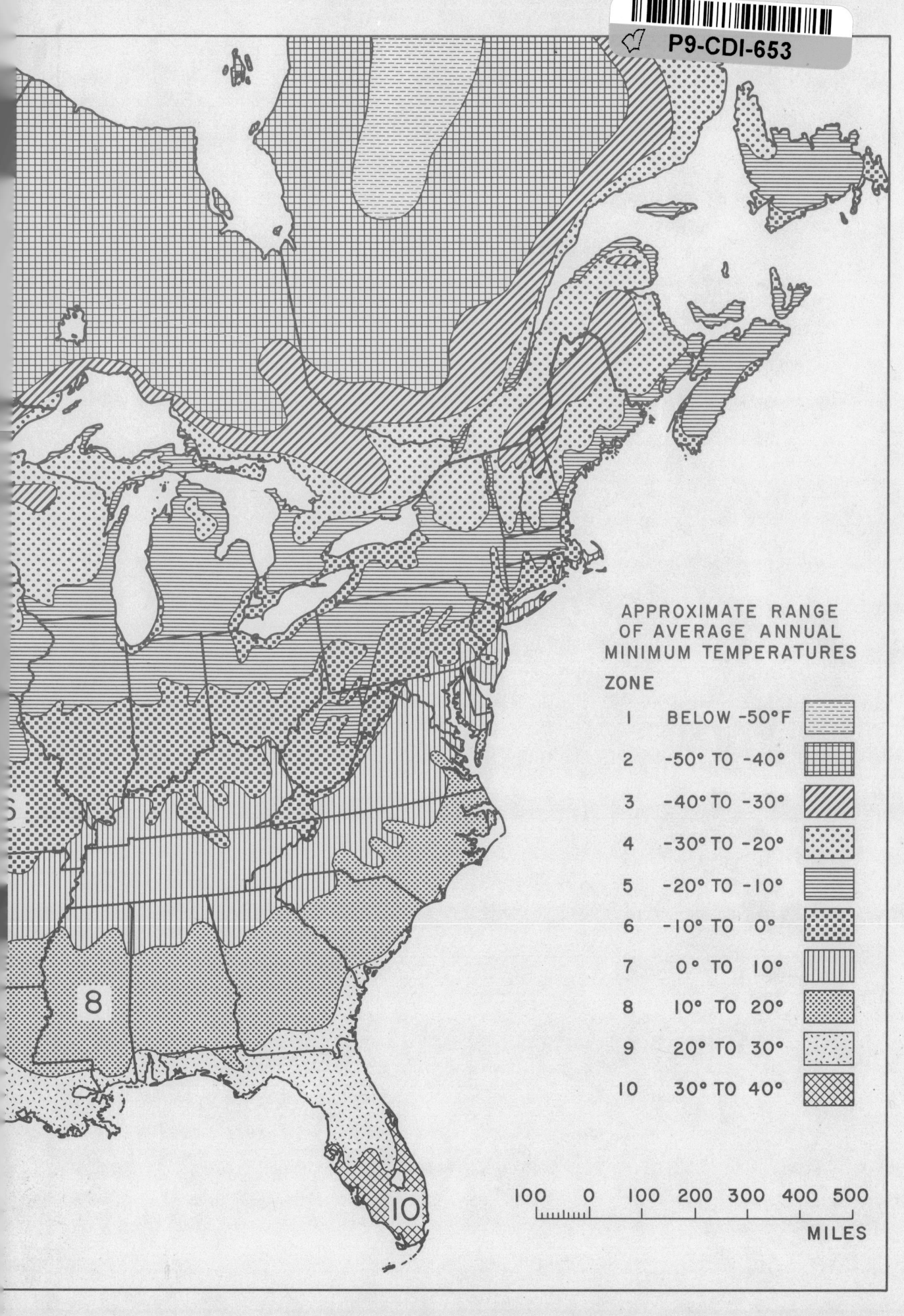

APPROXIMATE RANGE
OF AVERAGE ANNUAL
MINIMUM TEMPERATURES

ZONE

1	BELOW -50°F	
2	-50° TO -40°	
3	-40° TO -30°	
4	-30° TO -20°	
5	-20° TO -10°	
6	-10° TO 0°	
7	0° TO 10°	
8	10° TO 20°	
9	20° TO 30°	
10	30° TO 40°	

100   0   100   200   300   400   500

MILES

Hortus Third

Hortus Third

A Concise Dictionary of Plants Cultivated in the United States and Canada

Initially Compiled by
LIBERTY HYDE BAILEY
and **ETHEL ZOE BAILEY**

Revised and Expanded by
THE STAFF OF THE
LIBERTY HYDE BAILEY HORTORIUM
A Unit of the
New York State College of Agriculture and Life Sciences
a Statutory College of the
State University at Cornell University

MACMILLAN PUBLISHING COMPANY
New York
COLLIER MACMILLAN PUBLISHERS
London

Macmillan Publishing Company
866 Third Avenue, New York, N. Y. 10022
Collier Macmillan Canada, Inc.

20 19 18 17 16 15 14 13

Macmillan books are available at special discounts for bulk purchases for
sales promotions, premiums, fund raising, or educational use. For details,
contact:
Special Sales Director
Macmillan Publishing Company
866 Third Avenue
New York, New York 10022

Printed in the United States of America

For information about our audio products, write us at:
Newbridge Book Clubs, 3000 Cindel Drive, Delran, NJ 08370

Contents

Preface

Hortus Third is part of a long-standing program of research concerned with the systematics of cultivated plants that was initiated before the turn of the century by Liberty Hyde Bailey. Through the years this program was carried on by him, both alone and with the aid of his daughter, Ethel Zoe Bailey, and others, and since the founding of the Liberty Hyde Bailey Hortorium, it has provided focus to research in the Hortorium. The principal and continuing goal of the program has been to give horticulturists and others an inventory of accurately described and named plants of ornamental and economic importance. This goal has been realized through a succession of publications, among them the Cyclopedia of American Horticulture (1900–1902), the Standard Cyclopedia of Horticulture (1914–1917), Hortus (1930), Hortus Second (1941), and the Manual of Cultivated Plants (1924, 1949).

Hortus Third continues in the tradition of these publications. It provides a contemporary assessment of the kinds and the names of plants cultivated in the continental United States and Canada, Puerto Rico, and Hawaii. Initially planned as a simple revision of Hortus Second, Hortus Third evolved during its preparation into an essentially new work; for with the exception of some parts of the general articles, the entries have been rewritten and expanded. Many plants that were listed in earlier editions of Hortus have been omitted because they are no longer in cultivation or are not offered through the horticultural trade; however, many more plants have replaced them. Innovations included are: author or authors for each botanical name, illustrations of representative members of most families, a separate glossary of botanical terms, an index to common names, and a list of authors cited.

Since Hortus Second appeared, substantial change in the concepts underlying systematic botany has occurred, and a new system of nomenclature for cultivated variants of species has been developed. These, together with those changes resulting from the marked increase in the knowledge of the world's flora, are incorporated in Hortus Third. Not all groups of plants, however, are equally well known, nor have all been studied in a modern context. For these reasons, and because of the degree of freedom given to each contributor and exercised by each editor, there is some unevenness among treatments.

That publication of Hortus Third has become a reality is due to the foresight and labor of many individuals and to the strong support given the Hortorium by the New York State College of Agriculture and Life Sciences at Cornell University, of which the Hortorium is a unit. The conviction, so strongly held by Liberty Hyde Bailey, that knowledge in basic science should be made available to society as a whole led to the publication of his encyclopedic works and to his founding and gift to Cornell University in 1935 of the L. H. Bailey Hortorium. The Hortorium, established as a "place for the scientific study of garden plants, for their naming, for their classification, and their documentation," has expanded its activities somewhat beyond those originally envisioned by him, but even in so doing has maintained his conviction. The staff of the Hortorium feels honored to be able to carry on the work established by its founder.

It is also an honor to have as a friend and colleague Ethel Z. Bailey who, through many years, was her father's coworker and coauthor. Although she formally retired from the Hortorium in 1957, she remains no less active today, for she continues to work in the herbarium and library and, because of her long association with her father's work and the Hortorium, makes other valuable contributions. An index to sources of cultivated plants was begun by Miss Bailey over forty years ago and is still, with few exceptions, the result of her work. It is derived from horticultural trade catalogues and seed exchange lists of botanical gardens from the United States and other parts of the world. With more than 200,000 cards and many times that number of entries, it was the basic reference used to determine the species to be included in Hortus Third, and it continues to be used in other aspects of work at the Hortorium. It is a pleasure to express the appreciation of the Hortorium for her many contributions.

While the long-term success of the Hortorium ultimately rests on its programs, a favorable working climate is necessary for the achievement of its goals. The Hortorium has had strong program support from the College of Agriculture and Life Sciences. Financial support for the Hortus Third program has come from the State of New York, through the College and the New York State Experiment Station at Cornell University, and from the United States Department of Agriculture, through Hatch Project 401 "Taxonomic Studies of Cultivated Plants." Other funds for Hortus Third have come from the Liberty Hyde Bailey Memorial Fund, Macmillan Publishing Co., Inc., and National Science Foundation grants GB-1747 and GB-6619X, both entitled "Studies for a Dictionary and an Encyclopedia of Cultivated Plants," for which Harold

E. Moore, Jr. was principal investigator. In addition, gifts of funds or of plant materials from a large number of individuals and institutions have supported the research programs and thus helped in the preparation of *Hortus Third*. For this generous support and continued interest, the Hortorium is most grateful.

Hortus Third is the product of the collective talents and efforts of many individuals. It was initiated while L. H. Bailey was still director of the Hortorium and continued under George H. M. Lawrence, Harold E. Moore, Jr., and the present director. The taxonomic entries were prepared by the current professorial staff —David M. Bates, John W. Ingram, Jr., and Harold E. Moore, Jr.—together with the following who held appointments at or were otherwise associated with the Hortorium: George S. Bunting, Jr., Gordon P. DeWolf, Jr., Leslie A. Garay, George H. M. Lawrence, Elizabeth M. McClintock, Reid V. Moran, Philip A. Munz, Juan V. Pancho, and Claude Weber. In addition, it is a pleasure to acknowledge the work of many persons who reviewed or revised manuscripts of groups of plants of which they have special knowledge. These contributors included: Edward F. Anderson, Caroline K. Allen, Fred A. Barkley, Lyman D. Benson, Robert B. Clark, Lincoln Constance, Donovan S. Correll, Gilbert S. Daniels, Theodore R. Dudley, John E. Ebinger, Gene K. Eisenbeiss, John M. Fogg, Jr., Howard S. Gentry, Bernard E. Harkness, Charles B. Heiser, Jr., Barbara J. Hoshizaki, Peter A. Hyypio, Hugh H. Iltis, Duane Isely, Richard A. Jaynes, Baki Kasapligil, Linda M. Kohn, Walter H. Lewis, Tommie E. Lockwood, Joseph C. McDaniel, Frederick G. Meyer, Brian O. Mulligan, Albert E. Murray, Jr., Dan H. Nicolson, Timothy C. Plowman, John R. and Charlotte G. Reeder, Owen M. Rogers, Reed C. Rollins, Rainer W. Scora, Henry T. Skinner, Lyman B. Smith, Rolla M. Tryon, Jr., Heinrich W. E. van Bruggen, Susan E. Verhoek-Williams, Trevor Whiffen, and John J. Wurdack. The final taxonomic editing and revisions were done by the professorial staff of the Hortorium.

Walter H. Hodge, as a member of the Hortorium staff, contributed in many ways to the final preparation of the book, but especially by adding notes on culture, use, and economic properties, and by revising or reviewing the general articles. Others who generously contributed to the general articles were: Raymond C. Allen, Willard P. Bitters, Julian C. Crane, Chester E. Cross, Michael H. Dickson, Ernst P. du-Charme, John Einset, Elmer E. Ewing, Harold I. Forde, George L. Good, Hudson T. Hartmann, Donald

G. Huttleston, Haruyuki Kamemoto, Walter J. Kender, Dale E. Kester, Leon R. Kneebone, Harry B. Lagerstedt, Gerald A. Marx, Philip A. Minges, Henry M. Munger, Donald K. Ourecky, Howard M. Pidduck, Robert W. Schery, Nelson J. Shaulis, George L. Slate, Darrel Sparks, Dent Smith, Margaret H. Stone, John P. Tomkins, William E. Tomlinson, Jr., Harold B. Tukey, Jr., John P. Watson, and Roger D. Way.

The illustrations were derived from various sources. Most were taken from the Hortorium files and have not been previously published. Many, however, were taken from L. H. Bailey's *Manual of Cultivated Plants*, revised edition (Macmillan, 1949) and, with permission, from George H. M. Lawrence's *Taxonomy of Vascular Plants* (Macmillan, 1951) and *An Introduction to Plant Taxonomy* (Macmillan, 1955). The map inside the front and back covers was redrawn from the Plant Hardiness Zone Map (United States Department of Agriculture Miscellaneous Publication 814, 1960). The illustrations are principally the work of Marion Ruff Sheehan and Florence Mekeel Lambeth. Mitsu Nakayama and Barbara Bernstein have also made substantial contributions, and Elfriede M. Abbe and Margaret A. Lavery are each responsible for part of a single plate. The Hortorium was fortunate in having available the talents of these artists. Russell C. Mott and Clarence J. Newbury for many years provided expert care for many of the living plants that served as subjects for illustration and for taxonomic study.

Three persons who participated in the final stages of manuscript preparation and were of particular help were: Frederick B. Essig, Nancy E. Lee, and Margaret A. Marshall. Equally important was the work of Lucille S. Herbert, Heather D. Hyde, Marjorie P. Markell, and Luella M. Sullivan who deciphered seemingly indecipherable pages of edited manuscript to produce accurately typed final copy and assisted in a variety of other ways. Throughout the preparation of *Hortus Third* many persons helped with the great miscellany of tasks that inevitably accompany the production of a book of encyclopedic proportions. Although not all can be recognized individually, the contribution of each is appreciated.

It is inevitable that in a work of this scope, errors and omissions should occur. It is hoped that they are minimal, and that they will be brought to the attention of the Hortorium. Although *Hortus Third* could not have been completed without the help of all the contributors, responsibility for errors and omissions rests with the professorial staff of the Hortorium.

Ithaca, New York
January 1976

DAVID M. BATES
Director, L. H. Bailey Hortorium

Introduction

Hortus Third is a record of an astonishingly rich and diverse cultivated flora written from a botanical point of view for the horticultural community. The alphabetical arrangement of entries and the variety of typography are designed to provide the reader with ready access to information about the names and plants treated. The text, however, is of necessity somewhat technical, therefore some paragraphs of explanation seem desirable.

Scope of Hortus Third

Hortus Third accounts for the species of plants that have been available in North American horticulture over the past two decades. It is based largely on the index to cultivated plants mentioned in the Preface. Supplementary information has been obtained from horticultural journals, correspondence with horticulturists and botanists, specimens of cultivated plants at the Hortorium, and experience with plants grown in the Hortorium greenhouse and garden.

Hortus Third includes the description and correct botanical name with its author or authors for 281 families, 3,301 genera, and 20,397 species, as well as a large, but uncounted number of names of subspecies, varieties, forms, and cultivars. Botanical synonyms, common names, and notes on uses, methods of propagation, and culture are included in each entry when appropriate. Hardiness zones are included when known with reasonable certainty. Diagnostic illustrations, representing species of one genus or more, accompany most of the family descriptions. General articles deal with important crops, groups of plants, or methods of culture. Appendices include a glossary of botanical terms, a list of the authors cited and abbreviations for them, and an index to common names.

The geographical focus of *Hortus Third* is continental North America north of Mexico. Its limits, however, extend beyond those of previous editions to include Puerto Rico and Hawaii, so that tropical plants are more fully represented than in earlier editions of *Hortus*. Practical considerations have necessitated selection. In general, species known to be cultivated only in botanical gardens or in government test gardens have not been included. Only a selection of the enormous number of fancy-named cultivars has been included, largely those of woody plants which tend to persist over long periods. The constantly changing offerings of plants listed by specialized plant societies that are served by their own journals, newsletters, and registration authorities (see *Registration*) may not always be included since they are often transient in American horticulture.

Arrangement of Contents

The dictionary format in which *Hortus Third* is written restricts the information that can be included in each entry. Descriptions are written so as to provide a general understanding of the taxon described and usually to allow it to be distinguished from related taxa. (A taxon, plural taxa, is a taxonomic group of any rank, for example, family, genus, or species.) A conscious effort was made to use familiar terms; however, the use of some botanical terminology could not be avoided. Botanical terms are defined in the glossary. Similarly, measurements are in the English system, as being more familiar and because the metric system had not been accepted in the United States while *Hortus Third* was being written.

The names for taxonomic entries are governed by international codes of nomenclature and represent levels in a hierarchical classification of plants (see sections *Classification* and *Names*, which follow). Each taxonomic entry summarizes the descriptive characteristics and the geographical distribution of the plants included under the name and often also provides additional information on economic importance, culture, or notes on special taxonomic problems. If the name listed as an entry is a synonym, then the entry is followed by a colon and refers to the name or names under which a description or other information can be found. For example, the entry **ASSONIA:** *DOMBEYA* means that the generic name *Assonia* is a synonym of *Dombeya*. Information concerning *Assonia* or its species should be sought under the entry **DOMBEYA.**

Major Entries

The major entries in the text are alphabetized and set in boldface, upper case type. They include three categories, the first two taxonomic, the third general: (1) family names, as **VIOLACEAE**, the name for the violet family; (2) generic names, as **VIOLA,** the inclusive name for the violets, themselves; and (3) the key word or words of general articles, as **BLUEBERRY, CARNIVOROUS PLANTS.**

Family Entries

Family entries summarize basic family characteristics in descriptions that are usually supplemented by illustrations of representative species. They also list all genera of the family that are described in *Hortus Third,* so as to provide reference to generic treatments. The name of the family is followed by (1) the author or authors for that name, (2) synonyms, if any, set in italic type within brackets, and (3) the common name for the family set in capital and small capital letters. The description of the family then follows, beginning with a word or abbreviation that places the family in the context of a higher category, such as algae, ferns, gymnosperms, dicotyledons, or monocotyledons (the latter two abbreviated dicot. and monocot. respectively). Information about culture and economic use follows the description.

Generic Entries

Generic entries summarize the characteristics of the species that are included in the genus. This summary is mostly limited to a single description, but in the larger, more complex genera, for example, *Begonia* and *Rhododendron,* the genus is divided into lesser groups on the basis either of botanical or of horticultural characteristics. Notes on economic uses and cultural practices may be included for these groups. The name of the genus is followed by (1) the author or authors for that name, (2) synonyms, if any, set in italic type within brackets, (3) common names, if any, set in capital and small capital letters, and (4) the name of the family to which the genus belongs set in italic type.

Entries under Genus

Following each generic description, and listed alphabetically in sequence, are the botanical names (epithets) under which plants have been offered in that genus. These names are set in boldface, lower case type or, when capitalized, in lower and upper case, as **odorata** and **Rafinesquii** for two species of *Viola.* The names include those considered to be correct for species and hybrids, synonyms of species or hybrids, and names treated in catalogues as names of species, but having no botanical standing under the *International Code of Botanical Nomenclature.* Correct names are followed by (1) the author or authors for that name, (2) synonyms, if any, set in italic type within brackets, and (3) common names, if any, set in capital and small capital letters. Names listed in catalogues but having no botanical standing are followed by a colon, then usually a statement that they have no botanical standing, and, when their identity is known or conjectured, a reference to an appropriate entry where information may be found. When subordinate categories of a species are included, their names follow the accepted hierarchical arrangement of subspecies, varieties, forms, and cultivars (see section on *Classification* below). These are set in boldface type in upper and lower case, the cultivars within single quotation marks. Synonyms and common names, if given, and descriptions are treated as for the species.

General Articles

The general articles provide more extended and general accounts of particular species or groups of species than is possible in the taxonomic parts of the text, for example, citrus fruits; or they provide inventories of classes of plants that would not otherwise be brought together, for example, aquatic plants, conifers, or succulents; or they summarize basic horticultural practices, such as pruning and propagation, as these relate to home gardeners. A few explain terms, such as cultivar, or provide brief descriptions of such major categories of classification as dicotyledon and monocotyledon.

Classification

Living creatures have generally been divided into two major groups, the Plant Kingdom and Animal Kingdom, although the boundaries between and within these two groups are not always clear, and there is an increasing tendency to recognize as many as five kingdoms. For convenience of reference, the Plant Kingdom is used in the traditional sense in *Hortus Third,* and is subdivided into subordinate units, which are arranged in a hierarchy that attempts to reflect biological relationships. One of the earlier classifications, used here because of its relative simplicity and its usefulness for horticultural needs, recognizes four principal subdivisions called divisions: Thallophyta, Bryophyta, Pteriodophyta, and Spermatophyta.

Thallophytes and Bryophytes

The Thallophyta, or thallophytes, are the simplest plants. They are not differentiated into roots, stems, or leaves, and lack conducting tissue. In horticulture they are represented by a few algae (see *Algae*) and mushrooms (see *Fungi*), although many of the fungi are important in causing diseases in plants. The Bryophyta or bryophytes (see *Mosses and Liverworts*) are also represented in horticulture by only a few species. They may be differentiated into stem and leaves but lack true roots and conducting tissue.

Pteridophytes and Spermatophytes

The two divisions of importance in horticulture include plants that have roots, stems, leaves, and vascular conducting tissue. In the Pteridophyta or pterido-phytes, the ferns and their allies (see *Ferns and Fern Allies*), the plants reproduce by means of spores; in the Spermatophyta or spermatophytes, the plants reproduce by means of seeds. The spermatophytes provide most of our familiar cultivated plants. Two subdivisions, called classes, are recognized in the Spermatophyta: (1) the Gymnospermae (see *Gymnosperm*) which have ovules and seeds borne on the surface of a sporophyll, such as a cone scale, and include the conifers, cycads, and *Ginkgo;* and (2) the Angiospermae or flowering plants (see *Angiosperm*) which have ovules and seeds enclosed within an ovary borne in a flower that most often also includes sepals, petals, and stamens.

Subdivisions of Angiosperms

In a descending sequence, the angiosperm class is divided into two subclasses, the Dicotyledonae (see *Dicotyledon*) and Monocotyledonae (see *Monocotyledon*). These subclasses, in turn, are divided into orders, the names of which often terminate in *-ales,* as the Violales, the order that includes the family Violaceae together with such other related families as the Begoniaceae and Passifloraceae.

The next subordinate unit, the family, is the highest unit of the hierarchy described in the taxonomic entries in *Hortus Third*. It is composed of plants sharing certain characteristics of flower, fruit, and sometimes of leaf, but differing among themselves in characteristics that set them apart so that they can be recognized as lesser units or genera. The genus, in turn, consists of one or more species which, in large genera, may be arranged in subordinate units, such as subgenera and sections, as in the genus *Mammillaria* of the Cactaceae.

The species is, for the most part, the working unit of the horticulturist and botanist. In general, the individuals of a species resemble each other more than they do other plants, and they interbreed freely. A few, for example the maidenhair tree, *Ginkgo biloba,* are so distinctive that they are the sole representatives of such higher units as genus, family, or order; others, as some species of *Aster,* may be highly variable and difficult to distinguish from each other.

Further subcategories (infraspecific categories) within the species are sometimes used. These may be botanical or horticultural. The main botanical categories, in descending order in the hierarchy, are subspecies, variety *(varietas),* and form *(forma).* The subspecies is the principal subcategory and is used in contemporary schemes of classification when a species includes individuals that show minor but consistent morphological differences associated with distinct geographical or ecological distribution. The category variety is most often used today to designate variants that are not associated with distribution, but in some botanical works it is used as equivalent to subspecies, depending on the author, or the state of knowledge of the species, or both. The category form is usually reserved for such minor and sporadic variations as differences in color of flower or fruit.

Horticultural Categories

Two horticultural categories are used in *Hortus Third:* cultivar, the most frequently used, and group. A cultivar (from *cultivated variety*) is defined in the *International Code of Nomenclature of Cultivated Plants* as "an assemblage of cultivated plants which is clearly distinguished by any characters (morphological, physiological, cytological, chemical, or others), and which when reproduced (sexually or asexually), retains its distinguishing characters." The term is used internationally and replaces such words as "variety" in English, "varieté" in French, and "Sorte" in German. A group includes more than one cultivar of a particular kind as, for example, the cultivars of cabbage which together form the Capitata Group of *Brassica oleracea*.

For a number of reasons, both botanical and horticultural, the ideal hierarchical sequence is rarely encountered. Forms, for example, are less commonly used than previously, but more importantly, not all categories of the infraspecific hierarchy need be used. Thus, varieties of species are often described without the intervening category of subspecies. Infraspecific treatments in *Hortus Third* will be found to vary, depending on the group and the interpretation of the taxonomist who revised the group. Horticultural cultivars are often of unknown or hybrid origin and cannot be assigned to an appropriate infraspecific category. Moreover, special classification may be encountered in horticulturally complex species such as *Brassica oleracea,* which includes broccoli, kale, and kohlrabi, in addition to cabbage.

Names

The names used in *Hortus Third* are of three kinds: botanical names in Latin form, horticultural names (mostly those of cultivars), and common names. Botanical names of plants are governed by internationally accepted rules found in the *International Code of Botanical Nomenclature*. Horticultural names fall into two categories—those that are clearly of a horticultural origin, as cultivar, and whose formation and use is governed by the *International Code of Nomenclature of Cultivated Plants;* and those that

have a Latin spelling, but have never been published under the rules of the *International Code of Botanical Nomenclature*. Common names are not governed by any formal code of nomenclature.

Botanical Names

The botanical name of a family of plants may usually be recognized by the ending *aceae* attached to the stem of the name of a genus within the family—thus Violaceae, the name for the violet family, is composed of the stem *Viol* of the name for the violet genus, *Viola*, with the suffix *aceae*. Eight families have been known so long by names formed in another manner that either of two names may be used. These are: Compositae (Asteraceae), Cruciferae (Brassicaceae), Gramineae (Poaceae), Guttiferae (Clusiaceae), Labiatae (Lamiaceae), Leguminosae (Fabaceae), Palmae (Arecaceae), and Umbelliferae (Apiaceae).

Names of genera are singular nouns or words treated as such. They often are named after a real or mythical person, as *Linnaea* after Linnaeus, or *Arethusa*, after a nymph in Greek mythology; or they may be ancient Greek or Latin names for plants, as *Erica*. Generic names may also suggest some attribute of the genus, as *Spiranthes* from the Greek words for a coil *(speira)* and flower *(anthos)*, because of the spirally twisted spike, or they may be formed in a completely arbitrary manner, as *Muilla*, an anagram of *Allium*. The generic name, whatever its origin, is treated as Latin and its gender is usually that of the Greek or Latin word itself or, when formed from two or more such words, from the gender of the last.

The name of a species is a combination of the generic name with a specific epithet. Thus *albus* is the epithet for the species *Lupinus albus*. An epithet may be taken from any source or may be composed arbitrarily, but it is most often adjectival and so agrees in gender with the genus. Thus the Latin adjective *albus* (white) retains the masculine ending in *Lupinus albus*, because *Lupinus* is masculine, but the ending changes in other genera, as in *Nymphaea alba* (feminine) or *Sedum album* (neuter). Epithets may also be nouns in apposition, retaining their own endings, as in *Achillea Millefolium* and *Zea Mays*, or nouns in the genitive case, as in *Pandanus Veitchii*, that is, Veitch's pandanus. Adjectival endings such as *ana* may be added to personal or geographical names, as in *Calathea Veitchiana* and *Linum africanum*. When personal names end in a vowel, however, an *i* is added *(Heynei, Delavayi)* except when the name ends in *a* in which case *e* is added, as in *Balansae, Victoriae*. When a personal name ends in *er* the epithet is formed by adding a single *i* or *ana* as in *Berlandieri* or *Sanderana*. Some epithets are not declined, an example being *alpicola* ("dweller in the alps"). It is now recommended that all specific epithets commence with a lower case letter, but the practice of capitalizing the first letter of epithets derived from names of persons, former generic names, and common (non-Latin) names is still permitted and is followed in *Hortus Third* as a guide to those who wish to continue the practice.

The names of infraspecific taxa are combinations of the name of a species and an infraspecific epithet connected by a term denoting its rank, as *Asclepias asperula* subsp. *capricornu* or *Buxus microphylla* var. *japonica*. Epithets of infraspecific names are formed according to the same rules as those of species.

The names of hybrid plants are preceded by the multiplication sign (×), as in the hybrid genus ×*Guzvriesea* or the hybrid species *Acer* ×*coriaceum*. In *Hortus Third* the name of the hybrid is followed by a colon, then the names of the parents, arranged alphabetically and with the multiplication sign between them. Thus the parentage of ×*Guzvriesea* is expressed as *Guzmania* × *Vriesea* and that of *Acer* ×*coriaceum* as *A. monspessulanum* × *A. pseudoplatanus*. In speaking, the multiplication sign is expressed as "the hybrid genus" or "the hybrid species"—it is never pronounced like the letter *x*. Graft hybrids follow the same conventions as those used for normal hybrids except that the multiplication sign is replaced by a plus sign (+), as in the graft hybrid genus +*Laburnocytisus*.

A botanical name in *Hortus Third*, with the exceptions noted below, is followed by its author or authors, one or more names or abbreviations of names which indicate who published that name. For example, in *Hedera* L. and *Acer palmatum* Thunb., "L." is the abbreviation for Carolus Linnaeus and "Thunb." for Carl Pehr Thunberg (see appendix, *Authors Cited*). Names of joint authors are connected by an ampersand as in *Ancistrocactus* Britt. & Rose (for Nathaniel Lord Britton and Joseph Nelson Rose). If one botanist publishes a name proposed by another, their names are connected by *ex* as in *Anthurium tetragonum* Hook. ex Schott, Schott having published a name proposed by William Jackson Hooker.

When an author has transferred a species from one genus to another, or has changed the rank of a taxon—a variety to species, for example—the name of the original author is enclosed in parentheses followed by that of the author who made the transfer. Thus the species described by Linnaeus as *Agrostemma Coronaria* was transferred by Desrousseaux to the genus *Lychnis* so that the name is written *Lychnis Coronaria* (L.) Desr. Sometimes the same name is used independently by more than one author; then the name which was published first has priority and the later name or names must be replaced. This accounts for the entry **Viburnum Farreri** Stearn [*V. fragrans* Bunge, not Loisel.]. The name *Viburnum fragrans* Loisel. was published in 1824 and has priority over any other use of this name. Thus the name *Viburnum fragrans* Bunge, which was published in 1833 for a different plant, must be replaced by *V. Farreri*. In the last two examples, the names that are no longer used, *Agrostemma Coronaria* and *Viburnum fragrans*, are listed as synonyms of the accepted name and are listed in the text with a cross reference to the accepted name.

Names of subdivisions of genera (subgenera and sections) and those of infraspecific categories (subspecies, varieties, and forms) are not accompanied by an author citation when they repeat the name of the genus or the specific epithet, as *Rhododendron* subgenus *Rhododendron* or *Juniperus chinensis* var. *chinensis*.

Horticultural Names

Cultivar names published since January 1, 1959, must be fancy names that are markedly different from botanical names in Latin form, except that properly published botanical epithets proposed for forms, varieties, or even species, may be retained if they are subsequently considered to represent cultivars. Many older cultivar names are also retained in their Latin form. Regardless of the origin of the name of a cultivar, its initial letter is capitalized (with rare exceptions, depending on requirements of a modern language). It is further distinguished by placing the abbreviation cv. before it, as *Cupressus macrocarpa* cv. Golden Pillar, or by enclosing the name in single quotation marks, as *Cupressus macrocarpa* 'Stricta'. Cultivar names are not set in any special type; they are listed in boldface type in *Hortus Third* only to make them stand out as entries.

The name of a cultivar may be assigned to the species name, as above, or it may be assigned to a lesser category, as in *Juniperus communis* var. *depressa* 'Aurea'. In some instances, especially when cultivars are of hybrid or unknown origin, they may be assigned directly to a genus, as in *Ilex* 'Maplehurst'. When the usage is unambiguous, they may even be joined to a common name as in potato cv. Bake King.

When a species or an interspecific hybrid includes many cultivars, those which are similar may be arranged in groups. Cultivars of *Allium Cepa*, for example, may be assigned to the Aggregatum Group, the Cepa Group, or the Proliferum Group, depending on the presence or absence of bulbils or other means of vegetative reproduction. The name of the group is placed in parentheses when introduced between the name of the species and a cultivar, as *Brassica oleracea* (Capitata Group) 'King Cole'.

Horticultural names that have the form of botanical names are especially troublesome. Often they are no more than listings in catalogues or names used casually in the horticultural literature. Sometimes they are widely used in horticulture but apparently have never been properly described according to the *International Code of Botanical Nomenclature* and do not have standing as botanical names. Such names have been variously treated in *Hortus Third*. Most often

they are followed by the phrase "a listed name of no botanical standing," sometimes with additional information suggesting known, probable, or possible identity. Sometimes, however, they are identified as "a hort. name" or are referred directly to accepted names where they are listed as synonyms with the author indicated as Hort. (of gardens). Occasionally, however, a name, *Dracaena Baptisii* Hort., for example, has been appropriately described anonymously in the literature and cannot be distinguished from names of no botanical standing.

Common Names

Common names form an important part of our horticultural heritage. Many are names that are part of our everyday language—bean, marigold, oak, potato, or spinach. Others, however, may be used only in a limited region or by fanciers of special groups. Some common names are used in different ways in different regions, and many species have no common name at all, hence the desirability, among others reasons, of using botanical names.

The common names included in *Hortus Third* have been obtained from many published sources, but the list is not exhaustive. No attempt has been made to include mere translations of scientific names or other contrived common names. To economize space repeated portions of names are abbreviated when they occur in sequence, hence the common names for *Kalmia* are printed LAUREL, AMERICAN L. (laurel). The same device is used for species of a genus, as BOG L. (laurel), a common name for *Kalmia poliifolia*.

Generic names have sometimes become common names, as iris, kalmia, narcissus, and rhododendron. In *Hortus Third*, it was considered that any generic name may be used as a common name, as bog kalmia for *Kalmia poliifolia* or trailing abutilon for *Abutilon megapotamicum*. Generic names used as common names may also be abbreviated, hence bog kalmia appears as BOG K. (kalmia).

Abbreviations and Symbols

Aside from the usual abbreviations for geographical regions, countries, states, and provinces, those used in *Hortus Third* are as follows:

alt.	alternate
ann.	annual
arch.	archipelago
auth.	author
bien.	biennial
br., brs.	branch, branches
caps.	capsule
cent.	central
cult.	cultivated, cultivation
cv., cvs.	cultivar, cultivars
diam.	diameter
e.	east, eastern

fl.	flower, floral, flowering
fld.	flowered
fls.	flowers
fr., frs.	fruit, fruits
ft.	foot, feet
hort.	horticulture, horticultural
in.	inch, inches
infl., infls.	inflorescence, inflorescences
introd.	introduced
is.	island, islands
lf.	leaf
lft., lfts.	leaflet, leaflets
lvd.	leaved
lvs.	leaves
mts.	mountains
n.	north, northern

nat. . . . . naturalized
ne. . . . . northeastern
nw. . . . . northwestern
opp. . . . . opposite
pantrop. . . . . pantropical
pen. . . . . peninsula
per. . . . . perennial
prop. . . . . propagated, propagation
s. . . . . south, southern
se. . . . . southeast, southeastern
segm., segms. . . . . segment, segments
sp. . . . . species (singular)
spp. . . . . species (plural)

st., sts. . . . . stem, stems
subsp. . . . . subspecies (singular)
subspp. . . . . subspecies (plural)
subtrop. . . . . subtropical
sw. . . . . southwest, southwestern
temp. . . . . temperate
trop. . . . . tropical
var., vars. . . . . variety, varieties
w. . . . . west, western
× . . . . sign for a hybrid
+ . . . . sign for a graft hybrid
? . . . . possibly

Statistics*

Taxonomic categories

Families	1.	Described entries	281
	2.	Synonyms and cross references	13
Genera	1.	Described entries	3,301
	2.	Synonyms and cross references	753
Species	1.	Described entries	20,397
	2.	Synonyms and cross references	9,560
Total taxonomic entries exclusive of infraspecific categories			34,305

Other categories

General articles	187
Illustrations	260
Authors cited	3,293
Definitions in the glossary	1,105
Common names	10,408

* Some approximate.

Hortus Third

ABELIA R. Br. *Caprifoliaceae*. About 30 spp. of summer-flowering shrubs, native to Asia and Mex.; lvs. opp., simple, persistent or deciduous; fls. many, small, white or pink, in axillary or terminal cymes, sepals 2–5, large, purplish, corolla tubular to campanulate, 5-lobed, stamens 4, ovary inferior, 3-celled; fr. an achene, topped with persistent sepals.

Abelias thrive in a well-drained soil enriched with leaf-mold, and in a sunny, preferably protected, site. *A. floribunda* is sometimes grown in the greenhouse. Propagated by greenwood cuttings rooted under glass in the summer or by cuttings of ripe wood in autumn, rarely by seed. *A. ×grandiflora* and *A. Englerana* are hardy north; other species are less hardy.

chinensis R. Br. [*A. rupestris* Lindl.]. Deciduous, to 6 ft., or often prostrate, especially at base; lvs. ovate, to 1½ in. long; fls. in dense terminal panicles, white, funnelform, ½ in. long, fragrant, sepals 5. China. Zone 7. Plants grown under this name may be *A. ×grandiflora*.

Englerana (Graebn.) Rehd. Deciduous, to 6 ft.; lvs. ovate to elliptic-lanceolate, to 1½ in. long; fls. in few-fld. axillary clusters, rosy-purple or rosy-pink, funnelform, ¾ in. long, sepals 2. China. Zone 6.

floribunda (M. Martens & Galeotti) Decne. MEXICAN A. Evergreen, to 6 ft.; lvs. ovate, to 1½ in. long; fls. pendulous, solitary or in 2–3-fld. clusters, carmine-purple, tubular, 1½ in. long, sepals 5. Mex. Zone 9.

Gaucheri: see *Abelia* 'Edward Goucher' under *A. ×grandiflora*.

Graebnerana Rehd. Deciduous, to 10 ft.; lvs. ovate or narrowly so, to 2½ in. long, acuminate; fls. solitary or few, on short lateral brs., or axillary, pink or yellow inside. China. Zone 7.

×grandiflora (André) Rehd.: *A. chinensis* × *A. uniflora*. GLOSSY A. Half-evergreen, prostate or erect, to 6 ft.; lvs. ovate, to 1½ in. long, shining; fls. in loose terminal panicles, white flushed pink, bell-shaped, ¾ in. long, sepals 2–5. The common kind in cult.; often grown erroneously as *A. chinensis*. Zone 6. Cv. 'Prostrata'. A prostrate form. Cv. 'Sherwoodii'. A selected dwarf form, to 3 ft., lvs. and fls. somewhat smaller. *Abelia* cv. 'Edward Goucher' [*A. Gaucheri* Hort.]. A clone selected from a cross between *A. ×grandiflora* and *A. Schumannii*, with abundant lavender-pink fls. and showy reddish calyces.

integrifolia G. Koidz. Deciduous, to 6 ft.; lvs. broadly or narrowly oblanceolate, to 1¾ in. long; fls. white, to ½ in. long, sepals 4. Japan. Zone 8.

japonica: a listed name of no botanical standing.

rupestris: *A. chinensis*.

Schumannii (Graebn.) Rehd. Deciduous, slender shrub to 5 ft. or more; lvs. ovate to elliptic, to about 1 in. long, obtuse, mucronate; fls. several on short lateral brs., pink, corolla slender at base, sepals 2. China. Zone 7.

serrata Siebold & Zucc. Deciduous, to 4 ft.; lvs. ovate to ovate-lanceolate, to 1¾ in long, teeth few or none, sparsely hairy above and below or glabrous below; fls. in pairs at ends of short lateral brs., whitish or pale pink, corolla ½ in. long, funnelform, sepals 2. Japan. Zone 8.

spathulata Siebold & Zucc. Deciduous, to 4 ft., young shoots downy; lvs. elliptic-lanceolate to ovate, to 2 in. long, with few unequal teeth, margins reddish at first; fls. in pairs at ends of short lateral brs., whitish, corolla campanulate above with narrowly constricted short basal tube, to 1 in. long, sepals 5. Japan. Zone 8.

triflora R. Br. ex Wallich. Deciduous, to 12 ft.; lvs. lanceolate or ovate-lanceolate, to 3 in. long; fls. in terminal clusters 2 in. across, rosy-white, corolla salverform, tube slender, ½ in. long, sepals 5, nearly as long as corolla tube, with stiff marginal hairs. Himalayas. Zone 7.

uniflora R. Br. ex Wallich. Evergreen, to 6 ft.; lvs. ovate, to 1 in. long, acuminate, shining above; fls. pinkish-white, orange in throat, corolla funnelform, 1 in. long, lobes spreading widely, sepals 2. China. Zone 7. One of the parents of *A. ×grandiflora*.

Zanderi (Graebn.) Rehd. Deciduous, to 9 ft.; lvs. ovate to lanceolate, to 2½ in. long, sparingly hairy; fls. 2 on short lateral brs., whitish, corolla salverform, tube ⁵⁄₁₆ in. long, lobes spreading, sepals 4. China. Zone 6.

ABELIOPHYLLUM Nakai. *Oleaceae*. One sp., a deciduous shrub of Korea, allied to *Fontanesia*, but having petals united in a tube as long as the spreading lobes.

distichum Nakai. To 3 ft.; lvs. opp., ovate, to 2 in. long, entire, pubescent; fls. white, ¼ in. across, in short racemes; samara flattened, nearly orbicular, 1 in. across, winged all around. Early spring. Zone 6.

ABELMOSCHUS Medic. *Malvaceae*. From 6 to perhaps 20 spp. of ann. or per. herbs, in trop. and warm-temp. Asia; lvs. large, palmately lobed to divided or compound, rarely unlobed; fls. solitary in lf. axils or in terminal racemes, involucral bracts 4–16, often early deciduous; often included in *Hibiscus*, but having calyx thin, apically 5-toothed, spathaceous and longitudinally split, united basally to petals and staminal column and together with them dehiscent as a cap after flowering.

A. esculentus and *A. moschatus* are widely cultivated in the tropics and have become sparingly naturalized. In more temperate regions these, together with *A. Manihot*, are grown as annuals, *A. esculentus* for its edible fruit, the other two principally as ornamentals.

esculentus (L.) Moench [*Hibiscus esculentus* L.]. OKRA, GUMBO, GOBO, GOMBO, LADY'S-FINGER. Glabrate to bristly, rather stout-stemmed ann. herb, to 6 ft. or more; lvs. palmately divided to compound or scarcely lobed, often more than 12 in. across; fls. solitary in the upper lf. axils on stout pedicels, involucral bracts 8–12, linear, to 1 in. long, falling early, corolla white to yellow, purple or red at the base, to 3 in. across; caps. 3–8 in. long, 5-angled-cylindrical, beaked, bristly, then glabrescent. Trop., Asia. See *Okra*.

Manihot (L.) Medic. [*Hibiscus Manihot* L.]. Mostly hispid, erect, coarse per. herbs, to 6 ft. or more; lvs. 3-, 5-, or 7-lobed or -parted, the lowermost up to 18 in. long; fls. solitary or in racemes, involucral bracts 4–6, sometimes 8, ovate, to 1⅛ in. long, persistent in fr., corolla whitish- to sulphur-yellow, basally maroon, 3–5 in. across; caps. 2½ in. long, ovate-elliptic, deeply 5-angled, hispid, on pedicels to 2½ in. long. Trop. Asia.

moschatus Medic. [*Hibiscus Abelmoschus* L.]. MUSK MALLOW. Similar to *A. Manihot* but having involucral bracts 6–10, linear, mostly less than ⅝ in. long; caps. cylindrical or only slightly 5-angled, 2–3 in. long, on pedicels to 5 in. long. Trop. Asia. Sometimes grown for the musky seeds.

ABERIA: *DOVYALIS*. **A. Gardneri**: *D. hebecarpa*.

ABIES Mill. FIR. *Pinaceae*. About 40 spp. of large, coniferous, evergreen, monoecious trees, native to cooler, usually mountainous parts of N. Temp. Zone; 50 ft. and more in height, of conical habit, main axis or trunk not divided, brs. whorled; lvs. flat, linear, usually glossy above and with 2 white bands below; female cones erect, scales deciduous; seeds 2 to a scale, winged, maturing in 1 year. Distinguished from the spruces *(Picea)* in having lvs. flat, whitish beneath; branchlets smooth where leafless; and cones erect, with deciduous scales.

Hardy in cultivation from the central regions north, but does not thrive where the growing season is hot or where air is polluted. For culture see *Conifers*.

alba Mill. [*A. pectinata* (Lam.) DC.]. SILVER F. To 150 ft., branchlets brownish-pubescent; lvs. to 1¼ in. long, rounded and notched at apex, glossy dark green above; cones cylindrical, to 5½ in. long, turning reddish-brown. Cent. and s. Eur. Zone 5, but in the Northeast likely to lose its lower brs. and to become thin. Cvs. include: 'Columnaris', columnar; 'Compacta', dwarf, compact; 'Equitrojani', lvs. more pointed, cones oblong-cylindrical; 'Pendula', brs. drooping; 'Pyramidalis', columnar; 'Tortuosa', dwarf and compact, brs. crowded, lvs. glossy.

amabilis Dougl. ex J. Forbes. CASCADE F., PACIFIC SILVER F. To 200 ft. or more, branchlets densely pubescent; lvs. ¾–1½ in. long, notched or truncate at apex, pointed forward, glossy dark green above; cones oblong, to 5 in. long, purple. B.C. to Ore. Zone 6. Wood used for interior work and wood pulp.

arizonica: *A. lasiocarpa* var.

balsamea (L.) Mill. BALSAM F., FIR BALSAM. To 75 ft., branchlets pubescent; lvs. to 1 in. long, rounded or slightly notched at apex, dark green above; cones oblong, to 2½ in. long, violet-purple. Lab. to W. Va. and Iowa. Zone 3. Yields Canada balsam. Var. **balsamea** [var. *macrocarpa* A. Kent.]. The typical var.; cones with bracts shorter than the scales. Cv. 'Nana'. Dwarf habit. Forma **hudsonia** (Bosc ex Jacques) Fern. & Weatherby. Low or prostrate; lvs. shorter and broader. Var. **macrocarpa**: var. *balsamea*. Var. **phanerolepis** Fern. Cones with awns of mature bracts exserted and spreading.

brachyphylla: *A. homolepis.*

bracteata (D. Don) D. Don ex Poit. [*A. venusta* (Dougl.) C. Koch]. BRISTLE-CONE F., SANTA LUCIA F. To 150 ft., branchlets greenish, glabrous; lvs. to 2½ in. long, stiff, spine-tipped, glossy green above; cones ovoid, bristly, to 4 in. long, purplish-brown. Calif. Zone 7.

cephalonica Loud. [*A. cephalonica* var. *Apollinis* (Link) Beissn.]. GREEK F. To 90 ft., branchlets glossy red-brown; lvs. to 1 in. long, sharp-pointed, glossy deep green above; cones cylindrical, to 7 in. long, brownish. Mts., Greece. Zone 6.

chensiensis Van Tiegh. To 200 ft., branchlets glabrous; lvs. to 1½ in. long, usually rounded and notched at apex, glossy dark green above; cones ovoid-oblong, to 4 in. long, green, turning red-brown. Cent. China. Zone 6.

cilicica (Ant. & Kotschy) Carrière. To 90 ft., branchlets sparsely pubescent; lvs. about 1 in. long, slightly notched at apex, 2-ranked, forming a V-shaped trough, glossy bright green above; cones cylindrical, to 9 in. long, reddish-brown. Asia Minor, Syria. Zone 6.

concolor (Gord.) Lindl. ex Hildebr. WHITE F. To 100 ft. or more, branchlets yellowish-green, puberulent or glabrous; lvs. to 2 in. long, rounded or acute at apex, bluish-green above; cones cylindrical, to 5 in. long, greenish or purplish. Colo. to Mex. Zone 4. Wood used for general millwork and pulp. Cvs. include: 'Argentea', lvs. silvery-white; 'Aurea', lvs. golden-yellow when young; 'Brevifolia', lvs. short, thick; 'Compacta', densely branched; 'Conica', dwarf, conical; 'Glauca', a listed name; 'Globosa', dwarf, rounded; 'Lowiana', lvs. longer, notched at apex; 'Pendula', brs. drooping; 'Pyramidalis', conical; 'Violacea', lvs. bluish-white; 'Wattezii', lvs. pale yellowish, becoming silvery-white.

Delavayi Franch. [*A. Fabri* (M. T. Mast.) Craib.]. To 100 ft.; lvs. 2-ranked, forming a V-shaped trough, to 1 in. long, often strongly revolute at margins, glossy dark green above, bands beneath white, broad; cones barrel-shaped, to 4 in. long, dark violet-black. China.

Douglasii: *Pseudotsuga Menziesii.*

Ernesti Rehd. To 100 ft. or more; lvs. to 1¼ in. long, flat above, bands beneath pale; cones peduncled. W. China, probably Zone 6.

Fabri: *A. Delavayi.*

firma Siebold & Zucc. MOMI F., JAPANESE F. To 150 ft., branchlets grooved, puberulent; lvs. to 1½ in. long, apex rounded and notched, sharply 2-pointed when young, bands beneath inconspicuous; cones cylindrical, to 5 in. long, yellowish-green. Japan. Zone 6.

Fraseri (Pursh) Poir. SOUTHERN BALSAM F., FRASER F., SOUTHERN F., SHE BALSAM. To 75 ft., branchlets reddish-pubescent; lvs. to 1 in. long, rounded and notched at apex, glossy dark green above; cones oblong or ovoid, to 2¼ in. long, purple. Alleghany Mts. Zone 5. Cv. 'Horizontalis'. Dwarf, spreading. Cv. 'Prostrata'. Shrub, with spreading brs.

grandis (D. Don ex Lamb.) Lindl. GIANT F., LOWLAND F. To 200 ft. or more; lvs. to 2¼ in. long, rounded and notched at apex, glossy dark green above; cones cylindrical, to 4 in. long, bright green. Vancouver Is. to Calif. and Mont. Zone 6. Does not thrive in e. states. Wood valuable for timber and pulp. Cv. 'Nana'. Dwarf.

guatemalensis Rehd. To 100 ft. or more, branchlets brown; lvs. more or less comblike in arrangement, unequal, to 2¼ in. long, notched at apex, deep green above, glaucous beneath; cones to 4½ in. long, 2 in. in diam., bracts half as long as scales. Mts., Guatemala. Zone 7.

holophylla Maxim. NEEDLE F. To about 90 ft., branchlets glabrous; lvs. to 1½ in. long, rounded or acute at apex, spiny when young, glossy bright green above, bands beneath inconspicuous; cones cylindrical, to 6 in. long, green, becoming light brown. Manchuria, Korea. Zone 6.

homolepis Siebold & Zucc. [*A. brachyphylla* Maxim.]. NIKKO F. To nearly 100 ft., branchlets deeply grooved, glabrous; lvs. about 1 in. long, rounded and slightly notched at apex, glossy dark green above; cones cylindrical, 4 in. long, purple. Mts., Japan. Zone 5. Cvs. include:

'Scottiae', DWARF NIKKO F., a dwarf sport; 'Tomomi', less branched, lvs. shorter; 'Umbellata' [*A. umbellata* Mayr], young cones green.

Kawakamii (Hayata) T. Ito. To 50 ft.; lvs. broadly linear, flat, about ⅝ in. long, rounded-obtuse at apex; cones cylindrical or oblong, to 1⅝ in. in diam. Mts., Taiwan. Zone 8, where summers are cool.

koreana E. H. Wils. KOREAN F. To about 50 ft., branchlets puberulent then glabrous; lvs. to ¾ in. long, rounded and notched at apex, pointed when young, margins revolute, glossy green above; cones cylindrical, to 3 in. long, violet-purple. Korea. Zone 5. Cv. 'Prostrata'. Low, spreading.

lasiocarpa (Hook.) Nutt. ALPINE F. To 100 ft., sometimes more, branchlets gray, reddish-pubescent; lvs. to 1½ in. long, rounded or acute at apex, pale bluish-green; cones oblong-cylindrical, to 4 in. long, purple. Alaska to New Mex. Zone 3, but does not thrive in the East. Var. **arizonica** (Merriam) Lemm. [*A. arizonica* Merriam]. CORK F. Bark thick, corky. Zone 5. Cv. 'Compacta'. Dwarf. Cv. 'Glauca'. Lvs. glaucous.

magnifica A. Murr. RED F. To 180 ft. or more, branchlets reddish-pubescent; lvs. 4-sided, to 1½ in. long, rounded at apex; cones oblong-cylindrical, to 9 in. long, purplish-violet. Ore. to Calif. Zone 6. A source of timber and pulp. Var. **shastensis** Lemm. SHASTA RED F. Bracts of cone exserted. Cv. 'Argentea'. Lvs. bluish-white. Cv. 'Glauca'. AZURE F. Lvs. glaucous.

Mariesii M. T. Mast. To about 75 ft., branchlets not grooved, densely red-pubescent; lvs. to ¾ in. long, rounded or notched at apex, bluish-green and grooved above; cones ovoid to oblong, to 3½ in. long, dark purple. Mts., Japan. Zone 6. Probably much material listed under this name is *A. spectabilis*, which differs in having branchlets deeply grooved, pubescent in grooves only, and cones much larger.

Maxwellii: a listed name of no botanical standing for *Picea Abies* cv.

nidiformis: a listed name of no botanical standing for *Picea Abies* cv.

nobilis: *A. procera.*

Nordmanniana (Steven) Spach. To 150 ft., branchlets gray, pubescent; lvs. to 1½ in. long, rounded and notched at apex, glossy dark green above; cones cylindrical, to 6 in. long, reddish-brown. Greece, Caucasus, Asia Minor. Zone 5. Cvs. include: 'Aurea', lvs. yellow; 'Nana', dwarf; 'Tortifolia', some lvs. twisted.

numidica De Lannoy ex Carrière. ALGERIAN F. To 60 ft., branchlets glossy, glabrous; lvs. to ¾ in. long, rounded and slightly notched at apex, dark green above; cones cylindrical, to 7 in. long, purple. N. Afr. Zone 7.

obovata: *Picea obovata.*

Ohlendorffii: *Picea Abies* cv.

pectinata: *A. alba.*

Pindrow Royle. To 150 ft. or more, branchlets smooth, glabrous; lvs. to 2⅜ in. long, acute and notched at apex, glossy dark green above, bands beneath gray, inconspicuous; cones cylindrical, to 5½ in. long, deep purple. Himalayas. Zone 7.

Pinsapo Boiss. SPANISH F. To 75 ft., branchlets brown, glabrous; lvs. arranged radially around branchlets, to ¾ in. long, acute, thick, stiff, dark green above, bands beneath inconspicuous; cones cylindrical, to 5 in. long, purplish-brown. Spain. Zone 7. Cvs. include: 'Argentea', lvs. silvery-white; 'Glauca', lvs. glaucous; 'Nana', dwarf; 'Pendula', brs. drooping.

procera Rehd. [*A. nobilis* (Dougl. ex D. Don) Lindl., not A. Dietr.]. NOBLE F. To 150 ft. or more, branchlets reddish-pubescent; lvs. to 1½ in. long, rounded at apex, entire or slightly notched, bluish-green above; cones cylindric-oblong, to 10 in. long, green, becoming purplish-brown. Wash. to n. Calif. Zone 6, grows slowly in the East. Cv. 'Glauca'. Lvs. glaucous.

recurvata M. T. Mast. To 100 ft. or more, buds very resinous, branchlets glabrous, yellow-gray; lvs. ½–1½ in. long, acute, glossy green above, those on upper side somewhat recurved; cones 2–4 in. long, violet-purple, turning gray-brown. W. China. Zone 5b.

religiosa (HBK) Schlechtend. & Cham. To 100 ft. or more; lvs. spirally arranged, to 1¼ in. long, acute at apex, green above, glaucous beneath; cones cylindric-oblong, to 6 in. long, violet-blue. Mex.

sachalinensis (Friedr.Schmidt) M. T. Mast. SAKHALIN F. To 100 ft. or more, branchlets pubescent in a shallow groove; lvs. to 1½ in. long, entire or slightly notched and rounded at apex, bright green; cones cylindrical, to 3 in. long, greenish-purple to blackish-brown, bracts exserted and recurved. N. Japan, Sakhalin. Zone 3.

sibirica Ledeb. To 90 ft., branchlets gray, puberulent; lvs. to 1¼ in. long, rounded at apex, entire or notched, bright green and grooved above; cones cylindrical, to 3 in. long, bluish. N. Eurasia. Zone 3. Sometimes injured by hot dry summers.

spectabilis (D. Don) G. Don [*A. Webbiana* (D.Don) Lindl.]. HIMALAYAN F. To 100 ft. or more, brs. spreading, branchlets grooved, pubescent; lvs. to 2¼ in. long, rounded or notched at apex, glossy dark green above; cones cylindrical, to 7 in. long, violet-purple. Himalayas. Zone 6b. Material listed as this sp. may be *A. Mariesii*.

umbellata: *A. homolepis* cv.

Veitchii Lindl. To 75 ft.; branchlets densely pubescent; lvs. crowded, to 1 in. long, notched at apex, glossy dark green above; cones cylindrical, to 2½ in. long, bluish-purple, bracts exserted and reflexed. Japan. Zone 4. Var. **nikkoensis** Mayr. Cones smaller and bracts included.

venusta: *A. bracteata*.

Webbiana: *A. spectabilis*.

ABOBRA Naud. *Cucurbitaceae.* One sp., widely distributed in temp. S. Amer.; a dioecious vine with mostly forked tendrils; fls. small, green, axillary, solitary or racemose, fragrant, corolla rotate, 5-parted, woolly within, male fls. with 3 separate stamens, anthers flexuous, female fls. with 3-celled ovary, each cell with 2 erect basal ovules; fr. ovoid, berrylike.

tenuifolia (Gillies) Cogn. Per., 10–30 ft., with fleshy root and herbaceous sts.; lvs. broad-ovate in outline, 2–5 in. long and almost as wide, deeply 3–5-lobed and dissected, with linear segms., more or less white-dotted; fr. smooth, ⁵⁄₁₆–½ in. long, becoming bright red. Sometimes grown under glass for its ornamental fr. and finely cut lvs.

ABRONIA Juss. [*Tripterocalyx* (Torr.) Hook.]. SAND VERBENA. *Nyctaginaceae.* About 25 spp. of trailing or low, ann. or per. herbs, native to w. N. Amer.; sts. often viscid; lvs. opp.; fls. bisexual, fragrant, red, yellow, or white, verbenalike, in a peduncled showy head subtended by 5–8 bracts, calyx corollalike, salverform, with 4–5-lobed limb, stamens 4–5, stigma linear; fr. an achene, usually winged.

A few species are of minor importance for borders and flower gardens in sunny exposures. They are treated as annuals. For early summer bloom, seeds may be started indoors, but they are usually sown directly in the open ground; in mild climates seeds may be sown in the autumn. Remove the husk before planting; the seeds are often slow in germinating.

alba var. **platyphylla:** *A. umbellata* subsp. *platyphylla*.

arenaria: *A. latifolia*.

cycloptera A. Gray [*Tripterocalyx cyclopterus* (A. Gray) Standl.]. Erect or decumbent, to 2 ft., brs. sparsely scabrous or glabrate; lvs. to 3 in. long; fls. bright pink, to 1⅜ in. long; fr. hard, 3-winged, with 3 ribs between each 2 wings. Tex., New Mex., n. Mex.

fragrans Nutt. Erect per., to 10 in.; lvs. usually ovate, pale beneath; fls. white, to 1 in. long, night-blooming. B.C. to n. Mex.

latifolia Eschsch. [*A. arenaria* Menz.]. YELLOW S.V. Per., prostrate; fls. lemon-yellow. Coast, Calif. to B.C.

maritima Nutt. ex S. Wats. RED S.V. Prostrate herb, sts. succulent, somewhat villous; lvs. round to elliptic; fls. dark red; fr. with mostly 5 winglike lobes. Seashores, Calif. and Baja Calif.

pinetorum: *A. villosa* var. *aurita*.

pogonantha Heimerl. MOJAVE S.V. Trailing, glandular-villous per.; lvs. oblong-ovate to orbicular, to 1½ in. long; fls. 5-merous, pale lavender or purple; fr. usually 2-winged. Desert, Calif.

tripterocalyx: a listed name of no botanical standing, possibly referable to *A. cycloptera*.

umbellata Lam. PINK S.V., BEACH S.V. Per., prostrate, glabrous to viscid-puberulent; calyx rose or rarely whitish; fr. opaquely 2-4-5-winged, not veined. Coastal Calif. to B.C. The commonly cult. sp.; variable, with several subspp. Subsp. **platyphylla** (Standl.) Munz [*A. alba* Eastw. var. *platyphylla* (Standl.) Jeps.]. Sts. villous; lvs. irregular in outline; fr. with membranous wings. San Diego to Baja Calif. Cv. 'Grandiflora'. Fls. Larger. Cv. 'Rosea'. Fls. pale.

villosa S. Wats. DESERT S.V. Similar to *A. umbellata* but ann., with glandular-villous pubescence. Var. **villosa**. The typical var.; calyx purplish-rose, ½–⅝ in. long; fr. opaquely 3-4-winged, with coarse veins. Nev. and Calif., s. to Ariz. and Baja Calif. Var. **aurita** (Abrams) Jeps. [*A. pinetorum* Abrams]. Calyx longer, ⅝–1 in. long; fr. with almost no veins. Calif.

ABRUS L. *Leguminosae* (subfamily *Faboideae*). Four or more spp. of slender, more or less woody vines of pantrop. distribution; lvs. alt., pinnate, lfts. many, small; fls. in axillary racemes, small, papilionaceous, stamens 9, united; fr. a short legume.

Roots yield a licoricelike substance. Sometimes grown for the interesting seeds often made into necklaces. The seeds, however, are exceedingly poisonous if chewed and eaten, and a single seed can be fatal. Propagated by seeds which germinate more quickly if soaked, or by cuttings of firm shoots in sand under glass.

precatorius L. ROSARY PEA, LOVE P., INDIAN LICORICE, WILD L., LICORICE VINE, WEATHER PLANT, WEATHER VINE, PRAYER-BEADS, CORAL-BEAD PLANT, RED-BEAD VINE, CRAB'S-EYE. Twining, to 10 ft.; fls. rose to purple, rarely white; fr. oblong, to 1½ in. long, seeds glossy, scarlet, black at base, poisonous. Tropics, widely naturalized, including s. Fla. Zone 10b.

pulchellus Wallich. Twining, to 20 ft.; fls. pale purple; fr. linear, to 2 in. long. Trop. Afr. to Malay Pen.

ABUTILON Mill. FLOWERING MAPLE, PARLOR M., INDIAN MALLOW. *Malvaceae.* About 150 spp. of per. herbs, softwoody shrubs, or rarely ann. herbs, in trop. and most warm-temp. regions of the world; lvs. simple, often cordate-ovate and unlobed, or palmately 3-, 5-, or 7-lobed; fls. axillary, solitary or in cymes, sometimes in panicles, involucral bracts 0, petals 5, white, yellow, orange or reddish-purple, sometimes strikingly veined, stamens united in a tubular column, style brs. as many as the mericarps, stigmas terminal; fr. a schizocarp, mericarps 5 to many, in a single whorl, each with 2–9 seeds in a single, longitudinal row.

Abutilons are used as house plants and for bedding, and one species is cultivated in China for its fiber. *Abutilon megapotamicum* makes an attractive basket plant. Propagated by seeds or cuttings. For bloom in the winter and spring, plants grown in the open may be taken up in the autumn and half the new growth removed.

auratum: a listed name of no botanical standing.

Avicennae: *A. Theophrasti*.

grandiflorum G. Don. Softly velvety ann. or short-lived per., to about 5 ft.; lvs. cordate-ovate, to 6 in. long, long-acuminate, unlobed; fls. solitary, on axillary peduncles to 3 in. long, calyx about ⅝ in. long, lobed to about the middle, enlarging in fr., petals yellow, slightly longer than calyx; mericarps about 20, triangularly pointed or short-awned apically, 2–3-seeded. Cent. and s. Afr. Probably not in cult.; plants listed under this name are *A. hybridum*.

hybridum Hort. CHINESE-LANTERN. Cultigens; usually glabrate, soft-woody shrubs; lvs. unlobed or 3-, or 5-lobed, green or variegated; fls. mostly solitary, on elongate axillary peduncles, often nodding, calyx to about 1 in. long, petals to about 2 in. long, in various shades and patterns of white, red, yellow, and orange. Most garden and greenhouse variants belong here. Zone 9b.

indicum (L.) Sweet. Gray-pubescent per., to 6 ft.; lvs. to 4 in. long and wide, cordate, acuminate, unlobed or shallowly 3-lobed, serrate; fls. solitary on axillary peduncles 1½–3½ in. long, yellow, 1 in. across; fr. pubescent, yellow-green when young, black at maturity, mericarps about 20, apically rounded, 3-seeded. Trop., Old World; naturalized in Fla., W. Indies, trop. Amer.

insigne Planch. A reddish-pubescent shrub, to 4 ft.; lvs. cordate-ovate, 5 in. long or more, coarsely serrate-dentate, upper lvs. unlobed, lower lvs. shallowly 3-lobed; fls. 3–7 on flexuous, axillary peduncles, calyx tubular-campanulate, cleft only in the upper ⅓, corolla campanulate, petals to 2 in. long, whitish or rose, with heavier crimson veins, margins often erose. Colombia and Venezuela.

maximum: a listed name of no botanical standing. Plants offered under this name usually are *A. hybridum*, but the name has been used for *A. pictum* and *A. mollissimum*.

megapotamicum (K. Spreng.) St.-Hil. & Naud. [*A. vexillarium* E. Morr.]. TRAILING A. Slender-branched shrubs, 2–6 ft.; lvs. usually arrow-shaped, sometimes shallowly 3-lobed; fls. solitary, axillary, nodding, resembling a fuchsia, calyx tubular, red, petals closed, yellow, staminal column purplish, exserted. S. Brazil. Usually grown in the North as a winter- and spring-flowering basket plant, but will survive outdoors in the far South and s. Calif. Zone 9b. Cv. 'Variegata'. Lvs. mottled.

×**Milleri** Hort.: presumably *A. megapotamicum* × *A. pictum*. Similar to *A. megapotamicum*, but having lvs. perhaps broader and larger; fls. sometimes in axillary pairs, calyx greenish, with a rosy hue, slightly expanded, corolla campanulate, petals yellow with crimson veins, staminal column carmine.

mollissimum (Cav.) Sweet. Shrubby or subarborescent, 3–9 ft., upper brs. pilose with long, simple, spreading or reflexed hairs; lvs. to 6 in. long and nearly as broad, cordate, acuminate, unlobed or slightly 3-lobed; fls. 1–5 on long, axillary peduncles, about 1 in. across, corollas sulphur-yellow. S. Amer. Should be grown as a summer-flowering ann.

pictum (Gillies ex Hook. & Arn.) Walp. [*A. striatum* G. Dickson ex Lindl.]. Shrub or subarborescent, to 15 ft., brs. slender, glabrous; lvs.

maplelike 3-, 5-, or 7-lobed or sometimes unlobed in upper part of plant, 2–6 in. long and nearly as broad; fls. solitary, on axillary peduncles to 6 in. long, nodding, calyx deeply cleft, downy-pubescent, petals ¾–2 in. long, yellowish or yellow-orange with deep crimson veins, staminal column slightly longer than petals. Brazil; naturalized or perhaps native in other S. and Cent. Amer. countries also. Widely cult. in the tropics and may be grown outdoors in the s. U.S. and Calif. Cv. 'Thompsonii' [*A. Thompsonii* Hort. Veitch]. Lvs. variegated. Cv. 'Pleniflorum' [*A. pleniflorum* N.E.Br.]. Fls. double; lvs. green or variegated.

pleniflorum: *A. pictum* cv.

sanguineum: a listed name of no botanical standing, apparently belongs to *A. hybridum*.

Savitzii: a listed name of no botanical standing; offered as a plant with white and green foliage and belongs to *A. hybridum*.

speciosum G. Don. Apparently not in cult.; plants offered under this name are selections of either *A. hybridum* or *A. pictum*.

splendens: a listed name of no botanical standing; plants offered under this name are apparently *A. hybridum*.

striatum: *A. pictum*.

Theophrasti Medic. [*A. Avicennae* Gaertn.; *Sida Abutilon* L.]. VELVETLEAF, BUTTER-PRINT, PIE-MARKER, INDIAN MALLOW, CHINA JUTE. Ann. herb, 2–6 ft.; lvs. ovate-orbicular, up to 1 ft. across, acuminate, cordate, velvety-pubescent; fls. yellow, about 1½ in. across; mericarps about 15, long-awned apically, many-seeded. Trop. Asia; naturalized and weedy in U.S. An important fiber plant of n. China.

Thompsonii: *A. pictum* cv.

variegatum: a listed name of no botanical standing; has been used for forms of *A. hybridum, A. megapotamicum,* and *A. pictum* with mottled lvs.

vexillarium: *A. megapotamicum*.

vitifolium: *Corynabutilon vitifolium*.

ACACIA Mill. *Leguminosae* (subfamily *Mimosoideae*). Perhaps 800 spp. of shrubs and trees, mostly of dry trop. or warm-temp. regions, particularly Australia, where they are known as wattles; lvs. alt., 2-pinnate, or reduced to leaflike petioles (phyllodes) resembling simple lvs., stipules sometimes modified into spines; fls. mostly yellow, regular, 4–5-merous, arranged in peduncled heads or spikes, mostly in early spring, stamens indefinite, mostly many, filaments separate; fr. an ovate to linear legume, sometimes constricted between seeds.

Some species are important for timber, tanbark, dyewood, gums, or other commercial products. Ornamental acacias are grown extensively outdoors in warmer parts of the U. S, particularly on the West Coast (Zone 9) and in Hawaii, for their showy flowers and flowering branches; one species, *A. dealbata,* is sometimes marketed as mimosa by florists. Acacias are usually tender at temperatures below 18–20° F. They grow quickly, but are short-lived. In cold climates, plants are often grown under glass for spring bloom, but are not usually well-adapted to forcing. They need plenty of water and sunshine, and should be pruned after blooming and set outdoors for the summer.

Propagation is by seeds. Germination is hastened by softening the hard seed coats either by dropping seeds in boiling water and leaving them to soak in the cooling water until the seeds are inflated (mostly 4–5 days), or by putting them in hot ashes and leaving until cool. Propagated also by cuttings of half-ripened wood with a heel.

abyssinica Hochst. ex Benth. Tree, with flat-topped crown, sts. villous, spines very short or absent; lvs. 2-pinnate, lfts. linear, ⅛ in. long; heads 3–6 together, axillary; fr. 3–5 in. long, Ethiopia.

accola Maiden & Betche. Glabrous shrub, to 8 ft.; phyllodes linear, 3–5 in. long, 1-nerved; heads several in racemes 1½–2 in. long; fr. to 4 in. long, ½ in. wide, flat, with waxy luster. Australia, where it is known as WALLANGARRA. Probably not distinct from *A. adunca*.

achras: a listed name of no botanical standing.

acinacea Lindl. GOLD-DUST A. Diffuse shrub, 5–8 ft.; phyllodes oblong, to ½ in. long; fl. heads solitary or 2–4 together, as long as phyllodes; fr. curved, often twisted, to 1½ in. long, E. Australia.

aculeatissima Macbr. [*A. tenuifolia* F. J. Muell., not L.]. Diffuse shrub with drooping branchlets; phyllodes linear-awl-shaped, to 1 in. long; fl. heads solitary; fr. to 3 in. long. Se. Australia.

acuminata Benth. Tree, to 40 ft.; phyllodes long-linear, to 10 in. long, ¼ in. wide, with fine parallel nerves; fls. in sessile spikes to 1 ft. long; fr. linear, less than ¼ in. across, somewhat constricted between seeds. W. Australia, where it is known as the RASPBERRY-JAM TREE.

Adansonii: *A. nilotica* subsp.

adunca A. Cunn. Shrub, to 10 ft., with brown bark, young brs. cylindrical; phyllodes many, narrowly linear, acute, to 4⅜ in. long, less

than ⅛ in. wide; fl. heads globose, in 5–8-fld. axillary racemes, pale yellow; fr. 2–3 in. long, ¼ in. across, constricted between seeds. E. Australia.

alata R. Br. Differs from *A. glaucoptera* in having decurrent part of phyllodes linear-oblong, to 2 in. long and ½ in. wide, the lobes flaring, truncate, the lower angle tipped with slender spine, the upper tipped with a gland; heads 6–10-fld. W. Australia.

albida Delile. Tree, to 90 ft., young twigs white, spines straight, in pairs, 1 in. long; lvs. 2-pinnate, lfts. blue-green; fls. cream, in long spikes; fr. oblong, to 4 in. long, very twisted. Trop. Afr. to Transvaal. Known in Afr. as APPLE-RING A. and WINTER THORN.

aneura F. J. Muell. MULGA. Shrub or small tree; phyllodes narrow-linear, to 3 in. long; fls. in spikes to ¾ in. long; fr. oblong, to 1½ in. long. Australia.

angustissima (Mill.) O. Kuntze. Unarmed shrub, to 5 ft., sts. deeply grooved; lvs. 2-pinnate, lfts. linear-oblong, less than ¼ in. long; fls. white, tinged pink or lavender, in subracemose heads; fr. oblong, to 4 in. long. S. U.S., Mex. to Costa Rica.

arabica: *A. nilotica* subsp. *tomentosa.* Var. **tomentosa:** *A nilotica* subsp.

argophylla: a listed name of no botanical standing; possibly intended for *A. argyrophylla*.

argyrophylla Hook. Perhaps not specifically distinct from *A. brachybotrya,* but differing in having phyllodes with silvery hairs, golden while young, peduncles golden-pubescent. Australia.

armata R. Br. [*A. ornithophora* Sweet]. KANGAROO THORN. Bushy shrub, to 10 ft., spines ½ in. long; phyllodes semi-ovate, obliquely oblong or curved-lanceolate, to 1 in. long; fl. heads ¼ in. across, solitary; fr. to 2 in. long. New S. Wales (Australia). Zone 8b. Used as hedge or sand binder. Cv. 'Pendula' is listed. Var. **angustifolia** Benth. [var. *paradoxa* Hort.; *A. paradoxa* DC.]. Phyllodes narrower.

aspera Lindl. Spreading shrub, to 4 ft., very resinous and viscid; phyllodes oblong-linear, to 1½ in. long; fl. heads solitary or in pairs; fr. to 2 in. long, constricted between seeds. Se. Australia.

auriculiformis A. Cunn. ex Benth. Small tree; phyllodes oblong-curved, to 8 in. long; fl. heads in short, racemose spikes; fr. much-twisted. Trop. n. Australia.

Baileyana F. J. Muell. COOTAMUNDRA WATTLE, GOLDEN MIMOSA. shrub or small tree; lvs. 2-pinnate, lfts. to ¼ in. long, gray-glaucous; fl. heads about ⅛ in. across, in racemes to 3 in. long or more; fr. to 4 in. long, glaucous. Se. Australia. Cv. 'Purpurea'. Foliage purple-tinged.

Berlandieri Benth. Pubescent shrub, to 15 ft., armed with short spines; lvs. 2-pinnate, lfts. oblong-linear, less than ¼ in. long; fls. fragrant, white, in solitary, axillary heads; fr. flat, to 6 in. long, linear-oblong, velvety-pubescent. Tex., ne. Mex.

binervata DC. Shrub or tree, to 40 ft.; phyllodes curved, oblong to lanceolate, to 4 in. long; fl. heads in short racemes; fr. to 5 in. long. E. Australia.

binervia (H. L. Wendl.) Macbr. [*A. glaucescens* Willd.]. COASTAL MYALL, SALLY WATTLE. Tree, to 60 ft.; phyllodes lanceolate or curved, to 6 in. long, gray-pubescent; fls. in spikes to 2 in. long; fr. twisted or coiled, 2–3 in. long. E. Australia.

brachybotrya Benth. GRAY MULGA. Tall shrub, glaucous or silvery-pubescent; phyllodes obovate or oblong, to 1 in. long or more; fl. heads in short racemes or solitary; fr. linear. Australia.

Brownii: *A. juniperina* cv.

buxifolia A. Cunn. Shrub, brs. angular; phyllodes oblong-lanceolate, somewhat curved, mostly 1 in. long or less, thickish, veins not prominent; fl. heads globose, small; fr. flat, ⁵⁄₁₆ in. across or less. Se. Australia.

Bynoeana Benth. DWARF NEALIE. Viscous shrub, to 6 ft.; phyllodes linear or linear-lanceolate, nearly cylindrical, to 1 in. long, curved at tip; fl. heads solitary, or paired on a short common rachis; fr. linear, much-curved and often twisted, to 2½ in. long. E. Australia. Material cult. under this name may be *A. sclerophylla*.

caffra Willd. Tree, to 30 ft., with few, small, hooked spines in pairs below nodes; lvs. 2-pinnate, lfts. linear, ⁵⁄₁₆ in. long; spikes 2–3 in. long, solitary or 2–3 together; fls. pale yellow, darker in age; fr. flat, oblong, 4 in. long. Trop. Afr. to S. Afr.

calamifolia Sweet ex Lindl. BROOM WATTLE, WALLOWA. Tall shrub; phyllodes narrow-linear, to 4 in. long; fl. heads small, 3–4 in short racemes, or solitary; fr. to 6 in. long, constricted between seeds. Se. Australia.

cardiophylla A. Cunn. ex Benth. WYALONG WATTLE. Shrub, to 10 ft.; lvs. 2-pinnate, lfts. very small, soft-pubescent; fls. golden, in small heads in axillary racemes, nearly as long as lvs. Se. Australia.

Catechu (L.f.) Willd. CATECHU, WADALEE-GUM TREE, KHAIR, CUTCH, BLACK C. Tree, with short hooked spines; lvs. 2-pinnate, lfts.

¼ in. long; spikes to 5 in. long; fls. dark yellow, solitary or 2–3 together; fr. narrow, to 3 in. long. W. Pakistan to Burma. Heartwood yields the important brown khaki dye, black cutch.

Cavenia (Mol.) Mol. ESPINO-CAVAN. Shrub, to 20 ft., with stout spines; lvs. 2-pinnate; fl. heads clustered; fr. oblong. Chile. May not be specifically distinct from *A. Farnesiana.* Good for hedges because of stout spines.

confusa Merrill. Tree, to 50 ft., with cylindrical branchlets; phyllodes narrow-linear, to 5 in. long or more, rather obtuse, about 5-nerved; fl. heads axillary, solitary; fr. 3 in. long or more, somewhat inflated, more or less constricted. Philippine Is., Taiwan.

constricta Benth. Shrub, to 10 ft. or more, spiny; lvs. 2-pinnate, lfts. to ¼ in. long; fls. bright yellow, fragrant, in heads; fr. to 5 in. long, constricted between seeds. Tex to Ariz.; Mex.

cornigera (L.) Willd. [*A. spadicigera* Schlechtend. & Cham.]. BULL-HORN A., SWOLLEN-THORN A. Shrub or small tree, with large, paired, inflated, partly hollow spines resembling cattle horns, often twisted, usually round in cross section; lvs. 2-pinnate, with elongated petiolar nectaries, lfts. ¼ in. long; fls. yellow, in dense, very elongated spikes to 1½ in. long; fr. cylindrical, to 2½ in. long, beaked, indehiscent. Wet sites in lowlands, Mex. to Costa Rica; naturalized in W. Indies and subtrop. Fla. Zone 10b. A well-known trop. ant plant; where native, thorns always inhabited by biting ants, which protect plant against herbivores. Grown as a curiosity.

crassiuscula H. L. Wendl. Shrub, brs. slightly angled; phyllodes many, linear, obtuse or short-pointed, to 3 in. long, 1-nerved, thickish; fl. heads globose, 10–15-fld., in short, axillary racemes on thick peduncles; fr. linear, flat, ⅛ in. across. E. Australia, Tasmania.

cultriformis A. Cunn. KNIFE A. Tall shrub; phyllodes obliquely obovate, attached at one angle, with rib clearly paralleling lower side, to 1 in. long, gray-glaucous; fl. heads about ⅛ in. across, in long racemes at ends of brs.; fr. to 3 in. long, glaucous. E. Australia.

cuneata Benth. Tall shrub; phyllodes similar to *A. cultriformis,* but rib more central; fl. heads solitary, on peduncles nearly as long as phyllodes; fr. to 3 in. long, curved, hirsute. W. Australia.

cyanophylla Lindl. ORANGE WATTLE, GOLDEN WILLOW, PORT JACKSON W. Stoloniferous shrub, to 18 ft.; phyllodes linear-oblong to curved-lanceolate, 6–12 in. long; fl. heads ¼ in. across or more, in short racemes; fr. 5 in. long, constricted between seeds. W. Australia, where it is known as BLUE-LEAF WATTLE.

cyclopis A. Cunn. COASTAL WATTLE. Shrub, to 10 ft.; phyllodes narrow-oblong, to 3½ in. long; fl. heads solitary or in short racemes; fr. to 2½ in. long, curved or twisted. W. Australia.

dealbata Link. SILVER WATTLE, MIMOSA. Similar to *A. decurrens,* but bark, brs., and foliage silvery-gray; fls. highly scented. Tasmania, se. Australia. Zone 8b. Produces a gum arabic substitute. Profuse bloomer, cult. in s. France for perfumery. The sp. most frequently sold by florists as "mimosa." Sometimes considered a var. of *A. decurrens.*

Deanei (R. T. Bak.) R. T. Bak. ex Welch, Coombs, & McGlynn. Probably only a var. of *A. decurrens,* differing in having few pairs of lfts. and coarser pinnules. New S. Wales.

decipiens R. Br. Bushy shrub, to 12 ft.; phyllodes rigid, triangular to almost unequally 4-sided, to ⅝ in. long; fl. heads solitary or paired; fr. thick, to 2 in. long, much-curved. W. Australia.

decora Rchb. GRACEFUL WATTLE. Shrub, with angled branchlets; phyllodes lanceolate or linear, to 2 in. long, 1-nerved; fl. heads globose, in racemes longer than phyllodes; fr. flat, about ¼ in. across, scarcely constricted between seeds. E. Australia.

decurrens (J. C. Wendl.) Willd. [*A. decurrens* var. *normalis* Benth.]. Evergreen tree, to 60 ft. or more, bark olive-green to dark gray; lvs. dark green, 2-pinnate, lfts. in 16–70 pairs, to ½ in. long or more; fl. heads ¼ in. across, in racemes; fr. to 4 in. long. E. Australia. Most material cult. under this name is *A. Mearnsii.* Var. **mollis** Lindl.: *A. Mearnsii.* Var. **normalis:** typical *A. decurrens.*

dentifera Benth. Tall shrub; phyllodes narrowly linear, to 8 in. long; fl. heads solitary or paired; fr. straight or curved, flat, to 3 in. long, 5/16 in. across. W. Australia.

Dietrichiana F. J. Muell. Shrub, with viscid branchlets; phyllodes linear, to 3 in. long or more; fl. heads about ⅛ in. across, solitary; fr. 2½ in. long, constricted between seeds. Queensland (Australia). Material cult. under this name may be *A. suaveolens.*

diffusa Lindl. Shrub, to 6 ft., with pendent brs., branchlets angular; phyllodes stiff, linear, ¾ in. long; fl. heads mostly paired; fr. linear, to 4 in. long. Se. Australia.

discolor: *A. paniculata.*

dodonaeifolia (Pers.) Willd. Tall shrub; phyllodes lanceolate, to 4 in. long; fl. heads solitary or paired; fr. long and flat. S. Australia.

Drummondii Lindl. Shrub or small tree; lvs. 2-pinnate, lfts. ¼ in. long; fl. heads in dense, drooping spikes to 1½ in. long; fr. to 1 in. long. W. Australia.

eburnea Willd. Shrub, with spines to 2 in. long; lvs. 2-pinnate, lfts. to ⅛ in. long, gray-green; fl. heads less than ½ in. across, solitary; fr. narrow, to 6 in. long. Arabia to India and Ceylon.

elata: *A. terminalis.*

elongata Sieber ex DC. SWAMP WATTLE. Tall shrub; phyllodes narrow-linear, to 4 in. long; fl. heads solitary or paired; fr. to 2½ in. long. Se. Australia.

extensa Lindl. Shrub, to 5 ft.; phyllodes linear, to 4 in. long or more, resembling branchlets; fl. heads solitary or in short racemes; fr. to 4 in. long, constricted between seeds. W. Australia.

falcata Willd. Shrub or small tree; phyllodes curved-lanceolate, to 6 in. long or more; fl. heads to ¼ in. across, in short racemes; fr. to 3 in. long. E. Australia.

farinosa Lindl. Low shrub, with mealy branchlets; phyllodes broad-linear, often curved, to 1½ in. long; fl. heads paired; fr. linear, to 2 in. long, curved and twisted. Se. Australia.

Farnesiana (L.) Willd. SWEET A., POPINAC, OPOPANAX, HUISACHE, CASSIE, WEST INDIAN BLACKTHORN, SPONGE TREE. Thorny, much-branched shrub, to 10 ft.; lvs. 2-pinnate, lfts. to 3/16 in. long; fl. heads ¼–½ in. across, in small clusters, fls. very fragrant; fr. thick, to 3 in. long. Subtrop. and trop. Amer.; now pantrop. Widely cult. for the essential oil obtained from its fls. (cassie flowers) used in making perfume.

floribunda (Venten.) Willd. [*A. longifolia* var. *floribunda* (Venten.) F. J. Muell.]. Shrub or small tree; phyllodes linear-lanceolate, to 4½ in. long, ½ in. wide, with several prominent longitudinal nerves, margin without a gland; fls. in loose, axillary spikes, yellowish-white; fr. narrowly oblong, to 2½ in. long, constricted between seeds. Se. Australia. Much material offered under this name is *A. retinodes* cv. 'Floribunda'.

Galpinii Davy. Tree, to 80 ft., with short, hooked spines in pairs; lvs. large, 2-pinnate, lfts. obtuse, ¼ in. long, glaucescent; fls. light yellow, in spikes to 2½ in. long, racemosely clustered on short axillary brs.; fr. narrow, 3–8 in. long, flat. S. Afr.

giraffae Burchell. CAMEL THORN. Tree, to 40 ft., with straight, stout spines in pairs; lvs. 2-pinnate; fl. heads in clusters, often appearing before lvs.; fr. curved-ellipsoid, to 5 in. long, gray-velutinous, indehiscent, spongy inside. S. Afr., Rhodesia.

gladiiformis A. Cunn. ex Benth. Shrub, to 9 ft.; phyllodes linear-lanceolate, curved, 4–6 in. long; fl. heads 4–15, in racemes shorter than phyllodes; fr. straight, linear, to 2¾ in. long. Se. Australia.

glandulicarpa Reader. Shrub, 1–5 ft., young shoots viscid; phyllodes oblique, oblong-ovate to rhomboid, to ⅜ in. long, undulate; fl. heads solitary or paired; fr. viscid, with glandular, whitish hairs, constricted between seeds. Se. Australia.

glaucescens: *A. binervia.*

glaucoptera Benth. Shrub, to 8 ft.; phyllodes nearly triangular, glaucous, all in 1 plane, decurrent and united to sts. forming a continuous but notched wing to ¾ in. wide on each side of st., lobes directed forward, tipped by stout spine; fls. golden, in solitary or paired heads, ¼ in. across; fr. small, spiralled. W. Australia.

Gnidium Benth. Unarmed tree, to 15 ft., brs. erect; phyllodes many, rigid, narrowly linear, to 2 in. long; fl. heads golden. Ne. Australia.

Greggii A. Gray. CATCLAW A., TEXAS MIMOSA. Shrub, sometimes tree, to 20 ft.; lvs. 2-pinnate; fls. pale yellow, in spikes to 2¼ in. long; fr. to 4 in. long, twisted. Summer. Tex. to Ariz.; Mex.

gummifera Willd. MOROCCO GUM, BARBARY G. Tree, to 30 ft., with spines; lvs. 2-pinnate; fl. heads in spikes; fr. white-tomentose, constricted between seeds. Morocco.

hakeoides A. Cunn. ex Benth. Small tree or shrub; phyllodes linear-spatulate, rigid, to 5 in. long and ½ in. wide, usually obtuse, 1-nerved; racemes of 6–12 heads, nearly as long as phyllodes; fr. flat, usually curved, much constricted between seeds. E. Australia.

hastulata Sm. Shrub, to 3 ft.; phyllodes crowded, ovate-triangular to unequally 4-sided, to ¼ in. long, spine-tipped; fl. heads solitary, ⅛ in. across or less; fr. to 2 in. long, curved. W. Australia.

hemiglauca: a listed name of no botanical standing.

heteroclita Meissn. Shrub, to 4 ft. or more; phyllodes linear-oblong to spatulate, 1½–2 in. long; fls. yellow, in small, solitary or paired, axillary heads; fr. linear-oblong, 2–3 in. long. W. Australia.

holosericea A. Cunn. Shrub or tree, to 20 ft., with triangular branchlets, younger parts white-silky-pubescent; phyllodes obovate to elliptic-oblong, to 6 in. long or more, 4-nerved; fl. heads in spikes to 2 in. long; fr. twisted. Ne. Australia.

homalophylla A. Cunn. ex Benth. GIDGEE MYALL, FRAGRANT M., MYALLWOOD, YARRAN, VIOLETWOOD. Small tree; phyllodes lanceolate to linear, to 3 in. long; fl. heads paired or clustered; fr. linear, slightly curved. Australia.

horrida (L.) Willd. CAPE GUM. Low tree, with flat-topped crown, spines straight, to 2½ in. long; lvs. 2-pinnate, lfts. to ¼ in. long; fl. spikes many on leafless brs.; fr. oblong, to 2 in. long, flat, thin. India. Doubtfully in cult.; material offered under this name is probably *A. Karroo.*

Howittii F. J. Muell. STICKY WATTLE. Viscid shrub, with streaked pubescent branchlets; phyllodes ovate, to ¾ in. long, densely minutely ciliate; fl. heads small, solitary or paired; fr. oblong, compressed, 2 in. long, minutely ciliate. Se. Australia. May not be distinct from *A. verniciflua* A. Cunn.

implexa Benth. SCREW-POD WATTLE, LIGHTWOOD. Tree, to 50 ft.; phyllodes curved-lanceolate, to 6 in. long or more; fl. heads in short racemes; fr. narrow-linear, much twisted, constricted between seeds. Australia.

iteaphylla F. J. Muell. Shrub, with drooping brs.; phyllodes broadly linear, to 4 in. long, with short, curved spiny tip; fl. heads in slender racemes shorter than phyllodes, each at first enclosed in a large brown bract; fr. linear, flattened, to 4¾ in. long. S. Australia.

Jonesii F. J. Muell. Slender shrub, to 8 ft.; branchlets hairy; lvs. 2-pinnate, lfts. ¼ in. long or less, nearly or quite linear; fl. heads racemose; fr. compressed and narrow, to 3 in. long. Se. Australia.

Julibrissin: *Albizia Julibrissin.*

juniperina Willd. PRICKLY WATTLE. Shrub, to 12 ft.; phyllodes linear, to ½ in. long; fl. heads solitary; fr. to 2 in. long, constricted between seeds. E. Australia. Cv. 'Brownii' [*A. Brownii* Steud.]. Dwarf, compact shrub, to 2 ft.; fls. very large, golden.

Karroo Hayne [*A. horrida* of auth., not Willd.]. KARROO THORN. Shrub or small tree, with sharp, ivory-white spines of older parts to 3 in. long; lvs. 2-pinnate, lfts. obovate-oblong to ¼ in. long; fl. heads clustered, peduncles bracted at middle; fls. fragrant; fr. narrow, to 5 in. long, straight or curved. S. Afr. Useful as hedge or sand binder.

Kettlewelliae Maiden. BUFFALO WATTLE. Shrub or small tree, branchlets angular; phyllodes silvery, oblanceolate, 2–3 in. long; fl. heads in dense racemes shorter than phyllodes; fr. flat, broad, constricted between seeds, glaucous. Se. Australia.

Koa A. Gray. KOA. Tree, to 60 ft.; phyllodes curved, to 5 in. long; fl. heads usually in short racemes; fr. to 6 in. long and 1 in. wide. Hawaii.

laevigata: *Prosopis juliflora.*

latifolia Benth. To 15 ft. or more, branchlets 2–3-angled or nearly narrowly winged; phyllodes ovate-rhomboid or curved, to 6 in. long and 2 in. wide, glaucous; fl. heads in loose spikes to 2 in. long; fr. to 4 in. long. Ne. Australia.

leprosa Sieber. ex DC. CINNAMON WATTLE. Shrub or small tree, branchlets pendent; phyllodes linear-lanceolate, to 3 in. long; fl. heads paired or clustered; fr. curved. Se. Australia.

leptoclada A. Cunn. ex Benth. Shrub; lvs. 2-pinnate, lfts. about ⅛ in. long; fl. heads small, in racemes longer than lvs.; fr. linear, to 2 in. long. E. Australia.

ligulata A. Cunn. ex Benth. Shrub, to about 15 ft.; phyllodes linear or linear-oblong, to 4 in. long, ⁵⁄₁₆ in. wide, 1-nerved; fl. heads bright yellow, solitary or 2–5 in racemes shorter than phyllodes; fr. to 4 in. long, brittle, constricted between seeds. Australia.

linearis (H. L. Wendl.) Macbr. [*A. linifolia* (Venten.) Willd.]. Tall shrub; phyllodes linear, to 1½ in. long; fl. heads in short racemes; fr. to 4 in. long. E Australia. *Acacia linearis* Sims is *A. longissima.*

linifolia: *A. linearis.*

longifolia (Andr.) Willd. SYDNEY GOLDEN WATTLE. Shrub or small tree; phyllodes oblong-lanceolate, to 6 in. long; fl. heads in loose spikes to 2¼ in. long; fr. linear, to 5 in. long. E. Australia. Var. **floribunda:** *A. floribunda.* Var. **Sophorae** (R. Br.) F. J. Muell. [*A. Sophorae* R. Br.]. Phyllodes obovate-oblong, very obtuse, rarely to 3 in. long and 1 in. across.

longissima H. L. Wendl. [*A. linearis* Sims, not H. L. Wendl.]. Shrub; phyllodes narrow-linear, to 6 in. long or more; fl. heads in loose spikes to 2 in. long; fr. to 4 in. long. Se. Australia.

lophantha: *Albizia distachya.*

macracanthoides Bertero ex DC. Shrub or tree, to 40 ft., spines essentially cylindrical, mostly less than 1½ in. long; lvs. 2-pinnate, lfts. many, about ¼ in. long; fl. heads long-peduncled, mostly paired; fr. flat, 3 in. long or more, about ⁵⁄₁₆ in. across. W. Indies, Venezuela.

Mearnsii DeWild. [*A. decurrens* var. *mollis* Lindl.; *A. mollissima* of auth., not Willd.]. BLACK WATTLE. Similar to *A. decurrens,* but lfts. proportionately broader, less than ¼ in. long, softly tomentose, yellowish when young. Tasmania, se. Australia. Cult. widely as an important source of tanbark.

Meissneri Lehm. Tall shrub; phyllodes oblique, obovate-oblong, to 1 in. long; fl. heads solitary; fr. long and narrow. W. Australia.

melanoxylon R. Br. BLACKWOOD A., AUSTRALIAN BLACKWOOD. Large evergreen tree; phyllodes mostly oblong-lanceolate, to 4 in. long, 1 in. wide, obtuse, young shoots often with 2-pinnate lvs.; fl. heads ¼ in. across, in short racemes, fls. cream-colored; fr. to 5 in. long, twisted. Tasmania, s. Australia. Zone 8b. An important timber tree where native.

modesta Wallich. Much-branched shrub or small tree, to 12 ft., spines short, paired, straight; lvs. 2-pinnate, lfts. oblong or nearly obovate, about ½ in. long, obtuse, gray-glaucous; fls. white, becoming yellowish, in drooping spikes 3 in. long; fr. flat, linear-oblong, 1 in. long. N. India.

mollissima: *A. pubescens;* but material offered under this name is probably *A. Mearnsii.*

montana Benth. Viscid shrub, to 6 ft.; phyllodes linear-oblong, to 1 in. long, obtuse; fl. heads solitary or paired; fr. linear, to 2 in. long, densely tomentose. E. Australia.

myrtifolia (Sm.) Willd. Shrub, 3–6 ft.; phyllodes obovate to linear, somewhat curved, to 2 in. long or more; fl. heads, in short racemes, fls. cream-colored; fr. to 3 in. long, curved. Australia.

nigricans R. Br. Shrub, to 6 ft.; lvs. 2-pinnate, lfts. to ⁵⁄₁₆ in. long; fl. heads solitary; fr. to 1½ in. long. W. Australia.

nilotica (L.) Delile [*A. scorpioides* (L.) W. F. Wight]. GUM-ARABIC TREE, SUNTWOOD, BABUL. Small to large tree, to 75 ft., spines straight, to 3 in. long; lvs. 2-pinnate, lfts. linear-oblong, ³⁄₁₆ in. long; fl. heads axillary, 2–6 together; fr. linear, to 6 in. long, almost indehiscent. Trop. Afr.; widely naturalized in India, where it supplies the most important local tanbark, a substitute gum arabic, and a strong tough timber. Subsp. **nilotica.** The typical subsp.; fr. glabrous, very narrowly constricted between seeds. Subsp. **Adansonii** (Guillem. & Perrottet) Brenan [var. *Adansoniana* (Dubard) A. F. Hill; *A. Adansonii* Guillem. & Perrottet]. Fr. scarcely constricted between seeds and slightly pubescent to nearly glabrous. Subsp. **tomentosa** (Benth.) Brenan [*A. arabica* (Lam.) Willd.; *A. arabica* var. *tomentosa* Benth.]. GUM-ARABIC TREE, EGYPTIAN MIMOSA, EGYPTIAN THORN. Fr. persistent gray-pubescent; the wounded bark yields an inferior gum arabic; true gum arabic comes from *A. Senegal.*

obliqua A. Cunn. ex Benth. Straggling, much-branched shrub; phyllodes oblique-obovate or orbicular, to ½ in. long; fl. heads solitary or paired; fr. to 2 in. long, spirally coiled. S. Australia.

obtusata Sieber ex DC. Tall shrub; phyllodes stiff, oblong-linear, to 3 in. long, very obtuse; fl. heads in short racemes. Se. Australia.

ornithophora: *A. armata.*

Oxycedrus Sieber ex DC. Stiff, spreading shrub; phyllodes rigid, linear-lanceolate, to 1 in. long; fl. heads in dense spikes 1 in. long; fr. to 3 in. long, nearly cylindrical. Se. Australia.

paniculata (H. L. Wendl.) Macbr. [*A. discolor* (Andr.) Willd.]. SUNSHINE WATTLE. Shrub or small tree; lvs. 2-pinnate, lfts. ¼ in. long, pale beneath; fl. heads in racemes; fr. to 3 in. long. Tasmania, s. Australia.

paradoxa: *A. armata* var. *angustifolia.*

pendula A. Cunn. WEEPING MYALL. Small tree, branchlets pendent; phyllodes stiff, linear-lanceolate, to 3 in. long, silver-gray; fl. heads paired or clustered; fr. to 3 in. long, sutures narrowly winged. E. Australia. Wood is violet-scented and is used for veneer and fancy boxes. Cv. 'Glauca' is listed.

penninervis Sieber ex DC. MOUNTAIN HICKORY, BLACKWOOD. Tree, to 40 ft. or more; phyllodes oblong to curved-lanceolate, to 4 in. long or more; fl. heads pale yellowish, to ¼ in. across, in loose racemes; fr. to 5 in. long. E. Australia.

podalyriifolia A. Cunn. QUEENSLAND SILVER WATTLE, MT. MORGAN W., PEARL W. Tall, glaucous, pubescent shrub; phyllodes ovate or oblong, to 1½ in. long; fl. heads in long racemes; fr. to 3 in. long. Ne. Australia.

polybotrya Benth. Tall shrub; lvs. 2-pinnate, lfts. obtuse, ⁵⁄₁₆ in. long, with nerve on lower edge; fl. heads many, in racemes longer than lvs. or forming a terminal panicle; fr. about 3½ in. long, constricted between seeds. E. Australia.

pravissima F. J. Muell. OVENS A., OVENS WATTLE. Shrub or tree, to 20 ft., branchlets angular; phyllodes many, obliquely obovate to somewhat unequally 4-sided, to about ½ in. long, 2-nerved; fl. heads small, many, in racemes much longer than phyllodes; fr. flat. Se. Australia.

prominens A. Cunn. GOLDEN-RAIN WATTLE. Perhaps not specifically distinct from *A. linearis,* from which it differs in having broader phyllodes and fr. Se. Australia.

pruinosa A. Cunn. ex Benth. FROSTY WATTLE. Glaucous, small tree; lvs. 2-pinnate, lfts. to ¾ in. long; fl. heads in racemes; fr. to 3 in. long. Se. Australia. Material cult. under this name may be *A. schinoides.*

pubescens (Venten.) Ait. f. [*A. mollissima* Willd.]. HAIRY WATTLE. Differs from *A. decurrens* in having coarse, spreading pubescence on branchlets and lf. rachises, and pinnae shorter, glabrous on both surfaces, with only 11–15 pairs of lfts. Australia. Doubtfully in cult.

pycnantha Benth. GOLDEN WATTLE. Small tree; phyllodes curved-lanceolate, to 6 in. long, 1½ in. wide, sometimes to 4 in. wide in seedlings; fl. heads ¼–⅜ in. across, 35-fld. or more, fragrant, in short racemes; fr. linear, flat. Se. Australia. Cult. widely as a tanbark.

regenis: a listed name of no botanical standing; possibly intended for *A. rigens*.

retinodes Schlechtend. WIRILDA. Shrub or small tree; phyllodes linear-lanceolate, to 5 in. long, nearly straight, with gland near base; fl. heads ¼ in. across, in branched racemes shorter than phyllodes; fr. narrow, to 8 in. long. S. Australia. Zone 8b. Fls. throughout the year. Cv. 'Floribunda' is listed.

Riceana Hensl. Shrub or small tree; phyllodes dark green, linear, to 1½ in. long; fl. heads in loose spikes to 2 in. long; fr. linear, to 3 in. long, constricted between seeds. Tasmania.

rigens A. Cunn. NEEDLE-BUSH WATTLE. Tall shrub; phyllodes slender, cylindrical, to 5 in. long, pubescent when young; fl. heads nearly sessile, 1–3 in axils; fr. linear, curved, twisted, sparsely pubescent, 2½ in. long. Se. Australia.

Roemerana Scheele. Shrub or tree, to 15 ft., spines short, mostly recurved; lvs. 2-pinnate, lfts. blunt, oblong or obovate, to ½ in. long; fl. heads solitary, axillary; fr. oblong, thin and flat, to 4 in. long. Tex., n. Mex.

rubida A. Cunn. RED-STEM A., RED-LEAVED WATTLE. Tall shrub, brs. reddish, angular; phyllodes oblong-lanceolate, often curved, 3–6 in. long, rib and margins reddish, true lvs. often present, 2-pinnate, foliage reddish in winter; fl. heads small, bright yellow, in racemes shorter than phyllodes; fr. linear, to 5 in. long. E. Australia.

salicina Lindl. WILLOW A., COOBA. Shrub or tree, to 45 ft., with pendent brs. and foliage; phyllodes oblong-linear, to 5 in. long; fl. heads pale yellow, in short racemes or solitary; fr. to 3 in. long. Australia.

saligna (Labill.) H. L. Wendl. Shrub or small tree; phyllodes curved-lanceolate, to 8 in. long or more; fl. heads ½ in. across, in racemes; fr. to 5 in. long, constricted between seeds. W. Australia, where it is called WEEPING WATTLE.

schinoides Benth. Tree, brs. glaucous; lvs. 2-pinnate, lfts. in 15–20 pairs, elliptic-oblong, to ¾ in. long, ⁵⁄₃₂ in. wide, acute to minutely pointed; fl. heads yellow, in axillary racemes or terminal compound racemes; fr. oblong, undulate, to 2¾ in. long, ¼ in. across. Se. Australia.

sclerophylla Lindl. Sticky shrub; phyllodes oblong-oblanceolate, to 1 in. long, ⅛ in. wide, 3–5-nerved; fl. heads axillary, usually paired, 12–20-fld.; fr. linear, to 2 in. long, ⅛ in. across, hard. S. Australia.

scorpioides: *A. nilotica.*

Senegal (L.) Willd. GUM-ARABIC TREE, SUDAN GUM-ARABIC. Shrub or small tree, to 30 ft., with flattened crown, nodes swollen, with 3 short spines, the middle one recurved; lvs. 2-pinnate, lfts. gray-green; spikes axillary, 2–4 in. long, 1–3 together; fls. cream; fr. oblong, flat, to 4 in. long. Arid areas, Senegal to Nigeria. Tapped trees are a source of the true gum arabic of commerce.

Seyal Delile. GUM-ARABIC TREE, WHISTLING TREE, THIRTY THORN. Tree, to 30 ft., crown flat-topped, spines straight, to 2½ in. long, with short recurved prickles toward tips; lvs. 2-pinnate, lfts. to ³⁄₁₆ in. long; fls. fragrant, in heads, appearing before lvs.; fr. flat, narrow, 6 in. long. Egypt to Kenya. Yields a substitute gum arabic.

simplicifolia (L. f.) Druce. Unarmed tree, to 40 ft.; phyllodes broadly elliptic-ovate, to 4 in. long, several-veined; fl. heads small, globose, 1–3 in lf. axils; fr. to 6 in. long, somewhat constricted between seeds. New Hebrides, New Caledonia.

Sophorae: *A. longifolia* var.

spadicigera: *A. cornigera.*

spectabilis A. Cunn. ex Benth. GLORY WATTLE, MUDGEE W. Tall shrub, branchlets glaucescent; lvs. 2-pinnate, lfts. blue-green, obovate-oblong, to ½ in. long, obtuse, fleshy; fls. in many-headed racemes longer than lvs.; fr. to 4 in. long. E. Australia.

spinescens Benth. Rigid shrub, to 3 ft., branchlets mostly leafless, short, spine-tipped, sometimes retaining both phyllodes and lvs.; phyllodes to 2 in. long, lvs. pinnate; fl. heads sessile or very short-peduncled, along branchlets; fr. linear, curved, constricted between seeds, 1 in. long. E. Australia.

Steedmanii Maiden & Blakely. Shrub, to 4 ft., with angular branchlets; phyllodes lanceolate to broadly obovate, to 3½ in. long, obtuse; fl. heads in glaucous racemes shorter than phyllodes; fr. linear, glaucous, 2 in. long. W. Australia.

stenophylla A. Cunn. ex Benth. Tree; phyllodes linear, to 1 ft. long; fl. heads mostly in short racemes; fr. to 8 in. long, strongly constricted

between seeds. Australia, where known by the names DALBY MYALL and EUMONG.

suaveolens Willd. SWEET A. Shrub, to 6 ft.; phyllodes linear, to 6 in. long; fl. heads small, in racemes; fr. oblong, to 1½ in. long, glaucous. E. Australia.

subulata Bonpl. Shrub, to 10 ft.; phyllodes narrow-linear, to 6 in. long; fl. heads in slender racemes. Se. Australia.

Sutherlandii (F. J. Muell.) F. J. Muell. [*Albizia Sutherlandii* F. J. Muell.]. Tree, to 40 ft., with pendent branchlets; lvs. to 12 in. long, lfts. linear, to ⅛ in. long; fls. pale yellow, in solitary spikes to 2 in. long; fr. very thick, to 6 in. long, ¾ in. across. Ne. Australia.

tenuifolia: see *A. aculeatissima.*

terminalis (Salisb.) Macbr. [*A. elata* A. Cunn. ex Benth.]. CEDAR WATTLE, PEPPERMINT-TREE W. Tree, to 60 ft., young growth often golden-pubescent; lvs. 2-pinnate, lfts. to 2 in. long; fl. heads in racemes to 6 in. long; fr. to 6 in. long. Se. Australia.

texana: a listed name of no botanical standing; perhaps for *A. angustissima.*

tortuosa (L.) Willd. Shrub or low tree, to 15 ft., spines whitish, short; lvs. 2-pinnate, lfts. blunt, oblong-linear, ³⁄₁₆ in. long; fl. heads solitary or clustered; fr. nearly cylindrical, velvety, to 5 in. long. Mex., W. Indies.

torulosa Benth. Tall shrub or small tree, branchlets angular; phyllodes curved, linear-lanceolate, to 8 in. long; fl. spikes 1–3 together, to ¾ in. long; fr. long, oblong, constricted between seeds. Ne. Australia.

trineura F. J. Muell. Strongly scented, bushy shrub, branchlets glaucous; phyllodes cuneate-oblong, to 2 in. long, obtuse, mucronate; fl. heads 3–6 in very short racemes; fr. linear, 1 in. long, scarcely constricted between seeds. Australia.

undulifolia C. Fraser ex Lodd. Shrub or low bush, sometimes becoming large, fl. brs. long, pendent; phyllodes many, ovate to nearly orbicular, to 1 in. long or less, 1-nerved, undulate; fl. heads solitary, on slender peduncles often longer than phyllodes; fr. flat, to ¾ in. across. E. Australia.

verticillata (L'Hér.) Willd. Shrub or small tree; phyllodes in whorls, linear-subulate, to ¾ in. long; fl. heads in spikes 1 in. long; fr. to 3 in. long. Se. Australia. Zone 8b. In Victoria called PRICKLY MOSES.

vestita Ker-Gawl. WEEPING BOREE. Softly pubescent shrub, to 10 ft. or more; phyllodes many, gray-green, ovate-elliptic, slightly curved, undulate, about ½ in. long; fl. heads 10–20, in slender racemes much longer than phyllodes; fr. very flat, to 3 in. long. Se. Australia.

Victoriae Benth. BRAMBLE A., BRAMBLE WATTLE. Neat shrub, to 9 ft.; phyllodes glaucous, broad-linear, 1¼ in. long, sometimes with 2 spines ³⁄₁₆ in. long; fl. heads pale yellow, on slender, hoary peduncles in open racemes as long as phyllodes; fr. oblong, flattened, 2 in. long. E. Australia.

Visco Lorentz ex Griseb.: a name of uncertain application.

Woodii Davy. PAPER-BARK THORN. Large tree, young parts golden-tomentose, bark yellow-brown, flaking off, spines about ⅛ in. long; lvs. 2-pinnate, lfts. ³⁄₁₆ in. long; fls. heads solitary or paired, fls. cream; fr. woody, linear-oblong, to 6 in. long, dehiscent. S. Afr. By some considered a var. of *A. Sieberana* DC.

ACAENA L. *Rosaceae.* About 40 spp. of more or less woody or herbaceous, per. trailing plants, mainly in the mts. of the S. Hemisphere; lvs. pinnate; fls. inconspicuous, in globose heads or cylindrical spikes, sepals usually 4, petals 0; fr. a usually bristly or spiny achene.

Propagated by seeds, division, and cuttings. In mild climates used as a ground cover, sometimes in rock gardens.

anserinifolia (J. R. Forst. & G. Forst.) Druce [*A. Sanguisorbae* (L. f.) Vahl]. NEW ZEALAND BUR. Main sts. stout, woody, to 3 ft.; lvs. 2–3 in. long, lfts. 9–13, linear-oblong, toothed, brownish-green above, paler beneath; scapes ascending, to 4 in. or more, pilose heads, including spines, ⅝ in. in diam., spines 4, to ¼ in. long, brown or yellowish-green; anthers white. Australia, New Zeal.

argentea Ruiz & Pav. Sts. creeping, to 2 ft., densely hairy; lfts. 7–9, leathery, glabrous above, white-silky beneath, 1–1½ in. long, toothed; scape to 1 ft., head ½–1 in. in diam., including spines, spines 4, reddish, unequal. Andes.

Buchananii Hook. f. Main sts. subterranean, to 1½ ft.; lvs. 1–2 in. long, lfts. 11–13, densely hairy beneath, less so above, less than ³⁄₁₆ in. long, pale green; heads subsessile, ⅝–1 in. in diam., spines to ⅝ in. long, without barbs, pale to yellowish-green; anthers yellowish-white. New Zeal.

caesiiglauca (Bitter) Bergmans. Main sts. stout; lvs. 1½–2 in. long, lfts. 7–9, gray-glaucous, silky beneath; scapes to 6 in., pilose, heads to ¾ in. in diam., spines brown, to ³⁄₁₆ in. long; anthers white. New Zeal.

cylindristachys Ruiz & Pav. Sts. prostrate; lvs. 2–3 in. long, lfts. 9–11, nearly oblong, toothed, greenish above, silvery-silky beneath; scapes 4–8 in., heads spicate, ¾ in. long, spines 3–5, very unequal, ³⁄₁₆ in. long. Costa Rica to Bolivia.

fissistipula Bitter. Main sts. slender; lvs. 1–2 in. long, lfts. 7–11, broad, ⁵⁄₁₆ in. long, appressed-silky beneath; scapes 3 in., heads ⅜–¾ in. in diam., spines 4, pale red, barbed, ³⁄₁₆ in. long; anthers purple. New Zeal.

glabra J. Buchan. Main sts. to 1½ ft.; lvs. to 2 in. long, lfts. 7–11, incised-serrate, pale brownish-green; scapes often crowded, glabrous, to 4 in., heads to ¾ in. in diam., green to purplish, spines 4, to about ¹⁄₁₆ in. long; sepals 4, purple-margined. New Zeal.

glauca: a listed name of no botanical standing; said to be synonym of *A. caesiiglauca.*

glaucophylla: *A. magellanica.*

Hieronymii O. Kuntze. Like *A. pinnatifida*, but with achenes bristly at apex only. Argentina.

inermis Hook.f. Main sts. to 3 ft. or more; lvs. to 2 in. long, lfts. 7–15, glabrous to slightly hairy, ¼ in. long, crenate-dentate, purplish to olive- or bronze-green; scapes to 3 in., heads to ½ in. in diam.; sepals olive- to brownish-green, anthers white; achenes spineless. New Zeal.

magellanica (Lam.) Vahl [*A. glaucophylla* Bitter]. Sts. decumbent or creeping, to 3 ft. or more; lvs. to 4 in. long, lfts. about 15, pinnatifid, glabrous; anthers red. Patagonia.

microphylla Hook. f. Like *A. inermis*, but main sts. to 1 ft.; lvs. to 1 in. long, lfts. ⅛ in. long; scapes to 1 in., spines ⅜ in. long; stamens red. New Zeal. Zone 7?

myriophylla Lindl. Sts. ascending, very leafy, to 1½ ft.; lfts. 7–9, deeply cut, silky beneath; fls. green, in cylindrical spikes to 4 in. long; achene spines many, about ¹⁄₁₆ in. long, hooked. Chile.

novae-zelandiae T. Kirk. Main sts. stout, to 3 ft.; lvs. 2–4 in. long, lfts. 11–15, dark green and glabrous above, pale beneath, pilose on veins, ½ in. long; scapes 2–5 in., heads to 1½ in. in diam., including spines, these dark purple, to ⅜ in. long; anthers white. New Zeal.

ovalifolia Ruiz & Pav. Sprawling, densely leafy; lvs. 1½–4 in. long, lfts. 7–11, oblong, toothed, to 1 in. long or more, more or less hairy beneath; scape 3–5–(-10) in.; fls. in globose heads to ⅝ in. in diam., spines usually 2, purplish, sometimes to ½ in. long. Peru.

ovina A. Cunn. Lfts. ovate-oblong, deeply crenate, glabrous above, villous beneath; scapes to 9 in.; fls. in long interrupted spikes, anthers purple; achene with many short unequal prickles. Australia.

pinnatifida Ruiz & Pav. Lfts. 7–11, evergreen, deeply 3- or 5-parted into linear segms., glabrous above, hairy beneath; scapes erect, to 1 ft., spikes cylindrical, interrupted, to 9 in., spines several, stout, unequal, less than ³⁄₁₆ in. long, barbed throughout. Chile, where used medicinally.

Sanguisorbae: *A. anserinifolia.*

sericea Jacq.f. Lvs. rather long, lfts. 7–11, cuneate-oblong, silky beneath; scapes about 3 in., heads green, cylindrical. Patagonia.

ACALYPHA L. THREE-SEEDED MERCURY, COPPERLEAF. *Euphorbiaceae.* About 430 spp., mostly monoecious or dioecious shrubs, occasionally ann. or trees, with attractive foliage, native to subtrop. and trop. regions of both hemispheres; lvs. simple, alt., pinnately or palmately veined, petioled, usually toothed; fls. inconspicuous, usually in bracted, showy, axillary or terminal spikes or racemes, ovary usually 3-celled; fr. a caps.

Mostly conservatory ornamentals, also used for bedding, and for hedges and lawn specimens far south. Culture is simple. Propagated by cuttings taken from outdoor bedded plants in the autumn, from plants lifted in the autumn and cut back, and in summer from a stock kept from the previous season; the last is the best method, since cuttings may be obtained with a heel, which give excellent plants for use in the conservatory in autumn and winter.

Godseffiana: *A. Wilkesiana* cv.

hispida Burm.f. [*A. Sanderi* N. E. Br.; *A. Sanderana* Schum.]. CHENILLE PLANT, RED-HOT CATTAIL, RED CATTAIL, FOXTAIL, PHILIPPINE MEDUSA. Dioecious shrub, to 15 ft.; lvs. broadly ovate, to 9 in. long, acuminate, green; female spikes dense, pendent, to 1½ ft. long and 1 in. wide, red or purple. Probably originally native to the Malay Arch. Cv. 'Alba'. Fls. creamy-white.

Macafeeana: *A. Wilkesiana* cv.

marginata: *A. Wilkesiana* cv.

Miltoniana: a listed name of no botanical standing for *A. Wilkesiana* cv.

musaica: *A. Wilkesiana* cv.

obovata: *A. Wilkesiana* cv.

rhomboidea Raf. Monoecious ann., to 3 ft.; lvs. lanceolate to rhombic-ovate, 1–5 in. long, tapering to a blunt apex, coarse-toothed, essentially glabrous. Se. Canada, Minn. and Nebr., s. through Okla. and Fla.

Sanderi: *A. hispida.*

Sanderana: *A. hispida.*

tricolor: *A. Wilkesiana.*

Wilkesiana Müll. Arg. [*A. tricolor* Seem.]. JACOB'S-COAT, COPPERLEAF, FIRE-DRAGON, BEEFSTEAK PLANT, MATCH-ME-IF-YOU-CAN. Monoecious shrub, to 15 ft.; lvs. profuse, elliptic or ovate, 5–8 in. long, serrate, bronzy-green mottled with copper, red, or purple; spikes slender, 8 in. long, ¼ in. wide, reddish. Pacific Is. There are many cvs. in the trade, with lvs. variously colored: 'Godseffiana' [*A. Godseffiana* Hort. Sander ex M. T. Mast.], lvs. green with creamy-white margins; 'Macafeeana' [*A. Macafeeana* Hort. Veitch], lvs. red, marked crimson and bronze; 'Macrophylla', lvs. russet-brown; 'Marginata' [*A. marginata* Hort., not (Poir.) K. Spreng.], lvs. with crimson-colored or other-colored margins; 'Miltoniana', lvs. oblong, more or less drooping, with white, irregularly cut margins; 'Musaica' [*A. musaica* B. S. Williams], GIANT REDLEAF, lvs. green with orange and red markings; 'Obovata' [*A. obovata* Hort., not Benth.], lvs. becoming bronzy-green with rosy-pink margins. The many color strains of this plant are much planted in s. Fla. and the Amer. tropics, less in s. Calif.

ACANTHACEAE Juss. ACANTHUS FAMILY.˙Dicot.; about 250 genera and 2,500 spp. of mostly trop. herbs or shrubs, rarely trees of se. Asia, Afr., Brazil, Cent. Amer., the Medit. region, s. U.S., and Australia; lvs. opp., simple, mostly entire; infl. most commonly spicate, racemose, or glomerate, often with prominent, sometimes brightly colored bracts; fls. bisexual, calyx 4–5-parted, corolla somewhat regular to irregular, tubular, the limb 5-lobed or 2-lipped, stamens 2, or 4 in two pairs, ovary superior, 2-celled, each cell with usually 2–10 ovules, style slender; fr. mostly a 2-celled caps., sometimes dehiscing explosively, seeds in most genera, except *Thunbergia* among cult. genera, on small hooked stalks that aid in their dispersal. Cystoliths, seen as streaks or protuberances, especially on dried material, are usually present on sts. and lvs.

Classification has largely been based on such technical characters as anther shape and position and pollen surface, which exhibits a great variety of patterns; some genera and species are consequently difficult to identify accurately. The family is well known for its taxonomic problems. The cultivated genera are: *Acanthus, Anisacanthus, Aphelandra, Asystasia, Barleria, Chamaeranthemum, Crossandra, Dicliptera, Duvernoia, Dyschoriste, Eranthemum, Fittonia, Graptophyllum, Hemigraphis, Hygrophila, Hypoestes, Justicia, Lankesteria, Mackaya, Megaskepasma, Odontonema, Pachystachys, Peristrophe, Phlogacanthus, Pseuderanthemum, Ruellia, Ruspolia, Ruttya, Sanchezia, Schaueria, Sciaphyllum, Stenandrium, Strobilanthes, Thunbergia, Whitfieldia,* and *Xantheranthemum.*

ACANTHOCALYCIUM Backeb. *Cactaceae.* About 9 spp. of small cacti, native to n. Argentina; with habit of *Echinopsis*, but with a ring of hairlike staminodes below stamens and with fl. scales papery- to spiny-pointed, fls. mostly white or pink, tube short, fertile stamens in 1 series, filaments short. Perhaps referable to *Lobivia.*

For culture see *Cacti.*

chionanthum (Speg.) Backeb. Sts. to 3 in. high and 2½ in. thick, ribs 13–15, low; spines 7–9, radial, slender-awl-shaped, to ¾ in. long; fls. white, 1¾ in. long, staminodes brownish.

glaucum F. Ritter. Sts. to 6 in. high and 2¾ in. thick, glaucous, ribs 8–14; spines black, with pale base, radial spines 5–10, to ¾ in. long, central spines 0–2; fls. yellow, 2⅜ in. long, stamens white or yellow. Argentina.

Klimpelianum (Weidl. & Werderm.) Backeb. Sts. dark green, ribs about 19; spines brown to blackish, becoming gray, radial spines 6–8 (–10), unequal, central spines 1–4; fls. white, 1⅝ in. long. Argentina.

Peitscheranum Backeb. Sts. to 3³⁄₁₆ in. high and 4 in. thick, gray-green, ribs 17; spines light brown basally, almost black toward tip, radial spines 7–9, central spine 1; fls. whitish-lilac-rose, 2⅜ in. long. Argentina.

spiniflorum (K. Schum.) Backeb. [*Echinopsis spiniflora* (K. Schum.) A. Berger]. Sts. to 2 ft. high and 6 in. thick, ribs 17–20 or more; spines 10–20, awl-shaped, reddish-yellow, becoming gray, unequal, to 1 in. long, central spines 1–3, stouter; fls. rose, 1⅝ in. long, staminodes yellow.

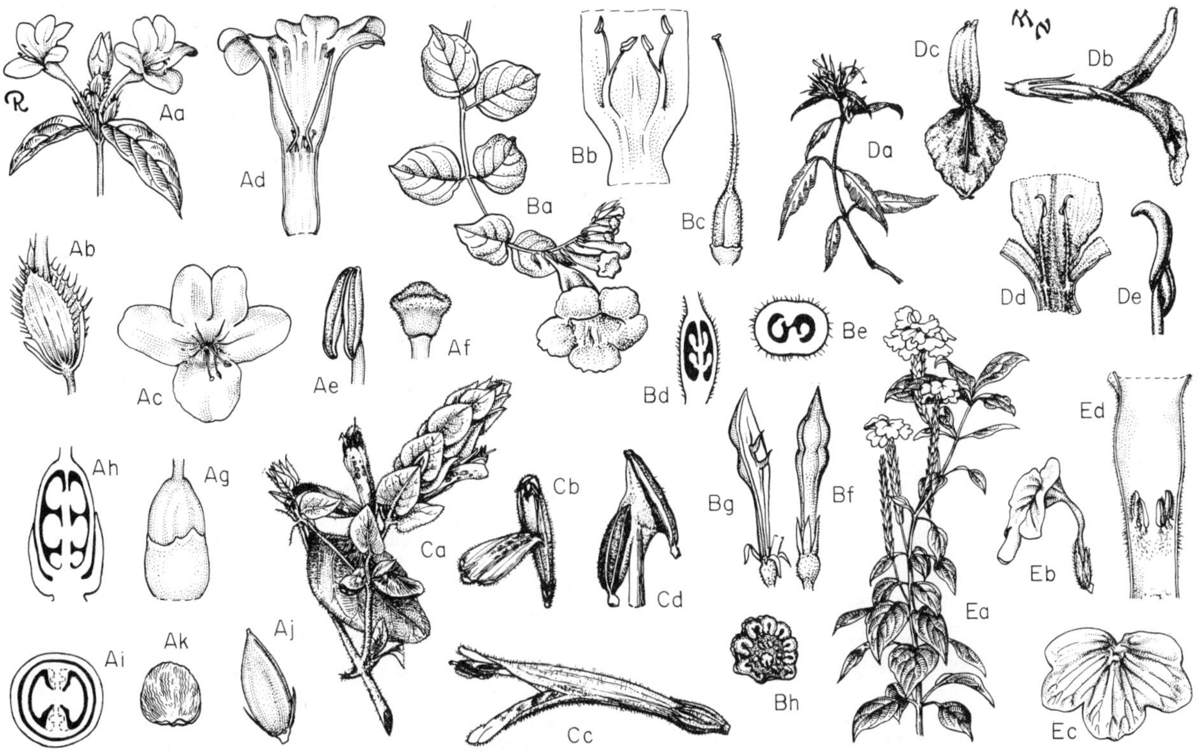

ACANTHACEAE. **A,** *Barleria cristata:* **Aa,** inflorescence, $\times \frac{1}{2}$; **Ab,** calyx, $\times$ 1; **Ac,** flower, face view, $\times$ 1; **Ad,** corolla, expanded, $\times$ 1; **Ae,** anther, $\times$ 5; **Af,** stigma, $\times$ 7; **Ag,** ovary, $\times$ 4; **Ah,** ovary, vertical section, $\times$ 5; **Ai,** ovary, cross section, $\times$ 6; **Aj,** capsule, $\times$ 1; **Ak,** seed, $\times$ 2. **B,** *Asystasia gangetica:* **Ba,** flowering stem, $\times \frac{3}{8}$; **Bb,** corolla tube, expanded, $\times$ 1; **Bc,** pistil, $\times$ 2; **Bd,** ovary, vertical section, $\times$ 4; **Be,** ovary, cross section, $\times$ 8; **Bf,** capsule, $\times \frac{3}{4}$; **Bg,** one valve of capsule, $\times \frac{3}{4}$; **Bh,** seed, $\times$ 2. **C,** *Justicia Brandegeana:* **Ca,** branch of inflorescence, $\times \frac{1}{2}$; **Cb,** flower, three-quarter face view, $\times$ 1; **Cc,** flower, side view, $\times$ 1; **Cd,** anther, $\times$ 5. **D,** *Peristrophe hyssopifolia* cv. 'Aureo-variegata': **Da,** flowering stem, $\times \frac{1}{8}$; **Db,** flower, side view, $\times$ 1; **Dc,** flower, face view, $\times$ 1; **Dd,** throat of corolla, expanded, $\times 1\frac{1}{2}$; **De,** anther, $\times$ 6. **E,** *Crossandra infundibuliformis;* **Ea,** flowering stem, $\times \frac{1}{10}$; **Eb,** flower, side view, $\times \frac{1}{2}$; **Ec,** flower, face view, $\times \frac{1}{2}$; **Ed,** tube of corolla, expanded, $\times$ 2. (Ca from Bailey, *Manual of Cultivated Plants,* ed. 2.)

thionanthum (Speg.) Backeb. Sts. to 5 in. high and 4 in. thick, ribs about 14, low; spines slender-awl-shaped, grayish, nearly equal, to $\frac{5}{8}$ in. long, radial spines 8–11, central spines 1–4; fls. yellow, $1\frac{3}{4}$ in. long, staminodes brownish.

violaceum (Werderm.) Backeb. VIOLET SEA-URCHIN. Sts. to 8 in. high and 5 in. thick, ribs about 15; spines 10–18, needle-shaped, yellow, becoming brown, to $1\frac{1}{4}$ in. long, central spines about 4; fls. lilac, 3 in. long, staminodes white.

ACANTHOCEREUS (Engelm. ex A. Berger) Britt. & Rose. *Cactaceae.* About 8 spp. of few-ribbed, clambering or rarely treelike cacti, native to N. and S. Amer.; ribs or angles mostly 3–5 on mature sts., often more on juvenile sts., obliquely crenate; fls. nocturnal, white, perianth persistent in fr., funnelform, stamens in 1 series, style slender; fr. spiny, tubercled, red, splitting at maturity, with colored flesh, seeds somewhat tubercled.

For culture see *Cacti.*

acutangulus (Hort. ex Pfeiff.) A. Berger. A poorly understood sp., said to be glossy-green with 3–4-angled sts.; spines ash-gray, radial spines 4–6, central spine 1, to $\frac{5}{8}$ in. long. Nativity not known.

colombianus: *A. Pitajaya.*

guatemalensis: a listed name of no botanical standing.

hondurensis: a listed name of no botanical standing.

horridus Britt. & Rose. Joints 3-angled or 3-winged, to $3\frac{1}{2}$ in. wide; areoles $1\frac{1}{4}$–$2\frac{1}{2}$ in. apart, spines brown or blackish, radial spines 1–6, conical, short, central spines 1–2, awl-shaped, to 3 in. long; fls. to 8 in. long; fr. $1\frac{1}{2}$ in. long. Mex., Guatemala. Close to *A. Pitajaya.*

occidentalis Britt. & Rose. Sts. forming thickets, 2 in. thick, 3–5-angled; areoles $\frac{3}{8}$–$1\frac{3}{16}$ in. apart, spines many, yellowish, needle-shaped, to $2\frac{3}{4}$ in. long; fls. to $7\frac{3}{16}$ in. long. W. Mex.

pentagonus (L.) Britt. & Rose [*A. tetragonus* (L.) Hummelinck; *Cereus pentagonus* (L.) Haw.]. Sts. clambering or arching, to 10 ft. long or more and 3 in. thick, 3–4-angled; spines needle-shaped to awl-shaped, radial spines 4–7, to $1\frac{1}{2}$ in. long, central spines 1 or more, longer; fls. fragrant, 6–8 in. long; fr. edible, 3 in. long, seeds $\frac{1}{8}$ in. long. Summer. S. Tex. and Mex. Cv. '**Monstrosus**' is listed.

Pitajaya (Jacq.) Dug. [*A. colombianus* Britt. & Rose; *Cereus Pitajaya* (Jacq.) DC.]. Sts. erect, to 10 ft. high and $3\frac{1}{2}$ in. thick, 3-winged; areoles 2 in. apart, radial spines 5–8, to $\frac{3}{16}$ in. long, central spines 1–2, awl-shaped, to 2 in. long; fls. 10 in. long, tube thick. Colombia.

subinermis Britt. & Rose. Sts. to 3 ft. long and 3 in. wide, 3–4-angled; areoles to $1\frac{1}{2}$ in. apart, spines 0 or 6–10, needle-shaped, to $\frac{5}{8}$ in. long; fls. 6–9 in. long; fr. $1\frac{1}{2}$ in. long. S. Mex.

ACANTHOLIMON Boiss. PRICKLY THRIFT. *Plumbaginaceae.* About 150 spp. of tufted, evergreen, per. herbs or subshrubs, extending from s. Greece and Crete e. through e. Eur. and cent. Asia to w. Tibet, mostly in mts. in gravelly, rocky places; lvs. in basal tufts or rosettes, linear, rigid, sharp-pointed, cylindrical or slightly 3-angled in cross section, the angles channelled; scape usually longer than lvs.; fls. in simple or compound panicles of 1- to many-fld. sessile spikelets, calyx tubular to funnelform, 5-ribbed, scarious, colored, petals united only at base, stamens 5, filaments separate, but united to petals at base, styles 5, separate, ovary fusiform or somewhat ovoid, gradually attenuate at apex to styles, stigmas globose; fr. 1-seeded, dehiscent.

The prickly thrifts are slow-growing plants for rock gardens and sandy places, needing sun and warmth. Propagated by cuttings taken in late summer and wintered under protection in a coldframe; also by layering.

acerosum (Willd.) Boiss. Low, woody per.; lvs. 3-angled in cross section, to 3 in. long, sharp-pointed, margins scabrous; fl. scape longer than lvs., spikelets many, loosely arranged; corolla white. Asia Minor.

albanicum: a listed name of no botanical standing.

Albertii Regel. Loose, cushionlike shrubs, to 2 ft.; lvs. 3-angled in cross section to nearly flat, to 1½ in. long, margins rough-ciliate; fl. scape longer than lvs., spikelets 1-fld., few on short lateral spikes; calyx funnelform, ⁵⁄₁₆ in. long, its expanded limb and corolla pink. Soviet cent. Asia.

androsaceum: *A. echinus.*

armenum Boiss. & Huet. Compact, cushionlike subshrub, to 8 in.; lvs. rigid, flat or nearly so, linear-lanceolate, to 1¼ in. long; fl. scape longer than lvs., strongly flexuous and zigzag, brittle, spikelets 1-fld.; calyx funnelform, to ½ in. long, tube densely hairy, the expanded limb white, corolla pink. Asia Minor.

aulieatense Czerniak. [*A. gramineum* Korovin]. Compact, cushionlike shrub; lvs. rigid, needlelike; fl. scapes to 12 in., much longer than lvs., spikelets remote, 1-fld. Soviet cent. Asia.

avenaceum Bunge. Loose, cushionlike subshrub; lvs. rigid, somewhat 3-angled in cross section, to 1¼ in. long, margins rough-ciliate; fl. scapes longer than lvs., to 10 in. or more, spikelets 1-fld. in loose spikes; calyx funnelform, to ⅜ in. long, tube sparsely hairy between nerves, the expanded limb purple to white, distinctly 10-nerved, corolla bright pink. Cent. Asia.

bracteatum (Girard) Boiss. Compact, cushionlike shrub; lvs. somewhat 3-angled in cross section, to nearly flat, to 2¼ in. long, margins rough-ciliate; scapes barely longer to much longer than lvs., spikelets 2–5-fld., in terminal somewhat capitate spikes; calyx funnelform, ½ in. long, the expanded limb and the corolla pink. Caucasus and Iran.

caryophyllaceum Boiss. Loose, cushionlike subshrub, to 12 in.; lvs. rigid, somewhat 3-angled in cross section, to 1½ in. long, minutely hairy, margins scabrous; fl. scapes minutely hairy, longer than lvs., strongly flexuous and zigzag, somewhat brittle in upper portion; calyx ½ in. long, funnelform, the expanded limb white, corolla pink. Caucasus, Armenia, Kurdistan.

creticum: *A. echinus* var.

echinus (L.) Boiss. [*A. androsaceum* (Jaub. & Spach) Boiss.]. Dense, cushionlike shrub; lvs. 3-angled in cross section, glabrous; scapes short, spikelets 3–7-fld.; calyx hairy, corolla purple. E. Medit. region. Var. **créticum** Boiss. [*A. creticum* (Boiss.) Rech. f.]. Lvs. pubescent.

glumaceum (Jaub. & Spach) Boiss. Loose, cushionlike subshrub; lvs. rigid, 3-angled in cross section, to 2½ in. long, usually hairy on lower half; fl. scapes to 6 in. long, somewhat hairy, slightly longer than lvs., spikelets 1-fld., densely 2-ranked in terminal spikes; calyx funnelform, to ¾ in. long, the expanded limb white, corolla pink. Caucasus, Armenia, Kurdistan.

gramineum: *A. aulieatense.*

Hohenackeri (Jaub. & Spach) Boiss. Compact, cushionlike subshrub; lvs. rigid, needle-shaped, to ¾ in. long; fl. scapes to 4 in., minutely hairy, spikelets 1-fld., loosely 2-ranked in spikes; calyx funnelform, to ½ in. long, the expanded limb white. Caucasus and Iran.

Karelinii (Shchegl.) Bunge. Loose, cushionlike subshrub; lvs. rigid, 3-angled in cross section, to 2 in. long, glabrous; fl. scapes to 12 in., much longer than lvs.; corolla bright pink. Differs from other spp. in having calyx nearly tubular with very narrow limb. Caucasus and Iran.

lepturoides (Jaub. & Spach) Boiss. Rather compact, cushionlike subshrub; lvs. rigid, to 1 in. long; fl. scapes to 8 in., longer than lvs.; spikelets 1-fld., remote, on jointed, somewhat zigzag ax.; calyx to ⅜ in. long, funnelform, the expanded limb white, corolla pink. Caucasus.

microcephalum: a listed name of no botanical standing.

pulchellum Korovin. Loose, cushionlike, somewhat rounded subshrub; lvs. somewhat 3-angled in cross section, to 1 in. long, glabrous; fl. scapes to 6 in., glabrous, spikelets 1-fld., 6–8 in compact terminal spikes; calyx ½ in. long, funnelform, the expanded limb white, corolla pink. Iran, Soviet cent. Asia.

spinosum: a listed name of no botanical standing.

subglabrum: a listed name of no botanical standing.

tataricum Boiss. Rather compact, cushionlike subshrub; lvs. narrowly linear-lanceolate, to 1 in. long, glaucous; fl. scapes hairy, to 6 in., longer than lvs., spikelets 2–4-fld., 5–10 in terminal spikes; calyx funnelform, to ½ in. long, tube pubescent, the expanded limb white, purple-veined, corolla bright pink. Soviet cent. Asia.

venustum Boiss. Loose, cushionlike; lvs. rigid, channelled on upper side, to ¾ in. long, gray-green; spikelets 1-fld., 12–20 in loose, terminal, 1-sided spikes; calyx narrowly funnelform, the expanded limb yellow-brown, corolla pink, much longer than calyx. Asia Minor.

ACANTHOLOBIVIA: *LOBIVIA.*

ACANTHOPANAX (Decne. & Planch.) Miq. *Araliaceae.* About 50 spp. of mostly deciduous, usually prickly shrubs or small trees of e. Asia, Malay Pen. and Philippine Is.; lvs. alt., palmately compound, lfts. mostly 3 or 5, serrate; fls. small and dull-colored, in globose umbels often arranged in large panicles, petals mostly 5, valvate, ovary 2–5-celled, styles 2–5, separate or united only at base; fr. a purple to black drupe.

Mostly hardy through Zone 6 or colder regions, but only *A. Sieboldianus* is commonly cultivated. Propagated by seeds sown as soon as ripe or stratified, by root cuttings over heat, and by hard wood cuttings.

divaricatus (Siebold & Zucc.) Seem. Shrub, to 10 ft., sts. with paired prickles; lfts. 5, to 3 in. long, pubescent beneath, long-petioluled; fls. brownish, in dense, short-stalked umbels; fr. black. Japan. Zone 6. Early deciduous.

Giraldii Harms. Shrub, to 9 ft., sts. densely prickly; lfts. 3–5, to 2 in. long, glabrous; umbels solitary; fls. greenish; fr. black. China. Zone 6.

Henryi (D. Oliver) Harms. Shrub, to 10 ft., sts. with short, conical prickles; lfts. mostly 5, to 4 in. long, rough above, pubescent beneath; fls. green, in dense umbels on stout, pubescent peduncles. China. Zone 6.

innovans (Siebold & Zucc.) Franch. & Sav. [*Kalopanax innovans* (Siebold & Zucc.) Miq.]. Small, unarmed tree, to 20 ft.; lfts. usually 3, to 6 in. long, nearly sessile, glabrous; umbels in panicles; fls. yellow-green, fr. black, globose, about ¼ in. in diam. Japan. Zone 7.

lasiogyne Harms. Shrub or small tree, to 20 ft., sts. gray, mostly unarmed; lfts. 3, ovate, to 2½ in. long, nearly entire, glabrous; fls. white-tomentose, in globose, headlike umbels; fr. black, abundant. W. China. Zone 7.

leucorrhizus (D. Oliver) Harms. Shrub, to 12 ft., sts. yellow-green, unarmed or with prickles at nodes; lfts. 3–5, to 5 in. long, glabrous; umbels solitary or clustered; fls. greenish; fr. purple-black. China. Zone 6. Var. **scaberulus** Harms & Rehd. Lfts. smaller, pubescent with bristles on veins beneath and petiolules.

pentaphyllus: *A. Sieboldianus.*

ricinifolius: *Kalopanax pictus.*

senticosus (Rupr. & Maxim. ex Maxim.) Harms. Shrub, to 15 ft., sts. erect, with abundant slender prickles; lfts. mostly 5, to 5 in. long, dark green above, pubescent; umbels many-fld., solitary or clustered; fls. purplish-yellow; fr. black. Ne. Asia. Zone 3.

sessiliflorus (Rupr. & Maxim. ex Maxim.) Seem. Shrub, to 12 ft., sparingly armed; lfts. 3–5, central one largest, to 7 in.. long; umbels headlike, globose; fls. purplish, sessile; fr. black. N. China to Korea. Zone 3.

setchuenensis Harms. Shrub, to 10 ft., sts. nearly unarmed, yellowish; lfts. 3, rarely 5, to 5 in. long, leathery, glaucous beneath; infl. of 3–7 umbels; fr. black. W. China. Zone 7.

Sieboldianus Mak. [*A. pentaphyllus* (Siebold & Zucc.) March.; *Aralia pentaphylla* Siebold & Zucc., not Thunb.]. Dioecious shrub, to 9 ft., sts. slender, arching, prickles short, usually sparse; lvs. somewhat clustered on spurs, lfts. 5, sometimes 7, to 1½ in. long, glossy beneath; umbels solitary on peduncles to 4 in. long; fls. unisexual, greenish-white; fr. black, but fertile fr. not seen in U.S., where male plants are not in cult. Japan. Zone 5. Cv. 'Variegatus'. Lvs. white-margined. Material of this sp. may be offered under the name *A. spinosus.*

Simonii Hort. Simon-Louis ex. C. K. Schneid. Shrub, to 9 ft., sts. greenish, smooth or with few recurved prickles; lfts. 3–5, the middle one longer, to 6 in. long, sharply toothed and bristly on both sides; umbels several; fls. greenish; fr. black. China. Zone 6.

spinosus (L.f.) Miq. [*Aralia pentaphyllus* Thunb., not Siebold & Zucc.]. Shrub, sts. prickly; lfts. 5, obovate, to 3 in. long, membranous, margins obscurely toothed, glabrous or with few appressed hairs above, pubescent beneath; umbels solitary, many-fld.; fr. black. Japan. Zone 6. Material offered under this name is usually *A. Sieboldianus.*

ternatus: *A. Wardii.*

trichodon Franch. & Sav. Shrub, to 10 ft., sts. grayish-white, prickly; lfts. 5, rhombic-ovate, 1–2½ in. long, acute, sparsely prickly on margin and veins above; umbels terminal, peduncles purple-red, glabrous, 1–2 in. long; fr. purple-black, ¼ in. long. Mts., cent. Japan. Zone 6.

trifoliatus (L.) Voss. Scandent shrub, to 20 ft.; sts. with scattered recurved prickles; lfts. usually 3, ovate, to 3 in. long, sparsely toothed; umbels in terminal whorls, peduncles slender. Mts., s. China, Philippine Is., Taiwan. Zone 8?

Wardii W. W. Sm. [*A. ternatus* Rehd.]. Shrub, to 6 ft., sts. grayish, unarmed, or with few straight prickles; lfts. 3, to 2 in. long, entire or sparsely toothed, glossy; umbels usually in clusters of 4–7; fls. greenish-white; fr. purple-black, much-compressed. China. Zone 6.

ACANTHOPHOENIX H. Wendl. BARBEL PALM. *Palmae.* Two spp. of trop., monoecious, single-stemmed palms of the Mascarene Is.; trunk to 60 ft. or more, closely ringed, spineless, with prominent crownshaft; lvs. pinnate, sheaths prickly, pinnae many, spreading, closely set, narrow, 2-cleft at apex, strongly veined; infl. below lvs., with 2 papery, deciduous bracts, peduncle short, prickly, rachis short, prickly, branched, the lower brs. again once-branched, rachillae with fls. in triads (2 male and 1 female) in the lower part and with paired or solitary male fls. in the upper part; male fls. larger than female, sepals small, acute, with petals acute, valvate, much longer than sepals, stamens 9–12; fr. about ½ in. long, with lateral remains of stigmas, seed with homogeneous endosperm.

　　Rarely cultivated outside the tropics. Zone 10b. For culture see *Palms*.

　　crinita (Bory) H. Wendl. Lvs. with rachis nearly smooth beneath, pinnae with veins nearly smooth beneath, the 2 lateral nearly as prominent as the midrib; peduncle tomentose, with long, undulate prickles; male fls. white to yellow or pink, 5⁄16 in. long; fr. oblong-ovoid.

　　rubra (Bory) H. Wendl. Lvs. to 12 ft. long, rachis prickly beneath; midrib of pinnae prickly beneath and more prominent than lateral veins; peduncle nearly glabrous, with straight prickles; male fls. reddish or purplish, ½ in. long; fr. globose.

ACANTHOPHYLLUM C. A. Mey. *Caryophyllaceae.*
About 50 spp. of per. herbs, subshrubs, or small shrubs, native to desert areas in sw. and cent. Asia and Siberia; lvs. opp., usually subulate, often needlelike and spiny, stiff; fls. in axillary or terminal heads, or sometimes in panicled or corymbose infls., bracts leaflike, spiny, calyx tubular or turbinate, with 5 prickly teeth, petals 5, white to pink, clawed, stamens 10, anthers often exserted, ovary 1-celled, with 4–5 ovules, styles 2; fr. a caps., seeds 1 or 2, reniform.

　　albidum Shishk. To about 1 ft., woody, with dense, short, gray hairs; lvs. spreading, needlelike, to ½ in. long; infl. of heads to 2 in. across, broadly corymbose; calyx tubular, crisply hairy, teeth subulate, petals white, faintly pink at base. Cent. Asia.

　　glandulosum Bunge ex Boiss. Plants generally viscid-glandular; lvs. erect to spreading, flat above, convex beneath; heads 1–3, dense, globose, peduncle short and thick, bracts oblong, viscid; calyx oblong-cylindrical, viscid, teeth triangular, mucronate, petals white, oblong. E. Elburz Mts. of ne. Iran to Turkestan and Pamir-Altai Mts.

　　gypsophiloides Regel. To 2½ ft., rhizomatous, sts. glabrous; lvs. linear-subulate, scarcely needlelike, to ¾ in. long, glabrous or rarely somewhat scabrous; infl. a loose panicle; calyx narrowly campanulate, teeth triangular, ¼ as long as calyx, petals white or roseate, obovate-oblong. Cent. Asia.

　　pungens (Bunge) Boiss. [*A. spinosum* C. A. Mey.]. To about 1 ft., sts. several, divaricately branched, short-hairy; lvs. subulate, stiff, to 1⅝ in. long; infls. corymbose, to 2 in. across; calyx tubular, teeth broadly triangular, petals reddish-pink, limb ovate, less than ⅛ in. wide. Cent. Asia.

　　sordidum Bunge ex Boiss. Plants generally glaucous, pubescent; lvs. flat above, convex beneath; heads solitary, sessile, terminal, globose, involucre leathery, bracts oblong; calyx oblong-cylindric, puberulous, teeth apiculate, ciliate, petals white, linear. Ne. Iran to Turkestan.

　　spinosum: *A. pungens.*

　　verticillatum (Willd.) Hand.-Mazz. [*Arenaria verticillata* Willd.]. Much-branched shrub, to 10 in., sts. ascending-erect, glabrous or papillose; lvs. needlelike, to ⅝ in. long, glabrous to papillose, spine-tipped; heads to ⅝ in. across, axillary and terminal; calyx tubular, teeth lanceolate, as long as the tube, petals white, linear to linear-lanceolate, ¼ in. long, retuse. E. Turkey, n. Iraq.

ACANTHORHIPSALIS (K. Schum.) Britt. & Rose. *Cactaceae.*
One or a few spp. of epiphytic cacti, native to S. Amer.; sts. branched, brs. flattened or 3-winged, crenate or serrate; areoles spiny; fls. solitary at lateral areoles, small, tube short, scales sometimes with axillary tufts of felt.

　　For culture see *Cacti.*

　　himantoclada: a listed name of no botanical standing; probably in error for *Disocactus himantocladus.*

　　micranthus (Vaup.) Britt. & Rose. Brs. 2–3-winged, to 8 in. long and ¾ in. wide, crenate; spines 3–10, spreading or hooked, to ⅜ in. long; fls. purple, about 1 in. long, scales with axillary tufts of felt; fr. globose, weakly winged and with few scales, short spines sometimes present. Peru.

　　monacantha: *Rhipsalis monacantha.*

ACANTHORRHIZA: *CRYOSOPHILA.* A. **aculeata**: *C. nana,* but the name *A. aculeata* often applied erroneously in hort. to *C. Warscewiczii.*

ACANTHOSTACHYS Klotzsch. *Bromeliaceae.*
One epiphytic sp., native to Brazil and Paraguay; lvs. semicylindrical, curled, spiny; infl. simple, scapose, appearing lateral, conelike, with broad bracts and compressed fls.; ovary partly superior, with apex rounded and protruding above insertion of the perianth; fr. a berry, seeds without appendages.

　　Can be grown in nearly full sun. For culture see *Bromeliaceae.*

　　strobilacea (Schult. f.) Klotzsch. Lvs. drooping; bracts to 2 in. long, orange-red; fls. yellow, to 1 in. long; fr. white, seeds few, large, sticky.

ACANTHUS L. BEAR'S-BREECH. *Acanthaceae.*
About 20 or more spp. of per. herbs or subshrubs, many xerophytic, mostly in Medit. region, extending to trop. and subtrop. Asia and Afr.; lvs. mostly basal, broadly lobed or pinnatifid, sometimes spiny; fls. showy, white or purplish, in long, erect spikes, subtended by large leaflike spine-tipped bracts, calyx 4-lobed, 2 lobes smaller than other 2, corolla with short tube and expanded 3-lobed lower lip, upper lip lacking, stamens 4; fr. a 2-celled caps., seeds 2 in each cell.

　　Their large decorative leaves make the acanthuses attractive ornamentals. They do best in rich well-drained soil. Propagated by seeds or by division in early autumn or spring. The bold leaves of acanthus have inspired important decorative features in Western art and architecture.

　　balcanicus Heyw. & I. Richardson [*A. longifolius* Host, not Poir.]. To 4 ft.; lvs. deeply pinnately lobed, lobes somewhat ovate and toothed, narrowed at their base; bracts ovate, dentate-spinose, slender-pointed; fls. usually rose-purple, lateral calyx lobes ovate-orbicular, margins scarious and glabrous. Se. Eur. Hardy north. See *A. mollis.*

　　latifolius: *A. mollis* cv.

　　longifolius: see *A. balcanicus.*

　　lusitanicus: *A. mollis* cv. 'Latifolius.'

　　mollis L. ARTIST'S A. Similar to *A. balcanicus* in habit, but lvs. less deeply lobed, the lobes not narrowed at their base, fls. usually white, lateral calyx lobes ovate-acute, margins pubescent. Medit. region. Not reliably hardy north. Cv. 'Latifolius' [*A. latifolius* Goeze; *A. lusitanicus* Hort.]. Lvs. large; said to be hardy. Cv. 'Oak Leaf' is listed.

　　montanus (Nees) T. Anderson. BEAR'S-BREECH, MOUNTAIN A., MOUNTAIN THISTLE. To 6 ft.; lvs. more or less deeply pinnatifid, with toothed, spinose lobes, dark glossy green above, paler beneath, papery; bracts and calyx segms. spinose, corolla rose or reddish, rarely white. W. Trop. Afr.

　　spinosissimus Pers. [*A. spinosus* L.]. To 4 ft.; differs from *A. montanus* in having lvs. rigid, leathery, deeply pinnatifid, with rigid-spinose teeth. Se. Eur.

　　spinosus: *A. spinosissimus.*

ACER L. [*Argentacer* Small; *Negundo* Boehmer ex Ludw.; *Rufacer* Small]. MAPLE. *Aceraceae.*
About 200 spp. of trees, sometimes shrubs, native mainly to n. temp. regions; mostly deciduous; flowering in later winter or early spring; lvs. opp., petioled, usually palmately lobed or sometimes compound, rarely entire; fls. in clusters, racemes, panicles, or corymbs, commonly unisexual, 5-merous, rarely 4-merous, stamens 4–10, usually 8, styles or stigmas 2; fr. a pair of long-winged samaras.

　　Maples are used extensively for lawn, park, and street plantings; some species provide a wood valuable for furniture and other uses requiring a hard dense wood; the sap of *A. saccharum* yields the well-known maple syrup and sugar. Most species are hardy in the northern states. They are strong- and free-growing, but shallow-rooted. Ordinary soil is satisfactory. Propagated by seeds sown soon after maturity or stratified and sown in spring. Rare species and cultivars may be budded in summer or winter-grafted by the veneer method on seedlings of the same or related species. Some shrubby species are propagated by layers or half-ripened green wood cuttings, or by cuttings in early spring from plants forced in greenhouses.

　　argutum Maxim. Shrub or tree, to 25 ft., twigs white-puberulent; lvs. 5- rarely 7-lobed, 2–4 in. across, long-acuminate, sharply and doubly serrate, downy underneath when young, petiole ¾–2⅜ in. long; fls. unisexual, greenish-yellow, female fls. in pendulous, many-fld. racemes; samaras ¾ in. long, wings diverging horizontally. Japan. Zone 6. Autumn foliage light yellow.

　　auratum: *A. Negundo* cv.

barbatum Michx. [*A. floridanum* (Chapm.) Pax; *A. saccharum* subsp. *floridanum* (Chapm.) Desmarais]. SOUTHERN SUGAR M., SUGAR TREE, FLORIDA M. To 50 ft., twigs grayish to purplish; lvs. 3–5-lobed, 1¼–3¾ in. long, 1½–4¼ in. wide, with rounded lobules, glaucescent and pubescent underneath; fls. greenish-yellow, with conspicuous long beard projecting from throat; samaras ⅝–1¼ in. long, wings diverging or sometimes nearly parallel. Fla. to e. Tex., n. to e. Va. and s. Mo. Zone 7.

barbinerve Maxim. Like *A. argutum*, but lvs. mostly 5- or rarely 3-lobed, petiole 1½–3½ in. long; female fls. yellow, usually in 7-fld. racemes; samaras 1¼ in. long, wings diverging at a right or obtuse angle. Manchuria, Korea. Zone 5.

Buergeranum Miq. [*A. trifidum* Hook. & Arn.]. TRIDENT M. To 50 ft., twigs glabrous; lvs. with 3 shallow, forward-pointing lobes, rarely entire, deep green above, pale green or whitish-glaucous underneath, 2¼–4 in. long, 1½–3 in. wide; fls. yellowish, in a broad-pyramidal, pubescent panicle; samaras ¾–1 in. long, wings parallel and connivent. China. Zone 6. Autumn foliage red and orange. Var. **ningpoense** (Hance) Rehd. Twigs, infl., and wings of samaras densely yellowish-green-tomentose.

caesium Wallich ex Brandis. To 80 ft., bark gray; lvs. 5-lobed, 4¾–6½ in. long, 7–8 in. wide, doubly serrate, glaucous underneath; fls. in large pyramidal corymbs; samaras 1½–2 in. long, wings diverging at a right or an acute angle. W. Himalayas. Zone 7.

californicum: *A. Negundo* subsp.

Campbellii Hook. f. & T. Thoms. Like *A. Oliveranum*, but 60–70 ft.; lvs. 5- to mostly 7-lobed, 3–6 in. long, 4–8 in. wide, sharply serrate, hairy on both surfaces when young. E. Himalayas. Zone 7.

campestre L. HEDGE M., FIELD M. Shrub or round-headed tree, to 35 ft., sometimes to 80 ft., twigs pubescent or glabrous when young, often corky; lvs. 3–5-lobed, 2–4 in. across, lobes broad, obtuse, entire or the middle one 3-lobed, petiole with milky juice; fls. greenish, in upright, pubescent corymbs; samaras 1–1½ in. long, pubescent or glabrous, wings diverging horizontally. Eur., n. Turkey, Caucasus, n. Iran. Zone 5. Autumn foliage clear yellow. Subsp. **campestre** [subsp. *hebecarpum* DC.]. The typical subsp.; fr. pubescent. Cv. 'Compactum' [forma *compactum* Schwer.]. Low, round bush of close growth. Cv. 'Schwerinii' [forma *Schwerinii* (Hesse) Schwer.]. Lvs. purple when young. Subsp. **hebecarpum**: subsp. *campestre*. Subsp. **leiocarpum** (Opiz) Pax. Fr. glabrous. E. Eur. and w. Asia.

capillipes Maxim. Tree, to 35 ft., twigs smooth, striped; lvs. red when unfolding, 3-lobed, 3–5 in. long, terminal lobe large, triangular, slender-pointed, veins and petiole red; fls. greenish-white, in glabrous, pendulous racemes; samaras ⅝–¾ in. long, wings diverging at an obtuse angle. Japan. Zone 6. Autumn foliage crimson.

cappadocicum Gled. Tree, 60–70 ft., twigs often bloomy when young, lustrous and green the second year; lvs. 5–7-lobed, 3–6 in. wide, lobes triangular, long, slender-pointed; fls. yellow, in corymbs; samaras 1⅛–2 in. long, wings diverging at an obtuse angle. Caucasus, n. Turkey, n. Iran, to Himalayas and w. China. Zone 6. Cvs. are: 'Aureum', lvs. yellow in spring and autumn; 'Rubrum' [var. *rubrum* (Kirchn.) Rehd.], lvs. blood-red when young; 'Tricolor' [var. *tricolor* (Carrière) Rehd.], lvs. blood-red and speckled with rose-pink when young.

carolinianum: *A. rubrum* var. *trilobum*.

carpinifolium Siebold & Zucc. HORNBEAM M. Tree, to 30 ft., twigs glabrous; lvs. ovate-oblong, 3–5 in. long, 1½–2½ in. wide, doubly serrate, pubescent on veins underneath when young; fls. greenish, on slender pedicels, in short, glabrous racemes; samaras 1¼ in. long, glabrous, wings diverging at a right or an obtuse angle, incurved at apex. Japan. Zone 6. Autumn foliage bright brownish-yellow.

caudatum Wallich [*A. papilio* King]. Shrub or tree, to 60 ft., twigs purplish when young; lvs. 5- or rarely 7-lobed, 3–5½ in. across, subcordate, lobes ovate, long-acuminate, incised-serrate; fls. yellowish-whitish, in upright, pubescent, racemose panicles; samaras 1 in. long, yellowish-brown, nutlets veined, wings diverging at an acute or a right angle. Himalayas and w. China. Zone 7. Subsp. **ukurunduense** (Trautv. & C. A. Mey.) E. Murr. [*A. caudatum* var. *ukurunduense* (Trautv. & C. A. Mey.) Rehd.; *A. ukurunduense* Trautv. & C. A. Mey.]. Lvs. usually rusty-tomentose beneath. N. China, Manchuria, Korea, e. to Sakhalin and Japan. Zone 6.

circinatum Pursh. VINE M. Shrub or round-headed, tree to 35 ft., twigs glabrous; lvs. almost orbicular, 7–9-lobed, 2–7 in. across; fls. in 6–20-fld. corymbs, sepals purple, petals white; samaras 1–1½ in. long, red, glabrous, wings diverging horizontally. B. C. to n. Calif. Zone 6. Autumn foliage red and orange.

circumlobatum: *A. japonicum* var.

cissifolium (Siebold & Zucc.) C. Koch [*Negundo cissifolium* Siebold & Zucc.]. Tree, to 30 ft., twigs downy when young; lvs. compound,

lfts. 3, ovate or obovate to elliptic, 2–3½ in. long, coarsely serrate toward apex; fls. yellowish, in slender, pubescent racemes; samaras ¾–1 in. long, glabrous, wings diverging at an acute angle. Japan. Zone 6. Autumn foliage red and orange.

×**coriaceum** Tausch [*A.* × *parvifolium* Tausch]: *A. monspessulanum* × *A. pseudoplatanus*. Shrub or small tree, of compact, rounded shape; lvs. mostly 3-lobed, 2–3½ in. across; fls. yellowish, in loose corymbs; samaras 1 in. long, wings diverging at an acute angle. Probably of hort. origin.

crataegifolium Siebold & Zucc. HAWTHORN M. Shrub or tree, to 20 ft., twigs glabrous, purplish, becoming striped with white; lvs. ovate, nearly unlobed or shallowly 3–5-lobed, 1–2½ in. long, slender-pointed; fls. yellowish-green, in 5–8-fld., glabrous racemes; samaras ¾–1 in. long, glabrous, wings diverging nearly at an angle of 180°. Moist, shaded woodlands, Japan. Zone 6.

dasycarpum: *A. saccharinum*.

Davidii Franch. Tree, 30–50 ft., twigs glabrous, striped; lvs. ovate to ovate-oblong, 3–7 in. long, 1½–4 in. wide, reddish-downy on veins underneath; fls. unisexual, yellowish, in slender, pendent racemes; samaras 1¼ in. long, wings diverging at an obtuse angle. China. Zone 6. Autumn foliage yellow and purple.

diabolicum Blume ex C. Koch. Round-headed tree, to 30 ft., twigs hairy when young; lvs. broadly ovate, 5-lobed, 4–7 in. long, remotely serrate, hairy on both surfaces when young; fls. on lateral branchlets, appearing before lvs., yellow, female fls. in few-fld. racemes, male fls. in pendulous clusters; samaras 1–1½ in. long, wings almost connivent. Japan. Zone 6. Autumn foliage not coloring. Var. **purpurascens** (Franch. & Sav.) Rehd. [*A. purpurascens* Franch. & Sav.]. Lvs. red when young; fls. purple; fr. purplish. Autumn foliage red.

×**Dieckii** (Pax) Pax: *A. Lobelii* × *A. platanoides*. Tree, to 60 ft.; lvs. 3–5-, rarely 7-lobed, 4–8 in. across, lobes entire; fls. yellow, in many-fld. corymbs; samaras 1½–2 in. long, wings diverging at an obtuse angle. A garden hybrid.

dissectum: *A. palmatum* var.

distylum Siebold & Zucc. Tree, to 50 ft., twigs puberulous when young; lvs. ovate, 4–7 in. long, deeply cordate, finely serrate; fls. yellowish, in panicles, styles divided to their base; samaras 1¼ in. long, wings diverging at an acute angle. Japan. Zone 7. Autumn foliage dark brown.

Douglasii: *A. glabrum* subsp.

Drummondii: *A. rubrum* var.

filicifolium: *A. japonicum* cv. 'Aconitifolium'.

floridanum: *A. barbatum*.

Forrestii Diels. Tree, 30–50 ft., bark rough, twigs purple when young; lvs. 3-lobed, 3–5½ in. long, 2–4½ in. wide, with long, acuminate middle lobe, cordate or subcordate at base, doubly serrate, deep green or purplish above, pale green underneath; fls. yellowish-green, in glabrous racemes; samaras ⅞–1 in. long, reddish-purple when young, wings diverging at an obtuse angle. China. Zone 7. Related to *A. pectinatum*.

Franchetii Pax. Related to *A. diabolicum* and *A. sterculiaceum;* lvs. 3-, rarely 5-lobed, cordate or subcordate; fls. yellowish-green, in downy lateral racemes; samaras ¾–1½ in. long, deep yellow, wings diverging at a nearly right angle. China. Zone 6.

fraxinifolium: *A. Negundo*.

Ginnala Maxim. [*A. Ginnala* var. *euginnala* Pax; *A. tataricum* var. *aidzuense* Franch.]. AMUR M. Shrub or tree, to 20 ft., twigs often purple when young; lvs. 3-, rarely 5-lobed, to 3½ in. long, 2½ in. wide, doubly serrate, middle lobe much longer than lateral lobes; fls. yellowish-white, fragrant, in small panicles; samaras ¾–1 in. long, wings nearly parallel. China, Mongolia, Manchuria, Korea, Japan. Zone 5. Autumn foliage scarlet. Cv. 'Durand Dwarf'. Shrub, spreading to 3 ft. Useful as a hedge.

glabrum Torr. ROCKY MOUNTAIN M. Shrub or tree, 20–30 ft.; lvs. 3–5-lobed or 2-parted, 2–5 in. across, subcordate, sharply serrate; fls. greenish-yellow, in racemose corymbs; samaras ¾–1 in. long, wings nearly parallel or diverging at an obtuse angle. Se. Alaska to Calif., e. to w. S. Dak. and New Mex. Zone 5. Autumn foliage yellow. Subsp. **glabrum**. The typical subsp.; lvs. usually deeply 3-lobed to trifoliolate. Cv. 'Microphyllum'. Lvs. smaller, lobes acutish, ¾–2⅜ in. long. Subsp. **Douglasii** (Hook.) Wesm. [*A. Douglasii* Hook.]. Twigs reddish; lvs. shallowly 3-lobed. Se. Alaska to Ore., e. to s. Alta. and Wyo. Var. **Torreyi** (Greene) Smiley. SIERRA M., MOUNTAIN M. Lvs. mostly 3- or obscurely 5-lobed. Sierras of Calif.

grandidentatum: *A. saccharum* subsp.

griseum (Franch.) Pax. PAPERBARK M. Large shrub or tree, 20–40 ft., bark cinnamon-brown, separating in thin, papery flakes, twigs pubescent when young; lvs. of 3 lfts., soft green above, silvery beneath, terminal lft. ovate-lanceolate, 1½–3 in. long, with 3–5 pairs of coarse teeth; fls. in few-fld., drooping cymes; samaras 1¼ in. long, wings diverging at an acute to right angle. China. Zone 6. Autumn foliage bright red and orange. Grown particularly for its unusual and attractive bark.

Grosseri Pax. Closely allied to *A. Davidii,* but smaller, 20–30 ft.; lvs. ovate-cordate, 3-lobed or unlobed, 2–5 in. long; samaras ¾–1¼ in. long, wings diverging at an obtuse angle or spreading horizontally. China. Zone 6. Var. **Hersii** (Rehd.) Rehd. [*A. Hersii* Rehd.]. Lvs. broadly ovate, 3- or rarely 5-lobed; fls. in shorter racemes. Autumn foliage red.

Heldreichii Orph. ex Boiss. BALKAN M. Tree, 40–50 ft., twigs dark red-brown; lvs. deeply 5-lobed, 4–7 in. across, lobes oblong, coarsely serrate, glaucous underneath; fls. yellow, in broad, upright corymbs; samaras 1–1¾ in. long, wings diverging at an obtuse to an acute angle. Albania, n. Greece, w. Bulgaria, se. Yugoslavia. Zone 6.

Hersii: *A. Grosseri* var.

Heyhachii: *A. japonicum* cv. 'Aconitifolium'.

Hookeri Miq. Tree, 35–50 ft., twigs red when young; lvs. oblong-ovate, 4–5½ in. long, cordate, acuminate, sharply serrate; fls. greenish-yellow, in long, slender racemes; samaras ¾ in. long, wings diverging at a right angle. Himalayas, Sikkim, Bhutan. Zone 7.

×**hybridum** Spach: *A. Opalus* × *A. pseudoplatanus.* Tree, 45–65 ft.; lvs. 3-lobed, 2½–6½ in. long, cordate, lighter green underneath than above; fls. yellow, in panicles; samaras to 1¾ in. long, wings nearly parallel.

hyrcanum Fisch. & C. A. Mey. [*A. Opalus* var. *hyrcanum* (Fisch. &. C. A. Mey.) Rehd.]. Tree, 20–30 ft., twigs pale when young, later striped with white; lvs. 5-lobed, 2–6 in. across, coarsely serrate, glaucous underneath; fls. greenish-yellow, in corymbs; samaras 1–1¾ in. long, wings nearly parallel or connivent. Se. Eur., to Turkey and n. Iran. Zone 7.

insigne: *A. velutinum* var. *glabrescens.* Var. **glabrescens:** *A. velutina* var. Var. **velutinum:** *A. velutinum.* Some material offered as *A. insigne* is *A. Trautvetteri.*

italum: *A. Ophalus.*

japonicum Thunb. JAPANESE M., FULL-MOON M. Shrub or tree, 20–30 ft., twigs glabrous; lvs. 7–13-lobed, 3–5½ in. long, lobes ovate, acuminate, doubly serrate; fls. purplish-red, in pendulous corymbs; samaras 1–2 in. long, pubescent when young, wings diverging at an obtuse angle or spreading horizontally. Japan. Zone 5. Autumn foliage crimson. Cv. '**Aconitifolium**' [var. *aconitifolium* Meehan; var. *filicifolium* Hesse; var. *Heyhachii* Mak.; *A. Heyhachii* Matsum. ex Mak.; var. *laciniatum* Van Houtte; var. *Parsonsii* Hort. Veitch ex Schwer.]. Lvs. divided nearly to the base, segms. 9–13, pinnately cut. Cv. '**Aureum**' [var. *aureum* Hort. Veitch ex Dipp.]. Lvs. pale golden-yellow. Cv. '**Vitifolium**'. Growth vigorous, brs. many; lvs. 10–12-lobed; fr. reddish. Var. **atropurpureum:** *A. palmatum* cv. Var. **circumlobatum** (Maxim.) G. Koidz. [var. *insulare* (Pax) Ohwi; *A. circumlobatum* Maxim]. Samaras spreading nearly horizontally. Var. **filicifolium:** cv. 'Aconitifolium'. Var. **Heyhachii:** cv. 'Aconitifolium'. Var. **insulare:** var. *circumlobatum.* Var. **Itaya:** var. *japonicum.* Var. **japonicum** [var. *Itaya* Hort.; var. *macrophyllum* Nichols.]. Lvs. 3–6 in. wide; samaras diverging at an obtuse angle. Var. **laciniatum:** cv. 'Aconitifolium'. Var. **macrophyllum:** var. *japonicum.* Var. **Parsonsii:** cv. 'Aconitifolium'.

laevigatum Wallich. Tree, twigs greenish; lvs. oblong-lanceolate, 3–6 in. long, acuminate, leathery, mostly entire, but serrate on young trees, reddish when young, strongly net-veined and green beneath; fls. yellow; samaras 1–2 in. long, wings diverging at an obtuse angle to spreading horizontally. E. Himalayas, s. China, se. Asia. Zone 7.

×**leucoderme:** *A. saccharum* subsp.

Lobelii Ten. Erect, columnar tree, 50–60 ft., twigs bloomy; lvs. usually 5-, rarely 3-lobed, to 7 in. across, lobes long-acuminate; fls. yellow, in corymbs; samaras 1–1⅛ in. long, wings diverging at an obtuse angle. Italy. Zone 8.

longipes Franch. ex Rehd. Tree, to 30 ft., twigs glabrous, green when young, bark of branchlets smooth; lvs. sometimes ovate and undivided, usually 3-, rarely 5-lobed, 4–6½ in. across, with long-acuminate, entire lobes, light green and soft-pubescent underneath, purplish when young; fls. yellowish-green, in glabrous, short-peduncled or loose corymbs; samaras 1–1¼ in. long, wings diverging at a right angle. China. Zone 7.

macrophyllum Pursh. OREGON M., CANYON M., BIG-LEAF M. To 100 ft., twigs stout, glabrous; lvs. 10–12 in. across, deeply 3–5-lobed, pubescent underneath when young, lobes with large secondary lobes, petiole 4–6 in. long; fls. yellow, in pendulous racemes, fragrant; samaras 1¾ in. long, red when young, hairy, wings diverging at a right angle or nearly parallel. Se. Alaska to Calif. Zone 7. Autumn foliage bright orange.

mandshuricum Maxim. Shrub or tree, to 30 ft., twigs glabrous; lvs. compound, 2–4 in. long, lfts. 3, oblong to oblong-lanceolate, acuminate, obtusely serrate, glaucous underneath, petiole ¾–4 in. long; fls. greenish-yellow, 3 or 5 in a cyme; samaras 1⅛–1½ in. long, nutlets reticulate, wings diverging at a right or an obtuse angle. Manchuria, Korea. Zone 5. Autumn foliage red. Sensitive to late frost in spring.

Matsumurae: *A. palmatum* var.

Maximowiczianum Miq. [*A. nikoense* auth., not (Miq.) Maxim.]. NIKKO M. Round-headed tree, to 50 ft., twigs pilose; lvs. compound, lfts. 3, ovate to elliptic-oblong, shallowly serrate, the middle lft. ovate, 3–5 in. long, petiole hairy; fls. appearing before the lvs., yellow, in 3-fld., nodding, pubescent cymes; samaras 1½–2 in. long, felted, wings nearly parallel to divergent. Japan, cent. China. Zone 6. Autumn foliage scarlet.

Mayrii: *A. truncatum* subsp.

micranthum Siebold & Zucc. Shrub or small tree, twigs reddish-brown; lvs. 5-, rarely 7-lobed, 2–3½ in. long, cordate, lobes ovate, long-acuminate, doubly serrate; fls. greenish-white, in slender racemes; samaras ½–¾ in. long, wings diverging at an obtuse angle to spreading nearly horizontally. Japan. Zone 6.

Miyabei Maxim. [*A. Shibatai* T. Nakai]. Tree, 30–40 ft., twigs pubescent when young, with slightly corky bark; lvs. 5-lobed, 4–6 in. wide, deeply cordate, with bluntly acuminate and bluntly dentate lobes, pubescent on both surfaces when young, petiole 1½–6 in. long, with milky juice; fls. greenish-yellow, in slender-peduncled corymbs; samaras 1–2 in. long, wings spreading horizontally. Japan. Zone 6. Autumn foliage yellow.

Mono: *A. truncatum* subsp. Var. **dissectum:** *A. truncatum* subsp. *Mono* cv. 'Dissectum'. Var. **Mayrii:** *A. truncatum* subsp. Forma **marmoratum:** *A. truncatum* subsp. *Mono* cv. 'Marmoratum'.

monspessulanum L. [*A. monspessulanum* var. *ibericum* (Bieb. ex Willd.) Tausch]. MONTPELLIER M. Shrub or round-headed tree, 20–30, rarely 50 ft.; lvs. somewhat leathery, 3-lobed, 1½–3 in. wide, reticulate underneath, lobes triangular-ovate, nearly entire, petiole without milky sap; fls. in corymbs, greenish-yellow, soon drooping; samaras ¾–1 in. long, reddish, wings connivent or overlapping. N. Afr., s. Eur., w. Asia. Zone 6.

neapolitanum: *A. Opalus* subsp. *obtusatum.*

Negundo L. [*Negundo fraxinifolium* (Raf.) DC.]. BOX ELDER, ASH-LEAVED M. Tree, 50–70 ft.; lvs. pinnate, lfts. 3–5, rarely 7 or 9, ovate, coarsely serrate, terminal lft. often 3-lobed; fls. appearing before the lvs., yellowish-green, the male in pendulous corymbs, the female in pendulous racemes; samaras 1–1½ in. long, glabrous, wings diverging at an acute angle. New Eng., s. to Fla., w. to Sask., Calif., s. to Guatemala; naturalized in the Maritime Provinces and e. Que. Zone 3. Widely cult. around the world.
Subsp. **Negundo.** The typical subsp.; twigs glabrous; lfts. 3–5, rarely 7 or 9, light green below and slightly pubescent when young, later nearly glabrous. Var. **Negundo.** The typical var. of subsp. *Negundo;* twigs green. Forma **Negundo.** Samaras green. Cvs. of subsp. *Negundo* var. **Negundo** include: '**Argenteo-variegatum**': 'Variegatum'; '**Auratum**' [forma *auratum* F. L. Späth], lvs. light green, yellow in autumn; '**Aureo-marginatum**' [cv. 'Elegans'; forma *aureo-marginatum* Dieck; forma *elegans* Schwer.], twigs whitish-green, lvs. small, with a yellow margin; '**Aureo-variegatum**' [forma *aureo-variegatum* F. L. Späth], lvs. blotched with yellow; '**Elegans**': cv. 'Aureo-marginatum'; '**Nanum**' [forma *nanum* Dieck], shrub of weak growth, lfts. asymmetrical; '**Pseudocalifornicum**' [var. *pseudocalifornicum* Schwer.], vigorous, twigs bloomy; '**Variegatum**' [cv. 'Argenteo-variegatum']; var. *variegatum* Jacques; forma *argenteo-variegatum* Bonamy], lvs. with a broad white margin. Forma **sanguineum** L. Martin. Samaras ox-blood-red when young. Ont. Var. **violaceum** (Kirchn.) H. Jaeg. Vigorous, twigs purplish or violet, with glaucous bloom. Mich. to Mont., s. to Mo., Kans. and Colo.; naturalized e. to New Eng. and N.J.
Subsp. **californicum** (Torr. & A. Gray) Wesm. [*A. californicum* (Torr. & A. Gray) D. Dietr.; *Negundo californicum* Torr. & A. Gray]. Twigs hoary-tomentose; lfts. 3, pubescent above, tomentose underneath when young, later merely densely pubescent. Calif. Most of cult. material grown as subsp. *californicum* is subsp. *Negundo* cv. 'Pseudocalifornicum'.

nigrum: *A. saccharum* subsp.

nikoense: see *A. Maximowiczianum.*

nipponicum Hara [*A. parviflorum* Franch. & Sav.]. Small tree, twigs rusty-brown; lvs. 3–5-lobed, 4–6 in. across, lobes broad-ovate, acute, doubly serrate; fls. in long, narrow, upright, puberulous panicles; samaras with wings usually diverging at an obtuse angle. Japan. Zone 6.

oblongum Wallich ex DC. Deciduous or semi-evergreen tree, 20–50 ft.; lvs. oblong or oblong-ovate, 2–4½ in. long, ¾–1½ in. wide, entire or, on young trees, 3-lobed, glaucous underneath; fls. greenish, in short panicles; samaras 1–1¼ in. long, wings diverging at a right angle or spreading nearly horizontally. Himalayas, China. Zone 7. Hardy in the North. Var. **biauritum**: *A. Paxii.* Var. **concolor** Pax. Lvs. green underneath. Cent. China.

obtusatum: *A. Opalus* subsp.

Oliveranum Pax. Tree, 15–30 ft., twigs glabrous, purplish; lvs. 5-lobed, 2–4 in. long, truncate or subcordate at base, glabrous underneath, lobes ovate, caudate-acuminate, finely serrate, middle lobes with 5–8 pairs of lateral veins; fls. whitish, few, in slender-peduncled corymbs; samaras 1 in. long, wings diverging nearly horizontally. China. Zone 6.

Opalus Mill. [*A. italum* Lauth; *A. opulifolium* Vill.]. Tree, 30–40 ft., twigs glabrous; lvs. shallowly 5-lobed, 2½–5 in. across, cordate or truncate, irregularly dentate, pubescent underneath when young; fls. yellow, in drooping corymbs; samaras glabrous, 1–1½ in. long, wings diverging at a right angle or connivent. S. Eur. Zone 6. Var. **hyrcanum**: *A. hyrcanum.* Var. **obtusatum**: subsp. *obtusatum.* Var. **tomentosum**: subsp. *obtusatum.* Subsp. **obtusatum** (Waldst. & Kit. ex Willd.) Gams [var. *obtusatum* (Waldst. & Kit. ex Willd.) A. Henry; var. *tomentosum* (Tausch) Rehd.; *A. neapolitanum* Ten.; *A. obtusatum* Waldst. & Kit. ex Willd.]. Lvs. to 6½ in. across, tomentose underneath. S. Italy, Yugoslavia, nw. Afr.

opulifolium: *A. Opalus.*

orientale L. Shrub, or rarely tree, 15–35 ft., deciduous or semievergreen, twigs glabrous; lvs. ovate to 3-lobed, ¾–2 in. long, entire or slightly crenulate-denticulate, leathery; fls. greenish-yellow, in few-fld., upright corymbs; samaras ¾ in. long, wings parallel or diverging at a right angle. E. Medit. region. Zone 7.

×**Osmastonii** Gamble: *A. Campbellii* × *A. laevigatum.* To 90 ft.; lvs. ovate-lanceolate to 3-lobed, 4–6 in. long, 2½–3 in. wide, acuminate, sharply serrate; fls. yellowish-white, in panicles; samaras with wings diverging at a right angle. Himalayas.

palmatum Thunb. [*A. polymorphum* Siebold & Zucc., not Spach]. JAPANESE M. Shrub or tree, 20–50 ft., twigs slender, glabrous; lvs. palmately and deeply 5–11-lobed or -parted to about the middle, 2–4 in. across, glabrous, lobes lanceolate to broadly ovate, acuminate, sharply doubly serrate; fls. reddish-purple, in small, glabrous corymbs; samaras glabrous, wings diverging at an obtuse angle, but incurved above. Korea, China, Japan. Zone 5. Autumn foliage scarlet. A very variable sp., especially under cult.; the variations in the wild may be accounted for in the following vars. Var. **palmatum** [var. *Thunbergii* Pax]. The typical var.; lvs. 1½–3 in. wide, 5–7-lobed, lobes lanceolate to broadly lanceolate, doubly serrate; wings of samara about ⅝ in. long including nutlet. Var. **heptalobum** Rehd. [var. *amoenum* (Carrière) Ohwi; var. *septemlobum* C. Koch, not *A. septemlobum* Thunb.]. Lvs. larger, 2½–5 in. wide, usually 7- sometimes 9-lobed, finely serrate; wings of samara ¾–1 in. long including nutlet. Forma **latilobatum** (G. Koidz.) Ohwi [var. *latilobatum* G. Koidz.]. A forma of var. *heptalobum*; lf. lobes broader, triangular-ovate. Var. **Matsumurae** (G. Koidz.) Mak. [*A. Matsumurae* (G. Koidz.) G. Koidz.]. Lvs. 5–9- but usually 7-lobed, 2–4 in. wide, lobes narrowly ovate to broadly lanceolate, strongly doubly or incisedly serrate; wings of samara ⅝–1 in. long including nutlet.

Named cvs. of the preceding vars. are numerous, and are themselves often listed as vars. In these the lvs. may be green, red to purple, yellowish, variegated, and may be variously dissected. Some of the better-known cvs. are grouped below according to general lf. color.

Cvs. with green lvs. include: 'Bonfire', lvs. dissected, red when young; 'Crispum' [forma *crispum* André], lvs. crinkled; 'Dissectum' [var. *dissectum* (Thunb.) Miq.; var. *multifidum* C. Koch], brs. weeping, lvs. dissected; 'Elegans' [forma *elegans* Nichols.], lvs. dissected, lobes subentire, usually 5; 'Hagoromo': 'Sessilifolium'; 'Koshimino': 'Sessilifolium'; 'Linearilobum' [var. *linearilobum* Miq.], lvs. dissected; 'Lutescens', lvs. yellow in autumn; 'Oginogare', lvs. crinkled; 'Okushimo', lvs. with upcurled margins; 'Ribesifolium', lvs. small, becoming bronzy when old; 'Rubellum', similar to 'Bonfire'; 'Sangokaku', bark coral to scarlet in winter; 'Scolopendriifolium' [forma *scolopendriifolium* Schwer.], lvs. dissected and crinkled; 'Seigai', lvs. crimson in early spring but becoming green in summer; 'Sessilifolium' [cvs. 'Hagoromo', 'Koshimino'; var. *sessilifolium* (Siebold & Zucc.) Maxim.], lvs. dissected; 'Shishigashira', dwarf shrub, lvs. crinkled; 'Sinuatum' [forma *sinuatum* Schwer.], lvs. dissected; 'Tsukumo', similar to 'Shishigashira'; 'Viride', lvs. bright green; 'Waterfall', lvs. dissected; 'Yatsufusa', lvs. very small, with a red margin in the spring and red in autumn.

Cvs. with red or reddish lvs. include: 'Atropurpureum' [var. *atropurpureum* (Van Houtte) Schwer.; forma *atropurpureum* Van Houtte]; 'Bicolor' [forma *bicolor* C. Koch]; 'Bloodgood'; 'Bonfire', lvs. dissected, becoming green in summer; 'Burgundy Lace', lvs. dissected; 'Chishio' [forma *Chisio* G. Koidz.]; 'Crimson Queen', lvs. dissected; 'Ever Red', lvs. dissected; 'Hillieri'; 'Mioun'; 'Nicholsonii'

[forma *Nicholsonii* Schwer.]; 'Nigrum' [var. *nigrum* Hort.], lvs. very large, dark purplish-black; 'Nomura Nishiki', brs. weeping, lvs. dark red, feathery; 'Ornatum' [forma *ornatum* Carrière], lvs. dissected; 'Oshio-beni', lvs. dissected; 'Purpureum'; 'Rosco Red'; 'Roseo-marginatum' [forma *roseo-marginatum* Van Houtte]; 'Rubellum' [forma *rubellum* Pax], similar to 'Bonfire'; 'Rubrum' [forma *rubrum* Hort. ex Schwer.]; 'Sanguineum' [forma *sanguineum* Carrière]; 'Scolopendriifolium Rubrum', lvs. dissected and crinkled; 'Seigai', crimson in early spring, becoming green in summer; 'Suminagashi', lvs. dissected; 'Tamukeyama' [forma *Tamukeyama* G. Koidz.], lvs. dissected and crinkled; 'Yatsufusa', lvs. green in summer; 'Yezo-nishiki', lvs. blood-red and vermilion.

Cvs. with yellow or golden lvs. include: 'Aoyagi'; 'Aureum': *A. japonicum* cv.; 'Osakazuki', lvs. blood-red in autumn.

Cvs. with variegated lvs. include: 'Aocha-nishiki', lvs. 9-lobed, green, cream, rose, and white; 'Argenteum', dwarf shrub with silver and pink lvs.; 'Aureo-variegatum', lvs. green and yellow; 'Dissectum Variegatum', brs. weeping, lvs. dissected, green and pink; 'Friderici-Guillelmi' [forma *Friderici-Guillelmi* Carrière], lvs. dissected, green, white, and pink; 'Laceleaf', lvs. deep green and yellow; 'Murakumo', lvs. green and yellow; 'Reticulatum' [forma *reticulatum* André], lvs. showing network of green veins on yellowish-white; 'Roseo-marginatum', lvs. green and pink; 'Roseum', lvs. green and deep pink; 'Sagara-nishiki', lvs. green, pink, and yellow; 'Tricolor' [var. *tricolor* Nichols.], lvs. green, pink, and white; 'Tsumagaki', lvs. yellowish-green and white; 'Versicolor' [forma *versicolor* Van Houtte], lvs. green, spotted, the spots pink at first, then white.

Cvs. 'Aconitifolium' and 'Filicifolium' are *A. japonicum* cv. 'Aconitifolium'.

papilio: *A. caudatum.*

parviflorum: *A. nipponicum.*

parvifolium: *A.* ×*coriaceum.*

Paxii Franch. [*A. oblongum* var. *biauritum* W. W. Sm.]. Tree, to 30 ft., evergreen; lvs. often apically 3-lobed, shining, thick, leathery, smooth above, distinctly reticulate underneath, lobes acuminate; fls. with long sepals, petals, and stamens; samaras with wings diverging at a right angle. Sw. China. Zone 7.

pectinatum Wallich ex Nichols. Tree; lvs. 3-lobed, 2½–3½ in. across, cordate, serrate, leathery, lobes acuminate, terminal lobe triangular; fls. in racemes; samaras ¾–1 in. long, nutlets flat, wings spreading horizontally. E. Himalayas, w. China, n. Burma. Zone 7. Related to *A. Forrestii.*

pensylvanicum L. [*A. striatum* Du Roi]. STRIPED M., PENNSYLVANIA M., WHISTLEWOOD, MOOSEWOOD. Tree, 15–20 or occasionally 35 ft., twigs green, brs. and young trunks green and conspicuously striped with white lines; lvs. roundish-obovate, 3-lobed at apex, 5–8 in. across, subcordate, serrulate, pubescent underneath when young, lobes acuminate; fls. yellow, in pendulous, glabrous racemes; samaras ¾–1 in. long, wings diverging at an obtuse angle. Que. to Wisc., s. to n. Ga. Zone 3. Autumn foliage clear yellow.

pictum: as originally published, a synonym of *Kalopanax pictus*, but later and in hort. misapplied to *A. truncatum* subsp. *Mono* cv. 'Marmoratum.' Var. **marmoratum**: *A. truncatum* subsp. *Mono* cv. Var. **parviflorum**: *A. truncatum* subsp. *Mono.*

platanoides L. NORWAY M. Round-headed tree, 60–70 or occasionally 90 ft., twigs glabrous; lvs. 5-lobed, glossy, lobes sharply acuminate, remotely dentate with pointed teeth, petiole with milky sap; fls. appearing before the lvs., greenish-yellow, in many-fld., upright corymbs; samaras pendulous, 1½–2 in. long, nutlet flat, wings spreading nearly horizontally. Eur., Caucasus, n. Turkey, n. Iran. Zone 4. Autumn foliage (in some areas) bright yellow. Cvs. are: 'Albescens' [forma *albescens* Dipp.], lvs. creamy-white in spring but reddish later; 'Albomarginatum', similar to 'Drummondii'; 'Albo-variegatum' [cv. 'Variegatum'; forma *albo-variegatum* Nichols.; var. *variegatum* Loud.], similar to 'Drummondii', but lvs. tinted with pink when young; 'Almira', low tree, of loose umbrella form; 'Argenteovariegatum', similar to 'Drummondii'; 'Ascendens': 'Erectum'; 'Atropurpureum Globosum' [cv. 'Globosum Atropurpureum'], similar to 'Crimson King'; 'Aureo-marginatum' [forma *aureo-marginatum* Pax], lvs. light green, slightly touched with pink; 'Charles F. Irish', large, round-headed tree, brs. upsweeping, lvs. small; 'Clarkei', similar to 'Drummondii'; 'Cleveland', upright oval tree, lvs. large and dark green, clear yellow in autumn; 'Columnare' [forma *columnare* (Carrière) Schwer.], columnar; 'Crimson King' [cvs. 'Nigrum', 'Schwedleri Nigrum'], lvs. dark maroon; 'Crispum' [var. *crispum* (Lauth) Spach], lvs. with crinkled margin; 'Cucullatum' [subvar. *cucullatum* Lauche], lvs. with short, crimped lobes; 'Dissectum' [forma *dissectum* Jacq.], growth weak, lvs. divided nearly to base, reddish-brown when young; 'Drummondii' [cv. 'Variegatum Drummond'], lvs. light green in center, silver-white at margins; 'Emerald Queen', lvs. glossy, dark green, leathery; 'Erectum' [cvs. 'Ascendens', 'Pyramidale'; forma *erectum* Slav.; *A. platanoides ascendens* Chadw.], growth weak, pyramidal, brs.

short, upright, lvs. larger and darker than in 'Columnare'; **'Faassen's Black'**, similar to 'Crimson King', but lvs. darker; **'Globe'**: 'Globosum'; **'Globosum'** [cv. 'Globe'; forma *globosum* Nichols.], dwarf, round, compact tree; **'Globosum Atropurpureum'**: 'Atropurpureum Globosum'; **'Goldsworth Purple'**, similar to 'Crimson King'; **'Harlequin'**, round-headed tree, lvs. variegated; **'Improved Columnar'** [cv. 'Roch'], graceful, columnar tree; **'Laciniatum'** [forma *laciniatum* Ait.], EAGLE-CLAW M., erect, slender, lvs. cuneate, lobes ending in slender, curved, clawlike points; **'Lorbergii'**: 'Palmatifidum'; **'Nigrum'**: 'Crimson King'; **'Olmsted'**, columnar tree, not exceeding 25 ft.; **'Palmatifidum'** [cv. 'Lorbergii'; var. *Lorbergii* Van Houtte; var. *palmatifidum* Tausch], lvs. divided nearly to base, light green; **'Purpurascens'**: 'Rubrum'; **'Pyramidale'**: 'Erectum'; **'Reitenbachii'** [forma *Reitenbachii* Nichols.; *A. Reitenbachii* Hort. ex Dipp.], lvs. deeply divided, bronzy-green, tinged with purple when young, dark purplish in summer; **'Roch'**: 'Improved Columnar'; **'Royal Red'**, well-shaped tree, lvs. remaining rich dark red and very glossy throughout growing season; **'Rubrum'** [cv. 'Purpurascens'; var. *purpurascens* Willk.; var. *rubrum* Herder], lvs. green in summer, rich red in autumn; **'Schwedleri'** [forma *Schwedleri* C. Koch; *A. Schwedleri* Hort.], SCHWEDLER M., lvs. soft red when young, later turning bronzy-green, then red in autumn; **'Schwedleri Nigrum'**: 'Crimson King'; **'Silver Variegated'**, lvs. green, with almost white edging; **'Stollii'** [forma *Stollii* F. L. Späth], lvs. shallowly 3-lobed, up to 9 in. across, red when young; **'Summer Shade'**, upright tree of rapid growth, lvs. large, very dark, very leathery; **'Undulatum'** [forma *undulatum* Dieck], lvs. deeply cordate, shortly and acutely serrate, lobes crisped; **'Variegatum'**: 'Albo-variegatum'; **'Variegatum Drummond'**: 'Drummondii'; **'Walderseei'** [forma *Walderseei* F. L. Späth], lvs. very densely speckled with tiny white dots.

polymorphum: see *A. palmatum*.

pseudoplatanus L. SYCAMORE, SYCAMORE M., MOCK PLANE. To 100 ft., twigs glabrous; lvs. 5-lobed, 3½–6½ in. across, cordate, lobes ovate, coarsely crenate-serrate, glaucescent underneath; fls. yellowish-green, in pendulous panicles; samaras glabrous, 1½–2 in. long, wings diverging at an acute or a right angle. Zone 5. Eur. and w. Asia. Var. **pseudoplatanus**. The typical var.; lvs. glabrous underneath. Cvs. are: **'Albo-variegatum'** [forma *albo-variegatum* Kirchn.], lvs. blotched and striped with white; **'Atropurpureum'** [cv. 'Purpurascens'; forma *atropurpureum* F. L. Späth; forma *purpurascens* Pax], lvs. maroon when young, later dark green above, deep red underneath, wings of samaras purplish; **'Erectum'**, pyramidal, brs. upright, lvs. green, cordate; **'Erythrocarpum'** [forma *erythrocarpum* Carrière], lvs. smaller, samaras bright red before maturity; **'Flavo-variegatum'** [forma *flavo-variegatum* Hayne], lvs. variegated with yellow; **'Handjery'**: 'Prinz Handjery'; **'Leopoldii'** [forma *Leopoldii* Lem.], lvs. dark rosy-pink when young, later variegated with yellowish-pink; **'Nervosum'** [forma *nervosum* Schwer.], growth weak, pyramidal, lvs. yellow between veins; **'Prinz Handjery'** [cv. 'Handjery'; forma *Handjeryi* F. L. Späth], growth weak, lvs. yellow to red when young, later with yellowish dots at base; **'Purpureum'** [forma *purpureum* Loud.], lvs. purple underneath; **'Purpurascens'**: 'Atropurpureum'; **'Pyramidale'** [forma *pyramidale* Nichols.], tree pyramidal, lvs. green, cordate; **'Quadricolor'** [var. *quadricolor* Schwer.], lvs. green, spotted with pure white and light rosy-buff when young; **'Rubrum'** [subvar. *rubrum* Schwer.], lvs. dark green above, wine-red underneath; **'Spaethii'** [forma *Spaethii* Schwer.; *A. Spaethii* Hort.], lvs. purplish-crimson underneath; **'Variegatum'** [forma *variegatum* Weston], lvs. variegated with white, reddish when young; **'Worleei'** [forma *Worleei* Ohlend. f.], lvs. orange-yellow when young, later deep yellow in the sun, green in the shade, petiole reddish. Var. **tomentosum** Tausch [*A. villosum* J. Presl & K. Presl]. Lvs. pubescent underneath.

pseudo-Sieboldianum (Pax) Kom. Like *A. Sieboldianum*, but lvs. 9–11-lobed, deeply serrate; fls. purple, on soon-glabrous peduncles. Manchuria, Korea. Zone 5.

purpurascens: *A. diabolicum* var.

pycnanthum C. Koch. Like *A. rubrum*, but tree smaller, twigs bluish; lvs. 3-lobed, 2–3½ in. long, 1¼ in. wide, lobes sometimes very short, doubly obtuse-serrate; samaras with wings nearly parallel. Japan. Zone 6.

Reitenbachii: *A. platanoides* cv.

rubrum L. [*A. sanguineum* Spach; *Rufacer rubrum* (L.) Small]. RED M., SCARLET M., SOFT M., SWAMP M. To 120 ft., open, twigs glabrous; lvs. 3–5-lobed, 3–6 in. across, more or less cordate, lobes triangular-ovate, short-acuminate, unequally crenate-serrate, lustrous above, glaucous underneath; fls. appearing long before lvs., male and female fls. often on separate trees, red, rarely yellowish, in short, dense clusters; samaras, ¾–1 in. long, glabrous, on pendulous stalks, wings bright red when young, diverging at an acute angle to connivent. Nfld. to Fla., w. to Minn., Iowa, Okla., and Tex. Zone 3. Autumn foliage scarlet and orange. A source of commercial wood. Var. **rubrum**. The typical var.; lvs. 3–5-lobed; fls. red or yellowish; samaras glabrous. Forma

pallidiflorum (C. Koch ex Pax) Fern. [var. *pallidiflorum* C. Koch ex Pax]. Fls. light yellow. Autumn foliage yellow. Forma **tomentosum** (Desf.) Dansereau [var. **tomentosum** (Desf.) Kirchn.]. Lvs. persistently pubescent beneath, those of fertile brs. somewhat cordate, suborbicular to triangular-ovate. Cvs. of var. **rubrum** are: **'Armstrong'**, tree narrowly columnar; **'Autumn Flame'**, dense, round-headed tree, lvs. becoming scarlet earlier and remaining longer; **'Bowhall'**, pyramidal tree, lvs. coloring well in autumn; **'Columnare'** [var. *columnare* Rehd.], upright, columnar tree, lvs. deep green, turning bronze to red in autumn; **'Conica Scanlon'**: 'Scanlon'; **'Gerling'**, broadly pyramidal tree; **'Globosum'** [var. *globosum* Rehd.], dwarf, compact tree, fls. bright scarlet; **'October Glory'**, lvs. lustrous, turning brilliant crimson in autumn and persisting longer; **'Palmatum'** [var. *palmatum* Hort. ex Schwer.], twigs pendulous, lvs. large, deeply 5-lobed, fls. male only; **'Paul E. Tilford'** [cv. 'Tilford'], globe-shaped; **'Pyramidale'**: 'Scanlon'; **'Scanlon'** [cv. 'Conica Scanlon'; cv. 'Pyramidale'], pyramidal, compact tree, lvs. turning orange, amber, and red in autumn; **'Schlesingeri'** [forma *Schlesingeri* Sarg. & Schwer.], vigorous, lvs. turning brilliant red earlier; **'Tilford'**: 'Paul E. Tilford.' Var. **Drummondii** (Hook. & Arn. ex Nutt.) Sarg. [*A. Drummondii* Hook. & Arn. ex Nutt.]. DRUMMOND M. Lvs. 5-lobed, more deeply cleft, more leathery, remaining pubescent underneath; samaras 1¼–1½ in. long, bright scarlet. Fla. to Tex., n. to Va., s. Ind., Ill. and Mo. Var. **tridens**: var. *trilobum*. Var. **trilobum** K. Koch [var. *tridens* A. Wood; *A. carolinianum* Walt.; *Rufacer carolinianum* (Walt.) Small]. Lvs. smaller, reniform to ovate, 3-lobed near apex, rounded or broad, cuneate at base, usually pubescent underneath. Fla. to Tex., n. to Nov. Sc., s. Que., and s. Ill.

rufinerve Siebold & Zucc. Tree, 30–40 ft., twigs glaucous; lvs. 3-lobed, 2½–6 in. long, unequally doubly serrate, rufous-pubescent on veins beneath when young; fls. pale green, in upright, rusty-pubescent racemes; samaras pubescent when young, ¾ in. long, wings diverging at an obtuse angle. Japan. Zone 6. Autumn foliage crimson. Cv. **'Albo-limbatum'** [var. *albo-limbatum* Hook.f.]. Lvs. broadly margined or wholly spotted with white. Less hardy than typical *A. rufinerve*. Cv. **'Erythrocladum'** has been listed. May be a cv. of *A. pensylvanicum*.

saccharinum L. [*A. dasycarpum* J. F. Ehrh.; *Argentacer saccharinum* (L.) Small]. SILVER M., SOFT M., WHITE M., RIVER M. Tree, 90–130 ft., bark gray, brs. pendulous; lvs. 5-lobed, 4–6 in. across, with acuminate, deeply and doubly serrate lobes, bright green above, silvery-white beneath, pubescent when young; fls. appearing long before lvs., pinkish, in short, dense clusters, petals 0; samaras 1½–2½ in. long, pubescent when young, wings diverging almost at a right angle, curved. Que. to Fla., w. to Minn., and Okla. Zone 3. Autumn foliage yellow and red. A source of commercial wood. Cvs. are: **'Albo-variegatum'** [forma *albo-variegatum* (F. L. Späth) Pax], lvs. flecked with white and pink; **'Beebe Cutleaf Weeping'** [cv. 'Laciniatum Beebe']; **'Blairii'**, well-shaped, of rapid growth, with stronger brs.; **'Crispum'** [forma *crispum* Schwer.], lvs. yellow-green, crisped; **'Fastigiatum'**: 'Pyramidale'; **'Heterophyllum'** [forma *heterophyllum* Hort. ex Schwer.], of upright habit, lvs. asymmetrical, dissected nearly to base; **'Laciniatum'**: 'Wieri'; **'Laciniatum Beebe'**: 'Beebe Cutleaf Weeping'; **'Longifolium'** [*A. dasycarpum* forma *longifolium* F. L. Späth], lvs. deeply 3-lobed; **'Lutescens'** [forma *lutescens* (F. L. Späth) Pax], lvs. orange when young, later yellowish, especially in the sun; **'Pyramidale'** [cv. 'Fastigiatum'; forma *pyramidale* (F. L. Späth) Pax], columnar; **'Silver Queen'**, large tree, of rapid growth, fls. male only; **'Skinneri'**, pyramidal, semiweeping tree, lvs. dissected; **'Tripartitum'** [forma *tripartitum* Schwer.], twigs with very large white lenticels, lvs. large, deeply 3-parted; **'Wieri'** [cv. 'Laciniatum'; forma *Wieri* (Wier) Schwer.; var. *laciniatum* Pax], pyramidal tree, lvs. symmetrical, dissected nearly to base.

saccharophorum: *A. saccharum*.

saccharum Marsh. [*A. saccharophorum* C. Koch]. SUGAR M., ROCK M., HARD M. To 130 ft., bark gray, furrowed, twigs glabrous, brown or gray; lvs. 3–5-lobed, 4–6 in. across, usually with narrow and deep sinuses, cordate, glabrous or pubescent beneath, lobes acuminate, sparingly coarsely dentate; fls. appearing before lvs., without petals, greenish-creamy-yellow, on pendulous hairy pedicels, in clustered corymbs; samaras glabrous, 1–1¾ in. long, wings slightly divergent. Que. to Fla. and Tex. Zone 3. Autumn foliage gold, orange, scarlet, or crimson. The chief source of commercial maple wood; sap yields maple syrup and maple sugar. Subsp. **saccharum**. The typical subsp.; bark usually gray; lvs. mostly 5-lobed, with acuminate lobules, light green to glaucescent beneath, glabrescent or pubescent, very variable. Nov. Sc. to Minn., s. to n. Ala. and Okla. Forma **Rugelii** (Pax) Palmer & Steyerm. Lvs. 3-lobed, usually broader than long, somewhat leathery, lobes entire. The cvs. of subsp. **saccharum** include: **'Columnare'**: 'Newton Sentry'; **'Erectum'**: 'Newton Sentry'; **'Globosum'**, shrub, broader than tall; **'Green Mountain'**, tree with oval crown, lvs. very thick, dark green all summer; **'Laciniatum'**: 'Sweet Shadow'; **'Monumentale'**: 'Temple's Upright'; **'Newton Sentry'** [cvs. 'Columnare', 'Erectum', 'Pyramidale'; forma *columnare* (Temple) Harkn.], often confused with 'Temple's Upright', but with strong central leader and few, ascending, stubby brs., lvs. leathery, undulate, dark green; **'Pyramidale'**: 'Newton Sentry'; **'Sweet Shadow'** [cv. 'Laciniatum'], lvs. deeply divided; **'Temple's Upright'** [cv, 'Monumentale'], often confused with 'Newton Sentry', but brs. many, ascending, with no dominant leader, lvs. not leathery, yellow-green. Subsp. **floridanum:** *A. barbatum.* Subsp. **grandidentatum** (Nutt. ex Torr. & A. Gray) Desmarais [*A. grandidentatum* Nutt. ex Torr. & A. Gray]. ROCKY MT. SUGAR M., BIG-TOOTH M. To 40 ft., bark dark brown; lvs. 3–5-lobed, usually hastate at the base or cordate. W. Mont. and Wyo. to n. Mex. in the mts. Subsp. **leucoderme** (Small) Desmarais [*A. leucoderme* Small]. CHALK M. To 30 ft., bark gray-brown to chalky; lvs. 3–5-lobed, 2–3½ in. across, usually acuminate, yellowish-green beneath. N.C. to Ga. and La. Subsp. **nigrum** (Michx.f.) Desmarais [*A. nigrum* Michx.f.]. BLACK M. Bark blackish, twigs mottled gray and brown; lvs. 3-lobed, to 7 in. across, with drooping sides, often with leafy stipules. Iowa to sw. Que., s. to N.C. Cv. **'Senecaense'** [*A.* × *senecaense* Slav.] is a hybrid between subsp. *leucoderme* and subsp. *saccharum;* a small, compact tree, similar to subsp. *grandidentatum.*

sanguineum: *A. rubrum.*

Schwedleri: *A. platanoides* cv.

scolpendriifolium: *A. palmatum* cv.

×**senecaense:** *A. saccharum* cv.

Shibatai: *A. Miyabei.*

Shirasawanum G. Koidz. Similar to *A. japonicum,* but lvs. usually cordate 11–13-lobed; petals pale yellow, sepals purple, ovary pubescent; samaras ¾ in. long, glabrous, wings diverging at a very obtuse angle, nutlet dark purple-brown. Japan. Zone 6.

Sieboldianum Miq. Shrub or small tree, twigs pubescent when young; lvs. 7–9-lobed, 2–6 in. across, cordate to nearly truncate at base, lobes ovate-oblong, acuminate, sharply serrate, petioles pubescent when young; fls. yellowish, on long, nodding, pubescent peduncles; samaras ¾ in. long, diverging almost horizontally. Japan. Zone 6. Autumn foliage red. Var. **microphyllum** Maxim. Lvs. smaller.

Spaethii: *A. pseudoplatanus* cv.

spicatum Lam. MOUNTAIN M. Shrub or small tree, to 30 ft., twigs grayish, pubescent; lvs. 3–5-lobed, 3–5 in. across, cordate, light green above, pubescent beneath, lobes ovate, acuminate, coarsely and irregularly serrate; fls. greenish-yellow, in upright, pubescent, narrow spikes; samaras ¾ in. long, pubescent when young, ribbed, yellowish to reddish, wings diverging at an acute or right angle. Nfld., s. to n. Ga., w. to e. Sask. and ne. Minn. Zone 3. Autumn foliage orange or scarlet to yellow.

stachyophyllum Hiern [*A. tetramerum* Pax; *A. tetramerum* var. *betulifolium* (Maxim.) Rehd.]. Tree, 20–30 ft., twigs glabrous; lvs. ovate, 2–3½ in. long, 1½–2 in. wide, acuminate, usually 3-nerved at base, unequally incised-serrate, sometimes also lobed or incised, slightly pubescent beneath; fls. 4-merous, yellow, male fls. 3–5 in short corymbs, female fls. in elongated racemes; samaras 1–1½ in. long, glabrous, wings diverging at an acute angle. E. Himalayas to w. China. Zone 7.

sterculiaceum Wallich [*A. villosum* Wallich, not J. Presl & K. Presl]. Tree, to 50 ft. or more, bark gray; lvs. 3–5-lobed, 3–7 in. across, cordate, remotely dentate, somewhat leathery, silky-hairy when young, glabrescent; infl. densely hairy, usually lateral; samaras to 2 in. long, with wings erect to divergent. Himalayas to w. China. Zone 7.

striatum: *A. pensylvanicum.*

tataricum L. TATARIAN M. Bushy shrub or small tree, to 30 ft., twigs glabrous; lvs. broadly ovate to ovate-oblong, 2–4 in. long, rounded to cordate, acuminate to acute, irregularly doubly serrate; fls. greenish-white, in upright, glabrous, long-peduncled panicles; samaras ¾–1¼ in. long, glabrous, reddish in later summer, wings nearly parallel. Se. Eur., w. Asia. Zone 5. Autumn foliage yellow. Var. **aidzuense:** *A. Ginnala.*

tegmentosum Maxim. Tree, to 30 ft., twigs glabrous, later striped white on green and brown; lvs. 3–5-lobed, generally hexagonal in shape, 3–6 in. across, cordate or subcordate, lobes acuminate, doubly serrulate; fls. yellowish-green, in pendulous racemes; samaras ¾–1⅛ in. long, wings spreading nearly horizontally. Manchuria and Korea. Zone 5. Autumn foliage yellow.

tenuifolium (G. Koidz.) G. Koidz. Related to *A. Shirasawanum,* with lvs. ovate, deeply and usually 9-, rarely 11-lobed, 1½–2½ in. wide, membranous; samaras loosely pubescent or glabrous, wings ascending. Japan. Zone 6.

tetramerum: *A. stachyophyllum.* Var. **betulifolium:** *A. stachyophyllum.*

Trautvetteri Medv. Tree, to 50 ft., twigs glabrous, dark red-brown at maturity; lvs. deeply 5-lobed, 4–8 in. across, cordate, glaucous beneath, lobes ovate-oblong, acuminate, irregularly dentate; fls. in

erect, pyramidal panicles; samaras to 2¼ in. long, pubescent when young, reddish, wings diverging at an acute angle to nearly connivent. Caucasus, n. Turkey. Zone 6. Often offered erroneously in the trade as *A. insigne.*

trifidum: *A. Buergeranum.*

triflorum Kom. Tree, 20–40 ft., bark peeling and flaking, tannish yellow-brown, twigs warty; lvs. trifoliolate, 2–4 in. long, dull green on both sides, sparsely hairy; samaras 1–1½ in. long, wings spreading nearly horizontally to diverging at an obtuse angle, nutlets densely pubescent. Manchuria and Korea. Zone 5.

truncatum Bunge. SHANTUNG M. Tree, 50–75 ft.; lvs. shallowly to deeply 5–7-lobed, 3–6 in. across, glossy, lobes acuminate; fls. in corymbs; samaras with wings merely diverging to spreading nearly horizontally, nutlets flattened. E.-cent. Asia. Zone 5. Autumn foliage golden-yellow to orange. Subsp. **truncatum.** The typical subsp.; tree, to 50 ft.; lvs. 5–7-lobed; fls. yellow-green; samaras 1–2 in. long. N. China. Subsp. **Mayrii** (Schwer.) E. Murr. [*A. Mayrii* Schwer.; *A. Mono* var. *Mayrii* (Schwer.) Nakai]. Tree, to 75 ft., brs. smooth, glaucous-green or -purplish to brown and gray; lvs. mostly 5-lobed, lobes usually not again lobed; fls. greenish-white; samaras 1–1¾ in. long. N. Japan and Sakhalin. Subsp. **Mono** (Maxim.) E. Murr. [*A. Mono* Maxim.; *A. pictum* var. *parviflorum* C. K. Schneid.]. Tree, to 60 ft., twigs becoming gray and slightly fissured the second year; lvs. mostly 5-lobed, lobes often again lobed; fls. greenish-yellow; samaras ¾–1¼ in. long. Manchuria, Korea, Sakhalin. Cv. **'Dissectum'** [*A. Mono* var. *dissectum* (Wesm.) Honda]. Lvs. divided beyond the middle, lobes long-acuminate. Cv. **'Marmoratum'** [*A. Mono* forma *marmoratum* (Nichols.) Rehd.; *A. pictum* var. *marmoratum* Nichols.]. Lvs. densely dotted and blotched with white.

Tschonoskii Maxim. Shrub or tree, 15–20 ft.; lvs. orbicular-ovate, 5-, rarely 7-lobed, 2–4 in. across, cordate, lobes sharply and doubly serrate, long-acuminate, rufous-pubescent along veins beneath when young; fls. yellowish-white, in glabrous racemes; samaras ¾–1¼ in. long, wings incurved, diverging at a right or an obtuse angle. Japan. Zone 6. Autumn foliage bright yellow.

ukurunduense: *A. caudatum* subsp.

velutinum Boiss. [*A. insigne* var. *velutinum* (Boiss.) Boiss. & Buhse]. PERSIAN M. Tree, to 120 ft.; lvs. 5-lobed, 5–7 in. across or more, slightly cordate, pubescent beneath, lobes ovate, coarsely and irregularly crenate-serrate; fls. yellowish-green, in upright panicles; samaras 1–2 in. long, puberulous, wings diverging at a right or an obtuse angle. Se. Caucasus and n. Iran. Zone 7. Var. **glabrescens** (Boiss. & Buhse) Rehd. [*A. insigne* Boiss. & Buhse; *A. insigne* var. *glabrescens* Boiss. & Buhse]. Lvs. larger, to 10 or 12 in. across, glaucous and glabrous beneath. Cv. **'Van Volxemii'** belongs here.

villosum: See *A. sterculiaceum* and *A. pseudoplatanus* var. *tomentosum.*

vitifolium: *A. japonicum* cv.

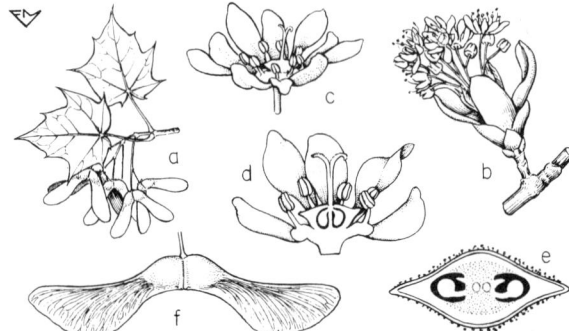

ACERACEAE. *Acer platanoides:* **a,** fruiting branch, × ⅙; **b,** inflorescence, × ½; **c,** flower, × 1½; **d,** flower, vertical section, × 2; **e,** ovary, cross section, × 5; **f,** fruit, × ½. (From Bailey, *Manual of Cultivated Plants,* ed. 2.)

ACERACEAE Juss. MAPLE FAMILY. Dicot.; 2 genera and about 200 spp. of trees and shrubs of n. temp. regions and of trop. mts.; lvs. opp., simple, petioled; infl. racemose, corymbose, or clustered; fls. bisexual or unisexual, sepals and petals 4–5, stamens 4–10, ovary superior, 2-celled; fr. a pair of samaras, separating when ripe. *Acer* is important in hort.

ACERANTHUS: *Epimedium.*

ACHILLEA L. YARROW. *Compositae* (Anthemis Tribe). Between 60 and 100 spp. of usually aromatic per. herbs, native to N. Temp. Zone of mainly the Old World; lvs. alt. or in basal rosettes, simple and toothed to pinnately dissected; fl. heads mostly in corymbs, rarely solitary, usually radiate, sometimes discoid, involucral bracts imbricate in several rows, dry and often scarious on margins, receptacle flat or convex or conical, scaly; fls. white, pink, or yellow, disc fls. tubular, bisexual, fertile, ray fls. female and fertile, sometimes absent; achenes strongly compressed, glabrous, not ribbed but with callose margins, pappus absent.

Yarrows are grown in borders and the smaller species in rock gardens, and bloom in spring and summer, often lasting until autumn. They are of easy culture, doing best in full sun. Propagated by division and rarely by cuttings; seeds should give blooming plants the second year.

ageratifolia (Sibth. & Sm.) Benth. Tufted, silvery-pubescent per., to 8 in.; lower lvs. in rosettes, linear to linear-lanceolate, to 1½ in. long, sharply toothed, often deeply so; heads solitary, to 1 in. across; ray fls. white. N. Greece. Var. **Aizoon** (Griseb.) Boiss. [*Anthemis Aizoon* Griseb.]. Lvs. entire or merely toothed. Greece.

Ageratum L. SWEET Y. Erect, essentially glabrous, woody-based per., to 1½ ft.; lvs. clustered, oblong, 1–2 in. long, blunt, toothed, upper lvs. sessile; heads to about ⅛ in. across, in compact corymbs to 1½ in. across; fls. yellow. S. Eur.

Aizoon: a listed name for *A. ageratifolia* var.

argentea: *Chrysanthemum isabellinum,* but material offered as *A. argentea* is probably *A. Clavennae.*

argentifolia: a listed name of no botanical standing; perhaps an error for *A. ageratifolia.*

atrata L. Scentless, tufted per., sts. erect to ascending, to 1 ft.; lvs. acutely and somewhat coarsely pinnately dissected into linear segms., essentially glabrous, deep glossy green; heads to ¾ in. across, 3–15 in loose corymbs, involucral bracts with black margins; fls. white. Cent. Eur. Subsp. **multifida** (DC.) Heimerl [*A. multifida* (DC.) Griseb., an illegitimate name]. Lvs. somewhat villous; heads to ½ in. across.

aurea: *A. tomentosa* cv.

chrysocoma Friv. Tufted, densely silky-hairy per., sts. erect, to 6 in., unbranched; lvs. linear-lanceolate, to about 1 in. long, hairy; heads to about ¼ in. across, in dense corymbs, involucral bracts with dry, brown margins; fls. yellow. Balkans.

Clavennae L. Tufted, hoary per., 4–10 in.; lvs. elliptic, 1–2-pinnatifid, white-silky-tomentose; heads to ¾ in. across, in loose corymbs; fls. white. S. and se. Alps.

Clusiana Tausch. Tufted per., to 8 in., sts. ascending; lvs. oblong in outline, to 2 in. long, 2–3-pinnately parted, almost glabrous; heads to ½ in. across, in simple corymbs; disc fls. yellow, ray fls. white. Alps. Considered by some taxonomists as not specifically distinct from *A. atrata,* or only a subsp. of it.

clypeolata Sibth. & Sm. Erect per., to 16 in., sts. unbranched; lvs. linear in outline, pinnately parted into elliptic or lanceolate, entire or slightly toothed segms., appressed-tomentose; heads to ⅛ in. across, in dense corymbs to about 2 in. across; disc fls. yellow, ray fls. few, yellow, with orbicular ligules. Albania, Yugoslavia, Greece.

compacta: see *A. coarctata.*

coarctata Poir. [*A. compacta* Willd., not L.; *A. sericea* Janka]. Silky-hairy to tomentose-woolly per., to 3 ft., unbranched or branched only in upper part; lvs. linear to linear-lanceolate, 2-pinnately dissected, to 8 in. long; heads about ⅛ in. across, in very compact corymbs; ray fls. yellow, ligules wider than long, 3-lobed. Cent. Eur., Asia Minor, s. Russia.

Eupatorium: *A. filipendulina.*

filipendulina Lam. [*A. Eupatorium* Bieb.]. FERN-LEAF Y. Stiff, erect per., 4–5 ft., sts. furrowed; lvs. to 10 in. long, progressively reduced upward, linear to elliptic, 1–2-pinnatifid into linear-lanceolate, toothed segms., hairy; heads about ³⁄₁₆ in. across, in dense, compound, convex corymbs to about 5 in. across; fls. all yellow. Asia Minor, Caucasus. Var. **alba** is listed as having white fls.

×**Fronmuelleri** Sünderm.: *A. abrotanoides* Vis. × *A. moschata.* Tufted per., to about 10 in.; lvs. ovate in outline, to 1½ in. long, pinnatifid; heads about ½ in. across, in loose corymbs; disc fls. yellow, ray fls. white. Of hort. origin.

Herba-rota All. Tufted, strongly but pleasingly aromatic per., to 8 in.; lvs. oblong to oblanceolate, to 1 in. long, cuneate, serrate to crenu-

late, glandular-dotted; heads about ½ in. across, in loose corymbs to about 1½ in. across; fls. white. Mts., cent. Eur.

impatiens L. [*A. nitida* Tausch]. Glabrous per., to 3–4 ft.; lvs. linear-lanceolate, to 2¾ in. long, pinnatifid; heads about ½ in. across, in a loose corymb to about 4 in. across; ray fls. white. Siberia, e. Eur.

×**Jaborneggii** Halácsy: *A. Clavennae* × *A. moschata.* Tufted per., to 6 in.; lvs. oblong, pinnatifid, green, silky; heads in a loose corymb; ray fls. white. Eur.

lanulosa: *A. Millefolium* var.

×**Lewisii** Ingw.: *A. Clavennae* × *A. tomentosa.* Tufted per., to 6 in.; lvs. linear, to about 1 in. long, gray, serrate; heads about ⁵⁄₁₆ in. across, in a rather dense corymb to 1½ in. across; fls. pale yellow, fading to creamy-white. Of hort. origin.

lingulata Waldst. & Kit. Hairy, erect per., to 1½ ft.; lower lvs. in a rosette, oblanceolate-spatulate, narrowed to a winged petiole, st. lvs. progressively reduced upward, irregularly toothed; heads about ⅜ in. across, in an umbellate corymb to about 4 in. across; disc fls. white to yellowish, ray fls. white, ligules 3-lobed at apex. E. Eur.

macedonica Rouy. White-hairy per., to about 10 in.; lvs. linear in outline, pinnately dissected; heads in a congested corymb; fls. light yellow. Balkans.

Millefolium L. COMMON Y., MILFOIL, SANGUINARY, THOUSAND-SEAL, NOSE-BLEED. Strongly aromatic, rhizomatous per., to 3 ft.; lvs. finely 2–3-pinnate, lower lvs. lanceolate to oblanceolate, to 8 in. long, long-petioled, upper lvs. lanceolate to linear, sessile; heads about ¼ in. across, in round to flat corymbs; fls. usually white. Eur., w. Asia; naturalized as a weed in N. Amer., Australia, and New Zeal. Dried lvs. and fls. have been used medicinally. Cv. **'Kelwayi'.** Fls. magenta-red. Cv. **'Rosea'.** Fls. pink. Cv. **'Rubra'.** Fls. deep pink. Var. **alpicola** (Rydb.) Garret. Sts. to 1 ft.; lvs. linear-lanceolate, gray; heads in flat corymbs, involucral bracts with black or dark brown margins. Alaska to cent. Calif., e. to Rocky Mts. Var. **arenicola** (Heller) Nobs [var. *maritima* Jeps.]. Sts. to 2 ft.; lvs. oblanceolate, gray; heads in round corymbs, involucral bracts with light brown margins. Coastal sands, n. Calif. to cent. Calif. Var. **lanulosa** (Nutt.) Piper [*A. lanulosa* Nutt.]. Sts. to 20 in., nearly cespitose; lvs. linear-lanceolate, gray, woolly; heads in a strongly convex corymb, involucral bracts with straw-colored to light brown margins. Que. to Yukon, s. to Okla., Calif., Mex. Var. **maritima:** var. *arenicola.*

moschata Wulfen. Tufted, erect per., to 6 in.; lvs. in rosettes, to 1½ in. long, pectinately parted, bright green, glabrous, glandular-punctate beneath; heads about ½ in. across, in loose corymbs; disc fls. yellow, ray fls. white. Eur. Used medicinally in home remedies.

multifida: *A. atrata* subsp.

nana L. Tufted, strongly aromatic, stoloniferous per., to 8 in.; lvs. in rosettes, narrowly elliptic, pinnatifid, densely woolly; heads ⅜ in. across, in a dense, rounded corymb; fls. dull white, ray fls. 6–9. S. Eur.

nitida: *A. impatiens.*

Ptarmica L. SNEEZEWORT, SNEEZEWEED. Rhizomatous per., to 2 ft.; lvs. sessile, simple, linear to linear-lanceolate, 1–4 in. long, finely serrate to subentire, essentially glabrous, heads to ¾ in. across, in a loose corymb; disc fls. greenish-white, ray fls. white. Eur., Asia; naturalized in e. N. Amer.

ptarmicifolia (Willd.) Rupr. ex Heimerl [*Pyrethrum ptarmicifolium* Willd.]. Per., to 2 ft.; lvs. narrowly linear, to 2¾ in. long, remotely serrate to nearly entire; heads to ⅜ in. across, in corymbs; ray fls. 8–9, white, ligules obovate. Caucasus.

rosea: *A. Millefolium* cv.

serbica Nym. [*A. ageratifolia* var. *serbica* (Nym.) Hayek]. Tufted per., to 10 in.; lvs. simple, linear, entire or minutely toothed, silvery-green, st. lvs. to 1½ in. long; heads to ¾ in. across, 2–5 in a corymb; ray fls. 12–13, to ¼ in. long, white. Balkans.

sericea: *A. coarctata,* but plants listed as *A. sericea* may be *A. Millefolium.*

sibirica Ledeb. Per., to 3 ft.; lvs. lanceolate, simple but deeply toothed, to 4 in. long, pubescent to nearly glabrous; heads to ⅜ in. across, in dense corymbs; disc fls. dull white, ray fls. 6–8, white. N. Asia, Japan. Considered by some auths. as not specifically distinct from *A. alpina* L.

sudetica Opiz. Stoloniferous per., sts. erect, to 10–12 in.; lvs. in rosettes, linear-lanceolate to oblong-lanceolate in outline, 1–4¾ in. long, 2-pinnately dissected, glabrous to sparsely woolly; heads ⅛ in. across, in open corymbs 1½–2¾ in. across; fls. pink to white. E. Eur.

taygetea Boiss. & Heldr. Herbaceous per., to 1 ft.; lvs. linear in outline, pinnately dissected into oblong segms., lower lvs. 2½ in. long, decreasing in size upward; heads about ¼ in. across, in compact corymbs to 1 in. across; fls. yellow. Greece.

tomentosa L. WOOLLY Y. Woolly, mat-forming, herbaceous per., to 1 ft.; lvs. linear-lanceolate in outline, 2-pinnately dissected, woolly; heads about ⅛ in. across, in dense corymbs; disc fls. yellow, ray fls. bright yellow. Eur., w. Asia. Cv. 'Aurea'. Fls. darker yellow. Cv. 'Nana' is listed.

umbellata Sibth. & Sm. Tufted, white-woolly per., 4–6 in. high; lvs. to about 1 in. long, ovate, pinnately toothed, silvery-tomentose; heads to ⅝ in. across, in dense, terminal corymbs about 1¼ in. across; fls. white. Greece.

×**Wilczekiana** Vacc.: *A. Herba-rota* var. *ambigua* Heimerl × *A. nana*. A natural hybrid, presumably intermediate in character between its parents. Nw. Italy. Use of this name in hort. may be an error for *A.* × *Wilczekii*.

×**Wilczekii** Sünderm.: *A. ageratifolia* × *A. lingulata*. Mat-forming per., to 6 in.; lvs. oblanceolate, to 2¾ in. long, gray-woolly-hairy, margins toothed; heads to about ⅝ in. across, in open corymbs. Of hort. origin.

×ACHIMENANTHA H. E. Moore: *Achimenes* × *Smithiantha*. Gesneriaceae.

A hybrid genus with few described "species" but many more hybrids not assigned to "species"; some have been given names under × *Eucodonopsis*, a name that is no longer of proper form for a hybrid genus.

For cultivation see *Gesneriaceae*.

naegelioides (Van Houtte) H. E. Moore [×*Eucodonopsis achimenoides* (Bartik) H. E. Moore]: *Achimenes glabrata* × *Smithiantha zebrina*. Much resembling *Achimenes glabrata* in habit, but the fls. intermediate between those of the parents and varying from pink to white or variously spotted, often flushed yellow.

ACHIMENES Pers. MONKEY-FACED PANSY, ORCHID P., JAPANESE P., CUPID'S-BOWER, MOTHER'S-TEARS, WIDOW'S-TEARS, NUT ORCHID, MAGIC FLOWER, KIMONO PLANT. Gesneriaceae.

About 26 spp. of per. herbs in Jamaica and from Mex. to Panama; roots fibrous, underground scaly rhizomes present and similar structures sometimes present also in lf. axils or in infl.; lvs. simple, opp. and those of each pair equal or strongly unequal, or whorled; fls. solitary or in pairs or in short cymes in lf. axils, calyx 5-lobed, corolla erect or oblique in the calyx, tubular to obliquely funnelform or salverform, sometimes spurred at base, limb spreading to suberect, 5-lobed, lobes entire or fringed, the upper 2 smaller than the lower 3, stamens 4, filaments separate, borne at base of corolla tube, the 4 anthers united apically into a square, disc at base of ovary ringlike, rarely interrupted, ovary half-inferior, 1-celled, with 2 parietal placentas, style elongating after pollen is shed, stigma mouth-shaped or 2-lobed; fr. a 2-valved caps.

For cultivation see *Gesneriaceae*.

Andersonii: *Achimenes* cv. 'Andersonii', a hybrid derivative of *A. longiflora;* rhizomes large, carrot-shaped; corolla light violet, with white splotch beneath throat.

Andrieuxii DC. Sts. pink-tomentose, short and with a few lvs. in a basal rosette in the wild, in cult. often longer and stouter and with more st. and basal lvs.; lf. blades elliptic to ovate, to 5 in. long, 2½ in. wide, crenate, lightly hairy above, densely pale-tomentose beneath; fls. solitary on peduncles to 2½ in. long, corolla obliquely funnelform, to ⅝ in. long, violet with purple-spotted white throat. S. Mex.

antirrhina (DC.) C. V. Mort. Sts. to 1 ft. or more; lvs. opp., those of each pair sometimes unequal and asymmetrical at base, ovate, to 4 in. long, 2 in. wide, serrate, softly hairy, sometimes reddish beneath; fls. solitary on short peduncles, tubular, straw-colored or yellow with red-brown or purple lines outside, yellow with red lines inside, lobes yellow outside, red inside, stigma mouth-shaped. W. Mex., Guatemala.

atropurpurea: *A. grandiflora* cv.

bella C. V. Mort. Sts. to 1 ft., densely long-hairy; lvs. opp., blades elliptic to ovate, to 5 in. long, 2½ in. wide, crenate-serrate, long-hairy on both surfaces, pale beneath; fls. solitary on peduncles to 2½ in. long, corolla obliquely funnelform, to 1⅛ in. long, violet with 3 yellow lines in throat, stigma mouth-shaped. W. Mex.

candida Lindl. Sts. to 1½ ft. but mostly shorter, hairy; lvs. opp., those of each pair sometimes unequal, blades ovate, to 2½ in. long, 1½ in. wide, serrate, with stiff, erect, short hairs above; fls. solitary or several on axillary peduncles, corolla tubular, ½ in. long, tube white, flecked with reddish-brown outside, with patches of yellow and lines of red dots in throat, limb white, lobes to ⅜ in. wide, stigma mouth-shaped. Guatemala.

Cettoana H. E. Moore. Sts. to 1 ft. in cult., densely strigose, rhizomes elongate; lvs. usually in whorls of 3–4, blades linear-lanceolate, to 2¾ in. long, ½ in. wide, serrate above middle, strigose; fls. solitary, corolla violet, tube laterally compressed, slender, minutely glandular, to 1 in. long, limb spreading obliquely, lobes to ¾ in. long, stigma 2-lobed. S. Mex.

coccinea: *A. erecta.*

Dentoniana: *Achimenes* cv. 'Dentoniana' [*Achimenes* cv. 'Variegata'], a hybrid derivative of *A. longiflora;* rhizomes carrot-shaped; corolla over 1½ in. wide, limb light violet, throat white with yellow splotch and minute red dots.

dulcis C. V. Mort. Sts. to 2 ft., densely puberulous; lvs. opp., blades ovate-lanceolate, to 4¼ in. long, 2 in. wide, dentate, appressed-pilose above; fls. solitary, to 2 in. long, corolla obliquely funnelform, white with yellow at base of throat, lobes to ⅜ in. long, stigma mouth-shaped. W. Mex.

Ehrenbergii (Hanst.) H. E. Moore. Sts. to 1½ ft., white-woolly; lvs. opp., blades ovate, to 6 in. long, 3 in. wide, crenate, pale-hairy above, white-woolly beneath; fls. solitary or in pairs, long-peduncled, corolla obliquely funnelform, to 1¾ in. long, lavender, with yellow and orange lines and spots in throat, lobes ½ in. long, stigma 2-lobed. S. Mex.

erecta (Lam.) H. P. Fuchs [*A. coccinea* (Scop.) Pers.; *A. pulchella* (L'Hér.) A. S. Hitchc.]. Sts. to 18 in., hairy; lvs. opp. or in whorls of 3, blades ovate to elliptic, to 2½ in. long, 1¼ in. wide, sparsely toothed, often red-veined or red-flushed beneath; fls. solitary or in pairs, corolla red or rose, tube cylindrical, to ¾ in. long, lobes to ⅜ in. long, stigma 2-lobed. Jamaica, Mex. to Panama. A tetraploid sp. dominant in hybrids.

×**Escherana** Lem.: *A. erecta* × *A. longiflora*. With habit of *A. erecta*, but fls. larger, corolla reddish-purple, with crimson-spotted yellow throat.

fimbriata Rose ex C. V. Mort. Sts. glabrous, to 1 ft.; lvs. opp., those of each pair usually unequal, blade ovate to ovate-lanceolate, to 2 in. long, 1½ in. wide, serrate, glabrous; fls. solitary, corolla obliquely funnelform, to ¾ in. long, white, spotted with violet, lobes to ¼ in. long, fringed, stigma mouth-shaped. W. Mex.

flava C. V. Mort. Sts. to 2 ft. in cult. but usually short in the wild, finely pilose; lvs. opp., those of each pair usually unequal, blades obliquely ovate, to 3¼ in. long, 1⅝ in. wide, serrate, finely pilose, green or red beneath; fls. solitary to several on short peduncles, corolla obliquely funnelform, to ⅞ in. long, yellow, spotted with red inside, lobes entire, stigma mouth-shaped. W. Mex.

Galatea: *A. longiflora* cv.

Ghiesbreghtii: *A. heterophylla*, but some material cult. under the name *A. Ghiesbreghtii* is *A. grandiflora*.

glabrata (Zucc.) Fritsch [*Gloxinia fimbriata* Brongn. ex Decne.]. Sts. to 1½ ft., glabrous or nearly so; lvs. opp., blades lanceolate to ovate, dentate, paler beneath, glabrous or nearly so; fls. solitary, corolla obliquely funnelform, to 2 in. long, white or lavender-flushed, clear yellow or spotted with purple in throat, limb broad, lobes to 1 in. wide, ½ in. long, stigma 2-lobed. W. Mex.

grandiflora (Schiede) DC. [*A. robusta* Hort.]. Sts. to 2 ft. or more, hairy; lvs. opp., blades ovate, to 6 in. long, 3½ in. wide, dentate, softly hairy, often reddish beneath; fls. solitary, in pairs, or sometimes several on a short peduncle, corolla oblique in the calyx, with short rounded spur, broadened toward the rounded throat, to 1¾ in. long, red-violet, with purple-dotted pale band in throat, lobes spreading, to ¾ in. wide, stigma 2-lobed. Mex. to Honduras. The name has been used erroneously for *A. longiflora* cv. 'Paul Arnold'. Several cvs. are listed; 'Atropurpurea' is dwarf, early. Some material grown as *A. Ghiesbreghtii* belongs here.

gymnostoma: *Gloxinia gymnostoma.*

Harveyi: *Achimenes* cv. 'Harveyi', a derivative of *A. erecta;* sts. weak, branching, red; lvs. narrow; corolla to 1 in. across, reddish-orange, throat yellow with red lines.

heterophylla (Mart.) DC. [*A. Ghiesbreghtii* Hort. ex Lindl.]. Sts. to 1 ft. or more, hairy; lvs. opp. or in whorls of 3, those in a pair often unequal, blades oblong-lanceolate, to 5 in. long, 3 in. wide, coarsely toothed; fls. solitary, corolla tubular, 1¼ in. long, smooth, bright orange-red or scarlet with yellow throat, rarely all yellow, lobes to ¼ in. long, stigma 2-lobed. W. Mex., Guatemala.

Jaureguia: *A. longiflora* cv. 'Alba'.

longiflora DC. Sts. to 1 ft. or more, pilose, rhizomes spherical or pear-shaped; lvs. opp. or in whorls of 3, blades ovate to lanceolate, to 3½ in. long, 1¼ in. wide, toothed, appressed-hairy, pale or reddish beneath; fls. solitary, corolla erect in calyx, tubular, slender, laterally compressed, to 2½ in. long, lilac or purple to rarely reddish or white, limb oblique, flattened, lobes to ¾ in. long, stigma 2-lobed. Mex. to

Panama. A variable sp. Several cvs. are offered: Cv. 'Alba' [var. *alba* F. A. Haage, Jr.; *A. Jaureguia* Warsz. ex F. A. Haage, Jr.; *A. maxima* Hort.]. Corolla white with yellow eye, and with dark purple line on each lobe. Cv. 'Ambroise Verschaffelt' [*A. Verschaffeltii* Hort.]. Similar to cv. 'Alba', but with heavy tracery of purple lines and dots from throat. Cv. 'Galatea'. Corolla violet with purple stain over throat and whitish patch underneath it, lobes not overlapping. Cv. 'Major'. Fls. large, to 3 in. across, corolla light violet, with darker purple above throat. Cv. 'Margarita' [*A. Margaritae* Hort.]. Similar to cv. 'Alba', but corolla pure white, throat yellow without markings. Cv. 'Paul Arnold'. To 16 in.; lvs. wine-red beneath; corolla deep purple, with yellow-stained white throat dotted with red.

magnifica: *Kohleria magnifica*, but plants grown as *A. magnifica* are probably some sort of *Achimenes*.

Margaritae: *A. longiflora* cv.

maxima: *A. longiflora* cv. 'Alba.'

mexicana (Seem.) Benth. & Hook. f. ex Fritsch [*A. mexicana* cv. 'Caerulescens'; *A. Scheeri* Hemsl.]. Sts. hairy, to 2 ft.; lvs. opp., blades ovate, to 5 in. long, 2½ in. wide, toothed, hairy; fls. solitary, corolla obliquely funnelform, to 2 in. long, purple or blue with pale throat, lobes spreading, stigma mouth-shaped. W. Mex. Some material grown under this name may be a cv. of *A. longiflora*.

Miltonii: *Achimenes* cv. 'Milton', probably a derivative of *A. heterophylla;* sts. to 18 in.; lvs. opp. or in whorls of 3; corolla tubular, tube velvety dark red, limb deep purplish-red.

miniata: *Achimenes* cv. 'Miniata'; sts. trailing, to 15 in. long; lvs. opp. or in whorls of 3; corolla tubular, limb oblique, deep purplish-red, shading to medium orange-yellow throat.

misera Lindl. Sts. to 8 in. in cult., softly hairy; lvs. opp., blades ovate, to 2¼ in. long, 1½ in. wide, toothed, softly hairy; fls. solitary or in pairs, corolla tubular, to ½ in. long, white, flushed with lilac patches beneath the lobes on inner surface, with 3 internal crests matched by external grooves, stigma mouth-shaped. Guatemala. *A. Warscewicziana* has been confused with this sp.

obscura C. V. Mort. Sts. to 6 in., minutely hairy; lvs. opp., blades obliquely ovate, to 4 in. long, 2¼ in. wide, crenate to serrate, minutely hairy; fls. solitary or in pairs, corolla obliquely funnelform, ½ in. long, white, spotted with purple inside, neither crested nor grooved, lobes small, suberect, stigma mouth-shaped. W. Mex.

patens Benth. Sts. to 1 ft. in cult., hairy; lvs. opp., those of each pair somewhat unequal, blades elliptic-ovate to ovate, to 3 in. long, 1½ in. wide, toothed, appressed-hairy, sometimes red beneath; fls. solitary, corolla oblique in the calyx, with a spur longer than calyx lobes, red-violet, flushed with yellow and dotted with violet in throat, tube to ¾ in. long, lobes minutely toothed, ½ in. long, stigma 2-lobed. W. Mex. Cv. 'Major'. Corolla with short, blunt spur and purplish-pink throat.

pedunculata Benth. Sts. to 3 ft., hairy, often with scaly propagules in lf. axils or on infl.; lvs. opp., blades ovate, to 3½ in. long, 3 in. wide, toothed, hairy; fls. solitary or several on peduncles usually longer than lvs., corolla oblique in calyx, tube enlarged upward to broad throat, vermilion, flushed with orange on lower side, lobes orange-red, with dark red lines and dots, throat yellow, dotted with red, stigma 2-lobed. Mex. to Honduras.

pulchella: *A. erecta.*

pulcherrima: *Achimenes* cv. 'Pulcherrima'; to 15 in., compact; corolla ruffled, strong reddish-purple.

robusta: *A. grandiflora.*

Scheeri: *A. mexicana.*

Skinneri Lindl. Sts. to nearly 3 ft., hairy; lvs. opp., blades ovate, to 3¼ in. long, 2¾ in. wide, sharply toothed, hairy; fls. 1–2 on peduncles usually longer than lvs., corolla tube expanded upward to the throat, to 1½ in. long, rose with yellow flush at throat, yellowish and minutely dotted with red inside, limb oblique, lobes minutely toothed, rose-lavender to rose, to ½ in. long, stigma 2-lobed. Guatemala.

tubiflora: *Sinningia tubiflora.*

variegata: *Achimenes* cv. 'Dentoniana.'

venusta: *Achimenes* cv. 'Venusta', an extinct cv. Material offered recently as *A. venusta* is *Achimenes* cv. 'Violacea Semiplena', with dark red upright sts. to 10 in.; lvs. very dark green; fls. semidouble, 1 in. long, stamens usually petaloid.

Verschaffeltii: *A. longiflora* cv. 'Ambroise Verschaffelt'.

violacea Hort. A name once used for *A. mexicana;* but material recently offered under this name is probably *Achimenes* cv. 'Violacea Semiplena', described under *A. venusta.*

Warscewicziana (Regel) H. E. Moore. Sts. to 1 ft. or mostly less, hairy; lvs. opp., blades elliptic-ovate to obliquely ovate, to 4½ in. long, 1¾ in. wide, toothed, sticky-hairy, especially beneath; fls. solitary or rarely in pairs or several on a peduncle, corolla obliquely funnelform,

⅜ in. long, white, spotted with red or red-brown to maroon, tube with 2 ridges on lower inner surface matched by 2 grooves externally, stigma mouth-shaped. S. Mex. to El Salvador.

Woodii C. V. Mort. Sts. to 1 ft. or more in cult., usually much shorter, hairy; lvs. opp., those of a pair strongly unequal to subequal, blades ovate, to 2 in. long, 1½ in. wide, toothed, minutely resinous-glandular and finely pilose, often red beneath; fls. solitary to several on short peduncles, corolla tube slender, white, flushed violet, 2-ridged inside, the ridges and corresponding external grooves yellow, spotted with purple, lobes spreading, white, stigma mouth-shaped. W. Mex.

ACHLYS DC. *Berberidaceae.* Two spp. of per. herbs native to w. N. Amer. and Japan; lvs. of 3 lfts., long-stalked; fls. in dense spikes on leafless scapes, minute, without petals or sepals, stamens 6–13, with long filaments.

triphylla (Sm.) DC. VANILLA LEAF, DEERFOOT. To 1 ft.; lfts. fan-shaped, to 6 in. across, wavy-toothed; spikes 1 in. long. Woods, B.C. to Calif. Sometimes planted in wild gardens or rock gardens.

ACHRAS: *MANILKARA.*

ACHYRANTHES L. *Amaranthaceae.* A few spp. of trop. herbs or subshrubs not known to be cult. in this country. Most material cult. under this name is *Alternanthera.*

Bettzickiana: *Alternanthera ficoidea* cv.

Herbstii: a listed name of no botanical standing for *Iresine Herbstii.*

philoxeroides: *Alternanthera philoxeroides.*

ACIDANTHERA Hochst. PEACOCK ORCHID. *Iridaceae.* About 33 spp. of tender, cormous herbs, native to trop. and S. Afr.; differing from *Gladiolus* in having perianth tube straight or essentially so, sometimes arched by the weight of perianth segms.; from *Babiana* in having corm with tunic of coarse fibers, lvs. not pleated, and spathe valves and bracts glabrous; and from *Tritonia* in having spathe valves green throughout, perianth tube longer than the segms. and somewhat dilated at the mouth.

About as hardy as *Tritonia;* of easy propagation by cormels produced at base of flowering-size corms, or by seeds. In temperate regions culture as for *Gladiolus.*

bicolor Hochst. Corms globose, scarcely 1 in. in diam., sts. branched, 12–24 in.; st. lvs. usually 3–4, linear, 6–15 in. long, glabrous; infl. loosely spicate, 2–4-fld. (10–12-fld. in cult.), outer spathe valve green, 2–3 in. long; fls. about 3 in. across, very fragrant, perianth tube 3–4 ½ in. long, slender, segms. sulphur-white, the 3 lower ones each with a chocolate brown blotch at base. Ethiopia. Var. **Murieliae:** *A. Murieliae.*

Murieliae Hort. [*A. bicolor* var. *Murieliae* Hort.]: a listed name of no botanical standing, used for plants differing from *A. bicolor* in having corms much flattened, infl. stiffy erect, 5–6-fld., perianth tube 4–5½ in. long, lower 3 segms. with purple-crimson blotches. Ethiopia.

ACINETA Lindl. *Orchidaceae.* About 15 spp. of epiphytes, native to Cent. and S. Amer.; pseudobulbs large; lvs. plicate; fls. in pendulous racemes on leafless lateral scapes, lip 3-lobed, fleshy, divided into hypochil and epichil by a transverse callus. For structure of fl. see *Orchidaceae.*

Warm greenhouse; for culture see *Orchids.*

Barkeri (Batem.) Lindl. Pseudobulbs to 6 in. long; lvs. 2–4, to 26 in. long and 3 in. wide; racemes to 18 in. long; fls. golden-yellow, lip spotted with red, about 1½ in. long, Autumn. Mex.

chrysantha (C. Morr.) Lindl. [*A. densa* Lindl. & Paxt.]. Similar to *A. Barkeri* in size, but fls. yellow, spotted with crimson outside, epichil warty at base. Costa Rica, Panama, Colombia.

densa: *A. chrysantha.*

Humboldtii: *A. superba.*

superba (HBK) Rchb. f. [*A. Humboldtii* Lindl.; *Anguloa superba* HBK]. Pseudobulbs to over 4 in. long; lvs. 3, to 16 in. long and 2¾ in. wide; racemes to 16 in. long; sepals and petals reddish-brown, spotted with red inside, lip yellow or brown-red, spotted with purple, about 3 in. across. Venezuela, Colombia, Ecuador.

ACINOS Mill. *Labiatae.* About 10 spp. of herbs, of temp. Eur. and Asia, closely related to *Calamintha*, sts. mostly square in cross section; lvs. opp., elliptic, small; fls. always in verticillasters, calyx tubular, 13-nerved, tube usually curved, constricted near middle and with a basal pouch, hairy inside, corolla 2-lipped, mostly violet, marked white, usually glabrous, stamens 4, usually shorter than corolla, curved and convergent apically, style brs. unequal; fr. of 4 ovoid, usually glabrous nutlets.

Grown in dry, sunny locations.

alpinus (L.) Moench [*Calamintha alpina* (L.) Lam.; *Satureja alpina* (L.) Scheele]. Decumbent per., usually diffusely branched; closely related to *A. thymoides,* but per. and having corolla ½–¾ in. long. Mts., cent. and s. Eur.

arvensis: *A. thymoides.*

thymoides (L.) Moench [*A. arvensis* (Lam.) Dandy; *Calamintha Acinos* (L.) Clairv. ex Gaud.-Beaup.; *Satureja Acinos* (L.) Scheele]. BASIL THYME, MOTHER OF T. Pubescent ann., to 12 in.; lvs. ovate, acute to obtuse, to ¾ in. long, entire or slightly crenate; whorls 3–8-fld.; calyx teeth subulate, corolla violet, to ¼–½ in. long. Summer. Eur.

ACIPHYLLA J. R. Forst. & G. Forst. *Umbelliferae.* About 30 spp. of usually dioecious, erect and usually spinescent, glabrous, per. herbs, native to New Zeal. and Australia; lvs. thick, pinnate; fls. small, in compound spiny-bracted umbels.

Grown in the rock garden or border.

Colensoi Hook. f. COLENSO'S SPANIARD. To 5 ft.; basal lvs. numerous, 1–2-pinnate, to 2½ ft. long, lfts. to 15 in. long and ½ in. wide, terminating in long, stout spine; fls. white, in narrowly cylindrical panicle, male infl. much looser than the female. New Zeal.

Dieffenbachii (F. J. Muell.) T. Kirk [*Coxella Dieffenbachii* (F. J. Muell.) Cheesem. & Hemsl.]. To 3 ft.; lvs. basal, 3–4-pinnate, 1–2 ft. long, gray-green, lfts. to 3 in. long; peduncles to 5 in. long; fr. ⅝ in. long. New Zeal.

ACKAMA A. Cunn. *Cunoniaceae.* Several spp. of polygamous shrubs or small trees to 40 ft., native to Australia and New Guinea, 1 in New Zeal.; lvs. opp., odd-pinnate, lfts. nearly sessile, serrate; fls. small, in showy panicles, sepals 5, united at base, valvate, petals 5, stamens 10, ovary superior, styles 2; fr. a 2-celled caps. Related to *Weinmannia,* which differs in having fls. in racemes and sepals imbricate.

rosifolia A. Cunn. Lvs. with 6–10 pairs of lfts., terminal lft. broadly lanceolate, to 2½ in. long, somewhat longer than lateral lfts.; panicles to 6 in. long. New Zeal.

ACMENA DC. *Myrtaceae.* About 11 spp. of mostly glabrous trees, native from se. China and Malay Arch. to Australia; lvs. opp., entire; fls. many, small, bisexual, in terminal or axillary panicles, petals minute, usually united into a deciduous cap, stamens many, anther sacs opening by terminal pores or slits, ovary inferior; fr. a berry. Closely related to *Eugenia* and *Syzygium,* but having anther sacs opening by a terminal slit or pore and cotyledons seemingly united.

Smithii (Poir.) Merrill & L. M. Perry [*Eugenia Smithii* Poir.] LILLY-PILLY. To 25 ft. or more; lvs. ovate to ovate-lanceolate, 2–3 in. long, punctate; fr. globular, to ½ in. across, whitish to purplish. Australia. Makes a good evergreen screen or hedge plant in warm areas. Recognized by the showy clusters of whitish to purplish (sometimes mauve), edible berries.

ACOELORRHAPHE H. Wendl. [*Paurotis* O. F. Cook]. *Palmae.* One sp., a variable palm of moist low ground in swampy, coastal areas in s. Fla., parts of W. Indies, Mex., and Cent. Amer.; trunks slender, clustered, often clothed with fibrous lf. sheaths; lvs. palmate, petioles armed with short spinelike teeth along margins; infl. among the lvs. and surpassing them, with persistent tubular-sheathing bracts, several-branched, the primary brs. 1–2 times branched; fls. small, yellow-green, in clusters of 2–3, bisexual, sepals nearly separate, about half as long as petals, stamens 6, in a ring, carpels 3, separate, except for united slender styles, usually only one carpel maturing; fr. black, globose, with apical stigmatic scar and basal abortive carpels, seed subglobose, with homogeneous endosperm.

Useful cluster palm for landscape plantings in full sun or shade, with roots in water (will tolerate some brackish water) or in dry areas of sand or limestone with a high water table. Also useful as a tub plant. For culture see *Palms.*

arborescens: *A. Wrightii.*

Wrightii (Griseb. & H. Wendl.) H. Wendl. ex Becc. [*A. arborescens* (Sarg.) Becc.; *Paurotis Wrightii* (Griseb. & H. Wendl.) Britt.]. EVERGLADES PALM, SILVER SAW P., SAW CABBAGE P. Trunks to 25 ft., occasionally taller; lvs. nearly orbicular, 2–3 ft. across or more, divided

to below middle into 40 or more, narrow, deeply 2-cleft, 1-ribbed segms., green above, generally silvery beneath; infl. arched, red-brown; fr. to ⅜ in. in diam. Coastal. Zone 9b.

ACOKANTHERA G. Don. BUSHMAN'S-POISON, POISON BUSH, POISON TREE. *Apocynaceae.* About 15 spp. of shrubs or small trees with milky sap, native to Arabia, e. trop. Afr., and S. Afr.; lvs. opp., entire, leathery; infl. axillary; fls. white or pinkish, fragrant, bisexual, sepals 4 or 5, corolla salverform, lobes overlapping to the left, stamens 4 or 5, separate, borne toward apex of corolla tube, with the anther tips often exserted, ovary 1, 2-celled; fr. a showy, leathery berry. Closely related to *Carissa,* but differing in having a highly toxic substance in the sap, the infl. axillary, the stamens borne toward the top of the corolla tube, and the anthers often exserted.

Several species yield arrow poisons and drugs. For cultivation see *Carissa.*

longiflora Stapf [*Carissa longiflora* (Stapf) G. H. M. Lawr.]. Tree, to 20 ft., glabrous except for new brs. and infls.; lvs. elliptic to elliptic-oblong, to 3½ in. long, acute, mucronate; fls. white, corolla tube about 1½ in. long, lobes scarcely ¼ in. long; berry plumlike, ellipsoid, to 2 in. long, purple, edible. E. Afr. Twigs and lvs. used by natives for making arrow poison.

oblongifolia (Hochst.) Codd [*A. spectabilis* (Sond.) Hook. f.; *Carissa spectabilis* (Sond.) Pich.]. WINTERSWEET. Shrub or small tree, to 15 ft.; lvs. ovate to elliptic, to 5 in. long, about 3 times longer than broad, acute or with short, sharp point, very dark green; infl. densely many-fld., about 1½ in. across; corolla white tinged with pink, tube to ¾ in. long or more, lobes acutish, ¼ in. long; berry ellipsoid to globose, to 1 in. long, black, 1–2-seeded. S.-W. Afr. Entire plant considered poisonous by natives.

oppositifolia (Lam.) Codd [*A. venenata* of auth., not G. Don; *Carissa Acokanthera* Pich.]. Differs from *A. oblongifolia* in having lvs. not more than twice as long as broad, and corolla tube scarcely ½ in. long. E. trop. Afr., S. Afr. Root used by natives to make arrow poison.

spectabilis: *A. oblongifolia.*

venenata: see *A. oppositifolia.*

ACOMASTYLIS: *GEUM.*

ACONITUM L. ACONITE, MONKSHOOD. *Ranunculaceae.* Probably 100 or more spp. of summer- or autumn-flowering per. herbs, with tuberous or thickened roots, native to the N. Temp. Zone; sts. erect, trailing, or half-climbing, mostly somewhat branched; lvs. palmately veined, lobed, or cleft; fls. irregular, blue, white, or sometimes yellow, in racemes or panicles, sepals 5, petaloid, upper sepal large and hoodlike or helmet-shaped, petals 2–5, small, the 2 upper spurlike and included in the helmet, the others minute or absent, stamens many, pistils 3–5; fr. of follicles.

Many species are poisonous or are a source of drugs. Aconites do best in a rich soil and partial shade is usually better than full sun. Once established, they should not be disturbed unless necessary. Useful at the back of borders and as specimen clumps. They can be propagated by seeds or by division. Seedlings flower in 2 or 3 years. Tall and slender kinds may need staking.

×**acuminatum** Rchb. Supposedly a hybrid. *A. compactum* × *A. paniculatum.* To 3 ft. or more, spreading-hairy in upper parts; helmet violet, 1 in. high, lateral edge of opening very concave.

acutum Rchb. Possibly a hybrid, *A. judenbergense* (Rchb.) Gáyer × *A. tauricum.* To 1½ ft., glabrous in upper parts; helmet erect, ⅝ in. high, lateral edge of opening almost straight.

anglicum Stapf. To 3 ft., crisp-puberulent in upper parts; lvs. 5–6 in. wide, ultimate lobes narrow; racemes dense, 8–20 in. long, almost simple; fls. mauve, helmet subhemispheric, ¾ in. high, somewhat beaked in front. England.

Anthora L. Low, mostly 1–2 ft., sts. mostly simple, crisp-pubescent in upper parts, densely leafy; lvs. roundish in outline, 2–5 in. wide, ultimate lobes linear; infl. almost simple, crowded; sepals persistent, pale yellow, helmet hemispheric, ⅝ in. high, with long marginal hairs and short beak. S. Eur.

autumnale: see *A. Henryi.*

Bakeri Greene. Closely related to *A. columbianum,* to 2 ft.; lvs. about 2 in. wide; spikes dark blue, helmet with profile strongly concave in front above the almost horizontal beak. Rocky Mts.

barbatum Pers. Erect, to 3 ft.; lvs. rounded in outline, 5-parted almost to base, ultimate lobes linear or oblong; fls. yellow to white, in a loose panicle of dense racemes, crisp-pubescent; helmet about 1 in. long, rounded in upper part, lower sepals yellow-bearded at margin. E. Asia.

×**bicolor** Schult. [*A. Stoerkianum* Rchb.]. Supposedly a hybrid, *A. Napellus* × *A. variegatum*. To about 3 ft., nearly glabrous; lvs. 2–3 in. wide, 5–7-parted, primary segms. rhombic in outline, often 3-lobed; center raceme loose, to 8 in., lateral ones few-fld.; fls. 1½ in. high, frequently white, with purple margins, helmet 1 in. high, strongly arched, lateral edge of opening strongly arcuate.

californicum: a listed name of no botanical standing, sometimes used for *A. Henryi.*

Carmichaelii Debeaux [*A. Fischeri* F. Forbes & Hemsl., not Rchb.; *A. Wilsonii* Stapf ex Mottet]. Sturdy, erect, to 6 ft. or more, crisp-pubescent in upper parts; lvs. leathery, dark green, 2–6 in. wide, 3-cleft, ultimate teeth large, broad; infl. a dense wandlike panicle, center raceme 1–8 in. long; fls. deep blue-purple, about 1½ in. high, helmet broad and rounded in upper part, about 1 in. high, lateral edge of opening almost straight. E. Asia. Often cult. under the name, *A. Fischeri.*

carneum: a listed name of no botanical standing.

chinense Paxt. [*A. Fortunei* Hemsl.; *A. sinense* Siebold ex Lindl. & Paxt.]. Like *A. Carmichaelii,* but having spreading, gland-tipped hairs on pedicels; helmet ⅝ in. high. E. Asia.

columbianum Nutt. Mostly erect and stout, to 5 ft.; glabrous in lower parts, but spreading-pubescent and somewhat viscid in infl.; lvs. thin, 2–4 in. wide, deeply 3–5-cleft, primary segms. rhombic-cuneate, laciniately toothed or cleft; infl. rather loose, racemose to paniculate; fls. purple or blue, helmet ⅝–1 in. long, conic-rounded in upper part, beak descending, lateral edge of opening concave. W. N. Amer.

compactum Rchb. Similar to *A. Napellus,* but lf. lobes linear to lanceolate, infl. axis, pedicels, and helmet short-appressed-hairy. W. Alps.

cordatum Royle. Erect, simple or branched, to 4 ft.; lower lvs. 5-lobed to about the middle, upper lvs. ovate-cordate, 2–4 in. wide; infl. finely villous; fls. green, veined with purple, helmet boat-shaped, ¾ in. high. Himalayas.

exaltatum Bernh. Possibly a hybrid, resembling *A. bicolor;* to 6 ft.; infl. glabrous, longer and narrower; fls. pale lilac, helmet narrow in upper part, gaping.

excelsum Rchb. Close to *A. Lycoctonum,* but differing in having lvs. more glabrous and pistils more hairy.

ferox Wallich ex Ser. Erect, to almost 3 ft., yellow-pilose in upper parts; lvs. scattered, 3–8 in. wide, 5-parted, ultimate lobes nearly acuminate, divergent; infl. a loose raceme; fls. blue, hairy, about 1½ in. high, helmet ¾ in. high, rounded in profile, beak long, descending, lateral edge of opening concave. N. India. Used medicinally in India.

Fischeri Rchb. About 3 ft., erect, leafy, somewhat strigulose in upper parts; lvs. more or less uniformly distributed, thin, almost glabrous, 2–6 in. wide, cordate at base, nearly equally 5-parted, segms. 3-lobed, then toothed or lobed; infl. compact to open; fls. mostly violet-purple, 1½ in. high or more, helmet ¾–1 in. high, strongly arched, short-beaked. E. Asia. Has been used medicinally. Material cult. under this name is largely *A. Carmichaelii.*

Fortunei: *A. chinense.*

Henryi E. Pritz. [*A. autumnale* Hort., not Rchb.]. Erect and stout in lower part, sinuous and freely branched in upper part, 3–6 ft. high, more or less crisp-pubescent; lvs. 2–6 in. wide, mostly 3-parted almost to base; panicle open; fls. mostly deep bluish-purple, 1–1½ in. high, helmet about ¾ in. high, profile rounded in upper part but almost straight in front, beak broad, short, inconspicuous, lateral edge of opening slightly concave. China. Much garden material labelled *A. autumnale, A. Napellus, A. californicum,* and *A.* cv. 'Spark's Variety' belongs here.

Howellii A. Nels. & Macbr. Close to *A. columbianum;* weak-stemmed, bulbiferous in upper lf. axils; helmet with a narrow horizontal beak ½ in. long. Ore.

japonicum Thunb. Robust, 2–6 ft., crisp-pubescent in upper parts, densely and uniformly leafy; lvs. 2–6 in. wide, 2–5-cleft; racemes few- to many-fld., flexuous or spreading; fls. bluish-purple, 1½ in. high, helmet about 1 in. high, slightly beaked, almost glabrous, lateral edge of opening concave. Japan. At least some garden material under this name seems to be *A. pyrenaicum,* and *A. uncinatum.*

Kusnezoffii Rchb. Nearly glabrous; lvs. truncate at base, 3–5-parted, primary segms. cuneate, 3-lobed, then pinnately toothed; fls. yellow, helmet beaked, lateral edge of opening concave, spur long, saccate at apex. E. Asia.

luridum: see *A. novoluridum.*

lutescens A. Nels. Like *A. Bakeri,* but having yellowish-white fls.

Lycoctonum L. [*A. septentrionale* Koelle]. WOLFSBANE. Tall; lvs. rounded to nearly reniform, 6–8 in. wide in lower parts, thin, 5–7-parted, divisions 3-cleft about halfway, sparsely hairy above, more so underneath; raceme elongate, glandular-villous; fls. purple-lilac, pubescent, helmet conic-cylindrical, ¾ in. high, pistils glabrous. N. Eur. Var. **pyrenaicum:** *A. pyrenaicum.*

moldavicum: *A. Vulparia.*

Napellus L. HELMET FLOWER, TURK'S-CAP, FRIAR'S-CAP, SOLDIER'S-CAP, BEAR'S-FOOT, GARDEN WOLFSBANE, GARDEN MONKSHOOD. Erect, rather slender, to almost 3 ft., crisp-pubescent in upper parts, rather leafy; lvs. 2–4 in. wide, 3-parted to base, lateral segms. again cut almost to their base, ultimate segms. lanceolate, at least ¼ in. wide; raceme dense, 2–8 in. long, pedicels appressed to axis; fls. violet, 1¼–1½ in. high, helmet hemispheric in upper part, about ¾ in. high, short-beaked, lateral edge of opening almost straight. N. Eur. Dried lvs. and roots yield the drug aconite, used medicinally. Much garden material offered under this name is *A. Henryi* or *A. pyramidale.* Var. **pyramidale** or **pyramidatum:** see *A. pyramidale.* Var. **tauricum:** *A. tauricum.*

novoluridum Munz [*A. luridum* Hook. f. & T. Thoms., not Salisb.]. Erect, to 2½ ft.; lvs. few, round-cordate to reniform, 2–4 in. wide, rather deeply 5-parted, segms. cuneate-obovate, sharply toothed; raceme to 16 in. long, rather dense, mostly simple, spreading-pubescent; fls. reddish to purplish, hairy, helmet ¼ in. high and about as wide; pistils hairy. E. Himalayas.

orientale Mill. With general habit of *A. Lycoctonum,* tall, sts. glabrous; lvs. large; infl. a large open panicle, appressed-pubescent; fls. yellowish-white, pubescent, helmet conic-cylindrical, ¾ in. high. Caucasus.

paniculatum Lam. Sts. 2–4½ ft., slender, with wide-spreading brs. and gland-tipped hairs in upper parts; lvs. evenly distributed, 5–7-parted, segms. cuneate-rhombic, 3-lobed near middle of sides, then pinnately lobed; infl. an open panicle 4–20 in. high, racemes few-fld.; fls. violet, somewhat pilose, 1–1½ in. high, helmet gaping, almost 1 in. high, broadly rounded and somewhat arched forward in upper half, lateral edge of opening very concave, beak projecting forward, almost ¼ in. long. S. Eur.

pyramidale Mill. [*A. Napellus* var. *pyramidale* (Mill.) Rouy & Foucaud; *A. Willdenowii* Rchb. ex Gáyer]. Close to *A. Napellus,* with crisped pubescence; lf. segms. broad, pedicels divergent, infl. elongate; infl. branched; helmet large, strongly arched. Much material cult. as *A. Napellus,* or *A. Napellus* var. *pyramidatum* Hort. belongs here.

pyrenaicum L. [*A. Lycoctonum* var. *pyrenaicum* (L.) Ser.]. St. 1–2½ ft. high, villous, mostly simple; lvs. rather few, round-reniform, divided almost to the base, segms. narrowly laciniate-incised; racemes long, simple or few-branched, rather compact; fls. yellow, helmet conic-cylindrical in profile, strongly indented in front, ¾ in. high. Pyrenees. Sometimes grown under the name *A. japonicum.*

reclinatum A. Gray. TRAILING WOLFSBANE. Trailing to diffusely erect, 1–7 ft. long; lvs. reniform in outline, 4–8 in. wide in lower parts, 3–7-cleft, segms. rhombic-obovate, somewhat 3-lobed; infl. a strigulose panicle of loose racemes; fls. white, helmet subconical, held almost horizontally, ½ in. high, ³⁄₁₆ in. wide in middle. S. Allegheny Mts.

rostratum Bernh. Close to *A. variegatum,* but differing in having lf. lobes nearly linear, and strict infl. with short, erect brs. Eur.

septentrionale: *A. Lycoctonum.*

sinense: *A chinense.*

Sparksii: a listed name of no botanical standing, probably refers to hort. form of *A. Henryi.*

Stoerkianum: *A. bicolor.*

tauricum Wulfen [*A. Napellus* var. *tauricum* (Wulfen) Ser.]. Close to *A. Napellus,* but having a glabrous infl. Se. Eur.

thyraicum: *A. Vulparia.*

uncinatum L. WILD M. Sts. slender, weak, ascending or climbing, 2–4 ft., glabrous, leafy; lvs. reniform-orbicular, 2–4 in. wide, 3–5-parted almost to the base, coarsely toothed; racemes few-fld., short; fls. deep blue, about 1 in. high, helmet ¾ in. high, rounded-conical in upper part, with somewhat curved lower margin and scarcely beaked. From Md. to S.C. Some cult. material of *A. japonicum* belongs here.

variegatum L. Sts. 3–4 ft., slender, flexuous, freely branching in upper part, glabrous; lvs. 2–4 in. wide, 5–7-parted, segms. cuneate-rhombic, then nearly pinnately lobed and sharply toothed; infl. usually open-paniculate, with few-fld., loose racemes; fls. 1½–2 in. high, violet, helmet gaping, 1 in. high or more, bulging forward in upper part. Se. Eur.

Vilmorinianum Kom. Sts. slender, climbing, branched, to 9 ft., crisp-pubescent in upper parts; st. lvs. 3-parted nearly to base, center segm.

broad-rhombic, then 3-lobed; racemes lateral and terminal, flexuous, loose; fls. 1½ in. high, dark purplish-blue, pubescent, helmet rounded in upper part, 1 in. high, lateral edge of opening concave, beak short, deflexed. China.

volubile Pall. ex Koelle. At first erect and slender, later usually climbing and twining, upper parts spreading-pilose; lvs. 3-parted, ultimate lobes lanceolate-linear; racemes loose, few-fld.; fls. 1–1½ in. high, purple, and green or blue, pilose, helmet round-conical in upper part, almost 1 in. high, lateral edge of opening concave, beak spreading. E. Asia.

Vulparia Rchb. [*A. moldavicum* Hacq. ex Rchb.; *A. thyraicum* Blocki]. Close to *A. Lycoctonum,* but infl. more openly branched, strigulose; fls. pale yellow, helmet slightly shorter. Cent. and s. Eur.

Willdenowii: *A. pyramidale.*

Wilsonii: *A. Carmichaelii.*

ACORUS L. *Araceae.* Two spp. of hardy, per. herbs of marshy places; lvs. arising from horizontal rhizomes, tufted, equitant, irislike or grasslike; peduncle and spathe a continuous leaflike unit bearing a green spadix above the middle; fls. bisexual, perianth 6-parted.

Sometimes planted in bog gardens; *A. gramineus* is used as an ornamental pot plant indoors. Propagated by division. The rhizome of *A. Calamus* is the source of medicinal calamus and has other uses.

Calamus L. SWEET FLAG, MYRTLE F., CALAMUS, FLAGROOT. To 6 ft., aromatic, rhizome stout, pinkish; lvs. to ¾ in. wide, with a prominent midrib; spadix stout, to 4 in. long. N. Hemisphere. Cv. **'Variegatus'** [*A. japonicus* Hort. var. *variegatus* Hort.]. Lvs. striped yellow. Var. **angustifolius** (Schott) Engl. Lvs. to 3/16 in. wide. India, Ceylon, Celebes Is.

gramineus Ait. GRASSY-LEAVED SWEET FLAG. To 18 in., not aromatic, rhizome slender; lvs. rarely more than ¼ in. wide, without a distinct midrib; spadix slender, to 3 in. long. China, se. Asia, Japan. Cv. **'Pusillus'** [var. *pusillus* (Siebold) Engl.]. A dwarf form. Japan. Cv. **'Albovariegatus'.** Lvs. striped white. Cv. **'Variegatus'** [*Carex variegata* Hort., not Lam. or Scheele]. Lvs. striped white.

japonicus var. **variegatus:** *A. Calamus* cv. 'Variegatus'.

ACRADENIA Kipp. *Rutaceae.* One sp., a shrub or small tree, native to Tasmania; lvs. opp., with 3 lfts., glandular-dotted; fls. white, in terminal corymbose cymes, sepals and petals 5; stamens 10–12; fr. a caps., 5-celled, 5-lobed, with a large gland terminating each lobe, 1–2-seeded.

Frankliniae Kipp. Shrub or small tree, to 10 ft.; lfts. sessile, lanceolate to oblong-lanceolate, to 3 in. long, serrulate to crenate, entire toward base; fls. white, 5/16 in. across; fr. downy.

ACROCARPUS Wight ex Arn. *Leguminosae* (subfamily *Caesalpinioideae*). Two spp. of unarmed trees of trop. se. Asia; lvs. alt., large, 2-pinnate; fls. small, red or orange, 5-merous, in racemes, stamens 5, separate, exserted; fr. a flat, long-stalked legume, seeds many.

Occasionally planted in wet tropical areas.

fraxinifolius Arn. SHINGLE TREE, PINK CEDAR, RED C. Deciduous tree, to 180 ft.; pinnae 12 in. long or more, lfts. glabrous, oblique-oblong, 3–4 in. long; fls. scarlet, in dense spikelike racemes, appearing before lvs.; fr. with wing along 1 suture. Mt. rain forests, India to Burma, where an important timber tree.

ACROCEPHALUS Benth. *Labiatae.* About 100 spp. of ann. or per. herbs of trop. Afr. to India, China, and Philippine Is.; lvs. opp., often appearing whorled because of axillary lvs., rather rigid, crenate-serrate, often hairy; fls. in verticillasters, arranged in spikes or congested into terminal heads, the upper lvs. forming an involucre, nearly sessile, small, calyx tubular, 2-lipped, upper lip entire, lower lip 4-toothed, corolla white, sometimes red, tube shorter than calyx, limb 2-lipped, 5-lobed, stamens 4, ovary 4-lobed; fr. of 4 glabrous nutlets.

sericeus Briq. Densely pubescent per., to 2 ft.; lvs. lanceolate, 1–3 in. long, attenuated at base, entire, sessile; fls. in globular heads 5/16 in. across, bracts orbicular, cuspidate, less than 3/16 in. long, calyx less than 3/16 in. long, corolla ¼ in. long. Angola.

ACROCLINIUM: *HELIPTERUM.*

ACROCOMIA Mart. GRU-GRU PALM. *Palmae.* More than 20 spp. of prickly, monoecious palms, native to trop. Amer.; trunk solitary, usually tall, cylindrical or swollen, unarmed and irregularly ringed in lower part but with persistent prickly petioles above, or armed with rings of stout spines and lvs. entirely deciduous; lvs. pinnate, pinnae 1-ribbed, acute; infl. among lvs., simply branched, lower bract short, upper bract woody, elongate, as long as infl., often densely hairy or prickly; rachillae with fls. in a few triads (2 male and 1 female) near the base and above these mostly solitary, densely crowded male fls., each set in a cup formed by united bractlets, together resembling cells in a honeycomb; male fls. with sepals separate, short, petals separate, asymmetrical, valvate, stamens 6, pistillode 3-lobed, female fls. with sepals separate, petals imbricate, staminodes in a ring, pistil 3-celled; fr. usually globose, smooth or minutely prickly, mesocarp fibrous, adherent to endocarp, this smooth, bony, with 3 pores at or above the middle, seed with homogeneous endosperm.

Fast-growing palms; a few species are planted in tropical and subtropical U.S. (Zones 9b and 10 in Fla.), but among gardeners and in the trade there is often confusion about the identity of species. Other species are important in local economies for the useful fruits, building materials, seed oil, and for making wine. For culture see *Palms.*

aculeata (Jacq.) Lodd. ex Mart. [*A. sclerocarpa* Mart.]. To 50 ft., trunk cylindrical or thickened toward top, with spines in rings; lvs. deciduous, to 9 ft. long, pinnae about 60 on each side, to 3 ft. long, green and finely hairy beneath; upper bract of infl. to nearly 6 ft. long, brown-felted, with few prickles; fr. 1½ in. in diam. or more. Dominica, Martinique. Zone 10.

armentalis: *Gastrococos crispa.*

belizensis: *A. mexicana.*

crispa: *Gastrococos crispa.*

fusiformis: *A. spinosa,* but material offered as *A. fusiformis* is sometimes *A. hospes.*

hospes L. H. Bailey. To 25 ft. or more, trunk cylindrical, irregularly ringed, unarmed except for persistent, prickly, petiole bases; pinnae to 1¼ in. wide, pale and puberulent beneath; upper bract of infl. to 4 ft. long or more, brown-felted, lacking prickles; fr. about 1⅜ in. in diam. Described from cult. Sometimes cult. under the name *A. fusiformis, A. sclerocarpa,* or *A. spinosa.*

mexicana Karw. ex Mart. [*A. belizensis* L. H. Bailey]. COYOLI PALM. To 30 ft., trunk cylindrical, irregularly ringed, unarmed except for persistent, prickly petiole bases; lvs. to 12 ft., pinnae in 2–3 planes, to 3 ft. long, 1¼ in. wide, pale and sparsely to densely hairy beneath; upper bract of infl. finely hairy, more or less prickly; fr. to 1⅝ in. in diam. Mex. to Brit. Honduras and Honduras. Zone 10.

sclerocarpa: *A. aculeata,* but the name *A. sclerocarpa* applied in hort. to *A. hospes* and in literature to Brazilian plants of uncertain identity.

spinosa (Mill.) H. E. Moore [*A. fusiformis* (Swartz) Sweet]. To 50 ft. or more, trunk swollen in upper part, with spines in rings; lvs. deciduous, to 9 ft. or more, pinnae 40 or more on each side, glabrous, grayish beneath; upper bract of infl. boat-shaped, to 6 ft. long or more, brown-felted, rarely prickly; fr. to 1⅝ in. in diam. Jamaica. The name has sometimes been applied erroneously to *A. hospes* in cult.

Totai Mart. GRU-GRU. To 45 ft. or more, trunk cylindrical, with spines in rings; lvs. deciduous, pinnae to 2 ft. long or more, ¾ in. wide, glabrous; upper bract of infl. reddish-felted, prickly near tip; fr. to 1¼ in. in diam. or more. N. Argentina and Paraguay, where it is an important source of palm kernel oil. The hardiest sp. of the genus. Zone 9b.

ACRODON N. E. Br. *Aizoaceae.* Three spp. of low, clump-forming succulents, native to S. Afr.; lvs. opp., 3-angled, in rosettes, dentate on margins or only near apex; fls. solitary, pedicelled, calyx 5–6-lobed, petals many, stamens many, erect, ovary inferior, 5-celled, stigmas 5, plumose; fr. a caps., with flexible wings on the valves, expanding keels ending in awnlike points, placental tubercles present.

Growth occurs in summer. Plants should be given a sunny location under glass with moderate moisture, but in winter they should be in a sunny, dry place with a relatively cool temperature of about 55° F. Propagated by seeds. See also *Succulents.*

bellidiflorus (L.) N. E. Br. To 3 in.; lvs. crowded, 4-ranked, spreading, recurved, gray-green, to 2 in. long, united basally in a sheath, 3-angled, laterally compressed toward apex, short-tipped, margins cartilaginous, toothed; fls. to 1⅝ in. across, petals white, red-margined. Cape Prov.

ACRONYCHIA J. R. Forst. & G. Forst. *Rutaceae.* About 40 spp. of polygamous trees and shrubs, native to Australia, trop. Asia, and Pacific Is.; lvs. alt. or opp., with 3 or 1 lft., glandular-dotted; fls. white to yellow, in cymes or panicles, bisexual or unisexual, calyx 4-cleft, petals 4, stamens 8, often dimorphic, staminodes sometimes present; fr. drupaceous or a 4-celled caps.

Baueri Schott. Tree; lvs. opp., with 1 lft., elliptic to obovate, 6 in. long; fls. very small, petals pubescent outside, in narrow, spikelike, axillary panicles; fr. ½ in. in diam. Australia. Planted in Calif.

ACROPERA: *GONGORA.* **A. Loddigesii:** *G. galeata.*

ACROSTICHUM L. SWAMP FERN. *Polypodiaceae.* Three spp. of large, coarse ferns with stout erect rhizomes, often forming massive tussocks in coastal mangrove swamps; lvs. tall, to 10 ft. or more, thick, leathery, 1-pinnate, pinnae entire or obscurely toothed; sporangia borne in a dense mass over the entire lower surface of the fertile pinnae.

Grown in the open far south or under glass. Useful for wet coastal sites in the tropics or Zone 10. See also *Ferns.*

aureum L. LEATHER FERN. Lvs. erect, 3–9 ft., only the upper pinnae fertile. Pantrop.

crinitum: *Elaphoglossum crinitum.*

daneifolium Langsd. & Fisch. [*A. excelsum* Maxon]. LEATHER FERN. Lvs. nearly erect, 5–12 ft., all or most of the pinnae fertile. Tropics, New World.

excelsum: *A. daneifolium.*

ACTAEA L. BANEBERRY, COHOSH, NECKLACEWEED. *Ranunculaceae.* About 8 spp. of erect, per. herbs of rich woods in the N. Temp. Zone; lvs. large, compound; fls. small, white, in terminal racemes, sepals 4–5, petaloid, falling early, petals 4–10, small, flat, spatulate, clawed, stamens many, pistil 1; fr. a berry, glossy.

Berries poisonous if eaten. Useful in the rock garden, wild garden, or border, doing especially well in shaded places like woods. Propagated by seeds sown in late autumn or spring; in spring division is the best method.

acuminata: *A. spicata* var.

alba: *A. pachypoda* for Amer. material, *A. spicata* for Eurasian.

arguta: *A. rubra* subsp.

Cimicifuga: *Cimicifuga foetida.*

japonica: *Cimicifuga japonica.*

pachypoda Elliott [*A. alba* of Amer. auth., not Mill.; *A. spicata* var. *alba* of auth., not L.]. WHITE B., WHITE C., DOLL'S-EYES. Resembling *A. rubra*, but having lfts. more cut and with more pointed teeth; raceme oblong; petals truncate at apex; fr. pedicels as thick as peduncle, berries usually white. Nov. Sc. to Ga., w. to Minn. and Mo.

rubra (Ait.) Willd. [*A. spicata* var. *rubra* Ait.]. RED B., SNAKEBERRY. Bushy, 1–2 ft.; lvs. ternate, lfts. mostly ovate, toothed to cleft or incised; raceme ovoid, pedicels slender, about ½ in. long; petals spatulate; berries mostly red, about ½ in. long. Nov. Sc. to N.J. and Penn., w. to S. Dak. and Nebr. Subsp. **arguta** (Nutt.) Hult. [*A. arguta* Nutt.]. Lvs. smaller, more incised; berries nearly spherical. W. N. Amer.

spicata L. [*A. alba* Mill.; *A. spicata* var. *alba* L.]. Lf. segms. lanceolate; fls. white to bluish; berries purplish-black. Eurasia. Var. **acuminata** (Wallich) Gürke [*A. acuminata* Wallich]. Lf. segms. long-acuminate. Se. Eur. to n. India. Var. **alba:** *A. spicata*, but the name *A. spicata* var. *alba* has been applied to *A. pachypoda.* Var. **rubra:** *A. rubra.*

ACTINEA: see *HYMENOXYS.* **A. simplex:** *H. acaulis.* **A. herbacea:** *H. acaulis* var. *glabra.* **A. angustifolia:** *H. scaposa.*

ACTINELLA: see *HYMENOXYS.* **A. lanata:** *H. acaulis* var. *caespitosa.* **A. fastigiata:** *H. scaposa* var. *linearis.*

ACTINIDIA Lindl. *Actinidiaceae.* About 36 spp. of climbing shrubs, native to Asia; pith solid or lamellate; lvs. alt., simple, petioled; fls. solitary or in axillary clusters, corolla cup-shaped, usually white; fr. a berry.

Actinidias grow equally well in sunny and semishady locations. Propagated by seeds sown in spring, also by cuttings of half-ripened wood in summer or of hardwood under glass, or even by layers. They are good vines for trellises and arbors. Several species, particularly *A. chinensis* and *A. arguta*, are cultivated for the edible fruits, with their greenish pulp of pleasant acid taste; others are grown as ornamental vines.

arguta (Siebold & Zucc.) Planch. ex Miq. BOWER A., TARA VINE, YANG-TAO. Pith lamellate, white to brown; lvs. broadly ovate, to 6 in. long, sharply serrate, rounded to subcordate, membranous, petioles 1–3 in. long; fls. in axillary cymes, white, 1 in. across, anthers blackish when dry; fr. subglobose, 1 in. in diam., greenish-yellow, edible. Temp. e. Asia. Zone 5.

Burbidgei: a listed name of no botanical standing.

chinensis Planch. CHINESE GOOSEBERRY, KIWI BERRY, YANG-TAO. Pith lamellate, whitish; lvs. ovate, to 7 in. long, rounded or somewhat cordate at base, upper surface dark green, puberulous, lower surface white-stellate-tomentose, petioles 1–2 in. long; fls. orange-yellow, 1½ in. across; fr. subglobose to ellipsoid, about 1⅛ in. in diam., edible. China and Taiwan. Zone 8. Cult. commercially in New Zeal. for the fr.

coriacea (Finet & Gagnep.) S. T. Dunn. Pith solid, whitish or yellowish; lvs. oblong to oblong-ovate, to 6½ in. long, leathery, both surfaces glabrous, lower surface pale, petioles to 1 in. long; fls. solitary or in 2–4-fld. cymes, reddish, about ¾ in. across, anthers yellow; fr. ovoid or globose, to ¾ in. in diam. China.

Kolomikta (Rupr. & Maxim.) Maxim. Pith lamellate, brown; lvs. ovate to oblong-ovate, to 6 in. long, cordate, membranous, with those near infl. often variegated with white or pink, glabrous on both surfaces, paler beneath, petioles to 1¼ in. long; fls. 1–3 together, white, ¾ in. across, anthers yellow; fr. globose, about ¾ in. in diam. Temp. e. Asia. Zone 5. Grown for the decorative foliage.

lanceolata S. T. Dunn. Pith lamellate, brown; lvs. lanceolate to ovate-lanceolate, to 2½ in. long, papery, upper surface minutely puberulent, the lower glaucescent with white-stellate tomentum, petioles about ½ in. long; fls. in 3–6-fld. cymes, greenish, ⅜ in. across, anthers yellow; fr. ovoid, ⅜ in. long. China.

melanandra Franch. Pith lamellate, whitish; lvs. ovate, to 2½ in. long, papery, lower surface with small tufts of rusty hairs in lf. axils, glaucous; fls. solitary or in few-fld. cymes, white, 1 in. across, anthers blackish when dry; fr. ovoid, 1¼ in. long, glabrous. China.

polygama (Siebold & Zucc.) Maxim. [*A. volubilis* (Siebold & Zucc.) Planch.]. SILVER VINE. Pith solid, white; lvs. ovate, to 6 in. long, rounded to subcordate at base, those near the infl. white above on upper half or yellowish, petioles slender, to 1½ in. long; fls. solitary or 2–3, white, about 1 in. across, anthers yellow or brown; fr. globose, 1 in. in diam., yellow. Temp. e. Asia. The decorative lvs. make this an ornamental vine. Lvs. and salted fr. eaten by the Japanese.

purpurea Rehd. Related to *A. arguta*, but differing in having lvs. longer, narrower, fls. generally smaller, and fr. ovoid or oblong, purplish. China.

volubilis: *A. polygama.*

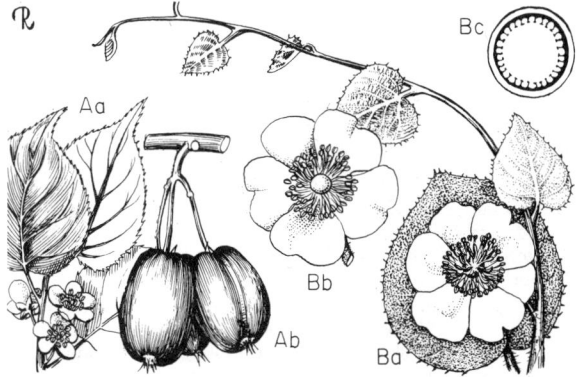

ACTINIDIACEAE. **A**, *Actinidia arguta:* **Aa**, flowering branch (male), × ¼; **Ab**, fruit, × ½. **B**, *A. chinensis:* **Ba**, flowering branch with bisexual flower, × ½; **Bb**, male flower, × ½; **Bc**, ovary, cross section, × 3. (From Bailey, *Manual of Cultivated Plants*, ed. 2.)

ACTINIDIACEAE Hutch. ACTINIDIA FAMILY. Dicot.; 4 genera and 285 spp. of trees, shrubs, or woody vines, native to trop. and temp. Asia and trop. Amer.; lvs. alt., simple; fls. usually in clusters, cymes, or panicles, sepals and petals 5, stamens usually many, anthers 2-celled, sometimes dehiscing by apical pores, ovary superior, carpels 3 or more, more or less united; fr. a berry or caps. *Actinidia* is cult. as an ornamental vine and for its edible fr.

ACTINODAPHNE Nees. *Lauraceae.* About 60–70 spp. of dioecious, evergreen shrubs or trees, native to e. and se. Asia; lvs. alt., nearly whorled, usually crowded at the st. apex, entire; infl. umbellate or clustered, axillary, sessile or peduncled, bracted; fls. small, perianth segms. 6, in 2 whorls, male fls. with (4–)6–9 usually fertile stamens, anthers introrse, 4-celled, female fls. with 9 staminodes; fr. a berry, subtended occasionally by a flat, shallowly concave structure or more commonly by a conspicuous cupule.

acuminata: *A. longifolia.*

longifolia (Blume) Nakai [*A. acuminata* (Blume) Meissn.]. Tree, to 40 ft., bark smooth; lvs. lanceolate, to 8 in. long, long-acuminate, powdery-white beneath, short-petioled; infl. a compound umbel; fr. ellipsoid, ¾ in. long, black. Cent. and s. Japan.

ACTINOMERIS: *VERBESINA.* **A. squarrosa**: *V. alternifolia.*

ACTINOPHLOEUS: *PTYCHOSPERMA.*

ACTINORHYTIS H. Wendl. & Drude. *Palmae.* One or perhaps a few spp. of solitary, unarmed, monoecious palms with prominent crownshaft, native to the Malay Arch., New Guinea, and the Solomon Is.; lvs. pinnate, pinnae acute at apex, with 1 principal rib; infl. below lvs., green, subtended by 2 thin deciduous bracts, peduncle short, rachis short, brs. spreading, the lower once-branched, rachillae with fls. in triads (2 male and 1 female) in the lower part and above these with paired or solitary male fls.; male fls. slightly asymmetrical, sepals imbricate, small, petals valvate, stamens 24–30, filaments inflexed at apex in bud, pistillode conical, female fls. larger, sepals and petals imbricate, ovary 1-celled; fr. large, ovoid, with apical stigmatic scar, endocarp operculate, seed with ruminate endosperm and basal embryo.

For culture see *Palms.*

calapparia (Blume) H. Wendl. & Drude ex Scheff. CALAPPA PALM. To 40 ft.; lvs. to 9 ft. long, arched at tip, pinnae regularly arranged, linear-lanceolate; fr. orange-yellow, to 3 in. long. Zone 10b in Fla.

ACTINOSTROBUS Miq. *Cupressaceae.* Two spp. of densely branched, coniferous, evergreen, monoecious shrubs, native to W. Australia; lvs. in whorls of 3, bluntly and thickly scalelike, appressed; male cones axillary, in several whorls, female cones globose or ovoid, scales 6, woody; seeds 1–2, winged; allied to *Callitris,* but differing in having many, minute, scalelike, sterile bracts about the base of female cones.

Propagated by seeds or cuttings. For culture see *Conifers.*

glaucus: a listed name of no botanical standing.

pyramidalis Miq. Pyramidal, *Cupressus*-like shrub, to 8 ft.; apical lvs. sometimes minutely needlelike, becoming scalelike; female cones ovoid, about ½ in. long, scales triangular, acute. Zone 10.

ACTINOTUS Labill. *Umbelliferae.* About 10 spp. of Australian and New Zeal. herbs; lvs. toothed to biternately divided; umbels simple, dense, headlike, subtended by an involucre of large bracts; fls. minute, petals 5 or 0, outer fls. sometimes male by abortion of pistil.

helianthi Labill. FLANNELFLOWER. Erect, woolly-tomentose per., to 2 ft.; lvs. 2–3-divided, segms. linear-oblong; involucre to 4 in. across, of 10–18 white-woolly petal-like bracts. Not hardy north, but may be treated as an ann.

ADA Lindl. *Orchidaceae.* Two spp. of epiphytes, native to Andes of Colombia; pseudobulbs clustered; lvs. 1–3; fls. in compact, arching racemes, not expanding except for the spreading sepal and petal tips, bright orange to cinnabar-red, sepals and petals linear-lanceolate, acute, lip shorter, oblong, acuminate, parallel to column. For structure of fl. see *Orchidaceae.*

Cool greenhouse; for culture see *Orchids.*

aurantiaca Lindl. Pseudobulbs to 4 in. long; lvs. to 9 in. long and ½ in. wide; racemes 5–13-fld., about as long as lvs.; fls. orange or cinnabar-red, 1½ in. long, lip 2-keeled. Late autumn to late spring. Var. **maculata** Hort. Infl. shorter; fls. larger, sepals and petals densely covered with small maroon-colored dots.

ADANSONIA L. *Bombacaceae.* Nine spp. of deciduous trees, native to Afr., Madagascar, and Australia; lvs. palmately compound, lfts. 3–9; fls. large, solitary, axillary, calyx deeply (3–)5-lobed, petals 5, stamens very many, united in a tube ½ their length, ovary 5-, 10- or rarely 15-celled, style elongate, stigma 5-, 10-, or 15-lobed; fr. large, woody, indehiscent, seeds many, large, angular, embedded in fibrous pulp.

digitata L. BAOBAB, MONKEY-BREAD TREE, DEAD-RAT TREE. To 60 ft., trunk relatively short, massive, to 30 ft. in diam.; brs. rather stout, leafy at the ends; lfts. 5–7, oblong-elliptic, to 5 in. long, acuminate, entire; fls. mostly pendulous on long peduncles, often opening before lvs. appear, petals white, obovate, to 4 in. long, reflexed or spreading, staminal column with large, dense crown of separate filaments and with exserted stigma; fr. more or less cylindrical, 4–16 in. long, velvety-tomentose. Trop. Afr., where bark yields fiber, young lvs. are eaten as a vegetable, and white pulp of the fr. is base for lemonadelike drink and febrifuge. Occasionally planted as a specimen tree in the tropics.

ADELOCARYUM Brand. *Boraginaceae.* Seven spp. of summer- and autumn-flowering, hairy per. or bien. herbs, native to Asia; lvs. simple, alt., basal and cauline; fls. blue or blue and white, in terminal cymes, calyx deeply 5-lobed, corolla campanulate, 5-lobed, corolla throat with scales, stamens 5, included; fr. of 4 nutlets with shortly barbed prickles, the surface concave. Differs from *Cynoglossum* in surface of nutlet concave and not flat or convex.

Rarely grown in the flower garden in warm countries.

anchusoides (Lindl.) Brand [*Lindelofia anchusoides* (Lindl.) Lehm.]. Hairy per., 1–3 ft.; basal lvs. elliptic-lanceolate, to 1½ ft. long, st. lvs. linear, few and smaller; fls. blue with rose-purple tube, ¼ in. long, in loose slender cymes. Cent. Asia.

coelestinum (Lindl.) Brand [*Cynoglossum coelestinum* Lindl.]. Somewhat hairy bien., to 5 ft.; basal lvs. broadly ovate, to 1 ft. long, upper lvs. becoming smaller; fls. blue, edged in white, ⁵⁄₁₆ in. across. India.

ADENANDRA Willd. *Rutaceae.* About 30 spp. of shrubs, native to S. Afr.; lvs. alt., rarely opp., simple, glandular-dotted; fls. white, pink, or red, terminal, sessile or pedicelled, calyx 5-parted, petals 5, stamens 5, staminodes 5, gland-tipped; fr. a 5-celled caps.

fragrans (Sims) Roem. & Schult. Glabrous, erect shrub, to 3 ft.; lvs. linear-oblong, to 1¼ in. long; fls. rose, to ¾ in. across, fragrant. Cult. in Calif. Zone 10.

ADENANTHERA L. BEAD TREE. *Leguminosae* (subfamily *Mimosoideae*). Four spp. of unarmed trees of trop. Asia and Australia; lvs. alt., large, 2-pinnate; fls. small, yellow or white, in long slender racemes, 5-merous, stamens 10, separate; fr. a narrow, curved legume, seeds bright-colored.

Grown as a street tree and for the ornamental seeds in the wet tropics and subtropics. Propagated easily by cuttings or by seeds that have been soaked in hot water.

pavonina L. CORALWOOD, REDWOOD, SANDALWOOD TREE, RED S.T., PEACOCK FLOWER-FENCE, BARBADOS-PRIDE, CORAL PEA. To 50 ft.; lfts. ¾–1½ in. long; racemes to 6 in. long; fls. ⁵⁄₁₆ in. long, white and yellow in same cluster; fr. to 9 in. long, much coiled after dehiscence, seeds lens-shaped, red, called "Circassian seeds." Se. Asia. The red heartwood used in cabinetwork and as a source of dye in s. India; seeds used for necklaces.

ADENIUM Roem. & Schult. *Apocynaceae.* About 4 spp. of fleshy-stemmed, spineless shrubs and small trees, native to trop. Afr.; lvs. alt., entire, rather fleshy, with several conspicuous glands in each axil; fls. in terminal corymbs, showy, 5-merous, bisexual, corolla pink or purple, tube funnelform from a short cylindrical base, lobes spreading, stamens short, borne toward base of corolla tube, hairy, anthers united, with long-filiform apical appendages and sagittate bases, pistil with 2 separate ovaries; fr. a pair of spreading or reflexed follicles, seeds many, linear-oblong, covered with retrorse hairs.

Rarely cultivated in this country; similar to other succulents in requiring hot, dry conditions. Propagated by cuttings of half-ripe shoots in sand.

arabicum: *A. obesum.*

obesum (Forssk.) Roem. & Schult. [*A. arabicum* Balf.f.]. DESERT ROSE. Variable shrub or small tree, to 15 ft., with swollen trunks; lvs. clustered at ends of brs., more or less sessile, obovate to oblong-obovate or elliptic, to 6 in. long, obtuse-truncate and mucronate, glabrous to densely tomentose; corolla deep pink at margin, paler toward center, to 2 in. or more across, downy outside, lobes undulate, apically rounded or with short sharp point. E. Afr. to s. Arabia.

ADENOCALYMNA Mart. ex Meissn. *Bignoniaceae.* More than 50 spp. of climbing shrubs, native to S. Amer., chiefly Brazil; lvs. opp., with 3 lfts., or with 2 lfts. and a terminal tendril; fls. showy, in racemes or panicles, calyx mostly 5-lobed, glandular outside, corolla funnelform, stamens 4; fr. a woody caps.

Grown under glass or in the open in warm regions, but little planted in the U.S. Propagated by cuttings.

inundatum Mart. ex DC. Lvs. ovate to ovate-oblong, to 6 in. long, shiny; fls. bright yellow, to 2 in. long. Brazil.

ADENOCARPUS DC. *Leguminosae* (subfamily *Faboideae*). Ten spp. of tender shrubs, native to the Old World; lvs. alt., small, of 3 lfts.; fls. yellow, papilionaceous, in terminal racemes, calyx 2-lipped, stamens united into a tube; fr. a flattened, linear, warty legume.

Culture as for *Cytisus.* Zone 9.

decorticans Boiss. Deciduous shrub or small tree, to 25 ft., with white bark; lfts. 5/16–3/4 in. long, revolute-folded; racemes short; fls. golden-yellow, calyx villous, not glandular, with nearly equal lips, teeth of lower lip equal; fr. 1–2¼ in. long. Spain.

foliosus (Ait.) DC. Densely branched, evergreen shrub, to 6 ft.; lvs. crowded, lfts. obovate-oblong; racemes compact; fls. many, calyx villous, teeth of lower lip equal. Canary Is.

viscosus Webb & Berth. Differs from *A. foliosus* in having lfts. folded, linear-oblong, and calyx glandular-pubescent, with median tooth of lower lip longer than laterals. Canary Is.

ADENOPHORA Fisch. LADYBELLS. *Campanulaceae.* Probably not more than 40 spp. of hardy, summer-blooming per. herbs, native to Eurasia and Japan; often confused with *Campanula,* and differing only in the presence of a tubular or glandular disk surrounding the base of the style beneath the expanded stamen filaments.

The taxonomy of *Adenophora* is poorly understood and plants offered under a species name are for the most part not correctly identified. Although plants are offered under the species names listed below, many are probably not in cultivation, for example, *A. Bulleyana.* Ladybells require the same treatment as campanulas. They are best propagated by seeds, for the fleshy roots should be disturbed as little as possible.

Bulleyana Diels. Sts. erect, to 3 ft., puberulent; upper lvs. oblong-ovate, to 3 in. long, serrate, hispidulous; infl. of several strict, densely fld., spicate brs.; fls. often borne in 3's, calyx lobes narrowly lanceolate, to 3/8 in. long, serrate, corolla pale blue, funnelform, to ½ in. long. W. China. Material offered under this name may be either *A. confusa* or *A. diplodonta.*

canescens: a listed name of no botanical standing.

chinensis: a listed name of no botanical standing for *A. sinensis.*

communis: *A. liliifolia.*

confusa Nannf. [*A. Farreri* Hort.]. Sts. erect, to 3 ft. or more, rigid, glabrous or sparsely pilose; st. lvs. many, alt., sessile and clasping or short-petioled and somewhat auricled, rhomboid-ovate to lanceolate-ovate, to 3 in. long, dentate-crenate; fls. in few-branched panicles, nodding, calyx lobes narrow-triangular, to 5/16 in. long, erect, then spreading, corolla deep blue, campanulate, to 7/8 in. long, style slightly exserted. W. China.

diplodonta Diels. Sts. erect, to 3 ft., puberulent; lvs. ovate, to 3 in. long, cuneate, doubly serrate, hirsute beneath; fls. in elongate racemes, sometimes paired, calyx lobes narrowly lanceolate, somewhat subfimbriate basally, corolla white to blue, funnelform, nearly 1 in. long, style exserted. W. China.

Farreri: a listed name of no botanical standing for *A. confusa.*

hakusanensis: *A. triphylla* var.

koreana Kitam. Sts. erect, to 3 ft., simple at base, branched above; lower st. lvs. more or less whorled, nearly sessile or short-petioled, oblong-obovate, to 5 in. long, acute or acuminate, nearly cuneate at the base, serrate, grading above to alt. and linear; fls. more or less nodding, in terminal panicles, calyx lobes lanceolate, about ¼ in. long, serrulate, corolla blue, open-campanulate, ½ in. long. Korea.

leucantha: a listed name of no botanical standing.

liliifolia (L.) Bess. [*A. communis* Fisch.; *A. stylosa* (Lam.) Fisch.]. Sts. erect, to 1½ ft., glabrous or sometimes puberulent; basal lvs. petioled, cordate-orbicular, st. lvs. petioled or sessile, ovate to lanceolate, to 3 in. long, cuneate, coarsely serrate; fls. many, nodding, in terminal racemes or panicles, calyx lobes serrulate or entire, corolla pale blue, open-campanulate, to 5/8 in. across. Cent. Eur. to Manchuria.

marsupiiflora: *A. stenanthina.*

Maximowicziana Mak. Sts. spreading, to 2 ft. long, glabrous; lvs. cordate-ovate, grading to linear-lanceolate above, 3–8 in. long; fls. few, in terminal, corymbose or paniculate infls., corolla blue, campanulate, to ½ in. long, style exserted. Japan.

nikoensis Franch. & Sav. Sts. to 1½ ft., glabrescent; lvs. sessile, linear to linear-lanceolate, 1–4 in. long, serrate; fls. in terminal racemes, calyx lobes usually linear, serrulate, corolla bluish, campanulate, 5/8–1 in. long, style sometimes exserted. Japan. Var. **stenophylla** (Kitam.) Ohwi [*A. nipponica* Kitam.]. Calyx lobes entire.

nipponica: *A. nikoensis* var. *stenophylla.*

ornata Diels. Sts. 1–4 ft., glabrous or puberulent; lvs. sessile, obovate to oblanceolate, to 2½ in. long, serrate; fls. usually in open panicles, corolla deep blue, funnelform, to 1 in. long, style included. W. China.

palustris Kom. Sts. erect, strict, to 3 ft., purplish; lvs. sessile, thickish, elliptic to oblong, to 3 in. long, serrate; fls. nodding, in narrow racemes, corolla pale lavender, campanulate, 3/8–7/8 in. long. China, Japan.

polymorpha Ledeb. An illegitimate name, originally used for a complex of spp.; material offered as *A. polymorpha* may be *A. liliifolia* or *A. nikoensis.*

Potaninii Korsh. Sts. weak or nearly scandent at the base, but becoming erect, to 3 ft. long or more, pilose; st. lvs. ovate-lanceolate to lanceolate, to 2 in. long, strongly toothed to nearly entire, pubescent; fls. nodding, in simple panicles, calyx lobes serrate to pinnatisect, corolla violet, broadly campanulate, to ¾ in. long and somewhat broader. W. China.

remotiflora (Siebold & Zucc.) Miq. Sts. erect or diffuse, to 3 ft., glabrous or sparsely pilose; lower st. lvs. petioled, cordate-ovate or narrower, to 8 in. long, acuminate, serrate or dentate, upper lvs. smaller, sessile; fls. nodding, in loose racemes or panicles, corolla bluish, narrow-campanulate, ¾–1¼ in. long, style usually not exserted. Japan, Korea, Manchuria.

sinensis A.DC. [*A. chinensis* Hort.]. Sts. erect, to 2½ ft., puberulent; lvs. sessile, lanceolate-ovate, to 3 in. long, doubly serrate, paler green beneath; fls. in racemes, corolla bluish-violet, open-campanulate, to ¾ in. long, style scarcely exserted. China.

stenanthina (Ledeb.) Kitag. [*A. marsupiiflora* (Roem. & Schult.) Fisch.]. Slender-stemmed, to 3 ft. or more; lower lvs. cordate-ovate, serrate, upper lvs. linear-lanceolate, to 3 in. long, nearly entire; fls. nodding, in panicles, calyx lobes entire, corolla bluish, narrowly campanulate, to 5/8 in. long, style long-exserted. U.S.S.R., Manchuria.

stricta Miq. Sts. very slender, erect, to 3 ft., strictly branched, sparsely white-pilose; basal lvs. long-petioled, reniform-cordate, st. lvs. sessile, ovate to oblong, to about 2½ in. long, coarsely serrate; fls. drooping, in dense spikes, calyx lobes narrowly lanceolate, entire, corolla violet, campanulate, to ¾ in. long, style slightly if at all exserted. Japan.

stylosa: *A. liliifolia.*

Takedae Mak. Sts. slender, declined, to about 2 ft., glabrous; st. lvs. linear to narrow-ovate, 1½–6 in. long, toothed or nearly entire; fls. in open, leafy racemes, on pedicels 1–2 in. long, calyx lobes glandular-toothed, corolla violet-blue, broadly campanulate, to 1 in. across, style not exserted. Japan.

Tashiroi (Mak. & Nakai) Mak. & Nakai. Sts. decumbent, to about 1 ft. long, nearly glabrous; lvs. broadly ovate, to 1½ in. long, coarsely toothed; fls. in racemes or sometimes solitary, corolla violet, campanulate, about 5/8 in. long, style not exserted. Japan.

Thunbergiana: *A. Triphylla* var.

triphylla (Thunb.) A. DC. [*A. verticillata* (Pall.) Fisch.; *A. verticillata* var. *angustifolia* Miq.]. Sts. erect, to 3 ft., glabrous or white-pilose; lvs. usually in whorls of 4, oblong to oblong-elliptic or linear, to 4 in. long, serrate; lower fls. usually in whorls on very slender pedicels, more paniculate above, corolla pale bluish-violet, narrowly urceolate-campanulate, about 3/8 in. long, style exserted. Japan, Taiwan, China to

U.S.S.R. Var. **hakusanensis** (Nakai) Kitam. [*A. hakusanensis* Nakai]. Sts. to about 1½ ft.; panicles more densely fld. Japan. Var. **japonica** (Regel) Hara [*A. Thunbergiana* Kudo]. Corolla more openly campanulate, to 1 in. long. Japan.

verticillata: *A. triphylla.* Var. **angustifolia:** *A. triphylla.*

ADENOROPIUM: *JATROPHA.* **A. hastatum:** *J. integerrima.*

ADENOSTOMA Hook. & Arn. *Rosaceae.* Two spp. of unarmed evergreen shrubs with resinous herbage, native to Calif.; lvs. small, entire, linear, rigid, many; fls. small, white, crowded in terminal panicles, stamens 10–15, in 2's or 3's, pistil 1, style lateral, not exserted; fr. an achene.

Sometimes planted in their native region or those of similar climate; needing a sunny, well-drained soil. Propagation largely by seeds.

fasciculatum Hook. & Arn. CHAMISE, GREASEWOOD. Diffuse shrub, 2–11 ft., bark reddish, shreddy only in age; lvs. linear to narrowly club-shaped, to ½ in. long, fascicled; panicles 2–5 in. long, bracts not scarious; petals obliquely truncate, $\frac{1}{16}$ in. long. Calif., n. Baja Calif.

sparsifolium Torr. RIBBONWOOD, REDSHANKS. Arborescent, to 20 ft., bark red-brown, exfoliating freely; lvs. scattered, filiform, to ⅝ in. long; panicles open, to 4 in. long, bracts scarious-margined; petals elliptic, $\frac{1}{16}$ in long. S. Calif. and Baja Calif.

ADHATODA: *JUSTICIA.* **A. Duvernoia:** *Duvernoia adhatodoides;* **A. Vasica:** *J. Adhatoda.*

ADIANTUM L. MAIDENHAIR FERN, MAIDENHAIR. *Polypodiaceae.* Two hundred or more spp. of dainty ferns, mostly of trop. Amer., a few spp. in temp. N. Amer. and e. Asia; lvs. thin, delicate, simple or divided into fan-shaped pinnules, petioles shiny black or purplish; sori borne at edges of pinnules, usually round or oblong, covered by a recurved marginal flap of the pinnule.

The tender species are popular greenhouse plants, which require a temperature of 60–65° F., a fairly moist atmosphere, protection from full exposure to sun, and soil of good loam and leaf mold. The native species may be grown in the open in places like their native habitat, protected from wind and the roots covered in winter. Propagation by spores or division of clumps. See also *Ferns.*

aemulum: *A. Raddianum.*

affine Willd. [*A. Cunninghamii* Hook.]. Lvs. 2-pinnate, to 15 in. long and 9 in. wide, pinnules oblong, to 1 in. long, lower surface convex, petioles black, glossy; sori many, reniform, along upper margin of each pinnule. New Zeal.

altadena: *A. Capillus-Veneris.*

Bausei: *A. tenerum* cv.

bellum T. Moore. BERMUDA M. F. Lvs. 4–6 in. long, tufted, 2-pinnate, pinnules to ¾ in. long, 2–3-lobed, erose; sori oblong, not curved. Bermuda. Material offered under the name *A. bellum* is generally *A. Raddianum* cv. 'Pacottii.'

californicum: *A. Raddianum* cv. 'Fragrantissimum'.

Capillus-Veneris L. [*A. altadena* Hort.; *A. Obrienii* Hort.]. SOUTHERN M., VENUS'S-HAIR, VENUS'S-HAIR FERN, DUDDER GRASS. Lvs. 2–3-pinnate, ovate to narrowly triangular, 18–24 in. long, to 10 in. wide, pinnules to 1 in. across, very variable, fan-shaped, upper margin 3–4-lobed or -cleft, then finely toothed, each vein ending at a marginal tooth; sori oblong, little or not at all curved. Worldwide in temp. and trop. regions. Cv. **'Mairisii'.** Lvs. broadly triangular to triangular, pinnules long-subrhombic to triangular.

cardiochlaenum: *A. polyphyllum.*

caudatum L. TRAILING M., WALKING FERN. Lvs. to 1½ ft. long, often rooting at apex, 1-pinnate, pinnae linear, attenuate, to ¾ in. long, half as wide, petioles short, brownish, hairy; sori lunate or oblong. Tropics, Old World. Tender.

chilense: Kaulf. Not cult.; material in the trade under this name is probably *A. Capillus-Veneris* cv. 'Mairisii'.

concinnum Willd. Lvs. 2–3-pinnate, long-triangular to lanceolate-ovate, to 1½ ft. long and 9 in. wide, pinnules long-rhomboid, fan-shaped, about ½ in. long, the 2 pinnules at base of pinnae on upper surface overlaid on rachis; sori mostly 6–12, roundish to reniform. W. Indies, Mex. to Venezuela and Peru. Cv. **'Latum'.** Lvs. stiff, upright, much larger.

Croweanum: *A. Raddianum* cv.

cuneatum: *A. Raddianum.*

Cunninghamii: *A. affine.*

curvatum Kaulf. Like *A. pedatum,* but pinnules longer, oblong, to ¾ in. long and ¼ in. wide, slightly recurved; sori 6–12, oblong, on apical margin. Brazil. Not in cult.; material in the trade under this name is apparently *A. Raddianum* cv. 'Lady Geneva'.

decorum: *A. Raddianum* cv. Cv. **'Weigandii':** *A. Raddianum* cv.

diaphanum Blume. Roots bearing small tubers; lvs. to 6 in. long, 1-pinnate, or to 3-pinnate at base, glabrous, pinnules to ⅜ in. long, oblong-rectangular, crenate; sori 4–5, in deep notches between teeth or lobes, horseshoe-shaped. Asia to Australia, New Zeal., and Melanesia.

elegans: *A. Raddianum* cv. 'Victoria's Elegans'.

emarginatum: *A. Jordanii.*

excisum Kunze. Lvs. to 1 ft. long and 4 in. wide, 2–3-pinnate, pinnules broadly cuneate to truncate at base, lobed; sori 2–5, round to horseshoe-shaped. Chile, Bolivia. Cv. **'Multifidum'.** Lvs. more finely cut.

farleyense: *A. tenerum* cv.

Fergusonii: *A. tenerum* cv.

formosum R. Br. AUSTRALIAN M. F. Lvs. broadly triangular, to 2 ft. long and 1½ ft. wide, to 4-pinnate, pinnules to ¾ in. long and ⅜ in. wide, mostly obtriangular, rachises hairy, petioles rough; sori mostly 4–6, on apical margin, reniform. Australia, New Zeal. Zone 10.

fragrantissimum: *A. Raddianum* cv.

Fritz-Luthii: *A. Raddianum* cv.

gracillimum: *A. Raddianum* cv.

Hemsleyanum Hort.: A cv. of *a. Raddianum,* closely related to cv. 'Fragrantissimum', but with more drooping habit and narrower segms. Material listed as *A. Hemsleyanum* in the U.S., however, has been identified as *A. Raddianum* cv. 'Lawsonianum'.

hispidulum Swartz [*A. pubescens* Schkuhr]. AUSTRALIAN M., ROUGH M. Lvs. forked into 2 spreading brs. and with about 5 narrow, oblong-lanceolate pinnae, pinnae 1-pinnate, pinnules rhombic-oblong, to ⅝ in. long, hairy, petioles and rachis hairy and rough; sori mostly 6–10, along apical margin, horseshoe-shaped. Tropics, Old World. Cult. in s. Calif.

hybridum: a listed name of no botanical standing; may refer to *A. Raddianum.*

Jordanii: K. Müll. Hal. [*A. emarginatum* Hook.]. CALIFORNIA M. F. Lvs. ovate, to nearly 2 ft. long, 2–3-pinnate, pinnules with apical margin rounded and finely toothed, entire with 1–4 deep clefts when fertile; sori 3–6, oblong, straight or curved. Ore. to s. Calif. Hardy.

Lathomii: see *A. tenerum* cv.

Legrandii: *A. Raddianum* cv.

lunulatum: *A. philippense.*

macrophyllum Swartz. Lvs. 1 ft. long, 1-pinnate, not rooting at tip, pinnae to 3 in. long, acute, petioles glossy; sori oblong, in a line along apical and basal margin. Trop. Amer.

microphyllum: material grown under this name is a form of *A. Raddianum* with very small pinnules.

Obrienii: *A. Capillus-Veneris.*

Pacottii: *A. Raddianum* cv.

pedatum L. AMERICAN M., MAIDENHAIR FERN, FIVE-FINGER F., NORTHERN M. Lvs. nearly orbicular, to 1½ ft. across, forked into 2 spreading brs., each br. bearing 4–12 or more narrow 1-pinnate pinnae, pinnules nearly rectangular, petioles smooth. Woods, N. Amer. and e. Asia. Forma **imbricatum** Hort. Lvs. compact, small, pinnules imbricate. Reportedly found in the wild in Wash. Var. **aleuticum** Rupr. ALEUTIAN M. Pinnules more oblique-triangular, bluish-green. Some material offered under this name is *A. pedatum* forma *imbricatum.*

pelicanii: *A. Raddianum* cv. 'Pelican'.

pentadactylon Langsd. & Fisch. Much like *A. trapeziforme,* but differing in having pinnules with more deeply cut, thinner lobes, fewer veins, and color of petiolule extending into blade and blending into color of veins. Brazil. Cv. **'Sanctae Catherinae'** [*A. Sanctae-Catherinae* Hort.]. Pinnules oblong-trapezoid to rhomboid-ovate, with lobes to $\frac{3}{16}$ in. deep.

peruvianum Klotzsch. Lvs. broadly ovate-triangular, 1 ft. long, 1-pinnate, sometimes 2-pinnate basally, pinnules to 2½ in. long, rhombic to nearly triangular, acuminate, broadly cuneate; sori many, short-oblong to lunate, along both margins. Ecuador to Bolivia.

philippense L. [*A. lunulatum* Burm. f.]. WALKING M. F. Lvs. 1 ft. long, rooting at apex, 1-pinnate, pinnae to ¾ in. long, apically obtuse, on slender stalks; sori in a single line along apical margin. Tropics.

polyphyllum Willd. [*A. cardiochlaenum* Kunze]. Lvs. erect, to 2 ft. long, 2–3-pinnate, pinnules oblong-rhombic, about 1 in. long and ⅜ in. wide, jointed at point of attachment; sori 3–8, horseshoe-shaped. Colombia, Venezuela.

princeps T. Moore. Like *A. tenerum,* but having rhizome with slightly ciliate, bright brown scales and lvs. with larger pinnules. Colombia.

pubescens: *A. hispidulum.*

Raddianum K. Presl [*A. aemulum* T. Moore; *A. cuneatum* Langsd. & Fisch.]. DELTA M. Lvs. deltoid to triangular, to 6½ in. long and wide, 3–4-pinnate, pinnules ¼ in. across, cuneate, apical margin like *A. Capillus-Veneris,* but each vein ending at a marginal sinus; sori round. Brazil. Frost-tender. There are many cvs.: '**Californicum**': 'Fragrantissimum'; '**Croweanum**' [*A. Croweanum* Hort.], large, vigorous, hardy; lvs. ovate-lanceolate to triangular-ovate, pinnules fan-shaped to almost rhombic or rounded; '**Decorum**' [*A. decorum* T. Moore], rather stiff, erect, petioles stout, to ¹⁄₁₆ in. thick, brown-black, lvs. 10 in. long, half or more as wide, dull green; '**Fragrantissimum**' [cv. 'Californicum'; *A californicum* Hort.; *A. fragrantissimum* T. Moore], fuller foliaged than typical, lvs. triangular; '**Fritz-Luthii**' [*A. Fritz-Luthii* Hort.], lvs. triangular, to 1 ft. long, pinnules cuneate; '**Gracillimum**' [*A. gracillimum* T. Moore], lvs. finely divided; '**Grandiceps**', TASSEL M. F., with tassel-like growths at ends of lvs.; '**Hemsleyanum**': see *A. Hemsleyanum;* '**Lawsonianum**', lvs. triangular, to 1 ft. long, 4-pinnate, pinnules narrowly wedge-shaped, ¾ in. long; '**Legrandii**' [*A. Legrandii* Hort. Veitch], similar to 'Gracillimum', but the segms. stouter, more numerous, and congested; '**Pacottii**' [*A. Pacottii* Bull], lvs. triangular, to 6 in. long, pinnae and pinnules densely overlapping; '**Pelican**' [*A. Pelicanii* Hort.], lvs. triangular, sterile; '**Tinctum**' [*A. tinctum* T. Moore; *A. Wagneri* Matt.], lvs. narrowly triangular, to 8 in. long, 2-pinnate, pinnules rounded to broadly fan-shaped or almost rhombic, sori oblong; '**Victoria's Elegans**' [*A. elegans* T. Moore], lvs. ovate or triangular-ovate, to 10 in. long, 4-pinnate, pinnules trapezoid or short-cuneate, to ⅛ in. long; '**Weigandii**' [*A. decorum* cv. 'Weigandii'; *A. Weigandii* T. Moore], pinnules broadly cuneate to rhombic; cvs. '**Deflexum**', '**Dissectum**', and many others are also listed.

rubellum T. Moore. Like *A. Raddianum* and probably a variant of it; lvs. reddish when young. Bolivia.

Sanctae-Catharinae: *A. pentadactylon* cv.

scutum: *A. tenerum* cv.

Siebrechtii: supposedly a cross between *A. decorum* and *A. Williamsii.*

tenerum Swartz. BRITTLE M., BRITTLE M.F., FAN M.F. Erect, to 3 ft.; lvs. triangular to ovate, 3-pinnate, pinnules ¾ in. across, deeply notched, obdeltoid to almost rhombic, disc present on apex of stalk of pinnule; sori several, oblong, on apical margin. Fla., W. Indies, Mex. to Peru. Cv. '**Bausei**' [*A. Bausei* Hort.]. A listed name. Cv. '**Farleyense**' [*A. farleyense* T. Moore]. FARLEY M.F., BARBADOS M.F., GLORY FERN. Lvs. sterile, drooping, to 3 ft. long and 2 ft. wide, delicate green, sometimes rose-tinted, pinnules deeply cut. The race of this cv. known as 'Gloriosa' produces indusia and is said to be fertile. Cv. '**Lathomii**' [*A. Lathomii* Hort.]. Not in cult.; material grown under this name is an otherwise unnamed cv. intermediate between *A. tenerum* and cv. 'Scutum'. Cv. '**Scutum**' [*A. scutum* Wigm.]. Lvs. deltoid to triangular, pinnules almost rhombic, crenate to shallowly lobed and finely dentate.

tinctum: *A. Raddianum* cv.

×**Tracyi** C. C. Hall: *A. Jordanii* × *A. pedatum.* TRACY'S M. Lvs. evergreen, ovate to reniform, 3-pinnate, first division tending to be pedate, pinnules and sori like *A. Jordanii.*

trapeziforme L. GIANT M. Lvs. 2-pinnate, to 1½ ft. long or more, pinnules oblong-rhombic, 1½–2 in. long, half as wide; sori many, oblong. Trop. Amer.

Wagneri: *A. Raddianum* cv. 'Tinctum'.

Weigandii: *A. Raddianum* cv.

Westleyanum: a listed name of doubtful status, probably belonging to *A. Raddianum.*

Wrightii: a listed name of no botanical standing; some material cult. under this name seems to be *A. tenerum,* but other material seems to be related to *A. tenerum* cv. 'Scutum'.

ADICEA: *PILEA.*

ADINA Salisb. *Rubiaceae.* About 20 spp. of shrubs or trees, native to trop. and subtrop. Afr. and Asia; lvs. opp., petioled; fls. in solitary or sometimes panicled rounded heads; corolla funnelform, tube long, stamens 5, borne in throat of corolla, filaments short; fr. a many-seeded caps.

rubella Hance. Shrub, to 10 ft., with slender, reddish-brown, pubescent branchlets; lvs. elliptic, to 1 in. long, glossy, green above, paler and pubescent along veins beneath; fl. heads solitary, axillary; fls. purplish, scented. S. China. Yields a durable building wood.

ADINOBOTRYS: *WHITFORDIODENDRON.*

ADLUMIA Raf. ex DC. *Fumariaceae.* One sp., an herbaceous bien. vine, native to e. N. Amer.; lvs. alt., 3–4-pinnate; fls. similar to those of *Dicentra,* in axillary panicles, bisexual, petals 4, united and persistent, enclosing stamens and ovary, stamens 6, united at base into a tube adherent to corolla, apically divided into 2 bundles; fr. a few-seeded caps.

Both foliage and flowers are ornamental; thrives in a cool, damp place protected from sun and wind, as in a thicket. Propagated by seeds in spring, often spontaneous thereafter.

fungosa (Ait.) Greene ex BSP. CLIMBING FUMITORY, MOUNTAIN-FRINGE, ALLEGHANY VINE. High-climbing, by petioles, lvs. delicate, fernlike, lowermost to 10 in. long, st. lvs. much smaller, ultimate divisions mostly less than ½ in. long; panicles drooping, 2–4 in. long; fls. white to purplish, ½ in. long or more, corolla narrowly cordate-ovate, persistent and enclosing oblong caps. Ont. to Mich., s. to N.C.

ADOLPHIA Meissn. *Rhamnaceae.* Two spp. of shrubs of sw. N. Amer. with opp., spinose twigs; lvs. opp., small, early-deciduous; fls. inconspicuous, 1 to several in axillary clusters, sepals 5, petals 5, hooded; fr. a caps. Related to *Colletia,* but always having cylindrical spines and fls. with petals and a cup-shaped calyx tube.

californica S. Wats. Intricately branched, to 3 ft.; lvs. ovate, to ½ in. long; fls. white, about ⅛ in. across. Chaparral, San Diego Co. (s. Calif.) and adjacent n. Baja Calif. Sometimes planted in dry areas.

ADONIDIA: *VEITCHIA.*

ADONIS L. PHEASANT'S-EYE. *Ranunculaceae.* Perhaps 40 spp. of temp., Eurasian herbs; lvs. alt., divided into narrow segms.; fls. solitary, terminal, mostly red or yellow, sepals 5, petals 5 to many, pistils many; fr. an achene.

A few are grown in the border and rock garden. Cultivation is simple; propagated by seeds, or perennial species by division in spring.

aestivalis L. Like *A. annua;* fls. crimson, but sepals appressed to spreading petals; achene with sharp tooth at base of inner side. Eur. Has been used medicinally. Forma **citrina** (Hoffm.) Voss [*A. citrina* Hoffm.]. Fls. citron-yellow.

aleppica Boiss. Habit of *A. aestivalis,* but only to 1 ft.; fls. to 1½ in. across, dark red. Asia Minor.

amurensis Regel & Radde. AMUR A. Per., to 1½ ft.; st. lvs. 3–6 in. long and wide, cut into linear segms.; fls. golden-yellow, varying to white or rose, 2 in. across, appearing before the lvs. are fully developed, petals 20–50, somewhat longer than sepals; achenes pubescent. Ne. Asia. Much used as a forced pot plant in Japan. Double-fld. forms occur.

annua L. [*A. autumnalis* L.]. Ann., with taproot, st. branched, 4–16 in., glabrous; lvs. 3-pinnate, ultimate segms. linear, acute; fls. ⅜–1 in. across, sepals 5, spreading, green or purplish, petals 5–8, suberect, scarlet, with dark basal spot; achenes not toothed at base on inner side. S. Eur. and sw. Asia.

autumnalis: *A. annua.*

Chrysocyathus Hook.f. & T. Thoms. Per., mostly 6–9 in.; lf. segms. linear to subcuneate; fls. golden-yellow, 2 in. across or more, sepals 7–8, petals 16–24, twice as long as sepals; achenes glabrous. Himalayas.

citrina: *A. aestivalis* forma.

flammea Jacq. Ann., 8–20 in., with scattered hairs; lvs. with linear segms; fls. 1–1½ in. across, scarlet, sepals pubescent; achenes pubescent. S. Eur. to Asia Minor.

Flos: a listed name of no botanical standing, perhaps *A. annua.*

pyrenaica DC. Per., 4–12 in., slightly pubescent; lower lvs. large, long-petioled; fls. yellow, smaller than in *A. vernalis,* sepals glabrous or nearly so, petals 8–10, obovate; achenes long-beaked. Pyrenees, Maritime Alps.

vernalis L. Per., to 1½ ft.; lower lvs. reduced to scales; fls. yellow, to 3 in. across, petals 10–15, narrow; achenes with a hooked beak. Cent. and s. Eur. Has been used medicinally. Cv. '**Alba**'. Fls. white.

ADOXA L. *Adoxaceae.* One sp.; characteristics those of the family.

Moschatellina L. MUSKROOT, MOSCHATEL. Delicate, musk-scented, single-stemmed herb, to 8 in.; radical lvs. long-petioled, ternately decompound, segms. rounded or ovate, 3-parted, st. lvs. in a single pair, 3-cleft to 3-divided; infl. a single, long-peduncled head, about 3/8 in. in diam.; fls. greenish or yellowish. Early summer. Sometimes grown in the rock garden.

ADOXACEAE J. Agardh. MOSCHATEL FAMILY. Dicot.; 1 genus, *Adoxa*, of small, per. herbs, native to n. regions of N. Amer., Eur., and Asia; rhizomes scaly; lvs. ternately decompound; fls. in heads, corolla rotate, 4–5-lobed, stamens 8–10, in pairs in the sinuses, filaments short, anthers 1-celled, ovary nearly inferior, 3–5-celled, style 3–5-branched; fr. a small, greenish drupe, seeds 3–5.

ADROMISCHUS Lem. *Crassulaceae*. About 50 spp. of succulent herbs and subshrubs, native to S. Afr.; sts. mostly short; lvs. alt. or nearly opp., commonly glabrous; infl. a terminal (rarely 2–3), commonly elongate raceme, spike, or spicate thyrse; corolla tube slender, much longer than lobes and sepals. Closely allied to *Cotyledon*, but infl. racemose and corolla tube slender.

For culture see *Succulents*.

Alectonii: a listed name of no botanical standing, perhaps an error for *A. Alstonii*.

Alstonii: *A. trigynus*.

alveolatus P. C. Hutchison. Root tuberous, sts. short; lvs. about 10, turgid but concave above, elliptic, to 1¼ in. long, ¾ in. wide, and ½ in. thick, surface rough, often pitted, petiole short; fl. st. to 7 in., pedicels stout, to ¼ in. long; corolla 5/8 in. long, lobes ovate, papillose. Namaqualand.

antidorcadum Poelln. Sts. papillose, becoming very rough; lvs. alt., ovate-lanceolate, ¾–1½ in. long, ¼–⅓ as wide, nearly cylindrical, somewhat furrowed above, obtusish, gradually narrowed to a short petiole, green with brownish-red flecks, papillose; fls. nearly sessile, corolla lobes short. Namaqualand. The name has been misspelled "anticordatum" and "antidorcatum."

Bolusii (Schönl.) A. Berger. Sts. to 5 in.; lvs. crowded, spatulate, to 1½ in. long and ¾ in. wide; pedicels ¼ in. long. Cape Prov. Close to *A. caryophyllaceus*.

caryophyllaceus (Burm.f.) Lem. Sts. branching, to 1 ft.; lvs. alt., obovate or spatulate to oblong-elliptic, ½–1½ in. long, obtuse, flattened above, rounded beneath; infl. compound; fls. pedicelled, corolla lobes white to purple. Cape Prov.

clavifolius (Haw.) Lem. Sts. densely covered with red-brown to gray aerial roots; lvs. alt., cylindrical, flattened and somewhat crisped at apex, 1–3 in. long, about ½ in. wide, glabrous, petioled; fl. st. to 1 ft.; fls. 1–3 at a node, nearly sessile, corolla ½ in. long, lobes ovate. Cape Prov. Sometimes grown as *A.* or *Cotyledon Van-der-Heydenii*.

Cooperi (Bak.) A. Berger [*Cotyledon Cooperi* Bak.]. PLOVER-EGGS. Sts. short; lvs. 5–15, obovate or mostly oblanceolate-spatulate, nearly cylindrical below, broadened in upper ¼ and with acute and often crisped margin, light green, usually with purplish spots, short-petioled; fl. st. 10 in.; fls. nearly sessile, corolla 3/8 in. long, lobes ovate, purplish-red, papillose. S. Cape Prov. Some material grown as *A. Cooperi* may be *A. festivus*. Cv. **'Brevifolia'** is listed.

cristatus (Haw.) Lem. CRINKLE-LEAF PLANT. Sts. short, branching, densely covered with red-brown aerial roots; lvs. alt., puberulent, ¾–2 in. long, blade obovate-truncate, flattened, to 1 in. wide and 3/8 in. thick, crisped at apex, usually abruptly narrowed to cylindrical petiole; fl. st. 16 in.; fls. nearly sessile, corolla ½ in. long, lobes ovate, papillose, white. Se. Cape Prov.

festivus C. A. Sm. Lvs. opp., club-shaped, 2 in. long, 5/8 in. wide, flattened at apex, spotted with purplish-brown, petioled; fl. st. to 14 in.; fls. sessile, to 5/16 in. long, lobes ovate, white or reddish, not papillose. Cape Prov. Formerly grown as *A. Cooperi*.

grandiflorus Uitew. Subshrub, to 6 in. or more; lvs. alt., scattered, obovate-cuneate, to 5/8 in. long, ¾ in. wide, and ¼ in. thick; fl. st. to 8 in.; fls. 2–5, thick-pedicelled, corolla 5/8 in. long, limb as wide, purplish. Sw. Cape Prov.

hemisphaericus (L.) Lem. Sts. to 8 in.; lvs. alt., obovate to nearly orbicular, semiglobose, ½–1½ in. long, half as wide, flattened above, rounded beneath, with acute margins, scaly; fl. st. to 16 in.; fls. nearly sessile, corolla ½ in. long, lobes ovate. Cape Prov.

Herrei (W. F. Barker) Poelln. Lvs. 10 or fewer, alt., ovoid-fusiform, about 1¼ in. long and ½ in. thick, acute or somewhat acuminate, papillose-roughened, petioled; fl. st. 2 in.; fls. 2–3, upright, pedicels ½ in. long. Namaqualand.

kleinioides C. A. Sm. [*A. mammillaris* var. *ruber* Poelln.]. Sts. to 2 ft.; lvs. scattered, spindle-shaped, 2–2½ in. long, acute, glaucous; fl. st. 1 ft.; fls. sessile, in 3's, corolla 5/8 in. long, limb dull red-brown, ¼ in. wide. Namaqualand.

maculatus (Salm-Dyck) Lem. CALICO-HEARTS. Sts. to 4 in.; lvs. alt., obovate-cuneate, to 2¾ in. long and 1½ in. wide, retuse to apiculate, brown-spotted; fl. st. 16 in.; fls. sessile, corolla ½ in. long, lobes lanceolate, ⅓ as long. Sw. Cape Prov. The name *A. maculatus* has been applied erroneously to *A. trigynus* in cult.

mammillaris (L.f.) Lem. Sts. creeping and rooting; lvs. alt., mostly remote, club-shaped, 1–3 in. long, round in cross section, obtuse to acute; fl. st. 1 ft.; fls. 1–3 at a node, nearly sessile, corolla ½ in. long, limb white or purplish. Sw. Cape Prov. Var. **ruber:** *A. kleinioides*.

Marianiae (Marloth) A. Berger. Lvs. few, nearly opp., oblong, to 2¼ in. long, turgid but channelled above, spotted purplish-brown; fl. st. 6 in.; fls. stout-pedicelled, corolla lobes white with rosy tip. W. Cape Prov.

Poellnitzianus Werderm. Sts. short, densely covered with red-brown aerial roots; lvs. alt., gradually narrowed to base, broadened, flattened, and often crisped at apex, 2–4 in. long, round in cross section, puberulent; fl. st. 16 in.; fls. 1–3 at a node, nearly sessile, corolla ½ in. long, lobes white tipped with red. Se. Cape Prov.

rhombifolius (Haw.) Lem. Lvs. opp., rhomboid-obovate, flat, mucronate, mealy, minutely dotted in the upper half. S. Cape Prov.

rotundifolius (Haw.) C. A. Sm. Sts. 2–8 in.; lvs. alt., scattered, nearly orbicular to obovate, ½–2 in. long, slightly concave above, convex beneath, greenish-white; fl. st. 10 in.; fls. short-pedicelled, corolla 5/8 in. long, limb pink. Sw. Cape Prov.

saxicola C. A. Sm. Sts. short, from thick root; lvs. alt., crowded, linear-oblong, to 1¼ in. long, 3/8 in. wide, and 3/16 in. thick; fl. st. 10 in., pedicels ¼ in. long; corolla 5/16 in. long, lobes short, purplish. Transvaal.

Schaeferanus: *Cotyledon Schaeferana*.

Schuldtianus (Poelln.) H. E. Moore. Sts. short; lvs. few, crowded, oblong to obovate, to 1 in. long, ½ in. wide, and 3/16 in. thick, biconvex, the upper margin cartilaginous, nearly undulate. Sw. Afr.?

sphenophyllus C. A. Sm. Lvs. a few opp. pairs, obovate-cuneate, to 4½ in. long and 2 in. wide, thickest at the middle or above, obtuse, with horny margin, glaucous with faint green flecks; fl. st. 1½ ft., often branching; fls. 1–3 at a node, sessile, corolla 3/8 in. long, lobes pink, 3/16 in. long. S. Cape Prov.

thyrsifolius: a listed name of no botanical standing.

tricolor C. A. Sm. Sts. short; lvs. opp., oblong-cylindrical, to 2½ in. long, ¼ in. wide, obtuse, gray-green with purplish-brown spots; fl. st. 10 in., often branched; fls. sessile, corolla 5/8 in. long, lobes white or purplish, ovate-lanceolate. W. Cape Prov.

Triebneri Poelln. Sts. to 4 in.; lvs. few, alt., obovate-cuneate, 1¼–2½ in. long, half as wide, green or reddish, with small spots especially toward apex, rounded to almost marginate, nearly petioled; fl. st. to 1½ ft.; fls. nearly sessile, corolla ½ in. long, limb narrow, reddish. Namaqualand.

triflorus (L.f.) A. Berger. Lvs. opp., obovate, about 2 in. long and half as wide, flattened; fl. st. 8 in.; fls. sessile, mostly 3 at a node, corolla ½ in. long, lobes ovate, short. W. Cape Prov.

trigynus (Burchell) Poelln. [*A. Alstonii* (Schönl. & Bak.f.) C. A. Sm.]. Lvs. alt., crowded, nearly orbicular, 1–1½ in. long, convex above and beneath, spotted all over with purple; fl. st. 10 in., pedicels ¼ in. long; corolla ½ in. long. Transvaal to S.-W. Afr. Sometimes grown under the name *A. maculatus*.

umbraticola C. A. Sm. Sts. to 5 in. high and ¾ in. in diam.; lvs. alt. to nearly opp., oblong to obovate-cuneate, to 2 in. long, ¾ in. wide, and 3/16 in. thick, rounded or sinuate at apex, glaucous; fl. st. simple to 3-branched, to 14 in., pedicels ¼ in. long; corolla limb purplish, ⅕ as long as tube. Transvaal.

Van-der-Heydenii: a listed name of no botanical standing for *A. clavifolius*.

violaceus: a listed name of no botanical standing.

AECHMEA Ruiz & Pav. [*Gravisia* Mez; *Hoplophytum* Beer; *Wittmackia* Mez]. AIR PINE, LIVING-VASE. *Bromeliaceae*. About 168 spp. of epiphytic herbs, native to trop. Amer.; lvs. stiff, spiny, mostly linear, in a basal rosette; fls. sessile or rarely pedicelled, yellow, red, or blue, borne in spikes, panicles, or racemes, or rarely in nearly sessile, abbreviated spikes, bracts often colored, sepals often mucronate, petals not united, usually with 2 scales inside at the base, ovary inferior, ovules usually caudate; fr. a berry, seeds without appendages.

Of easy culture and much grown as an ornamental in warm climates or in the greenhouse. Most require full sun or nearly full sun. For culture see *Bromeliaceae*. Hybrids have been made between several species, and some are extensively cultivated: 'Bert': *A. Fosterana* × *A. orlandiana*; 'Foster's Favorite': *A. Racinae* × *A. victoriana* var. *discolor*, lvs. bronze-red, infl. stiffly pendulous; 'Royal Wine': *A. miniata* var. *discolor* × *A. victoriana* var. *discolor*, more vigorous than the parents, lvs. glossy, bronze-red beneath.

Allenii L. B. Sm. Lvs. green, to 28 in. long, densely toothed, much longer than infl.; scape to 14 in. long, white-flocculose, infl. simple, 4 in. long, bracts pink; sepals spiny-tipped, petals white or pale lilac, 1³⁄₁₆ in. long. Panama.

amazonica: *A. Chantinii.*

angustifolia Poepp. & Endl. Lvs. few, stiffish, narrow, to 2 ft. long, ⅝ in. wide, light green, irregularly spotted with purple; infl. paniculate, long and narrow, fl. bracts very small, red; fls. sessile, ½ in. long, yellow; fr. white, turning blue. Costa Rica to Peru and Bolivia.

aquilega (Salisb.) Griseb. [*Gravisia aquilega* (Salisb.) Mez; *G. exsudans* (Lodd.) Mez]. To 3 ft. or more; lvs. strap-shaped, to 4½ ft. long, 2¾ in. wide; infl. of 10–20 heads, bracts lanceolate, reflexed, pink; fls. to 1½ in. long, sepals and bracts not waxy. Trinidad and Tobago to Brazil.

aureorosea: *A. nudicaulis* var.

Benrathii: *A. recurvata* var.

Blanchetiana (Bak.) L. B. Sm. Plant large; lvs. pale green, to 3 ft. long; infl. loosely branched, fl. bracts about as long as fls.; fls. to 1¼ in. long. Brazil.

Blumenavii Reitz. Lvs. 10–15, forming a tube, to 28 in. long, 1½ in. wide, white-scaly over green and horizontally banded, dark violet at apex; infl. loosely spicate; fls. ⅝ in. long, sepals rose, petals yellow. Brazil.

bracteata (Swartz) Griseb. To 5 ft. or more; lvs. to 3 ft. long and 4 in. wide, green; scape erect, bracts bright red, infl. paniculate, persistently pale-scaly, fl. bracts scarcely longer than ovary; fls. yellow, to ½ in. long, sepals separate, mucronate. Mex. to Colombia.

bromeliifolia (Rudge) Bak. [*A. tinctoria* (Mart.) Mez]. To 3 ft.; lvs. strap-shaped, in a tubular rosette, green above, pale beneath; infl. simple, white-woolly, dense, with only petals exposed at first; fls. greenish-yellow, turning black, sepals emarginate, petals with 2 scales well above the base. Guatemala to Argentina.

calyculata (E. Morr.) Bak. To 1 ft.; lvs. to 1 ft. long, rounded and cuspidate at apex, denticulate; infl. a globose head, scape bracts and fl. bracts entire; fls. bright yellow, sepals united ⅓, mucronate. Brazil and Argentina.

caudata Lindm. Lvs. to 3 ft. long and 3 in. wide, green, minutely spinose; infl. paniculate, sometimes simple toward apex, brs. and bracts pink, bracts recurved; fls. violet, to 1 in. long, sepals mucronate, united at base. Brazil. Cv. '**Variegata**' [*A. Forgettii* Hort.]. Lvs. white-striped; more commonly grown than the typical green-lvd. cv.

Chantinii (Carrière) Bak. [*A. amazonica* Ule]. Lvs. about 10, erect-spreading, broadly linear, 1 ft. long, 2 in. wide, rounded at tip, green, cross-barred with silvery-white, stoutly spiny; infl. short-pyramidal, branched, bracts orange-red; fls. yellow. Brazil. Cv. '**Pink Goddess**'. A large form; infl. stiff, pyramidal, bracts bright pink. Cv. '**Red Goddess**'. Similar, but bracts red.

coelestis (C. Koch) E. Morr. Similar to *A. caudata*, but lvs. to 1½ ft. long and 1¼ in. wide; infl. bracts and brs. erect or spreading; petals blue; berries sky-blue. Brazil. Cv. '**Albomarginata**'. Lvs. white-margined. Cv. '**Variegata**' is listed.

comata (Gaud.-Beaup.) Bak. [*A. Lindenii* (E. Morr.) Bak.]. Lvs. to 3 ft. long and 2¼ in. wide, densely spiny, sometimes striped; scape bracts entire, infl. simple, dense, with large, entire fl. bracts and a terminal tuft of sterile bracts; fls. yellow, changing to brown, to 1 in. long, sepals spine-tipped, only shortly united at base. Brazil. Cv. '**Makoyana**'. Lvs. broadly yellow-striped.

cylindrata Lindm. Lvs. 15–20, sparsely and minutely toothed, to 1½ ft. long, 2½ in. wide, blunt with short point; infl. simple, elongate, loose; fls. ¾ in. long, blue. Brazil.

dealbata E. Morr. ex Bak. Similar to *A. fasciata*, but bracts brown, with persistent, white, dense pubescence; infl. narrower; fls. coral-red. Brazil.

discolor: see *A. fulgens* var. or *A. miniata* var.

distichantha Lem. [*A. polystachya* (Vell.) Mez]. Lvs. to 3 ft. long and 1 in. wide, minutely spiny; infl. compound, fl. bracts winged-decurrent, forming pouches at base of fls.; fls. violet, to ⅝ in. long, sepals united at base, minutely spiny. Brazil. Var. **distichantha**. The typical var.; infl. loose, of many-fld., mostly spreading spikes. Var. **canaliculata** M. B. Foster. Lvs. channelled in center toward base. Var. **Schlumbergeri** E. Morr. ex Mez. Infl. dense, of few-fld., erect spikes.

fasciata (Lindl.) Bak. [*Billbergia rhodocyanea* Lem.]. URN PLANT. Lvs. in a tubular rosette, to 2 ft. long, toothed, streaked and marbled with white on black, inner lvs. rounded and mucronate at tip; infl. spicate or with 2–5 brs. and dense, bracts pale red, spiny; fls. sessile, sepals mucronate, united at base, petals pale blue, becoming red, appendaged. Brazil. Cvs. '**Albomarginata**', '**Purpurea**', '**Superba**', '**Variegata**' are listed.

filicaulis (Griseb.) Mez. Lvs. few, linear, minutely spiny; infl. branched, decurved; fls. sessile, 1¼ in. long with pink bracts, sepals scarcely mucronate, wing not extending beyond midrib, petals appendaged, white. Venezuela. Prefers shade.

Forgettii: a hort. name of no botanical standing for *A. caudata* cv. '**Variegata**'.

Fosterana L. B. Sm. Lvs. in a tubular rosette, to 2 ft. long and 4 in. wide, with broad, purplish-brown bands and a large, dark purple, apical spot; scape glabrous, dark purple, bracts entire, infl. compound, fl. bracts entire, longer than the ovary; fls. orange, to ⅝ in. long, sepals separate, tipped with a point. Brazil.

fulgens Brongn. CORALBERRY. Lvs. to 16 in. long and 3 in. wide, with small teeth, pale green; scape bright red, to ¾ in. long, panicles branched at base but simple in upper part, fl. bracts very small; sepals unarmed, petals bright blue. Brazil. Prefers shade. Var. **fulgens**. The typical var.; lvs. green. Var. **discolor** (C. Morr.) Brongn. ex Bak. Lvs. brownish or violet-red underneath.

gamosepala Wittm. Lvs. 15–20, suberect, linear, nearly spineless; infl. a many-fld. spike; fls. to ⅝ in. long, sepals united to middle, petals pale blue. Brazil.

hystrix: *A. ornata.*

Kienastii: *A. tillandsioides* var.

Kuntzeana Mez. Lvs. large, often to 3½ in. wide, spiny at margin and apex; infl. paniculate, rusty-tomentose, bracts large, spine-tipped; fls. more than 1 in. long. Brazil, Bolivia.

lagenaria: *A. Lamarchei.*

Lamarchei Mez [*A. lagenaria* Mez]. Lvs. many, linear, spiny, to 15 in. long, ¾ in. wide; infl. simple, cylindrical, to 2¾ in. long, bracts thin, ovate; fls. ⅞ in. long, sepals white, petals yellow, turning jet-black. Brazil.

Lasseri L. B. Sm. Stoloniferous; lvs. to 3 ft. long, dark green to reddish (in sun), distantly toothed with coarse spines; infl. pendulous, branched at base but spicate in the upper part, scape bracts tan-pink; fls. greenish-white, about 1¾ in. long. Venezuela.

Lindenii: *A. comata.*

lingulata (L.) Bak. [*Wittmackia lingulata* (L.) Mez]. Lvs. to 3 ft. long, ½ in. wide, densely spiny; infl. branched, scape bracts bright red, entire or finely toothed, fl. bracts about as long as ovary; fls. yellow-green, ¾ in. long; fr. white to red. W. Indies.

Lueddemanniana (C. Koch) Brongn. ex Mez. Lvs. to 1 ft. long, 1¾ in. wide, green and bronze (in sun); infl. paniculate, dense, bracts minute; fls. pedicelled, to ⅝ in. long, sepals green, petals rose; fr. blue and white, becoming purple, long-lasting. Mex., Brit. Honduras.

× **maginalii:** a hort. name of no botanical standing, used for a hybrid between *A. fulgens* var. *discolor* and *A. miniata* var. *discolor*, showing characteristics of both parents; lvs. apple-green above, maroon beneath; bracts salmon-red; fls. blue; fr. orange.

Mariae-Reginae H. Wendl. Plant large, rosette to 4 ft. across; lvs. to 3 ft. long and 4 in. wide, spiny-margined; dioecious, infl. a dense spike to 1 ft. long or more, scape bracts pendent, dentate-serrate, brilliant pink, fl. bracts minute, entire; fls. red, tipped with violet, sepals mucronate. Costa Rica.

marmorata: *Quesnelia marmorata.*

Mertensii (G. F. Mey.) Schult.f. Lvs. to 8 in. long, 3 in. wide at base, with brown spines; infl. densely paniculate, bracts rose to orange; fls. yellow to red; fr. blue. Trinidad to n. S. Amer. A variable sp.

mexicana Bak. Rosette large; lvs. to 2½ ft. long, 3⅛ in. wide, densely spiny; infl. many-fld., paniculate; fls. slender-pedicelled, red or lilac, to ⅞ in. long, sepals mucronate; berries white. Mex.

miniata (Beer) Hort. ex Bak. Lvs. spreading, to 18 in. long and 1⅜ in. wide, green, with many close-set teeth; fls. in branched panicles much longer than lvs., fl. bracts minute; sepals red, without spines, petals blue. Brazil. Var. **discolor** (Beer) Beer ex Bak. Lvs. purplish or brownish beneath.

Nallyi L. B. Sm. Lvs. about 10, in a funnel-shaped rosette, about 18 in. long, distantly toothed; infl. pyramidal, loosely 2-pinnate, scape bracts pink, reflexed; fls. sessile, sepals pale green, petals ¾ in. long. Peru.

nidularioides L. B. Sm. Lvs. to 2 in. wide, much longer than infl., loosely toothed; scape 6 in. long, infl. nearly globose, 6 in. long, bracts large, overlapping, rose, tipped with patches of white scales; fls. white. Colombia, Peru.

nudicaulis (L.) Griseb. Lvs. few, in a tubular rosette, to 1½ ft. long and 2⅜ in. wide; infl. simple, loose, scape bracts entire, red, fl. bracts minute; fls. yellow, sepals separate, mucronate, petals appendaged in upper part. Mex. and W. Indies to Brazil. Of very easy cult. Var. **aureorosea** (Ant.) L. B. Sm. [*A. aureorosea* (Ant.) Bak.]. Fl. bracts rather conspicuous, triangular; sepals tinged with red, petals red. Brazil. Var. **cuspidata** Bak. Fl. bracts rather conspicuous, triangular; sepals and petals yellow. Brazil.

organensis Wawra. Lvs. 10–20, suberect, to 14 in. long, 2¼ in. wide, dark green; infl. paniculate, densely and narrowly pyramidal; fls. to ¾ in. long, petals blue; fr. burnt orange. Brazil.

orlandiana L. B. Sm. FINGER-OF-GOD. Lvs. in a spreading rosette, to 1 ft. long and 1¼ in. wide, broadly dark-banded beneath; scape red, glabrous, bracts serrulate at apex, orange-red, infl. densely 2-pinnate, fl. bracts serrulate, longer than sepals; sepals not united at base, mucronate, petals yellow. Brazil.

ornata (Gaud.-Beaup.) Bak. [*A. hystrix* E. Morr.]. Lvs. many, linear, spiny, to 2 ft. long, 2 in. wide; infl. simple, similar to that of *A. Pineliana*, with apical tuft of spines; fls. ¾ in. long, sepals spine-tipped, petals pale red or rose, turning brown in age. Brazil.

Ortgiesii: *A. recurvata* var.

pectinata Bak. Lvs. to 1½ ft. long and 2½ in. wide, densely spiny; infl. simple, fl. bracts pectinate; fls. green, sepals acute-mucronate. Brazil.

penduliflora André. Lvs. entire or only minutely toothed at base, to 28 in. long, 1⅝ in. wide; scape bracts red, infl. paniculate, rather densely ellipsoid, fl. bracts red; fls. small, yellow; fr. white, becoming cobalt-blue. Costa Rica to Brazil. Foliage most colorful when grown in sun.

Pimentae-Velosoi Reitz. To 1 ft.; lvs. about 20, in a dense rosette, nearly tongue-shaped, recurving toward tip, to 1 ft. long, 1 in. wide, green, with brown spines, the sheath spotted with violet; infl. erect, to 20 in., simple, scape bracts ellipsoid, rose-colored, fl. bracts white, the uppermost red; fls. 1 in. long, yellow, tipped with violet. Brazil.

Pineliana (Brongn. ex Planch.) Bak. Lvs. gray to pink, to 3 ft. long and 1½ in. wide; infl. simple, with an apical tuft of yellow spines, scape bracts entire, pink, fl. bracts spine-tipped; fls. yellow, turning brown-black on drying, sepals minutely awned. Brazil.

Pittieri Mez. Lvs. broadly linear, to 2 ft. long or more, 3 in. wide, spiny-margined and tipped with a stout spine; infl. much-branched; fls. sessile, ½ in. long, ovary white-woolly. Costa Rica.

polystachya: *A. distichantha.*

pubescens Bak. Lvs. to 8 in. long and 1¼ in. wide; infl. 2–3-pinnate, scaly-pubescent at least when young, fl. bracts red, prominently veined, entire, about as long as fls.; fls. small, white or yellow, sepals mucronate, not united at the base or only shortly united; berries white, turning blue. Honduras to Colombia.

purpureorosea (Hook.) Wawra. Lvs. few, in a tubular rosette, to 2 ft. long and 2 in. wide, with stout dark spines to $^3/_{16}$ in. long, some blades narrowly triangular; infl. compound, bracts spine-tipped; sepals pink, awned, united at base, petals blue, fading red. Brazil.

pyramidalis Benth. Lvs. to 26 in. long, 1 in. wide, fiercely spiny; infl. paniculate, much-branched, pyramidal, bracts to $^5/_{16}$ in. long, prominently veined; fls. ⅝ in. long, petals yellow. Ecuador.

Racinae L. B. Sm. CHRISTMAS-JEWELS. Lvs. to 1 ft. long or more and 1½ in. wide, somewhat petioled, light green; infl. simple, pendulous, scape bracts reddish-green, fl. bracts minute; sepals without spines, orange-red, to ⅜ in. long, petals to ½ in. long, yellow with deep violet base. Early winter. Brazil. Prefers shade.

ramosa Mart. Lvs. about 12, toothed, to 8 in. long, 3 in. wide, light green with gray coating; infl. branched, fl. bracts red, entire, the emarginate spiny tip reaching to middle of calyx; fls. sessile, petals yellow, about ½ in. long. Brazil. Colorful for a long period.

recurvata (Klotzsch) L. B. Sm. Lvs. to 10 in. long or more, gradually tapering to acute apex; infl. simple, dense, on a short scape, fl. bracts red, nearly entire to serrate, as long as sepals; sepals mucronate, petals lavender-pink, to 1 in. long. Brazil, Uruguay. Var. **Benrathii** (Mez) Reitz [*A. Benrathii* Mez]. Lvs. and bracts essentially entire; infl. mostly included in lf. sheath. Var. **Ortgiesii** (Bak.) Reitz [*A. Ortgiesii* Bak.]. Lvs. and bracts serrate; infl. included in lf. sheath. Brazil.

rosea: plants grown under this name are probably *A. purpureorosea.*

Schultesiana Mez. Lvs. to 1½ ft. long and ¾ in. wide, rose-maroon and green; infl. paniculate, fl. bracts prominent, orbicular; sepals not united, not mucronate, petals appendaged; fr. white, becoming indigo-blue at maturity. Brazil.

Tessmannii Harms. Lvs. to 2½ ft. long or more, to 4 in. wide, thick, rigid, spiny, pale on both sides; infl. paniculate, to nearly 3 ft., orange-pink, fl. bracts oblong-ovate to ovate, to ¾ in. long, glossy; fls. to ¾ in. long, petals orange. Peru.

Thibautiana: a listed name of no botanical standing.

tillandsioides (Mart. ex Schult.) Bak. Lvs. few, narrowly linear, to 16 in. long and 1 in. wide; infl. loosely compound, with remote spikes, fl. bracts winged-decurrent, pouchlike; fls. dark purple, sepals mucronate, not united, petals with scales in upper part. Brazil to Colombia. Var. **Kienastii** (E. Morr. ex Mez) L. B. Sm. [*A. Kienastii* E. Morr. ex Mez]. Infl. simple or densely compound, with somewhat clustered spikes. Colombia to Mex.

tinctoria: *A. bromeliifolia.*

triangularis L. B. Sm. Similar to *A. bromeliifolia*, but differs in having lvs. caudate-acuminate, narrowly triangular, fl. bracts not retuse, sepals white, petals purple, turning jet-black after blooming. Brazil.

victoriana L. B. Sm. Lvs. to 1 ft. long and 1 in. wide, pale green, minutely spinose; infl. simple, loose, red, glabrous; fls. purple with white margin, sepals about ⅛ in. long, without spines. Brazil. Var. **discolor** M. B. Foster. Lvs. red underneath.

Weilbachii Didr. Lvs. to 2 ft. long and 1 in. wide, green with bronze tints; infl. paniculate, scape red, fl. bracts large, suborbicular; fls. blue and red, sepals not united, without spines. Brazil. Var. **leodiensis** André. Lvs. tinged with purple.

AEGLE Corrêa. *Rutaceae.* Three spp. of small, thorny, deciduous trees, native to trop. Asia; lvs. alt., with 3 lfts.; fls. white, in axillary panicles, calyx 4–5-lobed, petals 4–5, stamens 30–60; fr. a large, 8–15-celled berry, each cell many-seeded.

Propagated by seeds and suited to any good soil; may be grown in the warmer citrus regions, but little planted in the U.S.

Marmelos (L.) Corrêa. BAEL TREE, BAEL FRUIT, INDIAN BAEL, BENGAL QUINCE, BALL TREE, BELA TREE, BEL FRUIT, GOLDEN APPLE. Tree, to 10 ft.; lfts. ovate, 2–3 in. long, crenate; fls. fragrant; fr. greenish-white, globose to ovoid, 4–6 in. across, with very hard shell, pulp fragrant, mucilaginous, edible. India, Burma. Occasionally cult. in tropics. Zone 10. The pulp is used for making drinks and in India is considered a specific for dysentery.

sepiaria: *Poncirus trifoliata.*

AEGLOPSIS Swingle. *Rutaceae.* Two spp. of evergreen, spiny shrubs or small trees, native to trop. Afr.; lvs. alt., simple, glandular-dotted; fls. white, in small axillary panicles, sepals and petals 4–5, stamens 8–15; fr. subglobose to pear-shaped, hard-shelled, with a fragrant pulp or mucilage.

Chevalieri Swingle. Shrub or small tree, spines to 2¾ in. long; lvs. elliptic, 2–4¾ in. long, cuneate at base, glabrous; fls. white; fr. green, becoming yellowish, 6-celled, each cell 8–15-seeded. Coastal swamps, W. Trop. Afr. Grown experimentally in this country as a possible stock for citrus.

AEGOPODIUM L. *Umbelliferae.* About 5 spp. of coarse herbs of Eur. and Asia, with creeping rootstocks; lvs. biternate; fls. yellow or white, in compound umbels, involucre and involucels usually lacking.

Podagraria L. GOUTWEED, BISHOP'S WEED, HERB GERARD, ASHWEED, GROUND ASH, GROUND ELDER. To 14 in.; fls. white. June. Eur.; naturalized in N. Amer. Cv. **'Variegatum'.** Lvs. margined with white. Commonly planted, especially the variegated-lvd. cv., as an edging or ground cover; prop. by division. Either form is apt to become a bad weed unless controlled.

AELUROPUS Trin. *Gramineae.* Three spp. of per. grasses, native to Medit. region and Asia; lf. blades stiff, short, flat or involute, ligule a ridge of short hairs; spikelets compressed laterally, 4–11-fld., lemma ovate, keeled, short-pointed, palea as long as lemma, 2-keeled, 2-nerved, with broad flaps. For terminology see *Gramineae.*

littoralis (Gouan) Parl. MEDITERRANEAN SALT GRASS. Sts. to 20 in.; lf. blades flat, later involute, ligules consisting of a ring of hairs; infl. an oblong, compact, sometimes discontinuous spike; spikelets on very short, erect pedicels, glumes 3–5-nerved, short-pointed, lemma 5–9-nerved. Medit. Eur., sw. Asia, N. Afr. Cult. in Ariz. and New Mex.

AEONIUM Webb & Berth. *Crassulaceae.* About 38 spp. of succulent herbs and shrubs, mostly of the Canary Is.; lvs. alt., usually obovate or spatulate, often ciliate, mostly in rosettes at ends of brs.; panicles mostly terminal; fls. white, pink, or mostly yellow, 6–12-merous, petals separate, stamens twice as many, nectar glands usually present. *Aeonium* was formerly included in *Sempervivum*, from which it differs mainly in habit.

These plants are adapted to outdoor culture in Calif., and are interesting under glass. For culture see *Succulents*.

arborescens: a listed name of no botanical standing, probably intended for *A. arboreum*.

arboreum L. Shrub to 3 ft.; lvs. 2–3 in. long, ½–¾ in. wide, glabrous, glossy green; infl. 4 in. long, puberulous; fls. bright yellow. Winter. Morocco. Cvs. 'Atropurpureum' and 'Foliis Purpureis'. Lvs. dark purple.

balsamiferum Webb & Berth. Glabrous shrub, to 3 ft., with odor of balsam; lvs. in loose rosettes, 2–2½ in. long, 1–1½ in. wide; infl. 3–4 in. long, sticky; fls. yellow. Summer.

Barleyi: a listed name of no botanical standing.

Bethencourtianum: a listed name of no botanical standing, published as a synonym for *Aichryson Bethencourtianum*.

Burchardii Praeg. Shrub, to 1 ft. or more, with smooth brown bark; lvs. crowded or scattered, 3–4 in. long, 1 in. wide, thickened down the center, dark green; infl. glandular-pubescent, 3–4 in. long; petals buff with red midline. Spring.

caespitosum: *A. Simsii.*

canariense (L.) Webb & Berth. [*A. giganteum* Webb]. CANARY ISLAND A., VELVET ROSE, GIANT V.R. Velvety-pubescent, rosettes sessile, mostly solitary, to 2½ ft. wide; lvs. 4–12 in. long, 2–4 in. wide, pale green; infl. 1–1½ ft.; fls. pale yellow. Spring.

Castello-Paivae C. Bolle. Like *A. Haworthii*, but lvs. wholly gray-glaucous, rather soft and limp; fls. greenish-white. Late spring.

ciliatum (Willd.) Webb & Berth. [*Sempervivum ciliatum* Willd.]. Shrub, to 3 ft., sts. with a rhomboidal pattern of tubercles between lf. scars; lvs. about 4 in. long and 2 in. wide, glabrous; infl. pubescent, 6–12 in. long; fls. greenish-white. Spring.

Cooperi: a listed name of no botanical standing.

cuneatum Webb & Berth. Rosettes sessile, to 1½ ft. wide, offsets long-stemmed; lvs. to 10 in. long and 3 in. wide, acute, glabrous, often glaucous; infl. glandular, 1–2 ft. long; fls. golden. Spring.

decorum Webb. Like *A. Haworthii*, but sts. with hard, whitish, transverse, scalelike excrescences; lvs. green or reddish and narrower; fls. pinkish. Spring.

domesticum: *Aichryson domesticum.*

×**floribundum** A. Berger: *A. Simsii* × *A. spathulatum*. Bushy, to 1 ft.; lvs. oblong, sessile, 1–1½ in. long, ¼ in. wide, with prominent, longitudinal, immersed glands; infl. compact, 2–3 in. wide; fls. golden, ⅝ in. across, nectar glands none. Late spring. The plant commonly cult. in Calif. as *A. Tournefortii* Hort. seems referable here, though glands are present. Another hybrid (*A. Simsii* × ?), a coarser plant with pale yellow fls., is also cult. in Calif.

giganteum: *A. canariense.*

glutinosum (Ait.) Webb & Berth. Sticky throughout, rosettes loose, sessile; lvs. 3–4 in. long, 1½–2 in. wide, glabrous; infl. loose, to 1 ft. long and wide; fls. golden. Summer.

Goochiae Webb & Berth. Like *A. Lindleyi*, but lvs. ⅛ in. thick and fls. pink. Spring.

Haworthii Webb & Berth. PINWHEEL. Dense, rounded shrub, 1–2 ft. high and wide; lvs. 1–2 in. long, ¾–1¼ in. wide, blue-green, glaucous, often red-edged, firm; infl. 4–5 in. long; fls. cream-yellow or rose-tinged. Spring. Commonly grown.

hierrense (R. P. Murr.) Pit. & Proust. Unbranched, to 4 ft. when in fl., dying after flowering; lvs. 6–12 in. long, 2–3 in. wide, blue-glaucous or in cult. dark green, red-edged; infl. 1–2 ft. long and wide, pubescent; fls. white or pink. Spring.

holochrysum Webb & Berth. Like *A. arboreum*, but less branched; lvs. 3–6 in. long; infl. 6–12 in. long, glabrous. Winter.

Lindleyi Webb & Berth. Dense shrub to 1 ft., brs. tortuous; lvs. 1 in. long, ½–¾ in. wide, ¼ in. thick, glandular-pubescent, sticky; infl. flattish, 2–3 in. across; fls. yellow. Summer.

Manriqueorum C. Bolle. Like *A. arboreum*, but larger, to 6 ft.; lvs. 3–5 in. long; infl. 6–9 in. long; differing from *A. holochrysum* in having infl. puberulous. Winter.

nobile Praeg. Monocarpic, with fecal odor, rosettes solitary, short-stemmed, to 2 ft. wide; lvs. 8–12 in. long, 6–8 in. wide, ½ in. thick, yellowish-green; infl. flat, 1–2 ft. wide; fls. very many, orange-red. Early summer.

percarneum (R. P. Murr.) Pit. & Proust. Shrub, to 4 ft.; lvs. 3–4 in. long, 1½ in. wide, red-edged, coarsely ciliate, glabrous, green or with exposure purplish; infl. 10 in. long and wide; fls. pink. Spring.

pseudotabuliforme: a listed name of no botanical standing for *A. undulatum*.

sedifolium (Webb) Pit. & Proust. Dense, twiggy shrub, ½–1 ft.; lvs. ½ in. long, ¼ in. wide, glossy and sticky, striped with red; infl. 2 in. wide; fls. yellow, lacking nectar glands. Spring.

Simsii (Sweet) Stearn [*A. caespitosum* (C. A. Sm.) Webb & Berth.; *Sempervivum cespitosum* C. A. Sm.]. Cespitose; lvs. strap-shaped, 2½–3½ in. long, ¼ in. wide, light green, with prominent, longitudinal, immersed glands; fl. st. lateral, infl. flattish, 1½–2 in. wide; fls. golden. Spring. For hybrids see *A.* ×*floribundum.*

Smithii (Sims) Webb & Berth. Shrub, to 2 ft., brs. bristly-hairy; lvs. 1½–2 in. long, 1–1½ in. wide, with conspicuous, immersed, linear glands; infl. 2–2½ in. long; fls. yellow, ¾ in. wide, lacking nectar glands. Late spring.

spathulatum (Hornem.) Praeg. [*A. strepsicladum* Webb & Berth.]. Shrub, 1–2 ft.; lvs. obovate-spatulate, ½–1 in. long, ⅜ in. wide, puberulous, somewhat sticky, with conspicuous, immersed, longitudinal glands; fl. st. 6–8 in. long, infl. flattish, 2–4 in. wide; fls. golden-yellow, nectar glands none. Spring. Var. **cruentum** (Webb & Berth.) Praeg. Brs. straighter and more erect; lvs. cuneate-spatulate, more rounded, thickish. Early spring.

strepsicladum: *A. spathulatum.*

tabuliforme (Haw.) Webb & Berth. Rosettes sessile, mostly solitary, when sterile perfectly flat, 6–12 in. wide; lvs. 100–200, closely overlapping, 3–6 in. long, 1–1½ in. wide, pale green; fl. st. 1–2 ft. long; fls. pale yellow. Summer. Cv. 'Cristatum' is listed.

Tournefortii: a listed name of no botanical standing; see *A.* ×*floribundum.*

undulatum Webb & Berth. [*A. pseudotabuliforme* Hort.]. SAUCER PLANT. Sts. 3–10 ft., unbranched but suckering at base; lvs. 4–8 in. long, 1½–2½ in. wide, dark, glossy; infl. dense, 1–2 ft. long; fls. bright yellow. Spring.

urbicum (C. A. Sm.) Webb & Berth. Sts. unbranched, 2–7 ft.; lvs. 5–10 in. long, 1½–2 in. wide, green or glaucous; infl. glabrous, to 2½ ft. long; fls. greenish-white or pinkish. Spring.

virgineum Webb & Berth. Like *A. canariense* but smaller, branching, often reddish, velvety, rosettes to 10 in. wide; lvs. 4–6 in. long, 2–3 in. wide; infl. 8–12 in. long; fls. lemon-yellow. Early spring.

AERANGIS: *ANGRAECUM.*

AERIA: *GAUSSIA.*

AERIDES Lour. Orchidaceae. About 40 spp. of epiphytes, native to trop. Asia and Malay Arch.; lvs. thick, 2-ranked, sheathing the st. at their base; fls. in pendulous, lateral racemes, the 2 lateral sepals attached to base of column, the petals and upper sepal similar, lip 3-lobed, prolonged basally into a hollow, usually upturned spur. For structure of fl. see *Orchidaceae.*

Warm greenhouse; for culture see *Orchids.*

affinis: *A. multiflora.*

Ballantiniana: *A. odorata* var.

Brookei: *A. crispa.*

cornuta: *A. odorata.*

crassifolia C. Parish & Rchb.f. Lvs. to 8 in. long and 2 in. wide; racemes longer than lvs.; fls. rose-purple, 1½ in. long, spur greenish at tip. Late spring. Burma.

crispa Lindl. [*A. Brookei* Batem.]. Lvs. to 10 in. long, strap-shaped, retuse; racemes many-fld.; fls. large, sepals and petals white, tinged rose, lip 3-lobed, midlobe fringed, white at base, deep rose-purple at apex. Indonesia. Var. **Lindleyana** (Wight) Hort. Veitch. Racemes large, branching; fls. white and purplish-pink. Var. **Warneri** B. S. Williams. Fls. fragrant, sepals and petals white, flushed with rose, midlobe of lip deep magenta.

cylindrica: *A. vandarum.*

Ellisii: *A. odorata* var.

expansa: *A. falcata.*

falcata Lindl. & Paxt. [*A. expansa* Rchb.f.; *A. Larpentiae* Rchb.f.]. Similar to *A. crassifolia*, but sepals and petals white, spotted with purple, lip amethyst-red. Late spring. Burma. Var. **Houlletiana** (Rchb.f.) Hort. Veitch [*A. Houlletiana* Rchb.f.]. Sepals and petals yellowish-brown, lip creamy-white with magenta blotch at center. Var. **Leoniae** (Rchb.f. ex Godefr.) Hort. Veitch [*A. Leoniae* Rchb.f. ex

Godefr.]. Fls. larger than in typical var., lip white, spotted and edged with dark red.

Fieldingii E. Morr. Lvs. to 10 in. long and 1¾ in. wide; racemes longer than lvs.; fls. white, dotted and suffused with rose, 1½ in. across, spur white. Late spring. India.

Godefroyana: *A. multiflora* var.

Houlletiana: *A. falcata* var.

japonica Linden & Rchb.f. St. short; lvs. 3–4, close together; raceme loosely few-fld., to 6 in. long; fls. to 1¼ in. across, sepals and petals similar, ovate-oblong, cream or yellowish, with purplish transverse bars at base, lip 3-lobed, lateral lobes folded, midlobe round-ovate, greenish-white with purplish spots. Early summer. Japan.

Larpentiae: *A. falcata.*

Lawrenciae Rchb.f. Lvs. to 1 ft. long and 2 in. wide; racemes as long as lvs.; fls. 1½ in. across, sepals and petals white, tipped with amethyst-purple, lip white, midlobe purple, spur green. Summer. Philippine Is. Var. **Amesiana** Hort. Sander ex Kränzl. Fls. larger, light orange-yellow tipped with purple, midlobe of lip larger, with many radiating rows of purplish spots. Var. **Sanderana** Hort. Fls. usually lighter than in var. *Amesiana*, sepals and petals creamy-white, tipped with magenta, lip yellow, magenta, and creamy-white.

Lawrenciana: a listed name, in error for *A. Lawrenciae.*

Leoniae: *A. falcata* var.

Lobbii: *A. multiflora* var.

longicornu: *A. uniflora.*

multiflora Roxb. [*A. affinis* Wallich; *A. rosea* Hort. Lodd. ex Paxt.]. Lvs. to 9 in. long and ¾ in. wide; racemes longer than lvs.; fls. 1 in. across, sepals and petals white, spotted and tipped with purple, lip light purple, deeper purple in middle. Summer, early autumn. Himalayas to S. Vietnam. Var. **Godefroyana** (Rchb.f.) Hort. Veitch [*A. Godefroyana* Rchb.f.]. Differs from typical var. in having lvs. larger and heavier in texture, sepals and petals broader, more intensely colored. Var. **Lobbii** (Lem.) Hort. Veitch [*A. Lobbii* Lem.]. Differs from typical var. in having lvs. congested on a shorter st., infl. longer, occasionally branched, fls. more numerous, deeper in color.

odorata Lour. [*A. cornuta* Roxb.; *A. suavissima* Lindl.]. Lvs. to 8 in. long and 2 in. wide; racemes often longer than lvs.; fls. fragrant, to 1 in. long, sepals and petals white, with purple spot at tips, lip white, spotted with red, midlobe rose. Summer, early autumn. India to China, Philippine Is. Var. **alba** Hort. Fls. white. Var. **Ballantiniana** (Rchb.) Hort. [*A. Ballantiniana* Rchb.f.]. Racemes shorter than in typical var., fls. smaller, lip yellow, spotted with purple, midlobe purple. Var. **birmanica** Rchb.f. Fls. smaller than in typical var., lateral sepals with a purple line at apex on exterior, midlobe of lip narrow, purple, with a few marginal teeth. Var. **Dayana** Hort. Plant more robust; infl. very long. Var. **Ellisii** (B. S. Williams) Hort. [*A. Ellisii* Hort.]. Fls. somewhat larger than in other vars., sepals and petals flushed with purple, lip with pale magenta stripes. Var. **major** Hort. [*A. virens* Lindl.]. Racemes larger than in typical var. Var. **purpurascens** Hort. Plant very robust; lvs. dark green; racemes massive; fls. white, sepals and petals with bright pink tips. Var. **Sanderae** Hort. Racemes long; fls. pure white.

quinquevulnera Lindl. Differs from *A. odorata* in having midlobe of lip toothed on margins. Philippine Is. Var. **Roebelinii** (Rchb.f.) Hort. [*A. Roebelinii* Rchb.f.]. Base of sepals and petals greenish, lip rose, with yellow lateral lobes.

racemifera: *Sarcanthus pallidus.*

Roebelinii: *A. quinquevulnera* var.

rosea: *A. multiflora.*

Sanderana: *A. Lawrenciae* var.

sauvissima: *A. odorata.*

uniflora (Lindl.) Summerh. [*A. longicornu* Hook.f.]. Lvs. cylindrical, long, pendent; fls. solitary or 2 together, sepals and petals similar, lip 3-lobed, lateral lobes lacerate, midlobe notched in middle, spur twice as long as sepals. Nepal and Assam.

vandarum Rchb.f. [*A. cylindrica* Hook.]. Lvs. cylindrical, to 8 in. long; racemes 1–3-fld., shorter than lvs.; fls. 2 in. long, white, somewhat translucent, lateral lobes of lip finely toothed. Late winter. Himalayas.

virens: *A. odorata* var. *major.*

✕AERIDOVANDA Rolfe: *Aerides* ✕ *Vanda.* Orchidaceae. A group of bigeneric hybrids generally intermediate in character between the parent genera.

Culture as for *Aerides;* see also *Orchids.*

Mundyi Rolfe: *Aerides vandarum* ✕ *Vanda teres.* Fls. white, tinged with lilac.

AESCHYNANTHUS Jack [*Trichosporum* D. Don]. BASKET PLANT, BLUSHWORT. *Gesneriaceae.* More than 100 spp. of epiphytic subshrubs or vines, from India and s. China to New Guinea; sts. slender; lvs. opp. or in whorls of 3–4, usually entire, leathery or fleshy; fls. 1–2 in lf. axils or in a terminal cluster, calyx 5-lobed or of 5 sepals, deciduous or rarely persistent, corolla deep red to scarlet, orange, or greenish, tubular, usually curved toward the apex, 2-lipped, the upper 2 lobes usually shorter than the lower 3, stamens 4, usually exserted or at least as long as the corolla, anthers united in pairs by their tips, disc ringlike, ovary superior, elongate, style exserted, stigma capitate with a horizontal median groove; fr. an elongate, 2-valved caps., seeds many.

For cultivation see *Gesneriaceae.*

acuminatus Wallich ex A. DC. Lvs. elliptic, to 3½ in. long, ½ in. wide, cuneate at base, acuminate, waxy; fls. in terminal clusters, calyx divided nearly to the base, glabrous, corolla broadly tubular, straight, ½ in. long, yellow-green, upper lip yellow, lower lip deflexed, green or sometimes red-margined, filaments minutely glandular-pilose. E. Himalayas, Sikkim to Assam. Material cult. under this name may be *A. parasiticus.*

bracteatus Wallich ex A. DC. Lvs. variable, mostly elliptic, to 4 in. long, 1½ in. wide; fls. many in a terminal cluster, bracts red, to 1¼ in. long, longer than the red pedicels, calyx divided nearly to base, corolla slightly curved on upper side, to 1¾ in. long, red, lower lobes sometimes dark-spotted. E. Himalayas, Sikkim to Assam. Material cult. under this name may be *A. parasiticus* or *A. micranthus.*

ellipticus Lauterb. & K. Schum. Sts. densely short-reddish-hairy; lvs. elliptic, dark green; fls. solitary or several on puberulous pedicels, calyx divided to the base, 5/16 in. long, puberulous, corolla obliquely funnelform, to 2⅜ in. long, salmon-pink with darker hairs, yellowish-pink inside. New Guinea.

Evrardii Pellegr. Sts. glabrous; lvs. lanceolate, to 4½ in. long, 2¼ in. wide, glabrous; fls. axillary but more or less clustered at ends of brs., bracts small, calyx tubular, 1 in. long, ¼ in. wide, glabrous, lobes triangular, ¼ in. long, obtuse, corolla nearly funnelform, slightly curved at tip, to 3⅛ in. long, reddish-orange with yellow lower surface, lobes 3/16 in. long, sparsely glandular-pilose, striped with dark red, lower lobes yellow, filaments glandular-pilose; fr. to 16 in. long.

grandiflorus: *A. parasiticus.*

Hosseusianus Kränzl. Sts. glabrous; lvs. oblanceolate, to 1¾ in. long, ⅜ in. wide, green and pilose above, nearly white and velvety-hairy beneath; fls. mostly paired, terminal, calyx about 3/16 in. long, tubular for ⅓ its length, lobes linear, corolla slightly curved, contracted at throat, to 1¼ in. long, purple, sparsely pilose outside; fr. 2¼ in. long. Thailand.

javanicus: *A. radicans.*

Lobbianus: *A. radicans.*

longiflorus (Blume) A. DC. Sts. cylindrical; lvs. narrowly ovate to elliptic, to 6¼ in. long, 2 in. wide, acuminate, leathery, glossy dark green above, paler beneath; fls. 2–7 at tips of brs., pedicels short, minutely hairy, calyx divided nearly to base, the lobes linear, red, puberulous, corolla narrowly tubular, gradually enlarged upward and slightly curved at tip, 3¼ in. long, puberulous, deep red, the lower lobes to ⅜ in. long, with dark-margined, yellowish-red blotch at base, filaments and style purplish; fr. to 1 ft. long or more. Java.

marmoratus T. Moore [*A. zebrinus* Hort.]. Lvs. narrowly elliptic, to 4 in. long, 1½ in. wide, obscurely toothed, pale green with darker marbling above, pale and marked with red beneath; fls. solitary in axils near ends of brs., calyx divided nearly to base, the lobes very slender, ⅞ in. long, acuminate, hairy, corolla glabrous, curved, widening upward, 1½ in. long, yellow-green, splotched with chocolate on the short lobes; fr. to 7½ in. long. Burma, Thailand, Malay Pen.

micranthus C. B. Clarke. Sts. glabrous; lvs. elliptic, to 3½ in. long, 1 in. wide; fls. solitary or paired along st., calyx deeply divided, the lobes narrow, to ⅛ in. long, pilose, corolla tubular, slightly curved, 1 in. long, deep red, lobes very short, dark-spotted; fr. to 7½ in. long. Himalayas, Sikkim to Burma.

obconicus C. B. Clarke. Sts. glabrous; lvs. oblong-elliptic, to 3½ in. long, 1¼ in. wide, acuminate; fls. paired, on hairy pedicels to ⅜ in. long, calyx broadly obconical, to 5/16 in. long, ¾ in. wide, subentire, hairy, corolla slightly curved, ⅞ in. long, dark red, villous. Malay Pen.

parasiticus (Roxb.) Wallich [*A. grandiflorus* (D. Don) K. Spreng.; *A. parviflorus* (D. Don) K. Spreng.; *A. ramosissimus* Wallich]. Sts. glabrous; lvs. lanceolate, to 4 in. long, 1 in. wide; fls. usually clustered at tips of brs., calyx divided into lanceolate lobes about as long as tube, corolla curved, enlarged upward but contracted at throat, to 1⅜ in. long, pilose outside, orange-red with red lines from lobes, lobes orange-margined and splotched with red, filaments glandular-pilose; fr. to 10 in. long. India.

parviflorus: *A. parasiticus.*

parvifolius: *A. radicans.*

pulcher (Blume) G. Don. SCARLET BASKET VINE, RED-BUGLE VINE, ROYAL-RED BUGLER, LIPSTICK PLANT, PIPE PLANT, CLIMBING-BEAUTY. Similar to *A. radicans* but with fls. and pedicels glabrous except for a fringe of fine hairs along margin of corolla lobes, calyx green or purple-tinged, ⅞–1 in. long, corolla to 2½ in. long. Java.

pullobia: *Aeschynanthus* cv. 'Pullobia', a hybrid intermediate between its parents, *A. pulcher* and *A. radicans.*

radicans Jack [*A. javanicus* Hort. Rollisson ex Hook.; *A. Lobbianus* Hort. Veitch ex Hook.; *A. parvifolius* R. Br.]. LIPSTICK PLANT. Sts. minutely hairy to glabrous; lvs. ovate, elliptic, or obovate, to 1¾ in. long, 1 in. wide, entire or slightly toothed, sometimes purplish-margined; fls. paired on short peduncles toward ends of sts., calyx tubular, 1 in. long, longer than broad, flaring upward to very short, rounded lobes, dark green to deep blackish-purple, downy, corolla tubular but flared upward to throat, 2 in. long, hairy, bright red, lower lobes blotched with yellow at base; fr. to 14 in. long. Malay Pen., Java.

ramosissimus: *A. parasiticus.*

speciosus Hook. Lvs. opp. or in 3's, or those beneath the fls. in a whorl of 4–8, blades ovate-lanceolate, to 4 in. long, 1½ in. wide, acuminate, obscurely toothed; fls. 6–20 in cluster at ends of brs., calyx divided nearly to base, ⁵⁄₁₆ in. long, corolla expanded upward to a curved tip, slightly hairy, to 4 in. long, orange or yellow shading to orange, lobes short, with orange-yellow base separated from the scarlet tip by a deep red lunate bar. Malay Pen., Borneo, Java.

×**splendidus** T. Moore: *A. parasiticus* × *A. speciosus.* Similar to *A. speciosus,* but calyx tube about as long as lobes, corolla lobes with large blotches of deep maroon but no orange-yellow patch at base.

tricolor Hook. Sts. slightly hairy; lvs. ovate, to 1½ in. long, ½ in. wide, acute, slightly hairy on margin and beneath; fls. mostly paired on short, hairy peduncles, calyx tube to ½ in. wide, broader than long, obtusely and shallowly lobed, red, hairy, corolla to 2 in. long, scarlet streaked with bright yellow and black, glandular-hairy, limb oblique, large, about as broad as tube is long. Borneo.

zebrinus: *A. marmoratus.*

AESCULUS L. HORSE CHESTNUT, BUCKEYE. *Hippocastanaceae.* Thirteen spp. of deciduous shrubs or trees, native to N. Amer., se. Eur., and e. Asia; lvs. opp., palmately compound; fls. white, yellow, pink, or red, in erect, terminal panicles, calyx 5-lobed, petals 4 or 5, stamens 6–8; fr. a smooth, slightly scaly, or spiny caps.

Horse chestnuts are mostly hardy north (Zone 5), except for the Californian and Himalayan species. Propagated by seeds sown in the autumn or stratified, by side grafting, by budding on common species, and the shrubby kinds also by layers. *Aesculus parviflora* may be propagated by root cuttings.

arguta: *A. glabra* var.

californica (Spach) Nutt. CALIFORNIA H. C., CALIFORNIA B. Large shrub or tree, to 40 ft.; lfts. usually 5, ovate-lanceolate, oblong-lanceolate, or elliptic-oblong, to 7 in. long, acuminate, stalked; panicles to 8 in. long; fls. white to pale pink, stamens exserted. Calif.

×**carnea** Hayne [*A. × rubicunda* Loisel.]: *A. Hippocastanum* × *A. Pavia.* RED H.C. To 40 ft.; lfts. usually 5, cuneate-obovate, to 6 in. long, nearly sessile; panicles to 8 in. long; fls. flesh-colored to scarlet. Zone 4. Cv. 'Briotii'. Fls. scarlet. Cv. 'Rosea'. Fls. pink.

discolor: *A. Pavia.* Var. **Koehnei:** *A. Pavia.*

glabra Willd. [*A. glabra* var. *leucodermis* Sarg. and var. *Sargentii* Rehd.]. OHIO B. Large shrub or tree, to 30 ft. or more; lfts. 5–7, oblong-obovate or elliptic-obovate, to 6½ in. long, acute to long-acuminate, short-stalked; panicles to 6 in. long; fls. pale yellow or greenish-yellow, stamens exserted. W. Penn. to Iowa, s. to Ala., Ark., Miss. Var. **arguta** (Buckl.) B. L. Robinson [*A. arguta* Buckl.]. TEXAS B. Lfts. 7–11, ovate-lanceolate or elliptic, long-attenuate at both ends. Ne. Kans. to Tex. Wood used for artificial limbs and wood pulp.

glaucescens: *A. sylvatica.*

Hippocastanum L. COMMON H. C., EUROPEAN H. C. To 100 ft.; lfts. 5–7, obovate, to 12 in. long, sessile; panicles to 1 ft. long; fls. white, blotched with red and yellow; fr. spiny or warty. Balkan Pen. Wood used for various articles. Cvs. include: 'Alba', fls. pure white; 'Baumannii', fls. white, double; 'Rosea', fls. pink; 'Rubricunda', fls. red.

indica (Wallich ex Camb.) Hook. To 100 ft.; lfts. 5–9, oblong-lanceolate, to 9 in. long, short-stalked; panicles to 15 in. long; fls. white, uppermost petal yellow-blotched, lowermost tinged rose. Himalayas.

×**mutabilis** (Spach) Scheele: *A. Pavia* × *A. sylvatica.* Tree; lfts. elliptic-oblong, pale and hairy beneath; panicles 4–6 in. long; fls. yellow and red. Var. **Harbisonii** (Sarg.) Rehd. Panicles 6–8 in. long; fls. bright red. Var. **induta** Sarg. Lfts. densely hairy and glaucescent beneath.

neglecta: *A. sylvatica.* Var. **georgiana:** *A. sylvatica.* Var. **pubescens:** *A. sylvatica.* Var. **tomentosa:** *A. sylvatica.*

octandra Marsh. YELLOW B., SWEET B. To 90 ft.; lfts. 5–7, obovate-oblong to elliptic-oblong, to 8½ in. long, cuneate; panicles to 6 in. long, pubescent; fls. yellow, stamens included. Sw. Penn. to s. Ill., s. to Ga. and n. Ala. Wood used for various articles and for wood pulp.

parviflora Walt. [*A. parviflora* forma *serotina* Rehd.]. BUCKEYE, BOTTLEBRUSH B., DWARF H. C. Spreading shrub or small tree, to 15 ft.; lfts. 5–7, elliptic to oblong-obovate, to 11 in. long, acuminate, nearly sessile; panicle columnar, to 1 ft. long; fls. white, stamens exserted, straight. Ga. and Ala.

Pavia L. [*A. discolor* Pursh; *A. discolor* var. *Koehnei* Rehd.; *A. Pavia* var. *humilis* (Lodd. ex Lindl.) Mouill.; *A. splendens* Sarg.]. RED B. Shrub or small tree, to 12 ft. or rarely more; lfts. 5–7, oblong, lanceolate, narrowly elliptic, oblanceolate, or obovate; panicles oblong, to 10 in. long; fls. red to yellow. Mo. and s. Ill., s. to e. N.C. and Tex. Cvs. 'Alba' and 'Rubra' are listed.

×**rubicunda:** *A. × carnea.*

rubra: a listed name of no botanical standing, used for *A. Pavia.*

sinensis: *A. turbinata.*

splendens: *A. Pavia.*

sylvatica Bartr. [*A. glaucescens* Sarg.; *A. neglecta* Lindl.; *A. neglecta* vars. *georgiana* (Sarg.) Sarg., *pubescens* (Sarg.) Sarg., and *tomentosa* Sarg.]. Shrub or small tree, to 20 ft.; lfts. 5, oblong-obovate to elliptic, to 10 in. long, yellow-green; panicles to 6 in. long; fls. yellow, pedicels and calyx with few stalked glands. N.C. and Tenn. s. to Ga.

turbinata Blume [*A. sinensis* Bean]. JAPANESE H.C. To 100 ft.; lfts. 5–7, cuneate-obovate, to 15 in. long, sessile; panicles to 10 in. long; fls. yellowish-white with a red spot; fr. warty. Japan. Wood used for many purposes in Japan.

woerlitzensis Koehne. Tree; lfts. oblong-obovate, to 6¼ in. long, yellowish-green beneath; panicles to 5 in. long; fls. red. Of garden origin.

AETHEOPAPPUS: *CENTAUREA.*

AETHIONEMA R. Br. STONE CRESS. *Cruciferae.* About 30 or 40 spp. of glabrous, ann. or per. herbs, often low-growing, native to Medit. region; lvs. simple, sessile, often glaucous; fls. pink, lilac, yellow, or white, in showy terminal racemes, sepals and petals 4; fr. a silicle, flattened, usually winged, seeds few.

Useful in the border or rock garden, flowering mostly in spring; may also be used as cut flowers.

antitaurus: a listed name of no botanical standing.

arabicum (L.) Andrz. ex DC. [*A. Buxbaumii* Fisch. ex Hornem.; *A. cappodocicum* K. Spreng.]. Short-season ann., 3–6 in.; lvs. oblong, to 1 in. long; fls. minute, lilac. Grown for its erect racemes of large, thin, winged, overlapping silicles. Se. Eur. and sw. Asia.

armenum Boiss. Low-growing per., sts. many, simple, rarely branched, fl. sts. to 8 in.; lvs. linear-oblong, to ¾ in. long; fls. white or pink; silicles ovate-obovate, to ¼ in. long, 2-seeded. Turkey.

Buxbaumii: *A. arabicum.*

cappodocicum: *A. arabicum.*

coridifolium DC. [*Iberis jucunda* Schott & Kotschy]. LEBANON CRESS. Per., sts. many, mostly unbranched, fl. sts. to 6 in.; lvs. nearly linear, to ⅝ in. long, somewhat fleshy; fls. pink or rosy-lilac; silicles broadly ovate, to ½ in. long, cordate, concave-convex, 2-seeded. Mts., s. Turkey and Lebanon. See *A. grandiflorum.*

creticum: *A. saxatile.*

grandiflorum Boiss. & Hohen. [*A. pulchellum* Boiss. & Huet]. PERSIAN STONE CRESS. Many-stemmed per., fl. sts. simple or branched, to 12 in.; lvs. evenly distributed on st., linear-oblong, to 1½ in. long, or less; petals pink, to ½ in. long; silicles ovate or rounded, to ½ in. long, flat, 1- or 2-seeded. Turkey, Iraq, Iran. Variable in petal size and shape. Resembles *A. coridifolium,* and scarcely distinguishable in fl., but silicles flat.

iberideum (Boiss.) Boiss. Tufted, low per.; lvs. crowded, opp., 4-ranked, very narrow; fls. in short racemes, showy, white; silicles ovate-obcordate, to ¼ in. long, 2-seeded. Turkey, Greece.

jucundum: a listed name, used for *A. coridifolium.*

ovalifolium: *A. saxatile.*

persicum: a listed name of no botanical standing, used for a plant to 1 ft. high, with deep rose fls.; probably referable to *A. iberideum* or *A. saxatile*.

pulchellum: *A. grandiflorum*.

purpureum: a listed name of no botanical standing.

pyrenaicum: *A. saxatile*.

saxatile (L.) R. Br. [*A. creticum* Boiss.; *A. ovalifolium* (DC.) Boiss.; *A. pyrenaicum* Boutigny]. Ann., bien., or monocarpic per., sts. several, fl. sts. simple or branched, to 12 in.; lvs. usually ovate or oblong, obtuse; fls. in loose or dense racemes elongating in fr., petals white or pink, to ¼ in. long; silicles to ½ in. across. S. Eur., Asia Minor.

schistosum Boiss. & Kotschy. Low-growing, per., sts. many, fl. sts. simple or branched, to 4 in.; lvs. densely covering st., linear; fls. in a headlike infl. not elongating in fr., petals pink, to ¼ in. long, distinctly clawed; silicles ovate, ⅜ in. long, concave-convex, winged, 2-seeded. Turkey.

stylosum DC. Per., to 7 in., fl. sts. simple or branched; lvs. sessile or nearly so, ovate-lanceolate, to ¾ in. long; petals white or pale lilac, to ⁵⁄₁₆ in. long, silicles broadly ovate, to ⅜ in. long, with dentate, winged margins, 2-seeded. S. Turkey, w. Syria.

Thomasianum J. Gay. Closely related to *A. saxatile*, but more dwarf and having closely appressed, membranous-winged silicles. Nw. Italy.

×**warleyense** Bergmans: *A. armenum* × (probably) *A. grandiflorum*. Compact but spreading, 3–6 in.; lvs. steel-blue, broad; fls. large, to ¼ in. across, pale or brilliant rose-pink to rose-carmine.

AFRAEGLE (Swingle) Engl. *Rutaceae*. About 4 spp. of spiny trees or shrubs, native to trop. Afr.; lvs. alt., with 3 or sometimes 1 lft., glandular-dotted; fls. small, in small axillary panicles, (4–)5-merous, petals imbricate, linear, stamens, 15–20; fr. globose or pear-shaped, hard-shelled. Differs from *Balsamocitrus* in having more numerous stamens.

paniculata (K. Schum.) Engl. [*Balsamocitrus paniculata* (K. Schum.) Swingle]. Shrub or small tree, to 60 ft., often branched from near the base; lfts. 3, rarely 1, to 6 in. long, 2¾ in. wide, firm or nearly leathery; panicles 6–10-fld.; fls. white, 4-merous, fragrant; fr. globose or obovoid, to 3³⁄₁₆ in. in diam. W. Afr.

AFZELIA Sm. [*Pahudia* Miq.]. *Leguminosae* (subfamily *Caesalpinioideae*). Fourteen spp. of unarmed trees of trop. Afr. and Asia; lvs. alt., pinnate; fls. in terminal, simple or panicled racemes, calyx long, tubular, 4-lobed, petal 1, large, clawed, stamens 7 (or 5), staminodes 2; fr. a thick, woody, oblong to obovate-oblong, dehiscent legume, with transverse partitions between seeds.

Planted as ornamentals in warm regions; propagated by seeds.

africana Sm. ex Pers. [*Pahudia africana* (Sm. ex Pers.) Prain]. Large tree; lvs. even-pinnate, to 1 ft. long or more, lfts. in 3–5 pairs, elliptic or elliptic-oblong, to 5 in. long and 2¾ in. wide; panicles short; fls. hoary-pubescent, petals reddish, with white edges, ½–¾ in. long; fr. 4–6 in. long, 2½ in. across, seeds black, with orange aril. Senegal to Congo region. Wood useful in cabinetry.

cuanzensis Welw. MAKOLA. Medium-sized tree, differing from *A. africana* in its simple racemes of larger fls., blood-red standards to 1¼ in. long, and seeds with red aril. Nigeria to Angola and Mozambique. Often but incorrectly spelled *quanzensis*.

quanzensis: a misspelling of *A. cuanzensis*.

rhomboidea (Blanco) S. Vidal [*Pahudia rhomboidea* (Blanco) Prain]. To 80 ft.; lvs. even-pinnate, to 10 in. long, lfts. in 4 pairs, oblong to elliptic-ovate, to 3 in. long, acuminate; panicles pubescent, not longer than lvs.; petals yellowish-red; fr. about 8 in. long, to half as wide, seeds black, with orange-red aril. Philippine Is.

AGALINIS Raf. [*Gerardia* Benth., not L.]. GERARDIA. *Scrophulariaceae*. About 60 spp. of ann. or per. herbs, often more or less parasitic on roots of other plants, native to N. and S. Amer.; lvs. simple, opp., or the upper alt.; fls. pink, purple, or white, sometimes marked with yellow, in racemes, calyx 5-toothed or -lobed, corolla tube campanulate, nearly equally 5-lobed, stamens 4; fr. a caps.

pedicularia: *Aureolaria pedicularia*.

purpurea (L.) Penn. [*Gerardia purpurea* L.]. Glabrescent ann. to 4 ft.; lvs. linear, to 1½ in. long, entire; racemes 6–14-fld.; fls. rose-pink, corolla 1 in. long, with 2 yellow lines and red-purple spots in throat. Late summer. Mass. to Minn. and Nebr., s. to Fla. and e. Tex.

virginica: *Aureolaria virginica*.

AGALMYLA Blume. *Gesneriaceae*. More than 6 spp. of epiphytic subshrubs or vines with short roots along the st., native from Malay Pen. to New Guinea; lvs. opp., those of a pair strongly unequal, the smaller lf. stipulelike or with blade to ¾ in. long, margins with short, curved, more or less appressed hairs; fls. in subsessile to long-peduncled, congested, axillary cymes, calyx 5-lobed or 5-parted, corolla red, yellow in the throat, sometimes with black lines on the lobes, the tube nearly straight or arching, limb 5-lobed, 2-lipped or with lobes nearly equal, stamens 2 or 4, exserted, anthers united in pairs by their tips, disc ringlike, ovary superior, linear, stigma 2-lobed; fr. an elongate, cylindrical caps., seeds many.

For cultivation see *Gesneriaceae*.

parasitica (Lam.) O. Kuntze. SCARLET ROOT-BLOSSOM. Sts. climbing; smaller lf. of each pair stipulelike, large lf. with petiole to 9 in. long, hairy, blade elliptic, to 12 in. long, 4 in. wide, hairy beneath; cymes subsessile, calyx divided nearly to base, corolla to 1½ in. long, minutely hairy, vermilion to scarlet, lobes marked with purplish, tube light pinkish-yellow inside, filaments and styles magenta-rose; fr. to 14 in. long. Malay Pen. and Sumatra, e. to Borneo and Java.

AGAPANTHUS L'Hér. *Amaryllidaceae*. About 9 spp. of S. Afr. herbs with thick rhizomes; lvs. basal, often 2-ranked, deciduous or persistent, linear to strap-shaped; umbel terminal, subtended by membranous bracts (spathe valves); fls. tubular to campanulate, corona absent, stamens 6, exserted, ovary superior; fr. a loculicidal caps.

Popular as a tub plant or large pot plant, and for outdoors in warm regions. Does well in large tubs and will bloom for several years without repotting if given liquid fertilizer; will also force satisfactorily. The species hybridize readily and much garden material may be of mixed origin. Propagated by division or seeds.

africanus (L.) Hoffmanns. [*A. minor* Lodd.; *A. umbellatus* L'Hér., not Redouté]. AFRICAN LILY, BLUE A. L., LILY-OF-THE-NILE. To 20 in., evergreen; lvs. 8–18, persistent, linear-lanceolate, to ½ in. wide; umbel 12–30-fld.; fls. funnelform, deep violet-blue, to 1½ in. long. Often confused with *A. orientalis*, but less commonly cult.; cvs. listed under this sp. generally are referable to *A. orientalis*.

albidus: *A. orientalis* cv.

campanulatus Leighton. Lvs. deciduous; spathe valves deciduous; fls. ascending, campanulate, tube as long as or longer than the slightly undulate lobes.

globosus: a listed name of no botanical standing.

inapertus Beauverd [*A. Weilligii* Hort.]. To 2½ ft.; lvs. 5–8, deciduous, stiff, glaucous; spathe valves deciduous; umbel up to 100-fld.; fls. tubular, drooping, blue, to 1¼ in. long.

intermedius: a listed name of no botanical standing.

longispathus Leighton. To 2 ft.; lvs. deciduous, short, narrow; spathe valves persistent, green; fls. ascending, tube narrow, as long as or longer than spreading lobes.

minor: *A. africanus*.

Mooreanus: *A. orientalis* cv.

nanus: *A. orientalis* cv.

orientalis Leighton [*A. umbellatus* Redouté, not L'Hér.; *A. umbellatus* var. *maximus* S. T. Edw.]. To 2 ft. or more, evergreen; lvs. about 10, persistent, strap-shaped, to 2 in. wide; umbel 40–110-fld.; fls. funnelform, blue, to 2 in. long. The most commonly cult. sp. Several cvs. commonly listed under *A. africanus* or *A. umbellatus* probably belong here: 'Albidus', fls. white; 'Mooreanus', fls. dark blue, lvs. narrow; 'Nanus', dwarf and compact; 'Variegatus', lvs. striped.

pendulus L. Bolus. To 1½ ft.; lvs. deciduous, linear, to 15 in. long and 1½ in. wide; fls. dark purple outside, paler within, to 1½ in. long, pendulous, tubular, lobes scarcely spreading.

umbellatus: see *A. africanus* and *A. orientalis*.

Weilligii: *A. inapertus*.

AGAPETES D. Don ex G. Don [*Pentapterygium* Klotzsch]. *Ericaceae*. About 70 spp. of evergreen shrubs, sometimes epiphytic, native to se. Asia; lvs. alt., simple, leathery; fls. greenish-white, yellow, or red, solitary or in axillary clusters, calyx 5-lobed, sometimes 5-angled or 5-winged, corolla tubular, campanulate, or rarely urceolate, stamens 10, sometimes spurred, ovary inferior; fr. a 5-celled, many-seeded berry.

Grown in Calif.

serpens (Wight) Sleum. [*Pentapterygium serpens* (Wight) Klotzsch]. Shrub, to 3 ft., sts. densely glandular-hairy, drooping; lvs. lanceolate to oblong, to ½ in. long; calyx 5-angled, corolla tubular, ¾ in. long, bright red with darker V-shaped markings. Himalayas.

AGARICACEAE Fries. AGARIC FAMILY. Fungi; about 18 genera of fungi producing macroscopic fruiting bodies (basidiocarps) with stalk (stipe) and umbrella-shaped cap (pileus) bearing fertile layer (hymenium) on surface of gills (lamellae) beneath; hymenium, as seen microscopically, composed of basidia typically bearing 4 smooth or variously roughened spores; spores in deposit white, cream, light green, pink, ochre, brown, purple, or black. One sp. of *Agaricus* is cult.

AGARICUS L. ex Fries. *Agaricaceae.* About 60 spp. of fleshy, compact, usually large mushrooms on soil and dung, almost cosmopolitan; stalk provided with membranous ring (annulus) where cap was attached in button stage; gills not attached to stalk, usually pink when young; spores sepia- to purple-brown in deposit.

bisporus (J. E. Lange) Imbach [*A. campestris* of auth., not L. ex Fries]. Stalk white, 1¼–4¾ in. high, ⅜–¾ in. in diam.; cap white to brownish, dry, convex, becoming flat in old specimens, 1½–4¾ in. across, flesh white, firm, slightly reddened by exposure to air when young and fresh, becoming soft, elastic, and brown-spotted in age; gills pink when young, becoming brown and same color as spores in age; spores brown in deposit. Eurasia, N. Afr.; cult. worldwide for edible fruiting bodies.

campestris L. ex Fries. Not. cult.; see *A. bisporus.*

AGASTACHE Clayt. ex Gronov. [*Brittonastrum* Briq.; *Lophanthus* Benth.]. GIANT HYSSOP. *Labiatae.* About 30 spp. of coarse, robust, tall per. herbs of N. Amer., including Mex., and cent. and e. Asia; sts. mostly square in cross section; lvs. opp., serrate, petioled; fls. small, in many-fld. verticillasters arranged in interrupted terminal spikes, calyx tubular, oblique, 15-nerved, 5-toothed, upper teeth longer than lower, corolla 2-lipped, upper lip erect, 2-lobed, lower lip 3-lobed, the middle lobe crenate, stamens 4, exserted; fr. of 4 nutlets.

Plants large and used in garden borders for their bold effect.

anethiodora: *A. Foeniculum.*

breviflora (A. Gray) Epl. [*A. verticillata* Woot. & Standl.]. To 2 ft., rather pubescent, sts. woody at base, much-branched; lvs. ovate, to 1½ in. long, 1 in. wide, usually crenate; spikes 5 in. long; calyx teeth subulate, corolla rose, to ½ in. long. Ariz., New Mex., and n. Mex.

cana (Hook.) Woot. & Standl. [*Brittonastrum canum* (Hook.) Briq.; *Cedronella cana* Hook.]. MOSQUITO PLANT. To 2 ft., sts. woody at base, freely branching, glabrescent; lvs. ovate-lanceolate, to 1½ in. long, to ½ in. wide, serrate to entire; spikes to 12 in. long; calyx teeth narrowly triangular, corolla pinkish, to 1 in. long. New Mex. and w. Tex.

Foeniculum (Pursh) O. Kuntze [*A. anethiodora* Nutt. ex Britt.; *Lophanthus anisatus* (Nutt.) Benth.]. ANISE HYSSOP, BLUE G.H., FENNEL G.H., FRAGRANT G.H. To 3 ft., branched at top, glabrescent; lvs. ovate, to 3 in. long, 2 in. wide, acute, serrate, whitish beneath; spikes cylindrical, 4 in. long, bracts large, conspicuous, ovate, acuminate, often tinged violet; calyx teeth acute, corolla blue, to 5⁄16 in. long. N.-cent. N. Amer. Hardy; dried lvs. used for seasoning and for making a tea. A honey plant.

mexicana (Kunth) Lint & Epl. [*Brittonastrum mexicanum* (Kunth) Briq.; *Cedronella mexicana* (Kunth) Benth.; *Gardoquia betonicoides* Lindl.]. MEXICAN G.H. To 2 ft., branched at top, glabrescent; lvs. narrowly ovate to lanceolate, to 2½ in. long, to 1 in. wide, serrate; spikes 4 in. long; calyx teeth narrowly triangular, corolla red, to 1 in. long. Mex.

nepetoides (L.) O. Kuntze [*Lophanthus nepetoides* (L.) Benth.]. YELLOW G.H. Sts. stout, to 5 ft., glabrous; lvs. ovate, 2–5 in. long, acute, coarsely crenate; spikes to 5 in. long, bracts ovate, acute; calyx teeth ovate, obtuse, corolla yellowish-green. Que. and Ont., s. to Ga. and Kans.

rugosa (Fisch. & C. A. Mey.) O. Kuntze [*Lophanthus rugosus* Fisch. & C. A. Mey.]. WRINKLED G.H. Sts. to 3–4 ft., erect, branched at top, white-puberulent; lvs. ovate-cordate, 2–4 in. long, 1–3 in. wide, acuminate, cordate to rounded at base, serrate, nearly glabrous above, whitish beneath, petioled; spikes 2–6 in. long, ¾ in. in diam.; calyx ¼ in. long, teeth triangular, corolla purple, ⅜ in. long. Late summer, autumn. E. Asia.

rupestris (Greene) Standl. Related to *A. cana;* lvs. linear to linear-lanceolate, to 2 in. long, ¼ in. wide; calyx teeth triangular, corolla rose. Ariz., New Mex.

scrophulariifolia (Willd.) O. Kuntze [*Lophanthus scrophulariifolius* (Willd.) Benth.]. PURPLE G.H. Related to *A. Foeniculum,* but generally conspicuously pubescent; fls. rose to purple. New Eng. to Nebr., s. to N.C. and Mo.

urticifolia (Benth.) O. Kuntze. NETTLE-LEAF G.H. Related to *A. Foeniculum,* but corolla tube ⅜–⅝ in. long. B.C., s. to Mont. and Calif.

verticillata: *A. breviflora.*

AGATHAEA: *FELICIA.* **A. coelestis:** *F. amelloides.*

AGATHIS Salisb. DAMMAR PINE, KAURI. *Araucariaceae.* About 20 spp. of tall, evergreen, usually monoecious, coniferous trees, native from the Philippine Is. to Australia and New Zeal.; lvs. broad, entire, leathery; male cones cylindrical, female cones ovoid or globose, scales deciduous, seeds 1 to a scale, 1–2-winged, maturing second year. Identification of immature trees or mature trees without cones is often difficult, for the adult foliage of any sp. is variable, the juvenile lvs. differ from adult lvs. in form and arrangement and are always larger, and different spp. have closely similar juvenile foliage.

The genus includes important timber trees and is a source of certain of the hard resinous copals. Most can be grown outdoors only in the milder, frost-free parts of the country. Zone 10. For culture see *Conifers.*

alba: *A. Dammara.*

australis Hort. ex Lindl. KAURI, KAURI PINE. Juvenile lvs. opp., linear-oblong, somewhat curved, bronze-green, often spotted and reddish, to 2½ in. long, adult lvs. subopp., elliptic to broadly oblong, sessile, ½–1½ in. long, ¼–¾ in. wide, blunt; male cones ¾–1¼ in. long, ⅜ in. in diam., stalked, axillary, female cones subglobose, 2–3 in. in diam. New Zeal. One of the outstanding trees of the world in size, beauty, and timber value. Source of kauri gum or kauri copal. Rarely cult., because young trees have sparse yellowish foliage and poor habit; plants cult. under this name are usually *A. robusta.*

Dammara (Lamb.) L. Rich. [*A. alba* (Blume) Foxw.; *A. orientalis* (D. Don) Hook. ex Rehd.]. AMBOINA PINE. Lvs. mostly opp., broadly lanceolate to ovate, petioled, 2½–5 in. long; male cones 2–3 in. long, ¾–1 in. in diam., stalked, supra-axillary, female cones subglobose, about 4 in. in diam. Malay Pen. to Indonesia. Sometimes cult. in tropics. Resin is source of Manila copal.

orientalis: *A. Dammara.*

robusta (F. J. Muell.) F. M. Bailey. QUEENSLAND KAURI. Juvenile lvs. mostly opp., oblong-elliptic to ovate, to 4 in. long, subsessile, adult lvs. narrow-elliptic, 2–4 in. long, ¼–⅜ in. in diam., sessile, axillary, female cones ovoid or subglobose, 4–5 in. long, 3½–4½ in. in diam. Ne. Australia. Most frequently cult. sp., in tropics and subtropics.

AGATHOSMA Willd. [*Barosma* Willd.]. *Rutaceae.* About 134 spp. of polygamous, heathlike shrubs or subshrubs, native to S. Afr.; lvs. often crowded and overlapping, opp., whorled, or alt., simple; fls. white, red, or lilac, solitary or few in axils of upper lvs., but mostly in terminal clusters, bisexual or unisexual, calyx 5-parted, petals usually 5, sessile or clawed, stamens 5, staminodes 5, often gland-tipped; fr. a caps., separating into 1–5 sections, each usually horned at apex.

The dried leaves of two species have been the source of the diuretic buchu. Grown as ornamentals in warm regions (Calif.), sometimes in pots under glass. Propagated by cuttings from mature wood except *A. corymbosa,* which should be propagated like *Diosma.*

betulina (Bergius) Pillans [*B. betulina* (Bergius) Bartl. & H. L. Wendl.]. BUCHU. Much-branched, glabrous shrub; lvs. obovate, to ¾ in. long, cuneate, sharply and closely serrate; fls. pink, ½ in. across, solitary at ends of short, axillary branchlets, filaments hairy, carpels 5. Principal source of diuretic drug in S. Afr.

corymbosa (Montin) G. Don. [*A. Ventenatiana* (Roem. & Schult.) Bartl. & H. L. Wendl.; *A. villosa* (Willd.) Willd.; *Diosma purpurea* Hort. ex Bartl. & H. L. Wendl.]. Low shrub, 1–2 ft., with pubescent branchlets; lvs. lanceolate, 3⁄16 in. long, glabrous above, hairy beneath; fls. white, lilac, or purple, in terminal clusters, filaments glabrous, carpels 2.

crenulata (L.) Pillans [*Barosma crenulata* (L.) Hook.; *B. serratifolia* (Curtis) Willd.]. BUCHU. Shrub, 5–7 ft.; lvs. lanceolate or oblong- to ovate-lanceolate, to 1¼ in. long, serrate, glabrous; fls. white, ½ in.

across, solitary at ends of short axillary branchlets, filaments pubescent basally, carpels 5. A source of diuretic drug, buchu.

ovata (Thunb.) Pillans [*Barosma ovata* (Thunb.) Bartl. & H. L. Wendl.; *B. scoparia* Eckl. & Zeyh.]. Much-branched shrub, to 6 ft., with pubescent branchlets; lvs. variable in shape, to ½ in. long, mostly with glandular crenations; fls. white, less than ³⁄₁₆ in. long, 1–4 in axillary clusters, stamens glabrous, carpels 5.

pulchella (L.) Link. [*Barosma pulchella* (L.) Bartl. & H. L. Wendl.; *Diosma pulchella* L.]. Much-branched shrub, to 3 ft., with pubescent branchlets; lvs. lanceolate-ovate to ovate, to ¼ in. long, with glandular crenations, glabrous, glossy; fls. white to pale mauve, ⁵⁄₁₆ in. across, 1–2 in axils of upper lvs., stamens glabrous, carpels mostly 3.

Ventenatiana: *A. corymbosa.*

villosa: *A. corymbosa.*

AGATI: *SESBANIA.*

AGAURIA (DC.) Hook.f. *Ericaceae.* One extremely variable sp., a tree or shrub, native to trop. Afr., Madagascar and Mascarene Is.; lvs. nearly opp. or alt., simple, leathery, glabrous to pubescent, glandular or setose; infls. of 1-sided axillary or terminal racemes, often clustered toward ends of brs.; calyx 5-toothed, corolla cylindrical, deciduous, stamens 10, ovary superior; fr. a 5-valved caps., seeds many.

salicifolia (Comm. ex Lam.) Hook.f. ex D. Oliver. Shrub or tree, to 60 ft.; lvs. narrowly lanceolate to oblong or elliptic, to 6¾ in. long, entire, acuminate; fls. white, greenish or sometimes becoming red.

mature, flowering once and dying, often suckering, rhizome lacking; lvs. in a basal rosette or along a short stout st., long-lived, large, succulent, usually with sharp terminal spine, margins often toothed or sometimes thread-bearing; infl. a dense spike, raceme, or panicle, usually with a prominent bracted stalk; fls. bisexual, perianth tubular to shallowly funnelform, segms. 6, erect to curved, stamens 6, exserted, ovary inferior, 3-celled, each cell with many, axile ovules in 2 rows; fr. a loculicidal caps., seeds flattened, black. The name has 3 syllables.

Some species are cultivated for fiber (henequen, sisal) or for the sap, which in Mex. is fermented (for pulque) or distilled (for mescal and tequila), others are grown as ornamentals in semiarid regions or in succulent collections.

Agaves need a soil of mostly loam and sand, good drainage and firm potting. Most species can be propagated by seeds, but often the flowers must be artificially hand-pollinated to obtain seed; some kinds are propagated by the suckers around the old plants or by rhizomes, others by stem buds, and a few by the bulbils which are found in the flower clusters.

albicans Jacobi. Similar to *A. micracantha*; lvs. in a basal rosette, to 1 ft. long, 4 in. wide, terminal spine, soft, marginal teeth weak; infl. spicate; fls. reddish-green, to 1½ in. long. Probably Mex.

americana L. CENTURY PLANT, MAGUEY, AMERICAN ALOE. Lvs. in a basal rosette, to 5 ft. long, nearly 10 in. wide, gray, curved or reflexed at tip, margin toothed but not horny; infl. paniculate, tall; fls. pale yellow, to 3⅜ in. long, perianth segms. erect, to 1¼ in. long, ovary

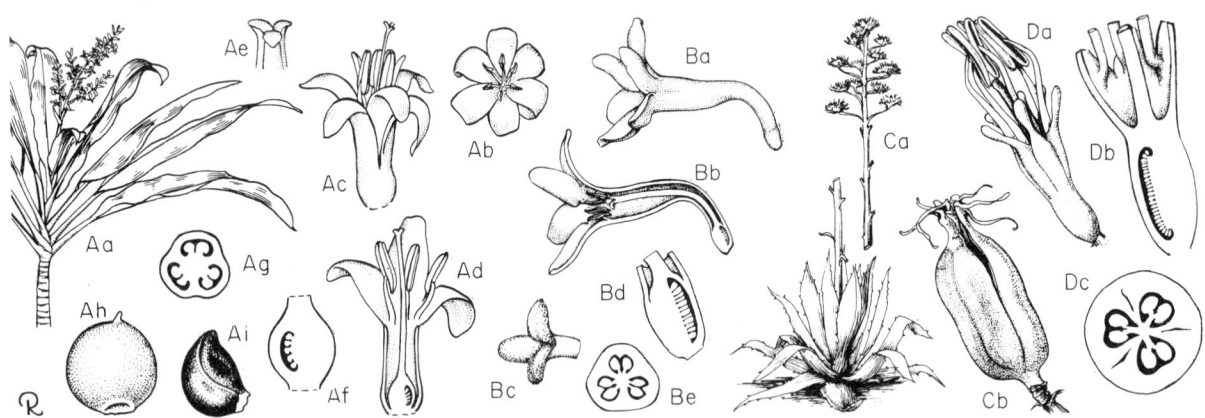

AGAVACEAE. **A,** *Cordyline terminalis:* **Aa,** upper part of flowering stem, × ¹⁄₁₂; **Ab,** flower, face view, × 1½; **Ac,** flower, side view, × 2; **Ad,** flower, vertical section, × 2; **Ae,** stigma, × 10; **Af,** ovary, vertical section, × 5; **Ag,** ovary, cross section, × 5; **Ah,** fruit, × 2; **Ai,** seed, × 5. **B,** *Polianthes tuberosa:* **Ba,** flower, × ½; **Bb,** flower, vertical section, × ½; **Bc,** stigma, × 2; **Bd,** ovary, vertical section, × 2; **Be,** ovary, cross section, × 2. **C,** *Agave americana:* **Ca,** leaf rosette and flowering scape, much reduced; **Cb,** capsule, × ½. **D,** *Agave* species: **Da,** flower, × ½; **Db,** flower, vertical section, × ½; **Dc,** ovary, cross section, × 2. (C from Bailey, *Manual of Cultivated Plants,* ed. 2.)

AGAVACEAE Endl. Monocot.; about 20 genera of dry regions, in warmer parts of both hemispheres; rhizomatous, per. herbs, long-lived rosette plants, or woody, branched treelike plants; lvs. mostly narrow, sometimes with marginal teeth, often congested in a basal rosette or at tips of sts.; infl. spicate to paniculate; fls. bisexual or unisexual, with perianth often united basally in a tube, stamens 6, ovary superior or inferior, 3-celled, ovules solitary to many on axile placentas; fr. usually a caps. or berry, seeds flattened. Genera in this family have been removed from the *Liliaceae* and *Amaryllidaceae.* Cult. representatives are: *Agave, Beaucarnea, Beschorneria, Cordyline, Dasylirion, Doryanthes, Dracaena, Furcraea, Hesperaloe, Manfreda, Nolina, Phormium, Polianthes, Sansevieria,* and *Yucca.*

Important fiber-producing genera, *Agave, Phormium, Sansevieria,* are included in the family as well as many ornamentals. They are mostly plants of dry regions and require a well-drained soil of loam and sand. Propagated by seeds, by suckers, or by cuttings of rhizomes.

AGAVE L. CENTURY PLANT. *Agavaceae.* Over 300 spp. native to N. Amer. and n. S. Amer., but sometimes naturalized elsewhere, rarely per., usually requiring many years to

shorter than perianth. Mex. Var. **americana.** The typical var.; lvs. long-acuminate, recurved to reflexed, terminal spine to 2 in. long, slender, marginal teeth larger, as long as or longer than their bases are wide. E. Mex. Cvs. include: 'Marginata', lf. margins yellowish-white to deep yellow; 'Medio-picta', lvs. with wide yellowish cent. stripe; 'Striata', lvs. striated with yellow or white; 'Variegata', lvs. dark green and yellow, twisted. Var. **expansa** (Jacobi) Gentry. Lvs. straight, short-acuminate, terminal spine short, to 1¼ in. long, thick, conical, marginal teeth shorter than their bases are wide. W. Mex. Cult. as a hedge plant and ornamental in sw. U.S.

andringitrensis: a listed name of no botanical standing.

angustifolia Haw. Sts. to 1½ ft.; lvs. to 3 ft. long, 3–4 in. wide, gray-green, terminal spine subulate-conical, black, marginal teeth black-brown when mature, ⅝–¾ in. apart; infl. paniculate, to nearly 9 ft.; fls. greenish, 2 in. long. Nativity unknown; cult. in tropics. Cv. 'Marginata' [cv. 'Variegata']. Lf. margins white.

applanata C. Koch. Lvs. many in a basal rosette, erect, stiff, to 4 ft. long, 4–6 in. wide, gray-green, terminal spine nearly 3 in. long, decurrent, margins horny, teeth curved; infl. paniculate, to more than 30 ft.; fls. yellow, 3 in. long. N. and e. Mex.

asperrima Jacobi. Lvs. few in a basal rosette, elongate-lanceolate, to 4 ft. long, 8 in. wide, dull dark green or with a whitish cast, rough on both sides, terminal spine to 2¼ in. long, decurrent, brown, margins sinuate-dentate, teeth triangular, curved, distant, mostly reflexed; infl. paniculate, very tall; fls. yellow, large. Tex. and n. Mex.

atrovirens Salm-Dyck [*A. latissima* Jacobi]. MAGUEY-DEL-CUMBRE. Lvs. in a massive basal rosette, spreading-erect, lanceolate, to 7 ft. long, 1 ft. wide, green to light glaucous gray, terminal spine 1½–2 in. long, decurrent on lf. margins and frequently in mid-apex of lf. also, margins nearly straight, with closely spaced moderate-sized teeth; infl. narrowly paniculate, to over 30 ft., with 20–30 globose umbels, fls. reddish, 3–3½ in. long. Mts. of Puebla-Veracruz border and Oaxaca (Mex.).

attenuata Salm-Dyck. Trunk to 5 ft.; lvs. elliptic, to 1½ ft. long or more, 10 in. wide, green to gray or whitish-coated, unarmed and with a soft tip; infl. spicate, to 5 ft. or more, sometimes bearing bulbils; fls. greenish-yellow, 2 in. long. Mex.

aurea Brandeg. Lvs. many in a basal rosette, narrowly lanceolate, to 3 ft. long, 3–4 in. wide, gray-green, terminal spine about 1–1½ in. long, decurrent, black-gray, marginal teeth many, straight or hooked; infl. paniculate, to 10 ft., fls. golden-yellow, 1½–2½ in. long, perianth segms. twice as long as tube. Baja Calif.

Bourgaei Trel. Lvs. in a basal rosette, repand, to 5 ft. long, 6 in. wide, gray, terminal spine conical, margins horny in upper third or more, teeth triangular, ⅜ in. apart; infl. paniculate, to 10 ft. or more; fls. to 3 in. long, perianth segms. nearly twice as long as tube. Cent. Mex.

bracteosa S. Wats. ex Engelm. Rosettes branching from lf. axils; lvs. to 22 in. long, 1½ in. wide at base, gray-green or pale green, tapering to a recurved tip without a terminal spine, marginal teeth minute; infl. spicate, about 3 ft.; fls. prominently bracted, without a tube, about 1 in. long, white, perianth segms. about as long as ovary. Ne. Mex.

brevispina Trel. Lvs. in a basal rosette, broadly lanceolate, to 40 in. or more long, 4 in. or more wide, dark green, dull, marginal teeth grooved, straight or recurved; infl. paniculate, to more than 12 ft.; fls. yellow, about 1⅝ in. long. Haiti.

candelabrum: *A. Cantala.*

Cantala Roxb. [*A. candelabrum* Tod.]. Stemless or short-stemmed; lvs. to 4½ ft. long, narrow at base, to 3¾ in. wide at middle, light or dark green, bright green and rough underneath, flexuous, tip often somewhat pendulous, terminal spine to ¾ in. long, grooved, not decurrent, black-brown, marginal teeth hooked, ⅜–1³⁄₁₆ in. apart; infl. paniculate, to 20 ft., with many adventitious plantlets on brs.; fls. to 2⅝ in. long. Nativity unknown.

carchariodonta Pamp. Lvs. in a basal rosette, ascending, to 14 in. long, 3⅝ in. wide, gray-green, terminal spine 1⅜ in. long, grooved, curved, decurrent, margins irregularly toothed to sinuate, teeth broadly triangular, hooked; infl. spicate, to 12 ft.; fls. nearly 1 in. long, perianth segms. 3 times as long as tube. Mex. An intermediate form between *A. lophantha* and *A. xylonacantha.*

caribaea Bak. An incompletely described sp.; material cult. under this name may represent more than one sp. and is not identified.

Celsii Hook. Lvs. in a basal rosette, soft-fleshy, spatulate, to 2 ft. long, 6 in. wide, abruptly narrowed to a slender tip, apple-green to gray-waxy, marginal teeth small, close-set, rather regular, brownish, a few or many, with forked tips; infl. spicate, to 4½ ft.; fls. yellow-green to light purple, 2 in. long. E. Mex.

chrysantha Peebles. Similar to *A. Palmeri*, but differing in having fls. yellow not tinged with purple; lvs. glaucous, marginal teeth to ⅜ in. long, ¾–1⅜ in. apart at middle of lf.; infl. paniculate, brs. ascending and about as long as fl. clusters; fls. many, congested. Ariz.

cochlearis Jacobi. Lvs. in a large, basal rosette, lanceolate-spatulate, to 6 ft. long, 14½ in. wide above the middle, olive-green, terminal spine to 2¾ in. long, partly grooved on upper surface, light gray-brown, marginal teeth pointing toward lf. base; infl. paniculate, to more than 25 ft., pyramidal; fls. yellow, 2⅜ in. long. Mex.

colimana Gentry. Lvs. many in a basal rosette, straight, linear, to 28 in. long, 1 in. wide, thin, flat above, terminal spine short, weak, margins brown-bordered, thread-bearing; infl. spicate, to 10 ft.; fls. pale yellow to lavender, to 2 in. long, perianth segms. recurved at flowering time. W. Mex.

colorata Gentry. Sts. short; lvs. few in a rosette, ovate, to 2 ft. long, 6¾ in. wide, often cross-banded and red-tinted, glaucous, terminal spine to 2 in. long, subulate, marginal teeth to ⁵⁄₁₆ in. long; infl. paniculate, to 10 ft.; fls. coppery-red to yellow, to 2¾ in. long, leathery, perianth segms. unequal. Sonora (Mex.).

connochaetodon: *A. margaritae.*

cubensis: *Furcraea hexapetala.*

cupreata Trel. & A. Berger. Lvs. in a basal rosette, obovate, to 30 in. long, light green, terminal spine 2 in. long, decurrent at sides, margins deeply sinuate, the large teeth irregularly arranged, with smaller ones between; infl. paniculate; fls. 2⅜ in. long. W. Mex.

decipiens Bak. FALSE SISAL. Lvs. erect to spreading, to 4½ ft. long, 4 in. wide, green, eventually covering a st. to 3 or rarely to 10 ft., terminal spine to ⅝ in. long, conical, not decurrent, black-brown, marginal teeth triangular, usually recurved, red-brown, ⅝–1¼ in. apart; infl. paniculate, to 20 ft., brs. with many adventitious plantlets; fls. greenish-yellow, 3 in. long. Nativity unknown.

deserti Engelm. Lvs. in a basal rosette, ascending, triangular-lanceolate, to 16 in. long, 2⅜ in. wide, gray-green, sometimes cross-banded, granular-roughened, terminal spine to 1¼ in. long, dark, marginal teeth straight or curved, pale, to ¼ in. long; infl. paniculate, to about 15 ft.; fls. yellow, 1⅜–2 in. long. Calif., Ariz., Baja Calif. and Sonora.

Desmettiana Jacobi [*A. miradorensis* Jacobi]. DWARF C. P. Lvs. in a basal rosette, linear-lanceolate, 20–40 in. long, 2¾–3½ in. wide, dark green to glaucous, terminal spine to ½ in. long, decurrent at sides, red-brown, margins unarmed or with minute teeth; infl. paniculate, to 10 ft.; fls. pale yellow, 1½ in. long. E. Mex.

falcata Engelm. Resembling *A. striata,* but lvs. stiffer, linear to falcate, to 20 in. long, ⅝ in. wide, light gray or often violet or red-brown, terminal spine to 1 in. long, very sharp, marginal teeth cartilaginous; infl. spicate, to 6 ft.; fls. to 1⅝ in. long. Mex.

Fenzliana Jacobi. Lvs. in a basal rosette, lanceolate, to 5 ft. long, 8 in. wide, greenish-yellow, terminal spine to 2¼ in. long, decurrent as much as 6 in., marginal teeth curved, dark brown, to ½ in. long; infl. paniculate, to more than 30 ft.; fls. yellow, about 3³⁄₁₆ in. long. Mex.

Fernandi-Regis A. Berger. Like *A. Victoriae-Reginae,* but lvs. more tapered, about 5 in. long, 2 in. wide at base, concave above, keeled beneath, dark green with white marginal stripes, terminal spine to ⅝ in. long, 3-angled, with 1–2 teeth at sides, black, margins not toothed, more or less detachable; infl. spicate; fls. as yet undescribed. Ne. Mex.

ferox C. Koch. Lvs. in a basal rosette, spreading, with recurved tip, or becoming prostrate, rigid, to 3¼ ft. long, 1¼ in. wide, keeled beneath, dark green, glossy, terminal spine to 3⅜ in. long, grooved toward base on upper surface, marginal teeth hooked, black-brown, to 1 in. long; infl. paniculate, to 30 ft. or more; fls. yellow, nearly 3⅝ in. long. Mex.

filifera Salm-Dyck. Lvs. in a basal rosette, lanceolate, 10–20 in. long, 1⅝ in. wide, clear green to dark green or purplish, terminal spine to ¾ in. long, margins thread-bearing, not toothed; infl. spicate, to more than 6 ft.; fls. greenish, becoming maroon, 2 in. long. E. Mex. Cv. **'Compacta'.** Lvs. to only 4 in. long.

fourcroydes Lem. HENEQUEN. Sts. to 4 ft., 10 in. in diam.; lvs. spreading, sword-shaped or oblanceolate, to 4½ ft. long, 4 in. wide, narrowed basally, gray-green or ashy, terminal spine 1¼ in. long, stiff, conical, black, marginal teeth often hooked; infl. paniculate, to 20 ft. or more, brs. with adventitious plantlets; fls. yellow-green, nearly 3 in. long. Yucatan (Mex.). An important fiber source.

Franzosinii Bak. Lvs. in a large basal rosette, erect, often arching, to nearly 8 ft. long, from nearly 7 in. wide and 6 in. thick at base to 16 in. wide at center, white-gray or blue-gray, rough, terminal spine to nearly 3 in. long, decurrent up to 8 in., margins somewhat undulate, teeth triangular, spiny, black-brown, to ¼ in. long; infl. paniculate, to more than 35 ft.; fls. yellow, to 2¾ in. long. Mex.

gracilispina: a listed name of no botanical standing.

guiengola Gentry. Lvs. few in a basal rosette, ascending, ovate to ovate-lanceolate, to 20 in. long, 10 in. wide, light gray or white-glaucous, densely papillate, terminal spine to 1¼ in. long, dark brown, marginal teeth blunt, with 1–2 apical cusps, dark brown, to ⅛ in. long; infl. spicate, to 12 ft. or more; fls. pale yellow or yellowish-white, to 1⅜ in. long, perianth segms. essentially separate. Oaxaca (Mex.).

heteracantha Zucc. Lvs. in a basal rosette, spreading-erect, rigid, broadly lanceolate, to 1 ft. long, 2½ in. wide, yellow-green, terminal spine about ½ in. long, chestnut-colored, margin chestnut-colored, horny, teeth white. Mex. The exact application of this name is not known; it has been variously applied, both botanically and horticulturally.

horrida Lem. ex Jacobi. Lvs. in a basal rosette without offsets, obovate-lanceolate, to 1 ft. long, nearly 3 in. wide, glossy dark green, terminal spine to 1⅝ in. long, red-brown becoming gray, margins with undulating horny border, teeth large, hooked, to ⅝ in. long. Morelos (Mex.).

huachucensis Bak. Lvs. in a basal rosette with offsets, ovate-lanceolate, to 16 in. long, 6 in. wide, light-gray-glaucous, terminal spine to 1⅜ in. long, grooved above, decurrent, brown, marginal teeth small or large, straight or flexuous, to ⅝ in. long; infl. paniculate, to 12 ft. or more; fls. bright lemon-yellow, to 2⅝ in. long. Ariz.

imperialis: a listed name of no botanical standing.

kaibabensis: *A. utahensis* var. *kaibabensis.*

Karwinskii Zucc. St. to 12 ft. or more; lvs. ascending to spreading, stiff, narrowly oblong to lanceolate, to 28 in. long, 1⅝ in. wide, green, terminal spine to 2 in. long, stout, black, marginal teeth stout, triangular, to 3/16 in. long, 1 to 1¾ in. apart; infl. paniculate, to 20 ft.; fls. red-brown, to 2⅜ in. long. Cent. Mex.

latissima: *A. atrovirens.*

Lecheguilla Torr. Lvs. in a basal rosette, falcately ascending, to 2 ft. long, 1¼ in. wide, green or bluish, often pale-striped on upper surface, terminal spine to 2 in. long, marginal teeth slightly recurved, confluent with narrow, detachable, horny border; infl. spicate, with short bracteoles. Tex. and n. Mex. Source of the fiber tula istle.

lophantha Schiede. Similar to *A. Lecheguilla*, but the lvs. spreading, rather thin, repand, infl. with long acicular bracteoles. E. Mex.

macroacantha Zucc. Lvs. in a basal rosette, elongate-lanceolate to linear-lanceolate, to 22 in. long, 1⅝ in. wide, stiff, gray-green to gray-white, terminal spine to 1¼ in. in. long, stout, somewhat decurrent, marginal teeth hooked, to 3/16 in. long; infl. paniculate, to 10 ft.; fls. reddish, flushed with gray, to 2¼ in. long. Mex.

margaritae Brandeg. [*A. connochaetodon* Trel.]. Lvs. in a basal rosette with offsets, nearly round to oblanceolate, 4–6 in. long and nearly as wide, dull green, with gray cross bands, terminal spine to 1 3/16 in. long, decurrent, marginal teeth 4–8, falcately curved; infl. paniculate, to 12 ft. or more; fls. light yellow, 2 in. long. Magdalena and Santa Margarita Is. (Baja Calif.).

Mariae-Reginae: a listed name of no botanical standing.

marmorata Roezl. Lvs. in a basal rosette, spreading, lanceolate to oblanceolate-spatulate, to 44 in. long, 10 in. wide, light gray to white or bluish, rough, terminal spine to ¾ in. long, rough, margins sinuate, teeth curved, small and large, to ¾ in. long; infl. paniculate; fls. golden-yellow, about 1¾ in. long. Cent. Mex.

micracantha Salm-Dyck. Lvs. in a basal rosette with offsets, ovate, to 18 in. long, 4⅝ in. wide, light green or grayish, terminal spine slightly bristly, marginal teeth many, small; infl. spicate, to 3 ft. or more; fls. green, to 2¼ in. long. Probably Mex.

miradorensis: *A. Desmettiana.*

missionum Trel. Lvs. in a basal rosette, broadly lanceolate, to more than 8 ft. long, 8 in. wide, dark green or gray-green, terminal spine to 1 in. long, decurrent, brown to gray, marginal teeth triangular, straight or slightly curved, to 3/16 in. long; infl. paniculate, to 20 ft. or more; fls. yellow, to 2¼ in. long. Virgin Is.

mitis Salm-Dyck. St. very short, ultimately with many rosettes; lvs. spreading, soft-fleshy, lanceolate, to 15 in. long, nearly 4 in. wide, dull green, terminal spine to 3/16 in. long, marginal teeth dense, minute, green, of 2 sizes; infl. spicate, to 5 ft. or more; fls. green-brown, to 1¾ in. long. Mex.

mitriformis Jacobi. Lvs. in a basal rosette, hard-fleshy, broadly elliptic, to nearly 30 in. long, 6 in. wide, dull blackish-olive, terminal spine to 3¼ in. long, slender, partly grooved, margins with a horny border below the terminal spine, teeth brown to gray, about ⅝ in. long; infl. paniculate. Mex.

mojavensis: a listed name of no botanical standing.

Murpheyi F. Gibs. Lvs. in a basal rosette with offsets, linear, to 26 in. long, 3¼ in. wide, light bluish-green to yellow-green, sometimes cross-banded, terminal spine to ¾ in. long, dark brown becoming grayish, margins undulate, teeth small, to ¼ in. long, ⅜–¾ in. apart; infl. paniculate, to 12 ft. or more, bearing bulbils; fls. pale waxy-green, with purplish to brownish tips, to 3 in. long. Ariz. and Sonora (Mex.).

neglecta Small. Lvs. in a basal rosette, ascending, then spreading, to nearly 10 ft. long, gray, terminal spine brown, marginal teeth many, narrow; infl. paniculate, to 40 ft. or more; fls. yellow-green, 2¼ in. long. Fla.

neomexicana Woot. & Standl. Lvs. in a compact basal rosette, oblong to ovate-lanceolate, to 1 ft. long, bluish-green, terminal spine brown-black becoming gray, margins horny, with 3–4 retrorsely hooked teeth in upper part, smaller ones in lower part; infl. paniculate, to 15 ft. or more; fls. dull brownish-red outside, deep yellow to orange inside, to 2⅜ in. long. New Mex.

nizandensis Cutak. Stoloniferous; lvs. 10–15 in a loose, nearly flat basal rosette, soft, to 14 in. long, 1¼ in. wide, dark green with a light central stripe, terminal spine ⅛ in. long, dark reddish, marginal teeth irregular, minute, pale; infl. paniculate, but brs. few, short, few-fld.; fls. yellowish-green, 2 in. long. Oaxaca (Mex.).

pachyacantha: *A. Shawii.*

Palmeri Engelm. Lvs. in a rosette with offsets, lanceolate, to 30 in. long, 4 in. wide, pale green to light glaucous-green or red-tinged, terminal spine to 2¼ in. long, brown to gray, marginal teeth regular, small, not more than 3/16 in., sometimes with smaller ones between; infl. paniculate, to 15 ft. or more, brs. horizontal, twice as long as fl. clusters; fls. pale greenish-yellow to white, reddish in bud, to 2¼ in. long. New Mex. and Ariz., s. to Sonora and Chihuahua (Mex.).

parrasana A. Berger. Lvs. in a basal rosette, obovate, to 1 ft. long, 6¼ in. wide, dull green with light gray-blue bloom, terminal spine 1 in. long, decurrent, brown, margins sinuate-dentate, teeth stout, curved, yellow-brown to gray, to ¾ in. long; infl. paniculate, to 12 ft., bracts purplish; fls. opening yellow. N.-cent. Mex.

Parryi Engelm. MESCAL. Lvs. in a basal rosette, stiff, erect or spreading, broadly oblong, to 1 ft. long, 4 in. wide, gray, terminal spine to 1 in. long, brown, marginal teeth linear or recurved, to ¼ in. long; infl. paniculate, to 15 ft. or more; fls. red in bud, opening creamy-yellow, to 1¼ in. long. Sw. U.S. to Mex.

parviflora Torr. Lvs. in a basal rosette, stiff, linear-lanceolate, to 4 in. long, ½ in. wide, dark green with white lines on upper surface, terminal spine 3/16 in. long, margins bearing short white threads, teeth few, basal; infl. spicate, to nearly 5 ft.; fls. yellow or greenish-yellow, small, ⅝ in. long. Ariz. and n. Mex. Subsp. **flexiflora** Gentry. Lvs. to 8 in. long. Sonora (Mex.).

Peacockii Crouch. Lvs. in a basal rosette, erect, becoming spreading, sword-shaped to obovate-lanceolate, to 2 ft. long, 4 in. wide, dark green, terminal spine 1 in. long, stout, brown, marginal teeth curved or hooked, irregularly spaced; infl. appearing spicate or racemose, to more than 15 ft.; fls. 3–5 on short brs., green, marked with red, to 2¼ in. long. Cent. Mex.

pendula Schnittsp. [*A. Sartorii* C. Koch]. Lvs. from a short st., narrowly lanceolate, to 2 ft. long, 2¾ in. wide, light green with pale central stripe, terminal spine 3/16 in. long, marginal teeth triangular, small, light brown; infl. spicate, to more than 3 ft.; fls. green 1¼ in. long. Mex.

picta Salm-Dyck. Lvs. in a basal rosette, curved upwards, lanceolate, to 6 ft. long, 8 in. wide at center, dark green or margined with yellow, terminal spine to 2 in. long, slender, marginal teeth triangular, red-dish-brown, distant; infl. paniculate, to 30 ft. or more; fls. pale yellow, to 3¼ in. long. Mex. Very similar to *A. americana.* The form with yellow-margined lvs. is prop. vegetatively, as seedlings have green lvs.

polyacantha Jacobi. Rosette dividing and branching from lf. axils; lvs. spreading, lanceolate, to 28 in. long, 4 in. wide, dark green or grayish, terminal spine ¾–1 in. long, black-brown, marginal teeth several, triangular, small, black-brown; infl. spicate, to 8 ft. or more; fls. red, 1½–2 in. long. E. Mex.

potatorum Zucc. [*A. Verschaffeltii* Lem.]. Lvs. in a basal rosette, fleshy, obovate, to 8 in. long, 4 in. wide, glaucous, terminal spine to 2⅜ in. long, grooved, brown, marginal teeth rust-brown, to 9/16 in. long; infl. paniculate, to 3 ft.; fls. greenish-yellow, 2¼ in. long. Puebla and Oaxaca (Mex.).

pumila Hort. De Smet ex Bak. Dwarf; lvs. in a basal rosette with offsets, erect, stiff, ovate-triangular, very short, gray-green, striped dark green beneath, terminal spine ¼ in. long, dark, marginal teeth hooked, distant, to 3/16 in. long. Probably Mex. Cv. **'Compacta'**, is listed.

Roseana Trel. Lvs. in a basal rosette, spreading, broadly lanceolate, to 20 in. long, 6 in. wide, glaucous gray-green, terminal spine, to 2¾ in. long, twisted, marginal teeth abruptly narrowed, curved, to 1 in. long; infl. paniculate, to 10 ft.; fls. to 2 in. long. Baja Calif.

Salmiana Otto ex Salm-Dyck. PULQUE A. Lvs. in a large basal rosette, spreading-erect with incurved tip, lanceolate, to 7 ft. long, 1 ft. wide, dark green, terminal spine 2 in. long, decurrent, margins sinuate-dentate, basal teeth confluent, cent. teeth separated; infl. paniculate, to 30 ft.; fls. greenish-yellow, 4 in. long. Cent. Mex.

Sartorii: *A. pendula.*

scabra Salm-Dyck [*A. Wislizenii* Engelm.]. Lvs. erect, rigid, oblong, concave above, to 3 ft. long, 6 in. wide, nearly white, terminal spine to ¾ in. long, slender, margins slightly sinuate-dentate, teeth stout, linear or hooked; infl. paniculate, to 12 ft.; fls. yellowish, to 2⅝ in. long. Mex.

schidigera Lem. Lvs. in a basal rosette without offsets, spreading, linear, to 20 in. long, ⅝ in. wide, light green, terminal spine to ½ in. long, margins with narrow horny border and many threads; infl. spicate, to 10 ft. or more; fls. red-brown, to 2¼ in. long. Mex.

Schottii Engelm. Lvs. in a basal rosette, with offsets, pliant and straight to falcate, narrowly linear, to 16 in. long, ½ in. wide, yellow-green to green, terminal spine to ½ in. long, grayish, margin with narrow brown border and few brittle threads; infl. spicate, to more than 8 ft.; fls. yellow, to 1¾ in. long. Ariz., s. to Sonora (Mex.).

Seemanniana Jacobi. Lvs. in a basal rosette, ovate to oblong-spatulate, to nearly 2 ft. long, 5–6 in. wide, glaucous to light green, terminal spine ¾–1½ in. long, margins sinuate, teeth fine, acutely triangular; infl. paniculate, to 12 ft., fls. yellow, to 2¼ in. long. Cent. Amer.

Shawii Engelm. [*A. pachyacantha* Trel.]. Sts. short to elongate, branching and forming clumps; lvs. elongate-spatulate, to 2 ft. long,

5 in. wide, dark green, terminal spine to 1½ in. long, stiff, somewhat curved, marginal teeth hooked, red, ⅛–⅜ in. long; infl. paniculate, to more than 10 ft.; fls. greenish-yellow, to 3½ in. long. S. Calif. and n. Baja Calif.

sisalana Perrine. SISAL HEMP, HEMP PLANT. St. to 3 ft.; lvs. spreading, narrowly lanceolate or sword-shaped, to 6 ft. long, 3 in. wide, stiff, bright green, terminal spine to 1 in. long, black-brown, margins unarmed or with a few teeth; infl. paniculate, to more than 20 ft.; fls. green, to 2⅝ in. long. E. Mex. Cult. for fiber.

sobria Brandeg. Lvs. in a basal rosette, lanceolate, to 2 ft. long, gray-green, marginal teeth narrowly triangular, curved, chestnut to glaucous, to ⅜ in. long; infl. paniculate, to 15 ft.; fls. light yellow, to 2 in. long. Baja Calif.

speciosa: a listed name of no botanical standing.

striata Zucc. St. short, branched in age; lvs. spreading, stiff, linear, to 18 in. long, ⅝ in. wide, gray-green with darker stripes, terminal spine to ⁵⁄₁₆ in. long, brown, margins entire; infl. spicate, to 12 ft.; fls. green, 1 in. long. Hidalgo (Mex.). Cv. 'Nana', is listed.

stricta Salm-Dyck. HEDGEHOG. St. thick, branched in age; lvs. spreading-erect to incurved, linear, to 14 in. long, ⁵⁄₁₆ in. wide, green, terminal spine to 1 in. long, very sharp, margin finely cartilaginous; infl. spicate, to 8 ft.; fls. to 1¼ in. long. Mex.

Toumeyana Trel. Lvs. in a basal rosette, subulate to linear, to 14 in. long, 1 in. wide, concave above, dark green, terminal spine ⅝ in. long, margins thread-bearing; infl. spicate; fls. greenish or pale yellow, to 1 in. long. Ariz.

triangularis Jacobi. Lvs. in a basal rosette, spreading, rigid, triangular-lanceolate, to 10 in. long, 2 in. wide, dull gray-green, terminal spine to 1 in. long, gray, margins gray-brown, horny, teeth slightly curved, to ⅝ in. long; infl. spicate. Mex. Var. **rigidissima** (Jacobi) Trel. Marginal teeth very many, small.

univittata Haw. Lvs. in a rosette with offsets, lanceolate or sword-shaped, to 2 ft. long, 2 in. wide, dull or glossy green with lighter central stripe, terminal spine about 1 in. long, brown, margins horny, teeth hooked, triangular, to ⅝ in. long; infl. spicate, to more than 10 ft.; fls. pale green, 2 in. long. Mex.

utahensis Engelm. Lvs. in a basal rosette usually with offsets, tapered upward, to 8 in. long, 1¼ in. wide, glaucous, terminal spine ⅜–8 in. long, marginal teeth small, triangular, ¹⁄₁₆ in. long or less; infl. to 8 ft. or more, paniculate but appearing spicate, with short-stalked clusters of about 4 fls. each; fls. yellow, to 1¼ in. long. Sw. U.S. Var. **utahensis**. The typical var.; cespitose, with rosette to 1 ft. across; lf. margin sinuate, terminal spine sessile. Utah. Var. **eborispina** (Hester) Breit. Lvs. olive-green, terminal spine 4–8 in. long, ivory-colored. Nev. Var. **kaibabensis** (McKelv.) Breit. [*A. kaibabensis* McKelv.]. Robust, with solitary rosette to 40 in. across, terminal spine decurrent for 4–6 in. Ariz. Var. **nevadensis** Engelm. ex Greenm. & Roush. Lvs. glaucous-green, terminal spine 1¼–3⅜ in. long, slender, dark brown. Calif.

variegata: *Manfreda variegata.*

Verschaffeltii: *A. potatorum.*

Victoriae-Reginae T. Moore. Lvs. in a basal rosette, stiff, to 6 in. long, 2 in. wide, blunt, dark green with white lines, terminal spine very small, sometimes with 2 smaller lateral spines, margins unarmed, white; infl. spicate, to 4 ft.; fls. pale green, to 2 in. long. Nuevo León and Coahuila (Mex.).

Vilmoriniana A. Berger. Lvs. in a loose rosette, erect to recurved, to 32 in. long, green, fleshy, to 3½ ft., terminal spine to 1⅝ in. long, more or less laterally compressed and decurrent, margins wavy, horny; infl. spicate. Nw. Mex.

virginica: *Manfreda virginica.*

Weberi J. F. Cels. Lvs. in a basal rosette, lanceolate-oblong, to 4 ft. long, 8 in. wide, green, terminal spine to 2 in. long, brown, margins entire or with few small teeth; infl. paniculate. Mex.

Wislizenii: *A. scabra.*

xylonacantha Salm-Dyck. Lvs. in a basal rosette, gradually tapering from base, to 3 ft. long, 3¼ in. wide, gray-green, terminal spine to 2 in. long, brown, margins undulate with large irregular teeth; infl. spicate, to more than 10 ft.; fls. greenish, to 1⅝ in. long. Cent. Mex.

AGDESTIS Moç. & Sessé ex DC. *Phytolaccaceae.* One sp., a vine with large, gray, tuberous root; lvs. alt., entire, long-petioled; fls. bisexual, white, in many-fld., axillary, loose panicles, sepals 4, petals 0, stamens 15–20, ovary partly inferior, 3–4-celled; fr. small, dry, 1-seeded, winged by persistent calyx segms.

Grown outdoors in southern U.S.; thrives in rich soil; propagated by seeds and offsets.

clematidea Moç. & Sessé ex DC. Climbing, to 50 ft., sts. slender, foliage ill-scented; lvs. cordate-ovate, to 3 in. long or more, petioles slender; panicles to 6 in. long; fls. fragrant, white, to ½ in. across, sepals oblong to obovate. S. Mex. to Honduras.

AGERATUM L. FLOSSFLOWER, PUSSY-FOOT. *Compositae* (Eupatorium Tribe). About 29 spp. of ann. herbs, subshrubs, and shrubs, native to s. Fla., W. Indies, and Mex. to S. Amer.; lvs. mostly opp., rarely alt., petioled or sessile, mostly ovate or lanceolate, usually serrate or crenate; fl. heads solitary or in irregular panicles or in cymose or corymbose clusters, discoid, involucres campanulate, hemispherical, or top-shaped, involucral bracts imbricate, in 2–3 rows, receptacle conical, naked or scaly; fls. all funnelform or tubular, bisexual, blue, purple, rose, or white; achenes 5-angled, pappus of 5–6 separate or united scales.

Ageratums require the culture usual for annuals; the dwarfer kinds are excellent for edging.

conyzoides L. Erect, pubescent ann., to 3 ft.; lvs. ovate, to 4¼ in. long including the pilose petiole, cuneate or rounded or rarely cordate basally, crenate, pilose to nearly glabrous above, pilose beneath; heads to ¼ in. across, in terminal cymose clusters, involucral bracts pilose to glabrous on back; fls. blue, lavender, or white. W. Indies, Mex., Cent. Amer., S. Amer.; a pantrop. weed.

Fraseri: Eupatorium rugosum.

Houstonianum Mill. [*A. mexicanum* Sims]. Ann., to 2½ ft.; lvs. ovate to triangular, to 4¾ in. long including the petiole, cordate to truncate at base, crenate or rarely dentate, pilose on both sides; heads to ⁵⁄₁₆ in. across, in cymose clusters, involucral bracts linear-lanceolate, glandular-ciliate; fls. blue, lilac, or lavender. Cent. and s. Mex. and adjacent Guatemala and Brit. Honduras. Cv. 'Album'. Fls. white.

Lasseauxii: Eupatorium Lasseauxii.

mexicanum: *A. Houstonianum.*

petiolatum (Hook. & Arn.) Hemsl. [*A. scabriusculum* (Benth.) Hemsl.]. Ann. or of longer duration, sts. to 2½ ft.; lvs. ovate to triangular, to 2¼ in. long including the pilose petiole, obtuse to slightly cordate basally, crenate, sometimes revolute, hairy on both sides; heads to ¼ in. across, in corymbose clusters, involucral bracts sparingly pubescent to almost glabrous; fls. lavender. Nicaragua to Panama.

scabriusculum: *A. petiolatum.*

AGLAOMORPHA Schott. *Polypodiaceae.* About 10 spp. of large epiphytic ferns, with fleshy, scaly rhizomes, native to trop. Asia; lvs. sessile, the basal part shallowly lobed, dry, harsh, brown, collecting humus, the upper part green, leathery, glabrous, deeply pinnatifid into broad, lanceolate, entire or undulate pinnae, veins netted, all with areoles having included veinlets; sori round, elongate, or in patches, indusium absent.

Cultivated as ornamentals in the tropics or as warm greenhouse plants. Propagated by spores or by division. Culture as for most epiphytes. See also *Ferns*.

coronans (Wallich) E. Copel. [*Polypodium coronans* Wallich]. Lvs. 2–4 ft. long, narrowed above brown base to wide green portion; sori oblong, often merging in a single row between main veins. Subtropics, Asia. Zone 10.

heracleum (Kunze) E. Copel. [*Polypodium heracleum* Kunze]. Lvs. 3–6 ft. long; sori round, in 2–3 rows between main veins, otherwise like *A. coronans.* Sumatra to New Guinea. Zone 10.

Meyeniana Schott [*Polypodium Meyeniana* (Schott) Hook.]. BEAR'S-PAW FERN. Like *A. coronans,* but lvs. 2–3 ft., fertile pinnae contracted almost to the midrib except for small lobes covered by round sori. Philippine Is. Zone 10.

AGLAONEMA Schott. *Araceae.* About 50 spp. of ascending or rhizomatous herbs, native to trop. Asia; lvs. inequilateral, oblong to lanceolate or ovate, mostly leathery, petioles sheathing; infls. several together, spathe expanded, greenish to yellow, short-convolute below, deciduous in age, spadix not united with spathe, covered with unisexual fls., the few female fls. lowermost; perianth absent; fr. an ellipsoidal, 1-seeded, orange or red berry.

For culture see *Dieffenbachia.*

angustifolium: *A. simplex* cv.

brevispathum (Engl.) Engl. Similar to *A. costatum* but lf. blades lanceolate, usually obtuse at base, petioles usually equalling or longer than blades; peduncle to ¾ as long as petiole, spathe 1½ in. long, spadix longer. Se. Asia. Forma **hospitum** (F. N. Williams) Nicols. [*A. hospitum* F. N. Williams]. Lvs. irregularly marked with small, white spots. Thailand.

commutatum Schott. Sts. ascending, 2–5 ft.; lf. blades mostly oblong-elliptic to lanceolate, usually less than 12 in. long and 4 in. wide, obtuse to subcordate, dark glossy green, more or less marked gray-green along primary veins, petioles shorter than blades, sheathing nearly to apex; peduncle to 6 in. long, spathe pale green, 1½–3½ in. long, spadix stalked, shorter than spathe; fr. to 1 in. long, turning yellow, then bright red. Philippine Is., ne. Celebes. Var. **commutatum** [*A. Cuscuaria* Hort., not (Aubl.) Miq.]. The typical var.; lvs. green, marked with a few, scattered, greenish-white spots. Var. **elegans** (Engl.) Nicols. [*A. elegans* Engl.; *A. marantifolium* Hort., not Blume]. Lf. blades to 10½ in. long and 3¾ in. wide, with narrow zones of pale green along primary veins on upper surface only, petioles to 8 in. long; spathe mostly 1¾–2¾ in. long. Cent. Luzon (Philippine Is.). Var. **maculatum** (Hook. f.) Nicols. [*A. marantifolium* var. *maculatum* Hook. f.]. Lf. blades to 8 in. long and 2¾ in. wide, medium green with pale green irregular stripes along primary veins on upper surface only, petioles to 5 in. long. Cent. Luzon (Philippine Is.). The common sort in cult. Cv. 'Albovariegatum'. Differs from var. *maculatum* in having white petioles, sts. and spathe. Var. **robustum** (Alderw.) Nicols. [*A. robustum* Alderw.]. Robust; lf. blades broadly elliptic, usually more than 10 in. long and over 4 in. wide, to 18 in. long and 8 in. wide, with pale green irregular zones along primary veins on upper surface only, petioles to 14 in. long; spathe to 4½ in. long. Known only in cult. Cv. 'Grafii': cv. 'Treubii'. Cv. 'Pseudobracteatum' [cv. 'White Rajah'; *A. pseudobracteatum* Hort.]. Sts. white, marked green; lf. blades green, with large irregular zones of gray-green and white adjacent to primary veins and with many scattered small white dots, spathes greenish-white. Cv. 'Treubii' [cv. 'Grafii'; *A. Treubii* Hort., not Engl.]. Plant relatively small; lf. blades narrowly lanceolate-oblong, to 10 in. long and only 2 in. wide, with large irregular blotches of pale green adjacent to primary veins on upper surface only. Cv. 'Tricolor' [*A. marantifolium tricolor* Hort.]. Lf. blade to 9½ in. long, dark green with pale blotches along primary veins above, mottled cream along the creamy midrib and main veins beneath, petiole as long as blade, pinkish; infl. ivory-pink, spathe succulent, margins inrolled. Cv. 'White Rajah': cv. 'Pseudobracteatum'.

costatum N. E. Br. SPOTTED EVERGREEN. Rhizomatous, sts. short, creeping; lf. blades ovate to lanceolate, to 6–12 in. long and 4 in. wide, acuminate, truncate to subcordate, typically black-green above with white midrib and few to many white spots, petioles usually shorter than blades, very short-sheathing at base; peduncle to 3 in. long. spathe about 1 in. long, spadix nearly as long, stout. Malay Pen. Var. **Foxii** Engl. Does not differ from the typical var. of the sp. Forma **immaculatum** (Ridl.) Nicols. Lvs. lack the white spots.

crispum (Hort. Pitcher & Manda) Nicols. [*A. Roebelinii* Hort. Pitcher & Manda; *Schismatoglottis Roebelinii* (Hort. Pitcher & Manda) Hort. Pitcher & Manda]. PAINTED DROP-TONGUE. To 4 ft.; lf. blades mostly elliptic, to 12 in. long and 5½ in. wide just above middle, obtuse to broadly acute at base, mostly greenish-gray, with dark green border and irregularly-margined zone along midrib, petioles to 8 in. long, long- and broad-sheathing, margins of sheath early scarious and ragged; peduncle to 4½ in. long, spathe to 2¾ in. long, spadix shorter, long-stalked; berries turning yellow, then red. S. Luzon (Philippine Is.).

Cuscuaria (Aubl.) Miq.: *Scindapsus Cuscuaria* (Aubl.) K. Presl, which is not in cult.; material offered as *A. Cuscuaria* is the typical var. of *A. commutatum*.

elegans: *A. commutatum* var.

hospitum: *A. brevispathum* forma.

integrifolium: *A. nitidum*.

marantifolium Blume, not Hort. [*A. oblongifolium* (Roxb.) Kunth, not Schott]. Sts. ascending, to 1 in. in diam.; lf. blades narrowly oblong to narrowly elliptic or oblanceolate, 10–13 in. long, 4–6 in. wide, obtuse-subtruncate at base, green, petioles as long as blades, long-sheathing; peduncle 5–7 in. long, spathe about 3 in. long, spadix long-stalked and ⅔ as long as spathe or less; berries red, to 1 in. long. Molucca Is. and New Guinea. Doubtfully in cult.; material offered under this name is *A. commutatum* var. *elegans*. [Var.] **tricolor:** *A. commutatum* var. *robustum* cv.

modestum Schott ex Engl. CHINESE EVERGREEN. Sts. green, ascending, to 2 ft.; lf. blades ovate to sublanceolate, to 8½ in. long and half as wide, long-acuminate, obtuse or rounded at base, crisped-undulate, glossy-green, petioles to 8 in. long, sheathing to above middle; peduncle to 4 in. long, spathe light green, to 3 in. long, spadix sessile, 1¾ in. long; pistils 9–13; berries orange, about 1 in. long. S. China to n. Thailand.

nitidum (Jack) Kunth [*A. integrifolium* (Link) Schott; *A. oblongifolium* Schott, not (Roxb.) Kunth]. Erect, to 3 ft.; lf. blades oblong to oblanceolate, to 18 in. long and 6 in. wide, cuspidate, cuneate at base, with 7–8 pairs of primary lateral veins, dark green, petioles to 10 in. long, sheathing nearly to apex, margins of sheath scarious and ragged; peduncle to 6 in. long, spathe to 2½ in. long, spadix stout, as long as spathe or longer. Burma, e. to Sumatra and Borneo. Cv. 'Curtisii' [var. *nitidum* forma *Curtisii* (N. E. Br.) Nicols.; *A. oblongifolium* var. *Curtisii* N. E. Br.]. The commonly cult. sort; lf. blades with silvery stripes along principle lateral veins.

oblongifolium: see *A. marantifolium* and *A. nitidum*; material in cult. under the name *A. oblongifolium* is *A. nitidum*.

pictum (Roxb.) Kunth [*Calla picta* Roxb.]. Sts. erect, to 2 ft., gray with age; lf. blade oblong to ovate, to 6½ in. long and 2½ in. wide, obtuse to rounded, finely crisped-undulate, upper surface dark blue-green with satin sheen and large, irregular, pale green and silvery blotches, midrib gray-green, petioles to 2½ in. long, broadly sheathing nearly or quite to blade, sheath translucent; peduncle 1–2 in. long, spathe inflated, dark green, becoming yellow, 1¼ in. long, spadix longer than spathe, stalked, the apical part obconoid-clavate, exserted, white. Sumatra. Cv. 'Tricolor' [var. *tricolor* N. E. Br. ex Engl.]. Lvs. spotted yellow and yellowish-green.

pseudobracteatum: *A. commutatum* cv.

robustum: *A. commutatum* var.

Roebelinii: *A. crispum*.

rotundum N. E. Br. Sts. decumbent in age; lf. blades orbicular-ovate, to 5 in. long and 4 in. wide, glossy dark green above with rose-pink to white midrib and primary veins, red-purplish beneath, petioles to 1¾ in. long, long-sheathing; peduncle and spathe each 2½ in. long, spadix strongly clavate, 1¼ in. long. N. Sumatra.

Schottianum var. **Brownii:** *A. simplex* cv. 'Angustifolium'.

simplex Blume. Long confused with *A. modestum,* but with sts. to 4 ft., lf. blades mostly oblong to narrowly elliptic or lanceolate, to 10 in. long and 4 in. wide, petioles shorter, to 4¾ in. long; peduncle to 3½ in. long, spathe to 2 in. long, spadix stalked, equalling or slightly longer than spathe; pistils 18–20; berries red, to ⅝ in. long. S. Burma, Malay Arch., Indonesia, Philippine Is. Cv. 'Angustifolium' [*A. angustifolium* N. E. Br.; *A. Schottianum* Miq. var *Brownii* Engl.]. Lf. blades narrow, to 7–10 times longer than wide.

Treubii Engl. A name of doubtful application; material grown under this name is *A. commutatum* cv. 'Treubii'.

AGNIRICTUS: *STOMATIUM.*

AGONIS (DC.) Lindl. WILLOW MYRTLE. *Myrtaceae.* About 12 spp. of evergreen trees and shrubs, native to W. Australia; lvs. alt.; fls. small, sessile, in dense, rounded heads, calyx lobes 5, petals 5, persistent, stamens 10 or 20, shorter than petals; fr. a 3-celled caps., seeds few. Allied to *Leptospermum,* but having fls. many, sessile, in heads, and ovules fewer (2–6) in each cell.

For culture see *Leptospermum.*

flexuosa (K. Spreng.) Schauer. PEPPERMINT TREE, AUSTRALIAN W. M. Tree, 25–35 ft., brs. pendulous, branchlets sometimes zigzag; mature lvs. lanceolate, entire, willowlike, to 4 in. long, inconspicuously 3-nerved, lvs. of immature trees broader, stiffer, usually prominently 3-nerved, borne on winged branchlets; fl. heads axillary, to ½ in. across, petals white, stamens usually 20. Spring–summer. The sp. most frequently seen and differing from others in its willowlike habit.

grandiflora Benth. Densely branched shrub, to 2 ft.; lvs. clustered, linear, to ½ in. long; fls. large, solitary or in 2–4-fld. heads, sessile in lf. clusters, calyx tube hairy, petals to ¼ in. long, obovate, stamens 20–30.

juniperina Schauer. Tall shrub or tree, to 25 ft. or more, brs. stiff, bark rough, stringy; lvs. clustered, linear, to ⅜ in. long, stiff; fl. heads ⁵⁄₁₆ in. across, terminal on short lateral branchlets, calyx tube hairy, petals broad-ovate, ⅛ in. long, stamens 10. Late winter–early summer.

linearifolia (DC.) Schauer. Shrub, to 12 ft. or more; lvs. linear to linear-lanceolate, to ½ in. long, obscurely 3-nerved; fl. heads small, axillary, petals short-clawed, stamens 10. Spring.

marginata Schauer. Shrub, to 12 ft., bark shredding; lvs. obovate-oblong, to 1 in. long, obtuse or mucronate at apex, obscurely 3-nerved, silky hairy, especially on margins; fl. heads to ¾ in. across, calyx tube hairy, petals white, stamens 10. Autumn and winter.

AGOSERIS Raf. MOUNTAIN DANDELION. *Compositae* (Cichorium Tribe). About 8 or 9 spp. of scapose, ann. or per. herbs with milky sap and well-developed taproot, native to

w. N. Amer., 1 in S. Amer.; lvs. mostly basal, glabrous or with evenly scattered hairs; fl. heads solitary, involucre nearly cylindrical to campanulate, involucral bracts nearly equal or imbricate; fls. all ligulate, bisexual, yellow to orange, anthers not tailed but sagittate at base; achenes beaked, pappus persistent, of 50 or more white, capillary bristles, not plumose.

aurantiaca (Hook.) Greene. Per., to 2 ft.; lvs. oblong-lanceolate, to 10 in. long, essentially entire to remotely pinnatifid; fls. burnt-orange, often turning purplish with age; achene with beak half as long as the body. B. C. and Alta., s. to Calif. and New Mex.

cuspidata: *Nothocalais cuspidata.*

glauca (Pursh) Raf. Per., to 2½ ft., essentially glabrous and somewhat glaucous; lvs. linear to oblanceolate, to 10 in. long, entire or with few teeth on shallow lobes; involucral bracts nearly equal, mostly sharp-pointed, sometimes with purple spots; fls. yellow, often turning pinkish with age; achenes hairy, with stout beak half as long as the body. B. C. to w. Ont., s. to Utah and Colo.

AGRIMONIA L. AGRIMONY, COCKLEBUR, HARVEST-LICE. *Rosaceae.* About 15 spp. of erect, per. herbs., mostly of the N. Temp. Zone; lvs. alt., interruptedly pinnate, lfts. crenate-serrate; fls. small, yellow, racemose, petals 5; fr. a bristly burr.

Sometimes grown in shady places or in the background for interest, but not particularly ornamental; also medicinal. Propagated by division in spring and by seeds.

Eupatoria L. To 5 ft., usually hirsute below; lvs. largely in lower part, lfts. 7–13, oblong to narrow-obovate, gray-hairy beneath, to 1 in. broad, rounded at base, with 6–13 teeth on each side; pedicels less than 3/16 in. long, lower bracts 3-lobed; petals golden-yellow, 3/16 in. long; fr. 5/16 in. long, obconic, deeply grooved throughout, with slightly spreading bristles. Eur., w. Asia, N. Afr. Herbage has been used medicinally; also a source of a golden-yellow dye.

odorata: *A. repens.*

parviflora Ait. Stout, to 6 ft., sts. densely hairy; lfts. 11–15, lanceolate-acuminate, gland-dotted beneath; fr. 3/16 in. long, outer bristles strongly spreading. Conn. to Ill., Nebr., s. to Tex.

pilosa Ledeb. Like *A. Eupatoria,* but lfts. with 3–7 teeth on each side, cuneate at base, pubescent beneath on veins only; calyx tube to 3/16 in. wide, petals pale yellow; bristles of fr. incurved, connivent apically. N. Asia, e. Eur.

repens L. [*A. odorata* Mill.]. To 40 in., villous, hairs not glandular; lvs. large, leathery, dark green above, grayish-green beneath, lfts. elliptic, to 2½ in. long; pedicels to ⅜ in. long, bracts often ovate, entire; calyx tube ⅜–½ in. wide, petals golden-yellow; lower bristles of fr. turned downward. Asia Minor.

AGRONOMY. Agronomy is an applied agricultural science dealing with the theory and practice of crop production and soil management in fields. Plantings of agronomic species usually occupy large acreages and may or may not be row crops. They include such crops as the food and fodder grasses, and plants (other than trees) producing textile and pulp fibers, sugar, seed oils, and numerous other products used mainly in industry.

AGROPYRON Gaertn. WHEATGRASS, DOG GRASS. *Gramineae.* Fewer than 40 spp. of usually per. grasses in temp. and cool regions of the N. and S. Hemispheres, often with creeping rhizomes, sts. usually erect; infl. spicate, green or purplish, usually erect; spikelets several-fld., sessile, flattened against the axis at each joint of a usually continuous rachis, rachilla at length disarticulating above the glumes and between the florets, glumes equal, firm, variously nerved, lemma convex on the back, rather firm, 5–7-nerved, acute or awned from the apex, palea about as long as the lemma. For terminology see *Gramineae.*

cristatum (L.) Gaertn. CRESTED W., FAIRWAY C. W. Distinguished from *A. sibiricum* in having spikes ovate-oblong or ovate, to 2¾ in. long, pectinate; spikelets crowded, divergent from rachis, horizontal to ascending, glumes and lemma short-awned, awn of lemma to 1 3/16 or rarely 1⅜ in. long; grain deeply grooved. Eurasia; introd. into the Great Plains; resistant to semiarid conditions. Adapted for hay and pasture use in the n. Great Plains.

desertorum: *A. sibiricum.*

elongatum (Host) Beauvois. TALL W. Sts. to 3 ft., with short rhizomes; lf. blades scabrous above, flat at first, then involute, narrow, stiff; spikes rather loose; spikelets 4–8-fld., 2-ranked, shorter than the internodes of the rachis, glumes ovate-oblong, rounded on the keel, obtuse, 5–7-nerved, half as long as the lemma, lemma truncate or notched at the apex. Eurasia; introd. for conservation and erosion control in the West.

inerme: *A. spicatum* var. *inerme.*

intermedium (Host) Beauvois. INTERMEDIATE W. Resembling *A. elongatum* but sts. to 4 ft., lf. blades short-involute, spikelets 3–8-fld., longer than the internodes of the rachilla, glumes about 5-nerved, lemma nearly always ending in a short point. Eurasia. Used for pasture, hay, and as soil binder in the West. The artificial hybrid *A. intermedium* × *A. trichophorum,* REE W., developed in S. Dak., is intermediate between the parents and not superior to either.

panormitanum Parl. Sts. erect, to 50 in.; lf. blades linear, flat, scabrous on both surfaces, 3-nerved; spikes slender, spikelets 2-ranked, few, large, loose, oblong-linear, 3–5-fld., glumes linear-lanceolate, as long as the florets, short-awned, 7-nerved. W. Medit. and Iran; introd. into Wash. Moderately drought-resistant.

pauciflorum: *A. trachycaulum.*

pectiniforme Roem. & Schult. Similar to *A. cristatum* but spikelets nearly glabrous, sometimes glabrate, midnerve of glume scabrous to long-ciliate. Russia; introd. as a range grass and escaped.

pseudoagropyron: *Elymus chinensis.*

repens (L.) Beauvois. QUACK GRASS, WITCHGRASS, COUCH GRASS, QUITCH G., QUICK G. Sts. to 3 ft. or more, erect or curved at base, with yellowish rhizomes; lf. blades flat, lax, usually sparsely pilose on the upper surface, mostly ¼–⅜ in. wide; spike 2–6 in. long; spikelets mostly 4–6-fld., with glabrous rachilla, ⅜–⅝ in. long, glumes shorter than spikelets, 3–7-nerved, stiffly pointed, lemma smooth, mostly 5/16–⅜ in. long, awn very short to as long as lemma. Eurasia; introd. and naturalized from Nfld. to Alaska, s. to N.C. and Calif.; Mex. A troublesome weed in the n. states.

sibiricum (Willd.) Beauvois [*A. desertorum* (Fisch.) Schult.]. SIBERIAN W., DESERT W., STANDARD CRESTED W. Sts. to 40 in., erect or bent at base, in dense clumps, without creeping rhizomes; lf. sheaths glabrous or the lower with spreading hairs, blades to ⅛ or rarely 3/16 in. wide; spikes linear, to 4 or rarely 6 in. long, not pectinate; spikelets ascending, nearly glabrous or somewhat pubescent, awnless or short-awned, glumes rigid, 1-keeled, awn of lemma to 1⅜ or rarely to 2 3/16 in. long; grain deeply grooved. Eurasia; introd. in Great Plains region for pasture and hay and naturalized, occasionally adventive in the East.

Smithii Rydb. WESTERN W. Sts. to 2 ft. or more, erect, with creeping rhizomes; lf. sheaths glabrous, blades stiff, usually flat when fresh but involute when dry, ⅛ in. wide or less, rough hairy or sometimes with long hairs on upper surface; spikes erect, 2¾–6 in. long, with rachis scabrous at the angles; spikelets closely overlapping, 6–10-fld., ⅜–¾ in. long, glumes rigid, tapering gradually to a short awn, ⅜–½ in. long, lemma hairy to nearly glabrous, about ⅜ in. long, acuminate to short-awned, palea rough-hairy on the keel. Ont., w. B. C., s. to Tenn. and ne. Calif.

spicatum (Pursh) Scribn. & J. G. Sm. BLUEBUNCH W. Sts. to 3 ft. or more, clustered, erect, often in large bunches, without creeping rhizomes; lf. sheaths glabrous, blades flat to loosely involute, mostly less than ⅛ in. wide, upper surface pubescent; spikes slender, mostly 3¼–6 in. long, the continuous rachis and the rachillae scaberulous on the angles; spikelets distant, usually more than 7 in a spike, mostly 6–8-fld., glumes rather narrow, usually about half as long as the spikelets, lemma about ⅜ in. long with strongly divergent awn ⅜–¾ in. long, palea as long as the lemma. N. Mich., w. to Alaska, s. to w. S. Dak., New Mex., and Calif. Var. **inerme** (Scribn. & J. G. Sm.) A. Heller [*A. inerme* (Scribn. & J. G. Sm.) Rydb.]. BEARDLESS W. Spikelets awnless. Mont. to B.C., s. to e. Ore. and w. Nebr.

tenerum: *A. trachycaulum.*

trachycaulum (Link) Malte [*A. pauciflorum* (Schweinitz) A. S. Hitchc.; *A. tenerum* Vasey]. SLENDER W. Green or glaucous, without creeping rhizomes; sts. to more than 3 ft., erect, clustered; lf. sheaths usually glabrous, rarely pubescent, blades mostly ⅛ in. wide or less; spikes erect or slightly nodding, slender, 4–10 in. long, sometimes 1-sided; spikelets scarcely to only slightly overlapping, few-fld., rachilla villous, glumes broad, nearly as long as the spikelet, not thin-margined, awnless, lemma glabrous, awnless or nearly so. Nfld. to Alaska, s. to Md. and Calif.

trichophorum (Link) K. Richt. PUBESCENT W., STIFF-HAIR W. Sts. with long rhizomes; lf. sheaths ciliate at the margins, blades rigid, prominently and closely ribbed on the upper surface, with scattered long hairs on both sides; spikes loose; spikelets falling entire at maturity, glumes very tough and rigid, oblong-lanceolate, very obtuse or more or less truncate at the apex, lemma hairy. S. Eur., sw. to cent. Asia; cult. for seed in the West and Southwest.

AGROSTEMMA L. CORN COCKLE. *Caryophyllaceae.* Three spp. of ann. herbs, native to the Medit. region; lvs. opp., entire; fls. solitary or in a loose, few-fld. dichasial cyme, bracts absent, calyx 10-ribbed, teeth 5, linear, leaflike, petals 5, clawed, stamens 10, ovary 1-celled, styles 5, alt. with calyx lobes; fr. a caps., dehiscing by 5 teeth, not stalked, seeds many, black.

atrosanguinea: *Lychnis Coronaria* cv.

Coeli-rosa: *Lychnis Coeli-rosa.*

Coronaria: *Lychnis Coronaria.*

Flos-Jovis: *Lychnis Flos-Jovis.*

Githago L. CORN COCKLE, PURPLE COCKLE. Silky ann. or bien., 1–3 ft., or more, much-branched; lvs. linear, to 4 in. long, to ¼ in. wide, entire, grayish, pubescent; fls., solitary, long-pedicelled, or in cymes, magenta-purple, rarely white, 1 in. across or more, calyx teeth longer than calyx, deciduous in fr., petals shorter than calyx, caps. with 5 teeth. E. Medit. region; naturalized in most temp. regions as a noxious weed in grain fields. The seeds are poisonous when eaten. Cv. 'Milas' [*A. Milas* Hort.]. Fls. to 3 in. across, rosy-purple.

gracilis Boiss. Similar to *A. Githago,* but smaller, more slender, less hairy; calyx teeth shorter than the tube, petals exceeding calyx, pale purplish, with black lines at base. Greece, Turkey.

hybrida: a listed name of no botanical standing used for *Lychnis* ×*Walkeri.*

Milas: *A. Githago* cv.

×**Walkeri:** *Lychnis* ×*Walkeri.*

AGROSTIS L. BENT, BENT GRASS. *Gramineae.* About 100 spp. of ann. or usually per. grasses, widely distributed; lf. blades flat or sometimes involute, scabrous; spikelets in open to contracted panicles, small, 1-fld., disarticulating above the glumes, rachilla usually not prolonged, glumes equal or nearly so, acute to awn-pointed, usually scabrous, lemma shorter, obtuse, mostly 3-nerved, awnless or dorsally awned, palea small to nearly lacking, nerveless or rarely 2-nerved. For terminology see *Gramineae.*

alba: *Poa nemoralis,* but the name has been universally misapplied to *A. gigantea* and *A. stolonifera.*

canina L. VELVET B., BROWN B. Per., sts. to 20 in., clustered; lf. blades to 2½ in. long, less than ⅛ in. wide; panicle 2–4 in. long, brs. spreading, scabrous, branched below middle; spikelets less than ⅛ in. long, glumes acute, the lower minutely scabrous on the keel, lemma a little shorter, awn exserted, bent, palea very small. Eur.; introd. and naturalized from Nfld. to Que., s. to Del., w. to W. Va. and Mich. Sometimes cult. for putting greens.

capillaris L. Per. sts. to 2 ft., erect, filiform; lf. blades narrow, flat, short, acute, margins scabrous; panicle open, spreading; spikelets not crowded, less than 1/16 in. long, pale or purplish, glumes obtuse, nearly spreading after flowering, lemma denticulate and awnless. Eurasia, N. Afr. Probably not cult. in the U.S. See *A. nebulosa* and *A. tenuis.*

gigantea Roth [*A. alba* of many auth., not L.; *A. stolonifera* var. *major* (Gaudin) Farw.]. REDTOP. Per., sts. to 5 ft., robust, erect or curved, from strong creeping rhizomes; lf. blades flat, 3/16–⅜ in. wide; panicle pyramidal, with spreading brs., reddish, to 8 in. long. Eurasia; cult. and extensively escaped in all the cooler parts of the U.S., where used for lawns and pastures.

maritima: *A. stolonifera* var. *palustris.*

nebulosa Boiss. & Reut. CLOUD GRASS. Ann., sts. to about 1 ft., slender, branching; foliage scant; panicle delicate, oblong, half as long as the plant, brs. whorled; spikelets less than 1/16 in. long. Spain. Cult. for dry bouquets. Sometimes erroneously called *A. capillaris.*

palustris: *A. stolonifera* var.

perennans (Walt.) Tuckerm. AUTUMN B., UPLAND B.G., BROWN B.G. Per., sts. to 3 ft., erect to somewhat decumbent, weak to rather stout, often with lax leafy shoots at base; lvs. many, blades flat, to 8 in. long and ¼ in. wide; panicle loose, pale to tawny, brs. spreading, again branched about the middle; spikelets to ⅛ in. long, sometimes aggregated toward the ends of branchlets, glumes acute or acuminate, lemma rarely awned, palea very small. Que. to Minn., s. to Fla. and e. Tex.; Mex.

pulchella: *Sporobolus pulchellus.*

stolonifera L. [*A. alba* of some auth., not L.]. CREEPING B. Per., sts. to 20 in., ascending from a decumbent and rooting base, rhizomes lacking; lf. blades flat, mostly ⅛ in. wide or less; panicle to 6 in. long, oblong, pale or purple, brs. ascending, some or all spikelet-bearing from near the base; spikelets less than ⅛ in. long, glumes scabrous on keel only, palea usually ½–⅔ as long as lemma. Nfld. to Alaska, s. to

Va. and Wash., introd. in S.C.; n. Eur. Var. **stolonifera.** The typical var.; sts. rather densely clustered; lf. blades mostly less than 2 in. long. Var. **compacta:** var. *palustris.* Var. **major:** *A. gigantea.* Var. **palustris** (Huds.) Farw. [*A. maritima* Lam.; *A. palustris* Huds.; *A. stolonifera* var. *compacta* Hartm.]. Sts. few, loosely stoloniferous; lf. blades mostly longer.

tenuis Sibth. [*A. vulgaris* With.]. COLONIAL B., RHODE ISLAND B.G. Per., sts. to 16 in., slender, erect, clustered, with short stolons but no rhizomes; lf. blades to 4 in. long and ⅛ in. wide; panicle to 4 in. long, open, delicate, with slender brs. naked at base; spikelets not crowded, glumes scabrous on keel only. Eur.; introd. and naturalized from Nfld., s. to N.C., W. Va. and Mich.; B.C. to Mont. and Calif. Has been confused with *A. capillaris.* Used for pasture and lawn.

vulgaris: *A. tenuis.*

AICHRYSON Webb & Berth. *Crassulaceae.* About 15 spp. of succulent subshrubs and ann. to triennial or per. herbs of the Canary Is., Azores, Madeira Is., and Morocco, erect and often shrublike, brs. often forking; lvs. alt., more or less spatulate, mostly thin; fls. 5–12-merous, mostly rotate, petals yellow, nearly separate, stamens twice as many, nectar glands 2-horned or digitate. Formerly included in *Sempervivum.*

For culture see *Succulents.*

Bethencourtianum C. Bolle. Densely soft-hairy per., to 6 in.; lvs. broad-spatulate, nearly petioled, ¾ in. long; fls. 8–9-merous, somewhat campanulate, golden, 5/16 in. wide. Canary Is.

dichotomum: *A. laxum.*

×**domesticum** Praeg. [*Aeonium domesticum* (Praeg.) A. Berger; *Sempervivum tortuosum* DC., not Ait.]: apparently *A. tortuosum* × *A. punctatum* (C. A. Sm.) Webb & Berth. YOUTH-AND-OLD-AGE. Sparingly hairy per., to 1 ft., divaricately branched from base; lvs. ¾ in. long and half as wide, blade tapering to the petiole; fls. 7–8-merous, golden, ⅝ in. wide. Early summer. Cv. 'Variegatum'. Lvs. broadly edged with white or some shoots wholly white.

laxum (Haw.) Bramw. [*A. dichotomum* (DC.) Webb & Berth.]. Robust, soft-hairy, ann. or bien., to 1 ft. or more, brs. forking; lvs. 1–3 in. long, blade nearly orbicular to somewhat rhomboidal, about as long as the petiole, widest near base; fls. 9–12-merous, pale yellow, ⅜ in. wide, sepals lanceolate. Late spring. Canary Is.

pygmaeum: *A. tortuosum.*

tortuosum (Ait.) Praeg. [*A. pygmaeum* C. A. Sm.]. Dense, viscid-downy per., to 6 in., sts. woody at base, much-branched; lvs. sessile, obovate-cuneate, ½ in. long, ¼ in. wide, fleshy; fls. 8-merous, golden, ⅜ in. wide. Late spring. Canary Is.

villosum (Ait.) Webb & Berth. Shaggy ann., erect, to 8 in.; lvs. ½–1¼ in. long, rhomboidal, blade longer than the petiole; fls. 6–9-merous, golden, ⅝ in. wide, sepals triangular. Late spring. Azores, Madeira Is.

AILANTHUS Desf. *Simaroubaceae.* About 15 spp. of tall, deciduous, polygamodioecious trees of e. Asia, E. Indies, Philippine Is., Solomon Is. and Australia; lvs. alt., odd-pinnate, ill-scented when bruised; fls. small, greenish, in terminal panicles, 5–6-merous, stamens 10–12, but 5–6 in bisexual fls., female fls. with deeply 2–5-parted ovary, style 1, stigmas 5–6, plumose; fr. a 2-winged samara.

One species, *A. altissima,* is widely planted as a yard and street tree; useful for its resistance to smog and freedom from insects and diseases. It grows on any upland soil and reproduces readily by seeds.

altissima (Mill.) Swingle [*A. glandulosa* Desf.]. TREE-OF-HEAVEN, COPAL TREE, VARNISH TREE. Rapid-growing tree, to 60 ft. or more; lvs. mostly 1–3 ft. long, lfts. 11–14, 3–5 in. long, oblong to lanceolate or ovate, entire except for 1–3 large, basal, gland-bearing or callus teeth, glabrous beneath; samara 1½–2 in. long, twisted, reddish-orange at maturity. China; naturalized in most of the U.S. except the extreme north. Only seed-producing plants should be planted, as the male fls. emit a sweetish to foetid odor. Var. **sutchuenensis** (Dode) Rehd. & E. H. Wils. [*A. sutchuenensis* Dode]. Petioles purplish, lfts. glaucous beneath. China.

excelsa Roxb. To 80 ft.; lvs. 1 ft. long or more, glandular-hairy, lfts. many, coarsely toothed; panicles often much-branched; samara to 2 in. long, ½ in. wide, twisted at base, copper-red, strongly veined. India.

glandulosa: *A. altissima.*

sutchuenensis: *A. altissima* var.

Vilmoriniana Dode. Tree, 20–50 ft.; lvs. 2–4 ft. long, lfts. 17–35, to 6 in. long, lanceolate to oblong-lanceolate, pubescent beneath; fls. greenish-yellow, in terminal panicles; samara 2 in. long. China. Cult. for food for silk worms.

AIPHANES Willd. [*Martinezia* of auth., not Ruiz & Pav.]. *Palmae*. About 35 spp. of prickly, monoecious palms of trop. Amer.; lvs. pinnate, pinnae truncate at apex, toothed; infl. among lvs., usually much-branched, rarely spicate, with 2 persistent bracts, the lower short, often concealed, the upper as long as infl., peduncle elongate, rachillae with fls. in triads (2 male and 1 female) near the base and above these with mostly paired, sessile or somewhat sunken, male fls.; male fls. with sepals small, acute, petals valvate, stamens 6, female fls. with sepals and petals nearly separate, staminodes in a ring

AIRA L. Not cult. **A. caespitosa:** *Deschampsia caespitosa*.

AIR LAYER: see *Propagation*.

AITONIA L.f. *Sapindaceae*. One sp., an evergreen shrub, native to S. Afr.; lvs. simple, alt. or in clusters; fls. purple, solitary and axillary, bisexual, sepals and petals 4, stamens 8, united in a tube, long-exserted; fr. a 4-angled, inflated caps.

    capensis L.f. Much-branched shrub, to 10 ft.; lvs. linear, linear-oblong, or spatulate, to 1½ in. long; caps. pink or purple, 1½ in. in diam.

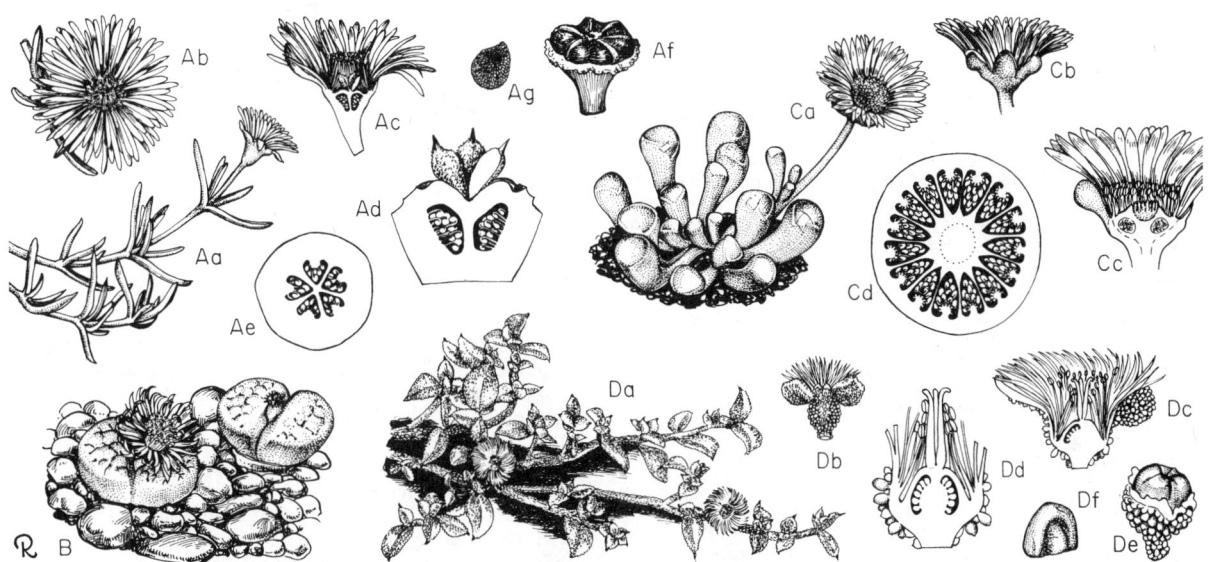

AIZOACEAE. **A,** *Lampranthus emarginatus:* **Aa,** flowering stems, × ¼; **Ab,** flower, × ½; **Ac,** flower, vertical section, × ½; **Ad,** pistil, vertical section, × 2; **Ae,** ovary, cross section, × 2; **Af,** fruit, × 1; **Ag,** seed, × 5. **B,** *Lithops gracilidelinata:* flowering plants among pebbles, × ½. **C,** *Fenestraria rhopalophylla:* **Ca,** plant in flower, × ½; **Cb,** flower, × ½; **Cc,** flower, vertical section, × 1; **Cd,** ovary, cross section, × 4. **D,** *Mesembryanthemum crystallinum:* **Da,** flowering stems, × ¼; **Db,** flower, × ½; **Dc,** flower, vertical section, × 1; **Dd,** pistil and base of flower, vertical section, × 2; **De,** fruit, × ¾; **Df,** seed, × 8.

united to petals, pistil 3-celled; fr. red, endocarp bony, often pitted, with 3 pores at or above middle.

    Tender palms grown in the tropics or in Zone 10b. For culture see *Palms*.

    acanthophylla (Mart.) Burret [*Bactris acanthophylla* Mart.; *Martinezia acanthophylla* (Mart.) Becc.]. To 15 ft. or more, trunk with sharp black spines; pinnae many, alt. or nearly opp., mostly not prickly, elongate, with nearly parallel sides below a somewhat broadened apex; upper bract of infl. prickly. Puerto Rico.

    caryotifolia (HBK) H. Wendl. [*Martinezia caryotifolia* HBK]. RUFFLE PALM, SPINE P. To 25 ft. or more; sheath, petiole, and lf. rachis prickly; pinnae in groups of 4–6 along rachis, wedge-shaped, broad and toothed at apex, prickly on veins at least underneath. N. S. Amer.

    corallina (Mart.) H. Wendl. [*Martinezia corallina* Mart.]. To 15 ft. or more, trunk densely spiny; pinnae many, alt. or nearly opp., with prickles on veins underneath, elongate with nearly parallel sides below the scarcely broadened truncate apex; upper bract of infl. prickly in lower half; endocarp prominently pitted. Martinique. Sometimes erroneously called *A. minima* in hort.

    erosa (Linden) Burret [*Martinezia erosa* Linden]. To 20 ft.; pinnae with nearly parallel sides, prolonged on upper margin, not prickly underneath; upper bract of infl. not prickly basally; endocarp not markedly pitted. Barbados.

    Lindeniana (H. Wendl.) H. Wendl. [*Martinezia Lindeniana* H. Wendl.]. To 15 ft. or more; lvs. with petiole and rachis black-prickly, pinnae in groups of 4–6 along the rachis, narrowly wedge-shaped, to 14 in. long, 1⅝ in. wide; infl. elongate, simply branched, with long rachillae; fr. rose-red. Colombia.

    minima: a name erroneously applied to *A corallina* in hort.

    truncata (Brongn. ex Mart.) H. Wendl. [*Martinezia truncata* Brongn. ex Mart.]. Lvs. 4–5 ft. long, pinnae in groups of 4–6 along the rachis, wedge-shaped; bracts densely prickly. Bolivia. A poorly known sp.; plants cult. under this name probably belong to another sp.

AIZOACEAE F. Rudolphi [*Ficoidaceae* Juss.; *Mesembryanthemaceae* Fenzl]. CARPETWEED FAMILY. Dicot.; about 130 genera and over 1200 spp. of mostly low, succulent herbs or subshrubs in trop. and subtrop. regions, especially abundant in S. Afr.; lvs. alt. or opp.; fls. regular, bisexual, calyx 4–8-parted, petals 0 or many, in 1 or more series, separate or united, or replaced by staminodes, stamens (1–)4–5 to many, ovary superior or inferior, 1–5-to many-celled, with 1 to many ovules in each cell, styles as many as ovary cells, separate or rarely united; fr. usually a caps. The plant is sometimes reduced to 2 or several fleshy, globular lvs. resembling large pebbles on a beach, particularly in arid desert regions such as S. Afr. At one time most of the spp. were included in *Mesembryanthemum*, formerly a large genus. Cult. as ornamental exotics are these genera: *Acrodon, Aloinopsis, Antegibbaeum, Aptenia, Argyroderma, Bergeranthus, Braunsia, Carpanthea, Carpobrotus, Carruanthus, Cephalophyllum, Chasmatophyllum, Cheiridopsis, Conicosia, Conophytum, Cylindrophyllum, Delosperma, Didymaotus, Dinteranthus, Dorotheanthus, Drosanthemum, Faucaria, Fenestraria, Frithia, Gibbaeum, Glottiphyllum, Hereroa, Herreanthus, Imitaria, Juttadinteria, Kensitia, Lampranthus, Lapidaria, Lithops, Maleophora, Mesembryanthemum, Monilaria, Nananthus, Neohenricia, Odontophorus, Oophytum, Ophthalmophyllum, Oscularia, Pleiospilos, Psammophora, Rabiea, Rhinephyllum, Rhombophyllum, Ruschia, Schwantesia, Semnanthe, Stomatium, Titanopsis, Trichodiadema,* and *Vanheerdia.*

Drainage and sun are of primary importance in their culture. They are tolerant of heat and mostly not hardy outdoors in the North. Propagated by seeds, by division, and by leaf cuttings.

AJUGA L. BUGLEWEED. *Labiatae.* About 40 spp. of ann. or per. herbs, of the temp. Old World, sts. mostly square in cross section; lvs. opp., often crenate to entire; fls. in verticillasters, arranged in terminal spikes; calyx campanulate, 5-toothed, corolla blue, white, or rose, tube exserted, with ring of hairs inside, limb 2-lipped, upper lip very short, lower lip 3-lobed, stamens 4, in 2 pairs, usually exserted; fr. of 4 obovoid, net-veined nutlets.

Ajugas reproduce vegetatively by runners, making them desirable as ground covers; they bloom in spring and early summer. Easily propagated by division. *Ajuga genevensis, A. pyramidalis,* and *A. reptans* hybridize readily.

alpina: *A. genevensis.*

Brockbankii: a listed name of no botanical standing for *A. genevensis.*

Chia Schreb. Decumbent, short-lived, to 12 in., glabrous to densely hairy; lvs. usually 3-parted, to 1 in. long, basal lvs. long-attenuate, st. lvs. short-attenuate; fls. 2–4 at each node, calyx cup-shaped, 5-toothed, to ³⁄₁₆ in. long, corolla to 1 in. long, yellow with red or purple markings; nutlets transversely rugose. Summer. Se. and e.-cent. Eur. Considered by some to be 1 of 2 subspp. of *A. Chamaepitys* (L.) Schreb., an ann., with smaller corolla, and reticulately veined nutlets.

genevensis L. [*A. alpina* L.; *A. rugosa* Host]. Rhizomatous, sts. 4–16 in., nearly glabrous to densely hairy; lower lvs. oblong-spatulate, to 4½ in. long, 2 in. wide; verticillasters distant, 6- to many-fld., bracts obovate, blue or violet-tinged; calyx ¼ in. long, teeth about as long as tube, corolla ½–¾ in. long, bright blue, rarely pink or white, tube longer than calyx, upper lip 2-toothed. Spring. Eurasia. Hardy; for the sunny rock garden. Cvs. are: 'Alba', fls. creamy-white; 'Rosea', fls. rose-pink; 'Variegata', lvs. mottled creamy-white.

metallica [var.] **crispa:** a listed name of no botanical standing for *A. pyramidalis* cv.

pyramidalis L. Rhizomatous, without stolons, sts. 2–12 in., nearly glabrous or hairy; basal lvs. spatulate, to 4 in. long, to 2 in. wide; verticillasters crowded, 4–8-fld.; calyx teeth as long as tube, corolla to ⅝ in. long, pale violet-blue, rarely pink or white, tube longer than calyx, upper lip entire. Early summer. Eur. Cv. 'Metallica Crispa' [*A. metallica crispa* Hort.]. To 5 in., lvs. purplish-brown, margin crisped.

repens: *A. reptans.*

reptans L. [*A. repens* N. Tayl.]. CARPET B. Stoloniferous, to 10 in., often less, pubescent; basal lvs. under 2½ in. long and 1 in. wide, st. lvs. smaller, ovate, usually nearly sessile; verticillasters crowded, usually 6-fld., bracts often tinged blue; calyx ¼ in. long, teeth about as long as tube, corolla blue, rarely pink or white, tube longer than calyx, upper lip entire. Spring. Eur. Cvs. are: 'Alba', fls. creamy-white; 'Albovariegata': 'Variegata'; 'Atropurpurea', lvs. bronze-purple, fls. dark purple; 'Compacta', of dense habit; 'Giant Bronze', lvs. large, metallic-bronze, crisped; 'Giant Green', lvs. bright green; 'Jungle Bronze', sts. tall, lvs. bronze, crisped, spikes to 10 in.;' 'Jungle Green', lvs. roundish, crisped, green; 'Multicoloris', lvs. mottled red, white, and yellow on green; 'Purpurea', lvs. purplish, fls. dark purple; 'Rosea', fls. rose-pink; 'Rubra', fls. purplish-red; 'Tottenhamii', lvs. turning bronze-purple in autumn, fls. purple; 'Variegata' [cv. 'Albovariegata'; probably *A. variegata* Hort.], lvs. mottled creamy-white.

rugosa: *A. genevensis.*

Tottenhamii: a listed name of no botanical standing for *A. reptans* cv.

variegata: probably *A. reptans* cv.

AKEBIA Decne. *Lardizabalaceae.* Two spp. of monoecious, hardy, twining shrubs, native to temp. e. Asia; lvs. half-evergreen, alt., palmately compound, lfts. 3–5, stalked, emarginate; fls. purplish, in axillary racemes, sepals 3, male fls. toward apex of the raceme, stamens 6, female fls. below, pistils 3–12; fr. an ovoid-oblong, bluish or purple berry, dehiscent along 1 side, seeds many, black.

Akebias thrive in sun and well-drained soil; propagated by seeds, hard wood and green wood cuttings, and root division. The edible but insipid fruit is seldom produced in cultivation.

lobata: *A. trifoliata.*

quinata (Houtt.) Decne. FIVE-LEAF A., CHOCOLATE VINE. Lfts. 5, entire; fls. fragrant. Spring. Japan, China, Korea.

trifoliata (Thunb.) G. Koidz. [*A. lobata* Decne.]. THREE-LEAF A. Lfts. 3, coarsely toothed or entire. Spring. Japan, China.

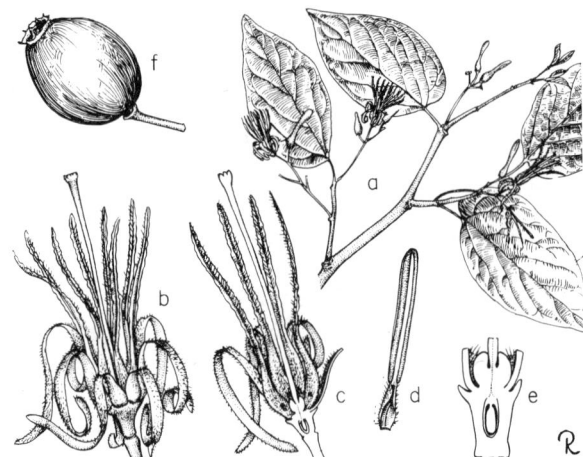

ALANGIACEAE. *Alangium chinense:* **a,** flowering branch, × ½; **b,** flower, × 1½; **c,** flower, vertical section, × 1½; **d,** upper part of stamen, × 2; **e,** ovary, vertical section, × 4; **f,** fruit, × 2. (From Lawrence, *Taxonomy of Vascular Plants.*)

ALANGIACEAE DC. ALANGIUM FAMILY. Dicot.; 1 genus, *Alangium,* of about 20 spp. of trees or sometimes shrubs or climbers, centered in s. Asia but reaching Afr., Australia, and Japan; lvs. alt., 2-ranked, simple, rarely lobed, without stipules; fls. in cymose, axillary clusters, bisexual, regular, calyx 4–10-toothed, petals as many as teeth of calyx, strap-shaped, valvate-cylindrical in bud, usually reflexed at flowering, stamens separate, as many as the petals and alternating with them or up to 6 times as many, filaments sometimes differentiated into an upper and lower portion, disc present above the ovary, ovary inferior, 1–2-celled, style simple, stigma expanded, elongate or 2–3-cleft; fr. drupaceous, crowned by the calyx teeth, seeds 1–2.

ALANGIUM Lam. *Alangiaceae.* Characteristics those of the family.

chinense (Lour.) Harms. Shrub or tree, to 50 ft.; lvs. rounded to oblong-ovate, to 12 in. long, often acuminate-toothed or -lobed, rarely palmately 3–5-parted; cymes 3–23-fld., peduncles ½–1½ in. long; petals 5–8, white, yellowish, or orangish, rarely red, to ¾ in. long, stamens as many as and nearly as long as petals, filaments bearded at tip of lower portion, glabrous above; fr. drupaceous, dark violet, to ½ in. long, seeds 1–2. Found nearly through the range of the genus, but not in Australia. May be confused with the closely related *A. platanifolium.* Probably hardy in the s. and Pacific states.

Lamarckii: *A. salviifolium.*

platanifolium (Siebold & Zucc.) Harms. Closely related to *A. chinense,* but having fls. longer and in 1–7-fld. cymes. Japan, Korea. Zone 8.

salviifolium (L. f.) Wanger. [*A. Lamarckii* Thwaites]. Climbing shrub to small tree, to 40 ft., often spiny; lvs. lanceolate to obovate, to 10 in. long, entire, not lobed; cymes 1–17-fld., nearly sessile; petals 5–10, white, greenish, or rarely yellow, to 1 in. long, stamens 10–32, filaments shorter than anthers, conspicuously divided into an upper and lower portion; fr. drupaceous, dark red, to ⅞ in. long, 1-seeded. Trop. Asia and Comoro Is.

ALBERTA E. H. Mey. *Rubiaceae.* Three to 5 spp. of shrubs or trees, 1 native to S. Afr., the others to Madagascar; lvs. opp., subsessile, stipules broad, cuplike; fls. in a terminal panicle, corolla funnelform, tube long, somewhat curved, corolla lobes 5, short, stamens 5, anthers sessile, included in corolla tube; fr. a drupe, made conspicuous by 2 enlarged, persistent calyx lobes.

magna E. H. Mey. Evergreen tree, to 30 ft.; lvs. elliptic to oblong, to 6 in. long; fls. red, corolla tube to 1¼ in. long, lobes to ⅛ in. long; drupe about ¼ in. long, persistent calyx lobes red, 1 in. long. Handsome tree with showy fls. and conspicuous frs. S. Afr.

ALBIZIA Durazz. (Often but not originally spelled *Albizzia.*) ALBIZZIA. *Leguminosae* (subfamily *Mimosoideae*). About 100–150 spp. of trees or shrubs, native to the Old

World; lvs. alt., deciduous, 2-pinnate; fls. in a plumelike or tassel-like head or spike, white, green-yellow, or pink, stamens many, exserted, united into a tube enclosing ovary; fr. a flat, straplike legume, without partitions.

Planted as an ornamental, mostly in tropics and subtropics. All species tender except *A. Julibrissin*. Culture as for *Acacia*.

amara (Roxb.) L. H. Boivin. Tree; lfts. linear, ⅛ in. long, obtuse; fl. heads on short peduncles, clustered at nodes of short lateral brs.; stamen tube reddish; fr. linear-oblong, to 8 in. long. Trop. Afr.

capensis: a listed name of no botanical standing.

coriaria Welw. ex D. Oliver. Tree, to 120 ft.; differs from *A. Lebbeck* in having lfts. usually ⅝ in. long; fls. sessile, corolla white, upper half of stamens red; fr. leathery, shorter, 5–8 in. long. Angola to Kenya.

distachya (Venten.) Macbr. [*A. lophantha* (Willd.) Benth.; *Acacia lophantha* Willd.]. PLUME ALBIZZIA. Shrub or tr/e, to 20 ft.; lfts. ⁵⁄₁₆ in. long; fls. yellow, in spikes 2 in. long; fr. 3 in. long. Australia.

Julibrissin Durazz. [*Acacia Julibrissin* (Durazz.) Willd.; *Mimosa Nemu* Poir.]. SILK TREE, MIMOSA, MIMOSA TREE. Tree, to 40 ft., with spreading crown; lvs 9–12 in. long or more, lfts. many, curved-oblong, ¼ in. long; fls. pink, in heads crowded toward ends of brs.; fr. thin, to 6 in. long and less than 1 in. wide, glabrous. Iran to Japan; now widespread and naturalized in se. U.S. Zone 7b. Cv. 'Alba'. Fls. white. Cv. 'Rosea' [var. *rosea* Mouill.]. Smaller; fls. bright pink. Var. **mollis** (Wallich) Benth. Lfts. broader, to ¼ in. wide, and densely pubescent, as are peduncles and calyces. N. India, Nepal. Var. **rosea:** cv. 'Rosea'.

Kalkora (Roxb.) Prain. Differs from *A. Lebbeck* in having lfts. oblong, corolla yellowish-white, stamens pink, and fr. to 6 in. long, on long stalk. India.

Lebbeck (L.) Benth. WOMAN'S-TONGUE TREE, LEBBEK TREE, SIRIS TREE. Tree, to 50 ft.; lfts. oblong, 1–1¾ in. long; fls. greenish-yellow, pedicelled, in heads on clustered peduncles; fr. 6–12 in. long, 1½–2 in. wide, remaining on tree long after lvs. fall. Trop. Asia; naturalized in W. Indies and Afr.

longipedata (Pitt.) Britt. & Rose. Large tree; lfts. oblique-obovate to oblong-ovate, to 1½ in. long, pubescent on both surfaces; fls. pedicelled, in umbels on peduncles to 3 in. long, stamens pink or white; fr. to 8 in. long, densely pubescent. Guatemala to Venezuela.

lophantha: *A. distachya*.

odoratissima (Willd.) Benth. Large tree; lfts. wide-oblong, strongly inequilateral, to 1½ in. long, glaucous beneath; fls. small, yellowish-white, sessile, in few-fld. heads in panicles 5–12 in. long; fr. to 9 in. long and 1½ in. across, the walls thin and embossed by the round seeds. Ceylon and India to Thailand. Sometimes called CEYLON ROSE-WOOD from the fragrant wood.

procera (Roxb.) Benth. Tree, to 80 ft.; lfts. elliptic-oblong, to 1 in. long, oblique; fls. greenish-white, in small heads in loose, terminal panicles; fr. narrow, to 7 in. long. Trop. Asia and Australia.

rhodesica Davy. Tree, to 30 ft., trunk to 12 in. in diam., bark peeling; lfts. to 1½ in. long, basally oblique; fls. white, in heads, these in groups of 2–6 on elongate peduncles; fr. stout, to 12 in. long. Rhodesia and Nyasaland, where called RED-PAPER TREE.

Richardiana (Wallich ex Voigt) King & Prain. Tree, to 80 ft.; lvs. to 7 in. long, lfts. linear, inequilateral, to ¼ in. long; fl. heads many-fld., in small panicles about 2 in. long; fr. thin, 4–5 in. long. Madagascar.

stipulata (Roxb.) L. H. Boivin. Tall tree; lfts. narrow, inequilateral, ¼–⁵⁄₁₆ in. long, glaucous beneath, stipules large, cordate; fl. heads in terminal, simple or compound racemes with densely pubescent brs.; fr. to 6 in. long, indehiscent. India and Ceylon to Burma.

Sutherlandii: *Acacia Sutherlandii*.

versicolor Welw. ex D. Oliver. Tree, to 40 ft.; lfts. obovate-elliptic to nearly orbicular, oblique, golden-tomentose beneath, the apical ones largest, to 2 in. long; fls. whitish, in heads on clustered peduncles, stamens crimson; fr. flat, thin, papery, to 10 in. long, 2 in. across. Trop. Afr. to S. Afr.

Zygia (DC.) Macbr. Tree, to 100 ft.; lfts. oblique-obovate to rhombic, the apical ones largest, to 2½ in. long, nearly equilateral; fls. in a corymbose raceme to 4 in. long, stamens red; fr. flat, to 6 in. long. Senegal to Angola.

ALBUCA L. *Liliaceae*. About 130 spp. of bulbous herbs, native to Arabia and Afr., but chiefly S. Afr.; bulb tunicate; lvs. nearly cylindrical to flat, basal; fls. yellow or white, in terminal racemes; perianth segms. 6, separate, the outer spreading, the inner erect, stamens 6; fr. a caps.

canadensis (L.) Leighton [*A. major* L.; *A. minor* L.]. To 3 ft.; lvs. 3–6, 8–24 in. long; fls. pale yellow to greenish-yellow, with wide, green median stripe, outer stamens sterile. S. Afr.

crinifolia Bak. To 2½ ft.; lvs. strap-shaped, 2–3 ft. long, membranous; perianth segms. 1 in. long, white, with reddish-brown median stripe, stamens all fertile. S. Afr.

major: *A. canadensis*.

minor: *A. canadensis*.

Nelsonii N. E. Br. To 5 ft.; lvs. 4 or 5, to 3½ ft. long; perianth segms. 1½ in. long, white, with dull red median stripe, stamens all fertile. S. Afr.

ALCEA L. HOLLYHOCK. *Malvaceae*. Perhaps as many as 60 spp. of mostly bien. or short-lived per. herbs from the e. Medit. region to cent. Asia; sts. usually erect, scarcely branched; lvs. simple, unlobed to palmately parted; infl. mostly elongate, racemose, naked or only leafy basally, involucral bracts generally united basally, often enclosing the bud; petals 5, usually more than 1 in. long, yellow, white, or pink to purple, stamens united in a tubular column, the column 5-angled, glabrous, style brs. filiform, stigmatic on inner edge, as many as the mericarps; fr. a schizocarp, mericarps about 40, in a single whorl, each indehiscent, nearly 2-celled, the upper cell sterile, the lower 1-seeded.

Hollyhocks are generally propagated by seeds or by rooting shoots developing about the root crown. Seeds are usually sown in June or July and the plants transplanted to their permanent location the following spring.

ficifolia L. [*Althaea ficifolia* (L.) Cav.]. Described by Linnaeus as having palmately compound lvs., but the identity of the sp. has not been established with any certainty; plants offered under this name may be forms of *A. rosea* with yellowish fls. and deeply lobed lvs., or *A. rugosa*.

pallida (Waldst. & Kit. ex Willd.) Waldst. & Kit. [*Althaea pallida* Waldst. & Kit. ex Willd.]. Tomentose and also usually hispid bien., to about 6 ft.; lvs. suborbicular, unlobed or shallowly 3- or 5-lobed; involucral bracts narrowly triangular, nearly as long as the calyx; corolla 2–3½ in. across, petals rose or lilac, not overlapping; mericarps with a deep, broad, dorsal furrow bordered by rugose wings. Se. and e.-cent. Eur.

rosea L. [*Althaea rosea* (L.) Cav.]. HOLLYHOCK. Bien. with strict, spirelike sts. to 10 ft., tomentose apically, glabrescent or thinly setose beneath; lvs. suborbicular, shallowly 3-, 5-, or 7-lobed, rugose; involucral bracts triangular to lanceolate, to ⅝ as long as calyx, corolla single or double, 2–4 in. across, petals white to pink or purple, sometimes yellowish, usually overlapping one another; mericarps with a narrow dorsal furrow, bordered by parallel wings. Probably native to Asia Minor; now cult. and naturalized in most parts of the world. There is an "annual" strain, which will flower the first summer if seed is sown indoors in Feb.

rugosa Alef. Similar to *A. rosea*, but having sts. persistently tomentose and villous with longer white hairs; lvs. deeply 3-, 5-, or 7-lobed; involucral bracts triangular, half as long as calyx, petals clear yellow or orange-yellow; mericarp wings divergent. Ukraine, s. Russia.

sulphurea (Boiss. & Hohen.) Alef. [*Althaea sulphurea* Boiss. & Hohen.]. Erect-stemmed, low, per. herbs; lvs. ovate to suborbicular, unlobed or shallowly 3-lobed, lower surface floccose; involucral bracts linear-lanceolate, as long as calyx; petals pale yellow; mericarps with a shallow dorsal furrow, without the border wings. Iraq and Iran. Plants offered under this name may be *A. rugosa*.

ALCHEMILLA L. LADY'S-MANTLE. *Rosaceae*. About 200 spp. of ann. or per. herbs, mostly of the N. Temp. Zone, difficult of classification, since much apomixis occurs; lvs. palmately lobed or divided; fls. small, greenish or yellowish, in mostly compound cymes, stamens 1–4, pistils 1–10, becoming achenelike and embedded in the dry persistent calyx tube.

Some species make good mats or low clumps with attractive foliage. Propagated by seeds or division.

alpina L. ALPINE L.-M. Per., with stolons, sts. to 8 in.; rosette lvs. to 2 in. long, lfts. 5–7, oblong-obovate, toothed at tip, silky-hairy, especially beneath, st. lvs. reduced; calyx tube strigose, stamens 4. Mts., Eur.

arvensis (L.) Scop. Spring or winter ann., to 1 ft., prostrate or ascending, pubescent; lvs. cauline, 3–5-cleft, to ½ in. long; calyx tube less than ¹⁄₁₆ in. long, sepals erect, ¹⁄₁₆ in. long, stamen mostly 1; achenes with lateral styles. Eur.; naturalized in N. Amer.

chirophylla Buser. Like *A. alpina*, but lacking stolons; lfts. 7–9, narrow-elliptic, toothed at tip, silky-hairy on both sides. Eur.

glaucescens Wallr. [*A. pubescens* of auth., probably not Lam.]. Per., long-pubescent throughout, to 8 in.; lvs. rounded, to 1½ in. wide, with

7–11 shallow, coarsely toothed lobes; fls. in glomerules, minute, yellowish. Eur.

gracilis Opiz [*A. micans* Buser]. Close to *A. vulgaris,* dark green, turning red in autumn, glabrescent. Eur.

micans: *A. gracilis.*

microcarpa Boiss. & Reut. PARSLEY-PIERT. Small ann., to 4 in.; lvs. deeply cleft, to ¼ in. wide; fls. fascicled in axils of dilated stipules, calyx tube minutely pubescent, scarcely ¹⁄₁₆ in. long. Eur.; naturalized in N. Amer.

pratensis Opiz. Not cult.; material cult. under this name is *A. xanthochlora.*

pubescens: see *A. glaucescens.*

speciosa Buser. Sts. spreading-hairy, to 2 ft.; lvs. more or less hairy above, spreading-hairy on petioles, lobed almost halfway to the base; infl. inconspicuous, yellow, very hairy; sepals longer than calyx tube. Caucasus.

vulgaris L. Per., to 1½ ft., hairy to nearly glabrous; lvs. mostly radical, with 7–11 rather shallowly toothed lobes, green on both sides; fls. to ⅛ in. across. Eur. Has been used medicinally.

xanthochlora Rothm. [*A. pratensis* of auth., not Opiz.]. Stout-based per., to 2 ft., spreading-hirsute; basal lvs. more or less reniform in outline, to 6 in. wide, with 5–9 rounded-oblong or short-ovate, serrate lobes, glabrous above; calyx tube campanulate, ¹⁄₁₆ in. long, glabrous, stamens 4. Eur., w. Asia; naturalized in e. N. Amer. Close to *A. vulgaris.*

ALCIMANDRA Dandy. *Magnoliaceae.* One sp., an evergreen tree, native to the Himalayas; lvs. alt., entire, stipules free from petiole; fls. terminal, small, solitary. Differs from *Michelia* in having terminal rather than axillary fls., and from *Magnolia* in having relatively small fls. with carpels not overtopping stamens.

Cathcartii (Hook. f. & T. Thoms.) Dandy [*Michelia Cathcartii* Hook. f. & T. Thoms.]. Tall tree, branchlets silky-hairy; lvs. oblong-lanceolate, to 4 in. long, pale beneath; fls. white, 1 in. across, with about 9 perianth segms.

ALDROVANDA L. *Droseraceae.* One sp., an herbaceous, carnivorous, rootless, floating aquatic, native from cent. Eur. to e. and se. Asia, Timor, and Queensland; st. jointed, leafy; lvs. whorled; fls. solitary, axillary, calyx 5-parted, petals 5, stamens 5; fr. a 5-valved, globose caps., seeds black, glossy.

Sometimes grown in aquaria as a curiosity.

vesiculosa L. Fine-textured, sts. weak, succulent; lvs. 6–9 in a whorl, to ⅜ in. long, the blade reniform, hinged, petiole terminating in 4–6 bristles on each side of the blade; fls. greenish-white. The lf. blades trap small aquatic organisms, functioning like those of *Dionaea.*

ALECTRYON Gaertn. *Sapindaceae.* About 20 spp. of evergreen trees of Australia, New Zeal., Pacific Is., and Hawaii; lvs. alt., pinnate; fls. in many-fld. axillary or terminal panicles, bisexual or unisexual, calyx 4–5-lobed, petals 0, stamens 5–8; fr. a subglobose, crested, 1-celled caps.

excelsus Gaertn. To 30 ft., bark nearly black; lvs. 14–18 in. long, lfts. 8–12, ovate-lanceolate to ovate-oblong, to 4 in. long, acuminate; panicles to 1 ft. long; caps. ½ in. long, pubescent. New Zeal. Wood used for utilitarian articles and cabinetry.

subcinereus (A. Gray) Radlk. SMOOTH RAMBUTAN. To 30 ft.; lvs. to 8 in. long, lfts. 2–6, oblong-elliptic to lanceolate, 3–5 in. long, glabrous; panicles loose, to 8 in. long; caps. nearly sessile, with globose lobes, to ⁵⁄₁₆ in. in diam. E. Australia.

ALETES J. Coult. & Rose. *Umbelliferae.* Six spp. of low, per. herbs of w. N. Amer., with persistent lf. bases; lvs. pinnate to ternate-pinnately decompound; fls. yellow, in compound umbels, involucre usually lacking, involucels of small bracts, calyx present; fr. compressed, not winged.

anisatus (A. Gray) Theob. & Tseng [*Pseudocymopterus anisatus* (A. Gray) J. Coult. & Rose; *Pteryxia anisata* (A. Gray) Mathias & Const.]. Stemless; scapes to 1 ft.; lvs. 2-pinnate, segms. rigid, acute; bractlets of involucels very conspicuous; fr. oblong, with some ribs winged. Colo.

ALETRIS L. STAR GRASS, COLICROOT. *Liliaceae.* About 10 spp. of per., fibrous-rooted herbs, native to e. N. Amer. and e. Asia; lvs. basal, grasslike, from a short, thick rhizome; fls. white or yellow, in erect, scapose, spikelike racemes, perianth 6-lobed, stamens 6; fr. a caps.

Star grass does well in moist, sunny locations; useful for colonizing. Propagated by seeds or division.

aurea Walt. YELLOW C. To 2½ ft.; lvs. pale yellowish-green, to 3 in. long, membranous; fls. yellow, campanulate; fr. nearly as long as perianth. Summer. S. Md. to Fla., w. to Tex.

farinosa L. UNICORN ROOT, CROW CORN, AGUEROOT. To 3 ft.; lvs. pale yellowish-green, to 6 in. long, firm; fls. white, tubular; fr. usually shorter than perianth. Late spring, summer. Me. to Minn., s. to Fla. and Tex.

ALEURITES J. R.. Forst. & G. Forst. *Euphorbiaceae.* Six spp. of trop. or subtrop., monoecious trees with milky juice, native to e. Asia, and the Hawaiian and Pacific Is.; young sts., foliage, and infl. with simple or stellate hairs; lvs. alt., simple, mostly palmately veined, ovate to cordate, often lobed; fls. in terminal, panicled cymes; fr. drupaceous.

Grown far south for the seeds, which yield valuable drying oils (Chinawood oils), and for shade. Propagated by seeds sown where plants are to stand, or seedlings transplanted when about 1 ft. high. Also propagated by hard wood cuttings. Trees begin to bear fruit in 3–6 years.

cordata (Thunb.) R. Br. JAPAN WOOD-OIL TREE. Tree, 25–30 ft.; lvs. broadly ovate-cordate, frequently 3–5-lobed or toothed; fls. ¾ in. long, ovary 3–4-celled; fr. warty. Se. Asia.

Fordii Hemsl. CHINA WOOD-OIL TREE or TUNG-OIL TREE. Tree, 15–40 ft.; lvs. ovate to cordate, sometimes 3-lobed, to 5 in. long, with 2 sessile glands at base; fls. white with red or orange veins, to 1 in. long, ovary 3–5-celled; fr. 2–3 in. in diam., smooth. Cent. Asia. Cult. commercially in Zone 9. Most important source of tung-oil, used in paints and quick-drying varnishes.

moluccana (L.) Willd. [*A. triloba* J. R. Forst. & G. Forst.]. CANDLE-NUT, CANDLENUT TREE, CANDLEBERRY TREE, VARNISH TREE, INDIAN WALNUT, COUNTRY W., OTAHEITE W. Large tree, to 60 ft., appearing frosty or whitish at a distance; lvs. ovate, to 8 in. long, sometimes 3–5-lobed, with stellate hairs; infl. to 9 in. long; fls. white, ovary 2-celled; fr. 2 in. in diam. or more. Se. Asia; cult. in China and Philippine Is. for oil, naturalized in tropics.

montana (Lour.) E. H. Wils. MU-OIL, MU TREE, TUNG. Flat-topped tree, to 25 ft.; lvs. ovate to cordate, sometimes 3–5-lobed, to 1 ft. long, with 2 stalked glands at base; fls. white, to 1 in. long, ovary 3-celled; fr. to 1¾ in. in diam. S. China, n. Burma. Cult. elsewhere. Oil of inferior quality.

triloba: *A. moluccana.*

ALGAE. Algae are largely aquatic and include some of the simplest organisms of the plant kingdom. As one group of the so-called thallus plants, they lack roots, stems, and leaves, do not flower, and are often grouped by their pigmentation, being green, brown, or red. Algae are immensely important because of their contribution as both primary and major producers of organic matter, being basic to the world's aquatic food chains through photosynthesis. Some species of the larger marine algae (seaweeds) have direct economic value as sources of food or industrial products, and in Japan several are intensively and widely cultivated for food in the shallow waters along the coasts. Algae are of little importance in American horticulture. However, where large quantities of seaweed drift over beaches, the material can be collected and used as compost to help build up the organic content of garden soil and as a source of potash and, to a lesser degree, nitrogen. Algae are also frequent contaminants in ponds, garden pools, or aquaria, where they cause "blooms," but they are readily controlled.

ALISMA L. WATER PLANTAIN. *Alismataceae.* About 6 or 7 spp. of widely distributed, aquatic, mostly per. herbs; lvs. basal, submersed or emersed, linear or often with broad, cordate blades, petioles basally sheathing; fls. small, bisexual, in whorls in scapose panicles, petals 3, white or rose-tinged, stamens 6, carpels 2 to many, in a single whorl, each 1-ovuled; fr. a head of achenes.

Sometimes grown about ponds and in bogs for the foliage and many small flowers. Propagated by division or seeds.

californica: *Machaerocarpus californicus.*

gramineum Lej. [*A. graminifolium* J. F. Ehrh.]. Lvs. linear, linear-lanceolate, or narrowly oblong, early lvs. scarcely petioled, to 20 in.

long; fls. in a panicle on stout st. to 1 ft. or more, style coiled; fr. broadest above middle. N. Amer., Eur., N. Afr., Asia.

graminifolium: *A. gramineum.*

Plantago: *A. Plantago-aquatica.*

Plantago-aquatica L. [*A. Plantago* auth.]. MAD-DOG WEED. Cormous per., to 3 ft.; lvs. long-petioled, emersed blades lanceolate or elliptic to broadly ovate, mostly to 6 in. long and half as wide, basally rounded to subcordate; pedicels erect, bracts scarious; fls. usually about ½ in. across, petals white, sometimes purple-tipped, ephemeral; fr. heads to ¼ in. in diam., achenes usually with 1 groove. Widespread, mainly in temp. zones. Var. **americanum** Schult. & Schult. f. [subsp. *brevipes* (Greene) Sam.; var. *brevipes* (Greene) Vict.; *A. triviale* Pursh]. Corolla pure white; fr. heads about 3/16 in. in diam. N. Amer., temp. e. Asia. Var. **brevipes;** var. *americanum.* Var. **parviflorum:** *A. subcordatum.*

subcordatum Raf. [*A. Plantago-aquatica* var. *parviflorum* (Pursh) Torr.]. Perhaps only a var. of *A. Plantago-aquatica,* from which it differs in having fls. smaller, with petals less than ⅛ in. long, and fr. heads less than 3/16 in. in diam. N.J. to Ga., w. to Nebr. and Tex.

triviale: *A. Plantago-aquatica* var. *americanum.*

ALISMACEAE: *ALISMATACEAE.*

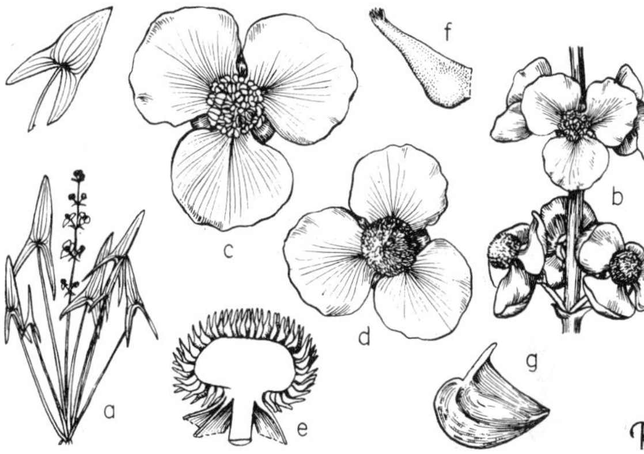

ALISMATACEAE. *Sagittaria sagittifolia:* **a,** plant, × 1/20; **b,** part of inflorescence, × ½; **c,** male flower, × 1; **d,** female flower, × 1; **e,** female flower, vertical section, perianth removed, × 3; **f,** pistil (carpel), × 12; **g,** achene, × 5. (From Bailey, *Manual of Cultivated Plants,* ed. 2.)

ALISMATACEAE Venten. [incorrectly spelled *Alismaceae*]. WATER PLANTAIN FAMILY. Monocot.; about 10 genera of marsh and aquatic herbs of worldwide distribution; submersed lvs. bladeless, emersed lvs. with linear to ovate-sagittate blades and petioles basally sheathing; fls. in racemes or panicles, often whorled, regular, bisexual or unisexual, sepals 3, green, persistent, petals 3 or none, stamens (3-)6 to many, separate, carpels 3 to many, usually not united, each with 1 to several basal or axile ovules; fr. a head of achenes. The cult. genera are: *Alisma, Echinodorus, Luronium, Machaerocarpus,* and *Sagittaria.*

Some species are cultivated as ornamentals in shallow ponds and along pool margins, or in aquaria; *Sagittaria sagittifolia* is grown in the Orient for its edible tubers.

ALLAGOPTERA Nees [*Diplothemium* Mart.]. *Palmae.* About 5 spp. of dwarf, mostly cespitose, unarmed, monoecious palms without emergent sts., native to Brazil and Paraguay; lvs. pinnate, pinnae acute but often splitting at tip in age, petiole not toothed along margin; infl. among lvs., erect, spicate, bracts 2, the upper woody and sulcate; fls. fragrant, cream-colored, in triads (2 male and 1 female); male fls. asymmetrical, pedicelled, sepals 3, slender, elongate, united basally, petals 3, valvate, much wider than thick, angled, stamens 6 or more, pistillode minute, female fls. with 3 imbricate sepals and petals, the sepals as long as the petals, staminodes united in a low cupule, pistil 3-celled, 3-ovuled; fr. 1-seeded, with apical stigmatic residue, mesocarp fibrous, endocarp thick with pores near base, seed with homogeneous endosperm.

For culture see *Palms.*

arenaria (Gomes) O. Kuntze. Lvs. long-petioled, rachis to more than 2 ft. long, pinnae about 50 on each side in groups of 2–4(–5) and borne in several planes, pale beneath; infl. with peduncle to nearly 3 ft. long, spike to 5 in. long; male fls. with 10–16 stamens; fr. with brown-woolly scales. Brazil. Warmer parts of Zone 9b, in Fla. Thrives in sandy sites, resistant to salt spray.

ALLAMANDA L. *Apocynaceae.* About 12 spp. of erect or clambering shrubs with milky sap, some lianalike, native to trop. Amer.; lvs. whorled or opp., entire; fls. in few-fld. cymes, large, showy, 5-merous, bisexual, calyx foliaceous, corolla funnelform, yellow or purplish, stamens borne on corolla, separate, included, ovary 1, 1-celled, ovules many, placentation parietal; fr. a globose, spiny caps., dehiscent by 2 valves, seeds many, dry, flattened, winged.

The cultivation of allamandas is simple, but they need extra feeding during the whole growing season. The plants should be kept nearly dry after growth ceases in late autumn until Feb. or Mar.; they should then be cut back and started in a moist atmosphere; all repotting should be done before the new growth is 6 in. long. Propagated from old and new wood cuttings. In warm countries they thrive in profusion on walls and fences.

cathartica L. COMMON A., GOLDEN-TRUMPET. Vigorous vine, to 50 ft. long; lvs. opp. or in whorls of 3–4, mostly oblanceolate to elliptic-oblong, to 4–6 in. long, short-acuminate, attenuate to a very short petiole; calyx lobes unequal, corolla bright yellow with paler throat, to 5 in. across, narrowed below into a slender tube to 1⅜ in. long and not swollen at base, lobes obovate and rounded; caps. about 1½ in. in diam., with spines about ⅜ in. long. Probably n. S. Amer.; now widespread. Zone 10b. Cv. **'Grandiflora'** [*A. grandiflora* Lam.]. Dwarf, compact, fls. lemon- or primrose-yellow, to 4½ in. across. Cv. **'Hendersonii'** [*A. Hendersonii* Bull]. Free-flowering; lvs. leathery, glabrous, fls. to 5 in. across, tinged brown outside in bud. Cv. **'Nobilis'** [*A. nobilis* T. Moore]. Fls. bright clear yellow, to 5 in. across, with magnolialike fragrance. Cv. **'Schottii'** [*A. Schottii* Pohl]. Young shoots and petioles slightly pubescent, fls. with dark-striped throat. Cv. **'Stansill's Double'.** A double-fld. sport of cv. 'Williamsii'. Cv. **'Williamsii'** [*A. Williamsii* Hort.]. Sts. pubescent, fls. yellow with reddish-brown throat.

grandiflora: *A. cathartica* cv.

Hendersonii: *A. cathartica* cv.

neriifolia Hook. BUSH A. Glabrous shrub, to 4–5 ft., sometimes with scandent brs.; lvs. 2–5 at a node; infl. paniculate, corolla golden-yellow, striped orange in the throat, to 2¼ in. across, tube short, only ½ in. long, swollen and angular at its base. S. Amer.

nobilis: *A. cathartica* cv.

purpurea: *A. violacea.*

Schottii: *A. cathartica* cv.

violacea G. Gardn. & Fielding [*A. purpurea* Hort.]. PURPLE A. Scandent shrub, young shoots and lvs. pubescent; lvs. usually in 4's, oblong or obovate-oblong, to 6 in. long, acuminate; calyx pubescent, corolla 2½–3½ in. long, 2–2½ in. wide, rose-pink to reddish-purple, deeper in throat, tube not swollen at base. S. Amer. Zone 10b. Thrives best when grafted on *A. cathartica* cv. 'Hendersonii' or cv. 'Schottii'.

Williamsii: *A. cathartica* cv.

ALLIONIA L. *Nyctaginaceae.* About 3 spp. of Amer. herbs, not in cult.

linearis: *Mirabilis linearis.*

nyctaginea: *Mirabilis nyctaginea.*

ALLIUM L. ONION. *Amaryllidaceae.* Perhaps 400 or more spp. of strongly odorous (when bruised), mostly per., rhizomatous or bulbous herbs, native primarily to the N. Hemisphere, sometimes producing bulblets at the tips of slender secondary lateral rhizomes from the base; bulbs either scarcely developed and borne on a stout horizontal rhizome, or densely clustered on a slender rhizome, or solitary, or clustered (through division of the bulb or production of bulblets) and borne on a scarcely persistent, short or poorly developed, more or less vertical rhizome; bulb coats either membranous, with the fibers sometimes parallel but sometimes forming distinctive patterns, or fibrous with the fibers parallel or reticulate; lvs. usually narrow, rarely with a distinct petiole and broad blade, basel or sheathing the scape to the middle or more, solid to hollow, flat, keeled, or semicylindrical to cylindrical; fls. small. borne in a few- to many-fld., sometimes bulbilliferous umbel terminating a scape and subtended by a spathe of 1–2, sometimes more, united valves; perianth segms. 6, separate or shortly united at the base, stamens 6, inserted basally, filaments sometimes broadened, and then sometimes with a tooth on each side, ovary superior, 3-celled, with 1–10 ovules in each cell, sometimes with crests on the ridges or with open nectaries in the hollows between the ridges; fr. a loculicidal caps., seeds black, flat or angled or rounded. The genus is complex and variously divided into subdivisions based largely on characters of rootstock, filaments, and ovary.

Several species are grown for food, others as ornamentals in the flower border, wild garden, or rock garden. The ornamental alliums require no special treatment and bloom in spring and summer; *A. neapolitanum* is used for cut flowers, and is grown in boxes or beds under glass. Propagation is by seeds sown in early spring, or by offsets, bulblets, or bulbils planted in autumn or spring. Most of the species are hardy north. It is doubtful that all the species offered to horticulturists are actually cultivated, many proving to be *A. fistulosum*, *A. Schoenoprasum*, or *A. senescens*.

acuminatum Hook. [*A. cuspidatum* Fern.]. Bulbs not on a rhizome, outer bulb coat membranous, netted with square or hexagonal meshes in rows, the mesh walls thick and uniform, forming pits; scape to 1 ft.; lvs. 2 or more, $\frac{3}{32}$–$\frac{1}{8}$ in. wide, shorter than scape; umbel several-fld., pedicels somewhat longer than fls.; perianth segms. deep rose-purple, $\frac{5}{16}$–$\frac{9}{16}$ in. long, the outer lanceolate, long-acuminate, with recurved tips, the inner shorter and finely toothed, filaments $\frac{2}{3}$ as long as segms., ovary obscurely 3-crested, without nectaries. B.C. to n. Calif., e. to Mont., Colo., and Ariz.

acutangulum: *A. angulosum.*

aflatunense B. Fedtsch. Bulb ovoid, solitary, outer bulb coat membranous, gray; scape robust, 2½–5 ft.; lvs. 6–8, strap-shaped, to $\frac{3}{8}$ in. wide, shorter than scape, glaucous, smooth, the sheaths surrounding the scape at base; umbel many-fld., subtended by short spathe, pedicels nearly equal, 2–4 times as long as fls.; perianth segms. light violet with darker nerve, to $\frac{5}{16}$ in. long, reflexed and twisted in age, filaments exserted, entire, united to segms. at base, anthers yellow, ovules several in each cell. Cent. Asia.

albidum: *A. denudatum.*

albopilosum: *A. Christophii.*

albopurpureum: a listed name of no botanical standing.

album: *A. neapolitanum*, but plants grown as *A. album* are probably *A. tuberosum.*

alleghaniense: *A. cernuum.*

alleghericum: a listed name of no botanical standing.

altaicum Pall. Similar to *A. fistulosum*, but bulbs on a rhizome, pedicels thick, nearly equal to, or the inner ones 1½ times as long as the fls., and the umbel headlike. Siberia, cent. Asia.

altissimum Regel. Bulb spherical, solitary, outer bulb coat membranous, grayish; scape 2½–5 ft.; lvs. 4–6, linear-lanceolate, ¾–1½ in. wide, shorter than scape, green, smooth; umbel many-fld., subtended by short spathe, pedicels unequal, 4–6 times as long as fls.; perianth starlike, segms. violet, with deeper nerve, to $\frac{5}{16}$ in. long, reflexed and twisted in age, filaments scarcely exserted, entire, united to segms. at base, more or less united above, anthers yellow, ovules several in each cell. Cent. Asia.

ammophilum: *A. flavescens.*

Ampeloprasum L. WILD LEEK. Variable, some forms with poorly developed bulbs, others with bulbs ovoid, of 2 cloves, often with smaller cloves among bases of lvs., outer bulb coat yellowish, membranous; scape to 3 ft. or more, leafy to middle; lvs. 6–9, flat, keeled, folded sharply lengthwise, to $\frac{3}{8}$ in. wide; umbel many-fld., sometimes with bulbils, spherical, pedicels unequal, longer than fls.; perianth segms. rose-pink to greenish, filaments not much exserted, inner ones with 2 lateral teeth, style exserted, ovary with nectaries. Eur., N. Afr., Asia. Three hort. groups are recognized: the Ampeloprasum Group, GREAT-HEADED GARLIC, LEVANT G., with large bulbs of many cloves used as seasoning; the Porrum Group [*A. Porrum* L.], LEEK, of which the poorly developed bulbs and leaf bases are eaten (see *Leeks*); and the Kurrat Group, KURRAT, small plants with poorly developed bulbs, the lvs. of which are eaten. The sp. is sometimes mistakenly grown under the name *A. giganteum.*

amplectens Torr. Bulbs not on a rhizome, outer bulb coat membranous, netted with horizontal V-shaped meshes in rows; scape to 18 in.; lvs. 2–4, narrow, becoming convolute-filiform, shorter than scape; umbel many-fld., spathe scarcely $\frac{3}{8}$ in. long, pedicels 1–2 times as long as fls.; perianth segms. white or tinged with pink, ¼–$\frac{5}{16}$ in. long, filaments included, slightly shorter than segms., ovary 6-crested, lacking nectaries. Wash. to s. Calif.

angulosum L. [*A. acutangulum* Schrad.]. MOUSE GARLIC. Bulbs slender, on a rhizome, outer bulb coat membranous; scape 1–2 ft.,

angular; lvs. 5–6, linear, keeled, $\frac{1}{8}$–$\frac{3}{16}$ in. wide, shorter than scape, glabrous; umbel many-fld., pedicels 2–3 times as long as fls.; perianth segms. rose-violet, oblong, acute, ¼ in. long, filaments and style included, ovary lacking nectaries. Meadows, Eur. to Siberia. Cv. 'Purpureum' is listed.

angustoprasum: a listed name of no botanical standing; plants grown under this name have proved to be *A. Schoenoprasum.*

anisopodium Ledeb. Bulbs slender, clustered on a slender rhizome, outer bulb coat slightly fibrous; scape 8–16 in.; lvs. 2–3, semicylindrical, very slender, shorter than scape; umbel many-fld., clustered, pedicels unequal, 3–7 times as long as fls.; perianth segms. rosy, about $\frac{3}{16}$ in. long, filaments entire, $\frac{2}{3}$ as long as perianth, the inner twice as wide as the outer, ovary lacking nectaries. Asia.

ascalonicum: a confused name used by Linnaeus for what was probably a cultigen, though said to be native to Asia Minor. The name has usually been applied to the shallot, now considered to belong to the Aggregatum Group of *A. Cepa*, but seeds or other material offered as *A. ascalonicum* sometimes prove to be other spp. The true shallot rarely flowers or sets seed.

Aschersonianum Barb. Bulbs ovate, outer bulb coat membranous; scape to 1½ ft.; lvs. strap-shaped, $\frac{3}{8}$–½ in. wide, denticulate-scabrid on margin; umbel many-fld., pedicels 3–4 times as long as fls.; perianth segms. rose, withering, reflexed and more or less twisted in age, filaments slightly longer than segms., ovules several in each cell. Asia Minor to Egypt. Plants grown under this name have proved to be *A. carinatum.*

atropurpureum Waldst. & Kit. [*A. nigrum* var. *atropurpureum* (Waldst. & Kit.) Vis.]. Allied to *A. nigrum*, but to 3 ft., the outer bulb coat blackish, lvs. narrower, perianth segms. smaller, dark purple to nearly black, filaments as long as segms. S. Eur.

atrorubens S. Wats. Bulbs not on a rhizome, outer bulb coat red-brown, membranous, not patterned; scape to 2½ in., cylindrical; lf. solitary, narrow, longer than the scape; umbel many-fld., pedicels somewhat longer than fls.; perianth segms. reddish-purple, $\frac{3}{8}$–½ in. long, filaments $\frac{2}{3}$ as long as segms., ovary with 6 prominent, toothed crests, lacking nectaries. Nev., e. Calif.

azureum: *A. caeruleum.*

Bakeri Regel. Bulbs slender, clustered on a slender rhizome, outer bulb coat membranous, with well-separated nerves; scape to 1½ ft., cylindrical; lvs. 2–4, linear, hollow, angular in cross section, $\frac{1}{16}$ in. wide, longer or shorter than the scape; umbel 6–30-fld., pedicels 2–4 times as long as fls. or more; perianth segms. rose-purple, obtuse, $\frac{3}{16}$ in. long, filaments to 1½ times as long as perianth, very shortly united at base, the inner with 1 or rarely 2 teeth on each side, ovary with nectaries, ovules 1–2 in each cell. E. India to China and Japan, where known as RAKKYO and cult. for pickles.

Beesianum W. W. Sm. Bulbs slender, clustered, outer bulb coat fibrous; scape to 1½ ft., leafy in lowermost $\frac{1}{3}$; lvs. flat, to $\frac{5}{16}$ in. wide, shorter than scape; umbel several-fld., usually nodding, pedicels shorter than fls.; perianth segms. deep blue edged with white, about $\frac{5}{8}$ in. long, filaments included, the inner broadened but not toothed at base, ovary with nectaries. China.

Bidwelliae: *A. campanulatum.*

bisceptrum S. Wats. Bulbs not on a rhizome, outer bulb coat membranous, netted with fine, horizontal oblong meshes in rows, vertical mesh walls thickest and sinuous; scapes often in pairs, to 8 in.; lvs. broadly linear, about as long as scape; umbel many-fld., pedicels twice as long as fls. or more; perianth segms. rose to nearly white, filaments slightly shorter than segms. to nearly as long, ovary conspicuously 6-crested, without nectaries. Idaho, Utah, Nev., s. Calif.

Bolanderi S. Wats. Bulbs not on a rhizome, outer bulb coat membranous, netted with horizontal, narrow, V-shaped meshes in rows; scape to 8 in.; lvs. 2, $\frac{1}{8}$ in. wide, shorter than scape; umbel many-fld., pedicels slightly longer than fls.; perianth segms. rose-pink to white, $\frac{3}{8}$ in. long, the outer ovate-lanceolate, long-acuminate, the inner with margins conspicuously serrulate, filaments about ½ as long as segms., ovary obscurely 6-crested, without nectaries. S. Ore., n. Calif. Var. **stenanthum** (E. Drew) Jeps. [*A. stenanthum* E. Drew]. Slightly taller; perianth segms. narrow, white or only pinkish.

brevistylum S. Wats. Bulb slender, at end of stout rhizome, outer bulb coat membranous; scape 1–2 ft.; lvs. several, linear, flat, $\frac{3}{8}$–¼ in. wide, shorter than scape, glabrous; umbel many-fld., pedicels 2–3 times as long as fls.; perianth segms. dark rose, lanceolate, acuminate, ¼–$\frac{5}{16}$ in. long, filaments included, stigma 3-lobed, ovary without nectaries. Montane woods and meadows, Mont., Colo., Utah.

Breweri S. Wats. Bulbs not on a rhizome, outer bulb coat membranous, not patterned; scape to 3 in., flattened, 2-winged; lvs. 2, sickle-shaped, $\frac{3}{16}$–$\frac{5}{16}$ in. wide, much longer than scape; umbel many-fld., pedicels somewhat longer than fls.; perianth segms. deep rose-purple,

⅜–½ in. long, obtuse to acute, or becoming acuminate in age, the inner entire or sometimes minutely glandular-serrate, filaments ⅔ as long as segms., ovary with 3 broadly triangular, sometimes lobed crests, without nectaries. Cent. Calif.

bulgaricum: *Nectaroscordum bulgaricum*, but material offered as *A. bulgaricum* is probably *A. sphaerocephalum* or some other sp. of *Allium*.

Bulleyanum Diels. Bulbs scarcely developed, outer bulb coat weakly fibrous; scape to 2 ft. or more; lvs. linear, ⅛–⅜ in. wide, to 1 ft. long; umbel many-fld., spathe deciduous, pedicels slender, 1 in. long; perianth segms. deep crimson, narrowly elliptic, to ¼ in. long, filaments included, entire, dilated and united at base. China.

Burbankii: a listed name for plants probably referable to *A. Schoenoprasum*.

caeruleum Pall. [*A. azureum* Ledeb.]. Bulbs nearly spherical, outer bulb coat membranous; scape to 2½ ft., leafy in lowermost ⅓; lvs. 3–4, 3-angled, ⅛–³⁄₁₆ in. wide, shorter than scape, scabrid; umbel many-fld., pedicels 2–5 times as long as fls.; perianth segms. blue, about ³⁄₁₆ in. long, filaments as long as segms. or slightly longer, of equal width and shortly united at base, entire, or the inner with 2 teeth near the base, style exserted, ovary with nectaries. Asia. Cv. 'Grandiflorum' has been listed under *A. azureum*. Var. **bulbilliferum** (Schrenk) Ledeb. [*A. viviparum* Kar. & Kir.]. Umbels bearing bulbils.

caesium Schrenck [*A. urceolatum* Regel]. Bulbs nearly globose, outer bulb coat membranous; scape to 2 ft., leafy in lowermost ¼–½; lvs. 2–3, semicylindrical, hollow, ¹⁄₁₆–⅛ in. wide, slightly longer or shorter than scape, scabrid; umbel many-fld., pedicels 2–3 or more times as long as fls.; perianth segms. dark azure-blue or rarely white, ³⁄₁₆–¼ in. long, filaments ¾ to nearly as long as segms., the inner broadened in the lower ⅔ and with 2 obtuse teeth, ovary with nectaries. Siberia, cent. Asia.

campanulatum S. Wats. [*A. Bidwelliae* S. Wats.]. Bulbs not on a rhizome, outer bulb coat membranous, netted with minute meshes in rows, the transverse walls inconspicuous, the vertical walls thick and sinuous; scape to 1 ft.; lvs. 2, ⅛–³⁄₁₆ in. wide, shorter than scape; umbel many-fld., pedicels twice or more as long as fls.; perianth segms. pale rose, ¼–⁵⁄₁₆ in. long, filaments about ¾ as long as segms., ovary with 6 prominent crests, without nectaries. Calif.

canadense L. WILD GARLIC, MEADOW LEEK, ROSE L., WILD ONION. Bulbs not on a rhizome, without basal bulblets, outer bulb coat a fibrous network of open meshes; scape to 1 ft. or more; lvs. usually 3 or more, to ³⁄₁₆ in. wide, shorter than scape; spathe valves 3–7-nerved, pedicels 2 to several times as long as fls.; perianth campanulate, segms. pink or white, withering in age, ³⁄₁₆–¼ in. long, filaments included, entire, ovary without nectaries or crests. A variable sp. of e. N. Amer. Var. **canadense** [*A. mutabile* Michx.]. The typical var.; most or all fls. replaced by bulbils. Var. **Fraseri** M. Ownb. [*A. Fraseri* (M. Ownb.) Shinn.]. Pedicels stout, fls. white. Var. **mobilense** (Regel) M. Ownb. [*A. mobilense* Regel]. Infl. without bulbils, pedicels slender, fls. pink.

carinatum L. Bulbs ovoid, outer bulb coat membranous; scape 10–18 in., leafy to middle; lvs. 3–4, narrow-linear, ¹⁄₁₆–⅛ in. wide, about as long as scape; umbel few-fld., bearing bulbils, ⅓ as long as spathe, pedicels all nearly the same length, 2–4 times longer than fls.; perianth ovoid-campanulate, segms. rose, with a dull bloom, about ³⁄₁₆ in. long, filaments 1½ times as long as segms., style exserted, ovary without nectaries. Eur.; escaped in N.J. and Penn. Material cult. as *A. carinatum* may be *A. Aschersonianum* or *A. pulchellum*.

Cepa L. ONION. To 4 ft., bulbs large, outer bulb coat membranous; scape hollow, swollen; lvs. 4–6, hollow, cylindrical except for groove on inner surface, shorter than scape; umbels large, pedicels with bracteoles, many times longer than fls.; perianth whitish-green, to ¼ in. long, filaments exserted, the inner ones broadened and 2-lobed or 2-toothed at base, ovary with nectaries. Known only in cult., in 3 principal groups. The Cepa Group includes onions with single bulbs and no bulbils in infl., and is usually produced by seed. The Aggregatum Group [*A. ascalonicum* of auth., not L.; *A. Cepa* vars. *aggregatum* G. Don, *solaninum* Alef., *multiplicans* L. H. Bailey] includes POTATO O., MULTIPLIER O., EVER-READY O., and SHALLOT, lacks bulbils in infl., is often sterile, and is prop. by lateral bulbs or shoots of underground bulb. The Proliferum Group includes TREE O., EGYPTIAN O., TOP O., CATAWISSA O., and is prop. by large bulbils borne in infl. See *Onion*.

cernuum Roth [*A. recurvatum* Rydb.; *A. alleghaniense* Small; *A. oxyphilum* Wherry]. NODDING O., WILD L., LADY'S LEEK. Bulbs elongate, clustered, outer bulb coat membranous; scape 1–2 ft.; lvs. several, linear, flat, ⅛–³⁄₁₆ in. wide, mostly shorter than scape; umbel many-fld., nodding in fl., pedicels 2–5 times as long as fls.; perianth segms. rose or white, ³⁄₁₆–¼ in. long, the outer filaments exserted, acute, entire, style exserted, ovary 6-crested, without nectaries. Rocky

slopes and dry hillsides, N.Y. to S.C., w. to B.C. and Calif. *A. alleghaniense*, with deep-purple perianth, and *A. oxyphilum*, which flowers in late summer and prefers acid soils, have been considered separate spp. by some authors. Cvs. 'Album' and 'Superbum' are listed.

Chamaemoly L. Bulbs ovoid, not on a rhizome, outer bulb coat brittle, honey-combed, brown; scape scarcely protruding above the ground, recurved in fr.; lvs. 2–4, flat, broadly linear, 4 in. to ⁵⁄₁₆ in. wide, much longer than scape, hairy; umbel few-fld., subtended by a spathe longer than the pedicels, pedicels recurved in fr.; perianth segms. white, with reddish nerves, linear-lanceolate, ⁵⁄₁₆ in. long, filaments ½ as long as segms., entire, style included, ovary without nectaries. S. Eur., N. Afr.

chinense G. Don. RAKKYO. Bulbs in clumps, similar to *A. Schoenoprasum*, but scape solid, lvs. sharply angled, spathe persistent, fls. in late summer with the new foliage, somewhat nodding, purple. Asia. Little cult. in U.S.

Christophii Trautv. [*A. albopilosum* C. H. Wright]. STARS-OF-PERSIA. Bulb spherical, solitary, outer bulb coat gray, membranous; scape stout, ½–2½ ft.; lvs. 3–7, strap-shaped, to 1 in. wide, as long as scape, somewhat glaucous, white-hairy beneath; umbel many-fld., spathe short, pedicels all nearly the same length, 3–5 or more times as long as fls.; perianth stellate, segms. lilac, ⅜–¾ in. long, narrow, becoming rigid after flowering, filaments included, entire, united to segms. basally and united to one another above, ovules several in each cell. Iran to Asia Minor.

ciliatum: *A. subhirsutum*.

cinereum: a listed name; plants cult. under this name have proved to be *A. cernuum*.

controversum: *A. sativum*.

Coryi M. E. Jones. Bulbs not on a rhizome, outer bulb coat a fibrous network of open meshes; scape to 1 ft.; lvs. 2–3, shorter than scape; umbel few-fld., pedicels much longer than fls.; perianth segms. chrome-yellow, sometimes tinged with red, ⅛–³⁄₁₆ in. long, filaments nearly as long as segms., ovary without crests or sometimes with flat, low crests, without nectaries. W. Tex.

Cowanii: *A. neapolitanum*.

crenulatum Wieg. [*A. vancouverense* Macoun]. Bulbs not on a rhizome, outer bulb coat membranous, not patterned; scape to 4 in., flattened, 2-edged, edges crenulate; lvs. 2, ⅛–¼ in. wide, longer than scape; umbel several- to many-fld., pedicels somewhat longer than fls.; perianth segms. deep rose-purple to pink or white, about ⁵⁄₁₆ in. long, filaments about ¾ as long as segms., ovary with 6 low dorsal crests, without nectaries. Vancouver Is., w. B.C., Wash., Ore.

crispum: *A. peninsulare* var.

Cusickii: *A. Tolmiei*.

cuspidatum: *A. acuminatum*.

Cuthbertii Small. STRIPED GARLIC. Bulbs not on a rhizome, outer bulb coat a fibrous network of open meshes; scape to 20 in.; lvs. 3 or more, to ⅛ in. wide, shorter than scape; umbel many-fld.; spathe valves 5–7-nerved, pedicels 2 or more times as long as fls.; perianth segms. white, acuminate, ¼–⁵⁄₁₆ in. long, withering in age, filaments included, ovary 6-crested, without nectaries. Coastal plain, N.C. to Fla. and Ala.

cyaneum Regel [*A. Purdomii* W. W. Sm.]. Bulbs slender, clustered, not producing bulblets on rhizomes, outer bulb coat fibrous; scape to 1 ft.; lvs. 1–3, filiform to very narrowly linear, to ⅛ in. wide, somewhat shorter than scape; umbel few- to many-fld., pedicels 1–2 times as long as fls.; fls. nodding, perianth segms. violet or purplish-blue, ¼–⁵⁄₁₆ in. long, obtuse, filaments exserted, the inner entire or 1–2-toothed at base, ovary with nectaries. China. Cv. 'Purpureum' is listed.

cyathophorum Bur. & Franch. The typical (cent. Asiatic) var. of the sp. is not known to be cult. here; it differs from var. *Farreri* in having the perianth segms. elliptic-oblong and subentire. Var. **Farreri** (Stearn) Stearn [*A. Farreri* Stearn]. Bulbs clustered on a short rhizome, greatly elongated, scarcely enlarged, outer bulb coat membranous, with few longitudinal fibers at base; scape to 1 ft., 3-angled; lvs. 4–6, narrowly linear, keeled, about ³⁄₁₆ in. wide, shorter than scape; umbel few- to many-fld., pedicels unequal, to 2 or more times as long as fls.; perianth segms. lanceolate, acuminate, red-purple, to ⅜ in. long, filaments entire, united to middle or nearly to apex, forming an urceolate tube, the free portions triangular, ovary without nectaries. Kansu (nw. China).

Cyrillii Ten. Allied to *A. nigrum*, but a smaller plant, with lvs. more narrow, perianth segms. linear, stamens fleshy, with dark purplish anthers. Italy to Asia Minor.

darwasicum Regel. Bulbs globose, outer bulb coat grayish, membranous; scape 4–18 in., ribbed; lvs. 1–2, linear, ³⁄₁₆–¾ in. wide, mostly shorter than scape, more or less scabrid on margin; umbel many-fld., dense, spathe short, pedicels as long as fls. or to 1½ times as long;

perianth segms. white with green nerve, 5/16–½ in. long, withering after flowering, filaments included, half as long as the segms., entire, united to perianth and to one another for ¾–⅔ their length, ovules several in each cell. Cent. Asia.

denudatum Redouté [*A. albidum* Fisch. ex Bess.]. Bulbs clustered on a rhizome, outer bulb coat membranous; scape to 1 ft., ribbed; lvs. 6, narrowly linear, flattish, channelled, 1/16–3/16 in. wide, shorter than scape, mostly smooth; umbel many-fld., pedicels all the same length, slightly longer than fls. or up to twice as long; perianth segms. white or reddish-tinged, oblong or oblong-elliptic, obtuse, 5/32–3/16 in. long, filaments as long as segms. or scarcely longer, style exserted, ovary without nectaries. Eurasia.

deserticola: *A. macropetalum.*

dichlamydeum Greene. Bulbs not on a rhizome, outer bulb coat membranous, netted with horizontal, narrow, V-shaped meshes in rows; scape to 1 ft.; lvs. narrow, shorter than scape; umbel many-fld., pedicels 1½–2 times as long as fls.; perianth segms. deep rose-purple, ⅜ in. long, the outer broadly oblong-ovate, abruptly acute, filaments ⅔ as long as segms., ovary 6-crested, without nectaries. Cent. Calif.

Douglasii Hook. Bulbs not on a rhizome, outer bulb coat membranous, not patterned; scape to 10 in., cylindrical; lvs. 2, ¼–5/16 in. wide, shorter than scape; umbel many-fld., pedicels about twice as long as fls.; perianth segms. pink or rarely white, about 5/16 in. long, filaments as long as segms. or slightly longer, style exserted, ovary not crested, without nectaries. Wash., Ore., Idaho.

Drummondii Regel [*A. Helleri* Small; *A. Nuttallii* S. Wats.]. Bulbs not on a rhizome, outer bulb coat a fibrous network of fine meshes with a membrane; scape to 1 ft.; lvs. 3 or more, to ⅛ in. wide, about as long as scape; umbel 10–25-fld., spathe valves 1-nerved; perianth campanulate, segms. white, pink, or red, ovate to lanceolate, ¼–5/16 in. long, becoming rigid in fr., filaments included, ovary without crests or nectaries. Tex. to New Mex. and n. Mex., n. to w. Nebr. Some material grown under this name is probably *A. canadense* var. *Fraseri.*

elatum Regel. Bulb ovoid, spherical, solitary, outer bulb coat blackish, membranous; scape 2–3½ ft., ribbed; lvs. 2–14, oblanceolate, ¾–2¾ in. wide, glabrous; umbel many-fld., spathe short, pedicels all nearly the same length, 3–8 times as long as fls.; perianth segms. violet, with darker nerves, ¼–5/16 in. long, unchanged after flowering, filaments exserted, entire, united to perianth and to one another at base, ovules several in each cell. Turkestan.

falcatum: a listed name of no botanical standing.

falcifolium Hook. & Arn. Bulbs not on a rhizome, outer bulb coat membranous, not patterned; scape to 4 in., flattened and 2-edged; lvs. 2, sickle-shaped, ⅛–3/16 in. wide, much longer than scape; umbel many-fld., pedicels as long as fls. or shorter; perianth segms. deep rose, narrowly lanceolate-attenuate and spreading, ⅜–9/16 in. long, the inner denticulate on the margin, filaments about half as long as segms., ovary with 3 narrow, central, entire crests, without nectaries. S. Ore., n. Calif.

fallax: *A. senescens.*

Farreri: *A. cyathophorum* var.

fibrillum M. E. Jones. Bulbs not on a rhizome, outer bulb coat membranous, netted with narrow, contorted meshes not in rows; scape to 4 in.; lvs. ⅛–3/16 in. wide, as long as or longer than scape; umbel many-fld., pedicels somewhat longer than fls.; perianth segms. white or pale rose, 5/16–½ in. long, filaments half as long as segms., ovary obscurely ridged, without nectaries. Idaho.

fibrosum: see *A. rubrum.*

fimbriatum S. Wats. Bulbs not on a rhizome, outer bulb coat membranous, not patterned; scape to 4 in., cylindrical; lf. solitary, ⅛ in. wide, longer than scape; umbel many-fld., pedicels 1½–2 times as long as fls.; perianth segms. rose-purple, 5/16–⅜ in. long, filaments about half as long as segms., ovary with 6 prominent fringed crests, without nectaries. Calif.

fistulosum L. WELSH O., CIBOULE, SPANISH O., JAPANESE BUNCHING O., TWO-BLADED O. Bulbs elongate, little or no thicker than the neck; scape robust, hollow, more than ¼ in. thick, leafy to upper part; lvs. hollow; umbel many-fld., spathes about as long as umbel, pedicels 2–3 times as long as fls., the inner ones longer, not bracteolate; perianth segms. yellowish-white, ¼–5/16 in. long, filaments exserted, broadened, entire, ovary with very narrow nectaries, ovules 2 in each cell. Of cult. origin. See *Onion.*

flavescens Bess. [*A. ammophilum* Heuff.]. Bulbs on a rhizome, outer bulb coat membranous; scape to 1 ft., often flexuous; lvs. 6–8, filiform, semicylindrical, shorter than scape, scabrid on margin, umbel many-fld., pedicels all the same length, 2–3 times as long as fls.; perianth segms. yellowish, oblong-lanceolate or oblong, ⅛–3/16 in. long, filaments as long as segms. or longer, style exserted, ovary without nectaries. Eurasia.

flavum L. Bulbs ovoid, outer bulb coat membranous; scape flexuous, 1½–2 ft., leafy to middle; lvs. narrow-linear, 1/16–⅛ in. wide; umbel many-fld., spathe valves 2, the longer 3–5 times as long as umbel, pedicels unequal, the shortest 2–3 times as long as fls.; perianth segms. bright yellow, 3/16 in. long, filaments 1½–2 times as long as segms., ovary without nectaries. S. Eur. to w. Asia. Cvs. **'Majus'**, **'Minus'**, **'Pulchellum'**, and **'Pumilum Roseum'** are listed.

Fraseri: *A. canadense* var.

frigidum Boiss. & Heldr. Bulb ovoid, outer bulb coat membranous; scape to 10 in.; lvs. 2–3, almost filiform; umbel many-fld., spathe about as long as pedicels, pedicels 4–7 times as long as fls.; perianth segms. reddish-yellow, 3/16 in. long, filaments slightly longer than segms., ovary without nectaries. Greece.

galanthum Kar. & Kir. Bulbs elongate, on a rhizome, outer bulb coat red-brown, membranous; scape to 20 in., robust, inflated, gradually tapered upward, leafy; lvs. 2–3, to ⅜ in. wide, ½–⅔ as long as scape; umbel many-fld., pedicels 2–3 times as long as fls.; perianth segms. white, 3/16 in. long, filaments scarcely exserted, united to perianth and to one another in a ring at base, entire or the inner with 2 short teeth at the base, ovary with nectaries. Siberia. Some of the material grown under this name is *A. fistulosum.*

Geyeri S. Wats. [*A. pikeanum* Rydb.]. Bulbs not on a rhizome, outer bulb coat a fibrous network of open meshes; scape to 20 in.; lvs. usually 3 or more, ⅛–3/16 in. wide, shorter than scape; umbel many-fld., spathe valves 1-nerved, pedicels often 3 or more times as long as fls.; perianth segms. pink or rarely white, ¼–5/16 in. long, filaments included, ovary with 6 rather prominent crests, without nectaries. Se. Ariz., w. Tex., n. to S. Dak. and Alta.

giganteum Regel. Bulbs ovoid, outer bulb coat membranous; scape to 4 ft.; lvs. 1½ ft. long, 2 in. wide, glaucous; umbels densely fld., globose, 4 in. across, pedicels all of nearly same length, many times longer than fls.; perianth segms. bright lilac, erect in fl. and fr., filaments exserted, entire, ovules several in each cell. Cent. Asia. Some material grown under this name is *A. Ampeloprasum.*

glaucum: *A. senescens.*

globosum Bieb. ex Redouté. Bulbs elongate, on a short rhizome, outer bulb coat splitting, not netted; scape to 2 ft., leafy in the lowermost ¼–⅓; lvs. 5–6, subulate, shorter than scape; umbel many-fld., spathe beaked, 2–3 or more times as long as umbel, pedicels 1½–2 times as long as fls.; perianth segms. deep rose, 3/16 in. long, filaments 1½–2 times as long as segms., entire, style exserted, ovary with nectaries. Caucasus.

haematochiton S. Wats. RED-SKINNED O. Bulbs. elongate, outer bulb coat membranous, reddish-purple; scape to 1½ ft., slightly 2-edged; lvs. several, linear, flat, 1/16–3/16 in. wide, about as long as scape; umbel many-fld., pedicels 2–3 times as long as fls.; perianth segms. deep purple or rose, ¼–5/16 in. long, filaments included, entire, style included, ovary 6-crested, without nectaries. Dry hillsides, s. Calif. to Baja Calif.

Heldreichii Boiss. Bulbs small, outer bulb coat membranous; scape to 1½ ft.; lvs. 2, cylindrical, hollow, longer than scape; umbel globose, pedicels shorter than to as long as fls.; perianth segms. 5/16 in. long, glossy, acuminate, filaments included, the inner with 2 teeth near the apex, ovary with nectaries. Greece.

Helleri: *A. Drummondii.*

Huteri: a listed name of no botanical standing; plants so named are a variant of *A. senescens.*

hymenorrhizum Ledeb. Bulbs 1 to few on a short rhizome, outer bulb coat brown, membranous; scape 1–3 ft., leafy nearly to middle; lvs. 4–6, linear, ⅛–3/16 in. wide, shorter than scape; umbel many-fld., pedicels all the same length, 1½–3 times as long as fls.; perianth segms. rosy, 3/16–¼ in. long, filaments 1½–2 times as long as segms., entire, style exserted, ovary with nectaries. W. Asia.

insubricum Boiss. & Reut. Similar to *A. narcissiflorum* and sometimes considered a var. of it, but differs in having outer bulb coat membranous, not netted, lvs. glaucescent, and fls. permanently nodding.

japonicum: *A. Thunbergii.*

kansuense Regel. Bulbs slender, clustered, fibrous, producing bulblets at the ends of short, slender rhizomes, outer bulb coat fibrous-netted; scape to 1 ft.; lvs. 3–5, linear, channelled, ⅛–3/16 in. wide, shorter than scape, minutely scabrid on margins; umbel many-fld., pedicels shorter than fls.; fls. nodding, perianth segms. blue, 3/16–5/16 in. long, filaments about ⅔ as long as segms., both inner and outer with 2 teeth near base, ovary with nectaries. Very similar to *A. sikkimense.* China.

karataviense Regel. Bulbs ovoid, outer bulb coat membranous; scape to 10 in.; lvs. broadly ovate to elliptic, 2–5 in. wide, longer than scape, glaucous; umbel many-fld., pedicels 2–5 times as long as fls.;

perianth segms. reddish, to 5/16 in. long, twisted and reflexed in fr., filaments as long as segms. or slightly longer, ovules several in each cell. Turkestan.

Kochii: *A. vineale* var.; but plants grown as *A. Kochii* have proved to be *A. fistulosum.*

Kunthii G. Don [*A. scaposum* Benth.]. Bulbs not on a rhizome, outer bulb coat membranous, not patterned; scape to 16 in., cylindrical; lvs. 2–4, 3-angled, channelled, about 1/8 in. wide, shorter than scape; umbel many-fld., pedicels 2–3 times as long as fls., perianth segms. white to pink, with red nerve, 3/16–1/4 in. long, filaments slightly shorter than segms., style not exserted, ovary not crested, without nectaries. New Mex. and Tex., s. to cent. Mex.

lacunosum S. Wats. Bulbs not on a rhizome, outer bulb coat membranous, netted with squarish or horizontally oblong meshes in rows, the mesh walls thick, uniform, enclosing pits; scape to 6 in.; lvs. narrow, about as long as scape; umbel several-fld., pedicels slightly longer than fls.; perianth segms. pale rose, 1/4–5/16 in. long, filaments nearly as long as segms., ovary obtusely 3-ridged at apex, without nectaries. Cent. and s. Calif.

Ledebourianum Roem. & Schult. [*A. uliginosum* Ledeb., not G. Don]. Bulbs clustered on a very small rhizome, outer bulb coat membranous; scape to 2½ ft., leafy to middle; lvs. 1–2, semicylindrical, hollow, 3/16–3/8 in. wide, shorter than scape; umbel many-fld., pedicels 1½–3 times as long as fls.; perianth segms. rose-violet, 1/4–1/2 in. long, filaments 2/3 to almost as long as segms., united to perianth and to one another at base, style exserted, ovary with nectaries. Siberia. Most cult. material so named is *A. Schoenoprasum.*

Lemmonii S. Wats. Bulbs not on a rhizome, outer bulb coat membranous, netted with vertical rows of fine, horizontally oblong meshes, with vertical mesh walls thickest and sinuous; scape to 6 in.; lvs. 2, 3/16 in. wide, about as long as scape; umbel many-fld., pedicels to twice as long as fls.; perianth segms. pale rose, to 5/16 in. long, filaments about as long as segms.; ovary with low, broad, obscure crests that are not evident in fr., without nectaries. Calif.

libani Boiss. Bulbs not on a rhizome, outer bulb coat membranous; scape to 3 in.; lvs. 3/16–1/2 in. wide, longer than the scape; umbel many-fld., pedicels 1½ times as long as fls.; perianth segms. 1/4 in. long, yellowish-white, with red nerve, filaments half as long as segms., ovary not crested, without nectaries. Asia Minor.

lineare L. Bulbs ovoid, outer bulb coat fibrous-netted; scape to 2 ft., leafy in lowermost 1/3–1/2; lvs. 3–4, narrowly linear, flat, 1/16–1/8 in. wide, shorter than scape, smooth or hispid on margin; umbel many-fld., pedicels 2–3 times as long as fls.; perianth segms. rose, 1/8–3/16 in. long, filaments 1½–2 times as long as segms., the inner with 2 teeth near base, stigma scarcely thickened, ovary with nectaries. Russia, Siberia.

macranthum Bak. Outer bulb coat membranous; scape 1–2 ft.; lvs. 6–9, 1/4–3/4 in. wide, shorter than scape; umbel many-fld., pedicels twice or more as long as fls.; perianth segms. dark purple, 1/4–1/2 in. long, filaments included, stigma headlike, style exserted. Sikkim Himalayas, Tibet, China.

macropetalum Rydb. [*A. deserticola* (M. E. Jones) Woot. & Standl.]. Bulbs ovoid, often clustered, outer bulb coat fibrous network of open meshes; scape to 8 in.; lvs. 2, to 1/8 in. wide, longer than scape; umbel 10–20-fld., spathe valves 3–5-nerved, pedicels 2–3 times as long as perianth; perianth segms. pink, with deeper colored nerve, 5/16–1/2 in. long, papery in fr., filaments included, entire, ovary 6-crested, without nectaries. Desert plains and hills, Colo. to Ariz. and w. Tex.

Mairei Lév. [*A. yunnanense* Diels]. Bulbs slender, clustered, outer bulb coat fibrous; scape to 16 in., leafy in lowermost 1/3; lvs. filiform, cylindrical, 1/16 in. wide, shorter than scape; umbel few-fld., pedicels unequal, 1–1½ times as long as fls.; perianth segms. pale pink or whitish, 3/8 in. long, filaments included, ovary with nectaries. China.

margaritaceum Sibth. & Sm. Bulb ovoid, outer bulb coat membranous; scape to 2 ft., leafy to middle; lvs. semicylindrical, to 1/8 in. wide; umbel many-fld., globose, outer pedicels 2–3 times as long as inner ones and many times longer than fls.; perianth segms. white, inner filaments with 2 teeth near apex, ovary with nectaries. S. Eur.

maritimum: *Muilla maritima.*

Mnuki: a listed name of no botanical standing.

mobilense: *A. canadense* var.

Moly L. LILY LEEK. Bulbs ovoid, not on a rhizome, outer bulb coat leathery, covered with a pale membrane obscuring a contorted network of meshes; scape to 1½ ft.; lvs. 2, basal, lanceolate, narrowed toward base and apex, 1/2–2 in. wide, to 12 in. long, glaucous; umbel several- to many-fld., pedicels 1–3 times as long as fls.; perianth segms. bright yellow, 3/8–1/2 in. long, papery and persistent, filaments about half as long as segms., entire, ovary without nectaries. S. Eur. Cv. **'Luteum'** is listed.

monadelphum Less. ex Kunth. Bulbs 1 to several on a rhizome; scape to 2 ft., leafy in lowermost 1/5–1/2; lvs. 1–2, hollow, cylindrical, 1/8–5/16 in. wide, shorter or longer than scape; umbel few-fld., pedicels unequal at flowering, 1/3–1/2 as long as fls., and in fr. up to twice as long; perianth segms. yellow, 4–6 times as long as wide, 5/16–3/8 in. long, filaments 1/3–1/2 as long as segms., united to the perianth almost halfway and united to one another for 2/3–3/4 their length, style included, stigmas 3, ovary with nectaries. Asia.

montanum: *A. senescens.*

moschatum L. Bulbs on a short rhizome, upper part of outer bulb coat more or less fibrous-netted; scape to 10 in.; lvs. 4–6, filiform, channelled, about as long as scape, scabrid on margin; umbel many-fld., spathe somewhat shorter than umbel, its beak usually longer than its expanded base, pedicels 2–3 times as long as fls.; perianth segms. rose, with purple nerve, about 1/4 in. long, filaments about 2/3 as long as segms., style not exserted, ovary with nectaries. Eur., Asia Minor, Caucasus.

multibulbosum: *A. nigrum.*

mutabile: *A. canadense* var. *canadense.*

nanhoense: a listed name of no botanical standing.

narcissiflorum Vill. [*A. pedemontanum* Willd.]. Bulbs slender, on a rhizome, outer bulb coat fibrous-netted; scape to 1 ft.; lvs. 4–6, basal, 1/8–3/16 in. wide, shorter than scape to nearly as long; umbel few-fld., nodding in bud, erect in fr., pedicels shorter than to somewhat longer than fls.; perianth segms. rose, 3/8–1/2 in. long, filaments about half as long as segms., entire, style included, stigma 3-lobed, ovary without nectaries. Italy.

neapolitanum Cyr. [*A. album* Santi; *A. Cowanii* Lindl.]. DAFFODIL GARLIC, FLOWERING O. Bulbs not on a rhizome, outer bulb coat membranous, netted with rectangular narrow meshes, the enclosed spaces shallow; scape to 1½ ft.; lvs. broadly linear, 5/16–1 in. wide, shorter than scape, often scabrid or short-ciliate on margin; umbel several- to many-fld., pedicels 2–3 or more times as long as fls.; perianth segms. white, broadly ovate or elliptic, obtuse, 3/8–5/8 in. long, becoming scarious, style entire, linear, ovary not crested, without nectaries. S. Eur., Asia Minor, N. Afr. Cvs. **'Albo-giganteum'**, **'Grandiflorum'**, and **'Roseum'** are listed.

Nevii S. Wats. Bulbs not on a rhizome, outer bulb coat membranous, netted with horizontal oblong meshes in rows, mesh walls fine, not forming pits; scape to 10 in.; lvs. 2, narrow, shorter than scape; umbel several-fld., pedicels to twice as long as fls.; perianth segms. light rose, filaments as long as segms., ovary with 6 low crests, without nectaries. Wash., Ore., Idaho.

nigrum L. [*A. multibulbosum* Jacq.; *A. speciosum* Cyr.]. Bulb ovoid, solitary, outer bulb coat membranous; scape to 2½ ft.; lvs. linear-lanceolate, 5/8–2⅜ in. wide, glabrous; umbel many-fld., spathe short, pedicels all nearly the same length, 4–5 times as long as fls.; perianth segms. elliptic, white or pale lilac, with green keel, 1/4–5/16 in. long, filaments 3/4 as long as segms., entire, united at base, anthers yellow, ovules several in each cell. N. Afr., s. Eur., w. Asia. Var. **atropurpureum:** *A. atropurpureum.*

nutans L. Bulbs on a stout rhizome, outer bulb coat membranous; scape 1–2 ft., 2-edged; lvs. 6–8, linear, flat, 5/16–5/8 in. wide, glabrous, glaucous; umbel many-fld., pedicels 1½–2 times as long as fls.; perianth segms. rose or rose-violet to white, oblong-ovate, 3/16 in. long, filaments united to one another and to perianth at base, 1½–2 times as long as segms., the inner twice as broad as the outer and usually with 2 teeth near the base, style exserted, ovary without nectaries. Siberia.

Nuttallii: *A. Drummondii.*

obliquum L. Bulb solitary, on a short rhizome, outer bulb coat membranous, reddish-brown; scape 2–5 ft., leafy in lower 1/3–1/2; lvs. 6–9, lanceolate, to 3/4 in. wide, shorter than scape; umbel many-fld., pedicels all nearly the same length, 2–3 times as long as fls.; perianth segms. greenish-yellow, 3/16 in. long, filaments 1½ times as long as segms., entire, united to perianth and to one another at base, style exserted, ovary with nectaries. Asia.

ochroleucum Waldst. & Kit. Bulbs on a short rhizome, outer bulb coat membranous, dark brown; scape 1 to, rarely, 2 ft., leafy at base or in lowermost 1/4; lvs. linear, 1/8–3/16 in. wide, shorter than scape; umbel many-fld.; pedicels all of the same length, 1–2 times as long as fls.; perianth segms. greenish-white, with reddish nerve, filaments about twice as long as segms., entire, ovary with nectaries. S. Eur.

odorum: *A. ramosum;* but see also *A. tuberosum.*

oleraceum L. FIELD GARLIC. Bulbs ovoid, outer bulb coat membranous; scape to 2 ft., leafy in lowermost 1/3–1/2; lvs. 3–4, narrow-linear, 1/16–1/8 in. wide, shorter than scape; umbel few-fld., bearing bulbils, spathe 2–3 times as long as umbel, pedicels unequal, 2–4(–6) times as long as fls.; perianth segms. greenish or rosy, 1/4 in. long, filaments as long as segms., style exserted, ovary without nectaries. Eur.

oreophilum C. A. Mey. Bulbs not on a rhizome, outer bulb coat membranous; scape to 4 in.; lvs. 2–3, ⅛–⁵⁄₁₆ in. wide, longer than scape, glaucous; umbel many-fld., pedicels to twice as long as fls.; perianth segms. purple, with darker nerve, ⅜ in. long, filaments included, ovary not crested, without nectaries. Caucasus, Turkestan, cent. Asia.

Ostrowskianum Regel. Bulbs not on a rhizome, outer bulb coat membranous, scape to 1 ft.; lvs. 2–3, linear-oblong, to ½ in. wide, longer than scape, glaucous; umbel many-fld., pedicels 2–3 times as long as fls.; perianth segms. rose, about ½ in. long, oblong-elliptic, filaments about ⅓ as long as segms., the inner linear, the outer broadly lanceolate-attenuate, ovary not crested, without nectaries. Turkestan. By some considered a var. or color form of *A. oreophilum*.

oxyphilum: *A. cernuum*.

pallens: a name of varied application, perhaps referable to *A. paniculatum*.

paniculatum L. Bulbs ovoid, outer bulb coat membranous; scape to 2 ft., leafy in lowermost ⅔; lvs. 3–4, narrow-linear, ¹⁄₁₆–⅛ in. wide, often longer than scape; umbel many-fld., spathe 2–4 times as long as umbel, pedicels 2–8 times as long as fls.; perianth segms. rose, ³⁄₁₆–¼ in. long, filaments about as long as segms., style scarcely exserted, ovary without nectaries. Medit., w. and cent. Asia.

Parishii S. Wats. Bulbs not on a rhizome, outer bulb coat membranous, not patterned; scape to 6 in.; lf. solitary, longer than scape; umbel few- to many-fld., pedicels shorter than to as long as fls.; perianth segms. rose-purple, ½–¾ in. long, lanceolate, filaments half as long as segms., ovary with 6 acutish, irregularly toothed crests, without nectaries. Calif.

parvum Kellogg. Bulbs not on a rhizome, outer bulb coat membranous, not patterned; scape to 2 in., cylindrical; lvs. 2, ³⁄₃₂–⅛ in. wide, twice as long as scape; umbel several- to many-fld., pedicels shorter than to as long as fls.; perianth segms. rose-purple, with dark nerve, ¼–⁵⁄₁₆ in. long, filaments about ⅔ as long as segms., ovary without nectaries. Calif., w. Nev.

pedemontanum: *A. narcissiflorum*.

peltatum: a listed name of no botanical standing.

peninsulare Lemm. Bulbs not on a rhizome, outer bulb coat membranous, netted with horizontal, narrow, V-shaped meshes in rows; scape to 1 ft.; lvs. 2–4, ¹⁄₁₆–⅛ in. wide, about as long as scape; umbel several-fld., pedicels 2–3 times as long as fls.; perianth segms. deep rose-purple, ⅜–½ in. long, outer segms. ovate-lanceolate, nearly twice as wide as the inner, filaments ⅔ as long as segms., ovary narrowly 6-crested, without nectaries. Calif. Var. **crispum** (Greene) Jeps. [*A. crispum* Greene]. Inner perianth segms. crisped along margins.

perdulce S. Fraser. Bulbs ovoid, often clustered, but not on a rhizome, outer bulb coat a fibrous network of open meshes; scape to 10 in.; lvs. 3 or more, to ⅛ in. wide, as long as or slightly shorter than scape; umbel 5–25-fld., spathe valves 5-nerved, pedicels 1–2 times as long as fls.; fls. urceolate, perianth segms. deep rose, to ⅜ in. long, enclosing ovary in fr., filaments included, ovary without crests. Se. S. Dak. and Iowa, s. to n.-cent. Tex. and e. New Mex. Sometimes grown under the name *A. reticulatum*.

pikeanum: *A. Geyeri*.

pilosum Sibth. & Sm. Bulbs subglobose, outer bulb coat membranous; scape to 3 in., leafy to middle; lvs. semicylindrical, narrowly linear, pilose; umbel densely many-fld., spathe as long as umbel or longer, pedicels all nearly the same length, 2–3 times as long as fls.; perianth segms. lilac, obtuse, without bloom, filaments about as long as perianth, entire, ovary without nectaries. E. Medit.

platycaule S. Wats. Bulbs not on a rhizome, outer bulb coat membranous, not patterned; scape to 6 in., flattened; lvs. 2, sickle-shaped, ⅜–¾ in. wide, longer than scape; umbel many-fld., spathe valves 3–4, long-acuminate, united basally; pedicels as long as fls. or somewhat longer; perianth segms. rose, ⅜–⁹⁄₁₆ in. long, long-acuminate, filaments as long as segms., ovary without nectaries. Ore., n. Calif.

Porrum: *A. Ampeloprasum* Porrum Group.

praecox Brandeg. Bulbs not on a rhizome, outer bulb coat membranous, netted with sinuous meshes in serrated rows; scape to 20 in.; lvs. 2–4, flat, to ³⁄₁₆ in. wide, shorter than scape; umbel 10–20-fld., pedicels 2–3 times as long as fls.; perianth segms. white, with rose-purple nerve, to ⅜ in. long, filaments ⅔ as long as segms., ovary without crest or nectaries. S. Calif.

prairiense: a listed name of no botanical standing.

Przewalskianum Regel. Bulbs very slender, densely clustered on a slender rhizome, outer bulb coat fibrous-netted; scape to 10 in.; lvs. filiform, semicylindrical, about as long as scape or longer; umbel many-fld., pedicels 2–3 times as long as fls.; perianth segms. rose-lilac, ⅛–³⁄₁₆ in. long, filaments 1½ times as long as segms., united to one another and to perianth basally, the inner with 2 teeth near the apex of the broad part, ovary without nectaries. China.

pulchellum G. Don. Bulbs ovoid, outer bulb coat membranous; scape 1–2 ft., leafy to middle; lvs. 3–4, semicylindrical, channelled, to ⅛ in. wide, usually shorter than scape; umbel many-fld., spathe 2–4(–5) times as long as umbel, pedicels very unequal, 2–10 times as long as fls.; fls. ellipsoid-campanulate, perianth segms. yellowish or more usually red-purple to rose, with lusterless bloom, ³⁄₁₆ in. long, filaments 1½–2 times as long as segms., style exserted, ovary without nectaries. S. Eur., w. Asia.

Purdomii: *A. cyaneum*.

Purdyi Eastw. Bulbs not on a rhizome, outer bulb coat membranous, not patterned; scape to 1 ft., cylindrical; lf. solitary, shorter than scape; umbel many-fld., pedicels 2–3 times as long as fls.; perianth segms. pale pink, with darker nerve, ¼ in. long, filaments included, ovary with 6 acute or acuminate crests, without nectaries. Calif.

pyrenaicum Costa & Vayr. Outer bulb coat membranous; scape to 1½ ft., leafy to middle; lvs. flat, about ½ in. wide, longer than scape; umbel several- to many-fld., spathe deciduous, long-beaked, pedicels 1–2 times as long as fls.; perianth segms. white, with green nerve, ¼–⁵⁄₁₆ in. long, acuminate, filaments included, with 2 teeth near the apex, ovary with nectaries. Pyrenees.

ramosum L. [*A. odorum* L.; *A. tartaricum* L.f.]. FRAGRANT-FLOW-ERED GARLIC. Bulbs elongate, on a stout rhizome, outer bulb coat fibrous-netted; scape to 20 in.; lvs. 4–9, slightly hollow, convex on the back, ⅛–⁵⁄₁₆ in. wide, shorter than scape; umbel many-fld., pedicels 2–3 times as long as fls.; fls. fragrant, perianth segms. white, with red nerve, ¼–⅜ in. long, filaments about half as long as segms., ovary without nectaries; caps. ovate, widest at base. Flowering in early summer in cult. Cent. Asia. Often confused with *A. tuberosum*.

recurvatum: *A. cernuum*.

reticulatum: *A. textile;* some material cult. as *A. reticulatum*, however, appears to be *A. perdulce*.

Rosenbachianum Regel. Bulb spherical, solitary, outer bulb coat blackish, membranous; scape 1½–2½ ft., strongly ribbed; lvs. 2–3, linear-lanceolate, ⅜–2 in. wide, shorter than scape, glabrous; umbel many-fld., spathe short, pedicels unequal, 3–9 times as long as fls.; perianth segms. dark violet, with darker nerve, narrow-linear, ¼–⅜ in. long, reflexed and twisted after flowering, filaments as long as segms., entire, united to perianth and to one another at base, anthers violet, ovules several in each cell. Turkestan. Cv. '**Album**' is listed. Material grown under this name may be *A. stipitatum*.

roseum L. Bulbs not on a rhizome, outer bulb coat membranous, netted with thick-walled, rounded meshes, the enclosed spaces deep; scape to 1½ ft.; lvs. broadly linear, to ⅜ in. wide, shorter than scape, smooth or scabrid on the margin; umbel several- to many-fld., pedicels 1½–3 times as long as fls.; perianth segms. rose or rarely white, elliptic-oblong, ⁵⁄₁₆–½ in. long, ovary without crests or nectaries. S. Eur., N. Afr., Asia Minor. Var. **bulbilliferum** Vis. Differs in bearing bulbils in the umbel.

rotundum L. Outer bulb coat dark, membranous, at least on bulb-lets and new bulbs; scape to 3 ft., leafy to middle; lvs. 3–5, flat, to ¼ in. wide; umbel dense, globose, outer pedicels very short, inner 1½–2 times as long as fls.; perianth segms. deep red-purple, filaments and style included, inner filaments with 2 lobes near apex, ovary with nectaries. Eur., w. Asia.

rubens Schrad. ex Willd. Bulbs crowded on a stout horizontal rhizome, outer bulb coat membranous; scape to 1 ft.; lvs. 5–6, basal, semicylindrical, to ⅛ in. wide but mostly less, minutely scabrid on the margin; umbel few-fld., pedicels 2–3 times as long as fls.; perianth segms. rosy-violet, ³⁄₁₆ in. long, obtuse, filaments as long as or scarcely longer than perianth, style included, ovary without nectaries. Ural Mts.

rubrum Osterh. [*A. fibrosum* Rydb., not Regel; *A. Rydbergii* Macbr.]. Bulbs not on a rhizome, outer bulb coat a fibrous network of open meshes; scape to 1 ft.; lvs. few, about ¼ in. wide or less, shorter than scape; umbel with bulbils and few or no fls., spathe valves 1-nerved, pedicels scarcely twice as long as fls.; perianth segms. ovate, obtuse, ¼ in. long, pink or white, filaments included, ovary inconspicuously crested with 6 low rounded knobs, without nectaries. New Mex. and Ariz. to B.C. and Alta.

Rydbergii: *A. rubrum*.

sativum L. [*A. controversum* Schrad.; *A. sativum* var. *controversum* (Schrad.) Regel and var. *Ophioscorodon* (Link) Döll]. GARLIC. Bulb ovoid or globose, usually divided into several cloves within the membranous coat, often bearing bulblets; scape to 2 ft., leafy to middle; lvs. 4–6, flat, to ½ in. wide; umbel bearing bulbils, spathe valves long-beaked, longer than fls., pedicels 2 or more times as long as fls.; perianth segms. white to pinkish, margins of outer segms. entire, filaments included, the inner with 2 lateral teeth near apex, the teeth longer than the central anther-bearing portion, ovary with nectaries. Variable cultigen, perhaps derived from an Asiatic sp. with intergrading forms. SERPENT GARLIC or ROCAMBOLE, a form with the scape coiled in bud, has been referred to as var. *Ophioscorodon* (Link) Döll. See *Garlic* and *Onion.*

scaposum: *A. Kunthii.*

Schoenoprasum L. CHIVE, CIVE, SCHNITTLAUCH. Bulbs clustered on a very small rhizome, outer bulb coat membranous; scape to 2 ft., hollow, leafy in lowermost ⅓–½; lvs. 1–2, hollow, cylindrical or semicylindrical, as long as scape or longer; umbel many-fld., pedicels unequal, shorter than fls.; perianth segms. rose to rose-violet, 4–6 times as long as wide, ¼–⅜ in. long, filaments ⅓–½ as long as segms., united to perianth and to one another ¼–⅓ their length, style included, ovary with nectaries. Eur., Asia. Var. **orientale** Regel. Umbels loose; perianth segms. lanceolate or linear-lanceolate, filaments nearly as long as segms. Siberia. See *Onion.* Var. **sibiricum** (L.) Hartm. [*A. sibiricum* L.]. Differs chiefly in having lvs. shorter than scape. Siberia, N. Amer.

Schubertii Zucc. Bulb spherical, solitary, outer bulb coat blackish, membranous; scape stout, to 1 ft.; lvs. linear-lanceolate, somewhat longer than scape, glaucous, crisped and scabrid on margins; umbel many-fld., spathe very short, pedicels unequal, thickened below fls., in 2 series, the fertile ones to 4 in., the sterile to 8 in. long; perianth segms. white to rose, with green or purplish nerve, to 5/16 in. long, rigid after flowering, filaments included, ovules several but of variable number in each cell. E. Medit., cent. Asia.

scilloides Dougl. An inadequately known and described sp. from the Columbia River valley, nw. U.S.

Scorodoprasum L. GIANT GARLIC, SPANISH G., SAND LEEK. Bulb ovoid or depressed-globose, to 1 in. thick, often bearing bulblets, outer bulb coat membranous, dark violet; scape to 3 ft., leafy to middle; lvs. 4–5, flat, 5/16 in. wide or more; umbel bearing bulbils, spathe valves short, pedicels 2 or more times as long as fls.; perianth segms. deep purple, margins of outer segms. minutely toothed, filaments included, with 2 lateral teeth near apex, the teeth longer than the central anther-bearing portion, ovary with nectaries. Eur., Asia Minor. Incorrectly called ROCAMBOLE, see *A. sativum.* For cult. see *Onion.*

senescens L. [*A. fallax* Roem. & Schult.; *A. glaucum* Schrad.; *A. montanum* F. W. Schmidt]. Bulbs on a stout rhizome, outer bulb coat membranous; scape 1–2 ft., 2-edged; lvs. 5–8, linear, flat, ⅛–⅜ in. wide, glabrous, more or less glaucous; perianth segms. rose to whitish, oblong-lanceolate to ovate, obtuse, 3/16 in. long, filaments united to perianth and to one another at base, slightly longer than segms. to 1½ times as long, the inner 1½ times as wide as the outer, generally entire, style exserted, ovary without nectaries. Eur. to Siberia. A variable sp. as to lvs. and size; common in cult. and grown under many names. Narrow-leaved forms are sometimes known as var. **calcareum** (Wallr.) Hyl. [*A. fallax; A. montanum*], or erroneously as *A. montanum* subsp. *petraeum* (DC.) Asch. & Graebn.; glaucous-leaved small forms are known as var. **glaucum** (Schrad.) Regel [*A. glaucum*].

serratum S. Wats. Bulbs not on a rhizome, outer bulb coat membranous, netted with horizontal, narrow, V-shaped meshes in rows; scape to 6 in.; lvs. 2–4, ⅛ in. wide, shorter than scape; umbel many-fld., pedicels as long as fls. to twice as long; perianth segms. rose-pink, 5/16 in. long, ovate-lanceolate, acuminate, filaments about ⅔ as long as segms., ovary with 6 narrow crests, without nectaries. Cent. Calif.

sibiricum: *A. Schoenoprasum* var.

siculum: *Nectaroscordum siculum.*

sikkimense Bak. Bulbs slender, clustered, outer bulb coat fibrous-netted; scape 4–12 in.; lvs. 2–3, narrowly linear, channelled, ½–¼ in. wide, shorter than scape; umbel few-fld., nodding, pedicels shorter than fls. to somewhat longer; perianth segms. lilac-purple, 5/16–½ in. long, filaments included, the inner with 2 teeth near the base, ovary with nectaries. Sikkim Himalayas.

sitchense: a listed name of no botanical standing.

speciosum: *A. nigrum.*

sphaerocephalum L. ROUND-HEADED GARLIC. Bulb ovoid, outer bulb coat membranous; scape to 2 ft., leafy to middle; umbel many-fld., globose, outer pedicels shorter than inner and 2–3 times as long as fls.; lvs. 3–5, semicylindrical, hollow, to ⅛ in. wide, much shorter than scape; perianth segms. red, inner filaments with 2 lateral teeth above the middle, the teeth about as long as the anther-bearing portion, filaments and style exserted, ovary with nectaries. N. Afr., Eur., w. Asia.

splendens Willd. ex Roem. & Schult. Bulbs ovoid, outer bulb coat fibrous-netted; scape to 20 in., cylindrical, leafy in lowermost ⅓–½; lvs. 3–4, linear, flat, 1/16–3/16 in. wide, scabrid on margin; umbel many-fld., pedicels 1½–2 times as long as fls.; perianth segms. bright rose-lilac, with purple nerve, 1/16–⅛ in. long, filaments 1½–2 times as long as segms., the inner 2–4-toothed near base, ovary with nectaries. Japan, e. Asia.

stellatum Ker. PRAIRIE O. Bulbs elongate, outer bulb coat membranous; scape to 1½ ft.; lvs. several, linear, flat, to 3/16 in. wide, mostly shorter than scape; umbel many-fld., pedicels 2–3 or more times as long as fls.; perianth segms. lavender-pink, 5/32–3/16 in. long, filaments exserted, entire, style exserted, ovary 6-crested, without nectaries. Rocky slopes or prairies, w. Ill. and Minn., w. to Nebr. and Kans. Cv. **'Album'** is listed.

Stelleranum Willd. Bulbs clustered on a rhizome, outer bulb coat membranous; scape to 1 ft.; lvs. 4–6, semicylindrical, narrowly linear, channelled, shorter than scape, scabrid on margin; umbel few-fld., pedicels as long as fls. to twice as long; perianth segms. yellow or rose-tinged, elliptic to ovate, 5/32–3/16 in. long, filaments slightly longer than segms. to 1½ times as long, style exserted, ovary without nectaries. Siberia.

stellulatum: a listed name, probably in error for *A. stellatum.*

stenanthum: *A. Bolanderi* var.

stipitatum Regel. Bulb spherical, solitary, outer bulb coat membranous, blackish; scape stout, 2–5 ft.; lvs. 4–6, strap-shaped, ¾–⅝ in. wide, hairy beneath; umbel many-fld., pedicels nearly equal, 3–6 times as long as fls.; perianth segms. lilac, about 5/16 in. long, reflexed and twisted after flowering, filaments as long as segms., entire, united to segms. at base and united to one another above, ovary stalked, ovules several in each cell. Cent. Asia. May be cult. mistakenly as *A. Rosenbachianum.*

striatum: *Nothoscordum bivalve.*

strictum Schrad. Bulbs ovoid, outer bulb coat fibrous-netted; scape to 2 ft., leafy in lowermost ⅓; lvs. 3–4, linear, flat, ⅛–3/16 in. wide, shorter than scape, scabrid on margin; umbel many-fld., pedicels 1½–2 or more times as long as fls.; perianth segms. rose, with purple nerve, 3/16 in. long, filaments as long as segms. to 1½ times as long, the inner with 2 teeth near base, stigma nearly headlike, ovary with nectaries. Eur., w. Asia.

subangulatum Regel. Bulbs clustered on a slender rhizome, outer bulb coat fibrous-netted; scape to 1 ft., leafy only near base; lvs. filiform, nearly cylindrical, shorter than scape, minutely ciliate-toothed on margin; umbel many-fld., pedicels shorter than fls. to 1½ times as long; perianth segms. rose-purple, ¼ in. long, filaments shortly united at base, slightly shorter than segms., the inner with 2 teeth near the apex. China?

subhirsutum L. [*A. ciliatum* Cyr.]. Bulbs not on a rhizome, outer bulb coat membranous, netted with squarish meshes, the enclosed spaces shallow; scape to 15 in.; lvs. linear, ¼–5/16 in. wide, shorter than scape, margin usually ciliate; umbel several- to many-fld., pedicels 1½–4 times as long as fls.; perianth segms. white, ¼–5/16 in. long, lanceolate, scarcely scarious in fr., ovary not crested, without nectaries. N. Afr., s. Eur., Asia Minor.

subroseum: a listed name of no botanical standing.

tanguticum Regel. LAVENDER GLOBE LILY. Bulbs ovate, outer bulb coat dark brown, with parallel fibers, inner coats membranous; scape to 16 in., leafy in lowermost ⅓; lvs. linear, flat, 1/16–⅛ in. wide, shorter than scape; umbel many-fld., pedicels 3 or more times as long as fls.; perianth segms. purplish, with dark nerves, ⅛ in. long, filaments entire, united to perianth and to one another, 1½–2 times as long as segms. W. China.

tartaricum: *A. ramosum.*

tenuissimum L. Bulbs slender, clustered on a slender rhizome, outer bulb coat membranous; scape 2–10 in.; lvs. 2–3, filiform, semicylindrical, nearly as long as scape; umbel hemispherical, few-fld., pedicels all nearly the same length, 1½–3 times as long as fls.; perianth segms. whitish or rosy, 3/16 in. long, filaments ⅔ as long as perianth, the inner twice as wide as the outer, entire, ovary without nectaries. Siberia. Plants cult. under this name appear to be *A. anisopodium.*

textile A. Nels. & Macbr. [*A. reticulatum* J. Fraser ex G. Don, not J. Presl & K. Presl]. Bulbs not on a rhizome, outer bulb coat a fibrous network of open meshes; scape to 1 ft.; lvs. usually 2, ⅛–3/16 in. wide, shorter than to as long as scape; umbel many-fld., spathe valves 1-nerved, pedicels unequal, 2–3 times as long as fls.; perianth segms. white, rarely to pink, with dark nerve, 3/16–¼ in. long, filaments included, ovary with 6 small, rounded crests, without nectaries. Minn. and Man. to Alta., s. to Colo., New Mex., and Utah.

Thunbergii G. Don [*A. japonicum* Regel]. Bulbs slender, clustered on a rhizome, outer bulb coat with nearly parallel fibers, inner coats membranous; scape to 2 ft., cylindrical; lvs. 2–3, linear, longer or shorter than scape; umbel many-fld., pedicels 2–3 times as long as fls.; perianth segms. purplish, 3/16 in. long, filaments separate, to 1½ times as long as perianth, entire, ovary with nectaries. Japan.

tibeticum Rendle. Differs from *A. sikkimense* in having fls. smaller, less campanulate, deep blue. Tibet. Probably not in cult.; most cult. material bearing this name is *A. cyathophorum* var. *Farreri.*

Tolmiei Bak. [*A. Cusickii* S. Wats.]. Bulbs not on a rhizome, outer bulb coat membranous, not patterned; scape to 6 in., flattened and 2-edged; lvs. 2, sickle-shaped, ⅛–½ in. wide, longer than scape; umbel many-fld., pedicels about twice as long as fls.; perianth segms. light rose-purple, ⁵⁄₁₆–⅜ in. long, filaments ½–¾ as long as segms., ovary with 6 obscure to prominent crests, without nectaries. Wash., Ore., Nev., w. to Idaho and Utah.

tricoccum Ait. WILD LEEK, RAMP. Bulbs single or clustered on a rhizome, elongate, outer bulb coat fibrous-netted; scape to 1 ft.; lvs. 2–3, elliptic-lanceolate, narrowed to a distinct petiole, without a sheathing base, to 2 in. wide, 5 in. long, withering before flowering; umbel many-fld., pedicels 2–3 times as long as fls.; perianth segms. greenish-white, about ³⁄₁₆ in. long, filaments included, ovary without nectaries, ovules 1 in each cell; seeds black, nearly spherical. New Bruns. to Minn., s. to N.C. and Iowa.

triquetrum L. Bulb solitary, ovoid, outer bulb coat membranous; scape to 1½ ft., 3-angled, decumbent and loosely sheathed basally; lvs. broadly linear, basal or somewhat sheathing, sharply keeled, to ⁵⁄₁₆ in. wide, ciliate on margin; umbel several-fld., pedicels 2–3 times as long as fls.; fls. campanulate-stellate, perianth segms. white with rosy keel to rose, to ½ in. long, coming together in fr., filaments in 2 series, about half as long as segms., entire, stigma trifid, ovary without nectaries; seeds with an aril. Medit. region.

tuberosum Rottl. ex K. Spreng. [*A. odorum* of many auth.; *A. uliginosum* G. Don, not Ledeb.]. CHINESE CHIVE, GARLIC C., ORIENTAL GARLIC. Bulbs elongate, on a stout rhizome, outer bulb coat fibrous-netted; scape to 20 in.; lvs. 4–9, not hollow, keeled on the back, ⅛–⁵⁄₁₆ in. wide, shorter than scape; umbel many-fld., pedicels 2–3 times as long as fragrant fls.; perianth segms. white, with greenish or brownish nerve, ³⁄₁₆ in. long, filaments from ⅘ to as long as segms., ovary without nectaries; caps. obovate, broader at apex. Se. Asia. This sp. and *A. ramosum* are often confused.

uliginosum: see *A. tuberosum* and *A. Ledebourianum*.

umbellatum: a listed name of no botanical standing applied to plants referable to *A. ramosum*.

unifolium Kellogg. Bulbs not on a rhizome, but producing bulblets at the tips of slender lateral rhizomes, outer bulb coat membranous, netted with horizontal, undulating meshes; scape to 2 ft.; lvs. 3–4, with short sheaths, broadly linear, flat, ⅛–⁵⁄₁₆ in. wide, shorter than scape; umbel loose, few- to many-fld., pedicels unequal, 1–3 times as long as fls.; perianth segms. bright rose, ⅜ in. long or more, filaments ½–⅔ as long as segms., entire, ovary without nectaries. Coast ranges, Calif.

urceolatum: *A. caesium*.

ursinum L. BEAR'S GARLIC, HOG'S G., GYPSY O., RAMSONS, BUCKRAMS. Bulbs on a short rhizome, elongate, outer bulb coat splitting longitudinally into parallel fibers; scape to 1½ ft., leafy at the base, sheathed less than ¼ its length; lvs. 2, narrowed to a distinct petiole, lanceolate or oblong, to 2 in. wide, shorter than scape, appearing with the fls.; umbel few-fld., pedicels 1½–2 times as long as fls.; perianth segms. white, ⅜–½ in. long, filaments about half as long as segms., ovary without nectaries; seeds black, nearly spherical. Eur., Asia.

validum S. Wats. SWAMP O. Bulbs slender, at the tip of a stout rhizome, bulb coat membranous; scape 1½–2½ ft., somewhat 2-edged; lvs. several, linear, ³⁄₁₆–⅝ in. wide, nearly as long as scape, glabrous; umbel many-fld., pedicels about twice as long as fls.; perianth segms. rose to nearly white, ¼–⁵⁄₁₆ in. long, lanceolate, narrowly long-acuminate, filaments and style exserted, ovary without nectaries. High mts., Wash. to Calif., e. to w. Nev. Cv. 'Purdyi': probably *A. Purdyi*.

vancouverense: a listed name of no botanical standing, sometimes applied to *A. crenulatum*.

Victorialis L. Bulbs single or clustered on a rhizome, elongate, bulb coat fibrous-reticulate; scape to 2 ft., leafy in the lowermost ⅓–½; lvs. 2–3, narrowed to a distinct petiole, elliptic-lanceolate, to 3 in. wide, appearing with the fls.; umbel many-fld., pedicels 2–3 times as long as fls.; perianth segms. greenish-white, about ³⁄₁₆ in. long, filaments exserted, ovary without nectaries; seeds black, nearly spherical. S. Eur., Asia, Aleutian Is.

vineale L. FIELD GARLIC, CROW G., STAG'S G. Bulbs ovate, often crowded, bulb coat membranous; scape to 3 ft. or more, leafy to middle; lvs. hollow, cylindrical at first, then channelled; umbel bearing bulbils, sometimes without fls., spathe 1-valved; fls., when present, pale rose to greenish or whitish, filaments much longer than perianth, the inner with 2 teeth near apex, ovary with nectaries. Eur. A weedy sp., naturalized in e. U.S. Subsp. **Kochii** (J. Lange) K. Richt. [*A. Kochii* J. Lange]. Outer filaments as long as perianth or only slightly longer. Denmark, Sweden. Probably not actually cult.

viviparum: *A. caeruleum* var. *bulbilliferum*.

Wallichianum Steud. [*A. Wallichii* Kunth]. Bulbs only slightly thickened, clustered, outer bulb coat membranous; scape to 20 in.; lvs.

linear to linear-lanceolate, ⅛–⅝ in. wide, longer than scape; umbel many-fld., pedicels 2 or more times as long as fls.; perianth segms. purple, ⁵⁄₁₆ in. long, filaments ⅔ as long as segms., entire. Temp. Himalayas, Kumaun to Sikkim.

Wallichii: *A. Wallichianum.*

Winkleranum Regel. Bulb globose, solitary, outer bulb coat membranous, blackish; scape ½–3 ft., ribbed; lvs. 1–2, linear-lanceolate, ³⁄₁₆–1 in. wide, shorter than scape, glabrous or scabrid on margin and nerves beneath; umbel many-fld., dense, spathe half as long to nearly as long as umbel, pedicels all nearly the same length, shorter than fls. or to 1½ times as long; perianth segms. rose-violet, with darker nerve, linear-oblong, withering after flowering, filaments included, entire, half as long as segms., united to perianth and to one another up to ½–⅔ their length, ovules several in each cell. Cent. Asia.

yunnanense: *A. Mairei.*

zebdanense Boiss. & Noë. Bulbs not on a rhizome, outer bulb coat membranous, pale, with scarcely discernible netted pattern; scape to 1 ft.; lvs. linear-lanceolate, ⅛–¼ in. wide, shorter than scape, smooth or scabrid on margin; umbel few- to many-fld., pedicels 1–2 times as long as fls.; perianth segms. white, with red nerve, ¼ in. long, oblong to elliptic, ovary without nectaries. Asia Minor.

Zenobiae Cory. Similar to *A. canadense* var. *mobilense*, but bearing sessile bulblets at the base of the bulb, more robust, having up to 175 lavender fls.; umbel to 2⅜ in. across, scape up to 2 ft., perianth segms. ¼ in. long. S.-cent. Tex.

ALLOPHYLUS L. *Sapindaceae.* About 175 spp. of polygamodioecious, evergreen shrubs and trees, native to trop. Amer., Afr., and Asia; lvs. alt., compound, with 1–3 lfts.; fls. white, in axillary or terminal racemes or panicles, irregular, sepals 4, the opp. ones paired, petals 4, stamens 8; fr. of 1 or 2 ovoid or globose, dry or fleshy sections.

africanus Beauvois. Tree, to 40 ft.; lvs. palmately compound, lfts. 3, oblong-cuneate, to 6 in. long, toothed toward apex, glabrous at maturity; fls. in axillary and terminal panicles; fr. blackish. Trop. Afr.

Dregeanus (Sond.) De Winter [*A. monophyllus* Radlk.]. Small tree; lft. 1, oblong-cuneate, to 4 in. long, leathery, glabrous; fls. in racemes to 4 in. long. Trop. and s. Afr.

monophyllus: *A. Dregeanus.*

ALLOPHYTON: *TETRANEMA.* **A. mexicanum**: *T. roseum.*

ALLOPLECTUS Mart. *Gesneriaceae.* Perhaps 70 spp. of terrestrial herbs or shrubs in trop. Amer.; roots fibrous, sts. erect or clambering; lvs. opp., entire or toothed, those of a pair equal or unequal; fls. solitary or few in lf. axils, or several on axillary peduncles, calyx lobes 5, usually colored, often broad, entire or toothed, corolla tubular, sometimes contracted at the throat, erect or oblique in the calyx, lobes small, nearly equal, erect or spreading, stamens 4, filaments united with each other and to corolla tube at base, the 4 anthers united by their tips and sides in a square, disc of a single, sometimes 2-lobed gland, at the back of the ovary, ovary superior, stigma 2-lobed or mouth-shaped; fr. a usually colored, conical or globose, tardily dehiscent, fleshy and berrylike caps. or rarely a white berry. The genus is not clearly separable from *Columnea*, especially those spp. with white berries.

For cultivation see *Gesneriaceae.*

ambiguus Urb. Sts. clambering; lvs. of a pair unequal, the larger twice the size of the smaller, blades oblong to elliptic, to 2½ in. long, 1¼ in. wide, crenate; fls. 2–3 in axils, calyx green or red, minutely hairy, lobed, the lobes toothed except the uppermost, corolla oblique in the calyx, to ⅞ in. long, yellow with red hairs, lobes to ³⁄₁₆ in. long, stigma 2-lobed, recurved; fr. a globose white berry. Puerto Rico.

bivittatus: a listed name of no botanical standing.

calochlamys J. D. Sm. Epiphytic subshrub; lvs. of a pair nearly equal, densely and softly appressed hairy, petioles to 1 in. long, blades elliptic, to 8 in. long, 2⅜ in. wide, serrate; fls. 1–4 in axils, bracts to ¾ in. long, slender, hairy, calyx long-persistent, orange-pink, hairy, tube ¼ in. long, lobes spreading in a star, ⅝ in. long, corolla ¾ in. long, tawny- or creamy-villous, lobes erect, deep maroon inside, ¹⁄₁₆ in. long; stigma mouth-shaped. Guatemala.

capitatus Hook. Terrestrial, erect, to 3 ft., sts. bluntly 4-angled, red-velvety; lvs. of a pair equal, petioles red-velvety, blades ovate, to 8 in. long, 4 in. wide, minutely toothed, deep green and velvety above, hairy and often purple beneath; fls. many in dense clusters on hairy axillary peduncles to 2 in. long, calyx blood-red, lobes spreading, to

¾ in. long, downy, corolla slightly longer than calyx, silky, yellow, stigma 2-lobed; fr. a blackish, fleshy caps., ⅜ in. in diam., with 4 pale lines. Andes of Venezuela and Colombia.

congestus Linden ex Hanst. Terrestrial, erect, hairy; lvs. of a pair nearly equal or unequal, petioles to 1½ in. long, blades ovate, to 5 in. long, 3 in. wide, serrate-crenate, somewhat rough-hairy, green above, red-veined or red beneath; fls. several in a cluster on reddish peduncles shorter than petioles, bracts broadly ovate to elliptic, to nearly 1 in. long, calyx spreading, red, lobes oblong-ovate, to ½ in. long, ⁵⁄₁₆ in. wide, with few teeth, corolla scarcely longer than calyx, yellow, hairy outside; fr. a dark, pointed, fleshy caps. Venezuela.

domingensis Urb. Epiphytic, sts. slender, clambering; lvs. of a pair equal or unequal, blades elliptic, to 2 in. long, ⅞ in. wide, toothed, red-hairy, green above, often red beneath; fls. solitary on red-hairy pedicels, calyx lobes to ½ in. long, toothed, red, corolla oblique in the calyx, short-spurred at base, slightly inflated, yellow, sparsely hairy, lobes ⅛ in. long. Hispaniola.

Lynchii: *Nautilocalyx Lynchii.*

Nummularia (Hanst.) Wiehl. [*Hypocyrta Nummularia* Hanst.]. Sts. slender, often swollen at nodes, brown, hairy; lvs. short-petioled, blades broadly ovate to nearly round or obovate, to 2½ in. long, 1¼ in. wide, toothed, often reddish; fls. solitary in axils, short-pedicelled, calyx lobes equal, linear, to ⅜ in. long, hairy, corolla erect in the calyx, ¾ in. long, vermilion, abruptly expanded into a pouch ½ in. deep, then narrowed to a violet-tinged neck ¹⁄₁₆ in. wide and short yellow lobes; fr. ⁵⁄₁₆ in. long, orangish, rupturing irregularly. Mex., Cent. Amer.

sanguineus: *Columnea sanguinea.*

Schlimii Planch. & Linden. Terrestrial, erect; lvs. of a pair nearly equal, blades ovate or ovate-oblong, to 4½ in. long, 2½ in. wide, oblique at base, shallowly toothed and fringed with red hairs, short-hairy, often red to wine-colored or red-veined beneath; fls. 1–4 on axillary, hairy pedicels, calyx red, lobes ovate, ⁷⁄₁₆ in. long, margins curved outward, corolla erect, nearly twice as long as calyx, densely hairy, yellow, throat red, lobes short, red, stigma mouth-shaped; fr. dark brown. Andes of Venezuela and Colombia.

strigosus: *Drymonia strigosa.*

Teuscheri (Raym.) Wiehl. [*Hypocyrta Teuscheri* Raym.]. Shrub, to 3 ft. or more, sts. 4-angled, hairy; lvs. equal in each pair, ovate, to 6 in. long, 3 in. wide, acuminate, finely toothed, hispid, bullate, deep green with a silvery band along midrib above, wine-red beneath; fls. many in lf. axils, subtended by red bracts, sepals red, ovate, to ½ in. long, dentate-ciliate, corolla lemon-yellow, to ¾ in. long, pouched below narrow throat, hairy, lobes crimson, small. Ecuador.

vittatus Linden & André. Terrestrial, erect, to 2 ft.; lvs. of a pair equal, blades broadly ovate, to 6 in. long, 3 in. wide, crenulate, rough-hairy and deep green with pale silvery-green along midvein and base of lateral nerves above, usually red-purple beneath; fls. several in clusters on red-bracted peduncles in axil of lvs., calyx red-purple, glabrous, sepals ⅝ in. long, toothed, corolla erect, somewhat longer than to nearly twice as long, yellow, densely hairy; fr. blackish. Peru.

ALMOND. The cultivated almonds are of two kinds, those grown for the "nut" or kernel in the stone or pit, and those grown as ornamentals, the flowering almonds. The almonds grown for their nuts belong to *Prunus dulcis,* probably native to western Asia. The fruit is a dryish drupe, the flesh more or less splitting at maturity and exposing the stone. The thin flesh is inedible for humans but is used as a livestock feed. Two varieties are recognized. The bitter almond (var. *amara*) is the source of oil of bitter almonds, a nondrying industrial oil. The sweet almond (var. *dulcis*) also yields an oil, but is grown primarily for its edible kernel; it may be either soft-shelled, as are most of the commercial kinds, or hard-shelled.

The almond tree is much like the peach and the culture is in general the same; however, the almond is self-incompatible, and two cultivars are needed for cross-pollination. Although the tree may be nearly as hardy as the peach, it blooms earlier and is therefore more subject to damage from spring frosts. Propagation of named cultivars is by budding either on almond seedlings (of the bitter variety or of the commercial cultivar 'Mission') or on peach seedlings. The almond is little grown commercially in North America outside California. Good cultivars in California are: 'Davey', 'Harpareil', 'Jordanolo', 'IXL', 'Ne Plus Ultra', 'Nonpareil', and 'Texas'.

The ornamental or flowering almonds include showy, double-flowered forms of *P. dulcis,* but most of the usual "flower-

ing almonds" are other species of *Prunus,* small spring-blooming shrubs prized for their single or double flowers in pink, rose, and white. Two species, *P. triloba* and *P. glandulosa,* are common, and *P. japonica* is sometimes grown. The dwarf Russian almond, *P. tenella,* with single pink or white flowers, is not much grown. Since these small ornamental almonds are commonly grown on plum stock, suckers from the plum root should be removed whenever they appear.

ALNUS B. Ehrh. ALDER. *Betulaceae.* About 30 spp. of deciduous, monoecious trees and shrubs native to the N. Hemisphere and Andes; lvs. alt., toothed; fls. in catkins, appearing before lvs. in many spp., male catkins long, female catkins short, becoming woody cones with 5-lobed scales; fr. a minute, winged nutlet. Most spp. spring-flowering but *A. maritima, A. nepalensis,* and *A. nitida* flower in autumn.

Alders are cultivated as ornamentals and the timber of the larger species is used for furniture and other articles. They are best suited to moist soils and cool or cold climates. Propagated by seeds dried in the autumn and sown in spring under a light covering; also by cuttings, suckers, and the rarer kinds by grafting on potted seedling stock under glass.

alnobetula: *A. viridis.*

barbata: *A. glutinosa* var.

californica: *A. rhombifolia.*

communis: *A. glutinosa.*

cordata (Loisel.) Duby [*A. cordifolia* Ten.; *A. tiliacea* Hort. ex Rehd.]. ITALIAN A. To 75 ft.; lvs. broad-ovate, to 4 in. long, cordate; male catkins to 3 in. long, 3–6 in a cluster; cones erect, ovoid, to 1 in. long, mostly in 3's. Corsica and s. Italy. A handsome tree; catkins appearing in spring before lvs.

cordifolia: *A. cordata.*

crispa (Ait.) Pursh [*A. Mitchelliana* M. A. Curt. ex A. Gray]. GREEN A., AMERICAN G.A., MOUNTAIN A. Shrub, to 10 ft.; lvs. ovate, to 3 in. long, rounded at base, aromatic when young; cones 3–6. Lab. to N.C. Var. **mollis** (Fern.) Fern. [*A. mollis* Fern.]. Young lvs. and branchlets pubescent underneath, lvs. to 3¾ in. long.

firma Siebold & Zucc. [*A. Sieboldiana* Matsum.]. Shrub or tree, to 10 ft.; lvs. ovate-oblong, to 5 in. long, rounded at base, with 10–24 straight, almost parallel lateral veins; male catkins to 2½ in. long, solitary or in pairs; cones solitary or in pairs, ovoid-ellipsoid, ¾ in. long. Japan. Var. **hirtella** Franch. & Sav. To 30 ft.; lvs. with 10–16 parallel lateral veins. Japan. Var. **multinervis:** *A. pendula.*

fruticosa Rupr. To 40 ft.; lvs. ovate, to 4½ in. long, lobed or somewhat so, glabrous underneath, with 5–10 pairs of veins; female catkins terminal. Ne. Asia.

glutinosa (L.) Gaertn. [*A. communis* Mirb.; *A. rotundifolia* Mill.; *A. vulgaris* Pers.]. BLACK A. To 80 ft., young growth very sticky; lvs. elliptic or nearly orbicular, to 4 in. long, broad at base, or lvs. variously laciniately lobed; cones 3–5, ovoid, to ⅝ in. long. Eur., N. Afr., Asia; sometimes escaped in e. N. Amer. Wood useful. Var. **barbata** (C. A. Mey.) Ledeb. [*A. barbata* C. A. Mey.]. Lvs. pubescent beneath. Caucasus. Var. **denticulata** (C. A. Mey.) Ledeb. Lvs. finely toothed, not or only slightly lobed. Medit. region. Var. **glutinosa.** The typical var.; includes the following cvs.: 'Aurea', lvs. yellow; 'Imperialis' [*A. imperialis* Hort.], lvs. deeply laciniately lobed; 'Incisa' [cv. 'Oxycanthifolia'; *A. incisa* Hort.], lvs. small, with broad, shallow lobes; 'Oxycanthifolia': 'Incisa'; 'Pyramidalis', of narrow pyramidal habit; 'Quercifolia', lvs. with broad, somewhat irregular lobes; 'Rubrinervia', lvs. glossy dark green with red nerves and petioles; 'Sorbifolia', lvs. small, with broad, deep lobes.

hirsuta (Spach) Rupr. [*A. tinctoria* Sarg.]. MANCHURIAN A. To 60 ft.; lvs. broad-ovate, to 6 in. long, rounded at base, shallowly lobed and doubly toothed, glaucous and reddish-pubescent underneath, with 9–12 pairs of veins; cones 3–4. Ne. Asia, and n. Japan. Var. **sibirica** (Spach) C. K. Schneid. [*A. sibirica* Fisch. ex Turcz.]. Lvs. densely pubescent underneath on midrib only, sparingly pubescent on veins.

hybrida: a name that has been applied to more than one hybrid.

imperialis: *A. glutinosa* cv.

incana (L.) Moench. WHITE A. Shrub or tree, to 60 ft.; lvs. ovate, to 4 in. long, rounded at base, entire or variously laciniately lobed, glaucous or grayish-green underneath, with 9–12 pairs of veins; male catkins to 4 in. long, 3–4 in a cluster. Asia, Eur., introd. in N. Amer. Cvs. include 'Acuminata', lvs. lobed about halfway; 'Aurea', lvs. yellow; 'Laciniata', lvs. lobed more than halfway, hardly distinct from cv.

'Acuminata'; **'Monstrosa'**, brs. much flattened; **'Pendula'**, brs. drooping; **'Pinnata'** [cv. 'Pinnatifida'], lvs. small, deeply lobed.

incisa: *A. glutinosa* cv.

japonica (Thunb.) Steud. JAPANESE A. To 80 ft.; lvs. narrow-elliptic, to 5 in. long, wedge-shaped at base, light green underneath, veins curved; cones 2–6, ellipsoidal, ¾ in. long. Ne. Asia and Japan.

latifolia: *A. rugosa.*

macrophylla: see *A. subcordata* and *A. rugosa.*

maritima (Marsh.) Nutt. SEASIDE A. Shrub or tree, to 30 ft.; lvs. oblong, to 4 in. long, wedge-shaped at base, glossy above, light green underneath, with 8–10 pairs of lateral veins; male catkins to 2½ in. long; cones ovate, to ½ in. long. Fls. in autumn. Se. U.S.

Matsumurae Callier. Tree; lvs. broad-elliptic or obovate, to 2½ in. long, serrate, grayish and sparsely pubescent underneath, with 8–9 pairs of veins; cones obovoid to ellipsoidal. Japan.

Maximowiczii Callier. Shrub or tree, to 30 ft.; lvs. broadly ovate, to 4 in. long, serrate, glabrous except for axillary tufts of hairs underneath, with 8–11 pairs of veins; male catkins to 2 in. long; cones ovoid or cylindrical, ½ in. long. Japan.

Mitchelliana: *A. crispa.*

mollis: *A. crispa* var.

multinervis: *A. pendula*

nepalensis D. Don. To 60 ft.; lvs. elliptic-lanceolate, to 7 in. long, shallowly toothed or nearly entire, glabrous above, downy on midrib and veins underneath, with 8–10 pairs of veins; male catkins to 6 in. long, often many, in drooping panicles. Fls. in autumn. E. Himalayas and w. China.

nitida (Spach) Endl. To 100 ft.; lvs. ovate to elliptic, to 6 in. long, slender-pointed, dark and glossy above, paler and glabrous underneath except for axillary tufts of hairs, with 9–12 pairs of veins; male catkins to 6 in. long, 1–4 in a cluster; cones oblong, to 1½ in. long. Fls. in autumn. W. Himalayas.

oregona Nutt. [*A. rubra* Bong., not Marsh.]. RED A., OREGON A. To 70 ft., slender, pyramidal in habit; lvs. ovate to elliptic, to 6 in. long, shallowly lobed or coarsely serrate, glabrous above, rusty-tomentose underneath, with 10–15 pairs of veins; male catkins to 6 in. long, 3–5 in a cluster; cones ellipsoidal, to 1 in. long. Stream banks and marshy places, w. N. Amer., where the wood is used for various articles.

pendula Matsum. [*A. firma* var. *multinervis* Regel; *A. multinervis* (Regel) Callier]. Shrub or tree, to 40 ft.; lvs. oblong-lanceolate, to 5 in. long, slender-pointed, cuneate or rounded at base, sharply toothed, with 18–26 pairs of veins; cones ½ in. long, 3–5 in pendulous, slender-stalked clusters up to 3 in. long. Japan. Similar to *A. firma*, but having smaller cones in pendulous racemes.

×**pubescens** Tausch: *A. glutinosa* × *A. incana.* Young twigs pubescent; lvs. obtuse to short-acuminate, usually pubescent, at least on veins; cones short-peduncled. Occurs naturally where the two parent spp. grow together.

rhombifolia Nutt. [*A. californica* Hort. ex H. J. Winkl.]. WHITE A. To 100 ft.; lvs. oblong-ovate or rhombic, to 4 in. long, acute to rounded at apex, cuneate, finely or coarsely serrate, dark green and glabrous above, light green and puberulent underneath, with 7–9 pairs of lateral veins; male catkins to 6 in. long; cones ellipsoidal, to ½ in. long. Mostly along streams, w. N. Amer.

rotundifolia: *A. glutinosa.*

rubra: *A. oregona.*

rugosa (Du Roi) K. Spreng. [*A. latifolia* Desf.; *A. macrophylla* Hort. in part; *A. serrulata* Willd.; *A. serrulata* Michx. f.]. HAZEL A., SMOOTH A., SPECKLED A. Shrub or tree, to 25 ft.; lvs. elliptic or obovate, to 4 in. long, rounded or short-pointed at apex, cuneate, glabrous above, nearly so underneath, with 10–12 pairs of lateral nerves; male catkins to 4 in. long; cones 4–10 in a cluster, ovoid, to ¾ in. long. E. N. Amer.

serrulata: *A. rugosa.*

sibirica: *A. hirsuta* var.

sinuata (Regel) Rydb. [*A. sitchensis* Sarg.]. Shrub or tree, to 50 ft.; lvs. ovate, to 4½ in. long, bright green, rounded or cuneate at base, lobed or nearly so, serrate, usually glabrous but sometimes somewhat pubescent underneath along midrib, with 5–10 pairs of veins; male catkins to 1 in. long, 2–4 in a cluster; cones several in a terminal raceme, ellipsoidal, to ¾ in. long. Alaska to n. Calif.

Sieboldiana: *A. firma.*

sitchensis: *A. sinuata.*

subcordata C. A. Mey. [*A. macrophylla* Hort. in part]. CAUCASIAN A. To 50 ft.; lvs. ovate or oblong-ovate, to 6 in. long, rounded at base, light green and pubescent on veins underneath, with 8–10 pairs of lateral veins; male catkins slender, to 6 in. long, 4 or 5 in a cluster; cones 1–5 in a cluster, to 1 in. long. Caucasus and Iran.

tenuifolia Nutt. MOUNTAIN A. To 30 ft.; lvs. ovate or ovate-oblong, to 4 in. long, mostly rounded at base, shallowly lobed and bluntly toothed, usually yellowish-green, with about 10 pairs of lateral veins; male catkins to 2 in. long, 3–4 in a cluster; cones narrowly ovoid, about ½ in. long. W. N. Amer.

tiliacea: *A. cordata.*

tinctoria: *A. hirsuta.*

tropicana: a listed name of no botanical standing.

viridis (Chaix) DC. [*A. alnobetula* B. Ehrh.]. EUROPEAN GREEN A. Shrub, to 10 ft., shoots sticky; lvs. ovate, to 3 in. long, sticky when young, abruptly pointed, sharply toothed, dark green and glabrous above, pubescent on veins underneath, with about 8 pairs of lateral veins; male catkins to 3 in. long; cones several in a cluster, ellipsoidal, to ½ in. long. Eur.

vulgaris: *A. glutinosa.*

ALOCASIA (Schott) G. Don. ELEPHANT'S-EAR PLANT. *Araceae.* About 70 spp. of erect, mostly rhizomatous per. herbs of trop. Asia, internodes short; lvs. entire to pinnatifid, often with basal lobes uppermost, sometimes beautifully marked or colored, petioles long, cylindrical; peduncle mostly much shorter than petiole, spathe greenish, tube short, convolute, blade long, expanded, fugacious, spadix densely-fld., terminated by sterile appendage; fls. unisexual, perianth absent, ovary 1-celled, ovules many. Differs from *Colocasia* in having basal ovules.

Favorite greenhouse plants requiring humid atmosphere, soils high in organic matter with excellent drainage, and temperatures above 60° F. Propagated by cuttings, stem pieces, or seeds. Through hybridization, many handsome forms have been produced. Some materials offered in the trade may be of mixed hybrid parentage, and so difficult to identify.

×**amazonica** André: *A. Lowii* × *A. Sanderana.* Differs from *A. Sanderana* in having lf. blades to 2 ft. long and 1 ft. wide, undulate.

×**argyraea** Hort. Sander: *A. longiloba* × *A.* × *Pucciana.* Lf. blades peltate, ovate, to 2 ft. long and 10 in. wide, sagittate, with basal lobes united ¼–⅓ their length, upper surface dark greenish-silvery with metallic sheen, lower surface shining red-brown, with prominent, green, primary lateral veins, petioles 2 ft. long, green.

atrovirens: a listed name of no botanical standing.

×**Chantrieri** André: *A. cuprea* × *A. Sanderana.* Suggestive of *A.* × *amazonica*, but lf. blades elliptic, elongate, with basal lobes united for ⅔ their length or more.

×**Chelsonii** Hort. Veitch: *A. cuprea* × *A. longiloba.* Lf. blades large, deep green and with metallic luster above, purple beneath.

cucullata (Lour.) G. Don. CHINESE TARO, CHINESE APE. Lf. blades spreading, peltate, ovate, to 16 in. long, 11 in. wide, cordate, glossy green on both surfaces, basal lobes united less than half their length, petioles to 3 ft. long, light green; spathe to 7 in. long. Ceylon and ne. India to Burma. Corms used for food in India.

cuprea (C. Koch & Bouché) C. Koch. GIANT CALADIUM. Lf. blades peltate, ovate-elliptic, to 18 in. long and 10–12 in. wide, with basal lobes blunt, united nearly their entire length, upper surface iridescent-purple or pale green between the black-green zones along the channelled midrib and main veins, lower surface red-violet, petioles to 2 ft. long, light green; spathe 4–6 in. long, tube green to red-purple, blade green, spadix with sterile appendage ¾ in. long. Borneo.

gigantea: *Colocasia gigantea.*

indica: *A. macrorrhiza.* Var. **metallica:** *A. plumbea.* Var. **violacea:** *A. macrorrhiza* cv.

Johnstonii: *Cyrtosperma Johnstonii.*

Korthalsii Schott [?*A. Lowii* var. *grandis* Hort. ex Nichols.; *A. Thibautiana* M. T. Mast.]. Lf. blades peltate, ovate, to 14 in. long and 7 in. wide, sagittate with basal lobes obtuse, connate almost half their length, upper surface dark olive-green with metallic luster, with midrib and the 4–5 pairs of primary lateral veins pale, these and margins grayish-bordered, lower surface purple, petioles to 18 in. long, green; spathe tube 2 in. long, blade twice as long, whitish. Borneo.

Lindenii: *Homalomena Lindenii.*

longiloba Miq. Similar to *A. Veitchii* but lf. blades green on both sides, or blue-green in juvenile lvs., and petioles green. Malay Pen., Indonesia.

Lowii Hook.f. Var. **grandis:** see *A. Korthalsii.* Vars. **picta** and **Veitchii:** *A. Veitchii.*

macrorrhiza (L.) G. Don [*A. indica* (Lour.) Spach]. PAI, TARO, APE, GIANT A. To 15 ft., aerial sts. stout, to 6 ft. or more; lf. blades erect or spreading, ovate, sagittate, mature lvs. not at all peltate, to 3 ft. long or more, petioles to 4½ ft. long, sheathing in basal half; peduncle to 1 ft. long, spathe 9½ in. long, spadix as long as spathe. Var. **macrorrhiza.** The typical var.; lf. blades with upper, main lobe wider than long, upper surface medium green, lower surface paler, with midrib and main veins greenish-cream; spathe with blade yellow-green, spadix with sterile appendage about 2 in. long. Ceylon, ne. India to Malay Pen. and Indonesia. Often confused with *A. odora.* Corms used for food. Cv. **'Variegata'** [var. *variegata* (C. Koch & Bouché) Furtado]. Lf. blades with large or small irregular splotches or zones of cream-white, gray-green, and darker green, petioles longitudinally striped green and cream, variegation unstable, sometimes reverting to green form. Cv. **'Violacea'** [*A. indica* (Lour.) Spach var. *violacea* Engl.]. Lf. blades pale violet. Var. **rubra:** *A. plumbea.*

Micholitziana Hort. Sander. Similiar to *A. Sanderana* but lf. blades pale green beneath, less deeply lobed, with basal lobes entirely free or very shortly united, midrib and veins pale green without silvery borders, and spadix almost as long as spathe. Philippine Is.

odora (Lodd.) Spach. Similar to *A. macrorrhiza* but lf. blades peltate, with basal lobes united about ⅕ their length or less. Ne. India to China, Philippine Is. Easily confused with *Colocasia gigantea,* but clearly separable on generic differences of ovary and sterile appendage of spadix.

picta: *A. Veitchii.*

plumbea C. Koch ex Van Houtte [*A. indica* var. *metallica* Schott ex Engl.; *A. macrorrhiza* var. *rubra* (Hassk.) Furtado]. Similar to *A. macrorrhiza* but lf. blades narrower, margins weakly sinuate, upper main lobes longer than wide, upper surface polished dark olive-green, lower surface purplish-silvery, with dark purple veins, petioles and peduncles purple; spathe with tube purple, to 1¾ in. long, blade white, spadix almost as long as spathe, with sterile appendage to 4½ in. long. Java.

porphyroneura H. G. Hallier ex Engl. [*A. princeps* Bull]. Lf. blades triangular, to 20 in. long and 8 in. wide, sagittate with basal lobes triangular, and nearly as long as upper main lobe, marginally sinuate, upper surface dark green, lower surface pale green with purple main veins and midrib, petioles to 2 ft., pale green with purple spots; peduncle purple-dotted, spathe with tube yellowish, blade yellow-green. Borneo.

Portei Schott [*Schizocasia Portei* (Schott) Engl.; *S. Regnieri* L. Linden & Rodig.]. To 10 ft. or more, sts. more than 1 ft. long and 5 in. in diam.; mature lf. blades ovate-sagittate, to 5 ft. long, deeply pinnatifid, marginally ruffled-undulate, segms. about 8 on each side, linear, obtuse, basal lobes 4–5-parted, petioles to 6 ft. long, finely marked red-purple, open-sheathing basally, juvenile lf. blades oblong-triangular, 5–7-lobed, the lobes short, obtuse, with flat margins. Philippine Is.

princeps: *A. porphyroneura.*

×**Pucciana** Hort. ex André: *A. Korthalsii* × *A. Putzeysii.* A parent of *A. argyraea,* not in cult.

Putzeysii N. E. Br. Differs from *A. Watsoniana* in having lf. blades smooth, with only 3 pairs of primary lateral veins from midrib, basal lobes triangular, united about ⅕ their length, and petioles cream-colored. Sumatra.

Regnieri: *A. Portei.*

Sanderana Bull. Lf. blades peltate, narrowly triangular, to 16 in. long and 7 in. wide, obtuse-lobed, with basal lobes flaring, triangular, united ⅕ their length, primary lateral veins widely spreading, upper surface black-green with metallic luster, ribs and primary veins silvery-gray, these and margin with narrow silvery borders, lower surface purple, petioles 2 ft. long; spathe 4¼ in. long, blade creamy, spadix with sterile appendage white, ⅞ in. long. S. Philippine Is.

×**Sedenii** Hort. ex M. T. Mast. & T. Moore: *A. cuprea* × *A. Veitchii.* Lf. blades peltate, ovate-elliptic, with basal lobes obtuse and united about ¾ their length, main veins widely spreading, upper surface dark green, with gray-green midrib, lower surface red-purple, petioles red-purple, becoming green apically.

Thibautiana: *A. Korthalsii.*

×**Uhinkii** Hort. ex Engl. & Kurt Krause [*A. Whinkii* Hort.]: perhaps *A. cuprea* × *A. plumbea.* Lf. blades spreading, peltate, ovate, to 22 in. long and 16 in. wide, sagittate, with basal lobes obtuse, and united more than half their length, dark green above, gray-violet with metallic luster beneath, petioles green, to 2 ft. long.

Veitchii (Lindl.) Schott [*A. Lowii* vars. *picta* Hook. f. and *Veitchii* Engl.; *A. picta* Hort.]. St. to 1 ft. long or more; lf. blades elongate elliptic- to ovate-triangular, peltate, to 30 in. long and half as wide, sagittate, with basal lobes triangular, and united ⅕–¼ their length, upper surface dark green, with midrib and main veins gray-green, these and margins with grayish borders, lower surface red-purple, petioles to 4 ft. or more, brown-purplish; spathe to 8 in. long, tube green, blade yellow, flushed reddish at apex, spadix shorter than spathe, with sterile appendage yellowish, 3 in. long. Borneo.

violacea: see *A. macrorrhiza* cv. and *Xanthosoma violaceum.*

Watsoniana Hort. Sander. Lf. blades peltate, elongate-ovate, to 3 ft. long and 2 ft. wide, sagittate, bullate, with basal lobes united more than half their length, upper surface dark olive-green, with midribs, primary, and some lesser veins pale green, these and margins bordered ivory-white, lower surface red-purple, petiole to 3 ft. long, pinkish. W. Malay Pen. and Indonesia.

Wavriniana: *Xenophya Lauterbachiana.*

Wentii Engl. & Kurt Krause. Sts. to about 18 in.; lf. blades oblong-triangular, to 3½ in. long and 2⅜ in. wide, nearly sagittate, rigid-leathery, dark green, petioles to 8 in. long, slender; peduncle 7 in. long, spathe 2¾ in. long, tube rose, spadix with sterile appendage clavate, 1⅜ in. long. New Guinea.

Whinkii: × *Uhinkii.*

zebrina C. Koch & Hort. Veitch. Lf. blades nearly erect, triangular, 18 in. long and half as wide, sagittate, with basal lobes triangular, blunt, green, petioles 1½ times longer than blade, transversely variegated black and light green, open-sheathing in basal ⅓; peduncle 10 in. long, variegated, spathe 7 in. long, blade whitish, spadix with sterile appendage rose, 2 in. long. Philippine Is.

ALOE L. *Liliaceae.* Between 200 and 250 spp. of succulent, per. herbs, shrubs, or trees, native to arid parts of the Old World, chiefly Afr.; usually stemless, but sometimes with simple or branched sts.; lvs. mostly in compact rosettes, thick, hard, sharp-pointed, mostly hard-toothed or spiny on margins; fls. usually red to yellow, in lateral or terminal racemes or panicles on scapes often much elevated above the lvs.; perianth tubular, segms. 6, separate or united at base, stamens 6, usually of 2 lengths; fr. a loculicidal caps. Not to be confused with the agaves, which are fibrous-lvd. and native to the New World. The scientific name *Aloe* has three syllables; the common name ALOE has two syllables.

Aloes are well-known pot plants and are also commonly planted about public buildings and parks in areas not subject to killing frost, especially s. Calif. They commonly thrive in the same pot for years when not grown for bloom. The resinous, yellow juice of the leaves of several species is the source of the purgative medicinal drug aloes. Propagated by suckers, sometimes by cuttings of new growths, and by seeds when available.

aculeata Pole-Evans. Usually stemless; lvs. about 30, in compact rosette, lanceolate, to 2 ft., attenuate, spiny beneath; fls. lemon-yellow, buds reddish-yellow, in compact racemes to 3 ft. high, sometimes branched near the base. S. Afr.

africana Mill. SPINY A. St. to 12 ft., clothed with persistent dead lvs.; lvs. about 30, in dense terminal rosette, to 20 in. long, dull green to glaucous, with scattered spines below and on margins; fls. yellow to yellow-orange, to 1½ in. long, much recurved, buds red, in dense racemes to 2½ ft. high. S. Afr.

albiflora Guillaum. Stemless; lvs. about 7, linear, to 4¾ in. long, attenuate, green with white tubercles; fls. campanulate, white, ⅜ in. long, brown at tips, in a slender raceme about 1 ft. high, stamens long-exserted. Madagascar.

andringitrensis Perr. Stemless; lvs. 10–20, to 20 in. long, roughened by small papillae, margin prickly; fls. yellow, ⅞ in. long, buds red-orange, in a panicle to 3 ft. high. Madagascar.

arachnis: a listed name of no botanical standing; material so offered may be referable to *Haworthia arachnoidea.*

arborescens Mill. CANDELABRA A., CANDELABRA PLANT, OCTOPUS PLANT, TORCH PLANT. Much-branched, arborescent shrub, 10–12 ft.; lvs. many, in terminal rosette, linear-lanceolate, to 2 ft. long and 2 in. wide, margins armed with firm, pale teeth; fls. scarlet, 1½ in. long, in dense racemes to 2½ ft. high. S. Afr.

aristata Haw. TORCH PLANT, LACE A. Stemless, usually in compact clumps; lvs. 100–150, narrowly lanceolate, to 4 in. long and ¾ in. wide, awned at apex, with transverse bands of white tubercles beneath, margins armed with soft white teeth; fls. reddish-yellow, 1¼ in. long, long-pedicelled, in simple or branched infls. to about 20 in. high. S. Afr.

ausana: *A. variegata.*

Bainesii Dyer. Tree, to 60 ft., trunk to about 9 ft. in diam., with forking brs.; lvs. in terminal rosettes, ensiform, 2–3 ft. long, margins bearing scattered prickles; fls. and buds rose to rose-pink, with greenish tips, 1½ in. long, in infl. 16–24 in. high, stamens exserted. S. Afr.

Bakeri Elliot. Stemless, plants forming dense clumps; lvs. to 3½ in. long; fls. shading from orange to yellow, with green tips, ¾ in. long, in simple, few-fld. racemes to 1 ft. high. Madagascar.

barbadensis Mill. [*A. perfoliata* L. var. *vera* L.; *A. vera* (L.) Webb & Berth.]. BARBADOS A., CURAÇAO A., MEDICINAL A., UNGUENTINE CACTUS. Stemless, stoloniferous, forming clumps; lvs. narrowly lanceolate, 1–2 ft. long, long-acuminate, glaucous-green, margins armed with whitish to reddish teeth; fls. yellow, about 1 in. long, in racemes to 3 ft. high. Medit. region. A major source of drug aloe, produced mainly in the Netherlands Antilles.

barbertoniae Pole-Evans. Stemless; lvs. lanceolate-attenuate, with dry, twisted apex, to 20 in. long, with irregular transverse bands of white spots, margins undulate, armed with stout, sharp, brown teeth; fls. dull pinkish-red, to 1½ in. long, cylindrical, inflated at base, in panicles to 3 ft. high. S. Afr.

× **Beguinii.** × *Gastrolea Beguinii.*

brevifolia Mill. Stemless, with basal offshoots; lvs. 30–40, triangular-lanceolate, to 3 in. long and 1 in. wide, glaucous, margins armed with white, horny teeth; fls. pale scarlet, 1½ in. long, in dense racemes to 16 in. high. S. Afr. Var. **humilis** is listed. Cv. 'Variegata'. Lvs. variegated.

Camperi G. Schweinf. [*A. Eru* A. Berger]. St. to 20 in.; lvs. in terminal rosette, ensiform, to 2 ft. long, very fleshy, margins armed with brown-tipped teeth; fls. reddish-yellow or red, to ¾ in. long, in dense racemes at ends of branched infl. to 3 ft. high. Trop. E. Afr. Cv. 'Maculata'. Lvs. narrow, smaller, spotted.

Chabaudii Schönl. Stemless or with very short sts., forming dense clumps; lvs. ovate-lanceolate, to 20 in. long, acuminate, dull gray-green to glaucous-green, margins armed with hooked teeth; fls. pale brick-red, to 1½ in. long, inflated at base, in loose panicles to 3 ft. high or less. S. Afr.

ciliaris Haw. CLIMBING A. Sts. runnerlike and climbing, to 15 ft. long or more; lvs. evenly spaced along st., linear-lanceolate, to 6 in. long, long-acuminate, slightly fleshy, sheathing at base, margins armed with cartilaginous white teeth, which diminish in size toward apex; fls. scarlet-red with yellowish-green tips, to 1¼ in. long, in simple racemes to 1 ft. high. S. Afr.

commutata Tod. Stemless; lvs. to 6 in. long and 2 in. wide, spotted; fls. pale red, 1¼ in. long, in a branched infl. Probably of garden origin; perhaps a hybrid between *A. grandidentata* and *A. saponaria.*

comosa Marloth & A. Berger. St. simple, to 6 ft., with persistent dead lvs.; lvs. in terminal rosette, lanceolate-ensiform, to about 2 ft. long, margins armed with brownish-red teeth; fls. deep pink to pinkish-ivory, to about 1¼ in. long, in racemes to about 8 ft. high. S. Afr.

cryptopoda Bak. Stemless; lvs. 40–50, lanceolate-ensiform, to 3 ft. long, margins armed with sharp reddish-brown teeth; fls. scarlet, with green tips, to 1½ in. long, in panicles to 6 ft. high. S. Afr.

Davyana Schönl. Stemless; lvs. about 12, triangular-lanceolate, the fleshy base to 4 in. long, the dry, twisted apical part to 4 in. long, spotted above, glaucous beneath, margins sinuate-dentate, armed with sharp brown teeth; fls. pink, to 1¼ in. long, in panicles to 3 ft. high. Transvaal.

dichotoma Masson. Tree, to 30 ft., 3–4 ft. in diam., with many forking brs.; lvs. in terminal rosettes, linear-lanceolate, to 14 in. long and 2 in. wide at base, glaucous-green, margins armed with small brownish-yellow teeth; fls. bright canary-yellow, 1¼ in. long, in panicles to 1 ft. high. S. Afr.

Dinteri A. Berger ex Dinter. Stemless; lvs. about 12, narrowly lanceolate, to 1 ft. long, acuminate, keeled, chocolate-brown to brownish-green, both surfaces with broken, transverse bands of spots, margins armed with white teeth; fls. pale rose-pink with white tips, to about 1¼ in. long, in panicles 20–34 in. high. S.-W. Afr.

distans Haw. JEWELLED A. St. to 9 ft., creeping and rooting, often forming dense clumps; lvs. lanceolate, to 6 in. long, glaucous-green, with scattered whitish tubercules, margins armed with yellow teeth; fls. dull scarlet, 1½ in. long, in capitate racemes in a forking panicle to 2 ft. high. S. Afr.

echinata: *A. humilis* var.

Ecklonis Salm-Dyck. Stemless, plants solitary or clumped; lvs. 14–20, to 16 in. long, dull green, unspotted, margins armed with firm white teeth; fls. yellow or red, to 1 in. long, in dense, capitate racemes to 20 in. high. S. Afr.

Eru: *A. Camperi.*

excelsa A. Berger. Tree, 15–20 ft., sts. clothed with persistent dead lvs.; lvs. in terminal rosette, lanceolate-ovate, to 8 in. long, acuminate, with apex recurved, spiny on margins and lower surface; fls. crimson, to ⅜ in. long, in dense panicles to 3 ft. high, stamens long-exserted. S. Rhodesia.

ferox Mill. CAPE A. St. usually to 6 ft., sometimes taller, clothed with persistent dried lvs.; lvs. 50–60, in dense terminal rosette, lanceolate-ensiform, to 3 ft. long, dull green with reddish tinge, often spiny, margins sinuate-dentate, armed with reddish teeth; fls. scarlet or orange, tipped brown, 1¼ in. long, in panicles to 4 ft. high. S. Afr. A source of drug aloe.

Fosteri Pillans. Usually stemless; lvs. 16–24, lanceolate-attenuate, the fleshy base 12–16 in. long, the dried, twisted apex to 4 in. long, with transverse bands of white spots above, green beneath, margin with brown teeth; lower fls. orange-red, upper golden-yellow, in panicles to 5 ft. high, perianth with basal swelling, constricted above ovary. S. Afr.

globosa: *A. humilis* cv.

globuligemma Pole-Evans. Stemless, forming clumps; lvs. lanceolate, to 20 in. long, attenuate, glaucous above, armed with brown-tipped white teeth; fls. sulphur-yellow to ivory, tinged red at base, to 2 in. long, in panicles to 3 ft. high, stamens almost black. S. Afr.

Greenii Bak. Stemless, but stoloniferous, forming dense clumps; lvs. linear-lanceolate, to 1½ ft. long, bright green, with irregular, wavy bands of confluent, oblong, whitish spots, margins sinuate-dentate, armed with pale brown to pink teeth; fls. flesh-pink, to 1¼ in. long, in panicles to 4 ft. high. S. Afr.

Hanburiana: *A. striata.*

harlana Reynolds. Stemless or with short st.; lvs. about 24, lanceolate, to 20 in. long, attenuate, margins sinuate-dentate, with horny reddish-brown teeth and edge; fls. deep red, to 1¼ in. long, in panicles to 3 ft. high, filaments pale lemon-yellow. Ethiopia.

hereroensis Engl. Stemless or with short, procumbent st.; lvs. about 30, triangular-lanceolate, to 1 ft. long, or sometimes to 20 in., margins sinuate, armed with short brown or reddish-brown teeth; fls. varying from yellow to orange, scarlet or dull red, to 1¼ in. long, clustered in corymbose panicles to 3 ft. high. S.-W. Afr.

humilis (L.) Mill. SPIDER A., HEDGEHOG, CROCODILE-JAWS. Stemless, forming dense clumps; lvs. ovate-lanceolate, to 4 in. long and ¾ in. wide, glaucous, tubercled, margins armed with white teeth; fls. red, tipped green, 1½ in. long, in racemes to 14 in. high. S. Afr. Cv. 'Globosa'. Lvs. glaucous-bluish, with tips turning purplish when grown in sun. Var. **brevifolia:** a listed name, for material perhaps referable to *A. brevifolia*. Var. **echinata** (Willd.) Bak. [*A. echinata* Willd.]. Lvs. smaller, with soft prickles but no tubercles on their upper surfaces. Var. **incurva** Haw. Larger, lvs. more fleshy, glaucous-green, with incurved, acuminate tips.

Jacksonii Reynolds. Sts. 4–8 in. long, sprawling, in large clumps; lvs. 5–7, narrowly subulate-attenuate, to 6 in. long, with 1 or 2 apical white spines, spotted, especially on underside, margins armed with isolated white teeth tipped with reddish-brown; fls. scarlet-red, with almost white tips, 1 in. long, in loose, few-fld. racemes to 1 ft. high. Ethiopia.

Juttiae: *A. microstigma.*

Krapohliana Marloth. Stemless or to 8 in., with persistent dead lvs.; lvs. 20–30, narrowly lanceolate, to 8 in. long, acuminate, incurved, glaucous, sometimes with transverse bands beneath, margins armed with small white teeth ⅜ in. apart; fls. scarlet-red with greenish tips, to 1⅜ in. long, in racemes to 16 in. high, filaments white, flattened, anthers orange, exserted. S. Afr.

latifolia: *A. saponaria.*

longistyla Bak. Stemless, plants solitary or 2–10 in a clump; lvs. lanceolate, to 6 in. long, glaucous, with white spines from tubercles, margins armed with horny, white, triangular teeth; fls. salmon-pink to rose-red, about 2 in. long, in stout-peduncled racemes to 8 in. high, styles exserted. S. Afr.

Marlothii A. Berger. St. 6–18 ft., clothed with persistent dead lvs.; lvs. 40–50, in terminal rosette, lanceolate, to about 5 ft. long, attenuate, with red-brown spines on both surfaces and margins; fls. orange to yellow-orange, to 1⅜ in. long, in 1-sided racemes in much-branched panicles to 2½ ft. high. S. Afr.

microstigma Salm-Dyck [*A. Juttiae* Dinter]. Sts. short or up to 1½ ft., plants solitary or in small clumps; lvs. triangular-lanceolate, to about 1 ft. long, usually spotted, margins sinuate-dentate, armed with reddish-brown teeth; fls. orange, fading to greenish-yellow, rarely dull red, about 1 in. long, in racemes 2–2½ ft. high. S. Afr.

Millotii Reynolds. Sts. decumbent, sprawling, to 10 in. long; lvs. triangular, to 4 in. long, in rather loose rosettes, with dull white spots beneath and a few toward base above, margins armed with white, widely spaced teeth; fls. scarlet, ⅞ in. long, in loose, 6–8-fld. racemes to 6 in. high. Madagascar.

mitriformis Mill. PURPLE-CROWN, PURPLE-AND-GOLD-CROWN. Sts. procumbent, sprawling, to 6 ft. long; lvs. ovate-lanceolate, to 8 in. long, ending in a simple or bifid spine, 4–6 spines on keel toward apex on lower surface, margins armed with pale, horny teeth that become dark in age; fls. dull scarlet, to 1¾ in. long, in dense, capitate racemes in a panicle to 2 ft. high. S. Afr.

×**mortolensis:** × *Gastrolea mortolensis.*

nobilis Haw. GOLDEN-TOOTH A., GREEN-AND-GOLD-CROWN. Similar to *A. mitriformis,* but lvs. less concave above; fls. red, to 1½ in. long, on pedicels 1–1½ in. long. S. Afr. Perhaps of hybrid origin, from *A. arborescens* × *A. mitriformis.*

obscura Mill. [*A. picta* Thunb.]. Short-stemmed; lvs. to 8 in. long and 3 in. wide, streaked and spotted with pale green, margins cartilaginous and spiny; fls. red, 1¼ in. long, in an infl. to 3 ft. high. Origin unknown.

parvibracteata Schönl. Stemless, but forming large, dense clumps; lvs. narrowly lanceolate, to 16 in. long, attenuate, with transverse bands of white spots above, unspotted beneath, margins armed with sharp, brown, widely spaced teeth; fls. red, to 1¼ in. long, in panicles to about 5 ft. high, perianth enlarged at base, constricted above ovary. S. Afr.

×**Paxii** A. Terracc. Reputed to be a hybrid between *A. stricta* and *A. commutata.* Stemless or nearly so; lvs. 12–18, oblong-lanceolate, 2–3 in. long, acuminate, margins armed with fleshy teeth; fls. yellow, suffused with pink, to 1½ in. long, in panicles to 3 ft. high.

×**perfectior:** × *Gastrolea Beguinii* var.

perfoliata var. **vera:** *A. barbadensis.*

Perryi Bak. SOCOTRINE A., ZANZIBAR A. St. to 1 ft.; lvs. 12–20, in terminal rosette, lanceolate, 10–12 in. long, acuminate and deeply concave, glaucous, margins armed with sharp brown spines; fls. red, with green tips, aging to yellow, to 1 in. long, in panicles to 2 ft. high. Socotra. A source of drug aloe.

×**pethamensis:** × *Gastrolea pethamensis.*

petricola Pole-Evans. Stemless, plants solitary or in clumps; lvs. 20–30, lanceolate, to 2 ft. long, attenuate, glaucous, often with a few spines on both sides, margins armed with sharp, dark brown teeth about ½ in. apart; fls. greenish-white to pale orange, about 1 in. long, the buds dull red, in densely fld. racemes, in panicles to 3 ft. high. S. Afr.

picta: *A. obscura.*

plicatilis (L.) Mill. Much-branched shrub or tree, 15–25 ft.; lvs. broadly linear to strap-shaped, 2-ranked on each br., to 1 ft. long, glaucous, margins horny, essentially entire; fls. scarlet, to 2¼ in. long, in racemes to 20 in. high. S. Afr.

pratensis Bak. Stemless, plants usually in clumps of 6; lvs. lanceolate to lanceolate-ovate, to 6 in. long, glaucous, usually with a few brownish spines arising from white tubercles on lower surface, margins armed with white, brown-tipped teeth; fls. rose-red, to 1½ in. long, in racemes to 2 ft. high, the peduncles essentially covered with ovate, imbricate bracts. S. Afr.

pretoriensis Pole-Evans. St. to 3 ft., clothed with persistent dead lvs.; lvs. 40–60, in terminal rosette, lanceolate, to 20 in. long, apex acuminate and 4 in. long, margins armed with sharp, reddish, horny teeth; fls. rose-pink to peach-red, in panicles 6–11 ft. high. S. Afr.

×**principis** (Haw.) Stearn [*A. Salm-Dyckiana* Schult. & Schult. f.]: *A. arborescens* × *A. ferox.* St. to 6 ft., clothed with persistent dead lvs., plants forming clumps; lvs. in terminal rosette, ensiform, to 2½ ft. long, yellow-margined; fls. light red, 1½ in. long, in panicles to 3 ft. high. S. Afr.

Reitzii Reynolds. Stemless, or st. procumbent and to 2 ft. high; lvs. lanceolate-ensiform, to 26 in. long, sharp-pointed, dull green, sometimes with 4–8 thorns beneath, margins armed with sharp brownish to brownish-red teeth; fls. red on upper side, yellow on underside, to 2 in. long, curved, in panicles to 4 ft. high. E. Transvaal.

rigens Reynolds & Bally. St. short; lvs. triangular-lanceolate, to 2½ ft. long, sharp-pointed, margins armed with isolated teeth; fls. rose-pink to dull scarlet, to 1¼ in. long, shortly hairy, with open mouth, in an open panicle to 5½ ft. high. Somali Republic.

rubrolutea Schinz. St. to 9 ft., clothed with persistent dead lvs.; lvs. in terminal rosette, lanceolate-ensiform, to 2 ft. long, sometimes spotted, margins armed with brown to reddish-brown teeth with white bases; fls. rose-red to bright red, turning yellow at mouth, to about 1¼ in. long, in many-branched panicles to 3 ft. high. S. Afr.

×**Salm-Dyckiana:** *A.* × *principis.*

saponaria (Ait.) Haw. [*A. latifolia* Haw.]. Stemless, or st. up to 20 in., plants solitary or forming clumps; lvs. lanceolate, 10–12 in. long, with dull white spots above, apex dried and twisted, margins armed with sharp, horny, brown teeth; fls. yellow to red, to 1¾ in. long, in corymbose-capitate racemes in forking-branched panicles to 3 ft. high. S. Afr.

secundiflora Engl. St. short; lvs. triangular-lanceolate, to 1½ ft. long, very fleshy, margins armed with horny, brown, wide-spaced teeth; fls. red, to 1 in. long, in 1-sided racemes in panicles to 2½ ft. high. E. Trop. Afr.

Sladeniana Pole-Evans. Stemless, forming clumps; lvs. 6–8, lanceolate, to 3¼ in. long, white-spotted, margins white-horny, armed with white teeth; fls. dull pink, to about 1¼ in. long, with basal swelling, in racemes or panicles, to 20 in. high, bracts 1-nerved. S.-W. Afr.

somaliensis C. H. Wright ex W. Wats. Stemless or with short st.; lvs. 17–20, lanceolate, to 6 in. long or sometimes longer, irregularly spotted, margins armed with red-tipped spines; fls. dull red, over 1 in. long, in panicles to 2½ ft. high. Somali Republic.

speciosa Bak. Much-branched tree, to 25 ft., sts. clothed with persistent dead lvs.; lvs. in terminal rosettes, ensiform, to 32 in. long, margins pink or pale red, armed with very small red teeth; fls. greenish-white, to 1¼ in. long, buds red, in cylindrical racemes to 20 in. high, exserted portion of filaments brownish-orange. S. Afr.

×**spinosissima** Hort. ex A. Berger. SPIDER A. Reputed to be a hybrid between *A. humilis* var. *echinata* and *A. arborescens* var. *pachythyrsa* A. Berger. St. to 3 ft. or more with age; lvs. lanceolate, to 1 ft. long, with few spines on both surfaces, margins armed with horny teeth; fls. orange-red, in dense, cylindric-conical racemes to 2 ft. high.

Steudneri G. Schweinf. Nearly stemless; lvs. lanceolate, to 2 ft. long, margins armed with rose-colored teeth; fls. red, with inner segms. yellow at tip, 2 in. long, in panicles to 3 ft. high. Ethiopia.

striata Haw. [*A. Hanburiana* Naud.]. CORAL A. St. procumbent, to 3 ft., clothed with persistent dead lvs.; lvs. 12–20, lanceolate, to 20 in. long, attenuate, striate, margins entire, with pink border; fls. coral-red, 1¼ in. long, with basal swelling, in corymbose panicles to 3 ft. high. S. Afr.

suprafoliata Pole-Evans. Stemless or with short st.; lvs. about 30, lanceolate, 12–16 in. long, glaucous, apex acuminate, becoming dry and twisted, margins armed with reddish-brown, sometimes bifid, teeth; fls. scarlet, green-tipped, to 2 in. long, in racemes to 3 ft. high. S. Afr.

Suzannae Decary. St. to 12 ft.; lvs. in loose rosette, to 3 ft. long, attenuated from base to apex, margins armed with yellowish teeth; fls. greenish-yellow, to 1¼ in. long, many, in dense, cylindrical racemes 6–9 ft. high, stamens exserted. Madagascar.

tenuior Haw. Sts. often branched, sprawling if unsupported, to 9 ft. long, forming clumps; lvs. in loose terminal rosette, linear-lanceolate, 4–6 in. long, glaucous, margins white, armed with minute white teeth; fls. yellow, about ½ in. long, in racemes to 14 in. high. S. Afr.

Thorncroftii Pole-Evans. Stemless or nearly so, plants always solitary; lvs. 25–30, lanceolate, to 1 ft. long, margins armed with horny, sharp, reddish-brown teeth; fls. dull rose-red to scarlet-red, to 2 in. long, in racemes to 3 ft. high, infl. sometimes branched. E. Transvaal.

Thraskii Bak. St. unbranched, 3–6 ft. or sometimes higher, clothed with persistent dead lvs.; lvs. in terminal rosette, lanceolate, to 5 ft. long, strongly recurved, sometimes with few spines beneath, margins reddish or brownish, armed with reddish teeth; fls. yellow to orange, to 1 in. long, in panicles to 2½ ft. high. Natal.

×**Todari** Borzi. Reputed to be a hybrid, with *A. humilis* as one parent; stemless or nearly so; lvs. 30–40, lanceolate, to 1 ft. long, spotted, margins armed with red teeth; fls. red, to 1½ in. long, in racemes to 1 ft. high.

Vaotsanda Decary. St. to 12 ft., clothed with persistent dead lvs.; lvs. in terminal rosette, perhaps to 3 ft. long, 6–8 in. wide at base, reddish-green, recurved, margins armed with triangular prickles; fls. yellow-orange, red at base, yellowish at tips, in panicles about 20 in. high, shorter than lvs. Madagascar.

variegata L. [*A. ausana* Dinter]. TIGER A., PARTRIDGE-BREAST, PHEASANT'S-WINGS, KANNIEDOOD A. Stoloniferous, stemless, to 9 in. high, forming large clumps; lvs. triangular-lanceolate, 4–6 in. long, with irregular transverse bands of white spots, margins white, horny, crenate-dentate; fls. pink to dull scarlet, to 1½ in. long, in racemes to 12 in. high, bracts 1-nerved. S. Afr.

vera: *A. barbadensis.*

virens Haw. Stemless, plants forming clumps; lvs. narrowly lanceolate, to 8 in. long, margins armed with fleshy, triangular, white teeth; fls. red, 1½ in. long, in racemes to 2 ft. high. S. Afr.

Wickensii Pole-Evans. Stemless or nearly so; lvs. 40–50, lanceolate-ensiform, to 32 in. long, pale green, incurved, margins armed with sharp brown to black teeth; fls. chrome-yellow with brownish tips, to 1¼ in. long, crowded in short racemes in panicles to 5 ft. high. S. Afr.

ALOINOPSIS Schwant. *Aizoaceae.* About 15 spp. of dwarf, tufted, per. succulents with a tuberous rhizome, native to S. Afr.; lvs. opp., in rosettes, linear-lanceolate to ovate, or spatulate, flattish above, nearly flat, convex or keeled beneath, glabrous, velvety-pubescent, punctate or even tubercled; fls. solitary or in groups of 2–3, calyx 5–6-lobed, petals yellow, salmon, flesh-pink or rose, many, in 1–3 series, stamens many, in a cone, ovary inferior, 7–12-celled, stigmas 7–12; fr. a caps., expanding keels winged, placental tubercles present.

Cultivate in deep pots in the greenhouse using a loamy-sandy soil, with careful watering and maximum light. Propagated by seeds. See also *Succulents*.

Jamesii L. Bolus [*Nananthus Jamesii* (L. Bolus) L. Bolus]. Lvs. 4–6 in a cluster, gray-green, rough-tubercled, to ¾ in. long, ³⁄₁₆ in. wide at base, ⅜ in. wide at middle, ⅛ in. thick, upper side slightly concave, lower side rounded at the base, keeled and broadened and 3-angled-tapered toward apex; fls. 1 in. across, sepals 5, petals golden-yellow, with red midrib. Cape Prov.

Lodewykii L. Bolus. Lvs. 6–8 on a br., erect or nearly so, glaucous-green to red-brown-green, prominently white-tubercled above, to ¾ in. long, with sheath to ³⁄₁₆ in. long, upper part reniform or semicircular in top view and to ¾ in. wide, lower part elongate and more slender; fls. on peduncle to ⅜ in. long, sepals 5–6, tubercled, petals coppery inside, pale salmon outside, to ⁵⁄₁₆ in. long. Cape Prov.

Luckhoffii (L. Bolus) L. Bolus [*Titanopsis Luckhoffii* L. Bolus]. Rosettes to 1½ in. across; lvs. bluish-green with coarse, gray-green, regularly arranged tubercles, to ¾ in. long, ³⁄₁₆ in. thick at base, to ½ in. wide and triangular in section at apex, the very tip slightly recurved, lower side rounded at the base, keeled toward the apex, margins with 5–6 large, pink, evenly spaced tubercles; fls. 1 in. across, sepals 6, petals light yellow. Cape Prov. Prefers a limy soil.

Malherbei (L. Bolus) L. Bolus [*Nananthus Malherbei* L. Bolus]. GIANT JEWEL PLANT. Lvs. erect with incurved apex, glaucous, to 1 in. long, broadly spatulate to fan-shaped and truncate, upper side flat, lower side flat to slightly rounded, apex with a row of white tubercles on the margin; fls. 1 in. across, on pedicels to 1 in. long, sepals 6, petals pale brown to flesh-colored. Cape Prov. Prefers a limy soil.

Orpenii (N. E. Br.) L. Bolus [*Nananthus Orpenii* (N. E. Br.) L. Bolus]. Clumps thick; lvs. erect, crowded, glabrous or minutely pubescent, bluish-green, dark-spotted, ¾ in. long, ⅜ in. wide, ¼ in. thick, ovate-lanceolate, upper side flat, lower side rounded at base, keeled and laterally compressed near the acute and somewhat recurved apex; fls. to ½ in. across, petals yellow with reddish tips. Cape Prov.

Peersii (L. Bolus) L. Bolus [*Nananthus Peersii* L. Bolus]. Lvs. 2–4, minutely pubescent, bluish gray-green and punctate, ascending from base, then suddenly spreading, to ⅞ in. long, ¼ in. thick, ⅜ in. wide at base, widened to ⅝ in. and tapered to a bluntly triangular tip, upper side flat, rounded and obtusely keeled at tip below; fls. solitary, yellow, 1 in. across. Cape Prov.

rosulata (Kensit) Schwant. Lvs. 5–6, dark green with whitish tubercles at tip, spreading, to 1³⁄₁₆ in. long, ⅜ in. wide at base, ⅝ in. wide at apex, spatulate, flattish on upper side, rounded basally and keeled toward apex on lower side, margins and tip rounded; fls. 1–3, to 1⅜ in. across, petals yellow. Cape Prov.

rubrolineata (N. E. Br.) Schwant. [*Nananthus rubrolineatus* (N. E. Br.) N. E. Br.]. Lvs. 4–6, 4-ranked, spreading-recurved, gray-green, white-tubercled in upper ⅓ on lower surface, to 1 in. long, ³⁄₁₆ in. thick, ⅜ in. wide at base, ¾ in. wide near middle, broadly triangular in outline, upper side flat, lower side rounded and obtusely keeled toward tip; petals yellow with central red stripe. Cape Prov.

Schooneesii L. Bolus [*Nananthus Schooneesii* (L. Bolus) L. Bolus]. Lvs. 6–8, erect or nearly so, glabrous, white or pale green below ground, briefly elevated above soil and there green or brown-green, punctate, to ⅝ in. long, ⅛ in. thick, ¼ in. wide, flat above, rounded beneath, dilated-truncate at the exposed tip; fls. solitary on peduncles to ½ in. long, sepals 5, petals pale coppery with red stripe. Cape Prov.

setifera (L. Bolus) L. Bolus [*Titanopsis setifera* L. Bolus]. Lvs. 4–6, glaucous to deep carmine, tubercled, to ¾ in. long, ⅛ in. thick, ¼ in. wide, upper side flattish, lower side rounded and somewhat keeled apically, tip obliquely rounded and triangular in outline, margins and both surfaces armed toward tip with elongate tubercles, some of these bristlelike and papillate; fls. 1 in. across, petals golden-yellow to salmon. Cape Prov.

spathulata (Thunb.) L. Bolus [*Nananthus crassipes* (Marloth) L. Bolus]. Brs. 1 or several, short; lvs. 6–10 on a br., gray-green or red-margined, densely and minutely tubercled, especially on margin at apex, erect, flattened, broadly spatulate from a narrow base; fls. solitary, sessile, petals deep pink, paler outside. Cape Prov.

Triebneri: a listed name of no botanical standing.

Villetii (L. Bolus) L. Bolus [*Nananthus Villetii* L. Bolus]. Lvs. 2 on a br. or with leaflike bracts and appearing as 4, erect, glaucous-green, densely tubercled, to ⅞ in. long, ⅝ in. wide, ¼ in. thick, broadly spatulate or the upper part nearly orbicular; fls. solitary, on peduncle to ⁵⁄₁₆ in. long, sepals 6, petals pale yellow, coppery toward tip inside, paler and pink toward tip outside. Cape Prov.

ALONSOA Ruiz & Pav. MASK FLOWER. *Scrophulariaceae.* About 7–10 spp. of ann. or per. herbs, or shrubs, native to trop. Amer.; sts. 4-sided; lvs. opp., or in 3's; fls. in terminal racemes, flat-rotate, with scarcely any corolla tube, turned upside down by twisting of the pedicel, stamens 4.

Propagated easily from seeds or cuttings. Grown in full sun, generally as annuals in the garden; or indoors for the showy winter bloom.

acutifolia Ruiz & Pav. Subshrubby, bushy per., to 3 ft.; lvs. narrowly lanceolate-elliptic, ¾–1¼ in. long, sharply serrate; fls. deep orange, ¾–1 in. across. Mts., Peru.

grandiflora: *A. Warscewiczii*, but also *A. incisifolia.*

incisifolia Ruiz & Pav. To 3 ft.; lvs. to 2½ in. long and 1¼ in. wide, deeply serrate; corolla deep scarlet, purple-black in throat, about ⅝ in. across. Chile. Some material cult. as *A. grandiflora* is this sp.

×**intermedia** Lodd. [*A. miniata* Hort.]: *A. incisifolia* × *A. linearis.* Shrubby plant; lvs. mostly ¾ in. long, weakly serrate to entire; fls. in shades of red.

linearis Ruiz & Pav. [*A. linifolia* Roezl]. Shrub, 2–3 ft.; lvs. linear, 1¼–1¾ in. long and less than ⅛ in. wide, sparingly serrulate; corolla brick-red, about ½ in. across. Peru.

linifolia: *A. linearis.*

miniata: *A. intermedia.*

Mutisii Steud. Not known to be cult.; material cult. under this name is *A. Warscewiczii.*

peduncularis (O. Kuntze) Wettst. Not known to be cult.; material listed under this name appears to be a cv. of *A. Warscewiczii.*

Warscewiczii Regel [*A. grandiflora* Hort.; *A. Mutisii* Hort., not Steud.]. MASK FLOWER. Much-branched shrub, 1–3 ft.; lvs. broadly ovate, often obtuse, finely and bluntly to crenately serrate; corolla usually in shades of red to orange, mostly ⅝–¾ in. across. Peru. Cv. 'Compacta'. Reported to have scarlet fls.

ALOPECURUS L. FOXTAIL. *Gramineae.* About 30 spp. of per. or ann. grasses in temp. N. Hemisphere; lf. blades flat; panicles soft, dense, spikelike; spikelets 1-fld., disarticulating below the glumes, strongly compressed laterally, glumes equal, usually united at base, ciliate on the keel, lemma 5-nerved, obtuse, margins united at base, awned dorsally from below the middle, awn slender, included or 2–3 times longer than the spikelet, palea 0. For terminology see *Gramineae.*

arundinaceus Poir. REED F., CREEPING F. Per., rhizomatous, sts. tall; lf. blades to ⅜ in. wide; infl. to 4 in. long and ⁵⁄₁₆ in. thick, often purplish; spikelets ¼ in. long, glumes sparsely hairy, keel long-ciliate, lemma about as long as glumes, awn to ⅛ in. long. Eurasia; introd. in Lab. and N. Dak.

pratensis L. MEADOW F. Per., sts. to 3 ft., erect; lf. blades to ¼ in. wide; infl. cylindrical, dense, to 2¾ in. long and ⅜ in. in diam.; spikelets to ¼ in. long, glumes ¼ in. long, keel conspicuously ciliate, sides pubescent, awn exserted, to ³⁄₁₆ in. long. Eurasia; naturalized in Nfld. and Lab. to Alaska, s. to Ore., Idaho, Mont., e. to Del. Occasionally cult. in meadows.

ALOPHIA Herb. [*Herbertia* Sweet, not S. F. Gray]. *Iridaceae.* About 10 spp. of cormous, per. herbs, native to Tex., s. Brazil, Uruguay, Argentina, and Chile; corm tunicate; lvs. basal, 2-ranked, linear to sword-shaped, pleated; fls. blue to violet, terminal, borne in a spathe, perianth tube none or very short, perianth segms. 6, spreading, the inner 3 much smaller than the outer, stamens 3, filaments united, style brs. 3, bifid near apex; fr. a caps.

Propagated by seeds and offsets.

amoena (Griseb.) O. Kuntze [*Herbertia amoena* Griseb.]. Corm subglobose, sts. to 1 ft.; lvs. linear, 3–10 in. long; fls. 1–2 in a spathe, violet, outer segms. ⅝ in. long; fr. to ½ in. long. Ne. Argentina, Uruguay.

Drummondii (R. C. Grah.) R. Foster [*Herbertia caerulea* (Herb.) Herb.; *H. Watsonii* Bak.]. Corm ovoid, sts. to 1 ft.; lvs. narrow-linear, to 1 ft. long; fls. 1–2 in a spathe, violet-blue, outer segms. white, spotted violet on the claws, to 1½ in. long; fr. ¾–1¼ in. long. Tex.

pulchella (Sweet) Benth. [*Herbertia pulchella* Sweet]. Corm globose, sts. to 9 in.; lvs. narrowly sword-shaped; fls. blue-purple, outer segms. white at base, with lilac dots. S. Brazil, Chile.

ALOYSIA Ort. *Verbenaceae.* About 30 spp. of aromatic shrubs, native to warm parts of N. and S. Amer.; lvs. opp. or whorled, simple; fls. small, spicate, the spikes axillary or panicled, calyx 4-toothed, enclosing the fr. at maturity, corolla 2-lipped, stamens 4; fr. dry, separating into 2 nutlets at maturity.

The lemon verbena is a popular greenhouse plant, which should be grown at a temperature of about 55° F. and the pots planted out in summer. Propagated by cuttings from the new growth.

citriodora: *A. triphylla.*

triphylla (L' Hér.) Britt. [*A. citriodora* (Cav.) Ort.; *Lippia citriodora* (Ort.) HBK; *Verbena citriodora* Cav.; *V. triphylla* L' Hér.]. LEMON VERBENA. Shrub, to 10 ft.; lvs. in whorls of 3 or 4, lanceolate, to 3 in. long, entire or toothed, glandular-dotted beneath, with odor of lemon; fls. white, in whorled, axillary spikes, or terminal panicle. Summer to autumn. Argentina, Chile. Commonly cult. in tropics.

ALPHITONIA Reiss. ex Endl. *Rhamnaceae.* Perhaps more than 5–6 spp. of trees or shrubs in Australia, the Philippine Is., Malay Arch. to sw. Pacific region; lvs. alt.; fls. ¼ in. across or less, in forking cymes; fr. dry, drupelike, the outer part often falling and leaving the 2 or 3 seeds standing on the receptacle.

excelsa Reiss. ex Endl. Tall tree, brs. whitish or rusty-tomentose; lvs. ovate to lanceolate, to 6 in. long, entire, leathery, white-tomentose beneath. N. Australia. Occasionally cult. in s. Calif.

ALPINES. Alpines are plants that grow above the tree line, but the term is frequently used for mountain plants in general, and alpine gardening is likely to mean only rock gardening. Alpines are primarily low, often cushionlike perennials, adapted to a short growing season. True alpine gardening attempts to approximate alpine conditions and is possible only in cool places, with a good supply of cold water and with soils similar to those of alpine regions; it is little attempted in North America outside of mountainous regions. The selection of plants requires experience and the handling of them demands skill.

ALPINIA Roxb. [*Catimbium* Lestib.; *Languas* J. König]. GINGER LILY. *Zingiberaceae.* Over 250 spp. of per. herbs in Asia; sts. leafy; infl. terminal on leafy sts. or rarely on separate leafless sts., a raceme, spike, or panicle; fls. often showy, calyx usually tubular, 3-toothed or 3-lobed, corolla 3-lobed, upper lobe often largest, tube at least as long as calyx, staminodial lip petal-like, lateral staminodes much reduced or absent, ovary inferior, 3-celled; fr. a caps. Sometimes divided into several genera, but the limits of these not clearly understood; the genus, therefore, is here retained in the broad sense for cult. material.

Alpinias are grown for their showy flowers and ornamental foliage and habit in the tropics, subtropics, and warm temperate regions, or in a moist greenhouse at a temperature of 60° F. or more. Plants require frequent watering. Propagated by division in spring; the plants make large clumps.

calcarata (Haw.) Roscoe. To 5 ft.; lvs. to 1 ft. long, 2 in. wide; infl. a dense panicle, to 4 in. long; fls. greenish-white, in axils of obtuse fl. bracts, the lip variegated with red and yellow. India. Similar to *A. Zerumbet,* but lvs. narrower, infl. usually erect. Some material grown under this name is *Brachychilum Horsfieldii.*

formosana K. Schum. [*A. Kumatake* Mak.]. Lvs. to 28 in. long, 4½ in. wide; infl. an erect panicle, to 6 in. long, axis glabrous; lip 1 in. long, crinkled. S. Japan, Taiwan. Zone 9. Similar to *A. Zerumbet,* but fl. bracts apiculate, infl. erect, and axis glabrous.

japonica (Thunb.) Miq. [*Languas japonica* (Thunb.) Sasaki]. To 24 in.; lvs. lanceolate or oblanceolate, to 16 in. long, 2¾ in. wide, glabrous above, minutely hairy beneath; fls. nearly sessile, 1–2 at each node of infl., with a small gland between them, calyx ½ in. long, corolla lobes and staminodial lip about ⅜ in. long. Cent. and s. Japan, Taiwan, China. Zone 8.

Kumatake: *A. formosana.*

mutica Roxb. [*Catimbium muticum* (Roxb.) Holtt.]. SMALL SHELL GINGER, ORCHID G. To 6 ft.; lvs. to 16 in. long, 1¾ in. wide; infl. terminating leafy st., about 6 in. long, with cincinni of 2–3 fls. at each node, short-hairy; fls. white, in axils of deciduous fl. bracts, lip to 1⅜ in. long, yellow, marked with red. Malay Pen. Material cult. under this name may be *Brachychilum Horsfieldii.*

nutans Roscoe: not known in cult., the name often used in error for *A. Zerumbet.*

purpurata (Vieill.) K. Schum. RED GINGER. To 15 ft.; lvs. lanceolate, to 2½ ft. long or more, to 6 in. wide, glabrous; infl. often pendulous, to nearly 3 ft. long, showy; fls. small, white, 1–2 in axils of persistent red bracts over 1 in. long. Pacific Is.

Rafflesiana Wallich ex Bak. To 4½ ft.; lvs. to 2 ft. long, 3¼ in. wide, short-hairy on both surfaces or almost glabrous above; infl. terminating st., with 1–3-fld. cincinni in axils of primary bracts; fls. subtended by reddish, funnelform bracts, calyx orange-red to rose, corolla tube longer than calyx, pale orange, lip to 1 in. long, orange-yellow to yellow, veined or flushed with crimson; fr. short-hairy. Malay Pen.

Sanderae Hort. Sander. VARIEGATED GINGER. Lvs. to 8 in. long and 1 in. wide, striped and marked with clear white. New Guinea. Botanical position uncertain; plant frequent in cult. but seldom flowering.

speciosa: *A. Zerumbet.*

tricolor Hort. Sander. To 8 ft.; lvs. oblong-lanceolate, to 10 in. long, 1¼ in. wide, green striped with white and yellow, or pale green; infl. loose; fls. white, in axils of 6–9 persistent, rose primary bracts and subtended by tubular fl. bracts, calyx ¾ in. long, 3-toothed, corolla lobes slender, ⅜ in. long, lip narrow. Solomon Is.

ventricosa: a listed name of no botanical standing; see *Renealmia ventricosa.*

vittata Bull. VARIEGATED GINGER. A name of doubtful standing; some plants grown under this name in the U.S. are *Renealmia ventricosa.*

Zerumbet (Pers.) B. L. Burtt & R. M. Sm. [*A. speciosa* (J. C. Wendl.) K. Schum.; *Catimbium speciosum* (J. C. Wendl.) Holtt.; *Languas speciosa* (J. C. Wendl.) Merrill]. SHELLFLOWER, SHELL GINGER, PINK PORCELAIN LILY. To 12 ft.; lvs. to 2 ft. long, 5 in. wide; infl. pendulous, hairy; fls. in axils of obtuse bracts, white, tinged with purple, fragrant, lip crinkled, yellow, variegated with red and brown. E. Asia. Commonly planted in warm regions but will withstand some frost. Zone 10. Has often been offered under the erroneous name of *A. nutans.*

ALSEUOSMIA A. Cunn. *Caprifoliaceae.* Eight spp. of evergreen shrubs, native to New Zeal.; lvs. alt., simple; fls. tubular or funnelform, fragrant, solitary or clustered in the axils, calyx and corolla 4–5-lobed, stamens 5, ovary inferior, 2–5-celled; fr. a crimson berry.

macrophylla A. Cunn. To 8 ft., glabrous; lvs. obovate to linear-oblong, to 7 in. long; fls. crimson, to 1½ in. long; berries ½ in. long. Cult. in Zone 10 in s. Calif.

ALSINE: *Arenaria.* **Alsine parnassica:** *Arenaria stellata.* **Alsine sedoides:** see *Arenaria sedoides* and *Arenaria verna.*

ALSINOPSIS: *ARENARIA.*

ALSOPHILA R. Br. [*Amphicosmia* G. Gardn.]. TREE FERN. *Cyatheaceae.* About 200 spp. of slender, evergreen, mostly trop., tree ferns; lvs. large, 2–3-pinnate, petioles smooth or spiny and with an early-deciduous scale at the spine apex, covered with broad, marginally differentiated scales bearing a black terminal bristle; sori on lower surface of pinnules, indusium absent or of minute basal scales.

One species is much cultivated as an ornamental outdoors in Zone 10, or often as a potted or tub plant for patio or greenhouse. Propagated by spores. For culture see *Ferns.*

australis R. Br. [*Cyathea australis* (R. Br.) Domin]. AUSTRALIAN T.F. To 20 ft., trunk straight; lvs. in a spreading head, to 12 ft. long, 3-pinnate, scales on petioles bright brown, scales on midribs of pinnules bullate and entire, fimbriate, or denticulate. Australia. Not cult.; material offered under this name is *Sphaeropteris Cooperi.*

Cooperi: *Sphaeropteris Cooperi.*

Cunninghamii (Hook.f.) Tryon [*Cyathea Cunninghamii* Hook.f.]. Trunk to 20 ft., slender; petioles slender, blackish-purple to dark brown, tubercled, scales of 2 kinds, linear and narrowly ovate; lvs. herbaceous, 3-pinnate, with stellate hairs beneath, rachises and ribs of pinnae with fawn to tan, stellate or much dissected scales appearing as wool. Australia, Tasmania, New Zeal. Zone 10.

Dregei (Kunze) Tryon [*Cyathea Dregei* Kunze]. Trunk to 4 ft.; lvs. 2-pinnate, acuminate, pinnules 2–3 in. long; sori on lower half of pinnules, immersed in rufous wool. Mts. of S. Afr. Zone 10.

Smithii (Hook.f.) Hook. [*Cyathea Smithii* Hook.f.; *Hemitelia Smithii* (Hook.f.) Hook.]. SOFT T.F. Petioles rough, lvs. soft, oblong-lanceolate, 2–3-pinnate, primary pinnae 16 in. long, 4 in. wide, rachis with red-stellate scales, pinnules crenate-serrate. New Zeal.

tricolor (Colenso) Tryon [*Cyathea dealbata* (Forst.) Swartz; *C. tricolor* Colenso]. SILVER T.F., SILVER-KING T.F. Trunk to 30 ft.; petioles broadening, finely fimbriate basally, scales glossy dark brown; lvs. 3-pinnate, powdery-white beneath in mature plants, pinnules dentate, rachises and midribs with fine, woolly, tan hairs. New Zeal. and Lord Howe Is. Pith of st. yields an edible sago.

Walkerae (Hook.) John Sm. [*Amphicosmia Walkerae* (Hook.) T. Moore; *Cyathea Walkerae* Hook; *Hemitelia Walkerae* (Hook.) K. Presl]. Petioles slightly muricate, lvs. very leathery, 2–3-pinnate, primary pinnae 1½ ft. long, the secondary pinnae remote, 3–4 in. long, deeply pinnatifid to 1-pinnate, pinnule oblong, very obtuse, entire to slightly crenate, scales deciduous; indusia often 2-lobed. Ceylon.

ALSTONIA R. Br. *Apocynaceae.* About 40 spp. of trees and shrubs with milky sap, native to se. Asia and Pacific Is.; lvs. mostly whorled, entire; fls. in corymbose cymes, 5-merous, bisexual, corolla salverform, the tube pubescent below stamens, stamens borne on upper part of tube, included, pistil with 2 separate ovaries; fr. a pair of slender follicles, seeds attached at their middle, ciliate.

macrophylla Wallich ex G. Don. Tree, to 60 ft. or more; lvs. oblanceolate or elliptic-lanceolate, to 1 ft. long, leathery, with 16–20 pairs of veins ½ in. apart, petioles to ¾ in. long; infl. large, many-fld.; calyx lobes short, obtuse, ciliate, corolla small, constricted at throat, tube to ³⁄₁₆ in. long, glabrous outside, villous in throat, lobes rounded, ciliate; follicles pendulous, to 18 in. long and ¼ in. in diam. Thailand and Malay Pen., e. to Philippine Is. and Indonesia.

scholaris (L.) R. Br. DEVIL TREE, PALI-MARA. Tree, to 60 ft. or more; lvs. spatulate to oblanceolate, rarely elliptic, to 8 in. long, usually obtuse, strongly leathery, with up to 50 pairs of veins spreading at right angles to midrib, petioles to ½ in. long; cymes very crowded; calyx densely tomentose outside, corolla greenish-white, to about ½ in. across, pubescent outside and in throat, lobes rounded and pubescent on both sides, ovaries hirtellous; follicles to 2 ft. long, ⅛ in. in diam. India to Indonesia, trop. Australia, and Afr. The bark is the source of an antimalarial drug.

venenata R. Br. Shrub, to 8 ft. or more, glabrous; lvs. petioled, oblong-lanceolate, to 8 in. long, finely acuminate, membranous, veins very slender and close together; corolla white, about 1 in. across, tube 1 in. long, lobes not ciliate; follicles to 6 in. long and ⅜ in. in diam., on a slender stalk about 1 in. long. India.

yunnanensis Diels. Shrub, to 10 ft.; lvs. nearly sessile, lanceolate, to 7 in. long, acuminate, hispidulous-pubescent beneath or at least on the many veins; infl. small, few-fld.; calyx lobes long-attenuate to an acute apex, ciliate, corolla white, about ½ in. across, tube about ⅜ in. long, densely bearded at throat, lobes ciliate; follicles to 1½ in. long, often slightly constricted at intervals, not stalked. W. China.

ALSTROEMERIA L. LILY-OF-THE-INCAS, PERUVIAN LILY. *Alstroemeriaceae.* Perhaps as many as 60 spp. of S. Amer. herbs; roots thick, elongate, fibrous; sts. leafy; fls. showy, red, violet, white, to yellow, in terminal bracted clusters, perianth segms. separate, nearly equal to markedly unequal, stamens 6, declinate, ovary inferior, 3-celled; fr. a caps.

Alstroemerias, except *A. aurantiaca,* are probably not hardy in the North but may be planted out in spring, lifted after blooming, and stored over winter. They should be set in semishady places in rich moist soil. May also be grown as pot plants in the greenhouse, but should be lifted and shaken out annually. Propagated by division of roots and by seeds.

aurantiaca D. Don ex Sweet. To 3 ft.; lvs. lanceolate, to 4 in. long, glabrous; peduncles about 5, each with 2–3 fls., rarely with more fls. or only 1; fls. bright orange or yellow, to 2 in. long, upper inner perianth segms. longest and spotted with red. Chile. Probably not specifically distinct from *A. versicolor.* Listed cvs. include: 'Angustifolia', 'Flava', 'Lutea', 'Major', 'Rubra', 'Splendens'.

brasiliensis K. Spreng. To 4 ft.; lvs. oblong-lanceolate, 2 in. long; fls. reddish-yellow, spotted with brown, 1¼ in. long. Brazil. Material cult. under this name may be *A. psittacina.*

caryophyllaea Jacq. To 1½ ft.; lvs. narrowly lanceolate, 1–3 in. long; peduncles about 5, each with 1 fl.; fls. with fragrance of carnations, perianth segms. graduated in length, the uppermost longest, the lowermost very short, the 3 upper white, spotted and streaked and tipped with red, the 3 lower red, sometimes tipped with white. Brazil.

chilensis: a confused name, sometimes applied to forms of *A. pulchra,* but not definitely assignable botanically.

Cooperi: a listed name of no botanical standing.

haemantha Ruiz & Pav. HERB LILY. To 3 ft.; lvs. lanceolate to linear, to 4 in. long, ciliate; peduncles 5–6, each with 2 fls.; fls. deep red, perianth segms. serrate, the upper inner segms. longest and streaked with yellow. Chile. Cv. 'Rosea'. Fls. rose.

Hookeri Lodd. Similar to *A. pulchra* and perhaps not specifically distinct, differing in having fls. pinkish and the upper inner segms. without red tips.

Ligtu L. To 1 ft.; lvs. linear-lanceolate, entire; peduncles 6–7, each with 2–3 fls.; fls. deep red, perianth segms. entire or minutely denticulate, the upper inner segms. longest and streaked with white. Chile. Cvs. 'Angustifolia', 'Pulchra', and 'Stinsonii' are listed.

Pelegrina L. To 2 ft.; lvs. lanceolate, to 2 in. long; fls. lilac, spotted with red-purple, outer perianth segms. broadly cordate-obovate with a central cusp, inner segms. narrower, not longer than the outer. Peru. Cv. 'Alba'. Fls. white.

peruviana, peruviensis: listed names of no botanical standing.

psittacina Lehm. To 3 ft.; lvs. lanceolate, to 3 in. long; peduncles 5–6, each with 1 fl.; fls. to 1¾ in. long, dark red, tipped with green and brown-spotted, perianth segms. graduated in length, the uppermost longest, the lowermost shortest. Brazil. Possibly identical with *A. pulchella.* Material cult. as *A. brasiliensis* may be this sp.

pulchella L.f. A poorly known sp.; most material grown under this name may be referable to *A. Ligtu* or *A. psittacina.*

pulchra Sims [*A. tricolor* Hook.]. To 1½ ft.; lvs. linear-lanceolate; peduncles several, each with 2–3 fls.; fls. white to pink, outer perianth segms. broadly obovate, usually entire with a green cusp, upper inner segms. longest, splotched with yellow and streaked and tipped with red or purple. Chile.

tricolor: *A. pulchra.*

versicolor Ruiz & Pav. To 1½ ft.; lvs. linear-lanceolate, petioled, to 4 in. long; peduncles 2–3, each with 1 fl.; fls. to 2 in. long, yellow or orange, with purple spots, outer segms. equal, inner segms. narrower and the 2 upper longest. Chile.

violacea: a name used in 3 senses botanically; the identity of plants cult. under this name has not been determined.

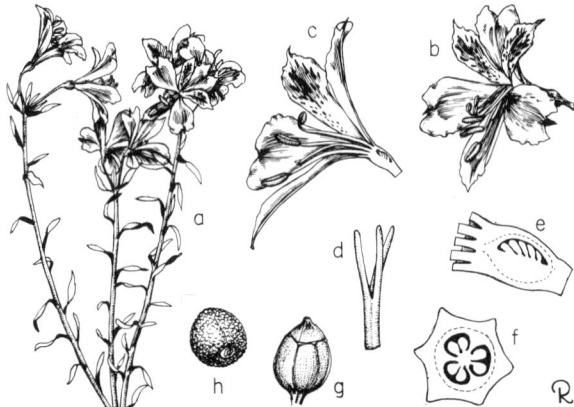

ALSTROEMERIACEAE. *Alstroemeria Pelegrina:* **a,** upper part of flowering stems, × ⅙; **b,** flower, × ⅓; **c,** flower, vertical section, × ½; **d,** apex of style, × 2; **e,** ovary, vertical section, × 2; **f,** ovary, cross section, × 2; **g,** fruit, × ½; **h,** seed, × 2.

ALSTROEMERIACEAE Dumort. ALSTROEMERIA FAMILY. Monocot.; 4 genera and over 180 spp. of rhizomatous herbs with fibrous roots or tubers and erect to climbing leafy sts., native to trop. and subtrop. Amer.; lvs. alt., parallel-veined, entire, often resupinate; fls. in a terminal bracted cluster or irregular raceme, bisexual, regular or nearly so, perianth segms. separate, in 2 series, stamens 6, anthers erect, ovary inferior, 1–3-celled, ovules many; fr. a caps. Formerly included in the Amaryllidaceae, but differing in having sts. leafy and infl. not strictly umbellate. *Alstroemeria* and *Bomarea* are cult.

ALTAMIRANOA: *VILLADIA.*

ALTERNANTHERA Forssk. [*Achyranthes* Hort., not L.; *Telanthera* R. Br.]. JOSEPH'S-COAT, COPPERLEAF. *Amaranthaceae*. More than 100 spp. of herbs or shrubs of warm or trop. countries; lvs. opp., entire, green, or variously colored or variegated; fls. bisexual, subtended by bracteoles, in small, dense, axillary, sessile or pedunceled heads, sepals usually 5, equal or unequal, petals none, stamens 3–5, filaments united basally into a tube, usually with staminodelike appendages between them, anthers 2-celled, ovary 1-celled, ovule 1, stalked; fr. a utricle.

The alternantheras in cultivation are herbs of the New World tropics. They are grown as bedding plants and not often allowed to reach the blooming stage, being usually kept low and compact by shearing. They grow best in warm, sunny locations. Propagated by division or by cuttings. Cuttings are usually made from strong plants in the garden in Aug., wintered over in hotbeds or the greenhouse and potted in Mar. or Apr.

amoena: *A. ficoidea* cv.

aurea nana: *A. ficoidea* cv.

axillaris (Hornem. ex Willd.) D. Dietr. [*A. spinosa* (Hornem.) Roem. & Schult.]. Erect or ascending, to 3 ft., branched; lvs. oblong-ovate or rhombic-ovate, to 2½ in. long, 1⅛ in. wide, rounded to acute at tip; fls. straw-colored, in axillary heads, sepals unequal, spinose-tipped, pilose, staminodelike appendages shorter than filaments, irregularly toothed to entire. Cuba.

Bettzickiana: *A. ficoidea* cv.

brilliantissima: *A. ficoidea* cv.

dentata (Moench) Stuchlík ex R. E. Fries. Erect, to 18 in. or more; lvs. ovate to linear-lanceolate, to 3½ in. long, 2 in. wide, green or sometimes colored; fl. heads white or greenish-white, to 1 in. long, on peduncles to 5 in. long or more, a few sometimes sessile, bracteoles as long as sepals, broadened and somewhat lacerate at tip. W. Indies to Brazil. Cv. 'Rubiginosa', INDOOR CLOVER. Lvs. red to purple. Cult. as a border or foliage plant; commonly grown erroneously under the names *A. ramosissima* or *A. ramosissima* cv. 'Versicolor'.

ficoidea (L.) R. Br. ex Roem. & Schult. Per., sts. procumbent or erect; lvs. elliptic to broadly ovate or obovate, tipped with a very short spine, green but in some cult. forms variously colored; fl. heads white or straw-colored, sessile in lf. axils; sepals unequal, the outer 3 broad, hairy, 3-ribbed at base, the inner 2 narrower, the staminodelike appendages longer than filaments, lacerate at tip. Mex. to Argentina. A variable sp., with several cvs. sometimes considered spp. Cult. for the ornamental foliage. Cvs. are: 'Amoena' [*A. amoena* (Lem.) Voss], PARROTLEAF, SHOOFLY JOYWEED, dwarf, lvs. lanceolate to elliptic, blotched and veined with red and orange; 'Aurea Nana', a selection from cv. 'Bettzickiana', lvs. yellow; 'Bettzickiana' [*Alternanthera Bettzickiana* (Regel) Nichols.; *Achyranthes Bettzickiana* (Regel) Standl.], CALICO PLANT, erect, with many ascending brs., lvs. narrowly spatulate, colored and blotched in shades of yellow and red; 'Brilliantissima', a selection from cv. 'Bettzickiana' with bright red lvs.; 'Rosea Nana', a selection from cv. 'Amoena', lvs. rose-colored; 'Sessilis', an 'Amoena' type, lvs. short-stalked; 'Versicolor', SNOWBALL, COPPER A., lvs. copper-red or blood-red, round-spatulate. Other named cvs. have been grown in Eur.

philoxeroides (Mart.) Griseb. [*Achyranthes philoxeroides* (Mart.) Standl.; *Telanthera philoxeroides* (Mart.) Moq.]. ALLIGATOR WEED. Aquatic per., sts. decumbent to ascending, often swollen, to 3 ft. long or more; lvs. lanceolate to obovate, to 4 in. long, ¾ in. wide; fl. heads usually on long peduncles, bracteoles less than half as long as sepals; sepals nearly equal, staminodelike appendages longer than stamens, lacerate. S. Amer. Introd. as an ornamental; now naturalized and weedy in s. U.S.

polygonoides (L.) R. Br. ex Roem. & Schult. [*Telanthera polygonoides* (L.) Moq.]. Per., sts. procumbent, branched; lvs. elliptic to ovate or obovate, to 1 in. long or more, to ⅝ in. wide; fl. heads white, globose to cylindric, sessile in lf. axils, bracteoles shorter than sepals; sepals unequal, outer 3 broader, 3-nerved, staminodelike appendages shorter than stamens. Mex. to Argentina.

ramosissima (Mart.) Moq. ex Chodat. Not in cult.; material grown under this name or as *A. ramosissima* cv. 'Versicolor' is *A. dentata* cv. 'Rubiginosa'.

rosea nana: *A. ficoidea* cv.

sessilis (L.) DC. Not in cult.; material offered under this name is *A. ficoidea* cv.

spinosa: *A. axillaris*.

versicolor: a listed name of no botanical standing for *A. ficoidea* cv.

ALTHAEA L. *Malvaceae*. About 12 spp. of ann. or per. herbs, from Eur. to cent. Asia; lvs. shallowly to deeply lobed or parted; fls. in racemes or panicles, usually distinctly peduncled or pedicelled, involucral bracts 6–9, united basally; petals 5, usually less than 1½ in. long, pink to bluish or purple, stamens united in a tubular staminal column, the column cylindrical, pubescent, style brs. filiform, stigmatic on inner edge, as many as the mericarps; fr. a schizocarp, mericarps about 20, in a single whorl, each indehiscent, 1-celled, 1-seeded.

Propagated by seeds or divisions of the rhizome. The generic name *Althaea* is often used as a common name for *Hibiscus syriacus* L. In the trade, cultivars of *H. syriacus* may be listed as "Althaeas." Among the Latin-named cultivars so listed are: 'Alba', 'Alba Plena', 'Amplissima', 'Anemoniflora', 'Meehanii', 'Paeoniflora', 'Purpurea', and 'Tota Alba'. Such listing rarely causes confusion, for in catalogues they clearly refer to the shrub *H. syriacus* and not to the herbaceous genera *Althaea* or *Alcea*.

armeniaca Ten. [*A. taurinensis* C. A. Mey., not DC.]. Erect, finely tomentose, per. herb, to about 4 ft.; lvs. palmately 3- or 5-parted, the divisions linear-lanceolate to obovate, coarsely toothed; fls. several on axillary peduncles as long or longer than the subtending lf., pinkish, to 1½ in. across, calyx lobes clasping the fr.; mericarps rugose, dorsal wall shallowly furrowed. E. Medit. region and se. Russia.

cannabina L. [*A. narbonensis* Pourr. ex Cav.]. Erect, pubescent, per. herb, to 5 ft.; lvs. palmately 3- or 5-parted, the divisions narrow, lacerate-toothed; fls. 1 to several on peduncles longer than subtending lf., sometimes in terminal panicles, purplish to rose, 1–2 in. across, calyx lobes erect in fr.; mericarps transversely rugose dorsally, with rounded edges. S. and e.-cent. Eur.

ficifolia: *Alcea ficifolia*.

frutex: *Hibiscus syriacus*.

kragujevacensis: *A. officinalis*.

narbonensis: *A. cannabina*.

officinalis L. [*A. kragujevacensis* Panč.; *A. taurinensis* DC., not C. A. Mey.]. MARSH MALLOW, WHITE MALLOW. Gray-velvety-pubescent per. herb, to 4 ft. or more; lvs. broadly ovate to ovate, unlobed or shallowly 3- or 5-lobed; fls. solitary or clustered in the lf. axils, shorter than subtending lf., bluish to pale rose, 1–2 in. across, calyx lobes clasping the fr.; mericarps pubescent, smooth, thin-walled. Eur.; naturalized in coastal marshes of e. U.S. Roots have medicinal properties.

pallida: *Alcea pallida*.

rosea: *Alcea rosea*.

sulphurea: *Alcea sulphurea*.

syriaca: *Hibiscus syriacus*.

taurinensis: see *A. armeniaca* and *A. officinalis*.

ALVESIA: see *BAUHINIA*.

ALYOGYNE Alef. *Malvaceae*. About 6 spp. of small shrubs from S. and W. Australia; lvs. unlobed to deeply divided or dissected; fls. axillary, solitary, on stout or elongate pedicels, involucral bracts 4–12, separate or more commonly basally united to form a toothed cup, calyx 5-lobed, longer than bracts, petals large, pale lilac, sometimes more deeply spotted at the base, usually 1-toothed at apex, stamens united in a tubular column, style unbranched, terminated by a 5-lobed or radiately 5-branched stigma; fr. a 5-celled, many-seeded caps.

Propagated by seeds or cuttings.

hakeifolia (Giord.) Alef. [*Cienfuegosia hakeifolia* (Giord.) Hochr.]. Erect shrubs, 3–10 ft., brs. slender, green, glabrous; lower lvs. 2-pinnate or ternately divided into linear, somewhat fleshy segms., upper lvs. narrowly linear; involucral bracts about ⅛ in. long, calyx about 1 in. long, petals 2–3 in. long, lilac-purple, with a deep purple basal spot; caps. ovoid, as long as the calyx, seeds woolly. S. and W. Australia.

Huegelii (Endl.) Fryx. [*Hibiscus Huegelii* Endl.]. Glabrescent or tomentose shrubs, most under 6 ft.; lvs. to about 3 in. long, 3- or 5-lobed or -parted, the lobes again lobed to deeply toothed; involucral bracts to ¼ in. long, united basally to form an 8–12-toothed cup, calyx ½–1 in. long, petals to 3 in. long, lilac or purple-red, deeply spotted at the base; caps. ovoid, pubescent, seeds glabrate. S. and W. Australia.

ALYSICARPUS Desv. ALYCE CLOVER. *Leguminosae* (subfamily *Faboideae*). About 16 spp. of herbs of Old World tropics; lvs. alt., of single lft.; fls. papilionaceous in few-fld. terminal racemes, small, blue or purple, standard clawed, wings united to keel, stamens 10, 9 united and 1 separate; fr. a nearly cylindrical, several-jointed legume.

vaginalis (L.) DC. Ann., sts. to 3 ft., spreading or erect; lfts. orbicular to lanceolate, ½–2 in. long, petioles slender, to ½ in. long, stipules subulate, as long as petioles; fls. ¼ in. long, in 4–12-fld. racemes to 3 in. long; fr. narrow, to ¾ in. long, nearly straight. Himalayas to Ceylon, Malay Pen.; naturalized in W. Indies and Fla. Grown in tropics and in the South as a forage plant. Will grow on more acid soil than most leguminous forage plants and is reported to have nutritive value equivalent to alfalfa. Prop. by seeds.

ALYSSOIDES Mill. [*Vesicaria* Adans.]. BLADDERPOD.

Cruciferae. Three spp. of per. herbs with stellate or branched hairs, in rocky places, on cliffs, or on walls, in cent. Eur. and Medit. region; lvs. entire; sepals 4, petals 4, yellow, long-clawed; fr. an inflated, saclike, more or less globose silicle. Differs from *Lunaria* and *Alyssum* in its inflated fr., and from *Alyssum* in its larger fls. with unequal sepals, the lateral ones saccate basally.

cretica (L.) Medic. [*Alyssum creticum* L.]. Diffuse, woody, much-branched at base; lvs. in basal rosettes, grayish-tomentose, oblanceolate to obovate; silicles sessile, pubescent. Crete.

graeca: *A. utriculata.*

sinuata (L.) Medic. [*Alyssum sinuatum* L.; *Vesicaria sinuata* (L.) Poir.]. Sts. to 18 in., little-branched, woody only at extreme base, sparsely to densely gray-pubescent; lvs. oblanceolate to lanceolate, lower lvs. sinuate-dentate; petals to ⅜ in. long; silicles sessile, to ½ in. across. Nw. Balkan Pen., e. Italy.

utriculata (L.) Medic. [*Alyssoides graeca* (Reut.) Jáv.; *Vesicaria utriculata* (L.) Lam.]. Sts. to 18 in., unbranched, woody at base; lvs. on nonflowering sts. crowded, petioled, obovate, stellate-hairy, of fl. sts. sessile, lanceolate, glabrous; petals to ¾ in. long; silicles stalked, to ½ in. across. Mts., cent. Eur.

ALYSSUM L. MADWORT. *Cruciferae.* About 160 spp. of

ann., bien., or per. herbs or subshrubs with sterile shoots and winter rosettes, native to Eur. and Asia, with the largest number in Turkey, plants mostly gray-pubescent with stellate, often scalelike hairs; lvs. alt., simple, entire; fls. usually yellow, rarely white, sepals and petals 4, long stamens usually with winged filaments, short stamens with an appendage; fr. a dehiscent or indehiscent silicle, with a distinct but often short style.

A few are grown in rock gardens and borders, in open or sunny sites. They require the usual culture for perennials and are propagated by seeds, cuttings, or division of the roots.

alpestre L. Usually procumbent per., to 6(–8) in.; basal lvs. obovate or oblong to linear, about ¼ in. long; fls. yellow, in short racemes. Mts., cent. Eur. Many plants grown as *A. serpyllifolium* may belong here.

alyssoides (L.) L. [*A. calycinum* L.]. Ann. or bien., to 10 in., mostly branching at base; lvs. narrow-oblong to spatulate, usually less than 1 in. long, gray-pubescent; fls. yellowish-white, in narrow terminal racemes, sepals persistent. Eur.; naturalized in N. Amer.

Arduinii: *Aurinia saxatilis.*

argenteum All. Not in cult.; material offered under this name is *A. murale.*

atlanticum Desf. Grayish-white, cespitose per., with nonflowering rosettes; basal lvs. sessile, oblong, st. lvs. lanceolate; fls. yellow, in simple racemes. Spain.

Benthamii: *Lobularia maritima.*

Bertolonii Desv. [*A. Janchenii* E. Nyár.]. Strictly erect per., to 2 ft.; st. lvs. oblanceolate, to 1 in. long; silicles orbicular-obovate or elliptic, to ¼ in. long, flattened, glabrous at maturity. Sw. Eur.

Borzaeanum E. Nyár. Per., to 2 in., with woody roots, sts. many, erect, stiff; lvs. obovate, sometimes nearly orbicular, white- or gray-pubescent; fls. yellow, in corymbs or racemes. Romania, Bulgaria, w. Turkey.

calycinum: *A. alyssoides.*

condensatum Boiss. & Hausskn. Per., sts. prostrate to ascending, to 8 in., woody at base, gray-pubescent; lvs. obovate-spatulate or oblanceolate; fls. in racemes; silicles elliptic, to ¼ in. long. Asia Minor.

Probably not cult.; plants offered under this name commercially are usually *A. cuneifolium.*

corymbosum: *Aurinia corymbosa.*

creticum: *Alyssoides cretica.*

cuneifolium Ten. Gray or nearly white, tufted per., to 6 in., with many nonflowering rosettes, fl. sts. diffuse, flexuous; basal lvs. oblong-obovate, attenuate to petiole, st. lvs. narrower, obtuse or subacute, lf. hairs crowded, multiradiate; fls. yellow, in short, dense racemes; silicles orbicular-elliptic, to ¼ in. long, densely gray-pubescent. Mts., s. Eur.

desertorum Stapf [*A. minimum* Willd., not L.]. Ann., to 4 in.; lvs. oblong, gray- or silvery-hairy; fls. pale yellow; silicles orbicular, to ³⁄₁₆ in. long, glabrous, in elongated racemes. Eur., Asia; naturalized in w. U.S.

diffusum Ten. Gray-green per., to 4 in., nonflowering sts. long, procumbent; basal lvs. elliptic or obovate, st. lvs. elliptic or lanceolate, cuneate; petals notched, to ¼ in. long; silicles round, inflated, in elongated racemes. Mts., s. Eur. Closely related to and sometimes offered as *A. montanum*, but differing in lf. shape.

edentulum: *Aurinia petraea.*

epiroticum: *A. sibiricum.*

floribundum Boiss. & Bal. Per., to 2 ft., gray-pubescent, woody at base; lvs. obovate, to ¾ in. long; fls. yellow; silicles obovate, to ½ in. long, flat, indehiscent, samaralike. Rare, confined to high-mountain serpentine, Turkey. Probably not cult.

gemonense: *Aurinia petraea.*

idaeum Boiss. & Heldr. Silvery-green per., sts. decumbent, short, unbranched; lvs. ovate-oblong, the basal about ½ in. long; fls. whitish, in a short panicle; silicles orbicular, to ¼ in. long, compressed-convex. Only on serpentine, Crete. Difficult to maintain under cult.; material offered under this name is usually *A. cuneifolium.*

incanum: *Berteroa incana.*

Janchenii: *A. Bertolonii.*

lutescens: a name of no botanical standing, used for a yellowish-fld. form of *Lobularia maritima.*

maritimum: *Lobularia maritima.*

Markgrafii O. E. Schulz. Per., to 1 ft., sts. stellate-pilose; lvs. narrowly linear-spatulate, to ¾ in. long; fls. to ³⁄₁₆ in. across, in dense panicles, petals bright yellow, narrow, nearly twice as long as calyx. Albania, Yugoslavia. Often confused with *A. murale.*

minimum: *Lobularia maritima*, but material offered as *A. minimum* is usually *A. desertorum.*

Moellendorfianum Asch. ex G. Beck. Silvery per.; lower lvs. more or less spatulate, upper lvs. ovate, all obtuse and about ½ in. long; fls. yellow, in an umbel-like head. Yugoslavia. Differs from *A. montanum* in being smaller, much more compact, and having flowering sts. always prostrate or procumbent, and silicles and pedicels silvery.

montanum L. [*A. pedemontanum* Rupr.]. Per., to 10 in., but commonly low and compact; lvs. obovate-oblong to linear, gray-pubescent; fls. yellow, fragrant, in short clusters elongating in fr.; silicles gray-pubescent or ashy-gray. Eur. Distinguished from *A. repens* by the absence of simple hairs among the stellate hairs of the pedicels.

murale Waldst. & Kit. [*A. argenteum* Vitm., not All.]. YELLOW-TUFT. Gray-green per., to 24 in.; basal lvs. obovate-spatulate, usually disappearing before flowering time, st. lvs. lanceolate or oblanceolate, to ¾ in. long; fls. yellow, small, many in terminal corymbs; silicles usually orbicular, each cell with 1 winged seed. E. Eur.; a variable sp.

orientale: *Aurinia saxatilis.*

ovirense A. Kern. Per., to 5 in., rarely to 1 ft., sts. ascending, woody at base; lower lvs. broadly obovate, tapering abruptly at base, upper lvs. lanceolate, all sparsely stellate-hairy and green; petals golden-yellow, hairy; silicles hairy, in elongated racemes. Cent. Eur. Often confused with *A. Wulfenianum.*

pedemontanum: *A. montanum.*

petraeum: *Aurinia petraea.*

podolicum: *Schivereckia podolica.*

procumbens: a listed name of no botanical standing; probably refers to *Lobularia maritima.*

repens Baumg. [*A. Rochelii* Andrz. ex Rchb.]. Diffuse or erect per., to 2 ft., with nonflowering sts. ending in rosettes; basal lvs. obovate-spatulate, st. lvs. lanceolate or linear-lanceolate. Related to *A. montanum* but fls. larger, orange, stellate-hairy and pedicels with long simple hairs intermixed with stellate hairs. Se. Eur. Sometimes incorrectly known as *A. Wierzbickii,* an entirely different sp., probably not in cult.

Rochelii: *A. repens.*

rostratum Steven. Not known to be in cult.; the name has been used erroneously for *A. montanum, A. murale,* and *A. repens.*

saxatile: *Aurinia saxatilis.*

scardicum Wettst. Spreading per., to 8 in., green or gray-green; lower lvs. elliptic-oblanceolate, st. lvs. linear; fls. pale yellow, in a dense head elongating in fr. Balkan Pen.

serpyllifolium Desf. Procumbent to erect per., to 12 in., with many nonflowering rosettes, basal lvs. oblanceolate or obovate-spatulate, to ⅜ in. long, gray or whitish beneath. Closely related to and sometimes confused with *A. alpestre,* but sts. longer, lvs. larger, and petals longer. Sw. Eur. Some plants cult. as *A. serpyllifolium* are *A. alpestre* or *A. alyssoides.*

sibiricum Willd. [*A. epiroticum* (Halácsy) E. Nyár.]. Erect or procumbent per., to 8 in., stout and woody at base; basal lvs. spatulate, to 2½ in. long, st. lvs. oblanceolate to suborbicular, gray-green. Se. Eur.

sinuatum: *Alyssoides sinuata.*

spinosum L. [*Ptilotrichum spinosum* (L.) Boiss.]. Small, spiny shrub, to 1 ft., silvery; lvs. long-lanceolate, to 2 in. long; fls. white or pinkish, in short racemes. Medit. region. Cv. 'Roseum'. Fls. deep rose-colored.

Wierzbickii Heuff. Usually bien., nonflowering sts. usually absent. Romania, Bulgaria, Yugoslavia. Probably not cult. See *A. repens.*

Wulfenianum Bernh. Gray-pubescent per.; differing from *A. montanum* mainly in silicles twice as large and only sparsely pubescent. S. Eur.

AMARACUS: *ORIGANUM.*

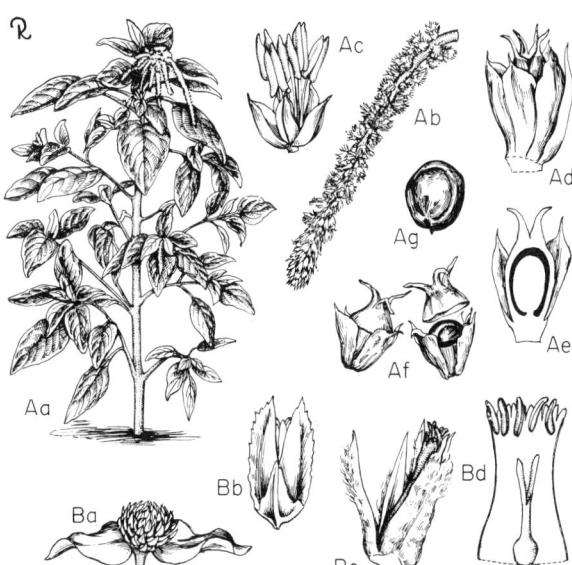

AMARANTHACEAE. **A,** *Amaranthus caudatus:* **Aa,** plant, × ¹⁄₂₀; **Ab,** branch of inflorescence, × ½; **Ac,** male flower, × 3; **Ad,** female flower, × 6; **Ae,** female flower, vertical section, × 6; **Af,** fruits, × 5; **Ag,** seed, × 8. **B,** *Gomphrena globosa:* **Ba,** inflorescence, × ½; **Bb,** bract of inflorescence, × 2; **Bc,** flower, × 3; **Bd,** pistil and expanded staminal tube, × 4.

AMARANTHACEAE Juss. AMARANTH FAMILY. Dicot.; more than 60 genera and over 800 spp., mostly of herbs of wide distribution; lvs. opp. or alt.; fls. small, unisexual or bisexual, subtended by dry scales, often showy in mass, perianth small, 2–5-parted, stamens 1–5, ovary superior; fr. a utricle, achene, or berrylike. The cult. genera are: *Alternanthera, Amaranthus, Celosia, Froelichia, Gomphrena,* and *Iresine.*

Many species are weedy, but some are grown as ornamentals or as green vegetables.

AMARANTHUS L. AMARANTH. *Amaranthaceae.* About 50 spp. of coarse ann. herbs, native in mild and trop. climates

in many parts of the world, some of them widely distributed as weeds of tilled lands and waste places; lvs. alt.; fls. unisexual, minute and inconspicuous, in chaffy, often colored heads or spikes, sepals mostly 5, stamens mostly 5, anthers 4-celled; fr. a 1-seeded utricle.

Cultivated for their ornamental colored foliage or heavy red or green spikes. In Asia some are grown as green vegetables or for their edible seeds. The species grow readily from seeds and do best in sunny locations; the leaf colors are likely to be less brilliant in very fertile soils. Some of the weedy kinds may be grown in collections for general interest.

abyssinicus: a listed name of no botanical standing for plants referable to *A. caudatus.*

albus L. TUMBLEWEED. To 3 ft., sts. whitish, much-branched; lvs. obovate to spatulate-oblong, to nearly 3 in. long; fls. greenish, in small clusters, bracteoles spinescent, much longer than calyx, sepals and stamens 3; fr. dehiscing horizontally. U.S.; now a semicosmopolitan weed.

caudatus L. LOVE-LIES-BLEEDING, TASSEL FLOWER. Stout, branching, upright, 3–5 ft.; infl. large, coarse, erect or sometimes nodding and tail-like, usually vividly colored. Tropics. Cult. in India as a food plant. Commonly cult. and sometimes escaped. Young lvs. and seeds are edible.

cruentus L. [*A. paniculatus* L.]. PURPLE A., RED A., PRINCE'S-FEATHER. To 6 ft.; lvs. long-petioled, to 12 in. long, ovate-lanceolate to rhombic; infl. a terminal panicle of red or purple spikes, lateral spikes mostly horizontally divergent. Probably a cultigen, and by some treated as a var. of *A. hybridus.*

fruticosus: a listed name of no botanical standing.

hybridus L. GREEN A., PIGWEED, WILD BEET. Common tall weed; similar to *A. cruentus* but brs. of infl. ascending and spikes green. Lvs. and seeds are edible. Var. **erythrostachys** Moq. [*A. hypochondriacus* L.]. PRINCE'S-FEATHER. The commonly cult. form; foliage often reddish; spikes red.

hypochondriacus: *A. hybridus* var. *erythrostachys.*

melancholicus: *A. tricolor.*

paniculatus: *A. cruentus.*

quadricolor: a listed name of no botanical standing.

retroflexus L. REDROOT, GREEN A., PIGWEED, WILD BEET. To 10 ft.; fls. green, in stout terminal panicles, with crowded lateral spikes to 2 in. long. U.S., Canada; now a semicosmopolitan weed.

salicifolius: *A. tricolor* var.

sanguineus: a listed name of no botanical standing for plants referable to *A. caudatus.*

tricolor L. [*A. melancholicus* L.]. TAMPALA. Erect, mostly much-branched, 1–4 ft.; lvs. elliptic or ovate, the main ones 2½–4 in. wide; fl. clusters small, globose, sessile, axillary, or borne along leafless axillary axes or in a narrow paniclelike infl. In cult., plants usually have lvs. blotched and colored, and are then known as JOSEPH'S-COAT. Tropics. Grown in the Orient as a green vegetable. Var. **salicifolius** (Hort. Veitch) Aellen [*A. salicifolius* Hort. Veitch]. FOUNTAIN PLANT. Lvs. narrow, to 7 in. long, ⅜ in. wide. Cv. 'Splendens'. Foliage deep red, uppermost lvs. brilliant light red.

×AMARCRINUM Coutts [×*Crindonna* Ragion.; ×*Crinodonna* Stapf]: *Amaryllis* × *Crinum. Amaryllidaceae.*

Howardii: ×*A. memoria-Corsii.*

memoria-Corsii (Ragion.) H. E. Moore [×*Amarcrinum Howardii* Coutts; ×*Crindonna memoria-Corsii* Ragion.; ×*Crinodonna Corsii* Stapf]: *Amaryllis Belladonna* × *Crinum Moorei.* Similar in habit to *Crinum,* with long-necked bulb; lvs. evergreen, 2-ranked, to 2 ft. long or more, 2 in. wide; fls. similar to *Amaryllis,* though with a distinct, narrow, curved tube and slightly curved limb. Autumn.

×AMARYGIA Ciferri & Giacom. [×*Brunsdonna* Hort. van Tuberg. ex Worsl.]: *Amaryllis* × *Brunsvigia. Amaryllidaceae.*

Bidwellii (Worsl.) H. E. Moore [×*Brunsdonna Bidwellii* Worsl.]: *Amaryllis Belladonna* × *Brunsvigia orientalis* (L.) Ait. ex Eckl. [*B. multiflora* Ait.]. Like ×*B. Parkeri,* but fls. said to be shorter and perianth segms. broader. Material cult. as *Brunsvigia multiflora* belongs here.

Parkeri (W. Wats.) H. E. Moore [*Amaryllis* ×*Parkeri* W. Wats.; ×*Brunsdonna Parkeri* (W. Wats.) Worsl.]: *Amaryllis Belladonna* × *Brunsvigia Josephinae.* NAKED-LADY LILY. Fls. clear deep rose suffused with carmine, or varying in various self-crosses and back-crosses.

AMARYLLIDACEAE. **A,** *Amaryllis Belladonna:* **Aa,** flowering plant and foliage, × ¹⁄₁₂; **Ab,** flower, × ¼; **Ac,** flower, vertical section, × ½; **Ad,** stigma, × 8; **Ae,** ovary, vertical section, × 1½; **Af,** ovary, cross section, × 2. **B,** *Galanthus nivalis:* **Ba,** flowering plants, × ¼, and bulb, vertical section, × ½; **Bb,** flower and spathe valves, × 1; **Bc,** flower, vertical section, × 1; **Bd,** anther, × 4; **Be,** ovary, cross section, × 3; **Bf,** fruit, × ¾; **Bg,** seed, × 4. **C,** *Narcissus Pseudonarcissus* hybrid; **Ca,** flowering plants, × ⅙; **Cb,** flower, vertical section, × ½. **D,** *Nothoscordum bivalve:* **Da,** umbel, × ½; **Db,** flower, × 1; **Dc,** fruit, × 2; **Dd,** seed, × 4. **E,** *Brodiaea elegans;* **Ea,** flowering plant, × ⅙; **Eb,** flower, × ½; **Ec,** flower, vertical section, × ½; **Ed,** perianth, expanded, × ½; **Ee,** pistil, × 1; **Ef,** ovary, cross section, × 3; **Eg,** seed, × 5. **F,** *Eucharis grandiflora:* **Fa,** flowering plant, × ¹⁄₁₂; **Fb,** flower, × ¼; **Fc,** flower, vertical section, × ⅓; **Fd,** stigma, × 2.

AMARYLLIDACEAE Jaume St.-Hil. AMARYLLIS FAMILY. Monocot.; over 90 genera and 1,200 spp. of temp. and warm regions, largely in S. Amer., S. Afr., and Medit. region, with tunicate bulbs or corms or rarely rhizomes; lvs. few, basal or very rarely on the scape; fls. 1 to many in a terminal umbel (subumbellate in *Ixiolirion*) subtended by 1 or more membranous bracts (spathe valves) on a hollow or solid scape, usually bisexual, regular or irregular, often showy, perianth 6-lobed, sometimes with a corona, stamens 6, opp. the lobes, filaments sometimes appendaged or united in a cup, ovary superior or inferior, 3-celled or rarely 1-celled by abortion, typically with axile placentation; fr. a caps. or berry. Closely allied to the Liliaceae, from which it differs in the umbellate infl. subtended by spathaceous bracts; and to the Iridaceae, from which it differs in having 6 stamens. The cult. genera are: *Agapanthus, Allium,* ×*Amarcrinum,* ×*Amarygia, Amaryllis, Ammocharis, Androstephium, Bessera, Bloomeria, Boophone, Brodiaea, Brunsvigia, Calostemma, Chlidanthus, Clivia, Crinum, Cybistetes, Cyrtanthus, Dichelostemma, Eucharis, Eustephia, Galanthus, Habranthus, Haemanthus, Hippeastrum, Hymenocallis, Ipheion, Ixiolirion, Leucocoryne, Leucojum, Lycoris, Milla, Muilla, Narcissus, Nectaros-* *cordum, Nerine, Nothoscordum, Pamianthe, Pancratium, Paramongaia, Petronymphe, Phaedranassa, Phycella, Sprekelia, Stenomesson, Sternbergia, Triteleia, Tulbaghia, Urceolina, Vallota, Worsleya,* and *Zephyranthes.*

The family furnishes vegetables used for food and seasoning in the genus *Allium* and many choice ornamental genera grown as pot plants or in the open in the South. Some of the groups are much hybridized, with many named cvs., and the cult. spp. are often confused. Numerous articles on Amaryllidaceae may be found in the journals *Herbertia* and *Plant Life.*

AMARYLLIS L. [*Callicore* Link; *Coburgia* Herb.]. *Amaryllidaceae.* One sp., a S. Afr. herb with tunicate bulb; lvs. basal, strap-shaped, appearing after fls.; umbel terminal on a solid scape, 6–12-fld. (or more in cult.), subtended by 2 membranous bracts (spathe valves); fl. tube short, lobes subequal, stamens 6, inserted at throat, declinate, anthers versatile, ovary inferior, ovules many, superposed; fr. globose, indehiscent or bursting irregularly, seeds 1 to few, green, globose.

The generic name *Amaryllis* has been applied in the U.S. to *Hippeastrum,* from which the amaryllis of horticulture is derived, but historically, and now by international accord, the name is correctly used as it is here. Plants grown as *A. Belladonna,* however, should be compared with the description of *Hippeastrum puniceum* to verify their identity.

Bulbs may be lifted and stored in a cool dry place during the winter, although they are hardy outdoors to central N.Y.

×**Ackermannii:** *Hippeastrum* ×*Ackermannii.*

advena: *Hippeastrum advena.*

Albertii: *Hippeastrum puniceum* cv. 'Semiplenum'.

ambigua: *Hippeastrum elegans* cv. 'Longiflorum'.

aulica: *Hippeastrum aulicum.*

aurea: *Lycoris africana.*

Bagnoldii: *Hippeastrum Bagnoldii.*

Barlowii: *Hippeastrum roseum.*

Belladonna L. [*A. blanda* Ker-Gawl.; *A. rosea* Lam.; *Brunsvigia rosea* (Lam.) Hann.; *Callicore rosea* (Lam.) Link; *Coburgia rosea* (Lam.) Gouws]. BELLADONNA LILY, CAPE BELLADONNA, NAKED-LADY L. To 1½ ft.; lvs. appearing in spring, dull green, to 1½ ft. long, ¾ in. wide; scape appearing in early autumn after lvs. have disappeared, pedicels 1–1½ in. long; fls. rose-red to whitish, 3–3½ in. long, tube ½ in. long or less. Several cvs. are listed, some of which may actually belong to *Hippeastrum puniceum.* Var. **barbata:** *Hippeastrum barbatum.* Var. **Parkeri:** ×*Brunsdonna Parkeri.* Hybrids with *Crinum* are ×*Amarcrinum;* with *Brunsvigia,* ×*Amarygia.*

bifida: *Hippeastrum bifidum.*

blanda: *A. Belladonna.*

bulbisperma: *Crinum bulbispermum.*

candida: *Hippeastrum argentinum.*

elegans: *Hippeastrum elegans.*

equestris: *Hippeastrum puniceum.*

Evansiae: *Hippeastrum Evansiae.*

formosissima: *Sprekelia formosissima.*

×**Garfieldii:** *Hippeastrum* × *Garfieldii.*

gracilis: a hort. name for a group of *Hippeastrum* cvs.

Hallii: *Lycoris squamigera.*

Hippeastrum: a listed name of no botanical standing; see *Hippeastrum.*

hybrida: a listed name of no botanical standing, used for various *Hippeastrum* hybrids.

immaculata: *Hippeastrum argentinum.*

×**Johnsonii:** *Hippeastrum* ×*Johnsonii.*

Josephinae: *Brunsvigia Josephinae.*

Leopoldii: *Hippeastrum Leopoldii.*

longifolia: *Cybistetes longifolia.*

maxima: a listed name of no botanical standing and of uncertain application.

miniata: *Hippeastrum miniatum.*

Moreliana: *Hippeastrum Morelianum.*

nivalis: a listed name of no botanical standing.

organensis: *Hippeastrum correiense.*

×**Parkeri:** ×*Amarygia Parkeri.*

phycelloides: *Phycella phycelloides.*

procera: *Worsleya Rayneri.*

psittacina: *Hippeastrum psittacinum.*

punicea: *Hippeastrum puniceum.*

purpurea: *Vallota speciosa.*

radiata: *Lycoris radiata.*

reticulata: *Hippeastrum reticulatum.*

reginae: *Hippeastrum reginae.*

rosea: *A. Belladonna.*

rubra: a listed name of no botanical standing and of uncertain application.

rutila: *Hippeastrum striatum.*

solandriflora: *Hippeastrum elegans.*

squamigera: a listed name, probably referable to *Lycoris squamigera.*

striata: *Hippeastrum striatum.*

×**Tubergenii:** a listed name of no botanical standing for ×*Amarygia Parkeri*

vittata: *Hippeastrum vittatum.*

AMBERBOA (Pers.) Less. *Compositae* (Carduus Tribe). About 20 spp. of ann. herbs, native from Medit. region to cent. Asia; lvs. alt., pinnatifid, not spiny; fl. heads mostly solitary, sometimes in pairs or small clusters, involucre ovate to globose, involucral bracts imbricate in several rows, scarious, often spine-tipped, receptacle flat, bristly; fls. all tubular, the outer row larger, raylike, sterile, anthers tailed; achenes obovate or oblong, 10–20-ribbed, hairy, pappus a persistent crown of several rows of scales.

muricata (L.) DC. [*Centaurea muricata* L.]. To 2 ft.; sts. straight, branched, furrowed; lower lvs. 3–5-lobed, upper lvs. entire or only toothed; heads to ¾ in. across; fls. pink to purple. Spain, Morocco, Algeria.

AMBLOSTOMA Scheidw. *Orchidaceae.* Four spp. of epiphytes, native to Cent. and trop. S. Amer.; st. fusiform, with few lvs. at apex; infl. a terminal, many-fld. raceme or panicle; fls. small, yellow or purple, sepals and petals spreading, lip 3-lobed, united to column, pollinia 4, globose. For structure of fl. see *Orchidaceae.*

For culture see *Orchids.*

tridactylum (Lindl.) Rchb.f. To 20 in. lvs. narrow, grasslike; panicle longer than lvs.; fls. ³/₁₆ in. across, yellow, sepals and petals fleshy, concave, lip 3-lobed, with 2 tubercles at base. Brazil.

AMBLYGONOCARPUS Harms. *Leguminosae* (subfamily *Mimosoideae*). One sp., an unarmed tree of trop. Afr.; lvs. alt., 2-pinnate; fls. small, in spikelike racemes, 5-merous, petals valvate, stamens 10, separate; fr. a woody, oblong-cylindrical or obtusely 4-angled legume, incompletely partitioned between seeds.

andongensis (Welw. ex D. Oliver) Exell & Torre [*A. obtusangulus* (Welw. ex D. Oliver) Harms]. To 75 ft.; lvs. to 10 in. long, lfts. ellipticoblong, to ⅞ in. long, emarginate at apex; racemes 4 in. long; fr. club-shaped, 4 in. long.

obtusangulus: *A. andongensis.*

AMBROSIA L. RAGWEED. *Compositae* (Helianthus Tribe). Weeds, mostly of N. and S. Amer., infamous as a common cause (through their pollen) of hay fever in human beings. Not ordinarily cult.

mexicana: *Chenopodium Botrys.*

AMBULIA: *LIMNOPHILA.*

AMELANCHIER Medic. SERVICEBERRY, SARVICEBERRY, JUNEBERRY, SHADBUSH, SHAD, SUGARPLUM. *Rosaceae.* About 25 spp. of shrubs and small trees of the N. Temp. Zone; lvs. alt., toothed; fls. white, mostly in terminal racemes, appearing in advance of the lvs. or with them, calyx tube bell-shaped, sepals 5, persistent, petals 5, often narrow; fr. a small dark purple or black pome, often edible.

Desirable because of the showy bloom in early spring; some are plants of good habit and have attractive, edible fruit. Amelanchiers are hardy in the North. Propagated by seeds sown when ripe or stratified, by suckers when produced, or rare kinds by budding. See *Juneberry.*

alnifolia Nutt. Stoloniferous shrub forming colonies, 3–20 ft.; lf. blades more or less truncate at tip, 1–2 in. wide, coarsely serrate-dentate with 5–12 broad teeth per in., prominently veined; fls. few, sepals ⅛ in. long, petals to ⅜ in. long, summit of ovary tomentose; fr. ⅜ in. thick. Var. **alnifolia.** The typical var.; petals usually less than ½ in. long; top of ovary usually strongly pubescent, styles usually 5. W. Ont. to Yukon, s. to Nebr., Colo., Idaho, Ore. Zone 6. Var. **Cusickii** (Fern.) C. L. Hitchc. [*A. Cusickii* Fern.]. Petals ⅝ in. long or more; top of ovary glabrous to hairy. E. Wash., ne. Ore., w. Idaho.

amabilis Wieg. Like *A. sanguinea,* sts. solitary or few; lvs. somewhat glaucous, with about 8 teeth per in.; petals ½–1 in. long. Sw. Que. and s. Ont. to N.Y.

arborea (Michx.f.) Fern. Close to *A. canadensis,* but more vigorous, 30–50 ft., more pubescent, with larger fls., racemes more pendulous. New Bruns. to Ont. and Minn., s. to Fla., La., Okla.

asiatica (Siebold & Zucc.) Endl. To 40 ft.; lvs. obovate, white-tomentose beneath when young, 1¾–2½ in. long, finely toothed; racemes 1–2 in. long, woolly; fls. nodding in age, 1¼ in. across, petals narrow-ovate. Temp. e. Asia. Zone 6.

Batchewana: a listed name of no botanical standing.

canadensis (L.) Medic. [*A. oblongifolia* M. J. Roem.]. Fastigiate shrub, to 25 ft.; lvs. scarcely half-grown at flowering time, then white-felty beneath, later oblong, 1–2 in. long, glabrate, finely serrate;

racemes 1–2 in., tomentose; sepals tomentose within, petals to ⅜ in. long, apex of ovary glabrous. Swamps, Que. to Ga. Zone 4. Fr. edible. Confused with *A. arborea*, which has larger fls.

Cusickii: *A. alnifolia* var.

florida Lindl. Like *A. alnifolia*, but lvs. obtuse, not truncate, becoming glabrous beneath; fls. larger, petals ½–1 in. long. S. Alaska to Idaho and n. Calif. Zone 2.

×**grandiflora** Rehd.: *A. arborea* × *A. laevis*. To 30 ft.; lvs. broad-elliptic, cordate; racemes pendent, pubescent; petals ⅝ in. long. Cv. 'Rubescens'. Fl. buds purple-red, petals pink.

humilis: *A. spicata.*

laevis Wieg. Fastigiate shrub or tree to 40 ft., resembling *A. canadensis*, but racemes flexuous or nodding, not ascending; lvs. essentially glabrous, acuminate; petals ⅜–¾ in. long. Nfld. to Ont., s. to Ga., Ohio, and Iowa. Zone 5. Cv. 'Rosea' is listed.

oblongifolia: *A. canadensis.*

ovalis Medic. [*A. rotundifolia* Dum.-Cours.; *A. vulgaris* Moench]. Shrubs to 8 ft., many-stemmed; lvs. ovate, rounded at ends, sharply toothed, woolly when young, later glabrous, 1–2 in. long; fls. 3–8, in erect racemes, styles separate, very short. Eur. Zone 5.

rotundifolia: *A. ovalis.*

sanguinea (Pursh) DC. Arched-ascending to straggling shrub, 3–10 ft., tending to form colonies, twigs reddish; lvs. elliptic-oblong to roundish, green, 1–2½ in. long, with 10–15 sharp teeth per in., primary veins mostly 12–15 pairs; sepals to ⅛ in. long, recurving from the middle, petals narrow-spatulate to linear, to ½ in. long, ovary tomentose above; fr. to ¼ in. in diam. Que. to Ont., s. to N.C., Iowa. Zone 5.

spicata (Lam.) C. Koch [*A. humilis* Wieg.]. Stoloniferous, sts. to 5 ft.; lvs. tomentose beneath at flowering time, 1–2 in. long, mostly oblong to obovate, entire to coarsely serrate-dentate to below middle, with 10–12 teeth per in.; racemes silky-tomentose, 1–2 in. long; petals oblong-obovate, to ⅜ in. long. Que. to Ont., s. to Penn., Ohio, S. Dak. Zone 5. Treated by some auths. as a hybrid of *A. canadensis* and *A. ovalis.*

stolonifera Wieg. Habit like *A. humilis;* lvs. with 15–20 teeth per in., dull green above, elliptic to round, 1–2 in. long; racemes ⅝–1⅝ in. long, pubescent; petals oblong, ⁵⁄₁₆ in. long, ovary tomentose at apex. Nfld. to Ont., s. to Va., Mich., Minn. Zone 5.

vulgaris: *A. ovalis.*

AMELLUS L. *Compositae* (Aster Tribe). About 15 spp. of ann. herbs or subshrubs, native to S. Afr.; lower lvs. opp., upper lvs. alt.; fl. heads radiate, solitary, peduncled, involucre ovoid, campanulate, or nearly hemispherical, involucral bracts imbricate in many rows, receptacle convex to subconical, scaly; disc fls. bisexual, fertile, ray fls. female, fertile; disc achenes wedge-shaped, compressed, pappus of inner disc achenes of 4–5 scabrous, deciduous bristles, pappus of outer disc achenes similar to that of ray achenes, ray achenes 4-angled, with pappus of few, short, unequal scales.

asteroides (L.) Druce [*A. lychnitis* L.]. Much-branched subshrub, to 1½ ft., with short, appressed hairs; lvs. linear or oblanceolate to obovate, to 1½ in. long, entire; heads to ½ in. across; ray fls. blue, sometimes white. S. Afr.

lychnitis: *A. asteroides.*

AMESIA: *EPIPACTIS.*

AMETHYSTEA L. *Labiatae.* One sp., an erect, nearly glabrous ann. herb of temp. Asia; sts. mostly square in cross section; lvs. opp., 3–5-parted, incised; fls. small, in verticillasters arranged in narrow terminal panicles, blue, pedicelled, calyx campanulate, 10-nerved, 5-toothed, corolla tube shorter than calyx, limb nearly regular, 4-lobed, stamens 2, anthers 2-celled; fr. of 4 obovoid nutlets.

caerulea L. To 3 ft., glabrous, sts. erect, branched; lower lvs. ovate to narrowly ovate, 1–2 in. long and wide, mostly 3-parted to sometimes 5-parted, cuneate, middle lobe lanceolate, incised, with obtuse apex, lateral lobes smaller, petioles to ¾ in. long, upper lvs. smaller, less lobed; calyx to ⅛ in. long, 5-lobed, lobes linear-lanceolate, corolla blue, slightly longer than the calyx; nutlets ¹⁄₁₆ in. long, rounded at apex, net-veined. Turkey to Japan.

AMHERSTIA Wallich. *Leguminosae* (subfamily *Caesalpinioideae*). One sp., an unarmed tree of Burma; lvs. alt., simple, pinnate; fls. racemose, calyx long-tubular, sepals 4, petals 3, stamens 10, 9 united and 1 separate, with 5 longer than the others; fr. a large, flat, semiwoody legume.

Grown sometimes in warm greenhouses and in protected sites in moist lowland tropics for its showy flowers. Requires rich, well-drained soil and high temperatures and humidity. Propagated by layering or by half-ripe cuttings with bottom heat. Seeds, when produced, are few and often infertile.

nobilis Wallich. To 40 ft., usually much smaller in cult.; lvs. to 3 ft. long, lfts. oblong, 6–12 in. long, green, but red or purplish and flaccid when young; racemes long, pendent, pedicels red, 2–4 in. long, buds enclosed by 2 persistent, red, petal-like bracts; petals bright red and yellow, the uppermost 2 in. across, staminal tube prominent; fr. to 7 in. long, wider toward apex.

AMIANTHIUM A. Gray [*Chrosperma* Raf.]. *Liliaceae.* One sp., a per., bulbous herb, native to e. N. Amer.; bulb tunicate; lvs. linear, mostly basal; fls. white, in terminal racemes; perianth segms. separate, spreading, without basal glands, stamens 6; fr. a caps.

Propagated by division or rarely by seeds.

muscitoxicum (Walt.) A. Gray [*Chrosperma muscitoxicum* (Walt.) O. Kuntze; *Zigadenus muscitoxicum* (Walt.) Regel]. FLY-POISON. To 4 ft.; lvs. to 2 ft. long and 1 in. wide; racemes to 5 in. long, peduncle with reduced lvs.; fr. abruptly 3-horned. Early summer. N.Y., s. to Fla., w. to s. Mo and Okla. Bulb very poisonous if eaten.

AMMI L. *Umbelliferae.* About 6 spp. of per., glabrous herbs of Medit. region, Chile, and Brazil; lvs. pinnate or ternately pinnate; fls. small, white, in compound, bracted umbels; fr. ovoid-oblong, only slightly compressed, with primary ridges prominent and blunt.

majus L. BISHOP'S WEED. To 2½ ft.; lvs. with sharply serrate margins; umbels to 6 in. across or more, spreading in fl. and fr., not borne on a disc, bracts of involucre to 1 in. long, trifid, those of involucels linear and acute; petals shorter than stamens, with lobes often unequal; fr. about ³⁄₃₂ in. long. Ne. Afr., Eurasia; naturalized in N. Amer. Widely cult. for cut-flower trade.

Visnaga (L.) Lam. BISNAGA. To 2½ ft.; lvs. finely divided into linear or threadlike segms.; umbels spreading in fl., contracted in fr., rays borne on a disc, 60–100, to 4 in. long, as long as the divided involucral bracts; fr. to ³⁄₃₂ in. long. S. Eur.; naturalized in N. Amer. Cult. for its potential as a drug.

AMMOBIUM R. Br. *Compositae* (Inula Tribe). Two or 3 spp. of herbs of Australia; lvs. alt.; fl. heads discoid, solitary, terminal on the brs., involucral bracts many, scarious, white, receptacle with chaffy scales between the fls.; fls. all tubular, yellow; achenes 4-angled, pappus of 2–4 teeth.

Of easy cultivation, sometimes treated as a biennial and the seeds sown in Sept., but usually grown as an annual, with seeds sown in spring. The flower heads remain white and are useful for dried arrangements if cut before full bloom and hung in a shady, airy place to dry.

alatum R. Br. WINGED EVERLASTING. Per., but grown as an ann., 2–3 ft., white-tomentose, sts. and brs. winged; basal lvs. ovate, long-tapering to the base, to 11 in. long, st. lvs. lanceolate, smaller, heads 1 in. across. Cv. 'Grandiflora'. Heads larger.

AMMOCALLIS: *CATHARANTHUS.*

AMMOCHARIS Herb. *Amaryllidaceae.* Five spp. of S. Afr. herbs, with tunicate bulbs; lvs. arranged in opp. fans, strap-shaped; umbel terminal on a lateral, compressed, erect scape, 1- to many-fld., subtended by 2 persistent bracts (spathe valves); fls. pedicelled, regular, not borne at an angle, white to red, perianth tube narrow-cylindrical, lobes clawed, often recurved, stamens 6, erect or divergent, exserted from the tube, ovary inferior, each cell with 4–30 ovules; fr. indehiscent, subglobose, seeds subglobose.

coranica (Ker-Gawl.) Herb. Bulb ovoid, to 6 in. in diam., 10 in. long; scape to 1 ft.; lvs. ¼–3 in. wide, to 3 ft. long or more, green or sometimes glaucous, margins papery and minutely erose; umbel 3–6-fld., pedicels to 2⅜ in. long; fls. pink to carmine, sometimes with white nerves, shiny, fragrant, perianth tube variable, ⅜–1 in. long, lobes to 4 in. long, spirally recurved toward apex. Sometimes confused with *Cybistetes longifolia*, but differs in having fls. regular. May be planted outdoors, and the bulbs stored in winter, or grown in pots in the greenhouse. Blooms in summer or autumn, or in winter under glass. Requires rich loamy soil.

falcata: *Cybistetes longifolia.*

heterostyla (Bullock) Milne-Redh. & Schweick. Bulb ovoid, to 3¾ in. in diam., 4½ in. long; lvs. 5–8, strap-shaped, to 14 in. long, 1 in. wide, glaucous; umbel 3–10-fld., scape to 5 in., compressed, pedicels to ⅞ in. long; fls. white with pink tube and pink line on lobes, tube variable, 1⅜–3 in. long, lobes to 1⅝ in. long, curved but not spiralled at apex. This has been offered under the name *Crinum parvum,* which is not cult. in N. Amer.

AMMOPHILA Host. BEACH GRASS, SAND REED, PSAMMA, MARRAM. *Gramineae.* Four spp. of tough, rather coarse, erect, per. grasses in Eur. and e. N. Amer.; creeping rhizomes hard, scaly; lf. blades long, tough, involute; infl. pale, dense, spikelike; spikelets 1-fld., compressed, rachilla disarticulating above the glumes and extended as a short bristle, glumes about equal, lemma similar but a little shorter, palea nearly as long. For terminology see *Gramineae.*

arenaria (L.) Link. EUROPEAN B.G. Distinguished from *A. breviligulata* in having sometimes thicker sts., thin ligule to 1¼ in. long, often thicker panicle, tapering to the apex, and slightly longer spikelets. Eur.; introd. as a sand binder and naturalized from Wash. to n. Calif.

breviligulata Fern. AMERICAN B.G. Sts. clustered, to 3½ ft., covered at base with many broad, overlapping sheaths, rhizome deep, extensively creeping; lf. blades elongate, soon involute, ligule firm, to ⅛ in. long; infl. nearly cylindrical, to 1 ft. long; spikelets pale, to ⅝ in. long, glumes scaberulous, lemma scabrous. Coastal, Nfld. to N.C.; on shores from Lake Ontario to Lake Superior and Lake Michigan.

AMOMUM Roxb. *Zingiberaceae.* Over 100 spp. of Asiatic per. herbs with creeping aromatic rhizomes; sts. leafy; infl. a dense, conelike spike borne on a separate st. arising from the rhizome beneath the foliage; fls. subtended by bracts, calyx tubular, usually 3-lobed, corolla with tube as long as calyx or longer, and 3 lobes as long as tube, upper lobe broadest, staminodial lip longer than corolla lobes, usually yellow or orange, lateral staminodes not petal-like, fertile stamen 1, shorter than lip, with usually 3-lobed anther crest; fr. berry-like or a caps., and dehiscent or indehiscent.

Grown as foliage plants in warm regions; sometimes seen in economic collections under glass, as some of the species yield spicy aromatic seeds used as substitutes for true cardamoms (see *Elettaria*). They require rich soil and abundant moisture. Propagated by division in spring.

Cardamomum: *Elettaria Cardamomum;* but see also *A. compactum.*

compactum Soland. ex Maton [*A. Cardamomum* of auth., not L.; *A. Kepulaga* T. Sprague & Burkill]. ROUND CARDAMOM. Leafy sts. to 3 ft.; lvs. sessile, linear-lanceolate, to 10 in. long, 3 in. wide; infl. short; corolla white or yellowish, lip to ¾ in. long, yellow with dark purple median band, or yellow-white with purple-margined median band; fr. with about 9 furrows, seeds with white aril. Java.

Kepulaga: *A. compactum.*

AMOMYRTUS (Burret) D. Legrand & Kausel. *Myrtaceae.* Two spp. of evergreen shrubs or trees, native to Chile; lvs. opp.; infl. a few-fld. raceme; calyx lobes and petals 5, stamens many, ovary 2-celled, each cell with 4–8 ovules. Has been placed in the genus *Myrtus* considered in the broad sense, but differs in having central and apical placentation and fewer ovules in cells of ovary.

Luma (Mol.) D. Legrand & Kausel [*Myrtus Lechlerana* (Miq.) Sealy; *M. Luma* Mol.]. Shrub or small tree, to 30 ft., young shoots grayish-hairy; lvs. ovate to broadly oval, to 1¼ in. long, bronze-green when young, dark green later; fls. white, 4–10 together in the upper lf. axils, petals nearly orbicular, ⅛ in. long; berry globose, to ¼ in. across, reddish at first, finally black. May be confused with *Luma apiculata,* but differs in having fls. smaller, 5-merous.

AMOORA Roxb. *A. Rohituka: Aphanamixis polystachya.*

AMOREUXIA Moç. & Sessé. *Cochlospermaceae.* Four spp. of herbs, native to sw. U.S. and Mex.; sts. short, from large tuberous roots; lvs. palmately lobed or parted; fls. few, in a terminal raceme, large, somewhat irregular, stamens many, in 2 series, one long and one short; fr. a large, thick caps.

Wrightii A. Gray. Lvs. 5-parted, segms. obovate, cuneate at the base; fls. yellow; fr. pendulous, oblong-ovoid, to 2 in. long, seeds obovoid, straight, smooth. S. and w. Tex.

AMORPHA L. FALSE INDIGO. *Leguminosae* (subfamily *Faboideae).* About 20 spp. of shrubs, native to N. Amer.; lvs. alt., odd-pinnate, deciduous, with many lfts.; fls. in dense, terminal, often panicled spikes, small, blue or white, sepals 5, petal 1, the standard enclosing the 10 exserted stamens; fr. a short, mostly glabrous, indehiscent legume.

Grown as ornamentals outdoors. Propagated by seeds, greenwood cuttings under glass, hardwood cuttings planted in sheltered location in autumn and left a year, suckers or layers. The cultivated species are mostly hardy in Zone 5.

angustifolia: *A. fruticosa* var.

brachycarpa Palmer. Erect, to 3 ft.; lfts. in 10–22 pairs, overlapping, oblong, to ⅝ in. long and ⁵⁄₁₆ in. wide; infl. paniculate, to 10 in. long; fr. to ³⁄₁₆ in. long. Mo.

californica Nutt. Differs from *A. fruticosa* in having branchlets and rachis of lvs. with pricklelike glands, calyx lobes longer, lanceolate, glandular-hairy, and fr. pubescent. Calif.

canescens Pursh. LEAD PLANT. To 4 ft., usually densely white-hairy; lfts. to ¾ in. long; spikes to 6 in. long; fr. densely villous-gray-pubescent. Summer. Man. to La. and New Mex.

croceolanata P. Wats. [*A. fruticosa* var. *croceolanata* (P. Wats.) Mouill.]. Allied to *A. fruticosa,* but differs in having twigs, lvs., and calyces densely tawny-pubescent. Mo. and Ky., s. to La. and Fla.

fragrans: *A. fruticosa* var. *angustifolia.* Var. **nana:** a listed name of no botanical standing, possibly drawn from *A. nana* Sims, not Nutt., a synonym of *A. fruticosa* var. *angustifolia.*

fruticosa L. BASTARD INDIGO, FALSE I., INDIGO BUSH. To 20 ft., branchlets and rachis of lvs. glabrous or somewhat pubescent, without glandular prickles; lfts. ovate or oblong, to 1½ in. long, obtuse at base, obtuse or slightly mucronate at apex, glandular; fls. in clustered spikes to 6 in. long, dark purple, varying to pale blue and white, calyx lobes short, obtuse; fr. glabrous, to ⁵⁄₁₆ in. long. Late spring. Sask., s. to Fla. and Mex. Forma **crispa** (Kirchn.) C. K. Schneid. [var. *crispa* Kirchn.]. Lfts. with crisped margins. Var. **angustifolia** Pursh [*A. angustifolia* (Pursh) Boynt.; *A. fragrans* Sweet; *A. nana* Sims, not Nutt.]. Lfts. usually elliptic or obovate, narrowed at base; fls. purple-blue. Ill., s. to Tex. and Mex. Var. **crispa:** forma *crispa.* Var. **croceolanata:** *A. croceolanata.* Var. **emarginata** Pursh. Lfts. usually larger, ovate, blunt or emarginate at apex. Var. **oblongifolia** Palmer. Lfts. many, crowded, narrowly oblong; fr. slightly larger. Var. **occidentalis** (Abrams) Kearn. & Peebles [*A. occidentalis* Abrams]. Spikes slender, usually single, to 10 in. long. Wyo. and w. Tex., w. to Calif. and Mex. Var. **tennessensis** (Shuttl.) Palmer [*A. tennessensis* Shuttl.]. Lfts. to ¾ in. long, noticeably pubescent when young; fls. violet-purple. N.C. to Fla., w. to Kans. and Tex.

glabra Desf. ex Poir. [*A. montana* Boynt.]. To 6 ft.; lfts. to 2 in. long; fls. blue, in racemes to 6 in. long, calyx lobes very short or nearly obsolete. Spring. N.C., s. to Ga. and Ala.

microphylla: *A. nana.*

montana: *A. glabra.*

nana Nutt. [*A. microphylla* Pursh]. FRAGRANT F.I. To 1 ft.; lfts. to ½ in. long; fls. purplish, in racemes to 6 in. long. Spring. Minn. to Rocky Mts. See also *A. fruticosa* var. *angustifolia.*

nitens Boynt. To 9 ft.; lfts. to 2½ in. long, glossy above; fls. in racemes to 10 in. long. Summer. Ga., Ala., Ill., Ark.

occidentalis: *A. fruticosa* var.

tennessensis: *A. fruticosa* var.

virgata Small. Similar to *A. fruticosa,* but shorter, more sparingly branched, and lfts. leathery, more broadly oblong, with glandular petiolules and reflexed margins. S. U.S.

AMORPHOPHALLUS Blume ex Decne. DEVIL'S-TONGUE, SNAKE PALM. *Araceae.* About 90 spp. of acaulescent, cormose, per. herbs, native to Old World tropics; lvs. produced after infl., large, solitary, umbrellalike, 3-parted, each division usually 2-pinnatifid, petioles stout, trunklike; spathe funnelform or hooded; fls. unisexual, perianth absent, spadix with zone of female fls. at base contiguous with zone of male fls., terminated by a prominent sterile appendage, this sometimes contorted and frequently emitting a disagreeable odor.

Often grown as a curiosity in greenhouses, or planted outdoors in mild climates. Plants thrive in rich loamy soil, in partial shade, and are most easily handled in pots or tubs. They should be dried off by withholding water gradually in Oct. until leaf withers, then stored at temperatures above 50° F. in winter. They can be brought into active growth again in late Mar. If corms are strong enough, a blossom will soon be produced. The leaf follows soon afterwards. Propagated by offsets and seeds.

bulbifer (Roxb.) Blume. To 3 ft.; petiole spotted brownish, rosy, or whitish, lf. blade to 2 ft. or more wide, bearing bulbils at major divisions; peduncle 10 in. long, colored like petiole, spathe widely expanded and hooded above, to 8 in. long, with greenish lines and spotted pink outside, rose in the throat and becoming flesh-colored upward inside, spadix shorter, the sterile appendage pinkish, 3 in. long, 1 in. thick. Ne. India.

campanulatus (Roxb.) Blume ex Decne. TELINGO POTATO. Lvs. 1 or 2, petiole to 30 in. long, smooth or prickly, spotted gray-green, lf. blade 3 ft. wide; peduncle to 4 in. long, spathe subcampanulate-funnelform, to 8 in. long and 10 in. across, widely expanded into ovate, undulate blade above, greenish and spotted white outside, reddish-purple in the throat and becoming whitish above inside, spadix to 12 in. long, dilated above, the sterile apex expanded, globose-conic, spongy, deep purple. Ne. India to Vietnam, Philippine Is., and New Guinea. Corms used for food.

Konjac: *A. Rivieri* cv.

Rivieri Durieu [*Hydrosme Rivieri* (Durieu) Engl.]. DEVIL'S-TONGUE, LEOPARD PALM, SNAKE P., UMBRELLA ARUM. To 4 ft., tuber to 10 in. in diam.; petiole brownish-green with dark purple spots, lf. blade to 4 ft. wide; infl. to 3 ft. high, spathe funnelform, to 16 in. long, the expanded ovate limb blackish-red and undulate, spadix much longer than spathe, the sterile appendage tapering, to 21 in. long. Se. Asia. Cv. 'Konjac' [var. *Konjac* (C. Koch) Engl.; *A. Konjac* C. Koch]. KONJAC. The commonly cult. form, with limb of spathe longer, oblong, and sterile appendage longer. Much grown from Indonesia to Japan for the edible corms. Zone 7.

Titanum Becc. TITAN ARUM. Similar to *A. Rivieri*, but much larger, corm about 18 in. in diam.; petiole 10–15 ft., lf. blade to 15 ft. wide; peduncle to 3 ft., spathe to 4 ft. across, spadix 6 ft. high. Sumatra. Not in general cult., but occasionally grown under glass at botanical gardens. Produces one of the largest infl. among herbaceous plants.

AMPELAMUS: *CYNANCHUM.* **A. albidus:** *C. laeve.*

AMPELODESMA: *AMPELODESMOS.*

AMPELODESMOS Link [*Ampelodesma* Beauvois ex Benth.]. VINE REED. *Gramineae.* One sp., a per. grass in the Medit. region; lf. blades curved at base, bent forward across the st., with upper surface downward; panicle large; spikelets flat, 2–5-fld., glumes somewhat unequal, keeled on the back, pointed, lemma and palea leathery, margins short-ciliate, palea nearly as long as the lemma, but narrower. For terminology see *Gramineae.*

mauritanicus (Poir.) T. Durand & Schinz. MAURITANIA V.R. Sts. to 10 ft., robust, solid, in large clumps; lf. blades elongate, wiry; panicle to 20 in. long, brs. slender, flexuous, very scabrous, naked at base, drooping; spikelets 2–5-fld., to ⅝ in. long, crowded toward ends of brs., lower part of lemma and rachilla joints densely white-hairy. Occasionally cult. as an ornamental and naturalized in Calif.

AMPELOPSIS L. Rich. *Vitaceae.* Perhaps 20 spp. of deciduous, woody vines or rarely shrubs, native to N. Amer. and Asia, bark not shredding, tendrils forked, without discoid tips; lvs. alt., simple or compound; infl. cymose, long-peduncled; fls. small, 5- or rarely 4-merous, greenish, petals falling separately, disc prominent, joined to the 2-celled, slender-styled ovary; fr. a small 1–4-seeded berry.

Ampelopsis is grown as a covering for walls and arbors, and is not particular as to soil. Propagated by seeds, also by cuttings and layers. Cuttings of hard wood may be taken in Sept. and propagated under glass or stored until spring like grape cuttings; those of soft wood can be struck in the summer.

aconitifolia Bunge. Brs. slender, glabrous, tendril-climbing; lvs. long-petioled, palmately 3–5-parted or compound, lfts. to 3 in. long, mostly toothed or strongly cut; fr. about ¼ in. in diam., orange or yellow, sometimes bluish. N. China. Zone 5. May be offered as *Vitis vinifera* cv. 'Ciotat'. Var. **glabra** Diels. Lvs. usually only 3-parted or trifoliolate.

arborea Koehne. PEPPER VINE. Bushy, more or less climbing, tendrils often small or absent; lvs. 2-pinnate, finely divided, lfts. mostly ovate, to 1½ in. long, deeply notched, hairy beneath; fls. 4–5-merous, in loose cymes; fr. to nearly ⅜ in. in diam., dark purple. Va. to Fla., Tex., and Mex. Zone 7.

brevipedunculata (Maxim.) Trautv. [*A. heterophylla* var. *amurensis* Planch.]. Tendril-climbing, young sts. and petioles pubescent; lvs. simple, thin, broadly ovate-cordate, to 5 in. long, with 3 coarsely toothed lobes, pilose beneath; cymes short, exceeded by the lvs.; fr. about ¼ in. in diam., lilac, becoming bright blue. Ne. Asia. Zone 5b. Var. **Maximowiczii** (Regel) Rehd. [*A. heterophylla* (Thunb.) Siebold & Zucc., not Blume; *Vitis heterophylla* Thunb.]. Brs. and lvs. glabrescent; lvs. deeply 3–5-lobed. E. China. Cv. 'Citrulloides'. Lvs. deeply 5-lobed, pilose beneath. Cv. 'Elegans'. Lvs. variegated with white, green, or pink.

Engelmannii: *Parthenocissus quinquefolia* cv.

heterophylla: *A. brevipedunculata* var. *Maximowiczii.*

humulifolia Bunge. Tendril-climbing, brs. mostly glabrous; lvs. sim-

ple, broadly ovate, to 5 in. long, 3–5-lobed, coarsely toothed, glossy above, whitish beneath; fr. pale yellow to bluish. N. China. Zone 6.

japonica (Thunb.) Mak. Root tuberous, brs. tendril-climbing, glabrous; lvs. compound, lfts. 3–5, pinnate or pinnately lobed, to 4 in. long, glossy above, rachis broadly winged; fr. about ¼ in. in diam., blue. Japan, China. Zone 6. Some of the material offered under this name may be *Parthenocissus tricuspidata.*

Lowii: *Parthenocissus tricuspidata* cv.

megalophylla Diels & Gilg. Robust, tendril-climbing, brs. glabrous, more or less glaucous; lvs. pinnate or 2-pinnate, 6–16 in. long, lfts. ovate to oblong-ovate, 2–5 in. long, serrate; cymes loose, slender; fr. ¼ in. in diam., black. W. China. Zone 7.

quinquefolia: *Parthenocissus quinquefolia.*

Saint-Paulii: *Parthenocissus quinquefolia* cv.

sempervirens: *Cissus striata.*

tricuspidata: *Parthenocissus tricuspidata.*

Veitchii: *Parthenocissus tricuspidata* cv.

AMPELOTHAMNUS: *PIERIS.*

AMPHIBLEMMA Naud. *Melastomataceae.* Fifteen spp. of herbs or small shrubs in W. Trop. Afr.; lvs. long-petioled, membranous, serrulate, 5–7-nerved; fls. showy, stamens 10, dimorphic, ovary inferior, 5-celled; fr. a caps.

Of easy culture under glass. Does well in partial shade, in loamy soil high in humus, kept moist, at a night temperature of about 60° F.

cymosum (Schrad. & J. C. Wendl.) Naud. Sparsely hairy subshrub, to 4 ft.; lvs. ovate-cordate, 3–7 in. long, acuminate, denticulate, 7–9-nerved, the veins depressed above; fls. in small, spreading, panicled, 1-sided cymes, to 1 in. across, rose to carmine-purple. W. Afr.

AMPHICARPAEA Elliott. HOG PEANUT. *Leguminosae* (subfamily *Faboideae*). Three spp. of twining, beanlike herbaceous vines, native to N. Amer., Afr. and Asia; lvs. alt., of 3 lfts.; fls. small, axillary, of 2 kinds, papilionaceous or apetalous; fr. of upper fls. a flat, linear-oblong, 3–4-seeded legume, fr. of lower fls. often underground, fleshy, 1-seeded.

bracteata (L.) Fern. Climbing, to 8 ft.; lfts. ovate, to 3 in. long; upper fls. racemose, papilionaceous, purplish or white, ½ in. long, the fr. to 1 in. long, mostly 3-seeded, lower fls. apetalous, the fr. strigose, 1-seeded, often underground. N. Amer.

AMPHICOME: *INCARVILLEA.*

AMPHICOSMIA: *ALSOPHILA.*

AMSONIA Walt. BLUESTAR. *Apocynaceae.* About 20 spp. of per. herbs with milky sap, native to N. Amer. and e. Asia; lvs. alt. or more or less whorled, entire; fls. in terminal thyrsoid or corymbose cymes, regular, 5-merous, bisexual, corolla salverform, villous inside, lobes ovate to lanceolate, spreading to nearly erect, stamens borne above middle of corolla tube, included, anthers obtuse at base, without appendages; fr. a pair of cylindrical follicles.

Amsonias are grown as ornamentals in shady locations in the hardy border. Propagated by division, seeds, or cuttings.

Amsonia: *A. Tabernaemontana.*

illustris Woodson. Differs from *A. Tabernaemontana* in having lvs. shining, strikingly leathery; calyx hirsute; and follicles spreading to pendulous, slightly constricted at intervals. Early spring. Mo., se. Kans., e. Okla., ne. Tex.

montana: a listed name of no botanical standing, probably for *A. Tabernaemontana*, but described as differing in its shorter, dense growth.

orientalis: *Rhazya orientalis.*

rigida Shuttl. To 5 ft.; lvs. many, alt., elliptic, to 2⅜ in. long, green above, glaucous or glaucescent beneath, distinctly petioled; cymes loose; corolla purplish-blue, tube ⅜ in. long, gradually dilated upward, glabrous outside, lobes scarcely longer than tube, wide-spreading; follicles to 4⅜ in. long, slender, attenuate. Spring. N. Fla. and s. Ga.

salicifolia: *A. Tabernaemontana* var.

Tabernaemontana Walt. [*A. Amsonia* (L.) Britt.]. To 3½ ft., usually forming clumps; lvs. alt., dull, thin, ovate to oblong-elliptic or lanceolate, lower ones obtuse to acuminate at base; cymes scarcely longer than lvs.; calyx glabrous, corolla light blue, tube to ⅜ in. long, pubescent outside, lobes spreading; follicles erect, rather abruptly acuminate, glabrous. Spring, early summer. Se. U.S.; escaped from Mass. to Del. Var. **salicifolia** (Pursh) Woodson [*A. salicifolia* Pursh]. Lvs. lanceolate to linear-lanceolate, 5–10 times longer than broad, acute to acuminate at both ends, glabrous; cymes loose, few-fld. Early summer. Va. to Mo., s. to Ga., and Tex.

ANACAMPSEROS L. *Portulacaceae.* Over 50 spp. of succulent herbs, native mostly to S. Afr., 1 to Australia; lvs. alt., fleshy; fls. solitary, or in more or less scorpioid terminal racemes, opening only in the sun, sometimes on long peduncles, sepals 2, petals 5, often showy, but falling early.

Several species occasionally grown in the greenhouse and in collections of succulents. Propagated by seeds or by stem and leaf cuttings.

albissima Marloth. Sts. white, branched, prostrate; lvs. minute, fleshy, covered by white, membranous stipules; fls. cream-colored, solitary, sessile, enclosed within apical stipules. S. and S.-W. Afr.

arachnoides (Haw.) Sims. Sts. branched, brs. densely leafy, to 2 in. long; lvs. ovate, $\frac{1}{4}$ in. long, cobwebbed, green and shining; fls. white, in 2–3-fld. racemes on scapes to 4 in. long. Var. **grandiflora:** *A. rufescens.*

Buderana Poelln. Sts. branched, branchlets to $\frac{1}{2}$ in. long; lvs. minute, covered by appressed, silvery-white stipules. S. Afr.

filamentosa (Haw.) Sims. Distinguished from *A. arachnoides* in having axillary hairs longer than the webby-pubescent lvs., and fls. larger, rose.

fissa Poelln. Sts. many, simple, erect, arising from a rootstock; lvs. spirally arranged, about half-covered by silvery stipules. S. Afr.

lanceolata (Haw.) Sweet. Sts. to 3 in. long; lvs. many, narrow-lanceolate to lanceolate, to 1 in. long, glabrous, with very long hairs in the axils; fls. 1–4, reddish. S. Afr.

rosulata: a listed name of no botanical standing.

rufescens (Haw.) Sweet [*A. arachnoides* var. *grandiflora* Sond.]. Sts. to 3 in. long, erect or creeping, forming mats; lvs. forming a basal rosette, obovate-lanceolate, $\frac{3}{4}$ in. long, thick, reddish-purple; fls. 2–4, pink. S. Afr.

telephiastrum DC. COPPER-LEAVES, LOVE PLANT, SAND ROSE. Forming mats when old; lvs. in a basal rosette, ovate, to $\frac{3}{4}$ in. long, thickish, glabrous; fls. reddish, in 2–4-fld. racemes on scapes to 6 in. long. S. Afr.

tomentosa A. Berger. Sts. often several, from a thick root, to 2 in.; lvs. elliptic, to $\frac{1}{2}$ in. long, thick, lower surface white-tomentose; fls. usually 3, pink, in infl. to $2\frac{1}{2}$ in. long. S.-W. Afr.

ustulata E. H. Mey. ex Sond. Sts. to $1\frac{1}{4}$ in., branchlets many, spirally leafy; lvs. small, reniform, covered by brownish-gray stipules; fls. solitary, sessile, terminal. S. Afr.

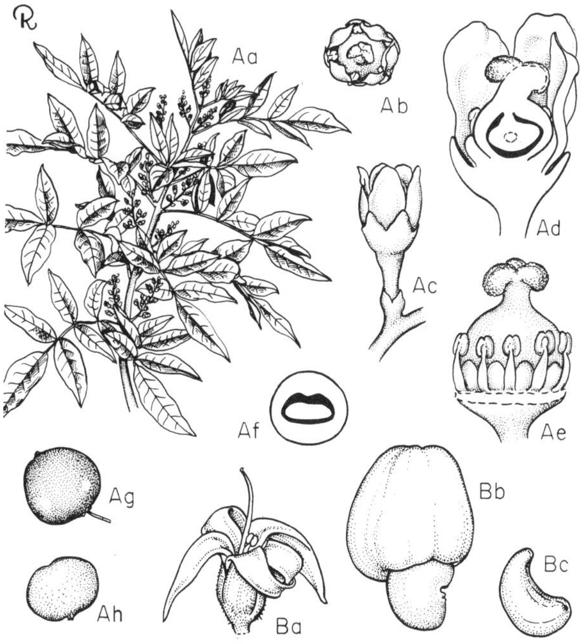

ANACARDIACEAE. **A,** *Schinus terebinthifolius:* **Aa,** flowering branch, $\times \frac{3}{8}$; **Ab,** flower, face view, $\times$ 6; **Ac,** flower, side view, $\times$ 6; **Ad,** flower, vertical section, $\times$ 12; **Ae,** stamens and pistil, $\times$ 12; **Af,** ovary, cross section, $\times$ 12; **Ag,** fruit, $\times$ 2; **Ah,** seed, $\times$ 2. **B,** *Anacardium occidentale:* **Ba,** flower, $\times 1\frac{1}{2}$; **Bb,** enlarged receptacle (above) with drupe, $\times \frac{1}{3}$; **Bc,** seed, $\times \frac{1}{2}$.

ANACARDIACEAE Lindl. CASHEW FAMILY. Dicot.; about 60 genera and 600 spp. of woody plants, sometimes evergreen, mostly trop., but extending into temp. zones; lvs. alt.; fls. usually regular, unisexual or bisexual, usually with annular disc between stamens and ovary, stamens 1–10, rarely more, ovary 1–6-celled, each cell 1-ovuled; fr. commonly drupelike or a nut. The following genera are cult.: *Anacardium, Astronium, Cotinus, Harpephyllum, Laurophyllus, Lithrea, Mangifera, Pistacia, Pleiogynium, Rhodosphaera, Rhus, Schinus, Semecarpus, Smodingium,* and *Spondias.*

Some species have tanning, medicinal, and poisonous properties; others yield materials for varnishes and lacquers; some are grown for their edible fruit, and still others as ornamentals.

ANACARDIUM L. *Anacardiaceae.* Fifteen spp. of trop. Amer. trees or shrubs; lvs. alt., simple, leathery, entire; petals and sepals 5, stamens 8–10, ovary 1-celled, 1-ovuled; fr. a kidney-shaped nut (drupe), subtended by a large, oblong, fleshy receptacle.

One species, *A. occidentale,* the cashew, widely cultivated for its edible seeds. Of easy cultivation in regions free from frost, thriving best in hot, semiarid climates. Propagated by seeds or choice varieties by shield-budding, bearing in 3–4 years.

occidentale L. CASHEW, CASHEW NUT, MARANON. Evergreen, spreading tree, to 40 ft., with milky, acrid juice; lvs. oblong-ovate to obovate; fls. in terminal panicles, yellowish-pink; fr. with receptacle $2–3\frac{1}{2}$ in. long, bright red or yellow, nut 1 in. long. Trop. Amer., naturalized widely in the tropics, cult. commercially for the nuts in India. Cult. in Zone 10, where the tree survives but fruits poorly. The receptacle is the edible cashew apple, from which candies and beverages are made.

ANACHARIS: *ELODEA.*

ANACYCLUS L. *Compositae* (Anthemis Tribe). About 20 spp. of ann., bien., or per. herbs, native to the Medit. region; lvs. alt., 1–3-pinnately dissected; fl. heads solitary or in pairs at ends of brs., usually radiate, sometimes discoid, involucre hemispherical or broadly campanulate, involucral bracts imbricate, in 2–3 rows, receptacle convex or conical, with chaffy scales; disc fls. tubular, bisexual, yellow, ray fls. female, sometimes sterile, white or yellow, often purple on the back, sometimes absent; achenes more or less flattened, glabrous, the outer ones 2-winged, pappus absent or a crown of scales.

atlanticus Litard. & Maire. White-hairy per., sts. prostrate, to $3\frac{1}{2}$ in. long; basal lvs. to $1\frac{3}{4}$ in. long, 2–3-pinnately dissected, segms. linear-lanceolate, st. lvs. to $\frac{3}{8}$ in. long; heads to $\frac{3}{8}$ in. across, hemispherical; ray fls. absent. Mts., Morocco.

depressus J. Ball. Bien. or per., sts. prostrate to ascending; lvs. to $1\frac{1}{2}$ in. long, 1–2-pinnately dissected, segms. lanceolate, acute; heads solitary or sometimes in pairs, to $1\frac{1}{8}$ in. across; ray fls. white above, purple on the back. Morocco.

maroccanus (J. Ball) J. Ball. Prostrate ann.; lvs. 2-pinnately dissected, segms. mucronate; heads to 2 in. across; ray fls. white above, purple on the back. Morocco.

radiatus Loisel. Erect ann., to 2 ft., villous to glabrescent; lvs. 2–3-pinnatisect, segms. linear-lanceolate, with mucronate apices; heads to $1\frac{1}{2}$ in. across; ray fls. yellow or white above, purplish on the back. Medit. region.

ANADENANTHERA Speg. *Leguminosae* (subfamily *Mimosoideae*). Two spp. of unarmed shrubs or trees of S. Amer.; lvs. 2-pinnate, pinnae opp. or nearly so, lfts. many, petiole with a gland above the base; fls. in globose heads, regular, 5-merous, calyx and corolla puberulous outside, stamens 10, exserted; fr. a straight legume, dehiscent along one margin only, seeds flat, elliptic to nearly orbicular, acutely margined but not winged.

colubrina (Vell.) Brenan. Shrub, or tree, to nearly 100 ft.; pinnae in 7–35 or more pairs, lfts. in 20–40 pairs, very small; heads to $\frac{3}{4}$ in. across, peduncles axillary, clustered, to $1\frac{5}{8}$ in. long; fls. white to orangish, anthers glandular in bud. Var. **colubrina.** The typical var.; lfts. linear, midrib more prominent than lateral veins; fr. 6 in. long or more, to $\frac{3}{4}$ in. wide, regularly constricted between seeds. Brazil, Argentina. Not cult. Var. **Cebil** (Griseb.) Altschul [*Piptadenia macrocarpa* Benth.]. Lfts. broadened in middle, lateral veins about as prominent as midrib; fr. 4 in. long or more, to $1\frac{3}{16}$ in. wide, irregularly constricted. Brazil to Peru and Argentina.

ANAGALLIS L. PIMPERNEL. *Primulaceae.* About 30 spp. of glabrous ann. or per. herbs, native to all continents, but most abundant in trop. Afr., sts. erect to prostrate, often rooting at nodes; lvs. simple, opp., whorled, or alt.; fls. red, blue, pink, or white, solitary and axillary, or in terminal racemes, calyx mostly 5-lobed, corolla nearly campanulate to rotate, mostly 5-lobed, stamens 5; fr. a caps. dehiscing horizontally.

Seeds of the annual species may be sown where the plants are to be grown. The perennials are propagated by division and cuttings.

arvensis L. POOR-MAN'S-WEATHERGLASS, COMMON P., SCARLET P., SHEPHERD'S-CLOCK. Spreading ann.; lvs. ovate, to ¾ in. long; fls. scarlet or white, about ¼ in. across, axillary. Widely distributed weed; naturalized from Eur. Used in home remedies. Forma **caerulea** (Schreb.) Baumg. [*A. caerulea* Schreb.]. Fls. blue.

    caerulea: *A. arvensis* forma.

    grandiflora: *A. Monelli* subsp. *linifolia.*

    linifolia: *A. Monelli* subsp.

    Monelli L. Per., to 1½ ft.; lvs. ovate or oblong, to 1 in. long; fls. blue, reddish beneath, ¾ in. across, axillary. Medit. region. Cv. 'Phillipsii'. To 1 ft.; fls. deep gentian-blue. Subsp. **linifolia** (L.) Maire [*A. grandiflora* Andr.; *A. linifolia* L.]. Lvs. linear or linear-laceolate.

    Phillipsii: a listed name of no botanical standing for *A. Monelli* cv.

ANAMOMIS: *MYRCIANTHES.*

ANANAS Mill. *Bromeliaceae.* Nine spp. of stiff, terrestrial per. herbs, native to trop. Amer.; lvs. long, slender, usually spiny, in basal rosettes; infl. borne on a scape, simple, forming a fleshy syncarp of fused inferior ovaries in fr., bearing a crown of leafy bracts, which often produces offsets at its base; petals separate, each with 2 funnelform scales.

The pineapple is grown in the tropics commercially for its fruit, and occasionally as an ornamental outdoors in sunny spots or as a pot plant under glass. For culture see *Bromeliaceae.*

    ananassoides (Bak.) L. B. Sm. Lvs. long, narrow, recurving, up to 1 in. wide, spiny; scape slender, elongate, terminating in a many-fld. infl., fl. bracts serrulate; fr. a many-seeded syncarp to 6 in. long. Brazil. Var. **nanus:** *A. nanus.*

    bracteatus (Lindl.) Schult. RED PINEAPPLE, WILD P. Similar to *A. comosus*, but fls. in showy red heads, with large, elongated, imbricate, spiny bracts usually concealing tops of ovaries. Brazil. Fr. seedy but edible. Var. **striatus** M. B. Foster. Lvs. with broad, white, marginal stripes.

    comosus (L.) Merrill [*A. sativus* Schult.]. PINEAPPLE. St. to 4 ft.; lvs. in rosettes, to 3 ft. long and 1½ in. wide, with spiny tips and prickly edges; fls. violet or reddish; fr. a fleshy and juicy syncarp becoming 1 ft. long or more. The most important pomological cvs. are: 'Smooth Cayenne', planted in Hawaii and 'Red Spanish', the commonest cv. in the W. Indies. A few cvs. with variegated lvs. are grown as ornamentals: 'Variegatus', with marginal, ivory stripes; 'Porteanus', with a central, yellow stripe. Cv. 'Cochin-chinensis' is listed, and is probably the same as cv. 'Variegatus'. For cult. see *Pineapple.*

    nanus (L. B. Sm.) L. B. Sm. [*A. ananassoides* var. *nanus* L. B. Sm.]. Similar to *A. ananassoides*, but apex of the scape tough, infl. few-fld., fr. only about 1½ in. long. Brazil.

    Porteanus: *A. comosus* cv.

    sativus: *A. comosus.*

ANAPHALIS DC. EVERLASTING, LIFE-EVERLASTING. *Compositae* (Inula Tribe). About 35 spp. of dioecious or polygamodioecious, gray- or white-woolly per. herbs, native to Eur., Asia, and N. Amer.; sts. leafy; fl. heads discoid, small, in corymbs, involucral bracts stiff, dry, white or gray; fls. all tubular, yellow; achenes oblong-obovate, pappus of capillary bristles.

Flowering stems sometimes cut before maturity, dried, and often dyed for use in winter bouquets.

    alpicola Mak. Tufted per., to 8 in.; lvs. of sterile shoots oblanceolate, to 4 in. long, grayish-woolly on both surfaces, lvs. of flowering sts. lanceolate, to 2⅜ in. long, sessile and decurrent; heads in dense corymbs. Japan.

    margaritacea (L.) Benth. & Hook. f. PEARLY E. Rhizomatous, sts. erect, to 3 ft., tomentose; lvs. sessile, linear-lanceolate to lanceolate, to 4 in. long, 1- or faintly 3-nerved, white-tomentose, but often greener above; heads many, ¼ in. across, involucre white. Summer, autumn. Widespread in N. Amer., e. Asia.

    nubigena: *A. triplinervis* var. *monocephala.*

    triplinervis (Sims) C. B. Clarke. Sts. tall, stout, tomentose; lvs. sessile, obovate to oblong-ovate, 3–8 in. long, ¾–2½ in. wide, 3–5-nerved, tomentose, but greener above; heads many, ½–¾ in. across, involucre white. Himalayas. Var. **monocephala** (DC.) Airy-Shaw. [*A. nubigena* DC.]. Low, tufted, gray-woolly, sts. 8 in. or less; lvs. oblanceolate to linear-lanceolate, mostly less than 1 in. long, to ³⁄₁₆ in. wide, 1-nerved, the uppermost with scarious appendages; heads solitary, or 2 or 3, ½–1 in. across, involucre white. Alpine Himalayas.

ANARRHINUM Desf. *Scrophulariaceae.* About 12 spp. of bien. or per. herbs, native to Medit. region; differing from *Antirrhinum* and *Linaria* in not having palate in corolla throat; basal lvs. in rosettes, st. lvs. alt.; fls. in slender spicate racemes, small, stamens 4; fr. a globose caps.

Of easy culture, propagated from seeds.

    bellidifolium (L.) Desf. Bien., 1½–2 ft., sts. simple or branched above middle; basal lvs. spatulate, 2–3½ in. long, rather sparsely but coarsely serrate; infl. erect, usually 4–8 in. long, tapering apically; calyx lobes green, corolla bluish-purple, limb sometimes tinged red. Sw. Eur.

    laxiflorum Boiss. Bien.; basal lvs. broadly ovate to spatulate, lower st. lvs. 3-lobed or toothed, upper lvs. entire and linear; calyx lobes with white margins, corolla white or very pale purple. Spain.

ANASTATICA L. *Cruciferae.* One sp., a small, ann., much-branched herb, native from n. Afr. to Arabia and Iran; lvs. deciduous after the fls. appear; fls. small, in sessile, axillary clusters, sepals and petals 4; fr. a silique.

Sometimes grown as a curiosity.

    hierochuntica L. RESURRECTION PLANT, ROSE-OF-JERICHO. Gray, unattractive plant, a few in. high; lvs. oblong-spatulate, toothed; fls. white, minute; fr. a small silicle. When the plant is mature and dead, the brs. curve inward and form a ball, which in the wild rolls over the desert, dispersing its seeds; the brs. open out again when moist. The balls are sometimes sold as curiosities; they open and close with moisture and dryness. The plant is easy to grown in warm, sunny locations.

ANCHUSA L. [*Buglossum* Gaertn.]. BUGLOSS, ALKANET. *Boraginaceae.* Between 30 and 40 spp. of coarse, hairy, erect, ann. or per. herbs of Eur., Asia Minor, and Afr.; lvs. simple, alt., basal and cauline; fls. blue, violet, white, or seldom yellow, tubular or funnelform, many, in leafy-bracted, paniculate or racemose, scorpioid cymes, calyx 5-lobed or -parted, corolla 5-lobed, with scales in the throat, stamens 5, included; fr. of 4 rough nutlets, each nutlet surrounded at the base by an annular rim.

Of easy cultivation in the flower garden or border. Propagated by seeds in spring or by division.

    affinis R. Br. Per., to 2 ft.; lvs. oblong to lanceolate-ovate or ovate; fls. blue, ¼ in. across; nutlets horizontal. Trop. Afr.

    angustifolia: *A. officinalis* cv.

    azurea Mill. [*A. italica* Retz.]. Hispid per., to 5 ft.; lvs. oblong to lanceolate and ovate-lanceolate; fls. bright blue, to ¾ in. across, calyx lobes parted almost to the base, linear, acuminate; nutlets erect. Medit. region; naturalized in N. Amer.

    Barrelieri (All.) Vitm. [*Buglossum Barrelieri* All.]. Per., to 2 ft.; lvs. spatulate to oblong-lanceolate or ovate-lanceolate; fls. bright blue, to ¼ in. across, calyx lobes obtuse; nutlets erect. Spring. Eur., Asia Minor.

    caespitosa Lam. Per. with decumbent cespitose sts., to 4 in.; lvs. narrowly linear; fls. blue with a white tube, few, calyx lobes linear, obtuse; nutlets erect. Summer. Crete.

    capensis Thunb. Bien., 1–2 ft.; lvs. linear to narrowly lanceolate, with bulbous-based hairs; calyx lobes triangular, corolla blue, margined with red, with a white throat, ¼ in. across; nutlets horizontal. Summer and autumn. S. Afr. Cv. 'Blue Bird'. Fls. blue. Cv. 'Pink Bird'. Fls. pink.

    italica: *A. azurea.*

    myosotidiflora: *Brunnera macrophylla.*

    officinalis L. BUGLOSS. Bien. or per., to 2 ft.; lvs. lanceolate; fls. bright blue or purple, ¼ in. across, calyx lobes cut below the middle, acute; nutlets horizontal. Summer and autumn. Eur., Asia Minor. Cv. 'Angustifolia' [*A. angustifolia* L.]. Lvs. narrowly lanceolate. Cv. 'Incarnata'. Fls. flesh-colored.

    riparia DC. Bien. or per., to 2½ ft.; lvs. narrowly-lanceolate, to 6 in. long, with hispid or setose hairs but those on lower surface not bulbous-based; fls. blue to purplish-red, about ⅛ in. across, calyx lobes obtuse; nutlets horizontal Summer. S. Afr. Distinguished from *A. officinalis* by its narrower lvs. and minute calyx lobes.

    sempervirens: *Pentaglottis sempervirens.*

ANCISTROCACTUS Britt. & Rose. HOOK CACTUS. *Cactaceae.* Four spp. of small, ellipsoid to ovoid or top-shaped, tubercled cacti, native to Tex. and Mex.; sts. solitary or few-branched, globose to oblong, tubercles slightly united, in about 13 spiral rows, adaxially grooved; radial spines 6–22, central spines 3–4, the lowest 1–3 hooked; fls. subapical, from the woolly groove, diurnal, funnelform, small, scales of ovary few, with naked axils; fr. greenish, thin-walled, seeds dark brown, truncate-papillose, hilum nearly basal, large, rimmed, micropyle closed. Resembling *Coryphantha* and *Thelocactus,* but with a hooked central spine and seeds otherwise.

For culture see *Cacti.*

brevihamatus: *A. Scheeri.*

crassihamatus (A. Web.) L. Bens. [*Ferocactus crassihamatus* (A. Web.) Britt. & Rose; *Thelocactus crassihamatus* (A. Web.) W. T. Marsh.]. Sts. to 6 in. thick, ribs divided into oblong tubercles; spines awl-shaped, radial spines 8, to 1 in. long, central spines 5, red, the lower 3 hooked; fls. purple, 1 in. long. Cent. Mex.

megarhizus: *A. Scheeri.*

Scheeri (Salm-Dyck) Britt. & Rose [*A. brevihamatus* (Engelm.) Britt. & Rose; *A. megarhizus* (Rose) Britt. & Rose]. FISHHOOK CACTUS. Sts. ellipsoid to oblong-obovoid, to 6 in. high and 4 in. thick; radial spines 12–18, spreading uniformly, needle-shaped, white or straw-colored, to 2 in. long, central spines 3–4, angled, to 1 in. long, the hooked one shorter; fls. greenish-yellow, 1 in. across. Spring. S. Tex. and n. Mex.

Tobuschii W. T. Marsh. ex Backeb. Sts. flat-topped or top-shaped, to 2 in. high and thick; radial spines 12–22, finely pubescent, spreading irregularly, to ⅜ in. long, central spines 6, to ⅞ in. long, the lowermost hooked; fls. light yellow, 1¼–1½ in. across. S. Tex.

uncinatus (Galeotti) L. Bens. [*Ferocactus uncinatus* (Galeotti) Britt. & Rose; *Hamatocactus uncinatus* (Galeotti) Borg; *Thelocactus uncinatus* (Galeotti) W. T. Marsh.]. Sts. cylindric-ovoid to ovoid, to 6 in. high and 4 in. thick; lower radial spines reddish or reddish-tan, some hooked, central spines reddish-tan to pinkish, the lower hooked one to 4½ in. long; fls. red, to 1¼ in. across. S. Tex., New Mex., n. Mex.

ANDIRA Juss. *Leguminosae* (subfamily *Faboideae*). About 25–35 spp. of trees of trop. Amer., 1 sp. also in W. Afr.; lvs. alt., odd-pinnate; fls. in terminal panicles, papilionaceous, fragrant, stamens 10, 9 united and 1 separate; fr. a drupelike, indehiscent legume, seed 1, large.

Grown as ornamentals for shade and for the attractive flowers. They require tropical temperatures and rich loamy soil. Propagated by cuttings over bottom heat when seeds are not available.

inermis (W. Wright) HBK ex DC. ANGELIN, ALMENDRO, CABBAGE BARK. To 60 ft.; lfts. oblong, to 2½ in. long; panicles dense, to 1 ft. long; fls. lilac or pale rose, petals ½ in. long; fr. nearly globose, 1½ in. long. Trop. Amer. and W. Afr. Wood useful.

ANDRACHNE L. *Euphorbiaceae.* About 20 spp. of monoecious shrubs and subshrubs, native to N. and S. Amer., Asia, and Afr.; lvs. alt., 2-ranked, simple, mostly entire; fls. small, axillary, on long pedicels, male fls. in clusters, with petals, female fls. solitary, sometimes without petals or with minute petals, ovary 3-celled; fr. a caps.

Propagated by seeds or by greenwood cuttings under glass.

colchica Fisch. & C. A. Mey. Shrub, to 2 ft., brs. many, simple, ascending; lvs. ovate, ½–1 in. long, glabrous, thin; fr. about ⅛ in. in diam. Asia Minor.

phyllanthoides (Nutt.) Müll. Arg. [*Savia phyllanthoides* (Nutt.) Pax & K. Hoffm.]. Shrub, to 3 ft., sts. simple; lvs. elliptic to broadly obovate, thin, pubescent beneath on the veins; fr. about ¼ in. in diam. Mo. to Ark. and Tex.

ANDROMEDA L. BOG ROSEMARY. *Ericaceae.* Two spp. of low, evergreen shrubs, native to N. Amer., Eur., and Asia; lvs. alt., simple, revolute, leathery; fls. pink to white, in nodding, terminal umbels, sepals 5, corolla urceolate, stamens 10, anthers awned, ovary superior; fr. a caps.

Grown in rock gardens and borders, and very hardy north. Propagated by seeds, cuttings of mature wood under glass, and by layers.

arborea: *Oxydendrum arboreum.*

cassinifolia: *Zenobia pulverulenta* forma *nitida.*

Catesbaei: *Leucothoe axillaris,* but material offered as *A. Catesbaei* is *Leucothoe Fontanesiana.*

floribunda: *Pieris floribunda.*

Forrestii: a listed name of no botanical standing for *Pieris Forrestii.*

glaucophylla Link. Sts. to 2½ ft., glaucous; lvs. linear to oblong, to 2½ in. long, white-puberulent beneath; fls. in umbels; caps. glaucous, wider than high, on pedicels usually less than twice as long. Ne. N. Amer. Zone 2.

japonica: *Pieris japonica.*

mariana: *Lyonia mariana.*

Polifolia L. To 1 ft., rhizomes creeping; lvs. linear to oblong, to 1½ in. long, glabrous and glaucous beneath; fls. in umbels, 1¼ in. long; caps. as broad as high, on pedicels 3 or 4 times as long. Eur., n. Asia, n. N. Amer. Cv. 'Montana'. More compact; lvs. darker. Cvs. listed are: 'Angustifolia', 'Compacta', 'Grandiflora Compacta', 'Major', 'Minima', and 'Nana'.

racemosa: *Leucothoe racemosa.*

speciosa: *Zenobia pulverulenta.*

ANDROPOGON L. BLUESTEM, BEARD GRASS. *Gramineae.* About 200 spp. of per. grasses in warm temp. and trop. regions of world; sts. solid, often coarse; infl. compound, of few to many peduncled, sheathed racemes or spikelets on a common peduncle and usually enclosed by a spathelike sheath, usually narrow, but sometimes in dense, nearly corymbose masses; spikelets in pairs at each node of an articulate rachis, one sessile and bisexual, the other pedicelled and either male, neuter, or reduced to a pedicel, rachis and pedicels of the sterile spikelets often villous, glumes of fertile spikelet nearly equal, the first nerved near margin, first lemma shorter than glumes, empty, hyaline, fertile lemma hyaline, narrow, usually awned from apex or from between lobes, awn bent and twisted, palea hyaline, small or 0, pedicelled spikelet awnless, about as large as sessile spikelet, sometimes consisting of 1–2 reduced glumes, sometimes only the pedicel present. For terminology see *Gramineae.*

annulatus: *Dichanthium annulatum.*

caricosus: *Dichanthium caricosum.*

caucasicus: *Bothriochloa caucasica.*

furcatus: *A. Gerardii.*

Gerardii Vitm. [*A. furcatus* Muhlenb.]. BIG B. Often glaucous, sts. to 7 ft., robust, usually sparingly branching toward the summit, often in large clumps, rhizomes short or absent; lower lf. sheaths and blades sometimes villous, blades flat, elongate, to ⅜ in. wide; infl. of mostly 3–6, usually purplish racemes 2–4 in. long on the long-exserted terminal peduncle, rachis straight, joints and pedicels stiffly ciliate, joints hispid at base; sessile spikelet to ⅜ in. long, the first glume slightly grooved, usually scabrous, awn geniculate and tightly twisted below, to ¾ in. long, pedicelled spikelet male, awnless. Que. to Sask., s. to Fla. and Ariz.; Mex.

Hallii Hack. SAND B. Distinguished from *A. Gerardii* in having pale or glaucous lvs., elongate creeping rhizomes, conspicuously villous, shorter racemes, the hairs grayish to pale golden, awn of the sessile spikelet rarely more than ¼ in. long, often nearly absent. N. Dak. and e. Mont., s. to Tex., Ariz., and Iowa.

intermedius: *Bothriochloa intermedia.*

Ischaemum: *Bothriochloa Ischaemum.*

littoralis: *Schizachyrium scoparium* var.

nodosus: *Dichanthium aristatum.*

scoparius: *Schizachyrium scoparium.*

ANDROSACE L. ROCK JASMINE. *Primulaceae.* About 125 spp. of tufted ann., bien., or per. herbs of Eur., Asia, and N. Amer.; lvs. simple, mostly basal; fls. red or white, in scapose umbels, or solitary, calyx 5-cleft, corolla funnelform or salverform, 5-lobed; fr. a 5-valved caps. Differs from *Primula* in having the corolla tube shorter than the calyx and constricted at throat. The generic name has 4 syllables.

Androsaces are sometimes grown in rock gardens or low borders. They require well-drained soil, which must not be allowed to dry out. Propagated by seeds, cuttings, or division.

albana Steven. Pubescent bien., to 6 in.; lvs. in dense basal rosettes, oblong to spatulate, to ⅝ in. long, with 2–3 teeth toward apex; fls. white, pink, or rose, in umbels. Caucasus.

alpina (L.) Lam. Loosely tufted per., to 3 in.; lvs. in rosettes at ends of brs., oblong-lanceolate, ³⁄₁₆ in. long, with branched hairs; fls. rose, ³⁄₁₆ in. across, solitary. Alps.

arachnoidea: *A. villosa* var.

armeniaca Duby. Bien., to 2 in.; basal lvs. oblong-lanceolate, to ⅝ in. long, usually acute, somewhat laciniate-dentate; fls. white, in 5–10-fld. umbel-like clusters. Asia Minor.

brigantiaca: *A. carnea* var.

carinata Torr. Hairy, tufted per., to 2½ in.; lvs. in basal rosette, linear to lanceolate or oblanceolate, often keeled, ciliate; fls. white to cream-colored, with orange to pinkish eye, in 2–5-fld. subcapitate umbels. High mts., Utah, Colo.

carnea L. Rhizomatous, more or less tufted per., to 3 in.; lvs. linear, to ¾ in. long; fls. rose to whitish, with a yellow eye, ⁵⁄₁₆ in. across, in 3–7-fld. umbels. Alps and Pyrenees. Var. **brigantiaca** (Jord. & Fourr.) R. Knuth [*A. brigantiaca* Jord. & Fourr.]. To 4 in.; lvs. narrower; fls. pink. Var. **Halleri** (L.) L. [*A. Halleri* L.]. Lvs. glossy, hairy, over 1 in. long. Var. **Laggeri** (Huet) R. Knuth [*A. Laggeri* Huet]. Densely tufted, to 1 in. or more; fls. bright pink.

Charpentieri Heer. Tufted per.; lvs. in rosettes at ends of brs., spatulate, downy; fls. rose, ³⁄₁₆ in. across, solitary, pedicels twice as long as lvs. N. Italy.

chumbyi: a listed name of no botanical standing for *A. primuloides* cv.

ciliaris: a listed name of no botanical standing.

ciliata DC. Per., to 3 in.; lvs. in rosettes, oblong-ovate, ¼ in. long, ciliate; fls. rose, ⁵⁄₁₆ in. across, solitary. Pyrenees.

coronopifolia: *A. lactiflora.*

cylindrica DC. Tufted per.; lvs. persistent, forming cylindrical rosettes toward ends of brs., linear-lanceolate. to ⁵⁄₁₆ in. long, downy; fls. white, ⁵⁄₁₆ in. across, solitary. Pyrenees.

Fedtschenkoi Ovchinn. To 2⅜ in.; lvs. in rosettes, linear-lanceolate or oblong-lanceolate, to ⅝ in. long, toothed, hairy; fls. white or pale yellow, ¼ in. across. Cent. Asia.

foliosa Duby ex Decne. Stoloniferous per., to 5 in.; lvs. basal but not in rosettes, elliptic to elliptic-oblong or obovate, 2–3 in. long, ciliate, and hairy on both sides; fls. pink, with yellow eye, to ½ in. across, in many-fld. umbels on stout scapes. W. Himalayas.

Halleri: *A. carnea* var.

hedraeantha Griseb. Tufted per., to ½ in.; lvs. in rosettes, oblong-lanceolate, ⁵⁄₁₆ in. long; fls. violet-red, in 5–10-fld. umbels. Balkans. Var. **Grisebachii** is listed.

helvetica (L.) Gaudin. Densely tufted per.; lvs. in dense rosettes, lanceolate, very small, hairy; fls. white, about ⅛ in. across, solitary, nearly sessile. Alps.

hirtella Dufour. Densely white-hairy, tufted per.; lvs. densely imbricate, linear, to ⁵⁄₁₆ in. long; fls. white, solitary. Pyrenees.

Hookeri: perhaps an error for *Hookerana.*

Hookerana Klatt. Stoloniferous, loosely tufted per., to 3 in.; lvs. in rosettes, obovate or elliptic, to ½ in. long, hairy; fls. pink, in a few-fld. umbel on solitary scape. Himalayas.

imbricata Lam. Densely tufted per.; lvs. oblong-lanceolate to linear-spatulate, very small, imbricate, and covering the brs., hairy; fls. white, to ³⁄₁₆ in. across, solitary. Alps.

lactea L. Tufted, glabrous per., to 8 in.; lvs. in rosettes, linear to linear-lanceolate, to ¾ in. long; fls. snow-white, ⁵⁄₁₆ in. across, in umbels, pedicels to 2 in. long. Mts., Eur.

lactiflora Pall. [*A. coronopifolia* Andr.]. Glabrous ann., to 1 ft.; lvs. in rosettes, linear-lanceolate, to 2 in. long, toothed toward apex; fls. white, to ½ in. across, in several, many-fld. umbels. Siberia.

Laggeri: *A. carnea* var.

lanuginosa Wallich. Prostrate per., covered with silky-white hairs; lvs. both basal and cauline, lanceolate-ovate, to ¾ in. long; fls. rose-colored, ⁵⁄₁₆ in. across, in umbels on scapes to 2–4 in. long. Himalayas. Var. **Leichtlinii** Darn. Fls. white, with yellow or crimson eye. Var. **oculata.** A listed name of no botanical standing for plants with lilac fls.

Mathildae Levier. Tufted per.; lvs. in rosettes, linear, to ½ in. long, glabrous; fls. white, about ⅛ in. across, solitary. Italy.

mucronifolia G. Watt. Loosely tufted, stoloniferous per.; lvs. imbricate, in rosettes, obovate, to ³⁄₁₆ in. long, obtuse, ciliate; fls. rose to lilac, usually in 3–6-fld. umbels on scapes to 1 in. long. Nw. Himalayas to Tibet.

occidentalis Pursh. Dwarf ann., to 3 in.; lvs. in basal rosettes, linear to oblong or elliptic-lanceolate, to ¾ in. long, with mostly simple hairs; fls. white, in umbels subtended by elliptic to ovate bracts. N. Amer.

oculata: a listed name of no botanical standing: see *A. lanuginosa* var.

✕pedemontana Rchb.: *A. carnea* ✕ *A. obtusifolia* All. Tufted per.; lvs. in rosettes, margins wavy-toothed; fls. in umbels, white with orange eye.

primuloides Duby [*A. sarmentosa* var. *primuloides* (Duby) Hook. f.]. Stoloniferous, the stolons to 6 in. long; lvs. in rosettes, oblanceolate, to ½ in. long, or the larger ones 2 in. or more, covered with silvery hairs; fls. pink, to ½ in. across, in umbels on scape to 4 in. high, bracts subtending umbels broadly lanceolate, calyx lobes half length of calyx. Himalayas. Cv. 'Chumbyi' [*A. chumbyi* Hort.; *A. sarmentosa* var. *chumbyi* Fitzh.]. More cespitose, and silky.

puberulenta: *A. septentrionalis* var.

pumila: a listed name of no botanical standing.

pyrenaica Lam. Densely tufted per.; lvs. imbricate on brs., linear, to ⅛ in. long, ciliate; fls. white with yellowish eye, solitary, on peduncles twice as long as lvs. Pyrenees.

salicifolia: a listed name of no botanical standing; material grown under this name is *A. lactiflora.*

sarmentosa Wallich [var. *Watkinsii* Hook. f.; var. *yunnanensis* R. Knuth]. Stoloniferous, the stolons to 5 in. long; lvs. in rosettes, lanceolate or ovate-lanceolate, to 1½ in. long, covered with silvery hairs when young; fls. rose-colored, ¼ in. across, in umbels on scapes to 5 in. high, bracts subtending umbels linear, calyx lobes ⅓ length of calyx. Himalayas. Var. **chumbyi:** *A. primuloides* cv. Var. **primuloides:** *A. primuloides.*

sempervivoides Jacquem. ex Duby. Stoloniferous, the stolons to 2 in. long; lvs. in rosettes on the stolons, ovate, to ¼ in. long, fleshy, ciliate; fls. rose, ¼ in. across, in umbels on scapes to 4 in. high. Himalayas.

septentrionalis L. Ann., to 8 in.; lvs. in rosettes, lanceolate to oblong, to ¾ in. long; fls. white or pink, to ³⁄₁₆ in. across, in umbels. Eur., Asia, n. N. Amer. Var. **puberulenta** (Rydb.) R. Knuth [*A. puberulenta* Rydb.]. Puberulent, to 6 in.; calyx lobes triangular to acuminate. Cent. and s. Rocky Mts., from Canada s. to Ariz. and New Mex. Var. **subulifera** A. Gray [*A. subulifera* (A. Gray) Rydb.]. To 3–10 in.; calyx lobes subulate to needle-shaped. Rocky Mts., B.C. to Ariz. and New Mex. Var. **subumbellata** A. Nels. [*A. subumbellata* (A. Nels.) Small]. To 2 in., almost glabrous. High mts., w. N. Amer.

spinulifera (Franch.) R. Knuth. Hairy per., to 1 ft., without stolons; lvs. in a rosette, first lvs. scalelike, later lvs. oblanceolate, to 6 in. long, with a sharp-pointed tip; fls. deep purple to rose, ½ in. across, in many-fld. umbels. China.

strigillosa Franch. Tufted per., to 1 ft.; lvs. in rosettes, narrowly oblong to obovate, to 3 in. long and ¾ in. wide, obtuse to acutish, usually hairy, base attenuated to petiole; fls. purple-violet, in 5–10-fld. umbels. Himalayas.

subulifera: *A. septentrionalis* var.

subumbellata: *A. septentrionalis* var.

villosa L. Densely white-hairy per., to 3 in.; lvs. in rosettes, lanceolate, minute; fls. white or rose, with yellowish-red throat, ⁵⁄₁₆ in. across, in umbels. Eur., Asia. Var. **arachnoidea** (Schott) R. Knuth [*A. arachnoidea* Schott]. To 1 in.; lvs. oblong-ovate.

Vitaliana: *Douglasia Vitaliana.*

Watkinsii: a listed name of no botanical standing for *A. sarmentosa.*

yunnanensis: a listed name of no botanical standing for *A. sarmentosa.*

ANDROSAEMUM: *HYPERICUM.*

ANDROSTEPHIUM Torr. *Amaryllidaceae.* Two spp. of herbs, native to N. and S. Amer.; corms fibrous-coated; lvs. basal, linear; fls. in an umbel terminal on a scape and subtended by several papery spathe valves, perianth segms. blue, united about halfway, filaments 6, united into a tube with short teeth between the anthers, ovary superior; fr. a loculicidal caps. One sp. is sometimes planted in the wild garden or border.

coeruleum (Scheele) Greene [*A. violaceum* Torr.]. BLUE FUNNEL LILY. To 8 in.; perianth lilac or violet, 1 in. long. Kans. to Tex.

violaceum: *A. coeruleum.*

ANEIMIA: see *ANEMIA.*

ANEMARRHENA Bunge. *Liliaceae.* One sp., a rhizomatous, per. herb, native to n. China; lvs. basal, grasslike; fls. in an elongated raceme; perianth segms. separate, not twisting spirally after flowering, stamens 3, anthers versatile; fr. a loculicidal caps.

asphodeloides Bunge. To 3½ ft.; lvs. to 2½ ft. long and ⅜ in. wide, long-tapering; fls. dull rose-purple, fragrant at night, segms. linear, about ¼ in. long.

ANEMIA Swartz (sometimes, but not originally, spelled *Aneimia*). FLOWERING FERN. *Schizaeaceae.* About 90 spp. of erect, terrestrial ferns, mostly of trop. Amer.; lvs. with basal pinnae fertile, erect, much longer than others and bearing panicles of many sporangia in 2 rows, sterile pinnae leafy, 1-pinnate to decompound.

Grown in the open in Zone 10 or under glass. For culture see *Ferns.*

adiantifolia (L.) Swartz. PINE FERN. To 3½ ft., rhizomes stout, creeping, brown-scaly; sterile pinnae triangular to ovate, about 1 ft. long, pinnately decompound, pinnules obovate to wedge-shaped, veins separate, petioles wiry. S. Fla., W. Indies, Cent. Amer.; frequently naturalized in warm regions.

Phyllitidis (L.) Swartz. To 2 ft.; sterile pinnae 1-pinnate, pinnae in 4–12 sessile pairs, ovate-oblong, mostly 2–4 in. long, veins netted. Trop. Amer.

rotundifolia Schrad. To 1½ ft.; sterile pinnae 1-pinnate, often rooting at tip, pinnae in 8–14 pairs, obtusely rhombic to flabellate, erosely serrulate, without midvein, veins radiating from base, separate. S. Brazil.

ANEMONE L. [*Pulsatilla* L.]. WINDFLOWER, LILY-OF-THE-FIELD. *Ranunculaceae.* About 120 spp. of per. herbs, native mostly to the N. Temp. Zone, often in high mts.; lvs. more or less divided or dissected, or even compound, st. lvs. forming a kind of involucre below fl., but often remote from it; fls. mostly solitary, sepals showy, yellowish, white, rose, red, to purplish and violet, petals absent, stamens many, shorter than sepals, pistils many, 1-ovuled; fr. an achene, with long plumose styles in the section *Pulsatilla*, not ribbed. The section *Pulsatilla* is sometimes treated as a separate genus. Some spp. flower very early, others in summer or autumn. As a Latin generic name, the word is pronounced Anemò-ne; as an English common name, Aném-one, both with 4 syllables.

Anemones are valuable in all types of gardens, thriving in rich sandy loam, many in partial shade. Except for the Japanese and florist's anemones, the species are used mostly in wild gardens and rock gardens. The tuberous, florist's anemones can be grown outdoors in mild climates. The Japanese anemones are good perennial herbs for autumn bloom. Most anemones can be propagated by seeds or by division, preferably in early spring. Seeds can be sown in the autumn, as soon as they have ripened.

albana Steven [*Pulsatilla albana* (Steven) Bercht. & J. Presl]. To 6 in.; lvs. bipinnatifid, segms. linear or oblong, white-villous, involucral lvs. united at base; fls. solitary, nodding, cream-yellow inside, purple and silky outside, to 3 in. across. Asia Minor to Baikal. Var. **georgica** Smirn. Lf. segms. narrower; sepals violet-rose. Caucasus.

alboviolacea: a listed name of no botanical standing for a plant of the section *Pulsatilla.*

alpina L. [*Pulsatilla alpina* (L.) Schrank]. Rhizome thick, strong, sts. simple, soft-hairy, 4–16 in.; lvs. large, basal, ternate, then 2-pinnate, long-petioled, involucral lvs. 3, much-divided; fls. solitary, 2–3 in. across, erect, sepals 6, white inside, tinged violet outside. Mts., Eur. Subsp. **sulphurea** (L.) Hegi [*A. sulphurea* L.]. Fls. sulphur-yellow.

altaica Fisch. ex Ledeb. To 6 in., resembling *A. nemorosa,* but having rhizome yellow, tuber-bearing; lvs. developing after fls., lf. tips blunter, toothed; fls. solitary, white with blue or violet veins, sepals 10–12, narrow. Altai in s. Siberia.

apennina L. Rhizome tuberous, sts. to 9 in.; basal lvs. 3-parted, segms. deeply incised, acute, weakly hairy; involucral lvs. ternate, petioled; fls. solitary, sky-blue, to 1½ in. across, sepals 12–18, narrow, pubescent on exterior. S. Eur. Cvs. include: 'Alba', fls. white; 'Allenii', fls. pale blue; 'Plena', fls. double; 'Purpurea', fls. mauve.

atrata: a listed name of no botanical standing for a plant of the section *Pulsatilla.*

baicalensis Turcz. Rhizome slender, branched, sts. 6–10 in.; lvs. hairy above and beneath, deeply cut; fls. solitary, white, sepals 6, strigose on exterior. Baikal.

baldensis L. Rhizome slender, elongate, sts. pubescent, 2–5 in.; lvs. 2-4-ternate, involucral lvs. petioled, remote from fl.; fls. solitary, to 2 in. across, sepals 6–10, acute, white, pubescent, sometimes rose-tinged on exterior; achenes woolly, in an ovoid-oblong head. Mts., se. Eur.

biflora DC. Rhizome tuberous, sts. glabrous, 2–8 in.; lvs. ternate, segms. linear, obtuse, somewhat incised, involucral lvs. 2–3, sessile, much-divided; fls. 2–3, nodding, deep crimson, sepals 5, hairy inside, to 1 in. long. Iran to Kashmir.

blanda Schott & Kotschy. Like *A. apennina,* 2–8 in. high, villous; fls. sky-blue, completely glabrous, sepals 9–14; fruiting head recurved. Se. Eur., Asia Minor. Cv. 'Atrocaerulea'. Fls. dark blue. Cv. 'Rosea'. Fls. pink. Var. **scythinica** Jenk. Fls. white inside, blue outside. N. Turkestan.

californica: *A. Drummondii.*

canadensis L. [*A. pensylvanica* L.]. Rhizome slender, sts. 1–2 ft., villous, usually branched; basal lvs. several, long-petioled, deeply 3-parted, segms. more or less incised, sharply toothed, involucral lvs. similar, but sessile; fls. 1–3, on long, stiff peduncles, white, to 2 in. across. Que. to B.C., s. to Md., Mo., New Mex.

caroliniana Walt. Rhizome tuberous, sts. to 1 ft.; lvs. ternate or 3-parted, petioled, segms. lobed, involucral lvs. sessile; fl. solitary, erect, purple or red to white, to 1½ in. across, sepals 10–20, hairy on exterior. E. U.S. Often cult. under the name *A. decapetala.*

caucasica Willd. ex Rupr. Resembling *A. blanda,* tubers short, ovoid; involucral lvs. short-petioled; sepals 8–10. Caucasus.

cernua Thunb. [*Pulsatilla cernua* (Thunb.) Bercht. & J. Presl]. Resembling *A. vernalis,* but having lfts. 5 and with larger teeth, and fls. nodding, sordid-claret. Japan, e. Asia. Used medicinally by the Chinese.

coronaria L. Rhizomes tuberous, sts. to 1½ ft.; basal lvs. petioled, 2-ternate; involucral lvs. sessile, much-divided; fls. solitary, to 2½ in. across, poppylike, sepals 6–8, elliptic, red, blue, to white. Medit. region. Most common sp. in the florist's trade. Cv. 'Chrysanthemiflora'. Fls. very double. Cv. 'Flore Pleno'. Fls. double.

cylindrica A. Gray. LONG-HEADED A., THIMBLEWEED. Sts. erect, 1–3 ft.; basal lvs. few to several, petioled, deeply 5-parted, segms. rhombic, involucral lvs. similar, 3–10; fls. 2–6, on erect peduncles 4–11 in. long, greenish-white, ¾ in. across; achenes woolly, in a cylindrical head. Me. to B.C., s. to N.J., Mo., Ariz.

dahurica Fisch. ex DC. [*Pulsatilla dahurica* (Fisch. ex DC.) K. Spreng.]. Close to *A. Pulsatilla;* lvs. ternate, terminal lft. with petiolule, 5-parted, lateral lft. sessile, unequally 3-lobed; sepals 6, erect, pink. Se. Siberia.

decapetala Ard. Resembling *A. multifida,* but lfts. merely crenate; fls. pink to greenish-white. S. Amer. Material cult. under this name is often *A. caroliniana.*

deltoidea Hook. Sts. slender, to 1 ft., sparsely hairy or glabrous; basal lvs. mostly solitary, petioled, with 3 lfts., lfts. ovate, 1–2½ in. long, involucral lvs. similar, but sessile; fls. 1–2, sepals white, mostly 5, ovate, ⅝–1 in. long. B.C. to n. Calif.

demissa Hook. f. & T. Thoms. Rhizome somewhat woody, tuberous, sts. 12–15 in., long-hairy; basal lvs. 3–5-parted, then 3–5-cleft, involucral lvs. sessile, 3-lobed; fls. 3–6, to 1½ in. across, white inside, purplish outside. Himalayas.

dichotoma L. Sts. branched, 1–2 ft.; basal lvs. 3-parted, segms. 2–3-parted, involucral lvs. sessile; infl. openly branched, somewhat drooping; fls. white, sepals narrow. Siberia to Japan.

Drummondii S. Wats. [*A. californica* Eastw.]. Rhizome stout, sts. 1 to several, to 1 ft., villous; basal lvs. several, petioled, 1–2 in. wide, 3–4-parted, ultimate segms. linear, involucral lvs. sessile; fls. usually solitary, on peduncles 1–4 in. long, sepals 5–8, ovate, ⁵⁄₁₆–⅝ in. long, white, tinged blue, villous outside. Alaska to Alta., Idaho, Calif.

elongata D. Don. Sts. 1–2 ft., hairy; lvs. as in *A. sylvestris,* hairy; fls. 1–3, dull white, to 1 in. across, sepals 4–6. Himalayas.

Farreri: a listed name of no botanical standing; said to be similar to *A. vitifolia.*

flaccida Friedr. Schmidt. Sts. 3–4 in.; lvs. thick, 3-parted, lateral segms. 2–3-parted, terminal segm. 3-cleft, coarsely toothed, segms. at first bronze-green, later dark green with gray spots at base of shallow lobes; fls. 1–3, cream-white, 1 in. across. Japan.

×fulgens (DC.) Rchb. Probably *A. hortensis* × *A. pavonina.* Like *A. pavonina;* sepals 15 or more, narrow, scarlet, stamens dark violet. Cv. 'Multipetala'. Fls. semidouble.

globosa: *A. multifida.*

Halleri All. [*Pulsatilla Halleri* (All.) Willd.]. To 12 in., silky-hairy; basal lvs. developing after fls., elongate-triangular, segms. linear, ¹⁄₁₆ in. wide, involucral lvs. sessile; fls. lilac-purple, sepals 1¼–1½ in. long, hairy on exterior. Alps.

Hepatica: see *Hepatica americana* and *H. nobilis.*

hirsutissima: *A. Nuttalliana.*

hortensis L. [*A. stellata* Lam.]. Resembling *A. pavonina;* fls. to 3 in. across, sepals 12–15, narrowly elliptic, lilac or rose-lilac, without a pale claw. Medit. region.

hudsoniana: *A. multifida.*

hupehensis Hort. Lemoine. JAPANESE A. Sts. 1–3 ft., sparsely hairy; lvs. ternate, lfts. elliptic, weakly 3–5-lobed, large-toothed, pointed; fls. to 15, cymose, 2–3 in. across, sepals 5–6, spreading, rose. China. Cvs. 'Rubra', 'Splendens', and 'Superba', are listed, but probably belong to *A.* ×*hybrida.* Var. **japonica** (Thunb.) Bowles & Stearn [*A. japonica*

(Thunb.) Siebold & Zucc., not Houtt.; *A. nipponica* Merrill]. To 2 or 3 ft.; sepals more than 20, pink, narrow. Japan.

× hybrida Paxt.: *A. hupehensis* var. *japonica* × *A. vitifolia*. JAPANESE A. Taller than *A. hupehensis* var. *japonica*, to 5 ft.; sepals 6–20, broad. Cvs. include: 'Alba', fls. white; 'Crispa', lvs. crisped; 'Lesseri', fls. crimson, early; 'Rosea Superba', fls. rose; 'Rubra', fls. waxy-red. This hybrid is generally offered under the name, *A. japonica*.

japonica: *A. hupehensis* var., but material offered as *A. japonica* is usually *A. × hybrida*.

lancifolia Pursh. Similar to *A. quinquefolia*, stouter, larger; terminal lft. of involucral lf. not incised; sepals ½–¾ in. long, white. Penn. to Ga.

Leveillei Ulbr. Roots fibrous, sts. to 2 ft.; lvs. reniform, 3-lobed, dentate; infl. open, well above lvs., pubescent; fls. 1–1½ in. across, white inside, lilac-pink outside, sepals rounded, bearded at tip. China.

lithophila Rydb. Sparingly silky, 4–8 in.; basal lvs. thickish, 3–5-parted, primary segms. about 1 in. long and the segms. again divided; sepals silky, yellowish-white, tinged with blue, ½ in. long, broadly elliptic. Mont. to Utah.

ludoviciana: *A. Nuttalliana*.

Lyallii: *A. quinquefolia* var.

magellanica: a listed name of no botanical standing, resembling *A. multifida;* about 6 in.; basal lvs. much divided; fls. cream-white, ½–1 in. across. S. Amer.

mexicana HBK. Sts. simple, 9–12 in.; lvs. with 3 lfts., lfts. rhombic-ovate, 3-parted, crenate-serrate, involucral lvs. 2–3, subsessile; fls. erect, 1–1½ in. across, sepals 5, white to pink or rose-purple, round-ovate, woolly on exterior. Mex.

montana Hoppe ex Sturm [*Pulsatilla montana* (Hoppe ex Sturm) Hoppe ex Rchb.]. Rhizome black, ascending, sts. 3–8 in.; basal lvs. dark green, long-petioled, 3-pinnatifid, segms. linear, involucral lvs. cut into linear segms.; fls. solitary, nodding, mostly dark violet, hairy on exterior, at first campanulate, later star-shaped. Cent. Eur.

multifida Poir. [*A. globosa* Nutt.; *A. hudsoniana* Richardson]. Stout, to 2 ft., villous in upper parts; basal lvs. several, long-petioled, deeply 2–3-ternate, the divisions linear-oblong, involucral lvs. similar, but sessile; fls. mostly solitary, sepals 5, white or yellowish, ³⁄₁₆–⅜ in. long. Nfld. to Alaska, s. to n. border states in the East and to Calif. and New Mex. in the West.

narcissiflora L. Like *A. demissa;* to 1½ ft., with more erect infl.; fls. white, to 1 in. across. Eurasia.

nemorosa L. EUROPEAN WOOD A. Rhizome woody, slender, brown, sts. simple, 6–10 in., slightly pubescent; lvs. 1–2, long-petioled, 3-parted, segms. 3–5-cleft and toothed, involucral lvs. similar, short-petioled; fls. white or rose, sepals 6–8, elliptic, glabrous, ½–¾ in. long. Eurasia. Cvs. include: 'Alba', fls. white, double; 'Allenii', fls. light blue, large; 'Major', fls. white; 'Rosea' and 'Rubra', fls. red-purple; 'Simplex', fls. white. Var. **Robinsoniana** Regel. Sepals powder-blue, yellowish outside.

nigricans: *A. pratensis* subsp.

nikoensis Maxim. Like *A. nemorosa*, but with lvs. more sharply toothed, and more divided; fls. solitary, white, almost 2 in. across. Japan.

nipponica: *A. hupehensis* var. *japonica*.

Nuttalliana DC. [*A. hirsutissima* (Britt.) MacMill.; *A. ludoviciana* Nutt.; *A. patens* var. *Wolfgangiana* (Bess.) C. Koch.; *Pulsatilla hirsutissima* Britt.; *P. Nuttalliana* (DC.) Bercht. & J. Presl]. PASQUE-FLOWER, WILD CROCUS, LION'S-BEARD, PRAIRIE-SMOKE, HARTSHORN PLANT. Resembling *A. patens,* but lvs. developing before fls., middle lf. segm. with petiolule, ultimate segms. less than ³⁄₁₆ in. wide. Alaska, s. to Wash., Utah, Nebr.

obtusiloba D. Don. Sts. 6–12 in., branched, usually hairy; lvs. in a rosette, with hairy petioles, palmately 3-parted, cordate, segms. broadly wedge-shaped, deeply crenate, involucral lvs. 3-cleft; fls. blue to violet or cream, silky on exterior, 1¼–1½ in. across, sepals 5–6, obtuse. Himalayas.

occidentalis S. Wats. [*Pulsatilla occidentalis* (S. Wats.) Freyn]. Stout, with thick, vertical root, sts. 1 to several, to 2 ft., villous when young; basal lvs. few, 2–3 in. wide, silky-villous, ternate, segms. 2-pinnately dissected, the divisions linear, involucral lvs. similar, sessile; fls. solitary, sepals 5–8, white or purplish, villous on exterior, 1 in. long. B.C. to Mont. and Calif.

oregana: *A. quinquefolia* var.

palmata L. Tuberous, to 12 in., basal lvs. cordate, 3–5-lobed, lateral lobes often bifid, involucral lvs. 3, sessile, united at base; fls. 1–2, golden-yellow, about 1 in. across, sepals 10–15, silky on exterior. W. Medit. region. Cv. 'Alba'. Lvs. violet underneath; fls. white. Cv. 'Flore Pleno'. Fls. double.

parviflora Michx. Rhizome slender, sts. to 1 ft.; basal lvs. deeply 3-parted, segms. cuneate-obovate; fls. solitary, sepals 5–6, white or bluish, ⁵⁄₁₆–½ in. N. N. Amer.

patens L. [*Pulsatilla patens* (L.) Mill.]. PASQUE FLOWER. To 8 in., taller in fr.; basal lvs. developing after fls., palmately 3-cleft, middle segm. sessile, ultimate lobes lanceolate, ¼ in. wide, involucral lvs. divided into many linear lobes; fls. solitary, 2–3 in. across, sepals blue-violet, hairy on exterior, styles 2 in. long in fr. N. Eur. Has been used medicinally. Var. **Wolfgangiana**: *A. Nuttalliana*.

Pavoniana Boiss. Similar to *A. baldensis*, but rootstock clothed with remains of old lvs., sts. to 12 in., only sparsely pubescent; fls. white, sepals 7–8, obtuse; achenes in a globose head. Spain. Probably not in cult.; material offered under this name is probably *A. pavonina*.

pavonina Lam. Rhizome tuberous, sts. 8–12 in.; lvs. 3–5-parted, involucral lvs. entire or slightly divided; fls. solitary, 1–2 in. across, sepals 20 or more, scarlet, with pale claws. S. Eur. May be cult. under the name *A. Pavoniana*. Var. **ocellata** (Moggr.) Bowles & Stearn. Sepals 7–12, scarlet with yellowish claws. Greece; naturalized on the Riviera. Var. **purpureoviolacea** (Boiss.) Halácsy. Sepals violet or rose, whitish at base.

pensylvanica: *A. canadensis*.

Piperi Britt. To 1 ft., sparingly appressed-silky; basal lvs. ternate, middle lobe rhombic, coarsely toothed, 1–3 in. long, lateral lobe broader, 2-cleft; sepals white, glabrous, ⅝ in. long. Wash. to Idaho.

polyanthes D. Don. Rhizome mostly woody, sts. 12–20 in.; basal lvs. long-petioled, 5–7-lobed, lobes broad, silvery-hairy, especially on lower surface, involucral lvs. 3-lobed, coarsely toothed; fls. white, 1–2 in. across, sepals 4–7, broad. Himalayas.

pratensis L. [*Pulsatilla pratensis* (L.) Mill.]. To 1 ft., silky; basal and involucral lvs. pinnatifid, segms. linear; fls. solitary, nodding, campanulate, light to dark violet, silky on exterior, sepals 6, reflexed at apex. N. Eur., Siberia. Has been used medicinally. Subsp. **nigricans** (Störck) A. Kern. [*A. nigricans* (Störck) Fritsch]. Sepals black-violet, 1 in. long, curved outward. Cent. Eur.

Pulsatilla L. [*Pulsatilla amoena* Jord.; *P. vulgaris* Mill.]. PASQUE-FLOWER. Soft-hairy, sts. ½ ft. in fl., becoming 1¼ ft. in fr.; basal lvs. developing after fls., 4–6 in. long, 3-pinnate, segms. linear, involucral lvs. 1 in. long, the lobes linear; fls. solitary, erect, blue to red-purple, to 2½ in. across, sepals 6. Eur. Has been used medicinally. Cvs. include: 'Alba', fls. white; 'Albicyanea', fls. bluish-white; 'Mallenderi', fls. deep purple; 'Rubra', fls. reddish-purple. Subsp. **grandis** (Wender.) Gürke. Lf. segms. broader, ⅛–¼ in., glabrous in age. Austria to Ukraine.

quinquefolia L. St. solitary, glabrous, to 1 ft.; single basal lf. with lfts. 3, seeming 5, rhombic, coarsely and unevenly toothed, involucral lvs. similar but smaller; fls. solitary, sepals 4–9, commonly 5, whitish, tinged pink or crimson, ¼–1 in. long, stamens 30 or more, in 2 or more series. Que. to N.C., Ohio, Ky. Var. **oregana** (A. Gray) B. L. Robinson [*A. oregana* A. Gray]. Sepals usually blue or pink, ⅜–¾ in. long. Wash. to n. Calif. Var. **Lyallii** (Britt.) B. L. Robinson [*A. Lyallii* Britt.]. Stamens 10–20, in a single series. B.C. to Ore.

ranunculoides L. Rhizome brown, somewhat tuberous, sts. 4–8 in.; basal lvs. long-petioled, 3-parted, segms. 2–3-cleft, involucral lvs. nearly sessile, palmately many-parted; fls. 1–2, golden-yellow, to 1 in. across. Eur., Caucasus, Siberia. Cv. 'Flore Pleno'. Fls. partly double. Cv. 'Superba'. Lvs. bronze-colored; fls. deep yellow.

reflexa Steph. Rhizome slender, horizontal, sts. to 9 in.; related to *A. nemorosa*, but sepals 5–6, greenish-white, curving back to peduncle. E. Asia.

Regeliana Maxim. [*Pulsatilla Regeliana* (Maxim.) Pavlov]. Basal lvs. broadly ovate, 3-pinnatisect, segms. usually sessile, lanceolate to linear, involucral lvs. laciniate; fls. blue-violet to rose, 1–1½ in. across, reflexed at apex. Mongolia.

riparia Fern. THIMBLEWEED. Resembling *A. cylindrica*, sts. 1–4, more or less villous, 1–10-fld.; basal lvs. 3–5-parted, segms. deeply cleft, involucral lvs. with mostly 3 divisions; fls. with central peduncle naked, the others with involucels, sepals 4–6, white, rarely red, ½–¾ in. long; achenes in a roundish cluster. Nfld. to B.C., s. to N.Y., Ill., Minn.

rivularis Buch.-Ham. ex DC. Rhizome short, woody, sts. coarse, 2–3 ft., silky-pubescent; lvs. long-petioled, 3-parted, pubescent, segms. cleft and toothed; cymes many-fld., pedicels slender; fls. white, 1½ in. across, sepals 5–8; achenes glabrous. India, Ceylon.

rupicola Camb. Like *A. sylvestris*, but with involucral lvs. sessile; fls. solitary, white, tinged purple on exterior, silky, sepals 1–1½ in. long. Himalayas, w. China.

serratifolia: a listed name of no botanical standing.

sibirica L. Lvs. roundish, ternate, lfts. palmately incised, petioles hairy, involucral lvs. 3, lobed, segms. lanceolate; fls. solitary, sepals roundish, yellow. Siberia.

slavica G. Reuss [*Pulsatilla slavica* G. Reuss]. Like *A. Pulsatilla,* but with involucral lvs. longer, to 1½ in., lf. segms. broader, to ½ in., and stamens fewer than 50. Carpathian Mts.

stellata: *A. hortensis.*

sulphurea: *A. alpina* subsp.

sylvestris L. Stoloniferous, to 1½ ft.; lvs. 2–6, petioled, pubescent, 5-parted, unequally dentate, involucral lvs. 3-parted, petioled; fls. 1–2, fragrant, often nodding, white, 1½–3 in. across, pubescent on exterior. Eur., Siberia. Cv. 'Flore Pleno'. Fls. double. Cv. 'Grandiflora'. Fls. large, white.

tetrasepala Royle. To 5 ft.; lvs. 3-parted, segms. 3-cleft and toothed, involucral lvs. 4, cymes with 5 brs., each bearing 3–5 white fls.; sepals 4. W. Himalayas.

thalictroides: *Anemonella thalictroides.*

tomentosa (Maxim.) P'ei. Sts. 12–20 in., densely woolly; lvs. 3-parted, large-toothed, densely woolly underneath; fls. in open cymes, bright pink, 2–3 in. across, sepals 5–6. Himalayas.

trifolia L. Sts. 8–10 in.; basal lvs. long-petioled, 3-parted or none, involucral lvs. 3, trilobed, toothed; fls. mostly solitary, white, 1–2 in. across, sepals usually 6, ovate. S. Eur.

tuberosa Rydb. Rhizome tuberous, sts. to 1 ft.; basal lvs. usually solitary, petioled, with 3 lfts., lfts. ovate, dentate, 1–2 in. long, involucral lvs. 3, simple, to 3 in. long, fls. solitary, sepals rose, linear-oblong, ½ in. long. New Mex. and Utah to e. Calif.

vernalis L. [*Pulsatilla vernalis* (L.) Mill.]. Sts. 2–6 in., with soft bronzy hairs; basal lvs. pinnate, lfts. 3–5, lobed, evergreen, 1–2 in. long, involucral lvs. with linear segms.; buds nodding, fls. erect, sepals 6, 1 in. long, white inside, violet in age. Eur.

verticillata: a listed name of no botanical standing.

virginiana L. THIMBLEWEED. Loosely villous, 1–1½ ft.; basal lvs. several, long-petioled, broadly rounded, deeply 3–5-parted, then toothed or incised, involucral lvs. similar, 3; fls. 1–3, white or greenish-white, to 1½ in. across. Nov. Sc. to S.C., w. to Kans.

vitifolia Buch.-Ham. ex DC. Sts. 1–3 ft.; lvs. large, 3–7-lobed; fls. in open cymes, white, 2–3 in. across, sepals 5, hairy on exterior. Nepal. Cv. 'Robustissima'. To 2½ ft.; fls. pale pink.

zephyra A. Nels. Doubtfully distinct from *A. narcissiflora;* lvs. less lobed; fls. usually solitary, lemon-yellow, ¾–1¼ in. across. Rocky Mts.

ANEMONELLA Spach. *Ranunculaceae.* One sp., a per herb of e. N. Amer., with tuberous roots and basal lvs., flowering in spring.

Grown in the rock garden and wild garden; propagated largely by division.

thalictroides (L.) Spach [*Anemone thalictroides* L.; *Thalictrum anemonoides* Michx.]. RUE ANEMONE. To 9 in., glabrous, delicate; lvs. 2–3-ternate, segms. ovate to oblong, ½–1 in. long, 3-toothed apically; umbel few-fld., subtended by 2–3 sessile, compound involucral lvs.; sepals white to pale pink-purple, ½ in. long, petals none; achenes ribbed. Tuberous roots are edible. Cv. 'Rosea'. Fls. reddish.

ANEMONOPSIS Siebold & Zucc. *Ranunculaceae.* One sp., a per. herb with underground rhizome, native to Japan.

Grown as a border plant; propagated by seeds and by division.

macrophylla Siebold & Zucc. FALSE ANEMONE. Sts. to 3 ft., simple; lvs. very long-petioled, to 10 in. across, triangular in outline, ternately compound, lfts. 2–4 in. long, incised; fls. in open racemes, nodding, rose to pale violet, 1½ in. across, sepals petaloid, staminodes many, petaloid. Late summer.

ANEMOPAEGMA Mart. ex Meissn. *Bignoniaceae.* About 40 spp. of climbing shrubs, native to trop. Amer., chiefly Brazil; lvs. opp., with 3 lfts., or with 2 lfts. and a terminal tendril; fls. creamy-white or pale yellow, in axillary racemes, calyx campanulate, entire, glandular, corolla funnelform, stamens 4; fr. a short caps.

Grown under glass or in the open in warm regions for the showy flowers.

Chamberlaynii (Sims) Bur. & K. Schum. [*Bignonia Chamberlaynii* Sims]. Lvs. with a terminal tendril, lfts. 2, oblong or ovate; fls. pale yellow, striped in throat with purple or white, to 3 in. long; fr. ellipsoid, to 6 in. long. Brazil.

ANEMOPSIS Hook. *Saururaceae.* One sp., a per. herb with thick, aromatic rootstocks, native to wet places of w. N. Amer.; lvs. mostly basal, entire; infl. on scapelike stalk, a dense terminal spike subtended by 6–8 involucral bracts; fls. small, each subtended by a bract, perianth none, stamens 6(–8), carpels 3, united, ovary 1-celled, sunken in rachis, stigmas 3; fr. dry, dehiscent.

Native in alkaline soils; propagated by division and seeds.

californica Hook. YERBA MANSA. To 2 ft. or more, forming colonies; basal lvs. elliptic-oblong, to 7 in. long, petioles long, sheathing at base, st. lf. broad, clasping, with 1–3 smaller lvs. in its axil; spike to 1½ in. long, involucral bracts white, to 1 in. long, each fl. subtended by small white bract. Calif. and Nev., s. to Baja Calif. and Tex. Rhizome has medicinal properties.

ANETHUM L. *Umbelliferae.* Two spp. of ann. or bien. herbs, native to the Old World, with strong odor; lvs. 3–4-pinnately divided into linear segms.; fls. small, yellow, in umbels, involucre and involucels usually lacking; fr. flattened.

One species grown for the leaves and seeds, which are used for flavoring. Easily grown from seeds, which should be sown in a sunny open place.

graveolens L. [*Peucedanum graveolens* (L.) C. B. Clarke]. DILL. To 3 ft.; lvs. very finely cut into threadlike divisions. Sw. Asia; naturalized in Eur. and N. Amer.

ANGELICA L. [*Archangelica* Hoffm.]. *Umbelliferae.* About 50 spp. of per. herbs, native to N. Hemisphere and New Zeal.; lvs. compound; fls. small, white or greenish, in terminal compound umbels with or without involucre or involucels; fr. compressed, usually winged.

Sometimes planted in borders for bold effects. Propagated by seeds and sometimes by division.

acutiloba (Siebold & Zucc.) Kitag. [*Ligusticum acutilobum* Siebold & Zucc.]. St. slender, to 4 ft.; lf. sheaths auriculate at apex, blades thin, more than 1 ft. long, ternately decompound, long-petioled, lfts. to 3 in. long, lanceolate, toothed; bracts of involucre few, bractlets of involucels many, umbels about 30-fld.; fr. ⅛ in. long. Japan.

Archangelica L. [*A. officinalis* Moench; *Archangelica officinalis* (Moench) Hoffm.]. ANGELICA, ARCHANGEL, WILD PARSNIP. Stout bien. or per., to 6 ft.; lvs. biternate, divisions pinnate, lfts. serrate, often 3-parted; fls. greenish. Low ground, Eur., Asia. The tender sts. and petioles are often candied, and the lvs. cooked as a vegetable.

atropurpurea L. GREAT A., ALEXANDERS, MASTERWORT. To 6 ft., st. dark purple; lvs. biternate to triternate, divisions pinnate, lfts. ovate, serrate; fls. white, in umbels to 10 in. across. Swamps, Nfld. to Del. and Minn. Sometimes grown for medicinal purposes.

Curtisii: *A. triquinata.*

Florenti: *A. Maximowiczii.*

Maximowiczii (F. Schmidt) Benth. [*A. Florenti* Franch. & Sav. ex Maxim.]. To 1 ft., glabrous; lvs. 2-pinnate, lfts. elongate, linear-lanceolate, petiole short or absent, upper lf. sheaths inflated; bracts of involucre few, bractlets of involucels many, about as long as fls. Japan.

officinalis: *A. Archangelica.*

Pancicii: *A. sylvestris.*

polyclada: *A. pubescens.*

pubescens Maxim. [*A. polyclada* Franch.]. To 10 ft.; lower lvs. 3-pinnately divided, lfts. ovate, serrate, acuminate, often 3-parted, upper lvs. reduced to inflated, hooded petioles; umbels 30–60-rayed, without involucre or involucels; fls. white, petals unequal; fr. flattened, winged. Japan.

triquinata Michx. [*A. Curtisii* Buckl.]. To 6 ft.; lvs. biternate, the divisions pinnate, lfts. serrate, upper lvs. often reduced to inflated petioles; umbels to 6 in. across, involucre lacking, involucels of linear bractlets; fls. white. Woods, Penn. to N.C.

sylvestris L. [*A. Pancicii* Vandas]. To 4½ ft.; lower lvs. triternate, with lfts. ovate-elliptic, acutely toothed, lower lfts. stalked, terminal lft. 2–3-lobed, upper lvs. biternate, with lfts. 2-pinnately divided; fls. small, white to pink. Bulgaria.

ANGELONIA Humb. & Bonpl. *Scrophulariaceae.* Thirty spp. of per. herbs or subshrubs, native to trop. Amer., mostly Brazil; lvs. opp., or the upper alt.; fls. blue to purple, solitary in axils or in terminal racemes, corolla 2-lipped, spurless, tube very short or seemingly none; fr. a caps.

Propagated easily from seeds or softwood cuttings. In the North usually grown under glass or set out as bedding plants; in areas having only a few degrees of frost, grown out of doors.

angustifolia Benth. Glabrous per., 1–1½ ft.; lvs. narrowly lanceolate, mostly 1½–3 in. long, acuminate, sharply fine-serrate; racemes long; fls. violet or purple, lower corolla lobes obovate. Mex. and W. Indies. Cv. 'Alba'. Fls. white.

grandiflora: *A. salicariifolia* cv.

salicariifolia Humb. & Bonpl. Sticky-pubescent per., 1½–2½ ft.; lvs. lanceolate to ovate-lanceolate, 1–3 in. long, acuminate to acute, remotely serrulate; racemes often branched, ¾ in. across; fls. bluish-purple, lower corolla lobes oblong. N. S. Amer. and W. Indies. Cv. 'Grandiflora' [*A. grandiflora* Hort.]. Said to have fls. 1 in. across.

ANGIOPTERIS Hoffm. TURNIP FERN. *Marattiaceae*. Perhaps 100 spp. of large, terrestrial woodland ferns, native to warmer parts of s. Japan to s. Polynesia and Madagascar; sts. short, thick, nearly globose; lvs. 2-pinnate, jointed, veins separate; sori elongate, near the margin, in double rows along the veins, sporangia separate, not fused in synangia. A complex group sometimes divided by botanists into many spp., but more frequently considered as a single but variable sp.

Grown in tropical greenhouses and also sometimes in greenhouse collections. Propagated by spores. For culture see *Ferns*.

evecta (G. Forst.) Hoffm. St. or root crown 2 ft. thick; lvs. ovate, 3–9 ft. long, pinnae to 1 ft. long, entire or toothed. S. Japan to Australia and Madagascar.

pruinosa Kunze. Probably a pruinose-nigrescent form of *A. evecta*. Java.

ANGIOSPERM (Angiospermae, one of the two main divisions of the seed plants). Plants producing flowers and reproducing by seeds enclosed within a carpel or female part of the flower are called angiosperms in contrast to the gymnosperms, which lack flowers and carpels. Most of the plants treated in *Hortus Third* belong to one of the two groups into which the angiosperms are divided. See *Dicotyledon* and *Monocotyledon*.

ANGOPHORA Cav. GUM MYRTLE. *Myrtaceae*. About 8 spp. of evergreen trees or shrubs, native to e. Australia; lvs. opp., entire, pinnately veined, leathery; fls. few to many in terminal panicles, fl. tube basally united to inferior ovary, calyx teeth and petals 5, small, stamens many, separate, showy; fr. an apically dehiscent, more or less ribbed caps., with persistent calyx teeth. Allied to and similar in appearance to *Eucalyptus*, but having petals separate.

Bakeri C. Hall. Small tree, to 30 ft., bark fibrous, rough, persistent; lvs. narrowly lanceolate, sickle-shaped, to 3 in. long, sessile or nearly so; fls. white, in short terminal panicles; fr. to ⅜ in. long. New S. Wales. Distinguished by its narrow lvs. and small fls. and frs.

cordifolia Cav. Shrub or small tree, to 15 ft., branchlets with stiff reddish hairs, bark rough and rather loose; lvs. ovate to oblong, to 4 in. long, cordate at base, sessile; fls. white, to 1½ in. across, in terminal corymbs; fr. to ¾ in. long. New S. Wales.

costata (Gaertn.) Britten [*A. lanceolata* Cav.]. Tall tree, to 80 ft., bark reddish, smooth, deciduous; lvs. lanceolate, to 5 in. long, short-petioled; fls. white, to 1 in. across, few to many in short panicles; fr. about ½ in. long, somewhat woody. Queensland and New S. Wales.

intermedia DC. Tree, to 40 ft. or more, bark fibrous, rough, persistent; lvs. oblong to lanceolate, to 5 in. long, short-petioled; fls. white, about ½ in. across, few to many in short panicles; fr. to ½ in. long, somewhat thin-walled. Queensland and New S. Wales.

lanceolata: *A. costata*.

ANGRAECUM Thouars [*Aerangis* Rchb. f.]. *Orchidaceae*. About 250 spp. of epiphytes, native to trop. Afr., Madagascar, Ceylon, Philippine Is.; sts. more or less elongate, densely leafy; lvs. very thick; fls. usually in racemes, sepals and petals similar, lip with lateral lobes small or lacking, midlobe entire, spur long, slender, united to the footless column, pollinia with undivided stalks. For structure of fl. see *Orchidaceae*.

Warm greenhouse; for culture see *Orchids*.

Arnoldianum: *A. Eichleranum*.

articulatum Rchb. f. [*A. descendens* Rchb. f.]. Sts. short; lvs. 3–5, long; racemes up to 15 in. long, many-fld.; fls. pure white with orange-brown pedicels, 1½ in. across, spur 3–4 in. long. Early spring. Madagascar.

citratum Thouars. Sts. short; lvs. few, blunt or retuse; racemes pendulous, up to 20 in. long, densely fld.; sepals and petals broadly rounded, yellow or straw-colored, to 1–2 in. long, spur slender, curved. Winter, spring. Madagascar.

descendens: *A. articulatum*.

distichum: *Mystacidium distichum*.

eburneum: *A. superbum*.

Eichleranum Kränzl. [*A. Arnoldianum* De Wild.]. Sts. pendulous, to 3 ft. long; lvs. to 5 in. long and 2 in. wide; fls. about 3 in. across, 1–3 together, on peduncles about as long as lvs., sepals and petals yellow-green, lip white, greenish-yellow near base, spur about 2 in. long. Early summer–early autumn. W. Trop. Afr.

Ellisii Rchb. f. Sts. heavy, to 10 in. high; lvs. leathery, up to 8 in. long; racemes arching, to 25 in. long, many-fld.; fls. white, 2½ in. across, sepals and petals similar, elliptic-oblong, lip somewhat broader than sepals, spur 5–7 in. long, slender. Early spring. Madagascar.

falcatum: *Neofinetia falcata*.

gracilipes Rolfe. Lvs. strap-shaped, to nearly 8 in. long, retuse; peduncles 1-fld., axillary, to nearly 8 in. long; fls. showy, white, to nearly 3 in. across, sepals and petals lanceolate, spreading, spur slender, about 2½ in. long. Madagascar.

infundibulare Lindl. Climbing, to 2 ft.; lvs. leathery, to 5 in. long, 1¼ in. wide; peduncles 1-fld.; fls. large, sepals and petals linear, reflexed, to 3 in. long, pale yellow, lip broadly ovate, white, green at base, 2½ in. long, prolonged basally into a reflexed spur, 4–5 in. long. Uganda.

Leonis: *Macroplectrum Leonis*.

modestum Hook. f. [*A. Sanderanum* Rchb. f.; *Aerangis modesta* (Hook. f.) Schlechter]. Lvs. to 6 in. long; racemes pendulous; fls. snow-white, about 1¼ in. across, spur to 3 in. long. Spring. Madagascar.

mystacidii Rchb. f. [*Aerangis mystacidii* (Rchb. f.) Schlechter]. Small epiphyte, sts. short; lvs. few; racemes arching, few-fld.; fls. white, about 1 in. across, sepals and petals similar, oblong-lanceolate, lip broadly ovate, spur slender, 2½ in. long. Natal (S. Afr.).

Sanderanum: *A. modestum*.

Scottianum Rchb. f. Sts. elongate, pendulous, to 20 in. long; lvs. cylindrical, to nearly 5 in. long; fls. 1–3 on peduncles about as long as lvs., 2 in. across, pale yellowish changing to white, spur pale reddish-brown, to 5 in. long. Late spring–late summer. Comoro Is. (E. Afr.).

sesquipedale: *Macroplectrum sesquipedale*.

superbum Thouars [*A. eburneum* Lindl.]. Sts. to 4 ft. high; lvs. to 2 ft. long and 2 in. wide; racemes 8–15-fld., longer than lvs.; fls. to 4 in. across, sepals and petals green, lip ivory-white, spur green, about 3 in. long. Early winter-early spring. Madagascar. Var. **virens** Hort. Veitch [*A. virens* Lindl.]. Fls. smaller than in typical var., center of lip greenish.

Veitchii: × *Macrangraecum Veitchii*.

virens: *A. superbum* var.

ANGULOA Ruiz & Pav. CRADLE ORCHID. *Orchidaceae*. About 250 spp. of terrestrial herbs, native to trop. S. Amer.; pseudobulbs 2–3-lvd.; lvs. plicate; fls. large, solitary, on long, erect scapes, sepals and petals fleshy, connivent, almost concealing the lip, lip smaller, 3-lobed, movably attached to column foot. For structure of fl. see *Orchidaceae*.

Cool greenhouse; for culture see *Orchids*.

Clowesii Lindl. Pseudobulbs to 6 in. long; lvs. to 2 ft. long; scapes to 1 ft. long; fls. yellow, lip white. Late spring. Colombia. Var. **eburnea:** *A. uniflora*.

eburnea: *A. uniflora*.

Ruckeri Lindl. Somewhat smaller than *A. Clowesii*; scapes to 8 in. long; fls. yellow-green, spotted with maroon inside. Late spring. Colombia. Var. **albiflora** Hort. Veitch. Fls. white. Var. **sanguinea** Lindl. Sepals and petals blood-red inside.

superba: *Acineta superba*.

uniflora Ruiz & Pav. [*A. Clowesii* var. *eburnea* (B. S. Williams) Hort. Veitch.; *A. eburnea* B. S. Williams]. Pseudobulbs to 7 in. long; lvs. 2–3, thin, 1–2 ft. long; scapes 8 in. long; fls. more open than in *A. Clowesii*, ivory-white, lip spotted with pink. Late spring. Peru.

ANIGOZANTHOS Labill. KANGAROO-PAW. *Haemodoraceae*. About 10 spp. of per. herbs with thick rootstocks, native to sw. Australia; lvs. linear or sword-shaped, basal; fls. red, purple, green, or yellowish, borne in 1-sided woolly racemes, spikes, or rarely panicles, perianth tube very long, split deeply on lower side, stamens 6, ovary inferior; fr. a caps.

Grown in the greenhouse or outdoors (in Zone 10) especially in southern Calif., preferably in a mixture of peat, loam, and sand, well-watered except during the winter rest period. Propagated by division of roots.

coccineus: *A. flavidus.*

flavidus Redouté [*A. coccineus* Paxt.]. To 4 ft., sts. nearly glabrous up to the branched infl.; fls. to 1¼ in. long, almost entirely red, anthers with appendages. Cv. '**Bicolor**' is listed.

humilis Lindl. To 1½ ft., sts. loosely woolly; lvs. to 6 in. long, ¼ in. wide; infl. a simple or forked spike; fls. nearly sessile, red to yellow, to 2 in. long, anthers shorter than filaments without appendages.

Manglesii D. Don. To 3 ft., sts. covered with red wool; lvs. broad; infl. simple or forked; fls. green, red at base, 3 in. long, perianth tube very narrow, woolly, anthers longer than filaments, without appendages.

viridis Endl. To 2 ft., sts. glabrous below the middle, woolly above; lvs. narrow; infl. simple or forked; fls. to 3 in. long, green or yellowish at base, anthers linear, as long as filaments, without appendages.

ANISACANTHUS Nees. *Acanthaceae.* Eight spp. of shrubs, in sw. U.S. and in Mex.; lvs. opp., entire; fls. usually red, in terminal spikes or axillary racemes, bracts mostly small, falling early, calyx 5-lobed, corolla funnelform, 2-lipped, 4-lobed, upper lip entire or nearly so, lower lip 3-lobed, stamens 2, anthers 2-celled, cells nearly equal, parallel; fr. a caps., slightly beaked, narrowed at base to form a stalk, seeds 2–4, each on a hooked stalk.

Thurberi (Torr.) A. Gray. CHUPAROSA, DESERT HONEYSUCKLE. To 4½ ft.; lvs. lanceolate, to 2 in. long; fls. in axillary racemes, calyx lobes ½–¾ in. long, linear; corolla to 1½ in. long. Ariz., New Mex., adjacent Mex. Perhaps not in cult.; material grown under this name in Calif. is *Justicia Leonardii.*

Wrightii (Torr.) A. Gray. To 4½ ft.; lvs. broadly lanceolate, to 2 in. long; fls. in terminal 1-sided spikes, calyx lobes ⅛ in. long, corolla 1½ in. long. Tex. and n. Mex.

ANISODONTEA K. Presl. *Malvaceae.* Nineteen spp. of suffruticose per. herbs or shrubs in S. Afr.; lvs. linear to transverse-elliptic in outline, mostly 3-, 5-, or 7-lobed or -parted, or rarely with 3 lfts.; fls. axillary, solitary or in few-fld. cymes, sometimes appearing corymbose or racemose, involucral bracts 3, separate or sometimes united basally or united to the calyx, petals white to deep magenta, often with a deeper spot basally at center, style brs. as many as the mericarps, stigmas terminal; fr. a schizocarp, mericarps 5–26, in a single whorl, each 1- or 2–6-seeded.

Propagated by seeds.

capensis (L.) Bates [*Malvastrum capense* (L.) A. Gray & Harv.; *M. virgatum* (J. Murr.) A. Gray & Harv.]. Suffruticose, to about 3 ft.; lvs. about 1 in. long, deeply 3- or 5-lobed, the lobes usually lobed; fls. 1–3 in the upper lf. axils, involucral bracts about ¼ in. long, slightly shorter than the calyx, petals about ⅝ in. long, spreading in a flat whorl, magenta, with darker veins and a basal spot; fr. about ¼ in. across, mericarps mostly 9–12, lateral walls fenestrate. Not in cult.; plants offered under the name *Malvastrum capense* are *A. scabrosa.*

scabrosa (L.) Bates [*Malvastrum scabrosum* (L.) Stapf]. Robust, soft-woody, often fragrant-viscid shrub, to 6 ft. or more; lvs. linear to orbicular, to about 3 in. long, mostly 3- or 5-lobed; fls. solitary, or few in loosely peduncled, axillary cymes, involucral bracts linear to ovate, to about ⅜ in. long, sometimes as long as the calyx, petals 5–8, to ¾ in. long, spreading in a flat whorl or forming a cuplike corolla, white to magenta, usually more deeply spotted basally at the center; fr. to ¼ in. across, mericarps 9–15, black, lateral walls striate.

ANISOSTICHUS: *BIGNONIA.*

ANNONA L. *Annonaceae.* About 100 spp. of trees and shrubs, native to trop. Amer.; lvs. alt., simple, entire; fls. solitary or clustered, 3-merous, bisexual, of odd dull colors, petals 6, in 2 series, mostly thick, fleshy, stamens and pistils many; fr. a large fleshy syncarp formed by the fusion of pistils and receptacle.

Grown for the edible dessert fruits. For culture see *Cherimoya.*

Cherimola Mill. CHERIMOYA, CHIRIMOYA, CUSTARD APPLE, CHERI-MALLA. To 25 ft., branchlets rusty-tomentose; lvs. ovate to ovate-lanceolate, to 10 in. long, velvety-pubescent beneath; fls. fragrant, yellow- to brown-tomentose outside, 1 in. long; fr. subglobose to conical, light green, to 5 in. long, smooth or with small tubercles. Andes

of Peru and Ecuador; widely cult. and naturalized in trop. highlands and in the subtropics. Zone 10. The best of the annonas.

diversifolia Saff. ILAMA, ANONA BLANCA. To 25 ft., branchlets glaucous, glabrous; lvs. elliptic to oblanceolate, to 5½ in. long; peduncles with leaflike bracts at base; fls. maroon, 1 in. long; fr. ellipsoid or globose, to 6 in. long, pale green or pink, with stout tubercles or sometimes smooth. Lowlands of Mex., and Cent. Amer. Very tender.

glabra L. POND APPLE. To 40 ft., evergreen, branchlets glabrous; lvs. ovate to oblong, to 7 in. long; fls. fragrant, yellowish, marked with red inside, 1 in. long or more; fr. ovoid, yellowish, smooth, to 4 in. long. Wet areas, s. Fla., trop. Amer., W. Afr. Fr. poor, insipid; grown as a grafting stock.

montana Macfady. MOUNTAIN SOURSOP, WILD S. Differs from *A. muricata* in having fr. slightly smaller, subglobose or broadly ovoid, with very small straight spinules, flesh yellowish, inedible. W. Indies.

muricata L. SOURSOP, GUANABANA, PRICKLY CUSTARD APPLE. To 20 ft., evergreen; lvs. obovate to elliptic, to 6 in. long; fls. solitary, yellow, 1 in. long or more; fr. ovoid, to 8 in. long, dark green, covered with long, curved, fleshy spinules, flesh white. Trop. Amer. Cult. widely in tropics. Very tender, warmest parts of Zone 10 in Fla. Used for sherberts and refreshing drinks.

paludosa Aubl. Shrub, to 5 ft., young branchlets densely rusty-tomentose; lvs. oblong to oblong-elliptic, to 8½ in. long, rusty-tomentose beneath; fls. axillary, 1–2 together, tawny-pubescent, petals wide, ovate, outer petals nearly 1 in. long; fr. ovoid, to 2 in. long, with short spinules. Fr. Guiana, and Pará, Brazil.

reticulata L. BULLOCK'S-HEART, CUSTARD APPLE. To 40 ft.; lvs. oblong-lanceolate to lanceolate, to 8 in. long; fls. axillary, yellowish, 1 in. long; fr. heart-shaped or ovoid, reddish-yellow or -brown, to 5 in. across, nearly smooth, the carpels outlined by slightly impressed lines. Trop. Amer. Widely cult. in lowland tropics. Zone 10. A poor fr.

senegalensis Pers. WILD CUSTARD APPLE. Sprawling, to 20 ft.; lvs. broadly elliptic, to 5 in. long, rounded at apex; fls. axillary, green turning yellow, softly pubescent outside; fr. globose, about 2 in. in diam., smooth, yellow, the outlines of carpels visible as lines. Cape Verde Is., e. to Gambia, n. Nigeria, Sudan.

squamosa L. SUGAR APPLE, CUSTARD A., SWEETSOP. To 20 ft., evergreen; lvs. oblong-lanceolate to lanceolate, to 4½ in. long; fls. greenish-yellow, to 1 in. long; fr. subglobose, cordate or conical, yellowish-green and glaucous, to 3½ in. across, tubercled, the carpels falling apart at maturity. Trop. Amer. Widely cult. in the lowland tropics and subtrop. Fla. Zone 10b. A dessert fr., the best of the trop. annonas.

ANNONACEAE. *Annona Cherimola:* **a,** flowering branch, × ⅙; **b,** flower, × 1; **c,** flower, vertical section, × 1½; **d,** flower, with sepals removed, × 2½; **e,** petal, × 5; **f,** anthers, two views, × 5; **g,** pistil, × 10; **h,** pistil, vertical section, × 10; **i,** syncarp, × ³⁄₁₀; **j,** seed, × ½.

ANNONACEAE Juss. ANNONA FAMILY. Dicot.; about 75 genera of mostly trop. trees and shrubs of wide distribution; lvs. alt., simple; fls. usually bisexual, sepals 3, petals 6, similar, in 2 series, stamens many, pistils few to many, separate; fr. a syncarp formed by union of pistils and receptacle, a berry or a caps. Grown as ornamentals, for their edible fr., and for use in perfumes. The cult. genera are: *Annona, Artabotrys,*

Asimina, Cananga, Cymbopetalum, Monodora, Polyalthia, Rollinia, and *Uvaria.*

ANNUALS. An annual is a plant that naturally completes its life cycle, from germination to seeding and death, within one year. Horticulturally the word frequently denotes a plant that blooms the first year from seed and is treated as an annual, whether or not it then completes its cycle and dies. Thus, the common bachelor button or cornflower *(Centaurea Cyanus)* is an annual, but four o'clock *(Mirabilis Jalapa)* is a tender perennial that blooms freely from seed the first year but, for horticultural purposes, is considered an annual. Similarly, the green or red pepper *(Capsicum annuum)* is grown as an annual because it is not hardy, but the plant is perennial in the tropics, where it is native.

Annuals are of simple cultural requirements as a rule. With few exceptions, they do best in full sun. In the northern states they can generally be grown with success if sown directly in the garden in well-prepared, sandy, warm soil when the weather becomes settled. In warm climates many of them are grown in the cool season. Late-blooming annuals, such as species of *Cosmos,* moonflower *(Ipomoea alba),* and the castor-bean *(Ricinus communis),* may be started indoors in pots or flats. Some kinds are classed as hardy, and can be sown before frosts have ceased; others are half-hardy, an intermediate, indefinite group that may be sown before the full warm weather comes; still others are tender and require the arrival of steady warmth before they can be sown outdoors, so that they are commonly started under glass.

Ordinarily the seeds of annuals are sown liberally. Many may not germinate, but even if they all come up, there is the advantage that the combined strength of the rising seedlings will break the crust on hard soils. In thinning the plants, only strong and promising ones are allowed to remain. Plants continue to bloom for a longer period if they are not allowed to produce seeds. The flowers should be picked, if possible, as soon as they begin to fade. Most annuals should be in good bloom at three months. Better effects are often obtained when the colors are in masses, especially if plants are grown in the bays of heavy shrub borders.

Wide choice is possible in the kinds of annuals, yet there are some groups considered to be standard or general-purpose plants, which are easily grown almost anywhere and are sure to give satisfaction. Other annuals are mostly of secondary value or adapted for particular purposes or uses.

General-purpose annuals: *Ageratum Houstonianum, Amaranthus tricolor, Antirrhinum majus, Calendula officinalis, Callistephus chinensis, Celosia cristata, Centaurea Cyanus, Chrysanthemum carinatum, Consolida ambigua, Coreopsis tinctoria, Cosmos bipinnatus, C. sulphureus, Delphinium grandiflorum, Dianthus chinensis, Eschscholzia californica, Heliotropium arborescens, Iberis amara, I. umbellata, Impatiens Balsamina, I. Wallerana, Ipomoea Nil, I. purpurea, I. tricolor, Lathyrus odoratus, Lobularia maritima, Matthiola incana* cv. 'Annua', *Papaver Rhoeas, Petunia* ×*hybrida, Phlox Drummondii, Portulaca grandiflora, Reseda odorata, Rudbeckia hirta* cv. 'Gloriosa Daisy', *Salpiglossis sinuata, Salvia azurea, S. farinacea, S. splendens, Scabiosa atropurpurea, Tagetes erecta, T. patula, Tropaeolum majus, Verbena* ×*hybrida, Zinnia elegans.* Some plants grown for their ornamental fruits belong with the annuals, as the gourds *(Cucurbita, Lagenaria)* and red pepper *(Capsicum).*

White-flowered annuals: *Ageratum Houstonianum, Ammobium alatum, Antirrhinum majus, Arctotis stoechadifolia, Argemone grandiflora, Brachycome iberidifolia, Callistephus chinensis, Centaurea americana, C. Cyanus, C. moschata, Chrysanthemum coronarium, C. segetum, Clarkia amoena, C. unguiculata, Consolida ambigua, Cosmos bipinnatus, Delphinium grandiflorum, Dianthus chinensis, Dimorphotheca pluvialis, Echinocystis lobata, Gomphrena globosa, Gypsophila elegans, Helichrysum bracteatum, Iberis amara, Impatiens Balsamina, I. Wallerana, Ipomoea alba, I. Nil, I. purpurea, I. tricolor, Lathyrus odoratus, Lavatera trimestris, Linaria maroccana, Lobelia Erinus, Lobu-*

laria maritima, Lupinus annual hybrids, *Lychnis Coeli-rosa, Malope trifida, Malcolmia maritima, Matthiola incana* cv. 'Annua', *Mirabilis Jalapa, Nemesia strumosa, Nicotiana alata, Nigella damascena, Papaver Rhoeas, Oenothera speciosa* (aging to pink), *Petunia* ×*hybrida, Phlox Drummondii, Portulaca grandiflora, Salvia farinacea, Scabiosa atropurpurea, Schizanthus pinnatus, Thunbergia alata, Verbena* ×*hybrida, Viola* ×*Wittrockiana, Zinnia elegans.*

Pink, rose-, and red-flowered annuals: *Abronia umbellata, Adonis aestivalis, A. annua, Amaranthus cruentus, A. tricolor* (red foliage), *Antirrhinum majus, Callistephus chinensis, Celosia cristata, Centaurea americana, C. Cyanus, C. moschata, Chrysanthemum carinatum, Clarkia amoena, C. unguiculata, Consolida ambigua, Coreopsis tinctoria, Cosmos bipinnatus, Dianthus chinensis, Emilia javanica, Eschscholzia californica, Gaillardia pulchella* var. *picta, Gomphrena globosa, Gypsophila elegans, Helichrysum bracteatum, Helipterum Manglesii, Iberis umbellata, Impatiens Balsamina, I. Wallerana, Ipomoea* ×*multifida, I. Nil, I. purpurea, I. Quamoclit, I. tricolor, Lathyrus odoratus, Lavatera trimestris, Linaria maroccana, Linum grandiflorum, Lupinus* annual hybrids, *Lychnis Coeli-rosa, Malcolmia maritima, Malope trifida, Matthiola incana* cv. 'Annua', *Mirabilis Jalapa, Nemesia strumosa, Nicotiana* ×*Sanderae, Oenothera speciosa, Papaver Rhoeas, Petunia* ×*hybrida, Phaseolus coccineus, Phlox Drummondii, Portulaca grandiflora, Salpiglossis sinuata, Salvia splendens, Schizanthus pinnatus, Tropaeolum majus, Verbena* ×*hybrida, Viola* ×*Wittrockiana, Zinnia elegans, Z. Haageana.*

Blue- lilac-, lavender-, and violet-flowered annuals: *Ageratum Houstonianum, Anagallis Monellii, Brachycome iberidifolia, Browallia americana, Callistephus chinensis, Centaurea Cyanus, Cobaea scandens, Consolida ambigua, Convolvulus tricolor, Delphinium grandiflorum, Echium Lycopsis, Gilia achilleifolia, G. capitata, G. tricolor, Heliotropium arborescens, Iberis umbellata, Ipomoea Nil, I. purpurea, I. tricolor, Lathyrus odoratus, Linaria maroccana, Lobelia Erinus, Lobularia maritima, Lupinus* annual hybrids, *Lychnis Coeli-rosa, Machaeranthera tanacetifolia, Malcolmia maritima, Matthiola incana* cv. 'Annua', *Nemesia strumosa, Nemophila maculata, N. Menziesii, Nierembergia hippomanica* var. *violacea, Nigella damascena, Nolana paradoxa, Petunia* ×*hybrida, Phacelia campanularia, P. minor, Phlox Drummondii, Salpiglossis sinuata, Salvia azurea, S. farinacea, S. patens, Scabiosa atropurpurea, Schizanthus pinnatus, Torenia Fournieri, Trachymene coerulea, Verbena* ×*hybrida, Viola* ×*Wittrockiana.*

Yellow- and orange-flowered annuals: *Baileya multiradiata, Calendula officinalis, Celosia cristata, Centaurea moschata, Chrysanthemum coronarium, C. segetum, Coreopsis tinctoria, Cosmos sulphureus, Dimorphotheca sinuata, Dyssodia tenuiloba, Emilia javanica, Erysimum Perofskianum, Eschscholzia californica, Gaillardia pulchella* var. *picta, Gamolepis Tagetes, Helianthus annuus, H. debilis* subsp. *cucumerifolius, Helichrysum bracteatum, Hunnemannia fumariifolia, Impatiens platypetala* subsp. *aurantiaca, Mirabilis Jalapa, Nemesia strumosa, Rudbeckia hirta* cv. 'Gloriosa Daisy', *Sanvitalia procumbens, Tagetes erecta, T. patula,* and their hybrids, *Tagetes tenuifolia, Thunbergia alata, Tithonia diversifolia, T. rotundifolia, Tropaeolum majus, T. peregrinum, Venidium fastuosum, Viola* ×*Wittrockiana, Xanthisma texanum, Zinnia angustifolia, Z. elegans, Z. Haageana.*

Annuals that continue to bloom after the first autumn frosts: *Abronia umbellata, Adonis aestivalis, A. annua, Antirrhinum majus, Argemone grandiflora, Calendula officinalis, Centaurea Cyanus, Chrysanthemum carinatum, C. coronarium, C. segetum, Convolvulus tricolor, Dianthus chinensis, Erysimum Perofskianum, Eschscholzia californica, Gaillardia pulchella* var. *picta, Iberis amara, I. umbellata, Lavatera trimestris, Lobularia maritima, Lychnis Coeli-rosa, Malcolmia maritima, Matthiola incana* cv. 'Annua', *Phlox Drummondii, Salvia farinacea, S. splendens, Verbena* ×*hybrida, Xanthisma texanum.*

Annuals adapted to edgings: *Abronia umbellata, Ageratum Houstonianum, Anagallis Monellii, Antirrhinum majus* (dwarf races), *Clarkia unguiculata, Coreopsis tinctoria* (dwarf races), *Dianthus chinensis, Eschscholzia californica, Gypsophila muralis, Iberis amara, Impatiens Wallerana* (dwarf races), *Lobelia Erinus, Lobularia maritima, Nemophila maculata, N. Menziesii, Nierembergia hippomanica* var. *violacea, Nigella damascena, Petunia ×hybrida* (dwarf races), *Phlox Drummondii* (dwarf races), *Portulaca grandiflora, Sanvitalia procumbens, Tagetes erecta* (dwarf races), *T. filifolia, T. insignis, T. patula, Tropaeolum majus* (dwarf races), *Verbena ×hybrida, Viola ×Wittrockiana, Zinnia elegans* (dwarf races).

Annuals climbing by means of tendrils or coiling petioles: *Cardiospermum Halicacabum, Momordica Balsamina, M. Charantia, Cobaea scandens, Cucurbita* species, *Eccremocarpus scaber, Echinocystis lobata, Lagenaria siceraria, Lathyrus odoratus, Tropaeolum majus, T. peregrinum.*

Annuals climbing by twining: *Dolichos Lablab, Humulus japonicus, H. Lupulus, Ipomoea alba, I. ×multifida, I. Nil, I. purpurea, I. Quamoclit, I. tricolor, Phaseolus coccineus, Thunbergia alata.*

ANODA Cav. *Malvaceae.* About 15 spp. of ann. or suffrutescent per. herbs of the New World, 1 sp. sparingly naturalized in the Old World; lvs. simple, often very variable even on the same plant, unlobed or palmately lobed, typically somewhat hastate basally; fls. solitary or in racemes or panicles, involucral bracts 0, petals 5, white, yellow, blue or violet, as long as or much longer than the calyx, stamens united in a tubular column, style brs. as many as the mericarps, stigmas terminal; fr. a discoid schizocarp, mericarps 5–20, each 1-seeded, unarmed or with a single, spreading or deflexed spine dorsally, the inner wall often separating from the outer wall and partly or completely enclosing the seed.

Grown under glass or in the open for summer and autumn bloom. Propagated by seeds.

acerifolia: *A. cristata.*

cristata (L.) Schlechtend. [*A. acerifolia* DC.; *A. Dilleniana* Cav.; *A. hastata* Cav.; *A. lavateroides* Medic.; *A. triangularis* (Willd.) DC.]. Glabrate to copiously hirsute, ann. or sometimes per. herb with erect or sprawling brs.; lvs. variable, unlobed to 3-, 5-, or 7-lobed, entire to coarsely serrate-dentate; fls. axillary, corolla ½–2 in. across, white, lavender, or purplish-blue; fr. ½–¾ in. in diam., mericarps 9–20, spines scarcely present to half as long as mericarp, inner wall white to black, reticulate and completely surrounding the seed to scarious, not reticulate, and covering only the upper portion of the seed. S. U.S., W. Indies to S. Amer.; naturalized elsewhere.

Dilleniana: *A. cristata.*

hastata: *A. cristata.*

lavateroides: *A. cristata.*

triangularis: *A. cristata.*

Wrightii A. Gray. Ann. to 2 ft.; herbage densely stellate-puberulent, often with a few simple hairs as well, sometimes viscid; lvs. ovate to oblong-ovate, scarcely lobed, subcordate to cordate; corolla about ¾ in. across, yellow-orange, often purple basally; mericarps 10–12, strongly reticulate on the back with black veins, hirsute. New Mex., Ariz., Mex. Plants offered as *A. Wrightii* are probably *A. cristata.*

ANOECTOCHILUS Blume. JEWEL ORCHID, KING-OF-THE-FOREST. *Orchidaceae.* About 25 spp. of terrestrial herbs with short rhizomes, native to trop. Asia, Australia, and Polynesia; sts. leafy; lvs. green or colored, often marked with another color along the reticulate veins; infl. a few-fld. raceme; fls. small, sepals and petals connivent, lip larger, variously fringed along margins, basally prolonged into a short spur. For structure of fl. see *Orchidaceae.*

Warm greenhouse; for culture see *Orchids.*

setaceus Blume. Sts. 6–8 in. high; lvs. dark brownish-green with yellow-green venation; bracts pink; fls. few to 6, about ½ in. long, sepals and petals greenish, lip white, 2-lobed at tip, spur 2-lobed, green. Early spring–autumn. Ceylon, Java, Borneo.

ANOGRA: *OENOTHERA.*

ANOMATHECA: *LAPEIROUSIA.* A. cruenta: *L. laxa.*

ANOPTERIS (Prantl) Diels. *Polypodiaceae.* One sp., a delicate fern, native to the Greater Antilles.

Sometimes grown under glass. For culture see *Ferns.*

hexagona (L.) C. Chr. [*Pteris heterophylla* L.]. Lvs. tufted, to 2 ft. long, 2–3-pinnate, somewhat dimorphic, fertile pinnules somewhat narrower than the sterile ones, the margins of sterile pinnules mostly sharply serrulate to serrate; sori continuous along each margin of pinnules, indusia slightly intramarginal, fixed to a vein and turned inward.

ANOPTERUS Labill. *Saxifragaceae.* Two spp. of tall evergreen shrubs or trees of Australia; lvs. alt., simple; fls. in terminal racemes; calyx tube short, united to base of ovary, calyx lobes, petals, and stamens 6–9; fr. an oblong-conical caps., seeds winged.

glandulosus Labill. TASMANIAN LAUREL. Tall shrub or tree, to 30 ft.; lvs. lanceolate-elliptic, to 7 in. long, rather thick and glossy, glabrous, narrowed to short, thick petioles; fls. white, to ¾ in. across. Tasmania.

Macleayanus F. J. Muell. Differs from *A. glandulosus* in being taller, to as much as 50 ft., and having lvs. longer, to 12 in. or more, of thinner texture. Queensland and New S. Wales.

ANOPYXIS Pierre ex Engl. *Rhizophoraceae.* One sp., a tree of trop. Afr.; lvs. in whorls of 3–4, or opp., leathery; infl. few-fld.; fls. bisexual, 5-merous, stamens 10, united into a tube, ovary sessile; fr. woody, indehsicent, seeds winged.

ealaensis: *A. klaineana.*

klaineana (Pierre) Engl. [*A. ealaensis* T. Sprague]. To 150 ft., crown dense and wide-spreading; lvs. oblong-oblanceolate, to 4 in. long; cymes short, axillary; calyx pubescent, petals yellow; fr. pubescent, narrowly ellipsoid, 1½ in. long. Sierre Leone to Cameroon and Dem. Rep. of Congo.

ANOTA Schlechter. *Orchidaceae.* Four or 5 spp. of epiphytes, native to Burma and Malay Arch.; sts. leafy; fls. in racemes, sepals and petals long-elliptic, lip entire, without auricles, contracted and lobed at the apex, spurred, with a pair of heavy raised veins. For structure of fl. see *Orchidaceae.*

For culture see *Orchids.*

densiflora (Lindl.) Schlechter [*Rhynchostylis densiflora* (Lindl.) L. O. Williams; *Saccolabium giganteum* Lindl.; *Vanda densiflora* Lindl.]. Sts. to 8 in. long; lvs. to 1 ft. long and 2 in. wide; racemes pendulous, dense, many-fld., to 16 in. long; fls. 1 in. across, sepals and petals white, spotted with violet-purple at base, lip violet-purple, white near base. Late autumn. Burma.

violacea (Lindl.) Schlechter [*Rhynchostylis violacea* (Lindl.) Rchb.f.; *Saccolabium violaceum* (Lindl.) Rchb.f.; *Vanda violacea* Lindl.]. Similar to *A. densiflora*, but racemes looser, sepals and petals white, spotted with violet-red, lip violet-red. Early winter–early spring. Philippine Is.

ANREDERA Juss. [*Boussingaultia* HBK]. *Basellaceae.* Five to 10 spp. of per. vines, native to trop. Amer.; lvs. alt., fleshy; fls. small, bisexual or unisexual, in axillary spikes or racemes, bractlets decussate, in 2 pairs, perianth segms. 5, united at base, stamens 5, ovary 1-celled; fr. globose, enclosed in perianth.

Grown as ornamentals out of doors in warm regions and under glass in cold regions, also root-hardy in the North. Propagated by seeds, division, and by planting the aerial tubers produced in the leaf axils.

baselloides (HBK) Baill. [*Boussingaultia baselloides* HBK]. Differs from *A. cordifolia* in having the styles undivided. Ecuador. Doubtfully in cult.; material offered under this name is probably *A. cordifolia.*

cordifolia (Ten.) Steenis [*Boussingaultia baselloides* Hook. and most other auth., not HBK; *B. gracilis* Miers; *B. gracilis* var. *pseudobaselloides* (Haum.) L. H. Bailey; *B. gracilis* forma *pseudobaselloides* Haum.]. MADEIRA VINE, MIGNONETTE VINE. Rapidly growing twiner, to 20 ft. or more, root tuberous; lvs. ovate or lanceolate, obtuse to long-acuminate, often with tubers in their axils; racemes 2–3 times as long as lvs.; fls. fragrant, perianth white, ⅛ in. long, style 3-cleft to base. Paraguay to s. Brazil and n. Argentina. Widely cult. in tropics.

ANSELLIA Lindl. *Orchidaceae.* Ten spp. of epiphytes, native to trop. Afr. and Natal; sts. canelike; lvs. 2-ranked, plicate; infl. terminal, many-fld.; fls. thin in texture, sepals and petals similar, lip 3-lobed, neither spurred nor saccate. For structure of fl. see *Orchidaceae*.

Warm greenhouse; for culture see *Orchids*.

africana Lindl. Sts. elongate; lvs. 4–7, linear, to 1 ft. long; panicles to 16 in. long; fls. yellowish, spotted with chocolate-brown, about 1 in. long, petals broader than sepals. Early winter–summer. Sierra Leone and Fernando Po (W. Afr.).

gigantea Rchb.f. [*A. nilotica* N. E. Br.; *Cymbidium Sandersonii* Harv.]. Similar to *A. africana*, but panicle to 20 in. long, sepals and petals similar in shape, 1½ in. long. Early winter–early summer. Natal (S. Afr.).

nilotica: *A. gigantea.*

ANTEGIBBAEUM Schwant. ex C. Web. *Aizoaceae*. One sp., a small, per., succulent herb in S. Afr., sts. branched from a root crown, brs. terminated by 1–4(–5) crowded pairs of lvs.; lvs. nearly equal or unequal, thick, flat on upper side, keeled on lower side; fls. large, terminal, subtended by 2 pairs of bracts, sepals 6, petals many, stamens white, staminodes lacking, disc ring-shaped; fr. a 6-celled caps.

Culture as for *Gibbaeum*. See also *Succulents*.

fissoides (Haw.) C. Web. [*Gibbaeum Nelii* Schwant.]. Lvs. gray-green or reddish, smooth or rugose, to 1¼ in. long, ⅜ in. wide, curved, angled and compressed toward the apex; fls. nearly sessile, to 2⅜ in. across, petals light violet-red. Cape Prov.

ANTENNARIA Gaertn. EVERLASTING, PUSSY-TOES, LA-DIES'-TOBACCO. *Compositae* (Inula Tribe). Variously estimated at 15–75 spp. of small, dioecious, white- or gray-woolly per. herbs, native in N. and S. Amer., and n. Eur. and Asia; sts. simple, erect; lvs. in basal rosettes and also alt. on sts.; fl. heads discoid, small, racemose to densely corymbose, sometimes solitary, involucral bracts imbricate, with white or colored scarious apex; fls. white, the female tubular, the male funnelform; pappus of capillary bristles, that in the male fls. have thickened tips. Male plants are usually smaller than female, and in some spp. are rare or even unknown, female plants often developing seeds parthenogenetically.

Sometimes grown for the dry flower heads or in rock gardens; adapted to poor soil. Propagated by seeds and division.

alpina (L.) Gaertn. Less than 5 in., with leafy stolons forming mats; rosette lvs. oblanceolate, to ¾ in. long, gray-tomentose beneath, becoming green and glabrous above, st. lvs. linear-oblong, the upper with a glabrous, flat appendage; heads usually 3, involucral bracts with brown or blackish-green apex. Circumboreal. Var. **media** (Greene) Jeps. [*A. media* Greene]. Lvs. tomentose on both sides. Mts., w. N. Amer., s. to Calif. and Colo.

aprica: *A. parvifolia.*

campestris: *A. neglecta.*

carpatica (Wahlenb.) R. Br. To 6 in., tufted, not stoloniferous, thinly tomentose; basal lvs. oblanceolate, to 3 in. long, 3-nerved, st. lvs. lanceolate; heads 2–6, involucral bracts with dark brown apex. Arctic regions and mts., Eur.

dioica (L.) Gaertn. To 10 in., stoloniferous; lvs. green and glabrate above, white-woolly beneath, 1-nerved, rosette lvs. spatulate, to 1 in. long, st. lvs. linear; heads 2–12, involucral bracts with white or rose apex. N. N. Amer., Eur., n. Asia. Var. **hyperborea** (D. Don) DC. [*A. hyperborea* D. Don]. Lvs. broader, white-tomentose on both surfaces. Scotland. Var. **rosea:** *A. rosea.* Cvs. 'Alba', 'Australis', 'Minima' are also listed. *A. tomentosa* Hort., which is esp. white-tomentose, probably should be treated as cv. 'Tomentosa' of this sp.

fallax: *A. plantaginifolia* var. *ambigens.*

gaspensis: *A. neglecta* var.

hyperborea: *A. dioica* var.

imbricata: *A. rosea.*

lanata (Hook.) Greene. To 8 in., compactly rhizomatous, gray-tomentose throughout; basal lvs. tufted, erect, oblanceolate, to 4 in. long, attenuate to a petiolelike base, usually 3-nerved, st. lvs. narrower, with expanded scarious apical appendage; heads several, involucral bracts brown or greenish-black, the innermost with white apex. Mts., B.C. to Ore., Wyo.

magellanica Schultz-Bip. To 2 in., many-stemmed, short-stoloniferous; lvs. spatulate to oblong-linear, tomentose; heads several in sessile corymbs, involucral bracts light brown. Straits of Magellan region (S. Amer.).

media: *A. alpina* var.

microphylla: see *A. rosea.*

monocephala DC. Dwarf, 1–6 in., short-stoloniferous, mat-forming; rosette lvs. narrowly spatulate, to ¾ in. long, thinly tomentose beneath, green and glabrous above, st. lvs. linear, with short, scarious, flat appendage; heads solitary, involucre ³⁄₁₆ in. long, involucral bracts with dark brown center and brownish or sordid-white apex. Mts., e. Siberia, Alaska, s. to B.C.

neglecta Greene [*A. campestris* Rydb.]. Three to 12 in., the slender stolons leafy at tip; rosette lvs. oblanceolate, tapering to the base, tomentose but soon becoming green and glabrate above, 1-nerved, to 2½ in. long, st. lvs. linear, the upper with a scarious appendage; heads several, involucral bracts green or purplish, with white apex. S. Canada to Calif. and Va. Var. **attenuata** (Fern.) Cronq. [*A. neodioica* Greene]. Stolons short, leafy; lvs. tardily glabrate, somewhat petioled, somewhat larger than in var. *gaspensis.* Range of the sp. Var. **gaspensis** (Fern.) Cronq. [*A. gaspensis* Fern.]. Stolons short, leafy; lvs. tardily glabrate, to ¾ in. long, ³⁄₁₆ in. wide. Nfld., Que., Me.

neodioica: *A. neglecta* var. *attenuata.*

nevadensis: a listed name of no botanical standing.

obovata: *A. plantaginifolia* var. *ambigens.*

oxyphylla: *A. rosea.*

parvifolia Nutt. [*A. aprica* Greene]. To 6 in., stoloniferous, densely tomentose; rosette lvs. spatulate or oblanceolate, to 1½ in. long, st. lvs. lanceolate to linear; heads several, involucre about ⁵⁄₁₆ in. long, involucral bracts with white, sometimes pink apex. Great Plains, w. to B.C., Wash., Ariz.

plantaginifolia (L.) Hook. To 15 in., stoloniferous; rosette lvs. elliptic to obovate, to 3 in. long, 3–5-nerved, tomentose but eventually glabrate above, petioled, st. lvs. lanceolate to linear, tomentose; heads several, involucral bracts pale green or sometimes purplish, with white apex. Que. to Minn., s. to Fla. and Tex. Var. **plantaginifolia.** The typical var.; female involucre ¼ in. long. Var. **ambigens** (Greene) Cronq. [*A. fallax* Greene; *A. obovata* E. E. Nels.]. Female involucre to ⁵⁄₁₆ in. long.

rosea Greene [*A. dioica* var. *rosea* Cockerell; *A. imbricata* E. E. Nels.; *A. microphylla* Rydb., not Gand.; *A. oxyphylla* Greene; *A. speciosa* E. E. Nels.]. To 15 in., stoloniferous, gray-tomentose throughout; rosette lvs. narrowly oblanceolate to spatulate, to 1 in. long, st. lvs. oblanceolate or linear; heads several, involucre about ¼ in. long, involucral bracts with white, pink, or rose apex. Alaska to Calif. and New Mex.

speciosa: *A. rosea.*

tomentosa: see *A. dioica.*

ANTHEMIS L. DOG FENNEL, CHAMOMILE. *Compositae* (Anthemis Tribe). About 100 spp. of mostly aromatic ann. or per. herbs, native to Eur., w. Asia, and N. Afr., but chiefly to the Medit. region and the Near East; sts. usually leafy; lvs. alt., incised-dentate to 1–3-pinnately dissected; fl. heads solitary, terminal on brs., radiate, or sometimes discoid, involucre saucer-shaped, the involucral bracts all nearly equal or imbricate in several rows, with usually dry margins, receptacle flat to conical, with more or less chaffy scales; disc fls. tubular, bisexual, yellow, ray fls. usually present, female or neutral, white or yellow; achenes cylindrical or ribbed, sometimes more or less compressed, pappus absent or a short crown.

A few kinds are useful in wild gardens and the border, blooming from midsummer to frost. Propagated by seeds and division.

Aizoon: *Achillea ageratifolia* var.

arabica: *Cladanthus arabicus.*

Barrelieri Ten. Per. herb, to about 5 in., gray-silky-tomentose, sts. decumbent; lower lvs. in a loose rosette, elliptic-oblong in outline, 2-pinnately dissected, st. lvs. pectinately parted; ray fls. white. Mts., Italy.

Biebersteiniana: *A. Marschalliana.*

Burnattii: a listed name of uncertain botanical standing.

carpatica Waldst. & Kit. ex Willd. Cushion-forming per., to 1 ft., sts. curving-ascending, sparsely hairy; lvs. ovate in outline, 1–2-pinnately dissected, lower lvs. petioled, upper lvs. sessile; heads to 1¾ in. across; ray fls. white. Mts., s. Eur.

cinerea Panč. Cushion-forming per., to 1 ft., sts. gray-pubescent or -tomentose; lvs. ovate in outline, 2-pinnately dissected, segms. oblong, obtuse; ray fls. white. Balkans.

Cota L. Erect ann., to 10 in., brs. spreading; lvs. oblong-ovate in outline, 2–3-pinnately dissected, sparsely hairy; heads to 1½ in. across; ray fls. white; achenes 10-ribbed. Balkans.

Cotula L. MAYWEED, STINKING C., COMMON D.F. Ill-smelling, erect ann., to 2 ft., sts. branching; lvs. ovate in outline, to 2¼ in. long, 2–3-pinnatifid, sparsely hairy; heads to 1 in. across, receptacle conical; ray fls. white, sterile; achenes with 10 tubercled ribs. Eur., n. and w. Asia; cosmopolitan weed.

Cupaniana Tod. ex Nym. Aromatic, cushion-forming per., to 3 ft. across and 8 in. high; lvs. 2-pinnately dissected, gray; ray fls. white. Italy.

frutescens: *Chrysanthemum frutescens.*

Haussknechtii Boiss. & Reut. Gray-green ann., to 10 in., sts. ascending to erect, with appressed hairs; lvs. ovate-oblong in outline, to 1 in. long, 3-pinnately dissected into filiform lobes; heads to 1 in. across, receptacle conical; ray fls. white. Syria, Iraq.

Kelwayi: *A. tinctoria* cv.

Marschalliana Willd. [*A. Biebersteiniana* (Adams) C. Koch; *A. Rudolphiana* Adams]. Much-branched per., to 1 ft., sts. ascending; lvs. oblong in outline, 2-pinnate, silvery-white-tomentose; heads to 1 in. across; ray fls. yellow. Caucasus.

montana L. Cushion-forming per., to 10 in., sts. curving-ascending; lvs. ovate in outline, 2–3-pinnatifid, pubescent; heads to 1½ in. across; ray fls. white; achenes slightly 4-angled. S. Eur.

nobilis: *Chamaemelum nobile.*

pallida: a listed name of no botanical standing, applied to a plant with lemon-yellow fls.

rigescens Willd. Erect, much-branched per., to about 2 ft.; lvs. broadly ovate-oblong in outline, to about 2 in. long, 2-pinnately dissected; heads to 2 in. across; ray fls. white. Balkans, Caucasus.

rosea Sibth. & Sm. Ann., sts. erect, rigid, pubescent; lvs. pinnately dissected, more or less lyrate; receptacle conical; ray fls. pink. Cyprus.

Rudolphiana: *A. Marschalliana.*

Sancti-Johannis Stoĭanov, Stefanov, & Turrill. Bushy per., to 3 ft., sts. erect, softly pubescent; lower lvs. oblong in outline, to 5½ in. long, reduced upward, 2–3-pinnately parted, the segms. with hard, white points; heads to 2 in. across, receptacle hemispherical, involucral bracts with black-brown margins; ray fls. deep orange; achenes 4-angled. Bulgaria.

tinctoria L. GOLDEN MARGUERITE. Bushy bien. or short-lived per., to 3 ft., sts. erect to ascending, angular, pubescent; lvs. to about 3 in. long, pinnately dissected, with pinnatifid segms., essentially glabrous above, white-woolly beneath; heads to 1½ in. across, receptacle hemispherical; ray fls. golden-yellow; achenes 4-angled. Cent. and s. Eur., w. Asia; sparingly naturalized in N. Amer. Fls. yield a yellow dye. Cv. **'Kelwayi'** [*A. Kelwayi* L. H. Bailey & N. Tayl.]. HARDY MARGUERITE. Foliage more finely cut; ray fls. bright yellow.

ANTHERICUM L. SPIDER PLANT. *Liliaceae.* Fifty or more spp. of per. herbs with fleshy or tuberous roots, native to Eur., trop. Amer., but chiefly to Afr.; rhizome short or absent; lvs. linear, basal; fls. white, in terminal racemes on slender scapes; perianth rotate, segms. separate, stamens 6; fr. a 3-celled caps., not sharply angled, seeds globose and angled.

Grown as border plants with protection, or in cool greenhouses in pots or benches. Of easy cultivation; propagated by stolons, divisions, and by seeds when available.

Bichetii: *Chlorophytum Bichetii.*

comosum: *Chlorophytum comosum.*

Liliago L. ST. BERNARD'S LILY. To 3 ft.; lvs. to 1 ft. long; scape unbranched; fls. about 1 in. across, ovary green. S. Eur.

Liliastrum: *Paradisea Liliastrum.*

Mandaianum: *Chlorophytum comosum* cv.

plumosum: *Trichopetalum plumosum.*

ramosum L. To 2 ft.; lvs. to 1 ft. long; scape branched; fls. about 1 in. across, ovary yellow. W. and s. Eur.

Renari: a listed name of no botanical standing.

ANTHOCEPHALUS A. Rich. *Rubiaceae.* About 3 spp. of trees, native to se. Asia; lvs. opp., petioled, stipules lanceolate, early-deciduous; fls. in terminal, solitary heads, calyx lobes of adjacent fls. confluent, corolla funnelform, tube long, lobes 5, stamens 5, borne at throat of corolla, filaments short; frs. united, embedded in fleshy receptacle.

About 3 species in Indomalayan region.

Cadamba (Roxb.) Miq. [*A. morindifolia* Korth.]. KADAM TREE. Large, deciduous tree; lvs. ovate, to 9 in. long, glabrous above, pubescent beneath, leathery, glossy; fl. heads to 2 in. across; fls. yellow to orange, scented at night; fr. fleshy, as large as an orange. Fast-growing tree; fr. said to be edible. Malay Arch., and New Guinea.

morindifolia: *A. Cadamba.*

ANTHOCERCIS Labill. *Solanaceae.* About 20 spp. of Australian shrubs; lvs. alt., sessile or subsessile, entire; fls. pedicelled, calyx 5-toothed, corolla campanulate, 5-lobed, white or yellow, fertile stamens 4, 1 staminode also often present; fr. an ovoid to globular caps., opening by 2 bifid valves, seeds reticulate.

Grown for ornament in mild climates. Propagated by seeds or cuttings.

albicans A. Cunn. GRAY RAYFLOWER. To 3 ft., white-stellate-pubescent; lvs. ovate or oblong, to ½ in. long, obtuse; fls. axillary, 2–3 in a cluster, corolla white, with purple streaks. Se. Australia. Zone 10.

ANTHOCLEISTA Afzel. ex R. Br. *Loganiaceae.* About 50 spp. of trees or shrubs, native to trop. Afr., Madagascar, and the Mascarene Is., 1 sp. in S. Afr.; lvs. opp., often large, more or less oblong, entire; fls. large, white or dull yellow, in terminal panicles, corolla 8–16-lobed; fr. a berry, seeds many, small.

grandiflora Gilg [*A. zambesiaca* Bak.]. Tree, to 90 ft., trunk straight, high-branched; lvs. obovate-oblong, to 27 in. long, clustered at ends of branchlets, veins prominent; fls. white or cream, about 1 in. long. S. Afr.

zambesiaca: *A. grandiflora.*

ANTHOGONIUM Wallich ex Lindl. *Orchidaceae.* Three spp. of terrestrial herbs, native to trop. Asia; sts. cormlike; lvs. 2–4, narrow, grasslike, plicate; scape radical; sepals and petals forming a long tube inserted on the pedicelled ovary at a right angle. For structure of fl. see *Orchidaceae.*

Cool greenhouse; for culture see *Orchids.*

gracile Lindl. To 1 ft.; sepals and petals rather delicate in texture, rose or magenta, ½ in. long, lip enveloping the column, obscurely 3-lobed, magenta with darker spots apically. Late summer. Himalayas, Burma.

ANTHOLYZA L. *Iridaceae.* Not cult. **A. paniculata:** *Curtonus paniculatus.*

ANTHOXANTHUM L. VERNAL GRASS. *Gramineae.* Fewer than 6 spp. of aromatic ann. or per. grasses in Eurasia and N. Afr.; lf. blades flat; panicles spikelike; spikelets with 1 terminal bisexual floret and 2 sterile lemmas attached to the fertile floret, the sterile lemmas shorter than glumes and awned from back, rachilla disarticulating above glumes, fertile lemma shorter than sterile lemma, awnless, palea 1-nerved, enclosed in the lemma. For terminology see *Gramineae.*

gracile Biv. Ann., distinguished from *A. odoratum* in having sts. to 8 in., pubescent lf. blades, silvery panicles, spikelets ½ in. long. Italy. Cult. for dry bouquets.

odoratum L. SWEET V.G. Per., sts. to 2 ft., clustered, slender; lf. blades glabrous, to $^{3}/_{16}$ in. wide; infl. long-stalked, brownish-yellow, to 2¼ in. long; spikelets to ⅜ in. long, glumes scabrous, sterile lemmas nearly equal, awned, golden-appressed-hairy, first lemma awned below apex, second awned from near base, awn twisted below and geniculate, fertile lemma less than ⅛ in. long, brown, smooth, glossy. Eurasia; introd. and naturalized, Greenland and Nfld., s. to Mich. and La., and from B.C. to Calif. Cult. to give fragrance to hay.

ANTHRISCUS Pers. *Umbelliferae.* About 12 spp. of herbs, native to Eur. and Asia; lvs. pinnate; infl. a compound umbel, with or without involucre, and with involucels of entire, usually reflexed bractlets; fls. small, white; fr. compressed, ovoid to linear, usually beaked.

Grown for the leaves, which are piquant and used like parsley. Of easy cultivation in any soil, thriving in shade; propagated by seeds.

Cerefolium (L.) Hoffm. CHERVIL, SALAD C. Ann., to 2 ft.; lvs. 2-pinnate, segms. ovate and deeply cut; fr. with beak ⅓ as long as body. Se. Eur., w. Asia; naturalized in N. Amer.

Chervil is a hardy annual, the leaves of which are used in salads and as a garnish. It is of simple culture and is grown as a spring or autumn crop, not thriving in the heat of summer. Usable leaves are obtained in 6 or 8 weeks after seeds are sown; the autumn sowing is sometimes carried over winter in frames, or in mild climates with a protection of mulch. Plants may stand 8–12 in. apart; they grow 1½ ft. or more.

sylvestris (L.) Hoffm. Per. or bien., to 3 ft.; lvs. 2-pinnate, segms. ovate-lanceolate, deeply cut; fr. with beak ⅙ as long as body. Eur., w. Asia; naturalized in N. Amer.

ANTHURIUM Schott. TAILFLOWER. More than 600 spp. of per., often epiphytic herbs, native to trop. Amer., sts. short or elongate; lvs. usually firm, with primary lateral veins mostly connected by well-defined vein running along inside and paralled to margin (antemarginal vein), smaller veins always reticulate, petioles geniculate; spathe persistent, spreading or reflexed, sometimes showy, spadix densely covered with bisexual fls., perianth 4-parted, ovary 2-celled with 1–2 ovules; fr. of berries, often colored and showy.

Anthuriums are popular foliage plants, and a few species produce blossoms of great beauty. They thrive under low light conditions, but high humidity is necessary for flowering. Terrestrial species grow well in moist, rich soil high in organic matter, while epiphytic species require good drainage, and are often potted in media containing chopped osmunda fiber or fir bark. Propagated by seeds, suckers, and stem cuttings.

acaule (Jacq.) Schott. Similar to *A. Hookeri* but lf. blades leathery, spatulate to narrowly elliptic-oblong, to 3 ft. long and 7½ in. wide, acute, cuneate to truncate or nearly auriculate basally, with very prominent reticulate veins, petioles angular, to 4 in. long; peduncle 2–3 ft. long, greenish, spathe linear-lanceolate, 5 in. long, spadix short-stalked, to 10–14 in. long. W. Indies.

aemulum Schott. Sts. climbing, internodes elongate; lf. blades reflexed, palmately compound, lfts. 5–7(–9), oblanceolate, to 9 in. long and 3 in. wide, outermost lfts. oblique, gibbous basally on outer side, lateral veins many, spreading, joining the distinct antemarginal connecting vein remote from margin, petioles to 18 in. long; peduncle 2 in. long, spathe lanceolate, to 4 in. long, spadix shorter than spathe, purple. Mex. to Costa Rica.

×**album:** *A.* × *roseum.*

Andraeanum Linden. FLAMINGO LILY, OILCLOTH FLOWER. Sts. to several ft., internodes short; lf. blades reflexed, ovate, 8–10 in. long and half as wide, sagittate, petioles somewhat longer than blades; peduncle 1½–2 times longer than petiole, spathe spreading, orbicular-ovate, 3–5 in long, cordate, puckered, polished, salmon-red, basal lobes semicircular, sometimes shortly united, spadix sessile, recurved, to 2¼ in. long, golden with an ivory zone. Colombia. One of the parents of a group of hybrids with large, showy, puckered spathes from black-red to red, salmon, pink, and white, usually incorrectly treated as vars. of the sp. Var. **album:** *A.* × *roseum* cv. Var. **atrosanguineum:** *A.* × *cultorum* cv. Var. **carneum:** *A.* × *carneum.* Var. **giganteum:** *A.* × *cultorum* cv. Var. **Reidii:** *A.* × *cultorum* cv. Var. **rhodochlorum:** *A.* × *cultorum* cv. Var. **roseum:** *A.* × *roseum* cv. Var. **salmoneum:** *A.* × *roseum* cv.

Bakeri Hook. f. Sts. stout, very short; lf. blades linear, to 2 ft. long and 2½ in. wide, tapering equally toward each end, dark green, petioles to 6 in. long; peduncle twice as long as petiole, spathe reflexed, oblong, to 2 in. long, green, spadix longer, to 8 in. long in fr., yellow-green; berries ovoid, ⅜ in. long, acute, scarlet. Costa Rica.

berriozabalense Matuda. Sts. very short; lf. blades reflexed, generally triangular, to 9½ in. long and nearly as wide, nearly hastate, basal lobes oblong, nearly as long as terminal lobe and separated by a broad sinus, petioles 16 in. long; peduncle half as long as petiole, spathe narrow, 2 in. long, green, spadix nearly as long. S. Mex. Material offered under this name differs in having the lvs. mostly sagittate, larger, to 13 in. long but only 8 in. wide, venation pattern different, petioles shorter, to 12 in. long, and peduncle longer than petiole.

caribaeum, caribbeum: *A. cordifolium.*

×**carneum** Hort. Chantrier ex Regel [*A. Andraeanum* var. *carneum* Hort.]: *A. Andraeanum* × *A. nymphaeifolium.* Similar to *A.* ×*ferrierense,* but spathes broader, to 7 in. long and 6 in. wide, rose-carmine, and spadix rosy.

×**chelseiense** N. E. Br.: *A. Andraeanum* × *A. Veitchii.* Similar to *A. Veitchii* but spathe wide-cordate, to 5 in. long and 3½ in. wide, smooth, crimson, spadix 3 in. long, and lf. blades with primary lateral veins fewer and spreading.

clarinervium Matuda. Differs from *A. crystallinum* in being much smaller, having lf. blades ovate, broader, 5 in. long and 4 in. wide, and petioles as long as blades. S. Mex.

Clevelandii: see *Spathiphyllum Clevelandii.*

cordifolium Kunth [*A. caribaeum* Hort.]. Sts. very short; lf. blades reflexed, ovate, to 22 in. long and 12 in. wide, cordate-sagittate, base of basal ribs marginal for ¾ in. in sinus, petioles somewhat longer than blades; peduncle to 31 in. long, spathe linear, to 7 in. long, green, spadix as long as spathe or longer, sessile, black-purple. W. Indies.

corrugatum Sodiro [*A. papilionense* Hort.; *A. papillosum* Hort. ex Markgr.]. Sts. climbing, internodes elongate; lf. blades reflexed, broadly ovate, to 2 ft. long and 16 in. wide, sagittate-cordate, closely puckered, with well-defined antemarginal vein; peduncle as long as petiole, spathe narrow, 8 in. long, green, spadix 6 in. long. Ecuador.

crassinervium (Jacq.) G. Don. Differs from *A. Hookeri* in having lf. blades narrower, acuminate, spadix longer, more slender, peduncle longer. Venezuela. See also *A. Hookeri.*

crystallinum Linden & André. CRYSTAL A., STRAP FLOWER. Sts. with internodes very short; lf. blades reflexed-pendent, broadly ovate-elliptic, to 21 in. long and 13 in. wide, shimmering emerald-green above with silvery midrib and lateral veins, basal lobes semicircular, petioles more or less cylindrical, to 17 in. long; peduncle to 2 ft. long, spathe reflexed, linear, 5 in. long, revolute, green, spadix stalked, longer than spathe, slender, yellow-green. Colombia.

cubense Engl. Similar to *A. Hookeri,* but having lvs. oblanceolate-spatulate, smaller, to 2 ft. long and 8 in. wide, more acuminate, more attenuate basally, decidedly thinner, and spadix sessile. Cuba.

×**cultorum** Birdsey. A name used for complex hybrids involving *A. Andraeanum, A. Lindenianum, A. nymphaeifolium,* and *A. ornatum.* Cvs. include: **'Atrosanguineum'** [*A. Andraeanum* var. *atrosanguineum* Hort.], spathes blood-red; **'Giganteum'** [*A. Andraeanum* var. *giganteum* Hort.], spathes large, salmon-red; **'Reidii'** [*A. Reidii* Hort.; *A. Andraeanum* var. *Reidii* Hort.], spathes very large, deep rose-pink; **'Rhodochlorum'** [*A. Andraeanum* var. *rhodochlorum* Hort.]., spathes huge, somewhat triangular or rhomboid, to 12 in. long, rose, but basal lobes green on outer half.

dentatum: *A. macrolobum.*

digitatum (Jacq.) G. Don. Sts. climbing, internodes short; lvs. peltate, palmately compound, lfts. 7–13, oblong-oblanceolate, to 12 in. long and 3½ in. wide, nearly cuneate, with distinct petiolules, antemarginal connecting veins close to margins, outermost lfts. nearly sessile, basally oblique to gibbous on outer margin, petioles to 2 ft. long; peduncle 2–3 in. long, spathe ovate-lanceolate, to 4½ in. long, red-purplish, spadix sessile, about as long as spathe, stout, purple. Venezuela.

Dussii Engl. Sts. thick, very short, with lvs. clustered; lf. blades elongate-elliptic, 14 in. long and 3½ in. wide, obtuse basally, with many parallel lateral veins, and well-defined antemarginal connecting vein, bright green, petioles 2½ in. long; peduncle 1 ft. long, spathe 4¾ in. long and ½ in. wide, spadix nearly sessile, as long as spathe, dark purple. Guadeloupe (W. Indies).

elegans: *A. fortunatum.*

enneaphyllum (Vell.) Stellf. [*A. variabile* Kunth]. Differs from *A. digitatum* in having lfts. narrower, ½–1½ in. wide, with outermost lfts. merely oblique at base, and spathe narrower, green. E. Brazil.

×**ferrierense** Bergman ex M. T. Mast. & T. Moore: *A. Andraeanum* × *A. ornatum.* Differs from *A. Andraeanum* in having lf. blades larger and broader, to 16 in. long and 10 in. wide, petioles to 3 ft. long; spathe ovate-cordate, to 6 in. long with smaller basal lobes, not puckered, pink-coral to rose-lilac, and spadix to 4 in. long, stouter, pinkish-white. Apparently indistinguishable from *A.* × *roseum.* Cv. **'Roseum'** is listed.

Forgetii N. E. Br. Differs from *A. crystallinum* in having lvs. peltate, broadly ovate, with basal lobes completely united, and spadix purplish. Colombia.

fortunatum Bunt. [*A. elegans* Engl. 1883, not 1881]. Differs from *A. palmatum* in having st. very short, lf. blades pedate-radiate, margins undulate-sinuate to lobed, middle lobe nearly twice as long as others, basal main ribs marginal for some distance along semicircular basal sinus, and spathe and spadix shorter. Colombia.

fraternum Schott. Sts. erect, internodes short; lf. blades elongate-ovate, to 16 in. long and 8 in. wide, deeply cordate, with 5–6 main veins on each side, petioles and peduncles as long as lf. blades, or longer; spathe oblong-elliptic, to 4 in. long and 1⅜ in. wide, caudate-acuminate, white or becoming green, spadix to 3 in. long, blunt, green or purplish. Guatemala. Material offered as *Spathiphyllum cordatum* appears to be related to this sp., but has lvs. elongate-triangular, cordate, with basal lobes separated by a very broad, open sinus, new lvs. with midribs and veins rosy, especially beneath; spadix white; and fr. yellow. Guatemala?

helleborifolium Schott. Differs from *A. pedatoradiatum* in having lvs. usually smaller, deeply divided into 7–11 narrower segms., the middle segm. cut nearly or quite to the base, to 2 in. long and wide, petioles to 2 ft. long, and spathe green, becoming brownish. E. Mex.

Hoffmannii Schott. Differs from *A. ornatum* in having lf. blades somewhat smaller and wider, 14 in. long and 10 in. wide, spathe lanceolate, to 4 in. long, whitish, and spadix nearly as long as spathe, purple-red. Costa Rica. Doubtfully in the trade.

Holtonianum Schott. Sts. climbing, internodes short; lf. blades reflexed, palmately compound, large, lfts. 5–9, pinnately lobed, middle one to 2 ft. long, all deeply 3–4-lobed on each side, petioles 3 ft. long; peduncle shorter than petiole, spathe oblong, to 16 in. long, spadix slightly longer. Colombia.

Hookeri Kunth [*A. crassinervium* Hook., not (Jacq.) D. Don.]. Sts. very short; lvs. clustered, blades parchmentlike, obovate-oblanceolate, to 3 ft. long and 14 in. wide, very short-acuminate, long-attenuate and acute basally, glaucous-green on upper surface, with about 10 primary lateral veins on each side of midrib, extending to margin, petioles stout, nearly 4-angled, about 4½ in. long; peduncle scarcely 6 in. long, spathe reflexed, ovate-lanceolate, purplish outside, spadix short-stalked, longer than spathe, 2¼ in. long or more, stout, lilac. Guiana. Considered by some auths. as conspecific with *A. crassinervium* (Jacq.) G. Don.

×**hortulanum:** see *A. Scherzeranum.*

Huegelii Schott. Differs from *A. Hookeri* in having lf. blades rounded to auriculate basally, bright green on upper surface, finely black-dotted on both surfaces, primary lateral veins strongly ascending-arching with uppermost pair sweeping uninterruptedly to apex, peduncle much longer, spathe linear-lanceolate, to 4½ in. long or more, and spadix to 6½ in long or more, slender, dark purple. Lesser Antilles, Trinidad, Venezuela. Long confused with *A. Hookeri.*

Kalbreyeri Hort. Veitch ex M. T. Mast. & T. Moore. Differs from *A. aemulum* in having lfts. larger, 1½–2 ft. long, sinuate, and only 3–4 pairs of primary lateral veins strongly ascending, but lacking a distinct antemarginal connecting vein, outermost lfts. strongly lobed at base on outside, and peduncle elongate. Colombia.

latihastatum Engl. ex Kurt Krause. Sts. elongate, internodes short; lf. blades hastate-trilobed, to 1 ft. long and 15 in. wide, middle lobe elongate-triangular, 3½ in. wide toward base, lateral lobes spreading, oblong, curved, to 8 in. long and 2¼ in. wide, petioles as long as blades; peduncle 8 in. long, spathe narrow, to 5 in. long, spadix shorter than spathe. Costa Rica.

Lindenianum: see *A. ornatum.*

longilaminatum Engl. Differs from *A. Dussii* in having lf. blades elliptic-oblong to 28 in. long and 5 in. wide, long-cuneate, petioles to 16 in. long; spathe 3 in. long, spadix more slender, twice as long as spathe. Brazil.

macrolobum Bull ex M. T. Mast. & T. Moore [*A. dentatum* André]. Differs from *A. pedatoradiatum* in having lf. blades lobed scarcely halfway, lobes 5–7, acuminate. Long considered a hybrid between *A. leuconeurum* Lem. and *A. pedatoradiatum,* but recently found in the wild in Mato Grosso, Brazil.

magnificum Linden. Differs from *A. crystallinum* in having petioles 4-angled, winged, peduncle winged toward apex, recurved, spathe longer, strongly undulate, and spadix longer, golden. Colombia.

microphyllum (Hook.) G. Don. Sts. very short; lf. blades elliptic-lanceolate or -ovate, to 6 in. long and 3 in. wide, truncate basally, petioles 6–8 in. long; peduncle 16 in. long, spathe reflexed, ovate-lanceolate, 1¼ in. long, yellow-green, spadix on a stalk to 1½ in., as long as spathe, deep purple. Brazil.

nymphaeifolium: see *A. ornatum.*

ornatum Schott. Sts. elongate, covered with brown scalelike lvs.; lf. blades reflexed, ovate, 2 ft. long, sagittate-cordate, petioles little longer than blades; peduncle 1 ft. long or more, spathe 6 in. long and 1½–2½ in. wide, subcordate-truncate basally, white or fading green or rose in age, spadix short-stalked, somewhat shorter than spathe, white to purplish. Venezuela, Colombia. Cv. 'Album' is listed. *A. nymphaeifolium* C. Koch & Bouché and *A. Lindenianum* C. Koch are very similar to this sp.

palmatum (L.) G. Don. Sts. climbing, to 3 ft. or more; lf. blades reflexed, nearly orbicular in outline, palmately cleft, segms. 7–11, oblong-spatulate or oblanceolate, to 18 in. long and 2–2¾ in. wide, petioles 2–3 times longer than lfts.; peduncle shorter than petioles, spathe to 10 in. long and 1 in. wide, green, spadix slightly longer than spathe, violet. W. Indies.

papilionense: *A. corrugatum.*

papillosum: *A. corrugatum.*

pedatoradiatum Schott. Sts. erect, very short; lf. blades nearly orbicular in outline, to 2 ft. wide, pedately cleft to basal 2–3 in., segms. 11–13, narrowly lanceolate to oblong, to 13 in. long and 3 in. wide, outer segms. strongly curved, petioles to 3 ft. long; peduncle to 2 ft. long, spathe reflexed, narrow, to 6 in. long, green, spadix short-stalked, nearly as long as spathe, purplish. E. Mex. Material offered under this name may be *A. helleborifolium.*

pentaphyllum (Aubl.) G. Don. Differs from *A. aemulum* in having lfts. generally 5, elliptic, and more nearly symmetrical. Guiana.

pictamayo: see *A. polyschistum.*

podophyllum (Cham. & Schlechtend.) Kunth [*A. polytomum* Schott]. Sts. erect, very short; lvs. peltate, pale green, lf. blades to 3 ft. wide, palmately divided nearly to base into 5–11 segms., each segm. narrowed toward base and acuminate into secondary segms., then linear, entire or repand to bifid or trifid, petioles longer than blades; peduncle nearly as long as petiole, spathe to 3 in. long, reddish, spadix twice as long as spathe, green. E. Mex.

polyschistum R. E. Schult. & Idrobo [*Anthurium* cv. 'Putumayo', sometimes incorrectly spelled 'Pictamayo']. Sts. climbing, to several ft., internodes about 3 in. long; lvs. peltate, palmately compound, lfts. 12–15, oblong, to 8 in. long and ¾ in. wide, acuminate at both ends, bright green, petioles furrowed, to 9 in. long; peduncle to 10 in. long, spathe narrow, to 4 in. long, greenish, spadix a little shorter than spathe. S. Colombia. In cult. material, lfts. are crisped-undulate.

polytomum: *A. podophyllum.*

putumayo: see *A. polyschistum.*

radicans C. Koch. Sts. stout, creeping and rooting, covered with brown scalelike lvs.; lf. blades ovate, 6 in. long, cordate, puckered, petioles shorter than blade; peduncle to 1½ in. long, spathe ovate, 1½ in. long, cordate, reddish, spadix on stalk ⅜ in. long or more, shorter than spathe, reddish. Brazil? Requires high temperature and atmospheric humidity.

Reidii: *A. ×cultorum* cv.

×**roseum** Hort. Makoy ex Closon [*A. ×album* (De Smet ex Pynaert) Hort. ex Engl.; *A. ×salmoneum* Garn.]: *A. Andraeanum* × *A. Lindenianum.* Differs from *A. Andraeanum* in having spathe flatter, less puckered, white to rose, and spadix more erect, white to pinkish. Cvs. include: 'Album' [*A. Andraeanum* var. *album* Hort.], spathe milky-white; 'Roseum' [*A. Andraeanum* var. *roseum* Hort.], spathe soft rose above, white-rose beneath, spadix whitish or rose; 'Salmoneum' [*A. Andraeanum* var. *salmoneum* Hort.], spathe yellow-salmon.

Rothschildianum: *A. Scherzeranum* cv.

rubrinervium: *A. sagittatum.*

sagittatum (Sims) G. Don [*A. rubrinervium* (Link) G. Don]. Sts. with internodes short; lf. blades reflexed, ovate-triangular, 15–18 in. long and 10 in. wide, sagittate, basal ribs marginal for some distance along open sinus, petioles as long as blades, veins, petioles, and peduncles reddish when young; peduncle to 1 ft. long, spathe to 4 in. long, green, spadix about as long as spathe, purplish. French Guiana.

×**salmoneum:** *A. ×roseum.*

Salviniae Hemsl. Sts. very short with lvs. clustered; lf. blades oblanceolate- or elliptic-oblong, to 2 ft. long and 4¾ in. wide, nearly truncate basally, petioles ⅕–⅙ as long as blade; peduncle slightly longer than lvs., spathe lanceolate, to 6 in. long, brown-purple, spadix as long as spathe. Guatemala.

scandens (Aubl.) Engl. Sts. slender, pendent, to 2 ft., clothed in brown scalelike lvs.; lf. blades elliptic to lanceolate, 3–7 in. long, petioles slender, ⅕–½ as long as blades; peduncle as long as petiole to 4 times longer, spathe inconspicuous, small, green, spadix longer than spathe, to 1½ in. in fr.; berries broadly obovoid, ⁵⁄₁₆ in. diam., translucent white or purplish. Trop. Amer.

Scherzeranum Schott. FLAMINGO FLOWER, PIGTAIL A., PIGTAIL PLANT. Sts. very short, with lvs. clustered; lf. blades oblong-elliptic to -lanceolate, to 9 in. long and 2 in. wide, petioles slender, to 10 in. long; peduncle reddish, spathe reflexed, broadly elliptic, to 2¾ in. long, nearly cordate, shiny, scarlet, spadix spirally contorted, vermilion. Guatemala, Costa Rica. By hybridization and selection, many cvs. have been produced, some having spathes to 5 in. long. The group name *A. ×hortulanum* Birdsey has been proposed for these cvs. Cv. 'Atrosanguineum'. Spathe dark red. Cv. 'Rothschildianum' [*A. ×Rothschildianum* Bergman & Veitch]. Spathe red, heavily peppered white, spadix yellow.

signatum C. Koch & Mathieu. Sts. elongate, internodes short, covered with fibers; lf. blades reflexed, hastate-trilobed, to 16 in. long and as wide at base, terminal lobe narrowly oblong-obovate, to 6 in. wide, basal lobes oblong-ovate, slightly curved, 4½ in. wide, rounded at apex, with 4 main lateral veins, petioles 2 ft. long; peduncle to 1 ft., spathe linear, 10 in. long, light green, spadix prominently stalked, as long as spathe, slender, golden. Venezuela.

Spathiphyllum N. E. Br. Differs from *A. Bakeri* in having lf. blades oblanceolate, very elongate, narrower, 1½ in. wide; peduncle shorter, spathe erect, ovate, broad, spadix as long as spathe, 1 in. long. Nativity unknown.

subsignatum Schott. Differs from *A. signatum* in having lf. blades nearly triangular, about 12 in. long and wide, sagittate-subhastate, with shorter basal lobes. Costa Rica. Doubtfully in cult.

tetragonum Hook. ex Schott. Differs from *A. Hookeri* in having peduncles 2 ft. long, and spadix about 6 in. long. Nativity uncertain.

trifidum D. Oliver. Differs from *A. signatum* in having lf. blades with terminal lobe oblong, narrower, lateral lobes shorter, each with 2 main lateral veins, and petioles, peduncle, spathe, and spadix reddish-brown. Trop. Amer.

undatum Schott ex Kunth. Differs from *A. aemulum* in having lfts. broader, to 4 in. wide, somewhat caudate, undulate, outermost ones more strongly gibbous and to 5 in. wide. Se. Brazil.

variabile: *A. enneaphyllum.*

Veitchii M. T. Mast. Sts. short; lf. blades reflexed-pendent, oblong, to 3 ft. long and 10 in. wide or more, sagittate, narrowed toward apex, with many downward-curving lateral veins, petioles slightly longer than blades, juvenile lvs. about twice as long as wide; peduncle to 20 in. long, spathe recurved, oblong-lanceolate, to 5 in. long, spadix sessile, about as long as spathe, rose-purplish. Colombia.

Warocqueanum T. Moore. Sts. climbing, internodes short; lf. blades reflexed-pendent, lanceolate, to 3 ft. long and 1 ft. wide, sagittate, shimmering emerald-green above, with midrib, lateral veins, and antemarginal connecting veins paler, petioles 2 ft. long; peduncle 1 ft. long, spathes reflexed, to 4 in. long, narrow, green, spadix nearly sessile, to 12 in. long. Colombia. Cv. 'Robustum' is an improved form.

watermaliense Hort. ex L. H. Bailey. Lf. blades reflexed, triangular, sagittate, undulate, basal lobes separated by a broad V-shaped sinus, petioles elongate; spathe to 10 in. long and almost half as wide, wrinkled, coppery-black, spadix brown. Colombia.

Wrightii: a listed name of no botanical standing. Material so listed may be *A. trifidum* or *A. signatum.*

Wullschlaegelii Engl. Lf. blades reflexed-pendent, ovate, 14 in. long and 9 in. wide, cordate, bright green on both sides, basal lobes overlapping, petioles somewhat longer than blades; peduncle 2 ft. long, spathe linear, 6 in. long, spadix about as long as spathe. Antigua (W. Indies).

ANTHYLLIS L. *Leguminosae* (subfamily *Faboideae*). About 50 or more spp. of ann. or per. herbs or shrubs, native to Eur., N. Afr., and w. Asia; lvs. alt., pinnate, or of 1 or 3 lfts.; fls. in dense cloverlike heads, papilionaceous, stamens 10, united into a closed tube; fr. a legume, enclosed by persistent, inflated calyx.

Sometimes grown as ornamentals, and *A. Vulneraria* for forage on poor soils in Eur. Propagated by seeds; shrubby kinds also by division and cuttings.

alpestris: *A. Vulneraria* subsp.

Gerardii L. Per. herb, sts. slender, to 3 ft. long; lfts. spatulate, to ⅝ in. long; heads ⅜ in. across; fls. rose; fr. 1-seeded. S. Eur.

Hermanniae L. Bushy, deciduous shrub, to 2 ft. or more, brs. crooked, ending in a spine; lvs. of 1 lft., linear-obovate, to 1 in. long; heads very short-stalked; fls. yellow, ⁵⁄₁₆ in. long, Medit. region. Zone 8.

montana L. Per. herb, to 1 ft.; lvs. pinnate, white-silky, lfts. many, small, elliptic or oblong; heads dense, involucrate; fls. purple or pink. Mts., Spain to Balkans. Cvs. 'Carminea', 'Rosea', and 'Rubra' are color forms.

tetraphylla L. Ann., mostly prostrate; lvs. with large terminal lft. and 2–4 small lateral lfts.; fls. yellowish-white, striped with pink. Medit. region.

Vulneraria L. KIDNEY VETCH, WOUNDWORT, LADIES'-FINGERS, LADY'S-FINGERS. Ann., bien., or per. herb, to 1 ft.; lower lvs. with terminal lft. 1 in. long, lateral lfts. smaller or none, upper lvs. odd-pinnate; fls. yellow to deep red. Eur., w. Asia. Food for livestock. Subsp. **Vulneraria**. The typical subsp.; calyx to ⁵⁄₃₂(–³⁄₁₆) in. wide, with small lateral teeth appressed to upper teeth; lfts. of upper st. lvs. equal. Pyrenees, Alps, Appennines. Subsp. **alpestris** (Hegetschw.) Asch. & Graebn. [*A. alpestris* Hegetschw.]. Calyx ³⁄₁₆ in. to nearly ⁵⁄₁₆ in. wide, with obvious lateral teeth not appressed to upper teeth; lfts. of upper st. lvs. unequal. Alps to mts. of Balkan Pen.

ANTIARIS Lesch. *Moraceae.* About 4 spp. of dioecious or monoecious, deciduous shrubs to large trees in trop. Afr., Madagascar, trop. Asia to Philippine Is. and Fiji Is.; bark fibrous, latex poisonous; lvs. alt., pinnately nerved, entire or serrate; fls. unisexual, the male in dense heads, the female solitary; fr. a fleshy drupe.

africana Engl. To 130 ft., branchlets rusty-tomentose; lvs. oblong-obovate to oblong, to 6 in. long, 4½ in. wide, base rounded to cordate, venation prominently reticulate beneath; male fls. on flat receptacle; drupe ellipsoid or pear-shaped, red or orange, to ⅝ in. long. Trop. Afr.

toxicaria (Pers.) Lesch. UPAS TREE. To 250 ft.; lvs. oblong-elliptic, to 8 in. long, entire or slightly toothed, the base unequal; drupe ellipsoid or pear-shaped, purple or red, to 1¾ in. long. Trop. Afr. and Asia to Philippine Is. and Fiji Is. The latex yields an arrow poison and the inner bark a strong fiber.

ANTICLEA: *ZIGADENUS.*

ANTIDESMA L. *Euphorbiaceae.* About 160 spp. of dioecious trees and shrubs, native to trop. Afr., Asia, Australia, and the Pacific Is.; lvs. alt., simple, short-petioled; fls. small, without petals, in long spikes or racemes; fr. a small fleshy drupe.

Sometimes cultivated as ornamentals in warm regions. Propagated by cuttings. The fruits of both species listed here are used for preserves.

Bunius (L.) K. Spreng. BIGNAY, CHINESE LAUREL. Evergreen tree, to 45 ft.; lvs. 3–7 in. long, elliptic to oblong, shining; fls. green, in spikes 2–7 in. long, ovary glabrous; fr. currantlike, red. India, Malay Arch.

Dallachyanum Baill. Small shrubby tree; lvs. ovate or lanceolate-elliptic, 2–4 in. long, thin; male fls. in spikes, female fls. in racemes, ovary pubescent; fr. red. Queensland (Australia).

ANTIGONON Endl. *Polygonaceae.* About 2–3 spp. of vines climbing with tendrils, native to trop. and subtrop. areas of Mex. and Cent. Amer.; lvs. alt., entire; fls. red, pink, white, or yellowish, in racemes terminating in a tendril, bisexual, sepals 5, stamens 8, styles 3; fr. an achene, large, 3-angled, in enlarged perianth.

Two species of easy cultivation; propagated by seeds and cuttings.

leptopus Hook. & Arn. MEXICAN CREEPER, CORALLITA, CONFEDERATE VINE, CORAL VINE, PINK VINE, LOVE VINE, CHAIN-OF-LOVE, MOUNTAIN ROSE, QUEEN'S-JEWELS, QUEEN'S-WREATH. Climbing, to 40 ft.; lvs. arrow-shaped or cordate-ovate, to 4 in. long; fls. bright pink, in axillary racemes, outer sepals ovate in fr.; achenes strongly angled at tip. Tubers are edible. Mex. Cv. 'Album'. Fls. white.

guatimalense Meissn. [*A. macrocarpum* Britt. & Small]. Similar to *A. leptopus*, but having lvs. thicker, more hairy, to 5 in. long, outer sepals orbicular in fr.; achenes with winged angles. Cent. Amer.; introd. in W. Indies and s. Fla.

macrocarpum: *A. guatimalense.*

ANTIRRHINUM L. SNAPDRAGON. *Scrophulariaceae.* About 40 spp. of erect or procumbent herbs of temp. areas of New and Old World, mostly per., but usually grown as anns.; fls. with corolla broadly tubular, 2-lipped, throat closed by a palate (personate), and base often swollen (saccate) on underside.

The common snapdragon grown in gardens and for cut flowers is *A. majus*, which with winter protection may remain perennial in all but the coldest parts of the country. For general garden use, treat as an annual and plant in full sun.

Asarina: *Asarina procumbens.*

calycinum Lam. Ann., 1–1½ ft.; glabrous; lvs. narrowly elliptic, 1–2 in. long, entire; corolla ¾ in. long, purple, much longer than calyx lobes. Portugal to Italy. Closely allied to *A. Orontium* and little cult.

Coulteranum Benth. CHAPARRAL S. Ann., erect or clambering, 1½–3 ft., glabrous except for pubescent infl., lateral brs. tendril-like; basal lvs. ovate-elliptic, to 1½ in. long, st. lvs. lanceolate-elliptic, entire; fls. in spikelike racemes, corolla whitish with yellowish palate, mostly ⅜–½ in. long. Calif.

filipes: *Asarina filipes.*

glandulosum: see *A. multiflorum.*

glutinosum Boiss. & Reut. Tender, suffrutescent per., 8–14 in., densely sticky-pubescent, sts. prostrate or decumbent; lvs. broadly ovate-elliptic, ¼–½ in. long; fls. showy, corolla about 1 in. long, yellowish-white, lip striped red, palate yellow. Spain.

majus L. COMMON S., GARDEN S. Erect per., mostly 2–3 ft. (or much shorter in dwarf cvs.), but to 6 ft. under glass, glabrous except for glandular-pubescent infl.; lvs. lanceolate to oblong-lanceolate, to 3 in. long; fls. in terminal racemes, purplish-red to white, but cvs. of shades of red, pink, yellow, and orange available, corolla mostly 1½–2 in. long. Medit. region; escaped in U.S. Many fancy and Latin-named cvs. available, classified by size and color groupings, amony them cvs. 'Maximum' [*A. maximum* Hort.], fls. large; 'Nanum Compactum' [*A. nanum-compactum* Hort.], dwarf.

maximum: *A. majus* cv.

molle L. Similar to *A. glutinosum*, but lacking viscid glands. Sw. France.

multiflorum Penn. [*A. glandulosum* Lindl., not Lej.]. WITHERED S. Viscid, erect, much-branched ann., 3–5 ft.; lvs. lanceolate, oblong to linear, ½–2½ in. long, obtuse at base, glandular-hairy, sessile; fls. in dense, showy, terminal racemes, light purple, to ¾ in. long. Calif.

nanum-compactum: *A. majus* cv.

Orontium L. LESSER S. Erect, mostly glabrous, diffusely branched ann., 9–15 in.; lvs. 1–1½ in. long, mostly linear-elliptic; fls. solitary, in lf. axils, corolla rose-pink, ⅝–¾ in. long, somewhat shorter than calyx lobes. Eur. and Asia; escaped in N. Amer. A weedy plant, not very showy.

ovatum Eastw. Erect, glandular-hairy ann., 12–16 in., with leafy brs.; lvs. oblong to ovate, ¾–1½ in. long, acute at base, petioled; fls. solitary in lf. axils, calyx lobes ⅔ as long as corolla, corolla nearly 1 in. long, purplish, upper lip pink, lower one white, palate yellowish. Calif.

pumilum Poir. ex Steud.: *Linaria flava* (Poir.) Desf.; but material offered as *A. pumilum* is mostly a cv. of *A. majus*.

speciosum: *Galvezia speciosa*.

ANUBIAS Schott. *Araceae*. About 15 spp. of herbs of Afr.; lvs. from short horizontal rhizomes, lanceolate or ovate, petioles geniculate; infl. long-peduncled, spathe green, loosely convolute below and expanded above; fls. unisexual, perianth absent, ovaries many-ovuled.

One species of wet habitats is offered for use in aquaria. It makes a satisfactory pot plant in diffuse sunlight in any good soil kept evenly moist, but will not tolerate low humidity.

Afzelii Schott [*A. lanceolata* Hort., not N. E. Br.]. AFRICAN CRYPTOCORYNE. To 2 ft. or more; lf. blades narrowed at each end, to 22 in. long and 7 in. wide, petioles 16 in. long, sheathed above the middle; peduncles as long as petioles, spathe to 2½ in. long, spadix stalked, to 4 in. long. Sierra Leone.

congensis N. E. Br. Lf. blades oblong-ovate, to 8 in. long and 4 in. wide, dark green, finely hairy beneath, petioles to 10 in. long, peduncle to 10 in. long, spathe to 2 in. long and ¾ in. wide, fleshy, green. W. Afr.

lanceolata N. E. Br. WATER ASPIDISTRA. Differs from *A. Afzelii* in having lvs. smaller, to 6 in. long, nearly orbicular basally, spathe about 2 in. long, spadix subsessile, about as long as spathe. Nigeria, Cameroons, Gabon. Doubtfully in cult.; material so listed is usually *A. Afzelii*.

nana Engl. Lf. blades ovate, to 2¼ in. long and 1⅛ in. wide, acuminate at apex, dark green, petioles about 2½ in. long; peduncle to 4 in. long, spathe lanceolate, to 1 in. long, pale green. Cameroons.

APHANAMIXIS Blume. *Meliaceae*. About 23 spp. of evergreen, dioecious, medium-sized trees, native to se. Asia, Philippine Is., and Malay Arch. to New Guinea; lvs. alt., odd-pinnate; fls. in axillary spikes or panicles, sepals 5, petals 3, anthers 3–6, filaments united in a tube, ovary 3-celled; fr. a leathery caps., seeds with an aril.

polystachya (Wallich) R. Parker [*A. Rohituka* (Wight & Arn.) Pierre; *Amoora Rohituka* Wight & Arn.]. Tree, 30–70 ft.; lvs. 1–3 ft. long, lfts. 9–15, oblong to elliptic-oblong, 3–9 in. long; male fls. in panicles to 12 in. long, female fls. in spikes 14–18 in. long, stamens 6; aril scarlet. Ceylon, se. Asia, Sumatra. Produces a useful timber and a semidrying oil from the seeds.

Rohituka: *A. polystachya*.

APHANANTHE Planch. *Ulmaceae*. Three or 4 spp. of monoecious, usually deciduous trees or shrubs, native to e. Asia, Malay Arch. and Australia; lvs. alt., petioled, serrate, 3-nerved at base; fls. unisexual, male fls. axillary, in dense corymbs near base of young branchlets, female fls. solitary, in axils of upper lvs.; fr. an ovoid to nearly globose drupe.

Propagated by seeds.

aspera (Thunb.) Planch. MUKU TREE. To 60 ft.; lvs. ovate, to 2½ in. long, scabrous above, appressed-pubescent and paler beneath; fr. globose, about ¼ in. across. Korea, e. China, Japan. A hardy, fast-growing, deep-rooted tree. Zone 6. Wood useful.

APHANIA Blume. *Sapindaceae*. About 23 spp. of polygamous shrubs or small trees, native to trop. Asia, Afr., and Indonesia; lvs. alt., pinnate; fls. in racemes or panicles, regular, sepals 4 or 5, petals 4–6, stamens 5–8; fr. drupaceous, usually deeply 2-lobed, seed without aril.

rubra (Roxb.) Radlk. [*Sapindus attenuatus* Wallich ex Hiern]. Shrub or tree; lvs. to 2 ft. long, lfts. 6–12, ovate-lanceolate, to 11 in. long; infl. to 20 in. long; fr. dark purple. N. India to Himalayas.

APHANOSTEPHUS DC. LAZY DAISY. *Compositae* (Aster Tribe). About 11 spp. of ann. or per. herbs or woody-based per., native from w. Fla., Ark., and Kans. to Ariz. and Mex.; lvs. alt., sessile or petioled, entire to deeply pinnatifid; fl. heads radiate, solitary, on peduncles with spreading to downwardly directed appressed hairs, involucre saucer-shaped to hemispherical, or even broadly urceolate, particularly so in fr., involucral bracts imbricate in 3–5 rows, scarious-margined, receptacle depressed-hemispherical to conical, roughened, naked; disc fls. bisexual, fertile, yellow, ray fls. female, fertile, white to lavender or rose-purple; achenes columnar, nearly cylindrical to 4-angled, not ribbed, glabrous to pubescent, pappus a crown of scales or hairs.

skirrhobasis (DC.) Trel. Ann., to 20 in., densely gray-pubescent, the hairs fine, soft; lower lvs. oblanceolate to oblong-elliptic, to 2⅜ in. long, on petioles to 2⅜ in. long, upper lvs. successively reduced, the uppermost sessile; ray fls. white, usually cherry-red to rose-purple on back, sometimes only streaked. Kans., Ark., Okla., Tex., New Mex.

APHELANDRA R. Br. *Acanthaceae*. About 80 spp. of shrubs or herbs in trop. Amer.; lvs. petioled, blades usually large; fls. red, yellow, orange, or white, sessile, in terminal spikes with large bracts, calyx divided nearly to base into 5 segms., corolla 2-lipped, tube straight, stamens 4, exserted, but not longer than upper lip of corolla, anther sac 1; fr. a caps., seeds 4, with silky hairs.

Aphelandras are grown under glass for the showy bracted spikes and are of easy cultivation. After blooming the plants should be rested. Propagated by cuttings of half-ripened wood or young growth with a heel, and by seeds when obtainable.

atrovirens: *A. bahiensis*.

aurantiaca (Scheidw.) Lindl. [*A. fascinator* Linden & André; *A. nitens* Hook. f.]. Herb or subshrub, to 4½ ft., glabrous; lvs. ovate-elliptic or oblong, 4–9 in. long, light green beneath; bracts stiffly erect, serrate; corolla orange or tinged scarlet, 2½ in. long. Mex. and n. S. Amer. Cv. 'Roezlii'. Lvs. large, veins marked with white.

bahiensis (Nees) Wassh. [*A. atrovirens* N. E. Br.]. Shrub; lvs. elliptic, to 4 in. long, dark green above, violet-purple beneath, veins sometimes mottled with light green; spikes almost cylindrical; corolla yellow, ¾ in. long. Brazil. Handsome foliage plant.

Chamissoniana Nees. Glabrous shrub; lvs. elliptic, 4–5 in. long, slender-pointed, veins marked with white; bracts yellow, 1½ in. long, slender-pointed, spiny; corolla bright yellow, 2 in. long. Brazil.

fascinator: *A. aurantiaca*.

ignea (Schrad.) Nees ex Steud. [*Stenandrium igneum* (Schrad.) Nees, not André]. Low-growing per.; lvs. cordate-ovate, to 4 in. long, petioled; corolla yellow, 1¼ in. long. S. Brazil. Not to be confused with *Xantheranthemum igneum*.

Leopoldii: *A. squarrosa* cv.

nitens: *A. aurantiaca*.

Sinclairiana Nees. Shrub or small tree, to 15 ft.; lvs. oblong-lanceolate, to 12 in. long; spikes solitary or several in a cluster, to 8 in. long, bracts broadly elliptic, to 1 in. long, orange-red; corolla rose-red or purplish-red, to 2½ in. long. Costa Rica and Panama.

squarrosa Nees. ZEBRA PLANT, SAFFRON-SPIKE. Shrub, robust, glabrous, more or less succulent; lvs. ovate to ovate-elliptic, 10–12 in. long, glossy green above, veins marked with white; spikes solitary or in 3's, bracts yellow or orange-yellow, 1–1½ in. long; corolla yellow, 1½ in. long. Brazil. Several cvs. with compact growth habit and lvs. variously marked with white are listed: 'Brockfeld', 'Dania', 'Fritz Prinsler', 'Leopoldii', 'Louisae'.

tetragona (Vahl) Nees. Shrub, to 3 ft., glabrous or nearly so; lvs. broadly ovate, to 9 in. long; spikes terminal and axillary, several, crowded, 4-sided, bracts small, ovate to lanceolate, ½ in. long or less; fls. much longer than bracts, corolla scarlet, 1½–2½ in. long, tube arched, upper lip hooded, middle lobe of lower lip curled backward, lateral lobes very short. Costa Rica to n. S. Amer.

APHYLLANTHES L. *Liliaceae*. One sp., a fibrous-rooted per. herb, native to Medit. region; lvs. reduced and membranous; fls. light blue or rarely white, subtended by chaffy bracts, usually terminal and solitary on leafless scapes, peri-

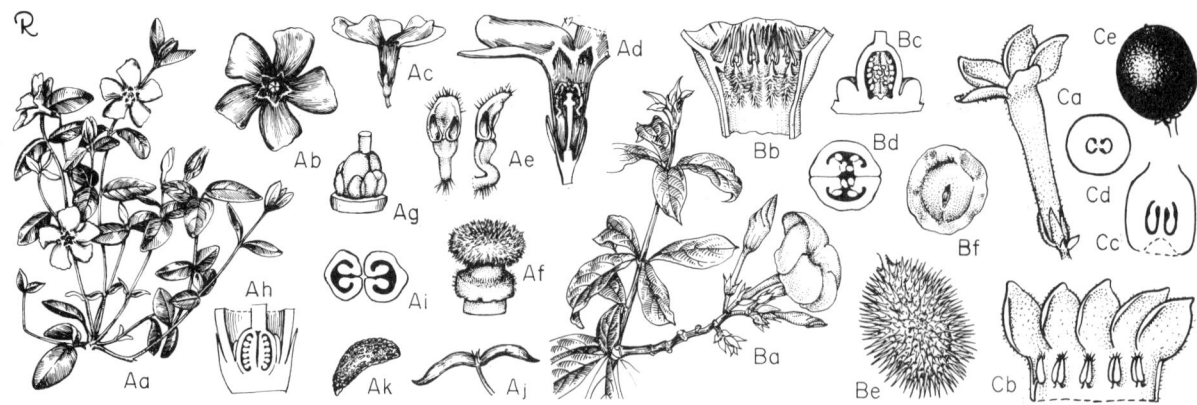

APOCYNACEAE. **A,** *Vinca minor;* **Aa,** plant, ×¼; **Ab,** flower, face view, ×½; **Ac,** flower, side view, ×½; **Ad,** flower, vertical section, ×1; **Ae,** stamen, two views, ×4; **Af,** stigma, ×5; **Ag,** ovaries and basal glands, ×4; **Ah,** base of flower, vertical section, ×4; **Ai,** ovaries, cross section, ×8; **Aj,** follicles, ×½; **Ak,** seed, ×2. **B,** *Allamanda cathartica:* **Ba,** flowering branch, ×¼; **Bb,** throat of corolla, expanded, ×1; **Bc,** ovary, vertical section, ×3; **Bd,** ovary, cross section, ×5; **Be,** capsule, ×⅓; **Bf,** seed, ×½. **C,** *Acokanthera oppositifolia:* **Ca,** flower, ×1½; **Cb,** throat of corolla, expanded, ×3; **Cc,** ovary, vertical section, ×10; **Cd,** ovary, cross section, ×8; **Ce,** berry, ×½.

anth 6-parted, persistent when withered, stamens 6; fr. a loculicidal caps.

monspeliensis L. Tufted per.; lvs. minute, basal; fls. to 1 in. across, on rushlike scapes to 10 in. high.

APIACEAE: see *UMBELLIFERAE.*

APICRA: *ASTROLOBA.*

APIOS Medic. *Leguminosae* (subfamily *Faboideae*). Eight to 10 spp. of tuberous-rooted, twining herbs, native to e. N. Amer. and Asia; lvs. alt., pinnate; fls. papilionaceous, in short racemes, stamens 10, 9 united, 1 separate; fr. a long, flat legume.

One species sometimes grown in the wild garden; propagated by tubers and by seeds.

americana Medic. [*A. tuberosa* Moench; *Glycine Apios* L.]. GROUNDNUT, POTATO BEAN, WILD B. To 8 ft.; roots with strings of tubers; lfts. 5–7, ovate-lanceolate, to 3 in. long; fls. brown, fragrant. Tubers edible. Late summer. New Bruns. to Fla., w. to Minn. and Tex.

tuberosa: *A. americana.*

APIUM L. *Umbelliferae.* About 20 spp. of herbs, native to N. and S. Amer., Eurasia, Australia, and New Zeal.; lvs. pinnate; umbels compound, with or without involucre and involucels; fls. small, white; fr. compressed.

One species is a common vegetable grown for the blanched leaf stalks, and a variety of it is grown for the edible roots.

dulce: *A. graveolens* var.

graveolens L. var. **dulce** (Mill.) Pers. [*A. dulce* Mill.]. CELERY. Bien., to 3 ft., strong-smelling; lvs. pinnate, lfts. 5–7, ternately lobed or compound, often again divided or toothed. Widely distributed. Var. **rapaceum** (Mill.) Gaud.-Beaup. [*A. rapaceum* Mill.]. CELERIAC, TURNIP-ROOTED CELERY. Root thickened, turniplike, edible. For cult. see *Celery.*

rapaceum: *A. graveolens* var.

APLECTRUM Nutt. *Orchidaceae.* One sp., a terrestrial herb, native to temp. N. Amer.; sts. cormlike; lf. solitary, broadly elliptic, plicate; scape radical; sepals and petals not united, ovary short-pedicelled. For structure of fl. see *Orchidaceae.*

For wild gardens; for culture see *Orchids.*

hyemale (Muhlenb. ex Willd.) Torr. [*A. spicatum* BSP]. PUTTYROOT, ADAM-AND-EVE. To 2 ft.; lf. to about 7 in. long and 3 in. wide, arising from the corm; scape leafless, to 20 in. high, racemes to 4 in. long; fls. yellowish-brown, sepals and petals narrow, lip 3-lobed. Late spring. S. Que. to N.C. and Ga., w. to Sask. and Ariz.

spicatum: *A. hyemale.*

APOCYNACEAE Juss. DOGBANE FAMILY. Dicot.; about 130 genera of herbs, shrubs, and trees, some scandent, often

with milky juice, of worldwide distribution but most abundant in tropics; lvs. opp., simple, without stipules; fls. regular, stamens borne on corolla, alternating with corolla lobes, pistil of 2 carpels completely united or with ovaries separate and styles united, the ovaries then 2, superior, closely appressed, each 1-celled; fr. a pair of follicles, 2 drupelets, or a caps. Differing from *Asclepiadaceae* in having filaments not united and pollen granular rather than agglutinated into waxlike masses. Besides many ornamentals the family yields drugs, minor kinds of rubber, and edible fr. The cult. genera are: *Acokanthera, Adenium, Allamanda, Alstonia, Amsonia, Apocynum, Aspidosperma, Beaumontia, Carissa, Catharanthus, Cerbera, Chonemorpha, Fosteronia, Holarrhena, Kopsia, Lanugia, Macrosiphonia, Mandevilla, Nerium, Ochrosia, Plumeria, Prestonia, Rauvolfia, Rhazya, Strophanthus, Tabernaemontana, Thenardia, Thevetia, Trachelospermum, Vallaris, Vallesia, Vinca,* and *Wrightia.*

APOCYNUM L. DOGBANE. *Apocynaceae.* Seven spp. of herbs native to temp. Amer.; sap milky, bark tough, fibrous; lvs. alt. or opp., entire; fls. in cymes, small, white or pink, 5-merous, bisexual, corolla campanulate to cylindrical, glabrous, with 5 scalelike appendages in base of tube, stamens borne at base of tube, alternating with appendages, pollen grains in persistent tetrads; fr. a pair of slender, cylindrical, spreading follicles, seeds many, with a tuft of hairs.

Sometimes planted in the hardy border. Propagated by seeds, but more commonly by division while dormant.

androsaemifolium L. COMMON D., SPREADING D. To 2 ft., brs. forking; lvs. opp., ovate to oblong-lanceolate, 1–4 in. long, drooping or spreading, pubescent to glabrous beneath, mostly petioled; corolla pink, mostly campanulate, to ⅜ in. long and broad, 2–3 times as long as calyx lobes; follicles to 6 in. long, straight, erect to pendulous at maturity. N. Amer.

cannabinum L. INDIAN HEMP, HEMP D. To 4 ft.; lvs. opp., ovate to lanceolate, to 6 in. long, ascending or slightly spreading, mostly petioled; corolla white to greenish, globoid-cylindrical, ⅛ in. long and broad, scarcely longer than calyx lobes; follicles to 8 in. long, usually falcate. U.S., Canada.

pumilum (A. Gray) Greene. ROCKY MT. D. Differs from *A. androsaemifolium* in having lvs. always glabrous, corolla nearly cylindrical to urn-shaped, to only ¼ in. long, at least 3 times as long as calyx lobes; follicles erect or nearly so at maturity. Mont. and Wyo., w. to Wash. and Calif.

APONOGETON L. f. [*Ouvirandra* Thouars.]. *Aponogetonaceae.* About 22 spp. of trop. and subtrop., aquatic, per. herbs, with characteristics of the family.

Aponogetons are grown in aquaria or less commonly in pools in the greenhouse, or *A. distachyus* outdoors in Zone 9. They should be potted and placed 1½–2 ft. under water. Temperatures of 65–70° F. should be maintained for *A. madagascariensis.* Propagated by division, offsets, or seeds when available.

Boivinianus Baill. ex Jumelle. Lvs. 2–12 in. long, ¾–3 in. wide, puckered; infl. a forked spike; fls. white or pinkish. Madagascar.

crispus Thunb. Lvs. 2–12 in. long, with 7–9 primary veins; infl. a simple spike, 4–6 in. long, peduncle not thickened toward infl.; perianth segms. about as long as stamens. Ceylon. Plants offered under this name may be *A. echinatus.*

desertorum Zeyh. ex K. Spreng. [*A. leptostachyus* E. H. Mey.]. Juvenile lvs. submersed, adult lvs. floating, blades lanceolate to oblong, to 4 in. long, 5–9-nerved, petioles to 1 ft. long; infl. a forked spike, 1–3 in. long; fls. yellow. S. Afr.

distachyus L. f. CAPE PONDWEED, WATER HAWTHORN, CAPE ASPARAGUS. Lf. blades floating, linear-oblong; infl. forked; fls. white, fragrant, perianth parts 1 or 2. Cape of Good Hope. Used for food in S. Afr. Cvs. are: **'Giganteus'**, a large form; **'Grandiflorus'**, perianth segms. larger than in typical form; **'Lagrangei'**, lvs. violet beneath, infl. larger, fls. violet; may not be distinct from cv. 'Grandiflorus'.

echinatus Roxb. Submersed lvs. oblong, to 10 in. long, 2 in. wide, membranous, floating lvs. slightly smaller; infl. a simple spike, to 5 in. long, peduncle thickened toward infl.; perianth segms. about as long as stamens; ovules 2; fr. mostly prickly. India. Often confused with *A. crispus.*

elongatus F. J. Muell. ex Benth. Lf. blades submersed, linear, to 1 ft. long, 1½ in. wide, margin crisped, petioles to 4 in. long; infl. a simple, narrow spike; fls. yellow or greenish-yellow. N. and e. Australia.

fenestralis: *A. madagascariensis.*

leptostachyus: *A. desertorum.*

madagascariensis (Mirb.) Van Brugg. [*A. fenestralis* (Pers.) Hook. f.; *Ouvirandra fenestralis* (Pers.) Poir.]. LACELEAF, LATTICELEAF, MADAGASCAR LACE PLANT, WATER YAM. Rhizome 3 in. long; lvs. submersed, broadly oblong, reduced to a lacelike network of veins. Madagascar. Grown mostly in aquaria, but difficult to grow.

natans (L.) Engl. & Kurt Krause. Juvenile lvs. submersed, lanceolate, to 3 in. long, very thin, adult lvs. floating, blades linear-oblong, to 5 in. long, 1¼ in. wide, cordate at base, petioles to 1 ft. long; infl. a simple, dense spike, to 3 in. long; fls. white, pink, or lilac, ovules about 8. Ceylon, e. India, e. Australia. Plants offered under this name are usually *A. echinatus.*

stachyosporus: *A. undulatus.*

ulvaceus Bak. Rhizome globose, 1 in. in diam.; lvs. submersed, to 14 in. long, 3 in. wide, linear-oblong, tapering basally, blade as long as petiole, undulate or contorted; infl. a forked spike, to 6 in. long; fls. minute, abundant, yellowish-white. Madagascar.

undulatus Roxb. [*A. stachyosporus* De Wit]. Lvs. submersed and also sometimes floating, blade 4–10 in. long, nearly twice as long as petiole, lanceolate, obtuse at base, undulate, with usually 2 primary veins, alternately transparent or opaque in an irregular pattern; infl. a simple spike, to 7 in. long, spathe persistent; fls. small, perianth segms. much longer than stamens, falling early. India to Malay Arch.

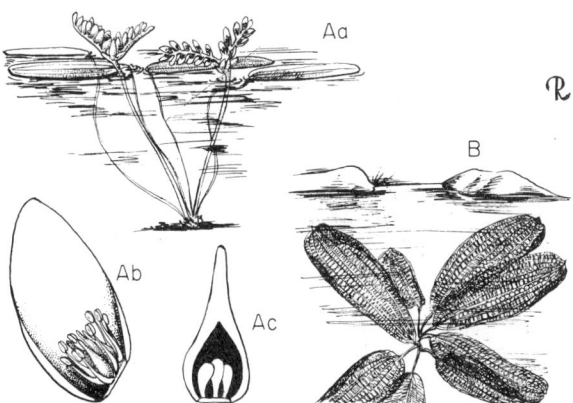

APONOGETONACEAE. **A,** *Aponogeton distachyus:* **Aa,** flowering plant, leaves floating, inflorescences emersed, × ⅛; **Ab,** flower, × 3; **Ac,** pistil, vertical section, × 6. **B,** *A. madagascariensis:* submersed plant, × ⅛. (From Bailey, *Manual of Cultivated Plants,* ed. 2.)

APONOGETONACEAE J. Agardh. APONOGETON FAMILY. Monocot.; 1 genus, *Aponogeton,* of aquatic, freshwater, rhizomatous, per. herbs, native to Old World tropics and subtropics; rhizomes tuberous; lvs. floating, submersed, or rarely emersed, mostly reticulate-veined; infl. bractless, spikelike, enveloped by a spathe when young; fls. bisexual or sometimes unisexual, perianth parts mostly 2, rarely 1, 3, 6, or 0, stamens 6, sometimes more, carpels 3–6, ovary superior, with 1 or more ovules; fr. a follicle.

APOPLANESIA K. Presl. *Leguminosae* (subfamily *Faboideae*). One or 2 spp. of trees of trop. Amer.; lvs. alt., odd-pinnate, lfts. many, glandular-dotted; fls. in panicles, small, papilionaceous, stamens 10, united basally; fr. a small, flat, nearly orbicular legume.

Cultivated as ornamentals; propagated by seeds.

paniculata K. Presl. To 30 ft.; lfts. ovate to oblong, to 2¾ in. long, apically rounded or emarginate, black-dotted, especially beneath; panicles dense, almost as long as lvs.; fls. white; fr. nutlike. Guatemala, Yucatan (Mex.).

APOROCACTUS Lem. *Cactaceae.* About 5 spp. of slender, creeping cacti, native to Mex.; sts. with aerial roots, pitted epidermis, and 5–14 low ribs; spines many but small; fls. pink or red, lasting several days, funnelform, often somewhat irregular, petaloid segms. spreading, often scattered along the tube, scales of the ovary and fr. with axillary bristles or spines.

For culture see *Cacti.*

Conzattii Britt. & Rose. Sts. ½–1 in. thick, ribs 8–10; areoles to ³⁄₁₆ in. apart, spines 15–20, needle-shaped, brown, to ½ in. long; fls. 3½ in. long, brick-red, perianth segms. acute, scales of the tube small, with axillary wool and a few bristly spines.

flagelliformis (L.) Lem. RATTAIL CACTUS. Sts. ½–1 in. thick, ribs 10–14; areoles to ⁵⁄₁₆ in. apart, spines 10–20, needle-shaped, brownish, about ¼ in. long; fls. crimson-pink, about 3 in. long, tube with narrow, spreading, petaloid segms. to below the middle, inner segms. apiculate; fr. globose, red, bristly, to ½ in. in diam. Presumably Mex. A good window, conservatory, and basket plant; widely grown and of easy cult., often grafted on erect cacti.

flagriformis (Zucc.) Lem. Similar to *A. flagelliformis,* but fls. 4 in. long, dark crimson, the outer segms. broader, the inner acuminate.

leptophis (DC.) Britt. & Rose. Sts. to ⅜ in. thick, ribs 7–8; areoles about ⅛ in. apart, spines 10–15, bristlelike, purplish, becoming yellow, to ½ in. long; fls. 2–3 in. long, tube with narrow petaloid segms. to the middle, inner segms. apiculate.

×**Mallisonii**: ×*Heliaporus Smithii.*

Martianus (Zucc.) Britt. & Rose. Sts. ½–¾ in. thick, ribs about 8; areoles ½ in. apart, spines 6–8, needle-shaped or bristlelike; fls. deep rose, to 4 in. long, tube with scales, petaloid segms. long-acuminate; fr. globular, greenish, spiny, ¾ in. in diam.

Ritteri: a listed name of no botanical standing.

APPLE. The taxonomy of the cultivated apples is obscured by centuries of breeding and selection by man, making it difficult to assign modern cultivars to any one species of *Malus.* The pomological, large-fruited apples are the descendants of *M. pumila,* native to southwestern Asia, or may be hybrids of *M. pumila* and *M. sylvestris* of Europe and southwestern Asia. The pomological crab apples are derivatives of *M. baccata,* and some cultivars have been produced by crossing *M. ioensis* with cultivated apples. The ornamental flowering crab apples are various species or hybrids between species.

Apples are the most important fruit grown in North America. They are produced primarily in commercial orchards but can also be grown in the home garden. Apples can be stored and used over a period of several months. Although growing a portion of one's apples can be interesting and satisfying, the home orchardist should not be misled into thinking that apple trees can be grown without effort and expense. The beginner should start with two to six trees; too big a planting can become a burden.

The methods of culture described here will be useful to the serious home gardener, but will not be adequate for the commercial apple grower, who should consult his state's agricultural experiment station to learn the best commercial practices.

Apples grow successfully in a wider range of climates than most other temperate-zone fruits, from as far south as Georgia and New Mexico, north to Maine, Wisconsin, and parts of Canada. Apples do not grow well in most of Florida, because there is insufficient winter cold to induce dormancy. Apples are grown on a commercial scale in localized, well-adapted regions in western New York, western Michigan, the Shenandoah-Cumberland Valley, the valleys of central Washington, and elsewhere. The gardener who is considering growing apples should first look to his neighbors and his local region, to be sure that apples are growing successfully nearby and to determine what cultivars perform best. A planting site with a gentle slope will provide air drainage, which will help reduce problems of blossom freezing by late spring frosts.

Soil is much less important than climate; apples will grow on any good agricultural soil that is fairly deep and well drained. Good drainage is necessary; a soil that stays wet late into the spring is unsatisfactory. Also, a very shallow soil which is only a few inches deep may become too dry and apple trees will not grow well in summers of limited rainfall. Rather heavy sandy or gravelly loams with good humus content are ideal.

Cultivars can be numbered in the hundreds. Those selected for the home orchard could be the same as commercially grown cultivars. Catalogs from local nurseries can be helpful in selecting appropriate types. 'Delicious' is the most important cultivar in the United States and in the world. Except in the coldest apple regions, it grows reasonably well in most areas of the country and best in central Washington. 'McIntosh' is grown extensively in the northeastern United States, but for the home orchard it has the disadvantage of being very susceptible to the most serious leaf and fruit fungus disease, apple scab. 'York' and 'Stayman' are important in the Shenandoah Valley, 'Jonathan' in the Midwest, and 'Gravenstein' in northern California. The earliest summer cultivars ripen in mid-July and the latest in early November. Although many cultivars can be grown successfully, the following list, in order of ripening, is recommended: for the period mid-July through the end of August, 'Quinte', 'Julyred', 'Jerseymac', 'Viking', 'Carroll', and 'Tydeman Early'; for September, 'Paulared', 'Earliblaze', 'Niagara', 'Prima' (scab-resistant), 'Jonamac', 'Wealthy', 'McIntosh'; for October 'Cortland', 'Macoun', 'Spartan', 'Jonathan', 'Rhode Island Greening', 'Empire', 'Priscilla' (scab-resistant), 'Delicious' (spur type), 'Golden Delicious', 'Idared', 'Red Rome', and 'Stayman'. Of course, the home orchardist would plant only a few of these.

New cultivars which can be grown successfully in home orchards include 'Beacon', 'Holly', 'Jonagold', 'Melrose', 'Milton', 'Monroe', 'Mutsu', and 'Spigold'. Some gardeners will elect to plant one of the old-fashioned apples such as 'Baldwin', 'Black Gilliflower', 'Chenango', 'Cox Orange', 'Early Harvest', 'Early McIntosh', 'Esopus Spitzenburg', 'Golden Russet', 'Gravenstein', 'Grimes Golden', 'Lodi', 'Maiden Blush', 'Northern Spy', 'Pound Sweet', 'Red Astrachan', 'Seek-no-further', 'Snow' ('Fameuse'), 'Twenty Ounce', 'Tolman Sweet', 'Turley', 'Wealthy', 'Winesap', or 'Yellow Transparent'.

'Delicious' has produced many good different red-colored sports. 'Delicious', 'Golden Delicious', 'McIntosh', and others have spur types which are usually preferred to nonspur types because they produce a smaller tree. Serious consideration should be given to planting the scab-resistant cultivars 'Prima' and 'Priscilla', because sprays to control scab are unnecessary. Nevertheless, even on these, fungicide sprays will be necessary to control mildew and cedar-apple rust.

Pollination must be provided for in all apple planting plans. All cultivars are self-incompatabile, but most cultivars can be effectively pollinated by almost any other cultivar. Apple pollen is carried from one tree to another by honey bees, which fly only when the temperature is above 60° F. Two cultivars should be separated by no more than 100 feet. For example, if a 'Prima' and a 'Delicious' tree are planted side by side, effective cross pollination and subsequent fruit set

will occur. Certain cultivars do not produce good pollen, and should not be relied on as pollenizers; some of these are 'Baldwin', 'Gravenstein', 'Mutsu', 'Rhode Island Greening', 'Stayman', and 'Winesap'. During cool springs, the spread in blooming period between early and late bloomers, e.g., 'Idared' (early) and 'Red Rome' (late), may be so long that they will not pollinate each other. Thus, selecting cultivars with the same blooming period is desirable.

Dwarf apple trees, first used at least 2,000 years ago, are very desirable for the home garden orchard as well as the commercial orchard. The majority of apple trees sold to the home orchardist are on dwarfing stock. They are easier to prune, spray, and harvest, and they begin to bear at a younger age. Each tree can yield up to two bushels. Dwarf trees are dwarf because they are budded on size-controlling rootstocks, which are not grown from seeds but are vegetatively propagated from suckers borne on mother plants called stool beds. The nurseryman producing commercial fruit trees removes these rooted suckers from the mother stool and plants them into the nursery row in the spring. In late summer, cultivars such as 'Delicious' are budded into them. Fully dwarfed apple trees are budded on 'Malling 9' rootstocks, and at maturity grow to about 8 feet tall. Semidwarf trees are on 'Malling 26', 'Malling 7', or 'Malling-Merton 106' rootstocks, and grow to about 13 feet tall when mature. Full-sized, nondwarfed trees are budded on seedling roots, and grow to a height of 26 feet or more. In certain small-growing cultivars, tree size is naturally small, regardless of rootstock, as in 'Idared' and spur cultivars of 'Delicious', whereas 'McIntosh', 'Cortland', and nonspur 'Delicious' are naturally very large, vigorous growers.

Propagation of apple cultivars in commercial nurseries is generally by budding onto the size-controlling rootstocks. Apple trees should be bought from a reliable nursery; cheap trees can be a poor investment. One-year-old dwarf, semidwarf, or spur-type trees are most satisfactory. Trees that have been grown in the nursery for two or three years do not grow any faster after planting than one-year-old trees, and they are more expensive. Older trees are inclined to be set back somewhat more than younger trees when planted bare root. A tree that has five different cultivars grafted onto it can be of interest to the home gardener, but it requires correct pruning to prevent the more vigorous cultivars from outgrowing the others.

Tree spacing in the row and between rows is dependent on the kind of rootstock, the kind of scion cultivar, and soil fertility. When spur cultivars are planted on a soil of average growing potential, these tree spacings are suggested for the following dwarf rootstocks: 'Malling 9' and 'Clark Dwarf' ('Malling 8' interstem), 6 × 12 feet; 'Malling 26', 10 × 18 feet; 'Malling 7', 12 × 22 feet; and 'Malling-Merton 106', 16 × 24 feet. For nonspur cultivars and in better soils, slightly wider spacing is used.

Planting is done in the early spring, even before the soil is fully dry; however, autumn planting is advantageous in milder climates. An area that is not shaded should be selected because apple trees need full sun. Before planting, the soil should be plowed and levelled. Extra-long roots or broken roots should be pruned back and the soil tamped firmly around the roots. Trees should not be fertilized at planting but they should be well watered.

Dwarf and semidwarf trees have very precise planting depth requirements. The bud union, which is the point at which the scion joins the rootstock, must be placed just at the soil surface or 1 inch above. If the union is planted beneath the soil surface, the scion top will send out vigorous, nondwarfing roots and all dwarfing effect will be lost. Trees having dwarfing and semidwarfing roots have poor anchorage and must be tied up to a stake. A 2 × 2 inch wooden stake should be driven into the ground at a distance of 4 inches from each trunk. Stakes should be 5 feet long, driven halfway into the ground. The tree should be tied near the top of the stake, using soft cloth. After a one-year-old nursery tree is planted, the top should be cut off, leaving the tree 30 inches high. This will encourage the growth of side buds, which will develop into the desired framework of branches.

Fertilizers should be applied before bloom each year, except in the year of planting, 4 ounces of ammonium nitrate for each year of tree age up to a maximum of 3.5 pounds. Thus, a four-year-old tree would receive about 1 pound. The amount of fertilizer applied should be regulated according to the rate of tree growth. If the previous year's shoots are more than 12 inches long, fertilizer should not be applied, but if growth was less than 12 inches the recommended application should be given. The fertilizer should be broadcast in a wide band under the tips of the branches, not next to the trunk. Potassium should be applied if it is deficient in the soil; apple trees do not benefit from phosphorous fertilizers. Fertilizer should not be applied in summer or early autumn since it will stimulate late growth and reduce winter hardiness. If ammonium nitrate is not available, a complete garden fertilizer such as 10–10–10 may be applied at three times the rate for ammonium nitrate.

Weed-control chemicals are sprayed on the soil, covering an area of a square yard under each tree. Keeping the soil under the tree completely free of weeds and grass promotes growth and helps discourage mouse invasion. Grass, such as meadow fescue *(Festuca pratensis)* or Merion blue grass (*Poa pratensis* 'Merion'), is seeded in the areas between the rows of trees to help prevent soil erosion and provide a good working area. It should be kept mowed as closely as a lawn. If only half a dozen trees are grown, it may be easier to control the weeds and grass by hoeing rather than by using weed-control sprays; for more than half a dozen, weed chemicals are easier. Mulches of hay or straw piled 6 inches deep and 12 inches wide in a band under the tips of the branches help suppress weed and grass growth and reduce soil drying, but they encourage mouse invasion.

Pruning in the first four years after planting should be kept to a minimum, except to train the branches to develop a tree structure having the desired placement of scaffold branches. Pruning delays bearing; prune as little as possible. Pruning is generally done in late winter, though summer pruning is also permissible. In the second and third years after planting, four or five good broad-angled branches widely spaced along the trunk should be selected and the rest removed. The tree should be shaped so that there is a strong central leader, kept taller than all the others, as the main axis through the center of the tree. Dead or diseased limbs, those that rub others badly, and suckers should be removed. Many cultivars, such as 'Delicious', tend to grow too upright, with side branches growing too close into the center and with resulting narrow branch angles. Young branches should be bent outward and held there with wire spreaders made of No. 9 wire, 8 inches long and sharpened to a point at each end.

Insect and disease control using chemical sprays is one of the most difficult problems facing the home orchardist. More insects and diseases, perhaps 400 kinds, attack apples grown in the northeastern United States than any other economic crop in the world. A dozen or more are serious pests and must be controlled. Each insect has its own unique life cycle, and there is a best chemical and best spray timing for the control of each. Commercial growers can afford to make special adjustments in spray programs to control each pest. The home orchardist, however, can obtain reasonably good control using a general fruit spray containing two insecticides, malathion and methoxyclor, and a fungicide, captan. Wettable sulphur and carbaryl (Sevin) are also common ingredients. None of these materials is toxic to humans when applied at the recommended rates, yet they give good control of pests and diseases. The first spraying is an oil spray to control San Jose scale and mites, applied while the trees are still dormant, just before the buds begin to enlarge. Then, there are seven sprayings of the general fruit spray: (1) when the buds have green tips, (2) when there are pink unopened blossoms, (3) when petals fall, and (4–7) cover sprays at ten-day intervals. The most important spraying is when petals fall; if only one spray is applied, it should be this one. Spraying should not

be done at full bloom, because it kills honey bees, which carry pollen from one cultivar to another. The last cover spray is completed about the end of June; but if apple maggot (railroad worm) is a pest, more than four cover sprays will be needed.

Mice, rabbits, deer, and birds can also be major pests on apples. Mice can girdle the bark completely around the bottom of the trunk on younger trees, killing the tree. Wire screen cut and formed into a cylinder about 5 inches in diameter and 12 inches high can be placed around the trunk and set into the soil. Bare soil without a covering of grass, weeds, or mulch will discourage mice. Commercial orchards annually apply mouse bait. Deer browse on growing shoots during late June and can often remove half the leaves from a young apple tree. Small bags of tankage suspended in the tree will repel deer. Birds may peck holes in the nearly ripe fruits of early-ripening cultivars.

The age at which apple trees begin to bear their first fruit depends on many factors. Dwarf trees on 'Malling 9' rootstock can begin bearing in the second year after planting, while semidwarf trees on 'Malling 7' rootstock may require four or more years. Cultivars differ. 'Golden Delicious' may bear in the third year, while 'Northern Spy' may require ten years. Rapid tree growth in the early years encourages early bearing. Healthy foliage, which can be kept healthy only by spraying even in the years before cropping begins, is essential for early bearing. Ringing the trunk induces early fruiting. In early June, a knife cut is made through the bark all the way around the trunk. This can cause flowering the following spring.

Thinning of fruits is sometimes necessary when a tree overcrops. Many cultivars have a strong tendency to bear a crop only in alternate years and as a result have small fruits because of overcropping. These include 'Early McIntosh', 'Golden Delicious', and 'Wealthy'. Overcropping can be corrected by thinning the fruits by hand in late June. When several fruits are borne in a cluster, all except one should be removed. From branches on which fruits have set too heavily, fruits should be removed until they are no closer than 6 inches apart. Commercial growers use naphthaleneacetamide or other chemicals as sprays to thin the blossoms to prevent overcropping.

Storage of apples in the cellar of a modern heated home is generally unsatisfactory. Unless controlled-atmosphere storage is available, apples keep best at 33° F and at high humidity. For the home orchardist, a large discarded kitchen refrigerator with its lock removed, buried with its back down in the ground, makes a good storage where apples will keep most of the winter. Long-keeping cultivars are 'Delicious', 'Empire', 'Idared', 'Mutsu', 'Northern Spy', 'Red Rome', and 'Stayman'; cultivars which are harvested in August or early September do not keep well.

APRICOT. The apricot is a stone fruit ripening mostly earlier than peaches, pubescent, or smooth at maturity, with a flat stone or pit that is not corrugated or furrowed on the side. It is much prized as a summer fruit in regions where it is grown and is canned and dried. The tree is about as hardy as the peach. The apricot, *Prunus Armeniaca,* is a variable species of eastern Asiatic origin. At least three varieties may be recognized. The typical variety, var. *Armeniaca,* is native to China and is the source of the commercial apricots. The other two varieties, var. *sibirica* and var. *mandshurica,* are found in more northerly regions and are adapted to more severe winters; var. *sibirica,* however, produces small, scarcely edible fruits. The Japanese apricot or Japanese flowering apricot, *Prunus Mume,* known as the winter-flowering "plum" of the Orient, has a few cultivars, such as 'Bungo' and 'Bungoume', that have fruits much used for pickles and sweet liqueur; it is also used in Japan for bonsai.

Because of the early blooming period and consequent damage from late spring frosts, apricot growing is confined mostly to regions where such frosts are not common. Apricots are grown commercially on the Pacific Coast and in some of the

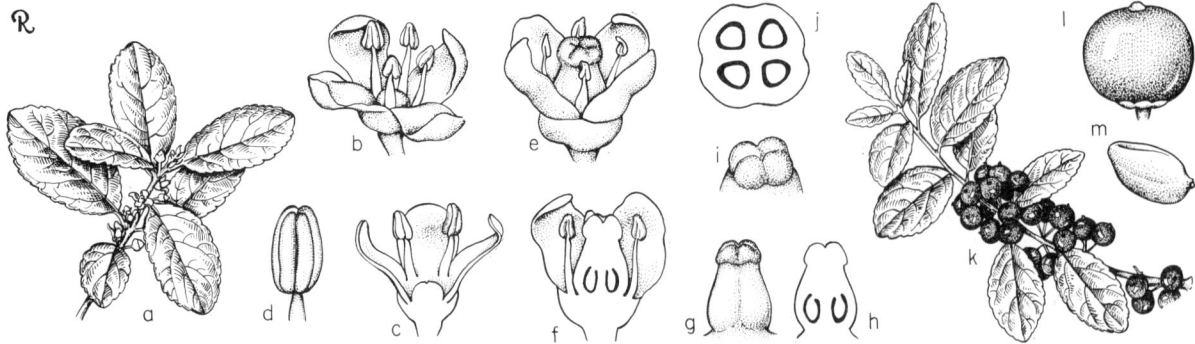

AQUIFOLIACEAE. *Ilex vomitoria:* **a,** flowering branch, female plant,×½; **b,** male flower,×5; **c,** male flower, vertical section, ×5; **d,** anther,×8; **e,** female flower,×5; **f,** female flower, vertical section,×5; **g,** pistil,×5; **h,** pistil, vertical section, ×5; **i,** stigma,×8; **j,** ovary, cross section,×10; **k,** fruiting branch,×½; **l,** fruit,×2½; **m,** pyrene,×3.

Rocky Mountain states, about 95 percent of the crop being produced in California. In home gardens they are planted sparingly wherever peaches thrive, and while not dependable in bearing, give occasional crops and in some cases may supply local markets.

Apricots are grown on several *Prunus* stocks, including apricot or peach seedlings, myrobalan plum, and 'Marianna' plum, but apricot seedlings are the preferred stocks except possibly under special conditions.

One- or two-year trees are planted in the early spring in the East and in late autumn in California. Soil and planting depend somewhat on the stock. Light soils are best for peach and apricot stocks, whereas plum stocks adapt the apricot for growth on heavier soils. Good drainage is necessary. Trees in home plantings should be mulched to keep down the grass, and if growth is not fairly vigorous they should be fertilized with manure or 2–3 pounds of nitrate to a tree, applied early in the spring. The young trees are pruned to give them a balanced head, and bearing trees require moderate thinning to assure renewal of fruit spurs and promotion of new growth.

In California, 'Blenheim', 'Royal', and 'Tilton' are the principal cultivars. Recently, as the result of apricot-breeding projects, new cultivars much superior to older ones have become available and are suggested for planting in the peach-growing regions of the North. Among them are 'Alfred', 'Earliril', 'Farmingdale', 'Goldcot', and 'Veecot'. For the northern limits of apricot growing, the less desirable but more winter-hardy 'Moongold' and 'Sungold' may be planted. 'Earliril', 'Moongold', and 'Sungold' are self-incompatible cultivars, so that each requires the presence of another cultivar for cross-pollination.

Curculio is a serious pest and bacterial leaf spot and brown rot are serious diseases of the apricot, difficult to control. The same control methods used for peaches are recommended.

APTENIA N. E. Br. *Aizoaceae.* Two spp. of small, somewhat shrubby, short-lived per. succulents, native to S. Afr., sts. prostrate, with distinct internodes; lvs. opp., flat; fls. solitary, axillary, pedicelled, calyx deeply and unequally 4-lobed, petals many, united basally into a short tube, stamens many, erect, from corolla tube, ovary inferior, 4-celled, stigmas 4; fr. a 4-valved caps., expanding keels without wings, placental tubercles absent.

Planted outdoors in summer in the rock garden or as bedding plants, but in winter they require a moderately dry place at a relatively cool temperature of about 45–55° F. Propagated by seeds, but much faster from cuttings for large planting outdoors. See also *Succulents.*

cordifolia (L. f.) Schwant. [*Mesembryanthemum cordifolium* L. f.]. BABY SUN ROSE. Brs. prostrate, to 2 ft. long, cylindrical, green, becoming gray, minutely papillate; lvs. 4-ranked, green, minutely papillate, to 1 in. long, nearly as wide, petioled, cordate-ovate; fls. terminal or lateral on a short peduncle, petals purple-red. E. coastal deserts, S. Afr. Cv. **'Variegata'.** Lvs. bordered with white.

AQUARIUM PLANTS. Plants used in aquaria are primarily freshwater aquatics from various parts of the world, usually submerged or free-floating species, grown to help maintain a proper biological balance and to provide a naturalistic and ornamental setting for the animals included (usually fish), as well as to supply them with food, shelter and protection, and areas for reproduction.

Aquarium plants require adequate light and proper nutrients to thrive. Lighting may be either natural daylight, equilavent artificial light, or an appropriate combination of both to satisfy the average ten hours of light per day required by most aquatics. Once an aquarium has been established, nutrients for the plantings are supplied by the animal life, but when setting up an aquarium for the first time, the plants will get a better start if small amounts of good garden soil are supplied beneath the gravel layer in which the aquatics are to be rooted.

To achieve an attractive effect one must be just as selective in choosing plant materials and as careful in their placement as in planning a landscape garden. In the miniature planting of the aquarium, however, the aquarist depends not on flowers for effect but rather on different growth habits of plants as well as variations in the form and color of foliage. Consideration is also given to whether the plants are for a warm-water tropical or cold-water tank. Slow-growing species should be used where a minimum of attention is desired, for fast-growing aquatics require regular pinching back or transplanting when they become overcrowded.

Details on maintaining aquaria and their plants should be sought in the specialized publications available. For descriptions of representative aquatics suited for culture as rooted aquarium plants see: *Aponogeton, Cabomba, Ceratopteris, Cryptocoryne, Echinodorus, Eichhornia, Eleocharis, Elodea, Fontinalis, Heteranthera, Hydrilla, Hygrophila, Isoetes, Lagenandra, Limnobium, Ludwigia, Marsilea, Myriophyllum, Nitella, Nuphar, Nymphaea, Nymphoides, Ottelia, Peplis, Sagittaria, Utricularia,* and *Vallisneria.* Free-floating plants belong to the genera *Azolla, Ceratophyllum, Ceratopteris, Eichhornia, Lemna, Pistia, Riccia, Salvinia, Spirodela, Stratiotes, Wolffiella,* and *Wolffia.* See also *Aquatics* and *Water Lily.*

AQUATICS. These plants live in deep, usually fresh, water, either rooted in soil or free-floating. The term is frequently used also for those plants with emergent stems and leaves that grow in bogs, swamps, and about the margins of ponds and lakes. Aquatic plants that are rooted in soil may be completely submerged (except for the inflorescence), as are *Aponogeton, Cryptocoryne, Elodea,* and *Vallisneria;* some may have a combination of submerged and floating leaves, as do *Cabomba* and *Potamogeton;* others may have all the leaves floating, as do the water lilies *(Nymphaeaceae).* Free-floating aquatics include *Azolla, Eichhornia, Lemna, Pistia,* and *Salvinia.* Aquatics are popular ornamental subjects for pools or ponds, and certain of the submerged and floating kinds are commonly used in aquaria. See *Aquarium Plants, Bog Plants, Water Lily.*

AQUIFOLIACEAE Bartl. HOLLY FAMILY. Dicot.; 2 genera and about 400 spp. of mostly dioecious or polygamodioecious shrubs and trees, primarily in temp. and trop. N. and S. Amer. and Asia; lvs. alt. or rarely opp., simple, with margins entire to toothed or spiny, often persistent, usually leathery, petioled, mostly stipuled; fls. regular, unisexual, rarely bisexual, very small, axillary, solitary or few or many in fascicles or cymes, calyx mostly 3–6-parted, usually persistent, petals mostly 4–6, separate or united at base, imbricate, deciduous, stamens as many as the petals or rarely more, separate or slightly joined to petals, ovary superior, 2–6 (rarely many) -celled; fr. drupaceous, mostly containing 3–8, rarely to 18, stony-covered seeds (pyrenes). *Ilex* and *Nemopanthus* are cult. for ornament, while some spp. of *Ilex* are used for medicine or drink.

AQUILEGIA L. COLUMBINE. *Ranunculaceae.* About 70 variable spp. of hardy, mostly erect, prominently branching, per. herbs of the N. Temp. Zone, many of them cult., as are many hybrids; lvs. 2–3-ternate; fls. white, yellow, blue, lavender, red, terminating the brs., showy, pendent or erect, sepals 5, petaloid, regular, petals with a short broad lip or lamina and usually a long hollow, backward-projecting spur, stamens many, the inner replaced by staminodes, pistils usually 5, free, sessile; fr. of many-seeded follicles.

Columbines are planted in rock gardens and perennial borders, doing best in a light sandy loam. Propagated by seeds or by division in the spring. The most common garden columbines are not species, but hybrids; those with hooked spurs usually indicate derivation from *A. vulgaris,* and those with long straight spurs from *A. caerulea* and *A. chrysantha.*

akitensis: *A. flabellata.* Var. **alba:** *A. flabellata* cv. Var. **kurilensis:** see *A. flabellata* var. *pumila.*

alba: a listed name of no botanical standing.

alpina L. To 1 or 2 ft., densely pubescent in upper parts, sts. 1–3-fld.; basal lvs. 2-ternate; fls. nodding, bright blue, sepals 1–2 in. long, limb of petals oblong, ⅝ in. long, spurs rather coarse, straight to curved, ⅝–1 in. long. Alps. Cvs. include: **'Alba'**, fls. white; **'Atroviolacea'**, probably a hybrid, fls. dark violet-purple; **'Caerulea'**, garden form of undetermined origin, fls. blue; **'Superba'**, close to the sp. but does not come true from seed.

atrata W. D. J. Koch. Close to *A. vulgaris,* but having stamens well exserted beyond the limbs of petals; fls. dark purple-violet, sepals ½ in. long, spurs ¾–1 in. long. Eur.

atropurpurea: *A. viridiflora.*

aurea Janka. To 15 in., sts. few-fld.; lvs. mostly basal, 2-ternate; fls. sulphur-yellow, suberect, spurs sharply hooked. Bulgaria, Macedonia.

Bernardii Gren. & Godr. To 2 ft., glandular-pubescent in upper parts; basal lvs. 2-ternate, glabrous; fls. nodding, pale blue, sepals spreading, 1 in. long or more, limb of petals obovate, ⅝ in. long. Corsica.

Bertolonii Schott [*A. Reuteri* Boiss.]. To 1 ft., glandular-pubescent in upper parts, sts. 1–3-fld.; basal lvs. few, 2-ternate, small; fls. nodding, violet-blue, sepals ⅝–1⁵⁄₁₆ in. long, limb of petals nearly truncate, ½ in. long, spurs straight to hooked, ½ in. long. S. Eur.

bicolor: *A. sibirica.*

brevistyla Hook. To 2½ ft., pilose and glandular in upper parts; basal lvs. few, 2-ternate, rather thin; fls. nodding, pilose, sepals blue, lanceolate, ½ in. long, limb of petals yellowish-white, ⁵⁄₁₆ in. long, spurs blue, hooked, ¼ in. long. Alaska, s. to B. C. and S. Dak.

Buergerana Siebold & Zucc. To 2½ ft.; basal lvs. 2-ternate, thickish; fls. nodding, sepals divergent, purple, to 1 in. long, limb of petals yellowish, truncate, about ½ in. long, spurs purplish, slightly curved, ½–⅝ in. long. Japan. Some plants offered under the name of *A. akitensis* belong here.

caerulea James. To 2½ ft.; basal lvs. 2-ternate, rather thin; fls. erect, sepals spreading, deep to light blue, ovate, 1–1½ in. long, limb of petals white, ⅝–1 in. long, spurs straight or curved outward, 1¼–2 in. long. Rocky Mts. State fl. of Colo. Important as a parent of many long-spurred aquilegias. Cvs. include: **'Alba'** and **'Candidissima'**, fls. white, do not breed true; **'Citrina'**, fls. citron-yellow; **'Cuprea'**, fls. copper-red; **'Rosea'**, probably a hybrid, fls. pink or red, often double. Var. **albiflora:** var. *ochroleuca.* Var. **alpina** A. Nels. Low, sepals pale blue, to ¾ in. Nw. Wyo. Var. **calcarea:** *A. scopulorum* var. *calcarea.* Var. **Daileyae** Eastw. Sepals blue, 1–1½ in., spurs lacking. Colo. Var. **Helenae:** *A.* ×*Helenae.* Var. **ochroleuca** Hook. [var. *albiflora* A. Gray]. Sepals whitish. W. Rocky Mts.

californica: *A. formosa* var. *truncata.*

canadensis L. WILD COLUMBINE, MEETING-HOUSES, HONEYSUCKLE. Mostly to 2 ft., sts. usually several-fld.; basal lvs. largely 2-ternate, not fleshy; fls. nodding, glandular-pubescent, sepals red, somewhat divergent, ovate, about ½ in. long, limb of petals yellow, to ⁵⁄₁₆ in. long, spurs red, straight, to 1 in. long. Nov. Sc. to Fla., w. to Minn. and Tenn. Cv. **'Nana'.** To 1 ft. Var. **latiuscula** (Greene) Munz [*A. latiuscula* Greene]. Basal lvs. often 3-ternate, lfts. deeply cleft. Nebr. to Tex.

caryophylloides: a listed name of no botanical standing for *A. vulgaris* cv.

caucasica: *A. olympica.*

chrysantha A. Gray. To 3½ ft., usually much-branched; basal lvs. mostly 3-ternate, rather thin; fls. erect, clear golden-yellow, somewhat glandular-pubescent, sepals spreading, lanceolate, 1–1½ in. long, limb of petals usually rounded at apex, spreading, ⁵⁄₁₆–⅝ in. long, spurs usually spreading, 1½–3 in. long. Ariz., New Mex., nw. Mex. Important parent of garden forms. Cvs. include: **'Alba'**, fls. whitish; **'Alba Plena'**, fls. double; white; **'Flore Pleno'**, fls. double, yellow; **'Grandiflora Sulphurea'**, sepals large, deep cream, petals cream-yellow; **'Nana'**, dwarf, fls. golden-yellow. Var. **Jaeschkanii:** *A.* ×*Jaeschkanii.* Much garden material named *A. longissima* is *A. chrysantha.*

clematiflora: a listed name of no botanical standing, applied to spurless derivative of *A. caerulea.*

dichroa Freyn. To 2 ft., sts. 1–2- to many-fld.; lvs. 2-ternate; fls. nodding, sepals blue, greenish at apex, ovate-lanceolate, acuminate, to ¾ in. long; limb of petals blue, white at apex, about ⁵⁄₁₆ in. long, spurs hooked, ½ in. long. Portugal.

discolor Levier & Leresche. Sts. to 1 ft., 1–2-fld.; basal lvs. 2-ternate, almost flat on the ground; fls. almost erect at flowering, nodding in bud, sepals blue, ½–¾ in. long, limb of petals whitish, ⁵⁄₁₆ in. long, spurs blue, somewhat incurved, to ⁵⁄₁₆ in. long. Spain.

ecalcarata Maxim. [*Semiaquilegia ecalcarata* (Maxim.) T. Sprague & Hutch.; *S. simulatrix* J. R. Drumm. & Hutch.]. To 2 ft., soft-pubescent; basal lvs. membranous, 2- or 3-ternate; fls. erect or somewhat nodding, wine-colored to rich purple, or whitish, sepals spreading, ½ in. long, limb of petals oblong, ½ in. long, spurs nearly or quite lacking. China. The name has also been applied to spurless forms of *A. micrantha* and *A. vulgaris.*

Einseleana F. W. Schultz. To 1½ ft., simple to few-branched; basal lvs. few, mostly 2-ternate, subcoriaceous; fls. nodding, blue-violet, sepals spreading, ⅝ in. long, limb of petals rounded at apex, ⁵⁄₁₆ in. long, spurs almost straight, pubescent, ⁵⁄₁₆ in. long. Austrian Alps.

elegantula Greene. Sts. to 16 in., 1- to few-fld.; basal lvs. 2-ternate; fls. nearly cylindrical, pendent, sepals red, often greenish or yellowish toward apex, ⁵⁄₁₆–½ in. long, limb of petals yellow, ⁵⁄₁₆ in. long, spurs red, straight, ⅝ in. long. Utah, Colo., New Mex.

erecta: a listed name of no botanical standing; plants double-fld., possibly derived from *A. atrata.*

eximia Van Houtte ex Planch. To 2–3 ft., densely glandular-pubescent throughout; basal lvs. 3-ternate; fls. nodding, viscid-puberulent, sepals reddish, ovate-lanceolate, ⅝–1 in. long, limb of petals lacking, spurs scarlet, yellowish at opening, to over 1 in. long. Calif. Garden plants under this name are often derivatives of *A. formosa.*

Fauriei: *A. flabellata.*

flabellata Siebold & Zucc. [*A. akitensis* Huth; *A. Fauriei* Lév. & Vaniot.; *A. japonica* Nakai & Hara]. To 1½ ft.; sts. with a few lvs., mostly 1–2-fld.; basal lvs. few, 2-ternate, sometimes ternate; fls. nodding, on glandular-pubescent pedicels, sepals blue-purple to lilac, about 1 in. long, divergent, limb of petals lilac, oblong, pale yellow at tip, ½ in. or longer, spurs lilac, strongly hooked, ⁵⁄₁₆–⅝ in. long. Japan. Cv. **'Alba'** [var. *alba* Hort.]. Fls. white. Cv. **'Nana Alba':** see var. *pumila.* Var. **kurilensis:** see var. *pumila.* Var. **pumila** Kudo [possibly cv. 'Nana Alba']. Sts. to 6 in.; limb of petals scarcely ½ in. long. Japan. Material of this var. is sometimes offered as *A. akitensis* var. *kurilensis* Hort.

flavescens S. Wats. To 2 ft., simple to several-branched; basal lvs. 2-ternate to almost 3-ternate, rather thin; fls. nodding, sparsely glandular-puberulent, sepals generally yellow, ½–1 in. long, limb of petals cream-colored, ¼–⁵⁄₁₆ in. long, spurs yellowish, more or less incurved at apex, ¼–¾ in. long. B. C. and Alta. to Ore. and Colo.

formosa Fisch. Sts. 2–3 ft., openly branched; basal lvs. 2-ternate, rather thin; fls. pendent, more or less pubescent, sepals wide-spreading, red, ovate-lanceolate, ⅝–1 in. long, limb of petals yellow, rounded or truncate, ⅛–¼ in. long, spurs red, rather stout, ⁵⁄₁₆–⅝ in. long. Alaska, s. to Mont., n. Calif., Utah. Cvs. include: **'Nana'**, dwarf, fls. shell-pink; **'Nana Alba'**, dwarf, fls. white; **'Rubra Plena'**, fls. double, red. Var. **hybrida** Hort. A name incorrectly used for a hybrid, *A.*

chrysantha × *A. formosa.* Fls. erect, sepals red, 1 in. long, spurs red, 1½ in. long. Var. **pauciflora** (Greene) Boothm. Sts. scapelike, to 1 ft.; lvs. mostly basal; limb of petals ¹⁄₁₆ in. long. Mts., Calif. Var. **truncata** (Fisch. & C. A. Mey.) Bak. [*A. californica* Hartweg ex Lindl.; *A. truncata* Fisch. & C. A. Mey.]. Sts. branched, to 40 in.; limb of petals ¹⁄₁₆ in. long. Nev. to s. Ore. and s. Calif.

fragrans Benth. To 2½ ft., brs. usually several; basal lvs. 2–3-ternate, thin; fls. several, fragrant, horizontal to somewhat nodding, sepals spreading, whitish to purplish, pubescent, 1 in. long, limb of petals somewhat paler, cuneate-oblong, ⅝ in. long, spurs straight or somewhat curved, ⅝ in. long. N. India.

glandulosa Fisch. ex Link. Sts. 6–24 in., 1–5-fld.; basal lvs. few to several, mostly 2-ternate; fls. suberect, sepals lilac-blue, spreading, 1–2 in. long, limb of petals mostly violet-blue, rounded to obtusish at apex, ⅝–1 in. long, spurs strongly hooked, ¼–½ in. long; seeds dull black. S.-cent. Siberia.

×**Helenae** Hort. [*A. caerulea* var. *Helenae* Hort.]: *A. caerulea* × *A. flabellata.* Fls. blue and white.

×**hybrida** Sims [*A. vulgaris* var. *hybrida* (Sims) Bak.]: *A. canadensis* × *A. vulgaris.* Sepals purplish, limb of petals white. The name *A.* ×*hybrida,* however, is more often used for long-spurred garden hybrids with a parentage involving *A. caerulea, A. chrysantha,* and possibly other spp.

×**Jaeschkanii** Hort. [*A. chrysantha* var. *Jaeschkanii* Hort.]: supposedly *A. chrysantha* × *A. Skinneri.* Sepals carmine-red, petals yellow.

japonica: *A. flabellata.*

Jonesii Parry. Dwarf, sts. scapelike, mostly 1–4 in. high, 1-fld.; lvs. in basal tufts, ternate to 2-ternate, subcoriaceous; fls. erect, sepals blue or purple, ⅝ in. long, limb of petals blue, ⁵⁄₁₆ in. long, spurs blue, straight, ⁵⁄₁₆–⅝ in. long. Mont., n. Wyo.

jucunda Fisch. & Avé-Lall. Like *A. glandulosa,* but having sepals blue, petals white, seeds shining. Siberia.

Kitaibelii Schott. To 1 ft., mostly 1–3-fld.; basal lvs. 2-ternate; fls. suberect, red-violet or blue-violet, sepals spreading, ⅝–¾ in. long, ciliate toward apex, limb of petals ½ in. long, spurs slightly curved, ¼–⁵⁄₁₆ in. long. Cent. Eur.

lactiflora Kar. & Kir. Sts. 16–30 in.; lvs. 2-ternate, thin; fls. 1 to several, nodding, sepals spreading to reflexed, almost white, ½–¾ in. long, limb of petals slightly rounded at apex, ⁵⁄₁₆ in. long, spurs almost straight ⅝–1 in. long. Sw. Asia.

latiuscula: *A. canadensis* var.

longissima A. Gray. To 3 ft., openly branched; basal lvs. 3-ternate, rather thin; fls. erect, pale yellow, somewhat glandular-puberulent, sepals spreading, acuminate, 1 in. long, limb of petals spreading, ⅝–1 in. long, spurs filiform, pendent, 3½–6 in. long. W. Tex., adjacent Mex. Much garden material bearing this name is *A. chrysantha.*

luteogigantea: a listed name of no botanical standing.

micrantha Eastw. [*A. rubicunda* Tidestr.]. Much-branched, viscid, 12–18 in.; basal lvs. 2–3-ternate, rather thin; fls. erect or nearly so, sepals spreading, white or pale blue to pinkish-lavender or reddish, ⁵⁄₁₆–⅝ in. long, limb of petals whitish or rarely reddish, erect, ¼–⁵⁄₁₆ in. long, spurs whitish or rarely reddish, straight or spreading, ⅝–1⅛ in. long. Utah, Colo., Ariz.

nevadensis Boiss. & Reut. To 2 ft., branched in upper parts; basal lvs. 2-ternate; fls. nodding, pale blue, smaller than in *A. vulgaris,* spurs straight or slightly curved. Spain.

nigricans Baumg. Like *A. atrata,* but sts. glandular-pubescent; sepals blue-violet, 1 in. long or more, spurs strongly hooked, ½–¾ in. long. Tyrol to Bulgaria, s. Yugoslavia. Some plants cult. as *A. Reuteri* belong here. Cv. **'Subalpina'** is listed.

olympica Boiss. [*A. caucasica* Ledeb. ex Rupr.]. Sts. to 2 ft., several-branched; basal lvs. 2-ternate, lfts. thin; fls. nodding, sepals spreading, light claret to lilac-purple, 1–2 in. long, limb of petals colored to whitish, ⁵⁄₁₆–⅝ in. long, spurs strongly hooked, ¾ in. long. S. Russia to n. Turkey and Iran.

Ottonis Orph. ex Boiss. Sts. 1–1½ ft., 1- to several-fld.; basal lvs. 2-ternate, membranous; fls. bicolored, sepals blue, ¼ longer than limb of petals, white, truncate, to ½ in. long, spurs blue, distinctly hooked. Greece, Italy.

oxysepala Trautv. & C. A. Mey. Sts. 2–3 ft., open-branched in upper parts; basal lvs. 2-ternate, thickish in texture; fls. horizontal to nodding, sepals divergent, 1 in. long, claret-red to violet, limb of petals oblong, ½ in. long, yellowish-white, spurs colored like sepals, strongly hooked, ⅝ in. long. Ne. Asia.

pubescens Cov. Tufted, 8–16 in.; basal lvs. ternate to 2-ternate, thickish; fls. erect, glandular-puberulent, sepals spreading, cream to yellow or pink, ⅝–¾ in. long, limb of petals oblong, mostly pale, to ½ in. long, spurs straight to spreading, 1–1½ in. long. Sierra Nevada, Calif.

pyrenaica DC. Sts. to 1 ft., 1–3-fld.; basal lvs. 2-ternate, thick; fls. nodding, bright lilac-blue, sepals spreading, ovate, 1–1½ in. long, limb of petals oblong-obovate, ½ in. long, pubescent outside, spurs slender, straight or slightly curved, pubescent, ⅜–¾ in. long. Pyrenees.

Reuteri: *A. Bertolonii,* but some material cult. as *A. Reuteri* is *A. nigricans.*

rubicunda: *A. micrantha.*

saximontana Rydb. Sts. many, 2–10 in., somewhat branched, almost completely glabrous, leafy; basal lvs. 2-ternate, rather thin; fls. nodding, glabrous, sepals blue, to ½ in. long, limb of petals yellowish, ⁵⁄₁₆ in. long, spurs blue, hooked, ¼ in. long. Colo.

scopulorum Tidestr. Sts. to 15 in., 1- to few-fld.; basal lvs. in a dense tuft, 2-ternate, glaucous, with glabrous petioles; fls. erect, sepals spreading, blue to white, sometimes red, ¾ in. long, limb of petals white to yellowish, blue, or red, ½ in. long, spurs straight, 1–1½ in. long. Nev., Utah. Var. **calcarea** (M. E. Jones) Munz [*A. caerulea* var. *calcarea* M. E. Jones]. Petioles glandular-pubescent. Wyo., Utah.

sibirica Lam. [*A. bicolor* J. F. Ehrh.]. Like *A. flabellata,* but having sts. nearly or quite leafless, pedicels glabrous, sepals blue to claret. Siberia, Mongolia. Cv. **'Flore Pleno'.** Fls. double.

Skinneri Hook. Sts. to 3 ft., usually openly branched; basal lvs. 3-ternate, thin; fls. pendent, puberulent, sepals erect to divaricate, yellowish-green, ¾–1 in. long, limb of petals greenish, rounded-truncate, ⁵⁄₁₆ in. long, spurs red, straight, 1½–2 in. long, ⁵⁄₁₆ in. in diam. at opening. New Mex. Cv. **'Flore Pleno'.** Fls. double.

×**Stuartii** Balf. f.: *A. glandulosa* × *A. olympica.* Sts. 6–9 in., fls. deep violet-blue, petals white at apex.

thalictrifolia Schott & Kotschy. Sts. to 2 ft., brs. slender, in upper part; basal lvs. few, mostly 2-ternate, glandular-pubescent; fls. nodding to nearly erect, blue-violet, sepals spreading, lanceolate, ¾ in. long, limb of petals cuneate-oblong, ½ in. long, spurs straight or somewhat curved, ⁵⁄₁₆ in. long. Tyrol and n. Italy.

truncata: *A. formosa* var.

viridiflora Pall. [*A. atropurpurea* Willd.]. Sts. 6–12 in., finely pubescent, the taller branched; basal lvs. 2-ternate, fairly thick; fls. inclined or nodding, sepals green, pubescent, ½ in. long, limb of petals yellow-green to brown-red to purplish, about as long as sepals, spurs straight or slightly curved, pubescent, ½–⅝ in. long. Siberia to China.

vulgaris L. EUROPEAN CROWFOOT, GARDEN C. Sts. mostly 1–2 ft., usually not glandular in upper parts; basal lvs. well developed, 2-ternate, green and glabrous above; fls. nodding, few to many, mostly violet, sepals spreading, lanceolate-ovate, ¾–1 in. long, limb of petals ½ in. long, rounded-truncate, spurs strongly hooked, ⅝–1 in. long. Widespread in Eur. Cvs. include: **'Alba Plena'**, fls. white, double; **'Atrorosea'**, fls. reddish; **'Caryophylloides'**, fls. white, flushed with red, semidouble; **'Erecta'**, fls. white, erect; **'Flore Pleno'**, fls. double; **'Nivea'**, fls. white; **'Stellata'**, spurs lacking. Var. **collina** K. Richt. & Gürke. Fls. violet, sepals much longer than overall length of petal. France. Var. **hybrida:** *A.* ×*hybrida.*

ARABIDOPSIS Heynh. MOUSE-EAR CRESS. *Cruciferae.* About 13 spp. of ann. or per. herbs, native mostly to Eur., Asia, and n. Afr.; lvs. simple, glabrous or pubescent with simple and branched hairs; fls. often white, sepals and petals 4; fr. a slender, linear silique, seeds many, small.

Thaliana (L.) Heynh. [*Arabis Thaliana* L.; *Sisymbrium Thalianum* (L.) J. Gay & Monn.]. Ann., to 18 in., usually branched; basal lvs. in rosettes, spatulate, to 2½ in. long, remotely toothed, sparsely stellate-hairy, st. lvs. few, sessile, oblong or linear; fls. in terminal racemes, petals white, ⅛ in. long; siliques to ¾ in. long. Temp. Eurasia, n. Afr.; naturalized in Calif. and from Tex. to the East Coast.

ARABIS L. ROCK CRESS. *Cruciferae.* More than 100 spp. of mostly low, ann., bien., or per. herbs, native to temp. N. Amer. and Eurasia; lvs. entire, lobed or pinnatifid, toothed; fls. white, pink, or purple, in terminal spikes or racemes, sepals and petals 4; fr. a long, narrow silique, valves flat, seeds sometimes winged.

Some of the rock cresses are alpine, grown in the border or rock garden and flowering mostly in spring or early summer. They require sun, but many of them thrive even in poor soil. Some produce attractive mats of late-season foliage. Propagated by division, seeds, or cuttings.

albida: *A. caucasica.*

Allionii DC. Per., to 18 in., sts. usually unbranched; lvs. ovate-oblong, somewhat toothed, glabrous, st. lvs. sessile, ovate; petals white, erect. Mts., cent. Eur.

alpina L. [*A. cenisia* Reut.]. MOUNTAIN R. C. Per., to 16 in., with vegetative rosettes, flowering sts. branched at base; basal lvs. oblong or obovate, dentate, attenuate-petioled, st. lvs. ovate, cordate to auricled at base; outer sepals conspicuously saccate at base, petals white, to ⅜ in. long; siliques to 1¼ in. long. Mts., Eur. Apparently not common in cult.; plants grown under this name are usually the closely related but more commonly cult. *A. caucasica.* Cvs. listed under this sp. include: **'Alba', 'Coccinea', 'Compacta', 'Grandiflora', 'Nana', 'Rosea', 'Superba', 'Variegata'.**

androsacea Fenzl. Per., to 3 in., densely cespitose, silvery-hairy, sts. mostly unbranched, leafy; basal lvs. mostly in dense rosettes, oblong-elliptic, nearly entire, st. lvs. linear; fls. white, in corymbose racemes; siliques to ½ in. long, erect, short-pedicelled. Mts., Turkey.

×**Arendsii** Wehrh.: *A. aubrietioides* × *A. caucasica.* Sts. creeping to ascending; lvs. elliptic, toothed, gray-hairy; fls. rose-red, in short clusters.

aubrietioides Boiss. Per., to 6 in., tufted, sts. erect; lvs. toothed, greenish, lower lvs. obovate, st. lvs. ovate, clasping; petals purplish-pink, to ½ in. long. Mts., Turkey.

Billardieri: *A. caucasica.*

blepharophylla Hook. & Arn. Per., to 8 in. or more, sts. unbranched; lvs. spatulate to oblong, toothed or entire, ciliate; fls. fragrant, petals rose-purple, ½ in. long. Cent. Calif.

Breweri S. Wats. Per., to 8 in., cespitose, pubescent, sts. much-branched; lvs. spatulate to lanceolate, usually entire; petals red-purple, ¼ in. long. N. Calif., s. Ore.

caerulea (All.) Jacq. Per., to 6 in., tufted, with taproot, st. with short stolons terminating in rosettes; basal lvs. spatulate to lanceolate-ovate, glabrous or sparsely pubescent, usually ciliate, thick, glossy-green; fls. in 5–8-fld., somewhat branched, erect infl., petals bluish-lilac, rarely white, to ¼ in. long; siliques small, about ¼ in. long. Bavarian and Salzburg Alps.

carduchorum Boiss. [*Draba gigas* Stur ex Boiss.]. Per., to 3 in.; lvs. in rosettes, linear, ciliate; petals white, to ¼ in. long. Turkey. Some material grown as *Draba fladnizensis* belongs here.

caucasica Schlechtend. [*A. albida* Steven ex Bieb.; *A. Billardieri* DC.]. WALL R. C. Per., to 12 in., tufted, procumbent, with many rosettes, usually whitish-soft-pubescent; basal lvs. usually obovate, tapering to base, st. lvs. auricled to sagittate at base; fls. in loose racemes, fragrant, petals white, ⅜–⅝ in. long; siliques 1½–2½ in. long. Se. Eur. to Iran. Not easily separable from *A. alpina,* but most reliably distinguished by its sagittate st. lvs. and its longer petals and siliques.

cenisia: *A. alpina.*

corymbiflora Vest. Bien. or per., to 12 in.; basal lvs. obovate, toothed, shortly attenuate-petioled, st. lvs. ovate to elliptic, rounded at base, entire or toothed; fls. about 30 in compact cluster, petals white, to 3/16 in. long. Mts., Eur.

cypria Holmb. Per., to 10 in., with basal rosettes; basal lvs. spatulate, rounded at apex, narrowed basally, coarsely toothed, st. lvs. few, oblong-elliptic, cordate-sagittate at base, sessile; fls. white, in terminal racemes; siliques linear, to 1½ in. long, spreading on slender pedicels. Mts., Cyprus.

Drummondii A. Gray. Bien. or per., to 3 ft., glabrous to sparingly hairy; lower lvs. oblanceolate, to 2½ in. long, entire or toothed, petioled, st. lvs. oblong to oblong-lanceolate, sessile, auricled, usually clasping; petals white or pink, to 5/16 in. long. Que., s. to Del., w. to Great Lakes region to Pacific Coast.

Ferdinandi-Coburgi Kellerer & Sünderm. Small per.; lvs. in gray rosettes that become green in winter; petals white, to 5/16 in. long. Bulgaria.

furcata S. Wats. Per., to 16 in.; basal lvs. obovate to spatulate, to 2 in. long, tapering to narrow petiole, st. lvs. smaller, obovate to oblong-lanceolate, sessile; petals white, to 5/16 in. long. Wash., Ore.

glabra (L.) Bernh. TOWER MUSTARD. Bien. or occasionally per., glaucous, sts. strict, erect, to 4 ft., glabrous above; lvs. oblong to oblanceolate, dentate, st. lvs. sagittate, sessile; fls. small, yellowish-white; siliques erect-appressed. Eur., Asia; widespread in N. Amer. but probably naturalized.

glauca: *A. serrata* var.

Holboellii Hornem. Bien. or per., to 3 ft.; basal lvs. linear-oblanceolate to broadly spatulate, mostly entire, densely stellate-hairy, st. lvs. lanceolate, sagittate at base; petals white or pink, to 5/16 in. long; siliques to 2½ in. long, on reflexed pedicels. Greenland and e. Canada, w. through Great Lakes region to Pacific Coast.

Jacquinii: *A. Soyeri* subsp.

japonica: *A. Stelleri* var.

×**Kellereri** Sünderm. *A. bryoides* Boiss. × *A. Ferdinandi-Coburgi.* Per., cushion-forming; distinguished by the small, deciduous, ash-gray, lanceolate lvs. hairy on both sides.

lusitanica Boiss. Bien., sparsely hairy; st. lvs. sagittate at base; infl. few-fld. Portugal.

Lyallii S. Wats. Per., to 10 in., cespitose, mostly glabrous; lvs. spatulate to narrow-oblanceolate, to 1 in. long, entire, st. lvs. narrow; petals rose, to ¼ in. long. Alta. and Wyo., w. to B.C. and Calif.

mollis Steven. Per., to 15 in., densely pubescent, sts. erect, little-branched; lvs. ovate or roundish, cordate, blunt-dentate, basal lvs. long-petioled, st. lvs. clasping; fls. white, in terminal racemes. Bulgaria. Material cult. under this name is usually *A. procurrens.*

muralis Bertol. [*A. rosea* DC.]. Per., to 12 in., tufted, pubescent; lvs. spatulate, dentate, st. lvs. oblong, sessile; fls. in elongating terminal racemes, petals white or rose, to ¼ in. long. Cent. and s. Eur.

oregana Rollins [*A. purpurascens* T. J. Howell ex Greene, not K. Presl]. Per., to 20 in., with coarse, branched hairs; basal lvs. obovate to oblanceolate, abruptly narrowed to a distinct petiole, st. lvs. oblong to ovate, sessile; outer pair of sepals saccate, petals purple, to ¾ in. long. N. Calif., s. Ore.

pauciflora (Grimm) Garcke. Per., to 3 ft., glabrous and glaucous; basal lvs. ovate, entire, long-petioled, st. lvs. sessile, the uppermost auricled and clasping; petals white or pink, ¼ in. long. Sw. Eur.

procurrens Waldst. & Kit. [*A. mollis* Hort., not Steven]. Per., to 1 ft., with creeping stolons; basal lvs. oblong to lanceolate or obovate, acuminate, entire, st. lvs. ovate, rounded at base; fls. in elongating racemes, petals white, 5/16 in. long. Mts., se. Eur.

pumila Jacq. Per., to 10 in., st. short, lateral shoots terminating in rosettes; basal lvs. obovate, ciliate, attenuate-petioled, st. lvs. ovate-lanceolate; petals white, ¼ in. long. Mts., cent. Eur.

purpurascens: *A. oregana.*

purpurea Sibth. & Sm. Per., st. distinctly woody at base; lvs. obovate to oblong-cordate, remotely toothed to entire; petals rose-pink to pale purple, about ¼ in. long. Greece.

rosea: *A. muralis.*

scabra: *A. stricta.*

serpillifolia Vill. Bien. or per., to 10 in., loosely cespitose; basal lvs. oblong, long-petioled, st. lvs. oblong-ovate, attenuate to rounded at base; petals white or rarely pink, to ¼ in. long. Mts., s. Eur.

serrata Franch. & Sav. Per., to 12 in., tufted with short, 2–4-branched hairs; basal lvs. in a rosette, to 2½ in. long, toothed, narrowed to a petiole, st. lvs. ovate to lanceolate, clasping; fls. white, few to many; siliques spreading to ascending. Japan. Var. **glauca** (Boiss.) Ohwi [*A. glauca* Boiss.]. Basal lvs. pilose above with 2-branched hairs.

Soyeri Reut. & Huet. Per., to 20 in., almost glabrous; basal lvs. obovate, dark green, glossy, attenuate-petioled; st. lvs. ovate to oblong-lanceolate, rounded at base, more or less clasping; petals white, ¼ in. long. Mts., cent. Eur. Subsp. **Jacquinii** (G. Beck) B. M. G. Jones [*A. Jacquinii* G. Beck]. Glabrous; st. lvs. not clasping.

Stelleri DC. var. **japonica** (A. Gray) Friedr. Schmidt [*A. japonica* A. Gray]. Sts. erect, stout, to 16 in.; basal lvs. oblong to oblanceolate, narrowed to broad petiole, st. lvs. auricled, clasping; petals white, 5/16 in. long. Korea, Amur, Japan, Sakhalin.

stricta Huds. [*A. scabra* All.]. Per., to 6 in., nearly glabrous; basal lvs. oblong, crenate, thickish and glossy, narrowed to a petiole, st. lvs. smaller, sessile; fls. yellowish-white, in short racemes. Eur.

Sturii Mottet. Related to *A. procurrens,* but a lower, more compact plant.

×**Suendermannii** Kellerer ex Sünderm.: *A. Ferdinandi-Coburgi* × *A. procurrens.* Lvs. lanceolate, twice as large as in *A. Ferdinandi-Coburgi.*

Thaliana: *Arabidopsis Thaliana.*

Turrita L. Bien. or per., to 2½ ft., pubescent; basal lvs. in rosettes, obovate, toothed, blue-violet beneath, long-petioled, st. lvs. cordate, clasping, sessile; fls. in many-fld. racemes, petals yellow, ¼ in. long. Cent. and s. Eur.

vochinensis K. Spreng. Per., to 6 in., cespitose, st. with many short stolons terminating in rosettes; basal lvs. obovate, obtuse, glabrous or sparsely pubescent beneath; fls. on erect, mostly unbranched, leafy sts., petals white, ¼ in. long. Mts., cent. Eur.

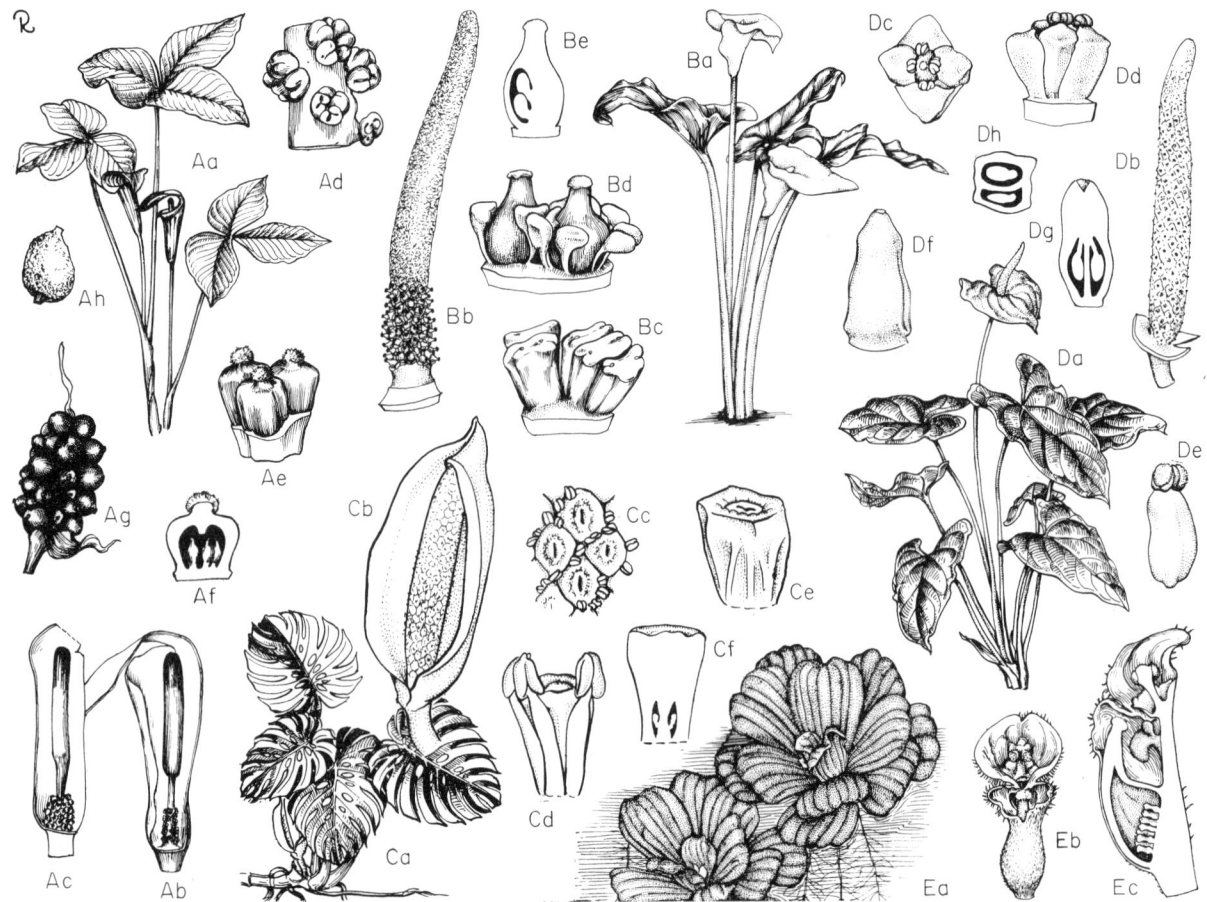

ARACEAE, **A**, *Arisaema triphyllum* subsp. *triphyllum:* **Aa**, two flowering plants, × ⅙; **Ab**, male inflorescence, part of spathe cut away, × ½; **Ac**, female inflorescence, part of spathe cut away, × ½; **Ad**, section of spadix with male flowers, × 4; **Ae**, section of spadix with female flowers, × 4; **Af**, pistil, vertical section, × 5; **Ag**, fruiting spadix, × ½; **Ah**, seed, × 2. **B**, *Zantedeschia aethiopica:* **Ba**, flowering plant, × ⅛; **Bb**, spadix, × ½; **Bc**, segment of spadix with male flowers, × 4; **Bd**, segment of spadix with female flowers, × 3; **Be**, pistil, vertical section, × 3. **C**, *Monstera deliciosa:* **Ca**, flowering plant, × ¹⁄₁₆; **Cb**, inflorescence, × ¼; **Cc** flowers, × 1; **Cd**, flower, side view, × 2; **Ce**, pistil, × 2; **Cf**, pistil, vertical section, × 2. **D**, *Anthurium Andraenum:* **Da**, flowering plant, × ¹⁄₁₀; **Db**, spadix, × ½; **Dc**, flower, face view, × 5; **Dd**, flower, side view, × 5; **De**, stamen, × 8; **Df**, pistil, × 8; **Dg**, pistil, vertical section, × 8; **Dh**, ovary, cross section, × 8. **E**. *Pistia stratiotes:* **Ea**, floating plants, × ⅙; **Eb**, inflorescence, × 2; **Ec**, inflorescence, vertical section, × 3.

ARACEAE Juss. ARUM FAMILY. AROIDS. Monocot.; about 15 genera and 2,000 spp. of per., often huge, herbs, of wide distribution, but mostly trop., including terrestrial, aquatic, and epiphytic spp.; plants stemless, with lvs. arising from corms or rhizomes, or with aerial sts. and the sts. erect, or climbing by means of aerial roots; lvs. in rosettes or alt. along st., entire to greatly dissected, generally with long, basally sheathing petioles; infl. mostly a densely-fld. spadix, subtended by a sometimes showy spathe either free from or surrounding spadix, or rarely united with it; fls. small, often reduced, bisexual, or unisexual and plants monoecious with female fls. toward base of spadix and male fls. above, or rarely intermixed, 2–3-merous, perianth scalelike or absent, stamens often modified and variously united; fr. a berry, or rarely dry, sometimes brightly colored. Genera in cult. include: *Acorus, Aglaonema, Alocasia, Amorphophallus, Anthurium, Anubias, Arisaema, Arisarum, Arum, Caladium, Calla, Callopsis, Colocasia, Cryptocoryne, Culcasia, Cyrtosperma, Dieffenbachia, Dracunculus, Epipremnopsis, Epipremnum, Gonatanthus, Helicodiceros, Homalomena, Lagenandra, Lysichiton, Monstera, Nephthytis, Orontium, Peltandra, Philodendron, Pistia, Pothos, Raphidophora, Rhektophyllum, Rhodospatha, Sauromatum, Schismatoglottis, Scindapsis, Spathicarpa, Spathiphyllum, Stenospermation, Steudnera, Symplocarpus, Syngonium, Taccarum, Thomsonia, Xanthosoma, Xenophya, Zamioculcas,* and *Zantedeschia.*

Several aroids are grown extensively in tropical regions for their edible tubers, the taro (dasheen) and yautia (tannia, malanga, ocumo) being starch staples in the diet of large segments of the population in the tropics of both hemispheres. One species of *Monstera* bears edible fruits. Many species are grown as ornamentals all over the world, especially for their handsome foliage or beautiful spathes, such as the florist's calla, and anthurium.

ARACHIS L. *Leguminosae* (subfamily *Faboideae*). About 12–15 spp. of mostly ann. herbs with procumbent sts., native to S. Amer.; lvs. alt., odd-pinnate, stipules united to base of petioles; fls. yellow, papilionaceous, in axillary spikes, stamens united in a closed tube; fr. a netted, indehiscent legume, ripening underground, seeds 1–3.

Peanuts are an important commercial crop in southeastern U.S., grown for food and as a source of an important nondrying oil. Sometimes grown in gardens and conservatories as a novelty. Peanuts should have sandy, fertile soil, and a long growing season. They are very tender to frost. Fruit may mature as far north as central N.Y. Propagated by seeds, preferably removed from the pods.

hypogaea L. PEANUT, COMMON P., GOOBER, GROUNDNUT, GRASS NUT, EARTH N., MONKEY N., PINDAR. Ann., sts. procumbent, to 20 in. long; lfts. 4, obovate or broadly oblong, to 2½ in. long; fr. on rigid stalks to 2½ in. long. S. Brazil. Widely grown in trop. and warm temp. regions.

ARACHNANTHE: *ARACHNIS.*

ARACHNIODES Blume [*Aspidium* Swartz]. *Polypodiaceae.* About 20 spp. of ferns with creeping rhizomes, native to tropics; lvs. rather thick, about 1–3 ft. long, 3–4-pinnate, broadly triangular or with enlarged basal pinnae; indusium laterally attached.

For culture see *Ferns.*

aristata (G. Forst.) Tindale [*Aspidium aristatum* (G. Forst.) Swartz; *Polystichum aristatum* (G. Forst.) K. Presl]. EAST INDIAN HOLLY FERN. Lvs. ovate-triangular, to 2 ft. long and 1 ft. wide, 2–4-pinnate basally, pinnules pinnatifid, finely bristle-toothed, glabrous, lowermost pinnae at base of lf. longer than others, petioles 1½ ft. long. Asia to Australia. Cv. 'Variegatum'. Pinnules banded with whitish-green.

Standishii (T. Moore) Ohwi [*Polystichum Standishii* (T. Moore) C. Chr.]. UPSIDE-DOWN FERN. Lvs. somewhat leathery, to 18 in. long, 9 in. wide, ovate-triangular, 3-pinnate, glabrous, lower pinnae the largest, somewhat triangular, unequal. E. Asia.

ARACHNIS Blume [*Arachnanthe* Blume; *Esmeralda* Rchb. f.]. SCORPION ORCHID. *Orchidaceae.* Seven spp. of epiphytes, native to China, Thailand, w. Malay Arch.; sts. long, leafy, often climbing and branched; infl. a few- to many-fld. raceme or panicle; fls. fleshy, sepals and petals similar, not united, lip much shorter and movable, attached to column. For structure of fl. see *Orchidaceae.*

For culture see *Orchids.*

Cathcartii (Lindl.) J. J. Sm. [*Vanda Cathcartii* Lindl.; *Esmeralda Cathcartii* Rchb. f.]. Fls. 3–4 in. across, sepals and petals broadly elliptic or obovate, closely banded transversely with dark maroon on yellowish ground, lip 3-lobed, fleshy, yellow, with a few purple bands. Early spring. Sikkim and Bhutan.

Clarkei (Rchb. f.) J. J. Sm. [*Arachnanthe Clarkei* (Rchb. f.) Rolfe; *Esmeralda Clarkei* Rchb. f.]. ESMARALDA. St. long, pendulous; lvs. to 6 in. long and 1½ in. wide; infl. 3–4-fld., to 8 in. long; fls. about 2½ in. across, sepals and petals spreading, yellow, banded transversely with brown, lip about the same length, yellow, spotted with brown. Summer. Himalayas.

flos-aeris (L.) Rchb. f. [*A. moschifera* Blume; *Arachnanthe flos-aeris* (L.) J. J. Sm.]. SPIDER ORCHID. Infl. paniculate, many-fld., to 5 ft. long; fls. yellow-green, with large dark maroon blotches, 3–4 in. across, sepals and petals similar, margins recurved, lip 3-lobed, with several smooth, orange ridges and a blunt, pouchlike spur at base. Late spring, late autumn. Malay Pen.

Hookerana Rchb. f. Infl. racemose, to 2 ft. long; fls. cream-colored, with small purplish spots, 2–2½ in. across, sepals and petals similar, margins recurved, lip 3-lobed, lateral lobes erect, midlobe entire, purple or purple-banded. Malay Pen. and Riouw Arch.

Lowii (Lindl.) Rchb. f. [*Arachnanthe Lowii* (Lindl.) Benth. & Hook. f.; *Renanthera Lowii* (Lindl.) Rchb. f.; *Vanda Lowii* Lindl.; *Vandopsis Lowii* (Lindl.) Schlechter]. To 6 ft.; lvs. to 2½ ft. long and 2 in. wide; infl. racemose, pendulous, many-fld., to 9 ft. long; fls. to 3 in. across, lower fls. orange-yellow, finely spotted with red, upper fls. with longer and narrower sepals and petals, greenish-yellow with large brown spots. Late summer–late autumn. Borneo.

×**Maingayi** (Hook. f.) Schlechter [*Renanthera* × *Maingayi* (Hook. f.) Ridl.]: *A. flos-aeris* × *A. Hookerana.* SPIDER ORCHID, PINK SCORPION O. Very similar to *A. flos-aeris,* but fls. somewhat smaller, sepals and petals off-white or pale pink, with large pink or light purple spots or bands, lip with a high keel. Malay Pen. and Borneo; known both as a natural and an artificial hybrid.

moschifera: *A. flos-aeris.*

ARALIA L. *Araliaceae.* Over 30 spp. of herbs, shrubs, or trees often with spiny sts., native to N. Amer., Asia, and Malay Pen.; lvs. alt., pinnate to 3-pinnate; fls. small, white or greenish, in umbels often arranged in panicles, petals 5, more or less imbricate, stamens 5, ovary 2–5-celled, styles 2–5, separate; fr. a drupe, pyrenes 2–5.

Planted outdoors, several species are nearly or fully hardy in Zone 5. The smaller species are woodland ground covers, and the foliage of the larger ones provides subtropical effects. They thrive in rich soil. Propagated by seeds in spring, or by root cuttings over heat.

Balfouriana: *Polyscias Balfouriana.*

cachemirica Decne. Erect, unarmed shrub, 5–10 ft.; lvs. large, 1–3-pinnate, lfts. of each pinna 5–9, stalked or sessile, oblong-ovate, 3–6 in. long, 1½–3 in. wide, toothed, sometimes lobed, paler beneath; infl. of many umbels in elongate panicles; fls. white; fr. black, ⅛ in. long. Himalayas. Zone 7.

californica S. Wats. ELK CLOVER. Unarmed per. herb, to 10 ft.; lvs. 2–3-pinnate, lfts. ovate to oblong, to 1 ft. long, serrate, thin; infl. of many-fld. umbels arranged in panicles to 1½ ft. long; fr. reddish-black, globose, less than ¼ in. long. Ore. to Calif. Zone 8. Distinguished from

A. racemosa in having thinner, more shallowly toothed lvs. and umbels of 20–75 fls.

chinensis L. Shrub or rarely small tree, to 30 ft., sts. prickly; lvs. 2–3-pinnate, 2–4 ft. long, lfts. ovate to broadly ovate, to 6 in. long, serrate, pubescent beneath, petiole and rachis mostly free of prickles; infl. of umbels arranged in panicles to 2 ft. long. China. Zone 8. Var. **nuda** Nakai. Lvs. much less hairy, more commonly cult. Cv. 'Variegata'. Lfts. white-margined.

cordata Thunb. [*A. edulis* Siebold & Zucc.]. UDO. Spineless per. herb, to 9 ft.; lvs. 2–3-pinnate, lfts. of each pinna 3–7, ovate, 2–6 in. long, unequally serrate; infl. of umbels arranged in large panicles. Japan, where the young blanched shoots are eaten. Recommended for culinary use but little grown in U.S.

edulis: *A. cordata.*

elata (Miq.) Seem. JAPANESE ANGELICA. Shrub or tree, to 45 ft., usually prickly; lvs. 2-pinnate, lfts. 5–9 on each pinna, ovate to elliptic, to 4 in. long, acuminate, irregularly toothed, pubescent above and beneath; infl. of umbels in spreading racemes to 1½ ft. long; fr. black, about ⅛ in. in diam. Manchuria, Korea, Japan. Zone 4. Cvs. include: 'Variegata', lfts. white-bordered; 'Aureo-variegata', lfts. yellow-bordered; 'Pyramidalis', brs. erect, lfts. smaller.

elegantissima: *Dizygotheca elegantissima.*

filicifolia: *Polyscias filicifolia.*

foliolosa (Wallich) Seem. Shrub or small tree, to 20 ft.; lvs. 2–3-pinnate, petiole and rachis prickly; infl. of umbels arranged in panicles to 18 in. long. S. China and India. Zone 9.

fruticosa: see *Polyscias fruticosa.*

Guilfoylei: *Polyscias Guilfoylei.*

hispida Venten. BRISTLY SARSAPARILLA. Suffruticose, with herbaceous, bristly sts. to 3 ft.; lvs. few, 2-pinnate, lfts. mostly 3–4 in. long, oblong to lanceolate; infl. glabrous, a loose cluster of usually 5–10 umbels; fr. black, globose, to ¼ in. in diam. Nfld. to N.C. and Minn. Zone 3.

japonica: *Fatsia japonica.*

Kerchoveana: *Dizygotheca Kerchoveana.*

laciniata: a listed name of no botanical standing, probably for *Dizygotheca elegantissima.*

Moseri: *Fatsia japonica* cv.

nudicaulis L. WILD SARSAPARILLA. Per., to 1 ft.; lvs. and scape arising from a rhizome, lvs. 2–3-pinnate, lfts. 3–5 on each pinna, elliptic to lanceolate, to 6 in. long, finely serrate; umbels 2–7, terminal on scape; fr. black. Nfld. to Ga. and Colo. Zone 3.

papyrifera: *Tetrapanax papyriferus.*

Pennockii: a listed name of no botanical standing for *Polyscias Balfouriana* cv.

pentaphylla: see *Acanthopanax Sieboldianus* and *Acanthopanax spinosus.*

racemosa L. SPIKENARD, AMERICAN S., PETTY MOREL, LIFE-OF-MAN. Per. herb, to 6 ft.; without prickles, becoming suffrutescent; lvs. few, to 2½ ft. long, 2–3-pinnate, lfts. ovate, to 8 in. long, sharply to mucronulately serrate; infl. of many umbels in axillary and terminal, dense racemes or panicles, mostly shorter than lvs.; fls. 10–25 in each umbel; fr. brown to purple. New Bruns. to N.C., w. to Ariz., Utah, and s. to n. Mex. Zone 4. Roots and rhizome used medicinally.

Sieboldii: *Fatsia japonica.*

spinosa L. DEVIL'S-WALKING STICK, HERCULES'-CLUB, ANGELICA TREE, PRICKLY ASH. Clump-forming shrub or tree, to 30 ft. or more, sts. mostly unbranched, with dense, stout prickles; lvs. mostly 2–6 ft. long, 2-pinnate, rachis usually prickly, swollen at nodes, lfts. 2–6 in. long, terminal lft. long-stalked; umbels many in large panicles often longer than lvs. Cent. Penn. to Fla. and Tex.; naturalized in N.Y. and Conn. Zone 5. Bark used medicinally.

ARALIACEAE Juss. ARALIA or GINSENG FAMILY. Dicot.; about 84 genera of herbs, shrubs, trees, or vines widely distributed in temp. and trop. regions; frequently bearing prickles, juvenile habit and lvs. sometimes different from the adult; lvs. alt., rarely opp. or whorled, simple or palmately or pinnately compound or decompound, often stellate-hairy; fls. small, in umbels or heads, often massed in compound infls., greenish-white or yellow, bisexual or unisexual, regular, calyx usually of 5 minute teeth, petals mostly 5–10, sometimes 4, often valvate in bud, stamens 5 to many, ovary inferior, 1 to several-celled, ovule 1 in each cell; fr. a drupe, pyrenes 1 to several. Cult. genera are: *Acanthopanax, Aralia, Boerlagiodendron, Brassaia, Brassaiopsis, Cussonia, Dendropanax,*

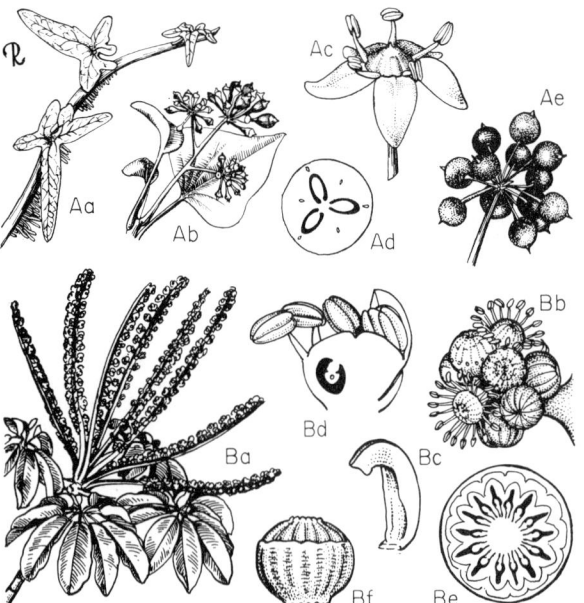

ARALIACEAE. **A,** *Hedera Helix* cv. 'Pedata': **Aa,** sterile leafy stem with aerial roots,×½; **Ab,** adult foliage with young fruiting inflorescence,×¼; **Ac,** flower,×2; **Ad,** ovary, cross section,×4; **Ae,** fruits,×½. **B,** *Brassaia actinophylla:* **Ba,** flowering branch,×¹⁄₁₀; **Bb,** umbel of buds and flowers,×¾; **Bc,** petal,×3; **Bd,** flower, vertical section (corolla largely abscised),×2; **Be,** ovary, cross section,×3; **Bf,** fruit,×2. (Aa–Ae from Bailey, *Manual of Cultivated Plants,* ed. 2.)

Didymopanax, Dizygotheca, Fatshedera, Fatsia, Hedera, Kalopanax, Meryta, Neopanax, Oplopanax, Oreopanax, Panax, Polyscias, Pseudopanax, Schefflera, Stilbocarpa, Tetrapanax, Tetraplasandra, Trevesia, and *Tupidanthus.*

Economically the family is of minor importance. Besides those species grown as ornamentals, *Tetrapanax papyriferus* is the source of Chinese rice-paper, and *Panax quinquefolius* provides ginseng roots, used in medicinal preparations. When grown as pot plants in the home, many species remain in similar juvenile stages and are difficult to identify.

ARAUCARIA Juss. *Araucariaceae.* About 15 spp. of tall, evergreen, usually dioecious, coniferous trees, native in S. Hemisphere from s. S. Amer. to Australia and Pacific Is.; brs. symmetrically whorled; lvs. stiff, awl-shaped or flat, usually closely overlapping; male cones solitary or in clusters, female cones large, woody; seeds 1 to a scale, mostly winged on each edge and united to the scales, maturing in 2 or 3 years. Young trees of different spp. may be closely similar and the juvenile form persists until trees are large, often to 20–50 ft. Old trees usually have flat, ragged heads above essentially naked trunks. Juvenile lvs. of all spp. are larger than adult lvs. and may differ from them also in form and arrangement.

Most species produce useful timber and one an edible seed. Araucarias are grown as ornamentals in warm regions and as pot plants in juvenile form. They can be planted in the open only in the warmer parts of the country, as in Fla. and Calif. (Zone 10), except *A. araucana,* which is much hardier. For culture see *Conifers.*

angustifolia (Bertol.) O. Kuntze [*A. brasiliana* A. Rich.; *A. brasiliensis* Lindl. var. *gracilis* Hort. ex Carrière; *A. gracilis* Hort.]. PARANÁ PINE, BRAZILIAN P. Lvs. loosely overlapping, oblong-lanceolate, sharp-pointed, glaucous-green, to 2¼ in. long on sterile brs., shorter and denser on fertile brs.; male cones 3–4 in. long, ½–¾ in. in diam. S. Brazil and adjacent Argentina, where an important timber tree. Zone 10.

araucana (Mol.) C. Koch [*A. imbricata* Pav.]. MONKEY-PUZZLE, MONKEY-PUZZLE TREE, CHILEAN PINE. Lvs. closely overlapping, ovate-lanceolate, 1–2 in. long, leathery, sharp-pointed; male cones erect, 3–5 in. long, 2 in. wide, female cones 4–7 in. long, 3–5 in. in diam. Chile, where it is the most important coniferous timber tree. Zone 7.

Bidwillii Hook. BUNYA-BUNYA, BUNYA-BUNYA PINE. Juvenile lvs. spreading, mostly in 2 rows, ovate- to oblong-lanceolate, to 2 in. long,

sharp-pointed, firm and glossy; adult lvs. overlapping, spiral, ovate, to ½ in. long, acute, rigid, woody; male cones 3–5 in. long, ⅜–½ in. in diam., female cones 7–9 in. long, 6–8 in. in diam. Ne. Australia. Zone 9.

brasiliana: *A. angustifolia.*

brasiliensis var. **gracilis:** *A. angustifolia.*

columnaris (G. Forst.) Hook. [*A. Cookii* R. Br. ex Endl.; *A. excelsa* (Lamb.) R. Br.]. NEW CALEDONIA PINE. To 200 ft., shedding lower brs. and developing short secondary brs., mature trees appearing columnar below an abruptly spreading short crown; juvenile lvs. awl-shaped, deep green, firm, to ½ in. long; adult lvs. overlapping, lanceolate-ovate to triangular, to ¼ in. long, obtuse, rigid, with blunt incurved apex and prominent midrib; male cones 1½–3½ in. long, ¹⁄₂–¾ in. in diam., female cones ovoid to ellipsoid, 4–5 in. long, the mucro at tip of scales elongate, recurved. New Caledonia, New Hebrides. Zone 10. Young trees, up to 25 ft. with only juvenile foliage, are difficult to separate from *A. heterophylla,* but the habit of mature trees is distinctive; *A. columnaris* has deeper green foliage and closer tiers of brs. and makes a better ornamental tree except in age. The name *A. excelsa* was long used incorrectly for *A. heterophylla.*

Cookii: *A. columnaris.*

Cunninghamii D. Don. HOOP PINE, MORETON BAY P. Mature tree with tufted twig clusters at ends of naked brs.; juvenile lvs. needlelike, laterally compressed, to ½ in. long, spiny-pointed, often recurved, adult lvs. awl-shaped to lanceolate, incurved, overlapping; male cones 2–3½ in. long, ½ in. in diam., female cones ovoid, 2½–3½ in. long, 1½–2½ in. in diam. E. Australia, where an important timber sp. Zone 10.

excelsa: *A. columnaris,* but most material cult. as *A. excelsa* is *A. heterophylla.*

gracilis: a listed name of no botanical standing, occasionally used for *A. angustifolia.*

heterophylla (Salisb.) Franco. NORFOLK ISLAND PINE, AUSTRALIAN P., HOUSE P. Mature trees to 200 ft., pyramidal; juvenile lvs. awl-shaped, incurved, laterally flattened, decurrent, light green, soft, to ½ in. long; adult lvs. closely overlapping, lanceolate to ovate-triangular with blunt incurved apex and obscure midrib; male cones 1½–2 in. long, female cones subglobose, 3–5 in. long, 3½–6 in. in diam., the mucro at tip of scales short, not recurved. Norfolk Is. Zone 10. Long known incorrectly as *A. excelsa.* The usual sp. grown by florists for indoor pot plants. Prop. by cuttings of vigorous, erect shoot tips.

imbricata: *A. araucana.*

ARAUCARIACEAE Henkel & Hochst. ARAUCARIA FAMILY. Gymnosperms; 2 genera of resinous, evergreen, coniferous trees, native to the S. Hemisphere; lvs. alt., awl-shaped to broadly ovate, often leathery; male cones cylindrical, female cones usually large, subglobose, scales woody, falling when seeds are ripe; differing from the *Pinaceae* in the lvs. and in having cone scales without distinct bracts and with only 1 ovule. The family includes some of the most important timber trees of the S. Hemisphere as well as species supplying hard resins for industry. *Agathis* and *Araucaria* are grown in conservatories or outdoors where climatic conditions permit.

ARAUJIA Brot. *Asclepiadaceae.* About 5 spp. of glabrous or mealy-pubescent, climbing shrubs, native to Argentina and Brazil; lvs. opp., simple; fls. in few-fld., peduncled, axillary cymes, calyx large and leafy, without glands, corolla salverform or campanulate, tube inflated at base, corona lobes attached to corolla tube, anthers terminated by small inflexed projection; fr. a follicle, leathery, sometimes inflated.

Grown under glass from cuttings or outdoors from seeds started indoors in early spring.

sericifera Brot. Lvs. oblong to triangular-oblong, to 4 in. long, broadly cuneate to somewhat sagittate, mucronate, dark green above, white-pubescent beneath; corolla white, often streaked with maroon inside, ¾–1 in. across; follicles inflated, deeply grooved, to 5 in. long, 3 in. broad. S. Brazil. Material offered as *Schubertia albens* may be this sp.

ARBORETUM. Literally, an arboretum is a collection of living trees; as now used, the term denotes a plantation of many kinds of woody plants permanently maintained for purposes of study, research, and education, as distinct from a grove, forest, nursery, or park. It is often part of a botanical garden.

ARBORICULTURE. Although defined as the cultivation of trees and shrubs, arboriculture implies the cultivation of the plants as individuals rather than as elements in a forest, the latter subject being silviculture and part of the larger domain of forestry. Arboriculture is to be distinguished also from the growing of trees for a particular product, as the raising of fruit, which is pomology.

ARBUTUS L. MANZANITA, STRAWBERRY TREE. *Ericaceae.* About 14 spp. of evergreen trees and shrubs, native to w. N. Amer., Medit. region, Canary Is.; bark red, smooth, flaking in thin plates; lvs. alt., simple, leathery; fls. pink or white, in terminal panicles, calyx 5-parted, corolla urceolate, stamens 10, anthers awned, ovary superior; fr. a red or orange berry.

Arbutuses are grown outdoors in warm regions or under glass in the North. They do best in well-drained soil with protection from the wind. Propagated by seeds, by cuttings of half-ripened wood in the autumn under glass, and also by layers, budding, or veneer grafting.

Andrachne L. To 40 ft.; lvs. ovate or oblong, to 4 in. long, usually entire; panicles to 4 in. long; fls. dull white; fr. orange. Se. Eur., Asia Minor.

canariensis Duh. To 30 ft.; lvs. oblong-lanceolate, to 6 in. long, serrate, glaucous beneath; panicles erect; fls. greenish-white, nearly ½ in. long; fr. bright orange. Canary Is.

Menziesii Pursh. MADRONA, MADRONE, MADRONO. To 50 or 100 ft.; lvs. elliptic to elliptic-ovate, to 6 in. long, entire, glaucous beneath; panicles erect, to 6 in. long; fls. white, urceolate, constricted in the middle, ⁵⁄₁₆ in. long; fr. orange or red. Late spring. B.C. to s. Calif. and Baja Calif. Zone 7. Bark has been used for tanning, and wood for making furniture.

microphylla: see *A. Unedo* cv.

texana: *A. xalapensis.*

Unedo L. STRAWBERRY TREE, CANE APPLES. To 30 ft.; lvs. oblong to obovate, to 4 in. long, serrate, shining above; panicles drooping, to 2 in. long; fls. white or pinkish, ¼ in. long; fr. scarlet. Autumn. S. Eur., Ireland. Hardy to Ga. in the East and on Pacific coast. Zone 8. Bark used in tanning and fr. used in preserves and alcoholic drinks. Cvs. are: '**Compacta**', a compact form; '**Integerrima**' [var. *integerrima* Sims], lvs. entire; '**Microphylla**' [*A. microphylla* Hort., not G. Forst.], lvs. smaller; '**Rubra**' [var. *rubra* Ait.], fls. deep pink.

xalapensis HBK [*A. xalapensis* var. *texana* (Buckl.) A. Gray; *A. texana* Buckl.; *Arctostaphylos rubescens* (Bertol.) Hemsl.]. To 45 ft.; lvs. oblong to lanceolate or ovate, to 4½ in. long, petioles 1–1½ in. long; fls. white to pinkish, corolla with inflated basal ring; fr. dark red. W. Tex., Mex., Guatemala.

ARCEUTHOBIUM: see *LORANTHACEAE.*

ARCHANGELICA: *ANGELICA.* Archangelica officinalis: *Angelica Archangelica.*

ARCHONTOPHOENIX H. Wendl. & Drude. KING PALM. *Palmae.* Two Australian spp. of solitary, unarmed, monoecious palms with prominent crownshaft; lvs. pinnate, pinnae acute, regularly arranged; infl. below lvs., subtended by 2 papery, deciduous bracts, peduncle short, rachis with several brs., the lower again 2-branched, rachillae with fls. in triads (2 male and 1 female) near the base and above these with paired or solitary male fls.; male fls. asymmetrical, sepals small, acute, imbricate, petals valvate, angled, stamens more than 6, filaments erect in bud, pistillode as long as stamens, female fls. symmetrical, with imbricate sepals and petals, ovary 1-celled; fr. red, with apical stigmatic scar, seed with ruminate endosperm and basal embryo.

King palms have a stately habit and are widely grown as ornamentals in the tropics and subtropics of both hemispheres (Zone 10). They are among the fastest growing of cultivated palms. Young plants make good pot or tub plants. Seeds germinate easily and rapidly. Can be transplanted only with great care. For culture see *Palms.*

Alexandrae (F. J. Muell.) H. Wendl. & Drude [*Ptychosperma Alexandrae* F. J. Muell.]. ALEXANDRA PALM, NORTHERN BANGALOW P. To 70 or 80 ft., where native, trunk enlarged toward base; pinnae to 2 in. wide, with prominent lateral veins, grayish-white beneath; fls. white or cream-colored; fr. about ½ in. long. N. Queensland. Zone 10b. Var. **Beatricae** (F. J. Muell.) C. T. White ex L. H. Bailey. STEP PALM. Bole enlarged at base and deeply ringed, so that trunk appears to have steps.

Cunninghamiana (H. Wendl.) H. Wendl. & Drude [*Ptychosperma Cunninghamianum* H. Wendl.]. PICCABEEN PALM, PICCABEEN BANGALOW P. Trunk not much enlarged at base; pinnae to 4 in. wide, green beneath, lateral veins not prominent; fls. lilac or purplish; fr. somewhat more than ½ in. long. Queensland, New S. Wales. Zone 10a. Sometimes grown under the erroneous name *Seaforthia elegans.*

ARCTERICA: *PIERIS.*

ARCTIUM L. BURDOCK, BEGGAR'S-BUTTONS, CLOTBUR. *Compositae* (Carduus Tribe). About 5 spp. of coarse, bien. or short-lived per. herbs with stout taproot, native to Eur. and Asia and naturalized as weeds in N. Amer., sts. unarmed; lvs. alt., mostly ovate-cordate, unarmed; fl. heads solitary, burlike, somewhat racemose or corymbose, involucre conical to globose, involucral bracts many, imbricate in many rows, usually terminating in a hooked spine, receptacle flat, bristly; fls. tubular, bisexual, purple to white, anthers tailed; achenes oblong, compressed, wrinkled, pappus of several rows of rough bristles.

One species is grown for its edible roots and one for medicinal purposes.

Lappa L. GREAT BURDOCK, EDIBLE B., CUCKOLD, HARLOCK. Stout, much-branched herb, to 10 ft.; lf. blades ovate-cordate, to 20 in. long, white-woolly beneath, petioles to 1 ft., solid; heads to 1¾ in. across, in corymbose clusters; fls. purplish-red. Eurasia; naturalized in N. Amer. Much cult. as a vegetable in Japan, where known as gobo; the slender roots are eaten when 2 ft. long or less. The plant may be treated as an ann., seeds sown in May producing edible roots by autumn, and those sown in autumn producing harvestable roots in spring. Thrives in deep, loose soil.

minus (J. Hill) Bernh. COMMON BURDOCK. Stout herb, to 5 ft.; lf. blades ovate-cordate, to 20 in. long, eventually glabrous beneath, petioles of lower lvs. hollow; heads to 1 in. across, racemose or nearly so; fls. pink or purplish. Eurasia; naturalized in N. Amer. Has been used medicinally.

ARCTOMECON Torr. & Frém. *Papaveraceae.* Three spp. of per. herbs with a long taproot, native to desert regions of the U.S.; lvs. mostly basal, wedge-shaped, toothed at apex, densely long-hairy, st. lvs., when present, alt. and entire; fls. large, showy, yellow or white, on long peduncles; fr. an obovoid caps.

Rarely cultivated, requiring conditions like those of native habitat.

californica Torr. & Frém. Sts. to 2 ft.; lvs. few; fls. yellow, several together. Nw. Ariz.

Merriamii Cov. DESERT POPPY. To 16 in., sts. sparsely leafy; fls. white, solitary on elongated peduncles. In creosote-bush desert, Death Valley, Calif., e. to adjacent Nev.

ARCTOSTAPHYLOS Adans. [*Arctous* (A. Gray) Niedenzu; *Mairania* Desv.; *Uva-ursi* Mill.]. BEARBERRY, MANZANITA. *Ericaceae.* About 50 spp. of evergreen, prostrate shrubs to small trees, native chiefly to w. N. Amer., but 2 spp. circumboreal; brs. crooked, smooth, red to brown; lvs. alt., simple, leathery; fls. white to pink, in terminal racemes or panicles, calyx 4–5-parted, corolla urceolate, stamens 10, anthers awned, opening by terminal pores, ovary superior; fr. a berrylike drupe, red to brown, smooth.

Culture as for *Arbutus.*

alpina (L.) K. Spreng. [*Arctous alpina* (L.) Niedenzu]. BLACK B., ALPINE B. Matted trailing shrub; lvs. obovate or oblanceolate, to 1½ in. long, turning red in autumn, withering with age; fls. white, tinged pink, less than ³⁄₁₆ in. long; fr. black. Late spring. N. Eur., n. Asia, n. N. Amer. Zone 2. Var. **japonica** (Nakai) Hult. [*Mairania japonica* (Nakai) Mak.]. Lvs. larger, more nearly spatulate, obtuse.

Andersonii A. Gray [*A. regismontana* Eastw.]. HEART-LEAF M. To 12 ft.; lvs. crowded, usually sessile, oblong or ovate, to 2¾ in. long, cordate, stomata on upper surface not visible with lens; infl. glandular-hairy; fls. white or pink, ovary pubescent; fr. red-brown, sticky-pubescent. Winter, early spring. Coastal, cent. Calif. Var. **auriculata:** *A. auriculata.* Var. **pallida** (Eastw.) J. E. Adams ex McMinn [*A. pallida* Eastw.]. Lvs. pale green, glabrous; fls. white; fr. bright red.

auriculata Eastw. [*A. Andersonii* var. *auriculata* (Eastw.) Jeps.]. To 12 ft.; lvs. sessile or nearly so, ovate to oblong-ovate, to 2 in. long, auriculate, stomata on upper surface visible with lens; infl. hairy but not glandular; fls. white or pinkish, ovary white-hairy; fr. red-brown or orange-brown. Late winter, early spring. Calif.

Bakeri: *A. Stanfordiana* subsp.

bicolor: *Xyloccocus bicolor.*

bracteosa: *A. tomentosa* var. *trichoclada.*

canescens Eastw. HOARY M. To 6 ft.; lvs. oblong-ovate to ovate, to 1½ in. long, pale green, white-pubescent; fls. white, ovary densely white-hairy. Winter, spring. S. Ore. to cent. Calif.

cinerea T. J. Howell. DEL NORTE M. To 6 ft., branchlets ash-colored; lvs. oblong-elliptic to obovate, to 1⅜ in. long, whitish-green; fls. white to pink, ovary hairy; fr. deep red-brown. Early to late spring. Sw. Ore. and adjacent Calif.

columbiana Piper. HAIRY M. Erect, often arborescent shrub, to 10 ft., branchlets densely pubescent; lvs. elliptic to oblong-ovate, to 2½ in. long, pale green; fls. white or pink, ovary tomentose; fr. bright red. Early to late spring. Coastal, B.C. to n. Calif.

crustacea Eastw. BRITTLE-LEAF M. To 6 ft., branchlets setose-bristly; lvs. petioled, oblong to ovate, to 1½ in. long, bright green; fls. white or pink, lower bracts leafy; fr. dark red. Late winter, spring. Calif. Var. **tomentosiformis:** *A. tomentosa* var.

Cushingiana: *A. glandulosa* var. Forma **repens:** *A. glandulosa* var. *Cushingiana.*

densiflora M. S. Bak. SONOMA M. Procumbent shrub, sts. blackish, rooting; lvs. elliptic, to 1¼ in. long, green, shining; panicles short, dense, many-fld.; fls. white or pink; fr. glabrous. Spring. Local, Sonoma Co. (Calif.).

diversifolia: *Comarostaphylis diversifolia.*

drupacea: *A. Pringlei* var.

Edmundsii J. T. Howell. LITTLE SUR M. Nearly prostrate, with rooting sts.; lvs. elliptic to broadly ovate, to 1¼ in. long, truncate to cordate; fls. pink, bracts leafy, ovary glabrous; fr. brown. Late autumn. Local, Monterey Co. (Calif.).

franciscana: *A. Hookeri* subsp.

glandulosa Eastw. EASTWOOD M. Erect spreading shrub, to 8 ft., sticky-glandular-hairy throughout; lvs. ovate to lanceolate-ovate, to 2 in. long; fls. white, bracts leafy, ovary glandular-hairy; fr. red-brown. Winter, early spring. Ore. to s. Calif. Var. **crassifolia** Jeps. Branchlets not glandular-hairy; lvs. dark green. Var. **Cushingiana** (Eastw.) J. E. Adams ex McMinn [*A. Cushingiana* Eastw.; *A. Cushingiana* forma *repens* J. T. Howell]. Branchlets grayish-tomentulose; lvs. slightly glaucous, infl. and ovary not glandular. Var. **Howellii** (Eastw.) J. E. Adams ex McMinn [*A. Howellii* Eastw.]. Branchlets not glandular; lvs. yellow-green; infl. and ovary glandular.

glauca Lindl. BIG-BERRY M. Erect, often arborescent shrub, to 18 ft.; lvs. oblong, elliptic, or ovate, to 1¾ in. long, glaucous, glabrous; fls. white or pink, ovary glandular; fr. brownish, to ⅝ in. in diam. Early winter to early spring. Calif. and Baja Calif.

hispidula: *A. Stanfordiana* subsp.

Hookeri G. Don. MONTEREY M. Procumbent shrub, forming mounds to 4 ft.; lvs. elliptic to ovate or obovate, to 1 in. long, bright green, shining, glabrous; fls. white or pinkish, ovary glabrous; fr. glossy, bright red. Late winter, early spring. Local, Monterey Co. (Calif.). Subsp. **franciscana** (Eastw.) Munz [*A. franciscana* Eastw.]. Branchlets prostrate, minutely puberulent; fls. and fr. slightly larger.

Howellii: *A. glandulosa* var.

insularis Greene. ISLAND M. Erect, much-branched shrub, to 10 ft.; lvs. ovate to elliptic, to nearly 2 in. long, bright green, shining, glabrous; fls. white, bracts shorter than pedicels; fr. light brown. Winter, early spring. Santa Cruz, Santa Rosa, and Santa Catalina Is. (Calif.).

intermedia: a listed name of no botanical standing.

Manzanita Parry. PARRY M. To 12 ft. and sometimes taller, brs. crooked; lvs. oblong to broadly elliptic, to 1¾ in. long; panicles drooping; fls. white or pink; fr. white, then red. Late winter, early spring. N. Calif. Jelly sometimes made from the fr. Zone 7?

Mariposa W. Dudl. MARIPOSA M. To 8 ft., arborescent, branchlets glandular; lvs. ovate to suborbicular, to 1¾ in. long, stiff, white-glaucous; fls. pink, ovary glandular-hairy; fr. light brown. Late winter, early spring. Cent. Calif.

media Greene. Spreading, prostrate shrub, to 2 ft.; lvs. obovate-cuneate, to 1 in. long, puberulent beneath; racemes terminal; fls. white or pale pink. Wash. Possibly a hybrid between *A. columbiana* and *A. Uva-ursi.* Cv. 'Grandiflora'. Fls. larger.

montana: *A. pungens* var.

morroensis Wiesl. & Schreib. MORRO M. To 8 ft.; lvs. oblong to oblong-lanceolate, to 1¼ in. long, gray-green to yellow-green, tomentose beneath; fls. white to pink, ovary densely tomentose; fr. orange-brown. Winter, early spring. Local, San Luis Obispo Co. (Calif.).

myrtifolia Parry. IONE M. Much-branched shrub, to 3 ft.; lvs. elliptic to ovate, to ¾ in. long, shining, light green; fls. white or pink, ovary with short stiff hairs; fr. green. Winter. Local, cent. Calif.

nevadensis A. Gray. PINE-MAT M. Mat-forming shrub, to 2 ft., with creeping, rooting sts.; lvs. elliptic, or lanceolate to obovate, to 1 in. long, mucronate, bright green; fls. white, ovary glabrous; fr. dark brown. Late spring, early summer. Nev., cent. Calif. to Wash.

Nummularia A. Gray. FT. BRAGG M. Prostrate to erect shrub, to 2 ft.; lvs. elliptic to oblong or ovate, to ¾ in. long, dark green, shining, glabrous; fls. white, 4-merous, ovary pubescent; fr. green. Early spring and spring. Coastal, n. Calif. Zone 7.

obispoensis Eastw. SERPENTINE M. Erect shrub, to 10 ft., bark purple-red; lvs. sessile or with short petioles, ovate to oblong-ovate, to 1¾ in. long, gray-hairy; fls. white or pink; fr. pale orange-brown. Late winter. Serpentine soils, cent. Calif.

otayensis Wiesl. & Schreib. OTAY M. Erect, to 8 ft., branchlets glandular-pubescent; lvs. elliptic to oblong, to 1½ in. long, gray-green to yellow-green, glandular; fls. white; fr. pale brown. Winter, early spring. Mts., San Diego Co. (Calif.).

pajaroensis J. E. Adams. PAJARO M. Erect, compact shrub, to 10 ft., branchlets bristly white-hairy; lvs. ovate-triangular, to 1¼ in. long, auriculate-clasping, mucronate, green, slightly glaucous, glabrous; fls. white, ovary white-hairy; fr. light red. Late winter. Local on sandy hills, n. Monterey Co. (Calif.).

pallida: *Arctostaphylos Andersonii* var.

patula Greene. GREEN-LEAF M. Much-branched shrub, to 6 ft., bark red-brown, branchlets glandular; lvs. ovate to suborbicular, to 2 in. long, bright green; fls. pink, ovary glabrous; fr. brown. Early spring to summer. S. Ore. to s. Calif., e. to Ariz., Utah, Colo. Zone 7?

pechoensis W. Dudl. ex Abrams. PECHO M. To 3 ft., branchlets white-tomentose, often bristly; lvs. nearly sessile, ovate to oblong-ovate, to 1½ in. long, auriculate or subcordate, tomentulose; fls. white to pink, ovary glabrous; fr. light brown. Winter. Cent. Calif. Var. **viridissima** Eastw. [*A. viridissima* (Eastw.) McMinn]. Lvs. glabrous, shining, dark green.

Pringlei Parry. Erect shrub, to 10 ft., branchlets glandular-hairy; lvs. oblong to ovate or suborbicular, to 2 in. long, pallid-green, glandular; fls. rose, ovary glandular; fr. dark red, separating into nutlets. Spring. Ariz. and Baja Calif. Var. **drupacea** Parry [*A. drupacea* (Parry) Macbr.]. PINK-BRACTED M. Fr. a solid stone, not separating into nutlets. Late winter, early spring. S. Calif., Baja Calif. (Mex.).

pumila Nutt. DUNE M. Prostrate shrub, to 3 ft., forming mats or mounds, branchlets finely-hairy; lvs. narrowly obovate to spatulate, to 1 in. long, dull green; fls. white to pink, ovary glabrous; fr. brown. Late winter, early spring. Around Monterey Bay (Calif.).

pungens HBK. MEXICAN M. Erect, 10 ft.; lvs. elliptic to oblong or obovate, to 1¼ in. long, bright green, becoming glabrous; fls. white, ovary glabrous; fr. brownish-red. Late winter. Calif., Nev. to Tex. and Mex. Var. **montana** (Eastw.) Munz [*A. montana* Eastw.]. Bushy to matlike, brs. often rooting. Local, Marin Co. (Calif.). Zone 7.

regismontana: *A. Andersonii.*

rubescens: *Arbutus xalapensis.*

rubra (Rehd. & E. H. Wils.) Fern. [*Arctous erythrocarpa* Small; *Arctous rubra* (Rehd. & E. H. Wils.) Nakai]. Differs from *A. alpina* in having lvs. brighter green, corolla narrower, entire, and fr. larger, bright red. Nw. N. Amer. and e. Asia. Zone 6?

rudis Jeps. & Wiesl. SHAGBARK M. To 5 ft.; lvs. elliptic to oblong, to 1½ in. long, bright green, becoming glabrous; fls. pink, pedicels and ovary glabrous; fr. brownish-red. Late autumn, winter. Coastal strand, San Luis Obispo and Santa Barbara Co. (Calif.).

×**Sherwoodii:** a name of no botanical standing; listed as a hybrid between *A. columbiana* and *A. nevadensis.*

silvicola Jeps. & Wiesl. SILVER-LEAF M. Erect, to 8 ft., branchlets silver-gray-hairy; lvs. elliptic to oblong-elliptic, to 1½ in. long; fls. white, bracts longer than pedicels; fr. light brown. Late winter. Local, Santa Cruz Mts., (Calif.).

Stanfordiana Parry. STANFORD M. To 6 ft., sts. dark red, branchlets glabrous or minutely pubescent; lvs. lanceolate-ovate to oblanceolate, to 2¾ in. long, bright green, shining, glabrous; fls. pink, ovary glabrous; fr. bright red. Late winter, early spring. N. Calif. Subsp. **Bakeri** (Eastw.) J. E. Adams [*A. Bakeri* Eastw.]. Branchlets with longer hairs; fls. larger. Subsp. **hispidula** (T. J. Howell) J. E. Adams [*A. hispidula* T. J. Howell]. Branchlets glandular-hispidulous; lvs. dull green. Se. Ore. and adjacent Calif.

tomentosa (Pursh) Lindl. WOOLLY M. To 6 ft., branchlets densely white-tomentose; lvs. oblong to elliptic or ovate, to 2 in. long, hoary-tomentose beneath; panicles loose, hairy but not glandular; fls. white, ovary densely tomentose; fr. light brown. Winter, early spring. Coastal, cent. Calif. Zone 7? Var. **tomentosiformis** (J. E. Adams) Munz [*A. crustacea* var. *tomentosiformis* J. E. Adams]. Branchlets densely white-tomentose with bristly hairs; lvs. white-tomentose beneath. Var. **trichoclada** (DC.) Munz [*A. bracteosa* (DC.) Abrams]. Lvs., bracts, branchlets, and pedicels glandular.

Uva-ursi (L.) K. Spreng. COMMON B., MEALBERRY, HOG CRAN-BERRY, KINNIKINICK, SANDBERRY, MOUNTAIN BOX, BEAR'S GRAPE, CREASHAK. Prostrate and creeping; lvs. obovate to spatulate, to 1 in. long, shining, glabrous; racemes terminal; fls. white or pink, ovary glabrous; fr. red. Late spring, early summer. Eur., n. Asia, N. Amer. Zone 2. Lvs. used medicinally, and for tanning in Sweden.

viridissima: *A. pechoensis* var.

viscida Parry. WHITE-LEAF M. To 12 ft.; lvs. elliptic to ovate or suborbicular, to 2 in. long, white-glaucous, glabrous; fls. white to pink, pedicels glandular-pubescent; fr. light brown or red. Late winter, early spring. Calif., Ore. Zone 7?

ARCTOTIS L. AFRICAN DAISY. *Compositae* (Arctotis Tribe). About 30 spp. of ann. and per. herbs, rarely subshrubs, native to S. Afr.; lvs. in basal rosette or alt. on sts.; fl. heads solitary on long, rather stout peduncles, radiate, involucral bracts imbricate in several rows, the inner bracts scarious, receptacle mostly bristly, pitted; disc fls. tubular, all bisexual or the innermost sometimes sterile, ray fls. ligulate, female; achenes usually 3–5-winged, with 2 or 3 cavities on their backs, pappus usually of 1–2 rows of scales, sometimes absent or reduced.

Propagated by seeds.

acaulis L. [*A. scapigera* Thunb.]. Stemless per. with stout, branching rhizome; lvs. in rosettes, variable in shape, 6–8 in. long, pinnately lobed or lyrate, with terminal lobe the largest, margins undulate, upper surface green and rough-hairy, lower surface woolly; heads to 3 in. across, on peduncles to 6 in. long; disc fls. purple-black, ray fls. yellow, reddish underneath.

breviscapa Thunb. Stemless ann.; lvs. oblong-lanceolate, pinnately lobed or lyrate, toothed or somewhat undulate, with scattered hairs above, white-woolly underneath; heads to 2 in. across, on hairy scapes shorter than lvs.; disc fls. dark brown, ray fls. orange-yellow above, coppery underneath. Var. **aurantiaca** Hort. Disc. fls. purple, ray fls. deep orange-yellow.

grandis: *A. stoechadifolia* var.

scapigera: *A. acaulis.*

stoechadifolia Bergius. BLUE-EYED A.D. Subshrubby per., grown as an ann., to 2½ ft., brs. leafy; lvs. oblong to obovate, to 4 in. long, pinnately lobed or lyrate, entire to irregularly toothed, white-woolly; heads to 3 in. across, on peduncles longer than lvs.; disc fls. violet, ray fls. creamy above, reddish underneath. Var. **grandis** (Thunb.) Less. [*A. grandis* Thunb.]. Lvs. to 6 in. long; peduncles to 1 ft. long.

ARCTOUS: *ARCTOSTAPHYLOS.* **Arctous erythrocarpa:** *Arctostaphylos rubra.*

ARDISIA Swartz [*Icacorea* Aubl.]. *Myrsinaceae.* About 250 spp. of trop. or warm temp. evergreen trees and shrubs, but rare in Australia and absent in Afr.; lvs. alt., simple, often leathery; fls. small, white or rose, in terminal or axillary cymes or panicles, calyx 4–5-parted, rotate, stamens 4 or 5; fr. a 1-seeded drupe.

Grown outdoors in warm climates in partially shady moist sites; one species a popular greenhouse subject. Propagated by seeds sown late in winter or early in spring; also by cuttings of half-matured wood over bottom heat.

acuminata: *A. guianensis.*

crenata Sims [*A. crenulata* Lodd.]. CORALBERRY, SPICEBERRY. Shrub, to 6 ft., glabrous; lvs. elliptic-lanceolate or oblanceolate, to 8 in. long, with 12–18 pairs of lateral veins, glabrous, margins crisped-undulate; fls. white or pink, about ¼ in. long; fr. coral-red. Japan to n. India. Slow-growing shrub, but grown as a pot plant in conservatories and homes for its abundant crop of long-lasting, bright red berries. Cv. 'Alba' is listed.

crenulata: *A. crenata.*

crispa (Thunb.) A. DC. Often confused with *A. crenata*, but differs in having twigs slightly pubescent when young, lvs. with about 8 pairs of lateral veins, and margins not crisped-undulate. Japan to s. China.

escallonioides Cham. & Schlechtend. [*A. paniculata* (Nutt.) Sarg., not Roxb.; *A. Pickeringia* Torr. & A. Gray; *Icacorea paniculata* (Nutt.) Sudw.]. MARLBERRY. Shrub or small tree, to 20 ft.; lvs. oblanceolate,

to 7 in. long, entire; fls. white; fr. black and glossy, smooth, 5⁄16 in. in diam. S. Fla., W. Indies, Mex.

glandulosa-marginata Ørst. Shrub or tree, to 25 ft.; lvs. elliptic to obovate-elliptic, to 4½ in. long, glandular-punctate, especially at margins; fls. creamy-white, calyx and pedicels lilac. About ¼ in. in diam., crimson when young, becoming black at maturity. Costa Rica.

guianensis (Aubl.) Mez [*A. acuminata* Willd.]. Small tree; lvs. oblong-elliptic, to 6 in. long, membranous, crenate; fls. typically 4-merous, white, calyx and corolla glandular-dotted; fr. black. Trinidad, the Guianas, and Venezuela to n. Peru.

japonica (Hornst.) Blume. MARLBERRY. Erect shrub, to 1½ ft.; lvs. elliptic, to 4 in. long, glossy, serrate, crowded at ends of brs.; fls. white; fr. red, ¼ in. in diam. Japan, China.

lanceolata Roxb. Large shrub or tree, to 40 ft.; lvs. elliptic-oblong or obovate, to 11 in. long, subentire; fls. rose-pink; fr. black. Se. Asia, Philippine Is.

macrocarpa Wallich. Shrub, to 4 ft.; lvs. narrowly lanceolate, to 6 in. long, acute at both ends, glabrous, crisped-crenulate; fls. pale pink; fr. bright red, dotted, to ½ in. in diam. Himalayas.

Oliveri: *A. opegrapha.*

opegrapha Ørst. [*A. Oliveri* M. T. Mast.]. Glabrous shrub; lvs. elliptic-lanceolate to oblanceolate, to 8 in. long, entire; fls. rose-purple, with white eye and yellow stamens; fr. black. Costa Rica.

paniculata Roxb., not Sarg. Tree; lvs. oblanceolate, to 14 in. long, glossy, alt., becoming whorled or crowded toward ends of brs.; fls. rosy-pink; fr. red, longitudinally ribbed. India. Probably not cult. in U.S.; material offered under this name is *A. escallonioides.*

Pickeringia: *A. escallonioides.*

primulifolia G. Gardn. & Champ. Stemless herb, rusty-hairy throughout; lvs. forming rosettes, elliptic to obovate, to 6 in. long, subentire; fls. cymose or more or less umbellate, on scapes to 4 in. long. S. China.

procepha: a listed name of no botanical standing.

punctata Lindl. Shrub, to 10 ft.; lvs. lanceolate, to 6 in. long, slightly wavy; fls. grayish-white, densely marked with purple spots. China.

pusilla A. DC. [*A. villosa* (Thunb.) Mez, not Roxb.]. Decumbent shrub, to 1 ft.; lvs. elliptic to elliptic-ovate, to 2 in. long, serrate, covered with rusty hairs; fls. pinkish-white; fr. red, to ¼ in. in diam. Japan, s. China.

solanacea Roxb. Glabrous shrub or small tree, to 20 ft.; lvs. oblong-lanceolate to oblanceolate, to 6 in. long; fls. rose; fr. black, ¼ in. in diam. India.

villosa: *A. pusilla.*

ARDISIANDRA Hook.f. *Primulaceae.* About 6 spp. of herbs, native to trop. Afr.; lvs. simple, alt.; fls. white, in clusters of 1–5, calyx 5-parted, corolla campanulate, stamens 5; fr. a 5–8-valved caps.

sibthorpioides Hook.f. Creeping herb, sts. pilose, to 14 in. long; lvs. widely ovate, to 1¼ in. long, cordate, lobed and dentate, pilose; fls. ¼ in. across, in 1–3-fld. clusters.

ARECA L. *Palmae.* About 50 spp. of slender, unarmed, monoecious palms of the wet tropics from India and Ceylon to the Philippine and Solomon Is.; lvs. pinnate or pinnately nerved, pinnae 1-ribbed or more commonly several-ribbed and toothed at apex; infl. below lvs., subtended by 1 deciduous papery bract, short-peduncled, branched, spicate or sometimes appearing spicate, especially in fr., rachillae with fls. in spirally arranged triads (2 male and 1 female) throughout, or in triads only in the lower part and above these with male fls. in 1-sided or 2-ranked pairs; male fls. asymmetrical, sepals small, separate or united, petals valvate, angled, stamens 3–24, filaments erect, pistillode minute, female fls. larger, with strongly imbricate sepals and petals, ovary 1-celled; fr. red or orange, with apical stigmatic scar, endocarp adherent to seed, not operculate, seed with ruminate endosperm and basal embryo.

The fruits (betel nuts) of *A. Catechu* are an important masticatory in the Old World tropics. Tender but sometimes planted as ornamentals in subtropical southern Fla. For culture see *Palms.*

Aliceae F. J. Muell. Described from Australia, but incompletely known; not found in wild state. Plants cult. under this name, and perhaps the sp. itself, are probably referable to *A. triandra.*

Baueri: *Rhopalostylis Baueri.*

Catechu L. BETEL PALM, BETEL-NUT P., ARECA-NUT P., CATECHU, PINANG. Slender palm, trunk solitary, to 100 ft., 6 in. in diam. below green crownshaft; lvs. few, 3–6 ft. long, pinnae many, broad, soft, several-ribbed, toothed at apex; infl. paniculate; female fls. few, large, basal on rachillae, male fls. above in 2-ranked pairs, stamens 6; fr. orange to red, ovoid to globose-ovoid, mostly 2 in. long or less, with thick, soft, fibrous mesocarp. Exact origin unknown, probably Malay Pen., but widely cult. in Old World tropics and elsewhere for the astringent kernel of the seed, which is chewed, either fresh or cured, with slaked lime, the lvs. of betel pepper, and various flavorings. Lvs. sometimes variegated. Shade-loving, especially in young stage; grows best in trop. areas with heavy rainfall; sensitive to cold and drought. Zone 10b.

concinna Thwaites. Sts. to 12 ft., clustered; lvs. few, to 3½ ft. long, with green sheaths and mostly 2- to several-ribbed pinnae; infl. paniculate; female fls. basal on rachillae, male fls. in 2-ranked pairs above, stamens 6; fr. scarlet, 1½ in. long, subfusiform and beaked. Ceylon. Nuts sometimes used as substitute for betel nut.

glandiformis Lam. Tall and slender, with ringed trunk and green crownshaft; lvs. to 8 ft., pinnae mostly several-ribbed; infl. compact, simply branched, appearing spicate in fr. when rachillae break off, female fls. basal on rachillae, male fls. in 2-ranked pairs above; stamens 6; frs. crowded. Moluccas.

Langloisiana: *A. vestiaria.*

lutescens: *Chrysalidocarpus lutescens.*

madagascariensis: a name used erroneously in hort. for *Chrysalidocarpus madagascariensis.*

rubra: a name used erroneously in hort. for *Dictyosperma album.*

sapida: *Rhopalostylis sapida.*

Tinkeri: a listed name of no botanical standing and uncertain application.

triandra Roxb. Sts. slender, clustered, green, to 10 ft. or more; lvs. 3–5 ft. long, bright green, pinnae several-ribbed; infl. paniculately branched, rachillae with female fls. near base, above these with male fls. in pairs on 1 side; stamens 3; fr. oblong, beaked, red or orange-red. India to Malay Pen. Zone 10a, marginal in warmest parts of 9b in Fla. Nuts used as substitute for betel nuts. Young plants make good tub plants.

vestiaria Giseke [*A. Langloisiana* Potzt.]. Sts. clustered, to 12 ft.; lf. sheaths bright orange, pinnae 14–15 on each side of rachis, green, mostly several-ribbed; infl. twice-branched, yellow, rachillae with fls. in spirally arranged triads in lower half, above these with male fls. in pairs; stamens 6; fr. ovoid, scarlet, 1 in. long. Celebes. Zone 10b in Fla. An attractive ornamental for trop. gardens.

ARECACEAE: see *PALMAE.*

ARECASTRUM

ARECASTRUM (Drude) Becc. *Palmae.* One sp., a solitary, unarmed, monoecious palm of subtrop. S. Amer.; lvs. pinnate, sheath fibrous, open, pinnae borne in groups of 1–5 and in several planes along the rachis, acute or acuminate, midrib prominent, petiole not toothed along the margin; infl. among the lvs., bracts 2, the lower 2-edged, open apically, usually concealed by sheaths, the upper fusiform in bud, woody, splitting abaxially, beaked, deeply sulcate externally, rachillae with fls. in triads (2 male and 1 female) nearly throughout, above these with paired or solitary male; male fls. with calyx 3-lobed, short, petals 3, valvate, much wider than thick, angled, much longer than sepals, stamens 6, pistillode minute, 3-cleft, female fls. with sepals 3, imbricate, petals 3, imbricate except short-valvate at apex, not much longer than sepals, staminodes united in a low membranous ring, pistil 3-celled, 3-ovuled; fr. ovoid, 1-seeded, mesocarp fleshy-fibrous, endocarp thick, bony, with 3 pores near the base and a prominent intrusion into the seed on one side, seed small, endosperm homogeneous, embryo at the base on one side.

Commonly planted as an ornamental in the tropics and in southern Calif. and Fla. Relatively short-lived, 35–40 years, in southern Calif. For culture see *Palms.*

australe: a listed name of no botanical standing, applied to *A. Romanzoffianum* var. *australe.*

Romanzoffianum (Cham.) Becc. [*Cocos Romanzoffiana* Cham.; *C. plumosa* Hook.]. QUEEN PALM. To 40 ft. or more, trunk gray-brown; lvs. many, arching or drooping, to 15 ft. long or more, petiole elongate, pinnae to 3 ft. long, 1¼ in. wide, tips usually bent over; infl. to 3 ft. long or more, male fls. yellow, to ⅜ in. long; fr. yellow, mostly about 1 in. long but to 1½ in. long. S. Brazil to Argentina. Zone 9b; but older

plants tolerate temperatures to 20° F. Considered the best substitute for royal palms where these cannot be grown. Commonest exotic palm in cent. Fla. A variable sp. in which several vars. have been recognized. Var. **Romanzoffianum.** The typical var.; fr. to 1 in. long, ¾ in. in diam., the endocarp not narrowed at either end. Var. **australe** (Mart.) Becc. [*Cocos australis* Mart.; *C. Datil* Griseb. & Drude]. Fr. with endocarp narrowed to both ends. Var. **botryophorum** (Mart.) Becc. Fr. larger, to 1½ in. long, 1½ in. in diam., endocarp thick, narrowed at both ends.

AREGELIA: see *NEOREGELIA.* **A. Marechalii:** *N. Carolinae.*

ARENARIA

ARENARIA L. [*Alsine* L.; *Alsinopsis* Small; *Minuartia* L.; *Moehringia* L.]. SANDWORT. *Caryophyllaceae.* About 150 spp. of low, often mat-forming, ann. or per. herbs of temp. N. Hemisphere, and common in arctic regions; lvs. opp., mostly narrow, without stipules; infl. terminal or axillary, often cymose and bracted; fls. usually white, small, sepals 4–5, separate, petals usually 5, rarely 0, entire or notched at apex, stamens 10, styles usually 3; fr. a caps., ovoid, seeds few to many.

The cultivated species are mostly perennials. Propagated by division, from seeds, and by cuttings. Usually grown in rock and wall gardens.

aculeata S. Wats. Mat-forming per., fl. sts. to 8 in., erect, many; lvs. stiff, subulate, to 1 in. long, pungent, glaucous, persistent; cymes few-fld.; fls. white, about ½ in. across, sepals ovate, acute, tipped pink, petals exceeding sepals. Arid mts., e. Ore. and e. Calif., e. to Mont. and Utah.

aggregata (L.) Loisel. Cespitose per., to 2 in.; lvs. mostly imbricate, lanceolate, to ⅛ in. long, acute, mucronate, recurved and folded; infl. capitate, 3–15-fld.; sepals lanceolate to linear-lanceolate, petals about as long as sepals. Sw. Europe.

aizoides (Boiss.) Fern. [*Minuartia aizoides* (Boiss.) Bornm.]. Per., forming many rosettes, fl. sts. 2–3 in.; lvs. stiff, subulate, to ½ in. long; infl. 1–3-fld., glandular-pubescent; sepals obtuse-lanceolate, petals to ¼ in. long. Mts., ne. Turkey and Caucasus.

Armeriastrum: *A. armerina.*

armerina Bory [*A. Armeriastrum* Boiss.]. Cespitose per., fl. sts. to 8 in.; lvs. ovate to linear, to ³⁄₁₆ in. long, obtuse, often puberulent; infl. a dense terminal cluster, subtended by linear bracts, often with 1–3 axillary fls. beneath; sepals linear-lanceolate, to ⁵⁄₁₆ in. long, acute, often somewhat woolly, petals to ½ in. long. Mts., s. Spain.

austriaca Jacq. [*Minuartia austriaca* (Jacq.) Hayek]. Cespitose per., to 10 in.; lvs. linear-lanceolate, to ¾ in. long, glabrous; fls. 1–3 together, sepals ovate-lanceolate, petals to ½ in. long, emarginate. E. Alps.

balearica L. CORSICAN S. Mat-forming per., fl. sts. to 2½ in.; procumbent, branched, scabrid to glabrous; lvs. broadly ovate, to ³⁄₁₆ in. long, pubescent, petioles ³⁄₁₆ in. long; fls. solitary, sepals ovate, pubescent, petals ¼ in. long. Shaded rocky slopes, w. Medit. Is.

Bauhinorum: *A. capillacea.*

Biebersteinii: *A. procera.*

blepharophylla Boiss. Tufted per., forming rosettes, fl. sts. to 1 ft., erect; lvs. long-ciliate, basal lvs. linear-setaceous, to 6 in. long, st. lvs. linear, to 2⅜ in. long, smaller toward apex; infl. a cymose panicle, peduncles glandular-pubescent; sepals ovate, to about ⅛ in. long, petals 1½ times longer than sepals. E. Turkey, nw. Iran. Var. **blepharophylla.** The typical var.; lf. margins usually long-ciliate; petals 1½ times as long as sepals. Turkey. Var. **parviflora** (Fenzl) McNeill [*A. Steveniana* Boiss.]. Lf. margins glabrous to very short-ciliate; sepals ovate to oblong-ovate, to a little more than ⅛ in. long; petals about twice as long as sepals. E. Turkey, Caucasus.

caespitosa: *A. verna.*

capillacea All. [*A. Bauhinorum* (J. Gay ex Lamotte) Bonnier & Layens; *Minuartia capillacea* (All.) Graebn.]. Cespitose per., fl. sts. to 1 ft., densely glandular-pubescent in upper part; lvs. linear-bristly, to about ¾ in. long, rigid; cymes 1–6-fld.; sepals ovate-oblong, about ¼ in. long, 3-veined basally, petals to ½ in. long; caps. to ½ in. long. Limy soils, s. and s.-cent. Eur.

capillaris Poir. [*A. formosa* Fisch. ex DC.]. Cespitose per., fl. sts. to 8 in.; lvs. crowded, linear, about 1 in. long, often scabrous-margined, nearly glaucous; infl. of 2–3-fld. cymes; sepals ovate, petals to ⁵⁄₁₆ in. long; caps. longer than calyx. Siberia, nw. N. Amer. Material cult. under this name may be *A. Kingii.*

caroliniana Walt. LONGROOT, PINE-BARREN S. Per., forming dense mats, fl. sts. to 12 in., taproot long; lvs. linear-subulate, to ⁵⁄₁₆ in. long;

infl. cymose, 1–13-fld.; sepals ovate, petals 5/16 in. long, white, green basally. Coastal plain, s. R.I. to nw. Fla.

cephalotes Bieb. Per., brs. woody, fl. sts. 8–20 in., stout; basal lvs. linear, 4–16 in. long; infl. a dense, hemispheric, terminal head, bracts showy, 5/8 in. long, leathery; fls. often nearly sessile, sepals lanceolate, 1/4 in. long. S. Ukraine and Moldavia.

circassica (Albov) Voronov [*Alsine pinifolia* of auth., not *Arenaria pinifolia* Bieb.; *Minuartia caucasica* (Adams ex Rupr.) Mattf.]. Resembling *A. aizoides*, but sts. tufted, fl. sts. to 8 in.; lvs. linear, to 1 in. long, margins scabrid; infl. 2–5-fld.; sepals oblong-spatulate, to 1/4 in. long, petals obovate-spatulate, more than twice as long as sepals. Caucasus.

congesta Nutt. ex Torr. & A. Gray. Per., woody at base, fl. sts. simple, 4–12 in., 4–6-lvd.; basal lvs. linear, to 2 in. long, often hispid-ciliate beneath; infl. terminal, globular, many-fld., sometimes 1–2 infls. in lf. axils beneath, bracts scarious; sepals ovate, less than 3/16 in. long, keeled, petals 1/4 in. long, stamens exserted. Arid mts., e. Wash. to cent. Calif., e. to Rocky Mts.

conimbricensis Brot. Ann., glandular-puberulent to pubescent, fl. sts. 2–6 in., branched; lvs. linear to oblanceolate, to 5/8 in., ciliate at base; cymes loose, pedicels glandular-hairy; sepals ovate, petals to 5/16 in., white, anthers dark red. Portugal and Spain.

foliosa Royle ex Edgew. & Hook.f. Per., branched at the base, glabrous, fl. sts. 2–6 in.; lvs. narrowly linear, bright green; cymes nearly umbel-like, long-peduncled, bracts ovate; sepals ovate-lanceolate, less than 3/16 in. long, 3-nerved, petals 1/4 in. long, white. W. Himalayas. Related to *A. juniperina.*

formosa: *A. capillaris,* but plants offered as *A. formosa* may be *A. Kingii.*

glaucovirens (Bertol.) Fern. [*Moehringia glaucovirens* Bertol.]. Tufted per., glaucous, glabrous, fl. sts. to 6 in.; lvs. threadlike, to 5/8 in. long; cymes 2–3-fld. or fls. solitary, pedicels slender; sepals ovate, 1-veined, petals longer than sepals; seeds black. S. Alps, n. Italy.

gothica Fries. Ann. or bien., fl. sts. to 6 in., scabrous; lvs. ovate, 1/4 in. long, ciliate toward base; cymes 1–8-fld., pedicels scabrous; sepals ovate, less than 3/16 in., ciliate at base, 3-veined, petals to 1/4 in. long. S. Sweden and w. Switzerland.

gracilis Waldst. & Kit. Cespitose per., fl. sts. 3–4 in., scabrous, glabrous at apex; lvs. lanceolate, to 3 in. long, denticulate, 1-veined, glabrous; cymes 1–3-fld., pedicels glabrous; sepals ovate, to 1/4 in. long, keeled, glabrous, petals to 1/2 in. S. and w. Yugoslavia.

graminifolia Ard. Per., fl. sts. unbranched, to about 6 in.; lvs. linear-lanceolate, to 1 5/8 in. long, rigid; infl. a 2–7-fld. cyme; sepals lanceolate, to 3/8 in. long, 5–7-veined, acute, petals longer than sepals, white. S. Eur. Probably not cult. Material offered under this name is usually *A. procera.*

grandiflora L. [*Alsine grandiflora* (L.) Crantz]. Cespitose per., fls. sts. to 6 in., hairy; lvs. linear-lanceolate, to 3/8 in. long, aristate, margins and midrib leathery; cymes 1–6-fld., pedicels glandular-pubescent; sepals ovate, 1/4 in. long, glandular-hairy, petals to 1/2 in., white. Portugal to Czechoslovakia.

groenlandica (Retz.) K. Spreng. MOUNTAIN DAISY, MOUNTAIN S. Per., forming dense mats, fl. sts. to 6 in., glabrous; lvs. linear, to 5/8 in. long; cymes 1–30-fld., pedicels to 1 in. long; sepals ovate, to 1/4 in. long, petals to 3/8 in., white, rarely 0. Greenland, s. to New Eng., and in mts., s. to Ga. and Tenn.

Hookeri Nutt. ex Torr. & A. Gray. Suffrutescent per., much-branched, fl. sts. to 12 in., glandular-puberulent; lvs. rigid, linear-subulate, to 1 1/2 in. long, pungent; cymes dense, bracts conspicuous, scarious; sepals rigid, 1/4 in., petals longer than sepals. Rocky Mts.

imbricata Bieb. Densely tufted per., fl. sts. to 4 in., glabrous to sparsely hairy; lvs. linear to linear-lanceolate, to 1/4 in. long, long-ciliate; fls. solitary, sepals oblong, to 1/4 in. long, petals obovate-spatulate, to 1/2 in. long. Caucasus.

juniperifolia: probably a misspelling for *A. juniperina.*

juniperina L. [*A. juniperifolia* Hort.; *Minuartia juniperifolia* Hort.; *M. juniperina* (L.) Maire & Petitm.]. Cespitose per., glabrous to glandular-pubescent, fl. sts. to 8 in., rigid, nodes thickened; lvs. with axillary clusters of smaller lvs., rigid, cylindrical, to 1 in. long, spiny; cymes 4- to many-fld.; sepals lanceolate, less than 3/16 in. long, petals 1/4 in. long, white. Greece, to perhaps w. Iran.

Kingii (S. Wats.) M. E. Jones. Suffrutescent per., fl. sts. 4–8 in., glandular-pubescent; lvs. needlelike, to 3/4 in. long; cymes few-fld., pedicels to 1 in., glandular-pubescent; sepals elliptic, less than 3/16 in. long, glandular-pubescent, petals longer than sepals, entire or emarginate, white. Mts., e. Calif., w. Nev.

Kitaibelii: *A. laricifolia* subsp.

Kotschyana Fenzl. Cespitose per., glabrous or pubescent, fl. sts. to 8 in.; lvs. linear, to 1 in. long, cymes 1–6-fld.; sepals ovate, less than 3/16 in. long, keeled, petals elliptic, 1/4 in. long, slightly clawed. Turkey.

laricifolia L. [*Alsine laricifolia* (L.) Crantz; *Minuartia laricifolia* (L.) Schinz & Thell.]. Cespitose per., woody at base, fl. sts. to 12 in.; lvs. rigid, linear, curved, ciliate; cymes 1–6-fld., pedicels and sepals crisped-hairy; sepals linear-oblong, 1/4 in. long, margin reddish, petals to 1/2 in. long. Subsp. **laricifolia.** The typical subsp.; sepals sometimes glandular; seeds rugose on back. Mts., cent. Spain to Carpathians. Subsp. **Kitaibelii** (Nym.) Mattf. [*A. Kitaibelii* (Nym.) Bonnier; *Minuartia Kitaibelii* (Nym.) Pawl.]. Sepals glandless; seeds tubercled on back. Limy soils, e. Austrian Alps and Carpathian Mts.

lateriflora L. [*Moehringia lateriflora* (L.) Fenzl]. Rhizomatous per., fl. sts. to 8 in., erect, pubescent; lvs. elliptic, to 1 in. long, ciliate, veins hairy; cymes axillary, 1–4-fld., pedicels puberulent; sepals elliptic, nearly 1/8 in. long, glabrous, petals to 1/4 in. long. Scandinavia and Russia.

Ledebouriana Fenzl. Spiny per., fl. sts. to 10 in., glabrous to glandular-pubescent; lvs. subulate, to 3/8 in., ciliate, spiny, often glaucous to purplish; infl. a panicle of 1–10, 2–5-fld. cymes, bracts triangular; sepals ovate, less than 3/16 in. long, petals 5/16 in. long. Turkey.

macrophylla Hook. Related to *A. lateriflora;* fl. sts. to 6 in.; lvs. lanceolate, to nearly 3 in. long, almost glabrous; peduncles 1–2-fld., either terminal or lateral, to 1 in. long, bracts linear-aristate; sepals lanceolate, 1/4 in. long, petals 1/4 in. long. Labrador to New Eng., w. to s. B.C. and s. Calif.

montana L. Robust per., gray-green, pubescent, fl. sts. to 12 in.; lvs. oblong to linear, to 1 in. long; cymes 1–10-fld.; sepals ovate, 5/16 in. long, petals to 5/8 in. long, white; caps. shorter than or equal to sepals. Portugal to cent. and nw. France.

nevadensis Boiss. & Reut. Ann., glandular-puberulent, purple at base, fl. sts. to 3 in., branched; lvs. to 5/16 in. long, 3-veined, basal lvs. spreading, ovate, upper lvs. erect, linear-lanceolate; corymbs dense, pedicels erect, to 1/2 in. long; sepals lanceolate-acuminate, to 1/4 in. long, petals shorter than sepals, white; caps. ovoid, shorter than sepals. Sierra Nevada of s. Spain.

norvegica Gunnerus. Cespitose, ann. or per., to 3 in.; lvs. oblanceolate, to 1/4 in. long, glabrous to ciliate beneath; cymes 1–4-fld., pedicels to 1/2 in. long; sepals ovate, about 1/8 in. long, petals to 1/4 in. long, anthers white. Mts., Brit. Is., Norway, w. Sweden.

obtusiloba (Rydb.) Fern. [*Alsinopsis obtusiloba* Rydb.]. Woody per., much-branched, fl. sts. to 2 in., glandular-pubescent; lvs. rigid, subulate, to 1/4 in. long; cymes 1–3-fld.; sepals elliptic, 3/16 in. long, glandular-pubescent, petals 1/4 in. long, white. Rocky Mts., Alta. and B.C., s. to New Mex.

octandra (Siebold ex K. Spreng.) Fern. Cespitose per., fl. sts. to 2 in., branched; lvs. elliptic, 1/8 in. long, 3-veined; fls. solitary, sepals lanceolate, 1/8 in. long, petals shorter than sepals, sometimes 0. Cent. and e. Alps.

pindicola: a listed name of no botanical standing.

pinifolia: see *A. circassica.*

polaris: *A. procera* subsp. *glabra.*

procera K. Spreng. [*A. Biebersteinii* Schlechtend.; *A. graminifolia* of auth., not Ard.]. Suffrutescent per., fl. sts. to 16 in., erect, thick; basal lvs. linear, to 5 in. long, acuminate, st. lvs. shorter, broader; infl. panicled to clustered, pedicels to 3/4 in. long; sepals ovate, 1/4 in. long, petals about 1/2 in. long or less. Subsp. **procera.** The typical subsp.; infl. brs. and pedicels glandular-pubescent. Ukraine, s. Russia. Subsp. **glabra** (F. N. Williams) J. Holub [*A. polaris* Shishk.]. Infl. brs. and pedicels glabrous. Cent. and e. Eur. to Siberia.

propinqua: *A. rubella.*

pungens Clemente ex Lag. Cespitose per., fl. sts. to 8 in., branched, viscid-puberulent; lvs. stiff, linear-subulate, 4-angled, to about 1 in. long, spiny; cymes 1–3-fld., pedicels about 1 in. long, viscid-puberulent; sepals linear-lanceolate, to 1/2 in. long, spiny, viscid-puberulent, petals shorter than sepals, white. Mts., s. Spain and Morocco.

purpurascens Ramond ex DC. [*Cerastium purpurascens* (Ramond ex DC.) Fenzl, not Adams]. PINK S. Diffuse per., fl. sts. to 4 in., glabrous at base, to puberulent towards apex; lvs. elliptic, to 3/8 in. long; cymes 1–4-fld., pedicels to 1/4 in., pubescent; sepals lanceolate, to 1/4 in. long, 3–5-veined, glabrous, petals to 1/2 in. long, white to pale purplish; caps. to 1/2 in. long. Pyrenees and Cantabrian Mts., n. Spain and sw. France.

recurva All. [*Minuartia condensata* (J. Presl & K. Presl) Hand.-Mazz.; *M. recurva* (All.) Schinz & Thell.]. Cespitose per., fl. sts. to 5 in., woody, blackish at base; lvs. falcate, to 3/8 in. long, 3-veined; cymes 1–8-fld., pedicels to 3/4 in. long; sepals ovate-lanceolate, to 1/4 in. long, 5–7-veined, petals slightly longer than sepals. Mts., Portugal to Romania.

rigida Bieb. Suffrutescent per., glabrous, fl. sts. to 16 in., erect; basal lvs. linear, to 5 in. long, st. lvs. shorter, broader; infl. panicled, pedicels about 1/4 in. long; sepals lanceolate, to 1/4 in. long, petals slightly longer than sepals, white. S. Ukraine to Romania and Bulgaria.

Rossii R. Br. [*Alsinopsis Rossii* (R. Br.) Rydb.]. Cespitose per., fl. sts. to 2 in.; lvs. linear, to 5/16 in. long, glabrous; fls. mostly solitary, sepals 1/8 in. long. Arctic-alpine regions, Alaska to N. W. Terr., s. to Wash. and Colo.

rotundifolia Bieb. Cespitose per., sts. slightly puberulent; lvs. elliptic to nearly orbicular, to 1/4 in. long, petioles short, ciliate; cymes 2–5-fld.; sepals about 1/8 in. long, petals shorter than sepals. Mts., Caucasus, Turkey, n. Greece, Bulgaria.

rubella (Wahlenb.) Sm. [*A. propinqua* Richardson; *Minuartia rubella* (Wahlenb.) Hiern]. Mat-forming per., glandular-hairy to glabrous, fl. sts. to 8 in.; basal lvs. linear-subulate, to 1/2 in. long, 3-veined; cymes 1–7-fld., pedicels to 1 in. long; sepals lanceolate-ovate, to 1/4 in. long, 3-veined, petals shorter than sepals. Arctic-alpine regions, N. Amer. and n. Eurasia.

sajanensis Willd. ex Schlechtend. Cespitose per., to 5 in., glandular towards apex; lvs. linear, 5/16 in. long, keeled; cymes 1–3-fld.; sepals oblong, 1/4 in. long, often purplish-tipped, petals about 1/4 in. long, anthers white. Arctic regions, N. Amer. and Eurasia.

Saxifraga Friv. [*Minuartia Saxifraga* (Friv.) Graebn.]. Cespitose per., fl. sts. erect, glandular-pubescent; lvs. ovate-lanceolate, mostly less than 1/2 in. long; cymes 1–7-fld.; sepals lanceolate, 1/4 in. long, glandular-pubescent, petals longer than sepals. Mts., cent. Bulgaria, w. Turkey.

sedoides (L.) F. J. Hanb. [*Alsine sedoides* (L.) Kittel, not Froel. ex W. D. J. Koch; *Minuartia sedoides* (L.) Hiern]. Cushion-forming per., glabrous; lvs. linear-lanceolate, 1/4 in. long, 3-veined, margins scabrous; fls. solitary, barely above the foliage, sepals less than 1/4 in. long, stamens or ovary may abort. Pyrenees, Alps, Carpathians, mts. of Scotland.

serpyllifolia L. THYME-LEAVED S. Ann. or bien., robust, scabrous, fl. sts. to 12 in., much-branched; lvs. ovate, to 5/16 in. long, 3–5-veined, basal lvs. petioled, upper lvs. sessile; infl. diffuse; sepals ovate, to 1/4 in. long, 3–5-veined, petals shorter than sepals, white. Widespread, Eur.

stellata (E. D. Clarke) Maire & Petitm. [*Alsine parnassica* Boiss. & Sprun.]. Cespitose per., forming rosettes, fl. sts. columnar, glandular-pubescent; basal lvs. triangular-lanceolate, to 3/8 in. long; cymes 1–4-fld.; sepals lanceolate, 1/4 in. long, 5-veined, glandular-pubescent, petals 3/8 in. long. Mts., Greece and s. Albania.

Steveniana: *A. blepharophylla* var. *parviflora.*

stricta Michx. [*Minuartia stricta* (Michx.) Hiern]. ROCK S. Diffuse, loosely tufted ann. or per., fl. sts. to 10 in., wiry, branched, leafy at base; lvs. rigid, subulate, to 5/8 in. long; cymes 3–30-fld.; sepals ovate, to 1/4 in. long, 3–5-ribbed, petals 3/8 in. long. Dry rocky ledges, New Eng., w. to Nebr., s. to S.C. and Tex. Var. **texana** B. L. Robinson [*A. texana* (B. L. Robinson) Britt.]. Plants stiffer, to 8 in. or more; lvs. to 3/8 in. long, the opp. pairs united; sepals lanceolate, margins inrolled. Tex. and Ark., n. to Nebr. and Ohio.

tetraquetra L. Cushion-forming per., nearly glabrous; lvs. ovate, less than 3/16 in. long, ciliate at base, glabrous; fls. solitary, about 5/16 in. above foliage, sepals lanceolate, 1/4 in. long, petals to 3/8 in. long. Cent. and e. Pyrenees, and mts. of e. and se. Spain.

texana: *A. stricta* var.

tmolea Boiss. Cespitose per., to 3 in., glandular-pubescent; lvs. ovate, to 5/8 in. long; sepals slightly keeled, petals oblanceolate. Similar to *A. Kotschyana.* Mt. Tmolus (w. Turkey).

verna L. [*A. caespitosa* J. F. Ehrh.; *Alsine sedoides* Froel ex W. D. J. Koch, not (L.) Kittel; *Minuartia verna* (L.) Hiern]. Cushion-forming per., sts. glandular-pubescent toward apex; lvs. linear-lanceolate, to 3/4 in. long, glabrous to glandular-pubescent, rarely scabrid; cymes few- to many-fld.; sepals ovate, glandular-pubescent, petals longer than sepals. Spain to n. Russia. A very variable sp. Cv. **'Aurea'.** Lvs. yellowish-green.

verticillata: *Acanthophyllum verticillatum.*

Villarsii Balb. ex Schlechtend. [*Minuartia flaccida* Schinz & Thell.; *M. Villarsii* (Balb. ex Schlechtend.) Chenev.]. Similar to *A. austriaca* in habit, glabrous to hairy; lvs. broader, to nearly 1/8 in. wide; cymes 2–7-fld.; sepals 3/16 in. long, petals about 1/4 in. long. Mts., Spain to sw. Alps.

villosula: a listed name of no botanical standing.

ARENGA Labill. [*Didymosperma* H. Wendl. & Drude ex Hook. f.]. *Palmae.* About 17 spp. of dwarf to large, solitary or cespitose, usually monocarpic, monoecious palms of trop. Asia; flowering from the top downward and then dying, rarely flowering from the base upward; lvs. pinnate or rarely undivided, pinnae often pale underneath, linear to cuneate or rhomboidal, toothed and often lobed along the margins and at the blunt apex; infls. 1 or several at a node, rachillae usually with fls. in triads (2 male and 1 female), more rarely the infls. unisexual; male fls. with sepals imbricate, petals valvate, stamens many, female fls. with sepals imbricate, petals valvate, united to about middle, pistil 3-celled, 2–3 cells fertile; fr. 1–3-seeded, seeds with homogeneous endosperm.

Several ornamental species are frequently cultivated and *A. pinnata* is important economically as a source of starch, sugar, and alcohol in the Old World tropics. Most are cluster palms, producing new stems as old ones die. Propagated by seeds and with difficulty by suckers. The juicy pulp of the fruit is irritating to skin. See also *Palms.*

Ambong Becc. Sts. several, to 10 ft. or more; lvs. to 15 ft. long, pinnae to 2 ft. long or more, 5 in. wide, irregularly undulate and lobed, often auricled at base; infls. large, several at a node; male fls. maroon, 3/4 in. long, stamens 100–150, anthers aristate; fr. globose-oblong, 1 5/16 in. long, nearly as broad, seeds 3. Philippine Is.

brevipes Becc. Sts. several, short; lvs. to 20 ft. long, pinnae elongate-cuneate, to 30 in. long or more, 6 in. wide, lower pinnae in clusters, central ones sometimes auricled at base; male fls. 9/16 in. long, anthers 100, not aristate; fr. not known. Borneo.

Engleri Becc. Sts. clustered, to 6 ft.; lvs. to 5 ft. long, petiole 2 1/2–3 ft. long, pinnae about 28–32 pairs in one plane, nearly linear, to 18 in. long, 1 1/8 in. wide, not auricled at base, toothed only near the apex; infls. solitary; male fls. maroon, intensely fragrant, 3/4 in. long, stamens many, apiculate, not aristate, female fls. on rachillae about 10 in. long or less; fr. globose, red, 3/4 in. in diam., seeds 3. Taiwan, Ryukyu Is. Zone 9b. Hardiest sp. in the genus.

microcarpa Becc. Sts. clustered, to 24 ft.; lvs. long-petioled, blade to 10 ft. long or more, pinnae linear, to 30 in. long, 1 1/4 in. wide, rounded to auricled at the base, lower pinnae in 2 ranks and sometimes clustered in separated groups of 4–5; male fls. yellow-green, 3/8 in. long, stamens 50–70, not aristate; fr. red, 1/2–3/4 in. in diam., 3-seeded. New Guinea.

mindorensis: *A. tremula.*

nana (Griff.) H. E. Moore [*Didymosperma nanum* (Griff.) H. Wendl. & Drude ex Hook. f.]. Dwarf, sts. cespitose, to 2 ft.; lvs. to 2 ft. long, pinnae in 2–3 pairs, angularly lobed, grayish, cuneate at base; infls. solitary, spicate or with 2–3 brs.; male fls. with about 14 stamens, female fls. with pistil 2-celled; fr. white, obliquely oblong, 9/16 in. long, 1-seeded. Assam, India.

obtusifolia Mart. Sts. tardily cespitose, to 30 ft., 1 ft. in diam., annulate except below crown, where needlelike fibers and fibrous sheaths persist; lvs. to 16 ft. long, petiole 3 ft. long, pinnae linear, to 3 ft. long or more, to 2 1/2 in. wide, apex obtuse and entire or 2-cleft, base auricled; infl. brs. to 2 ft. long or more; male fls. maroon, 1/2 in. long, stamens 150–200 or more, aristate; fr. ellipsoid, depressed at tip, 2 in. long or more. Java. Sumatra.

pinnata (Wurmb) Merrill [*A. saccharifera* Labill.]. SUGAR PALM, GOMUTI P., BLACK-FIBER P., ARENG P. St. solitary, to 30 ft., 1 ft. in diam., covered with fibrous sheaths and long needlelike fibers; lvs. to 20 ft. long, pinnae linear, auricled at base, in several ranks and more or less clustered, about 60 on each side; infls. solitary, unisexual, to 4 ft. long; male fls. maroon, to 1 in. long, stamens 60–80, aristate; fr. 2 in. long, depressed-oblong or nearly globose. Malay Arch.; probably naturalized elsewhere. Zone 10b. Cult. in tropics of both hemispheres and especially on Malay Pen. where the male spadices are regularly tapped for the syrupy sap used to produce palm sugar, or when fermented, toddy.

porphyrocarpa (Blume) H. E. Moore [*Didymosperma porphyrocarpum* (Blume) H. Wendl. & Drude ex Hook. f.]. Sts. several, reedlike, to 6 ft.; lvs. to 8 ft. long, long-petioled, pinnae 5–6 on each side, to 20 in. long, 7 in. wide, deeply lobed, cuneate at base; infls. several at each node, few-branched; male fls. maroon, stamens 16–20 or more; fr. oblong-ovoid, red, to 3/4 in. long, 1–2-seeded. Java.

saccharifera: *A. pinnata.*

tremula (Blanco) Becc. [*A. mindorensis* Becc.]. Sts. cespitose, to 10 ft.; lvs. many, to 20 ft. long, pinnae recurved, elongate, narrow; infl. brs. to 3 ft. long; male fls. yellow-green, stamens 20–30, not aristate; fr. globose, to 3/4 in. in diam. Philippine Is.

undulatifolia Becc. Sts. tardily cespitose, to 20 ft., 8 in. in diam.; lvs. to 18 ft. long, pinnae to 3 ft. long or more, 6 in. wide, margins sinuate-undulate, base auricled; infls. usually several at each node, rachillae to 1 ft. long or more, stout; male fls. maroon, to 3/4 in. long, stamens about 150, aristate; fr. 3-seeded, oblong-ellipsoid, to 2 in. long, 1 1/2 in. in diam. Borneo, Celebes.

Westerhoutii Griff. Sts. usually several, to 30 ft., not covered with fibers; lvs. to 18 ft., pinnae to 5 ft. long, 3 in. wide, similar to *A. pinnata* but in 80–90 pairs and 2-ranked; infl. 1½ ft. long; male fls. ¾ in. long, stamens about 70, aristate; fr. oblong-ellipsoid, depressed at top, 2 in. long, 1½–2½ in. in diam., 3-seeded, seeds 1⅜ in. long. Malay Pen. The sp. has been considered identical with *A. obtusifolia* by some writers, but is distinct in stamen number.

AREQUIPA: *BORZICACTUS.* **A. erectocylindrica:** *B. leucotrichus.* **A. myriacantha:** *B. aurantiacus.* **A. Rettigii:** *B. leucotrichus.*

ARETHUSA L. *Orchidaceae.* One sp., a low terrestrial herb, native to e. N. Amer.; sts. small, cormlike; lf. solitary; scapes lateral, 1-fld.; sepals and petals connivent to form a hood, lip reflexed, bearded. For structure of fl. see *Orchidaceae.*

Sometimes planted in cool, moist, protected places; for culture see *Orchids.*

bulbosa L. SWAMP PINK, WILD P., DRAGON'S MOUTH, BOG ROSE. To 1 ft.; lf. linear, grasslike, developing after the fl.; fls. to 2 in. long, sepals and petals rose-purple, lip whitish, with 3 fringed ridges and yellow and purple markings. Late spring–late summer. Sphagnum bogs and acid meadows, e. Canada, s. to S.C., w. to Minn. and n. Ill., also La.

ARGANIA Roem. & Schult. *Sapotaceae.* One sp., an evergreen tree with hard wood, to 20 ft., often with spiny brs.

May be planted in southern Calif. Zone 10. Propagated by layers and cuttings.

Sideroxylon: *A. spinosa.*

spinosa (L.) Skeels [*A. Sideroxylon* Roem. & Schult.]. ARGAN TREE, MOROCCO IRONWOOD. Lvs. small, lanceolate-spatulate, entire, glabrous; fls. greenish-yellow, in clusters, sepals spirally arranged, corolla 5-parted, without appendages, staminodes alt. with corolla lobes; fr. an oblong berry. Morocco. The seeds yield oil.

ARGEMONE L. PRICKLY POPPY, ARGEMONY. *Papaveraceae.* About 30 spp. of ann. or per. herbs, and 1 shrub not in cult., with yellow or orange sap, native to N. and S. Amer., and Hawaii, *A. mexicana* a pantrop. weed; lvs. pinnatifid, spine-tipped; fls. large, to 6 in. across, sepals usually 3, often horn-tipped, petals white, yellow, or lavender, usually 6; fr. a caps., more or less prickly. Latin name pronounced in 4 syllables.

Grown as annuals in the flower garden. They thrive in any good soil and sunny exposure.

alba: *A. polyanthemos.*

grandiflora Sweet. Ann. or short-lived per.; basal and lower st. lvs. deeply lobed, the middle and upper st. lvs. less deeply lobed, clasping; fls. white, 2½–4 in. across; caps. more or less prickly, the surface always visible through the prickles. Mex. A form with yellow fls. is listed.

hispida A. Gray [*A. platyceras* var. *hispida* (A. Gray) Prain]. Per.; lower st. lvs. lobed to ¾ the distance to the midrib or more, uppermost lvs. not clasping; fls. white, 2½–4 in. across; caps. densely prickly, the prickles nearly obscuring the surface. Rocky Mts.

intermedia: *A. polyanthemos.*

mexicana L. MEXICAN POPPY. Ann., to 3 ft.; lvs. glaucous, with light blue conspicuous markings over veins, lower lvs. lobed half or more of the distance to the midrib, upper lvs. more shallowly lobed, middle and upper lvs. clasping; fls. 1½–2½ in. across, yellow; caps. more or less spinescent, surface visible through spines. W. Indies, and probably Cent. Amer. and Fla.; a cosmopolitan trop. and subtrop. weed. Argemone oil, a minor semidrying oil is obtained from the seeds. Cvs. **'Alba'** and **'Sanguinea'** are listed.

munita E. Durand & Hilg. Ann. or per., 2–5 ft.; lower lvs. lobed about half way to midvein, upper lvs. more shallowly lobed and clasping; fls. 2–5 in. across, white; caps. sparsely to densely prickly, the surface clearly visible to obscured by prickles. Calif. and n. Baja Calif., e. to New Mex.

ochroleuca Sweet. Ann. or short-lived per., 1–3 ft.; lvs. glaucous, with light blue conspicuous markings over veins, basal and st. lvs. deeply lobed nearly to midrib, middle and upper lvs. not clasping or only uppermost slightly clasping; fls. 1¼–2½ in. across, yellow; caps. with large and smaller spines, surface visible through spines. Mex.

platyceras Link & Otto. Ann. or may be longer-lived, usually 1–2½ ft., with weak spines; lvs. bluish, lowermost lobed to ⅔ the distance to the midrib, upper lvs. more shallowly lobed, often clasping; fls. 4–5 in. across, white or often pale yellow; caps. more or less densely prickly, surface nearly or completely obscured by spines. Mex. Distinguished by the weak and sparse spines of the st. and lvs. and the dense spines of the caps. Var. **hispida:** *A. hispida.* Var. **rosea:** *A. sanguinea.*

polyanthemos (Fedde) G. Ownb. [*A. alba* James; *A. intermedia* Eastw.]. Ann. or bien., with a deep taproot, to 3 ft. (sometimes 4 ft.); lvs. glaucous, succulent, the lowermost lobed ⅔ the distance to midrib, uppermost more shallowly lobed and clasping, upper surface of lvs. without prickles; fls. 2½–4 in. across, white; caps. with stout spines interspersed with smaller ones, surface clearly visible. E. base of Rocky Mts., sw. S. Dak. and e. Wyo., s. to New Mex. and Tex. Distinguished by the sparingly prickly lvs., absence of prickles on upper lf. surface, and the usually sparsely prickly caps.

sanguinea Greene [*A. platyceras* var. *rosea* J. Coult.]. Ann., bien., or short-lived per., to 3 (sometimes 4) ft.; lvs. glaucous, veins with light blue lines, basal and lower st. lvs. deeply lobed almost to midrib, middle and upper st. lvs. less deeply lobed, not definitely clasping; fls. 2–3½ in. across, white to lavender; caps. with large and smaller spines, surface clearly visible. S. Tex., s. to ne. Mex.

ARGENTACER: *ACER.*

ARGETA: *GIBBAEUM.*

ARGYREIA Lour. [*Lettsomia* Roxb.]. *Convolvulaceae.* About 90 spp. of twining or climbing, seldom nearly erect, pubescent or tomentose shrubs or per. herbs, in trop. Asia, Malay Arch., and Queensland; lvs. alt., simple, orbicular; fls. showy, purple or rose, in peduncled, axillary cymes, corolla funnelform, with hairy stripes outside; fr. indehiscent, globose or ellipsoid, pulpy and fleshy or thick-walled and leathery.

Grown under glass, and in the open far south.

capitata (Vahl) Choisy [*Lettsomia capitata* (Vahl) Miq.; *L. strigosa* Roxb.]. Tall, hairy twiner; lvs. ovate to orbicular, to 6 in. long; cymes dense, capitate; fls. purple, to 2 in. long; fr. ¼ in. across, orange-red or reddish-brown. India to Malay Arch.

nervosa (Burm. f.) Bojer [*A. speciosa* (L. f.) Sweet]. WOOLLY MORNING-GLORY. Large climber; lvs. ovate-cordate, to 1 ft. across, white-tomentose beneath; fls. rose, 2–3 in. long, on pedicels to 6 in. long. India. Reported as escaped in Fla. Used medicinally in India.

speciosa: *A. nervosa.*

splendens (Roxb.) Sweet. SILVER MORNING-GLORY. Tall climber; lvs. elliptic, to 7 in. long and 4 in. across, angular or rounded, never cordate at base, white-silky-hairy beneath; fls. rose, 1½ in. long, on pedicels 1–4 in. long. India.

ARGYRODENDRON: *HERITIERA.*

ARGYRODERMA N. E. Br. [*Roodia* N. E. Br.]. *Aizoaceae.* About 50 spp. of stemless, usually clump-forming, per. succulents, native to S. Afr.; lvs. 4-ranked, 1–3 pairs on a shoot, members of a pair united basally, nearly cylindrical and fingerlike, or the lower surface convex and the pair of lvs. pressed together at their flat upper surfaces, forming a subglobose or elongate-ovoid body (growth), separating apically when in fl., surface bluish-white to whitish-gray-green, with or without dots; fls. solitary, terminal, on bracted peduncles, sepals 6, united into a tube, petals and stamens many, arising from calyx tube, ovary inferior, 10–24-celled; fr. a 10–24-valved caps., the expanding keels with membranous wings, awned, placental tubercles present.

Growth and flowering occur in summer, the plants requiring maximum sunlight. In winter, grown at a relatively cool temperature of about 60° F., with scarcely any watering, although young seedlings must be kept moist even in winter. Propagated easily by seeds, but growth is slow. See also *Succulents.*

angustipetalum L. Bolus. Forming thick clumps, often with 6–8 shoots; lvs. 2–4 on a shoot, smooth, gray-green or reddish toward base inside, to 1¼ in. long, 1⅛ in. wide, ¾ in. thick, half-ovoid, upper side flat to slightly concave, rounded-triangular in outline, to ⅝ in. long, lower side rounded and arching toward tip, tips separated by about ⅜ in.; fls. sessile, to 1¼ in. across, petals yellow, very narrow. Cape Prov.

blandum L. Bolus. Sts. 1 each year; lvs. spreading, ⅞ in. apart at tip in fl., about 1 in. long, with sheath ⅜ in. long, 1³⁄₁₆ in. wide at sheath, upper side reniform, rounded on the back and about ¾ in. thick above middle; fls. with compressed receptacle ½ in. long, petals rose or rose-purple, to 1 in. long, stamens white. Cape Prov.

Braunsii (Schwant.) Schwant. [*Cheiridopsis Braunsii* Schwant.]. Branching in age; lvs. 2–4 on a shoot, erect, slightly laterally curved, smooth, blue-green to gray or reddish in age, to 2¾ in. long, to ½ in. across, fingerlike in appearance, upper side flat or convex, lower side rounded, arched over the tip; fls. nearly sessile. Cape Prov.

brevipes (Schlechter) L. Bolus [*Roodia digitifolia* N. E. Br.]. Forming loose clumps, with a few underground brs.; lvs. 2 on a br., opp., erect, smooth, glabrous, green or often reddish at tip, to 4 in. long, to ½ in. thick, semicylindrical, nearly flat on upper side, rounded on lower side; fls. ½ in. across, on pedicels to 1½ in. long, petals light magenta-red. Cape Prov.

citrinum L. Bolus. Sts. woody, ½ in. thick; lvs. pale but flushed with pink at apex, to ⅞ in. long, 1⅛ in. wide, united basally for ¼ in., separated about ¼ in. at apex in fl., the free part semicircular in section, inconspicuously keeled on lower side; fls. 1¼ in. across, nearly sessile, petals lemon-yellow. Cape Prov.

formosum L. Bolus. Shoots 1 each year; lvs. spreading, 1¼ in. long, with sheath ½ in. long, 1¼ in. wide at top of sheath, 1⅜ in. apart at tip, upper surface nearly kidney-shaped, tip rounded, lower side obscurely keeled; petals rose-purple, to 1 in. long, stamens white or pale yellow. Cape Prov.

Kleijnhansii L. Bolus. Sts. about 5, cespitose; lvs. erect, unequal, to 1⅞ in. long, united into basal sheath to ½ in. long, ¼–⅜ in. wide, ⅜ in. thick, to ¾ in. apart at tips, ellipsoid, upper side flat, lower side rounded, apex rounded; fls. on pedicels ¼ in. long, petals yellow, to ½ in. long. Cape Prov.

Lesliei: *A. octophyllum.*

Nortieri L. Bolus. Sts. to 11 each year, forming mats; lvs. ascending, thick, to 1½ in. long, with sheath ½ in. long, 1–1⅛ in. wide at top of sheath, to ⅝ in. in diam. at center, ⅝ in. in diam. at rounded tips where separated 1–1¼ in. in fl., upper side nearly ovate in outline, sides rounded or concave, lower side rounded or acute; fls. on peduncle to ¼ in. long, bracts half as long as ovary, sepals 6, petals yellow, to nearly ½ in. long. Cape Prov.

octophyllum (Haw.) Schwant. [*A. Lesliei* N. E. Br.]. SILVER-SKIN. Lvs. 2 or 4, smooth, blue-green, to 1³⁄₁₆ in. long, 1 in. wide, ⅝ in. thick, upper side flat, nearly semicircular to somewhat ovate in outline, slightly keeled at tip; fls. sessile, to 1⅜ in. across, petals yellow, to ⅛ in. wide, often spirally curved. Cape Prov.

orientale L. Bolus. Sts. to 19 each year in a clump; lvs. 4 on a shoot, olive-green, purple-pustulate beneath, to 1¾ in. long, with sheath ½ in. long, ½ in. wide at top of sheath, 1–1⅜ in. apart at tips, about ¼ in. thick, upper side flat or somewhat rounded, lower side rounded, slightly keeled, tip rounded; fls. on peduncle to 1½ in. long, bracts to ⅝ in. long, petals rose, to ⅝ in. long. Cape Prov.

ovale L. Bolus. Sts. (1–)2–10 each year; lvs. to ¾ in. long with sheath ⅜ in. long, about ⅝ in. wide at top of sheath, upper surface elliptic in outline, keeled on lower side at tip where about ⅜ in. thick, with a large, suborbicular pustule on the back; fls. on peduncle about ¼ in. long, bracts ½ in. long, petals rose-purple, to ½ in. long. Cape Prov.

patens L. Bolus. Sts. to 8 each year; lvs. ashy-glaucous, to 1³⁄₁₆ in. long, with sheath ⅜ in. long, to 1³⁄₁₆ in. wide, ⅝ in. thick at middle, 1³⁄₁₆–1¾ in. apart at tips, upper side broadly elliptic in outline, lower side rounded, obtusely keeled, margins conspicuous; fls. sessile, petals yellow or coppery in age, to ⅝ in. long. Cape Prov.

Pearsonii (N. E. Br.) Schwant. [*A. testiculare* var. *Pearsonii* N. E. Br.]. Like *A. testiculare*, but fls. sessile or nearly so, outer petals magenta-red, inner petals ocher, striped with red. Cape Prov.

reniforme L. Bolus. Lvs. 2, with a pustule half as long as blade, blade to 1 in. long, with sheath to ⅝ in. long, 1¾ in. wide at tip of sheath, 1 in. thick at apex, appressed to soil dorsally, reniform in top view; fls. on peduncle ⅜ in. long, petals rose-purple, emarginate, to nearly ½ in. long. Cape Prov.

roseum (Haw.) Schwant. Brs. 1–2 each year; lvs. 2–4 on a br., blue-green to white, to 1⅜ in. long and united halfway, to 1½ in. long, 1 in. thick, upper side flat, lower side and tip strongly rounded; fls. to 3½ in. across, sessile, petals rose-violet. Cape Prov.

Schlechteri Schwant. Lvs. 2, white to bluish-green, to ¾ in. long, ⅝ in. wide, united half their length, little separated at the tips, upper side somewhat concave, lower side rounded, extended and curved into the tip; fls. 1³⁄₁₆ in. across, petals rose-red. Cape Prov.

Schuldtii Schwant. Lvs. 4, 4-ranked, blue to gray-green, to ¾ in. long, 1³⁄₁₆ in. wide, ⅝ in. thick, round-ovate in outline, upper side flat, lower side and tip rounded; fls. small, pink. Cape Prov.

strictum L. Bolus. Brs. several each year; lvs. erect, to about 1 in. long, with sheath ⅝ in. long, ½ in. wide at sheath, ¼ in. thick at apex, about ³⁄₁₆ in. apart at tips in fl., oblong-elliptic in outline in top view, pustule half as long as free part of blade, tip and back rounded; fls.

on peduncle ⅝ in. long, bracts elongate, petals brownish-yellow suffused with orange. Cape Prov.

subrotundum L. Bolus. Lvs. 2, to nearly 1 in. long, with sheath ¼ in. long, to 1 in. wide, ⅝ in. thick a little above the middle, about ¾ in. apart at tips in fl., upper side more or less rounded, lower side rounded; fls. on peduncle ⅛ in. long, petals apricot-yellow, to ⅝ in. long. Cape Prov.

testiculare (Ait.) N. E. Br. Lvs. 2, whitish, to 1⅜ in. long and 1½ in. thick, ovate or hemispherical in outline; fls. to 1⅝ in. across, sessile or nearly so, petals white or cream. Cape Prov. Probably not cult.; most material cult. under this name is *A. octophyllum.* Var. **Pearsonii:** *A. Pearsonii.*

Villetii L. Bolus. Brs. to 30 each year; lvs. paired, to ¾ in. long and united for ⅜ in., ¾ in. wide, scarcely separated at the tips, hemispherical in section, rounded and keeled on lower side; fls. to 1³⁄₁₆ in. across, on peduncle ⁵⁄₁₆ in. long, petals pink. Cape Prov.

ARIKURYROBA Barb.-Rodr. ARIKURY PALM. *Palmae.* One or a few spp. of solitary, unarmed, monoecious palms in Brazil; lvs. pinnate, sheath fibrous, open, pinnae obliquely 2-cleft at apex, midrib prominent, petiole armed with stout teeth along the margin; infl. among the lvs., long-peduncled, bracts 2, the lower 2-edged, open at the apex, the upper fusiform in bud, beaked, splitting abaxially, deeply sulcate externally, rachis elongate, rachillae many, simple, with fls. in triads (2 male and 1 female) in lower ⅓ and above these with paired or solitary male fls.; male fls. somewhat asymmetrical, sepals 3, acute, imbricate basally, petals 3, valvate, much longer than sepals, much wider than thick, angled, stamens 6, filaments slightly inflexed at apex in bud, pistillode small, 3-cleft, female fls. with sepals 3, broadly imbricate, petals 3, broadly imbricate except short-valvate at apex, only slightly longer than sepals, staminodes joined in a low cupule, pistil 3-celled, 3-ovuled; fr. 1-seeded, mesocarp fleshy-fibrous, endocarp bony, acute at both ends, 3-ridged with 3 shining lines inside and pores near the base, seed with ruminate endosperm, embryo near the base.

For culture see *Palms.*

schizophylla (Mart.) L. H. Bailey. To 10 ft. or more; lvs. to more than 4 ft. long, petiole to 3 ft., pinnae 40–50 on each side, to 18 in. long, 1³⁄₁₆ in. wide; infl. to 4 ft. long or more, rachillae to about 1 ft. long; fls. cream-colored, male to ¼ in. long, female to ⁵⁄₁₆ in. long; fr. orange, 1¼ in. long, ¾ in. in diam. Zone 10a in Fla.

ARIOCARPUS Scheidw. [*Neogomesia* Castañeda; *Roseocactus* A. Berger]. LIVING-ROCK CACTUS. *Cactaceae.* Six spp. of small cacti, native to s. Tex. and Mex.; st. simple, depressed, crowned by a globose to flattened rosette of overlapping, triangular or prismatic, leaflike tubercles; sterile part of areoles an apical or subapical woolly point, or a central woolly furrow, or lacking, with or without spines, the wool and spines usually deciduous, fl.-bearing part of areoles axillary, woolly; fls. diurnal, white, yellow, or magenta, rotate-campanulate, sometimes becoming tubular, ovary naked; fr. fleshy becoming dry, globose to oblong, naked. Resembling *Mammillaria*, but with cartilaginous tubercles and usually lacking spines at maturity.

For culture see *Cacti.*

agavoides (Castañeda) E. F. Anderson [*Neogomesia agavoides* Castañeda]. Subglobose, 1⅝–3³⁄₁₆ in. wide, tubercles often not clearly erect, 4 or more times as long as broad, greenish-brown; areoles ³⁄₁₆– ½ in. below tip of tubercle, spines 0 or 2; fls. magenta, ⅝ in. across, outer perianth segms. with greenish margins. N. Mex.

elongatus: *A. retusus.*

fissuratus (Engelm.) K. Schum. [*Roseocactus fissuratus* (Engelm.) A. Berger]. Depressed-globose, 2–4(–6) in. wide, tubercles spreading, brownish-green, ⅜–¾ in. long, upper surface convex and fissured, areole in central groove; fls. light magenta, to 1¾ in. across. Var. **fissuratus.** LIVING-ROCK, STAR CACTUS. The typical var.; upper surface of tubercles grooved parallel to outer edges, strongly roughened. S. Tex. Var. **Lloydii** (Rose) M. T. Marsh. [*A. Lloydii* Rose; *Roseocactus Lloydii* (Rose) A. Berger]. Upper surface of tubercles not grooved parallel to outer edges, only slightly roughened. N. Mex.

furfuraceus: *A. retusus.*

intermedius: a listed name of no botanical standing for *A. fissuratus* var. *Lloydii.*

Kotschoubeyanus (Lem.) K. Schum. [*A. sulcatus* (Salm-Dyck) K. Schum.; *Rosecactus Kotschoubeyanus* (Lem.) A. Berger]. Depressed-globose, to 3 in. wide, tubercles spreading, dark olive-green, ³⁄₁₆–½ in. long, upper surface flattened, slightly roughened, not fissured, areole in central groove; fls. rose to light purple or white, to 1 in. across Cent. Mex. Cv. 'Albiflorus' is listed.

Lloydii: *A. fissuratus* var.

Macdowellii: a listed name of no botanical standing for a small form of *A. Kotschoubeyanus.*

retusus Scheidw. [*A. elongatus* (Salm-Dyck) Wettst.; *A. furfuraceus* (S. Wats.) C. H. Thomps.]. SEVEN-STARS. Globose, to 6 in. wide, tubercles crowded, divergent, gray- or blue-green, to 1⅝ in. long, sharply 3-edged, the upper surface flat or slightly concave, not fissured; areole nearly apical, sometimes apparently absent; fls. 1¼ in. long, perianth segms. white with reddish midline, white, or the inner rarely magenta. N. Mex.

scapharostrus Böd. Globose, to nearly 4 in. wide, tubercles few, not crowded, divergent, erect, about twice as long as wide, gray-green, boat-shaped, to 2 in. long and ¾ in. wide, sharply 3-angled, not fissured; areole apparently lacking; fls. violet-rose, 1½ in. across. N. Mex.

strobiliformis: *Pelecyphora strobiliformis.*

sulcatus: *A. Kotschoubeyanus.*

trigonus (A. Web.) K. Schum. Globose, to 6 in. wide, tubercles many, not crowded, divergent, erect and incurved, about twice as long as wide, dark green, to 3 in. long and 1 in. wide, convex on upper surface, keeled on lower surface, not fissured; areoles terminal, soon inconspicuous; fls. yellowish or cream-colored, 2 in. across. N. Mex.

ARISAEMA Mart. *Araceae.* More than 190 spp. of stemless, tuberous herbs, native mostly to Old World; lvs. 1–3, 3-lobed or 3-parted, to pedately dissected with 5–19 segms., petioles long; spathe convolute below, expanded above into a narrow to very broad blade often colored or marked with purple; fls. unisexual, spadix monoecious or dioecious, terminated by a prominent elongate sterile appendage, this occasionally, bearing filiform, sterile, rudimentary fls.; perianth absent, ovaries 1-celled, ovules 1–9, basal.

Hardy species are often planted out in partly shaded locations for their curious spring blooms, handsome summer foliage, and colorful fruits. They thrive in rich, well-drained soils high in organic matter, with a continuous supply of soil moisture during the growing season. Tubers must be planted deep enough to accommodate the roots, which grow from their tops. Propagation by seeds and natural offsets. The American species, and some Asian ones indicated below, are winter-hardy. Tender kinds are grown in the home or greenhouse, or outside in summer, dried off in autumn, and stored with little soil moisture in a frost-free place during the dormant period.

amurense Maxim. Tuber small; lvs. pedate, segms. 5, to 4 in. long, middle one obovate, lateral ones oblong-lanceolate, petioles 12–24 in. long; peduncle stout, shorter than petioles, spathe 4½ in. long, tube pale green margined with purple, blade erect, 2–2½ in. long, greenish and sometimes purple-striped, or violet, spadix with terminal appendage cylindric, 1½ in. long. Japan, Korea, N. China and adjacent U.S.S.R. Zone 6.

atrorubens: *A. triphyllum.*

Dracontium (L.) Schott. GREEN-DRAGON, DRAGONROOT. Tuber oblong; lf. solitary, pedate, segms. 7–19, oblong to elliptic, to 10 in. long, middle one shorter and broader than adjacent lateral ones, petiole to 3 ft.; peduncle shorter than petiole, spathe to 3 in. long, green, hood erect, spadix with sterile appendage erect, cylindrical, slender, 5–6 in. longer than spathe; berries reddish. Me. to Fla., w. to Kans., Tex., ne. Mex. Spring to early summer. Zone 6.

Griffithii Schott. Tuber to 4½ in. in diam.; lvs. 2, segms. 3, sessile, broadly elliptic or trapezoid-ovate, to 12 in. long, petioles stout, 2 ft. long; peduncle to 10 in., spathe with tube 4–6 in. long, fluted, dark purple and white-striped, suddenly widened into blade, the blade 6–10 in. across, 2-lobed, bent forward and centrally convex, and checkered brown-purple with prominent green veins, spadix with sterile appendage brown-purple, the apex threadlike, 12–20 in. long. Sikkim, Bhutan, and adjacent India.

Jacquemontii Blume. Differs from *A. Dracontium* in having 2 lvs., radiately 5–7-parted, petioles sheathing nearly ⅘ their length, spathe 3–5 in. long, green, white-striped, with caudate tip either erect or bent forward and ½–3 in. long, and spadix with sterile appendage 1½–3½ in. long, with a knob near base. Nw. Pakistan and Kashmir to Bhutan.

Pradhanii C. E. Fisch. Probably not specifically distinct from *A. Griffithii*, from which it has been distinguished in having lf. segms.

veined purplish beneath, petioles and peduncle purplish, warty, and spathe with blade wider and looser. Sikkim.

speciosum (Wallich) Mart. COBRA LILY. Differs from *A. triphyllum* in having tuber horizontal-cylindric, lvs. solitary, blades sometimes twice as large, with reddish veins, petioles spotted purple, spathe suberect, 3–10 in. long, acuminate-caudate, and spadix with sterile appendage dilated basally, the apex a pendent, filiform tail 12–28 in. long. Nepal and Sikkim.

Stewardsonii: *A. triphyllum* subsp.

Thunbergii Blume. Differs from *A. Dracontium* in having tubers subglobose, lvs. with the middle segm. largest, petioles and peduncles variegated with red or purple, spathe tube white, striped pale purplish-brown, blade nearly caudate, bent forward, broader, dark brown and with paler veins inside, and spadix with sterile appendage fusiform with threadlike tip 8–12 in. long. Japan. Zone 8. Var. **Urashima** (Hara) Mak. Spadix with sterile appendage densely tubercled just above the thickened part. Japan.

triphyllum (L.) Torr. [*A. atrorubens* (Ait.) Blume]. JACK-IN-THE-PULPIT, INDIAN TURNIP, DRAGONROOT. Tuber subglobose; lvs. mostly 2, segms. 3, sessile, elliptic, to 9 in. long, petioles to 2 ft.; peduncle shorter than petiole, spathe 4–7 in. long, green to purple outside, tube long, inside variously striped purple and green or white, blade bent forward, spadix with sterile appendage nearly cylindrical, short, green to purple, slightly exserted beyond tube; berries red, ⅜ in. in diam. Subsp. **triphyllum.** The typical subsp.; lvs. glaucous beneath, lateral lfts. strongly to moderately oblique or lobed; spathe with flange at top of tube only slightly reflexed, not rolled under. New Bruns. and Nov. Sc. to Minn., s. to Fla. and Tex. Dried corms have been used medicinally. Late spring. Zone 5. Cv. 'Zebrinum' (forma *zebrinum* (Sims) Fern.]. Spathe purple to bronze and with whitish longitudinal stripes inside. Subsp. **Stewardsonii** (Britt.) Huttl. [*A. Stewardsonii* Britt.]. Blooming somewhat later; lf. segms. narrower, darker green above, not glaucous beneath; spathe with tube strongly fluted, flange at top strongly reflexed and inrolled. Nov. Sc. to N.C.

Wallichianum Hook.f. Lvs. solitary, segms. 3, rhombic-orbicular, middle lobe 3½ in. long and 2¾ in. wide, lateral lobes to 5–8 in. long and 3 in. wide, petiole 6–12 in. long; peduncle shorter than petiole, spathe to 8 in. long, striped purple and pale green, caudate and bent forward at apex, blade as long as tube, spadix with sterile appendage 5–6 in. long, dilated below and becoming long filiform above. Nw. Himalayan India to Sikkim.

ARISARUM A. Targ.-Tozz. *Araceae.* Three spp. of small, stemless, tuberous or rhizomatous herbs, native to Medit. region; lvs. long-petioled, ovate-sagittate or -subhastate; spathe with tube united at margins, the blade expanded and hooded; fls. unisexual, spadix terminated by sterile appendage, with zones of male and female fls. contiguous, the female fls. few, perianth absent.

For culture see *Arisaema.*

proboscideum (L.) Savi [*Arum proboscideum* L.]. MOUSE PLANT. Rhizome creeping; lvs. solitary, blades ovate- or oblong-subhastate, 3–5 in. long, petioles 8–12 in. long; peduncle 2–6 in. long, spathe with tube inflated, ½ in. long, the blade olive-green outside, deep purple in the mouth, hood ¾ in. long, with green, ascending, tail-like tip 4–6 in. long. Italy.

ARISTEA Ait. *Iridaceae.* About 50 spp. of fibrous-rooted herbs, native to trop. and S. Afr.; lvs. mostly basal, 2-ranked; fls. generally blue, in spikes, racemes, or corymbs, perianth regular, tube very short or none, segms. of nearly equal size, twisting spirally after flowering, filaments separate, style filiform, with obscure stigmatic lobes; fr. an oblong to obovoid, short-stalked caps. Allied to *Sisyrinchium.*

Grown under glass, or in the open in Pacific coast areas; propagated by seeds and division. Plants once established do not readily recover from being moved.

capitata Ker-Gawl. Robust, sts. to 4½ ft.; basal lvs. 20–40 in. long, to ⅝ in. wide, rigid, st. lvs. 3–5, erect, to 15 in. long; infl. an elongated, much-branched panicle, bracts brown, scarious; perianth blue, outer segms obovate-cuneate, ⅝ in. long; caps. nearly rectangular in outline, ⅝ in. long, seeds about ¼ in. long. S. Afr. Closely allied to *A. thyrsiflora*, and some cult. material offered as *A. capitata* may be that sp.

Ecklonii Bak. A variable, sp.; robust sts. 1½–3 ft., rhizome about ⅜ in. in diam.; basal lvs. 1–2 ft. long, ½ in. wide, st. lvs. flexuous, slightly smaller; infl. paniculate, bracts linear-lanceolate, entire, scarious-margined; perianth bright blue, outer segms. mostly ⁵⁄₁₆ in. long; caps. oblong, 3-lobed, ½–¾ in. long, seeds ¹⁄₁₆ in. long or less. S. Afr. to trop. Afr.

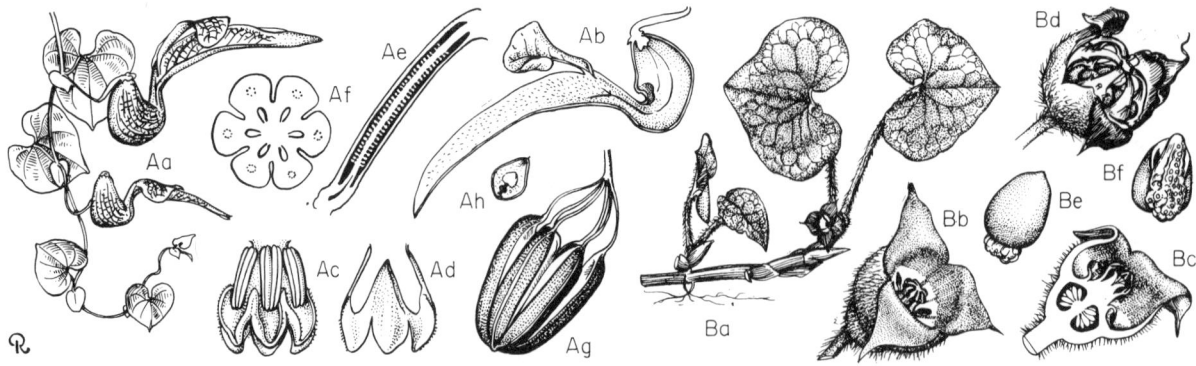

ARISTOLOCHIACEAE. **A.** *Aristolochia ringens:* **Aa,** flowering stem, × ¹⁄₁₆; **Ab,** flower, vertical section, × ¼; **Ac,** stamens, style, and stigmas, × 2; **Ad,** style and stigmas, vertical section, × 2; **Ae,** ovary, vertical section, × 1; **Af,** ovary, cross section, × 4; **Ag,** capsule, × ¼; **Ah,** seed, × 4. **B,** *Asarum canadense:* **Ba,** plant, × ¼; **Bb,** flower, × 1; **Bc,** flower, vertical section, × 1; **Bd,** capsule, × 1; **Be, Bf,** seed, two views, × 3.

thyrsiflora (D. Delar.) N. E. Br. Robust, sts. 3–5 ft., cylindrical or obtusely angled, ½ in. in diam. or more at base; basal lvs. in dense rosettes 3–4½ ft. long, ½–¾ in. wide, suberect, with brownish margins; infl. spicate to closely paniculate, bracts linear-lanceolate, to ½ in. long, entire, white-margined; perianth blue, outer segms. ⅝ in. long, obovate; caps. short-oblong, 3-winged, nearly ½ in. long, seeds ³⁄₁₆ in. long. S. Afr. Some material cult. as *A. capitata* may belong here.

ARISTIDA L. Not cult. *A. pennata: Stipagrostis pennata.*

ARISTOLOCHIA L. BIRTHWORT. *Aristolochiaceae.* About 200 spp. of mostly trop. climbing shrubs or per. herbs; lvs. petioled, often cordate; peduncles axillary, usually with prominent bracts at base or below ovary; fls. solitary, clustered, or in racemes, the calyx corrollalike, tubular, usually peculiarly shaped, very irregular, the tube bent, often constricted at mouth, stamens usually 6, ovary inferior; fr. a caps.

The tender kinds do best in the greenhouse in rich soil. Propagated by cuttings of ripened wood over heat, layering, and seeds.

altissima Desf. Evergreen, slender climber, to 18 ft., sts. 6-angled; lvs. ovate-oblong, to 3 in. long; fls. solitary, 1½ in. long, yellow inside, pale yellow-brown striped with dark red-brown outside, tube curved, globose at base, gradually expanded into the oblique, ovate limb. E. Medit. Root frost-hardy.

brasiliensis Mart. [*A. ornithocephala* Hook.]. Climbing; lvs. reniform-orbicular, to 8 in. across; fls. solitary, calyx dingy-yellow, veined with purple, tube inflated, limb 2-lipped, the upper lip narrow, to 4 in. long, the lower lip expanded into a reniform lobe to 4 in. long and 7 in. across. Se. Brazil.

californica Torr. Woody, deciduous climber, to 12 ft.; lvs. ovate, to 6 in. long; calyx greenish-purple, tube strongly bent, about 1½ in. long, limb 2-lipped, the upper lip 2-lobed. Calif.

cymbifera var. **labiosa:** *A. labiosa.*

durior J. Hill [*A. macrophylla* Lam.; *A. Sipho* L'Hér.]. DUTCHMAN'S-PIPE, PIPE VINE. Deciduous, woody climber, to 30 ft.; lvs. reniform-orbicular, to 1 ft. long; fls. solitary, calyx yellowish-green, tube U-shaped, to 3 in. long, glabrous, limb 3-lobed, to 1 in. across, brownish-purple; caps. cylindrical, to about 3 in. long. Penn. to Ga. and Kans. Hardy north; a rapid grower, good for covering buildings and as a screen for porches.

elegans M. T. Mast. CALICO FLOWER. Slender woody climber; lvs. triangular-reniform, to 3 in. long; fls. solitary, calyx tube inflated, to 1½ in. long, yellow-green, limb nearly orbicular, entire, to 3 in. across, white veined with purple outside, rich purple-brown marked with white inside. Brazil.

fimbriata Cham. Sts. climbing or prostrate; lvs. suborbicular-reniform, to 3½ in. across; bracts absent; fls. solitary, calyx tube green, strongly curved, inflated at base, limb erect, 1-sided, cordate, to 1 in. across, ciliate with long hairs, greenish-brown outside, purple-brown veined with yellow inside. Argentina, Paraguay, s. Brazil.

gigantea Mart. & Zucc., not Hook. Differs from *A. elegans* in having calyx tube oblong-ovoid, to 3 in. long, and limb much larger, to 20 in. long and 14 in. across, deeply cordate at base. Se. Brazil. *A. gigantea* Hook. is a synonym of *A. grandiflora* var. *Hookeri.*

gigas: *A. grandiflora.*

grandiflora Swartz [*A. gigas* Lindl.]. PELICAN FLOWER. High-climbing; lvs. broadly ovate, to 10 in. long, acuminate or acute; fls. solitary, pendent, with offensive odor, calyx tube U-shaped, inflated, yellowish-green, limb broadly ovate-cordate, to 6 in. across or more, with a long-hanging tail, whitish, veined with purple and with deep purple ring about the mouth of the tube. Caribbean trop. Amer. Var. **Hookeri** Duchartre [*A. gigantea* Hook., not Mart. & Zucc.]. Fls. with short tail. Var. **Sturtevantii** W.Wats. Fls. to 2 ft. wide, 3 ft. long, with a tail to 3 ft. long.

labiosa Ker-Gawl. [*A. cymbifera* Mart. & Zucc. var. *labiosa* (Ker-Gawl.) Duchartre]. Glabrous twiner; lvs. reniform-suborbicular, to nearly 3 in. wide, obtuse at apex; fls. solitary, large, with offensive odor, calyx tube saccate, expanded into a 2-lipped limb, the shorter lip lanceolate, acuminate, the larger lip rotund-reniform, 2-lobed, to 4 in. across, limb cream with purple veins, the throat purple, covered with hairs. S. Brazil.

macrophylla: *A. durior.*

manshuriensis Kom. Very similar to *A. durior,* but limb of calyx with abruptly acuminate lobes, caps. much larger, to 4⅜ in. long. Korea, Manchuria, adjacent Russia.

moupinensis Franch. Differs from *A. tomentosa* in having lvs. usually pointed, and limb of fls. yellow dotted with purple. W. China.

ornithocephala: *A. brasiliensis.*

paulistina Hoehne. Tall, glabrous twiner; lvs. triangular-ovate, obtuse or slightly emarginate, to 6 in. long; fls. solitary, calyx tube bent, the upper part funnelform, purplish-yellow, truncate, but extending into a narrow caudate lip to 7 in. long with pendent tail. Se. Brazil.

racemosa Brandeg. Sts. twining; lvs. hastate-ovate, acuminate, to 4 in. long and a little wider; fls. in axillary racemes, calyx about 1 in. long, tube funnelform above, expanded into a lip with attenuate apex, brownish-purple outside. E. Mex.

ringens Vahl. Similar to *A. brasiliensis,* but fls. with upper lip of calyx obovate, much smaller, to only 3 in. long and half as wide, lower lip linear-lanceolate and channeled, to 7 in. long. Costa Rica to the Amazon, and Jamaica.

sempervirens L. Similar to *A. altissima,* but sts. only 1 ft. long; lvs. smaller, to 1¼ in. long, more acuminate; and fls. smaller, on pendent peduncles. E. Medit.

Serpentaria L. VIRGINIA SNAKEROOT. Erect herb, to 3 ft.; lvs. ovate, cordate; calyx about 1 in. long, greenish, tube curved, limb short, slightly 3-lobed. Conn., s. to Fla. and La.

Sipho: *A. durior.*

tomentosa Sims. Woody, deciduous climber, to 30 ft.; lvs. orbicular-ovate, to 8 in. long, usually rounded at apex; fls. solitary, about 1½ in. long, calyx tube greenish-yellow, U-shaped, pubescent outside, with a narrow purple mouth, limb 3-parted, reflexed, ¾ in. across, yellow. N.C., w. to Mo., s. to Fla.

ARISTOLOCHIACEAE Juss. BIRTHWORT FAMILY. Dicot.; 5 genera of herbs or, usually, climbing woody plants, of trop. and warm temp. regions; lvs. alt., petioled, often cordate; fls. bisexual, calyx corrollalike, 3-lobed, of various colors and irregular form; stamens 3–36, ovary usually inferior, 4–6-celled; fr. a caps. *Aristolochia* and *Asarum* are cult.

ARISTOTELIA L'Hér. *Elaeocarpaceae*. About 11 spp. of evergreen, sometimes polygamous trees or shrubs, native to S. Hemisphere; lvs. opp. or nearly so, simple, symmetrical; fls. small, sepals 4–5, petals 4–5, imbricate in bud; fr. a berry.

Planted in southern Calif. as an ornamental. Propagated by cuttings of ripe wood under glass.

chilensis (Mol.) Stuntz [*A. Macqui* L'Hér.]. Shrub, to 7 ft.; lvs. oblong, about 3 in. long, toothed, shining and sometimes variegated; fls. greenish, solitary or in few-fld. cymes. Chile. Fr. is edible.

fruticosa Hook. f. Shrub, to 8 ft., much-branched; lvs. obovate, to 1 in. long, entire or lobed, or on young plants pinnatifid, leathery; fls. solitary or in 3–6-fld. cymes. New Zeal.

Macqui: *A. chilensis.*

racemosa Hook. f. NEW ZEALAND WINEBERRY. Tree, to 25 ft.; lvs. ovate, to 5 in. long, deeply sharp-toothed; fls. rose, in many-fld. panicles; berry dark red or nearly black, size of pea. New Zeal. Wood used for various purposes.

ARMATOCEREUS: *LEMAIREOCEREUS.* **A. armatus, A. chalaensis, A. giganteus, A. Larabei, A. mocupensis, A. nazcensis, A. solitarius** are listed names of no botanical standing.

ARMERIA Willd. [*Statice* Mill. and of L. in part]. THRIFT, SEA PINK. *Plumbaginaceae*. Perhaps as many as 35 spp. of per., evergreen, low-growing, tufted, herbs or subshrubs, mostly in alpine situations, mt. meadows, and maritime shores of Eur., Asia Minor, and n. Afr., also in the extreme ne. and on the Pacific Coast of N. Amer., and in Chile; sts. often much-branched; lvs. in rosettes on ends of the short brs., linear to lanceolate; fl. scapes usually cylindrical, bearing a solitary, terminal, globose fl. head subtended by involucral bracts, the outermost bracts united and forming a sheath enclosing the uppermost portion of scape; fls. bisexual, 5-merous, calyx funnelform, 5-lobed, 10-ribbed, scarious, colored, base sometimes prolonged into a spur, petals united only at base, styles 5, stigmas capitate; fr. 1-seeded.

The species differ only in small technical characters, few of which are easily seen and usable in distinguishing them. The calyx has several useful characters such as length of spur when present, and presence or absence of pubescence on the ribs and the areas between. The leaves are of some use but are not entirely reliable. There has consequently been much confusion in recognizing the species, both in the wild and in cultivation, and many names have been used for minor variants. Most cultivated plants belong to the highly variable *A. maritima.*

Thrifts are useful in the border and rock garden, and are sometimes used as edging plants. They succeed in any soil, doing best in a well-drained location in full sun; the true alpine forms, such as *A. juniperifolia*, require complete surface drainage, especially during the summer months. Propagated by seeds or cuttings. Many of the species and their varieties hybridize freely and much of the material in the trade represents mixtures of various trade binomials and not the species indicated.

alliacea (Cav.) Hoffmanns. & Link [*A. allioides* Boiss.; *A. juncea* Wallr., not Girard]. A name of doubtful application, apparently referring to a plant closely related to *A. maritima*, but with lvs. broader, lanceolate to broadly oblong-lanceolate. Spain, Portugal.

allioides: *A. alliacea.*

alpina: *A. maritima.* Var. **alba:** a listed name of no botanical standing; probably refers to a white-fld. form of *A. maritima.* Var. **nana:** *A. maritima.*

arborea: a listed name of no botanical standing.

arctica: see *A. maritima.* Var. **californica:** *A. maritima.*

berlengensis Daveau. Similar to *A. mauritanica*, but with calyx tube entirely hairy. Portugal.

bottendorfensis: *A. maritima.*

caesalpina: a listed name of no botanical standing, used for a dwarf form said to be a natural hybrid between *A. juniperifolia* and *A. plantaginea.*

caespitosa: *A. juniperifolia.*

canescens (Host) Ebel [*A. majellensis* Boiss.]. Resembling *A. maritima*, but with outer lvs. shorter and wider than inner ones, inner lvs. ¾ in. long, flat, glabrous. S.-cent. Eur.

cantabrica: *A. maritima.*

caucasica: a listed name of no botanical standing.

cephalotes: *A. pseudarmeria.* Var. **rubra:** a listed name of no botanical standing; perhaps refers to a color form of *A. pseudarmeria.*

chilensis var. **majellanica:** *A. maritima.*

corsica: a listed name of no botanical standing, used for a form of *A. leucocephala.*

echioides: a listed name of no botanical standing.

elongata: *A. maritima.*

formosa: *A. pseudarmeria.* Formosa alba, formosa carnea, formosa grandiflora, formosa hybrida: listed names of no botanical standing.

grandiflora: *A. pseudarmeria.*

Halleri: *A. maritima.*

japonica: a listed name of no botanical standing, used for a form of *A. maritima.*

juncea Girard [*A. setacea* Delile ex Nym. may belong here]. Low, tufted plant to 10 in.; resembling *A. maritima*, but with outer lvs. shorter and wider than inner ones, inner lvs. to ½ in. wide and 1¼ in. long, often glaucous-blue; fls. pink. Cv. 'Alba'. Fls. white. S. Eur.

juncifolia: a listed name of no botanical standing.

juniperifolia (Vahl) Willd. ex Hoffmanns. & Link [*A. caespitosa* (Quer ex Cav.) Boiss.; *Statice caespitosa* Quer ex Cav.]. Densely tufted, with many rosettes, to 6 in.; resembling low-growing forms of *A. maritima*, but with lvs. shorter, usually less then ¾ in. long, sharply mucronate. Spain.

juniperina: a listed name of no botanical standing.

kurilensis: a listed name of no botanical standing.

labradorica: *A. maritima.*

latifolia: *A. pseudarmeria.*

Laucheana: *A. maritima.* Laucheana alba, Laucheana nana, Laucheana rosea: listed names of no botanical standing, used for forms of *A. maritima.*

leucocephala Salzm. ex W. D. J. Koch [*A. leucocephala* var. *procera* Boiss.]. Resembling *A. maritima*, with lvs. linear, to 4 in. long, sometimes limp, or stiff and erect, glabrous or pubescent on both surfaces; fls. white to rose. Corsica and Sardinia.

macrophylla: *A. pinifolia.*

majellanica: *A. maritima.*

majellensis: *A. canescens.*

maritima (Mill.) Willd. [*A. maritima* var. *californica* (Boiss.) G. H. M. Lawr.; *A. maritima* var. *Willkommiana* Bernis; *A. maritima* forma *Laucheana* Voss; *A. alpina* Willd.; *A. alpina* var. *nana* Bolz.; *A. arctica* Wallr., in part; *A. arctica* var. *californica* (Boiss.) S. F. Blake; *A. bottendorfensis* Wein; *A. cantabrica* Boiss. & Reut.; *A. chilensis* Boiss. var. *majellanica* Boiss.; *A. elongata* (Hoffm.) W. D. J. Koch; *A. Halleri* Wallr.; *A. labradorica* Wallr.; *A. Laucheana* Hort.; *A. majellanica* Hort.; *A. patagonica* Phil.; *A. ruscinonensis* Girard; *A. sibirica* Turcz. ex Boiss.; *A. vulgaris* Willd.; *A. Willkommiana* Hort.; *Statice Armeria* L., in part; *S. maritima* Mill.]. Plant cespitose, to 12 in. or more; lvs. linear, to 4 in. long or more, 1-nerved; fl. scapes glabrous or pubescent; fls. pink or white, in heads to 1 in. across, involucral bracts in 1 or more rows, interfloral bracts present, calyx variously pubescent, basal spur very short or absent. Widely distributed throughout the range of the genus. An exceedingly polymorphic sp. with geographical variants. Such variants, however, are not easily recognizable among plants in cult.

mauritanica Wallr. Glabrous, glaucous, tufted, to 2 ft.; lvs. oblong-lanceolate to spatulate, to 7 in. long, 3–5-nerved, margin white-scarious; fls. pink, in heads to 2 in. across, interfloral bracts usually as long as or longer than calyx tube, calyx with basal spur projecting downward, ribs sparsely hairy to glabrous. Spain and N. Afr.

montana: *A. plantaginea.* Vars. **alpina** and **rosea:** listed names of no botanical standing.

patagonica: *A. maritima.*

pinifolia (Brot.) Hoffmanns. & Link [*A. macrophylla* Boiss. & Reut.]. To 2 ft.; lvs. narrowly lanceolate to linear, generally more than 2½ in. long to as much as 6–10 in. long, usually 1-nerved; fls. usually pink, in heads about 1 in. across, involucral bracts generally more than 17, thin and scarious, glabrous, or brown-hairy, calyx tube with hairs on and between ribs, spur usually ½–⅔ as long as calyx tube. Spain and Portugal.

plantaginea Willd. [*A. montana* Wallr.; *A. rigida* Wallr.; *A. stenophylla* Girard]. Resembling *A. pseudarmeria*, but with lvs. narrowly lanceolate, to ¼ in. wide, margins rarely scarious, and sheath to 2 in. long. Cent. and s. Eur.

pseudarmeria (J. Murr.) Mansf. [*A. cephalotes* (Ait.) Hoffmanns. & Link; *A. formosa* Hort. Vilm.-Andr.; *A. grandiflora* Boiss.; *A. latifolia*

Willd.; *Statice pseudarmeria* J. Murr.]. Resembling *A. maritima*, but with lvs. broader, lanceolate, to 10 in. long, ¾ in. wide, 5–7-nerved, margins narrowly scarious; involucral sheath to 4 in. long; fls. white to dark rose-pink. Portugal. The commonly cult. broad-lvd. thrift.

rigida: *A. plantaginea.*

Rouyana Daveau. To 1 ft., forming mats; lvs. filiform or linear, channelled, 1-nerved, to 4 in. long; interfloral bracts pubescent at least on basal half, usually as long as or longer than calyx tube, calyx spur more than half as long as calyx tube, calyx hairy on and between ribs, fls. rose-pink. Portugal.

rumelica Boiss. Lvs. stiff, 3–5-nerved, of 2 kinds, outer lvs. broadly linear, shortly acuminate, inner lvs. narrowly linear; fls. purplish-pink. Balkan Pen.

ruscinonensis: *A. maritima.*

setacea: see *A. juncea.* Var. **alba:** a listed name, probably referring to *A. juncea* cv.

sibirica: *A. maritima.*

splendens: *A. juniperifolia.*

stenophylla: *A. plantaginea.*

Sundermanii: a listed name of no botanical standing, used for a form of *A. maritima.*

vulgaris: *A. maritima.* Vars. **nana** and **splendens:** listed names of no botanical standing, used for forms of *A. maritima.*

Walterana: a listed name of no botanical standing.

Welwitschii Boiss. [*A. Welwitschii* var. *stenophylla* Daveau]. Tufted, subshrubby, to 1 ft., glabrous, somewhat glaucous; lvs. linear, to 4 in. long, channelled or flat, obscurely 1-nerved; fls. pink, calyx with basal spur. Portugal.

Willkommiana: *A. maritima.*

ARMORACIA P. Gaertn., B. Mey. & Scherb. *Cruciferae.* About 3 spp. of glabrous per. herbs, with deep roots or rhizomes, native to Eur. and Asia; lvs. simple to pinnatifid, basal lvs. large and often docklike, variously dissected; fls. white, small, sepals and petals 4; fr. a globose to ellipsoidal silicle.

One species is widely grown as a condiment plant, the fleshy roots being grated for use as a pungent relish or appetizer with meats. Does not mature viable seeds; propagated by root cuttings planted in spring, and best treated as an annual crop, the roots harvested in late autumn of the same year.

rusticana P. Gaertn., B. Mey. & Scherb. [*Cochlearia Amoracia* L.; *Nasturtium Amoracia* (L.) Fries; *Radicula Amoracia* (L.) B. L. Robinson; *Rorippa Amoracia* (L.) A. S. Hitchc.]. HORSERADISH, RED COLE. Deep-rooted, strong per.; lower lf. blades to 15 in. long and 9 in. across, crenate-dentate or jagged, sometimes dissected into linear segms., upper st. lvs. lanceolate to oblong; fls. in terminal panicle. Spring. Se. Eur.; naturalized in N. Amer.

ARNEBIA Forssk. *Boraginaceae.* Not cult. **A. Echioides:** *Echioides longiflorum.*

ARNICA L. *Compositae* (Senecio Tribe). About 30 spp. of rhizomatous, pubescent and also usually glandular per. herbs, native to Eur., Asia, and N. Amer., sts. simple or branched above; lvs. opp.; fl. heads radiate or discoid, 1 to several, rather large, long-peduncled, involucral bracts in 2 rows, herbaceous; disc and ray fls. yellow; achenes slender, cylindrical, pappus of minutely barbed or almost plumose bristles.

Arnicas are grown in the rock garden or border or are colonized in woodsy places. Tincture of arnica, derived from *A. montana*, has medicinal uses. Propagated by seeds or division.

alpina (L.) Olin. To 4–15 in.; st. lvs. 1–4 pairs, lanceolate or oblanceolate, to 4–5 in. long, nearly entire, sessile or the lowermost petioled; heads usually solitary, to 2 in. across, involucre woolly; anthers yellow; pappus white. Circumboreal.

amplexicaulis Nutt. To 2 ft., viscid; st. lvs. 4–10 pairs, ovate to broadly elliptic-lanceolate, to 5 in. long, serrate-dentate, sessile; heads 3–9, 1½ in. across; anthers yellow; pappus tan. W. U.S. to Alaska.

betonicifolia: *A. latifolia.*

Chamissonis Less. To 2 ft.; st. lvs. 5–8 pairs, lanceolate-oblong to oblanceolate, to 6 in. long, denticulate or dentate, all sessile and clasping, or the lower ones short-petioled; heads 3–9, 2 in. across; anthers yellow; pappus tan. Nw. U.S. to s. Alaska. Subsp. **foliosa** (Nutt.) Maguire [*A. foliosa* Nutt.]. Lvs. usually entire, the lower ones distinctly petioled. Wyo. and Colo., w. to Calif. and Canada.

Clusii: *Doronicum Clusii.*

cordifolia Hook. To 18 in.; st. lvs. 2–3 pairs, the lower broad-lanceolate to ovate, cordate, long-petioled, mostly coarsely dentate, blades 2–3 in. long, the upper reduced, ovate or lanceolate, sessile; heads solitary, or sometimes 3, 2–3 in. across; anthers yellow; achenes pubescent their whole length, pappus white. S. Dak. to New Mex., w. to Calif., n. to Yukon, also n. Mich. The most desirable sp.

foliosa: *A. Chamissonis* subsp.

fulgens Pursh [*A. pedunculata* Rydb.]. Rhizomes short, rooting, with tufts of tan hairs in axils of old lf. bases, sts. 1–2 ft.; st. lvs. 4 or 5 pairs, oblanceolate, the lower crowded near base, petioled, to 6 in. long, nearly entire, the upper much-reduced, sessile; heads usually solitary, 2–3 in. across; anthers yellow; pappus whitish or light tan. B.C. to Sask., s. to n. Calif. and Colo.

latifolia Bong. [*A. betonicifolia* Greene]. To 2 ft.; st. lvs. 2–4 pairs, ovate to elliptic-lanceolate, 1–3 in. long, dentate, all sessile or the lowermost petioled; heads mostly 1–3; anthers yellow; achenes glabrous or hirsute only in upper half, pappus white. Wyo. and Colo., w. to Calif., n. to s. Alaska.

Lessingii Greene. To 10 in., without glands; lvs. 4–5 pairs in a rosette toward base of st., lanceolate or oblanceolate, 2–4 in. long, entire or denticulate, sessile or short-petioled; heads solitary, nodding, 2 in. across; anthers purple; pappus tan. Alaska, Kamchatka.

longifolia D. C. Eat. Sts. in clumps, to 2 ft.; st. lvs. 5–7 pairs, lanceolate to lanceolate-elliptic, to 4 in. long, entire or denticulate, viscid, sessile; heads 7–30, to 2 in. across; anthers yellow; pappus straw-colored or tan. Mts., Calif. and Colo., n. to Wash. and Mont.

mollis Hook. To 2 ft.; st. lvs. 2–4 pairs, ovate, lanceolate, obovate, or oblanceolate, to 6 in. long, denticulate, sessile or the lower ones petioled; heads mostly 1–3, to about 3 in. across; anthers yellow; pappus tan. Colo. to Calif., n. into Canada, also N.Y. and New Eng. to Gaspé Pen.

montana L. To 2 ft.; st. lvs. about 3 pairs, broadly lanceolate, ovate, or obovate, entire or obscurely denticulate, sessile, upper pair much reduced, the others in a basal rosette, to 5 in. long; heads 1–3 or more, to 3 in. across; anthers yellow; pappus tan. Cent. Eur., s. Scandinavia.

pedunculata: *A. fulgens.*

sachalinensis (Regel) A. Gray. Nearly glabrous, 12–30 in.; st. lvs. 12–20 pairs, lanceolate or oblanceolate, to 6 in. long, serrate, sessile and united; heads 5–15, to 2½ in. across; anthers purple; pappus tan. Sakhalin Is.

saluensis: a listed name; perhaps for *A. sachalinensis.*

unalaschcensis Less. To 3–12 in.; st. lvs. 3–5 pairs, mostly broadly lanceolate or oblanceolate, to 4 in. long, serrulate, the upper sessile, the lower petioled; heads solitary, about 1½ in. across; corolla tube glabrous, anthers purple; pappus tan. Japan and islands of Bering Sea. Var. **Tschonoskyi** (Iljin) Kitam. & Hara. Corolla tube pubescent. Japan.

ARONIA Medic. CHOKEBERRY. *Rosaceae.* A few spp. of low, deciduous shrubs of N. Amer.; lvs. alt., simple, short-petioled, finely serrate; fls. small, pink or white, in terminal cymes, calyx tube urceolate, sepals 5, petals 5, concave, spreading, styles 3–5, united at base; fr. a small berrylike pome. Often considered a subgenus of *Pyrus.*

Propagated by seeds sown when ripe or stratified, and by suckers, layers, and cuttings of green wood under glass. Useful for colonizing in low places; showy in bloom and the fruit attractive in autumn.

arbutifolia (L.) Pers. [*Pyrus arbutifolia* (L.) L.f.]. CHOKEBERRY, RED C. Shrub, tending to form colonies, to 12 ft. or more, young growth tomentose; lvs. broadly oblanceolate to wider, pointed, green and glabrous above, tomentose and pale beneath, crenate-serrate, 1–3½ in. long; fls. 2–25, about ⅜ in. across, calyx tube tomentose, sepals with stipitate glands; fr. red, ³⁄₁₆ in. in diam. Nov. Sc. to Ont., Mich., s. to Tex., Fla. Zone 6.

atropurpurea: *A. prunifolia.*

floribunda: *A. prunifolia.*

melanocarpa (Michx.) Elliott [*A. nigra* (Sarg.) Koehne; *Pyrus melanocarpa* (Michx.) Willd.]. Like *A. arbutifolia*, but young twigs, lower lf. surfaces, and calyx tube glabrous, sepals essentially glabrous; fr. black, ⁵⁄₁₆ in. in diam. Nfld. to Minn., S.C., Tenn.

nigra: *A. melanocarpa.*

prunifolia (Marsh.) Rehd. [*A. floribunda* (Lindl.) Spach; *Pyrus atropurpurea* (Britt.) L. H. Bailey]. Like *A. arbutifolia*, but sepals glandless or nearly so; fr. purple or purple-black, ⁵⁄₁₆ in. in diam. Nfld. to Ont., s. to Va. and Ind. Zone 5.

ARPOPHYLLUM Llave & Lex. HYACINTH ORCHID. *Orchidaceae*. Two spp. of epiphytes, native to Cent. Amer., W. Indies, and n. S. Amer.; pseudobulbs slender, with 1 terminal lf.; infl. a dense raceme; fls. red or purplish, sepals and petals similar, lip concave, slightly 3-lobed. For structure of fl. see *Orchidaceae*.

Intermediate greenhouse; for culture see *Orchids*.

giganteum: *A. spicatum.*

spicatum Llave & Lex. [*A. giganteum* Hartweg ex Lindl.]. To 2 ft. or more, pseudobulbs to 8 in. high or more; lvs. linear, to 1 ft. long; racemes dense, stiff, erect, to 1 ft. long; fls. small, light rosy-red, lip somewhat darker. Spring–early summer. Mex., Cent. Amer., Jamaica.

ARRABIDAEA DC. *Bignoniaceae*. over 50 spp. of vines or shrubs, native to trop. Amer.; lvs. opp., with 2 lfts. or ternately compound, often with terminal tendril; fls. showy, white to pinkish-purple, in terminal or axillary paniculate clusters, rarely solitary, calyx truncate or 5-toothed, corolla campanulate to funnelform, stamens 4; fr. a linear caps.

magnifica: *Saritaea magnifica.*

rotundata (DC.) Bur. ex K. Schum. [*Bignonia rotundata* DC.]. Small tree; lvs. leathery, with 3 lfts., lfts. orbicular, to 1 in. long, pubescent; fls. pale red, funnelform, to about 1 in. long. Brazil.

ARRACACIA E. N. Bancr. *Umbelliferae*. About 40 spp. of stout, per. herbs native from Mex. to Peru and Bolivia; lvs. pinnate or ternately compound; fls. small, white or dark purple, in compound umbels; fr. compressed.

One species is grown in the mountains of the tropics for the thick, edible roots. Propagated by the large buds that form at the bases of the leaf stalks.

esculenta: *A. xanthorrhiza.*

xanthorrhiza E. N. Bancr. [*A. esculenta* DC.]. PERUVIAN CARROT, APIO, R'ACCACHA, ARRACACHA. Roots branching, with starchy, yellow flesh; lvs. biternately compound or 2-pinnate; fls. greenish-white to purplish-brown. N. S. Amer.

ARRHENATHERUM Beauvois. OAT GRASS. *Gramineae*. Six spp. of per. grasses in Medit. region; lf. blades flat; panicles narrow; spikelets 2-fld., lower floret male, upper one bisexual, rachilla disarticulating above the glumes, glumes broad and papery, the first 1-nerved, the second 3-nerved, lemmas 5-nerved, the lower awned near the base, awn twisted, geniculate, exserted, the upper awned below the tip, awn short, straight, slender. For terminology see *Gramineae*.

bulbosum: *A. elatius* var. *bulbosum*. Var. **variegatum:** *A. elatius* cv.

elatius (L.) Beauvois ex J. Presl & K. Presl [*Avena elatior* L.]. TALL O.G. Sts. to 5 ft., erect, slender; lf. blades flat, scabrous, soft, to ⅜ in. wide; panicle pale green or purplish, glossy, to 1 ft. long, narrow, brs. short, whorled, usually bearing spikelets from the base; spikelets ⁵⁄₁₆ in. long, glumes minutely scabrous, male floret with awn about twice as long as lemma. Eur.; introd. Cult. in the n. humid region of the U.S. as a meadow grass; escapes frequently from cult., especially in the n. and e. states. Cv. 'Variegatum' [*A. bulbosum* var. *variegatum* A. S. Hitch.; *A. tuberosum* cv. 'Variegatum']. Lf. blades variegated. Var. **bulbosum** (Willd.) Spenn. [*A. bulbosum* (Willd.) K. Presl; *A. tuberosum* (Gilib.) Schultz-Bip.]. TUBER O.G. Base of st. with short, subglobose, cormlike internodes to ⅜ in. in diam. Eur. Occasionally cult.

tuberosum: *A. elatius* var. *bulbosum*. Cv. 'Variegatum': *A. elatius* cv. 'Variegatum'.

ARROJADOA Britt. & Rose. *Cactaceae*. Two spp. of slender, low-ribbed, jointed cacti, native to Brazil; ribs 10–12, joint apex with persistent long hairs and slender, needle-shaped spines; fls. nocturnal, pinkish, cylindrical, small, in subapical clusters among bristles, tube naked, perianth segms. short, stamens and style included, ovary naked; fr. slender top-shaped, naked, juicy, seeds small, minutely pitted.

For culture see *Cacti*.

rhodantha (Gürke) Britt. & Rose. Sts. erect to nearly decumbent, to 6 ft. long and 2 in. thick; spines brownish, becoming gray, radial spines about 20, to ½ in. long, central spines 5–6, to 1¼ in. long; fls. waxy, violet-pink, to 1½ in. long; fr. red, ¾ in. long.

ARSENOCOCCUS: *LYONIA*. **A. frondosus:** *L. ligustrina* var. *foliosiflora.*

ARTABOTRYS R. Br. TAIL GRAPE. *Annonaceae*. Over 100 spp. of climbing shrubs, native to Old World tropics; lvs. alt., simple; hooked peduncles adapted to climbing borne opp. lvs.; fls. bisexual, 3-merous, petals 6, yellow or white, valvate, in 2 series, inflated beneath and covering the many closely packed stamens and pistils; fr. 2-seeded, in clusters on the hardened receptacle.

Grown in greenhouses or in the open. Requires fertile soil. Propagated by seeds.

hexapetalus (L.f.) Bhand. [*A. odoratissimus* R. Br.; *A. uncinatus* (Lam.) Merrill]. CLIMBING ILANG-ILANG. Climbing shrub, to 12 ft. long; lvs. narrowly oblong-lanceolate, to 6 in. long; fls. not showy but very fragrant, 1–2 together on long peduncles, sepals reflexed, yellow, petals about 1 in. long; fr. narrowly obovoid, yellow, 1½ in. long, sessile, in dense clusters 20 in. long. Ceylon and s. India. Cult. widely in the tropics. Zone 10.

odoratissimus: *A. hexapetalus.*

uncinatus: *A. hexapetalus.*

ARTEMISIA L. SAGEBRUSH, MUGWORT, WORMWOOD. *Compositae* (Anthemis Tribe). About 200 spp. of mostly aromatic, ann., bien., or per. herbs or shrubs, native mostly in dry areas in the N. Hemisphere, a few in w. S. Amer., 1 in S. Afr.; lvs. alt., entire to lobed or dissected; fl. heads in spikes, racemes, or panicles, radiate or discoid, involucre cylindrical to globose, involucral bracts imbricate in several rows, dry, at least the inner ones scarious or with scarious margins, receptacle flat or hemispherical, naked or with long hairs; disc fls. white, yellow, brownish, or purplish, ray fls. female and fertile, or absent; achenes ellipsoid or ovoid to nearly prismatic, 2–5-angled to faintly ribbed, pappus absent or only a short crown.

Artemisias are grown as ornamentals and for their medicinal and aromatic qualities. They thrive even in poor, dry soil. Usually increased by division; also by seeds when obtainable.

Abrotanum L. [*A. procera* Willd.]. SOUTHERNWOOD, OLD-MAN. Subshrub to 6 ft., much-branched, glabrous, green, aromatic; lvs. 1–3-pinnately dissected, the segms. revolute, filiform or linear; heads to ³⁄₁₆ in. across, nearly globose, nodding, in loose panicles, receptacle naked; fls. yellowish-white; achenes 4–5-angled. S. Eur.; adventive in e. U.S.

Absinthium L. ABSINTHE, COMMON W. Coarse, per. herb, to 4 ft., aromatic, sts. erect, silky-hairy; lvs. orbicular-ovate in outline, 2–3-pinnatifid into oblong segms., silvery-silky; heads ⅛ in. across, nodding, many in leafy panicles, receptacle with many long hairs. Eur.; naturalized in n.e. U.S. and adjacent Canada. Used in making absinthe; dried lvs. used medicinally.

albula: *A. ludoviciana* var.

annua L. SWEET W. Ann. to 10 ft., much-branched, glabrous, sweetly aromatic; lvs. to 4 in. long, 2–3-pinnatifid, the segms. linear to lanceolate, short-toothed; heads about ¹⁄₁₆ in. across, often nodding, in a loose panicle; fls. yellow; achenes only faintly nerved. Asia and e. Eur.; naturalized in waste places in e. and cent. N. Amer.

arborea: a listed name, perhaps in error for *A. arborescens.*

arborescens L. Shrubby per., to 3½ ft.; lower lvs. 3-pinnately dissected, upper lvs. 1–2-pinnately dissected into linear, obtuse segms., silky-hairy on both surfaces; heads to ¼ in. across, in leafy panicles, receptacle with long hairs; fls. bright yellow; achenes glandular. Medit. region.

arbuscula Nutt. LOW S. Low, evergreen shrub, to 1 ft.; lvs. cuneate to fan-shaped, to ½ in. long, usually 3–5-toothed or -lobed at apex or rarely entire, silvery-pubescent or almost glabrous in age; heads to ³⁄₁₆ in. across, in erect, narrow, often spikelike panicles; fls. brownish; achenes resinous-glandular. Rocky Mts., and Sierra Nevada from Alpine Co., Calif., to Wash.

borealis: *A. campestris* subsp. Var. **Wormskioldii:** *A. campestris* subsp. *borealis.*

californica Less. CALIFORNIA S. Grayish, much-branched shrub, 1½–7 ft.; lvs. sessile, lower lvs. to 2 in. long, 1–2-palmately parted into linear-filiform segms., upper lvs. frequently in clusters, often entire, densely gray-pubescent or ashy-gray, margins revolute; heads to ³⁄₁₆ in. across, in racemose panicles; fls. yellow, disc fls. 15–30, ray fls. 6–10; achenes oblong-turbinate. Coastal n. Calif. to Baja Calif.

campestris L. Tufted, scentless per., to 2 ft. high, sts. decumbent to ascending, silky-hairy to almost glabrous; lower lvs. 2–3-pinnatifid, to 4 in. long, upper lvs. sessile, the uppermost linear and entire, all silky-hairy but finally glabrous; heads ⅛ in. across, many in elongated, racemose panicles; fls. yellow or reddish; achenes glabrous. Eur., Asia. Subsp. **borealis** (Pall.) H. M. Hall & Clements [*A. borealis* Pall.; *A. borealis* var. *Wormskioldii* Bess.; *A. canadensis* Michx.]. Per. herb, to 16 in.; lvs. 1–2-ternately parted, the lobes linear to linear-filiform; heads to ³⁄₁₆ in. across; disc fls. 15–30, ray fls. 10–25. N. Mont. and Wash., and Siberia.

camphorata Vill. Camphor-scented subshrub, to 2½ ft.; lvs. 2–3-pinnately dissected into linear-filiform segms., essentially glabrous; heads ¼ in. across, nodding, in panicles, receptacle hairy; fls. yellow. S. Eur., N. Afr.

cana Pursh. Freely branching shrub, to 3 ft., sometimes to 5 ft.; lvs. linear to linear-oblanceolate, to 2⅜ in. long, entire or rarely toothed, silvery–gray-pubescent; heads to ³⁄₁₆ in. across, in loose panicles, rarely nearly spicate; fls. yellow; achenes dotted with granules. Sierra Nevada of Calif., n. to se. Ore., e. to Colo., N. Dak., and adjacent Canada.

canadensis: *A campestris* subsp. *borealis*.

canariensis (Bess.) Less. Aromatic shrub, to about 2½ ft.; lvs. crowded, to 4 in. long, broadly ovate in outline, 2-pinnately dissected, segms. linear to linear-lanceolate, hoary-tementose; heads to about ¼ in. across, in loose panicles; fls. pale yellow; achenes obovate, glabrous. Canary Is.

caucasica Willd. Cespitose shrub, sts. ascending, to 6 in. in fl., silky-tomentose; lvs. to about 1¼ in. long, palmately multifid into linear, acute segms., gray-green, silky-hairy; heads to ¼ in. across, in loose panicles, receptacle hairy; fls. yellow. Caucasus.

chamaemelifolia Vill. Aromatic shrub, to 2½ ft.; lvs. sessile, glabrous or nearly so, 2–3-pinnately dissected, segms. linear to linear-filiform; heads in leafy, dense panicles. S. Eur.

discolor: *A. Michauxiana*.

Douglasiana Bess. [*A. vulgaris* var. *heterophylla* (Nutt.) Jeps.]. Rhizomatous per. herb, sts. stout, to 5 ft., sometimes taller, usually unbranched or branched only above; lvs. to 6 in. long, lanceolate to elliptic and entire, or oblanceolate to obovate and with few coarse teeth or lobes toward apex, dark green and nearly glabrous on upper surface, gray-tomentose on lower surface; heads about ⅛ in. across, in dense, narrow panicles; disc fls. 10–25, ray fls. 6–10; achenes ellipsoid. Wash. to Baja Calif., e. to Idaho and w. Nev.

Dracunculus L. [*A. Redowskii* Ledeb.]. TARRAGON, ESTRAGON. Rhizomatous per., to 5 ft., almost scentless to strongly aromatic, sts. erect, glabrous to hairy; lvs. linear to lanceolate, to 6 in. long, entire or sometimes 2–5-cleft, lower lvs. commonly deciduous; heads ⅛ in. across, in loose, spreading panicles; fls. whitish-green; achenes ellipsoid, glabrous. S. Eur., Asia, U.S. w. of Mississippi R. The lvs. are used for seasoning. Var. **sativa** is listed.

filifolia Torr. SAND SAGE. Freely branching shrub or subshrub, to about 5 ft.; lvs. alt. or frequently clustered, to 3⅛ in. long, filiform or ternately parted into filiform segms., grayish or gray-pubescent; heads about ³⁄₃₂ in. across, many in narrow, leafy panicles; achenes glabrous. Nebr. to Nev., s. to Tex. and Mex.

frigida Willd. Aromatic, mat-forming per., to 16 in., from a woody crown; lvs. clustered, to ½ in. long, 2–3-ternately parted into linear or linear-filiform segms., silky-hairy; heads ⅛ in. across, nodding, in panicles or sometimes in racemes, receptacle long-hairy; fls. yellow; achenes at most obscurely nerved. Kans. and sw. Wisc., s. to Ariz. and w. to Wash., Alaska, also in Siberia.

glacialis L. Strongly aromatic, tufted, shrubby per., sts. to 6 in., gray-pubescent; lvs. to 1¼ in. long, palmately dissected into linear-lanceolate segms.; heads ¼ in. across, in dense corymbs to ¾ in. across, receptacle pubescent; fls. 30–40, golden-yellow. Alps.

Gmelinii Webb ex Stechm. [*A. sacrorum* Ledeb.]. RUSSIAN W. Ann. or bien. subshrub, 3–5 ft., gray-pubescent; lvs. elliptic, 1–3 in. long, 2-pinnate, long-petioled, rachis winged; heads 15–20-fld., about ⅛ in. across, in leafy, terminal panicles to 10 in. long. S. Russia to Siberia and ne. Asia. Cv. 'Viridis'. SUMMER FIR. To 10 ft., pyramidal; lvs. rich green, much dissected.

gnaphalodes: *A. ludoviciana*.

Haussknechtii Boiss. Bushy per., to 6 in., rhizomatous, white-hairy; lvs. dense, 2-pinnatifid into linear-oblong, attenuate segms.; heads very small, nodding, receptacle tomentose. Iran.

japonica Thunb. [*Chrysanthemum japonicum* Thunb.]. Per. herb, to about 3 ft.; lvs. spatulate, to 3⅛ in. long, pinnately lobed and toothed, silky-hairy; heads in panicles; fls. yellow-green. Japan, e. Asia, Taiwan.

lactiflora Wallich ex DC. WHITE M. Erect, per. herb, to 4–5 ft., sts. grooved, glabrous; lower lvs. to 9 in. long, pinnatifid into ovate-lanceolate, coarsely toothed or lobed segms. to 3 in. long, upper lvs. shorter, lower surface paler; heads about ¹⁄₁₆ in. across, many, in loose panicles to 2 ft.; fls. white. China.

lanata Willd. [*A. pedemontana* Balb. ex Loisel.]. Tufted, shrubby per.; lvs. to 1 in. long, palmately cut into linear segms., downy; heads to ¼ in. across, in spikes to 8 in. long; fls. yellow. Mts., s. and cent. Eur.

laxa (Lam.) Fritsch [*A. Mutellina* Vill.]. ALPINE W. Tufted shrub, to 8 in., strongly aromatic; lower lvs. to 1 ft. long, palmately divided into linear segms., gray-pubescent, upper lvs. shorter; heads to ³⁄₁₆ in. across, in racemes, receptacle pubescent; fls. 12–15, yellow. Alps.

longifolia Nutt. Per., to 3 ft., white-tomentose, sts. woody at base, clustered; lvs. linear-lanceolate, to 4¾ in. long, mostly entire, thinly hairy to almost glabrous above, persistently white-hairy beneath, revolute; heads to ¼ in. across, erect, in a narrow, compact panicle; fls. yellow. Nebr. to Mont. and adjacent Canada.

ludoviciana Nutt. [*A. ludoviciana* var. *gnaphalodes* (Nutt.) Torr. & A. Gray; *A. gnaphalodes* Nutt.; *A. Purshiana* Bess.]. WESTERN M., CUDWEED, WHITE SAGE. Per. herb, to 3 ft., rhizomatous, aromatic, sts. simple, branched only in the infl.; lvs. lanceolate to elliptic-lanceolate, to 4¼ in. long, entire or merely lobed, white-tomentose beneath, almost glabrous above when old; heads to ⅛ in. across, usually in rather dense panicles. Mich. to Wash., s. to Ark., Tex., and Mex. Var. **albula** (Woot.) Shinn. [subsp. *albula* (Woot.) Keck; *A. albula* Woot.]. SILVER-KING A. Lvs. lanceolate, mostly to ¾ in. long, white-tomentose on both surfaces. S. Colo., s. to s. Calif., w. Tex., and adjacent Mex.

maritima L. [*A. nutans* Willd.]. WORMSEED. Strongly aromatic subshrub, fl. sts. to 2 ft.; lvs. to 2 in. long, essentially woolly on both surfaces, 2-pinnately dissected, segms. linear to filiform, obtuse; heads ³⁄₃₂ in. across, in leafy panicles; fls. yellowish or reddish. Eur., Asia.

Michauxiana Bess. [*A. discolor* Dougl. ex Bess.]. Per., to 1½ ft., woody at base; lvs. to 1 in. long, 1–2-pinnatifid into linear or lanceolate segms., usually green above, white-tomentose beneath; heads to ⅛ in. across, in narrow or spicate panicles. B. C. to Calif., e. to Alta., Wyo., and Utah.

Mutellina: *A. laxa*.

nana Gaudin. Per. herb, to 8 in.; lvs. to 1½ in. long, 2-pinnatifid into linear segms., pubescent to almost glabrous; heads to ¼ in. across, in racemes; fls. pale greenish-yellow. Alps.

nutans: *A. maritima*.

pedemontana: *A. lanata*.

pontica L. Erect, shrubby per., to 4 ft.; lvs. to 2 in. long, 2–3-pinnately dissected into linear segms., gray-pubescent on both surfaces; heads to ⅛ in. across, nodding, in long, open panicles; fls. whitish-yellow. Se. Eur.; naturalized in e. N. Amer.

procera: *A. Abrotanum*.

Purshiana: *A. ludoviciana*.

pycnocephala (Less.) DC. Per., to 2 ft., sts. erect to ascending, woody at base; lvs. crowded, to 2¾ in. long, 1–3-pinnately dissected into linear or linear-spatulate segms., silky-tomentose; heads to about ⅛ in. across, in dense, spicate, narrow panicles; fls. yellow. Coastal cent. Calif., n. to cent. Ore.

Redowskii: *A. Dracunculus*.

sacrorum: *A. Gmelinii*.

Schmidtiana Maxim. Rhizomatous, tufted per., to 2 ft.; lvs. to 1¾ in. long, twice palmately divided into linear segms., with silvery-white silky hairs, uppermost lvs. linear; heads to ³⁄₁₆ in. across, in pyramidal panicles, receptacle with dense white hairs. Japan. Cv. 'Nana'. Listed as a dwarf form.

splendens Willd. Tufted, per., to 10 in., sts. woody at base, silky-pubescent; lvs. to 1 in. long, palmately divided into linear segms., silky-pubescent; heads about ¼ in. across, in long, loose racemes. Caucasus, Armenia, Iran.

Stellerana Bess. BEACH W., OLD-WOMAN, DUSTY-MILLER. Rhizomatous, per. herb, to 2½ ft., not aromatic, sts. felty-white; lvs. to 4 in. long, oblong to ovate in outline, pinnately lobed, felty-white; heads to ¼ in. across, in often dense, narrow panicles; fls. yellow. Ne. Asia; naturalized in e. N. Amer. and in Eur.

tridentata Nutt. COMMON S., BASIN S. Rounded, evergreen shrub, to 10 ft., strongly aromatic, sts. silvery-gray-pubescent; lvs. to 1 in. long, cuneate, usually with 3 blunt apical teeth, sometimes entire or 4–9-toothed, silvery-gray-pubescent; heads to ⁵⁄₁₆ in. across, in panicles. Dry areas, B.C. to Baja Calif., and Rocky Mts. Var. **trifida:** *A. tripartita*.

tripartita Rydb. [*A. tridentata* var. *trifida* (Nutt.) McMinn]. Rounded, much-branched, evergreen shrub, to 2½ ft., aromatic; lvs. to 1¼ in. long, cuneate, with 3 narrow, sometimes 3-cleft, apical lobes, or sometimes linear and entire, gray-pubescent; heads ⅛ in. across, in panicles. Dry areas, e. Wash., adjacent Ore., e. to w. Mont. and Wyo.

versicolor: a listed name for a plant described as dwarf, with silvery foliage.

vulgaris L. MUGWORT, FELON HERB. Rhizomatous, per. herb, to 6 ft., essentially glabrous below infl., aromatic; lvs. mostly ovate or obovate in outline, to 4 in. long, 1–2-pinnatifid into oblong, toothed or entire segms., dark green above, white-tomentose beneath; heads to ⅛ in. across, in dense, leafy panicles; fls. mostly reddish-brown. Eur., Asia; naturalized in e. N. Amer. Dried lvs. used as a condiment. Var. **heterophylla:** *A. Douglasiana.*

ARTHROCEREUS A. Berger. *Cactaceae.* Four spp. of small cacti, native to Brazil; sts. jointed or not, ribs 8–18, low; fls. nocturnal, white or pinkish, slender, scales of ovary and tube small, scattered, with axillary hairs, perianth persistent in fr., stamens in 2 series; fr. fleshy. Probably referable to *Trichocereus,* but fls. slender.

For culture see *Cacti.*

Campos-Portoi (Werderm.) Backeb. Sts. solitary or cespitose, cylindrical, prostrate or half-erect, joints to 6 in. long and 1³⁄₁₆ in. thick, ribs about 12; areoles close together, radial spines 25–35, spreading, dark brown, central spines 0–2, to 1⅝ in. long; fls. white, to 3⅜ in. long.

microsphaericus (K. Schum.) A. Berger. Sts. of globose to ellipsoid joints to 2 in. long and 1 in. thick, ribs 8–11; spines bristlelike, to ⁵⁄₃₂ in. long, radial spines about 12, white, central spines 4–12, thickened at base, brownish; fls. white, to 5 in. long; fr. pear-shaped, ½ in. in diam.

mirabilis: *Setiechinopsis mirabilis.*

Rondonianus Backeb. & Voll. Sts. cylindrical, to 30 in. high and 1 in. thick, ribs 12–18; areoles to ⅜ in. apart, spines 40–50, bristlelike to needle-shaped, yellow, ¼–¾ in. long, central spines 0–2, to 3 in. long; fls. pink, fragrant, to 4½ in. long.

ARTHROPODIUM R. Br. *Liliaceae.* About 10 spp. of tufted, per. herbs, native to Australia, New Zeal., and New Caledonia; roots fibrous and fleshy; lvs. basal; fls. white or purplish, in racemes or panicles, perianth segms. separate, spreading, stamens 6, filaments bearded; fr. a 3-valved caps.

Grown in southern Calif. Propagated by division or seeds.

candidum Raoul. Slender herb, to 14 in.; lvs. narrow-linear, to 10 in. long and ¼ in. wide, grasslike; fls. white, ¼ in. across, in simple racemes. New Zeal.

cirrhatum (G. Forst.) R. Br. Stout herb, to 3 ft.; lvs. lanceolate or oblanceolate, to 2 ft. long and 2½ in. wide, rather fleshy; fls. white, to 1 in. across, in panicles to 1 ft. long; filaments with 2 tendril-like appendages. New Zeal.

ARTHROPTERIS John Sm. *Polypodiaceae.* About 20 spp. of epiphytic ferns, mostly in the temp. and trop. parts of the S. Hemisphere; rhizomes slender, scandent, scaly; petioles remote, jointed at or above the point of attachment to the rhizome, lvs. 1-pinnate, pinnae jointed to rachis, oblique, veins free; sori in one row on each side of midvein, indusia round-reniform or absent.

Propagated by spores or cuttings of rhizomes. For culture see *Ferns.*

tenella (G. Forst.) John Sm. Petiole short, brown, lvs. narrow-lanceolate, long, 1-pinnate, pinnae alt., stalked, long-elliptic or lanceolate, serrate or lobed; sori small, round, one in center of each lobe. New Caledonia, Australia, New Zeal.

ARTHROSTEMA Ruiz & Pav. *Melastomataceae.* About 12 spp. of fragile, succulent, dichotomously branched, per. herbs of trop. Amer.; lvs. opp., petioled, membranous, ovate to ovate-lanceolate, serrulate, 5–7-nerved, those of a pair equal; fls. in loosely branched terminal cymes, calyx lobes broad and short, petals 4, stamens 8; fr. a caps. Distinguished from *Heterocentron* by the calyx lobes and from *Centradenia* by the shape of the lvs.

ciliatum Ruiz & Pav. [*A. fragile* Lindl.]. Sts. weak, to 3 ft. long or more; lvs. 1¼–2½ in. long; fls. 1½ in. across, bright pink, ovary very sparsely glandular-puberulous. Cuba, Jamaica, s. Mex. to Bolivia.

fragile: *A. ciliatum.*

ARTIFICIAL-LIGHT GARDENING: See *House Plants* and *Photoperiod.*

ARTOCARPUS J. R. Forst. & G. Forst. *Moraceae.* About 50 spp. of evergreen or deciduous, monoecious trees, native from trop. Asia to Polynesia; lvs. alt., entire or lobed, pinnately nerved; male fls. in stiff spikes, female fls. in heads; fr. embedded in the fleshy perianth forming a heavy syncarp.

Several species are grown in the tropics for valuable timber or for their edible fruits which are cooked as vegetables. For culture see *Breadfruit.*

altilis (Parkins.) Fosb. [*A. incisus* L.f.]. BREADFRUIT. Evergreen tree, to 60 ft. or more; lvs. ovate, pinnately lobed, to 2 ft. long or more, dark green, shining, thick and leathery; male spikes yellow, club-shaped, to 1 ft. long; fr. round or ovoid, to 8 in. in diam., yellow when ripe, covered with prickles. Malay Pen., now widely cult. in the wet trop. lowlands, especially Polynesia. A highly ornamental tree. The starchy fr. is much used, and the common cvs. are seedless.

elasticus Reinw. ex Blume. Tree, to 100 ft., twigs stout; lvs. ovate, entire to lobed or, when young, 2-pinnately divided, to 16 in. long and 10 in. wide, hairy, petioles 1–3 in. long. Java.

heterophyllus Lam. [*A. integer* (Thunb.) Merrill; *A. integrifolius* of auth., not L.f.]. JACKFRUIT. Tree, to 50 ft. or more, trunk straight; lvs. elliptic to obovate, to 8 in. long, stiff and glossy, entire; fls. borne on trunk and thick brs., male spikes cylindrical or club-shaped, to 4 in. long; fr. oblong, to 2 ft. long, greenish-yellow, turning brownish, covered with hard points. India to Malay Pen., cult. occasionally throughout wet lowland tropics. Requires deep, rich soil. Prop. by seeds but does not transplant easily and should be planted where it is to stand. The unripe fr. is used as a vegetable, the ripe fr. is eaten fresh for the pulp surrounding the seeds. The wood is durable and of good quality.

hirsutus Lam. Tall evergreen tree, to 80 ft.; lvs. broadly elliptic, 6–9 in. long, rough beneath, nearly entire; male spikes pendulous; fr. erect, 2–3 in. long, spines ¼ in. long, perforated, seeds ovoid, hirsute, to ¾ in. long. S. India. Yields an important teaklike timber.

hypargyraeus Hance ex Benth. Tree, brs. rusty-pubescent; lvs. oblong, 3–5 in. long, narrowly acuminate, entire to sinuately toothed, glabrous, shiny above, rough white-tomentose and with primary veins prominently raised beneath; fl. heads obovoid, solitary, on tomentose peduncles, male heads to ½ in. long. S. China, Hong Kong.

incisus: *A. altilis.*

integer: *A. heterophyllus.*

integrifolius: see *A. heterophyllus.*

Lakoocha Roxb. MONKEY JACK. Deciduous tree, to 60 ft., crown dense, brs. villous-tomentose; lvs. oblong or elliptic, 6–12 in. long, entire, pubescent beneath; fr. globose, to 3 in. across, smooth or wrinkled. India to Burma. Cult. for the edible fr. and the durable wood.

odoratissimus Blanco. Tree; lvs. 7–9-lobed, villous beneath, pilose along the veins above, lobes lanceolate; male fls. in a common receptacle, conical; fr. small, globose, with many seeds. Philippine Is.

ARUM L. *Araceae.* Twelve spp. of tuberous, stemless herbs, native to Old World; lvs. oblong to ovate, mostly subhastate to hastate at base, petioles long; spathe showy, loosely convolute below, the blade broad and expanded; fls. unisexual, spadix with a short zone of filiform, rudimentary, sterile fls. above the zone of female fls. and also above the zone of male fls., terminated by a sterile appendage, perianth absent.

Hardy species are noted below. For culture see *Arisaema.*

cornutum: *Sauromatum guttatum.*

creticum Boiss. & Heldr. Tuber subglobose; lf. blades ovate-hastate or -sagittate, 4–5 in. long, petioles 6–9 in. long, widely sheathing to above the middle; peduncle 10–14 in. long, spathe about 7 in. long, tube short, pale green inside, blade to 5½ in. long and 2 in. wide, whitish, spadix with sterile appendage fusiform, to 4 in. long, pale, Crete.

crinitum: *Helicodiceros muscivorus.*

Dracunculus: *Dracunculus vulgaris.*

hygrophilum Boiss. [*Zantedeschia hygrophila* Hort.]. Differs from *A. palaestinum* in having lf. blades oblong-hastate, elongate, spathe with blade smaller, greenish, merely margined purplish, spadix with a sterile appendage slender, cylindrical, and intermediate sterile rudimentary fls. globose at base. Israel to s. Turkey and Cyprus.

italicum Mill. ITALIAN A. A variable sp.; tubers mostly cylindrical or ovoid; lf. blades oblong- to triangular-subhastate, to 12 in. long, midrib pale yellow-green, veins pale and very conspicuous, petioles to 16 in. long; peduncle mostly shorter than petiole, spathe with tube 1½–4 in. long, white to violet, blade 6–12 in. long, pale green or yellowish, variously marked purplish to solid purple, spadix not extending beyond middle of spathe blade, sterile appendage 1–3 in. long, yellow to red-violet; berries scarlet, ⅜ in. in diam. Eng. to s. Eur., Algeria, Turkey, Syria. Frost-hardy. Cv. '**Marmoratum**' [var. *marmoratum* Hort.]. Lf. blades marbled with yellow- to whitish-green, spathes sordid yellow-green, becoming purple toward base. Greece.

maculatum L. CUCKOOPINT, LORDS-AND-LADIES, ADAM-AND-EVE. Similar to *A. italicum* but blooming earlier, and having lf. blades smaller, to but 8 in. long, often black- or purple-spotted, with dark green midrib; peduncle as long as or longer than petiole, spathe to 10 in. long, with sterile appendage often extending beyond middle of spathe blade, dull purple or rarely yellow; berries ³⁄₁₆ in. in diam. Eur. Frost-hardy. Tubers edible if properly cooked. Cv. '**Immaculatum**' [var. *immaculatum* Hort.]. Lf. blade unspotted; spathe with tube basally white inside, spotted purple above, blade solid green or margined purplish inside. Austria.

orientale Bieb. A variable sp. differing from *A. italicum* in having tubers discoid or subglobose, petioles and peduncles green or purple; spadix with sterile appendage purple or reddish to rusty. Yugoslavia to Turkey and Turkmen. Frost-hardy.

palaestinum Boiss. [*Arum sanctum* Hort. Dammann]. BLACK CALLA, SOLOMON'S LILY. Tuber discoid; lf. blades ovate to oblong, sagittate-hastate, to 8 in. long, very veiny, petioles to 12 in. long, flecked with red; peduncle shorter than petiole, spathe to 8 in. long, green outside, tube green or purple inside, blade about 6 in. long, recurved, dark purple on inner surface, spadix with sterile appendage stalked, black-purple, intermediate rudimentary sterile fls. filiform, to ⅜ in. long, laterally compressed at base. Israel.

pictum L.f. BLACK CALLA. Tuber subglobose; lf. blades oblong-ovate, 10 in. long and 3 in. wide, cordate, midrib ⅜ in. wide; petioles stout, 8–10 in. long; peduncle 2–3 in. long, spathe 7 in. long, tube green to white, blade to 8 in. long, purple, spadix extending beyond middle of spathe blade, with no intermediate rudimentary sterile fls., the sterile appendage clavate, 4½ in. long, dark purple. Corsica, Sardinia, Balearic Is.

proboscideum: *Arisarum proboscideum.*

sanctum: *A. palaestinum.*

ARUNCUS Adans. GOATSBEARD. *Rosaceae.* Two or 3 spp. of tall, dioecious, per. herbs of the N. Hemisphere; lvs. 2–3-pinnate, long-petioled; fls. small, white, unisexual, in spikes forming large panicles, sepals and petals 5, stamens many; pistils mostly 3; frs. of separate follicles.

These plants thrive in moist, partially shaded locations; attractive because of the upright panicles of many small flowers. Propagated by seeds.

dioicus (Walt.) Fern. [*A. sylvester* Kostel.; *Spiraea Aruncus* L.]. Four to 7 ft., glabrous or somewhat pubescent; lvs. large, much-divided, lfts. ovate to oblong-lanceolate; panicles 4–16 in. long; fls. ⅛ in. across; fr. body ⅛ in. long. A variable sp., with a number of intergrading geographical and morphological vars. Eurasia and N. Amer. Cv. '**Kneiffii**'. Foliage finely dissected.

sylvester: *A. dioicus.*

ARUNDINA Blume. *Orchidaceae.* Three spp. of terrestrial herbs, native to se. Asia, Ceylon, nw. Malay Arch.; sts. cane-like, leafy; lvs. 2-ranked; infl. terminal; sepals and petals similar, not united, lip large, enclosing column, with fringed keels. For structure of fl. see *Orchidaceae.*

For culture see *Orchids.*

bambusifolia: *A. graminifolia.*

graminifolia (D. Don) Hochr. [*A. bambusifolia* Lindl.]. BAMBOO ORCHID. Sts. erect, to 6 ft.; lvs. linear-lanceolate; sepals and petals white, suffused with pink, to 2 in. long, lip magenta, commonly yellow in throat. Flowering throughout the year. Malay Arch.; cult. and naturalized in Hawaii.

ARUNDINARIA Michx. [*Pleioblastus* Nakai]. BAMBOO, CANE. *Gramineae.* More than 30 spp. of woody grasses of rhizomatous habit in N. Amer. and e. and s. Asia, sts. to 30 ft., erect, branched, flowering branchlets with nearly or quite bladeless sheaths borne in fascicles on the main st. or on

primary brs., bladeless flowering shoots also arising from the rhizomes, flowering sts. apparently dying after setting seed; lf. sheaths on basal part of shoots and primary brs. 6–10, loose, papery, blades narrow, rudimentary, to ¾ in. long, not petioled at base, upper lvs. 4–10, large, petioled, crowded, sheaths overlapping, blades tessellate; spikelets 6–12-fld., large, compressed, rachilla joints rather thick, appressed-hirsute, glumes unequal, shorter than lemma, the first sometimes lacking, lemma papery, rather thin, about 11-nerved, acute to awn-tipped, palea prominently 2-keeled, stamens 3. For terminology see *Gramineae.*

Flowering occurs at infrequent intervals, usually each species over a wide area simultaneously and the flowering period apparently continuing for about a year. Propagated by division or cuttings of underground rhizomes taken in early to late winter before new shoots appear. See *Bamboos.*

amabilis McClure. TONKIN B., TONKIN C., TSINGLI C. Resembles *Pseudosasa japonica*, but differs in having taller (to 40 ft.), more massive (to 2½ in. in diam.), straighter sts., stiffly erect infl., 5–14-fld., distinctly flattened spikelets to 2¾ in. long, borders of all glumes, lemmas, and paleas bearing a fringe of hairs of varying length. China. Known only in cult. Zone 8b. Sts. are the preferred kind for the best split-bamboo fishing rods.

argenteostriata (Regel) Ohwi [*Bambusa argenteostriata* Regel]. Sts. to nearly 10 ft. high, about ½ in. in diam., nodes densely hairy at first, becoming glabrous; st. sheath ciliate; lvs. few to 13, blades lanceolate, variegated or green, 1 ft. long, 1⅜ in. wide, rounded to acute at base, acuminate at apex; spikelets 5–9-fld., to 2¾ in. long. Japan.

disticha Pfitz. [*Bambusa disticha* Mitf.; *B. nana* Hort., not Roxb.; *Sasa disticha* (Mitf.) E. Camus]. DWARF FERN-LEAF B. Sts. slender, to 30 in., fistulose; st. sheaths tessellate, the upper ones tinged with purple; lf. blades to 6 in. long and ⁵⁄₁₆ in. wide, 4–6-nerved, slender-pointed, narrowed into a short petiole, setose-serrulate, bright green on both sides. Japan. Zone 7 (on coasts).

falcata: *Chimonobambusa falcata.*

Falconeri (Hook.f. ex Munro) Benth. & Hook.f. ex Duthie. Sts. tall, internodes to 8 in. long, brs. slender, to about 6 in. long, fascicled at nodes; lvs. thin, blades to 4 in. long and ½ in. wide, striate above, inconspicuously tessellate, sheath glabrous, with elongate ligule but not fringed; infl. brs. to more than 1 ft. long; spikelets with 1 bisexual and a sterile floret in simple racemes, spathes long, sheathing. Nepal.

Fortunei: *A. variegata.*

gigantea (Walt.) Muhlenb. CANEBRAKE B., SOUTHERN C. Sts. to 15 ft. or more, ¾ in. in diam., from rhizomes with or without air canals, sheaths at middle of st. shorter or longer than internodes, brs. several at a node; lf. blades to 1 ft. long and ³⁄₁₆ in. wide or more, rounded at base, densely pubescent on both surfaces or nearly glabrous above; infl. a raceme or simple panicle on shoot from rhizome, crowded toward ends of slender, angled brs.; spikelets few to many on each br., 5–15-fld., to 2 in. long, compact, glumes obtuse to acuminate, lemma scarcely keeled. Se. U.S. Subsp. **gigantea**. The typical subsp.; rhizomes without air canals, not usually turning up at apex to form a st.; sheaths at middle of st. shorter than internode, deciduous; lf. blades nearly glabrous above. Not listed as in cult. Subsp. **tecta** (Walt.) McClure [*A. tecta* (Walt.) Muhlenb.]. SWITCH C., SMALL C. Rhizomes with air canals, usually turning up to form st.; sheaths at middle of st. longer than internode, not deciduous; lf. blades pubescent on both sides; lemma often purplish.

humilis Mitf. [*Pleioblastus humilis* (Mitf.) Nakai; *Sasa humilis* (Mitf.) E. Camus]. Sts. to 3 ft., very slender, narrowly fistulose, green, brs. usually 2–3 at each node; st. sheaths purplish at first; lf. sheaths with 2 clusters of bristles at apex, blades to 6 in. long and ¾ in. wide, 6–10-nerved, long-pointed, rounded at base, scarcely hairy, pale green. Japan.

japonica: *Pseudosasa japonica.*

Metake: *Pseudosasa japonica.*

pumila Mitf. [*Pleioblastus pumilus* (Mitf.) Nakai; *Sasa pumila* (Mitf.) E. Camus]. DWARF B. Sts. slender, to 2 ft., fistulose; st. sheaths tessellate, the upper ones tinged with purple; lf. blades to 6 in. long and ¾ in. wide, 8–10-nerved, usually abruptly long-pointed, rounded at base, serrulate, bright green, slightly hairy on both sides. Japan. Zone 8.

pygmaea (Miq.) Asch. & Graebn. [*Bambusa pygmaea* Miq.; *Sasa pygmaea* Hort.]. PYGMY B. Rhizomatous, sts. to 1 ft., bright green, purple and flattened at top, very slender, cylindrical, internodes about 1 in. long, zigzag, nodes purple, prominent, with a protective band of waxy bloom around the base, brs. 1–2, rather long; lf. blades to 5 in. long and ¾ in. wide, pubescent, bright green, tessellated, petiole well-defined, margins serrate. Japan. Zone 8. One of the smallest bamboos; useful as a ground cover.

Simonii (Carrière) A. Rivière & C. Rivière [*Pleioblastus Simonii* (Carrière) Nakai]. SIMON B. Sts. to 25 ft., hollow, to 1¼ in. in diam. at base, outer ones arching outward; st. sheaths to 10 in. long, purplish when young, rather persistent; lf. blades to 1 ft. long and 1¼ in. wide, 8–14-nerved, long-pointed, broadly cuneate at base, bright green above, often striped white or whitish, glaucescent beneath on 1 side of the midrib, nearly green on the other. Japan. Zone 8. Var. **variegata** Hook.f. [*Pleioblastus Simonii* var. *variegatus* (Hook.f.) Nakai]. Lf. blades striped white.

tecta: *A. gigantea* subsp.

variegata (Siebold ex Miq.) Mak. [*A. Fortunei* (Van Houtte ex Munro) A. Rivière & C. Rivière; *Pleioblastus Fortunei* (Van Houtte ex Munro) Nakai; *P. variegatus* Hort.; *Sasa Fortunei* Hort.]. DWARF WHITE-STRIPE B. Dwarf, with vigorous rhizomes, sts. to 3 ft., internodes to 1 in. long; lf. blades to 5 in. long and ¾ in. wide, 6–10-nerved, striped with white. Japan. Zones 7 and 8, on coasts.

viridistriata (Siebold ex André) Mak. ex Nakai [*Pleioblastus viridistriatus* (Siebold ex André) Mak.]. Sts. to 2½ ft., slender, dark purplish-green, fistulose; lf. sheaths minutely and irregularly ciliate, sparsely fimbriate or naked at apex, blades to 8 in. long and 1¼ in. wide, 10–12-nerved, abruptly long-pointed, rounded at base, serrulate, striped green and golden-yellow, at first sparingly puberulous above, softly pubescent beneath. Japan. Zone 8. Prefers partial shade; needs winter mulch in the North. The same material may also be known by the hort. names *Bambusa argentea*, *Phyllostachys argentea*, or *P. argenteostriata*.

ARUNDINELLA Raddi. *Gramineae.* More than 50 spp. of usually per. grasses in warmer regions of both hemispheres; infl. an open or contracted panicle or raceme; spikelets 2-fld., glumes unequal, 3–5-nerved, lemma of upper floret glabrous, usually scaberulous, minutely 2-lobed at the apex, with the lobes sometimes prolonged into short capillary bristles, awned between the lobes or awnless, callus hairy, lower floret male. For terminology see *Gramineae.*

Ecklonii: *A. nepalensis.*

nepalensis Trin. [*A. Ecklonii* Nees]. Sts. to 4 ft., erect, glabrous; lf. blades flat or convolute, linear, tapering to a fine point, to over 1 ft. long, to ⁵⁄₁₆ in. wide, rigid, glabrous, the margins rough; panicle linear-oblong to oblong, contracted or open, to 1 ft. long, brs. solitary or in pairs, rarely 3–4 in a whorl, stiff, scabrous; spikelets ¼ in. long, lower glume ovate-oblong, mucronate, to ¼ in. long, 3-nerved or rarely 4–5-nerved, upper glume ovate-lanceolate, to ⅜ in. long, 7-nerved, palea linear-oblong, shorter, keels winged below, scaberulous above, awn tenuous, minutely bearded. S. Afr.

ARUNDO L. *Gramineae.* About 6 spp. of tall per. reeds in trop. and subtrop. Old World; lf. blades broad, linear; panicles large, plumelike, terminal; spikelets several-fld., summits of all florets about equal, rachilla glabrous, disarticulating above the glumes and between the florets, glumes thin, 3-nerved, narrow, tapered, about as long as the spikelet, lemma thin, 3-nerved, long-pilose, gradually tapered, awned from central nerve, other nerves ending in slender teeth. For terminology see *Gramineae.*

conspicua G. Forst.: *Chionochloa conspicua* (G. Forst.) Zotov. Not cult. Material cult. as *Arundo conspicua* is *Cortaderia Richardii.*

Donax L. GIANT REED, CARRIZO, CAÑA BRAVA. Sts. to 18 ft., stout, in large clumps, little-branched, rhizomes thick; lf. blades many, conspicuously 2-ranked, elongate, to 2¾ in. wide, margin scabrous; panicle to 2 ft. long, greenish or purplish, dense; spikelets ½ in. long. Medit. region; introd. and naturalized in Ark. and Tex., w. to s. Calif., occasionally on e. coast from Md. s.; also in trop. Amer. Often planted to control erosion; sts. are a source of reeds for musical instruments and are much used in wattlework. Var. **variegata:** var. *versicolor.* Var. **versicolor** (Mill.) J. Stokes [var. *variegata* Hort. Vilm.-Andr.]. Blades with white stripes.

ASARINA Quer [*Lophospermum* D. Don; *Maurandya* Ort.]. *Scrophulariaceae.* About 15 spp. of tender, per. herbs, of N. Amer. and Eur.; mostly climbing by means of coiling petioles; lvs. triangular or halberd-shaped; fls. axillary, showy, 2-lipped, white, rose, purple and blue. Distinguished from *Antirrhinum* by their climbing habit and symmetrical (not oblique) caps.

Asarinas flower freely in winter in a cool greenhouse; but if the seed is sown early, they bloom the first summer and may be grown in baskets or window boxes in the open. Propagated by seeds or cuttings, the cuttings taken any time after mid-Jan.

antirrhinifolia (Humb. & Bonpl.) Penn. [*Maurandya antirrhinifolia* Humb. & Bonpl.]. Plant glabrous; lvs. deltoid, ¾–1¼ in. long, hastate at base, entire; corolla about ¾ in. long, purple or white, with distinct, yellow palate. Tex. to Calif., through Mex. Grows mostly in limey soils.

Barclaiana (Lindl.) Penn. [*Maurandya Barclaiana* Lindl.]. Lvs. mostly ¾ in. long, broadly hastate at base, glabrous, entire; calyx segms. long-attenuate, glandular-pilose, corolla 1–1¼ in. long, pink, becoming deep purple, purple-downy outside, palate lacking. Mex. A showy vine growing to 10 ft. or more in fl.

erubescens (D. Don) Penn. [*Maurandya erubescens* (D. Don) A. Gray]. CREEPING GLOXINIA. Plant densely soft-glandular-pubescent, grayish-green; lvs. 1½–3 in. long, deltoid-toothed; calyx lobes ¾–1 in. long, leaflike, corolla 2–3 in. long, rose-pink, lobes obtuse or notched; seeds winged. Mex. Much material grown as *A. scandens* or *Maurandya scandens* is this sp.

filipes (A. Gray) Penn. [*Antirrhinum filipes* A. Gray]. Slender, glabrous twiner; lvs. linear, ¼–⅜ in. long; fls. on threadlike pedicels 2–3 in. long, resembling miniature snapdragon fls., corolla about ½ in. long, yellow with black-dotted throat. Ariz. and Utah. w. to Pacific Coast.

Lophospermum (L. H. Bailey) Penn. [*Lophospermum scandens* D. Don; *Maurandya Lophospermum* L. H. Bailey; *M. scandens* (D. Don) A. Gray, not (Cav.) Pers.]. Differs from *A. erubescens* in having plant glabrate or weakly pubescent, green; and fls. rose-purple. Mex.

procumbens Mill. [*Antirrhinum Asarina* L.]. Procumbent sticky-pubescent per.; lvs. 1–2 in. long, reniform, coarsely dentate; fls. solitary in lf. axils, on pedicels as long as fl.; corolla 1¼–1½ in. long, pale to rose-pink. Iberian Pen. Hardy to Philadelphia; suited to rock garden and can be grown as ann.

Purpusii (Brandeg.) Penn. [*Maurandya purpurea* Hort.]. Glabrous per., flopping but not climbing; lvs. deltoid, coarsely dentate; fls. in lf. axils, on pedicels longer than corollas, calyx lobes ½ in. long, broadly oblong, leaflike, corolla 1½–1¾ in. long, rose-red, lacking palate. Mex. Cult. as an ann.; attractive, but not much cult.

purpurea: *A. Purpusii.*

scandens (Cav.) Penn. [*Maurandya scandens* (Cav.) Pers.]. Similar to *A. Barclaiana*, but having calyx lobes glabrous, corolla funnelform, 1½–2 in. long, lavender, with tube paler than the spreading lobes. Mex. Most material listed as *A. scandens* or *Maurandya scandens* is *A. erubescens.*

ASARUM L. [*Hexastyles* Raf.]. WILD GINGER, ASARA-BACCA. *Aristolochiaceae.* About 75 spp. of N. Temp. Zone (mainly Japanese), per., rhizomatous, stemless herbs; lvs. mostly cordate, long-petioled; fls. purplish or brown, borne singly near surface of ground, calyx corollalike, campanulate, regular, 3-parted, corolla vestigial or none, stamens 12; fr. a fleshy, globose caps.

Planted in shaded wild gardens. They require moist rich soil and are propagated by division and by seeds.

arifolium Michx. [*Hexastylis arifolia* (Michx.) Small]. Evergreen; lvs. arrow-shaped, to 5 in. long, usually mottled, petioles to 8 in. long; fls. 1 in. long, contracted at throat. Late spring. Va., s. to Fla. and Ala.

canadense L. WILD GINGER, SNAKEROOT. Deciduous; lvs. 2, to 7 in. across, pubescent, petioles to 1 ft. long; fls. brownish-purple, 1 in. across. Spring, New Bruns., s. to N.C. and Mo.

caudatum Lindl. Evergreen, rhizome slender, elongate; lvs. 2, to 6 in. across, petioles to 7 in. long; fls. brownish-purple, calyx lobes prolonged into tails to 2 in. long. Summer. B.C. to Calif.

europaeum L. Evergreen; lvs. 2, to 3 in. across, uniformly green, glossy, petioles to 5 in. long; fls. greenish-purple or brown, ½ in. long. Eur.

Hartwegii S. Wats. Evergreen, rhizome stoutish, rather closely scaly; lvs. to 5 in. across, mottled with white, petiole to 8 in. long; fls. brownish-purple, ½ in. across, calyx lobes prolonged into tails to 2½ in. long. Ore. and Calif.

Shuttleworthii Britten & Bak.f. [*Hexastylis Shuttleworthii* (Britten & Bak.f.) Small]. Evergreen; lvs. 1–2, to 3 in. across, usually mottled, petioles to 8 in. long; fls. mottled with violet inside, to 2 in. long. Early summer. Va., s. to Ga. and Ala.

virginicum L. [*Hexastylis virginica* (L.) Small]. Evergreen; lvs. 1–3, to 3 in. across, usually mottled, petioles to 7 in. long; fls. purple, to 1 in. long. Late spring. Va., s. to S.C. and Tenn.

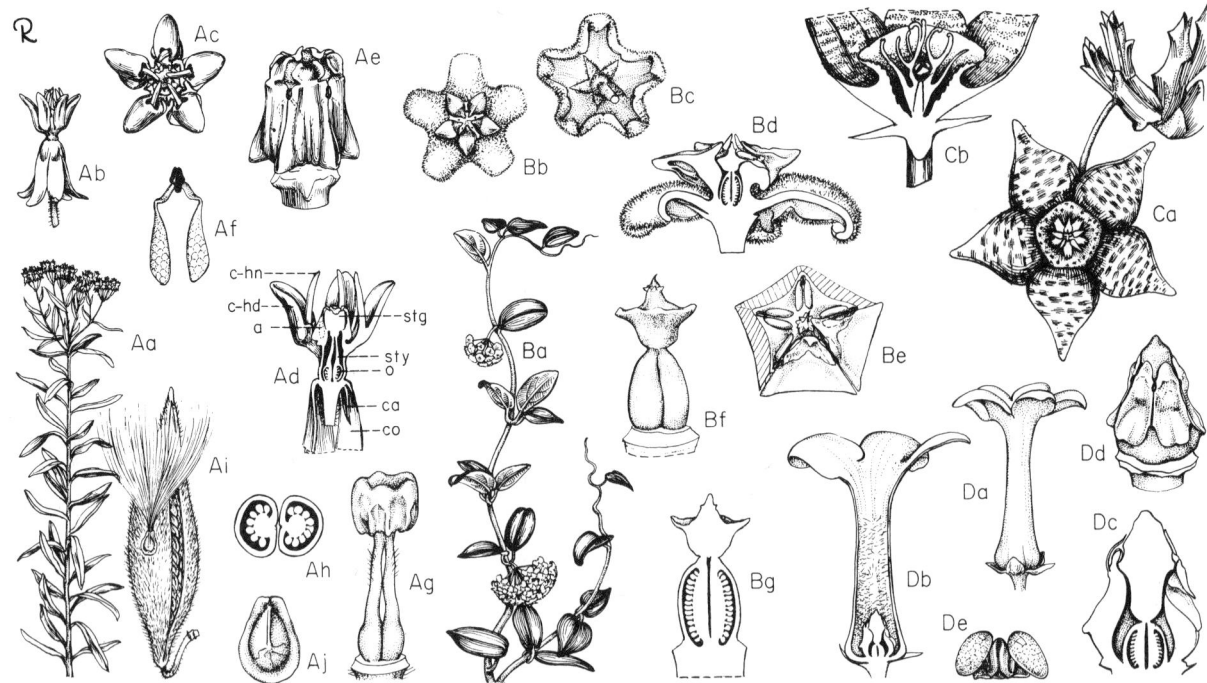

ASCLEPIADACEAE. **A,** *Asclepias tuberosa:* **Aa,** flowering stem, much reduced; **Ab,** flower, side view, × 1; **Ac,** flower, face view, × 2; **Ad,** flower, vertical section (corolla partly cut away), × 2; **Ae,** anthers, × 5; **Af,** pair of pollinia connected by gland, × 8; **Ag,** pistil, × 5; **Ah,** ovaries, cross section, × 10; **Ai,** fruit and seed with tuft of hairs, × ½; **Aj,** seed, × 2. **B,** *Hoya carnosa:* **Ba,** flowering stem, much reduced; **Bb,** flower, face view, × 1; **Bc,** flower, back view, × 1; **Bd,** flower, vertical section, × 2; **Be,** detail of center of flower (three corona lobes removed to show pollinia and stigma), × 5; **Bf,** pistil, × 5; **Bg,** pistil, vertical section, × 5. **C,** *Stapelia variegata:* **Ca,** flowering branch, × ½; **Cb,** flower, vertical section, × 1. **D,** *Stephanotis floribunda:* **Da,** flower, × ½; **Db,** flower, vertical section, × ⅗; **Dc,** corona, staminal column, and pistil, vertical section, × 3; **Dd,** anthers and stigma, × 2½; **De,** pollinia, much enlarged. (a anther, ca calyx, co corolla, c-hn corona horn, o ovary, stg stigma, sty style.) (Ca, Cb from Bailey, *Manual of Cultivated Plants,* ed. 2.)

ASCLEPIADACEAE R.Br. MILKWEED FAMILY. Dicot.; about 130 genera and 2,000 spp. of per. herbs, shrubs, and vines, often succulent and with reduced or obsolete lvs., mostly with milky sap, widely distributed, particularly in the tropics and subtropics; lvs. generally opp. or whorled, simple, usually entire, without stipules; infl. cymose, but often appearing umbelliform; fls. regular, bisexual, calyx deeply 5-lobed, corolla 5-lobed, often with an annulus at the throat, stamens 5, filaments coherent into a tube basally, united to the corolla tube and bearing 1 or 2 whorls of appendages of various forms that are collectively termed the corona, anthers winged, united to the stigma, sometimes with apical appendages, pollen of each anther cell aggregated into a waxy mass (pollinium), ovaries superior, 2, the 2 carpels being free at the base but joined at the apex in a common stigma; fr. a pair of follicles (or 1, by abortion), seeds mostly many, with tuft of hairs at apex. The cult. genera are: *Araujia, Asclepias, Calotropis, Caralluma, Ceropegia, Cryptostegia, Cynanchum, Diplocyatha, Dischidia, Duvalia, Echidnopsis, Edithcolea, Gonolobus, Hoodia, Hoodiopsis, Hoya, Huernia, Huerniopsis, Marsdenia, Matelea, Oxypetalum, Pectinaria, Periploca, Piaranthus, Sarcostemma, Stapelia, Stapelianthus, Stephanotis, Stultitia,* and *Tavaresia.*

ASCLEPIAS L. [*Asclepiodora* A. Gray]. MILKWEED, SILKWEED, BUTTERFLY FLOWER. *Asclepiadaceae.* About 200 spp. of mostly per. herbs, widely distributed, but principally in N. Amer. and Afr.; sap generally milky; lvs. simple, opp., or sometimes whorled or more or less alt.; fls. in axillary or terminal umbellate cymes, rarely solitary, corolla white, yellowish, red, or purple, rotate, lobes 5, valvate, generally reflexed and hiding the calyx at flowering, corona present, with 5 hoodlike lobes variable in size, shape, and position, each with or without a horn; follicles generally paired and erect on deflexed or erect pedicels, seeds usually with tuft of hairs.

Mostly summer blooming; of easy cultivation in the wild garden or border; may have an attractive habit, showy flowers, and ornamental fruits. Propagated by division or by seeds.

amplexicaulis Sm. Per. herbs, to 3 ft., sts. stout, simple; lvs. opp., sessile, often clasping, ovate to oblong-lanceolate; infl. usually terminal, peduncles longer than lvs., corolla greenish or suffused purple or rose, lobes nearly ½ in. long, hoods stalked, tubular-cucullate, indistinctly toothed, to ¼ in. long, each with a horn half again as long; follicles narrow-fusiform, 4–6 in. long. New Eng. to Nebr., s. to Fla. and Tex.

asperula (Decne.) Woodson. Low per. herbs, sts. clustered from stout rootstock; lvs. irregularly alt., linear to linear-lanceolate, 4–8 in. long; infl. terminal, many-fld., corolla yellowish-green, sometimes flushed purple, lobes ⅜–½ in. long, hoods broadly clavate-falciform, abruptly deflexed but with ascending tips; follicles narrow-fusiform, 2–5 in. long, smooth. Subsp. **asperula** The typical subsp.; lvs. mostly linear-lanceolate; infl. peduncled; hoods dark purple. Idaho and Colo., s. to New Mex. Subsp. **capricornu** (Woodson) Woodson [*Asclepiodora decumbens* (Nutt.) A. Gray]. Lvs. more broadly lanceolate; infl. sessile or subsessile; hoods usually greenish-cream. Kans. to cent. and e. Tex.

Cornuti: *A. syriaca.*

curassavica L. BLOODFLOWER. Glabrescent ann., to 3½ ft., sts. simple or branched; lvs. opp., elliptic-lanceolate, to 5 in. long; infls. axillary, corolla bright crimson, rarely yellow or white, lobes about ⅜ in. long, hoods orange, cucullate, each with a needlelike horn nearly ¼ in. long; follicles fusiform, about 4 in. long. Probably native to S. Amer., now a pantrop. weed.

eriocarpa Benth. Hoary-tomentose per., to 3 ft., sts. simple; lvs. opp. or whorled, nearly sessile, oblong to ovate, to 8 in. long; infls. axillary, corolla greenish or yellowish, sometimes flushed rose on exterior, lobes to ⅜ in. long, hoods about ⅛ in. long, ovate, each with a curved horn completely fused to it; follicles fusiform, to 4 in. long, smooth, densely white-tomentose. Calif. and Baja Calif.

exaltata L. [*A. phytolaccoides* Pursh]. Stout-stemmed per., to 3 ft.; lvs. opp., ovate to oblong-elliptic, to 8 in. long; infls. subterminal, peduncles shorter than lvs., corolla white, usually flushed rose or purple on exterior, lobes to ½ in. long, hoods stalked, tubular-cucullate, more or less minutely toothed, to ⅛ in. long, each with a horn about

¼ in. long and fused to it below the middle; follicles fusiform, 5–6 in. long. Me. to Ga., w. to Minn. and Iowa.

fruticosa L. [*Gomphocarpus fruticosa* (L.) R. Br.]. Branching, suffrutescent per., 3–6 ft.; lvs. opp., subsessile, lanceolate to oblanceolate, to 5 in. long; infls. axillary, corolla white, lobes about ¼ in. long; hoods folded, with 2 curved lobes at apex, without horns; follicles ovoid, to 3 in. long, softly filiform-spinescent. Afr.; naturalized in waste places in Jamaica and S. Amer.

Hallii A. Gray. Distinguished from *A. purpurascens* by its more or less alt., lanceolate to narrowly ovate, acute or acuminate lvs. and slightly smaller fl. parts. Wyo. to Colo., s. to Nev. and n. Ariz.

incarnata L. SWAMP M. Rather stout-stemmed per., to 5 ft.; lvs. opp., linear to ovate-elliptic, 2–6 in. long; infls. usually in pairs in the upper axils, corolla pink, rarely white, lobes about ⅛ in. long, hoods stalked, cucullate, each with a curved horn; follicles erect on erect pedicels, fusiform, to about 3½ in. long. Wet areas; Nov. Sc. to Fla. and Utah. Subsp. **pulchra** (J. F. Ehrh. ex Willd.) Woodson [*A. pulchra* J. F. Ehrh. ex Willd.]. Generally pubescent, sts. little-branched; lvs. mostly broadly ovate to ovate-elliptic. Nov. Sc. to S.C.; adventive further s. and inland.

lanceolata Walt. Per., to 4 ft., rootstock tuberous, sts. slender; lvs. opp., linear-lanceolate, to 10 in. long; infl. terminal, few-fld.; corolla dull red, lobes to ⅜ in. long, hoods broadly oblong with incised margins, to ¼ in. long, longer than the horns; follicles fusiform, about 4 in. long. N.J., s. to Fla. and e. Tex.

latifolia Raf. Per., to 2 ft., sts. mostly simple; lvs. opp., scarcely petioled, broadly rounded-obovate, to 6 in. long, often retuse; infls. nearly sessile in the upper axils, corolla pale green, sometimes tinged purple, lobes to ⅜ in. long, hoods 4-angled, about ⅛ in. long, each with a horn entirely fused to it; follicles broadly fusiform, to 3 in. long, smooth, glabrous. Nebr. to sw. U.S.

mexicana Cav. Per., to 2½ ft., sts. slender; lvs. in whorls of 4–6, elliptic or elliptic-lanceolate, to 5 in. long; infls. clustered or paired in upper axils, fls. small, corolla white but more or less suffused purple, lobes to ¼ in. long, hoods stalked, cucullate, longer than the needlelike horns; follicles fusiform, 3–4 in. long. Cent. Mex.

ovalifolia Decne. Similar to *A. syriaca,* but with sts. more slender, lvs. to 3 in. long, fls. in loose clusters, corolla greenish-white to purple-tinged, and follicles smooth. Sask., Man., Wisc., s. to N. and S. Dak.

physocarpa (E. H. Mey.) Schlechter [*Gomphocarpus physocarpus* E. H. Mey.]. White-pubescent, suffrutescent per., to 6 ft.; lvs. linear-lanceolate to lanceolate, 2–4 in. long; infls. axillary, corolla white, lobes about ¼ in. long, hoods 4-angled, short-lobed at the apex, about ⅛ in. long, without horns; follicles solitary, subglobose, inflated, to 2½ in. in diam., soft-bristly. S. Afr.

phytolaccoides: *A. exaltata.*

pulchra: *A. incarnata* subsp.

pumila (A. Gray) Vail. Cespitose per., to 1 ft.; lvs. alt. or the lower ones whorled, sessile, ascending, filiform, to 1¾ in. long; infls. terminal and in upper axils, corolla white or faintly suffused rose or yellowish-green, lobes to ⅛ in. long, hoods stalked, cucullate, about 1⁄16 in. long, each with a horn twice as long; follicles narrow-fusiform, 1¾–3 in. long. Great Plains, N. Dak. to Wyo., s. to New Mex. and Tex.

purpurascens L. PURPLE M. Per., to 3 ft.; lvs. opp., ovate to oblong-lanceolate, to 8 in. long, dark green above, densely pubescent beneath; infls. usually terminal, corolla deep rose, lobes to ⅜ in. long, hoods oblong-elliptic, acute or acuminate, about ¼ in. long; follicles narrow-fusiform, to 6 in. long, smooth. Thickets and open woods, s. Ont., New Hamp. to Va. and e. Kan.

quadrifolia Jacq. Per., mostly less than 2 ft., sts. slender; lvs. opp. or congested and appearing whorled, ovate to ovate-elliptic, to 6 in. long; infl. terminal, corolla pale pink or cream, lobes about ¼ in. long, hoods stalked, cucullate, with pronounced small marginal lobes, 3⁄16 in. long, each hood with a slightly longer horn; follicles fusiform, 3–5 in. long. Ont. and N.Y. to Ga. and e. Tex.

rubra L. Per., to 3 ft., sts. slender; lvs. opp., sessile or subsessile, narrowly lanceolate to ovate, to 6½ in. long; infls. terminal and axillary, corolla dull red to purplish or lavender, lobes to ⅜ in. long, hoods stalked, lanceolate, marginally incised, to ¼ in. long, each with a somewhat shorter horn; follicles fusiform, to 5 in. long. N.J. to Ga. and Tex.

speciosa Torr. Similar to *A. purpurascens,* but densely white-tomentose, and having infls. axillary, corolla purple-rose, lobes sometimes more than ½ in. long, hoods spreading, ⅜–½ in. long, and follicles smooth or spiny. Canada and w. U.S.

subulata Decne. *Ephedra*-like undershrubs, to 6 ft.; lvs. linear or filiform, soon deciduous; infls. axillary, corolla yellowish-white, lobes nearly ½ in. long, hoods tapering to a solid stalk, broadly obovate-fan-shaped, to ½ in. long, each with a horn fused to it and reduced to an

undulate crest; follicles on pendulous or subpendulous pedicels, fusiform, to 5 in. long. Deserts, Calif., Ariz., Nev.; Baja Calif., Sonora (Mex.).

Sullivantii Engelm. ex A. Gray. Per., to 3 ft., sts. stout, glabrous, often glaucous; lvs. opp., sessile or nearly so, ovate to oblong-lanceolate, to 6 in. long; infls. axillary, corolla purplish-rose, lobes nearly ½ in. long, hoods broadly ovate, cucullate, each with a slightly shorter horn; follicles about 4 in. long, more or less spiny. Ont. to Minn., s. to Nebr., and Okla.

syriaca L. [*A. syriaca* var. *kansana* (Vail) Palmer & Steyerm.; *A. syriaca* forma *leucantha* Dore; *A. Cornuti* Decne.]. Coarse, per. herbs, 3–6 ft., sts. mostly simple; lvs. opp., ovate to oblong-elliptic, 3–12 in. long; infls. solitary in upper axils, corolla rose or purple, rarely white, lobes to ⅜ in. long, hoods stalked, ovate, nearly ¼ in. long, each with a shorter horn; follicles narrowly to broadly fusiform, 3–5 in. long, smooth or soft-spinulose. New Bruns. to Man., s. to Ga. and Okla.

tuberosa L. BUTTERFLY WEED, PLEURISY ROOT, TUBERROOT, IN-DIAN PAINTBRUSH, CHIGGER FLOWER. Mostly hispid per., to 3 ft., sts. stout, rootstock woody; lvs. more or less spiral and crowded, narrowly lanceolate to oblanceolate, to 4½ in. long; infls. in upper axils, corolla orange or occasionally red or yellow, lobes to 5⁄16 in. long, hoods cucullate, stalked, lanceolate, to ¼ in. long, with short tooth on each lateral margin; follicles narrowly fusiform, to 6 in. long. New Eng. to N. Dak., s. to Fla., Ariz., n. Mex. Dried root has medicinal properties.

verticillata L. HORSETAIL M. Similar to *A. mexicana,* but having lvs. chiefly 3–4 in a whorl, rarely opp., linear, to 3 in. long; infls. solitary or paired in upper axils; hoods usually shorter than stigma, horns twice as long as hoods. E. and cent. U.S.

vestita Hook. & Arn. Per., to 2 ft., sts. simple, clustered from the rootstock, tomentose when young; lvs. opp., short-petioled, lanceolate to ovate-elliptic, to 5 in. long, somewhat succulent; infls. mostly terminal, corolla yellowish-white, suffused purple, lobes ¼–⅜ in. long, hoods obtriangular, truncate, 1⁄16–⅛ in. long, each with a curved horn; follicles broadly fusiform, apiculate, to 3½ in. long. Calif.

viridifolia Raf. Per., to nearly 3 ft., sts. unbranched; lvs. opp. or more or less alt., linear to suborbicular, to 5 in. long; infls. subterminal, corolla pale green, lobes to ¼ in. long, hoods deeply saccate, oblong, about 3⁄16 in. long, without horns; follicles fusiform, to 6 in. long. Mass. to Ga., w. to Man., Ariz., n. Mex.

ASCLEPIODORA: *ASCLEPIAS.* Asclepiodora decumbens: *Asclepias asperula* subsp. *capricornu.*

ASCOCENTRUM Schlechter. *Orchidaceae.* Five spp. of epiphytes, native to se. Asia and Malay Arch.; st. short, leafy; lvs. many, linear; infl. an erect, lateral, densely many-fld., short-peduncled raceme; sepals and petals similar, lip spurred, 3-lobed, lateral lobes erect, pressed against column, midlobe strap-shaped. For structure of fl. see *Orchidaceae.*

For culture see *Orchids.*

ampullaceum (Lindl.) Schlechter [*Saccolabium ampullaceum* Lindl.]. St. to 10 in. long, usually much shorter; lvs. leathery, linear, deeply toothed at apex, to 6 in. long; racemes dense, shorter than lvs.; fls. ¾–1 in. across, bright rose-carmine, sepals and petals ½ in. long, oblong, midlobe of lip 3⁄16 in. long, tongue-shaped. Early spring–early summer. Himalayas, Burma, China.

curvifolium (Lindl.) Schlechter [*Saccolabium curvifolium* Lindl.]. St. to 4 in. long; lvs. very fleshy, to 8 in. long, lobed and toothed at apex; infl. to 5 in. long; fls. ¾ in. across, bright orange or orange-yellow, sepals and petals ¼ in. long, elliptic, lateral lobes of lip triangular, midlobe bent downwards, ¼ in. long. Himalayas to Java.

Hendersonianum (Rchb.f.) Schlechter [*Saccolabium Hendersonianum* Rchb.f.]. Vegetatively similar to *A. ampullaceum,* but lvs. fleshy, tongue-shaped, to 5 in. long, pointed; racemes dense, to 5 in. long; fls. to ¾ in. across, sepals and petals obovate or elliptic, carmine, lip white, midlobe reduced to a small tooth. Late spring–summer. Borneo.

miniatum (Lindl.) Schlechter [*Saccolabium miniatum* Lindl.]. Lvs. smaller and stiffer than in *A. ampullaceum;* fls. nearly 1 in. across, orange-red or clear yellow, sepals and petals elliptic, lip with oblong midlobe ¼ in. long. Winter–early summer, autumn. Java, Philippine Is.

ASCOTAINIA Ridl. *Orchidaceae.* Ten spp. of terrestrial herbs, native to India, China, w. Malay Arch.; pseudobulbs 1-lvd.; infl. a raceme on scape arising from rhizome; sepals and petals similar, lip entire or 3-lobed, usually with 3–5 keels. For structure of fl. see *Orchidaceae.*

For culture see *Orchids.*

viridifusca (Hook.f.) Schlechter [*Tainia viridifusca* (Hook.f.) Benth.]. Lvs. up to 20 in. long and 3 in. wide; scapes 1½ ft. or more high; sepals and petals brownish-olive-green, lip yellowish-white. Late winter. China, Burma.

ASCYRUM: *HYPERICUM.*

ASIMINA Adans. *Annonaceae.* Eight spp. of shrubs and small trees, native to N. Amer.; lvs. alt., simple; fls. axillary, nodding, white or purplish, bisexual, sepals 3, petals 6, in 2 series, stamens many, short, pistils 3–15; fr. an ellipsoid to oblong berry.

One species is sometimes cultivated. It thrives in rich moist soil and is hardy in Zone 5. Propagated by seeds sown in autumn or stratified, and by layering or root cuttings.

triloba (L.) Dunal. PAWPAW. Deciduous tree, to 30 ft.; lvs. obovate-oblong, to 1 ft. long, drooping; fls. purple, to 2 in. across, appearing before the lvs.; fr. fleshy, edible, 3–5 in. long, green becoming brown, seeds compressed. N.Y. to Fla. and Tex.

ASPALATHUS L. *Leguminosae* (subfamily *Faboideae*). Over 200 spp. of evergreen shrubs or subshrubs, native to S. Afr.; lvs. mostly needlelike, in groups of 3's, or solitary, or in clusters; fls. in terminal racemes or spikes, or solitary and lateral, mostly yellow, papilionaceous, stamens 10, united basally; fr. a small, somewhat flat legume, seeds few.

Ornamental, grown in cool greenhouse, or outdoors in mild climates; propagated by seeds.

sarcodes Vogel ex Benth. Glabrous shrub, to 4 ft. high and wide; lvs. linear, to ½ in. long, mucronate; fls. 1 or 2, terminal, with broadly ovate bracteoles, sepals obtuse, broadly ovate, corolla ¾ in. long; fr. oblique, lanceolate, 1 in. long. S. Afr.

ASPARAGUS L. [*Myrsiphyllum* Willd.]. *Liliaceae.* Between 100 and 300 spp. of per. herbs, woody vines, or shrubs, native to the Old World, rootstock matted or tuberous-rooted, sts. spreading, erect, or climbing; true lvs. scalelike, subtending narrow, green, leaflike branchlets (cladophylls); fls. bisexual or unisexual, greenish, white, or yellowish, solitary, paired, or in racemes or umbels; perianth segms. 6, separate or united basally, stamens 6, filaments arising from base of perianth segms., anthers versatile; fr. a berry.

The decorative kinds are of easy culture, but most are tender, and are commonly grown under glass or other cover. Propagated by seeds and division, and woody kinds also by cuttings. One species, *A. officinalis,* is an important vegetable; for its culture, see *Asparagus.*

acutifolius L. Branching shrub, to 5 ft., with wiry, somewhat woody sts.; cladophylls in clusters of 4–12, cylindrical, ¼ in. long, spine-tipped; fls. unisexual, yellow, solitary or paired; fr. olive-green, waxy. Medit. region.

africanus Lam. [*A. Cooperi* Bak.]. Sts. woody, spiny, forming low bushes to 3 ft., or climbing to 40 ft.; roots fibrous; cladophylls in clusters of 8–20, subulate, to ⅜ in. long; fls. bisexual, mostly in axillary clusters of 2–3, but sometimes up to 20, white; fr. red. S. Afr. and S.-W. Afr.

asparagoides (L.) W. F. Wight [*A. medeoloides* (L.f.) Thunb.; *Medeola asparagoides* L.; *Myrsiphyllum asparagoides* (L.) Willd.; *Smilax asparagoides* Hort.]. SMILAX A., SMILAX of florists. Tuberous-rooted branching vine; cladophylls alt., ovate, to 2 in. long, leathery, with many longitudinal veins; fls. bisexual, solitary or paired, stamens orange; fr. red. S. Afr. Cv. **'Myrtifolius'** [*Smilax myrtifolia* Hort.]. BABY SMILAX. A more graceful form, with smaller cladophylls.

Cooperi: *A. africanus.*

crispus Lam. Tuberous-rooted small shrub, with climbing, flexuous, herbaceous sts.; cladophylls in clusters of 3, linear; fls. bisexual, solitary, whitish, anthers orange or vermilion; fr. whitish. S. Afr.

cupressoides: *A. setaceus* cv.

deflexus Bak. Sts. woody, much-branched, climbing; lvs. modified into deflexed, spurlike spines, cladophylls in clusters of 6–10, subulate, to ⅜ in. long; fls. 1–2 in lf. axils. Angola. Material offered under this name may be *A. scandens* var. *deflexus.*

densiflorus (Kunth) Jessop [*A. myriocladus* Bak.; *A. sarmentosus* Bak., not L.]. Tuberous, sts. woody, erect, weakly decumbent, or weakly twining, finely ridged, glabrous, to 3 ft., somewhat spiny; cladophylls solitary or sometimes 3 or more at a node, linear, usually flattened, slightly curved, 1-nerved; fls. bisexual, white or pale pink, in axillary racemes; fr. red. S. Afr. A very variable sp. The typical form, with cladophylls usually solitary, to ⅝ in. long, is probably not in cult. Cv. **'Myers'** [*A. Myersii* Hort.]. Sts. stiffly erect or spreading, very densely short-branched, to 2 ft., forming narrow plumes to 2½ in. wide, tapering very gradually to the apex; cladophylls 3–4 at a node, to ⅜ in. long, dark green. Cv. **'Sprengeri'** [*A. Sprengeri* Regel]. SPRENGER A., SPRENGERI, EMERALD FERN, EMERALD-FEATHER. Sts. flexuous and drooping, loosely branched, to 3 ft., brs. spreading, to 5 in. long; cladophylls 1–6 but usually 3 at a node, ⅜–1¼ in. long. This cv. is the most commonly cult. of all ornamental asparaguses; grown for its graceful, airy masses of "foliage" in pots, urns, hanging baskets, and window boxes. Cv. **'Sprengeri Deflexus'** [*A. Sprengeri* cv. 'Deflexus']. Similar to cv. 'Sprengeri', but cladophylls broader, with metallic luster. Cv. **'Sprengeri Nanus'** [*A. Sprengeri* cv. Nanus']. Similar to cv. 'Sprengeri', but dwarfer. Cv. **'Sprengeri Robustus'** [*A. Sprengeri* cv. 'Robustus']. Stronger-growing than cv. 'Sprengeri'.

falcatus L. SICKLE THORN. Sts. woody, climbing, to 40 ft.; true lvs. modified into rigid spines; cladophylls in clusters, linear-lanceolate, curved, to 2 in. long, bright green, 1-nerved; fls. bisexual, white, fragrant, in racemes to 2 in. long; fr. brown. Ceylon, trop. and se. Afr.

filicinus Buch.-Ham. ex D. Don. Sts. tall, erect, unarmed; cladophylls in clusters of 2–5, to 5/16 in. long, curved; fls. bisexual and unisexual, green, spreading, solitary or paired, stamens white; fr. black. India, China.

Macowanii Bak. Fibrous-rooted, sts. erect, to 6 ft., woody, smooth or somewhat grooved, glabrous, white, branched; cladophylls clustered, many, cylindrical, curved, to ½ in. long; fls. clustered. S. Afr. Commonly but mistakenly cult. under the names *A. myriocladus* and *A. retrofractus.*

medeoloides: *A. asparagoides.*

Myersii: *A. densiflorus* cv.

myriocladus: *A. densiflorus,* but material cult. as *A. myriocladus* is usually *A. Macowanii.*

officinalis L. COMMON A., GARDEN A. Rhizomatous herb, to 5 ft., sts. ann., much-branched, unarmed; cladophylls up to 10 in a cluster, filiform, to ½ in. long; fls. unisexual, yellow or yellow-green, in clusters of 1–4; fr. red. Eur., Asia, N. Afr.; naturalized locally in N. Amer. Var. **pseudoscaber** (Grec.) Asch. & Graebn. [*A. pseudoscaber* Grec.]. More graceful in habit. Romania.

plumosus: *A. setaceus.*

pseudoscaber: *A. officinalis* var.

racemosus Willd. [*A. tetragonus* Bresl.]. Tuberous, sts. climbing to 20 ft., spineless; cladophylls in whorls of 3–8, linear, 3–4-angled, to ¾ in. long; fls. bisexual, white or pink, fragrant, in racemes to 4 in. long, from the old wood; fr. red. S. Afr. through e. Afr. to Asia.

retrofractus L. Fibrous-rooted, sts. scrambling or weakly climbing, to 6 ft. or more, zigzagging, branched, white and grooved when young, later brown and smooth; cladophylls clustered, cylindrical, curved, ¼–1⅛ in. long, not all the same length; fls. mostly 2–6 together in the axils, white, anthers orange; fr. orange. S. Afr. Material grown under this name may be *A. Macowanii.*

sarmentosus L. A name of uncertain application, used for a plant said to have come from Ceylon. Material grown under this name may belong to *A. densiflorus.*

scandens Thunb. Sts. herbaceous, weak, climbing to 3 ft. or more; cladophylls in whorls of 3, spreading in 1 plane, linear-lanceolate, curved, to ½ in. long; fls. bisexual, white, nodding, 1–3 in lf. axils, anthers yellow; fr. scarlet. S. Afr. Var. **deflexus** Bak. Small form, with zigzag sts. and deflexed brs. S. Afr.

setaceus (Kunth) Jessop [*A. plumosus* Bak.]. ASPARAGUS FERN, LACE F. Evergreen, with tall-climbing woody or wiry sts.; true lvs. modified into spines with reflexed tips, cladophylls in clusters of 8–20, to ¼ in. long, bright green, the many clusters arranged in nearly a single plane to form a flat, leaflike spray, triangular in outline; fls. bisexual, whitish, spreading, in clusters of 1–4; fr. purple-black. S. Afr. The long fernlike brs. are cut for decoration, and are much used by florists. Cv. **'Cupressoides'**. Of dense, cypresslike habit. Cv. **'Nanus'** [var. *nanus* Nichols.]. DWARF A. F. Smaller; cladophylls more numerous and shorter. Cv. **'Pyramidalis'**. Of loose pyramidal habit. Cv. **'Robustus'**. Especially vigorous.

Sprengeri: *A. densiflorus* cv. Cv. **'Deflexus'**: *A. densiflorus* cv. 'Sprengeri Deflexus'. Cv. **'Nanus'**: *A. densiflorus* cv. 'Sprengeri Nanus'. Cv. **'Robustus'**: *A. densiflorus* cv. 'Sprengeri Robustus'.

tetragonus: *A. racemosus.*

trichophyllus Bunge. Sts. flexuous, to 5 ft., much-branched, with curved prickles; cladophylls many, in whorls, setose, to 1 in. long; fls. unisexual, white, usually solitary. Hardy. Siberia and n. China.

verticillatus L. Rootstock woody, sts. ann., climbing to 15 ft., somewhat woody, prickly; cladophylls in whorls of 3–8, filiform, to 2 in. long; fls. unisexual, funnelform, 1–4 in lf. axils; fr. red. Hardy. Iran to Siberia.

virgatus Bak. Rhizomatous, sts. erect, to 6 ft., much-branched; cladophylls in whorls of 3, to ¾ in. long, stiff, dark green; fls. bisexual, greenish-white, spreading, solitary; fr. dull orange-red. S. Afr.

ASPARAGUS, GARDEN. The cultivated plant is a developed or improved form of the native *Asparagus officinalis* of the seacoasts of Europe, North Africa, and Asia. It is a hardy perennial, grown for its edible spring shoots, which are tender and can be injured by frost; it has frequently escaped in waste places and in saline areas. The indigenous plant in its native countries is short-branched and more or less prostrate at the base, whereas the cultivated asparagus is strongly erect, to 3 feet or more. The genus also includes many ornamental species (see *Asparagus*).

The edible asparagus is a favorite vegetable in the spring and is extensively cultivated. In a few districts, like the Imperial Valley of California, asparagus is sometimes forced into autumn production. A planting will produce well for 12 years or more on good, deep soil, if the weeds are kept under control, sufficient time is allowed for replenishing the food reserves in the crowns, and good aerial growth is maintained by proper fertilization and adequate control of diseases and pests.

Although direct field seeding is practiced by a few growers in California, most asparagus plantings are started by planting one-year-old crowns or plants. The crowns are grown in a nursery by sowing three to six seeds per foot in rows 24–30 inches apart in early spring. The following spring the plants are dug, separated, sorted to cull small crowns, replanted in the permanent beds, and set about 18 inches apart in furrows 6–8 inches deep, with rows spaced 5–8 feet apart. In home gardens, 50–100 feet of row is needed to supply a family. After planting, the crowns are first covered with 2–3 inches of soil and then the furrow is gradually filled in as the plants grow. The tops should be allowed to grow without cutting for the first two seasons in order to develop strong crowns. Harvesting of spears may begin the third spring. The length of the harvest season will vary for different regions, ranging from about five or six weeks in the northeastern states to 12 weeks or longer in California, where harvest begins in March. Green asparagus should be cut when the spears are 8–10 inches high and while the heads are still tight. In cutting off the spears, care must be taken to avoid injury to younger shoots.

Best quality of spears develops when night temperatures four to five days before harvest are in the range of 60°–65°F and day temperatures are moderate. Cool night temperatures (below 55°F) tend to increase toughness and purpling.

The main cultivars are 'Mary Washington', of which there are several strains, and 'Waltham Washington', planted in the eastern United States because of its fair resistance to rust. Several new lines of 'Washington' are used in the West. All are similar in type with only minor variations in coloring, spear size, and earliness.

Since asparagus is a perennial, control of weeds, particularly perennial weeds, is important for maintaining good yields over a long period. A combination of tillage before and after the cutting season plus appropriate use of herbicides will give satisfactory control.

The common and the spotted asparagus beetles, the most common pests, can be controlled by judicious use of appropriate chemicals. The garden symphylan and thrips are other insect pests. Two troublesome diseases, rust and *Fusarium* root rot, can be controlled by use of resistant cultivars.

Asparagus can be blanched by hilling soil over the row and cutting the spears deep in the ridge when the tips appear at the surface. This white asparagus is popular in Europe and some canned white asparagus is consumed in the United States.

ASPASIA Lindl. *Orchidaceae.* Five spp. of epiphytes, native from Cent. Amer. to Brazil; pseudobulbs oblong, 2-edged, with sheathing basal lvs. and 1–2 terminal lvs.; fls. in a lateral, erect, few-fld. raceme shorter than lvs.; sepals and petals spreading, lip entire or 3-lobed, united up to the middle to the column and at right angles to it. For structure of fl. see *Orchidaceae.*

Culture as for *Oncidium*, in the greenhouse, in a moist atmosphere and shady position. See also *Orchids.*

epidendroides Lindl. Lvs. lanceolate, narrow, to 1 ft. long; racemes loose, 2–10-fld.; fls. about 1½ in. across, sepals and petals greenish-yellow, transversely streaked with brown, lip white or yellowish, with purplish-brown spots. Nicaragua to Panama. Var. **principissa** (Rchb.f.) P. Allen [*A. principissa* Rchb.f.]. To 1½ ft.; racemes 2–7-fld.; fls. to nearly 3 in. across, sepals and petals greenish, with chocolate-brown longitudinal lines, lip white, tinted with rose. Costa Rica, Panama.

lunata Lindl. To 1 ft.; sepals and petals greenish-yellow, with maroon blotches, to 1½ in. long, lip fan-shaped, finely toothed, white with maroon dots. Winter–spring. Brazil.

principissa: *A. epidendroides* var.

variegata Lindl. To 1 ft.; sepals and petals to 1½ in. long, light green or cream, with dark maroon longitudinal lines on yellowish-brown crossbars, lip 3-lobed, white, spotted with maroon, and with yellow callus at base. Late autumn. Trinidad, Guyana, Brazil.

ASPERULA L. WOODRUFF. *Rubiaceae.* About 90 spp. of ann. and per. herbs, with square sts., native to Eur., Asia, Australia; lvs. whorled; fls. in forking cymes, small, many, mostly 4-merous, corolla funnelform; fr. indehiscent, leathery, seldom fleshy. Closely related to *Galium* from which it has traditionally been separated only on the length of the corolla tube. Recent workers consider *Asperula* an unnatural assemblage of heterogeneous spp. of plants and several spp. of *Asperula* are here placed in *Galium.*

Woodruffs are grown in borders or rock gardens, where they thrive in shady locations in moist soil, although *A. orientalis* does well in the open flower garden. Propagated by seeds and by division of the roots and clumps.

affinis Boiss. & Huet [*A. pontica* Boiss.]. Plants loosely cespitose, with underground runners, glabrous to scarcely hirsute, often blackening on drying; fl. heads stalked, terminal, subtended by narrow, leaflike bracts, the bracts often more than half as long as the corolla. Asia Minor.

azurea: *A. orientalis.*

cespitosa: *A. lilaciflora.*

ciliata Rochel. Per., to 2 ft.; lvs. usually in 4's, linear-lanceolate, to 1¼ in. long, acute, margins revolute, setose-ciliate, midrib often setose beneath; fls. white, in a paniculate cyme, corolla tube as long as lobes. Cent. and e. Eur. Very similar to *A. tinctoria*, but having lvs. setose-ciliate, and corolla lobes longer.

cynanchica L. Per., sts. decumbent or ascending, to 16 in.; lvs. in 4's, linear, to ⅝ in. long; fls. white or pink, few in paniculate cymes, corolla tube longer than lobes. Eur., Asia.

Gussonei Boiss. [*A. suberosa* Guss., not Sibth. & Sm.]. Low, tufted per.; lvs. in pairs, ovate-oblong to linear-lanceolate; fls. pinkish-white, inconspicuous. Sicily.

hexaphylla All. Per., sts. slender, ascending, to 2 ft. or more; lvs. in 6's, linear; fls. white, corolla tube 3 times as long as lobes. S. Eur.

hirta Ramond. Hairy, mat-forming per., to 8 in.; lvs. in 6's, linear; fls. pinkish, small, corolla tube slightly longer than lobes. Pyrenees.

humifusa: *Galium humifusum.*

lilaciflora Boiss. [*A. cespitosa* Boiss.]. Per., to 1 ft.; lvs. in 4's, linear, to ¾ in. long; fls. lavender. Asia Minor.

longifolia: *Galium longifolium.*

Neilreichii G. Beck. Per., to 6 in.; lvs. opp., not whorled, linear; fls. small, to ³⁄₁₆ in. long. Cent. Eur.

odorata: *Galium odoratum.*

orientalis Boiss. & Hohen. [*A. azurea* Jaub. & Spach; *A. azurea* var. *setosa* Regel.]. Branched ann., to 1 ft.; lvs. in 8's, lanceolate; fls. blue, ⅜ in. long, in terminal headlike clusters subtended by leafy bracts. Eur., Asia.

pontica: *A. affinis.*

scutellaris Vis. Per., to 1 ft.; lvs. filiform, covered with translucent dots, margins revolute; fls. pale yellow, solitary, axillary and terminal, on short peduncles. Albania.

setosa Jaub. & Spach. Ann.; lvs. 4–6, linear; fls. pale blue, otherwise similar to *A. orientalis.* Asia Minor.

suberosa: *A. Gussonei.*

tinctoria L. DYER'S W. Per., to 2 ft., roots reddish; lvs. in 4's and 6's, linear, margins revolute, glabrous; fls. white or reddish. Eur.

verticillata: a listed name of no botanical standing.

ASPHODELINE Rchb. JACOB'S-ROD. *Liliaceae.* About 18 or 20 spp. of rhizomatous, per. herbs with fibrous or sometimes fleshy roots, native from the Medit. region to the Caucasus; sts. leafy; lvs. linear; fls. yellow or white, in dense, long, cylindrical racemes; perianth segms. 6, united near base, spreading, stamens 6, filaments alternately of two different lengths; fr. a globose caps. The name has five syllables.

Hardy and of easy cultivation in any soil; useful for border or wild garden. The flowers open in the afternoon. Propagated by division and by seeds.

liburnica (Scop.) Rchb. [*Asphodelus liburnicus* Scop.]. To 2 ft., sts. leafy only in the lower ⅓ or ½; lvs. to 4 in. long; fls. yellow, the subtending bracts small, to ¼ in. long. Greece, Austria, Italy, Yugoslavia.

lutea (L.) Rchb. [*Asphodelus luteus* L.]. ASPHODEL, KING'S-SPEAR. To 4 ft., sts. leafy up to the infl.; lvs. linear, to 1 ft. long; fls. yellow, fragrant, 1 in. long, the subtending bracts large, membranous, about ¾ in. long. Medit. region.

taurica (Pall.) Kunth. To 2 ft., sts. leafy throughout; lvs. 3–9 in. long, narrowly linear, erect, sharp-pointed; fls. white, segms. with pinkish-tan midnerve. Greece through Asia Minor to the Caucasus.

ASPHODELUS L. ASPHODEL. *Liliaceae.* Ten to 15 spp. of ann., bien., or per. herbs, with fibrous or thickened roots, native from Canary Is. through Medit. region to India, and on Mauritius; lvs. all basal; fls. white to pink, in cylindrical racemes or in panicles terminating leafless scapes, segms. 6, united at base, stamens 6, filaments of equal length, dilated at base; fr. a caps.

Of easy culture in the open, in the border or wild garden. Propagated by division and by seeds.

acaulis Desf. Stemless per.; lvs. in a dense rosette, linear, to 1 ft. long; infl. sessile, shorter than lvs., lower fls. on long pedicels; fls. white to pink, funnelform, to 1½ in. long. N. Afr. Not hardy north.

albus Mill. Per., to 3 ft. or more, with tuberous roots; lvs. linear, 3-angled, to 2 ft. long; fls. white to pale pink, to about ¾ in. long, in racemes, the subtending bracts brown; caps. less than ½ in. long, with 4–6 transverse ridges on its valves. Portugal to Greece. Var. **delphinensis:** *A. delphinensis.*

cerasiferus J. Gay [*A. ramosus* L., in part]. Per., 4–5 ft. high, with tuberous roots; lvs. linear, to 14 in. long, strongly keeled; fls. white, to 1 in. long, in much-branched panicles; caps. subglobose, ⅝–¾ in. long. Portugal, Spain, s. France, Corsica, Balearic Is.

delphinensis Gren. & Godr. [*A. albus* var. *delphinensis* (Gren. & Godr.) Asch. & Graebn.; *A. Villarsii* J. Verl. ex Jord.]. Per.; lvs. linear, to about 2 ft. long; fls. white, about ¾ in. long, in racemes, the subtending bracts blackish-brown; caps. ⅜–⅝ in. long or less, with 6–8 transverse ridges on its valves. Pyrenees to Bulgaria.

fistulosus L. Bien. or short-lived per., to 2 ft., with hollow sts. and fibrous roots; lvs. cylindrical and hollow, to 1 ft. long, glabrous except on margins; fls. white to pale pink, about ½ in. long, in panicles; caps. about ⅜ in. long. Canary Is., N. Afr.; adventive in Australia and New Zeal.

liburnicus: *Asphodeline liburnica.*

luteus: *Asphodeline lutea.*

microcarpus Salzm. & Viv. [*A. ramosus* L., in part]. Per., to 3 ft., with tuberous roots; lvs. linear, to 14 in. long; fls. white, to ¾ in. long, in a much-branched panicle; caps. obovoid, usually not over ⅜ in. long. Canary Is. to Asia Minor.

ramosus: material offered under this name is either *A. cerasiferus* or *A. microcarpus.*

tenuifolius Cav. Ann., to 20 in. or more; lvs. semicylindrical, hollow, to about 8 in. long, scabrous on nerves; fls. white to pale pink, to ½ in. long, in panicles; caps. about ¼ in. long. N. Afr. and s. Eur. to India, and on Mauritius.

Villarsii: *A. delphinensis.*

ASPIDISTRA Ker-Gawl. *Liliaceae.* About 8 spp. of evergreen, per. herbs, native to e. Himalayas, Taiwan, China, and Japan; stemless, with thick roots and rhizomes; lvs. basal, leathery, glossy; fls. dull brown or brown-purple to green, borne singly at ground level and often obscured by the foliage, perianth 6–8-lobed, stamens 6 or 8, pistil mushroom-shaped, ovary 4-celled; fr. a berry.

Aspidistras withstand neglect, dull light, and poor soil. Propagated by division in early spring.

elatior Blume [*A. lurida* Hort., not Ker-Gawl.]. BARROOM PLANT. Lvs. to 2½ ft. long, to 4 in. across, oblong-elliptic, solitary from a basal sheath; fls. campanulate, brown-purple, 1 in. across, stamens 8. Japan. Cv. 'Variegata'. Lvs. striped green and white.—Because of its ability to persist under difficult conditions, sometimes called CAST-IRON PLANT or IRON PLANT.

lurida Ker-Gawl. Lvs. elongate-lanceolate, 2 or 3 from a basal sheath; fls. uniformly purple inside, stamens 8. China. Material offered under this name is probably *A. elatior.*

ASPIDIUM: *ARACHNIODES.* A. **acrostichoides:** *Polystichum acrostichoides;* A. **Bootii:** *Dryopteris Bootii;* A. **cristatum:** *D. cristata;* A. **falcatum:** *Cyrtosmium falcatum;* A. **falcatum** var. **Fortunei:** *C. Fortunei;* A. **Filix-mas:** *Dryopteris Filix-mas;* A. **Goldianum:** *D. Goldiana;* A. **marginale:** *D. marginalis;* A. **munitum:** *Polystichum munitum;* A. **noveboracense:** *Thelypteris noveboracensis;* A. **spinulosum:** *Dryopteris austriaca* var. *spinulosa;* A. **Thelypteris:** *Thelypteris palustris;* A. **tsus-simense:** *Polystichum tsus-simense;* A. **violescens:** *Thelypteris dentata.*

ASPIDOSPERMA Mart. & Zucc. *Apocynaceae.* About 50 spp. of trees native to trop. Amer.; sap usually milky or reddish; lvs. mostly alt., simple; fls. in axillary clusters shorter than lvs., many, small, 5-merous, bisexual, calyx lobes sometimes unequal, corolla salverform or funnelform, stamens borne above middle of corolla tube, separate, included, ovaries 2; fr. 1 or 2, stalked, woody, obliquely obovoid, usually laterally flattened follicles, seeds many, flattened, with a papery wing.

australe Müll. Arg. Tree, to 60 ft.; lvs. ovate- to narrowly oblong-elliptic, to 4½ in. long, glabrous, or minutely pilose beneath when young, petioles to 2 in. long; infl. puberulent; corolla to ⁵⁄₁₆ in. long, greenish or yellowish, densely white-silky outside, lobes ovate, ⅓ as long as tube; follicles grayish, flattened, nearly circular, to 1½ in. long, without a midrib, essentially glabrous. S. Brazil and n. Argentina, w. to Bolivia.

ASPLENIUM L. SPLEENWORT. *Polypodiaceae.* About 700 spp. of ferns of cosmopolitan distribution; lvs. usually evergreen, simple, deeply cut, or compound; sori oblong to linear, straight or nearly so, on the veinlets, indusia attached along 1 side, opening toward apex of pinnule.

Hybrids and polyploids are common. Some species are hardy, but most cultivated kinds are tropical and grown in the greenhouse. They require no special handling, but under glass should not be exposed to strong sunshine; if kept too wet they may lose color in the period when they are not in active growth. Propagated by spores or some species by division, or from bulblets or plantlets. See also *Ferns.*

acrostichoides: *Diplazium acrostichoides.*

adiantoides: *A. falcatum.*

angustifolium: *Diplazium pycnocarpon.*

aurium: a listed name of uncertain application.

australe: *Diplazium australe.*

Belangeri (Bory) Kunze. Lvs. evergreen, long and narrow, to 1½ ft. long and 4 in. wide, often with bulblets in axils of pinnae, 2-pinnate, upper pinnule at base of each pinna forked, the others ¼ in. long, entire; sori marginal. Malay Arch.

Bradleyi D. C. Eat. BRADLEY'S S. Lvs. evergreen, oblong-lanceolate, 1½–8 in. long, 1-pinnate, pinnae oblong-ovate, ¼–1 in. long, obtuse, incised or pinnatifid, petioles chestnut-brown. N.Y. to Ga. and Okla.

bulbiferum G. Forst. MOTHER S., HEN-AND-CHICKENS FERN, KING-AND-QUEEN F., MOTHER F., PARSLEY F. Lvs. to 4 ft. long and 1 ft. wide, with bulblets or plantlets on upper surface, 2–3-pinnate, pinnae to 1½ ft. long, once more pinnately divided into obovate to oblong pinnules. New Zeal., Australia, India. Var. **laxum** (R. Br.) Hook.f. Smaller, with more finely divided lvs.

caudatum G. Forst. Tufted, ½–2 ft. long, 4–8 in. wide, 1-pinnate, pinnae 2–4 in. long, lanceolate, often caudate, serrate or lobed; sori in 2 parallel rows along midvein. Tropics.

cryptolepis: see *A. Ruta-muraria.*

daucifolium Lam. [*A. viviparum* (L. f.) K. Presl]. Lvs. to 2 ft. long and 8 in. wide, 1–4-pinnate, often bearing bulblets, pinnules usually filiform; sori marginal or nearly so. Mauritius, Réunion Is.

ebeneum: *A. platyneuron.*

falcatum Lam. [*A. adiantoides* (L.) C. Chr.]. Like *A. caudatum,* but pinnae broader at base, margins variable, usually irregularly lobed then finely toothed; sori many, slender. Madagascar, India, Malay Arch., Australia, New Zeal., Polynesia.

Filix-femina: *Athyrium Filix-femina.* Var. **cyclosorum:** *Athyrium Filix-femina* var. *sitchense.*

gemmiferum Schrad. Lvs. leathery, to 2 ft. long and 8 in. wide, 1-pinnate, pinnae to 5 in. long, slightly wavy-toothed. E. to S. Afr.

Goeringianum: *Athyrium Goeringianum.*

Hemionitis L. Lvs. 6 in. long and wide, hastate, with terminal lobe triangular. Spain, Canary Is.

longissimum Blume. Lvs. to 8 ft. long, rooting at tips, 1-pinnate, pinnae mostly 50–70 pairs, to 4½ in. long, slightly toothed, nearly equal basally on each side of midrib, petioles to 1 ft. long, blackish. Malay Pen.

lucidum: *A. Lyallii.*

Lyallii Hook.f. [*A. lucidum* G. Forst., not Salisb. or Burm. f.]. Lvs. leathery, to 3 ft. long and 14 in. wide, 1-pinnate; pinnae mostly 30–50 pairs, narrowly ovate, to 6 in. long, wavy-toothed, narrowed abruptly at base of apical margin, petioles to 1½ ft. long, scaly, grayish. New Zeal.

montanum Willd. MOUNTAIN S. Lvs. triangular-ovate, 1–2-pinnate, pinnae ovate, toothed or cut, petioles dark brown at base. Conn., s. to Ga. and Ark.

nidus L. [*A. nidus-avis* Hort.]. BIRD'S-NEST FERN, NEST F. Large epiphytic plant; lvs. stiff, erect, simple, to 4 ft. long, 8 in. wide, entire, wavy, or slightly lobed, bright green. Trop. Asia, Polynesia.

nidus-avis: *A. nidus.*

parvulum: *A. resiliens.*

pinnatifidum Nutt. LOBED S., PINNATIFID S. Lvs. tufted, lanceolate-caudate, 2–15 in. long, pinnatifid or rarely 1-pinnate basally, pinnae obtuse, coarsely erose, petioles black. An acid-soil rock fern, se. Penn. to Ga., w. to Okla.

platyneuron (L.) Oakes [*A. ebeneum* Ait.]. EBONY S. Lvs. to 15 in. long and 3 in. wide, 1-pinnate, pinnae many, oblong-linear, auricled on apical margin, petioles purplish-brown. Me. to Ga., w. to Tex. and Colo.; S. Afr. Hardy.

pycnocarpon: *Diplazium pycnocarpon.*

resiliens Kunze [*A. parvulum* M. Martens & Galeotti, not Hook.]. LITTLE EBONY S., BLACK-STEM S. Lvs. linear-elliptic, to 10 in. long, 1-pinnate, pinnae elliptic, entire or slightly crenate, auricled at base, petioles blackish, glossy. On limestone, Penn. to Fla. and Mex.; S. Amer.

Ruta-muraria L. WALL RUE. Lvs. ovate-lanceolate to triangular, to 3 in. long, 2–3-pinnate, pinnules narrowly cuneate or roundish-obovate, toothed at apex; petioles green. On limestone, e. U.S., Eur., Asia. The Amer. plants have been separated from those of the Old World as *A. cryptolepis* Fern. [*A. Ruta-muraria* subsp. *cryptolepis* (Fern.) R. T. Clausen & Wahl] and are distinguished by several minute and somewhat integrating technical characters.

serratum L. BIRD'S-NEST FERN, WILD B.-N. F. Lvs. simple, narrowly oblanceolate, to 30 in. long, short-acuminate, cuneate at base, crenate-serrate above the middle, sometimes incised, petioles somewhat scaly, green; sori slenderly elongate, following the veins at end of frond. Fla. to trop. Amer.

squamulatum Blume. Not known to be cult.; plants offered under this name are *Polypodium punctatum.*

×**Stotleri** Wherry: *A. Bradleyi* × *A. pinnatifidum* × *A. platyneuron.* Differs from each presumed parent in pinnae margins rounded instead of sharply toothed.

thelypteroides: *Diplazium acrostichoides.*

Trichomanes L. MAIDENHAIR S. Lvs. evergreen, clustered, to 8 in. long and ¾ in. wide, 1-pinnate, pinnae round to oblong, about ½ in. long, cuneate to truncate at base, slightly toothed. N. Amer., Eur., Asia. Hardy. Var. **vespertinum:** *A. vespertinum.*

vespertinum Maxon [*A. Trichomanes* var. *vespertinum* (Maxon) Jeps.]. WESTERN S. Like *A. Trichomanes,* but margins more deeply crenate and shallowly auricled on apical margin. Calif.

viride Huds. GREEN SPLEENWORT. Lvs. to 8 in. long and ½ in. wide, 1-pinnate, pinnae mostly ovate-orbicular, to ½ in. long; petioles brownish, rachis green. N. N. Amer., Eur., Asia.

viviparum: *A. daucifolium.*

ASSONIA: *DOMBEYA.*

ASTELIA Banks & Soland. ex. R. Br. *Liliaceae.* About 25 spp. of dioecious, tufted, rhizomatous herbs native to Ré-union, Australia, New Zeal., New Guinea, Polynesia to Hawaii, and Chile; lvs. linear, mostly basal, sheathing at base; fls. unisexual, yellow, green, brownish-green, white, rose, or crimson, in scapose racemes or panicles, perianth segms. united into a short tube, stamens 6; fr. a 1- or 3-celled berry, seeds black and lustrous.

Cockaynei Cheesem. Lvs. 2–6 ft. long, 1–1½ in. wide, silky above, scaly and woolly beneath, with 2 secondary longitudinal nerves on each side of midrib; fls. in slender panicles to 6 in. high, on scapes 16 in. long. New Zeal.

nervosa Banks & Soland. ex Hook.f. Plant robust; lvs. to 8 ft. long, 1½–4 in. wide, becoming glabrous above, scaly and woolly beneath, with one secondary longitudinal nerve on each side of midrib; panicles much-branched, to 1 ft. high, on scapes to 2 ft. long; fls. green to greenish-purple, fragrant, to ½ in. across. New Zeal.

ASTER L. [*Sericocarpus* Nees]. MICHAELMAS DAISY, STAR-WORT, FROST FLOWER. *Compositae* (Aster Tribe). Between 250 and 500 spp. of mostly per. herbs, rarely ann. or bien. or shrubs, native to N. and S. Amer., Eur., Asia, and Afr., sts. frequently rhizomatous, or fibrous-rooted; lvs. alt., simple, entire to toothed; fl. heads usually radiate, rarely solitary, usually many in racemes, corymbs, or panicles, involucre campanulate, hemispherical or turbinate, involucral bracts equal or imbricate in many rows, herbaceous or scarious, receptacle flat, pitted, naked; disc fls. bisexual, yellow, sometimes orange, whitish, or purple, ray fls. in 1 row, rarely absent, female or neutral, purple, blue, violet, pink, or white, style brs. flattened; achenes more or less compressed, not ribbed, glabrous or hairy, pappus persistent, of many, nearly equal, capillary bristles, sometimes with a few short outer scales or bristles also.

Asters are mostly summer or autumn flowering and are used in the border, for colonizing, and for bold clumps. Most perennial kinds thrive best in a medium-rich soil. The named cultivars are increased usually by division or cuttings, since seeds do not reproduce true to type. The more common native asters may be propagated by seeds sown in spring for bloom the following year, or by division in spring. The common annual or China aster is *Callistephus chinensis.*

acris: *A. sedifolius.*

acuminatus Michx. Rhizomatous per., to 2½ ft., sts. slightly flexuous, hairy; lower lvs. reduced, deciduous, the others elliptic or obovate, to 6¾ in. long, long-acuminate, sharply toothed, glabrous to sparingly scabrous above, sticky-hairy beneath; heads to 1½ in. across, in a corymbose panicle; ray fls. white or purplish. Sw. Nfld. and Que., s. to Ga. and e. Tenn.

×**alpellus** Hort.: *A. alpinus* × *A. Amellus.* Sts. to 1 ft.; disc fls. orange, ray fls. blue.

alpigenus (Torr. & A. Gray) A. Gray. Per., from a little-branched root crown, sts. to 7 in., decumbent, scapose; lvs. mostly in a basal tuft, linear-spatulate or oblanceolate, to 6 in. long, leathery, obtuse or rounded at apex, entire, glabrous; heads to 1⅜ in. across, solitary; ray fls. 20–38, deep violet to purple. Mts., Ore. and Wash. Var. **Haydenii** (T. C. Porter) Cronq. [*A. Haydenii* T. C. Porter]. Sts. more slender, to 6 in.; lvs. linear to linear-elliptic, to 4 in. long, acute; ray fls. 10–30. E. Ore. and ne. Nev. to w. Mont. and w. Wyo.

alpinus L. Per. from a root crown, sts. to 9 in.; lvs. mostly basal, lanceolate-spatulate, to 2 in. long, entire; heads to 2 in. across, solitary, rarely as many as 3–4; ray fls. blue to violet. Spring. Mts., Eur., Asia. Cvs. are: 'Albus', fls. white; 'Coeruleus', sts. to 10 in., ray fls. blue; 'Roseus', sts. to 6 in., ray fls. pale rose; 'Rubra', ray fls. rosy-purple; 'Superbus', heads larger and more showy, ray fls. purple. Var. **dolomiticus** G. Beck. Sts. to 8 in., foliage with fine appressed hairs. Balkan Pen. Var. **himalaicus:** probably *A. himalaicus.* Var. **polycephalus** Anzi. Heads several on a st., terminal heads much larger than lateral ones. Switzerland. Var. **speciosus** Regel. Sts. to 20 in.; heads larger; ray fls. dark violet. Cent. Asia. Var. **Wolfii** Favrat. Sts. to 1 ft. or more; ray fls. blue. Switzerland.

altaicus: *Heteropappus altaicus.*

Amellus L. ITALIAN A. Per., to 2 ft., rough-hairy; basal lvs. oblanceolate to obovate, to 5 in. long, entire or nearly so, st. lvs. oblong to lanceolate; heads to 2 in. across, in a corymb, rarely solitary; ray fls. bluish-lilac. Cent. and se. Eur., w. Asia. Cv. 'Elegans'. Lower and free-flowering. Var. **bessarabicus** (Bernh. ex Rchb.) DC. Gray-hairy, sts. to 2 ft.; basal lvs. to 4¾ in. long; ray fls. dull purple. Bessarabia.

Var. **ibericus** (Steven) DC. [*A. ibericus* Steven]. Ray fls. dark blue. Asia Minor and Caucasus.

asteroides (DC.) O. Kuntze [*A. likiangensis* Franch.]. Erect per. herb, to 6 in., rarely taller, with a tuberous rhizome, sts. villous, glandular-pubescent; basal lvs. ovate or elliptic, to 1½ in. long, entire to 1–2-toothed, petioles to 1¼ in. long, upper st. lvs. nearly sessile, linear to lanceolate; heads about 2 in. across, solitary; ray fls. dark blue-purple or mauve. Early summer. Se. Tibet, Bhutan, w. China.

azureus Lindl. Erect, stiff per., to 5 ft., sts. scabrous-pubescent to almost glabrous; lvs. ovate-lanceolate to oblong, to 5 in. long, nearly cordate to cordate at base, often crenate-serrate, scabrous-hispid, upper lvs. linear to lanceolate, sessile; heads to ½ in. across, many in panicles; ray fls. deep blue to blue-violet. S. Ont. and w. N.Y. to Minn., s. to Ala. and Tex.

Batesii Rydb. Rhizomatous per., to 2 ft., sts. many, ascending; lvs. sessile, linear, to 1¼ in. long, spinose-apiculate apically, hispidulous-strigose, rough-ciliate; heads about ⅜ in. across, in panicles; ray fls. sky-blue. Nebr.

Bigelovii: *Machaeranthera Bigelovii.*

brachytrichus Franch. Rhizomatous per., to 1 ft., sts. hairy; lvs. oblong-spatulate to obovate, to 2¼ in. long, entire, hairy, lower lvs. often deciduous in age; heads to 2 in. across, solitary; ray fls. violet. China.

capensis: *Felicia aethiopica*, but plants grown as *A. capensis* are likely to be *Felicia amelloides*.

caucasicus Willd. Per., to 2 ft.; lvs. sessile, ovate to oblong-lanceolate, to 3½ in. long, remotely serrate, rough; heads to 2 in. across, solitary; ray fls. purple. Caucasus.

chilensis Nees [*A. leucopsis* Greene; *A. Menziesii* Lindl.]. Per., to 3 ft., sts. ascending to erect; lvs. entire to serrulate, lowest lvs. oblanceolate to obovate, to 4¾ in. long, narrowed to a winged petiole, middle st. lvs. sessile, linear-lanceolate, to 3½ in. long, uppermost lvs. bractlike; heads to 1 in. across, in racemes or racemose panicles; ray fls. violet to purple or whitish. Coastal, n. Ore., s. to Santa Barbara Co. (Calif.).

ciliolatus Lindl. [*A. Lindleyanus* Torr. & A. Gray; *A. Saundersii* Burgess]. Rhizomatous per., to 4 ft., hirsute to essentially glabrous; basal and lower st. lvs. lanceolate to ovate, to 4¾ in. long, petioled, cordate to nearly so, sharply serrate, often deciduous, the upper successively reduced, their petioles becoming winged, the uppermost lvs. sessile, entire; heads about 1 in. across, in a panicle; ray fls. blue. Que., Me., N.Y., w. to Mackenzie Dist. (B.C.) and Mont.

commutatus: *A. falcatus.*

concolor L. Per., with a short root crown, often also rhizomatous, sts. to 2½ ft., little-branched, hairy; lvs. elliptic-oblong to lanceolate, to 2 in. long, entire, silky or glabrate in age, basal lvs. deciduous, st. lvs. sessile; heads to 1 in. across, in an elongated, wandlike, spicate raceme; ray fls. blue to violet-blue, occasionally pink. Mass. to Fla. and Miss., occasional in Tenn. and Ky.

conspicuus Lindl. Stoloniferous per., to 2 ft., sts. stout, glandular; lvs. sessile, clasping, oblong-ovate to elliptic or obovate-elliptic, to about 7 in. long, sharply toothed toward apex, scabrous on both sides, veiny; heads to 1½ in. across, in cymes or cymose panicles; ray fls. violet. S. Dak. and Wyo. to Sask., w. to e. Wash. and ne. Ore.

cordifolius L. BLUE WOOD A. Per., with short root crown or rhizome, sts. to 6 ft.; lf. blades ovate, to 5 in. long, thin, cordate at base, sharply serrate, scabrous above, hirsute beneath, basal lvs. long-petioled, upper lvs. successively reduced; heads to ¾ in. across, in large, loose panicles; ray fls. violet or blue. Nov. Sc. to Minn., s. to Ga. and Mo.

corymbosus: *A. divaricatus.*

Curtisii Torr. & A. Gray. Glabrous, erect, clump-forming per., to 5 ft.; basal lvs. mostly deciduous, st. lvs. linear to elliptic-lanceolate or elliptic, to 6 in. long, acuminate, serrate to crenate, glabrous or sometimes pubescent beneath; heads to 1 in. across, in panicles; ray fls. violet-blue. Mt. woodlands, N.C., Ga., Tenn.

diplostephioides (DC.) C. B. Clarke. Erect, viscid, rhizomatous per., to 1½ ft.; basal lvs. oblanceolate, to 5 in. long including the 2¾ in.-long petiole, entire to occasionally distantly denticulate, st. lvs. linear to lanceolate, successively reduced upward; heads to 3 in. across, solitary; disc fls. yellow or orange, lobes externally blackish or brownish, ray fls. blue or pale purple. Early summer. Himalayas.

divaricatus L. [*A. corymbosus* Ait.]. WHITE WOOD A. Rhizomatous per., to 3 ft., sts. glabrous, often flexuous; lower lvs. lanceolate-ovate to ovate or triangular, to 7 in. long, on petioles to 5 in. long, thin, glabrous, acuminate, cordate at base, margins coarsely and sharply serrate, upper lvs. successively reduced upward, the uppermost sessile; heads to 1 in. across, in a broad corymb; disc fls. yellow or red, ray fls. white. Mt. woodlands, n. New Hamp., w. to Ohio, s. to n. Ga. and e. Ala.

Douglasii: *A. subspicatus.*

dracunculoides Lam. Per., to 3 ft., sts. much-branched, very leafy; lvs. linear-oblong to lanceolate, to 3 in. long, heads to ⅜ in. across, in corymbs; ray fls. blue. S. Eur., w. Asia.

dumosus L. Per., with stout root crown or creeping rhizomes, sts. to 3 ft., usually puberulent; lvs. sessile, linear to linear-lanceolate or narrowly elliptic, to 4½ in. long, entire, often revolute, firm, more or less scabrous above, glabrous beneath; heads to ½ in. across, many in a loose panicle; ray fls. pale lavender to blue or white. Sw. Me. to Fla. and La.

elongatus: *Felicia elongata.*

ericoides L. [*A. multiflorus* Ait.]. HEATH A. Rhizomatous, hairy per., to 3 ft.; lvs. sessile, basal lvs. many, spatulate, st. lvs. linear or oblong, to 3 in. long, the upper successively reduced upward and becoming spreading, lower to middle lvs. early-deciduous; heads ½ in. across, many in panicles with divergent to recurved 1-sided brs.; ray fls. white, sometimes blue or pink. Me. to Ga., e. to Minn., S. Dak., New Mex., and adjacent Mex.

falcatus Lindl. [*A. commutatus* (Torr. & A. Gray) A. Gray]. Rhizomatous per., to 2 ft.; lvs. sessile and clasping, linear, to 2⅜ in. long, firm, cuspidate, entire, hirsute, lower to middle lvs. early-deciduous; heads to ⁵⁄₁₆ in. across, in racemes or panicles with brs. not 1-sided; ray fls. white. S. Wisc. to B.C. and e. Wash., s. to New Mex., Utah, and Ariz.

Farreri W. W. Sm. & J. F. Jeffr. Tufted, per. herb, to 2 ft. or more, from a short rhizome; basal lvs. lanceolate, to 6 in. long, petioled, dark green, hairy, entire, ciliate, st. lvs. successively reduced upward, sessile; heads to 3 in. across, solitary; disc fls. orange, ray fls. purplish-blue. Early summer. W. China, Tibet.

Fendleri A. Gray. Tufted per., from a root crown, sts. erect, to 16 in.; lvs. sessile, sometimes with axillary tufts of lvs., linear, to 1¾ in. long, firm, finely serrate to spinulose-ciliate; heads to ¾ in. across, in short racemes; ray fls. bluish. High plains, Kans. to Colo., s. to Tex. and New Mex.

flaccidus Bunge [*A. Purdomii* Hutch.; *A. tibeticus* Hook.f., in part]. Tufted per. herb, to 6 in., sts. white with villous hairs, often also glandular; lvs. mostly basal, spatulate or obovate, to 2½ in. long, slightly cuneate, villous or almost glabrous, margins ciliate; heads to 2½ in. across, solitary; ray fls. blue or mauve. Early summer. Siberia, n. China, cent. Asia, Himalayas.

foliaceus Lindl. ex DC. Per., from a root crown or creeping rhizome, glabrous to pubescent, sts. to 2 ft.; lower lvs. oblanceolate to obovate, to 8 in. long including petiole, often early-deciduous, middle st. lvs. sessile, clasping, to 4¾ in. long, entire; heads to 1 in. across, in a broad, open, cymose panicle; ray fls. rose-purple to blue-violet. Alaska to Wash.

Forrestii: *A. Souliei.*

Fremontii: *A. occidentalis.*

×**Frikartii** Frikart: *A. Amellus* × *A. Thomsonii*. Much-branched per., to 2½ ft.; heads to 3 in. across, solitary on brs.; ray fls. violet-blue.

fruticosus: *Felicia fruticosa.*

fuscescens Bur. & Franch. Rhizomatous per. herb, sts. erect, to 2 ft.; basal lvs. broadly ovate, to 5 in. long, cordate basally, thin, soft, hairy, on petioles to 6 in. long, deciduous by flowering time, middle and upper lvs. to 3 in. long, on petioles to 1¼ in. long; heads about 1¼ in. across, in corymbs; disc fls. yellow or orange, ray fls. bluish to purple. W. China, se. Tibet, ne. Burma.

Geyeri: *A. laevis* var.

gracilis Nutt. Per., from a cormlike woody base, sts. to 2 ft.; basal lvs. elliptic, to 2½ in. long, thick, firm, essentially entire, on petioles longer than blade, st. lvs. narrower, to 3½ in. long, sessile; heads about ¾ in. across, many in a corymb; ray fls. blue-violet to rose-purple. Dry, sandy areas, N.J. to S.C.

grandiflorus L. Rhizomatous per., to 5 ft., sts. slender, hispid; lowest lvs. oblong to oblanceolate, to 3 in. long, early-deciduous, st. lvs. sessile, linear to oblong, to about ⅝ in. long, hard, scabrous, ciliate; heads to 2 in. across, solitary at ends of long, corymbose brs.; ray fls. deep violet. E. Va., N.C.

Greatae Parish. Rhizomatous per., to 4 ft., sts. leafy, sparsely coarse-pubescent, but often glabrous in lower part; basal lvs. oblanceolate, petioled, early-deciduous, st. lvs. lanceolate-elliptic, clasping, to 6 in. long, thin, acuminate, entire to serrulate, successively reduced upward; heads about ½ in. across, in cymose panicles; ray fls. light purple. S. Calif.

Haydenii: *A. alpigenus* var.

himalaicus C. B. Clarke. Rhizomatous, sparingly stoloniferous per. herb, to 10 in., sts. arising laterally from base of rosette; basal lvs. of nonflowering shoots obovate, oblanceolate, or elliptic, to 1⅜ in. long, narrowing to the 1¾-in. petiole, entire to 2–3-toothed, lower st. lvs. absent or withered at flowering time, upper st. lvs. on flowering shoots sessile, oblong, obovate, or lanceolate, to 2 in. long; heads 1½ in. across, usually solitary; ray fls. purplish-blue. Early summer. Tibet, Nepal, Sikkim, Bhutan, Assam, and Burma.

hybridus Hort. A name of uncertain application, but often applied to a garden race of dwarf forms in a wide assortment of colors, to which many cv. names have been given. Var. **luteus:** × *Solidaster luteus.*

ibericus: *A. Amellus* var.

incisus: *Boltonia incisa.*

integrifolius Nutt. Per., from a short, woody, densely fibrous-rooted rhizome, sts. to 2½ ft., nearly glabrous to densely villous; basal lvs. broadly oblanceolate to elliptic, to 4¾ in. long, on slender petioles as long as blades, lower st. lvs. oblanceolate to elliptic, narrowed to clasping base, upper st. lvs. reduced, elliptic to lanceolate-linear; heads to 1¾ in. across, in a cymose, racemose, or paniculate infl.; ray fls. purple or violet. Se. Wash. to n. Calif., e. to Mont. and Colo.

japonicus: see *Boltonia japonica* and *Erigeron Thunbergii.*

junceus: a confused name of uncertain application.

junciformis Rydb. Rhizomatous, slender per., to 3 ft., sts. glabrous in lower part, but hairy above in decurrent lines from lf. bases; lvs. sessile, usually slightly clasping, linear to oblong-linear or lanceolate-linear, to 5 in. long, long-acuminate, margins entire or subentire but generally scabrous; heads about 1 in. across, in racemes or panicles, rarely solitary; ray fls. white to pale blue or lavender. N.J. and Que., w. to Colo., Idaho, and Alaska.

Kumleinii: *A. oblongifolius.*

laevis L. Per., to 3½ ft., from a branched root crown or stout rhizome, glabrous, often glaucous; lvs. lanceolate, elliptic, ovate, or oblanceolate, to 5 in. long, thick, mostly entire, basal lvs. tapering to a winged petiole, upper lvs. sessile and usually more or less auriculate-clasping; heads to 1 in. across, in a thyrsoid, racemose-paniculate, or paniculate infl., involucral bracts with short, more or less rhombic, green tips; ray fls. blue or pale purple. Yukon to ne. Ore. and New Mex., e. to Me. and Ga. Var. **Geyeri** A. Gray [*A. Geyeri* (A. Gray) T. J. Howell]. Involucral bracts with narrower and longer, green tips. E. Wash. and Alta. to S. Dak. and Colo.

lateriflorus (L.) Britt. Per., to 4 ft., from a branched root crown or stout rhizome, sts. villous to glabrous; basal lvs. and lower st. lvs. petioled, obovate to nearly orbicular, often early-deciduous, upper lvs. essentially sessile, linear, lanceolate, lanceolate-elliptic, or subrhombic, to 6 in. long, serrate or entire, reduced upward; heads ⁵⁄₁₆ in. across, many, in panicles with 1-sided brs.; ray fls. white or pale purple. Se. Canada to Minn., s. to Fla., Mo., and Tex.

ledophyllus (A. Gray) A. Gray. Per., to 3 ft., from a stout woody root crown; lowest lvs. scalelike, the others sessile, oblong or lanceolate-elliptic to oblong-elliptic, to 2¼ in. long, entire, green and glabrous above, hairy beneath; heads to 1½ in. across, in corymbs or thyrses; ray fls. lavender-purple. N. Calif. to n. Wash.

leucopsis: *A. chilensis.*

likiangensis: *A. asteroides.*

linearifolius L. Per., to 2 ft., from a short root crown, sts. wiry, hairy; lvs. linear, to 1½ in. long, firm, entire but with scabrous-ciliate margins, lowest lvs. early-deciduous; heads 1 in. across, in a corymb, rarely solitary; ray fls. violet. Que. and Me. to Fla., w. to Wisc., Mo., and Tex. Cv. 'Albus'. Ray fls. white. Cv. 'Purpureus'. Ray fls. purple. Cv. 'Roseus'. Ray fls. pink.

Lindleyanus: *A. ciliolatus.*

Linosyris (L.) Bernh. GOLDILOCKS. Erect per., to 2 ft., sts. stiff, glabrous; lvs. sessile, very numerous, narrowly linear, to 2 in. long, rough-margined, glabrous, punctate; heads about ½ in. across, in dense corymbs; disc fls. bright yellow, ray fls. absent. Eur., N. Afr., Caucasus.

Lipskii Kom. Per., to 1½ ft., sts. erect, slender, with short hairs; basal lvs. broadly lanceolate, long-petioled, irregularly toothed; heads to 2⅜ in. across, solitary; ray fls. deep violet. Early summer. Tibet.

luteus: × *Solidaster luteus.*

Maackii Regel. Rhizomatous per., to 3 ft., rough-hairy; basal lvs. and lower st. lvs. early-deciduous, middle st. lvs. sessile, lanceolate, to 4 in. long, with scattered teeth, upper lvs. reduced, oblong, ¾ in. long; heads about 1½ in. across, in loose corymbs; ray fls. bluish. Japan, Korea, Manchuria.

macrophyllus L. Rhizomatous per., to 4 ft., sts. glabrous or rough-hairy, glandular at least in infl.; basal lvs. on sterile shoots cordate, to 8 in. long, long-petioled, crenate or serrate, upper lvs. of fertile shoots ovate, lanceolate, or elliptic, successively less cordate, the uppermost sessile; heads about 1 in. across, many in flat- or round-topped cor-

ymbs; ray fls. pale blue or violet. Que. to Minn., s. to Ga., Tenn., and Ill.

Menziesii: *A. chilensis.*

meritus: *A. sibiricus* var.

modestus Lindl. Stoloniferous per., to 3 ft., sts. usually solitary, very leafy, covered with dense, stalked glands at least in upper part; lvs. sessile and more or less auriculate-clasping, linear-lanceolate to oblong-lanceolate, to 6 in. long, thin, entire to sharply and remotely serrate, rough to smooth above, glabrous or hairy beneath, lowest lvs. early-deciduous; heads about 1¼ in. across, cymose; ray fls. violet or purple. Sw. Ore. to Alaska, e. to Minn. and w. Ont.

mongolicus Franch. Erect per., to 3 ft., sts. paniculately branched, rough-hairy; lower and middle lvs. lanceolate in outline, pinnatifid into oblong, entire lobes, upper lvs. successively reduced upward, the uppermost toothed and finally linear and entire, middle lvs. about 3 in. long, all smooth to sparsely hispid on both sides, margined with short, strigose-hispid hairs; heads about 1¼ in. across, solitary at ends of brs.; ray fls. bright lavender-blue. Dry areas, e. Asia.

multiflorus: *A. ericoides.*

natalensis: *Felicia rosulata.*

nebraskensis: *A. praealtus* var.

nemoralis Ait. Rhizomatous per., to 2 ft., sts. slender, harshly puberulent; lower lvs. much reduced, early-deciduous, the others sessile, linear or linear-lanceolate to elliptic or oblong, to 2 in. long, firm, essentially entire, usually revolute, scabrous above, more or less hairy beneath; heads to 1½ in. across, solitary or corymbose; ray fls. pink or lilac-purple. Acid bogs, Nfld. to N.J., w. to Hudson Bay and Mich.

novae-angliae L. NEW ENGLAND A. Per., to 6½ ft., from a woody root crown or thick rhizome, sometimes creeping, sts. clustered, the upper part much-branched, hairy, glandular; lower lvs. early-deciduous, the others sessile and auriculate-clasping, lanceolate, to 5 in. long, entire, scabrous or with stiff hairs above, with softer hairs beneath; heads to 2 in. across, crowded toward ends of brs. in corymbose clusters; ray fls. usually deep violet-purple, but variable. Vt. to Ala., w. to N. Dak., Wyo., and New Mex. An important autumn-blooming garden aster, with many named cvs. Cv. 'Albus'. Ray fls. white. Cv. 'Roseus'. Ray fls. rose-pink.

novi-belgii L. Rhizomatous per., to 4½ ft., varying from small and slender to large and stout, sts. glabrous or with lines of hairs; lvs. sessile and more or less auriculate-clasping to winged-petioled, lower lvs. reduced, early-deciduous, the others linear-lanceolate to lanceolate or elliptic, to 7 in. long, firm and thick, glabrous, margins entire to sharply serrate, scabrous-ciliate; heads about 1 in. across, cymose-paniculate; ray fls. blue-violet. Mostly coastal, Nfld. to Ga.

oblongifolius Nutt. [*A. oblongifolius* var. *rigidulus* A. Gray; *A. Kumleinii* Fries]. Rhizomatous per., to 16 in., sts. brittle, glandular, more or less hairy or scabrous; lower lvs. early-deciduous, the others sessile and often auriculate-clasping, oblong to lanceolate-oblong, to 4 in. long, entire, hairy, scabrous or even sometimes glabrous; heads about 1¼ in. across, loosely corymbose; ray fls. violet. Ind., w. to N. Dak., Ark., Wyo., New Mex. Cv. 'Roseus'. Ray fls. rose-pink.

occidentalis (Nutt.) Torr. & A. Gray [*A. Fremontii* A. Gray]. Slender per., to 1½ ft., from creeping rhizomes; lower lvs. usually persistent, linear-oblanceolate to oblanceolate, narrowed to a winged, ciliate petiole, middle st. lvs. sessile, linear-lanceolate; heads about 1 in. across, in a cyme or cymose-panicle; ray fls. lavender or violet. Mts., cent. Calif. to B.C., e. to Colo. and Idaho.

oreophilus Franch. Per., to 1½ ft., sts. purplish; basal lvs. oblanceolate or spatulate, to 5 in. long including the narrowly winged petiole, entire to shallowly serrate, upper lvs. successively reduced upward, the uppermost oblong-linear, sessile; heads to 2 in. across, 1 or 2 together; ray fls. pale lilac to blue-mauve. Early summer. W. China.

paniculatus Mill., not Lam. The application of this name has not been determined; material cult. as *A. paniculatus* is *A. simplex* var. *ramosissimus.*

Pappei: *Felicia amoena.*

patens Ait. Per., to 5 ft., from a short root crown, sometimes also rhizomatous, sts. brittle, slender, hairy; lower lvs. early-deciduous, the others persistent, sessile and cordate-clasping, ovate to oblong, to 6 in. long, entire, hairy or scabrous; heads to 1 in. across, solitary on divaricate brs. of infl.; ray fls. blue, rarely pink. S. New Hamp. and Mass., s. to Ga., Ala., and se. Mo.

paternus Cronq. [*Sericocarpus asteroides* (L.) BSP]. Per., sts. to 2 ft., from branched root crown; basal and lower st. lvs. persistent, petioled, oblanceolate to obovate, sometimes elliptic, to 4 in. long, upper st. lvs. sessile, some lvs. toothed, all ciliate; heads about ¾ in. across, in flat-topped, loose corymbs; ray fls. 3–8, white, sometimes pink; achenes densely silky. Dry woods, Me. to Fla., e. to s. Ohio and s. Ala.

Pattersonii: *Machaeranthera Bigelovii.*

paucicapitatus (B. L. Robinson) B. L. Robinson. Per., to 1½ ft., from a stout root crown, often with a taproot, glandular and with pilose hairs; lowest lvs. reduced and scalelike, the others sessile or nearly so, elliptic or elliptic-oblong to lanceolate-elliptic, to 1⅜ in. long, entire; heads 1½ in. across, 1–4 together; ray fls. white. Olympic Pen. (Wash.) and adjacent Vancouver Is.

praealtus Poir. [*A. salicifolius* Ait.]. Rhizomatous per., to 6 ft.; lower lvs. early-deciduous, the others sessile or nearly so, lanceolate to lanceolate-elliptic, to 5 in. long, firm, glabrous to scabrous, margins entire, slightly revolute; heads to 1 in. across, many in densely leafy panicles; ray fls. bluish-purple or white. Mich. to Ga., w. to Nebr., s. Ariz., and n. Mex. Var. **nebraskensis** (Britt.) Wieg. [*A. nebraskensis* Britt.]. Sts. more pubescent; lvs. with conspicuous, spreading hairs beneath. Nebr.

ptarmicoides (Nees) Torr. & A. Gray. WHITE UPLAND A. Clump-forming, fibrous-rooted per., to 2½ ft., from a branched root crown covered with persistent lf. bases; lower lvs. linear-oblanceolate, to 8 in. long, petioled, entire, glabrous or scabrous, upper lvs. successively reduced, the uppermost linear, sessile; heads to 1 in. across, corymbose; disc and ray fls. white. W. Que. and Vt., s. to Ga., w. to Sask., S. Dak., Colo., and Ark.

puniceus L. Per., to 8 ft., from a stout rhizome or root crown, sts. stout, reddish, hispid; lower lvs. early-deciduous, the others sessile and auriculate-clasping, lanceolate to oblong or elliptic-oblong, to 6½ in. long, serrate or entire, nearly glabrous to scabrous above, glabrous or with spreading hairs on midrib beneath; heads to 1½ in. across, many in leafy, cymose panicles; ray fls. blue-violet to lilac, pink, or white. Swamps, Nfld. to s. Man., s. to Ga. and Ala.

Purdomii: *A. flaccidus.*

pyrenaeus DC. Stout per., to 2 ft., sts. rough-pubescent; lvs. sessile, semiclasping, oblong-lanceolate, distantly toothed; heads 2½ in. across, solitary, or few in a corymb; ray fls. bluish-lilac. Pyrenees.

radula Ait. Rhizomatous per., to 4 ft., sts. very leafy, glabrous except below infl.; lower and middle st. lvs. reduced, early-deciduous, the others sessile, elliptic to oblong or oblong-lanceolate, to 4 in. long, more or less serrate, rugose-veiny, scabrous above, hairy to subglabrous beneath; heads 1½ in. across, 1–40 in a corymb; ray fls. violet. Swamps, Nfld. to W. Va. Var. **stricta** (Pursh) A. Gray. Plants more slender, smaller; heads 1–8. Lab. and Nfld. to n. New Eng.

sagittifolius Wedem. ex Willd. Per., to 4 ft., from a branched root crown or short rhizome; lowest lvs. lanceolate-ovate or ovate, to 6 in. long, thick, scabrous or glabrous above, glabrous or more or less villous-hirsute below, margins shallowly toothed, petioles winged, to 4 in. long; heads ¾ in. across, many in a panicle; ray fls. pale blue or lilac, occasionally white. Sw. Vt. to Minn., s. to Fla., Ga., and Miss.

salicifolius: *A. praealtus.*

salsuginosus: *A. sibiricus.*

Saundersii: *A. ciliolatus.*

scopulorum A. Gray. Tufted per., to 5 in., from a densely branched, woody root crown, sts. erect, many, unbranched; lvs. sessile, spatulate or elliptic to oblong or linear, to ⅝ in. long, spinulose-tipped, rigid, hispidulous-scabrous, margin entire; heads to 1 in. across, solitary; ray fls. violet or purple. E. Ore. to Mont. and Wyo., s. to Calif. and cent. Nev.

scaber Thunb. Per., to 5 ft., from a short, thick rhizome; lower lvs. ovate, to 10 in. long, including the long petiole, acuminate, cordate basally, scabrous on both sides, coarsely toothed, lvs. successively reduced upward and becoming less cordate; heads about 1 in. across, in loose corymbs; ray fls. white. China, Manchuria, Korea, Japan.

sedifolius L. [*A. acris* L.]. Erect, very leafy per., to 3 ft., roughish-hispid; lvs. linear or lanceolate-linear, to 1½ in. long, attenuate at apex and base, strongly punctate, entire; heads to 1¼ in. across, in corymbs; ray fls. blue. S. Eur.

sericeus Venten. Per., to 2 ft., from a short, branched root crown, sts. much-branched, wiry, brittle, thinly silky to almost glabrous; basal and lower st. lvs. oblanceolate, petioled, early-deciduous, the others sessile, lanceolate or lanceolate-ovate to oblong or elliptic, to 1½ in. long, silky, entire; heads 1½ in. across, many, corymbose or paniculate; ray fls. deep violet to rose-purple. Mts., N.C. and Ga., and Mich. to S. Dak., s. to Tenn. and Tex.

Shortii Lindl. Per., to 4 ft., from a short, branched root crown, sts. glabrous below, hairy above; lvs. ovate to ovate-lanceolate, petioled, to 6 in. long, cordate to nearly so at base, glabrous to scaberulous above, hairy beneath, mostly entire, successively reduced upward; heads 1 in. across, many in an open, leafy-bracted panicle; ray fls. blue or infrequently rose-red or white. Sw. Penn. and Va., w. to se. Minn. and adjacent Iowa, s. to Ga. and Ala.

sibiricus L. [*A. salsuginosus* Richardson]. Per., to 16 in., from a branched, creeping rhizome; lvs. sessile to somewhat petioled, oblanceolate to elliptic, oblong, or oblong-lanceolate, to 4 in. long, glabrous above, glabrous to downy beneath, serrulate to almost entire; heads to ¾ in. across, solitary, or few and cymose; ray fls. purple or blue. Circumboreal. Var. **meritus** (A. Nels.) Raup [*A. meritus* A. Nels.]. Plants taller, sts. more branched, less pubescent; heads more numerous. E. Ore. to B.C. and Alta., e. to Wyo. and S. Dak.

sikkimensis Hook. Per., to 2½ ft., from a somewhat woody base, usually pubescent, sts. purplish, flexuous; basal lvs. lanceolate, to 9 in. long, petiole indistinctly winged, upper lvs. sessile, lanceolate, to 5 in. long, semiclasping basally, with scattered glands beneath, denticulate, lower st. lvs. early-deciduous; heads about 1 in. across, in large corymbs; ray fls. blue, purple, rose, or white. Sikkim and Nepal.

simplex Willd. Rather stout per., to 5 ft., from a rhizome, forming colonies; lvs. sessile, oblong-lanceolate to oblanceolate, to 8 in. long, ⅜–1⅜ in. wide, somewhat scabrous or glabrous above, serrate or sometimes entire; heads ¾ in. across, in leafy panicles; ray fls. white, sometimes tinged blue or lavender. Nfld. to N.C., w. to Sask. and Kans. Var. **ramosissimus** (Torr. & A. Gray) Cronq. [*A. paniculatus* Lam., not Mill.]. Lvs. linear, to 6 in. long, ⅛–½ in. wide. Que. to Va., w. to Minn., Iowa, and Mo.

sinensis: *Callistephus chinensis.*

Souliei Franch. [*A. Souliei* var. *limitaneus* (W. W. Sm. & Farrer) Hand.-Mazz.; *A. Forrestii* Stapf]. Erect, scapose per., to 1 ft., sts. more or less glabrous to pubescent; basal lvs. spatulate, oblanceolate, or obovate, to 4¼ in. long, pubescent or glabrous above, pilose beneath on veins, entire to obscurely crenate, usually ciliate, st. lvs. reduced, sessile; heads to 3 in. across, solitary; ray fls. blue or mauve. Early summer. Se. Tibet, nw. Yunnan.

spectabilis Ait. Rhizomatous per., to 3 ft., sts. usually densely glandular at least above; lvs. usually persistent, elliptic, to 4¾ in. long, glabrous or scabrous above, firm, entire or shallowly toothed, somewhat reduced upward, the uppermost sessile; heads 1½ in. across, in leafy-bracted corymbs; ray fls. violet-purple. Mass. to S.C.

stenomeres A. Gray. Tufted, fibrous-rooted per., to 1 ft., sts. many, simple, densely leafy; basal lvs. reduced, spatulate, the others sessile, linear, to 1⅜ in. long, rigid, scabrous-hispidulous, entire; heads to 2 in. across, solitary; ray fls. violet. Mts., ne. Wash. and se. B.C. to cent. Idaho and adjacent Mont.

subcoeruleus: *A. tongolensis.*

subspicatus Nees [*A. Douglasii* Lindl.]. Slender per., to 3 ft., from a fibrous-rooted root crown, sts. pubescent in lines; lowest lvs. oblanceolate, to 6 in. long, narrowed to a winged, clasping petiole, upper lvs. sessile, lanceolate, serrate and scabrous-ciliate; heads 1½ in. across, in cymose panicles; ray fls. violet. Cent. Calif. to Alaska, e. to Mont.

tanacetifolius: *Machaeranthera tanacetifolia.*

tataricus L.f. TARTARIAN A. Rhizomatous per., to 6 ft., minutely setose; basal lvs. spatulate-oblong, to 2 ft. long, including the long, winged petiole, early-deciduous, st. lvs. lanceolate, elliptic, or ovate-lanceolate, to 1 ft. long including petiole, uppermost lvs. nearly sessile, linear; heads about 1¼ in. across, in large corymbs; ray fls. blue-purple. Japan, Korea, Manchuria, n. China, Mongolia, Siberia.

Thomsonii C. B. Clarke. Rhizomatous per., to 2 ft., sts. usually more or less flexuous, glandular and hairy above; basal lvs. early-deciduous, st. lvs. sessile, elliptic-ovate, to 4 in. long, acute to acuminate, cuneate basally, hairy, usually glandular beneath, margins with 4–6 shallow or coarse teeth on each side; heads to 2½ in. across, solitary or few; ray fls. pink or purplish. Early summer. W. Himalayas.

tibeticus Hook.f. A name based on mixed material of *A. flaccidus* and *Erigeron multiradiatus.* Plants cult. as *A. tibeticus* may be forms of *A. alpinus.*

tongolensis Franch. [*A. subcoeruleus* S. L. Moore]. Stoloniferous per., to 1 ft.; lvs. sessile, oblong or oblong-oblanceolate, to 3½ in. long, often pubescent, entire or nearly entire; heads about 2 in. across, solitary; ray fls. pale blue. Early summer. W. China.

tortifolius: *Machaeranthera tortifolia.*

Tradescantii L. Rhizomatous per., to 2 ft., sts. with hairs in lines in upper part, glabrous below; basal lvs. linear to linear-lanceolate or lanceolate-elliptic, to 4 in. long, petioled, the other lvs. successively reduced upward, the uppermost sessile, all glabrous and entire to shallowly toothed; heads ½ in. across, in an elongated, open panicle. S. Nov. Sc. to n. N.Y. and n. Mich.

tricephalus C. B. Clarke. Rhizomatous per., to 16 in., often with sterile rosettes on robust stolons; basal lvs. absent or withered at flowering time, st. lvs. sessile and semiclasping, oblanceolate, elliptic, or lanceolate, to 2½ in. long, entire or with few teeth, lvs. of sterile rosettes spatulate, to 2½ in. long; heads about 2 in. across, 1–3, rarely more; ray fls. white or blue. Early summer. Nepal, Sikkim.

trinervius D. Don. Rhizomatous per., to 6 ft., sts. usually hairy, at least in upper part; basal lvs. early-deciduous, lower st. lvs. elliptic, lanceolate, or ovate, to 4 in. long, on petioles to ¼ in. long, upper st. lvs. sessile, lanceolate or ovate, to 2 in. long, all acuminate, entire to serrulate; heads ½ in. across, many in corymbs or loose corymbose panicles; ray fls. usually white, sometimes pink, bluish, or purplish. Nepal, n. China, Japan.

Tripolinum L. Glabrous ann. or short-lived per., to 3 ft.; basal lvs. oblanceolate to obovate, to 4¾ in. long, st. lvs. linear or narrowly oblong, all fleshy, entire to obscurely toothed; heads ¾ in. across, many in corymbs; ray fls. blue-purple to almost white. Eur. and N. Afr. to n. and cent. Asia and Japan.

umbellatus Mill. Rhizomatous per., to 8 ft., sts. puberulent, or glabrous below infl.; lower lvs. reduced, early-deciduous, the others elliptic to elliptic-ovate, to 6½ in. long, acuminate, tapering to a short petiole or nearly sessile base, scabrous above, glabrous or puberulent beneath, entire; heads ¾ in. across, in a dense, flat-topped corymb; ray fls. white. Moist areas, Nfld. to Ga., w. to Ill. and Minn.

undulatus L. Per., to 4 ft., from a branched root crown or short rhizome, sts. hairy to almost glabrous below infl.; lvs. lanceolate-ovate to ovate, to 5½ in. long, scabrous to glabrous above, usually hairy beneath, lowest lvs. cordate, petioled, upper lvs. with enlarged petioles or sessile and cordate-clasping; heads ¾ in. across, many in open panicles with more or less spreading, bracted brs.; ray fls. blue or lilac. Me. to n. Fla., e. to se. Ind. and e. Miss.

Vahlii (Gaud.-Beaup.) Hook. & Arn. Rhizomatous per., to 14 in., glabrous to sparsely hairy; lower lvs. oblanceolate to obovate, or sometimes elliptic-oblanceolate, to 2 in. long, ciliate, tapering to the ciliate, 2 in.-long petiole, upper lvs. sessile, linear-oblanceolate to linear, to 3½ in. long, nearly entire; heads to about 1½ in. across, usually solitary, rarely 2 or 3 or more; ray fls. pale purple, rarely white. Falkland Is., s. S. Amer.

×**versicolor** Willd.: *A. laevis* × *A. novi-belgii*. Glabrous per., to 3 ft.; lvs. oblong-lanceolate, slightly toothed; heads ½ in. across, corymbose; ray fls. blue-violet, or white changing to purple.

vimineus Lam. Rhizomatous per., to 5 ft., sts. glabrous or hairy in lines; lvs. linear or narrowly lanceolate, to 4½ in. long, glabrous or somewhat scabrous, entire or nearly so, lvs. of infl. much reduced; heads ⅜ in. across, many in an open panicle; ray fls. white or infrequently purplish. Me. to Ont. and Mich., s. to N.C., Ind. and Mo.

yunnanensis Franch. Rhizomatous per., to 2 ft., sts. hairy and with dark glands, base of sts. covered with fibrous remains of old lvs.; basal lvs. lanceolate or oblanceolate, to 6½ in. long, to 1½ in. wide, st. lvs. sessile, ovate, to 5 in. long, to 1¾ in. wide, all lvs. pilose and glandular, cordate basally, entire to denticulate and ciliate; heads 2½ in. across, 2–6, rarely solitary; ray fls. blue-mauve. Early summer. W. China, se. Tibet.

ASTERACEAE: see *COMPOSITAE*.

×**ASTERAGO**: ×*SOLIDASTER*.

ASTERANTHERA Klotzsch & Hanst. *Gesneriaceae*. One sp., a woody climber, in temp. rain forests of Chile; lvs. opp., those of a pair often unequal, toothed; fls. 1–2 on bracted peduncles longer than lvs., calyx deeply 5-lobed, corolla narrowly funnelform, limb 2-lipped, oblique, stamens 4, exserted, anthers united in a starlike cluster, disc ringlike, poorly developed, ovary superior, incompletely 2-celled; fr. a fleshy caps.

For cultivation see *Gesneriaceae*.

ovata (Cav.) Hanst. Lvs. ovate-elliptic to nearly orbicular, to 1½ in. long, ¾ in. wide, hairy; corolla raspberry-red, to 2¼ in. long, lower lip striped with yellow; fr. green and purple.

ASTERISCUS Mill. [*Odontospermum* Schultz-Bip.]. *Compositae* (Inula Tribe). About 15 spp. of ann. or per. herbs or shrubs, native in the Canary Is. and in the Medit. region to Iran; lvs. opp.; fl. heads radiate, solitary or corymbose, involucre hemispherical or broadly campanulate, involucral bracts imbricate in several rows, receptacle slightly convex, with chaffy scales; disc fls. tubular, bisexual, anthers tailed, ray fls. female; disc achenes cylindrical, ribbed, ray achenes 3-angled, pappus of many separate scales.

Propagated by cuttings or seeds.

maritimus (L.) Less. [*Odontospermum maritimum* (L.) Schultz-Bip.]. Silky-woolly, mound-forming, subshrubby per., to 1 ft.; lvs. oblong-spatulate, spatulate, or oblanceolate, to 2 in. long, gray-hairy; heads to about 1½ in. across, solitary, sessile; fls. yellow. Medit. region.

sericeus (L.f.) DC. [*Odontospermum sericeum* (L.f.) Schultz-Bip.]. Shrub, to 4 ft.; lvs. oblanceolate, to 2½ in. long, often cuneate, silkyhairy, sessile; heads to 2 in. across, solitary, terminal and axillary, sessile; fls. yellow. Canary Is.

ASTEROGYNE H. Wendl. *Palmae*. A few spp. of short, solitary, unarmed monoecious palms without a crownshaft, in Cent. Amer. and n. S. Amer.; lvs. pinnately ribbed, elongate-wedge-shaped, undivided except at 2-cleft apex; infl. among lvs., long-peduncled, subtended by 2 basally inserted bracts, spicate or branched, then the rachis very short and rachillae 2–8, nearly fascicled, simple; fls. white, in triads (2 male and 1 female) sunken in pits arranged in vertical rows; male fls. with sepals imbricate, petals united basally, valvate above, stamens 6, anthers 2-cleft, pistillode elongate, female fls. with sepals imbricate, petals united basally, valvate above, staminodes 6, spreading, ovary 3-celled; fr. with basal stigmatic scar, endocarp not operculate, seed with homogeneous endosperm and basal embryo.

For culture see *Palms*.

Martiana (H. Wendl.) H. Wendl. ex Hemsl. To 8 ft.; lvs. to 2 ft. long or more; infl. to 3 ft. long, orange in fr., rachillae mostly 5; fls. white; fr. black, about 3/8 in. long. Zone 10b.

ASTILBE Buch.-Ham. ex D. Don [*Hoteia* C. Morr. & Decne.]. SPIRAEA, PERENNIAL S. *Saxifragaceae*. About 14 spp. of per. herbs, 2 in N. Amer., the rest in e. Asia; lvs. 2–3-ternately compound, lfts. toothed or cut; fls. panicled, white or pink, bisexual or unisexual, calyx small, usually 4–5-parted, petals 4–5 or more, or 0, stamens as many or twice as many as the petals, pistils 2 or 3, separate or variously united; fr. a dehiscent follicle. Sometimes confused with *Aruncus* and *Filipendula* of the Rosaceae, but those genera have many stamens and 3 to many separate pistils.

Astilbes are of easy cultivation and grow best in rich soil, with plenty of water. Propagated by division or by seeds. They may be grown in the open or partly shaded border or forced under glass. They require 10–14 weeks to come into bloom when forced, and need abundant moisture.

The florist's astilbes are likely to be hybrids, the result of crossing *A. japonica*, *A. chinensis* var. *Davidii*, *A. Thunbergii*, and a plant called "*A. astilboides.*"

×**Arendsii** Arends. A collective name for a series of hybrids between *A. chinensis* var. *Davidii* and various other spp.; fls. range in color from purplish to nearly white.

astilboides (Maxim.) E. Lemoine: *Aruncus dioicus* var. *astilboides* (Maxim.) Mak., which is not known to be in general cult. Material grown as *Astilbe astilboides* is probably a variant of *A. japonica* with larger panicles of densely arranged white. fls.

biternata (Venten.) Britt. [*A. decandra* D. Don]. FALSE GOATS-BEARD. To 6 ft.; lvs. to 2 ft. across, lfts. ovate, to 5 in. long, cordate to rounded at base, sharply serrate; fls. many, yellowish-white, fertile fls. with minute stamens and none. Mts., Ky. and Va. to Ga.

chinensis (Maxim.) Franch. To 2 ft.; lvs. 2–3-ternately compound, lfts. ovate-oblong, double serrate; axis of infl. densely woolly, panicles narrow-branching; fls. white, rose-tinged, or purplish, sessile. China, Japan. Var. **Davidii** Franch. [*A. Davidii* (Franch.) A. Henry]. Fls. rosepurple; one parent of some hybrid races, including *A.* ×*Arendsii*.

×**crispa** (Arends) Bergmans. A race of garden hybrids.

Davidii: *A. chinensis* var.

decandra: *A. biternata*.

grandis Stapf ex E. H. Wils. To 6 ft.; lvs. ternately pinnate or 3-pinnate, lfts. ovate, to 4 in. long, doubly toothed, somewhat hairy; panicles densely fld., to 3 ft. long, with spreading brs.; fls. creamy-white. Cent. China.

japonica (C. Morr. & Decne.) A. Gray. SPIRAEA (of florists). To 3 ft.; lvs. 2–3-ternately compound, lfts. narrow- to lanceolate-ovate, cuneate, sharp-toothed; panicles erect, terminal and axillary; fls. small, white, petals narrowly spatulate, usually longer than stamens. Cv. 'Morheimii' is listed.

koreana Nakai. To 2 ft.; lvs. pinnate or 2-pinnate; panicles many-fld., arching; fls. small, rose-pink in bud, creamy-white when open. Korea.

×**Lemoinei** E. Lemoine: "*A. astilboides*" × *A. Thunbergii*. A race of garden hybrids.

rivularis Buch.-Ham. ex D. Don. To 5 ft., with creeping rhizome; lvs. 2-ternately compound, lfts. ovate, to 3 in. long, toothed; panicles large with spikelike brs.; fls. yellowish-white, petals 0. Nepal.

×**rosea** Hort. van Waveren & Kruijff: *A. chinensis* × *A. japonica.* Similar to *A. japonica* in habit, but fls. pinkish. The best-known cvs. are: **'Peach Blossom'**, fls. pale peach-pink; **'Queen Alexandra'**, fls. deep pink.

×**rubella** Hort. Lemoine: *A. chinensis* var. *Davidii* × *A.* ×*Lemoinei.* Similar to *A.* ×*Lemoinei* but fls. rose-colored; panicle more compact than in *A. chinensis.*

sikokumontana: *A. Thunbergii* var.

simplicifolia Mak. Not over 1 ft.; lvs. simple, ovate, deeply lobed or cut, 3 in. long; panicle slender, narrow; fls. starlike, white. Japan.

sinensis: a listed name of no botanical standing, perhaps in error for *A. chinensis.*

Thunbergii (Siebold & Zucc.) Miq. To 2 ft.; lvs. 2–3-pinnate, lfts. ovate, to 3½ in. long, toothed, hairy; panicles spreading; fls. white, often becoming pink. Japan. Var. **fujisanensis** (Nakai) Ohwi. Lvs. small, doubly serrate, firm; petals short, nearly as long as stamens. Var. **sikokumontana** (G. Koidz.) Murata [*A. sikokumontana* G. Koidz.]. Lfts. narrow, doubly incised-serrate.

tomentosa: a listed name of no botanical standing, perhaps for *Spiraea tomentosa.*

ASTRAGALUS L. MILK VETCH. *Leguminosae* (subfamily *Faboideae*). Perhaps 1,000 spp. of herbs, mostly of temp. regions of the N. Hemisphere; lvs. alt., odd-pinnate, lfts. entire, stipules prominent; fls. purple, white, or yellow, papilionaceous, 5-merous, stamens 10, 9 united and 1 separate; fr. a 1–2-celled, leathery, fleshy or papery legume, not much swollen.

Certain species are the source of gum tragacanth. Ornamental species are occasionally planted in the border or rock garden. Propagated by seeds or division in spring.

adsurgens Pall. Sts. erect, nearly glabrous; lfts. in 11–12 pairs, lanceolate, acute; peduncles longer than lvs., spikes oblong, narrow; fls. blue-purple; fr. oblong-cylindrical, somewhat 3-angled. E. Asia, w. N. Amer. Var. **adsurgens.** The typical var.; standard 3–4 times as long as calyx tube. E. Asia. Var. **robustior** Hook. [*A. striatus* Nutt.]. Standard less than 3 times as long as calyx tube. W. N. Amer.

agrestis Dougl. [*A. goniatus* Nutt.]. Tufted per., to 10 or 12 in., with cespitose root crown; lfts. in 7–10 pairs, linear-oblong to elliptic, about ⁵⁄₁₆ in. long, sometimes retuse; spikes short; fls. purple; fr. 2-celled, ovoid, to ⅜ in. long, villous. Calif., n. to Yukon, e. to Man., and New Mex.

alopecuroides L. Erect per., to 5 ft., pubescent; lfts. ovate-oblong, 1 in. long, acute; spikes dense, ovate to cylindrical; fls. yellow; fr. erect, ovoid, pubescent, without grooves, enclosed in woolly calyx. Siberia and cent. Eur.

alpinus L. Per., sts. often decumbent, to 8–15 in. long; lfts. in 6–11 pairs, to ½ in. long; racemes short; fls. violet; fr. 1-celled, black-pubescent. Mts., n. Eur., Asia, N. Amer.

Barrii Barneby. Differs from *A. tridactylicus* in having glabrous stipules and fls. larger, to ⅝ in. long. S. Dak.

bisulcatus (Hook.) A. Gray. Per., sts. often decumbent, to 2½ ft. long; lfts. to 1 in. long; racemes dense, spikelike; fls. purple; fr. 1-celled, 2-grooved on upper side. Alta., s. to New Mex. and Nebr.

canadensis L. Per., to 5 ft.; lfts. in 10–13 pairs, oblong; spikes long, dense; fls. greenish-cream; fr. crowded, 2-celled, cylindrical, to ½ in. long, glabrous. Que., s. to Ga., w. to Calif. and Tex.

caryocarpus: *A. crassicarpus.*

coccineus Brandeg. Low, tufted per., sts. densely tomentose; lfts. in 3–7 pairs; calyx tube reddish, ½ in. long, petals scarlet, to 1½ in. long; fr. ovoid or fusiform, to 1½ in. long, silky-pubescent. Calif., Ariz.; nw. Mex.

crassicarpus Nutt. [*A. caryocarpus* Ker-Gawl.; *A. succulentus* Richardson]. GROUND PLUM. Pubescent per., sts. often decumbent, to 15 in. long; lfts. to ½ in. long; racemes short; fls. violet-purple; fr. stalked, nearly globose, to ¾ in. in diam. Minn. to Tex. Var. **crassicarpus.** The typical var.; sts. arising together from root crown. Miss. Valley, w. nearly to foothills of Rocky Mts. Var. **Berlandieri** Barneby [*A. mexicanus* A. DC.]. Sts. arising singly or a few together from widely creeping rhizomes. Tex.

depressus L. Sts. very short, to 4 in. long, spreading; lvs. to 6 in. long, lfts. in 10–12 pairs, obovate, obtuse to retuse, to ⁵⁄₁₆ in. long, white-pubescent beneath; peduncles very short or to 3 in. long, racemes short; fls. small, lilac to whitish; fr. oblong, inflated, glabrous. Mts., s. Eur., n. to Switzerland; Morocco.

exscapus L. Tufted, densely tawny-hairy in all parts, sts. very short; lvs. erect, to 12 in. long, long-petioled, lfts. in 12–28 pairs, elliptic to ovate, to 1¼ in. long; peduncles mostly very short, racemes dense,

headlike; fls. yellow, to 1 in. long, calyx large, thin; fr. to ¾ in. long. Spain to s. Russia.

falcatus Lam. Per., to 2 ft.; lfts. in 16–20 pairs, elliptic-oblong, acute to mucronate; infl. a spike; fls. greenish-yellow; fr. pendent, curved, 2-celled, appressed-pilose. Siberia.

gilviflorus E. P. Sheld. Tufted, silvery-pubescent per., to 4 in.; lvs. of 3 lfts., lfts. ⅝ in. long; fls. yellowish, few in axils; fr. oblong, less than ½ in. long, acute, strigose. Man. to Mont., s. to Nebr. and Colo.

glareosus: *A. Purshii.*

goniatus: *A. agrestis.*

mexicanus: *A. crassicarpus* var. *Berlandieri.*

missouriensis Nutt. Per., to 5 ft.; lvs. to 5 in. long, silky-pubescent, lfts. to ½ in. long or less; spikes short, loose, few-fld.; fls. violet-purple; fr. sessile, leathery, 1-celled, cylindric-oblong, to 1 in. long. Sask., s. to Kans. and New Mex.

monspessulanus L. Per., sts. trailing, to 10 in. long; lfts. in 18–25 pairs, broadly elliptic, to ⁵⁄₁₆ in. long; peduncles long, ascending; racemes short; fls. purple or violet; fr. nearly cylindrical, almost glabrous. Eur., N. Afr.

Nuttallii (Torr. & A. Gray) J. T. Howell. Bushy per., white-villous to almost smooth; lvs. to 6 in. long, lfts. cuneate-obovate to oblong, to 1 in. long, retuse; peduncles to 6 in. long, racemes dense; fls. greenish-white, ½ in. long; fr. inflated, 1–2 in. long. Calif.

Onobrychis L. Per., sts. decumbent or ascending, to 1½ ft. long, gray-pubescent; lfts. to ½ in. long; racemes short; fls. bright violet, about 1 in. long; fr. short, villous. Eur., w. Asia.

Purshii Dougl. ex Hook. [*A. glareosus* Dougl. ex Hook.]. White-woolly, mat-forming per.; lvs. to 2½ in. long, lfts. in 4–9 pairs, to ½ in. long; fls. in clusters of 3–5, white, or white and blue, to 1 in. long; fr. oblong, to ¾ in. long, woolly. Rocky Mts.

shiroumaensis Mak. Per., to 1 ft., white-pubescent; lvs. to 2½ in. long, lfts. in about 7 pairs, elliptic, sometimes retuse; peduncles longer than lvs., racemes about 1 in. long; fls. ½ in. long. Japan.

spatulatus E. P. Sheld. Tufted per.; lvs. simple or with 3–5 lfts., lvs. or lfts. linear-oblanceolate, to 2 in. long, appressed-silky-hairy; racemes short, 2–10-fld. or more; fls. about ⁵⁄₁₆ in. long; fr. about ½ in. long, finely strigose. Sask. s. to Nebr., Colo., and Utah.

striatus: *A. adsurgens* var. *robustior.*

succulentus: *A. crassicarpus.*

tridactylicus A. Gray. Stemless, tufted per., about 2 in. high, densely white-silky; lvs. alike or dimorphic, lfts. 3, oblanceolate, to ¾ in. long, those of the early lvs. usually broader and shorter, stipules, at least the early ones, pubescent beneath; fls. pink-purple, to ⁷⁄₁₆ in. long; fr. globose-ovoid, hoary. Colo., Wyo.

Wootonii E. P. Sheld. Slender ann., to 1 ft.; lfts. in 5–9 pairs, oblanceolate to linear-oblong; racemes short, loose, 4–10-fld.; fls. whitish; fr. ovoid-ellipsoid, to 1 in. long, strigose. Tex. to Calif., n. Mex. Causes loco disease in animals.

ASTRANTIA L. MASTERWORT. *Umbelliferae.* About 9 spp. of polygamous herbs of Eur. and w. Asia; lvs. palmately lobed or dissected; fls. small, in umbels subtended by leafy involucres; fr. nearly cylindrical.

A few species are sometimes planted in the border; propagated by seeds and by division.

bavarica F. W. Schultz. Per., to 1½ ft.; lvs. 5-parted to base or nearly so, lobes toothed; involucral bracts 3-nerved, mostly entire, longer than fls. Bavarian Alps.

Biebersteinii Trautv. Per., to 1 ft. or less; lvs. 3-parted, middle section more or less 3-lobed, oblong, serrate; fls. whitish, calyx lobes pinkish, as long as petals. Caucasus. By some authors treated as a var. of *A. major*, differing in having basal lf. segms. smaller and more obtuse, and involucral bracts oblanceolate.

carniolica Vul'f. Per., similar to *A. bavarica*, but only 1 ft., lvs. 3–5-parted to middle, involucral bracts shorter than fls. Eur.

helleborifolia: *A. maxima.*

major L. Per., to 3 ft.; lvs. mostly basal, with 3–5 deeply toothed lobes; involucral bracts showy, usually lanceolate, longer than fls., often tinged purplish; fls. pinkish, rose, or white. Eur. Adapted to stream-side planting.

maxima Pall. [*A. helleborifolia* Salisb.]. Per., to 30 in.; lvs. 3–4-parted, with finely toothed lobes; involucral bracts ciliate-serrate, longer than fls., often tinged with pink. S. Eur., Caucasus.

minor L. To 16 in.; lvs. long-petioled, divided into 7–9 toothed, narrow segms.; involucral bracts entire or 3-toothed, about as long as fls. Eur.

trifida Hoffm. To 18 in. or more; lvs. long-petioled, mostly divided into 3 rather broad, toothed segms.; involucral bracts 3–5-nerved, entire or minutely toothed, slightly longer than fls. Caucasus.

ASTRIPOMOEA Meeuse [*Astrochlaena* H. G. Hallier, not Corda, or Garcke]. *Convolvulaceae* Three spp. of erect to decumbent, sometimes prostrate but never climbing, ann. or per., stellate-pubescent herbs or subshrubs of S. Afr.; lvs. usually ovate, entire to coarsely dentate-sinuate; fls. in few- to many-fld., or occasionally 1-fld. cymes; fr. a dehiscent, usually glabrous caps.

malvacea (Klotzsch) Meeuse [*Astrochlaena malvacea* (Klotzsch) H. G. Hallier]. Per., erect or decumbent, sts. more or less densely white- or tan-stellate-pubescent; lvs. to 3 in. long, densely white-tomentose beneath; fls. mauve or purple; caps. subglobose, ¼ in. across.

ASTROCARYUM G. F. Mey. *Palmae.* More than 40 spp. of monoecious palms from Mex. to Brazil, prickly on most or all parts; trunks solitary to cespitose; lvs. pinnate, pinnae acute or apically toothed, 1- or several-ribbed, often pale underneath; infl. among lvs., long-peduncled, simply branched but in fr. sometimes appearing spicate, bracts 2, the upper enclosing the infl. in bud, usually prickly, more or less persistent, fls. in basal part of rachilla either in 1 to few triads (2 male and 1 female) or the female solitary, above these male fls. many, paired or solitary, seated in cups formed by united bractlets, together resembling a honeycomb; male fls. with sepals united, petals valvate, stamens 6, female fls. with calyx cupular or tubular, corolla tubular, staminodes in a ring or separate, pistil 3-celled; fr. smooth or prickly, sometimes angled, mesocarp fleshy, endocarp bony with 3 pores near the middle, seed with homogeneous endosperm.

Several of the Brazilian species have been important sources of oilseeds. For culture see *Palms.*

aculeatum G. F. Mey. [*A. aureum* Griseb. & H. Wendl.]. TUCUMA. St. solitary, to 75 ft. or more, 1 ft. in diam., densely spiny; lvs. ascending, to more than 10 ft. long, pinnae about 100 per side, in groups and in several planes, 1-ribbed; infl. erect, to 6 ft. long or more, rachillae to 300, bearing 2–4 female fls.; fr. subglobose to ovoid, beaked, yellow-orange, to 2³⁄₁₆ in. long. Trinidad, n. S. Amer. Frs. yield a palm oil.

aureum: *A. aculeatum.*

mexicanum Liebm. To 15 ft. or more, spiny; lvs. spreading, 3 ft. long or more, pinnae in 1 plane, unequal in width, 1- to several-ribbed, pale underneath; infl. 1 ft. long or more; rachillae several, bearing a single female fl.; fr. prickly, to 2 in. long. Mex. to Honduras. Warmer parts of Zone 10a.

Standleyanum L. H. Bailey. To 45 ft. or more, spiny; lvs. spreading, to 12 ft. long or more, pinnae many, in groups and in more than 1 plane, 1-ribbed; rachillae many, bearing 2–3 female fls.; fr. orange, beaked, to 1¾ in. long. Cent. Amer.

ASTROCHLAENA: see *ASTRIPOMOEA.*

ASTROLOBA Uitew. [*Apicra* Haw., not Willd.]. *Liliaceae.* About 12 spp. of succulent aloelike per. herbs, native to S. Afr.; sts. short; lvs. crowded or arranged in spirals; fls. usually greenish, in loose, spikelike racemes, perianth tubular, regular, stamens 6; fr. a caps.

For culture see *Succulents.*

aspera (Haw.) Uitew. [*Apicra aspera* (Haw.) Willd.]. St. to 6 in.; lvs. broadly triangular, ⅝ in. long and wide, warty on underside; fls. greenish, tinged pink, ⅜ in. long, in racemes to 1 ft. high.

deltoidea (Hook.f.) Uitew. [*Apicra deltoidea* (Hook.f.) Bak.]. St. to 6 in.; lvs. broadly triangular, to 1 in. long, in 5 rows; fls. yellow-green, in racemes to 1 ft. long.

Dodsoniana Uitew. Old sts. decumbent, to 8 in. long; lvs. ovate-lanceolate, to 1⅜ in. long, long-acuminate, sharp-pointed; fls. white with green nerves and yellow tips, somewhat urceolate, about ⅜ in. long.

foliolosa (Haw.) Uitew. [*Apicra foliolosa* (Haw.) Willd.]. St. to 1 ft.; lvs. broadly-triangular, to ¾ in. long; fls. greenish-yellow, pink at tips, ½ in. long, in racemes over 1 ft. long.

pentagona (Haw.) Uitew. [*Apicra pentagona* (Haw.) Willd.; *Haworthia pentagona* Haw.]. St. to 1 ft.; lvs. lanceolate-triangular, to 1½ in. long and about ¾ in. wide, in 5 vertical rows; infl. to 1½ ft. high, simple or occasionally branched; fls. greenish, ½ in. long.

Skinneri (A. Berger) Uitew. [*Apicra Skinneri* A. Berger; *Haworthia Skinneri* (A. Berger) Resende]. St. erect; lvs. ovate-triangular, to 1½ in. long and about 1 in. wide, with many tubercles beneath.

ASTROLOMA R. Br. *Epacridaceae.* About 20 spp. of low shrubs, native to Australia; lvs. alt.; fls. axillary, solitary, 5-merous, corolla tubular, the lobes valvate and hairy inside, tube much longer than lobes, with 5 tufts of hairs or scales inside below the middle, stamens inserted on throat of tube, not exserted, ovary 5-celled, 1-ovuled; fr. a more or less succulent drupe.

Cultivation as for *Erica.*

humifusum (Cav.) R. Br. CRANBERRY HEATH, AUSTRALIAN CRANBERRY. Small prostrate shrub; lvs. linear to narrowly lanceolate, to ½ in. long, sharp-pointed, ciliate, scabrous; corolla bright red, ½–1 in. long; fr. globose-ovoid, to nearly ½ in. in diam., greenish, sweet and edible. Temp. Australia. Zone 10 in Calif.

major: a listed name of no botanical standing; applied to a plant having umbels of rose to white fls., with purple-tinged showy bracts.

ASTRONIUM Jacq. *Anacardiaceae.* About 13 spp. of trop. Amer. trees, usually dioecious; lvs. alt., pinnate; fls. small, in axillary or terminal panicles, unisexual, petals longer than sepals in male fls., shorter than sepals in female fls.; fr. a drupe. Distinguished from *Rhus* by the enlarged winged calyx enveloping the fr.

Balansae Engl. To 30 ft.; lvs. of 10–17 lfts., these lanceolate-acuminate, 2–2½ in. long; panicles large, as long as the lvs.; fr. nearly globose, to ³⁄₁₆ in. in diam. Paraguay and Argentina. Zone 9b.

ASTROPHYTUM Lem. STAR CACTUS. *Cactaceae.* Six spp. of few-ribbed cacti, native to Mex.; sts. mostly solitary, hemispherical to short-cylindric, mostly scaly or floccose, the crown not woolly, ribs mostly 5 or 8; armament none or sparse; fls. subapical, opening on successive days, short-funnelform, yellow, often with red center, scales of tube and ovary pungent, their axils woolly; fr. globose, seeds dark, glossy, hilum with a large shallowly cuplike collar. Many vars. and hybrids have been listed.

For culture see *Cacti.*

asterias (Zucc.) Lem. [*Echinocactus asterias* Zucc.]. SEA-URCHIN CACTUS, SAND-DOLLAR, SILVER-DOLLAR. Sts. hemispherical, to 1½ in. high and 3 in. wide, ribs mostly 8, low and rounded; areoles prominent, round, woolly, spineless; fls. yellow, 1½ in. across; fr. opening at base. Spring, S. Tex., n. Mex.

capricorne (A. Dietr.) Britt. & Rose. Sts. globose to ovoid, to 10 in. high and 4 in. thick, with white, starlike scales, ribs mostly 8, acute; spines 5–10, flat, twisted, weak, brown, to 3 in. long; fls. 3 in. long; fr. opening at base. N. Mex. Cvs. are: **'Aureum'**, young spines yellow; **'Crassispinum'**, spines 6–8, thick, dark, the lowest pair strongest, curved to the sides; **'Majus'**: perhaps 'Crassispinum'; **'Minus'**, smaller, to 5 in. high, with fewer, shorter, more nearly cylindrical spines; **'Senile'**, larger, to 14 in. high and 6 in. thick, with few scales, the spines 15–20, nearly cylindrical.

coahuilense (H. Moell.) Kayser [*A. myriostigma* var. *coahuilense* (H. Moell.) Borg]. Sts. globose to cylindrical, with gray-white scales, ribs 5; fls. sulphur-yellow with orange to scarlet center; fr. purple-red, opening at the bottom. N. Mex.

myriostigma (Salm-Dyck) Lem. BISHOP'S CAP, BISHOP'S-HOOD, MONKSHOOD. Sts. solitary or cespitose, globose to cylindrical, to 2 ft. high and 8 in. thick, grayish with scales, ribs 4–10, mostly 5, broad; areoles brown-woolly, spineless; fls. to 2½ in. long and wide; fr. vertically dehiscent. N.-cent. Mex. Var. **coahuilense:** *A. coahuilense.* Var. **potosinum** (H. Moell.) Borg. Fls. yellow; fr. dry, green, few-seeded, splitting at apex. Cv. **'Columnare'**. St. cylindrical. Cv. **'Nudum'**. St. green. Var. **quadricostatum** (H. Moell.) Borg. [var. *tetragonum* Hort.]. Broader than high, green, ribs 4; fls. yellow; fr. dry, green, few-seeded, splitting at apex. Tamaulipas (Mex.). Var. **tetragonum:** a listed name of no botanical standing for var. *quadricostatum.*

ornatum (DC.) Britt. & Rose. STAR CACTUS, BISHOP'S-CAP, ORNAMENTAL MONKSHOOD. Sts. short-cylindric, to 14 in. high and 6 in. thick, white-floccose, ribs mostly 8, acute; areoles remote, spines 5–11, awl-shaped, little-curved, pungent, yellow, becoming brown, to 1¼ in. long; fls. yellow, to 3½ in. wide; fr. splitting longitudinally. Cent. Mex. Cv. **'Mirbellii'**. Spines golden-yellow.

ASYNEUMA Griseb. & Schenk. *Campanulaceae.* About 40–50 spp. of per. herbs, native mostly to se. Eur. and Asia Minor, sometimes united with *Phyteuma,* from which it is distinguished by the loose spicate-paniculate infls.; distinguished from *Campanula* by the deeply divided corolla with more or less linear-oblong, tardily separating lobes.

campanuloides (Bieb.) Bornm. [*Phyteuma campanuloides* Bieb.]. Sts. erect, simple, 1–2 ft.; lower lvs. petioled, ovate, crenate, grading above to sessile and lanceolate; fls. in terminal, often compound racemes, corolla deep violet-blue. Caucasus.

canescens (Waldst. & Kit.) Griseb. & Schenk [*Phyteuma canescens* Waldst. & Kit.]. To 3 ft., sts. simple or branched basally, grayish-pubescent or nearly glabrous; lvs. ovate, short-petioled in lower part, sessile above, lanceolate to linear; fls. nearly sessile, paniculate at base of infl., remotely spicate above, pale lilac, to ⁵⁄₁₆ in. long. Yugoslavia to Greece.

limonifolium (L.) Janch. [*Campanula phyteumoides* Sibth. ex Zuccagni; *Phyteuma limonifolium* (L.) Sibth. & Sm.]. Erect, to 2 ft., glabrous or scabrous; lvs. basal, with slender petiole, 2–8 in. long, spatulate or elliptic, denticulate or entire; fls. sessile or nearly so, in elongate, naked, simple spikes, blue, about ¼ in. long. Yugoslavia to Turkey.

lobelioides (Willd.) Hand.-Mazz. [*Phyteuma lobelioides* Willd.]. Erect, to 2 ft.; lvs. principally in basal rosettes, narrowly lanceolate, to 5 in. long, wavy-toothed, a few grading to linear along the lower st.; fls. long-pedicelled, in loose, spikelike racemes, lilac-blue, ¼–⁵⁄₁₆ in. long. Asia Minor.

ASYSTASIA Blume. *Acanthaceae.* About 70 spp. of herbs or shrubs, in the Old World tropics; lvs. opp., entire; fls. usually opp., sometimes alt., in spikes or racemes, bracts and bractlets small, calyx divided into 5 linear lobes, corolla tube short to long, funnelform, ventricose, or narrow, lobes 5, subequal, stamens 4, didynamous, anther sacs 2, parallel, minutely spurred at base, ovary pubescent, ovules 4, stigma slightly 2-parted or subcapitate; fr. an elliptic caps., 2- or 4-seeded above, contracted at base, seeds flat, round, glabrous.

bella: *Mackaya bella.*

coromandeliana: *A. gangetica.*

gangetica (L.) T. Anderson [*A. coromandeliana* Nees]. Sparsely pubescent per., sts. procumbent or clambering, 1–4 ft. long; lvs. ovate, 1–4 in. long; fls. in 1-sided racemes to 4 in. long, calyx lobes shorter than corolla tube, corolla lavender, purple, to yellowish, to 1½ in. long and 1 in. across, lobes spreading; caps. 1 in. long. India, Malay Pen., Afr. Grown as a ground cover in s. Fla. and the tropics.

ATALANTIA Corrêa. *Rutaceae.* Not cult. A. buxifolia: *Severinia buxifolia.*

ATALAYA Blume. *Sapindaceae.* About 10 spp. of polygamous trees and shrubs, native to Australia, Timor, and S. Afr.; lvs. alt., pinnate; fls. in large axillary or terminal panicles, sepals and petals 5, stamens 8; fr. separating into 1-seeded, long-winged samaras.

hemiglauca (F. J. Muell.) F. J. Muell. ex Benth. Small tree; lfts. 2–6, linear to oblong, 2½–8 in. long, glabrous, glaucous; fls. white, sepals ovate or orbicular; samaras to 1½ in. long. Australia.

ATAMOSCO: *ZEPHYRANTHES.*

ATHANASIA L. [*Hymenolepis* Cass.]. *Compositae* (Anthemis Tribe). About 40 spp. of pungently scented shrubs in S. Afr.; lvs. alt., simple or pinnate; fl. heads small, in corymbs, discoid, involucral bracts imbricate, scarious, receptacle with chaffy scales; fls. all tubular, ray fls. absent; achenes oblong, 5-angled, pappus of short scales or stout hairs.

parviflora L. Much-branched shrub, to over 3 ft.; lvs. to 4 in. long, pinnately divided into few, long, linear lobes; heads many, small, cylindrical, 3–4-fld., in dense corymbs. S. Afr.

ATHROTAXIS D. Don. *Taxodiaceae.* Three spp. of densely branched, monoecious, coniferous, evergreen trees, native to Tasmania, allied to *Cryptomeria;* lvs. small, crowded, scalelike or lanceolate; male cones solitary, female cones globose, scales 10–16, woody; seeds 3–6, 2-winged, maturing in 1 year.

Sometimes grown in frost-free climates with cool growing season, as the Pacific Coast (Zone 10). For culture see *Conifers.*

cupressoides D. Don. To 40 ft.; lvs. imbricate, appressed, of 2 kinds, those on young twigs scalelike, rhombic-ovate, to ⅛ in. long, others oblong, ¼–½ in. long; female cones to ½ in. across, with 5–6 pairs of decussate scales. Zone 9. Pacific Coast.

laxifolia Hook. To 25 ft.; lvs. looser than in *A. cupressoides,* ovate-lanceolate, ¼ in. long, acute or obtuse; female cones ¾ in. across, with many spirally arranged scales.

selaginoides D. Don. To 100 ft.; lvs. in dense spirals, looser than in the other spp., oblong-lanceolate, to ½ in. long, spiny-pointed; female cones to 1 in. across, with spirally arranged, abruptly acuminate, spine-tipped scales.

ATHYRIUM Roth. *Polypodiaceae.* About 25 spp. of ferns, widely distributed, mostly in the tropics; lvs. similar to some spp. of *Asplenium,* with which this genus has sometimes been united, but not evergreen, and differing in petiole anatomy, and the sori oblong to linear, usually curved, sometimes more or less horseshoe-shaped, mostly crossing a veinlet.

A few species are cultivated. For culture see *Ferns.*

acrostichoides: *Diplazium acrostichoides.*

alpestre (Hoppe) Ryl. Lvs. tufted, from a short rhizome, elliptic-lanceolate to ovate-lanceolate, to 3 ft. long, 2-pinnate, pinnae oblong or lanceolate, pinnules sharply toothed; sori orbicular, small, seemingly without indusia, spores blackish, reticulate. Eur., Asia, Iceland, Nfld. Var. **americanum** Butters [*A. americanum* (Butters) Maxon; *A. alpestre* var. *gaspense* Fern.]. Pinnae very narrow, more distant; indusia absent. Que., Alaska to Calif.

americanum: *A. alpestre* var.

angustifolium: *Diplazium pycnocarpon.*

angustum: *A. Filix-femina* var. *Michauxii.*

asplenioides: *A. Filix-femina* var.

australe: *Diplazium australe.*

cyclosorum: *A. Filix-femina* var. *sitchense.*

Filix-femina (L.) Roth. [*Asplenium Filix-femina* L.]. LADY FERN. Lvs. to 3 ft. long, bright green; 2-pinnate, pinnae deeply cut or toothed; sori mostly lunate to horseshoe-shaped. Temp. N. Hemisphere. Hardy. The Amer. representatives all in cult. are now generally treated as follows: Var. **asplenioides** (Michx.) Farw. [*A. asplenioides* (Michx.) Eat.]. SOUTHERN L. F. Rhizomes horizontal, creeping, with minute deciduous scales; lvs. widest toward the base; indusia with gland-tipped cilia. Mass. to Fla., w. to Okla. and Tex. Var. **californicum:** var. *sitchense.* Var. **cyclosorum:** var. *sitchense.* Var. **Michauxii** (K. Spreng.) Farw. [*A. angustum* (Willd.) K. Presl.; *Asplenium Michauxii* K. Spreng.]. NORTHERN L. F. Rhizomes somewhat ascending, with persistent chaffy scales to ⅝ in. long; lvs. widest near the middle; indusia with cilia not gland-tipped. Ne. N. Amer. Var. **sitchense** Rupr. [*A. Filix-femina* var. *californica* Butters; *A. cyclosorum* Rupr.; *Asplenium Filix-femina* var. *cyclosorum* Ledeb.]. Rhizomes strongly ascending to erect; indusia minute, spores warty, not smooth. Boreal N. Amer. and s. to Calif. Cvs. derived from material of Eur. origin include: 'Coronatum', 'Corymbiferum', 'Craigii', 'Crispum', 'Cristatum', 'Frizelliae', 'Grandiceps', 'Laciniatum', 'Latifolium', 'Multifidum', 'Plumosum', 'Pulcherrimum', 'Setigerum', 'Victoria'.

Filix-mas: a listed name, probably in error for *A. Filix-femina* or *Dryopteris Filix-mas.*

Goeringianum (Kunze) T. V. Moore. Lvs. deciduous, usually drooping, to 1½ ft. long, 1-pinnate, pinnae toothed or cut. Japan. Hardy. Cv. 'Pictum'. Lvs. with central gray stripe, petioles purplish.

japonicum: *Diplazium japonicum.*

Michauxii: *A. Filix-femina* var.

pycnocarpon: *Diplazium pycnocarpon.*

stenopteris: a listed name of no botanical standing.

thelypteroides: *Diplazium acrostichoides.*

umbrosum: *Diplazium australe.*

ATRAGENE: *CLEMATIS.*

ATRAPHAXIS L. *Polygonaceae.* About 18 spp. of deciduous subshrubs, native to N. Afr. and Greece, w. to cent. Asia; lvs. small; fls. white or pinkish, in terminal racemes, bisexual, sepals 4–5, stamens 6–8; fr. an achene, surrounded by enlarged sepals.

They thrive on rather dry soil in sunny positions. Propagated by seeds in spring, by layers, and by cuttings of young wood in early summer under glass.

buxifolia: *A. caucasica.*

caucasica (Hoffm.) Pavlov [*A. buxifolia* (Bieb.) Jaub. & Spach]. To 2 ft. or more; lvs. obovate-cuneate, to nearly 1 in. long, obtuse, with crisp margin, yellowish- to brownish-green; fls. rose-pink. Cent. U.S.S.R. to Caucasus.

frutescens (L.) C. Koch [*A. lanceolata* (Bieb.) Meissn.]. To 3 ft.; lvs. oblong to lanceolate, to 1¼ in. long, grayish-green; fls. whitish, in racemes to 3 in. long. Summer to autumn. S. U.S.S.R. to cent. Asia. Hardy far north.

lanceolata: *A. frutescens.*

ATRIPLEX L. SALTBUSH, ORACH. *Chenopodiaceae.* About 100 or more spp. of cosmopolitan mealy or scurfy herbs or shrubs; lvs. alt. or opp.; fls. in clustered spikes, small, unisexual, male fls. with 3–5-parted calyx, no bracts, and 3–5 stamens, female fls. usually with no calyx, but 2-bracted, the bracts enlarging and covering the fr., ovary 1-celled, with 2 very slender styles; fr. a utricle.

Often occuring natively in saline soils. One species, *A. hortensis,* is grown for greens; others are grown as ornamentals, or for forage in desert regions. Propagated by seeds.

Breweri: *A. lentiformis* subsp.

californica Moq. Prostrate, gray-scurfy, monoecious per.; sts. much-branched, to 20 in. long; lvs. alt. or the lowest ones opp., crowded, sessile, lanceolate to oblanceolate, to ¾ in. long, entire. Coastal Calif. and Baja Calif.

canescens (Pursh) Nutt. FOUR-WING S., CENIZO, CHAMISO, CHAMIZA. Shrub, to 6 ft., gray-scurfy, dioecious; lvs. alt., sessile, linear-spatulate to narrowly oblong, to 2 in. long, margins revolute; bracts in fr. with 4 conspicuous wings or crests. Wash. to Mex., e. to S. Dak., Kans., and Tex.

confertifolia (Torr. & Frém.) S. Wats. SPINY S., SHADSCALE, SHEEP-FAT. Shrub, to 3 ft., spiny, gray-scurfy, dioecious; lvs. crowded, alt., entire, circular-ovate to -obovate or elliptic, to ¾ in. long, apically obtuse, subsessile. E. Ore. to N. Dak., s. to n. Mex.

Halimus L. SEA ORACH. Shrub, to 6 ft., silvery-white; lvs. alt., persistent, ovate-rhomboid to oblong, to 2½ in. long, entire. Medit. region.

hortensis L. ORACH, GARDEN O., MOUNTAIN SPINACH. Ann., to 6 ft.; lvs. triangular-ovate or arrow-shaped, to 5(–8) in. long, entire to denticulate. Asia; established in Eur. and N. Amer. Grown for greens and for ornament. The lvs. are typically green, but vary to yellowish and to dark red. Var. **atrosanguinea:** cv. 'Rubra'. Cv. **'Cupreatorosea'** [cv. 'Cupreata']. Lvs. and sts. red with a coppery luster. Cv. **'Rosea'.** Lvs. light red with darker veins and petioles. Cv. **'Rubra'** [var. *atrosanguinea* Hort. ex L. H. Bailey; var. *rubra* L.]. Lvs. blood-red.

hymenelytra (Torr.) S. Wats. DESERT HOLLY. Compact shrub, to 3 ft., white-scurfy, dioecious; lvs. alt., silvery, persistent, circular to rhombic, rounded to subcordate at base, to 1⅜ in. long, irregularly and deeply toothed, petioled; fl. bracts entire. Deserts, Calif. to Utah and New Mex., n. Mex.

lentiformis (Torr.) S. Wats. QUAILBUSH, LENS-SCALE, WHITE THISTLE. Spreading shrub, to 10 ft. or more, spiny, gray-scurfy; lvs. alt., ovate-triangular to arrow-shaped, silvery, to 2 in. long, sessile or short-petioled, entire or dentate. Subsp. **lentiformis.** The typical subsp.; dioecious; lvs. to 1½ in. long and 1 in. wide; fr. bracts flattish, to ⅛ in. long. Deserts, Calif. to Utah and New Mex., n. Mex. Subsp. **Breweri** (S. Wats.) H. M. Hall & Clements [*A. Breweri* S. Wats.]. Monoecious or dioecious; lf. blades larger, to 2 in. long and nearly as wide; fr. bracts convex, to ¼ in. long. Calif.

Nummularia Lindl. Shrub, to 10 ft., gray-scurfy, monoecious or some plants dioecious; lvs. alt., many, blue-green, circular-spatulate, to 2½ in. across, obtuse, entire to toothed, short-petioled; fls. in dense panicles, bracts sinuate-dentate, thick and corky in fr. Australia; naturalized in s. Calif.

Nuttallii S. Wats. Per., to 20 in., woody at base, white- to gray-scurfy, usually dioecious; lvs. alt., many, spatulate-oblong to obovate, to 2 in. long, entire, obtuse, basally cuneate, short-petioled. Nebr. to n. Calif., Alta. and Man.

ATROPA L. *Solanaceae.* About 4 spp. of tall, much-branched, glabrous or pubescent herbs, native from Eur. and the Medit. region to cent. Asia and Himalayas; lvs. mostly alt., entire; fls. axillary, usually solitary, rarely 2 or more, calyx 5-parted, spreading, enlarged in fr., corolla campanulate, slightly 2-lipped, stamens usually 5, borne at base of corolla tube, anthers separate, stigma peltate; fr. a 2-celled berry, seeds many.

One species yields the important drug belladonna and its constituent alkaloids, atropine and hyoscyamine. Sometimes cultivated in collections of drug plants. Propagated by seeds.

Belladonna L. BELLADONNA, DEADLY NIGHTSHADE. Per., mostly 2–3 ft., from a thick rhizome, young growth pubescent, sap red; lvs. alt. or opp., petioled, ovate-elliptic, to 6 in. long, acute; fls. solitary or in pairs, nodding, corolla about 1 in. long, dull purple-brown; berry black, glossy, nearly globose, about ½ in. in diam. Eurasia, N. Afr. All parts of the plant are poisonous if eaten. Cv. **'Lutea'** [cv. 'Lutescens']. Fls. pale greenish-yellow.

ATTALEA HBK. *Palmae.* About 30 spp. of palms in trop. Amer. resembling *Maximiliana, Orbignya, Scheelea,* but differing in having male fls. with valvate petals much wider than thick, stamens 6 to many, shorter than petals, anthers straight. One Brazilian sp. is a source of commercial fiber.

Cohune: *Orbignya Cohune.*

macrosperma: a listed name of no botanical standing and of uncertain application.

AUBRIETA Adans. *Cruciferae.* About 12 spp. of mat-forming, montane or alpine per. herbs from s. Eur. to Iran; pubescent with stellate or simple hairs, rarely glabrous; lvs. simple; fls. many, lilac-magenta to bright purple, sepals 4, petals 4, long-clawed; fr. a silique, short-oblong to globose. Closely allied to and resembling *Arabis,* but style much more slender than the ovary and often as long.

Several species are cultivated for their many colorful spring flowers.

aureo-variegata: a listed name of no botanical standing for a variegated-lvd. plant, probably a form of *A. deltoidea.*

Bougainvillei: see *A. deltoidea.*

Campbellii: see *A. deltoidea.*

Columnae Guss. To 6 in., more or less cespitose to straggling, green, loosely hairy; lvs. long-spatulate, to ½ in. long; fls. pale purple, large, to ¾ in. across, on short sts., not exceeding foliage; fr. to ¾ in. long, elliptic, stellate-hairy, style as long as ovary. Se. Eur. Subsp. **croatica** (Schott, Nym. & Kotschy) Mattf. [*A. croatica* Schott, Nym. & Kotschy]. Lvs. obovate- to rhombic-cuneate; infl. exceeding the foliage; style of fr. less than half as long as ovary. Nw. Balkan Pen.

croatica: *A. Columnae* subsp.

deltoidea (L.) DC. To 6 in., occasionally 1 ft., spreading, bushy, compact; lvs. rhombic- to obovate-cuneate; infl. usually much exceeding foliage; fls. rose-lilac to purple, to ¾ in. across, calyx cylindrical; fr. to ¾ in. long, broadly elliptic, somewhat swollen, covered with simple and forked hairs, styles usually only to ⅓ as long as ovary. Sicily, Greece to Asia Minor. Var. **graeca** (Griseb.) Regel [*A. graeca* Griseb.]. Larger and bushy; calyces and petals large; fr. with styles ½–¾ as long as ovary. A variable sp. Many names in the trade are probably hort. variants or intervarietal hybrids of this sp., including: *Bougainvillei, Campbellii, Eyrei, gloriosa, grandiflora, Hendersonii, Leichtlinii, Marschallii, Moerheimii, purpurea, rosea, tauricola, variegata, violacea.*

Eyrei: see *A. deltoidea.*

gloriosa: see *A. deltoidea.*

gracilis Sprun. ex Boiss. To 4 in., sts. slender and prostrate, forming thin carpets or tufts; lvs. narrowly lanceolate, to ⅜ in. long, entire; fls. ⅝ in. across, calyx saccate; fr. to 1 in. long or more, narrowly linear, flat, finely stellate-hairy to glabrescent, style to ¼ in. long. Greece, Albania. Variants with toothed lvs. and densely hairy fr. are known, but may not be in cult.

graeca: *A. deltoidea* var.

grandiflora: see *A. deltoidea.*

Hendersonii: see *A. deltoidea.*

×**hybrida** Hausskn.: *A. gracilis* × *A. intermedia* Heldr. & Orph. Differs from *A. gracilis* in lvs. toothed, and the many-fld. infl. much exceeding the foliage. Material listed as *A. hybrida* in the trade, however, may be hort. forms of *A. deltoidea.*

Leichtlinii: see *A. deltoidea.*

Moerheimii: see *A. deltoidea.*

purpurea: see *A. deltoidea.*

rosea: see *A. deltoidea.*

tauricola: see *A. deltoidea.*

variegata: see *A. deltoidea.*

violacea: see *A. deltoidea.*

AUCUBA Thunb. *Cornaceae.* About 3–7 spp. of dioecious, evergreen shrubs, native to temp. areas from the Himalayas to Japan; lvs. opp., simple, entire to dentate; fls. purple, in terminal panicles, calyx 4-toothed, petals 4, stamens 4, or ovary inferior, 1-celled; fr. a berrylike drupe.

Aucubas are grown for their ornamental foliage and colorful berries outdoors in mild climates or in a cool greenhouse. They thrive in a partly shaded location in moist, well-drained soil. Easily propagated by cuttings of half-ripened wood, by seeds, or the cultivars by grafting.

crotonifolia: *A. japonica* cv.

himalaica Hook.f. & T. Thoms. HIMALAYA LAUREL. To 15 ft.; lvs. lanceolate or broader, to 8 in. long, finely toothed; fr. orange to scarlet. Himalayas. Zone 9.

japonica Thunb. JAPANESE A., JAPANESE LAUREL. To 15 ft.; lvs. ovate or oblong, to 7 in. long, coarsely toothed above the middle, dark green and glossy; fr. scarlet, rarely yellow or white, ripening in early winter. Early spring. Himalayas to Japan. Zone 8. Smog-resistant. Cvs. are: 'Angustifolia': 'Longifolia'; 'Aureo-maculata': 'Picturata'; 'Crotonifolia' [*A. crotonifolia* Hort.], lvs. white-spotted; 'Dentata', lvs. smaller, coarsely toothed; 'Fructu Albo', foliage silver-variegated, fr. pale pinkish-buff; 'Goldieana', lvs. mostly yellow; 'Latimaculata': 'Picturata'; 'Longifolia' [cvs. 'Angustifolia', 'Salicifolia'], lvs. deep green, narrow, to 5 in. long; 'Macrophylla', lvs. large, broad; 'Maculata': 'Variegata'; 'Nana', compact and dwarf; 'Picturata' [cvs. 'Aureo-maculata,' 'Latimaculata'], lvs. with large yellow blotch in center; 'Salicifolia': 'Longifolia'; 'Serratifolia', lf. margins serrate; 'Variegata' [cv. 'Maculata'], GOLD-DUST TREE, GOLD-DUST PLANT, lvs. yellow-spotted; 'Viridis', robust form, lvs. green.

AULAX Bergius. *Proteaceae*. Three spp. of dioecious, evergreen shrubs of S. Afr.; lvs. scattered, simple, entire, leathery; male fls. in spikelike bracted racemes terminal on short leafy branchlets, female fls. in involucrate heads, fls. yellow or whitish-yellow; fr. an indehiscent, bearded nut.

pallasia Stapf. Shrub, to 4 ft.; lvs. linear-filiform to linear, flat or semicylindrical and channelled above, to 5 in. long, acute to obtuse, long-attenuate at base; male racemes to 1½ in. long, female heads to ¾ in. long.

pinifolia Bergius. Shrub, to 6 ft., differing from *A. pallasia* in having lvs. more or less needle-shaped, semicylindrical, and longer; male racemes shorter, about 1 in. long, female heads larger, about 1 in. long.

AULIZA: *EPIDENDRUM.*

AUREOLARIA Raf. *Scrophulariaceae*. Eleven spp. of N. Amer. herbs, parasitic on roots of *Quercus;* lvs. entire or bipinnatifid; fls. on axillary peduncles or in a terminal leafy raceme or panicle, corolla yellow, with spreading lobes; fr. a caps.

Sometimes grown from seed in the oak-woodland garden or transferred from the wild; requires acid soil. Rarely cultivated.

flava (L.) Farw. [*A. glauca* (Eddy) Raf.; *Gerardia flava* L.]. Per., to 4 ft.; lvs. mostly oblong-lanceolate, 4–6 in. long, pinnately cut or lobed; corolla yellowish-orange, 1½–2 in. long, glabrous outside. Summer. Me. to Wisc., s. to Ga. and Miss.

glauca: *A. flava.*

pectinata (Nutt.) Penn. Ann., 15–24 in., mostly much-branched; ¾–1½ in. long, 2-pinnatifid, glandular-pubescent, segms. toothed; corolla yellow, tinged with brown, about 1½ in. long, glandular-pubescent outside. Summer, autumn. Ky. to Fla., w. to Mo., and Okla.

pedicularia (L.) Raf. [*Agalinis pedicularia* (L.) S. F. Blake]. FALSE FOXGLOVE. Ann., mostly 2–4 ft., much-branched; lvs. 2-pinnatifid, puberulent, segms. mostly obtusely or bluntly toothed; corolla yellow tinged with brown, about 1½ in. long. Me. to Ga., w. to Minn.

virginica (L.) Penn. [*Agalinis virginica* (L.) S. F. Blake; *Gerardia virginica* (L.) BSP]. DOWNY FALSE FOXGLOVE. Per., mostly 1½–3 ft., sts. puberulent, not much-branched; lvs. elliptic, simple, entire to weakly toothed; fls. in terminal, leafy, tapering racemes, corolla clear yellow, 1½–2 in. long. Spring, autumn. New Hamp. to Fla., w. to Mich. and La.

AURINIA Desv. *Cruciferae*. About 7 spp. of bien. or per. herbs, native to cent. and s. Eur. and Turkey; basal lvs. many in tufted rosettes, margins repand, sinuate, dentate, or pinnatifid, petioles long, deeply grooved, st. lvs. reduced; fls. yellow or white, racemose or paniculate, sepals and petals 4; fr. a silicle, flattened or somewhat inflated. Included until recently in *Alyssum*, which differs in basal lvs. in looser rosettes and rarely more than 1 in. long, with entire margins and cylindrical petioles, and st. lvs. essentially as large as rosette lvs.

For culture see *Alyssum.*

corymbosa Griseb. [*Alyssum corymbosum* (Griseb.) Boiss.]. Per., to 18 in.; lvs. spatulate or lanceolate, usually dentate, yellow, to ¼ in. long; silicle globose, to ⅜ in. long, glabrous, each cell 4-seeded. Se. Eur.

petraea (Ard.) Schur [*Alyssum edentulum* Waldst. & Kit.; *A. gemonense* L.; *A. petraeum* Ard.]. Whitish per., 1 ft. or less, woody at base, not much branched; basal lvs. oblong-oblanceolate to spatulate, sinuate or pinnatifid; fls. yellow, in racemes; silicle elliptic to obovate, to ³⁄₁₆ in. long, somewhat inflated. Se. Eur.

saxatilis (L.) Desv. [*Alyssum Arduini* Fritsch; *A. orientale* Ard.; *A. saxatile* L.]. BASKET-OF-GOLD, GOLDENTUFT MADWORT, GOLDEN-TUFT ALYSSUM, GOLD-DUST, ROCK MADWORT. Mat-forming per. with woody roots, stellate-hairy, lower lvs. spatulate, sinuate to repand-dentate, st. lvs. linear-oblanceolate; fls. pale yellow, in a panicle; silicle orbicular, compressed, glabrous. S. and cent. Eur., Turkey. Used in rock gardens for its bright yellow fls. Cvs. 'Citrina', 'Compacta', 'Lutea', 'Nana', 'Sulphurea' have been offered.

AUSTROCACTUS Britt. & Rose. *Cactaceae*. About 8 spp. of small, solitary or cespitose, elongate-globose to oblong, ribbed cacti, native to Argentina and Chile; spines sometimes hooked; fls. nearly apical, campanulate, scales of tube and ovary sharp-pointed, with axillary hairs and bristles, perianth inrolled, persistent in fr., stamens included, mostly inserted at base of tube, a distinct series at the mouth; fr. globose, dry, seeds many, snail-shaped, soft.

For culture see *Cacti.*

hibernus F. Ritter. Sts. cespitose, prostrate, ascending at tip, to 4 in. long and 1³⁄₁₆ in. thick, green, ribs 7–8, to ¼ in. high; areoles pale yellow, radial spines 5–8, the lower ones whitish, very slender, to ⅜ in. long, the upper ones yellow-brown, thicker, needle-shaped, to ¾ in. long, central spines 1–4, to 1³⁄₁₆ in. long; fls. diurnal, often unisexual, white or rose, to 2 in. long. Mts., Chile.

AUSTROCEDRUS Florin & Boutelje. *Cupressaceae*. One sp., a coniferous, evergreen, monoecious tree, with frondlike, 2-ranked, compressed branchlets, native to Chile and adjacent Argentina; lvs. scalelike, obtusely tipped, 4-ranked, of 2 kinds, the marginal lvs. longitudinally grooved, overlapping the smaller facial lvs.; male cones globose to oblong, female cones ovoid, scales in 2 pairs, erect, valvate, with a minute tubercle on the back below the apex, only the upper ones fertile; seeds 1–2 to each scale, unequally winged, 1 wing longer than the seed.

Requires moist, well-drained soils; propagated by cuttings or seeds. For culture see *Conifers.*

chilensis (D. Don) Florin & Boutelje [*Libocedrus chilensis* (D. Don) Endl.]. CHILEAN INCENSE CEDAR. Pyramidal to spreading, to 60 ft. high; marginal lvs. with silvery line on side; female cones ½ in. long. Zone 8, where summers are cool.

AUSTROCEPHALOCEREUS: *CEPHALOCEREUS.*

AUSTROCYLINDROPUNTIA: *OPUNTIA* section *Austrocylindropuntia.*

AVENA L. OAT (or OATS). *Gramineae*. Fewer than 50 spp. of mostly ann. grasses in Medit. Eur. and N. Afr. to cent. Asia; panicles narrow or open, usually few-fld.; spikelets large, 2–3-fld., rachilla bearded, disarticulating above the glumes and between the florets, glumes thin, 7–9-nerved, longer than the lower floret, usually exceeding the upper floret, lemma 5–9-nerved, with 2 teeth and a usually bent, twisted, dorsal awn. For terminology see *Gramineae.*

barbata J. F. Pott ex Link. SLENDER WILD O. Distinguished from *A. fatua* by very slender curved pedicels, narrow spikelets, 7-nerved lemmas with fine-pointed teeth. Introd. from s. Eur. for hay, naturalized on the Pacific coast.

elatior: *Arrhenatherum elatius.*

fatua L. WILD O., TARTARIAN O., POTATO O., FLAVER, DRAKE. Sts. to 3 ft., stout; lf. blades flat, to ⁵⁄₁₆ in. wide, scabrous; panicle loose and open, to 12 in. long; spikelets broad, usually 3-fld., glumes to 1 in. long, florets readily falling from the glumes, lemma hairy at base, about ¾ in. long, 9-nerved, awn to 1⅜ in. long. Eurasia; introd. and rare from Me. to Penn., w. to Mo. but a common weed in the Pacific states. Planted for hay.

sativa L. OATS. Distinguished from *A. fatua* by mostly 2-fld. spikelets, florets not readily separating from the glumes, glabrous lemmas, usually straight awn, or the awn absent. Medit. Widely cult., adapted to cool, moist climates. Probably derived from *A. fatua.*

sempervirens: *Helictotrichon sempervirens.*

sterilis L. ANIMATED O. Distinguished from *A. fatua* by spikelets to 1¾ in. long with awns to 2¾ in. long. Medit.; cent. Asia. The awns of the fr. twist and untwist when laid on a moist surface; for this reason used as flies in fishing and sometimes cult. as a curiosity.

AVERRHOA L. *Oxalidaceae.* Two spp. of evergreen trees of trop. se. Asia; lvs. alt., odd-pinnate, somewhat sensitive; fls. small, fragrant, in clusters, sepals and petals 5, stamens 10, alternately long and short, sometimes only 5 fertile; fr. an oblong, fleshy, edible berry, seeds few to many.

Grown in the tropics for the edible, astringent fruit which is eaten fresh, when sweet, or used to make pickles, jams, jellies, or drinks. They thrive in deep rich soil in moist tropical climates. Propagated by seeds or by budding.

Bilimbi L. BILIMBI, BLIMBING, CUCUMBER TREE, TREE SORREL. To 50 ft.; lfts. 23–45, lanceolate to oblong-lanceolate; fls. red-purple, borne on the trunk or brs., fertile stamens 10; fr. greenish-yellow, to 4 in. long, with 5 obscure angles, flesh acid, juicy, edible. Nativity uncertain, probably the Malay region. Cult. or naturalized in some trop. regions.

Carambola L. CARAMBOLA, CARAMBA, BLIMBING, COUNTRY GOOSEBERRY. Handsome ornamental tree, to 30 ft.; lfts. 5–11, ovate to elliptic; fls. variegated white and purple, borne in lf. axils, fertile stamens 5; fr. yellow or golden-brown, to 5 in. long, with 3–5 deep ribs, edible. Malay region; cult. and often naturalized in the tropics. Zone 10b, in Fla. This the better of the 2 spp., and forms with sour and sweet fr. are known.

AVOCADO. This is the large, pear-shaped, oblong, or nearly globose fruit of *Persea americana,* an evergreen, broad-leaved tree of tropical America. A highly nutritious fruit, it has long been a staple food and common dooryard tree in many parts of tropical America. Besides being rich in fat, carbohydrates, and vitamins, it also has more protein than any other fruit. During the present century, the avocado has become a market fruit of considerable importance in southern California and southern Florida. In those states it is grown in orchard plantings, the trees standing 20–30 feet apart either way, on well-drained fertile open land. Spacing distance varies with the vigor of the cultivar and the richness of the soil. Trees reach a height of 30 feet or more and are naturally very long-lived.

Cultivars are propagated by shield budding (in California) or side grafting (in Florida, using West Indian type stock), in autumn or spring, on seedling avocado stocks (planted in gallon or five-quart containers).

The transplanting of young grafted stock is commonly undertaken in spring and early summer, a ball of earth always being removed with the tree. In two or three years most kinds begin to bear, though not heavily until after five to eight years. Once established, an avocado tree can stand almost any hardship except flooding or freezing.

Pollination presents a special problem with the avocado because the period of pollen shedding of one group of cultivars does not overlap the period of receptivity of the pistils of that group. Plantings should include several cultivars chosen for their pollen value. Orchards may be grown under mulch or with cultivation and cover crops.

Horticulturists classify avocado cultivars as West Indian, Guatemalan, or Mexican. The West Indian group, the only one originally found in the Antilles, to which it was probably carried by the Spaniards from Central America, comprises the strictly tropical avocados; these can be grown in the continental United States only in the warmest parts of Florida (Zone 10b). West Indian cultivars are early-ripening (July through October) and include 'Fuchs', 'Pollock', 'Simmonds', 'Trapp', and 'Waldin'. The Guatemalan group, originally from the highlands of Guatemala, is hardier and can be grown in Zone 10a in California and Florida; typical cultivars are 'Hass' and 'Nabal'. The Mexican group is from Mexico, where it is the most common avocado type, and is the hardiest generally (about as hardy as the sweet orange), and so useful for culture in southern California. Superior cultivars include 'Duke', 'Mexicola', and 'Topa Topa'. Hybrids between the groups also exist as important cultivars, of which

'Booth' (nos. 1, 7, 8), 'Choquette', 'Hall', 'Hickson', 'Lula', 'Simpson'—all West Indian × Guatemalan crosses—are important avocados in Florida, ripening later than pure West Indian kinds. 'Fuerte', a Mexican × Guatemalan hybrid, is an important commercial avocado in California (December to July).

California requires only a few standard avocado cultivars, for the climate permits fruit maturation over a long period of time. Fruiting seasons for avocado cultivars under Florida conditions are short, so that a larger number of cultivars, maturing at different times, is required to assure a constant supply of commercial fruit during the normal avocado season (July–January). Avocados commonly planted in Florida and listed in order of their season include: 'Fuchs' (July), 'Pollock' (mid-July through August), 'Trapp' (September to mid-October), 'Waldin' (mid-September through October), 'Booth 8' (mid-October through November), 'Booth 7', 'Collinson', and 'Hickson' (November to mid-December), 'Lula' (mid-October through December), 'Booth 5' (December), 'Booth 1' and 'Taylor' (December to mid-January).

Annual yield of avocado trees varies widely depending on the cultivar (Guatemalan group cultivars tend to alternate between heavy and light crops in successive years) and on weather conditions during the March–April blossoming period. Over several years and under good conditions, an average of three bushels per tree is considered a conservative estimate for plantings ten or more years old in California. In Florida similar yields are obtained from the cultivars 'Booth 7', 'Booth 8', and 'Lula', classed as heavy producers; most other Florida avocados are medium (two bushels) to light (one bushel) producers.

AXONOPUS Beauvois. *Gramineae.* About 60 spp. of per. or rarely ann. grasses in trop. regions, mostly Amer.; sts. stoloniferous or clustered; lf. blades flat or folded, rounded or somewhat pointed at tip; infl. of slender, spikelike racemes borne digitately or racemosely along the main axis; spikelets solitary, subsessile and alt., in 2 rows on one side of a 3-angled rachis, depressed-biconvex, usually obtuse, back of fertile lemma turned away from rachis, first glume absent, second glume and sterile lemma equal, palea absent, fertile lemma and palea hard, the oblong-elliptic lemma usually obtuse, with margins slightly inrolled. For terminology see *Gramineae.*

affinis Chase. CARPET GRASS, COMMON C.G. Per., sts. tufted or stoloniferous, slender, glabrous, 14 in. high or rarely more, sometimes forming dense mats, nodes glabrous; lf. sheaths compressed, keeled, blades to 1 ft. long, usually much less, to ¼ in. wide; racemes 2–4, to 4 in. long, ascending; spikelets ⅛ in. long, oblong-elliptic, nearly acute, sparsely appressed-silky, second glume and sterile lemma scarcely or not pointed beyond the fr. N.C. to Fla., w. to Okla. and Tex.; Cuba, s. Mex., S. Amer.; naturalized in Australia.

compressus (Swartz) Beauvois. Per., stoloniferous, sts. to 20 in., relatively stout, compressed, usually densely pubescent at nodes, stolons elongate, with short internodes and short, broad, obtuse blades; lf. blades on st. to 8 in. long, mostly to ½ in. wide but the uppermost small, margins ciliate; racemes 2–5, mostly to 2¾ in. long, ascending, the upper two paired, the remainder separated; spikelets to ⅛ in. long, sparsely pilose, the second glume and sterile lemma distinctly pointed beyond the fr. S. Fla. and La.; Mex., W. Indies, S. Amer.

AYLOSTERA: *REBUTIA.* **A. floccosa, A. robustispina:** listed names of no botanical standing.

AZALEA: see *RHODODENDRON.* See under *Rhododendron* for comments on hybrid azalea groups.

×**altaclerensis** Gowen. One of the Ghent Hybrid Azaleas *(R. ×gandavense);* not to be confused with *R. ×altaclerense* Lindl.

balsaminiflora (balsaminaeflora): *R. indicum* cv.

cantabilis: *Rhododendron* cv. 'Cantabile'. A Glenn Dale Hybrid Azalea; corolla white. Not to be confused with *R. cantabile* Balf.f. ex Hutch., a synonym of *R. russatum.*

cardinalis: *Rhododendron* cv. 'Cardinale'. A Kaempferi Hybrid Azalea; corolla phlox-pink.

carminita splendens: *Rhododendron* cv. 'Carminitum Splendens'. A Kurume Hybrid Azalea.

coccinea major: *Rhododendron* cv. 'Coccineum Majus'. Two cvs. of this name are known: one is a Ghent Hybrid Azalea with blood-red corolla; the other an Indian Hybrid Azalea of low, spreading habit, with single, orange-red corolla to 2½ in. across.

coccinea speciosa: *Rhododendron* cv. 'Coccineum Speciosum'. A Ghent Hybrid Azalea; corolla orange-red.

Daviesii: *Rhododendron* cv. 'Daviesii'. A Ghent Hybrid Azalea, derived from *R. molle* and *R. viscosum;* corolla pale yellow to white, with yellow blotch, 2¼ in. across.

dilatata: *R. reticulatum.*

imbricata: *Rhododendron* cv. 'Imbricatum'. An Indian Hybrid Azalea; corolla double, white with green stripes and margin.

indica: *R. indicum.* [Var.] **alba:** *R. mucronatum.* Var. **balsaminiflora (balsaminaeflora):** *R. indicum* cv. Var. **Cavendishii:** *Rhododendron* cv. 'Cavendishii'. Of hybrid origin, probably *R. indicum* × *R. Simsii;* corolla single, red, with darker blotch, white margins, and dark red stripes. Var. **coccinea major:** *Rhododendron* cv. 'Coccineum Majus'. An Indian Hybrid Azalea, probably involving *R. calendulaceum;* corolla orange-red. Var. **concinna:** *Rhododendron* cv. 'Concinnum'. An Indian Hybrid Azalea; corolla rosy-lilac. Var. **formosa:** *Rhododendron* cv. 'Formosum'. An Indian Hybrid Azalea, involving *R. pulchrum;* corolla violet-red with red blotch. Var. **Iveryana:** *R. indicum* cv. Var. **laciniata:** *Rhododendron* cv. 'Laciniatum'. An Indian Hybrid Azalea; corolla deeply 5-parted. Var. **phoenicea:** *R. pulchrum* var. Var. **praestantissima:** *Rhododendron* cv. 'Praestantissimum'. An Indian,' Hybrid Azalea; corolla single, violet-red with darker blotch (there is also a Ghent Hybrid Azalea cv. named 'Praestantissimum', with corolla orange-red). [Var.] **rosea:** *R. mucronatum* cv. 'Indicum Roseum'. Var. **rosiflora (rosaeflora):** *R. indicum* cv. 'Balsaminiflorum'. Var. **violacea rubra:** *Rhododendron* cv. 'Violaceum Rubrum'. An Indian Hybrid Azalea, perhaps involving *R. pulchrum;* corolla violet-red with crenate margins. Var. **lateritia:** *R. indicum.* Var. **vittata:** *R. Simsii* cv.

japonica: *R. japonicum.* Var. **alba:** *R. mucronatum* cv. 'Amethystinum'.

lateritia: *R. indicum.*

ledifolia: *R. mucronatum.* Cv. '**Magnifica**': *R. mucronatum* cv. 'Sekidera'. Forma **Sekidera:** *R. mucronatum* cv. Var. **amethystina:** *R. mucronatum* cv. Var. **lilacina:** *R. mucronatum* cv. Var. **Noordtiana:** *R. mucronatum* cv. Var. **purpurea:** *R. pulchrum* var. *calycinum.* Var. **rosea:** *R. mucronatum* cv.

macrantha: *R. indicum.*

macrosepala: *R. linearifolium* var.

magnifica: a name, properly to be treated as *Rhododendron* cv. 'Magnificum', used for at least 4 different cvs.: a Ghent Hybrid Azalea with soft red corolla; or another Ghent Hybrid with orange-blotched cream-colored corolla changing to pale rose; or an Indian Hybrid Azalea with rose corolla; or a synonym of *R. mucronatum* cv. 'Sekidera'. Not to be confused with *R. magnificum* F. K. Ward.

narcissiflora: *Rhododendron* cv. 'Narcissiflorum'. A Ghent Hybrid Azalea; corolla double, yellow.

nudiflora: *R. periclymenoides.*

orchidiflora: *Rhododendron* cv. 'Orchidiphillum' [*R.* cv. 'Orchidiflorum']. An Indian Hybrid Azalea; corolla orchid.

pontica: *R. luteum.*

poukhanensis: *R. yedoense* var. *poukhanense.*

procumbens: *Loiseleuria procumbens.*

rosea: *R. prinophyllum.*

rosiflora (rosaeflora): *R. indicum* cv. 'Balsaminiflorum.'

rustica flore pleno: *R.* × *mixtum.*

rosmarinifolia: *R. mucronatum* (not *R. rosmarinifolium*). Var. **alba:** *R. mucronatum.*

sinensis: *R. molle.*

sublanceolata: *R. scabrum.*

×**Vuykiana:** *R.* × *Vuykianum.*

Yodogava: *R. yedoense.*

AZALEASTRUM: *RHODODENDRON.*

×AZALEODENDRON: *RHODODENDRON.*

AZARA Ruiz & Pav. *Flacourtiaceae.* About 12 spp. of evergreen trees and shrubs, native to Chile; lvs. alt., simple, with a leaflike stipule at base of each lf.; fls. small, fragrant, in axillary racemes or clusters, petals none, stamens usually many and conspicuous; fr. a berry.

Grown as ornamentals in mild temperate regions (Zone 9, primarily on the Pacific coast) and sometimes under glass. Propagated by seeds or ripened cuttings.

celastrina D. Don. Much-branched shrub, to 9 ft.; lvs. ovate-elliptic, to 2 in. long, obscurely serrate-crenate, glabrous or slightly pubescent above.

dentata Ruiz & Pav. Shrub, to 10 ft.; lvs. elliptic to ovate, to 1½ in. long, serrate, glabrous and glossy above, hairy beneath; fls. yellow, in corymbs.

Gilliesii: *A. petiolaris.*

integrifolia Ruiz & Pav. GOLDSPIRE. Shrub or small tree, to 30 ft.; lvs. obovate or oblong, to 1½ in. long, entire or nearly so, short-petioled; fls. in racemes, bright yellow.

lanceolata Hook.f. Shrub or small tree, to 20 ft.; lvs. lanceolate, to 2½ in. long, coarsely serrate, short-petioled; fls. many, in axillary clusters; berry violet.

microphylla Hook.f. Shrub or small tree; lvs. obovate, to ¾ in. long, remotely toothed; fls. small, greenish, stamens 5; berry orange.

petiolaris (D. Don) I. M. Johnst. [*A. Gilliesii* Hook. & Arn.]. Shrub or small tree, to 15 ft.; lvs. ovate, to 3 in. long, with few teeth, dark shining green above, paler beneath, petioles long; fls. many, yellow, in racemes about 1 in. long.

AZOLLA Lam. MOSQUITO FERN, WATER F., FAIRY MOSS. *Salviniaceae.* Six spp. of mosslike, free-floating ferns, widely distributed through tropics and subtropics and some extending into temp. regions; lvs. uniform, minute, in 2 rows, 2-lobed, each with a floating leafy upper lobe and a usually larger submerged lower lobe; sori enclosed in sporocarps, in pairs in lf. axils near the lower lobe.

Azollas live symbiotically with the blue-green alga, *Anabaena*, which inhabits a small cavity found in the base of each leaf. Readily propagated asexually by self-division, often grown in pools and aquaria. See also *Ferns.*

caroliniana Willd. MOSQUITO PLANT. Plants forming colonies, sts. to about ½ in. long, green or becoming reddish in bright sun, upper lf. lobes not imbricate, orbicular, scarcely 1/32 in. long, smooth. Mass. to Wisc., s. to W. Indies. Some cult. material may be the more trop. *A. filiculoides.*

filiculoides Lam. Plants to 1 in. long, frequently reddish, easily fragmenting; lvs. appressed and imbricate, oblong to ovate, 1/16 in. long, deeply 2-lobed, upper lobe papillate-hairy. Wash. to Mex.; S. Amer.

AZTEKIUM Böd. *Cactaceae.* One sp., a small cactus, native to Mex.; distinguished by having low, 3-ridged secondary ribs without areoles between the main ribs, main and secondary ribs closely cross-furrowed, sts. woolly at the crown; areoles contiguous, forming a woolly midline on each main rib, spines small, soon deciduous; fls. nearly apical, funnelform, small, with slender, naked tube; fr. small, naked, seeds small, pear-shaped, tubercled, with aril.

For culture see *Cacti.*

Ritteri (Böd.) Böd. Sts. simple or cespitose, depressed-globose, to 2 in. wide, main ribs 9–11, about 5/16 in. wide and high; spines 1–3, to 5/32 in. long; fls. white, ⅜ in. long; fr. white. Ne. Mex.

AZUREOCEREUS Akers & J. H. Johnson. *Cactaceae.* Two spp. of columnar cacti, native to Peru; sts. sparsely branched, ribs low, nearly tubercled; fls. nocturnal, white, cylindrical, curved, tube and ovary densely scaly, scales overlapping, fringed, naked in the axils; perianth segms. spreading; fr. ovoid, scaly, seeds black, glossy. Perhaps not distinct from *Browningia.*

For culture see *Cacti.*

ayacuchensis: a listed name of no botanical standing; probably *A. Hertlingianus.*

Hertlingianus (Backeb.) Backeb. [*A. nobilis* Akers]. Sts. to 26 ft. high and 6 in. thick, blue-green, ribs about 15; radial spines 15–20, to 1½ in. long, central spines 1–3, deflexed, to 4 in. long; fls. 4 in. long, scales ½ in. long; fr. black, 1 in. in diam., scales not sharp-pointed and spreading.

imperator, imperialis: listed names of no botanical standing; probably *A. Hertlingianus.*

nobilis: *A. Hertlingianus.*

viridis Rauh & Backeb. Sts. to 30 ft. high or more, dark green, ribs about 12–14; spines short, to ¾ in. long, not deflexed; fr. with sharp-pointed, spreading scales.

BABIANA Ker-Gawl. BABOON FLOWER, BABOONROOT. *Iridaceae.* About 61 spp. of cormous herbs with soft fibrous tunics, native to s. Afr., 1 sp. to Socotra; lvs. several, pleated, strongly veined and ribbed, sometimes petioled; infl. often 2-ranked, spicate, spathe valves variously hairy; fls. regular or irregular, sometimes 2-lipped, often fragrant, perianth tube straight or curved, segms. equal or unequal, style brs. short, unbranched, often apically flattened; fr. a caps.

Spring-blooming; may be grown in the open in mild, temperate regions of southern U.S.; grown in shallow pots under glass in colder climates. Propagated by seeds or cormels; of easy culture.

ambigua (Roem. & Schult.) G. J. Lewis [*B. plicata* of auth., not Ker-Gawl.]. St. short, erect to decumbent, sometimes branched, to 6 in. below ground, 2 in. above ground; lvs. 3–6, linear or lanceolate, longer than fls., to 3$^3/_{16}$ in. long, ⅜ in. wide, pubescent; spike short, 4–5-fld., bracts herbaceous; fls. blue or mauve-blue, perianth 2-lipped, tube to ¾ in. long, slightly widened upward, lobes more or less clawed, lanceolate to spatulate, uppermost to 1¾ in. long, lower lateral ones to 1$^1/_{16}$ in. long, with white or pale yellow area and purple W-shaped mark, ovary glabrous or puberulous on the ribs. Cape Prov.

erectifolia: *B. stricta* var.

hypogaea Burchell. Sts. 6–12 in. below ground, 1–4 in. above ground; lvs. several, linear, 12–18 in. long, ⅛–¼ in. wide, ribbed, hairy; infl. of 1–3 dense, 3–6-fld. spikes, bracts about 2 in. long, attenuate, green apically, hairy; fls. 2-lipped, nearly white to dark blue or mauve, about 4½ in. long, perianth tube very slender, about 2$^3/_{16}$ in. long, lobes more or less oblanceolate, to 2⅜ in. long, lower lateral ones usually with a white or yellow area near the middle. S.-W. Afr. to Rhodesia.

macrantha: *B. pygmaea.*

nana (Andr.) K. Spreng. [*Gladiolus nanus* Andr.]. Sts. to nearly 4 in. below ground, to 4 in. above ground; lvs. 5–7, usually spreading like a fan, petiole to 2$^3/_{16}$ in. long, blade obovate to oblanceolate-oblong, narrowed to acute tip, not much pleated, to nearly 5 in. long, 1$^3/_{16}$ in. wide, hairy; spike short, 2–6-fld., bracts herbaceous, villous; fls. irregular, blue to rose-pink, widely campanulate, perianth tube to ⅝ in. long, lobes ovate-oblong to elliptic-oblong, the upper somewhat longer than lower, to 1⅝ in. long, lower lateral ones with small pale yellow or whitish area near middle and purple or reddish-purple arrow-shaped mark near base, ovary glabrous or puberulous on the ribs. Cape Prov.

plicata Ker-Gawl. Sts. erect, usually flexuous, to 8 in., longer than lvs., sometimes branched; lvs. 6–8, usually spreading like a fan, lanceolate to sword-shaped, to nearly 5 in. long, ¾ in. wide, pubescent; spike 4–10-fld., bracts herbaceous; fls. irregular, violet to pale blue or white, perianth tube to 1 in. long, lobes spreading, upper somewhat longer than lower, to 1 in. long, lower lateral ones usually with a yellow area marked with 2 purple dots at base, ovary villous or sericeous above the base. Cape Prov. Has been confused with *B. ambigua.*

purpurea (Jacq.) Ker-Gawl. [*Gladiolus purpureus* (Jacq.) Willd.]. Sts. erect, often flexuous, to 6 in., unbranched or with 1–3 brs.; lvs. 6–7, ascending to nearly erect, lanceolate, to nearly 5 in. long, ⅜ in. wide, pubescent; spike 4–10-fld., bracts herbaceous; fls. regular, mauve-purple to deep purple-pink, perianth tube to 1$^1/_{16}$ in. long, lobes obovate to oblong, to ¾ or rarely 1 in. long, ½ in. wide, with a purple line at center outside, anthers dark. Cape Prov.

pygmaea (Burm.f.) Bak. [*B. macrantha* MacOwan]. Sts. to 2⅜ or rarely 6 in.; lvs. 4–6, 2-ranked, petiole to 2 in. long, blade oblique-lanceolate or sword-shaped, to nearly 5 in. long, ⅞ in. wide, pubescent; spike 2–5-fld., bracts herbaceous; fls. regular, sulphur-yellow with purple-maroon center, perianth tube straight, to 1 in., or rarely 1$^3/_{16}$ in. long, lobes obovate, nearly equal, spreading, to 2 in. long, 1$^3/_{16}$ in. wide near top, outer ones mucronate. Cape Prov.

rubrocyanea (Jacq.) Ker-Gawl. [*B. stricta* var. *rubrocyanea* (Jacq.) Ker-Gawl. ex Bak.]. Sts. to 6 in. or rarely 8 in.; lvs. lanceolate or sword-shaped, to 4 in. long, ¾ in. wide, pubescent; spike 5–10-fld., bracts green; fls. regular, perianth tube straight, to ¾ in. long, lobes equal, to 1 in. long, clawed and scarlet in lower ⅓, obtuse, bright blue and spreading above. Cape Prov.

sambucina (Jacq.) Ker-Gawl. Sts. mostly to ¾ in. above ground; lvs. 5–6, erect or nearly so, linear to sword-shaped, to nearly 6 in. long, to ¼ in. wide, hairy; spike short, 2–6-fld., bracts herbaceous; fls. irregular, pale blue-mauve to purple, perianth tube straight, to 2 in. long, lobes nearly equal, elliptic-oblong to obovate-oblong, to 1⅜ in. long, lower lateral ones with white mark near middle. Cape Prov.

stricta (Ait.) Ker-Gawl. Sts. erect or bent down, often flexuous, to 8 in. or rarely 1 ft.; lvs. 6–8, linear to lanceolate or sword-shaped, to nearly 5 in. long, ½ in. wide, pubescent; spike short, 4–8-fld., bracts herbaceous; fls. regular, purple to mauve-blue or yellow, perianth tube straight, to ¾ in. long or more, lobes oblong or obovate-oblong, to 1 in. long, 2 lower or all 3 inner lobes usually paler, sometimes yellowish, lower lateral ones with small purple marks at base. Cape Prov. Var. **stricta.** The typical var.; sts. usually erect; lvs. spreading like a fan, lanceolate or sword-shaped; fls. pale to deep blue or mauve. Var. **erectifolia** (G. J. Lewis) G. J. Lewis [*B. erectifolia* G. J. Lewis]. St. usually erect; lvs. erect, linear-lanceolate to subulate; fls. pale to deep blue or mauve. Var. **rubrocyanea:** *B. rubrocyanea.* Var. **sulphurea** (Jacq.) Bak. [*B. sulphurea* (Jacq.) Ker-Gawl.]. St. usually bent down; lvs. spreading like a fan, lanceolate or sword-shaped; fls. yellow.

sulphurea: *B. stricta* var.

BACCHARIS L. *Compositae* (Aster Tribe). Probably 350 spp. of dioecious, sometimes evergreen shrubs, in N. and S. Amer.; lvs. alt., sometimes lacking; fl. heads small, discoid, in panicles; fls. all tubular, white or yellowish; achenes 4–10-nerved, pappus of white capillary bristles, many in the female fls., few in the male.

The species are sometimes transferred to grounds for their more or less persistent foliage, or the profuse white or yellowish flowers and conspicuous white pappus. Some of them require well-drained soil and a sunny location, others are marsh plants. Propagated easily both by seeds and by cuttings rooted under glass.

angustifolia Michx. FALSE WILLOW. To 8 ft.; lvs. linear, to 3 in. long, entire or nearly so, leathery. Autumn. Brackish marshes, N.C. to Fla. and Tex., W. Indies.

glomeruliflora Pers. To 9 ft.; lvs. spatulate or obovate, to 2 in. long, toothed above the middle or entire, leathery, light green; heads clustered and sessile in lf. axils. Autumn. Swamps and salt marshes, N.C. to Fla. and W. Indies.

glutinosa Pers. STICKY B., SEEP WILLOW, WATER W., WATER-MOTIE, WATER-WALLY. Evergreen, to 10 ft.; lvs. lanceolate, to 4 in. long, glossy, glutinous, toothed; heads panicled at ends of main brs. Summer. Along watercourses, Colo. to Tex. and Calif., Mex., Chile. May be planted for erosion control.

halimifolia L. GROUNDSEL TREE, GROUNDSELBUSH, SEA MYRTLE, CONSUMPTION WEED, SILVERLING. To 12 ft.; lvs. oblong to obovate, to 2½ in. long, toothed, or entire, gray-green; heads clustered on peduncles, panicled. Autumn. Coastal marshes, Mass. to Fla. and Tex., Cent. Amer. Resistant to salt spray, and thus useful in seaside plantings.

neglecta Britt. To 9 ft. or more; lvs. linear to narrowly oblanceolate, to 3 in. long, entire or denticulate; heads clustered on short peduncles. Late summer. Prairies, Nebr. to Tex., w. to Ariz. and n. Mex.

pilularis DC. DWARF B., COYOTE BRUSH, CHAPARRAL BROOM. Spreading evergreen shrub, to 1 ft. high and to 10 ft. across; lvs. cuneate-obovate, to ¾ in. long, dark green and slightly glutinous, sinuately toothed; heads mostly solitary in axils of lvs. at ends of twigs. Late summer. Coastal bluffs, Calif. Often planted as a ground cover. Var. **consanguinea** (DC.) O. Kuntze. Upright, to 10 ft.; lvs. to 1½ in. long. Coastal and inland hills, Calif. and s. Ore.

viminea DC. MULE-FAT. Evergreen, to 12 ft.; lvs. narrowly lanceolate to oblong, to 4 in. long, dull green, not glutinous, entire or slightly denticulate; heads panicled on short lateral brs. as well as at end of main sts. Spring. Along watercourses, Calif. Sometimes planted for erosion control.

BACKHOUSIA Hook. f. & Harv. SAND-VERBENA MYRTLE. *Myrtaceae.* Six spp. of trees or shrubs, native to e. Australia; lvs. opp., pinnately veined, evergreen; fls. white, in axillary or terminal cymes or umbels, calyx lobes 4, scarious, persistent, petals 4, stamens many, separate in several series, ovary inferior; fr. a caps.

Occasionally planted in southern Fla.

anisata Vickery. Glabrous tree, to 50 ft., bark rather thin, rough, subfibrous; lvs. lanceolate, to 4 in. long, with anise odor when crushed; fls. cream-white, in few-fld. axillary or terminal clusters, fragrant. New S. Wales.

citriodora F. J. Muell. Small tree, to 25 ft.; lvs. lanceolate, to 4 in. long, leathery, lemon-scented when crushed; fls. small, white, in umbel-like clusters. Queensland. Yields a commercial oil.

BACOPA Aubl. [*Herpestis* C. F. Gaertn.; *Hydrotrida* Small]. WATER HYSSOP. *Scrophulariaceae*. About 60 spp. of summer-flowering aquatic or semiaquatic per. herbs, mostly native to temp. and trop. N. and S. Amer., but some to Asia, Afr., and Australia; sts. creeping to ascending or erect, often rather succulent; lvs. opp.; fls. white or blue, axillary, calyx 5-parted, corolla campanulate, salverform, or 2-lipped, stamens usually 4; fr. a caps.

amplexicaulis: *B. caroliniana.*

caroliniana (Walt.) B. L. Robinson [*B. amplexicaulis* (Michx.) Wettst.; *Herpestis amplexicaulis* (Michx.) Pursh; *Hydrotrida caroliniana* (Walt.) Small]. Stoloniferous per., to 2 ft., sts. creeping to ascending, hairy at summit, little branched; lvs. ovate, to 1 in. long, clasping, palmately 3–13-nerved, punctate, lemon-scented when bruised; fls. blue, to ⅜ in. long, solitary, on pedicels to ¾ in. long. Shallow streams and banks of pools in pinelands, se. Va. to Fla., w. to e. Tex. An aquarium plant.

Monnieri (L.) Penn. WATER HYSSOP. Mat-forming per., sts. glabrous, succulent; lvs. spatulate to cuneate-obovate, to ¾ in. long, usually entire, 1-nerved; fls. white to pale blue, subtended by 2 bracts, on pedicels to 1 in. long. Pantrop.; in U.S. from se. Va. to Fla. and Tex. Grown in aquaria.

BACTRIS Jacq. ex Scop. [*Guilielma* Mart.]. SPINY-CLUB PALM. *Palmae.* More than 100 spp. of mostly cespitose, small to moderate, monoecious palms of trop. Amer., usually prickly or spiny in some or all parts; lvs. pinnate or sometimes only pinnately ribbed, pinnae acute to acuminate, very rarely oblique and toothed at apex; infl. among lvs., spicate or branched, bracts 2, the lower short, the upper enclosing the infl. in bud, splitting at and more or less persistent after flowering, both inserted near base of the short peduncle, rachillae simple, few to many, with fls. all in triads (2 male and 1 female) or in triads with male fls. interspersed; male fls. with calyx cupular, petals valvate, stamens 6–12, female fls. with calyx cupular to tubular, corolla tubular to urceolate, staminodes separate or united, pistil 3-celled; fr. fleshy, sometimes prickly, endocarp bony, with 3 pores at or near the middle, seed with homogeneous endosperm.

Several species yield edible fruits and oilseeds, and the tough fibrous wood (chonta) has been the common source of material for bows, spears, and blowgun darts for the lowland Indian tribes of tropical S. Amer. For culture see *Palms.*

acanthophylla: *Aiphanes acanthophylla.*

balanoidea: *B. major.*

Gasipaes HBK [*Guilielma Gasipaes* (HBK) L. H. Bailey; *G. utilis* Ørst.]. PEACH PALM, PEJIBAYE. Sts. several, to 60 ft., densely spiny; lvs. to 12 ft. long, pinnae many, deep green above, lighter beneath, arranged in groups and in several planes; infl. large; fr. to 2 in. long, red, orange, or yellow, sometimes seedless. Origin uncertain, possibly Amazonian Peru. Widely grown as dooryard food plant in lowland humid tropics of the New World, with some small commercial plantings in Cent. Amer. Cult. as an ornamental in Hawaii. An important food plant of trop. Amer. The mealy flesh of the pericarp, boiled in salted water, is highly nutritious. Easily prop. by seeds, bearing after 3–4 years. Mature palms very productive, yielding 4 or 5 fr. bunches annually.

guineensis (L.) H. E. Moore [*B. horrida* Ørst.; *B. minor* Jacq.]. TOBAGO CANE, PRICKLY-POLE. Sts. several, to 12 ft.; lvs. to 3 ft. long or more, light green, with vicious spines on petiole, pinnae 20–30 per side, regularly arranged; short and narrow; infl. to 8 in. long, upper bract setose-prickly, rachillae many; fr. black, to ⅝ in. long, with distinct staminodes at base. S. and Cent. Amer. Fr. edible.

horrida: *B. guineensis.*

major Jacq. [*B. balanoidea* (Ørst.) H. Wendl.]. PRICKLY PALM. Sts. many, to 25 ft., 2 in. in diam., at first prickly but becoming smooth with age; lvs. to 8 ft. long, dull green, glabrous, with densely prickly petiole, pinnae 30 or more on each side, regularly arranged; fr. ellipsoid, about 2 in. long, purplish, surrounded at base by a ring of united staminodes. Cent. and n. S. Amer. Planted as an ornamental in tropics.

mexicana Mart. Sts. clustered, to 15 ft., armed with black spines; lvs. to 8 ft. long, rachis with long black spines, pinnae to 18 in. long, 1¾ in. wide, tapered to a long-acuminate apex; infl. recurved, rachillae several, with more male fls. than female; fr. turbinate, red, ½ in. in diam., with distinct staminodes at base. Mex.

minor: *B. guineensis.*

trichophylla Burret. Sts. clustered, to 25 ft., 2½ in. in diam., armed with slender blackish prickles; lvs. to 6 ft. long, pinnae about 25 on each side, in groups toward the base, to 2 ft. long, 1½ in. wide, pubescent beneath; fr. depressed-globose, ⁹⁄₁₆ in. in diam., red, with distinct staminodes at base. Guatemala, Br. Honduras.

BACULARIA: *LINOSPADIX.*

BAECKEA L. *Myrtaceae.* About 70 spp. of glabrous, sometimes heathlike shrubs, mostly in Australia, a few in se. Asia and sw. Pacific; lvs. opp., entire glabrous; fls. small, usually white, either solitary or several together in lf. axils, 5-merous; fr. a caps., partly enclosed in calyx tube, opening at apex, 2–3-celled, each cell 1–2-seeded.

camphorata R. Br. To 4 ft. or more, conspicuously gland-dotted; lvs. oblong, to ¼ in. long; fls. white, 1–3, on short pedicels, petals rounded, to ⅛ in. long. Se. Australia.

virgata Andr. To 12 ft.; lvs. linear-lanceolate, to 1 in. long; fls. white, several in loose umbel on peduncle to ½ in. long, petals rounded, clawed, to ⅛ in. long. E. Australia.

BAERIA: *LASTHENIA.* B. aristata: *L. coronaria.* B. californica: *L. coronaria.* B. chrysostoma and subspp. gracilis and hirsutula: *L. chrysostoma.* B. gracilis: *L. chrysostoma.* B. hirsutula: *L. chrysostoma.*

BAIKIAEA Benth. *Leguminosae* (subfamily *Caesalpinioideae*). Five spp. of unarmed trees of Afr.; lvs. alt., pinnate; fls. in stout racemes, mostly large, with tomentose pedicels and calyces, petals 5, separate, stamens 10, 9 united, 1 separate; fr. a flat, brown or black, tomentose, dehiscent legume.

Sometimes planted in the tropics for the attractive flowers. Propagated by seeds.

insignis Benth. To 75 ft. or more; lfts. 3–8, mostly alt., leathery, obliquely elliptic or oblong-elliptic, to 10 in. long; racemes to 4 in. long; petals 6–8 in. long, white, the largest marked yellowish; fr. obovate-lanceolate, 12–18 in. long. Wet forests, Fernando Po and Nigeria to the Congo region. Subsp. **insignis.** The typical subsp.; petals 4–8 in. long. Subsp. **minor** (D. Oliver) J. Léonard [*B. minor* D. Oliver]. Petals 2–4⅝ in. long.

minor: *B. insignis* subsp.

plurijuga Harms. RHODESIAN TEAK. To 50 ft., differing from *B. insignis* in having lvs. even-pinnate, lfts. in 5 pairs, mostly opp., to 2½ in. long, racemes to 6 in. long; fls. smaller, petals crisped, mauve-pink; fr. much smaller. Arid or desert soils, Angola, n. and s. Rhodesia. Yields a valuable timber valued for flooring. Has not been successfully cult. in U.S.

BAILEYA Harv. & A. Gray ex Torr. DESERT MARIGOLD, WILD M. *Compositae* (Helenium Tribe). Three or 4 spp. of densely woolly herbs, native to deserts and dry regions of w. N. Amer.; lvs. alt.; fl. heads radiate, solitary; disc and ray fls. yellow, the latter becoming papery with age; achenes club-shaped, pappus none.

multiradiata Harv. & A. Gray ex Torr. Ann. or per., to 20 in.; lvs. basal and along lower part of sts., pinnatifid, the uppermost entire; heads to 2 in. across, long-peduncled; ray fls. 20–50. Spring-autumn. Utah to s. Calif., Tex., n. Mex.

BAILLONIA Bocq. ex Baill. *Verbenaceae.* Not cult. B. juncea: *Diostea juncea.*

BALAKA Becc. *Palmae.* About 20 spp. of small to moderate, solitary, unarmed, monoecious palms with a slender crownshaft, in the Fiji Is. and Samoa; lvs. pinnate, pinnae with 1 principal rib, generally narrowly to broadly wedge-shaped with truncate or obliquely toothed apex; infl. below lvs., subtended by 2 thin deciduous bracts, the upper extending beyond the lower, peduncle and rachis short, rachillae several, simple, forked or once-branched, with fls. in triads (2 male and 1 female) near the base and above these with paired or solitary male fls.; male fls. with sepals imbricate, rounded, petals valvate, boat-shaped, stamens more than 6, filaments erect, anthers attached by back, pistillode elongate, female fls. with imbricate sepals and petals, ovary 1-celled; fr. with apical stigmatic scar, endocarp not operculate, seed 4-angled, with homogeneous endosperm, basal embryo.

For culture see *Palms.*

Seemannii (H. Wendl.) Becc. Small palm with slender dark st., to 5 ft. or more; lvs. few, with about 8 narrowly wedge-shaped pinnae to 6 in. long on each side; infl. small, to about 15 in. long, with lower brs. forked or divided into 3 rachillae; male fls. with about 21 stamens; fr. about ¾ in. long. Fiji Is. This sp. has been listed in cult. but most or all plants so named belong to the genus *Ptychosperma.*

BALFOURODENDRON Méllo ex D. Oliver. *Rutaceae.* One sp., a small tree, native to s. Brazil; lvs. alt. or opp., with 3 lfts., glandular-dotted; fls. small, in many-fld. terminal panicles, sepals and petals 4, stamens 4; fr. dry, leathery, indehiscent, 3–4-winged.

Riedelianum (Engl.) Engl. Lfts. elliptic-oblong to oblanceolate, 3–5 in. long; fr. 2½ in. wide, veiny. Wood is used for various articles.

BALLOTA L. *Labiatae.* About 35 spp. of per. herbs or small shrubs of Eur., the Medit. region, and w. Asia; sts. mostly square in cross section; lvs. opp.; fls. in few- to many-fld. verticillasters, fl. bracts subulate, calyx funnelform, 10-nerved, 5–16-toothed, corolla tube ringed with hairs inside, limb 2-lipped, stamens 4, exserted; fr. of 4 nutlets.

nigra L. BLACK HOREHOUND. To 3 ft., more or less pubescent; lvs. petioled, blade ovate to lanceolate, to 2 in. long, cordate, deeply and irregularly crenate; verticillasters many-fld.; calyx tubular, 5-toothed, to ⅜ in. long, corolla purplish or white, about ½ in. long. Eur., N. Afr., w. Asia; naturalized in ne. U.S.

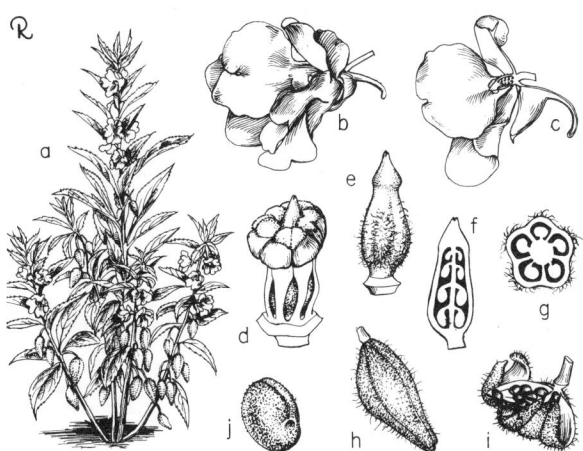

BALSAMINACEAE. *Impatiens Balsamina:* **a,** plant, × ¹⁄₁₆; **b,** flower, × ½; **c,** flower, vertical section, × ½; **d,** stamens surrounding pistil, × 3; **e,** pistil, × 3; **f,** pistil, vertical section, × 3; **g,** ovary, cross section, × 8; **h,** capsule, × ½; **i,** capsule, dehisced, × ½; **j,** seed, × 3.

BALSAMINACEAE A. Rich. BALSAM or TOUCH-ME-NOT FAMILY. Dicot.; 2 genera with over 500 spp. of herbs or subshrubs, widely distributed, particularly in trop. and subtrop. Asia and Afr.; sts. mostly succulent, often swollen at nodes; lvs. simple, alt. or opp., or whorled, generally without stipules; fls. bisexual, strongly irregular, solitary or in axillary or terminal clusters, sepals 3, rarely 5, the upper 2 small, the lower 1 petaloid, asymmetrically funnelform, usually with a nectariferous spur, petals 5, the uppermost one flat or hel-

met-shaped, the 4 lower ones usually united in lateral pairs, stamens 5, alt. with the petals and united toward the top, ovary superior, 5-celled; fr. a 5-valved, elastically and explosively dehiscent caps., rarely a berry. *Impatiens* is cult.

BALSAMITA: *CHRYSANTHEMUM.*

BALSAMOCITRUS Stapf. *Rutaceae.* One sp., a spiny tree, native to trop. e. Afr.; lvs. alt., with 3 lfts., glandular-dotted; fls. small, greenish-yellow, in short, axillary panicles, sepals and petals 5, stamens 10; fr. ovoid-globose, hard-shelled.

Dawei Stapf. To 50–60 ft. or more in its native habitat; lfts. stalked, elliptic-ovate to ovate, to 5 in. long; fr. yellow-orange, 4–6 in. in diam., 8-celled, many-seeded. Sometimes grown as possible stock for citrus.

paniculata: *Afraegle paniculata.*

BALSAMORHIZA Nutt. BALSAMROOT, SUNFLOWER. *Compositae* (Helianthus Tribe). About 12 spp. of taprooted per. herbs, in w. U.S., sts. scapose or occasionally with opp. bracts; lvs. basal, entire to pinnatifid, long-petioled; fl. heads radiate, solitary or more rarely several, large, involucral bracts imbricate, herbaceous, receptacle scaly; disc fls. bisexual, yellow, ray fls. female, fertile, yellow, rarely purplish; pappus lacking.

Sometimes planted as ornamentals; spring- and summer-blooming. Propagated by seeds, the best method of propagation; slow-growing and taking several years to come to flowering size.

deltoidea Nutt. To 3 ft.; basal lvs. triangular-hastate, to 1 ft. long or more, entire or crenate, green on both sides, hirsute; heads 2½–4 in. across, solitary or 2–3. B.C. to s. Calif.

incana Nutt. To 2 ft.; basal lvs. pinnatifid, to 18 in. long, silky-tomentose; heads 3–4 in. across, solitary. Wash. and Ore., e. to Mont. and Wyo.

sagittata (Pursh) Nutt. OREGON S. To 2½ ft.; basal lvs. triangular-hastate or -cordate, entire, white-tomentose beneath when young, becoming nearly glabrous and green with age; heads 2½–4 in. across, solitary. S. Dak. and Colo., w. to s. B.C. and s. Calif.

serrata Macbr. & A. Nels. To 1 ft.; basal lvs. triangular-ovate, to 1 ft. long, sharply serrate and sometimes some also pinnatifid, green, rough-hispidulous; heads 2–3 in. across, solitary. S. Wash. and Ore.

BAMBOO. Bamboos are various, often giant, long-lived, woody, evergreen grasses, members of the family Gramineae, tribe Bambuseae, mostly of the genera *Arundinaria, Bambusa, Chimonobambusa, Dendrocalamus, Phyllostachys, Pseudosasa, Sasa, Semiarundinaria,* and *Shibataea,* as known in this country. These genera are mainly Asian but some species of *Arundinaria* and *Bambusa* are native to the Western Hemisphere, one of the species in North America ranging to Missouri and Maryland.

The bamboos are adapted mainly to the warmer parts of the country. The tropical and subtropical clump-forming bamboos, such as *Bambusa* and *Dendrocalamus,* are mostly very tender and are killed or severely injured by even a few degrees of frost, although a few can endure temperatures down to 16° F without serious injury. The frost-hardy running bamboos, like *Phyllostachys* and *Sasa,* include species of warm-temperate lands and develop best in hardiness Zone 9; however, some of them can be grown successfully in Zone 8, and a few *(Phyllostachys aureosulcata, P. nuda, Pseudosasa japonica)* can be planted in sheltered sites in Zone 7 along the east coast perhaps as far north as Long Island, New York.

Bamboos range from timber-producing species the size of trees (principally in the tropics, in such genera as *Bambusa* and *Dendrocalamus,* and in extratropical *Phyllostachys*) to shrubs *(Arundinaria, Bambusa, Chimonobambusa, Phyllostachys, Pseudosasa, Sasa, Semiarundinaria)* or ground cover plants *(Arundinaria, Phyllostachys, Sasa, Shibataea).* Apart from the many uses of their stems in the Orient and elsewhere, the bamboos have much to offer as ornamental specimens in the landscape, as groves established for ornament or erosion control, as hedges and ground covers, and as tub or pot plants for patio or greenhouse. The strong stems of many species, particularly of the genus *Phyllostachys,* can be cut and cured when mature (three years or older) to yield excellent garden stakes, poles, or material for fencing. Species of *Bambusa* and especially *Phyllostachys* can also provide the home with the fresh edible bamboo sprouts so much used in oriental cookery; these are dug just as the new sprout tips are breaking through the soil.

Based on the nature of their underground rhizomes, most bamboos can be classified as either clump-forming bamboos (e.g., *Bambusa*) or running bamboos (e.g., *Phyllostachys*). The former class, in which the plant consists of a single dense clump of stems, includes mainly tropical genera; new shoots of clumping bamboos appear in summer or autumn or, in their native tropics, at the initiation of a rainy season following a relatively dry period. The running bamboos, so-called because their shoot-producing rhizomes spread extensively underground to form rather open colonies or groves, are mostly species of temperate regions and do not usually thrive in the warm tropics; their new shoots are produced annually in the spring.

With some exceptions, most of the bamboo species cultivated in this country flower only after intervals of many years; thus, vegetative propagation is required. This is accomplished usually by simple division of the clump or colony, the propagules dug preferably at the periphery of the mother plant. Rhizome cuttings may also be made, but propagation by stem cuttings is usually practiced only with the larger tropical clumping bamboos such as *Bambusa* and *Dendrocalamus*. Whole stems two or three years old, trimmed of branches, may be staked down horizontally and covered with soil 6–8 inches deep, or stem segments 3 feet long, taken at the base of stems that are three or more years old, may be trimmed of all lateral branches and buried in the ground at an angle, with the tip at ground level and the base about 12 inches deep. Division of bamboos or propagation by cuttings is best done a month or two before the appearance of the new annual shoots, which occurs in late summer or autumn in clumping species or early to late spring in the running bamboos.

All kinds of propagation material as well as newly established plants must not be allowed to dry out during their first year's growth. All bamboos are heavy feeders and require a well-drained but moist, fertile soil. Some species thrive along water courses, where they can be useful soil-binders. With age and thorough establishment of the rhizomes, after six or seven years, bamboo clumps or groves become conspicuous or even commanding landscape objects but may have to be kept under control, especially the running kinds. The latter are sometimes restricted by use of natural or special underground barriers. A bamboo planting may be easily eliminated simply by cutting off at ground level all aerial growth and new shoots as they appear.

BAMBURANTA: *HYBOPHRYNIUM.* **B. Arnoldiana:** *H. Braunianum.*

BAMBUSA Schreb. BAMBOO. *Gramineae.* About 100 spp. of stout, tall, clump-forming per. grasses in trop. and subtrop. Asia, a few from Mex. to S. Amer., sts. erect or climbing, woody, sometimes bearing spines; lvs. short-petioled, the blade articulated with the sheath; spikes combined in glomerules on the brs. of panicles; spikelets 2- to many-fld., bisexual or unisexual, the 3–4 lower glumes empty, stamens 6, rachilla jointed below the florets. For terminology see *Gramineae.*

Besides their value as ornamentals, the larger species produce stems used in the tropics as timber and sources of pulp and the young stem sprouts of some are edible. Most species are tender and to be grown largely in tropical areas or in the warmer parts of Zone 10. Propagated by clump division or by stem cuttings or stem layering, all propagation being best done in the spring. See *Bamboos.*

Alphonse-Karrii: *B. glaucescens* cv. 'Alphonse Karr'.

argentea: a name of no botanical standing; see *Arundinaria viridistriata* and *B. glaucescens.*

argenteostriata: *Arundinaria argenteostriata,* but see also *B. glaucescens* cv. 'Silverstripe'.

argenteovittata: a name of no botanical standing, see *B. glaucescens* cv. 'Silverstripe'.

arundinacea (Retz.) Willd. GIANT THORNY B. Sts. to 100 ft. high, 5½ in. in diam., in dense clumps, green and glossy, zigzag when young, becoming straight and golden-yellow, brs. graceful, bearing spines on lower branchlets; lf. blades to 8 in. long, ½ in. wide or more, nearly glabrous; panicle of great size; plant dying after fruiting. India; introd. widely in tropics and locally in subtrop. Fla. Shoots edible, appearing in autumn.

aurea: a listed name of no botanical standing for *Phyllostachys aurea.*

Bambos (L.) Voss: a confused name not clearly applicable, but sometimes used for *B. arundinacea.*

Beecheyana Munro [*Sinocalamus Beecheyana* (Munro) McClure]. BEECHEY B. Sts. to 40 ft. high, 4 in. in diam., fistulose, unarmed, bright green; lf. sheaths glabrous, blades lanceolate, acuminate, slightly cordate, subsessile, to 4¾ in. long and 1 in. wide, 12-nerved, not tessellate; panicle with 4 nodes, not rigid; spikelets in glomerules, hidden by bracts, ovate to oblong, 7–11-fld., lemma 18–20-nerved, mucronate, palea long-fimbriate. Se. China. Cult. in Hawaii, s. Calif., and s. Fla.; hardy in Zone 10. An important source of commercial bamboo sprouts in s. China.

Castillonii: *Phyllostachys bambusoides* cv. 'Castillon'.

disticha: *Arundinaria disticha;* but the name may be used also for *B. glaucescens* cv. 'Fernleaf' or 'Stripestem Fernleaf.'

falcata: *Chimonobambusa falcata.*

glaucescens (Willd.) Siebold ex Holtt. [*B. argentea* Hort.; *B. multiplex* of auth., not (Lour.) Räuschel; *B. nana* Roxb.]. HEDGE B., ORIENTAL H. B. Sts. to 10 ft. high, 1¼ in. in diam., shrubby, nearly solid, unarmed, glabrous, green then yellow; lf. blades linear-lanceolate, sessile, sheaths rather short, ciliate at the throat; panicle with few spikelets; spikelets 3–5-fld. China. A very variable sp. Introd. widely as an ornamental and for hedges or as tubbed specimens. Hardy in warmer parts of Zone 9. Cv. **'Alphonse Karr'** [*B. Alphonse-Karrii* Mitf. ex Satow; *B. nana* var. *Alphonse-Karrii* (Mitf. ex Satow) Mak. ex Shiras]. ALPHONSE KARR B. Sts. yellow, striped with green, to 35 ft. high. Cv. **'Fernleaf'** [*B. disticha* Hort.]. FERN-LEAF H. B. Usually dwarf, sts. rarely to 20 ft. high, foliage fernlike. Cv. **'Silverstripe'** [*B. argenteostriata* Hort.; *B. argenteovittata* Hort.; *B. nana* var. *variegata* E. Camus; *B. vittatoargentea* Hort.]. SILVER-STRIPE H.B. Sts. with internodes often narrowly striped with yellow, to 40 ft. high; lvs. yellowish or striped with white. Cv. **'Stripestem Fernleaf'** [*B. disticha* Hort.]. Sts. yellowish, striped with green, to 10 ft.; lvs. green, fernlike. Var. **Alphonse-Karrii:** cv. 'Alphonse Karr'. Var. **Riviereorum** Maire. CHINESE-GODDESS B. Dwarf, solid-stemmed, fern-lvd. Se. China. Foliage resembles cvs. 'Fernleaf' and 'Stripestem Fernleaf', but this var. has solid sts. Var. **variegata:** cv. 'Silverstripe'.

longispiculata Gamble ex Brandis. Sts. clustered, to 40 ft. high, 3 in. in diam.; lf. blades to 1 ft. long, 2½ in. wide, 24–31-nerved; infl. erect, bladeless, often branching, to 15 in. long; spikelets 6–12-fld., glumes 1 in. long. Burma.

Metake: *Pseudosasa japonica.*

mitis: a name used in several senses, but some hort. material may be *Phyllostachys bambusoides* cv. 'Allgold' or *P. viridis.*

multiplex (Lour.) Räuschel. A name of doubtful application. Material grown under this name is *B. glaucescens.*

nana: *B. glaucescens,* but see also *Arundinaria disticha.* Var. **Alphonse-Karrii:** *B. glaucescens* cv. 'Alphonse Karr'. Var. **variegata:** *B. glaucescens* cv. 'Silverstripe'.

nigra: *Phyllostachys nigra.*

Oldhamii Munro [*Sinocalamus Oldhamii* (Munro) McClure]. OLDHAM B. Clumps moderately open, sts. to 55 ft. high, 3¼ in. in diam., much-branched, unarmed, nearly herbaceous, very fistulose, pale green; st. sheaths glabrous, blades lanceolate, very acute, 10–12-nerved, not tessellate; lf. sheaths striate, hirsute, the margins fimbriate; panicle terminal, nearly simple, sometimes nearly a spike; spikelets ovate-lanceolate, 6–10-fld., palea hyaline, membranous, fimbriate. China, Taiwan. Cult. in Hawaii, hardy in Zone 10. Plants of this sp. when first introd. to s. Fla. and Calif. were erroneously identified as *Dendrocalamus latiflorus* Munro, which is apparently not cult.

pallescens: *B. tuldoides.*

palmata: *Sasa palmata.*

polymorpha Munro. Clumps very dense, sts. to 90 ft. high, 6 in. in diam., with bluish waxy surface, the lower portion free of brs. in mature clumps; st. sheaths stiff, densely covered with stiff, appressed hairs, auricles prominent, margined with long, stiff bristles; lvs. small, slender, to 7½ in. long, 7/16 in. wide. Bengal to Burma. Cult. in the tropics and locally in Zone 10 in Fla.

pygmaea: *Arundinaria pygmaea.*

Sasa: a listed name of no botanical standing, perhaps for a sp. of *Pseudosasa* or *Sasa.*

textilis McClure. Cespitose, clumps compact, sts. erect, but the tips arcuate or slightly pendulous, to 50 ft. high and 2⅜ in. in diam., nodes not prominent, internodes elongate, cylindrical, slightly farinose, brs. fasciculate; apex of st. sheaths narrow, the sheath blade nearly equalling the width of the sheath apex, twice as long as wide; lvs. on primary brs. to 8 in. long, 1 in. wide, smaller elsewhere, blades erect, narrowly triangular; infl. not known. S. China. Hardy in Zone 10; one of hardiest spp. of the genus. Split sts. are much used in China for handicrafts.

Thouarsii: see *B. tuldoides.*

tulda Roxb. Sts. to 70 ft. high, 3 in. in diam.; st. sheaths brown-hairy on outside, broad at apex with sheath blade broadly triangular, nearly equalling the width of the sheath apex and broader than high; lvs. to 10 in. long, 1⅛ in. wide. India. Cult. in tropics and locally in Zone 10 in Fla. Sts. outstanding for furniture and articles requiring split bamboo.

tuldoides Munro [*B. pallescens* (Döll) Hack.]. PUNTING-POLE B. Sts. slender, erect, straight, to 55 ft. high, 2½ in. in diam., fistulose, unarmed; apex of st. sheath broad, the base of the sheath blade nearly equalling the width of the sheath apex; lf. blades dark green, oblong, on older sts. to 5 in. long, to ⅝ in. broad, pale and hirsute on the lower surface, sheaths glabrous; flowering branchlets near top of the panicle alt. and leafy, nearly whorled below; spikelets pale, not glossy, glomerules more or less distant to densely aggregate, lower palea somewhat obtuse, abruptly mucronate. S. China; naturalized in Brazil. An important economic sp. in s. China. Hardy in Zone 10. Has been grown in s. Calif. and Fla. as *B. Thouarsii* Kunth, a misidentification.

Veitchii: *Sasa Veitchii.*

ventricosa McClure. BUDDHA B., BUDDHA'S-BELLY B. Sts. thick-walled, to 55 ft. high, 2¼ in. in diam.; st. sheaths not glaucous, apex broadly and symmetrically rounded, the sheath blade much shorter than sheath, broadly ovate in outline, subcordate at base; lf. blades to 7 in. long, not or scarcely glaucous on lower surface. S. China. Hardy in Zone 10 but also used as a greenhouse plant. This sp. can be much dwarfed by cult. in pot or tub or in dry sterile soil. When grown thus, the sts. are short (to 8 ft.), the lvs. are smaller, and the internodes are shortened and swollen, the reason for the common names.

verticillata Willd.: a name of uncertain application.

viridiglaucescens: *Phyllostachys viridiglaucescens.*

vittatoargentea: a name of no botanical standing; see *B. glaucescens* cv. 'Silverstripe'.

vulgaris Schrad. ex J. C. Wendl. COMMON B. Clumps rather open, sts. to 60 ft. high and 5 in. in diam., bright green, arching with age, brs. many, striate, unarmed; apex of st. sheath very wide, the base of the sheath blade much narrower than the apex; lf. blades to 10 in. long and 1¼ in. wide, not tessellate, margins and lower surface rough; panicle large, leafy, with large clusters of spikelets at the nodes. Known only in cult., but widely cult. and naturalized in the tropics; tender, withstands little or no frost, cult. locally in warmest parts of Zone 10. The great strength of its sts. and its easy culture make this bamboo adaptable to many uses. Among color forms of the sts. are those that are all yellow, green with yellow stripes, and green blotched with black.

BANANA. Bananas, of Old World origin, are among the most important tropical fruits. They are widely grown throughout the wet tropics, for home and local use as a staple food, and for export as a dessert fruit to markets in temperate regions. The major centers for commercial production have been the lowlands of tropical America, principally Central America, the West Indies, and northern South America, where production methods are highly sophisticated. Large commercial plantings are increasing elsewhere, especially in Taiwan and the Philippine Islands.

The banana plant is a perennial herb but the leaf sheaths produce a trunklike structure called a pseudostem, usually several present at a time. Depending upon the kind, the plant may attain a height of 20–30 feet with a crown of very large long leaves and a heavy cluster of fruits. The common edible bananas of commerce are cultivars of *Musa acuminata,* either diploids, like 'Bande' and 'Paka', or triploids, like 'Dwarf Cavendish', 'Grand Nain', 'Gros Michel', 'Lacatan', and 'Valery'. Some others are hybrids between *M. acuminata* and *M. Balbisiana,* these hybrids being referred to *M.* ×*paradisiaca.* Cultivars of *M.* ×*paradisiaca* may be diploid, like 'Ney Poovan', triploid, like 'French Plantain', 'King', 'Nadan', and 'Silk', or tetraploid, like 'Tiparoot'. Fruits of some clones are eaten fresh, and are usually referred to as common or dessert bananas; fruits of others, often called cooking bananas or plantains, are used as a staple vegetable and require cooking.

Many forms of edible bananas are grown as dooryard or home garden plants in the tropics, especially in the Old World. However, the highly developed commercial banana plantations of the New World represent plantings of a very few cultivars selected or bred primarily for their resistance to diseases or pests and to wind damage. Blowdown by wind is the single most serious threat to the plantation. For this reason the tall-growing and disease-susceptible cultivar 'Gros Michel', for many years the standard commercial banana, has been replaced by more dwarf, disease-resistant cultivars such as 'Grand Nain', 'Lacatan', and 'Valery'.

Representatives of another edible banana, known as the fehi or fe'i banana, are occasionally cultivated for ornament, but the fruit, palatable only when cooked, is not important outside Polynesia and Melanesia. The correct name for this banana is not certain but it is often referred to as *Musa Fehi.*

Mature banana plants consist of a clump of pseudostems, which arise successively from the underground rhizome system. Each pseudostem at maturity produces a single bunch of fruit ("stem"), after which it dies. In plantation practice, the pseudostem is cut off at the time the bunch of bananas is harvested, thus encouraging growth of the younger shoots. Under plantation culture the next oldest pseudostem will produce fruit ten months later but a longer period is required for plants grown in a greenhouse. About 100 days is required for a fruit bunch to mature after the young inflorescence bud "shoots" or first appears from the leaf sheaths.

Because edible hybrid bananas are seedless, propagation is by vegetative means. Usually entire corms ("heads") or parts ("bits") of the corm, each piece weighing 6–8 pounds and having a bud ("eye"), are used. Rooted suckers may also be planted. Dwarf bananas, such as *M. acuminata* 'Dwarf Cavendish', may be set as close as 8–10 feet either way but the ordinary large kinds should stand 14–20 feet apart in plantings. Bananas require a hot and humid climate, moist, deep, well-drained, fertile soil, and protection from wind. Surplus suckers are removed to control the succession of fruiting and to space the fruiting trunks.

Within the continental United States, edible bananas are seldom grown commercially, except for 'Dwarf Cavendish', although they are sometimes planted for home use, ornament, and interest in Zone 10 or in the warm greenhouse. The aerial portion of banana plants is destroyed by frost but new shoots arise from the rhizomes if the freezing is not too severe.

Several smaller inedible-fruited banana species, especially *M. coccinea* and *M. velutina,* are grown in tropical gardens or in the warm greenhouse for the colorful bracts of their long-lasting erect inflorescences. Another species, *M. Basjoo,* is root-hardy outdoors in sheltered sites in Zone 9. The Abyssinian banana, hardy in Zone 10, is *Ensete ventricosum.*

BANKSIA L.f. *Proteaceae.* About 50 spp. of evergreen trees or shrubs, native to Australia, 1 sp. in New Guinea and Aru Is.; lvs. alt.; fls. yellowish or occasionally reddish, in pairs in dense terminal spikes, becoming woody and spikes conelike in fr.

Sometimes grown in southern U.S. Propagated by cuttings under a belljar or with difficulty from seeds.

Baxteri R. Br. Tall shrub; lvs. to 4 in. long, divided to midrib into triangular segms. 1 in. long and ¾ in. wide at base, pale beneath; spikes globular, to 3 in. across. W. Australia.

Caleyi R. Br. Shrub, to 6 ft.; lvs. linear or oblong-lanceolate, 6–12 in. long, regularly toothed or cut, pale beneath; spikes nearly globular, to 3 in. long. W. Australia.

coccinea R. Br. Shrub, to 15 ft.; lvs. obovate to orbicular, to 2½ in. long, prickly-toothed, stiff; spikes globular, 2 in. across; fls. red. W. Australia.

collina R. Br. Shrub, to 12 ft.; lvs. linear, to 3 in. long or more, sharply toothed, white-tomentose beneath; spikes to 6 in. long; fls. yellowish, styles exserted, greenish-yellow to red to black. Queensland, New S. Wales, Victoria.

ericifolia L.f. Shrub or small tree, to 14 ft.; lvs. narrowly linear, about ½ in. long, notched or truncate at apex, margins entire, revolute; spikes to 10 in. long; fls. golden-yellow. New S. Wales.

grandis Willd. Tree, to 40 ft.; lvs. to 1 ft. long, divided to midrib into triangular segms. to 2 in. long and 1 in. wide at base, pale and tomentose beneath; spikes to 1 ft. long; fls. yellowish. W. Australia.

integrifolia L.f. Tree, to 30 ft.; lvs. scattered, oblong to lanceolate, to 8 in. long and 1 in. wide, entire or sometimes toothed, white-tomentose beneath; spikes to 6 in. long; fls. yellowish. Queensland, New S. Wales, Victoria. Bark yields tannin.

latifolia: *B. robur.*

littoralis R. Br. Tree, to 40 ft.; lvs. linear, to 8 in. long, usually toothed, white-tomentose beneath; spikes to 10 in. long; fls. yellowish or orange, styles exserted, purplish or yellowish. W. Australia.

marginata Cav. Shrub, to 15 ft.; lvs. oblong-lanceolate, to 2 in. long, usually entire, white beneath, margins recurved; spikes to 3 in. long; fls. yellowish. Se. Australia and Tasmania.

Meissneri Lehm. Low, spreading shrub, to 3 ft. across; lvs. crowded, linear, to ¼ in. long, revolute, white-hairy beneath; spikes ovoid; fls. to ¼ in. long, styles about ¾ in. long, hooked. W. Australia.

Menziesii R. Br. Tree, to 40 ft.; lvs. to 1 ft. long and 1 in. wide, truncate at apex, rusty-tomentose beneath; spikes to 5 in. long. W. Australia.

nutans R. Br. Shrub; lvs. narrow-linear, to 1 in. long, glabrous, margins entire, revolute; spikes to 2 in. long, sometimes nodding. W. Australia.

occidentalis R. Br. Shrub, to 5 ft.; lvs. linear, to 4 in. long, notched or toothed at apex, white beneath, margins recurved; spikes to 6 in. long; fls. red. W. Australia.

pulchella R. Br. Shrub; lvs. linear, to ½ in. long, margins entire, revolute; spikes to 1½ in. long. W. Australia.

quercifolia R. Br. Shrub, to 6 ft., glabrous; lvs. oblong, to 4 in. long, truncate at apex, deeply toothed or cut; spikes to 4 in. long; fls. orange-yellow. W. Australia.

repens Labill. Prostrate shrub; lvs. long-petioled, to 1 ft. long, deeply pinnatifid, thick and stiff; spikes to 4 in. long. W. Australia.

robur Cav. [*B. latifolia* R. Br.]. Low, stout shrub, brs. densely tomentose; lvs. obovate-oblong, 4–8 in. long, irregularly serrate, minutely tomentose beneath; spikes cylindrical, to 5 in. long; fls. greenish, metallic-green in bud. Queensland, New S. Wales.

serrata L.f. Tree, to 20 ft.; lvs. oblong-lanceolate, to 6 in. long and 1 in. wide, deeply toothed, tomentose beneath, leathery; spikes to 6 in. long; fls. blue-gray at first, later yellowish. Queensland, New S. Wales, Victoria. Wood used for furniture and window frames and ships.

speciosa R. Br. Tall shrub, 15–20 ft., sts. dense, tomentose; lvs. pinnately divided, 8–12 in. long, with segms. rounded to triangular, becoming larger toward base of lf., white-hairy beneath; spikes dense, oblong, to 5 in. long; fls. greenish, to 1 in. long, style incurved at base. W. Australia.

sphaerocarpa R. Br. Shrub, to 4 ft., tomentose; lvs. linear, 1–3 in. long, margins entire, revolute; spikes globular, to 3 in. across; fls. lemon-yellow. W. Australia.

verticillata R. Br. Small tree, to 15 ft.; lvs. whorled, oblong-lanceolate, to 3 in. long, white beneath, margins recurved; spikes to 8 in. long; fls. yellow. W. Australia.

BAPHIA Lodd. *Leguminosae* (subfamily *Faboideae*). About 60–65 spp. of trees and shrubs, native to Afr. and Madagascar; lvs. alt., simple, entire; fls. papilionaceous, in axillary racemes, clusters, or panicles, stamens 10, separate; fr. a flat, linear-lanceolate legume, narrowed to apex.

Grown as an ornamental.

obovata Schinz. Tree, to 25 ft.; lvs. obovate, to 2½ in. long, obtuse and mucronate, whitish-pubescent, petioles very short; fls. 2–4 together at often leafless nodes, white, with standard ¾ in. across. S.-W. Afr., Angola, Rhodesia.

racemosa (Hochst.) Walp. CAMWOOD. Broad shrub, to 12 ft. or more; lvs. broadly oblong-lanceolate, 2½–4 in. long, pointed, petioles ½–¾ in. long; fls. in short, panicled, leafy clusters, white, with purple veins, standard nearly ½ in. across; fr. 2 in. long. S. Afr., where known as TREE VIOLET.

BAPTISIA Venten. FALSE INDIGO, WILD I. *Leguminosae* (subfamily *Faboideae*). About 30–35 spp. of per. herbs, native to N. Amer.; lvs. alt., mostly of 3 lfts.; fls. papilionaceous, in racemes, stamens 10, separate; fr. a short, inflated legume. Native in dry regions.

Adapted to borders and wild gardens. Propagated by division and seeds.

alba (L.) Venten. To 3 ft.; lfts. oblong to lanceolate; racemes lateral, long-peduncled; fls. white, to ½ in. long. Va. to Fla.

australis (L.) R. Br. [*B. caerulea* Michx.; *B. versicolor* Lodd.]. BLUE F.I., PLAINS F.I., WILD BLUE I. To 6 ft., forming huge clumps; lfts. oblanceolate to ovate, to 2½ in. long; racemes long, terminal; fls. indigo-blue, to 1 in. long. Summer. Penn., s. to N.C. and Tenn.

bracteata Muhlenb. ex Elliott. To 2½ ft.; lfts. oblanceolate to obovate, to 4 in. long, softly pubescent; fls. white or cream-colored. Spring. N.C., s. to Ga. and Ala.

caerulea: *B. australis.*

leucantha Torr. & A. Gray. PRAIRIE F.I., WHITE F.I. To 4 ft.; lfts. obovate to cuneate, to 2 in. long; racemes lateral; fls. white, to nearly 1 in. long. Early summer. Ohio to Minn., s. to Miss. and Tex. Plant has medicinal properties.

leucophaea Nutt. Differs from *B. bracteata* in having lfts. narrowly oblanceolate-spatulate and villous. Mich. to Minn., Ark., and Tex.

minor Lehm. Distinguished from *B. australis* by its divaricate brs., and lfts. ⅝–2 in. long. Mo. and Kans., s. to Tex.

tinctoria (L.) Venten. HORSEFLY, HORSEFLY WEED, RATTLEWEED, WILD INDIGO. To 4 ft.; lfts. to 1 in. long; fls. bright yellow. Summer. Mass. to Fla., w. to Minn. A dye plant.

versicolor: *B. australis.*

villosa (Walt.) Nutt. To 4 ft., pubescent throughout, especially when young; lvs. nearly sessile, lfts. to 4 in. long, cuneate at base, entire; racemes lateral, to 1 ft. long; fls. yellow, to 1 in long. Early summer. Va. to S.C.

BARBAREA R. Br. [*Campe* Dulac]. WINTER CRESS, UPLAND CRESS. *Cruciferae*. About 12 spp. of bien. to per., erect, branching herbs in the N. Hemisphere; lvs. pinnatifid or pinnatisect, st. lvs. clasping; fls. small, yellow, in terminal racemes, sepals 4, petals 4, clawed; fr. a 4-angled, elongate, erect or spreading silique.

Some species are field and roadside weeds; a few are sometimes grown as edible cress, and more rarely as ornamentals.

praecox: *B. verna.*

rupicola Moris. Per., forming mats or sods, st. to 1 ft.; basal lvs. with large, cordate terminal segm., st. lvs. pinnatifid; fls. relatively large, pedicels longer than sepals. Corsica, Sardinia. Grown as an ornamental.

verna (Mill.) Asch. [*B. praecox* (Sm.) R. Br.]. EARLY W.C., BELLE ISLE CRESS, AMERICAN C., LAND C., UPLAND C., SCURVY GRASS. Bien., to 2 ft.; lvs. irregularly pinnatifid, basal lvs. with mostly 4–8 pairs of segms.; silique 1½ in. long or more, sharply 4-angled, on pedicel nearly or quite as thick as itself, the beak short and thick. Early spring. Eur.; naturalized in N. Amer. Sometimes grown for its lvs. used as salad, seasoning, or garnishing.

vulgaris R. Br. WINTER CRESS, ROCKET, YELLOW R. Glabrous bien. or per., to 3 ft.; lvs. with 1–5 pairs of lateral lobes; silique 1 in. long or less, obtusely angled, on relatively slender pedicels, the beak commonly very slender. Late spring. Eur.; naturalized in N. Amer., and occasionally a noxious weed in new meadows and cult. land.

BARKERIA: *EPIDENDRUM.* B. spectabilis: *E. Lindleyanum.*

BARKLYA F. J. Muell. *Leguminosae* (subfamily *Faboideae*). One sp., an Australian tree; lvs. alt., simple; fls. nearly regular, stamens 10, separate; fr. a flat, thin, stalked legume.

Propagated by seeds and by stem or root cuttings.

syringifolia F. J. Muell. GOLD-BLOSSOM TREE. To 60 ft.; lvs. evergreen, broadly triangular-ovate, cordate, to 4 in. long, palmately veined, petioles 1–2 in. long; fls. small, golden-yellow, in dense racemes to 9 in. long forming terminal panicles. Queensland and New S. Wales. Zone. 10.

BARLERIA L. Acanthaceae. About 230 spp. of trop. shrubs and herbs, many xerophytic, erect, glabrous or pubescent, sometimes spiny; fls. showy, blue or white, axillary or in terminal spikes with large, often spinose bracts, calyx 4-parted, 2 segms. large, 2 small, corolla tube slender, upper part broad, lobes 5, spreading, broad, mostly subequal, stamens 4, didynamous; fr. a caps., seeds flat, covered with hygroscopic hairs.

Grown under glass or in the open in warm climates. Propagated by cuttings of young wood over heat.

caerulea: a name of uncertain application; plants so listed may be *B. strigosa.*

cristata L. PHILIPPINE VIOLET. To 4 ft.; lvs. to 4 in. long; fls. axillary, sessile or nearly so, the 2 outer calyx segms. larger, ovate, veiny, spiny-margined, the 2 inner segms. linear, entire, corolla blue or white, 2 in. long, lobes obtuse. India and Burma.

lupulina Lindl. To 2 ft.; sts. with nodal spines; lvs. lanceolate, to 4 in. long; fls. in terminal hoplike spikes, bracts broadly ovate, overlapping, corolla yellow, 1 in. long, tube straight. Mauritius.

obtusa Nees. To 3 ft., lacking spines; lvs. elliptic, rarely as much as 3 in. long; fls. in loose axillary cymes, corolla mauve, 1¼ in. long. S. Afr.

strigosa Willd. To 4 ft.; lvs. ovate, to 5½ in. long or more, sessile or short-petioled, decurrent on st.; fls. in dense, 1-sided spikes, bracteoles lanceolate, to ⅝ in. long, outer calyx segms. 1 in. long, corolla blue, 2 in. long. India.

BAROSMA: *AGATHOSMA.* **B. scoparia:** *A. ovata.* **B. serratifolia:** *A. crenulata.*

BARRINGTONIA J. R. Forst. & G. Forst. *Barringtoniaceae.* About 40 spp. of mostly glabrous, evergreen trees, native to the Old World tropics; lvs. crowded near the ends of the brs., simple, entire or slightly crenate-serrate; infls. terminal and lateral, elongate racemes or spikes; calyx lobes 2–5, valvate or imbricate, petals 4, rarely 5, stamens many in several series, protruding beyond the petals, ovary inferior, 2–4-celled; fr. 1-seeded, drupaceous.

Suitable for seaside plantings in Zone 10.

acutangula (L.) Gaertn. INDIAN OAK. To 40 ft.; lvs. oblanceolate to obovate, to 5 in. long, entire or finely toothed; fls. in pendulous racemes to about 1 ft. long, calyx lobes usually 4, imbricate, petals 4, red, about ⅜ in. long, stamens red; fr. oblong-quadrangular, narrowed at both ends, to 1½ in. long. India to n. Australia.

asiatica (L.) Kurz [*B. speciosa* J. R. Forst. & G. Forst.]. Glabrous, to 15 ft.; lvs. sessile, obovate, to 15 in. long, entire, glossy; fls. in short, erect racemes, calyx funnelform, petals white, to 2½ in. long, stamens purplish; fr. 4-angled, to 3 in. in diam. Madagascar to Pacific Is.

racemosa (L.) K. Spreng. Glabrous, to 50 ft.; lvs. oblanceolate to obovate, to 10 in. long, slightly crenate-dentate; fls. in pendulous racemes to 18 in. long, calyx lobes mostly 2–3, valvate, petals apparently white or red, to about ½ in. long; fr. ovoid, slightly 4-angled, to 1½ in. long. Malay Pen., Pacific Is.

speciosa: *B. asiatica.*

BARRINGTONIACEAE F. Rudolphi. BARRINGTONIA FAMILY. Dicot.; 8 genera of trees or treelike shrubs of the Old World tropics; lvs. large, alt., simple; fls. bisexual, regular, calyx 2–5-lobed, petals 4, sometimes 5 or 0, stamens many, more or less united basally and attached on the outer edge of a thickened ring or disc above the 2–4-celled, inferior ovary; fr. a drupe or berry. Closely related to the *Lecythidaceae* and often included in that family, but differ in lacking a specialized androphore. *Barringtonia* and *Napoleona* are occasionally cult.

BARTONIA: *MENTZELIA.* **B. aurea:** *M. Lindleyi.*

BARTSCHELLA: *MAMMILLARIA* subgenus *Bartschella.*

BARTSIA L. *Scrophulariaceae.* About 40 spp. of per. herbs, native to n. temp. regions of Eur. and the Andes; lvs. opp.; infl. racemose; calyx 4-parted, corolla 2-lipped, upper lip concave, with 2 lobes, lower lip 3-lobed, stamens 4; fr. a flattened loculicidal caps., seeds winged.

Plants parasitic on roots of grasses.

alpina L. ALPINE B., VELVET-BELLS. Ann., sts. to 8 in., from a rhizome, pubescent; lvs. sessile, ovate, to ¾ in. long, serrate; infl. few-fld., bracts purplish; corolla about twice as long as calyx, dull purple, upper lip longer than the lower. Early summer. Arctic regions and mts., Eur.

BASELLA L. MALABAR NIGHTSHADE. *Basellaceae.* Five variable spp. of twining, herbaceous, glabrous vines, native to trop. Afr. and Asia; lvs. fleshy, ovate to ovate-lanceolate, petioled; fls. bisexual, in mostly simple spikes, perianth urceolate, fleshy, enlarging and enclosing the fr., styles 3.

Grown in tropical and warm countries as potherbs. In the North, seeds must be started indoors.

alba L. MALABAR SPINACH, INDIAN S. Rampant vine, to 30 ft. long; lvs. oblong to broadly ovate, to 4¾ in. long, acute to slightly obtuse, shallowly cordate to truncate, green or purplish, petioles to 1⅛ in. long; fls. white; fr. black, glossy. Probably native to Afr. and se. Asia; distribution now pantrop. Cv. 'Rubra' [*B. rubra* L.]. Sts., petioles, and fls. reddish. Occasionally used as a hot-weather potherb or substitute for spinach.

rubra: *B. alba* cv.

BASELLACEAE. *Basella alba* cv. 'Rubra': **a,** flowering stems, × ⅙; **b,** inflorescence, × ½; **c,** flower, × 4; **d,** flower, vertical section, × 4; **e,** fruit, × 2; **f,** seed, × 2.

BASELLACEAE Moq. BASELLA FAMILY. Dicot.; allied to the *Chenopodiaceae;* 4 genera of climbing or decumbent herbs, native to trop. and subtrop. Amer., Asia, E. Afr. and Madagascar; lvs. alt., fleshy; fls. small, regular, bisexual or unisexual, in spikes, racemes, or panicles, bractlets 2 or 4, united basally with perianth, perianth segms. 5, remaining closed, stamens 5, inserted on perianth, ovary superior, 1-celled; fr. indehiscent, enclosed by persistent, often fleshy perianth. *Basella* is sometimes grown for food, and *Anredera* as an ornamental. ULLUCO (*Ullucus tuberosus* Caldas), a tuber food of the high Andes, is seldom grown in N. Amer.

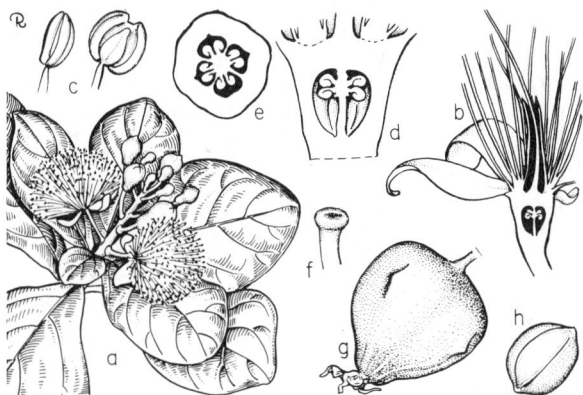

BARRINGTONIACEAE. *Barringtonia asiatica:* **a,** flowering branch, × ⅛; **b,** flower, vertical section, with apices of stamens and style and two petals cut off, × ¼; **c,** anthers, two views, × 5; **d,** ovary, vertical section, × 1½; **e,** ovary, cross section, × 1½; **f,** stigma, × 1½; **g,** fruit, × ¼; **h,** seed, × ⅙.

BASKET PLANTS. Plants suitable for planting in hanging baskets or pots are of more or less vining, trailing, or diffuse habit and of simple cultural requirements. Plants thus grown are commonly used on patios and porches, in windows, or in the conservatory. Some of them are annuals of simple culture; others are perennials, often propagated by means of cuttings. Among the more commonly used basket subjects are *Abutilon megapotamicum, Asparagus densiflorus, Campanula isophylla, Chlorophytum comosum, Coleus pumilus, Epipremnum aureum, Ficus pumila, Gynura aurantiaca* cv. 'Purple Passion', *Hoya bella, Othonna capensis, Pelargonium peltatum, Philodendron scandens, Saxifraga stolonifera, Sedum Morganianum, Senecio mikanioides, Syngonium podophyllum,* and various species and cultivars of the genera *Achimenes, Begonia, Browallia, Cissus, Columnea, Episcia, Fuchsia, Hedera, Impatiens, Oxalis, Petunia, Plectranthus, Rhipsalis, Schlumbergera, Tradescantia, Tropaeolum, Vinca, Zebrina,* and the many cacti known as epiphyllum hybrids. Several genera of epiphytic ferns also furnish material suitable for basket planting. Selection of the subject must depend upon the temperature conditions under which the subject is to be grown and whether the basket is to be hung in sun or shade.

BASSELINIA Vieill. *Palmae.* About 10 spp. of small, unarmed, monoecious palms in New Caledonia; sts. solitary or clustered, ringed; lvs. pinnate, sheaths at first tubular, splitting opposite petiole, not forming a crownshaft, pinnae acute; infl. among lvs. or persisting below them, with 2 deciduous bracts, 2–3-branched, rachillae slender, hairy, with fls. in triads (2 male and 1 female); male fls. smaller than female, sepals 3, imbricate, petals 3, valvate, stamens 6, filaments awl-shaped, inflexed at apex in bud, pistillode thick, columnar, as long as stamens in bud; female fls. with sepals and petals 3, imbricate, staminodes 3, minute, pistil 1-celled, 1-ovuled; fr. globose to nearly reniform, with lateral stigmatic residue; seed with homogeneous endosperm, embryo basal.

May be grown as ornamentals. For culture see *Palms.*

eriostachys (Brongn.) Becc. To nearly 20 ft., sts. usually clustered, to 2 in. in diam.; lvs. spreading, sheaths deep red-violet to nearly black, orange inside, pinnae 10–11 on each side, deep green; infls. with orangish bracts, rachillae gray- to red-brown-tomentose; fls. very small; fr. ¼ in. in diam., globose.

BATEMANNIA Lindl. *Orchidaceae.* Five spp. of epiphytes, native to trop. S. Amer.; pseudobulbs few-lvd.; lvs. plicate; infl. a lateral, pendulous, loosely few-fld. raceme; upper sepals and petals similar, spreading-erect, lateral sepals with inrolled margins, directed downward, base of petals running down long column foot, lip 3-lobed, lateral lobes folded up along column, midlobe with basal, transverse callus. For structure of fl. see *Orchidaceae.*

Intermediate to warm greenhouse; for culture see *Orchids.*

Burtii: *Huntleya meleagris.*

Colleyi Lindl. [*Maxillaria Colleyi* Hort. ex Planch.]. Pseudobulbs compressed, ovate to oblong, obtusely 4-angled, 1–3-lvd. at summit; lvs. oblanceolate-elliptic or obovate-oblong; raceme 10-fld., to 6 in. long; sepals and petals green outside, dull brownish-purple inside, lip 3-lobed, white or whitish-yellow, dotted with red. Trinidad, Guyana.

BATRACHIUM: *RANUNCULUS.*

BATSCHIA: *LITHOSPERMUM.*

BAUERA Banks. *Saxifragaceae.* Three spp. of evergreen shrubs of Australia; lvs. opp., sessile, of 3 toothed lfts., resembling a whorl of 6 small lvs.; fls. small, solitary in the axils of upper lvs., calyx tube united with ovary, sepals and petals 4–10, stamens as many as petals or numerous, ovary half-inferior; fr. a many-seeded caps.

One species is grown in the cool greenhouse and blooms throughout winter and spring. Propagated by cuttings of half-ripened wood in spring.

rubioides Andr. Shrub to 2 ft.; lfts. lanceolate, to ½ in. long; fls. pink or white, on slender pedicels to ¾ in. long. New S. Wales.

BAUHINIA L. [*Alvesia* Welw. 1858, not 1869; *Piliostigma* Walp.]. *Leguminosae* (subfamily *Caesalpinioideae*). Perhaps 300 spp. of trees, shrubs, and woody vines and lianas, sometimes armed, native to warm temp. and trop. regions; lvs. alt., usually 2-lobed or 2-parted; fls. in racemes, panicles, or corymbs, petals 5, nearly equal, stamens 10 or fewer; fr. a flat, linear or oblong legume.

Grown as ornamentals in warm regions or sometimes elsewhere under glass. Propagated by seeds, suckers, air layering, and cuttings over heat.

acuminata L. DWARF WHITE B. Shrub, to 10 ft.; lvs. lobed less than halfway; fls. in racemes, showy, 4 in. across, petals broad, white, stamens 10, fertile; fr. to 5 in. long. Summer. India, China, Malay Pen.

alba: *B. variegata* cv. 'Candida'.

binata Blanco. Shrub, brs. scandent, with tendrils; lvs. to 1½ in. long, much broader than long, divided to base; fls. in dense corymbs, small, white, to 2 in. across, petals oblong-spatulate, pubescent, stamens 10. Late spring. Philippine Is.

Blakeana S. T. Dunn. Evergreen tree, to 40 ft. or more; lvs. 6–8 in. across, lobed ¼–⅓ their length; fls. in long racemes, to 6 in. across, fragrant, petals obovate or elliptic, reddish or rose-purple; fr. sterile, not setting seed. Possibly of hybrid origin. Winter. All cult. plants originated from a single tree discovered in Canton, China; prop. vegetatively.

candicans: *B. forficata.*

candida: *B. variegata* cv.

Carronii F. J. Muell. Similar to *B. Cunninghamii,* but petals white, obovate, and fr. narrower, to 1½ in. wide. Queensland (Australia), where called QUEENSLAND EBONY.

Championii Benth. Climber, with tendrils; lvs. to 2 in. long or more, lobed to ⅓ their length, pubescent beneath; fls. in axillary racemes 4–8 in. long, very small, white, fertile stamens 3; fr. 3 in. long, 1 in. wide. Hong Kong.

corymbosa Roxb. ex DC. PHANERA. Climbing by tendrils; lvs. 1–2 in. long, lobed to about middle; fls. in loose racemes, pinkish to rose, or white with pink veins, 1 in. across, fertile stamens 3; fr. to 5 in. long, less than 1¾ in. wide. Se. Asia.

Cunninghamii Benth. Erect, to 20 ft. or more; lvs. to 1½ in. long, bifid to base; fls. 2–3 together, massed along brs., small, rosy-red, petals ovate, less than 1 in. long, silky-tomentose, stamens 10; fr. thin, 6 in. long and 2 in. wide. Queensland (Australia).

forficata Link [*B. candicans* Benth.]. Erect, to 30 ft., brs. pendent, with spines to ¼ in. long; lvs. to 4 in. long, 3½ in. wide, lobed to middle, glaucous beneath; fls. 2–4 opp. lvs., 4–5 in. across, petals white, narrow, stamens 10; fr. 6–8 in. long, ¾ in. wide. Summer. Peru to Argentina and Brazil.

Galpinii: *B. punctata.*

glauca (Wallich ex Benth.) Benth. Slender climber, with puberulous tendrils; lvs. 3 in. long, lobed to middle; fls. in dense terminal corymbs 1 in. long, small, cream, stamens 3; fr. thin, 6–8 in. long, 2 in. wide, indehiscent. Se. Asia.

grandiflora: a listed name of no botanical standing, applied to various spp. of *Bauhinia.*

Hookeri F. J. Muell. Spreading tree, to 50 ft.; lvs. bifid to base; fls. in short racemes, petals white, edged in crimson, ovate, 1½ in. long, stamens 10. Ne. Australia, where known as MOUNTAIN EBONY.

insignis: a listed name of no botanical standing.

integrifolia Roxb. Scandent, with tendrils, rusty-pubescent; lvs. to 6 in. long, with triangular apical sinus; fls. in long, dense panicles, petals obovate, rusty-silky; fr. 5–6 in. long, 2 in. wide. Malay Pen.

Kappleri: *B. monandra.*

Kurzii Prain. Scandent shrub; lvs. to 5 in. across, lobed to ⅓ their length, tawny-puberulous beneath; fls. in terminal corymbose racemes, small, rose, petals obovate-linear, ⅝ in. long, pubescent. Burma.

malabarica Roxb. MALABAR B. Spreading tree, to 50 ft.; lvs. broader than long, lobed ¼ their length or less; fls. in short, sessile, dense racemes, crowded near tips of st., pale yellow, to ¾ in. long, calyx tubular, petals scarcely longer than calyx, stamens 10; fr. to 12 in. long. India to Java.

megalandra Griseb. Tree, to 15 ft.; lvs. to 5 in. wide, lobed to ⅓ their length; fls. solitary, or the uppermost racemose, petals white, linear, to 3 in. long, stamens 10. Winter. W. Indies, Trinidad, Venezuela.

mollicella S. F. Blake. Thorny tree, to 15 ft.; lvs. lobed to ⅓ their length, soft-pubescent beneath; fls. 1–5 together, showy, 3–4 in. across, petals broad, white, becoming cream, stamens 10. Summer. Venezuela.

monandra Kurz [*B. Kappleri* Sagot]. BUTTERFLY FLOWER, JERUSALEM DATE. Shrub or small tree, to 20 ft., differing from *B. variegata* in having fls. in terminal racemes, pinkish, with the median petal heavily marked with red-purple, and only 1 fertile stamen. Summer. Burma; naturalized in trop. Amer.

natalensis D. Oliver. Small, slender shrub; lvs. 1 in. long, bifid to base; fls. 1–2 together opp. lvs., to 1½ in. across, petals white, obovate-oblong, the 3 upper ones smaller, with reddish midveins, stamens 10; fr. 3 in. long. Natal. Doubtfully in cult.

Pauletia Pers. RAILWAY-FENCE B. Erect, to 25 ft., brs. long, slender, with short stout spines; lvs. to 2¼ in. long, lobed to ⅓ their length; fls. inconspicuous, petals greenish-cream, linear, 3 in. long, stamens 5; fr. linear, to 9 in. long. Mex., s. to Panama, Venezuela, Trinidad; escaped in Puerto Rico.

Petersiana C. Bolle. Shrub, sts. spreading, climbing; lvs. about 3 in. across, lobed to middle; fls. in few-fld. corymbs, petals white or pale yellow, narrow-oblanceolate, to 2½ in. long, fertile stamens 5. Mozambique.

picta DC. Erect; lvs. roundish-elliptic, lobes nearly ovate, acutish; fls. in terminal racemes, white, petals oblong. Colombia. Doubtfully in cult.; material offered under this name may be *B. tomentosa* cv.

piliostigma: a listed name of no botanical standing; probably for *B. Thonningii.*

polycarpa Wallich ex Benth. Erect, to 12 ft.; lvs. to 4 in. long, lobed about ⅓ their length; fls. in narrow, dense racemes, 3–5 in. long, inconspicuous, petals yellow-green, ¼ in. long, stamens 10; fr. linear, 3–4 in. long. Burma.

porosa L. H. Boivin ex Baill. Scandent, glabrate; lvs. orbicular or short-ovate, to 4 in. long, lobed to middle or entire; fls. in short racemes, petals slightly unequal, long-clawed; fr. 8 in. long. Madagascar.

punctata C. Bolle [*B. Galpinii* N. E. Br.]. RED B., NASTURTIUM B. Low, spreading shrub, to 10 ft., brs. scandent; lvs. lobed less than halfway; fls. in few-fld. racemes, brick-red, 2½ in. across, fertile stamens 3; fr. to 5 in. long. Summer. Trop. Afr.

purpurea L. [*B. triandra* Roxb.]. BUTTERFLY TREE, ORCHID TREE. Often confused with *B. variegata*, but much earlier-flowering, with petals not overlapping, narrower, oblanceolate, and fertile stamens 3–4. Autumn. India to Malay Pen. No variant with pure white fls. is known.

racemosa Lam. Small bushlike tree, brs. drooping; lvs. to 2 in. long, broader than long, bifid nearly or quite to base; fls. in loose racemes, small, yellowish, stamens 10; fr. 6–12 in. long, 1 in. across. Ne. India.

reticulata DC. Differs from *B. Thonningii* by its smaller lvs. to 4 in. long and 4¾ in. across, quite glabrous between veins beneath; fls. white with green centers. Egypt, Sudan. Used where native for food, fiber, blue and black dyes, and for making soap. *B. reticulata* of most auths. is *B. Thonningii.*

rufescens Lam. Differs from *B. racemosa* in its smaller lvs., less than 1 in. across, and much smaller fr., to 3½ in. long and ½ in. across; fls. fragrant. Senegal to Ethiopia. Used where native for fiber, tanning, carpentry, and for medicine.

scandens L. Climber, to more than 100 ft., with tendrils; lvs. deeply cordate, very shallowly to obviously lobed, lobes acuminate; fls. in panicled racemes, petals white, small; fr. 1½–2 in. long. India to Malay Arch. The name has been variously applied and material in hort. may be misidentified.

sinensis: a listed name of no botanical standing.

taitensis Taub. Shrub, to 5 ft.; lvs. pubescent, less than 1 in. long, lfts. obtuse; fls. many, small, cream-white. Kenya.

Thonningii Schumach. [*B. reticulata* of auth., not DC.; *Piliostigma Thonningii* (Schumach.)) Milne-Redh.]. Erect, to 60 ft.; lvs. to 6 in. long and 8 in. wide, pubescent between veins beneath; fls. in racemes, white, drooping, 1 in. long, fragrant, petals crinkled, puberulous, stamens 10; fr. oblong, to 12 in. long and 2 in. wide, indehiscent. Trop. Afr.

tomentosa L. [*Alvesia tomentosa* (L.) Britt. & Rose]. ST. THOMAS TREE, YELLOW B., BELL B. Erect, to 15 ft.; lvs. nearly orbicular, to 2¼ in. long, lobed to ⅓ their length, villous beneath; fls. campanulate, bright yellow to white, with a brown or red blotch at base of upper petal, 2 in. long, fertile stamens 10; fr. 5 in. long. India to China, trop. Afr.; naturalized in W. Indies. Cv. 'Picta' [*B. picta* Hort., not DC.]. Fls. light yellow, almost whitish.

triandra: *B. purpurea.*

Vahlii Wight & Arn. MALU CREEPER. Climber, to 100 ft., trunks to 4 in. in diam.; lvs. to 12 in. long and wide, lobed to ⅓ their length; fls. white, becoming yellowish, to 2½ in. across, fertile stamens 3; fr. to 1 ft. long. Summer. Foot of Himalayas.

variegata L. ORCHID TREE, MOUNTAIN EBONY. Tree, to 20–40 ft.; lvs. 4–6 in. across, lobed about ⅓ their length; fls. in short racemes lateral at tips of brs., appearing as lvs. fall, 4–5 in. across, petals overlapping, broad, lavender to magenta, purple, or white, the central one marked dark purple, fertile stamens 5. Winter. India, China. Used for food, medicine, dyeing, tanning, as a gum, and for farm implements. Most commonly grown sp. Cv. 'Candida' [*B. alba* Buch.-Ham.; *B. candida* Ait.]. Fls. pure white, with greenish veins.

violacea: a listed name of no botanical standing for *B. purpurea.*

BEAN. Various species of *Phaseolus* are commonly known as beans, namely: common, kidney, or snap bean, *Phaseolus vulgaris;* lima bean, *P. limensis;* sieva or civet bean, *P. lunatus;* these species are annual twiners, but also have bush or dwarf forms. White Dutch runner bean, *P. coccineus* cv. 'Albus', and scarlet runner bean, *P. coccineus,* are perennial twiners, also with bush forms, but are grown as annuals. All these plants are tender, to be planted only after the weather is warm and settled. Broad, Windsor, or horse bean, *Vicia Faba,* is a stiffly erect hardy annual grown in North America mostly in Canada, and especially in the maritime districts; it does not thrive in hot, dry summers. Other kinds of beans are grown for ornament, for forage, and special purposes. See *Canavalia, Dolichos, Glycine, Pachyrhizus, Phaseolus, Vicia,* and *Vigna.*

The present statements about culture of beans apply to the kinds of *Phaseolus* mentioned above. In respect to their uses, they may be divided into three categories: those used as green or snap beans, the entire pod being eaten ('Astro', 'Bush Blue Lake', 'Contender', 'Harvester', 'Midas', 'Provider', 'Tender crop'); those used as shell beans, the full-sized but immature beans being shelled from the pod, and cooked (French horticultural); dry beans, or those used in their dry or winter condition.

Beans will grow in most soils, but the best results may be expected in ground well enriched and in good physical condition. Little is to be gained by planting bean seed before the soil has become warm (50° F). No vegetable seed decays more quickly than beans, and the delay caused by waiting for the ground to become warm and free from excessive moisture will be more than made up by the rapidity of growth when finally they are planted. The beans may be dropped 1 inch deep in shallow drills, the seeds to lie 2 inches apart. Cover to the surface of the soil, and if the ground is dry, firm it with the foot or the back of the hoe. For the bush varieties, allow 2–2½ feet between the drill rows. Pole beans are given more room, and support must be provided. The bush varieties may be planted at intervals of two weeks from the first planting until about two months before the average date of the first frost in autumn. Each planting may be on ground previously occupied by some early-maturing crop. Thus, the first to third plantings may be on ground from which has been harvested a crop of spinach *(Spinacia),* early radish *(Raphanus)* or lettuce *(Lactuca);* after that, on ground where early peas *(Pisum)* have been grown; and the later sowings where beets *(Beta)* or early potatoes *(Solanum tuberosum)* have grown. Snap beans for canning are commonly taken from the last crop. One pound of seed will plant about 100 feet of drill.

Lima bean cultivars often fail to mature in the northern states. The land should not be very rich in nitrogen (or stable manure), else the plants will run too much to vine and be too late. Choose a fertile sandy or gravelly soil with warm exposure, use a general fertilizer, and give them the best of culture. Aim to have the pods set before the droughts of midsummer come. The pole limas, such as cultivar 'Fordhook', are commonly planted in hills that are 2–4 feet apart in the rows; 1 pound of beans plants about 100 hills. Good trellises for beans are made by strong twine stretched between two horizontal wires, one of which is drawn 1 foot and the other 6 or 7 feet above the ground. Dwarf limas, such as cultivars

'Kingston' and 'Thorogreen', are more desirable for small gardens than the pole varieties, as they may be planted much closer, the bother of procuring poles and twine is avoided, and the garden will have a more sightly appearance; they are grown in rows that are about 2½ feet apart. Dwarf limas and pole limas require a longer season than the common garden bush beans and usually only one planting is made.

Beans are attacked by a number of diseases and insects, for the control of which the grower should consult the latest bulletins and books.

BEAUCARNEA Lem. BOTTLE PONYTAIL. *Agavaceae.* About 6 spp. of dioecious or polygamodioecious, treelike plants, native to dry regions of Tex. and Mex., with tall trunks usually much swollen at base; lvs. long, linear, stiff, entire or scaberulous-margined; infl. paniculate; fls. small, whitish, perianth segms. 6, stamens 6, ovary superior, 1-celled, with 2–3 ovules; fr. a 3-winged caps. Sometimes retained in the genus *Nolina.*

Suitable for outdoor planting in warm dry regions. Cultivation as for *Yucca.*

gracilis Lem. [*Dasylirion gracile* (Lem.) Macbr.; *Nolina gracilis* (Lem.) Ciferri & Giacom.] Differs from *B. stricta* in having lvs. to 20 in. long, ⅛–¼ in. wide, seeds only ⅛ in. long. Puebla (Mex.).

recurvata Lem. [*Nolina tuberculata* Hort.]. ELEPHANT-FOOT TREE, PONYTAIL. To 30 ft.; lvs. to 6 ft. long, ¾ in. wide, thin, nearly flat, green, recurving, with smooth grooves and nearly smooth margins; fr. long-pedicelled. Mex. Var. **intermedia** Hort. ex Bak. Lvs. less than 3 ft. long. This appears to be the var. most commonly cult. in Calif.

stricta Lem. To 20 ft. or more; lvs. firm, keeled, glaucous, straight, to about 2 ft. long, 5/16–9/16 in. wide, with papillose grooves and scaberulous yellowish margin; fr. short-pedicelled, seeds ⅛–3/16 in. long.

BEAUMONTIA Wallich. NEPAL TRUMPET FLOWER. *Apocynaceae.* About 8 spp. of woody vines, native from India to Java; lvs. opp., entire, membranous; fls. in terminal cymes, large, 5-merous, bisexual, calyx large, corolla funnelform to campanulate, stamens borne in upper part of corolla tube, filaments long, anthers sagittate, acute at apex, connivent and adhering to stigma; fr. a pair of long-cylindrical, woody follicles.

Planted as ornamentals in tropics and subtropics, Zone 10, and sometimes under glass. Beaumontias require rich loamy soil and do not thrive in pots. Propagated by cuttings.

grandiflora (Roxb.) Wallich. HERALD'S-TRUMPET, EASTER-H.-T., EASTER-LILY VINE. To 10 ft. or more, brs. rusty-pubescent; lvs. elliptic to obovate-oblong, to 8 in. long, abruptly acuminate, glabrous above, slightly pubescent beneath, veins greenish-white and prominent beneath, petioles to about 1 in. long; fls. fragrant, calyx lobes foliaceous, broadly ovate-elliptic, to 1¾ in. long, margins often tinged red, corolla trumpet-shaped, to 4 in. across and 4 in. long, tube much longer than lobes. Himalayas.

Jerdoniana Wight. Similar to *B. grandiflora,* but smaller in all its parts, calyx lobes lanceolate, corolla funnelform, about 3 in. long. India.

BECIUM: *OCIMUM.*

BEDDING. This is a more or less technical term to denote the growing of plants in beds or masses in contrast to placing them singly or in lines or hills. It is commonly employed to designate the close massing of plants in the open for the making of striking displays of flowers or foliage. Bedding is ordinarily a more or less temporary recourse for spring, summer, or autumn show, although the name is sometimes given to assembled effects of perennials, as of grasses, and even of low evergreens. Sometimes the bed is of short duration even though the plants are perennial, as with the spring bulbs. It is evident that for temporary or seasonal effects the site must be well chosen and the ground carefully prepared so that results are obtained speedily and at the desired date.

In spring bedding, the plants are commonly bulbs such as *Crocus, Hyacinthus, Tulipa,* or other early-flowering plants. In this case, the ground is usually occupied later in the season by other plants. These latter may be annuals, the seeds of which are sown among the bulbs as soon as the season is far enough advanced; or the annuals may be started in boxes and the plants transplanted among the bulbs as soon as the weather permits. Heavy early over-planting of this kind, however, is likely to weaken the bulbs or prevent their proper maturation.

Summer bedding is often made with perennial plants carried over from the preceding year, or better, propagated for that particular purpose in February and March. Such plants as ageratum, coleus, geranium, heliotrope, lobelia, scarlet salvia, and sweet alyssum may be grown for these beds. Many low-growing and compact continuous-flowering annuals are excellent for summer bedding effects.

Bedding of another type attempts to make patterns or designs; it is carpet bedding. Comparatively few species are adapted to this purpose, for the plants must be such as will stand shearing and have very strong and constant colors of foliage. The most popular carpet-bedding plants are alternanthera, coleus, iresine, various dusty millers, and such succulent plants as *Sempervivum* and *Echeveria.* Some annuals may also be used for strong color effects, as lobelia and sweet alyssum. Ordinarily the making of carpet beds should be left to professional gardeners, since it requires much skill and care to make and keep the beds in perfect condition; a ragged or imperfect carpet bed is worse than no bed at all. Carpet beds are really curiosities, and they have no more legitimate place in the general landscape design than painted stones or sheared evergreens. Therefore, they should be placed by themselves, at one side, where they do not interfere with the general design of the place. In public parks they make a very useful attraction when set off by themselves, the same as topiary work, floral clocks, or other specialties.

Bold subtropical effects can be produced by planting in the open such plants as bananas, caladiums, cannas, crotons, and palms, as well as castor beans and other quick growers. Plants like the palms and bananas, which are normally kept in pots, are better left in the pots and plunged to the rims rather than turned out directly into the ground. To attain quick and continuous effects, it is advisable to set the plants rather closely. As these plants are likely to be injured by strong winds, it is well to have subtropical beds in somewhat protected places. Care must be taken to provide a good water supply, for the effects depend largely on luxuriant growth and clean foliage.

BEET. One species of beet, *Beta vulgaris,* is widely grown for the edible roots and leaves, and as a commercial source of sugar. It is of easy cultivation in any good soil; the seeds may be sown early in spring and at intervals of a few weeks throughout the summer to provide a continuous crop. Long-rooted cultivars should be planted only in open, well-tilled soil, or roots will be misshapen.

BEFARIA Mutis ex L. (sometimes spelled *Bejaria*). *Ericaceae.* About 15 spp. of evergreen shrubs or trees, native to Fla., Cuba, and Mex. to S. Amer.; lvs. alt., simple; fls. white, pink, yellow, or red, in terminal racemes, corymbs, or panicles, calyx 6–7-lobed, petals 6 or 7, stamens 12–14, anthers opening by terminal pores, ovary superior; fr. a 6–7-valved caps.

racemosa Venten. TARFLOWER, FLY-CATCHER. To 6 ft. or sometimes taller; lvs. oblong to elliptic, to 2 in. long, leathery; fls. white, to 2 in. across, in showy racemes to 8 in. long. Spring, summer. Sandy soil and low places, s. Ga. and Fla. Sometimes planted in Fla.

BEGONIA L. *Begoniaceae.* Over 1,000 spp. in tropics and subtropics of both hemispheres, but less abundant in islands of Pacific Ocean; monoecious herbs or shrubs, usually per., fibrous-rooted, rhizomatous, tuberous, or bulbous, sts. erect or procumbent, sometimes climbing, succulent or woody, sometimes absent; lvs. alt., variable in size and shape, usually oblique or asymmetrical, petioled, with 2 stipules; fls. unisexual, white, pink, red, orange, or yellow, usually in axillary cymes, with sometimes showy bracts; male fls. with 2–4 sepals and 0–2 petals, the sepals and petals of different size and shape but similarly colored and usually referred to as tepals, stamens many, forming a yellow globose mass or rarely a column in center of fl., female fls. with 2–5 equal tepals, ovary inferior, usually 3-celled and 3-angled, the angles extended into 3 often unequal wings, styles usually 3, stigmas twisted; fr. a caps., opening loculicidally below perianth, or rarely fleshy, berrylike, and bursting irregularly, seeds very many, minute, with net-veined coat.

The many species, not all now in cultivation, have given rise, through crossing and by selection, to over 10,000 recorded hybrids and cultivars. Many of these bear Latin names as if they were species, thus adding to the confusion of the nomenclature. The many kinds bearing only vernacular names are not included in this account.

Since the botanical classification of *Begonia* into sections is based on the type of placentation and is impractical for horticultural purposes, begonias are divided by horticulturists into 3 large groups, according to their rootstock: fibrous-rooted, rhizomatous, and tuberous, the last including the bulbous *B. socotrana* and its derivatives. These 3 main divisions are generally again divided into smaller subdivisions for convenience and exhibition purposes, but the lines between these subdivisions are often rather indefinite or overlapping. Some species or cultivars do not fit into any of these subdivisions, and at flower shows or in nursery catalogues are grouped together as "odd and rare types."

The fibrous-rooted begonias are divided into the wax begonia or Semperflorens-Cultorum group, including the derivatives of *B. semperflorens*, used most often outdoors in the summer as bedding plants; the cane types or angel-wing begonias, including *B. corallina* and closely related species, several of which are hardy in the South; and the hairy or hirsute begonias with feltlike leaves, which are greenhouse or house plants, grown for their ornamental leaves and flowers.

The rhizomatous-rooted begonias are divided into the Rex-Cultorum group, including derivatives of *B. rex* and its allied species, grown for their brightly colored foliage; and the remaining rhizomatous group, subdivided by the size, type, or hairiness of the leaves. The flowers are usually small and inconspicuous.

The tuberous-rooted begonias are divided into the Tuberhybrida group, derived from the crossing of several Andean species, and grown outdoors in the summer for bedding, window decoration, or hanging baskets, blooming from early summer to the first frosts; and greenhouse plants flowering during the winter, subdivided into the Cheimantha group, the result of crosses between *B. socotrana* and *B. Dregei*, an Afr. species, and the Elatior group, including cultivars produced by the crosses of *B. socotrana* and tuberous species of Andean origin, or *B.* × *tuberhybrida*. The tuberous begonias are grown for their many, colorful, and usually large flowers. They have a resting period in summer or winter, depending on the species they are derived from.

The monthly journal *The Begonian*, published by the American Begonia Society, Inc., is a source of further information on the genus.

Begonias are mostly tender plants, and do not tolerate dry conditions. Unless otherwise stated, they are subjects for greenhouse, window-garden, or lathhouse, requiring protection from strong sunlight, although many kinds are useful for bedding-out in protected areas and one species, *B. grandis*, will overwinter in Zone 7. The fibrous-rooted kinds with stems are propagated readily from cuttings of firm, half-ripened wood, and the rhizomatous kinds by division of the rhizomes. All the species are easily raised from seeds under cover; the heavy-leaved kinds, such as the Rex-Cultorum Hybrids, may be propagated from leaf cuttings. The tuberous kinds are propagated mostly by seeds, although large tubers may be divided. In the summer-flowering kinds, tubers usually produce their best blooms in the second year from seeds, although they may be dried off when the flowers are past and growth is fully mature, and used again for several years. Seeds of begonias are very small, so they must be sown on the surface of the soil or other medium, or covered over only very lightly, and always treated with care in a humid, protected seedbed.

acetosa Vell. [*B. cantareira* Hort.]. Fibrous-rooted; lvs. to 1 ft. across, obliquely cordate, with rounded basal lobes, deep coppery olive-green and white-hairy above, deep wine-red underneath, petioles 1 ft. long; fls. white, in many-fld. clusters on peduncles 1½ ft. long. Brazil.

acida Vell. [*B. brasiliensis* or *B. braziliensis* Hort., not *B. brasiliensis* Klotzsch]. Rhizomatous, hairy, stemless; lvs. to 9 in. across, nearly orbicular, rugose, bright green; fls. ⅝ in. across, creamy-white to pale pink, in clusters nodding in bud, then erect. Winter to spring. Brazil.

aconitifolia A. DC. [*B. Faureana* Linden ex Garn.]. Fibrous-rooted, sts. stout, few-branched; lvs. 5–7 in. long, ovate, palmately 4–6-lobed, cordate basally, toothed, dark glossy green with white blotches above, red underneath; fls. inconspicuous, white or pink-tinged, in many-fld. clusters. Autumn. Brazil. Some material offered under this name is *B. sceptrum*. Cv. 'Metallica' [cv. 'Hildegard Schneider'; *B. Faureana* var. *metallica* Rodig.]. Lvs. bronzy, less markedly white-blotched.

acuminata: *B. acutifolia.*

acutangula: *B. stipulacea* cv.

acutangularis: *B. stipulacea* cv. 'Acutangula'.

acutifolia Jacq. [*B. acuminata* Dryand.]. HOLLY-LEAF B. Fibrous-rooted, sts. 12–16 in., bushy, succulent, reddish-brown with green streaks; lvs. 3 in. long, 1½ in. wide, obliquely ovate, long-pointed, crinkled, toothed, glossy green, sparsely hairy above, hairy on veins underneath; fls. large, white, male fls. with 4 tepals, female with 5, ovary pubescent, with 2 short and 1 very long wing. Spring to autumn. Jamaica.

alba perfecta: *B. undulata.*

alba scandens: *B. glabra.*

albo-coccinea Hook. ELEPHANT'S-EAR B. Rhizomatous; lvs. large, obliquely broad-ovate, peltate, thick, glabrous, glossy green, short-petioled; fls. white inside, coral-red outside, with 4 tepals, in many-fld. clusters on tall, coral-red, brown-tomentose peduncles. India.

albo-picta Bull. GUINEA-WING B. Fibrous-rooted, shrubby, sts. branched, drooping; lvs. 2 in. long, elliptic-lanceolate, glossy green with silvery-white spots, short-petioled; fls. small, greenish-white. Summer. Brazil. Cv. 'Rosea'. More vigorous; fls. larger, pink, pendulous.

×**Alleryi** Hort. A name of no botanical standing for *Begonia* cv. 'Alleryi': *B. gigantea* × *B. metallica*. Fibrous-rooted, sts. to 6 ft. or more, bushy, white-hairy; lvs. obliquely ovate, pointed, deeply and irregularly toothed, bronzy-green, purple-veined underneath; fls. many, rosy-pink. Summer to autumn.

alnifolia A. DC. ALDER-LEAF B. Fibrous-rooted, glabrous, sts. climbing to erect, bushy, woody; lvs. 4–6 in. long, 1½–3 in. wide, obliquely elliptic-obovate, short-acuminate, lobed, toothed, green, sparsely bristly-hairy, short-petioled; fls. pink, in few-fld., branched clusters. Colombia.

amoena Wallich. Tuberous, stemless or sts. to 1 ft.; lvs. 3 in. long, 2 in. wide, ovate to oblong, long-pointed, symmetrically cordate basally, toothed, glabrous; fls. in forking cymes, male fls. with 4 tepals, female with 2 large opp. tepals and 1 smaller lateral one, all enlarged and persistent in age, ovary with nearly equal wings; seeds very elongate. Himalayas.

Andersonii Hort. A name of no botanical standing; plants of this name are tuberous, with lvs. obliquely ovate, lobed to serrate, gold- and red-hairy above, white underneath; fls. in compact clusters, on peduncles shorter than foliage. Said to be native to India.

andina Rusby. Fibrous-rooted, medium-sized, brown-scurfy, sts. rather weak, drooping or spreading; lvs. obliquely ovate, pointed, fleshy, dull green; fls. white. Winter to spring. Bolivia.

angularis: *B. stipulacea.*

annulata C. Koch [*B. Griffithii* Hook.; *B. picta* Hort. Henders. ex A. DC., not Sm.]. Similar to *B. rex*, but lvs. olive-green, with broad zone of gray, tinged with red underneath; fls. white, outer tepals tinged with pink, ovary crinkled along the angles. Assam.

×**argenteo-guttata** V. Lemoine: *B. albo-picta* × *B. olbia*. TROUT-LEAF B., TROUT B., ANGEL-WING B. Fibrous-rooted, sts. 2–4 ft. high, stout, branching, glabrous; lvs. 4–6 in. long, ovate, acuminate, shallowly lobed, toothed, glabrous, glossy green, thickly dotted with silver; fls. white, tinged pink, ovary rosy-pink.

argyrostigma: *B. maculata.*

aridicaulis Ziesenh. Rhizomatous, rhizome woody, appearing shriveled, creeping; lvs. to 2½ in. long, obliquely ovate, pointed, deeply cordate basally, entire, light green with silvery veins above, with reddish-brown hairs on veins underneath; fls. white, with 2 round tepals, in few-fld. axillary cymes. Late winter. Mex.

×**ascotiensis** J. B. Web. [*Begonia* cv. 'Corbeille de Feu'; cv. 'Vesuvius']: *B. cucullata* var. *Hookeri* × *B. foliosa* var. *miniata*. Fibrous-rooted, shrubby, sts. many, 2–3 ft. or more, erect, bushy, slender, glabrous, reddish; lvs. 1½ in. long, 1 in. wide, ovate, thick, cupped, toothed, ciliate, glossy green, red at the margin, short-petioled; fls. 1 in. across, bright red, 10–12 in drooping cymes on red peduncles. Used for bedding and greenhouses.

auriculata Hook.f. Rhizomatous, glabrous, sts. to 1 ft., stout; lvs. in 2 ranks, small, obliquely obovoid or lanceolate, long-acuminate, cordate basally with a large rounded auricle, entire or shallowly toothed, wavy, cupped, glossy olive-green, marked silvery-green in center, long-petioled; fls. in short, subterminal cymes, with 2 nearly orbicular tepals, ovary 3-winged. Summer. W. Trop. Afr.

Bakeri Knowles & Westc. Fibrous-rooted, brown-scurfy, sts. to 2 ft., rigidly erect, few-branched; lvs. to 6 in. wide, broad-ovate, pointed, shallowly lobed, with overlapping basal lobes, toothed, bright green, reddish at margin; fls. large, pink, in branched, showy clusters, on red peduncles 1 ft. high. Spring. Mex.

Bartonea Hort. A name of no botanical standing for *Begonia* cv. 'Winter Jewel'. Fibrous-rooted, sts. to 1½ ft., bushy, sparsely hairy; lvs. obliquely ovate, pointed, toothed, rich deep green and glistening red at margin above, rusty-brown underneath; fls. bright pink, in many-fld., short clusters. Said to be native to Puerto Rico.

Baueri: *B. Boweri.*

Beddomei Hook.f. Rhizomatous; lvs. obliquely ovate to orbicular, cordate basally, shallowly lobed, toothed, ciliate, green with silver spots and yellowish at margin above, red underneath; fls. to 1½ in. across, pink, in few-fld. cymes; male fls. with 4 tepals, female with 8, ovary pink. Winter. Assam. Apparently not now in cult., but one parent of *B.* ×*Lesoudsii.*

×**Bertinii:** *B.* ×*intermedia* cv. However, the name is sometimes incorrectly used to refer to the Bertinii Hybrids; see under *B.* ×*intermedia* cv. 'Bertinii'.

bhotanensis: *B. deliciosa.*

biserrata Lindl. [*B. palmaris* A. DC.]. Tuberous, sts. erect; lvs. to 8 in. long, orbicular, usually palmately divided into triangular lobes, acute, toothed, sometimes merely once-cleft between base and apex, ciliate, green, hairy above and on veins underneath; fls. white, with serrate tepals, in dense, axillary cymes, shorter than foliage. Summer. S. Mex. and Guatemala.

boliviensis A. DC. Tuberous, sts. 2–3 ft., ann., erect at first, then drooping, branching, succulent, green, slightly hairy; lvs. 3–5 in. long, lanceolate to narrow-ovate, acuminate, serrate; fls. cinnabar-red, fuchsialike, usually in pairs on short axillary peduncles, 1 fl. male, with stamens in an elongated column, the other fl. female, half as long as the male, with 3-winged ovary. Summer. Bolivia. Has entered into the parentage of many hybrid tuberous begonias.

Boweri Ziesenh. (sometimes misspelled *Baueri*). EYELASH B., MINIATURE B. Like *B. strigillosa*, but with straight, scattered, single hairs on petioles, lf. margin, and peduncles; lvs. narrower, long-pointed, light green, wavy-margined, ciliate, with irregular, triangular brown blotches; fls. pink with obovoid tepals. Winter to early spring. Mex. Cv. '**Major**'. Larger; lvs. with blotches not so pronounced. Cv. '**Nigromarga**'. Lvs. mint-green with chocolate blotches.

Bowringiana: see *B. laciniata* var. and *B. cathayana.*

Bradei Irmsch. [*B. laeteviridis* Hort.; *B. macrocarpa* Hort., not Warb.]. Fibrous-rooted, hirsute, sts. erect or procumbent; lvs. 3½–4½ in. long, 1–2 in. wide, oblong, cordate basally, bronzy-green above, red underneath; fls. large white. Summer. Brazil. Cv. '**Pubescens**' [also known as *Begonia* cv. 'Alto da Serra']. Lvs. velvety-dark-green with red margin, underneath.

brasiliensis: *B. polygonifolia.* Material cult. as *B. brasiliensis* (or *B. braziliensis*), however, is *B. acida.*

Brooksii: *B. plebeja* cv. 'Brooks'.

buddleiifolia A. DC. [*B. Pilderia* A. DC.; *B. urticifolia* Hort. ex Klotzsch, not Sm.]. Fibrous-rooted, sts. 2–3 ft., branched, woody, rusty-villous; lvs. obliquely broad-oblong, long-acuminate, irregularly toothed, ciliate, green, villous on veins on both surfaces; fls. white, in many-fld. cymes, male fls. with 4 tepals, female with 5, ovary with nearly equal wings. Venezuela to Peru.

Bunchii: *B. erythrophylla* cv.

caffra: *B. Dregei* var.

×**camellia**, ×**camelliiflora:** *Begonia* Tuberhybrida Hybrids, Camellia Group; see under *B.* ×*tuberhybrida.*

cantareira: *B. acetosa.*

caraguatatubensis Brade. Fibrous-rooted, sts. to 1 ft., erect, brownish, glabrous; lvs. 5–7½ in. across, obliquely broad-ovate, pointed, cordate basally, light glossy green, glabrous, petioles with leafy scales around the apex; fls. ¼ in. across, in many-fld. cymes, male fls. with 4 tepals, female with 3 long, contorted styles, ovary with nearly equal wings. Brazil.

caroliniifolia Regel. Rhizomatous; sts. thick, succulent; lvs. orbicular in outline, palmately compound, lfts. 6–8, stalked, lanceolate to obovate, coarsely toothed; fls. small, pink, in cymes on long peduncles, ovary with 3 unequal wings. Spring. S. Mex. and Guatemala.

carpinifolia Liebm. [*B. salvadorensis* Irmsch.; *B. udisilvestris* C. DC.]. Fibrous-rooted, sts. to 1 ft. long; lvs. small, obliquely ovate, acuminate, lobed, blunt with basal lobes, toothed, dark green, sparsely bristly-hairy above, glabrous underneath; fls. white or light pink, male fls. with 4 tepals, female with 3, ovary unequally 3-winged. Winter. Cent. Amer.

×**catalina** Hort. A name of no botanical standing for *Begonia* cv. 'Catalina' [*Begonia* cv. 'Improved Digswelliana'; *B.* cv. 'Lady Waterlow']. A seedling of *B.* ×*Digswelliana*, from which it differs in being sparsely stiff-hairy, with brs. spreading, lvs. with depressed veins, margin undulate, ciliate, darker green, petioles red, fls. white on the inside, pink on the outside. Autumn to spring.

cathayana Hemsl. [*B. Bowringiana* Hort., not Champ. ex Benth.]. Fibrous-rooted, sts. 2–3 ft., erect, few-branched, with soft-crimson hairs; lvs. hanging, obliquely ovate, pointed, cordate basally, toothed, olive-green with crimson veins above, mottled crimson underneath; fls. orange-vermilion, sometimes white, in axillary cymes. Autumn or spring. China.

Cathcartii Hook.f. & T. Thoms. Fibrous-rooted, sts. unbranched, petioles and peduncles with scattered hairs; lvs. ovate, acuminate, cordate basally, glabrous; fls. white to pink, male fls. with 4 tepals, female with 5, ovary pubescent. Himalayas.

×**cheimantha** T. H. Everett ex C. Web.: *B. Dregei* × *B. socotrana.* Alternatively, *Begonia* Cheimantha Hybrids. CHRISTMAS-FLOWERING BEGONIAS, CHRISTMAS B., BLOOMING-FOOL B., LORRAINE B. Fibrous-rooted (though derived from 2 semituberous spp.), sts. ann., herbaceous, branched; lvs. nearly orbicular, usually cordate basally, toothed, green; infl. a loose cyme held above foliage, peduncles, pedicels, and bracts pink; fls. large, usually pink, nearly all male, with 4 tepals. Winter. This hybrid complex includes such cvs. as 'Gloire de Lorraine', 'Glory of Cincinnati', 'Lady Mac', 'Melior'.

circumlobata Hance. Rhizomatous, sts. bushy, dull red, white-hairy; lvs. 8 in. across, lobed about half their length, serrate, red when young, later glossy green, red-tinged only at the margin, rough above, long-petioled; fls. ¼ in. across, pink, in few-fld. cymes, male fls. with 4 tepals, female with 5. China.

Clarkei Hook.f. Tuberous, sts. to 2 ft., erect, ann., succulent, puberulent; lvs. 4–7 in. long, ovate, cordate basally, serrate, green, short-petioled; fls. 2 in. across, cinnabar-red, in pendulous racemes. Bolivia. Has contributed to the hybrid tuberous begonias.

coccinea Hook. [*B. rubra* Hort., not Blume]. ANGEL-WING B. Fibrous-rooted, sts. 3–4 ft., erect, branched, succulent, glabrous; lvs. 4–6 in. long, obliquely oblong to ovate, serrate, thick, green with wavy red margin above, reddish underneath; fls. coral-red, waxlike, very persistent, in axillary, pendulous racemes on red peduncles, male fls. ½ in. across, with 4 unequal tepals, female with long, red ovary nearly equally 3-winged. Summer. Brazil. Cv. '**Fragrans**': *B. corallina* cv.

compta Bull. Similar to *B. stipulacea*, but smaller; lvs. narrower, with a conspicuous gray center and more silvery veins above, bright red underneath; fls. white, but the sp. is a shy bloomer. Brazil. Perhaps only a var. of *B. stipulacea.* Cv. '**Robinson's Vedderi**': *Begonia* cv. 'Robinson's Vedderi'; see under *B.* ×*Vedderi.*

conchifolia A. Dietr. Rhizomatous, rhizome creeping, succulent; lvs. to 2½ in. long, ovate, pointed, cordate basally, cupped, fleshy, glossy green above, light green with brown tomentum on the veins underneath; fls. pale pink to nearly white, fragrant, in erect clusters. Spring. Honduras, Costa Rica, Panama.

concinna Schott [*B. peltata* Schott ex A. DC., not Otto & A. Dietr.]. Rhizomatous, rhizome short; lvs. 2½–5½ in. long, 2–4 in. wide, peltate, obliquely obovate, shortly acuminate, wavy-margined, bright green, hairy; fls. white, in short forking cymes. Brazil.

convolvulacea A. DC. [*B. scandens* Klotzsch, not Swartz]. Fibrous-rooted, sts. to 7 ft., succulent, thickened at nodes, climbing by adventitious roots, green, glabrous; lvs. 3½–4½ in. long, broadly cordate, pointed, irregularly and shallowly 5–7-parted, dark glossy green above; fls. white, male fls. with 4 tepals, female with 5, ovary glabrous, with 3 unequal wings. Spring. Brazil.

Cooperi C. DC. Fibrous-rooted, sts. to 3 ft., erect, branched, densely reddish-brown-hairy; lvs. to 4 in. long, long-ovate, sharply toothed, glossy-green, crinkled, with a few scattered, long hairs above, hairy on veins underneath, petiole short, hairy; fls. many, white, on short, hairy peduncles. Costa Rica.

corallina Carrière. Often confused with *B. coccinea*, from which it differs in having sts. 8–10 ft., needing support, brownish when old, lvs. 3–8 in. long, lanceolate, glossy green with white spots above, red underneath, greener toward margin, fls. larger and more numerous. Spring. Brazil. Cv. '**Fragrans**' [*B. coccinea* Hook. cv. 'Fragrans']. Fls. white, fragrant. Cv. '**Odorata**' [*B. rubra odorata* Hort.]. Fls. rosy-pink, fragrant. This sp. has given rise, through hybridization, to many good cvs., having in common sts. canelike, slender, less branched than in *B. corallina*, lvs. lobed to various depths, usually silver-spotted. Among the older and better-known cvs. are the following. *Begonia* cv. '**Lucerna**' [*B.* cv. 'Luzerna'; *B.* cv. 'Corallina de Lucerna']. ANGEL-WING B. A seedling of *B.* cv. 'Madame Charrat'; sts. to 8 ft. or more; lvs. to 1 ft. long, olive-green, silver-spotted; fls. deep pink to bright red, drooping, in massive clusters, ovary white with carmine wings. *Begonia* cv. '**Madame Charrat**': *B. corallina* × *B. Teuscheri. Begonia* cv. '**President Carnot**': *B. corallina* × *B. olbia. Begonia* cv. '**Rossii**'. A seedling of *Begonia* cv. 'Lucerna'; lvs. large, almost as broad at apex as at base, light green, flushed with bronzy-red towards margin, irregularly silver-spotted; fls. delicate-pink with deeper pink wings, in large and pendulous clusters. *Begonia* cv. 'Veitch's Carmine': *B. corallina* × *B. Dregei*. The *Begonia* Superba Hybrids are derived from the cross *B. aconitifolia* × *Begonia* cv. 'Lucerna'; see *B.* × *superba*.

cordifolia Thwaites. Tuberous, stemless; lvs. 2–3 in. across, ovate-orbicular, cordate basally, toothed, pilose above, pubescent on veins underneath; fls. in forking cymes, male fls. with 4 unequal tepals, female with 3, ovary with nearly equal wings. India. Not in cult. The name *B. cordifolia* has been applied to several spp., but material so called in cult. is *B. glabra* var. *cordifolia*.

coriacea A. DC. Tuberous, lvs. few, reniform, shallowly lobed, crenately toothed, leathery; fls. with 4 tepals, female with 5. Bolivia. Not in cult. Material called **B. coriacea flora alba** by horticulturists [*B. peltifolia* Hort.] is a hybrid, probably *B. incana* × *B. venosa*, and has been renamed *Begonia* cv. 'Society'; fibrous-rooted, sts. to 5 ft., succulent; lvs. to 6 in. long, 3½ in. wide, fleshy, ovate, pointed, cupped, dark glossy green above, brown-tomentose underneath; fls. creamy-white, on axillary, arching peduncles.

×**Credneri** Hort. Haage & Schmidt [*B.* × *pictaviensis* Bruant ex André]: *B. metallica* × *B. Scharffiana*. Fibrous-rooted, medium-sized, sts. bushy, soft-white-hairy; lvs. ovate, olive-green above, reddish underneath; fls. pink, on erect peduncles.

×**crestabruchii** Hort. A name of no botanical standing for *Begonia* cv. 'Crestabruchii': *B. manicata* cv. 'Crispa' × *B.* × *ricinifolia* cv. 'Sunderbruckii'. LETTUCE-LEAF B. Rhizomatous; lvs. broad-ovate, ruffled, glossy green, margin crested, ciliate, veins and margin rose-colored, petiole long, hairy; fls. pink, in erect panicles. Spring.

×**crispa**: *Begonia* Tuberhybrida Hybrids, Crispa Group. **B.** ×**crispa marginata**: *Begonia* Tuberhybrida Hybrids, Marginata Group. See under *B.* × *tuberhybrida*.

×**crispei** Hort. A name of no botanical standing for *Begonia* cv. 'Crispei': *B. crispula* × *B. Dregei*. Fibrous-rooted, sts. 1–2 ft., branched; lvs. orbicular, shallowly lobed, dark green, quilted, with red veins and red sinus above, red underneath; fls. small, white, on short peduncles.

crispula Brade. Rhizomatous, rhizome short; lvs. 5–6 in. across, spreading on surface of soil, orbicular, cordate basally, crisped, dark glossy green, short-petioled; fls. ½ in. across, white, pinkish on exterior, in few-fld. clusters on reddish, appressed-hairy peduncles. Brazil.

cristata Koord. Herbaceous, glabrous; lvs. obliquely ovate-oblong, acuminate, cordate basally, toothed; fls. in cymes, ovary 3-angled. Celebes. Not in cult. *B.* × *cristata* of hort. is *Begonia* Tuberhybrida Hybrids, Cristata Group; see under *B.* × *tuberhybrida*.

cubensis Hassk. CUBAN HOLLY, HOLLY-LEAVED B., HOLLY-LEAF B. Fibrous-rooted, sts. branched, suffruticose, reddish-brown-hairy; lvs. 1–2 in. long, obliquely ovate, acuminate, toothed, hairy on veins; fls. ¼ in. across, white, on short peduncles, male fls. with 4 tepals, female with 5, ovary with 3 unequal wings. Winter. Cuba.

cucullata Willd. Fibrous-rooted, stoloniferous, glabrous, succulent, sts. to 3 ft., little-branched, reddish-green; lvs. to 4 in. long and almost as wide, obliquely broad-ovate, obtuse, mostly truncate or rounded basally, finely serrulate, ciliate, glossy green, slender-petioled; fls. pink, in axillary and terminal cymes, male fls. with 2 large and 2 smaller tepals, female with 4–5 nearly equal tepals, ovary with 3 unequal wings. Summer. Var. **cucullata**. The typical var.; lvs. with margins somewhat inrolled at base; tepals of male fls. up to about ¼ in. long; seeds acute at apex. Guiana, Colombia, Brazil, Paraguay, Uruguay, Argentina. Not cult. Var. **Hookeri** (A. DC.) L. B. Sm. & Schub. [*B. semperflorens* Link & Otto]. Lvs. flat, not inrolled at base; tepals of male fls. up to ¾ in. long; seeds obtuse at apex. Se. Brazil, ne. Argentina. Perhaps no longer in cult. in its pure state, having been supplanted by its hybrids. Most material cult. as *B. semperflorens* or its cvs. actually belongs to the *Begonia* Semperflorens-Cultorum hybrid complex.

cuspidata: *B. multinervia*.

×**cypraea** Hort. A name of no botanical standing for *Begonia* cv. 'Cypraea'. A hybrid, with *B. metallica* as one parent, and similar to it, but white-hairy, lvs. olive-green with dark green veins above, fls. large, white or pale pink, pink-bearded.

daedalea: *B. strigillosa*.

Davisii Hort. Veitch. ex Hook.f. DAVIS B. Tuberous, stemless; lvs. 4 in. long, spreading, obliquely ovate, cordate basally, crenately toothed, thin, hairy, glossy green above, crimson underneath; fls. bright red, in a 6-fld., erect umbel, peduncles and pedicels bright red, male fls. with 4 tepals, female with 5, ovary with 3 unequal wings. Summer. Peru. Has contributed to the hybrid tuberous begonias.

Dayi: *B. glandulosa*.

decandra Pav. ex A. DC. Fibrous-rooted, sts. to 1 ft., erect, branched, glabrous; lvs. 3½ in. long, 2 in. wide, ovate, pointed, undu-

late and toothed, stiffly sparsely hairy, dark green, veins depressed; fls. white to pinkish, 6–8 in a terminal or axillary cluster. Puerto Rico, Cent. Amer.

decora Stapf. Rhizomatous, sts. 5–6 in., herbaceous, covered with thick papillae and short hairs, branched; lvs. 3–5 in. long, obliquely ovate, acute, crenately toothed, deep glossy green, hairy above, crimson underneath; fls. pink, fragrant. Summer. Malay Pen.

deliciosa Böhme [*B. bhotanensis* Hort.]. Rhizomatous, sts. 1–2 ft., erect, succulent, greenish-red to brown; lvs. 6–10 in. long, 5–7½ in. wide, obliquely cordate, deeply palmately 6–8-lobed, toothed, dark olive-green, heavily gray-spotted above, red underneath; fls. ¾ in. across, soft pink, fragrant, usually in pairs. Late summer to winter. Borneo.

diadema Hort. Linden. Rhizomatous, sts. to 2 ft., succulent; lvs. many, deeply and irregularly palmately lobed, toothed, glossy green with white blotches, petioles red; fls. white or pink, in cymes enveloped in a dark red sheath before opening, male fls. 2 in. across, with 4 tepals, female smaller, with 5 tepals. Autumn to winter. Borneo. [Var.] **erecta**: *B. sceptrum*.

×**dicalata**, ×**diclata**, ×**diculata** Hort.: various names for the hybrid correctly named *Begonia* cv. 'Diclata': *B. dichroa* × *B. undulata*. Fibrous-rooted, sts. canelike; lvs. very dark green, variably silver-spotted; fls. red.

dichotoma Jacq. KIDNEY B. Fibrous-rooted, sts. usually 2–3 ft., occasionally to 12 ft., semisucculent; lvs. 3–12 in. long, 4 in. wide, nearly orbicular to ovate, shallowly lobed, serrulate, green; fls. small, white, in long-peduncled clusters, ovary with 1 sharply triangular wing. Winter. Venezuela.

dichroa T. Sprague. Fibrous-rooted, low, spreading, sts. woody; lvs. 8–12 in. long, 3½–5½ in. wide, obliquely ovate, pointed, cordate basally, flecked above with white when young, later glossy green; fls. orange, in dense clusters, male fls. with 4 tepals, female with 5, ovary orange, glabrous, with 1 large wing. Winter. Brazil.

Dietrichiana Irmsch. Fibrous-rooted, sts. erect, suffruticose; lvs. 2–2½ in. long, obliquely elliptic-oblong, acuminate, cordate basally, toothed, green above, red underneath; fls. light pink, in forking cymes, male fls. with 4 unequal tepals, female with 5. Brazil.

×**Digswelliana** Dombr. [*B.* × *Saundersonii* Hort.]: probably *B. foliosa* var. *miniata* × *B. odorata*. Fibrous-rooted, sts. spreading or erect, brs. drooping; lvs. 2–4 in. long, elliptic-ovate, acuminate, irregularly and coarsely toothed, glossy green; fls. small, white, in many-fld. short clusters.

dipetala R. C. Grah. [*B. malabarica* Lam. var. *dipetala* C. B. Clarke; *Begonia* cv. 'Mrs. W. S. Kimball']. Similar to *B. malabarica*; sts. to 2 ft., erect, rarely branched; lvs. finely toothed, green above, red underneath; fls. light pink, with 2 tepals, drooping, in few-fld. axillary cymes. All year. India.

discolor: *B. grandis*.

domingensis A. DC. PEANUT-BRITTLE B. Fibrous-rooted, sts. to 1 ft., branched, pilose; lvs. 1 in. long, ovate, long-pointed, cordate basally, lobed, leathery, crinkled, glossy green, petioles and veins underneath brownish-pilose; fls. white or pink, in compact cymes. Hispaniola.

dominicalis A. DC. Fibrous-rooted, sts. erect, much-branched; lvs. large, obliquely ovate, acuminate, toothed, glossy green; fls. small, greenish-white, tinged with light pink, in cymes, female fls. larger than male. Winter. Dominica.

Dregei Otto & A. Dietr. [*B. parvifolia* R. C. Grah., not Schott or Klotzsch]. GRAPE-LEAF B., MAPLE-LEAF B. Tuberous or semituberous, glabrous; st. 1–3 ft., ann., succulent, red; lvs. 3 in. long, ovate or rhombic, shallowly lobed, toothed, thin, light green with purple veins and slightly spotted with gray above, reddish underneath; fls. few, white, on axillary peduncles. Summer. S. Afr. Cv. 'Macbethii', [*B. Macbethii* Hort.]. DEWDROP B., MAPLE-LEAF B., St. to 1½ ft., more slender; lvs. smaller, deeply notched to lobed, green-veined; fls. smaller. Cv. 'Macbethii Obtusa' [*B. multangula* Hort., not Blume]. More compact than cv. 'Macbethii', which it resembles in shape of lvs., but having the purple veins of the sp. Var. **caffra** (Meissn.) A. DC. [*B. caffra* Meissn.] Lvs. glossy green; fls. white to pink; caps. larger.

×**Drostii** Hort. [*B. Haageana* Hort. ex W. Wats. cv. 'Drostii'; *B. Scharffii* Hook. f. cv. 'Drostii']. A name of no botanical standing for *Begonia* cv. 'Drostii'. A hybrid with *B. Scharffii* as one parent; sts. to 5 ft. or more, white-hairy; lvs. cupped; fls. light pink, red-bearded, as is the ovary.

×**Druryi** Hort. A name of no botanical standing for *Begonia* cv. 'Druryi': *Begonia* cv. 'Cypraea' × *B. sanguinea*. Fibrous-rooted, white-hairy, sts. to 6 ft., erect, bushy; lvs. ovate-lanceolate, pointed, glossy olive-green above, deep red underneath; fls. small, creamy-white, red-bearded, in few, erect, soon-drooping clusters.

×**Duartei** Hort. A name of no botanical standing for *Begonia* Rex-Cultorum cv. 'Duartei'. Lvs. with 1 lobe spirally rolled, dark green with silver streaks, densely red-hairy.

×**Duchartrei** Bruant ex André: *B. echinosepala* × *B. Scharffiana.* Fibrous-rooted, white-hairy, sts. 2–3 ft., branched; lvs. 5–8 in. long, ovate-lanceolate, acuminate, cordate basally, toothed, deep green above, green with red veins underneath; fls. large, waxy-white, red-bearded, in tall, compact clusters. An earlier homonym, *B.* ×*Duchartrei* Hort. Lemoine, was apparently not validly published. It was used for a hybrid tuberous begonia (*B. Pearcei* × *B. subpeltata* Wight) with bronzy-green, yellow-veined lvs. and yellow fls., no longer in cult.

echinosepala Regel. Fibrous-rooted, bushy, hairy, sts. erect, green with reddish nodes; lvs. small, ovate-oblong, pointed, coarsely toothed, glossy green with darker veins above, purple underneath; fls. pink, pink-bearded on exterior, on axillary peduncles. Summer. Brazil.

ecuadoriensis: *B. rigida.*

Edmundoi Brade. Sts. to 3 ft., erect, suffruticose, branched, glabrous; lvs. 4–5 in. long, 1–1½ in. wide, lanceolate, long-acuminate, short-petioled; fls. 2 in. across, white, in few-fld. clusters on axillary peduncles, male fls. with 4 unequal tepals, female with 5, ovary glabrous, with 3 equal wings. Brazil.

egregia N. E. Br. [*B. quadrilocularis* Brade]. Fibrous-rooted; lvs. 6–11 in. long, 2–3 in. wide, lanceolate, somewhat cupped, brittle, pebbled, gray-green; fls. white, many, ovary 4-celled, 4-winged. Winter. Brazil.

×**elatior:** *Begonia* Elatior Hybrids; see *B.* ×*hiemalis.* The name is based on an early hybrid cv. of this group, cv. 'Elatior'.

×**eminenta** Hort. A name of no botanical standing for *Begonia* Rex-Cultorum cv. 'Eminenta'. Lvs. to 1 ft. across or more, ciliate on margin, blackish-maroon or blackish-olive, with variable zone of dark green.

Eminii Warb. Similar to *B. Mannii,* but more robust; lvs. with red margins. E. Trop. Afr.

Engleri Gilg. Fibrous-rooted, sts. 3–5 ft., sparsely branched, green with purple spots; lvs. 3–5 in. across, ovate, coarsely toothed, green with purplish veins; fls. clear pink, in arching, flat panicles, ovary red and red-hairy. Spring. E. Trop. Afr.

epipsila Brade. Fibrous-rooted, red-hairy; sts. 15–20 in., erect, branched, woody; lvs. 2–3¼ in. long, 3–4 in. wide, obliquely ovate, acuminate, cordate basally, entire, dark glossy green, glabrous above, red and rusty-woolly underneath; fls. white, male fls. with 2 tepals, female with 5, in many-fld. cymes. Spring. Brazil.

×**Erfordia:** *B. pictavensis* cv.

×**erythrophylla** J. Neumann [*B.* ×*Feastii* Hort. ex L. H. Bailey]: *B. hydrocotylifolia* × *B. manicata.* BEEFSTEAK B., KIDNEY B. Rhizomatous, rhizome thick; lvs. 2½–3 in. across, nearly orbicular, peltate, thick, with shaggy white hairs on margins, red underneath, petioles red-hairy; fls. light pink, on long peduncles, male fls. soon dropping. Winter and spring. Cv. '**Bunchii**'. LETTUCE-LEAF B. A sport of *B.* ×*erythrophylla;* lvs. with crested and frilled margin. Cv. '**Helix**' [*B.* ×*Feastii* cv. 'Spiralis']. WHIRLPOOL B., POND-LILY B. Also a sport of *B.* ×*erythrophylla;* lvs. with basal lobes rolled in a spiral.

estrellensis C. DC. ex J. D. Sm. Fibrous-rooted, sts. woody, branched; lvs. 3 in. long, 1 in. wide, ovate-elliptic, long-pointed, toothed, green, short-petioled; fls. ½ in. across, white, in axillary clusters, male fls. with 4 tepals, female with 2–3, ovary with 3 unequal wings. Winter. Costa Rica.

Evansiana: *B. grandis.*

Faureana: *B. aconitifolia.* Var. **metallica:** *B. aconitifolia* cv.

×**Feastii:** *B.* ×*erythrophylla.* Cv. 'Spiralis': *B.* ×*erythrophylla* cv. 'Helix'.

Fernandoi-Costae Irmsch. Fibrous-rooted, sts. erect; lvs. 4½–7 in. long, broad-ovate, acuminate, cordate basally, entire or shallowly toothed, very hairy, bright green above, rosy-pink underneath, petiole scaly; fls. white, with 4 tepals, in large, erect, forking cymes above foliage. Summer to autumn. Brazil.

ferruginea L. f. [*B. magnifica* Hort. Linden]. Fibrous-rooted, bushy, sts. spreading, woody when old, brs., petioles, and peduncles hairy; lvs. to 6 in. long or more, 4 in. wide, ovate, pointed, semicordate basally, toothed, ciliate, glossy green above, dotted with small red spots and with veins red-hairy underneath; fls. large, red, in very large clusters on red peduncles. Colombia.

fimbriata Liebm. Rhizomatous; lvs. obliquely ovate, acuminate, cordate basally, toothed, ciliate, reddish-hairy; fls. red, with 2 tepals, ovary pilose. Mex. Not in cult. Material cult. as *B.* ×*fimbriata* is *Begonia* Tuberhybrida Hybrids, Fimbriata Group; see under *B.* ×*tuberhybrida.*

floccifera Beddome. Rhizomatous; lvs. ½–3 in. long, nearly orbicular, cordate basally, toothed or nearly entire, leathery, whitish- or yellowish-hairy on both surfaces when young; fls. ¼ in. across, in compound cymes, male fls. with 2 tepals, female with 4, ovary with nearly equal wings. India.

floribunda: *B. foliosa* var. *miniata* cv. 'Rosea'. The name *B.* ×*floribunda* has also been applied to *Begonia* Tuberhybrida Hybrids, Multiflora Group; see under *B.* ×*tuberhybrida.*

florida: *B. Popenoei* cv.

foliosa HBK. Fibrous-rooted, shrubby; sts. to 3 ft. or more, slender-branched, succulent, glabrous; lvs. ½–2 in. long, many, densely 2-ranked on short, shaggy branchlets, ovate-oblong, slightly toothed, dark green to bronzy-green; fls. in many terminal or axillary panicles, white to red, male fls. with 4 tepals, female with 5. Early summer, or autumn and winter. Colombia and Venezuela. A very variable sp. Var. **foliosa**. FERN B., FERN-LEAF B., FERN-LEAVED B. The typical var.; lvs. ½–1½ in. long; peduncles very slender, 1–2-fld.; fls. white, to ½ in. across, anthers linear to oblong, mostly longer than filaments. Colombia. Var. **miniata** (Planch.) L. B. Sm. & Schub. [*B. fuchsioides* Hook.; *B. miniata* Planch.]. FUCHSIA B., CORAZÓN-DE-JESÚS. Lvs. ¾–2 in. long; peduncles stouter, 2–30-fld.; fls. red or rose, ½–1¼ in. across, anthers ellipsoid, shorter than filaments. Venezuela. Cv. '**Coccinea**'. Fls. red. Cv. '**Rosea**' [cv. 'Floribunda'; *B. floribunda* Carrière; *B. multiflora rosea* Hort.]. Fls. rose-pink.

Francisii Ziesenh. NASTURTIUM-LEAF B. Rhizomatous, rhizome creeping, ascending, branched; lvs. 3 in. long, 2 in. wide, oblong-ovate, pointed, peltate, cupped, fleshy, green, red at margin above, with reddish-brown hairs on veins underneath; fls. ¼ in. across, white, with 2 orbicular tepals, in few-fld. cymes. Summer. Mex.

Franconis Liebm. Fibrous-rooted, ann., sts. to 6 in., erect, branched, hairy; lvs. to 2 in. long, obliquely ovate, somewhat cordate basally, toothed, ciliate, yellow-green; fls. white or pink-tinged, in small, few-fld. clusters. S. Mex. and Guatemala. May be used as a hanging-basket or bedding plant; becoming weedy in the greenhouse.

friburgensis Brade. Rhizomatous, sts. red; lvs. orbicular, folded and resembling cockscombs when young, thick, leathery or rubbery, dark glossy green above, red underneath; fls. white and pink, in compact clusters. Winter. Brazil.

Froebelii A. DC. Tuberous, stemless; lvs. 6–12 in. long, 3–8 in. wide, many, orbicular, acuminate, cordate basally, with fleshy purplish hairs on both surfaces; fls. vivid crimson, in drooping cymes, on erect, red peduncles above foliage, male fls. 2 in. across, with 4 ovate tepals, female smaller, with 5 tepals, ovary woolly, 3-angled, winged. Ecuador. Winter-flowering in greenhouse, or used for summer bedding.

×**frondosa** Hort. A name of no botanical standing for *Begonia* cv. 'Frondosa'. A hybrid, with *B. Scharffii* as one parent; sts. to 4 ft., vigorous; lvs. glossy, dark green above, harder-textured than in *B. Scharffii,* purple underneath; fls. pink, red-bearded.

×**frutescans** Hort. A name of no botanical standing for *Begonia* cv. 'Frutescans'. An apparent hybrid, showing relationship to *B. sanguinea,* differing in being low and spreading, with lvs. half as large, thinner, cupped, wavy-margined, darker olive-green above and darker red underneath; fls. small, white. Hanging-basket plant.

×**frutescaria** Hort. A name of no botanical standing for *Begonia* cv. 'Frutescaria'. Related to *B.* cv. 'Frutescans', differing in having lvs. more oblique, not wavy-margined, lighter gray-green in color, with more pronounced veins; fls. white.

fruticosa A. DC. Fibrous-rooted, sts. to 2 ft., erect, woody, reddish-green; lvs. 3 in. long, 1½ in. wide, obliquely oblong-ovate, acuminate, serrate, ciliate, glossy green on both surfaces, veins reddish underneath; fls. white, male fls. with 4 tepals, female with 5, ovary purplish. Brazil.

fuchsioides: *B. foliosa* var. *miniata.*

fusca Liebm. [*B. maxima* Hort. ex Klotzsch]. Rhizomatous, succulent; lvs. 6–11 in. long, 3–9 in. wide, obliquely broad-ovate, acuminate, cordate basally, lobed, green above, pubescent above and underneath, petioles long, hairy; fls. pink or white, bearded on exterior, male fls. with 2 tepals, female with 2 or 3, ovary pubescent, with 3 very unequal ciliate wings. Summer. S. Mex. and Guatemala.

×**fuscomaculata** A. Lange [*B.* ×*rubella* Bull, not. *B. rubella* Buch.-Ham. ex D. Don; *B.* ×*rubellina* L. H. Bailey]: *B. heracleifolia* × *B. strigillosa.* Rhizomatous, rhizome creeping; lvs. broad-ovate, with pointed lobes, toothed, dark olive-green spotted with chocolate-brown, petioles long, white-hairy, red at base; fls. greenish-white, in few-fld., erect clusters. Cv. '**Reichenheim**' [*B.* ×*Reichenheimii* Bartsch, not Gouas or Hort. Makoy]: *B.* ×*fuscomaculata* × *B. heracleifolia.* Lvs. palmately lobed halfway to center, green with light bronzy areas along veins; fls. bright pink, in tall, pyramidal panicles.

gigantea Wallich. Semituberous, rootstock woody, sts. 2–3 ft., rarely branched; lvs. 9–12 in. long, 3–4 in. wide, ovate, caudate-acuminate, wavy-margined to toothed; fls. white or pale pink, in terminal clusters, male fls. with 2 tepals, female with 3, ovary with 2 cells and 1 wing. Sikkim. The name *Begonia* ×*gigantea* has been applied to *Begonia* Tuberhybrida Hybrids, Single Group; see under *B.* ×*tuberhybrida.*

×**Gilsonii** Hort. A name of no botanical standing for *Begonia* cv. 'Gilsonii'. Hybrid of unknown parentage; fibrous-rooted, sts. to 2 ft., thick, more or less procumbent, green with white longitudinal lines; lvs. ovate-attenuate, shallowly lobed, toothed, glossy green above, petioles and veins underneath hairy; fls. ½–1 in. across, light pink, male fls. double or crested, with petaloid stamens, on long, erect, red peduncles axillary in upper lvs. Winter to summer.

glabra Aubl. [*B. alba scandens* Hort.; *B. radicans* Hort., not Vell.; *B. scandens* Swartz; *B. scandens alba* Hort.]. Fibrous-rooted, sts. trailing, rooting at nodes, branched; lvs. small, symmetrically ovate-lanceolate, short-acuminate, obtuse at base, irregularly crenately toothed, glossy green, veins depressed; fls. ¼ in. across, white, in short, few-fld. cymes. Summer. Mex. and W. Indies to Peru and Bolivia. Cv. **'Cordifolia'** [*B. cordifolia* Hort.; *B. scandens* Swartz var. *cordifolia* C. DC.]. Lvs. larger, lighter green, cordate. Cv. **'Coralipetiolis'** [*B. scandens* Swartz cv. 'Coralipetiolis']. Similar to cv. 'Cordifolia' but petioles pale pink to coral-red, carmine at the nodes.

glandulosa A. DC. ex Hook. [*B. nigro-venia* Regel; *B. Dayi* Hort.]. Rhizomatous; lvs. obliquely orbicular-cordate, acuminate, wavy-margined, toothed, glossy yellow-green with deep chocolate-brown veins above, dark red underneath; fls. small, greenish-white, fragrant, male fls. with 2 tepals, female with 5, ovary unequally 3-winged. Winter to spring. Mex. Very similar to *B. lobata,* and perhaps not specifically distinct.

glaucophylla: *B. Limmingheiana.*

goegoensis N. E. Br. FIRE-KING B. Rhizomatous, compact, rhizome short, thick, greenish-red; lvs. 6–9 in. long, ovate-orbicular, peltate, cupped, blistered or puckered, green with dark bronzy blotches and paler veins above, red underneath, petioles 4-angled; fls. small, rosy-pink, in compact clusters on erect peduncles as long as petioles, male fls. with 4 tepals, female with 5. Summer to autumn. Sumatra.

gracilis HBK. HOLLYHOCK B. Tuberous, sts. 2–3 ft., erect, mostly unbranched, succulent, glabrous; lvs. variable in size, orbicular to lanceolate, crenately toothed, very fleshy, pale green; fls. large, pink, on short axillary peduncles, male fls. with 2 large, obovate, serrate tepals and 2 smaller ones, female smaller, ovary green, 3-angled. Summer. Mex. and Guatemala. Bulblets present in lf. axils, and may be used for prop. Var. **Martiana:** *B. Martiana.* The name *B.* ×*gracilis* has also been applied to *Begonia* Semperflorens-Cultorum Hybrids, Gracilis Group; see under *B.* ×*semperflorens-cultorum* var. *gracilis.*

grandis Dryand. [*B. discolor* Ait.; *B. Evansiana* Andr.]. HARDY B. Tuberous, sts. 2–3 ft., erect, ann., succulent, branched, red, glabrous; lvs. obliquely ovate, acuminate, somewhat cordate basally, lobed, green with red-tinted veins, red-hairy, with bulblets in lf. axils; fls. 1½ in. across, flesh-color, fragrant, in drooping cymes, male fls. with 4 unequal tepals, female with 2 broad tepals, ovary pink, 3-winged. Summer. Malay Pen., China, Japan. Zone 7, hardy farther north, with protection. Cv. **'Alba'**. Fls. white. Some material in cult. called *B.* ×*grandis* is *Begonia* Rex-Cultorum cv. 'Grandis' (probably *B. rex* × *B. robusta*).

Griffithii: *B. annulata.*

Haageana: *B. Scharffii.* Cv. **'Drostii'**: see *B.* ×*Drostii.*

Handelii Irmsch. Rhizomatous, reddish-pilose, sts. unbranched; lvs. 4–6 in. long, 2½–4½ in. wide, obliquely broad-ovate, acuminate, toothed, green; fls. to 4 in. across, pink, with 4 tepals, ovary top-shaped, 4-celled, wingless. Early spring. Vietnam, s. China.

Handroi Brade. Fibrous-rooted, sts. to 1 ft., arching, branched, sparsely hairy; lvs. to 4½ in. long, 2½ in. wide, obliquely ovate, acuminate, cordate basally, minutely toothed, fleshy, dark green and hairy above, red underneath; fls. 1½ in. across, white, in short, few-fld. cymes, male fls. with 4 tepals, female with 5, ovary with nearly equal wings. Brazil.

Hemsleyana Hook.f. Tuberous, sts. to 1½ ft., erect, sparingly branched, succulent, slightly hairy, rosy-pink; lvs. 4–5 in. across, orbicular, palmately parted, segms. 7–9, lanceolate, acuminate, irregularly serrate, upper surface bright green, sometimes with red margin when young, petioles long; fls. to 1½ in. across, light pink, male fls. with 4 tepals, female with 5, in separate cymes. Summer. China.

hepatica maculata: *B. stigmosa.*

×**heracleicotyle** Hort. Veitch: *B. heracleifolia* × *hydrocotylifolia.* Like *B.* ×*erythrophylla,* but lvs. with several shallow, round lobes, toothed, fleshy, green; fls. deep pink, set closer together.

heracleifolia Cham. & Schlechtend. STAR B., STAR-LEAF B. Rhizomatous, rhizome thick, plant hairy; lvs. 1 ft. across or more, 5–9-lobed, lobes deep and narrow, toothed, extending to middle of blade or beyond, bronzy-green, petioles 10–18 in. long, stout, succulent, tinged with red; fls. to 1 in. across, white or rosy-pink, fragrant, on peduncles 2–4 ft. long, male and female fls. with 2 ovate tepals, ovary 3-angled, with 1 long wing. Spring to autumn. S. Mex., Guatemala, Brit. Honduras. Cv. **'Pyramidalis'**. Lvs. light green. Var. **nigricans** Hook. [*B. nigricans* Klotzsch; *B.* ×*ricinifolia* A. Dietr. cv. 'Sunderbruchii Nigricans']. Lvs. tinged with black near margin. Var. **punctata** (Link & Otto) Nichols. [*B. punctata* Link & Otto]. Lvs. green, reddish near margin; fls. rosy-pink with reddish spots. Var. **'Sunderbruchii'**: *B.* ×*ricinifolia* cv.

herbacea Vell. Rhizomatous, rhizome shaggy; lvs. 4–6 in. long, symmetrically lanceolate, attenuate, serrate, light green with silver spots, short-petioled; fls. white or pink, male fls. heart-shaped in bud, with 2 tepals, in clusters on peduncles shorter than foliage, female with 3, rarely 4 tepals, solitary, sessile at base of lvs. All year. Brazil.

×**hiemalis** Fotsch. [*B.* ×*elatior* Hort.]. Alternatively, the *Begonia* Elatior Hybrids. WINTER-FLOWERING BEGONIAS. A group of hybrid cvs., derived from crossing *B. socotrana* with various Andean tuberous spp. or with *B.* ×*tuberhybrida* cvs. These combine the winter-flowering habit of *B. socotrana* and the large, colorful fls. of the Andean tuberous begonias; fls. white to pink, red, orange, or yellow, single or double. There are many named cvs.

hirsuta Aubl. Fibrous-rooted, sts. branched, pilose; lvs. ovate, acute, somewhat cordate basally, toothed to shallowly lobed; fls. white, in forking cymes, male fls. with 4 tepals, female with 5, ovary with 3 unequal wings. Guyana.

hirtella Link. Fibrous-rooted, white-hairy, sts. 1–3 ft., ann., branched; lvs. 1–4½ in. long, 1–2 in. wide, obliquely broad-ovate, acuminate, cordate basally, irregularly toothed, ciliate, green, petioles reddish; fls. small, greenish-white to pinkish, with 4–6 tepals, in short, few-fld., forking, drooping cymes. Winter. Brazil, Peru. Variable sp., of little decorative value. Var. **nana** (Walp.) A. DC. Plant smaller, with fewer fls. Brazil, Peru.

hispida Schott ex A. DC. Fibrous-rooted, hairy, sts. to 5 ft., stout, branched, glabrous; lvs. 3½ in. long, obliquely broad-ovate, acuminate, cordate basally, shallowly lobed to deeply toothed, pale green, soft-downy; fls. white. Brazil. The typical var. is not in cult. Var. **cucullifera** Irmsch. PIGGY-BACK B. Lvs. bearing many adventitious leaflets along the veins on the upper side.

hispidivillosa Ziesenh. Rhizomatous, rhizome creeping or ascending, green with red blotches below nodes, glabrous; lvs. to 7 in. long, 5 in. wide, obliquely ovate, acute, cordate basally, ciliate, green, with long stiff hairs; fls. red, with 2 oblong tepals, ovary with 3 unequal wings. Autumn to winter. Mex.

×**Houghtonii** Hort. [*B. Scharffii* Hook.f. cv. 'Houghtonii']. A name of no botanical standing for *Begonia* cv. 'Houghtonii'. A hybrid, probably with *B. Scharffii* as one parent, but bushier than that sp.; lvs. ovate, long-attenuate; fls. light pink, bearded with deeper red. A dwarf form of this exists.

Huegelii (Klotzsch) Hort. ex A. DC. Fibrous-rooted, densely soft-hairy, sts. erect, branched, green; lvs. ovate-oblong, shallowly lobed, toothed, green above, red underneath; fls. white, white-bearded, in large, loose clusters, male fls. 1¼ in. across, female ½ in. across. Summer. Brazil.

humilis Ait. Fibrous-rooted, sts. 2–3 ft., ann., branching at base, sparsely hairy above, green; lvs. 2–4½ in. long, obliquely ovate, acuminate, cordate basally, shallowly lobed, serrate, ciliate, pilose above, short-petioled; fls. white, male fls. with 2–4 tepals, female with 5, in few-fld. cymes. Winter. Mex. to Brazil, and W. Indies.

hydrocotylifolia Otto ex Hook. PENNYWORT B., MINIATURE POND-LILY B. Rhizomatous, hairy; lvs. 1½–2½ in. long, orbicular to cordate, glossy green above, red underneath, short-petioled; fls. in cymes on peduncles to 1½ ft. long, fls., pedicels, and peduncles rosy-pink. Spring to summer. Mex.

×**illustrata** Hort.: *Begonia* Rex-Cultorum cv. 'Illustrata' (*B. imperialis* × *B.* Rex-Cultorum cv. 'Speculata'). Similar to *B. imperialis,* but coarsely-hairy, lvs, ovate, metallic-green with lighter green or reddish veins and occasional purple overtones, fls. dull pinkish-white. Winter.

imperialis Lem. [*B. imperialis maculata* Hort.]. Rhizomatous, rhizome thick, short, plant low, very hairy; lvs. 4–6 in. across, cordate, brown with irregular bands of bright green along the veins, petioles 4–6 in. long; fls. ½ in. across, white, in infls. not overtopping foliage, male and female fls. with 2 ovate tepals, ovary broad, green, 3-angled, with 1 long wing. All year. Mex. Var. **smaragdina** Lem. ex A. DC. Lvs. wholly bright green.

incarnata Link & Otto. Fibrous-rooted, sts. 2–3 ft., erect, succulent, swollen at nodes, reddish, spotted; lvs. 4–10 in. long, obliquely cordate to lanceolate, acuminate, shallowly lobed, green, often more or less spotted or feathered above, reddish-green underneath; fls. many, to 1½ in. across, rose-pink, on arching, rose-colored peduncles, male fls. with 2 ovate and 2 narrow tepals, female smaller, with 5 equal tepals, ovary 3-angled, wings unequal. Early winter. Mex. Variable sp. with several cvs. Cv. 'Purpurea'. Lvs. purplish. Not now in cult., but a parent of several cvs. Cv. 'Sandersii'. Fls. more numerous, larger, light pink.

inciso-serrata A. DC. Fibrous-rooted, tawny-hairy, sts. stout, branched; lvs. palmately 5–9-parted, segms. oblong, acuminate, irregularly serrate, curling at margin and apex when mature, glossy green, scabrous above; fls. in few-fld. cymes. Brazil.

×**Ingramii** T. Moore [*B.* × *robusta* Hort., not. *B. robusta* Blume]: *B. foliosa* var. *miniata* × *B. minor*. Fibrous-rooted, sts. to 3 ft., with horizontal flowering brs.; lvs. small, ovate, toothed, sparsely hairy, green, tinged with red in the sun; fls. rosy-pink, in drooping clusters on red peduncles. It has been suggested that *B. acutifolia* or *B. fruticosa* is more likely than *B. minor* as the second parent.

×**intermedia** Hort. Veitch ex Van Houtte: *B. boliviensis* × *B. Veitchii*. Similar to *B. boliviensis*, but fls. larger, light scarlet, less pendent. Cv. 'Bertinii' [*B.* × *Bertinii* Hort. ex Legros]: *B. boliviensis* × *B.* × *intermedia*. A backcross hybrid; tuberous, compact, sts. several, to about 1 ft.; lvs. 4–5 in. long, obliquely ovate-lanceolate, toothed, hairy; fls. many, about 1¼ in. long, vermilion, drooping, in pairs on long peduncles. The *Begonia* Bertinii Hybrids [*B.* × *multiflora Bertinii* Hort.], with long, drooping, fuschialike fls. in shades of red, pink, and scarlet, are derived from this cv. Technically, they form a subgroup in the *Begonia* Tuberhybrida Hybrids, Multiflora Group; see under *B.* × *tuberhybrida*.

involucrata Liebm. Rhizomatous, sts. bushy, covered with red-brown fuzz; lvs. 6–7½ in. across, broad-ovate, palmately 3–5-lobed, toothed, bright green, softly white-hairy; fls. white, in compact axillary cymes. Spring. Guatemala to Panama.

isoptera Dryand. Fibrous-rooted, sts. 1½–2 ft., glabrous, brs. spreading; lvs. to 3½ in. long, strongly obliquely ovate-oblong, somewhat cordate basally, wavy-margined, toothed, red; fls. inconspicuous, greenish edged with pink, male fls. in terminal cymes, female in 2's or 3's between male infl. and the opp. lf. Summer. Java.

Johnstonii D. Oliver. Fibrous-rooted, sts. branched, trailing, succulent, pale green, streaked with red; lvs. broad-ovate, crenately lobed, basal lobes overlapping, glossy green above, paler underneath, with minute soft hairs along veins; fls. large, soft pink, in few-fld. clusters on arching peduncles. Summer. Trop. Afr.

Josephii A. DC. Tuberous, stemless; lvs. small, ovate to orbicular, sometimes lobed, toothed, usually peltate when young; fls. small, white or rosy-pink. Himalayas.

Karwinskiana A. DC. Rhizomatous; lvs. obliquely ovate-orbicular, cuspidate, deeply cordate basally, shallowly lobed to toothed, wavy-margined, ciliate; fls. white in forking cymes. Mex.

×**Kathlayana** Hort.: *Begonia* Rex-Cultorum cv. 'Kathlayana' (*B. cathayana* × *Begonia* cv. 'Mrs. H. G. Moon'). Lvs. long-pointed, lobed, heavily speckled with silver, green along veins.

Kellermanii: *B. peltata*.

Kenworthyi Ziesenh. Rhizomatous, rhizome to 6 in., erect, unbranched, thick, succulent, green, with lvs. only at tip; lvs. to 12 in. long, 8 in. wide, unequally sharply lobed, cordate basally, serrate, red-ciliate, fleshy, slate-gray, veins green, covered with a gray bloom; fls. ½ in. across, white, with 2 orbicular tepals, in many-fld. axillary cymes. Winter. Mex.

×**kewensis** Hort. Lemoine. Perhaps better treated as *Begonia* cv. 'Kewensis': *B. coccinea* × *B. undulata*. Resembling *B. undulata*, but brs. spreading or drooping, lvs. to 6 in. long, 2 in. wide at base, wavy-margined, fls. greenish-white, ½ in. across, in large clusters. Hanging-basket plant.

Kunthiana Walp. Fibrous-rooted, sts. 12–18 in., erect, slender, swollen at nodes, glabrous, purple-brown; lvs. 3 in. long, lanceolate, serrate, glabrous, dark green above, crimson underneath, short-petioled; fls. white, in 2 groups of 3 on short peduncles, male fls. 1½ in. across, with 2 large and 2 small tepals, female with 5 equal tepals, ovary 3-angled, with large nearly equal wings. Summer. Venezuela.

laciniata Roxb. Rhizomatous, rhizome 1–2 ft., erect, later straggling, green; lvs. 5–8 in. long, broad-ovate, cordate basally, nearly glabrous, except on margins, angled to sharply lobed to laciniate, purplish-black with broad green band between margin and center above, reddish underneath; fls. white, similar to those of *B. rex*. India, Burma, S. China. Var. **Bowringiana** (Champ. ex Benth.) A. DC. [*B. Bowringiana* Champ. ex Benth., not Hort.]. Fls. smaller, pubescent. Probably not

now in cult. Var. **flava** Hook. [*B. laciniata* cv. 'Lutea']. Lvs. smaller, thinner, green above with brown along center and margin, greenish underneath; fls. yellow, bearded on exterior. Cv. '**Lutea**': var. *flava*.

laeteviridis: *B. Bradei*.

lepidota: *B. manicata*.

leptotricha C. DC. MANDA'S WOOLLY-BEAR B., WOOLLY-BEAR. Fibrous-rooted, sts. to 1 ft., rusty-woolly; lvs. 1½–3 in. long, obliquely ovate, pointed, crenately toothed, fleshy, glossy green and cobwebby-hairy above, rusty-woolly underneath; fls. white, many, in short, few-fld. clusters, tepals irregular, male fls. with 4 tepals, female with 5; seeds obtuse. Perpetually in bloom. Paraguay. Has been confused with *B. subvillosa*.

×**Lesoudsii** André: *B. Beddomei* × *B. diadema*. Rhizomatous; lvs. large, shallowly lobed, dark green, mottled with pea-green and with wider silver band along margin above, petioles red, scaly, hairy; fls. large, pink.

×**lettonica** Hort. A name of no botanical standing for *Begonia* cv. 'Lettonica': *B. heracleifolia* × *B. nelumbiifolia*. Rhizomatous, rhizome thick, ascending, plant large; lvs. obliquely ovate, acuminate, cordate basally, shallowly lobed, toothed, fringed with brown hairs, green above, reddish underneath, long-petioled; fls. clear pink.

Liebmannii: *B. ludicra*.

Liminghii: *B. Limmingheiana*.

Limmingheiana C. Morr. [*B. glaucophylla* Gower; *B. glaucophylla scandens* Hort. P. Henders.; *B. Liminghii* C. Koch; *B. undulata* Hort., not Schott]. SHRIMP B. Rhizomatous, rhizome short, sts. 6–8 ft. long, creeping, drooping, or climbing, green spotted with white; lvs. 3–5 in. long, obliquely ovate to oblong-lanceolate, wavy, reddish in bud, glaucous-green spotted with white above, purple underneath, short-petioled; fls. to 1 in. across, brick-red, variegated in bud, in compact, axillary clusters on short peduncles, male fls. with 2 ovate and 2 linear tepals, female with 5 equal tepals, ovary large, 3-winged. Winter. Brazil. Hanging-basket plant. Cv. '**Purpurea**'. Lvs. with bronze tinge; fls. fragrant, female white with purplish-red center.

Lindleyana Walp. [*B. pilifera* (Klotzsch) A. DC.; *B. vitifolia* Lindl., not Schott or Hort.]. Rhizomatous, covered with red felt when young, rhizome usually erect, to 12 in. long; lvs. 3–8 in. long, obliquely broad-ovate, cordate basally, acuminate, toothed, entire or broadly lobed and toothed, soon glabrous above; fls. white, male fls. with 2 or 4 tepals, female with 2–3, in broad, few- to many-fld. cymes on hairy peduncles above foliage. Early spring to summer. S. Mex. to Colombia.

×**Lloydii**: *Begonia* Tuberhybrida Hybrids, Pendula Group; see under *B.* × *tuberhybrida*.

lobata Schott. HONEY-BEAR B. Fibrous-rooted, villous except at base, st. fruticose; lvs. ovate, pointed, cordate basally, shallowly lobed to crenately toothed, soft-hairy, bronzy-green; fls. white; caps. pubescent. Brazil. Cv. '**Variegata**' [*B. lobulata* A. DC. cv. 'Variegata']. Lvs. with silver spots.

longibarbata Brade. Sts. branched; lvs. 7–10 in. long, 12–16 in. wide, obliquely broad-ovate, acuminate, cordate basally, wavy-margined, toothed, ciliate, green with red basal sinus, slightly hairy above, purplish underneath; fls. white, with 4 tepals, in few-fld. cymes. Brazil.

longipes: *B. reniformis*.

Lubbersii E. Morr. Rhizomatous, rhizome short, ascending, sts. 2 ft., erect, thick; lvs. 2 in. wide, peltate, obliquely lanceolate, dark green with silver blotches above, crimson underneath, petioles 5 in. long; fls. 1½ in. across, white, on short axillary peduncles, male fls. with 2 broad and 2 rudimentary tepals, female much smaller, with 5 tepals. Flowering the year around. Brazil.

Lucerna: *Begonia* cv. 'Lucerna'; see under *B. corallina*.

ludicra A. DC. [*B. Liebmannii* A. DC.]. Rhizomatous, rhizome slender, erect or creeping; lvs. obliquely ovate to subpalmate, sharply lobed, entire or toothed, green, blotched with silver and glabrous to sparsely pilose above, purple tinged underneath; fls. large, greenish-white, in short, erect, few-fld. cymes; caps. with unequal wings. Spring. S. Mex. to Panama.

Ludwigii Irmsch. Fibrous-rooted, sts. very thick, slightly bulbous at base; lvs. to 14 in. across, nearly orbicular, shallowly palmately lobed, acuminate, doubly serrate, green with red veins in center above, with short white bristles on both surfaces, petioles with collar of hairs at apex; fls. 1 in. across, creamy-white, streaked with green and rose on exterior, in cymes on white-flecked peduncles, 1½ ft. long, tepals orbicular, ruffled when young, male fls. with 4, female with 5. Spring to summer. Ecuador.

×**Lulandii** Hort. A name of no botanical standing for *Begonia* cv. 'Lulandii': *B. corallina* cv. 'Lucerna' × *B. Sutherlandii*. Tuberous, low-spreading, bushy, sts. swollen at nodes, light red; lvs. similar to those of *B. Sutherlandii* but wider and not as long, crinkled, light green, with a red line along margin; fls. few, large, bright pink. Hanging-basket plant.

×**luminosa:** *Begonia* Semperflorens-Cultorum Hybrid, Gracilis Group, cv. 'Luminosa.' A hybrid, with lvs. bronzy-red, fls. large, bright scarlet-red. See under *B.* × *semperflorens-cultorum* var. *gracilis.*

lutea L. B. Sm. & Schub. Tuberous, stemless; lvs. to 5 in. across, obliquely broad-ovate to suborbicular, shortly acuminate, cordate basally, toothed, sparsely tomentose, green with reddish veins; fls. ½ in. across, yellow, in few-fld. cymes on pubescent peduncles, male fls. with 4 tepals, female with 5, ovary with 3 unequal wings. Colombia.

luxurians Scheidw. PALM-LEAF B. Fibrous-rooted, sts. 1 ft., succulent, red, soft-hairy; lvs. palmately compound into 7–17 lfts., 3–6 in. long, lanceolate, serrate, hairy, reddish above, green underneath; fls. small, cream-colored, in long-peduncled cymes. Summer. Brazil. Used medicinally in Brazil.

Luzerna: *Begonia* cv. 'Lucerna'; see under *B. corallina.*

Lyncheana Hook.f. [*B. Roezlii* Hort. Benary ex Lynch, not Regel]. Somewhat tuberous, sts. to 3 ft., erect, little branched, glabrous; lvs. to 8 in. long, obliquely broad-ovate, cordate basally, shallowly angulately lobed, ciliate-toothed, glabrous, bright green above with basal red blotch at juncture of nerves, paler with red veins underneath; infl. many-fld., enclosed when young in 2 large bracts; fls. scarlet, male fls. 1½ in. across, with 2 orbicular tepals, female smaller, with 2–4 tepals, stigmas capitate, ovary with 3 unequal wings. Early to late winter. Mex.

Macbethii: *B. Dregei* cv. [Var.] **obtusa:** *B. Dregei* cv. 'Macbethii Obtusa.'

Macdougallii Ziesenh. Rhizomatous, rhizome ascending to erect, succulent; lvs. 2 ft. across or more, palmately compound, with 7–10 lanceolate leaflets, fleshy, asymmetrical, green, petioles 3 ft. long, brown-hairy; fls. ¼ in. across, greenish-white, with 2 orbicular tepals, ovary with 3 unequal wings. Spring. Mex.

macrocarpa Warb. Rhizomatous, sts. herbaceous, procumbent; lvs. 2-ranked, 4–5½ in. long, 2–3 in. wide, obliquely ovate-elliptic, acute to acuminate, serrate, dark glossy olive-green, sparsely bristly-hairy; fls. red, in axillary, few-fld. cymes. Cameroon. Material cult. under the name *B. macrocarpa* may be *B. Bradei.*

maculata Raddi [*B. argyrostigma* Fisch. ex Link & Otto]. Fibrous-rooted, sts. 2–3 ft., erect, branched, woody when old, glabrous; lvs. 4–6 in. long, obliquely lanceolate, cordate basally, wavy-margined, green with roundish white spots above, crimson at margin and underneath; fls. many, pale rose or white, on drooping axillary peduncles, male fls. ½ in. across, with 2 orbicular and 2 very narrow tepals, female fls. more numerous, with 5 equal tepals, ovary with broad, nearly equal wings. Summer. Brazil. Very variable sp. Cv. '**Wightii**'. Sts. 6–8 ft.; lvs. large, much-spotted; fls. 1 in. across, white.

magnifica: *B. ferruginea;* but material offered as *B. magnifica* may be a *Begonia* Rex-Cultorum cv.

malabarica Lam. Fibrous-rooted, sts. to 2 ft., suffruticose, glabrous; lvs. 3–6 in. long, oblong-ovate, acuminate, cordate basally, reddish-brown; fls. large, white, in clusters of 2–6, male fls. with 2 tepals, female with 5, ovary and wing white. Summer to autumn. India, Ceylon. Var. **dipetala:** *B. dipetala. Begonia malabarica* Roxb. is *B. Roxburghii.*

manicata Brogn. ex Cels [*B. lepidota* Liebm.]. Rhizomatous, mostly glabrous except on lf. margins and petioles, sts. short, succulent; lvs. 4–8 in. long, short-ovate, fleshy, wavy-margined, toothed, glossy green above, reddish underneath except for veins, petioles long, with collar of coarse hairs at apex; fls. pink, in loose panicles on peduncles 1 ft. long or more, male and female fls. with 2 tepals, ovary with nearly equal wings. Winter. S. Mex. and Guatemala. Cv. '**Aurea Crispa**': 'Aureo-maculata Crispa'. Cv. '**Aurea Cristata**': cv. 'Aureo-maculata Crispa'. Cv. '**Aureo-maculata**'. LEOPARD B. Lvs. light green, with large, yellowish-white, occasionally rosy-red blotches. Cv. '**Aureo-maculata Crispa**' [cvs. 'Aurea Crispa', 'Aurea Cristata']. Lvs. light green, mottled with yellow, margin crested, becoming pink in the sun. Cv. '**Crispa**'. Lvs. light green, margin crested.

Mannii Hook.f. [*B. parva* T. Sprague, not Merrill; *B. Spraguei* C. Web.]. Fibrous-rooted, sts. to 6 ft., scandent, branched, slender, woody, rusty-tomentose; lvs. 4–5 in. long, nearly symmetrically ovate, pointed, shallowly lobed or toothed, wavy-margined, leathery, dark glossy green, glabrous above, rusty-tomentose underneath; fls. pale red, female fls. with 4 tepals, ovary cylindrical, wingless. Spring. Congo region.

×**margaritacea** Hort. Veitch: *Begonia* cv. 'Arthur Mallet' × *B. coccinea.* Sts. to 1½ ft., not very erect, branched; lvs. 4½–6 in. long, 2–3½ in. wide, obliquely ovate, pointed, toothed, bronzy-green with silver to rose flecks and hairy above, wine-red underneath.

×**Margaritae** Hort. ex Fotsch: *B. echinosepala* × *B. metallica.* Fibrous-rooted, sts. 1–2 ft., purple, soft-hairy; lvs. very small, ovate, acuminate, wavy-margined, toothed, olive-green above, veins purple underneath; fls. large, rosy-pink, pink-bearded. Summer.

×**marginata:** *Begonia* Tuberhybrida Hybrids, Marginata Group; see under *B.* × *tuberhybrida.*

×**marmorata:** *Begonia* Tuberhybrida Hybrids, Marmorata Group; see under *B.* × *tuberhybrida.*

Martiana Link & Otto [*B. gracilis* HBK var. *Martiana* A. DC.]. HOLLYHOCK B. Similar to *B. gracilis*, but sts. not as high, stouter; lf. margin entire; fls. 2 in. across, fragrant, tepals not fringed. Mex. *Begonia* cv. 'Martiana Grandiflora' is a hybrid, *B. Martiana* × *B. racemiflora*, with sts. green, fls. large, rose-carmine. Summer.

Masoniana Irmsch. IRON-CROSS B. Rhizomatous; lvs. to 4 in. long, obliquely broad-cordate, toothed, ciliate, wrinkled, with conelike elevations on the surface, each elevation carrying a red hair, upper surface green with palmately lobed central star of chocolate-brown, the rays of the star radiating along the deeply sunken main veins and broadened apically, petioles curly-haired; fls. reddish, in many-fld. cymes., male fls. with 4 tepals, female with 3. Probably native to China.

Maxiae: *B. Mexiae.*

maxima: *B. fusca.* The name has also been applied, in hort., to *Begonia* Tuberhybrida Hybrids, Multiflora Group; see under *B.* × *tuberhybrida.*

Mazae Ziesenh. Fibrous-rooted, sts. to 1½ ft., rarely branched, becoming woody; lvs. obliquely orbicular to ovate, acuminate, cordate basally, dull green with small green and red dots above, yellowish-green at margin, oxblood-red underneath; fls. ¼ in. across, white to pale pink, with 2 orbicular tepals, in many-fld. cymes. Winter to spring. Mex. Cv. '**Nigricans**'. Lvs. green, shading to black in center and on veins.

megaptera A. DC. Rhizomatous, rhizome ascending to erect, thick, green with white stripes, like the petioles; lvs. 5–7 in. long, obliquely broad-ovate, sharp-pointed, irregularly lobed, dark glossy green with silver blotches above, dark reddish-purple underneath; fls. many, 2 in. across, apple-blossom pink, on long peduncles, male fls. with 4 tepals, female with 7. Himalayas.

metallica W. G. Sm. METALLIC-LEAF B. Fibrous-rooted, hairy, sts. 3–4 ft.; lvs. to 6 in. long, obliquely ovate, angled or lobed, sinuate-serrate on margins, olive-green with metallic-purple veins above, paler underneath; fls. to 1½ in. across, blush-white to light rose, in large, many-fld. cymes, male fls. with 2 large, broad tepals and 2 small, narrow ones, female fls. smaller, with 4 reddish-bearded tepals. Summer to autumn. Brazil.

Mexiae Standl. Rhizomatous, stemless; lvs. to 7½ in. long, 5 in. wide, obliquely round-ovate, acute, cordate basally, entire to shallowly toothed, apple-green, petioles long, covered with white scurf; fls. white or pink, in loose, many-fld. forking cymes, male fls. with 2 ovate to orbicular tepals, ovary with 3 unequal wings, largest wing white. Mex. Sometimes misspelled *B. Maxiae.*

micranthera Griseb. Tuberous, sts. erect, usually unbranched; lvs. to 12 in. long, obliquely ovate, acuminate, cordate basally, shallowly lobed, thin, serrate, ciliate; peduncles axillary, erect, 2-fld., fls. to 1 in. across, white or light pink, ovary with 1 large and 2 small wings. Argentina. Var. **fimbriata** L. B. Sm. & Schub. Sts. to 20 in., branched; lvs. to 6½ in. long; peduncles 3- or more-fld., fls. pink, fimbriate. S. Bolivia. Var. **foliosa** L. B. Sm. & Schub. Sts. branched; lvs. many, smaller, firmer; peduncles 2-fld., ovary with 3 or often 4 cells. Ne. Argentina, s. Bolivia. Var. **Venturii** L. B. Sm. & Schub. Lvs. blackish-hairy; peduncles 3- or more-fld. Ne. Argentina, s. Bolivia.

miniata: *B. foliosa* var. *miniata.*

minor Jacq. [*B. nitida* Ait.]. Fibrous-rooted, glabrous, sts. 3–6 ft., erect, branched; lvs. 4–6 in. across, obliquely ovate or reniform, cordate basally, wavy-margined, crenately toothed, glossy green; fls. white or pale pink, crowded on long axillary peduncles, male fls. to 2 in. across, with 2 broad and 2 narrow tepals, female smaller, with 5 equal tepals, ovary with 1 large and 2 small wings. Summer. Jamaica. The first begonia to be introd. into cult. in Eur. Cv. '**Rosea**' [*B. nitida rosea* Hort.; *B. odorata rosea* Hort.]. Fls. deep rose, fragrant.

multangula Blume. Rhizomatous, hairy; lvs. obliquely reniform to orbicular, acuminate, cordate basally, lobed; male fls. with 4 tepals, female with 3-angled, glabrous ovary with rudimentary wings. Java. Not in cult. Material cult. under this name is *B. Dregei* cv. 'Macbethii Obtusa'.

multiflora Benth. Fibrous-rooted, sts. woody; lvs. 2 in. long, obliquely oblong, toothed, nearly sessile; male and female fls. in separate cymes. Colombia. Not in cult. Material offered as *B.* × *multiflora, B.* × *multiflora Bertinii, B.* × *multiflora gigantea, B.* × *multiflora* *grandiflora,* or *B.* × *multiflora maxima* is *Begonia* Tuberhybrida Hybrids, Multiflora Group; see under *B.* × *tuberhybrida. B. multiflora rosea* is *B. foliosa* var. *miniata* cv. 'Rosea'.

multinervia Liebm. [*B. cuspidata* C. DC.]. Rhizomatous, rhizome thick, erect, sts. to 9 ft., sparsely branched, woody; lvs. to 9 in. long, 5½ in. wide, obliquely cordate, wavy-margined, sometimes coarsely toothed, glossy green with reddish-brown veins above, lighter green with occasional reddish spots underneath, petioles short, hairy; fls. large, white or pink-tinged, in large, compact, forked cymes. Winter. Costa Rica and Panama.

muricata Blume [?*B. tuberosa* Lam.]. Rhizomatous; lvs. far apart, to 6½ in. long, obliquely ovate, pointed, cordate and incised basally, dark green, long-hairy above and underneath or glabrous above; fls. up to 1¼ in. across, white or pink, male with 4 tepals, female with 2 or 3, ovary with 3 nearly equal wings. E. Indies. Not in cult. Material cult. as *B.* × *tuberosa* is *Begonia* Tuberhybrida Hybrids; see under *B.* × *tuberhybrida.*

× **narcissiflora:** *Begonia* Tuberhybrida Hybrids, Narcissiflora Group; see under *B.* × *tuberhybrida.*

natalensis Hook. Tuberous, sts. 3–6 ft., ann., branched, succulent, glabrous; lvs. 2–3 in. long, obliquely cordate, lobed, wavy-margined, green, sometimes mottled with gray, veins reddish above; fls. many, 1 in. across, bluish-white, on slender, axillary peduncles, male fls. with 2 ovate tepals, female with 5, ovary 3-angled, with 2 long and 1 short wing. Winter. Natal.

nelumbiifolia Cham. & Schlechtend. LILY-PAD B., POND-LILY B. Rhizomatous, rhizome thick, short, ascending; lvs. to 18 in. long, peltate, round-ovate to nearly orbicular, short-pointed, serrulate, ciliate, green; fls. to ½ in. across, white or pink-tinged, in tall, erect, forking cymes. Winter to spring. S. Mex. to Colombia. Cv. 'Glabra'. Plant smaller; lvs. more pointed, pea-green.

nigricans: *B. heracleifolia* var.

nigro-venia: *B. glandulosa.*

nitida: *B. minor.* **B. nitida odorata alba:** *B. suaveolens.* **B. nitida rosea:** *B. minor* cv.

obscura Brade. Fibrous-rooted, sts. to 2 ft., erect, bushy, rusty-pilose when young; lvs. 3–4 in. long, 1 in. wide, obliquely oblong, long-acuminate, doubly serrate, green, villous on veins underneath; fls. ¾ in. across, white, bearded on exterior, male with 4 tepals, female larger, with 5 tepals, ovary with 3 unequal wings. Winter. Brazil.

octopetala L'Hér. Tuberous, stemless; lvs. to 8 in. long, cordate, lobed, toothed, green, on stout, fleshy petioles 12–18 in. long; fls. ivory-white, in 6–20-fld. corymbs on peduncles 1–2 in. long, male fls. 2–3 in. across, with 6–10 tepals, female smaller, with 6 tepals, ovary top-shaped, 3-angled, with 3 unequal wings. Autumn or winter. Peru.

odorata Paxt. [*B. odorata alba* Hort.; *B. nitida odorata alba* Hort.]. Similar to *B. minor,* but sts. shorter, more slender, more branched, red at base when young; lvs. smaller, flatter, glossier, shorter-petioled; fls. white or pink-tinged, fragrant, male with 4 tepals, often dropping before expanding, female larger, with 5 tepals, continuously produced. *B. odorata rosea* is *B. minor* cv.

olbia Kerch. MAPLE-LEAF B. Fibrous-rooted, sts. short, erect, mostly branched, stout, succulent; lvs. to 5 in. long, obliquely ovate, cordate basally, shallowly lobed, coarsely toothed, white- or red-hairy, bronzygreen with white dots above, red along margin, red underneath; fls. ¾ in. across, greenish-white, in short, drooping, axillary clusters. Spring. Brazil.

Olsoniae L. B. Sm. & Schub. [*B. Vellozoana* Brade, not *B. Velloziana* Walp.]. Fibrous-rooted, sts. to 5½ in. long, ascending; lvs. 4–5 in. long, 5–8 in. wide, obliquely broad-ovate to nearly orbicular, cordate basally, bronzy-green with ivory or pink midrib, pilose on both surfaces; fls. whitish or rosy-pink on exterior, in few-fld. cymes, male fls. with 4 tepals, female with 5, ovary with 3 unequal wings. Winter. Brazil.

ovatifolia A. DC. Tuberous, nearly stemless; lvs. ovate, acuminate, somewhat cordate basally, wavy-margined, toothed; fls. few, white or rosy-pink, on arching peduncles. Sikkim.

oxyphylla A. DC. Fibrous-rooted, sts. erect, woody, reddish-tomentose when young; lvs. small, obliquely narrow-oblong, acuminate, shallowly toothed, green and waxy above, petioles and veins on lower surface red-tomentose; fls. white, in pubescent cymes. Brazil.

palmaris: *B. biserrata.*

palmifolia: *B. vitifolia.*

parilis Irmsch. ZIGZAG B. Fibrous-rooted, sts. to 5 ft., slender, branched, arching, zigzag; lvs. long-ovate, leathery, glossy brownish-green; fls. white, in drooping clusters. Brazil.

parva Merrill. Rhizomatous, softly brown-hairy; lvs. 1–1½ in. long, ¾–1 in. wide, obliquely oblong-ovate or narrowly oblong, cordate basally, entire; fls. 1 in. across, pink, with 4 tepals, in few-fld. cymes just above foliage, ovary with 1 large wing. Philippine Is. Not in cult. Material cult. under this name is *B. Mannii.*

parvifolia: see *B. Dregei.*

paulensis A. DC. Rhizomatous, soft-hairy, rhizome 3 in. long, ascending, succulent; lvs. 8–9 in. long, 6 in. wide, oblong, acuminate, irregularly toothed, glossy green, with lighter veins forming a spiderweb pattern, petioles hairy, with collar of red hairs at apex; fls. 1½–2 in. across, white with fleshy maroon hairs on exterior, in panicles, male fls. with 4 tepals, female with 5, ovary 3-angled, covered with fleshy, maroon hairs, with 1 large, red wing. Brazil.

Pearcei Hook.f. Tuberous, sts. 1 ft., ann., branched, succulent, pubescent; lvs. 4–6 in. long, obliquely ovate, acuminate, cordate basally, toothed, glabrous, green above, tomentose and dull red beneath; fls. 1½ in. across, yellow, on erect, axillary peduncles, male fls. with 2 orbicular and 2 ovate tepals, female smaller, with 5 equal tepals, ovary green, 3-angled, with 3 nearly equal wings. Summer. Bolivia. This sp. is the source of yellow fl. color in the hybrid tuberous begonias.

× **Pearlii** Hort.: *Begonia* Rex-Cultorum cv. 'Pearlii'. Lvs. dull silver, pebbled.

peltata Otto & A. Dietr. [*B. incana* Lindl.; *B. Kellermanii* C. DC.]. LILY-PAD B. Fibrous-rooted, sts. 1–2 ft., erect, succulent, hairy; lvs. 4–9 in. long, peltate, ovate, acuminate, thick, felted, whitish underneath; fls. 1 in. across, white, in cymes on long, erect peduncles. Winter. S. Mex. and Guatemala. *B. peltata* Schott ex A. DC. is *B. concinna.*

peltifolia: see under *B. coriacea.*

pendula Ridl. Rhizomatous, rhizome creeping; lvs. 2–2½ in. long, lanceolate, acute, rounded at base, entire to irregularly toothed, glabrous; fls. few, very small, reddish-pink, male with 2 tepals, in terminal cymes, female with 3 tepals, solitary at base of lvs. Sarawak. Not in cult. Material offered under the name *B.* × *pendula* is *Begonia* Tuberhybrida Hybrids, Pendula Group; see under *B.* × *tuberhybrida.*

peponifolia Hort. ex Vis. Rhizomatous; lvs. 10–16 in. long, nearly orbicular, obliquely cordate basally, wavy-margined, toothed, glabrous above, scurfy on veins underneath, petioles long, scurfy; fls. many, ¾ in. across, white, with 2 tepals, in forking cymes on stout peduncles 3 ft. long or more. Probably Mex. Not now in cult., but one of the parents of *B.* × *ricinifolia.*

× **perfectiflora:** *B. undulata* cv.

philodendroides Ziesenh. Rhizomatous, rhizome creeping, succulent; lvs. 4 in. long, 5½ in. wide, palmately divided into acuminate, serrate lobes, cordate basally, glossy green above, sparsely reddish-brown-hairy and prominently veined underneath; fls. white, ovary with 3 long wings, peduncles green, striped and dotted with oxblood-red. Autumn. Mex.

phyllomaniaca Mart. [*Begonia* cv. 'Jessie']. CRAZY-LEAF B. Fibrous-rooted, shrubby, sts. erect, branched, rarely succulent, shaggy-hairy, producing, as do the lvs., many buds and leafy growths; lvs. 4–8 in. long, obliquely cordate, attenuate, slightly laciniate and fringed; fls. 1 in. across, pale pink, in hanging clusters, male fls. smaller than female, ovary with 1 large wing. Winter. Brazil. The buds and leafy growths can be used for propagation. Cv. 'Templinii' [*B. Templinii* Hort.]. Lvs. with yellow blotches.

picta Sm. [*B. picta* cv. 'Rosea']. Tuberous, st. to 1 ft. or more; lvs. 3–5 in. long, 2½ in. wide, ovate, pointed, cordate basally, toothed, hairy, dark green and mottled with lighter green and metallic-bronze above, villous on veins underneath; fls. clear pink, ovary pubescent. Summer. Himalayas. [Var.] **alba:** *B. undulata. B. picta* Hort. Henders. ex A. DC. is *B. annulata.*

× **pictavensis** Bruant ex André: *B. cucullata* var. *Hookeri* × *B. Schmidtiana.* Similar to the *Begonia* Semperflorens-Cultorum Hybrids, but less variable. Cv. 'Erfordia' [*B. semperflorens* Link & Otto cv. 'Erfordia'; *B.* Semperflorens-Cultorum cv. 'Erfordia'; *B.* × *Erfordia* Hort.]: *B. cucullata* var. *Hookeri* cv. 'Vernon' × *B. Schmidtiana.* Fls. rose-carmine. Used for bedding.

× **pictaviensis:** *B.* × *Credneri.*

Pilderia: *B. buddleiifolia.*

pilifera: *B. Lindleyana.*

pinetorum A. DC. Rhizomatous; lvs. obliquely ovate, long-pointed, cordate basally, wavy-margined, green and glabrous above, reddish-brown-tomentose underneath, petioles red-tomentose; fls. pink, male with 2 tepals, female with 5, in many-fld., erect panicles. Winter. Mex.

plebeja Liebm. Rhizomatous, rhizome ascending, thick, succulent, branched; lvs. 3–6 in. long, obliquely cordate, acute, irregularly toothed, ciliate, green and glabrous above, with white dots and pilose underneath, long-petioled; fls. white, in forking cymes, male and female fls. with 2 tepals, ovary glabrous, with 3 unequal wings. Autumn or winter. S. Mex. and Cent. Amer. Cv. 'Brooks' [*B. Brooksii* Hort.]. Lvs. mottled chocolate-brown, with light green veins.

Poggei Warb. Similar to *B. Mannii*, but brs. stubby, woody, lvs. green, fls. greenish-white. Trop. Afr.

polygonifolia A. DC. [*B. brasilensis* Klotzsch]. Fibrous-rooted, sts. erect, hairy near apex, glabrescent at base; lvs. obliquely ovate, acute, cordate basally, lobed, lobes crenately toothed; fls. pink, in few-fld. cymes, ovary with 3 equal wings. Brazil. Probably not in cult.; material offered as *B. brasiliensis* is *B. acida*.

Popenoei Standl. Rhizomatous, rhizome very thick, ascending; lvs. large, orbicular, pointed, irregularly toothed, ciliate, sparsely hairy, bright green, red-tinged at margin above; fls. large, white, in tall, erect panicles. Spring and summer. Honduras. Cv. 'Florida' [*B. florida* Hort.]. Larger, more vigorous; lvs. larger, sometimes partly peltate, darker green, more stiffly hairy; not as free-flowering.

princeps Hort. ex Klotzsch. Fibrous-rooted, sts. to 2 ft., erect to spreading, bushy, branched from base, white-hairy; lvs. 10–12 in. long, 6–8 in. wide, obovate, nearly peltate, acuminate, cordate basally, leathery, dark glossy green and glabrous above, hairy and red with paler veins underneath, margin ciliate, curled under, petioles red-hairy; fls. 1½ in. across, white, male fls. with 4 tepals, female with 5, ovary small, white, with 3 pinkish wings. Winter. Brazil.

pruinata A. DC. [*B. pruinosa* Hort.]. Rhizomatous, sts. to 1 ft., erect, sparsely branched; lvs. to 3 in. long, ovate, pointed, cordate basally, green and glistening above, hairy near the veins and glaucous-light-green underneath; fls. white, many, in cymes on peduncles 1 ft. tall. Winter. Cent. Amer.

pruinosa: *B. pruinata*.

×**prunifolia** Hort. A name of no botanical standing for seedlings of *B.* × *Viaudii*. Similar to *B. Scharffiana*, but differing in having lvs. to 6 in. long, deep purple underneath, fls. white or pink, bearded, in large, drooping clusters. It is suggested that the white-fld. form be called *Begonia* cv. 'White Prunifolia' and the pink-fld. one *Begonia* cv. 'Pink Prunifolia'.

pseudolubbersii Brade. Fibrous-rooted, sts. to 2½ ft., erect, somewhat woody; lvs. 3–5 in. long, 1½ in. wide, obliquely oblong-lanceolate, cordate basally, shallowly toothed, green with silver dots; fls. to 2 in. across, in few-fld. cymes, male fls. with 4 tepals, female smaller, with 5–6 tepals, ovary with 3 nearly equal wings. Brazil.

×**pseudophyllomaniaca** A. Lange: possibly *B. heracleifolia* × *B. incarnata*. Fibrous-rooted, sts. rhizomelike, erect, stout; lvs. ovate, pointed, 5-lobed, toothed, glossy green with reddish margin, sparsely hairy above; fls. pink, in large panicles.

pseudovalerii: a name of no botanical standing.

punctata: *B. heracleifolia* var.

purpurea Swartz. Fibrous-rooted, sts. 2–4 ft., woody, glabrous; lvs. 2–4½ in. across, obliquely oblong-elliptic to oblong-lanceolate, acuminate, cordate basally, irregularly toothed; fls. pink or purple, male fls. with 4 unequal tepals, female with 5, ovary with 1 large wing. Jamaica.

pustulata Liebm. [*B. pustulata* cv. 'Argentea']. Rhizomatous, stemless; lvs. 3–6 in. long, obliquely broad-ovate, acuminate, cordate basally, blistered, toothed, ciliate, nile-green with silvery-white markings, on long reddish-hairy petioles; fls. pink, in few-fld. clusters. S. Mex. and Guatemala. Cv. 'Argentea': *B. pustulata*.

quadrilocularis: *B. egregia*.

radicans: see *B. glabra*.

×**Reichenheimii:** see *B.* ×*fuscomaculata* cv. 'Reichenheim'.

relmifolia: a name of no botanical standing, used for a hanging-basket plant with "fernlike" lvs. and white fls.

reniformis Dryand. [*B. reniformis* cv. 'Petiolata'; *B. longipes* Hook.]. Fibrous-rooted, sts. 3 ft. or more, erect, branched, thick, green, with short red hairs or glands; lvs. large, obliquely obovate, cordate basally, serrate, glossy yellowish-green above, hairy or glandular underneath, long-petioled; fls. small, white, in many-fld. clusters, male fls. with 4 tepals, female with 5, ovary with 1 large, white wing. Winter. Brazil, Colombia. Cv. 'Petiolata': *B. reniformis*.

rex Putz. KING B., PAINTED-LEAF B. Rhizomatous, rhizome succulent, creeping below ground; lvs. 8–12 in. long, 6–8 in. wide, obliquely ovate, wavy-margined, wrinkled, rich metallic-green with a 1-in.-wide zone of silvery-gray above, reddish underneath, petioles red, hairy; fls. pale rosy-pink, in cymes above foliage, male fls. 2 in. across, with 4 unequal tepals, female smaller, with nearly equal tepals, ovary 3-angled, with 1 long and 2 short wings. Winter. Assam. The principal

progenitor of the *Begonia* Rex-Cultorum Hybrids; perhaps no longer in cult. as a pure sp.

×**rex-cultorum** L. H. Bailey. REX B., BEEFSTEAK GERANIUM. Nomenclaturally perhaps better treated as *Begonia* Rex-Cultorum Hybrids. Of various habit, but commonly rhizomatous; lvs. mostly obliquely ovate to lanceolate-ovate, unlobed to sinuately or sharply lobed, boldly or subtly zoned, marbled, blotched, or spotted in various patterns of green, purple, reddish-brown, bronze, gray, or silver; fls. mostly white or pink, variable, usually not showy.

A group of interrelated cvs. of often complex hybrid origin, derived mostly from *B. rex* and related rhizomatous spp., including *B. annulata*, *B. decora*, *B. diadema*, *B. laciniata*, *B. robusta*, *B. rubro-venia*, *B. xanthina*, and others. Some fibrous-rooted and tuberous spp., such as *B. cathayana*, *B. Dregei*, *B. grandis*, *B. imperialis*, and *B. incarnata*, have also been successfully crossed with *B. rex* and its hybrids, and have contributed to this complex. Assignable here are hundreds of named cvs., varying in habit, plant size, and lf. size, shape, pubescence, and coloration. They are grown primarily for their highly ornamental foliage. As a group, they require more protection from the sun and more warmth and humidity than most begonias.

Richardsiana: *B. suffruticosa*.

Richardsoniana: *B. suffruticosa*.

Richardsonii: *B. suffruticosa*.

×**richmondensis** Hort. A name of no botanical standing for *Begonia* cv. 'Richmondensis'. A hybrid of unknown parentage; fibrous-rooted, sts. stout; lvs. small, ovate, acute, toothed, wavy-margined, glossy green, slightly hairy; fls. large, bright pink. Winter. [Var.] **purpurea:** *Begonia* cv. 'Black Richmondensis'. Lvs. dark bronzy-green; fls. white or pink.

×**ricinifolia** A. Dietr.: *B. heracleifolia* × *B. peponifolia*. CASTOR-BEAN B., STAR B., BRONZE-LEAF B. Like *B. heracleifolia*, but lvs. 1 ft. long, orbicular in outline, lobed less than about ⅓ depth of blade, convex, dark green above, purplish-red underneath; fls. rosy-pink, tepals netted. Cv. 'Sunderbruckii' [*B.* × *Sunderbruckii* Hort.; *B. Sunderbruckii* Hort.; *B. heracleifolia* Cham. & Schlechtend. var. *Sunderbruchii* Hort. ex C. Cheval.]: *B. heracleifolia* × *B.* × *ricinifolia*. FINGER-LEAF B. Like *B. heracleifolia*, but lvs. with rarely more than 7 lobes, bronzy-green, with silver bands along veins, purple underneath; fls. pink. Cv. 'Sunderbruckii Nigricans': *B. heracleifolia* var. *nigricans*.

rigida Regel ex A. DC. [*B. ecuadoriensis* Hort.]. Fibrous-rooted, sts. to 2 ft., erect, rarely branched, very stout; lvs. large, orbicular, palmately lobed, toothed, sparsely white-hairy, olive-green with red veins above, tinged with red underneath; fls. creamy-white or pale pink, with 4 tepals, 15 together in erect clusters on peduncles 1 ft. long. Spring. Ecuador.

robusta Blume [*B. splendida* Hort. Rollisson ex A. DC.]. Rhizomatous, sts. 2 ft., succulent, red-hairy; lvs. obliquely suborbicular to ovate, acuminate, cordate basally, wavy-margined, green; fls. white, red-bearded on exterior, male fls. with 2 large ovate and 2 very small tepals, female with 5 equal tepals. Spring. Java. Not now in cult. Material cult. as *B.* × *robusta* is *B.* × *Ingramii*.

Roezlii Regel. Fibrous-rooted, sts. erect, little-branched; lvs. obliquely ovate, cordate basally, shallowly angulately lobed, ciliate-toothed, glabrous, bright green above with red spot at juncture of veins; fls. many, pale pink in axillary cymes, male fls. ¾ in. across, with 2 nearly orbicular tepals, female with 2 tepals, stigmas spiral, ovary with 3 unequal wings. Winter. Peru. *B. Roezlii* Hort. Benary ex Lynch is *B. Lyncheana*.

×**Rogeri** Hort. A name of no botanical standing for *Begonia* cv. 'Rogeri'. A hybrid of unknown parentage; like *B.* × *Thurstonii*, but smaller, more compact, lvs. occasionally indented at margin.

rosiflora: *B. Veitchii*. Some material offered as *B.* × *rosiflora* may belong to the *Begonia* Tuberhybrida Hybrids, Rosebud Group; see *B.* × *tuberhybrida*.

×**Rossii:** *Begonia* cv. 'Rossii'; see under *B. corallina*.

rotundifolia Lam. Rhizomatous, rhizome slender, short, creeping; lvs. to 2½ in. across, almost orbicular, crenately lobed, the 2 basal lobes usually overlapping, glossy, light yellowish-green, petioles red; fls. white or pink, in erect clusters. Blooming for a long period. Haiti. Hardy in the South, where it is used as a rock-garden plant.

Roxburghii A. DC. [*B. malabarica* Roxb., not Lam.]. Fibrous-rooted, sts. to 4 ft., branched, thick, succulent, brown-tomentose; lvs. to 8 in. long, 6 in. wide, irregularly ovate, acuminate, cordate basally, cupped, deeply veined, bristly-hairy, glossy green; fls. 1 in. across, white, opening one at a time; fr. 4-celled, succulent. Himalayas.

rubella Buch.-Ham. ex D. Don. Lvs. obliquely cordate, acuminate, toothed, on filiform petioles; fls. small, red, in many-fld. panicles. Not in cult. Material grown under this name is *B. fuscomaculata*.

×**rubellina:** *B.* ×*fuscomaculata.*

rubra Blume: *B. robusta* var. *rubra* (Blume) A. DC., which is not in cult. Material grown as *B. rubra* may be *B. coccinea,* but the name may also refer to the so-called *Begonia* Rubra Hybrids or Angel-wing Hybrids (BAMBOO BEGONIAS), developed from *B. coccinea,* with tall, bamboolike sts., long, narrow, winglike lvs., and white, pink, or red fls. *B. rubra odorata* is *B. corallina* cv. 'Odorata'.

rubro-venia Planch. Rhizomatous, rhizome slender, creeping, sts. low, erect, branched; lvs. obliquely oblong, long-pointed, shallowly scalloped, dark glossy green, brown-tomentose on veins on both surfaces, petioles long, grooved; fls. 1 in. across, in few-fld. clusters, greenish-white, larger tepals of male fls. red-veined on exterior. Spring. Himalayas.

rupicola Miq. Rhizomatous, rhizome slender, creeping; lvs. to 3 in. long, ovate, acuminate, toothed, green with yellowish margin; fls. pale pink, in few-fld., short clusters. Java.

salicifolia A. DC. Fibrous-rooted, sts. fruticose; lvs. 3–4 in. long, obliquely narrow-lanceolate, acuminate, shallowly toothed, green, on very short petioles; fls. ¾ in. across, white. Winter. Brazil.

salvadorensis: *B. carpinifolia.*

sanguinea Raddi. Fibrous-rooted, glabrous, glossy throughout, sts. 1½ ft., woody at base, red; lvs. 4–6 in. long, obliquely cordate, pointed, nearly peltate, minutely toothed, fleshy, bright green above, crimson underneath; fls. white, in forking cymes on peduncles 1 ft. high, male fls. to ¾ in. across, with 4 unequal tepals, female with 5 nearly equal tepals, ovary 3-angled, green. Spring. Brazil. Used medicinally in Brazil.

Sartorii Liebm. [*B. lobulata* A. DC.; *B. vitifolia* Hort., not Schott or Lindl.]. GRAPE-LEAF B. Fibrous-rooted, sts. erect, sparsely branched, light green; lvs. large, broad-ovate, shallowly lobed, finely toothed, glossy green above, brown-tomentose underneath; fls. white or pale pink, in erect clusters. Spring. S. Mex. and Guatemala. Cv. '**Variegata**': *B. lobata* cv.

×**Saundersonii:** *B.* ×*Digswelliana.*

scabrida A. DC. Fibrous-rooted, rough-hairy, sts. erect, stout, branched; lvs. obliquely broad-ovate, cordate basally, toothed, bright green; fls. many, ¾ in. across, white, in erect, forking cymes. Winter to spring. Venezuela.

scandens: see *B. glabra* and *B. convolvulacea. B. scandens alba* is *B. glabra.*

sceptrum Bull. Fibrous-rooted, sts. erect, thickened at base; lvs. obliquely ovate, deeply 4-lobed, with 1 lobe longer than the others, lobes again divided, toothed, upper surface green with silver streaks and spots, lower surface lighter green and rose-tinged; fls. large, white tinged with pink, on short, slightly pendulous peduncles. Brazil. Sometimes erroneously offered under the names *B. aconitifolia* or *B. diadema erecta.*

Scharffiana Regel. Fibrous-rooted, sts. 1–3 ft., stout, softly white-hairy; lvs. to 8 in. long, broad-ovate, pointed, olive-green above, bright red underneath; fls. to 1 in. across, waxy-white, with red flecks and red hairs when young, in few-fld. clusters, male fls. with 2–4 tepals, female with 4–5, ovary with 1 long wing. Brazil.

Scharffii Hook.f. [*B. Haageana* Hort. ex W. Wats.]. Fibrous-rooted, red-hairy, sts. 2–4 ft., woody; lvs. to 10 in. long, obliquely ovate, pointed, cordate basally, shallowly lobed, bronzy-green with red veins above, red underneath; fls. white, red-bearded on exterior, in large, drooping, many-fld. clusters, male fls. about 2 in. across, with 4 tepals, female smaller, with 5 tepals, ovary with nearly equal wings. Blooming all year. Brazil. Cv. '**Drostii**': see *B.* ×*Drostii.* Cv. '**Houghtonii**': see *B.* ×*Houghtonii.*

Schmidtiana Regel [*B. Schmidtii* Hort. Haage & Schmidt]. Fibrous-rooted, sts. usually 1 ft. or less, herbaceous, branched, hairy, red-tinged; lvs. to 3 in. long, obliquely ovate, acuminate, lobed, toothed, green above, hairy, reddish underneath; fls. many, ⅝ in. across, white tinted with rose, on short, axillary peduncles, male fls. with 4 tepals, female with 5 unequal tepals, ovary 3-angled, wings equal. Brazil. Used for summer bedding, or in the greenhouse in winter.

Schmidtii: *B. Schmidtiana.*

Schulziana Urb. & Ekm. Rhizomatous, rhizome slender, creeping, plant low, spreading; lvs. to 3 in. long, broad-ovate, sharply 5–7-lobed more than halfway to the center, white-scurfy; fls. pink, in erect, few-fld. clusters. Late autumn. Haiti.

secreta: *B. Seretii.*

×**sementacea** Hort.: *Begonia* Rex-Cultorum cv. 'Sementacea'. Lvs. irridescent, with very prominent veins.

semperflorens: *B. cucullata* var. *Hookeri.*

×**semperflorens-cultorum** Hort. Nomenclaturally perhaps better treated as *Begonia* Semperflorens-Cultorum Hybrids. BEDDING B., WAX B., WAX PLANT. Fibrous-rooted, bushy, sts. branching, succulent; lvs. ovate to broad-ovate, more symmetrical than in *B. cucullata* var. *Hookeri,* glossy, usually glabrous, occasionally sparsely hairy, green to bronzy-red or mahogany-red, or green variegated with white; fls. single or double, white to shades of pink or red, in small, axillary clusters. Blooming almost continuously, and very popular as summer bedding plants, in sun or shade, and as year-round pot plants for home or greenhouse.

A group of cvs. of hybrid origin, derived originally from *B. cucullata* var. *Hookeri* (formerly known as *B. semperflorens*) and *B. Schmidtiana,* but now including also descendants of crosses between these hybrids and such spp. as *B. foliosa* var. *miniata, B. gracilis, B. minor,* and *B. Roezlii.* Many strains and cvs. are known, varying chiefly in size and compactness of the plant, foliage color, and size, color, and degree of doubling of the fls. The nomenclature of these is sometimes rather confused.

Var. **gracilis** Hort. [*B.* ×*gracilis* Hort. Vilm.-Andr., not *B. gracilis* HBK; *B. semperflorens* Link & Otto var. *gracilis* Hort.]. This is nomenclaturally better treated as *Begonia* Semperflorens-Cultorum Hybrids, Gracilis Group. It originally included cvs. derived from crossing *B. gracilis* HBK with hybrids of *B. cucullata* var. *Hookeri* and *B. Schmidtiana,* but is now often more loosely applied to include any cv. of the *B.* Semperflorens-Cultorum complex which resembles the original *B. gracilis* hybrids. Plants dwarf, compact; lvs. glossy; fls. white to dark red.

Begonia Semperflorens-Cultorum cvs. with lvs. green, marbled with white, with the youngest lvs. emerging pure white and inrolled at the lower margins, and thus resembling miniature calla lilies, are known as CALLA-LILY B., or, less commonly, as YOUTH-AND-OLD-AGE B. These vary somewhat, from cv. to cv., in vigor, size of plant and lf., and color and doubleness of fls., but all are less vigorous and usually more difficult to grow than the relatively undemanding green- or reddish-lvd. cvs.

Seretii De Wild. [*B. secreta* Hort.]. Fibrous-rooted, glabrous, sts. to 1 ft., irregularly branched, succulent; lvs. to 7½ in. long, 9 in. wide, obliquely reniform, acute, cordate basally, palmately 5-lobed, toothed, sometimes ciliate, green above, red underneath; fls. pink, striped with red, with 2 tepals, ovary 3-angled, wingless. Winter. Congo region. Cv. 'Macrocarpa' is listed.

serratipetala Irmsch. Fibrous-rooted, sts. 2 ft., arching, bushy; lvs. small, obliquely ovate, long-pointed, sharply cut, crinkled, double-toothed, dark olive-green with deep pink raised dots above; fls. pink, female fls. with red-toothed tepals, in short, few-fld. clusters. New Guinea.

sikkimensis A. DC. Tuberous, tuber woody, sts. 1 ft. or more, erect, unbranched, succulent; lvs. to 6 in. long, obliquely broad-ovate, acuminate, 5–7-lobed, toothed, ciliate, fls., pedicels, and bracts bright red. Sikkim. Cv. '**Gigantea**'. Plant larger. Cv. '**Maculata**': 'Variegata'. Cv. '**Variegata**' [cv. 'Maculata']. Lvs. irregularly blotched.

socotrana Hook.f. Semituberous, sts. 6–12 in., ann., somewhat branched, slender, succulent, sparsely hairy, bearing at their base many fleshy bulblike buds; lvs. 4–10 in. across, centrally peltate, orbicular, depressed in center, margin rolled or scalloped; fls. many, rosy-pink, on slender, axillary peduncles, male fls. 2 in. across, with 5 nearly equal concave tepals, female with 5–6 equal tepals, ovary green, 3-angled, with 1 long wing. Winter. Socotra. *B. socotrana* has entered into the parentage of many important cvs. For example, crossed with *B. Dregei,* it has produced *Begonia* cv. 'Gloire de Lorraine', the first of the *Begonia* Cheimantha Hybrids; with *B. incarnata* cv. 'Purpurea', it has produced *Begonia* cv. 'Gloire de Sceaux'; with *B. Roezlii, Begonia* cvs. 'Triomphe de Lorraine' and 'Triomphe de Nancy'; with *B. strigillosa, Begonia* cv. 'Triomphe de Lemoine'; and with *Begonia* Tuberhybrida cv. 'Viscountess Doneraile', *Begonia* cv. 'John Heal', the first of the *Begonia* Hiemalis Hybrids.

sparsipila Bak. Rhizomatous, covered with short, fine, feltlike, rusty hairs; lvs. 8–9 in. long, 5–6 in. broad, peltate, obliquely ovate, acute, bright green and glabrous above; fls. ¾ in. across, pink, with 2 tepals, in many-fld., drooping corymbs, ovary with 3 nearly equal wings. Cent. Amer.

×**speculata** Hort.: *Begonia* Rex-Cultorum cv. 'Speculata'. GRAPE-LEAF B. Rhizomatous, low, hairy; lvs. crowded, to 8 in. across, obliquely broad-ovate to nearly orbicular, acuminate, lobed up to halfway to center, blistered, dull gray and speckled with gray above, reddish underneath; fls. 1 in. across, white, drooping, on long peduncles.

spinibarbis Irmsch. SEERSUCKER B. Fibrous-rooted, sts. 8 in. long, arching, sparsely branched, reddish, pilose; lvs. 3½–5½ in. long, broad-ovate, pointed, attenuate at base, entire to shallowly toothed, fleshy, golden-green above, red underneath, short-petioled; fls. to ¼ in. long, white, bearded with tiny spines on exterior, male fls. with 4 tepals, female with 5 toothed tepals, ovary pubescent. Brazil.

splendida: *B. robusta.*

Spraguei: *B. Mannii.*

squamosa: *B. vestita.*

squarrosa: see *B. stigmosa.*

stigmosa Lindl. [*B. hepatica maculata* Hort.; *B. squarrosa* Seem., not Liebm.]. Rhizomatous; lvs. small, orbicular, thick, light yellow-green, blotched with liver-colored markings above, scaly on the main nerves and hairy on finer veins underneath; fls. small, white to pinkish. Winter. S. Mex. to Colombia.

stipulacea Willd. [*B. angularis* Raddi; *B. zebrina* Hort.]. Fibrous-rooted, glabrous, sts. to 8 ft. long, spreading or drooping, bushy; lvs. 4–6 in. long, 1–3 in. wide, obliquely ovate, slender-pointed, glossy green with white veins above, tinged reddish underneath; fls. ⅝ in. across, white or pink, in large clusters above foliage. Winter. Brazil. Cv. 'Acutangula' [*B. acutangula* Hort.; *B. acutangularis* Hort.]. ANGEL-WING B. Larger, more erect, stouter, sts. thick, deeply grooved; lvs. larger, more coarsely toothed, more rounded at the tips, sometimes red underneath.

strigillosa A. Dietr. [*B. daedalea* É. Lemoine]. Rhizomatous, bushy, with clumps of hairs on veins, petioles, and peduncles; lvs. 3–6 in. long, 2½–3½ in. wide, obliquely ovate, acuminate, cordate basally, toothed, olive-green above, netted with brown veins; fls. white to pink, on peduncles shorter than foliage. Guatemala, Costa Rica.

subvillosa Klotzsch. [*Begonia* cv. 'Scotch Luxurians']. Fibrous-rooted, sts. 1–2 ft., rusty-villous or -tomentose; lvs. 1½–5 in. long, obliquely ovate, acute, obliquely cordate basally, ciliate, dark green and bristly-villous above, densely rusty-velvety underneath; fls. white, on axillary peduncles, bearded on exterior, male fls. with 2 large and 2 smaller tepals, female with 5, ovary pubescent, unequally 3-winged; seeds acuminate. Summer. Brazil.

suffruticosa Meissn. [*B. Richardsiana* T. Moore; *B. Richardsoniana* Houll.; *B. Richardsonii* Hort.]. MAPLE-LEAF B. Similar to *B. Dregei*, but smaller; lvs. smaller, more finely palmately lobed and toothed, with a red spot at sinuses of lobes; fls. white or light pink. Summer. Natal.

sulcata Scheidw. Fibrous-rooted, sts. to 3½ ft., glabrous; lvs. 2–4 in. long, 1½–3 in. wide, obliquely ovate, acute, cordate basally, shallowly lobed, doubly toothed, ciliate, bright green, short-petioled; fls. to ½ in. across, white, male fls. with 4 tepals, female with 5, ovary with 3 unequal wings. Colombia.

×suncana Hort. A name of no botanical standing, for *Begonia* cv. 'Suncana': *B. incana* × *B.* ×*ricinifolia* cv. 'Sunderbruckii'. Rhizomatous; lvs. ovate, pointed, shallowly and rather roundly lobed, green but brown-tomentose; fls. white, in clusters on tall peduncles.

×Sunderbruchii, ×Sunderbruckii: *B.* ×*ricinifolia* cv. 'Sunderbruckii'.

×superba Hort. Nomenclaturally, preferably treated as *Begonia* Superba Hybrids. A group of cvs. derived from crossing *B. aconitifolia* and *Begonia* cv. 'Lucerna'. Fibrous-rooted, sts. tall, canelike, vigorous, glabrous; lvs. narrow-ovate, irregularly lobed, bright green; fls. large, clear pink. Cv. 'Superba Azella'. Tall, vigorous; lvs. deeply lobed, green with paler veins, splashed with silver, the margin red; fls. pink. Cv. 'Superba Kenzii'. Lvs. less deeply and sharply lobed, sometimes sparsely splashed with silver; fls. white.

Sutherlandii Hook.f. Tuberous or semituberous, sts. 1–2 ft., ann., herbaceous, bright red; lvs. 4–6 in. long, lanceolate, deeply lobed at base, serrate, green with red margin and veins, petioles slender, red; fls. many, coppery- or salmon-red, in axillary or terminal cymes, male fls. with 4 unequal tepals, female with 5 equal tepals, ovary with 3 equal wings. Summer. Natal. Cv. 'Major'. Lvs. larger.

Templinii: *B. phyllomaniaca* cv.

tenuifolia Dryand. Rhizomatous, sts. 2 ft., ascending, thick, stubby, short-branched; lvs. obliquely broad-ovate, acuminate, obscurely lobed, toothed, bright green, long-petioled; fls. large, soft pink, male with 4 tepals, female with 5, in few-fld. clusters, not surpassing foliage. Autumn and winter. Java.

tessaricarpa C. B. Clarke. Similar to *B. Roxburghii*, but lvs. green with reddish flush in center, fls. much smaller, infls. shorter, caps. less succulent. Assam.

Teuscheri Hort. Linden. Fibrous-rooted, pilose, sts. to 6 ft., erect, branched; lvs. large, ovate-lanceolate, shallowly lobed, serrate, olive-green with grayish blotches or dots and red margin above, red and prominently veined underneath; fls. deep pink, in axillary clusters. Malay Pen.

×Thurstonii Hort. ex Kennedy: *B. metallica* × *B. sanguinea*. Fibrous-rooted, nearly glabrous, sts. 2 ft., bushy, glossy; lvs. 8–10 in. long, 5 in. wide, orbicular, acuminate, glossy bronzy-green above, red underneath; fls. 1½ in. across, pink, reddish-bearded, in erect clusters. Summer.

tomentosa Schott. Fibrous-rooted, white-hairy, sts. unbranched, woody; lvs. 4–6 in. long, ovate, acuminate, cordate basally, entire to toothed, thick, cupped when young, light green with a fine red line along margin; fls. many, 1 in. across, white or pink, bearded on exterior. Brazil.

×tuberhybrida Voss [*B.* ×*tuberosa* Hort., not *B. tuberosa* Lam.]. Alternatively, and preferably, called the *Begonia* Tuberhybrida Hybrids. HYBRID TUBEROUS B. A group of cvs. derived, through hybridization and selection, from several Andean spp., including *B. boliviensis*, *B. Clarkei*, *B. Davisii*, *B. Pearcei*, *B. rosiflora*, *B. Veitchii*, and perhaps *B. Froebelii*, *B. gracilis* and others. Tuberous, stemless or st. short, erect or procumbent; fls. in a wide range of colors, white or shades of pink, rose, red, yellow, or orange, borne in 3's with 1 male fl. between 2 female, or in pairs, male fls. up to 6 in. across or more, single or double, of varied form, sometimes fragrant, female fls. smaller, single. Normally summer flowering, planted outdoors in summer, dormant during winter; occasionally forced under artificial light at other seasons. Named cvs. are known but are seldom offered or grown in Amer., most plants being unnamed seedlings. Begonias of this hybrid complex are usually divided into several groups based on plant habit or form or color of the male fls. There is some overlapping among these groups:

1. Single Group [*B.* ×*gigantea* Hort., not Wallich]. Fls. large, single, with 4 usually flat tepals.

2. Crispa or Frilled Group [*B.* ×*crispa* Hort.]. Fls. large, single, with margins of tepals frilled and ruffled.

3. Cristata or Crested Group [*B.* ×*cristata* Hort., not Koord.]. Fls. large, single, with a frilled tuft or crest near center of each tepal.

4. Narcissiflora or Daffodil-flowered Group [*B.* ×*narcissiflora* Hort.]. Fls. large, more or less double, with central tepals spreading-erect and forming a "trumpet" reminiscent of that in daffodils.

5. Camellia or Camelliiflora Group [*B.* ×*camellia* Hort.; *B.* ×*camelliiflora* Hort.]. Fls. large, double, resembling camellias, of various solid colors and unruffled.

6. Ruffled Camellia Group. Fls. as in the Camellia Group, but ruffled.

7. Rosebud or Rosiflora Group [*B.* ×*rosiflora* Hort., not Hook.f.]. Fls. large, double, with a raised rosebudlike center.

8. Fimbriata Plena or Carnation Group [*B.* ×*fimbriata* Hort., not Liebm.]. Fls. large, double, carnationlike, with tepals fringed on margin.

9. Picotee Group. Fls. large, usually double and of camellia form, with tepals margined with a different shade or color blending with the dominant color.

10. Marginata Group [*B. crispa marginata* Hort.; *B.* ×*marginata* Hort.]. Fls. as in the Picotee Group, but tepals edged with a precise line of a color different from the dominant color.

11. Marmorata Group [*B.* ×*marmorata* Hort.]. Fls. as in the Camellia Group, but rose-colored, blotched or spotted with white.

12. Pendula or Hanging-basket Group [*B.* ×*Lloydii* Hort.; *B.* ×*Lloydii pendula* Hort.; *B.* ×*pendula* Hort., not Ridl.]. Sts. trailing or pendant; fls. many, small to large, single or double.

13. Multiflora [*B.* ×*floribunda* Hort.; *B.* ×*maxima* Hort.; *B.* ×*multiflora* Hort., not Benth.; *B.* ×*multiflora gigantea* Hort.; *B.* ×*multiflora grandiflora* Hort.; *B.* ×*multiflora maxima* Hort.; *B.* ×*tuberosa floribunda* Hort.; *B.* ×*tuberosa multiflora* Hort.]. Plants low, bushy, compact; fls. many, relatively small, single to double.

tuberosa Lam.: probably *B. muricata*. Material cult. as *B.* ×*tuberosa* is *Begonia* Tuberhybrida Hybrids; see under *B.* ×*tuberhybrida*. *B.* ×*tuberosa floribunda* and *B.* ×*tuberosa multiflora* are *Begonia* Tuberhybrida Hybrids, Multiflora Group; see under *B.* ×*tuberhybrida*.

udisilvestris: *B. carpinifolia.*

ulmifolia Willd. ELM-LEAF B. Fibrous-rooted, sts. to 6 ft., erect, branched, grooved, light green; lvs. to 5 in. long, ovate-oblong, doubly serrate, somewhat rough-hairy, green; fls. many, ½ in. across, white, male fls. with 2 tepals, female with 5. Spring. Venezuela.

undulata Schott [*B. alba perfecta* Hort.; *B. picta alba* Hort.]. Fibrous-rooted, sts. 3–6 ft., branching freely, thick at base, succulent till old; lvs. 3–3½ in. long, 1–1½ in. wide, oblong-lanceolate, acuminate, wavy, glabrous, glossy green; fls. 1 in. across, in pendulous clusters, white, male fls. with 2 large and 2 very small tepals, ovary of female fls. with 3 nearly equal wings. Summer to autumn. Brazil. The name *B. undulata* has also been used by horticulturists for *B. Limmin-*

gheiana. Cv. **'Perfectiflora'** [*B. alba perfecta* cv. 'Grandiflora'; *B. perfectiflora* Hort.]. Fls. larger, ovary and wings white.

urophylla Hook. Fibrous-rooted, sparsely soft-bristly-hairy, stemless; lvs. large, broadly cordate, long-pointed, margin incised-dentate; fls. white, slightly flushed pink, with 2 tepals, very concave, in large, many-fld. panicles, female fls. about ¼ as large as male, ovary with 1 large wing. Spring. Origin unknown.

urticifolia Sm.: *B. urticae* L.f., a sp. not in cult. Material cult. under the name *B. urticifolia* is *B. buddleiifolia.*

valdensium A. DC. PHILODENDRON-LEAF B. Fibrous-rooted, sts. erect; lvs. to 12 in. long, obliquely broad-ovate, acuminate, cordate basally, flat to slightly wavy, grass-green, with prominent ivory veins above, petiole with a fringed collar at apex; fls. pinkish to white. Summer. Brazil.

Valerii Standl. Rhizomatous, rhizome procumbent, very thick; lvs. to 1 ft. across, orbicular, shallowly lobed, serrate, rippled, dark green, sparsely hairy above, more densely brown-hairy underneath, petioles 1 ft. long, covered with dense, long, brown hairs; fls. white, in panicles. Costa Rica.

×**Vedderi** Hort. A name of no botanical standing for *Begonia* cv. 'Vedderi'. Parentage unknown; fibrous-rooted, sts. 3–6 ft., erect, soft-hairy; lvs. 6–8 in. long, 2–3 in. wide, ovate-lanceolate, crenately lobed, toothed, dull olive-green, red-tinged underneath, with red veins; fls. white to pale pink, pink-bearded. Autumn. Raised by Chauncey Vedder, Calif., 1922. Another *B.* × *Vedderi* Hort., a seedling of *B. compta* raised by A. D. Robinson, Calif., 1933, has been renamed *Begonia* cv. 'Robinson's Vedderi'. This has sts. to 3 ft., bushy, hairy; lvs. triangular-ovate, with 1 prominent lobe between base and apex, wavy-margined, crenately toothed, green above, gray-green and red-veined underneath; fls. pink, pink-bearded on exterior.

Veitchii Hook.f. [*B. rosiflora* Hook.f.]. Tuberous, sts. very short, succulent, green; lvs. 2–4 in. long, nearly orbicular, lobed and toothed, ciliate, sparsely pubescent to glabrous and green above with main veins radiating from a bright carmine spot, glaucous and often densely pubescent underneath; fls. 2½ in. across, cinnabar-red. Peru. Not now in cult., but has entered into the parentage of many *Begonia* Tuberhybrida cvs.

Vellozoana: *B. Olsoniae.*

venosa Skan ex Hook.f. Fibrous-rooted, white-scurfy, sts. erect, thick, hidden by large, thin, papery stipules; lvs. reniform, depressed at center, not peltate, fleshy, appearing frosted; fls. white, fragrant, on long, arching peduncles covered with soft, white hairs. Late summer to spring. Brazil.

×**Verschaffeltiana:** *B.* ×*Verschaffeltii.*

×**Verschaffeltii** Regel [*B.* ×*Verschaffeltiana* É. Lemoine]: *B. caroliniifolia* × *B. manicata.* Rhizomatous; lvs. 10–12 in. long, ovate, acuminate, lobed, toothed, green; fls. rose, in large clusters. Winter.

versicolor Irmsch. FAIRY-CARPET B. Rhizomatous, rhizome short, red-pilose; lvs. 3–5 in. across, obliquely broad-ovate or oblong, short-acuminate, minutely toothed, ciliate, dark green with silver markings, and with red along the veins above, red underneath; fls. red, bearded on exterior, in dichotomous cymes, ovary with 2 cells. Yunnan.

vestita C. DC. [*B. squamosa* C. DC.]. Rhizomatous, rough-scaly; lvs. to 3 in. across, cordate to reniform, pointed, cordate basally, toothed, fleshy, bright green, hairy on veins underneath; fls. white or pink, in few-branched, few-fld. clusters. Costa Rica, Panama.

×**Viaudii** André: *B.* × *Credneri* × *B.* × *Duchartrei.* Fibrous-rooted, medium-sized, hairy; lvs. ovate, olive-green, shallowly toothed; fls. large, white, white-bearded, on long, red peduncles.

vitifolia Schott [*B. palmifolia* Hort.]. Fibrous-rooted; lvs. ovate or orbicular, cordate basally, lobed, finely serrate, hairy; fls. white. Brazil. Not in cult.; material cult. as *B. vitifolia* may be *B. Lindleyana* or *B. Sartorii.*

Wallichiana Steud. Fibrous-rooted, shortly glandular-hairy, sts. to 1 ft., branched, bushy; lvs. 2–3 in. long, obliquely broad-ovate, cordate basally, toothed, viscid-pubescent on both surfaces; fls. ½ in. across, white or tinged with pink, pilose on exterior, male fls. with 4 unequal tepals, female with 5 equal tepals, ovary with 3 nearly equal brown wings; seeds ellipsoid. Autumn. India.

×**weltoniensis** Hort. ex André [*B.* ×*weltoniensis* cv. 'Rosea']: *B. Dregei* × *B. Sutherlandii.* MAPLE-LEAF B., GRAPEVINE B. Tuberous or semituberous, sts. to 3 ft., branched, reddish, with bases much swollen; lvs. 3 in. across, ovate, acuminate, shallowly lobed, toothed, dark glossy green with purple veins above, lighter green underneath; fls. pink or white, many, on short peduncles. Cv. 'Alba'. Lvs. with green veins, less deeply lobed; fls. white. Cv. 'Rosea': *B.* ×*weltoniensis.*

×**Wettsteinii** Weick ex Wettst. Said to be a hybrid between *B. corallina* and *B.* ×*ascotiensis.* Fibrous-rooted, glabrous, sts. short, erect but weak; lvs. small, ovate-lanceolate, wavy-margined, coarsely toothed, green; fls. coral-red, in small, drooping clusters.

Wrightiana A. DC. Fibrous-rooted, sts. to 3 ft. or more, woody; lvs. obliquely ovate, acuminate, cordate basally, toothed, pilose; fls. pink, ovary with 3 unequal wings. Cuba.

xanthina Hook. Similar to *B. rex,* but lvs. glossy green above, purplish underneath, fls. 1½ in. across, bright yellow, tinged with red on exterior, male fls. larger than female. Spring. Himalayas.

zebrina: *B. stipulacea.*

×**Zugensis** Hort. A name of no botanical standing, used for hybrids between *B.* × *Credneri* and *B. paulensis.*

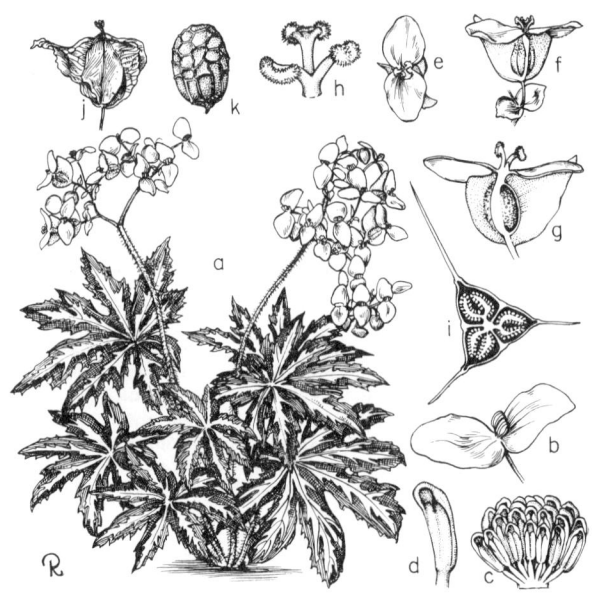

BEGONIACEAE. *Begonia heracleifolia:* **a,** plant, × ⅛; **b,** male flower, × 1; **c,** stamens, × 3; **d,** single anther, × 6; **e,** female flower, face view, × ½; **f,** female flower, side view, × ½; **g,** female flower, vertical section, × ¾; **h,** stigmas, × 2; **i,** ovary, cross section, × 2; **j,** fruit, × 1; **k,** seed, × 30.

BEGONIACEAE Agardh. BEGONIA FAMILY. Dicot.; 3 genera and over 1,000 spp., in the tropics and subtropics of both hemispheres; monoecious herbs, usually per., sometimes shrublike, mostly more or less succulent; lvs. alt., usually oblique at base and asymmetrical, stipuled; fls. unisexual, radially or bilaterally symmetrical, tepals separate, stamens many, ovary inferior, usually 3-celled and 3-winged, stigmas usually twisted; fr. a caps. with axile placentation, seeds many, minute, usually anatropous, without albumen. *Begonia,* which includes all but about 15 of the spp. of the family, is the only genus in general cult. It is distinguished from the other 2 genera, *Hillebrandia* D. Oliver and *Symbegonia* Warb., by the number, position, and distinctness of the perianth parts and their attachment on the ovary.

BEILSCHMIEDIA Nees. *Lauraceae.* Over 200 spp. of evergreen trees and shrubs, native mostly from s. and se. Asia to Australia and New Zeal., but several spp. in Amer.; lvs. alt. or opp., leathery, venation pinnate, often conspicuous, reticulate; infl. paniculate; fls. bisexual, calyx tube short, deciduous, fertile stamens 9, in 3 whorls, anthers in whorls 1 and 2 introrse, in whorl 3 extrorse; fr. a berry on naked pedicel, not enclosed by calyx tube.

Anay (S. F. Blake) Kosterm. Tree, to 60 ft. and more; lvs. alt., elliptic, to 8 in. long; infl. axillary, somewhat pubescent; fls. small; fr. narrowly pear-shaped, to 6 in. long, glossy, purplish-black. Guatemala. Fr. somewhat like an avocado in appearance and flavor.

Miersii (C. Gay) Kosterm. Tree, to 50 ft., lvs. nearly opp., leathery, ovate, to 4 in. long, entire, venation conspicuously reticulate. Chile.

Tawa (A. Cunn.) Benth. Tree, to 100 ft., branchlets slender, glabrous or nearly so; lvs. alt., occasionally nearly opp., lanceolate, to 4 in. long, entire, thinly leathery, midvein and main veins evident, not obscured by reticulation; infl. to 3 in. long. New Zeal.

BELAMCANDA Adans. [*Pardanthus* Ker-Gawl.]. *Iridaceae.* Two spp. of hardy per. herbs, with stout rhizomes, native to China and Japan; lvs. broad, irislike, infl. loosely corymbose; fls. twisting spirally as they fade, perianth segms. 6, not united, about equal, style brs. 3, flattened and emarginate at apex; fr. a caps., valves reflexing and exposing column covered with glossy black seeds resembling a blackberry.

Often planted in gardens and of easy culture; propagated by seeds or division.

chinensis (L.) DC. [*Pardanthus chinensis* (L.) Ker-Gawl.]. BLACKBERRY LILY, LEOPARD FLOWER. Sts. 3–4 ft.; lvs. basal and cauline, to 10 in. long, 1 in. wide; fls. deep orange with red dots, to 2 in. across, starlike, perianth segms. acute, filaments reddish-purple. China, Japan. Thrives in full sun and sandy loam. Used medicinally by the Chinese.

flabellata Grey. Sts. 12–20 in.; basal lvs. glaucous, about 8 in. long, 1½ in. wide; infl. stout, leafy; fls. light yellow, about 2½ in. across, perianth segms. obtuse, spotted orange at base, filaments white. Reported as first collected in Japan. Does well in partial shade, with abundant moisture.

BELLEVALIA Lapeyr. *Liliaceae.* About 45 spp. of bulbous, scapose, per. herbs, native to the Medit. region, Turkestan, and n. Afghanistan; bulbs tunicate; lvs. more than 2, all basal, linear to lanceolate, margins membranous, often ciliate or scabrous; fls. campanulate, funnelform, or tubular, never constricted, white, lilac, or violet, fading to brown, in racemes, perianth deeply 6-lobed, stamens 6, arising from base of lobes; fr. a 3-lobed, loculicidal caps. with prominent ribs, seeds black to bluish, with a waxy bloom.

Culture as for *Hyacinthus.*

ciliata (Cyr.) Nees [*Hyacinthus ciliatus* Cyr.]. To about 1½ ft.; lvs. 3–5, lanceolate, margins strongly ciliate; fls. campanulate, lilac, with greenish lobes, to ½ in. long, in a loose, 30–50-fld., conical raceme, anthers purple; fruiting pedicels to 4 in. long. Nw. Afr., s. Eur., w. Asia Minor.

romana (L.) Rchb. [*Hyacinthus romanus* L.]. To about 1½ ft.; lvs. 3–6, linear, longer than scape, margins glabrous; fls. campanulate, white or slightly tinged with blue, to about ⅜ in. long, in a 20–30-fld., cylindrical raceme, anthers violet; fruiting pedicels to ⅝ in. long. S. France to Greece.

Saviczii Voronov [*Hyacinthus Saviczii* (Voronov) Vved.]. To about 16 in.; lvs. 3–6, oblong-lanceolate, to 10 in. long, glaucous above, margins ciliate to scabrous; fls. campanulate, white turning grayish-brown, to ⅜ in. long, in a loose, 15–30-fld., conical raceme, anthers violet; lower fruiting pedicels to 2 in. long. Region e. of Caspian Sea, s. to Afghanistan and s. Iran.

BELLIS L. DAISY. *Compositae* (Aster Tribe). About 15 spp. of ann. or per. herbs, native to Eur. and Medit. region, cespitose or with branching sts.; lvs. alt. or all basal; fl. heads radiate, solitary, peduncled, involucre hemispherical or campanulate, involucral bracts leaflike, equal or unequal, in 2 rows, receptacle convex to conical, naked; disc fls. bisexual, yellow, ray fls. female, white to pink or purple; achenes compressed, with thick margins, not ribbed, pappus absent.

English daisies are easily raised from seeds sown in the spring for flowers the following year. The cultivars are propagated by division in cool weather, since the seeds do not reproduce true to type. The plants are favorites for edging and colonizing in lawns; they should have fertile moist soil.

caerulescens, coerulescens: *B. rotundifolia* var.

monstrosa: *B. perennis* cv.

perennis L. ENGLISH DAISY. Per.; lvs. in a basal rosette, spatulate to obovate, usually 1–2 in. long, crenate-toothed, glabrous to pubescent; fl. heads to 2 in. across, on scapes 3–6 in. or occasionally to 8 in. high; ray fls. white to rose. Spring, early summer. Eur., w. Asia; adventive and more or less established as a weed in lawns and waste places in much of U.S. Cvs. are: 'Monstrosa', heads large, ray fls. dark red;

'Prolifera', secondary heads proliferating from axils of involucral bracts, appearing like hen-and-chickens; 'Rosea', ray fls. rose-pink; 'Tubulosa', ray fls. quilled, rose.

rotundifolia Boiss. & Reut. Per.; lvs. in a basal rosette, ovate to orbicular, to 1¼ in. long, sinuate-toothed, on petioles to 3 in. long; heads to 1¼ in. across; ray fls. white. Algeria, Morocco. Var. **coerulescens** Hook.f. [*B. caerulescens* Coss. ex J. Ball]. Ray fls. blue. Algeria, Morocco.

BELLIUM L. *Compositae* (Aster Tribe). About 4 spp. of ann. or per. herbs, native to Medit. region; lvs. all basal; fl. heads radiate, solitary on long scapes, involucre hemispherical, involucral bracts imbricate in 2 rows, receptacle naked; disc fls. bisexual, fertile, yellow, ray fls. female, white; achenes somewhat compressed, pappus of an outer row of white scales alternating with an inner row of long, rough bristles.

bellidioides L. Stoloniferous per.; lvs. spatulate, blade to ¼ in. long, entire, on pubescent petioles to ½–¾ in. long; heads to ⅛ in. across; ray fls. white to pinkish. Balearic Is., Corsica, Sardinia.

minutum L. Ann.; lvs. ovate-spatulate, entire, long-petioled; heads to ½ in. across, on scapes to about 3 in. long; disc fls. yellow, the lobes purplish on back, ray fls. white. Greece, Asia Minor.

BELOPERONE: *JUSTICIA.* **B. Amherstiae:** *J. brasiliana;* **B. comosa:** *J. fulvicoma;* **B. guttata:** *J. Brandegeana;* **B. longispicua, B. lutea, B. tomentosa:** see *J. Brandegeana;* **B. violacea:** *J. carthaginensis.*

BELOTIA A. Rich. *Tiliaceae.* Perhaps not more than 3 spp. of trees, native to Cent. Amer. and W. Indies; lvs. alt., simple, serrulate; fls. in axillary cymes near ends of brs., sepals 5, petals 5, with blue or violet, nectariferous spot at base, androgynophore present, ciliate at apex, stamens many, separate; fr. a caps., flattened, 2-celled, cells with several biseriate, ciliate seeds.

grewiifolia A. Rich. Tree, 25–60 ft., bark light gray, rather smooth; lvs. ovate to oblong-ovate, 4–8 in. long, narrowly long-acuminate, green above, tomentose beneath; cymes few- to many-fld., shorter than lvs.; sepals pink, about ¼ in. long, petals violet, bifid at apex, as long as sepals; caps. nearly ½ in. long, hirsute, truncate and beaked at apex. Cuba, Cent. Amer.

mexicana (DC.) K. Schum. Similar to *B. grewiifolia,* but having sepals ⅜ in. long or more and caps. ½–¾ in. long. S. Mex., Cent. Amer.

BENINCASA Savi. *Cucurbitaceae.* One sp., an ann., hairy, monoecious pumpkinlike tendril-bearing vine probably native to Malay Arch.; fls. solitary, axillary, calyx lobes toothed, reflexed, leaflike, corolla rotate, male fls. with 3, separate stamens, borne on the short tube, anthers flexuous, female fls. with ovary inferior, placentas 3, parietal; fr. large, fleshy, indehiscent, seeds many, horizontal.

Grown in southern and eastern Asia for the large fruit, which is used as a vegetable when young and in making preserves and sweet pickles when ripe. Cultivation as for pumpkin and squash.

cerifera: *B. hispida.*

hispida (Thunb.) Cogn. [*B. cerifera* Savi]. WAX GOURD, WHITE G., ASH G., ZIT-KWA, TUNKA, CHINESE WATERMELON, CHINESE PRESERVING MELON, WHITE PUMPKIN. Long-running vine; lvs. broadly cordate-ovate, angled or somewhat lobed and toothed; corolla yellow, veiny, nearly rotate, to 3 in. across; fr. oblong to cylindrical, to 16 in. long, hairy, white-waxy, flesh white, seeds oblong, pointed, white, 5⁄16–½ in. long. Se. Asia. Has been grown erroneously as CASSABANANA, which is *Sicana odorifera.*

BENSONIA: *BENSONIELLA.*

BENSONIELLA C. V. Mort. [*Bensonia* Abrams & Bacig.]. *Saxifragaceae.* One sp., a slender, per. herb of s. Ore.; lvs. mostly basal; fls. small, white, sepals, petals, and stamens 5, filaments and styles elongated; fr. a caps., dehiscing before mature. Similar to *Mitella,* but with elongate filaments and styles.

oregona (Abrams & Bacig.) C. V. Mort. [*Bensonia oregona* Abrams & Bacig.]. Lvs. broadly ovate to 2½ in. long, cordate at base, 5–9-lobed, petioles 3–5 in. long; fls. in racemes on stalks 12–16 in. long.

BENZOIN: LINDERA. **B. aestivale:** *L. Benzoin.* **B. praecox:** *Parabenzoin praecox.* **B. trilobum:** *Parabenzoin trilobum.*

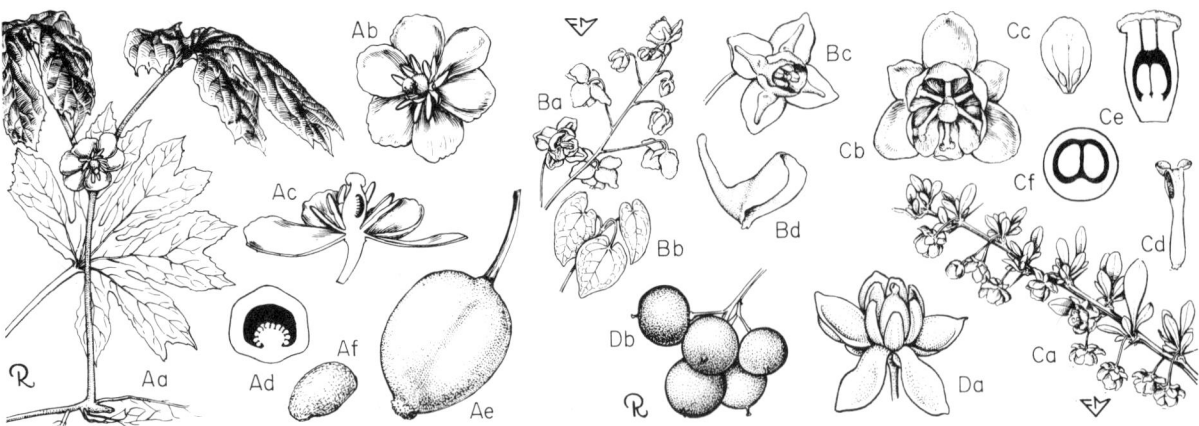

BERBERIDACEAE. **A,** *Podophyllum peltatum:* **Aa,** plant and leaf, × ⅙; **Ab,** flower, × ⅓; **Ac,** flower, vertical section, × ½; **Ad,** ovary, cross section, × 1½; **Ae,** fruit, × ½; **Af,** seed, × 2. **B,** *Epimedium versicolor* cv. 'Sulphureum': **Ba,** part of inflorescence, × ½; **Bb,** part of compound leaf, × ¼; **Bc,** flower, × 1; **Bd,** petal, × 2. **C,** *Berberis Thunbergii:* **Ca,** flowering branch, × ½; **Cb,** flower, × 2; **Cc,** petal with two basal glands, × 2; **Cd,** stamen, × 4; **Ce,** pistil, vertical section, × 5; **Cf,** ovary, cross section, × 8. **D,** *Nandina domestica:* **Da,** flower, × 2; **Db,** fruits, × 1. (B, C from Bailey, *Manual of Cultivated Plants,* ed. 2.)

BERBERIDACEAE Juss. BARBERRY FAMILY. Dicot.; 10 or more genera of herbs and shrubs, native to the N. Temp. Zone; lvs. radical, or cauline and alt., simple or compound; fls. solitary or in racemes or panicles, bisexual, sepals and petals often similar, usually imbricate in 2 or more series, stamens as many as petals to twice as many, ovary superior, 1-celled; fr. a berry, or dry and irregularly or obliquely dehiscent. The genera in cult. are: *Achlys, Berberis, Bongardia, Caulophyllum, Diphylleia, Epimedium, Jeffersonia, ×Mahoberberis, Mahonia, Nandina, Podophyllum, Ranzania,* and *Vancouveria.*

BERBERIDOPSIS Hook.f. *Flacourtiaceae.* One sp., a somewhat climbing evergreen shrub, native to Chile; lvs. alt.; fls. in terminal racemes, sepals and petals spirally arranged, intergrading, the inner parts longer than the outer, stamens 5–15; fr. a berry.

Grown outdoors in Calif. Zone 9. Propagated by seeds, green wood cuttings in spring, or layers in autumn.

corallina Hook.f. Lvs. ovate-cordate, to 3 in. long, coarsely sharp-toothed; fls. ⁵⁄₁₆ in. long, on long pedicels, the bracts, sepals, and petals red.

BERBERIS L. BARBERRY. *Berberidaceae.* Nearly 500 spp., most numerous in S. Amer. and e. Asia, also in N. Amer., Eur., and n. Afr.; usually spiny shrubs with yellow wood, the mature first-year sts. yellow or red to nearly black; lvs. deciduous and brightly colored in autumn, or evergreen, simple, often with spiny margins, in fascicles or whorls on short shoots usually subtended by simple or divided spines; fls. yellow to red, solitary or in axillary subumbellate fascicles or racemes, sepals and petals usually 6, in 2 series, the sepals petal-like, stamens 6, ovary 1-celled; fr. a red, yellow, or black berry, style often persistent.

Barberries are widely grown as hedges and as specimen bushes for their foliage or for the attractive flowers in spring and the fruits in autumn and winter. Most of the evergreen species are not hardy in the northern states. They do best in moist, well-drained soils, but the deciduous species tolerate drier soils. All are of easy cultivation. Propagated by seeds, which should be separated from the pulp and sown in autumn, and which germinate the following spring; by layers; by cuttings of young wood in early June planted in sand in a shaded hotbed; sometimes by suckers removed from the parent plant; and rare kinds by grafting on common stocks.

The stem rust of wheat, oats, barley, and rye passes one stage of its development on susceptible kinds of barberry, and many states have adopted a program to eradicate these kinds. The most susceptible species is *B. vulgaris,* but *B. canadensis* is also attacked, as well as some of the hybrids between *B. Thunbergii* and *B. vulgaris.*

aggregata C. K. Schneid. SALMON B. Deciduous, to 5 ft., mature sts. pale yellow, grooved, spines 3-parted; lvs. to 1 in. long, spiny-margined, dull yellow-green above; fls. in sessile panicles to 1 in. long; fr. pale red, style short. W. China. Var. **Prattii:** *B. Prattii.*

amurensis Rupr. Deciduous, to 11 ft., mature sts. pale yellow to gray, angled and grooved, spines 3-parted; lvs. to 3 in. long, densely spinulose-toothed; fls. in drooping racemes to 4 in. long; fr. red or bluish at base, style lacking. Manchuria. Var. **japonica:** *B. Regeliana.*

Aquifolium: *Mahonia Aquifolium.*

aristata DC. Evergreen, to 12 ft., mature sts. pale yellow, spines mostly 3-parted toward base of st.; lvs. to 3 in. long or more, entire or with few spiny teeth; fls. in 3–25-fld. racemes; fr. bright red, with slightly blue bloom, style evident. Nepal. Most plants cult. under this name are *B. floribunda.*

atrocarpa C. K. Schneid. Evergreen, dense, to 8 ft., mature sts. finely black-roughened, angled and grooved, spines 3-parted, to 2 in. long; lvs. thick, green, paler and dull beneath; fls. in 5–9-fld. fascicles; fr. black, style short. W. China.

Beaniana C. K. Schneid. Deciduous, compact, to 8 ft., mature sts. pale yellow-gray, angled and grooved, spines 3-parted, to 1 in. long; lvs. to 2 in. long, with 5–12 marginal spines, deep green; fls. in loose panicles; fr. dark red, with heavy mauve bloom, style lacking. W. China.

bidentata Lechl. Evergreen, to 5 ft., mature sts. grayish, cylindrical, spines 3-parted; lvs. lanceolate, with reflexed margins and 2 spiny teeth at apex, glaucous beneath; fls. in few-fld. corymbs longer than lvs.; fr. violet. Chile.

brachypoda Maxim. Deciduous, to 4 ft., mature sts. yellow-gray, spines 3-parted; lvs. to 3 in. long, with 25–40 marginal spines, dull light green; fls. in 20–30-fld. racemes, petals longer than inner sepals, fr. blood-red, style short. China. Most material grown under this name is *B. mitifolia.*

buxifolia Lam. MAGELLAN B. Evergreen, to 7 ft., mature sts. red-brown, spines present or absent, weak; lvs. entire, leathery, dull dark green; fr. globose, blue, style absent. S. S. Amer. Var. **buxifolia.** The typical var.; spines weak; pedicels to ⅜ in. long; fr. ¼–⁵⁄₁₆ in. long. Var. **nana** Mouillef. Similar, but compact, 2 ft. Var. **papillosa** C. K. Schneid. [*B. dulcis* Paxt.]. Lvs. minutely warty beneath; pedicels to 1³⁄₁₆ in. long; fr. to ⅝ in. long. Cv. 'Pygmaea' has been listed.

calliantha Mullig. Evergreen, to 3 ft., mature sts. red-brown, spines ⅜–¾ in. long; lvs. to 2 in. long, with 10–20 spiny teeth, lustrous deep green above with impressed reticulate veins, waxy-white beneath; fls. in fascicles to 1 in. across, nodding; fr. black, with a bloom. Tibet.

canadensis Mill. AMERICAN B., ALLEGHANY B. Deciduous, to 6 ft., mature sts. dull, angled, spines 3-parted; lvs. to 2 in. long, with 1–9 spiny teeth, grayish-white beneath; fls. bright yellow, in racemes to 1¾ in. long; fr. scarlet. Va., s. to Ga. and Mo.

candidula (C. K. Schneid.) C. K. Schneid. Evergreen, dwarf shrub, to 3 ft., 5 ft. across, spines long, 3-parted; lvs. lustrous dark green above, white beneath; fls. solitary; fr. pale gray. China.

×Chenaultii Ahrendt: *B. Gagnepainii* × *B. verruculosa.* Similar to *B. Gagnepainii,* but differing in having foliage shiny, brs. arching, and petals subentire.

chinensis Poir. Deciduous, to 6 ft., mature sts. dark red to brown, spines weak; lvs. to 1⅜ in. long, entire; fls. in subumbellate racemes; fr. dark red. Caucasus.

circumserrata (C. K. Schneid.) C. K. Schneid. Deciduous, to 3½ ft., mature sts. yellow, spines simple to 5-parted, to 1 in. long; lvs. to 1½ in. long, with 15–40 minute marginal spines, dull gray beneath; fls. in fascicles; fr. pale red or yellowish-red. Nw. China.

corallina: *B. ×stenophylla* cv.

cretica L. Deciduous, to 5 ft. or procumbent, mature sts. dark red or purple, spines 3-parted; lvs. about ¾ in. long, entire; fls. in short 2–7-fld. racemes; fr. purplish-black. Greece, Crete, Cyprus.

Darwinii Hook. DARWIN'S B. Evergreen, to 8 ft., mature sts. dark brown, spines 3–5-parted; lvs. to about ¾ in. long, with 2 spiny teeth on each margin, rigid, lustrous dark green above, paler beneath; fls. orange-yellow to red on red pedicels, in 10–30-fld. racemes; fr. black, with blue bloom. Chile, Argentina. Suitable only for the South and Calif. Cvs. **'Depressa'** and **'Nana'** are dwarf forms.

diaphana Maxim. Deciduous, to 6 ft., mature sts. pale yellow, spines 3-parted; lvs. to 1¼ in. long, with 4–12 spiny teeth, dull gray-green above, gray beneath; fls. bright yellow, solitary or in fascicles or racemose; fr. bright or dark red, style short. W. China.

dictyota: *Mahonia dictyota.*

Dielsiana Fedde. Deciduous, to 9 ft., mature sts. dark red, spines simple; lvs. to 3 in. long or more, entire or inconspicuously toothed, dull deep green above; fls. in 10–20-fld. racemes; fr. red. W. China.

dulcis: *B. buxifolia* var. *papillosa.*

×**emarginata** Willd.: reputedly *B. sibirica* Pall. × *B. vulgaris.* Deciduous, sts. red-brown, spines weak; fls. racemose or somewhat fasciculate; fr. ellipsoid, deep red. Perhaps no longer cult.

floribunda Wallich ex G. Don. Evergreen, mature sts. pale yellow, nearly cylindrical, spines absent, if present simple, or rarely 3-parted with short laterals; lvs. to 2 in. long, mostly entire, dull green; fls. in racemes; fr. dark red or almost purple, with blue bloom, style short. Nepal. Often erroneously grown under the name *B. aristata.*

Fremontii: *Mahonia Fremontii.*

Gagnepainii C. K. Schneid. Evergreen, to 6 ft., spines 3-parted; lvs. to 4 in. long, spiny-margined, pale beneath; fls. bright yellow, in 3–7-fld. fascicles; fr. bluish-black, with a bloom. W. China. Var. **lanceifolia** Ahrendt. Lvs. narrow, pedicels to ⅞ in.; probably the most commonly cult. var. Var. **praestans** Ahrendt. Lvs. narrow, scarcely undulate, margins finely spinulose or nearly entire.

Gilgiana Fedde. Deciduous, mature sts. red-brown to purple, spines simple; lvs. to 1⅝ in. long, entire or with 2–9 spiny teeth, dull pale green on both sides; fls. in spikelike racemes; fr. red. China.

gracilis: *Mahonia gracilis;* but plants offered as *B. gracilis* are probably a cv. of *Mahonia Aquifolium.*

Higginsiae: *Mahonia Higginsiae.*

Hookeri Lem. Evergreen, mature sts. yellow, spines 3-parted; lvs. to 2⅜ in. long, with 7–15 spiny teeth, deep green above, white or green beneath; fls. in 3–6-fld. clusters; fr. black-purple. Himalayas. Var. **latifolia:** see *B. manipurana.*

Horvathii: a listed name of no botanical standing and uncertain application.

hypokerina Airy-Shaw. VIOLET-BEAD B. Evergreen, to 2½ ft., mature sts. dark red, spines absent; lvs. to nearly 5 in. long with 6–15 spiny teeth, silvery-white beneath; fls. in 6–12-fld. fascicles; fr. black with white bloom, or bluish-violet. Burma.

ilicifolia G. Forst. HOLLY B. Evergreen, to 8 ft., mature sts. pale yellow, spines 3–5-parted; lvs. to 2 in. long or more, with 2–6 spiny teeth, lustrous gray-green above, paler beneath; fls. orange-yellow, in 4–7-fld. clusters; fr. black with blue bloom. S. Chile, Argentina. Plants cult. under this name are usually ×*Mahoberberis Neubertii.*

×**Irwinii** Byhouwer. A hybrid similar to *B. ×stenophylla*, but differing in having stamens much exserted, conspicuously and slenderly apiculate.

Julianae C. K. Schneid. WINTERGREEN B. Evergreen, to 7 ft., mature sts. yellow, spines 3-parted; lvs. to 4 in. long, with 12–20 spiny teeth; fls. in 15–20-fld. fascicles; fr. black, with heavy white bloom. China. Cvs. **'Nana'**, **'Pyramidalis'**, and **'Sargentii'** are listed.

Knightii (Lindl.) C. Koch. A poorly known sp.; material cult. under this name is usually *B. manipurana.*

koreana Palib. Deciduous, to 4 ft., mature sts. dark red, spines leaflike, or simple to 3–7-parted; lvs. to 2⅝ in. long, with 10–20 spiny teeth, dull light green, but often mottled or veined in red when young, becoming red in autumn; fls. in 10–20-fld. racemes to 2⅜ in. long; fr. glossy red. Korea.

levis Franch. A Chinese sp. not in cult.; plants offered under this name are usually *B. atrocarpa.*

linearifolia Phil. Evergreen, to 8 ft., mature sts. pale yellow, spines absent or 3-parted; lvs. narrow, to 2 in. long, entire, revolute, somewhat glaucous beneath; fls. orange or crimson, in few-fld. fascicles; fr. blue-black. Chile.

×**lologensis** Sandw.: apparently *B. Darwinii* × *B. linearifolia.* Evergreen; lvs. varying from rhombic-elliptic with few teeth to linear and entire; fr. black, with blue bloom.

lucida Schrad. Similar to *B. vulgaris* and perhaps only a form of it; lvs. finely toothed, dark green and glossy above; fr. red.

Lycium Royle. Deciduous, to 12 ft., mature sts. pale yellow-gray, spines 3-parted; lvs. oblanceolate, entire or with 1–2 spiny teeth, dull gray-green above; fls. bright yellow, usually in racemes to 4 in. long; fr. black, with heavy gray-white bloom. Himalayas. Suitable only to the far South.

manipurana Ahrendt. Evergreen, to 10 ft., mature sts. yellowish-brown, spines 2-parted; lvs. to 3⅜ in. long, with 10–20 minute, spiny teeth, pale green beneath; fls. in 6–12-fld. fascicles; fr. black, with blue bloom. Assam. Often cult. under erroneous names such as *B. Knightii, B. Hookeri* var. *latifolia* Bean, *B. xanthoxylon.*

×**mentorensis** L. Ames: *B. Julianae* × *B. Thunbergii.* Evergreen, to about 3 ft.; lvs. about 1 in. long, spiny-toothed; fr. dark dull red.

mitifolia Stapf. Deciduous, to 8 ft., mature sts. yellow and black-roughened, spines 3-parted; lvs. to 2⅜ in. long, with 15–25(–40) marginal spines, yellow-green; fls. in 20–30-fld. racemes, petals shorter than inner sepals; fr. red, style lacking. China. Often grown under the name *B. brachypoda.*

nervosa: *Mahonia nervosa.*

Nevinii: *Mahonia Nevinii.*

oblonga (Regel) C. K. Schneid. Deciduous, to 7 ft., mature sts. dark red or purple, spines 3-parted, yellow-brown; lvs. to 2⅜ in. long, entire, rarely with a few minute marginal spines, dull pale gray-green above, gray beneath; fls. in loose 10–20-fld. racemes; fr. black, with blue bloom, style short. Turkestan.

×**ottawensis** C. K. Schneid.: *B. Thunbergii* × *B. vulgaris.* Deciduous, sts. yellowish-brown; lvs. about 1 in. long, entire or finely toothed; fls. umbellate; fr. red.

panlanensis Ahrendt. Evergreen, mature sts. yellow, grooved, spines 3-parted; lvs. narrowly oblong, to 1⅝ in. long, with 3–8 or more appressed, spiny teeth, dull gray-green above, lustrous deep yellow-green beneath; fls. solitary or paired; fr. black, without bloom. China.

pinnata: *Mahonia pinnata.*

Piperana: *Mahonia Piperana.*

Poiretii C. K. Schneid. Deciduous, to 6 ft., mature sts. dark, spines weak or absent; lvs. to 1⅝ in. long, entire, bright green above; fls. bright yellow, in racemes; fr. bright red. Siberia, n. China.

Potaninii Maxim. Deciduous, spines simple or 3-parted; lvs. to 1⅜ in. long, with 1–2 spiny teeth, pale beneath; fls. in racemes to 1½ in. long; fr. red. W. China.

Prattii C. K. Schneid. [*B. aggregata* var. *Prattii* (C. K. Schneid.) C. K. Schneid.]. Deciduous, to 10 ft., mature sts. pale yellow, grooved, spines simple to 3-parted; lvs. to 1³⁄₁₆ in. long, with 3–8 spiny teeth, light yellowish-green above; fls. in panicles; fr. bright pink, style short. W. China.

pruinosa Franch. Evergreen, to 5 ft., mature sts. pale yellow, spines 3-parted; lvs. to 2 in. long, entire or with 2–20 spiny teeth; fls. in fascicles; fr. bluish-black, with a bloom. China.

Regeliana Koehne ex C. K. Schneid. [*B. amurensis* var. *japonica* (Regel) Rehd.]. Deciduous, to 6 ft., mature sts. pale yellow-gray, grooved, spines 3-parted; lvs. to 2³⁄₁₆ in. long, closely spiny-toothed, gray-bloomy beneath; fls. in racemes; fr. red, style lacking. Japan.

repens: *Mahonia repens.*

×**rubrostilla** Chitt. Probably a hybrid of garden origin; deciduous, to 4 ft.; lvs. oblanceolate, to ¾ in. long, with 4–6 spiny teeth, reticulate, gray beneath; fls. in 2–4-fld. umbellate racemes; fr. ovoid, red.

sanguinea Franch. A Chinese sp. not in cult.; plants so named are *B. panlanensis.*

Sargentiana C. K. Schneid. Evergreen, to 7 ft., mature sts. dark red, sometimes black-roughened, shoots bright red, spines 3-parted, to 2⅜ in. long; lvs. oblong-elliptic, to 4 in. long, with 15–25 spiny teeth, lustrous dark green above, paler dull yellow-green underneath; fls. pale greenish, in mostly 4–8-fld. fascicles; fr. black, without bloom, style lacking. China.

shensiana Ahrendt. Deciduous, to 6 ft., mature sts. dark red, shoots red, spines 3-parted; lvs. obovate, to 1⅝ in. long, with 4–12 spiny teeth; fls. in 6–15-fld. racemes; fr. purple, style short. China.

Sieboldii Miq. Deciduous, compact, to 3 ft., mature sts. dark red or purple, spines weak; lvs. rhombic-ovate, to nearly 3 in. long, attenuate, open-reticulate, with 50–150 spiny teeth, bright green above, paler beneath; fls. in 3–6-fld. umbellate racemes; fr. globose, deep red. Japan.

Soulieana C. K. Schneid. Evergreen, to 5 ft., mature sts. pale yellow, grooved, spines 3-parted; lvs. oblong to oblong-ovate, -elliptic or -obovate, to 3³⁄₁₆ in. long, with mostly 6–10 spiny teeth, deep bright green above, paler beneath; fr. mauve, with a bloom. China.

Stapfiana: *B. Wilsoniae* var.

×**stenophylla** Lindl. *B. Darwinii* × *B. empetrifolia* Lam. Evergreen, to 10 ft., brs. arching, mature sts. dark red-brown, spines simple; lvs. in fascicles of 5–6, narrowly elliptic to linear-elliptic, to ⅝ in. long, entire, revolute; fls. in 7–14-fld. racemes, stamens scarcely exserted; fr. globose, black with a blue bloom, style present. Cvs. listed are: '**Coccinea**', lvs. broad, fls. red outside; '**Corallina**' [*B. corallina* Hort.], lvs. narrow, fls. red in bud; '**Diversifolia**', some lvs. narrow and entire, some broad and with 2–3 minute marginal spines, fls. golden-yellow; '**Gracilis**', of low habit, some lvs. narrow and entire, some broad and 3-toothed, fls. golden-yellow; '**Irwinii**': *B.* ×*Irwinii.*

subcaulialata: *B. Wilsoniae* var.

Thunbergii DC. JAPANESE B. Deciduous, dense, compact, to about 5 ft., mature sts. dark red, grooved; lvs. rhombic-ovate, to ¾ in. long, entire, dull yellow-green to red or variegated above, somewhat glaucous beneath; fls. reddish outside, in mostly 2–5-fld. umbellate fascicles; fr. ellipsoid, red, lustrous. Cvs. include: '**Argenteo-marginata**', lvs. on new shoots with white margins; '**Atropurpurea**', lvs. dark purple; '**Aurea**', lvs. citron-yellow; '**Erecta**', TRUEHEDGE B., sts. and brs. upright; '**Maximowiczii**', lvs. narrower, acute, green beneath; '**Minor**', to 2 ft.; '**Pluriflora**', infl. 5–12-fld. Cvs. '**Compacta**', '**Fastigiata**', '**Inermis**', and '**Nana**' are also offered.

triacanthophora Fedde. Native to China, apparently not in cult.; plants so named are *B. wisleyensis.*

trifoliata: *Mahonia trifoliolata.*

vernae C. K. Schneid. Deciduous, to 4 ft., mature sts. dark red, warty, spines simple, to 1¾ in.; lvs. oblanceolate, to 1⅜ in. long, entire, green; fls. in 15–35-fld. racemes to 1¾ in. long; fr. globose, pale red, style lacking. China.

verruculosa Hemsl. & E. H. Wils. Evergreen, to 3 ft., mature sts. yellow, cylindrical, warty, pubescent, spines 3-parted; lvs. obovate-elliptic, to ⅞ in. long, with 2–4 spiny teeth, dark green above, grayish-white or green beneath; fls. solitary; fr. oblong-ovoid, black with blue bloom, style lacking. China.

virgetorum C. K. Schneid. Deciduous, to 6 ft., mature sts. pale yellow, slightly angled, spines simple; lvs. oblong-rhombic, to 4 in. long, longer than infl., entire, dull yellow-green above; fls. in mostly 5–10-fld. racemes or near-umbels; fr. oblong-ellipsoid, red, style lacking. China.

vulgaris L. COMMON B., JAUNDICE BERRY, PIPRAGE. Deciduous, to 7 ft., mature sts. yellow, angled or grooved, spines simple to 3-parted; lvs. oblong to elliptic, to 2⅜ in. long, with 18–36 spiny teeth, dull green to purple above; fls. in 15–25-fld. racemes to 2⅜ in. long; fr. red, oblong, style lacking. Eur. Cv. '**Atropurpurea**'. Lvs. purple.

Wilsoniae Hemsl. Semievergreen, to 3 ft., 6 ft. across, mature sts. dark red, grooved, puberulous or glabrous, spines 3-parted; lvs. obovate-spatulate, to 1 in. long, reticulate, dull; fls. in 4–7-fld. fascicles; fr. soft pinkish-red. China. Var. **Stapfiana** (C. K. Schneid.) C. K. Schneid. [*B. Stapfiana* C. K. Schneid.]. Lvs. oblong-spatulate; lvs. yellow-green; fr. ovoid or oblong-ovoid. Var. **subcaulialata** (C. K. Schneid.) C. K. Schneid. [*B. subcaulialata* C. K. Schneid.]. Sts. glabrous; lvs. blue-green; fr. globose.

wisleyensis Ahrendt. Evergreen, the mature sts. yellow, somewhat angled, spines 3-parted; lvs. linear-lanceolate, to 2³⁄₁₆ in. long, with 2–5 spiny teeth; fls. in 2–6-fld. fascicles; fr. oblong-ovoid, black with blue bloom, style lacking. Cult.; probably of Chinese origin. Plants distributed as *B. triacanthophora* belong here.

xanthoxylon Hassk. ex C. K. Schneid. A sp. native to Java, not in cult.; plants offered under this name are probably *B. Julianae* or *B. manipurana.*

BERCHEMIA Neck. ex DC. SUPPLEJACK, RATTAN VINE. *Rhamnaceae.* About 12 or more spp. of twining, deciduous shrubs in s. and e. Asia, e. Afr., and N. Amer.; lvs. alt., entire, with conspicuous parallel veins; fls. small, in terminal panicles; fr. drupaceous.

The species thrive in any soil but are not reliable far north. Propagated by seeds and root cuttings in spring or by layers and cuttings of ripe wood in autumn.

racemosa Siebold & Zucc. Lvs. ovate, to 2½ in. long, subcordate, somewhat glaucous underneath; panicles to 6 in. long; fls. greenish; fr. red, turning black, to ¼ in. long. Japan and Taiwan. Zone 6. Cv. '**Variegata**' is listed.

scandens (J. Hill) C. Koch [*B. volubilis* (L.f.) DC.]. SUPPLEJACK. Lvs. elliptic to oblong-ovate, rounded at base; panicles to 1½ in. long; fls.

greenish-white; fr. bluish-black. Va. and Ky., s. to Fla. and Tex. Zone 6.

volubilis: *B. scandens.*

BERGENIA Moench [*Megasea* Haw.]. *Saxifragaceae.* Twelve or more spp. of per. herbs of temp. Asia; plants with thick rhizomes, developing into large clumps or colonies; lvs. large, thick, wavy, entire or toothed, with glandular pits, petioles sheathed at base; fls. in scapose infl., large, pink or white, sepals and petals 5, stamens 10, ovary superior, styles 2; fr. a caps. Closely related to *Saxifraga.*

Grown for the showy, early flowers, and as a ground cover, the leaves being ornamental and more or less evergreen. Propagated by division or by seeds.

bifolia: *B. crassifolia.*

ciliata (Haw.) Sternb. [*B. ligulata* Engl.; *Megasea ciliata* Haw.; *Saxifraga ligulata* Wallich]. WINTER BEGONIA. Lvs. orbicular, or sometimes broadly obovate, broadly ovate, or elliptic, 8–14 in. long, denticulate or crenate, ciliate, densely and coarsely hairy; infl. to 12 in., often several from one rosette of lvs., scape and brs. of infl. green, pinkish-crimson, or flushed reddish; fls. usually few, white or pink. W. Pakistan.

cordifolia (Haw.) Sternb. [*Saxifraga cordifolia* Haw.]. Lvs. orbicular, to 10 in. long, rounded or cordate at base, crenulate-serrate, glabrous, often bullate; infl. to 16 in. long, sometimes much longer than lvs. in wild plants but usually not so in cult. Siberia and Mongolia.

crassifolia (L.) Fritsch [*B. bifolia* Moench; *Saxifraga crassifolia* L.]. SIBERIAN TEA. Lvs. elliptic, obovate, or oblong, to 8 in. long, shallowly serrate, glabrous; infl. to 18 in., as long as lvs. or longer; fls. medium rose-purple to deep reddish-purple. Siberia and Mongolia.

Delavayi: *B. purpurascens.*

gigantea: a listed name of no botanical standing.

Leichtlinii: a listed name, probably for *B.* ×*Schmidtii.*

ligulata: *B. ciliata.* Var. **Leichtlinii:** *B.* ×*Schmidtii.*

×**media** (Haw.) Engl. [*Saxifraga aemula* Tausch]. A hybrid, probably *B. cordifolia* × *B. crassifolia;* plants often dwarf; lvs. broadly ovate, rounded or cordate at base; infl. usually longer than lvs.; fls. rather dense.

ornata: *B.* ×*Schmidtii.*

purpurascens (Hook.f. & T. Thoms.) Engl. [*B. purpurascens* var. *Delavayi* (Franch.) Engl. & Irmsch.; *B. Delavayi* (Franch.) Engl.; *Saxifraga Delavayi* Franch.; *S. purpurascens* Hook.f. & T. Thoms.]. Lvs. elliptic or ovate-elliptic, to 10 in. long, glabrous, more or less suffused with purple; fls. few to many, nodding, deep purplish-red or bright pink. E. Himalayas, w. China, n. Burma.

×**Schmidtii** (Regel) Silva-Tar. [*B. ornata* Stein ex Guillaum.; *Saxifraga ligulata* Wallich var. *speciosa* B. Verlot; *S.* ×*Schmidtii* Regel; the following names are probably also referable here: *B. ligulata* var. *Leichtlinii* Hort. ex Wehrh.; *Saxifraga* ×*Leichtlinii* Hort.; *S.* ×*speciosa* Leichtl.]: *B. ciliata* × *B. crassifolia,* a hybrid of garden origin; lvs. broadly obovate to obovate-elliptic, to 8 in. long, rounded or shallowly cordate at base, ciliate-denticulate, often drooping; fls. at first nodding, in branched panicles, bright rose-pink. Probably cult. in temp. regions throughout the world, and the largest, commonest, and most vigorous *Bergenia* in cult.

speciosa: probably *B.* ×*Schmidtii.*

Stracheyi (Hook.f. & T. Thoms.) Engl. [*Saxifraga Stracheyi* Hook.f. & T. Thoms.]. Lvs. obovate or obovate-cuneate, mostly to 8 in. long, serrulate or doubly serrulate, ciliate or rarely lacking cilia, glabrous; infls. often several from one rosette, to 8 in. long, as long as lvs. or shorter; fls. rather numerous, nodding, white becoming pink-tinged, or pink, or yellowish. E. Afghanistan and w. Pakistan, e. to Kashmir, Nepal, w. Tibet.

BERGERANTHUS Schwant. *Aizoaceae.* About 11 spp. of stemless, per., succulent herbs with fleshy rhizomes, native to S. Afr.; lvs. 4-ranked, densely crowded, smooth, gray-green, sometimes minutely dark-punctate, nearly triangular to nearly cylindrical in section, upper surface flat to concave, lower surface rounded, keeled toward apex, and sometimes extended over upper surface like a chin, margins entire; fls. 3–5 in a group, pedicelled, expanding in the afternoon, calyx lobes 5, narrow, petals yellow, many, in several series, stamens many, erect, ovary 5-celled, stigmas 5; fr. a caps., placental tubercles large.

Growth occurs in summer. In winter the plants require a fairly dry condition at a relatively cool temperature of about 55° F. Free-flowering plants easily propagated by seeds or cuttings. See also *Succulents.*

multiceps (Salm-Dyck) Schwant. Cespitose; lvs. 6–8 in rosettes, spreading, smooth, green, not punctate, to 2 in. long, ⅜ in. wide at the center, 3-angled in section, acuminate, minutely awned; fls. to 1¼ in. across, on pedicels to 1¾ in. long, petals yellow, somewhat reddish on outside. Cape Prov.

scapiger (Eckl. & Zeyh.) Schwant. Cespitose; lvs. dark green with a smooth, pale, cartilaginous edge, to 4¾ in. long, ⅝ in. wide, one lf. of each pair shorter and gradually tapered, the other longer, keeled; fls. 3–4, to 2 in. across, on pedicels to 1¾ in. long, petals golden-yellow, reddish outside. Cape Prov.

vespertinus (A. Berger) Schwant. Cespitose; lvs. erect at first, becoming procumbent, to 2½ in. long, ¼ in. wide, flat above, semicylindrical in section at the base, keeled and 3-angled in section toward apex, tapered; fls. 3–5, on pedicels to 1¼ in. long, petals yellow. Cape Prov.

BERGEROCACTUS Britt. & Rose. *Cactaceae.* One sp., a slender cactus of coastal s. Calif. and n. Baja Calif.; sts. branching from the base, ribs many, low; spines golden; fls. diurnal, yellow, small, with a short tube, scales of ovary and tube with axillary spines; fr. globose, spiny, extruding pulp and seeds.

For culture see *Cacti.*

Emoryi (Engelm.) Britt. & Rose [*Cereus Emoryi* Engelm.]. Sts. erect or decumbent, to 6 ft. long or more, 1–2 in. thick, forming thickets, ribs 14–21; areoles close-set, spines 35–50, yellow, becoming brown, needle-shaped, to 2½ in. long; fls. about 2 in. long.

BERLANDIERA DC. GREEN-EYES. *Compositae* (Helianthus Tribe). Six or 7 spp. of per. herbs in s. U.S. and Mex.; lvs. alt., crenate or pinnatifid; fl. heads radiate, peduncled, involucral bracts leafy, in 3 rows, receptacle beset with green bracts; disc fls. few, sterile, brown or yellow, ray fls. fertile, yellow; achenes of ray fls. flat, usually joined to 1 involucral and 2 receptacular bracts, pappus lacking or of 2 short awns.

Easily propagated by seeds.

lyrata Benth. Erect, branched, to 20 in.; lf. blades oblong, to 7 in. long, deeply pinnately lobed in lower half, whitish beneath; disc fls. maroon, ray fls. yellow above, brownish beneath. Heads expanded in the morning. Spring, summer. Kans. and Ark., w. to Ariz. and n. Mex.

BERRYA Roxb. *Tiliaceae.* About 3–5 spp. of trees, native to trop. Asia and Malay Arch.; lvs. alt., simple, usually entire; fls. small, in cymose panicles terminating the branchlets, calyx irregularly 2–3-lobed, petals 4–5(–6), stamens many, all fertile, ovary 3–5-celled, cells 1–6-ovuled; fr. a caps., 3–5-valved, valves 2-winged, cells 1–4-seeded.

Ammonilla: *B. cordifolia.*

cordifolia (Willd.) Burret [*B. Ammonilla* Roxb.]. Large tree; lvs. cordate-ovate, to 10 in. long, acute-acuminate; fls. white or pinkish, to 1¼ in. across, ovary 3–4-celled, cells 4-ovuled, style filiform, stigma 3-lobed; caps. stellate-pubescent, 6–8-winged, wings asymmetric, oblong, 1 in. long or more, seeds hairy. India to Malay Arch. Wood used for construction.

javanica (Turcz.) Burret [*B. quinquelocularis* Teysm. & Binnend. ex Koord. & Val.]. Similar to *B. cordifolia,* but petals bright rose-colored, greenish-yellow at base, ovary (4–)5-celled, cells 6-ovuled, style thick, elongate-conical; caps. (8–)10-winged, seeds glabrous. Java.

quinquelocularis: *B. javanica.*

BERTEROA DC. *Cruciferae.* Several spp. of ann. or per. herbs of stony or rocky places in Eur. and Asia, with hairs stellate or stellate and unbranched, intermixed; fls. white or pale yellow, sepals 4, petals 4, deeply bifid; fr. a silicle, seeds 2–6 in each cell. Related to *Alyssum* but petals bifid and silicles often somewhat inflated.

incana (L.) DC. [*Alyssum incanum* L.]. HOARY ALYSSUM. Ann. or per., to 2 ft., erect, gray-green; lvs. oblong or lanceolate, to 2 in. long, usually entire; fls. in terminal racemes, petals white, to ¼ in. long. Eur.; naturalized in N. Amer. Sometimes grown in sunny places as an ornamental.

BERTHOLLETIA Humb. & Bonpl. *Lecythidaceae.* One or 2 spp. of large, evergreen trees in trop. S. Amer. and the W. Indies; lvs. large, alt., simple, without stipules; fls. in spikes, calyx 2-parted, petals 6, stamens many, clustered on a disclike androphore, arranged on 1 side of the fl. and forming an overarching hood, ovary inferior, 4-celled; fr. large, woody, with thick walls and an apical plug formed of the hardened calyx, seeds 18–30, large, 3-angled.

Suited only for tropical climates, but small specimens may be seen in collections of economic plants under glass. Propagated by seeds or layers.

excelsa Humb. & Bonpl. BRAZIL NUT, PARA N., CREAM N. To 100 ft.; lvs. oblong, to 20 in. long, wavy-margined, leathery; fls. creamy-white; fr. globose, to 5 in. in diam., seeds 1½–2½ in. long. Amazonian S. Amer. The seeds are the Brazil nuts of commerce.

BERTOLONIA Raddi. *Melastomataceae.* About 14 spp. of dwarf, creeping herbs of Brazil; lvs. simple, 3–11-nerved; infl. of 1-sided cymes; fls. white, rose, or purple, ovary superior, 3-celled; fr. a caps.

Grown in the greenhouse for the foliage, which is often purplish beneath, with various metallic colors above. Propagated by cuttings over heat and by seeds.

argyraea: a listed name of no botanical standing.

Houtteana Van Houtte. Stemless, or nearly so; lvs. ovate to elliptic, 4–7 in. long, the upper surface olive-green, striped bright rose along primary veins and on many cross veins, sparsely strigose; petals pink. Of cult. origin; not producing seeds.

maculata Mart. ex DC. Sts. decumbent; lvs. broadly ovate, 2–3 in. long, obtuse, hairy, upper surface velvety-green, with a purple or magenta band bordering veins; infl. racemose, 4–6 in. long; fls. ¾ in. across, rose, opening in the morning. Flowering several times a year. Ne. Brazil. Cv. 'Wentii'. Lvs. zoned silvery along veins.

marmorata Naud. Sts. decumbent, hairy; lvs. ovate-oblong, acute, slightly hairy, streaked with white along veins; fls. to 1 in. across, purple. N. Brazil. Cv. 'Sanderana'. Lvs. zoned silvery-green along primary veins above. Var. **aenea** (Naud.) Cogn. Lvs. coppery-tinged, only slightly spotted.

pubescens: a listed name of no botanical standing for *Triolena pustulata.*

Sanderana: a listed name of no botanical standing for *B. marmorata* cv.

Wentii: a listed name of no botanical standing for *B. maculata* cv.

BERZELIA Brongn. *Bruniaceae.* About 12 spp. of small shrubs, native to S. Afr.; lvs. closely set or imbricate, usually keeled; fls. small, in bracted, globose heads, fl. tube united to ovary, petals separate, stamens subequal or equal, exserted, ovary 1-celled, 1-ovuled, style unbranched.

Suitable for Zone 10 in southern Calif.

lanuginosa (L.) Brongn. To 6 ft.; lvs. linear-lanceolate to acicular, mostly less than ¼ in. long; fl. heads to about ⅜ in. across, terminating short branchlets, bracts nearly equalling fls.; petals cream, erect, about ¹⁄₁₆ in. long, shorter than stamens.

BESCHORNERIA Kunth. *Agavaceae.* About 10 spp. of small evergreen herbs of Mex., sts. rhizomatous, thickened; lvs. in a basal rosette, fleshy, lanceolate to sword-shaped; infl. an erect raceme or panicle; fls. green or red, funnelform, in bracted clusters, segms. 6, erect, stamens 6, with slender filaments and versatile anthers, ovary inferior, 3-celled, with many ovules, style slender; fr. a caps.

Cultivation as for *Yucca.*

tubiflora Kunth. Lvs. more or less sword-shaped, to 2 ft. long, glaucous-green, scabrous beneath, margins denticulate; scape green or brown-tinged, to 4 ft.; fls. green, tinged brown-purple outside, drooping, subtended by purple bracts.

yuccoides Hook. Lvs. to 2 ft. long, glaucous above, scabrous beneath; infl. to 4 ft., much branched, red; fls. green, to 2 in. long, glabrous, subtended by bright red bracts.

BESSERA Schult.f. [*Pharium* Herb.]. *Amaryllidaceae.* Two spp. of herbs native to Mex.; corm membranous-coated; lvs. 1–2 or more, linear, concave-convex to rounded in cross section; infl. an umbel terminal on a scape and subtended by 3–4 spreading spathe valves; fls. jointed to the pedicels, perianth campanulate to cylindrical, tube short or long, with 6 lobes, stamens 6, united at the base or to the middle, ovary superior, 3-celled, borne on a short 3-angled stalk united at the angles to the perianth tube; fr. a loculicidal caps., seeds flattened, black.

elegans Schult.f. [*Pharium elegans* (Schult.f.) Steud.]. CORAL-DROPS. To 3 ft.; lvs. green, to 32 in.; umbel 2–30-fld., fls. nodding, campanulate, to 1³⁄₁₆ in. long, scarlet to purple, with green nerves outside, white-striped inside, perianth tube shorter than or as long as the spreading lobes, stamens united half their length, exserted. *Milla biflora* has sometimes been grown under this name.

BESSEYA Rydb. KITTEN-TAILS. *Scrophulariaceae.* Nine spp. of rhizomatous, per. herbs of w. U.S., one in Great Lakes region; basal lvs. long-petioled, crenate or crenate-serrate, st. lvs. alt., reduced, sessile; fls. violet-purple, white or yellow, in bracted spikelike racemes, calyx 2- or 4-lobed, corolla 2-lipped, sometimes rudimentary or absent, stamens 2, exserted; fr. a flattened loculicidal caps. Allied to *Synthyris,* but differing in fl. color, corolla shape, and in having several to many bractlike lvs. below infl.

alpina (A. Gray) Rydb. [*Synthyris alpina* A. Gray]. To 6 in., hairy, becoming glabrate; basal lvs. cordate-ovate to elliptic, to 2 in. long, crenate-serrate; fls. violet-purple, to ⅜ in. long, densely crowded. Mts., Wyo. and Utah, s. to New Mex.

cinerea (Raf.) Penn. [*Synthyris cinerea* Hort.; *S. wyomingensis* (A. Nels.) A. Heller]. To 1 ft., soft-pubescent throughout; basal lvs. ovate to oblong, to 6 in. long, crenate; calyx 2-lobed, corolla absent, filaments bright purple. S. Dak. to Alta., s. to Utah and Colo.

plantaginea (James) Rydb. [*Synthyris plantaginea* (James) Benth.]. To 1 ft. or more, tomentose; basal lvs. ovate to ovate-oblong, to 6 in. long, crenate; fls. white or tinged purplish, to ⅜ in. long. Wyo. to New Mex.

Ritterana (Eastw.) Rydb. [*Synthyris Ritterana* Eastw.]. To 1 ft., pubescent to glabrate; basal lvs. elliptic to oblong, to 6 in. long, crenate; fls. pale lemon-yellow, ¼ in. long. Mts., Colo.

rubra (Dougl. ex Hook.) Rydb. [*Synthyris rubra* (Dougl. ex Hook.) Benth.]. To 1½ ft., loosely hairy and reddish-tinged, lvs. becoming glabrate; basal lvs. ovate, to 9 in. long, truncate to cordate at base, crenate; calyx 4-lobed, corolla absent, stamen filaments dark red. W. Mont. to e. Wash. and Ore.

BETA L. BEET. *Chenopodiaceae.* About 12 spp. of herbs in the Old World; lvs. simple, in a basal rosette or alt. on st.; fls. small, in panicled spikes, usually bisexual, greenish or reddish, bracted, calyx 5-lobed, petals none, stamens 5, ovary sunken in a disc, stigmas 3; fr. developing mostly from aggregates of 2 or more fls. cohering at base and forming very irregular dry structures (the "seeds" of commerce) with hardened, woody calyx.

For culture see *Beet.*

dracaenifolia: *B. vulgaris* cv.

vulgaris L. BEET, SEA B. Bien. or ann.; sts. to 4 ft., produced the second year; lvs. ovate to oblong-ovate, basal ones long-petioled, to 18 in. long or more, st. lvs. progressively reduced in size upward along st.; calyx lobes spatulate to linear, more or less keeled, appressed to the mature fr. Canary Is., Madeira Is., Atlantic coast of Eur., Medit. region to s. Russia, Syria, Iraq. The cult. kinds fall into 2 groups. The Cicla Group [var. *Cicla* L.; convar. *vulgaris*], includes the kinds grown as leafy vegetables, known as LEAF BEET, SPINACH B., CHARD, SWISS C., and a few grown for their ornamental foliage; root not fleshy-thickened; lvs. much-developed, blades to 15 in. long and 10 in. wide, or larger, sometimes ruffled and puckered, often highly colored, and in some races, as Swiss chard, with midribs and petioles very thick. Cv. 'Dracaenifolia'. Lvs. narrow, dark crimson; grown as an ornamental. The Crassa Group [convar. *crassa* (Alef.) J. Helm], includes the kinds grown chiefly for their roots, used as a vegetable, forage, or source of sugar, and known as GARDEN BEET, RED B., YELLOW B., SUGAR B., BEETROOT, MANGEL, MANGEL-WORZEL, MANGOLD; root short or long, greatly fleshy-thickened, whitish, yellow, or pink to red-purple.

BETONICA: *STACHYS.* **B. macrantha:** *S. grandiflora.*

BETULA L. BIRCH. *Betulaceae.* About 50 or 60 spp. of deciduous, monoecious trees and shrubs, native to the N. Hemisphere; lvs. alt., toothed; fls. unisexual, borne in catkins, male catkins forming in autumn, remaining naked during the winter, and opening in spring, female catkins becoming conelike, with 3-lobed scales. Closely related to *Alnus,* but fruiting catkins shattering when ripe.

Birches are cultivated as ornamentals and for timber used for furniture and other articles; one species is the major source of oil of wintergreen. They are graceful, mostly short-lived trees with pendent branches, suitable for northern climates. The bark is silvery or grayish-white in some species, but in others yellowish-orange, orange-red, reddish-brown, or almost black.

They thrive in moist sandy soil, or some species in drier locations. Propagated by seeds sown as soon as mature or after stratification, in sandy soil that is kept moist and shady. Seedlings should be transplanted when about a year old. Also propagated by layers, green wood cuttings under glass, and grafting or budding on seedling stock.

alascana: *B. papyrifera* var. *humilis.*

alba: *B. papyrifera* or *B. pendula.* Var. **elegans laciniata:** *B. pendula* cv. 'Gracilis'. Var. **atropurpurea:** *B. pendula* cv. 'Purpurea'. Var. **dalecarlica:** *B. pendula* cv. Var. **pyramidalis:** *B. pendula* cv. 'Fastigiata'. Var. **Youngii:** *B. pendula* cv.

albo-sinensis Burkill. To 100 ft., bark flaking, orange-red, branchlets somewhat glandular, not pubescent; lvs. ovate-oblong, to 2¾ in. long, acuminate at apex, obtuse-truncate to subcordate at base, doubly serrate, glabrous and dark yellowish-green above, paler and somewhat pubescent at least along midrib below, veins 9–14 pairs. China. Var. **septentrionalis** C. K. Schneid. Bark brownish-orange; lvs. to 3¼ in. long, more silky beneath. W. China.

alleghaniensis Britt. [*B. excelsa* Hort. not Ait.; *B. lutea* of auth.]. YELLOW B., GRAY B. To 90 ft., bark peeling in thin flakes, yellowish or silvery-gray, reddish-brown on old trunks, that of twigs and young lvs. aromatic and somewhat bitter; lvs. ovate, to 5 in. long, glabrous or pubescent underneath, veins 9–11 pairs; cones oblong, about 1 in. long. Mostly in moist woods, Nfld., s. to Ga. and Tenn. A valuable timber tree.

alnoides Buch.-Ham. ex D. Don [*B. cylindrostachys* Wallich]. To 60 ft., bark brown or grayish, outer bark peeling in thick patches; lvs. ovate-oblong, to 6 in. long, rounded or cuneate at base, with appressed teeth, nearly glabrous; cones several, to 3½ in. long. Himalayas.

aurata Borkh. Reputed to be a hybrid, *B. pendula* × *B. pubescens*; shrub or small slender tree, habit more like that of *B. pubescens*, young branchlets more or less hairy and glandular; lvs. mostly rhomboid, to 2 in. long, finely toothed.

Bhojpattra: *B. utilis.*

communis: a listed name, probably referable to *B. papyrifera.*

corylifolia Regel & Maxim. ex Regel. To 70 ft., bark grayish-white, branchlets glabrous or nearly so, purplish-brown; lvs. ovate to elliptic or obovate, to 3 in. long, glaucous and hairy underneath, veins 10–14 pairs; cones cylindrical, to 2 in. long. Japan.

costata Trautv. To 100 ft., bark papery, flaking; lvs. ovate, to 3 in. long, long-acuminate; cones ellipsoid, ¾ in. long. Ne. Asia.

cultriformis: a listed name of no botanical standing.

cylindrostachys: *B. alnoides.*

davurica Pall. To 70 ft., bark flaking and peeling, purplish-brown, branchlets pubescent, glandular; lvs. ovate, to 3¼ in. long, acute or acuminate, more or less pubescent underneath, glabrous above at maturity; veins 6–8 pairs; cones to 1¼ in. long. Ne. Asia and Japan.

Ermanii Cham. To 60 ft., bark flaking, grayish-white to reddish; lvs. triangular-ovate, to 4 in. long, acuminate, coarsely toothed, light green underneath, veins 7–11 pairs; cones oblong, about 1 in. long. Ne. Asia and Japan.

excelsa: see *B. alleghaniensis* and *B. pumila.*

fastigiata: *B. pendula* cv.

fontinalis: *B. occidentalis.*

fruticosa Pall. Shrub, to 15 ft.; lvs. ovate, to 2 in. long, slightly pubescent on veins underneath, veins 5–6 pairs; cones oblong-cylindrical, to 1 in. long. Ne. Asia. Differs from *B. humilis* in having twigs less glandular, and lvs. more finely and sharply serrate.

glandulosa Michx. DWARF. B. Shrub, to 6 ft., branchlets resinous, glandular, glabrous; lvs. nearly orbicular to obovate, to 1 in. long, pale and glandular underneath; cones cylindrical, to ¾ in. long. N. U.S., Canada, Alaska.

globispica Shirai. To 60 ft., bark flaking, nearly white; lvs. broad-ovate, to 3 in. long, short-acuminate, nearly round at base, veins about 10 pairs; cones globose-ovoid, to 1¼ in. long. Japan.

grandis: *B. papyrifera.*

grossa Siebold & Zucc. [*B. ulmifolia* Siebold & Zucc.]. JAPANESE CHERRY B. To 80 ft., bark smooth, but fissured on trunks of old trees, dark gray to black, twigs glabrous, yellow to chestnut-brown; lvs. ovate, to 4 in. long, acuminate, basally subcordate, coarsely doubly serrate, lower side glandular, veins silky, 10–15 pairs; cones to 1 in. long. Japan.

humilis Schrank. Shrub, to 10 ft., branchlets pubescent, glandular; lvs. usually ovate to elliptic, to 1¼ in. long, acute, rarely obtuse, dentate-serrate to entire, glabrous above and beneath, veins 4–5 pairs; cones to ¾ in. long. Eur., and w. Asia.

× **Jackii** C. K. Schneid.: *B. pumila* × *B. lenta.* Shrub, bark aromatic; lvs. ovate, to 2 in. long, glabrate, veins about 7 pairs; cones to ¾ in. long.

Jacquemontii Spach. Tree, bark white, branchlets pubescent, slightly glandular; lvs. ovate, to 2½ in. long, glandular underneath,

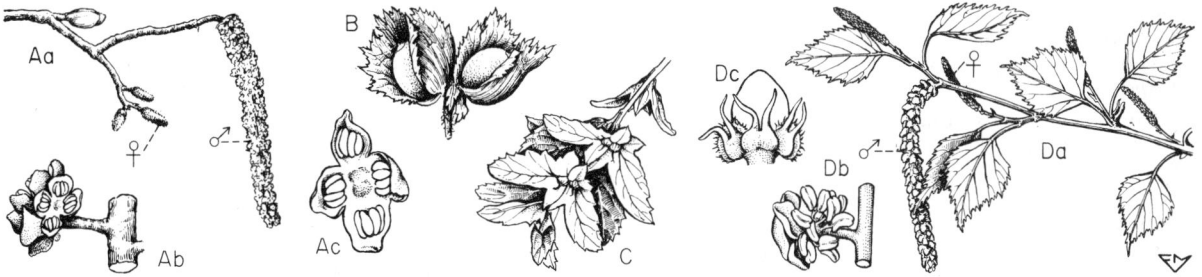

BETULACEAE. **A,** *Alnus rugosa:* **Aa,** twig with male (♂) and female (♀) catkins, × ½; **Ab,** part of axis of male catkin with flowers, × 3; **Ac,** single male flower, × 5. **B,** *Corylus Avellana:* fruit, × ½. **C,** *Carpinus caroliniana:* fruiting raceme, × ½. **D,** *Betula pendula:* **Da,** twig with male (♂) and female (♀) catkins, × ½ **Db,** part of axis of male catkin with flowers, × 3; **Dc,** female flowers, × 10. (From Bailey, *Manual of Cultivated Plants,* ed. 2.)

veins hairy, 7–9 pairs; cones on long pubescent stalks. Himalayas. Related to *B. utilis,* but having bark white and lvs. with fewer pairs of veins.

japonica: *B. platyphylla* var.

kenaica: *B. papyrifera* var.

laciniata: *B. pendula* cv. 'Dalecarlica'.

latifolia: see *B. platyphylla* and *B. papyrifera.*

lenta L. CHERRY B., SWEET B., BLACK B., MAHOGANY B., MOUNTAIN MAHOGANY. To 75 ft., bark not peeling, fissured into thick plates on old trunks, almost black, that of twigs and young brs. aromatic and of agreeable flavor; lvs. oblong-ovate, to 5 in. long, silky-pubescent underneath when young, veins 9–12 pairs; cones ovoid-oblong, to 1½ in. long. Moist woods, Me. to Ala. The wood is used for various articles, and the young twigs and bark are the main source of oil of wintergreen.

lutea Michx.f.: the sp. commonly known by this name is *B. alleghaniensis,* but the name is technically a synonym of *B. pumila.*

macrophylla: the name of a fossil sp.; cult. material of this name may be *B. pubescens.*

mandshurica: *B. platyphylla.*

Maximowicziana Regel. MONARCH B. To 100 ft., bark flaking, gray or orange-gray; lvs. broad-ovate, to 6 in. long, cordate at base, veins 10–12 pairs; cones 2–4 in a raceme, drooping, cylindrical, to 2¾ in. long. Japan. The large cordate lvs. give this birch the appearance of some lindens *(Tilia).*

nana L. Spreading, branching shrub, to 2 ft.; lvs. orbicular to ½ in. long, sticky and pubescent underneath when young; cones to ½ in. long. N. Asia, n. Eur., Alaska.

neoalaskana: *B. papyrifera* var. *humilis.*

nigra L. [*B. rubra* Michx.f.]. RIVER B., BLACK B., RED B. To 100 ft., bark peeling in papery flakes, reddish-brown or silvery-gray on younger brs.; lvs. rhombic-ovate, to 3 in. long, whitish underneath, veins 7–9 pairs; cones oblong-cylindrical, 1½ in. long. By streams and in bottomlands, Mass., s. to Fla. and Kans. Graceful tree with bark appearing torn and ragged. The wood is used for various articles.

occidentalis Hook. [*B. papyrifera* var. *occidentalis* (Hook.) Sarg.; *B. fontinalis* Sarg.]. WATER B. Tall shrub or tree, to 40 ft., bark not peeling, reddish-brown, shining, branchlets rough with large resinous glands; lvs. broad-ovate, to 2 in. long, veins 3–4 pairs; cones about 1 in. long. Pacific Coast, e. to Colo.

odorata: *B. pubescens.*

papyracea: *B. papyrifera.*

papyrifera Marsh. [*B. alba* L., in part; *B. grandis* Schrad.; *B. latifolia* Tausch; *B. papyracea* Ait.]. CANOE B., PAPER B., WHITE B. To 100 ft., bark flaking, papery, white, young branchlets pubescent and somewhat glandular, becoming glabrous and less noticeably glandular with age; lvs. ovate, to 4 in. long, acuminate, basally cuneate or obtuse to cordate, coarsely serrate, usually somewhat pubescent on veins underneath, but glabrous above, veins 6–10 pairs; cones cylindrical, to 2 in. long. Light soils on rocky land, n. N. Amer. Wood has many uses and bark a former source for canoes of aborigines. Var. **commutata** (Regel) Fern. [var. *Lyalliana* (Koehne) C. K. Schneid.]. Bark not freely flaking, often reddish; lvs. to 3 in. long. Ne. and nw. N. Amer. Var. **cordifolia** (Regel) Fern. Small tree or shrub; lvs. broadly ovate, doubly serrate, veins pubescent underneath. Lab. to Minn. Var. **humilis** (Regel) Fern. & Raup [var. *neoalaskana* (Sarg.) Raup; *B. alascana* Sarg., not *B. alaskana* Lesq. (a fossil sp.); *B. neoalaskana* Sarg.]. Twigs resinous-glandular. Sask. to Alaska. Var. **kenaica** (W. H. Evans) A. Henry [*B. kenaica* W. H. Evans]. To 40 ft., bark furrowed, dark brown to nearly black; lvs. to 2 in. long, veins about 4 pairs. Kenai Pen. (Alaska). Var. **Lyal-**

liana: var. *commutata.* Var. **minor** (Tuckerm.) S. Wats. & J. Coult. Shrub or low bushy tree; lvs. to 1½ in. long, glabrous beneath, glutinous. Lab. to New Hamp., w. to Minn. Var. **neoalaskana:** var *humilis.* Var. **occidentalis:** *B. occidentalis.* Var. **subcordata** (Rydb.) Sarg. Small tree, sts. with crystalline glands, bark silvery-gray, tinged with purple; lvs. to 2 in. long. Se. Wash., adjacent Ore., and Idaho.

pendula Roth [*B. alba* L., in part; *B. verrucosa* J. F. Ehrh.]. EUROPEAN WHITE B., WHITE B. To 60 ft., bark white and flaking off in layers, but toward base usually dark and dissected into rectangular sections, brs. usually drooping, branchlets with appressed, peltate resin glands; lvs. rhombic-ovate, to 2½ in. long, veins 6–9 pairs; cones cylindrical, about 1 in. long. Eur., and Asia Minor. Compare with *B. pubescens.* Cv. 'Dalecarlica' [*B. alba* var. *dalecarlica* L.f.; *B. laciniata* Wahlenb.]. Lvs. deeply lobed. Cv. 'Fastigiata' [var. *fastigiata* C. Koch; *B. alba* var. *pyramidalis* Hort.; *B. pyramidalis* Hort.]. Of columnar habit. Cv. 'Gracilis' [*B. alba* var. *elegans laciniata* Hort.]. Brs. drooping, lvs. finely dissected. Cv. 'Purpurea' [*B. alba* var. *atropurpurea* H. Jaeg.]. Lvs. purple. Cv. 'Tristis'. Brs. drooping, forming a round head. Cv. 'Youngii' [*B. alba* var. *Youngii* Hort.]. YOUNG'S WEEPING B. Brs. drooping, very slender, forming an irregular head.

platyphylla Sukachev [*B. latifolia* Kom., not Tausch; *B. mandshurica* (Regel) Nakai]. To 60 ft., bark white, branchlets glandular; lvs. ovate to triangular-ovate, to 2½ in. long, acuminate, basally mostly broadly cuneate, unequally serrate; cones pendulous, cylindrical. Manchuria and Korea. Var. **japonica** (Miq.) Hara [*B. japonica* Siebold; *B. Tauschii* (Regel) G. Koidz.]. JAPANESE WHITE B. Lvs. broadly ovate-triangular, truncate to subcordate. Japan and n. China.

populifolia Marsh. GRAY B., WHITE B., FIRE B., OLD FIELD B. Tree, to 30 ft., bark chalky; lvs. triangular-ovate, to 3 in. long, acuminate, basally truncate or rarely cuneate, glossy above; cones cylindrical, about 1 in. long. Nov. Sc. to Del. Small, graceful tree, useful for dry, poor, and even boggy sites. Cvs. are: 'Laciniata', lvs. pinnately lobed; 'Pendula', brs. drooping; 'Purpurea', lvs. purple when young.

pubescens J. F. Ehrh. [*B. odorata* Bechst.]. Shrub or tree, to 60 ft., bark flaking, grayish or brownish, eventually becoming dark at base of trunk, branchlets downy, without resin glands; lvs. ovate, to 2 in. long, usually pubescent underneath, veins 5–7 pairs; cones cylindrical, 1 in. long. Eur., Siberia. Compare with *B. pendula.* Cv. 'Urticifolia' [*B. urticifolia* Lodd.]. Lvs. coarsely toothed or lobed. Cv. 'Fastigiata': a listed name. Cv. 'Variegata'. Lvs. variegated.

pumila L. [*B. excelsa* Ait., not of auth.; *B. lutea* Michx.f.]. LOW B., SWAMP B. Shrub, to 15 ft.; lvs. orbicular to obovate, about 1 in. long, densely pubescent underneath when young; cones cylindrical-oblong, 1 in. long. Nfld., s. to N.J. and Minn.

purpurea: *B. pendula* cv.

pyramidalis: *B. pendula* cv. 'Fastigiata'.

rubra: *B. nigra.*

Sargentii: a listed name of no botanical standing.

Tauschii: *B. platyphylla* var. *japonica.*

ulmifolia: *B. grossa.*

urticifolia: *B. pubescens* cv.

utilis D. Don [*B. Bhojpattra* Lindl. ex Wallich]. To 60 ft., bark flaking, dark brown; lvs. ovate to 3 in. long, veins 10–14 pairs, pubescent underneath; cones cylindrical, peduncled, 1 in. long. Himalayas.

verrucosa: *B. pendula.*

BETULACEAE S. F. Gray [*Corylaceae* Mirb.]. BIRCH FAMILY. Dicot.; 6 genera and over 100 spp. of deciduous, mostly monoecious trees and shrubs, native mostly to N. Hemisphere; lvs. alt., simple; male fls. in long drooping catkins, female fls. in short catkins or clusters, stamens 2–10 in the axils of bracts, ovary inferior, 2-celled; fr. a nut or nutlet. The cult. genera are *Alnus, Betula, Carpinus, Corylus,* and *Ostrya.*

The family furnishes ornamentals, valuable timber, and some edible nuts; the bark of some species was once used for canoes and writing paper.

BIDENS L. BEGGAR-TICKS, BUR MARIGOLD, WATER M., PITCHFORKS, SPANISH-NEEDLES, STICK-TIGHTS, TICKSEED. *Compositae* (Helianthus Tribe). About 200 spp. of cosmopolitan ann. and per herbs; lvs. opp., toothed, cut, or divided; fl. heads usually radiate, sometimes discoid, solitary or clustered, involucre double, outer involucral bracts leafy, the inner membranous, receptacle scaly; disc fls. yellow, ray fls. mostly white or yellow, sometimes lacking; pappus of few, mostly retrorsely barbed awns. Closely allied to *Cosmos* and *Coreopsis.*

Some species are grown from seeds in the flower garden. Native wild species are usually weedy.

atrosanguinea: *Cosmos atrosanguineus.*

bipinnata L. [*B. tenuifolia* Tausch]. Ann., to 5 ft.; lvs. mostly 2–3-pinnate, segms. ovate to lanceolate, toothed; heads radiate, slender, only ¼ in. across; ray fls. inconspicuous, pale yellow. E. U.S., Asia; a pantrop. weed.

connata Muhlenb. Similar to and perhaps conspecific with *B. tripartita,* but barbs at the base of the achene upward-pointing. Wet places, e. N. Amer.

coronata (L.) Britt. [*B. trichosperma* (Michx.) Britt.; *Coreopsis trichosperma* Michx.]. Ann. or bien., to 5 ft.; lvs. to 5 in. long, pinnately cut, segms. lanceolate to linear, incised; heads radiate, to 2½ in. across; ray fls. golden-yellow. N. Amer.

ferulifolia (Jacq.) DC. FERN-LEAVED B.-T. Ann. or bien., to 3 ft. or more; lvs. pinnate or 2-pinnate, segms. linear; heads radiate, about 1 in. across, corymbose; fls. bright yellow. S. Ariz. and Mex.

grandiflora: *B. serrulata.*

humilis: *B. triplinervia* var. *macrantha.*

pilosa L. Ann., to 5 ft.; lvs. mostly 3–7-parted, segms. serrate, glabrate to tomentose-pilose; heads discoid or radiate, long-peduncled; variable and widespread sp., pantrop. Cult. only in the var. **radiata** Schultz.-Bip., which is shorter and has heads about 1 in. across, with 5–6 white, yellow, or pinkish ray fls. Tropics, Amer., Afr., Asia.

serrulata (Poir.) Desf. [*B. grandiflora* Balb.]. Ann., to 2½ ft., somewhat glaucous; lvs. 2–5 or more times pinnately divided, segms. linear or lanceolate, entire or toothed; heads radiate, 1½–2½ in. across; fls. golden-yellow. Mex.

tenuifolia: *B. bipinnata.*

trichosperma: *B. coronata.*

tripartita L. Ann., to 6 ft.; lvs. simple or more commonly 3–5-parted, segms. ovate to lanceolate, toothed; heads discoid, rarely with inconspicuous rays, disc less than 1 in. across; fls. yellow. Eur., Asia; naturalized in e. N. Amer.

triplinervia HBK. Diffuse per.; lvs. simple, serrate; heads radiate, 1–2½ in. across, long-peduncled; fls. yellow. S. Mex., to n. S. Amer. Only var. **macrantha** (Wedd.) Sherff [*B. humilis* HBK] is offered, differing in its pinnate to 3-pinnate lvs. with linear segms. S. Mex. to Chile.

BIENNIALS. These are plants that live for two years from seed, blooming only or mostly the second year. Some perennials are so short-lived that they become practically biennial in cultivation and may be so listed. Examples of plants that are actually or essentially biennial are *Alcea rosea, Brassica oleracea, Campanula Medium, Daucus Carota, Digitalis purpurea, Pastinaca sativa,* forms of *Trifolium pratense,* most *Verbascum* species, and *Viola ×Wittrockiana.* Of most ornamental kinds, bloom may be obtained from seeds sown the previous midsummer, the seedlings being transplanted promptly to insure continuous growth.

BIFRENARIA Lindl. [*Lindleyella* Schlechter]. *Orchidaceae.* Ten spp. of epiphytes, native to Cent. and S. Amer.; pseudobulbs 1-lvd.; lvs. leathery; fls. in lateral racemes, sepals and petals similar, lateral sepals decurrent on

column foot, forming a spur, lip usually 3-lobed, with a callus or ridges. For structure of fl. see *Orchidaceae.*

Intermediate or cool greenhouse; for culture see *Orchids.*

atropurpurea Lindl. Pseudobulbs to 3 in. long; lvs. linear-lanceolate, to 10 in. long; racemes 3–5-fld., to 3 in. long; fls. about 2 in. across, very fragrant, sepals and petals wine-red, with yellow center, lip entire, whitish, tinged with rose, with linear callus. Early summer. Brazil.

aurantiaca Lindl. [*Lindleyella aurantiaca* (Lindl.) Schlechter]. Pseudobulbs to 2 in. long; lvs. plicate, elliptic, to 10 in. long and 3 in. wide; racemes 7–13-fld., to 8 in. long; fls. yellow, spotted with purple, lip with a bright yellow callus between the wide lateral lobes. Winter–early spring. Trinidad, Guyana.

Harrisoniae (Hook.) Rchb.f. [*Lycaste Harrisoniae* Hort.]. Pseudobulbs to 3 in. long; lvs. narrow, elliptic, to 1 ft. long; racemes short, 1–3-fld.; fls. about 2¾ in. across, sepals and petals yellowish, tinged with red, lip violet-red, with hairy, yellow callus, base of column and lateral sepals prolonged into spur over 1 in. long. Spring. Brazil.

inodora Lindl. Similar to *B. Harrisoniae,* but fls. to 3 in. across, sepals and petals narrower, greenish-yellow, lip purple, with glabrous callus. Brazil.

tetragona (Lindl.) Schlechter [*Lycaste tetragona* Lindl.]. Pseudobulbs ovate, acutely 4-angled, to 4 in. long; lvs. to 18 in. long; racemes 3–4-fld., to 4 in. long; fls. 2 in. across, sepals and petals light yellow-green, streaked with red-brown, lip fleshy, whitish, sometimes yellowish-green beneath, deep maroon-violet toward base inside. Early summer. Brazil.

vitellina Lindl. Pseudobulbs to 1½ in. long; lvs. to 1 ft. long and 1½ in. wide; racemes 5–8-fld., to 8 in. long; fls. 1 in. across, orange-yellow, lip with purple spot. Early summer. Brazil.

BIGNONIA L. [*Anisostichus* Bur.]. *Bignoniaceae.* One sp., a woody, evergreen climber, native to e. N. Amer.; lvs. opp., compound, lfts. 2 with terminal tendril; fls. large, in axillary cymes, calyx truncate at apex or slightly 5-toothed, corolla funnelform, slightly 2-lipped, stamens 4; fr. a linear caps., flattened parallel to partition.

Grown as a wall cover in the South and sometimes in the greenhouse. Propagated by cuttings, and by seeds when available.

aequinoctialis: *Cydista aequinoctialis.*

australis: *Pandorea pandorana.*

callistegioides: *Clytostoma callistegioides.*

capensis: *Tecomaria capensis.*

capreolata L. [*B. crucigera* L., in part; *Anisostichus capreolatus* (L.) Bur.; *Campsis capreolata* Hort.; *Doxantha capreolata* (L.) Miers]. CROSS VINE, QUARTER V., TRUMPET FLOWER. Climbing, to 50 ft.; lfts. ovate or oblong, to 6 in. long, entire, tendrils branched; fls. yellow-red, paler inside, 2 in. long; caps. to 7 in. long. Spring. Woods and swamps, Va. and Fla., w. to Ill., La., e. Tex., but root-hardy farther north. Cv. 'Atrosanguinea' [*Bignonia capreolata* var. *atrosanguinea* Hook.f.]. Lfts. longer and narrower; fls. darker.

Chamberlaynii: *Anemopaegma Chamberlaynii.*

Cherere: *Distictis buccinatoria.*

chinensis: *Campsis grandiflora.*

crucigera: see *B. capreolata.*

grandiflora: *Campsis grandiflora.*

ignea: *Pyrostegia venusta.*

jasminoides: see *Pandorea jasminoides.*

laurifolia: a listed name for evergreen vine with lavender fls.

leucoxylon: *Tabebuia riparia.*

linearis: *Chilopsis linearis.*

magnifica: *Saritaea magnifica.*

muricata: *Pithecoctenium echinatum.*

pandorana: *Pandorea pandorana.*

pentaphylla: *Tabebuia riparia.*

purpurea: *Clytostoma binatum.*

radicans: *Campsis radicans.*

rotundata: *Arrabidaea rotundata.*

spathacea: *Dolichandrone spathacea.*

speciosa: *Clytostoma callistegioides.*

stans: *Tecoma stans.*

×**Tagliabuana:** a listed name of no botanical standing, used for *Campsis* ×*Tagliabuana.*

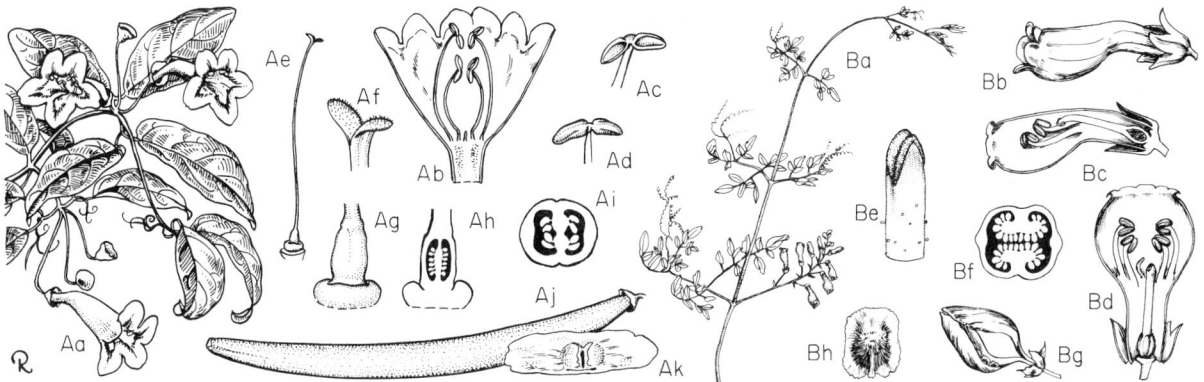

BIGNONIACEAE. **A,** *Bignonia capreolata:* **Aa,** flowering branch, × ⅓; **Ab,** corolla, expanded, × ½; **Ac, Ad,** anther, two views, × 1½; **Ae,** pistil, × ¾; **Af,** stigma, × 4; **Ag,** ovary with basal disc, × 3; **Ah,** ovary, vertical section, × 3; **Ai,** ovary, cross section, × 6; **Aj,** fruit, × ⅜; **Ak,** seed, × ½. **B,** *Eccremocarpus scaber:* **Ba,** flowering stem, × ⅛; **Bb,** flower, × 1; **Bc,** flower, vertical section, × 1; **Bd,** flower, with calyx and corolla expanded, × 1; **Be,** apex of style and stigma, × 5; **Bf,** ovary, cross section, × 6; **Bg,** fruit, × ½; **Bh,** seed, × 3.

Tweediana: *Macfadyena Unguis-cati.*

Unguis-cati: *Macfadyena Unguis-cati.*

venusta: *Pyrostegia venusta.*

violacea DC.: apparently a sp. of *Arrabidaea,* but material cult. as *B. violacea* is *Clytostoma callistegioides.*

BIGNONIACEAE Juss. BIGNONIA FAMILY. Dicot.; about 110 genera and 750 spp., of trees, shrubs, woody vines, rarely herbs, mostly trop. and subtrop. in distribution, a few spp. extending into temp. regions; lvs. opp. or rarely alt., simple or compound; infl. various; fls. bisexual, irregular, showy, calyx truncate to 5-toothed, sometimes spathelike, corolla funnelform to campanulate, often 2-lipped, stamens borne on petals, sometimes 2 or 5, but typically 4 in 2 pairs, staminodes 1–3 if present, ovary superior, 2-celled with axile placentation, sometimes 1-celled with parietal placentation; fr. usually a 2-valved caps., or infrequently indehiscent and gourdlike, seeds usually winged. Several genera yield important trop. timbers but the cult. genera, mainly ornamentals, include: *Adenocalymna, Anemopaegma, Arrabidaea, Bignonia, Campsis, Catalpa, Chilopsis, Clytostoma, Crescentia, Cybistax, Cydista, Delostoma, Deplanchea, Distictis, Dolichandra, Dolichandrone, Eccremocarpus, Enallagma, Fernandoa, Godmania, Haplophragma, Incarvillea, Jacaranda, Kigelia, Macfadyena, Markhamia, Millingtonia, Newbouldia, Oroxylum, Pandorea, Parmentiera, Paulownia, Pithecoctenium, Podranea, Pyrostegia, Radermachera, Rhigozum, Saritaea, Spathodea, Stereospermum, Tabebuia, Tecoma, Tecomaria, Tecomella,* and *Tisserantodendron.*

BILDERDYKIA: *POLYGONUM.*

BILLARDIERA Sm. *Pittosporaceae.* About 8 spp. of small shrubs with twining brs., native to Australia; lvs. alt.; fls. mostly yellow or purple, solitary or clustered, anthers not coming together around style, shorter than filaments, ovary 2-celled; fr. a berry.

Grown under glass or outdoors in mild climates (Zone 9). Propagated by cuttings under glass or by seeds.

longiflora Labill. Lvs. varying from ovate to linear, to 1½ in. long, entire; fls. greenish-yellow or becoming purple, solitary, drooping from slender pedicels to ½ in. long; berries blue or violet, sometimes pale.

BILLBERGIA Thunb. VASE PLANT. *Bromeliaceae.* About 52 spp. of stemless, epiphytic herbs, native to trop. Amer., especially e. Brazil; lvs. stiff, spinose, in generally tall and slender rosettes or clusters; infl. a spike or panicle, scapose, often pendent; fls. of short duration, usually sessile, with showy bracts, mostly irregular, petals green or blue, appendaged, ovary inferior; fr. a berry, seeds without appendages.

Grown as ornamentals outdoors in warm areas, or under glass, or as house plants. Of easy culture, preferring bright light for best development of foliage color and form. For culture see *Bromeliaceae.*

Numerous hybrids have been made, with *B. amoena, B. nutans, B. pyramidalis,* and *B. vittata* as chief parents of older crosses. Fancynamed, more recent hybrids include: 'Elvenia Slosson', lvs. deep green, becoming purplish-bronze in the sun, bracts red, fls. deep purple; 'Fantasia' [*B. pyramidalis* × *B. Saundersii*], flowering in the autumn or early spring, with habit of *B. pyramidalis,* lvs. blotched with white, green, and rose; 'Henry Teuscher' [*B. pyramidalis* × *B. venezuelana*], resembling *B. pyramidalis;* 'Muriel Waterman' [*B. Euphemiae* var. *purpurea* × *B. horrida* var. *tigrina*], lvs. plum-colored, banded with silvery-gray, bracts dull pink, fls. steel-blue; 'Thelma Darling Hodge', like *B. Porteana,* bracts rose, fls. yellowish-green, reflexed; 'Theodore L. Mead', of unknown parentage, a luxuriant grower, lvs. soft green, infl. drooping, bracts rose, fls. blue; 'Violet Beauty', lvs. blue-green, bracts rose, fls. violet.

Alberti: a listed name of no botanical standing.

amoena (Lodd.) Lindl. [*B. pallescens* C. Koch; *B. pallida* (Ker-Gawl.) Beer; *B. speciosa* Thunb.]. Lvs. linear, to 2 ft. long and 1½ in. wide, the inner truncate; infl. glabrous, paniculate at least in the lower half, upper fl. bracts minute, the lower sometimes red and expanded; fls. to 3 in. long, pale green, with lavender spots at apex. Brazil. A variable sp. Var. **rubra** M. B. Foster. Lvs. rich red, spotted with white and yellow. Var. **viridis** L. B. Sm. Fls. entirely green, with pink bracts.

angustifolia C. Koch. A dubious sp., incompletely known.

Bakeri: *B. distachia* var. *Straussiana.*

brasiliensis L. B. Sm. [*B. Leopoldii* of auth., not C. Koch]. Lvs. in a tubular rosette, to 3 ft. long and 1⅝ in. wide, spiny-margined, with broad silvery bands; infl. pendent, many-fld., white-mealy, densely spicate, with large rose bracts; fls. to 2⅝ in. long, blue-violet. Brazil.

Bucholtzii Mez. Lvs. to 16 in. long and 2½ in. wide, violet on inner face; infl. paniculate, glabrous, with minute fl. bracts above; fls. to 2¾ in. long, blue-violet. Brazil?

calophylla: a listed name of no botanical standing, once used for *B. vittata.*

Canterae: *B. zebrina.*

chiapensis Matuda. To 3 ft. or more; lvs. densely white-scaly; infl. pendent, mealy, fl. bracts erect; sepals ⅝ in. long, petals ¾ in. long. S. Mex. Drought-resistant.

corina: a listed name of no botanical standing.

distachia (Vell.) Mez. Lvs. few, in a short-tubular rosette, linear, minutely spiny, to 2½ ft. long and 1½ in. wide; infl. paniculate, simple, glabrous, few-fld., nodding; fls. to 2½ in. long, green with pale blue tinted tips; sepals acute. Brazil. Var. **Straussiana** (Wittm.) L. B. Sm. [*B. Bakeri* E. Morr.]. Inner lvs. unarmed; sepals rounded. Cvs. 'Albertii' and 'Rubra' have been listed.

Eipperi: a listed name of no botanical standing.

elegans: a listed name of no botanical standing.

Enderi: *Quesnelia lateralis.*

ensifolia Bak. Lvs. few, narrowly linear above a short-tubular rosette, brown-spiny; infl. unbranched, nodding, glabrous, few-fld.; fls.

not pedicelled, to 2¾ in. long, green, petals blue-tipped, not coiled after flowering. Brazil.

Euphemiae E. Morr. Stoloniferous; lvs. in a tubular rosette, to 1 ft. long and 2 in. wide, gray; infl. pendent, axis geniculate, unbranched, few-fld., densely white-mealy, with minute pink fl. bracts in upper part; fls. deep violet, to 1⅝ in. long, ovary white-mealy. Brazil. Var. **purpurea** M. B. Foster. Lvs. reddish-purple, without gray bands. Var. **saundersioides** L. B. Sm. Lvs. pale-spotted, but not banded.

horrida Regel. Lvs. in a tubular rosette, to 2 ft. long and 2 in. wide, green, with stout spines to ¼ in. long; infl. glabrous, unbranched, erect, with minute rose fl. bracts; fls. white or pale green, tipped with blue. Cv. 'Tigrina'. Lvs. brown, banded with white on back.

gothensis: a listed name of no botanical standing.

iridifolia (Nees & Mart.) Lindl. Stemless or nearly so; lvs. to 1½ ft. long, lanceolate, undulate, spiny, dark green above and purplish-green beneath; infl. unbranched, glabrous, fl. bracts rose-red, as long as fls.; fls. sessile, petals yellowish-green. Brazil. Fast-growing, excellent for hanging baskets. Var. **concolor** L. B. Sm. Lvs. entirely green. Brazil.

Leopoldii: *B. brasiliensis,* but material cult. as *B. Leopoldii* is *B. vittata.*

leptopoda L. B. Sm. PERMANENT-WAVE PLANT. Lvs. to 1 ft. long and 1⅜ in. wide, pale, scaly, spotted beneath, spiny; infl. unbranched, glabrous, erect, fl. bracts rose, longer than ovaries; fls. pedicelled, green, with dark blue tips. Brazil.

Lietzii E. Morr. Lvs. 6–10, cylindrical, to 1 ft. long, 1 in. wide, minutely spiny, not striped; infl. unbranched, few-fld., glabrous, erect or nodding; fl. bracts rose, not much shorter than ovary; sepals pale red, petals green or blue, not spirally recoiled, ovary glabrous. Brazil.

macrocalyx Hook. Lvs. erect or recurved, concave, to 2½ ft. long and 1⅝ in. wide, acute, somewhat spinose-serrate, dark green, with scattered pale green spots; infl. unbranched, erect, densely white-mealy, fl. bracts rose-red; fls. pedicelled, petals yellowish-green, tipped with blue. Brazil.

macrolepis L. B. Sm. To 3 ft.; lvs. linear-triangular, with large sheaths, to 4 ft. long, remotely spiny, gray-green, white-spotted beneath; infl. unbranched, to 16 in. long, curved downward, scape bracts imbricate, white-cottony; fls. bronze-green, to about 2 in. long. Costa Rica, Panama.

marmorata: *Quesnelia marmorata.*

Meyeri Mez. Lvs. in a tubular rosette, to 20 in. long and 2 in. wide, minutely spiny, dark gray-brown, gray-banded; infl. pendent, scape bracts pink, fl. bracts slightly shorter than sepals; fls. to 3 in. long, sepals lilac, petals green, blue- or violet-tipped, spirally coiled at apex after flowering. Brazil.

minarum L. B. Sm. To 3 ft.; lvs maroon-green, mottled with cream-white spots; scape curved, infl. pendent, upper fl. bracts minute; sepals and petals green, blue-tipped. Brazil.

Morelii Brongn. Lvs. to 16 in. long and 2 in. wide, with small spiny teeth; fls. in drooping, few-fld., dense, white-mealy spikes, scapes suberect, to 1 ft. long, with long red bracts, fl. bracts minute, sepals red, petals lilac, to 2 in. long. Brazil. Much material so named may be *B. Euphemiae.*

nobilis: a listed name of no botanical standing.

nutans H. Wendl. FRIENDSHIP PLANT, QUEEN'S-TEARS. Lvs. to 1½ ft. long and ½ in. wide, forming an open rosette, finely toothed, or the inner ones without teeth; scapes to 1 ft. long, infl. unbranched, bracts bright rose; fls. few, drooping, sepals about 1 in. long, rose, margined blue, petals green, edged with blue. Brazil. One of the commonest spp. in cult. and much used in hybridization.

organensis: a listed name of no botanical standing.

pallescens: *B. amoena.*

pallida: *B. amoena.*

pallidiflora Liebm. Lvs. arching, to 2 ft. long, spiny-toothed; scape arching, white-mealy, fl. bracts short; fls. sessile, petals green, partially coiled, to 2 in. long. S. Mex. to Nicaragua.

Porteana Brongn. ex Beer. Lvs. few, tubular, with recurved tips, to 3 ft. long, 2¼ in. wide, spiny-margined, more or less striped on back; infl. pendent, loosely fld., fl. bracts minute; fls. to 3 in. long, sepals acute, petals green, becoming spirally coiled after flowering. Brazil.

pyramidalis (Sims) Lindl. [*B. thyrsiflora* Hort. ex Gentil; *B. thyrsoidea* Mart. ex Schult.]. FOOLPROOF PLANT. Lvs. to 3 ft. long and 2½ in. wide, finely spiny-toothed; infl. a dense, white-mealy, pyramidal spike, to 4 in. long, bracts bright orange-red; petals red, tipped with violet. Brazil. Var. **concolor** L. B. Sm. Petals entirely red.

rhodocyanea: *Aechmea fasciata.*

rosea Beer. Lvs. very stiff, banded, more or less reddish; infl. pendent, mealy, densely cylindrical, fl. bracts small; fls. sessile, to 3⅜ in. long, sepals unequal, petals yellow-green, spirally twisted. Trinidad.

rubrocyanea: a listed name of no botanical standing; *B. Saundersii* has been grown and listed under this name.

Sanderana E. Morr. Lvs. leathery, about 1 ft. long and 2½ in. wide, spiny-toothed; panicles glabrous, loose, to 10 in. long, on nodding scapes, fl. bracts rose, about ⅓ as long as ovary; sepals entire, tipped with blue, petals blue, with yellowish-green claw. Brazil.

Saundersii Hort. ex C. Koch. RAINBOW PLANT. Lvs. in a short-tubular rosette, green above, reddish beneath, with red spines and white blotches; infl. white-mealy, unbranched, nodding, with minute fl. bracts in upper part; fls. pedicelled, greenish, tipped with blue. Brazil.

speciosa: *B. amoena.*

thrysiflora: *B. pyramidalis.*

thyrsoidea: *B. pyramidalis.*

venezuelana Mez. Lvs. in a tubular rosette, to 3 ft. long, rigid, mottled or banded with maroon and silver; infl. very showy, pendent, mealy, lower fl. bracts larger than sepals, pink; fls. sessile, to 2¾ in. long, petals and stamens purple, coiled. Venezuela. One of the most ornamental sp. in the genus.

vittata Brongn. [*B. Leopoldii* C. Koch.] To 3 ft.; lvs. to 3 ft. long, 2½ in. wide or more, transversely banded beneath, apex recurved, obtuse, and abruptly pointed with red spine; infl. paniculate, glabrous, fl. bracts red, conspicuous; sepals awned, petals deep blue, recurved. Brazil. A variable sp.

×**Windii** Hort. Makoy ex E. Morr.: *B. decora* Poepp. & Endl. × *B. nutans.* Lvs. to nearly 3 ft. long, 1¼ in. wide, weakly toothed, green, indistinctly gray-banded beneath; infl. simple, pendent, bracts light rose to carmine; fls. green, tipped with blue and margined with red.

zebrina (Herb.) Lindl. [*B. Canterae* André]. Lvs. to 3 ft. long and 3 in. wide, prickly-toothed, spotted and banded with white; infl. a white-mealy spike on drooping scape shorter than lvs., bracts pink or salmon, fl. bracts minute; fls. green or yellowish-green, petals spirally twisted at tip after flowering. Brazil.

×**BILTANTHUS**: ×*CRYPTBERGIA.*

BILTIA: *RHODODENDRON.*

BINGHAMIA: *ESPOSTOA.* **B. chosicensis**: *Haageocereus chosicensis.*

BIOPHYTUM DC. *Oxalidaceae.* About 50 spp. of trop., caulescent herbs and subshrubs, native to Asia, Afr., and Amer.; lvs. pinnate, crowded toward tip of sts.; fls. yellow or pink, in umbellate or capitate infls., regular, sepals 5, petals 5, stamens 10, in 2 series; fr. a caps., the valves separating at maturity.

sensitivum (L.) DC. LIFE PLANT. Sts. simple, to 10 in.; lvs. to 5 in. long, lfts. 8–17 pairs, rectangular to cuneate-obovate, to ½ in. long, sensitive to touch. Trop. Afr. and Asia.

BIOTA: *PLATYCLADUS.*

BIRDS (PLANTINGS FOR). Birds and gardens go together, for most plants shelter or are hosts to insects, which are the usual food for many birds. Birds in the garden and on the home grounds thus assure one kind of natural biological pest control. The person who enjoys the presence of native songbirds can, with a little extra planning, make his permanent plantings even more attractive to avian visitors by supplying plant materials that offer additional attractants to birds. Just how attractive some plants can be is known all too well by the gardener who grows such small fruits as blueberries, cherries, or strawberries, whose natural dispersal is dependent upon the appeal of the fruits to birds.

The three basic life requirements of wild birds are natural food, nesting sites, and protective cover or hiding places. For most field, forest, or woodland birds these requirements are largely supplied by plants. Where grounds are spacious, it is often wise to make mass plantings or thickets of the native species, usually trees, shrubs, and vines, that are locally favored by birds. Where garden space is limited, exotic woody ornamentals may be used and can be equally attractive to birds. Carefully selected plantings can serve the avian population throughout the year particularly in the production of fruits and seeds that are especially sought by many birds. Some woody species with early-appearing soft fruits, like those of the juneberries *(Amelanchier),* provide food for fledglings in the nesting season; later-maturing fruits of the several dogwoods *(Cornus)* or woodbine *(Parthenocissus)* are attractive to migrants flocking in late summer and early autumn; and, finally, plants like birch *(Betula),* holly *(Ilex),* tulip tree *(Liriodendron),* and fire thorn *(Pyracantha)* supply berries and seeds sought by birds resident during the winter.

A considerable literature is available detailing by regions plants that attract and shelter birds. The interested person may locate such references through local chapters of the Audubon Society and state or federal departments of agriculture.

BISCHOFIA Blume. *Euphorbiaceae.* One sp. of dioecious, evergreen or partly deciduous trees, native to trop. Asia; lvs. alt., long-petioled; fls. without petals, ovary 3- or rarely 4-celled; fr. berrylike.

javanica Blume [*B. trifoliata* (Roxb.) Hook.]. TOOG. To 75 ft.; lvs. compound, lfts. 3, ovate-acuminate, 2–5 in. long, serrulate, bronzy-green; fls. small, greenish, in many-fld. racemes; fr. yellow, brown, reddish, or blue-black, size of a pea. Sometimes planted in the extreme South. Zone 10. Important timber tree.

trifoliata: *B. javanica.*

BISCUTELLA L. *Cruciferae.* About 40 spp. of ann. or per. herbs in cent. Eur., Medit. region, and se. Asia, sts. mostly slender; basal lvs. entire to pinnatifid; fls. small, yellow, sepals 4, petals 4, usually clawed; fr. a silicle, with 2 flattened, orbicular, winged lobes.

laevigata L. Per., to 2 ft., sts. simple or branched; lvs. variable, basal lvs. often in a rosette, long-oblong and toothed; fls. in terminal racemes; silicle about ⁵⁄₁₆ in. across. Spring and summer. Cent. and s. Eur. Sometimes planted as an ornamental because of its interesting twin frs.

BISMARCKIA Hildebrandt & H. Wendl. *Palmae.* One sp., a solitary, moderately tall, stout, dioecious palm of Madagascar; lvs. costapalmate, petioles elongate, margins armed with minute spinelike teeth; infls. among lvs., peduncle elongate, sheathed by several tubular bracts, primary brs. several, each sheathed by a tubular bract and with few, digitately arranged, catkinlike flowering brs. covered with imbricate bractlets in male plants, flowering brs. similar but reduced to 1–2 in the female plants, fls. sunken in pits formed by the bractlets; male fls. in clusters of 3, calyx deeply 3-lobed, petals united in a solid base with 3 separate, imbricate lobes, stamens 6, pistillode minute, female fls. solitary, stalked, sepals and petals 3, similar, imbricate, staminode a 6-lobed ring, pistil 3-celled, 3-ovuled; fr. stalked, globose-ovoid, dry and fibrous, endocarp bony, with many longitudinal internal ridges penetrating the seed, endosperm homogeneous.

A majestic ornamental fan palm with attractive blue foliage. Should not be moved bare-rooted. For culture see *Palms.*

nobilis Hildebrandt & H. Wendl. [*Medemia nobilis* (Hildebrandt & H. Wendl.) Gallerand]. To 25 ft. or more, sts. 10 in. in diam.; lf. blades waxy blue-gray, to 4 ft. long or more, segms. about 75, stiff, 1-ribbed; infls. to 4 ft. long or more; brs. of male infl. to 9 in. long, ⅛ in. in diam., with 4–7 red-brown rachillae, brs. of female infl. slightly longer and thicker; fr. to 1⅜ in. long on a stalk to ¾ in. long. Planted as an ornamental in the tropics and in warmer parts of Zone 10a in s. Fla.

BIVONEA: *CNIDOSCOLUS.*

BIXA L. *Bixaceae.* One sp.; characteristics those of the family.

Orellana L. ANNATTO, LIPSTICK TREE, ACHIOTE. To 20 ft.; lvs. ovate, to 7 in. long; fls. pink or rose to white, to 2 in. across, stamens yellow; caps. reddish-brown to crimson, to 2 in. long, covered with soft spines, seeds with a thin, waxy, bright red aril. Prop. by seeds and cuttings. Grown in s. Fla. as an ornamental for the colorful red fr. Zone 10b. A major source of red body paint for Indian tribes of trop. Amer.; now much planted in the tropics for the bright yellow, nearly tasteless dye (annatto) extracted from the arils of the seeds and used as a food colorant.

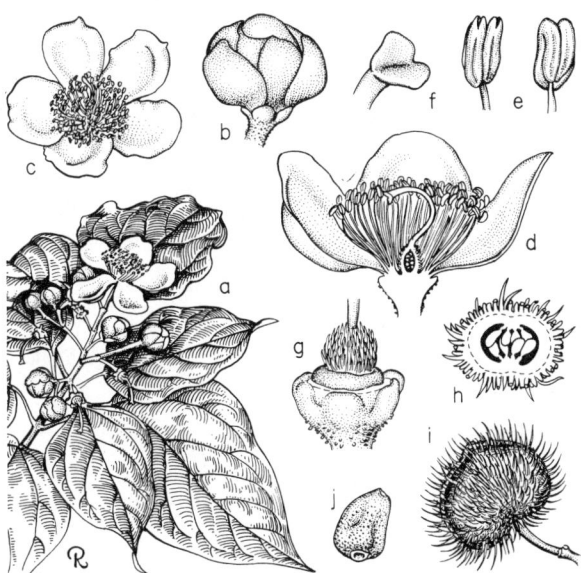

BIXACEAE. *Bixa Orellana:* **a,** flowering branch, × ¼; **b,** flower bud, × 1; **c,** flower, × ½; **d,** flower, vertical section, × 1; **e,** anther, two views, × 5; **f,** stigma, × 5; **g,** calyx, ovary, and base of style, × 2; **h,** ovary, cross section, × 4; **i,** fruit, × ½; **j,** seed, × 2.

BIXACEAE Link. BIXA FAMILY. Dicot.; 1 genus, *Bixa,* allied to Cochlospermaceae; a shrub or small tree, native to trop. Amer. and naturalized in tropics of Old World; lvs. alt., simple, palmately veined, stipuled; fls. in panicles, regular, bisexual, sepals and petals 5, imbricate, stamens many, ovary superior, 1-celled, with 2 parietal placentas; fr. a caps.

BLACKBERRY. Most blackberry cultivars have been developed from species indigenous to North America. Species are found all over the continent and quantities of fruit are gathered from the wild throughout their natural ranges. The cultivated blackberries of North America can be classified into five major groups: (1) the erect or nearly erect types, like cultivars 'Early Harvest' and 'Eldorado', of the eastern United States; (2) the eastern trailing types without red hairs on the canes, similar to cultivar 'Lucretia', with a distribution similar to that of the erect types; (3) the southeastern trailing types with red hairs on the canes, found along the Atlantic and Gulf Coasts from Delaware to Texas; (4) the trailing types of the Pacific Coast, from which cultivar 'Logan' was derived; (5) the semitrailing evergreen types of the Pacific Coast. Although the pomological blackberries and dewberries in North America are derived from native species, the cultivars cannot now always be referred to their original sources. Trailing blackberries are frequently called dewberries, ground blackberries, or running blackberries, and have canes that are not self-supporting; in cultivation they must be tied to poles or to a trellis. Fruit clusters of trailing blackberries are smaller and more open than those of the erect types and ripen earlier.

The culture of the blackberry is limited by the cold winters of the northern and plains states and by drought and dry heat in the Southwest. Almost any good soil will grow blackberries, provided that it is well drained and retentive of moisture and has a good humus content.

Propagation of cultivars is by suckers, which come up from the roots and, for more rapid increase, by root cuttings. Roots are cut into sections 3–4 inches long, buried in soil or placed in cold storage during the winter to form a callus, and planted in the nursery row in early spring. Some of the trailing cultivars root at the tips of the canes. Planting is done in very early spring, the erect tpes 2–3 feet apart in rows 7–9 feet apart, or in hills 3–4 feet apart; the vigorous trailing or semitrailing types (such as 'Smoothstem', 'Thornfree', and 'Thornless

Evergreen') 8–12 feet apart in rows 10 feet apart; and other trailing types 4–6 feet apart in rows 7–9 feet apart.

Shallow, clean cultivation is essential for successful culture of blackberries. Home plantings may be mulched to combat weeds and to retain moisture. Suckers outside the row or hill must be destroyed or the plantings will become a thicket. Blackberries respond to the application of manure or complete fertilizer on poor soils. Care should be taken not to stimulate the plants to excessive vigor.

Pruning consists of cutting out the fruiting canes soon after the fruit is picked and thinning out the new canes in the early spring to space them about 1 foot apart in the row or five to six to the hill. The canes are biennial, growing from the ground one year and fruiting the next year. Canes of the erect types may be topped at 5 feet if very vigorous, stimulating lateral branching. The lateral branches may then be pruned in early spring to 8–12 inches in length. Trailing types should be trained on a trellis in early spring before growth starts. For fresh fruit, hand picking is required, and fruit for home use should become soft-ripe on the plants. Most commercial plantings are harvested mechanically.

In choosing cultivars, adaptation to climate is important. Useful hardy older cultivars now seldom offered include: 'Ebony King', 'Eldorado', 'De Soto', and 'Snyder'.

Select modern cultivars recommended by area are: for the northeastern United States, 'Bailey' and 'Darrow'; for Maryland, Arkansas, and the central United States, 'Black Satin', 'Cherokee', 'Comanche', 'Dirksen Thornless', 'Ranger', 'Raven', 'Smoothstem', and 'Thornfree'; for Georgia, Florida, and the Gulf states, 'Flint', 'Flordagrand', 'Gem', 'Georgia', 'Oklawaha', and 'Thornless'; for Texas and the Southwest, 'Brazos', 'Dallas', 'Humble', and 'Mayes'; for Washington and Oregon, 'Aurora', 'Cascade', 'Chehalem', 'Marion', and 'Olallie'.

Care should be taken to plant only disease-free plants. If rust is prevalent, the only remedy is to plant resistant cultivars or to weed out diseased plants systematically. Insect, disease, and weed control measures are similar to those of the raspberry.

BLANDFORDIA Sm. *Liliaceae.* Four spp. of fibrous-rooted, per. herbs of Tasmania and e. and se. Australia; lvs. 2-ranked, mostly basal, linear; fls. funnelform to almost campanulate, 6-lobed, drooping, in terminal, bracted racemes, stamens 6, united to perianth; fr. a stalked caps., seeds many.

Adapted to mild climates. Propagated by seeds and occasionally by division of roots.

Cunninghamii Lindl. To 3 ft.; lvs. 1–2 ft. long, about ⅜ in. wide, upper lvs. erect, with subulate tips; fls. 6–18 in dense racemes, on pedicels equalling the bracts, red with yellow tips, 2 in. long, tube narrow below, abruptly expanding in upper part, stamens attached below middle of perianth tube. New S. Wales.

flammea: *B. grandiflora.*

grandiflora R. Br. [*B. flammea* Lindl. ex Paxt.]. To 3 ft. or more; lvs. linear, to 1½ ft. long; fls. in loose, few-fld. racemes, yellow to orange, suffused red at base, 1½ in. long or more, almost campanulate, on pedicels 1½–2 in. long and much longer than bracts. Queensland and New S. Wales.

marginata: *B. punicea.*

nobilis Sm. To 3 ft.; lvs. to 1½ ft. long and ³⁄₁₆ in. wide; fls. in few-fld. loose racemes, brownish-red with yellow lobes, to 1¼ in. long, longer than pedicels, perianth tube narrow, abruptly expanded. New S. Wales.

punicea (Labill.) Sweet [*B. marginata* Herb.]. Rather stout, 2–3 ft.; lvs. to 1½ ft. long, and 1½ in. wide, suberect, with rough margins; fls. in dense racemes, brick- to copper-red outside, yellowish inside, to 1½ in. long, tapering toward the base, on pedicels as long as the bracts, stamens attached well above middle of perianth tube. Tasmania.

BLECHNUM L. *Polypodiaceae.* Over 200 spp. of rather coarse ferns, cosmopolitan, but mainly in S. Hemisphere; lvs. pinnatifid or 1-pinnate, dimorphic or uniform, sterile pinnae with veinlets free, not netted; sori in a line close to midrib of segm., indusium present.

A few species are cultivated in greenhouses, or outdoors in warmer climates. Propagated by spores except in the species that develop

plantlets at the ends of the creeping rhizomes. Blechnums require a rather dry atmosphere, but plenty of moisture at the roots, and a temperature of 60°–65° F. Species with creeping rhizomes are useful in borders; others, as *B. Spicant,* may be grown singly as specimen plants. See also *Ferns.*

auriculatum Cav. [*B. hastatum* Kaulf.; *B. remotum* K. Presl]. Rhizomes short, stout, scaly; lvs. lanceolate, to 2 ft. long, 2–4 in. wide, 1-pinnate; pinnae 20–40 pairs, upper side of pinnae cordate with a large ear; sori in a line midway between midrib and margin. Temp. S. Amer.

brasiliense Desv. [*B. corcovadense* Raddi var. *crispum* of some auth.]. Trunk to 3 ft., dark brown, scaly; lvs. to 3 ft. long, 15 in. wide, oblong-lanceolate, deeply pinnatifid, tapering basally, pinnae usually connected at the base. Brazil, Peru. Cv. 'Crispum'. Lvs. smaller, red when young, pinnae crowded, with undulate margins.

capense (L.) Schlechtend. Rhizomes stout, scaly; lvs. dimorphic, sterile lvs. to 3 ft. long, 1 ft. wide, 1-pinnate, with a terminal pinna, pinnae to 20 pairs, linear, 3–12 in. long, ½–1 in. wide, serrate, gradually narrowed at apex. S. Afr.

corcovadense var. **crispum:** *B. brasiliense.*

crispum: *Cryptogramma crispa.*

discolor (G. Forst.) Keyserl. Rhizomes stout; lvs. dimorphic, sterile lvs. oblong-lanceolate, to 3 ft. long, 6 in. wide, deeply pinnatifid, tapering gradually at base, petioles black, glossy. Australia, New Zeal.

fluviatile (R. Br.) Salomon. Trunkless or nearly so; lvs. dimorphic, linear, to 2½ ft. long, 1½ in. wide, 1-pinnate, midrib densely scaly throughout, pinnae obtuse, the sterile ones oblong, fertile ones linear. Australia, New Zeal.

fraxineum Willd. Rhizomes slender, creeping; lvs. 1-pinnate, the blade to 1 ft. long, to 8 in. wide, terminal pinna large, lateral pinnae 3–6 on each side, strongly curved, petioles slender, 6–12 in. long. Tropics, N. and S. Amer.

gibbum (Labill.) Mett. Trunk to 5 ft., scaly, black; lvs. dimorphic, sterile lvs. oblong-lanceolate, to 3 ft. long, 1 ft. wide, deeply pinnatifid, tapering gradually at base, lowest pinnae not connected to each other at the base. New Caledonia, Aneityum (New Hebrides) and Isle of Pines in S. Pacific. Material in the trade as *B. Moorei* [*B. Moorei* Hort., not C. Chr.] is a hardier variant of this sp. with fewer, more erect lvs., pinnae ⅝ in. wide or more, midveins and petioles reddish-pink when young. Cv. 'Platyptera'. Larger, more erect, fertile lvs. predominating.

hastatum: *B. auriculatum.*

lineatum C. Chr. Trunk stout, to 4 in., scaly; lvs. dimorphic, sterile lvs. oblong to narrowly lanceolate, to 5 ft. long, to 1½ ft. wide, 1-pinnate, with a terminal pinna, pinnae 20–40 pairs, curved, serrate, somewhat revolute, grayish-green. Tropics, N. and S. Amer.

Moorei C. Chr. Trunk to 12 in., to 1½ in. thick; lvs. dimorphic, sterile lvs. ovate-oblong, to 2 ft. long, to 1 ft. wide, deeply pinnatifid, narrowed basally, pinnae lobed, apex truncate, notched, or bifid, bearing a fringe of cilia, lowest pinnae often separate, petioles blackish. New Caledonia. Perhaps not in cult.; material in the trade under this name is referable to a variant of *B. gibbum.*

occidentale L. HAMMOCK FERN. Rhizomes creeping underground, stoloniferous; lvs. ovate-acuminate, to 1½ ft. long, 4–8 in. wide, 1-pinnate in lower half, pinnatifid above, pinnae 12–24 pairs, linear, curved, narrowed to a bluntish point, the lower ones cordate, the lowest deflexed, not much smaller than those above. Trop. Amer.

orientale L. Trunk stout, to 2 ft. or more; lvs. ovate, to 5 ft. long, to 3 ft. wide, 1-pinnate, pinnae many, linear, narrowed to a long point, the lowest reduced to very small auricles. Australia, Malay Pen., China, Himalayas.

remotum: *B. auriculatum.*

serrulatum L. Rich. SAW FERN., SWAMP F. Rhizomes widely creeping underground; lvs. 2–3 together, linear to broadly oblong, to 2 ft. long, to 1 ft. wide, 1-pinnate throughout, pinnae many, jointed at point of attachment, narrowly oblong to linear, acute or acutish at apex, inequilateral at base, spinulose-serrulate. N. and S. Amer.

Spicant (L.) Roth. [*Struthiopteris Spicant* (L.) Weiss]. DEER FERN. Rhizomes erect; lvs. evergreen, dimorphic, sterile lvs. lanceolate-linear, to 3½ ft. long, to 1½ in. wide, deeply pinnatifid; pinnae many, close, oblong to oblong-linear, obtuse to acute, the lowest often separate from one another at the base and broadly joined to midrib. Alaska to Calif.; Eur., Asia. Hardy. Var. **californica.** A listed name of no botanical standing.

virginicum: *Woodwardia virginica.*

unilaterale Swartz. Rhizomes creeping, stoloniferous; lvs. lanceolate, to 2 ft. long, to 3 in. wide, pinnate at base, pinnatifid in upper part, pinnae many, spreading, linear, ¾–1 in. long, the lower distant, small, broader than long, irregularly triangular, entire or nearly so. Trop. Amer.

BLEPHARIGLOTTIS: *HABENARIA.* **B. grandiflora:** *H. psychodes.*

BLEPHILIA Raf. *Labiatae.* Two spp. of per. herbs, of e. N. Amer.; sts. mostly square in cross section; lvs. opp., simple; fls. in axillary or terminal, globose verticillasters; calyx tubular, 13-nerved, 2-lipped, upper lip with 3 awned teeth, lower lip with 2 awnless teeth, tube naked in throat, corolla inflated at throat, limb 2-lipped, upper lip erect, entire, lower lip 3-lobed, middle lobe emarginate, lateral lobes ovate, larger than middle lobe, stamens 4, exserted, upper pair minute or absent; fr. of 4 nutlets. Resembling *Monarda*, but corolla smaller, more dilated, and calyx tube 13-nerved.

Adapted to the wild garden; propagated by seeds or division.

ciliata (L.) Benth. To 2 ft., somewhat pubescent, rarely branched; lvs. ovate to oblong-lanceolate, to 3 in. long, narrowed at base, remotely dentate, almost sessile; verticillasters terminal, in a spikelike infl., lowermost distant from the ones above, bracts several below each verticillaster, ovate-acuminate, to ½ in. long, ¼ in. wide, colored, ciliate; calyx ⁵⁄₁₆ in. long, upper lip longer than lower, corolla bluish-purple, rarely white, to ½ in. long. Dry woods, Vt. to Wisc., s. to Ga. and e. Tex.

hirsuta (Pursh) Benth. WOOD MINT. To 2½ ft., hairy, branched; lvs. lanceolate, to 3½ in. long, rounded or cordate at base, dentate, long-petioled, uppermost lvs. and bracts linear-subulate; calyx longer than bracts, long-haired, corolla pale lavender-blue, spotted purple. Moist shady places, Vt. to Minn., s. to Ga. and e. Tex.

BLETIA Ruiz & Pav. *Orchidaceae.* About 45 spp. of erect, terrestrial herbs, native to trop. Amer.; allied to *Calanthe*, but differing in having lip not spurred, and only jointed to, not fused with, base of column; lvs. plicate, 2–4, long and narrow; scape erect, arising from side of corm, leafless; fls. few to many, in terminal, often branched racemes, sepals and petals similar, often not spreading very widely, lip usually 3-lobed, with longitudinal crests or ridges. For structure of fl. see *Orchidaceae.*

For culture see *Orchids.*

alta: *B. purpurea.*

catenulata Ruiz & Pav. [*B. Sherrattiana* Batem. ex Hook.f.]. To 6 ft.; scape loosely few-fld.; fls. large, blood-red, pink, or purple, sepals and petals spreading, to 1½ in. long, lip 3-lobed, lateral lobes spreading and not enfolding column, midlobe transverse, 2-lobed, more intensely colored than other segms. Early spring–early autumn. Ecuador, Peru, Bolivia, Brazil.

florida: *B. purpurea.*

hyacinthina: *Bletilla striata.*

patula Hook. To 2 ft.; scape loosely few-fld.; fls. pink or light magenta, sepals and petals spreading, 1 in. long, lip marked with white, entire or obscurely lobed, base partially enfolding column. Flowering throughout the year. W. Indies.

purpurea (Lam.) DC. [*B. alta* A. S. Hitchc.; *B. florida* R. Br.; *B. Shepherdii* Hook.; *B. verecunda* R. Br.]. PINE PINK. To 4 ft.; infl. racemose or paniculate, loosely many-fld.; sepals and petals spreading, rose-purple or crimson, to 1 in. long, lip distinctly 3-lobed, midlobe narrow and cleft at apex. Flowering throughout the year. Trop. and subtrop. Amer.

Shepherdii: *B. purpurea.*

Sherrattiana: *B. catenulata.*

striata: *Bletilla striata.*

tuberosa: *Calopogon tuberosus.*

verecunda: *B. purpurea.*

BLETILLA Rchb.f. *Orchidaceae.* Nine spp. of terrestrial herbs with tuberous rhizomes, confined to temp. e. Asia; lvs. plicate, rather thin; fls. in terminal racemes on leafless scapes, sepals and petals similar, lip separate, 3-lobed. For structure of fl. see *Orchidaceae.*

Sometimes planted outdoors in the woodland garden; for culture see *Orchids.*

hyacinthina: *B. striata.*

striata (Thunb.) Rchb.f. [*B. hyacinthina* (Sm.) Rchb.f. ex Pfitz.; *Bletia hyacinthina* (Sm.) R. Br.; *B. striata* (Thunb.) Druce]. To 2 ft.; lvs. 3–5; racemes longer than lvs., 3–7-fld.; fls. purple, about 1 in. long. Early summer. China, Japan. Zone 8. Cv. 'Alba'. Fls. white.

BLIGHIA K. König. *Sapindaceae.* Four spp. of evergreen, mostly dioecious trees and shrubs, native to trop. Afr.; lvs. alt., pinnate; fls. usually in axillary racemes, regular, unisexual, sepals and petals 5, stamens 8–10; fr. a fleshy, 3-valved caps.

Akees withstand a few degrees of frost when well established. They succeed on moist loamy soils; usually propagated by seeds.

sapida K. König [*Cupania sapida* (K. König) Voigt]. AKEE. Tree, to 40 ft.; lfts. 6–10, oblong or obovate, to 6 in. long; fls. small, greenish-white; fr. straw-colored to magenta-red, 3 in. long, splitting into 3 parts, each with 1 shining seed having a white fleshy aril at base. W. Afr. Cult. and naturalized widely in tropics and subtropics including Fla. Zone 10. The arils are edible when fresh and ripe; the pink raphe attaching the aril to the seed and the arils of unripe or fallen fr. are poisonous.

BLOOMERIA Kellogg. *Amaryllidaceae.* Two spp. of herbs native to Calif.; corms fibrous-coated; lvs. basal, grasslike; infl. an umbel terminal on a scape and subtended by several papery spathe valves; fls. yellow, wheel-shaped, perianth segms. separate, or nearly so, filaments filiform, with cup-shaped, winged, often 2-pointed appendage around the base, ovary superior; fr. a loculicidal caps.

Bloomerias withstand several degrees of frost. The plants thrive in sandy, well-drained soil, and a sunny exposure. The corms should be dug after ripening and replanted in autumn; they are good summer bloomers. Propagated by seeds.

aurea: *B. crocea* var.

crocea (Torr.) Cov. GOLDEN-STARS. To 1½ ft.; lvs. solitary, ¼–½ in. wide; fls. orange-yellow, striped with darker lines, ½ in. long, filaments papillose, with 2 short teeth at apex. Var. **aurea** (Kellogg) J. Ingram [*B. aurea* Kellogg]. Filaments with 2 awnlike points at apex.

BLUEBERRY. Certain species of the genus *Vaccinium* in North America are known as blueberries or sometimes locally as huckleberries, but are not to be confused with the true huckleberries of the genus *Gaylussacia*. The latter, unlike the species of *Vaccinium*, have blackish, spicy fruits with ten large stony seeds and foliage usually spotted with resinous dots. The native blueberries may be classified as lowbush and highbush species; the latter, the source of our horticulturally important cultivars, have a more southeastern center of abundance.

The lowbush species are not ordinarily cultivated, but native stands (blueberry barrens) of the northernmost low sweet blueberry, *Vaccinium angustifolium*, and the velvet-leaf blueberry, *V. myrtilloides*, in New England and maritime Canada are sources of commercial fruit gathered in large quantities and utilized for canning, freezing, and the fresh-fruit market. Wild lowbush blueberries form extensive colonies by subterranean rhizomes. They grow to a height of only 1–2 feet and thrive in areas that have been cut and burned. Lowbush blueberries are pruned every two or three years by burning, a process which removes all the tops and most of the competing weeds. Plants produce their fruiting wood the first growing season after burning and the first crop appears the following year. Fields are burned while the soil is still frozen and before any growth takes place in the spring.

Most cultivated blueberries are largely derived from two native highbush species, the common highbush blueberry, *V. corymbosum*, and the rabbit-eye blueberry, *V. Ashei*. Of these, the former is the more important and is the principal type cultivated in the major blueberry-producing states—New Jersey, Michigan, North Carolina, Washington, and Oregon. Highbush and rabbit-eye blueberries have been greatly improved in productiveness and size of fruit by selection and breeding. While bush blueberries are found in many different parts of the country, they have very exacting soil and climatic requirements. However, rabbit-eye cultivars are less sensitive to soil type and are more heat- and drought-resistant than cultivars of the common highbush blueberry. The latter requires moist acidic soil (pH 4.0–5.2) with good drainage and aeration. Higher pH may result in chlorosis due to iron deficiency or lack of the ammonia form of nitrogen. The addition of sulfur to soils may correct this condition. High organic matter (3–15 percent) is also important. Highbush blueberries will not tolerate temperatures below −20° F and are killed to the ground at −30° F. For best performance, a growing season of at least 160 days is required. The southern limit for cultivars of *V. corymbosum* is about 300 miles north of the Gulf of Mexico. Plants start to bear well in their third year and with proper care are long-lived, reaching a height of 6–8 feet when mature. Besides their primary importance in producing edible fruits, highbush blueberries are also valued for their bloom and for the attractive, if subdued, color of their foliage in autumn. Because of this, in areas where azaleas or other ericaceous shrubs thrive, blueberries are sometimes effectively combined as ornamentals in plantings because of their similar cultural needs. Berries produced by such plants may be harvested for home use or left to attract birds to the garden.

When grown for their fruits, highbush plants are set at either a 4 × 9 feet or a 4 × 10 feet spacing. In home plantings it is advisable to set plants in ample holes or trenches about 1 foot deep in a mixture of peat or partially decomposed sawdust mixed with sand. Clean cultivation is generally practiced to protect them from competing weeds. Since they are naturally adapted to lowland soils, attempts to adapt blueberry plants to drier soils of a higher pH and lower organic matter have necessitated the use of mulches. Sawdust, peat, oak leaves, pine needles, or other material is satisfactory for this purpose and useful in home or other small plantings. Good drainage and aeration are required but a uniform and adequate supply of soil moisture is essential for proper growth. If natural soil water is inadequate, irrigation is required. Blueberry plants have been found to respond more to nitrogen than to any other fertilizer element and it has a profound effect on growth. Chemical fertilizers like ammonium sulfate that have an acid reaction in the soil are recommended. To prevent bird depredation, home plants may be covered with protective nettings when the fruits mature. Propagation of the blueberry is by dividing the clumps or rhizomes, by layering, or by cuttings. The last, used to produce nursery-grown plants, are usually hardwood cuttings taken in late winter or early spring from shoots produced the previous season.

Important cultivars derived mainly from *V. corymbosum* are 'Berkeley', 'Bluecrop', 'Blueray', 'Bluetta', 'Collins', 'Coville', 'Darrow', 'Dixi', 'Earliblue', 'Herbert', 'Jersey', 'Lateblue', 'Pemberton', and 'Rubel'. 'Angola', 'Croatan', and 'Wolcott' are recommended for North Carolina. These blueberries require cross-pollination for maximum crops.

Rabbit-eye *(V. Ashei)* cultivars are mainly seedling selections dug from the wild in northern Florida, Alabama, and Georgia. These produce mostly small, black, and grittyfleshed berries. Rabbit-eye types have a shorter cold requirement and are much better adapted to highland conditions than the cultivars of *V. corymbosum*. Recommended rabbit-eye cultivars are 'Callaway', 'Coastal', 'Garden Blue', 'Homebell', 'Menditoo', 'Tifblue', and 'Woodward'. These cultivars are nearly self-sterile and two different cultivars must be planted together to insure adequate cross pollination.

BLUMENBACHIA Schrad. *Loasaceae.* About 6 spp. of square-stemmed ann. or bien. herbs, with stinging hairs, native to S. Amer.; lvs. opp., lobed; fls. solitary, axillary, petals 5, hooded, stamens many, in clusters opp. petals, staminodes 10, threadlike, alt. with petals; fr. a globose caps., opening by 3–10 spirally twisted valves.

Propagated by seeds sown under glass, and seedlings transplanted after danger of frost is over.

Hieronymii Urb. Bien.; lvs. ovate, nearly palmately 5-lobed, toothed; fls. white, to 1½ in. across, on peduncles to 4½ in. long, calyx lobes ovate, toothed to pinnatifid. Argentina.

insignis Schrad. Ann. or grown as such, twining, sts. to 2 ft. or more; lvs. to 3 in. across, deeply palmately 5-lobed, lobes pinnatifid-toothed; fls. white, 1 in. across, calyx lobes linear to triangular-lanceolate, entire, petals hooded, with thick yellow basal scales spotted with red. Brazil to Argentina.

lateritia: *Cajophora lateritia.*

BLYXA Noronha ex Thouars. *Hydrocharitaceae.* About 10 spp. of submersed, stoloniferous aquatic herbs, native to tropics of Old World; lvs. alt., linear, with prominent midrib; fls. unisexual or bisexual, enclosed within a spathe, sepals 3, petals 3, longer than sepals, fringed, stamens 3, 6, or 9, ovary beaked; fr. indehiscent, submersed.

echinosperma (C. B. Clarke) Hook.f. Monoecious, lvs. basal, sheathing, to 1 ft. or sometimes longer, dark green; fls. bisexual, white, 1 or rarely 2 in a spathe, stamens 3; fr. linear, to 2¾ in. long. Philippine Is. and s. and e. Asia, s. to E. Indies and trop. Australia.

BOCCONIA L. *Papaveraceae.* About 9 spp. of trop. and subtrop. trees, shrubs, or per. herbs with yellowish juice, native to trop. Amer.; lvs. alt., mostly pinnately lobed or parted; fls. small, borne in terminal, branching panicles, petals lacking; fr. fleshy, opening from the base upward, seed 1. Related to the Asiatic genus *Macleaya*.

Planted in warmer parts of U.S. for tropical effect of the large leaves.

arborea S. Wats. Shrub or tree, to 25 ft., bark corky; lvs. clustered toward ends of brs., 4–18 in. long, glabrous above, glabrous or tomentose beneath, lobes narrow, attenuate, few or many. Mex. and Cent. Amer. Source of a yellow dye used by aborigines.

cordata: *Macleaya cordata.*

edulis: a listed name of no botanical standing.

frutescens L. Shrub or tree, to 25 ft., bark smooth and pale; lvs. 5–15 in. long or more, tomentose or glaucous beneath, lobes broad, acute, dentate; fls. purplish. Trop. Amer.

japonica: *Macleaya cordata.*

microcarpa: *Macleaya microcarpa.*

spectabilis: a listed name of no botanical standing.

BOEA Comm. ex Lam. *Gesneriaceae.* More than 50 spp. of per. stemless or stemmed herbs in s. Asia to Australia and Polynesia; lvs. opp. or basal; fls. in few- to many-fld., loose cymes on axillary peduncles, calyx deeply 5-lobed, corolla small, broadly campanulate, somewhat swollen at base, limb 5-lobed, 2-lipped, lobes ovate, obtuse, the 2 lower stamens fertile, the 2 upper stamens reduced to staminodes, anthers often coherent by their tips and face to face, their cells often confluent, disc lacking, ovary superior; fr. a linear caps.

For cultivation see *Gesneriaceae.*

hygroscopica F. J. Muell. Sts. short; lvs. congested, blades ovate, to 6 in. long and 4½ in. wide, crenate, rugose, densely hairy above with hairs of several lengths, paler and with prominent reticulate nerves and long glandless and short glandular hairs beneath, petioles to 3 in. long, villous with brown-tipped hairs; fls. many on peduncles longer than petioles, calyx green, ⅛ in. long, corolla deeply 2-lobed, violet with yellow-green star at throat, the lower lobe with deeper violet margining the green, tube ⅛ in. long, lobes to ¼ in. long, spreading, stamens exserted, filaments inflated, yellow-green, anthers united by tips and aligned face to face, style violet, stigma mouth-shaped; fr. 1⅜ in. long. Queensland.

BOEHMERIA Jacq. FALSE NETTLE. *Urticaceae.* About 50 spp. of monoecious or dioecious herbs, shrubs, or small trees, without stinging hairs, widely distributed in trop. and temp. regions; lvs. alt. or opp., simple, toothed; infl. axillary; fls. in globose or spikelike clusters arranged in spikes or panicles or sessile, male fls. with 3–5-parted calyx, female fls. with tubular or urceolate, 2–4-toothed calyx, style filiform; fr. an achene enclosed by the calyx.

Grown under glass or in the open in the South for the ornamental foliage. One species, *B. nivea,* is an important fiber plant in most warm regions, but the difficulties in getting and spinning the fiber have limited its use in this country. Propagated by division or seeds.

argentea Linden. Small tree, to 30 ft.; lvs. alt., ovate, to 1 ft. long, acuminate, upper surface rugose, bluish-green, often with silvery margins; panicles few-branched, drooping, to 10 in. long. Mex.

cylindrica (L.) Swartz. BOG HEMP. Per. herb, to 3 ft.; lvs. opp., elliptic to lanceolate, to 5 in. long, acuminate, rounded at base; spikes axillary, erect, usually leafy toward apex. S. U.S. to W. Indies and S. Amer.

nivea (L.) Gaud.-Beaup. RAMIE, CHINESE SILK PLANT, CHINA GRASS. Coarse, hispid-stemmed per., 3–5 ft. high or more; lvs. alt., broadly ovate, to 6 in. long or more, acuminate, cuneate or rounded at base, white-tomentose underneath; panicles densely branched, mostly shorter than subtending petiole. Trop. Asia, where cult. as a fiber plant. Has been grown to some extent in s. U.S. and Calif.; it requires fertile, well-drained soil. Var. **tenacissima** (Gaud.-Beaup.) Miq. RHEA. Lvs. green on both sides. Malay Pen.

BOENNINGHAUSENIA Rchb. ex Meissn. *Rutaceae.* One sp., a per. herb, native from Assam to cent. Japan; lvs. alt., 2–3-pinnate, glandular-dotted; fls. white, in terminal, leafy, many-fld. cymes, calyx 4-lobed, petals 4, stamens 6–8, unequal, ovary stalked, 3–5-celled and -lobed; fr. of 3–5, several-seeded, separate sections.

albiflora (Hook.) Meissn. Diffuse per., to 2 ft.; lvs. long-petioled, 3–6 in. long, glaucous-gray, lfts. obovate to obcordate, to ¾ in. long, terminal lft. largest; fls. white, to ½ in. across. Zone 8.

BOERLAGIODENDRON Harms. *Araliaceae.* About 40 spp. of unarmed, glabrous, evergreen trees and shrubs of se. Asia, abundant in Malay Pen. and Philippine Is.; lvs. large, palmately lobed or incised, petiole bases swollen, with raised, spiral, ringlike stipule scars; fls. in terminal, 3-branched, cymose infls. with those of the central br. sterile, and of the lateral brs. bisexual and fertile, petals 4–8, variously united, stamens 5–30, ovary 5- to many-celled, stigmas radiating from a short column; fr. a drupe, pyrenes many.

eminens (Bull) Merrill. Little-branched tree, 15–40 ft.; lvs. 2–3 ft. long, on stout petioles as long or longer than the blades, blades glabrous, dark glossy green above, palmately 9–15-lobed, lobes lanceolate-acuminate, coarsely incised. Philippine Is. Zone 10 in s. Fla.

BOG PLANTS. Plants called bog plants in horticulture differ from aquatics in that they do not live permanently in deep water but rather in wet places, as about lakes and ponds and in bogs. Usually they are native plants transferred to wet places in grounds and sometimes colonized. For the most part they are easily grown if the natural habitat is understood and imitated. Commonly they are perennials that take care of themselves when once established. *Alisma, Cyperus, Juncus, Pontederia,* and *Sagittaria* are common genera of bog and swamp plants, as well as some species of *Eupatorium, Lysimachia,* and *Lythrum.* Any region outside deserts and plains yields interesting material for the appreciative planter.

BOISDUVALIA Spach. *Onagraceae.* About 8 spp. of erect or decumbent ann. or bushy per. herbs of w. N. Amer. and s. S. Amer.; fls. 4-merous, calyx tube short or long, petals purplish or reddish to whitish, ovary inferior; fr. a caps., 4-celled.

Propagated by seeds.

densiflora (Lindl.) S. Wats. [*Oenothera densiflora* Lindl.]. Erect ann., 1–4 ft., pubescent, leafy throughout; lvs. lanceolate, 1–3 in. long, reduced to leafy bracts in the terminal spikes; petals deeply notched, ¼–½ in. long, rose-purple to pink. B.C., s. to Idaho and Calif.

BOLANDRA A. Gray. *Saxifragaceae.* Two spp. of per. herbs of the nw. U.S.; rhizome short, bulbiferous, sts. leafy; st. lvs. with leaflike stipules; fls. in few-fld., bracted, terminal panicles, calyx tube not united to ovary, calyx lobes 5, linear-lanceolate, spreading, petals 5, linear, erect or slightly spreading, stamens 5, shorter than calyx lobes and petals, carpels 2, united about ⅓ basally and tapering gradually into the styles.

oregana S. Wats. Sts. 16–24 in.; basal and lower st. lvs. reniform, to 2½ in. across, coarsely and irregularly toothed, on slender petioles to 6 in. long, upper st. lvs. smaller, ovate, toothed, on shorter petioles or sessile; calyx to ¾ in. long, petals linear, purple, about as long as calyx lobes; caps. to ⅜ in. long. Se. Wash., ne. Ore. Useful in the rock or wild garden.

BOLBOXALIS: *OXALIS.* **B. cernua:** *O. Pes-caprae.*

BOLDEA: *PEUMUS.*

BOLDOA: see *PEUMUS.* **B. fragrans:** *P. Boldus.*

BOLLEA Rchb. f. *Orchidaceae.* Ten spp. of cespitose, epiphytic herbs, native to n. S. Amer.; pseudobulbs lacking; lvs. plicate, with imbricate sheaths; infl. lateral, scape 1-fld.; sepals and petals spreading, lip fleshy, with many-ridged callus (or crest) under the hoodlike column. For structure of fl. see *Orchidaceae.*

Intermediate greenhouse; for culture see *Orchids.*

coelestis Rchb. f. [*Zygopetalum coeleste* (Rchb. f.) Rchb. f.]. Lvs. to 12 in. long and 2 in. wide; fls. solitary, to 4 in. across, blue-violet, lip with large semicircular callus. Late spring–summer. Colombia.

Lalindei Rchb. f. [*Zygopetalum Lalindei* Rchb. f.]. Lvs. to about 12 in. long and 1½ in. wide; fls. solitary, to 3 in. across, sepals and petals rose, darker above, lip and callus yellow to orange. Late summer. Colombia.

BOLTONIA L'Hér. [*Kalimeris* Cass. (usually incorrectly cited as *Calimeris* Nees)]. *Compositae* (Aster Tribe). About 10 spp. of glabrous, leafy-stemmed, asterlike per. herbs, in e. and cent. U.S. and e. Asia; lvs. alt., sessile, linear to lanceolate, mostly entire; fl. heads radiate, peduncled, in panicles; disc fls. yellow, ray fls. white, purplish, or violet; disc achenes flattened, winged marginally, ray achenes 3-angled, pappus of short bristles and 2–3 longer awns.

Boltonias are often planted in the border or used for colonizing; they are of the easiest culture. Propagated by division in the spring, also by seeds. They resemble wild asters.

asteroides (L.) L'Hér. [*B. glastifolia* (J. Hill) L'Hér.]. To 6 ft. or more, branched above; lvs. linear to oblanceolate, to 5 in. long, glaucous; heads usually fewer than 25 on a st., on longish brs. of an open panicle, involucral bracts linear, acute to acuminate; ray fls. white, lilac, to purplish. E. U.S. Var. **decurrens:** *B. decurrens.* Var. **latisquama** (A. Gray) Cronq. [*B. latisquama* A. Gray]. Heads many in a denser, short-branched corymb, involucral bracts oblong to narrowly obovate, obtusish. Mo., Kans., Okla. Cv. 'Nana'. Listed as a dwarfer form of this var. Var. **recognita** (Fern. & Grisc.) Cronq. [*B. latisquama* A. Gray var. *recognita* Fern. & Grisc.]. Involucral bracts linear, acute. E. and cent. U.S.

decurrens (Torr. & A. Gray) A. Wood [*B. asteroides* var. *decurrens* (Torr. & A. Gray) Engelm.]. Similar to *B. asteroides* var. *recognita* but lvs. more numerous, broader, decurrent on st. Ill., Mo.

glastifolia: *B. asteroides.*

incisa (Fisch.) Benth. [*Aster incisus* Fisch.; *Kalimeris incisa* (Fisch.) DC.]. Rhizomatous per., to 5 ft.; lower and middle st. lvs. sessile, oblong-lanceolate to lanceolate, to 4 in. long, acuminate, toothed, lustrous above, glabrous beneath, toothed to incised, upper lvs. linear-lanceolate; heads to 1⅜ in. across, on long peduncles; ray fls. purple to almost white. Siberia, n. China, Manchuria, Korea, Japan.

japonica (Miq.) Franch. & Sav. [*Aster japonicus* (Miq.) Franch. & Sav., not Less.]. Rhizomatous per., to 3 ft.; basal lvs. cordate, to 3½ in. long, acuminate, pilose on both sides, coarsely incised-serrate, long-petioled, upper lvs. reduced, becoming successively ovate, then lanceolate, short-petioled; heads to 1 in. across. Japan.

laevigata: a listed name of no botanical standing; perhaps for *B. asteroides.*

latisquama: *B. asteroides* var.

BOLUSANTHUS Harms. *Leguminosae* (subfamily *Faboideae*). One sp., a tree, native to Afr.; lvs. alt., odd-pinnate; fls. in racemes, papilionaceous, stamens 10, separate, not equal; fr. a flat, oblong-linear legume.

Handsome tree, propagated by seeds.

speciosus (H. Bolus) Harms. To 20 ft.; lvs. deciduous, lfts. inequilateral, lanceolate, to 4 in. long; racemes loose, 9 in. long or more; fls. violet, ⅞ in. long; fr. a legume, sordid-cream, 2½ in. long. S. Afr., Rhodesia; in the latter called RHODESIAN WISTARIA or WILD W.

BOMAREA Mirb. *Alstroemeriaceae.* Over 100 spp. of twining herbs, native to mostly highland parts of trop. Amer.; lvs. parallel-veined; fls. tubular, borne in drooping bracted clusters, perianth segms. equal or in 2 unequal series, stamens 6, erect, ovary 3-celled; fr. a caps.

Bomareas may be grown outdoors in the South in partial shade, or in a cool greenhouse. They require abundant water and fertilizing in the growing season. The roots may be left in the soil over winter, the tops being cut off. Propagated by division of the roots or by seeds over heat.

acutifolia (Link & Otto) Herb. Lvs. lanceolate to ovate-lanceolate, to 4 in. long, 1½ in. wide, pubescent on the veins beneath; umbels compound; fls. few or several, segms. equal, ¾ in. long, outer segms. red, inner segms. orange or yellow and spotted with brown. Mex.

Caldasiana: *B. Caldasii.*

Caldasii (HBK) Asch. & Graebn. [*B. Caldasiana* Herb.]. Lvs. with distinct petiole, oblong-acute, to 6 in. long, puberulent or glabrescent on lower side; umbels simple, pedicels to 2 in. long; fls. to 1½ in. long, outer segms. short, reddish-brown, inner segms. longer, bright yellow. N. S. Amer.

conferta: *B. patacocensis.*

edulis (Tussac) Herb. WHITE JERUSALEM ARTICHOKE. Lvs. lanceolate, to 5 in. long, 1 in. wide, glabrous or puberulent beneath; umbels compound, the rays glabrous, mostly long and slender; fls. to 1³⁄₁₆ in. long, perianth segms. nearly equal, outer segms. pink, inner segms. vivid green or yellowish, purple-spotted. W. Indies, Mex., and Cent. Amer., s. to Brazil.

formosissima (Ruiz & Pav.) Herb. Lvs. broadly lanceolate, to 10 in. long and 2 in. wide, acuminate, glabrous, petiole winged; umbels dense, 60–80-fld., pedicels densely reddish-pubescent; fls. to 1½ in. long, perianth segms. equal, outer segms. red, inner segms. yellow, spatulate; fr. dehiscent. Peru.

frondea M. T. Mast. Lvs. oblong, to 5 in. long, pubescent beneath; umbel simple, dense, many-fld.; perianth segms. unequal, outer segms. to 1½ in. long, yellow, inner segms. 2 in. long, bright yellow, dark-spotted. Colombia.

multiflora (L. f.) Mirb. Lvs. oblong, to 4 in. long; umbels dense, many-fld.; fls. 1 in. long, perianth segms. nearly equal, outer segms. tinged red, inner segms. reddish-yellow, spotted with brown. Colombia and Venezuela.

oligantha Bak. Lvs. oblong, to 4 in. long; umbels simple, 6–8-fld.; fls. to 1¼ in. long, perianth segms. equal, outer segms. red, inner segms. yellow and spotted with reddish-brown. Ecuador.

patacocensis Herb. [*B. conferta* Benth.]. Lvs. oblong-lanceolate, to 6 in. long; fls. with unequal segms., outer segms. about 1¼ in. long, orange, inner segms. to 2½ in. long, chrome-yellow, with chocolate spotting and orange tips. Andes of Colombia and Ecuador. Plants grown under this name are probably *B. racemosa.*

racemosa Killip. Lvs. lanceolate or ovate-lanceolate, to 5 in. long, 1⅜ in. wide, minutely pilose beneath; umbels simple, 20–60-fld., pedicels stout, tomentulose, to 4 in. long; perianth segms. scarlet, unequal, outer segms. about 2 in. long, inner segms. 1½–3 in. long, spotted with dark brown, yellow at base. Colombia. This sp. has been grown and illustrated as *B. papacocensis.*

BOMBACACEAE. **A,** *Ceiba pentandra:* **Aa,** fruiting branch, × ⅙; **Ab,** flowering branch, × ⅛; **Ac,** flower, × ½; **Ad,** stigma, × 8; **Ae,** segment of ovary, cross section, × 2; **Af,** dehiscing fruit, × ¼; **Ag,** seed, × 1. **B,** *Pseudobombax ellipticum:* **Ba,** flower, × ¼; **Bb,** base of flower, vertical section, × ½. **C,** *Ochroma pyramidale:* **Ca,** flower, × ¼; **Cb,** apex of staminal tube, with spiralled anthers and protruding stigma, × ½.

BOMBACACEAE Kunth. BOMBAX FAMILY. Dicot.; about 27 genera of trees or rarely shrubs, sometimes with stout spines, native principally to trop. regions of both hemispheres; lvs. alt., stipuled, simple or palmately compound; fls.

regular or slightly irregular, bisexual, calyx cupular, 2–5-lobed or truncate, sometimes deciduous after flowering, epicalyx (involucre) present or absent, petals mostly 5, rarely 0, stamens 5 to many, usually united into a tube in lower part and united to the petals, anthers 1- to many-celled, separate or coherent, ovary superior, 2–5- or 10- or rarely 15-celled, each cell with 2 to many ovules; fr. mostly a loculicidally dehiscent caps., sometimes drupelike or berrylike, or rarely winged, the inner walls glabrous or woolly. The family yields the kapok of commerce, food products, timber, and several striking ornamentals. *Adansonia, Bombacopsis, Bombax, Cavanillesia, Ceiba, Chiranthodendron, Chorisia, Durio, Fremontodendron, Kydia, Ochroma, Pachira* and *Pseudobombax* can be cult. in trop. and subtrop. areas.

BOMBACOPSIS Pitt. *Bombacaceae.* About 21 spp. of deciduous or evergreen, sometimes spiny shrubs or trees, native to New World tropics; lvs. palmately compound, lfts. 3–7, articulate at base; fls. solitary or in few- to many-fld. cymes, regular, calyx truncate or 3–5-lobed, persistent; petals 5, strap-shaped to narrowly oblanceolate, stamens 100–1000 in 1 or apparently 2 whorls, clustered in 5, 10, or 15 groups joined basally into a common tube; fr. a 5-celled caps., woody or nearly so, sparsely to densely whitish- or reddish-pubescent inside, seeds few to many.

Fendleri (Seem.) Pitt. [*B. quinata* of auth., not (Jacq.) Dugand]. To about 100 ft., usually massively buttressed, trunk and brs. with stout spines; lfts. mostly 5, usually obovate, to 7 in. long, glabrous; calyx about ½ in. long, truncate or undulate, petals linear, to 4½ in. long, about ¼ in. wide, brownish outside, whitish inside, stamens 100–166, in 5 groups, 2–3½ in. long; caps. oblong-obovoid, 5-angled, blunt at apex, 1½–4 in. long, densely yellowish-brown- to brown-pubescent inside, seeds many. Lowland wet forest, from Nicaragua to Colombia. Sometimes planted in tropics.

quinata: technically a synonym of *Bombax Ceiba,* but the name *Bombacopsis quinata* has generally been applied to *B. Fendleri.*

BOMBAX L. [*Salmalia* Schott & Endl.]. *Bombacaceae.* Eight or more spp. of sometimes spiny, deciduous trees, native to trop. Asia, Afr., and Australia; lvs. alt., palmately compound, lfts. articulate at base; fls. large, red, yellowish, purplish, or white, clustered near ends of brs., calyx truncate or shallowly lobed, deciduous with petals and stamens after flowering, stamens very many, separate to near the base; fr. a 5-celled, woody caps., seeds many, small, embedded in wool.

angulicarpum: *B. buonopozense.*

buonopozense Beauvois [*B. angulicarpum* Ulbr.]. GOLD COAST B. To 120 ft. in the wild, trunk with large, conical spines, lfts. 5–9, oblong-ovate, to 7 in. long; fls. axillary, solitary or up to 6 in clusters, calyx about ½ in. long, petals red, oblong, to 3½ in. long, stamens about 180, in 2 whorls, tube scarcely present; caps. oblong, 4–7 in. long, 5-angled, acute at apex. W. Afr.

Ceiba L. [*B. malabaricum* DC.; *Salmalia malabarica* (DC.) Schott & Endl.]. RED SILK-COTTON TREE. To 75 ft. or more, spiny; lfts. 3–7, elliptic-obovate, to 10 in. long, acute-acuminate; fls. solitary, but clustered near ends of brs., calyx 3–6-lobed, about 1 in. long, petals dull to bright red, oblong-obovate, 2–4 in. long, recurved, stamens in 2 whorls, the outer whorl divided into 5 bundles of 9–20 each, the inner whorl of 10–15 stamens; caps. oblong, slightly angled, acute at apex, to 6 in. long. Trop. Asia. Widely cult. elsewhere. Zone 10.

cyathophorum: *Pseudobombax grandiflorum.*

ellipticum: *Pseudobombax ellipticum.*

malabaricum: *B. Ceiba.*

BOMMERIA E. Fourn. *Polypodiaceae.* Four spp. of small, evergreen rock ferns of N. Amer.; lvs. triangular, pinnate to pinnatifid, or 3-pinnatifid, entire, hairy; sporangia in series along veins, indusia absent.

For culture see *Ferns.*

hispida (Mett.) Underw. HAIRY BOMMARA. Rhizome elongate; lvs. pinnatifid to 3-pinnatifid, to 6 in. long, covered with brown scales darkening in age, very hairy. W. Tex. to Ariz. and Mex.

BONGARDIA C. A. Mey. *Berberidaceae.* One sp., a per. herb native from Greece to Afghanistan; lvs. radical, from

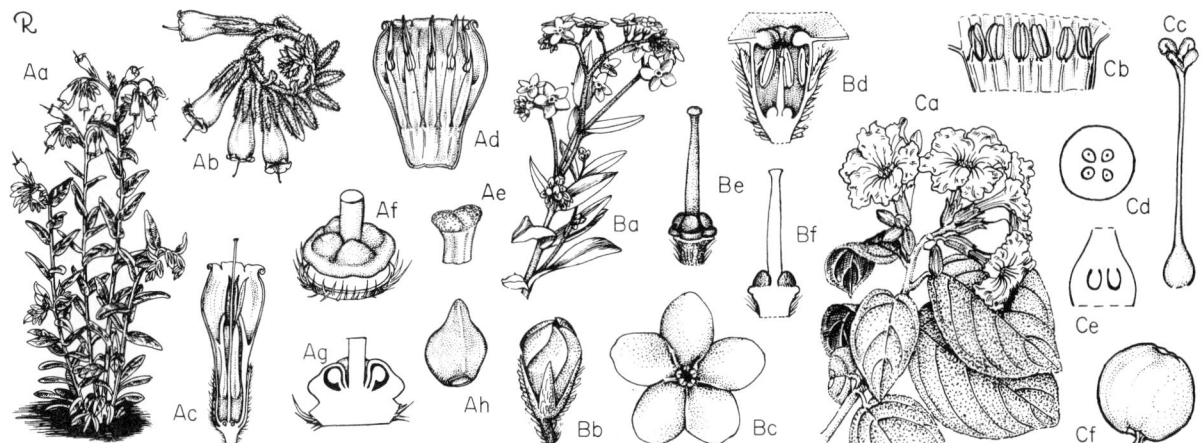

BORAGINACEAE. **A,** *Onosma stellulata:* **Aa,** flowering plant, × ⅙; **Ab,** branch of inflorescence, × ½; **Ac,** flower, vertical section, × 1; **Ad,** corolla, expanded, × 1; **Ae,** stigma, × 12; **Af,** base of pistil, × 8; **Ag,** base of pistil, vertical section, × 8; **Ah,** nutlet, × 4. **B,** *Myosotis sylvatica:* **Ba,** flowering branch, × ½; **Bb,** flower bud, × 2; **Bc,** flower, × 2; **Bd,** flower, vertical section (part of corolla cut away), × 5; **Be,** pistil, × 8; **Bf,** pistil, vertical section, × 8. **C,** *Cordia Sebestena:* **Ca,** flowering branch, × ½; **Cb,** throat of corolla, expanded, × 2; **Cc,** pistil, × 2; **Cd,** ovary, cross section, × 5; **Ce,** ovary, vertical section, × 4; **Cf,** fruit, × ½.

tuberous base; fls. in a panicle, sepals 3–6, petals 6, stamens 6, ovary with 5–6 ovules; fr. a membranous follicle, rupturing irregularly at apex.

Chrysogonum (L.) Griseb. To 10 in.; lvs. pinnate, segms. in 3–8 pairs or ternately arranged or whorled along rachis, to 1½ in. long, cuneate, apically toothed, often reddish at base; fls. yellow, to 1 in. across.

BONSAI. A Japanese word (pronounced *bone-sigh*) meaning "tray planting," bonsai refers to the highly specialized Japanese horticultural practice of growing woody plants, usually trees, as naturally or artificially dwarfed and picturesque specimens in appropriate pots or containers. In a densely populated land like Japan, where both living space and garden space are minimal, the development of the culture of miniature trees for enjoyment in the home is understandable. The culture of bonsai (the word is also used for the dwarfed trees themselves, and is both singular and plural) is now widespread in many parts of the world.

Favorite woody plant materials used for bonsai in Japan include conifers such as *Chamaecyparis obtusa, Juniperus chinensis* var. *Sargentii, Picea jezoensis, Pinus densiflora, P. parviflora, P. Thunbergiana,* and *Taxus cuspidata;* broadleaf evergreens such as the Kurume hybrid azaleas, *Cycas revoluta, Trachycarpus Fortunei,* and various bamboos; and various deciduous trees and shrubs such as *Acer buergeranum, A. palmatum, Chaenomeles japonica, C. speciosa, Fagus crenata, Ilex serrata, Malus prunifolia, Prunus incisa, P. Mume, P. serrulata, P. subhirtella,* and *Zelkova serrata.* Plants in wide variety throughout the world, however, are suitable for use as bonsai. Plants for a bonsai collection should be selected to ensure seasonal variety and year-round enjoyment and might include both evergreen and deciduous trees, plants for showy spring flowers or colorful autumnal fruits or foliage, and species with interesting form of trunk and branches. The production and cultivation of bonsai require creativity, horticultural skill, and patience. Those interested in the subject should seek out the detailed literature now widely available.

BONTIA L. *Myoporaceae.* One sp., an evergreen shrub or small tree, native to W. Indies and n. S. Amer.; lvs. alt., fleshy, entire; fls. small, purplish, peduncled. Much like *Myoporum,* but fls. deeply 2-lipped; fr. a drupe.

Sometimes grown as ornamental in subtropical Fla. and in tropics.

daphnoides L. Sometimes to 30 ft.; lvs. willowlike, oblong or lanceolate, to 4 in. long; fls. solitary or clustered, yellow, spotted with purple, ¾ in. long; fr. yellow, pointed, ½ in. long. Useful in seaside gardens since it resists damage by salt spray.

BOOPHONE Herb. *Amaryllidaceae.* A few spp. of bulbous S. Afr. per. herbs; lvs. sword- or strap-shaped; infl. a many-fld. umbel terminal on a scape and subtended by 2 separate, ovate spathe valves, pedicels elongating in fr.; fls. regular, salverform, tube short, lobes equal, linear or lanceolate, stamens 6, straight, ovary inferior, cells 1–6-ovuled; fr. a loculicidal caps., seeds solitary, globose. (*Boophone* is pronounced with 4 syllables; sometimes incorrectly spelled *Buphone.*)

disticha (L.f.) Herb. GIFBOL. To 1 ft.; lvs. 8–16, 2-ranked, to 1½ ft. long; umbel dense, to 1 ft. in diam., pedicels 2–4 in. long; fls. red, tube ¼–½ in. long, lobes linear, ¾–1 in. long. Foliage poisonous if eaten.

BORAGINACEAE Juss. BORAGE FAMILY. Dicot.; about 100 genera and 2,000 spp. of herbs, shrubs, trees or rarely lianas, of wide range on all continents; plants mostly with hispid hairs or sometimes glabrous; lvs. simple, mostly alt., basal and cauline; fls. blue, purple, pink, white, yellow, orange, or red, mostly bisexual and regular, usually in a coiled infl. which unrolls and straightens as the fls. mature (often referred to as a cincinnus or a helicoid or scorpioid cyme), calyx mostly deeply 5-lobed, corolla 5-lobed, stamens 5, exserted or included, ovary superior, 2- or 4-celled; fr. mostly of 4 nutlets, rarely 1–4-seeded drupes or nuts. The family furnishes timber trees, medicinal plants and dyes, and also many ornamental subjects in the genera: *Adelocaryum, Anchusa, Borago, Bourreria, Brunnera, Buglossoides, Cerinthe, Cordia, Cryptantha, Cynoglossum, Echioides, Echium, Ehretia, Eritrichium, Hackelia, Heliotropium, Lappula, Lindelofia, Lithodora, Lithospermum, Mattiastrum, Mertensia, Moltkia, Myosotidium, Myosotis, Omphalodes, Onosma, Pentaglottis, Plagiobothrys, Pulmonaria, Solenanthus,* and *Symphytum.*

BORAGO L. BORAGE. *Boraginaceae.* Three spp. of hairy ann. or per. herbs, native to the Medit. region; sts. erect or decumbent; lvs. simple, alt.; fls. blue, in open, leafy cymes, calyx and corolla 5-lobed, corolla throat filled by short scales, stamens 5, attached near the base of corolla, anthers erect, exserted, connivent into a cone, appendaged on the back; fr. of 4 erect nutlets.

One or two species grown in the flower garden, and *B. officinalis* sometimes as a potherb and for bees. Propagated by seeds sown in spring, and by division or cuttings.

laxiflora (DC.) Fisch. Sts. decumbent, hispid, herbaceous, from a per. root; lvs. oblong to ovate; fls. pale blue, drooping, on long pedicels, corolla campanulate. Corsica. Good for the rock garden.

officinalis L. TALEWORT, COOL-TANKARD. Coarse, thick, ann., 1½–2 ft.; lvs. oblong or ovate; fls. blue or purple, to ¾ in. across, many, rotate. Eur., N. Afr.

BORASSUS L. *Palmae.* Seven spp. of tall, stout, solitary dioecious palms of trop. Afr., Asia, and Malay Arch.; lvs. large, costapalmate, petiole elongate, margin usually armed with coarse spinelike teeth; infls. among the lvs., with elongate peduncles sheathed by several tubular bracts, unlike in male and female plants, the male with several large primary brs. along an elongate axis, each sheathed basally by a tubular bract and divided into 1–3 catkinlike secondary brs., fls. in clusters, sunken in pits formed by large imbricate bractlets, the female with a single axis or rarely divided into a few brs. at about the same point, fls. solitary, sessile, subtended by large bractlets; male fls. with sepals 3, separate or united to the middle, petals united in a long slender solid base with 3 separate, imbricate lobes, stamens 6 at base of corolla lobes, pistillode minute or 0, female fls. very much larger than male, sepals and petals 3, similar, imbricate, staminodes forming a lobed ring, pistil globose-ovoid, 3-celled, 3-ovuled; fr. large, globose or oblong, fleshy-fibrous, with 1–3 seeds inside a hard, thick endocarp, endosperm homogeneous, embryo apical.

Seeds are planted where the trees are to grow, or if they are planted in containers, care must be taken not to damage primary root when planting out. For culture see *Palms.*

aethiopum Mart. Similar to *B. flabellifer* but the trunk often swollen in some part and male fls. with sepals united to the middle. Trop. Afr.

flabellifer L. PALMYRA PALM, TODDY P., WINE P., TALA P., DOUB P. To 40–60 (occasionally 100) ft., with straight trunk to 3 ft. in diam.; lf. blades to 5 ft. long, segms. about 80, 1-ribbed; male infl. to 5 ft. long, with about 7 primary brs., secondary brs. to nearly 1 ft. long, ¾ in. in diam., fls. with separate sepals; female infl. with flowering portion to 1 ft. long, 1 in. in diam., fls. 8–16, spirally arranged, about 2 in. in diam.; fr. to 6 in. in diam. Drier areas of India, Burma and Ceylon. Often planted where native for its many uses; cult. elsewhere in the tropics and in s. Fla., Zone 10a. A primary source of toddy, the popular drink of trop. Asia.

BORDER. In the horticultural sense, a border is a narrow planting along a boundary or division line such as a walk or road, or against a building or wall or foot of slope, although the term is sometimes inaccurately employed for any long, narrow strip planting even though it has no relation to margins or confines. Ordinarily it is 5 feet broad or less so that it can be planted and tended from one side, but it may be broader if there is easy access from both sides. A border is properly not only a place in which plants can be conveniently grown, but it has relation to the layout and subdivision of the home property. A good border, well placed for the growing of plants, provides an attractive receiving plot for accessions, and should afford a never-ending variety in bloom and vegetation.

The border receives different designations, depending on the kinds of plants; it may be a shrub border, a flower border, a hardy border for native and other hardy plants, or a vine border. As a rule, the most effective planting is that which is massed, for one plant reinforces the other, and the flowers have a good setting or background. Very striking displays of foliage and flowers and plant forms can be made when massed. Plants are more easily grown when planted in a border, since the whole area can be kept cultivated with ease; and if a plant becomes weak or dies, its place is readily filled by neighboring plants spreading into it. The border may be mixed—that is, composed of a great variety of plants—or it may be made up of one species in considerable quantity. In long and very striking borders, it is often best to have the background—that is, the back row—of one general type of plant in order to give continuity and strength to the whole group. In front of this a variety of plants may be set. Shrub borders are sometimes planted of one species only for continuous, bold effect.

For best results in border planting the land should be fertile. The whole area should be plowed or spaded. If the border is composed of shrubs, and is large, a power cultivator may be run in and out between the plants for the first two or three years, since the shrubs will be set 2–4 feet apart. Ordinarily, however, cultivation is done with hand tools. After the plants are once established and the border is filled,

it is best to dig up as little as possible, for the digging disturbs the roots and breaks off the crowns. It is usually best to pull out the weeds and give the border a topdressing of well-rotted manure each autumn. If the ground is not very rich, an application of wood ashes or some commercial fertilizer may be given from time to time. The border may be planted thickly to allow the plants to run together, thereby giving one continuous effect. Most shrubs should be set 3 feet apart. Those as large as lilacs *(Syringa)* may go 4 feet and sometimes even more. Common herbaceous perennials, such as *Campanula, Delphinium, Dicentra,* and the like, should be spaced 12 to 18 inches apart. The front edge of the border is an excellent place for annual and tender flowering plants. These may be planted far enough apart to allow full development. Spring- and summer-flowering bulbs may find good conditions in a well-made border. Into the heavy borders about the boundaries of the property the autumn leaves will drift and afford an excellent mulch. If these borders are planted with shrubs, the leaves may be left there to decay, and not all raked off in the spring.

BORONIA Sm. *Rutaceae.* Between 60 and 70 spp. of shrubs or subshrubs, rarely ann., native to Australia; lvs. opp., simple or pinnate or ternately compound, glandular-dotted; fls. white, pink, red, blue, or purple, solitary or in cymes or umbels, often fragrant, sepals and petals 4, stamens 8, but 4 often sterile, ovary 4-parted, styles 4; fr. of 2–4, 2-valved sections.

Grown in a cool greenhouse in well-drained soil and outdoors in Calif. Plants should be cut back after flowering to make them bushy, and should be replaced by new plants after two years. Propagated by seeds and cuttings of half-ripened wood.

elatior Bartl. Much-branched shrub, 4–6 ft., brs. with thick, spreading hairs; lvs. pinnate, to 1½ in. long, lfts. 5–13, linear; fls. rose-red to purplish, about ¼ in. long, solitary and axillary, not opening widely. W. Australia.

heterophylla F. J. Muell. Much-branched, glabrous shrub, to 6 ft.; lvs. whorled, sometimes simple, linear, to 2 in. long, sometimes pinnate, lfts. 3–5, linear; fls. pink or scarlet, drooping, solitary on axillary peduncles, to ½ in. across, not opening widely. W. Australia.

ledifolia (Venten.) J. Gay. Erect shrub, brs. glandular-tomentose; lvs. revolute and hoary beneath, either simple, to 1 in. long, or pinnate, lfts. 3–7, linear, lanceolate, or oblong, ½ in. long; fls. pink, ¾ in. across, on 1–fld., axillary peduncles. E. Australia.

megastigma Nees ex Bartl. SCENTED BORONIA. Slender shrub, to 2 ft.; lvs. pinnate, lfts. 3–5, linear, ¾ in. long; fls. ½ in. across, solitary and axillary, rather open, very fragrant, corolla brown-purple outside, yellow inside. W. Australia. Source of oil used in making perfume.

serrulata Sm. Glabrous shrub, to 4 ft.; lvs. dense, simple, obovate, to ¾ in. long, serrate toward apex; fls. bright rose, ⅝ in. across, in terminal clusters. Se. Australia.

BORZICACTELLA: a listed name of no botanical standing. **B. prostrata:** a listed name of no botanical standing for *Borzicactus serpens.* **B. viperina:** a listed name of no botanical standing for *Borzicactus tenuiserpens.*

BORZICACTUS Riccob. [*Arequipa* Britt. & Rose; *Clistanthocereus* Backeb.; *Loxanthocereus* Backeb.; *Maritimocereus* Akers & Buin.; *Matucana* Britt. & Rose; *Morawetzia* Backeb.; *Oreocereus* (A. Berger) Riccob.; *Seticereus* Backeb.; *Submatucana* Backeb.]. *Cactaceae.* About 10 spp. of slender, ribbed cacti, native from Ecuador to n. Argentina; sts. erect or procumbent, ribs 8–20, low; fls. diurnal, red or orange, tubular or funnelform, mostly slightly to strongly irregular, rarely regular, slender, tube longer than the segms., limb mostly oblique, usually only the lower segms. spreading; fr. globose.

For culture see *Cacti.*

acanthurus (Vaup.) Britt. & Rose [*B. eriotrichus* (Werderm. & Backeb.)Backeb.; *B. Faustianus* Backeb.; *Loxanthocereus acanthurus* (Vaup.) Backeb.; *L. eriotrichus* (Werderm. & Backeb.) Backeb.; *L. Faustianus* (Backeb.) Backeb.]. Sts. sprawling, to 1 ft. long and 1½ in. thick, ribs 15–18, rounded, cross-furrowed; flowering areoles white-woolly, spines many, slender, yellowish, to ½ in. long; fls. scarlet, 2 in. long, 1 in. wide; fr. ¾ in. in diam. Peru.

aurantiacus (Vaup.) Kimnach & P. C. Hutchison [*Arequipa myriacantha* (Vaup.) Britt. & Rose; *Submatucana aurantiaca* (Vaup.) Backeb.; *S. calvescens* (Kimnach & P. C. Hutchison) Backeb.]. Sts. cespitose, globose, to 6 in. high and thick, dark green, with octagonal tubercles; areoles woolly, spines 20–30, radial spines and central spines intergrading, dark chestnut-brown with yellow tips, becoming brownish-gray, radial spines to 1 in. long, recurved at tip, central spines 3–7, to 1⅝ in. long; fls. tubular-funnelform, orange-yellow to dark red, to 3⅜ in. long; fr. nearly globose, to ¾ in. in diam. Peru.

Celsianus (Lem. & Salm-Dyck) Kimnach [*Oreocereus Celsianus* (Lem. ex Salm-Dyck) Riccob.; *O. Celsianus* var. *Bruennowii* (Ferd. Haage) Britt. & Rose; *O. neocelsianus* Backeb.]. OLD-MAN-OF-THE-MOUNTAINS, SOUTH AMERICAN OLD-MAN. Sts. erect, to 5 ft., ribs 10–17, hairs matted; spines yellow to reddish, radial spines about 9, stiff, central spines 1–4, stouter, to 3 in. long; fls. red, 3½ in. long, tube compressed; fr. oblong, opening basally. S. Bolivia. Cv. 'Giganteus' is listed. Cv. 'Lanuginosior'. Hair abundant, not matted; spines yellow.

Doelzianus (Backeb.) Kimnach [*Morawetzia Doelziana* Backeb.; *Oreocereus Doelzianus* (Backeb.) Borg]. Sts. erect, to 3 ft. high and 3½ in. thick, ribs 9–11, flowering sts. club-shaped, with larger hairs and spines; spines yellow to dark brown, needle-shaped, to 1¾ in. long, central spines stronger, scarcely distinguishable from radial spines; fls. red, 2–3 in. long, tube not compressed. Cent. Peru.

eriotrichus: *B. acanthurus.*

Faustianus: *B. acanthurus.*

Fieldianus Britt. & Rose. Sts. erect, to 20 ft., light or dark green, forming thickets, ribs perhaps 6–7; spines 6–10, white, awl-shaped, unequal, to 2 in. long; fls. red, nearly straight, only slightly irregular. Peru.

fossulatus (Labour.) Kimnach [*Oreocereus fossulatus* (Labour.) Backeb.]. MOUNTAIN CEREUS. Sts. erect, to 6 ft. high and 3 in. thick, ribs 9–14, transversely furrowed above the areole, hairs not matted; spines about 14, amber, central spines to 2 in. long; fls. greenish-rose. Bolivia.

Haynei (Otto ex Salm-Dyck) Kimnach [*Matucana Blancii* Backeb.; *M. breviflora* Rauh & Backeb.; *M. cereoides* Rauh & Backeb.; *M. comacephala* F. Ritter; *M. elongata* Rauh & Backeb.; *M. Haynei* (Otto ex Salm-Dyck) Britt. & Rose; *M. Herzogiana* Backeb.; *M. hystrix* Rauh & Backeb.; *M. multicolor* Rauh & Backeb.; *M. yanganucensis* Rauh & Backeb.]. Sts. globose to oblong, to 20 in. high and 5 in. thick, ribs 25–30; areoles close-set, woolly; spines white or gray, dark-tipped, needle-shaped, to 1½ in. long, radial spines 28–30, central spines 6–8; fls. orange-red, to 3 in. long, 2½ in. across, scales of tube with naked axils. Peru.

Hendriksenianus (Backeb.) Kimnach [*Oreocereus Hendriksenianus* Backeb.]. Sts. erect, to 5 ft., ribs about 10, lightly grooved between areoles, hairs brown, becoming white; radial spines 8–9, to ¾ in. long, central spines 1–4, yellow, to 3 in. long; fls. carmine; fr. yellow-green. S. Peru.

Humboldtii: *B. icosagonus.*

icosagonus (HBK) Britt. & Rose [*B. Humboldtii* (HBK) Britt. & Rose; *Seticereus Humboldtii* (HBK) Backeb.; *S. icosagonus* (HBK) Backeb.]. Sts. creeping, to 2 ft. long and 2 in. thick, ribs 18–20; spines yellow, radial spines about 30, to ½ in. long, central spines on old sts. sometimes to ¾ in. long; fls. orange, to 3 in. long; fr. yellowish, ¾ in. in diam. S. Ecuador.

jajoianus Backeb. [*Loxanthocereus jajoianus* (Backeb.) Backeb.]. Sts. cespitose, erect or decumbent, to 2 ft. long and 2½ in. thick, ribs about 12, broadened at the areoles and cross-furrowed between; spines pale yellow, radial spines about 20, to ¼ in. long, central spines 1–4, bulbous at base, to 2½ in. long; fls. orange, 2½ in. long. S. Peru.

leucotrichus (Phil.) Kimnach [*Arequipa erectocylindrica* Rauh & Backeb.; *A. leucotricha* (Phil.) Britt. & Rose; *A. Rettigii* (Quehl) Oehme]. Sts. solitary or cespitose, globose to oblong, to 2 ft. high and 4 in. thick, ribs about 20, low, tubercled; spines needle-shaped, brittle, pilose on young plants, radial spines about 30, white, to ⅜ in. long, central spines about 10, shorter; fls. to 2½ in. long; fr. globose, ¾ in. in diam. S. Peru.

Madisoniorum P. C. Hutchison. Sts. solitary, globose or short-columnar, to 10 in. high and 4 in. thick, gray-green, ribs 7–12, obscure, flattened; spines 0–3 or 5, brown, becoming whitish, to 2⅜ in. long, curved or twisted; fls. orange-red, regular, narrowly funnelform, to 4 in. long. Peru.

Morleyanus: *B. sepium.*

sepium (HBK) Britt. & Rose [*B. Morleyanus* Britt. & Rose; *Cleistocactus Roezlii* (F. A. Haage, jr.) Backeb.; *Seticereus Roezlii* (F. A. Haage, jr.) Backeb.]. Sts. simple, to 5 ft. high and 1½ in. thick, ribs 8–11, obtuse, crenate; areoles to ¾ in. apart, spines dark red, becoming gray, radial spines 8–10, slender, to ⅜ in. long, central spine 1, to

¾ in. long; fls. scarlet, 1½ in. long, tube with woolly ring below stamens; fr. ¾ in. in diam., flesh white. Peru.

serpens (HBK) Kimnach. Sts. creeping, brs. elongate, to ¾ in. thick or more, ribs 8–11; areoles somewhat gray-woolly, radial spines 10–15, spreading, to ⅝ in. long, central spine 1, to 1³⁄₁₆ in. long; fls. flesh-colored, to 2 in. long. N. Peru. Has been offered under the listed name *Borzicactella prostrata.*

Sextonianus (Backeb.) Kimnach [*Maritimocereus gracilis* Akers & Buin.]. Sts. trailing, to 6 ft. long and 2 in. thick, ribs about 11, low, nearly tubercled, grooves between ribs zigzag; spines stout, yellow, needle-shaped, radial spines about 8, to ⅜ in. long, central spines 1–3, to ¾ in. long; fls. orange-red, about 2 in. long, lasting several days, tube somewhat curved, scales sparsely hairy in the axils; fr. globose, to 1½ in. in diam., splitting. S. Peru.

Strausii: *Cleistocactus Strausii.*

tenuiserpens (Rauh & Backeb.) Kimnach. Sts. much-branched, to 6 ft. long, brs. very slender, ⁵⁄₁₆–⅜ in. thick, green, ribs 9–10; marginal spines 10–11, pale, to ⁵⁄₁₆ in. long, central spines 0–1. Peru. Has been offered under the listed name *Borzicactella viperina.*

Trollii (Kupper) Kimnach [*Oreocereus Trollii* (Kupper) Backeb.]. OLD-MAN-OF-THE-ANDES. Sts. erect, to 2 ft. high and 5 in. thick, ribs 15–25; spines about 15, light yellow or reddish, awl-shaped, to 2 in. long; fls. rose. S. Bolivia and n. Argentina.

BOTANICAL GARDEN. A botanical garden is a controlled and staffed institution for the maintenance of a living collection of plants under scientific management for purposes of education and research, together with such libraries, herbaria, laboratories, and museums as are essential to its particular undertakings. Each botanical garden naturally develops its own special field of interests depending on its personnel, location, extent, available funds, and the terms of its charter. It may include greenhouses, test grounds, an herbarium, an arboretum, and other departments. It maintains a scientific as well as a plant-growing staff, and publication is one of its major modes of expression.

The botanical garden may be an independent institution, a governmental operation, or affiliated with a college or university. If a department of an educational institution, it may be related to the teaching program. In any case, it exists for scientific ends and is not to be restricted or diverted by other demands. It is not merely a landscaped or ornamental garden, although it may be artistic, nor is it an experiment station or yet a park with labels on the plants. The essential element is the intention of the enterprise, which is the acquisition and dissemination of botanical knowledge.

BOTANY. This is the branch of biology that deals with plants, as opposed to zoology, which deals with animals. Broadly speaking, botany is concerned with fundamental studies of all plants, from the simplest unicellular forms to the most highly advanced and more familiar flowering plants. It includes, among others, studies in morphology, anatomy, cytology, physiology, chemistry, ecology, paleobotany, geographical distribution (floras), evolution, systematics, and nomenclature. The principles of botany are basic to the development of applied sciences of many kinds and especially such agricultural disciplines as agronomy, horticulture, and plant breeding.

BOTHRIOCHILUS Lem. *Orchidaceae.* Four spp. of epiphytes, native to Cent. Amer.; pseudobulbs several-lvd.; lvs. plicate, terminal; infl. a lateral raceme, scape covered by an inflated sheath; fls. only partially opening, dorsal sepal separate, lateral sepals united to column foot. For structure of fl. see *Orchidaceae.*

Intermediate greenhouse; for culture see *Orchids.*

macrostachyus (Lindl.) L. O. Williams [*Coelia macrostachya* Lindl.]. To 3 ft., pseudobulbs to 3 in. long; lvs. linear-lanceolate, 3 ft. long; scape to 20 in. long, raceme densely fld.; sepals and petals connivent, white or pale rose, ½ in. long, lip white, tongue-shaped, with 2 short basal sacs. Summer. Mex., Costa Rica, Panama, Colombia.

BOTHRIOCHLOA O. Kuntze. *Gramineae.* About 50 spp. of per. grasses in the Old World, distinguished from *Andropogon* by ascending racemes, 1 pair of spikelets rarely unisexual, glumes sometimes pitted, upper lemma of the sessile spikelet not cleft, often stipitate and passing into the awn. For terminology see *Gramineae.*

caucasica (Trin.) C. E. Hubb. [*Andropogon caucasicus* Trin.]. CAUCASIAN BLUESTEM. Distinguished from *B. intermedia* by spikelets about ⅛ in. long, lower lemma of the sessile spikelet about half the length of the lower glume. Russia, nw. India; introd. into the s. Great Plains area for dry-land grazing and for hay.

intermedia (R. Br.) A. Camus [*Andropogon intermedius* R. Br.]. AUSTRALIAN BLUESTEM. Primary axis of the panicle simple, mostly 1¼–2¾ in. long, all brs. of the panicle simple or rarely one of the lower divided, the lower shorter than the rachis; racemes to 2¾ in. long; sessile spikelets to 1¾ in. long, lower glumes of sessile spikelets glabrous, lower lemma nearly as long as the glume. India, China, Malay Arch.; introd. for reseeding of dry range country in the Southwest and for grazing in Fla.

Ischaemum (L.) Keng [*Andropogon Ischaemum* L.]. YELLOW BLUESTEM, TURKESTAN B. Per., sts. to 3½ ft., nodes glabrous; racemes nodding, few to several, on slender peduncles clustered or somewhat distant on a slender axis, to 2 in. long; sterile spikelets as conspicuous as the fertile, lower glumes of sessile spikelets hairy below the middle, rachis and pedicels silky-ciliate, awns slender, twisted and bent, about ⅝ in. long. Eurasia, N. Afr.; naturalized in Tex., introd. in Kans., Tenn., and N.Y.

BOTRYCERAS: *LAUROPHYLLUS.* **B. laurifolius:** in error for *B. laurinum.* **B. laurinum:** *L. capensis.*

BOTRYCHIUM Swartz. GRAPE FERN, MOONWORT. *Ophioglossaceae.* About 40 spp. of mostly somewhat fleshy ferns, native chiefly to temp. regions of both hemispheres, many in the U.S.; rhizomes short, each bearing a single lf. with a 1–3-pinnate sterile blade and an erect, fertile, paniclelike blade; sporangia sessile, in grapelike clusters.

Most species are not showy and are not easily or commonly cultivated. See also *Ferns.*

dissectum K. Spreng. DISSECTED G.F. Evergreen, to 1½ ft., fruiting usually in autumn; sterile blades long-stalked, to 6 in. across, ternately compound, the main divisions 1–3-pinnate, pinnules acuminate. Nov. Sc. and Que., s. to S.C. and Mo. Var. **obliquum** (Muhlenb.) Clute [*B. obliquum* Muhlenb.]. Blades ternately compound, the main divisions 1–2-pinnate, pinnules to 1 in long, entire or finely toothed.

Lunaria (L.) Swartz. MOONWORT. Deciduous, to 10 in.; sterile blades 1-pinnate, pinnae lunate, entire or toothed. N. and S. Amer., Eurasia, Australia.

matricariifolium A. Braun. DAISY-LEAVED G.F. Deciduous, to 1 ft.; sterile blades sessile or short-stalked, 1–2-pinnate, pinnae 2–7 pairs, toothed or divided, glabrous. N. Amer., Eurasia.

multifidum (S. G. Gmel.) Rupr. LEATHERY G.F. Evergreen, very variable, 2 in.–1½ ft.; sterile blades long-stalked, thick, ½ in.–1 ft. wide, ternately compound, the pinnae 1–3-pinnate, pinnules rounded to obtuse; fruiting usually in summer. N. Amer.; Eurasia. Subsp. **californicum** (Underw.) R. T. Clausen [*B. californicum* Underw.]. A large, loose plant. Calif. Subsp. **silaifolium** (K. Presl) R. T. Clausen [var. *intermedium* (D. C. Eat.) Farw.; *B. silaifolium* K. Presl; *B. ternatum* (Thunb.) Swartz var. *intermedium* D. C. Eat.]. Blades large, leathery. The common plant of n. and w. U.S. and s. Canada

obliquum: *B. dissectum* var.

silaifolium: *B. multifidum* subsp.

ternatum (Thunb.) Swartz. Native to e. Asia; not cult. Plants cult. under this name are *B. dissectum* var. *obliquum.*

virginianum (L.) Swartz. RATTLESNAKE FERN. Deciduous; sterile blades sessile, to 2½ ft. high, broadly triangular, ternately compound, the 3 pinnae 1–2-pinnate, pinnules acutely toothed. N. Amer., Eurasia.

BOTTIONEA: *TRICHOPETALUM.* **B. thysanthoides:** *T. plumosum.*

BOTTOM HEAT: see *Hotbed.*

BOUGAINVILLEA Comm. ex Juss. *Nyctaginaceae.* Perhaps 14 spp. of shrubs, vines, or small trees in S. Amer., usually armed with spines; lvs. alt.; fls. solitary and with 3 bracts, or in axillary clusters of 3 and each fl. attached by the pedicel to a large, persistent, often showy bract, calyx tubular with shallowly 5-lobed limb, stamens 5–10; fr. an elongate, 5-ribbed achene. The generic name was originally spelled *Buginvillaea,* a Latinization of the personal name De Bougainville, but the corrected spelling has been conserved.

The cultivated kinds are grown as woody vines, but may be trained as standards in the open far south and in greenhouses north. Many forms bear Latin names as though they were species. Of easy cultivation in any soil, thriving best in full sunshine; in the North grown as pot plants in a cool greenhouse. Propagated by cuttings, some kinds more easily than others; *B.* × *Buttiana* and *B. spectabilis* flower well only after dry weather outdoors or when given dry conditions indoors.

americana: a listed name of no botanical standing.

arborea: a listed name of no botanical standing.

brasiliensis: a listed name of no botanical standing, which has been applied to both *B. glabra* and *B. spectabilis.*

×**Buttiana** Holtt. & Standl.: probably *B. glabra* × *B. peruviana.* Lvs. broadly ovate; bracts crimson or orange, fading to purple or mauve, much crisped, calyx distinctly angled, with very short, upwardly curved hairs. Cvs. include: '**Golden Glow**', bracts lemon-yellow, fading to apricot; '**Louis Wathen**', bracts orange, fls. lacking starlike limb; '**Mrs. Butt**' [cv. 'Crimson Lake'], bracts crimson, fls. all with starlike limb; '**Mrs. McClean**', bracts orange, fls. starlike; '**Praetoria**', sport from cv. 'Mrs. Butt', with bracts yellow, turning to golden-salmon, perhaps same as cv. 'Golden Glow'; '**Scarlet Queen**', similar to cv. 'Mrs. Butt', but lacking starlike limb.

glabra Choisy. PAPER FLOWER. Weakly spinose, glabrous or nearly so; lvs. almost evenly elliptic, narrow at base, pointed at apex; bracts purple or magenta, running into lighter shades in cvs., changing little in color on aging and little crisped on the edges, calyx distinctly angled, with very short, upward-curved hairs. Brazil. Flowering nearly continuously. Cv. 'Sanderana'. Floriferous, bracts bright purple; lvs. shortly hairy on both sides.

Harrisii: a listed name of no botanical standing; used for plants with dark green lvs. marbled with creamy-white.

lateritia: *B. spectabilis* cv.

peruviana Humb. & Bonpl. Vine, with stout spines; lvs. broadly ovate to suborbicular, becoming nearly glabrous; bracts rose to light magenta-pink, ⅞–1¼ in. long, calyx glabrous except back of lobes, very slender, to 3⁄32 in. in diam., not angled. Colombia to Peru. A parent of *B.* × *Buttiana,* but rarely cult. in U.S.; known elsewhere as 'Ecuadorean Pink', 'Lady Hudson', or 'Princess Margaret Rose'.

praetoria: *B.* × *Buttiana* cv.

rosea-speciosa: a listed name of no botanical standing.

Sanderana: *B. glabra* cv.

spectabilis Willd. Often with stout spines; lvs. more or less ovate, velvety-hairy beneath and often above; bracts purple, pink, or light brick-red, calyx not distinctly angled, with many spreading hairs to 1⁄32 in. long or more. Brazil. The sp. typically has purple bracts about 2 in. long. Cv. '**Lateritia**'. Bracts light brick-red, fading to orange, less than 2 in. long.

Thomasii: *B. spectabilis* cv.

variegata: a listed name, perhaps referable to *B. glabra* cv.

BOURRERIA P. Br. *Boraginaceae.* About 40 or more spp. of trees of trop. Amer.; sts. glabrous or hairy; lvs. simple, alt., glabrous or hairy; fls. in corymbose cymes, calyx and corolla 5-lobed, stamens 5; fr. a drupe.

ovata Miers. STRONGBACK. Shrub or small tree, to 50 ft.; lvs. elliptic to obovate, to 3 in. long; fls. white, fragrant, in 15–20-fld. cymes; fr. orange-red, ½ in. in diam. S. Fla., W. Indies.

BOUSSINGAULTIA: *ANREDERA.* **B. gracilis:** *A. cordifolia.*

BOUTELOUA Lag. GRAMA, GRAMMA, GRAMA GRASS, GRAMMA G., MESQUITE G. *Gramineae.* About 50 spp. of per. or ann. grasses from cent. U.S. to Argentina; spikes 2 to several, racemose on a common axis, or sometimes solitary; spikelets few to many, rarely solitary, pectinate, or more loosely arranged and appressed, 1-fld., with rudiments of 1 or more florets above, in 2 rows along 1 side of the rachis which is often naked at the tip, glumes 1-nerved, acuminate or awn-tipped, the first shorter and narrower, lemma 3-nerved, nerves extending into short awns or mucros, the tissue between the nerves usually extending into lobes or teeth, palea sometimes 2-awned. For terminology see *Gramineae.*

curtipendula (Michx.) Torr. SIDEOATS G. Per., sts. erect, clustered, to 32 in., base with scaly rhizomes; lf. blades flat or nearly involute, about ⅛ in. wide, scabrous; spikes 35–50, to ¾ in. long, purplish, spreading or pendulous, mostly along one side of a slender axis 6–10 in. long; spikelets 5–8 in each spike, appressed or ascending, to ⅜ in. long, fertile lemma acute, mucronate. Me., w. to Mont., s. to Va., Ariz. and s. Calif.; introd. in S.C.; Mex. to Argentina. Pasture grass.

eriopoda (Torr.) Torr. BLACK G. Per., sts. clustered, to 2 ft. long, slender, wiry, decumbent or stoloniferous, white-woolly, swollen at base; lf. blades 1/16 in. wide, flexuous; spikes 3–8, but mostly 4–5, loosely ascending, to 1¼ in. long; spikelets 12–20, not crowded and pectinate, to ⅜ in. long, narrow, fertile lemma with a terminal awn. Okla. and Tex., w. to s. Calif.; n. Mex. Pasture grass.

filiformis: *B. repens.*

gracilis (HBK) Lag. ex Steud. BLUE G. Per., sts. in dense clusters, erect, to 20 in. high, base leafy; lf. blades flat or loosely involute, less than ⅛ in. wide; spikes 1–3, usually 2, to 2 in. long, curved-spreading, rachis not prolonged; spikelets to 80, about ¼ in. long, glumes not or only slightly tubercled, fertile lemma pilose, awn slender. Wisc. to Man. and Alta., s. to Ark., Tex. and s. Calif.; Mex. Pasture grass.

hirsuta Lag. HAIRY G. Per., sts. to 24 in., in dense clusters, glabrous, erect, leafy at base; lf. blades flat or nearly involute, less than ⅛ in. wide, flexuous; spikes 1–4, usually 1⅜–2 in. long, rachis prolonged into a slender point; spikelets 35–45, about ¼ in. long, second glume black-tubercled-hirsute, fertile lemma 3-cleft, awn-tipped, the divisions and margins pubescent. Wisc. and N. Dak. to Tex. and Calif., s. through Mex.; also s. Fla.

repens (HBK) Scribn. & Merrill [*B. filiformis* (E. Fourn.) Griffiths]. SLENDER G. Sts. to 2½ ft., erect or geniculate at the base, little-branched, rhizomes lacking; spikes 4–12, ascending to spreading, mostly about ⅝ in. long, but sometimes longer; spikelets mostly 3–9, glumes broad, glabrous, fertile lemma 3-awned, hard at the center. S. New Mex. to s. Calif.; W. Indies, Cent. and n. S. Amer. Pasture grass.

BOUVARDIA Salisb. *Rubiaceae.* About 30 spp. or more, mostly shrubs or herbs, native to Mex. and Cent. Amer.; lvs. opp. or whorled, stipules interpetiolar, united into a sheath; fls. usually large, red, yellow or white, in terminal cymes, sometimes solitary, corolla tubular, 4-lobed; fr. a caps., seeds many.

Bouvardias are grown outdoors in warm regions or in the greenhouse. They thrive in a temperature of about 55° F. in rich soil with abundant water. Propagated by root cuttings and cuttings of fresh shoots taken with a heel and placed over bottom heat.

corymbiflora: *B. longiflora.*

Harlandii: a listed name of no botanical standing.

Humboldtii: *B. longiflora.*

Jacquinii: *B. ternifolia.*

leiantha Benth. Lvs. in whorls of 3–5, ovate, to 3 in. long, pubescent beneath; fls. deep red, ½ in. long, glabrous outside. S. Mex. and Cent. Amer.

longiflora (Cav.) HBK [*B. corymbiflora* Hort.; *B. Humboldtii* Hort.]. To 5 ft.; lvs. opp., ovate or lanceolate, to 2 in. long; fls. white, to 3½ in. long, glabrous outside. Mex. The showy fls. have a jasminelike fragrance.

ternifolia (Cav.) Schlechtend. [*B. Jacquinii* HBK; *B. triphylla* Salisb.]. To 6 ft.; lvs. in 3's and 4's, lanceolate to ovate; fls. red, to 1¼ in. long, pubescent outside. Mex., w. Tex.

triphylla: *B. ternifolia.*

BOWENIA Hook. ex Hook.f. *Zamiaceae.* Two spp. of cycads with underground sts., native to Australia; lvs. pinnately decompound, in a rosette; male and female sporophylls (cone scales) arranged in vertical rows in stalked or subsessile cones; seeds with fleshy outer coat.

Sometimes grown as ornamentals in Zone 10. For culture see *Cycads.*

serrulata (Bull) Chamberl. St. bearing at its crown 5–20, short, slender, lf.- and cone-bearing brs.; lvs. 5–30, to 6 ft. long, but usually smaller, pinnules to about 30 on each pinna, to 6 in. long, sharply serrate; male cones ovoid, to 2 in. long, female cones oblong-globose, to 4 in. long, scales in about 8 rows. Queensland.

spectabilis Hook. ex Hook. f. St. bearing at its crown 1–5, short, slender, lf.- and cone-bearing brs.; lvs. few, 1–7, to 6 ft. long, but usually smaller, pinnules 7–30 on each pinna, to 6 in. long, entire or sometimes with a few lacerations; cones as in *B. serrulata.* Queensland.

BOWIEA Harv. ex Hook.f. [*Schizobasopsis* Macbr.]. *Liliaceae.* Two spp. of bulbous, per. herbs, native to S. Afr. and E. Trop. Afr.; sts. rather fleshy, twining, leafless; fls. small, green to greenish-white, on long pedicels, perianth segms. 6,

separate, persistent, stamens 6, filaments dilated at base, ovary superior, 3-celled; fr. a loculicidal caps., seeds black, several in each locule.

Grown in greenhouses as curiosities, because of their large exposed bulbs and twining, leafless stems. Plants should be kept dormant from May to early Oct., at which time the bulbs should be repotted and kept well watered. Propagated by seeds or sometimes by division of the bulbs.

volubilis Harv. ex Hook.f. CLIMBING ONION, ZULU POTATO. Bulb fleshy, to 7 in. across, sts. 5–15 ft. long, the single main st. branching, the many brs. repeatedly forked; fls. to ⅝ in. in diam., perianth segms. becoming reflexed. S. Afr.

BOWKERIA Harv. *Scrophulariaceae.* Five or 6 spp. of shrubs or trees of S. Afr.; lvs. sessile or short-petioled, usually in whorls of 3; fls. in axillary or nearly terminal infl., calyx 5-parted, corolla 2-lipped, lower lip inflated, stamens 4, in 2 pairs; fr. a caps., seeds many.

Gerrardiana Harv. ex Hiern. Shrub, to 10 ft., hairy or glabrous in lower part; lvs. elliptic-lanceolate, to 6 in. long, finely toothed, paler beneath; corolla white, upper lip to ½ in. long and ⅝ in. wide.

BOYKINIA Nutt. *Saxifragaceae.* About 8 spp. of per. herbs, mostly in mts. and woods in e. Asia and N. Amer., mostly w. U.S.; rhizomes scaly, creeping; lvs. mostly basal, reniform, toothed or lobed, petioled, usually with stipules; fl. st. leafy, branched, calyx tube united to lower half of ovary, calyx lobes 5, petals 5, white, early-deciduous, stamens 5, with short filaments, ovary 2-celled, styles 2, forming divergent beaks; fr. a 2-celled caps.

Summer-flowering; easily grown in the wild garden or rock garden in moist shady places. Propagated by seeds or division.

elata (Nutt.) Greene [*B. occidentalis* Torr. & A. Gray]. To 2 ft.; lvs. 1–4 in. across, deeply lobed and toothed, stipules evident, often reduced to bristles; petals much longer than calyx lobes. Calif.

heucheriformis: *Telesonix Jamesii.*

Jamesii: *Telesonix Jamesii.*

major A. Gray. To 3 ft.; lvs. 4–8 in. across, cut and toothed, stipules large, leaflike, often clasping or united; petals slightly longer than calyx lobes. Ore. and Calif.

occidentalis: *B. elata.*

rotundifolia Parry. To 2 ft.; lvs. 2–7 in. across, shallowly lobed and toothed, stipules not evident; petals only slightly longer than calyx lobes. Calif.

tellimoides: *Peltoboykinia tellimoides.*

BOYSENBERRY. The boysenberry is a cultivar of *Rubus ursinus* var. *loganobaccus,* as are also the loganberry and youngberry. The exact origin of the boysenberry is obscure; it was named in 1923 after Rudolf Boysen, who was instrumental in its introduction. The boysenberry closely resembles the youngberry but ripens later. The fruits are often 2 inches in length, ¾–1 inch in diameter, dark wine-red to almost black, juicy, soft when ripe, tart in flavor. The torus separates with the fruit as it does in the blackberry. The boysenberry is much grown in the Pacific Coast states. It is not hardy in the northeastern United States, where it requires winter protection. The new canes are thorny and grow along the ground, often reaching 8–10 feet in length. In spring, the trailing canes are trained on a trellis, along a single wire or in a coil between two wires. For general culture see *Blackberry.*

BRACHIARIA (Trin.) Griseb. SIGNAL GRASS. *Gramineae.* About 50 spp. of branching and spreading ann. or per. grasses in the Old World; lf. blades linear; racemes several, spreading or appressed, approximate along a common axis; spikelets solitary or rarely paired, subsessile, in 2 rows on one side of a 3-angled, sometimes narrowly winged rachis, first glume turned toward the rachis, second glume and sterile lemma about equal, 5–7-nerved, the lemma enclosing a hyaline palea and sometimes a male floret, fertile lemma hard, usually papillose-rugose, with inrolled margins. For terminology see *Gramineae.*

subquadripara (Trin.) A. S. Hitchc. Per., sts. to 24 in. long, creeping; lf. blades flat, to 4 in. long and 5/16 in. wide; racemes mostly 3–5, spreading, separated; spikelets about ⅛ in. long, elliptic, glabrous. Asia; widely distributed in trop. Old World. Occasionally planted in s. Fla. as a forage grass.

BRACHYCHILUM (R. Br.) Petersen. *Zingiberaceae.* Two spp. of per. herbs in Java and the Moluccas, with aromatic rhizomes; sts. leafy; infl. terminal on leafy st., loose, spicate, with sheathing bracts; fls. several, in axils of bracts, calyx tubular, corolla tube elongate, slender, corolla lobes pendulous, twisted, linear, staminodial lip very short, deeply 2-parted, lateral staminodes petal-like, stamen filament long, anther sacs not spurred; fr. a 3-valved caps., splitting to reveal a mass of red-arillate seeds.

Culture as for *Alpinia.*

Horsfieldii (R. Br.) Petersen. To 2 ft. or more; lvs. lanceolate or linear-lanceolate, to 1 ft. long, 2½ in. wide, ligule ⅝ in. long; spike erect; fls. usually 2–4 in axil of each bract, white or yellowish, to 3 in. long, stamen filament orange; caps. orange inside, seeds dark, with fringed red aril. Java. Frequently mistakenly cult. under the names *Alpinia calcarata* and *A. mutica.*

BRACHYCHITON Schott & Endl. BOTTLE TREE. *Sterculiaceae.* About 12 spp. of tall shrubs or trees, often with swollen trunks, native to Australia and perhaps New Guinea; differing from *Sterculia* chiefly in having seeds in compartments of the hairy, honeycomblike endocarp within the follicles.

Planted as ornamentals in Zone 10, particularly in Calif.; propagated by seeds and cuttings of ripened wood.

acerifolius (A. Cunn.) F. J. Muell. [*Sterculia acerifolia* A. Cunn.]. FLAME TREE, FLAME B.T. To 100 ft. or more in the wild, 20–40 ft. in cult., leafless when in fl.; lvs. deeply 3–5–7-lobed or sometimes nearly entire, to 12 in. across, glossy above; fls. in loose racemes or panicles, calyx bright scarlet, campanulate, to ¾ in. long, glabrous; follicles blackish, to 4 in. long, long-stalked. Queensland to New S. Wales.

australis (Schott & Endl.) A. Terracc. [*Sterculia Trichosiphon* Benth.]. BROAD-LEAVED B.T., FLAME TREE. Deciduous, glabrous tree, leafless when in fl.; lvs. 4–8 in. long and wide, 5–7-lobed, lobes ovate-acuminate to lanceolate; fls. in short racemes, calyx about ¾ in. long, glabrous, tubular-campanulate, the lobes shorter than the tube, column swollen and hairy in the middle; follicles smooth, 2–3 in. long, short-stalked. Queensland, n. Australia.

Bidwillii Hook. [*Sterculia Bidwillii* (Hook.) Hook. ex Benth.]. Similar to *B. paradoxus,* but having lvs. deeply 3-lobed and calyx narrow-tubular, to 1½ in. long. Queensland.

discolor F. J. Muell. [*B. luridus* C. Moore ex F. J. Muell; *Sterculia discolor* (F. J. Muell.) F. J. Muell ex Benth.; *S. lurida* (C. Moore ex F. J. Muell.) F. J. Muell. ex Benth.]. SCRUB B. T., QUEENSLAND LACE-BARK, HAT TREE. To 100 ft., deciduous in cooler regions; lvs. 3–5–7-lobed or -angled, 4–8 in. across, white- or yellowish-tomentose underneath; fls. clustered in the axils, calyx pink or pale red, campanulate, to 2 in. long, tomentose; follicles 4–6 in. long, densely rusty-pubescent. N. Australia, Queensland, New S. Wales.

diversifolius R. Br. Not known to be in cult.; cult. material so named is *B. populneus.*

Gregorii F. J. Muell. DESERT KURRAJONG. Tree, probably deciduous, glabrous except for fls.; lvs. deeply 3–5-lobed, lobes linear-lanceolate, acuminate; fls. in small axillary panicles, calyx pale yellow, margined red, broadly campanulate, to ¾ in. long; follicles to 2 in. long. S., cent., and w. Australia. Trees cult. under this name in Calif. are probably *B.* × *hybridus* or *B. populneus.*

×hybridus Hort.: *B. acerifolius* × *B. populneus.* Intermediate between the parents; lvs. mostly unlobed; fls. somewhat paler than in *B. acerifolius.* In Calif., has been grown as *B. Gregorii* and under the hort. name *Sterculia Sextonii.*

luridus: *B. discolor.*

paradoxus Schott & Endl. [*B. ramiflorus* R. Br.]. Tomentose shrub or small tree; lvs. cordate-ovate to nearly orbicular, up to 6 in. long, entire or angularly or obscurely 3–5-lobed; fls. few, nearly sessile in axillary clusters, calyx red, open-campanulate, to 1½ in. long; follicles glabrous outside, to 4 in. long. N. Australia, Queensland.

populneus (Schott & Endl.) R. Br. [*B. diversifolius* Hort., not R. Br.; *Sterculia diversifolia* G. Don]. KURRAJONG. To 60 ft., with a dense, heavy crown; lvs. ovate, entire or 3–5-lobed, to 3 in. long, glossy, glabrous; fls. in short panicles, calyx white or greenish-yellow and puberulent outside, yellowish or red inside; follicles long-stalked, glabrous, to 3 in. long. Queensland, New S. Wales.

ramiflorus: *B. paradoxus.*

rupestris (Lindl.) K. Schum. [*Sterculia rupestris* (Lindl.) Benth.]. QUEENSLAND B. T., NARROW-LEAVED B. T. Large tree with swollen trunk; lvs. of mature trees simple, oblong-linear to lanceolate, 3–6 in. long, those of young trees digitately 3–9-divided, the lfts. sessile, linear-lanceolate, to 6 in. long or more; fls. in tomentose panicles, calyx campanulate, to ⅜ in. long; follicles to 1½ in. long, as long as or shorter than the stipes. Queensland.

Trichosiphon: a listed name of no botanical standing, used for *B. australis.*

BRACHYCOME Cass. *Compositae* (Aster Tribe). About 70 spp. of ann. or per. herbs or rarely subshrubs, native chiefly to Australia and New Zeal., sts. scapose or branched; lvs. basal or alt. on sts., entire to variously dissected; fl. heads radiate, solitary to several in a loose cluster at ends of brs., involucre usually hemispherical, involucral bracts in 2–3 rows, scarious-margined, receptacle flat to convex, naked, sometimes pitted; disc fls. bisexual, fertile, yellow, ray fls. in 1 row, female, white, blue, lilac, pink, or sometimes yellow; achenes compressed or more or less 4-angled, sometimes winged, pappus of separate or united bristles or absent.

Of easy culture. Propagated by seeds.

aculeata (Labill.) Less. More or less branched per., to 2 ft.; basal lvs. spatulate to oblanceolate, to 4 in. long, crenate or with remote, sharp teeth, st. lvs. successively reduced upward, the uppermost linear and sessile; heads to 1½ in. across, solitary on scapes or axillary peduncles; ray fls. white, blue, or lilac. Se. Australia, Tasmania.

iberidifolia Benth. SWAN RIVER DAISY. Much-branched ann., to 1½ ft., glandular-pubescent to nearly glabrous; lvs. to 3 in. long, pinnately dissected into linear segms., rarely entire; heads to 1 in. across, on slender peduncles to 3⅜ in. long; ray fls. blue, rose, or white. W. Australia to n. S. Australia.

nivalis F. J. Muell. Erect per., to 1 ft., glabrous except for the sparsely glandular petioles and part of the scape; lvs. mostly in basal rosette, 2-pinnately dissected, to 6 in. long including the petiole; heads 1–3, to ¾ in. across; ray fls. white. Se. Australia, Tasmania. Var. **alpina** (F. J. Muell. ex Benth.) G. L. Davis. Basal lvs. linear to narrowly spatulate, entire or irregularly pinnatifid. New S. Wales and Victoria.

rigidula (DC.) G. L. Davis. Much-branched, many-stemmed per., to 15 in., sts. densely leafy, glandular-hairy; lvs. to ¾ in. long, pinnately dissected, segms. linear, sharp-pointed; heads about 30, to ⅜ in. across, on glandular, scapose peduncles; ray fls. blue. Se. Australia, Tasmania.

scapigera (Siebold ex K. Spreng.) DC. Erect, glabrous per., to 1½ ft.; lvs. in a loose, basal rosette, linear to oblanceolate, to 7½ in. long, entire; heads to ½ in. across, solitary on the long scape; ray fls. white or mauve. S. Queensland to Victoria.

BRACHYGLOTTIS J. R. Forst. & G. Forst. *Compositae* (Senecio Tribe). One or 2 spp. of shrubs or small trees of New Zeal., white-tomentose except for green upper surfaces of lvs.; lvs. large, ovate-oblong, sinuate; fl. heads radiate, small, many in terminal panicles, involucral bracts in 1 row, linear, scarious; disc and ray fls. white; achenes papillose, pappus of capillary bristles.

Sometimes planted in Calif.

Rangiora J. Buchan. To 14 ft.; lvs. to 15 in. long, glossy above; involucral bracts purplish; otherwise very like *B. repanda* and perhaps only a var. of it.

repanda J. R. Forst. & G. Forst. To 20 ft.; lvs. to 12 in. long, dull above; heads ⅛ in. across, involucral bracts whitish, glossy.

BRACHYSEMA R. Br. *Leguminosae* (subfamily *Faboideae*). About 15 spp. of shrubs, native to Australia; lvs. simple; fls. solitary or clustered in axils, mostly red, papilionaceous, stamens 10, separate; fr. an ovoid or elongate legume.

Cultivated outdoors in southern Calif. Zone 10.

acuminatum Hort. ex Jacques. Subshrub, with scandent brs.; similar to *B. lanceolatum,* but lvs. ovate-elliptic. W. Australia.

lanceolatum Meissn. To 3 ft.; lvs. usually opp., lanceolate, to 4 in. long, silvery-gray-pubescent beneath; fls. in clusters; fr. about ½ in. long. W. Australia.

BRACHYSTEGIA Benth. *Leguminosae* (subfamily *Caesalpinioideae*). About 30 spp. of unarmed trees, native to Afr.; lvs. alt., even-pinnate; racemes paniced or simple, shorter than lvs.; buds enclosed in a pair of sepal-like bracteoles; fls.

inconspicuous, perianth minute, stamens about 10, united; fr. a flat, oblong, woody legume at right angles to stalk.

Excellent shade tree for tropical plantings. Propagated by seeds.

spiciformis Benth. To 50 ft. or more; lvs. deciduous, lfts. usually in 3–4 pairs, with the terminal pair largest, obliquely ovate-elliptic, 1–3 in. long, new lvs. pink-red; racemes spikelike, densely fld., bracteoles to ⁵⁄₁₆ in. long; fls. very fragrant; fr. to 4½ in. long, explosively dehiscent. Angola to Mozambique. In Rhodesia called MSASA.

BRAHEA Mart. [*Erythea* S. Wats.]. ROCK PALM, HESPER P. *Palmae.* About 12 spp. of mostly low or medium palms with bisexual fls. in limestone areas of Mex. and Cent. Amer.; sts. solitary or rarely clustered by basal sprouting; lvs. briefly costapalmate, petiole margins smooth or armed with spinose teeth, blade divided into 1-ribbed, 2-cleft segms. about an undivided base; infl. elongate, among and often exceeding lvs., with tubular bracts sheathing peduncle and base of the several primary brs., these 2–3 times branched; fls. solitary or in clusters of 3, at least at base of rachillae, sepals 3, separate, petals 3, separate or briefly united basally, stamens 6, carpels 3, separate except united styles, usually only 1 maturing; fr. ellipsoid to subglobose but usually somewhat flattened on 1 side, with subapical stigmatic residue and basal abortive carpels, seed with homogeneous endosperm intruded on 1 side by seed coat.

Several species are grown as ornamentals for street or garden planting. Mostly slow-growing. Need full sun for best development. Acid soil should receive applications of agricultural lime. For culture see *Palms.*

armata S. Wats. [*Erythea armata* (S. Wats.) S. Wats.; *E. Roezlii* Becc.]. BLUE H. P., GRAY GODDESS, BLUE FAN P., MEXICAN BLUE P. To 40 ft. or more, robust; lvs. long-persistent if not cut or burned, waxy blue, deeply divided into about 50 segms., petiole armed with stout curved teeth; infl. much longer than lvs., to 15 ft. long, arched with pendulous brs.; fls. in clusters of 3 on softly hairy rachillae; fr. globose, about ¾ in. long, yellow, fleshy. Baja Calif. Zone 10a. Very slow-growing, but popular because of its attractive blue-gray lvs.

Brandegeei (C. Purpus) H. E. Moore [*Erythea Brandegeei* C. Purpus]. SAN JOSÉ H.P. To about 40 ft., trunk slender; lvs. long-persistent when not cut or burned, petiole elongate, armed with curved or hooked spinose teeth to about ¼ in. long, blade to 3 ft. wide or more, dull green above, glaucous beneath, soft, the 50–60 segms. deeply 2-cleft, often drooping at apex; infl. not exceeding the lvs.; fls. in clusters of 3 on softly hairy rachillae; fr. brown and yellow, to ¾ in. long, flattened on 1 side. S. tip of Baja Calif. Zone 10a. Faster growing than *B. armata.*

calcarea: *B. dulcis* but material cult. under this name is usually *B. nitida.*

dulcis (HBK) Mart. [*B. calcarea* Liebm.]. Trunk to 20 ft. or more, solitary and erect or sometimes leaning or nearly procumbent and suckering at the base; lvs. not long-persistent, petiole armed with short, hooked teeth, blades stiff, to 5 ft. long, green above, often glaucescent beneath, segms. about 60, briefly 2-cleft; infl. exceeding lvs., to 7 ft. long; fls. solitary, partly immersed in yellowish tomentum of flexuous rachillae; fr. yellow, succulent, about ⅝ in. long. W. and cent. Mex. to Guatemala. Zone 10a.

edulis H. Wendl. ex S. Wats. [*Erythea edulis* (H. Wendl. ex S. Wats.) S. Wats.]. GUADALUPE PALM. Trunk stout, to 30 ft. or more; lvs. not long-persistent on trunk, petiole stout, to 4½ ft. long, 2½ in wide, armed with very short, spinose teeth, blade green on both sides, to 6 ft. wide, soft, segms. 80 or more, briefly 2-cleft; infl. not exceeding the lvs.; fls. in clusters of 3 on softly hairy rachillae; fr. black at maturity, 1 in. in diam. or more. Guadalupe Is. (Mex.). Zone 9b. Relatively slow-growing.

elegans (Franceschi ex Becc.) H. E. Moore [*Erythea elegans* Franceschi ex Becc.]. FRANCESCHI PALM. Small tree; lvs. thinly glaucous on both surfaces, petiole armed with stout, curved or hooked teeth; infl. exceeding lvs.; fls. in clusters of 3 on softly hairy rachillae; fr. yellow, nearly globose or pear-shaped, to ⅞ in. long. An imperfectly understood sp. described from cult. and said to have come from Sonora (Mex.). Zone 10a.

nitida André. St. solitary, erect, to 30 ft. or more; lvs. not long-persistent, petiole lacking teeth on edges, blade green above, prominently waxy glaucous beneath, segms. 50–70, briefly 2-cleft; infl. exceeding lvs.; fls. solitary, hairy in bud on softly hairy rachillae or both fls. and rachillae eventually becoming nearly glabrous; fr. to ¾ in. long, yellow. W. Mex. and Guatemala. Zone 10a. This sp. has been confused in hort. and in literature with *B. calcarea.*

Pimo Becc. To 15 ft., trunk with fibrous sheaths at top; long-persistent, petiole densely hairy when young, armed with short, spinose teeth, blade green on both sides, with minute scales beneath, segms. 50 or more, briefly 2-cleft; infl. somewhat exceeding the lvs.; fls. in clusters of 3 on lightly hairy rachillae, sepals and petals white-canescent; fr. yellow, ¾ in. long, ⅝ in. in diam. Nayarit to Guerrero (Mex.). Zone 10a.

Roezlii: a listed name of no botanical standing for *B. armata.*

salvadorensis H. Wendl. ex Becc. To 20 ft., trunk with fibrous sheaths at top; lvs. not long-persistent, petiole hairy when young, armed with acute, spinose teeth, blade green on both sides, with minute scales beneath, segms. about 70, briefly 2-cleft; infl. not exceeding the lvs.; fls. in clusters of 3 on softly hairy rachillae, sepals and petals glabrous or nearly so. Guatemala, El Salvador, Honduras.

BRASENIA Schreb. *Nymphaeaceae.* One cosmopolitan sp. of aquatic herbs, often in deep water; rhizomes creeping, rooted in mud, sts. slender, branched; lvs. alt., floating, petioled; fls. small, axillary, sepals 3–4, persistent, petals as many as sepals, similar, stamens 12–18 or more, carpels 4–18, separate; fr. leathery, indehiscent, 1–3-seeded.

Propagated by seeds or division of roots.

Schreberi J. F. Gmel. WATER-SHIELD, PURPLE-WAN DOCK. Sts. trailing, several ft. long; lf. blades ovate to elliptic, 2–5 in. long, bright green above, often purplish beneath; fls. purple, to ¾ in. across; fr. beaked. Submersed parts with thick, transparent, gelatinous coating.

BRASILIOPUNTIA: *OPUNTIA* subgenus *Brasiliopuntia.*

BRASSAIA Endl. *Araliaceae.* About 40 spp. of trees or shrubs, native from India to the Malay Pen., Philippine Is., ne. Australia, and Hawaii; lvs. crowded, long-petioled, palmately compound; infl. of headlike umbels arranged in panicles or racemes; sepals 5, falling early, petals 5 or more, valvate, joined at the apex, stamens as many as the petals, ovary mostly 10–12-celled; fr. a subglobose drupe, pyrenes 1 to several.

actinophylla Endl. [*Schefflera actinophylla* (Endl.) Harms]. AUSTRALIAN UMBRELLA TREE, QUEENSLAND U. T., QUEEN'S U. T., AUSTRALIAN IVY PALM, OCTOPUS TREE, STARLEAF. Evergreen tree, to 40 ft., sts. usually simple, with few short brs. at the top; lvs. spreading, 2–4 ft. long, lfts. mostly 7–16, radiating from the apex of the elongate petiole, oblong, 4–12 in. long, glossy, entire or sparsely dentate on juvenile plants; fls. small, red, crowded in umbels arranged in elongate, divergent racemes standing out above the foliage; fr. purplish-red. Queensland. Zone 9b. Widely cult. as a landscape tree in Hawaii, s. Fla., and Calif., elsewhere indoors in tubs. May be kept multiple-stemmed and bushy by cutting back. Prop. by seeds, cuttings, or air-layers.

BRASSAIOPSIS Decne. & Planch. *Araliaceae.* Twenty or more spp. of tall, variously armed or unarmed shrubs or trees, native in trop. Asia; lvs. palmately compound, lfts. whorled; infl. of umbels arranged in tomentose racemes or large compound panicles; petals 5, valvate, stamens 5, styles 2, ovary 2-celled; fr. a drupe, pyrenes 1–2.

glomerulata (Blume) Regel [*B. speciosa* Decne. & Planch.]. Tree, to 30 ft., with prickly, rusty-tomentose branchlets; lfts. 5–9, oblong, entire or serrulate, glabrous, glaucous beneath; umbels in panicles to 1 ft. long. S. China to Java. Zone 10.

speciosa: *B. glomerulata.*

BRASSAVOLA R. Br. [*Rhyncolaelia* Schlechter]. *Orchidaceae.* About 15 spp. of epiphytes, native to trop. Amer.; pseudobulbs stemlike; lvs. solitary, terminal, fleshy; fls. solitary or in short, terminal racemes, sepals and petals narrow, spreading, lip entire or often toothed or even fringed, attached to base of a very short finely toothed column. For structure of fl. see *Orchidaceae.*

For culture see *Orchids.*

acaulis Lindl. & Paxt. Large, pendent, to 3 ft. long; lvs. cylindrical, to ¾ in. wide; fls. 1 or 2, on short peduncle arising from rhizome, sepals and petals green or greenish-white, similar, linear, 3 in. long, acuminate, lip white, broadly ovate, acute, the base enfolding the column. Costa Rica, Panama.

cordata Lindl. To 20 in.; lvs. fleshy, nearly cordate in cross section, raceme shorter than lf., few-fld.; sepals and petals spreading, greenish-white, filiform, to 2 in. long, lip white, cordate-obovate, with long, involute, serrate claw. Autumn. W. Indies.

cucullata (L.) R. Br. Pseudobulbs cylindrical, with a bulbous thickening at base; lvs. filiform, cylindrical, fleshy, to 1 ft. long; fls. 1–2 on peduncles to 8 in. long, sepals and petals white to greenish-white, aging to yellowish, spreading and pendulous, linear, acuminate, to 3 in. long, lip to 3 in. long, white, short-clawed, semicircular, with finely toothed margins, apically prolonged into a slender, acuminate lobe. Late spring–early winter. Trop. Amer.

Digbyana Lindl. [*Laelia Digbyana* (Lindl.) Benth.; *Rhyncholaelia Digbyana* (Lindl.) Schlechter]. Pseudobulbs elongated, jointed, club-shaped; lvs. leathery, elliptic, glaucous-green, to 8 in. long; infl. 1-fld.; fl. showy, fragrant, 4–6 in. across, sepals and petals elliptic, pale green-yellow, lip large, 3 in. long, obscurely 3-lobed, nearly orbicular, involute at base and enveloping column, cream-white with greenish suffusion, upper margins deeply lacerate-fringed, disc with several fleshy ridges. Spring–summer. Cent. Amer. Frequently used as a parent in crosses with spp. and cvs. of *Cattleya, Laelia,* and *Sophronitis,* the resultant hybrids possessing large, fringed lips.

fragrans Barb.-Rodr. To 20 in.; lvs. fleshy, cylindrical; raceme much shorter than 1f., few-fld., flexuous; fls. fragrant, yellowish-white, with a few purple spots, to 2 in. long, sepals and petals filiform, lip recurved, somewhat shorter than sepals. Autumn. Brazil.

glauca Lindl. [*Laelia glauca* (Lindl.) Benth; *Rhyncholaelia glauca* (Lindl.) Schlechter]. Pseudobulbs club-shaped, to 4 in. long; lvs. leathery, oblong-elliptic, glaucous, to 5 in. long; fls. solitary, nodding, fragrant, on peduncle 4 in. long, sepals linear-elliptic, to 2½ in. long, olive-green to white or lavender, petals similar to sepals in shape and length, olive-green to whitish, lip to 2 in. long, white or yellowish with rose-pink spot over several reddish stripes in throat, 3-lobed, midlobe squarish-oblong, apiculate at apex. Winter–early spring. Cent. Amer.

nodosa (L.) Lindl. LADY-OF-THE-NIGHT. Pseudobulbs 1–4 ½ in. long; lvs. to 9 in. long; fls. solitary, short-peduncled, sepals and petals linear, to 3 in. long, greenish-yellow or white, lip white, not toothed. Winter. W. Indies, Cent. Amer., Colombia, Venezuela, Surinam.

Perrinii Lindl. To 10 in., with ascending rhizome; lvs. fleshy, cylindrical; peduncle shorter than lf., 1-fld.; fls. to 2 in. long, sepals and petals greenish-yellow, spreading, filiform, lip white, with yellow-green throat, ovate, short-clawed, acute at apex. Brazil, Paraguay.

BRASSIA R. Br. *Orchidaceae.* About 50 spp. of epiphytes, native to trop. Amer.; pseudobulbs 1–3-lvd.; fls. in lateral racemes, sepals and petals narrow, long-pointed, often tail-like, lip entire, shorter than sepals. For structure of fl. see *Orchidaceae.*

Intermediate greenhouse; for culture see *Orchids.*

Allenii L. O. Williams ex C. Schweinf. Pseudobulbs not developed; lvs. many, forming a broad fan, to 1 ft. long; raceme several-fld., from lf. axils, shorter than lvs.; fls. fragrant, sepals and petals similar, spreading, reddish-tan to olive-ochre, 1½ in. long, linear-lanceolate, lip nearly orbicular, yellow, with band of reddish-tan and a white disc, cuspidate at apex. Autumn. Panama.

brachiata: *B. verrucosa.*

caudata (L.) Lindl. Pseudobulbs to 6 in. long; lvs. oblong or oblong-elliptic, to 11 in. long, acute; infl. to 1½ ft. long, 6–15-fld.; sepals and petals greenish-yellow, with brown spots on basal half, lateral sepals to 6 in. long, petals to 1 in. long, lip light yellow with brown spots, with 2 small teeth at apex of callus. Winter–late summer. Trop. Amer., from Fla. to S. Amer.

chlorops Endres & Rchb.f. To 1 ft.; lvs. lanceolate; infl. to 10 in. long, shorter than lvs., loosely few-fld.; fls. small, ¾ in. long, greenish, sepals and petals lanceolate, acuminate, lip linear-lanceolate, with 2 pubescent keels at base. Costa Rica, Panama, Colombia.

Gireoudiana Rchb.f. & Warsz. Pseudobulbs to 5 in. long, 2-lvd.; lvs. oblong or elliptic-oblong, to over 17 in. long; infl. over 2 ft. long, usually 7–10-fld.; sepals linear-lanceolate, to 6 in. long, tapering, cream-colored or greenish-yellow, spotted with brown on basal ⅓, petals to 2½ in. long, yellow, spotted with brown on lower half, lip light yellow, spotted with brown. Early winter–late spring. Costa Rica, Panama.

guttata: *B. maculata.*

Keiliana Rchb.f. ex Lindl. Pseudobulbs much-compressed, to 2 in. long, 1-lvd.; lvs. narrowly ovate, strap-shaped, to 10 in. long; infl. as long as lvs. or longer, few- or many-fld.; fl. bracts as long as pedicelled ovary or longer; fls. yellow, spotted with brown, sepals to 3 in. long, petals to 1¾ in. long, lip whitish. Late spring. Colombia, Venezuela.

Lanceana Lindl. [*B. pumila* Lindl.]. Pseudobulbs strongly flattened, 1–3-lvd.; lvs. lanceolate-oblong, to 12 in. long; infl. longer than lvs., densely many-fld.; sepals and petals yellow, with brown markings, sepals 2½ in. long, petals 1¼ in. long, lip oblong-pandurate, yellowish-

white, flecked with brown, acute, with a pair of white calluses at base. Surinam, Venezuela.

Lawrenceana Lindl. Pseudobulbs over 2 in. long, 2-lvd.; lvs. oblong or lanceolate, to 8 in. long; infl. to 2 ft. long or more; sepals and petals greenish- or bright yellow, spotted with brown, sepals almost 3 in. long, petals 1½ in. long, lip light yellow, without flecks. Late spring. Guyana, Surinam. Var. **longissima**: *B. longissima.*

longissima (Rchb.f.) Nash [*B. Lawrenceana* var. *longissima* Rchb.f.]. Pseudobulbs to 5 in. long, 1- or 2-lvd.; lvs. to 15 in. long and 2½ in. wide; infl. to 2 ft. long, 10–15-fld.; sepals and petals golden-yellow or greenish-yellow, spotted with brown at base, lateral sepals to 12 in. long, petals about 3 in. long, lip acuminate, pale yellow or white, spotted with red-brown. Late winter–autumn. Costa Rica.

maculata R. Br. [*B. guttata* Lindl.]. Differs from *B. longissima* in having lateral sepals only 2–3 in. long, petals smaller, and lip much broader, acute. Spring–summer, autumn. W. Indies and Cent. Amer.

pumila: *B. Lanceana.*

verrucosa Batem. [*B. brachiata* Lindl.]. Pseudobulbs to 3 in. long or more, 2-lvd.; lvs. oblong or elliptic-oblong, to 1 ft. long; infl. to about 2½ ft. long, 4–16-fld.; sepals and petals green or yellowish, spotted with brown at base, sepals 3–5 in. long, petals to 2 in. long, lip white, warty, spotted with dark green toward base. Spring–early summer. Mex., Guatemala, Honduras, Venezuela.

BRASSICA L. [*Sinapis* L.]. COLE, MUSTARD. *Cruciferae.* Probably more than 40 spp. of mostly ann., bien., or sometimes per. herbs or small shrubs of Old World origin, but the nativity of many unknown; plants erect, tall, branched, and for the most part glabrous, often glaucous; lower lvs. variously pinnatifid or lyrate or strongly toothed; fls. in terminal racemes, yellow, yellowish-white or sometimes white, sepals 4, petals 4, clawed, lateral nectaries prismatic, deep green; fr. an elongate silique, valves convex, with prominent midvein.

acephala: *B. oleracea,* Acephala Group.

alba: *B. hirta.*

alboglabra: *B. oleracea,* Alboglabra Group.

arvensis: *B. Kaber.*

botrytis: *B. oleracea,* Botrytis Group.

bullata: see *B. oleracea,* Capitata Group.

campestris: *B. Rapa.*

capitata: *B. oleracea,* Capitata Group.

cauliflora: *B. oleracea,* Botrytis Group.

caulorapa: *B. oleracea,* Gongylodes Group.

chinensis: *B. Rapa,* Chinensis Group.

fimbriata: *B. Napus,* Pabularia Group.

gemmifera: *B. oleracea,* Gemmifera Group.

hirta Moench [*B. alba* (L.) Rabenh., not Gilib.; *Sinapis alba* L.]. WHITE M. Ann., to 4 ft., sparsely hairy; lvs. elliptic to obovate, deeply divided at the sides; fls. yellow, about ½ in. long; siliques spreading, to 1½ in. long, lower part seed-bearing and nodulose, beak flat. Medit. region, w. Asia; naturalized in N. Amer. Cult. for its mustard- and oil-producing seeds, also for greens.

japonica: *B. juncea* var.

juncea (L.) Czerniak. [*B. rugosa* Hort.; *Sinapis juncea* L.]. BROWN M., INDIAN M., LEAF M., MUSTARD GREENS. Ann., to 4 ft., green but st. sometimes slightly glaucous; lower lvs. elliptic to obovate, lyrate-lobed or divided, toothed or scalloped, rather thin, st.-lvs. narrowed at base but not clasping; fls. bright yellow; siliques to 1½ in. long. Eur., Asia. Much cult. for spring greens and as an oilseed, also spontaneous and a weed in N. Amer. Var. **crispifolia** L. H. Bailey [*B. japonica* Hort., not Thunb.]. CURLED M., SOUTHERN C. M., OSTRICH-PLUME. Lvs. cut, curled, crisped. The commonest leaf mustard for greens. Var. **foliosa** L. H. Bailey. BROAD-LEAVED M. Lvs. very large. Grown for greens. Var. **longidens** L. H. Bailey. Lvs. long, narrow, with large, pronglike teeth. Var. **multisecta** L. H. Bailey. Lvs. finely divided. See *Mustard.*

Kaber (DC.) Wheeler [*B. arvensis* (L.) Rabenh., not L.; *Sinapis arvensis* L.; *S. Kaber* DC.]. CHARLOCK, CALIFORNIA RAPE. Ann., to 3 ft. or more, green, commonly hispid toward base and sometimes above; lvs. ovate to oblong-ovate, variously lobed or lyrate, not clasping; fls. yellow, small; siliques about ¾ in. long or less, nodulose, beak often ½ in. long or more. Probably native in Medit. region. Sometimes cult. for mustard, but seeds not pungent; an early-flowering weed of waste places and grain fields.

Napobrassica: *B. Napus,* Napobrassica Group.

Napus L. RAPE, COLZA. Ann., but late-sown plants overwintering and flowering the following spring, making thin taproot; lvs. glaucous, lower lvs. lyrate-pinnatifid, sparsely bristly, petioled, middle and upper lvs. oblong-lanceolate, thick, clasping and sessile; fls. pale yellow; siliques to 4¼ in. long, ascending, on rather slender pedicels, beak to 1 in. long. Nativity unknown. In N. Amer. sown late as a forage and cover crop for late autumn and early spring. Elsewhere ann. or summer races of rape are grown for the seed, used for oil and as birdseed. See *Rape.*

Napobrassica Group [*B. Napobrassica* Mill.; *B. Napobrassica* var. *solidiflora* L. H. Bailey]. RUTABAGA, SWEDE, SWEDISH TURNIP. Thickened root with solid yellow or white flesh and with long neck or crown often withstanding winter in the North; siliques much spreading, on short pedicels, the beak short, stout. See *Rutabaga.*

Pabularia Group [*B. fimbriata* (Mill.) DC.; *B. oleracea* var. *fimbriata* Mill.]. SIBERIAN KALE, HANOVER SALAD. Low, dwarf bien., producing much edible herbage for winter and spring use, then going to seed; lvs. oblong or narrower, deeply lobed at the sides, curled or fringed, glaucous-blue, sometimes purplish. See *Kale.*

narinosa L. H. Bailey. BROAD-BEAKED M. Stout, low, bien., glabrous, not glaucous; lower lvs. in short clusters, orbicular-ovate, small, mostly entire, puckered, petioles broad, white, st. lvs. very broad, entire, clasping; fls. yellow; siliques very thick, ¾ in. long or less, ½ or ⅓ as broad, beak very short, stout. Probably Asia. Grown as a potherb by Chinese.

nigra (L.) W. D. J. Koch [*Sinapis nigra* L.]. BLACK M. Much-branched ann., to 6 ft. and more, mostly hispid-hairy at least below, green, little if at all glaucous; lvs. pinnatifid to lyrate, dentate, petioled; fls. yellow, in many short racemes; siliques appressed to rachis, 1 in. long or less, 4-sided. Eurasia. Widespread weed; cult. as a main source of pungent table mustard.

oleracea L. WILD CABBAGE. Stout ann. to per., sometimes bien., glabrous, glaucous; lvs. thick, lower lvs. rounded or obovate, to 20 in. long, lobed at base, st. lvs. narrow, long, sometimes clasping; fls. whitish-yellow or cream-yellow, to 1 in. long; siliques spreading, to 4 in. long, seeds large, round. Coastal, w. and s. Eur. Represented in cult. by many forms, including several common vegetables. All forms, herein assigned to groups, have similar cult. requirements, including a cool growing season and deep, fertile soil capable of holding abundant moisture. Var. *fimbriata*: *B. Napus*, Pabularia Group.

Acephala Group [var. *acephala* DC.; *B. acephala* of auth.]. KALE, TALL K., CABBAGE K., TREE K., DECORATIVE K., FLOWERING K., KITCHEN K., ORNAMENTAL K., ORNAMENTAL-LEAVED K., SCOTCH M., FLOWERING CABBAGE, COW C., COLLARDS, COLE, COLEWORT, BORECOLE, BRASCHETTE. St. usually unbranched, lvs. separate or only in loose rosettes, not making solid heads, thick, glaucous. The kales are planted in late spring or in late summer to produce either an autumn or early spring crop. Where winters are mild the plants may stand for a year or more. The ornamental kale, with rosettes of variously colored white, pink, or purplish lvs., often with fringed margins, is similarly planted from seed to produce autumn or winter bedding plants. See *Collard* and *Kale.*

Alboglabra Group [var. *alboglabra* (L. H. Bailey) Musil; *B. alboglabra* L. H. Bailey]. CHINESE KALE. Ann., sometimes overwintering, to 3 ft., glabrous, very glaucous; lvs. thick, lower lvs. elliptic, to 10 in. long, sinuate, upper st. lvs. long-oblong and petioled or at least not clasping; fls. white; siliques 2–3 in. long. Probably native to Asia, where grown as a potherb.

Botrytis Group [var. *botrytis* L.; *B. botrytis* (L.) Mill.; *B. cauliflora* Gars.]. BROCCOLI, CAULIFLOWER. Low, with stout, short st.; infl. a dense, terminal head formed of thickened, modified fl. clusters overtopped by lvs. Cult. of cauliflower and broccoli is similar to that of cabbage, but the plants are more tender to frost and less tolerant of heat and dryness. Broccoli requires a longer growing season than cauliflower. See *Broccoli* and *Cauliflower.*

Capitata Group [var. *capitata* L.; *B. capitata* of auth.]. CABBAGE, HEAD C. Low, with stout, short st., bearing dense, terminal head of lvs. In one form, the SAVOY CABBAGE [var. *bullata* DC.; *B. bullata* of auth.], the lvs. are blistered and puckered. Cvs. differ in season of maturity and in color, size, and shape of the head. In all stages of development they withstand considerable frost, although young plants from hotbeds must be hardened off. See *Cabbage.*

Gemmifera Group [var. *gemmifera* Zenk.; *B. gemmifera* of auth.]. SPROUTS, BRUSSELS S. St. simple, erect, to 3 ft., with small, compact, edible buds. See *Brussels sprouts.*

Gongylodes Group [*B. caulorapa* Pasq.]. KOHLRABI. Low, stout bien., st. enlarging just above ground into a turniplike, edible tuber; lvs. elliptic, 10 in. long or less, long-petioled; fls. cream-yellow; siliques 2–3 in. long, beak short, thick. There are green- and purplish-stemmed cvs. Cult. as for turnips. Tubers should be harvested when 2 or 3 in. in diam. See *Kohlrabi.*

Italica Group [var. *italica* Plenck]. ITALIAN BROCCOLI, ASPARAGUS B., SPROUTING B. Differs from Botrytis Group in the fl. brs. thickened, but not condensed into a solid head.

Tronchuda Group [var. *Tronchuda* L. H. Bailey]. TRONCHUDA KALE, PORTUGUESE K., TRONCHUDA CABBAGE, PORTUGUESE C. Low, cabbagelike plant, without compact heads of lvs., with fleshy petiole and broad midribs. Lvs. used much like celery.

parachinensis L. H. Bailey. FALSE PAK-CHOI. Like *B. Rapa*, Chinese Group, but with basal lvs. more nearly orbicular, petiole not margined, and st. lvs. narrowed to base, not clasping. Probably e. Asia. Grown by Chinese as a potherb.

pekinensis: *B. Rapa*, Pekinensis Group.

perviridis: *B. Rapa*, Perviridis Group.

Rapa L. [*B. campestris* L.]. FIELD M. Ann. or bien., root flat or globose, without a long neck or crown; lvs. lyrate-pinnatifid, to 20 in. long, soft but hispid, clasping; fls. yellow; siliques 2½ in. long or less. Eur. Var. **lorifolia**: Rapifera Group. Var. **septiceps**: Rapifera Group. See *Mustard.*

Chinensis Group [*B. chinensis* L.]. PAK-CHOI, CELERY MUSTARD, CHINESE M. Ann. or bien., glabrous, somewhat glaucous at maturity; lower lvs. glossy, making a rather compact cluster to 20 in. high, but not a head, obovate, entire or nearly so, petiole thickened, succulent, white, narrowly winged or margined but not jagged, st. lvs. clasping; fls. pale yellow, ¾ in. long; siliques to 2½ in. long. In habit of growth resembling garden celery or chard. Much cult. in Asia for its succulent lvs.

Pekinensis Group [*B. pekinensis* (Lour.) Rupr.]. PE-TSAI, CHINESE CABBAGE, CELERY C. Ann., glabrous or essentially so; lvs. soft, green, basal lvs. large, very broad, undulate or obscurely toothed, petiole broad, flat, with jagged wings, st. lvs. petioled or clasping; fls. light yellow; siliques 2½ in. long. Grown as a cool-season vegetable, the lvs. forming a more or less solid head.

Perviridis Group [var. *perviridis* L. H. Bailey; *B. perviridis* (L. H. Bailey) L. H. Bailey]. TENDERGREEN, SPINACH M. Ann. or perhaps bien., to 6 ft. in fr., branching above; lower lvs. many, spatulate-oblong, nearly entire, glossy green, tender, petiole not lobed; seeds small, somewhat angled. Grown in N. Amer. for its edible foliage, but the thick, tuberous crown to 3 in. across, pickled in Asia.

Rapifera Group [var. *lorifolia* L. H. Bailey; var. *septiceps* L. H. Bailey; *B. septiceps* (L. H. Bailey) L. H. Bailey]. TURNIP, SEVEN-TOP T., RAPINI. Stout bien., glaucous, very leafy and floriferous, with several tall sts. from root crown; lower lvs. with few deep lobes, st. lvs. clasping; fls. small, in short clusters; seeds small, angled or irregular. One of the oldest root crops. Turnips are short-season plants for cool climates. The roots are many sizes and shapes, with white or yellow flesh. Growing shoots used as greens. For use as a salad plant it is usually sown in late summer and early autumn. Sometimes called BROCCOLI or ITALIAN KALE. See *Turnip.*

Ruvo Group [*B. Ruvo* L. H. Bailey]. RUVO KALE, TURNIP BROCCOLI, ITALIAN TURNIP, BROCCOLI RAAB. Ann. if sown in spring, bien. if sown in autumn, 2½–3½ ft. at maturity, with taproot; lvs. lyrate-pinnatifid, with lobes on petioles, dark green, often glossy; fls. small, in close clusters; siliques small, about 2 in. long. Not to be confused with Italian broccoli, *B. oleracea*, Italica Group.

rugosa: *B. juncea.*

Ruvo: *B. Rapa*, Ruvo Group.

septiceps: *B. Rapa*, Rapifera Group.

BRASSICACEAE: see *CRUCIFERAE.*

BRASSIOPHOENIX Burret. *Palmae.* Two spp. of solitary, unarmed, monoecious palms of New Guinea; lvs. pinnate, sheaths tubular, forming a prominent crownshaft, pinnae cuneate, 3-pronged at apex with prominent midrib and marginal veins; infl. below lvs., somewhat long-peduncled, bracts 2, the upper protruding from the lower in bud, rachillae with fls. in triads (2 male and 1 female); male fls. symmetrical, sepals 3, imbricate, petals 3, valvate, stamens many, anthers attached by base, pistillode shorter than the stamens, female fls. with sepals and petals imbricate, staminodes about 6, small, dentiform, pistil ovoid, 1-celled, 1-ovuled; fr. ovoid with terminal stigmatic residue, scarlet or yellowish-orange, endocarp hard, 5- or 9-ribbed, seed 5-sulcate, endosperm homogeneous.

For culture see *Palms.*

Schumannii (Becc.) Essig. To 30 ft.; lvs. 5–9 ft. long, rachis conspicuously dark-scaly, pinnae 9–10 on each side; infl. stout, few-branched, dark scaly; fls. cream-colored, male buds ⅜–½ in. long; fr. yellowish-orange, 1¼–1¾ in. long.

×**BRASSOCATTLAELIA**: ×*BRASSOLAELIOCATTLEYA.*

× **BRASSOCATTLEYA** Rolfe: *Brassavola* × *Cattleya. Orchidaceae.* A group of bigeneric hybrids, generally intermediate in character between the parents; lip usually large, fringed or ruffled. There are many named cvs.

For culture see *Orchids.*

Cliftonii Hort.: ×*Brassocattleya Veitchii* × *Cattleya Trianaei.* Fls. magenta, lip darker, up to 5 in. across. Cv. 'Magnifica'. Lip deeper colored.

digbyano-mossiae: × *B. Veitchii.*

heatonensis Hort.: *Brassavola Digbyana* × *Cattleya* ×*Hardyana.* Fls. light magenta, lip darker, fringed.

Lindleyana (Rchb.f.) Rolfe [*Laelia Lindleyana* (Rchb.f.) Nichols.]: *Brassavola tuberculata* Hook. × *Cattleya intermedia.* A natural hybrid; plant small; fls. white with pink blush, lip spreading. Brazil.

speciosa Hort.: ×*Brassocattleya digbyano-mendelii* Hort. × *Cattleya Schroderae.*

Thorntonii Hort.: *Brassavola Digbyana* × *Cattleya Gaskelliana.* Fls. white, lip marked with purple.

Veitchii Rolfe [×*Brassocattleya digbyano-mossiae* Hort.]: *Brassavola Digbyana* × *Cattleya Mossiae.* Fls. rose-pink, lip purple at apex, fringed.

× **BRASSOLAELIA** Rolfe: *Brassavola* × *Laelia. Orchidaceae.* A group of bigeneric hybrids generally intermediate between the parents; fls. small, often many in a compact raceme.

For culture see *Orchids.*

digbyano-purpurata: × *B. Veitchii.*

Jessopii Hort.: *Brassavola Digbyana* × *Laelia xanthina.* Fls. small, greenish-yellow, lip fringed.

Veitchii Hort. [× *B. digbyano-purpurata* Hort.]: *Brassavola Digbyana* × *Laelia purpurata.* Sepals and petals blush-white, lip purple.

× **BRASSOLAELIOCATTLEYA** Hort. [× *Brassocattlaelia* Hort.]: *Brassavola* × *Cattleya* × *Laelia.* A group of trigeneric hybrids with large, often vividly colored fls. with (when *Brassavola Digbyana* is involved) large, ruffled lip. There are many named cvs.

For culture see *Orchids.*

BRAUNERIA: *ECHINACEA.*

BRAUNSIA Schwant. [*Echinus* L. Bolus, not Lour.]. *Aizoaceae.* Five spp. of dwarf, erect or creeping, succulent shrubs, native to S. Afr., sts. often rooting at the nodes, roots fine, fibrous; lvs. 1–2 pairs on a br., opp., crescent-shaped in general outline, 3-angled, keeled, members of the pair united ¼–½ their length, glabrous or velvety-hairy; fls. solitary or in cymes, terminal on br., pedicelled or sessile, bracted, calyx 5-lobed, petals many, in 4–5 series, stamens many, staminodes present, ovary inferior, 5-celled, stigmas 5; fr. a caps., with reflexed cell lids, expanding keels lying close and parallel to one another, and broadly winged valves.

Difficult to grow. See also *Succulents.*

apiculata (Kensit) L. Bolus [*Echinus apiculatus* (Kensit) L. Bolus]. To 10 in., velvety-hairy, sts. covered with old lvs., internodes to ⅝ in. long, ¼ in. thick, brs. short; lvs. ascending or spreading, to 1 in. long, ⅜ in. across, flat or convex above, sharply keeled beneath, the keel entire, pale, horny, with small brown hairs, margins pale, apex sharply pointed; fls. ¾ in. across, on pedicels ¼ in. long, petals pink. Cape Prov.

edentula: *Mesembryanthemum edentulum.*

geminata (Haw.) L. Bolus [*Echinus Mathewsii* (L. Bolus) N. E. Br.]. Subshrub, brs. ascending, forked, to 6 in. long; lvs. erect, smooth, with white cartilaginous margins, to 1 in. long, ⅝ in. wide where united, ¼ in. wide where separate, about ⅝ in. thick, 3-angled in section; fls. 1½ in. across, petals white. Cape Prov.

BRAVOA: *POLIANTHES.*

BRAYODENDRON: *DIOSPYROS.*

BREADFRUIT. The breadfruit is the great, rough syncarp of *Artocarpus altilis*, native probably in the Malay Archipelago but now widely dispersed in the tropics, especially in the islands of the South Pacific; it is boiled, baked, or fried for eating. The tree is large and, with its large lobed leaves, is attractive as an ornamental. The yellow-green fruit is borne on small branches; it is commonly 4–8 inches in diameter when full-grown, spheric or short-oblong. The tree is sometimes seen in economic collections under glass, but its real culture is confined to low moist regions in the tropics. The usual breadfruit is seedless and is propagated by means of suckers and root-cuttings. The seed-bearing form, usually called breadnut, may be propagated by seeds; this is grown for the seeds, which are roasted or boiled.

BREVOORTIA: *DICHELOSTEMMA.*

BREXIA Noronha ex Thouars. *Saxifragaceae.* One or 2 spp. of trees in Madagascar; lvs. alt., simple; fls. greenish, in axillary, few-fld. umbels, sepals and petals 5, stamens 5, borne along margins of a fringed disc, ovary conical, about as long as stamens; fr. a woody, indehiscent, pear-shaped stone fr., seeds many.

madagascariensis (Lam.) Noronha. Tree, to 20 ft.; lvs. obovate or oblong, to 6 in. long, narrowed to short, thick petioles; fls. to ¾ in. across; fr. to 2 in. long.

BREYNIA J. R. Forst. & G. Forst. *Euphorbiaceae.* Between 20 and 30 spp. of monoecious shrubs and trees, native to se. Asia, Pacific Is., and Australia; lvs. alt., simple; fls. axillary, without petals, usually solitary, but male fls. sometimes in clusters, ovary 3-celled; fr. a berry. Differs from *Phyllanthus* in lacking a disc around the base of the pistil and stamen.

Grown as an ornamental and hedge in the warmest parts of the country, and in greenhouses in the North. Propagated by green wood cuttings and roots.

disticha J. R. Forst. & G. Forst. [*B. nivosa* (W. G. Sm.) Small; *Phyllanthus nivosus* W. G. Sm.]. SNOWBUSH, FOLIAGE FLOWER. Shrub, 3–4 ft., brs. zig-zag, dark red; lvs. ½–2 in. long, variegated green and white, elliptic to ovate or obovate, somewhat 2-ranked, entire, short-petioled; fls. small, greenish, on long pedicels. Pacific Is.; more or less naturalized in s. Fla. and the tropics. Cv. 'Atropurpurea'. Lvs. dark purple. Cv. 'Roseo-picta' [*Phyllanthus roseopictus* Hort.]. Lvs. mottled with pink and red.

nivosa: *B. disticha.*

BRICKELLIA Ell. *Compositae* (Eupatorium Tribe). About 100 spp. of herbs or shrubs, in N. and S. Amer.; lvs. alt. or opp.; fl. heads discoid, in panicles or corymbs, involucre narrow, of imbricated bracts; fls. all tubular, bisexual, white, yellowish, or pinkish; achenes 10-ribbed, pappus of many smooth or minutely barbed bristles.

Propagated by cuttings over heat.

californica (Torr. & A. Gray) A. Gray. Woody-based per., to 3 ft.; lvs. ovate, to 1½ in. long, crenate; heads about ½ in. long, densely clustered on short lateral brs., 8–18-fld.; fls. creamy. S. Ore. and Calif., e. to Colo. and w. Tex.

grandiflora (Hook.) Nutt. TASSEL FLOWER. Herbaceous per., to 3 ft.; lvs. triangular-ovate, to 4 in. long, dentate; heads slightly smaller than in *B. californica*, nodding in loose clusters on short lateral brs., mostly 20–38-fld.; fls. whitish. Western half of U.S. Thrives in shady, moist locations.

incana A. Gray. Woody-based per., to 3 ft.; lvs. ovate, to 1¼ in. long, serrulate or entire, white-tomentose; heads solitary on brs., about 1 in. long, about 60-fld.; fls. creamy. Deserts of s. Calif., w. Nev., Ariz.

BRIGGSIA Craib. *Gesneriaceae.* About 23 spp. of stemless or rarely stemmed per. herbs with thick rhizomes, in high mts. of India and s. China; lvs. subsessile or petioled, basal or opp., entire or toothed, usually hairy; fls. bracted, solitary or in many-fld., peduncled, umbel-like cymes in lf. axils, calyx deeply 5-lobed, corolla cylindrical at base, more or less swollen toward throat, limb 2-lipped, upper lip 2-lobed, lower 3-lobed, stamens 4, included, anthers at first coherent in pairs, becoming free at dehiscence, cells parallel to filaments, the latter not spirally retracted, disc ringlike, conspicuous, ovary superior; fr. an elongate, 2-valved caps.

For cultivation see *Gesneriaceae.*

Kurzii (C. B. Clarke) W. E. Evans [*Chirita Kurzii* (C. B. Clarke) C. B. Clarke]. Sts. short; lvs. opp. or more or less alt., congested, blades elliptic, to 8 in. long, 4 in. wide, strongly toothed; fls. several on each long axillary peduncle, calyx lobes ⁹⁄₁₆ in. long, corolla to 1¼ in. long, yellow, spotted with orange-brown in the throat. Sikkim Himalayas.

muscicola (Diels) Craib. Stemless; lvs. many in a dense rosette, petiole flattened, to 1½ in. long, with short white and longer brown hairs, blade narrowly elliptic-lanceolate, to 2½ in. long, 1 in. wide, crenulate, white-velvety above, 7–8-nerved and short-white-hairy between the long-hairy nerves beneath; cymes 2–6-fld., peduncles hairy, to 2 in. long; pedicels pilose, calyx deeply divided, the lobes to ¼ in. long, short-white-hairy, with a few long brown hairs intermixed, corolla tube ½ in. long, ⅜ in. wide, yellowish-green outside and around the 2 pouches where lower filaments are attached, golden-yellow and spotted and marbled with purple inside; fr. nearly 2 in. long. Yunnan (China) and Bhutan to se. Tibet.

BRIMEURA Salisb. *Liliaceae*. Two spp. of bulbous, scapose, per. herbs, native to s. Eur.; bulb tunicate, renewed yearly; lvs. 4–8, all basal; fls. blue, rose, or white, campanulate, in a bracted, few- to many-fld. raceme, perianth 6-lobed, stamens 6, arising from perianth tube; fr. a 3-valved, loculicidal caps., seeds black, 2–3 per cell.

Culture as for *Hyacinthus*.

amethystina (L.) Salisb. [*Hyacinthus amethystinus* L.; *Scilla amethystina* (L.) Salisb., not Vis.]. To about 10 in.; lvs. 6–8, linear, to 8 in. long; fls. light blue, to ⅜ in. long, nodding, not fragrant, in a loose, 4–15-fld. raceme, anthers yellow, filaments nearly sessile. Spain. Cv. 'Alba'. Fls. white.

BRITTONASTRUM: *AGASTACHE*.

BRIZA L. QUAKING GRASS. *Gramineae*. About 20 spp. of ann. or per. grasses in temp. regions throughout the world; lf. blades flat; panicles usually open, showy; spikelets several-fld., on often capillary pedicels, florets broad, often cordate, crowded and spreading horizontally, rachilla disarticulating above the glumes and between the florets, glumes about equal, papery, with thin margins, lemma several-nerved, papery, with thin, spreading margins, palea much shorter than lemma. For terminology see *Gramineae*.

gracilis: a listed name of no botanical standing for *B. minor*.

major: *B. maxima*.

maxima L. [*B. major* K. Presl]. BIG Q. G. Ann., sts. to 2 ft., erect or decumbent at base; lf. blades with a ligule to ³⁄₁₆ in. long; panicle with few spikelets; spikelets on slender, drooping pedicels, ovate, ½ in. long or more, ⅜ in. broad, 7–20-fld., glumes and lemma with usually purple or brown margins, lemma sparsely hairy to glabrous. Medit. region. Sometimes cult. for ornament and sparingly escaped in Calif. and Tex.

media L. Per., sts. to 2 ft.; lf. blades to ¼ in. wide, ligule short, truncate; panicle erect, to 4 in. long, the brs. naked below, rather stiff, ascending; spikelets 5–12-fld., orbicular, about ¼ in. long. Eurasia; naturalized from Ont. to Conn. and Mich.

minima: *B. minor*.

minor L. [*B. minima* Hort. ex Nichols.]. LITTLE Q. G. Ann., sts. to 16 in., erect; upper lf. blades to ⅜ in. wide, ligule ¼ in. long, acute; panicle to 4¾ in. long, brs. stiffly ascending; spikelets pendulous, triangular-ovate, 3–6-fld., ⅛ in. long. Eurasia; naturalized from Canada to Fla., Ark. and Tex., common on the Pacific Coast, especially Calif.

BRIZOPYRUM: *DESMAZERIA*.

BROCCOLI. Broccoli is one of the allies and derivatives of the cabbage. Classified along with cauliflower as *Brassica oleracea*, Botrytis Group, it differs from cauliflower in that its abortive flower heads are smaller and the leaves larger, the whole plant remaining green. The green buds and stems are the edible portion. Broccoli is a cool-season vegetable and requires a long growing period. Culture is similar to that of cauliflower (see *Cauliflower*). 'Waltham 29', 'Spartan Early', 'Atlantic', 'Topper', and 'Medium' are common open-pollinated cultivars. Hybrids are now available, including 'Green Comet', 'Duchess', 'Gem', and 'Premium Crop'. For spring planting, transplants 4–5 weeks from seeding are used to start the crop in the garden. For autumn harvest, the seed can be planted directly in the garden in rows 2–3 feet apart and the plants later thinned to 15–18 inches apart. The central heads

are ready to use when the buds are well formed and before they begin to show any yellow color. Side shoots form after the central heads are cut, and these can continue to be harvested for several weeks.

A related plant, making a loose, more or less leafy panicle of edible flower shoots, is the asparagus broccoli or sprouting broccoli (*B. oleracea*, Italica Group). Turnip broccoli is *B. Rapa*, Ruvo Group.

BRODIAEA Sm. [*Hookera* Salisb.]. *Amaryllidaceae*. About 10 spp. of w. N. Amer.; per. herbs with dark brown fibrous-coated corm; lvs. 2–5, elongate, rounded on underside and not keeled, flat or concave on upper side; infl. an umbel terminal on a slender, rigid, cylindrical scape and subtended by an involucre of small scarious spathe valves; fls. jointed to the pedicels, perianth tube funnelform, inflated, or campanulate, lobes 6, mostly longer than the tube, widely flaring, fertile stamens 3, erect, appressed to style, anthers dorsifixed near their sagittate base, rarely with 2 dorsal appendages, staminodes 3 and attenuate, or rarely absent, ovary superior, stigma 3-parted, with long recurved lobes; fr. a loculicidal caps., seeds black, slightly longer than thick, obtusely angled, longitudinally striate, with a ridge moderately developed on one side.

Brodiaeas are only occasionally reliably hardy outside the Pacific and southern states; they are useful in borders, and are sometimes grown in pots, blooming in spring and summer. They thrive in any soil that is not wet or heavily manured. Propagated by seeds, or by offsets if produced.

bicolor: *Triteleia grandiflora* var. *Howellii*.

Bridgesii: *Triteleia Bridgesii*.

californica Lindl. Scape to 1½ ft.; perianth lilac to violet or rarely pink, to 1¾ in. long, lobes 2½–3 times as long as tube, anthers without appendages, staminodes narrow, to 1 in. long, closely folded about stamens, perianth tube splitting in fr. Wooded hills and open plains, cent. Calif.

candida: *Triteleia laxa*.

capitata: *Dichelostemma pulchellum*.

coccinea: *Dichelostemma Ida-Maia*.

congesta: *Dichelostemma congestum*.

coronaria (Salisb.) Engl. [*B. grandiflora* Sm.; *Hookera coronaria* Salisb.]. HARVEST B. Scape to 1 ft.; perianth violet to lilac, to 1¼ in. long, lobes 1–2 times as long as tube, anthers without appendages, staminodes with inrolled margins, usually leaning inward, longer than the stamens and often folded around them. Vancouver Is. to s. Calif. The name has often been misapplied to *B. elegans*. Var. **macropoda** (Torr.) Hoover [*B. terrestris* Kellogg]. Scape wholly subterranean or to 2 in. high; fls. smaller. Mostly coastal, Ore., Calif.

crocea: *Triteleia crocea*.

Douglasii: *Triteleia grandiflora*.

Eastwoodiae, Eastwoodiana, Eastwoodii: names of no botanical standing, generally applied to *Triteleia pendunculars*.

elegans Hoover [*B. coronaria* of auth., not (Salisb.) Engl.; *B. grandiflora* of auth., not Sm.]. HARVEST B. Scape to 16 in.; perianth violet, rarely pink, to 1½ in. long, lobes 1–2 times as long as tube, strongly recurved, anthers without appendages, staminodes flat, usually shorter than the stamens and distant from them. Ore., Calif.

grandiflora: *B. coronaria;* but the name *B. grandiflora* has also been applied to *B. minor*, *B. elegans*, *Dichelostemma multiflorum*, and *Triteleia grandiflora*.

Hendersonii: *Triteleia Hendersonii*.

hyacinthina: *Triteleia hyacinthina*.

Ida-Maia: *Dichelostemma Ida-Maia*.

inodora: a listed name, possibly referable to *Nothoscordum inodorum*.

ixioides: see *Triteleia ixioides* and *Leucocoryne ixioides*. Var. **lugens:** *Triteleia lugens*.

lactea: *Triteleia hyacinthina*.

laxa: *Triteleia laxa*.

Leachiae: *Triteleia Hendersonii* var. *Leachiae*.

minor (Benth.) S. Wats. [*B. grandiflora* Sm. var. *minor* Benth.; *B. Purdyi* Eastw.]. Scape slender, to 1 ft., pedicels often horizontally spreading in fr.; perianth violet, to 1 in. long, lobes about twice as long as the apically constricted tube, rotate, somewhat recurved, anthers

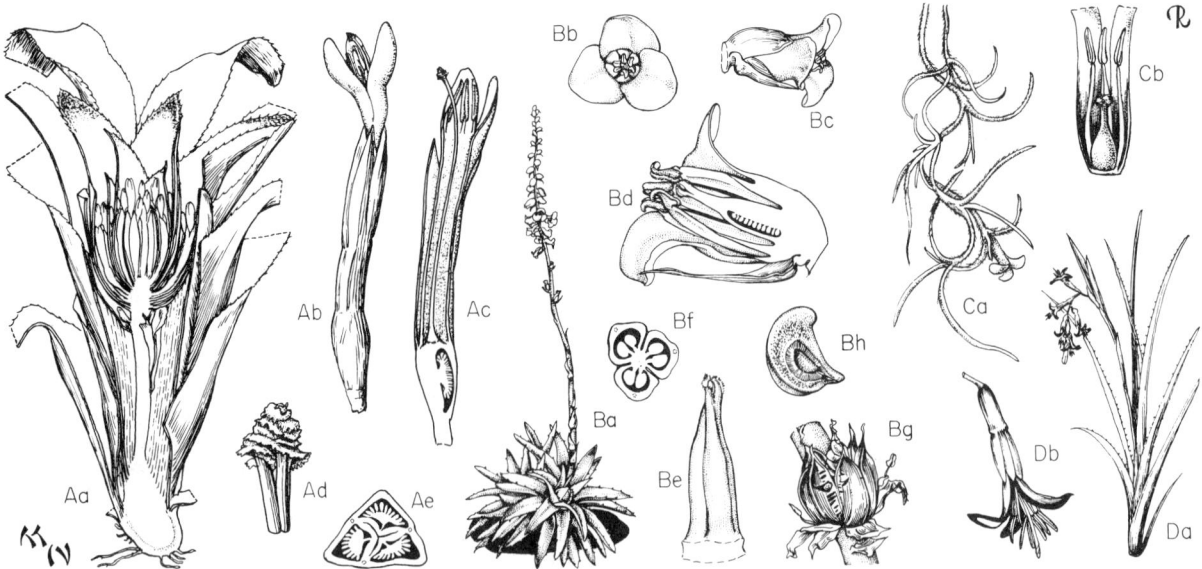

BROMELIACEAE. **A,** *Nidularium Innocentii:* **Aa,** flowering plant, vertical section (apices of many leaves cut off), × ¼; **Ab,** flower, × 1; **Ac,** flower, vertical section, × 1; **Ad,** stigmas, × 4; **Ae,** ovary, cross section, × 2. **B,** *Dyckia brevifolia:* **Ba,** flowering plant, × ⅛; **Bb,** flower, face view, × 1; **Bc,** flower, side view, × 1; **Bd,** flower, vertical section, × 2; **Be,** pistil, × 3; **Bf,** ovary, cross section, × 5; **Bg,** capsule, × 1; **Bh,** seed, × 3. **C,** *Tillandsia usneoides:* **Ca,** flowering stems, × ½; **Cb,** part of flower, × 2. **D,** *Billbergia nutans:* **Da,** flowering plant, × ¹/₁₀; **Db,** flower, × ½. (C, D from Bailey, *Manual of Cultivated Plants,* ed. 2.)

without appendages, staminodes folded about stamens at base, curved outward at the apex. Calif.

multiflora: *Dichelostemma multiflorum.*

Orcuttii (Greene) Bak. Scape to 16 in.; perianth violet, to 1 in. long, lobes spreading, about twice as long as tube, anthers without appendages, staminodes absent. S. Calif.

peduncularis: *Triteleia peduncularis.*

pulchella: *Dichelostemma pulchellum.*

Purdyi: *B. minor.*

stellaris S. Wats. Scape to 16 in.; perianth violet, to 1 in. long, lobes spreading, 1–2 times as long as campanulate tube, anthers with 2 broad appendages on the back, deeply notched at apex, staminodes loosely folded about stamens, with inrolled margins, the apex retuse and inflexed. Calif.

terrestris: *B. coronaria* var. *macropoda.*

Tubergenii: a listed name of no botanical standing, used for a blue-fld. hybrid.

uniflora: *Ipheion uniflorum.*

volubilis: *Dichelostemma volubile.*

BROMELIA L. *Bromeliaceae.* About 48 spp. of terrestrial herbs, native to trop. Amer.; lvs. in basal rosettes, stiff, spiny-margined; fls. in sessile or pedunculed heads or panicles, petals united to the filament tube, but with margins separate, pollen smooth, ovary inferior; fr. a berry, seeds not appendaged.

Planted outdoors in the tropics and subtropics and sometimes in greenhouses. Grown in full sun. For culture see *Bromeliaceae.*

antiacantha Bertol. To 2 ft.; lvs. rigid and arching, to 5 ft. long, with stout, antrorse and recurved, triangular spines; infl. peduncled, paniculate; fls. violet, to 1 in. long, subtended by inconspicuous bracts, sepals rounded at apex; fr. lemon-yellow, ovoid, to ⅞ in. long. Often grown as *B. fastuosa.* Brazil.

Balansae Mez. HEART-OF-FLAME. Lvs. to 4½ ft. long, 1¼ in. wide; infl. paniculate, short-peduncled, white-woolly; fls. maroon or violet, to 2 in. long, subtended by conspicuous scarlet bracts to 1¼ in. long, sepals rounded at apex. Argentina. Sometimes grown as *B. serra.* The commonest sp. in cult. Cv. **'Variegata'** is listed.

fastuosa Lindl. A poorly known sp., perhaps referable to *B. Pinguin;* but most material grown as *B. fastuosa* is *B. antiacantha.*

Pinguin L. PINGUIN. Lvs. to 6 ft. long and 1½ in. wide, light green, with hooked prickles; infl. a mealy panicle shorter than lvs., fl. bracts long-attenuate; fls. white or pinkish, to 2 in. long, sepals acute, petals tomentose at apex. W. Indies, S. Amer. Fr. edible.

serra Griseb. Lvs. to 4½ ft. long, 1½ in. wide; infl. headlike, on a very short scape; fls. red-violet to white, to 2 in. long, sepals white. Bolivia and Brazil to Argentina. Yields a useful fiber. Plants cult. under this name may be *B. Balansae.* Cv. **'Variegata'.** HEART-OF-FLAME. Lvs. white-margined.

BROMELIACEAE Juss. BROMELIA or PINEAPPLE FAMILY, BROMELIADS. Monocot.; about 45 genera and 2,000 spp. of trop. Amer., with 1 sp. in Afr.; herbs or subshrubs, epiphytic or less frequently terrestrial; lvs. usually long, stiff, often in rosettes, the bases sheathing one another and forming a tube or cup; fls. regular, bisexual or rarely unisexual, in spikes, heads, racemes, or branching panicles, often with showy colored bracts and sometimes with showy fls., sepals 3, petals 3, often with single or paired scales or folds on inner surface, stamens 6, ovary superior to inferior, 3-celled; fr. a berry or caps., seeds with or without appendages. The cult. genera are: *Acanthostachys, Aechmea, Ananas, Billbergia, Bromelia, Canistrum, Catopsis, Cryptanthus,* ×*Cryptbergia, Deuterocohnia, Dyckia, Fascicularia, Fosterella, Guzmania, Hechtia, Hohenbergia, Neoglaziovia,* ×*Neomea,* ×*Neophytum, Neoregelia, Nidularium, Ochagavia, Orthophytum, Pitcairnia, Portea, Pseudananas, Puya, Quesnelia, Ronnbergia, Streptocalyx, Tillandsia, Vriesea,* and *Wittrockia.*

The pineapple *(Ananas)* is grown commercially as an important fruit crop, some bromeliads supply useful fibers, but most are grown in the home, in greenhouses, or outdoors in warm climates, for their handsome foliage or showy inflorescences.

Epiphytic bromeliads are grown in pots, in hanging wooden or wire baskets, or attached to boards, as is done with some orchids, or the terrestrial kinds in well-drained soil. They require a well-drained neutral to acid medium using such materials as osmunda fiber, German peat, leafmold, or sawdust lightened with an equal part of coarse builder's sand or crushed granite. Water requirements vary with the region and species; generally light and frequent waterings are necessary. Water retained in the cups formed by leaf bases of many species should ordinarily be left, although in Calif. it has been found practical to let this water dry off during the winter months. Thick-leaved kinds such as *Ananas, Dyckia, Hechtia,* and *Puya* like full sun; most others require good light but protection from full exposure. Most do well at night temperatures of about 50° F.; a very few will withstand near-freezing or freezing temperatures. Propagation is by offsets or seeds. More detailed cultural notes are to be found in the cultural handbook and *Journal* published by the Bromeliad Society.

BROMUS L. BROME, BROMEGRASS, CHESS. *Gramineae*. About 100 spp. of ann. or per. grasses, native mostly to the temp. regions of the N. Hemisphere; lvs. with closed sheaths, blades usually flat; infl. an open or contracted panicle of large spikelets; spikelets several- to many-fld., rachilla disarticulating above the glumes and between the florets, glumes unequal, acute, the first 1–3-nerved, the second usually 3–5-nerved, lemma 5–9-nerved, 2-toothed, awned between the teeth or awnless, convex on the back, or keeled, palea usually shorter than the lemma, keel ciliate. For terminology see *Gramineae*.

anomalus Rupr. ex E. Fourn. Per., sts. tall and slender; lf. blades flat; panicles to 1 ft. long, open, drooping; spikelets flattened, about 1¼ in. long, mostly purplish, lemma keeled, awned. Mex. Occasionally cult. as an ornamental.

briziformis Fisch. & C. A. Mey. RATTLESNAKE C. Ann., sts. to 2 ft.; lf. sheaths and blades pilose; panicle to 6 in. long, with few, loose, drooping brs.; spikelets oblong-ovate, to 1 in. long and ⅜ in. wide, glumes broad, obtuse, the first 3–5-nerved, the second 5–9-nerved, twice as long as the first, lemma ⅜ in. long, very broad, inflated, obtuse, smooth, nearly or quite awnless. Eur.; naturalized in Canada and Alaska, occasional from Wash. to Calif., rare eastward. Sometimes cult. for use in dry bouquets.

canadensis Michx. [*B. ciliatus* of auth., not L.]. FRINGED BROME. Per., sts. to 4 ft., slender, rhizomes lacking; lf. sheaths glabrous or the lower ones short-pilose, blades rather lax, to ⁵⁄₁₆ in. wide, glabrous to sparsely pilose on both surfaces; panicles open, to 10 in. long, brs. slender, drooping; spikelets not strongly flattened, 3–9-fld., to 6 in. long, sometimes bronze- or purple-tinged, first glume 1-nerved, second 3-nerved, lemma to ½ in. long, pubescent on margin and lower part of back, awn to ¼ in. long. Nfld. to Wash., s. to N.J., Tenn., and Calif.; Mex.

carinatus Hook. & Arn. [*B. laciniatus* Beal]. CALIFORNIA BROME. Ann. or mostly bien., sts. to 3 ft.; lf. sheaths scabrous to rather sparsely pilose, blades flat, to 12 in. long and ⅜ in. wide, scabrous or sparsely pilose; panicle to 1 ft. long, brs. spreading or drooping; spikelets strongly flattened, to 1¼ in. long, mostly 6–10-fld., florets not overlapping, rachilla exposed, glumes keeled, acuminate, the first to ⁵⁄₁₆ in. long, the second longer, lemma compressed-keeled, to ⅛ in. wide and ¾ in. long, palea acuminate, the teeth short-awned. B.C. and Idaho, s. to Baja Calif., e. to New Mex.

catharticus Vahl: a confused name based on an apparent mixture; plants so named in cult. are *B. unioloides*.

ciliatus L. Not cult.; but the name has been used in error for *B. canadensis*.

erectus Huds. ERECT BROME. Per., sts. to 3 ft., clustered, erect, slender, rhizomes lacking; lf. sheaths sparsely pilose or glabrous, blades narrow, sparsely pubescent; panicle to 8 in. long, narrow, brs. erect; spikelets 5–10-fld., not strongly flattened, glumes acuminate, the first to ⁵⁄₁₆ in., the second to ⅜ in. long, lemma not compressed-keeled, to ½ in. long, glabrous or evenly scabrous, awn ¼ in. long. Eur.; naturalized from Me. to Wisc., s. to Ky. and Ala., Wash. to Calif.

inermis Leyss. SMOOTH BROME, AWNLESS BROMEGRASS, HUNGARIAN B. Per., sts. to 3 ft., erect, from creeping rhizomes; lf. blades smooth or nearly so, to ⅜ in. wide; panicle to 8 in. long, erect, brs. whorled, ascending or spreading; spikelets to 1 in. long, first glume to ¼ in. long, second to ⁵⁄₁₆ in. long, lemma glabrous to pubescent, to ½ in. long, obtuse to short-awned. Eurasia; naturalized from Minn. to Kans. and Wash. to Calif., occasional eastward. Cult. as a pasture and hay grass.

japonicus Thunb. JAPANESE C. Ann., sts. to 2 ft. or more, erect or geniculate at base; lf. sheaths and blades pilose; panicle to 8 in. long, broadly pyramidal, diffuse, brs. somewhat drooping; spikelets not strongly flattened, to 1 in. long, glumes rather broad, the first acute, 3-nerved, to ¼ in. long, the second obtuse, 5-nerved, to ⁵⁄₁₆ in. long, lemma broad, rounded, obtuse, smooth, to ⁵⁄₁₆ in. long, 9-nerved, awn to ⅜ in. long, usually somewhat twisted, palea less than ⅛ in. long. Eurasia; naturalized from Mich. to Wash., s. to Mo. and Nebr., occasional in New Eng.

laciniatus: *B. carinatus.*

lanceolatus Roth [*B. macrostachys* Desf.]. MEDITERRANEAN BROME. Ann., sts. to 2 ft., erect; lf. blades flat, blades and sheaths pilose; panicle narrow, compact; spikelets few, large, 8–20-fld., glabrous or pubescent, glumes and lemma unequal, awns twisted and spreading, about 1¼ in. long. Medit. region.

macrostachys: *B. lanceolatus.*

madritensis L. Distinguished from *B. rubens* in having sts. smooth below the contracted but scarcely dense panicles, lf. sheaths mostly smooth, blades puberulent to glabrous, lemma with teeth to ⅛ in. long, awn to ⅞ in. long. Medit. region; escaped in Ore. and Calif. Occasionally cult. as an ornamental.

marginatus Nees ex Steud. MOUNTAIN BROME. Per., sts. to 4 ft.; lf. sheaths mostly conspicuously retrorse-pilose, blades commonly pubescent, to ½ in. wide; panicles erect, rather narrow, to 8 in. long; spikelets mostly closely fld., lemma compressed-keeled, pubescent, awns ¼ in. long or less. B.C. to S. Dak., s. to New Mex. and Calif.; introd. in a few other states.

mollis L. SOFT C. Ann., softly pubescent throughout, sts. to 40 in., erect; panicle dense, with erect brs., to 4 in. long; spikelets thick, glumes broad, obtuse, the first 3–5-nerved, to ¼ in. long, the second 5–7-nerved, to ⁵⁄₁₆ in. long, lemma broad, rounded, soft, obtuse, 7-nerved, deeply 2-dentate, ⁵⁄₁₆ in. long, margin and apex hyaline, awn to ⁵⁄₁₆ in. long, palea about ¾ as long as lemma. Eur.; naturalized in Canada and Alaska, Pacific Coast, rarer eastward to Nov. Sc. and s. to N.C.

rubens L. FOXTAIL C. Ann., sts. to 16 in., pubescent below the panicle; lf. sheaths and blades pubescent; panicle erect, contracted, dense, ovoid, to 4 in. long, usually purplish; spikelets 4–11-fld., 1 in. long, first glume to ⁵⁄₁₆ in. long, second to ½ in. long, lemma narrow, acuminate, scabrous to coarsely pubescent, to ⅝ in. long, bifid with teeth to ¼ in. long, awn to ⅞ in. long, somewhat spreading at maturity. Wash. to Calif., e. to Idaho and Ariz., also in Mass. and Tex.

unioloides HBK [*B. catharticus* of auth., not Vahl]. RESCUE GRASS, PRAIRIE BROME, RESCUE B. Ann. or bien., sts. to 3 ft., erect or spreading; lf. sheaths glabrous or pubescent, blades narrow, glabrous or sparsely pilose; panicle to 8 in. long, open, brs. to 6 in. long, naked at base; spikelets to 1¼ in. long, 6–12-fld., glumes keeled, acuminate, ⅜ in. long, lemma compressed-keeled, glabrous, scabrous or sometimes pubescent, acuminate, ⅝ in. long, closely overlapping, awnless or with an awn to ⅛ in. long, palea ⅔ as long as the lemma. S. Amer.; introd. and escaped in the s. states. Grown for forage.

BROSIMUM Swartz. *Moraceae*. About 50 spp. of trees with abundant milky sap, native to trop. Amer.; lvs. alt., pinnately nerved, entire, leathery; male fls. many, of a single stamen, female fls. and frs. immersed in the fleshy receptacle.

Grown in the lowland Caribbean region for the seeds, cooked for food, and the leaves, cut for fodder. Propagated by cuttings over heat.

Alicastrum Swartz. BREADNUT. To 100 ft., bark gray; lvs. oblong, to 7 in. long and 2½ in. wide, glabrous, entire, lateral nerves about 14 pairs; fr. globose, about 1 in. in diam., yellow, with a single large seed which is eaten and roasted. Mex., Cent. Amer., W. Indies.

BROUGHTONIA R. Br. *Orchidaceae*. One sp., a small W. Indian epiphyte, similar to *Epidendrum*, but the lip free from column and extended basally into a spur united to the ovary; ovary prolonged above into a long hollow neck. For structure of fl. see *Orchidaceae*.

Intermediate greenhouse; for culture see *Orchids*.

domingensis: *Laeliopsis domingensis.*

lilacina: *Laeliopsis domingensis.*

sanguinea (Swartz) R. Br. Pseudobulbs to 2 in. long, 2-lvd.; lvs. stiff, hard, fleshy, 3–4 in. long; racemes terminal, to 16 in. long, densely few-fld.; fls. crimson, sepals and petals spreading, not united, to 1 in. long, petals broader than sepals, lip broadly ovate or nearly orbicular, emarginate at apex, margins finely toothed. Winter–late spring, early autumn. Cuba, Jamaica.

BROUSSONETIA L'Hér. ex Venten. *Moraceae*. About 7 spp. of deciduous trees or shrubs with milky sap, native to e. Asia and Polynesia; lvs. alt., toothed, often lobed; male fls. in drooping catkins, female fls. in globose heads; fr. a small syncarp composed of orange-red drupelets.

The inner bark of one species yields fiber used in the Orient for making paper and in Polynesia for tapa cloth. Propagated by seeds, suckers, and cuttings of green or ripe wood in a cool greenhouse, root cuttings over slight bottom heat, and by layers. Cultivars may be budded in the summer or grafted in spring in the greenhouse on roots of the type.

papyrifera (L.) Venten. PAPER MULBERRY, TAPA-CLOTH TREE. Small to medium-sized tree; lvs. ovate, to 8 in. long, either unlobed or very deeply lobed with an open to closed sinus, usually rough to scabrous and olive-green above, velvety pubescent and grayish beneath, toothed; syncarp globose, tomentose, to ¾ in. in diam. Temp. e. Asia to Polynesia. Widely cult. as an ornamental; naturalized in

Zone 6 in the e. U.S., hardy in Zone 5 where protected. Cvs. are: **'Laciniata'**, lvs. finely dissected; **'Leucocarpa'**, fr. white; **'Variegata'**, lvs. variegated white or yellow.

BROWALLIA L. BUSH VIOLET. *Solanaceae.* About 8 spp. of ann. or per. herbs of trop. Amer.; lvs. mostly simple; infl. racemose, or fls. solitary in lf. axils; calyx usually 5-toothed, corolla blue, violet, or white, somewhat irregular, salverform, 5-lobed, tube 15-nerved, stamens 4, borne on the corolla, didynamous, anthers of shorter pair with 1 cell not developed, 1 staminode also often present; fr. a caps., included in calyx.

Grown in the greenhouse or as tender annual in the garden for the attractive flowers; easily propagated by seeds, or the cultivars from cuttings.

americana L. [*B. elata* L.]. To 2 ft., slightly viscid; lvs. ovate, mostly 2½ in. long, bluntly acute or acuminate; fls. 1 to several in upper axils, calyx hairy, corolla bluish-purple, with pale yellow eye, tube ½–¾ in. long, lobes 2-cleft or notched, ½–1 in. across. Lowlands, trop. Amer. Cvs. are: **'Caerulea'**, fls. bluish; **'Grandiflora'** and **'Major'**, fls. large; **'Nana'**, plants dwarf.

elata: *B. americana.*

grandiflora D. Don. Diffuse, glabrous ann.; lvs. ovate to elliptic-ovate, to 6 in. long, acuminate, shiny; fls. in short terminal racemes, corolla lobes white to pale lilac, somewhat 2-cleft, 1–2 in. across. Peru. Material offered under this name may be *B. americana* cv.

speciosa Hook. Suffrutescent per., to 5 ft., brs. somewhat pendent; lvs. narrowly ovate, to 2½ in. long, obtuse to acute; fls. solitary in upper lf. axils, pedicels about 1 in. long, calyx to ⅜ in. long, glandular-hairy, corolla dark purple or in some cvs. blue, violet, or white, mostly 2 in. across, tube about 1 in. long, lobes not notched or 2-cleft. Colombia. Used in window boxes and hanging baskets. Cv. **'Major'**. SAPPHIRE FLOWER. Fls. large.

viscosa HBK. Very similar to *B. americana,* but shorter, to 1 ft., with young growth and calyx sticky- or clammy-viscid and the fls. more numerous. Peru. Cv. **'Alba'**. Fls. white. Cv. **'Compacta'**. Plants compact.

BROWNEA Jacq. *Leguminosae* (subfamily *Caesalpinioideae*). About 25 spp. of evergreen, mostly small and spreading, trees of lowlands in trop. Amer.; lvs. alt., even-pinnate, leathery, limp and colorless or reddish when young; fls. in large headlike spikes, narrow, red or pink, regular, 5-merous, stamens 10 or more; fr. a flat legume.

Grown in moist, lowland tropics for the very showy flowers borne at the tips of branches or pendent among the leaves along the older branches. Propagated by marcots, or cuttings (slow-rooting, in closed frame). Seeds seldom produced.

capitella Jacq. Lfts. 9 in. long or more, long-acuminate; fl. heads orange-red, about 11 in. across, stamens long-exserted. Venezuela.

coccinea Jacq. SCARLET FLAME BEAN. Tree, short-spreading with pendent brs. and lvs.; lvs. 6–8 in. long, lfts. in 2–5 pairs, ovate-oblong, acuminate; fl. heads small, many, borne on sts. and older brs., pendent; fls. scarlet, petals 1¼ in. long, stamens nearly twice as long. Venezuela.

grandiceps Jacq. ROSE-OF-VENEZUELA. Handsome tree, sometimes to 60 ft., with stout, tomentose branchlets; lfts. to 11 pairs, oblong or lanceolate, to 7 in. long, caudate, petioles pubescent; fl. heads dense, nearly globose, 8–9 in. across, borne at the ends of brs.; fls. bright red, stamens scarcely exserted. Venezuela.

grandiflora: a listed name of no botanical standing, applied to a medium-sized tree with hanging fl. heads 4–5 in. across, stamens exserted ½–¾ in.

latifolia Jacq. Lfts. in 1–3 pairs, ovate or obovate, to 4 in. long, cuspidate; fl. heads small; stamens slightly exserted. Trinidad, Venezuela.

macrophylla Linden ex M. T. Mast. Small tree, to 30 ft., brs. and petioles brown-tomentose; lfts. in 3–6 pairs, elliptic-lanceolate, to 12½ in. long; fl. heads on trunk and brs., 8–10 in. across; fls. fire-red, stamens long-exserted. Panama, Colombia.

BROWNINGIA Britt. & Rose. *Cactaceae.* One sp., a treelike cactus of s. Peru and n. Chile; trunk erect, spiny, ribs many, low; brs. almost spineless, naked or bristly, erect to drooping; fls. nocturnal, white, funnelform, perianth persisting in fr., scales of ovary and tube overlapping, broad, naked in the axils; fr. fleshy.

For culture see *Cacti.*

candelaris (Meyen) Britt. & Rose. To 18 ft., trunk to 1 ft. thick, ribs 30–34; spines 20–50, brownish, becoming gray or black, unequal, to 4 in. long, yellow, spines on flowering brs. weak; fls. 3–5 in. long; fr. 2½ in. long.

BRUCEA J. F. Mill. *Simaroubaceae.* About 8 spp. of polygamous shrubs and trees of Old World tropics, with bitter bark; lvs. alt., odd-pinnate; fls. in axillary, cymose panicles, sepals, petals, and stamens 4, ovary deeply 4-lobed or of 4 separate carpels, disc 4-lobed; fr. an ovoid drupe.

javanica (L.) Merrill [*Rhus javanica* L.]. Shrub, to 9 ft.; lvs. to 14 in. long, lfts. 5–9, lanceolate to ovate, to 3½ in. long, serrate; fls. small, purple, in narrow panicles. India to China, E. Indies, Malay Arch., trop. Australia.

BRUCKENTHALIA Rchb. *Ericaceae.* One sp., an evergreen heathlike shrub, native to s. Eur. and Asia Minor; lvs. simple, crowded; fls. pink, in racemes, calyx 4-lobed, corolla campanulate, longer than calyx, stamens 8, inserted at base of corolla, ovary superior; fr. a caps.

Adapted for the rock garden and hardy north. Propagated by seeds and cuttings.

spiculifolia (Salisb.) Rchb. SPIKE HEATH. To 10 in.; lvs. linear, to ³⁄₁₆ in. long, bristle-pointed; racemes to ¾ in. long; fls. very small, style long-exserted. Summer. Zone 6.

BRUGMANSIA Pers. ANGEL'S-TRUMPET. *Solanaceae.* Five spp. of per. shrubs or small trees of S. Amer., mainly Andean, 10–20 ft., occasionally to 35 ft.; lvs. alt., simple, entire to coarsely dentate; fls. pedicelled, pendulous or nodding, 6–20 in. long, very fragrant in the evening (except *B. sanguinea*), calyx spathelike or 2–5-toothed, deciduous after flowering or enlarging and enclosing fr., corolla plicate-convolute in bud, 5-toothed, generally flaring at mouth, with reflexed teeth, white, yellow, apricot-peach, pink, or red, stamens 5, equal, borne on the corolla; fr. a large, fleshy, indehiscent berry, 2-celled, globose to ovoid, oblong-cylindric, or long-fusiform, seeds usually large, with a corky seed coat in some spp. Sometimes included in *Datura.*

Grown as an ornamental throughout the tropics and subtropics (including Zone 10b) or under glass, and some species also by S. Amer. aborigines for the narcotic alkaloids. Propagated by seeds and by cuttings, the latter preferably taken with a heel.

arborea (L.) Lagerh. [*Datura arborea* L.; *D. cornigera* Hook.]. MAIKOA. Shrub or small tree, 6–15 ft., with young sts., lvs., calyx, and fr. velvety-pubescent; lvs. ovate, entire to coarsely dentate; fls. small, 5–6½ in. long, nodding, not completely pendulous, calyx 4–5½ in. long, spathelike, extending at apex into a long, spreading tip, sometimes remaining as a dry husk at base of fr.; corolla white, teeth separated by distinct sinuses or notches; fr. globose to ovoid, 2½–3½ in. long. Andes (10,000–12,000 ft.), cent. Ecuador to n. Chile. In its natural range will not grow at low elevations; not commonly cult., and most material listed as *B. arborea* or *Datura arborea* is *B. × candida.* Source of a narcotic used by aborigines.

aurea Lagerh. Small tree, occasionally to 35 ft.; lvs. glabrous to somewhat pubescent, those on juvenile plants sometimes coarsely dentate, those on mature plants entire; fls. large, 6–10 in. long, nodding to pendulous, calyx 2–5-toothed, corolla white or golden-yellow, flaring at mouth, teeth recurved; fr. ovoid to oblong-cylindric, 3–6 in. long, seeds large, with corky seed coat. Andes (9,000–11,000 ft.), cent. Colombia to s. Ecuador, where most commonly cult.

× candida Pers. [*Datura × candida* (Pers.) Saff.]: *B. aurea × B. versicolor.* Small tree, 10–20 ft., with young sts., lvs., and calyx pubescent; lvs. ovate to oblong-elliptic, entire to coarsely dentate; fls. large, usually 10–12 in. long, pendulous, calyx spathelike, corolla about twice as long as calyx, white, rarely yellow or pink, not constricted beyond calyx, flaring at mouth, teeth 2½–4½ in. long, recurved; frs. rare, variable in size and shape, oblong-cylindric to fusiform, 5–6 in. long. Ecuador. Widely cult. in tropics; most material cult. as *B. arborea* or *Datura arborea* belongs here.

× insignis (Barb. Rodr.) Lockw.: *B. suaveolens × B. versicolor.* A second generation hybrid backcrossed to *B. suaveolens* and often misidentified as that sp., from which it differs in having a longer corolla and corolla teeth, and pubescent calyx, corolla white or pink, and anthers connivent or not. Lower e. slopes of the Andes of Peru. Cult. in Ecuador, coastal Peru, and through Cent. Amer. and s. Mex.

sanguinea (Ruiz & Pav.) D. Don. RED A.-T. Shrub or small tree, to 35 ft., with young sts., lvs. and calyx soft-pubescent; lvs. of juvenile plants coarsely dentate, lvs. of mature plants nearly entire; fls. large, generally 8–10 in. long, calyx with 1–4 acute to obtuse teeth, often slightly inflated, persistent and enclosing the fr., corolla typically red at mouth, fading to yellow and yellowish-green towards base, tubular, not trumpet-shaped or greatly flaring at mouth, teeth less than 1 in. long, recurved to strongly reflexed; fr. ovoid, 3–5 in. long. Andes (10,000–12,000 ft.), n.-cent. Colombia to n. Chile. Commonly cult. within its natural range. Source of a narcotic used by aborigines. Forms with golden-yellow, orange, and yellow-green fls. are common.

suaveolens (Humb. & Bonpl. ex Willd.) Bercht. & J. Presl. [*Datura Gardneri* Hook.f.]. Shrub or small tree, 6–15 ft., glabrous to minutely pubescent; lvs. ovate to narrowly-elliptic, entire; fls. large, 8–12 in. long, nodding but not completely pendulous, calyx 2–5-toothed, slightly inflated, persistent and generally enclosing fr., corolla white, more campanulate than trumpet-shaped, constricted for a short distance beyond the calyx, teeth 1½ in. long or less, flaring but not recurved, anthers connivent; fr. fusiform, 4–6 in. long, somewhat rugose. Se. Brazil Zone 10b. Cult. and naturalized in many parts of the tropics at low elevations. Material cult. under this name may be *B.* ×*insignis*. A rare yellow form is known from Jamaica.

versicolor Lagerh. [*Datura mollis* Saff.]. Small graceful tree, 8–15 ft.; lvs. oblong-elliptic, entire, glabrous to soft-pubescent; fls. very large, 12–20 in. long, pendulous, calyx spathelike, rarely persistent on fr., corolla typically white, turning apricot-peach with age, tube constricted well beyond the calyx, teeth long, flaring and recurved; fr. fusiform, 6–12 in. long. Guayaquil Basin (Ecuador). Frequently cult. at low elevations throughout the tropics. A pure white form is common and a pink form occurs in s. Ecuador.

BRUNFELSIA L. *Solanaceae*. About 40 spp. of shrubs or small trees of trop. Amer.; lvs. alt., simple, entire; fls. showy, often fragrant, in loose or dense terminal cymes, sometimes solitary, calyx tubular or campanulate, 5-toothed or -cleft, corolla white, becoming yellow with age, or purple fading to white, salverform, limb 5-lobed, fertile stamens in 2 pairs, borne on the corolla, anthers 1-celled, all alike, ovary superior, 2-celled, ovules many in each cell; fr. a dry or fleshy caps.

Several species are grown as ornamentals; none are frost-hardy. Brunfelsias require a soil rich in compost and respond to liberal feeding during the growing season. When under glass, they require a night temperature of 50° F. and bloom best when pot-bound. Propagated by cuttings from new growth.

americana L. [*B. fallax* Duchass. ex Griseb.; *B. violacea* Lodd.]. LADY-OF-THE-NIGHT. Shrub or small tree, to 20 ft.; lvs. elliptic to obovate, 2–5 in. long, acute to retuse; fls. solitary at ends of lateral brs., fragrant at night, calyx campanulate, about ¼ in. long, corolla white, tube 2–2½ in. long, limb 1½–2½ in. across; caps. orange, to ¾ in. in diam. W. Indies.

australis Benth. [*B. Hopeana* var. *australis* (Benth.) J. A. Schmidt; *B. paraguayensis* Chodat]. PARAGUAY JASMINE, MORNING-NOON-AND-NIGHT, YESTERDAY-TODAY-AND-TOMORROW, YESTERDAY-AND-TODAY. Shrub, to 12 ft.; lvs. broadly elliptic to obovate, 1½–5 in. long, bluntly acute to rounded; fls. 1–3, fragrant, calyx inflated-campanulate, to ½ in. long, corolla purple, with white ring at mouth, fading to white, tube 1–1¼ in. long, limb 1¼–1½ in. across. Argentina, Paraguay, s. Brazil. Most material cult. as *B. latifolia* belongs here.

calycina: *B. pauciflora* var. Var. **eximia:** *B. pauciflora* cv. Var. **floribunda:** *B. pauciflora* var. *calycina* cv. Var. **macrantha:** *B. pauciflora* var. *calycina* cv.

eximia: *B. pauciflora* cv.

fallax: *B. americana.*

floribunda: *B. pauciflora* var. *calycina* cv.

grandiflora D. Don. Shrub or small tree, to 12 ft.; lvs. lanceolate to oblong, 2½–9 in. long, acuminate; fls. 5 to many in dense or loose cymes, calyx tubular-campanulate, to ½ in. long, corolla purple, with white eye, tube to 1½ in. long, limb to 2 in. across. W. S. Amer., Venezuela to Bolivia. Subsp. **Schultesii** Plowm. Fls. smaller, corolla tube about 1 in. long, limb to 1¼ in. across.

Hopeana: *B. uniflora.* Var. **australis:** *B. australis.*

hydrangeiformis (Pohl) Benth. [*B. macrophylla* (Cham. & Schlechtend.) Benth.]. Shrub, to 6 ft.; lvs. oblanceolate to somewhat spatulate, 5–12 in. long, acuminate, usually abruptly so; fls. up to 50 in capitate cymes, pedicels about ¼ in. long, calyx tubular, often as long as corolla tube, corolla purple, tube ¾–1½ in. long, limb ¾–1½ in. across. Brazil.

lactea Krug. & Urb. Shrub or small tree, to 25 ft.; lvs. leathery, elliptic to obovate, 2–6 in. long; fls. 1–3, fragrant, calyx ¼–½ in. long, corolla white, tube 2–3½ in. long, limb to 2½ in. across. Mts., Puerto Rico.

latifolia (Pohl) Benth. [*B. maritima* Benth.]. Low shrub, 1–3 ft.; lvs. elliptic to oblong, 1½–3½ in. long, obtuse to bluntly acute; fls. 5–13, without scent, calyx ¼–½ in. long, pale green, corolla pale violet, with white eye, tube ¾ in. long, limb to 1¼ in. across. Brazil. *Most material cult. under this name is B. australis.*

Lindeniana: *B. pauciflora* var. *calycina* cv. 'Macrantha'.

macrantha: *B. pauciflora* var. *calycina* cv.

macrophylla: *B. hydrangeiformis.*

maritima: *B. latifolia.*

nitida Benth. Shrub, to 6 ft.; lvs. leathery, obovate, 2–3 in. long, obtuse to short-acuminate, glossy on upper surface; fls. solitary in uppermost lf. axils, fragrant, calyx deeply cleft, to ½ in. long, corolla white, tube 3½–4½ in. long, limb to 2 in. across; caps. orange, to ¾ in. in diam. Cuba.

paraguayensis: *B. australis.*

pauciflora (Cham. & Schlechtend.) Benth. Shrub, to 9 ft.; lvs. leathery, oblong to oblong-lanceolate, 3–6 in. long; fls. 1–10 in terminal cymes, calyx to 1¼ in. long, deep green, minutely tomentose, corolla purple, with prominent white eye at mouth surrounded by bluish ring, tube 1¼–1½ in. long, limb 1¼–3 in. across. Brazil. Cv. 'Eximia' [*B. calycina* var. *eximia* (Scheidw.) L. H. Bailey & Raffill; *B. eximia* (Scheidw.) Bosse]. MORNING-NOON-AND-NIGHT, YESTERDAY-TODAY-AND-TOMORROW, YESTERDAY-AND-TODAY. Fls. larger, corolla fading to white. Var. **calycina** (Benth.) J. A. Schmidt [*B. calycina* Benth.]. Differs from the typical form in having somewhat larger and very glabrous calyx. Cv. 'Floribunda' [*B. calycina* var. *floribunda* L. H. Bailey & Raffill; *B. floribunda* Hort.]. Rather dwarf and free-flowering. Cv. 'Macrantha' [*B. calycina* var. *macrantha* (Lem.) L. H. Bailey & Raffill; *B. Lindeniana* (Planch.) Nichols.; *B. macrantha* Lem.]. Fls. very large.

pilosa Plowm. Shrub; lvs. lanceolate to obovate, 1½–3 in. long, acuminate, pilose at midrib; fls. mostly solitary, calyx inflated, ½–¾ in. long, purplish, pilose, corolla deep purple, with white ring at mouth, tube 1–1¼ in. long, limb 1¼–1¾ in. across. S. Brazil.

undulata Sw. RAIN TREE. Slender, evergreen shrub, to 12 ft.; lvs. oblong-lanceolate, 3–7 in. long, acute to acuminate; fls. to about 20 in terminal cymes, calyx inflated, ½ in. long, light green, corolla white, tube 3½–4½ in. long, limb to 2 in. across, undulate; caps. globose, orange, to 1¼ in. in diam. Jamaica.

uniflora (Pohl) D. Don. [*B. Hopeana* (Hook.) Benth.]. MANACÁ, VEGETABLE MERCURY. Shrub; lvs. oblong-elliptic to lanceolate or obovate, to 3 in. long, acute to acuminate; fls. solitary, calyx tubular, ½–¾ in. long, corolla blue-violet, tube to 1 in. long, limb ¾–1¼ in. across. Brazil, Venezuela.

violacea: *B. americana.*

BRUNIA L. *Bruniaceae*. Seven spp. of shrubs or subshrubs, native to S. Afr., brs. ascending; lvs. closely set or imbricate, sessile or short-petioled; fls. small, in bracted heads, fl. tube united to ovary, petals separate, stamens exserted, more or less unequal, ovary imperfectly 2-celled, rarely 1-celled, each cell 1–2-ovuled, styles 2, free; fr. mostly 2-seeded, dehiscent, to woody.

Suitable for Zone 10 in southern Calif.

albiflora E. P. Phillips. Six to 10 ft.; branchlets villous; lvs. crowded, petioled, linear-lanceolate, mostly less than ½ in. long, curved upwards at apex; fl. heads globose, about ⅝ in. across, in corymblike clusters, calyx lobes with deciduous, apical spine, petals white, about ¼ in. long, ovary 2-celled, each cell 1-ovuled.

nodiflora L. Usually less than 3 ft.; lvs. imbricate, about ⅛ in. long; fl. heads about ½ in. across, usually in panicles, petals cream, reflexed, to ⅛ in. long, stamens much exserted, conspicuously unequal in length, cells of ovary 2-ovuled.

BRUNIACEAE DC. BRUNIA FAMILY. Dicot.; 12 genera of shrubs and subshrubs, native to S. Afr.; lvs. small, often imbricate; fls. bisexual, rarely slightly irregular, axillary or in terminal heads, rarely in spikes or panicles, calyx 5-lobed, petals 5, usually thickened inside and either separate or united into a tube basally, white to pink, mauve, or red, stamens 5, equal or unequal in length, ovary superior to inferior, 1–3-celled, each cell with 1–12 pendulous ovules, styles 1–3, free or united; fr. not well known but apparently 1-seeded, indehiscent, or septicidally dehiscent into the component carpels. *Berzelia* and *Brunia* are offered and are most suited to cult. in s. Calif.

BRUNNERA Stev. *Boraginaceae.* Three spp. of per. herbs of w. Siberia and e. Medit. region; sts. hairy; lvs. simple, alt., ovate, conspicuously veined; fls. blue, many, in bractless paniculate cymes, calyx and corolla 5-lobed, corolla throat with scales, stamens 5; fr. of 4 nutlets.

macrophylla (Adams) I. M. Johnst. [*Anchusa myosotidiflora* Lehm.]. SIBERIAN BUGLOSS. Sts. slender, to 1½ ft.; basal lvs. ovate, cordate or reniform, long-petioled, cauline lvs. ovate, sessile or with short petiole; fls. blue, ¼ in. across. Summer. Caucasus, w. Siberia.

BRUNONIA Sm. *Brunoniaceae.* One sp., of Australia and Tasmania, with characteristics of the family.

Cultivated as an ornamental. Propagated by seeds.

australis Sm. BLUE PINCUSHION. To 1 ft.; lvs. oblanceolate, to 4 in. long, entire, long-petioled; fls. small, blue, tubular, in a head to ¾ in. across, subtended by small bracts. Zone 10, in Calif.

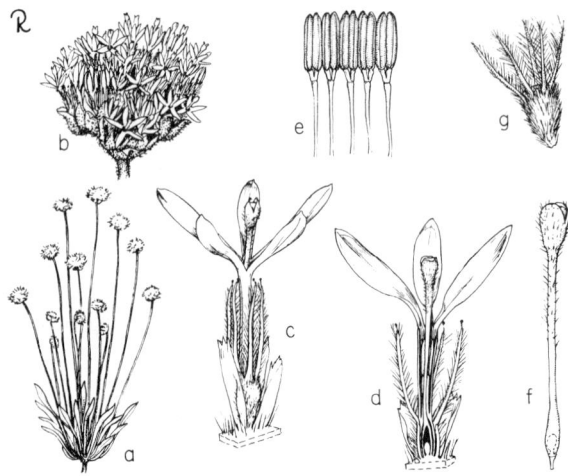

BRUNONIACEAE. *Brunonia australis:* **a,** plant, × ⅛; **b,** inflorescence, × 1½; **c,** flower with subtending bracts, × 4; **d,** flower, vertical section, × 4; **e,** upper part of stamens, with anthers united, × 5; **f,** pistil, × 6; **g,** fruit, × 3. (From Lawrence, *Taxonomy of Vascular Plants.*)

BRUNONIACEAE Dumort. BRUNONIA FAMILY. Dicot.; 1 genus, *Brunonia,* with a single sp., a per. herb, native to Australia and Tasmania; lvs. basal; fls. in heads on scapes, bisexual, nearly regular, calyx and corolla lobes 5, stamens 5, borne on corolla near its base, anthers coherent around style, pistil 1, stigma surrounded by a cuplike structure (pollen cup), ovary superior, 1-celled, 1-ovuled; fr. a nutlet enclosed in calyx tube. Often included in the Goodeniaceae, but differing in having almost regular fls. and seeds without endosperm.

×**BRUNSDONNA:** ×*AMARYGIA.* ×**B. Tubergenii:** a listed name of no botanical standing for ×*A. Parkeri.*

BRUNSVIGIA Heist. *Amaryllidaceae.* Nearly 20 spp. of S. Afr. herbs with tunicate bulbs; lvs. basal, strap-shaped, appearing after the fls.; umbel terminal on a solid, leafless scape, 3–60-fld., subtended by 2 separate spathe valves; fls. red or pink, funnelform, erect to usually declinate, ovary inferior, ovules many; fr. a 3-valved, 3-angled, turbinate, loculicidal caps., seeds many, rounded. Under natural conditions, the umbel and scape break from the bulb as a unit and are blown about by the wind like tumbleweed.

Brunsvigias require rich sandy soil, together with heat and sunlight. After flowering, the bulbs should be rested in a cool, dry place, except on the West Coast, where they are usually planted outdoors.

Josephinae (Redouté) Ker-Gawl. [*Amaryllis Josephinae* Redouté]. JOSEPHINE'S LILY. To 1½ ft.; lvs. somewhat glaucous, 2–3 ft. long, 2 in. wide; umbels 20–30- or to 60-fld., pedicels 6–12 in. long; fls. bright red, 2½–3 in. long, tube curved, 1½ in. long.

multiflora: plants offered in hort. under this name are referable to ×*Amarygia Bidwellii.*

rosea: *Amaryllis Belladonna.*

×**Tubergenii:** a listed name of no botanical standing for ×*Amarygia Parkeri.*

BRUSSELS SPROUTS. One of the allies and derivatives of the cabbage, Brussels sprouts (botanically, *Brassica oleracea,* Gemmifera Group) is a biennial in which the axillary buds on the main stem develop into miniature heads instead of branches. The edible little heads or "sprouts" appear the first year, and flowers and seed the second year. Culture is essentially that for kale, except that Brussels sprouts is always an autumn crop, the seeds being sown in spring in a seed bed and the young plants set in the field in late spring or summer, 18–30 inches apart in rows 30–36 inches apart. The sprouts attain a diameter of 1 or 2 inches; they are gathered as they mature along the stem from the bottom upwards, and a good plant should yield about 1 quart. As the sprouts attain form and considerable size, the leaf subtending each sprout is removed, the terminal crown of foliage maintaining the vigor of the plant. The crop is desired to mature after frosty weather comes. The little sprouts or buttons are among the most delicate products of the cabbage tribe; they are best when not too large, perhaps an inch or even less in diameter. The insects and diseases are those of the cabbage.

'Improved Long Island' and 'Jade Cross' (a hybrid) are the main cultivars now grown.

BRYONIA L. BRYONY. *Cucurbitaceae.* About 10 spp. of mostly dioecious, tendril-bearing, climbing herbs of temp. Eur. and w. Asia, with per., more or less fleshy or tuberous root; fls. in racemes, not large, male fls. with perianth rotate, stamens 3, free, borne on short perianth tube, anthers flexuous, female fls. aggregated or rarely solitary in axils; fr. a small, mostly indehiscent berry, seeds few, horizontal.

Occasionally grown as an ornamental or arbor vine.

alba L. WHITE BRYONY. Monoecious, to 12 ft. or more, from light yellow, thick root; lvs. 5-angled or -lobed; fls. greenish-white, to ½ in. across; fr. a blackish berry, to ⁵⁄₁₆ in. in diam. Eur. to n. Iran. Dried roots have been used medicinally.

dioica Jacq. RED BRYONY, WILD HOP. Dioecious, to 10 or 12 ft., from fleshy tuber or roots; lvs. palmately 5-lobed, rough; fls. greenish, to ¾ in. across; fr. a glabrous red berry, ¼ in. in diam. Eur., N. Afr., w. Asia. Dried roots have been used medicinally.

BRYONOPSIS Arn.: *KEDROSTIS* Medic., which is not in general cult.

laciniosa (L.) Naud.: *Cayaponia laciniosa* (L.) C. Jeffr., a sp. not in general cult.; material grown as *B. laciniosa* is *Diplocyclos palmatus.*

BRYOPHYLLUM: *KALANCHOE.* **B. calycinum:** *K. pinnata.* **B. crenatum:** *K. laxiflora.* **B. scandens:** *K. Beauverdii* var. *parviflora.*

BUCHLOE Engelm. *Gramineae.* One sp., a per., stoloniferous, monoecious or dioecious grass of N. Amer.; lvs. with short curly blades; male fls. in 2–3 short spikes on slender, erect sts., female fls. in sessile heads partly hidden among the lvs.; male spikelets 2-fld., sessile and closely imbricate in 2 rows on 1 side of a slender rachis, glumes somewhat unequal, rather broad, 1-nerved, acutish, lemma longer, 5-nerved, rather obtuse, whitish, palea as long as lemma; female spikelets usually 4–5 in a short spike or head that falls entire, heads usually 2 to the infl., peduncle short and included in the somewhat inflated sheaths of the upper lvs., the thickened, hard rachis and broad second glume forming a stiff, white, rounded structure crowned by green-toothed tips of the glumes, first glume narrow, thin, mucronate, variable and prominent to nearly lacking in spikelets of a single head, second glume firm, thick and rigid, expanded in the middle, enveloping the floret, abruptly contracted, acuminately 3-lobed, lemma firm-membranous, flattened, 3-nerved, tip narrow, 3-lobed, green, palea broad, obtuse, surrounding the fr. For terminology see *Gramineae.*

dactyloides (Nutt.) Engelm. BUFFALO GRASS. Blades gray-green, rather sparsely pilose, less than ⅛ in. wide; sts. forming a dense sod 2–4 in. thick, male sts. slender, to 8 in. high, with spikes to ⅝ in. long; female heads about ⅛ in. thick. W. Minn. to cent. Mont., s. to w. La., Ariz.; s. Mex. Sometimes planted in lawns or to cover exposed dry banks.

BUCHNERA L. BLUEHEARTS. *Scrophulariaceae.* About 100 spp. of per. herbs of se. N. Amer., se. Asia, and S. Hemisphere; lvs. simple, lower lvs. opp., upper lvs. usually alt.; fls. white, blue, violet, rose or rarely scarlet, usually in terminal spikes, rarely solitary in lf. axils, calyx mostly 5-lobed, 5–10-nerved, or -ribbed, corolla salverform, limb spreading, nearly equally 5-lobed, stamens 4, anthers 1-celled; fr. a caps.

Often parasitic on roots.

Henriquesii Engl. Dwarf, hairy, woody-based herb, to 10 in.; lvs. linear or lanceolate, to 1¾ in. long; fls. in terminal spikes, corolla blue, violet, rose, or white, to ½ in. long. Trop. Afr.

BUCIDA L. *Combretaceae.* About 6 spp. of trop. trees, sometimes spiny, native to Fla., Cent. Amer., and W. Indies; lvs. alt., simple, leathery, usually crowded on swollen ends of brs.; fls. in axillary spikes, small, 5-merous, petals 0, stamens 10, exserted; fr. a small drupe.

buceras L. BLACK OLIVE. To 50 ft. or more; brs. often armed with spines 1 in. long; lvs. obovate to elliptic, to 3½ in. long, obtuse or notched, with a pair of glands at base; fls. in spikes to 4 in. long, greenish-yellow; fr. ⁵⁄₁₆ in. long. Fla., W. Indies, Mex. to Panama.

BUCKINGHAMIA F. J. Muell. *Proteaceae.* One sp., a tree, native to Queensland; lvs. alt.; fls. small, white, in long terminal racemes; fr. a compressed follicle, seeds 4 or fewer, flat, thin, narrowly winged.

celsissima F. J. Muell. To 60 ft.; lvs. elliptic-oblong, to 5 in. long or more, entire, or on young trees deeply 3-lobed or more, glaucous or silvery beneath; racemes to 8 in. long; follicle about 1 in. long.

BUCKLANDIA: see *EXBUCKLANDIA.*

BUCKLEYA Torr. *Santalaceae.* Three spp. of large, dioecious, deciduous, parasitic shrubs, native to e. Asia and N. Amer.; lvs. opp., entire; male fls. in umbels, sepals and stamens 4, female fls. terminal, solitary, with 4 persistant bracts and 4 small deciduous sepals at apex of inferior ovary; fr. a drupe.

Since the cultivated species is parasitic on the roots of hemlock (*Tsuga*), seeds must be sown in a pot with a hemlock, and set out with the host plant. Hardy in New Eng.

distichophylla Torr. To 12 ft.; lvs. ovate to ovate-lanceolate, to 2½ in. long, sessile; fls. greenish, small; drupes ellipsoid, yellowish-green or dull orange, about ½ in. long. N.C. and Tenn.

BUDDING: see *Grafting.*

BUDDLEIA L. [*Chilianthus* Burchell; *Nicodemia* Ten.]. BUTTERFLY BUSH. *Loganiaceae.* About 100 or more spp. of deciduous or evergreen shrubs or sometimes small trees, rarely herbs, with stellate, glandular, or scaly pubescence, native to tropics and subtropics of N. and S. Amer., Afr., and Asia; lvs. mostly opp., lanceolate; fls. in heads, panicles, or spikes, calyx and corolla 4-lobed; fr. a 2-valved caps. or a berry. Spelled *Buddleja* by Linnaeus but now correctly spelled *Buddleia.*

Some species have been used as a fish poison, some for medicinal purposes; a number are planted as ornamentals. Even when buddleias are not hardy north, the roots may survive with winter protection, but some of the species stand the winter in Zone 5. They thrive in sunny locations in rich well-drained soil. Propagated by seeds sown over heat in spring, by green wood cuttings, and by cuttings of ripe wood kept over winter in a frost-proof room.

alnifolia: a listed name of no botanical standing; probably a corruption of *alternifolia.*

alternifolia Maxim. Deciduous, to 12 ft. or more, brs. drooping or arching; lvs. alt., to 4 in. long, gray-tomentose beneath; fls. lilac-purple, in dense clusters to ¾ in. long. Summer. Nw. China. Distinguished by its alt. lvs., a condition rare not only in this genus but in the family as well. Cv. 'Argentea' is listed.

amplissima: a listed name of no botanical standing.

asiatica Lour. Evergreen shrub or small tree; lvs. to 8 in. long, entire or fine-toothed, white- or yellow-tomentose beneath; fls. white, fragrant, in drooping spikes to 9 in. long. Winter–spring. W. Pakistan and cent. India to s. China, Taiwan, s. to Malay Arch. and Mariana Is. Zone 10. Also grown under glass. Where native, it is used as a fish poison.

auriculata Benth. Evergreen shrub, to 9 ft.; lvs. lanceolate-oblong, to 4 in. long, thinly white-tomentose beneath; fls. fragrant, white and orange, in a leafy panicle. Late summer–winter. S. Afr. Zone 10. Also grown under glass.

brasiliensis Jacq.f. Erect shrub, to 10 ft. or more; lvs. oblong-lanceolate, to 8 in. long, dentate-crenate, white-tomentose beneath, blade decurrent to a winged, auriculed petiole; fls. yellow-orange to reddish-orange, in many-fld., leafy racemes. Brazil. Zone 10.

candida S. T. Dunn. Lvs. lanceolate or lanceolate-oblong, to 7 in. long, pubescent above, densely woolly beneath; fls. violet, in dense, spikelike infl. to 5 in. long. E. Himalayas.

caryopteridifolia W. W. Sm. Deciduous shrub, to 6 ft.; lvs. ovate to oblong, to 2½ in. long, with large irregular teeth, tomentose; fls. lavender, in narrow panicles to 3 in. long, on the year-old, smaller-lvd. shoots. Early summer. W. China. Zone 9.

Colvilei Hook.f. & T. Thoms. Shrub or small tree, to 30 ft.; lvs. elliptic-lanceolate, to 7 in. long, toothed, pubescent; fls. about 1 in. long, purple or crimson, with white eye, in drooping panicles to 1½ ft. long. Himalayas. Zone 9. Has the largest fls. of all cult. spp.

crispa Benth. [*B. paniculata* C. B. Clarke, not Wallich]. Deciduous shrub, to 15 ft., brs. white- or tawny-villous-tomentose; lvs. lanceolate, to 5 in. long, coarsely toothed, pubescent above, white- or yellow-tomentose beneath; fls. lilac, with white eye, fragrant, in panicles to 4 in. long. Summer. Himalayas. Zone 9.

curviflora: see *B. japonica.*

Davidii Franch. [*B. variabilis* Hemsl.]. SUMMER LILAC, ORANGE-EYE B. Deciduous shrub, to 15 ft.; lvs. to 10 in. long, finely toothed, dark green above, white-tomentose beneath; fls. lilac, with orange eye, fragrant, in spikes to 10 in. long. Late summer. A variable sp. with several vars. China; naturalized locally in Calif. Zone 5. Vigorous, one of the hardiest and probably the commonest sp. Var. **magnifica** Rehd. & E. H. Wils. [*B. magnifica* Hort.]. Infl. very large, densely-fld. W. China. Var. **nanhoensis** (Chitt.) Rehd. [*B. nanhoensis* Hort.]. Relatively small, to 5 ft.; lvs. to 4½ in. long. Cent. China. Var. **superba** (De Corte) Rehd. & E. H. Wils. Similar to var. *magnifica*, but panicles larger. W. China. Var. **Veitchiana** (Hort. Veitch) Rehd. Early-flowering, fls. mauve, spikes dense. Cent. China. Var. **Wilsonii** (E. H. Wils.) Rehd. & E. H. Wils. Fls. rose-lilac, spikes drooping, to 2 ft. long. There are many named cvs. of garden origin.

Fallowiana Balf. f. & W. W. Sm. Deciduous shrub, to 12 ft., branchlets white-tomentose; lvs. lanceolate, to 10 in. long, toothed, dull above, densely white-tomentose beneath; fls. lavender, fragrant, in terminal panicles on current season's shoots. W. China. Zone 9.

×**Farquharii** Farringt.: *B. asiatica* × *B. officinalis*. Lvs. yellow-tomentose beneath; fls. pale pink, in spikes. Zone 9.

Farreri Balf. f. & W. W. Sm. Deciduous shrub, to 12 ft., branchlets densely white-tomentose; lvs. ovate, to 12 in. long, slightly cordate to cuneate at base, white-hairy above at first, becoming green and glabrous, white-tomentose beneath; fls. pale lavender, in narrow panicles to 5 in. long, from axils of previous season's shoots. Spring. W. China. Zone 9.

Forrestii Diels. Deciduous shrub, to 10 ft.; lvs. lanceolate, to 10 in. long, toothed, dull above, pale and thinly stellate-tomentose beneath; fls. maroon and mauve, fragrant, in cylindrical panicles to 8 in. long. Summer. W. China. Zone 9.

Fortunei: a listed name of no botanical standing.

globosa Hope. Semievergreen shrub, to 15 ft.; lvs. lanceolate, to 10 in. long, wavy-toothed, wrinkled above, yellow-tomentose beneath; fls. orange, fragrant, in dense, long-stalked heads ¾ in. across. Summer. Chile, Peru. Cult. on Pacific Coast. Zone 9.

Hartwegii: a listed name of no botanical standing; has been used for a cv. of *B. Davidii.*

×**intermedia** Carrière: *B. japonica* × *B. Lindleyana.* Lvs. to 6 in. long; fls. violet, in drooping panicles to 8 in. long. Cv. 'Insignis'. Fls. rose-violet, in erect, dense spikes.

japonica Hemsl. [*B. curviflora* André, not Hook. & Arn.]. Deciduous shrub, to 6 ft., branchlets 4-winged; lvs. to 8 in. long, slightly toothed, tomentose beneath when young; fls. lilac, in drooping panicles to 8 in. long. Summer. Japan. Zone 9.

Lindleyana Fort. ex Lindl. Shrub, to 6 ft., branchlets 4-angled; lvs. to 4 in. long, slightly toothed, nearly glabrous beneath; fls. purplish-violet, in erect spikes to 8 in. long. Summer. China; sometimes naturalized in se. U.S. Zone 8.

madagascariensis Lam. [*Nicodemia madagascariensis* (Lam.) R. Parker]. Straggling shrub, to 20 ft.; lvs. to 5 in. long, dark green above, white- or yellow-tomentose beneath; fls. orange, in panicles. Winter. Madagascar. Zone 10. Grown in Calif. and in other mild climates.

magnifica: *B. Davidii* var.

microphylla: *B. parviflora.*

myriantha Diels. Shrub, sts. 4-angled, thinly tomentose, slender; lvs. lanceolate, to 6 in. long, auriculed, serrate, white- or yellow-tomentose beneath; fls. purple, in slender spikes to 8 in. long. Se. Tibet, w. China, Burma.

nanhoensis: *B. Davidii* var.

nivea Duthie. Deciduous shrub, to 10 ft., brs. white-tomentose; lvs. ovate-lanceolate, to 10 in. long, coarsely toothed, dark green above, white-tomentose beneath; fls. lilac or purple, in dense spikes to 6 in. long, corolla tomentose outside. Late summer. China. Zone 8. Var. **yunnanensis** Rehd. & E. H. Wils. Lvs. pubescent above, yellow-tomentose beneath; spikes usually solitary.

officinalis Maxim. Evergreen or semideciduous shrub, to 10 ft.; lvs. to 6 in. long, entire or fine-toothed, gray-pubescent above, white- or yellow-tomentose beneath; fls. lilac, with orange eye, fragrant, in panicles 6 in. long. Winter–spring. W. China. Zone 9. Also grown under glass.

paniculata: *B. crispa.*

parviflora HBK [*B. microphylla* HBK]. Shrub or small tree, to 20 ft.; lvs. narrowly lanceolate to ovate, to 4 in. long, serrate or entire, usually glabrate above, densely tomentose beneath; fls. small, white, in few-fld. heads in small or large panicles. Mex.

× **Pikei** H. R. Fletch.: *B. alternifolia* × *B. caryopteridifolia.* Shrub; lvs. alt. or opp., ovate, oblong, or lanceolate, to 6 in. long, irregularly lobed to sinuate-dentate, stellate-pubescent beneath; fls. lavender-pink.

saligna Willd. [*Chilianthus arboreus* (L. f.) A. DC.]. Shrub or small tree, to 20 ft., brs. more or less 4-angled; lvs. lanceolate, linear, or oblong, to 4 in. long, with entire, inrolled margins, green and nearly glabrous above with veins reticulate and impressed, densely scurfy-tomentose beneath with veins prominent; fls. small, whitish, in large, many-fld. panicles, stamens and styles prominently exserted. S. Afr.; locally naturalized in s. Calif. Zone 10.

salviifolia (L.) Lam. Evergreen shrub, to 15 ft., sts. tomentose, more or less 4-angled; lvs. lanceolate, to 5 in. long, green, finely toothed, lightly pubescent and wrinkled above, rusty-tomentose beneath; fls. from white to yellowish to lilac, with orange throat, in terminal panicles to 6 in. long. S. and trop. Afr.

stenostachya Rehd. & E. H. Wils. Deciduous shrub, to 10 ft., brs. densely white-tomentose; lvs. lanceolate to oblong-ovate, to 8 in. long, crenate-serrate or nearly entire, dull green and nearly glabrous above, densely white-tomentose beneath; fls. lilac, many, usually borne in 3's, in slender, cylindrical, terminal spikes, up to 18 in. long. Late summer. W. China.

Sterniana Cotton. Shrub, to 10 ft., much-branched; lvs. ovate to ovate-oblong, to 3¼ in. long, cordate at base, coarsely dentate, glabrous above when mature, white-tomentose with stellate hairs beneath, petiole 1¼ in. long; fls. pale lavender with orange eye, in compact, narrow clusters to 2 in. long. China.

variabilis: *B. Davidii.*

BUETTNERIACEAE: *BYTTNERIACEAE.*

BUGLOSSOIDES Moench. *Boraginaceae.* About 7 spp. of hairy ann. or per. herbs or subshrubs, native to s. Eur., N. Afr., and Asia; lvs. alt., simple, entire; fls. purple, blue to white, in cymes, calyx and corolla 5-lobed, corolla with 5 distinct vertical lines of hairs and glands, stamens 5, borne at or below the middle of corolla and included, style shorter than mature nutlets; fr. of 1–4 nutlets. Differs from *Lithospermum* in having 5 vertical rows of hairs or glands in the corolla.

Propagated from seeds and cuttings. Planted in borders and rock gardens.

purpureocaeruleum (L.) I. M. Johnst. [*Lithospermum purpureocaeruleum* L.; *L. purpurascens* Gueldenst.]. Per., sts. procumbent, from a dense rhizome, to 2 ft.; lvs. lanceolate, 1–3 in. long; fls. first purple then blue, ½ in. across, in a pair of terminal cymes, anthers twice as long as filaments; nutlets smooth, white. Eur.

BUGLOSSUM: *ANCHUSA.*

BULBINE Willd. [*Bulbinopsis* Borzi]. *Liliaceae.* About 25 spp. of ann. or per. herbs, native to Afr. and Australia; rhizome of per. spp. woody or tuberous; lvs. linear or lanceolate, fleshy; fls. yellow or white, in racemes, perianth segms. 6, 1-nerved, stamens 6, anthers versatile, filaments hairy, or sometimes only the inner 3 hairy; fr. a 3-valved, loculicidal caps., each cell with 4 seeds. The name has three syllables.

These plants are occasionally grown under glass, or in the open in warm regions; they bloom in spring and summer.

alooides (L.) Willd. Stemless per., to 16 in., with tuberous rhizome; lvs. lanceolate, to 9 in. long; fls. bright yellow, ¼ in. long, in dense racemes to 1 ft. long. S. Afr.

annua (L.) Willd. Stemless ann.; lvs. cylindrical, to 1 ft. long; fls. bright yellow, ¼ in. long, in loose racemes to 6 in. long on long scapes. S. Afr.

caulescens L. To 2 ft. or more, st. distinct, to 1 ft. high, simple or branched; lvs. cylindrical, to 1 ft. long, crowded toward upper part of st.; fls. bright yellow, in dense racemes to 1 ft. long. S. Afr.

latifolia (L.f.) Schult. & Schult.f. Tufted, stemless per.; lvs. oblong-lanceolate, to 1 ft. long and 2–3 in. wide; fls. bright yellow, 5/16 in. long, in dense racemes to 1 ft. long. S. Afr.

semibarbata (R. Br.) Haw. [*Bulbinopsis semibarbata* (R. Br.) Borzi]. Stemless per., to 2 ft., without tubers; lvs. cylindrical, to 1 ft. long; fls. yellow, only the inner 3 filaments hairy. Australia.

Triebneri Dinter. Per., to 3 ft.; lvs. linear, flat, to 16 in. long; fls. white, 5/16 in. long, many, in racemes to about 1½ ft. long. S.-W. Afr.

BULBINELLA Kunth [*Chrysobactron* Hook.f.]. *Liliaceae.* About 13 spp. of per. herbs, native to S. Afr. and New Zeal.; rhizome woody, compressed, with fibrous to fleshy tuberous roots; lvs. basal; fls. unisexual or bisexual, yellow to white, in a dense terminal raceme, perianth 6-parted, stamens 6, anthers versatile, filaments glabrous; fr. a 3-valved, loculicidal caps., seeds 2 in each cell.

Grown in the border, where they do best in rich moist soil; useful in warm regions. Propagated by division or seeds.

floribunda (Ait.) T. Durand & Schinz [*B. robusta* Kunth; *B. robusta* var. *latifolia* (Kunth) Bak.]. To 2½ ft.; lvs. strap-shaped, to 2 ft. long; fls. bisexual, yellow, cream-colored, or white, racemes to 6 in. long on long scapes. S. Afr.

Hookeri (Colenso ex Hook.) Cheesem. [*Chrysobactron Hookeri* Colenso ex Hook.]. To 2½ ft. or more; lvs. linear, to 1 ft. long; fls. bisexual, yellow, 5/16 in. across, racemes to 10 in. long, on long scapes. New Zeal.

robusta: *B. floribunda.* Var. **latifolia:** *B. floribunda.*

BULBINOPSIS: *BULBINE.*

BULBOCODIUM L. *Liliaceae.* Two spp. of spring-flowering, crocuslike, cormous, per. herbs, native from the Alps to the Caucasus; lvs. basal; fls. violet-purple, 1–3 from each corm, borne close to the ground, perianth segms. 6, long-clawed, separate to the base, stamens 6, anthers versatile, style 1, 3-lobed; fr. a 3-valved, septicidal caps. Differs from *Colchicum* by its distinctly clawed perianth segms. and its single, 3-lobed style, and from *Crocus* by its 6 stamens and superior ovary.

vernum L. [*Colchicum Bulbocodium* Ker-Gawl.; *Colchicum vernum* (L.) Ker-Gawl.]. SPRING MEADOW SAFFRON. To 4–6 in. high, from a corm 1 in. in diam., with nearly black scales; lvs. 3, lanceolate, obtuse; flowering before lvs. are fully developed.

BULBOPHYLLUM Thouars [*Cirrhopetalum* Lindl.; *Megaclinium* Lindl.]. *Orchidaceae.* About 1,200 spp. of pantrop. epiphytes; pseudobulbs with 1 or 2 terminal lvs.; fls. in a raceme or sometimes solitary, on a scape arising from the rhizome; petals smaller than sepals, lip fleshy, mobile, column with 2 arms. For structure of fl. see *Orchidaceae.*

Warm greenhouse; for culture see *Orchids.*

appendiculatum (Rolfe) J. J. Sm. [*Cirrhopetalum appendiculatum* Rolfe]. Pseudobulbs ¾ in. long, spaced along the rhizome, 1–2-lvd.; lvs. thick, 2 in. long; fls. solitary, about 8 in. long, petals and dorsal sepal pale yellow, streaked with purple and tipped with purple fringe, lip thick, bright purple. India, Burma.

barbigerum Lindl. Pseudobulbs to 1 in. long, 1-lvd.; lvs. to 3 in. long and 1 in. wide; racemes many-fld.; fls. to 4 in. long, sepals dull purple, petals minute, lip green with yellow markings, hairy and fringed apically with long purple hairs. Early summer. Trop. Afr.

Careyanum K. Spreng. [*B. cupreum* Hook.]. Pseudobulbs to 2½ in. long, 1-lvd.; lvs. to 10 in. long and 1½ in. wide; racemes dense, nodding, to 3 in. long; fls. yellow, thickly spotted with red-brown. Autumn–early winter. Himalayas.

cupreum: *B. Careyanum.*

cylindraceum Lindl. Rhizome creeping, pseudobulbs cylindrical, 1-lvd.; lvs. to 9 in. long; scape erect, rachis of raceme nodding, to 18 in. long, densely many-fld.; fls. very small, shorter than subtending bracts, sepals dull red, dorsal sepal separate, lateral sepals connivent, petals very short, lip ovate, fleshy, nearly black. India.

falcatum (Lindl.) Rchb.f. [*Megaclinium falcatum* Lindl.]. Rhizome creeping, pseudobulbs widely spaced, to 2 in. long, 2-lvd.; lvs. to 3 in. long and ½ in. wide; raceme with flattened rachis, to 6 in. long; fls. green and yellow or dark reddish-purple and orange. Spring–early summer, autumn. W. Afr.

leopardinum (Wallich) Lindl. Rhizome creeping, pseudobulbs close-set, to 2 in. long; lvs. fleshy, petioled, to 8 in. long; scape short, stout, 1–3-fld.; fls. globose, to 1 in. across, sepals and petals connivent, yellowish-green with pink suffusion, densely covered with small maroon dots, lip fleshy, deep crimson-red with darker red spots. India, Assam.

Medusae (Lindl.) Rchb.f. [*Cirrhopetalum Medusae* Lind.]. Pseudobulbs spaced along the rhizome, 1½ in. long, 1-lvd.; lvs. to 6 in. long and 2 in. wide; infl. a many-fld. umbel; fls. pale yellow, spotted at base with red, lateral sepals prolonged into tails 6 in. long. Winter. Malay Pen., Thailand, Borneo.

ornatissimum (Rchb.f.) J. J. Sm. [*Cirrhopetalum ornatissimum* Rchb.f.]. Pseudobulbs ovoid, to 2 in. long, 1-lvd.; lvs. leathery, to 6 in. long; infl. umbellate, on stout scape longer than lvs.; fls. to 4 in. long, yellowish, greenish, or pale purplish-brown, with dark purple stripes and reticulations, lip crimson-purple. Himalayas, Philippine Is.

pachyrrhachis (Rchb.f.) Griseb. To 16 in., pseudobulbs close-set, 2-lvd.; scape erect or arching, fleshy, thickened in upper ⅓; fls. small, fleshy, greenish, dorsal sepal separate, lateral sepals connivent, sharply pointed, petals small, toothlike, lip fleshy and blunt. Trop. Amer.

picturatum (Lodd.) Rchb.f. [*Cirrhopetalum picturatum* Lodd.]. Pseudobulbs ovoid, 1–2 in. long, 1-lvd.; lvs. to 6 in. long and 1½ in. wide; infl. an umbel of about 10 fls.; fls. about 2 in. long, sepals and petals green, spotted with red, upper sepal with a terminal red filiform appendage, lip dark red. Autumn, spring. Burma.

refractum (Zoll.) Rchb.f. [*Cirrhopetalum refractum* Zoll.]. WINDMILL ORCHID. Pseudobulbs 1 in. long, 2-lvd.; lvs. lanceolate, to 5 in. long; raceme to 15 in. long; fls. 2½ in. long, yellow, lip spotted with red. Himalayas, Java.

Reinwardtii: *B. uniflorum.*

umbellatum Lindl. [*Cirrhopetalum guttulatum* Hook.f.]. To 8 in., pseudobulbs spaced on short rhizome, 2 in. long, 1-lvd.; lvs. 6–8 in. long, 1 in. wide; infl. slender, corymbose, many-fld.; sepals and petals spreading, obtuse, to ¾ in. long, yellowish-green, dotted with deep maroon-purple, lip fleshy, deep purple. Autumn. India, Nepal.

uniflorum Hassk. [*B. Reinwardtii* Rchb.f.]. Pseudobulbs to 4 in. long, 1-lvd.; lvs. elliptic, to 9 in. long; fls. about 4 in. long, yellowish, tinged with brownish-red. Java, Malay Pen.

BULBS. When defined as a horticultural class, bulbs are ornamental, partial-season, mostly simple-stemmed plants arising from bulbs, corms, tubers, or thickened rhizomes. The term is used more loosely and imprecisely in horticulture than it is in botany: it includes many kinds of *Allium, Anemone, Begonia, Brodiaea, Caladium, Colchicum, Crinum, Crocus, Cyclamen, Dahlia, Endymion, Eranthis, Erythronium, Freesia, Fritillaria, Galanthus, Gladiolus, Gloxinia, Hippeastrum, Hyacinthus, Iris, Ixia, Leucojum, Lilium, Lycoris, Muscari, Narcissus, Oxalis, Scilla, Sternbergia, Tulipa, Zantedeschia,* and many other genera of lesser importance. It often connotes spring-blooming subjects, but there are bulbs for all seasons and climates and for sun or shade. Because of their quick growth and showy bloom, bulbs are unceasing favorites with gardeners. Many of them flower very early when few other plants are able to grow and bloom outdoors. Many, however, require a cold period and are unsuitable for growing in frostless regions.

The outdoor culture of the common bulbs is simple. Success depends on good stock to begin with. Not only should

the cultivars be good and true to name, but the bulbs themselves should be well ripened and firm. While the so-called Dutch or Holland bulbs thrive in almost any kind of soil, all do better in deep, sandy ground well enriched with well-rotted manure; but the manure should not come into direct contact with the bulb. Even heavy clay may be fitted for the growing of bulbs by the addition of sharp sand, either worked into the soil or placed directly under the bulb when planted.

To make a bulb bed, choose, if possible, a loose or loamy soil and throw out the top earth to the depth of 6 inches. Put into the bottom of the bed about 2 inches of well-rotted (not fresh) manure and spade it into the soil. Throw back half of the top soil, level it off nicely, set the bulbs firmly on this bed and then cover them with the remainder of the soil; in this way one will have the bulbs from 3 to 4 inches below the surface and of uniform depth. In the North, when the weather is cold enough to freeze a hard crust on the soil, the bed should have a winter covering. This may be straw, hay, cornstalks, or leaves, spread over the bed to the depth of 6 inches if the material is coarse; if leaves are used, 3 inches will be enough, because the leaves lie close together and may smother out the frost that is in the ground and let the bulbs start. If they start too early, the hard freezes of March and early April will spoil the beauty of leaves or flowers near or above the surface. Early in April, in Zone 5, the covering may be removed gradually, and should all be off the beds before the leaves show above the ground. Some bulbs may be readily naturalized in grassy and untilled areas, including *Crocus, Muscari, Narcissus,* and *Tulipa.* They are usually massed irregularly for pleasing and striking effect. The area may be fertilized in autumn with top dressing.

The growing of flowering bulbs in northern winters adds variety to the list of house plants. *Crocus, Hyacinthus, Narcissus,* and *Tulipa* can be made to flower in the winter without difficulty. Pot the bulbs by the middle or last of October—if earlier, all the better. The soil should be rich, sandy loam, if possible; if not, the best one can get, to which add about one-fourth the bulk of sand and mix thoroughly. If ordinary flower pots are to be used, put in the bottom a few pieces of broken pot, charcoal, or small stones for drainage, then fill the pot with earth so that when the bulbs are set on it the top of the bulbs is even with the rim of the pot. Fill around them with soil, leaving just the tips of the bulbs showing. If the soil is heavy, a good plan is to sprinkle a small handful of sand under the bulbs to carry off the water, just as in beds outdoors. If one does not have pots, boxes may be used, and excellent flowers are sometimes obtained from bulbs planted in old cans. If boxes or cans are used, care must be taken to have holes in the bottoms for drainage. A large size *Hyacinthus* bulb will do well in a 5-inch pot. The same size pot will do for three or four bulbs of *Narcissus* or eight to twelve of *Crocus. Hyacinthus* and *Narcissus* bulbs may also be grown in water in specially shaped glasses. After the bulbs are planted they should be placed in a cold pit or cellar, or on the shady side of a building, or, better yet, plunged or buried up to the rim of the pot in a shady border. This is to force the roots to grow before the top appears, as only bulbs with good roots will give good flowers. When the weather is so cold that a crust is frozen on the soil, the pots should be covered with a little straw, and as the weather becomes colder more straw must be added. In six to eight weeks after planting the bulbs, they should have made roots enough to grow the plant, and the pots may be taken up and placed in a cool room for a week or so, after which, if plants have started into growth, they may be taken into a warmer room where they have plenty of light. They will then grow very rapidly and will need much water. When just coming into bloom, the plants may have full sunlight part of the time to help bring out the color of the flowers. *Crocus* and *Tulipa* open only in sunlight. After blooming in the house, the bulbs are usually discarded and new ones purchased for the following year, although it is possible to grow them on for future blooming. If it seems desirable to save the hardy bulbs for planting outdoors later, the plants must be cared for and given light and regular watering until the foliage shows a tendency to turn yellow. At that point watering should become less frequent, and, when the foliage has nearly died down, the bulbs, still in their pots, may be stored in a cool, dry place until one is ready to plant them outdoors. Forced bulbs often require a year or two of restorative growth in the garden before they are able to flower again.

BULNESIA C. Gay. *Zygophyllaceae.* About 9 spp. of shrubs and trees, with sts. enlarged at nodes, native to S. Amer.; lvs. opp., pinnate; fls. terminal, showy, solitary or in pairs, sepals 5, petals 5, clawed, stamens 10, with fringed appendages basally; fr. a 3–5-celled caps.

   arborea (Jacq.) Engl. Tree, 30–40 ft. and more; lvs. to 4 in. long, lfts. 7–14, to 1⅜ in. long, oblong to ovate; fls. in pairs, yellow; caps. stalked. Colombia, Venezuela. Valuable timber tree.

BUMELIA Swartz. *Sapotaceae.* About 25 spp. of evergreen or deciduous, often thorny shrubs and trees, with very hard wood, native to s. U.S. and southward; lvs. alt. to nearly opp., small, often clustered or crowded on short spurs; fls. small, white, clustered in axils, sepals spirally arranged, corolla with lateral appendages, staminodes alternating with corolla lobes, ovary superior; fr. small, black, drupelike, seeds with small scar.

   lanuginosa (Michx.) Pers. CHITTAMWOOD, SHITTIMWOOD, FALSE BUCKTHORN, GUM-ELASTIC, BLACK HAW. Deciduous tree, to 45 ft.; lvs. persisting late, oblong-obovate, 2–3 in. long, entire, reticulate-veiny, tomentose underneath, thick; fr. about 5⁄16 in. long. Woods and copses, Va. to Fla., w. to Kans., Tex., n. Mex.

   lycioides (L.) Pers. BUCKTHORN, SOUTHERN B., IRONWOOD, MOCK ORANGE, SHITTIMWOOD. Deciduous or partly evergreen shrub or small tree, to 30 ft., often thorny; lvs. elliptic or elliptic-lanceolate, to 5 in. long, glabrous or with a few hairs along midvein beneath; fls. 20–60 in a cluster; fr. about ½ in. long. River banks and wet or dry woods, s. Va. to Fla., w. to Ark. and e. Tex.

   reclinata (Michx.) Venten. var. **rufotomentosa** (Small) Cronq. [*B. rufotomentosa* Small]. Evergreen shrub, to 6 ft., young twigs red-tomentose; lvs. obovate or ovate, to 2 in. long, somewhat red-hairy beneath; fls. mostly less than 20 in a cluster; fr. about 5⁄16 in. long. Fla.

   rufotomentosa: *B. reclinata* var.

BUNCHOSIA L. Rich. *Malpighiaceae.* Between 40 and 50 spp. of trees and shrubs, native to trop. Amer.; foliage glabrous or pubescent, lvs. opp., simple, entire; fls. in axillary racemes, calyx with 8–10, sessile, persistent glands on exterior, petals yellow or white, clawed, stamens 10, all fertile, filaments united at base, glabrous; fr. a drupe, varying in color.

   lanceolata Turcz. Tree, 12–20 ft.; lvs. oblong, elliptic, or oblong-lanceolate, 2½–8 in. long, bright green, shining, short-petioled; racemes 12–18-fld.; fls. yellow. Mex., s. to Bolivia.

BUNIAS L. *Cruciferae.* About 6 spp. of ann., bien., or per. herbs in Eur. and Asia, glabrous or with glandular hairs; lvs. entire to pinnatifid; fls. white or yellow, sepals 4, petals 4, not clawed; fr. an indehiscent, ovoid silicle on erect-spreading pedicel.

   orientalis L. TURKISH ROCKET, HILL MUSTARD. Per., to 2 ft., coarsely branched above; basal rosette lvs. oblong-elliptic, lyrate-pinnatifid, st. lvs. lanceolate-elliptic, upper lvs. merely toothed; fls. yellow, in dense, branched racemes; silicles ovoid-apiculate, scarcely ¼ in. long, on stout ascending pedicels about ½ in. long. Cent. Eur., e. to Siberia. Often weedy when well established.

BUPHTHALUM L. OXEYE. *Compositae* (Inula Tribe). Two spp. of per. herbs, native to Eur. and Asia Minor; lvs. alt.; fl. heads radiate, solitary, involucral bracts imbricate in 2–3 rows, receptacle flat to convex, scaly; disc fls. bisexual, anthers tailed, ray fls. female, fertile; disc achenes cylindrical or somewhat compressed, ray achenes 3-angled and winged, pappus of short bristles.

   Of easy culture in the border and mostly hardy north. Propagated by division; also by seeds, and sometimes blooming first year.

   grandiflorum: *B. salicifolium.*

   salicifolium L. [*B. grandiflorum* L.]. Erect per., to 2½ ft.; lvs. oblong-lanceolate to lanceolate, to 7 in. long, glabrous to white-hairy, entire to remotely toothed, basal lvs. petioled, upper lvs. sessile and clasping; heads to 2⅜ in. across; fls. yellow. Cent. Eur.

   speciosum: *Telekia speciosa.*

BUPLEURUM L. THOROUGHWAX. *Umbelliferae.* About 100 spp. of mostly Old World herbs or shrubs; lvs. simple, entire; fls. yellow to purplish, in compound umbels; fr. compressed.

   Suitable for dry, sterile soils in warm climates; grown as ornamentals.

   americanum J. Coult. & Rose. Per., to 16 in., green and glabrous; lvs. linear to oblong-lanceolate, to 6⅜ in. long; bractlets of involucels not so long as fls. and fr.; fls. yellow or purplish; fr. to 3⁄16 in. long. Alaska to Wyo. and Mont.

   Candollii Wallich ex DC. To 3 ft.; lvs. linear-oblong to ovate, to 5 in. long; involucral bracts few or lacking, rays 5–8; fr. to ⅛ in. long. Himalayas.

   falcatum L. var. **scorzonerifolium** (Willd.) Ledeb. [*B. scorzonerifolium* Willd.]. HARE'S-EAR. Per., to nearly 3 ft., green and glabrous; lvs. linear to oblong-spatulate, to 8 in. long, st. lvs. narrowed at base; bractlets of involucels not so long as fls. and frs.; fls. yellow; fr. to 3⁄16 in. long. Japan and Siberia to India.

   fruticosum L. Subshrub, to 6 ft., evergreen or partly so; lvs. oblong, to 3½ in. long, leathery; umbels to 4 in. across, involucral bracts deflexed. S. Eur.

   longifolium L. Per., to 3 ft., sts. erect, mostly unbranched; lvs. oblong-ovate or lanceolate, pinnately and reticulately veined; involucre and involucels each of about 5 ovate bracts with branched nerves. Eur. to N. China.

   nipponicum Koso-Pol. Per., to 2 ft., glaucous, glabrous, rhizomatous; lvs. linear to oblong-lanceolate, to 7 in. long; bractlets of involucels as long as or longer than the yellow or purplish fls.; fr. to 3⁄16 in. long. Japan.

   ranunculoides L. Per., to 2 ft., sts. flexuous; lvs. lanceolate or linear, 3–7-nerved; involucels with 5–6 elliptic bracts, not deflexed. Cent. and sw. Eur.

   rotundifolium L. Ann., to 2 ft., sts. stiff, glabrous, branching; lvs. broadly ovate or elliptic, to 1½ in. long, obtuse or mucronate, perfoliate; umbels to 1 in. across, involucral bracts large, yellowish-green. Eur.; naturalized in cult. fields of U.S.

   scorzonerifolium: *B. falcatum* var.

BURCHELLIA R. Br. *Rubiaceae.* One sp., an evergreen shrub, native to S. Afr.; lvs. opp., ovate, stipules broad, interpetiolar; fls. scarlet, 3–4 in a terminal head, corolla tube more or less cylindrical, lobes 5, short, stamens 5, filaments very short; fr. a berry.

   bubalina (L. f.) Sims [*B. capensis* R. Br.]. BUFFALO-HORN. To 5 ft. or more; lvs. to 4 in. long; corolla to 1 in. long. The wood is extremely hard.

   capensis: *B. bubalina.*

BURSARIA Cav. *Pittosporaceae.* Three spp. of mostly spiny shrubs or small trees, native to Australia; lvs. alt., simple; fls. small, in terminal panicles; fr. a thinly leathery, flattened caps., seeds 1–2, not winged.

   spinosa Cav. BOX THORN. Spiny shrub or small tree; lvs. to 1 in. long; fls. white; caps. about ¼ in. in diam. Zone 9.

BURSERA Jacq. [*Elaphrium* Jacq.]. *Burseraceae.* About 40 spp. of deciduous, aromatic, polygamodioecious, trop. and subtrop. shrubs and trees, with resinous sap, native to the New and Old Worlds; lvs. alt., simple or compound; fls. in racemes or panicles, sepals and petals 3–6, stamens 8–10, separate; fr. a berry, 1-celled and 1-seeded by abortion.

   microphylla A. Gray. ELEPHANT TREE, TOROTE. Small tree, 4–10 ft. or more, older brs. cherry-red; lvs. to 1½ in. long, pinnate, lfts. 13–33, to ¼ in. long, oblong-linear; fls. in 1–3-fld. clusters, 5-merous, appearing before the lvs. Sw. Ariz., se. Calif., nw. Mex.

   Simaruba (L.) Sarg. [*Elaphrium Simaruba* (L.) Rose; *Pistacia Simaruba* L.]. WEST INDIAN BIRCH, GUMBO-LIMBO, GUM ELEMI. Tree, 20–60 ft., wood soft, bark reddish; lvs. 4–8 in. long, pinnate; lfts. 3–7, ovate or elliptic to obovate, 1–2 in. long; fls. in many-fld. racemes, 5-merous. S. Fla., W. Indies, Mex., Cent. Amer.

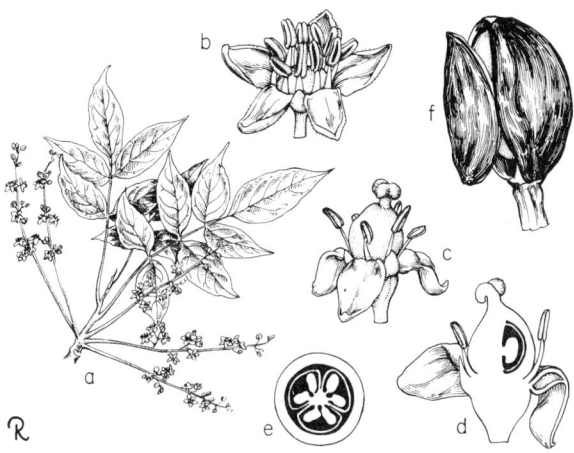

BURSERACEAE. *Bursera Simaruba:* **a,** flowering branch, × ⅓; **b,** male flower, × 4; **c,** female flower, × 4; **d,** female flower, vertical section, × 5; **e,** ovary, cross section, × 6; **f,** fruit, × 2. (From Lawrence, *Taxonomy of Vascular Plants.*)

BURSERACEAE Kunth. TORCHWOOD FAMILY.

Dicot.; about 20 genera and 600 spp. of aromatic, deciduous, trop. and subtrop. shrubs and trees, most numerous in ne. Afr. and trop. Amer., often polygamodioecious; lvs. alt., pinnate or 2-pinnate, rarely reduced to 1 lft., rachis often winged; fls. regular, solitary or racemose, or panicled, sepals and petals 3–5, stamens 6–10, disc present, cup-shaped or annular, ovary superior, 2–5-celled; fr. a 1–5-seeded berry, often referred to as drupaceous or a drupe. *Bursera* and *Garuga* are cult.

Several Old World genera yield useful resins, such as myrrh (*Commiphora* Jacq.) and frankincense (*Boswellia* Roxb. ex Colebr.), and another genus yields edible pili nuts (*Canarium* L.).

BUTEA Roxb. ex Willd. *Leguminosae* (subfamily *Faboideae*). About 7 spp. of trees or climbing shrubs of trop. Asia; lvs. alt., of 3 lfts.; racemes dense; fls. large, orange or red, papilionaceous, stamens 10, 9 united and 1 separate; fr. a flat legume, with 1 seed near apex.

One species planted in the tropics and subtropics for its showy flowers appearing before the new leaves; frost-hardy and drought-resistant and endures saline soil. Propagated by seeds or root suckers.

frondosa: *B. monosperma.*

monosperma (Lam.) Taub. [*B. frondosa* Roxb. ex Willd.]. FLAME-OF-THE-FOREST. Tree, to 50 ft., trunk generally crooked, twigs gray or brown silky-pubescent; petioles to 6 in. long, lfts. rhombic with terminal one more rounded, to 8 in. long, leathery, silky beneath; racemes to 6 in. long; fls. bright orange-red, corolla silvery-tomentose outside, to 1 in. across or more; fr. silvery-gray-pubescent, to 8 in. long and 2 in. wide. India to Burma. Zone 10b. Source of the gum "Bengal Kino."

BUTIA (Becc.) Becc. *Palmae.* About 12 spp. of trop. to subtrop. solitary, monoecious palms from Brazil to Argentina; lvs. pinnate, sheath open, fibrous, petiole armed with stout, sharp teeth along margin, pinnae acute, midrib prominent; infl. among the lvs., bracts 2, the lower 2-edged, open apically, usually concealed, the upper fusiform in bud, beaked, splitting abaxially, smooth or woolly but not deeply sulcate externally, rachillae simple, with fls. in triads (2 male and 1 female) in lower part and above these with paired or solitary male fls.; male fls. with sepals 3, small, acute, basally united, petals 3, valvate, much wider than thick, angled, stamens 6, pistillode minute, 3-cleft, female fls. with sepals 3, broadly imbricate, petals 3, imbricate except valvate tips, not much longer than sepals, staminodes united in a low cupule, pistil 3-celled, 3-ovuled; fr. 1-seeded, mesocarp fleshy, endocarp acute at both ends, slightly 3-ridged, with pores near base, seed with homogeneous endosperm and embryo near the base.

Several species of these relatively hardy palms (Zone 9a) are grown for their graceful arching foliage. For culture see *Palms.*

australis: a listed name of no botanical standing, probably for *B. capitata.*

Bonnetii Becc. [*Cocos Bonnetii* Hort.]. To 4 ft.; pinnae regularly arranged, narrow; infl. about 2 ft. long, with glabrous upper bract; perianth to ⅜ in. long in fr.; fr. conic-ovoid, about ¾ in. long. Brazil? A poorly known sp. described from cult. material and probably not distinct from *B. capitata.* The name *B. Gaertneri* may also have been used for plants representing this sp.

capitata (Mart.) Becc. JELLY PALM, SOUTH AMERICAN J.P. To 20 ft. or more, trunk to 1½ ft. in diam., often covered with persistent lf. bases; lvs. elongate, curving, pinnae regularly arranged or sometimes clustered, ascending from the rachis, usually whitish beneath or glaucous, to about 2½ ft. long, ¾ in. wide or more; infl. to 5 ft. long or more, rachis 2½ ft. long or more, upper bract 3 ft. long or more, smooth; fls. yellow to red, perianth to about ⅜ in. long; fr. ovoid or conic-ovoid to depressed-globose, to 1 in. long, 1⅜ in. in diam. Sheltered sites in Zone 8b. The best known of the butias and one of the 3 hardiest exotic palms. A variable sp., sometimes grown under the erroneous names *Cocos australis* and *C. campestris,* with a number of vars. distinguished in cult. Var. **capitata.** The typical var.; lvs. glaucous; fr. ovoid, acute, yellow, to 1 in. long, ¾ in. in diam. Var. **Nehrlingiana** (G. Abbott ex Nehrl.) L. H. Bailey [*B. Nehrlingiana* (G. Abbott ex Nehrl.) L. H. Bailey; *Cocos Nehrlingiana* G. Abbott ex Nehrl.]. Lvs. glaucous; female fls. red-violet; fr. small, bright red. Var. **odorata** (Barb.-Rodr.) Becc. Lvs. glaucous; fr. yellow, depressed-globose, ¾ in. long, 1 in. in diam. Var. **pulposa** (Barb.-Rodr.) Becc. Lvs. glaucous; fr. yellow, depressed-globose, pulpy, to 1⅜ in. in diam. Var. **strictior** L. H. Bailey. Lvs. bluish, strongly ascending.

eriospatha (Mart. ex Drude) Becc. [*Cocos eriospatha* Mart. ex Drude]. WOOLLY B. PALM. To 10 ft.; pinnae green above, more or less glaucous beneath, regularly arranged along the rachis, petiole tomentose on margin at base; upper bract of infl. densely brown-tomentose outside; fr. yellow, depressed, 1 in. long, to ¾ in. in diam. Brazil.

Gaertneri: a listed name of no botanical standing for *Syagrus coronata,* but cult. material is probably *B. Bonnetii.*

Nehrlingiana: *B. capitata* var. *Nehrlingiana.*

Yatay (Mart.) Becc. [*Cocos Yatay* Mart.]. YATAY PALM, JELLY P. To 20 ft. or more, trunk to 1½ ft. in diam.; pinnae more or less regularly arranged, glaucescent beneath; upper bract of infl. smooth; perianth ⅓ as long as the fr. or more; fr. dark yellow to orange or flushed with red, ovoid, to 1⅜ in. long, ¾ in. in diam. Argentina. Fr. edible.

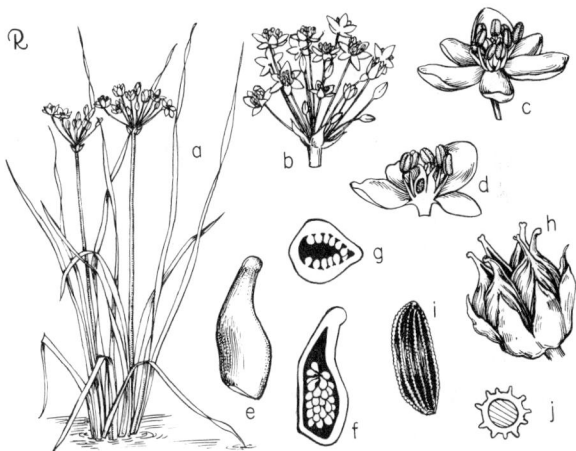

BUTOMACEAE. *Butomus umbellatus:* **a,** plant, × ⅛; **b,** inflorescence, × ¼; **c,** flower, × 1; **d,** flower, vertical section, × 1; **e,** single pistil, × 4; **f,** pistil, vertical section, × 4; **g,** ovary, cross section, × 5; **h,** fruit, × 2; **i,** seed, × 10; **j,** seed, cross section, × 10.

BUTOMACEAE L. Rich. FLOWERING RUSH FAMILY.

Monocot.; 4 or 5 genera of widely distributed, per., rhizomatous herbs of wet or aquatic habitats, usually with milky sap; lvs. linear to orbicular, petioled; fls. solitary or in umbels, bisexual, regular, sepals 3, green or sometimes colored, petals 3, stamens 5 to many, separate, carpels 3–6 or more, separate or basally united, ovules many, scattered over inner walls; fr. dehiscent, seeds many. *Butomus, Hydrocleys,* and *Limnocharis* are cult. as ornamentals for pool or pond margins, or in aquaria.

BUTOMUS L. *Butomaceae.* One sp., an erect, aquatic, rhizomatous per. herb; lvs. in tufts, long, linear; fls. in scapose umbels, perianth segms. 6, colored, stamens 9, pistils 6, coherent at base, ovules many; fr. of 6 follicles.

Well suited to naturalizing at back of pool, readily forming colonies. Propagated by seeds and division.

umbellatus L. FLOWERING RUSH, GRASSY R., WATER GLADIOLUS. To 4½ ft. high, producing many tiny tubers in autumn; lvs. erect, rushlike, to 3 ft. long, basally 3-angled; pedicels slender, to 3 in. long; fls. showy, 1 in. across, perianth rose-colored, anthers and young pistils dark red. Eurasia; naturalized in. ne. N. Amer.

BUTTERNUT: see *Walnut.*

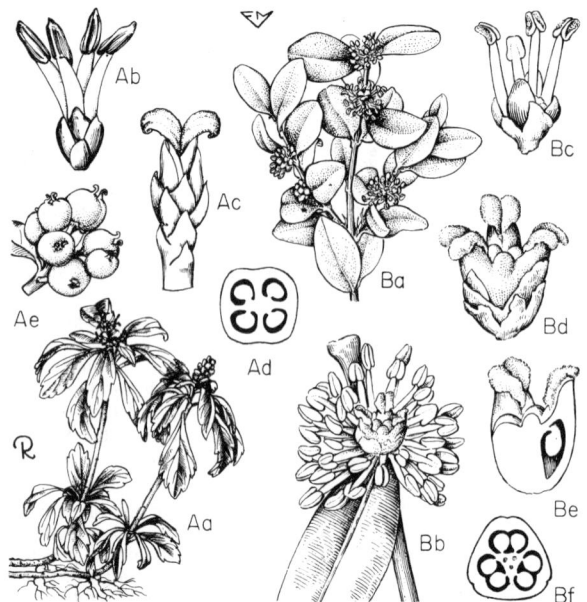

BUXACEAE. **A,** *Pachysandra terminalis:* **Aa,** plant, × ⅙; **Ab,** male flower, × ½; **Ac,** female flower, × 3; **Ad,** ovary, cross section, × 8; **Ae,** fruits, × ½. **B,** *Buxus sempervirens:* **Ba,** flowering branch, × ½; **Bb,** axillary inflorescence, × 2; **Bc,** male flower, × 3; **Bd,** female flower, × 3; **Be,** pistil, vertical section, × 3; **Bf,** ovary, cross section, × 5. (B from Bailey, *Manual of Cultivated Plants,* ed. 2.)

BUXACEAE Dumort. BOX FAMILY. Dicot.; about 7 genera and 40 spp. of monoecious or dioecious shrubs, trees, or sometimes per. herbs with watery sap and mostly persistent foliage, widely distributed in temp. and subtrop. regions; lvs. alt. or opp., simple, without stipules; fls. unisexual, calyx lobes usually 4, sometimes 4–12, in female fls., or calyx none, petals 0, stamens mostly 4, opp. the sepals, ovary superior, mostly 3-celled, with as many style brs.; fr. a caps. or berrylike. *Buxus, Pachysandra, Sarcococca,* and *Simmondsia* are cult. as ornamentals.

BUXELLA: *GAYLUSSACIA.*

BUXUS L. BOX, BOXWOOD. *Buxaceae.* About 30 spp. of monoecious, evergreen shrubs or small trees, native to w. Eur., Medit. region, temp. e. Asia, W. Indies, and Cent. Amer.; lvs. opp., entire, leathery; fls. in axillary or terminal clusters consisting of a terminal female fl. and several male fls. below in the axils of bracteoles, petals none, male fls. with 4 sepals and stamens, female fls. with 4–6 sepals and 3-celled ovary; fr. a caps., with 3 two-horned valves.

Box is extensively used for hedges and edgings, as the plants stand pruning and shearing well. It is suited to any well-drained soil and thrives in partial shade. Plants may be set out in spring or in Aug. or Sept. Propagated by hard wood cuttings, suckers, division, or layering. Seeds may be sown, but the plants grow very slowly. Dwarf forms may also be propagated by division.

balearica Lam. Shrub or small tree, to 30 ft., brs. 4-angled, slightly downy when young; lvs. elliptic to ovate-oblong, ¾–1½ in. long, ¼–¾ in. wide, emarginate or sometimes mucronate, cuneate. Balearic Is., Sardinia, Spain. Zone 8.

Harlandii Hance. Shrub, branchlets pubescent; lvs. nearly sessile, oblong to obovate, ¾–1¼ in. long, rounded or emarginate, cuneate.

China. Probably not in cult.; material offered under this name being misidentified.

japonica: *B. microphylla* var.

microphylla Siebold & Zucc. Compact shrub, to about 3 ft. or sometimes prostrate, glabrous, brs. sharply quadrangular; lvs. obovate to lanceolate-obovate, to 1 in. long, rounded or emarginate, cuneate; fl. clusters mostly terminal. Japan. Zone 6. Var. **japonica** (Müll. Arg.) Rehd. & E. H. Wils. [*B. japonica* Müll. Arg.]. JAPANESE B. To 6 ft., brs. spreading; lvs. light green; fl. clusters mostly axillary. Japan. The most commonly cult. var. Cvs. of this var. are: **'Richardii'**, a fast-growing form, **'Rotundifolia'**, lvs. broader. Var. **koreana** Nakai. KOREAN B. To about 2 ft., young brs. pilose; lvs. less than ½ in. long, pubescent underneath at base of midrib; fls. both axillary and terminal. Korea. Var. **sinica** Rehd. & E. H. Wils. Brs. short-pilose; lvs. elliptic to orbicular, to 1⅜ in. long, usually emarginate, with puberulent midrib. China. The dwarf cvs. **'Compacta'** and **'Nana'** are not referable to a var.

sempervirens L. COMMON B. Shrub or tree, 6–15(–30) ft., brs. quadrangular, puberulous; lvs. elliptic to lanceolate-oblong, broadest below the middle, ½–1⅜ in. long, mostly dark green and lustrous above; fls. in axillary clusters. Eur., N. Afr., w. Asia. Zone 6. The hard dense wood is the Turkish boxwood of commerce. Named cvs., probably not always distinct, include: **'Albo-marginata'**, lvs. white-margined; **'Angustifolia'**, lvs. narrow, oblong; **'Arborescens'**, of tree-like habit. Typical of the sp.; **'Argentea,'** lvs. white or white-variegated; **'Argenteo-variegata'**, white-variegated, slow-growing; **'Aurea'**, lvs. yellowish; **'Aureo-variegata'**, lvs. yellowish-variegated; **'Bullata'**, lvs. large, bullate; **'Columnaris'**, erect, columnar; **'Conica'**, erect, conical; **'Cronii'**, strong-growing, hardy; **'Elegans'**, lvs. white-variegated, oblong; **'Elegantissima'**, lvs. white-variegated; **'Fastigiata'**, erect, columnar; **'Glauca'**, pyramidal, lvs. blue-green; **'Handsworthiensis'** [cv. 'Handsworthii'], erect, dense, bushy, lvs. large; **'Latifolia'**, lvs. suborbicular; **'Longifolia'**, lvs. long, narrow; **'Marginata'**, lvs. yellowish-margined; **'Myosotidifolia'**, dwarf, lvs. small; **'Myrtifolia'**, dwarf, lvs. small; **'Navicularis'**, upright; **'Pendula'**, arborescent, weeping; **'Prostrata'**, spreading; **'Pyramidata'**, erect, pyramidal; **'Rosmarinifolia'**, dwarf, lvs. small; **'Rotundifolia'**, lvs. suborbicular; **'Salicifolia'**, lvs. long, narrow; **'Suffruticosa'**, EDGING B., dwarf, lvs. small; **'Variegata'**, lvs. white- or yellowish-variegated; **'Variifolia'**, lvs. light green; **'Welleri'**, strong-growing, hardy.

BYRNESIA: *GRAPTOPETALUM.* B. **Weinbergii:** *G. paraguayense.*

BYRSONIMA L. Rich. *Malpighiaceae.* Over 100 spp. of trees or shrubs, often scandent, native to trop. Amer.; lvs. opp., simple, entire; fls. in terminal racemes, calyx 5-parted, usually with 10 glands on exterior, petals yellow to yellow-orange, clawed, stamens 10, all fertile; fr. a drupe.

cotinifolia: *B. crassifolia.*

crassifolia (L.) HBK [*B. cotinifolia* HBK]. Shrub or tree, to about 30 ft., very variable in hairiness and lf. shape; lvs. elliptic, oblong, obovate, to ovate, to 6 in. long, thick, short-petioled; drupe yellow, ½ in. in diam., edible. W. Indies and Mex., s. to n. S. Amer. Wood used for making charcoal.

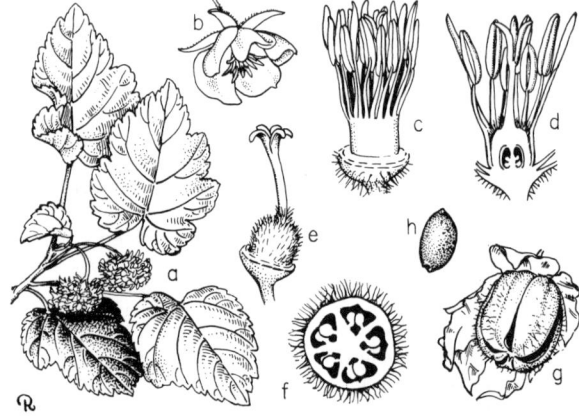

BYTTNERIACEAE. *Dombeya Wallichii:* **a,** flowering branch, × ⅙; **b,** flower, × ½; **c,** stamens and staminodes, × 1½; **d,** flower, vertical section (perianth cut away), × 1½; **e,** pistil, × 1½; **f,** ovary, cross section, × 3; **g,** capsule, × 1½; **h,** seed, × 3.

BYTTNERIACEAE R. Br. [*Buettneriaceae* of auth.]. BYTTNERIA FAMILY. Dicot.; about 50 genera of mostly trop.

shrubs and trees, rarely herbs; sometimes included in the Sterculiaceae, but distinguished from that family in having fls. bisexual, petals 5, stamens 5 to many, arranged singly or in groups alternating with petaloid staminodes, or, if staminodes absent, then stamens 5, separate or united into a tube basally; fr. a caps., mostly loculicidally dehiscent, mostly 5-celled, 5-valved. The family furnishes cocoa, chocolate, timber, ornamental subjects, and many locally important products. The cult. genera are: *Corchoropsis, Dombeya, Helicteres, Hermannia, Kleinhovia, Pterospermum, Reevesia, Theobroma, Triplochiton,* and *Waltheria.*

CABBAGE. One of the standard garden vegetables and truck crops, cabbage (*Brassica oleracea* Capitata Group) is essentially a cool-season plant but grows continuously through the summer; in all stages it withstands considerable frost, although young plants from hotbeds must be hardened off. Soil should be deep and fertile, and it should be capable of holding abundant moisture to supply the heavy demands in growth. The cabbages of many kinds have been developed through the centuries apparently from *Brassica oleracea* of coasts of western Europe. The cultivars differ in season, in color, and in size and shape of head. The Savoy cabbages, which are of excellent quality, are a race with puckered or blistered (bullate) leaves. It is usual to classify cabbage by season into three groups: early, midseason, late or winter. Consult experiment station bulletins for recommended cultivars.

For early and very early crops, such as 'Golden Acre' and 'Copenhagen Market', seeds are usually sown in a hotbed or indoors at least a month before hard frosts are expected to cease. The seedlings may be transplanted into flats or into other frames, to keep them stocky. They should be given plenty of air, with reduction of temperature, to harden them for the field. In the field the plants are placed about 12 inches apart in rows 30–36 inches apart.

For the later and midseason crops, such as 'Greenback', 'King Cole', 'Roundup', 'Market Prize', and 'Red Head', seeds are commonly sown in the open in seed beds six to eight weeks before time for planting in the field, in rows 3 inches or more apart; from these rows they are usually transplanted directly to the field, or more often they are direct-seeded, with seeds spaced 4–6 inches apart and later thinned to 15–18 inches.

The autumn and storing kinds, such as 'Danish Ballhead', 'Rio Verde', 'Market Prize', 'Green Winter', and 'Storing Strain 4409', are transplanted in July, in the North, spaced 12–18 inches apart in rows 30 inches apart.

For winter storage, only the long-keeping cultivars ('Green Winter') should be employed; the heads should be mature and solid, free from injury and disease, internally moist and plump, but the center of the head should be free of water. They should be stored at 31° F or as close to that as possible, and the humidity kept as high as possible.

In the midsouthern parts of the United States cabbage plants are often started in autumn and carried over winter in the field; they are then ready for growth in earliest spring. In the southern states cabbage is treated as a winter or early spring crop, being grown continuously in the cool season.

Many insects and fungi attack cabbages. The grower should keep in touch each year with the new advice issuing from the experiment stations. The root maggot is often a serious pest; young plants in seed beds as well as transplants may be protected by treatment with diazinone in the row. The club-root fungus is controlled by long rotations in which related plants (crucifers) are not grown; also by liming to bring the soil reaction to neutral (pH 7.4) or slightly alkaline, and by use of Terraclor in transplant water. For cabbage worm and aphid control, see current experiment station recommendations.

CABOMBA Aubl. FANWORT, WATER-SHIELD. *Nymphaeaceae.* Seven spp. of Amer. aquatic herbs; floating lvs. often alt., entire, submersed lvs. opp. or whorled, finely divided; fls. very small, sepals 3, petals 3, stamens 3–6, carpels 3(2–4), separate; fr. indehiscent, leathery, 3-seeded, rarely 1-seeded.

Sometimes grown in ponds and aquaria; propagated by cuttings set in soil in 1–2 ft. of water, by division of plants, and by seeds.

caroliniana A. Gray. WASHINGTON GRASS, FISH GRASS, FANWORT. Sts. to 6 ft. long; floating lvs. linear-oblong, ¾ in. long, submersed lvs. 1–2 in. across, with filiform segms.; fls. axillary, ½ in. across, white with 2 yellow spots at base of each petal. Ponds and slow streams, Mich. to Fla. and Tex. Forms with purple fls. occur. Var. **pulcherrima:** *C. pulcherrima.*

aquatica Aubl. Internodes yellow-hairy when young; submersed lvs. finely divided into linear segms., never red, floating lvs. broad-elliptic, to ¾ in. wide; fls. to ⅜ in. long, yellow, petals triangular-lanceolate, narrowed toward apex, auricled basally. Guyana to mouth of Amazon.

australis Speg. Internodes red-hairy when young; submersed lvs. finely divided into linear segms., with many red lines, floating lvs. to ⅝ in. wide; fls. to ½ in. long, white, yellow toward center, petals oblong or obovate, rounded at apex, auricled basally. Paraguay and s. Brazil to e. Argentina.

pulcherrima (R. M. Harper) Fassett [*C. caroliniana* var. *pulcherrima* R. M. Harper]. Internodes red-hairy when young; submersed lvs. finely divided into many, often red-streaked or red-flecked segms., floating lvs. to 1¼ in. wide; fls. to ⅜ in. long, purple, sepals and petals emarginate, petals auricled at base. N. Fla., Ga., s. S.C.

CABOMBACEAE: see *NYMPHAEACEAE.*

CACALIA L. *Compositae* (Senecio Tribe). About 50 spp., mostly per. herbs, chiefly in e. Asia; not in cult.

aurea: *Emilia javanica* cv. 'Lutea'.

coccinea: *Emilia javanica.*

sagittata: *Emilia javanica.*

sonchifolia: *Emilia sonchifolia.*

CACALIOPSIS: *LUINA.*

CACTACEAE Juss. CACTUS FAMILY. Dicot.; 50–220 genera and 800–2,000 spp. of mostly spiny, succulent, per. herbs, shrubs, vines, or small trees, sometimes epiphytic, native mostly to drier regions of N. and S. Amer., *Rhipsalis* also in Afr., Madagascar, Mascarene Is., Seychelles Is., and Ceylon; sts. fleshy, simple or usually branched at base or above, cylindrical to flattened or triangular, often jointed or tubercled or ribbed, bearing cushions (areoles) spirally arranged or at tips of tubercles or along summits of ribs and usually with straight or hooked spines in the middle (central spines) and at the edges (radial spines) and/or hairs or minute, barbed bristles (glochids); lvs. broad, flat, and more or less persistent, or usually cylindrical or rudimentary and soon falling; fls. bisexual, sessile or stalked, solitary or rarely clustered, on areoles or in axils of tubercles, perianth of intergrading leaflike (scales), sepal-like (sepaloid), and petal-like (petaloid) segms. forming a tube, the lower part united to the inferior ovary, the upper part short or long, stamens many on the inside of the tube, ovary 1-celled, with 2 to many parietal placentas, ovules many, style elongate, stigmas several; fr. a berry. The family is subdivided into 3 tribes: the *Pereskia* tribe (Pereskieae Britt. & Rose) with persistent, flat, broad lvs. and no glochids includes *Maihuenia* and *Pereskia;* the *Opuntia* tribe (Opuntieae Britt. & Rose) with usually cylindrical lvs. falling early and glochids includes *Opuntia, Pereskiopsis,* and *Quiabentia;* the *Cactus* or more commonly the *Cereus* tribe (Cacteae) with rudimentary lvs. and no glochids includes the remaining cult. genera. Generic and specific limits are not always clear, e.g., *Cereus* might well include *Bergerocactus, Carnegiea, Cephalocereus, Hylocereus, Lemaireocereus, Lophocereus, Peniocereus, Pilocereus, Selenicereus,* and *Wilcoxia.* Many of these names are well established in the literature and they and others are retained pending definitive studies of genera.

The following genera are cult.: *Acanthocalycium, Acanthocereus, Acanthorhipsalis, Ancistrocactus, Aporocactus, Ariocarpus, Arrojadoa, Arthrocereus, Astrophytum, Aus-*

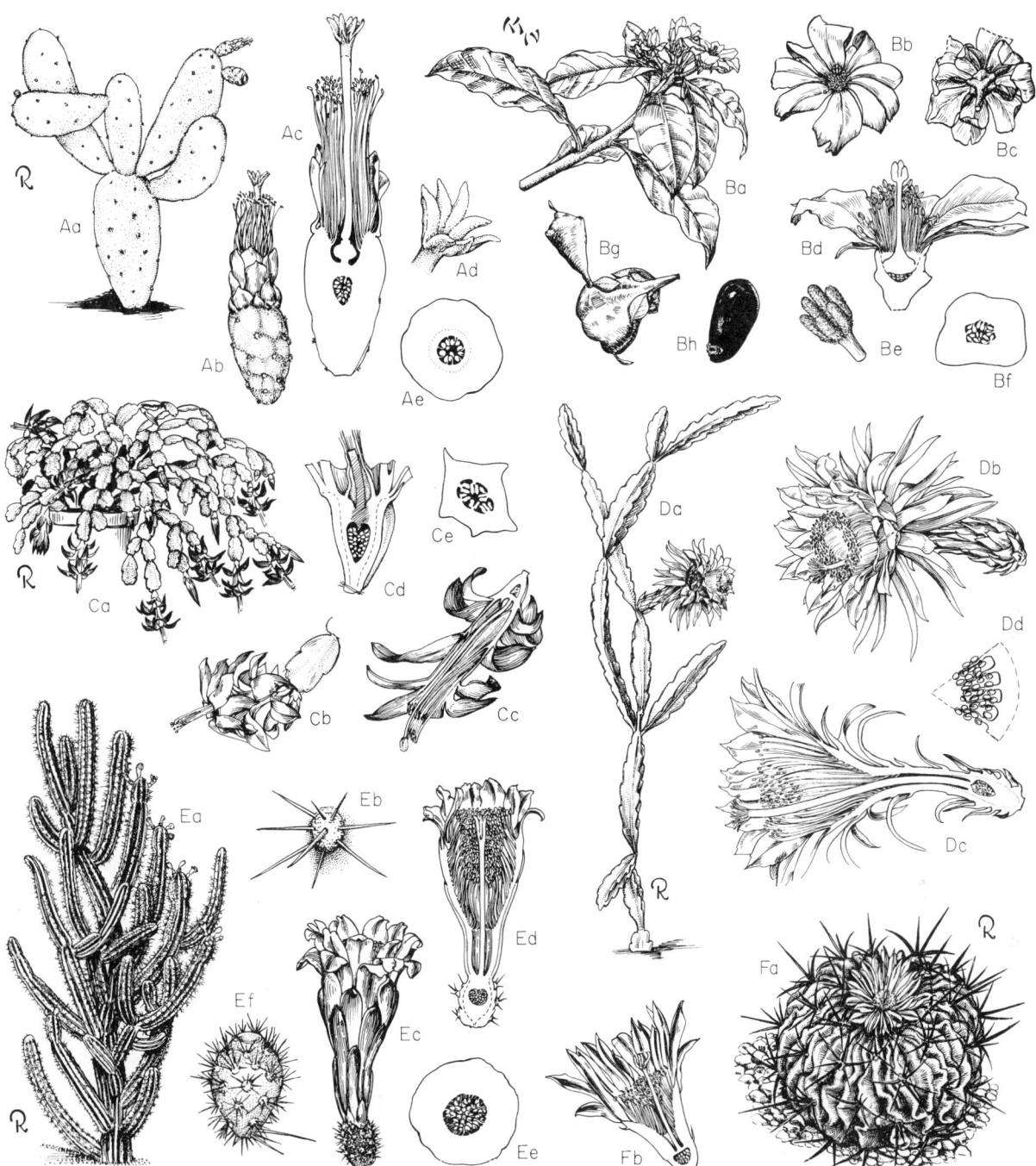

CACTACEAE. **A,** *Nopalea cochenillifera:* **Aa,** flowering plant, × ¹/₁₂; **Ab,** flower, × ½; **Ac,** flower, vertical section, × ¾; **Ad,** stigma, × 2; **Ae,** ovary, cross section, × 1. **B,** *Pereskia grandifolia:* **Ba,** flowering branch, × ¼; **Bb,** flower, face view, × ½; **Bc,** flower, back view, × ½; **Bd,** flower, vertical section, × 1; **Be,** stigma, × 3; **Bf,** ovary, cross section, × 1½; **Bg,** fruit, × ⅙; **Bh,** seed, × 2. **C,** *Schlumbergera Bridgesii:* **Ca,** flowering plant, × ¹/₁₀; **Cb,** joint of stem with flower, × ¼; **Cc,** flower, vertical section, × ½; **Cd,** ovary and base of flower, vertical section, × 1½; **Ce,** ovary, cross section, × ¾. **D,** *Hylocereus undatus:* **Da,** flowering plant, × ¹/₁₂; **Db,** flower, three-quarters face view, × ⅙; **Dc,** flower, vertical section, × ⅙; **Dd,** excised segment of ovary, cross section, × 2. **E,** *Lemaireocereus pruinosus:* **Ea,** flowering plant, × ¹/₄₀; **Eb,** areole with spines, × ½; **Ec,** flower, × ½; **Ed,** flower, vertical section, × ½; **Ee,** ovary, cross section, × 1½; **Ef,** fruit, × ½. **F,** *Echinofossulocactus* sp.: **Fa,** flowering plant, × ½; **Fb,** flower, vertical section, × ¾.

trocactus, *Aztekium, Azureocereus, Bergerocactus, Borzicactus, Browningia, Carnegiea, Cephalocereus, Cereus, Chamaecereus, Cleistocactus, Cochemiea, Copiapoa, Corryocactus, Coryphantha, Cryptocereus, Deamia, Denmoza, Discocactus, Disocactus, Eccremocactus, Echinocactus, Echinocereus, Echinofossulocactus, Echinopsis, Epiphyllanthus, Epiphyllum, Epithelantha, Erdisia, Eriosyce, Erythrorhipsalis, Escontria, Espostoa, Eulychnia, Ferocactus, Frailea, Gym-* nocalycium, *Haageocereus, Harrisia, Hatiora, ×Heliaporus, Heliocereus, Hylocereus, Lemaireocereus, Leuchtenbergia, Lobivia, Lophocereus, Lophophora, Maihuenia, Mammillaria, Mammillopsis, Melocactus, Mila, Monvillea, Morangaya, Myrtillocactus, Neolloydia, Neoporteria, Neoraimondia, Neowerdermannia, Nopalea, Nopalxochia, Notocactus, Nyctocereus, Obregonia, Opuntia, Oroya, Pachycereus, Parodia, Pediocactus, Pelecyphora, Peniocereus, Pereskia,*

Pereskiopsis, Pfeiffera, Pterocactus, Quiabentia, Rathbunia, Rebutia, Rhipsalidopsis, Rhipsalis, Schlumbergera, Sclerocactus, Selenicereus, Setiechinopsis, Stetsonia, Strombocactus, Tacinga, Thelocactus, Trichocereus, Weberocereus, Werckleoцereus, Wigginsia, and *Wilcoxia.*

Members of the Cactaceae are grown as ornamentals or some for the edible fruit *(Cereus, Hylocereus, Lemaireocereus, Opuntia)* and edible stems *(Opuntia),* as host to cochineal insects *(Opuntia),* or as the source of narcotic alkaloids *(Lophophora).* The ornamentals are grown in the greenhouse, outdoors as garden or hedge plants in warm, dry areas, or the smaller ones as window garden plants. For culture see *Cacti.*

CACTI. Cacti include the many genera of almost exclusively New World plants belonging to the family Cactaceae. The majority are succulent, arid-land plants of varied habit but with thickened stems, which, besides functioning as water-storage organs, serve the plants also as photosynthetic organs, replacing the leaves, which are mostly either minute or early deciduous. Spines are usually present and plants should be handled with care. The succulent habit is not unique to the cacti but is shared by other kinds of plants of desert and other dry habitats. Many other succulents are also grown as ornamentals and are often confused by the layman with cacti. See *Succulents.*

Although most of the cacti are desert or dry-country plants, they need a liberal supply of water in their growing period. For the most part they bloom in summer and are more or less dormant in winter, when care should be taken not to overwater them, but they soon suffer in pots if allowed to be dry for any length of time, and they should not be grown close to hot pipes. Soils should be open in texture to insure proper drainage; sand and sometimes pounded brick are often added to the soil, and care should be taken not to have much fresh organic material in it. In summer, if placed outdoors, the plants are usually plunged rather than turned out of the pots.

Propagation is by offsets in the species that produce them, and most kinds grow readily from cuttings made of the stems or joints. The severed or cut surface should be allowed to dry in the air for several days, until it is seared or a corky layer has formed; the cutting is then inserted shallowly in sand in a pot or pan. Cacti start quickly from seeds, when they are available, and seed-grown plants commonly are more amenable under glass than those transplanted directly from the wild. Seeds should be sown only in sterilized soil. Seeds of some cacti, as of *Opuntia* and *Echinocactus,* germinate in a few days. The seedlings may remain in their pots or pans for several months or more before transplanting. When large enough, they are transplanted to other pots or pans; the shifting may then proceed as required, being careful not to use too large pots.

The cacti are easily grafted on other stocks. This practice is employed in order to provide weeping kinds with straight stout stems or standards, and also to propagate the many crested and contorted forms, and sometimes to elevate small globose kinds. *Pereskia* stocks are often employed, and also some of the strong columnar kinds of the *Cereus* group. The cacti graft rather indiscriminately. Any method of applying the cut surfaces of stock and scion together is satisfactory if the surfaces are held firmly in place by cords or thongs. Wax is not employed. The cleft graft is perhaps most commonly used, but when small globose forms are grafted on columnar stocks it is necessary only to cut off squarely the top of the stock and the base of the scion and to set one on the other, and tie the parts firmly together.

CACTUS: *MAMMILLARIA.* **C. Melocactus:** *Melocactus communis.*

CAESALPINIA L. [*Libidibia* Schlechtend.; *Poinciana* L.]. *Leguminosae* (subfamily Caesalpinioideae). About 70 spp. or more of trop. or subtrop. trees and shrubs, sometimes scandent; lvs. alt., 2-pinnate; fls. in racemes or panicles, bisexual or sometimes unisexual, red or yellow, not papilionaceous, stamens 10, separate; fr. a legume, mostly flat.

Some species planted as ornamentals in warm regions or under glass. Propagated by seeds, which will germinate more readily if soaked in warm water several hours before sowing. Transplanted into pots as soon as seedlings show first true leaf. In frost-free regions plants may soon be set permanently outdoors. Source of valuable commercial tannins and dyewoods.

Conzattii (Rose) Standl. Small tree; lfts. in 4–5 pairs, oblong to obovate; racemes sessile; fls. yellow-red to brilliant red; fr. curved, pubescent. Mex.

coriaria (Jacq.) Willd. DIVI-DIVI. To 30 ft.; lfts. many, small; fls. white or yellowish; fr. oblong, curved, about 1 in. long. Trop. Amer. Pods are source of the tannin divi-divi.

echinata Lam. BRAZILWOOD. Tree, with prickly trunk; lfts. many, rhombic-oblong; fls. yellow; fr. oblong, 3 in. long. Trop. Amer. Heartwood yields a red dye.

ferrea Tulasne. BRAZILIAN IRONWOOD. Tall shrub, or tree to 50 ft., unarmed; pinnae 3–4 pairs, lfts. in 4–8 pairs, oblong to nearly obovate, to 1 in. long, obtuse or retuse; racemes short, in dense terminal panicles; fls. 4-merous, petals scarcely longer than calyx; fr. thick, elliptic-oblong, to 3 in. long. E. Brazil.

Gilliesii (Wallich ex Hook.) Benth. [*Poinciana Gilliesii* Wallich ex Hook.]. BIRD-OF-PARADISE, BIRD-OF-PARADISE SHRUB. Straggling shrub or small tree, unarmed, branchlets glandular-pubescent; lfts. many, very small; fls. light yellow, stamens bright red; fr. to 4 in. long. Argentina, Uruguay. Zone 8.

japonica Siebold & Zucc. Doubtfully distinct from *C. sepiaria;* distinguished by being nearly glabrous, and having fls. in looser racemes, with red stamens and red marking on upper petal. Japan.

mexicana A. Gray. Shrub or small tree, to 30 ft., unarmed; lfts. oblong to nearly orbicular; fls. yellow; fr. 2½ in. long. Mex.

pectinata: *C. spinosa.*

peltophoroides Benth. SIBIPIRUNA, FALSE BRAZILWOOD. Tree, to 35 ft., unarmed; pinnae 6–10 pairs, lfts. many, somewhat curved-oblong to rhomboid, about ¼ in. long; racemes densely fld., terminal, shorter than lvs., rusty-tomentose; fls. small, petals yellow, filaments almost as long as petals. E. Brazil.

pulcherrima (L.) Swartz [*Poinciana pulcherrima* L.]. BARBADOS-PRIDE, PRIDE-OF-BARBADOS, FLOWER-FENCE, BARBADOS F.-F., DWARF POINCIANA. Shrub, to 10 ft., more or less prickly, glabrous; lfts. to ¾ in. long; petals red with yellow margins, becoming deep red, stamens bright red, to 2½ in. long, or fls. rarely rose or pure yellow; fr. to 4 in. long. W. Indies. Zone 10. Much planted in tropics.

punctata Willd. [*Libidibia punctata* (Willd.) Britt.]. To 40 ft.; lvs. to 1 ft. long, lfts. in 3–5 pairs, elliptic or obovate, to ¾ in. long; 1 petal orange-variegated; fr. straight, woody, 2 in. long. Venezuela, where called QUEBRAHACHA.

Sappan L. BRAZILWOOD, SAPPANWOOD. Tree, to 15 ft., prickly; lfts. many, rhombic-oblong; panicles almost as long as lvs.; fls. yellow; fr. to 3½ in. long, beaked. India, Malay Pen. Heartwood yields a red dye.

sepiaria Roxb. MYSORE THORN. Scrambling shrub, prickly; lfts. oblong; fls. yellow; fr. oblong, to 3 in. long, beaked. India.

spinosa (Mol.) O. Kuntze [*C. pectinata* Cav.; *C. tinctoria* (Dombey ex HBK) Benth. ex Taub.]. TARA. Tree or large shrub, trunk covered with short, sharp tubercles; lfts. oblong; racemes dense, to 8 in. long; fls. yellow, lower calyx lobe greatly enlarged, with comblike margin; fr. reddish, to 4½ in. long and 1 in. wide. Deserts, w. S. Amer. Pods yield important tannin.

tinctoria: *C. spinosa.*

CAILLIEA: *DICHROSTACHYS;* **C. glomerata:** *D. cinerea;* **C. nyassana:** a listed name of no botanical standing for *D. cinerea* subsp.

CAIOPHORA: *CAJOPHORA.*

CAJANUS DC. *Leguminosae* (subfamily *Faboideae*). Two spp. of shrubs of the Old World tropics; lvs. alt., of 3 lfts.; fls. in axillary racemes, rather large, papilionaceous, stamens 10, 9 united, 1 separate; fr. a flat, linear legume.

Grown as an annual or perennial in warm areas. Propagated by seeds, or in the greenhouse by cutting. Thrives in Zone 10b.

Cajan (L.) Huth [*C. indicus* K. Spreng.]. CAJAN, CATJANG, CATJANG PEA, PIGEON P., CONGO P., ANGOLA P., NO-EYE P., RED GRAM, DAHL. Erect, to 10 ft.; lfts. elliptic to lanceolate, to 4 in. long, soft-hairy, glandular-dotted beneath; fls. to ¾ in. long, yellow or orange, standard often purplish outside; fr. hairy, to 3 in. long, constricted between seeds; seeds small, truncate-orbicular, somewhat flattened. Probably native to trop. Afr. Widely cult. in trop. countries for the edible seeds, as a cover crop, and for green manure.

indicus: *C. Cajan.*

CAJOPHORA K. Presl (also spelled *Caiophora*). *Loasaceae.* About 70 spp. of S. Amer. herbs, usually with stinging hairs, sts. round; lvs. opp.; fls. yellow, white, or red, stamens many, in clusters opp. hooded petals; fr. a spirally twisted caps.

Propagated by seeds and cuttings.

lateritia Klotzsch [*Blumenbachia lateritia* (Klotzsch) Griseb.; *Loasa aurantiaca* Hort. ex Lilja; *L. lateritia* (Klotzsch) Gillies ex Arn.]. Ann., twining to 20 ft.; lvs. pinnately toothed or lobed, to pinnate; fls. orange-red, to 2 in. across, on very long pedicels. Argentina.

CALADIUM Venten. MOTHER-IN-LAW PLANT, ELEPHANT'S-EAR, ANGEL-WINGS. *Araceae.* About 15 spp. of tuberous, stemless, per. herbs, native to trop. Amer.; lvs. tufted, often beautifully marked with red, white, or other colors, petioles long; spathe convolute, constricted above tube, the blade partly expanded; fls. unisexual, spadix included, covered with fls., ovary with sessile stigmas.

Popular potted and bedding plants. Tubers may be started in boxes of peat or sphagnum at temperatures of 70–85° F.; when roots appear, tubers should be potted in rich loam to which bonemeal has been added. In summer or warm climates they may be planted directly outdoors in well-worked soil. Propagated by division or seeds.

argyrites: *C. Humboldtii.*

bicolor (Ait.) Venten. HEART-OF-JESUS. Lf. blades peltate, ovate, to 14 in. long and 6½ in. wide, basally bifid with lobes mostly obtuse, red with broad green border, petioles variegated, nearly as long as or to 1½ times longer than blades; spathes to 4 in. long, tube green outside, greenish-white inside, the limb whitish. Para (Brazil). Probably the chief parent of the *C.* × *hortulanum* group.

bulbosum: a listed name of no botanical standing.

candidum: *C.* × *hortulanum* cv.

esculentum: *Colocasia esculenta.*

×**hortulanum** Birdsey. FANCY-LEAVED C. Of mixed hybrid origin; lf. blades sometimes peltate, ovate to lanceolate in outline, basally bifid, cordate, or truncate, flat, undulate or ruffled, variously variegated with red, rose, salmon, white, and green, petioles as long as or several times longer than blades. Cv. 'Candidum' [*C. candidum* Hort.]. Lf. blade white, with dark green veins, margin green.

Humboldtii Schott [*C. argyrites* Lem.]. Slender; lf. blades peltate, ovate, to 4¼ in. long and 2½ in. wide, with rounded basal lobes, splotched and spotted white between primary lateral veins, petioles to 18 in. long, variegated. S. Venezuela.

marmoratum Mathieu. Differs from *C. bicolor* in having lf. blades green, irregularly spotted gray, yellow-green, and whitish, glaucousgreen beneath, with primary lateral veins wide-spreading, petioles nearly twice as long as blade, variegated. Ecuador.

picturatum C. Koch & Bouché. Differs from *C. bicolor* in having lf. blades peltate, lanceolate, to 12 in. long and 4 in. wide, with basal lobes acute, petioles commonly elongate, to 18 in. long, and spathe with tube basally purple inside. Trop. Amer.

Schomburgkii Schott. Lf. blades scarcely or not at all peltate, obliquely wide-triangular-ovate, to 8 in. long and 6 in. wide, basally truncate or emarginate, with spreading primary lateral veins pale or silvery or red, petioles to 2 ft. long. Guiana. Cv. 'Changjur' belongs here. Var. **venosum** (N. E. Br.) Engl. [*C. rubescens* N. E. Br.; *C. venosum* N. E. Br.]. Lvs. lanceolate, narrower, 2–3 in. wide, with undulate to ruffled margins and strongly ascending veins, variously variegated, petioles as long as blades. Brazil.

venosum: *C. Schomburgkii* var.

CALAMINTHA Mill. CALAMINT. *Labiatae.* About 7 spp. of per. herbs of Eur. and Asia; sts. mostly square in cross section, sometimes woody at base; lvs. opp., simple; fls. in axillary, usually peduncled cymes, calyx tubular, 13-nerved, 2-lipped, upper lip erect, 2-toothed, lower lip 2-toothed, longer than upper, tube straight, not swollen on one side, hairy in throat, corolla 2-lipped, upper lip entire or notched, lower lip 3-lobed, stamens 4; fr. of 4 nutlets. Sometimes included in *Satureja*, which has calyx campanulate, 10-nerved, not 2-lipped.

Acinos: *Acinos thymoides.*

alpina: *Acinos alpinus.*

ascendens: *C. sylvatica* subsp.

chinensis: *Clinopodium chinense.*

Clinopodium: *Clinopodium vulgare.*

georgiana: *Satureja georgiana.*

glabella: *Satureja glabella.*

grandiflora (L.) Moench [*Satureja grandiflora* (L.) Scheele]. To 18 in., glabrescent; lvs. ovate, to 2½ in. long, 1¼ in. wide, acute, coarsely dentate to serrate with 6 or more teeth on each side; cymes 1–5-fld.; calyx to ½ in. long, corolla twice as long as calyx, pink. Summer. S. Eur.

Nepeta (L.) Savi [*Clinopodium Nepeta* (L.) O. Kuntze; *Satureja Calamintha* (L.) Scheele; *S. Nepeta* (L.) Scheele]. Rhizomatous, bushy, to 2 ft., gray-pubescent; lvs. broadly ovate, to ¾ in. long, ⅜ in. wide, obtuse, subentire or shallowly to deeply crenate-serrate, with up to 9 teeth on each side; calyx to ¼ in. long, hairs in throat exserted after flowering, corolla to ⅝ in. long, white or lilac. Summer. S. Eur. and Medit. region. Subsp. **Nepeta** [*C. nepetoides* Jord.]. The typical subsp.; more robust; lvs. over ¾ in. long, with 5–9 teeth on each side; cymes 10–20-fld. Subsp. **glandulosa** (Req.) P. W. Ball [*C. officinalis* Moench]. Lvs. less than ¾ in. long, with up to 5 teeth on each side; cymes 5–11-fld.

nepetoides: *Calamintha Nepeta* subsp. *Nepeta.*

officinalis: *Calamintha Nepeta* subsp. *glandulosa;* but the name has often been applied to *C. sylvatica* subsp. *ascendens.*

sylvatica Bromf. To 32 in., pubescent, stoloniferous; lvs. ovate or round-ovate, green, sparsely hairy, nearly entire to coarsely toothed, with 5–10 teeth on each side; cymes 3–9-fld.; calyx to ⅜ in. long, lower calyx teeth to ⁵⁄₃₂ in. long, long-ciliate, corolla to ⅞ in. long, pink or lilac with white spots on lower lip. Eur. Subsp. **sylvatica.** The typical subsp.; to 32 in.; lvs. to 2¾ in. long, coarsely toothed or crenate-serrate; corolla ⅝–⅞ in. long. Subsp. **ascendens** (Jord.) P. W. Ball [*C. ascendens* Jord.]. To 24 in.; lvs. to 1⅝ or rarely 2 in. long, nearly entire to shallowly crenate-serrate; corolla ⅜–⅝ in. long.

vulgaris: see *Clinopodium vulgare.*

CALAMPELIS: *ECCREMOCARPUS.*

CALAMUS L. RATTAN PALM, WAIT-AWHILE VINE. *Palmae.* More than 300 spp. of usually spiny, climbing or cespitose and shrublike, dioecious palms of humid forests in trop. Afr., Asia, Malay Arch. to Australia, Solomon Is., Philippine Is., and Taiwan, sts. slender; lvs. pinnate, sheath tubular, often with a ligule at apex, usually armed with solitary or clustered to whorled spines, in some spp. with united infl. modified as climbing organ (flagellum), petiole and lf. blade usually spiny or clawed, pinnae acute or rarely toothed at apex, rachis prolonged in a clawed climbing organ (cirrus) in many spp., infl. united to sheath of lf. above, often armed with claws and with a sterile clawed tip, bracts persistent, tubular or rarely splitting, sheathing peduncle and base of each primary br., primary brs. usually 1–3 times branched into slender rachillae with sheathing bractlets; male fls. usually solitary, calyx tubular, 3-lobed, corolla deeply divided, stamens 6, female fls. usually accompanied by an early deciduous neuter fl., similar to male fls. but usually smaller, staminodes in a ring, ovary 3-celled; fr. covered with imbricate scales, usually 1-seeded, seed with homogeneous or ruminate endosperm.

The long, strong, flexible sts. of a number of the high-climbing species form the common canes or rattans of commerce. A few species are sometimes grown in tropical economic gardens and in Zone 10b. For culture see *Palms.*

formosanus Becc. Climbing; lvs. more than 3 ft. long, terminating in a cirrus, pinnae about 18 on each side, in groups of 2–3; male fls. ¼ in. long. Taiwan.

Margaritae: *Daemonorops Margaritae.*

ornatus Blume. Climbing; sts. to nearly 3 in. in diam.; lvs. with flagellum to 30 ft. long, blade to 12 ft. long or more, pinnae many, equidistant, to 2 ft. long or more; fr. large, to 1⅜ in. long. Indonesia, Malay Pen. to Philippine Is. Fr. edible.

Rotang L. [*C. Roxburghii* Griff.]. RATTAN CANE. Sts. climbing, slender; lvs. to about 3 ft. long, flagellum slender, pinnae many, equidistant; fr. globose, ½ in. in diam. Ceylon, s. India. An important Indian source of rattan cane used in furniture. Young shoots and flesh of frs. edible.

Roxburghii: *C. Rotang.*

CALANDRINIA HBK. ROCK PURSLANE. *Portulacaceae.* More than 150 spp. of rather fleshy low herbs, native mostly to w. N. and S. Amer.; lvs. basal, or alt., narrow; fls. red or rose, ephemeral, in racemes or panicles; fr. a caps.

Suitable for borders or rock gardens. Cultivated as annuals and propagated by seeds or cuttings.

caulescens: *C. ciliata.*

ciliata (Ruiz & Pav.) DC. [*C. caulescens* HBK]. REDMAIDS. Ann., to 1 ft.; lvs. linear-spatulate, to 1⅜ in. long; fls. purple, or white fading to purple, to ⅝ in. across, solitary, axillary. Peru, Ecuador. Var. **Menziesii** (Hook.) Macbr. [*C. Menziesii* (Hook.) Torr. & A. Gray; *C. speciosa* Lindl.]. Sts. diffuse or erect, to 2 ft.; lvs. oblanceolate to linear, to 3 in. long; fls. crimson or rose-red, about ⁵⁄₁₆ in. long. W. N. Amer. Lvs. may be eaten as a garnish or as greens.

grandiflora Lindl. Per., to 3 ft., but grown as an ann.; lvs. elliptic, to 8 in. long; fls. light purple. Chile.

Menziesii: *C. ciliata* var.

speciosa: *C. ciliata* var. *Menziesii.*

umbellata (Ruiz & Pav.) DC. Per., to 6 in., but grown as an ann.; lvs. basal, linear; fls. bright crimson-magenta. Peru, Chile.

CALANTHE R. Br. *Orchidaceae.* About 120 spp. of terrestrial or epiphytic herbs with pseudobulbs, native to warm-temp. and subtrop. Asia, Afr., Oceania, Cent. and S. Amer., and W. Indies; lvs. broad, plicate, deciduous; fls. in racemes on erect or nodding scapes, white, rose, or yellow, sepals and petals similar, lip with claw united to the column, usually 3-lobed and prolonged basally into a spur. For structure of fl. see *Orchidaceae.*

Warm greenhouse; for culture see *Orchids.*

alismifolia Lindl. Rhizome short, with close-set pseudobulbs; lvs. erect, elliptic, to 1 ft. long, including the long petioles; scape lateral, shorter than lvs., bearing a few-fld. raceme; fls. white, tinged with pink, sepals greenish, sepals and petals connivent, scurfy on the exterior, to ½ in. long, lip 3-lobed, lateral lobes narrow, midlobe deeply cleft at apex, with a bright yellow callus, spur long, slender. Late spring–late summer. Himalayas.

×**bella:** *C.* × *Veitchii* cv.

biloba Lindl. Robust, to 2½ ft., pseudobulbs cylindrical, stemlike, leafy at top; raceme from lf. axils, erect, many-fld.; fls. 1½ in. across, sepals and petals spreading, ochre-colored, mottled with purple-brown, lip cream-colored, with purplish apex, ovate, 2-lobed at apex, long-clawed basally, spur conical. Autumn. Nepal.

brevicornu Lindl. To 2 ft., pseudobulbs small, ovoid, leafy; raceme erect, loosely many-fld.; sepals and petals spreading, acute, brownish-purple, to 1 in. long, lip 3-lobed, purple, yellow in middle, lateral lobes linear, sickle-shaped, midlobe nearly square, spur very short. Late spring. Himalayas.

densiflora Lindl. Erect, to 10 in., from a stout rhizome, pseudobulbs small, 2–3-lvd.; lvs. petioled, to 18 in. long; raceme dense, subcapitate, many-fld., to 10 in. long; fls. pendent, yellow, sepals and petals connivent, to ¾ in. long, lip 3-lobed, midlobe shallowly 2-lobed, spur long, conical. Autumn. Himalayas.

discolor Lindl. Lvs. 2–3, broadly lanceolate-elliptic, to 12 in. long, acute, strongly striate; raceme erect, to 16 in. long, 6–12-fld.; sepals and petals lanceolate-elliptic, wine-red, lip 3-lobed, white, suffused or dotted with pale pink, midlobe bifid. Japan. Forma **Sieboldii** (Decne.) Ohwi [*C. Sieboldii* Decne.; *C. striata* var. *Sieboldii* (Decne.) Maxim.]. Fls. clear yellow. Japan.

Elmeri Ames. To 2 ft.; lvs. deciduous, absent during flowering; scape erect, pubescent, loosely many-fld.; sepals and petals spreading, pubescent, purple, to ½ in. long, lip 4-lobed, flabellate, spur slender, curved, pubescent. Early winter–early spring. Philippine Is.

furcata Batem. ex. Lindl. [*C. veratrifolia* R. Br.]. Lvs. lanceolate-elliptic, to about 2 ft. long; racemes many-fld., to 3 ft. high or more; fls. almost 2 in. across, snow-white, lip 4-lobed, often yellow at base, spur slender. Winter. India, Pacific Is., Australia.

gracilis Lindl. Similar in appearance to *C. biloba;* raceme lateral, below the lvs., short, to 10 in. long, loosely fld.; sepals and petals semierect, white, to ½ in. long, lip 4-lobed, cuneate at base, white with yellow throat, without a spur. Autumn. Sikkim.

herbacea Lindl. Pseudobulbs conical, close-set; lvs. erect, petioled, to 2 ft. long; raceme erect, many-fld.; fls. on pedicels 2 in. long, sepals and petals reflexed, yellowish-green to bronze, to ¾ in. long, lip deeply 4-lobed, white, yellow in center, spur filiform, 2 in. long. Early summer. Sikkim.

Masuca Lindl. Similar to *C. herbacea* in growth and appearance, but fls. to 1 in. long, sepals and petals deep violet, lip 3-lobed, magenta or rich purple, lateral lobes oblong, midlobe flabellate, 2-parted at apex. Late summer. Sikkim. Var. **grandiflora** B. S. Williams. Raceme to 4 ft. and blooming continuously for 3 months. India.

nipponica Mak. To 8 in.; lvs. narrow-lanceolate; raceme longer than lvs., few-fld.; sepals and petals spreading, purplish, to ¾ in. long, lip triangular-ovate, shallowly 3-lobed, spur short, club-shaped. Early summer. Japan.

oculata: *C. vestita.*

puberula Lindl. To 1½ ft.; lvs. 1–5, petioled; raceme as long as or shorter than lvs., loosely fld.; fls. pale lavender, to 1 in. across, sepals ovate-lanceolate, petals linear, lip 3-lobed, lateral lobes sickle-shaped, midlobe ovate, finely toothed, spur lacking. Summer. Himalayas.

reflexa Maxim. Similar to *C. puberula;* to 16 in.; fls. smaller, to ¾ in. across, white, tinged with purple, sepals and petals reflexed, lip projecting forward, 3-lobed, midlobe cuneate-elliptic, mucronate at apex, spur lacking. Late summer. Japan.

Regnieri: *C. vestita* cv.

rosea (Lindl.) Benth. To 1½ ft.; lvs. lanceolate, plicate; scape hirsute, raceme loosely fld.; fls. large, to 2 in. across, sepals and petals spreading, rose to pink, lip flat, oblong, entire, retuse at apex, spur horizontal, straight, blunt. Early winter. Thailand, Java.

×**Sandhurstiana:** *C.* × *Veitchii* cv.

×**Sedenii:** *C.* × *Veitchii* cv.

Sieboldii: *C. discolor* forma.

striata var. **Sieboldii:** *C. discolor* forma *Sieboldii.*

Turneri: *C. vestita* cv.

×**Veitchii** Lindl.: *C. rosea* × *C. vestita.* To 3 ft.; fls. large, rich rose, lip with white spot at base. Very variable in color. Winter. Garden hybrid. Cv. 'Bella' [*C.* × *bella* Rchb.f.]. Sepals white, petals white, suffused with pale pink, lip blush-pink, with rose-carmine spot at base. Cv. 'Sandhurstiana' [*C.* × *Sandhurstiana* Gosse ex Rchb.f.]. Fls. deep rose-carmine, sepals paler than petals, lip with a deeper spot at base. Cv. 'Sedenii' [*C.* × *Sedenii* Rchb.f.]. Fls. deep rose-carmine, lip with a deeper carmine spot, bordered with white at base.

veratrifolia: *C. furcata.*

vestita Lindl. [*C. oculata* Hort.]. Pseudobulbs 3 in. long; lvs. broad-lanceolate, to 1½ ft. long; racemes on scapes to 2½ ft. long, 6–12-fld.; fls. white or cream, 2½ in. across, lip 4-lobed, orange-yellow at base, spur slender. Early winter. Burma, Malay Arch. Cv. 'Gigantea'. Plant and fls. larger throughout. Cv. 'Luteo-oculata'. Lip with orange-red spot at base. Cv. 'Nivalis'. Fls. pure white. Cv. 'Regnieri' [*C. Regnieri* Rchb.f.]. Lip less deeply lobed than in typical form, with purple spot at base. Cv. 'Rubro-oculata'. Lip with a deep red-purple blotch at base. Cv. 'Turneri' [*C. Turneri* Rchb.f.]. Similar to cv. 'Rubro-oculata', but with later flowering season. Cv. 'Williamsii' [*C. Williamsii* F. W. Moore]. Sepals and petals white, with rose margins, lip deep rose.

Williamsii: *C. vestita* cv.

CALATHEA G. F. Mey. *Marantaceae.* About 100 spp. of herbs, with attractively marked, mostly basal lvs. in clumps, native to trop. Amer.; infl. a dense, bracted spike or raceme, borne on a scape among the lvs.; fls. irregular, sepals 3, corolla 3-parted, tube almost equal to or longer than sepals, fertile stamen 1, staminodes 3, the outer one usually larger than petals, ovary inferior, 3-celled; caps. usually 3-seeded.

A leaf wax and edible tubers are obtained from species of this genus. Calatheas should be grown in a humid greenhouse shaded from the direct rays of the sun and with a night temperature not below 65° F. In subtropical climates (Zone 10), they may be grown outside with winter protection. They require good drainage and loamy soil mixed with leafmold and sand. Leaf colors are likely to differ in young and old plants. Propagated by division of crowns, by tubers, and by cuttings in spring.

Albertii (Pynaert & Van Geert) L. H. Bailey. Similar to *C. Lietzei*, but lvs. broader, gray-green, feathered with olive-green. Nativity unknown.

amabilis: a listed name of no botanical standing for *Stromanthe amabilis.*

argyraea Körn. To 8 in.; lf. blades oblong-lanceolate, narrowed toward each end, to 5 in. long and 1½ in. wide or larger, dark green with silver-gray bands above, purple beneath, petioles short. Nativity unknown. This name has been applied by some authors to a plant somewhat similar to *C. bella.*

Bachemiana E. Morr. Lf. blades spreading or reflexed, long-lanceolate to 10 in. long and 2 in. wide, upper surface gray-green, with dark green elliptic-lanceolate spots along main lateral veins, and medium green smaller veins, midrib, and margin, lower surface sometimes slightly purplish, petioles to 1 ft. long; fl. spikes about 3 in. long. Brazil.

bella (Bull) Regel [*C. Kegeliana* Hort.; *Maranta Kegeljanii* E. Morr.]. Lvs. few, velvety at apex, blades spreading, elliptic-ovate, to 1 ft. long and 5½ in. wide, markedly unsymmetrical, cordate, gray-green, with markings as in *C. Bachemiana*, margin to 1 in. wide, petioles to 6 in. long. Brazil? By some authors considered a variant of *C. Bachemiana.*

Clossonii: a listed name of no botanical standing, applied to a plant with lvs. lanceolate, rounded at base, yellow-green above, with short almond-shaped green blotches on each side of midrib. Brazil.

cylindrica (Roscoe) K. Schum. [*C. grandifolia* Lindl.]. To 5 ft. or more; lf. blades spreading, elliptic or oblong, to 18 in. long and 10½ in. wide, abruptly short-acuminate, green; peduncles 9 in. long, spikes dense, cylindrical, to 6 in. long, fls. yellowish. Se. Brazil.

discolor: *C. lutea.*

fasciata: *C. rotundifolia* cv.

glabra: a listed name of no botanical standing for *Ctenanthe glabra.*

grandifolia: *C. cylindrica.*

insignis Petersen. RATTLESNAKE PLANT. To 6 ft. or more; lf. blades oblong, to 18 in. long and 9 in. wide, green on both sides; spikes compact, to 10 in. long, with many bronzy bracts; fls. yellow. Mex. to Ecuador. Doubtfully in cult.; material offered under this name is probably *C. lancifolia.*

Kegeliana: *C. bella;* variant spelling of Kegeljanii.

lancifolia Boom [*C. insignis* Bull, not Petersen; *Maranta insignis* H. W. Ward]. To 20 in.; lf. blades erect, narrowly lanceolate, very undulate, upper surface light green with darker midrib and alternating large and small, dark green, elliptic spots along lateral veins, lower surface purple-red. Plants offered as *C. insignis* probably belong here.

Lietzei E. Morr. [*Maranta Lietzei* Hort.]. To 2 ft.; lf. blades spreading, ovate-lanceolate, to 9 in. long, obtuse, undulate, dark velvety-green and with olive-green stripes between lateral veins above, purple beneath; peduncles longer than lvs., spikes small, cylindrical, subtended by solitary lf. Brazil.

Lindeniana Wallis [*C. Lindenii* Wallis & André]. To 3 ft.; lf. blades elliptic, to 16 in. long, upper surface dark green with olive-green zone on each side of midrib and along margin, lower surface glaucescent-green and with purple zone along midrib and margin. Brazil.

Lindenii: *C. Lindeniana.*

Louisae Gagnep. To 3 ft.; lf. blades elliptic-ovate, to 1 ft. long, narrowed toward each end, green and feathered with greenish-white along midrib above, tinted purple-red beneath; spikes sessile, 2⅜ in. long, pure white, bracts 5–10. Nativity unknown.

Luciani Nichols. To 3 ft.; lvs. elliptic-acuminate, to 1 ft. long, metallic-green and with wide band of silver-white along midrib above, gray-green beneath. Trop. Amer.

lutea (Aubl.) G. F. Mey. [*C. discolor* G. F. Mey.]. CAUASSÚ. To 15 ft.; lf. blades ovate to obovate, to 5 ft. long and 2 ft. wide, waxy beneath; infl. of several spicate brs. to 8 in. long, bracts reddish-brown; fls. yellow. Trop. Amer. A good wax similar to carnauba wax is obtained from the dried lvs., which are also used in basketry.

macrosepala K. Schum. Robust plant; lf. blades lanceolate or lanceolate-oblong, to 14 in. long and 6 in. wide, acute at base, subcaudate at apex; peduncles 4 in. long, spikes ellipsoid, 2¾ in. long, bracts straw-colored, pubescent. Costa Rica.

Makoyana E. Morr. PEACOCK PLANT, CATHEDRAL-WINDOWS, BRAIN PLANT. To 20 in. or more; lf. blades ovate, upper surface cream-colored or olive-green with dark green, elliptic to oblong spots along the lateral veins and dark green border, lower surface purple, repeating the pattern, petioles red-purple, puberulent. Brazil.

mediopicta E. Morr. To 20 in.; lf. blades oblong-elliptic, to 8 in. long and 3½ in. wide, dark green and feathered with white along midrib above, pale green beneath, long-petioled; peduncles short, spikes subglobose, to 2 in. long. Brazil.

micans (Klotzsch) Körn. To 8 in.; lf. blades nearly oblong or oblong-lanceolate, to 5 in. long and 1½ in. wide, shining green and feathered with white above, pale green beneath, petioles and peduncles 5 in. long; spikes slender, ¾ in. long. Cent. Amer. to Guyana and Bolivia.

musaica (Bull) L. H. Bailey. Dwarf plant; lf. blades ovate, to 6 in. long, cordate, with many transverse connecting veins, shining yellow-green above, with lateral and transverse veins deep green. Brazil.

ornata (Linden) Körn. To 3(–9) ft.; lvs. oblong-lanceolate, to 2 ft. long or more, rich green above, dull purple-red beneath, young lvs. often marked with pink and white lines along lateral veins; peduncles to 14 in. long, spikes ovoid, 3 in. long; petals violet. Guyana, Colombia, Ecuador. Cv. '**Roseo-lineata**' [var. *roseolineata* Lem. ex Regel]. Young lvs. marked with rose lines. Cv. '**Sanderana**' [*C. Sanderana* Linden ex L. H. Bailey]. Lvs. slightly wider.

picta (Bull) Hook. f. To 4 ft.; lf. blades oblong-lanceolate, to 8 in. long and 2½ in. wide, obtuse at base, velvety-green and feathered paler green between lateral veins above, purple-red beneath, petioles long-sheathing, almost equalling lf. blades; peduncles long, spikes cylindrical, to 4 in. long, subtended by lvs.; bracts yellowish, purple-margined; fls. white. Brazil.

picturata (Linden) C. Koch & Linden. To 15 in.; lf. blades elliptic, to 6 in. long and half as wide, acute at both ends, upper surface dark green, with white stripe along midrib and near margin, lower surface purple; spikes narrow, 4 in. long. Brazil. Cv. '**Vandenheckei**' [*C. Vandenheckei* (Lem.) Regel]. Juvenile phase of this sp. Cv. '**Argentea**'. Lf. blade greenish-white, with dark green border. Venezuela.

princeps (Linden) Regel. Robust, to 3 ft. or more; lf. blades almost equalling petioles, oblong or elliptic-lanceolate, light green and with broad black-green central band above, violet-purple beneath, petioles to 18 in. long. N. Brazil.

propinqua (Poepp. & Endl.) Körn. [*C. trifasciata* (C. Koch) Körn.]. To 2 ft., producing tubers ¾ in. long; lf. blades oblanceolate to obovate, to 13 in. long and 6 in. wide, acute at base, upper surface silvery-gray, with margin and stripes between lateral veins dark green and midrib pubescent, lower surface pale green and appressed brown-pubescent; spikes sessile, ovoid, 2 in. long; fls. yellow. Venezuela, Guianas, n. Brazil.

roseolineata: a listed name of no botanical standing for *C. ornata* cv.

roseopicta (Linden) Regel. To 8 in.; lvs. elliptic, to 9 in. long and 6 in. wide, upper surface dark green, with red midrib and a zone of bright red near margin fading silvery-pink, lower surface purple; peduncles 6 in. long, spikes cylindrical, 3½ in. long. Brazil.

rotundifolia (C. Koch) Körn. [*Maranta orbifolia* Linden]. To 1 ft.; lvs. spreading, suborbicular, to 12 in. long, dark green and with whitish bands between main lateral veins, paler beneath, petioles 6 in. long. Cv. '**Fasciata**' [*C. fasciata* Körn.]. Lvs. with silvery-white bands.

rufibarba Fenzl. Brown-hairy throughout except the fls.; lvs. linear-oblong to linear-lanceolate, to 7 in. long, undulate, bright green above, bluish-green with purplish cast beneath, petioles long, red-brown; peduncles 2 in. long, spikes dense, to 3 in. long; fls. golden, about 1 in. across. Brazil.

Sanderana: *C. ornata* cv.

setosa: a listed name of no botanical standing for *Ctenanthe setosa.*

tricolor: a listed name of no botanical standing and uncertain application.

trifasciata: *C. propinqua.*

undulata Linden & André. To 8 in.; lvs. oblong, to 4 in. long and 2 in. wide, rounded at base, undulate, shining dark green and with central white stripe above, purplish beneath; peduncle 3 in. long; fls. white. Peru.

Vandenheckei: *C. picturata* cv.

Veitchiana Hook.f. To 4 ft.; lvs. ovate-elliptic, to 1 ft. long and half as wide, rounded at base, dark green above, with yellow-green blotches along midrib and a pale green scalloped band about midway between midrid and margin, the dark green areas purple underneath; peduncles to 8 in. long, spikes to 3 in. long; fls. white and pale purple. Trop. S. Amer.

violacea (Roscoe) Lindl. To 3 ft.; lvs. elliptic-lanceolate, to 18 in. long and 6 in. wide, green above, glaucescent or purplish beneath; peduncles to 10 in. long, spikes ellipsoid, 2½ in. long, subtended by solitary lf.; fls. purple. Se. Brazil. Young fls. used for food.

vittata (C. Koch) Körn. To 3 ft.; lvs. oblong to ovate-oblong, to 18 in. long and 9 in. wide, but usually smaller, light green and striped with white between the lateral veins above, tinted yellowish-green beneath; infl. short, spikes ovoid; fls. yellow. Colombia.

Warscewiczii (Mathieu ex Planch.) Körn. To 3 ft.; lvs. oblong-lanceolate, to 1 ft. long and 5 in. wide, acute at base, velvety-green and feathered along midrib with yellow-green above, purple beneath; peduncles pubescent, to 4 in. long, spikes ellipsoid, to 2⁵⁄₁₆ in. long. Costa Rica.

Wiotii (E. Morr.) Regel. Small plant; lvs. ovate-oblong, to 4 in. long and 1½ in. wide, rounded or subcordate at base, light green and with almond-shaped dark green spots on each side of midrib above, purplish beneath. Nativity unknown.

zebrina (Sims) Lindl. ZEBRA PLANT. To 3 ft.; lf. blades elliptic, to 2 ft. long and 1 ft. wide, velvety-green and with yellow-green veins and midrib above, purplish-red beneath. Se. Brazil. Cv. '**Binotii**' [var. *Binotii* Hort. ex L. H. Bailey]. Larger; lvs. darker colored, to 4½ ft. long.

CALCEOLARIA L. SLIPPERWORT, SLIPPER FLOWER, POCKETBOOK F., POUCH F. *Scrophulariaceae.* About 500 spp. of herbaceous and shrubby plants, native from Mex. s. in the Andes to Chile and Argentina; lvs. opp., or whorled, simple or pinnate, petiole often winged; fls. showy, in irregular cymes, calyx 4-parted, corolla usually yellow, sometimes purple, often variously spotted, 2-lipped, saccate, upper lip small and more or less pouched, lower lip, in cult. forms, very large and inflated and somewhat slipperlike, stamens 2; fr. a caps.

Plants cultivated in greenhouses in the North and in the open in warmer regions. The herbaceous calceolarias are grown from seeds sown from late spring to early autumn for plants for the next winter and spring. Soil should be finely sifted, preferably containing leafmold. Seeds should be watered carefully as they are very small; subirrigation is the best method. A temperature of 60° F. is recommended, and no direct sun till the plants are rather large. The shrubby types are grown from seeds, or from cuttings of firm wood. These are usually taken when plants are trimmed in later summer or early autumn, cut down to two joints, and given a temperature of 45–50° F. and protection from the sun.

biflora Lam. Herbaceous per.; lvs. in a basal rosette, ovate or spatulate, to 2½ in. long, toothed; corolla yellow, ½ in. long, ¾ in. across. Chile and Argentina.

crenatiflora Cav. Stout, pubescent, per. herbs, to 2½ ft.; lvs. ovate, to 8 in. long, coarsely toothed; basal lvs. petioled, st. lvs. becoming smaller and sessile toward upper part of st.; fls. drooping, corolla to 1 in. long and across, yellow, lower lip with orange-brown spots, inflated, crenate. Chile. Much grown by florists in different races; probably the parent of cvs. sometimes known collectively as *C. herbeohybrida* Voss [*C. hybrida* Hort.], with plant usually dwarf or small, 2 ft. or less, fls. with large inflated pouches of many colors.

Darwinii Benth. Low, glabrous, cespitose per.; lvs. oblong, to 3 in. long, minutely toothed and wavy, glossy; fls. solitary, on scapes 6 in. long, corolla to 1 in. wide, yellow, with large reddish-brown spots and waxy-white bar across lower lip. Patagonia. Said to be hardy on Pacific Coast, n. to Vancouver, B.C.

fruticohybrida: see *C. integrifolia.*

gracilis: *C. tripartita.*

grandiflora Penn. Pubescent, loose, scrambling herb, to about 7 ft.; lvs. ovate, 3–5 in. long, toothed, petiole winged, the wings connate-perfoliate; corolla yellow, 1¼ in. long. Ecuador. Not known to be in cult.; material cult. as *C. grandiflora* or *C. grandiflora tigrina* is probably *C. crenatiflora.*

herbeohybrida: see *C. crenatiflora.*

hybrida: see *C. crenatiflora.*

integrifolia J. Murr. [*C. rugosa* Ruiz & Pav.]. Becoming a subshrub, sts. woody, to 6 ft.; lvs. oblong or elliptic, to 3 in. long, crenate-serrate, rugose; corolla yellow to red-brown, spotted, ½ in. across. Chile. Common under glass or planted out. Cv. 'Stewartii' [*C. Stewartii* Hort.] is listed. Some forms cult. under this name are probably hybrids of obscure derivation; the name *C. fruticohybrida* Voss has been applied to these.

mexicana Benth. Glandular-hairy ann., to 1½ ft.; lower lvs. 3-parted or -lobed, upper lvs. pinnate, to 2½ in. long or more, segms. ovate, toothed; corolla pale yellow, ½ in. long and ¼ in. across. Mex. and Cent. Amer.

multiflora Cav. Low shrub; lvs. ovate, to ½ in. long, toothed; fls. 3–4 in terminal clusters, corolla yellow, to ⅜ in. long. Peru. The material listed in the trade as *C. multiflora nana* or *C. hybrida multiflora nana* is probably a small-fld., floriferous form of *C. crenatiflora.*

pinnata L. Pubescent ann., to 3 ft.; lvs. pinnate, to 3 in. long; corolla pale yellow, ½ in. long and across. Peru, Chile, Bolivia.

polyrrhiza Cav. Sparsely hairy, dwarf, tufted per., to 2 in.; lvs. crowded, basal, lanceolate, to 2½ in. long; fls. solitary, on scapes to 4 in. long, corolla yellow, spotted purple, 1 in. long and ½ in. across. Chile. One of the hardiest sp., grown with protection in N.Y.

rugosa: *C. integrifolia.*

scabiosifolia: *C. tripartita.*

Stewartii: *C. integrifolia* cv.

tenella Poepp. & Endl. Sparsely hairy, low, creeping subshrub, to 8 in.; lvs. broadly ovate, to ½ in. long, remotely toothed, glossy, very short-petioled to almost sessile; fls. usually 2–3 on peduncles to 6 in. long, corolla yellow, spotted orange-red inside, to ½ in. long. Chile. Hardy on Pacific Coast, if protected.

tigrina Hort. Material cult. under this name is probably a strain of *C. crenatiflora.*

tomentosa Ruiz & Pav. Per. herb, to 3 ft. or more; lvs. triangular-ovate, to 6 in. long, petiole winged, the wings perfoliate, doubly dentate; fls. yellow, 1½ in. long and across. Peru.

tripartita Ruiz & Pav. [*C. gracilis* HBK; *C. scabiosifolia* Roem. & Schult.]. Glandular-pubescent, much-branched ann., to 2 ft.; lvs. variously pinnatisect or pinnate, to 8 in. long, bases of petioles connate-perfoliate, lfts. or segms. in 2–3 pairs, ovate to lanceolate, toothed or cut; fls. pale yellow, ½ in. long and ⅜ in. across. Colombia to Chile. An extremely variable sp.

CALENDULA L. *Compositae* (Calendula Tribe). About 15 spp. of more or less glandular-pubescent ann. or per. herbs, sometimes shrubs, native from the Canary Is. through s. and cent. Eur. and N. Afr. to Iran; lvs. alt., simple; fl. heads solitary, on terminal peduncles, radiate, involucral bracts imbricate in 1–2 rows, often with scarious margins, receptacle naked or rarely sparsely bristly; disc fls. tubular, bisexual, sterile, ray fls. commonly ligulelike, female, fertile; achenes incurved, glabrous, sometimes prickly on back, pappus absent.

Calendulas are of easy culture in the greenhouse as well as in the border. Propagated quickly from seeds, and special color types by cuttings.

arvensis L. FIELD MARIGOLD. Ann., to 1 ft., sts. ascending, finely glandular-pubescent; lvs. lanceolate to oblong-lanceolate or narrowly oblanceolate, to 2¾ in. long, entire to remotely toothed, middle and upper lvs. sessile, lower short-petioled; heads to 1½ in. across; ray fls. yellow; achenes from strongly incurved to almost a complete circle, strongly muricate on back. Cent. Eur. and Medit. region; established in waste places in Calif. and elsewhere.

officinalis L. POT MARIGOLD. Coarse, much-branched ann., to 2 ft.; lvs. oblong to oblong-obovate, entire to remotely toothed, more or less clasping; heads 1½–4 in. across, closing at night; ray fls. pale yellow to deep orange; achenes mostly boat-shaped, muricate. S. Eur.; occasionally escapes from gardens in Calif. A favorite garden ann., blooming for the entire season and enduring several frosts and light snow in autumn; grown under glass for cut fls. in winter; also used medicinally. Cv. 'Chrysantha'. Fls. double, buttercup-yellow.

CALIMERIS: see *BOLTONIA.*

CALLA L. *Araceae.* One sp., a hardy, per. herb, growing in bogs in N. Temp. Zone, sts. prostate; lvs. simple; spathe open, spadix subtended by spathe, short, covered with bisexual fls., perianth absent. The florist's or garden calla or calla lily is a sp. of *Zantedeschia.*

Sometimes transplanted to pond margins and wet places.

palustris L. WATER ARUM, WILD C., WATER-DRAGON. Lf. blades ovate-cordate, to 6 in. long and nearly as wide, petioles to 10 in. long; spathe green outside, white inside, about 2 in. long and 1½ in. wide, spadix much shorter; berries red. Midsummer. Temp. N. Amer., Eur., Asia.

picta: *Aglaonema pictum.*

CALLIANDRA Benth. POWDERPUFF. *Leguminosae* (subfamily *Mimosoideae*). About 150 spp. or more of trop. shrubs and trees; lvs. alt., 2-pinnate; fls. in globose heads, regular, 5-merous, petals small, stamens 10–100, long, conspicuous; fr. a flat legume, with thickened margins.

Grown for their showy flowers outdoors in tropical and subtropical regions and in greenhouses in the North. Propagated by cuttings over bottom heat when seeds are not available.

anomala (Kunth) Macbr. Distinguished from *C. Houstoniana* by having lvs. with usually 15–20 pairs of pinnae, and lfts. rounded or very obtuse and not curved. Mex.

brevipes Benth. Lvs. short-petioled, with 1 pair of pinnae, lfts. many, oblong-linear, ⁵⁄₃₂ in. long, curved; heads solitary, short-peduncled; fls. 1 in. long, stamens red toward apex. Brazil.

calothyrsus Meissn. Distinguished from *C. Houstoniana* by being nearly glabrous, and having lvs. with usually 15–20 pairs of pinnae, lfts. rounded or very obtuse, not curved, and corolla glabrous. Mex. to n. S. Amer.

confusa T. Sprague & Riley. Shrub, rarely a tree to 18 ft., scarcely branched; lvs. with about 15 pairs of pinnae, lfts. many, linear; petals green, inconspicuous, stamens purple-red, 1½ in. long. Cent. Amer.

emarginata (Humb. & Bonpl.) Benth. Low, dense shrub, or tree to 15 ft.; lvs with 1 pair of pinnae, each with 3 lfts., these oblong or obovate, to 2 in. long, sometimes emarginate; heads solitary; petals to ¼ in. long, stamens bright red, 1 in. long. S. Mex. to Honduras.

eriophylla Benth. MOCK MESQUITE, MESQUITILLA, FAIRY-DUSTER. Low, woody shrub, to 1½ ft. or more; lvs. less than 1 in. long, usually with 2–3 pairs of pinnae, lfts. many, to ⁵⁄₃₂ in. long, pubescent beneath; heads axillary, few-fld.; fls. red-purple, pubescent; fr. densely pubescent. W. Tex. to se. Calif.; Mex.

Guildingii Benth. Unarmed tree, to 30 ft.; lvs. with 1 pair of pinnae, lfts. 3–4 pairs, the uppermost largest, to 4 in. long, and 1¼ in. wide; heads solitary; petals greenish-white, stamens 10, crimson, to 3 in. long. Trinidad and St. Vincent.

haematocephala Hassk. [*C. inaequilatera* Rusby]. RED P. Shrub, or small tree to about 16 ft.; lvs. with 2 pairs of pinnae, lfts. (4-)5–8(-10) pairs on each pinna, terminal lfts. largest, to 3⅜ in. long, heads about 2 in. in diam.; fls. bisexual or functionally male, corolla reddish, stamens about 25, filaments white basally, red toward apex, united basally in a tube, as long as or longer than corolla, with an irregular fringe internally; fr. linear-oblanceolate, to 4¾ in. long. Bolivia.

haematoma Benth. Straggling shrub, or low spreading tree to 12 ft.; lvs. with 1 pair of pinnae, lfts. few, oblong, ¼ in. long; heads axillary, mostly solitary; stamens purple, 1 in. long; fr. tomentose. Jamaica, Hispaniola, Bahama Is.

Houstoniana (Mill.) Standl. Slender shrub, to 10 ft., sts., petioles, and rachises rusty-hairy; lvs. with 7–12 pairs of pinnae, lfts. 30–40 pairs, oblong-linear, somewhat curved, to ¼ in. long, acute; heads clustered at intervals along rachis in terminal, racemelike infl. to 14 in. long; fls. to 2 in. long, perianth rusty-hairy, stamens purple-red; fr. to 4¾ in. long, densely brown-hispid. S. Mex. to Honduras.

inaequilatera: *C. haematocephala.*

portoricensis (Jacq.) Benth. Shrub, or tree to 20 ft.; lvs. with 2–6 pairs of pinnae, lfts. oblong-linear, to ⅝ in. long; heads axillary; corolla green, very short, stamens many, white, to ¾ in. long; fr. to 5 in. long. W. Indies, s. Mex. to Panama.

surinamensis Benth. Spreading shrub; lvs. with 1 pair of pinnae, lfts. 8–12 pairs, oblong-lanceolate, about ½ in. long; heads axillary; stamens rose apically. Guyana and Brazil.

Tweedii Benth. [*Inga pulcherrima* Cerv. ex Sweet]. MEXICAN FLAMEBUSH. To 6 ft.; lvs. with 3–4 pairs of pinnae, lfts. many, oblong-linear, ⁵⁄₃₂ in. long; heads solitary; calyx and corolla yellowish-green, villous, stamens red; fr. to 2 in. long, villous. Brazil.

CALLIANTHEMUM C. A. Mey. *Ranunculaceae.* Several spp. of mostly low, glabrous, per. herbs of high mts. of Eur. and Asia, with short, heavy rhizomes; sts. 1 or more, naked or with 1–2 small, dissected lvs.; basal lvs. long-petioled, somewhat glaucous, decompound, repeatedly pinnatifid; fls. 1–3, terminal, white or rose, sepals 5 or 10, deciduous, petals 5–15, showy, yellowish at base, with basal nectaries, stamens many, pistils usually 6.

Occasional in the trade as a rock garden or low border plant suited to cool climates. Difficult to grow from seeds.

angustifolium Witasek. Like *C. coriandrifolium,* but having lvs. narrower, elliptic in outline, with 3–4 pairs of pinnae, the lowest considerably shorter than half the lf. length; fls. 1–1½ in. across, sepals rose, petals white. Siberia.

coriandrifolium Rchb. St. single, mostly 2–8 in.; basal lvs. developing before or with fls., ovate, with 2–3 pairs of pinnae, the lowest about half the lf. length; fls. white, ½–1¼ in. across, nectaries broad-ovate, white. Pyrenees to Bosnia.

rutifolium (L.) C. A. Mey. [*Ranunculus anemonoides* Zahlbr.]. Like *C. coriandrifolium,* but basal lvs. developing after fls.; nectaries narrow, reddish. Tyrol.

CALLICARPA L. BEAUTYBERRY. *Verbenaceae.* About 135 spp. of polygamous, deciduous or evergreen shrubs and trees, often with stellate or scurfy pubescence, native to tropics and subtropics of Asia, Australia, N. and Cent. Amer.; lvs. opp., simple, entire or toothed, often acuminate; fls. pink, bluish, red, purple, or whitish, in axillary cymes, calyx 4-toothed, rarely 4-parted or 5-toothed, corolla 4-lobed or rarely 5-parted, stamens 4 or rarely 5, ovary 4-celled, 4-ovuled; fr. drupaceous.

Callicarpas can be grown in a light airy place in the greenhouse in a compost of loam and peat. Propagated by cuttings, layers, and seeds. They are raised for both the ornamental flowers and clusters of colored fruits. Those from northerly regions may be hardy in Zone 5, and if the tops die back, new shoots usually bloom and fruit.

americana L. FRENCH MULBERRY, BEAUTYBERRY. Shrub, to 6 ft.; lvs. elliptic-ovate to ovate-oblong, to 6 in. long, toothed, white- or rusty-tomentose beneath, to 6 in. long, toothed, white- or early summer. Va. to Tex. and W. Indies. Zone 7. Var. **lactea** F. J. Muell. [var. *alba* Rehd.]. Fr. white.

Bodinieri Lév. [*C. Giraldiana* Hesse var. *subcanescens* Rehd.]. Shrub, to 10 ft.; lvs. elliptic to elliptic-ovate or lanceolate-oblong, to 5 in. long, toothed, pubescent beneath; cymes dense, to 1½ in. across; fls. lilac; fr. violet. Summer. Cent. and w. China. Zone 5. Var. **Giraldii** (Hesse ex Rehd.) Rehd. [*C. Giraldiana* Hesse]. Glabrescent.

dichotoma (Lour.) C. Koch. [*C. koreana* Hort. Vilm.-Andr.; *C. purpurea* Juss.]. Shrub, to 4 ft.; lvs. elliptic or obovate, to 3 in. long, toothed

above the middle; fls. pink; fr. lilac-violet. Summer. E. and cent. China, Japan; sparingly naturalized in e. U.S. Zone 5.

Giraldiana: *C. Bodinieri* var. *Giraldii.* Var. **subcanescens:** *C. Bodinieri.*

japonica Thunb. Shrub, to 5 ft., lvs. elliptic to ovate-lanceolate, to 5 in. long, long-acuminate, finely toothed; fls. pink or whitish; fr. violet. Summer. Japan, Taiwan, China. Zone 5. Var. **angustata** Rehd. Lvs. narrower. Cv. 'Leucocarpa'. Fr. white.

koreana: *C. dichotoma.*

longifolia Lam. Shrub, to 15 ft.; lvs. oblong-lanceolate or oblong, to 8 in. long, long-acuminate, toothed toward apex, pubescent beneath; fls. rose or purple; fr. white or dark pink. Himalayas and Japan, s. to Philippine Is., Malay Pen., Java, trop. Australia.

Loureiri Hook. & Arn. Shrub, to 12 ft., branchlets densely hairy, conspicuously 4-angled; lvs. 4-ranked, elliptic, to 9½ in. long, toothed except at base, densely pubescent beneath; fls. pinkish-purple, China, Japan, Taiwan.

mollis Siebold & Zucc. [*C. Shirasawana* Mak.]. Shrub; lvs. lanceolate to oblong or elliptic, to 5 in. long, sharply toothed except at base and apex, densely hairy beneath; fls. purplish-rose; fr. violet-purple. Japan and Korea.

nudiflora Hook. & Arn. Shrub or tree, to 30 ft.; lvs. oblong or elliptic-oblong, varying to oblong-lanceolate, to 9 in. long, acute or acuminate, toothed except at base, pubescent beneath, densely resinous-dotted; cymes to 6 in. across; fls. red or purple; fr. blue. China, India, Malay Pen.

pedunculata R. Br. Shrub; lvs. 4-ranked, oblong or oblong-elliptic, to 6 in. long, sharply toothed except at apex and base, densely hairy on both sides; fr. purple or deep lilac to white. India, Malay Arch., to trop. Australia.

purpurea: *C. dichotoma.*

Shirasawana: *C. mollis.*

vestita Wallich ex C. B. Clarke. Tree, to 30 ft.; lvs. ovate, to 10 in. long, nearly entire, white-hairy beneath; fls. pinkish to pale purple. Nepal, Sikkim, ne. India.

CALLICOMA Andr. *Cunoniaceae.* One sp., an evergreen shrub or small tree, native to Australia; lvs. opp., simple; fls. small, in many-fld. globular heads, sepals 4–5, petals 0, stamens 8–15, filaments long, ovary superior, styles 2, filamentous; fr. a caps.

serratifolia Andr. To 40 ft.; lvs. oblong to ovate-lanceolate, to 4 in. long, coarsely toothed, glossy above, tomentose beneath; stamens much exserted. Queensland and New S. Wales.

CALLICORE: *AMARYLLIS.* C. rosea: *A. Belladonna.*

CALLIOPSIS: *COREOPSIS.* Calliopsis Drummondii: *Coreopsis basalis.* Calliopsis bicolor: *Coreopsis tinctoria.*

CALLIPRORA: *TRITELEIA.*

CALLIRHOE Nutt. POPPY MALLOW. *Malvaceae.* About 8 spp. of ann. or per. herbs in the U.S. and n. Mex., the per. herbs with a thickened taproot and several spreading to ascending sts.; basal lvs. few, mostly more or less orbicular, st. lvs. smaller, usually more deeply and narrowly lobed; fls. solitary or few in axils of upper lvs., involucral bracts 3 or 0, petals white to deep red-purple, apically truncate, mostly erose, stamens united in a tubular column, style brs. filiform, stigmatic on inner edge, as many as the mericarps; fr. a schizocarp, mericarps 10–25, in a single whorl, each apically rounded or short-beaked, sometimes slightly dehiscent, with small upper sterile cell and 1-seeded lower cell.

Seeds should be sown where the plants are to stand; the perennials may also be propagated by division.

alcaeoides (Michx.) A. Gray. Resembles *C. digitata,* but with strigose pubescence, especially the pedicels and mericarps, lf. divisions mostly unlobed or only 3-lobed; pedicels usually less than 2 in. long at flowering; fls. mostly white. Spring. Ill. to Nebr., s. to Tenn. and Tex.

digitata Nutt. Glabrous or sparsely pubescent per., 1–4 ft.; lvs. suborbicular in outline, usually divided to the base into 3–9, pinnately parted divisions; involucral bracts 0, fls. mostly solitary, on pedicels up to 6 in. long or more, white to purple-red, 1–2 in. across; mericarps rugose, glabrous. Spring–early summer. Mo. and Kan., s. to Ark. and Tex.

involucrata (Torr. & A. Gray) A. Gray. POPPY MALLOW. Mostly hirsute, procumbent per., about 1 ft.; lvs. orbicular in outline, deeply

5-, or 7-parted, the divisions oblanceolate to obovate, lobed or incised, stipules commonly ½–1 in. long; involucral bracts mostly linear-lanceolate, ½–1 in. long, borne at the base of the calyx, fls. solitary, erect on elongate pedicels, deep red or paler, to 2½ in. across. Spring–early summer. Mo. to Wyo., s. to Tex.

Papaver (Cav.) A. Gray. Closely resembling *C. involucrata*, but having lf. divisions unlobed or with only 1 or 2 teeth, stipules less than ½ in. long, involucral bracts usually less than ⅜ in. long and one usually borne about ⅛ in. beneath the calyx. Spring–early summer. Ga. and Fla. to Tex.

triangulata (Leavenw.) A. Gray. Harshly stellate-pubescent per., 2–3 ft.; basal lvs. mostly triangular, acute, truncate to nearly sagittate at base, crenate, upper lvs. narrower, sometimes cleft; involucral bracts spatulate or obovate, fls. crowded at the ends of axillary peduncles, deep purple, about 2 in. across. Summer. Ind. to Wisc., s. to Nebr. and Mo.

CALLISIA L. [*Spironema* Lindl.]. INCH PLANT. *Commelinaceae*. About 8 spp. of creeping, sprawling, or suberect herbs of trop. Amer.; lvs. cordate to oblong-lanceolate, sheathing at base; brs., when present, emerging from orifice of lf. sheath; infl. of sessile, paired cincinni, in axils of lvs. or bracts toward end of st.; fls. sometimes fragrant, sepals 3, chaffy, petals 3, equal, white, pink, or blue, stamens 3–6, those opp. the petals longer than the others or the only ones present, filaments glabrous, anthers with broad connectives, ovary 2–3-celled, each cell with 2 ovules, style filiform, stigma brushlike or somewhat capitate; fr. a caps.

Grown mostly under glass or indoors. Propagated by seeds and cuttings.

elegans Alexand. ex H. E. Moore. STRIPED I.P. Densely puberulent throughout, sts. ascending, to 2 ft.; lvs. ovate to broadly lanceolate, to 3 in. long, 1⅛ in. wide, dark green, striped with silvery-white above, generally purple beneath; infl. unbranched or with short basal brs.; fls. white, petals longer than sepals, stamens 6, stigma brushlike. S. Mex. Has been erroneously listed as *Setcreasea striata*.

fragrans (Lindl.) Woodson [*Spironema fragrans* Lindl.]. Sts. fleshy, to 3 ft., loose, branched, bearing long stolons at base; lvs. elliptic-lanceolate, to 10 in. long, 1½ in. wide; infl. branched; fls. fragrant, white, petals not much longer than sepals, stamens 6, stigma brushlike. Mex. Makes a good basket plant. Sometimes cult. as *Tradescantia dracaenoides*. Cv. 'Melnickoff'. Lvs. inconstantly striped in white or pale yellow. Has been offered erroneously as *Spironema Melnickoffii*.

tehuantepecana Matuda. Similar to *C. elegans*, but lvs. green, lanceolate, fls. bright pink. S. Mex.

CALLISTEMON R. Br. BOTTLEBRUSH. *Myrtaceae*. About 20 spp. of shrubs or small trees, in Australia; lvs. alt., simple, entire; fls. red or yellow, in showy heads or spikes, the long-exserted stamens making the infl. resemble a bottlebrush, stamens many, separate or rarely shortly united in a basal ring, calyx tube ovoid, campanulate, or urceolate, calyx lobes and petals 5, deciduous; fr. a caps. embedded in enlarged calyx tube, dehiscent at top. Closely resembles *Melaleuca*, but has the stamens separate or united only at the base. The spp. closely resemble each others and are difficult to differentiate, particularly since hybrids apparently occur both in the wild and in cult.

Suitable for cultivation in the milder parts of the Pacific Coast states, particularly Calif. Heavy pruning every three years is recommended for maximum flowering. The species are not particular as to soil requirements, some thriving in moist soils and others being very tolerant of dry conditions. Propagated by seeds or hardwood cuttings. Seeds are gathered in summer by allowing the capsule to open in boxes or on sheets of paper and are sown the next spring.

acuminatus Cheel. To 10 ft., with silky hairs on young shoots and infl., few persisting on older brs. and midrib of lvs.; lvs. broad-lanceolate, to 4 in. long, acuminate, undulate, lateral venation and intramarginal veins somewhat prominent, oil glands scattered or sometimes not visible; spikes dense; fls. dark crimson, calyx tube and persistent calyx lobes covered with silky hairs, petals hairy; frs. depressed-globose, to ⅜ in. across, more or less pubescent. New S. Wales. May be confused with *C. citrinus*.

australis: *C. salignus* var. *australis*.

brachyandrus Lindl. To 6 ft., soft hairs on young brs. sometimes persisting; lvs. narrow-linear, to 1½ in. long, rigid, cylindrical or slightly flattened or channelled; spikes to 3 in. long; fls. rose-pink, stamens ¼ in. long, anthers yellow. New S. Wales and Victoria. Tolerant of semiarid conditions.

citrinus (Curtis) Stapf [*C. lanceolatus* (Sm.) DC.]. CRIMSON B. Shrub or small tree, to 25 ft., young brs. silky-hairy; lvs. lanceolate, sometimes broadly so, to 3 in. long, somewhat rigid, glabrous, lateral veins, midrib and oil glands prominent; spikes to 4 in. long; fls. crimson, calyx tube pubescent, becoming glabrous, stamens to 1 in. long, anthers dark red; fr. depressed-globose, to ⅜ in. across, glabrous. Se. Australia. Zone 9. The most commonly used and showiest sp. Cv. 'Splendens' [var. *splendens* Stapf]. Lvs. linear-lanceolate; spikes cylindrical, dense.

coccineus: *C. macropunctatus*.

Cunninghamii C. Koch. Name of uncertain application, used for a garden plant.

hybridus: a listed name of no botanical standing.

lanceolatus: *C. citrinus*.

lilacinus Cheel. Name of uncertain application, used for a plant with lavender stamens.

linearifolius (Link) DC. Lvs. linear to linear-lanceolate, to 5½ in. long, lateral veins not reaching margin; spikes to 5 in. long; fls. red; fr. ¼ in. across. New S. Wales. Similar to *C. rigidus*, but having lvs. somewhat broader and lateral veins not reaching margins.

linearis (Schrad. & J. C. Wendl.) DC. To 9 ft.; lvs. linear, to 5 in. long, channelled, often pungent; spikes to 4 in. long; fls. red, stamens to 1 in. long. New S. Wales. Zone 9.

macropunctatus (Dum.-Cours.) Court [*Callistemon coccineus* F. J. Muell.; *C. rugulosus* (Willd. ex Link) DC.]. To 12 ft., glabrous except the young silky-hairy lvs.; lvs. narrow-lanceolate, to 2¼ in. long, rigid, pungent, more or less punctate, midrib and margins thickened; spikes to 4 in. long; fls. red, stamens to 1 in. long; fr. globular-truncate, to ¼ in. across. S. Australia. Zone 9.

paludosus: *C. salignus* var. *australis*.

parviflorus: a listed name of no botanical standing.

phoeniceus Lindl. To 8 ft.; lvs. narrow-lanceolate, to 4 in. long, thick, lateral veins not visible; spikes to 4 in. long, not dense; fls. red, stamens to 1 in. long. W. Australia. Resembles *C. citrinus*, but has lvs. thicker, without conspicuous veins. A prostrate form is listed.

pinifolius (J. C. Wendl.) DC. To 6 ft.; lvs. linear-filiform, to 4 in. long, cylindrical, more or less distinctly channelled above, punctate; spikes to 2½ in. long; fls. greenish-yellow, stamens to 1 in. long; fr. globose, to ¼ in. across. New S. Wales. Cv. 'Viridis'. Fls. bright green.

pumilus: a listed name of no botanical standing.

rigidus R. Br. To 15 ft.; lvs. linear, to 5 in. long, flat, not channelled, acute-acuminate; spikes to 4 in. long; fls. red, stamens to 1 in. long. New S. Wales. Zone 9. Similar to *C. linearifolius*, but having lateral veins reaching lf. margins and forming distinct ridges.

rugulosus: *C. macropunctatus*.

salignus (Sm.) DC. To 15 ft., or sometimes a small tree to 30 ft.; lvs. narrow-lanceolate, to 3 in. long, midrib, lateral veins and margins prominent; spikes to 3 in. long; fls. pale yellow or pink, stamens to ½ in. long, anthers yellow-green; fr. ovoid-truncate, to ¼ in. across. New S. Wales and S. Australia. Zone 9. Var. **australis** Benth. [*C. australis* (Benth.) Cheel; *C. paludosus* (Schlechtend.) F. J. Muell.; *Melaleuca paludosa* Schlechtend., not R. Br. ex Ait.]. Lvs. with lateral veins almost invisible. E. and S. Australia.

speciosus (Sims) DC. [*Metrosideros speciosus* Sims, not Colenso]. Shrub or small tree, to 20 ft.; lvs. lanceolate, to 3 in. long, midrib and lateral veins prominent; spikes to 6 in. long, dense; fls. scarlet-red, stamens to 1 in. long, filaments shortly united at the base; fr. globose, to ¼ in. across. W. Australia. Zone 9. Does well in Fla., where it is sometimes incorrectly known as *Melaleuca genistifolia*.

villosus: a listed name of no botanical standing.

viminalis (Soland. ex Gaertn.) Cheel. WEEPING B. Tree, to 20 ft. or more, with graceful weeping habit; lvs. lanceolate, to 4 in. long, punctate, bronze-green when young; spikes to 3 in. long, dense; fls. scarlet-red, stamens to 1 in. long, filaments shortly united at base; fr. globose, to ¼ in. across. New S. Wales. Its weeping habit is distinctive. Common in Fla., occasional in Calif.

violaceus: a listed name of no botanical standing, used for a plant to 12 ft. with violet fls.

CALLISTEPHUS Cass. *Compositae* (Aster Tribe). One sp., a late summer- and autumn-blooming, strongly scented ann. herb, native to China; sts. erect, rather stiff; lvs. alt.; fl. heads usually radiate, large, solitary, terminal on the brs., involucral bracts in several rows, the outer herbaceous, the inner membranous-scarious, receptacle pitted, naked; disc fls. bisexual, fertile, yellow, ray fls. female, of various shades of violet to rose or white; achenes compressed, pappus of 2 rows of bristles.

Grown from seeds; for early bloom seed is sown indoors in late spring, but the main crop may be sown directly in the open.

chinensis (L.) Nees [*Aster sinensis* Hoffm.]. CHINA ASTER, ANNUAL A. Erect, to 2½ ft., sts. branching, hispid-hairy; lf. blades broadly ovate to triangular-ovate, to 3½ in. long, sometimes longer, deeply and irregularly toothed, decurrent to the petiole, upper lvs. spatulate; heads showy, to 5 in. across; disc fls. yellow, ray fls. in 1–2 rows in wild plants. China. There are many cvs., varying in height, season of bloom, and composition of the head; the ray fls. may be very numerous, and frequently replace most of the disc fls., showing a wide range in size, shape, and color—violet, purple, blue, red, rose, pink, white, and even pale yellow.

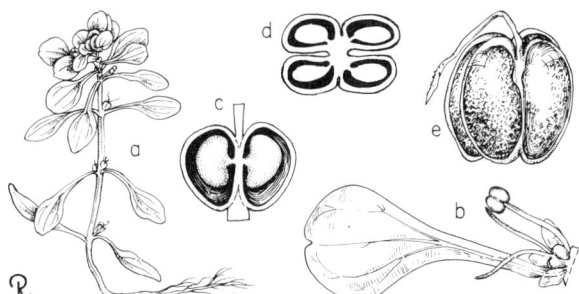

CALLITRICHACEAE. *Callitriche heterophylla:* **a,** flowering stem, × 1; **b,** leaf with axillary male flower and female flower and bracts, × 5; **c,** ovary, vertical section, × 25; **d,** ovary, cross section, × 25; **e,** fruit, × 15. (From Lawrence, *Taxonomy of Vascular Plants.*)

CALLITRICHACEAE Link. WATER STARWORT FAMILY. Dicot.; 1 genus, *Callitriche*, of weak-stemmed, monoecious, aquatic or terrestrial herbs, essentially cosmopolitan in distribution; sts. delicate; lvs. simple, opp., entire, without stipules; fls. unisexual, usually solitary, axillary, perianth none, stamen 1, pistil 1, ovary superior, 2-lobed, 2-carpelled, styles 2; fr. separating into 2 or 4 segms. when mature.

CALLITRICHE L. WATER STARWORT, WATER CHICK-WEED. *Callitrichaceae*. About 26 spp.; characteristics those of the family.

Sometimes grown in aquaria.

autumnalis: *C. hermaphroditica.*

hamulata: *C. intermedia* subsp.

hermaphroditica L. [*C. autumnalis* L.]. Plant submersed, sts. to 20 in., branched; lvs. linear-lanceolate, to ¾ in. long, metallic-green with white margins; fr. about 1⁄16 in. in diam., compressed, narrowly winged, irregularly pitted. N. Amer., Eur.

heterophylla Pursh. Aquatic, sts. to 10 in. long; floating lvs. obovate, ¼ in. long, submersed lvs. linear; fr. somewhat heart-shaped in outline. Widespread in N. and Cent. Amer.

intermedia Hoffm. Sts. to 2½ ft.; lower lvs. submersed, linear, to 1 in. long, emarginate, upper lvs. in floating rosette, narrowly oblanceolate-spatulate, to 1 in. long; fr. subglobose, to about 1⁄16 in. in diam. Iceland, Greenland, Eur. Subsp. **hamulata** (Kütz. ex W. D. J. Koch) Clapham [*C. hamulata* Kütz. ex W. D. J. Koch]. Lvs. wider toward apex, more deeply emarginate; fr. more ellipsoidal, sessile. Eur., Greenland.

palustris: *C. verna.*

stagnalis Scop. Sts. to 2 ft.; lower lvs. submersed, elliptic or spatulate, upper lvs. in floating rosette, elliptic to orbicular, to ¾ in. long; fr. subglobose, about 1⁄16 in. in diam. S. Eur., N. Afr., Canary Is.

verna L. [*C. palustris* L.]. Sts. to 10 in.; submersed lvs. linear, upper lvs. in floating rosette, lf. blades obovate, to ¼ in. long, petioles ¼ in. long; fr. obovoid, winged toward apex. N. Amer., Eur., Asia.

CALLITRIS Venten. CYPRESS PINE. *Cupressaceae*. Sixteen spp. of coniferous, evergreen, monoecious shrubs or trees, native to Australia and Tasmania; branchlets jointed, mostly angled; lvs. scalelike, appressed in alternating whorls of 3; male cones catkinlike, ovoid or cylindrical, female cones woody, scales 6–8, unequal, whorled, seeds 2–9 on each scale, broadly 1–3-winged.

Useful in arid regions of Zone 10. For culture see *Conifers.*

arenosa: *C. columellaris.*

calcarata: *C. Endlicheri.*

columellaris F. J. Muell. [*C. arenosa* A. Cunn. ex R. T. Bak. & H. G. Sm.; *C. glauca* R. Br. ex R. T. Bak. & H. G. Sm.]. WHITE C. P. To 60 ft., branchlets in thick clusters; lvs. rounded dorsally, green or greenish-blue to glaucous; female cones solitary, on slender branchlets, ovoid to depressed-globose, to ¾ in. in diam., scales separating nearly to base at maturity. Australia.

cupressiformis: *C. rhomboidea.*

cupressoides: *Widdringtonia cupressoides.*

Endlicheri (Parl.) F. M. Bailey [*C. calcarata* R. Br. ex F. M. Bailey]. BLACK C.P., RED C.P. To 80 ft.; lvs. prominently keeled dorsally, green or glaucous, about 1⁄8 in. long; female cones solitary or clustered on slender branchlets, ovoid to globose, to ¾ in. in diam., scales with small dorsal point. Se. Australia.

glauca: *C. columellaris.*

Muelleri (Parl.) F. J. Muell. MUELLER'S C.P. To less than 50 ft., or shrubby with fastigiate brs.; lvs. keeled dorsally, usually 1⁄8–3⁄8 in. long, dark green; female cones solitary or clustered on branchlets, depressed-globose, to 1¼ in. in diam., scales with small dorsal point. Se. Australia.

quadrivalvis: *Tetraclinis articulata.*

Preissii Miq. [*C. robusta* (A. Cunn. ex Parl.) R. Br. ex F. M. Bailey]. ROTTNEST ISLAND PINE. Tree or shrub; lvs. usually about 1⁄8 in. long, rounded dorsally; female cones solitary, or several on stout, often clustered branchlets, ovoid to depressed-globose, to 1⅜ in. in diam., scales not separating near the base at maturity. Se. Australia. Subsp. **Preissii.** The typical subsp.; female cones usually 1 in. in diam. or more. Subsp. **verrucosa** (A. Cunn. ex Endl.) J. Gard. [*C. verrucosa* (A. Cunn. ex Endl.) F. J. Muell.]. MALLEE PINE. Female cones usually less than 1 in. in diam.

rhomboidea R. Br. ex L. Rich. [*C. cupressiformis* F. J. Muell.; *C. tasmanica* (Benth.) R. T. Bak. & H. G. Sm.]. OYSTER BAY PINE, PORT JACKSON P. To 40 ft. or less, or shrubby; lvs. keeled dorsally, to 1⁄8 in. long, often glaucous; female cones usually several, on clustered branchlets, ovoid to depressed-globose, to ¾ in. in diam., scales with short, broadly conical, dorsal protuberances. Se. Australia, Tasmania.

robusta: *C. Preissii.*

tasmanica: *C. rhomboidea.*

verrucosa: *C. Preissii* subsp.

CALLOPSIS Engl. *Araceae*. One sp., a per. herb, native to Afr.; lvs. arising from short rhizomes, cordate, petioles long; infl. long-peduncled, spathe expanded; fls. unisexual, spadix subtended by spathe and shorter, the lower (female) part united to spathe on one side, perianth absent.

Propagated by division or seeds; plants thrive in soil high in organic matter kept evenly moist, in diffuse sunlight, but will not tolerate low humidity.

Volkensii Engl. MINIATURE CALLA. To 10 in.; lf. blades ovate, to 5½ in. long and 3 in. wide, obtuse-apiculate at apex, rugose; peduncle to 7 in. long, spathe white, ovate-elliptic, to 1¼ in. long, spadix shorter, yellow. Tanzania.

CALLUNA Salisb. HEATHER, SCOTCH H., LING. *Ericaceae*. One sp., an evergreen shrub, native to Eur. and Asia Minor and adventive in N. Amer.; lvs. opp., 4-ranked; fls. in terminal, one-sided, spikelike racemes, calyx 4-lobed, colored, corolla campanulate, shorter than calyx, stamens 8, ovary superior; fr. a caps.

Culture as for *Erica.*

vulgaris (L.) Hull [*Erica vulgaris* L.]. To 3 ft.; lvs. scalelike, overlapping; infl to 10 in. long; fls. purplish-pink, corolla and calyx persistent. Summer, early autumn. Bee plant. Zone 5. There are many cvs.: **'Alba'** [cvs. 'Elata', 'Minima', 'Minor', 'Pilosa', 'Rigida', 'Tenella'], fls. white; **'Alportii'**, tall and vigorous, fls. carmine; **'Argentea'**, lvs. pale; **'Atrorubens'**, fls. crimson; **'Aurea'** [cv. 'Aureifolia'], dwarf, lvs. golden; **'Aureifolia'**: 'Aurea'; **'Camla'**, fls. double, rose; **'Carnea'**, fls. pink; **'Coccinea'**, fls. deep red; **'Compacta'**, of compact habit; **'Cuprea'**, lvs. golden, turning bronze; **'Decumbens'** [cv. 'Prostrata'], brs. prostrate, fls. pink; **'Elegantissima'**, fls. lilac; **'Foxii'**, dwarf and matted; **'Hammondii'**, taller, lvs. brighter green than cv. 'Alba', fls. white; **'Hirsuta'** [cv. 'Tomentosa'], lvs. gray-tomentose; **'Humilis'**, low, fls. white; **'Hypnoides'**, to 1 ft., fls. deep pink; **'Johnsonii'**, lvs. medium green, fls. purple; **'Kupholdii'**, prostrate, fls. pink; **'Multiplex'**: 'Plena'; **'McKayi'**, fls. soft pink; **'Monstrosa'**, lvs. bright green, fls. pink; **'Nana'** [cv. 'Pygmaea'], to 4 in., fls. purple; **'Plena'** [cv. 'Multiplex'], fls. double, pink; **'Prostrata'**: 'Decumbens'; **'Purpurea'** [cv. 'Rubra'], fls. dark purple; **'Pygmaea'**: 'Nana'; **'Pyramidalis'**, of pyramidal habit, fls. white; **'Rosea'**, fls. pink; **'Rubra'**: 'Purpurea'; **'Searlei'**, late-blooming, fls. white; **'Seri-**

cea', late-blooming, fls. white; 'Spicata', fls. deep pink; 'Tomentosa': 'Hirsuta'; 'Variegata', lvs. somewhat variegated with white.

CALOCARPUM: *POUTERIA.* **C. mammosum** (L.) Pierre is an illegitimate name synonymous with *Manilkara Zapota*, but the name *C. mammosum* has been universally misapplied to *Pouteria Sapota*.

CALOCEDRUS Kurz [*Heyderia* C. Koch]. *Cupressaceae.* Three spp. of monoecious, coniferous, evergreen trees, native to w. N. Amer., Taiwan, s. China, and Burma; branchlets 2-ranked, flattened; lvs. of sterile branchlets scalelike, 4-ranked, flattened, decurrent, free only at apex, the pairs about equal in length, the lateral lvs. keeled, overlapping the narrower facial lvs., lvs. of fertile branchlets similar or smaller, in spirals; male cones ovoid or oblong, female cones oblong, scales in 3 pairs, imbricate, woody, the lower pair short, recurved, the upper pair linear and united, the middle pair fertile, seeds 2 to each scale, 2-winged, the larger wing nearly as long as scales.

For culture see *Conifers.*

decurrens (Torr.) Florin [*Heyderia decurrens* (Torr.) C. Koch.; *Libocedrus decurrens* Torr.]. CALIFORNIA INCENSE CEDAR. To 100 ft.; female cones to 1 in. long, on short flattened branchlets with lvs. similar to those of sterile branchlets. W. Ore. to Baja Calif. Zone 6. Cv. 'Compacta'. Dwarf, compact.

formosana (Florin) Florin [*Libocedrus macrolepis* auth., not Benth. & Hook.f.]. FORMOSA INCENSE CEDAR. Large trees; female cones to ¾ in. long, on short flattened branchlets with lvs. similar to those of sterile branchlets. Taiwan. Zone 10.

macrolepis Kurz [*Libocedrus macrolepis* (Kurz) Benth. & Hook.f.]. To 100 ft.; female cones ¾ in. long, on elongate rounded branchlets, lvs. in spirals, smaller than those of sterile branchlets. S. China, Burma. Material from Taiwan under this name is *C. formosana*. Doubtfully cult. in U.S.

CALOCEPHALUS R. Br. *Compositae* (Inula Tribe). About 10 spp. of ann. or per. herbs, rarely subshrubs or small shrubs, native to Australia; lvs. alt. or opp., entire; infl. a compound head composed of many 2–3-fld. individual heads crowded together in an ovoid or globose cluster on a common globose or conical receptacle, but lacking a common involucre; fls. all tubular, bisexual, anthers usually tailed; achenes usually compressed, pappus of separate or united scales or bristles.

Propagated by cuttings.

Brownii (Cass.) F. J. Muell. CUSHIONBUSH. Much-branched, white-woolly shrub, to 3 ft.; lvs. alt., appressed, linear, to ³⁄₁₆ in. long; infl. globose, about ½ in. cross; fls. yellow. Seacoasts, temp. Australia.

citreus Less. Hoary per., to 16 in.; lvs. mostly opp., linear, to 3 in. long; infl. ovoid to oblong, to about ⅝ in. long; fls. yellow. S. Australia, Tasmania.

CALOCHORTUS Pursh [*Cyclobothrya* D. Don]. MARIPOSA, MARIPOSA LILY, SEGO L., GLOBE TULIP, STAR T., BUTTERFLY T. *Liliaceae.* About 60 spp. of bulbous, per. herbs, native to w. N. Amer. from the Dakotas to B.C., s. to Guatemala; bulbs tunicate, coats usually membranous, sometimes fibrous-reticulate, sts. leafy or scapose; lvs. basal and cauline, the basal lf. usually very long; fls. white, yellow, orange, red, lavender, purple, or sometimes brownish or bluish, erect or nodding, solitary or in subumbellate clusters, sepals 3, petals 3, often bearded, usually with a somewhat flattened gland on the basal ⅓ of the inside of each petal, stamens 6, anthers basifixed; fr. a septicidal, 3-winged or 3-angled caps.

Calochortuses should have a light, porous soil, not too rich, with perfect drainage. They withstand fairly low temperatures, but not alternate thawing and freezing. Winter protection of leaves should be provided. Planting should be late in autumn, and outside of their native region, bulbs should be lifted after ripening the following season. They are useful in borders and rock gardens and are sometimes flowered indoors. Propagated by natural increase and by seeds when obtainable.

albus Dougl. ex Benth. FAIRY-LANTERN, GLOBE LILY. St. erect, to 2½ ft., branched; basal lf. 1–2 ft. long, st. lvs. lanceolate to linear, 2–10 in. long; fls. globose to globose-campanulate, white, nodding, petals 1¼ in. long; caps. elliptic-oblong, 3-winged, nodding, to 1½ in. long.

Calif. Var. **rubellus** Greene. Fls. tinged with rose. Santa Cruz Mts. to Santa Lucia Mts., Calif.

amabilis Purdy. GOLDEN FAIRY-LANTERN, GOLDEN GLOBE TULIP. Sts. rather stout, erect, to 20 in., branched; basal lf. to 20 in. long, st. lvs. lanceolate to linear, to 8 in. long; fls. triangular in outline, nodding, petals deep, clear yellow, 1¼ in. long, fringed; caps. oblong, 3-winged, nodding, about 1⅛ in. long. Coast Ranges, n. Calif.

amoenus Greene. PURPLE GLOBE TULIP. Sts. slender, erect, rather flexuous, to 20 in.; basal lf. to 20 in. long, st. lvs. lanceolate, to 6 in. long; fls. narrow-campanulate, nodding to erect, petals ¼ in. long, deep rose; caps. elliptic, narrowly 3-winged, nodding, to about 1⅛ in. long. W. foothills, Sierra Nevada, cent. Calif.

apiculatus Bak. St. stout, scapose, erect, to 1 ft.; basal lf. 1 ft. long; fls. 1–9 from a single bulb, campanulate, petals ¾ in. long, yellowish-white, with orbicular glands; caps. elliptic, 3-winged, nodding. Alta. and B.C., s. to e. Wash., n. Idaho, and nw. Mont.

argillosus: a listed name; material offered under this name may be *C. superbus.*

aureus: *C. Nuttallii* var.

barbatus (HBK) Painter [*Cyclobothra flava* (Schult.f.) Lindl.; *C. lutea* Lindl.]. St. flexuous, branched, to 2 ft., bulb coats fibrous-reticulate; basal lf. linear, shorter than st., st. lvs. linear to linear-lanceolate; fls. campanulate, nodding, in 2's, petals to ¾ in. long, yellow, fringed and bearded; caps. 3-angled, erect. Mex.

catalinae S. Wats. St. erect, rather zigzag, to 2 ft.; lvs. linear, to 10 in. long, reduced upward along st.; fls. bowl-shaped, petals 2 in. long, white, tinged with lilac or light purple, with purple spot at base; caps. narrow-oblong, narrowly 3-winged, erect, 1 in. long. Santa Barbara Is. and s. Calif.

citrinus: *C. Weedii.*

clavatus S. Wats. St. coarse, zigzag, to 40 in.; lvs. linear, to 8 in. long, reduced upward along st.; fls. cup-shaped, erect, lemon-yellow, petals 2 in. long, with transverse red-brown line above the gland and club-shaped hairs in lower half; caps. lanceolate-linear, 3-angled, erect, 2½–3½ in long. Calif.

coeruleus (Kellogg) S. Wats. BEAVERTAIL GRASS, CAT'S-EAR. St. erect or flexuous, to 6 in., scapose; basal lf. 4–8 in. long; fls. open-campanulate, erect to ascending, petals ½ in. long, bluish, hairy just above the gland, anthers acute; caps. elliptic, 3-winged, nodding, ⅝ in. long. W. side of Sierra Nevada, n. Calif.

concolor (Bak.) Purdy. GOLDEN-BOWL MARIPOSA. St. stout, erect, to 2 ft.; lvs. linear, 4–8 in. long, reduced upward along st.; fls. campanulate, erect, petals to 2 in. long, yellow, often tinged purple on drying, with a few long yellow hairs near gland; caps. lanceolate-linear, 3-angled, erect, to 3¼ in. long. S. Calif. and n. Baja Calif.

Dunnii Purdy. Erect, branched, to 2 ft.; basal lvs. to 8 in. long, st. lvs. reduced; fls. open-campanulate, erect, petals about 1¼ in. long, white or flushed pink, with red-brown spot above the hairy gland; caps. linear, 3-angled, erect, 1¼ in. long. Mts., s. Calif. to n. Baja Calif.

elegans Pursh. St. flexuous, scapose, to 6 in.; basal lf. to 8 in. long, usually much longer than st.; fls. open-campanulate, petals ¾ in. long, greenish-white, papillose, hairy and fringed, with purple crescent above the depressed gland, anthers long-apiculate; caps. elliptic to orbicular, 3-winged, nodding, ¾ in. long. Cent. Idaho and adjacent Wash. and Ore. Var. **selwayensis** (St. John) M. Ownb. Petals only moderately hairy, glands shorter, nearly straight, not depressed. W. Mont. and adjacent Idaho.

eurycarpus: *C. nitidus.*

Gunnisonii S. Wats. St. erect, unbranched, to 1½ ft.; lvs. linear, reduced upward along st.; fls. campanulate, erect, petals 1¾ in. long, white to purple, bearded with glandular, branched hairs, often purple-banded above gland; caps. linear-oblong, 3-angled, erect. Cent. Mont. and w. S. Dak., s. to ne. Ariz. and cent. New Mex.

invenustus Greene [*C. Nuttallii* var. *australis* Munz]. St. simple, to 20 in.; lvs. linear, to 8 in. long, reduced upward along st.; fls. campanulate, erect, petals 1⅜ in. long, white or dull lavender to purple, sometimes with purple spot below gland; caps. lanceolate-linear, erect, 3-angled, to 3¾ in. long. Calif.

Kennedyi T. C. Porter. DESERT MARIPOSA. St. erect, simple, to 8 in. or more; lvs. linear, to 8 in. long, glaucous, reduced upward along st.; fls. campanulate, petals to 1½ in. long, vermilion to orange, often with brown-purple spot at base; caps. lanceolate-linear, 3-angled, erect, longitudinally striped, to 2¼ in. long. Deserts, se. Calif. to Nev. and Ariz., s. to Sonora (Mex.). Var. **aurea** is listed.

Leichtlinii Hook.f. St. erect, simple, to 16 in. or more; lvs. linear, to 6 in. long, reduced upward along st.; fls. campanulate, erect, petals 1¼ in. long, white, tinged smoky-blue or pink, with dark spot above gland; caps. lanceolate-linear, erect, to 2¼ in. long. Mts., w. Nev. and adjacent cent. and n. Calif.

Lobbii Purdy [*C. subalpinus* Piper]. St. erect or flexuous, scapose, to 1 ft.; basal lf. 1 ft. long; fls. broadly campanulate, nearly erect, sepals with purple, glandular spot on inside of base, petals about 1 in. long, yellowish-white, sometimes tinged lavender, often with a purple crescent above the gland; caps. elliptic, 3-winged, nodding, to 1 in. long. W. Ore. and sw. Wash.

longebarbatus S. Wats. St. erect, to 1 ft.; basal lf. 1 ft. long; fls. campanulate, erect, petals to 1¼ in. long, lavender-pink, with purplish-red spot above gland; caps. broadly elliptic, 3-winged, erect, to 1 in. long. Ne. Calif. to se. Wash.

luteus Dougl. ex Lindl. [*C. luteus* var. *citrinus* of auth., not S. Wats.]. YELLOW M. St. erect, slender, to 20 in.; lower lvs. linear, to 8 in. long, reduced upward along st.; fls. campanulate, erect, deep yellow, petals to 2 in. long, often with red-brown lines and red-brown blotch; caps. lanceolate-linear, 3-angled, erect, to 2⅜ in. long. Cent. to n. Calif. Var. **citrinus:** *C. superbus*, but generally misapplied by most authors to typical *C. luteus*. Var. **Vestae:** *C. Vestae*.

Lyallii Bak. St. erect, simple, to 20 in.; basal lf. to 1 ft. long; fls. erect or spreading, petals triangular-lanceolate and clawed, white or purplish-tinged, papillose inside, fringed with long slender hairs, usually with a purple crescent above gland; caps. elliptic, 3-winged, nodding. Wash. and s. B.C.

macrocarpus Dougl. GREEN-BANDED M. St. stout, simple, to 20 in.; lvs. linear, to 4 in. long, involute, recurved at tip; fls. campanulate, erect, petals to 2 in. long, purple, with longitudinal median green stripe, hairy and sometimes purple-banded above gland; caps. lanceolate-linear, 3-angled, erect, to 2 in. long. B.C. and Mont., s. to n. Calif. and n. Nev.

Maweanus: *C. Tolmiei*.

nitidus Dougl. [*C. eurycarpus* S. Wats.]. St. erect, to 20 in.; basal lf. to 1 ft. long, st. lf. solitary, at about middle of st.; fls. erect, petals 1½ in. long, creamy-white to lavender, with red-purple blotch in middle; caps. elliptic-oblong, 3-winged, erect, about 1 in. long. Sw. Mont. to se. Wash. and Ore., s. to ne. Nev.

nudus S. Wats. SIERRA S.T. St. erect, to 10 in., scapose; basal lf. to 8 in. long; fls. open-campanulate, erect, petals to ⅝ in. long, white to pale lavender, erose-denticulate at apex; caps. elliptic, 3-winged, erect, to ¾ in. long. Mts., n. Calif.

Nuttallii Torr. SEGO LILY. St. erect, simple, to 1½ ft.; lvs. linear, reduced upward along st.; fls. campanulate, erect, petals to 1¾ in. long, white, tinged with lilac, yellow at base, marked with reddish-brown or purple spot above gland; caps. lanceolate-linear, 3-angled, erect, to 2⅛ in. long. S. Dak., e. N. Dak. and Mont., s. to n. New Mex., n. Ariz., and Nev. Var. **aureus** (S. Wats.) M. Ownb. [*C. aureus* S. Wats.]. Fls. lemon-yellow, petals with a maroon blotch above gland. Nw. New Mex. through s. Utah and n. Ariz. Var. **australis:** *C. invenustus*.

Palmeri S. Wats. St. erect, to 2 ft., often branched; basal lvs. to 8 in. long, st. lvs. reduced; fls. campanulate, erect, petals to 1 in. long, white to lavender, sometimes with brownish spot above gland; caps. linear, 3-angled, erect, to 2 in. long. S. Calif.

Plummerae Greene. St. erect, branched, bulb coats fibrous-reticulate; basal lf. to 16 in. long, usually withered before flowering, st. lvs. linear, reduced upward along st.; fls. broadly companulate, erect, petals to 1½ in. long, pink to rose, erose-dentate, bearded with long yellow hairs in median band; caps. linear, 3-angled, erect, to 3⅛ in. long. S. Calif.

splendens Dougl. ex Benth. LILAC M. St. erect, branched, to 2 ft.; basal lvs. to 6 in. long, st. lvs. reduced; fls. campanulate, erect, petals to 2 in. long, deep lilac, petals and sepals sometimes with purple spot; caps. linear, 3-angled, erect, to 2¾ in. long. Coast Ranges, cent. Calif. to n. Baja Calif.

striatus S. Parish. St. erect, to 1½ ft.; basal lvs. linear, to 8 in. long; fls. campanulate, erect, petals to 1 in. long, lavender with purple veins; caps. linear, 3-angled, erect, to 2 in. long. Desert, s. Calif. and s. Nev.

subalpinus: *C. Lobbii*.

superbus Purdy ex J. T. Howell [*C. luteus* var. *citrinus* S. Wats.; *C. venustus* var. *citrinus* Bak. and var. *oculatus* Hort. ex Purdy & L. H. Bailey]. St. erect, often branched, to 2 ft.; lvs. linear, to 10 in. long, reduced upward along st.; fls. campanulate, erect, petals white to yellowish or lavender, usually streaked with purple lines at base, with brown or purple blotch surrounded by zone of bright yellow; caps. linear, 3-angled, erect, to 2⅜ in. long. Calif.

Tolmiei Hook. & Arn. [*C. Maweanus* Leichtl.]. PUSSY-EARS. St. somewhat flexuous, to 16 in.; basal lf. to 16 in. long; fls. open-campanulate, erect or spreading, petals to 1 in. long, white or cream, sometimes tinged rose or purple, hairy inside to apex, fringed; caps. elliptic-oblong, 3-winged, nodding, 1⅛ in. long. Sw. Wash. to cent. Calif.

uniflorus Hook. & Arn. St. barely coming above ground; basal lf. to 16 in. long, st. lvs. 1–3, linear; fls. on long pedicels to 4 in. long, lilac,

petals 1 in. long, with purple spot above gland; caps. oblong, 3-winged, nodding, to 1 in. long. Coast Ranges, sw. Ore., s. to cent. Calif.

venustus Dougl. ex Benth. [*C. venustus* var. *purpurascens* Bak. and var. *roseus* Reuthe]. WHITE M. St. erect, stiff, branched, to 10 in., or sometimes 2–4 ft.; basal lvs. linear, to 8 in. long, st. lvs. reduced; fls. campanulate, petals 2 in. long, white to yellow, purple, or dark red, with scattered hairs in lower part and a median dark red blotch; caps. linear, 3-angled, erect, to 2¼ in. long. Mts., cent. Calif. Var. **citrinus:** *C. superbus*. Var. **oculatus:** *C. superbus*.

Vestae Purdy [*C. luteus* var. *Vestae* (Purdy) Jeps.]. St. erect, stout, to 20 in.; lvs. linear, to 8 in. long; fls. campanulate, erect, petals to 1⅝ in. long, white to purplish, with red to purple lines and a central red-brown blotch surrounded by a pale yellow zone, with a few hairs near gland; caps. linear, 3-angled, erect. Coast Ranges, n. Calif.

Weedii A. Wood [*C. citrinus* Bak.]. WEED'S M. St. slender, branched, 2–3 ft., bulb coats fibrous-reticulate; basal lf. to 16 in. long, st. lvs. reduced; fls. open-campanulate, erect, orange-yellow, petals to 1¼ in. long, bearded with long yellow hairs, minutely flecked and margined with red-brown; caps. linear, 3-angled, erect, to 2 in. long. S. Calif. Var. **intermedia** M. Ownb. Fls. purplish, petals fringed with yellow or dark hairs. S. Calif.

CALODENDRUM Thunb. *Rutaceae.* Two spp. of evergreen trees, native to trop. and S. Afr.; lvs. opp. or whorled, simple, glandular-dotted; fls. white to mauve-pink, in large terminal panicles, calyx 5-parted, petals 5, stamens 5, staminodes 5, petal-like, ovary 5-lobed, stalked; fr. a caps., 5-valved, woody, tubercled.

Adapted to cultivation in Fla. and Calif.; grown for the dark green foliage and showy flowers. Propagated by cuttings of young wood over heat.

capense (L.f.) Thunb. CAPE CHESTNUT. Tree, 40–70 ft.; lvs. ovate, to 5 in. long, parallel-veined; fls. to 5 in. across, petals linear-oblong, 1½ in. long. S. Afr.

CALONCOBA Gilg. *Flacourtiaceae.* About 15 spp. of trees and shrubs, native to trop. Afr.; lvs. alt., large, scaly or thinly hairy, petioled; infl. few-fld., axillary; fls. white; fr. berrylike, smooth or prickly, sometimes edible.

echinata (D. Oliver) Gilg. Glabrous shrub; lvs. elliptic-oblong, to 6 in. long, thinly leathery; fls. small, axillary, solitary or 2–3 together on short peduncles; fr. about 1 in. in diam., densely spinose. Trop. Afr. Zone 10b. The root, bark, lvs. and seeds have medicinal uses; the seeds contain an oil rich in chaulmoogric acid.

Schweinfurthii Gilg. Shrub or small tree; lvs. broadly ovate, to 6 in. long, long-petioled; fls. about 1 in. across; fr. smooth, broadly ellipsoid, to 2½ in. long, pulpy. E. Trop. Afr. Zone 10b.

CALONYCTION: *IPOMOEA.* **C. aculeatum:** *I. alba.* **C. grandiflorum:** *I. tuba.*

CALOPHACA Fisch. ex DC. *Leguminosae* (subfamily *Faboideae*). About 10 spp. of low shrubs or herbs of Asia; lvs. alt., odd-pinnate; fls. papilionaceous, in racemes or solitary, yellow or violet, stamens 10, 9 united and 1 separate; fr. a cylindrical legume.

Grown in borders or on rocky slopes in well-drained soil. Propagated by seeds, or sometimes grafted high on *Laburnum*.

wolgarica (L.f.) Fisch. ex DC. Shrub, 3 ft.; lfts. in 5–8 pairs, orbicular, 12 in. long; fls. in racemes, bright yellow, 1 in. long; fr. to 1¼ in. long. S. Russia, Turkestan. Hardy north.

CALOPHANES: *DYSCHORISTE.*

CALOPHYLLUM L. *Guttiferae.* About 100 spp. of polygamous trees or sometimes shrubs, native to trop. Asia and Amer.; lvs. opp., petioled, entire, leathery, with many lateral, parallel veins usually at right angles to midvein; fls. in axillary or terminal panicles or racemes, sepals and petals 4–12, in 2–3 whorls, not clearly distinguished, stamens many, ovary 1-celled, style elongate, stigma shield-shaped or wavy-toothed; fr. a 1-seeded drupe.

Several species yield oil and gum or wood for cabinet work; sometimes planted as ornamentals in tropics.

antillanum: *C. brasiliense*.

brasiliense Camb. [*C. antillanum* Britt.; *C. calaba* Jacq., not L.]. MARIA, SANTA M. To 65 ft. or more; lvs. elliptic, to 6 in. long; fls. in few-fld. axillary racemes to 2 in. long, white, about ½ in. across, fragrant; fr. about 1 in. in diam. W. Indies and Mex., s. to n. S. Amer.

calaba: see *C. brasiliense.*

inophyllum L. ALEXANDRIAN LAUREL, INDIAN L., LAURELWOOD. To 60 ft.; lvs. evergreen, broadly elliptic-oblong, to 6½ in. long; fls. in upper lf. axils, in 4–15-fld. erect racemes to 8 in. long, white, about ¾ in. across, very fragrant; fr. to 1½ in. in diam. Coastal, s. India to Malay Pen. Zone 10b in Fla. Much planted in the tropics as an ornamental for its handsome lvs. and fragrant fls. Resists salt spray.

CALOPOGON R. Br. SWAMP PINK, GRASS P. *Orchidaceae.* Four spp. of tuberous, terrestrial per. herbs of N. Amer.; lvs. grasslike; fls. in racemes on naked scapes, sepals and petals similar, spreading, lip long-clawed, dilated and bearded above. For structure of fl. see *Orchidaceae.*

Planted in bog or rock gardens; for culture see *Orchids.*

pulchellus: *C. tuberosus.*

tuberosus (L.) BSP [*C. pulchellus* (Salisb.) R. Br.; *Bletia tuberosa* (L.) Ames; *Limodorum tuberosum* L.]. To 1½ ft.; lvs. linear, to 10 in. long; racemes many-fld.; fls. pink to rose-purple, 1½ in. across, lip bearded with golden-yellow hairs. Summer. Acid bogs, swamps, and wet pinelands, Nov. Sc. and Que., s. to Fla., w. to Minn. and Tex., also Cuba and Bahama Is.

CALOSTEMMA R. Br. *Amaryllidaceae.* A few spp. of Australian herbs with tunicate bulbs; lvs. linear to oblong; umbel terminal on a scape, many-fld., subtended by large, separate spathe valves; fls. narrowly funnelform, lobes ascending, stamens inserted at throat, filaments united into a cup in lower half, ovary 1-celled by abortion, ovules 2–3; fr. a caps., seed solitary, globose.

purpureum R. Br. To 2 ft.; lvs. linear, sessile, to ¼ in. wide, appearing after the fls.; umbel 10–20-fld.; fls. dark purple, to ½ in. long, tube shorter than lobes. New S. Wales and s. Australia.

CALOTHAMNUS Labill. NETBUSH, ONE-SIDED BOTTLEBRUSH. *Myrtaceae.* About 24 spp. of evergreen shrubs, confined to W. Australia; lvs. scattered, linear-lanceolate or linear, 1 in. long or more; fls. showy, red, in more or less 1-sided clusters or spikes, calyx lobes 4–5, persistent or deciduous, petals 4–5, spreading, stamens united into bundles, long-exserted; fr. a caps., enclosed in the hardened and enlarged calyx tube, opening by 3–4 valves. Distinguished from *Melaleuca* and *Callistemon* by the 1-sided fl. clusters.

For culture see *Callistemon.*

asper Turcz. ROUGH N. To 7 ft., pubescent; lvs. linear, to 1 in. long, stiff, rough to touch; fls. 4-merous, staminal bundles more or less equal.

coccineus: a listed name of no botanical standing.

Gilesii F. J. Muell. GILES N. To 7 ft.; lvs. needlelike, to 1½ in. long, sharp-pointed; fls. 4-merous, staminal bundles more or less equal.

homalophyllus F. J. Muell. To 6 ft.; lvs. oblong-cuneate to oblanceolate, to 1½ in. long; fls. 4-merous, staminal bundles more or less equal.

longissimus F. J. Muell. To 3 ft.; lvs. cylindrical, to 12 in. long; fls. 4-merous, calyx hairy, more or less sunken in st., staminal bundles in 2 unequal pairs.

quadrifidus R. Br. To 8 ft.; lvs. needlelike, to 1 in. long; fls. 4-merous, calyx glabrous, lobes shorter than tube, staminal bundles equal.

rupestris Schauer. To 5 ft.; lvs. linear-cylindrical, to 1 in. long, mostly upwardly curved and crowded, finely pubescent but becoming glabrous; fls. 4-merous, calyx hairy, staminal bundles more or less equal.

sanguineus Labill. To 8 ft.; lvs. needlelike, to 1½ in. long, silky-hairy; fls. 4-merous, calyx hairy, staminal bundles red, in 2 unequal pairs, the upper broad and flat with many filaments, the lower united nearly to apex, without anthers.

validus S. L. Moore. To 6 ft.; lvs. linear, cylindrical, to 1 in. long, pungent; fls. 4-merous, calyx sparsely short-hairy, lobes about as long as tube, staminal bundles equal; fr. woody with 2 persistent calyx lobes bent inward and meeting. Allied to *C. quadrifidus* but having larger fls. and calyx lobes as long as fl. tube.

villosus R. Br. WOOLLY N. To 4 ft. or more, shoots hairy; lvs. cylindrical, to 1½ in. long, gray-hairy; fls. 5-merous, calyx hairy, staminal bundles equal.

CALOTROPIS R. Br. *Asclepiadaceae.* About 6 spp. of shrubs or small trees, native to trop. Afr. and Asia; lvs. opp., simple, nearly sessile; fls. 5-merous, in umbellate or racemose cymes, corolla campanulate-rotate, lobes more or less valvate, corona a massive column, the lobes 5, fleshy, laterally compressed, spurred on exterior and tubercled at apex; fr. a horned follicle.

Greenhouse plants, requiring moderate drainage. Propagated by cuttings in sand over heat. Both *C. gigantea* and *C. procera* produce a strong bark fiber, their milky juice dries to rubber similar to gutta-percha, and the silk of the seeds may be used in weaving or as a stuffing material.

gigantea (L.) Ait.f. MUDAR, MADAR, BOWSTRING HEMP, CROWN PLANT. Small trees, to 15 ft., shoots and lower lf. surfaces white-woolly; lvs. 4–8 in. long, obovate to obtriangular, cordate at base, clasping; cymes umbellate, bracted, long-peduncled, corolla 1–2 in. across, rose to purple inside, lobes eventually reflexed, corona lobes purplish, white-pubescent; follicle 3–4 in. long. India to Indonesia. Lvs. used medicinally and for food, and floss for stuffing.

procera (Ait.) Ait.f. MUDAR, MADAR. Shrubs, mostly less than 6 ft., but up to 15 ft.; similar to *C. gigantea,* but lvs. oblong to elliptic, corolla usually about 1 in. across with lobes more erect, corona lobes glabrous or pubescent, and follicle 4–5 in. long. India to Iran and Afr.

CALPURNIA E. H. Mey. *Leguminosae* (subfamily *Faboideae*). Six or 7 spp. of trees or shrubs of Afr. and India; lvs. alt., odd-pinnate; fls. in racemes, yellow, papilionaceous, keel petals united, stamens 10, separate or united at base; fr. a flat, slightly winged legume.

Grown as an ornamental in subtropical climates or in greenhouses in the North; propagated by cuttings under glass or by seeds.

aurea (Ait.) Benth. [*C. lasiogyne* E. H. Mey.]. EAST AFRICAN LABURNUM. Shrub, to 15 ft.; lfts. elliptic to oblong, to 1¾ in. long, rounded at each end; racemes many, as long as lvs.; fls. about ½ in. long, ovary glabrous or silky-pubescent; fr. linear, 3 in. long, sparsely pubescent. Afr., s. India. Subsp. **aurea.** The typical subsp.; lower surface of lfts. and ovaries appressed-pubescent. Ethiopia to S. Afr. Subsp. **sylvatica** (Burchell) Brumm. [*C. sylvatica* (Burchell) E. H. Mey.]. Lower surface of lfts. and the ovaries glabrous. S. Afr.

lasiogyne: *C. aurea.*

sylvatica: *C. aurea* subsp.

villosa Harv. Differs from *C. aurea* in having petioles, twigs, and peduncles villous-tomentose, lfts. smaller, to ½ in. long, appressed-silky beneath, peduncles few-fld., with fls. ¼ in. long, S. Afr.

CALTHA L. MARSH MARIGOLD. *Ranunculaceae.* About 15–20 spp. of low, fleshy, per. herbs of the cold marshes of the N. and S. Temp. Zone; lvs. alt., petioled, entire or serrate; fls. axillary or terminal, peduncled, sepals 5–9 or more, petaloid, yellow, white, or pink, petals none, stamens many, pistils 4 to many; fr. of follicles.

Grown in moist, boggy places; propagated by division of roots and by seeds.

asarifolia DC. Sts. leafy, decumbent; lvs. round-reniform, 1–3 in. broad, crenate; fls. 1–3, sepals 5–7, bright yellow, ⅝–¾ in. long; follicles sessile. Alaska to Ore.

biflora DC. To 10 in., sts. 1-lvd., 2-fld.; lvs. long-petioled, round-reniform, 2–3 in. broad, not as long, crenate; sepals 6–9, white; follicles stipitate. Alaska to Ore.

Chelidonii Greene [*C. uniflora* Rydb.]. Dwarf, 2–4 in.; lvs. short-petioled, blades ½ in. long or less, round-cordate, acutish, somewhat crenate, basal sinus open; fl. solitary, white or bluish, sepals 5–8, ½ in. long, B.C. to Mont.

leptosepala DC. [*C. rotundifolia* (Huth) Greene]. Sts. scapose, 1-fld., or with a lf. or bract and 2-fld.; lvs. oblong-cordate, longer than broad, coarsely dentate; sepals 6–12, white; follicles short-stipitate. Alaska to Alta., s. to Ore. and New Mex.

palustris L. [*C. parnassifolia* Raf.]. MARSH MARIGOLD, COWSLIP, MEADOW-BRIGHT, KINGCUP, MAY-BLOB. Sts. hollow, 8–24 in., branched in upper parts; basal lvs. long-petioled, the petioles becoming progressively shorter in upper parts, lf. blades to 7 in. wide, basal sinus open; fls. bright yellow, to 2 in. across, sepals elliptic to obovate; follicles subsessile. Nfld. to Alaska, s. to N.C. and Tenn.; Eurasia. Herbage sometimes used as a potherb, and the pickled fl. buds as a substitute for capers. Cv. **'Monstruosa'** [cv. 'Monstrosa Plena']. Fls. double.

parnassifolia: *C. palustris.*

rotundifolia: *C. leptosepala.*

scaposa Hook.f. & T. Thoms. Sts. many, scapose, 3–6 in.; lvs. 1–1½ in. long, elliptic-oblong, cordate, nearly entire to minutely crenate; sepals yellow, suborbicular, ⅜ in. long; follicles many, stalked. Himalayas, w. China.

uniflora: *C. Chelidonii.*

CALVOA Hook.f. *Melastomataceae.* About 25 spp. of ann. or per. herbs or small shrubs of trop. Afr., often succulent, brs. with nodes thickened; lvs. ovate, 3–5-nerved, long-petioled; fls. in cymes, stamens 10, equal, or almost so, ovary inferior, 5-celled; fr. a caps.

orientalis Taub. Per., 12–18 in.; lvs. ovate, 2–4 in. long, serrulate; infl. a terminal panicle 3–5 in. long with scorpioid brs.; fls. ¾ in. across, rose-purple. Spring. W. Afr.

sessiliflora Cogn. ex De Wild. & T. Durand. Ann., sts. to 8 in., with few brs., puberulous toward apex; lvs. ovate, 1–3 in. long, 1–1½ in. wide, sinuately denticulate, remotely ciliate, 3–5-nerved, sparsely setose above, scurfy beneath, petioles to ¾ in. long; cymes to 1½ in. long, often forked, 1- to few-fld.; fls. sessile, calyx glabrous to scurfy; fr. a caps., to ¼ in. long and wide. Congo.

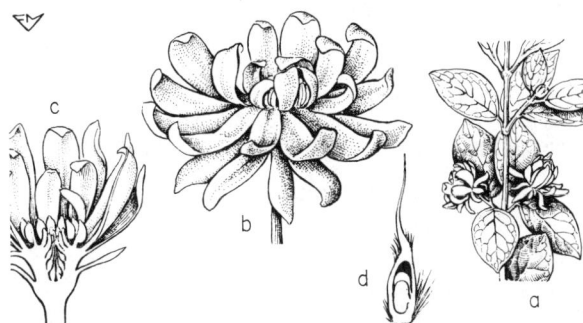

CALYCANTHACEAE. *Calycanthus floridus:* **a,** flowering branch, × ¼; **b,** flower, × 1; **c,** flower, vertical section, × 1; **d,** pistil, vertical section, × 5. (From Bailey, *Manual of of Cultivated Plants,* ed. 2.)

CALYCANTHACEAE Lindl. CALYCANTHUS FAMILY. Dicot.; 2 genera and about 6 spp. of shrubs with aromatic bark, native to temp. N. Amer. and e. Asia; lvs. opp., entire; fls. solitary, bisexual, sepals and petals many, similar, stamens 5 to many, all borne on the fl. tube; fr. of many achenes enclosed by the capsulelike fl. tube. *Calycanthus* and *Chimonanthus* are cult. as ornamentals.

CALYCANTHUS L. SWEET SHRUB. *Calycanthaceae.* Four spp. of deciduous shrubs, native to N. Amer.; lvs. opp., entire; fls. large, fragrant, reddish-brown, borne at tips of short branchlets, bisexual, sepals and petals many, similar, stamens many, all borne on fl. tube; fr. of many achenes enclosed by the urceolate fl. tube.

Hardy in the North, except *C. occidentalis.* They thrive in rich, well-drained soil. Propagated by seeds, layers, suckers, and division.

fertilis Walt. CAROLINA ALLSPICE. To 10 ft.; lvs. ovate to oblong, to 6 in. long, glaucous and nearly glabrous beneath; fls. brown, to 2 in. across, fl. tube contracted at mouth. Penn. to Ga. and Ala. Zone 5.

floridus L. CAROLINA ALLSPICE, PINEAPPLE SHRUB, STRAWBERRY S. To 10 ft.; lvs. ovate or elliptic, to 5 in. long, densely pubescent and pale beneath; fls. dark reddish-brown, 2 in. across, fl. tube contracted at mouth. Va. to Fla. Zone 5. Cv. '**Purpureus**'. Lvs. purple.

occidentalis Hook. & Arn. To 12 ft. or more; lvs. ovate to oblong-lanceolate, to 8 in. long, green and only slightly pubescent beneath; fls. light reddish-brown, to 3 in. across, fl. tube 1¾ in. long, not contracted at mouth. Calif. Zone 8.

praecox: *Chimonanthus praecox.*

CALYCOPHYLLUM DC. *Rubiaceae.* About 6 spp. of trees, native to S. Amer. and W. Indies; lvs. opp., stipules interpetiolar, deciduous; fls. in terminal cymes, small, usually white, 4–8-merous, one of calyx lobes sometimes leaflike, stamens and styles often exserted; fr. a caps., seeds small, winged.

The wood of some species is useful for construction and cabinet work.

candidissimum (Vahl) DC. DEGAME. To 60 ft.; lvs. rounded-elliptic or ovate, to 5 in. long, glabrous or nearly so; leaflike calyx lobes of some fls. white, ovate. Cuba and Mex., s. to n. S. Amer. A source of commercial lancewood.

Spruceanum (Benth.) Hook.f. ex K. Schum. To 75 ft.; lvs. oblong to oblong-ovate, to 7 in. long; fls. all alike. Peru, Bolivia, w. Brazil.

CALYPSO Salisb. *Orchidaceae.* One sp., a circumboreal terrestrial orchid of cool bogs; sts. small, cormlike; lf. solitary, plicate; scape lateral, 1-fld., with 2 or more basal sheaths; sepals and petals reflexed, lip pendent, saccate. For structure of fl. see *Orchidaceae.*

For culture see *Orchids.*

borealis: *C. bulbosa.*

bulbosa (L.) Oakes [*C. borealis* (Swartz) Salisb.]. FAIRY-SLIPPER, CALYPSO, CYTHEREA, PINK SLIPPER ORCHID. Lf. petioled, round-ovate, to 3½ in. long, persisting through the winter; scape to 9 in. high; sepals and petals narrowly lanceolate, to 1 in. long, purple, lip oblong, about 1 in. long, the sac whitish to purple and streaked with red-brown, but apical upper surface white, spotted with purple, and with yellow or white beard. Spring. Cool forests and bogs, circumboreal, s. in N. Amer. to n. U.S. in east and Calif. and New Mex. in west.

CALYPTRIDIUM Nutt. [*Spraguea* Torr.]. *Portulacaceae.* About 6 spp. of ann. or per. herbs, native to w. N. Amer.; basal lvs. spatulate, st. lvs. alt.; fls. small, mostly in scorpioid spikes, petals 2–4, more or less coherent and carried up on the caps.; fr. a membranous, 2-valved caps., seeds many.

One species suitable for the rock garden.

multiceps: *C. umbellatum.*

umbellatum (Torr.) Greene [*C. multiceps* Hort.; *Spraguea umbellata* Torr.; *S. multiceps* J. T. Howell]. PUSSY-PAWS. Ann. to per., sts. several, spreading to suberect, to 10 in.; basal lvs. to 2½ in. long, st. lvs. reduced; fls. white or pink. Mts., B.C. to Calif., e. to Rocky Mts.

CALYPTROCALYX Blume. *Palmae.* About 40 spp. of solitary or clustered, unarmed, monoecious palms lacking a crownshaft, native in the Moluccas and New Guinea; lvs. pinnate or blades 2-cleft at apex and pinnately ribbed, pinnae acute, 1-ribbed; infl. among lvs., of 1 or several long-peduncled spikes, each spike surrounded by a thin, cylindrical bract in bud, fls. in triads (2 male and 1 female) sunken in pits; male fls. with sepals imbricate, petals valvate, stamens 6 or more, with filaments erect or inflexed in bud, pistillode about as long as stamens, female fls. with sepals and petals imbricate, ovary 1-celled; fr. with apical stigmatic scar, endocarp not operculate, seed with homogeneous or ruminate endosperm and basal embryo.

For culture see *Palms.*

spicatus (Lam.) Blume. To 40 ft.; lvs. evenly pinnate, to 12 ft. long, pinnae 30 in. long or more; spikes 1–3 in each lf. axil, to 9 ft. long; male fls. with stamens 100 or more; fr. ovoid, red.

CALYPTROGYNE H. Wendl. *Palmae.* About 5 spp. of small, usually stemless, clustered, unarmed, monoecious palms without a crownshaft, native from Mex. to Panama and Colombia; lvs. variously pinnate or blades 2-cleft at apex and pinately ribbed; infl. among lvs., erect, spicate, long-peduncled, subtended by 2 bracts, the upper cylindrical and inserted at base of spike, fls. in triads (2 male and 1 female) sunken in pits arranged in vertical rows; male fls. with sepals imbricate, petals united basally in a soft tube, valvate above, stamens 6 with erect filaments united at base and sagittate anthers, female fls. with sepals imbricate, petals united basally in a soft tube, valvate above, staminodes in an urceolate tube at flowering, pistil 3-celled; fr. with basal stigmatic residue, endocarp not operculate, seed with homogeneous endosperm and basal embryo.

Sometimes planted as ornamentals. For culture see *Palms.*

Ghiesbreghtiana (Linden & H. Wendl.) H. Wendl. St. not evident or to 3 ft. long; lvs. to more than 3 ft. long, irregularly pinnate, with 1-ribbed and several-ribbed pinnae; infl. to 4½ ft. long; fr. obovoid, to ⅝ in. long. Mex. to Honduras.

Swartzii: *Calyptronoma occidentalis.*

CALYPTRONOMA Griseb. MANAC PALM. *Palmae.* Three spp. of moderately stout, unarmed, solitary, monoecious palms without a crownshaft, in the W. Indies; lvs. pinnate, pinnae with 1 principal rib, acute; infl. among lvs., subtended by 2 unequal, thick bracts, the upper longer than the lower but shorter than expanded infl., peduncle elongate, rachis prominent, brs. simple or the lower once-branched, rachillae with fls. in triads (2 male and 1 female) sunken in pits; male fls. with sepals imbricate, petals briefly united basally, valvate above, stamens 6, filaments erect, united basally, anthers sagittate, female fls. with sepals imbricate, petals united basally, valvate and circumscissile apically, staminodes united in an urceolate tube, pistil 3-celled; fr. with basal stigmatic residue, mesocarp with thickened curved fibers, endocarp not operculate, seed with homogeneous endosperm and basal embryo.

Sometimes cultivated as ornamentals in tropical and tropical gardens. Zone 10b. For culture see *Palms.*

dulcis (Wright ex Griseb.) L. H. Bailey. CUBAN MANAC. To more than 20 ft.; lvs. to 9 ft. long or more, pinnae many on each side; infl. to 3 ft. long or more, pits with lips shorter than mouth; fr. subglobose, to ½ in. in diam. Cuba.

occidentalis (Swartz) H. E. Moore [*Calyptrogyne Swartzii* (Griseb.) Becc.]. JAMAICAN MANAC, LONG-THATCH. To nearly 40 ft., trunk 9 in. in diam. or more; lvs. bright green, to 9 ft. long or more, pinnae 30 or more on each side; infl. to 3 ft. long, pits with lips as long as mouth; fr. to ⅝ in. long. Jamaica.

CALYSTEGIA R. Br. BINDWEED. *Convolvulaceae.* About 25 spp. of prostrate or twining per. herbs, in temp. and trop. regions of both hemispheres; lvs. petioled, mostly glabrous, entire or lobed, sagittate to hastate basally; fls. axillary, usually solitary, bracts 2, mostly large and leaflike, sepals 5, enclosed by bracts, corolla campanulate to funnelform, white or pink, rarely yellowish, with 5 stripes outside, stigma 2-lobed, lobes mostly oblong or elliptic, ovary and fr. 1-celled or with an imperfect cross wall. Sometimes included in *Convolvulus*, but having bracts usually large, fls. solitary, style brs. oblong, more or less elliptic, and fr. 1-celled.

hederacea Wallich [*Calystegia japonica* (Thunb.) Miq., not Choisy; *Convolvulus japonicus* Thunb.]. JAPANESE B. Per., sts. twining; lvs. narrowly arrow-shaped, to 2½ in. long, long-petioled; fls. solitary, on winged peduncles, corolla rose-colored, to 1½ in. long. E. Asia. Cv. 'Flore Pleno' [cv. 'Plena'; *Calystegia pubescens* Lindl.; *Convolvulus pellitus* Ledeb. forma *anestius* Fern.]. CALIFORNIA ROSE. Fls. very double, sterile. Much more commonly cult. than the single-fld. form; naturalized in e. U.S.

japonica: material cult. under this name is *C. hederacea.*

macrostegia (Greene) Brumm. Per., sts. twining or trailing, 3–12 ft. long, more or less woody at base; lf. blades fleshy, triangular-hastate, 2–4 in. long, petioles as long as blades or longer; bracts below fls. ¾–1¼ in. long; corolla white, aging to pink, 2–2⅜ in. long. Coastal is. of Calif. The typical subsp. is probably not cult. Subsp. **cyclostegia** (House) Brumm. [*Convolvulus cyclostegius* House]. Lf. blades less fleshy, ovate to triangular-lanceolate, to 2 in. long, petioles usually shorter than blades; bracts ⅜–⅝ in. long; corolla white, often striped purple outside, ¾–1¾ in. long. Coastal, s. Calif.

occidentalis (A. Gray) Brumm. [*Convolvulus occidentalis* A. Gray]. Per., somewhat woody in lower part, climbing to 10 ft. or more; lvs. triangular to lanceolate, to 3 in. long, sagittate at base, glabrous and glaucous above; corolla purplish and white, to 2 in. long. Calif.

pubescens: *C. hederacea* cv. 'Flore Pleno.'

sepium (L.) R. Br. [*Convolvulus sepium* L.]. WILD MORNING-GLORY, BINDWEED, HEDGE B., RUTLAND-BEAUTY. Per., sts. twining; lvs. deltoid-ovate to deltoid, to 3 in. long, subhastate, long-petioled; fls. solitary, with peduncles not winged, corolla rose-colored, to 2½ in. long. Eur., Asia, N. Amer. Weedy.

Soldanella (L.) R. Br. ex Roem. & Schult. [*Convolvulus Soldanella* L.]. SEA B. Per., sts. creeping, prostrate; lvs. reniform, broader than long, to 2 in. wide, long-petioled; fls. solitary, on long peduncles, corolla pale pink, 2½ in. across. Seashores around the world. The seeds are distributed by sea currents.

spithamaea (L.) Pursh [*Convolvulus spithamaeus* L.]. LOW B. Sts. erect, at least the fl. part, the nonflowering part often elongating and declinate; lvs. oblong to oblong-ovate, to 3 in. long, rounded or cordate at base, upper lvs. sessile, those subtending fls. on petioles shorter than the lf. blades; fls. solitary, corolla pink or white, to 2½ in. long. E. N. Amer.

CALYTRIX Labill. (sometimes but not originally spelled *Calythrix.*). *Myrtaceae.* About 40–50 spp. of heathlike shrubs in Australia; lvs. small, semicylindrical or 3- or 4-angled, stiff; fls. solitary in upper lf. axils or in terminal leafy heads, calyx

tube elongated, often slender, 10-ribbed, calyx lobes 5, the midrib prolonged into a long bristlelike awn, petals 5, stamens usually many, ovary inferior, 1-celled; fr. dry, indehiscent, 1-seeded. Allied to *Lhotskya*, but having calyx lobes with bristlelike awn.

Sullivanii F. J. Muell. To 8 ft.; lvs. linear, to ¼ in. long, 3-angled; fls. pink or white, in terminal or lateral heads or short spikes, calyx awns less than ¼ in. long. Victoria. Has been confused with *Lhotskya brevifolia.*

tetragona Labill. To 5 ft.; lvs. linear, to ½ in. long, erect or spreading, 3-angled or convex underneath, petiole very short; fls. pink or white, subsessile in the upper axils forming leafy heads, calyx awns over ¼ in. long. Australia and Tasmania.

CAMARIDIUM: *MAXILLARIA.*

CAMAROTIS: *SARCOCHILUS.*

CAMASSIA Lindl. [*Quamasia* Raf.]. CAMASS, CAMAS. *Liliaceae.* Five spp. of per., scapose, bulbous herbs, native to N. Amer.; bulbs tunicate, with brown or black coats; lvs. basal, linear; fls. regular to slightly irregular, white, blue, or blue-violet, in terminal racemes, perianth segms. 6, separate, 3–9-nerved, stamens 6, anthers yellow, blue-violet, or brown, versatile; fr. a 3-valved, loculicidal caps.

Camassias are hardy and do well in loamy soils. Bulbs should be planted 3–4 in. apart in early autumn and not disturbed; also propagated by seeds. Useful in borders.

azurea: *C. Quamash* subsp.

Cusickii S. Wats. Bulbs large, clustered; lvs. to 20 in. long, ¾–1½ in. wide, rather succulent; scapes to 3 ft.; fls. slightly irregular, pale blue to blue-violet, 1–1⅜ in. long, perianth segms. not twisted together after pollination; caps. subglobose. Ne. Ore.

esculenta: *C. Quamash.*

Fraseri: *C. scilloides.*

Leichtlinii (Bak.) S. Wats. To 4 ft.; lvs. to 2 ft. long and 1 in. wide; fls. regular, creamy-white, 1–1⅜ in. long, usually only 1–2 fls. open at a time, perianth segms. twisted together after pollination; caps. ovate, to 1 in. long. Endemic to Umpqua R. valley, Douglas Co., Ore. Subsp. **Suksdorfii** (Greenm.) Gould [var. *caerulea* Hort.]. Fls. light to bright blue, or, in cv. 'Atrocaerulea', deep blue-violet, or, in cv. 'Alba', white. B.C. to n. Calif.

Quamash (Pursh) Greene [*C. esculenta* Lindl.]. QUAMASH, COMMON C., CAMOSH. To 2½ ft.; lvs. to 20 in. long, glaucous above; fls. irregular, white, pale blue, to blue-violet, to 1¼ in. long, perianth segms. not twisted together after pollination; caps. ovate or oblong. S. Alta. and se. B.C., s. to w. Mont., n. Idaho, n. Ore. Subsp. **azurea** (A. Heller) Gould [*C. azurea* A. Heller; *Quamasia azurea* A. Heller]. To 2 ft.; lvs. to 16 in. long; fls. light blue-violet and almost regular. Alluvial plains, w. Wash.

scilloides (Raf.) V. L. Cory [*C. Fraseri* Torr.; *Quamasia hyacinthina* (Raf.) Britt.]. EASTERN C., WILD HYACINTH, MEADOW H., INDIGO SQUILL. To 2½ ft.; lvs. to 24 in. long; fls. regular, white, blue, or blue-violet, to ⅝ in. long, perianth segms. not twisted together after pollination, anthers bright yellow; caps. subglobose. S. Penn. to s. Minn., s. to W. Va., Ga., and Tex.

CAMELLIA L. [*Thea* L.]. *Theaceae.* About 80 spp. or more of evergreen shrubs and small trees of e. Asia; lvs. alt., simple, toothed, leathery, petioles short; fls. usually showy, bisexual, solitary or clustered, axillary or seeming terminal, peduncles generally with 4–5 bracteoles, sepals 5, petals 5(–8–14), stamens many, joined into a short tube below and also united with petals basally, ovary 3–5-celled; fr. a caps., 1- to several-seeded.

The genus is the source of tea of commerce and of valuable seed oils. Camellias are popular ornamental shrubs especially outdoors in the Southeast and on the Pacific Coast (Zones 8 and 9). When grown in a greenhouse, a temperature of 50–60° F is required during the flowering season. Camellias thrive in partial shade and serve admirably in landscape plantings in areas where they are hardy. They prefer well-drained, neutral to slightly acid soil rich in organic matter. Propagated from cuttings of current season's growth in summer, and by grafting on suitable rootstock.

Especially in *C. japonica*, seedlings produce flowers of unique form and color, and sports (mutations) frequently occur in existing cultivars. Double flowers result when stamens become petal-like, and various types of double forms are recognized, such as: semidouble, with mostly 14–20 petals and a central mass of stamens; incompletely double, with many petal-like stamens intermixed with fertile stamens; and completely double, having no apparent stamens, with many petals regularly arranged and then either imbricate (formal) or tiered, irregularly arranged in a convex mass. The many combinations of form and color in camellia flowers have attracted great interest, and there are several societies devoted expressly to camellia culture and knowledge.

Bohea: C. sinensis.

cuspidata (Kochs) Hort. Veitch ex R. Pearson. Shrub, to 15 ft.; lvs. lanceolate, to 3 in. long, long-acuminate; bracteoles distinct from sepals, fls. white, to 1½ in. across, petals 6–7. Late spring. China.

fraterna Hance. Shrub, to 15 ft., young sts. densely hairy; lvs. elliptic, to 3 in. long, long-acuminate; peduncles, bracteoles, and sepals villous, bracteoles distinct from sepals, fls. white, flushed with pink outside, to 1½ in. across, outer stamens united ½–⅔ their length. China.

Granthamiana Sealy. Small tree, about 10 ft.; lvs. oblong-elliptic, mostly about 3½ in. long and 1–1½ in. wide, blunt-acuminate; bracteoles and sepals similar, 12 or more, persistent, fls. to 5½ in. across, white, petals 8, notched, styles united, hairy. Autumn to winter. Hong Kong.

hiemalis Nakai. Probably only a form of C. Sasanqua, having fls. semidouble, rose, 2 in. across. China.

irrawadiensis Barua. Tall, open shrub, to 20 ft.; lvs. mostly elliptic, to 4½ in. long or more and 1½ in. wide, bluntly acuminate; bracteoles deciduous, fls. to 1½ in. across, white, petals 7–8(–10), styles 4–5-cleft; caps. depressed-globose, about 1½ in. in diam. Winter to spring. Burma.

japonica L. COMMON C. To 45 ft., branchlets glabrous; lvs. broadly elliptic, to 4 in. long, short-acuminate, dark green and glossy above, petioles to ½ in. long; bracteoles and sepals similar, in a single series, deciduous, fls. single or double, red to pink, white, or variegated, to 5 in. across, petals 5–6, stamens strongly fused with petals, mostly 1 in. long or more, the outer united for ½–⅔ their length into a ring, often petal-like, pistil glabrous; fr. to 1⅜ in. long, 2–3-celled. Near coasts, Japan, s. Korea, Taiwan, widely cult. in warm temp. regions. Zone 8. Over 2,000 named cvs. are known; the more common Latin-named cvs. and synonyms are: **'Alba Fimbriata':** 'Fimbriata'; **'Alba Plena',** fls. white, completely double, formal, to 3½ in. across; **'Alba Plena Fimbriata':** 'Fimbriata'; **'Alba Superba',** fls. white, semidouble to incomplete double, 3 in. across; **'Althaeiflora',** fls. dark crimson, incompletely double, of medium size; **'Amabilis',** fls. white, single, to 4 in. across, petals undulate and notched; **'Anemoniflora Alba',** fls. white, incompletely double, to 4¼ in. across; **'Angustifolia',** fls. red, blotched pink; **'Aspasia MacArthur':** 'Paeoniiflora'; **'Bealii Rosea',** often, but not originally, spelled 'Bealei Rosea', fls. rose-pink, completely double, incompletely imbricate, to 2¼ in. across; **'Brooklynia',** fls. deep rose irregularly blotched white, completely double, formal, to 3 in. across; **'Candida Elegantissima'** [cv. 'Nagasaki'], fls. rose-red irregularly marked with white, semidouble, about 4½ in. across; **'Candidissima',** fls. white, completely double, formal or tiered, to 3 in. across; **'Campbellii',** fls. white, spotted red, some material offered under this name is cv. 'Margherita Coleoni'; **'Chandleri Elegans':** 'Elegans'; **'Chandleri Alba',** pure white form of 'Elegans'; **'Chandleri Rosea',** pure deep rose-pink form of 'Elegans'; **'Chandleri Rubra',** form of 'Elegans' with fls. rose-red, sometimes spotted white; **'Cliveana',** fls. carmine-rose, mostly incompletely double, to 3½ in. across, not to be confused with old cv. 'Cliviana' with completely double cherry-red fls., to 4½ in. across or more; **'Collettii'** [cv. 'Collettii Maculata'], fls. boldly variegated red and white, incompletely double, to 3 in. across; **'Coquettii',** fls. variegated bright red and white, large, completely double, irregular, some material offered under this name is cv. 'Glen 40'; **'Darsii',** fls. cherry-red, with few white spots, incompletely double, to 3¾ in. across; **'Delectissima',** fls. mostly white with few long stripes of rose, single, to 4 in. across; **'Derbyana',** fls. red to purplish-red, incompletely double, to 3½ in. across; **'Diversiflora Plena',** fls. light rose-pink, blotched white, completely double, formal, of medium size; **'Donckelardii',** fls. cherry-red, variously marked with white, semidouble, to 5 in. across; **'Elata'** [cv. 'Enrico Bettoni'], fls. rose-pink, incompletely double, to 4 in. across; **'Elegans'** [cvs. 'Chandleri Elegans', 'Elegans Chandleri'], fls. rose-pink, often spotted white, incompletely double, to 4 in. across; **'Emperor Wilhelm':** 'Gigantea'; **'Enrico Bettoni':** 'Elata'; **'Feastii',** fls. white, with few rose flecks, completely double, formal, to 4¾ in. across; **'Festiva'** [cv. 'Maria Morren'], fls. rose-pink, veined darker, double, formal, of medium size; **'Fimbriata'** [cvs. 'Alba Fimbriata', 'Fimbriata Plena', 'Fimbriata Alba', 'Alba Plena Fimbriata'], fls. white, completely double, formal, petals conspicuously fringed, 3 in. across; **'Fimbriata Alba':** 'Fimbriata'; **'Fimbriata Plena':** 'Fimbriata'; **'Fimbriata Superba'** [cv. 'Fred Sander'], fls. crimson, sometimes spotted white, semidouble, to 4 in. across, petals marginally creped and laciniate; **'Fred Sander':** 'Fimbriata Superba';

'Gigantea' [cv. 'Emperor Wilhelm'], fls. red, variegated with white, semidouble to incompletely double, to 5 in. across; **'Gigantea Red',** fls. cherry-red, incompletely to irregularly completely double, to 4⁵⁄₁₆ in. across; **'Glen 40',** fls. cherry-red, completely double and formal, or incompletely double, to 4½ in. across; **'Grandiflora Rosea'** [cv. 'Lady Clare'], fls. deep pink, with darker veins, sometimes spotted white, semidouble to incompletely double, to 5 in. across, petals wavy; **'Gunnellii',** fls. white, irregularly double; **'Haemanthus',** fls. deep red, veined purple, sometimes blotched white, incompletely double, of medium size; **'Horkan':** 'Variabilis'; **'Ignescens',** fls. deep orange-red, semidouble, some material offered under this name is cv. 'Rose Emery'; **'Imbricata Rubra Plena'** [cv. 'Pope Pius IX'], fls. rose-red, completely double, formal, to 4⁵⁄₁₆ in. across; **'Jacksonii',** fls. red, striped white, some material offered under this name is cv. 'Gigantea Red'; **'Japonica Alba',** fls. white, single, of medium size; **'Kelvingtoniana',** fls. rose-red, heavily blotched white, incompletely double, to 4⁵⁄₁₆ in. across; **'Lady Clare':** 'Grandiflora Rosea'; **'Latifolia',** fls. crimson, semidouble, to 4 in. across; **'Leana Superba',** sometimes, but not originally, spelled 'Leeana Superba', fls. red, sometimes blotched and streaked white, completely double, incompletely imbricate, 4 in. across; **'Leucantha'** [cv. 'Tricolor Sieboldii White'], fls. pure white, semidouble, to 3½ in. across; **'Lilyi',** fls. white, sometimes with red stripes or areas, completely double, incompletely imbricate, to 3 in. across; **'Magnoliiflora',** fls. pale pink, semidouble, to 4 in. across, petals erect and recurved; **'Magnoliiflora Alba',** a white-fld. sport of cv. 'Magnoliiflora'; **'Margherita Coleoni',** fls. deep rose-pink, completely double, incompletely imbricate, to 3 in. across; **'Maria Morren':** 'Festiva'; **'Mathotiana'** [cv. 'Mathotiana Rubra'], fls. rosy-crimson, becoming purple-violet in age, completely double, formal, to 5 in. across, plants cult. under this name may not be this cv; **'Mathotiana Alba',** fls. white, sometimes streaked or tinged pink, completely double, formal; **'Mathotiana Rosea',** fls. red-pink, completely double, incompletely imbricate, to 4 in. across; **'Mathotiana Rubra':** 'Mathotiana'; **'Mathotiana Variegata',** fls. scarlet, flecked or blotched with white, completely double, incompletely imbricate; **'Nobilissima',** fls. white, yellowish toward center, incompletely double, to 2¾ in. across; **'Nobilissima Rosea',** fls. pink, with shape of cv. 'Nobilissima'; **'Paeoniiflora'** [cv. 'Aspasia MacArthur'], fls. white, flecked rose, incompletely double to irregularly completely double, to 4 in. across; **'Pope Pius IX':** 'Imbricata Rubra Plena'; **'Prattii',** fls. rose-pink, with white stripe in center of each petal, completely double, formal, of large size; **'Rose Emery',** fls. fiery-red, completely double, irregular; **'Rosea Superba',** perhaps the same as cv. 'Mathotiana Rosea'; **'Rosularis',** fls. white, heavily blotched rose-pink, completely double, irregular, large; **'Rubens',** fls. deep rose-pink with broad white bands down center of petals, completely double, formal, 4 in. across; **'Rubra Virginalis',** fls. bright pink, completely double, irregular, of medium to large size; **'Speciosa',** fls. deep crimson, with some white blotches, completely double, irregular, 3½ in. across, material offered under this name may represent another cv. having cherry-pink fls. with pale areas; **'Storeyii',** fls. completely double, formal, of small size, petals deep rose with central white stripe; **'Strata',** fls. rose-red, occasionally mottled white, incompletely double, of large size; **'Sweetii Vera',** fls. light pink, flecked rose-pink, incompletely double, 4 in. across; **'Traversii Plenissima',** fls. red, completely double, formal, of moderate size; **'Tricolor'** [cv. 'Tricolor Sieboldii'], fls. white or pinkish, streaked and flecked with crimson, semidouble, 3–4 in. across, not to be confused with cv. 'Tricolor California' having petals white, striped with rose, or an occasional one solid rose; **'Tricolor Sieboldii':** 'Tricolor'; **'Tricolor Sieboldii White':** 'Leucantha'; **'Tricolor Superba',** fls. from solid white to solid red, often pink and striped or splashed rose or red, semidouble, to 4 in. across; **'Variabilis'** [cv. 'Horkan'], fls. white or flushed pinkish, usually with broad red stripes on petals or solid red, incompletely double, 4 in. across or more; **'Variegata',** plant spreading, fls. rose-red, blotched white, incompletely double, to 3½ in. across; **'Wilderi',** fls. light pink, complete double, formal. Subsp. **rusticana** (Honda) Kitam. [C. rusticana Honda]. Differs from the typical subsp. in having petioles shorter, to ⁵⁄₁₆ in. long, bracteoles, sepals, and stamens shorter, the stamens to only ¹⁄₁₆ in. above union with petals. W. Honshu (Japan).

maliflora Lindl. Shrub, to 8 ft. and nearly as broad, young sts. finely villous; lvs. elliptic, to 2 in. long, acute or short-acuminate, minutely denticulate, very thin-leathery, midrib villous above; bracteoles intergrading into sepals, fls. double, white shaded with rose, about 1½ in. across, fertile stamens 1–2, pistil deformed. China. Known only from original stock brought into cult. in 1818. Apparently the same as Camellia cv. 'Betty McCaskill'.

oleifera Abel [C. oleosa (Lour.) Y. C. Wu]. TEA-OIL PLANT. Shrub or small tree, to 20 ft., differing from C. Sasanqua in having lvs. larger, to 3(–5) in. long and to 1⅜(–2⅜) in. wide, acute to acuminate, serrulate; bracteoles and sepals tomentose to densely villous on outside, stamens erect, compact; caps. and seeds somewhat larger. China, where cult. for its seeds, which yield commercial tea oil.

Pitardii Cohen-Stuart. To 25 ft.; lvs. oblong-elliptic to elliptic, mostly to 4 in. long and 1⅜ in. wide, acute to abruptly acuminate or caudate, often prominently serrulate or subserrate; bracteoles and sepals similar, corolla 1–2 in. long, rose to white, united at base with the broad, fleshy staminal tube about ½ in.; caps. to 2 in. in diam. Winter–spring (and autumn?). China.

reticulata Lindl. To 35 ft. or more, young sts. glabrous; lvs. elliptic, to 4½ in. long and 2 in. wide, acute to short-acuminate, leathery, often dull green above; bracteoles and sepals similar, in a single series, inner sepals sometimes petal-like, fls. rose, or rose and white, to deep red, often double, to 6½ in. across, petals 5–6(–7), stamens united ⅓–¾ of length into a fleshy, yellowish tube or cup, ovary tomentose. Autumn to spring. China. Zone 9.

rosiflora Hook. Similar to *C. maliflora,* but having lvs. to 3 in. long and 1 in. wide, more acuminate, more widely crenulate-serrulate, thicker; fls. single, soft pinkish-rose, pistil normal, glabrous. Known only in cult.

rusticana: *C. japonica* subsp.

salicifolia Champ. ex Benth. Shrub or small tree, branchlets slender, pendulous tawny-villous; lvs. oblong-elliptic, to 4 in. long, 1 in. wide, long-acuminate to caudate, with black-tipped serrulations, firm-papery, villous beneath; bracteoles and sepals villous, persistent, fls. white, 2 in. across, petals 5–6, acuminate to rounded, pubescent outside, stamens about ½ in. long, outer filaments united in basal ⅔, free part hairy, pistil hairy; fr. usually 1-seeded. China, Taiwan.

saluenensis Stapf ex Bean. Compact shrub, to 15 ft.; lvs. oblong to elliptic, to 2 in. long and half as wide, glossy deep green above; bracteoles and sepals grading into one another, in a single series, deciduous, fls. mostly pinkish to deep rose-pink, petals 6–7, to 1¾(–2) in. long, stamens united in basal ⅔–¾ into a deep fleshy cup, ovary white-tomentose. Autumn to spring. China.

Sasanqua Thunb. SASANQUA C., SASANQUA. To 15 ft., twigs very slender; lvs. elliptic, to 2(–3) in. long, acute, with tip blunt or cuspidate, crenulate, thin-leathery, bright glossy green above; bracteoles and sepals grading into one another, inner sepals pubescent on outside, all deciduous, fls. white to rose, petals 6–8, mostly separate to base, stamens spreading, scarcely fused at base, ovary densely silky; fr. globose, to ¾ in. in diam. Autumn to winter. Japan and Ryukyu Is. Zone 7b. Seeds yield a nondrying oil. Many cvs. are known; included are cvs.: **'Alba'**, fls. white, single; **'Floribunda'**, fls. white, edged lavender, single, to 3½ in. across; **'Grandiflora Alba'** [cv. 'Gulf Glory'], fls. white, single, to 3¾ in. across; **'Rosea'**, fls. deep rose-pink, single, to 3⁵⁄₁₆ in. across; **'Rubra Simplex'**, fls. rose-red, single; **'Tricolor Magnifica'**: cv. 'Versicolor'; **'Versicolor'** [cv. 'Tricolor Magnifica'], fls. white at center, becoming pink, margined lavender, single, to 3 in. across.

sinensis (L.) O. Kuntze [*C. Bohea* (L.) Sweet; *C. Thea* L.; *Thea Bohea* L.; *T. sinensis* L.; *T. sinensis* vars. *Bohea* (L.) C. Koch and *viridis* (L.) Pierre]. TEA, TEA PLANT. Variable shrub or tree, 3–50 ft., young sts. rather stout; lvs. elliptic, mostly 2–5½ in. long and ¾–2 in. wide, dark glossy green; fls. nodding, to nearly 1 in. across, peduncles exposed, to ⅜ in. long, sepals 5–6, persistent, corolla cup-shaped, petals 7–8, white, stamens ½ in. long, shortly united below, ovary white-hairy. Autumn. Se. and e. Asia. The processed young lvs. yield commercial tea, the world's most important caffeine beverage. Tea is cult. mainly in warm temp. parts of e. and s. Asia. The seeds also yield an oil. Var. **sinensis.** The typical var.; lvs. mostly to 3½ in. long and 1¼ in. wide, apically obtuse. China. A useful ornamental hedge plant; a form with rose-colored fls. is cult. Var. **assamica** (J. W. Mast.) Kitam. [*Thea assamica* J. W. Mast.]. More tender, makes a tree to 50 ft.; lvs. relatively broader, usually larger, to 8½ in. long and 3 in. wide, bluntly acuminate, thinly leathery. Se. Asia.

spectabilis: *Tutcheria spectabilis.*

Thea: *C. sinensis.*

vernalis (Mak.) Mak. Similar to *C. Sasanqua,* from which it differs only by its later flowering period. Spring. Described from a cult. plant at Tokyo.

CAMOENSIA Welw. ex Benth. & Hook.f. *Leguminosae* (subfamily *Faboideae*). Two spp. of woody climbers of trop. Afr.; lvs. alt., of 3 lfts.; fls. in axillary racemes, papilionaceous, stamens 10, separate; fr. a flat legume.

maxima Welw. ex Benth. Lfts. obovate-oblong, to 6 in. long; calyx tubular, to 7 in. long, red-woolly, petals white, frilled and edged with gold, standard 4 in. wide; fr. to 8 in. long, rusty-woolly. Congo region and Angola.

CAMPANEA: *CAPANEA.*

CAMPANULA L. BELLFLOWER. *Campanulaceae.* About 300 spp. of ann., bien., or per. herbs, distributed throughout the N. Hemisphere, but principally in the Caucasus, Balkan, and Medit. region, varying from small rosette or mat-forming plants to coarse, erect spp.; lvs. alt., without stipules, the basal or rosette lvs. often longer, broader, and with much longer petioles than the st. lvs.; fls. usually in racemes, sometimes solitary or in spikes, heads, or narrow panicles, bisexual, calyx tube regular, united to the ovary, with needle-shaped to triangular lobes, often with a reflexed lobe or appendage in each sinus, corolla violet-blue to purplish, white or pink, campanulate to rotate, 5-lobed, stamens 5, filaments flattened at the base, borne on the base of the corolla tube, anthers separate, ovary 3–5-celled, ovules many, style elongate, stigma 3–5-lobed; fr. a caps., dehiscing by basal or lateral pores or slits.

Because of their diversity in size and form and their generally large and showy flowers, bellflowers provide many species suitable for the flower garden, rock garden, and border. One species, *C. Rapunculus* is used as a vegetable, the first-year roots and leaves sometimes being eaten as a salad. The perennial species are propagated by seeds under glass and transplanted to the open after the danger of frost is past, and by cuttings and divisions. Seeds are sometimes sown in the summer to produce blooming plants the following season. This procedure is followed with the biennials such as canterbury bells. The annuals are propagated by seeds sown outdoors or under glass.

abietina Griseb. & Schenk. Slender-stemmed, erect, glabrous ann. or short-lived per., to 2 ft.; st. lvs. few, narrowly elliptic to lanceolate or oblanceolate, less than 2 in. long, crenulate to entire; fls. few near apex of st., erect or ascending, on bracted peduncles to 2 in. long, calyx without appendages, lobes awl-shaped, to ½ in. long, corolla light violet, rotate, deeply lobed, 1–1½ in. across, stigma 3–lobed. Carpathians.

Adria: a listed name of no botanical standing; material offered under this name is *C. Elatines.*

adsurgens Levier & Leresche. Probably not in cult.; differs from *C. Elatines,* from which it is probably not specifically distinct, in having lvs. cordate-orbicular, crenate, fls. in short terminal racemes, calyx lobes erect, and fr. obconical. Spain.

affinis Roem. & Schult. [*C. Bolosii* Vayr.]. Erect bien., to 2½ ft.; rosette lvs. sessile, oblanceolate, to 8 in. long, coarsely ciliate, lvs. many, sessile, narrowly lanceolate; fls. many in leafy racemes, calyx with appendages about as long as calyx lobes, to ½ in. long, triangular, acute, corolla white to pink or pale violet, broadly campanulate-rotate, to 2 in. across. Spain.

afra: *C. dichotoma.*

alaskana: a listed name of no botanical standing for *C. rotundifolia.*

alata Desf. Erect per., to 5 ft., sts. thick, glabrous; st. lvs. decurrent, to 6 in. long, ovate to lanceolate, dentate; fls. in dense terminal spikes or racemes, calyx without appendages, the tube short-hispid, lobes lanceolate, corolla to 1¾ in. long, broadly campanulate, lobed to the middle. Algeria, Tunisia. Cv. **'Alba'** is offered.

alliariifolia Willd. Erect, gray-pubescent per., to 4 ft.; rosette lvs. similar to st. lvs., but sometimes hastate, on petioles to 10 in. long or more, st. lvs. cordate-ovate to nearly reniform, to 5 in. long, acute, irregularly crenate-dentate; fls. nodding, in dense, 1-sided, terminal racemes, calyx to ½ in. long, with acute appendages, corolla 1–2 in. long, white, tubular-campanulate, stigma 3–lobed. Asia Minor, Caucasus.

Allionii Vill. [*C. alpestris* All.]. Dwarf per., with creeping rhizome, rosette lvs. sessile, linear or lanceolate, to 2 in. long, entire, pubescent; st. lvs. few, nearly erect in upper part of st.; fl. sts. 2–5 in. high, each with single, erect or declined fl., calyx about ½ in. long, lobed to near the base, with appendages, corolla blue or white, to 1¾ in. long, broadly tubular-campanulate, style included, 3-lobed. Mts., s. France, n. Italy.

alpestris: *C. Allionii.*

alpina Jacq. Dwarf, tufted, short-lived per., 3–6 in.; lvs. linear to oblanceolate, to 2 in. long, entire, hairy; fls. long-pedicelled, 1 or few on each st., ascending or nodding, calyx white-hairy, with minute appendages, lobes spreading, lanceolate, half to nearly as long as the corolla, corolla pale to dark blue, to 1 in. long, campanulate, with short lobes, style included, 3-lobed. Alps and Carpathians, Eur.

amabilis: *C. persicifolia.*

americana L. TALL B. Erect, simple or few-branched ann., to 6 ft., glabrous or pubescent; st. lvs. lanceolate to ovate-elliptic, to 6 in. long, narrowed at both ends, serrate; fls. 1–3 in the axils, in long spikes, calyx lobes linear, to ⅜ in. long, corolla blue or white, to 1 in. across, rotate, style 3-lobed. Moist, shady places, e. N. Amer.

aparinoides Pursh. MARSH B. Decumbent per., sts. weak, 1–3 ft., the angles usually minutely scabrous; lvs. sessile, very narrowly elliptic, to 1½ in. long; fls. on elongate, filiform, leafy-bracted peduncles, corolla white or bluish, to ⁵⁄₁₆ in. long, broadly campanulate. Swamps and grassy swales, e. U.S.

ardonensis Rupr. Tufted, glabrate, grasslike per., 3–4 in.; lower lvs. linear, to 2 in. long, upper lvs. filiform; fls. solitary on sts., scarcely exceeding lower lvs., corolla deep blue, ½–¾ in. long, narrowly campanulate. Caucasus. Probably not in cult.

arvatica Lag. Tufted per., sts. glabrous, to 8 in. long, spreading and only reaching 2–3 in. high; lvs. ovate to rhomboidal, to ⁵⁄₁₆ in. long, upper lvs. deeply dentate; fls. few on a st., calyx lobes about ¼ in. long, each usually with 1–2 teeth near the middle, corolla blue or white, to 1 in. across, rotate-campanulate. Mts., n. Spain. Not always hardy north. Material offered under this name may be *C. Aucheri*.

attica; *C. ramossisima.*

Aucheri A. DC. Tufted per., similar to *C. tridentata,* 4–5 in.; lvs. mostly downy-pubescent, the lower broadly ovate to spatulate, 2–3 in. long, dentate apically, the upper smaller, linear to lanceolate; fls. mostly solitary, erect, calyx lobes with acute appendages longer than the tube, corolla violet-blue to pale blue, to 1 in. across, broadly campanulate, pubescent. Mts., Armenia to Iran.

aurita Greene. Tufted per., sts. erect, to 6 in., scabrous, leafy, 1-fld.; lvs. sessile, oblong-lanceolate, to 1 in. long, entire or with few coarse teeth; calyx lobes with 2 erect teeth at base, corolla violet, to ¾ in. long, campanulate, with spreading, lanceolate lobes. Alaska.

Autraniana Albov. Somewhat tufted, glabrous per.; lower lvs. long-petioled, cordate-ovate to lanceolate, to 3 in. long, acute, irregularly crenate-dentate, st. lvs. sessile, linear; fl. sts. slender, to 8 in., scapose, 1 to few-fld., calyx with minute appendages, lobes spreading, triangular, to ¼ in. long, corolla purple-blue, to 1 in. long, broadly tubular-campanulate. W. Caucasus.

barbata L. Tufted, hairy per., sts. to about 12 in., scapose, erect, mostly unbranched; rosette lvs. sessile, lanceolate to oblanceolate, 2–6 in. long, entire, or serrulate; fls. nodding, in open, often 1-sided racemes, calyx up to ½ in. long, with appendages, corolla pale blue, to 1 in. long, campanulate with short, spreading, ciliate lobes. Mts., Norway, Alps. Cv. 'Alba' is offered.

Bellardii: *C. cochleariifolia:* but plants offered as *C. Bellardii* are likely to be *C. caespitosa,* and material grown from seed said to be *C. Bellardii* has proven to be *C. rapunculoides.*

bellidifolia Adams. Tufted, glabrate per., similar to *C. tridentata;* rosette lvs. long-petioled, ovate-orbicular, to ½ in. across, coarsely crenate, st. lvs. smaller, spatulate; fl. sts. many, slender, erect, 1-fld., calyx with lanceolate appendages as long as the tube, corolla deep violet, campanulate. Caucasus. Most of the material offered as *C. bellidifolia* in the trade is *C. patula* or *C. Aucheri.*

betulifolia C. Koch. Tufted, glabrous or puberulent per., sts. thin, erect to decumbent, to 8 in. long; lvs. long-petioled in lower part, nearly sessile above, thickish, ovate, to 1½ in. long, laciniate-serrate, glossy; fls. long-pedicelled, erect, to 12 on a st., calyx with lanceolate appendages, corolla white or blue, flushed with pink outside, 1–1½ in. long, campanulate. Armenia.

Billardieri: *C. Cymbalaria.*

Bolosii: *C. affinis.*

bononiensis L. Erect, glabrous to canescent bien., to 2–3 ft.; rosette lvs. long-petioled, cordate-ovate, st. lvs. sessile, ovate, serrate, 2–3 in. long in lower part, progressively smaller above; fls. in terminal, naked, spicate infls., calyx without appendages, corolla bluish, about ¾ in. long. E. Eur., sw. Asia.

Broussonetiana: *C. lusitanica.*

Burghaltii: a listed name of no botanical standing; perhaps a hybrid between *C. latifolia* and *C. punctata* or even only a form of the latter; erect, to 3 ft., sts. with large, pendent fls. apically; corolla pale lavender to grayish-blue, to 3 in. long, campanulate.

caespitosa Scop. Tufted, taprooted, glabrous per., sts. many, slender, erect, 4–8 in.; lowest lvs. tapering to a short petiole, ovate, to 1½ in. long, with a few deep serrations, upper lvs. smaller, sessile, linear, entire; fls. in racemes above the lvs., ascending or declined, calyx without appendages, corolla blue, ribbed, to ¾ in. long, urceolate-campanulate, with very short lobes. Mts., Eur. Cv. 'Alba'. Fls. white.

calamenthifolia Lam. Grayish-pubescent, short-lived per. with rosette of lvs., sts. radiating, decumbent, to about 8 in. long; lvs. petioled, ovate to spatulate or orbicular, to ½ in. long, dentate; fls. many, erect, solitary, in axils, calyx with acute appendages, corolla blue or white, campanulate-rotate, to 1 in. across, tomentose outside. Greece.

californica (Kellogg) A. Heller. Erect per., to 1½ ft., sts. slender, simple or few-branched, leafy, more or less retrorsely scabrous; lvs. sessile or nearly so, ovate to elliptic, about 1 in. long, minutely crenate;

calyx with appendages, corolla pale blue, to ⅝ in. long, campanulate. Coastal fresh water swamps, n. Calif.

calycanthema: a listed name of no botanical standing for *C. Medium* cv.

campanulata: a listed name of no botanical standing. Var. **Moesiaca.** May refer to *C. Moesiaca.*

carpatica Jacq. [*C. turbinata* Schott]. TUSSOCK B. Glabrous, clump-forming per., 8–18 in., sts. slender, spreading, leafy at base; lvs. long-petioled, ovate-triangular to broadly lanceolate, 2 in. long or less, deeply serrate, long-petioled; fls. erect on long, slender, naked, axillary pedicels, calyx without appendages, corolla blue-lilac, 1–2 in. across, broadly campanulate, style exserted. Carpathians. Material offered as *C. Raineri* is often a dwarf form of this sp. Represented in cult. by many cvs., including color variants, 'Compacta', 'Nana', and 'Turbinata'. Other fancy-named cvs. are also listed.

cashmeriana Royle. Small, tufted per., sts. many, zigzag, decumbent to erect, to about 8 in. long; lvs. sessile, elliptic, to 1 in. long, entire, velvety-pubescent, greenish above, grayish beneath; fls. solitary in the axils, few to many, corolla blue, to ⅝ in. long, narrow-campanulate. Himalayas. Probably not hardy north.

Celsii A. DC. Small, grayish-velvety bien., with dense rosette; lvs. long-petioled, ovate, irregularly lobate-dentate; fl. sts. several, erect to decumbent, to 8 in. long, racemes many-fld., calyx with small, acute appendages, corolla lavender, to 1 in. long, tubular-campanulate with spreading lobes, style 5-lobed. Cyclades Is. (Greece).

celtidifolia: *C. lactiflora.*

cenisia L. Glabrous or slightly hairy, creeping per., 2–3 in.; rosette lvs. spatulate to broadly obovate, ¼–⅝ in. long, often apiculate, entire, mostly minutely ciliate; fls. solitary, terminal, erect, calyx without appendages, corolla bright blue, twice as long as calyx, about ¾ in. long, tubular-campanulate. Above 7,500 ft., Alps.

cephallenica Feer. Similar to *C. Elatines,* but with looser habit, remote lvs., and few-fld. racemes. Is. of Cephalonia (Greece).

Cervicaria L. Pilose, erect bien., to 2½ ft., sts. simple; lvs. linear to lanceolate, to 6 in. long, serrate, petioles often winged; fls. bracted, in dense axillary and terminal cluster, calyx without appendages, corolla blue, to ⅝ in. long, narrow-campanulate. Cent. and n. Eur. Rarely cult.

Chamissonis Fedorov. Per., sts. to 6 in.; lower lvs. somewhat in a rosette, long-petioled, oblanceolate to oblong, to 1¾ in. long, obtuse, glabrous or with few hairs marginally or on the veins beneath; fls. solitary, terminal, calyx pubescent, with minute, awl-shaped appendages, corolla blue, to 1¾ in. long, campanulate, softly white-hairy on the margins and within. E. Siberia, n. Japan, Kurile and Aleutian Is. The names *C. dasyantha* and *C. pilosa* have sometimes been misapplied to this sp.

cochleariifolia Lam. [*C. Bellardii* All., *C. pusilla* Haenke]. Similar to and often confused with *C. caespitosa,* but spreading rather than tufted and lower lvs. long-petioled, basally broadly cuneate to cordate. Mts., Eur. Cv. 'Alba'. Fls. white. Cv. 'Miranda'. Of dwarf habit.

collina Bieb. Clump-forming per., sts. many, erect, to 1 ft., scapose; lvs. clustered basally, the lowermost long-petioled, blades ovate-oblong, 2–3 in. long, serrate; fls. few, in 1-sided racemes, nodding, calyx without appendages, to about ⅜ in. long, often drying bluish, corolla deep purplish-blue, to 1½ in. long, broadly campanulate. Caucasus.

colorata Wallich ex Roxb. Much-branched, slender-stemmed, spreading-hairy ann. or short-lived per., to 2 ft.; upper lvs. remote, ovate-lanceolate, to 1½ in. long, few-toothed; fls. solitary on elongate, axillary or terminal pedicels, calyx without appendages, corolla deep purple-blue, to ⅝ in. long, closed-campanulate with spreading lobes, somewhat hairy outside. Himalayas, Kashmir to w. Tibet. Not hardy north.

cretica: *Symphyandra cretica.*

Cymbalaria Sibth. & Sm. [*C. Billardieri* A. DC.]. Doubtfully per., glabrous or puberulous, sts. decumbent to erect, to 1 ft. long; lvs. ovate to reniform-cordate, to 1 in. long, toothed; fls. long-pedicelled, in 1–3-fld. clusters in axillary racemes, calyx without appendages, corolla blue, to ½ in. long, twice as long as calyx, campanulate. Bulgaria, Greece.

dasyantha Bieb. [*C. pilosa* Pall. ex Roem. & Schult.]. Pilose per., 2–6 in.; basal lvs. lanceolate to linear-spatulate, to about 1 in. long, acute, glabrous, st. lvs. sessile; fls. 1–3 on a st., calyx pilose, with ovate, acute appendages, corolla violet, to 1 in. long, funnelform with acute, flaring lobes. Altai Mts., Mongolia to Alaska. Cvs. 'Elegantissima' and 'Superba' are listed. Often confused with *C. Chamissonis,* but differs in its acute, pubescent, narrower basal lvs. Material grown under the name *C. dasyantha* may be *C. Chamissonis.*

dichotoma L. [*C. afra* Cav.]. Diffuse, spreading or ascending, leafy ann., 4–18 in. high, sts. pilose, often appearing dichotomously branched; lvs. more or less elliptic, to 1½ in. long, minutely crenate to entire; fls. many, often in 3's and terminal, calyx conspicuously ciliate, with large, lanceolate appendages, corolla purplish-pink fading to deep blue, to ¾ in. long, tubular-campanulate. Medit. region.

dichroantha: a listed name of no botanical standing.

divaricata Michx. [*C. flexuosa* Michx., not Waldst. & Kit.]. SOUTHERN HAREBELL. Freely branching, glabrous per., 1–3 ft.; lvs. ovate-lanceolate to narrow-lanceolate, 1–6 in. long, sharply toothed; fls. nodding, in many-fld. slender-branched panicles, corolla pale blue, to ½ in. long, style exserted. Woods, Md. to Ky., s. to Ala. and Ga.

Elatines L. ADRIATIC B. Glabrous or pubescent per., sts. slender, spreading from a root crown; lower lvs. long-petioled, cordate-ovate to -orbicular, to 1 in. long and broad, very sharply toothed; fls. several to many in racemes or narrow panicles, calyx without appendages, lobes linear or awl-shaped, corolla white or blue, to ½ in. across or more, nearly rotate. A variable sp. of the Adriatic region and eastward. Although several botanical vars. and several cvs. have been recognized, the garden plants and not easily referable to them. Cvs. '**Alba**', '**Glaberrima**', '**Glabra**', and '**Hirsuta**' have been listed. Var. **elatinoides** (Moretti) Fiori [*C. elatinoides* Moretti]. Of dense, compact habit, lvs. somewhat fleshy, white-tomentose. Italian Alps. Var. **fenestrellata** (Feer) L. H. Bailey [*C. fenestrellata* Feer]. Basal lvs. glabrous, glossy; fl. pedicels mostly 5–9 times longer than the calyx. Italy to Yugoslavia. Cv. '**Alba**'. Var. **garganica** (Ten.) Fiori [*C. garganica* Ten.]. Basal lvs. mostly ovate, acute, green, with minute pubescence; corolla ⅛–⅜ in. long. S. Italy. Cvs. '**Alba**', '**Erinus**', '**Hirsuta**', '**Major**', '**Pallida**', and '**Villosa**' have been listed. Var. **istriaca** (Feer) Fiori [*C. istriaca* Feer]. Lvs. broadly orbicular, gray-pubescent; corolla to ½ in. long or more. Yugoslavia.

elatinoides: *C. Elatines* var.

elegans Roem. & Schult. Sts. pubescent, simple, to 1 ft. or more; lvs. sessile, linear-lanceolate, entire, the lower ones broader, shortly petioled; fls. in interrupted spikes, calyx lobes very narrow, and as long as the corolla. Siberia. A dubious sp.; plants cult. under this name are *C. rapunculoides*.

Erinus L. Much-branched, downy-pubescent ann., 6–15 in.; lvs. oblong or ovate, to 1 in. long, somewhat toothed, upper lvs. often with only 1 pair of deep teeth; fls. axillary, nearly sessile, corolla reddish-violet to white, to about ¼ in. long, scarcely longer than calyx. Medit. region. Material offered under this name is rarely this sp.

excisa Schleich. ex Murith. Spreading, glabrous per., 3–8 in., sts. slender; lvs. linear or nearly spatulate basally, to 1½ in. long, entire; fls. pendent, solitary or few toward the apex, calyx without appendages, lobes filiform-awl-shaped, less than ⅓ as long as corolla, corolla violet, to ¾ in. long, campanulate with a hole at the base of each sinus. Alps, Switzerland and Austria.

fenestrellata: *C. Elatines* var.

×**Fergusonii** Hort. ex André. Thought to be a hybrid between *C. carpatica* and *C. pyramidalis*, but similar to *C. carpatica*; to 6 in.; fls. erect, campanulate.

filicaulis Durieu. Tufted, glabrate per., sts. decumbent, angular; basal lvs. obovate, to 1½ in. long, narrowed to a winged, ciliate base, st. lvs. similar, about ½ in. long; fls. solitary on slender pedicels, calyx with minute appendages, corolla bluish, about ½ in. long, rotate. Morocco, Algeria. Probably not in cult.; some of the material listed under this name is *C. sarmatica*.

flexuosa: see *C. divaricata* and *C. Waldsteiniana*; material offered as *C. flexuosa* is probably *C. Waldsteiniana*.

Formanekiana Degen & Dörfl. Monocarpic, silvery-pubescent, erect, to 2 ft. or sometimes without a main st.; rosette lvs. winged-petioled, blade abruptly expanded, ovate or triangular, to 1½ in. long, coarsely toothed, st. lvs. sessile; fls. in leafy panicles, ascending to nodding, calyx with appendages, lobes serrate, corolla white, to 1½ in. long, narrow-campanulate with reflexed lobes. N. Greece to Albania. Some material listed under this name is *C. Poscharskyana*.

fragilis Cyr. Decumbent, pubescent herb, sts. to 1½ ft. long; basal lvs. long-petioled, reniform to ovate, to ¾ in. long, coarsely toothed; fls. axillary, more or less terminal, calyx without appendages, corolla bluish-purple, whitish toward the center, to 1½ in. across, rotate. S. Italy. Not hardy in colder regions.

garganica: *C. Elatines* var.

glomerata L. CLUSTERED B. Erect, rather coarse per., 1–3 ft., sts. simple or branched; lvs. ovate-oblong to lanceolate, to 5 in. long, minutely serrate, the lowest long-petioled; fls. in dense terminal and axillary clusters, calyx without appendages, corolla blue or white, ¾–1 in. long. Eurasia. Var. **acaulis** Rehn. Fl. clusters on short sts. barely

longer than the rosette. Var. **dahurica** Fisch. ex Ker-Gawl. [*C. speciosa* Hornem.]. Fl. clusters larger, to 3 in. across. Cv. '**Alba**' is listed. Cv. '**Superba**'. A more showy strain.

grandiflora: *Platycodon grandiflorus;* see also *C. Medium*.

grandis: *C. persicifolia*.

Grossekii Heuff. Coarse, erect per., to 3 ft., sts. often angled, bristly-hairy; lower lvs. long-petioled, broadly cordate-ovate, to 6 in. long, very coarsely double-toothed, upper lvs. sessile, narrow-ovate, obtuse; fls. solitary or in few-fld. clusters along the sts., calyx setose, without appendages, corolla blue, 1–1½ in. long, narrow-campanulate, the principal veins setose. Hungary. Often confused with *C. Trachelium*.

×**Hallii** Hort.; *C. cochleariifolia* × *C. Portenschlagiana*. Intermediate between the parents; fls. erect, white, rotate, mostly solitary on short sts.

Hawkinsiana Hausskn. & Heldr. ex Hausskn. Glabrous or glabrate, mat-forming ann. or short-lived per., sts. slender, ascending, to 6 in.; lvs. orbicular to ovate, about ¼–½ in. long, 1–2-toothed; fls. terminal, erect, calyx without appendages, corolla blue, to 1 in. across, rotate-campanulate. Mts., Albania and Greece.

×**haylodgensis** Hort.: *C. carpatica* × *C. cochleariifolia*. Sprawling, glabrous, slender-stemmed; lvs. ovate, sharply serrate; fls. few on long pedicels, near the ends of sts., corolla blue, single or double, about ½ in. long, broadly campanulate. Cv. '**Warley White**' [*C. Warleyensis* Hort.]. Fls. white.

Hemschinica C. Koch. Bien., sts. erect, to 1–1½ ft.; lower lvs. narrow-oblong, on short, slender petioles, upper lvs. sessile and clasping the st., oblong-lanceolate; fls. few, more or less terminal on the brs., on short, strict pedicels, calyx without appendages, corolla blue, to 1 in. long, tubular-campanulate. Mts., e. Eur.

hercegovina Degen & Fiala. Lax herbs, 6–12 in., sts. slender; lower lvs. long-petioled, ovate, nearly cordate at base, 2–3-toothed, progressively narrower and shorter-petioled in upper part of st.; fls. on filiform pedicels, in loose panicles, calyx without appendages, corolla blue-violet, to ¾ in. long, campanulate. Mts., Yugoslavia.

heterodoxa: see *C. rotundifolia*.

Hohenackeri: *C. siberica*.

Hostii: *C. linifolia*, but material offered as *C. Hostii* is usually *C. rotundifolia*.

hybrida: *Legousia hybrida*.

imeretina Rupr. Hispid per., to 6 in. or more, lower lvs. obovate, narrowed at base to a winged petiole, upper lvs. sessile, ovate, to 1 in. long, scarcely crenate; fls. erect, few in a more or less dichotomously branched, terminal infl., calyx with acute appendages, lobes broadly lanceolate, corolla violet-blue, about ½ in. long. Caucasus. Plants grown under this name have proved to be *C. rapunculoides*.

imperialis: a listed name of no botanical standing.

incurva Aucher ex A. DC. [*C. Leutweinii* Heldr.]. Prostrate or ascending, pubescent, monocarpic, with sts. 1–1½ ft. long; lower lvs. ovate-oblong to reniform, cordate at base, crenate to serrate, upper lvs. more usually ovate, narrowed basally to winged petioles; fls. erect, axillary near the ends of brs., calyx with large, triangular appendages, corolla white to pale violet, to 2 in. long, campanulate. Greece.

Innesii: a listed name of no botanical standing.

isophylla Moretti. ITALIAN B., STAR-OF-BETHLEHEM, FALLING-STARS. Glabrous or grayish-pubescent per., sts. slender, trailing; lower lvs. long-petioled, broadly cordate-ovate, to 1½ in. long, deeply serrate, upper lvs. often more lanceolate; fls. erect, many, in short, corymbose panicles, calyx without appendages, corolla violet-blue, grayish toward the center, to 1–1½ in. across, rotate-campanulate. Italy. Cvs. are: '**Alba**', fls. white; '**Caerulea**', fls. blue; and '**Mayi**', grayish-pubescent, large-fld. All make excellent basket plants.

istriaca: *C. Elatines* var.

×**Jenkinsae** Hort. Presumed to be a hybrid between *C. carpatica* cv. '**Alba**' and *C. rotundifolia*. Fl. sts. erect, to 12 in.; racemes loose, few-fld.; fls. white, open-campanulate.

kachethica Z. Kantsch. Erect per., sts. to 1 ft., leafy, hirsute, 1-fld.; lower lvs. long-petioled, blade oblong-ovate, to 2 in. long, nearly cordate at base, st. lvs. shorter-petioled, ovate, less deeply serrate; calyx with obscure appendages, corolla whitish-rose to rose-violet, to ¾ in. long, narrowly campanulate. Caucasus.

Kantschavelii Zagar. Grayish per., sts. many, to 1 ft.; similar to *C. kachethica*, but fls. in loose, racemose cymes, sometimes with the calyx lobe and appendage margins bristly-pubescent, corolla deep lavender, to 1 in. long, tubular-campanulate. Caucasus.

Kemulariae Fomin. Clump-forming per.; basal lvs. long-petioled, cordate-ovate, doubly serrate, of rather hard, shiny texture, st. lvs. reduced; fl. sts. to 1 ft. long, often decumbent, many-branched, calyx with prominent triangular appendages, corolla pale mauve, to 1 in. long, broadly campanulate. Transcaucasus.

Kolenatiana C. A. Mey. ex Rupr. Monocarpic, usually bien.; similar to *C. sarmatica*, but lvs. green rather than grayish-pubescent, the calyx broad with bristly, subdentate, lanceolate, recurved appendages, corolla violet-blue. Caucasus.

Komarovii Maleev. Per., with woody rhizomes; rosette lvs. winged-petioled, spatulate, obscurely toothed, hairy; fl. sts. several, ascending, with terminal, few-fld. racemes, calyx densely white-setose, with large, ovate, reflexed appendages, corolla deep violet, to 2 in. long, broadly campanulate. Caucasus, Black Sea region of U.S.S.R.

lactiflora Bieb. [*C. celtidifolia* Boiss.]. Per., sts. several, to 4 ft.; basal lvs. sessile, ovate, to 5 in. long, serrate; fl. sts. with progressively smaller lvs., often nearly naked, with many-fld. terminal panicles; fls. erect, calyx without appendages, the lobes serrate, corolla pale blue or nearly white, to about 1 in. across, campanulate-rotate. Caucasus. Cv. 'Alba'. Fls. white. Cv. 'Caerulea'. Fls. blue.

lanata Friv. [*C. velutina* Velen.]. Monocarpic, densely grayish-silky-tomentose; basal lvs. tufted, cordate-ovate, about 4 in. long, serrate, petioles as long as the blades, winged, upper lvs. smaller; fl. sts. several, to 3 ft.; fls. many, axillary and terminal, calyx with minute, lanceolate appendages, corolla white, pale yellow, or even pinkish, to 1¼ in. long, broadly campanulate. Mts., n. Greece and Bulgaria.

lasiocarpa Cham. Nearly glabrous, tufted, dwarf per., 3–6 in.; lvs. spatulate, obovate, or linear, to 1¾ in. long, serrate; fls. erect, terminal on scapose sts., calyx without appendages, often woolly between the toothed lobes, corolla dark violet-blue, to 1 in. long, broadly campanulate. W. N. Amer. and Japan.

latifolia L. [*C. macrantha* Fisch.]. Coarse per. herb, glabrous or sparsely pubescent; basal lvs. cordate-ovate, deeply dentate-serrate, blade to 6 in. long, with petioles nearly as long, st. lvs. smaller; fl. sts. erect, simple, with fls. nearly erect in the upper lf. axils and in terminal clusters, calyx smooth, without appendages, glabrous or woolly pubescent at the base, lobes lanceolate, corolla purplish-blue, 1½–3 in. long, broadly campanulate. N. England, Eur., and Asia. Cv. 'Alba'. Fls. white. Cv. 'Macrantha'. Fls. larger.

latiloba: *C. persicifolia*.

Leutweinii: *C. incurva*; but some of the material listed as *C. Leutweinii* is *C. Grossekii* or *C. rapunculoides*.

lingulata Waldst. & Kit. Bristly-pubescent bien., with several fl. sts. to 15 in.; lvs. oblong-spatulate, to 2 in. long, undulate-toothed, the uppermost clasping; fls. few, in terminal and axillary, bracted heads, calyx with appendages, lobes oblong-obtuse, corolla violet, to 1 in. long, narrow campanulate, hispid on the angles. Hungary, se. Eur.

linifolia Scop. [*C. Hostii* Baumg.; *C. pulla* Baumg. ex Steud., not L.; *C. Scheuchzeri* Vill.; *C. valdensis* All.]. Loosely tufted per., sts. erect or decumbent, with erect brs. to 10 in.; lower lvs. petioled, cordate-reniform, st. lvs. abundant, sessile, linear to linear-lanceolate, to 2 in. long, entire or obscurely toothed, often ciliate; fls. terminal, solitary or in few-fld. racemes, calyx without appendages, lobes entire nearly as long as the corolla, corolla lilac to rose-violet, ⅝ in. long, funnelform. Alps, Eur. Material offered under this name may be *C. rotundifolia*.

Loeflingii: *L. lusitanica*.

longiflora: a listed name of no botanical standing.

longistyla Fomin. Erect bien., to 1½ ft. or more; rosette lvs. petioled, ovate, st. lvs. narrow-elliptic to ovate, to 2 in. long, the uppermost sessile; fls. nodding, many, in racemes or panicles, calyx with ovate, acute appendages, corolla deep blue, to 1½ in. long, campanulate, somewhat constricted above the middle. Caucasus.

lusitanica L. ex Loefl. [*C. Broussonetiana* Roem. & Schult.; *C. Loeflingii* Brot.]. Much-branched ann., to about 1 ft., nearly glabrous or sparsely bristly; st. lvs. often clasping, ovate-lanceolate, 1–2 in. long; fls. many, on long, filiform pedicels, calyx without appendages, lobes linear-lanceolate, corolla blue-violet, whitish at the base, twice as long as calyx, to ¾ in. long, broadly campanulate with flaring lobes. Spain, Portugal, nw. Afr.

macrantha: *C. latifolia*.

macrorhiza J. Gay ex A. DC. Tufted per., with thick rhizomes; basal lvs. petioled, cordate-orbicular, dentate, st. lvs. sessile or nearly so, linear-lanceolate, to about 1½ in. long; fl. sts. several, erect, simple or branched, to about 1 ft., many-fld.; fls. erect, calyx without appendages, lobes linear-lanceolate, reflexed, corolla violet-blue, to 1 in. long, open-campanulate. S. France.

macrostyla Boiss. & Heldr. Bristly-pubescent ann., to 1 ft.; lvs. lanceolate-elliptic, to about 2 in. long, nearly entire; fls. few, terminal on apical brs., calyx with deflexed, bladdery appendages, enlarging in fr., lobes ¾ as long as the corolla, corolla purplish, mottled inside, about 2½ in. across, very open-campanulate, style exserted, stigma lobes prominent, to ½ in. long. Cent. Turkey.

Makaschvilii E. Busch. Similar to *C. alliariifolia*, but smaller, to about 1½ ft., less hairy, and with smaller calyx lobes and appendages. Caucasus.

Marchesettii: *C. rotundifolia*.

Medium L. [*C. grandiflora* Lam., not Jacq.]. CANTERBURY-BELLS. Hairy bien., to 3 ft.; rosette lvs. ovate to obovate, to 10 in. long, crenate-undulate, roughish, petioles winged, st. lvs. sessile, smaller; fls. 1–2 together in very open racemes, calyx bristly-ciliate, with large, ovate appendages, corolla white to blue, to 2 in. long, campanulate, somewhat inflated at the base. S. Eur. Cvs. 'Alba', 'Caerulea', and 'Rosea' are color variants; cv. 'Nana' is a dwarf form. Cv. 'Calycanthema' [var. *calycanthema* T. Moore, *C. calycanthema* Hort.]. CUP-AND-SAUCER. Calyx petal-like, deeply or shallowly lobed, and up to 3 in. across. Var. **calycanthema**: 'Calycanthema'.

mirabilis Albov. Monocarpic, much-branched, to 1 ft.; rosette lvs. ovate, serrate, smooth, glossy, petioles winged, to about 6 in. long, st. lvs. reduced, the uppermost clasping; fl. sts. erect, fls. ascending, 1–4 on short, axillary brs., calyx with appendages, ciliate, corolla pale lilac-blue, to 2 in. across, campanulate. Caucasus.

Moerheimii: a listed name of no botanical standing for *C. persicifolia* cv.

moesiaca Velen. Low, soft-pubescent bien.; rosette lvs. oblong, serrate, abruptly narrowed to winged petioles; fl. sts. erect, with fls. in dense, terminal and sometimes axillary, bracted clusters, calyx without appendages, lobes triangular-lanceolate, corolla lilac-blue, to 1¼ in. long, campanulate. Subalpine, Balkans.

Morettiana Rchb.f. Somewhat mat-forming, grayish-pubescent per.; lvs. cordate-orbicular, about ½ in. long, mostly few-toothed; fl. sts. erect, 2–3 in., each usually bearing a simple, erect fl., calyx without appendages, corolla violet-blue, to 1 in. long, campanulate. Mts., n. Italy, Tyrol. Plants offered under this name are likely to be *C. rotundifolia*.

muralis: *C. Portenschlagiana*.

nitida: *C. persicifolia*.

oblongifolia (C. Koch) Charadze. Grayish-pubescent per., to 3 ft.; rosette and lower st. lvs. long-petioled, oblong to elliptic, upper st. lvs. sessile and more or less clasping at base, more ovate, all finely toothed and scabrous; fls. sessile in bracted, few-fld., interrupted spikes, calyx whitish-pubescent, corolla about twice as long as calyx, to 1 in. long, tubular to funnelform. Caucasus.

ochroleuca (Kem.-Nat.) Kem.-Nat. Per., to 2½ ft.; rosette lvs. long-petioled, triangular-cordate, to 5 in. long, st. lvs. sparse, very much reduced toward infl.; fl. sts. with spicate-racemose infls., calyx with appendages to ⅓ as long as corolla, lobes lanceolate, short, hairy, corolla pale ochre-yellow, large, narrowly campanulate. Caucasus.

olympica Boiss. Creeping per. producing rosettes of elliptic to obovate, crenulate lvs. and erect, simple sts. 1–2 ft. high at ends of stolons; fls. erect, few, in racemes, calyx without appendages, lobes lanceolate, usually toothed at the base, corolla pale violet-blue, to 1¼ in. long, funnelform. Mt. Olympus (Greece). Other plants may be offered under this name, especially *C. rotundifolia* cv. 'Olympica'.

Parryi A. Gray [*C. planiflora* Engelm., not Lam. or Hort.]. Mostly glabrous per., sts. erect, 3–10 in., from slender rhizomes; rosette lvs. oblanceolate to spatulate, to 2 in. long, entire or denticulate, st. lvs. linear; fls. erect, usually solitary, terminal, calyx without appendages, the lobes usually denticulate near the base, corolla violet-blue, about 1 in. across, funnelform-rotate. Subalpine, Rocky Mts., s. Wyo. to New Mex. and Ariz. Cv. 'Alba'. Fls. white. Var. **idahoensis** McVaugh. Lvs. and calyx lobes entire, fls. generally smaller on short pedicels, and calyx tube often puberulent.

patula L. Bien., sts. erect, to 2 ft., much-branched, often hispidulous on the angles; rosette lvs. spatulate to oblanceolate, to 3 in. long, st. lvs. remote, sessile, mostly linear to lanceolate; fls. erect, in open panicles, calyx without appendages, lobes linear-lanceolate, spreading, corolla whitish to bluish-purple, 1–1½ in. across, broadly funnelform. Cent. and s. Eur.

pentagonia *Legousia pentagonia*.

peregrina L. Erect, rather bristly-stemmed bien., 2–3 ft.; rosette lvs. ovate to spatulate, to 4 in. long, crenate, rugose, st. lvs. sessile, ovate, acute; fl. sts. simple, fls. in spikes, calyx ciliate, without appendages, lobes broad, corolla deep violet toward the center with lighter lobes, funnelform. Medit. region.

persicifolia L. [*C. amabilis* Leichtl.; *C. grandis* Fisch. & C. A. Mey.; *C. latiloba* A. DC.; *C. nitida* Ait.; *C. phyctidocalyx* Boiss. & Noë; *C. planiflora* Hort., not Lam. or Engelm.; *C. subpyrenaica* Timb.-Lag.]. WILLOW B., PEACH-BELLS. Per., sts. erect, to 3 ft., mostly unbranched; rosette lvs. oblong-lanceolate, to 8 in. long, entire or serrulate, smooth, st. lvs. linear; fls. axillary, solitary or in few-fld. racemes, calyx without appendages, corolla campanulate, to 1½ in. long, white to deep blue. Eur. to ne. Asia. A very variable sp. including many cvs. among which are: 'Alba'; 'Alba Superba'; 'Caerulea'; 'Grandiflora'; 'Grandiflora Alba'; 'Humosa', fls. double; 'Moerheimii', fls. double, white; and 'Pfitzeri'. Material offered under the names *C. nitida, C. planiflora, C. amabilis,* and *C. phyctidocalyx* is dwarf; that offered as *C. grandis* and *C. latiloba* has large, sessile fls. and hispid calyx; and that as *C. subpyrenaica* has large fls. in loose racemes and white-pubescent calyces.

petiolata: *C. rotundifolia.*

petrophila Rupr. Tufted, glabrous or pubescent per.; basal lvs. broadly ovate, to about ⅝ in. long, entire or 3-toothed apically, st. lvs. more sessile or nearly so, narrowly ovate; fl. sts. slender, decumbent, about 4 in. long, generally terminated by a solitary, erect. fl., calyx with obscure appendages, corolla blue, ¾ in. long, tubular to broadly campanulate. Caucasus.

phyctidocalyx: *C. persicifolia.*

phyteumoides: *Asyneuma limonifolia.*

pilosa: see *C. dasyantha* and *C. Chamissonis.*

Piperi T. J. Howell. Tufted per., sts. 1 or more, lax, to 4 in.; basal lvs. more or less obovate, to 1 in. long, spiny-toothed; fls. 1 to few, calyx hispidulous, with minute appendages, corolla bright blue, about ½ in. across, funnelform. Olympic Mts. (Wash.). Cvs. 'Alba' and 'Sovereigniana'. Fls. white.

planiflora Lam., not Engelm. or Hort. Based on a plant of unknown identity, but usually presumed to be *C. pyramidalis;* material offered in the trade as *C. planiflora* is *C. Parryi, C. persicifolia,* or *Symphyandra Hoffmannii.*

polymorpha Witasek. A Russian sp. near *C. rotundifolia,* but apparently not in cult.; material listed as *C. polymorpha* may be *C. rotundifolia, Wahlenbergia trichogyna,* or *W. gracilis.*

Portenschlagiana Roem. & Schult. [*C. muralis* Portenschl.]. Per., somewhat evergreen, similar to *C. Elatines,* but with corolla more funnelform, not lobed beyond the middle, and up to ¾ in. long. N. Yugoslavia.

Poscharskyana Degen. Perhaps not distinct from *C. Elatines,* but having stronger, more rampant growth, corolla to 1¼ in. across, broadly funnelform, calyx lobes lanceolate. N. Yugoslavia.

prenanthoides E. Durand. Per., sts. clustered, erect, to 2½ ft., glabrous or sparsely hairy; lvs. sessile or nearly so, ovate to elliptic, to about 2 in. long, deeply but remotely serrate; fls. few, in interrupted spikes, racemes, or narrow panicles, corolla pale blue, about ½ in. long, funnelform with linear-lanceolate lobes, style curved, much longer than corolla. B. C. to cent. Calif.

primulifolia Brot. Rather coarse, hairy per.; rosette lvs. broadly ovate to obovate, to 6 in. long and erect, doubly serrate, winged-petioled; fl. sts. to 3 ft., leafy below the many-fld., narrow-paniculate infls., calyx without appendages, lobes ciliate, corolla blue, whitish toward the center, to 2 in. across, broadly campanulate. Spain, Portugal.

×**pseudoraineri** Hort. Thought to be a hybrid between *C. carpatica* and *C. Raineri,* but differs from the former only in its slightly grayer foliage.

pulcherrima: a listed name of no botanical standing; material so offered has been *C. rapunculoides.*

pulla L. Glabrate, dwarf per.; rosette lvs. ovate, about 1 in. long, crenate, glossy; fl. sts. 2–6 in. long, with solitary, nodding fls., calyx without appendages, lobes linear, corolla deep purple-blue, about ¾ in. long, campanulate. Se. Eur. Other spp., especially *C. cochleariifolia,* are grown under this name. *C. pulla* Baumg. ex Steud. is *C. linifolia.*

×**pulloides** Hort. Reported to be a hybrid between *C. carpatica* and *C. pulla;* plants to 8 in.; corolla blue-purple, very large and broad.

punctata Lam. Coarsely hirsute per., sts. erect, to 2½ ft., apically branched; rosette lvs. cordate-ovate, coarsely serrate, st. lvs. sessile or winged-petioled, ovate to lanceolate, about 3 in. long; fls. nodding, solitary in the axils, calyx with appendages, lobes lanceolate to ovate, corolla whitish to rose-purple or darker, spotted and flecked purple within, to 2 in. long, tubular-campanulate. E. Siberia, n. Japan.

pusilla: *C. cochleariifolia.*

pyramidalis L. CHIMNEY B. Strict, glabrous per., to 5 ft.; lower lvs. long-petioled, ovate to oblong-ovate, serrate, st. lvs. progressively shorter-petioled and smaller to below the infl.; fls. in elongate, race-mose-paniculate infls., calyx without appendages, corolla white to pale blue, to 1 in. across, campanulate-rotate, style exserted. S.-cent. Eur. Cvs. are 'Alba', fls. white; 'Caerulea', fls. blue; 'Compacta', dwarf, dense, fls. large.

×**pyraversi** Hort. Cayeux & Le Clerc: *C. pyramidalis* × *C. versicolor.* Erect, to about 3 ft.; fls. of the same size and shape as *C. versicolor.*

Raddeana Trautv. Glabrous or glabrate per., to 1 ft.; lvs. ovate to lanceolate, coarsely serrate, the lowest long-petioled, cordate, to 1½ in. long; sts. much-branched, with nodding fls. toward the apex, calyx with large, acute appendages, lobes strigose-ciliate, corolla dark purple, ¾ in. long, campanulate. Caucasus.

Raineri Perp. Tufted per.; lvs. sessile or nearly so, ovate to obovate, dentate, grayish; fl. sts. leafy, 1–4 in. high, each usually bearing a solitary, erect. fl., calyx without appendages, lobes ovate-acuminate, serrate or entire, corolla blue, as long as calyx lobes, to 1¼ in. long, broadly campanulate. Alps, n. Italy. Cv. 'Alba'. Fls. white. Material offered as *C. Raineri* is often *C. carpatica.*

ramosissima Sibth. & Sm. [*C. attica* Boiss. & Heldr.]. Nearly glabrous ann., to about 1 ft.; lvs. obovate to lanceolate, to 1 in. or sometimes 2 in. long, entire or serrulate; fls. erect, solitary on each br., calyx tube white-pilose, calyx without appendages, lobes lanceolate, corolla blue, whitish at the center, 1–2 in. across, funnelform to rotate. Greece, Italy.

rapunculoides L. ROVER B., CREEPING B. Erect, sparsely pubescent per., to about 3 ft.; basal lvs. very long-petioled, cordate-ovate, serrate, st. lvs. sessile, narrow-ovate to lanceolate, to 4 in. long; fls. nodding, in elongate, more or less naked, terminal racemes, calyx without appendages, corolla violet-purple, to 1 in. long or more, funnelform. Eurasia. A vigorous, persistent sp. spreading by rhizomes and seeds; naturalized about properties and roadsides throughout the U.S. Often offered under the names of other spp.; to be avoided in gardens as an almost ineradicable weed.

Rapunculus L. RAMPION. Bien., with thick taproot; sts. erect, to 3 ft., rosette lvs. mostly with long, winged petioles, ovate-spatulate, to about 4 in. long, entire to undulate-serrate, st. lvs. linear-lanceolate; fls. in racemes or narrow panicles, short-pedicelled, calyx without appendages, corolla lilac, about ¾ in. long. E. Eur. and w. Asia. First year roots and basal lvs. sometimes used as a salad.

Reiseri Halácsy. Soft-puberulous bien., with erect central st. 9–12 in. and procumbent to ascending lateral sts.; basal lvs. cordate-ovate, serrate, roughish, with winged, sometimes lobed petioles, st. lvs. ovate-spatulate, serrate, the uppermost sessile; fls. in short racemes, erect, calyx with obscure appendages, lobes broadly lanceolate, corolla violet, tubular-campanulate, the exserted style 5-lobed. S. Greece.

Reuterana Boiss. & Bal. Erect, bristly-hairy ann., sts. 1–1½ ft., appearing dichotomously branched in upper part; lvs. sessile, oblong, entire; fls. mostly terminal on the brs., erect or ascending, calyx with short, ovate appendages, lobes lanceolate, setose, corolla lavender-blue, campanulate. Turkey to Iran. Some material so listed is *C. glomerata.*

Reutermanniana: a listed name of no botanical standing; plants grown under this name have been identified as *C. Grossekii.*

rhomboidalis L. Erect, nearly glabrous per., to 2 ft.; lower lvs. long-petioled, ovate, crenate, upper lvs. sessile, to 2 in. long; fls. nodding to ascending, in terminal racemes, calyx without appendages, corolla bluish-purple, campanulate, to 1 in. long. Eur. Cv. 'Alba'. Fls. white.

rotundifolia L. [*C. heterodoxa* Hort., not Vest ex Roem. & Schult.; *C. Marchesettii* Witasek; *C. petiolata* A. DC.; *C. rotundifolia* var. *alaskana* A. Gray; *C. sacajaweana* Peck]. BLUEBELL, HAREBELL, COMMON H. A polymorphic aggregate of per. forms, typically producing a loose rosette of lvs. and stolons, eventually forming a mat from which arise erect fl. sts. 3–18 in. high; rosette lvs. long-petioled, ovate to orbicular, to about 1 in. across, entire or toothed, st. lvs. sessile, linear to lanceolate-ovate; fls. in loose, terminal racemes or sometimes solitary, erect in bud, nodding to ascending in flower, calyx without appendages, lobes short, usually spreading, corolla white to deep lavender-blue, about 1 in. long, campanulate. Many cvs. have been offered, among them 'Alba', 'Hostii', 'Linifolia', 'Nana', 'Olympica', and 'Superba'. Var. **alaskana:** *C. rotundifolia.*

sacajaweana: *C. rotundifolia.*

sarmatica Ker.-Gawl. Grayish-green, pubescent, clump-forming per.; lower lvs. long-petioled, hastate-ovate, to 3 in. long, unequally dentate, st. lvs. smaller, more oblong; fl. sts. mostly simple, to 1–2 ft.; fls. nodding, in nearly naked racemes, calyx with white-villous, small appendages, corolla pale gray-blue, about 1 in. long, hairy outside. Caucasus.

sarmentosa Hochst. ex A. Rich. Tufted per.; rosette lvs. sessile, obovate, obtuse, bristly-ciliate; fl. sts. erect, slender, much-branched, to 1 ft., each with a few-fld. raceme, calyx with acute appendages, lobes lanceolate, ciliate, corolla violet-blue, campanulate. Ethiopia.

Sartorii Boiss. & Heldr. Monocarpic, procumbent bien., sts. to about 10 in. long; basal lvs. cordate-orbicular, about ¾ in. across; fls. solitary in the lf. axils, erect, calyx without appendages, corolla white or pinkish, to ½ in. long, funnelform, style long-exserted. Is., e. Medit., Greece.

saxatilis L. Tufted, glabrous per.; rosette lvs. petioled, oblong-spatulate, to 2 in. long, toothed; fl. sts. erect, to 6 in., glabrous, with racemes of clustered fls., calyx with short, obtuse appendages, corolla pale blue with darker veins, to ½ in. across, tubular-campanulate. Crete.

Saxifraga Bieb. Tufted per., to 6 in.; differing from *C. tridentata* in its generally greater pubescence and green rather than grayish-green lvs. usually with only 3 or 5 serrations near the apex. Caucasus.

scabrella Engelm. Scabrellous or hirtellous, tufted per., to about 4 in.; basal lvs. spatulate, upper lvs. linear, all entire, to 1½ in. long; fls. erect, solitary or 2–5, corolla blue, to ½ in. long. Nw. U.S.

Scheuchzeri: *C. linifolia;* but some material offered as *C. Scheuchzeri* may be *C. rotundifolia.*

Scouleri Hook. ex A. DC. Similar to *C. prenanthoides*, but having sts. shorter, 3–12 in., st. lvs. mostly petioled, the lowermost broadly ovate, and corolla tubular-campanulate, lobed only to about the middle. Alaska to n. Calif.

siberica L. [*C. Hohenackeri* F. Fisch. & C. A. Mey.]. Coarsely pubescent bien., sts. several, erect, to 18 in.; basal lvs. obovate to spatulate, to about 4 in. long, minutely crenate, st. lvs. sessile, lanceolate-acuminate; fls. more or less pendulous, in racemes or narrow panicles, calyx bristly-pubescent, with reflexed, ovate-acute appendages, corolla violet-blue, to 1 in. long, tubular-campanulate. Eurasia. Cvs. 'Alba', and 'Major' are listed.

spathulata: *C. Sprunerana.*

speciosa: *C. glomerata* var. *dahurica.*

Speculum: see *Legousia Speculum-Veneris.*

Speculum-Veneris: *Legousia Speculum-Veneris.*

spicata L. Coarse, hispid-pubescent bien., sts. erect, simple, to 2 ft., basally leafy; rosette lvs. oblanceolate, st. lvs. oblong to linear or lanceolate, to 6 in. long; fls. in dense, elongate, bracted spikes, corolla blue-violet, narrow-funnelform, deeply and narrowly lobed, bearded within. Mts., cent. and s. Eur.

Sprunerana Hampe [*C. spathulata* Sibth. & Sm.]. Diffuse, slender-branched per., to about 1 ft., basally pilose; basal lvs. long-petioled, spatulate to obovate, upper lvs. sessile, lanceolate to linear, to about 2 in. long; fls. erect, solitary on elongate pedicels, calyx without appendages, lobes linear-lanceolate, half or more as long as the corolla, usually dentate basally, corolla pale blue to whitish, to 1 in. long; broadly campanulate to funnelform. Yugoslavia to Greece.

×**Stansfeldii** Hort. Apparently a hybrid, *C. carpatica* × *C. Waldsteiniana*, mat-forming, sts. ascending, to 5 in. high; lvs. petioled, lanceolate-ovate, to 2 in. long, coarsely serrate; fls. many, more or less pendent, corolla violet-blue, about ¾ in. across, broadly campanulate.

Stevenii Bieb. Mat- or clump-forming per., with stolons producing small rosettes; rosette lvs. obovate to oblanceolate, to 2 in. long; fl. sts. slender, mostly simple, 1- to few-fld.; fls. erect, calyx without appendages, lobes linear-lanceolate, half as long as the corolla, corolla lilac, about 1 in. long, broadly campanulate. E. Caucasus. Cv. 'Nana'. A dwarf, more freely flowering form.

subpyrenaica: *C. persicifolia.*

teucrioides Boiss. More or less prostrate per.; rosette lvs. short-petioled, ovate, to about ½ in. long, dentate to pinnatifid, grayish; fls. 1–5 in 1-sided spikes, calyx with somewhat inflated appendages, lobes triangular, ciliate, corolla bluish or lilac, to ½ in. long, tubular-campanulate. W. Asia Minor.

thessala Maire. Decumbent, grayish-pubescent per.; basal lvs. oblong, lyrately lobed, st. lvs. sessile, oblong-obovate, toothed; fls. in loose racemes, calyx with minute appendages, lobes triangular-lanceolate, corolla pale violet, to 1 in. long, tubular-funnelform. Greece. Material offered under this name has been *C. rotundifolia.*

thessalica: a listed name of no botanical standing, probably for *C. thessela.*

thyrsoides L. Coarse, monocarpic; rosette lvs. lanceolate to linear, to 6 in. long, stiff-hairy; fl. sts. erect, simple, very leafy, to 2½ ft., terminating in dense, but elongate, bracted spikes, corolla cream or yellowish, to 1 in. long. Alps, Eur. Cv. 'Carniolica' is offered.

Tommasiniana W. D. J. Koch ex F. W. Schultz. Glabrous per., sts. mostly several, spreading to erect, slender, to 6 in. high or more; lvs. short-petioled, linear-lanceolate to lanceolate, to 2 in. long, minutely serrate; fls. axillary, nodding, mostly exceeding the lvs., calyx without appendages, lobes linear, corolla pale violet, to ¾ in. long, tubular-campanulate. Yugoslavia. Often confused with *C. Waldsteiniana.*

Trachelium L. NETTLE-LEAVED B., THROATWORT. Erect, hispid per., to 2 or 3 ft.; lower lvs. broadly ovate to triangular, cordate at base, irregularly toothed, st. lvs. narrow, to 5 in. long, obtuse at base; fls. in leafy panicles, ascending or nodding, calyx hispid, without appendages, lobes lanceolate-ovate, corolla blue-purple, to 1½ in. long, campanulate. Eurasia; naturalized in N. Amer. Cv. 'alba'. Fls. white.

Trautvetteri Grossh. ex Fedorov. Mostly pubescent per., 4–12 in.; rosette lvs. petioled, ovate-oblong, minutely serrate, abruptly narrowed at base, st. lvs. smaller, the uppermost clasping; fls. borne in terminal, bracted heads, calyx lobes lanceolate, corolla lilac, ¾–1½ in. long. E. Caucasus.

tridentata Schreb. Tufted, usually hairy per.; rosette lvs. obovate to spatulate, usually 3- or 5-toothed apically, grayish-green; fls. decumbent, to about 5 in. long, each terminated in a solitary, erect fl., calyx without appendages, the tube often lanate, lobes broadly lanceolate obtuse, corolla pale to deep blue, white at base, to 1¼ in. long, campanulate or funnelform. Caucasus, widely distributed and quite variable.

turbinata: *C. carpatica.*

×**Tymonsii** Hort. Presumed to be a hybrid between *C. carpatica* and *C. pyramidalis;* similar to *C. carpatica* and probably synonymous with *C.* ×*Fergusonii.*

uniflora L. Nearly or quite glabrous, tufted per., sts. weak, more or less erect; basal lvs. oblanceolate, obtuse, nearly entire, st. lvs. linear to linear-lanceolate; fl. sts. 1–2 in. long, each with a solitary, erect, terminal fl., calyx without appendages, lobes awl-shaped, corolla dark violet, to ½ in. long. Northern regions and high mts., N. Hemisphere.

valdensis: *C. linifolia.*

×**VanHouttei** Carrière. Possibly a hybrid between *C. latifolia* and *C. punctata;* similar to *C. punctata*, but with more tufted habit and darker fls.

Vaumeri: a listed name of no botanical standing.

velutina: *C. lanata.*

versicolor Sibth. & Sm. Erect per., to about 3 ft.; basal lvs. oblong to ovate, nearly cordate at base, deeply serrate, petioles longer than blades, st. lvs. narrower, sometimes nearly entire, the uppermost nearly sessile; fls. more or less erect, in spicate racemes, calyx without appendages, lobes often serrulate, corolla pale blue then lighter above the deep violet throat, 1 in. across or more, rotate. Mts., cent. Italy to Greece.

Vidalii H. Wats. Shrubby per., sts. glossy, grooved; lvs. fleshy, ovate-spatulate, 3–4 in. long, coarsely serrate; fls. pendent, in terminal racemes, corolla yellowish or white with a yellow or orange ring at base, to 2 in. long, tubular. Azores.

Waldsteiniana Roem. & Schult. [*C. flexuosa* Waldst. & Kit., not Michx.]. Similar to *C. Tommasiniana*, but fls. erect and corolla rotate-campanulate rather than nodding and tubular-campanulate. Nw. Yugoslavia.

Wanneri: *Symphyandra Wanneri.*

Warleyensis: *C.* ×*haylodgensis* cv. 'Warley White'.

×**Wockii** Hort. Presumed to be a hybrid between *C. pulla* L. and *C. Waldsteiniana;* fls. pendent. Material so offered appears to be *C. Waldsteiniana.*

Zoysii Wulfen. Tufted, short-lived per., rosette lvs. petioled, nearly orbicular to ovate, to ½ in. long, entire, st. lvs. few, smaller, oblanceolate; fl. sts. slender, 1–6-fld., to 4 in. high, corolla pale lilac, urceolate, lobes incurved and marginally joined. Alps, Austria and Italy.

CAMPANULACEAE Juss. BELLFLOWER FAMILY. Dicot.; about 40 genera and more than 700 spp. of herbs or sometimes shrubs or trees, mostly with milky sap, widely distributed in temp. and trop. regions of the world; lvs. alt., without stipules, simple and only rarely lobed or divided; fls. solitary or in spicate to paniculate infls.; bisexual, regular or nearly so, usually 5-merous, calyx tube usually joined to the ovary, the limb parted, corolla lobed, lilac to blue or purple, sometimes white, stamens 5, sometimes inserted slightly on the corolla, separate or united, ovary, except in *Cyananthus*, inferior, mostly 2-5-celled, style 1, stigmas as many as the carpels; fr. a variously dehiscent caps., sometimes berrylike. Genera grown as ornamentals are: *Adenophora, Asyneuma, Campanula, Canarina, Codonopsis, Cyananthus, Edraianthus, Jasione, Legousia, Mindium, Ostrowskia, Phyteuma, Platycodon, Symphyandra, Trachelium, Triodanis,* and *Wahlenbergia.*

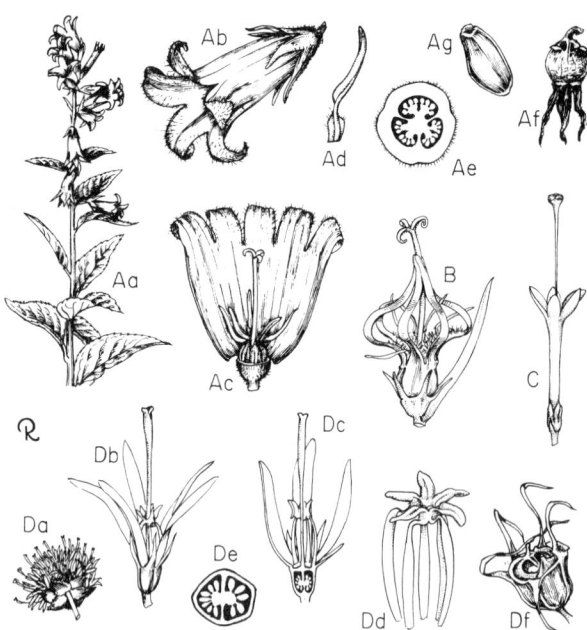

CAMPANULACEAE. **A,** *Campanula latifolia:* **Aa,** flowering stem, × ⅛; **Ab,** flower, × ½; **Ac,** flower, corolla expanded, × ½; **Ad,** stamen, × 1; **Ae,** ovary, cross section, × 2; **Af,** capsule, × ½; **Ag,** seed, × 5. **B,** *Phyteuma Scheuchzeri:* flower, × 1½. **C,** *Trachelium caeruleum:* flower, × 2. **D,** *Jasione perennis:* **Da,** inflorescence, × ½; **Db,** flower, × 2; **Dc,** flower, vertical section, × 2; **Dd,** stamens, × 4; **De,** ovary, cross section, × 6; **Df,** capsule, × 3.

CAMPELIA L. Rich. *Commelinaceae.* One sp., a robust erect or decumbent herb, native to W. Indies and from Mex. to Brazil; brs. breaking through the lf. sheaths at the nodes; lvs. alt., with sheathing base; fls. in paired sessile cincinni subtended by 2 leafy bracts at tip of elongate lateral peduncles, sepals becoming fleshy around the caps., petals separate, stamens 6, nearly equal, filaments bearded, anthers dehiscing longitudinally, ovary 3-celled; fr. with 1–2 seeds in each cell.

Grown indoors or under glass. Propagated by seeds or cuttings.

Zanonia (L.) HBK. To 6 ft.; lvs. broadly elliptic to oblanceolate, to 10 in. long, 2½ in. wide, narrowed to a slender petiolelike base; fls. white. Cv. '**Mexican Flag**'. Lvs. variegated, white-striped and narrowly margined with red. Sometimes erroneously offered as *Dichorisandra reginae.* What is probably this plant has been illustrated as *C. Zanonia* 'Albolineata' and *Dichorisandra* 'Albomarginata'.

CAMPHORA: *CINNAMOMUM.* **Camphora officinalis:** *Cinnamomum Camphora.*

CAMPSIDIUM Seem. *Bignoniaceae.* Not in cult. **C. australis:** a listed name; material offered under this name may be *Pandorea pandorana.*

CAMPSIS Lour. TRUMPET CREEPER, TRUMPET FLOWER, CROWN PLANT. *Bignoniaceae.* Two spp. of deciduous shrubs, climbing by aerial rootlets, 1 native to N. Amer., and 1 to e. Asia; lvs. opp., odd-pinnate, lfts. toothed; fls. orange or scarlet, in terminal cymes or panicles, calyx unequally 5-toothed, corolla funnelform, 5-lobed slightly 2-lipped, stamens 4; fr. a long caps.

The trumpet creepers are showy-flowered vines that thrive in fertile soil in sunny locations. Both *C. grandiflora* and *C. radicans* do well in southern U.S. and *C. radicans* is fairly hardy north. Propagated by seeds, cuttings of green wood under glass, layers, and cuttings of roots or mature wood.

capreolata: a listed name of no botanical standing; material offered under this name is *Bignonia capreolata.*

chinensis: *C. grandiflora.*

grandiflora (Thunb.) K. Schum. [*C. chinensis* (Lam.) Voss; *Bignonia chinensis* Lam.; *B. grandiflora* Thunb.; *Tecoma chinensis* (Lam.) C. Koch; *T. grandiflora* (Thunb.) Loisel.]. CHINESE T.C., CHINESE T.F.

Lfts. 7–9, ovate or ovate-lanceolate, to 2½ in. long, glabrous beneath; fls. to 2 in. across, calyx deeply 5-lobed, corolla scarlet, tube only slightly longer than calyx. China. Zone 8. Cv. '**Thunbergii**'. Fls. orange, corolla tube short, lobes reflexed. Var. **sanguinea**. A listed var.

radicans (L.) Seem. ex Bur. [*Bignonia radicans* L.; *Tecoma radicans* (L.) Juss.]. TRUMPET CREEPER, TRUMPET VINE, COW-ITCH, TRUMPET HONEYSUCKLE. Lfts. 9–11, elliptic to ovate-oblong, to 2½ in. long, pubescent at least on midrib beneath; fls. to 2 in. across and 3 in. long, calyx short-toothed, corolla orange with scarlet limb, tube 3 times as long as calyx. Late summer. Penn. to Fla., w. to Ill., se. Iowa, Tex. Zone 5. Cv. '**Flava**'. Fls. orange-yellow. Var. **floribunda** is listed. Var. **speciosa** (Parsons) Rehd. Lfts. smaller, elliptic; fls. orange-red.

×**Tagliabuana** (Vis.) Rehd. [*Bignonia* × *Tagliabuana* Hort.]: *C. grandiflora* × *C. radicans.* Fls. to 3 in. long and 2 in. across; intermediate between the parents.

CAMPTOSORUS Link. WALKING FERN, WALKING LEAF. *Polypodiaceae.* Two spp. of hardy, small, evergreen ferns growing usually on limestone rock, in N. Amer. and n. Asia; lvs. simple, long-pointed, rooting at the tip; sori linear or oblong, irregularly scattered.

Transplanted sometimes to rock and wild gardens when limey conditions can be provided. Propagated by spores or plantlets. See also *Ferns.*

rhizophyllus (L.) Link. WALKING FERN. Lvs. lanceolate, to 9 in. long, cordate at base, tapering caudately to a long, often filiform tip. Que. to Ga., w. to Okla. and Ala.

CAMPTOTHECA Decne. *Nyssaceae.* One sp., a polygamous, deciduous tree, native to China; lvs. alt., simple; fls. small, in solitary or racemose heads, calyx 5-toothed, petals 5, stamens 10; fr. a samara.

Grown in s. Calif. Zone 10.

acuminata Decne. To 75 ft., quick-growing; lvs. ovate, to 6 in. long, acuminate; stamens white, long-exserted; samara about 1 in. long, brown and shining.

CAMPYLANTHUS Roth. *Scrophulariaceae.* About 8 spp. of shrubs, native to Canary Is., Cape Verde Is., and sw. Asia; lvs. alt., entire; fls. in terminal racemes, calyx 5-lobed or -parted, corolla tubular, 5-lobed, stamens 2; fr. a caps.

salsoloides Roth. Shrub, to 6 ft.; lvs. linear, to 1 in. long, thick, glabrous; racemes to 4 in. long, fls. pink, sticky-pubescent, on recurved pedicels. Canary Is.

CAMPYLONEURUM: *POLYPODIUM.*

CAMPYLOTROPIS Bunge. *Leguminosae* (subfamily *Faboideae*). More than 60 spp. of deciduous shrubs and subshrubs, native to Asia; differing from *Lespedeza* in having pedicels mostly solitary in the axils of usually deciduous bracts and jointed below the calyx.

macrocarpa (Bunge) Rehd. To 3 ft.; lfts. 3, oblong, to 2 in. long, blunt, silky beneath; fls. in dense racemes to 3 in. long, purple, about ⁵⁄₁₆ in. long. China. Hardy north.

CANANGA (DC.) Hook.f. & T. Thoms., not Aubl. [*Canangium* Baill.]. *Annonaceae.* Two spp. of trees, native to trop. Asia; lvs. alt., simple; fls. in axillary clusters, large, 3-merous, petals 6, in 2 series, stamens and pistils many; frs. many, oblong, fleshy, borne on the receptacle, each containing 6–12 or rarely fewer seeds in 2 rows. Differs from *Polyalthia* in having apiculate stamen connectives, and fr. with more seeds.

odorata (Lam.) Hook.f. & T. Thoms. [*Canangium odoratum* (Lam.) King]. ILANG-ILANG. To 80 ft.; lvs. oblong-ovate, long-acuminate, to 8 in. long; fls. greenish-yellow, drooping, very fragrant, petals narrow, to 2 in. long; fr. stalked, greenish, nearly 1 in. long. Trop. Asia to n. Australia. Grown as an ornamental in the tropics and in the Philippine Is. for the perfume oil distilled from the fls.

CANANGIUM: *CANANGA.*

CANARINA L. CANARY BELLFLOWER. *Campanulaceae.* Three spp. of per. herbs, native to the Canary Is. and trop. E. Afr. which differ from *Campanula* in having lvs. opp. or ternate, fls. usually 6-merous, and fr. a berry.

They may be grown in a cool greenhouse or in the open in the far South, perhaps with winter protection.

campanula: *C. canariensis.*

canariensis (L.) O. Kuntze [*C. campanula* L.]. Sts. semiscandent, slender, 6–8 ft. long, from a fleshy tuber; lvs. petioled, narrowly ovate-to lanceolate-oblong, about 3 in. long, lobed and somewhat hastate at the base, coarsely toothed; fls. pendent, solitary in the axils, calyx leaflike, with spreading or reflexed lobes, corolla yellowish, with brick-red or purplish-brown lines, campanulate, to 2 in. long, lobes short, reflexed. Canary Is.

CANAVALIA DC. *Leguminosae* (subfamily *Faboideae*). About 50 spp. of trop. herbs, scandent or nearly erect; lvs. alt., of 3 lfts.; fls in axillary racemes, papilionaceous, stamens 10, 9 united in a tube and the upper one separate only at base; fr. a large, flat, woody legume, strongly ribbed or winged near one margin.

Sometimes grown in warm countries as ornamentals, stock feed, a green-manure crop, and the beans for human food. Adapted to about the same climatic conditions as cotton and requires a long season.

ensiformis (L.) DC. JACK BEAN, WONDER B., GIANT STOCK B., HORSE B., SWORD B. Nearly erect ann., 3–6 ft.; lfts. to 8 in. long; fls. pink-purple, standard more than 1 in. long; fr. linear, to 14 in. long and 1⁵⁄₁₆ in. wide, tan, seeds white. Trop. Amer. Fresh immature seeds are considered to be poisonous.

gladiata (Jacq.) DC. SWORD BEAN. Twining or nearly erect ann., similar to *C. ensiformis*, but fr. to 2 in. wide with seeds usually dark red, pink, or brown. Tropics of Old World.

CANDOLLEA: *HIBBERTIA.*

CANELLA P. Br. *Canellaceae.* One sp., an evergreen, aromatic tree, native to s. Fla. and W. Indies; lvs. alt., entire; fls. in terminal corymbs, petals 5, stamens 10–20, united; fr. a berry.

Winterana (L.) Gaertn. WILD CINNAMON. To 45 ft., often shrubby, bark gray, aromatic; lvs. obovate or spatulate, to 4 in. long, obtuse, glossy above; fls. purple, red, or violet, to ¾ in. long, anthers yellow; berries crimson, ¼ in. in diam., with gelatinous pulp. Zone 10b. Source of canella bark. Used as a spice and also medicinally.

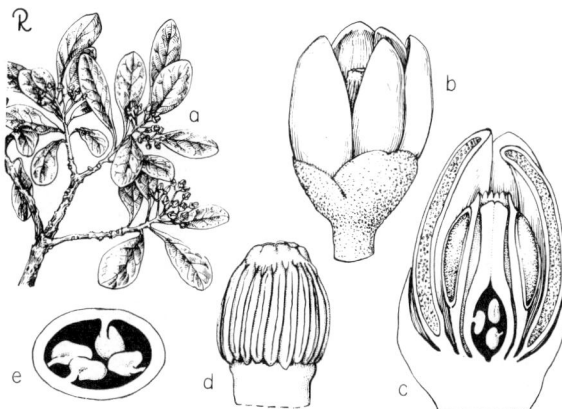

CANELLACEAE. *Canella Winterana:* **a,** flowering branch, × ¼; **b,** flower, × 4; **c,** flower, vertical section, × 7; **d,** staminal tube, × 7; **e,** ovary, cross section, × 10. (From Lawrence, *Taxonomy of Vascular Plants.*)

CANELLACEAE Mart. CANELLA FAMILY. Dicot.; 5 genera of aromatic trees and shrubs, native to trop. Amer. and Afr.; lvs. alt., entire; fls. bisexual, sepals 3, petals 4–12 or 0, stamens many, filaments united into tube, ovary superior, 1-celled; fr. a berry. *Canella* may be grown in s. Fla. or s. Calif.

CANISTRUM E. Morr. *Bromeliaceae.* Seven spp. of epiphytic or rarely rock-inhabiting herbs, native mostly to Brazil; lvs. usually spiny, in a basal rosette; fls. green, yellow, or blue, in a nearly sessile, dense, compound, central infl. subtended by colored bracts, petals separate with scales inside,

pollen sculptured, ovary inferior; fr. a berry, seeds without appendages.

Occasionally cultivated outdoors in tropical gardens or in the greenhouse. Require filtered light. For culture see *Bromeliaceae.*

amazonicum: *Wittrockia amazonica.*

Lindenii (Regel) Mez [*Nidularium Lindenii* Regel]. Lvs. to 2 ft. long, 3 in. wide, finely toothed, green, spotted with darker green; fl. bracts acute; fls. pure white, in dense heads. Var. **roseum** (E. Morr.) L. B. Sm. [*C. roseum* E. Morr.]. Bracts rose to bright red; fls. 50–90.

roseum: *C. Lindenii* var.

CANNA L. *Cannaceae.* About 60 spp. of tall, erect, per. herbs, native to tropics and subtropics, with thick, branching rhizomes and mostly simple main sts.; lvs. large, simple, entire, with sheathing petioles; fls. 3-merous, irregular, sepals and petals small, petals united into a tube at base, fertile stamen 1, petal-like, bearing a half anther on one side, staminodes 1–4, petal-like, an inner one reflexed and forming a lip, ovary inferior; fr. a 3-valved, roughish caps.

Most cannas are cultivated as ornamentals and are hybrids of mixed parentage; one species is important as a tropical food plant and source of an arrowroot starch. They are of easy cultivation in any fertile moist soil, especially soils high in humus. In the North the roots should not be planted until danger of frost is past, and they should be dug before the first freeze and stored over winter in a warm dry place. Propagation is usually by division of rhizomes, each piece with a bud; in the North these divisions may be started indoors 1 month or more before planting outside. New varieties can be obtained from seeds, which should be soaked in warm water before sowing, or the seed coat notched or filed.

edulis Ker-Gawl. EDIBLE C., QUEENSLAND ARROWROOT, ACHIRA, TOUS-LES-MOIS. To 10 ft., sts. purple; lvs. to 2 ft. long, purplish beneath; fls. bright red, outer staminodes 3, uppermost in fl., varying to orange and 2½ in. long. W. Indies, S. Amer. Produces edible tuberous rhizomes, which are used for food in Andean S. Amer. and grown in Queensland for the starch.

flaccida Salisb. To 5 ft., sts. and foliage green; lvs. to 2 ft. long and 5 in. wide; fls. tubular at base, yellow, petals strongly reflexed, outer staminodes 3, to 3 in. long, S.C. to Fla. The most important parent of the orchid-fld. cannas, *C.* ×*orchiodes.*

×**generalis** L. H. Bailey. COMMON GARDEN C. Varying in height and color of foliage, but usually glaucous; fls. not tubular at base, in many colors, to 4 in. across, petals not reflexed, 3 staminodes and lip commonly erect or spreading. Of garden origin. The original Crozy or French cannas are included in this group.

gigantea: *C. latifolia.*

indica L. INDIAN-SHOT. To 4 ft., sts. and foliage green; lvs. to 1½ ft. long and 8 in. wide; fls. bright red, the lip orange, spotted with red, outer staminodes 3, to 3 in. long. Trop. Amer.; naturalized far s. in U.S., and in tropics.

iridiflora Ruiz & Pav. To 10 ft., sts. and foliage green; lvs. to 4 ft. long and 1½ ft. wide; fls. large, rose, drooping, corolla tube 2½ in. long. Peru.

latifolia Mill. [*C. gigantea* Desf.]. Stout, to 16 ft., pubescent; lvs. ovate or ovate-oblong, green, but purple-margined when young, to 4 ft. long; racemes paniculate; fls. scarlet, petals 2 in. long, staminodes united into a tube, brick-red; caps. large. S. Amer.

×**orchiodes** L. H. Bailey. ORCHID-FLOWERED C. Fls. very large, tubular at base, yellow to red, striped and splashed, to 6 in. across, petals reflexed after first day, outer staminodes 3, large, lip larger than outer staminodes. Of garden origin.

Strelitziana: a listed name of no botanical standing.

Vanderi: a listed name of no botanical standing.

Warscewiczii A. Dietr. To 5 ft., sts. and foliage purplish or brown-purple; lvs. about twice as long as broad; fls. scarlet, often tinged with blue, outer staminodes 2 or 3, to 3 in. long. Costa Rica, S. Amer.

CANNABACEAE Endl. [*Cannabinaceae* Lindl.]. HEMP FAMILY. Dicot.; 2 genera and 3 spp. of the N. Hemisphere, dioecious, scabrous, aromatic, sometimes climbing herbs, with watery juice; lvs. palmately veined, and usually divided, stipules separate; male fls. in panicles, female fls. in leafy-bracted spikes or dense, often conelike clusters, pistil 2-carpelled, 1-celled; fr. a glandular achene. *Cannabis* and *Humulus,* each with important economic spp., are cult.

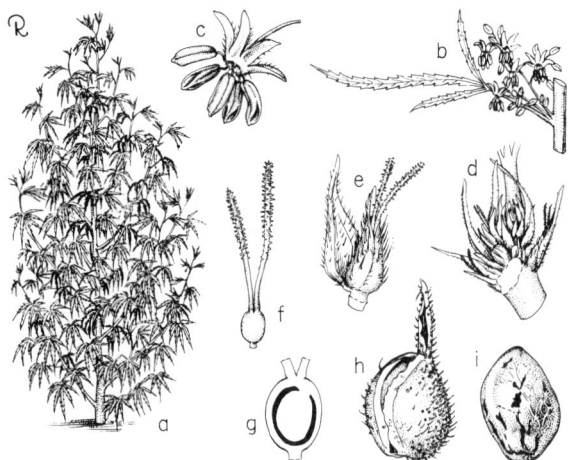

CANNABACEAE. *Cannabis sativa:* **a,** plant, × ¹/₄₀; **b,** male inflorescence, × ½; **c,** male flower, × 1½; **d,** female inflorescence × 2; **e,** female flower, × 6; **f,** pistil, × 8; **g,** ovary, vertical section, × 20; **h,** achene enclosed in bract, × 3; **i,** achene, × 3.

CANNABINACEAE: *Cannabaceae.*

CANNABIS L. HEMP. *Cannabaceae.* One sp., a tall, coarse, viscid-pubescent, dioecious, ann. herb of temp. cent. Asia; lvs. alt., palmately divided; male fls. green, in axillary or terminal panicles, sepals 5, petals 0, stamens 5, female fls. spicate or densely clustered, bracted, ovary 1-celled, styles 2, filiform; fr. a small achene.

gigantea: *C. sativa.*

sativa L. [*C. gigantea* Crevost]. TRUE H., SOFT H., MARIJUANA, GALLOW GRASS. Plants 6–12 ft., scabrous, with tough fibrous inner bark; lf. segms. 3–7, narrowly lanceolate, mostly 3–6 in. long, toothed; male fls. in panicles 9–15 in. long, female spikes about ¾ in. long, leafy. Cent. Asia; naturalized widely, including parts of N. Amer.

An important economic plant in many countries. The sts. supply a strong, durable bast fiber (true hemp); the fr. yields a drying oil (hempseed oil) and bird feed; and the dried flowering and fruiting tops of female plants produce drugs (marijuana or cannabis, hashish or charas, bhang, and ganja). Methods of cult. vary depending upon the product desired. The sp. is usually grown for fiber in temp. regions and for drug production in warmer regions. In the U.S., it can be grown only under government permit.

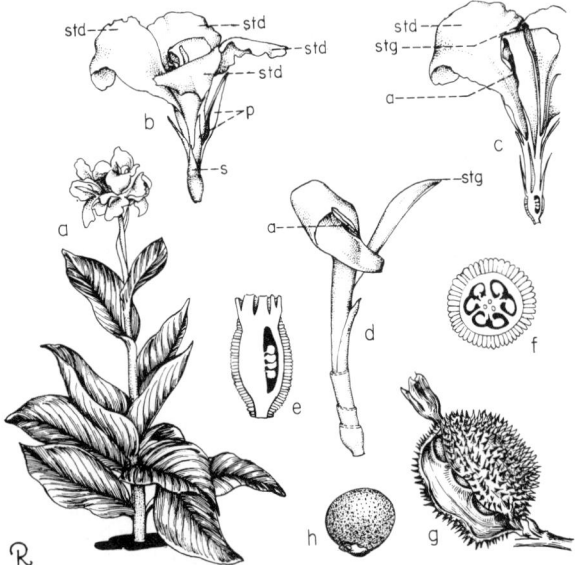

CANNACEAE. *Canna* × *generalis:* **a,** plant, × ⅛; **b,** flower, × ¼; **c,** flower, vertical section, × ¼; **d,** stamen and stigma, × ½; **e,** ovary, vertical section, × 1; **f,** ovary, cross section, × 1½; **g,** capsule, × ¾; **h,** seed, × 2. (a anther, p petal, s sepal, std staminode, stg stigma.)

CANNACEAE Juss. CANNA FAMILY. Monocot.; 1 genus, *Canna,* native to trop. and subtrop. regions; lvs. alt., entire, with sheathing petioles; fls. in terminal spikes, racemes, or panicles, red or yellow, of peculiar structure, sepals 3, small, overlapping, petals 3, erect or reflexed, sepal-like, more or less united basally, green or colored, fertile stamen 1, petal-like, bearing a half anther on one side, staminodes 1–4, petal-like, an inner one reflexed and forming a lip, ovary inferior; fr. a caps.

CANTALOUPE: see *Melon.*

CANTHIUM Lam. *Rubiaceae.* About 200 spp. of shrubs, vines, or trees, native to trop. Old World, occasionally with axillary spines; lvs. opp., stipules acuminate from broad base; fls. crowded in short panicles or cymes, 4–5-merous, stamens exserted or included, style exserted; fr. a drupe.

attenuatum R. Br. ex Benth. Shrub or small tree; lvs. oblong-elliptic to narrow-lanceolate, to 6 in. long; fls. small, corolla tube ¹/₁₆ in. long, lobes longer, anthers exserted. Queensland (Australia).

glabrifolium: *C. subcordatum.*

subcordatum DC. [*C. glabrifolium* Hiern]. Tree, to 30 ft. or more, brs. horizontal near crown; lvs. broadly ovate, to 8 in. long, sparsely hairy or glabrous; fls. white, scented, somewhat larger than *C. attenuatum,* anthers included. W. Trop. Afr.

CANTUA Lam. *Polemoniaceae.* Six spp. of shrubs and trees, native to Andean S. Amer.; lvs. simple, alt.; fls. red, violet, or white, solitary or in terminal, many-fld. corymbs, calyx 5-lobed, corolla long-tubular, with 5 short lobes, stamens 5; fr. a many-seeded caps.

Grown in a cool greenhouse or outdoors in mild climates. Propagated by seeds or by cuttings under glass.

bicolor Lam. Hispid shrub, to 4 ft.; lvs. oblong or elliptic, to 1½ in. long, entire; fls. solitary, to 1½ in. long, corolla with yellow tube and scarlet lobes. Bolivia.

buxifolia Juss. ex Lam. MAGIC FLOWER, SACRED-FLOWER-OF-THE-INCAS, MAGIC-FLOWER-OF-THE-INCAS, SACRED-FLOWER-OF-PERU. Glabrous or hairy shrub, to 10 ft.; lvs. elliptic or obovate, to 1 in. long, entire or with few teeth; fls. in terminal corymbs, to about 3 in. long, corolla pinkish-red, striped yellow, anthers dark purple. Peru, Bolivia, n. Chile.

pyrifolia Juss. ex Lam. Shrub or small tree; lvs. elliptic to obovate, to 3 in. long, entire or toothed; fls. in dense terminal corymbs, to 1 in. long, corolla with yellow tube and white lobes, anthers yellow. Ecuador, Peru, Bolivia.

CAPANEA Decne. (frequently but apparently incorrectly spelled *Campanea*). *Gesneriaceae.* About 10 spp. of large herbs, shrubs, or vines, in Cent. and n. S. Amer.; lvs. opp., equal, usually toothed; fls. 1 to several on an axillary peduncle, calyx 5-lobed, tube ribbed, corolla obliquely campanulate, 5-lobed, stamens 4, anthers united, disc of 5 glands, ovary half-inferior, stigma mouth-shaped.

For cultivation see *Gesneriaceae.*

Humboldtii (Klotzsch) Ørst. Shrub or vine, to 6 ft., softly brown-hairy; lvs. oblong-lanceolate, to 7½ in. long, 3⅛ in. wide, fls. 1–4 on peduncles 4–6 in. long, brown-hairy outside, calyx lobes ⁹/₁₆ in. long, 5-nerved, corolla to 2 in. long, yellowish-green inside, spotted with purple at throat. Cent. Amer.

Oerstedii (Klotzsch) Ørst. Similar to *C. Humboldtii,* but herbaceous, to 3 ft., lvs. smooth or only short-hairy above, calyx lobes 3-nerved. Costa Rica.

CAPPARACEAE Juss. CAPER FAMILY. Dicot.; about 37 trop., subtrop., and temp. genera of herbs, shrubs, or trees; lvs. alt., simple or palmately compound; fls. mostly bisexual, irregular, sepals and petals 4(–8), or rarely petals 0, stamens (4–)6 to many, ovary superior, 1-celled, sessile or more usually stalked; fr. an elongate caps. or berry. *Capparis, Cleome, Crateva,* and *Polanisia* are cult.

CAPPARIS L. CAPER BUSH. *Capparaceae.* Perhaps 300 spp. of trop. or subtrop. shrubs or trees; lvs. simple; fls. usually large, white or yellowish, in corymbs or solitary, petals and sepals 4, stamens many, long, ovary usually long-stalked; fr. berrylike or podlike.

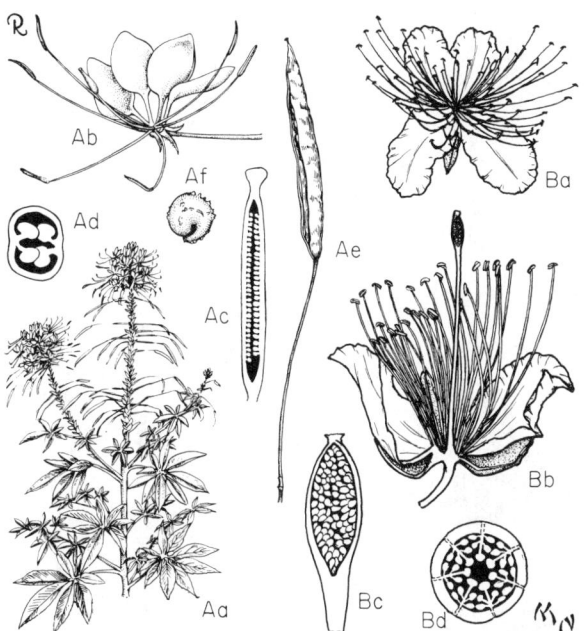

CAPPARACEAE. **A,** *Cleome Hasslerana:* **Aa,** upper part of flowering plant, × ¹⁄₁₆; **Ab,** flower, × ½; **Ac,** pistil, vertical section, × 3; **Ad,** ovary, cross section, × 8; **Ae,** capsule on long stipe, × ½; **Af,** seed, × 3. **B,** *Capparis spinosa:* **Ba,** flower, × ½; **Bb,** flower, vertical section, × ¾; **Bc,** pistil, vertical section, × 3; **Bd,** ovary, cross section, × 6.

One species *(C. spinosa)* is grown for the flower buds, which are pickled and sold as capers. Propagated by cuttings or by seeds. Not hardy north, but may be grown as an annual.

cynophallophora L. [*C. jamaicensis* Jacq.]. JAMAICA CAPER TREE. Shrub or small tree, bronze-scurfy throughout; lvs. elliptic or ovate, 1½–4 in. long, leathery; fls. solitary, about 1¼ in. across; fr. a beanlike, fleshy berry, 3–10 in. long. Caribbean and s. Fla.

inermis: *C. spinosa* var.

jamaicensis: *C. cynophallophora.*

rupestris: *C. spinosa.*

spinosa L. [*C. rupestris* Sibth. & Sm.]. CAPER BUSH, CAPER. Spiny, essentially glabrous shrub, to 5 ft.; lvs. roundish, to 2 in. long; fls. solitary, 2–3 in. across, on long pedicels; fr. an ovoid or round berry. Rocky, dry places, Medit. region. The pickled fl. buds are the pungent condiment capers of commerce. A very variable sp. Var. **inermis** Turra. Stipular prickles lacking.

umbonata Lindl. Shrub, brs. pubescent; lvs. lanceolate, 3–8 in. long, leathery; fls. about ¾ in. across; fr. globose, small, on slender stalks. Australia.

CAPRIFOLIACEAE Juss. HONEYSUCKLE FAMILY. Dicot.; about 12–15 genera and 400–450 spp. of shrubs, or sometimes woody climbers, rarely herbaceous, native mostly to temp. regions of the N. Hemisphere, extending to New Zeal. and into the Andes in S. Amer.; lvs. opp., simple or pinnate; fls. few and in cymes or many and in flat-topped or rounded clusters, bisexual, calyx 4–5-toothed, corolla 4–5-lobed, sometimes irregular, stamens 4–5, ovary inferior, usually 1–5-celled; fr. a berry, drupe, achene, or caps. The family furnishes many ornamentals in the genera: *Abelia, Alseuosmia, Diervilla, Dipelta, Kolkwitzia, Leycesteria, Linnaea, Lonicera, Sambucus, Symphoricarpos, Triosteum, Viburnum,* and *Weigela.*

CAPSICUM L. PEPPER, GREEN P., RED P., CHILI P. *Solanaceae.* About 20 spp. of much-branched, glabrous, shrubby, per. herbs, native to trop. Amer.; lvs. alt., simple, ovate to elliptic, entire; fls. axillary, solitary or in 2's or 3's, pedicelled, calyx campanulate, short, entire or 5-toothed, corolla whitish or greenish, sometimes tinged violet, nearly rotate, 5-lobed, stamens 5, usually bluish, ovary 2–3-celled, stigma capitate; fr. a podlike, many-seeded berry, becoming red, orange, or yellow, varying in size, shape, and pungency.

The genus yields one of the world's best known spices. Four species are widely cultivated in tropical Amer., where they are native, but only 2 are grown in the U.S. Cultivated capsicums are usually treated as annuals and propagated by seeds. Plants are tender when young but endure some frost in autumn. For culture see *Pepper.*

annuum L. [*C. frutescens* of auth., not L.]. To 30 in. in cult., glabrous or pubescent; lvs. lanceolate, 1–5 in. long; fls. solitary, rarely 2 at a node, calyx rotate, 5-toothed, corolla clear-white or dingy-white, rarely purple, 5-lobed, to ½ in. across; fr. varied in shape, size, color, and pungency, early-maturing, seeds ⅛ in. in diam. Var. **annuum.** The typical var.; includes most of the cult. peppers of N. Amer. and n. S. Amer. Five groups can be distinguished, each with many cvs., certain cvs. of the first 3 groups being grown as ornamentals: Cerasiforme Group. CHERRY P. Fr. erect or declined, globose, to 1 in. across, yellow or purplish, very pungent. Conoides Group. CONE P. Fr. usually erect, conical or oblong-cylindric, to 2 in. long. Fasciculatum Group. RED C.P., CLUSTER P. Fr. erect, clustered, very slender, to 3 in. long, red, very pungent. Grossum Group. BELL P., SWEET P., GREEN P., PIMENTO. Tall, stout; fr. large, thick-fleshed, inflated with depression at base, sides usually furrowed, broadly oblong bell-shaped or -apple-shaped, red or yellow when mature, nonpungent, mild in flavor. The vegetable and salad peppers and the source of pimento. Longum Group. CAPSICUM P., CAYENNE P., CHILI P., LONG P., RED P. Fr. mostly drooping, elongate, to 1 ft. long, tapering to apex, often 2 in. across at base, very pungent. The principal condiment pepper, source of chili powder, paprika and medicinal capsicum. Var. **glabriusculum** (Dunal) Heiser & Pickersg. BIRD P. Includes the wild or spontaneous forms, ranging from s. U.S. and Mex. to Colombia.

frutescens L. TABASCO P., TABASCO-SAUCE P. Similar to *C. annuum,* but fls. frequently paired or several at a node, corolla greenish-white or yellowish-white; fr. always pungent, generally late-maturing, seeds ¹⁄₁₆–⅛ in. in diam. Trop. Amer. Apparently not widely cult. Used in commercial production of hot sauces, grown principally in the Gulf states.

CARAGANA Lam. PEA TREE, PEA SHRUB. *Leguminosae* (subfamily *Faboideae*). More than 60 spp. of hardy shrubs and small trees of temp. cent. Asia, sometimes armed; lvs. alt., even-pinnate, spine- or bristle-tipped, lfts. small, entire; fls. mostly yellow, solitary or in few-fld. clusters, papilionaceous, standard erect, long-clawed, stamens 10, 9 united and 1 separate; fr. a linear, straight, cylindrical legume.

Grown for their showy flowers, pea trees should be planted in sunny locations in sandy soil. Propagated by seeds sown outdoors in autumn, or in spring after being soaked in warm water; also by softwood cuttings in early June, root cuttings, layering, or grafting on *C. arborescens.*

arborescens Lam. [*C. sibirica* Medic.]. SIBERIAN P.T. To 20 ft., variable; stipules usually spiny, lvs. 2–3½ in. long, lfts. in 3–6 pairs, obovate to elliptic-oblong, to 1 in. long; fls. 1–4 together, to ⅞ in. long, calyx teeth very short, as long as broad; fr. stalked, to 2 in. long. Late spring. Siberia, Manchuria. Valued for windbreaks. Forma **Lorbergii** Koehne [*C. Lorbergii* Hort.]. Graceful; lfts. linear, about 1 in. long and ³⁄₃₂ in. wide; standard and wings narrower; fr. rarely setting seeds. Var. **crasse-aculeata** (Bois) R. J. Moore [*C. Boisii* C. K. Schneid.]. Spreading, to 6 ft.; stipules woody, to ⅜ in. long. Var. **nana** H. Jaeg. Dwarf shrub, branchlets contorted. Var. **pendula** Carrière. Brs. strongly pendent, usually grafted high on the typical var.

aurantiaca Koehne. Similar to *C. pygmaea,* but of more upright, compact habit, with grayish bark, and fls. orange-yellow, the auricle of the wing petals at least half as long as claw. Late spring. Siberia to Afghanistan.

Boisii: *C. arborescens* var. *crasseaculeata.*

Chamlagu: *C. sinica.*

decorticans Hemsl. To 18 ft., dense, with yellow bark, branchlets green; stipules spinescent, lvs. about ¾ in. long, rachis spine-tipped, lfts. in 3–5 pairs, elliptic-obovate or oblong, mucronate, with prominent veins, rachises spine-tipped; calyx teeth spinulose, wing petals short-auricled; fr. flat. Early summer. Afghanistan.

frutescens: *C. frutex.*

frutex (L.) C. Koch [*C. frutescens* DC.]. RUSSIAN P.S. Erect, glabrous shrub, to 10 ft.; lvs. petioled, lfts. in 1 or 2 pairs, close together and appearing palmately arranged, obovate, obtuse, to more than 1 in. long, dull green, rachises persistent; fls. 1–3 together, bright yellow, 1 in. long; fr. to 2⅜ in. long. Spring. Turkestan to Siberia. Cv. 'Globosa'. Smaller, very compact, of globose form. Var. **macrantha** Rehd. Lfts. and fls. slightly larger, rachises early deciduous.

jubata (Pall.) Poir. SHAG-SPINE P.S. Shrub, to 3–8 ft., sts. little-branched, branchlets thick, densely woolly; lvs. clustered, lfts. in 4–7 pairs, oblong, to ¾ in. long, lf. rachises crowded, persistent, spiny; fls.

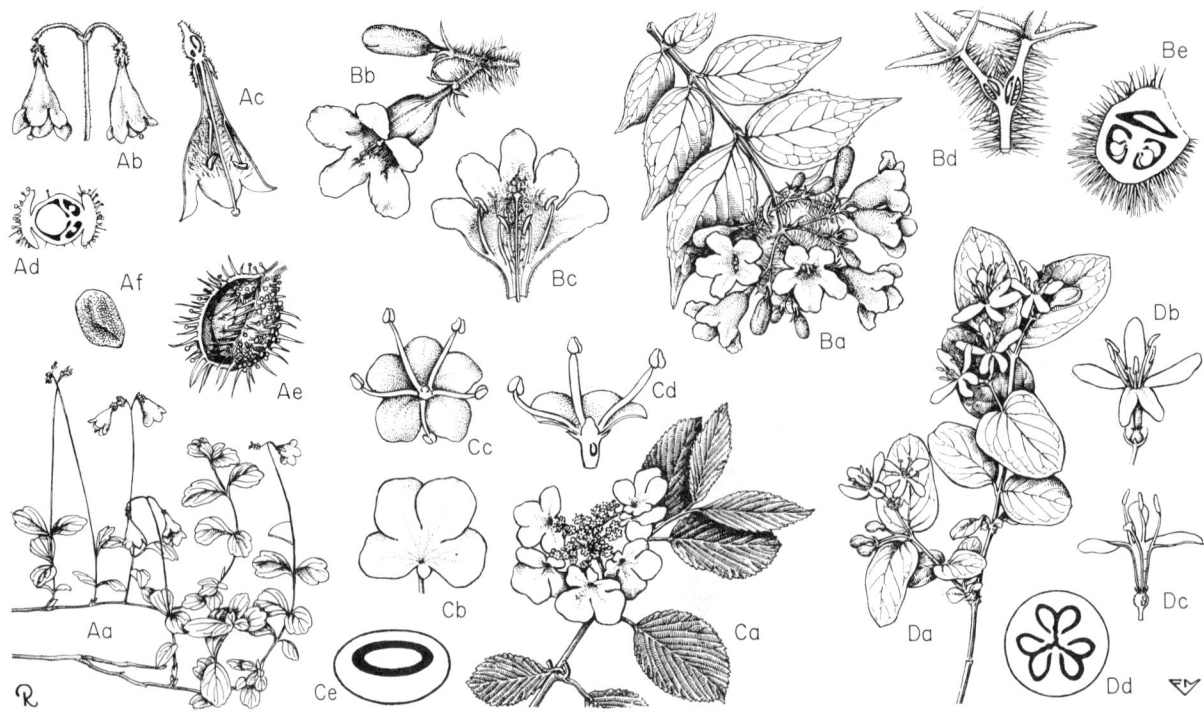

CAPRIFOLIACEAE. **A,** *Linnaea borealis:* **Aa,** plant, × ½; **Ab,** flowers, × 1; **Ac,** flower, vertical section, × 2; **Ad,** ovary, cross section, × 6; **Ae,** fruit, × 10; **Af,** seed, × 30. **B,** *Kolkwitzia amabilis:* **Ba,** flowering branch, × ½; **Bb,** flower and bud, × 1; **Bc,** corolla, expanded, × 1; **Bd,** ovaries, vertical section, × 2; **Be,** ovary, cross section, × 10. **C,** *Viburnum plicatum* forma *tomentosum:* **Ca,** flowering branch, × ¼; **Cb,** sterile flower, × ½; **Cc,** bisexual flower, × 1½; **Cd,** bisexual flower, vertical section, × 3; **Ce,** ovary, cross section, × 18. **D,** *Lonicera tatarica:* **Da,** flowering branch, × ½; **Db,** flower, × 1; **Dc,** flower, vertical section, × 1; **Dd,** ovary, cross section, × 7. (B, C, D from Bailey, *Manual of Cultivated Plants,* ed. 2.)

solitary, white or rosy, often more than 1 in. long, wing petals very long-auricled at base on one side. Cent. Asia.

Lorbergii: a listed name of no botanical standing for *C. arborescens* forma.

Maximowicziana Kom. To 5 ft., spreading, densely branched; stipules spinescent, lfts. in 2–3 pairs, oblong-lanceolate, ⅜ in. long, rachises persistent, short, spiny; fls. bright yellow, to 1 in. long, wing petals not auricled. W. China.

microphylla Lam. To 3 ft., spreading; differing from *C. arborescens* in having lvs. scarcely longer than 1 in., lfts. to ⅜ in. long and about ³⁄₃₂ in. wide, fls. solitary or in pairs, calyx longer than broad, and corolla larger. Late spring. Siberia, n. China.

pygmaea DC. Erect, to 4 ft., or occasionally prostrate, with golden-yellow bark; lvs. nearly sessile, lfts. in 2 pairs, linear-oblanceolate, to ⅜ in. long, acute, rachis spine-tipped; fls. solitary, ¾ in. long, wing petals very short-auricled. Late spring. Nw. China, Siberia. Cv. '**Pendula**' is listed.

sibirica: *C. arborescens.*

sinica (Buc'hoz) Rehd. [*C. Chamlagu* Lam.]. Bushy, to 6 ft., differing from *C. frutex* in having lfts. in 2 pairs, remote from one another, dark green, glossy, fls. solitary, reddish-yellow, 1¼ in. long, and fr. slightly flat. Spring. N. China.

×**sophorifolia** Tausch: *C. arborescens* × *C. microphylla.* Differs from the parents in having lfts. usually in 6 pairs, elliptic to oblong, basally cuneate, mucronate at apex, and fr. ¾ in. long.

tibetica (Maxim.) Kom. Prostrate, brs. ascending, to 10 in.; lvs. crowded, lfts. in 3–6 pairs, linear-oblong, to ⅜ in. long, acute, silky-pilose, rachises persistent; fls. pale yellow, calyx teeth short, wing petals short-auricled. W. China.

tragacanthoides (Pall.) Poir. Related to *C. Maximowicziana,* but differing in having lfts. in 2–5 pairs, obovate to oblanceolate, larger, to more than ½ in. long, and fls. slightly larger, with calyx teeth spinulose, and wing petals auricled. Cent. Asia.

turkestanica Kom. Differs from *C. decorticans* in having lvs. about 1½ in. long, and lfts. larger, with scarcely prominent veins. Turkestan.

CARALLUMA R. Br. *Asclepiadaceae.* About 100 spp. of dwarf, succulent, leafless herbs, native from India to the Medit. region and S. Afr.; sts. mostly 4–6-angled, the angles toothed; fls. usually in fascicles, corolla 5-lobed, tube open-campanulate, without an inner secondary tube or cushionlike annulus, corona of 2 whorls, sometimes appearing 1-whorled, the outer 5 lobes separate or united into a cup, the inner 5 lobes often united to the outer whorl; fr. a follicle.

For culture see *Succulents.*

avastmontana: a listed name of no botanical standing.

Baldratii A. C. White & Sloane. Sts. 4-angled, with large spreading teeth; fls. solitary or in fascicles at apex of st., corolla about 1 in. across, narrow-lobed to near the base, cream or light reddish-brown at center, sometimes red-spotted, lobes deep reddish-brown, corona appearing 1-whorled. E. Ethiopia.

Burchardii N. E. Br. Sts. to 1½ ft., 4-angled, with deflexed teeth; fls. sessile, in fascicles at apex of st., corolla about ½ in. across, olive-brown, with long white hairs, outer whorl of corona cup-shaped, 10-toothed, yellow. Canary Is. Var. **maura** Maire. Fls. pedicelled, corolla about ⅜ in. across. Sw. Morocco.

Dalzielii N. E. Br. To 1 ft., branching from the base, sts. 4-angled; fls. pendulous, in 2–3-fld. fascicles, corolla about ½ in. across, whitish or yellowish with purple spots at base, lobes lanceolate, dark purple, purple-ciliate. N.-cent. Afr.

europaea (Guss.) N. E. Br. Sts. 4-angled, procumbent to erect; fls. 5–8 in umbels at apex of st., corolla rotate, about ¾ in. across, pale yellow, striped purple in lower part, lobes entirely purple at tips, outer whorl of corona of 5 dark purple pouches, each bearing 2 globose, yellow knobs at the rim. N. Afr., Spain. Several vars. are recognized, based principally on floral differences.

hesperidum Maire. Sts. simple or branching, irregularly purple-mottled, scarcely 4-angled, with large conical teeth; fls. 2–10, in fascicles at apex of st., corolla about ¾ in. across, dark brownish-purple, velvety-papillate, tube yellowish inside, outer whorl of corona cup-shaped. Morocco.

hottentotorum (N. E. Br.) N. E. Br. Sts. 4–6 in. high, bluntly 4-angled, with stout, conical teeth; fls. in clusters along st., corolla about ¼–⅝ in. across, pale greenish-yellow, corona small, yellow. S. Afr. Var. **minor** Lückh. Corolla about ¼ in. across.

Keithii R. A. Dyer. Sts. to 4 in., mottled reddish-brown, 4-angled, with large, flattened, alt. teeth; fls. 1–3 in a cluster, corolla ⅝ in. across, with a raised, angled annulus, purplish, with irregular white spots, papillate, outer whorl of corona cuplike, 5-lobed, each lobe deeply bifid. Swaziland.

Knobelii (E. P. Phillips) E. P. Phillips. Sts. spreading, branched; fls. many, in umbellate clusters halfway up the st.; corolla to 1¼ in. across, white in lower part, greenish at margins of lobes, mottled with purple throughout, ciliate with purple, clavate hairs, lobes of outer whorl of corona 4-angled, striped. S. Afr. Var. **Langii** (A. C. White & Sloane) A. C. White & Sloane. Pedicels longer, corolla with a yellower ground color.

lateritia N. E. Br. Sts. broadly toothed; fls. clustered near base, corolla 3–3½ in. in diam., deeply and narrowly 5-lobed, brownish-maroon, papillate-rugulose, purple-ciliate, outer whorl of corona bowl-shaped, the lobes denticulate. S. Afr.

Lugardii N. E. Br. Branching, 2–3 in.; fls. axillary, corolla 1½–1¾ in. across, bright chocolate, lobes long, linear-attenuate, sometimes olive-green at apex, outer whorl of corona 15–20-toothed, inner whorl dull orange. S. Afr.

lutea N. E. Br. Sts. to 4 in.; fls. in dense, many-fld. clusters near middle or base of the st., mostly opening at same time; corolla 1½–2½ in. across, narrowly and deeply lobed, yellow, purple-ciliate. Mozambique to S. Afr.

mammillaris (L.) N. E. Br. Bushy, to 1½ ft., brs. spirally 5–6-ridged, thick; fls. in fascicles in the grooves, corolla about 1½ in. across, narrowly and deeply lobed, papillate, upper part of tube and lobes velvety purple-black, tube pale yellow, dotted purple inside, outer whorl of corona cup-shaped, 1–15-toothed. S. Afr.

melanantha (Schlechter) N. E. Br. Sts. to 4 in., 4-angled, angles strongly toothed; fls. in clusters of 3–5 near middle of sts., corolla rotate, to 2 in. across, rugose, deep purple-black, purple-ciliate, outer whorl of corona of 5 broad, flat, spreading lobes. S. Afr. and s. Rhodesia.

Nebrownii A. Berger. Sts. to 8 in., mottled red; fls. in clusters of 15–30, corolla nearly rotate, deeply and narrowly lobed, to 4 in. across, transversely rugose, deep red-brown to blackish-brown, glabrous, outer whorl of corona bowl-shaped, the lobes 5, broadly rectangular. S.-W. Afr. Var. **pseudonebrownii** (Dinter) A. C. White & Sloane [*C. pseudonebrownii* Dinter]. Fls. in clusters of 5–15, corollas marked with yellow.

piaranthoides Oberm. Sts. to 4 in., with large teeth; fls. 2–5, near apex of st., corolla about ⅝ in. across, yellow, spotted wine-red, tubercled and papillate, corona cream-colored. S. Rhodesia.

Pillansii N. E. Br. Bushy, to 1 ft.; fls. in fascicles along st., corolla 1½ in. across, purplish-gray, spotted purple-brown, corona very small, dark purple-brown. S. Afr.

plicatiloba Lavr. Sts. to 4 in., up to 1 in. in diam., 4- or rarely 5-angled, with large, ovoid teeth; fls. 5–12 in sessile, axillary umbels, corolla to ⅝ in. across, yellowish, transversely marked with purple, the lobes purple, white-pubescent, revolute at margins, corona yellow-orange. Aden.

pseudonebrownii: *C. Nebrownii* var.

ramosa (Masson) N. E. Br. Bushy, about 1 ft., sts. 4-angled, angles scarcely toothed; fls. in small fascicles along grooves of st., corolla about ⅝ in. across, tube whitish, lobes blackish-purple, corona lobes minute. S. Afr.

retrospiciens (Ehrenb.) N. E. Br. Sts. thick, with compressed angles, to 2 ft.; fls. in terminal, globose, compound umbels, corolla ⅝–¾ in. across, minutely rugose, purple-black. Ne. Afr. Var. **tombuctuensis** (A. Cheval.) A. C. White & Sloane. Sts. to 3 or even 4 ft., with teeth horizontal rather than deflexed. N.-cent. Afr.

Rogersii (L. Bolus) E. A. Bruce. Sts. about 4 in.; fls. in 3–4-fld. clusters along st., corolla to 1½ in. across, pale yellow, lobes slender, ascending-incurved, inner whorl of corona with filiform, erect lobes. S. Afr.

tsumebensis Oberm. Sts. to 10 in., mostly 5-angled, spotted red; fls. in many-fld. fascicles at base of st., corolla about 2½ in. across, velvety-chocolate-brown, outer whorl of corona cup-shaped. S.-W. Afr.

Turneri E. A. Bruce. Sts. to 18 in., thick and 4-angled toward the base, slender and less prominently angled above, sometimes branched; fls. in clusters of 2–4 along upper part of sts., corolla to ¾ in. across, rotate, deeply divided, lobes about ⅛ in. wide, undulate, yellowish, transversely banded violet-brown, pubescent at the base. Kenya.

umdausensis Nel. Sts. 4-angled; fls. solitary or in pairs along the upper part of sts., erect on pedicles to 1 in. long, corolla to 1 in. across, open-campanulate, glabrous, tube reddish-purple with radiating white stripes merging into the greenish-yellow of the lobe apices. S.-W. Afr.

variegata: a listed name of no botanical standing.

CARDAMINE L. *Cruciferae.* More than 100 spp. of ann. or per. herbs of temp. regions of both hemispheres, glabrous or with unbranched hairs; lvs. simple to pinnate; fls. white to purple, sepals and petals 4; fr. an elongate, flat, dehiscent silique, with valves coiling spirally from the base at dehiscence.

Some species are showy, but appear not to be in general cultivation.

lyrata Bunge. Stoloniferous herb, to 20 in.; lower lvs. sessile, with 11–13 lfts., lateral lfts. ovate, to ⅜ in. long, terminal lft. orbicular-cordate, to ¾ in. long, upper lvs. with 5–7 lfts.; fls. white, in many-fld. racemes; siliques to 1⅛ in. long, seeds winged. Japan, Korea, n. China, e. Siberia. Sometimes grown in aquaria.

pratensis L. LADY'S-SMOCK, CUCKOOFLOWER, MAYFLOWER, MEADOW CRESS, BITTER C. Erect per., to 20 in.; lvs. pinnate, lfts. of basal lvs. 3–7 pairs, elliptic to rounded, lfts. of upper lvs. smaller, narrower; fls. white to rose-colored, often double. Circumboreal, widely distributed in Eur., Asia, n. N. Amer. Adapted to rock gardens and moist cool borders or to margins of bogs. Lvs. said to be used as a cress in parts of Eur. Prop. usually by offsets, but may be started from seeds.

CARDIANDRA Siebold & Zucc. *Saxifragaceae.* Several spp. of subshrubs of e. Asia; lvs. mostly alt.; infl. terminal, corymbose; marginal fls. sterile, consisting of 3 colored, petal-like calyx lobes, central fls. fertile, small, many, calyx tube short, partly united to ovary, calyx lobes 4–5, petals 5, stamens many, ovary partly inferior, styles 3.

Not hardy north; propagated by cuttings of young wood under glass.

alternifolia Siebold & Zucc. Sts. to 24 in.; lvs. alt., broadly lanceolate to oblong, to 8 in. long; fls. white. Japan. Zone 8. Closely related to *Hydrangea,* but with alt. lvs.

CARDIOCRINUM (Endl.) Lindl. *Liliaceae.* Three spp. of bulbous herbs, native to Asia; principal bulb dying after flowering and fruiting, but plant remaining per. by offset bulbs, sts. leafy, not rooting above bulb; lvs. cordate, long-petioled, with reticulate venation; fls. funnelform and sometimes somewhat irregular, greenish to creamy-white, in racemes, perianth segms. 6, stamens 6; fr. a loculicidal caps., the valves fringed with teeth, seeds many, flat.

Requiring a cool, partly shaded location. Bulbs should be planted shallowly, as for *Lilium candidum.*

cathayanum (E. H. Wils.) Stearn [*Lilium cathayanum* E. H. Wils.]. St. to 4½ ft.; lvs. mostly in a loose whorl at middle of st., blades oblong-ovate, to 8 in. long, reniform-cordate; fls. somewhat irregular, greenish-white outside, creamy inside with few purple dots near tip, to 4½ in. long, in a 1–5-fld. raceme. E. and cent. China.

cordatum (Thunb.) Mak. [*Lilium cordatum* (Thunb.) G. Koidz.; *L. cordifolium* Thunb.; *L. Glehnii* Friedr. Schmidt]. St. to 5 ft., stout, hollow; lvs. in a loose whorl toward lower half of st., blades ovate, to 1 ft. long, deeply cordate; fls. somewhat irregular, slightly fragrant, creamy-white, the lower segms. with reddish-brown spots and yellow inside at base, to 6 in. long, in a 4–24-fld. raceme. Japan.

giganteum (Wallich) Mak. [*Lilium giganteum* Wallich, not Hort.]. St. to 12 ft.; lvs. in basal rosette and along entire st., blades broadly ovate, to 1½ ft. long; fls. regular, fragrant, white, striped with red-purple inside, to 6 in. long, in a few- to 20-fld. raceme. Himalayas and se. Tibet. The EASTER LILY, commonly called *L. giganteum* in the trade, is *Lilium longiflorum* var. *Takeshima.*

CARDIOSPERMUM L. HEARTSEED, BALLOON VINE. *Sapindaceae.* About 12 spp. of herbaceous or shrubby vines, native mostly to trop. Amer., with a few in trop. Afr. and Asia; lvs. alt., mostly 2-ternate, coarsely toothed; fls. in axillary corymbs with a pair of opp. tendrils, irregular, sometimes unisexual, sepals 4 or 5, petals 4, stamens 8; fr. an inflated caps., seeds black with heart-shaped white spot near the hilum.

These vines are grown as ornamentals and for covering trellises and bushes. Propagated by seeds sown where plants are to grow and treated as annuals; in mild regions they may self-sow.

grandiflorum Swartz. Herbaceous vine, sts. usually hairy; lvs. variously hairy especially underneath; fls. cream-white, to ⅜ in. long, fragrant; fr. elliptic or obovate, more or less 3-angled, to 2½ in. long, usually nearly glabrous. Trop. Amer. and Afr. Forma **hirsutum** (Willd.) Radlk. [*C. hirsutum* Willd.]. Sts. and petioles hirsute-setose.

Halicacabum L. BALLOON VINE, HEART PEA, WINTER CHERRY. Woody per., to 10 ft., but mostly grown as an ann. or bien.; lvs. glabrous; fls. white, to ¼ in. long; fr. nearly globular but 3-angled, much inflated, about 1 in. long and broad, pubescent. Bermuda, Fla., to Tex., trop. Amer.; but naturalized in many parts of the world and commonly cult.

hirsutum: *C. grandiflorum* forma.

CARDUUS L. PLUMELESS THISTLE. *Compositae* (Carduus Tribe). More than 100 spp. of stout herbs in Eur., Asia, N. Afr., Canary Is.; sts. usually winged by decurrent lf. bases; lvs. sessile, spiny-toothed or -lobed; fl. heads solitary or in panicles, involucre spiny; fls. all tubular, purple or white. Distinguished from *Cirsium* by the rough but not plumose pappus bristles. None appear to be in general cult. in the U.S. today.

benedictus: *Cnicus benedictus.*

Marianus: *Silybum Marianum.*

CAREX L. SEDGE. *Cyperaceae.* About 2,000 spp. of rhizomatous, mostly monoecious, grasslike, per. herbs, cosmopolitan, but most common in temp. and cold regions; fl. sts. (culms) 3-angled, solid; lvs. 3-ranked, the lower lvs. mere bladeless sheaths or nearly so, or with well-developed blades, sheaths, and ligules, the uppermost lvs. (called bracts) subtending the spikes or absent; infl. of one or more spikes which are entirely male, or entirely female, or with male fls. above and female fls. below, or with female fls. above and male fls. below; fls. solitary in the axil of a scale, perianth absent, male fls. with stamens 3 (rarely 2), female fls. with pistil 1, enclosed in a saclike or bladderlike perigynium, style 1, stigmas 2 or 3; achene 3-angled, lens-shaped or flattened-convex, completely surrounded by the persistent perigynium.

Sedges of this genus are sometimes planted as edgings in greenhouses or as pot plants. Many of the species with pendant spikes make attractive clumps in the wild garden and pond borders. Some of the smaller evergreen species are ideal for the rock garden. The forage value of some is comparable to grasses and they are important as food and cover for wildlife and in erosion control. Propagation is by division or seeds sown in the autumn.

conica F. Boott. Sts. tufted, 8–20 in.; lvs. ¾–1½ in. wide, flat, stiff, dark green; bracts short, with long, inflated, often purplish-brown sheaths; spikes 3–5, erect, the terminal ones male, brown, the others female, short-cylindrical, ⅜–1 in. long; perigynia light green, with abruptly recurved beak. Spring to early summer. Open woods, Japan, s. Korea.

Fraseri: *Cymophyllus Fraseri.*

Grayi J. Carey. Sts. tufted, 1–3 ft.; lvs. many, ¼–½ in. wide, upper lvs. and bracts similar, prolonged, overtopping sts.; male spikes terminal, female spikes 1–2, globose 1–1½ in. in diam.; perigynia 6–30, radiating widely from a common center, inflated, many-ribbed, lanceovoid with short beak, ½–¾ in. long, achenes obtusely triangular. Summer, autumn. Moist meadows and woodlands, Vt. to Wisc., s. to Ga. and Mo.

Morrowii F. Boott. Sts. tufted, 12–24 in.; lvs. clustered, basal sheaths dark reddish-brown, blades ³⁄₁₆–⅜ in. wide, flat, thick, stiff, deep lustrous green, bracts short-bladed and long-sheathing basally; spikes 4–6, distant, on long erect peduncles, the upper male, the lower female; perigynia ⅛ in. long, spreading to divergent. Spring. Woods in low mts., Japan. The typical var. is not cult. Var. **albomarginata:** var. *expallida* Ohwi [var. **albomarginata** Mak.; cv. 'Variegata']. JAPANESE SEDGE GRASS. Lvs. striped white, a garden cv. useful for pots or border. Zone 5. Cv. '**Variegata**': var. *expallida.*

pendula Huds. SEDGE GRASS. Sts. tufted, from stout rhizomes, 2–5 ft., nodding at the top; lower lvs. bladeless, the sheaths brownish-red, upper lvs. with blades ½–¾ in. wide, shorter than sts., more or less keeled, yellow-green above, glaucous beneath, lower bracts leaflike, as long as infl., long-sheathing; upper spikes 2½–4 in. long, male, lower spikes 4–5, female, distant, pendulous, 2¾–6 in. long. Spring–summer. Damp woods and shady places near water usually on clayey soils, Brit. Is., Eur. from Denmark s. to N. Afr., w. Asia. A handsome sedge recognized by its large size, broad lvs., and long drooping spikes.

plantaginea Lam. Sts. tufted, 1–2 ft., arising laterally from old bases and bearing bladeless purple sheaths only; lvs. of sterile rosettes evergreen, broad, ⅜–1¼ in. wide, sometimes longer than the sts., the basal ones reduced to sheaths, purple; upper spikes male, long-peduncled, purple, stamens yellow; lower spikes 2–4, female, distant, the peduncles scarcely exserted from purple sheathing bracts. Rich deciduous woods, New. Bruns. to se. Man., s. to Ala. and Tenn. Early spring to early summer. Conspicuous by broad evergreen lvs. and purple sheaths.

variegata: a name used in various senses, but material cult. under this name is *Acorus gramineus* cv.

CARICA L. PAPAYA. *Caricaceae.* About 25 spp. of more or less succulent trees or, rarely, vines, native to trop. and subtrop. Amer., commonly dioecious or often imperfectly so, with straight trunks bearing a crown of palmately lobed lvs. at summit; fr. a large berry resembling a melon; fl. characters as for the family.

One species, *C. Papaya,* is widely grown in the lowland tropics for the popular edible fruits, and for the protein-digesting enzyme, papain, which is extracted from the fruits and other parts of the plant. Papayas require tropical temperatures, but withstand a few degrees of frost. They do best in rich, well-drained loam. Trees bear within a few months after planting, but are short-lived. Care must be taken to have both male and female plants, although some varieties have bisexual flowers. Propagated by seeds, or sometimes by cuttings or grafting. See also *Papaya.*

candamarcensis: *C. pubescens.*

Papaya L. PAPAYA, PAWPAW, MELON TREE. To 25 ft., glabrous; lvs. to 2 ft. across, deeply palmately 7-lobed, the lobes pinnately lobed; fls. yellowish, to 1 in. long or more, male fls. slender, long-tubed, in long-peduncled, axillary racemes to 3 ft. long, female fls. broader, solitary or few together, on short peduncles; male plants sometimes bearing a few female or bisexual fls.; fr. elongate to globose, with central cavity, greenish-yellow to orange, to 20 in. long, with thick, yellow or orange flesh, seeds many, black. Lowland trop. Amer. Widely cult. in tropics. Zone 10b in Fla.

pubescens Lenné & C. Koch [*C. candamarcensis* Hort. ex Hook.f.]. MOUNTAIN P. To 20 ft., differing from *C. Papaya* in its stouter trunk, pubescent lvs., green, pubescent fls. in subsessile clusters, and smaller fr. very aromatic, elliptic, deeply 5-ribbed, sharply pointed at apex, deep yellow to orange, about 4 in. long, the center filled with seeds and their gelatinous arils. Highland tropics, Andes of Ecuador and Colombia. Hardier than the common papaya; fr. inferior, eaten only when cooked with sugar.

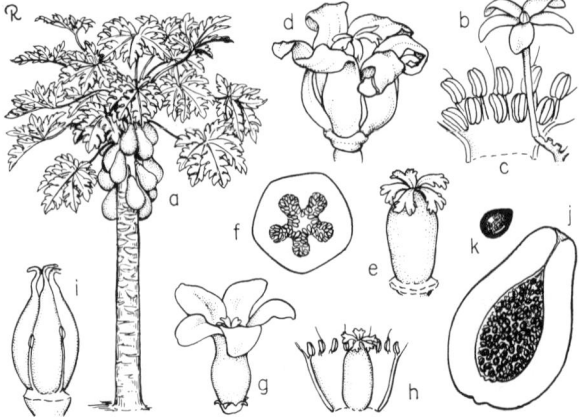

CARICACEAE. *Carica Papaya:* **a,** plant, much reduced; **b,** male flower, × ½; **c,** throat of expanded male corolla, × 1½; **d,** female flower, ×½; **e,** pistil, × ½; **f,** ovary, cross section, × 1; **g,** bisexual flower (*elongata* type), × ½; **h,** same, with corolla expanded, × ½; **i,** pistil and stamens of bisexual flower (*pentandria* type), × ½; **j,** fruit, × ⅛; **k,** seed, × ½.

CARICACEAE Dumort. PAPAYA FAMILY. Dicot.; 2 genera of mostly dioecious trees or, rarely, vines, native to the tropics and subtropics, sap milky; lvs. in terminal crowns, palmately lobed; fls. with calyx and corolla 5-lobed, stamens 10, ovary superior, 1-celled; fr. a berry. *Carica* is grown for the edible fr.

CARISSA L. *Apocynaceae.* About 35 spp. of much-branched, evergreen, often spiny, shrubs or small trees, native to Old World tropics; sap milky; lvs. opp., entire, leathery; fls. subsessile in few to many-fld. terminal or pseudoaxillary clusters, white or pinkish, fragrant, 4–5-merous, bisexual, corolla salverform, stamens borne on corolla, lobes overlapping to the right or left, separate, pistil with a single 2-celled ovary; fr. a showy, leathery berry.

Widely cultivated in tropics and subtropics for foundation plantings and hedges, and for the tart, edible fruits. Of easy culture in full sun. Propagated by seeds and cuttings.

Acokanthera: *Acokanthera oppositifolia.*

acuminata: *C. bispinosa.*

Arduina: *C. bispinosa.*

bispinosa (L.) Desf. ex Brenan [*C. acuminata* A. DC.; *C. Arduina* Lam.]. HEDGE THORN. To 10 ft., glabrous, spines simple to repeatedly forked, to 1½ in. long; lvs. ovate to oblong, to 3 in. long, acute, mucronulate; fls. white, ½ in. across, corolla tube ⁵⁄₁₆ in. long, lobes much shorter, ovules 1 in each cell; berry ½ in. long, red, 1–2-seeded, edible. S. Afr.

Carandas L. KARANDA. Shrub or small tree, spines 1–2 in. long; lvs. ovate-elliptic to oblong, to 3 in. long, mostly obtuse; fls. crowded in terminal cymes, white or pink, ½ in. across, corolla tube to ¾ in. long, lobes acute, about half as long as tube; berry ellipsoid, to 1 in. long, red, then black, 4- or more-seeded. India to Indonesia.

edulis (Forssk.) Vahl. Straggling or clambering shrub, to 10 ft., spineless or with simple or branched spines; lvs. ovate to sublanceolate, to 2 in. long, mostly acute, often mucronulate; fls. white inside, purple to red outside, ½ in. across, corolla tube to ¾ in. long, lobes acute, about half as long as tube; berry globose, about ⁵⁄₁₆ in. in diam., red to red-purple, 2–4-seeded, edible. Trop. Afr. to s. Iraq. Var. **tomentosa** (A. Rich.) Stapf. Branchlets and lvs. tomentose when young. E. Ethiopia to w. S. Afr.

grandiflora (E. H. Mey.) A. DC. NATAL PLUM, AMATUNGULU. Dense shrub, to 18 ft. high and broad, spines mostly forked, to 1½ in. long; lvs. ovate, to 3 in. long and 2 in. wide, dark green; fls. white, 2 in. across, corolla tube to ½ in. long, lobes much longer, broad, rounded at apex; berry ovoid-ellipsoid, to 2 in. long, scarlet, 6–16-seeded, edible. S. Afr. Valuable hedge plant; fr. used in jellies and preserves. Cvs. are: 'Horizontalis', exceptionally compact and prostrate; 'Minima', dwarf, lvs. and fls. smaller; 'Nana', more compact, lvs. smaller; 'Nana Compacta', listed name; 'Prostrata', low and spreading; 'Tuttlei', very compact and spreading.

longiflora: *Acokanthera longiflora.*

minima: *C. grandiflora* cv.

spectabilis: *Acokanthera oblongifolia.*

spinarum A. DC. Probably not specifically distinct from *C. Carandas*, differing in having spines shorter, more slender, lvs. acute, berry globose, ¼ in. in diam. India and Ceylon to Burma.

CARLINA L. *Compositae* (Carduus Tribe). About 20 spp. of ann., bien., or per. herbs, native to Eur., w. Asia, and Canary Is.; lvs. in rosettes, pinnatifid, spiny; fl. heads solitary or in corymbs, involucre broadly campanulate, involucral bracts imbricate in several rows, spinose, the outer row leaf-like, the inner row papery, glossy, receptacle flat, scaly; fls. all tubular, bisexual, anthers tailed, filaments separate; achenes cylindrical, with appressed, forked hairs, pappus deciduous, 1 row of plumose hairs united basally in groups of 2–4.

acanthifolia All. ACANTHUS-LEAVED THISTLE. Similar to *C. acaulis*, but lvs. white-tomentose beneath, heads solitary, to 5½ in. across, fls. yellowish to white. S. Eur. to w. Asia.

acaulis L. [*Cirsium acaule* (L.) All.]. Stemless per., or sometimes with sts. to about 9 in. or more; lvs. in a rosette, oblong in outline, to 6 in. long, pinnatifid, glabrous or sparsely cobwebby, the lobes spiny; heads solitary, sometimes more, 2–5 in. across; fls. white or reddish. Eur.

CARLUDOVICA Ruiz & Pav. *Cyclanthaceae*. Three spp. of tall, erect, nearly stemless plants, with watery sap; lvs. fan-shaped, deeply parted; fls. unisexual, male and female fls. alternating spirally in an elongate, cylindrical, or ellipsoid spadix subtended by 3–4 crowded spathes; male fls. fleshy, massive, with 15–20 perianth lobes arranged in 4's about each female fl.; female fls. becoming partly united.

Carludovicas are cultivated as ornamentals in the tropics or as a source of fiber; they are sometimes grown under glass in the North and require abundant water and good drainage. Propagated by division or by seeds sown on surface of finely chopped sphagnum after the pulp has been washed off.

atrovirens: *Dicranopygium atrovirens.*

palmata Ruiz & Pav. PANAMA-HAT PLANT, PANAMA-HAT PALM. Lvs. long-petioled, to 10 ft. or more, blades to nearly 3 ft. long, 3–5-parted nearly to base, the segms. cut, the tips drooping. Cent. Amer.

to Bolivia. Often cult. in trop. gardens. In Ecuador the lvs. are collected for making Panama hats.

CARMICHAELIA R. Br. *Leguminosae* (subfamily *Faboideae*). More than about 40 spp. of shrubs, native to New Zeal. and Lord Howe Is., with branchlets often flat and green, functioning as lvs.; lvs. absent or early-deciduous, of 1 lft. or pinnate and then with 3–7 lfts., the lfts. usually obcordate; fls. few in lateral racemes, small, papilionaceous, standard reflexed, stamens 10, 9 united and 1 separate; fr. a small legume, or both valves separating from the partition, the margins and seeds remaining in place.

Occasionally cultivated in mild, frost-free regions as ornamentals. Zone 9 on Pacific Coast.

arborea (G. Forst.) Druce [*C. australis* of auth., probably not R. Br.]. Shrub, to 15 ft., branchlets leafless at maturity, flat, about ¹⁄₁₆ in. wide; lfts. mostly 3, obcordate, ¼ in. long; racemes many, 3–6-fld.; fls. white, standard with purple veins and base; fr. 2–4-seeded, seeds pale or yellowish-green, mottled black. New Zeal.

arenaria Simps. To 20 in., main sts. procumbent, branchlets flat; lfts. 3–5, to ³⁄₁₆ in. long; fls. in umbellate racemes, 3–5 on very short peduncles, standard dark purple centrally, striped toward sides, other petals whitish, tipped purplish; fr. elliptic-oblong, to ½ in. long, with straight beak, seeds 2–4, dark red, mottled black. New Zeal.

australis R. Br. A name impossible to apply precisely; most material under this name is *C. arborea*.

compacta Petrie. To 3 ft., leafless at maturity, branchlets crowded, wiry, cylindrical; racemes many, loose, to ¾ in. long; standard dark purple basally, purple-veined above; fr. flattened, beak turned up abruptly, seeds 1–2, yellowish, mottled brown or black. New Zeal.

Enysii T. Kirk. Leafless, much-branched, forming dense patches to 2 in. high and 4 in. across, branchlets thin, flat; racemes 1–3-fld.; standard purplish, with darker veins; fr. flat, to ⁵⁄₁₆ in. long, nearly orbicular, with recurved beak, seeds dull black, usually solitary. New Zeal.

odorata Colenso ex Hook.f. To 6 ft., usually leafy in spring and summer, branchlets pendent, flattened, pubescent; lvs. many, lfts. 3–7, ⅛ in. long, silky-hairy; racemes erect, 5–10-fld.; standard white, with purple veins; fr. flat broadly ovate to suborbicular, to ¼ in. long, long-beaked, seeds 1–2, pale brown to yellowish, usually dark-blotched. New Zeal.

Solandri Simps. To 10 ft., spreading, leafless at maturity, branchlets flattened, about ³⁄₃₂ in. wide, glabrous; lfts. 3–5, ¾ in. long; peduncles pilose, somewhat umbellately 3–7-fld.; calyx teeth red-tipped, standard purple-striped, keel white, tipped purple, wing petals white; fr. elliptic-oblong, ⁵⁄₁₆ in. long, short-beaked, seeds red, marked with black. New Zeal.

subulata T. Kirk. A name impossible to apply precisely.

CARNATION. In North America, the name carnation is ordinarily understood to mean the florist's plant, *Dianthus Caryophyllus*, grown under glass for cut flowers, but it rightly belongs to all the forms of the species. The highly developed large-flowered forms are of two general groups, the border or outdoor carnations and the glasshouse or florist's carnations. Interest in carnations is represented by the American Carnation Society.

The border carnations are little grown or esteemed in North America although they are pleasing plants when well grown. These are commonly propagated by means of cuttings to perpetuate particular cultivars and sometimes by means of layers. The florist's, winter-flowering, or perpetual carnations have long been favorites. They may be considered either as house plants or as florist's stock grown in glass ranges. The propagation and general cultural requirements are the same in either case, although the extent of the operations may be very different. Propagation of carnations for window garden and greenhouse is by means of cuttings taken from the strong shoots that arise at the base, the side shoots of the flowering stem, or the main shoots before they show flower buds. The cuttings from the base make the best plants in most cases, or from the middle of strong flower stems.

For window garden use, the cuttings may be taken at any time in autumn or winter, rooted in sand and potted up, to be held in pots until planted out in spring, usually in April, or any time when the ground is ready to work. Care should be taken to pinch out the tops of young plants when they are growing in the pot, and later in the ground, to make them grow stocky and send out new growth along the stem. The young plants should be grown cool, 50° F suiting them well. The cuttings should be syringed each day while in the house to keep down red spider. In summer, the plants may be grown in the field. The soil in which they are to be planted should be moderately rich and loose. The plants should be taken up in September, potted firmly, watered well, and then set in a cool, partly shaded location until root growth has started. On approach of cold weather they are taken indoors to bloom. The humidity and temperature of the usual home conditions are not suited to carnations and care must be taken to overcome the heat and dryness. Pick off most or all of the side buds, to increase the size of the leading flowers. It is probably advisable in most cases to purchase plants from a florist, and after blooming either throw them away or store them for planting in the spring, when they will bloom in the summer.

CARNEGIEA Britt. & Rose. *Cactaceae.* One sp. of s. Ariz., se. Calif., and nw. Mex.; sts. large, columnar, ribbed, usually with a few erect brs.; fls. nocturnal, funnelform, tube thick-walled, scales broad, perianth segms. recurved, stamens very many, not declined; fr. often weakly spiny, pulpy, splitting, seeds many.

For culture see *Cacti.*

gigantea (Engelm.) Britt. & Rose [*Cereus giganteus* Engelm]. SAGUARO, GIANT S., SAHUARO, ARIZONA-GIANT, GIANT CACTUS. St. to 60 ft. high and 2 ft. thick, ribs 12–30; spines 20–25, gray, needle-shaped to awl-shaped, ½–3 in. long, needle-shaped, yellow in upper areoles; fls. white, to 5 in. long, closing next afternoon; fr. oblong, red, to 3 in. in diam., edible. Spring and summer. Sometimes transplanted from the wild, but not thriving in cult.

CARNIVOROUS PLANTS. Sometimes called insectivorous plants, these are plants which have evolved special mechanisms, through transformation of their leaves, for trapping and digesting animal prey, which consists mainly but not exclusively of small insects. Most of these plants are perennial herbs inhabiting very humid but sunny, boggy, sheltered locations where, under acid conditions, decay of organic matter is slow and available nitrogen is thus in short supply. Their adaptations for carnivory allow such species to obtain extra nitrogen in sites where competition from other plants is often low.

Carnivorous-plant traps are of various sorts, including the pitfalls of pitcher plants *(Aldrovanda, Cephalotus, Darlingtonia, Heliamphora, Nepenthes, Sarracenia),* the sticky flypaperlike leaves of sundews and butterworts *(Byblis, Drosera, Drosophyllum, Pinguicula),* and the spring-traplike leaf mechanism of Venus's flytrap *(Dionaea).*

Some species of carnivorous plants, principally in the genera *Nepenthes* and *Sarracenia,* have been grown for years and numerous hybrids were at one time developed by horticulturists, especially abroad. The bizarre nature of these plants has also made them popular subjects for display or study at botanical gardens and in school laboratories but they are now being grown also by increasing numbers of gardening hobbyists throughout the world. *Byblis* Salisb., *Cephalotus* Labill., and *Heliamphora* Benth. are rare and seldom cultivated in this country and so are not treated in *Hortus Third* other than in this article. The cultivated carnivorous plants are treated under the genera *Aldrovanda, Darlingtonia, Dionaea, Drosera, Drosophyllum, Nepenthes, Pinguicula,* and *Sarracenia.*

Several of the genera cultivated *(Darlingtonia, Dionaea, Drosera, Pinguicula,* and *Sarracenia)* are native to the continental United States and so are frequently planted in this country, often being simply transplanted from the wild. Most are of rather easy culture provided the growing conditions given are similar to those of their native habitats. Nearly all carnivorous plants require high humidity and good light for best development. The relatively small size of some makes them easily adapted to terrarium or greenhouse culture and they also thrive under fluorescent lights designed for growing plants indoors. Several of the natives *(Drosera anglica, D. intermedia, D. rotundifolia, Pinguicula vulgaris, Sarracenia purpurea),* in their very hardy northern forms, occur naturally in hardiness Zones 1 and 2, but most of the other species in these genera, plus *Darlingtonia* and *Dionaea,* require a mild climate (Zone 9). Certain of the exotic taxa (in *Byblis, Cephalotus, Drosera, Drosophyllum)* should also be hardy in Zone 9, especially where a Mediterranean climate prevails, but species of *Heliamphora* and most species of *Nepenthes* are strictly tropical and best suited to the protection of the warm, humid conservatory where the minimum night temperature is 65° F. Some of the exotics are difficult in culture and are not recommended for the novice gardener.

Many species of *Dionaea, Drosera, Pinguicula,* and *Sarracenia* are grown in strong light or full sun, potted in live sphagnum (or fibrous dried sphagnum) or in peat topped with sphagnum. The pots, preferably of an inert material, not clay, usually stand in saucers of water to assure ample and constant boglike conditions. Care must be taken that the sphagnum does not overgrow smaller species such as the sundews. All require constant high humidity and copious water (rain water or distilled water should be used where tap water is alkaline). Wherever possible, the temperature regimes prevailing where a species is native should be duplicated under culture. Species that undergo dormancy in nature, with lower temperatures and shorter photoperiods in winter, such as those of *Sarracenia,* require the same in cultivation. Special care must be taken not to use insecticidal sprays where carnivorous plants are grown; the glandular leaves of various kinds of *Drosera* are especially susceptible to such pesticides.

Propagation is by seeds or cuttings. Genera like *Byblis* and *Drosophyllum,* which are usually available for culture only as seeds, are best planted in pure ground sphagnum. *Drosophyllum* seed is usually lightly scratched with fine sandpaper and soaked overnight in water before planting; a biennial, it flowers the second year from planting and is best grown as single plants in 5-inch pots. Species of *Byblis* will flower four to five months from seed. Both genera need hand pollination of the flowers to assure seed set, required to maintain additional plant generations. Plants of other carnivorous genera are usually propagated vegetatively by offshoots or rhizome cuttings *(Nepenthes, Sarracenia)* or leaf cuttings *(Drosera, Pinguicula),* both types of propagules being placed in or on sphagnum covered with plastic, and shaded.

Species of *Nepenthes* are semiscandent tropical epiphytes, better suited to culture in large hanging pots or baskets filled either with pure sphagnum or with a peat, sphagnum, and sand or perlite mix, and under highly humid conditions (50–80 percent). They require good light but protection from full sun. Day temperatures of 70–85° F are optimal with a 65° F minimum at night. Pitchers are produced on new growth only under photoperiods of 12 hours or longer; for year-round pitcher development in temperate latitudes a 16–18-hour light schedule must be maintained.

CAROLINEA: *PACHIRA.* C. princeps: *P. aquatica.*

CARPANTHEA N. E. Br. *Aizoaceae.* Two spp. of hairy, branched, succulent ann. herbs, native to S. Afr.; lvs. opp., flat, united basally, basal or on lower part of brs.; fls. solitary, or 2–3 in a group, terminal, pedicelled, expanding in the afternoon, calyx unequally 5-lobed, petals and stamens many, staminodes present, ovary inferior, 12–20-celled, stigmas 12–20; fr. a many-celled, 12–20-valved caps., with cell lids set obliquely, expanding keels awned but without marginal wings.

Seeds may be sown directly in the garden or the seedlings transplanted. See also *Succulents.*

pomeridiana (L.) N. E. Br. [*Mesembryanthemum pomeridianum* L.]. To 1 ft., sts. erect, branched, white-hairy; lvs. spreading or ascending, petiole grooved, blade spatulate or lanceolate-spatulate, to 4 in. long, 1 in. wide, minutely ciliate; fls. to 2¾ in. across, 1–3 on hairy pedicels to 4 in. long, petals golden yellow. Cape Prov.

CARPENTARIA Becc. *Palmae.* One sp., a solitary, unarmed, monoecious palm with a crownshaft, in N. Territory of Australia; lvs. pinnate, sheaths tubular, pinnae oblique to truncate and toothed at apex; infl. below the lvs., with 2 deciduous bracts of about equal size, peduncle short, lower brs. twice-branched into slender rachillae, these bearing fls. in triads (2 male and 1 female); male fls. symmetrical, sepals 3, imbricate, petals 3, valvate, stamens many, filaments erect in bud, anthers attached by back, pistillode ovoid with elongate style, female fls. with sepals and petals 3, imbricate, staminodes 3, 2-lobed, pistil 1-celled, 1-ovuled; fr. subglobose with apical stigmatic scar, mesocarp with stout fibers, seed circular in cross-section, endosperm homogeneous, embryo basal.

For culture see *Palms.*

acuminata (H. Wendl. & Drude) Becc. Trunk gray, to 40 ft., 8 in. in diam., crownshaft 4 ft. long; lvs. spreading, petiole to 6 in. long, pinnae about 88 on each side of rachis about 10 ft. long; infl. yellowish; fls. cream-colored, stamens about 33; fr. bright crimson in yellow calyx, to ¾ in. long.

CARPENTERIA Torr. *Saxifragaceae.* One sp. of the cent. Sierra Nevada, Calif., an evergreen shrub; lvs. opp., leathery; fls. large, solitary or in few-fld., terminal cymes, calyx tube shallow, united to ovary, sepals and petals 5–7, stamens many, ovary partly inferior, style short, with lobed stigma; fr. a leathery, dehiscent caps., seeds many.

Requires a well-drained, light and sandy soil, and a sunny, sheltered location; excess water in winter is especially harmful, probably more than the cold. Propagated by greenwood cuttings under glass in summer, by suckers, which are freely produced, and by seeds sown in spring.

californica Torr. TREE ANEMONE. To 6 ft. or more; lvs. oblong, to 4 in. long, green and glabrous above, gray beneath, appressed-tomentose; fls. pure white, to 3 in. across. One of the most handsome native shrubs. Calif. Zone 7.

CARPINUS L. HORNBEAM, IRONWOOD. *Betulaceae.* About 35 spp. of deciduous, monoecious trees of medium or small size, native to the N. Hemisphere; bark scaly or smooth, gray; lvs. alt., toothed; fls. unisexual, in catkins, always appearing in spring; fr. a small achenelike nut subtended by a 3-lobed leafy bract.

Hornbeams make interesting ornamentals; the strong heavy wood is useful in turning and for making levers and tool handles. They are hardy north (Zone 4) and thrive in moist soils. Propagated by seeds in autumn; if seeds do not germinate, the next spring the bed should be covered with moss and kept moist until the remaining seeds sprout. Varieties may be grafted or budded on seedling stocks.

americana: *C. caroliniana.*

Betulus L. EUROPEAN H. To 70 ft.; lvs. ovate or ovate-oblong, to 4 in. long, veins 10–13 pairs; fruiting catkins to 5 in. long, bracts to 2 in. long, middle lobe much larger. Eur. to Iran. A large handsome tree. Wood used for tool handles. Cvs. include: **'Carpinizza'**, lvs. small, often cordate, with 7–9 pairs of veins; **'Columnaris'**, of slender, pyramidal habit; **'Compacta'**, a listed name; **'Fastigiata'**, of pyramidal habit, not as slender as cv. 'Columnaris'; **'Incisa'**, lvs. deeply lobed; **'Pendula'**, brs. drooping; **'Purpurea'**, young lvs. purple; **'Quercifolia'**, lvs. with deeply toothed lobes.

caroliniana T. Walt. [*C. americana* Michx.]. AMERICAN H., BLUE BEECH, WATER B. To 40 ft., but usually smaller, bark ashy-gray; lvs. ovate-oblong, to 4 in. long, veins 10–14 pairs; fruiting catkins to 4 in. long, bracts about 1 in. long, the middle lobe largest. Md. to Fla., w. to s. Ill. and e. Tex. Wood useful. Var. **virginiana** (Marsh.) Fern. The northern form, bark blue-gray. New Eng. to N.C., w. to Minn. and Ark.

cordata Blume [*C. erosa* Blume]. To 50 ft., bark scaly; lvs. ovate or oblong-ovate, cordate, to 5 in. long, veins 15–24 pairs; fruiting catkins to 3 in. long, bracts overlapping, nut covered by base of bract. N. Asia. Wood useful. Compare with *C. japonica.*

erosa: *C. cordata.*

japonica Blume. To 50 ft., bark scaly; lvs. oblong-ovate or oblong-lanceolate, to 4 in. long, veins 20–24 pairs; fruiting catkins to 2½ in. long, bracts ovate, ¾ in. long, overlapping, nut covered by base of bract. Japan. Compare with *C. cordata.*

laxiflora (Siebold & Zucc.) Blume. To 50 ft.; lvs. usually ovate, to 2¾ in. long, cordate, pubescent only in axils of veins underneath, veins 13–15 pairs; fruiting catkins loose, to 2¾ in. long. Japan. Wood useful.

orientalis Mill. Shrub or tree, to 20 ft.; lvs. usually ovate, to 2 in. long, veins 11–15 pairs; fruiting catkins to 2½ in. long. Se. Eur. and Asia Minor.

populifolia: a listed name of no botanical standing.

Tschonoskii Maxim. [*C. yedoensis* Maxim.]. To 50 ft., young brs. densely pubescent; lvs. ovate or oblong-ovate, to 3½ in. long, veins 10–14 pairs; fruiting catkins to 3 in. long, bracts lobed on one side. N. Asia.

Turczaninovii Hance. Small tree, to 20 ft., young brs. closely pubescent; lvs. ovate, to 2½ in. long, veins 9–12 pairs; fruiting catkins to 2 in. long. N. China and Korea. Graceful, shrubby tree with small lvs.

yedoensis: *C. Tschonoskii.*

CARPOBROTUS N. E. Br. *Aizoceae.* About 29 spp. of succulent subshrubs, native to Afr., Australia, Tasmania, and N. and S. Amer.; sts. prostrate, 2-angled, stout; lvs. opp., 3-angled, curved, thick; fls. solitary, large, terminal, calyx 5-lobed, petals many, stamens many, erect, ovary inferior, 8–16-celled, stigmas 8–16, feathery, radiating; fr. indehiscent, fleshy or pulpy, edible.

Naturalized in Eur. Rooted cuttings planted out in spring in rich soil will cover a large area in short time. Propagated by seeds, but very easy and best from cuttings. See also *Succulents.*

acinaciformis (L.) L. Bolus. HOTTENTOT FIG. Sts. to 5 ft., lateral brs. short, compressed when young; lvs. spreading, pustulate near base, light gray-green, to 3½ in. long, ⅜ in. wide, ¾ in. thick, saber-shaped, keel prominent on lower side, edges cartilaginous, entire or slightly undulate-roughened; fls. to 4¾ in. across, opening at noon, petals bright carmine-purple; fr. 10–15-celled. Cape Prov.

aequilaterus (Haw.) N. E. Br. [*Mesembryanthemum aequilaterum* Haw.]. PIG'S-FACE. Like *C. edulis,* but smaller; lvs. shorter and narrower; fls. to 2¾ in. across, red, stamen filaments white; fr. 8–10-celled, to 2 in. long, usually red. Tasmania, Australia. Probably not cult.; material offered under this name is usually *C. chilensis.*

chilensis (Mol.) N. E. Br. [*Mesembryanthemum aequilaterale* Hort., not Haw.; *M. chilense* Mol.]. SEA FIG. Sts. to 3 ft. long or more, forming extensive mats; lvs. 1¼–2 in. long, 3-angled in section; fls. to 3½ in. across, sessile or nearly so, sepals unequal, the larger leafy, petals magenta, stamen filaments yellow; fr. 8–10-celled. Coastal Ore. to Baja Calif., Chile.

edulis (L.) L. Bolus. HOTTENTOT FIG. Brs. to 3 ft. long or more; lvs. green, spreading and slightly bent inward, to 4¾ in. long, ⅝ in. thick, equally 3-angled in section, keeled beneath, the keel minutely serrate; fls. to 4 in. across, opening at noon, petals light yellow, yellowish-pink, or purple; fr. 10–15-celled, edible. Cape Prov. Escapes easily in suitable areas, as Calif.

Mellei (L. Bolus) L. Bolus. Lvs. united basally, bluish to glaucous, to 3 3/16 in. long, ⅜ in. wide, ⅝ in. thick, nearly saber-shaped; fls. to 2 3/16 in. across, on 2-bracted pedicel to 1¾ in. long, bracts to 1 in. long, petals pink to pale pink. Cape Prov.

Muirii (L. Bolus) L. Bolus. Lvs. incurved at tip when young, becoming erect or spreading, green, united basally, to 2¾ in. long, ¼ in. wide, ¼ in. thick; fls. to 3⅝ in. across, on 2-bracted pedicels to 1⅝ in. long, bracts to 1⅝ in. long, petals pink-purple. Cape Prov.

CARPODETUS J. R. Forst. & G. Forst. *Saxifragaceae.* Several spp. of shrubs or small trees, 1 in New Zeal., the others in New Guinea; lvs. alt.; fls. small, in few-fld. panicles, sepals, petals, and stamens 5–6, calyx tube united to ovary, ovary half-inferior; fr. globose, indehiscent, seeds many.

serratus J. R. Forst. & G. Forst. Small tree, to 30 ft.; juvenile plants and reversion shoots with lvs. broad-elliptic to nearly orbicular, to 1¼ in. long, membranous, lvs. of adult plants ovate-elliptic to broad-elliptic, to 2¼ in. long, thinly leathery, often mottled, margins distantly serrate; fls. white, to ¼ in. across; fr. to ¼ in. in diam. New Zeal.

CARPODIPTERA Griseb. *Tiliaceae.* Up to 6 spp. of trees, 2 native to Afr., the others to W. Indies and Cent. Amer.; similar to *Berrya,* but having style short or obsolete, stigma large, 2-lobed, spreading, fr. a caps., 2-celled, 4-winged, cells 1- or rarely 2-seeded.

Ameliae Lundell. Tree, 30–75 ft.; lvs. ovate to ovate-lanceolate, to 8 in. long, acute or obtuse-acuminate, truncate to subcordate, entire, usually undulate, veins sometimes pubescent beneath; fls. many, unisexual, in peduncled, cymose panicles, calyx 2–3-lobed, less than ¼ in. long, petals purple, to ½ in. long; wings of caps. oblong, 1 in. long or more. Cent. Amer. Cult. in s. Fla.

CARRIEREA Franch. *Flacourtiaceae.* Three spp. of deciduous trees, native to e. Asia; lvs. alt., long-petioled; fls. in terminal infl., sepals 5, petals none; fr. a caps.

Propagated by seeds and by greenwood cuttings and roots.

calycina Franch. Tree, to 20–30 ft.; lvs. ovate, glabrous, serrate, 3-nerved from base; fls. in erect panicles, sepals white, cordate, forming a cup 1½ in. across and 1¼ in. deep; caps. spindle-shaped, to 2½ in. long. China.

CARROT. The carrot, *Daucus Carota* var. *sativus,* is a biennial or sometimes annual plant, grown for the thick edible root. It is an esteemed garden vegetable and also a farm crop raised for stock feed.

Carrots require deep, friable soil for the largest and most shapely roots. They are hardy and easily grown. The extra-early cultivars may be forced in a hotbed, or seeds may be sown as soon as the ground is fit to work in the spring. The stump-rooted or half-long cultivars are sown for the early garden crop. Well-enriched mellow loam, deeply dug or plowed, is best suited to the requirements of carrots. The time of planting of the seeds for the main crop is determined by the appearance of the several broods of carrot rusty fly maggots. In the North (Zone 5), plantings made after the first week of June will avoid the early brood. These carrots can be harvested in September before the late brood of maggots does much damage. Sow thickly, thinning to 3–4 inches in the row. The rows, if in a garden that is hand-worked, may be 12 inches apart. If the cultivation is by tractor, the rows should be 2–3 feet apart. One ounce will sow 100 feet of drill. Seeds germinate slowly, and they should not be placed in land that is likely to become hard and crusted.

CARRUANTHUS (Schwant.) Schwant. ex N. E. Br. *Aizoaceae.* Two spp. of tufted succulents with fleshy rhizome, native to S. Afr.; lvs. 4-ranked, crowded, 3-angled in section, toothed; fls. mostly solitary, calyx 5-lobed, petals many, stamens many, ovary inferior, 5-celled, stigmas 5; fr. a caps., cell lids soft, not quite covering the seeds, placental tubercles absent.

Growth occurs in summer. In winter the soil should be quite dry and the plants grown at a relatively cool temperature of about 55° F. Propagated by seeds or cuttings. See also *Succulents.*

caninus: *C. ringens.*

ringens (L.) Boom [*C. caninus* (L.) Schwant.]. Short-stemmed, cespitose; lvs. spreading to nearly erect, smooth, gray-green, to 2½ in. long, ¾ in. wide, narrower at base, upper side somewhat concave, lower side strongly keeled, the keel expanded and rounded to tip, margins dentate toward tip; fls. to 2 in. across, petals yellow, reddish outside. Cape Prov.

CARTHAMUS L. [*Kentrophyllum* Neck.]. *Compositae* (Carduus Tribe). About 20 spp. of stiff ann. herbs, native from Canary Is. and Medit. region to cent. Asia; lvs. alt., spiny; fl. heads terminal, solitary or corymbose, outer involucral bracts spreading, leafy, inner bracts spiny, receptacle scaly; fls. all tubular, yellow, purple, blue, or whitish; achenes glabrous, usually 4-ribbed, pappus of scales or lacking.

Several species are cultivated, primarily as economic crops, for edible oil and dye.

tinctorius L. FALSE SAFFRON, BASTARD S., SAFFLOWER. To 3 ft., glabrous, sts. branching above; lvs. sessile, broadly oblanceolate to ovate, minutely spiny-toothed; heads about 1 in. across, involucral bracts green, constricted above a papery base; fls. orange-yellow; achenes white, pappus lacking. Probably Eurasia; known only as a cultigen. Much cult. in the Old World and to some extent in Calif., primarily as an oilseed crop, but tender shoots are edible and fl. heads yield an important dye.

CARUM L. *Umbelliferae.* About 30 spp. of mostly Old World herbs; lvs. pinnate or ternately compound; fls. small, white or pinkish, in compound umbels; fr. somewhat compressed.

Of easy culture in any garden soil; propagated by seeds sown in spring.

Carvi L. CARAWAY. Ann. or bien., to 2 ft., roots thick; lvs. pinnately cut into linear or threadlike segms.; bractlets of involucels absent or minute; fls. white or pinkish. Eur.; naturalized in N. Amer. Grown for its seeds, which are used as flavoring.

Gairdneri: *Perideridia Gairdneri.*

Petroselinum: *Petroselinum crispum.*

CARUMBIUM: *HOMALANTHUS.*

CARYA Nutt. [*Hicoria* Raf.]. HICKORY. *Juglandaceae.* About 20–25 spp. of deciduous, monoecious trees, mostly native to e. N. Amer., s. to Cent. Amer., and a few in e. Asia, twigs with solid pith; lvs. alt., odd-pinnate; fls. unisexual, male fls. in drooping catkins, female fls. in 2- to 10-fld. terminal racemes; fr. a drupe with a stone or nut enclosed in a thick green husk that splits into 4 valves.

Several species are grown as ornamentals, and for the edible nuts and strong hard wood. Any of the native hickories can be grown in parks and private grounds. They are of slow growth and not readily transplanted. Propagated by seeds stratified and sown in spring, by root sprouts, or special varieties by grafting. See *Hickory Nut.*

alba: see *C. ovata* and *C. tomentosa.*

amara: *C. cordiformis.*

aquatica (Michx.f.) Nutt. BITTER PECAN, WATER H. To 90 ft.; lfts. 7–13, lanceolate, to 5 in. long, yellow-tomentose when young; nut broad-obovoid, compressed, 4-angled, reddish-brown. Along coastal plain, in river bottoms and swamps, Va. to Fla. and Tex. Zone 7?

cathayensis Sarg. CHINESE H. To 60 ft.; lfts. 5–7, ovate to ovate-lanceolate, to 6 in. long, yellowish beneath; nut ovoid, slightly angled. China.

cordiformis (Wangenh.) C. Koch [*C. amara* Raf.]. BITTERNUT, PIGNUT, SWAMP H. To 90 ft.; lfts. 5–9, ovate-lanceolate to lanceolate, to 6 in. long; nut almost globose, nearly smooth, gray. Que. to Fla. and La. Zone 5.

glabra (Mill.) Sweet [*C. microcarpa* Nutt.; *C. porcina* (Michx.f.) Nutt.; *Hicoria microcarpa* (Nutt.) Britt.]. PIGNUT, PIGNUT H., SMALL-FRUITED H., BROOM H. To 40 ft., bark close, not shaggy; lfts. mostly 5, oblong or somewhat oblanceolate, to 6 in. long, acuminate, serrate; nut obovoid, somewhat ridged, to 1 in. long, kernel astringent. Me. and Ont., s. to Fla. Zone 5.

illinoinensis (Wangenh.) C. Koch (not "*illinoensis*") [*C. oliviformis* (Michx.) Nutt.; *C. Pecan* (Marsh.) Engl. & Graebn.; *Hicoria Pecan* (Marsh.) Britt.]. PECAN. To 150 ft.; lfts. 11–17, oblong-lanceolate, to 7 in. long; nut ovoid or oblong, smooth, light brown. Ind., Ill., Iowa, s. to Mex. Zone 6. For cult. see *Pecan.*

laciniosa (Michx.f.) Loud. [*C. sulcata* Pursh]. SHELLBARK H., KING NUT, BIG SHELLBARK. To 120 ft.; lfts. 7–9, oblong-lanceolate, to 8 in. long, pubescent beneath; nut nearly globose, compressed and angled, yellow or reddish. N.Y. to Penn., sw. to Okla. Zone 6.

microcarpa: *C. glabra.*

oliviformis: *C. illinoinensis.*

ovata (Mill.) C. Koch [*C. alba* Nutt., not C. Koch]. SHAGBARK H., SHELLBARK H. To 120 ft., bark shaggy; lfts. usually 5, elliptic, to 6 in. long; nut ellipsoid, slightly angled, white. Que., s. to Fla. and Tex. Zone 5.

pallida (Ashe) Engl. & Graebn. [*Hicoria pallida* Ashe]. SAND H., PALE H. To 110 ft., bark very rough; lfts. 7–9, oblong-lanceolate, to 5 in. long, with silvery scales and scurfy-pubescent beneath when young; nut subglobose to obovoid, to 1¼ in. long, thin-shelled. Coastal plain, often in sandy soil, s. N.J. and Tenn., s. to nw. Fla. and La. Zone 6.

Pecan: *C. illinoinensis.*

porcina: *C. glabra.*

sulcata: *C. laciniosa.*

tomentosa Nutt. [*C. alba* (Mill.) C. Koch, not Nutt.]. MOCKERNUT H., WHITE-HEART H., MOCKERNUT, SQUARENUT. To 90 ft.; lfts. 7–9, oblong, to 7 in. long, tomentose beneath; nut nearly globose, angled, light brown. Mass., s. to Fla. and Tex. Zone 5.

CARYOPHYLLACEAE Juss. [*Illecebraceae* R. Br.]. PINK FAMILY. Dicot.; about 70 genera of herbs and a few subshrubs of wide distribution; sts. often swollen at the nodes; lvs. opp., simple, entire, veins parallel; fls. in terminal, dichasial cymes or solitary, regular, white or brightly colored, sepals 4–5, separate or united, petals 4–5, stamens 8–10, ovary superior, 1–5-celled, styles 2–5; fr. usually a many-seeded caps., rarely

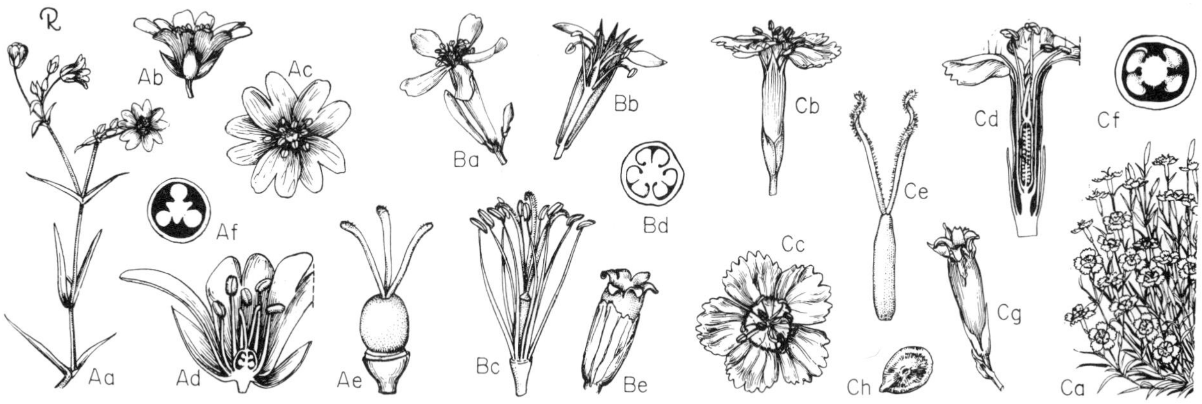

CARYOPHYLLACEAE. **A.** *Stellaria Holostea:* **Aa,** flowering stem, × ½; **Ab,** flower, side view, × 1; **Ac,** flower, face view, × 1; **Ad,** flower, vertical section, × 2; **Ae,** pistil, × 4; **Af,** ovary, cross section, × 5. **B,** *Silene Armeria:* **Ba,** flower and buds, × 1; **Bb,** flower, vertical section, × 1; **Bc,** stamens and pistil, × 2; **Bd,** ovary, cross section at base, × 10. **C,** *Dianthus deltoides:* **Ca,** flowering plant, × ⅕; **Cb,** flower, side view, × 1; **Cc,** flower, face view, × 1; **Cd,** flower, vertical section, × 1½; **Ce,** pistil, × 2; **Cf,** ovary, cross section, × 8; **Cg,** capsule, × 1; **Ch,** seed, × 10.

an indehiscent, 1-seeded nutlet, or even berrylike in *Cucubalus.* The cult. genera include: *Acanthophyllum, Agrostemma, Arenaria, Cerastium, Cucubalus, Dianthus, Drypis, Gypsophila, Herniaria, Lychnis, Paronychia, Petrocoptis, Petrorhagia, Sagina, Saponaria, Scleranthus, Silene, Spergula, Spergularia, Stellaria, Telephium,* and *Vaccaria.*

Cultivated as ornamentals, usually grown outdoors, but the carnation *(Dianthus Caryophyllus)* extensively grown as a commercial cut flower in greenhouses. Of the outdoor species, some are annuals, others biennial, and many are dwarf perennials well-suited to rock walls, rock gardens, and the perennial border. Some are not long-lived, but they are readily propagated by seeds, cuttings, layers, and division. They thrive in full sun and with good drainage; many do better in a limestone soil.

CARYOPTERIS Bunge. BLUEBEARD. *Verbenaceae.* About 6 spp. of glabrous or hairy, deciduous shrubs, subshrubs, or per. herbs, native to e. Asia; lvs. opp., simple, entire or toothed; fls. blue, lavender, or white, in axillary, or terminal and panicled cymes, calyx deeply 5-lobed, enlarging in fr., corolla 5-lobed, tube short, limb spreading, with 1 segm. larger and fringed, stamens 4, exserted; fr. dry, 4-valved, separating into 4 somewhat winged nutlets.

Grown in pots in the greenhouse in a compost of peat and loam. Not fully hardy out of doors in the North, but in the southern states may bloom from root shoots. Propagated by seeds in spring or by cuttings in autumn under glass.

×**clandonensis** A. Simmonds ex Rehd.: *C. incana* × *C. mongholica.* Shrub, to 3 ft.; lvs. elliptic-lanceolate to lanceolate, to 4 in. long, entire or occasionally with few teeth; fls. blue, to ⅜ in. long, in many-fld. cymes. Zone 5.

Giraldii: a listed name of no botanical standing.

incana (Thunb.) Miq. [*C. Mastacanthus* Schauer; *C. tangutica* Maxim.]. Shrub, to 5 ft., but often dying back and treated as a per. herb; lvs. ovate to oblong-ovate, to 3 in. long, grayish-tomentose beneath; fls. violet-blue, to ¼ in. long, in dense cymes. Autumn. China, Japan. Zone 7. Known in the nursery trade as BLUE SPIRAEA. Cv. **'Candida'.** Fls. white.

Mastacanthus: *C. incana.*

mongholica Bunge. Shrub, to 3 ft.; lvs. linear-lanceolate to linear, to 2 in. long, nearly entire; fls. blue, to ½ in. long, in few-fld., loose cymes. N. China, Mongolia. Zone 3.

tangutica: *C. incana.*

CARYOTA L. FISHTAIL PALM. *Palmae.* A small genus of solitary or cespitose, monoecious palms, native in the Asiatic tropics, distinguished from all other palms by the 2-pinnate lvs. with cuneate to trapeziform ("fishtail-like") pinnules toothed at the often oblique tip; sts. flowering from top to base and dying; infl. once-branched or rarely spicate, rachillae with fls. in triads (2 male and 1 female); male fls. with imbricate sepals, petals valvate, stamens 6–100 or more, female fls. with sepals imbricate, petals valvate, united in a short tube at base, pistil 3-celled, but only with 1–2 fertile; fr. 1–2-seeded, with irritant flesh, seed with ruminate endosperm. The spp. of *Caryota* are very insufficiently known botanically; they are often misidentified and probably hybridize in cult.

One species, *C. urens,* is an economically important palm in India. These palms are often planted in the tropics as ornamentals and the cespitose species are also used for their ornamental foliage under glass as well as outdoors in warmest regions of the U.S. (Zone 10 in Fla.).

aequatorialis (Becc.) Ridl. Sts. solitary, to 60 ft., 1 ft. in diam.; lvs. to 18 ft. long, pinnules obcuneate, toothed, to 1 ft. long, 2½ in. wide; infl. to 12 ft. long, with many rachillae; male fls. with more than 100 stamens; fr. globose. Malay Pen.

Alberti: *C. Rumphiana.*

Cumingii Lodd. ex Mart. Sts. cespitose, to 25 ft., 8 in. in diam.; pinnules erect-spreading, half rhomboidal; infl. brs. short, hairy-scurfy; male fls. ¼ in. long, stamens about 9; fr. globose, 1-seeded, to ¾ in. in diam. Philippine Is. Most material cult. under this name is misidentified.

furfuracea: *C. mitis.*

Griffithii: *C. mitis.*

mitis Lour. [*C. furfuracea* Blume; *C. Griffithii* Becc.; *C. sobolifera* Wallich ex Mart.]. BURMESE F.P., CLUSTERED F.P., TUFTED F.P. Sts. clustered, 12–40 ft., 4 in. in diam.; pinnules obliquely wedge-shaped; infl. brs. short, scurfy; male fls. to ½ in. long, stamens 12–16; fr. 1-seeded, 9/16 in. in diam. Burma to Malay Pen., Java, and Philippine Is. Much planted as an ornamental in the tropics and often seen in greenhouse collections.

ochlandra Hance. Sts. solitary, to 4 ft. or more; pinnules half rhomboidal; infl. brs. green, to 9 ft. long; male fls. 9/16 in. long, stamens 110–155; fr. blood-red, 1–2-seeded, 1 in. in diam. S. China.

plumosa: a listed name of no botanical standing, used for a clustering palm not satisfactorily identified with any known sp.

Rumphiana Mart. [*C. Alberti* F. J. Muell. ex H. Wendl. & Drude]. St. solitary, to 75 ft., 1 ft. in diam.; pinnules half rhomboidal, variable; infl. brs. glabrous, to 4½ ft. long; male fls. to ¾ in. long, stamens 10–50; fr. 1–2-seeded, to ⅝ in. in diam. or more. Solomon Is. to Australia, India, and Philippine Is.

sobolifera: *C. mitis.*

urens L. WINE PALM, JAGGERY P., SAGO P., TODDY P., KITTUL TREE. St. solitary, to 40 ft.; pinnules obliquely wedge-shaped; infl. brs. elongate, pendulous, to 20 ft.; male fls. with 40–45 stamens; fr. reddish, 1–2-seeded, to ¾ in. in diam. India, Ceylon, Malay Pen. Fast-growing and much planted as an ornamental in trop. gardens. Where native, the sp. is an important source of a strong fiber (kittul), of toddy, sago, and timber.

CASIMIROA Llave. *Rutaceae.* About 6 spp. of large shrubs or trees, native to the highlands of Mex. and Cent. Amer.; lvs.

alt., palmately compound, sometimes of 1 lft., glandular-dotted; fls. mostly small, in axillary or terminal panicles or corymbs, sepals, petals, and stamens usually 5; fr. drupaceous, green or yellow, 2–5-celled, 2–5-seeded.

One species is grown in warm countries for its edible fruit. The white sapote is subtropical, thriving on any well-drained soil, preferably a sandy loam. Propagated by seeds sown in flats or pots. Seedlings should not be planted out until about 3 ft. high and should then receive liberal watering. The terminal bud should be pinched off to induce branching. For quick results and to reproduce cultivars superior in quality and productivity, shield budding should be practiced.

edulis Llave. WHITE SAPOTE, MEXICAN APPLE, ZAPOTE BLANCO. To 50 ft.; lvs. long-petioled, lfts. mostly 5, elliptic to ovate, to 5 in. long, glabrous on both surfaces; fls. greenish, fragrant; fr. 3–4 in. across, yellowish-green, pulp soft, cream-colored, edible, very sweet. Mex. Grown as a dooryard tree in Mex. and Cent. Amer. above 3,000 ft., and in subtrop. Fla. and Calif. Var. **Wilsonii** is listed.

tetrameria Millsp. MATASANO. To 30 ft.; lfts. mostly 5, oblong-ovate to elliptic, to 6 in. long, green and glabrous above, densely pubescent beneath; fls. white or cream-colored; fr. like *C. edulis,* sometimes rather bitter. Cent. Amer.

CASSANDRA: see *CHAMAEDAPHNE.*

CASSIA L. [*Chamaefistula* G. Don]. SENNA, SHOWER

TREE. *Leguminosae* (subfamily *Caesalpinioideae*). Perhaps more than 500 spp. of trees, shrubs, and ann. or per. herbs, mostly of trop. or subtrop. regions; lvs. alt., even-pinnate; fls. in often large racemes, sometimes corymbose, panicled, clustered, or solitary, showy, nearly regular, 5-merous, mostly yellow, stamens mostly 10 (rarely 5), with 7 fertile and 3 abortive anthers; fr. a flat or cylindrical legume, sometimes winged. By some auths. divided into several genera.

A number of species are medicinal, supplying drugs such as senna; a few yield important tanbarks. Many are ornamental and certain of the woody cassias are among the showiest of tropical flowering trees. Most of the woody species require a tropical or subtropical climate (Zone 10b) and can be grown only under glass in the North; propagated by division and cuttings. The herbaceous kinds are grown in the border from seed or by division.

abbreviata D. Oliver. Shrub, or tree to 25 ft.; lfts. in 8–12 pairs, elliptic, to 2 in. long, obtuse or emarginate; corymbs to 6 in. long, with crowded, persistent bracts; fls. fragrant, petals 1 in. long; fr. slender, nearly cylindrical, 1–3 ft. long, with transverse seeds and partitions, mostly densely pubescent. Somalia Republic to Uganda, Mozambique, and S.-W. Afr. Zone 9b. In Rhodesia called LONG-TAIL C. Subsp. **abbreviata**. The typical subsp.; lfts. with hairs not appressed beneath; fr. rarely almost glabrous. Subsp. **Beareana** (Holmes) Brenan [var. *granitica* (Bak.f.) Bak.f.; *C. Beareana* Holmes]. Lfts. with minute appressed hairs beneath or rarely glabrous; petals sometimes veined red or brown; fr. velvety to glabrous.

aculeata Pohl ex Benth. Differs from *C. alata* in having branchlets, petioles, and rachises prickly; lfts. glabrous; fr. flat, 3–4 in. long and ¾ in. wide. E.-cent. Brazil.

acutifolia Delile. ALEXANDRIAN S. Shrub or subshrub; lfts. in 3–7 pairs, ovate or lanceolate, acute; racemes longer than lvs.; fr. broad, oblong, to 2¼ in. long. Egypt, Sudan to Nigeria. Cult. in India. A source of the drug senna.

alata L. RINGWORM C., CANDLESTICK S., EMPRESS CANDLE PLANT, CHRISTMAS-CANDLE. Shrub, to 8 ft.; lvs. very large, lfts. in 8–14 pairs, oblong or obovate, to 2½ in. long, obtuse, pubescent; racemes stout, elongate, spikelike, petals yellow, veiny, ⅞ in. long, fertile anthers 6–7, dehiscing by apical pores; fr. winged, to 6 in. long. Tropics. Zone 8b.

angulata Vogel. Differs from *C. speciosa* in being taller, and in having branchlets pendent or scandent, lfts. mostly 1–2 in. long, and fls. in smaller, narrow panicles. Brazil.

armata S. Wats. Bushy shrub, to 5 ft., sts. yellow-green, leafless much of year; lvs. to 6 in. long, lfts. in 1–4 pairs, remote, oblong-ovate, to ⁵⁄₁₆ in. long; racemes dense, terminal, to 6 in. long; fr. yellowish, spongy, to 1½ in. long. Calif. and Ariz.

artemisioides Gaud.-Beaup. ex DC. WORMWOOD S., FEATHERY C. Shrub, to 4 ft., silky-gray-pubescent; lfts. in 3–8 pairs, needlelike, 1 in. long; fls. sulphur-yellow; fr. flat, to 3 in. long. E. Australia.

auriculata L. AVARAM, TANNER'S C. Tall shrub, brs. and lvs. gray-puberulous beneath; lvs. to 4 in. long, lfts. in 8–12 pairs, obovate-oblong, to 1 in. long, obtuse to emarginate-mucronate, stipules large, leafy, persistent; racemes corymbose; fls. 1 in. long; fr. thin, to 5 in. long and ⅝ in. wide. India and Ceylon. One of the principal native tanbarks of s. India.

australis Sims. Tall shrub; lfts. in 8–10 pairs, oblong-lanceolate to linear, to 1 in. long; fls. in clusters of 2–6, petals broad, ½ in. long; fr. to 4 in. long. Australia.

Beareana: *C. abbreviata* subsp.

bicapsularis L. [*C. Candolleana* Vogel]. Erect shrub, to 12 ft., sts. weak, straggling; differs from *C. corymbosa* in having 3–5 pairs of obovate or oblong-obtuse lfts. and slender pods to 6 in. long. Trop. Amer.; now pantrop.

Brewsteri F. J. Muell. Tree, to 40 ft. or more, usually glabrous throughout; lfts. in 2–4 pairs, varying from ovate to obovate and ¾ in. long to oblong or oblong-lanceolate and 2 in. long; racemes to 6 in. long; petals narrow, ovate, ⁵⁄₁₆ in. long, golden to golden-orange, the longer 3 filaments globose-dilated near middle; fr. thick, flat, 1 ft. long, 1 in. wide, with transverse partitions, the margins remaining after inside falls away. Queensland (Australia).

Candolleana: *C. bicapsularis.*

capsularis: a listed name of no botanical standing; perhaps intended for *C. bicapsularis.*

Carnaval Speg. Deciduous tree, to 20 ft.; golden-rusty-pubescent; lfts. in 10–15 pairs, ovate to lanceolate, to 2¾ in. long, densely pubescent beneath; racemes much shorter than lvs.; fls. to 1½ in. across, petals unequal, veiny, the lowermost very oblique and twice as large as the upper ones, stamens equal, much shorter than petals, anthers dehiscent by apical pores; fr. 4–8 in. long, ⅜ in. across, seeds transverse. Argentina, where called CARNAVAL. Zone 9b. Perhaps not specifically distinct from *C. excelsa.* Some material offered as *C. Carnaval* may be *C. leptophylla.*

Chamaecrista L. Per., sts. often woody at base, prostrate or ascending, to 1 ft. long; lfts. in 5–16 pairs, linear-oblong; fls. few, ¼ in. long, in short axillary clusters, fertile anthers 5–7; fr. narrow, flat, to 1¼ in. long. W. Indies, Mex. Probably not cult. in U.S.; material offered under this name is likely to be *C. fasciculata.*

corymbosa Lam. Shrub, to 10 ft.; lfts. mostly in 3 pairs, oblong-lanceolate, to 2 in. long and less than ½ in. broad, obtuse or nearly acute; fls. in axillary corymbs, petals less than ½ in. long; fr. cylindrical, 3–4½ in. long. N. Argentina, Uruguay, s. Brazil; naturalized in s. U.S. and frequently cult. Zone 8. Var. **plurijuga** Benth. [*C. floribunda* Hort.]. Lfts. in 4–5 pairs; all racemes in corymbose panicles.

Covesii A. Gray. DESERT S. Shrubby, to 2 ft., densely white-pubescent; lfts. in 2–3 pairs, oblong to obovate, to 1 in. long; racemes axillary, few-fld.; petals conspicuously veined; fr. flat, to 2 in. long. Ariz., Calif., Baja Calif.

didymobotrya Fresen. [*C. nairobensis* Hort.]. Shrub, to 10 ft.; lvs. about 1 ft. long, lfts. in 8–16 pairs, oblong to ovate-elliptic, to 2 in. long, mucronate, stipules ovate, ¼ in. long; racemes erect, to 1 ft. long; fls. to ¾ in. long; fr. flat, to 4 in. long, ¾ in. wide, indehiscent. Trop. Afr.; naturalized locally in s. Fla. and trop. Amer.

eremophila A. Cunn. ex Vogel [*C. nemophila* A. Cunn. ex Vogel]. Bushy shrub; lfts. in 1 or 2 pairs, linear, cylindrical, narrow, usually 1 in. long or more, petioles cylindrical or laterally flattened, lower lvs. reduced to flattened phyllodes; fls. in axillary, nearly corymbose racemes much shorter than petioles, fertile anthers 10; fr. 3–4 in. long, ⁵⁄₁₆ in. wide. Australia, where called DESERT CASSIA. A very variable sp., sometimes approaching *C. artemisioides.* Var. **zygophylla** (Benth.) Benth. Lfts. flat, linear, about ¹⁄₁₆ in. wide.

excelsa Schrad. Tall shrub, or tree to 30 ft., branchlets, petioles, and infl. softly pubescent; lfts. in 10–20 pairs, elliptic-oblong to 1½ in. long; fls. in axillary racemes shorter than lvs. or in terminal panicles to 6–12 in. long, petals oblique, veiny, nearly 1 in. long; fr. cylindrical, to 6 in. long, ½ in. in diam., with transverse seeds separated by partitions. E. Brazil. Zone 10b.

fasciculata Michx. [*C. Chamaecrista* Walt., not L.]. PARTRIDGE PEA, PRAIRIE S., GOLDEN C. Ann., to 1½ ft.; lfts. in 12–44 pairs, sensitive, linear-oblong, to ⅝ in. long; fls. yellow, clustered in axils, to ¾ in. long, fertile anthers 10; fr. flat, linear, to 1½ in. long. Me. to Fla., w. to S. Dak., Tex., Mex.

fastuosa Willd. ex Vogel. Differs from *C. ferruginea* in having lfts. glossy above, pale and scarcely puberulous beneath, stipules rather wide, and petals more than 1 in. long. N. Brazil.

ferruginea Schrad. ex DC. Small tree, or sometimes to 60 ft.; lfts. in 10–20 pairs, narrowly oblong, soft-pubescent, especially beneath, stipules narrow, petioles and infl. reddish-pubescent; racemes mostly pendent, almost as long as lvs., to 12 in. long; petals scarcely ¾ in. long. E. Brazil.

fistula L. GOLDEN-SHOWER, INDIAN LABURNUM, PURGING FISTULA, PUDDING-PIPE TREE, GOLDEN-RAIN. Tree, to 30 ft., nearly or quite glabrous; lvs. large, lfts. in 4–8 pairs, ovate, to 6 in. long; racemes pendent, 12–18 in. long, bracts minute, falling early; fls. before the lvs., pale yellow; fr. cylindrical, to 2 ft. long. Spring. India. Zone 10. Dried fr. has medicinal properties.

floribunda Cav. [*C. grandiflora* Desf.; *C. laevigata* Willd.]. Shrub, to 6 ft.; lfts. in 3–4 pairs, ovate-lanceolate, acuminate or acute, the larger terminal lfts. to 3 in. long; fls. in short, somewhat corymbose racemes in terminal panicles; fr. cylindrical, to 3½ in. long. Tropics. Seeds have medicinal properties. Some material offered as *C. floribunda* may be *C. corymbosa* var. *plurijuga.*

florida: *C. siamea.*

gigantea: *C. siamea.*

glandulosa L. Shrubby, to 3 ft.; lvs. to 3 in. long, lfts. usually in 10–16 pairs, oblong-linear to nearly lanceolate, to ¾ in. long, oblique basally; fls. axillary, solitary or 2–3 together, sepals to ⅜ in. long, petals longer, fertile anthers 10; fr. oblong-linear, to 1½ in. long. Brazil.

glauca: *C. surattensis.*

goratensis: *C. singueana.*

grandiflora: *C. laevigata.*

grandis L.f. PINK-SHOWER, HORSE C. Tree, to 50 ft.; lfts. in 8–20 pairs, oblong, to 2½ in. long, tomentose beneath; racemes lateral, to 7 in. long; fls. before the lvs., petals yellow, becoming peach-colored or salmon; fr. nearly cylindrical, to 2 ft. long, rough, with transverse seeds in a malodorous pulp. Trop. Amer.

hebecarpa Fern. WILD S. Distinguished from *C. marilandica* by its linear-bristly stipules, slenderly club-shaped gland near base of petiole, and fr. with sections as long as wide. New Eng. to Wisc., s. to N.C. and e. Tenn.

hirsuta L. Per., to 6 ft.; lfts. in 3–5 pairs, ovate to ovate-lanceolate, to 3 in. long, acute or acuminate, hirsute; racemes short, axillary; fls. to ¾ in. long; fr. linear, to 6 in. long, densely hairy. Trop. Amer.

javanica L. APPLE-BLOSSOM C., APPLE-BLOSSOM S. Low tree, with broad-spreading crown; differs from *C. nodosa* in having larger stipules, to ½ in. long, usually obtuse lfts., to 2 in. long; fls. mostly larger, of short duration, calyx brown to reddish, petals to 1$\frac{5}{16}$ in. long, at first pale red, changing to dark red, and finally paling. Indonesia. Zone 10b. Hybrids with *C. nodosa* occur in cult.

leptocarpa Benth. Erect herb, to 3 ft., very pilose; lfts. in 4–7 pairs, ovate to elliptic, to 4 in. long, acute, usually pilose; petals ⅝ in. long, fertile anthers 6–7; fr. linear, sometimes pilose, to 1 ft. long, scarcely ⅛ in. wide. Cuba, s. Mex. to S. Amer.

leptophylla Vogel. Differs from *C. ferruginea* in having lfts. in 8–12 pairs, ovate-lanceolate, nearly acute, and the 3 longer filaments thickened above the middle. Se. Brazil. Zone 9b. Fls. of this sp. are yellow, not pink as described by some auths.

Lindheimerana Scheele. Differs from *C. Covesii* in having 4–8 pairs of lfts., anthers red, and fr. to 2¼ in. long. Tex. to Ariz., s. to n. Mex.

Mannii D. Oliver. Tree, to 75 ft.; lfts. in 5–6 pairs, elliptic to oblong, to 2½ in. long, acute; fls. in corymbs to 4 in. long, petals elliptic, violet-rose to white, to 1 in. long; fr. cylindrical, indehiscent, to 2 ft. long, 1 in. in diam. W. Trop. Afr. to Uganda and Tanzania.

marginata: see *C. Roxburghii.*

marilandica L. [*C. Medsgeri* Shafer]. WILD S. Per., to 4 ft., glabrous or nearly so; lfts. oblong or oblong-lanceolate, nearly acute, stipules linear-lanceolate, petiolar gland short-cylindrical to conic-ovoid; fr. flat, thickish, to 3½ in. long, sections much shorter than broad. Penn. to Fla., w. to Iowa, Kans., Tex.

Medsgeri: *C. marilandica.*

montana B. Heyne. Shrub; lvs. to 6 in. long, lfts. in 10–15 pairs, oblong, to 1½ in. long, bristle-tipped; corymbs axillary, or the terminal ones panicled; fr. thin, flat, to 5 in. long, ¾ in. wide, glossy. India.

moschata HBK. BRONZE-SHOWER. Differs from *C. fistula* in having lfts. in 10–18 pairs, nearly opp. to alt., oblong, 1½–2 in. long and ½ in. wide, soft-pubescent; racemes shorter, 6–10 in. long; fls. yellow, becoming orange- or brick-red with age; fr. smaller, 12–18 in. long, pulp surrounding seeds with musky odor. Panama and Colombia.

multijuga A. Rich. Tree, to 20 ft.; lfts. in 18–40 pairs, linear-oblong, to ¾ in. long, obtuse; fls. to 2 in. across, in large panicles; fr. flat, 6 in. long. Brazil and Guyana; naturalized in W. Indies.

nairobensis: a listed name of no botanical standing for *C. didymobotrya.*

nemophila: see *C. eremophila.*

nicaraguensis Benth. Glabrous shrub, or tree to 15 ft.; lfts. in 10–20 pairs, oblong, to 3 in. long; racemes as long as lvs. or longer; petals yellow, with darker veins, 1 in. long; fr. linear, flat, to 4½ in. long. S. Mex. to Panama.

nictitans L. WILD SENSITIVE PLANT. Ann., to 18 in., erect or decumbent, somewhat pubescent; lvs. sensitive, lfts. in 6–22 pairs, linear, to ⅜ in. long; fls. very small, axillary, only 1 petal longer than calyx, fertile anthers usually 5; fr. to 1¾ in. long, pubescent. Me. to Ga., w. to Ind. and Tex.; W. Indies.

nodosa Buch.-Ham. ex Roxb. PINK-AND-WHITE-SHOWER, JOINT-WOOD. Tree, to 50 ft. or more; lfts. in 5–12 pairs, elliptic-ovate to oblong, to 4 in. long, usually acute; racemes dense; calyx green, petals at first pale, becoming bright pink, ¾ in. long, the 3 longest filaments thickly dilated near middle; fr. cylindrical, to 2 ft. long, with transverse partitions. E. Himalayas to Malay Pen. Zone 10b. May not be specifically distinct from *C. javanica.*

occidentalis L. COFFEE S., STYPTICWEED, STINKING WEED. Differs from *C. leptocarpa* in being glabrous or only puberulent throughout and having fr. to 4½ in. long, $\frac{3}{16}$–$\frac{5}{16}$ in. wide. Va. to Ind., s. to Fla. and Tex.; W. Indies, Mex. to S. Amer.; naturalized in Old World tropics. Used medicinally.

oligophylla F. J. Muell. Tall shrub, glabrous or minutely pubescent; lfts. in 2 (rarely 1) pairs, leathery, broadly obovate, to 1 in. long; racemes short, axillary, densely fld.; fertile anthers 10; fr. to 2½ in. long and nearly ¾ in. wide. N. Australia.

pleurocarpa F. J. Muell. Erect, glabrous shrub; lfts. usually in 4–5 pairs, oblong-linear, to 2 in. long; fls. in axillary, loose racemes, stamens on short filaments; fr. flat, 2 in. long and ½ in. wide, thin, with longitudinal ridge above each seed. Australia.

quinquangulata L. Rich. [*Chamaefistula antillana* Britt. & Rose]. Shrubs, or low trees to 25 ft. or more, brs. vinelike, 5-angled; lfts. in 2 pairs, obliquely ovate, to 4 in. long, acute-acuminate; petals orbicular-ovate, to ¾ in. long, veiny; fr. linear, to 7 in. long, turgid when mature. W. Indies, Venezuela to Brazil.

renigera Wallich ex Benth. Deciduous, to 25 ft., branchlets drooping, soft-pubescent; distinguished from *P. Roxburghii* in having lfts. oblong-strap-shaped, only slightly oblique, to 2½ in. long, broadly rounded at each end, velvety on both surfaces, stipules prominent, persistent, reniform, very oblique, to 1 in. across, cuspidate; racemes axillary, 6 in. long, rachis velvety; fls. pink or yellow; fr. cylindrical, to 2 ft. long, 1 in. in diam., smooth. Burma.

reticulata Willd. Tall shrub, to 15 ft., differing from *C. alata* in having fr. flat, ⅝ in. wide, with prominent margins. Cent. Amer. to Brazil.

robusta Pollard. Herb, to 6 ft., sts. densely pubescent; lfts. in 10–15 pairs, elliptic, to ¾ in. long, obtuse, stipules leafy, broadly lanceolate; fls. large, 1–3 in axils; fr. linear, pubescent, to 1½ in. long. Ky., s. to Ala. and La.

Roemerana Scheele. Per., to 1½ ft.; lfts. in 1 pair, linear-lanceolate, to 2½ in. long; racemes terminal, corymbose; fls. orange-yellow; fr. about 1 in. long. Tex. and New Mex., Mex.

Roxburghii DC. [*C. marginata* Roxb., not Willd.]. Tree, with densely tomentose branchlets; lvs. to 1 ft. long, lfts. in 15–20 pairs, oblong, strongly oblique, to 1½ in. long, emarginate, downy beneath; racemes short, axillary, or the terminal ones panicled; petals small, rose, fertile anthers 10; fr. cylindrical, indehiscent, with transverse partitions between the seeds. India and Ceylon.

siamea Lam. [*C. florida* Vahl; *C. gigantea* Bertero ex DC.]. KASSOD TREE. Tree, to 40 ft.; lfts. in 8–9 pairs, oblong, to 3 in. long; fls. in corymbs forming large terminal panicles, petals to ⅝ in. long; fr. flat, to 9 in. long. Indonesia, Malay Pen.; naturalized in Amer. tropics.

Sieberana DC. Tree, to 60 ft., brs. silky-pubescent at apex; differs from *C. fistula* in its smaller lfts., to 3 in. long, and bracts of infl. to ⅝ in. long, persistent. Senegal to Uganda. Roots have medicinal properties.

singueana Delile [*C. goratensis* Fresen.]. Shrub, or tree to 35 ft.; lvs. to 8 in. long, lfts. in 5–8 pairs, elliptic, emarginate; racemes axillary, 5 in. long; petals reddish-yellow with brown veins, obovate, more than 1 in. long; fr. linear, to 6 in. long. Trop. Afr.

speciosa Schrad. Shrub, or medium-sized tree, mostly with petioles and infl. tawny-hairy; lfts. in 2 pairs, obliquely ovate-oblong, soft-pubescent beneath, the upper pair to 2 in. long, the lower pair nearly as long or shorter; racemes corymbose, forming wide, terminal panicles; petals to 1½ in. long, pubescent on outside; fr. cylindrical, to 1 ft. long, with transverse seeds and partitions. E. Brazil.

spectabilis DC. Tree, rarely to 60 ft., branchlets softly pubescent; lfts. in 8–15 pairs, oblong-lanceolate, to 3 in. long, pubescent beneath; racemes to 2 ft. long; fls. bright yellow, 1½ in. across; fr. cylindrical, 1 ft. long. Trop. Amer. Zone 10b. Closely related to *C. excelsa.*

splendida Vogel. GOLDEN-WONDER. Shrub, to 10 ft.; lfts. in 2 pairs, elliptic to oblong, to 3 in. long; racemes panicled; fls. large; fr. nearly cylindrical, to 1½ in. long. Brazil. Zone 9b.

Sturtii R. Br. Bushy shrub, usually white-glaucous or -tomentose; lfts. usually in 3–5 pairs, or only 2 on lower lvs., thick, linear to lanceolate, cuneate, elliptic, or almost obovate, to 1 in. long; racemes axillary, short, dense; fertile anthers 10; fr. ½ in. wide. Australia.

sulcata DC. Differs from *C. leptocarpa* in having obtuse lfts. 1–2 in. long. S. Brazil.

surattensis Burm.f. [*C. glauca* Lam.]. Tall shrub or tree; lfts. in 6–10 pairs, obovate, about 1½ in. long; racemes umbel-like; fls. large, fertile anthers 10; fr. flat, to 6 in. long. Trop. Asia, Australia, Polynesia.

tomentosa L.f. Shrub, to 12 ft., brs. tomentose; lfts. in 6–8 pairs, oblong, to 2 in. long, yellowish-tomentose beneath; racemes shorter than lvs.; fls. deep yellow; fr. thick, flat, to 5 in. long. S. Mex. and Guatemala, w. S. Amer. Zone 9b.

Tora L. SICKLEPOD. Erect ann., to 3 ft.; lfts. in 2–4 pairs, oblong-ovate to obovate, to 2 in. long; racemes axillary, few-fld.; fertile anthers 6–7; fr. linear, 4-angled, to 8 in. long, with thick margins. Va. to Ind., s. to Fla., and Ark.; W. Indies, Cent. and S. Amer.

turrialba: a listed name of no botanical standing.

CASSINE L. [*Elaeodendron* Jacq.f. ex Jacq.]. *Celastraceae.* Perhaps 80 spp. of sometimes polygamous trees and shrubs, native mostly to trop. and subtrop. regions of the Old World, rarer in the New World; lvs. opp. or alt., simple, leathery; fls. small, greenish or white, in axillary cymes or panicles, calyx 4–5-parted, petals and stamens 4 or 5; fr. drupaceous, seeds not surrounded by aril.

Grown in tropical or warm regions or, in the juvenile state, under glass. Propagated by cuttings.

australis (Venten.) O. Kuntze [*Elaeodendron australe* Venten.]. Tree, to 40 ft.; lvs. ovate to oblong-lanceolate, 2–5 in. long, entire to crenate; fls. 4-merous; fr. bright red, about ½ in. long. Australia.

capensis L. Shrub or tree, to 30 ft.; lvs. oblong or ovate, to 2¾ in. long, serrate, veins translucent; fls. 4–5-merous, in cymes half as long as lvs.; fr. black or dark purple, to 5/16 in. long. S. Afr.

glauca (Pers.) O. Kuntze [*Elaeodendron glaucum* Pers.]. CEYLON TEA. Tree, to 45 ft.; lvs. elliptic, ovate, or orbicular, to 6 in. long, nearly entire, serrate, or crenate; fls. 5-merous, yellow-green; fr. yellow-green, ½ in. long. India.

Laneana (A. H. Moore) J. Ingram [*Elaeodendron Laneanum* A. H. Moore]. BERMUDA OLIVE-WOOD BARK. Evergreen tree, to 45 ft.; lvs. oblanceolate, to 4 in. long, shallowly toothed; fls. unisexual, 5-merous; fr. yellowish-white, to 1 in. long. Bermuda.

orientalis (Jacq.) O. Kuntze [*Elaeodendron orientale* Jacq.]. FALSE OLIVE. Shrub or small tree, 10–30 ft.; juvenile lvs. long, narrow, with dark red midrib, gradually passing into mature lvs., mature lvs. lanceolate, oblong to obovate, to 3 in. long, cuneate at base, crenate; fls. 5-merous, yellow-green; fr. about size of olive. Mauritius and, doubtfully, Madagascar.

papillosa (Hochst.) O. Kuntze [*Elaeodendron capense* Eckl. & Zeyh.; *E. papillosum* Hochst.]. Shrub, to 18 ft.; lvs. lanceolate-elliptic, to 2½ in. long, spiny-toothed, slightly revolute; fls. small, 4-merous, green; fr. yellow, about ½ in. long. S. Afr.

quadrangulata (Schrad.) O. Kuntze [*Elaeodendron quadrangulatum* (Schrad.) Reiss.]. Tree; lvs. elliptic to ovate, to 6 in. long, serrate; fls. 4-merous, white. Brazil.

CASSINIA R. Br. *Compositae* (Inula Tribe). About 20 spp. of evergreen shrubs, rarely herbs, native to Australia, New Zeal., and S. Afr.; lvs. alt., entire; fl. heads discoid, very small, in dense corymbs or panicles, involucral bracts imbricate, scarious, receptacle with scales among the fls.; fls. all tubular; pappus of capillary bristles.

A few species are grown outdoors in Calif.

fulvida Hook.f. Much-branched shrub, to 6 ft.; lvs. crowded, linear-spatulate, to ⅝ in. long, revolute, green and sticky above, yellowish-tomentose beneath; heads 1–2 in. across, 5–8-fld., in rounded corymbs, inner involucral bracts white-tipped, receptacular scales none or few; fls. white. New Zeal.

Vauvilliersii Hook.f. Differs from *C. fulvida* in having lvs. yellowish- or white-tomentose beneath, heads 8–15-fld., and receptacular scales many; fls. white. New Zeal.

CASSIOPE D. Don [*Harrimanella* Cov.]. *Ericaceae.* About 12 spp. of low, evergreen shrubs, native to the Himalayas, n. Asia, n. Eur., and n. N. Amer.; lvs. 4-ranked, scalelike, mostly thick and overlapping; fls. white or pinkish, nodding, solitary, axillary or terminal, calyx 4–5-lobed, corolla campanulate, stamens 8–10, anthers awned, ovary superior; fr. a 4–5-celled caps.

Cassiopes should be planted in moist, partly shady locations or rock gardens, in peaty or sandy soil. Propagated by cuttings of mature wood in Aug. under glass, also by layers and seeds.

fastigiata D. Don. Densely tufted, much-branched shrub, 6–12 in.; lvs. sessile, ovate-oblong, grooved on the back, margins scarious, ciliate; fls. white, broadly campanulate, to 5/16 in. long. Himalayas. Zone 7?

hypnoides (L.) D. Don. Sts. densely tufted, branched, ascending, to 3 in. or more; lvs. linear-subulate, less than 3/16 in. long, not grooved; fls. pure white or tinged pink, corolla 5-cleft, pedicels terminal, to 1 in. long. Arctic regions of N. Hemisphere. Zone 2.

lycopodioides (Pall.) D. Don. Sts. creeping, filiform; lvs. ovate, about 1/16 in. long, not grooved, margins scarious; fls. white, to ¼ in. long, style slender. Ne. Asia, Japan, Alaska. Zone 2.

Mertensiana (Bong.) D. Don. WHITE HEATHER. Tufted, to 1 ft.; lvs. ovate to lanceolate, to ¼ in. long, not grooved; fls. white to pinkish, to ¼ in. long, pedicels puberulent. Idaho, Mont., n. Calif. to Alaska. Zone 6. Var. **gracilis** (Piper) C. L. Hitchc. Sts. and pedicels glabrous.

selaginoides Hook.f. & T. Thoms. Tufted shrublet, to 10 in.; lvs. lanceolate to lanceolate-oblong, to ⅛ in. long, grooved on the back, bristle-tipped; fls. white, to ⅜ in. long. Himalayas. Zone 7?

Stellerana (Pall.) DC. [*Harrimanella Stellerana* (Pall.) Cov.]. Spreading, with matted sts.; lvs. spreading, oblong to linear-oblong, ⅛ in. long; fls. on terminal pedicels, white, ¼ in. long, corolla deeply lobed. Alaska to Wash.

tetragona (L.) D. Don. Sts. erect or ascending, to 1 ft.; lvs. oblong-ovate, to ¼ in. long, grooved on the back, usually pubescent when young; fls. on pedicels to 1 in. long, white, to ¼ in. long. Ore. to Alaska and eastward. Zone 2.

CASTALIA: *NYMPHAEA.* **C. flava:** *N. mexicana.* **C. minor:** *N. odorata* var.

CASTALIS Cass. *Compositae* (Calendula Tribe). Three spp. of per. herbs, woody at base, native to S. Afr.; lvs. alt., entire to pinnatifid; fl. heads solitary on terminal peduncles, radiate, involucral bracts in 1–2 rows, scarious-margined, receptacle naked; disc fls. tubular, bisexual, anthers sagittate, ray fls. ligulate, sterile; achenes obcordate to nearly orbicular, with thickened margins, smooth, pappus absent.

nudicaulis (L.) Norl. [*Dimorphotheca nudicaulis* (L.) DC.]. Sts. to 1 ft., more or less erect, glandular-hairy; lvs. in a basal rosette and also on the sts., oblong-lanceolate to narrowly obovate, to 2¾ in. long, remotely toothed to sinuate-toothed; heads to 2½ in. across; disc fls. purple, ray fls. white above, purple or brown underneath. Cape Prov. Var. **graminifolia** (L.) Norl. [*Dimorphothca nudicaulis* var. *graminifolia* (L.) Harv.]. Lvs. linear, usually entire.

spectabilis (Schlechter) Norl. [*Dimorphotheca spectabilis* Schlechter]. Sts. erect, to 16 in., glandular-pubescent; lvs. sessile, lanceolate to narrow-elliptic, to 2¾ in. long, almost clasping, essentially entire; heads to 2½ in. across; disc fls. yellow, tipped purple, ray fls. lilac-purple on both sides. Transvaal.

Tragus (Ait.) Norl. [*Dimorphotheca aurantiaca* DC., not Hort.]. Sts. to 1 ft., erect to ascending, glabrous; lvs. linear or linear-oblong to narrowly spatulate, to 2¾ in. long, margins entire or slightly sinuate-dentate, scabrous-ciliate; heads to 2½ in. across; disc fls. golden-brown, tipped in blue, ray fls. orange-yellow. Little Namaqualand.

CASTANEA Mill. CHESTNUT. *Fagaceae.* About 12 spp. of hardy, deciduous trees and shrubs, native to n. temp. regions; lvs. alt., oblong or lanceolate, toothed; fls. unisexual, male fls. in catkins, female fls. at base of male catkins or in separate lf. axils; fr. 1–7 large brown nuts enclosed in a prickly, dehiscent involucre or bur.

Chestnuts are grown as ornamentals and for the edible nuts. They are naturally tolerant of acid soils and present no special cultural difficulties on well-drained land. The chestnut blight may be injurious or fatal to susceptible species and weevils may be troublesome. Trees often bear nuts two or three years after planting. Propagation is by budding or grafting on chestnut stocks. Seedlings of the Chinese species are suitable stocks for varieties of Oriental origin. Breeding of chestnuts for blight resistance has received considerable attention. See *Chestnut.*

alnifolia Nutt. [*C. nana* Elliott]. BUSH CHINQUAPIN, DOWNY C. Low shrub, to 2 ft., with creeping rootstock; lvs. oblong or narrowly elliptic, to 6 in. long, sparsely pubescent; nuts solitary, ½–¾ in. long. Se. U.S. Zone 7.

americana: *C. dentata.*

crenata Siebold & Zucc. [*C. japonica* Blume; *C. pubinervis* C. K. Schneid.]. JAPANESE C. To 30 ft.; lvs. to 6 in. long, closely toothed, with rounded sinuses between, commonly tomentose beneath; nuts usually 2–3, about 1 in. across. Japan, where much planted for the nuts and useful wood. A blight-resistant sp. Zone 6.

dentata (Marsh.) Borkh. [*C. americana* Raf.]. AMERICAN C. To 100 ft.; lvs. to 10 in. long, mostly tapering or narrow at base, coarsely toothed, glabrous beneath; nuts usually 2–3, to 1 in. across. Me. to Miss. Zone 5. Once an important tree for its durable timber, tan bark and the sweet edible nuts. The sp. is now almost extinct because of the chestnut bark disease or blight. It persists mostly as sprouts coming up from the old stumps in the native forests. The hardiest of the chestnuts and produces the best quality nuts.

Henryi (Skan) Rehd. & E. H. Wils. To 90 ft.; lvs. ovate to lanceolate, to 6 in. long, acuminate, tapered or broadly obtuse to cordate basally, sharply dentate, glabrous; nut usually solitary, about ½ in. across. China. Zone 6. An important Chinese timber sp.

japonica: *C. crenata.*

koraiensis: a listed name of no botanical standing.

mollissima Blume. CHINESE C. To 60 ft.; lvs. to 6 in. long, coarsely toothed, pubescent beneath; nuts usually 2–3, about 1 in. across. China and Korea. Zone 5. A blight-resistant sp.

nana: *C. alnifolia.*

pubinervis: *C. crenata.*

pumila (L.) Mill. CHINQUAPIN. Shrub or tree, to 45 ft.; lvs. to 5 in. long, coarsely toothed, white-tomentose beneath; nut usually solitary, to ½ in. across. Penn., s. to Fla. and Tex. Zone 6. Wood durable and used for posts and railroad ties.

sativa Mill. [*C. vesca* Gaertn.]. SPANISH C., EUROPEAN C., EURASIAN C. To 100 ft.; lvs. to 8 in. long, mostly rounded or broad at base, with coarse spreading teeth, pubescent beneath when young; nuts 1–3, 1 in. across or more. S. Eur., N. Afr., w. Asia. Zone 6. Blight susceptible. Cvs. include forms with variegated lvs., and cv. **'Aspleniifolia'**, lvs. narrow, often linear and irregularly lobed; cv. **'Macrocarpa'**, fr. large.

Seguinii Dode. Tree or shrub, to 30 ft.; lvs. lanceolate, elliptic or obovate, to 5½ in. long, acuminate, obtuse to cordate, pubescent on veins beneath; nuts usually 3, about ½ in. across. China. Warmer parts of Zone 7.

tamba: a listed name of no botanical standing.

vesca: *C. sativa.*

CASTANOPSIS (D. Don) Spach. CHINQUAPIN. *Fagaceae.* About 110 spp. of monoecious, evergreen trees and shrubs, native to Asia, 2 in w. N. Amer.; lvs. alt., entire or dentate; fls. unisexual, the female usually at base of male catkins; fr. of 1–3 nuts enclosed in a spiny or tubercled involucre.

Not hardy in cold climates. For culture see *Castanea.*

caudata Franch. Shrub, to 20 ft., much-branched; lvs. usually glaucescent, leathery, and glossy. China. Zone 8?

chrysophylla (Dougl.) A. DC. GIANT C. To 100 ft. or more, although sometimes shrublike, bark heavily furrowed; lvs. oblong, to 6 in. long, entire, shining dark green above, with golden-yellow scales beneath; fr. with spiny husk. Wash. to Calif. Zone 8.

cuspidata (Thunb.) Schottky [*Quercus cuspidata* Thunb.]. JAPANESE C. Tree; lvs. ovate or oblong, to 3 in. long, entire, or toothed toward tip, gray-tomentose beneath; fr. with tubercled husk, nuts edible. Japan and Korea. Zone 8? Much used in gardens and parks in Japan.

Delavayi Franch. Lvs. stiff, elliptic to obovate, to 4½ in. long, toothed or crenate, glabrous at maturity, grayish beneath; fr. about ½ in. across, spiny. W. China. Zone 8?

sclerophylla: *Lithocarpus chinensis.*

sempervirens (Kellogg) W. Dud. BUSH C. Shrub, to 8 ft., bark smooth; lvs. oblong or oblanceolate, to 3 in. long, subentire; yellowish-gray-green above, rusty-tomentose beneath; female fls. ill-smelling; fr. with spiny husk ¾-1¼ in. across. S. Ore. to Calif. Zone 8.

CASTANOSPERMUM A. Cunn. *Leguminosae* (subfamily *Faboideae*). One sp., an evergreen tree, native to Australia; lvs. alt., large, odd-pinnate; fls. in lateral racemes, large, papilionaceous, petals nearly equal, stamens 10, separate, long-exserted; fr. a large, somewhat woody legume, spongy inside between the large, nearly globose seeds.

Propagated by seeds.

australe A. Cunn. & C. Fraser. MORETON BAY CHESTNUT, BLACK BEAN. To 60 ft.; lfts. in 5–7 pairs, oblong, to 5 in. long; racemes to 6 in. long, on old wood; fls. yellow to orange and reddish, standard 1 in. across, emarginate, recurved; fr. cylindrical, to 9 in. long, 2 in. in diam. E. Australia. Tender.

CASTILLA Sessé. *Moraceae.* About 10 spp. of trees with milky sap in lowland trop. Amer.; lvs. large, alt., deciduous; fls. unisexual, in dense heads. The generic name is often misspelled *Castilloa.*

Several species have been secondary sources of rubber and were formerly cultivated in plantations. Sometimes planted in the tropics. Propagated by seeds; the seedlings should be transplanted to a permanent position when about 1 ft. high.

elastica Sessé. PANAMA RUBBER TREE, CASTILLA R.T. Tree, to 60 ft., brs. fulvous-pilose; lvs. elliptic-obovate, 8–18 in. long, shallowly cordate, densely pubescent beneath, petioles under 1 in. long; male infl. about 1 in. wide and long, club-shaped, female infl. nearly sessile; fr. about 1 in. long, red or orange when ripe, seeds about $\frac{5}{16}$ in. long. S. Mex. to n. S. Amer. In 19th century, an important rubber source; supplanted by the Para rubber tree *(Hevea).*

CASTILLEJA Mutis ex L.f. PAINTED-CUP, PAINTBRUSH. *Scrophulariaceae.* About 200 spp. of per. herbs of N. and S. Amer., one sp. in n. Asia, partly parasitic on roots of other plants; lvs. alt.; fls. mostly greenish, in yellow-, purple-, or red-bracted, spikelike racemes, calyx 4-lobed, corolla 2-lipped, upper lip helmetlike, stamens 4; fr. a caps.

Seldom grown in gardens.

californica Abrams. INDIAN-PAINTBRUSH. Hairy per., to 2½ ft.; lvs. linear, entire or 2–4-lobed; fl. bracts and calyces tipped with scarlet or scarlet-red, corolla to 1¾ in. long, lower lip dark green or becoming dark brown. Coastal Calif. to n. Baja Calif.

chromosa A. Nels. [*C. collina* A. Nels.]. Puberulent, hispid-villous per., to 16 in.; lvs. linear, to 2¾ in. long, entire, or 3–5-parted in upper part of plant, segms. linear; fl. bracts and calyces green at base, tipped with scarlet, corolla to 1¼ in. long, green, crimson-edged. Ore. and Calif., e. to Wyo. and New Mex.

coccinea (L.) K. Spreng. INDIAN-PAINTBRUSH, SCARLET P. Hairy ann. or bien., to 2 ft.; basal lvs. obovate or oblong, to 3 in. long, mostly entire, st. lvs. 3–5-lobed; fl. bracts scarlet, corolla to about 1 in. long, pale yellow. New Hamp. to s. Man., s. to n. Fla., La., Okla.

collina: *C. chromosa.*

foliolosa Hook. & Arn. WOOLLY PAINTED-CUP. White-woolly, much-branched, woody-based per., to 2 ft.; lvs. linear or oblong-linear, to 1 in. long, entire; fl. bracts and calyces scarlet-tipped, corolla ¾ in. long, yellowish or greenish. Calif., and n. Baja Calif.

Haydenii (A. Gray) Cockerell. Tufted per., to 6 in., finely pubescent or glabrous below infl.; lvs. linear, to 3 in. long, entire or 3–5-lobed; fl. bracts crimson, corolla to 1 in. long, green tipped dark crimson. Mts., Colo. and n. New Mex.

hispida Benth. ex Hook. Hairy per., to 1½ ft.; lvs. lanceolate to ovate, entire in lower part of plant, 3–5-lobed toward apex; fl. bracts and calyces scarlet, rarely crimson or yellow, corolla 1 in. long, lower lip dark green. Wash. and Ore. to w. Mont.

latifolia Hook & Arn. SEASIDE PAINTED-CUP. Much-branched, rough-hairy per., to 1½ ft.; lvs. oblong, to 1 in. long, usually shorter, mostly entire; fl. bracts and calyces scarlet-tipped, sometimes yellow, corolla about ¾ in. long. Coastal cent. Calif.

miniata Dougl. ex Hook. Per., to 2½ ft. or more, glabrous or pubescent, lvs. lanceolate, to 2 in. long, entire or 3-lobed; infl. villous-pubescent, fl. bracts and calyces scarlet-red-tipped, corolla to 1¼ in. long. B.C. to s. Calif., e. to Alta., Mont., Colo. Var. **oblongifolia:** *C. oblongifolia.*

oblongifolia A. Gray [*C. miniata* var. *oblongifolia* (A. Gray) Munz]. Hairy per., to 2 ft.; lvs. oblong, to 2 in. long, entire; fl. bracts and calyces red-tipped, corolla to 1¾ in. long. S. Calif.

pallida (L.) K. Spreng. Glabrous or puberulent per., to 16 in.; lvs. linear to linear-lanceolate, to 2¾ in. long; fls. bracts yellow- or white-tipped, corolla about 1 in. long. N. Asia and Alaska.

pulchella Rydb. Villous, cespitose per., to 6 in.; lvs. linear-lanceolate, to 1½ in. long, entire or the upper lvs. 3-cleft; calyx yellowish, corolla to ¾ in. long. Mont. and Wyo.

septentrionalis Lindl. [*C. sulphurea* Rydb.]. Glabrous or slightly hairy per., to 1½ ft.; lvs. linear to lanceolate, entire; fl. bracts pale yellow or varying to white or purplish, corolla to 1 in. long. Lab., Nfld., Me., w. to Alta., B.C., Wash., s. to Utah and New Mex.

sulphurea: *C. septentrionalis.*

CASUARINA L. ex Adans. BEEFWOOD, AUSTRALIAN PINE, SHE OAK. *Casuarinaceae.* About 30 spp. of trees or shrubs, native to Australia and the Pacific Is., branchlets slender, jointed, striate, superficially resembling horsetail *(Equisetum);* lvs. whorled, reduced to minute scales or teeth; fls. unisexual, male fls. borne in spikes, female fls. in dense heads, each fl. subtended by a bract and 2 bracteoles which become woody in fr. and enclose the 1-seeded samara, the head at maturity forming a "cone."

Some of the species are important for timber where native and are grown for this purpose or for fuel elsewhere in the tropics. Much planted in Fla. and Calif. and other warm regions, both as street and as specimen trees. The species in cultivation are difficult to identify because under cultivation trees continue to produce only shoots of juvenile form from even quite old trees, and because hybrids occasionally occur in Fla. among *C. equisetifolia, C. glauca,* and *C. Cunninghamiana,* and in Calif. between *C. glauca* and *C. Cunninghamiana.* Some confusion is also due to the mistaken belief that *C. cristata* has been introduced into Fla. and that *C. equisetifolia* is commonly grown in Calif. *Casuarina cristata, C. Deplancheana, C. distyla, C. Fraserana, C. Huegeliana, C. paludosa* are probably not cultivated in the U.S.; plants bearing these names are probably not correctly identified.

burmensis: a listed name of no botanical standing.

campestris Diels & E. Pritz. Shrub, to 6 ft.; lf. scales on branchlets of adult growth usually 8 in a whorl; cones subsessile, narrowly-oblong, 1–1½ in. long, ½–¾ in. wide. W. Australia.

corniculata F. J. Muell. [*C. horrida* D. A. Herb.]. Shrub, to about 10 ft., branchlets many, erect, rigid; lf. scales on branchlets of adult growth mostly 10–12 in a whorl; cones globular, depressed, ½ in. in diam. W. Australia. May not be in cult.

cristata Miq. [*C. lepidophloia* F. J. Muell.]. To 45 ft., branchlets ascending, hoary, striate; lf. scales on branchlets of adult growth 9–10 in a whorl; cones subglobular to oblong, to 1¼ in. long. W. and s. Australia. May not be in cult.

Cunninghamiana Miq. To 70 ft., branchlets about ⅟₃₂ in. in diam.; lfs. scales on branchlets of adult growth usually 8 in a whorl, occasionally 7 or 9, terminal portion of scales withering to a whitish color beyond a marked transverse brownish band; cone subglobose, to ½ in. long, ⅜ in. in diam., grayish, samara ⅛–³⁄₁₆ in. long. E. Australia. Cult. in both Calif. and Fla. Valuable timber tree.

Deplancheana Miq. Tree, to 35 ft.; lf. scales on branchlets of adult growth 4 in a whorl; cones broader than long, bracts enclosing samaras strongly beaked and prominent. New Caledonia. Probably not in cult. Valuable timber tree.

distyla Venten. [*C. Fraserana* Miq.]. Diffusely branched shrub; lf. scales on branchlets of adult growth usually 7 in a whorl, rarely 6 or 8, very short; cones usually whorled, narrow-cylindrical or globular, to 1¼ in. long. Australia, probably limited to Tasmania and Victoria. May not be in cult.

equisetifolia J. R. Forst. & G. Forst. HORSETAIL TREE, SOUTH SEA IRONWOOD, MILE TREE. To 70 ft., branchlets about ⅟₃₂ in. in diam.; lf. scales on branchlets of adult growth 6 or 7 in a whorl, not withering as in *C. Cunninghamiana;* cones broadly oblong, to ¾ in. long, ½ in. in diam., grayish, samara ¼ in. long. A seashore pioneer tree widespread from se. Asia to Pacific Is. to n. and ne. Australia. Cult. widely in tropics; Zone 10b in Fla., where sometimes naturalized. Good for hedges, windbreaks, and seaside plantings.

Fraserana: *C. distyla.*

glauca Sieber ex K. Spreng. To 50 ft.; branchlets ⅟₃₂–⅟₁₆ in. in diam.; lf. scales on branchlets of adult growth 14–16 in a whorl; cone subglobose, ⅜–½ in. long, grayish, samara ³⁄₁₆ in. long. E. and s. Australia.

horrida: *C. corniculata.*

Huegeliana Miq. Related to *C. stricta* and *C. glauca,* from which it differs in having more compact cones and small, thick, scarcely projecting bracts enclosing the samaras. W. Australia. Probably not in cult.

lepidophloia: *C. cristata.*

littoralis Salisb. [*C. suberosa* Otto & A. Dietr.]. To 50 ft., branchlets ⅟₃₂ in. in diam.; lf. scales on branchlets of adult growth 6–7 in a whorl; cones globose, to ¾ in. in diam., dark glossy brown to blackish, samara to ⁵⁄₁₆ in. long. E. Australia and Tasmania.

obesa Miq. Tree, branchlets ⅟₃₂–⅟₁₆ in. in diam.; lf. scales on branchlets of adult growth 11–13 in a whorl; cones subglobose, ½–¾ in. long, grayish, samara ³⁄₁₆ in. long. E. Australia.

paludosa Sieber ex K. Spreng. Low, erect shrub; lf. scales on branchlets of adult growth 6 in a whorl, rarely 7; cones oblong, less than ¾

in. long. E. Australia. Related to *C. distyla,* but differing in its smaller stature and smaller cones. May not be in cult.

quadrivalvis: *C. stricta.*

sinensis: a listed name of no botanical standing.

stricta Ait. [*C. quadrivalvis* Labill.]. Tree, to 30 ft., branchlets ⅟₃₂–⅟₁₆ in. in diam., pubescent; lf. scales on branchlets of adult growth 10–12 in a whorl, rarely 9; cones subglobose, 1–1½ in. long, dark glossy brown to blackish, samara ⅝ in. long. S. Australia. Valuable timber tree.

suberosa: *C. littoralis.*

torulosa Ait. Tree, branchlets very fine, slightly less than ⅟₃₂ in. in diam., bronze-green; lf. scales on branchlets of adult growth 4 in a whorl; cones oblong, to 1 in. long, dark glossy brown to blackish, samara ⅜ in. long. E. Australia. Valuable timber tree.

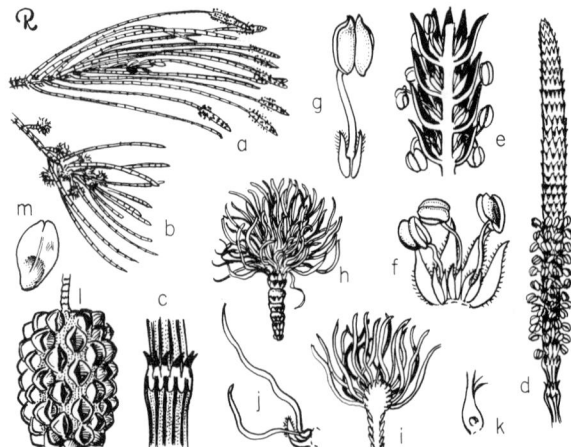

CASUARINACEAE. *Casuarina equisetifolia:* **a,** branch with male inflorescences, × ¼; **b,** branch with female inflorescences, × ¼; **c,** node of twig, with toothed leaf sheath, × 6; **d,** male inflorescence, × 1; **e,** part of male inflorescence, vertical section, × 4; **f,** three male flowers, × 5; **g,** single male flower, × 7; **h,** female inflorescence, × 1; **i,** same, vertical section, × 1; **j,** single female flower, × 5; **k,** ovary, vertical section, enlarged; **l,** fruiting "cone," × 1; **m,** samara, × 1½.

CASUARINACEAE R. Br. CASUARINA FAMILY. Dicot.; 1 genus of monoecious trees or shrubs, native to Australia and the Pacific Is., branchlets slender, jointed, striate; lvs. whorled, reduced to minute scales; fls. unisexual; fr. heads dry, conelike. *Casuarina* is planted as an ornamental in frost-free regions.

CATALPA Scop. CATAWBA, INDIAN BEAN. *Bignoniaceae.* About 13 spp. of deciduous or rarely evergreen trees, native to N. Amer. and e. Asia; lvs. opp. or sometimes whorled, simple, long-petioled; fls. white, pinkish, or yellowish, in terminal racemes or panicles, calyx 2-lipped or splitting irregularly, corolla campanulate, 2-lipped, stamens 2; fr. a long narrow caps. separating into 2 valves, seeds with a tuft of hairs at each end.

Catalpas are popular lawn and avenue trees and very showy when in bloom in late spring and early summer; sometimes planted for small timber. Mostly hardy north, they do well in any good soil. Propagated by seeds in spring and cuttings of mature wood; also by layers, root cuttings, cuttings of young wood in early summer; and named varieties by grafting on seedlings or by cuttings of young trees.

bignonioides Walt. [*C. Catalpa* (L.) Karst.]. COMMON C., INDIAN BEAN. Rounded tree, to 60 ft.; lvs. ovate, to 8 in. long, abruptly short-acuminate, pubescent beneath, ill-smelling when bruised; fls. in panicles to 10 in. long, corolla white, with 2 yellow stripes and brown spots, 2 in. across. Ga., s. to Fla. and Miss.; naturalized further north. Zone 5. Cv. 'Aurea'. Lvs. yellow. Cv. 'Nana' [*C. Bungei* Hort., not C. A. Mey.]. Dwarf, usually grafted on upright boles, forming standards with dense umbrellalike heads.

Bungei C. A. Mey. Small pyramidal tree, to 30 ft.; lvs. triangular-ovate, to 6 in. long, long-acuminate, sometimes toothed or angled near the base, glabrous; fls. in a 3–12-fld. raceme, corolla white, spotted purple, to 1½ in. long. N. China. Zone 6. This name is often mistakenly applied to *C. bignonioides* cv. 'Nana'.

Catalpa: *C. bignonioides.*

Duclouxii: *C. Fargesii* forma.

Fargesii Bur. To 60 ft., young sts. stellate-pubescent; lvs. ovate, to 6 in. long, long-acuminate, 3-lobed on young plants, pubescent beneath with branched hairs; fls. with corolla pink or purple, spotted brown, 1½ in. long. W. China. Zone 6. Forma **Duclouxii** (Dode) Gilm. [*C. Duclouxii* Dode]. Glabrous, corolla rose, marked with orange.

×**hybrida** Hort. ex F. L. Späth [*C. Teasii* Penh.]: *C. bignonioides* × *C. ovata.* HYBRID C. Intermediate in character between parents; lvs. larger than in *C. ovata,* sometimes angled or shallowly lobed, mostly purplish when young; fls. resembling *C. bignonioides,* but smaller. Much planted.

Kaempferi: *C. ovata.*

longissima (Jacq.) Dum.-Cours. To 50 ft.; lvs. elliptic-lanceolate to elliptic, 4–5 in. long, less than half as broad; fls. to 1 in. long, corolla white, with fine pink or purple lines; caps. very slender, to 18 in. or more. W. Indies. Planted in s. Fla.

ovata G. Don [*C. Kaempferi* Siebold & Zucc.]. CHINESE C. Spreading tree, to 30 ft. or more; lvs. broad-ovate, sometimes 3–5-lobed, to 10 in. long, abruptly acuminate, pubescent on veins beneath; fls. in panicles to 10 in. long, corolla yellowish-white, marked with orange and violet, to ¾ in. long. China; escaped and naturalized from Conn. to s. Ont., s. to Md. and Ohio. Zone 5.

speciosa Warder ex Engelm. WESTERN C., CATAWBA, CIGAR TREE, INDIAN BEAN. Pyramidal tree, to 100 ft.; lvs. ovate to ovate-oblong, to 1 ft. long, long-acuminate, densely pubescent beneath, odorless; fls. in panicles 6 in. long, corolla white, spotted with brown, 2½ in. across. S. Ind. and se. Iowa, s. to Ark. and Tex. Zone 5. Wood used for posts, telephone poles, railroad ties, furniture and interior finishing.

Teasii: *C.* × *hybrida.*

CATANANCHE L. CUPID'S-DART. *Compositae* (Cichorium Tribe). Five spp. of bien. or per. herbs with milky sap, native to Medit. region; lvs. alt., crowded near base of st., linear, lanceolate, or oblanceolate; fl. heads solitary on long peduncles, involucral bracts in several rows, scarious toward apex, receptacle bristly; fls. all ligulate, bisexual, blue, white, or yellow; achenes oblong, usually villous or bristly, pappus of bristles or lanceolate, long-acuminate scales.

One species is cultivated in the herbaceous border, and as an everlasting. It grows well in average garden soil and under the usual treatment for perennials. Propagated by seeds sown in spring and blooming the same year; also by division.

bicolor: a listed name of no botanical standing for *C. caerulea* cv.

caerulea L. Per., to 2 ft.; lvs. lanceolate to oblanceolate, to 1 ft. long, entire to few-toothed, tomentose; heads to 2 in. across; fls. blue, the ligule toothed. Summer. S. Eur. Cvs. are: '**Alba**', fls. white; '**Bicolor**', fls. blue edged with white; '**Major**', sts. to 20 in., fls. deep violet-blue.

CATASETUM L. Rich. ex Kunth. *Orchidaceae.* About 70 spp. of terrestrial or epiphytic orchids, native to trop. Amer.; pseudobulbs with 2 or more lvs.; lvs. plicate; fls. in racemes, bisexual or, in most spp., unisexual and dimorphic, the male and female then on separate infls., pollen masses ejected suddenly and forcibly when appendages of column are touched. In the spp. that have unisexual fls., the descriptions below are for male fls., since the female fls. are seldom produced, and are not always distinctive. For structure of fl. see *Orchidaceae.*

Cultivated in the warm greenhouse, commonly suspended and given a resting period; for culture see *Orchids.*

album: a listed name of no botanical standing.

barbatum (Lindl.) Lindl. Pseudobulbs 2–6 in. long; lvs. to 1 ft. long; racemes semierect to pendent, loosely 15–20-fld., to 18 in. long; fls. unisexual, male fls. with sepals and petals narrow-oblong, about 1¼ in. long, green, spotted with dark purple, petals and upper sepal erect, connivent, lateral sepals spreading, lip oblong, green, spotted with red, saccate in middle, margins fringed. Spring–summer. Guyana, Brazil, e. Peru.

bicolor Klotzsch. Lvs. deciduous; racemes pendent, few-fld.; fls. unisexual, male fls. with sepals and petals to 1½ in. long, brownish-green to dark reddish-brown, petals and upper sepal erect, connivent, lateral sepals spreading, lip short, fleshy, saccate, white or pale yellow, with palmately lacerate margin. Late summer. Panama, Colombia.

Bungerothii: *C. pileatum.*

cernuum (Lindl.) Rchb.f. Racemes pendent, loosely 10–15-fld., to 1 ft. long; fls. unisexual, male fls. with sepals and petals oblong, about 1¼ in. long, green, spotted with dark brown, lip broadly wedge-shaped, 3-lobed toward the front, lateral lobes horizontal, entire, midlobe much shorter. Spring–summer. Brazil. Var. **Rodigasianum** (Rolfe) Mansf. [*C. Rodigasianum* Rolfe; *C. tenebrosum* Rolfe]. Lip shorter, lateral lobes erect or somewhat involute, fringed, midlobe scarcely developed. Brazil.

Christyanum: *C. saccatum* var.

decipiens Rchb.f. Pseudobulbs to 5 in. long; lvs. narrow, to 10 in. long; racemes pendent, loosely fld.; fls. unisexual, male fls. with sepals and petals spreading, to 1½ in. long, maroon, lip saccate, subglobose, with revolute margins, yellow-orange. Venezuela.

dilectum Rchb.f. Pseudobulbs to 3 in. long; lvs. to 12 in. long; racemes arching, as long as or longer than lvs., many-fld.; fls. bisexual, small, sepals and petals reflexing, to ¾ in. long, erect, lip fleshy, entire, to 1 in. long, saccate at base, sac yellow inside, spotted with brown. Panama, Colombia, Ecuador.

fimbriatum (C. Morr.) Lindl. & Paxt. Large; racemes pendent, loosely many-fld., to 18 in. long; fls. unisexual, male fls. large, green with brown blotches, to 2 in. across, sepals and petals spreading, pointed, lip saccate at base, recurved in front, with deeply lacerate-fimbriate margins. Early autumn. Brazil, Uruguay, Paraguay, Bol. Cv. '**Aureum**'. Differs from typical var. in having sepals and petals yellowish with small purplish dots, lip with bright orange callus. Brazil.

gnomus André. Robust, pseudobulbs to 6 in. long; lvs. several, narrow; racemes pendent, loosely many-fld., to 2 ft. long; fls. unisexual, male fls. fleshy, to 2½ in. across, sepals spreading, rust-brown with small darker spots, petals parallel with column, green, barred with dark maroon, lip saccate, with lobed, revolute margins, green, spotted maroon inside. Late autumn. Brazil.

integerrimum Hook. [*C. Oerstedii* Rchb.f.]. Racemes 6–12-fld., to 16 in. long; fls. unisexual, male fls. with sepals and petals bright green, often spotted with purple, lip green outside and sometimes purple-spotted, suffused with purple inside. Winter. Mex., Cent. Amer.

longifolium Lindl. Pseudobulbs to 8 in. long; lvs. to 3 ft. long; racemes pendent, loosely fld.; fls. unisexual, male fls. with sepals and petals broadly ovate, to ¾ in. long, greenish inside, purple outside, petals ciliate, lip saccate, fleshy, nearly globose, orange with small yellow dots, dark maroon and ciliate at apex. Guyana.

macrocarpum L. Rich. ex Kunth [*C. tridentatum* Hook.]. JUMPING ORCHID. Pseudobulbs oblong, to 8 in. long; lvs. elliptic-lanceolate, keeled, to 16 in. long; racemes erect or arching, few-fld., 16 in. long; fls. unisexual, male fls. with sepals and petals yellowish-green, spotted with red or purple, lip bright yellow with greenish to bright green apex, usually purple-spotted inside. Trinidad, S. Amer. Fl. color somewhat variable.

microglossum Rolfe. Lvs. to 1 ft. long; racemes pendent, to 2 ft. long; fls. unisexual, male fls. with petals and upper sepal erect, lateral sepals spreading, all about 1 in. long, purplish, lip small, saccate, yellow, densely covered with toothlike calluses. Summer. Peru.

Mooreanum: a listed name of no botanical standing, for a plant with racemes with up to 20 fls., fls. yellow-green to yellow.

Oerstedii: *C. integerrimum.*

pileatum Rchb.f. [*C. Bungerothii* N. E. Br.]. Pseudobulbs slender, 4–8 in. long; racemes several- to many-fld., to 1 ft. long; fls. unisexual, male fls. white or yellow-greenish-white or light rose, sometimes purple-spotted, sepals about 2 in. long, lip transversely oblong or semiorbicular, short-saccate. Early summer. Trinidad, Venezuela, Brazil. Cv. '**Aurantiacum**'. Sepals and petals white, lip yellow. Cv. '**Aureum**'. Fls. entirely yellow.

Rodigasianum: *C. cernuum* var.

Russellianum Hook. Pseudobulbs conical, 2–3 in. long; racemes pendent, many-fld., nearly 1½ ft. long; fls. bisexual, sepals and petals oblong, about 1½ in. long, pale green, lip saccate, with a double fringe of teeth. Late summer. Mex., Cent. Amer.

saccatum Lindl. Pseudobulbs 3–6 in. long; racemes erect, 6–10-fld.; fls. unisexual, male fls. large, 4 in. across or more, green, spotted with purplish-brown, petals and upper sepal erect, connivent, lateral sepals spreading, lip deeply saccate at base, 3-lobed in front, lateral lobes rounded, green, midlobe ovate or oblong-ovate, purplish-brown, all lobes reflexed and fimbriate. Summer. Guyana, Brazil, e. Peru. Var. **Christyanum** (Rchb.f.) Mansf. [*C. Christyanum* Rchb.f.]. Fls. smaller, sepals and petals red-brown, lip smaller, midlobe obovate, abruptly acuminate, green, marked with purple. Brazil, e. Peru. Var. **incurvum** (Klotzsch) Mansf. Lip larger, ovate or suborbicular-ovate. E. Peru.

scurra: *C. Warczewitzii.*

×**Sumanii** Hort.: *C. pileatum* × *C. saccatum.* Fls. cream to yellow, margin of lip serrate.

tenebrosum: *C. cernuum* var. *Rodigasianum.*

thylaciochilum Lem. Pseudobulbs to 4 in. long; lvs. to 16 in. long; racemes pendent, densely many-fld., to 8 in. long; fls. bisexual, fleshy, greenish-white, with darker green veins, sepals and petals spreading, to 1 in. long, lip concave, saccate at base. Spring. Mex.

tridentatum: *C. macrocarpum.*

viridiflavum Hook. Pseudobulbs oblong, to 5 in. long; lvs. to about 1 ft. long; racemes shorter than lvs., up to 12-fld.; fls. unisexual, male fls. with petals wider than sepals, both uniformly yellow-green, lip yellow or yellow-green outside, deep yellow inside, ciliate. Panama.

Warczewitzii Lindl. & Paxt. [*C. scurra* Rchb.f.]. Small, pseudobulbs to 2 in. long; lvs. deciduous, absent at flowering time; racemes pendent, few-fld.; fls. bisexual, pale straw-color or white with green veins, fragrant, to ¾ in. across, lip with lateral lobes and apex of protuberant midlobe fringed. Cent. Amer., Colombia, Venezuela, Guyana.

CATESBAEA L. *Rubiaceae.* About 16 spp. of spiny shrubs or small trees, native to W. Indies; lvs. opp. or whorled, stipules small, interpetiolar, deciduous; fls. solitary, white, corolla funnelform or campanulate, 4-lobed; fr. a white berry.

spinosa L. LILY THORN. To 15 ft., with spines 1 in. long or more; lvs. ovate, to 1 in. long; fls. creamy, to 6 in. long, much longer than lvs.; fr. to 2 in. long. Cuba. Sometimes cult. in s. Fla. and other warm regions.

CATHA Forssk. *Celastraceae.* One sp., an evergreen shrub or tree, native to mts. of trop. E. Afr.; lvs. opp., rarely alt. on sterile shoots; fls. small, bisexual, in axillary cymes, sepals, petals, and stamens 5; fr. a leathery, 3-valved caps.

edulis (Vahl) Forssk. ex Endl. CHAT, KHAT, KAT, CAFTA, QAT, ARABIAN TEA, ABYSSIAN T., SOMALI T. To 20 ft., (occasionally to 50 ft.); lvs. opp., to 4 in. long, toothed; fls. white; fr. 3-angled, about ¼ in. long. Probably Ethiopia. Cult. in Ethiopia and in Somalia, Yemen, and Zambia for the lvs. and tender shoots, which are chewed fresh by Moslems as a favorite daily stimulant. Formerly used as a tea. Zone 10. Planted in s. Fla. and Calif., also sometimes under glass for its economic interest.

CATHARANTHUS G. Don [*Ammocallis* Small; *Lochnera* Rchb., not *Lochneria* Scop.]. PERIWINKLE. *Apocynaceae.* About 5 spp. of erect ann. and per. herbs, native to Old World tropics; lvs. opp., entire, deciduous; fls. solitary, or 2-3 in axillary cymes, 5-merous, bisexual, corolla salverform, throat closed by bristlelike hairs, stamens borne just below throat of tube, anthers elongate, without appendages, style uniformly slender; fr. a pair of narrow-cylindrical follicles, seeds 15-30 or more. Sometimes included in *Vinca,* but quite distinct.

Propagated by seeds.

roseus (L.) G. Don [*Ammocallis rosea* (L.) Small; *Lochnera rosea* (L.) Rchb.; *Vinca rosea,* L.]. ROSE P., MADAGASCAR P., OLD-MAID. Per., to 2 ft., often cult. as an ann.; lvs. oblong-lanceolate, 1-2 in. long, glossy; fls. typically rose-pink, varying to mauve and white, to 1½ in. across, tube about 1 in. long; fr. to 1½ in. long. Madagascar to India; naturalized pantropically. Has medicinal properties, and is poisonous when eaten by cattle. Cv. 'Albus' [*C. roseus* var. *albus* Sweet]. Fls. white. Cv. 'Ocellatus'. Fls. white with rose-pink to carmine-red eye.

CATHARTOLINUM: *LINUM.*

CATIMBIUM: *ALPINIA.*

CATOPSIS Griseb. *Bromeliaceae.* About 18 spp. of epiphytic herbs, native to trop. Amer.; lvs. in a basal rosette, entire; infl. scapose, terminal, simple to compound; fls. small, in several rows, yellow to yellow-green, bisexual or functionally unisexual, sepals asymmetrical, petals separate, without appendages, ovary superior; fr. a caps., seeds with plumose, apical, folded tail.

Infrequently cultivated, requiring growing conditions used for *Tillandsia.* Require filtered light. For culture see *Bromeliaceae.*

floribunda L. B. Sm. To 2½ ft.; lvs. many, stiff and suberect, to 16 in. long, 1¼ in. wide, green or brownish toward the base, obscurely and minutely scaly; scape erect, terminating in a loosely branched infl. of long-stalked, loosely fld. spikes to 6 in. long; fls. white, sepals ⅛-¼ in. long. S. Fla., W. Indies, Cent. Amer. to Venezuela.

nutans (Swartz) Griseb. [*C. nutans* var. *stenopetala* (Bak.) L. B. Sm.]. To 16 in.; lvs. erect or spreading, to 1 in. wide, green or whitish beneath; scape usually pendulous; fls. yellow, to 5/16 in. long, sepals ⅝ in. long. W. Indies, Cent. Amer., n. S. Amer.

subulata L. B. Sm. To 2 ft.; lvs. to 1 ft. long and ½ in. wide; scape erect, very short, infl. densely fld.; fls. white, functionally unisexual, sepals to 3/16 in. long. Mex. to Honduras.

CATTLEYA Lindl. *Orchidaceae.* About 60 spp. of epiphytic orchids, native to trop. Amer.; pseudobulbs 1-3-lvd.; lvs. very thick, stiff; infl. emerging from a terminal spathe; fls. in racemes, rarely solitary, often large, sepals similar, petals broader, lip 3-lobed, lateral lobes forming tube around column, midlobe spreading. For structure of fl. see *Orchidaceae.*

Cultivated in the intermediate greenhouse; for culture see *Orchids.*

Aclandiae Lindl. Pseudobulbs to 6 in. long, 2-lvd.; lvs. broadly elliptic, to nearly 3 in. long; fls. 1 or 2, to 4 in. across, sepals and petals yellowish-green, spotted with purple-brown, lip with short, whitish-rose lateral lobes and wavy, magenta midlobe. Late spring, autumn. Brazil. Cv. 'Nigrescens'. Sepals and petals almost uniformly dark brown.

×**amabilis** Hort.: *C. labiata* × *C. Warscewiczii.* Fls. large, rosy-purple, lip with 2 yellow spots in throat.

amethystoglossa Linden & Rchb.f. [*C. guttata* var. *Prinzii* Rchb.f.]. Pseudobulbs 2-lvd.; lvs. elliptic-oblong, to over 8 in. long; racemes 5-8-fld.; fls. about 4 in. across, sepals and petals white, suffused with rose and spotted with deep rose, lip with whitish lateral lobes and bluish-violet midlobe. Late autumn-summer. Brazil. Cv. 'Sanderae'. An albino form.

×**armainvillierensis** Hort.: *C. Mendelii* × *C. Warscewiczii.* Fls. large, sepals and petals white, tinged with pale lilac, midlobe of lip and margins of lateral lobes purple.

×**Armstrongiae** Hort.: *C.* ×*Hardyana* × *C. Harrisoniana.* Sepals and petals rose, lip with orange disc and apical rose-purple blotch.

aurantiaca (Batem.) P. Don [*Epidendrum aurantiacum* Batem.]. To 1 ft., pseudobulbs cylindrical, 2-lvd.; racemes shorter than lvs., few-fld.; fls. campanulate, to 1 in. long, deep orange. Early winter-late spring. Mex., Cent. Amer.

aurea: *C. Dowiana* var.

×**Ballantiniana** Rchb.f.: *C. Trianaei* × *C. Warscewiczii.* Fls. large, sepals and petals pale rose, lip rose, deeper colored on margins toward base, white inside, yellow in throat.

×**Bertii** Hort.: *C. Harrisoniana* × *C. labiata.* Fls. large, sepals and petals rose-lilac, lip entire, pale yellow, with deep yellow disc, rose-purple apically.

bicolor Lindl. Pseudobulbs slender, 15-30 in. long, 2-lvd.; lvs. oblong-lanceolate, to about 6 in. long; racemes 2-8-fld.; fls. 3-4½ in. across, sepals and petals bronze-green, lip rose-purple, sometimes edged with white, toothed, without lateral lobes. Winter-spring, autumn. Brazil.

Bowringiana Hort. Veitch. Pseudobulbs 12-14 in. long, 2-lvd.; lvs. oblong or elliptic-oblong, to 8 in. long; racemes 5-13-fld.; fls. about 3 in. across, sepals and petals rose-violet, lip deeper rose-violet, with brownish spot in throat. Autumn–early winter. Cent. Amer. Cv. 'Grandiflora'. Fls. larger than in typical var. Cv. 'Splendens'. Fls. larger than in typical var., more richly colored. Cv. 'Triumphans'. Fls. rich purple.

×**Chapmanii** Hort.: *C. Bowringiana* × *C. Warneri.* Fls. small, rose-lavender, lip maroon.

chocoensis André. Pseudobulbs and lvs. as in *C. labiata;* fls. medium-sized, campanulate, not expanded, cream or greenish-white, with ruffled margins, lip yellow in throat, stained in front with rich magenta-purple. Colombia.

citrina Lindl. TULIP C. Downward growing, pendent, pseudobulbs small, globular, sheathed in silvery-white membrane, 2-lvd.; lvs. strap-shaped, to 9½ in. long; fls. usually solitary, campanulate, citron-yellow, fragrant, lip white-margined, undulate. Spring–early summer. Mex. Cv. 'Gigantea'. Plants and fls. larger.

×**Deckeri** Klotzsch [*C.* ×*guatemalensis* T. Moore; ×*Epicattleya guatemalensis* (T. Moore) Rolfe]: *C. aurantiaca* × *C. Skinneri.* A natural hybrid; pseudobulbs club-shaped, to 6 in. long, 2-lvd.; racemes short, few- to many-fld.; sepals and petals spreading, to 2 in. long, yellow to rose, lip red-magenta to carmine-pink, with yellow throat. Autumn–late winter. Cent. Amer.

×**dolosa** Rchb.f. [*C. Walkerana* var. *dolosa* Hort. Veitch]: *C. Loddigesii* × *C. Walkerana.* A natural hybrid; pseudobulbs 4-6 in. long, usually 2-lvd.; peduncle 1- or 2-fld.; sepals and petals rose-purple to lilac, lip amethyst-purple. Late spring. Brazil.

Dormaniana Rchb.f. Pseudobulbs cylindrical, to 8 in. long, 2–3-lvd.; racemes about as long as lvs., few-fld.; fls. pendent, to 2 in. long, olive-green with purple spots, lip intense rose to purple. Winter. Brazil.

Dowiana Batem. [*C. labiata* var. *Dowiana* (Batem.) Hort. Veitch]. QUEEN C. Pseudobulbs to 1 ft. long, 1-lvd.; lvs. to 1 ft. long; racemes 2–6-fld.; fls. to nearly 7 in. across, sepals and petals nankeen-yellow, lip dark purple with radiating gold veins. Spring, summer. Cent. Amer. Cv. 'Johnsoniana'. Sepals and petals very deep, rich yellow, lip with bright orange veins. Cv. 'Rosita'. Sepals creamy-white, tinged with purple, petals rose-purple, suffused with yellow. Var. **aurea** (Linden) B. S. Williams & T. Moore [*C. aurea* Linden]. Differs from typical *C. Dowiana* in having sepals and petals deeper yellow, lip velvety purple-crimson, with more pronounced and intricate gold venation. Colombia.

×**Dupreana** Hort.: *C. Warneri* × *C. Warscewiczii*. Fls. large, to 5 in. across, magenta.

Eldorado Linden [*C. labiata* var. *Eldorado* (Linden) Hort. Veitch]. Pseudobulbs to 8 in. long, stout, 1-lvd.; lvs. oblong or elliptic-oblong, to 12 in. long; fls. fragrant, to about 6 in. across, pale rosy-lilac shading to white, lip crisped, with orange blotch at center and purple margins. Summer–early autumn. Brazil. Cv. 'Crocata'. Fls. white or pale rose, lip with deep orange disc. Cv. 'Wallisii' [var. *Wallisii* (Linden) E. S. Rand; *C. Wallisii* Linden]. Fls. white, lip with orange-yellow spot.

elongata Barb.-Rodr. Pseudobulbs elongate, to 2 ft. long, 2-lvd.; lvs. elliptic, to 6 in. long; racemes 2–8-fld.; fls. 3–4 in. across, sepals and petals red-brown or orange, undulate, lip magenta with darker lines. Early spring, autumn. Brazil.

Forbesii Lindl. Pseudobulbs stemlike, to 1 ft. long, 2-lvd.; lvs. elliptic-oblong, to 5 in. long; racemes 2–5-fld., or fls. solitary; fls. 3–4 in. across, sepals and petals olive- or yellow-green, lip white or pale yellow outside, yellow inside, often marked with red. Late spring–autumn. Brazil.

Gaskelliana Rchb.f. ex B. S. Williams [*C. labiata* var. *Gaskelliana* (Rchb.f. ex B. S. Williams) Hort. Veitch]. SUMMER C. Pseudobulbs to 1 ft. long, 1-lvd.; lvs. oblong, to almost 1 ft. long; racemes 2–3-fld.; fls. to 7 in. across, sepals and petals purple-violet, suffused with white, lip purple-violet with a saddle-shaped yellow blotch, crisped on margin. Late spring–early autumn. Venezuela, Brazil. Cv. 'Alba'. Fls. white, lip with yellow patch in throat. Cv. 'Caerulea'. Fls. pure white, lip bluish in throat. Cv. 'Delicata'. Fls. pale purple-violet. Cv. 'Hodgkinsonii'. Sepals and petals white, lip with crimson disc.

gigas: *C. Warscewiczii*.

granulosa Lindl. Pseudobulbs stemlike, to 2 ft. long, 2-lvd.; lvs. elliptic-oblong, to 6 in. long; racemes 5–8-fld.; fls. to 4 in. across, sepals and petals olive-green, more or less spotted with red-brown, lip white, dotted with purple, midlobe undulate, the claw yellowish, marked with red. Late summer. Brazil. Cv. 'Buyssoniana' [var. *Buyssoniana* O'Brien]. Sepals and petals without spots. Var. **Russelliana** Lindl. Fls. larger, sepals and petals broader, lateral lobes of lip orange-yellow, midlobe spotted with crimson-purple papillae. Var. **Schofieldiana** (Rchb.f.) Hort. Veitch. Fls. large, spreading, sepals and petals yellow, spotted with crimson-purple, midlobe of lip covered with magenta-purple papillae.

×**guatemalensis**: *C.* × *Deckeri*.

guttata Lindl. Pseudobulbs cylindrical, 2-lvd.; lvs. oblong-elliptic, to 9 in. long; racemes 4–6-fld.; fls. fleshy, to 4 in. across, sepals and petals green, spotted with red-purple, lateral lobes of lip rose or white, midlobe violet-purple. Spring–autumn. Brazil. Var. **Leopoldii**: *C. Leopoldii*. Var. **Prinzii**: *C. amethystoglossa*.

×**Hardyana** Sander: *C. Dowiana* var. *aurea* × *C. Warscewiczii*. A natural hybrid; similar to *C. Warscewiczii* in habit; fls. fragrant, to 8 in. across, sepals and petals deep rosy-purple, lip magenta-crimson, with 2 yellow eyes in throat. Late summer. Colombia. Cv. 'Alba'. Sepals and petals white.

Harrisoniana Batem. Pseudobulbs to 20 in. long, 2-lvd.; lvs. oblong-lanceolate, to 6 in. long; racemes 2–5-fld.; fls. to 4 in. across, rose-lilac, midlobe of lip whitish-rose, with yellow spot. Winter, summer–autumn. Brazil. Cv. 'Alba'. Sepals and petals white, lip white with lemon-yellow spot in throat. Cv. 'Candida'. Sepals and petals white, lip white with yellow disc. Cv. 'Gigantea'. Fls. larger. Cv. 'Maculata'. Sepals and petals with purple dotlike spots. Cv. 'Superbissima'. Fls. large, sepals and petals dark rose, lip creamy-white. Cv. 'Violacea'. Sepals and petals dark violet, lip with orange spot.

×**highburiensis** Hort.: *C. Harrisoniana* × *C. Mossiae*. Fls. large, to 5 in. across, sepals and petals pale lavender, lip with magenta disc.

intermedia R. C. Grah. Pseudobulbs cylindrical, 2-lvd.; lvs. oblong, to 6 in. long; racemes usually 3–5-fld.; fls. to 5 in. across, pale rose,

midlobe of lip purple, crisped. Spring–early summer, autumn. Brazil. Cv. 'Alba'. Fls. pure white. Cv. 'Parthenia'. Robust, pseudobulbs twice as long as in typical var.; fls. large, glistening snow-white. Cv. 'Punctatissima'. Sepals and petals spotted and dotted with deep rose.

Jenmanii Rolfe. Pseudobulbs to 7 in. long, 1-lvd.; racemes short, 2–3-fld.; fls. to 3 in. long, sepals and petals rosy-mauve, lip to 2½ in. long, midlobe crimson at apex, disc yellow, with radiating red-brown veins. Guyana.

×**Kienastiana** Hort.: *C. Dowiana* × *C. Luddemanniana*. Sepals and petals rose, lip pink with yellow throat, veined with purple-red and with purple-rose blotch in center.

labiata Lindl. AUTUMN C. Pseudobulbs 1-lvd.; lvs. oblong, to 10 in. long; racemes 2–5-fld.; fls. to 6 in. across, rose-lilac, lip violet-purple bordered with rose-lilac, with yellow in throat. Autumn–early spring. Brazil. Cv. 'Alba'. Fls. large, to 6 in. across, white, lip with yellow throat. Cv. 'Amesiana'. Sepals and petals white, lip lilac. Cv. 'Autumnalis'. Fls. large, to 6 in. across, deep rose, lip with a deeper spot on disc and yellow throat. Cv. 'Beyrodtiana'. Fls. white, lip pale yellow in throat, with splash of purple at apex. Cv. 'Cooksoniae'. Fls. white, with crimson lip and white margins. Cv. 'Rosea'. Fls. very pale rose. Cv. 'Superba'. Fls. large, sepals and petals deep rose, lip deep crimson-purple. Var. **chocoensis**: *C. chocoensis*. Var. **Eldorado**: *C. Eldorado*. Var. **Luddemanniana**: *C. Luddemanniana*. Var. **Mendelii**: *C. Mendelii*. Var. **Mossiae**: *C. Mossiae*. Var. **Percivaliana**: *C. Percivaliana*. Var. **Trianaei**: *C. Trianaei*. Var. **Warneri**: *C. Warneri*. Var. **Warscewiczii**: *C. Warscewiczii*.

Lawrenceana Rchb.f. Pseudobulbs to 15 in. long, 1-lvd.; lvs. oblong or elliptic-oblong, to 9 in. long; racemes 5–7-fld.; fls. to 5 in. across, rose-purple, lip with purple disc and maroon band, throat white. Winter–spring. Venezuela, Guyana.

Leopoldii Hort. Versch. [*C. guttata* var. *Leopoldii* (Hort. Versch.) Linden & Rchb.f.]. Pseudobulbs 2–3-lvd.; lvs. oblong-elliptic, to 8 in. long; racemes densely 10–25-fld.; fls. to 4 in. across, sepals and petals brown to green, dotted with purple-red, lip white in throat, purple apically, undulate. Autumn. Brazil.

lobata: *Laelia lobata*.

Loddigesii Lindl. Pseudobulbs cylindrical, to 1 ft. long, 2-lvd.; lvs. elliptic-oblong, to 5 in. long; fls. to 4 in. across or more, rose-lilac, lip white inside, yellow at base, crisped on margins. Late summer. Brazil. Cv. 'Alba'. Fls. white, lip with light yellow throat. Cv. 'Delicata'. Fls. white, suffused with pale pink. Cv. 'Innocens'. Fls. milk-white. Cv. 'Splendens'. Sepals and petals bright purplish-rose, lip white inside, pale lilac outside, disc and lateral lobes pale yellow.

Luddemanniana Rchb.f. [*C. labiata* var. *Luddemanniana* Hort.; *C. speciosissima* Hort.]. Pseudobulbs to 1 ft. long, 1-lvd.; lvs. oblong or elliptic-oblong, to 10 in. long; racemes 2–5-fld.; fls. to 6 in. across, rose-purple, lip undulate, amethyst-purple, throat spotted with yellow or white. Summer–early autumn. Brazil, Venezuela. Cv. 'Alba'. Fls. white. Cv. 'Stanleyi'. Fls. white, midlobe of lip with yellow disc streaked with purple.

luteola Lindl. Pseudobulbs 2–3 in. long, 1-lvd.; lvs. oblong-elliptic, to 9 in. long; racemes 2–6-fld.; fls. to 2 in. across, citron-yellow, sometimes with lilac stripes, midlobe of lip whitish and wavy. Late autumn–late summer. Ecuador, Peru, Brazil, Bolivia.

×**Mantinii** Mantin: *C. Bowringiana* × *C. Dowiana* var. *aurea*. Sepals and petals rose-purple, lip darker, with golden veins.

×**Marstersoniae** Rchb.f.: *C. labiata* × *C. Loddigesii*. Fls. large, sepals and petals deep rose, lip rich purple with 2 yellow blotches in front of throat.

maxima Lindl. Pseudobulbs to 1 ft. long, 1-lvd.; lvs. oblong, to 10 in. long; racemes 3–7-fld.; fls. to 5 in. across, lilac or pale rose, the limb of lip wavy, whitish to crimson-purple, with darker veins and orange-yellow central band. Spring–summer, autumn. Colombia, Ecuador, Peru.

Mendelii Backh. [*C. labiata* var. *Mendelii* (Backh.) Rchb.f.]. VIRGIN'S C. Pseudobulbs to 16 in. long, 1-lvd.; lvs. oblong, to 10 in. long; racemes 2–3-fld.; fls. to 8 in. across, white or rosy, limb of lip very wavy, white or rosy at base, purple near apex, yellow in throat. Early spring–autumn. Colombia. Cv. 'Bertii'. Fls. tinted with rose. Cv. 'Bluntii'. Fls. white, lip with small yellow spot. Cv. 'Dixoniae'. Fls. large, sepals and petals delicate pink. Cv. 'Hackbridgensis'. Fls. large, petals blotched with crimson. Cv. 'Lachneri'. Lip with unusual color pattern, midlobe with broad marginal band of dark purple sparingly blotched with white and an inner band of lighter purple. Cv. 'Lambeanana'. Fls. white. Cv. 'Leucoglossa'. Sepals and petals bluish, lip whitish. Cv. 'Lowiae'. Lip white, with pale purple apex. Cv. 'Macroziana'. Fls. very large. Cv. 'Majestica'. Fls. large, white. Cv. 'Maudeae'. Fls. white, lip with rose markings. Cv. 'Pietiae'. Fls. whitish, lip marked with pink. Cv. 'Wisetonensis'. Lip rich rose-purple, delicately veined, throat yellow, veined with reddish-purple.

Mossiae Hook. [*C. labiata* var. *Mossiae* (Hook.) Lindl.]. EASTER C., SPRING C. Pseudobulbs to 15 in. long; lvs. oblong, to 8 in. long; racemes 3–5-fld.; fls. 5–8 in. across, rose, lip frilled, with purple limb variegated with violet and edged with rose, throat yellow and orange. Early spring–late summer. Venezuela. Cv. 'Alba'. Fls. white. Cv. 'Alexandra'. Fls. pale blush, lip white, spotted and veined with purple, throat orange, marked with purple. Cv. 'Aurea'. Fls. smaller than typical, sepals and petals pale pink, lip white or suffused with pink, marked with buff-orange at base. Cv. 'Aureola'. Fls. large, brilliant white. Cv. 'Boelensis'. Fls. of a deep, dark shade. Cv. 'Caerulea'. Sepals and petals blue-violet. Cv. 'Coelestis'. Fls. tinted lavender. Cv. 'Condoniensis'. Fls. large, intensely colored. Cv. 'Dulcis'. Fls. rose-tinted, lip ruffled, with orange center and rich rose-crimson blotch at apex. Cv. 'Floryae'. Fls. large, white. Cv. 'Goosensiana'. Sepals and petals white, lip deep reddish-violet, with ruffled white margin. Cv. 'Grandiflora'. Fls. large, sepals and petals pale pink, lip deep, rich purple-rose, with orange throat and pale blush margins. Cv. 'Reineckiana'. Sepals and petals and tube of lip white, limb of lip mauve-lilac, bordered with white, throat yellow, veined with purple-violet. Cv. 'Rouseleana'. Fls. rose. Cv. 'Wageneri'. Fls. white, lip with small yellow spot.

nobilior Rchb.f. [*C. Walkerana* var. *nobilior* (Rchb.f.) Hort. Veitch]. Pseudobulbs to 5 in. long, 2-lvd.; fls. 1–3, from base of pseudobulb, rosy-lilac, lip with primrose-yellow blotch. Winter–early spring. Brazil.

Percivaliana (Rchb.f.) O'Brien [*C. labiata* var. *Percivaliana* Rchb.f.]. CHRISTMAS C. Similar to *C. Mossiae*, but fls. smaller, somewhat darker colored; pseudobulbs to 1 ft. long, 1-lvd.; sepals and petals rose-lilac, lip small, fringed, purple-crimson with yellow to orange throat. Winter. Venezuela. Cv. 'Alba'. Fls. white, lip with orange stain in throat. Cv. 'Grandiflora'. Fls. larger, sepals and petals bright rose, lip maroon-purple with orange-yellow throat. Cv. 'Roeblingiana'. Fls. white, lip rose-purple. Cv. 'Summitensis'. Sepals and petals pale, delicate pink.

rex O'Brien. Pseudobulbs to 14 in. long, 1-lvd.; lvs. oblong, to 1 ft. long or more; racemes 3–6-fld.; fls. 6–7 in. across, sepals and petals yellowish-white, lip wavy, yellow with crimson limb edged with white. Summer–early autumn. Peru.

Sanderana: *C. Warscewiczii.*

Schillerana Rchb.f. Pseudobulbs to 5 in. long; lvs. elliptic, to 4 in. long; fls. 1 or 2 together, to 4 in. across, sepals and petals wavy on margin, brownish-green to green, spotted with brown, lip yellow inside near base, purplish-crimson at apex, fimbriate. Spring, autumn. Brazil.

Schroederae: *C. Trianaei* var.

Schroederana: *C. Trianaei* var. *Schroederae.*

Skinneri Batem. Pseudobulbs to 10 in. long; lvs. elliptic, to 8 in. long; racemes 4-(rarely)13-fld.; fls. 4–5 in. across, rose-purple, lip yellowish-white in throat. Summer. Cent. Amer. Cv. 'Alba'. Fls. white. Var. **autumnalis** P. Allen. Differs from typical var. in flowering in autumn; fls. smaller. Panama.

speciosissima: *C. Luddemanniana.*

×**suavior** Rchb.f. ex Hort. Veitch: *C. intermedia* × *C. Mendelii.* Sepals and petals pale rose-lilac, lip frilled, amethyst-purple, with cream-white disc.

superba: *C. violacea.*

Trianaei Linden & Rchb.f. [*C. labiata* var. *Trianaei* (Linden & Rchb.f.) Duchartre]. CHRISTMAS ORCHID, WINTER C. Pseudobulbs to 1 ft. long, 1-lvd.; lvs. oblong, to 8 in. long; racemes 2–3-fld.; fls. to 7 in. across, rose, lip with wavy dark purple limb and yellow throat. Winter. Colombia. Cv. 'Alba'. Fls. white. Cv. 'Mariae'. Sepals and petals silvery-white, veined with pink, lip deep magenta-crimson toward apex, with 2 yellow eyes in throat. Cv. 'Mooreana'. Sepals and petals light rosy-lilac, lip ruby-claret, orange at base. Var. **Schroederae** Rchb.f. [*C. Schroederae* Sander; *C. Schroederana* Rchb.f.]. Fls. fragrant, white to rose or light purple, segms. crisped, lip with an orange area. Colombia. Cvs. of var. *Schroederae* include: 'Alba', fls. white with yellow blotch in throat; 'Albescens', fls. white, tinted pink; 'Coerulea', lip bluish-purple.

velutina Rchb.f. Pseudobulbs 2-lvd.; lvs. broadly lanceolate, to 10 in. long; racemes 2–8-fld.; fls. fragrant, 3½–4 in. across, sepals and petals orange-yellow, spotted with purple, lip whitish, with purple lines, throat yellow. Late winter–late spring, late summer–autumn. Brazil.

violacea (HBK) Rolfe [*C. superba* Schomb. ex Lindl.]. Pseudobulbs to 10 in. long, 2-lvd.; lvs. elliptic, to 6 in. long; racemes 3–6-fld.; fls. fragrant, 4–5½ in. across, sepals and petals rose-purple, lip deep purple, throat with a central band of yellow separating 2 white blotches. Winter. Colombia, Venezuela, Guyana, s. to Peru and Brazil. Cv. 'Splendens'. Fls. paler.

Walkerana G. Gardn. Pseudobulbs to 5 in. long, furrowed, 1- or 2-lvd.; lvs. elliptic-oblong, to 5 in. long; fls. 1–3, to 5 in. across, sepals

and petals pale to deep lilac-purple, disc of lip yellow streaked with purple and with a deep border of purple. Brazil, Bolivia. Var. **dolosa:** *C.* ×*dolosa.* Var. **nobilior:** *C. nobilior.*

Wallisii: *C. Eldorado* cv.

Warneri T. Moore ex Warner [*C. labiata* var. *Warneri* (T. Moore ex Warner) Hort. Veitch]. Pseudobulbs to 8 in. long, 1-lvd.; lvs. oblong, to 7 in. long; racemes 3–5-fld.; fls. to 8 in. across, rosy, lip carmine, very wavy, throat yellow. Late spring–summer. Brazil. Cv. 'Alba'. Fls. white, throat of lip yellow.

Warscewiczii Rchb.f. [*C. gigas* Linden & André; *C. labiata* var. *Warscewiczii* (Rchb.f.) Rchb.f.; *C. Sanderana* Hort.]. Pseudobulbs 1-lvd.; lvs. oblong, to 10 in. long; racemes 2–3-fld.; fls. to 9 in. across, sepals and petals violet-rose, lip wavy, deep purple, with 2 yellow spots in throat. Spring–summer. Colombia. Cv. 'Alba'. Fls. white.

×**Wavriniana** Hort.: *C. granulosa* × *C. Warscewiczii.* Sepals and petals yellowish, tinged with rose, lip rose, veined with purple.

CAULARTHRON Raf. [*Diacrium* (Lindl.) Benth.]. *Orchidaceae.* Two spp. of epiphytes of trop. Amer.; pseudobulbs with a few lvs.; fls. in racemes, mostly white, sepals and petals similar, petals notched, lip separate, 3-lobed, with 2 horns on the upper surface, column winged, not united to the lip. For structure of fl. see *Orchidaceae.*

For culture see *Orchids.*

bicornutum (Hook.) Raf. [*Diacrium bicornutum* (Hook.) Benth.; *Epidendrum bicornutum* Hook.]. VIRGIN ORCHID, VIRGIN MARY O. Pseudobulbs long-cylindrical, to 1 ft. long, 3–5-lvd.; lvs. to 10 in. long; racemes erect, to about 2½ ft. long, including peduncle, 5–20-fld.; fls. about 2 in. across, white, lip finely spotted with purple. Early winter–spring. S. Amer. n. of the Amazon to Trinidad and Tobago.

bilamellatum (Rchb.f.) R. E. Schult. [*Diacrium bilamellatum* (Rchb.f.) Hemsl.; *D. indivisum* (Bradf. ex Griseb.) Broadw. ex Rolfe; *Epidendrum indivisum* Bradf. ex Griseb.]. LITTLE VIRGIN. Pseudobulbs long-fusiform, 2–9 in. long, 2–3-lvd.; lvs. strap-shaped to linear-oblong, 2–9 in. long; infl. erect, to 6 in. long, few- to many-fld.; fls. to 1½ in. across, white or tinged with pink or lavender, lip fleshy, as long as petals, the horns lamellalike. Early winter–late spring. Cent. Amer., Panama, n. S. Amer.

CAULIFLOWER. Cauliflower, botanically classified along with broccoli in *Brassica oleracea,* Botrytis Group, is a biennial plant related to the cabbage but more tender to frost and unfavorable conditions, the edible part being a head formed of the condensed and thickened malformed flower cluster rather than an aggregation of leaves. If the old plant is set out the following year, good flowering and seed-bearing shoots will arise from the stump and from such parts of the head as may not have been removed, as in the cabbage.

Cauliflower is not as cosmopolitan as to conditions as cabbage, or as easy to grow. It does best in a rather cool, moist soil and under equable conditions; only highly selected seeds should be used and plants must be kept continuously thrifty. Insects and diseases are the same as those of cabbage and are similarly controlled.

The great heat and dryness of midsummer are to be avoided as far as possible at heading time, if the crop is to be grown in difficult regions. To this end, very early cultivars may be grown, starting them under glass and harvesting the crop in June or early summer. The plants are handled as are cabbages, and the distances for the early kinds may be 18 inches in the row. For the late or main crop, seeds may be sown in seed beds in late spring or early summer, and since these types make bigger plants the distances should be 2 feet in the row or even more for the larger kinds. In the southern states, the crop may be grown for early spring use from seeds sown in autumn. In parts of California, the crop is grown in winter. Wherever irrigation is available, many of the difficulties of cauliflower-growing may be overcome.

A continuous steady growth from high-quality seeds and well-grown plants should produce a solid head of regular shape, without "buttons" or breaks or straggling branches. To whiten the head, the outer leaves are sometimes tied together over it, but openings should be left on the sides for ventilation or the head may decay from the accumulation of moisture. Heads should be harvested as fast as they mature or they may crack or become discolored or develop decayed spots. In harvesting, a good circle of leaves should go with the head, and these leaves are trimmed a little above the head to serve as a protection, and to provide a cup in which the head sits attractively.

×CAULOCATTLEYA Hort. [×*Diacattleya* Hort.]: *Caularthron × Cattleya*. Orchidaceae. A group of bigeneric hybrids, generally intermediate in character between the parents.

For culture see *Orchids*.

CAULOPHYLLUM Michx. *Berberidaceae*. Two spp. of erect, rhizomatous herbs, 1 in e. N. Amer., 1 in e. Asia; lvs. ternately compound; fls. small, in clusters, appearing with unfolding lvs., sepals 6, petals 6, thick and smaller than sepals, stamens 6, ovary bursting early, exposing the 2 seeds; seeds drupelike at maturity.

thalictroides (L.) Michx. BLUE COHOSH, PAPOOSEROOT. To 3 ft.; fls. yellow-green, about ½ in. across; mature seeds globose, ⁵⁄₁₆ in. across, with thin, fleshy, blue seed coat. Early spring. Deep woods; New Bruns. to S.C. and Mo. Requires shade.

CAUTLEYA Hook. *Zingiberaceae*. About 5 spp. of per., aromatic terrestrial or epiphytic herbs in the Himalayas; sts. clustered, from a short rhizome; lvs. lanceolate or oblong, 2-ranked, with sheaths open opp. blade; infl. a terminal, loose spike; fls. yellow, solitary in axils of bracts, calyx tubular, split on one side, corolla funnelform, tube short, lobes 3, nearly equal, the upper petal and lateral petal-like staminodes forming a hood, staminodial lip broadly cuneate, emarginate or 2-lobed, stamen filament short, erect, anther sacs spurred, ovary 3-celled; fr. a 3-valved caps.

For culture see *Zingiberaceae*.

gracilis (Sm.) Dandy [*C. lutea* Royle]. To 16 in.; lvs. 4–6, sessile, ovate to lanceolate, to 8 in. long, 1½ in. wide, glabrous, purplish beneath; spike loosely 2–8-fld., axis red, bracts green; fls. yellow, calyx longer than bracts, ¾ in. long, about half the length of the fl.; fr. red.

lutea: *C. gracilis*.

spicata (Sm.) Bak. To 6 in.; lvs. often petioled, lanceolate or oblong-lanceolate, to 14 in. long, 3¼ in. wide, acuminate, glabrous, green; spike densely fld., bracts red, about 1 in. long; calyx shorter than bracts, corolla lobes about 1 in. long, lip yellow.

striata: a listed name of no botanical standing.

CAVANILLESIA Ruiz & Pav. *Bombacaceae*. About 4 spp. of large trees, native to Cent. and S. Amer., trunk sometimes enlarged at middle; lvs. simple, palmately nerved and usually lobed; fls. in umbellate cymes, appearing before lvs., calyx 5-parted, petals 5, glandular at base inside, stamens many, united basally in a column, ovary 3–5-celled, with 2 ovules in each cell; fr. indehiscent, with 3–5 large, membranous wings, the cells usually 1-seeded.

platanifolia (Humb. & Bonpl.) HBK. CUIPO. To 125 ft. or more, bark smooth, pale, crown open; lvs. mostly 3-, 5-, or 7-lobed, to 1 ft. wide; petals reddish inside, about ⅞ in. long, stamens exserted, about 1 in.; ear-fusiform, to 5 in. long, wings 5, membranous, semicircular, to 6 in. long and 3 in. wide. Panama to Peru, where the wood is used for making floating rafts and canoes.

CEANOTHUS L. REDROOT. *Rhamnaceae*. About 55 spp. of deciduous or evergreen shrubs or small trees, sometimes spiny, mostly in w. N. Amer., a few spp. in e. N. Amer.; lvs. alt. or opp., often 3-nerved at base; fls. small, blue or white, many in showy umbels, racemes, or panicles, bisexual, 5-merous; fr. a 3-lobed caps.

The genus includes many ornamentals, among them hybrids of European origin and many named cultivars. Most Pacific Coast species and their derivatives are not hardy in regions colder than Zone 8. Ceanothus thrives in light, well-drained soil in sunny locations. Propagated by seeds sown in spring, layers, and some cultivars by grafting on roots of *C. americanus* in spring under glass; also by cuttings of mature wood in autumn or softwood cuttings in spring from forced plants. Species native in the eastern part of the country are sometimes transferred to gardens in that region.

americanus L. NEW JERSEY TEA, WILD SNOWBALL, MOUNTAIN-SWEET. Shrub, to 3½ ft.; lvs. alt., ovate, finely toothed; fls. white. Me. to S.C., w. to Tex. Zone 4. Has been used in Eur. to develop hybrids.

arboreus Greene. CATALINA C., CATALINA MOUNTAIN LILAC, FELT-LEAF C. Evergreen shrub or tree, to 20 ft.; lvs. alt., ovate, finely toothed, white-tomentose beneath; fls. pale to deep blue, fragrant. Is. off Calif. coast.

austromontanus: *C. foliosus*.

×Burtonensis: a listed name of no botanical standing; used for *Ceanothus* cv. 'Burtonensis', a natural hybrid between *C. impressus* and *C. thyrsiflorus*.

californicus: *C. integerrimus*.

coeruleus Lag. Shrub or small tree, to 20 ft. and more; lvs. alt., oblong-lanceolate to ovate, finely toothed, rusty-tomentose beneath; fls. blue or nearly white. Mex., Guatemala. Has been used in Eur. to develop hybrids.

cordulatus Kellogg. SNOWBUSH. Spiny shrub, to 4 ft., much-branched, forming flattened clumps; lvs. alt., ovate, entire or finely toothed; fls. white. Ore., Calif. Zone 7.

crassifolius Torr. HOARY LEAF C. Shrub, to 6 ft., stiffly branched, young sts. pubescent; lvs. opp., elliptic to obovate, to 1 in. long, usually dentate and revolute, somewhat fleshy, white-pubescent beneath; fls. white. S. Calif. and n. Baja Calif. Var. planus Abrams. Lvs. entire, not revolute.

cuneatus (Hook.) Nutt. BUCKBRUSH. Rigid, erect, evergreen shrub, to 8 ft.; lvs. opp., spatulate-obovate, to 1 in. long; fls. white, lavender, or blue. Ore., Calif., Baja Calif. Zone 7.

cyaneus Eastw. SAN DIEGO C. Evergreen shrub, to 10 ft.; lvs. alt., ovate-elliptic, to 2 in. long, entire to glandular-toothed, glossy; fls. dark blue, becoming paler, in clusters to 1 ft. long. S. Calif. Zone 8. The large clusters of dark blue fls. make this an attractive ornamental. Cv. 'La Primavera'. A selected garden seedling.

×Delilianus Spach: *C. americanus × C. coeruleus*. To 3 ft.; lvs. alt., ovate, finely toothed; fls. pale or deep blue. Zone 7. Cv. 'Gloire de Versailles'. One of the best-known selections.

dentatus Torr. & A. Gray. Evergreen, to 3 ft., densely branched; lvs. alt., obovate, revolute; fls. blue. Calif.

divaricatus: see *C. leucodermis*.

divergens Parry. Low shrub, brs. slender, arching; lvs. oblong to obovate, to 1 in. long, undulate, coarsely toothed, somewhat revolute; fls. blue, in small umbels. Cent. Calif.

Fendleri A. Gray. To 1½ ft., spiny; lvs. alt., ovate, entire, silky beneath; fls. white. S. Dak. to Wyo., s. to n. Mex. Zone 5.

foliosus Parry [*C. austromontanus* Abrams]. WAVY LEAF C. Evergreen, to 1 ft. or more, densely branched; lvs. alt., oblong to ¾ in. long, usually more or less undulate, pale beneath; fls. blue. Calif. Zone 8. Var. vineatus McMinn. VINE HILL C. Lvs. obovate to broadly elliptic, with nearly plane margin.

gloriosus J. T. Howell. POINT REYES C., POINT REYES CREEPER. Prostrate, evergreen shrub, to 1 ft.; lvs. opp., broadly elliptic to round, to 1½ in. long, usually spiny-toothed, leathery, dark green; fls. deep blue to purple. N. Calif. Zone 8. Var. exaltatus J. T. Howell. NAVARRO C. Sts. erect, to 12 ft. Var. porrectus J. T. Howell. MOUNT VISION C. Low, sprawling, branchlets slender, not very rigid.

Greggii A. Gray. Shrub, to 6 ft.; lvs. elliptic-oblong, to ⅝ in. long, grayish on both sides, entire or with 1–3 small teeth near the base, rarely concave above; fls. white, in small umbels. New Mex. and s. Calif., s. to n. Mex. Zone 7. Var. perplexans (Trel.) Jeps. [*C. perplexans* Trel.]. CUP LEAF C. Lvs. yellowish-green, broadly elliptic to obovate, to ¾ in. long or more, usually more sharply pointed.

griseus (Trel.) McMinn. Erect, spreading to prostrate, evergreen shrub, to 8 ft. or more; lvs. alt., broadly ovate, to 1¾ in. long, undulate, revolute, pubescent beneath; fls. blue, in panicles to 2 in. long. Coastal, cent. Calif. Zone 8. Var. griseus [*C. thyrsiflorus* var. *griseus* Trel.]. CARMEL C. The typical var.; sts. erect. Var. horizontalis McMinn. YANKEE POINT C., CARMEL CREEPER. Low and spreading to more or less prostrate.

impressus Trel. SANTA BARBARA C. Spreading, evergreen shrub, to 5 ft.; lvs. alt., broadly elliptic to round, to ½ in. long, loosely villous, strongly revolute; fls. dark blue. S. Calif. Zone 8. Var. nipomensis McMinn. NIPOMO C. To 8 ft., and spreading to 20 ft.; lvs. to 1 in. long, not revolute.

incanus Torr. & A. Gray. Erect evergreen, to 12 ft., bark white; lvs. alt., ovate, usually entire, whitish-pubescent beneath; fls. white. Calif.

insularis Eastw. [*C. megacarpus* Nutt. var. *insularis* (Eastw.) Munz]. Erect, evergreen shrub, to 9 ft., stiffly branched; lvs. opp. or alt., elliptic, to 1½ in. long, entire; fls. white or with bluish centers; caps. globose, without horns or crests. Islands off s. Calif.

integerrimus Hook. & Arn. [*C. californicus* Kellogg]. DEERBUSH, DEERBRUSH. Loosely branched, to 12 ft.; lvs. alt., ovate, to 2 in. long, entire; fls. white, rarely pale blue or pink. Calif.

Jepsonii Greene. Low, evergreen, spreading shrub, to 4 ft., intricately branched; lvs. opp., elliptic, to ¾ in. long, leathery, somewhat hollylike; fls. white or blue. N. Calif. Var. **purpureus:** *C. purpureus.*

Lemmonii Parry. Low, evergreen, spreading shrub, to 3 ft.; lvs. alt., elliptic to oblong, to 1¼ in. long, toothed, pale and pubescent beneath; fls. pale blue. N. Calif.

leucodermis Greene [*C. divaricatus* of auth., not Nutt.]. Evergreen shrub, to 2 ft.; lvs. alt., elliptic-oblong to ovate, to 1½ in. long, 3-veined from base, entire to serrulate, glabrous; fls. pale blue to white; fr. globose. Calif. and n. Baja Calif.

×**Lobbianus** Hook. Probably a natural hybrid between *C. dentatus* and *C. griseus.* Evergreen shrub, to 10 ft.; lvs. alt., oblong, remotely toothed, whitish beneath; fls. dark blue.

macrocarpus: *C. megacarpus.*

Masonii McMinn. BOLINAS RIDGE C. Erect to spreading shrub, to 6 ft.; lvs. opp., broadly elliptic to nearly orbicular, to ¾ in. long, obtuse to notched at apex, thick, leathery; fls. dark blue to purple, many in umbels. Cent. Calif.

megacarpus Nutt. [*C. macrocarpus* Nutt., not Cav.]. Evergreen shrub, to 12 ft.; lvs. mostly alt., cuneate-obovate, to 1 in. long, truncate or notched at apex; fls. white, in small clusters; fr. globose, to ½ in. in diam., with large dorsal horns. S. Calif. Var. **insularis:** *C. insularis.* Var. **pendulus** McMinn. Brs. long, slender, arching or drooping.

microphyllus Michx. Shrub, to 2 ft., sts. erect, diffuse; lvs. alt., suborbicular to elliptic, to ¼ in. long, entire, somewhat fleshy; fls. white, to ⅛ in. across, in loose terminal and axillary panicles. Ga. to Fla. and Ala. Sometimes cult. in se. U.S.

oliganthus Nutt. Evergreen shrub, to 12 ft.; lvs. alt., ovate, finely toothed, pale green or brown beneath; fls. deep blue or purplish. Calif. Var. **Orcuttii** (Parry) Jeps. [*C. Orcuttii* Parry]. Fls. pale blue.

olivaceus: a listed name of no botanical standing for *C. tomentosus* var.

Orcuttii: *C. oliganthus* var.

ovatus Desf. Shrub, to 3 ft.; lvs. alt., oblong or elliptic, to 2½ in. long, toothed, glossy above; fls. white. Vt. to Colo. and Tex. Zone 5. Similar and closely related to *C. americanus.*

×**pallidus** Lindl. Presumably a hybrid between *C. ×Delilianus* and *C. ovatus;* to 3 ft. or less; lvs. alt., oblong, finely toothed; fls. light blue. Var. **roseus** (Spach) Rehd. Fls. pink. Cv. '**Marie Simon**' belongs here.

Palmeri Trel. Partly deciduous shrub, to 12 ft.; lvs. ovate to oblong, to 1½ in. long, entire, firm and leathery, pale beneath; fls. white, in erect showy clusters to 5 in. long. Mts., s. Calif. and n. Baja Calif.

papillosus Torr. & A. Gray. WART LEAF C. Evergreen, to 6 ft.; lvs. alt., oblong to linear, revolute, papillose above, pubescent beneath; fls. blue. Cent. and s. Calif. Var. **Roweanus** McMinn. Sometimes sprawling, to 3 ft. or more; lvs. usually less than ⅜ in. wide. Cv. '**Supressus**' is listed as a prostrate form.

Parryi Trel. Evergreen, to 6 ft. or more; lvs. alt., oblong, to 2 in. long, finely toothed, becoming revolute, tomentose beneath; fls. blue. Calif.

perplexans: *C. Greggii* var.

porrectus: a listed name of no botanical standing, perhaps for *C. gloriosus* var.

prostratus Benth. [*C. prostratus* vars. *divergens* (Parry) K. Brandeg., and *laxus* Jeps.]. MAHALA-MAT. Prostrate evergreen; lvs. opp., obovate, coarsely spiny-toothed; fls. blue. Wash. to Calif. Zone 7. Var. **occidentalis** McMinn. Lvs. usually cuneate-spatulate, undulate, with long, sharply spinose teeth.

pumilus Greene. SISKIYOU-MAT. Prostrate, evergreen shrub, to 8 in. or less, much-branched, forming mats; lvs. cuneate to obovate, to ½ in. long, finely white-pubescent beneath, nearly sessile; fls. blue to white. S. Ore., n. Calif.

purpureus Jeps. [*C. Jepsonii* var. *purpureus* (Jeps.) Jeps.]. HOLLY-LEAF C. Erect or spreading, evergreen shrub, to 4 ft.; lvs. opp., orbicular to broadly elliptic, to ¾ in. long, sinuate, dark green, glossy; fls. deep blue to purple, in umbellate clusters to 2 in. across. Calif. Zone 7b.

ramulosus (Greene) McMinn. COAST C. Evergreen, to 4 ft., brs. spreading, arching, or procumbent; lvs. opp., oblanceolate, obovate, or nearly orbicular, to ⅝ in. long, nearly sessile; fls. blue, lavender, or white, in small umbels. Calif. Var. **fascicularis** McMinn. LOMPOC C. Lvs. usually narrowly oblanceolate, some in clusters.

repens: a listed name of no botanical standing for *C. thyrsiflorus* var.

rigidus Nutt. MONTEREY C. Evergreen, to 6 ft., stiffly branched; lvs. opp., obovate, ½ in. long, cuneate, entire, or toothed near tip, thick and leathery; fls. bright blue. Calif. Cv. '**Albus**'. Fls. white.

Roweanus: a listed name of no botanical standing for *C. papillosus* var.

sanguineus Pursh. WILD LILAC. Shrub, to 10 ft., twigs greenish, long-pubescent, older sts. reddish; lvs. alt., elliptic, to 2¼ in. long, obtuse at apex; fls. white. B.C., s. to Mont. and Calif. Zone 5.

sorediatus Hook. & Arn. JIM BUSH, JIM BRUSH. Evergreen, to 7 ft., stiffly branched; lvs. alt., ovate, to 1 in. long, finely toothed, pale beneath; fls. blue or nearly white. Calif.

spinosus Nutt. RED-HEART, GREEN-BARK C. Evergreen shrub, to 10 ft., sometimes a tree to 24 ft., often spiny; lvs. alt., oblong, to 1¼ in. long, entire or finely toothed; fls. pale blue or white. Calif.

thyrsiflorus Eschsch. BLUEBLOSSOM. Evergreen shrub, to 8 ft., or tree to 25 ft.; lvs. alt., oblong, to 2 in. long, finely toothed, glossy above; fls. blue or rarely white. Ore. to Calif. Zone 8. Var. **griseus:** *C. griseus.* Var. **repens** McMinn. CREEPING BLUEBLOSSOM. Prostrate.

tomentosus Parry. WOOLLY LEAF C. Evergreen shrub, to 8 ft., branchlets rusty-tomentose; lvs. alt., elliptic to broadly ovate, to 1 in. long, glandular-serrulate, whitish- or brownish-tomentose or pubescent beneath; fls. blue to white. Calif. Var. **olivaceus** Jeps. Lvs. glandular-denticulate.

×**Veitchianus** Hook. Appears to be a natural hybrid between *C. griseus* and probably *C. rigidus;* evergreen, to 10 ft.; lvs. alt., obovate, remotely toothed, glossy above, whitish beneath; fls. deep blue.

velutinus Dougl. Evergreen, to 15 ft.; lvs. alt., elliptic, to 2½ in. long, finely toothed, glossy above, tomentose beneath; fls. white. B.C. to Calif. and Colo. Zone 5.

verrucosus Nutt. Evergreen shrub, usually to 8 ft., occasionally more, brs. rigid, roughened; lvs. alt., obovate, to ½ in. long, entire or slightly toothed, pale beneath; fls. white, with dark centers. S. Calif. and n. Baja Calif.

vineatus: a listed name of no botanical standing for *C. foliosus* var.

CECROPIA Loefl. *Moraceae.* About 100 spp. of fast-growing, dioecious trees, native to humid trop. Amer.; sts. and brs. hollow with septa at internodes, sap milky; lvs. large, usually palmately lobed, more or less peltate, long-petioled; fls. unisexual, in dense spikes.

Sometimes planted for ornament in the tropics or in Zone 10. Where native, the hollow stems are usually inhabited by biting ants.

angustifolia Trécul [*C. digitata* Klotzsch]. To 40 ft. or more, bark pale, crown spreading; lvs. peltate, 14–16-lobed, rough above, white-tomentose beneath, lobes 6–10 in. long, 2–3 in. wide, elongate, narrow, ligulate, entire, nearly obtuse to acute, petioles cylindrical, 12–16 in. long, striate, pilose; male infls. many, female infls. 2–4, to 1½ in. long; fr. oblong, acute. Andes, Peru.

digitata: *C. angustifolia.*

palmata Willd. SNAKEWOOD TREE. To 50 ft., with soft wood; lvs. borne at ends of brs., 7–11-lobed to the middle or deeper, scabrous to glabrescent above, white-tomentose beneath, lobes ovate-oblong, blunt. W. Indies, n. S. Amer.

peltata L. TRUMPET TREE. To 60 ft.; lvs. orbicular, to 1 ft. across or more, 7–9-lobed, dark green and scabrous above, densely white-tomentose beneath, lobes ovate, somewhat pointed, petioles often longer than blade; male infls. many, under 2 in. long, female spikes 2–6, sessile, yellowish; fr. 1–2 in. long, thick, succulent. Lowland, Caribbean trop. Amer.

CEDRELA P. Br. [*Toona* M. J. Roem.]. *Meliaceae.* About 20 spp. of trees with soft, light-colored wood, native to trop. Amer., and from China to India, s. through Malay Arch. to Australia; lvs. alt., pinnate; fls. in terminal or axillary panicles, calyx 4- or 5-lobed, petals 4 or 5, stamens 4–6, filaments separate, ovary 5-celled; fr. a 5-celled, 5-valved, woody or leathery caps., seeds winged.

The wood furnishes valuable timber, that of *C. odorata* has been used extensively for cigar boxes; several are also grown as ornamentals. Cedrelas thrive in fertile loamy soil; propagated by seeds, cuttings of mature wood, and root cuttings, over heat.

Dugesii S. Wats. Large tree; lfts. 6–10, ovate or lanceolate-ovate, caudate-attenuate, conspicuously ciliolate; panicles dense; fr. to 1 in. long. Mex.

fissilis Vell. Tree, 50–60 ft., lfts. 16–26, oblong lanceolate to oblong ovate, densely pubescent beneath; fls. yellowish, velvety, in pubescent panicles; fr. to 1 in. long or more, seeds winged in upper part. Trop. N. and S. Amer. Wood used for general carpentry.

odorata L. WEST INDIAN CEDAR, SPANISH C., CIGAR-BOX C., BARBADOS C. Timber tree, to 100 ft., with smooth bark and reddish-brown, aromatic heartwood; lfts. 12–20, ovate-lanceolate, entire, glabrous; fls. yellowish, in panicles shorter than lvs.; fr. to 1½ in. long, seeds winged in lower part. W. Indies, S. Amer. One of the most important timbers for domestic use in trop. Amer.; wood repels insects so has been much used for closets and cigar boxes.

serrata Royle. To 60 ft.; lfts. 15–25, elliptic-oblong or oblong-lanceolate, toothed; fls. pink, fetid, in panicles longer than lvs.; seeds winged in upper part. W. Himalayas.

sinensis Juss. [*Toona sinensis* (Juss.) M. J. Roem.]. Deciduous tree, to 50 ft., bark shaggy; lfts. 10–20, oblong or oblong-lanceolate, serrate or entire, pubescent beneath; fls. white, in pendulous panicles much longer than lvs.; fr. 1 in. long, seeds winged in upper part. China. Planted as an ornamental in temp. areas. Zone 6.

Toona Roxb. ex Rottl. Nearly evergreen, to 70 ft.; lfts. 10–20, lanceolate to ovate-lanceolate, entire or wavy; fls. white, fragrant, in panicles shorter than lvs.; fr. to 1 in. long, seeds winged at both ends. Himalayas. Planted in s. Fla., Zone 10. Valuable wood with many uses.

CEDRONELLA Moench. *Labiatae*. One sp., a per. sub-shrub of Madeira and the Canary Is.; sts. square in cross section; lvs. opp., of 3 lfts.; fls. in false whorls arranged in dense, terminal, racemes or heads, the lowest verticillaster often remote, bracts simple, calyx tubular-campanulate, 13–15-nerved, 5-toothed, corolla tube longer than calyx, limb 2-lipped, upper lip 2-lobed, lower lip 3-lobed, middle lobe longest, stamens 4, about as long as corolla, style brs. nearly equal. Differs from *Dracocephalum* in regular calyx.

For the flower garden; propagated by seeds or cuttings.

cana: *Agastache cana.*

canariensis (L.) Webb [*C. triphylla* Moench]. BALM-OF-GILEAD, CANARY BALM. Shrubby, 3–5 ft.; lfts. oblong-lanceolate, 2–4 in. long, acuminate, crenate, petiole glandular-fringed or ciliate; verticillasters often in upper lf. axils; calyx to ½ in. long, corolla ¾–1 in. long, lilac to violet. Canary Is. Cult. in s. Calif.

cordata: *Meehania cordata.*

mexicana: *Agastache mexicana.*

triphylla: *C. canariensis.*

CEDRUS Trew. CEDAR. *Pinaceae*. Four or fewer spp. of large, monoecious or dioecious, coniferous, evergreen trees, native to mts. of N. Afr. and Asia; brs. wide-spreading; lvs. stiff, needle-shaped, 4-angled, clustered on short, stout, lateral spurs; male cones ovoid, erect, female cones small, scales closely imbricate, deciduous, seeds 2 to a scale, winged, maturing in 2 or 3 years.

Mostly trees for the milder parts of the country, but perhaps except for *C. brevifolia*, all can be grown in favorable, sheltered locations in Zone 7 and *C. libani* in Zone 6. For culture see *Conifers*.

atlantica (Endl.) G. Manetti ex Carrière [*C. libani* subsp. *atlantica* (Endl.) Franco]. ATLAS C. To 100 ft. or more; lvs. less than 1 in. long, bluish-green; cones to 3 in. long. N. Afr. Zone 7. Some cvs. are: 'Argentea', lvs. silvery-white; 'Aurea', lvs. yellowish; 'Fastigiata', narrow-conical; 'Glauca', lvs. glaucous; 'Pendula', branchlets drooping.

brevifolia (Hook.f.) Dode [*C. libani* var. *brevifolia* Hook.f.]. CYPRUS C. Closely allied to *C. libani*, but lvs. shorter, glaucous, cones shorter. Cyprus. Zone 7?

Deodara (D. Don) G. Don. DEODAR. To 150 ft.; branchlets drooping, densely pubescent; lvs. to 2 in. long, dark bluish-green; cones to 5 in. long, rounded apically. Himalayas. Zone 7. An important timber tree in India. Cvs. are: 'Aurea', lvs. yellow; 'Compacta', slow-growing, dense, rounded; 'Fontinalis' (probably the same as 'Pendula'), shoots elongated, flexible; 'Glauca' and 'Nana', listed names; 'Pendula', brs. long, drooping; 'Prostrata', low-lying; 'Repandens' and 'Repens', listed names; 'Robusta', more vigorous, lvs. stiffer; 'Verticillata', compact, lvs. bluish-white; "Viridis', lvs. deeper green.

libani A. Rich. [*C. libanotica* Link]. CEDAR-OF-LEBANON. To 100 ft. or more, main brs. spreading or ascending; lvs. 1 in. long, dark or bright green; cones to 4 in. long. Asia Minor. Zone 6. Subsp. **atlantica:** *C. atlantica*. Var. **brevifolia:** *C. brevifolia*. Cvs. include: 'Aurea', lvs. yellowish-green; 'Compacta', dense; 'Comte de Dijon': 'Nana'; 'Glauca', lvs. blue or silvery-white; 'Nana' [cv. 'Comte de Dijon'], dwarf, compact; 'Pendula', brs. drooping; 'Sargentii', slow-growing, sts. erect, short, brs. dense, pendulous.

libanotica: *C. libani.*

CEIBA Mill. [*Eriodendron* DC.]. *Bombacaceae*. About 10 spp. of usually large, deciduous, mostly spiny trees, native to

tropics of Amer. and perhaps Afr.; lvs. palmately compound; fls. showy, solitary or in axillary clusters, calyx cupular, truncate or irregularly lobed, petals 5, somewhat incurved at apex, stamens 5, united basally in a tube, each with 1–3 anthers; fr. a 5-celled, leathery or woody caps.; seeds many, embedded in a cottonlike fiber, the kapok of commerce.

Planted as a specimen tree in the tropics.

aesculifolia (HBK) Britt. & Bak.f. [*C. grandiflora* Rose]. Medium or large tree, trunk spiny; lfts. 5–8, elliptic to oblanceolate, to 5 in. long, acuminate, usually serrulate; fls. opening before lvs. appear, calyx 1–1½ in. long, petals white, brownish-tomentose outside, 4–6 in. long, stamens white to purple-red, about as long as petals; caps. ellipsoid, to 7 in. long. Mex., Guatemala.

Casearia: *C. pentandra.*

grandiflora: *C. aesculifolia.*

pentandra (L.) Gaertn. [*C. Casearia* Medic.; *Eriodendron anfractuosum* DC.]. SILK-COTTON TREE, WHITE S.-C. T., KAPOK T. To 150 ft. or more, brs. widely spreading, spiny trunk often to 9 ft. in diam., with thin buttresses sometimes extending some 30 ft.; lfts. 5–7, oblong-lanceolate, to 6 in. long, entire; fls. usually opening before lvs. appear, calyx 4–5-lobed, to ½ in. long, petals yellowish, rose, or white, oblong-obovate, to 1⅜ in. long, tomentose outside; caps. ellipsoid to fusiform, 4–10 in. long. Pantrop. Cult. for kapok, produced commercially mainly in Ceylon, Java, and Philippine Is.

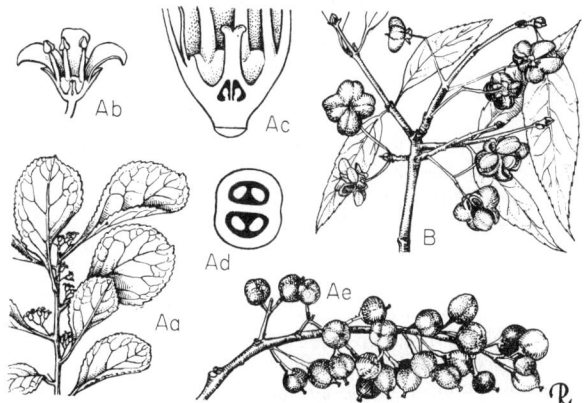

CELASTRACEAE. **A,** *Celastrus orbiculatus*: **Aa,** flowering branch, × ¼; **Ab,** male flower, vertical section, × 2; **Ac,** base of female flower, vertical section, × 6; **Ad,** ovary, cross section, × 20; **Ae,** fruits, × ½. **B,** *Euonymus Hamiltoniana* var. *Maackii*: fruiting branch, × ½. (From Bailey, *Manual of Cultivated Plants*, ed. 2.)

CELASTRACEAE R. Br. STAFF-TREE FAMILY. Dicot.; about 55 genera and 800 spp. of evergreen or deciduous, polygamous trees or shrubs, often scandent, native in most of the world except the Arctic; lvs. alt., opp., or whorled, simple; fls. small, bisexual or unisexual, regular, in cymes or panicles, sepals, petals, and stamens usually 4–5, disc present around ovary, pistil 1, compound, ovary superior, 2–5-celled; fr. a caps., drupe, samara, or berry, often brightly colored, seeds often enclosed in a brightly colored aril, which is exposed when fr. dehisces in the autumn. Genera cult. as ornamentals are: *Cassine, Catha, Celastrus, Euonymus, Maytenus, Paxistima, Putterlickia,* and *Tripterygium*.

Catha is the source of an important masticatory much used as a stimulant in Ethiopia, and *Tripterygium* has insecticidal properties.

CELASTRUS L. BITTERSWEET, SHRUBBY B. *Celastraceae*. About 31 spp. of usually deciduous, twining, polygamous shrubs, native to N. and S. Amer., Oceania, e. Asia, and Madagascar; lvs. alt., simple; fls. small, greenish, yellowish, or white, in axillary or terminal cymes, racemes, or panicles, calyx 5-parted, petals and stamens 5; fr. a yellow to orange caps., seeds 2 in each cell, enclosed in a yellow, orange, vermilion, or crimson aril, showy when ripe.

Suitable for covering walls, trellises, and the like. They thrive in ordinary soils. Propagated by seeds sown in autumn or stratified, by suckers, by cuttings of young or mature wood, and by root cuttings.

angulatus Maxim. [*C. angulatus* var. *latifolius* Hort.; *C. latifolius* Hemsl.]. To 20 ft., brs. angular; lvs. ovate to orbicular, to 7 in. long; fls. in terminal panicles to 6 in. long; aril vermilion. China. Zone 7.

articulatus: *C. orbiculatus.*

flagellaris Rupr. To 25 ft., brs. with paired spiny stipules; lvs. elliptic to ovate, to 2 in. long; fls. in few-fld. axillary cymes; aril vermilion. N. China, Korea, Japan. Zone 7.

gemmatus Loes. Winter buds to ½ in. long, pointed; lvs. elliptic, to 4¼ in. long, acuminate, toothed, glossy above; fls. in few-fld., axillary cymes; fr. ½ in. in diam. Cent. and w. China. Zone 7?

latifolius: *C. angulatus.*

Loeseneri: *C. Rosthornianus.*

orbiculatus Thunb. [*C. articulatus* Thunb.]. ORIENTAL B. To 30 or 40 ft., brs. spiny when young; lvs. broadly obovate to nearly orbicular, to 4 in. long, crenate; fls. in few-fld., axillary cymes; aril scarlet. Japan, China; naturalized in e. U.S. Zone 5. Var. **punctatus** (Thunb.) Rehd. Less vigorous; lvs. smaller.

Rosthornianus Loes. [*C. Loeseneri* Rehd. & E. H. Wils.]. To 20 ft.; lvs. narrowly elliptic to elliptic-oblong, to 3 in. long, acuminate, toothed; fls. 1–3, in lf. axils; aril scarlet. Cent. and w. China. Zone 7?

scandens L. AMERICAN B., FALSE B., CLIMBING B., SHRUBBY B., STAFF VINE, WAXWORK. To 25 ft.; lvs. ovate to ovate-lanceolate, to 4 in. long, toothed; fls. in terminal racemes or panicles to 4 in. long; aril scarlet to crimson. Que., s. to N.C. and New Mex. Zone 4.

CELERY. Celery, *Apium graveolens* var. *dulce,* is a biennial or perennial herb grown for the edible leaf stalks. It is raised from seeds, coming to horticultural maturity the same year, but flowers are normally produced the second year although the plant sometimes runs to seed the first year. The leaf stalks are blanched in the field but the process is often completed in the storage cellar for the late kinds.

Ordinary, deep, fertile, mellow garden land will produce good celery. The soil must be thoroughly prepared, and if not naturally retentive of moisture it should be supplemented with a system of irrigation or watering for dry times. The commercial growing of celery is an important industry on reclaimed lands, particularly on muck and other lowlands that can be drained. Under such conditions a uniform moisture supply can be assured and the ground readily provides the proper tilth. In such areas celery-growing has become a special skilled industry of great importance.

Celery should make a continued rapid growth. It is especially important that the plants get a "quick" start. Stimulation by some form of available nitrogen, as in nitrate of soda, is advisable. This nitrate may be applied to seed beds, about 1 teaspoon to a gallon of water. Heavy applications of well-rotted stable manure are advisable on uplands, and a chemical fertilizer of a 4–8–12 analysis on muck lands, liberally applied. Side dressing the plants with nitrate of soda once or twice during their growth is usually advantageous.

For the home garden, celery may be planted in shallow trenches to facilitate blanching, but this method is now less used than formerly. The plants are commonly set 6 inches apart in rows 28–40 inches apart. Blanching may be accomplished by banking with earth late in the season until only the tops are visible, by shading with boards placed on edge on either side, or by tying with paper, or a drain tile may be put over each plant. The late crop may be packed in boxes, the roots covered with earth, and placed in the cellar to complete the blanching. Self-blanching may also be practiced, which consists of setting the plants very close together; this requires very rich soil and plenty of moisture; the plants may be set 5 or 6 inches apart in rows 10–24 inches apart.

Propagation is entirely by seeds, which for the early crop should be sown in boxes or hotbeds; seedlings should be transplanted once before being permanently set out. Seeds for the late crop should be sown in a well-prepared seed bed, from which the seedlings should be transplanted to the garden or field. It requires 8–10 weeks for the plants to reach the proper size for setting in the field, depending on the temperature.

Celery is harvested by cutting the plants just beneath the crown. This is accomplished with a spade in small areas, and

by special garden tractor or hand tools in large plantations. The plants are usually trimmed slightly in the field. They may be packed there in crates for storage or taken to a packing shed, where they are trimmed and washed, then tied in bunches or crated for local market or shipment. Storage of celery may be combined with the blanching of it, as already indicated. Plants are placed closely in crates; the storage house or cellar should not freeze but there should be good ventilation and clean sanitary conditions. For late autumn or early winter use, late celery may be stored and bleached in field trenches, the tops being covered with straw or similar material.

The celery crop is subject to devastation by early and late blight, which produce spots and holes on the foliage. These diseases may be prevented by spraying thoroughly every week or ten days with bordeaux mixture, beginning in the seed bed. Other diseases and pests are frequent, and the grower should avail himself of the latest books and bulletins.

Celeriac (*A. graveolens* var. *rapaceum*) is grown the same as celery, for the thickened edible crown, except that no blanching is required; the leaf stalks are not eaten as they are in celery.

CELMISIA Cass. *Compositae* (Aster Tribe). About 60 spp. of per. herbs, subshrubs, or shrubs, native chiefly to New Zeal., with a few in Australia and Tasmania; lvs. all basal, with their sheaths usually tightly enfolding one another and forming a pseudostem, or imbricate on the sts., or in rosettes at ends of brs., usually leathery, petiole present or the blade narrowing directly into a sheath; fl. heads radiate, solitary, involucre broadly hemispherical, involucral bracts imbricate in several to many rows, receptacle flat or convex, pitted; disc fls. bisexual, usually yellow, ray fls. in 1 row, female, usually white, sometimes pale mauve, rarely pale yellow; achenes linear, slightly compressed or angled, hairy to glabrous, pappus usually of many minutely barbed bristles.

Planted somewhat in the Pacific Coast states. Propagated by seeds, which apparently are viable for only a relatively short time.

angustifolia Cockayne. Densely tufted subshrub, brs. covered with remains of old lvs.; lvs. in rosettes at ends of brs., linear to linear-spatulate, to 2 in. long, viscid and glabrous above, with dense, appressed, silvery-white hairs beneath, sheath about ⅝ in. long, glabrous; heads to 1½ in. across, on slender, viscid scapes to 6 in. long. New Zeal.

argentea T. Kirk. Densely branched subshrub, forming a cushion to 8 in. high and 8 in. across, brs. covered with remains of old lvs.; lvs. many, imbricate, linear-subulate, to ½ in. long, with grayish-white, appressed hairs on both sides, sheath about ½ in. long, silky-hairy on back; heads ½ in. across, essentially sessile, sunk among the upper lvs. New Zeal.

Armstrongii Petrie. Tufted herb; lvs. all basal, linear-lanceolate to linear-ensiform, 6–18 in. long, rigid, upper surface longitudinally ribbed, yellow-green, with a yellow or orange longitudinal stripe on each side of midrib, and with a delicate, silvery epidermis, lower surface with appressed, satiny hairs, margins entire, recurved; heads to 2 in. across, scapes to 10 in. long, white-floccose. New Zeal.

asteliifolia: *C. longifolia.*

coriacea (G. Forst.) Hook.f. Clump-forming, tufted per., spreading by offsets from branched runners; lvs. all basal, lanceolate to lanceolate-oblong or ovate-oblong, to 2 ft. long, entire, upper surface with longitudinal furrows and a delicate, silvery epidermis, lower surface with appressed, white, satiny hairs; heads to 4¾ in. across, scapes to 16 in. long, stout, covered with white, satiny hairs. New Zeal. Var. **stricta** Cockayne. Clumps to 6 ft. across; lvs. narrower, more rigid, more silvery above. New Zeal.

densiflora Hook.f. Tufted herb; lvs. narrowly linear-oblong, to 6 in. long, glabrous above, pubescent with appressed, white, satiny hairs beneath, margins crenate-sinuate, very slightly recurved; heads to 2 in. across, scapes to 1½ ft. long, stout, glabrous, glandular-viscid, purplish. New Zeal.

discolor Hook.f. Subshrub, sts. prostrate to sprawling, often forming broad flat-topped cushions to 3 ft. across, brs. covered with remains of old lvs.; lvs. in rosettes at ends of brs., oblong-spatulate to obovate-spatulate, to 1½ in. long, with soft appressed hairs or thin epidermis above, and very dense, appressed, white, satiny hairs beneath, margins denticulate; heads to 1¼ in. across, scapes to 6 in. long, slender, glandular-pubescent, often white-tomentose. New Zeal.

Durietzii Cockayne & Allan ex W. Martin. Robust subshrub, brs. covered with remains of old lvs.; lvs. in rosettes at ends of brs., narrow obovate to elliptic-obovate or subspatulate, to 2⅜ in. long, glabrous above, with dense, appressed, silky, soft hairs below, gradually narrowed to a 1¼ in.-long petiole; heads to 1½ in. across, scapes to 8 in. long, rather stout, stiff. New Zeal.

gracilenta Hook.f. Slender, tufted herb; lvs. all basal, linear, to 8 in. long, acute, often apiculate, upper surface with silvery epidermis, lower surface with appressed, white, almost satiny hairs, margins entire, recurved to midrib; heads to ¾ in. across, scapes to 16 in. long, slender, white-hairy. New Zeal.

Haastii Hook.f. Viscid, rather stout, low-growing subshrub forming patches to 2½ ft. across, brs. covered with the remains of old lvs.; lvs. in rosettes at ends of brs., obovate-spatulate, to 3⅛ in. long, gray-green, glabrous and usually with longitudinal grooves above, with appressed, satiny hairs beneath, margins minutely denticulate, slightly recurved; heads to 1½ in. across, scapes to 6 in. long, glabrous to densely tomentose. New Zeal.

Hectori Hook.f. Much-branched subshrub, forming patches to 3 ft. across, brs. covered with remains of old lvs.; lvs. in rosettes at ends of brs., linear-oblong to spatulate-oblong, or linear-obovate, to 1 in. long, with a dense, appressed, scurfy, white tomentum above, and appressed, satiny, white tomentum beneath; heads to 1¼ in. across, scapes to 4 in. long, rather stout, densely floccose. New Zeal.

Hookeri Cockayne. Tufted herb; lf. blades broad-lanceolate to oblong or spatulate-oblong, to 1 ft. long or sometimes longer, dark green and glabrous or thinly floccose above, with dense, appressed, lustrous, soft, white to buff hairs beneath, narrowed to a petiole or sheath to 2¾ in. long; heads to 4 in. across, scapes to 1 ft. long, stout, silky-hairy. New Zeal.

incana Hook.f. Subshrub, forming mats to about 5 ft. across, sts. stout, woody, to 4 in. in diam., covered by persistent, reflexed old lvs.; lvs. in rosettes at ends of brs., obovate-oblong, to 1⅝ in. long, both surfaces with appressed, white hairs; heads to 1⅜ in. across, scapes to 4 in. long, floccose-hairy. New Zeal.

insignis W. Martin. Tufted herb; lvs. all basal, linear to linear-oblong, to 6 in. long, sometimes even to 1 ft., rigid, upper surface dark green when fresh, but drying white-silvery, lower surface with dense, appressed, white, satiny hairs, margin entire; heads to 1½ in. across, scapes to 1 ft. long, rather stout, white-hairy. New Zeal.

lanceolata Cockayne. Tufted herb; lvs. all basal, oblong to narrow-lanceolate, to 1 ft. long, rigid, longitudinally ribbed, upper surface with a thin, loose epidermis, midrib yellowish to orange, lower surface with dense, appressed, satiny, white tomentum, margins entire, recurved, sheath about 6 in. long; heads to about 2¾ in. across, scapes to 1 ft. long, stout, more or less compressed, white-floccose. New Zeal.

longifolia Cass. [*C. asteliifolia* Hook.f.]. Tufted per.; lvs. all basal, linear or linear-lanceolate, to 15 in. long, older lvs. glabrous and glossy above, white-tomentose beneath, revolute; heads to about 1 in. across, scapes to 1½ ft. long, white-tomentose. Se. Australia, Tasmania.

Lyallii Hook.f. Tufted herb; lvs. all basal, rigid, narrow-ensiform, to 1½ ft. long, sharp-pointed, glabrous and finely striate above, almost glabrous or with thin, appressed, satiny, white hairs beneath, entire, sheath 1¼–3 in. long; heads to 2 in. across, scapes to 1 ft. long, rather slender, white-floccose. New Zeal.

Mackaui Raoul. Tufted herb, spreading by offsets from rhizomes; lvs. all basal, lanceolate to linear-lanceolate, to 20 in. long, long-acuminate, almost membranous, glabrous, rather bluish-green above, entire, petiole to 6 in. long; heads to 2 in. across, scapes to 2 ft. long, stout, nearly glabrous. New Zeal.

major Cheesem. Tufted herb; lvs. all basal, narrow-linear, to 8 in. long or sometimes to 16 in., grooved and with a thin epidermis above, with dense, appressed, silvery-white hairs beneath, margins recurved, sheath about 2⅜ in. long; heads to 1¼ in. across, scapes to 8 in. long, stout, hairy. New Zeal. Var. **brevis** Allan. All parts smaller; lvs. to 6 in. long, sheath about 1⅛ in. long; heads to 1⅜ in. across. New Zeal.

Monroi Hook.f. Tufted per.; lvs. all basal, lanceolate-elliptic to elliptic-oblong, to 6 in. long, stiff, with a silvery epidermis above, with dense, appressed, white-silvery hairs beneath, margins essentially entire, recurved, sheath to 4 in. long; heads to 1½ in. across, scapes to 8 in. long, rather stout, densely floccose. New Zeal.

petiolata Hook.f. Large, tufted herb; lvs. all basal, elliptic-oblong to narrow-oblong or lanceolate-oblong, usually 3–6 in. long, but sometimes to 1 ft., almost acute, apiculate, upper surface bright green, smooth and silky, lower surface with appressed, white or brownish, satiny hairs and purple midrib, petiole to 1¼ in. long, flat, purple, winged, widening into the ribbed, thin, 2 in.-long sheath; heads to 2¾ in. across, scapes to 8 in. long, purplish, more or less villous. New Zeal.

Petriei Cheesem. Stout, tufted herb; lvs. all basal, linear-lanceolate, 8–12 in. long, sometimes to 20 in., straight, rigid, acuminate, upper surface glabrous, with 2 longitudinal ribs more prominent than the midrib, lower surface with densely appressed, white, satiny hairs, sheath to 3⅛ in. long; heads to 1½ in. across, scapes to 20 in. long, stout, woolly. New Zeal.

prorepens Petrie. Much-branched, stout herb, brs. covered with remains of old lvs., creeping, rooting at nodes, forming patches to 3 ft. across; lvs. in rosettes at ends of brs., elliptic-oblong to obovate-oblong, to 2 in. long, but sometimes to 3⅛ in. long, both sides longitudinally wrinkled, upper glabrous, lower with thin, deciduous epidermis, margins serrate, slightly recurved, sheath very viscid; heads to 1½ in. across, scapes to 8 in. long, angled, viscid. New Zeal.

pseudolyallii (Cheesem.) Cockayne. Probably a hybrid, perhaps *C. Lyallii* × *C. spectabilis*. Tufted herb; lvs. all basal, narrow-lanceolate to narrow-oblong, to 1½ ft. long, not sharp-pointed, dark green, upper surface pleated but without regular grooves and ridges; heads to 2 in. across, scapes to 1 ft. long. New Zeal.

ramulosa Hook.f. Subshrub or small shrub, sts. procumbent to ascending; lvs. densely imbricate, linear-oblong to subulate, to ⅜ in. long, pale green and glabrous above, with dense, soft, white hairs beneath, margins strongly revolute; heads to 1 in. across, scapes to 1½ in. long, slender, densely glandular-pubescent. New Zeal.

sessiliflora Hook.f. Robust, densely branched subshrub, to 4 in., often forming patches to 3 ft. across; lvs. in compact rosettes, linear to linear-subulate, ¾–1¼ in. long, rather rigid, both sides with dense, matted, white hairs; heads to ¾ in. across, almost sessile, but scapes increasing to 2 in. in fr. New Zeal.

spectabilis Hook.f. Stout, tufted herb, bearing offsets from rhizomes and forming large patches; lvs. all basal, linear-oblong to ovate-oblong, to 6 in. long, sometimes to 10 in., very leathery, obtuse to nearly acute, usually apiculate, glabrous and glossy above, with dense, felty, yellowish or buff to white hairs beneath; heads to 2 in. across, scapes to 10 in. long, stout, densely white-floccose. New Zeal. Var. **magnifica** Allan. Very robust; lvs. to 14 in. long; scapes with long, white, glossy hairs. New Zeal.

Traversii Hook.f. Tufted herb; lvs. all basal, oblong or broad-oblong to almost lanceolate, to 10 in. long, sometimes to 16 in., glabrous above, with dense, brown, velvety hairs beneath, petioles to 6 in. long, purple; heads to 2 in. across, scapes to 20 in. long, stout, flattened, brown-velvety-hairy. New Zeal.

viscosa Hook.f. Stout subshrub, forming patches to 3 ft. across, older brs. covered with remains of old lvs.; lvs. in rosettes at ends of brs., linear-subulate to narrow-oblong, to 3⅛ in. long, sometimes to 6 in., rigid, very viscid, green and often glabrous above, with dense, appressed, soft, white, felted hairs beneath, margins minutely denticulate; heads to 1½ in. across, scapes 6–8 in. long, sometimes to 1 ft., stout, densely glandular-pubescent. New Zeal.

Walkeri T. Kirk. Mat-forming, sprawling shrub, main sts. to 6 ft. long, brs. stout, woody, covered by persistent lf. sheath; lvs. erect, then becoming reflexed, narrow-oblong to narrowly obovate-oblong, to 2 in. long, glabrous and more or less viscid above, with appressed, soft, white hairs beneath; heads to 1½ in. across, scapes to 8 in. long, slender, more or less glandular-pubescent. New Zeal.

CELOSIA L. WOOLFLOWER. *Amaranthaceae.* About 60 spp. of ann. or per. herbs, native to warm region of Amer. and Afr.; lvs. alt., entire or lobed; fls. small, not individually showy, in dense chaffy spikes, sepals 5, white or colored, petals none, stamens 5, anthers 4-celled, filaments united into a tube; ovules 2 to many.

Celosias thrive in fertile soil with plenty of moisture. Propagated by seeds.

argentea L. Ann., to 3 ft.; lvs. linear to ovate-lanceolate, to 2 in. long; fls. silvery-white, in erect or drooping spikes 1–4 in. long. A polyploid complex; rarely cult., but weedy and widely distributed in tropics. Var. *cristata: C. cristata.*

Childsii: *C. cristata* Childsii Group.

cristata L. [*C. argentea* var. *cristata* (L.) O. Kuntze]. COCKSCOMB. A tetraploid cultigen similar to *A. argentea;* sts. and brs. terminated by usually enlarged spikes variously crested, plumed, or feathered, ranging from white to yellow, purple, and shades of red; lvs. sometimes variegated. There are many cvs., most of which fall into groups such as the Childsii Group, with ball-like knobs at end of each br.; Nana Group, plants dwarf; the Plumosa Group, FEATHERED AMARANTH, infl. feathery; the Spicata Group, fls. silvery-rose, in slender spikes.

globosa Schinz. Not in cult.; material offered under this name is referable to *C. cristata.*

spicata (Thouars) K. Spreng. Not in cult.; but material offered under this name is referable to *C. cristata.*

CELSIA L. *Scrophulariaceae.* Between 30 and 40 spp. of ann., bien., or per. herbs, chiefly from the Medit. region and Asia, one from S. Afr.; allied to *Verbascum* but differing in having 4 stamens instead of 5.

Propagated by seeds sown in the greenhouse, the plants set out in the open after all danger of frost is past; also by cuttings.

Arcturus (L.) Jacq. CRETAN BEAR'S-TAIL. Pubescent bien. or per., to 1½ ft.; upper lvs. alt., ovate, toothed, lower lvs. lyrate-pinnatifid; fls. long-pedicelled, in loose racemes, corolla yellow, filaments violet-bearded. Crete, Asia Minor.

betonicifolia Desf. Hairy or subglabrous per., to 3 ft.; lvs. oblong-ovate to oblong-lanceolate, toothed, glabrous or subglabrous above, hairy beneath; fls. on long pedicels, in racemes, corolla yellow, to 1½ in. across, shorter filaments densely yellow- or purple-bearded, longer ones glabrous, hairy at base. N. Algeria.

cretica L.f. CRETAN MULLEIN. Stout, hairy bien., to 6 ft.; upper lvs. ovate, clasping, toothed, lower lvs. lyrate-pinnatifid; fls. almost sessile in loose racemes, corolla yellow, marked with purple, shorter filaments violet-bearded, longer ones glabrous. Medit. region.

horizontalis Moench. Ann., bien., or per., to 2½ ft.; lvs. opp., lyrate-pinnatifid, to 10 in. long, dentate; fls. in many-fld. racemes, corolla yellow, with 5 purple-brown spots in throat, about 1 in. across, filaments with white hairs at apex and purple-violet hairs in the middle. E. Medit. region.

orientalis L. Puberulent or glabrous ann., to 3 ft., sts. slender, very leafy; lvs. 2-pinnate, segms. linear to oblong; fls. in long, loose racemes, corolla yellow, filaments yellow-hairy. N. Medit. region.

pontica Boiss. Hairy bien., to 5 ft.; lower lvs. oblong, to 9 in. long, obtuse, somewhat cordate, petioled, upper lvs. ovate, acuminate; fls. in racemes to 2 ft. long, calyx glandular-hairy, corolla yellow. Armenia.

CELTIS L. HACKBERRY, NETTLE TREE, SUGARBERRY. *Ulmaceae.* About 70 spp. of trees or sometimes shrubs, usually deciduous, native to temp. regions of N. Hemisphere, a few spp. in the tropics; lvs. alt., elmlike, asymmetrical at base, often 3-nerved, rough above; fls. small, unisexual or bisexual; fr. a small, round or ovoid drupe, solitary on a slender stalk. The cult. spp. are difficult to distinguish.

Useful as a shade tree; the leaves turn yellow in autumn. Most species hardy in the northern and north-central states. They are not particular as to soil. In a few species the small fruits are sweet and edible. Propagated by seeds, layers, and cuttings in the autumn, or sometimes grafted on *C. occidentalis.*

australis L. MEDITERRANEAN H., EUROPEAN N.T., LOTE TREE, HONEYBERRY. To 80 ft.; lvs. lanceolate to ovate-lanceolate, to 6 in. long, long-acuminate, rounded or cordate, sharply toothed, scabrous above, grayish-green and pubescent beneath; fr. globose, to ¼ in. across, dark purple, peduncle to 1¼ in. long. Medit. region. Zone 7.

Bungeana Blume. Tree, to 50 ft.; lvs. ovate to ovate-lanceolate, to 3 in. long, slightly toothed only above middle, greenish on both surfaces, glossy above; fr. black, round, to ¼ in. across, peduncle to ¾ in. long, stone white. Ne. Asia. Zone 6. Var. **jessoensis**: *C. jessoensis.*

Douglasii: *C. reticulata.*

japonica: *C. sinensis.*

jessoensis G. Koidz. [*C. Bungeana* var. *jessoensis* (G. Koidz.) Kudo]. Tree, brs. puberulous; lvs. ovate, to 4 in. long, acuminate, rounded to obtuse, teeth incurved except near base, mostly glabrous above, glaucous and pubescent beneath, especially on nerves; drupe black, to ¼ in. across, peduncle to 1 in. long. Japan, Korea. Zone 6.

Kraussiana Bernh. To 70 ft.; twigs reddish, ferruginous-pubescent when young; lvs. ovate, to 3 in. long, acuminate, asymmetrical at base, serrate, or often entire below middle; fr. rounded, to ¼ in. across, peduncle to 1 in. long. Arabia, trop. and s. Afr. Wood used for various purposes.

laevigata Willd. [*C. mississippiensis* Spach]. SUGARBERRY, MISSISSIPPI H. To 100 ft.; lvs. to 4 in. long, long-acuminate, usually entire, thin; fr. orange-red, becoming dark purple. Fla., w. to s. Ind., Tex., ne. Mex. Zone 6.

mississippiensis: *C. laevigata.*

occidentalis L. [*C. occidentalis* var. *crassifolia* (Lam.) A. Gray; *C. pumila* Pursh]. NETTLE TREE, SUGARBERRY. To 120 ft.; lvs. to 5 in. long, toothed, shining above, paler beneath; fr. orange-red to dark purple. Que. to N.C. and Ala. Zone 4. Wood used for various purposes.

pumila: *C. occidentalis.*

reticulata Torr. [*C. Douglasii* Planch.]. To 40 ft.; lvs. ovate, to 2½ in. long, acute or acuminate, rounded or subcordate, entire, or with few coarse teeth above middle, scabrous above, reticulate and slightly pubescent beneath; fr. orange-red, to ⅜ in. across, peduncle to ⅜ in. long. W. U.S. and nw. Mex. Zone 6.

sinensis Pers. [*C. japonica* Planch.]. JAPANESE H. To 60 ft.; lvs. to 4 in. long, wavy-toothed, pubescent beneath when young; fr. dark orange. China, Korea, Japan. The warmer parts of Zone 7.

Tournefortii Lam. To 20 ft.; lvs. to 3 in. long, toothed, bluish- or grayish-green; fr. reddish-yellow. Se. Eur., w. Asia.

CENTAUREA L. [*Aetheopappus* Cass.]. KNAPWEED. *Compositae* (Carduus Tribe). Between 400 and 500 spp. of ann., bien., or per. herbs, or rarely subshrubs, native chiefly in the Medit. region and Near East, with 2 spp. in N. Amer., 1 in Australia, a few in n. Asia and n. Eur., some spp. common in temp. regions as introduced weeds, sts. unbranched to corymbosely branched; lvs. basal or alt. on the sts., entire to pinnately dissected, usually not spiny; fl. heads solitary at ends of brs., long-peduncled to sessile, and partly surrounded by uppermost lvs., or sometimes in small clusters, involucre campanulate, ovoid, globose, or cylindrical, involucral bracts imbricate in several rows, entire or more frequently with ciliate to pectinate or spiny appendage, often scarious or scarious-margined, receptacle flat, densely bristly; fls. blue to shades of purple, or yellow to white, all tubular and bisexual, or the outer enlarged, raylike, and sterile, anthers tailed or not; achenes often compressed, with an oblique or lateral point of attachment, smooth and shiny, pappus absent or of several graduated rows of bristles or scales.

The genus offers a wide variety of ornamentals, from flower garden annuals to bedding and foliage plants, basket plants, and stout thistle-like species for background effects. The annuals are grown from seeds sown directly in the garden or started earlier indoors. *C. Cineraria* and other foliage types are increased from cuttings taken in Sept. and carried over winter indoors or from seeds sown in late winter. *C. Cyanus*, the bachelor's-button, is an easily grown hardy annual.

aggregata Fisch. & C. A. Mey. ex DC. Bien. or per., to 3 ft., sts. wandlike, cobwebby; basal lvs. lyrate, st. lvs. oblong, sessile; heads 2–7 in clusters, involucre oblong-cylindrical, involucral bracts glabrous, fringed; fls. purple, the outer not enlarged, none raylike. Asia Minor to Iran.

alpestris: *C. Scabiosa* subsp.

amara L. Per., to 2 ft., sts. decumbent to erect; lower lvs. oblanceolate, to 6 in. long, sinuate-denticulate, petioled, upper lvs. linear to linear-lanceolate, to about 4 in. long, sessile, successively reduced upward, the uppermost shorter than involucre; heads to 1¼ in. across, involucre ovoid, involucral bracts with orbicular, erose appendage; fls. purplish, the outer enlarged, raylike; pappus absent. Medit. region.

americana Nutt. BASKET FLOWER, THORNLESS THISTLE, CARDO-DEL-VALLE. Stout, erect ann., to 6 ft., sts. often enlarged directly below head; lvs. to 4 in. long, mostly entire, gland-dotted, scabrous, sessile, lower lvs. narrowly obovate, upper lanceolate; heads solitary, to 4 in. across, involucre campanulate, involucral bracts with lanceolate-triangular, straw-colored appendage fringed with 4–6 pairs of lateral teeth; fls. rose, the outer enlarged, raylike. Mo. to La., w. to e. Ariz. and adjacent Mex.

atrata: *C. Triumfettii.*

austriaca: *C. phrygia.*

Behen L. Bien. or per., to 5 ft., sts. sparingly papillose-pubescent, winged by decurrent lf. bases; basal lvs. oblong, entire or pinnatifid to lyrate, to 1 ft. long, petioled, st. lvs. successively reduced upward, oblong, entire, sessile, decurrent, all lvs. veiny with elevated nerves; heads to 1½–2 in. across, involucre ovoid-conical, involucral bracts leathery, straw-colored, glabrous, entire, mucronate; fls. yellow. Asia Minor and s. Russia to Iran.

bella Trautv. Per., to 16 in., forming a broad, low cushion, sts. cobwebby; lvs. lyrate-pinnatifid, to 5 in. long, with entire, elliptic to obovate segms., glandular-punctate above, white-tomentose beneath, heads about 1¾ in. across, involucre ovoid, involucral bracts with orbicular, scarious, lacerate appendage; fls. pinkish-lavender to pale purple, outer fls. enlarged, raylike. Caucasus.

candidissima: *C. Cineraria*, but plants cult. as *C. candidissima* are usually *Senecio Vira-vira.*

Cineraria L. [*C. candidissima* Lam.]. DUSTY-MILLER. Erect, branching, white-tomentose per., to 3 ft.; lvs. to about 1 ft. long, 1–2-pinnatifid, segms. obtuse; heads about 1½ in. across, involucre round-ovoid, involucral bracts with an ovate appendage with black, scarious, long-ciliate margins and a terminal thickened bristle; fls. purple, the outer raylike but only slightly larger than the inner; pappus copious. S. Eur.

conifera: *Leuzea conifera.*

Crupina: *Crupina vulgaris.*

Cyanus L. CORNFLOWER, BACHELOR'S-BUTTON, BLUEBOTTLE. Slender ann. or winter ann., to 2 ft., sts. wiry, cottony when young; lower lvs. lyrate-pinnatifid or narrowly oblanceolate, entire or with few remote teeth, petioled, upper lvs. linear or linear-lanceolate, entire, sessile, all with grayish, cottony hairs; heads to 1½ in. across, involucre ovoid, outer involucral bracts with white teeth, the inner with brown teeth; fls. usually blue, sometimes purple or pink, the outer enlarged, raylike. Eur., Near East; now a cosmopolitan weed, escaped from cult. Cv. 'Alba'. Fls. white.

dealbata Willd. Per., to 2½ ft.; lvs. 1–2-pinnatifid, glabrous above, white-tomentose beneath, lower lvs. to 1½ ft. long, petioled, st. lvs. sessile or nearly so; heads solitary, 2 in. across or more, involucre ovoid-globose, involucral bracts with deeply fringed, scarious margins; fls. rose-purple to pink, the outer enlarged, raylike. Caucasus. Cv. 'Rosea'. Foliage silvery; fls. rose-pink. Cv. 'Steenbergii' [*C. Steenbergii* Hort.]. Inner fls. white, outer fls. purplish-red.

depressa Bieb. Ann., to 2 ft., sts. and foliage grayish, cobwebby; lower lvs. oblong to oblong-spatulate, to 9¼ in. long, lyrate-pinnatifid to entire, petioled, upper st. lvs. linear-lanceolate; heads about 1½ in. across, involucre ovoid, involucral bracts with white to tawny, scarious, toothed margins; fls. blue-violet, the outer enlarged, raylike. Caucasus, Iran.

diffusa Lam. Ann. or bien., to about 2 ft., sts. diffusely and divaricately branched; basal lvs. 1–2-pinnatifid, to about 5 in. long, petioled, deciduous, st. lvs. oblong-lanceolate, pinnatifid, to 1½ in. long, successively reduced upward, all cobwebby at first, then sparsely scabrous-puberulent; heads solitary or in clusters of 2–3, to about ⅜ in. across, involucre cylindrical, involucral bracts spinose-ciliate, with a slender apical spine; fls. yellowish, white, or red, the outer not enlarged; pappus absent. Se. Eur.; sporadic as a weed in N. Amer.

Fritschii Hayek. Per., to 6 ft.; lvs. pinnately dissected, segms. linear-lanceolate, toothed or entire, glabrous and glossy above, scabrous on margins and on nerves beneath; heads solitary, about 2 in. across, involucre ovoid-globose to globose, involucral bracts tomentose, with a fimbriate, black apex; fls. rose to purple. Balkans.

gymnocarpa Moris & De Not. DUSTY-MILLER. Bushy, subshrubby per., to 3 ft., felty-white-tomentose throughout; lvs. 1–2-pinnately dissected, to 8 in. long, lower petioled, upper reduced, sessile; heads to about 1½ in. across, involucre ovoid, involucral bracts with ciliate appendage; fls. rose-violet or purple, the outer enlarged, raylike; pappus absent. Capri.

hypoleuca DC. Erect per., to 1½ ft.; lower lvs. lyrate, to 1 ft. long, upper lvs. oblong, all dull green and glabrous above, white-tomentose beneath; heads solitary, involucre ovoid, involucral bracts with a dark, oblong-lanceolate, deeply fimbriate-margined appendage; fls. rosy-pink, the outer enlarged, raylike. Asia Minor.

iberica Trevir. ex K. Spreng. Cobwebby-pubescent per., to about 3 ft., sts. divaricate; basal lvs. lyrate-pinnatifid to pinnatifid, to 6 in. long, st. lvs. reduced, sessile; heads to about 1 in. across, involucre ovoid, outer involucral bracts leathery, with a terminal stout spine to ¾ in. long, the inner scarious, unarmed; fls. purplish-pink. S. Eur., w. Asia; an infrequent weed in Calif.

imperialis Hausskn. ex Bornm. Not in cult.; material grown under this name is *C. moschata* cv.

Jacea L. BROWN K. Per., to 4 ft.; basal lvs. lanceolate to ovate, elliptic or oblanceolate, to 4 in. long, entire to somewhat pinnatifid, petioled, st. lvs. reduced, lanceolate, sessile, all glabrous to somewhat cobwebby; heads solitary, to 1½ in. across, involucre ovoid-globose, involucral bracts with tan to dark brown, scarious, irregularly lacerate margins; fls. rose-purple, the outer enlarged, raylike; pappus absent. Eur., N. Afr., n. and w. Asia; rather well-established weed in N. Amer.

kopetdaghensis Iljin. Per., to 20 in.; sts. erect, usually many, branched, cobwebby; lvs. oblong, entire; heads solitary, about ½ in. across, involucre ovoid to oblong-ovoid, outer and middle involucral bracts blackish-brown with whitish, ciliate margins and a terminal spine; fls. yellow. Turkmen S.S.R.

Kotschyana Heuff. Erect per., to 3 ft.; lower lvs. obovate-oblong, to about 7 in. long, coarsely toothed to lyrate or pinnatifid into lanceolate, dentate or lobed segms., usually scabrous beneath on veins, petioled, upper lvs. oblong, usually dentate or entire; heads to 1½ in. across, involucre globose, involucral bracts with black, triangular appendage with whitish, ciliate margin; fls. dark purple, the outer not enlarged. Balkans.

macrocephala Pushk. ex Willd. Erect per., to 3 ft., sts. simple, hollow, hairy, enlarged below the heads; lvs. oblanceolate, lanceolate-ovate, or elliptic, entire to shallowly serrate, scabrous, the lower to 1 ft. long, petioled, the upper reduced, slightly decurrent; heads solitary, 3–4 in. across, involucre globose, involucral bracts rusty, scarious, fringed; fls. golden-yellow, the outer not enlarged. Caucasus.

maculosa Lam. Bushy bien. or short-lived per., to 4 ft., sts. wiry, wandlike, with paniculate-corymbose branching, scabrous; lower lvs. pinnate to pinnatifid into linear or lanceolate segms., gray-pubescent, upper lvs. reduced; heads to 1 in. across, involucre ovoid or oblong, involucral bracts striate, unarmed, scarious-margined, with pectinate, black apex; fls. pink to pale purple, the outer enlarged, raylike. Eur.; commonly established weed in N. Amer.

Margaritae: *C. moschata* cv. 'Alba'.

maritima Dufour. Erect, branched per., to 2 ft., sts. white-cottony-hairy; lvs. lyrate-pinnatifid, spiny-dentate, white-hairy beneath, upper lvs. semiclasping, decurrent; involucre globose, involucral bracts with 5–7, spreading, apical spines; fls. purple, the outer not enlarged and raylike. Spain. Cv. 'Diamond': *Senecio Cineraria*.

Marschalliana K. Spreng. Per., to 1 ft., sts. procumbent to ascending, gray-tomentose; basal lvs. ovate-lanceolate, to about 5 in. long, pinnatifid, petioled, upper lvs. reduced, lyrate, green and pubescent above, gray-tomentose beneath; heads to ⅝ in. across, involucre globose, involucral bracts with triangular-ovate, recurved, dentate, dark brown appendage; fls. pink, the outer enlarged, raylike. E. Eur. to Siberia.

montana L. MOUNTAIN BLUET. Per., to about 1½ ft., often stoloniferous, sts. usually unbranched; lvs. lanceolate or elliptic to obovate-oblanceolate, entire, cobwebby or silvery-tomentose, lower lvs. to 7½ in. long, petioled, the upper successively reduced, the uppermost sessile, decurrent; heads solitary, to 3 in. across, involucre ovoid, involucral bracts with black, fringed margins; fls. blue-violet, outer fls. enlarged, raylike, to 1 in. long. Cent. Eur. Cv. 'Alba'. Fls. white, Cv. 'Coerulea'. Fls. blue.

moschata L. [*C. suaveolens* L.]. SWEET-SULTAN. Erect ann., to 3 ft., sts. bright green, branched in lower part; lvs. lyrate to pinnatifid to simple and only toothed, sparsely pubescent; heads solitary, long-peduncled, to 2 in. across, involucre ovoid-globose, involucral bracts entire; fls. yellow, white, pink, or purple, fragrant, the outer much enlarged, raylike. Orient. Cv. 'Alba' [*C. Margaritae* Hort.]. Fls. white. Cv. 'Imperialis' [*C. imperialis* Hort., not Hausskn. ex Bornm.]. Resulting from crossing typical *C. moschata* with cv. 'Alba', sts. 4 ft.; fls. white, rose lilac, or purple. Cv. 'Purpurea'. Fls. purple. Cv. 'Rosea'. Fls. rose-pink to purplish-pink.

muricata: *Amberboa muricata.*

nigra L. BLACK K., HARDHEADS, SPANISH-BUTTONS. Coarse, rough-pubescent per., to 2½ ft.; basal lvs. elliptic-lanceolate to elliptic, to 6 in. long, sinuate, petioled, st. lvs. reduced, oblong-lanceolate, sessile; heads to 1½ in across, involucre ovoid-globose, involucral bracts dark brown to black, usually deeply pectinate; fls. rose-purple, the outer mostly not enlarged. Eur.; naturalized in N. Amer. Var. **radiata** DC. Involucral bracts mostly tawny; outer fls. slightly larger than inner. Eur.; naturalized in ne. N. Amer.

orientalis L. Erect, branched per., to 3 ft., sts. sparsely cobwebby; lvs. leathery, 1–2-pinnatifid, lower lvs. to 1 ft. long, petioled, the upper successively reduced, glabrous to scabrous, sessile; heads solitary, to 2½ in. across, involucre ovoid-globose, involucral bracts chestnut-brown, with tan or reddish, long-ciliate margins; fls. yellow, the outer enlarged, raylike. Se. Eur.

phrygia L. [*C. austriaca* Willd.]. Erect per., to 2½ ft., sts. corymbosely branched in upper part or sometimes simple, rough-hairy; lower lvs. broadly ovate to lanceolate-ovate, to 1 ft. long, hairy, petioled, upper lvs. successively reduced, rounded or nearly cordate at base, sessile; heads to 2 in. across, involucre ovoid or ovoid-globose, involucral bracts with brownish-black, pectinate-ciliate appendage recurved at apex; fls. rose, the outer enlarged, raylike. Scandinavia to the Balkans and Russia.

pulcherrima Willd. [*Aetheopappus pulcherrimus* (Willd.) Cass.]. Erect per., to 2½ ft., sts. simple; lvs. pinnately dissected, to 7 in. long, green above, gray-tomentose beneath, petioled, the upper successively reduced, the uppermost sessile; heads solitary, to about 2–3 in. across, long-peduncled, involucre globose, involucral bracts scarious, the inner white, the outer brown, fringed; fls. purple, the outer enlarged, raylike. Caucasus, Asia Minor.

ragusina L. DUSTY-MILLER. Per., to 2 ft., sts. short; lvs. crowded, in rosettes, first lvs. broadly ovate, entire to toothed, later lvs. pinnatifid, to about 8 in. long, densely white-tomentose and felty on both sides, petioled; heads solitary or in clusters of 2–3, to about 2 in. across, long-peduncled, involucre globose, involucral bracts with a short brown to black, ciliate appendage terminating in a long spine; fls. bright yellow, the outer not enlarged. Dalmatia.

Rothrockii Greenm. Ann., to 3½ ft., sts. erect, sparingly branched above, essentially glabrous; lvs. lanceolate to oblong-lanceolate, to about 5 in. long, sessile, often clasping; heads solitary, to 6 in. across, involucre somewhat campanulate, involucral bracts chestnut-brown at apex, with 8–12 slender marginal teeth; inner fls. yellow, the outer enlarged, raylike, purple. Se. Ariz., sw. New Mex. to Oaxaca (Mex.).

ruthenica Lam. Glabrous per., to 5 ft., sts. wandlike, corymbosely branched; lvs. pinnately dissected, segms. serrate, lower lvs. to 10 in. long, the upper successively reduced; heads solitary, to 2½ in. across, long-peduncled, involucre ovoid-globose, outer involucral bracts rounded, the inner elliptic, all brown at apex, scarious-margined but not fringed; fls. sulphur-yellow. Romania to Caucasus and Siberia.

Scabiosa L. Per., to 5 ft., sts. erect, usually branched above middle, root crown enclosed by persistent lf. bases; basal lvs. oblanceolate in outline, to 10 in. long, pinnatifid or toothed, st. lvs. reduced, sessile, all usually hispid on both sides; heads solitary, to 2 in. across, involucre ovoid-globose, involucral bracts with blackish-brown, horseshoe-shaped, fringed appendage; fls. purple, the outer usually enlarged, raylike. Eur., Caucasus, w. Asia; naturalized locally in e. U.S. Cv. 'Splendens'. Fls. violet. Subsp. **alpestris** (Hegetschw.) Hayek. Sts. to 2½ ft., usually unbranched; fls. purple-red. Cent. Eur.

simplicicaulis Boiss. & Huet. Rhizomatous per., to about 1½ ft., sts. decumbent, unbranched; lvs. mostly basal, pinnately dissected, to 5 in. long including petiole, glabrous above, white-hairy beneath, lvs. reduced upward; heads solitary, to about 2 in. across, long-peduncled, involucre ovoid, involucral bracts with a wide, dark brown appendage with white, hyaline, lacerate margin; fls. pale rose-purple, the outer enlarged, raylike. Armenia.

Steenbergii: *C. dealbata* cv.

stenolepis A. Kern. Erect per., to 3 ft., sts. cobwebby; lvs. simple, elliptic, lanceolate, or ovate, the lower to 10 in. long, petioled, upper lvs. reduced, sessile, all more or less cobwebby-gray-pubescent; heads solitary or clustered, to about 1½ in. across, involucre ovoid, involucral bracts with a dark, attenuated, plumose appendage; fls. purplish, the outer enlarged, raylike. Cent. and e. Eur.

stenophylla Dufour. Slender, much-branched per., to 2½ ft. or more; lvs. narrowly ovate-oblong to lanceolate-linear, lyrate to pinnatifid or sinuate; heads about 1 in. across, involucre ovoid-oblong, involucral bracts with 3 yellowish spines; fls. purple, rarely white. Spain, Portugal. By some authorities considered to be only a var. of *C. aspera*.

suaveolens: *C. moschata*.

Szovitsiana Boiss. Bien. or per., to 3 ft., sts. corymbosely branched; basal lvs. to 1 ft. long, petioled, pinnately parted into 7–8 pairs of lanceolate segms., terminal segm. triangular, divaricately 3-parted, st. lvs. oblong to ovate, all scabrous on margins; heads to about ¾ in. across, enclosed by oblong-ovate, leafy bracts, involucre ovoid-conical, involucral bracts entire, sometimes with a small, early-deciduous appendage; fls. pale yellow. Russian Armenia.

Triumfettii All. [*C. atrata* Willd.]. Stoloniferous per., to 2 ft., sts. erect, unbranched; lvs. linear-lanceolate to ovate-lanceolate, white-tomentose-lanate on both sides, entire or the lower lvs. sometimes sinuate-dentate or lobed, lowest lvs. petioled, the upper lvs. successively more nearly sessile and decurrent; heads solitary, to 2½ in. across, involucre ovoid, involucral bracts with brown to black, triangular, pectinate-ciliate-margined appendage; fls. blue to purple-red, the outer enlarged, raylike. Cent. and s. Eur.

uliginosa Brot. Erect per., to 5 ft., sts. usually unbranched; lower lvs. lanceolate, to 1 ft. long, dentate, pubescent, petioled, st. lvs. linear-lanceolate, nearly entire, nearly sessile, the uppermost decurrent; heads about 1¼ in. across, involucre globose, involucral bracts entire except for 3–7 apical teeth; fls. blue. Portugal.

uniflora L. Per., to about 1½ ft., forming a woody root crown with age, sts. unbranched; lvs. simple, silvery-white-pubescent, lower lvs. linear-lanceolate to oblanceolate, toothed, petioled, upper lvs. lanceolate, entire, sessile; heads solitary, to 2 in. across, sessile, involucre nearly globose, involucral bracts with long, linear-subulate, plumose, reflexed appendage; fls. purple, the outer enlarged, raylike. S. Eur.

CENTAURIUM J. Hill [*Erythraea* Borkh.]. CENTAURY. *Gentianaceae*. About 30 spp. of slender, mostly ann. or bien. herbs, widely distributed in the N. Hemisphere, one extending s. to Chile and another to Australia; lvs. opp., simple, entire; fls. red or rose, in cymes, usually 4-merous, anthers often spirally twisted after flowering, style with 2-lobed, capitate stigma; fr. a caps.

Sometimes cultivated in the rock garden and in borders. They thrive in light sandy loam and require protection from sun and frost. Propagated by seeds, the perennials by cuttings and division.

Beyrichii (Torr. & A. Gray) B. L. Robinson. Sts. erect, to 8 in.; lvs. to 1 in. long; corolla deep pink, 1 in. across, tube at first as long as calyx, becoming twice as long. Ark. to Tex.

chilense (Pers.) Druce [*Erythraea chilensis* Pers.]. Sts. erect, to 10 in., usually branched above; lvs. elliptic-lanceolate, 1-nerved; fls. on short pedicels. Chile, Uruguay.

chloodes (Brot.) Samp. [*C. confertum* (Pers.) Druce; *Erythraea chloodes* (Brot.) Gren. & Godr.]. Ann. or bien. forming rosettes, sts. many, to 4 in.; lvs. oblong, obtuse; fls. rose. Eur.

confertum: *C. chloodes*.

Erythraea Rafn [*C. minus* of auth., not Moench; *C. umbellatum* Hort.; *Erythraea Centaurium* of auth., not (L.) Pers.]. CENTAURY. Bien., to 20 in., sts. solitary or several, usually branched above; lvs. of basal rosette obovate to elliptic, to 2 in. long, ¾ in. wide, attenuate towards base, st. lvs. smaller, narrower; fls. in corymblike cymes, calyx usually ½–¾ as long as corolla lobes, corolla pink to pink-purple or white. Eurasia.

exaltata (Griseb.) W. F. Wight. Sts. simple or branched to 14 in.; lvs. of basal rosette oblong-elliptic to oblong-lanceolate, to 1¼ in. long, st. lvs. smaller; fls. pedicelled, terminal on brs. and in forks, calyx lobes to ⅜ in. long, corolla pink to white, tube to ⅜ in. long. E. Wash., s. to Baja Calif., e. to Idaho, Nev., Utah, Ariz.

floribundum (Benth.) B. L. Robinson. Sts. usually several from base, to 20 in.; basal lvs. not in a rosette, obovate, to ¾ in. long, st. lvs. oblong-ovate to oblong-linear; fls. pedicelled and sessile, in cymes, corolla pink. Calif.

Massonii: *C. scilloides*.

minus: see *C. Erythraea*.

Muehlenbergii (Griseb.) W. F. Wight. Sts. erect, unbranched or branched, to 12 in.; lvs. lanceolate-oblong to ovate, to 2 in. long; fls. sessile or nearly so, corolla pink, tube about ½ in. long. Calif., Ore.

portense: *C. scilloides*.

pulchellum (Swartz) Druce [*C. ramosissimum* (Vill.) Druce; *Erythraea ramosissima* (Vill.) Pers.]. Sts. slender, unbranched to much-branched, to 6 in.; lvs. lanceolate to elliptic, to ¾ in. long, sessile; fls. on short pedicels, corolla pink, about ¼ in. across, tube slightly longer than calyx. Eur., w. and cent. Asia; naturalized in N. Amer.

ramosissimum: *C. pulchellum*.

scilloides (L.f.) Samp. [*C. Massonii* Hort.; *C. portense* Brot. ex Butch.; *Erythraea Massonii* Hort.; *E. scilloides* (L.f.) Chaub. ex Puel]. Tufted per., sts. erect or semiprostrate, 2–3 in. or more; lvs. orbicular to oblong-lanceolate, usually concave, to ¾ in. long, sessile; fls. bright pink or deep rose to white. W. Eur. and Azores.

umbellatum: see *C. Erythraea*.

venustum (A. Gray) B. L. Robinson [*Erythraea venusta* A. Gray]. Ann., sts. erect, usually branched above, 6 in. to as much as 10 in.; lvs. oblong to oblong-ovate, to 1 in. long, sessile; corolla pink, about 1 in. across, lobes as long as tube. Calif.

CENTRADENIA G. Don. *Melastomataceae*. About 5 spp. of herbs or subshrubs, native to s. Mex. and Cent. Amer.; lvs. lanceolate, entire, with oblique bases, those of a pair unequal; fls. small, pink or white in often panicled cymes, calyx lobes broad and short; fr. a caps.

Centradenias are grown in greenhouses for the showy, colored leaves and flowers. They thrive in soil composed of rich leafmold and sharp sand. Propagated by cuttings.

floribunda Planch. Small shrub, sts. obscurely angled, wiry, pubescent; lvs. narrowly lanceolate, 1–3 in. long, 3-nerved, glaucous-green beneath; infl. panicled, 1½–4 in. long; fls. ⁵⁄₁₆ in. across, white inside, pink outside. Spring. Guatemala.

grandifolia (Schlechtend.) Endl. Shrub, to 5 ft., sts. 4-winged; lvs. oblong-lanceolate, 3–6 in. long, curved, very unequal-sided, minutely ciliate, red beneath; cymes on very slender peduncles; fls. ⅝ in. across, rose-pink. Spring. S. Mex. and Guatemala.

CENTRANTHUS DC. [*Kentranthus* Neck.]. CENTRANTH. *Valerianaceae*. About 12 spp. of ann. or per. herbs or subshrubs, native to Eur. and the Medit. region; lvs. opp., simple; fls. small, white or red, in dense terminal clusters, calyx pappuslike, with 5–15 narrow divisions, corolla tubular, 5-parted, spurred at base, stamen 1, ovary inferior; fr. a 1-celled, 1-seeded nut.

A few species are grown in the flower garden, *C. ruber* being common. Propagated by seeds and division.

albus: a listed name of no botanical standing, probably *C. ruber* cv.

angustifolius (Mill.) DC. Per., to 2 ft.; lvs. linear to linear-lanceolate, to 3 in. long, entire; fls. rose, to ½ in. long, fragrant. S. Eur.

macrosiphon Boiss. LONG-SPURRED VALERIAN. Ann., to 2 ft.; lvs. ovate, to 3 in. long, toothed to lobed, glaucous; fls. deep rose, about ½ in. long. Spain.

ruber (L.) DC. [*Kentranthus ruber* (L.) Druce; *Valeriana coccinea* Hort.; *V. rubra* L.]. RED VALERIAN, JUPITER'S-BEARD, FOX'S-BRUSH. Compact per., to 3 ft., glaucous, glabrous; lvs. lanceolate to ovate, to 4 in. long, slightly toothed to entire, sessile; fls. many, crimson to pale red, about ½ in. long, fragrant. Eur. and N. Afr. to Asia Minor; escaped and naturalized locally in Calif. Cvs. are: '**Albus**', fls. white; '**Atrococcineus**', fls. deep red; '**Roseus**' [*Valeriana rosea* Hort.], fls. rose.

CENTROLOBIUM Mart. ex Benth. *Leguminosae* (subfamily *Faboideae*). Three spp. of trees of trop. Amer.; lvs. alt., large, odd-pinnate, the terminal lfts. largest; fls. papilionaceous, in large, terminal panicles, calyx 4-parted nearly to middle, standard orbicular, reflexed, stamens 10, united; fr. an ovoid or globose, spiny legume, with large wing, samaralike, seeds few.

tomentosum Guillem. ex Benth. Large tree, with foliage and infl. rusty-pubescent; lfts. in 6–8 pairs, leathery, ovate or oblong, to 6 in. long, acuminate; fls. rose, standard ⅝ in. long; fr. with wing to 6 in. long, rusty-tomentose. E. Brazil.

CENTROPOGON K. Presl. *Lobeliaceae*. Over 200 spp. of robust herbs to small shrubs, native to trop. Amer.; lvs. alt., toothed; fls. pedicelled, solitary in axils of lvs. or bracts, or racemose, corolla mostly red but varying to orange, pink, white, or yellowish-green, 2-lipped, tube elongate, not split, often expanded apically, filaments united at base of corolla, anther tube exserted, often curved apically, lower 2 anthers tufted-pubescent or triangular-appendaged at apex; fr. berrylike, many-seeded. See *Hypsela*.

Particularly well-suited for hanging baskets in a warm greenhouse; propagated by cuttings over heat.

Austin-Smithii: *C. solanifolius*.

costaricensis: a listed name of no botanical standing, possibly for *C. costaricae* (Vatke) McVaugh or *C. ferrugineus* var. *costaricanus* (Planch. & Ørst.) McVaugh.

solanifolius Benth. [*C. Austin-Smithii* Standl.]. Herb or suffrutescent, to 5 ft.; lvs. ovate to elliptic, 3–6 in. long; fls. in racemes or clustered, bracts leafy, corolla scarlet, with yellowish lobes, 1¼–2¼ in. long, filaments yellow, anther tube ¼–⅜ in. long, gray-violet, with darker stripes, lower anthers appendaged at tip with a triangular brush of hairs; fr. depressed-globose, ¼–½ in. in diam. Costa Rica and Venezuela, s. to Ecuador.

CENTROSEMA (DC.) Benth. BUTTERFLY PEA, CONCHITA. *Leguminosae* (subfamily *Faboideae*). About 45–50 spp. of mostly scandent herbs of W. Hemisphere; lvs. alt., pinnate, usually of 3 lfts.; fls. axillary, large, showy, purplish to pink or white, standard broad, flat, spurred near base; fr. a linear, flat legume, with thickened margins.

Propagated by seeds.

virginianum (L.) Benth. Per.; lfts. ovate to linear-lanceolate, to 2 in. long; fls. purple to whitish; fr. to 5 in. long and ⅛ in. wide. E. N. Amer., trop. Amer.; Afr.

CEPHAELIS Swartz. *Rubiaceae*. About 100 spp. of usually shrubs or small trees, native to trop. Amer., but also trop. Afr. and Asia; lvs. opp., stipules separate or united, usually persistent; fls. in terminal heads subtended by involucral bracts, corolla funnelform or salverform, tube straight, lobes 5; fr. a drupe, seeds 2.

The dried rhizomes and roots of *C. Ipecacuanha* (Brot.) A. Rich. of tropical Amer. are the source of the drug, IPECAC.

tomentosa (Aubl.) Vahl. Shrub, to 15 ft., hairy; lvs. lanceolate to elliptic, to 10 in. long, long-acuminate; bracts bright red, to 2 in. across; fls. yellow; fr. blue. Mex. to Bolivia.

CEPHALANTHERA L. Rich. *Orchidaceae*. About 14 spp. of terrestrial herbs, native to n. temp. Eurasia; sts. erect, leafy; fls. in a terminal, loosely fld. spike, campanulate to spreading, sepals and petals similar, lip divided into hypochil and epichil, pouched at base, column without a rostellum. For structure of fl. see *Orchidaceae*.

For culture see *Orchids*.

falcata Lindl. Lvs. up to 8, 2-ranked, lanceolate, strongly nerved; spikes to 5 in. long; fls. sessile, yellow. China, Japan.

CEPHALANTHUS L. BUTTONBUSH. *Rubiaceae*. Six or more spp. of shrubs or small trees, native to temp. N. Amer., Asia, Afr.; lvs. opp. or whorled, stipules small, interpetiolar; fls. small, in dense, globose, showy heads, corolla tubular, 4-lobed, styles long-exserted.

Of easy cultivation in good land if moist. Propagated by seeds and by cuttings of mature wood in autumn or green wood in spring.

occidentalis L. Deciduous, to 20 ft.; lvs. ovate to elliptic-lanceolate, to 6 in. long, glossy above; fls. creamy, in long-stalked heads about 1 in. across. Summer, early autumn. Swamps and along streams, e. and w. N. Amer. There are narrow-lvd. and pubescent forms.

CEPHALARIA Schrad. ex Roem. & Schult. *Dipsacaceae*. About 65 spp. of ann. or per. herbs, native to Eur., w. Asia, N. Afr., Ethiopa, and S. Afr.; lvs. opp., simple or compound; fls. white, yellowish, or bluish, in long-stalked, prominent, involucrate heads, calyx cup-shaped to saucer-shaped, many-toothed, enveloped by a pappuslike epicalyx, corolla 4-parted, stamens 4, borne on petals; fr. a ribbed achene.

Easily propagated by seeds.

alpina (L.) Roem. & Schult. [*Scabiosa alpina* L.]. Coarse per., sts. to 6 ft., ribbed; lvs. pinnatisect, irregularly toothed; heads to 1¼ in. across; fls. sulphur-yellow. Alps.

corniculata: *C. uralensis*.

flava (Sibth. & Sm.) Szabó [*C. graeca* Roem. & Schult.]. Per. to 2 ft.; lvs. pinnatisect, segms. ovate to oblong, often dentate or incised; heads to 1½ in. across; fls. yellow. Greece, se. Yugoslavia.

gigantea (Ledeb.) Bobrov [*C. tatarica* Hort., not (L.) Roem. & Schult.]. Coarse per., sts. to 6 ft. or sometimes taller, ribbed, hairy in lower part; lvs. pinnately divided, segms. oblong to elliptic-lanceolate, decurrent, toothed; heads to 2 in. across; fls. cream or yellow, marginal fls. enlarged. Caucasus.

graeca: *C. flava*.

radiata Griseb. & Schenk. Per., to 4 ft.; lvs. pinnatisect, pubescent, segms. elliptic to lanceolate, terminal segm. largest; involucral bracts obtuse; fls. yellow to white. Hungary.

scabra (L.f.) Roem. & Schult. [*Scabiosa scabra* L.f.]. Per., to 3 ft., scabrous-hairy; lvs. pinnatifid to 2-pinnatifid, segms. linear, toothed, revolute; fls. white. S. Afr.

tatarica: *Knautia tatarica*, but material offered as *C. tatarica* is *C. gigantea*.

Tchihatchewii Boiss. Per., to 3 ft., sts. with spreading setose-hispid hairs; lvs. lyrate-pinnatifid, segms. oblong-lanceolate, 3–5-parted; fls. yellow. Armenia.

uralensis (J. Murr.) Roem. & Schult. [*C. corniculata* (Waldst. & Kit.) Roem. & Schult.]. Per., to 3½ ft.; lvs. pinnately lobed, segms. oblong, entire; fls. pale yellow, usually double. Autumn. Se. Eur. to w. Siberia.

CEPHALOCEREUS Pfeiff. [*Austrocephalocereus* Backeb.; *Coleocephalocereus* Backeb.; *Neobuxbaumia* Backeb.; *Neodawsonia* Backeb.; *Pilocereus* Lem.; *Pilosocereus* Byles & Rowley; *Stephanocereus* A. Berger]. *Cactaceae*. About 50 spp. of ribbed, cylindrical cacti, native to trop. and subtrop. Amer.; sts. mostly erect, columnar, ribs 12–30; flowering region (cephalium) lateral or terminal, of several adjacent ribs whose areoles differ from sterile ones in having more wool and sometimes longer spines, these ribs sometimes suppressed or broken into tubercles; fls. nocturnal, relatively small, tubular-campanulate, white to red, perianth persistent in fr., tube thick-walled, scales of tube and ovary 0 or few, with mostly naked axils, stamens in 1 series; fr. often topshaped, seeds black, tubercled. Many spp. have been separated as the genus *Pilosocereus* [*Pilocereus* K. Schum, not Lem.].

Propagated by seeds and cuttings. For culture see *Cacti*.

alensis (A. Web.) Britt. & Rose. Sts. to 20 ft., slender, branching from base, ribs 12–14, nearly tubercled; spines 10–14, brownish, needle-shaped, ½ in. long; cephalium with white or yellowish hairs to 2 in. long; fls. purplish. Mex.

apicicephalium Dawson [*Neodawsonia apicicephalium* (Dawson) Backeb.]. To nearly 10 ft. high and 3 in. thick, gray-green, often branching from the base and sometimes above, ribs 22–25; areoles with grayish felt, radial spines 9–12, gray-white, needle-shaped, to ¾ in. long, central spines 1–4, pale rose or reddish-yellow to gray or nearly black; cephalium terminal, with long, woolly, corrugated hairs; fls. rose, tinted yellow, narrowly campanulate, to 2⅜ in. long. Mex.

Arrabidae (Lem.) Britt. & Rose [*Pilocereus Arrabidae* Lem.]. To 10 ft., branching from base, brs. 2½–4 in. thick; areoles close-set, at first long-woolly, spines 5–10, stout-needle-shaped to awl-shaped, brownish or yellowish, the upper short, 1–2 central, to 1½ in. long; flowering areoles not woolly; fls. white, to 3 in. long; fr. depressed-globose, to 2½ in. in diam. Brazil.

Backebergii (Weing.) Borg [*Pilocereus Backebergii* (Weing.) Backeb.]. Treelike, to 18 ft., brs. 3–5 in. thick, ribs 9–15; areoles at first with white silky hairs, radial spines 6–12, needle-shaped, ½ in. long, central spine 1, to 2 in. long; fr. depressed-globose, reddish. Venezuela.

catingicola (Gürke) Britt. & Rose [*Pilocereus catingicola* (Gürke) Werderm.]. Treelike, to 35 ft., brs. 3–5 in. thick, ribs 4–5, to 1½ in. high; areoles 3–4 in. apart, mostly gray-woolly, spines awl-shaped, yellow, radial spines 8–12, to ⅜ in. long, central spines 5–8, to 4 in. long; fls. white, odorless, to 3 in. long; fr. depressed-globose, to 3 in. in diam., flesh purple. Brazil.

chrysacanthus (A. Web.) Britt. & Rose [*Pilocereus chrysacanthus* A. Web.]. GOLDEN-SPINES, GOLDEN OLD-MAN. Shrubby, to 18 ft., brs. erect or ascending, ribs 9–12; areoles ⅜ in. apart, spines 12–15, yellow, to 1½ in. long; cephalium discontinuous, of long white wool; fls. rose, 3 in. long; fr. red, to 1½ in. in diam., flesh red. S. Mex.

chrysomallus: *C. militaris.*

chrysostele (Vaup.) Borg [*Pilocereus chrysostele* (Vaup.) Werderm.]. Shrubby, to 18 ft., brs. ascending, to 3½ in. thick, ribs 20–30, ¼ in. high; areoles close-set, often with a few long hairs, spines about 30, yellow, needle-shaped or bristlelike, to ¾ in. long; cephalium with white wool and yellow bristles to 2 in. long; fls. whitish, 2 in. long; fr. depressed-globose, green, to 1½ in. in diam. Brazil.

Collinsii Britt. & Rose. To 10 ft., few-branched, sts. to 1½ in. thick, ribs about 7, obtuse; areoles ⅝ in. apart, long-woolly, spines about 15–20, needle-shaped, to 1½ in. long; fls. subapical, 2 in. long; fr. depressed-globose, 1¼ in. in diam. S. Mex.

columna-Trajani (Karw.) K. Schum. [*Cephalocereus Hoppenstedtii* (A. Web.) K. Schum.]. Sts. simple, columnar, to 35 ft. high and 16 in. thick, tapering upward, ribs 20 or more, low; areoles close-set, radial spines 14–18, white, short, central spines 5–8, brownish, to 4 in. long; cephalium 4–8 in. wide, with dense yellowish wool to 2½ in. long and yellowish bristles; fls. yellowish, to 3 in. long; fr. ovoid, to 1¼ in. in diam. S. Mex.

cometes (Scheidw.) Britt. & Rose [*Pilocereus cometes* (Scheidw.) F. M. Knuth]. Sts. cylindrical, ribs 12–15, obtuse; areoles close-set, woolly, spines brownish, to ¾ in. long; flowering areoles with yellow hair longer than spines. Cent. Mex.

Dybowskii (Rol.-Goss.) Britt. & Rose [*Austrocephalocereus Dybowskii* (Rol.-Goss.) Backeb.]. To 15 ft., branched at base, brs. 3 in. thick, ribs 18–26, low; areoles close-set, with white, cobwebby hairs, spines needle-shaped, yellow, radial spines many, short, central spines 2–3, to 1¼ in. long; cephalium narrow, to 2 ft. long, with long white wool; fls. white, 1½ in. long; fr. globose, pink, 1 in. in diam. Brazil.

euphorbioides: *Lemaireocereus euphorbioides.*

fluminensis (Miq.) Britt. & Rose [*Coleocephalocereus fluminensis* (Miq.) Backeb.]. Sts. erect or decumbent, to 7 ft. long and 4 in. thick, branching from base, ribs 10–17, broad, to ⅝ in. high; areoles close-set, white-woolly, spines yellow, needle-shaped, to 1¼ in. long, the upper shorter, 2–7 in lower areoles and 2–10 in upper areoles stouter than others; cephalium 1–2 in. across, to 3 ft. long, with white wool to 1¼ in. long and yellow bristles to 3 in. long, ribs suppressed; fls. white, 2 in. long; fr. top-shaped, red to purple, 1 in. in diam. Brazil.

fulviceps (A. Web.) H. E. Moore. MEXICAN-GIANT. To 60 ft. high and 1 ft. thick, in age fastigiately many-branched, brs. bluish, about 6 in. thick, ribs 11–14; areoles close-set or confluent, the fertile upper ones densely brown-woolly, radial spines about 12, slender, central spines 1–3, the longest to 5 in. long; fls. white, to 3¼ in. long, stamens in 1 series, the lower somewhat united at base, style exserted. S. Mex. The names *C. chrysomallus* and *Pachycereus chrysomallus* have been widely misapplied to this sp.

glaucescens (Labour.) Borg [*Pilocereus glaucescens* Labour.]. Treelike, to 20 ft., brs. blue-glaucous, to 4 in. thick, ribs 8–10, obtuse, to

⅝ in. high; areoles close-set, with some pendulous white hairs to ¾ in. long, spines needle-shaped, yellowish, to ⅝ in. long, radial spines 13–18, central spines 5–7, stouter, thickened at base; fls. white, to 3 in. long. Brazil.

glaucochrous (Werderm.) Borg. Sts. erect, little-branched, to 15 ft. high and 3 in. thick, blue-glaucous, ribs about 9, ½ in. high; areoles with silky hair to 1¼ in. long, spines needle-shaped, straw-yellow, radial spines 9–12, to ¾ in. long, central spines 3–4, to 2 in. long; fls. white to pink, 2 in. long; fr. depressed-globose, to 2 in. in diam. Brazil. Apparently intergrading with *C. pentaedrophorus*.

Gounellei (A. Web.) Britt. & Rose [*Pilocereus Gounellei* A. Web.]. Shrubby, to 20 ft., sometimes sprawling, brs. to 3 in. thick, ribs 10–11, grooves undulate; areoles large, ½ in. apart, with pendulous wool to 2 in. long, spines awl-shaped, brownish, radial spines 15–25, central spines 4–6, to 4 in. long; fls. white, to 3½ in. long; fr. depressed-globose, reddish, to 2½ in. in diam. Brazil.

Hoppenstedtii: *C. columna-Trajani.*

keyensis: *C. Robinii.*

lanuginosus (L.) Britt. & Rose [*Pilocereus lanuginosus* (L.) Rümpler]. Simple or much-branched and treelike, sts. bluish, ribs 9–13, rounded; areoles woolly, spines needle-shaped, yellow; fls. white, to 2½ in. long; fr. depressed-globose, red. Curaçao.

leucocephalus (Poselg.) Britt. & Rose [*Pilocereus leucocephalus* Poselg.]. To 25 ft., branching below, brs. 2½–4 in. thick, ribs 10–12; areoles white-woolly, spines about 10, needle-shaped, brown, to ¾ in. long; fls. whitish, 2½ in. long; fr. globose, purplish, to 1½ in. in diam. Mex.

leucostele (Gürke) Britt. & Rose [*Pilocereus leucostele* (Gürke) Werderm.; *Stephanocereus leucostele* (Gürke) A. Berger]. Sts. little-branched, erect, to 10 ft. high and 3 in. thick, of a few long joints, each with a crown of bristles which remains as a ring around the st., ribs 12–18, low; areoles ½ in. apart, white-woolly, radial spines to 20, slender-needle-shaped, white, to ⅝ in. long, central spines several, whitish to yellow, to 2 in. long, bristles of crown yellow, to 3 in. long; fls. from new or old crown, white, to 2½ in. long; fr. globose or depressed-globose, to 2 in. in diam., flesh white. Brazil.

Maxonii Rose. Shrubby, to 10 ft., brs. about 4 in. thick; upper areoles with dense white wool to 2 in. long, spines 10, slender, yellow, central spine 1, to 1½ in. long; fls. purple, 1½ in. long; fr. depressed-globose, 1½ in. in diam. Guatemala.

mezcalensis Bravo [*Neobuxbaumia mezcalensis* (Bravo) Backeb.]. Sts. simple, columnar, yellow-green, to 20 ft. high or more and 1 ft. thick, ribs 15 or more, narrow, ¾ in. high; areoles with yellow wool, radial spines 6–7, white or pale yellow, to ⅜ in. long, central spine 1, slightly larger; fls. white, to 2¾ in. long and 1½ in. across. Cent. Mex.

militaris (Audot) H. E. Moore [*Cephalocereus chrysomallus* (Lem.) K. Schum.; *Pachycereus chrysomallus* (Lem.) Britt. & Rose]. Not cult.; both synonyms have been widely misapplied to *C. fulviceps.*

nobilis (Haw.) Britt. & Rose. Sts. erect, branched from base, to 15 ft. high and 3 in. thick, ribs 5–10; areoles white-woolly, spines needle-shaped, yellow or brown, radial spines about 9, to ½ in. long, central spines 2–4, to 1½ in. long; fls. white or purplish, to 2½ in. long, stigma exserted; fr. depressed-globose. W. Indies.

Palmeri Rose [*Pilocereus Palmeri* (Rose) F. M. Knuth]. BALD OLD-MAN, YELLOW O.-M., WOOLLY TORCH CACTUS. To 20 ft., branching, brs. bluish, 2–3 in. thick, ribs 7–9, obtuse; upper areoles with dense white wool to 2 in. long, radial spines 8–12, slender, central spine 1, longer, to 1¼ in. long; fls. purplish to brownish, 2½ in. long; fr. globose, to 2½ in. in diam. E. Mex.

pentaedrophorus (Labour.) Britt. & Rose [*Pilocereus pentaedrophorus* (Labour.) Console]. Sts. erect, often unbranched, to 35 ft. high, rarely 4 in. thick, ribs 4–6, low, sinuses somewhat sinuate; areoles without wool, spines various, 6–12, needle-shaped, yellowish to brown, to 1½ in. long; fls. white, to 2 in. long, stigma exserted; fr. depressed-globose, to 2 in. in diam., flesh purple. Brazil.

piauhyensis (Gürke) Britt. & Rose [*Pilocereus piauhyensis* (Gürke) Werderm.]. Treelike, to 35 ft., brs. many, slender, bluish, ribs 12–16, to ⅜ in. high; areoles ⅜ in. apart, the upper woolly, spines needle-shaped, yellow-brown, radial spines 20, to ½ in. long, central spines 5–7, stouter, to 1¼ in. long; fls. white, 1½ in. long; fr. depressed-globose, red, to 2 in. in diam. Brazil.

polylophus (DC.) Britt. & Rose [*Neobuxbaumia polylopha* (DC.) Backeb.]. Sts. simple, columnar, to 45 ft., ribs 25–40, compressed; spines slenderly needle-shaped, yellow, radial spines 7–8, to ¾ in. long, central spine 1, longer; fls. pink to purplish, to 3 in. long, scales decurrent, mucronate; fr. depressed-globose, 1½ in. in diam. E. Mex.

purpureus Gürke [*Austrocephalocereus purpureus* (Gürke) Backeb.]. Sts. columnar, to 18 ft. high and 5 in. thick, unbranched, ribs

12–25, to ⅜ in. high; radial spines 15–20, white, needle-shaped, to ½ in. long, central spines 5–10, yellowish-brown, to 2 in. long, awl-shaped in lower areoles; cephalium to 5 in. wide and 3 ft. long with thick gray wool and curved, reddish-brown to black bristles to ¾ in. long; fls. white or pinkish, 1½–2 in. long; fr. top-shaped, purple, ¾ in. long. Brazil.

Purpusii Britt. & Rose. Sts. erect, simple or branched, to 10 ft. high and 1½ in. thick, ribs 12, ¼ in. high; areoles close-set, at first with silky white hairs, spines many, needle-shaped, thickened at base, yellow, to 1¼ in. long; fls. pink, to 3 in. long; fr. globose, 1 in. in diam. W. Mex.

Robinii (Lem.) Britt. & Rose [*C. keyensis* Britt. & Rose]. Treelike, to 25 ft., with a broad, dense crown, brs. ascending, to 4 in. thick, ribs 10–13; areoles ½ in. apart, short-woolly, spines 15–20, needle-shaped, yellow, to 1 in. long; fls. white, 2 in. long, with odor of onion, stigma exserted; fr. depressed-globose, red, to 1½ in. in diam. S. Fla. and Cuba.

Royenii (L.) Britt. & Rose. Treelike, to 30 ft., ribs 7–11, high; areoles close-set, soft-woolly, spines needle-shaped, ½–2½ in. long; fls. white, 2 in. long; fr. depressed-globose, 2 in. in diam., flesh red. W. Indies.

Sartorianus Rose [*Pilocereus Sartorianus* (Rose) Backeb. & F. M. Knuth]. Similar to *C. leucocephalus* and perhaps a var. of it having 6–8 ribs. E. Mex.

senilis (Haw.) Pfeiff. OLD-MAN CACTUS. Sts. columnar, to 50 ft. high and 1 ft. thick or more, mostly simple, ribs 20–30, low; areoles close-set, at first woolly, with many gray bristles that become 1 ft. long, spines 3–5, yellow, to 1½ in. long; cephalium at first lateral, becoming terminal, with dense tawny wool to 2½ in. long and gray bristles to 5 in. long; fls. rose, to 2 in. long or more; fr. obovoid, rose, to 1¼ in. long. Cent. Mex.

Tetetzo (A. Web.) Vaup. [*Neobuxbaumia Tetetzo* (A. Web.) Backeb.; *Pachycereus Tetetzo* (A. Web.) Ochot.]. Sts. branching, columnar, to 40 ft., ribs 13–17, rounded, 1 in. high; radial spines 8–12, needle-shaped, to ½ in. long, central spines 1–3, awl-shaped, to 2 in. long, spines of upper areoles fewer, weaker, shorter; fls. subapical, greenish-white, 2½ in. long, scales narrow, not overlapping, decurrent, papery-tipped; fr. ovoid, 1½ in. long. S. Mex.

CEPHALOPHYLLUM N. E. Br. *Aizoaceae.* More than 70 spp. of dwarf succulents, native to S. Afr., sts. short or decumbent to prostrate with distinct internodes; lvs. opp., crowded, in tufts on main st. and ends of brs., nearly cylindrical to 3-angled, minutely dotted; fls. solitary or 2–3 in a group, terminal, usually expanding at noon, calyx 5-lobed, petals many, stamens many, ovary inferior, 12–20-celled, stigmas 12–20; fr. a many-celled, 12–20-valved caps., with well-developed valve wings and large placental tubercles.

Of easy culture in summer, the plants making a good covering for stones or dry walls. In winter the plants require an airy, sunny place, a relatively cool temperature of about 55° F. and fairly dry soil. Propagated by seeds and cuttings. See also *Succulents.*

Alstonii Marloth ex L. Bolus. Brs. prostrate, to 2 ft. long or more, gray in age, internodes 2 in. long; lvs. erect, curved inward, gray-green, dark-dotted, to 2¾ in. long, ⅜ in. across, nearly cylindrical, the upper side somewhat flattened, apex briefly acuminate; fls. to 3³⁄₁₆ in. across, petals dark ruby-red, stamens violet. Cape Prov.

anemoniflorum (L. Bolus) Schwant. [*Mesembryanthemum anemoniflorum* L. Bolus]. Glabrous, procumbent, internodes to 1 in. long, brs. erect; lvs. 2–6, erect to spreading, curved inward, blue-green or sometimes reddish, to 1½ in. long, semicylindrical at the center becoming 3-angled toward apex, abruptly narrowed to a short point at apex, narrowed toward the base; fls. 2 in. across, on pedicels to ¾ in. long, petals salmon-pink. Cape Prov.

aureorubrum L. Bolus. Sts. decumbent, to nearly 7 in. long and ⅛ in. in diam.; lvs. glaucous-green, smooth, to 2⅜ in. long, with sheath ¼ in. long, to ⁵⁄₁₆ in. broad and thick, obtuse, more or less semicircular in section, upper side flat, lower side rounded; fls. 2–3, the lateral on 2-bracted pedicels, bracts to 1 in. long, petals in 3 series, narrowed and orange below the middle, red above and rounded or emarginate at tip. Cape Prov.

confusum (Dinter) Dinter & Schwant. Brs. forming cushions to 8 in. wide, 3³⁄₁₆ in. high; lvs. curved, to 1½ in. long, ³⁄₁₆ in. thick, united ⅛ in. at base, nearly round to somewhat 3-angled in section, apex obtuse; fls. to 1³⁄₁₆ in. across, on pedicels to ⅝ in. long, petals golden-yellow. S.-W. Afr.

cupreum L. Bolus. Sts. to 22 in. long, ½ in. in diam., internodes to 1³⁄₁₆ in. long; lvs. light glaucous-green, to 2⅝ in. long, ½ in. wide and thick, convex above and laterally, obscurely keeled, apex acute; fls. solitary, on peduncle to 1¾ in. long, sepals unequal, petals coppery and yellow basally inside, nearly rose or pale outside, to 1⅜ in. long, ³⁄₁₆ in. wide. Cape Prov.

decipiens (Haw.) L. Bolus. Sts. to 16 in. long, greenish or reddish, becoming gray in age, brs. stiff; lvs. arched, green or reddish at sheath and finely rough-dotted, to 2 in. long or more, ³⁄₁₆ in. wide at base, semicylindrical but narrowed and becoming 3-angled toward the apex where briefly acuminate; fls. solitary, on pedicels to ⅛ in. long, petals yellow. Cape Prov.

frutescens L. Bolus. Sts. erect, stiff, to 2 ft. high; lvs. 4 on a br., ascending, glaucous, to 3⅜ in. long, ¼ in. in diam. or more, nearly cylindrical, upper side flat to slightly rounded, obscurely keeled on lower side; fls. about 2⅜ in. across, on pedicels to nearly 4 in. long, petals yellow. Cape Prov.

procumbens (Haw.) L. Bolus. Sts. stout, elongate, rooting, often purplish, internodes ⅝ in. or rarely to 1³⁄₁₆ in. long; lvs. ascending or incurved-spreading, glaucous-rose, purplish beneath, to 2 in. long, ³⁄₁₆ in. in diam., nearly round in section, acute; fls. to 2 in. across, often solitary, petals golden-yellow. Cape Prov.

spongiosum (L. Bolus) L. Bolus. Shrubby, to more than 10 in., sts. more than 1 ft. long, ⅝ in. thick, yellow-brown, white and spongy inside, internodes to 2 in. long, brs. ascending to erect; lvs. 2–6 on a br., whitish, to 4⅜ in. long, ½ in. wide, ¾ in. thick, nearly saber-shaped, flat above, keeled beneath, apex blunt or briefly acuminate; fls. to 2⅜ in. across, on pedicels to 2³⁄₁₆ in. long, petals scarlet. Cape Prov.

subulatoides (Haw.) N. E. Br. Brs. crowded in rosettes; lvs. spreading, light gray-green, transparent-dotted, to 2¾ in. long, ⅜ in. wide, semicylindrical, keeled on the lower surface, the keel and sometimes the edges cartilaginous; fls. to 1⅝ in. across, on pedicels to 2¾ in. long, petals purple-red. Cape Prov.

CEPHALOTAXACEAE Neger. PLUM-YEW FAMILY. Gymnosperms; 1 genus, *Cephalotaxus,* of evergreen, resinous, mostly dioecious, coniferous trees or shrubs, native to temp. e. Asia; brs. opp. or in whorls; lvs. alt., linear, pointed, with 2, broad, glaucous-green lines beneath; male cones axillary, subglobose, with 3–8 sporangia, female cones stalked, bracts opp., with 2 ovules at base, but only 1 ovule in each cone maturing; seeds large, drupelike with outer fleshy coat and inner woody coat maturing the second year.

CEPHALOTAXUS Siebold & Zucc. PLUM YEW. *Cephalotaxaceae.* Seven spp. of evergreen, dioecious or infrequently monoecious trees and shrubs, native to e. Asia, with characters of the family.

Hardy in Zone 6 in protected sites. For culture see *Conifers.*

drupacea: *C. Harringtonia* var.; var. **Harringtonia** and var. **pedunculata:** *C. Harringtonia.*

Fortunii Hook. CHINESE P.Y. To 30 ft.; lvs. spreading horizontally from branchlets, 2–3 in. long, tapering to a fine point, with about 20 rows of stomata on each glaucous band beneath; seeds purple. China. Zone 7. Usually remains a bush with spreading and pendulous brs.

Harringtonia (D. Don) C. Koch [*C. drupacea* var. *Harringtonia* (D. Don) Pilg. and var. *pedunculata* (Siebold & Zucc.) Miq.; *C. pedunculata* Siebold & Zucc.]. HARRINGTON P.Y. Shrub or tree, to 30 ft.; lvs. 1–1½ in. or rarely 2 in. long, abruptly mucronulate at apex, dark green above, with about 15 rows of stomata on each glaucous band below, 2-ranked and forming a V-shaped trough on branchlets; seeds green, almond-shaped, about 1 in. long. Japan. Var. **Harringtonia.** The typical var.; known only in cult., lvs. 1½–2 in. long; male cones in clusters of 2–5 on stalks ½–¾ in. long. Zone 6. Var. **drupacea** (Siebold & Zucc.) G. Koidz. [*C. drupacea* Siebold & Zucc.]. JAPANESE P.Y., PLUM-FRUITED YEW, COW'S-TAIL PINE. Lvs. about 1 in. long; male cones in clusters, on stalks ⅛–¼ in. long. Japan. Var. **nana** (Nakai) Rehd. Low, spreading by suckers. Japan. Var. **sinensis:** *C. sinensis.* Cv. **'Fastigiata'.** Lvs. spirally arranged. Cv. **'Sphaeralis'.** Seeds spherical.

pedunculata: *C. Harringtonia.*

sinensis (Rehd. & E. H. Wils.) H. L. Li [*C. Harringtonia* var. *sinensis* (Rehd. & E. H. Wils.) Rehd.]. Similar to *C. Harringtonia,* but a shrub to 14 ft.; lvs. 1–1⅝ in. long, thinly leathery, narrowly lanceolate, gradually tapering to a short acute or acuminate tip. China.

CERASTIUM L. MOUSE-EAR CHICKWEED. *Caryophyllaceae.* About 60 spp. of cosmopolitan, ann. or per. herbs, mostly mat-forming or cespitose, mostly hairy, sts. sometimes slightly woody basally; lvs. opp., usually gray to gray-green or green; infl. cymose, sometimes solitary; sepals 5, rarely 4, separate, petals white, 5, rarely 4, sometimes 0, often bifid or emarginate, stamens 5–10, styles usually 5; fr. a caps., cylindrical, dehiscent, with 10 teeth, seeds many, reniform or spherical.

Cerastiums are readily grown in rock walls and rock gardens, on embankments, and in the garden border. Propagated by seeds, division, and from cuttings taken after flowering.

alpinum L. Per., to 8 in.; lvs. obovate, to ⅜ in. long, woolly to glabrous; infl. 1–5-fld., peduncles under 2 in., bracts acute, margin scarious; sepals acute, to ⅜ in. long, truncate at base, petals to ¾ in. long. Arctic, N. Amer. and Eur., mts. of Eur. Subsp. **alpinum**. The typical subsp.; plants grayish-green; lvs. evenly hairy. Subsp. **lanatum** (Lam.) Asch. & Graebn. [*C. lanatum* Lam.]. Plants woolly; lvs. with tangled hairs at apex.

arvense L. [*C. strictum* L.]. FIELD M.-E.C., STARRY GRASSWORT. Cespitose per., to 12 in., sts. procumbent, rooting at lower nodes; lvs. linear to elliptic, ½ to 1 in., variable; bracts ciliate, margins scarious; petals 2–3 times longer than sepals, white. Most of Eur., except far north. Cv. 'Compactum'. Low, compact form.

Biebersteinii DC. Mat-forming per., to 12 in., white-woolly, apical internode to 4 in. long, much longer than other internodes; lvs. linear-lanceolate, to 2 in. long; cymes 3–5-fld., pedicels to ¾ in., bracts lanceolate, tomentose, margins scarious; sepals similar to the bracts, to ⅜ in. long, tomentose, petals to ¾ in. long. Crimea.

candidissimum Corr. Cespitose per., to 12 in., white- to yellowish-woolly, internodes about equal; lvs. lanceolate, to ¾ in. long, revolute; cyme dense, bracts ovate, margin scarious; sepals ¼ in. long, white-tomentose, petals to ⅜ in. long, auricled to truncate. Mts., w. and s. Greece.

carinthiacum Vest. Matted per., to 8 in.; lvs. ovate to lanceolate, to 1 in. long, often glabrous or glossy; cymes few- to 7-fld.; sepals ¼ in. long, obtuse. E. Alps and Carpathians.

Columnae: *C. tomentosum.*

decalvans Schloss. & Vuk. [*C. lanigerum* Clementi, not Desv.]. Per., to 16 in.; lvs. elliptic-lanceolate, ⅛–¼ in. wide, attenuate, sparsely tomentose, midrib conspicuous, yellow; bracts lanceolate, margins scarious; sepals lanceolate, to ⁵⁄₁₆ in. long, pubescent, petals spreading. Mts., Balkan Pen.

fontanum Baumg. Short-lived per., to 24 in., basal shoots short, nonflowering; lvs. sessile, to 1 in. long; bract with margins usually scarious; sepals to ⅜ in. long, petals about as long as sepals. Eur. Subsp. **fontanum**. The typical subsp.; sepals ¼ in. long or more. Not cult. Subsp. **triviale** (Link) Jalas [*C. holosteoides* Fries]. Cespitose, 2–20 in.; sepals to ³⁄₁₆ in. long.

glaciale: *C. uniflorum.*

glomeratum Thuill. Ann., 12–18 in., sts. hairy, sometimes glandular-hairy; lvs. to 1 in. long, basal lvs. obovate, st. lvs. ovate, hairy; cymes compact; sepals lanceolate, to ¼ in. long, hairy at apex, petals as long as sepals or shorter, bifid in apical ¼, stamens 10. Eur.

holosteoides: *C. fontanum* subsp. *triviale.*

lanatum: *C. alpinum* subsp.

lanigerum: *C. decalvans.*

latifolium L. Cespitose per., to 4 in., glandular-pubescent; lvs. sessile, rigid, ovate, to 1 in. long, bluish-green; cymes 1–3-fld., bracts herbaceous; sepals ¼ in. long, margins scarious, petals ½ in. long, slightly bifid. Alps, n. Appenines.

maximum L. Stoloniferous per., 8–16 in., puberulent, glandular toward apex; lvs. linear-lanceolate, to ⁵⁄₁₆ in. long; cymes 3–13-fld., umbel-like; petals 2–3 times longer than sepals. Arctic Russia, Siberia, Arctic N. Amer.

moesiacum Friv. Cespitose per., to 16 in., basal shoots tomentose, apical internode to 4 in. long, slightly longer than the others; lvs. elliptic to obovate, to 1 in. long; cymes many-fld., bracts obtuse, hairy, margins scarious; sepals obtuse, petals twice as long as sepals. Balkan Pen.

purpurascens Adams. Cespitose per., sts. erect, to 12 in., pilose; lvs. lanceolate, pilose; cymes many-fld., loose; sepals ⅜ in., pilose, margins scarious, petals to ¾ in. long, white, the claws pilose. Caucasus, n. Turkey, n. Iran. Some material offered under this name may be *Arenaria purpurascens.*

schizopetalum Maxim. Densely tufted per., pubescent, sts. to 8 in., branched at base; lvs. linear-lanceolate, to ¾ in. long; cymes few-fld., glandular-pilose, pedicels to ¾ in.; sepals ovate, under ¼ in. long, glabrous, margin scarious, petals to ½ in. long, bifid, the lobes 2–3-lobed. Alpine regions, cent. Japan.

strictum: *C. arvense.*

tomentosum L. [*C. Columnae* Ten.]. SNOW-IN-SUMMER. Per., mat-forming, white-woolly, sts. 6–10 in., rarely longer; lvs. lanceolate, to 1 in. long, white-woolly, showy; cymes 3–15-fld.; fls. nearly 1 in. across, showy, petals notched. Mts. of Italy, to Sicily. Commonly cult. in the rock garden.

uniflorum Clairv. [*C. glaciale* Gaudin ex Ser.]. Per., to 4 in.; lvs. obovate, to ¾ in. long, bright green; cymes 1–3-fld.; sepals ¼ in. long, petals ½ in. long, bifid halfway. Alps, w. Carpathians, mts. of Yugoslavia.

CERATIOLA Michx. *Empetraceae.* One sp., a dioecious, heathlike evergreen shrub, native to se. U.S.; lvs. simple, whorled; fls. axillary, sessile, sepals 4, corolla none, male fls. with 2 exserted stamens, female fls. with superior, 2-celled ovary, style 1, stigmas 3 or 4, flattened and deeply cut; fr. red or greenish-yellow, drupaceous.

ericoides Michx. ROSEMARY. To 6 ft., brs. roughened by persistent lf. bases; lvs. linear, to ½ in. long, spreading; sepals about ¹⁄₁₆ in. long; fr. ⅛ in. in diam. Coastal plain, S.C. to Fla. and Miss.

CERATODACTYLIS John Sm. *Polypodiaceae.* Not in cult. *C. osmundioides: Llavea cordifolia.*

CERATONIA L. *Leguminosae* (subfamily *Caesalpinioideae*). One sp., an evergreen tree, with dense crown, native to e. Medit. region; lvs. alt., even-pinnate; fls. small, in short, lateral racemes on old wood, bisexual or unisexual, calyx tubular, 5-lobed, petals 0, stamens 5; fr. a flat, leathery, indehiscent legume, edible, filled with sweet pulp between seeds.

The carob sometimes withstands a few degrees of frost, but is generally adapted to the same range as the orange. It will grow on any well-drained soil. The pods are eaten by livestock and as human food; carob flour is made from the fruits, and carob gum is obtained from the seeds. Propagated by seeds, preferably under glass, the seedlings afterwards budded; or by cuttings over bottom heat.

Siliqua L. CAROB, ST. JOHN'S-BREAD, ALGARROBA BEAN, LOCUST B. To 50 ft.; lfts. in 2–3 pairs, orbicular to obovate, to 4 in. long, obtuse or emarginate, glossy; fls. small, red; fr. to 1 ft. long.

CERATOPETALUM Sm. *Cunoniaceae.* Five spp. of shrubs or trees, native to e. Australia and New Guinea; lvs. opp., of 1 or 3 lfts.; fls. small, white or rose, in terminal cymes or panicles, sepals 4 or 5, small at first, becoming enlarged, colored, and woody in fr., petals 4 or 5, or 0, stamens 10, ovary half-inferior; fr. indehiscent.

Grown under glass or outdoors in the South. Propagated by cuttings of half-ripened wood.

apetalum D. Don. To 60 ft., bark silvery; lfts. usually 1, ovate-lanceolate, to 5 in. long or more, toothed; petals 0, calyx to ¼ in. long in fr. New S. Wales, se. Queensland.

gummiferum Sm. To 40 ft.; lfts. 3, lanceolate, to 1½ in. long or more, toothed; petals deeply lobed; calyx to ½ in. long in fr. New S. Wales.

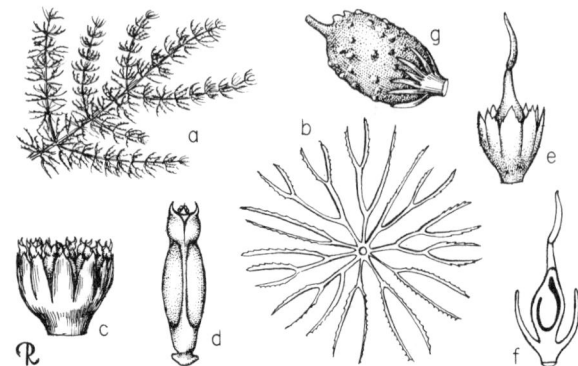

CERATOPHYLLACEAE. *Ceratophyllum demersum:* **a,** branching stem, × ⅙; **b,** whorl of leaves, × 1; **c,** male flower, × 12; **d,** stamen, × 25; **e,** female flower, × 12; **f,** female flower, vertical section, × 12; **g,** fruit, × 15. (From Bailey, *Manual of Cultivated Plants*, ed. 2.)

CERATOPHYLLACEAE S. F. Gray. HORNWORT FAMILY. Dicot.; 1 cosmopolitan genus, *Ceratophyllum*, of submersed aquatic herbs, with floating, leafy brs.; lvs. whorled, finely dissected into threadlike divisions; fls. minute, solitary, sessile, unisexual, male and female fls. at separate nodes, perianth thin, many-parted, stamens 10–20, nearly sessile, with connectives extended into thick, often colored, appendages, ovary sessile, 1-celled, ovule 1, pendulous; fr. an achene.

CERATOPHYLLUM L. HORNWORT. *Ceratophyllaceae.* Three or 4 spp. of aquatic herbs, growing in ponds and lakes in temp. and trop. regions; with characteristics of family.

Popular plants for aquaria and pools. Of easy cultivation; propagated by cuttings.

demersum L. Sts. elongate, branched; lvs. to 1 in. long, 3-forked, divisions serrate along 1 side; fr. ellipsoid, ¼ in. long, with spinelike beak and 2 spines near base. Quiet waters, N. Amer.

echinatum A. Gray. Sts. elongated, freely branching; lvs. 2–4-forked, segms. entire, capillary; fr. to ¼ in. long, with roughened surface, and basal and lateral spines. E. and s. U.S., n. Mex.

submersum L. Sts. elongated, with softer texture than *C. demersum;* lvs. to 1⅜ in. long, 3-forked, segms. sparsely serrate, light green; fr. warty but spineless. Eur., N. Afr., Asia.

CERATOPTERIS Brongn. WATER FERN, FLOATING F. *Parkeriaceae.* Four spp. of ann., aquatic or semiaquatic, pantrop. ferns, floating on the water with roots often extending to and growing into the muddy substrate; lvs. dimorphic, sterile lvs. simple to 3-pinnate, fertile lvs. larger than sterile lvs., 4–5-pinnate, much contracted; sporangia in 1–4 rows along the veins and enclosed in revolute lf. margins.

The leaves are succulent, and those of one species are much used as a vegetable in Asia, where it is often common in flooded rice fields. These ferns are useful in ponds and aquaria, either free-floating or planted in pots which are slightly submerged. Propagated by buds which are formed on all parts of the leaves. See also *Ferns.*

cornuta (Beauvois) Lepr. Sterile lvs. lanceolate, 4–6 in. long, pinnate to 2-pinnately parted, pinnules to 1½ in. long, irregular in shape and lobing, fertile lvs. 8–12 in. long, 2-pinnate, pinnules linear. Trop. Afr. and Madagascar, w. Asia to Burma, Indonesia, and N. Australia.

deltoidea: *C. Richardii.*

pteridoides (Hook.) Hieron. FLOATING FERN. Petioles short, centrally inflated; sterile lvs. floating, to 8 in. long, simple and palmately 3-lobed or pinnately 5-lobed, fertile lvs. erect, to 16 in. long, 1–4-pinnate. Fla. to Brazil.

Richardii Brongn. [*C. deltoidea* Bened.]. TRIANGLE W.F. Sterile lvs. triangular to ovate or lanceolate, to 1 ft. long, 1-pinnate-pinnatifid to 2-pinnate, triangular, long-petioled, fertile lvs. shaped like sterile lvs., to 10 in. long or more, 4–5-pinnate basally, 2-pinnate apically, pinnules triangular, or linear or lanceolate toward apex; sporangia in 1–4 rows, enclosed by inrolled margins of segms. Pantrop.

siliquosa: *C. thalictroides.*

thalictroides (L.) Brongn. [*C. siliquosa* (L.) E. Copel.]. WATER FERN. Sterile lvs. not floating, oblong, 1–2-pinnatifid into triangular pinnules, long-petioled, fertile lvs. similar but pinnules linear. S. Japan to Polynesia, Malay Arch., and India; naturalized in Jamaica. Lvs. edible, widely eaten in the Orient.

CERATOSTIGMA Bunge. *Plumbaginaceae.* About 8 spp. of per. herbs or shrubs, native in the Himalayas, China, Ethiopia, and Somaliland; lvs. alt., ciliate, sometimes bristly; fls. usually blue, in dense terminal or axillary, bracted heads; calyx tubular, 5-lobed, corolla with slender tube and 5 spreading lobes, stamens 5, borne in middle of corolla tube; fr. a caps., splitting into 5 parts.

Used as border and bedding plants; prized for their blue flowers. Propagated by division and cuttings.

Griffithii C. B. Clarke. Evergreen shrub, to 2 ft., much-branched, sts. weakly ribbed, reddish-pubescent, with some stellate hairs; lvs. obovate, to 1½ in. long, ciliate, with appressed bristles on both surfaces; corolla to ¾ in. long, azure-blue. Himalayas of Tibet and Bhutan.

Larpentiae: a listed name of no botanical standing, used for *C. plumbaginoides.*

minus Stapf ex Prain. Deciduous shrub, to 3 ft., sts. weakly ribbed or not ribbed, mostly appressed-strigose-hairy; lvs. obovate to spatulate, to 1½ in. long, glabrous above or at least less hairy than beneath; corolla to ⅝ in. long, tube usually reddish-purple, lobes dark blue. W. China.

plumbaginoides Bunge [*Plumbago Larpentiae* Lindl.]. Per. herb, to 20 in., sts. woody at base, glabrous or sparsely setose, somewhat zigzag; lvs. mostly obovate, to 3½ in. long, ciliate, glabrous on both surfaces; corolla to 1 in. long, dark blue. W. China. Distinguished by its glabrous, herbaceous sts.

Willmottianum Stapf. CHINESE PLUMBAGO. Deciduous shrub, to 4 ft., sts. angled, bristly-hairy; lvs. elliptic to oblanceolate, to 2 in. long, ciliate, bristly hairy on both surfaces; fls. in terminal or axillary heads,

corolla about 1 in. long, tube reddish-purple, lobes pale blue. W. China and Tibet.

CERATOTHECA Endl. *Pedaliaceae.* About 6 spp. of ann. or per. herbs, native to trop. and s. Afr.; lvs. opp., simple or 3-lobed; fls. pink to lavender, solitary, axillary, calyx 5-parted, corolla 2-lipped, stamens 4, included; fr. a 4-celled caps., horned at apex.

triloba E. H. Mey. ex Bernh. Softly hairy ann., to 6 ft., sts. obtusely 4-angled; lvs. ovate-cordate to triangular and 3-lobed, to 6 in. long, coarsely crenate-dentate; fls. rose-lavender, with darker lines, to 3 in. long, pendent. S. Afr.; naturalized in Fla.

CERATOZAMIA Brongn. *Zamiaceae.* Two spp. of cycads with short trunks, native to Mex.; lvs. stiff, pinnate, borne in a crown, petioles persistent; sporophylls (cone scales) in cones, the scales V-shaped or 2-horned at the ends.

Sometimes grown in the greenhouse or outdoors in partial shade in Zone 10. Relatively easy to hand pollinate. For culture see *Cycads.*

Fisheri: a listed name of no botanical standing, perhaps for *Zamia Fischeri.*

Kuesterana Regel. Trunk globose to subcylindrical, branched at the base; lvs. 2–4 ft. long, erect or spreading, pinnae narrowly lanceolate, curved, 5–12 in. long, leathery, margin revolute; male cones subcylindrical, 4–16 in. long.

latifolia: *C. mexicana* var.

longifolia: *C. mexicana* var.

mexicana Brongn. MEXICAN HORNCONE. To 4 or rarely 6 ft., trunk short, usually simple; lvs. erect to spreading, gracefully recurved, 3–9 ft. long, pinnae narrowly to broadly lanceolate, 4–16 in. long, ½–3 in. wide; male cones subcylindrical, 4–6 in. long, female cones ellipsoid, to 6 in. long. A variable sp., including the following poorly marked vars. Var. **mexicana.** The typical var.; pinnae more or less equal, broadly lanceolate, 6–14 in. long. Var. **latifolia** (Miq.) J. Schuster [*C. latifolia* Miq.]. Pinnae more or less equal, lanceolate, 8–12 in. long, 1–2 in. wide, lower margin incised toward apex. Var. **longifolia** (Miq.) J. Schuster [*C. longifolia* Miq.]. Pinnae unequal, narrowly lanceolate, 8–16 in. long, to 1¼ in. wide. Var. **Miqueliana** (H. Wendl.) J. Schuster [*C. Miqueliana* H. Wendl.]. Pinnae obovate, 5–12 in. long, 1–3 in. wide, abruptly acuminate, base obliquely cuneate, lower margin sinuate near apex.

Miqueliana: *C. mexicana* var.

plumosa: a listed name of no botanical standing.

Purpusii: a listed name of no botanical standing for a plant with erect lvs. and narrow pinnae.

recurvata: a listed name of no botanical standing, probably for *C. mexicana.*

spinosa: a listed name of no botanical standing.

spiralis: a listed name of no botanical standing for a plant with erect lvs. and very narrow pinnae.

CERBERA L. *Apocynaceae.* About 6 spp. of large shrubs and trees with milky sap, native to Madagascar, trop. Asia, Australia, and Pacific Is.; lvs. alt., entire, crowded at ends of brs., drying black; fls. regular, in terminal cymes with large deciduous bracts, 5-merous, bisexual, calyx lobes fugacious, corolla salverform, tube swollen in upper part, with 5 scales in throat, stamens 5, borne on corolla, included, pistil with 2 separate ovaries and a single glabrous style; fr. of 1 or 2 drupelets, each with thick, fibrous endocarp and 1–2 seeds.

Sometimes planted in warm regions as an ornamental. Propagated by cuttings of ripe shoots.

Odollan Gaertn. Shrub or tree, to 50 ft.; lvs. obovate-oblong, to 12 in. long, acuminate, long-attenuate at base, lateral veins many, at right angles to midrib; fls. in compound cymes, pedicels to 1 in. long; calyx lobes recurved-spreading, about ⅝ in. long, corolla with yellow eye, to 2⅜ in. across, tube to 1 in. long or more, stamens borne near middle of tube; drupes mostly subglobose, 2–4 in. long, red. India to Pacific Is.

CERCIDIPHYLLACEAE Engl. CERCIDIPHYLLUM or KATSURA TREE FAMILY. Dicot.; 1 genus, *Cercidophyllum,* of deciduous, dioecious trees, native to temp. e. Asia; lvs. opp. or subopposite on the vegetative shoots, solitary on the short fl. spurs, palmately veined, petioled; fls. unisexual, sepals 4, petals none, male fls. solitary or in clusters, stamens 15–20, filaments long, female fls. with 4–6 slender pistils, ovary superior; fr. a follicle, seeds many, winged.

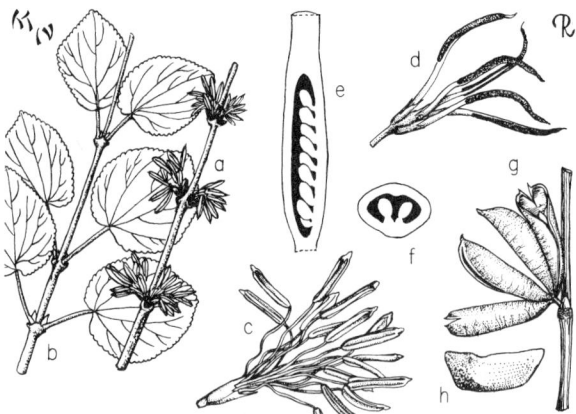

CERCIDIPHYLLACEAE. *Cercidiphyllum japonicum:* **a,** segment of flowering branch of male tree, × ½; **b,** segment of branch in leaf, × ¼; **c,** male flower, × 2; **d,** female flowers, × 1; **e,** ovary, vertical section, × 10; **f,** ovary, cross section, × 10; **g,** follicles, × 1; **h,** seed, × 5. (c–h from Bailey, *Manual of Cultivated Plants,* ed. 2.)

CERCIDIPHYLLUM Siebold & Zucc. *Cercidiphyllaceae.* One or 2 spp. of trees, native to temp. e. Asia, with the characters of the family.

Handsome ornamental for park or specimen planting. Grows best in rich, moist soil. Propagated by seeds, cuttings of greenwood in spring, and by layers.

japonicum Siebold & Zucc. ex J. Hoffm. & H. Schult. KATSURA TREE. Upright branching tree, to 100 ft., trunk often branched above the base; lvs. orbicular to ovate, to 4 in. long, cordate, crenate-serrate, glabrous, dark green above, glaucescent beneath, becoming yellow or scarlet in autumn; fls. before lvs.; follicles about ¾ in. long. Japan, China. Zone 5. Wood used for general construction in Japan. Var. **sinense** Rehd. & E. H. Wils. Taller, usually with a single trunk; lvs. somewhat hairy on veins beneath. China.

magnificum Nakai. Differing from *C. japonicum* in having lvs. much wider, to about 3 in. long and 2⅜ in. wide. Japan. Cv. 'Pendulum' is listed.

CERCIDIUM Tulasne. *Leguminosae* (subfamily *Caesalpinioideae*). About 10 spp. of small trees and shrubs with sharp spines and green brs., native to warmer parts of W. Hemisphere; lvs. alt., 2-pinnate, with opp. lfts., deciduous; fls. yellow, nearly regular, 5-merous, in short axillary corymbs, stamens 10, separate; fr. a linear or oblong legume.

floridum Benth. ex A. Gray [*C. Torreyanum* (S. Wats.) Sarg.; *Parkinsonia Torreyana* S. Wats.]. PALO VERDE. Small bushy tree, to 30 ft., with smooth, blue-green bark, leafless most of year; lvs. with 1 pair of pinnae, lfts. in 2–4 pairs, to ⁵⁄₁₆ in. long, pale; fls. to ¾ in. across; fr. to 3 in. long, more than ½ in. wide, glabrous. Ariz., s. Calif., nw. Mex.

macrum I. M. Johnst. Differs from *C. floridum* in having dull green brs., green lvs., and very flat fr. to ⅜ in. wide. Se. Tex., ne. Mex.

microphyllum (Torr.) Rose & I. M. Johnst. [*Parkinsonia microphyllum* Torr.]. Differs from *C. floridum* in having bark yellowish-green, lvs. pubescent, with 4–8 pairs of minute lfts., fls. smaller, with pale yellow petals, and fr. cylindrical, puberulous. S. Calif., Ariz., nw. Mex.

Torreyanum: *C. floridum.*

CERCIS L. REDBUD, JUDAS TREE. *Leguminosae* (subfamily *Caesalpinioideae*). Seven spp. of deciduous, small trees and shrubs, native to N. Amer., s. Eur., and Asia; lvs. alt., simple, entire, palmately-veined, petioles slender; fls. before or with lvs., clustered or racemose, pink to mauve or white, petals 5, the 3 upper smaller than the 2 lower, stamens 10, separate; fr. a thin, flat legume, narrowly winged on the lower edge.

Redbuds are planted for their showy early flowers. They thrive in fertile sandy loam. *C. canadensis* is the most hardy. Propagated by seeds sown in spring, or by layering, softwood cuttings in spring, or *C. chinensis* by soft cuttings in summer under glass.

canadensis L. REDBUD. Tree, to 40 ft.; lvs. broadly ovate to nearly orbicular, to 4 in. across or more, usually cordate basally; fls. in clusters, rosy-pink, ½ in. long; fr. to 3½ in. long. E. U.S. Zone 5. Forma **alba** Rehd. Fls. white. Cv. 'Rosea' is listed.

chinensis Bunge [*C. japonica* Planch.]. CHINESE R. Differs from *C. canadensis* in having lvs. deeply cordate, with a transparent thickened margin, glossy beneath when young, and fls. more than ½ in. long. Cent. China. Zone 8. Often shrubby in cult. Cvs. 'Arborea' and 'Nana' have been listed.

japonica: *C. chinensis.*

occidentalis Torr. Shrub, to 15 ft.; lvs. reniform, to 2¾ in. across, emarginate; fls. in clusters, reddish, ½ in. long; fr. 3 in. long and ¾ in. wide. Calif. Zone 8.

racemosa D. Oliver. Differs from *C. canadensis* in having lfts. abruptly short-acuminate, basally truncate or nearly cordate, pubescent beneath, racemes many-fld., pendent, to 4 in. long, and fr. to 4 in. long. Cent. China. Zone 8.

reniformis Engelm. Shrub or tree, to 40 ft.; lvs. broad-ovate to reniform, to 3 in. across, obtuse or emarginate; fls. in clusters, ½ in. long; fr. to 4 in. long, ½ in. wide. Tex., New Mex. Zone 8.

Siliquastrum L. JUDAS TREE, LOVE TREE. To 40 ft.; lvs. nearly orbicular, to 4¾ in. across, deeply cordate, apically obtuse or emarginate; fls. in clusters, purplish-rose, ¾ in. long; fr. to 4 in. long. S. Eur., w. Asia. Zone 7. Var. **alba** Weston. Fls. white.

CERCOCARPUS HBK. MOUNTAIN MAHOGANY. *Rosaceae.* A few spp. of evergreen shrubs or low trees of N. Amer.; lvs. simple, more or less leathery, straight-veined; fls. small, solitary or fascicled, calyx tube salverform, the lower nearly cylindrical part persistent, the upper bowl-shaped part deciduous, sepals 5, petals 0; fr. an elongate achene with a long, silky-plumose style.

Sometimes planted for shrubbery where native or in similar places; they succeed in dry soils, and mostly with sunny exposure. Propagated by seeds or cuttings.

alnifolius: *C. betuloides* var. *Blancheae.*

betulifolius: *C. betuloides.*

betuloides Nutt. ex Torr. & A. Gray [*C. betulifolius* Nutt. ex Hook.]. Erect, open, to 25 ft., bark smooth, gray; lvs. obovate to broadly elliptic, to 1 in. long, serrate toward tip, glabrous above, paler and pubescent beneath, with 3–6 lateral veins on each side of midrib; fls. ¼–½ in. across; styles of fr. 2–3½ in. long. Ore. to n. Baja Calif. Zone 7? Var. **Blancheae** (C. K. Schneid.) Little [*C. alnifolius* Rydb.]. Lvs. 1½–2½ in. long, flexible, with 6–10 lateral veins on each side of midrib; calyx tube not densely white-woolly. Is. off s. Calif. Var. **Traskiae** (Eastw.) Dunkle [*C. Traskiae* Eastw.]. Lvs. 1–2½ in. long, leathery, with 6–10 lateral veins on each side of the midrib, the upper surface with impressed veins; calyx tube densely white-woolly. Catalina Is., Calif.

intricatus S. Wats. Intricately branched, to 10 ft.; lvs. entire, linear, to ½ in. long, margins revolute almost to the midrib; styles ⅜–¾ in. long. E. Calif. to Utah, Ariz.

ledifolius Nutt. Bark red-brown, plants to 30 ft.; lvs. entire, lanceolate-elliptic, to 1 in. long, margins slightly revolute; styles 2–3 in. long. E. Calif. and Wash., e. to Mont., Colo., Ariz.

minutiflorus Abrams. Like *C. betuloides,* but lvs. greenish-yellow, glabrous beneath, fls. ¹⁄₁₆–³⁄₁₆ in. across. San Diego Co., Calif., n. Baja Calif.

montanus Raf. [*C. parvifolius* Nutt. ex Hook. & Arn.]. Close to *C. betuloides,* with brownish bark; lvs. with coarse-ovate, rather than triangular-apiculate teeth, finely tomentose beneath; fls. ¼ in. across. Rocky Mts. Zone 6.

parvifolius: *C. montanus.*

Traskiae: *C. betuloides* var.

CEREALS: see *Grasses.*

CEREUS Mill. [*Piptanthocereus* (A. Berger) Riccob.; *Subpilocereus* Backeb.]. *Cactaceae.* About 36 spp. of ribbed, cylindrical cacti of the W. Indies and e. S. Amer.; sts. prostrate to more or less erect, often robust, ribs mostly 4–8, often high and thin; spines straight; fls. from unspecialized areoles, nocturnal, mostly white, tube and ovary with few or no scales, perianth soon abscissing from the ovary; fr. fleshy, mostly splitting, the flesh red, purple, or white. Some 1,000 names have been used in *Cereus,* a genus formerly held to include many elements now thought to be not so closely related. The word "cereus" is most popularly known in the name "night-blooming cereus," but the plants commonly so called are now placed in such genera as *Hylocereus, Nyctocereus,* and *Selenicereus.*

Propagated readily by seeds and cuttings. For culture see *Cacti.*

aethiops Haw. [*C. coerulescens* Salm-Dyck]. Sts. to 7 ft., slender, bluish or purplish, ribs 7–8, low, nearly tubercled; areoles close-set, spines slender, black, radial spines 9–12, to ½ in. long, central spines 1–4, to ¾ in. long; fls. white, 9 in. long; fr. brownish. N. Argentina.

alacriportanus Pfeiff. Sts. erect, to 10 ft., bluish at apex, ribs 5–6, to 1¼ in. high; areoles 5/16–1 in. apart, spines needle-shaped, light yellow, 5/16–¾ in. long, radial spines 6–8, central spine 1; fls. white, tinged rose, to 9 in. long. S. Brazil, Paraguay.

argentinensis Britt. & Rose. Tree, to 40 ft., brs. 4–6 in. thick, green, ribs 4–5, 2 in. high, ½ in. thick; areoles to 1½ in. apart, spines slenderly awl-shaped, brownish, radial spines 3–8, ⅜–2 in. long, central spines 1–2, 1–4 in. long; fls. white, 7–9 in. long, odorless. N. Argentina. Plants cult. under this name may be *C. glaucus.*

azureus Parm. Sts. erect, slender, blue-glaucous, ribs 6–7, weakly sinuate; areoles remote, with brown tomentum and grayish wool, radial spines 8–12, white, dark-tipped, central spines 1–3, stouter, brown; fls. white, 4–5 in. long. Brazil.

caesius: *C. validus;* see also *C. pseudocaesius.*

chalybaeus Otto. Sts. to 10 ft., glaucous, ribs 6, high, sinuate; areoles ¾ in. apart, black, spines needle-shaped, dark, to ¾ in. long, radial spines 7 to many, central spines several; fls. white, 8 in. long; fr. golden-yellow. N. Argentina.

coerulescens: *C. aethiops.*

Dayamii Speg. Tree, to 80 ft., brs. 3–5 in. thick, pale green, ribs 5–6, thin, 1¼ in. high; areoles 1 in. apart, spines 3–5, yellow, 5/32–½ in. long; fls. white, odorless, 10 in. long; fr. red, to 3 in. long, flesh white. N. Argentina.

diffusus: *Monvillea diffusa.*

Emoryi: *Bergerocactus Emoryi.*

Engelmannii: *Echinocereus Engelmannii.*

euphorbioides: *Lemaireocereus euphorbioides.*

fernambucensis Lem. [*C. formosus* C. F. Först.]. Sts. erect or sprawling, to 1½ ft. high and 3 in. thick, pale green, ribs 3–5, crenate, to 1 in. high; areoles 1 in. apart, spines 4–11, yellowish, needle-shaped, central spines 3–4, often stouter, to 2 in. long; fls. white, to 7 in. long; fr. red, flesh white. Coastal, s. Brazil, Uruguay. Sometimes spelled "pernambucensis," but originally "fernambucensis" and correctly so, since the place was formerly often called Fernambuco. Cv. **'Monstrosus'** [*C. formosus* cv. 'Monstrosus']. Ribs tubercled or irregularly interrupted.

Forbesii Otto. Sts. erect, to 10 ft., grayish, ribs 5–7, about 1¼ in. high; areoles about 1¼ in. apart, spines stoutly needle-shaped, radial spines 5–6, to 1½ in. long, central spines 3–4, to 2½ in. long; fls. 7 in. long, the limb cup-shaped, inner segms. white, the middle ones pink-tipped; fr. purple, 2½ in. long, flesh red. N. Argentina.

formosus: *C. fernambucensis.*

geometrizans: *Myrtillocactus geometrizans.*

giganteus: *Carnegiea gigantea.*

glaucus Salm-Dyck. Treelike, to 20 ft., brs. 3–7 in. thick, bluish, ribs 6–8, mostly 7, platelike, 2–4 in. high, crenate; areoles 1–2 in. apart, spines 5–15, yellowish, needle-shaped, to 1 in. long, more numerous and to 4 in. on old sts.; fls. white, to 11 in. long; fr. red, 4 in. long or more, flesh white. Brazil. Material offered as *C. argentinensis* may belong to this sp.

grandiflorus: *Selenicereus grandiflorus.*

Greggii: *Peniocereus Greggii.*

hexagonus (L.) Mill. [*C. lepidotus* Salm-Dyck]. Treelike, to 50 ft., brs. 4–6 in. thick, gray-green, ribs 4–6, thin, undulate, 1½–2½ in. high; areoles ¾–1½ in. apart, spines 2–3, to ⅛ in. long, 5–10 on mature sts., central spine to 2½ in. long; fls. white, 8–10 in. long; fr. reddish, to 5 in. long, flesh whitish. W. Indies and n. S. Amer.

Hildmannianus K. Schum. Treelike, to 20 ft., brs. to 5 in. thick, blue-glaucous, ribs 5–6, relatively thin and flat, crenate, to 2½ in. high; areoles about 1 in. apart, spines 0 or 6–12 on large, old sts., dark, radial spines to 5/16 in., central spine to ¾ in. long; fls. white, 8–9 in. long. Brazil.

horridus Otto. Shrubby, brs. 4 in. thick, green, ribs 5–9, 1½–2½ in. high; areoles 1½ in. apart, radial spines about 5, central spines 3, to ¾ in. long, or on old sts., 15–20, the longest to 4 in. long; fls. white, to 9 in. long; fr. red, 3 in. long, flesh whitish. Venezuela.

Huntingtonianus Weing. Shrubby, to 10 ft. high, brs. 4 in. thick, bluish, ribs 5–7, 1 in. high; areoles 1 in. apart, radial spines 3–4, to ⅝ in. long, central spines 1 or more, to 4 in. long; fls. 7 in. long, limb cup-shaped, middle segms. pink-tipped; fr. purplish, to 2½ in. long, flesh red. Origin unknown; probably a var. of *C. Forbesii.*

insularis Hemsl. [*Monvillea insularis* (Hemsl.) Britt. & Rose]. Sts. creeping or clambering, to 1¼ in. thick, ribs 6–8, low; spines 12–15, yellow-brown, needle-shaped, to ⅜ in. long; fls. yellow, 5 in. long, tube slender. Brazil.

Jamacaru DC. Treelike, to 40 ft., brs. 4–5 in. thick, often glaucous, ribs 4–10, mostly about 5, 1½ in. high; areoles 1–2 in. apart, spines 10–15, yellow to brown, needle-shaped, short, sometimes 20–30 on old sts., some to 8 in. long; fls. white, 8–12 in. long; fr. red, 4–8 in. long, flesh white, seeds to 5/32 in. long. Brazil. Extremely variable; sometimes almost spineless.

Knuthianus: a listed name of no botanical standing.

lepidotus: *C. hexagonus.*

Llanosii: a listed name of no botanical standing.

marginatus: *Lemaireocereus marginatus.*

Milesimus Rost. Shrubby, brs. 3–5 in. thick, bluish, ribs 9–12, platelike, 1–2 in. high; areoles ¾ in. apart, radial spines 4–6, awl-shaped, ¾ in. long, a few bristly on older sts., central spines 1–3, ascending, to ¾ in. long; fls. white, about 7 in. long; fr. orange-red, to 3 in. long, flesh whitish. Brazil. More commonly grown is the cv. **'Monstrosus',** which has ribs irregularly broken into segms. that may be laterally displaced.

mohavensis: *Echinocereus triglochidiatus* var.

monstrosus: *C. peruvianus* cv. 'Monstrosus'.

obtusus Haw. Sts. low, 1–2 in. thick, ribs 3, obtuse; spines reddish, to 5/16 in. long, radial spines about 4, central spine 1; fls. diurnal?, white, about 8 in. long. Brazil?

pentagonus: *Acanthocereus pentagonus.*

pernambucensis: see *C. fernambucensis.*

peruvianus (L.) Mill. [*Piptanthocereus peruvianus* (L.) Riccob.]. PERUVIAN APPLE, APPLE CACTUS, PERUVIAN A. C. Shrubby, to 10 ft., or perhaps treelike, brs. about 4 in. thick, green, becoming grayish, ribs 6–8, scarcely crenate, ¾–2 in. high, to 2 in. thick at base; areoles about 1 in. apart; spines needle-shaped, radial spines 4–6, to ¾ in. long, the upper short or none, central spine 1, to 2 in. long in age; fls. white, to 6½ in. long, lightly fragrant, tube short, often ridged, stigma often exserted before flower opens; fr. depressed-globose, yellow or flushed red, 2½ in. in diam., flesh white. Se. S. Amer. Cv. *'Longispinus'* is listed. Cv. **'Monstrosus'** [*C. monstrosus* Steud.]. GIANT-CLUB, CURIOSITY PLANT. Ribs about 12, irregularly divided into tubercles. Cv. **'Reclinatus'.** Fls. to 9 in. long, outer perianth segms. reflexed.

Pitahaya, Pitajaya: *Acanthocereus Pitajaya;* but the names *C. Pitahaya* and *C. Pitajaya* are sometimes misapplied to *C. fernambucensis* or *C. variabilis.*

pseudocaesius Werderm. Shrubby, brs. glaucous, to 4½ in. thick, ribs 6–8, thick, first to 1 in., later to 3 in. high; areoles ½–1½ in. apart, spines about 14 or to 20 or more on old sts., yellow-brown, becoming gray, to ½–2 in. long, slenderly needle-shaped, mostly in lower half of areole; fls. white, 11 in. long; fr. reddish, to 3½ in. long, flesh whitish, seeds ⅛ in. long. Described from cult. Commonly misnamed *C. caesius.*

repandus (L.) Haw. [*Subpilocereus repandus* (L.) Backeb.]. Treelike, to 40 ft. high and 16 in. thick, much-branched, gray- or bluish-green or reddish, ribs 8–12, to ¾ in. high; areoles with gray or brown hairs, spines 8–20 or rarely more, gray-white, dark-tipped, radial spines 7–13, central spines 1–7, to 2⅜ in. long; fls. white, or greenish, or sometimes rose, to 4⅜ in. long; fr. red-violet, cylindrical to ovoid, to 2 3/16 in. long, flesh white or rose. W. Indies.

Thurberi: *Lemaireocereus Thurberi.*

trigonodendron K. Schum. Erect, to 50 ft., ribs 3, thin; areoles woolly, spines mostly 6, black, to ¼ in. long, central spine 1; fls. red, 4 in. long. E. Peru.

validus Haw. [*C. caesius* Salm-Dyck]. Sts. erect, to 10 ft., glaucous, ribs 3–8, compressed; areoles 1¼ in. apart, spines yellow-brown, needle-shaped, radial spines 5, to ¾ in. long, central spines 2–4, to 2 in. long; fls. white or pinkish, 9 in. long; fr. yellowish, 3 in. long, flesh white. N. Argentina.

variabilis Pfeiff. Creeping or to 14 ft. high, brs. 1½–3 in. thick, green or glaucescent, ribs 3–5, nearly compressed; areoles to ⅝ in. apart, spines rigid, radial spines 6–8, to 1 in. long, central spines 1–2, to 2 in. long; fls. white, 8–11 in. long. Brazil.

xanthocarpus K. Schum. Treelike, to 20 ft., little-branched, brs. to 4½ in. thick, ribs 5, to 2 in. high and 5/16 in. thick; areoles ¾–1½ in. apart, spines 0 or 3–5, conical, brown, central spine to ⅜ in. long; fls. white, 5 in. long; fr. yellowish, to 3 in. long, flesh white. Paraguay.

CERINTHE L. HONEYWORT. *Boraginaceae.* About 14 spp. of ann. or per. herbs, native to Medit. region; sts. glabrous;

lvs. simple, alt., often glabrous and glaucous, sometimes rough; fls. yellow or yellow and purple, in leafy, terminal, scorpioid cymes, calyx deeply 5-cleft, corolla 5-toothed, throat without scales, glands, or hairs, tube much longer than lobes, stamens 5, anthers sagittate at the base, papillate; fr. of 2 nutlets.

Of easy cultivation; propagated by seeds.

major L. Ann., to 1–2 ft.; lvs. oblong to ovate, cordate, clasping, ciliate; fls. yellow at the base, purple above, ½–¾ in. long, anthers about same length as corolla lobes, filaments about same length as anthers. Medit. region.

CEROPEGIA L. *Asclepiadaceae.* About 150 spp. of upright or twining herbs or subshrubs, native to trop. Asia, Afr., and Madagascar, with 1 sp. reaching New Guinea and n. Australia; lvs. opp., sometimes lacking; fls. in axillary cymes, corolla tubular, often inflated at the base, lobes mostly erect or inflexed over mouth of tube and united only at the apex, but sometimes free and recurved, corona of 2 whorls; fr. a follicle.

Ceropegias are greenhouse plants requiring a moderate temperature and well-drained soil. Propagated by cuttings or seeds, though seeds are not often produced.

africana R. Br. Delicate, tuberous-rooted twiners; lvs. ovate-acuminate or ovate-acute, to 2 in. long; corolla about 1⅛ in. long, very slender, greenish, flushed purple on the slightly expanded base, lobes erect, linear, joined at apex, dark purple-gray, pubescent. S. Afr.

ampliata E. H. Mey. Climbing, with thickish, glabrous brs.; lvs. small, deciduous before flowering; cymes 2–4-fld., corolla to 2½ in. long, tube white with green nerves outside, the base banded purplish, somewhat lobate, to 1 in. across, lobes erect, joined at apex, greenish, with darker green spots. S. Afr.

barbertonensis: *C. Woodii.*

Barkleyi Hook.f. Small, slender-stemmed, scrambling herbs, from tuberous rootstocks; lvs. sessile or nearly so, fleshy, ovate-acuminate, to 2 in. long, white-veined; corolla to 2 in. long, tube globose and greenish at base, slender, purplish, funnelform above, the lobes as long as the tube, filiform, pale green, purple-reticulate inside, basally incurved, then outcurved above, the apices abruptly horizontal and united. S. Afr.

bulbosa Roxb. Glaucous, glabrous herbs, sts. twining, slender, from a small tuberous root; lvs. fleshy, linear to orbicular, to 4 in. long; fls. in 5-fld. umbels shorter than lvs., corolla to about 1 in. long, yellow-green tinged with purple, tube inflated at base, lobes erect, connivent, purple inside. India.

caffrorum: *C. linearis.*

cimiciodora Oberm. Succulent climbers with rudimentary lvs., distinguished from *C. stapeliiformis* by its truncate-triangular corolla lobes united in a short cone. S. Afr.

crassifolia Schlechter [*C. Thorncroftii* N. E. Br.]. Glabrous twiners, from white, clustered roots; lvs. ovate to elliptic, to 2¼ in. long, undulate; cymes many-fld.; corolla tube white, spotted purple, to 1 in. long, broadly inflated then constricted at the base, lobes erect, to ⁵⁄₁₆ in. long, connivent at apex, purplish outside, margins reflexed, showing green inner surface. S. Afr.

debilis N. E. Br. Sts. several, weak, very slender, twining, from a flat tuber; lvs. nearly sessile, linear, nearly cylindrical; corolla tube to ¾ in. long, slightly bent above the inflated base, greenish-white tinged purple, lobes erect, to ¼ in. long, linear, united at apex, each with a blackish-purple, retrorsely pubescent keel inside. Malawi and s. Rhodesia.

dichotoma Haw. Succulent subshrubs, to 4 ft., sts. appearing to be dichotomously branched, jointed; lvs. linear, early-deciduous; fls. in clusters of 3–6 at upper nodes, corolla pale yellow, about 1 in. long. Canary Is.

elegans Wall. [*C. similis* N. E. Br.]. Twining shrubs, brs. slender, glabrous, somewhat fleshy, from fibrous roots; lvs. remote, oblong, to 3 in. long, acute; cymes few-fld., open, long-peduncled, umbellate; corolla about 1½ in. long, greenish-white, spotted purple, tube slightly swollen at base, curved, flaring at apex, lobes united at apex, purple-tipped, ciliate with purple-black hairs. India and Ceylon.

fusca C. Bolle. Bushy, succulent, erect or decumbent shrubs, similar to *C. dichotoma,* but having corolla 1⁵⁄₁₆ in. long, reddish-brown, the lobes to ½ in. long, triangular, acuminate, the tips joined at first then more or less spreading. Canary Is.

hastata: *C. Woodii.*

Haygarthii Schlechter. Glabrous, fleshy climbers; lvs. petioled, ovate to lanceolate-ovate, to 1½ in. long; fls. 1–2 at the nodes, corolla tube to 1½ in. long, curved at right angles to the slightly inflated base, whitish or pinkish, spotted purple, lobes abruptly inflexed over throat of tube, united at apex to form a slender, erect column to ½ in. long, with an ellipsoid, purplish, ciliate apex. S. Afr.

×**hybrida** N. E. Br.: *C. elegans* × *C. Sandersonii.* Sts. trailing, fleshy, glabrous; lvs. sessile, ovate, to ⅜ in. long; corolla tube 1–2 in. long, curved and narrow above the slightly inflated base, then abruptly funnelform, to ¾ in. across at the throat, white, striped and spotted dark green, lobes to 1 in. long, erect, oblong, united at apex, blackish-red.

linearis E. H. Mey. [*C. caffrorum* N. E. Br.]. Similar to *C. debilis,* but distinguished by its slightly smaller fls. and ciliate but otherwise glabrous corolla lobes. Mozambique and S. Afr.

mozambicensis: *C. nilotica.*

nilotica Kotschy [*C. mozambicensis* Schlechter]. A very variable sp.; sts. twining, often 4-angled, from tuberous roots; lvs. petioled, ovate to lanceolate or suborbicular, to 2 in. long; fls. few, in axillary, sometimes somewhat racemose cymes, corolla tube ⅞–2½ in. long, abruptly constricted at base, greenish-white to dark reddish-brown, lobes erect, ⅜–1 in. long, triangular, united at the apex, purplish-pubescent, often yellow-spotted inside at base. Ethiopia to S. Afr.

radicans Schlechter. Sts. prostrate, fleshy, rooting at the nodes; lvs. ovate to elliptic or oblong, to 1¾ in. long; cymes 1- or few-fld., fls. erect on slender pedicels, corolla tube 1⅜–2 in. long, expanded at base, whitish, spotted purple, lobes to 1¼ in. long, triangular, then abruptly long-linear, connivent at apex, purple-brown, banded white and green, purple-ciliate. S. Afr. Var. **Smithii** (M. R. Henders.) H. Huber [*C. Smithii* M. R. Henders.]. Corolla lobes obovate to spatulate, to ⅝ in. long. S. Afr.

Rendallii N. E. Br. Sts. very slender, twining, glabrous; lvs. linear to ovate, to 1¼ in. long; fls. few, axillary, erect, corolla whitish, tube to ⅞ in. long, expanded at base, and usually curved, lobes erect, linear at base, united and abruptly dilated above, forming an umbrellalike covering over throat of tube. S. Afr.

Sandersonii Hook.f. UMBRELLA FLOWER, PARACHUTE PLANT. Glabrous, stout, succulent climbers; lvs. remote, cordate-ovate, to 2 in. long; cymes 2–4-fld., corolla mottled light and dark green, to 2½ in. long, tube slightly expanded at base, broadly flaring at the throat, lobes narrow basally, then abruptly dilated and united above and inflexed to form a flattened umbrellalike cap to 2 in. across, with upturned margins, ciliate with translucent hairs. Mozambique to Natal.

similis: *C. elegans.*

Smithii: *C. radicans* var.

stapeliiformis Haw. Sts. trailing, succulent, glabrous, up to ¾ in. in diam.; lvs. inconspicuous; fls. 1–2 at nodes, corolla 2–3 in. long, tube slightly swollen at base, white with purple spots, lobes spreading, ⅝ as long to nearly as long as tube, purple, but the margins strongly reflexed, showing white, pubescent inner surface. S. Afr.

Thorncroftii: *C. crassifolia.*

Woodii Schlechter [*C. barbertonensis* N. E. Br.; *C. hastata* N. E. Br.]. ROSARY VINE, HEARTS-ON-A-STRING, STRING-OF-HEARTS, HEART VINE, HEARTS-ENTANGLED. Sts. filamentous, creeping or pendulous, tubercled at the nodes; lvs. opp., short-petioled, reniform to ovate or broadly lanceolate, to 1 in. long, dark green marbled with white on the upper surface; cymes 2–3-fld., corolla about 1 in. long, tube flesh-colored, lobes erect, connivent at apex, blackish. S. Rhodesia to S. Afr.

CEROPTERIS: *PITYROGRAMMA.*

CEROTHAMNUS: *MYRICA.* **C. caroliniensis:** *M. pensylvanica.*

CEROXYLON Bonpl. *Palmae.* Fifteen or more spp. of moderate to very tall, solitary, unarmed, dioecious palms, without crownshafts but often with waxy trunks, in the Andes from Venezuela and Colombia to Peru and Bolivia; lvs. pinnate, pinnae acute; infl. among lvs., long-peduncled, paniculate, bearing many sheathing bracts; male fls. with sepals short, united, petals acute, united basally, stamens 6–15, filaments erect, pistillode small, female fls. similar but anthers reduced, ovary 3-celled; fr. globose with basal stigmatic scar, endocarp not operculate, seed with homogeneous endosperm and basal embryo.

Includes the tallest of palms, some 190 ft. Several species have been introduced into southern Calif. but have not yet succeeded. One has been listed but its identity is uncertain. Probably requires uniform frost-free coolness and high humidity throughout the year. See also *Palms.*

alpinum Bonpl. [*C. andicola* Humb. & Bonpl.]. WAX PALM. Very tall, trunk ringed and incrusted with wax; lvs. to 20 ft. long, pinnae many, narrow, deep green above, densely silvery-tomentose underneath; fr. purplish. A poorly known sp. from Colombia.

andicola: *C. alpinum.*

CESTRUM L. *Solanaceae.* About 150 spp. of shrubs and trees of trop. Amer.; lvs. simple, mostly narrow, entire; fls. in terminal or axillary clusters, calyx 5-toothed, small, corolla salverform, red, yellow, white, or greenish, stamens 5, borne on corolla, ovary 2-celled, ovules 3–6 in each cell; fr. a berry.

Planted in warm regions or under glass for the attractive and often very fragrant flowers. Propagated by seeds, or in mid to late winter, by cuttings kept at a warm temperature.

album: *C. diurnum.*

aurantiacum Lindl. More or less climbing shrub or small tree, 6–20 ft., glabrous; lvs. lanceolate or ovate, to 6 in. long, acute or acuminate, entire, long-petioled, with strong odor when crushed; infl. terminal, paniculate; fls. orange, to 1 in. long, glabrous, calyx to ⅜ in. long, with 5 subulate teeth; fr. white, globose, spongy, limb about ½ in. across. Guatemala. Cv. 'Album'. Fls. white.

diurnum L. [*C. album* Ferrero ex Dunal]. DAY JESSAMINE, DAY-BLOOMING C. Pubescent shrub or small tree, to 15 ft. or more, sometimes scandent; lvs. oblong or oblong-elliptic, to 4½ in. long, obtuse or acute, entire; fls. in short clusters on long axillary peduncles, fragrant by day, calyx campanulate, to ⅛ in. long, corolla greenish-white to yellowish, to ¾ in. long; fr. glossy black. W. Indies. Zone 10.

elegans (Brongn.) Schlechtend. [*C. purpureum* (Lindl.) Standl.]. More or less climbing shrub, to 10 ft. or more, pubescent; lvs. ovate to ovate-lanceolate, to 5 in. long, acute to acuminate, entire; fls. in rather loose terminal clusters, more or less nodding, calyx glabrous, about ¼ in. long, corolla crimson to reddish-purple, to ⅞ in. long, glabrous; fr. red. Mex. Cv. 'Smithii' [*C. purpureum* var. *Smithii* L. H. Bailey]. Continuous-blooming; fls. blush-rose.

fasciculatum (Schlechtend.) Miers. Shrub, to 10 ft.; similar to *C. elegans*, but larger in all its parts; calyx 4–5-toothed, pubescent, corolla purplish-red, pubescent. Mex.

Newellii (Hort. Veitch) Nichols. Similar to *C. fasciculatum*, but fls. bright crimson, about 1 in. long, and calyx glabrous. Free-flowering. Known only from cult.; may be a hybrid of *C. elegans* × *C. fasciculatum.* Some material listed as *C. Newellii* is *C. fasciculatum.*

nocturnum L. NIGHT JESSAMINE. Scandent or spreading shrub, to 12 ft.; similar to *C. diurnum*, but glabrous; fls. in axillary, elongating but not long-peduncled clusters, very fragrant at night, calyx to 3/16 in. long, corolla greenish-white to cream-colored, to 1 in. long; fr. white. W. Indies.

Parqui L'Hér. WILLOW-LEAVED JESSAMINE. Similar to *C. diurnum*, but glabrous; lvs. narrowly lanceolate, to 5 in. long; fls. profuse in axillary and terminal clusters, fragrant at night, calyx 5-toothed, to ¼ in. long, corolla greenish-white to greenish-yellow or brownish, to ⅞ in. long; fr. black. S. S. Amer. Zone 10. Probably the hardiest sp. in cult.; poisonous to cattle and sheep.

purpureum: *C. elegans.* Var. **Smithii:** *C. elegans* cv.

CHAENACTIS DC. *Compositae* (Helenium Tribe). About 25 spp. of ann., bien., or per. herbs in w. N. Amer.; lvs. alt., entire or dissected; fl. heads discoid, 10–50-fld.; solitary or corymbose, peduncled, involucral bracts in 1–3 rows, green; fls. yellow, white, or pink, all tubular, but the outer fls. expanded, sometimes raylike; achenes slender, blackish, pappus of 4–20 hyaline scales.

Propagated by seeds or division.

alpina (A. Gray) M. E. Jones [*C. Douglasii* var. *alpina* A. Gray]. Tufted per., to 8 in.; lvs. elliptic, pinnatifid, to 2 in. long, thinly woolly or glabrate; heads mostly solitary, to ¾ in. across; fls. white or pinkish; pappus scales 10, of 2 lengths. Mts., e. Ore. to Mont., s. to Calif. and Colo.

Douglasii (Hook.) Hook. & Arn. Bien. or short-lived per., sts. stout, erect, corymbose, to 18 in.; lvs. in a basal rosette and on sts., ovate, 2–3-pinnatifid, to 4 in. long, thinly tomentose; heads several, to ¾ in. across; fls. white to pink; pappus scales 10, of 2 lengths. B.C. to Mont., s. to Calif. and Ariz. Var. **alpina:** *C. alpina.*

Fremontii A. Gray. Ann., to 10 in., nearly glabrous; lvs. to 2 in. long, pinnatifid or entire, the few segms. cylindrical and succulent; infl.

sparingly branched, heads several, ½ in. across; fls. white; pappus scales 4. Deserts, Nev. and Utah, s. to Baja Calif. and Ariz.

glabriuscula DC. Ann., sts. to 16 in., leafy, branching; lvs. ovate, to 3 in. long, once pinnatifid into flat, linear segms., puberulent; heads ½ in. across; fls. yellow; pappus scales 4. Calif. Var. **Orcuttiana** (Greene) H. M. Hall [*C. Orcuttiana* (Greene) S. Parish]. Lower, much-branched, brs. fleshy, leafy; lvs. succulent, to 2 in. long, 2–3-pinnatifid into short blunt lobes. Coastal dunes, s. Calif., n. Baja Calif.

Orcuttiana: *C. glabriuscula* var.

CHAENOMELES Lindl. FLOWERING QUINCE. *Rosaceae.* A genus of 3 spp. of deciduous or semievergreen shrubs of e. Asia; lvs. alt., toothed, stipules reniform; fls. solitary or clustered, showy, waxy, appearing in early spring before the lvs., petals 5, stamens 20 or more, pistils 5, styles 5, united at the base; fr. a hard, quincelike pome.

These are attractive ornamental subjects and mostly hardy north. The fruits of some kinds are occasionally used for making preserves. Propagated by seeds stratified and sown in the spring, by root cuttings or cuttings of half-ripe wood under glass, by layers, and rare kinds by grafting on *C. speciosa* or *Cydonia oblonga.*

×**californica** W. Clarke ex C. Web.: *C. cathayensis* × *C.* ×*superba.* Usually to 6 ft., with stiff, erect brs. strongly armed with spurs; lvs. lanceolate; fls. large, pink or rosy-red. Not hardy north.

cathayensis (Hemsl.) C. K. Schneid. [*C. lagenaria* var. *Wilsonii* Rehd.]. To 10 ft., brs. few, erect, straight, stiff, armed, young shoots more or less pubescent; lvs. elliptic to lanceolate, tomentose beneath when young, sharply serrate, each tooth with an awnlike tip; fls. white to pink, 1½ in. across; fr. abundant, ovoid, 6–8 in. long. China.

×**Clarkiana** C. Web.: *C. cathayensis* × *C. japonica.* Low in growth, with erect-spreading brs. and many long spines, young shoots pubescent; lvs. intermediate between those of the parents; fls. large, pink to rose.

japonica (Thunb.) Lindl. ex Spach. LESSER F.Q. Dwarf shrub, 3–4 ft., brs. widely spreading, with short, slender spines, young shoots scabrous-tomentose; lvs. obovate to spatulate, glabrous, coarsely crenate, 1–2 in. long; fls. usually salmon to orange, 1–1¼ in. across; fr. like small gnarled apples, to 1½ in. in diam. Japan. Zone 5. Var. **alpina** Maxim. Dwarf; lvs. ⅜–¾ in. long, almost round. Var. **pygmaea** Maxim. Plant dwarf, trunk subterranean, brs. nearly spineless. Plants grown under this name in this country probably do not represent this var. Cvs. include: 'Alba': 'Zoge'; 'Maulei', fls. single, salmon-pink to orange; 'Sargentii', dwarf, fls. single, salmon-pink to orange; 'Zoge' [cv. 'Alba'], fls. cream-white.

lagenaria: *C. speciosa.* Var. **Wilsonii:** *C. cathayensis.*

Maulei: *C. japonica* cv.

sinensis: *Cydonia sinensis.*

speciosa (Sweet) Nakai [*C. lagenaria* (Loisel.) G. Koidz.]. JAPANESE QUINCE, FLOWERING Q. Shrubby, usually 6 or sometimes 10 ft., with many, erect to spreading, spiny brs., young shoots glabrous or nearly so; lvs. ovate to oblong, mostly glabrous, sharply serrate, 1½–3½ in. long; fls. normally red, but also white or pink, 1½–2 in. across; fr. variable, globose to pear-shaped, 2–2½ in. long, fragrant. China. Zone 5. Favorite pot or bonsai subject in Japan. Quite hardy. Cvs. include: 'Alba': 'Candidissima' or 'Nivalis'; 'Atrococcinea', fls. single, red; 'Baltzii', fls. single, rose, fr. apple-shaped; 'Candida', fls. single, pure white; 'Candidissima' [cv. 'Alba'], fls. single, white, tinged with pink; 'Cardinalis', fls. bright red, single or semidouble; 'Contorta', brs. and spines tortuous, fls. white, tinged pink; 'Grandiflora', fls. large, white, tinted with pink and lemon, single or slightly double; 'Kermesina', fls. single, carmine-red; 'Macrocarpa', fls. single, rosy-red; 'Marmorata', fls. single, marbled white and pink; 'Moerloosei', fls. single, white, striped rose-pink; 'Nana': 'Umbilicata Nana'; 'Nivalis' [cv. 'Alba'], fls. pure white, single; 'Rosea Plena', fls. pink to coral-pink, semidouble, fr. ribbed; 'Rubra Grandiflora', fls. large, single, deep crimson-red; 'Sanguinea Plena', fls. rosy-red, semidouble; 'Simonii', semihorizontal, fls. small, semidouble; 'Umbilicata', fls. rosy-red, single, fr. apple-shaped; 'Umbilicata Nana' [cv. 'Nana'], dwarf, almost spineless, fls. orange-red, single; 'Versicolor', fls. white and two shades of pink, single. See also *Quince.*

×**superba** (Frahm) Rehd.: *C. japonica* × *C. speciosa.* To 4 or 5 ft., with many erect-spreading brs. and slender spines, young shoots tomentose; fls. medium-sized, white, pink, orange, or red; fr. apple-shaped. Cvs. include: 'Columbia' [cv. 'Semperflorens'], fls. single, pink to rosy-red, often mostly female; 'Corallina', fls. strong red-orange; 'Foliis Rubris', fls. coral-pink, single, fr. ovoid, 'Fruticosa Alba', fls. white, tinted with pink, single; 'Semperflorens': 'Columbia.'

vedrariensis: *C.* × *Vilmoriana* cv.

×**Vilmoriana** C. Web.: *C. cathayensis* × *C. speciosa*. Shrubs 7–8 ft., with many, stiff, erect brs. and nearly glabrous young twigs; lvs. elliptic to ovate, slightly serrate; fls. large, white, suffused with pink; frs. few, ovoid. Cv. 'Vedrariensis' [*C. vedrariensis* Hort.]. Lvs. short and broad; fls. single, white, tinted with pink; fr. obovoid.

CHAENORRHINUM (DC.) Rchb. DWARF SNAPDRAGON. *Scrophulariaceae*. About 20 spp. of ann. and per. herbs, native to Medit. region and Asia; sts. branching; lvs. opp. or alt., entire; fls. white, blue, or purple, in lf. axils or loose racemes, calyx 5-parted, corolla 2-lipped, shortly spurred at base, stamens 4; fr. an asymmetrical caps., dehiscing by narrow openings at top. Differing from *Linaria* in the dehiscence of caps.

glareosum (Boiss.) Willk. [*Linaria glareosa* (Boiss.) Boiss. & Reut.]. Per., sts. many, to 1 ft., stolons with minute scale lvs.; lvs. ovate to ovate-orbicular, to ½ in. long, ¼ in. wide, glabrous; racemes few-fld.; calyx lobes linear-spatulate, corolla to 1 in. long, violet, tinged pink or yellow, lips violet to lilac, palate yellow. S. Spain.

minus (L.) J. Lange [*Linaria minor* (L.) Desf.]. Much-branched ann., to 1 ft.; lvs. sessile, oblong to linear-lanceolate, glandular-pubescent; fls. long-stalked, in loose, leafy racemes, corolla lilac, to ¼ in. long. Eur.; naturalized in N. Amer.

origanifolium (L.) Fourr. [*Linaria origanifolia* (L.) Cav.]. Per., to 10 in.; lvs. oblong to obovate, glandular-hairy; corolla ½ in. long, pale purple to white, with yellow palate, spur shorter than corolla tube. S. Eur. Some material listed under this name is *Anarrhinum bellidifolium*.

villosum (L.) J. Lange [*Linaria villosa* (L.) DC.]. Diffuse per., to 1 ft.; lvs. elliptic to ovate, glandular-pubescent; corolla lilac or yellowish, with violet stripes. Spain.

CHAENOSTOMA: *SUTERA*.

CHAEROPHYLLUM L. *Umbelliferae*. About 35 spp. of herbs, native to Eur., cent. Asia, and N. Amer.; lvs. pinnate or ternately compound; fls. small, white, in compound umbels; fr. flattened.

One species is grown for the edible root.

bulbosum L. TURNIP-ROOTED CHERVIL, PARSNIP C. Bien., to 3 ft., root tuberous, gray or blackish, with yellowish-white flesh; lvs. decompound into linear segms. Eur.; naturalized in Washington, D.C.

A hardy biennial, producing a carrotlike edible root. Seeds sown in Aug. or Sept., after ripening, usually do not germinate until spring, the roots then maturing 4–6 months later; culture otherwise as for carrot. It is better to stratify the seeds in autumn and to sow them in spring. If kept dry, as with most seeds, they may not germinate until the second spring if at all.

dasycarpum: *C. Tainturieri* var.

procumbens (L.) Crantz. Glabrous or slightly hispid ann., sts. spreading, to 30 in.; lvs. ternate-pinnately dissected, to 5 in. long, segms. linear to ovate; bractlets of involucels shorter than pedicels; fr. to ⅜ in. long. N.Y. to Va., w. to Iowa, Kans., Ark.

Tainturieri Hook. Ann., to 3 ft.; lvs. ternate-pinnately dissected into ovate segms.; bractlets of involucels spreading, usually longer than pedicels; fr. narrowly oblong, to 5⁄16 in. long. Va. to Fla., w. to Tex. and Kans. Var. **dasycarpum** S. Wats. [*C. dasycarpum* Nutt., in syn.]. Differs from the typical var. in being pubescent. Ala., Tex.

CHALCAS: *MURRAYA*. C. exotica: *M. paniculata*.

CHAMAEBATIA Benth. MOUNTAIN-MISERY. *Rosaceae*. Two spp. of glandular-pubescent, evergreen shrubs of Calif. and n. Baja Calif.; lvs. 2–3-pinnate, lfts. many, minute; fls. white, cymose-panicled, sepals and petals 5, pistil 1; fr. an achene.

Adapted to rock gardens in warm parts of the U.S., doing best in sunny locations in sandy, well-drained soil. Propagated by seeds or by cuttings of green wood under glass.

foliolosa Benth. To 3 ft.; lvs. viscid, 1–4 in. long; petals to 5⁄16 in. long. Sierra Nevada, Calif. Zone 7?

CHAMAEBATIARIA (T. C. Porter) Maxim. FERNBUSH. *Rosaceae*. One sp. of w. N. Amer., an aromatic, semideciduous shrub; lvs. 2-pinnate, stellate-pubescent; fls. white, panicled, sepals and petals 5, pistils 5, united below; fr. 5 dry follicles.

Growing best in a sunny, well-drained place. Propagated by cuttings of half-ripened wood and by seeds.

millefolium (Torr.) Maxim. Stout, densely branched, to 6 ft.; lvs. 1–1½ in. long with 15–20 pairs of pinnate pinnae; panicle 1–4 in. long; petals ¼ in. long. Ore., e. Calif., e. to Wyo. and Ariz. Zone 6.

CHAMAECEREUS Britt. & Rose. *Cactaceae*. One sp., a small cactus of Argentina; sts. slender, decumbent; fls. lateral, diurnal, red, funnelform, scales of tube and ovary with axillary hairs, stamens in 1 series; fr. small, dry, hairy, seeds black, dotted. Allied to *Lobivia*.

For culture see *Cacti*.

giganteus: a listed name of no botanical standing; applied to a plant with erect sts. 2 ft. high and 1½ in. thick; perhaps a sp. of *Lobivia*.

Sylvestri (Speg.) Britt. & Rose. PEANUT CACTUS. Sts. clustered, at first erect, to 6 in. long or more and ½ in. thick, ribs 6–9, mostly 8, low; spines 10–15, white, bristlelike, to 3⁄32 in. long; fls. to 3 in. long. Cvs. 'Aureus' and 'Crassicaulis' are listed.

CHAMAECYPARIS Spach [*Retinispora* Siebold & Zucc.]. FALSE CYPRESS. *Cupressaceae*. Seven or 8 spp. of large, coniferous, evergreen, monoecious trees of pyramidal to columnar habit, native to N. Amer. and Asia, some attaining 100 ft. or more in native habitats, branchlets flattened; lvs. opp., entire, scalelike, appressed or the juvenile lvs. awl-shaped or needlelike and spreading in some spp.; male cones yellow or red, female cones small, globose, woody, scales 6–12, peltate, having a point or prominence in middle; seeds 2–5 to each scale, winged, maturing in 1 year. Retinisporas (or retinosporas) are juvenile forms of *Chamaecyparis* and *Thuja*.

The genus yields important commercial timbers. Excellent as small ornamental trees, most of them are hardy in the North; widely variable. For culture see *Conifers*.

andelyensis: *C. thyoides* cv.

coralliformis: *C. obtusa* cv. 'Coralliformis'.

decussata: *Platycladus orientalis* cv.

filifera: *C. pisifera* cv.

formosana: *C. obtusa* var.

formosensis Matsum. To 150 ft. or more in native habitat, branchlets flattened; lvs. dull green, tinged brown, sometimes whitish beneath, ovate, mucronate, keeled or with a glandular pit; female cones ellipsoid, to ⅜ in. in diam., scales wrinkled, brownish, with a quadrangular process, seeds 2 to each scale, maturing the first year. Taiwan. Zone 8?

funebris (Endl.) Franco [*Cupressus funebris* Endl.]. MOURNING CYPRESS. To 60 ft. or more, brs. drooping, branchlets flattened; lvs. acute, light green; female cones about ⅝ in. in diam., maturing in 2 years. Zone 8. China.

Henryae: see *C. thyoides*.

Lawsoniana (A. Murr.) Parl. [*Cupressus Lawsoniana* A. Murr.]. LAWSON CYPRESS, PORT ORFORD CEDAR. To 100 ft. or more, brs. usually drooping, the branchlets frondlike; lvs. obtuse, with a gland or pit on the back and indistinct white markings beneath, acute; male cones pink or crimson, female cones ¼–⅜ in. in diam., green becoming brown, scales with a small ridgelike process. Sw. Ore. to nw. Calif. Zone 6. One of the important commercial timber spp. of the Pacific Northwest. Much grown in mild climates and prized for its many very ornamental forms. Some of the cvs. offered are: 'Allumii', columnar, lvs. very glaucous; 'Argentea', lvs. silvery; 'Aurea', lvs. golden-yellow when young; 'Bowleri', compact, branchlets drooping at tips; 'Coerulea', lvs. blue-green; 'Columnaris', narrowly columnar; 'Compacta', compact; 'Drummondii' and 'Elegantissima', listed names; 'Ellwoodii', dwarf, slow-growing, lvs. of juvenile form glaucous, gray-green; 'Erecta', narrowly conical, lvs. bright green; 'Erecta Glauca', one of several color forms of 'Erecta', lvs. glaucous; 'Filiformis', branchlets drooping; 'Fletcheri', dense, broadly columnar, lvs. of juvenile form, glaucous; 'Forsteckensis', low, branchlets twisted into coxcomblike heads; 'Fraseri', columnar, lvs. dark blue; 'Gimbornii', dwarf, lvs. blue-green; 'Glauca', lvs. steel-blue; 'Globosa', dwarf, globose shrub; 'Gracilis', branchlets drooping, lvs. light green; 'Grandis' a listed name; 'Hillieri', vigorous, lvs. yellow, branchlets somewhat drooping at tips; 'Hollandii', erect, shrubby, lvs. dark green; 'Intertexta', pyramidal, lvs. bluish-green; 'Knowfieldensis', low, subglobose, lvs. glaucous to sage-green; 'Lane', narrowly columnar, lvs. yellow-gold above; 'Lutea', young growth bright yellow; 'Lutescens', a listed name; 'Lycopodioides', brs. irregular, branchlets twisted; 'Minima Glauca', dwarf, lvs. steel-blue; 'Monumentalis', to 30 ft., branchlets erect, lvs. bluish; 'Nana', dwarf, globose; 'Nana Glauca', similar to 'Nana', but lvs. bluish-green; 'Nidiformis', horizontal brs. radiating from dense center; 'Pendula', branchlets drooping; 'Pendula Vera', branchlets drooping; '**Pottenii**', conical, ultimate br. systems dense and compact; '**Pyramidalis**', columnar; '**Pyramidalis Alba**', columnar, young growth white; '**Robusta**', broadly columnar, to 60 ft., lvs. dark green; '**Rosenthalii**', a listed name; '**Stewartii**', young shoots with deep yellow lvs.; '**Stricta**', narrow, fastigiate; '**Tortuosa**', conical, brs. and twigs thick; '**Variegata**', a listed name; '**Versicolor**', lvs. variegated, white, yellow, and light green; '**Westermannii**', stiffly pyramidal, lvs. light yellow; '**Wisselii**', columnar, brs. tufted, lvs. glaucous.

leptoclada: *C. thyoides* cv. 'Andelyensis'.

Lindleyi: a listed name of no botanical standing; perhaps a cv. but of unknown sp. affinity; said to be broadly pyramidal with blue-green lvs.; see also *Cupressus lusitanica*.

minima: *C. Lawsoniana* cv. 'Minima Glauca'.

nootkatensis (D. Don) Spach. NOOTKA CYPRESS, ALASKA CEDAR. To 100 ft. or more; branchlets drooping; lvs. acute, dark green, without white markings; male cones yellow; female cones ½ in. in diam., green, tinged purple, scales 4–6, each bearing a sharp triangular process. Alaska to Ore. Zone 5, but needs protection from winter winds. Where native is an important commercial wood. Cvs. are: '**Compacta**', dwarf, globose; '**Glauca**', lvs. very glaucous; '**Pendula**', brs. drooping; '**Viridis**', narrowly columnar, lvs. fresh green.

obtusa (Siebold & Zucc.) Endl. [*Cupressus obtusa* (Siebold & Zucc.) C. Koch; *Retinispora obtusa* Siebold & Zucc.; *Thuja obtusa* (Siebold & Zucc.) M. T. Mast.]. HINOKI CYPRESS, HINOKI F.C., JAPANESE F.C. To 120 ft., bark reddish-brown; branchlets flattened and frondlike, drooping; lvs. unequal, obtuse, glossy above, with whitish lines beneath; female cones to ⅜ in. in diam., orange-brown when maturing, the scales depressed with a minute central ridge. Japan. Zone 5. Source of an important commercial wood in Japan. Var. **formosana** (Hayata) Rehd. Lvs., cones, and seeds smaller than in the typical var. Taiwan. Zone 8.—Some of the cvs. are: '**Aurea**', lvs. golden-yellow when young; '**Breviramea**', pyramidal, brs. short; '**Caespitosa**', very dwarf, dense, lvs. dark green; '**Compacta**', dwarf, brs. and branchlets dense; '**Coralliformis**', compact, slow-growing, branchlets contorted, lvs. scalelike; '**Crippsii**', lvs. pale yellow; '**Cyanoviridis**': *C. pisifera* cv. 'Cyanoviridis'; '**Erecta**', brs. strictly ascending; '**Ericoides**', low, lvs. linear, bluish-gray; '**Filicoides**', branchlets short, frondlike; '**Gracilis**', pyramidal, lvs. dark green; '**Gracilis Aurea**', lvs. bright yellow when young; '**Juniperoides**', TENNIS-BALL C., dwarf, globose, very slow-growing; '**Keteleeri**', similar to 'Crippsii'; '**Kosteri**', a listed name; '**Lutea**', lvs. yellow; '**Lycopodioides**', dwarf, shrubby; '**Magnifica**', vigorous, lvs. glossy bright green; '**Mariesii**', slow-growing, broadly conical shrub, brs. white to yellowish-green; '**Minima**', GOLF-BALL C., dwarf, slow-growing, globose, to 15 in. in diam.; '**Nana Aurea**', as in 'Nana', but lvs. golden-yellow when young; '**Pygmaea**', very dwarf, brs. almost creeping; '**Sanderi**', dwarf, conical shrub, lvs. of juvenile form, bluish-green; '**Tetragona**', dwarf, branchlets 4-angled, partly golden-yellow; '**Viridis**' and '**Youngii**', listed names.

pisifera (Siebold & Zucc.) Endl. [*Cupressus pisifera* (Siebold & Zucc.) C. Koch; *Retinispora pisifera* Siebold & Zucc.]. SAWARA CYPRESS. To 120 ft., branchlets flattened and slightly drooping; lvs. acuminate, glossy above, with whitish lines below; female cones about ¼ in. in diam., scales depressed in the center with a minute point. Japan. Zone 5, but likely to suffer in exposed places. The many cvs. include: '**Aurea**', lvs. golden-yellow; '**Cyanoviridis**', compact, broadly conical, lvs. of juvenile form, very glaucous, bronze in winter; '**Ericoides**', lvs. small; '**Filifera**', brs. threadlike, drooping, with several related cvs. of different habits and lf. colors; '**Globosa**', slow-growing, dense, rounded; '**Nana**', dwarf, spreading shrub; '**Plumosa**' dense, conical, branchlets feathery, with related cvs. of various lf. colors; '**Pygmaea**', dwarf; '**Squarrosa**', tree or dense shrub, branchlets feathery, lvs. glaucous, with several related cvs. of different habits and lf. colors.

thyoides (L.) BSP [*Cupressus thyoides* L.]. WHITE CEDAR, SOUTHERN W.C., SWAMP W.C., ATLANTIC W.C. To 90 ft., branchlets flattened, not drooping; lvs. acute, light green or glaucous; female cones ¼ in. in diam. Cool acid bogs; Me. to Fla. and Miss. Zone 5. A source of commercial cedarwood. The southern element from n. Fla. to Miss. has recently been considered a distinct sp., *C. Henryae* H. L. Li, differing in having bark smoother, lvs. on secondary brs. mostly lacking glands, juvenile lvs. green below, male cones pale. Some cvs. are: '**Andelyensis**' [*C. leptoclada* (Zucc.) Hochst.], upright, but smaller, brs. crowded, fan-shaped, lvs. loosely appressed; '**Ericoides**', dense shrub, lvs. spreading, with 2 glaucous lines beneath; '**Glauca**', lvs. nearly silvery-white; '**Variegata**', branchlets variegated yellow.

CHAMAEDAPHNE Moench [*Cassandra* D. Don, not Spach]. *Ericaceae*. One sp., a low, evergreen shrub, growing in bogs, native to n. Eur., n. Asia, and N. Amer.; lvs. alt., simple; fls. white, nodding, in one-sided, terminal, leafy racemes, sepals 5, corolla urceolate, stamens 10, awnless, ovary superior; fr. a caps.

A good shrub for the rock garden, where it does best in a moist soil of sand and peat. Propagated by seeds only slightly covered, by cuttings of ripe wood under glass, by layers, and by suckers.

calyculata (L.) Moench [*Cassandra calyculata* (L.) D. Don]. LEATHERLEAF, CASSANDRA. To 5 ft.; lvs. elliptic to oblong-lanceolate, to 2 in. long, rusty-scaly beneath; fls. ¼ in. long, in racemes to 5 in. long. Spring. Zone 2. Cv. '**Nana**'. To 1 ft.

CHAMAEDOREA Willd. [*Collinia* (Liebm.) Liebm. ex Ørst.; *Eleutheropetalum* (H. Wendl.) H. Wendl. ex Ørst.]. *Palmae*. More than 100 spp. of solitary or cespitose, unarmed, slender, dioecious understory palms usually of trop. rain forests, principally in Mex. and Cent. Amer.; lvs. pinnate or blades 2-cleft at apex and pinnately ribbed, sheaths tubular but often splitting and not forming a crownshaft, pinnae linear to doubly or singly curved, usually with the midrib most prominent; infls. among or below lvs., usually solitary but sometimes several at a node, sometimes penetrating sheaths, branched or spicate, bracts 3 or more, usually tubular, rachillae with fls. mostly solitary and spirally arranged but male fls. sometimes clustered or arranged in vertical rows, female fls. not clustered but sometimes in vertical rows, rachillae of female infls. usually becoming orange in fr.; male fls. symmetrical, calyx cupular and entire or 3-lobed or 3-parted or of 3 imbricate sepals, petals 3, free and valvate, or united basally with valvate tips, or united apically and opening by lateral slits, stamens 6, pistillode usually prominent, female fls. with calyx cupular or 3-parted or sepals separate and imbricate, petals separate, imbricate or subvalvate, rarely united, staminodes 0–6, minute, pistil 3-celled, 3-ovuled; fr. usually 1-seeded, black or red, with basal stigmatic residue, seed with homogeneous endosperm and lateral embryo.

Chamaedoreas are highly ornamental small palms with neat, green, bamboolike stems. Besides being useful for moist, shady sites in tropical and subtropical gardens (Zone 10), they are among the most popular of palms for house plants because they thrive in poor light (in fact, they should not be grown in full sun) and survive neglect in watering. They offer much variety in foliage, size, and general habit, some maturing when only a few in. tall, while the cespitose species, when planted in a large pot or tub, form attractive clumps 8 ft. tall or more. All produce floral branches and flowers in the home, but the fruits usually are not matured unless both male and female plants are grown together and the female flowers are hand-pollinated. One species, *C. elegans*, produced commercially in great numbers in Fla. and elsewhere, is the most widely grown house palm. It is used, when mature, either as a solitary or grouped pot plant or, when juvenile, as a feature subject in diminutive dish gardens. Among the other more attractive single-stemmed species are *C. Ernesti-Augusti, C. geonomiformis*, and *C. Klotzschiana*. The most popular cespitose species are *C. costaricana, C. erumpens*, and *C. Seifrizii*. Propagated by seeds or by clump division in the cespitose species. Most species are very susceptible to nematodes. See also *Palms*.

adscendens (Dammer) Burret. Solitary, to 8 ft.; lvs. with 1–6, dull velvety green pinnae on each side, to 6½ in. long, 1 in. wide; infls. solitary, long-peduncled, penetrating sheaths, ascending to erect, bracts 8–9, male rachis short with 2–5 pendulous rachillae to 6 in. long, female rachis spicate; male fls. with petals separate above the base, anthers entire at apex, longer than filaments, pistillode columnar, female fls. with petals imbricate; fr. black, globose or ovoid, ⁵⁄₁₆ in. long. Brit. Honduras, Guatemala.

alternans H. Wendl. Sometimes cespitose, with few sts., but usually solitary, to 10 ft. or more; lvs. spreading, petiole and rachis pale beneath, pinnae 8–12 on each side, the central to 15 in. long, 2½ in. wide, each with 5 or more prominent veins; infls. below lvs., male 2–5 and female 1–3 at each node, bracts 4, the upper broad and yellow inside; male fls. densely arranged in rows, calyx short, ringed, petals joined basally with spreading valvate tips, filaments cylindrical, longer than ovoid anthers, pistillode shorter than stamens and briefly 3-cleft apically or sometimes lacking, female fls. with imbricate petals; fr. black at full maturity, ellipsoid, to ¾ in. long, ⅜ in. wide. Mex.

Arenbergiana H. Wendl. Solitary, to 12 ft. or more; lvs. dark green, rachis pale beneath, pinnae 8–10 on each side, to 2 ft. long, 4 in. wide, each with several prominent veins; infls. spicate or forked, bracts 5, fls. densely crowded; male fls. with calyx shallowly lobed, petals united basally, valvate and spreading above, pistillode columnar, as long as stamens, female fls. with calyx 3-lobed, nearly as high as imbricate petals; fr. black, crowded, to ½ in. long. Guatemala to Panama.

brachypoda Standl. & Steyerm. Cespitose or colonial, to 4 ft., sts. very slender; lvs. undivided except at 2-cleft apex, to 6 in. long, 4 in. wide, 11–13-ribbed on each side, rachis pale beneath; infls. rupturing old sheaths, short-peduncled, bracts 6, very short, rachillae 5–8; male fls. yellow, calyx shallowly lobed, petals valvate above a united base, anthers 2-cleft apically, pistillode swollen at middle, 3-angled, female fls. with petals imbricate; fr. ellipsoid, black. Guatemala. Zone 10. Sometimes grown under the name *C. stolonifera.*

cataractarum Mart. Cespitose by branching of procumbent sts.; lvs. pinnate, erect, petiole and rachis pale beneath, pinnae 13–16 on each side, partly decurrent at base, to 11 in. long, 1 in. wide, each 1-ribbed with a prominent vein on each side; infls. erect among lvs., male with up to 6 rachillae to 3 in. long, female spicate or with 2–3 rachillae to 4 in. long; male fls. densely 4-ranked, calyx annular, petals united basally, valvate above, filaments prominent, pistillode columnar, briefly 3-cleft, female fls. with petals imbricate; fr. black, globose, ¼ in. in diam. S. Mex. Zone 10. Some material grown under this name is *C. oreophila.*

costaricana Ørst. Cespitose, to 10 ft.; lvs. pinnate, pinnae to 40, linear-lanceolate; infl. long-peduncled, rachillae 10–25, to 6 in. long; fr. globose. Costa Rica. Zone 10.

elatior Mart. Cespitose, subscandent; lvs. to 9 ft. long, deep green, undivided and 2-cleft on juvenile plants, pinnate on adults with pinnae toward apex usually reflexed and hooklike, pinnae to 14 in. long, 1¼ in. wide; infl. breaking through sheaths, bracts 3–4, rachillae several; female fls. with calyx deeply lobed, petals imbricate; fr. globose, black with glaucous bloom, ⅜ in. in diam. Mex., Guatemala.

elegans Mart. [*C. humilis* Mart.; *Collinia elegans* (Mart.) Liebm. ex Ørst.]. PARLOR PALM, GOOD-LUCK P. Solitary, to 6 ft.; lvs. deep green, pinnae 11–20 on each side of a pale-backed rachis, linear to narrowly lanceolate, to 8 in. long, ¾ in. wide; infls. long-peduncled, erect, bracts 4–9, rachillae simple or sometimes branched, spinose-tipped; male fls. pale yellow, calyx lobed, petals united except for triangular opening, pistillode 6-angled at apex, female fls. similar to male but with depressed-globose pistil; fr. globose, black, ¼ in. in diam. Mex., Guatemala. Zone 10. This sp., one of the most commonly cult., has often been listed under the invalid name *Neanthe bella.*

Ernesti-Augusti H. Wendl. [*Eleutheropetalum Ernesti-Augusti* (H. Wendl.) H. Wendl. ex Ørst.]. Solitary, to 6 ft.; lvs. broadly cuneate-obovate, deeply 2-cleft, otherwise undivided, rachis to 1 ft. long, ribs 13–16 on each side; infls. among lvs., long-peduncled, erect, bracts 5, the male with many rachillae, the female spicate; male fls. orange, calyx 3-lobed, petals valvate above united base, anthers deeply 2-cleft, pistillode columnar with 6-angled, truncate apex, female fls. with petals orange, basally imbricate but valvate above, hood-shaped; fr. ellipsoid, black, to 9/16 in. long, 5/16 in. in diam. Mex. to Honduras. Zone 10.

erumpens H. E. Moore. BAMBOO PALM. Cespitose, to 10 ft.; lvs. with green rachis, pinnae 5–15, deep green, lanceolate, to 11 in. long, 1 3/16 in. wide; infl. short-peduncled, rupturing sheaths, peduncle to 2¾ in. long, bracts 5, rachillae 4–11; fls. yellow, the male with sepals imbricate above base, petals valvate, anthers 2-cleft at tip, pistillode columnar, 3-lobed at apex, female with sepals and petals imbricate; fr. black, globose, about 5/16 in. in diam. Brit. Honduras, Guatemala. Zone 10. Useful for screening purposes in shady enclosed patios.

falcifera H. E. Moore. Solitary, to 18 ft.; lvs. pinnate, rachis pale beneath, pinnae 3–4 on each side, doubly curved, to 6 in. long, 1¼ in. wide; infls. below lvs., long-peduncled, bracts 3–4, rachillae 4–8; male fls. yellowish-green, corolla opening by lateral slits, female fls. with petals imbricate; fr. sickle-shaped, orange, to 9/16 in. long, ⅛ in. in diam. Guatemala.

fragrans (Ruiz & Pav.) Mart. Cespitose, to 5 ft. or more, very slender; lvs. deeply 2-cleft, otherwise undivided; infls. short, rachillae few; male fls. orange, intensely fragrant. Peru.

geonomiformis H. Wendl. Solitary, to nearly 6 ft.; lvs. deeply 2-cleft at apex, otherwise undivided, oblanceolate in outline, ribs 9–12 on each side; infls. among lvs., the male with 2–6 rachillae, the female spicate, bracts 5, fls. yellow; male fls. opening by lateral slits, female fls. with sepals and petals imbricate; fr. globose, blue-black, to nearly ½ in. in diam. Brit. Honduras to Honduras.

glaucifolia H. Wendl. Solitary, to 15 ft.; lvs. pinnate, more or less glaucous, elongate, pinnae 46–80 on each side in groups of 2–4, borne in different planes and directions, narrowly linear, to 14 in. long, ⅜ in. wide; infl. below lvs. or among old sheaths, long-peduncled, erect, solitary at nodes, bracts 6, male infl. with many pendulous rachillae, the female with 16–30 stiff rachillae, fls. solitary; male fls. opening by lateral slits, female fls. with petals imbricate; fr. globose, black. S. Mex.

graminifolia H. Wendl. Solitary; lvs. pinnate, pinnae about 30, regularly arranged, narrowly linear, to 12 in. long, ½ in. wide; infls. long-peduncled, male rachillae about 12, pendulous, to 12 in. long; male fls. opening by lateral slits, female fls. and fr. not known. Guatemala? Zone 10. Material grown under this name is usually misidentified; the sp. was described from cult. and is incompletely known.

humilis: *C. elegans.*

Karwinskyana H. Wendl. Cespitose; petiole and rachis pale beneath, pinnae 27–33 on each side, elongate-lanceolate; infls. below lvs., spreading, rachillae 18–26; male fls. yellow, with separate petals; fr. oblong in outline, black. Mex.

Klotzschiana H. Wendl. Solitary, to 8 ft. or more; lvs. pinnate, pinnae about 14–15 on each side in groups of 2–4, somewhat doubly curved, to 10 in. long, 2⅛ in. wide; infl. long-peduncled, bracts about 6, tubular, rachillae about 12, to 9 in. long; fls. solitary; male fls. opening by lateral slits, female fls. with petals imbricate; fr. black, globose, about ⅜ in. in diam. Mex. Zone 10.

lepidota H. Wendl. Solitary, to 1½ ft. or more, sts. ¾ in. in diam.; lvs. pinnate, to 3½ ft. long, minutely pale lepidote, petiole and rachis green, pinnae about 13 on each side, elongate-lanceolate, to 9 in. long, 1¾ in. wide; infls. below lvs., long-peduncled, bracts 7, male rachillae about 26, to 7 in. long, female rachillae 18–24, the lower sometimes branched; male fls. opening by lateral slits, female fls. with petals imbricate; fr. black, globose, ¼ in. in diam. Mex.

metallica O. F. Cook ex H. E. Moore. Similar to *C. Ernesti-Augusti* but differing in deep green lvs. with metallic sheen, often cupped upward toward the tip, sometimes partly pinnate, with 8–9 ribs on each side; female infl. spreading-erect, with spike at an angle to peduncle; fr. black, ½ in. long, about ⅜ in. in diam. Mex. Sometimes grown under the name *C. tenella.*

microspadix Burret. Cespitose, to 8 ft., sts. ⅜ in. in diam.; lvs. pinnate, petiole and rachis green, pinnae velvety green above, glaucous beneath, about 9 on each side of rachis or fewer when the terminal pair broader, to 10 in. long, 1¼ in. wide; infls. short, to 9 in. long, bracts 4–5, rachis to 1 in. long, with 3–4 green rachillae; male fls. in clusters of 2–4, creamy-white, petals valvate with spreading tips, filaments prominent, anthers shallowly 2-cleft at apex and base, female fls. solitary along rachillae, calyx 3-lobed, half as long as imbricate petals; fr. orange-red or red, globose, ⅜ in. in diam. E. Mex. Relatively cold-tolerant, warmer parts of Zone 9a. Resistant to nematodes.

neurochlamys Burret. Solitary, to more than 12 ft.; lvs. pinnate, rachis pale beneath, pinnae 6–8 on each side, narrowly rhombic, doubly curved, to 13 in. long, 2⅝ in. wide; infls. among or below lvs., long-peduncled, bracts 5–6, rachillae 10–25; male fls. opening by lateral slits, female fls. with petals imbricate; fr. subreniform, orange, about ⅜ in. long, 3/16 in. in diam. Mex. to Honduras.

oblongata Mart. Solitary, to 10 ft. or more; lvs. pinnate, rachis pale beneath, pinnae 6–9 on each side, somewhat leathery, rhombic-lanceolate and doubly curved, to 16 in. long, 4 in. wide; infls. below lvs., long-peduncled, bracts 5–7, rachillae 6–25; male fls. greenish, calyx 3-lobed, petals valvate, spreading, stamens white, pistillode cylindrical, female fls. with calyx deeply lobed, petals imbricate; fr. black, ellipsoid or slightly lunate, to 9/16 in. long, 5/16 in. in diam. Mex. to Nicaragua.

oreophila Mart. Solitary, or perhaps rarely cespitose, to 6 ft., sts. to ½ in. thick; lvs. pinnate, rachis more or less pale beneath, pinnae narrow, straight, 11–18 on each side, to 8 in. long, ½ in. wide, not decurrent, midrib prominent; infls. erect, spicate, the male 5 at a node, to 9 in. long, the female solitary, to 5½ in. long, peduncle to 2 ft. long, bracts about 6; male fls. densely crowded, petals separate, filaments cylindrical, elongate, pistillode slender, as long as stamens, female fls. crowded, petals imbricate; fr. red. Mex.

Pacaya Ørst. Solitary, to 6 ft.; lvs. pinnate, petiole and rachis pale beneath, pinnae strongly doubly curved, 5–8 on each side, to 7 in. long, 2 in. wide; infl. among or below lvs., long-peduncled, rachillae few; fr. orange, ellipsoid or obovoid, to ½ in. long. Costa Rica, Panama.

pochutlensis Mart. Cespitose, to 10 ft. or more; lvs. pinnate, petiole and sheath each to 1 ft. long, rachis to 32 in. long, pinnae 20–24 on each side, regularly arranged, somewhat curved-acuminate, to 16 in. long, 1 in. wide; infls. erect below lvs., long-peduncled, bracts 7, rachillae green; fls. solitary, male fls. bright yellow, calyx lobed, petals acute, spreading, stamens shorter than pistillode, anthers not deeply 2-cleft at apex, pistillode columnar, 3-lobed at apex, female fls. with sepals and petals imbricate; fr. globose, black with glaucous bloom, to ½ in. in diam. W. Mex.

radicalis Mart. Solitary or rarely cespitose, decumbent or sometimes erect; lvs. arched, pinnate, deep green, petiole and rachis green, pinnae straight, narrow, about 18 on each side, to 13 in. long, ⅝ in. wide, not decurrent at base, midrib prominent beneath; infls. erect, peduncle to 32 in. long or more, bracts about 7, rachis to 1½ in. long, male rachillae to about 9, to 8 in. long, female rachillae fewer, shorter; male fls. mostly in pairs, sepals broadly imbricate, nearly as long as valvate petals, filaments as long as pistillode, female fls. solitary, calyx cupular, petals imbricate; fr. ellipsoid to nearly globose, red, ⅜ in. long. Ne. Mex. Cold-tolerant, warmer parts of Zone 9a. Somewhat resistant to nematodes.

Sartorii Liebm. Solitary, to 10 ft., sts. to ¾ in. in diam.; lvs. pinnate, petiole to 16 in. long, pale beneath as is rachis, pinnae 6–8 on each side, doubly curved, to 16 in. long, 3¼ in. wide; infls. long-peduncled, solitary and erect from sheaths, bracts 5–6, male infl. with many pendulous green rachillae to 7¼ in. long, the female with 4–6 erect rachillae; male fls. with calyx lobed, petals orange, valvate, female fls. with sepals imbricate, petals lightly imbricate basally, orange and subvalvate above; fr. black, ellipsoid, to ⅝ in. long. Mex. to Honduras.

Schiedeana Mart. Solitary, to 10 ft., sts. to 1 in. in diam.; lvs. pinnate, petiole and rachis green, pinnae 13–14 on each side, narrowly doubly curved, acuminate, to 1 ft. long, 1⅝ in. wide, midrib and marginal veins prominent; infls. below lvs., long-peduncled, to 32 in. long, bracts 6–7, rachillae 10–15; fls. solitary, spirally arranged, male fls. opening by lateral slits, female fls. with petals imbricate; fr. globose, glaucous, black, about ¼ in. in diam. E. Mex.

Schippii Burret. Colonial, to 9 ft.; lvs. pinnate, rachis green with about 30 narrowly linear, straight pinnae on each side, these to 1 ft. long, ¾ in. wide; infls. erect from below lvs., long-peduncled, bracts about 5, rachillae many, the male pendulous, the female stiffish; male fls. opening by lateral slits, female fls. with petals imbricate; fr. globose, black, ⁵⁄₁₆ in. in diam. Brit. Honduras.

Seifrizii Burret. Similar to *C. erumpens* but pinnae 13–18 on each side of rachis, straight, narrow, stiffish, to 14½ in. long, ⅝ in. wide; male fls. fragrant. Yucatan Pen. Zone 10. Useful for low hedges, 4–5 ft. Can withstand more sun than most chamedoreas but susceptible to nematodes.

stolonifera H. Wendl. Colonial, to 3 ft., sts. to ¼ in. in diam.; lvs. few, petiole short, rachis pale beneath, to 4¼ in. long, blade undivided except the deeply 2-cleft apex, to 6⅜ in. long on upper margin; infl. below lvs., short, to 6 in. long, bracts 3–4, rachillae 1–2 on female or 2–7 on male infls.; fls. orange, the male with petals valvate, pistillode as long as stamens, the female with petals briefly imbricate basally, valvate above; fr. globose, black, to about ⅜ in. in diam. Mex. Much material so named in cult. is *C. brachypoda.*

tenella H. Wendl. Solitary, to 2 ft. or perhaps more; lvs. 2-cleft apically, otherwise undivided, rachis to about 6½ in. long, blade narrow, 1½–3 in. wide, toothed along lateral margin, ribs 11–12 on each side; infls. short, bracts 4, male infl. with 1–4 rachillae to 4½ in. long, the female spicate; fls. solitary, spirally arranged, yellow, male fls. opening by lateral slits, female fls. with petals imbricate; fr. globose, black, ⁵⁄₁₆ in. in diam. Mex. Much material so named may be *C. metallica.*

Tepejilote Liebm. [*C. Wendlandiana* (Ørst.) Hemsl.]. PACAYA. Solitary or rarely cespitose, to 20 ft. or more, often with prop roots; lvs. pinnate, large, rachis pale beneath, with 12–25 pinnae on each side, these with 1 rib and several prominent veins, broadly linear-lanceolate, to 28 in. long, 3 in. wide, apex narrowed, curved; infls. solitary at nodes, bracts 3–5, the upper hoodlike, rachillae of male infls. 18–50, spreading or pendulous, with fls. crowded in 4–7 rows, rachillae of female infls. 4–17, stiffish, with fls. separate; male fls. yellow, petals united basally, apices spreading, valvate, female fls. with petals imbricate; fr. ovoid to ellipsoid, blue-green maturing black, to ¾ in. long, ⁵⁄₁₆ in. in diam. Mex. to Colombia. A variable sp., sometimes cult. (especially in Guatemala) for the edible unopened male infl.

Wendlandiana: *C. Tepejilote.*

CHAMAEFISTULA: *CASSIA.* Chamaefistula antillana: *Cassia quinquangulata.*

CHAMAELAUCIUM: *CHAMELAUCIUM.*

CHAMAELIRIUM Willd. DEVIL'S-BIT. *Liliaceae.* One sp., a dioecious, per. herb, native to e. N. Amer.; roots tuberous; lvs. basal and cauline; fls. unisexual, white, drying yellowish, in terminal, spikelike racemes, perianth segms. 6, 1-nerved, stamens 6; fr. a 3-valved, loculicidal caps.

Sometimes planted in shady locations in the garden.

luteum (L.) A. Gray. BLAZING-STAR, FAIRY-WAND, RATTLESNAKE ROOT. St. erect, 1–4 ft., female plants taller and more leafy than male plants; basal lvs. spatulate to obovate, 3–6 in. long, st. lvs. progressively reduced and narrowed upward along st. Mass. to s. Ont. and Mich., s. to Fla. and Ark. Dried roots used medicinally.

CHAMAEMELUM Mill. *Compositae* (Anthemis Tribe). Three spp. of per. herbs, native to w. Eur. and Medit. region; sts. leafy; lvs. alt., 1–3-pinnately parted; fl. heads solitary, terminal on brs., radiate; disc fls. with base of corolla saccate,

covering top of achene, ray fls. present; achenes laterally compressed, not ribbed.

Propagated by seeds and division.

nobile (L.) All. [*Anthemis nobilis* L.]. CHAMOMILE, GARDEN C., RUSSIAN C. Pleasantly aromatic, creeping, much-branched per., to 1 ft., sts. decumbent or ascending, downy; lvs. to 2 in. long, sparsely hairy, 2–3-pinnately divided, the segms. linear-bristly or filiform; heads to 1 in. across, receptacle conical; disc fls. yellow, ray fls. white; achenes 3-angled. W. Eur., Azores, N. Afr.; occasionally escaped from cult. in N. Amer. Fl. heads are used medicinally.

CHAMAENERION: *EPILOBIUM.*

CHAMAEPERICLYMENUM: *CORNUS.*

CHAMAERANTHEMUM Nees. *Acanthaceae.* Four spp. of per. herbs or subshrubs of Cent. and S. Amer.; lvs. opp., usually large, sometimes variegated; fls. white, in terminal panicles or spikes, bracts small, corolla tube long, slender, lobes nearly equal, stamens 4, included, didynamous, the longer pair with 2 anther sacs, the shorter with 1 or 2 sacs; fr. a caps., seeds 4.

Sometimes grown as houseplants for their attractive foliage.

alatum: *Pseuderanthemum alatum.*

Gaudichaudii Nees. Prostrate; lvs. ovate, to 3 in. long, cordate, sometimes variegated; fls. small, in terminal spikes. Brazil. An attractive foliage plant.

igneum: *Xeranthemum igneum.*

venosum M. B. Foster ex Wassh. & L. B. Sm. Sts. prostrate or ascending, tomentose; lvs. ovate, to 3 in. long, rounded or subcordate at base, sometimes variegated; fls. in terminal spikes, corolla white, suffused with lavender, about ½ in. long. Brazil.

CHAMAEROPS L. FAN PALM. *Palmae.* One sp., a dioecious or polygamo-dioecious palm in Medit. region of Eur. and N. Afr., sts. usually suckering and forming a low clump but sometimes arborescent, clothed with more or less persistent fibrous lf. sheaths; lvs. palmate, petiole armed with short, straight spinose teeth pointing toward the blade, blade deeply divided into 1-ribbed segms.; infl. among lvs., bearing a single completely keeled bract at the base, smaller bracts subtending the few brs.; fls. borne singly, sepals united in a low, 3-lobed cupule, petals 3, imbricate, stamens or staminodes 6, carpels 3 and separate or reduced to pistillodes; fr. globose to oblong-ellipsoid, fleshy, seed with marginally ruminate endosperm and deeply intruded seed coat on one side.

One of the hardier palms, thriving in full sun or partial shade in Zone 9. Not particular as to soil but responding best to deep rich loam. Forms clumps which are excellent landscape or garden subjects or for making low informal hedges; often used in tubs for patio or cool greenhouse. Easily propagated by seeds, germinating rather quickly, but slow-growing unless fertilized. The several varieties and cultivars propagated by suckers. See also *Palms.*

canariensis: a listed name of no botanical standing, probably for a form of *C. humilis.*

elegans: a listed name of no botanical standing, probably for a form of *C. humilis.*

excelsa: a name applied incorrectly in hort. to *Trachycarpus Fortunei;* botanically, the name is a synonym of *Rhapis excelsa.*

Fortunei: *Trachycarpus Fortunei.*

humilis L. EUROPEAN F.P. Sts. to 5 ft. or rarely to 20 ft. in arborescent forms or when suckers are pruned; lvs. stiff, small, 2–3 ft. wide, green or rarely glaucous; fr. variable in size and shape. The only palm native to Eur., widely cult. in areas with Medit. type climates. Zone 9. Cvs. '**Canariensis**' and '**Robusta**' are listed. Var. **arborescens** (Pers.) Steudel. Arborescent. Var. **elatior** Guss. [var. *macrocarpa* (Tineo ex Guss.) Becc.]. Fr. large. Var. **macrocarpa:** var. *elatior.*

Ritchiana: *Nannorrhops Ritchiana.*

CHAMAESYCE: *EUPHORBIA.*

CHAMBEYRONIA Vieill. *Palmae.* Two spp. of tall, solitary, unarmed, monoecious palms with a prominent crownshaft, native in New Caledonia; lvs. pinnate, pinnae acute; infl. below lvs., paniculate, peduncle short, bearing 2 nearly equal, caducous bracts, rachillae with fls. large, in triads (2 male and 1 female) near the base and above these with paired or solitary male fls.; male fls. with sepals imbricate, petals valvate, asymmetrical, stamens many, filaments erect, female fls. with sepals and petals imbricate, ovary 1-celled; fr. ovoid-ellipsoid with apical stigmatic scar, endocarp not operculate, seed with homogeneous endosperm and basal embryo.

For culture see *Palms.*

macrocarpa (Brongn.) Vieill. To 60 ft. or more; lvs. large, reddish when young, green in age, pinnae many, wide, with strong marginal veins; fr. dark red, about 1½ in. long.

CHAMELAUCIUM Desf. [*Chamaelaucium* DC.]. WAX-FLOWER. *Myrtaceae.* About 12 spp. of heathlike shrubs in W. Australia; lvs. opp., linear, sessile; fls. white, pink, or red, 5-merous, in the axils of upper st. lvs., or few in terminal racemes, stamens 10, dehiscing longitudinally; fr. dry, inde-hiscent, enclosed in the persistent calyx base.

ciliatum Desf. CAMEO PINK. To 2 ft. or more; lvs. to ⅜ in. long, obtuse; fls. very small, calyx lobes fringed, petals to ⅛ in. long. Perhaps not cult.; material offered under this name is probably *C. uncinatum.*

roseum: a listed name of no botanical standing.

uncinatum Schauer. GERALDTON W., GERALDTON WAX PLANT. Shrub, to 15 ft. or more; lvs. to 1 in. long, with a hooked tip; fls. white, pink, or lilac, in few-fld. cymes, petals orbicular, ⅜ in. long. Late spring. Often grown under the name *C. ciliatum.*

CHARACEAE Agardh. STONEWORT FAMILY. Algae; 5 or 6 genera and about 215 spp. of nonvascular green plants allied to the green algae and forming a group rather inter-mediate between green algae and mosses; axis erect, divided into nodes and internodes, with whorls of filiform, leaflike, branched axes at the nodes, the entire plant body sometimes incrusted with calcium carbonate; reproduction oogamous, with eggs produced in oogonia and sperm in antheridia. *Nitella* is cult.

CHARIEIS Cass. *Compositae* (Aster Tribe). One sp., an ann. herb of S. Afr.; lvs. oblong-spatulate, the lower opp., the upper alt.; fl. heads radiate, solitary, on long peduncles, in-volucre broad, involucral bracts in 1 row, green, scarious-margined, receptacle naked; disc fls. tubular, ray fls. ligulate; achenes obovate, flat, with a thickened margin, pappus of disc achenes of deciduous plumose bristles, pappus of ray achenes none.

heterophylla Cass. [*C. Neesii* Hort.]. Sts. 6–12 in., branching near base; lvs. entire or remotely toothed, sparsely hairy; heads about 1 in. across; disc fls. blue or yellow, ray fls. blue.

Neesii: *C. heterophylla.*

CHASMANTHE N. E. Br. *Iridaceae.* About 9 spp. of cor-mous herbs, native to trop. and S. Afr.; corm tunicate, with thin fibers, sts. usually simple; lvs. 2-ranked, linear or sword-shaped, soft, not pleated; fls. in a terminal spike or panicle with a straight axis, spathe valves entire, shorter than the tube, perianth tube curved, constricted near the middle or below, limb 2-lipped, upper lip slightly hooded, lower lip slightly shorter, of 5 segms. of equal length, stamens 3, fila-ments borne on the perianth tube, not united, style brs. 3; fr. a 3-valved caps.

Cultivation as for *Gladiolus.*

aethiopica (L.) N. E. Br. Corm globose, tunic membranous, sts. to 4 ft., often branched; lvs. stiffly erect, 12–24 in. long, mostly ½–1 in. wide, bright green; infl. erect, dense, many-fld.; fls. curved, about 2 in. long, perianth tube constricted abruptly below dilated part into a short, narrow, basal part, upper segm. orange-red, the other 5 segms. greenish, half as long.

floribunda (Salisb.) N. E. Br. Differs from *C. aethiopica* in having lvs. 1–1¾ in. wide or more, and the perianth tube tapering or rounding off from the dilated part into the narrow basal part.

paniculata: a listed name of no botanical standing.

CHASMANTHIUM Link. *Gramineae.* Five spp. of per. grasses in e. and se. U.S., sts. simple or branched, clustered or colonial from rhizomes; lf. blades flat, serrate; infl. panicu-late, spikelets 2- to many-fld., laterally compressed, rachillas disarticulating above the glumes and between the florets; glumes 2, keeled, 3–7-nerved, lemmas 5–15-nerved, keeled,

lower 1–4 empty, keels serrate or ciliate, florets bisexual, with 1 stamen. For terminology see *Gramineae.*

latifolium (Michx.) Yates [*Uniola latifolia* Michx.]. WILD OATS. Sts. to 5 ft., rarely branched, leafy to ⅘ their height; lf. blades broadly lanceolate, to 9 in. long, ¾ in. wide; panicle open, nodding or droop-ing, brs. with few spikelets; spikelets mostly 6–17-fld., long-pedicelled, to 2 in. long, ¾ in. wide. Woodlands, Penn., w. to Man., s. to n. Fla., New Mex., and n. Mex.

CHASMATOPHYLLUM Dinter & Schwant. *Aizoaceae.* About 6 spp. of shrubby succulents, native to S. Afr., sts. erect or ascending at first, later creeping or prostrate; lvs. 4-ranked, surface with whitish tubercles, sometimes with 1–2 blunt teeth on margins and lower side toward apex; fls. solitary, terminal, bractless, calyx unequally 5-lobed, petals yellow, many, in 2 series, stamens many, ovary inferior, 5-celled, stigmas 5; fr. a 5-valved caps., expanding keels broadly winged, placental tubercles absent.

Growth occurs in summer when the plants need a sunny location and moderate moisture. In winter they require a light, dry place with a relatively cool temperature of about 55° F. Propagated easily by seeds or cuttings. See also *Succulents.*

musculinum (Haw.) Dinter & Schwant. Sts. forming dense mats; lvs. spreading, slightly incurved, gray-green, minutely rough-dotted, to ¾ in. long, ¼ in. wide, equally 3-angled in section to semicylindrical, upper side slightly rounded, lower side with a blunt keel, the keel and edges usually armed with 1–2 small teeth, apex bluntly acuminate; fls. ⅝ in. across, petals yellow, reddish at tip on the outside. S.-W. Afr., Cape Prov., Orange Free State.

Nelii Schwant. Sts. gray; lvs. spreading, gray-green, white-tubercled beneath and near apex above, to ½ in. long, about ⅛ in. wide and thick, more or less spatulate in outline, upper side flat or slightly rounded, lower surface rounded, keeled toward blunt, 3-angled, toothless apex; fls. about ½ in. across, petals golden-yellow. Cape Prov.

CHAYOTE. The chayote is a cucurbit, *Sechium edule,* grown for the edible fruits and root tubers, both used as vegetables. It is native to tropical America, probably Mexico and Central America, is widespread in the western tropics and elsewhere as a cultivated plant, and is adaptable also to the coastal parts of the United States from South Carolina southward and to southern California. The roots survive the winter if given protection in regions where the ground does not freeze more than an inch or so deep. If grown only as an annual each year from seeds, the plant may be raised to the fruiting stage farther north, although a long season of at least five or six months is required. Two or more plants should be grown to insure pollination.

The chayote is propagated from seeds, the entire ripe, usu-ally sprouting fruit being planted in spring, or perhaps in autumn in southern Florida; the fruit is placed with the broad end sloping downward and the stem end slightly exposed. There is one seed in each fruit. The plants are started where they are to stand. They should be 8–12 feet apart, with a trellis or other support provided. Special or named cultivars are propagated by cuttings of shoots taken at the crown of the plant, and struck under glass or other protection. If the soil is fertile, a plant should produce 50–100 or more fruits in a season. The fruits are boiled, and prepared in various ways for eating. In tropical countries the large root tubers are eaten like potatoes; the tubers are usually harvested after the second year's growth. If the tubers are left in the ground in regions where they do not freeze, the plant is, of course, perennial. Under such conditions the stems of the plant are usually pruned back to a length of about 6 feet between fruiting seasons. The chayote fruit is much prized in tropical America, where it may be known also as christophine and chuchu, and in some places as mirliton and vegetable pear. The herbage supplies good forage, and the young parts are sometimes used like asparagus and spinach.

CHEILANTHES Swartz. LIP FERN. *Polypodiaceae.* About 180 spp. of small ferns, widely distributed in temp. and trop. regions, in dry rocky situations; often hairy, woolly, or scaly; lvs. 1–3-pinnate; sori on ends of veins, marginal, with margins of pinnules recurved over them.

Greenhouse and semihardy ferns; under glass the foliage should be kept dry. For culture see *Ferns.*

alabamensis (Buckley) Kunze. ALABAMA L.F. Lvs. to 10 in. long, lanceolate, 2-pinnate, nearly glabrous, petioles black. Va. to Ala. and Ariz.

californica (Hook.) Mett. CALIFORNIA L.F. Lvs. to 15 in. long, pentagonal-triangular, 3–4-pinnate, glabrous, petioles to 1 ft. long, brownish. Calif.

Clevelandii D. C. Eat. CLEVELAND'S L.F. Lvs. few, to 30 in. long, glabrous above, scaly-hairy beneath, 3–4-pinnate, pinnae curved, pinnules somewhat cordate-orbicular, nearly entire; sori several. S. Calif.

Covillei Maxon. COVILLE'S L.F. Lvs. tufted, to 20 in. long, 3-pinnate, glabrous above, densely covered with white or brown ciliate scales beneath, longer than the pinnules. S. Calif., Nev., Utah, Ariz.

densa: *C. siliquosa.*

Feei T. Moore [*C. lanuginosa* Nutt.]. SLENDER L.F., FÉE'S L.F. Lvs. to 12 in. long, linear-oblong to ovate, 2–3-pinnate, hairy above, densely woolly beneath, without scales. Wisc. to B.C., s. to Tex. and Calif.

Fendleri Hook. FENDLER'S L.F. Lvs. to 10 in. long, 3-pinnate, glabrous above, brown-scaly, not tomentose beneath, pinnules nearly orbicular, often with 1 broad central scale beneath, petioles brown. Sw. U.S. from Colo. to Mex.

gracillima D. C. Eat. LACE FERN. Lvs. to 12 in. long, 2-pinnate, with a few small scales above, densely woolly beneath, margins of pinnules strongly reflexed, petioles to 6 in. long, dark brown. B.C. to Calif.

hispanica Mett. Lf. blade 1–1½ in. long, ¾ in. wide, triangular, 2–3-pinnate, pinnae opp., the lowest largest, oblong or branched on lower side; pinnules roundish-oblong, pinnatifid, petioles with wiry linear-filiform scales at base. Portugal, Spain.

lanosa (Michx.) D. C. Eat. [*C. tomentosa* Link]. HAIRY L.F., WOOLLY L.F. Lvs. to 20 in. long, 2-pinnate-pinnatifid, densely rusty-hairy on both sides, pinnules oblong, deeply lobed, petioles villous-hispidulous, brown-woolly. Va. to Ga., Okla., Ariz. and Mex. Not to be confused with the more n. *C. vestita.*

lanuginosa: *C. Feei.*

myriophylla Desv. Lvs. densely tufted, to 9 in. long, 3–4-pinnate, densely scaly and woolly beneath, petioles brown. Mex. to S. Amer.

siliquosa Maxon. [*C. densa* (Brackenr.) Fée; *Cryptogramma densa* (Brackenr.) Diels; *Pellaea densa* (Brackenr.) Hook.]. INDIAN'S-DREAM. Lvs. somewhat dimorphic, triangular to nearly pentagonal, to 18 in. long, 3-pinnate, glabrous, sterile lvs. smaller, on shorter petioles, and short-lived; sori narrow-linear, glossy-brown. Que., Ont., B.C. to Calif. Some authors now place this plant in *Cryptogramma* or in *Pellaea.*

tomentosa: *C. lanosa.*

vestita (K. Spreng.) Swartz. HAIRY L.F. Confused with *C. lanosa;* but lvs. hairy, not woolly, to 10 in. long, petioles sparsely villous-hirsute. Conn. to Ga., w. to Mo. and Tex.

viscida Davenp. VISCID L.F. Lvs. many, to 18 in. long, 2-pinnate, minutely glandular-viscid; sori solitary on lobes of ultimate segms. S. Calif.

CHEIRANTHUS L. *Cruciferae.* About 10 spp. of per. herbs from the Madeira and Canary Is., e. to Himalayas, sometimes woody at base, more or less grayish-pubescent; lvs. narrow, nearly or quite entire; fls. mostly yellow or orange, sometimes brownish, sepals 4, petals 4, long-clawed; fr. a long silique.

The species ordinarily cultivated is the wallflower, *C. Cheiri,* a spring-blooming, low, erect perennial, much like stock but with flowers yellow, yellow-brown, red, to red-black. It is much prized in Eur., where it is native, but less popular in this country. In England it is a frequent inhabitant of fence walls and quarries. It requires a cool season for best bloom, and in the northern U.S. the unflowered plants must usually be carried over in a frame. Their free flowering, rich deep colors, and pleasant fragrance make wallflowers good plants for very early spring bloom, or for winter bloom in mild climates. Special color forms are propagated by means of cuttings, but plants are usually grown from seeds. Since plants should be strong and bushy to go through the winter well, seeds are best sown early in the year, the plants transplanted once or twice, ready for bloom the following spring. If wanted for bedding-out, they may be carried over winter dormant in pots, and turned out as soon as the ground is open. Seeds planted later, in late spring or early summer, may give satisfactory spring-blooming plants if the season and all other conditions are favorable to them, but it is better to sow seeds earlier. Some of the strains give bloom the first year from seeds if started early, the plants being practically annual.

Allionii: a confused name; plants known by this name in the trade probably belong to *Erysimum hieraciifolium.*

alpinus: plants known by this name in the trade probably belong to *Erysimum hieraciifolium.*

asper: *Erysimum asperum.*

Cheiri L. [*C. fruticulosus* L.; *C. Senoneri* Heldr. & Sartori]. WALLFLOWER, ENGLISH W. To 2½ ft., strongly erect; lvs. lanceolate or narrower, to 3 in. long, acute; fls. yellow to yellow-brown, to 1 in. long, fragrant. Spring. S. Eur. An old garden favorite, variously colored and often double.

fruticulosus: *C. Cheiri.*

×**kewensis** Hort.: *C. Cheiri* × *C. mutabilis.* WINTER WALLFLOWER. Branched subshrub; fls. in upright racemes, about 1 in. across, fragrant, petals brownish-orange inside and reddish-brown outside, becoming pale purple.

linifolius: *Erysimum linifolium.*

maritimus: *Malcolmia maritima.*

mutabilis L'Hér. Madeira and Canary Is. Not in general cult., but one parent of *C.* × *kewensis.*

Senoneri: *C. Cheiri.*

CHEIRIDOPSIS N. E. Br. *Aizoaceae.* About 100 spp. of dwarf, clump-forming succulents, native to S. Afr.; lvs. opp., 1–3 pairs on a shoot, successive pairs usually differing in form, size, and growth, surface green, glaucous-green, or white, sometimes dotted, lf. sheath drying and often partly or entirely covering the next pair of lvs. during resting period; fls. solitary, terminal, pedicels with sheathing bracts, calyx 4–5-lobed, petals many, stamens many, ovary partly superior becoming inferior in fr., 8–19-celled, stigmas 8–19, usually plumose; fr. a caps., cell lids present, expanding keels awned and incurved at tip, usually without marginal wings, placental tubercles large.

Growth occurs for most species during early summer when they require a light, sunny location with moderate moisture. During autumn watering should be gradually decreased, and when completely dry, the plants should be kept at a relatively cool temperature of about 55–60° F. Young seedlings must be kept dry during winter. Propagated by seeds; cuttings are very difficult. See also *Succulents.*

acuminata L. Bolus. Minutely papillate-velvety, robust, brs. light brown, to ⅝ in. in diam.; lvs. 4 on sterile brs., 2 on fertile brs., all alike, lower ones to 3 in. long or more, ⅝ in. wide at middle, upper ones to 2⅝ in. long with sheath ⅜ in. long, ⅜ in. wide and thick; fls. to 2½ in. across, on bracted pedicels ¼ in. long, petals pale yellow, stigmas 9. Cape Prov.

aspera L. Bolus. Stiff, sts. and lvs. roughened, green or slightly glaucous, becoming reddish in age; lvs. 4 on sterile brs., 2 on fertile brs., lower ones unequal, the larger in a pair to 1⅜ in. long above sheath ³⁄₁₆ in. long, about ¼ in. wide and thick at middle, semicylindrical, flattish above, rounded on the sides and obscurely keeled beneath, keel and edges minutely ciliate, apex acute or rarely obtuse, upper lvs. equal, to 1⅝ in. long; fls. 2 in. across, on pedicels to 1¾ in. long, petals yellow, stigmas 10. Cape Prov.

Braunsii: *Argyroderma Braunsii.*

brevis L. Bolus. Brs. and lvs. minutely velvety, glaucous-green; lvs. 4 on sterile brs., 2 on fertile brs., lower ones to ¾ in. long, ¼ in. wide and thick, upper side flat, rounded on the back and obtusely keeled toward the truncate tip, upper ones to nearly ¾ in. long, acutely keeled and obtuse; fls. about 1³⁄₁₆ in. across, on pedicel about ⅜ in. long, opening at midday, petals yellow or golden-yellow, stigmas 10. Cape Prov.

candidissima (Haw.) N. E. Br. GOAT'S-HORNS, VICTORY PLANT. Mat-forming; lvs. 2–4 on a br., nearly erect, gray-white, dotted with dark green, to 4 in. long, ½ in. wide, ⅝ in. thick, elongate boat-shaped, upper side flat, lower side wide, rounded and obtusely keeled toward apex, tip with a reddish point; fls. 2 in. across, on pedicels 3 in. long, petals white or light pink, stigmas 17–19. Cape Prov.

Caroli-Schmidtii (Dinter & A. Berger) N. E. Br. Mat-forming; lvs. in several pairs on a br., all similar but of unequal length, light gray, transparent-dotted, to 1⅝ in. long, 1 in. wide, ⅝ in. thick, semicylindrical, united basally for ⅓ their length in a solid body, upper side flat, lower side rounded, obtusely keeled toward the rounded and minutely mucronate apex, keel cartilaginous; fls. 1½ in. across, on pedicels ½ in. long, petals golden-yellow. S.-W. Afr.

Comptonii: a listed name of no botanical standing, once used for a form of *C. Pillansii.*

crassa L. Bolus. Velvety; lvs. 4 on a br., pale glaucous-green, lower ones to 1³⁄₁₆ in. long, 1 in. wide, ⅞ in. thick, upper surface flat, lower surface rounded on the sides and curved to tip where rounded-triangular in section, upper lvs. to 1³⁄₁₆ in. long, about ⅝ in. wide and thick;

fls. on pedicels $\frac{5}{8}$ in. long, petals pale straw-colored, to $1\frac{1}{4}$ in. long, stigmas 17. Cape Prov.

cuprea (L. Bolus) N. E. Br. Cushion-forming; lvs. 4 on a br., lower ones to $1\frac{1}{8}$ in. long, $\frac{3}{8}$ in. wide, united basally in a sheath $\frac{5}{8}$ in. long, flat on upper side, 3-angled in section, truncate, upper lvs. to $1\frac{1}{4}$ in. long, $\frac{1}{8}$ in. wide, 3-angled in section, truncate, angles minutely serrate; fls. $1\frac{1}{2}$ in. across, on pedicels to 3 in. long, bracts 2, united, petals yellow at the base shading upward to coppery-red in the upper half, stigmas 12. Cape Prov.

denticulata (Haw.) N. E. Br. St. not evident; lvs. gray, slender, rounded and dentate on keel toward tip beneath, 3-angled in section toward tip; fls. to $3\frac{3}{16}$ in. across, on pedicels to $\frac{5}{16}$ in. long, petals pale straw-colored. Cape Prov.

Duplessii L. Bolus. Cushion-forming, much-branched, brs. to $1\frac{5}{8}$ in. long, covered with old lvs.; lvs. minutely velvety-papillate, dotted, glaucous or nearly white to green, 4–6 on sterile brs., 4 on fertile brs., lower lvs. to 2 or even 3 in. long, $\frac{1}{2}$ in. wide, $\frac{3}{8}$ in. thick, truncate or nearly rounded at tip, central lvs. to 1 in. long above a sheath to 1 in. long and about $\frac{1}{8}$ in. wide and thick; fls. to $2\frac{1}{2}$ in. across, on pedicels to $1\frac{1}{2}$ in. long, bracts sheathing, to $1\frac{1}{4}$ in. long, petals yellow to golden-yellow, stigmas 10–12. Cape Prov.

Herrei L. Bolus. Sts. and lvs. minutely velvety-papillate; lvs. 4 on sterile brs., 2 on fertile brs., glaucous or dull gray-brown, to $\frac{3}{4}$ in. long above a sheath $\frac{1}{2}$ in. long, about $\frac{1}{2}$ in. wide and thick at the middle, upper side flat, sides rounded but compressed toward apex and the lower side obtusely keeled and abruptly curved to a truncate tip, with a large pustule; fls. to $2\frac{3}{8}$ in. across, on pedicels to $\frac{3}{8}$ in. long, petals yellow, at length orangish, reddish toward tip outside, stigmas 10. Cape Prov.

longipes L. Bolus. Lvs. 6 on sterile brs., 2 on fertile brs., lower lvs. spreading, glaucous-green, minutely velvety, minutely dotted, to $2\frac{1}{2}$ in. long, above a sheath $\frac{3}{8}$ in. long and to about $\frac{5}{16}$ in. wide and thick, more or less equal, some acute, others obtusely keeled to apex, central lvs. to 2 in. long, $\frac{1}{8}$ in. wide, $\frac{5}{16}$ in. thick, upper lvs. sometimes longer than the central; fls. to $2\frac{3}{8}$ in. across, on pedicels to nearly 4 in. long, petals yellow, reddish on outside, stigmas 11. Cape Prov.

Luckhoffii L. Bolus. Sts. and lvs. minutely velvety, pale glaucous; lvs. 4 on sterile brs., 2 on fertile brs., dissimilar, lower ones slender, to $\frac{3}{8}$ in. long, included in dry sheath, others to about 1 in. long, to $\frac{1}{4}$ in. wide and thick, rounded or nearly truncate at tip, obscurely keeled, upper about $\frac{1}{4}$ in. long with sheath to $\frac{1}{2}$ in. long; fls. $1\frac{3}{16}$ in. across, on pedicels to $\frac{3}{4}$ in. long, opening during the day, petals yellow, stigmas 9. Cape Prov.

peculiaris N. E. Br. Sts. not evident, single or in clumps, deep-rooted; lvs. about 8 on a br., nearly glaucous-green to gray-green or tinted with purple, dotted with dark green, the outer pair spreading flat, ovate in outline, to 2 in. long and wide, $\frac{3}{8}$ in. thick, upper side flat, lower side slightly rounded, second pair shorter, united half their length, triangular-ovate in outline, flat above, keeled beneath, tips ascending or spreading, third pair to $1\frac{3}{4}$ in. long, about $\frac{3}{8}$ in. wide, united half their length, triangular, flat above, keeled beneath, tips ascending-spreading, fourth pair to 2 in. long, $\frac{3}{8}$ in. wide and half as thick, scarcely united, elongate-triangular, flat above, keeled beneath; fls. to 2 in. across, terminal, solitary, on a pedicel to $2\frac{1}{2}$ in. long, petals yellow, stigmas 14–15. Cape Prov.

Pillansii L. Bolus. LOBSTER-CLAWS. Clump-forming, sts. very short; lvs. 1–2 pairs on a br., whitish-gray, dark-dotted, to nearly 2 in. long, not widely separated, compressed laterally, upper side flat, lower side rounded and obtusely keeled toward apex, the pairs, when appressed, ovoid; fls. to $2\frac{1}{2}$ in. across, petals bright yellow, stigmas 11. Cape Prov.

purpurea L. Bolus. Lvs. 2 on fertile brs., briefly papillate, glaucous or pale or weakly rose-colored, to $1\frac{3}{8}$ in. long above a sheath $\frac{3}{8}$ in. long, about $\frac{1}{2}$ in. thick and $\frac{3}{8}$ in. wide, flat above, sides slightly rounded, keeled and expanded toward apex on lower side, 3-angled in section at least toward base; fls. $1\frac{3}{8}$ in. across, nearly sessile, petals rose-purple, paler on outside, stigmas 11. Cape Prov.

rostratoides (Haw.) N. E. Br. Mat-forming, sts. to nearly 2 in. long in age; lvs. spreading or incurved, minutely roughened, to about 1 in. long above sheath, $\frac{3}{8}$ in. wide, $\frac{1}{8}$ in. thick, 3-angled in section, rounded at tip; fls. yellow, stigmas 9. S. Afr.

scabra L. Bolus. Lvs. 6 on sterile brs., 2 on fertile brs., pale glaucous-green, lower ones often nearly spreading, to $1\frac{3}{8}$ in. long above a sheath $\frac{3}{16}$ in. long, about $\frac{5}{8}$ in. wide, $\frac{3}{8}$ in. thick, flat above, rounded beneath and keeled toward apex, scabrous or punctate beneath, the keel scabrid and crenulate, middle pair to $\frac{3}{4}$ in. long above a sheath $\frac{1}{2}$ in. long, usually with a large pustule, about $\frac{1}{4}$ in. wide and thick, upper pair about $\frac{5}{8}$ in. long; fls. on pedicels nearly $\frac{3}{4}$ in. long, petals pale yellow, rosy on the back, to nearly $\frac{7}{8}$ in. long. Cape Prov.

tuberculata (Mill.) N. E. Br. St. not evident; lvs. blue or gray to green or reddish, transparent-dotted, to $4\frac{3}{8}$ in. long, $\frac{1}{2}$ in. wide, $\frac{1}{4}$ in. thick, united in a sheath to $1\frac{3}{8}$ in. long, blades flat above, rounded beneath, keeled toward apex, blunt or mucronate at tip, semicircular in section; fls. $1\frac{3}{4}$ in. across, on pedicels to 4 in. long, petals yellow, stigmas 10–12. Cape Prov.

velutina L. Bolus. Lvs. 4 on sterile brs., 2 on fertile brs., velutinous, pale glaucous-green, inconspicuously green-dotted, lower ones to $2\frac{5}{8}$ in. long, above a sheath about 1 in. long, flat or slightly rounded above, sides rounded, keeled toward the obtuse or nearly truncate apex, keel serrulate; fls. to $2\frac{3}{8}$ in. across, on pedicels to $2\frac{3}{8}$ in. long, petals yellow. Cape Prov.

CHELIDONIUM L. CELANDINE. *Papaveraceae.* Two or perhaps more spp. of Eurasian bien. or per. herbs with orange-colored sap; lvs. deeply pinnatifid; fls. medium-sized, in few-fld. umbels, petals 4, stamens many; fr. a cylindrical caps.

One species grown in wild gardens and somewhat weedy. Propagated by seeds or division of roots.

Franchetianum: *Dicranostigma Franchetianum.*

majus L. To 4 ft.; lvs. deeply pinnatifid, glaucous beneath; fls. yellow, to $\frac{5}{8}$ in. across, sometimes double; caps. to 2 in. long. Eur. and Asia; naturalized in e. U.S. Lvs. closely resemble those of *Stylophorum.* Var. **laciniatum** (Mill.) Syme. Lvs. deeply incised.

CHELONE L. TURTLEHEAD, SNAKEHEAD. *Scrophulariaceae.* About 5 or 6 spp. of summer-flowering, hardy, per. herbs of N. Amer.; closely allied to *Penstemon;* plants mostly glabrous; lvs. opp., serrate; fls. white or purple, in spikelike racemes, sepals 5, imbricate, corolla 2-lipped, lower lip bearded inside, fertile stamens 4, woolly, staminode 1, shorter; fr. a caps., seeds many, winged.

Thrive in partial shade and in soil that is not too dry, as they are native mostly in swampy places and damp woods. Propagated by seeds or by division.

barbata: *Penstemon barbatus.*

Cuthbertii Small. To 5 ft.; lvs. lanceolate to oblong-ovate, to 4 in. long, rounded, subcordate at base, sessile; fls. 4-ranked, corolla purple, to 1 in. long, staminode purple. Va. and N.C.

glabra L. TURTLEHEAD, SNAKEHEAD, BALMONY. To 6 ft.; lvs. lanceolate to ovate, to 6 in. long, subsessile or with short, winged petiole; corolla white or pinkish, 1 in. long, lower lip white-bearded, staminode white or greenish. Nfld. to Ga., w. to Minn. and Mo. Var. **elatior** Raf. [var. *montana* Hort.; *C. montana* (Raf.) Penn. & Wherry]. Corolla purple or rose at apex and throat. Var. **montana:** var. *elatior.*

Lyonii Pursh. To 3 ft.; lvs. ovate, to 7 in. long, petiole to $1\frac{1}{2}$ in. long; corolla rose-purple, to 1 in. long, lower lip yellow-bearded. Mts., N.C., S.C., Tenn. Hardy north.

montana: *C. glabra* var. *elatior.*

obliqua L. To 2 ft.; lvs. lanceolate to lanceolate-elliptic, short-petioled; corolla purple, 1 in. long, lower lip pale yellow-bearded, staminode white. Tenn. and Md., s. to Fla. and Miss.

Pentstemon: *Penstemon laevigatus.*

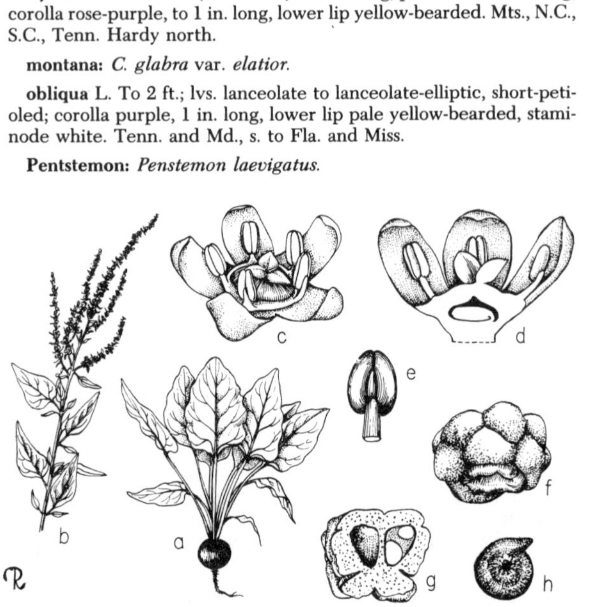

CHENOPODIACEAE. *Beta vulgaris:* **a,** plant with basal leaves and thickened root, $\times \frac{1}{12}$; **b,** flowering stem, $\times \frac{1}{20}$; **c,** flower, $\times$ 10; **d,** flower, vertical section, $\times$ 12; **e,** anther, dorsal view, $\times$ 20; **f,** fruit, $\times$ 3; **g,** fruit, vertical section, $\times$ 3; **h,** seed, $\times$ 3. (From Bailey, *Manual of Cultivated Plants,* ed. 2.)

CHENOPODIACEAE Venten. GOOSEFOOT FAMILY. Dicot.; about 75 genera of herbs and shrubs of wide distribution, many weedy; lvs. mostly alt. and simple; fls. small and inconspicuous, bisexual or unisexual, often bracted, having no perianth or only a 1–5-lobed calyx, stamens 1–5, opp. the calyx lobes, ovary usually superior, 1-celled, with 1 ovule; fr. a utricle or achene. Several genera have spp. grown as vegetables or as ornamentals. The genera treated here are: *Atriplex, Beta, Chenopodium, Kochia, Salicornia, Sarcobatus,* and *Spinacia.*

CHENOPODIUM L. GOOSEFOOT, PIGWEED. *Chenopodiaceae.* About 250 spp. of mostly weedy herbs of wide distribution, usually mealy or glandular, often with strong odor; lvs. alt.; fls. small, mostly bisexual, in spikes or panicles, bractless, calyx usually 5-parted, corolla none, stamens 5 or fewer, ovary 1-celled, with 2–5 very slender stigmas; fr. a utricle, enclosed in the dryish, persistent calyx.

A few species grown as potherbs, for the nutritious seeds, or as ornamentals; one is medicinal. Of easy culture; propagated by seeds.

album L. LAMB'S-QUARTERS, PIGWEED, WHITE G. Ann., to 10 ft.; lvs. rhombic-ovate to lanceolate, to 4 in. long, entire or toothed or lobed, glaucous, often white-mealy beneath. Eur., Asia, N. Amer. Sometimes gathered for edible greens.

amaranticolor Coste & Reynier. Ann., to 8 ft.; lvs. triangular-ovate to rhomboid, to 5 in. long, irregularly toothed and notched, those toward top of plant violet-red. Of unknown origin.

ambrosioides L. MEXICAN TEA, SPANISH T., WORMSEED, AMERICAN W. Ann. or per., to 3½ ft., with strong odor; lvs. oblong to lanceolate, to 5 in. long, coarsely toothed or cut; calyx gland-dotted. Trop. Amer.; naturalized in N. Amer., Eur., Asia. Cult. for the essential oil, oil of chenopodium, which has medicinal properties.

Bonus-Henricus L. GOOD-KING-HENRY, MERCURY, ALLGOOD, FAT-HEN, GOOSEFOOT, WILD SPINACH. Coarse per., to 2½ ft.; lvs. arrow-shaped, to 3 in. long or more, entire or repand. Eur.; naturalized in e. N. Amer. Sometimes used as a potherb.

Botrys L. FEATHER GERANIUM, JERUSALEM OAK. Ann., to 2 ft., glandular-pubescent and viscid, aromatic; lvs. ovate-elliptic to oblong, to 4 in. long, lobed to pinnatifid; panicles narrow and elongate. Eur., Asia, Afr.; naturalized in N. Amer. Sometimes cult. under the name *Ambrosia mexicana* Hort.

capitatum (L.) Asch. STRAWBERRY BLITE, INDIAN-PAINT. Ann., to 1½ ft.; lvs. triangular-ovate to subhastate, toothed; fls. in dense heads, which become bright red and berrylike in fr. Eur. Sometimes grown as a potherb.

Quinoa Willd. QUINOA, QUINUA. Ann., to 5 ft.; lvs. triangular-ovate, angular-toothed or pinnatifid; infl. a dense terminal panicle. Andes. The seeds are a staple "cereal" food of the Andean highlands. Fruiting takes place only under short day length.

CHERIMOYA. The cherimoya is a small tree of the Andes of Ecuador and northern Peru, *Annona Cherimola,* cultivated in mild frostless regions for the delicious edible fruit, which is heart-shaped or conical, averaging about 1 pound or less in weight. A number of species of *Annona* are grown for fruit, but this is by far the best. The flesh is white, soft and melting, containing black beanlike seeds. It is a dessert fruit, with a subacid flavor somewhat suggestive of the pineapple. There are several cultivars, superior to the average run of seedlings offered by nurseries in California and Australia. It is not strictly a fruit of the warm tropics, being native in more or less elevated cool regions, and requires a relatively dry climate. It does not thrive under lowland tropical conditions. It has been planted in a small way in parts of southern California, but it does not endure temperatures much below freezing without injury; the climate of Florida does not suit it.

The cultivation of the cherimoya is similar to that of the citrus fruits. Trees are planted 20–30 feet apart. Choice cultivars are multiplied by shield budding or grafting on seedlings of cherimoya, although other species of *Annona* may be employed as stocks. Trees begin to bear in three or four years after planting. The scant yield of some trees of cherimoya is probably the result of insufficient pollination.

CHERRY. A number of species of the genus *Prunus* of the *Rosaceae* are known as cherries. The common fruit-producing cherries are of two species, the sweet cherry, *Prunus avium,* and the sour cherry, *Prunus Cerasus;* the duke cherries, with the habit of *P. avium* but bearing acid fruit, are *P. × effusus,* a hybrid between the two species. The dwarf cherry or western sand cherry of the Plains region is *Prunus Besseyi,* a native species; this is sometimes employed as a stock for sour cherries in cold regions. The Nanking cherry, *Prunus tomentosa* of eastern Asia, and some other species also yield edible cherry fruits.

The sweet and sour cherries differ markedly in their ability to succeed under a wide range of climatic and soil conditions. The sweet cherry is much the more restricted of the two and can be grown to advantage only in the more favored fruit regions that have an equable climate, as, for example, the Hudson Valley of New York, the shores of the Great Lakes, and the Pacific Coast. It is about as tender to injury from winter cold and late frosts as is the peach and does not endure heat as well. The sour cherry, on the other hand, can be grown over a much wider territory extending north of the sweet cherry belt and south into the Mississippi Valley and along the Atlantic Coast. The largest sour cherry plantings are in New York, Michigan, and Wisconsin.

Soils are of less importance than climate in cherry growing. Sour cherries thrive on most well-drained soils, either light or heavy, and withstand rather dry conditions. Sweet cherries are more exacting, and reach their best development in deep, well-drained, sandy or gravelly loams.

Propagation of both sweet and sour cherries is by budding on seedling stocks. The sweet cherry grows best on mazzard stock although mahaleb stocks are used in many cases with fair results. Sour cherries are commonly budded on the mahaleb stock, which is preferred by nurserymen because it makes a better nursery tree. Mazzard stocks make better orchard trees under most conditions.

Orchard treatment is not unusual. One- or two-year nursery trees are set in very early spring or, in the milder climates, in the late autumn. Sour cherries are placed about 18 × 18 feet apart, although 24 × 24 feet is better for the more vigorous sorts on good soil. Sweet cherries may be set 25 × 25 feet apart, or 30 × 30 feet in favorable situations. Sour cherries succeed best commercially under clean cultivation and cover crops, as described for the apple, although in the home garden considerable fruit will be produced on trees growing in sod or under almost total neglect. Sweet cherries withstand sod culture even better than the sour kinds. Fairly vigorous terminal growth is necessary for crop production with both sweet and sour cherries. This can be stimulated by a nitrogenous fertilizer applied early in the spring at the rate of 3–5 pounds to the mature tree.

Pruning is begun when the two-year tree is set out; all but the leader and two well-spaced laterals should be removed. The remaining branches should not be headed back. For the mature sweet cherry, the spreading type of tree with several large scaffold branches is the most desirable. The main branches may be headed back when they become too high for convenient harvesting. Sour cherries are pruned rather lightly at first, but as soon as growth begins to get short and spurry the branches must be thinned out and renewal pruning practiced to keep up the vigor of growth.

Most cultivars of sweet cherries need a pollinizer, so at least two kinds should be planted near together. This matter should receive careful attention, for some cultivars, as, for example, 'Napoleon' ('Royal Anne'), 'Lambert', and 'Bing', will not pollinate each other, but may be pollinated by such cultivars as 'Black Tartarian', 'Black Republican', and 'Windsor'. Sour cherries do not need a pollinizer but yields are increased by placing honeybees in the orchard to pollinate the blossoms.

The following are listed in approximate order of ripening: black sweet cherries—'Vista', 'Viva', 'Schmidt', 'Bing', 'Stella', 'Ulster', 'Van', 'Windsor', 'Hedelfingen', 'Compact Lambert', and 'Hudson'; white sweet cherries—'Rainier',

'Emperor Francis', 'Napoleon', and 'Gold Sweet'; sour cherries—'Montmorency', 'Northstar', 'Meteor', and 'English Morello'.

Viruses and mycoplasmas in cherries are controlled by planting virus-free trees from the nursery. Bacterial canker can be reduced by planting resistant cultivars. Chemical sprays will control the cherry leaf-spot disease, brown rot of blossoms and fruits, as well as the cherry fruit fly and the plum curculio, both of which cause wormy cherries. Without sprays, every cherry could have a worm in it.

A general purpose fruit spray for home garden orchards generally sold at garden stores usually contains two insecticides, malathion and methoxyclor, and a fungicide, captan. Directions for spray application are given on the container. The most important cherry spray is the prebloom one, just after the buds begin to show color. Spray applications of insecticides during flowering should be avoided because they kill honey bees, which are needed for effecting cross pollination. Following the prebloom spray, the general purpose spray is applied at petal fall and in four additional cover sprays at ten-day intervals. Thorough coverage of the foliage is essential.

Birds are a serious menace to growing sweet cherries in the home garden. The problem of controlling them is almost insurmountable. In commercial sweet cherry orchards, birds remove only a small percentage of the crop, but in home gardens they often take 90 percent of the crop, just as the fruits begin to turn red and long before they are fully black and ripe. Trees can be covered with netting, but sweet cherry trees may grow to a height of 15 feet before they begin bearing fruits. Such big trees are difficult to cover with a net. Sweet cherry trees with dwarfing rootstocks are, unfortunately, not generally sold by nurseries.

CHESTNUT. The attractive trees of the genus *Castanea* are grown for their edible nuts and to some extent for shade and ornament. The native chestnut, *Castanea dentata,* formerly covered large areas of the eastern United States, but this species has been nearly exterminated by the chestnut bark disease or blight, *Endothia parasitica* (Murrill) P. J. Anderson & H. W. Anderson, which was introduced from Asia in the late 1800's. This tree, valued not only for its edible nuts but even more for its very durable timber and as a source of tannins, was the most important deciduous species in the forests of the eastern United States. It persists mostly as sprouts, coming up from the old stumps in the native forests. The European chestnut, *C. sativa,* has been introduced and rather widely distributed, but plantings of this species also have succumbed to the bark disease.

More recently the Japanese chestnut, *C. crenata,* and the Chinese chestnut, *C. mollissima,* have been introduced. Both of these species are more resistant to the blight than the American or European sorts and promise by hybridization to give rise to acceptable cultivars that can be grown in the blight-infested area. The Chinese chestnut and hybrids with it are being propagated for their nuts; cultivars being tried in the East include 'Crane', 'Eaton', 'Nanking', 'Orrin', and 'Sleeping Giant'. Although not immune to the blight, they are sufficiently resistant to persist in spite of blight infection.

The American species excels the others in hardiness to cold and quality of nuts, although these are much smaller in size. The larger-fruited species usually are not as sweet, but a few of the cultivars are noted for their good quality. The Chinese chestnut and its hybrids are generally adapted to areas where peaches can be grown, and are subject to winter injury where the temperatures reach −15° F or lower. The European kinds are less hardy.

There are a few commercial chestnut orchards in the East, notably in Georgia and Maryland. Chinese chestnut seedlings are widely grown in the East. They are distributed by mail-order nurseries and state nurseries for yard and game-food plantings.

Chestnuts are naturally tolerant of acid soils and present no special cultural difficulties on well-drained land. Blight is

the limiting factor, though weevils may become troublesome. The trees are precocious, often bearing nuts two or three years after planting.

Propagation by grafting on chestnut stocks is practiced, and recent research indicates that cuttings can be rooted. Seedlings of the Chinese species are suitable stocks for cultivars of oriental origin. Expert workmanship is essential for a high percentage of "take." The breeding of chestnuts for blight resistance, both as forest trees and nuts, is receiving much attention from federal and other agencies and enough progress has been made to indicate that, in the future, chestnuts again may be grown in the United States in spite of the blight.

CHIAPASIA: *DISOCACTUS.*

CHIASTOPHYLLUM (Ledeb.) Stapf. *Crassulaceae.* One sp., a glabrous succulent per. herb of the w. Caucasus, perhaps best included in *Umbilicus,* but with creeping rhizomes and opp. lvs.; fls. 5-merous, sepals separate, petals united to the middle, hooded, stamens 10.

For culture see *Succulents.*

oppositifolium (Ledeb.) A. Berger [*Cotyledon oppositifolia* Ledeb.; *C. simplicifolia* Hort.; *Umbilicus oppositifolius* (Ledeb.) Ledeb.]. Brs. creeping and rooting; lvs. 6–8, basal, elliptic to ovate, 1–1¾ in. long, obtuse, coarsely crenate, petioled; fl. st. terminal, ½–1 ft., infl. of several elongate racemes; fls. creamy, ⅛–³⁄₁₆ in. long. Late spring.

CHICORY. Chicory, *Cichorium Intybus,* is a perennial native to Europe and grown for the roots and also as salad. The same plant has also extensively run wild in North America along roadsides and in neglected fields, where it is conspicuous for its attractive azure-blue flowers.

The thick roots are employed as substitute for coffee. For this purpose, chicory is grown as a field crop, in deep, well-prepared soil. Seeds are sown in spring in drills about 18 inches apart, good tillage is provided, and the hard, parsnip-like roots are harvested in autumn.

Chicory is also grown for the foliage, used as greens or salad. The best-known product is witloof, which is the crown of uncolored leaves forced in winter or spring from stored roots. Seeds of the strain of chicory mostly employed for the production of witloof are sown in drills in spring and thinned to about 6 inches in the row. At the close of the season the roots are lifted, the tops cut off above the crown, and the roots stored in a cellar in the same way as other root crops. For the production of the crown of leaves known as witloof, the roots are trimmed on the lower end to 8 or 9 inches long, then placed upright in soil or sand in a box and the crowns covered with about 8 inches of sand; temperature is kept at about 60° F, and in a fortnight the white salad witloof should be ready, a good "head" being 6 inches long.

Sometimes the leaves of chicory are blanched in the field late in the season by banking as for celery; or the same treatment may be applied in spring to the new leaves arising from roots remaining in the ground over winter. Some persons force the stored roots in darkness to obtain the blanched tops. The unblanched leaves are also sometimes used as greens.

CHILENIA: *NEOPORTERIA.* **C. acutissima:** *N. subgibbosa.*

CHILIANTHUS: *BUDDLEIA.* **C. arboreus:** *B. saligna.*

CHILITA: *MAMMILLARIA* section *Chilita.*

CHILOPSIS D. Don. *Bignoniaceae.* One large shrub or small tree of sandy washes or springs, native from sw. U.S. to Mex.; lvs. simple, alt., or lower ones opp. or whorled; fls. in terminal racemes, calyx 2-lipped, inflated, corolla white, pink, lilac, lavender, or purple, with 2 yellow stripes or mottled inside, funnelform-campanulate, 2-lipped, with 5 crimped lobes, stamens 4; fr. a cylindrical, linear caps.

Planted in the South.

linearis (Cav.) Sweet [*Bignonia linearis* Cav.]. DESERT WILLOW, FLOWERING W. To 20 ft. or more; lvs. linear to linear-lanceolate, to 8 in. long, often curved, entire; fls. to 2 in. long. Summer. Tex., s. Nev., and s. Calif., s. to Mex. Zone 8.

CHIMAPHILA Pursh. PIPSISSEWA, WINTERGREEN, WAX-FLOWER, PRINCE'S PINE. *Pyrolaceae.* About 7 or 8 spp. of glabrous, evergreen, woodland herbs or small subshrubs with creeping sts., native to the temp. N. Hemisphere; lvs. in irregular whorls, simple, toothed; fls. white to rose-pink, in few-fld. terminal corymbs, sepals and petals 5, stamens 10, filaments expanded at base, hairy at middle; fr. a 5-celled caps.

Chimaphilas are grown in the wild garden, where they thrive in partial shade. Propagated by division of the creeping underground rootstocks.

maculata (L.) Pursh. SPOTTED WINTERGREEN. To 10 in.; lvs. lanceolate to ovate-lanceolate, to 2 in. long, variegated white above along the veins; fls. white, fragrant, Summer. E. U.S.

Menziesii (R. Br. ex D. Don) K. Spreng. To 6 in.; lvs. often not distinctly whorled, ovate to lanceolate-oblong, to 1⅜ in. long, sometimes variegated, dark green above, pale beneath; fls. white, fading pink. Summer. B.C. and Idaho, s. to s. Calif.

umbellata (L.) W. Barton. To 10 in.; lvs. oblong-obovate, to 2 in. long, broadest above the middle, not variegated; fls. pink, calyx lobes longer than broad. Eurasia. Lvs. used medicinally. Var. **cisatlantica** S. F. Blake. PRINCE'S PINE, PIPSISSEWA. Lvs. 1½–2¾ in. long, conspicuously veined beneath; calyx lobes broader than long. E. N. Amer. Var. **occidentalis** (Rydb.) S. F. Blake. Lvs. to 3½ in. long, obscurely veined or without veins beneath; calyx lobes longer than broad. W. N. Amer. and n. Mich.

CHIMONANTHUS Lindl. *Calycanthaceae.* Four spp. of shrubs, native to China; lvs. opp., entire; fls. yellow, axillary, sepals and petals many, stamens 5–6, all borne on fl. tube; fr. of many achenes, enclosed in cup-shaped fl. tube constricted at the mouth.

Requires winter protection in the North. Propagated by seeds sown in spring and by layering in autumn.

fragrans: *C. praecox.*

praecox (L.) Link [*Chimonanthus fragrans* Lindl.; *Calycanthus praecox* L.]. WINTERSWEET. To 10 ft., deciduous; lvs. elliptic-ovate to oblong-lanceolate, 6 in. long; fls. fragrant, about 1 in. long, outer perianth segms. yellow, inner ones striped purplish-brown. Zone 7. Flowering before lvs., often in midwinter in mild climates. Var. **grandiflorus** (Lindl.) Mak. Lvs. larger; fls. purer yellow, larger, less fragrant.

CHIMONOBAMBUSA Mak. BAMBOO. *Gramineae.* Twelve spp. of evergreen, per., rhizomatous, woody grasses with somewhat running habit, native to e. and s. Asia; sts. nearly solid, cylindrical, brs. several at each node; st. sheaths with conspicuous appendages, deciduous; lf. sheaths with smooth bristles at apex; spikelets racemose, lemma prominently nerved, not tessellate, stamens 3, styles 2. For terminology see *Gramineae.*

Propagated by plant division, taken well before new shoots appear. See *Bamboos.*

falcata (Nees) Nakai [*Arundinaria falcata* Nees; *Bambusa falcata* Hort. ex Vilm.] SICKLE B. Sts. to 20 ft., slender, not over ½ in. in diam., covered with a bluish-white-waxy coating when young, eventually yellow-green; lf. sheaths glabrous, striate, ciliate at the ligule, blades to 6 in. long, about 5/16 in. wide, light green, striate-veined. Himalayas. Often confused with *Arundinaria Falconeri.* Zone 8.

marmorea (Mitf.) Mak. Sts. to 10 ft. high, to ⅝ in. in diam., smooth, cylindrical, lower nodes lacking prominent air roots; st. sheaths membranous, spotted brownish-purple; lf. sheaths promptly deciduous, lf. blades lanceolate, to 6 in. long, to ½ in. wide. Warm temp. e. Asia. Hardy in Zone 8. Useful for hedges.

quadrangularis (Fenzi) Mak. SQUARE B., SQUARE-STEM B. Sts. slender, to 30 ft. high, to 1 in. in diam., roughened, dark green shading to purple, square when old; lower nodes with prominent air roots, nodes 4–5 in. apart, square, but rounded at the corners, very prominent, with a deep purple band on the lower side, densely fringed with yellow-brown bristles; brs. 6–7, breaking off readily when the st. is dry, leaving a little raised scar, often depressed in the center; st. sheaths loosely tessellate, thin and delicate, shading to purple; lf. blades 8 in. long, 1 in. wide, deep green, serrated on both edges, ligule minute. China. Cult. in Japan, Eur., and U.S. Hardy in Zone 8. Prefers sun and moist soil.

CHINESE CABBAGE. This is an annual leaf vegetable, included in *Brassica Rapa* Pekinensis Group, much grown in the Orient under the name pe-tsai. The heading type of Chinese cabbage is the one commonly grown in the United States, where under moderate temperatures it produces a close mass of foliage making a relatively solid head with good flavor. In the North (Zone 5) it is best to plant seed in the garden in June or July, for then plants will attain the heading stage during the shorter days and more desirable temperatures of early or mid-autumn. If planted earlier, the plants often develop flowers before a good head is formed, and heads that mature in hot weather often have poor texture and a strong, undesirable flavor. Cultivars include 'Michihli', a tall cylindrical plant with dark green leaves that heads from 75 to 85 days after seeding, and 'Wong Bok', a later, shorter plant. Plants should be spaced 8–10 inches apart in rows 2–3 feet apart.

Related biennial cabbages are pak-choi, also included in *Brassica Rapa* Chinensis Group, and false pak-choi, *B. parachinensis.* These plants do not produce the solid head typical of the Chinese cabbage. All three are probably natives of temperate eastern Asia. See *Brassica.*

CHIOCOCCA P. Br. SNOWBERRY. *Rubiaceae.* About 20 spp. of shrubs or vines, native to s. Fla., W. Indies, trop. Amer.; lvs. opp., leathery; fls. in axillary racemes, small, yellow or white, 5-merous; corolla tube relatively short, lobes shorter; fr. a globular white drupe.

alba (L.) A. S. Hitchc. [*C. racemosa* L.]. Shrub, to 10 ft., or vine; lvs. elliptic or ovate, to 3 in. long; fls. yellow, to ¼ in. long. S. Fla. and W. Indies.

racemosa: *C. alba.*

CHIOGENES: *GAULTHERIA.* **C. serpyllifolia:** *G. hispidula.*

CHIONANTHUS L. FRINGE TREE. *Oleaceae.* About 3–4 spp. of deciduous, polygamodioecious trees or shrubs, 2 in e. N. Amer. and 1 or 2 in e. Asia; lvs. opp., entire; fls. many, small, white, in showy panicles, petals 4, linear, united only at base; fr. a dark blue drupe.

Fringe trees are hardy north with some protection. They succeed in sunny locations in moist sandy loam. Propagated by seeds in autumn or stratified, by layers and cuttings of forced plants, and by grafting or budding on ash.

retusus Lindl. & Paxt. To 20 ft.; lvs. ovate or elliptic, to 4 in. long; panicles terminal, to 4 in. long; petals ¾ in. long; fr. ½ in. long. Early summer. China. Zone 6. Var. **serrulatus** (Hayata) G. Koidz. Lvs. serrulate; considered a distinct sp. by some. Taiwan.

virginicus L. OLD-MAN'S-BEARD. To 30 ft.; lvs. mostly oblong or obovate-oblong, to 8 in. long; panicles lateral, to 8 in. long; petals 1 in. long; fr. ⅝ in. long. Late spring. Penn. to Fla., w. to Tex. Zone 5.

CHIONODOXA Boiss. GLORY-OF-THE-SNOW. *Liliaceae.* Five or six spp. of alpine or subalpine, early-spring-blooming, scapose, bulbous, per. herbs, native to Crete, Cyprus, and Asia Minor; bulbs tunicate; lvs. basal; fls. blue, white, or pink, in terminal racemes, perianth segms. 6, united into tube at base, stamens 6; fr. a 3-valved, loculicidal caps.

Chionodoxas thrive in any soil, but need plenty of moisture and light. Bulbs should be planted approximately 3 in. deep and replanted about the third year. Propagated by offsets or seeds.

gigantea: *C. Luciliae* cv.

Luciliae Boiss. To 3–6 in., becoming higher in fr.; lvs. linear to oblanceolate; fls. mostly 4–6, bright blue with white center, to 1 in. across. Asia Minor. Cvs. are: **'Alba'**, fls. white; **'Gigantea'** [*C. gigantea* Hort. ex L. H. Bailey], fls. larger and more numerous; **'Rosea'**, fls. pink; **'Tmoli'**, late-blooming.

sardensis Hort. Barr & Sugden. To 6 in.; lvs. linear-oblanceolate, to 5 in. long; fls. ¾ in. across, entirely sky-blue, filaments white. Asia Minor.

tmoli: *C. Luciliae* cv.

CHIONOGRAPHIS Maxim. *Liliaceae.* Four or five spp. of per. herbs allied to *Chamaelirium,* native to Asia; rhizome thick; lvs. basal and on st., elliptic to oblanceolate or ovate, often long-petioled, st. lvs. much smaller, sessile; fls. bisexual, white, in terminal spikes, perianth segms. 3–6, unequal, stamens 6, filaments stout and short, or absent; fr. a 3-valved, loculicidal caps., each cell 2-seeded.

japonica Maxim. To 1 ft., basal lvs. to 3 in. long, irregularly toothed to entire, st. lvs. linear to 1½ in. long; fls. to ¾ in. across, in spikes to 4–5 in. long, perianth segms. linear and spreading. Japan.

Koidzumiana Ohwi. To 8 in., basal lvs. oblong-ovate to ovate, to 1¼ in. long, wavy-margined, on petioles to 1⅜ in. long, st. lvs. 3–6, lanceolate, to ¾ in. long; fls. greenish, in dense spikes to 1⅜ in. long. Japan.

CHIONOPHILA Benth. SNOW-LOVER. *Scrophulariaceae.* Two spp. of per. herbs, native to the Rocky Mts. of Idaho, Colo., Mont., and Wyo.; lvs. mostly basal; fls. in one-sided spikes or racemes, calyx 5-lobed, corolla tubular, 2-lipped, stamens 4, staminode 1, glabrous; fr. a caps.

Jamesii Benth. Glabrous or finely pubescent per., to 6 in.; basal lvs. spatulate or oblanceolate, thick, st. lvs. linear; fls. greenish-white to cream-colored, ½ in. long. Colo. and Wyo. Sometimes grown in rock gardens.

CHIRANTHODENDRON Larreat. *Bombacaceae.* One sp., a tree native to Mex. and Guatemala; lvs. long-petioled, simple, cordate, mostly 3-, 5-, or 7-lobed; fls. solitary, on peduncles, opp. the lvs., calyx campanulate, deeply 5-lobed, 2–3-bracted at base, petals 0, stamens united basally into a curved tube but divided apically into 5 exserted, linear-acuminate divisions, each division with 2 linear 1-celled anthers on the outside below the apex; fr. a 5-valved, woody caps., seeds many.

pentadactylon Larreat. [*C. platanoides* (Humb. & Bonpl.) Baill.]. MEXICAN HAND PLANT. From 35 to 100 ft. or more; lvs. to 12 in. long, green above, tomentose beneath; calyx to 2 in. long, brown-woolly outside, glabrous, reddish and with basal nectar-secreting pits inside, stamens and style rose-red; caps. to 6 in. long, deeply 5-lobed. A rapidly growing tree cult. in s. Calif. for shade and the curious fls.

platanoides: *C. pentadactylon.*

CHIRITA Buch.-Ham. ex D. Don. *Gesneriaceae.* More than 100 spp. of ann. or per., mostly low herbs, native to tropics of Asia; sts. fleshy; lvs. opp. to whorled, rarely alt., sometimes those of a pair unequal; fls. 1 or more on axillary, bracted peduncles, or on peduncles united to petioles, or in axillary clusters, or scapose, calyx 5-lobed, corolla tubular-funnelform or swollen, limb 5-lobed, more or less 2-lipped, lower 2 stamens fertile, staminodes 2–3, anthers touching or united at tips, disc low, ringlike, ovary superior, linear, stigma obliquely shield-shaped, 2-lobed or -notched; fr. a linear, loculicidal caps.

For cultivation see *Gesneriaceae.*

anachoreta Hance. Per., to more than 1 ft.; lvs. of a pair equal, blades obliquely elliptic-ovate, to 7 in. long, 3½ in. wide, sharply toothed; fls. few on each short peduncle, calyx tube yellow-green, ½ in. long, lobes about as long, corolla to 2 in. long, sulphur-yellow. China.

asperifolia (Blume) B. L. Burtt [*C. Blumei* C. B. Clarke]. Per., to nearly 3 ft., branched; lvs. obliquely elliptic to ovate-elliptic, to 7 in. long, 3¾ in. wide, toothed, rough-hairy; fls. few to many in clustered, peduncled cymes, calyx ⅜ in. long, tube twice as long as lobes or more, corolla 1¾ in. long, lavender-purple, with white limb and pale lavender throat, or sometimes white with pale yellow throat. Java.

barbata T. Sprague. Bien., to 2 ft., hairy; lvs. opp., ovate-oblong, to 6 in. long, 2½ in. wide, with 8–10 pairs of nerves, hairy, petioles to 1 in. long; peduncle united to petiole, fls. 4–8 on hairy pedicels appearing to arise from petiole, calyx lobes longer than tube, ½ in. long, corolla 1 in. long or more, swollen toward throat, bluish-lilac with yellow band in floor of throat, anthers bearded; fr. more than 2 in. long. E. Indies.

Blumei: *C. asperifolia.*

Elphinstonia Craib. Ann., to 3 ft., branched, sts. glabrous or nearly so; lvs. opp., elliptic or oblong, to 6 in. long, 3½ in. wide, with more than 20 pairs of nerves, softly hairy above; peduncles united to petiole, fls. on ascending pedicels appearing to arise from petiole, calyx lobes linear-lanceolate, to ⁷⁄₁₆ in. long, corolla yellow with purple spots at attachment of stamens, tube ⁹⁄₁₆ in. long, anthers white-bearded. Thailand.

hamosa R. Br. Usually less than 1 ft.; lvs. opp., ovate or elliptic, to 6 in. long, 4 in. wide, obscurely crenate, with 12–16 pairs of veins, hairy; peduncle united to petiole, fls. appearing to arise from petiole,

calyx deeply lobed, ⁵⁄₁₆ in. long, corolla ¾ in. long, pale blue to nearly rose, anthers not bearded; fr. 2–3 in. long. India, Burma. Material grown under this name is probably misidentified.

Kurzii: *Briggsia Kurzii.*

lavandulacea Stapf. Ann., succulent, sts. to 3 ft., light green, much-branched; lvs. opp., blades elliptic to elliptic-oblong, to 8 in. long, 5 in. wide, with 12–14 pairs of veins, light green, hairy; fls. few to many on glandular, axillary pedicels, calyx ¼ in. long, lobes linear-lanceolate, corolla to 1¼ in. long, whitish outside and in throat, with lavender-blue limb, anthers bearded; fr. to 2½ in. long. Asia, but precise region not known.

macrophylla Wallich. Sts. to 20 in., branched, hairy; basal lvs. long-petioled, st. lvs. short-petioled, blades ovate or elliptic, to 6 in. long, 3⅛ in. wide; fls. several on axillary, 2-bracted peduncles to ¾ in. long, calyx to 1 in. long, divided to middle or below, the lobes ovate-lanceolate or lanceolate, corolla to 2¼ in. long, yellow; fr. 4 in. long or more. Himalayas.

micromusa B. L. Burtt. Ann., to 1 ft., succulent; lowest lf. derived from a cotyledon, petiole ¾ in. long, blade to 10 in. long, 5 in. wide, cordate at base, with about 15 pairs of veins, the rest of the lvs. similar but smaller; peduncle united to petiole, fls. 7–20, appearing to arise from top of petiole, calyx deeply divided, the lobes linear-lanceolate, ⅜ in. long, corolla ⁹⁄₁₆ in. long, lemon-yellow and densely hairy outside, burnt-orange in throat, with orange-yellow limb, stamens attached at top of corolla tube, anthers with tuft of wine-colored hairs; fr. about 1¾ in. long. Thailand.

pumila D. Don. Sts. to 20 in.; lvs. opp., those of a pair often unequal, blades elliptic, to 5½ in. long, 2 in. wide, toothed, hairy, blotched; fls. 1–5 on axillary peduncles to 2 in. long, calyx ½ in. long, lobes lanceolate, to ⁵⁄₁₆ in. long, corolla 1¼ in. long, white suffused with purple-blue and with yellow streaks in throat; fr. 4 in. long or more. Himalayas.

sinensis Lindl. Lvs. basal, petioled, blades elliptic or ovate-lanceolate, to 8 in. long, 2 in. wide, coarsely rugose, dark green or irregularly variegated with silvery-green, hairy; fls. 1–4 on red-purple-villous scapes to 6 in. long, bracts at base of pedicels long, calyx divided nearly to base, corolla to 1⅜ in. long, white, streaked and blotched with yellow in throat, lobes suffused rose-purple; fr. nearly 4 in. long. Hong Kong.

urticifolia Buch.-Ham. ex D. Don. Sts. to 18 in.; lvs. opp., those of a pair more or less unequal, elliptic, to 5 in. long, 2 in. wide, toothed, sparsely hairy; fls. 1–4 on axillary peduncles, calyx divided to middle, corolla to 1¾ in. long, purple, with yellow lines inside, hairy. Himalayas. Material cult. under this name is probably misidentified.

CHIRONIA L. *Gentianaceae.* More than 15 spp. of herbs or subshrubs in s. and trop. Afr. and Madagascar; lvs. opp., simple, sessile; fls. in a loose cyme or sometimes solitary, corolla pink, 5-lobed, anthers sometimes spirally twisted; fr. a caps. or berrylike.

baccifera L. Subshrub, to 1½ ft. or more; lvs. linear, to ¾ in. long; fls. terminal, solitary, or in 1–3-fld. cymes, corolla to ⅝ in. long; fr. a berrylike, reddish-orange caps. S. Afr.

ixifera: *C. linoides.*

linoides L. [*C. ixifera* Hort.]. Subshrub, to 3 ft.; lvs. linear to linear-lanceolate, to 2 in. long; fls. terminal, or on upper lateral branchlets, in loose, 1–3-fld. cymes, corolla to ¾ in. long; fr. a caps., black at first, turning brown when ripe. S. Afr.

palustris Burchell. Herb, to 28 in.; basal lvs. persistent or not, oblong-cuneate to obovate-oblong, to 3½ or rarely 8 in. long, ⅞ in. wide, st. lvs. sessile, linear-lanceolate to oblong-elliptic; fls. in terminal, open panicles of 2–3-fld. cymes, corolla pink to white, to 1¼ in. long, tube shorter than lobes. S. Afr. Subsp. **palustris.** The typical subsp.; to 2 ft.; basal lvs. persistent in a rosette, st. lvs. much reduced, separated; fls. to 1 in.; not cult. Subsp. **transvaalensis** (Gilg) Verd. [*C. transvaalensis* Gilg]. Sts. leafy, forming clumps, to 28 in. high; basal lvs. not persistent, st. lvs. linear-lanceolate to narrowly oblong-lanceolate, to 3¼ in. long, ¼ or rarely to ½ in. wide, glaucous; fls. usually less than 1 in. long. Swaziland and Transvaal.

transvaalensis: *G. palustris* subsp.

CHIVE: see *Onions.*

CHLIDANTHUS Herb. *Amaryllidaceae.* Two spp. of trop. Amer. bulbous herbs; lvs. basal, strap-shaped; scape solid, umbel few-fld., subtended by 1–2 separate spathe valves; fls. fragrant, yellow, tube long and slender, lobes lanceolate, stamens 6 at throat of tube, anthers erect, basifixed, stigma trifid, ovary inferior, ovules many; fr. a caps., seeds flat, black.

One species introduced in Calif. and hardy when well mulched. Propagated by offsets or seeds.

fragrans Herb. PERFUMED FAIRY LILY. To 10 in.; lvs. present with the fls., glaucous; fls. to 3 in. long. Summer. Andes.

CHLORAEA Lindl. *Orchidaceae.* About 80 spp. of terrestrial herbs, native to temp. S. Amer.; sts. erect, enveloped by tubular, membranous sheath; lvs. basal; infl. a 1- to many-fld. terminal raceme; fls. green or yellow, segms. spreading, sepals all alike, petals often with callosities, lip entire or lobed, profusely adorned with callosities, column without a rostellum. For structure of fl. see *Orchidaceae.*

For culture see *Orchids.*

Bergii Hieron. To 8 in.; lvs. few; fls. solitary, large, to 1¼ in. long, sepals and petals similar, acuminate, reticulately veined, lip entire, densely ciliate. Autumn. Argentina, Brazil.

CHLORIS Swartz. FINGER GRASS, WINDMILL G. *Gramineae.* About 70 spp. of per. or ann. grasses cosmopolitan in trop. and subtrop. regions, sts. usually clustered; lf. blades flat or folded, scabrous; infl. of 2 to several spikes aggregated at summit of the st.; spikelets sessile, in 2 rows along one side of a continuous rachis, the rachilla disarticulating above the glumes, extending beyond and bearing 1 to several reduced florets above the usually single, bisexual floret, glumes somewhat unequal, the first shorter, narrow, acute, lemma keeled, usually broad, 1–5-nerved, often villous on the keel or marginal nerves, with a slender awn or only a point from between the short teeth of a bifid apex. For terminology see *Gramineae.*

Berroi Arech. URUGUAY C., GIANT F.G. Per., sts. to 26 in., in dense clusters, leafy; spikes mostly 2–5, usually 2–2¾ in. long, digitate or nearly so, but the rachises adherent to form a subcylindrical silky infl.; spikelets crowded, about ⅛ in. long. Uruguay. Occasionally cult. in Okla. and Tex.

Gayana Kunth. RHODES GRASS. Sts. to 5 ft., tough and wiry, internodes compressed, stolons long, stout, leafy; lf. blades to ¼ in. wide; spikes several to many, erect or ascending, to 4 in. long; spikelets crowded, pale tawny, lemma ⅛ in. long, hispid on the margin toward the apex, more or less hispidulous below, the awn to ¼ in. long. Afr. Cult. as a meadow grass, mostly in irrigated regions but also escaped from N.C. and Fla. to s. Calif.; trop. Amer.

truncata R. Br. STAR GRASS, CREEPING W.G. Per., stoloniferous, sts. erect, to 1 ft.; spikes 6–10, to 6 in. long, horizontal or reflexed; spikelets ⅛ in. long with awns to ½ in. long. Australia. Occasionally cult. for ornament.

ventricosa R. Br. AUSTRALIAN W.G. Sts. to 3 ft. long, straggling and rooting at the nodes; spikes 3–5, to 4 in. long, flexuous, spreading or drooping; spikelets about ¼ in. long, fertile lemma rather hard, brown, truncate, awned, glabrous except for the pubescent callus, awn to ¼ in. long. Australia. Occasionally cult. in Va. and Okla.

CHLOROGALUM (Lindl.) Kunth. SOAP PLANT, AMOLE. *Liliaceae.* Five spp. of bulbous, per. herbs, native to w. N. Amer. from s. Ore. to n. Baja Calif.; bulb coats membranous or fibrous; lvs. mostly basal; fls. white, pink, or blue, in terminal panicles; perianth segms. 6, separate, 3-nerved, twisting together after pollination, stamens 6, anthers versatile; fr. a 3-valved, loculicidal caps.

Culture as for *Camassia.*

angustifolium Kellogg. Slender per., to 2 ft., bulb to 2 in. long, with membranous coat; lvs. to 1 ft. long, about ¼ in. wide; fls. white with greenish-yellow midvein, to ½ in. long, opening in afternoon, pedicels about ⅛ in. long. N. and cent. Calif.

pomeridianum (DC.) Kunth. SOAP PLANT, WILD POTATO. Stout per., 2–8 ft., bulb to 6 in. long, with fibrous coat; lvs. to 2½ ft. long, to 1 in. wide, wavy-margined; fls. white, with green or purple midvein, to 1 in. long, opening in the afternoon, pedicels to 1 in. long or more. S. Ore. to s. Calif. Var. **minus** Hoover. Bulb coats mostly membranous, sts. only 12–16 in. high. N. Calif. The bulbs yield a lather, which can be used as a soap substitute.

CHLOROPHORA Gaud.-Beaup. *Moraceae.* About 5 spp. of dioecious trees with milky sap, native to trop. Amer. and trop. Afr.; lvs. alt., entire or toothed, pinnately nerved; male fls. in dense catkinlike spikes, female in dense heads; fr. a syncarp containing many achenes.

Occasionally planted in tropics.

tinctoria (L.) Gaud.-Beaup. ex Benth. & Hook.f. FUSTIC. To 60 ft., crown spreading, bark light brown, brs. often spiny; lvs. lanceolate to elliptic, to 5 in. long, acuminate, entire or toothed. Tropics, circum-Caribbean. Zone 10b. The heartwood yields the important dye, fustic.

CHLOROPHYTUM Ker-Gawl. ST. BERNARD'S LILY. *Liliaceae.* About 215 spp. of per., rhizomatous herbs, native to all continents except N. Amer. and Eur.; lvs. basal, sessile and linear, or lanceolate to ovate and petioled; fls. small, white or greenish, in bracted racemes or panicles, perianth rotate, segms. 6, separate, stamens 6; fr. a 3-winged, -lobed, or -angled, loculicidal caps.

Grown as house plants, in greenhouses, and outdoors in warm regions; they are generally easy to cultivate. Propagated by division or by seeds.

amaniense Engl. Lf. blades broadly lanceolate, to 1 ft. long, glossy, 20–26-nerved, petioles to 6 in. long, channelled, and, like lower margins of blade, pinkish-orange-buff; fls. greenish, shorter than subtending bract, in dense, terminal racemes to 5 in. long, on scapes less than 2 in. long. E. Afr.

arundinaceum Bak. Lf. blades oblanceolate, to 1½ ft. long, 20–30-nerved, petioles to 4 in. long, channelled; fls. crystalline-white, in dense, terminal racemes to 8 in. long, on scapes to 1 ft. long. E. Himalayas.

Bichetii (Karrer) Backer [*Anthericum Bichetii* (Karrer) Encke]. Dwarf plant, to 8 in.; lvs. tufted, linear-lanceolate, to 8 in. long, striped yellowish-white, particularly along margin, distinctly petioled; fls. white, in loose infl. shorter than lvs., pedicels jointed below middle. Gabon.

capense (L.) Voss [*C. elatum* (Ait.) R. Br.]. Plant only rarely proliferous; lvs. lorate, to 2 ft. long, firm, glaucous, forming a rosette; scape compressed, fls. white, in a loose, much-branched panicle; seeds about 10 in each cell. S. Afr.

comosum (Thunb.) Jacques [*C. Sternbergianum* (Schult. & Schult. f.) Steud.; *Anthericum comosum* Thunb.]. SPIDER IVY, SPIDER PLANT, RIBBON P., WALKING ANTHERICUM. Plant proliferous; lvs. linear to linear-lanceolate, to 1½ ft. long and ¾ in. wide, soft, green, loosely arranged; fls. white, in a loose panicle, scape cylindrical; seeds 3–5 in each cell. S. Afr. Cv. 'Mandaianum' [*C. Mandaianum* Hort.; *Anthericum Mandaianum* Hort.]. Plant dwarf, lvs. to 6 in. long, ½ in. wide, with bright yellow central stripe. Cv. 'Picturatum' [*C. picturatum* Hort.]. Lvs. to 1 ft. long, with central yellow stripe. Cv. 'Variegatum'. Lvs. margined with white. Cv. 'Vittatum' [*C. vittatum* Hort.; *C. elatum* (Ait.) R. Br. var. *vittatum* Hort.]. Lvs. recurved, with a central white stripe.

elatum: *C. capense.* Var. **variegatum**: probably *C. comosum* cv. Var. **vittatum**: *C. comosum* cv.

macrophyllum (A. Rich.) Asch. ex Bak. Lvs. lanceolate, to 2½ ft. long, narrowing into winged, somewhat petiole-like base, 30–40-nerved; fls. white, on scapes to 14 in. long, in terminal racemes to 16 in. long, pedicels jointed near apex. Trop. Afr.

Mandaianum: *C. comosum* cv.

nepalense (Lindl.) Bak. Lvs. linear-lanceolate, to 1½ ft. long, light green above, glaucous beneath, not petioled; fls. white, in panicles to 3 ft., on pedicels jointed at or below middle. Nepal and Sikkim.

orchidastrum Lindl. Lf. blades oblong to ovate-lanceolate, to 10 in. long, 14–24-nerved, glossy, tapering into a distinct, channelled petiole to 10 in. long; fls. greenish, in panicles. Sierra Leone.

picturatum: *C. comosum* cv.

Sternbergianum: *C. comosum.*

vittatum: *C. comosum* cv.

CHLOROXYLON DC. SATINWOOD. *Rutaceae.* One sp., a deciduous tree, native to s. India and Ceylon; lvs. alt., pinnate, glandular-dotted; fls. small, in axillary or terminal panicles, calyx 5-lobed, petals 5, stamens 10; fr. an oblong, 3-celled caps., each cell with 4 winged seeds.

Swietenia DC. EAST INDIAN S. To 50 ft.; lvs. 5–9 in. long, lfts. 20–40, ovate to rhombic, to 1 in. long, oblique at base; fls. whitish. Source of excellent furniture and cabinetwood.

CHOISYA HBK. *Rutaceae.* Seven spp. of evergreen shrubs, native to Ariz. and Mex.; lvs. opp., palmately compound, glandular-dotted; fls. white, solitary or in axillary or terminal cymes, sepals and petals 4 or 5, stamens 8 or 10; fr. 3–5-valved caps.

Grown under glass, and outdoors in the South and Calif. where it withstands a few degrees of frost. Propagated by cuttings of young wood over heat or of older wood in a cold frame.

ternata HBK. MEXICAN ORANGE. To 10 ft.; lvs. with 3 lfts., lfts. elliptic to oblanceolate, to 3 in. long; fls. about 1 in. across, conspicuous above the foliage, fragrant. Mex.

CHONDRORHYNCHA Lindl. *Orchidaceae.* Not in general cult. **C. aromatica:** *Cochleanthes aromatica.* **C. discolor:** *Cochleanthes discolor.*

CHONEMORPHA G. Don. *Apocynaceae.* About 14 spp. of robust vines, native from India to Malay Arch.; sap milky; lvs. opp., entire, with stipules; fls. large, in cymes, 5-merous, bisexual, calyx tubular, 5-lobed, corolla white, funnelform, lobes broad, twisted to the right, stamens borne on corolla tube, filaments short, broad, anthers basally spurred, united to stigma; fr. a pair of long, straight, hairy follicles, seeds ovate, flat, beaked, with apical tuft of hairs.

Grown in Fla. and Calif. as ornamentals and for the fragrant flowers; propagated by cuttings.

fragrans (Moon) Alston [*C. macrophylla* (Roxb.) G. Don; *Rynchospermum fragrans* Hort.; *Trachelospermum fragrans* Hort., not Wallich ex Hook.f.; *T. fragrans* Hort. var. *grandiflorum* Hort.; *T. grandiflorum* Hort.]. Lvs. ovate to elliptic, to 15 in. long and 9 in. wide, rounded at base, slightly hairy above, densely pubescent beneath; fls. many, to 3 in. long, fragrant, calyx tube longer than lobes, glabrescent. Late spring, summer. India to Malay Pen. and Java. Zone 10.

macrophylla: *C. fragrans.*

CHORDOSPARTIUM Cheesem. *Leguminosae* (subfamily *Faboideae*). One sp., a tree, with leafless brs., native to New Zeal.; fls. racemose, papilionaceous, stamens 10, 9 united, 1 separate; fr. a short, turgid, indehiscent legume.

Stevensonii Cheesem. To 20 ft. or more; brs. long, slender, pendent, nearly cylindrical; racemes solitary or 2–5 together, to 1½ in. long, many-fld., rachis densely woolly; fls. purple, ³⁄₁₆ in. long, standard orbicular, darker-veined, reflexed; fr. ovoid, ³⁄₁₆ in. long, 1-seeded. South Is. (New Zeal.). Zone 9, where summers are cool.

CHORISIA HBK. FLOSS-SILK TREE. *Bombacaceae.* About 3 spp. of deciduous trees, native to S. Amer.; trunks usually with many short, stout spines; lvs. alt., palmately compound; similar to *Ceiba,* but staminal tube bearing a whorl of staminodes above the base and a whorl of 5 pairs of sessile anthers at the apex.

Occasionally grown as large specimen trees in the tropics and subtropics because of their bizarre form. Seeds rarely set in the continental U.S., and otherwise difficult to propagate.

africana: a listed name of no botanical standing; probably refers to *C. speciosa.*

insignis HBK. Slender-branched tree to 50 ft. tall, with bottle-shaped trunk to 6 ft. in diam., bark smooth, green; lfts. oblong-obovate, to 5 in. long, abruptly acuminate, serrate; petals white to yellow, oblong-obovate, 2–3 in. long, to 1 in. wide, obtuse, entire or undulate, canescent; caps. to 5 in. long. Peru. Zone 10.

speciosa St.-Hil. To 50 ft. or more, trunk enlarged at base; lfts. lanceolate, to 5 in. long, serrate; fls. often opening before lvs. appear, 3–5 in. across, petals pubescent, variously colored, white or yellowish to reddish or violet above, shading to white or cream in lower part, usually spotted at base; caps. to 8 in. long. Brazil, Argentina. Widely cult. in the tropics and subtropics. Warmer regions of Zone 9. The silky seed floss is used for stuffing pillows.

CHORIZANTHE R. Br. ex Benth. *Polygonaceae.* About 50 spp. of ann. and per. herbs, native to sw. U.S., Mex., and Chile; lvs. usually in basal rosettes, st. lvs. reduced to bracts; fls. usually solitary, in an involucre, involucres arranged in heads or cymes, calyx 6-lobed, stamens 9, 6, or 3, styles 3; fr. an achene, 3-angled.

Palmeri S. Wats. To 12 in., erect or prostrate; lvs. linear to oblong-spatulate, to 1¼ in. long, sessile or nearly so; fls. rose-pink, calyx lobes rounded, the inner ones fringed. S. Calif.

staticoides Benth. TURKISH-RUGGING. To 10 in., brs. spreading, reddish or purplish; lvs. oblong, to ¾ in. long, long-petioled; fls. very small, rose or white, lobes not fringed. S. Calif.

CHORIZEMA Labill. *Leguminosae* (subfamily *Faboideae*). About 15 spp. of evergreen shrubs or subshrubs, native to Australia; lvs. simple, mostly alt.; fls. usually in terminal racemes, orange or red, papilionaceous, petals clawed, standard broad, emarginate, stamens 10, separate; fr. an ovoid, short legume.

Planted outdoors in the South (Zone 10) or grown in greenhouses; they require plenty of sunlight. Propagated by cuttings.

cordatum Lindl. AUSTRALIAN FLAME PEA, FLOWERING OAK. Shrub, to 10 ft., brs. weak; lvs. ovate-lanceolate, to 2½ in. long, basally cordate, with small prickly teeth; racemes loose or open, to 6 in. long; fls. orange-red, with purplish wing petals. W. Australia.

ilicifolium Labill. Differs from *C. cordatum* in being a low, weak subshrub, with rigid, hollylike lvs. with spiny margins; racemes axillary, loose, to 4 in. long; fls. orange-red, with crimson wing petals. W. Australia.

varium Benth. Erect shrub, to 6 ft., with downy shoots; lvs. ovate, cordate, with prickly teeth; racemes short, dense; standard light orange, ½ in. wide, wing petals and keel purple-red. W. Australia.

CHROSPERMA: *AMIANTHIUM.*

CHRYSALIDOCARPUS H. Wendl. *Palmae.* About 20 spp. of unarmed, monoecious palms of Madagascar, Comoro Is., and Pemba Is.; sts. solitary or clustered, slender or stout, usually ringed, lacking a true crownshaft; lvs. pinnate, pinnae many, slender, acute; infl. among the lvs., bearing 2 unequal bracts basally, the upper longer than the lower, deciduous or more or less persistent, rachillae with small fls. in triads (2 male and 1 female) near the base and above these with paired or solitary male fls.; male fls. with sepals 3, imbricate, petals 3, valvate, stamens 6, filaments briefly inflexed at apex in bud, pistillode prominent, female fls. with sepals and petals 3, imbricate, ovary 3-celled, 1-ovuled; fr. ovoid to ellipsoid or obovoid, with basal stigmatic scar; endocarp not operculate, adherent to seed, seed with homogeneous endosperm, embryo lateral.

For culture see *Palms.*

Cabadae H. E. Moore. Sts. clustered, to 30 ft. or more, 5 in. in diam., erect, bamboolike, with green internodes; lvs. ascending, curved at apex, sheaths glaucous, pinnae narrow, to 2 ft. long, 1 in. wide, 24–60 on each side, borne in 1 plane and regularly arranged; fr. ellipsoid, bright red, ⅜ in. long. Known only from cult.; origin not certain.

lucubensis: *C. madagascariensis* var.

lutescens H. Wendl. [*Areca lutescens* Bory]. YELLOW PALM, ARECA P., BUTTERFLY P., YELLOW B.P., CANE P., GOLDEN-FEATHER P. Sts. many, clustered, slender and sometimes branching, to 30 ft. or more; lvs. ascending, curved at apex, sheaths and petioles mostly yellowish or orange-tinged, pinnae narrow, 40–60 on each side, borne in 1 plane and regularly arranged; fr. oblong-ellipsoid, violet-black, about ¾ in. long. Madagascar. Widely grown in the tropics and subtropics, and as a tub plant indoors. Zone 10b in Fla., but barring killing frosts, will thrive in warmest parts of Zone 9b.

madagascariensis Becc. [*Areca madagascariensis* Hort.; *Dypsis madagascariensis* Hort.]. Sts. stoutish, gray-brown, obscurely ringed, to 30 ft.; lvs. with more than 100 pinnae on each side, these arranged in groups and in several planes; infl. rusty-tomentose; fr. about ¾ in. long. Often grown under the name *Dypsis decipiens.* Var. **madagascariensis.** The typical var.; sts. few, in clumps. Madagascar. Var. **lucubensis** (Becc.) Jumelle & Perr. [*C. lucubensis* Becc.]. Sts. solitary. Nossi Bé Is. (Madagascar).

CHRYSAMPHORA: *DARLINGTONIA.*

CHRYSANTHEMUM L. [*Balsamita* Desf.; *Leucanthemum* DC.; *Pyrethrum* Zinn]. *Compositae* (Anthemis Tribe). Between 100 and 200 spp. of often aromatic ann. or per. herbs or subshrubs, native mostly to the N. Hemisphere, chiefly Eur. and Asia, a few in S. Afr.; lvs. alt., sometimes in a basal rosette, entire, toothed, or sometimes pinnatifid; fl. heads usually radiate, solitary or in corymbs, involucral bracts more or less imbricate in 2–5 rows, dry to scarious at least at apex and margins, receptacle flat or convex, naked; fls. white, yellow, orange, pink, red, or purple, disc fls. all bisexual, usually fertile, ray fls. female, fertile, sometimes absent; achenes nearly cylindrical or ribbed to angled or somewhat winged, often dimorphic, pappus absent or a short crown.

Chrysanthemums are grown primarily as ornamentals; several species are cultivated as sources of the important insecticide, pyrethrum; and one species is grown in the Orient as a leaf vegetable.

Cultivated chrysanthemums are hardy or half-hardy, mostly aromatic, coarse plants, with flowers in a wide range of colors; they usually bloom late in the season in the open. A half dozen cultural classes may be distinguished, as follows:

1. Annual chrysanthemums. These are suitable for mass color in late summer and autumn. They are raised readily from seeds, which commonly are sown as soon as the ground is fit, directly where the plants are to grow; for best blooms they should be thinned to 12–24 in. apart. Provide an open, sunny position. Three species are involved: *C. coronarium* is the tallest, and single large plants sometimes need staking; *C. carinatum* is the usual flower-garden kind, in many colors; *C. segetum* yields good clear yellows.

2. Feverfews. These are forms of *C. Parthenium,* sometimes known as pyrethrum. All are perennial, hardy, of the simplest culture, and persistent. They are grown for the abundant little white-rayed heads with yellow discs, or the dwarf compact forms for the foliage, which is sometimes crisped and yellow-tinged. They grow readily from seeds, blooming the second year, and frequently seed themselves; offsets may be taken from the clumps.

3. Pyrethrums. These are derived from *C. coccineum,* and bloom in late spring and summer. They are useful for cutting and are used as a florist's flower. The stems are long and simple, from a crown of attractive foliage; the daisylike heads are bright white, rose, carmine, lilac, and other shades. Propagated by seeds, blooming the second year, and named cultivars by offsets or division.

4. Marguerite chrysanthemums. These belong to *C. frutescens* and are frequently known as Paris daisy. They are planted out in the warm climates, but are tender in the North, and are grown in pots and tubs for late winter and spring bloom. Propagated by cuttings, like the florist's chrysanthemum; cuttings taken in spring should give blooming plants for the following winter and spring.

5. Perennial border daisies. These are hardy, strong plants, propagated by division, and by seeds, which give blooming plants the second year; if necessary, they may be multiplied by short cuttings of young firm shoots. They require sunny positions. Some of the recent introductions belong to *C. Zawadskii.*

6. Common chrysanthemums of florists (*C. × morifolium*). These are known in two types; the kinds developed for very large flower heads, for pot culture, and the hardy, bushy, border kinds that remain permanently in the perennial garden. These two types are not essentially different, however, as the large flower heads of the florist's kinds are developed not only by selection but by extra care in propagation, culture, pruning, and disbudding; they reflect the skill of the grower, for if left to themselves to produce bushy plants, the florist's kinds bear many small or medium-sized heads. All are essentially more or less hardy perennials, propagated by seeds, cuttings, and division.

The usual propagation of the common or florist's chrysanthemums is by cuttings taken in spring from shoots that arise from crowns of plants that have been carried through the winter. When the plants begin to stool or to send up new growth, the shoots are cut 2 or 3 in. long, and inserted in sand in boxes or on a bench. The cuttings should be trimmed of their lower leaves and the upper leaves are usually cut in half to reduce the evaporating surface; as soon as the cuttings are rooted, they are placed in small pots, say 2½ in.

The young plants may be carried through the summer in pots, after two or three repottings, or planted in the ground and lifted in Oct. or Nov. Pains should be taken to keep the plants growing without check or insect or fungus injury. If one does not care to make cuttings, one may purchase plants in late spring or early summer that have been potted and are well rooted and stocky. By the time the plants are to bloom, they should be in 6 in. or larger pots, in 10–12-in. pots if very large bushy plants are desired.

For cut flowers, the plants are usually grown by florists in benches under glass from first till last, after the cuttings are turned out of their first small pots; if to be grown to single stems for very large bloom, the plants may be set 8–12 in. apart each way on the benches, and are tied, trained, and disbudded as they grow, only the terminal bud being retained.

For display or show, the amateur usually prefers bushy plants with a good number of smaller heads, and so allows the plants to branch. All weak growths should be removed as they appear, and when buds begin to show they should all be removed except the terminal one on the branch; in this way there will be as many heads as branches, perhaps one to two dozen depending on the size and vigor of the plants and the wish of the grower. The heads will be approximately all the same size. The plants may be flowered in pots 6 in. or larger. They are discarded after blooming unless one wants to propagate a new lot for the following year; in this case, the tops are cut down and the pot placed in a cellar and kept cool and moist enough to maintain life and strength but not to encourage growth or induce decay. In Feb. or Mar. the plants may be brought to warmth and light and given water, whereupon shoots for cuttings will soon start. Plants should be grown cool when in the house.

Chrysanthemums may now be had as flowering pot plants or as cut flowers the year around, chiefly through control of the "day length" to which plants are subjected. Flower bud initiation may be induced at any time of the year by regularly covering the plants with black cloth or by otherwise shortening the hours of daylight to which they are subjected, over a prescribed period of time. Different cultivars respond somewhat differently to variations in such treatment and many have been tested and selected as being most responsive to particular conditions. Names of suitable cultivars and details of the culture necessary for such controlled flowering should be sought in the catalogues of commercial chrysanthemum specialists and in the horticultural literature. Such techniques are more likely to be practiced by the commercial grower.

alpinum L. Tufted per., to 6 in., sparingly white-woolly; lvs. essentially entire to deeply pinnately lobed, basal lvs. to 2 in. long, st. lvs. shorter; heads to 1½ in. across, solitary; disc fls. orange, ray fls. white to pink. High Alps.

anserinifolium (Hausskn. & Bornm. ex Hausskn.) J. Ingram & Dress [*Pyrethrum anserinifolium* Hausskn. & Bornm. ex Hausskn.]. Per., to 1½ ft., grayish-white-woolly-tomentose; lvs. elliptic-oblong in outline, pinnately dissected to pinnate, segms. deeply pinnately cut into lanceolate-oblong, acuminate lobes; heads to 1½ in. across, solitary on long peduncles in a loose corymb; disc fls. yellow, ray fls. white. Asia Minor.

arcticum L. ARCTIC C., ARCTIC DAISY. Base of sts. creeping, sts. to 1 ft.; lvs. spatulate in outline, pinnatifid, 3–7-lobed toward apex, st. lvs. linear, progressively reduced upward; heads to 2 in. across, solitary; disc fls. yellow, ray fls. white. Coastal Alaska and Kamchatka.

atlanticum J. Ball. Rhizomatous per., to about 3–4 in., nearly cespitose; lvs. basal, to 1½ in. long, 3-parted, each part mostly 3–4-lobed; heads to 1¼ in. across, solitary, long-peduncled; disc fls. pale yellow, ray fls. white, flushed pink at first on lower surface; achenes 10-winged. Morocco.

atratum Jacq. [*Leucanthemum coronopifolium* (Vill.) Schur.]. Mat-forming per., to 1 ft.; lvs. mostly linear, to 3 in. long, fleshy, brittle, dentate, petiole winged; heads to 1¾ in. across, solitary; disc fls. yellow, ray fls. white. Alps.

atrococcineum: *C. carinatum.*

Balsamita L. [*C. majus* (Desf.) Asch.; *Tanacetum Balsamita* L.]. COSTMARY, MINT GERANIUM, ALECOST. Coarse per., to 3 ft., from a stout root crown, aromatic; lvs. silvery-hairy, crenate, lower lvs. oblong or elliptic, 6–12 in. long, petioles about as long as blades, upper lvs. 1½–5 in. long, the uppermost sessile; heads to about ½ in. across, many in corymbs; disc fls. yellow, ray fls. minute, white. Eur., w. Asia; escaped from cult. and naturalized locally in N. Amer. Var. **tanacetoides** (Boiss.) Boiss. ex W. Mill. Heads to ⁵⁄₁₆ in. across; ray fls. absent. Eur., w. Asia.

boreale Mak. Per., spreading by short rhizomes, sts. to 4 ft.; lvs. to about 3 in. long, ovate to oblong-ovate in outline, pinnately parted into incisely toothed segms., pubescent; heads to ⅝ in. across, corymbose; fls. all yellow. Siberia, n. China, Korea, Japan.

Burnatii (Briq. & Cavillier) J. Ingram [*Leucanthemum Burnatii* Briq. & Cavillier]. Tufted, glabrous per., sts. slightly glaucous, petioles with white, scarious, sheathing bases, early lvs. linear-oblong, entire to slightly toothed, later lvs. linear-filiform to filiform, essentially entire; heads to 1½ in. across, involucral bracts more or less fimbriate; disc fls. yellow, ray fls. white. French maritime Alps.

Burridgeanum: *C. carinatum* cv.

carinatum Schousb. [*C. atrococcineum* Hort.; *C. tricolor* Andr.]. TRICOLOR C. Glabrous ann., 2–3 ft., sts. simple or forked; lvs. more or less succulent, pinnatifid into linear lobes; heads to 2½ in. across, solitary, long-peduncled, involucral bracts keeled; disc fls. purple, ray fls. white, yellow, red, or purple, often with band of different color at base; achenes winged. Morocco. Cv. 'Burridgeanum'. Ray fls. with red band at base. Cv. 'Dunnettii' [*C. Dunnettii* Hort.]. Often double-fld.; fls. bronze, yellow, or crimson.

Catananche J. Ball [*Leucanthemum Catananche* (J. Ball) Maire]. Tufted per., to 6 in.; lvs. basal, to 2½ in. long, irregularly lobed, silvery-gray; heads to 2 in. across, solitary on peduncles to 4 in. long, involucral bracts white, transparent; disc fls. yellow, ray fls. yellow, with blood-red band toward base. Morocco.

cinerariifolium (Trevir.) Vis. [*Pyrethrum cinerariifolium* Trevir.]. PYRETHRUM, DALMATIA P., DALMATIAN INSECT FLOWER. Glaucous, tufted per., to 15 in., sts. slender; lvs. oblong to elliptic in outline, pinnatifid, to 1 ft. long including petiole, silvery-silky-hairy beneath; heads to 1½ in. across, solitary on long peduncles; disc fls. yellow, ray fls. white. Yugoslavia. Now cult. in a number of countries, including Japan and the U.S. The dried infls. are the primary source of the insecticide, pyrethrum.

coccineum Willd. [*C. roseum* Adams; *Pyrethrum atrosanguineum* Hort.; *P. carneum* Bieb.; *P. coccineum* (Willd.) Vorosh.; *P. hybridum* Hort.]. PYRETHUM, PAINTED DAISY, PERSIAN INSECT FLOWER. Per., to 2 ft., sts. usually unbranched; lvs. thin, 1- or 2-pinnatifid, fernlike; heads to 3 in. across, solitary, sometimes "double-fld.," peduncles mostly unbranched; disc fls. yellow, ray fls. white, pink, or red. Sw. Asia. The dried fl. heads are a source of commercial pyrethrum. Cv. 'Roseum'. Fls. rose-pink.

coreanum Nakai: a name of unknown application; material cult. under this name in the past has been *C. Zawadskii* [*C. sibiricum*].

coronarium L. GARLAND C., CROWN DAISY. Stout, branched ann., to 4 ft.; lvs. 2-pinnately parted into sharply toothed segms., not succulent, auricled at base, glabrous; heads 1½ in. across, many, often double-fld., involucral bracts dry, not keeled; ray fls. yellow or yellowish-white; achenes angled. Medit. region. Much grown in the Orient, for the young lvs. eaten as greens; the fl. heads are also eaten in Japan.

corymbosum L. Stout per., 1–4 ft., sts. much-branched in upper part, essentially glabrous; lvs. 2-pinnately dissected, to 6 in. long; heads to 1 in. across; disc fls. yellow, ray fls. white. Caucasus.

densum (Labill.) Steud. Velvety-hairy subshrub, to 16 in., sts. simple, rigid; lvs. elliptic in outline, pinnately dissected, 1–2 in. long, woolly; heads to ½ in. across, few in corymbs; disc and ray fls. yellow. Syria.

depressum (J. Ball) H. Lindb. Somewhat cespitose per., to about 8 in.; lvs. crowded, to 1½ in. long, pinnately parted, finely hairy; heads to about ¾ in. across, solitary on long scapes, involucral bracts with wide scarious margins; disc fls. yellow, ray fls. pinkish-white above, reddish beneath. Great Atlas Mts., N. Afr.

Dunnettii: *C. carinatum* cv.

erubescens: *C. Zawadskii* var. *latilobum*.

frutescens L. [*Anthemis frutescens* Hort.]. MARGUERITE, WHITE M., PARIS DAISY. Bushy, woody-based, glabrous per., to 3 ft., lvs. oblong to ovate in outline, 2-pinnatifid, 2–4 in. long; heads to 2 in. across, solitary, involucral bracts with wide, hyaline margins; disc fls. yellow, ray fls. white or lemon-yellow. Canary Is. Cv. 'Chrysaster'. BOSTON YELLOW DAISY. Ray fls. yellow.

Haradjanii Rech.f. Subshrub, to 1½ ft., with dense, white, woolly-tomentose hairs; lvs. oblong-elliptic to ovate in outline, 2–3-pinnatifid, to 2 in. long, upper lvs. progressively reduced; heads to ⅛ in. across, in loose corymbs; fls. all tubular, ray fls. lacking. Syria.

hosmariense (J. Ball) J. Ingram [*Leucanthemum hosmariense* (J. Ball) Font Quer]. Rhizomatous, spreading, bushy per., to 1 ft., sts. with appressed, downward-pointing silvery hairs; lvs. sessile, lower lvs. 3-parted, to 2¾ in. long, with silvery hairs, upper lvs. linear; heads to 1½ in. across, solitary on peduncles to 6 in. long, involucral bracts silvery with dark margins; disc fls. yellow, ray fls. white. Morocco.

indicum L. Stoloniferous, much-branched per., 2–3 ft., sts. leafy; lvs. soft, ovate to oblong-ovate in outline, pinnately cleft, to 3 in. long or more, felty-gray beneath; heads to about 1 in. across, many in loose terminal corymbs; disc and ray fls. yellow. Japan, China.

inodorum: *Tripleurospermum maritimum* subsp.

isabellinum (C. Koch) Rech.f. [*Achillea argentea* Lam.]. Cespitose per., to 1 ft., sometimes taller, with silvery-silky hairs; lvs. ovate in outline, pinnately dissected into 5–7 cuneate segms., segms. parted into 3–7 linear-oblong divisions; heads in dense corymbs; ray fls. white; achenes 4–5-ribbed. W. Asia.

japonicola: *C. Makinoi*.

japonicum: *Artemisia japonica*.

lacustre Brot. PORTUGUESE C., PORTUGUESE DAISY. Robust per., 3–6 ft., branched in upper part; lvs. ovate-lanceolate, to 5 in. long, serrate-dentate, clasping; heads 2–3 in. across, usually solitary on long peduncles, sometimes in 3's; disc fls. yellow, ray fls. white. Portugal.

Leucanthemum L. [*Leucanthemum vulgare* Lam.]. OXEYE DAISY, WHITE D., MARGUERITE, WHITEWEED. Slender, erect per., to 3 ft., rhizomatous, essentially glabrous, sts. simple or sparingly branched; basal lvs. spatulate to obovate, to 6 in. long including petiole, toothed, st. lvs. oblong, toothed to pinnatifid, sessile; heads 1–2 in. across, solitary on long peduncles; disc fls. yellow, ray fls. white. Eur., Asia; naturalized as a weed in N. Amer.

macrophyllum Waldst. & Kit. [*Tanacetum macrophyllum* (Waldst. & Kit.) Schultz-Bip.]. TANSY C. Erect, rhizomatous per., 2½–3½ ft.; lvs. to 8 in. long, coarsely pinnatifid into coarsely toothed segms., pubescent; heads about ¼ in. across, in dense corymbs; disc fls. yellow, ray fls. white tinged with yellow. Se. Eur. to Caucasus.

majus: *C. Balsamita*.

Makinoi Matsum. & Nakai [*C. japonicola* Mak.]. Stoloniferous, somewhat shrubby per., to 2½ ft., sts. gray-tomentose; lvs. ovate to nearly orbicular in outline, to 2 in. long, 3-lobed, usually cuneate at

base, toothed, somewhat glaucous, densely hairy beneath; heads to 1½ in. across, solitary, or few in terminal corymbs; disc fls. yellow, ray fls. white. Japan.

Marshallianum: a listed name of no botanical standing; applied to a plant described as 1½ ft. high, with yellow heads, resembling a giant *Anthemis tinctoria*.

Mawii Hook.f. Subshrubby per., to 1½ ft.; lvs. triangular to oblong in outline, to 1 in. long, pinnatifid or upper lvs. entire, with soft, loose, woolly hairs; heads to 1½ in. across, solitary on long peduncles; disc fls. brown, ray fls. white, rose on lower surface; pappus tubular, elongated on 1 side into a translucent auricle, as long as or longer than tube of fl. Great Atlas Mts., N. Afr.

maximum Ramond, not Hort. MAX C., DAISY C. Glabrous per., to 2 ft., sts. simple, rigid; lvs. serrate-dentate, lower lvs. spatulate, to 1 ft. long including the long, winged petiole, upper lvs. lanceolate to linear, to 1 in. long, sessile; heads to about 2⅜ in. across, solitary on long peduncles; disc fls. yellow, ray fls. white; pappus lacking. Pyrenees. Most of the material cult. as *C. maximum* is probably *C. × superbum*.

×morifolium Ramat. FLORIST'S C., MUM. Assumed to be a hybrid involving *C. indicum*, *C. japonense* (Mak.) Nakai, *C. Makinoi*, *C. ornatum* Hemsl., and perhaps even other spp.; stout, subshrubby per., 2–5 ft., sts. erect or spreading; lvs. thick, strongly aromatic, lanceolate to ovate, to 3 in. long, lobed, lobes entire to coarsely toothed, lower surface gray-pubescent; heads of various sizes and shapes, typically clustered; disc fls. yellow, ray fls. longer than the disc, white, yellow, bronze, pink, reddish, or purple. Probably of Chinese origin.

multicaule Desf. Glabrous, glaucous ann., to 1 ft., sts. many, simple; lvs. variable in outline, often linear to spatulate, lobed and coarsely toothed or sometimes 3-parted or pinnately dissected, to 3 in. long; heads to 2½ in. across, solitary on long peduncles; disc and ray fls. golden-yellow. Algeria.

nipponicum (Franch. ex Maxim.) Sprenger. NIPPON C., NIPPON DAISY. Shrubby per., to 3 ft., sts. branched; lvs. crowded, sessile, thick, spatulate to oblong, to 3½ in. long, coarsely toothed toward apex, entire toward base, dark green above, paler beneath; heads to 3¼ in. across, solitary; disc fls. greenish-yellow, ray fls. white. Japan.

Nivellei Br.-Bl. & Maire. Erect ann., to about 1 ft., sts. simple or with few brs.; lvs. thickish, obovate in outline, to about 4 in. long including petiole, pinnately parted, margins toothed; heads to 1¼ in. across, solitary on long peduncles; disc fls. yellow, ray fls. white. Mts., Morocco.

partheniifolium (Willd.) Pers. [*Pyrethrum partheniifolium* Willd.]. Erect, aromatic per., to about 2½ ft., sts. branched; lvs. ovate in outline, 2-pinnately dissected, hairy, petioled; heads to 1⅜ in. across, in broad, loose corymbs; disc fls. yellow, ray fls. white. Caucasus.

Parthenium (L.) Bernh. [*Matricaria capensis* Hort., not L.; *M. eximia* Hort.; *M. parthenoides* Hort.]. FEVERFEW. Erect, bushy, aromatic per., to 3 ft.; lvs. oblong to broadly ovate in outline, blade 3 in. long, pinnatifid, lower lvs. petioled, hairy at least beneath; heads to ¾ in. across, many in corymbs; disc fls. yellow, ray fls. white, sometimes lacking. Se. Eur. to the Caucasus; introd. in N. and S. Amer. Dried fls. are medicinal. Cv. 'Aureum'. GOLDEN-FEATHER. Lvs. golden-yellow. Cv. 'Selaginoides' [*C. selaginoides* Hort.]. Sts. to 8 in.; lvs. more or less slashed.

primavera: a listed name of no botanical standing; used for a plant described as everblooming, with yellow fls.

ptarmiciflorum (Webb) Brenan [*Cineraria candicans* Hort.; *C. candidissima* var. *candicans* Hort.; *C. maritima* var. *candicans* Hort.; *Pyrethrum ptarmiciflorum* Webb]. DUSTY-MILLER, SILVER-LACE. Shrubby, white-tomentose per., to about 2 ft.; lvs. elliptic to oblong-ovate in outline, to 4 in. long including petiole, 2-pinnately parted; heads to about 1¼ in. across, in broad, rather dense corymbs; disc fls. yellow, ray fls. white. Grand Canary Is.

roseum: *C. coccineum*.

×rubellum: *C. Zawadskii* var. *latilobum*.

segetum L. CORN C., CORN MARIGOLD. Glabrous, glaucous, erect ann., to 2 ft., sts. simple or branched; lvs. oblong to spatulate or ovate in outline, to about 3 in. long, pinnatifid or coarsely toothed, somewhat fleshy; heads to 2½ in. across, solitary on peduncles thickened toward summit; disc and ray fls. golden-yellow. Eur., w. Asia; established in N. and S. Amer. and N. Afr.

selaginoides: *C. Parthenium* cv.

serotinum L. [*C. uliginosum* (Waldst. & Kit. ex Willd.) Pers.; *Pyrethrum uliginosum* Waldst. & Kit. ex Willd.]. HIGH DAISY, GIANT D. Erect, bushy per., 4–7 ft.; lvs. long-lanceolate, to 4 in. long, sharply and coarsely toothed; heads to 3 in. across, several terminating brs.; disc fls. yellow, ray fls. white. Cent. Eur.

sibiricum: *C. Zawadskii*.

×**superbum** Bergmans ex J. Ingram [*C. maximum* Hort., not Ramond]. SHASTA DAISY. Presumably a hybrid between *C. lacustre* and *C. maximum* Ramond; robust, glabrous per., to 3 ft. or more; lvs. coarsely toothed, lower lvs. oblanceolate, to 1 ft. long including petiole, upper lvs. lanceolate, sessile; heads to 4 in. across, solitary on long peduncles; disc fls. yellow, ray fls. pure white. Extremely variable and including many cvs. The Laciniata Group (var. *laciniata* Hort.) includes cvs. with fringed ray fls.

Tchihatchewii: *Tripleurospermum Tchihatchewii.*

tricolor: *C. carinatum.*

uliginosum: *C. serotinum.*

vulgare: *Tanacetum vulgare.*

Weyrichii (Maxim.) Miyabe. Stoloniferous per., to 1 ft.; lower lvs. nearly orbicular, palmately 5-cleft or 5-parted, fleshy, long-petioled, upper lvs. lobed or linear and entire; heads to 1¾ in. across, solitary on long peduncles; ray fls. white to pink. Japan.

yezoense T. Maek. Stoloniferous per., to about 20 in., sts. purplish, slightly pubescent; lower lvs. ovate-cuneate, to 1½ in. long, on long petioles, pinnately cleft or 3-cleft, fleshy, almost glabrous, upper lvs. spatulate; heads to 2½ in. across, solitary on long peduncles; ray fls. white. Japan.

Zawadskii Herbich [*C. sibiricum* Fisch. ex F. Forbes & Hemsl.]. Per., to 1½ ft., with woody, purplish rhizomes; lower lvs. broadly ovate in outline, to 1½ in. long, on petioles to 1¾ in. long, 2-pinnate, glandular-dotted, slightly pubescent to glabrous, upper lvs. reduced; heads to 2⅜ in. across, solitary; disc fls. yellow, ray fls. white. Japan, Korea, n. China, Manchuria, Siberia, and Carpathians. Var. **latilobum** (Maxim.) Kitam. [*C. erubescens* Stapf; *C.* × *rubellum* Sealy]. Sts. stout, to 3 ft.; heads to 3¼ in. across; disc fls. yellow, ray fls. pink. Japan, Korea, n. China, Manchuria. This sp., hybridized with *C.* × *morifolium* cvs., has given rise to the so-called Korean chrysanthemums, an especially hardy group, originally with heads daisylike, 2–3 in. across, with only 1 or few rows of ligules, but now also "double," with ray fls. of various colors.

CHRYSOBACTRON: *BULBINELLA.*

CHRYSOBALANACEAE R. Br. CHRYSOBALANUS FAMILY.

Dicot.; 17 genera and about 430 spp. of subshrubs to trees, pantrop. in distribution; lvs. alt., simple, entire, pinnately veined, with stipules; infl. of cymose panicles or terminal and axillary cymules; fls. mostly bisexual, sepals 5, petals 5 or 0, stamens many, staminodes sometimes present, disc lining the fl. tube, ovary superior, usually 1-celled, ovules 2; fr. a fleshy or dry drupe. *Chrysobalanus* is cult.

CHRYSOBALANUS L. *Chrysobalanaceae.*

Four spp. of shrubs or small trees native to trop. Amer. and Afr.; lvs. alt., simple, leathery; fls. small, white or greenish, in cymes or panicles; fr. a pulpy drupe.

Planted somewhat in the subtropical U.S. Propagated by seeds.

Icaco L. COCO PLUM, ICACO. Evergreen, to 30 ft.; lvs. entire, broad-obovate to nearly round, to 3 in. long, obtuse or emarginate, shining above; fls. white, in short cymes, sepals 5, petals 5, ¼ in. long; fr. to 1½ in. long. Coastal, s. Fla. to n. S. Amer. Zone 10b. Fr. edible but insipid.

CHRYSOCOMA L. *Compositae* (Aster Tribe).

About 10 spp. of small shrubs or herbs in S. Afr.; lvs. alt., linear or pinnatifid; fl. heads discoid, globose, short-peduncled, terminating the brs., receptacle naked; fls. all tubular, bisexual, yellow; pappus of 1 row of rough bristles.

Coma-aurea L. Shrublet, to 1½ ft., sts. erect, fastigiately branching; lvs. linear, about ⅜ in. long, flat, glabrous, entire; heads ½ in. across, on slender peduncles about 1½ in. long. Spring. Grown in Calif.

CHRYSOGONUM L. *Compositae* (Helianthus Tribe).

One sp., a low per. herb, native from Penn. to Fla. and La.; lvs. opp.; fl heads radiate, involucre in 2 rows, outer 5 involucral bracts green, inner 5 bracts chaffy, receptacle scaly; disc fls. many, sterile, ray fls. usually 5, fertile; achenes obovate, 4-angled, pappus a short crown.

Propagated by division or by seeds.

virginianum L. Plant hairy, sts. short early in season, later branching and elongating, to 10–12 in.; lvs. petioled, ovate or oblong, 1–3 in. long, toothed; heads to 1½ in. across; fls. yellow. Spring to autumn.

CHRYSOLARIX: *PSEUDOLARIX.* C. amabilis: *P. Kaempferi.*

CHRYSOPHYLLUM L. *Sapotaceae.*

About 80 spp. of trop., evergreen trees, native to N. and S. Amer., W. Afr., Australasia; lvs. alt., entire; fls. small, in clusters, sepals 5, imbricate, corolla mostly 5-lobed, stamens usually 5, staminodes lacking, ovary superior; fr. a berry, 1- to several-seeded.

Ornamental trees, also grown for their edible fruits. Require tropical temperatures and a humid atmosphere but no special type of soil. Propagated by seeds, by cuttings of ripe wood over heat, and probably by budding.

albidum G. Don. To 60 ft.; lvs. oblanceolate-oblong, to 10 in. long, 3 in. wide, bright green above, pale reddish- or whitish-hairy beneath; fls. on pedicels to ⅛ in. long; fr. 1½ in. thick, 5-celled. Trop. Afr.

Cainito L. STAR APPLE, CAIMITO. To 50 ft.; lvs. elliptic or oblong, to 6 in. long, shining above, golden-brown and silky beneath; fls. purplish-white; fr. globose, to 4 in. in diam., smooth, purple or light green, seeds 3–8, shining, embedded in white, translucent, edible pulp, star-shaped in transverse section. Trop. Amer., where commonly cult. as a handsome dooryard tree. Zone 10b, in Fla. Fr. eaten fresh but must be fully ripe.

monopyrenum: *C. oliviforme.*

oliviforme L. [*C. monopyrenum* Swartz]. SATINLEAF, DAMSON PLUM (of Jamaica). To 30 ft.; lvs. mostly smaller than in *C. Cainito,* densely brown- or reddish-tomentose underneath; fr. about ¾ in. long, purple, usually 1-seeded. S. Fla., trop. Amer. Zone 10b.

CHRYSOPOGON Trin. *Gramineae.*

About 20 spp. of ann. or per. grasses in Asia, Afr., and Australia, 1 in Fla. and Cuba; panicles open; spikelets borne in 3's at the ends of long, slender, naked brs., 1 sessile and bisexual, the other 2 pedicelled and sterile, or sometimes paired fertile and sterile below, fertile spikelet cylindrical, glumes leathery, sterile and awned fertile lemmas thin and hyaline. For terminology see *Gramineae.*

fulvus (K. Spreng.) Chiov. [*C. montanus* Trin. ex K. Spreng.]. Lvs. not 2-ranked, glabrous, occasionally with a few tubercle-based hairs; sessile spikelet to ¼ in. long, the second glume keeled, pectinate-ciliate in the lower ⅔–¾ with long, golden or golden-brown, rigid hairs, pedicelled spikelets ⅛ in. long, the first glume pubescent and awned, pedicels shorter than half the length of the sessile spikelet. Trop. Asia, E. Afr.; introd. into Fla. for fodder and hay.

montanus: *C. fulvus.*

CHRYSOPSIS (Nutt.) Elliott. GOLDEN ASTER. *Compositae*

(Aster Tribe). About 30 spp. of summer- and autumn-flowering ann., bien., or per. herbs, native to N. Amer.; sometimes stoloniferous, sts. leafy, erect to decumbent; lvs. alt., simple, usually entire, pinnately veined, variously pubescent, progressively reduced upward along st.; fl. heads few to many in corymbose infl., involucre campanulate to hemispherical, involucral bracts imbricate in several rows, partly herbaceous, receptacle naked; disc and ray fls. yellow; achenes obovoid, compressed, pappus double, the inner of bristles, the outer of shorter bristles or scales.

Occasionally grown in border, wild garden, or rock garden; of easy culture, preferring full sun. Propagated by seeds or, in some species, by division.

amplifolia: *C. villosa* var. *foliosa.*

camporum Greene [*C. villosa* var. *camporum* (Greene) Cronq.; *Heterotheca camporum* (Greene) Shinn.]. Coarse, hispid, short-rhizomatous per., sts. erect, thick, to 3½ ft.; lvs. sessile, lanceolate-oblong, more or less toothed, ciliate basally; heads to 2½ in. across, long-peduncled, involucre hispid to nearly glabrous, minutely glandular. Mo., s. Ill., and Ind.

falcata: *Pityopsis falcata.*

graminifolia: *Pityopsis graminifolia.*

gossypina (Michx.) Elliott [*Heterotheca gossypina* (Michx.) Shinn.]. White-tomentose or -woolly per. or bien., not stoloniferous, sts. curving-erect or decumbent, to 3 ft. long; lvs. sessile, oblanceolate or elliptic, to 2½ in. long, obtuse, the lower to 4 in. long, attenuate basally; heads few, to 1¾ in. across, in loose infl., involucre woolly. Sandy soil, se. Va. to Fla.

mariana (L.) Elliott [*Heterotheca mariana* (L.) Shinn.]. Short-stoloniferous per., sts. erect or curving-erect, 1–3 ft. high, silky-hairy, often purplish; lvs. silky-hairy, later nearly glabrous, the lowermost petioled, spatulate or oblanceolate, to 9 in. long, entire or toothed, upper lvs. reduced, sessile, lanceolate, entire; heads 1½ in. across, in compact infl., involucre and peduncles stipitate-glandular. Sandy soil, e. N.Y. to Ohio, s. to Fla. and e. Tex.

microcephala: *Pityopsis graminifolia*.

nervosa: *Pityopsis nervosa*.

pinifolia: *Pityopsis pinifolia*.

Rutteri: *C. villosa* var.

verticillata: a listed name of no botanical standing.

villosa (Pursh) Nutt. [*Heterotheca villosa* (Pursh) Shinn.]. Very variable; tap-rooted, sts. erect to decumbent, often woody at base, 6–40 in. long, variously pubescent, often much-branched; lvs. oblong-elliptic to linear-oblanceolate, obtuse or acute, entire, seldom toothed; infl. dense to loose, heads ¾–1½ in. across, involucre variously pubescent or glandular-viscid. Wisc. to B.C., s. to Tex. and Calif. Var. **villosa**. The typical var.; to 16 in.; lvs. somewhat petioled, oblanceolate, green, villous to hirsute; heads clearly peduncled. Range as in sp. Var. **camporum**: *C. camporum*. Var. **foliosa** (Nutt.) D. C. Eat. [*C. amplifolia* Rydb.; *C. foliosa* Nutt.; *Heterotheca foliosa* (Nutt.) Shinn.]. To 2 ft.; lvs. sessile, broadly oblong to obovate, gray-pubescent with short, appressed, silky hairs; heads subtended by leafy bracts. Minn. to Wash. and Ariz. Var. **prostrata**: a listed name of no botanical standing, used for a low, decumbent form of *C. villosa*. Var. **Rutteri** Rothr. [*C. Rutteri* (Rothr.) Greene; *Heterotheca Rutteri* (Rothr.) Shinn.]. Lvs. lanceolate, densely silvery-pubescent with appressed, silky hairs; heads subtended by leafy bracts. Ariz.

CHRYSOSPLENIUM L. GOLDEN SAXIFRAGE. *Saxifragaceae*. About 55 spp. of small, semiaquatic, creeping or prostrate herbs in ne. Asia, Eur., N. Amer., a few in N. Afr. and s. S. Amer.; fls. very small, greenish; calyx tube united to ovary, sepals 4, spreading, petals 0, stamens 4–8, borne on margin of an 8-lobed disc, ovary partly inferior, styles 2, short.

Sometimes used as a cover on moist ground, in bog gardens or near pools.

alternifolium L. Sts. to 6 in. long, from an underground rhizome; lvs. alt., orbicular-reniform, coarsely toothed. Early spring. Eur., n. Asia.

americanum Schweinitz. WATER-MAT, WATER-CARPET. Glabrous, sts. creeping, to 8 in. long; lvs. opp., or the upper alt., ovate or orbicular, to ¾ in. long; fls. solitary in the axils, sepals greenish, anthers red. Spring. Que. to Ont., s. to Va. and Ind.

oppositifolium L. Loosely cespitose, pubescent, sts. decumbent, rooting, leafy, to 8 in. long; lvs. opp., orbicular; sepals greenish-yellow or yellow, anthers yellow. Late spring. Eur.

CHRYSOTHAMNUS Nutt. RABBITBRUSH. *Compositae* (Aster Tribe). Thirteen spp. of shrubs or subshrubs, native to w. U.S., 1 sp. in Mex.; sts. erect, much-branched; lvs. alt., never clustered, sometimes glandular-dotted, entire; fl. heads discoid, many in racemes, cymes, or panicles, mostly 5-fld., involucre cylindrical, involucral bracts imbricate, usually in 5 rows; disc fls. all tubular, bisexual, fertile, yellow or white; achenes cylindrical, angled, or compressed, glabrous or silky-hairy, pappus of many capillary bristles.

Suitable for dry regions.

graveolens: *C. nauseosus* subsp.

nauseosus (Pall.) Britt. Shrub, to about 7 ft., with several much-branched sts. arising from the base, twigs usually densely leafy, often strongly scented, with felty, persistent, gray or whitish hairs; lvs. linear-filiform to linear-oblanceolate, to 2¾ in. long, nearly glabrous to tomentose; heads in dense, rounded cymes or elongated, round-topped thyrses; fls. yellow. Sask. to B.C., s. to Tex., Sonora, and Baja Calif. Subsp. **nauseosus** [*C. plattensis* (Greene) Greene]. The typical subsp.; low shrub, to 2 ft., foliage not strongly scented; lvs. linear, to 2 in. long, white-tomentose; heads in a cymose or elongated infl. Sask. to B.C., s. to Colo. and Utah. Subsp. **graveolens** (Nutt.) H. M. Hall & Clements [*C. graveolens* Nutt.]. Robust shrub, to 5 ft., foliage mildly ill-scented; lvs. broadly linear, to 2⅜ in. long; heads crowded in a round to flat-topped cyme. N. Dak. and Idaho., s. to New Mex. and n. Ariz. Subsp. **hololeucus** (A. Gray) H. M. Hall & Clements. Shrub, to 7 ft., with white, gray, or yellow twigs, foliage sweet-scented; lvs. linear, to 1¼ in. long; heads in a rounded, often compact cyme. E. Calif. and Nev.

plattensis: *C. nauseosus* subsp. *nauseosus*.

CHRYSOTHEMIS Decne. [*Tussaca* Rchb.]. *Gesneriaceae*. Seven spp. of tuberous, per. herbs in Amer. tropics; lvs. opp.,

equal, usually toothed; fls. in few-fld., axillary cymes, calyx tubular, sometimes angled, lobes much shorter than tube, corolla cylindrical, limb spreading, short, lobes rounded, stamens 4, filaments united to each other and to the corolla basally, anthers united, disc of a single, sometimes 2-lobed gland at the back of the ovary, ovary superior; fr. a globose caps.

For cultivation see *Gesneriaceae*.

Friedrichsthaliána (Hanst.) H. E. Moore [*Tussaca Friedrichsthaliana* Hanst.]. Sts. to 1 ft.; lvs. oblong to nearly lanceolate, to 1 ft. long, 5 in. wide, decurrent on petiole, thin, with short, pale hairs; peduncles 3- or more-fld., to 1 in. long; calyx 5-angled and seemingly winged, inflated at base, ¾ in. long, green or yellow, lobes triangular, broader than long, corolla 1¼–1½ times as long as calyx, orange or yellowish, lobes faintly red-striped. Cent. Amer. and w. Colombia.

pulchella (J. Donn ex Sims) Decne. Similar to *C. Friedrichsthaliana*, but with calyx campanulate, not inflated at base, red, and corolla 1½–3½ times as long as calyx. W. Indies, Panama, ne. S. Amer. to Amazonian Brazil.

CHYSIS Lindl. *Orchidaceae*. Three spp. of epiphytic orchids, native to Cent. and S. Amer.; sts. pendent, jointed, fusiform, leafy in the upper part; lvs. plicate, imbricate; infl. a lateral, many-fld. raceme; fls. fleshy, sepals and petals similar, lip 3-lobed, with a many-ridged callus at base, column basally elongated into a foot. For structure of fl. see *Orchidaceae*.

For culture see *Orchids*.

aurea Lindl. Infl. to 6 in. long, several-fld.; fls. campanulate, to 2 in. across, sepals and petals similar, golden-yellow, paler toward base, lip yellow with red stripes, the midlobe with 5 prominent keel-like crests. Late winter–late summer. Cent. and S. Amer. Forma **Limminghii** (Linden & Rchb.f.) P. Allen [*C. Limminghii* Linden & Rchb.f.]. Sepals and petals marked with reddish-brown. Mex. Var. **bractescens** (Lindl.) P. Allen [*C. bractescens* Lindl.]. Racemes drooping, bracts prominent, more than 1 in. long; fls. to 3 in. across, sepals and petals white, lip yellow with crimson stripes. Winter–late spring. Mex., Guatemala.

bractescens: *C. aurea* var.

×**chelsoni** Rchb.f.: *C. aurea* forma *Limminghii* × *C. laevis*. Infl. arching, loosely few-fld.; sepals and petals yellow with a large red-brown spot at apex, lip white, finely spotted with purple.

laevis Lindl. Infl. few-fld.; fls. fleshy, large, to 2½ in. across, sepals and petals similar, spreading, yellow with orange flush toward apex, lip white with red veins and blotches, midlobe with 3 keel-like crests. Early winter. Mex., Costa Rica.

Limminghii: *C. aurea* forma.

CIBOTIUM Kaulf. TREE FERN. *Dicksoniaceae*. About 15 spp. of tree ferns of Mex., Cent. Amer., trop. Asia, and Polynesia, trunk stout, apically covered with limp, soft hairs; lvs. arching, triangular, 1–3-pinnate; indusium marginal, 2-valved, both valves similar in texture and distinctly different from the green blade.

The cut trunks of the Hawaiian species are much utilized in horticulture for making pots and planters useful for potted vines and epiphytes. Several species are cultivated as ornamentals in tropical or subtropical gardens (Zone 10), or under glass. Propagated by spores. The Hawaiian species can be maintained for long periods by placing the severed trunks in containers with pebbles and water. See also *Ferns*.

Barometz (L.) John Sm. SCYTHIAN-LAMB. Trunk prostrate, very short, densely covered with glossy brown hairs; lvs. to 6 ft. long, glaucous beneath, ribs appressed-hairy; sori on lower half of the pinnae, indusia with the inner valve ⅔ as wide as the outer. China, Malay Pen.

Chamissoi Kaulf. [*C. Menziesii* Hook.]. HAWAIIAN T.F., HAPUU-II. Trunk to about 25 ft., with yellowish-brown hairs; petioles tubercled with yellowish-brown hairs basally and stiff, long, blackish hairs above, lvs. leathery, to 12 ft. long, glabrous or with minute tufts of hair beneath. Hawaii. The name *C. Chamissoi* was long mistakenly applied by botanists to *C. splendens*. Material grown as *C. Chamissoi* is mostly *C. glaucum*.

glaucum (Sm.) Hook. & Arn. Like *C. splendens*, but the trunk hairs lustrous, lvs. somewhat leathery, glaucous and glabrous beneath, the lowest pair of pinnules usually auricled and deflexed. Hawaii. Most of the material offered as *C. Chamissoi* belongs here.

Menziesii: *C. Chamissoi*.

regale Versch. & Lem. Trunk to 30 ft., covered with hairs; petioles hairy at base; lvs. to 12 ft. long, with conspicuous white bloom beneath, veins of pinnules 2–3-forked. Mex.

Schiedei Schlechtend. & Cham. MEXICAN T.F. Trunk to 15 ft. in the wild, trunk and base of petioles covered with somewhat lustrous, yellow-brown silky hairs; lvs. to about 5 ft. long, membranous, pale green, glaucous beneath; pinnules small, to 5 in. long, ribs covered with long, silky hairs; sori protuding beyond margin, making fertile pinnules crenate. Mex. and Guatemala. A graceful slow-growing tree fern, often grown for decoration as a tub plant under glass.

splendens (Gaud.-Beaup.) Kraj. ex Skottsb. [*C. Chamissoi* of auth., not Kaulf.]. HAPUU, BLOND T.F., MAN T.F., HAWAIIAN T.F., MAN FERN. Trunk to 16 ft.; trunk and base of petioles covered with mass of dull, yellowish-brown, matted hairs; lvs. to 8 ft. long, slightly glaucous or green and covered with pale cobwebby hairs beneath. Hawaii.

CICCA: *PHYLLANTHUS.* C. disticha: *Phyllanthus acidus.*

CICER L. *Leguminosae* (subfamily *Faboideae*). About 14 spp. of herbs of w. Asia; lvs. pinnate, lfts. toothed; fls. solitary or few together in axils, inconspicuous, papilionaceous, white or purplish, stamens 10, 9 united and 1 separate; fr. a short, inflated legume, with large seeds.

Propagated by seeds planted 8–12 in. apart in rows 2 ft. apart. Thrives best on light loamy soils.

arietinum L. CHICK PEA, EGYPTIAN P., GARBANZO, GRAM. Ann., to 2 ft.; lvs. odd-pinnate, lfts. 9–17, opp. or alt., obtuse, elongate, to ⅝ in. long; fr. to 1 in. long and ½ in. wide, with 1 or 2 globose seeds. Sw. Asia. Widely cult. for the nutritious seeds; the most important leguminous crop in India.

CICERBITA: *LACTUCA.*

CICHORIUM L. CHICORY. *Compositae* (Cichorium Tribe). Nine spp. of deep-rooted ann., bien., or per. herbs with milky sap, native mostly to Medit. region; sts. branched, with reduced lvs.; lvs. mostly basal, alt.; fl. heads mostly sessile and axillary, involucral bracts in 2 rows, receptacle naked; fls. all ligulate, bisexual, blue, purple, pink, or white; achenes glabrous, striate-nerved, pappus of 2–3 rows of chaffy scales.

Two species are important as salad plants.

Endivia L. ENDIVE. Glabrous ann. or bien., to 3 ft.; lvs. many in a basal rosette, brittle, oblong, lobed or greatly cut and curled, st. lvs. successively reduced; heads about 1½ in. across, some subtended by leafy bracts usually longer than heads; fls. violet-blue. Probably India. Widely cult. as a hardy salad plant. For cult. see *Endive.*

glandulosum Boiss. & Huet. Ann., to 1 ft., sts. stiff, white, glandular; lower lvs. ovate-oblong, finely toothed, upper lvs. lanceolate; involucral bracts glandular-ciliate; fls. blue. Near East.

Intybus L. COMMON C., BLUE-SAILORS, SUCCORY, WITLOOF, BARBE-DE-CAPUCHIN. Per., 3–5½ ft., sts. stout, stiff, almost leafless in upper part; basal lvs. broadly oblong to oblanceolate, pinnatifid or toothed, bristly-hairy beneath, short-petioled, upper lvs. lanceolate, clasping; heads 1½ in. across, subtended by leafy bracts shorter than heads; fls. azure-blue, rarely pink or white. N. Afr., Eur., w. Asia; established as a cosmopolitan weed. Cult. especially in Eur., for greens, and the root used as a substitute for or an adulterant of coffee. For cult. see *Chicory.*

pumilum Jacq. Ann., to 3 ft., sts. erect, stiff; lower lvs. runcinate or dentate, minutely setose, upper lvs. minute, linear; involucral bracts not glandular but sometimes ciliate; fls. blue, 3 times as long as involucre. S. Eur., Near East.

CICUTA L. WATER HEMLOCK. *Umbelliferae.* About 8 spp. of per., heavy-scented herbs of Eurasia and N. Amer., with poisonous roots; lvs. decompound; fls. very small, white, in terminal compound umbels; fr. slightly flattened.

Sometimes transplanted to the wild garden or bog garden. Members of this genus have been said to be among the most violently poisonous plants (when eaten) of the north temperate region.

maculata L. MUSQUASH ROOT, SPOTTED COWBANE, BEAVER-POISON. To 6 ft.; lvs. 2- or 3-pinnate, segms. lanceolate, to 5 in. long. Swamps, Prince Edward Is., Que., s. to N.C., w. to N. Dak. and Tex.

CIENFUEGOSIA Cav. C. hakeifolia: *Alyogyne hakeifolia.*

CIMICIFUGA L. BUGBANE, RATTLETOP. *Ranunculaceae.* About 15 spp. of tall, upright, per. herbs of the N. Temp. Zone; lvs. large, ternately decompound; fls. small, white, many, in long racemes, sometimes panicled, sepals 2–5, petal-

oid, falling early, petals 1–8 or none, small, clawed, mostly 2-lobed, stamens many, pistils 1–8, sessile or stipitate, many-ovuled; fr. of follicles.

Plants usually of rich woods, sometimes planted at the back of the border or in partially shaded places in the wild garden. Propagated by seeds or by division.

acerina: *C. japonica* var.

americana Michx. AMERICAN B., MOUNTAIN B., SUMMER COHOSH. Sts. slender, 2–6 ft.; lvs. 2–3-ternate, then pinnate with 3–5 lfts., lfts. ovate, oblong, incised, acuminate, 1–3 in. long; infl. loose, elongate; petals 2-horned, with basal concave nectary; follicles 3–8, shorter than slender stipes. Penn. and W. Va. to Ga. and Tenn.

cordifolia: *C. racemosa* var.

dahurica (Turcz.) Torr. & A. Gray ex Maxim. Sts. 3–5 ft.; lvs. 2–3-ternate, lfts. pinnatifid or lobed at base, toothed, terminal lft. cordate, mostly 2½–4 in. long; infl. paniculate; fls. cream-white; follicles 2–3, sessile. Se. Siberia, Amur R. region, Japan.

elata Nutt. Sts. 3–6 ft., more or less pubescent; lvs. 2–3-ternate, pubescent, lfts. round-ovate, deeply cordate, with broad lobes and teeth, ¾–2 in. long; infl. paniculate, petals none; follicle mostly solitary, pubescent, nearly sessile. Wash., Ore.

foetida L. [*Actaea Cimicifuga* L.]. Sts. 3–6 ft., leafy, branched and tomentose in upper parts; lvs. ternate, then 2-pinnate, lfts. 2–3 in. long, deeply toothed, terminal lft. often 3-lobed; sepals mostly 4, greenish, petals more or less bifid; follicles 4–8, pubescent, ½ in. long, stipitate. Se. Eur., Siberia. Used medicinally by the Chinese.

japonica (Thunb.) K. Spreng [*Actaea japonica* Thunb.]. Sts. about 3 ft.; lvs. basal, ternate, shining above, lfts. long-petioled, cordate, 3–5-lobed, lobes acuminate; raceme long, sometimes branched at base; fls. sessile; follicles stipitate. Japan. Var. **acerina** (Siebold & Zucc.) Huth [*C. acerina* (Siebold & Zucc.) T. Tanaka]. Lvs. maplelike, with long-pointed lobes. Japan. Var. **obtusiloba** (Siebold & Zucc.) Mak. Lvs. duller, blunter, both ternate and 2-ternate. Japan.

laciniata S. Wats. Sts. 3 ft. or more, glabrate; lvs. 2–3-ternate, lfts. 1–2½ in. long, ovate, acuminate, incised and laciniately toothed; infl. paniculate, pubescent; petals less than 3⁄16 in.; follicles 2–4, pubescent, ¼ in. long, stipes half as long. Ore.

racemosa (L.) Nutt. BLACK COHOSH, BLACK SNAKEROOT. Sts. 3–8 ft.; lvs. 2–3-ternate, then often pinnate, lfts. cuneate to cordate at base, 1–4 in. long; racemes few, wandlike, erect, 1–3 ft.; petals 1–2-horned; follicle 1, sessile. Mass. to Ont., s. to Ga., Tenn., Mo. Used medicinally. Var. **cordifolia** (Pursh) A. Gray [*C. cordifolia* Pursh]. Lfts. few (about 9), 4–10 in. long, at least the terminal lft. deeply cordate. Va., N.C., Tenn.

rubifolia Kearn. Sts. 2–4 ft.; terminal lfts. 5–7-lobed, 4–12 in. wide; follicles 1–2, glabrous, 5⁄16 in. long, sessile. Tenn.

simplex (DC.) Turcz. Like *C. foetida*, but st. simple, 2–4 ft.; lvs. 4–12 in. across; racemes 1, rarely 2, closely pubescent; follicles glabrous, stipes long. Se. Siberia, Manchuria, Kamchatka, Japan.

CINCHONA L. QUININE. *Rubiaceae.* About 40 spp. of trees or shrubs, native mostly to Andean S. Amer., n. to Costa Rica; lvs. opp., stipules large, often red-veined, deciduous; fls. small, rose or yellowish-white, many in a terminal panicle with opp. brs., 5-merous, corolla salverform; fr. a caps., opening from base, seeds many, winged. The spp. are difficult to distinguish and their nomenclature is confused.

The bark of several species, formerly called sacred bark and Jesuits' bark, is the source of several important alkaloids, especially the antimalarial quinine. Despite the development of synthetic antimalarial drugs, quinine is still required for certain types of malaria. The species are native to cool, wet, montane tropical regions, and similar conditions should be provided when they are grown under glass, as ornamentals and for economic interest. Propagated by seeds or by cuttings of ripe wood.

Calisaya Wedd. [*C. Ledgerana* Moens ex Trimen]. CALISAYA. Tree, bark white, with strong lateral fissures; lvs. oblong-elliptic, to 7 in. long; corolla pale pink, ½ in. long. E. slopes of Andes, s. Peru, Bolivia. The inner bark is the yellow calisaya or Ledger quinine bark of commerce. This sp. is main source of high-yielding cvs. developed in Indonesia and elsewhere.

Condaminea: see *C. officinalis.*

Ledgerana: *C. Calisaya.*

micrantha Ruiz & Pav. HUÁNUCO. Tall tree, with mature bark gray-brown, often warty; lvs. elliptic to obovate, thin, large, glabrous beneath except along midrib; corolla whitish, about ¼ in. long. Montane rainforests, s. Ecuador to Bolivia. The inner bark is the gray cinchonine bark of commerce.

officinalis L. Tree, bark rough, brown; lvs. ovate-lanceolate, mostly firm-leathery, to 4 in. long; corolla deep pink, to 5/8 in. long. Variable, local from Colombia to n. Peru. The bark is the crown or Loja quinine bark of commerce. *C. Condaminea* Humb. & Bonpl. may be a synonym or a form of *C. officinalis.*

pubescens Vahl. Tall tree; lvs. elliptic, to 18 in. long, thin, usually pubescent beneath; corolla rose-pink, ½ in. long. Variable and widespread, Costa Rica and Venezuela, s. to Bolivia. Inner bark is red quinine bark of commerce. *C. succirubra* Pav. ex Klotsch probably belongs here as a well-marked var.

succirubra: see *C. pubescens.*

CINERARIA: *SENECIO.* **C. candicans:** *Chrysanthemum ptarmiciflorum.* **C. candidissima:** see *S. Vira-vira.* **C. candidissima** var. **candicans:** *Chrysanthemum ptarmiciflorum.* **C. grandiflora:** a listed name, perhaps referring to *S. × hybridus.* **C. maritima:** *S. Cineraria.* **C. maritima** var. **candicans:** *Chrysanthemum ptarmiciflorum.* **C. maritima** var. **candidissima:** *S. Vira-vira.* **C. nana:** a listed name, perhaps referring to a dwarf race of *S. ×hybridus.* **C. stellata:** a listed name, perhaps referring to *S. ×hybridus.*

CINERARIA. *Senecio × hybridus,* the cineraria of florists, is much grown under glass for its abundant flowers in many colors (except yellows), well set off by heavy, attractive foliage. The plant is perennial but it is commonly grown as an annual, since strong, well-grown, new stock produces the most profuse flowers. The single-flowered kinds are usually preferred, being raised each year from seeds. For autumn and early winter bloom, seeds may be sown in May, or, for winter and spring bloom, in late summer or early autumn. The main lot is usually started in midsummer. The young plants are pricked off into pots and afterwards shifted to maintain continuous growth, and not allowed to bloom until in their final 5- or 6-inch pots, or in 8-inch pots for very large specimens. The double-flowered kinds are propagated by cuttings of strong shoots that arise after the flowering tops are removed. Cinerarias must be grown cool, as cool as carnations, or they will not give good results. If broad, bushy plants are desired, the center may be pinched out when the flower buds begin to show. The cineraria is subject to aphids; if fumigation cannot be practiced, nicotine sprays may be employed. Cinerarias are adapted to window garden culture if care is taken not to stunt them by growing them too hot or by neglecting to water them.

Other plants known as cinerarias are some of the dusty millers. See *Senecio Cineraria* and *S. Vira-vira.*

CINNAMOMUM Trew. [*Camphora* Fabr.]. *Lauraceae.* About 250 spp. or more of aromatic trees and shrubs, native from e. and se. Asia to Australia; lvs. evergreen, nearly opp., leathery, strongly 3-nerved from base except in *C. Camphora;* fls. small, bisexual or unisexual, usually in axillary panicles, perianth tube short, with 6 lobes, stamens 9, in 3 whorls, anthers 4-celled, introrse in whorls 1 and 2, in whorl 3 extrorse; fr. a berry, subtended by a shallow but conspicuous cupule.

Several species are important as sources of essential oil, the bark yielding spices used in flavoring, perfumery, and medicine. Grown in the South as ornamentals; likely to be found in collections of economic plants. Propagated by seeds and by cuttings of half-ripened wood in spring with heat under glass.

Burmanii (Nees) Blume [*C. pedunculatum* Nees]. PADANG CASSIA. Tree; lvs. opp., sometimes alt., ovate-oblong, acuminate. Bark is aromatic and a source of cassia. Se. Asia and Indonesia.

Camphora (L.) J. Presl [*Camphora officinalis* Nees ex Steud.; *Laurus Camphora* L.]. CAMPHOR TREE. Handsome tree, to 100 ft., brs. yellow-brown, buds enclosed by large imbricate scales; lvs. alt., ovate-elliptic, to 5 in. long, acuminate, whitish beneath, shed in early spring and immediately replaced by new lvs.; panicles shorter than lvs.; fls. yellow; fr. globose, black. China, Taiwan, Japan. Thrives in s. Calif. and in southernmost states; useful as a specimen tree for parks or for row plantings along streets. The wood much used in cabinetwork in the Orient; twigs, lvs., and wood distilled to produce camphor.

Cassia (Nees) Nees & Eberm. ex Blume. CASSIA-BARK TREE, CASSIA, CHINESE CINNAMON. Tree, to 40 ft.; lvs. opp., oblong to lanceolate, to 6 in. long, long-acuminate; panicles as long as lvs. Burma. Cult. in s. China and Indonesia. Source of one of the oldest spices; the bark used like cinnamon.

glanduliferum (Wallich) Nees [*Laurus glandulifera* Wallich]. Small tree; lvs. alt., elliptic or lanceolate, to 5 in. long, caudate-acuminate; panicles 2 in. long. Cent. Himalayas.

japonicum Siebold ex Nees [*C. pseudoloureirii* Hayata]. Medium-sized tree; lvs. ovate-lanceolate to oblong, to 3½ in. long, acute to acuminate, reticulate, glabrous, petioles ½ in. long; infl. of long-peduncled umbels; fr. ellipsoid, black. Temp. e. Asia.

kotoense: *C. myrianthum.*

Loureirii Nees. CASSIA-FLOWER TREE, SAIGON CINNAMON. Medium-sized tree; lvs. alt. or opp., elliptic to oblong, to 5 in. long; fls. greenish-yellow. Se. Asia. Bark is an official cinnamon.

micranthum (Hayata) Hayata. To 90 ft.; lvs. obovate, to 4 in. long, abruptly acuminate, short-caudate at base, 3-nerved, green and glossy above, hairy in vein axils beneath; panicles few-fld., axillary; fls. small. Taiwan.

myrianthum Merrill [*C. kotoense* Kaneh. & Sasaki]. Tree; lvs. opp. to subopp., ovate-oblong, to 6 in. long, acute, rounded at base, 3-nerved, glabrous, glossy above, smooth beneath, not hairy in vein axils; infl. cymose, cymes axillary and terminal, short, stout, few-fld.; fr. ellipsoid, about ½ in. long. Philippine Is. and Taiwan.

nobile: a listed name of no botanical standing.

pedunculatum: *C. Burmannii.*

pseudoloureirii: *C. japonicum.*

zeylanicum Blume. CINNAMON, CEYLON C. Small tree, to 30 ft.; lvs. ovate to ovate-lanceolate, to 7 in. long, obtuse or acute; panicles as long as lvs.; fls. inconspicuous, yellowish. Ceylon and sw. India. Cult. in other trop. areas. Dried bark yields the commercially important spice, cinnamon.

CIPURA Aubl. *Iridaceae.* Not cult. **C. martinicensis:** *Trimezia martinicensis.*

CIRCAEA L. ENCHANTER'S NIGHTSHADE. *Onagraceae.* About 12 spp. of per. herbs with underground rhizomes and slender sts., mostly of woods in the N. Hemisphere; lvs. opp., delicate; fls. small, 2-merous, in bracted racemes, ovary inferior; fr. small, indehiscent, with hooked bristles.

Sometimes grown in shaded or moist rock gardens.

alpina L. Like *C. lutetiana,* but the open fls. clustered at end of raceme; fr. 1-celled. N. Amer., Eurasia.

canadensis: *C. lutetiana.*

lutetiana L. [*C. canadensis* (L.) J. Hill]. To 2 ft.; lvs. oblong-ovate, 2–4 in. long, rounded or cordate at base; open fls. scattered along racemes, sepals scarcely 1/8 in. long, purplish, petals slightly longer; fr. 2-celled. E. U.S., Eurasia.

CIRRHOPETALUM: *BULBOPHYLLUM.* **C. guttulatum:** *B. umbellatum.*

CIRSIUM Mill. THISTLE, PLUME THISTLE. *Compositae* (Carduus Tribe). Between 100 and 200 spp. of spiny ann., bien., or per. herbs, native to the N. Hemisphere; lvs. in rosettes or alt. on the sts., simple or more frequently pinnately lobed or divided, margins usually prickly or spiny; fl. heads solitary on ends of brs. or clustered, involucre campanulate to globose, ovoid, or cylindrical, involucral bracts imbricate in several rows, at least some usually spine-tipped, receptacle flat to subconical, densely bristly; fls. all tubular, bisexual or female, white, yellowish, red, or purple, anthers tailed; achenes compressed or 4-angled, glabrous, pappus of plumose bristles united basally in a ring and falling as a unit.

A few species are grown as ornamentals, being adapted to bold effects.

acaule: *Carlina acaulis.*

acaulescens: *C. foliosum.*

arizonicum (A. Gray) Petrak. Per., to 4 ft.; lvs. linear in outline, pinnatifid, floccose above, white-tomentose beneath, margins with weak, yellow spines, lower lvs. to 1 ft., st. lvs. reduced, semiclasping; heads to 1½ in. across, solitary or clustered; fls. crimson. Mts., Ariz. and Utah.

arvense (L.) Scop. CANADA T. Per., to 3 ft., sometimes taller, with a creeping rhizome, mostly dioecious; lvs. oblong to lanceolate, sinuate-pinnatifid, to 4¾ in. long, prickly-margined; heads to 1 in. across, solitary or irregularly corymbose; fls. pinkish-purple to whitish. Noxious weed, Eur.; naturalized in N. Amer.

Coulteri Harv. & A. Gray. Stout bien., to 4 ft., from a taproot; lvs. lanceolate, shallowly pinnatifid, cobwebby-tomentose, prickly-margined, basal lvs. to 1 ft. long, petioled, st. lvs. reduced, sessile; heads to 2¾ in. across, solitary on cymose brs.; fls. dark crimson or rarely white, longer than involucre. Calif.

diacantha (Labill.) DC. FISHBONE T. Bien., to 3 ft.; lvs. linear-lanceolate, to 8 in. long, glabrous or sparingly cobwebby on upper surface, white-tomentose beneath, sessile, half-clasping, margin dentate, each tooth ending in 1 or 2 stiff yellow spines; fls. purplish. Asia Minor.

edule Nutt. Bien. or short-lived per., to 6 ft., sts. often stout and hollow, rather succulent; lvs. weakly pubescent or almost glabrous, lower lvs. oblanceolate, to 16 in. long, pinnately divided, ultimate divisions oblong or triangular, spine-tipped, st. lvs. reduced, semiclasping, more stoutly spiny; heads to 1½ in. across, solitary or 2–4 in congested clusters; fls. rose-purple or lavender-rose. Nw. Ore. to s. B.C.

eriocephalum: *C. scopulorum.*

eriophorum (L.) Scop. Bien., to 5 ft., sts. not prickly, from a thick taproot; basal lvs. broadly lanceolate in outline, to 2 ft. long, deeply pinnatifid, white-tomentose beneath, margins undulate, spiny, st. lvs. reduced, sessile, clasping but not decurrent; heads 1½–2¾ in. across, solitary; fls. light red-purple. Eur.

foliosum (Hook.) DC. [*C. acaulescens* K. Schum.]. Bien. or short-lived per., stemless or st. up to 3 ft. high, succulent, hollow, from a thick taproot; lvs. narrowly oblanceolate, to 20 in. long, pinnately lobed, hairy, spinulose-ciliate, the upper lvs. reduced, more spiny, clasping but not decurrent, uppermost lvs. bractlike, surrounding the heads; heads to 2 in. long, solitary or somewhat spicate; fls. lavender-pink or rose to white, shorter than involucre. Mts., n. Baja Calif. n. to Yukon Terr., e. to Rocky Mts.

heterophyllum (L.) J. Hill. Stoloniferous per., to about 4 ft., sts. cottony, not winged; lvs. green above, felty beneath, margins with soft prickles, basal lvs. elliptic-lanceolate, to 16 in. long, lower st. lvs. sometimes pinnatifid, upper st. lvs. lanceolate, clasping; heads to 2 in. across, solitary or in clusters of 2 or 3; fls. red-purple or sometimes white. Eur., Asia.

japonicum DC. Per., to 3 ft. rarely to 6 ft.; basal lvs. obovate-oblong, to 1 ft. long, pinnately cut or lobed, spiny-toothed, sparsely pubescent above, pubescent on nerves beneath, st. lvs. oblong, pinnately cut, clasping; heads to 1½ in. across, solitary or in clusters of 2 or 3; fls. purplish or rose. Japan.

lanceolatum: see *C. vulgare.*

occidentale (Nutt.) Jeps. Bien., to 3 ft., occasionally taller; lvs. oblong-elliptic, narrowly oblanceolate or lanceolate, pinnatifid, to 1 ft. long, floccose or cobwebby to white-lanate beneath, lobes and teeth spiny, the upper lvs. successively reduced upward, the uppermost sessile and decurrent; heads to 2¾ in. across, solitary; fls. purplish-red, rarely white, only slightly longer than involucre. Coastal, cent. Calif. to Santa Barbara Co. Var. **candidissimum:** *C. pastoris.*

pastoris J. T. Howell [*C. occidentale* var. *candidissimum* (Greene) Macbr.]. Bien., to 5 ft., from a stout taproot; lvs. oblong to oblanceolate or lanceolate, to 1 ft. long, pinnately lobed or parted into 3–5-lobed segms., white-lanate, the hairs felty, upper lvs. reduced, decurrent; heads to 2⅜ in. across, solitary; fls. pink to bright red or crimson. Sw. Ore., n. Calif., w. Nev.

scopulorum (Greene) Cockerell [*C. eriocephalum* (A. Gray) A. Gray]. Per., to 2 ft.; lvs. lanceolate to oblong-lanceolate, pinnatifid into triangular or ovate segms., green and glabrous above, more or less tomentose beneath; heads to 1⅜ in. across, in clusters; fls. yellowish-white to white. Mts., Mont., Wyo., Colo., Utah.

spinosissimum (L.) Scop. Per., to 1½ ft., sts. densely leafy; lvs. linear to lanceolate, to 6 in. long, pinnately parted, hairy, spiny-toothed, uppermost lvs. paler, longer than the heads and surrounding them; heads to 1¼ in. across, clustered; fls. pale yellow. Mts., cent. Eur.

vulgare (Savi) Ten. [*C. lanceolatum* Scop., not J. Hill]. BULL T. Coarse bien., to 5 ft., sts. winged by the spiny decurrent lf. bases; basal lvs. oblanceolate to elliptic, to 1 ft. long, pinnatifid, prickly-hairy above, tomentose beneath, margins spiny, st. lvs. sessile, decurrent; heads to 1½ in. across, solitary or in a cluster of 2 or 3; fls. rose-purple, rarely white. Eur., w. Asia, N. Afr.; widespread as a weed in N. Amer.

CISSUS L. GRAPE IVY, TREEBINE, IVY. Vitaceae. Perhaps 350 spp. of trop. and subtrop. vines or shrubs, most bearing tendrils, with herbaceous or woody sts., often somewhat fleshy; lvs. deciduous or persistent, alt., simple or palmately compound; infl. mostly of axillary, umbellate cymes; fls. bisexual or unisexual, 4-merous, petals expanding, separate, disc 4-lobed; fr. a 1–2-seeded, usually inedible berry.

Cissus rhombifolia and *C. antarctica* are important as foliage plants in the home where they survive under conditions of low light and little humidity. These and other species are important ground covers and lattice coverings in southern Calif. and other almost frost-free areas. *C. striata* of Chile will withstand occasional frost. Propagated by cuttings or by seeds.

adenopoda T. Sprague. PINK C. Herbaceous climber, with tuberous root; lvs. trifoliolate, lfts. elliptic, to 6 in. long, coarsely toothed, pilose-hairy, green to purplish-red above, brighter red beneath; fls. pale yellow, in clusters to 4 in. long. Trop. W. Afr.

albo-nitens: *C. sicyoides* cv.

amazonica Linden. Woody climber; lvs. simple, linear-lanceolate, to 2 in. long on young plants, becoming broadly ovate-lanceolate, to 6 in. long on mature plants, glabrous, glaucous-green with silvery-white veins above, pale purplish-red beneath; fls. and fr. not known. Reportedly from Brazil, but known only in cult.

antarctica Venten. [*Vitis antarctica* (Venten.) Benth.]. KANGAROO VINE. Woody climber; lvs. simple, somewhat fleshy-leathery, ovate to oblong, 3–4 in. long, acuminate, entire to irregularly toothed, glossy green; fls. greenish, in dense, hairy, umbellate cymes. Queensland, New S. Wales (Australia). Zone 10. Cv. 'Minima'. Dwarf and very slow growing, with mostly horizontal brs.

Bainesii (Hook.f.) Gilg & M. Brandt. AFRICAN TREE GRAPE. Succulent, trunk fleshy, bottle-shaped, to 5 ft. high and 18 in. in diam., with several short, erect, herbaceous brs. at apex; lvs. glabrous, mostly trifoliolate, lfts. ovate to oblong, 3–6 in. long, broadly cuneate at base, lateral lfts. sessile; cymes terminal, glandular; fr. coral-red. S.-W. Afr.

braziliensis: a listed name of no botanical standing, sometimes used for *Mikania scandens.*

capensis: *Rhoicissus capensis.*

discolor Blume. TRAILING BEGONIA, CLIMBING B., REX-BEGONIA VINE, BEGONIA C. Sts. slender, climbing; lvs. simple, ovate, 4–7 in. long, serrate, rugose, velvety-green with silvery-white or pale pink blotches between the veins; fls. greenish-yellow, in cymes shorter than lvs. Indonesia. Cv. 'Mollis'. Lvs. uniformly green and hirtellous above; fls. pale rose-red, in larger, long-stalked cymes.

erosa L. Rich. Sts. slender, climbing, glabrous, becoming woody, striate to ribbed or winged; lvs. trifoliolate, lfts. subsessile, ovate to obovate, crenate-serrate. Trop. Amer.

gongylodes (Bak.) Burchell ex Planch. Sts. somewhat fleshy, climbing, pubescent, strongly winged; lvs. pilose, trifoliolate, 2–7 in. long, lfts. sessile, serrate, terminal lft. rhombic; infl. of several, dense, globose cymules. Brazil, Paraguay.

Henryana: *Parthenocissus Henryana.*

himalayana (Royle) Walp. [*C. neilgherrensis* (Wight) Wight; *Vitis himalayana* (Royle) Brandis]. Sts. woody, robust, without tendrils, new growth somewhat fleshy; lfts. 3, 2–5 in. long, sharply serrate, usually glossy; cymes as long as the lvs.; fr. black, about ¼ in. in diam. Himalayas. Zone 10.

hypoglauca A. Gray [*Vitis hypoglauca* (A. Gray) F. J. Muell.]. Climbing, but lacking tendrils; lvs. 4–5-foliolate, lfts. oblong-lanceolate, obtuse at base, pale green above, glaucous beneath when young, petiolules about 1 in. long; fls. yellow, minute, but showy. Victoria and New S. Wales (Australia).

incisa (Nutt.) Desmoul. MARINE I., MARINE VINE, POSSUM GRAPE. Sts. scrambling or climbing, stout; lvs. deciduous or semievergreen, fleshy, deeply 3-lobed to trifoliolate, lfts. ovate, to 2 in. long, coarsely toothed or lobed; fls. in umbellate cymes; fr. black, obovoid, to ⅜ in. long. Mo., s. to Fla. and Ariz. Zone 6b.

Juttae Dinter & Gilg ex Gilg & M. Brandt. Small succulent tree, trunk fleshy, columnar, bottlelike, to 10 ft. high and 3 ft. in diam., brs. at top short, fleshy, herbaceous; lvs. trifoliolate, lfts. coarsely serrate, veins often reddish beneath, lateral lfts. strongly decurrent; infl. long-peduncled. S.-W. Afr.

neilgherrensis: *C. himalayana.*

oblonga (Benth.) Planch. Evergreen tree, to 25 ft., tendrils occasional; lvs. simple, 2 in. long, leathery-fleshy, ovate to oblong, obtuse, entire, weakly 3-veined; cymes repeatedly forking. Queensland (Australia).

quadrangula L. [*Vitis quadrangula* (L.) Wallich ex Wight & Arn.]. VELDT GRAPE. Vine, sts. strongly 4-ribbed to 4-winged, often nearly leafless; lvs. simple, broadly cordate-ovate, sometimes 3-lobed, to 2 in. long; fls. greenish, in short cymes; fr. red. Trop. and s. Afr., and much of trop. Asia. The epithet is often incorrectly spelled *quadrangularis.*

rhombifolia Vahl [*Vitis rhombifolia* (Vahl) Bak.]. VENEZUELA T. Vine, sts. long, hairy, with forked tendrils; lvs. evergreen, trifoliolate, lfts. rhombic-ovate, 1–4 in. long, margins coarsely serrate, glossy above, often with sparsely appressed silky hairs, pilose beneath, petioles and young sts. rufous-pilose; fls. greenish-hairy outside. Mex. to Colombia, Brazil, and W. Indies. Zone 10. Cv. 'Mandaiana'. Sts. erect, without tendrils at first, later becoming scandent; lvs. glabrous above, more leathery. Material of this sp. may be offered as *Rhoicissus rhomboidea*, a S. Afr. vine of similar foliage, but with tendrils not forked, or *Vitis rhomboidea*.

sicyoides L. PRINCESS VINE. Vine, pubescent to glabrous; lvs. green, simple, fleshy, ovate to oblong, to 4 in. long, not lobed, acuminate, mostly cordate basally, margins usually with minutely bristle-tipped teeth; fls. greenish-white to purplish. Fla. and trop. Amer. Cv. 'Albo-nitens' [*C. albo-nitens* Nichols.]. Lvs. of young plants with peculiar metallic silver-gray luster on upper surface. Said to come from Brazil.

striata Ruiz & Pav. [*Ampelopsis sempervirens* Hort.; *Vitis striata* (Ruiz & Pav.) Miq.]. MINIATURE G.I. Small evergreen vine; lfts. 4–5, sessile, obovate, to 1 in. long, coarsely toothed; fls. in forking cymes. S. Chile and s. Brazil. Used as a screen on lattices in s. Calif.

trifoliata (L.) L. POSSUM GRAPE. Vine, low-climbing, with long stout tendrils; lvs. fleshy, mostly trifoliolate, toothed at tip; fls. in cymes about as long as lvs.; fr. purple to black. Trop. Amer.

Voinieriana: *Tetrastigma Voinieranum.*

vomerensis: a listed name of no botanical standing for a robust form of *Tetrastigma Voinieranum.*

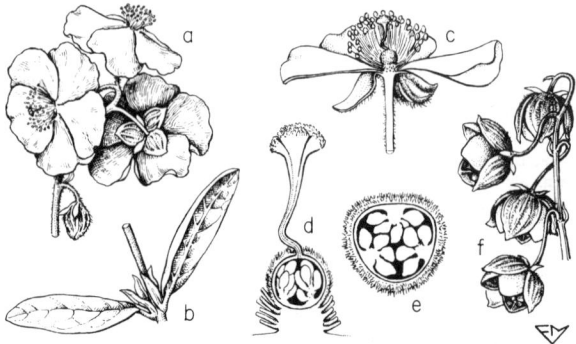

CISTACEAE. *Helianthemum nummularium* subsp. *grandiflorum:* **a**, flowers, × ½; **b**, stem node with opposite leaves, × 1; **c**, flower, vertical section, × 1; **d**, pistil, vertical section, × 4; **e**, ovary, cross section, × 6; **f**, capsules, × 1. (From Bailey, *Manual of Cultivated Plants*, ed. 2.)

CISTACEAE Juss. ROCK ROSE FAMILY. Dicot; about 8 genera and 175 spp. of herbs or shrubs, native to warmer parts of N. Hemisphere, but most abundant in Medit. region, often stellate-hairy; lvs. mostly opp., simple; fls. solitary or in cymes or racemes, regular, sepals 3–5, often unequal, petals usually 5, soon deciduous or ephemeral, stamens many, ovary superior, 1-celled, or with 3 or more incomplete cells; fr. a caps. *Cistus, Fumana,* × *Halimiocistus, Halimium, Helianthemum, Hudsonia,* and *Tuberaria* are grown as ornamentals.

CISTUS L. ROCK ROSE. *Cistaceae.* Seventeen spp. of shrubs of low or medium height, native to Medit. region, evergreen or mostly so; lvs. opp., simple, entire; fls. in terminal cymes or solitary, showy, white or purple, often with yellowish or dark blotch at base of petals; fr. a 5–10-valved caps. There are many garden and natural hybrids.

Rock roses prefer well-drained limestone soil and sunny exposures and will not stand many degrees of frost. Propagated by seeds, which should be sown in pots as seedlings do not transplant well. Also increased by layers or cuttings under glass. The species are useful in Calif. and are grown in the southern states. They are plants long known to horticulture.

acutifolius: *C. hybridus.*

×**Aguilari** Pau: *C. ladanifer* × *C. populifolius.* Upright shrub, to 6 ft.; lvs. lanceolate, to 4 in. long, shiny; infl. cymose, 3-fld.; fls. white, opening flat, to 3½ in. across, sepals tinged red. Occurs naturally in Spain and Morocco. Cv. 'Maculatus'. Petals with dark blotch at base.

albidus L. To 6 ft.; lvs. sessile, oblong to elliptic, to 2½ in. long, 3-veined, not undulate, tomentose; infl. cymose, 3–8-fld.; fls. lilac or rose, 2½ in. across, sepals 5, tomentose. Portugal to Italy, w. N. Afr.

algarvensis: *Halimium ocymoides.*

Atchleyi Hort. Name used for a plant described as low, semiprostrate; lvs. oblong, venation reticulate; fls. white, 2 in. across.

×**canescens** Sweet: *C. albidus* × *C. villosus.* Lvs. oblong-lanceolate, gray-tomentose, short-petioled; fls. dark purple. Cv. 'Albus'. Fls. white.

Clusii Dunal [*C. Libanotis* of auth., not L.; *C. rosmarinifolius* Pourr. in part, not All.]. To 3 ft.; lvs. subsessile, linear, to 1 in. long, undulate, white-tomentose beneath; infl. cymose, 1–12-fld.; fls. white, 1 in. across, sepals 3. S. Spain to se. Italy.

corbariensis: *C. hybridus.*

coridifolius: *Fumana ericoides.*

creticus: *C. incanus* subsp.

crispus L. To 2 ft., sts. hirsute; lvs. sessile, oblong to elliptic, to 1½ in. long, undulate, 3-nerved, villous-tomentose, with some stellate hairs; infl. cymose, to 7-fld.; fls. rose, to 2 in. across, sepals 5, densely villous. Portugal to Italy, w. N. Afr.

×**cyprius** Lam.: *C. ladanifer* × *C. laurifolius.* To 6 ft.; lvs. petioled, oblong-lanceolate, to 3 in. long, white-tomentose beneath; infl. an umbel, 2- to many-fld.; fls. 3 in. across, petals white, with purple blotch at base.

×**florentinus** Lam.: *C. monspeliensis* × *C. salviifolius.* Lvs. petioled, lanceolate, to 1½ in. long; infl. 2- to many-fld.; fls. white, 2 in. across.

formosus: *Halimium lasianthum.*

halimiifolius: *Halimium halimiifolium.*

hirsutus: *C. psilosepalus.*

×**hybridus** Pourr. [*C. acutifolius* Sweet; *C. corbariensis* Pourr.]: *C. populifolius* × *C. salviifolius.* Lvs. ovate, to 2 in. long; fls. white, 1½ in. across. Medit. region.

incanus L. [*C. villosus* of auth., not L.]. To 3 ft.; lvs. ovate to ovate-oblong, to 3 in. long, pinnately veined, veins impressed above and prominent beneath, petioles winged; infl. terminal, 1–4-fld.; fls. rose-pink, to 2½ in. across, sepals 5, ovate-lanceolate, densely covered with long simple hairs mixed with stellate hairs. S. Eur. Subsp. **incanus** [*C. tauricus* K. Presl]. The typical subsp.; sts. and pedicels densely white-villous; lvs. flat; sepals with many long hairs covering the stellate hairs. Corsica to the Crimea. Subsp. **creticus** (L.) Heyw. [*C. creticus* L.]. Lvs. undulate-crispate. Greece and Aegean region.

ladanifer L. [*C. ladanifer* forma *maculatus* (Dunal) Dansereau]. LAUDANUM. To 5 ft., lvs. sessile, lanceolate, to 4 in. long, 3-nerved in lower ⅓, dark green, viscid above, white-tomentose beneath; fls. solitary, to 3½ in. across, sepals 3, rounded, petals white with basal, reddish-brown blotch. Portugal to France, w. N. Afr. Yields a resin used in perfumery. Forma **albiflorus** (Dunal) Dansereau [cv. 'Immaculatus']. Fls. pure white.

laurifolius L. To 5 ft.; lvs. ovate or ovate-cordate, to 3 in. long, 3-nerved, dark green and glabrous above, white-tomentose beneath, petioles to 1 in. long; infl. cymose, to 6 in. long, 2–7-fld.; fls. white, to 3 in. across, sepals 3, ovate. Portugal to Italy.

Libanotis: see *C. Clusii.*

Loretii: *C. stenophyllus.*

maculatus: a name applied to blotched variants of those spp. in which petals are sometimes blotched, sometimes unblotched.

monspeliensis L. To 3 ft., brs. and infl. hirsute; lvs. sessile, lanceolate, to 2 in. long, 3-nerved, viscid, green and sparsely pubescent above, densely stellate-tomentose beneath; infl. scorpioid, 2–10-fld.; fls. white, to 1 in. across, sepals 5, the outer ovate. S. Eur.

×**obtusifolius** Sweet: *C. hirsutus* × *C. salviifolius.* Dwarf, to 1½ ft.; lvs. sessile, oblong, resembling those of *C. salviifolius* in color and rough surface; infl. several-fld., terminal; fls. white, 1¾ in. across, sepals 5, cordate.

ocymoides: *Halimium ocymoides.*

Palhinhae C. Ingram. ST. VINCENT C. To 1½ ft.; lvs. subsessile, obovate-spatulate, to 1½ in. long, often almost rounded at apex, tapering toward base, veins impressed above and prominent beneath; fls. solitary, white, large, to 4 in. across, sepals 3, ovate. Closely related to *C. ladanifer.* Portugal.

parviflorus Lam. To 3 ft., gray-pubescent, lvs. short-petioled, ovate, to 1½ in. long, 3-nerved in basal half, gray-tomentose; infl. cymose, 1–6-fld.; fls. pink, to 1¼ in. across, sepals 5. E. Medit. region.

populifolius L. To 4½ ft.; lvs. cordate-ovate, to 4 in. long, petioles glabrous, to 2 in. long; infl. axillary, to 6 in. long, 2–6-fld.; fls. white, 2 in. across, sepals 5, the outer 2 cordate. Portugal to s. France.

psilosepalus Sweet [*C. hirsutus* Lam. 1786, not 1778]. To 3 ft., lvs. sessile, elliptic-lanceolate, to 2½ in. long, 3-nerved, not undulate, ciliate; infl. corymbose, 1–7-fld.; fls. white, 1½ in. across, sepals 5, the outer cordate. Portugal, Spain.

×**pulverulentus** Pourr.: *C. albidus* × *C. crispus.* To 2 ft.; lvs. sessile, ovate, undulate; fls. cymose, rose-red.

×**purpureus** Lam.: *C. ladanifer* × *C. villosus.* To 4 ft.; lvs. lanceolate, to 2 in. long; fls. 3 in. across, petals purple, yellow at base with maroon blotches.

rosmarinifolius: *C. Clusii.*

salviifolius L. To 3 ft.; lvs. petioled, elliptic to oblong, to 1¾ in. long, stellate-tomentose, scabrous and rugose above; infl. 1–3-fld.; fls. white, to 2 in. across, sepals 5, cordate. S. Eur.

×**stenophyllus** Link [*C. Loretii* Rouy & Foucaud]: *C. ladanifer* × *C. monspeliensis.* Lvs. linear-lanceolate, to 2½ in. long, sticky, gray-pubescent beneath; infl. 2-fld. or more; fls. to 2½ in. across, petals white, with crimson blotch at base.

symphytifolius: *C. vaginatus.*

tauricus: *C. incanus* subsp.

verticillatus: *Halimium verticillatum.*

villosus: see *C. incanus.*

vaginatus Ait. [*C. symphytifolius* Lam.]. To 6 ft.; lvs. subsessile to petioled, ovate, to 4 in. long, 3-nerved; infl. cymose-paniculate, 2–9-fld.; fls. pink, 2 in. across, sepals 5, ovate. Canary Is.

CITHAREXYLUM Mill. *Verbenaceae.* Over 70 spp. of shrubs or trees, native to trop. N. and S. Amer.; twigs sometimes spiny, sometimes 4-angled; lvs. opp., simple, often leathery; fls. white or yellow, in racemes, fragrant, calyx 5-lobed, corolla nearly equally 5-lobed, stamens 4 or 5, the fifth often rudimentary or sterile; fr. a berrylike drupe separating into 2 nutlets.

Planted out of doors in the South and Calif. They have the appearance of wild cherry trees, and are seen frequently in warm countries.

barbinerve: *C. montevidense.*

Berlandieri B. L. Robinson. Shrub or tree, to 30 ft.; lvs. oblong to ovate or rhombic, to 3 in. long, mostly entire, rarely coarsely toothed; racemes short; fls. white. S. Tex., Mex.

fruticosum L. FIDDLEWOOD. Shrub or small tree, to 30 ft.; lvs. elliptic or oblong-ovate, to 6 in. long, entire; racemes to 5 in. long; fls. white. Flowering throughout the year. W. Indies. Produces a useful timber.

ilicifolium HBK. Shrub, to 10 ft. or more; lvs. lanceolate or elliptic to oblong, to 2 in. long, entire or spiny-toothed; racemes short, to 1 in. long; fls. white. Ecuador.

montevidense (K. Spreng.) Moldenke [*C. barbinerve* Cham.]. Shrub or small tree, with few spines; lvs. elliptic, to 5 in. long; racemes to 4 in. long; fls. yellow. Brazil, Uruguay.

spinosum L. FIDDLEWOOD. Tree, to 50 ft.; lvs. elliptic or oblong-elliptic, to 8 in. long, entire or coarsely toothed; racemes slender, to 1 ft. long; fls. white. W. Indies.

×**CITROFORTUNELLA** J. Ingram & H. E. Moore: *Citrus* × *Fortunella. Rutaceae.* Evergreen trees; lvs. with 1 lft., petiole narrowly winged; fls. and fr. more or less intermediate between parents.

floridana J. Ingram & H. E. Moore: *Citrus aurantiifolia* × *Fortunella japonica.* LIMEQUAT. Lfts. dark green above, lighter beneath, 2–3 in. long; fls. white or streaked with pink; fr. ovoid to subglobose, light yellow, segms. 6–9. Cv. 'Eustis'. Fls. pure white; fr. 1⅛–1½ in. in diam. An excellent acid limequat suitable for home gardens where true limes are not hardy. Cv. 'Lakeland'. Fls. white, streaked with pink; fr. about 1¾ in. in diam.

mitis (Blanco) J. Ingram & H. E. Moore [*Citrus mitis* Blanco]: *Citrus reticulata* × *Fortunella* sp. (?*F. margarita*). CALAMONDIN, PANAMA ORANGE. Small dense-topped tree, spineless or with very short prickles; lfts. elliptic, 2–4 in. long, petioles very narrowly winged; fls. 1–2 in axils of lvs.; fr. borne at ends of brs., bright orange, globose or depressed-globose, to 1¼ in. in diam., with loose skin and acid pulp. Fr. used like limes and lemons. One of the hardiest citrus frs.; an attractive ornamental, the colorful frs. holding throughout the winter. Zone 9b. The name *Citrus madurensis* has been misapplied to this hybrid.

Swinglei J. Ingram & H. E. Moore: *Citrus aurantiifolia* × *Fortunella margarita.* LIMEQUAT. Lfts. lanceolate; fls. pink in bud; fr. obovoid to ovoid or subglobose, light cadmium-yellow, segms. 7–8. Cv. 'Tavares'. Fr. obovoid or ellipsoid, 1¼–1⅞ in. in diam., pulp mustard-yellow.

×**CITRONCIRUS** J. Ingram & H. E. Moore: *Citrus* × *Poncirus. Rutaceae.* Evergreen or semideciduous trees; lvs. with

3 lfts. or occasionally 1 lft.; fls. and fr. more or less intermediate between parents.

Webberi J. Ingram & H. E. Moore: *Citrus sinensis* × *Poncirus trifoliata.* CITRANGE. Fr. 2–3 in. in diam., acid, bitter. Hardier than *C. sinensis* and on *Poncirus* stock may be grown in s. Ga. The frs. are used for ades and culinary purposes. Cv. 'Troyer' [cv. 'Carrizo']. Vigorous, erect-spreading, brs. thorny; lvs. with 3 lfts. or 1 lft. Much used as a stock for other citrus frs. Additional named cvs. are: 'Coleman', 'Morton', and 'Rusk'.

CITROPSIS (Engl.) Swingle & Kellerm. AFRICAN CHERRY ORANGE. *Rutaceae.* About 10 spp. of spiny shrubs or small trees, native to trop. Afr.; lvs. alt., pinnate, with 3, or sometimes 1 lft., glandular-dotted, rachis and petiole broadly winged; fls. white, in short racemes or axillary clusters, calyx 4–5-lobed, petals 4 or 5, stamens 8 or 10; fr. limelike, small, in clusters.

Of interest as a stock for citrus trees and for hybridizing.

Schweinfurthii (Engl.) Swingle & Kellerm. Lfts. 3–5, oblong or lanceolate, to 5 in. long, cuneate, acute; fls. white, to 1 in. across, fragrant; fr. 1½ in. in diam., sweet.

CITRULLUS Schrad. *Cucurbitaceae.* Three spp. of ann. and per., monoecious or dioecious vines with branched tendrils, native to S. and trop. Afr. and probably Asia; fls. solitary in axils, corolla 5-parted, rotate or broadly campanulate, male fls. with 3 separate stamens, anthers flexuous, female fls. with inferior ovary, placentas 3; fr. a berry, seeds many, horizontal.

lanatus (Thunb.) Matsum. & Nakai [*C. vulgaris* Schrad.]. WATERMELON. Ann., monoecious, long-running, hairy; lvs. pinnately divided or dissected; fls. yellow, about 1½ in. across; fr. globose to oblong or cylindrical, dark or light green or mottled or striped, flesh red, orange, yellow, or white, sweet, edible. Trop. and S. Afr.; runs wild in various parts of W. Hemisphere. Many cvs. Var. **citroides** (L. H. Bailey) Mansf. CITRON, PRESERVING MELON. Fr. small, flesh white, hard, seeds not marked or marbled as sometimes in the watermelon. Used only for preserving. For cult. see *Watermelon.*

vulgaris: *C. lanatus.*

CITRUS L. *Rutaceae.* About 16 spp. of evergreen, usually spiny shrubs or small to medium-sized trees, native to s. and se. Asia and Malay Pen.; lvs. alt., compound, but reduced to 1 simple lft., thick, leathery, glandular-dotted; fls. white or purplish, solitary, in pairs or axillary cymes, usually fragrant, mostly bisexual, calyx 4–5-lobed, petals usually 5, stamens 20–60, united in bundles; fr. an aromatic, leathery-skinned berry (a hesperidium), glandular-dotted, with 8–15 cells or internal segms. with juicy pulp.

Several kinds are important citrus fruits of commerce, such as the orange, mandarin, lemon, lime, grapefruit, and citron; they are also useful in the home garden for fruit or ornament and some are grown indoors as pot plants. Propagated by seeds and subsequent grafting of selected stock onto the seedlings. See also *Citrus Fruits, Fortunella, Poncirus.*

aurantiifolia (Christm.) Swingle. LIME. Much-branched, spiny shrub or small tree; lfts. elliptic-ovate, to 3 in. long, petioles narrowly winged; fls. white, in racemose clusters; fr. greenish-yellow, ovoid, to 3 in. long, 2½ in. in diam. or less, thin-skinned and smooth, very acid, very tender. Probably India and se. Asia; naturalized in the tropics. The most tender sp. in the genus; much grown in the W. Indies (especially Dominica and Montserrat), Mex., and India, and somewhat in subtrop. Fla. for culinary purposes, for juice, and for oil of lime expressed from the rind. Limes are of two kinds, with either a very acid pulp, acid limes, or an insipid sweet pulp, sweet limes. Sweet limes are little known in the U.S., but popular in India and Latin Amer.

The common acid lime of subtrop. Fla. and the Caribbean is produced by seedling trees named for their place of growth or origin (MEXICAN L., KEY L., WEST INDIAN L.); fr. produced the year round is variable, usually small, oblong or ovoid, to 2¼ in. long, with nipple small, if present. Cvs. listed include: 'Bears', fr. of medium size, seedless, grown in Calif., possibly a seedling of the following; 'Tahiti', PERSIAN L., fr. large, broadly ovoid, to 3 in. long, with broad nipple, produced in autumn and winter. Hybridizes with *Fortunella* to produce limequats, × *Citrofortunella* hybrids.

Aurantium L. SOUR ORANGE, BITTER O., SEVILLE O., BIGARADE. Spiny tree, 20–30 ft.; lfts. ovate-oblong, to 4 in. long, petioles broadly winged; fls. white; fr. orange to reddish, globose, somewhat flattened, to 3¼ in. in diam., the segms. separating when ripe and forming a hollow center, pulp acid and bitter. S. Vietnam. Now cult. or naturalized in many subtrop. and trop. regions, including Fla. The lvs. when crushed and the cut fr. have a characteristic aromatic pungent odor. The fls. yield neroli oil, used in perfumery; the fr. is important in marmalade manufacture. Until recently much used as a rootstock because of its disease resistance, but now shown susceptible to the virus disease, "tristeza"; also, prized as an ornamental because of the lush dark foliage and bright-colored fr. Cv. 'Bouquet': see under subsp. *Bergamia*. Subsp. **Bergamia** (Risso & Poit.) Wight & Arn. BERGAMOT, BERGAMOT ORANGE. Fls. small, sweet-scented; fr. globose to pear-shaped, bright yellow, skin smooth, highly aromatic. Long cult. in s. Italy and elsewhere for oil of bergamot, obtained from the rind and used in perfumery. Probably not grown in the U.S., the so-called bergamot orange of Calif. and Fla. representing the sour orange cv. 'Bouquet'.

australis: *Microcitrus australis.*

decumana: *C. maxima.*

grandis: *C. maxima.*

japonica: *Fortunella japonica.*

Limon (L.) Burm.f. LEMON. Small tree, to 20 ft., usually with short, stout spines; lfts. oblong to elliptic-ovate, to 4 in. long, petioles not winged; fls. reddish-tinted in bud, to 2 in. across; fr. yellow, ovoid or oblong, 3–5 in. long, with a terminal nipple, very acid. Probably se. Asia. Now widely cult., especially in Italy and Calif. Zone 10. The most utilitarian of the citrus frs., with many culinary uses; the rind produces commercial lemon oil, and the pulp citrate of lime, citric acid, and juice. Both acid and nonacid cvs. of lemons are grown, but the former are those cult. in the U.S. and exemplified by the following: Cv. 'Eureka'. Open, spreading, thornless; lfts. dark green, rounded or short-pointed; fr. lemon-yellow, ellipsoid. Important commercial cv. in Calif. Cv. 'Lisbon'. Dense, upright; lfts. light green, long-pointed; fr. lemon-yellow, ellipsoid. Important commercial cv. in Calif. Cv. 'Meyer' [*C. Meyeri* Y. Tanaka]. MEYER L., CHINESE DWARF L., DWARF L. Hardiest lemon; fr. large, to 3 in. in diam., rounded, lacking a pronounced nipple, skin thin, very smooth. Grows readily from cuttings; excellent for the home garden and also as a pot or tub plant. Cv. 'Ponderosa' [*C. ponderosa* Hort.]. WONDER L., AMERICAN W.L., GIANT L. Fr. orange-yellow, rounded, large, to 4½ in. in diam., skin thick and rough. Grows readily from cuttings. Often used ornamentally as a garden or pot plant. Cv. 'Rough'. Fr. orange-yellow, rounded, lacking prominent nipple, medium-sized, to 2¾ in. in diam., skin rough and bumpy. Important rootstock for citrus spp.; naturalized in s. Fla. Cv. 'Villafranca'. Open, spreading, thorny; lfts. dark green, rounded or short-pointed. Similar to cv. 'Eureka', but more vigorous and with denser foliage. Important commercial cv. in Fla.

× **limonia** Osbeck [*C. Limon* × (probably) *C. reticulata*]. LEMANDARIN, RANGPUR, RANGPUR LIME, MANDARIN L. Medium-sized tree, brs. spreading and drooping, thorns few, small; lvs. dull green; fl. buds and petals tinged with purple; fr. variable, but usually depressed-globose to round or broadly obovate, often with a short nipple, rind yellowish to reddish-orange, thin, moderately loose, segms. 8–10, orange, easily separating from each other, strongly acid, seeds rather numerous. The OTAHEITE ORANGE [*C. otaitensis* Risso & Poit.; *C. taitensis* Risso] is believed to be a low-acid or sweet form of *C.* × *limonia;* a small thornless bush; lfts. oblong to elliptic, finely crenulate, petioles narrowly winged; fls. fragrant, petals purplish outside; fr. orange or deep yellow, depressed-globose to globose, about 2 in. in diam., segms. 8 or 9, juice with sweet, insipid flavor; often grown as a pot plant, the common potted ornamental orange of florists, much grown for the Christmas trade.

maxima (Burm.) Merrill [*C. decumana* (L.) L.; *C. grandis* (L.) Osbeck]. SHADDOCK, POMELO, PUMELO, PUMMELO, POMMELO, POMPELMOUS. Rounded tree, 15–30 ft.; lfts. oblong-ovate to elliptic, 4–8 in. long, somewhat pubescent beneath, petioles broadly winged; fr. borne singly, yellow to orange, globose to pear-shaped, very large, skin very thick, with few, large oil glands, segms. 11–14, often separating readily, with coarse-grained pulp. Probably Malay Pen. and Polynesia. Now cult. as a popular fr. in China and se. Asia. Grown in the U.S. as an ornamental or curiosity for its giant frs., sometimes weighing up to 20 lbs. Very tender. Zone 10.

medica L. CITRON. Large thorny shrub or small tree, to 10 ft.; lfts. oblong to elliptic-ovate, 4–7 in. long, serrate, petioles not winged; fls. clustered, purplish in bud; fr. yellow, oblong, 6–10 in. long, rough or warty, with very thick rind and scant acid pulp. India. Cult. in se. Asia, Medit. region, and W. Indies. Zone 10. Sometimes planted in Fla. and Calif. for the striking fr. The oldest known citrus fr.; grown for its thick rind, which is candied. Cv. 'Etrog' [var. *Ethrog* Engl.]. Fr. fragrant, size of a lemon, but more elongate; used by people of the Jewish faith in ceremonies associated with the Feast of Tabernacles.

Meyeri: *C. Limon* cv. 'Meyer'.

madurensis: *Fortunella japonica*, but the name *C. madurensis* has been misapplied to the calamondin (see under × *Citrofortunella mitis*).

mitis: × *Citrofortunella mitis.*

× **nobilis** Lour.: *C. reticulata* × *C. sinensis*. TANGOR. More or less intermediate between parents. Cv. 'King'. KING ORANGE, KING MANDARIN, KING-OF-SIAM. Small tree, often nearly thornless; lfts. lanceolate, to 4½ in. long, petioles nearly wingless; fr. orange-yellow to orange, globose to depressed-globose, to 3¾ in. in diam., skin rough and warty, thick, easily removed, segms. 10–12, seeds many, fruiting in early spring. S. Vietnam. One of the best-flavored citrus frs. Cv. 'Temple'. TEMPLE ORANGE. Fr. medium to large, deep orange-red, in Jan.-Apr. Much grown in Fla. *C. nobilis* Andr. is *C. reticulata.*

otaitense: see under *C.* × *limonia.*

× **paradisi** Macfady.: *C. maxima* × *C. sinensis*. GRAPEFRUIT. Tree, 30–50 ft.; lfts. ovate, 3–7½ in. long, crenate, glabrous, petioles broadly winged; fls. 2–20 in clusters; frs. borne close together in clusters, light yellow to yellow-orange, globose to depressed-globose, large, skin with many small oil glands, segms. 11–14, with fine-grained pulp. Genetic origin unknown, probably shaddock × sweet orange F_1, backcrossed to shaddock; arose as seedling sport in W. Indies. Zone 10 and warmer parts of Zone 9. Much grown in U.S., especially Fla. and Tex. Many cvs., including: 'Duncan', seeded, with large juice sacs, superior in quality, hardiest, late season; 'Marsh' [cv. 'Marsh's Seedless'], fr. nearly seedless, with pink-fleshed forms, midseason; 'Ruby', like cv. 'Marsh', but fr. with deeper pink-colored flesh, early to midseason; 'McCarty' [cv. 'Indian River'], frs. large, borne singly on brs., of excellent quality, midseason.

ponderosa: *C. Limon* cv.

reticulata Blanco [*C. nobilis* Andr., not Lour.]. MANDARIN ORANGE, SATSUMA O., TANGERINE. Small, spiny tree, brs. slender; lfts. narrowly lanceolate to ovate-lanceolate, to 1½ in. long, petioles very slightly winged; fr. orange-yellow to deep orange-red, depressed-globose, to 3 in. in diam., segms. 10–14, readily separating from each other and from the smooth, loose, thin skin, pulp sweet, embryos in seeds greenish. Se. Asia. Zone 9. Now widely grown in most citrus areas of the world. Grown principally as a specialty commercial fr. or in the home garden for fr. or as an ornamental. The name mandarin orange is considered the preferable all-inclusive name for this sp.

Among the cvs. are: Cv. 'China' [cvs. 'Kid Glove', 'Willow Leaf']. Tree willowy in growth; fr. depressed-globose, medium-sized, in Nov.-Dec. Cv. 'Clementine'. Fr. globose to elliptic, deep orange-red, smooth, glossy, in Nov.-Dec. Cv. 'Cleopatra'. SPICE TANGERINE. Fr. small, depressed-globose, with seeds, of good quality, in Jan.-Feb. An excellent ornamental. Cv. 'Dancy'. Fr. of medium size, almost tomato-red, with seeds, of excellent quality, in Dec.-Jan. The common commercial tangerine in Fla. Cv. 'Ponkan'. Fr. large, globose to depressed-globose, in Dec.

SATSUMA ORANGES are a hort. class of mandarin oranges from Japan and are the hardiest of commercial citrus frs.; of these, cv. 'Owari', with small seedless fr. in Oct.-Nov., is listed.

sinensis (L.) Osbeck. SWEET ORANGE. Compact tree, to 40 ft., usually with stout spines; lfts. elliptic to oblong-ovate, to 4 in. long, petioles narrowly winged; fls. 1–6 in a cluster; fr. orange, globose or depressed-globose, with solid core, skin smooth, segms. 10–14, pulp sweet, embryo in seeds white. China or S. Vietnam. Zone 10. Widely cult. in trop. and subtrop. regions. The most important citrus fr. and among the finest of the world frs., the pulp used fresh or for juice, and the essential oil of orange extracted from the skin.

There are many cvs. of the sweet orange, but they are classified horticulturally into 1 of 4 groups, based either on geographical ancestry (MEDITERRANEAN ORANGES, SPANISH ORANGES) or on fr. characteristics (BLOOD ORANGES, NAVEL ORANGES). Common cvs. of sweet oranges in the U.S. are: Cv. 'Hamlin'. Fr. with very smooth skin, few seeds, abundant juice, of excellent flavor, in Oct.-Nov.; a heavy bearer. Cv. 'Homassassa'. Fr. of excellent quality, in Dec.-Feb. Cv. 'Lue Gim Gong'. Fr. large, oblong, deep orange-red, of very good quality, persists on tree, in June-Sept.; hardiest of all cvs. of sweet orange. Cv. 'Parson Brown'. Fr. round to oblong with abundant juice, in Oct.-Nov. Cv. 'Pineapple'. Fr. deep orange, of high quality and flavor, in Jan.-Feb.; most important mid-season commercial orange in Fla. Cv. 'Ruby'. Fr. with blood-red flesh when fully ripe, of finest quality, in Feb.-Mar. Cv. 'Valencia'. Fr. thin-skinned, seeds about 6, in Apr.-Sept. Originally from Spain. The important late-season juice orange in Calif. and Fla. Cv. 'Washington' [cv. 'Bahia']. Fr. large, seedless, thick-skinned, with prominent navel at one end formed by additional carpels produced inside the flesh, in Nov.-Apr. Originally from Brazil. Grown principally in Calif., where one of the 2 main commercial oranges.

Tachibana (Mak.) T. Tanaka. TACHIBANA ORANGE. Tall, glabrous shrub, to 20 ft., with short spines; lfts. elliptic-ovate, petioles not winged; fr. yellow, flattened-globose, 1¼ in. in diam., segms. 6–7, juice bitter and inedible. S. Japan to Taiwan. Considered a sacred plant by the Japanese since earliest times.

taitensis: see under *C.* × *limonia*.

×**Tangelo** J. Ingram & H. E. Moore: *C.* × *paradisi* × *C. reticulata*. TANGELO. Variable but more or less intermediate between parents; fr. highly colored, aromatic, rind thin, smooth, only moderately loose. Among listed cvs. are: '**Minneola**', fr. large, usually with prominent neck, segms. 10–12, pulp orange, juicy, tart, seeds few; '**Orlando**', fr. medium-large, without neck, segms. 12–14, pulp orange, juicy, mildly sweet, seeds many; '**Sampson**', fr. medium-sized, often somewhat necked, pulp dull orange, somewhat acid; '**Seminole**', fr. medium-large, deep reddish-orange, pulp orange, juicy, acid, seeds many; '**Thornton**', fr. medium-large, often somewhat necked, pulp pale orange, juicy, mildly sweet. Cvs. '**Minneola**' and '**Orlando**' are grown commercially and require another cv. for pollination.

trifoliata: *Poncirus trifoliata*.

CITRUS FRUITS. Fruits of the genera *Citrus, Fortunella*, and *Poncirus* and of the intergeneric hybrids × *Citrofortunella* and × *Citroncirus* are collectively known as citrus fruits. The present article presents a general discussion of these genera from the pomological point of view, and then separate discussions of certain fruits as follows (see also × *Citrofortunella*, × *Citroncirus, Citrus, Fortunella*, and *Poncirus*):

Calamondin, page 279
Citrus as ornamentals, page 279
Citrus hybrids, page 279
Grapefruit, page 278
Kumquat, page 278
Lemon, page 278
Lime, page 278
Mandarin, page 278
Shaddock, page 278
Sour orange, page 278
Sweet orange, page 279
Trifoliate orange, page 279

Among subtropical fruits, those belonging to the citrus groups are the most important, and they are grown the world over in regions suited to them. In the continental United States, the major areas of production are principally within plant hardiness Zone 9b: California, Florida, the Rio Grande Valley in Texas, and to a lesser extent Arizona and the warmer sections of the Gulf states.

None of these citrus regions is free from the effects of frost, and the extension of culture northward is definitely limited by winter temperatures. Within the group, which includes the lime *(Citrus aurantiifolia)*, lemon *(C. Limon)*, grapefruit *(C.* × *paradisi)*, orange *(C. sinensis)*, mandarin or tangerine *(C. reticulata)*, calamondin (× *Citrofortunella mitis)*, and kumquat *(Fortunella)*, there is a marked variation in cold resistance. Roughly, these are of increasing hardiness in the order in which they have been named, and, while the lime requires an almost frostless climate and succeeds well in the tropics, the kumquat has withstood temperatures down to about 12° or 15° F. Mandarin fruits are more susceptible to freezing injury than oranges, though the wood is more hardy. Indeed, it is doubtful whether the best citrus fruits of some kinds can be grown outside those regions in which frosts occur at intervals during their ripening season. Orchard heating or use of wind machines is standard procedure to combat frost damage in the intensive citrus districts in California, Florida, and Texas.

Soils varying from very light sands to heavy, sticky clays are capable of producing citrus. The latter soils are difficult to handle and are likely to be poorly drained. The necessity for adequate drainage must be emphasized, as nothing is more inimical to the welfare of the trees than the presence of stagnant water. A deep, mellow, rather open soil is desirable. Most Florida citrus is grown on light, sandy soils.

Propagation of citrus trees is by budding desired varieties on one- or two-year seedling stocks of the same or other species. Seedling stocks of many kinds have been employed, but stocks now used are sour orange *(C. Aurantium)*, rough lemon *(C. Limon* cv. 'Rough'), rangpur lime *(C.* × *limonia)*, Cleopatra mandarin *(C. reticulata* cv. 'Cleopatra'), sweet orange *(C. sinensis)*, trifoliate orange *(Poncirus trifoliata)*, and the citrange (× *Citroncirus Webberi* cv. 'Troyer'). Of these, sour orange is used for lands of good quality, rough lemon for light, sandy soils in warmer areas, and trifoliate orange for heavier soils with good moisture supply in the colder districts. Seeds are sown in rows or drills. They are liberally supplied with fertilizer and usually the seed beds are irrigated. At the end of 12–18 months, the seedlings are large enough to plant out in a nursery row. Selection is made at time of transplanting and only the most vigorous seedlings saved. In the nursery row they are grown for a year, when they are budded.

Planting in Florida is mostly done in spring and early summer, in California, from March to May. Planting distances vary considerably but are usually 15–25 feet for oranges and grapefruit, to 15–25 feet for mandarins and lemons, and to 15 feet for kumquats. It is important that trees should be set no deeper than they grew in the nursery, with earth well packed about the roots, and in the drier districts they should be watered copiously.

The necessary weed control in orchards formerly was largely handled by regular tillage. Discing, chopping, and mowing is still utilized to some extent, but use of chemical herbicides is now the more common practice.

Irrigation is essential in the West and Southwest, which have an insufficient rainfall of about 25 inches; sufficient water is added to meet the requirements of the trees. Thus, a total of 40–45 inches is secured. Irrigation and cultivation are alternated. In Florida, irrigation is also used heavily to increase production, with about six irrigations applied annually, most in the dry spring months.

Fertilizers are applied to citrus plantings to supply nitrogen, phosphorus, and potash. In some sections, as in Florida, the use of commercial fertilizer is an important part of successful citrus culture, because citrus is grown largely on light, sandy soils. In California, on the other hand, soils commonly contain sufficient phosphorus and potash and only fertilizers containing nitrogen are useful.

The common practice in Florida is to make two applications each year. A standard formula for young trees in Florida contains 2 percent phosphoric acid, 8 percent potash, and 8 percent nitrogen, while a mixture for fruiting trees will contain about 20 percent phosphoric acid, 20 percent potash, and 20 percent nitrogen. The amount required will depend on the size and age of the trees and the crop carried. It will vary from 4 or 5 pounds each for young trees to 50 pounds or more for old trees in full bearing. Certain trace elements are also applied to the trees, either to the soil or in the form of a foliage spray, to control certain physiological disorders in both Florida and California. Zinc, copper, iron, boron, manganese, and magnesium are the principal trace element supplements used.

Pruning nursery trees one to three years old consists of cutting back to 18–24 inches at time of planting, thus insuring low-branched heads. No further pruning is undertaken for a year or two except for the removal of sprouts that have come from below the bud union. The first pruning after the trees are well established consists in removing all branches from the original stem except for four or five chosen to form the framework of the tree.

It is the habit of citrus trees to grow with shapely, symmetrical heads and comparatively little pruning is required to secure this end, especially in dooryard plantings. Sprouts that are too numerous are removed from time to time. Dead branches are taken out. If these are the result of frost injury, it is best to allow sufficient time for new shoots to grow before pruning away the dead parts; by so doing, much unnecessary labor is avoided. Neglected or out-of-condition trees can often be rejuvenated by heading back.

Insects and diseases are numerous, although many of them

are of minor importance. Most of the damage from year to year is credited to black scale, whitefly, and rust mite among insects, and to stem-end rot, scab, melanose, anthracnose, brown rot, and greasy spot among diseases. The fungus diseases are more troublesome in moist climates than in dry ones, and insects more difficult to control in dry climates than in moist ones. In damp climates, insects may be held in check to a considerable extent by fungi parasitic on them. The latest detailed information is available from agricultural extension offices in all major citrus-producing areas. On the home grounds, citrus fruit usually can be grown successfully without recourse to a regular pest-control program. The eye appeal of the whole fruit may suffer but the internal quality will not be affected.

Grapefruit

Once believed to be of the same species as the shaddock, the grapefruit or pomelo *(Citrus × paradisi)* is now considered to be a hybrid between that species and the sweet orange. The culture of grapefruit, essentially an American enterprise, has been developed in Florida to a greater extent than in other citrus districts of the continental United States, although also important in southern Texas and California. The fruit was unknown to early European citrus growers; there is evidence that it originated in the West Indies, and its introduction into the United States, probably about 1809, was much more recent than that of the sour or sweet orange.

Most fruit now marketed is the product of budded trees. The cultivars are mainly of Florida origin, selections from earlier plantings of seedling trees. The number of cultivars introduced from time to time is much smaller than that of sweet oranges. Present plantings are usually made with 'Duncan' or 'Marsh'. Other cultivars are 'Thompson', 'Foster', and 'Ruby'. The last two are pink and early kinds. 'Marsh' is the favorite cultivar in California. When cultivars containing seeds are held late on the trees, the seeds sprout and the flavor of the fruit is impaired. 'Marsh' is favored as a late grapefruit because it is seedless. 'Duncan' is hardy and unsurpassed in quality, but very seedy. Several pink-fleshed cultivars, including 'Foster', 'Thompson' ('Pink Marsh'), and 'Ruby', are grown somewhat in groves and as garden fruits, and commercially in Texas.

Lemon

Of the acid citrus fruits, the lemon *(Citrus Limon)* is the most widely and largely grown in commercial plantings.

The lemon is hardier than the lime but, except for the cultivar 'Meyer', less hardy than the orange; consequently, unless adequate protection can be given, its cultivation is limited to warmer locations than are required for the orange. The lemon is perhaps also less resistant to certain diseases than either the orange or grapefruit.

The principal kinds planted in California are 'Lisbon' and 'Eureka', with the latter the favorite. In Florida, cultivars usually planted are Sicilian types, including 'Lisbon'. 'Meyer' is best for the home garden because of its cold tolerance and productivity.

Lime

The lime *(Citrus aurantiifolia)*, whether of sweet or acid type, is a distinctly tropical fruit. It is grown in the tropics the world around and, because it is very tender, its culture does not extend far outside that region. Only acid types of limes are grown in the United States. In southern California, they are grown as home-garden fruits, while in extreme southern Florida they are a crop of considerable importance. They are also grown in the latter state as a garden fruit for considerable distances north of the commercial areas.

The greater part of the limes are the product of seedling trees. Usually this fruit is named for the point of origin, as Key, West Indian, or Mexican lime. The trees are very thorny and very thick-headed and receive a minimum of attention in pruning, cultivation, and fertilizer; they are much like wild trees. The fruit is thin-skinned, round-oblong, about 1½ inches in diameter, and very acid. It is produced to some extent throughout the year, but the season of heaviest production is the summer months. Cultivar 'Tahiti' is larger, resembling a small-fruited lemon, and on rough lemon stock is grown in small plantings for home use and local market in Florida. 'Bears', grown in California, may be a selection of 'Tahiti'. The rangpur lime *(C. × limonia)* from northwest India, used as a lime, is not a true lime but an acid mandarin orange. It is much hardier than true limes, is orange-red in color, aromatic, and very acid.

Kumquat

The kumquats, the smallest in size of fruit among the citrus in cultivation in America, are of the genus *Fortunella*, closely related to the genus *Citrus*. Commonly they are grown as shrubs, the largest reaching a height of 12 feet or so, with a head diameter of about 8 feet, but on certain stocks they grow much larger. The tops are dense and when well fruited the plants are very ornamental and excellent garden subjects.

Two kinds representing as many species are currently grown. These are the nagami kumquat *(Fortunella margarita)* and the marumi kumquat *(F. japonica)*. A third, the Meiwa kumquat, is thought to be a hybrid; it may sometimes be grown. The fruits of nagami are oblong, 1¼ by 1½ inches, with acid juice; those of marumi are round, 1¼ inches in diameter, acid; those of Meiwa are round, 1½ inches in diameter, with sweet rind and almost juiceless pulp. Kumquats are grown as ornamental shrubs, and the fruits are used for decoration and in the making of jellies and fine marmalades. The whole fruit, skin and pulp, can also be eaten fresh. The species are propagated on *Citrus Limon* cv. 'Rough' and *Poncirus trifoliata* stocks, and are commonly planted 15 feet apart when grown in orchards.

Mandarin orange

The mandarin oranges *(Citrus reticulata)*, including tangerines and Satsuma oranges, are of main importance, particularly cultivar 'Dancy', which is planted commercially in Florida and is usually available on northern markets in early winter. The Satsuma orange, a mandarin type from Japan, is one of the hardiest citrus fruits when grown on *Poncirus trifoliata* stock and has been planted in northern Florida and the coastal regions of the Gulf states. Severe freezes make the growing of even this hardy horticultural group precarious outside the citrus regions of Florida, but it is now somewhat common in California.

Several mandarin × sweet orange hybrids *(C. × nobilis)* are now popular commercial fruits, especially in Florida. Best known is the Temple orange *(C. × nobilis* 'Temple'), in season from January to April. The high quality king orange *(C. × nobilis* 'King'), with a green color and rough skin, is now rarely grown as a fancy fruit.

Shaddock

This fruit *(Citrus maxima)* takes it name from a Captain Shaddock, who is credited with having brought it to Barbados sometime before 1707. It is also properly called pummelo and is regarded as one of the parent species of the grapefruit. It is of no commercial importance in North America, but is occasionally found in the warmer citrus districts, where its large, glossy foliage and huge fruits (sometimes weighing 15–20 pounds) make it an interesting and valued garden plant. Since it is tender, its cultural range is limited. In southern and southeastern Asia, the shaddock is highly esteemed and it is used regularly by the Chinese as a decoration at their New Year festival.

Sour orange

In Spain the sour orange *(Citrus Aurantium)* is grown for the products that are made from its fruit and some of the most beautiful plantings in that country are of this species. In America, however, the sour orange is not a cultivated fruit in the usually accepted sense of the term. Such trees as occur here and there are either those that are feral on the shores of lake and river or in similar locations, as in Florida, or those that are found in plantings of sweet oranges when the top variety has died out and the stock has sprouted and taken its place. Under these conditions, the trees are usually neglected and ill-kept. The fruit of the sour orange is valuable in the making of orangeade and marmalade. It is widely and largely employed for the latter purpose and the quality of the product is scarcely surpassed by that obtained from any other citrus. Seedlings are largely used for stock on which to grow many other kinds of citrus. The stock is adapted to heavy and moist soils of good depth; it is very hardy, and remarkably resistant or immune to foot rot and gum diseases. A high quality fruit is produced when it is used as a stock, and worldwide it has been more commonly used than any other stock. However, susceptibility to the virus disease tristeza now restricts its use.

Sweet orange

The sweet oranges of grove cultivation and of the markets are botanically *Citrus sinensis,* of numerous cultivars. Their cultivation in California and Florida goes back to the earliest beginnings of fruit-growing, and orange culture with its related industries has become a commercial enterprise of vast proportions.

A large number of cultivars, such as 'Jaffa', 'Majorca', 'Ruby', and 'Valencia', were introduced from Mediterranean countries and elsewhere. Few of these have gained a permanent place in grove plantings. As the growing of citrus fruits has become a great commercial enterprise, the standardization of cultural practices and marketing procedure has made it necessary to limit more recent plantings to a smaller number of cultivars of proved merit.

Climatic conditions in California make it possible to cover a 12-month shipping season with two cultivars, the 'Washington' navel (from Brazil) covering the period from November to April and May, and 'Valencia' (from Spain) covering the season from May or June to November.

It is necessary to use a large number of cultivars in Florida to cover the season from October to July. In order of their ripening, from early to late, the cultivars commonly planted are 'Washington', 'Hamlin', 'Pineapple', and 'Valencia'. 'Hamlin' and 'Pineapple' are seedling cultivars of local origin.

Additional cultivars suitable for dooryard plantings are 'Parson Brown' (early midseason) and 'Queen' and 'Ruby' (midseason).

Trifoliate orange

The trifoliate (strictly, trifoliolate) or "three-leaved" orange is *Poncirus trifoliata* (formerly *Citrus trifoliata*). The fruit is not eaten, but the plant is prized for its hardiness as an ornamental and a hedge plant (Zone 7), for use as stocks on which to work sweet and mandarin oranges, and as a parent in hybridization in the procuring of hardy races and of fruits superior for the making of ades. Trifoliate seedlings are extensively grown as orange stocks, to be employed on the northern limits of orange culture and for moist, deep, rich soils.

Citrus hybrids

There are other *Citrus* hybrids besides *C.* × *limonia, C.* × *nobilis, C.* × *paradisi,* and *C.* × *Tangelo,* but they are not important in horticulture. Intergeneric hybrids are listed under × *Citrofortunella* (calamondin, limequats) and × *Citroncirus* (citrange).

Calamondin

The calamondin (× *Citrofortunella mitis*) is the hardiest of the acid citrus hybrids now grown in America. Its dense head of bright green leaves, upright habit, and small fruits resembling mandarins in shape and color make it one of the most ornamental of the *Citrus* allies. The fruits are bright orange,

1–1½ inches in diameter, with deep orange flesh, and remain on the tree through the winter. The juice is well flavored and very acid. It is a valuable garden fruit, adapted to those regions where the Satsuma orange and the kumquat are grown. Among ade-making fruits it is unsurpassed.

Citrus as ornamentals

A number of the plants mentioned above make excellent shrubs or trees for landscaping home grounds and are attractive for their evergreen foliage, fragrant flowers, and ornamental as well as edible fruits, which often stay on the tree for lengthy periods. The calamondin (× *Citrofortunella mitis*), a limequat (× *Citrofortunella floridana* cv. 'Eustis'), and Cleopatra mandarin (*Citrus reticulata* cv. 'Cleopatra'), and species of *Fortunella* can all be grown as small specimens or accent shrubs or for foundation or border plantings. The trifoliate orange *(Poncirus trifoliata)* is much used for hedges, deciduous but impenetrable; hedges or screens made from the calamondin are evergreen. Where *Citrus* is not hardy, many kinds can be grown as attractive fruit-producing pot or tub plants in the moist greenhouse or home conservatory, but the climate of the average house is too dry for these plants. In years past, especially in Europe, the orangery, a special greenhouse for growing *Citrus,* was not uncommon.

Potted *Citrus* must be grown from cuttings, for plants produced from seed will seldom blossom or fruit. The Otaheite orange (see *Citrus* × *limonia*), widely grown as a dwarf ornamental pot plant, lemons, especially *Citrus Limon* cv. 'Meyer', and citron *(Citrus medica)* are easiest to root and can be grown by being budded onto stock, once the latter has attained a diameter slightly larger than a lead pencil. Most *Citrus* species and hybrids can be budded in this way, but especially recommended are *Citrus reticulata,* particularly the Satsuma oranges, which flower profusely, and species of *Fortunella.* For more details on culture, see a standard reference on *Citrus.*

CLADANTHUS Cass. *Compositae* (Anthemis Tribe). One sp., an aromatic, ann. herb, native in s. Spain and from Morocco to Libya; sts. branching in false whorls immediately below fl. heads; lvs. alt., 1–2-pinnately parted; fl. heads solitary, terminal, radiate, involucre hemispherical, involucral bracts imbricate in 2 rows, receptacle hemispherical; fls. yellow, disc fls. fertile, each subtended by a scale or bract with a tuft of apical hairs, ray fls. female or neuter, sterile; achenes nearly cylindrical, pappus absent.

arabicus (L.) Cass. [*Anthemis arabica* L.]. Sts. to 2½ ft. or more, much-branched; lvs. sessile, to 1¾ in. long, glandular-dotted; heads to about 2½ in. across.

CLADOTHAMNUS Bong. *Ericaceae.* One sp., a deciduous shrub, native from nw. Ore. to Alaska; lvs. alt., simple, sometimes crowded toward ends of brs.; fls. copper-colored, solitary or sometimes in axillary clusters, calyx 5-lobed, petals 5, separate, stamens 10, anthers opening by slits, ovary superior; fr. a 5–6-valved caps.

pyroliflorus Bong. To 10 ft.; lvs. nearly sessile, oblanceolate to elliptic-oblanceolate, to 2 in. long, entire; fls. to 1 in. across. Zone 7?

CLADRASTIS Raf. YELLOWWOOD. *Leguminosae* (subfamily *Faboideae*). Four spp. of hardy, deciduous trees, native to temp. e. Asia and e. N. Amer.; lvs. alt., odd-pinnate, lfts. alt.; fls. usually in panicled racemes, white, papilionaceous, stamens 10, nearly separate; fr. a thin, flat, dehiscent legume.

Planted as ornamentals. Propagated by seeds in spring, or by root cuttings kept over winter in moderately cool and moist sand or moss.

amurensis: *Maackia amurensis.*

lutea (Michx.f.) C. Koch [*C. tinctoria* Raf.]. YELLOWWOOD, VIRGILIA. To 50 ft.; bark smooth; lfts. 7–11, ovate, to 4 in. long; panicles pendent, 10–12 in. long; fls. fragrant, 1 in. long; fr. 3–4 in. long. Early summer. Se. U.S. Heartwood yields a yellow dye. Cv. **'Rosea'**. Fls. pinkish.

platycarpa (Maxim.) Mak. Differs from *C. lutea* in having 7–15 lfts. with short stalks, panicles erect, to 6 in. long; fls. ½ in. long, white with yellow spot at base; fr. to 3 in. long, winged marginally. Japan. Zone 8.

sinensis Hemsl. To 80 ft., differing from *C. lutea* in having lfts. 9–13, pubescent beneath, petioles and rachises pubescent, and fls. smaller, ½ in. long, in upright panicles. China.

tinctoria: *C. lutea.*

CLAPPERTONIA Meissn. [*Honckenya* Willd.]. *Tiliaceae.* Three spp. of shrubs or small trees, native to trop. Afr.; lvs. mostly palmately lobed; fls. in axillary or terminal cymes, sepals 4–5, with apical or subapical gland, petals 4–5, clawed, glandless, stamens many, only about 12 fertile; fr. a caps., 4–8-celled and -valved, elliptic or oblong-ovoid, bristly, many-seeded.

ficifolia (Willd.) Decne. [*Honckenya ficifolia* Willd.]. Shrubs, 6–9 ft., young brs., petioles, and peduncles densely reddish-stellate; lvs. oblong to ovate, to 6 in. long, lobes 3–7, rounded, serrate; sepals lanceolate-oblong, 1–1½ in. long, with dark glandular tip, petals pinkish-mauve or white, longer than sepals, fertile stamens with large, elongate anthers, longer than sterile stamens, stigmas 4–8, purplish, reflexed; caps. about 2 in. long. Trop. Afr. Furnishes a jutelike fiber.

CLARKIA Pursh [*Eucharidium* Fisch. & C. A. Mey.; *Godetia* Spach]. FAREWELL-TO-SPRING, GODETIA. *Onagraceae.* Some 33 spp. of ann. herbs, of w. N. Amer. and s. S. Amer.; lvs. simple, linear to ovate; infl. a leafy spike or raceme, the fl. buds erect, deflexed or pendulous; fls. mostly showy, ½–4 in. across, calyx tube short, sepals 4, petals 4, sessile or clawed at the base, stamens 8 or 4, ovary inferior; fr. a caps., club-shaped to cylindrical, often grooved.

Clarkias should have sunny exposure and fairly light soil. Propagated by seeds sown where plants are to grow or under glass for transplanting.

amoena (Lehm.) A. Nels. & Macbr. [*Godetia amoena* (Lehm.) G. Don; *G. vinosa* Lindl.]. SATIN FLOWER. Coarse, mostly sprawling, to 3 ft.; lvs. lanceolate, ½–2 in. long; buds erect, fls. more or less congested, calyx tube ¼–5⁄16 in. long, petals 1–1½ in. long, pink to lavender, usually with some bright red in center; immature caps. 4-grooved. Coastal, n. Calif. Subsp. **Lindleyi** (Dougl.) F. H. Lewis & M. E. Lewis [*Godetia grandiflora* Lindl.; *G. Lindleyana* Spach]. Erect, 3–6 ft.; petals 1–1½ in. long, lavender, with or without central spot. Interior, Wash. and Ore. Subsp. **Whitneyi** (A. Gray) F. H. Lewis & M. E. Lewis [*Godetia Whitneyi* (A. Gray) T. Moore]. Coarse, 1–1½ ft.; lvs. lanceolate to almost ovate; petals 1¾–2½ in. long, with central red spot; immature caps. 8-grooved. Coastal bluffs, nw. Calif.

biloba (E. Durand) A. Nels. & Macbr. Erect, simple or branched, to 3 ft.; lvs. linear to lanceolate, to 2⅜ in. long; buds pendulous, calyx tube less than 3⁄16 in. long, sepals pink to greenish, pushed to one side in fl., petals wedge-shaped, to 1 in. long, emarginate to 2-lobed, lavender to pink, often flecked with red; caps. 4-sided. Calif.

Bottae (Spach) F. H. Lewis & M. E. Lewis [*Godetia Bottae* Spach]. Erect, usually branched, 8–18 in.; lvs. lanceolate to lanceolate-linear, 1–2 in. long; buds pendulous, calyx tube ⅛ in. long, petals ½–1¼ in. long, pinkish-lavender, sometimes with darker flecks; immature caps. 4-grooved. Monterey (Calif.).

Breweri (A. Gray) Greene [*Eucharidium Breweri* A. Gray]. FAIRY-FANS. Much like *C. concinna,* but petals about as long as broad, the middle lobe narrower than the lateral lobes, filaments club-shaped. Calif.

concinna (Fisch. & C. A. Mey.) Greene [*C. grandiflora* (Fisch. & C. A. Mey.) Greene; *Eucharidium concinnum* Fisch. & C. A. Mey.; *E. grandiflorum* Fisch. & C. A. Mey.]. RED-RIBBONS. Erect, 8–16 in.; lvs. lanceolate-ovate to broadly elliptic, ½–2 in. long; petals twice as long as broad, ⅜–1 in. long, deep bright pink, the middle lobe spatulate, equal to 2 lateral lobes, filaments flattened, not club-shaped. Calif.

Dudleyana (Abrams) Macbr. Erect, simple or branched, to 28 in.; lvs. narrowly lanceolate to lanceolate, to nearly 3 in. long; buds pendulous, calyx tube ⅛ in. long, petals fan-shaped, to 1 in. long, lavender-pink, often red-flecked; fr. 4–8-sided. Calif.

elegans: see *C. unguiculata.*

grandiflora: *C. concinna.*

pulchella Pursh. Erect, to 20 in.; lvs. linear to lanceolate, 1–4 in. long; sepals green to reddish, ½–1 in. long, petals ⅜–1 3⁄16 in. long, bright pink to lavender, 3-lobed, the lateral lobes usually narrower than the middle one. Rocky Mts. to Pacific Coast. Forms with notched or toothed petals are cult.

purpurea (Curtis) A. Nels. & Macbr. Erect or decumbent, simple or branched, to 30 in. or rarely more; lvs. linear to narrowly oblanceolate or even ovate, to 2¾ in. long and ¾ in. wide; buds erect, calyx tube to ⅜ in. long, petals fan-shaped, to 1 in. long, lavender, pink, purple, or wine-red to rarely white; caps. 4-angled. Wash. to Ariz., Baja Calif. Subsp. **purpurea.** The typical subsp.; sts. erect, glabrous basally; lvs. broadly lanceolate to elliptic or ovate, to 1¾ in. long, to ¾ in. wide; infl. congested; petals to 1 in. long, lavender to purple or purplish-red, often with dark spot near apex. S. Ore., Calif. Subsp. **quadrivulnera** (Dougl.) F. H. Lewis & M. E. Lewis [*Godetia quadrivulnera* (Dougl.) Spach]. Sts. erect; lvs. linear to lanceolate, 1–2 in. long, to ¼ in. wide; infl. loose or congested; petals ¼–⅝ in. long, lavender to purple, often deep red, often with a wedge-shaped or shield-shaped purple spot. Wash. to Ariz., Baja Calif. Subsp. **viminea** (Dougl.) F. H. Lewis & M. E. Lewis [*Godetia Goddardii* Jeps.; *G. viminea* (Dougl.) Spach]. Sts. erect or decumbent; lvs. linear to linear-lanceolate, 1–3 in. long, to 5⁄16 in. wide; infl. loose; petals ⅝–1 in. long, lavender to purple, usually with a dark spot in the upper part. Calif.

rubicunda (Lindl.) F. H. Lewis & M. E. Lewis [*Godetia rubicunda* Lindl.]. Slender, erect or somewhat decumbent; lvs. lanceolate, to 5⁄16 in. wide; infl. loose; petals 5⁄16–1 in. long, lavender, usually with a basal red spot. Coastal, cent. Calif.

speciosa F. H. Lewis & M. E. Lewis. Erect to decumbent, sts. to 2 ft. long; lvs. linear to narrowly lanceolate, ½–2 in. long; buds erect, petals ½–1 in. long, purplish-red to lavender, with bright red spot. S. Coast Ranges, Calif.

unguiculata Lindl. [*C. elegans* Dougl., not Poir.]. Erect, to 3 ft., glabrous and glaucous; lvs. lanceolate to ovate, ½–2 in. long; infl. erect; buds deflexed, petals triangular to rhombic, ⅜–¾ in. long, lavender-pink to salmon or purple, with long slender basal claws. Calif. Cvs. with double fls. and of many colors are in cult.

CLASSIFICATION. The living world, both plant and animal, is divided into categories in a hierarchical scheme for purposes of reference. Major units of the plant kingdom are division (e.g., seed plants), class (e.g., flowering plants), subclass (see *Dicotyledon, Monocotyledon*), order (composed of one or more families), and family (see *Family*). The rank of family is the first that receives extended treatment in *Hortus Third.* A family comprises one or, more usually, several to many genera (see *Genus*), and a genus comprises one or more species (see also *Species*).

CLAUSENA Burm.f. *Rutaceae.* About 23 spp. of spineless trees of trop. Asia, Australia, and trop. and S. Afr.; lvs. alt., pinnate, glandular-dotted; fls. white or greenish-white, in axillary or terminal racemes or panicles, calyx 4–5-lobed, petals 4 or 5, stamens 10, ovary 2–5-celled, stalked; fr. small, globose, berrylike.

Lansium (Lour.) Skeels [*C. punctata* (Sonn.) Rehd. & E. H. Wils.; *C. Wampi* (Blanco) D. Oliver]. WAMPI. Small tree; lvs. to 10 in. long, lfts. 5–9, lanceolate, ovate-elliptic, or ovate, to 5 in. long; fr. about 1 in. long, pubescent. China. Widely cult. in tropics and subtropics as fr. tree, and sometimes planted far south as an ornamental. Can be grafted on *Citrus.*

punctata: *C. Lansium.*

Wampi: *C. Lansium.*

CLAYTONIA L. SPRING-BEAUTY. *Portulacaceae.* About 15–20 spp. of glabrous, small, succulent, spring-flowering per. herbs, with taproots, corms, or stolons, native mostly to w. N. Amer., elsewhere in S. Amer. and Old World; basal lvs. 1 or more, st. lvs. opp., usually 1 pair; fls. white or rose, in terminal racemes; fr. a caps.

Sometimes transplanted from the wild to moist shady locations and rock gardens.

caroliniana Michx. With globose corm, sts. weak, to 1 ft.; lvs. broadest in middle, to ¾ in. wide, obtuse, st. lvs. with distinct petiole; fls. 2–15, in a raceme, pink to white, marked with pink. E. N. Amer.

flagellaris: *C. parvifolia* var.

lanceolata Pursh. Mostly with globose corm, sts. to 10 in.; basal lvs. absent, st. lvs. elliptic-lanceolate to ovate, sessile or nearly so, 3–6 ribbed; fls. 1–15, in a raceme to 4 in. long, pink to white, marked with pink, sometimes blotched with yellow, petal tips emarginate to retuse. E. U.S.

megarhiza (A. Gray) Parry ex S. Wats. Taproot long, to 1 in. thick; basal lvs. spatulate, to 6 in. long, petioles margined, st. lvs. oblanceolate to linear; fls. in a dense raceme, white to light and dark pink. Wash. to New Mex. Var. **nivalis** (English) C. L. Hitchc. [*C. nivalis* English]. Fls. deep rose. Wash.

nivalis: *C. megarhiza* var.

parvifolia Moç. ex DC. [*Montia parvifolia* (Moç. ex DC.) Greene]. Often stoloniferous, sts. spreading or decumbent, slender, to 12 in.; basal lvs. in a rosette, obovate to oblanceolate, to 2¼ in. long, st. lvs. becoming smaller upwards, sometimes bearing bulblets in the axils; fls. 1–8, at end of sts., pink to white, marked with pink. W. N. Amer. Plants may be eaten for greens. Var. **flagellaris** (Bong.) R. J. Davis [*C. flagellaris* Bong.; *Montia flagellaris* (Bong.) B. L. Robinson; *M. parvifolia* subsp. *flagellaris* (Bong.) Ferris]. With well-developed, fine, flagellate runners; fls. larger, petals to ¾ in. long. Coastal, Alaska to s. Ore.

perfoliata: *Montia perfoliata.*

rosea Rydb. Closely related to *C. lanceolata,* but having basal lvs. present, st. lvs. linear to linear-lanceolate, narrower, and petal tips rounded to acute. Rocky Mts.

sibirica: *Montia sibirica.*

virginica L. SPRING-BEAUTY. Corms globose, sts. 1 to many, to 12 in.; basal lvs. none to many, linear or linear-lanceolate, to 5 in. long, about ½ in. wide; fls. as many as 15, in a raceme to half as long as st., white tinged with pink. E. N. Amer.

CLEISTANTHUS Hook.f. *Euphorbiaceae.* About 130 spp. of monoecious, rarely dioecious shrubs and trees, native to Afr., se. Asia, Pacific Is., and Australia; lvs. simple, pinnately veined, short-petioled; fls. in axillary clusters, ovary 3-celled; fr. a caps.

collinus (Roxb.) Benth. Small deciduous tree, brs. rigid; lvs. orbicular to obovate, 1½–4½ in. long, glaucous-green; fls. sessile, in axillary clusters, ovary glabrous; fr. dry, glabrous, smooth, ½–¾ in. long. India, Ceylon.

CLEISTES L. Rich. *Orchidaceae.* About 30 spp. of terrestrial herbs, native to temp. N. Amer. and n. S. Amer., closely allied to *Pogonia* and *Isotria;* differing from *Pogonia* in having pollen grains cohering in groups of 4, and from *Isotria* in having lvs. solitary or alt., not whorled. For structure of fl. see *Orchidaceae.*

For culture see *Orchids.*

divaricata (L.) Ames [*Pogonia divaricata* (L.) R. Br.]. SPREADING POGONIA, LILY-LEAVED P., FUNNEL-CREST, ROSEBUD ORCHID. To 2½ ft.; lf. solitary, oblong or lanceolate-elliptic, to 6 in. long; petals pale salmon-pink, elliptic-lanceolate, sepals narrower, darker colored, lip convolute, greenish with purple veins, not bearded. Spring–summer. Coastal plain, N.J. to Fla. and Miss., w. to e. Ky.

CLEISTOCACTUS Lem. *Cactaceae.* About 28 spp. of slender, ribbed cacti, native to S. Amer.; sts. mostly erect, ribs 9–24, low; fls. mostly red, tubular, often somewhat S-shaped, scales of the tube and ovary close-set, appressed, with woolly axils, perianth segms. like the scales, small, not spreading, stigmas and sometimes stamens exserted; fr. globose.

For culture see *Cacti.*

areolatus (Mühlenpf.) Riccob. Sts. erect, to 10 ft. high, 1½–3 in. thick, ribs 12–15, furrowed obliquely upward from the areoles; spines yellowish, about 1 in. long, radial spines 9–10, needle-shaped, central spines 2–4, stouter; fls. carmine, 1¾ in. long, narrowed upward. Bolivia.

Baumannii Lem. SCARLET-BUGLER. Sts. erect, to 6 ft. high, ¾–1½ in. thick, ribs 12–16; spines 15–20, yellow or brown, to 1½ in. long; fls. scarlet to orange, 2–3 in. long, S-shaped, with oblique limb, stamens somewhat exserted; fr. red, ½ in. in diam. N. Argentina, Paraguay, Uruguay.

Buchtienii Backeb. Sts. erect, to 2 in. thick, ribs about 18, cross-furrowed above the areoles; spines about 12, needle-shaped, to 1¼ in. long; fls. wine-red, 2½ in. long. Bolivia.

dependens Cardenas. Sts. prostrate to climbing or pendulous, to 1⅜ in. thick, ribs 10–12, low; areoles white-hairy above, black-hairy below, radial spines 8–13, very short, red-gray, central spines 3–4, darker, 1 dark-tipped and to ⅝ in. long; fls. light green to white, to 1¾ in. long. Bolivia.

Herzogianus Backeb. Treelike, to 6 ft., with a dense crown, brs. 2 in. thick, ribs 11–14, weakly furrowed above the areole; spines yellow, radial spines 8, about ¼ in. long, central spine 1, to ¾ in.; fls. bright red, straight, 1–1½ in. long, perianth segms. rudimentary; fr. orange. Bolivia.

hyalacanthus (K. Schum.) Rol.-Goss. Sts. erect, to 3 ft. high, about ¾ in. thick, ribs about 20, hidden by spines; spines 25 or more, mostly white and slender, to ¾ in. long, 1 or 2 of them later becoming stronger, gray-black, microscopically hairy; fls. bright red, somewhat curved, 1½ in. long. N. Argentina.

jujuyensis (Backeb.) Backeb. [*C. Strausii* var. *jujuyensis* Backeb.]. Sts. erect, to 3 ft. high or more and 2⅜ in. thick, branched from the base, ribs about 20; areoles small, brownish- to white-hairy, spines many, very slender, white or yellowish-white, radial spines 25–30, central spines somewhat stouter and longer, golden-yellow to brown, to 1³⁄₁₆ in. long; fls. light red, to 1⅝ in. long. N. Argentina.

laniceps (K. Schum.) Rol.-Goss. Sts. erect, to 12 ft. high and 2 in. thick, ribs 9, blunt; areoles large, gray-woolly, spines usually 3, gray, in upper part of areole, to ⅝ in. long; fls. to 1⅜ in. long. Bolivia.

luminosus: a listed name of no botanical standing.

luribayensis Cardenas. Sts. columnar or branched and treelike, to 10 ft. high and 2⅜ in. thick, ribs about 19, low; spines 16–22, white to brownish, marginal spines to ⅝ in. long, central spines to 1⅝ in. long; fls. rose, 1³⁄₁₆ in. long. Bolivia.

Morawetzianus Backeb. Sts. erect, to 6 ft. high and 2½ in. thick, ribs 14–16, with a V-shaped furrow above the areole; spines many, yellow to white, short, central spines 1–3, to ¾ in. long; fls. slightly curved, whitish, 2 in. long. Peru. The only sp. with white fls.

Roezlii: *Borzicactus sepium;* but the name *Cleistocactus Roezlii* in cult. may apply to an unidentified sp.

smaragdiflorus (A. Web.) Britt. & Rose. Sts. about 3 ft. high and 1 in. thick, ribs 12–14; spines many, central spines to ¾ in. long; fls. straight, to 2 in. long, inner perianth segms. green. N. Argentina.

Strausii (Heese) Backeb. [*Borzicactus Strausii* (Heese) A. Berger]. SILVER-TORCH. Sts. erect, to 6 ft. high and about 2½ in. thick, ribs about 25; areoles close-set, with 30–40 white, bristlelike spines to ¾ in. long and about 4 yellowish, stouter spines; fls. red, to 3½ in. long, nearly straight. Bolivia and Argentina. Var. **jujuyensis:** *C. jujuyensis.*

tominensis (Weing.) Backeb. Sts. erect, to 7 ft. high and 2 in. thick, ribs 18–22, low; areoles to ⁵⁄₁₆ in. apart, spines 8–9, yellow, becoming gray, weak, the longest to ¾ in. long, the others ⁵⁄₁₆ in. long; fls. red with green, 1 in. long. Bolivia.

tupizensis (Vaup.) Backeb. Sts. to 4 ft. high and 2½ in. thick, branching from the base, ribs 22–24; spines 15–20, bristlelike, to 1¼ in. long; fls. salmon-red, to 4 in. long. S. Bolivia.

CLEISTOCALYX Blume. *Myrtaceae.* About 21 spp. of evergreen trees and shrubs, native from Burma, se. China, Malay Arch., to n. Australia, Lord Howe Is., New Caledonia, and Fiji; long included in *Eugenia* but having calyx lobes united to form a cap (calyptra or operculum) over the fl. bud and falling in one piece by irregular circumscissile dehiscence.

operculatus (Roxb.) Merrill & L. M. Perry [*Eugenia operculata* Roxb.]. Tree, 20–50 ft.; lvs. lanceolate to broadly ovate-elliptic, 5–8 in. long; fls. small, white, in 3's; fr. pealike, ripening from dark red to purple, edible. S. China, se. Asia, n. Australia.

CLEMATIS L. [*Atragene* L.; *Clematitis* L.; *Clematopsis* Bojer ex Hook.; *Viorna* Rchb.; *Viticella* Dill. ex Moench]. VIRGIN'S BOWER, LEATHER FLOWER, VASE VINE. *Ranunculaceae.* Over 200 spp. of per. herbs or woody climbing vines native to N. Temp. Zone; lvs. opp., compound or simple; fls. solitary or panicled, urceolate, campanulate, or opening flat, sepals petaloid, petals none, stamens many; fr. an achene, commonly with a long feathery style. In the description of the spp. that follow, the fls. may be considered as opening flat unless described otherwise.

Many species of *Clematis* are much prized as ornamentals. Some are perennial herbs and should be so treated in the border. Others are small-flowered woody vines not much modified by cultivation, planted for permanent cover of fences, arbors, and porches; while others are large-flowered vines used extensively in the development of horticultural hybrids.

These hybrids are segregated into 3 groups, with the divisions based on the kind of growth and time of blossoming. They are: (1) the Florida Group, flowering on old wood in summer; (2) the Patens Group, flowering on old wood in spring; and (3) the Jackmanii Group (including also those of *C. lanuginosa* and *C. Viticella* parentage) flowering on new wood during summer and autumn. The plants of all 3 groups should be grown on trellises or posts.

Plants of the Florida Group should be pruned lightly and not too frequently. Cultivars of this group include: 'Belle of Woking', 'Duchess of Edinburgh', 'Enchantress'.

Plants of the Patens Group should be treated like those of the Florida Group. This group includes the cultivars: 'Bees Jubilee', 'Barbara Dibley', 'Barbara Jackman', 'Guiding Star', 'Miss Bateman', 'La-surstern', 'Mrs. Bush', 'Mrs. George Jackman', 'Mrs. P. B. Truax', 'Mrs. Spencer Castle', 'Nelly Moser', 'President'.

Those plants that bloom on wood of the current season, including the Jackmanii Group, should be pruned to the ground during the dormant period. Generally speaking, these plants are more resistant to extreme cold than are the other large-flowered hybrids. This group includes the cultivars: 'Ascotiensis', 'Blue Gem', 'Comtesse de Bouchard', 'Crimson King', 'Daniel Deronda', 'Duchess of Albany', 'Elsa Späth', 'Ernest Markham', 'Etoile Violette', 'Fairy Queen', 'Gipsy Queen', 'Hagley', 'Huldine', 'King Edward VII', 'Lady Betty Balfour', 'Little Nell', 'Lord Neville', 'Marie Boisselot', 'Minuet', 'Mme. André', 'Mrs. Cholmondeley', 'Prins Hendrik', 'Ramona', 'Ville de Lyon', 'W. E. Gladstone', 'William Kennett'.

Clematises do best in fertile, light, loamy soil that is well drained. The hybrids succeed best when planted in partial shade, in soil to which some lime has been added. It is advisable to provide the base of the stems with some protection against mechanical injury until plants are well established. Clematises are sometimes affected by a nematode disease, but not seriously so in regions where the ground freezes about the roots. Propagated by stratified seeds, layers, division, or cuttings rooted under glass in summer. Cultivars can be grafted on roots of *C. Flammula* or *C. Viticella;* these roots should be taken from plants outdoors to avoid nematode infection, and the scions taken from plants grown in a greenhouse.

Addisonii Britt. Suberect, to 3 ft.; lvs. simple, nearly sessile, broadly ovate, 2–4 in. long, obtuse, glaucous underneath, or compound, the lfts. in 2–3 pairs, round-ovate; fls. much as in *C. Viorna.* W. Va.

aethusifolia Turcz. Climbing, to 6 ft.; lvs. 1–2-pinnate, lfts. small, narrow, deeply cut; fls. in few-fld. clusters, pale yellow, campanulate, ½–¾ in. long, sepals 4, oblong. China, Manchuria. Var. **latisecta** Maxim. Lvs. pinnate, ultimate lobes broader; fls. whitish. Manchuria.

afoliata J. Buchan. Climbing or prostrate shrub, branchlets often grooved, glabrous, bound together by lf. tendrils; lvs. reduced to petioles and petiolules to 2 in. long, lf. blades developing in shade and on young plants, small, ovate, entire; fls. solitary or in clusters of 2–5, sepals mostly 4, about ¾ in. long, greenish-yellow; fr. with styles ¾ in. long. New Zeal.

alpina (L.) Mill. [*Atragene alpina* L.]. Per., sts. climbing, to 6 ft. or more; lvs. 2-ternate, rarely simply ternate, lfts. lanceolate to ovate; fls. solitary, long-peduncled, nodding, sepals usually 4, divergent, stamen filaments flat, petal-like, the outer wider and with reduced or no anthers. Eurasia. Var. **alpina.** The typical var.; lfts. crenate-serrate; sepals lanceolate, acuminate, usually violet-blue, sometimes white or rose-violet, staminodes rounded, covering stamens. Alps, n. Balkan Pen. Cvs. of this var. are: '**Columbine**', fls. campanulate, soft lavender-blue, sepals extra long, pointed; '**Frances Rivis**', sepals ovate, to 2 in. long, bluebird-blue; '**Gravetye Form**', fls. large, cream-white, early; '**Pamela Jackman**', sepals rich deep azure, outer staminodes bluish; '**Pauline**', fls. deep blue; '**Ruby**', fls. soft rosy-red. Var. **occidentalis:** *C. occidentalis* var. *occidentalis,* but most material cult. as *C. alpina* var. *occidentalis* is *C. columbiana.* Var. **ochotensis** (Pall.) S. Wats. Lfts. nearly entire to coarsely toothed; sepals ovate, acute, violet-blue. Korea and Japan to e. Siberia. Var. **sibirica** (L.) C. K. Schneid. [*C. sibirica* (L.) Mill.]. Lfts. irregularly incised-serrate, sepals lanceolate, white or yellowish-white, rarely faintly blue-tinged, acuminate. N. Eur. to Siberia.

angustifolia Jacq. Stiff, erect, per. herb, to 3 ft.; lvs. compound, lfts. few to many, linear, entire, glabrous; fls. many, yellowish-white, 1½–2 in. across, sepals 5–6. Asia, s. Eur.

apiifolia DC. Deciduous climber resembling *C. grata,* but lfts. 3, toothed or lobed; fls. in axillary panicles, dull white, about ½ in. across. Japan.

aristata R. Br. Close to *C. microphylla,* but having lfts. usually 3, broader, toothed; fls. in clusters of 4–7, white, campanulate, to ¾ in. across. Australia.

Armandii Franch. Evergreen, to 16 ft.; lvs. compound, lfts. 3, narrow-lanceolate, 3–5 in. long, entire, leathery; fls. in axillary panicles, white, 2–2½ in. across. China. Cv. '**Farquhariana**'. Fls. light pink.

× **aromatica** Lenné & C. Koch: *C. Flammula* × *C. integrifolia.* Upright, to 6 ft.; lvs. 3-lobed to pinnate; fls. in terminal cymes, on long peduncles, bluish-violet, fragrant, 1–1½ in. across.

australis T. Kirk. Dioecious climber, branchlets slender, grooved, more or less pubescent; lvs. compound, lfts. 3, stalked, 1–1½ in. long, pinnate below, pinnatifid above; fls. unisexual, solitary or few in panicles, sepals of male fls. 5–8, white or pale yellow, ¾ in. long, silky, sepals of female fls. pale yellow, shorter; achenes pubescent only when young. New Zeal.

Baldwinii Torr. & A. Gray [*Viorna Baldwinii* (Torr. & A. Gray) Small]. PINE HYACINTH. Erect herb, to 2 ft.; lvs. simple, elliptic to

lanceolate or linear, to 4 in. long, the upper lvs. sometimes with 3 lfts.; fls. solitary, nodding, purple or pinkish, urceolate, about 1 in. long; fr. with styles to ½ in. long. Fla.

balearica L. Rich. Climbing; lvs. compound, lfts. 3-toothed or 3-lobed; fls. subtended by a remote pair of united bracts, greenish-yellow, spotted inside with red. Corsica, Minorca.

Beadlei (Small) Erickson [*Viorna Beadlei* Small]. Climber, sts. pubescent at least at nodes; lvs. pinnate, lfts. ovate to lanceolate, to 3 in. long, usually lobed, acute to acuminate, thinnish, finely reticulate in age; fls. on bracted pedicels, to 1 in. long. Mts., Tenn. to Ga.

brachiata Thunb. Woody climber; lvs. pinnate, usually with 5 lfts., rarely 2-pinnate, lfts. rounded to ovate, coarsely toothed; fls. many, cream or white, sepals ½–1 in. long. S. Afr.

brevicaudata DC. Climber; lvs. 1–2-pinnate, lfts. toothed or entire; fls. in axillary cymes, white, to ¾ in. across. Mongolia, Manchuria, n. China.

Buchananiana DC. Large, woody, hoary or coarsely hairy climber; lvs. pinnate, lfts. 5–7, broadly ovate to rounded-cordate, 2–3 in. long; fls. many, creamy-yellow, 2–3 in. across, tomentose. Himalayas, sw. China.

californica: a hort. name; probably *C. ligusticifolia* var.

campaniflora Brot. Like *C. Viticella,* but weaker and more delicate; lvs. 2-pinnate, lfts. entire or lobed; fls. more open, sepals obovate, to ⅜ in. long, pale blue, whitish, or greenish. Portugal, Spain.

Catesbyana Pursh. Minutely pubescent climber; lvs. 2-ternate, lfts. lobed or entire, membranous; fls. in panicled cymes, white, 1 in. across, sepals linear to cuneate. S.C. to Fla. and La.

chinensis Retz. Vigorous deciduous climber, to 1 ft., branchlets ribbed; lvs. compound, lfts. 5, ovate to cordate, 1½–3 in. long, entire, downy on midrib; fls. in axillary panicles, fragrant, white, ½–¾ in. across, sepals 4, narrow, with downy margins. China.

chrysocoma Franch. [*C. Spooneri* Rehd. & E. H. Wils.]. Deciduous, shrubby or climbing, to 10 ft., densely yellowish-pubescent; lvs. ternate, lfts. 3-lobed, 1–2½ in. long; fls. in clusters, white or pinkish, 2 in. across, sepals 4, short-pointed. China. Var. **sericea** (Franch.) C. K. Schneid. To 20 ft.; fls. white, 3–4 in. across, sepals broadly obovate. China.

cirrhosa L. Evergreen climber, to 10 ft.; lvs. simple, narrow or broad, pointed or blunt, entire or sometimes lobed; fls. 1–2, in the axils, on peduncles 1–2 in. long, yellowish-white, 1½–2½ in. across. Medit. region.

coccinea: *C. texensis.*

columbiana (Nutt.) Torr. & A. Gray [*C. alpina* var. *occidentalis* of auth., not (Hornem.) A. Gray; *C. pseudoalpina* (O. Kuntze) A. Nels.; *Atragene columbiana* Nutt.]. Half-woody climber with slender branchlets; lvs. compound, lfts. 3, broadly ovate, 1–1½ in. long, usually cordate, pointed, entire or coarsely toothed, thin; fls. solitary, on a bractless peduncle, sepals lanceolate, 1–2 in. long, purple or blue; fr. with styles 1–2 in. long. B.C. to Alta., s. to Colo. and Ore.

connata DC. Deciduous climber, to 25 ft.; lvs. pinnate, lfts. 3, 5, or 7, ovate-cordate, 2–5 in. long, slender-pointed, toothed or rarely 3-lobed, glabrous; fls. on axillary peduncles, fragrant, yellow, campanulate, ¾–1 in. long, sepals 4, reflexed at apex. Himalayas, China.

crispa L. BLUE JASMINE, MARSH C., CURLY C., CURLFLOWER. Climber; lvs. pinnate, lfts. 5–9, ovate to cordate or lanceolate, entire or 3–5-parted, glabrous; fls. solitary, blue-purple, 1–2 in. long, calyx cylindrical below, upper half dilated and widely spreading, with broad, wavy, thin margins. Va. to Mo., s. to Fla. and Tex. Var. **Walteri** (Pursh) A. Gray. Lfts. linear or lanceolate-linear.

Davidiana: *C. heracleifolia* var.

Delavayi Franch. Erect, to 5 ft.; lvs. pinnate, 1–4 in. long, lfts. sessile, ovate, ½–¾ in. long, silky underneath; fls. 1 to several, white, 1 in. across, silky on exterior, sepals 4–6. W. China.

dioscoreifolia Lév. & Vaniot. Tall, glabrous climber; lvs. compound, lfts. 5, ovate, cordate, entire or rarely with a lateral lobe, leathery, terminal lft. on a longer stalk than the laterals; fls. in corymbiform panicles, sepals ⅜–⅝ in. long, white, densely pubescent along margins on exterior; fr. with styles 1 in. long. Korea. Sometimes cult. as *C. paniculata.* Var. **robusta** (Carrière) Rehd. [*C. paniculata* Thunb., not J. F. Gmel.]. Lfts. 3–5, ovate, 1–3 in. long, entire; fls. 1¼ in. across. Japan. Some material cult. as *C. paniculata* is *C. dioscoreifolia.*

Douglasii: *C. hirsutissima.*

Drummondii Torr. & A. Gray. Climbing or straggling, ashy-pubescent; lvs. pinnate, lfts. coarsely cleft or parted, ½–1 in. long, the segms. pointed; fls. few, white, ¾ in. across, silky on exterior; fr. with styles very slender, 2–4 in. long. Tex. to Ariz.

× **Durandii** O. Kuntze: *C. integrifolia* × *C.* ×*Jackmanii.* To 6 ft.; lvs. simple, ovate, entire, 3–6 in. long; fls. 1–3, nodding, dark violet, open-urceolate, sepals 4 or more.

erecta: error for *C. recta.*

eriophora Rydb. [*Viorna eriophora* (Rydb.) Rydb.]. White-villous, 1–1½ ft.; lvs. 2-pinnate, segms. ½–1 in. long; fls. solitary, campanulate, sepals oblong, 1 in. long, purplish; fr. with styles 1½ in. long. Rocky Mts.

× **eriostemon** Decne. [*C.* ×*intermedia* Carrière]: *C. integrifolia* × *C. Viticella.* Subshrub to 8 ft.; lvs. simple to pinnate, lfts. ovate, to 2 in.; fls. solitary, on peduncles 3–4 in. long, fragrant, sepals ¾–1¼ in. long, blue.

Fargesii: *C. Potaninii* var.

Flammula L. Climbing, sts. ribbed, 6–15 ft.; lvs. 2–3-pinnate, lfts. ovate, 1–2 in. long, entire or lobed; fls. many, white, 1 in. across, with the odor of bitter almonds. Medit. region to Iran. Cv. 'Rosea-purpurea'. Fls. rose. Var. **rotundifolia** DC. Lfts. broader, almost round.

florida Thunb. Woody climber, 6–12 ft.; lvs. usually 2-ternate, lfts. lanceolate-ovate, 1–2 in. long, entire or few-toothed; fls. on peduncles with 2 leaflike bracts, cream-white, 2–3 in. across, sepals 4–8, lanceolate or broader, 1–3 in. long, with a green stripe down the back. China, Japan. Cv. 'Plena'. Fls. double. Var. **bicolor:** forma *Sieboldii.* Forma **Sieboldii** (D. Don) Rehd. [var. *bicolor* Lindl.; var. *Sieboldii* D. Don; *C. Sieboldii* (D. Don) Paxt.]. With purple staminodes.

foetida E. F. A. Raoul. Climber, young branchlets grooved, fulvous-tomentose; lvs. compound, lfts. 3, stalked, ovate, 1–2 in. long, entire to crenate, dark green; fls in panicles, fragrant, yellow, to 1 in. across, sepals 5–8; fr. with styles 1 in. long. New Zeal.

Forsteri J. F. Gmel. Close to *C. paniculata,* but lfts. crenately toothed, brighter green, thinner, sepals 1 in. long, white; fr. with style 1 in. long. New Zeal.

Fremontii S. Wats. [*Viorna Fremontii* (S. Wats.) A. Heller]. FRE-MONT'S CROWFOOT. Stout, erect, to 1½ ft.; lvs. crowded, subsessile, round to oblong, 2–5 in. long, sparingly villous-tomentose, thickish; fls. solitary, peduncled, 1 in. long, glabrous on exterior; fr. with styles ½–1 in. long and woolly at base. Nebr., Kans.

fruticosa Turcz. Erect shrub; lvs. simple, lanceolate, entire or serrate; fls. in clusters of 1–4, yellow. Cent. Asia.

fusca Turcz. Climbing, semiwoody, to 15 ft.; lvs. compound, lfts. 5 or 7, 1½–2½ in. long, entire, glabrous; fls. solitary, nodding, violet, brownish-pubescent on exterior, 1 in. long. Ne. Asia. Var. **violacea** Maxim. Fls. violet on exterior.

Gattingeri Small [*Viorna Gattingeri* (Small) Small]. Glandular-pubescent climber; lvs. pinnate, lfts. lanceolate to lanceolate-ovate, 1–3 in. long, thin, not reticulate; fls. on bracted peduncles, purple, campanulate, ½ in. long; fr. with plumose styles. Tenn.

gentianoides DC. Sts. prostrate or creeping, to 4 ft. long; lvs. simple, or compound, the lfts. 3, lanceolate or lanceolate-ovate; fls. white, solitary or few, sepals 4, oblong. Tasmania.

glauca Willd. Like *C. orientalis,* but lfts. entire; sepals glabrous on both sides. China, Siberia. Var. **akebioides** (Maxim.) Rehd. & E. H. Wils. Lfts. broadly toothed; fls. bronze-yellow. W. China. Var. **angustifolia** Ledeb. Lfts. narrow. Siberia.

Gouriana Roxb. Vigorous climber, pubescent on young parts; lvs. compound, lfts. 5 or 7, acuminate, shining above; fls. in large panicles, white, ½ in. across; achenes pubescent. Himalayas, China. Var. **Finetii:** *C. Peterae.*

grandiflora DC. Slender climber; lvs. usually pinnate, lfts. 5, lanceolate-ovate, to 6 in. long, broadly crenate-toothed to denticulate, teeth mucronate; fls. solitary, axillary, greenish, to 1¾ in. long, sepals sub-erect. Trop. Afr.

grata Wallich. Hoary-pubescent, woody climber, sts. deeply furrowed; lvs. compound, lfts. about 5, broadly ovate, sometimes cordate, 1–2 in. long, acute to acuminate, incised-serrate or 3-lobed; fls. in decompound panicles, ¾–1 in. across, cream-colored, sepals spreading. Himalayas. Var. **argentilucida** (Lév. & Vaniot) Rehd. Lfts. larger, more coarsely toothed; fls. to 1 in. across. W. China.

graveolens: *C. orientalis.*

grewiiflora DC. Densely tomentose climber; lvs. pinnate, lfts. 3 or 5, broadly ovate-cordate, 3–4 in. long, usually deeply 5-lobed, more or less serrate; fls. in many-fld. panicles, tawny-yellow, 1½ in. long, densely tomentose outside, pubescent inside. Himalayas.

Henryi D. Oliver. Climber; lvs. simple, petioled, oblong-ovate, 3½–5 in. long, cordate, 3–5-nerved; fls. solitary, axillary, pale flesh-colored to ivory, 1 in. long; fr. with plumose styles. Cent. China. Cult. material offered under this name may be *C.* ×*Lawsoniana* cv. 'Henryi'.

heracleifolia DC. Subshrub, to 3 ft., sts. slightly downy; lvs. compound, lfts. 3, coarsely toothed, terminal lft. ovate, to 5 in. long; fls. in short axillary clusters, tubular, ¾–1 in. long, sepals blue, recurved at apex. E. China. Var. **Davidiana** (Decne. ex B. Verl.) Hemsl. [*C. Davidiana* Decne. ex B. Verl.]. To 2 ft.; fls. light violet-blue, fragrant, sepals not recurved at apex. N. China.

Hilarii K. Spreng. Vigorous, dioecious climber; lvs. compound, lfts. 3-toothed or -lobed, 1–3 in. long, leathery; fls. in few-fld. panicles, white, ¾–1 in. across; fr. with styles 2–3 in. long. Brazil to Argentina.

hirsutissima Pursh [*C. Douglasii* Hook.]. Erect, villous per., 1–2 ft., sts. 1 to several; lowest lvs. reduced, the others 2–3-pinnate, petioled, the ultimate divisions linear or lanceolate-linear; fls. solitary, on a naked peduncle, nodding, sepals 4, 1–2 in. long, brown-purple, leathery, villous on exterior; fr. with styles 2–2½ in. long. B.C. to Ore., Mont., Wyo.

Hookerana Allan. Like *C. paniculata,* but having lfts. deeply lobed, sepals greenish to pale yellow, male fls. to 1 in. across. New Zeal.

indivisa: *C. paniculata.*

instricta: a listed name of no botanical standing.

integrifolia L. Erect, to 3 ft.; lvs. simple, sessile, 2–4 in. long, entire, thin; fls. solitary, nodding, blue, open-urceolate, to 1½ in. long; fr. with styles to 2 in. long. Eur., Asia.

× **intermedia:** *C.* ×*eriostemon.*

× **Jackmanii** T. Moore: *C. lanuginosa* × *C. Viticella.* Climbers, to 10 ft.; lvs. pinnate or the upper simple; fls. usually in 3's, blue-purple to reddish, to 6 in. across, sepals usually 4. Cvs. include: 'Alba', fls. grayish-white; 'Purpurea Superba', fls. dark violet-purple; 'Rubra', fls. purplish-red.

× **Jouiniana** C. K. Schneid.: *C. heracleifolia* var. *Davidiana* × *C. Vitalba.* Vigorous climber, to 12 ft. or more; lfts. 3 or 5, ovate, 2–4 in. long, coarsely toothed; fls. in compound panicles, sepals 4, ¾ in. long, yellowish-white, aging to pale blue.

jubata Bisch. Herbaceous, to 3 ft.; lvs. simple, ovate or cordate, glaucous when young; fls. in large terminal panicles, white or cream, fragrant. Nativity unknown.

koreana Kom. Deciduous, prostrate shrub; lvs. compound, thinly hairy, lfts. 3, cordate-ovate, 1½–3½ in. long, middle lft. 3-parted or 3-lobed; fls. solitary, on peduncles 4–6 in. long, yellow or reddish to dull violet, sepals elliptic-lanceolate, downy on margins, 1–1¼ in. long. Korea. Cv. 'Lutea'. Fls. fragrant, cream-yellow, with dark centers.

lancifolia Bur. & Franch. Shrub, to 15 in.; lvs. lanceolate to lanceolate-ovate, leathery, deep green; fls. solitary, 1 in. across. China.

lanuginosa Lindl. Climbing, to about 6 ft., branchlets hairy; lvs. simple or compound, then lfts. 3, ovate, entire, 2–4 in. long, tomentose when young; fls. solitary or in groups of 2 or 3, arranged in a false cyme, on bractless peduncles, 1–2½ in. across, sepals 6, to 2 in. wide in the middle, hairy on exterior, lavender or white; achenes with styles to 3 in. long. China. Cv. 'Alba'. Fls. white.

lasiandra Maxim. Deciduous climber, 10–15 ft.; lvs. ternate or 2-ternate, 3–8 in. long, lfts. ovate to lanceolate, 2–4 in. long, coarsely toothed; fls. 1–3, dull purple, campanulate, ½ in. long. China.

lasiantha Nutt. Woody climber; lvs. compound, lfts. 3, broadly ovate, 1–2 in. long, somewhat 3-lobed, coarsely crenate; fls. 1, 3, or 5, on bracted peduncles, sepals broadly oblong, white; achenes with styles about 1 in. long. Calif.

× **Lawsoniana** T. Moore & Jackm.: a group of hybrids, *C. lanuginosa* × *C. patens.* Lvs. usually ternate; fls. solitary, rose-purple with darker veins, to 6 in. across, sepals usually 6–8. Cv. 'Henryi'. Fls. very large, cream-white, sepals long, pointed.

ligusticifolia Nutt. To 20 ft., much like *C. virginiana;* lvs. pinnate, lfts. 5–7, ½–1½ in. wide, thickish, firm; achenes densely pilose, styles to 2 in. long. Man. to B.C., s. to Mo., New Mex., Calif. Var. **californica** S. Wats. Lvs. canescent. S. Calif.

lilacina floribunda: a listed name of no botanical standing used for a cv. resembling *C. lanuginosa* with fls. pale grayish-lilac.

macropetala Ledeb. Climbing, to several ft.; lvs. 2–3-pinnate, lfts. deeply cut or lobed; fls. solitary, nodding, violet, 3–3½ in. across. China, Siberia. Cvs. are: 'Ballet Blanc', fls. white, staminodes many; 'Lagoon', fls. deep lavender, semidouble; 'Maidwell Hall', fls. clear lavender-blue, semidouble, to 2 in. across; 'Markham's Pink', sepals rose, suffused with purple at base; 'Rodklokke', fls. pink; 'White Moth', fls. white.

mandshurica: *C. recta* var.

marata J. B. Armstr. Dioecious climber, branchlets extremely slender; lvs. compound, lfts. 3, linear, ½–1 in. long, entire or 3-lobed, pubescent; fls. greenish-yellow, ½–1 in. across, sepals 4. New Zeal.

Meyeniana Walp. Evergreen climber, to 20 ft. or more, branchlets glabrous; lvs. compound, lfts. 3, entire, leathery, 3-veined; fls. in open, drooping panicles, white, 1 in. wide, sepals 4, notched at apex. Se. China.

microphylla DC. Woody climber, lvs. long-petioled, lvs. 2–3-ternate, with linear or lanceolate-oblong segms.; fls. in short panicles, sepals 4, cream-colored, ⅝–1 in. long; fr. with styles 1–1½ in. long. Australia.

missouriensis: *C. virginiana* var.

montana Buch.-Ham. ex DC. Woody climber, to 25 ft.; lvs. fascicled at the nodes, lfts. 3, ovate, toothed or incised; fls. in 1–5-fld. clusters, fragrant, white, turning pink, 2 in. across; fr. with plumose styles. Himalayas, China. Cvs. include: **'Alba'**, fls. white; **'Lilacina'**, fls. bluish-lilac; **'Perfecta'**, fls. large, bluish-white; **'Platyphylla'**; **'Rosea'**, fls. rose; **'Superba'**. Cv. **'Undulata'** is *Clematis* cv. 'Undulata', a hybrid: *C. gracilifolia* Rehd. & Wils. × *C. montana;* fls. large, bluish-white. Var. **rubens** E. H. Wils. Lvs. purplish, fls. rose or pink. Var. **Wilsonii** T. Sprague. Fls. white, to 3 in. across, sepals narrow. China.

occidentalis (Hornem.) DC. Sts. woody, climbing or trailing; lvs. ternate, lfts. lanceolate-ovate to triangular or nearly round; fls. solitary, long-peduncled, nodding, sepals 4, divergent, prominently veined, stamen filaments flat, petaloid, pubescent, the outer spatulate, wider than the inner, usually with anthers; achenes with plumose styles. Ne. and nw. N. Amer. Var. **occidentalis** [*C. alpina* var. *occidentalis* (Hornem.) A. Gray; *C. verticillaris* DC.]. The typical var.; sts. 3 ft. or more; lfts. unlobed, sometimes 2–3-lobed, nearly entire to serrate; sepals rose-violet, to 2⅜ in. long, obtuse to acute. Que. to Ont., s. to N.C. and Iowa. Var. **dissecta** (C. L. Hitchc.) Pringle. Sts. usually less then 3 ft.; lfts. deeply incised; sepals reddish-violet or violet-blue, to 1¾ in. long, rarely more, acute to acuminate. Cascade Mts. of Wash. Var. **grosseserrata** (Rydb.) Pringle. Sts. usually more than 3 ft.; lfts. unlobed, sometimes 2–3-lobed, nearly entire to serrate; sepals violet-blue or rarely white, to 2⅜ in. long, acuminate to attenuate. Mts., Sask. to Yukon, s. to Colo.

ochroleuca Ait. [*Viorna ochroleuca* (Ait.) Small]. CURLY-HEADS. Erect, 1–2½ ft., young growth silky; lvs. ovate, to 4 in. long and half as wide, entire; fls. solitary, campanulate, sepals 1 in. long or more, dull yellow to purplish, gray-pubescent on exterior; fr. with styles yellowish-brown, 1–2 in. long. N.Y. to Ga.

Olgae: a listed name of no botanical standing, applied to a plant said to resemble *C. integrifolia.*

orientalis L. [*C. graveolens* Lindl.]. Woody climber; lvs. pinnate or 2-pinnate, lfts. 1–2 in. long, sharply and coarsely toothed; fls. 1 or 3, yellow, 1–2 in. across, sepals 4, villous at least on exterior, somewhat reflexed; fr. with plumose styles. Iran to Himalayas.

paniculata J. F. Gmel. [*C. indivisa* Willd.]. Climber, branchlets stout, glabrous; lvs. compound, lfts. 3, broadly ovate, 1–4 in. long, entire to crenate, or basally lobed, leathery; male fls. white, 2–4 in. across, female fls. smaller; fr. with styles 1–2 in. long. New Zeal. Some material cult. under this name is *C. dioscoreifolia* or *C. dioscoreifolia* var. *robusta.*

Parkmanii: a listed name of no botanical standing, applied to a plant with large purple fls.

patens C. Morr. & Decne. Climbing, to 12 ft.; lower lvs. with 2 widely separated pairs of lfts., upper lvs. with 3 lfts. or simple, lfts. round-ovate to lanceolate; fls. terminal, solitary, on bracted peduncles, 4–6 in. across, sepals 8 or more, violet to white. China. Cvs. include: **'Fortunei'**, fls. double, greenish-white, 3–5 in. across; **'Grandiflora'**, fls. large; **'Standishii'**, lfts. 3, fls. lilac-blue.

pauciflora Nutt. Low, dioecious, woody climber, lvs. compound, lfts. 3 or 5, cordate to cuneate-obovate, ⅜–¾ in. long, usually 3-toothed or 3-lobed, glabrous to silky-tomentose; fls. solitary to few in panicles, sepals lanceolate-oblong, about ½ in. long. S. Calif., n. Baja Calif.

Peterae Hand.-Mazz. [*C. Gouriana* var. *Finetii* Rehd. & E. H. Wils.]. Pubescent woody climber; lvs. pinnate, lfts. ovate or elliptic, 1–3 in. long, rounded or somewhat cordate at base, acuminate, entire or 1–4-toothed; fls. in many-fld., loose panicles, white or yellowish, sepals oblong, to ½ in. long; fr. with styles about 1 in. long. China.

Pitcheri Torr. & A. Gray [*Viorna Pitcheri* (Torr. & A. Gray) Britt.]. High climber, more or less pubescent; lvs. pinnate, lfts. 3–9, ovate or subcordate, entire or 3-lobed; fls. solitary, dull purplish, campanulate, ½-1 in. long; fr. with styles 1 in. long. Ind. to Nebr., s. to Tenn. and Tex.

Potaninii Maxim. var. **Fargesii** (Franch.) Hand.-Mazz. [*C. Fargesii* Franch.]. Climbing, to 20 ft.; lvs. 2-pinnate, lfts. cut or lobed; fls. solitary or cymose, white, to 2 in. across. China.

pseudoalpina: *C. columbiana.*

pseudoflammula Schmalh. ex Lipskiĭ. Upright, to 5 ft.; fls. fragrant, cream-white. Caucasus.

pubescens Benth. Climber; lfts. 3, acuminate, subcordate, entire or coarsely toothed, silky-pubescent; fls. 1–3 on a peduncle, white, small, sepals ovate, soft-hairy. Mex.

recta L. Herbaceous, erect or ascending, to 5 ft.; lfts. 5–9, on a stalk, ovate-lanceolate, 1–2½ in. long, pointed, entire; fls. many in a panicle, white, fragrant, to 1 in. across. S. Eur. Cvs. include: **'Grandiflora'**, semierect, fls. pure white, starry, borne in profusion; **'Plena'**, fls. double; **'Recta Purpurea'**, like cv. 'Grandiflora', but foliage purple. Var. **mandshurica** (Rupr.) Maxim. [*C. mandshurica* Rupr.]. Sts. longer, decumbent; peduncles terminal and axillary. E. Asia.

Rehderana Craib. Deciduous climber, to 20 ft.; lvs. pinnate, lfts. 1½–3 in. long, toothed or 3-lobed, silky underneath; fls. in short panicles, nodding, fragrant, pale yellow, ½ in. long, sepals recurved at apex. China.

reticulata Walt. [*Viorna reticulata* (Walt.) Small]. Climber, more or less pubescent; lfts. 3–7, rounded and mucronate apically, entire, leathery, coarsely reticulate-veined; fls. solitary, on peduncle with petioled bracts, nodding, urceolate, sepals ¾ in. long, yellowish outside, pale violet inside, closely hairy. S.C. to Fla. and Tex.

Scottii T. C. Porter [*Viorna Scottii* (T. C. Porter) Rydb.]. Sts. to 2 ft., erect, simple or nearly so, glabrous in age; lvs. petioled, the upper pinnate or 2-pinnate, 3–6 in. long, lfts. lanceolate to ovate; fls. solitary, peduncled, nodding, purple, nearly 1 in. long; fr. with styles 1–2 in. long. S. Dak. and Idaho to Nebr. and Colo.

serratifolia Rehd. Like *C. tangutica,* but fls. smaller, to 2 in. across, yellow, with purple stamens. Korea.

serrulata: a listed name of no botanical standing, perhaps referable to a var. of *C. orientalis* or *C. serratifolia.*

sibirica: *C. alpina* var.

Sieboldii: *C. florida* forma.

songarica Bunge. Shrub, to 5 ft.; lvs. simple, lanceolate, toothed or slightly pinnatifid near the base; fls. in terminal cymes, yellowish-white, 1 in. across. Asia.

Spooneri: *C. chrysocoma.*

Stanleyi Hook. [*Clematopsis Stanleyi* (Hook.) Hutch.]. Tall, stout, much-branched shrub, with silky, spreading hairs; lvs. 3-pinnate, lfts. divided into narrowly linear segms.; fls. in panicles, purplish or bluish, 1½ in. across. S. Afr.

stans Siebold & Zucc. Erect, dioecious herb, to 6 ft.; lvs. compound, lfts. 3, large, coarsely toothed or lobed; fls. unisexual, in long terminal panicles and axillary clusters, white or bluish, tubular, about ½ in. long. Japan.

tangutica (Maxim.) Korsh. Climbing, to 10 ft., branchlets pubescent at first; lvs. pinnate or 2-pinnate, lfts. toothed or lobed, green; fls. usually solitary, bright yellow, to 4 in. across. Mongolia, n. China. Cv. **'Farreri'**. Fls. golden-yellow. Var. **obtusiuscula** Rehd. & E. H. Wils. Lfts. smaller, sepals more obtuse.

tenuiloba A. Gray [*Atragene tenuiloba* (A. Gray) Britt.]. Vine, mostly trailing; lvs. 2-ternate, lfts. to 1 in. long, usually divided to near the midrib into lanceolate or ovate divisions; sepals spreading, acuminate, 1–1½ in. long, blue or purple; fr. with styles 2 in. long. S. Dak. to Ariz.

texensis Buckl. [*C. coccinea* (A. Gray) Hook.f.]. Tall climber; lvs. many, mostly pinnate, lfts. broadly to narrowly ovate, to 2½ in. long, entire or rarely lobed, glaucous, thick; fls. nodding, scarlet or purple-red, ovoid, about ¾ in. long; fr. with styles 1–2 in. long. Tex.

Thunbergii Steud. Pubescent climber; lvs. pinnate or ternate, lfts. widely spaced, ovate, toothed or cut; fls. many, in panicles, to 2 in. across, sepals spreading, lanceolate-acuminate. S. Afr.

troutbeckiana: *C. versicolor.*

×vedrariensis Hort. Vilm.-Andr.; *C. chrysocoma* × *C. montana.* Lfts. 3, ovate, 1–2½ in. long, often 3-lobed, very pubescent; fls. mauve-pink or rose, 2 in. across. Cv. **'Rosea'**. Fls. shell-pink.

Veitchiana Craib. Much like *C. Rehderana,* deciduous, to 10 ft.; lvs. 2-pinnate, lfts. more deeply cut; fls. yellowish-white, ½ in. long, China.

versicolor Small [*C. troutbeckiana* Spring.]. LEATHER FLOWER. Climbing, to 12 ft., sts. nearly cylindrical; lvs. pinnate, lfts. elliptic, 1–3 in. long, blunt, reticulate, leathery; fls. solitary on peduncle with 2 bracts near the base, dull purple or bluish-lavender, with greenish tips, ovoid-campanulate, 1 in. long, glabrous on exterior, the upper margin pilose; fr. with styles 2 in. long. Ky. and Tenn., w. to Mo., Ark., Okla.

verticillaris: *C. occidentalis* var. *occidentalis.*

Viorna L. [*Viorna Viorna* (L.) Small]. LEATHER FLOWER, VASE VINE. Climbing, to 10 ft., sts. angled; lvs. compound, lfts. 3–7, ovate to lanceolate, 2–4 in. long, acute, nearly glabrous, bright green, membranous; fls. solitary, on naked or 2-bracted peduncle, purple, ovoid-campanulate, sepals thickish, ⅝–1 in. long; fr. with styles 1–2 in. long. Penn. to Ga., w. to Ill., Iowa, Tex.

virginiana L. WOODBINE, LEATHER FLOWER, VIRGIN'S BOWER, DEVIL'S-DARNING-NEEDLE. Climber, to 10 or 20 ft.; lvs. compound, lfts. 3, similar, ovate, acuminate, incised, the teeth few, lower surface glabrous or nearly so; fls. many, in corymbiform panicles, cream-white, sepals ¼–½ in. long, pubescent at least on exterior; fr. with styles 1–1½ in. long. Nov. Sc. and Que. to Man., s. to La. and Ga. Var. **missouriensis** (Rydb.) Palmer & Steyerm. [*C. missouriensis* Rydb.]. Lfts. often 5, soft-silky underneath. Ont. to Minn., s. to Nebr. and Mo.

Vitalba L. Woody climber, to 30 ft. or more; lvs. pinnate, lfts. 3–5, rather distinct, narrow-ovate, rounded or subcordate, entire or coarsely toothed; fls. in panicles, greenish-white, fragrant, about 1 in. across, densely pubescent on exterior. Eur., sw. Asia, N. Afr. Young sprouts sometimes eaten in Eur. Var. **taurica** Bess. Less hairy, lfts. lobed or asymmetrically toothed.

Viticella L. [*Viticella Viticella* (L.) Small]. Climbing, to 12 ft., lvs. 1–2-pinnate, lfts. 1–2 in. long, inequilateral, entire or 3-lobed, thin; fls. solitary or in 3's, blue, purple, or rose-purple, 1–2 in. across, sepals spreading; fr. with styles not plumose. S. Eur., w. Asia. Cvs. include: 'Albiflora' or 'Alba', fls. white; 'Caerulea', fls. blue-violet; 'Kermesina', fls. wine-red; 'Purpurea' [cv. 'Rubra'], fls. red-purple; 'Rubra': 'Purpurea'.

CLEMATITIS: *CLEMATIS.*

CLEMATOPSIS: *CLEMATIS.*

CLEMENTSIA: *SEDUM.*

CLEOME L. [*Gynandropsis* DC.; *Isomeris* Nutt.; *Neocleome* Small; *Pedicellaria* Schrank]. SPIDER PLANT. *Capparaceae.* About 200 spp. of trop., subtrop., or rarely temp. herbs, subshrubs, or shrubs, usually with a fetid odor; lvs. simple or palmately compound; fls. white, green, yellowish, or purple, in usually bracted racemes or solitary, petals 4, usually clawed, stamens usually 6 and long, ovary usually on a long stipe or sessile; fr. a narrow caps., seeds several to many.

One annual species (*C. Hasslerana,* commonly known as *C. spinosa*) is frequently cultivated in the flower garden and border for its rose-purple to light pink or white flowers; it is raised from seeds usually sown where the plants are to stand.

arborea HBK. Pubescent, glandular, giant herb; fls. green. Venezuela. Perhaps not specifically distinct from *C. viridiflora.* The *C. arborea* of the trade is *C. Hasslerana.*

gigantea; *C. viridiflora;* as used in the trade, *C. gigantea* is usually *C. Hasslerana,* but may be *Polanisia trachysperma* or *P. uniglandulosa.*

grandis: generally *C. Hasslerana,* but may be *Polanisia trachysperma* or *P. uniglandulosa.*

gynandra L. [*C. pentaphylla* L.; *Gynandropsis gynandra* (L.) Briq.; *G. pentaphylla* (L.) DC.; *Pedicellaria pentaphylla* (L.) Schrank]. SPIDER-WISP. Ann., to 3 ft. or more; lvs. compound, lfts. 3–7, obovate to oblanceolate, somewhat glandular-puberulent when young, minutely toothed; fls. solitary, white to purplish, stamens 6, attached to stipe halfway between petals and the elongate ovary. Old World tropics; naturalized weed throughout the tropics.

Hasslerana Chodat [*C. arborea* Hort., not HBK.; *C. gigantea* Hort., not L.; *C. grandis* Hort.; *C. pungens* of auth., not Willd.; *C. spinosa* of auth., not Jacq.; *Neocleome spinosa* (L.) Small]. SPIDER FLOWER. Glandular-pubescent, erect, strongly scented ann., to 5 ft.; lvs. compound, usually with pairs of short spines at base, lfts. 5–7, long-acuminate; fls. in bracted racemes, usually dark pink, fading to nearly white by noon, stamens 2½ in. long; caps. long-stalked, slender, 1–2 in. long. Se. Brazil to Argentina; sometimes runs wild in e. U.S. Cvs. include: 'Great Pink', 'Pink Queen', 'Rosea', fls. pink; 'Alba' and 'Snow Crown', fls. white, similar to and confused with the true *C. spinosa* Jacq.

Isomeris Greene [*Isomeris arborea* Nutt.]. BLADDERBUSH, BURRO-FAT. Glabrous, per., rounded shrubs or small trees, to 9 ft.; lvs. compound, lfts. 3, small, thickish; fls. yellow, sepals united, petals ½ in. long, stamens 1 in. long; caps. 1–2 in. long, more or less inflated, on stipe ½–1 in. long, seeds few, large, smooth. Deserts, cent. Calif. to Baja Calif.

integrifolia: *C. serrulata.*

lutea Hook. YELLOW C., YELLOW BEE PLANT, GOLDEN C. Glabrous ann., to 5 ft.; lvs. compound, lfts. 5, acute to rounded, to 1½ in. long; fls. yellow; caps. narrow, 1–2 in. long. Wash., s. to Calif. and Colo.

pentaphylla: *C. gynandra.*

pungens: *C. spinosa;* material commonly cult. as *C. pungens,* however, is *C. Hasslerana.*

serrulata Pursh [*C. integrifolia* (Nutt.) Torr. & A. Gray]. ROCKY MOUNTAIN BEE PLANT, STINKING CLOVER. Glabrous ann., 2–5 ft.; lvs. compound, lfts. 3, narrowly lanceolate-elliptic, 1–2½ in. long, acute to obtuse; fls. deep pink, rarely white, in very dense, showy racemes; otherwise very similar to *C. lutea.* W. Canada through w. U.S., s. to Mex. At one time planted as a bee plant.

speciosa Raf. [*C. speciosa* HBK; *C. speciosissima* Deppe ex Lindl.; *Gynandropsis speciosa* (HBK) DC.]. Robust, succulent ann., to 5 ft. or less, nearly glabrous, without spines; fls. showy, pink or white, stamens borne on a stipe about ¼–½ in. above the petals and 1–2½ in. below the ovary; very similar to *C. Hasslerana* [*C. spinosa* of auth.]. Mex. to n. S. Amer. Grown as ornamental in warm countries.

speciosissima: *C. speciosa.*

spinosa Jacq. [*C. pungens* Willd.]. Very similar to, and confused with the widely cult. *C. Hasslerana,* but having fls. sordid-white, less showy, petals and caps. more or less pubescent, stipes shorter, and caps. deflexed. S. Mex. to Venezuela and Caribbean Is. Not cult. in N. Amer.

trachysperma: *Polanisia trachysperma.*

uniglandulosa: *Polanisia uniglandulosa.*

viridiflora Schreb. [*C. gigantea* L.]. Giant herb, to 12 ft., glandular-pubescent; lvs. large, compound, lfts. 5–12 in. long; racemes few, erect, very long, open, bractless; fls. green, narrow, 1–2 in. long, glandular-hairy; caps. 3–6 in. long, seeds smooth, glossy. Trop. Amer.

CLERODENDRUM L. [*Siphonanthus* L.; *Volkameria* L.]. GLORY-BOWER, KASHMIR-BOUQUET, TUBEFLOWER. *Verbenaceae.* Over 450 spp. of deciduous or evergreen trees or shrubs, sometimes climbing, native to the tropics, but mostly to the E. Hemisphere; lvs. opp. or whorled, simple, toothed, lobed, or entire; fls. white, yellow, orange, red, blue, or violet, in corymbs or cymes, the cymes sometimes in panicles, calyx 5-toothed or -lobed, sometimes colored and showy, corolla funnelform or salverform, limb somewhat unequally 5-lobed, stamens 4, long-exserted, curved; fr. a drupe, subtended or enclosed by persistent calyx.

Clerodendrums are grown in the greenhouse or out of doors in the South and Calif. Those native to temperate regions may be hardy to Zone 6. Propagated by seeds or cuttings of half-ripened wood kept at a temperature of about 70° F.

aculeatum (L.) Schlechtend. [*Volkameria aculeata* L.]. Vinelike shrub, to 10 ft., armed with paired spines; lvs. oblong to elliptic-obovate, to 2 in. long, entire; cymes axillary; fls. white. Summer and autumn. W. Indies.

Balfourii: *C. Thomsoniae.*

Bungei Steud. [*C. foetidum* Bunge]. Spreading shrub, to 6 ft.; lvs. long-petioled, broadly ovate, to 1 ft. long, coarsely toothed, reddish-pubescent beneath, strong-scented; corymbs dense, capitate, to 8 in. across; fls. rose-red, ¾ in. across. China. Zone 9.

Colebrookianum Walp. Shrub, to 8 ft. or more; lvs. long-petioled, cordate-ovate, to 15 or 20 in. long, entire; fls. white, to 1 in. long, in corymbs; fr. blue, subtended by fleshy red calyx. Se. Asia.

cyrtophyllum Turcz. Shrub; lvs. oblong-ovate to lanceolate, to 11 in. long, usually long-acuminate, glabrous, pale beneath; cymes long-peduncled; fls. white. China.

delectum: *C. Thomsoniae* cv.

fallax: *C. speciosissimum.*

foetidum: *C. Bungei.*

Fargesii: *C. trichotomum* var.

floribundum R. Br. Shrub or small tree; lvs. elliptic to lanceolate or ovate, 2–6 in. long, glabrous or tomentose when young; fls. to 1¼ in. long; fr. black, subtended by red calyx. Australia.

fragrans: *C. philippinum.*

Gaudichaudii Dop. Tree, to 20 ft.; lvs. elliptic, oblong, or obovate to elliptic-obovate, to 9 in. long, entire or irregularly toothed, glabrous; cymes in panicles; fls. yellow; fr. black, subtended by red calyx. Indochina.

glabrum E. H. Mey. Shrub or small tree, to 15 ft.; lvs. opp. or whorled, oblong-ovate, to 5 in. long, entire, glossy above, glabrous or slightly hairy on veins beneath; cymes dense; fls. white or pinkish, fragrant; fr. white. S. Afr. Zone 9.

indicum (L.) O. Kuntze. [*C. Siphonanthus* R. Br.; *Siphonanthus indicus* L.]. TUBEFLOWER, TURK'S-TURBAN. Shrub or woody herb, to 8 ft.; lvs. mostly whorled, lanceolate-oblong, to 6 in. long, entire, glabrous; cymes axillary or in panicles; fls. white, corolla tube to 4 in. long;

fr. red or purple, subtended by red-brown calyx. Malay Arch.; naturalized in s. U.S.

japonicum (Thunb.) Sweet. Shrub, to 10 ft.; lvs. ovate-cordate, to 9 in. long or more, acuminate, glabrous above, scaly beneath, margins glandular-toothed; fls. bright red to scarlet, to ¾ in. long. China, Japan; naturalized in Md. Zone 6.

Kaempferi (Jacq.) Siebold [*C. squamatum* Vahl]. Shrub, to 8 ft.; lvs. ovate, to 1 ft. long or more, cordate at base, entire or toothed, scaly beneath; fls. bright scarlet, to 1½ in. long, in large, narrow panicles. China, India.

minahassae Teysm. & Binnend. Shrub or small tree; lvs. elliptic, oblong to obovate, to 8 in. long, entire, glabrous; fls. in cymes, white, to 4 in. long; fr. subtended by fleshy red calyx. Malay Arch.

myricoides (Hochst.) R. Br. ex Vatke. Shrub, to 6 ft.; lvs. opp. or whorled, lanceolate or obovate, to 3½ in. long, cuneate, coarsely toothed, particularly above the middle, or entire; cymes in panicles; corolla with 4 upper lobes nearly equal, white or pale blue, lower lobe much larger, usually blue-violet. Trop. and S. Afr.

nilgaricum: a listed name of no botanical standing.

nutans Wallich. Glabrous shrub, to 7 ft.; lvs. lanceolate to oblanceolate, to 8 in. long, acuminate, entire; panicles few-fld., loose, terminal; fls. white; fr. purple. Assam to Himalayas.

paniculatum L. PAGODA FLOWER. Shrub, to 4 ft.; lvs. orbicular to ovate, 5-lobed, to 6 in. long, cordate; cymes in terminal panicles, to 1 ft. long; fls. scarlet, corolla tube to ½ in. long. Se. Asia.

philippinum Schauer [*C. fragrans* Willd., *C. fragrans* var. *pleniflorum* Schauer]. Subshrub, 5–8 ft.; lvs. long-petioled, broadly ovate, to 10 in. long or more, truncate or cordate at base, coarsely toothed; corymbs terminal, resembling the florist's hydrangea; fls. pink or white, 1 in. across, fragrant, double. The single-fld. wild form is seldom seen. China, Japan; naturalized in s. U.S. and throughout tropics.

rubrum: a listed name of no botanical standing.

Siphonanthus: *C. indicum.*

speciosissimum Van Geert. [*C. fallax* Lindl.]. Erect shrub, to 12 ft., branching after flowering; lvs. ovate, to 1 ft. long, cordate, entire or toothed, densely pubescent; cymes in panicles to 1½ ft. long; fls. bright scarlet, to 2 in. long, Java.

× **speciosum** Dombr.: *C. splendens* × *C. Thomsoniae.* JAVA GLORY BEAN, PAGODA FLOWER. Corolla dull red, persistent, calyx pale red.

splendens G. Don. Twining shrub; lvs. oblong or elliptic, to 6 in. long; cymes many-fld.; fls. bright scarlet or yellow, 1 in. across. Trop. Afr.

squamatum: *C. Kaempferi.*

Thomsoniae Balf. [*C. Balfourii* Hort.]. BLEEDING G.-B., TROPICAL BLEEDING-HEART, BLEEDING-HEART VINE, GLORY TREE, BAGFLOWER. Twining, glabrous, evergreen shrub; lvs. ovate to oblong-ovate, to 5 in. long, acuminate, entire; fls. in cymes, calyx large, white, corolla crimson. W. Trop. Afr. Grown in greenhouses. Cv. 'Delectum'. Fls. in very large clusters, rose-magenta.

tomentosum (Venten.) R. Br. Tree, to 30 ft.; lvs. lanceolate to ovate-elliptic, to 4 in. long, tomentose; fls. in cymes, corolla white, tube to ¾ in. long, anthers yellow. Australia.

trichotomum Thunb. Shrub, to 10 or 20 ft.; lvs. ovate, to 5 in. long, entire or toothed, pubescent; cymes long-peduncled, in upper l. axils; fls. white, fragrant; fr. bright blue, subtended by fleshy red calyx. Japan. Zone 5. Var. **Fargesii** (Dode) Rehd. [*C. Fargesii* Dode]. Lvs. smaller, nearly glabrous. China.

tuberculatum A. Rich. Shrub, sts. cylindrical, covered with small tubercles; lvs. elliptic, rounded on both ends, leathery, rusty-hairy beneath; cymes axillary, shorter than the lvs.; fls. white. Cuba.

ugandense Prain. Glabrous shrub, to 10 ft.; lvs. elliptic or narrowly obovate, to 4½ in. long, coarsely toothed; fls. to 1 in. long, calyx lobes crimson, rounded, corolla with 3 lobes pale blue and 1 lobe violet-blue, filaments purple, anthers blue. Trop. Afr.

CLETHRA L. WHITE ALDER, SUMMER-SWEET. *Clethraceae.* About 30 spp. of shrubs or small trees, native to e. Asia, e. N. Amer., Madeira Is., and the neotropics; lvs. alt., simple; fls. white or rarely pink, fragrant, in terminal racemes or panicles, calyx 5-lobed, petals 5, stamens 10; fr. a 3-valved caps., enclosed in the enlarged calyx.

Propagated by seeds sown in pans in spring, greenwood cuttings under glass, or layers and division. Several of the species listed here are hardy in northern or north-central states.

acuminata Michx. To 15 ft.; lvs. elliptic or oblong, to 8 in. long, acuminate, finely serrate, thin, pale underneath; racemes nodding,

solitary, bracts longer than fls., deciduous. Summer. Va. to Ga. and Ala. Zone 6.

alnifolia L. [*C. alnifolia* var. *paniculata* (Ait.) Rehd.; *C. paniculata* Ait.]. SWEET PEPPERBUSH, SUMMER-SWEET. To 10 ft.; lvs. obovate, to 4 in. long, obtuse or acute, cuneate, sharply serrate; racemes erect, usually panicled, bracts shorter than fls. Summer to autumn. Me. to Fla. Zone 5. Cv. 'Rosea'. Fls. pinkish.

arborea Ait. To 25 ft., evergreen; lvs. elliptic, to 5 in. long, acuminate, shining above; racemes panicled. Summer to autumn. Madeira Is. Zone 9.

barbinervis Siebold & Zucc. To 30 ft.; lvs. obovate, to 5 in. long, acuminate, sharply serrate, pubescent; racemes panicled. Summer to autumn. Japan. Zone 7.

Delavayi Franch. To 45 ft.; lvs. elliptic-oblong to oblanceolate, to 6 in. long, hairy underneath; racemes solitary, 1-sided; calyx red, petals ciliate. Summer. W. China. Zone 5.

Fargesii Franch. To 12 ft.; lvs. ovate-oblong to elliptic-oblong, to 5½ in. long, serrate, nearly glabrous; racemes panicled, to 8 in. long; fls. white. Summer. Cent. China. Zone 5.

lanata M. Martens & Galeotti. To 40 ft.; lvs. obovate, to 7 in. long, rounded or subacute at apex, densely rusty-hairy underneath; racemes panicled. S. Mex. to Panama.

monostachya Rehd. & E. H. Wils. To 20 ft.; lvs. elliptic-oblong to oblong-lanceolate, to 5½ in. long, cuneate, thin, nearly glabrous; racemes usually solitary, to 8 in. long; petals glabrous. Summer. Cent. China. Zone 5.

paniculata: *C. alnifolia.*

tomentosa Lam. To 8 ft.; lvs. obovate, to 4 in. long, acute or acuminate, tomentose underneath; racemes erect, solitary or few. Late summer. N.C. to Fla. and Ala. Zone 8.

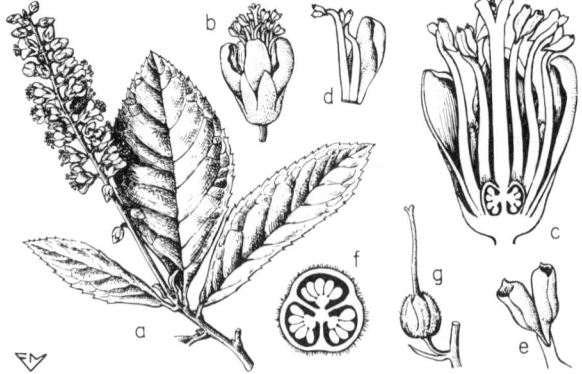

CLETHRACEAE. *Clethra alnifolia:* **a,** flowering branch, × ½; **b,** flower, × 2; **c,** flower, vertical section, × 4; **d,** petal with stamens, × 2; **e,** anther, × 10; **f,** ovary, cross section, × 8; **g,** capsule, × 2. (From Bailey, *Manual of Cultivated Plants,* ed. 2.)

CLETHRACEAE Klotzsch. WHITE ALDER FAMILY. Dicot.; 1 genus, *Clethra,* of evergreen or deciduous shrubs or small trees, native to e. Asia and e. N. and S. Amer. and Madeira; mostly with stellate hairs; lvs. alt., simple; fls. regular, bisexual, calyx 5-lobed, petals 5, stamens 10, ovary superior, 3-celled; fr. a caps.

CLEYERA Thunb. *Theaceae.* About 17 spp. of trop. and subtrop. small trees and shrubs; lvs. alt., simple, entire or serrulate, short-petioled; peduncles elongate, sturdy; fls. axillary, solitary or in clusters, bisexual, sepals 5, unequal, ciliate, petals 5, united just at base, stamens about 25, in 1 series, anthers distinctly setose, basifixed, ovary 2–3-celled; fr. indehiscent, berrylike, globose to ovoid, many-seeded.

Suitable for greenhouse culture or outside in the South. Zone 8. Propagated by cuttings, transplants easily. Thrives in half-shaded sites. For culture see *Camellia.*

Fortunei: *C. japonica* cv. 'Tricolor'.

japonica Thunb. [*C. ochnacea* DC.; *Eurya ochnacea* (DC.) Szysz.]. Glabrous, evergreen shrub, to 15 ft.; lvs. elliptic to narrowly obovate,

3–6 in. long and ¾–2 in. wide, acuminate but blunt at tip, usually entire; peduncles to ½ in. long or more; fls. 1–5 in axils of lvs., creamy-white, to ¾ in. across, fragrant; fr. black, ⅜ in. long. Temp. e. Asia. In Japan cut leafy brs. used in Shinto rituals. Not to be confused with *Eurya japonica*. Forma **tricolor:** cv. 'Tricolor'. Cv. **'Tricolor'** [forma *tricolor* (Nichols.) Kobuski; *C. Fortunei* Hook.f.; *Eurya japonica* var. *variegata* Hort.]. Lvs. thinner, bright green, variegated with golden-yellow and rose toward margins.

ochnacea: *C. japonica.*

CLIANTHUS Soland. ex Lindl. *Leguminosae* (subfamily *Faboideae*). Two spp. of erect or trailing, tender shrubs or herbs, native to Australia and New Zeal.; lvs. alt., odd-pinnate, with many small lfts.; fls. large, red (rarely pink to white), papilionaceous, in short, pendent, axillary racemes, standard acuminate, reflexed over calyx, keel petals long and beaklike, stamens 10, 9 united and 1 separate; fr. a cylindrical, inflated legume.

Grown for their spectacular flowers. *Clianthus puniceus* is of easy culture in the greenhouse or outdoors in the South; *C. formosus* is a desert plant suitable for growing outdoors in southern Calif., often quite difficult to cultivate; greater success has been obtained by grafting onto roots of *Colutea arborescens*. Propagated generally by seeds and cuttings.

Dampieri: *C. formosus.*

formosus (G. Don) Ford & Vickery [*C. Dampieri* A. Cunn. ex Lindl.; *C. speciosus* (G. Don) Asch. & Graebn.]. DESERT PEA, STURT D.P., GLORY P. Sometimes per., sts. procumbent or erect, to 4 ft., herbage gray-pubescent; lfts. to 1 in. long; fls. to 3 in. long, standard with a large purple-black blotch at base; fr. to 2½ in. long. W. Australia. Zone 10.

puniceus (G. Don) Soland. ex Lindl. GLORY PEA, PARROT'S-BILL, PARROT'S-BEAK. Semiwoody, to 6 ft.; fls. to 3 in. long, standard usually without dark blotch; fr. to 3 in. long, seeds yellowish, speckled dark brown. New Zeal., where also called RED KOWHAI.

speciosus: *C. formosus.*

CLIFTONIA Banks ex C. F. Gaertn. *Cyrillaceae.* One sp., an evergreen shrub or small tree, native to swamps along coastal plain from La. to n. Fla. and Ga.; lvs. alt., simple, entire; fls. small, pinkish to white, in terminal or axillary racemes, sepals 5, petals 5, stamens 10, in 2 whorls of 5; fr. dry, 2–5-winged.

monophylla (Lam.) Britt. ex Sarg. BUCKWHEAT TREE, BUCKWHEAT BRUSH, TITI, BLACK T., IRONWOOD. To 24 ft. or more; lvs. elliptic-oblanceolate to oblanceolate-obovate, to 2¼ in. long, leathery, glossy above, glaucous underneath; racemes to 3½ in. long; fls. white, fragrant. A bee plant. Cv. 'Rosea'. Fls. pink.

CLINOPODIUM L. *Labiatae.* About 4 spp. of per. herbs of temp. regions; sts. mostly square in cross section; lvs. opp., usually toothed, the upper ones bractlike, fls. in dense, many-fld. verticillasters, calyx tubular, 13-nerved, 2-lipped, upper lip spreading, 3-toothed, lower lip 2-toothed, tube often pilose inside throat, corolla often inflated, limb 2-lipped, upper lip entire or retuse, lower lip 3-lobed, stamens 4, in 2 pairs; fr. of 4 globose, glabrous nutlets. Differs from *Calamintha* in having false whorls dense, many-fld., and calyx tube curved.

Propagated by seeds or division.

carolinianum: see *Satureja georgiana.*

chinense (Benth.) O. Kuntze [*Calamintha chinensis* Benth.; *Satureja chinensis* (Benth.) Briq.]. Sts. erect, 10–30 in. long, white-pilose; lvs. ovate, to 1½ in. long, to 1 in. wide, acute, rounded basally, petioles to ¾ in. long; fl. bracts to ⁵⁄₁₆ in. long, pilose; corolla pale rose-purple, to ½ in. long, puberulent. Late summer. E. Asia.

georgianum: *Satureja georgiana.*

Nepeta: *Calamintha Nepeta.*

vulgare L. [*Calamintha Clinopodium* (Benth.) Benth.; *Calamintha vulgaris*(L.) Halácsy, not Clairv.; *Satureja vulgaris*(L.) Fritsch]. BASIL, WILD B., BASILWEED, DOG MINT. To 2½ ft., pubescent; lvs. broadly ovate, to 1¾ in. long, obtuse, shallowly crenate; verticillasters 1 in. across, distant or the uppermost crowded, fl. bracts almost as long as calyx, long-ciliate; corolla rose-purple, about twice as long as calyx. Summer. Eurasia.

CLINOSTIGMA H. Wendl. *Palmae.* Perhaps 10–12 spp. of solitary, stout, unarmed, monoecious palms with a prominent

crownshaft, sometimes with stilt roots, native in Fiji Is., Samoa, Micronesia to Bonin Is.; lvs. pinnate, pinnae regularly arranged, acute; infl. below lvs., paniculate, peduncle short, bearing 2 nearly equal, deciduous bracts, rachillae with fls. in triads (2 male and 1 female) near the base and above these with paired or solitary male fls.; male fls. with sepals and petals acute, asymmetrical, stamens 6, filaments inflexed at apex in bud, pistillode shortly 3-cleft, female fls. with sepals and petals imbricate, ovary 1-celled; fr. globose to ovoid or ellipsoid, with stigmatic scar subapical or lateral, endocarp operculate, seed with homogeneous endosperm and basal embryo.

For culture see *Palms.*

Mooreanum: *Lepidorrhachis Mooreana.*

samoense H. Wendl. To 60 ft. or more; lvs. large; fr. globose, ⅜ in. in diam., with lateral stigmatic scar. Samoa.

CLINTONIA Raf. *Liliaceae.* About 6 spp. of per., rhizomatous, scapose herbs, native to N. Amer. and e. Asia; sts. erect; lvs. mostly basal; fls. white to greenish-yellow or rose-purple, in terminal umbels, rarely solitary or racemose, perianth segms. 6, separate, stamens 6, anthers basifixed; fr. a blue or black berry.

Clintonias should be planted in moist shady and woodsy places. Propagated by division of roots in spring, or by seeds.

alpina Kunth. To 2 ft.; lvs. 4–9, oblanceolate to obovate, 2–4 in. long; fls. white, ⁵⁄₁₆ in. long, infl. racemose to umbellate; fr. many-seeded. Temp. Himalayas.

Andrewsiana Torr. To 20 in.; lvs. 5–6, oblanceolate to broadly elliptic, 6–10 in. long, 4¾ in. wide; fls. deep rose-purple, ⅝ in. long, in a terminal umbel and often in one or more lateral umbels; fr. blue. Cent. and n. Calif.

borealis (Ait.) Raf. CORN LILY, BLUEBEAD L. To 1½ ft.; lvs. 2–5, oblong to elliptic or obovate, to 1 ft. long, glossy green, ciliolate; fls. greenish-yellow, nodding, ¾ in. long, in loose 3–8-fld. umbels, sometimes also in secondary umbels; fr. blue, rarely white. E. N. Amer.

udensis Trautv. & C. A. Mey. To 2 ft.; lvs. 3–4, oblong, to 1 ft. long; fls. white, ½ in. long, 3–4 and umbellate, or 5–8 and subumbellate; fr. blue, with 4–6 seeds in each cell. E. Siberia, Japan.

umbellulata (Michx.) Morong. SPECKLED WOOD LILY. To 1½ ft.; lvs. 2–5, oblong, oblanceolate, or obovate, to 1 ft. long, ciliolate; fls. white, spotted with green and purple, ³⁄₁₆ in. long, erect, in 5–30-fld. umbels; fr. black, each cell 2-seeded. N.J., w. N.Y., and e. Ohio, s. to Tenn. and Ga.

uniflora (Schult.) Kunth. BRIDE'S-BONNET, QUEENCUP. To 8 in.; lvs. 2–3, oblanceolate to obovate, to 6 in. long; fls. white, erect, 1 in. long, usually solitary; fr. blue, each cell 2–3-seeded. Mts., cent. Calif. to B.C.

CLISTANTHOCEREUS: *BORZICACTUS.* **C. samnensis:** a listed name of no botanical standing.

CLITORIA L. BUTTERFLY PEA, PIGEON-WINGS. *Leguminosae* (subfamily *Faboideae*). About 30 spp. of mostly tender per. herbs or shrubs, often climbing, native to warm regions of the world; lvs. alt., pinnate; fls. racemose or axillary, showy, papilionaceous, standard large, emarginate, wing petals adherent to the incurved keel, stamens 10, similar, united or 1 separate; fr. a linear, flat, dehiscent legume.

Mostly grown as ornamentals outdoors far south (Zone 10b) and under glass. Propagated by seeds or cuttings.

amazonum Mart. Nearly erect, or tall scandent shrub; lfts. 3, ovate, to 5 in. long, acuminate, pale beneath, petioles shorter; racemes short, few-fld.; standard to 3 in. long, white or pale rose, with darker lines; fr. to 6 in. long, ⅝ in. wide. N. Brazil. Zone 10b.

cajanifolia Benth. Herb, to 2 ft.; lfts. 3, oblong, retuse or emarginate, gray-pubescent beneath; fls. pale violet, to 1½ in. long; fr. to 2½ in. long. Tropics, where grown as a cover crop and for green manure.

mariana L. To 3 ft., often twining; lfts. 3, ovate to obovate; fls. lilac, 2 in. long; fr. to 2 in. long. Early summer. N.J., s. to Fla., Tex., Mex. Zone 6.

Ternatea L. Slender twiner; lfts. 5–7, ovate or oblong; fls. solitary, bright dark blue, with lighter markings, 2 in. long; fr. to 4½ in. long. Pantrop., probably native to Asia. Zone 10b. Double-fld. as well as white-fld. forms are known.

CLIVIA Lindl. [*Imantophyllum* Hook.]. KAFFIR LILY. *Amaryllidaceae.* A few spp. of S. Afr. herbs with fleshy roots, the expanded lf. bases forming bulblike parts in some spp.; lvs. narrow, evergreen; fls. in an umbel terminal on a solid scape, umbel subtended by several separate spathe valves, perianth reddish-yellow or scarlet, the tube short, stamens declinate, ovary inferior, cells 5–6-ovuled; fr. a red, pulpy berry, seeds globose.

Clivias are good greenhouse or house plants. Plants should be kept in the same pots for several years and given liquid manure. Water should be practically withheld during resting period. In the subtropics, they should be grown in the shade. Propagated by seeds or by division.

caulescens R. A. Dyer. Sts. to 12 or 18 in.; lvs. about 15, strap-shaped, 1–6 ft. long, 1–2 in. wide; umbel 15–20-fld.; fls. drooping, curved, to 1⅜ in. long, deep salmon, tipped with green and yellow.

× **cyrtanthiflora** (van Houtte) Wittm.: *C. miniata* × *C. nobilis*. Habit of *C. nobilis*, but lvs. larger, fls. fewer, pendulous, intermediate between parents in size, shape, and color.

grandiflora: a listed name referable to *C. miniata* cv.

hybrida: a listed name of uncertain application, perhaps *C.* ×*cyrtanthiflora*.

miniata Regel [*Imantophyllum miniatum* (Regel) Hook.]. Stemless; lvs. to 1½ ft. long and 2 in. wide, thick and glossy; umbel 12–20-fld.; fls. erect, scarlet, yellow inside, to 3 in. long; berries bright red, 1 in. long. Cvs. 'Grandiflora' and 'Lindenii' are listed.

nobilis Lindl. Stemless; lvs. 1–1½ ft. long, to 1½ in. wide; umbel 40–60-fld.; fls. drooping, curved, narrower and shorter than in *C. miniata*, red and yellow, tipped with green.

CLONE, CLON. A plant propagated by asexual or vegetative means, including divisions, buds, cuttings, layers, etc. Such methods are used especially with plants that do not "come true" from seeds. Horticultural cultivars of *Citrus*, *Dianthus*, *Fragaria*, *Malus*, and *Rosa* are clones, and also the cultivated forms of *Hemerocallis* and *Hosta* that do not produce seeds. Clone is a horticultural rather than taxonomic term.

CLUSIA L. *Guttiferae*. About 145 spp. of dioecious trees and shrubs, occasionally more or less epiphytic or stranglers, native to trop. and subtrop. Amer., brs. usually horizontal; lvs. leathery, without conspicuous lateral veins; fls. differing from those of *Calophyllum* and *Mammea* in having ovary many-ovuled, style absent or very short, and fr. an inedible fleshy caps.

rosea Jacq. BALSAM APPLE, CUPEY, COPEY, SCOTCH-ATTORNEY. Tree, 20–50 ft., growing on other trees and rocks; lvs. obovate, to 8 in. long, cuneate; fls. pink and white, to nearly 2 in. across; fr. greenish-white, globose, to 3 in. in diam. Subtrop. Fla., W. Indies, and s. Mex., s. to n. S. Amer. Zone 10. Resists salt spray. Seeds contain a sticky resin which is extracted and used as a birdlime or caulking for the seams of boats.

CLUSIACEAE: see *GUTTIFERAE*.

CLYTOSTOMA Miers ex Bur. *Bignoniaceae*. About 8 spp. of evergreen climbing shrubs, native to trop. S. Amer.; lvs. opp., simple, with 3 lfts., or with 2 lfts. and a terminal simple tendril; fls. in axillary or terminal pairs, or in panicles, calyx 5-toothed, corolla funnelform-campanulate, 2-lipped, stamens 4; fr. a broad prickly caps.

Clytostomas are grown under glass in the North and in the open in warm regions. They thrive in fertile soil. Propagated by cuttings.

binatum (Thunb.) Sandw. [*C. purpurea* (Lodd. ex Hook.f.) Rehd.; *Bignonia purpurea* Lodd. ex Hook.f.]. Lfts. 2, ovate to elliptic or oblong-lanceolate, to 3 in. long or more, usually entire, glabrous; fls. to 2¼ in. long and wide, corolla mauve with white throat. Venezuela, Guiana, Brazil, Paraguay.

callistegioides (Cham.) Bur. [*Bignonia callistegioides* Cham.; *B. speciosa* R. C. Grah.; *B. violacea* Hort., not DC.]. ARGENTINE TRUMPET VINE, LOVE-CHARM. Lfts. 1 or 2, elliptic-oblong, to 4 in. long, undulate, glabrous; fls. to 3 in. long and wide, corolla lavender and streaked violet. S. Brazil, Argentina.

purpurea: *C. binatum*.

CNEORACEAE Link. Dicot.; 1 genus, *Cneorum*, of small shrubs, native to the Canary Is. and Medit. region; lvs. simple;

fls. bisexual, regular, solitary or cymose, sepals, petals, and stamens 3–4, pistil 1, ovary superior, 3–4-celled; fr. drupaceous, of 1–4 separable segms.

CNEORIDIUM Hook.f. *Rutaceae*. One sp., an evergreen shrub, native on hills of s. Calif.; lvs. opp. or in clusters, simple, glandular-dotted; fls. white, in axillary clusters, calyx 4-lobed, petals 4, stamens 8; fr. drupelike, globose, 1-celled.

dumosum (Nutt.) Hook.f. BUSH RUE. Stiffly twiggy shrub, to 6 ft.; lvs. linear to oblong, to 1 in. long, glabrous, entire; fr. drying red-brown, about ¼ in. in diam. Adapted to cult. where native.

CNEORUM L. *Cneoraceae*. Three spp. of shrubs of the Canary Is. and Medit. region; lvs. alt., leathery, entire; fls. yellow, 3–4-merous, solitary or cymose; fr. drupaceous, of 1–4 separable segms.

Cultivated in mild climates.

tricoccon L. SPURGE OLIVE. Glabrous shrub, to 4 ft.; lvs. oblong, to 2 in. long, glossy; fls. deep yellow; fr. red-brown. S. Eur. Zone 9.

CNICUS L. BLESSED THISTLE. *Compositae* (Carduus Tribe). One sp., a branching, thistlelike ann. herb of the Medit. region and Near East, sparingly naturalized in the U.S.; fl. heads terminal on brs., subtended by spiny, leafy bracts, involucral bracts with pinnately divided spiny appendages; fls. all tubular; achenes ribbed, glabrous, pappus of a toothed crown and 2 rows of bristles, the inner ones shorter.

Easily grown from seeds.

benedictus L. [*Carduus benedictus* (L.) Steud.]. To 2 ft., thinly hairy; lvs. oblong, pinnately spiny-lobed, veiny; heads about 1 in. across; fls. yellow.

CNIDOSCOLUS Pohl [*Bivonea* Raf.; *Jussieuia* Houst.]. TREAD-SOFTLY, SPURGE NETTLE. *Euphorbiaceae*. About 75 spp. of monoecious or rarely dioecious per. herbs, shrubs, or small trees, native to N. and S. Amer., with milky juice; lvs. alt., petioled, entire, lobed, toothed, or divided, mostly stinging-bristly; fls. in cymes, calyx showy, white, without petals; fr. an ovoid caps., separating into 2-valved carpels. Distinguished from *Jatropha* by pubescence, lack of petals, calyx always white, and repeatedly forked stigmas.

Chayamansa McVaugh [*Jatropha urens* var. *inermis* Calvino]. Succulent, nearly glabrous shrub, to about 7 ft., with few stinging hairs; lvs. broader than long, 3-lobed to below the middle, lateral lobes often divided about ⅓ their length, petioles fleshy, much shorter than the blades; fls. white, small, glabrous. Mex. to Brazil.

stimulosus: see *C. texanus*.

texanus (Müll. Arg.) Small [*Jatropha texana* Müll. Arg.]. To 2 ft., copiously armed with stiff yellowish hairs; lvs. to 6 in. wide, deeply divided into 3–5 toothed or cut lobes, petioles as long as or longer than the blades; fls. on peduncles to 5 in. long, white, small, male calyces bristly. Ark. to Tex. *C. stimulosus* (Michx.) A. Gray, a closely related sp., not known to be in cult., has stinging hairs and calyces of male fls. mostly glabrous at maturity. Va. to Fla., e. to Tex. and Okla.

urens (L.) Arth. [*Jatropha urens* L.]. SPURGE NETTLE, TREAD-SOFTLY. From 3–15 ft., with stinging hairs; lvs. to 7 in. across, 3–5-lobed, toothed or entire, petioles as long as or longer than the blades; fls. white, peduncles to 2 in. long, calyces hairy. Fls. and frs. produced throughout the year. Lesser Antilles and s. Mex., s. to Argentina.

COBAEA Cav. *Polemoniaceae*. About 10 spp. of shrubby climbers, native to trop. Amer.; lvs. alt., pinnate, terminating in a branched tendril; fls. violet to bright green, solitary, axillary, calyx 5-parted, leaflike, corolla campanulate, 5-lobed, stamens 5, exserted; fr. a caps., seeds winged.

Grown under glass and in the open; treated as annuals in northern gardens. Propagated by seeds.

scandens Cav. MEXICAN IVY, MONASTERY-BELLS, CUP-AND-SAUCER VINE. Glabrous climber, to 25 ft.; lfts. 4–6, elliptic or oblong, to 4 in. long; fls. on peduncles to 10 in. long, violet or greenish-purple, to 2 in. long and 1½ in. across. Autumn. Mex. Cv. 'Alba'. Fls. white.

COBURGIA: *AMARYLLIS*. *C. rosea*: *A. Belladonna*.

COCCINEA Wight & Arn. *Cucurbitaceae*. About 30 spp. of tendril-bearing, mostly dioecious per. vines from trop. Asia and Afr.; lvs. angled or lobed; fls. with corolla campanulate, male fls. solitary or racemose, stamens 3, filaments united, anthers flexuous, female fls. solitary, ovary with 3 parietal placentas; fr. somewhat berrylike, small, roundish to oblong, indehiscent, seeds many, horizontal.

cordifolia: see *C. grandis.*

grandis (L.) Voigt [*C. cordifolia* of auth., not (L.) Cogn.; *C. indica* Wight & Arn.]. IVY GOURD, SCARLET-FRUITED G. Climbing or prostrate, to 6 ft. or more, glabrous, root per.; lvs. broadly triangular-ovate, angled, 2–4 in. across; fls. solitary, corolla white, about 1½ in. long, with sharp lobes; fr. ovoid or oblong, smooth, scarlet. Asia and Afr.; naturalized in trop. Amer. Grown as an ornamental or arbor vine. Shoots and fr. eaten in the Old World.

indica: *C. grandis.*

COCCOCYPSELUM P. Br. *Rubiaceae.* About 20 spp. of prostrate pubescent herbs, native to trop. Amer.; lvs. opp., stipules interpetiolar; fls. small, white, purplish or blue, 4-merous; fr. an ovoid, blue berry, seeds many.

guianense (Aubl.) K. Schum. Ann., sts. slender, decumbent, rooting at nodes; lvs. ovate, to 2½ in. long, hairy; fls. purplish, small; fr. a blue berry, about ¾ in. long. Fla., W. Indies, Trinidad, n. S. Amer. Suitable as a ground cover or as a hanging-basket plant.

COCCOLOBA P. Br. *Polygonaceae.* About 150 spp. of trees, shrubs, and vines, native to trop. and subtrop. Amer.; lvs. alt., entire, often very large, evergreen or deciduous; fls. unisexual, in racemes, spikes, or panicles, in which the male are in clusters, the female solitary at nodes, sepals 5, greenish-white, stamens 7–8, ovary 1-celled or incompletely 3-celled; fr. an achene, ridged, surrounded by fleshy calyx.

Grown outdoors in warm and frostless climates and under glass northward. They do best in rich sandy soil. Propagated by seeds, cuttings of ripe wood, and layering.

diversifolia Jacq. [*C. floridana* Meissn.; *C. laurifolia* Lindau, not Jacq.]. PIGEON PLUM, SNAILSEED. Small tree; lvs. oblong, 2–4 in. long, entire; racemes short; fr. pear-shaped, about ⁵⁄₁₆ in. long, edible. S. Fla. and the Carribean.

floridana: *C. diversifolia.*

grandifolia: *C. pubescens.*

laurifolia: *C. diversifolia.*

pubescens L. [*C. grandifolia* Jacq.]. Tree, to 80 ft.; lvs. orbicular, to 3 ft. across, with prominent veins, rusty-pubescent beneath; fls. greenish, in erect terminal racemes to 2 ft. long. Grown in its juvenile stage as a pot plant for the large ornamental lvs.

Uvifera (L.) L. SEA GRAPE, KINO, PLATTERLEAF. Tree, to 20 ft. or more; lvs. orbicular, to 8 in. across, cordate, leathery, glossy, veined red; fls. white, in dense racemes to 10 in. long; fr. purple, resembling bunches of grapes. S. Fla., s. to S. Amer. A characteristic tree of the ocean beach margin; fr. used for jelly.

COCCOTHRINAX Sarg. FAN PALM, SILVER P. *Palmae.* Over 30 spp. of small or slender, solitary, unarmed palms with bisexual fls., from s. Fla. through W. Indies and Mex. to Brit. Honduras; lvs. palmate, sheath fibrous, not splitting at base of petiole, sometimes with long free fibers or with stout marginal spinelike processes; infl. mostly shorter than lvs., with several tubular bracts at base and 1 sheathing each primary br., brs. again branched into slender rachillae bearing solitary, sessile or pedicelled fls. in spiral arrangement; fls. small, whitish, or yellowish, perianth 5–7-lobed, stamens 6–12 or perhaps more, carpel 1-celled, 1-ovuled; fr. usually purplish or black, fleshy, seed deeply and irregularly sulcate, endosperm homogeneous.

The leaves of many of the species are used where native for hats and basketry. Slow-growing, sun-loving palms, adapted to growth in open sites in Zone 10. For culture see *Palms.*

acuminata: *C. Miraguama.*

alta (O. F. Cook) Becc. To 30 ft.; lvs. large, deeply divided into about 40 segms., blade silver beneath; infl. with 3–4 brs.; fls. with stamens 12; fr. globose, ¼ in. in diam., briefly pedicelled. Puerto Rico. Planted in s. Fla., where it has been called *Thrinax altissima* and may also appear under the names *Thrinax radiata* or *Coccothrinax radiata.*

anomala: *Zombia antillarum.*

argentata (Jacq.) L. H. Bailey [*C. Garberi* (Chapm.) Sarg.]. SILVER P., FLORIDA S.P. To 20 ft., but often fruiting when nearly trunkless; lvs. small, very deeply divided into 15–20 segms., silvery beneath;

stamens 9–12; fr. ⅜–⅝ in. in diam., short-pedicelled, black. S. Fla. to Bahama Is. Hats and baskets are made from the lvs.

argentea (Lodd. ex Schult. & Schult.f.) Sarg. ex Becc. [*Thrinax argentea* Lodd. ex Schult. & Schult.f.]. SILVER THATCH, BROOM PALM. To 30 ft. or more; lvs. silvery beneath, divided into about 60 segms.; stamens 7–9; fr. to ⅜ in. diam., blackish-purple, sessile. Hispaniola. Material cult. under this name is usually misidentified.

barbadensis (Lodd.) Becc. A name for a sp. described from foliage only and not identified precisely, but the name is used for *C. Dussiana* and perhaps other spp. in cult.

crinita Becc. THATCH PALM. To 30 ft. or more, trunk 8 in. in diam., covered with very long hairlike fibers, at length becoming smooth basally; lvs. divided about to the middle into about 52 segms., to 3 ft. long; infl. to 6 ft. long; stamens 12; fr. pedicelled, to ¾ in. in diam., whitish maturing pink. Cuba. Very slow-growing.

Dussiana L. H. Bailey. To 50 ft.; lvs. large, green above, silvery beneath, divided ⅔ to the base into slender-tipped segms.; infl. with 4–5 primary brs.; fls. pedicelled, stamens 9–12; fr. ⅜ in. in diam. Guadaloupe (Fr. W. Indies). Sometimes grown under the name *C. barbadensis.*

Eggersiana Becc. To about 15 ft.; lvs. large, with many stiff segms., green above, pale beneath, to 28 in. long; infl. large, rachillae glabrous, to about 3 in. long; fls. sessile on short tubercles, stamens 9. Virgin Is.

fragrans Burret. To 20 ft. or more; lvs. green above, pale below, divided ⅔ to the base into about 50 segms. with acuminate tips; infl. with 4–5 primary brs.; fls. pedicelled, fragrant, stamens 12. E. Cuba, Haiti.

Garberi: *C. argentata.*

Martii Becc. Trunk of moderate size; lvs. rigid, sheath fibrous, blade deeply divided into about 30 segms., to 30 in. long, 1¼ in. wide, silvery beneath; fls. with stamens 12; fr. blackish, ⁵⁄₁₆ in. in diam., on short pedicels less than ⅛ in. long. Cuba.

Miraguama (HBK) Becc. [*C. acuminata* Sarg. ex Becc.]. To 15 ft. or more, trunk 4 in. in diam.; lvs. stiff, sheath fibrous, petiole slender, blade orbicular, more or less silvery beneath, segms. 42–48, to 26 in. long; infl. to 28 in. long; fls. on pedicels to ¼ in. long, stamens 6–9; fr. globose, about ⁵⁄₁₆ in. in diam. Cuba.

radiata: *Thrinax radiata;* but the name is sometimes applied to plants representing *C. alta* in cult.

spissa L. H. Bailey. Trunk thick and often swollen, to 24 ft., 1 ft. in diam.; lvs. green above, gray beneath, to 30 in. long, divided ⅔ to the base into 40 or more narrow segms. with deeply forked, pendulous tips; infl. short, rachillae to 4 in. long; fls. short-pedicelled, stamens 6; fr. about ½ in. in diam. Hispaniola.

COCCULUS DC. *Menispermaceae.* Eleven spp. of dioecious, twining or rarely erect shrubs of wide distribution, primarily trop.; lvs. alt., entire or lobed; infl. a raceme or panicle; fls. small, inconspicuous, unisexual, sepals and petals 6, male fls. with 6–9 stamens, female fls. with 6 or 0 staminodes and 3–6 separate ovaries; fr. drupaceous, to ⅜ in. long.

Easily cultivated in moist soil. Propagated by seeds or cuttings of half-ripened wood under glass.

carolinus (L.) DC. CAROLINA MOONSEED, RED M., RED-BERRIED M., CORAL-BEADS, SNAILSEED. Twining, to 12 ft.; lvs. ovate, to 4 in. long, entire or 3–5-lobed, pubescent beneath; panicles to 5 in. long; fr. showy, red, ¼ in. in diam., in dense clusters. Se. U.S. Zone 7.

laurifolius (Roxb.) DC. Evergreen shrub, to 15 ft., glabrous, erect; lvs. oblong, to 6 in. long, with 3 prominent veins from base, leathery and shining; panicles to 2 in. long; fls. small, yellow; fr. black. S. Japan to Himalayas. Zone 9. Bark yields alkaloids.

trilobus (Thunb.) DC. Deciduous, scandent shrub, more or less pubescent; lvs. ovate to broadly ovate, sometimes hastate or shallowly 3-lobed, to 5 in. long and 4 in. wide; fls. small, yellow-white; fr. about ¼ in. in diam., black, glaucous. Temp. and trop. e. Asia. Zone 8.

COCHEMIEA (K. Brandeg.) Walton. *Cactaceae.* Five spp. of low, tubercled cacti, native to Baja Calif.; sts. cespitose, cylindrical, with watery sap; areoles on ungrooved tubercles, axils of tubercles bearing wool and sometimes bristles; fls. axillary, red, tubular, often somewhat oblique, perianth segms. red, petaloid, spreading or recurved, stamens and style red, exserted, stigma lobes erect, ovary naked; fr. red, naked, seeds black, reticulate.

For culture see *Cacti.*

Halei (Brandeg.) Walton. Sts. to 2 ft. high and 3 in. thick, densely spiny; spines straight, white, becoming dark gray, radial spines 10–20,

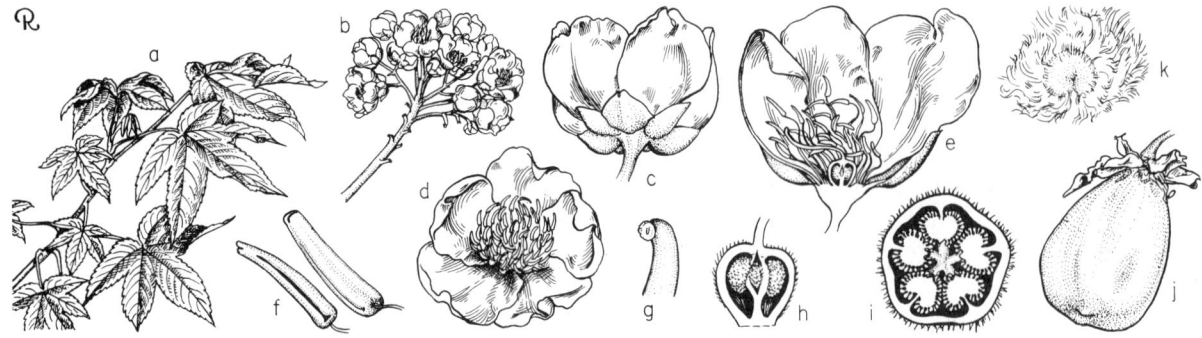

COCHLOSPERMACEAE. *Cochlospermum vitifolium:* **a,** leafy branch, × ⅛; **b,** inflorescence, × ¹⁄₁₂; **c,** flower, exterior, × ⅓; **d,** flower, face view, × ⅓; **e,** flower, vertical section, × ½; **f,** anthers, two views, × 4; **g,** apex of style and stigma, × 5; **h,** ovary, vertical section, × 1½; **i,** ovary, cross section, × 3; **j,** fruit, × ¼; **k,** seed, × 1½.

to ½ in. long, central spines 3–4, to 1 in. long; fls. to 2 in. long; fr. clavate, to ¾ in. long. Magdalena and Santa Margarita Is.

maritima G. Lindsay. Sts. to 20 in. high and 3 in. thick; spines reddish-brown, radial spines 10–15, to ½ in. long, central spines 4, the lower to 2 in. long, hooked; fls. 1¼ in. long; fr. globose. Cent. Baja Calif.

Pondii (Greene) Walton. Sts. to 16 in. high and 2½ in. thick, densely spiny, axils of tubercles bristly; spines brownish, radial spines 15–24, central spines 8–11, 1–3 of these hooked and to 1½ in. long; fls. 2 in. long; fr. obovoid, to 1 in. long. Cedros and Natividad Is.

Poselgeri (Hildm.) Britt. & Rose. Sts. trailing, to 6 ft. long and 1¾ in. thick, tubercles remote; spines brown, radial spines 7–9, to ½ in. long, central spine 1, hooked, to 1 in. long; fls. 1¼ in. long; fr. pear-shaped, ⁵⁄₁₆ in. long. S. Baja Calif.

setispina (Engelm. ex J. Coult.) Walton. Sts. to 2 ft. high and 4 in. thick, densely spiny; spines slender and flexuous, white with brown tips, radial spines 10–12, to 1½ in. long, central spines 1–4, to 2 in. long, the lower hooked; fls. to 3 in. long; fr. obovoid, 1 in. long. Cent. Baja Calif.

COCHLEANTHES Raf. *Orchidaceae.* About 15 spp. of epiphytic orchids, native to trop. Amer.; sts. short, not pseudobulbous, completely covered by imbricating lf. sheaths; lvs. 2-ranked, forming an open fan, fleshy; infl. lateral, 1-fld.; fls. large, sepals and petals spreading, lip simple or lobed, often concave, with ridged callus at base, column fleshy, cylindrical, pollinia 4. For structure of fl. see *Orchidaceae.*

For culture see *Orchids.*

aromatica (Rchb.f.) R. E. Schult. & Garay [*Chondrorhyncha aromatica* (Rchb.f.) P. Allen; *Warscewiczella aromatica* Rchb.f.; *W. Wendlandii* (Rchb.f.) Schlechter; *Zygopetalum Wendlandii* Rchb.f.]. Lvs. linear-strap-shaped to elliptic-lanceolate, to 12 in. long; scape to 4 in. high; sepals and petals spreading, pale green or yellowish-green, to 1 in. long, lip flattened out but reflexed at apex, disc lavender, with a many-grooved, violet-blue callus. Costa Rica, Panama.

discolor (Lindl.) R. E. Schult. & Garay [*Chondrorhyncha discolor* (Lindl.) P. Allen; *Warrea discolor* Lindl.; *Warscewiczella discolor* (Lindl.) Rchb.f.; *Zygopetalum discolor* (Lindl.) Rchb.f.]. Similar vegetatively to *C. aromatica;* scape to 6 in. high; sepals and petals spreading, white, yellowish toward apex, lip hooded, deep violet-purple, often with whitish margins, the base enveloping the column, disc with a many-grooved callus. Costa Rica, Panama.

COCHLEARIA L. SCURVY GRASS. *Cruciferae.* About 25 spp. of ann. to per. herbs in the N. Hemisphere, glabrous or sparsely hairy; lvs. simple; fls. racemose, sepals 4, petals 4, short-clawed, filaments straight; fr. a laterally compressed silicle with convex valves.

One species, a sometime medicinal plant, has been grown as a salad plant but the tarry flavor is unappetizing to most people. For salad, it is grown as an annual, the leaves being ready 2–3 months after sowing; successive sowings may be made. Thrives in a cool location, or a partly shaded one.

Armoracia: *Armoracia rusticana.*

officinalis L. SCURVY GRASS, SPOONWORT. Bien. or grown as an ann., about 12 in. when in fl.; early basal lvs. cordate or reniform; fls. small, white; silicles globose to ovoid-ellipsoid, to ¼ long. Spring. Eur.

saxatilis: *Kernera saxatilis.*

COCHLIODA Lindl. *Orchidaceae.* Four spp. of epiphytes, native to the Andes of S. Amer.; pseudobulbs well developed; infl. a lateral, many-fld. raceme; sepals and petals similar, spreading, rose or scarlet, lip recurved, lobed, column with 2 separate stigmas. For structure of fl. see *Orchidaceae.*

Culture as for *Odontoglossum;* see also *Orchids.*

densiflora Lindl. [*C. Noezliana* Rolfe]. Pseudobulbs to 2 in. long; lvs. linear-oblong; fls. orange-scarlet or rose-red, about 1¼ in. across, lip 3-lobed, midlobe with yellow disc. Peru, Bolivia.

Noezliana: *C. densiflora.*

COCHLIOSTEMA Lem. *Commelinaceae.* Two spp. of epiphytic herbs of trop. Amer.; lvs. large, in a bromeliadlike rosette; fls. in axillary, spreading to pendulous, bracted thyrses of unpaired cincinni, sepals 3, petals 3, separate, the lower one longer and narrower than the upper 2, fertile stamens 3, filaments united in a stalked hood enclosing 3 spirally twisted anthers, staminodes 2, lateral, villous, ovary 3-celled, ovules many; fr. a caps.

Grown in the greenhouse. Culture as for bromeliads and orchids (see *Bromeliaceae, Orchids*).

Jacobianum: *C. odoratissimum.*

odoratissimum Lem. [*C. Jacobianum* C. Koch & Linden]. Lvs. many, to 4 ft. long, 6 in. wide, green, narrowly margined with purple; infl. to 1 ft. long, bracts whitish, opp. or whorled, as long as the whitish peduncles, cincinni 5–8-fld.; sepals lilac, 1 in. long, petals longer, blue-violet, fringed, stamen-hood blue-violet, filaments tufted with yellow hairs, staminodes violet-bearded. Wet lowland forests, Costa Rica to Bolivia.

COCHLOSPERMACEAE Planch. COCHLOSPERMUM FAMILY. Dicot.; 2 or 3 genera of herbs and woody plants, native mostly to trop. regions, separated from the Bixaceae by the lobed or divided lvs. and characters of the endosperm. *Amoreuxia* and *Cochlospermum* are cult.

COCHLOSPERMUM Kunth [*Maximilianea* Mart. & Schrank]. *Cochlospermaceae.* About 15 spp. of trop. mostly xerophytic trees or shrubs; lvs. palmately lobed or divided; fls. in racemes or panicles, appearing at end of dry season before lvs.; stamens many, all of same length, ovary 1-celled except at base; fr. a caps., seeds covered with floss.

Two species widely grown in the tropics and introduced in southern Calif. and Fla. (Zone 10b) for their large attractive yellow flowers.

Gossypium: *C. religiosum.*

religiosum (L.) Alston [*C. Gossypium* (L.) DC.]. SILK-COTTON TREE. Small tree, to 18 ft., soft-wooded; lvs. alt., deeply 3–5-lobed, to 8 in. across, green and glabrous above, gray-tomentose beneath; fls. bright yellow, stamens many; caps. to 3 in. in diam. Burma, India, where important as a source of an important gum, used industrially as a substitute for gum tragacanth.

vitifolium (Willd.) K. Spreng. To 40 ft.; lvs. alt., deeply 5-, rarely 3- or 7-lobed, to 1 ft. across, the lobes toothed, green above and beneath, with sparse hairs on the veins beneath or glabrous; fls. in terminal clusters, bright yellow, 4 in. across or more; caps. to 3 in. long, velvety-pubescent. Mex., cent. Amer., n. S. Amer.

COCONUT. The coconut is the fruit of *Cocos nucifera*, a widespread tropical palm and one of the world's most economically important trees. The products of the coconut tree are mainly four: toddy or beverage derived from the sap, which is obtained by incising the flower clusters and which may also be a source of sugar; coir, the fiber from the husk of the nut, much used in cordage and in the making of brushes and mats and otherwise; copra, the dried meat of the nut, employed in the making of coconut oil, the most widely used industrially of all edible fatty oils; and the mature edible nut itself.

Coconuts thrive in the lowland tropics, usually but not necessarily on the seacoast. They grow well in Hawaii and in southern Florida (Zone 10b), where they are now spontaneous on some of the Keys. In this country, the nuts are used less as an article of commerce than for propagating purposes; in both Florida and Hawaii they are planted for ornament and home use. The tree is grown only from seeds, the whole fruit ordinarily being planted in a shaded seed bed, with the husk not completely covered, and preferably once or more transplanted before being set in a permanent place. When only a few trees are desired, the fruit may be planted where the plant is to grow if quick effects are not desired. For fruit bearing, the trees are planted when perhaps three or four years old. About 25 feet apart each way is a good spacing for a commercial grove. Ordinarily coconuts receive little attention in tillage or fertilizing but they respond to good treatment as well as do other plants. Fruits may be borne in four or five years. A good tree on fertile ground should yield 75 or more nuts a year, when fully mature, but the average is probably not more than one-third of this number. There are many cultivars of coconuts in the tropics, some of which have proved highly susceptible to lethal yellowing disease; 'Golden Malay Dwarf' appears to be resistant. In growing any cultivar, the grower should choose nuts from trees producing abundantly of choice fruits if he expects the best product.

COCOS L. *Palmae*. One sp., a solitary, unarmed, monoecious palm thought to be of Old World Origin but widely cult. in tropics of both hemispheres; lvs. pinnate, sheath fibrous, open, petiole not toothed marginally, rounded below, channelled above, pinnae many, 1-ribbed, regularly arranged, stiff, acute; infl. among the lvs., simply branched or rarely spicate, bracts 2, the lower 2-edged, open apically, the upper woody, fusiform in bud, splitting abaxially, beaked, striate but not deeply sulcate, rachillae with fls. in one or a few triads (2 male and 1 female) at the base and above these with paired or solitary male fls.; male fls. fragrant, sepals 3, imbricate, acute, petals 3, valvate, much wider than thick, angled, much longer than sepals, stamens 6, pistillode small, 3-cleft, female fls. much larger than male, sepals and petals 3, imbricate, staminodes united in a low ring, pistil 3-celled, 3-ovuled; fr. large, normally 1-seeded, mesocarp (husk) fibrous, endocarp thick, bony, with 3 pores near the base, seed adherent to the endocarp, endosperm homogeneous, hollow, embryo near the base.

australis: *Arecastrum Romanzoffianum* var. *australe,* but material cult. as *C. australis* is usually *Butia capitata.*

Bonnetii: *Butia Bonnetii.*

campestris: *Syagrus campestris,* but material cult. as *C. campestris* is probably *Butia capitata.*

Datil: *Arecastrum Romanzoffianum* var. *australe.*

eriospatha: *Butia eriospatha.*

flexuosa: *Syagrus flexuosa,* but material cult. as *C. flexuosa* is probably *Arecastrum Romanzoffianum* var. *australe.*

Nehrlingiana: *Butia capitata* var. *Nehrlingiana.*

nucifera L. COCONUT, COCONUT PALM. Trunk to 80 ft., usually somewhat curved from a thickened base; lvs. to 20 ft. long, pinnae to 3 ft. long; infl. more than 3 ft. long; male fls. to 5/16 in. long, female fls. about 1 in. across; fr. to 1 ft. long. Origin not certain, but probably trop. Melanesia, widely planted in lowland tropics mainly close to sea coasts. Zone 10b in s. Fla. One of the most valuable plants of the tropics, the coconut is the world's chief source of vegetable fat, ob-

tained from oil expressed from the dried endosperm. It also provides fiber (coir) from the husk of the fr., sugar, and alcohol from the sap of the tapped infl., and the endosperm and "milk" which fills the cavity are used fresh or in cooking. Trees are usually grown commercially in plantations but are also widely used as ornamentals. See also *Coconut.*

plumosa: *Arecastrum Romanzoffianum.*

Romanzoffiana: *Arecastrum Romanzoffianum.*

Weddelleiana: *Microcoelum Weddellianum.*

Yatay: *Butia Yatay.*

CODIAEUM A. Juss. [*Phyllaurea* Lour.]. VARIEGATED LAUREL, CROTON (of florists; not to be confused with the genus *Croton*). *Euphorbiaceae.* Six spp. of monoecious trees and shrubs, native to Malay Pen. and Pacific Is.; lvs. alt., simple, rarely lobed, leathery, glabrous, petioled; fls. small, in axillary racemes, ovary 3-celled; fr. a caps. Cult. material belongs to one very variable sp., *C. variegatum.* Other names in the trade or hort. literature ought to be considered cvs. of this and are listed as such below.

Extensively grown in the tropics, far south, and under glass for the colored ornamental foliage. Any good soil is suitable for crotons. They develop better coloring if planted in sunny locations. Propagated by seeds, but named cultivars should be increased by cuttings of half-ripened wood over bottom heat. Separate plants may be produced from large branches by air layering.

variegatum (L.) Blume var. **pictum** (Lodd.) Müll. Arg. [*Croton pictum* Lodd.]. GARDEN CROTON. Shrub to 6 ft. or more; lvs. linear to ovate-lanceolate, entire or lobed, sometimes cut almost to the midrib, variously variegated with white, yellow, or red; fls. white. Many cvs. are offered: **'Andreanum'**, lvs. broad, yellow; **'Angustissimum'**, lvs. narrow, with yellow margins and ribs; **'Anietumense'**, lvs. narrow; **'Aucubifolium'**, lvs. broad, yellow, red- blotched; **'Aureo-maculatum'**, lvs. green, spotted yellow; **'Bogoriense'**, lvs. oblong, truncate, variegated yellow; **'Bruxelense'**, lvs. broad; **'Craigii'**, lvs. 3-lobed; **'Delicatissimum'**, lvs. narrow; **'Edmontonense'**, lvs. narrow, bright-colored; **'Gloriosum'**, lvs. linear, with practically no red coloration; **'Graciosum'**, lvs. linear; **'Grusonii'**, lvs. narrow, with light midrib; **'Interruptum'**, lvs. yellow, with red midrib, sometimes twisted; **'Linearis Nigrescens'**, lvs. dark, linear; **'Montefontainense'**, lvs. 3-lobed; **'Punctatum'**, a listed name; **'Punctatum Aureum'**, lvs. narrow; **'Reidii'**, lvs. yellow, variegated with red; **'Sanderi'**, lvs. broad, irregularly blotched; **'Schattii'**, lvs. broad; **'Spirale'**, lvs spirally twisted, red and green; **'Warrenii,'** lvs. yellow, variegated with red; **'Weismannii,'** lvs. narrow, wavy-margined, variegated with yellow, petiole red.

CODONANTHE (Mart.) Hanst. *Gesneriaceae.* About 15 spp. of epiphytic subshrubs or vines in trop. Amer., usually associated with aerial ant nests; lvs. opp., those of a pair equal or rarely unequal, usually somewhat fleshy, glossy, frequently with red nectar-secreting glands on lower surface; fls. 1 or more in succession in lf. axils or on short axillary peduncles, calyx deeply 5-lobed, rarely 2-lipped, sometimes with red glands in sinuses, corolla tubular, oblique in the calyx, spurred at the base, waxy, stamens 4, filaments united to one another and to corolla basally, anthers broader than long, coherent in pairs, dehiscing by irregular or rounded pores, disc a solitary gland at back of ovary, ovary superior; fr. a caps., 2-valved, fleshy, tardily dehiscent, often berrylike.

For cultivation see *Gesneriaceae.*

crassifolia (Focke) C. V. Mort. Sts. creeping and rooting at nodes; lvs. ovate-elliptic to elliptic, to 2 in. long, 7/8 in. wide, entire, fleshy, glabrous, with red glands beneath, midnerve evident only underneath; fls. 1–3, axillary, calyx lobes linear-lanceolate, to 3/16 in. long, puberulous, the lower 3 with red glands at base of sinuses, corolla white or the limb sometimes pinkish, tube about 1/2 in. long, rounded basally, gradually expanding to a throat 3/16 in. wide, lobes to 3/16 in. long, filaments and style glabrous; fr. ovoid-subglobose, to 5/16 in. long, red. Cent. Amer. to Venezuela and Peru. *C. macradenia* has been grown under this name.

macradenia J. D. Sm. Sts. creeping and rooting at nodes; lvs. elliptic, to 1¼ in. long, ¾ in. wide, obscurely toothed above middle, fleshy, with red glands underneath, midnerve evident only underneath; fls. 1 or several, calyx lobes linear-lanceolate, to ¼ in. long, corolla very narrow above the base, then compressed and arcuately expanded on upper side, flattish with 2 grooves and a central ridge on lower side, white, spotted with red on lower surface inside, lobes to 3/16 in. long, filaments and style prominently hairy; fr. ovoid, ½ in. long, red. Cent. Amer.

purpurea: a listed name of no botanical standing.

CODONOPSIS Wallich. BONNET BELLFLOWER. *Campanulaceae.* About 32 or more spp. of per. or sometimes ann. herbs, native to cent. and e. Asia, mostly with tuberous roots and usually low to twining in habit, herbage often strong-smelling when crushed; lvs. alt. to opp., simple, mostly ovate; fls. generally solitary, often on elongate, naked peduncles, calyx 5-lobed, the lobes sometimes leaflike, corolla rotate to campanulate or tubular, 5-lobed, yellowish-green to pale blue, usually darker veined or spotted, especially within, stamens 5, separate, filaments dilated at base, ovary inferior or partially so, 3–5-celled; fr. a dry or sometimes fleshy caps., beaked and dehiscent at the apex.

Most species of *Codonopsis* require winter protection in the North and should be provided with good drainage, doing best in fairly acid, sandy loam. Propagated by seeds and otherwise cultivated as for *Campanula.*

affinis Hook.f. & T. Thoms. Sts. twining; lvs. oblong-ovate, 2–4 in. long, deeply cordate, nearly entire, villous beneath; fls. solitary or few on lateral branchlets, calyx lobes awl-shaped, to ⅜ in. long, corolla greenish with purple markings, campanulate, to ¾ in. across; fr. about ½ in. across. E. Himalayas, Sikkim.

assuriensis: a listed name of no botanical standing; probably referring to *C. ussuriensis.*

cardiophylla Diels ex. Kom. Erect per., to 1½ ft., leafy-stemmed, moderately pilose; lvs. thickish, ovate to oblong-ovate, to 1½ in. long, margins revolute and sometimes whitish; fls. solitary or in few-fld. racemes, calyx lobes oblong-ovate, to ½ in. long, corolla white or flushed blue, spotted purple inside, broadly campanulate, to 1 in. long. Cent. China to Tibet.

clematidea (Schrenk ex Fisch. & C. A. Meyer) C. B. Clarke. Erect, but eventually sprawling and tending to twine; lvs. lanceolate-ovate to ovate, to about 1 in. long, cordate, entire, pubescent; fls. mostly nodding, solitary and terminal or few in the upper lf. axils, calyx lobes oblong-ovate, spreading or reflexed, about ½ as long as the corolla, not ciliate or ciliate only at apex, corolla pale blue with darker veins, with two rings of purple inside, broadly campanulate, to 1 in. long; fr. about ½ in. across. Cent. w. Asia.

convolvulacea Kurz [*C. vinciflora* Kom.]. Glabrous per., sts. to 8 ft. long, slender, little-branched, creeping or twining; lvs. linear-lanceolate to ovate, to 3 in. long, entire or coarsely toothed; fls. solitary, on elongate, twining peduncles, calyx lobes ovate, to ¾ in. long, corolla violet-blue, rotate, lobed to near the base, 1–2 in. across. Himalayas, w. China.

cordifolia Kom. Sts. slender, branched, twining, glabrous; lvs. ovate, to 3 in. long, acuminate, deeply cordate; fls. solitary, on short, axillary peduncles, calyx lobes spreading, oblong-lanceolate, to ½ in. long, corolla greenish-yellow, faintly marked purplish, campanulate, to 1 in. long. Yunnan (China).

Handeliana Nannf. Stems clambering or twining, to 3 ft. or more, puberulent; lvs. ovate to triangular-ovate, cordate at base, crenulate; fls. on naked peduncles, calyx lobes triangular-ovate, entire, corolla greenish-yellow, flushed purplish, broadly campanulate, about ¾ in. long. Yunnan (China).

lanceolata (Siebold & Zucc.) Trautv. Sts. twining, glabrous; lvs. crowded or nearly whorled at ends of short lateral brs., lanceolate to ovate-elliptic, to 3 in. long, narrowed at the apex and base, entire or nearly so; calyx lobes leaflike, to 1 in. long, corolla light blue or lilac, with violet lines or spots inside, campanulate, to 1½ in. long; fr. to 1 in. across, seeds winged on 1 side. China, Japan.

meleagris Diels. Sts. erect, scapose, to 2 ft.; lvs. crowded at the base, sessile or nearly so, elliptic or oblong, to 3 in. long, mostly cuneate, sinuate to coarsely crenate; fls. nodding, solitary or few on nearly naked peduncles, calyx lobes about ¼ in. long, corolla cream to bluish, with a network of chocolate-colored veins outside, and purple-violet, sometimes spotted yellow inside, broadly campanulate, to 1⅜ in. long. Yunnan (China).

mollis Chipp. Tufted, many-stemmed, to 3 ft.; differing from *C. thalictrifolia* in having lvs ovate, to 1½ in. long, gray-green, soft-hairy, and corolla tubular, to 1½ in. long, blue, with purple throat and veining. S. Tibet.

ovata Benth. Similar to and often confused with *C. clematidea,* but sts. more scapose, with solitary nodding fls.; calyx lobes less than ⅖ as long as the corolla, minutely ciliate, usually revolute, corolla pale blue, sometimes with darker veins. Himalayas, S. China.

pilosula (Franch.) Nannf. [*C. silvestris* Kom.]. Sts. twining, to 6 ft. long or more; lvs. ovate, mostly less than 1½ in. long, cordate or obtuse at base, entire or nearly so, pilose; fls. on leafy lateral branchlets, calyx lobes ovate, ⅜–½ in. long, corolla pale greenish, flushed purple apically, campanulate, about 1 in. long; fr. to 1 in. across. Ne. Asia.

rotundifolia Royle. Ann., sts. twining, to 3 ft. long, sometimes more; lvs. mostly basal on sts., ovate, 1–2 in. long; fls. solitary, on axillary peduncles 1–6 in. long, calyx lobes leaflike, ½ to as long as corolla, entire or toothed, corolla yellowish-green, veined purple, broadly campanulate, to 1 in. long. W. Himalayas.

silvestris: *C. pilosula.*

Tangshen D. Oliver. Similar to *C. pilosula,* but lvs. sometimes nearly glabrous, fls. often on less leafy brs., calyx divided almost to the base, and corolla perhaps more conspicuously spotted inside. W. China.

thalictrifolia Wallich. Tufted and more or less erect, with filiform brs.; lvs. ovate-orbicular to reniform, about 5/16 in. long, nearly entire, densely hairy; fls. solitary, on terminal peduncles 2–6 in. long, calyx lobes to ¼ in. long, corolla bluish, narrowly tubular, with a somewhat flaring mouth, to 1 in. long. Nepal, Sikkim, Tibet.

tubulosa Kom. Glabrous, sts. twining, remotely leafy; lvs. lanceolate-ovate to oblong-ovate, to 2 in. long, narrowed at base and apex; fls. solitary, terminal, calyx slightly inflated, lobes broadly ovate, to ⅜ in. long, corolla tubular, about 1½ in. long. N. Burma, sw. China.

ussuriensis (Rupr. & Maxim.) Hemsl. Similar to *C. lanceolata,* but smaller and more delicate, with lvs. less than 2 in. long; calyx lobes less than ⅝ in. long, corolla deep purple above and spotted purple at the base inside, about 1 in. long; fr. about ½ in. across, seeds not winged. Japan, Manchuria.

vinciflora: *C. convolvulacea.*

viridiflora Maxim. Weakly erect or twining, to 4 ft. or more; lvs. lanceolate to ovate, about 1 in. long, subcordate, margin sinuate and revolute; fls. terminal on long peduncles, calyx lobes ovate, irregularly serrate, corolla yellowish-green, dotted purple at base inside, campanulate, about ½ in. long. Cent. to e. Asia.

COELIA Lindl. *Orchidaceae.* One sp., an epiphyte, native to Cent. Amer. and W. Indies; pseudobulbs 2–4-lvd.; lvs. plicate; infl. lateral, racemose, with sheathing dry bracts; fls. fleshy, sepals and petals connivent, lateral sepals forming a mentum with the column-foot, pollinia 8; caps. prominently winged. For structure of fl. see *Orchidaceae.*

For culture see *Orchids.*

Bauerana: *C. triptera.*

macrostachya: *Bothriochilus macrostachyus.*

triptera (Sm.) G. Don ex Steud. [*C. Bauerana* Lindl.]. To 1 ft., pseudobulbs to 2 in. long, 3–4-lvd.; lvs. linear-lanceolate; fls. white, ¼ in. long, in dense racemes, ovary ellipsoidal, sharply 3-winged, about ½ in. long. Spring. Cuba, Jamaica, Mex.

COELOGLOSSUM: *HABENARIA.* **C. bracteatum:** *H. viridis.*

COELOGYNE Lindl. *Orchidaceae.* About 200 spp. of epiphytes, native to trop. Asia, Malay Arch., and Oceania; pseudobulbs usually spaced at intervals along the rhizomes, in the cult. spp. usually 2-lvd.; fls. showy, in racemes, sepals and petals similar, spreading or reflexed, lip concave at base, usually 3-lobed, with longitudinal crests. For structure of fl. see *Orchidaceae.*

Grown mostly in the intermediate greenhouse; for culture see *Orchids.*

asperata Lindl. Lvs. lanceolate, to 2½ ft. long, 3–6 in. wide, acute; raceme drooping, to 16 in. long, several- to many-fld.; fls. to 3 in. across, white or cream-white, fragrant, lip marked with yellow, orange, and brown, wavy on margins. Early spring–late summer, early winter. E. Indies, Philippine Is., Malay Pen.

barbata Lindl. ex Griff. Lvs. broadly lanceolate, to 18 in. long; racemes as long as lvs., erect, densely fld., compact; fls. to 2 in. across, white, sepals and petals spreading, lip 3-lobed, lateral lobes enclosing column, midlobe fringed with brown and with 3 fringed brown crests. Autumn–winter. Himalayas.

×**burfordiense** Hort.: *C. asperata* × *C. pandurata.* Racemes densely fld.; fls. similar to those of *C. pandurata,* but longer-lasting, lip with black markings that turn brown with age.

carinata Rolfe. Lvs. 4–5 in. long; racemes 4–5-fld.; sepals and petals whitish-green, to 1 in. long, lip paler, splashed with orange-brown basally and with orange-brown area on basal half of midlobe and apex of lateral lobes. Early summer. New Guinea.

cinnamomea Teysm. & Binnend. Lvs. oblong-lanceolate; racemes recurved, 6–8-fld.; fls. ¾ in. long, yellowish or yellowish-white, lateral lobes of lip yellowish-brown with white margins. Java.

corrugata: *C. nervosa.*

corymbosa Lindl. Lvs. to 6 in. long; racemes shorter than lvs., 2–3-fld.; fls. fragrant, white, to 2 in. across, sepals and petals spreading, lip 3-lobed, the lobes with brown markings. Spring–late summer. Himalayas.

cristata Lindl. Lvs. to 1 ft. long, 1 in. wide; racemes drooping, 5–9-fld.; fls. large, 3–4 in. across, fragrant, snow-white, lip with 5 deep yellow keels. Winter–spring. Himalayas. Cv. 'Chatsworthii'. Fls. and pseudobulbs larger than typical. Cv. 'Hololeuca'. Fls. pure white, without yellow on lip. Cv. 'Citrina' [cv. 'Lemoniana']. Flowering later than the typical var.; center of lip stained a delicate lemon color, not deep yellow. Cv. 'Lemoniana': 'Citrina'. Cv. 'Major' [cv. 'Maxima']. Fls. very large, with broader sepals and petals, superior to typical var. in form. Cv. 'Maxima': 'Major'.

Dayana Rchb.f. Lvs. to nearly 1½ ft. long and 4 in. wide; racemes drooping, to 40 in. long, loosely many-fld.; fls. to 2½ in. across, whitish or pale yellow, lip blotched with chocolate-brown inside and with 6 fringed crests. Late spring–late summer. Malay Pen.

elata Lindl. Lvs. to 1½ ft. long and 3 in. wide; racemes erect, to 16 in. long, to 14-fld.; fls. to ¾ in. long, white or cream-white, lip with orange or yellow spot and 2 crests edged with red. Winter–late spring. Himalayas.

fimbriata Lindl. Lvs. to 5 in. long, to 1½ in. wide; racemes 1–4-fld.; fls. to 1 in. across, white or greenish-yellow, lip dingy yellow, fringed, with 2 deep brown, fringed crests. Summer–late autumn. Himalayas, China.

flaccida Lindl. Lvs. to 1 ft. long and 1 in. wide; racemes to 10 in. long, to 12-fld.; fls. 1½ in. across, white or cream-white, lateral lobes of lip with brownish streaks, midlobe with central yellow spot and 3 yellow keels. Late winter–spring. Himalayas.

Foerstermannii Rchb.f. To 2 ft., rhizome prominent; lvs. to 18 in. long; racemes loosely many-fld.; sepals and petals white, to 1½ in. long, sepals keeled, lip white, midlobe with yellow-brown stain on disc and with 3 longitudinal, toothed crests. Sunda Is. (Malay Arch.)

fuliginosa Lindl. Lvs. to 7 in. long and about 1 in. wide; racemes shorter than lvs., to 5-fld.; fls. to 2 in. across, brownish-yellow or brownish-white, lip red-brown, blotched with deep brown, fringed. Late summer–late autumn. Himalayas, Burma, Java.

fuscescens Lindl. Lvs. to 10 in. long; racemes drooping, shorter than lvs., 5–7-fld.; fls. not fully expanded, to 2½ in. across, pale orange-red or buff, of translucent texture, lip buff, bordered inside with red, with 3 broad, raised, reddish-brown crests converging to apex. Winter. Himalayas.

Huettnerana Rchb.f. Lvs. to about 10 in. long and 1½ in. wide; racemes shorter than lvs., drooping, 8–10-fld.; fls. to 1 in. long, white or cream-white, fragrant, lip spotted with citron-yellow. Early spring–early summer. Burma, Thailand. Var. **lactea** (Rchb.f) Pfitz. [*C. lactea* Rchb.f.]. Fls. milk-white, petals smaller, lip without yellow spots. Burma.

lactea: *C. Huettnerana* var.

Lawrenceana Rolfe. Lvs. to about 11 in. long and 1 in. wide; racemes to 8 in. long, 1–3-fld.; fls. large, to 4 in. across, greenish-yellow or brownish-white, lip very large, lateral lobes brown-veined, midlobe white, with yellow spot on disc and large, reddish-brown basal blotch, and with 3 warty crests. Spring. Vietnam.

lentiginosa Lindl. Lvs. to 8 in. long and 1½ in. wide; racemes to 4 in. long, about 4–8-fld.; fls. straw-yellow or yellow-green, lip white, lateral lobes edged with brown, midlobe blotched with orange. Early winter–early spring. Burma.

Massangeana Rchb.f Lvs. to 20 in. long and 6 in. wide; racemes pendent, to 2 ft. long, loosely many-fld.; fls. to 2¼ in. across, pale yellow, lateral lobes of lip streaked with brown and yellow, midlobe brown and white. Early spring–early summer, autumn. Assam, Malay Pen., Java.

Mayerana Rchb.f Rhizome ascending, thick, pseudobulbs widely spaced, to 2 in. long, 2-lvd.; lvs. to 8 in. long and 1 in. wide; racemes to 1 ft. long, to 10-fld.; fls. to 2½ in. across, green, lip streaked with dark brown. Early spring, autumn. Malay Pen.

Mooreana Hort. Sander ex Rolfe. Lvs. to 20 in. long and 2 in. wide; fls. large, to 3 in. across; racemes erect, to 16 in. long, loosely several-fld.; fls. white, lip with lemon-yellow spot and dark orange hairy crests. Winter. S. Vietnam.

nervosa A. Rich. [*C. corrugata* Wight]. Lvs. to 6 in. long or more and about 1 in. wide; racemes 3–6-fld.; fls. to 2½ in. across, white, lip striped red inside, midlobe with yellow disc and 3 fringed, white keels. Late summer. India.

nitida (Roxb.) Hook.f. [*C. ocellata* Lindl.]. Rhizome ascending, pseudobulbs to 1 in. long; lvs. to 10 in. long and 1½ in. wide; racemes

3–6-fld.; fls. to 2 in. across, white, lip spotted with golden-yellow, and with 5 crests on midlobe. Spring, autumn. Himalayas, Burma, Vietnam. Cv. 'Maxima'. More robust; racemes longer, 6–10-fld.; fls. larger, to 1½ in. long.

occultata Hook.f Lvs. to 3 in. long; racemes 3–4-fld.; fls. half concealed by sheaths, to 2 in. across, white, lip streaked with dull red, midlobe with 2 very thick, yellow, crenate crests on disc. Himalayas.

ocellata: *C. nitida.*

ochracea Lindl. Pseudobulbs to 2½ in. long, 2–3-lvd.; lvs. 6–8 in. long; racemes shorter than lvs., 5–7-fld.; fls. fragrant, pure white, to 2 in. across, lip ochraceous-yellow, with 2 large orange-bordered blotches on disc. Spring. N. India.

ovalis Lindl. Pseudobulbs 2–3 in. long; lvs. 3–4 in. long; scape 1-fld.; fls. variable in size, to 2 in. across, yellowish-brown, lip yellow-brown, fringed and covered with flexuous purple hairs, and with 2 crests on each side of median stripe. Autumn. Sikkim, China.

pandurata Lindl. BLACK ORCHID. Lvs. to about 26 in. long and 2½ in. wide; racemes nearly as long as lvs., arching, pendent, loosely several-fld.; fls. to 4 in. across, pale green, lip marked with blackish-brown or black, warty. Winter, late spring–summer. Malaya, Borneo.

Parishii Hook.f. Pseudobulbs to 5 in. long; racemes terminal, 6-fld.; fls. resembling those of *C. pandurata,* but smaller, about 2½ in. across, yellowish-green, lip green, with a few black spots and fringed crests. Spring. Moulmein (Burma).

prolifera Lindl. Rhizome prominent, pseudobulbs to 1 in. long; lvs. narrow, to 8 in. long; racemes terminal, loosely few-fld.; fls. small, to 1½ in. across, greenish-yellow, midlobe of lip wavy-margined. Early spring. Himalayas, Thailand, Burma.

Rhodeana Rchb.f. Lvs. to 14 in. long and 1 in. wide; racemes to 4 in. long, 3–5-fld.; fls. to ¾ in. across, greenish-white, lip dark brown, midlobe with 2 yellow stripes. Molucca Is.

rigida C. Parish & Rchb.f Pseudobulbs large, narrowly oblong, 4–6-lvd.; lvs. elliptic-lanceolate; racemes drooping, loosely fld.; fls. to ½ in. long, sepals and petals yellow, lip saccate, yellow, with 2 long and 1 short, red, crenulate crests. Moulmein (Burma).

Sanderana Rchb.f Pseudobulbs to 2 in. long; lvs. to 15 in. long and 3 in. wide; racemes as long as lvs., to 9-fld.; fls. to 4 in. across, white, lateral lobes of lip marked with brown, midlobe yellow. Spring. Sunda Is., Borneo.

sparsa Rchb.f. Lvs. to 4 in. long and 1 in. wide; racemes arching, 7½ in. long or less, to 7-fld.; fls. to 1 in. across, whitish, lip with brown mottling on lateral lobes and orange blotch on midlobe. Winter–late spring, autumn. Philippine Is.

speciosa Lindl. Pseudobulbs 1-lvd.; lvs. to 15 in. long, 2 in. wide or more; racemes shorter than lvs., 1–4-fld.; fls. to 4 in. across, greenish- or yellowish-brown, lip yellowish-white, heavily marked with dark brown. Winter–summer, autumn. Java. Cv. 'Alba'. Fls. white.

tomentosa Lindl. Lvs. to 20 in. long and 3 in. wide; racemes pendent, hairy, to 18 in. long, 2- or more-fld.; fls. to 4 in. across, light olive-green or red-brown, lateral lobes of lip streaked with brown, midlobe yellow with brown margins. Late spring. Malay Pen.

COFFEA

COFFEA L. COFFEE. *Rubiaceae.* About 40 spp. of shrubs or trees, native to Old World tropics; lvs. opp., stipules interpetiolar; fls. in axillary clusters, whitish, 5–7-merous; corolla salverform or funnelform; fr. a small, 2-seeded berry.

Widely grown in the tropics around the world for the coffee beans, (really the seeds within the pulpy fruit), source of beverage coffee. In the U.S. coffee is grown only occasionally as an ornamental for its attractive flowers and colorful fruits and for general interest; it is sometimes seen under glass. Propagated by cuttings of ripe wood, and in the tropics by seeds from which the pulp is removed.

arabica L. COFFEE, COMMON C., ARABIAN C., ARABICA C., ARABIAN COFFEE PLANT. Shrub, to 15 ft.; lvs. elliptic, to 6 in. long, glossy dark green; fls. pure white, fragrant, corolla 5-lobed, ¾ in. long; fr. red, ½ in. long, becoming soft and fleshy. Trop. Afr. Major source of quality coffee and principal sp. grown in Latin Amer. Cvs. 'Columnaris', 'Erecta', and 'Excelsa' are listed.

canephora Pierre ex Froehn. [*C. robusta* L. Linden]. ROBUSTA C., WILD R.C. Shrub or small tree, to 12 ft. or sometimes more; lvs. broadly elliptic or obovate, to 12 in. long; fls. white, to ¾ in. long, many in each lf. axil, fragrant; fr. red, to ½ in. long. W. Trop. Afr. Important in Old World where red coffee rust exists.

liberica Bull ex Hiern. LIBERIAN C. Shrub or tree; lvs. obovate, to 1 ft. long, glossy; corolla 6–7-lobed, 1 in. long; fr. black, ¾ in. long, remaining hard and fibrous. Trop. Afr. Produces an inferior coffee.

racemosa Lour. Much-branched small tree; lvs. mostly deciduous, ovate-lanceolate, scabrous; fls. in subterminal, erect racemes; fr. red, subglobose. Trop. e. Afr.

robusta: *C. canephora.*

zanguebariae Lour. ZANZIBAR C. Tree, to 6 ft.; lvs. elliptic or obovate, to 4 in. long; fls. in axillary clusters, corolla white, 6–7-lobed; fr. red, turning black, ½ in. long, longitudinally nerved. Trop. Afr.

COGSWELLIA: *LOMATIUM.* C. trinervata: see *L. triternatum.*

COIX L. *Gramineae.* About 4 spp. of tall, branched, monoecious ann. grasses in Asia; lvs. flat; infls. many on long stout peduncles, these clustered in the axils of lvs.; spikelets unisexual, male spikelets 2-fld., in pairs or 3's on the continuous rachis, glumes membranous, obscurely nerved, lemma and palea hyaline, stamens 3, female spikelets in 3's, 1 fertile and 2 sterile at the base of the infl., glumes of fertile spikelet several-nerved, pointed, the first glume wide and enfolding the spikelet, second glume keeled, narrower than the first, sterile lemma similar but a little narrower, fertile lemma and palea hyaline, sterile spikelets consisting of a single, narrow, tubular glume as long as the fertile spikelet. For terminology see *Gramineae.*

Lacryma-Jobi L. JOB'S-TEARS. Sts. usually over 3 ft. high; lf. blades to 1⅝ in. wide; fr. white to bluish-gray, sometimes mottled or striped, globular or ovoid, to ½ in. long. Se. Asia. Cult. as an ornamental and for the fr., used for food in se. Asia and as beads for necklaces and rosaries. Var. **frumentacea** Mak. Fr. ellipsoid, short-beaked.

COLA Schott & Endl. *Sterculiaceae.* About 110–125 spp. of monoecious or polygamous trees, native to trop. Afr.; lvs. alt., simple, entire or palmately lobed or compound; fls. in axillary clusters or panicles, calyx 4–5(–7)-lobed, petals 0, male fls. with 10–24 anthers in 1 or 2 superposed whorls near the apex of the column, female and bisexual fls. with (3–)4–5(–10), mostly many-ovuled carpels in a ring above the either abortive or fertile anthers; fr. of 3 or more woody or leathery follicles, with 1 to many seeds.

Several species grown in the tropics, especially of the Old World, for the caffeine-containing seeds ("nuts") which are used fresh as a masticatory in tropical W. Afr., and for flavoring cola beverages. Colas are sometimes planted in tropical gardens where they do best in sandy loam soil. They are propagated by seeds, preferably planted singly in pots, and then set out permanently, as they do not transplant well; also by cuttings of mature wood over heat.

acuminata (Beauvois) Schott & Endl. COLA, ABATA C., COLA TREE, GOORA NUT. Evergreen tree, 60 ft. or more in the wild; lvs. entire, obovate to elliptic, short-acuminate, to 8 in. long, leathery; calyx yellowish, about ½ in. across, anthers in 2 whorls, 10–12 in each whorl; follicles 3–6(–8) in. long, seeds about 1 in. long. A source of cola nuts.

COLCHICINE: see *Plant Hormones.*

COLCHICUM L. *Liliaceae.* Between 60 and 70 spp. of cormous, per. herbs of Eur., N. Afr., and w. and cent. Asia; st. and scape underground; lvs. linear, lanceolate, oblong, or strap-shaped, appearing either with the fls. or afterward—in the cult. autumn-flowering spp., appearing in spring; fls. crocuslike, usually white to purple, rarely yellow, perianth segms. 6, joined basally into a long tube extending underground, stamens 6, anthers versatile or very rarely basifixed, ovary superior, styles 3; fr. a septicidal caps. The drugs colchicum and colchicine are obtained from *C. autumnale.*

Colchicums do well in sunny locations and loamy soil. Corms should be planted 2–3 in. deep in Aug. or Sept. and not disturbed until they show signs of deterioration. Propagated by division of corms and by seeds.

agrippinum Bak. Lvs. 3–4, in spring, linear-lanceolate, 4–6 in. long, slightly wavy; fls. 2–3, lilac-purple, checkered, the tube white, anthers purple. Autumn. Not known in the wild.

atropurpureum Stapf ex Stearn [*C. autumnale* var. *atropurpureum* Hort.]. Lvs. 3–5, in spring, linear to lanceolate, to 10 in. long, dark green and somewhat glaucous; fls. usually 2, pale violet at first, changing to deep magenta-red, anthers golden-yellow. Autumn. Not known in the wild.

autumnale L. AUTUMN CROCUS, FALL C., MEADOW SAFFRON, MYSTERIA, WONDER BULB. Lvs. 3–8, in spring, lanceolate, to 1 ft. long; fls. 1–4, purple to white, sometimes double, to 4 in. across, anthers yellow. Autumn. Eur., N. Afr. The dried corms and seeds are the source of

medicinal colchicum and colchicine, the latter valuable in plant-breeding work. Cvs. are: 'Album', fls. white; 'Majus', more robust; 'Minus', a dwarf form; 'Roseum', fls. rose-pink. Var. **atropurpureum:** *C. atropurpureum.*

Bornmuelleri: *C. speciosum* var.

Bulbocodium: *Bulbocodium vernum.*

byzantinum Ker-Gawl. Lvs. 5–6, in spring, oblong, to 16 in. long, to 4 in. wide; fls. up to 20, pale pinkish-lilac, to 4 in. across, anthers dull yellow. Autumn. Se. Eur.

cilicicum (Boiss.) Dammer. Lvs. about 5, elliptic-oblong to broadly strap-shaped, to 1 ft. long, very dark green; fls. up to 25, rose-lilac with yellowish-white keel on back, to 3 in. across, anthers golden-yellow. Autumn. Asia Minor.

Doerfleri Halácsy. Lvs. 2, in spring, linear-lanceolate, hairy beneath; fls. 1–5, white to rose-pink, anthers brown; fr. hairy. Spring. Macedonia.

fasciculare (L.) R. Br. [*C. illyricum* Stokes]. Lvs. 5–7, in spring, linear-lanceolate, to 8 in. long, arcuate-reflexed; fls. many, white or pale rose, anthers brown. Spring. N. Syria.

giganteum Leichtl. ex S. Arn. [*C. speciosum* var. *illyricum* Hort.]. Lvs. 4–6, in spring, to 16 in. long; fls. 3–4, large, soft rosy-purple, white at base, perianth segms. on stout tubes. Autumn. Asia Minor.

illyricum: *C. fasciculare;* but material offered as *C. illyricum* may be *C. giganteum.*

luteum Bak. Lvs. 2–5, in spring, linear-lanceolate, to 1 ft. long; fls. 1–4, yellow, to 1½ in. across, anthers yellow. Spring. Himalayas.

Parkinsonii: *C. variegatum.*

Sibthorpii Bak. Lvs. 3–8, in spring, prostrate on ground, linear, to 8 in. long, dull bluish-green, wavy-margined; fls. 1–4, lilac-purple, checkered, anthers yellow, pollen green. Autumn. S. Greece.

speciosum Steven. Lvs. 4–6, in spring, widely oblong, to 16 in. long; fls. rose to purple, with white throat, to 4 in. across, globose and tapering to the 6–12 in.-long tube, anthers yellow or brown. Autumn. Caucasus, Asia Minor, e. Medit. Cv. 'Album'. Fls. white. Cv. 'Atrorubens'. Fls. dark red. Var. **Bornmuelleri** (Freyn) Bergmans [*C. Bornmuelleri* Freyn]. Fls. larger and earlier. Var. **illyricum:** *C. giganteum.*

variegatum L. [*C. Parkinsonii* Hook.f.]. Lvs. 3–4, in spring, lanceolate, to 6 in. long, wavy-margined, prostrate on ground; fls. rose, checkered, to 4 in. across, tube white, anthers brown. Autumn. Greece and Asia Minor.

vernum: *Bulbocodium vernum.*

COLDFRAME: see *Hotbed.*

COLEOCEPHALOCEREUS: *CEPHALOCEREUS.*

COLEONEMA Bartl. & H. L. Wendl. *Rutaceae.* About 5 spp. of heathlike shrubs, endemic to S. Afr.; lvs. alt., simple, linear, glandular-dotted; fls. white or red, solitary, axillary, toward ends of brs., calyx 5-parted, petals 5, clawed, stamens 5, staminodes 5, concealed in claws; fr. a 5-carpelled caps., each carpel horned.

Sometimes planted in warm climates and grown under glass in pots. For cultivation see *Diosma.*

album (Thunb.) Bartl. & H. L. Wendl. [*Diosma alba* Thunb.]. Much-branched shrub, to 6 ft.; lvs. linear, ½ in. long, straight-pointed; fls. white, about ⁵⁄₁₆ in. across, calyx lobes ovate, thin, ciliate.

ericoides: a listed name of no botanical standing, used for *Diosma ericoides.*

pulchrum Hook. Much-branched shrub, 4–6 ft., brs. wandlike; lvs. to 1½ in. long; fls. red, to ¾ in. across.

COLEOSPADIX: *DRYMOPHLOEUS.* C. oninensis (Becc.) Becc.: *D. oninensis* (Becc.) H. E. Moore, a sp. not known to be cult.; material grown as *C. oninensis* is *Ptychosperma Schefferi* or a hybrid derived from it.

COLEUS Lour. FLAME NETTLE, PAINTED LEAVES. *Labiatae.* About 150 spp. of ann. or per., usually succulent herbs of the Old World tropics; sts. mostly square in cross section; lvs. opp., crenate-serrate or doubly crenate-serrate, gland-dotted beneath; fls. in 6- to many-fld. verticillasters crowded at apex and progressively more distant toward the base, arranged in terminal panicles, bracts falling early, calyx campanulate, 5–10-nerved, 2-lipped, upper lip entire, broad, lower lip 4-lobed, corolla bluish or lilac to violet, tube longer than calyx, limb 2-lipped, upper lip short, 2–4-lobed, lower

lip entire, boat-shaped, stamens 4, ovary 4-parted, glabrous, style 2-lobed; fr. of 4 smooth, glabrous nutlets. Differs from *Plectranthus* in having filaments united basally into a tube split along one side.

Coleus is commonly cultivated indoors in the home and also outdoors as a bedding plant for its colorful foliage. Most species are tender. Choice cultivars are readily propagated from cuttings; seedlings often produce colorful variations. There are many hybrids resulting from two species in particular: *C. Blumei* and *C. pumilus*, but other species are also presumed to be involved. Because of the uncertainty of origin, these hybrids are probably best treated as *C.* × *hybridus*.

amboinicus Lour. [*C. aromaticus* Benth.]. SPANISH THYME, INDIAN BORAGE, COUNTRY B. Aromatic per., 1½–3 ft.; lvs. fleshy, ovate, mostly 1½–2½ in. long, crenate, pilose; fls. pale purple. From cult. in India to Malay Arch.; nativity uncertain. The aromatic shoots are sometimes sold for culinary purposes in markets of trop. Amer.

aromaticus: *C. amboinicus.*

Autranii Briq. Per., 2–3 ft., nodes villous; lvs. broadly ovate-lanceolate, 3–5 in. long, dark dull green and pilose above, pale green and hispidulous beneath; fls. in 6–12-fld. verticillasters arranged in panicles 6–10 in. long, corolla pale to heliotrope purple, ½ in. long. W. Ethiopa. Cult. outdoors in s. Calif.

Blumei Benth. PAINTED NETTLE. Glabrous per., 3–6 ft., becoming subshrubby; lvs. membranous, ovate, 3–8 in. long, mostly acuminate, coarsely crenate; fls. in close verticillasters, these sessile or on very short peduncles, corolla pale to dark blue. Java. Var. **Verschaffeltii** (Lem.) Lem. [*C. Verschaffeltii* Lem.]. BUTTERFLY C. More robust and much-branched; lvs. acute, variously colored. This sp. itself may not be in cult., and material so listed is likely to be of hybrid origin. See *C.* × *hybridus.*

candidus: a listed name of no botanical standing for *C.* × *hybridus* cv.

carnosus: see *C. repens.*

Frederici G. Tayl. Fleshy per., 3–4 ft.; lvs. broadly ovate, to 3 in. long, dentate, lower lvs. strongly decurrent; fls. on very slender pedicels, in open, terminal panicles 6–5 in. long, corolla deep blue, about ¾ in. long. Angola.

× **hybridus** Voss. A name given to the hybrid assemblage comprising the cvs. of common garden coleus. Among the 200 or more named cvs. are: 'Brilliancy', 'Candidus', 'Christmas Cheer', 'Defiance', 'Goldbound', 'Golden Bedder', 'Klondyke', 'Metallicus', 'Mrs. Harding', 'Pink Rainbow', 'Sunset'. In much of the literature these cvs. are listed under *C. Blumei*, but their hybrid origin involves other spp., and it is incorrect to treat them as derivatives of any single sp.

laciniatus (Blume) Benth. A name based on Javanese material of presumed hort. origin and probably representing only a form of *C. Blumei* or *C. scutellarioides;* said to differ in having lvs. incised, serrate to laciniate.

lanuginosus Hochst. ex Benth. Per., roots producing tubers; lvs. ovate, to 3 in. long, densely pubescent; fls. in short-peduncled verticillasters arranged in long, loose panicles, corolla lilac. Cent. Afr.

macrophyllus (Blume) Benth. Per.; lvs. orbicular-ovate, to 3 in. long, acute, cuneate, usually puberulous; fls. in peduncled verticillasters arranged in open panicles. Some material so listed is *C. Blumei*, or may be still other spp. Of doubtful status; may be a sp. of *Plectranthus*.

metallicus: a listed name of no botanical standing for *C.* × *hybridus* cv.

pumilus Blanco [*C. Rehneltianus* A. Berger]. Per., 1½–3 ft., sts. mostly creeping and ascending; lvs. ovate to orbicular, ¾–1½ in. long, acute to obtuse, deeply crenate-dentate, with central, pinkish, basal zone, or in cult. material with a conspicuous often 3-colored pattern and only the margins green; fls. fragrant, in few-fld. verticillasters arranged in an open spikelike infl. 6–15 in. long, corolla bright blue, about ⅝ in. long. Philippine Is. to Indonesia.

Rehneltianus: *C. pumilus.*

repens Gürke [*C. carnosus* A. Cheval., not Hassk.]. More or less succulent, pubescent per., sts. creeping or ascending; lvs. nearly orbicular, to 1 in. across, deeply crenate; fls. in short racemes. W. Afr.

salicifolius: a listed name of no botanical standing, possibly a cv. of *C.* × *hybridus.*

shirensis Gürke. Robust per., 4–7 ft., sts. woody at base, hispid; lvs. ovate, 3–6 in. long, acuminate, very coarsely crenate, puberulous to pilose on both sides, petioles hispidulous; fls. in many loose verticillasters forming a showy panicle 8–15 in. long, corolla bluish-mauve, about ¾ in. long. Swampy, shaded areas, trop. e. Afr.

spicatus Benth. Semisucculent per., 1–1½ ft., minty-aromatic, sts. often decumbent, puberulent; lvs. mostly orbicular, 1–2½ in. across,

obtuse, weakly crenate; fls. in congested terminal verticillasters arranged in a spicate infl. 2–4 in. long, corolla azure-blue, about 1 in. long. E. India.

thyrsoideus Hook.f. FLOWERING BUSH C. Per., 2–3½ ft., sts. woody at base, viscid; lvs. broadly ovate, 2–3 in. long, crenately incised, weakly erose, dull green above, gray-green beneath; fls. produced profusely, verticillasters on long slender peduncles arranged in a showy panicle 8–15 in. long, corolla gentian- to indigo-blue, about ⅜ in. long, upper lip 4-lobed. Cent. Afr.

Verschaffeltii: *C. Blumei* var.

COLLANDRA: *COLUMNEA*. **Collandra picta**: see *Columnea sanguinea.*

COLLARD. A large kale, *Brassica oleracea* Acephala Group, grown in the South for greens. It is biennial or potentially perennial, producing a hard stalk 1–2 feet high and bearing a loose crown of cabbagelike leaves (but not a solid head), which are eaten. Sometimes collards are grown as a winter annual for spring use, and sometimes the leaves are taken as needed and the plant allowed to stand for a year or more where winters are very mild. The usual procedure is to sow seeds in spring in a seed bed, transplant to 3 or 4 feet apart in the field, till through the season, and harvest the crop in autumn. The plant endures hot weather better than cabbage. If seed is wanted, the stocks may be allowed to stand where climate permits, or they may be stored for the winter and planted out the next year as are cabbage stumps.

Sometimes young cabbage plants, or related things, are erroneously called collards when used for greens.

COLLETIA Comm. ex Juss. *Rhamnaceae*. About 17 spp. of stiff, spiny shrubs of s. S. Amer., with thickened often flattened, paired branchlets; lvs. opp., usually absent or very small; fls. yellowish or white, calyx tubular, petals 0; fr. a leathery 3-lobed caps. Related to *Adolphia* but having showy, tubular, calyx lobes and no petals.

Occasionally planted as ornamentals, grown outdoors in warm regions or under glass as a curiosity. Propagated by seeds or cuttings of half-ripened wood.

armata Miers. To 8 or 10 ft., brs. and spines usually pubescent, spines straight or slightly curved, to 1½ in. long; lvs. small. Autumn. Chile. Zone 7?

cruciata Hook. ANCHOR PLANT. To 10 ft., brs. flattened, with very broad spines; lvs. few, small; fls. yellowish-white. Autumn. S. Brazil and Uruguay. Zone 7? Occasionally grown in Fla. and Calif. Distinguished from *C. armata* in having flattened branchlets; rarely, however, it will produce a shoot having the cylindrical spines of that sp.

COLLINIA: *CHAMAEDOREA.*

COLLINSIA Nutt. *Scrophulariaceae*. Over 20 spp. of attractive, hardy ann. herbs, native to N. Amer., chiefly from w. U. S.; lvs. opp. or in whorls of 3–5; fls. white, lilac, rose to violet, or bright blue, solitary or in umbel-like clusters appearing whorled in lf. axils, calyx 5-cleft, corolla 2-lipped, stamens 4; fr. a caps.

Collinsias require only the usual treatment for annuals; the seeds may be sown outdoors in autumn, if well protected in winter, but preferably in spring in the North.

bicolor: *C. heterophylla.*

candidissima: *C. heterophylla* cv.

grandiflora Dougl. ex Lindl. BLUELIPS. To 15 in., pubescent or glabrous; lvs. oblong to linear, to 1¾ in. long, toothed or entire; fls. on pedicels about as long as fls., corolla to ¾ in. long, tube shorter than the lips, lower lip deep blue or violet, upper lip purple or white. B.C. to Calif.

heterophylla Buist ex R. C. Grah. [*C. bicolor* Benth.]. CHINESE-HOUSES. To 2 ft., glabrous, pubescent, or sometimes glandular-pubescent; lvs. lanceolate to oblong, to 2 in. long, toothed or entire; fls. nearly sessile, corolla to 1 in. long, lower lip violet or rose-purple, upper lip white. N. Calif. to n. Baja Calif. Cvs. 'Alba' and 'Candidissima' [*C. candidissima* Hort.] have white fls.

parviflora Dougl. ex Lindl. [*C. pusilla* T. J. Howell]. Erect or spreading, to 16 in., pubescent; lvs. oblong-lanceolate to linear-lanceolate or ovate, to 2 in. long, toothed or usually entire, upper lvs. often in whorls of 3–5; fls. to ⅜ in. long, axillary, usually solitary, on pedicels usually longer than fls., corolla tube longer than lips, lower lip violet-blue, upper lip white or violet-blue. B.C. to s. Calif. and Ariz., e. to Ont., Vt., and Colo.

pusilla: *C. parviflora.*

tinctoria Hartweg. To 2 ft., glandular-pubescent, especially in infl., producing an iodinelike stain; lvs. oblong, lanceolate, or ovate, to 4 in. long, serrate or entire; fls. nearly sessile, corolla ⅝ in. long, pale purplish or nearly white and streaked, upper lip very short. Calif.

verna Nutt. BLUE-EYED MARY, INNOCENCE. To 2 ft., sts. hairy in lines; lvs. ovate to ovate-lanceolate, to 2 in. long, upper lvs. partly clasping; fls. on pedicels longer than fls., corolla ½ in. long, lower lip bright blue, upper lip white or purplish. N.Y. to Wisc., s. to Ky., n. Ark., e. Kans.

violacea Nutt. To 15 in., sts. evenly hairy; lvs. lanceolate or oblong-lanceolate, to 2 in. long, entire or toothed, upper lvs. sessile; fls. on pedicels longer than fls., corolla to ½ in. long, lower lip violet, upper lip pale. E. Kans. and Mo., s. to Tex.

COLLINSONIA L. HORSE BALM, HORSEWEED. *Labiatae.* Five spp. of strongly aromatic per. herbs of e. N. Amer.; sts. mostly square in cross section; lvs. opp., large, ovate; fls. yellowish, in verticillasters arranged in a panicle, calyx ovoid, 2-lipped, upper lip 3-toothed, lower lip 2-parted, corolla elongate, with inflated throat, tube with a bearded ring inside, limb 2-lipped, upper lip 4-lobed, lower lip lacerated, stamens 2, exserted, anther cells spreading; fr. of 4 nutlets.

Propagated by seeds or division; useful in the wild garden.

canadensis L. CITRONELLA, RICHWEED, STONEROOT. Rhizome very hard, sts. 1–4 ft., glabrous; lvs. petioled, ovate, 4–10 in. long, coarsely serrate, lemon-scented when crushed, especially in spring; panicles 8–15 in. long; fls. to ⅝ in. long, lemon-scented. Rich moist woods, Vt. to Ont. and Wisc., s. to Fla. and Ark.

COLLOMIA Nutt. *Polemoniaceae.* About 15 spp. of prostrate to erect, sometimes rhizomatous ann. or per. herbs, native to w. N. Amer. and from Bolivia to Patagonia; lvs. mostly linear or lanceolate, entire to dissected; fls. pink, scarlet, yellowish, white, or purplish, mostly in cymes, or congested in headlike, leafy-bracted clusters, calyx 5-toothed, enlarging in fr., corolla trumpet-shaped to funnelform, 5-lobed, stamens 5, equally or unequally inserted; fr. a caps., seeds often becoming mucilaginous when wet. Differs from *Gilia* in that mature caps. does not rupture calyx.

Of easy cultivation in any garden soil. Propagated by seeds sown where plants are to stand, in open exposure.

biflora: *C. Cavanillesii.*

Cavanillesii Hook. & Arn. [*C. biflora* (Ruiz & Pav.) Brand]. Ann., to 2 ft.; lvs. linear, to 2 in. long, toothed or cut near tip; fls. scarlet, tinged with buff outside. Bolivia, Chile, Argentina.

debilis (S. Wats.) Greene. Tufted, rhizomatous, erect or decumbent per., to 8 in.; lvs. to 1½ in. long, entire, to 3–7-toothed or -lobed, glandular-villous; fls. pink, blue to white, drying purple, to 1 in. long. Summer. High mts., Wash. and Mont., s. to Ore. and Utah.

grandiflora Dougl. ex Hook. Erect, often coarse ann., to 3 ft.; lvs. lanceolate to elliptic, to 4 in. long, entire; fls. salmon-yellow to cream or nearly white. Spring to late summer. B.C. to s. Calif., e. to Rocky Mts.

COLOCASIA Fabr. ELEPHANT'S-EAR, ELEPHANT'S-EAR PLANT. *Araceae.* About 6 spp. of large, per. herbs, native to trop. Asia; lvs. peltate, mostly ovate, notched at base, petioles long; spathe convolute, constricted between the inflated tube and the expanded blade, spadix densely fld., terminated by short or long, sterile appendage; fls. unisexual, perianth absent, ovaries 1-celled, ovules many, parietal, in 2–4 rows.

Colocasias are widely grown for food and as ornamentals. They are of easy culture in rich, well-drained soil supplied with abundant water. Many varieties are grown in warm climates for their edible tubers and young leaves. Tubers are planted 2–3 in. deep about 2 ft. apart in 4-ft. rows, and are ready to harvest in about seven months. The young shoots of certain varieties, forced and blanched, are used as a winter vegetable. Taro is widely grown for food throughout the tropics; in Hawaii and other Pacific Islands where eaten particularly in the form of "poi." It is often grown as an ornamental in pools, where it thrives when planted in several in. of water.

antiquorum: *C. esculenta* var. *antiquorum.* Var. **esculenta:** *C. esculenta.* Var. **typica:** *C. esculenta* var. *antiquorum.* For other vars. of *C. antiquorum,* see cvs. of *C. esculenta.*

esculenta (L.) Schott [*C. antiquorum* var. *esculenta* Schott; *Caladium esculentum* Hort.]. TARO, KALO, DASHEEN, EDDO. A variable sp., 3–7 ft.; lvs. all basal from a corm, blades to 2 ft. long, upper surface velvety green to bluish-black between pale primary veins, petioles green to violet or reddish; spathe to 15 in. long, basally green or red-purple, blade expanded, reflexed, yellow. Runs into many forms, of which the following are listed: Var. **antiquorum** (Schott) F. T. Hubb. & Rehd. [*C. antiquorum* Schott var. *typica* Engl.]. CULCAS, EGYPTIAN TARO. Lvs. green, spadix with a very long, terminal sterile appendage. India. The following cvs. are grown as ornamentals: cv. **'Euchlora'** [var. *euchlora* (C. Koch & H. Sello) A. F. Hill; *C. antiquorum* var. *euchlora* (C. Koch & H. Sello) Schott]. Lvs. dark green, with violet margins, petioles violet, basal shoots short. Cv. **'Fontanesia'** [var. *Fontanesii* (Schott) A. F. Hill; *C. antiquorum* var. *Fontanesii* Schott; *C. violacea* Hort. ex Hook.f.]. VIOLET-STEMMED TARO. Differs from cv. 'Euchlora' in having lvs. large, purple-veined. Ceylon? Cv. **'Illustris'** [var. *illustris* (Bull) A. F. Hill; *C. antiquorum* var. *illustris* (Bull) Engl.]. IMPERIAL TARO, BLACK CALADIUM. Lvs. large, marked bluish-black or black-purple between primary veins. The following cvs. are grown for food: cv. **'Globulifera'** [var. *globulifera* (Engl. & Kurt Krause) R. A. Young; *C. antiquorum* var. *globulifera* Engl. & Kurt Krause]. Probably identical to cv. 'Trinidad'. Cv. **'Sacramento'.** Differs from cv. 'Trinidad' in having corms larger, more regular, producing 10–15 larger, but more uniform tubers of variable quality. Cv. **'Trinidad'.** To 7 ft., with many short side-shoots, corms subglobose to ovoid, each producing 20 or more ovoid to elongate tubers; lvs. dark green, petioles dark green, marked with maroon lines; spadix with very short appendage. Cult. in Fla. for its tubers of superior quality, and its edible shoots. Cv. **'Ventura'.** Differs from cv. 'Trinidad' in having corms slightly smaller, more regular, with fewer, more uniform tubers of excellent quality, and petioles basally more reddish. Var. **aquatilis** Hassk. Stoloniferous, the stolons slender, reddish, to 6 ft. long, rhizome not enlarging. Java; established as a weed along streams and lakes in s. U.S. See *Taro.*

fallax Schott. Differs from *C. esculenta* in having tubers solitary, lf. blades ovate to rotund-ovate, to 8 in. long, basally emarginate, spathe 3–6 in. long, and spadix with sterile appendage 2 in. long. Himalayas.

gigantea (Blume) Hook.f. [*C. indica* of auth., not (Lour.) Kunth; *Alocasia gigantea* Hort.]. St. to 2 ft. or more; lf. blades white-glaucous beneath, basal lobes shortly united, petioles stout, glaucous; spathe to 8 in. long, blade erect, hooded, white, spadix with sterile appendage less than ½ in. long, stigmas 4-lobed, covering apex of pistils. Malay Pen., Java. Doubtfully in cult.; material so listed may be a form of *C. esculenta,* or of *Alocasia odora* with green lvs.

indica: see *C. gigantea.*

multiflora: a listed name of no botanical standing; material so listed may be a form of *C. esculenta* with purple petioles.

violacea: *C. esculenta* cv. 'Fontanesia'.

COLPOTHRINAX Griseb. & H. Wendl. ex Siebert & Voss. *Palmae.* Two spp. of slow-growing, medium-sized palms with bisexual fls., native in Cuba and Cent. Amer., trunk solitary, swollen in one sp.; lvs. briefly costapalmate, petiole margins smooth, blade divided about halfway into 1-ribbed segms.; infl. among lvs., bracts tubular, sheathing peduncle and base of several primary brs.; fls. solitary, sepals united in a low cupule, petals 3, united with stamens at base, separate above, stamens 6, carpels 3, separate except united styles; fr. globose, seed with homogeneous endosperm and lateral embryo.

Perhaps occasionally planted in tropical gardens but does not thrive in southern Fla. For culture see *Palms.*

Wrightii Griseb. & H. Wendl. ex Siebert & Voss. BOTTLE PALM, BARREL P., CUBAN BELLY P. To 40 ft., trunk much swollen near the middle at maturity; lvs. to 5 ft. wide; fls. yellowish; fr. globose, ½ in. in diam. or more, black at maturity. Cuba.

COLQUHOUNIA Wallich. *Labiatae.* About 6 spp. of erect or twining, sometimes tomentose shrubs of e. Himalayas to sw. China; sts. mostly square in cross section; lvs. opp., remotely crenate; fls. small, scarlet, in many-fld., loose verticillasters arranged in terminal spikes, fl. bracts minute, calyx tubular-campanulate, 10-nerved, 5-toothed, glabrous inside throat, corolla tube incurved, longer than calyx, limb 2-lipped, upper lip erect, entire, lower lip 3-lobed, stamens 4, in 2 pairs, style 2-lobed; fr. of 4 glabrous nutlets. Related to *Stachys* but having upper lip of corolla entire or emarginate, and shorter than lower lip.

coccinea Wallich. Tomentose shrub, 4–10 ft., usually sprawling and half-climbing; lvs. ovate to lanceolate, 2–8 in. long, sharply wavy-toothed; spikes dense, 6–15 in. long; corolla funnelform, about 1 in. long, pale pink to scarlet to dark red, yellowish inside. Himalayas to sw. China. Var. **vestita** (Wallich) Prain [*C. vestita* Wallich]. Lvs. coarsely crenate, densely white-tomentose beneath, tomentum often floccose; fls. to 1¼ in. long, corolla pink. Var. **mollis** (Schlechtend.) Prain. Always erect; lvs. rusty-tomentose beneath, not floccose; fls. large, corolla orange-red.

vestita: *C. coccinea* var.

COLUBRINA L. Rich. ex Brongn. *Rhamnaceae.* About 30 spp. of trees or shrubs, mostly in Mex., S. Amer., a few in Malay Arch., trop. Australia, Pacific Is., E. Afr., and Mauritius; lvs. alt., 3-nerved at base or pinnately nerved; fls. small, in axillary cymes or clusters, calyx with 5 spreading lobes, petals 5, hooded, stamens 5, included in hooded petals; fr. a drupe.

arborescens (Mill.) Sarg. [*C. ferruginosa* Brongn.]. WILD COFFEE. Shrub or small tree, to 20 ft. or more, young brs. reddish-tomentose; lvs. elliptic to ovate-lanceolate, to 6 in. long, pinnately nerved, dark green above, paler, reddish-pubescent and black-glandular beneath; fls. white, reddish-pubescent, in axillary cymes; fr. nearly globose, to ⅜ in. in diam., blackish. Fla., W. Indies, Mex., Cent. Amer.

asiatica (L.) Brongn. Large shrub or small tree, glabrous, brs. often slender and flexuous; lvs. ovate, to 3 in. long, pinnately 3-nerved; fls. greenish, small, in axillary cymes. Widespread in trop. Asia, Pacific Is., Queensland.

ferruginosa: *C. arborescens.*

COLUMNEA L. [*Collandra* Lem.; *Trichantha* Hook.]. *Gesneriaceae.* More than 100 spp. of epiphytic shrubs or vines, native to Amer. tropics; lvs. opp., or in whorls, those of a pair equal or very unequal, the smaller sometimes stipulelike; fls. solitary or clustered in lf. axils, subtended by small bracts, sepals 5, corolla tubular, spurred at the base, limb nearly regular or, mostly, strongly 2-lipped, the upper 4 lobes united in a helmetlike hood (galea) with prominent lateral lobes, stamens 4, filaments attached to corolla, anthers united in a square, dehiscing by slits, disc of a single gland at back of ovary or rarely of 5 glands, ovary superior; fr. a berry, seeds many.

For cultivation see *Gesneriaceae.* Many interspecific hybrids and cultivars are now offered. The most recent list of these appears in The Gesneriad Register 1966, *Columnea,* published by the American Gloxinia Society, Inc.

affinis C. V. Mort. Sts. stout, velvety with red-purple hairs when young; lvs. of a pair very unequal, the larger asymmetrically oblanceolate to a winged base, to 9 in. long, 2½ in. wide, the smaller less than 1 in. long, blades dark green above, paler beneath, velvety with red-purple hairs; fls. 2–3 in axils of orange bracts, sepals ¾ in. long, 2–3-toothed, densely hairy, orange, corolla slightly curved, cylindrical, about 1¼ in. long, yellow, with dense orange-red hairs, lobes equal, short, ³⁄₁₆ in. long, filaments glabrous; berry yellowish. Venezuela.

Allenii C. V. Mort. Sts. slender, pendulous in cult., slightly pale-hairy; lvs. of a pair equal, oblong-elliptic, ¾ in. long, ½ in. wide, rounded or short-pointed at apex, dark green, smooth, glossy above, paler beneath; fls. solitary on red-hairy pedicels, sepals 1 in. long, entire, reddish, hairy only along the edges where they touch one another, corolla strongly 2-lipped, red to orange, with yellow at throat, 2¾–3 in. long, tube 1 in. long, galea to 2 in. long, with triangular lateral lobes, lower lip 1 in. long, filaments glabrous. Panama.

argentea Griseb. Sts. stout, pale-silky-hairy when young; lvs. of a pair nearly equal, narrowly elliptic, to 5 in. long, 2 in. wide, remotely toothed, gray-hairy; fls. 1–4 in axils of small bracts, pedicels to 1 in. long, silky, sepals narrowly lanceolate, to ¾ in. long, ⅛ in. wide, silky, corolla strongly 2-lipped, pale yellow and densely white-silky outside, tube about 1 in. long, galea 1 in. long, notched at middle, with narrowly triangular lateral lobes, lower lip ¾ in. long, filaments glabrous; berry pink, ½ in. long. Jamaica.

arguta C. V. Mort. Sts. slender, pendulous in cult., red-hairy when young; lvs. opp. or in whorls of 3, to 1 in. long, ⁵⁄₁₆ in. wide, sharply pointed, smooth except for red-hairy margins, often reddish beneath; fls. solitary in axils, pedicel short, sepals ½ in. long, toothed, hairy, corolla strongly 2-lipped, orange-red, yellow at throat and in lines down tube, to 2⅜ in. long, tube 1½ in. long, galea ¾ in. long, 1 in. wide, with lateral lobes ½ in. long, lower lip ¾ in. long, filaments glabrous. Panama.

aureonitens Hook. Similar to *C. affinis,* but lvs. to 10 in. long, 4 in. wide, new growth and corolla with golden hairs. Costa Rica and Colombia.

×**Banksii** Lynch: *C. Oerstediana* × *C. Schiedeana.* Sts. stoutish, pendulous or trailing; lvs. ovate or oblong-ovate, small, to 1¾ in. long, ¾ in. wide; corolla strongly 2-lipped, scarlet with obscure yellow lines at mouth.

Barkleyi: a listed name of no botanical standing.

brevifolia: a listed name of no botanical standing.

brevipila Urb. Sts. to ⁵⁄₁₆ in. thick, minutely hairy when young; lvs. of a pair nearly equal, narrowly elliptic, to 5 in. long, 2 in. wide, obscurely toothed, green, with very short hairs, prominently veined beneath; fls. 1–5 in axils, pedicels to 1 in. long, sepals narrowly lanceolate, to 1¼ in. long, entire, green, corolla strongly 2-lipped, yellow, with long hairs outside, to 2 in. long, tube 1 in. long, galea 1 in. long, with spreading-ascending lateral lobes, lower lip ⅝ in. long, filaments glabrous. Jamaica.

consanguinea Hanst. Sts. stoutish, pale-hairy; lvs. of a pair very unequal, the larger asymmetrically oblanceolate, to 7 in. long, 1½ in. wide, entire, glabrous above, occasionally red-spotted beneath, the smaller to 1 in. long; fls. 1 to several in axils of conspicuous green bracts, sepals lanceolate, ⅝ in. long, entire, green, minutely hairy, corolla with nearly regular limb, yellow, densely silky, a little longer than calyx, to ¾ in. long. Costa Rica.

costaricensis: see *C. Raymondii.*

crassifolia Brongn. [*C. stenophylla* Standl.]. Sts. stiff, hairy when young; lvs. of a pair equal, very narrowly elliptic, to 4 in. long, ½ in. wide, shining dark green and smooth above, paler with few hairs beneath; fls. solitary on short pedicels, sepals slender, ¾ in. long, green, corolla strongly 2-lipped, bright red, hairy, 3 in. long, tube 1¾ in. long, galea 1¼ in. long, with upturned lateral lobes, lower lip ½ in. long; berry whitish, tinged pink, ¾ in. long. S. Mex., Guatemala.

erythrophaea Decne. ex Houll. Sts. thick, pale-hairy when young; lvs. of a pair nearly equal, asymmetrically elliptic, to 2½ in. long, ⅝ in. wide, green and smooth above, paler beneath, hairy on margins and on nerves beneath; fls. solitary on red-hairy pedicels to 1½ in. long, sepals ovate, to ⅞ in. long, recurved and with a few teeth beneath, dull rose and green, corolla strongly 2-lipped, orange-red with yellow lines at throat and yellow near base, tube 2 in. long, galea 1¼ in. long, with narrow, strongly recurved, lateral lobes, lower lip deflexed, ¾ in. long, filaments red-hairy. S. Mex.

×**euphora** H. E. Moore: *C. gloriosa* × *C. lepidocaula.* Intermediate between parents, with sts. pendulous but robust and branching; lvs. of a pair equal, ovate, to 2¼ in. long, 1¼ in. wide, densely hairy; fls. solitary, sepals as in *C. gloriosa,* but variable in size; corolla 2¾ in. long, as in *C. lepidocaula,* but red and filaments hairy. Cv. 'Ithacan'. Lvs. and sepals dull green. Cv. 'Othello'. Lvs. suffused with red-purple, sepals larger, purplish, corolla tube completely yellow on lower side.

Fawcettii (Urb.) C. V. Mort. Sts. stiff, whitish-hairy; lvs. of a pair equal to unequal, elliptic to ovate, to 4 in. long, 1¾ in. wide, green above, paler beneath, short-hairy; fls. 1–3 in axils of small bracts, sepals narrowly lanceolate, to 1⅛ in. long, toothed, densely hirsute, red, corolla strongly 2-lipped, red with longitudinal yellow stripes, pale-hairy, to 2 in. long, tube 1 in. long, galea 1⅛ in. long, with narrow spreading lateral lobes, lower lip ¾ in. long, filaments slightly hairy. Jamaica.

flaccida Seem. Sts. slender, pendulous in cult.; lvs. of a pair nearly equal, ovate or elliptic-ovate, to 1¼ in. long, ¼ in. wide, sparsely hairy; fls. solitary, pedicels purple, red-hairy, sepals to ⅝ in. long, deeply toothed, red-hairy, red externally, corolla strongly 2-lipped, rose-red with a little yellow at throat, red-hairy outside, to 2⅜ in. long, tube 1½ in. long, galea 1 in. long, with short, spreading lobes, lower lip ½ in. long, filaments glabrous. Costa Rica, Panama.

flava M. Martens & Galeotti. Similar to *C. Schiedeana,* but fls. yellow, not spotted, pedicels white-hairy. S. Mex.

glabra Ørst. Sts. stiff, branched, minutely hairy; lvs. of a pair nearly equal, oblanceolate or elliptic, to 1 in. long, ⅜ in. wide, fleshy, glabrous; fls. solitary on short pedicels, sepals narrowly elliptic, ½ in. long, green, minutely hairy basally, corolla strongly 2-lipped, red, softly hairy, 2 in. long, tube 1½ in. long, with spreading, lateral lobes, lower lip ⅜ in. long, filaments glabrous. Costa Rica.

glauca: a listed name of no botanical standing, used for *C. Moorei.*

gloriosa T. Sprague. Sts. slender, pendulous in cult., branching and somewhat flexuous, densely hairy; lvs. of a pair equal or unequal, short-petioled, ovate or ovate-oblong, to 1¼ in. long, ⅝ in. wide, green with dense purplish or reddish hairs above or purplish-red and hairy beneath; fls. solitary on pedicels to 1 in. long, sepals ovate, ½ in. long, hairy, green, corolla strongly 2-lipped, scarlet with bright yellow at throat and on lower side of tube, white-hairy, to 3 in. long, tube 1 in. long, galea 2 in. long, with short, triangular lateral lobes, lower lip 1 in. long, filaments glabrous; berry dull white with purplish hairs. Costa Rica. Cv. **'Diminutifolia'**: *C. microphylla.* Cv. **'Superba'** [cvs. 'Purpurea', 'Rubra', 'Splendens']. Lvs. intensely colored.

Harrisii (Urb.) Britt. ex C. V. Mort. Sts. stiff, whitish-hairy; lvs. of a pair equal or unequal, green, silky, the longer blade asymmetrical, narrowly elliptic-oblong, to 5¼ in. long, 2 in. wide, shallowly toothed, the smaller blade broader; fls. 1–3 in axils, sepals lanceolate, entire or with 1–2 minute teeth on each side, green, silky, corolla strongly 2-lipped, yellow striped with red, white-hairy outside, to 2 in. long, tube a little longer than calyx, galea 1 in. long, with narrow, spreading, lateral lobes, lower lip ⅝ in. long, filaments glabrous. Jamaica.

hirsuta Swartz. Sts. robust, densely long-hairy; lvs. of a pair unequal, toothed, green, with long hairs on both sides and on margins, the larger blade elliptic to obovate, to 4¾ in. long, 2¼ in. wide, the smaller blade about half as large; fls. 1–3 in axils, on long-hairy pedicels, sepals linear, to ¾ in. long or more, remotely toothed, red or green, densely hairy, corolla strongly 2-lipped, red with wide yellow stripes, densely long-hairy outside, to 2 in. long, tube ¾ in. long, galea 1 in. long, with narrow, spreading, lateral lobes, lower lip ⅞ in. long, reflexed, filaments sparsely hairy. Jamaica.

hirsutissima C. V. Mort. Sts. stiff, red-hirsute; lvs. of a pair strongly unequal, the larger blade oblong or narrowly oblong, to 4 in. long, 1⅜ in. wide, obscurely toothed, green, densely hirsute on both sides, the smaller blade about ⅜ in. long; fls. 1–2 in axils, sepals linear, ¾ in. long, remotely glandular-toothed, red-hairy, corolla strongly 2-lipped, rose striped with white at base, short-hairy outside, glandular inside, to 3 in. long, galea 1 in. long, with short, spreading, lateral lobes, lower lip ½ in. long, filaments glandular at base. Panama.

hirta Klotzsch & Hanst. Sts. stiff, reddish-hairy; lvs. of a pair nearly equal, oblong, to 1½ in. long, ⅜ in. wide, green, densely hairy; fls. solitary on short pedicels with linear bracts, sepals linear-lanceolate, ⅝ in. long, entire or with 2 pairs of teeth, hairy, corolla strongly 2-lipped, vermilion, long-hairy, to 2⅜ in. long, tube 1½ in. long, galea 1 in. long, with lanceolate lateral lobes, lower lip ¾ in. long, recurved, filaments glabrous. Costa Rica.

hispida Swartz. Sts. stout, hispid; lvs. of a pair unequal, blades elliptic to obovate, asymmetrical, remotely toothed, dark green above, paler beneath, long-reddish-hairy above, on margins, and on veins beneath, the larger blade long-petioled, to 6 in. long, 2¾ in. wide, the smaller blade to 2⅜ in. long, 1⅜ in. wide; fls. 1–3 in axils on short, hispid pedicels, sepals narrow, to ⅝ in. long in flower, entire, corolla strongly 2-lipped, dull yellow, hispid, 1 in. long, tube ⅜ in. long, galea ⅝ in. long, with rounded lateral lobes, lower lip ⅜ in. long, filaments minutely hairy. Jamaica.

illepida H. E. Moore. Sts. stiff, hairy; lvs. of a pair very unequal, the larger oblanceolate to obovate, hairy, green above, red-blotched or entirely red beneath, the smaller stipulelike; fls. several in axils on slender, hairy pedicels, sepals linear, to ¾ in. long, pectinate-toothed, corolla weakly 2-lipped, 2 in. long, tube dull yellow, striped with maroon, lobes to ¼ in. long, yellow-margined, striped or spotted with maroon, with short yellow appendages between the lobes. Panama. Has been offered as cvs. **'Butcher's Gold'**, **'Butcher's Panama Gold'**, **'Panama Gold'**.

jamaicensis Urb. Sts. slender, pendulous in cult., reddish-hairy when young; lvs. of a pair unequal, narrowly ovate to ovate, asymmetrical, dark green above, paler beneath, sparsely hairy, the longer blades to 2¼ in. long, ⅞ in. wide, the smaller to 1¼ in. long, ⅝ in. wide; fls. solitary, pedicels to 1¼ in. long, sepals ovate or lanceolate, to ½ in. long in flower, green or reddish, sparsely hairy, corolla weakly 2-lipped, orange-yellow, striped with orange-red or yellow, to 1¼ in. long, galea about ⅜ in. long, lower lip 5/16 in. long; berry white. Jamaica.

kewensis: a listed name of no botanical standing, used for plants probably of hybrid origin.

lepidocaula Hanst. Sts. stiff, brown, checked with pale brown when old; lvs. of a pair nearly equal, fleshy, elliptic to ovate, to 3½ in. long, 1⅛ in. wide, deep green; fls. solitary, sepals oblong-lanceolate, to 1 in. long, green, appressed-hairy at base, corolla strongly 2-lipped, orange shading to yellow at throat and lower side, to 3 in. long, tube to 1½ in. long, galea to 1½ in. long, lower lip 5/16 in. long, filaments densely and minutely hairy. Costa Rica.

linearis Ørst. Sts. thick; lvs. of a pair equal, linear, to 3½ in. long, ⅜ in. wide, glossy dark green; fls. solitary, sepals ovate-lanceolate, to ¾ in. long, corolla strongly 2-lipped, rose-pink, finely pale-hairy, 1¾ in. long, tube about as long as calyx, lower lip ½ in. long, filaments finely hairy. Costa Rica.

magnifica Klotzsch ex Ørst. Sts. stiff, hairy; lvs. of a pair nearly equal, oblanceolate, to 3½ in. long, green, softly hairy; fls. solitary on pedicels as long as sepals or longer, sepals ½ in. long, basally toothed, green, hairy, corolla strongly 2-lipped, scarlet, softly hairy, 2½ in. long, tube 1¼ in. long, galea 1¼ in. long, lower lip 1 in. long, filaments shortly and densely hairy. Costa Rica.

microphylla Klotzsch & Hanst. ex Ørst. [*C. gloriosa* cv. 'Diminutifolia']. Sts. slender, pendulous in cult., densely red-brown-hairy; lvs. of a pair equal, blades broadly ovate or nearly round, short-petioled, to ⅜ in. long, green or often reddish, densely red-hairy; fls. solitary, sepals ⅜ in. long, entire or slightly toothed, green or red-flushed, white-hairy, corolla strongly 2-lipped, scarlet with a bright yellow patch at throat and base of lower lip, 2½–3¼ in. long, tube 1–1¼ in. long, galea 1½–2 long, lower lip 1 in. long, filaments glabrous. Costa Rica. Cv. **'Diminutifolia'** is only a hort. name for the sp.

minor (Hook.) Hanst. [*Trichantha minor* Hook.]. Similar to *C. Teuscheri,* differing only in having lvs. glabrous except near margin and only minutely strigose beneath. Colombia. Probably not in cult.; *C. Teuscheri* was originally introd. to cult. under this name.

Moorei C. V. Mort. Sts. slender, pendulous in cult., minutely hairy; lvs. of a pair equal, short-petioled, broadly elliptic, to ⅝ in. long, ½ in. wide, dark green and shining above, light green beneath; fls. solitary on elongate, red-hairy pedicels, sepals to ⅝ in. long, ½ in. wide, deeply pectinately toothed, red-hairy, corolla weakly 2-lipped, tube red, with long red hairs, to 2¼ in. long, galea 2-lobed, red, lower lip 3-lobed, yellow, lobes to 3/16 in. long, with minute yellow appendages between them, filaments glabrous; berry white, with reddish hairs. Panama.

Mortonii Raym. Similar to *C. hirta,* but lf. blades less than twice as long as broad, bracts of the pedicel triangular, sepals to ½ in. long, with 1 pair of inconspicuous teeth, corolla 3¼–3⅜ in. long, filaments strongly glandular-pilose. Panama. Has been offered as cvs. **'Butcher's Panama Red'**, **'Butcher's Panama Rose'**, **'Butcher's Red'**, **'Butcher's Rose'**, **'Panama Red'**.

nicaraguensis Ørst. Sts. to 2½ ft., stiff, brownish-hairy; lvs. of a pair very unequal, the larger blade ovate to elliptic, to 5 in. long, 2 in. wide, dark green with fine hairs above, paler and with nerves prominently hairy beneath, the smaller blade often stipulelike or soon deciduous; fls. 3 in axils, sepals lanceolate, to 1 in. long, entire, corolla strongly 2-lipped, scarlet with yellow on lower side of tube, densely appressed-hairy, to 3 in. long, tube 1¼ in. long, galea 1¾ in. long, the lateral lobes reflexed and with recurved margins, lower lip 1 in. long, filaments finely hairy. Nicaragua to Panama.

Oerstediana Klotzsch ex Ørst. Sts. slender, pendulous in cult., appressed-hairy; lvs. of a pair equal, short-petioled, blades ovate or broadly elliptic, ½ in. long, 5/16 in. wide, glabrous above; fls. solitary, sepals ovate, ⅜ in. long, toothed below the middle, green or with reddish margins, corolla strongly 2-lipped, red, softly hairy, 2¾ in. long, tube 1½ in. long, galea 1¼ in. long, lower lip ⅞ in. long, filaments glabrous. Costa Rica.

percrassa C. V. Mort. Sts. loose, pendulous in cult.; lvs. of a pair nearly equal, short-petioled, blades elliptic to more or less rhombic, to 1¼ in. long, ⅝ in. wide, thick and fleshy, dark green and glossy; fls. solitary, calyx 5-angled, the sepals broadly triangular, to ½ in. long, recurved, green, inconspicuously glandular-toothed, corolla strongly 2-lipped, scarlet, red-hairy, to 2¼ in. long, tube about 1⅛ in. long, orange-red, with yellow line from throat on lower side, galea to ⅞ in. long, lower lip 5/16 in. long, filaments glabrous, ovary glabrous basally. Panama. Has been offered as cvs. **'Butcher's Canal Zone'** and **'Canal Zone'**.

pilosissima Standl. Similar to *C. hirta,* but sts. with colorless hairs, sepals less densely hirsute, corolla larger, to 3⅝ in. long, lateral lobes reflexed, and filaments glabrous. Honduras.

querceti Ørst. Similar to *C. verecunda,* but sepals oblong-lanceolate, ⅛–3/16 in. wide at base. Costa Rica.

Raymondii C. V. Mort. [*C. costaricensis* Raym., not O. Kuntze]. Very similar to *C. nicaraguensis,* but sepals triangular, reddish-tipped, corolla with spreading, not appressed, hairs, galea blood-red rather than scarlet, lateral lobes and lower lip horizontal rather than reflexed, and with flat rather than recurved margins. Costa Rica.

rubricaulis Standl. Sts. pilose, new growth sometimes reddish; lvs. sometimes in whorls of 3 and somewhat unequal, blades linear-oblong, to 2½ in. long, ⅜ in. wide, attenuate, glabrous above; fls. solitary on red-hairy pedicels to 2 in. long, sepals to 5/16 in. long, acuminate, minutely toothed basally, green, corolla strongly 2-lipped, vivid orange, sparsely appressed-pilose, 2⅝ in. long, tube 1½ in. long, galea 1 in. long, with reflexed lateral lobes, lower lip ⅜ in. long, filaments pilose; berry globose, pink. Honduras, Nicaragua.

rutilans Swartz. Sts. stiff, reddish-hairy when young; lvs. of a pair unequal, blades lanceolate or narrowly lanceolate, remotely toothed, dark green and minutely hairy above, red-veined or red and hairy beneath, the larger to 7¼ in. long, 2⅜ in. wide, the smaller to 1¾ in. long, 1 in. wide, soon falling; fls. 1–4 in axils, sepals to 1 in. long in flower, pinnately toothed, with 3 acute teeth on each margin, red-hairy, corolla strongly 2-lipped, red with longitudinal orange stripes, to 2¼ in. long, tube covered by calyx, galea to 1¼ in. long, lower lip to 1 in. long, filaments slightly hairy. Jamaica.

salmonea Raym. Sts. arching-pendulous in cult., hirsute; lvs. of a pair equal, short-petioled, blades ovate, to 1 in. long, ⅝ in. wide, green and sparsely pilose above, paler and veined beneath, and margined with wine-red beneath; fls. solitary in axils, sepals united in lower ⅓, lanceolate, to ⅝ in. long, entire, white-hairy, corolla strongly 2-lipped, salmon, pilose outside, 2¾ in. long, tube 1¼ in. long, galea ¾ in. long, lower lip 1 in. long; berry white-pilose, marked with blue. Costa Rica.

sanguinea (Pers.) Hanst. [*Alloplectus sanguineus* (Pers.) Mart.; *Collandra picta* Klotzsch & Hanst., not Lem.]. Sts. to 4½ ft., stiff, hairy; lvs. of a pair very unequal, the larger nearly sessile, oblong-lanceolate, to 12 in. long, 4¾ in. wide, with a large red blotch below the apex, the smaller to 2 in. long, 1 in. wide; fls. 2–3 in axils, sepals lanceolate, to ¾ in. long, with about 4 teeth on each side, hairy, corolla nearly regular, pale yellow, hairy, to 1¼ in. long, lobes erect, nearly equal, about ⅛ in. long, filaments slightly hairy. Var. **sanguinea.** The typical var.; corolla ¾–⅞ in. long. Hispaniola. Var. **trinitensis** C. V. Mort. Corolla 1–1¼ in. long. Trinidad.

sanguinolenta Hanst. Sts. erect in cult.; lvs. of a pair strongly unequal, the larger oblanceolate, to 4¾ in. long, 1½ in. wide, green above, sometimes red-spotted beneath, the smaller stipulelike; fls. solitary on elongate, hairy pedicels, sepals to 1¼ in. long, deeply pectinately fringed, densely hairy, corolla nearly regular, scarlet, 1½ in. long, limb oblique, lobes small, rounded. Costa Rica, Panama.

scandens L. Sts. pendulous in cult., hairy on new growth; lvs. of a pair equal, short-petioled, blades ovate to nearly orbicular, to 1⅝ in. long, ¾ in. wide, entire or obscurely toothed above middle, strigose; fls. solitary in axils, on short pedicels, sepals linear-lanceolate, to ½ in. long, entire or the 3 upper with a single tooth, corolla strongly 2-lipped, red, sparsely hairy, to 2¼ in. long, tube 1¼ in. long, galea ¾ in. long, lower lip ⅜ in. long, filaments glabrous. Var. **scandens.** The typical var.; lf. blades ovate to suborbicular, about 1½ times as long as wide and more or less toothed. Martinique, Montserrat. Var. **aripoensis** (Britt.) C. V. Mort. Lf. blades ovate to oblong, 2–2½ times as long as wide. Trinidad, Tobago.

Schiedeana Schlechtend. Sts. to 3 ft., stiffly spreading; lvs. of a pair unequal, blades obliquely lanceolate or oblong, green, pale-hairy, red or red-veined beneath, the longer to 5 in. long, 1½ in. wide; fls. 1–2 in axils, on red-hairy pedicels, sepals ovate, reddish, to ⅞ in. long, softly hairy, corolla strongly 2-lipped, dull yellow, with maroon spots and lines, to 2¼ in. long, tube 1½ in. long, galea 1 in. long, lower lip ¾ in. long, filaments glabrous. Mex.

splendens: *Nematanthus longipes,* but plants originally offered as *C. splendens* were a sp. of *Columnea.*

stenophylla: *C. crassifolia.*

subcordata C. V. Mort. Sts. stout, hispid when young; lvs. of a pair unequal, green, hirsute, the larger blades oblong-elliptic, to 5½ in. long, 2⅜ in. wide, sometimes subcordate at base, the smaller blades ovate or obovate, to 1⅜ in. long, ¾ in. wide; fls. 2–4 in axils, calyx 2-lipped, of 1 free sepal and 4 others joined at the base for ³⁄₁₆–⁵⁄₁₆ in., to ⅞ in. long, hispid, corolla strongly 2-lipped, light yellow, glandular-hairy, to 1⅞ in. long, tube not much longer than calyx, galea 1 in. long, lower lip ⅝ in. long, filaments glabrous.

Teuscheri (C. V. Mort.) H. E. Moore. Sts. very slender, pendulous in cult., red-hairy; lvs. of a pair strongly unequal, the larger petioled, lanceolate-elliptic, to 3⅜ in. long, 1½ in. wide, dark green, hirsute, the smaller minute and stipulelike, or more rarely to 1¼ in. long; fls. 1–3 in axils, on red-hairy pedicels to 1¼ in. long, sepals to ¾ in. long, deeply cut marginally into linear lobes, red-hairy, green or red, corolla weakly 2-lipped, maroon with longitudinal yellow stripes, tube to 1¾ in. long, lobes rounded, with conspicuous yellow appendages between them, the upper 2 maroon, united, the lower 3 yellow, spreading, filaments glabrous; berry white. Ecuador. Originally introd. to cult. as *C. minor,* but differing in having hirsute lvs. and smaller calyx.

tigrina: *C. zebrina.*

translucens Raym. Sts. stiff, densely hairy with glandular, orange-red hairs; lvs. of a pair unequal, the larger asymmetrically elliptic-oblong, to 2 in. long, 1¼ in. wide, softly hairy, the smaller to ¾ in. long, ⅜ in. wide; fls. 1–3 in axils, on short pedicels, sepals ⅞ in. long, remotely toothed, orange with green base, densely hairy, corolla nearly regular, orange, translucent, densely orange-hairy, to 2 in. long, lobes yellow, ⅛–³⁄₁₆ in. long, filaments glabrous. Panama.

triplinervia: a listed name of no botanical standing.

tulae Urb. Sts. hairy; lvs. of a pair equal, elliptic or oblong, to 1¾ in. long, ¾ in. wide, green, softly and densely hairy; fls. solitary in axils, sepals lanceolate, to ½ in. long, entire, green or red, corolla strongly 2-lipped, yellow, orange, or red, to 2 in. long, tube 1¼ in. long, finely

hairy, galea ½ in. long, lower lip ¼ in. long. Puerto Rico. Fls. vary in color. Cv. **'Flava'.** Corolla yellow. Cv. **'Rubra'.** Corolla red.

Urbanii Stearn. Sts. stout, hirsute when young; lvs. of a pair nearly equal, short-petioled, broadly elliptic to broadly obovate or nearly orbicular, to 4¾ in. long, 2¼ in. wide, light green, hirsute above, strigose beneath; fls. 1–2 in axils, sepals lanceolate, to ⅝ in. long in flower, entire, green, densely hirsute, corolla strongly 2-lipped, pale yellow, hirsute on upper side, 2 in. long, tube ⅞ in. long, galea to 1 in. long, lower lip ¾ in. long, filaments glabrous. Jamaica.

×**vedrariensis** Hort. Vilm. ex Mottet: *C. magnifica* × *C. Schiedeana.* Sts. slender, to 3 ft.; lvs. elliptic-lanceolate, to 4 in. long, green, with red midrib; fls. 1–2 in axils, on red pedicels, sepals toothed, red, corolla scarlet, streaked with yellow.

verecunda C. V. Mort. Sts. to 2½ ft., stiff; lvs. of a pair very unequal, the larger oblong-lanceolate, to 4¼ in. long, 1¼ in. wide, deep green and smooth above, green or burgundy-red and with short hairs on veins beneath, the smaller slender, to ¼ in. long; fls. several in axils, sepals narrow, ⅝ in. long, ⅛ in. wide, finely hairy, corolla strongly 2-lipped, yellow or pale red, pale-appressed-hairy, 1½ in. long, tube and lower lip about ½ in. long, not much longer than sepals, galea ½ in. long, filaments pilose. Costa Rica. Cv. **'Florence Carrell'.** Lvs. broad, burgundy-red beneath; fls. yellow.

×**Vilmoriniana** Meuniss.: *C. gloriosa* cv. 'Superba' × *C.* ×*vedrariensis.* Combines characters of the parents. Material now cult. under this name may not represent the original hybrid.

Warscewicziana (Klotzsch) Hanst. Sts. stiff, densely hairy; lvs. of a pair strongly unequal, the larger asymmetrically oblanceolate or elliptic, to 4¾ in. long, 1½ in. wide, sharply toothed, hairy, the smaller stipulelike, to about 1 in. long; fls. solitary in axils on green pedicels to 1⅝ in. long, sepals lanceolate, ¼ in. long, entire or with a few slender teeth, green, hairy, corolla weakly 2-lipped, swollen on one side, red, to 2 in. long, limb oblique, lobes small, rounded, upper 2 united, ¼ in. long, lower 3 spreading. Costa Rica, Panama.

×**Woodii** H. E. Moore: *C. crassifolia* × *C. nicaraguensis.* Sts. ascending; lvs. of a pair nearly equal, lanceolate, large; fls. 1–3 in axils, corolla red with yellow throat, appressed-pale-hairy outside.

zebrina Raym. [*C. tigrina* Raym.]. Sts. stiff, strigillose; lvs. of a pair unequal, the larger subsessile, elliptic-ovate, to 6 in. long, glabrous above, the smaller stipulelike, to 1 in. long; fls. 2–4 in axils, on short pedicels, sepals ovate, ¾ in. long, pilose, corolla strongly 2-lipped, lemon-yellow, striped with deep red, 3 in. long, galea 1¼ in. long, lower lip 1 in. long, filaments glabrous; berry white. Panama.

COLUTEA L. BLADDER SENNA. *Leguminosae* (subfamily *Faboideae*). About 25 spp. of shrubs or small trees from the Medit. region and Ethiopia to the Himalayas; lvs. alt., deciduous, odd-pinnate, lfts. mostly ovate to elliptic, retuse; fls. papilionaceous, on axillary, few-fld. peduncles, standard reflexed, somewhat orbicular, with 2 folds or swellings above claw, stamens 10, 9 united and 1 separate; fr. an inflated, bladderlike legume.

Grown mostly in mild climates, Zone 8. Propagated by seeds, cuttings in autumn, or choice varieties by grafting on *C. arborescens.*

arborescens L. To 15 ft.; lfts. in 4–5 pairs, silky beneath; fls. yellow, standard with red markings, wings about as long as keel; fr. to 3 in. long. S. Eur., n. Afr.

cilicica Boiss. & Bal. Differs from *C. arbocescens* in having fls. with the wings longer than the keel. Asia Minor.

×**media** Willd. [*C.* ×*orientalis* Lam.]: probably *C. arborescens* × *C. cruenta* Ait. To 10 ft.; fls. orange or reddish-yellow.

×**orientalis:** *C.* ×*media.*

persica Boiss. To 8 ft.; lfts. in 3 pairs; fls. yellow, wing petals longer than keel; fr. to 2 in. long. Kurdistan.

COLVILLEA Bojer. *Leguminosae* (subfamily *Caesalpinioideae*). One sp., a tree, native to Madagascar; lvs. alt., large, 2-pinnate, with many lfts.; fls. racemose, showy, irregular, with large 2-parted calyx, standard convolute, much shorter than the 4 other petals, stamens 10, separate; fr. an elongate, turgid legume.

Propagated by seeds.

racemosa Bojer. To 50 ft., with thick trunk; lvs. to 3 ft. long, pinnae in 20–30 pairs, lfts. oblong, ½ in. long; racemes drooping, in groups of 4–12 near st. tips, to 18 in. long; fls. crowded, buds red, velvety, petals orange-red, to ¾ in. long, stamens exserted, yellow; fr. to 6 in. long. Zone 10b.

COMANDRA Nutt. BASTARD TOADFLAX. *Santalaceae.* Six spp. of glabrous, sometimes parasitic, herbs with creeping rhizomes, native to N. Amer. and se. Eur.; lvs. alt., sessile or nearly sessile; fls. in terminal clusters, whitish, bisexual, calyx 4–5-lobed, petals none, stamens 4–5, ovary inferior; fr. drupaceous, dry or fleshy.

pallida A. DC. To 16 in.; lvs. linear to lanceolate, many, thick, pale and glaucous; fls. in panicles; fr. ovoid, to ⁵⁄₁₆ in. long. W. N. Amer. Parasitic on the roots of other plants; sometimes transplanted from the wild.

COMAROSTAPHYLIS Zucc. *Ericaceae.* About 20 spp. of evergreen, erect or spreading shrubs, native chiefly to Mex., 1 in Calif.; lvs. alt., simple, often revolute; fls. in terminal racemes or panicles, calyx 4- or 5-lobed, corolla urceolate, stamens usually 10, ovary superior; fr. fleshy, drupelike, warty.

Culture as for *Arbutus.*

diversifolia (Parry) Greene [*Arctostaphylos diversifolia* (Parry) Parry ex A. Gray]. To 20 ft.; lvs. oblong to elliptic, to 3 in. long, strongly revolute, green and shining above, hairy beneath; fls. white, ovary pubescent; fr. red. Late spring. S. Calif., Baja Calif. Var. **planifolia** Jeps. Lvs. not revolute. Spring. Zone 7.

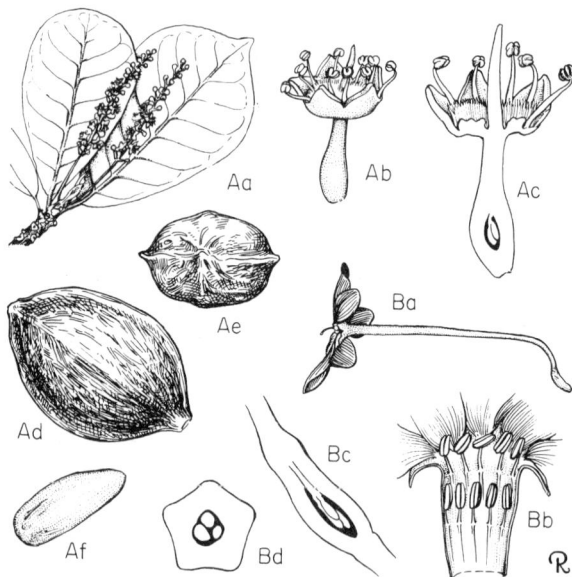

COMBRETACEAE. **A,** *Terminalia Catappa:* **Aa,** flowering branch, × ⅙; **Ab,** flower, × 2; **Ac,** flower, vertical section, × 3; **Ad,** fruit, side view, × ½; **Ae,** fruit, end view, × ½; **Af,** seed, × ¾. **B,** *Quisqualis indica:* **Ba,** flower, × ½; **Bb,** throat of corolla, expanded, × 1½; **Bc,** ovary, vertical section, × 3; **Bd,** ovary, cross section, × 6. (Aa from Bailey, *Manual of Cultivated Plants,* ed. 2.)

COMBRETACEAE R. Br. COMBRETUM FAMILY. Dicot.; about 15 genera of trees and shrubs, some climbing, of wide distribution in the tropics; lvs. simple; fls. bisexual or unisexual, 4–5-merous, stamens 8–10, ovary inferior, 1-celled; fr. dry or drupaceous, often winged. *Bucida, Combretum, Conocarpus, Pteleopsis, Quisqualis,* and *Terminalia* are cult. as ornamentals and *Terminalia* also for its frs., used for tannins or edible oil.

COMBRETUM L. *Combretaceae.* Perhaps 350 spp. of widely distributed, polygamous, trop. trees and large, often climbing, shrubs; lvs. mostly opp., entire; fls. in spikes, racemes, or panicles, 4–5-merous, stamens 8–10, long-exserted; fr. dry, leathery, 4–6-winged.

Grown in tropical and subtropical gardens for the showy flowers.

celastroides Welw. ex M. Laws. Somewhat scandent shrub; lvs. opp., broadly lanceolate, about 2 in. long, very short-petioled; racemes longer than lvs.; fls. small, 5-merous; fr. subglobose, ⅝ in. long, scaly, with papery wings. Angola.

erythrophyllum Sond. BUSH WILLOW. Graceful tree to 40 ft., without spines, bark smooth, gray or greenish; lvs. opp. or alt., lanceolate, acute, glabrous, drooping, turning bright gold and red in autumn and

winter; spikes axillary, globose, shorter than lvs.; fls. greenish-white, stamens 8; fr. ½ in. long, 4-winged. S. Afr. St. yields a gum.

grandiflorum G. Don. Vine, to 20 ft.; lvs. oblong to obovate-elliptic, to 6 in. long, short-acuminate, pubescent, becoming glabrous; spikes short, dense, 1-sided; fls. showy, 5-merous, red, about 1 in. long; fr. thin, broadly ellipsoid, 1½ in. long. Gambia and Guinea to Ghana.

microphyllum Klotzsch. BURNING BUSH. Large, rambling shrub; lvs. opp. or alt., broadly ovate, about 1 in. long, notched; racemes axillary, shorter than lvs.; fls. 4-merous, scarlet, pubescent; fr. 4-angular, ellipsoid. Mozambique, where called FLAME CREEPER.

paniculatum Venten. Vine, attaining great length, branchlets pubescent, with short spines; lvs. alt., broadly elliptic to suborbicular, to 8 in. long, pubescent beneath when young, petioles persistent, becoming recurved spines; panicles large, terminal; fls. 4-merous, coral-red, often appearing when plant is leafless; fr. pink or orange, to 1½ in. long. Trop. Afr.

COMMELINA L. DAYFLOWER. *Commelinaceae.* Perhaps over 100 spp. of widely distributed herbs; sts. jointed; lvs. alt., entire; fls. irregular, mostly blue, short-lived, in cincinni subtended by a hooded or folded leafy bract, the cincinni solitary or paired—if paired, the outer one much reduced, with male fls. only, stamens 5–6, the lower 2–3 fertile, with elliptic anthers, the upper 2–3 sterile, with cross-shaped anthers; fr. a caps.

Grown in greenhouses or outdoors, often as ground cover. Propagated by seeds, cuttings over heat, or division of the tubers if these are produced.

angustifolia: *C. erecta* var.

benghalensis L. Sts. straggling and rooting at nodes; lvs. ovate to ovate-lanceolate, to 1¼ in. long, rarely to 2½ in., blunt, pubescent; infl. bracts with the margins united, pubescent, several together in axils of upper lvs.; fls. to ⅝ in. across, upper petals pale violet or bluish-violet, lower small and colorless; caps. 5-seeded, seeds reticulate. Trop. Asia, Afr. Cv. **'Variegata'** is listed.

clandestina Kunth. A confused name of uncertain application.

coelestis Willd. BLUE SPIDERWORT. Per., with tuberous roots, to 1½ ft.; lvs. lanceolate-oblong, to 7 in. long, 2 in. wide; infl. bracts with free margins; fls. deep blue, to 1 in. across; caps. 5-seeded. Mex. A frequent greenhouse plant. Sometimes offered as *C. sikkimensis* or *C. tuberosa.* Cv. **'Alba'.** Fls. white. Cv. **'Variegata'.** Fls. blue and white.

communis L. Ann., sts. becoming diffuse and rooting; lvs. ovate-lanceolate, to 4 in. long, 1¼ in. wide; upper infl. bracts with separate margins; fls. with upper petals blue, lower pale and smaller; seeds 4 in 2 cells, rugose. E. Asia; naturalized and weedy in e. U.S., and sometimes cult.

crispa: *C. erecta* var. *angustifolia* forma.

diffusa Burm.f. [*C. nudiflora* of auth., not L.; *C. Sellowiana* Schlechtend.]. Creeping per., sts. rooting at joints; fls. blue, to ½ in. across, lower petal smaller and often paler than upper petals, fertile stamens 3, yellow, sterile stamens 2; caps. 5-seeded, seeds reticulate. Asia, Afr., S. Amer., N. Amer., as far north as N.J. Grown in the open garden.

elegans HBK. Similar to *C. erecta,* but with sts. procumbent, to 2 ft. long or more, lvs. lanceolate-oblong, to 2 in. long or more. Trop. Amer.

erecta L. Sts. erect or ascending, to 3 ft. or more; lvs. lanceolate or narrower in the vars., to 6 in. long, 1½ in. wide, the sheath with usually white-haired auricles; infl. bracts with united margins; fls. with 2 blue petals and 1 short white petal; caps. 3-seeded. N.Y. to Fla., w. to Tex. Var. **angustifolia** (Michx.) Fern. [*C. angustifolia* Michx.]. Not as tall as typical var.; lvs. linear to linear-lanceolate, to ¾ in. wide. A form of this var., forma **crispa** (Woot.) Fern. [*C. crispa* Woot.], has the bracts white-villous.

nudiflora: see *C. diffusa.*

sativa: a listed name of no botanical standing; possibly referable to *C. tuberosa.*

Sellowiana: *C. diffusa.*

sikkimensis C. B. Clarke. Creeping per.; lvs. lanceolate, to 3 in. long, unequal and usually obtuse at base, sheath glabrous or nearly so; fls. blue, usually 6–12 in terminal cincinni. Himalayas. Material cult. under this name may be *C. coelestis.*

tuberosa L. Diffusely branching from tuberous root; lvs. narrowly lanceolate, to 3 in. long, sheath pubescent; fls. blue. Mts., Mex. When planted in the open, tubers should be lifted and stored in dry sand over winter. Plants in cult. under this name are usually *C. coelestis.*

virginica L. To 4 ft.; lvs. lanceolate, to 8 in. long and 1½ in. across, sheath pubescent with rusty hairs; infl. bracts with united margins; fls. blue, to 1 in. across, petals nearly equal; caps. 5-seeded. Penn. to Mo., s. to Fla. and Tex.

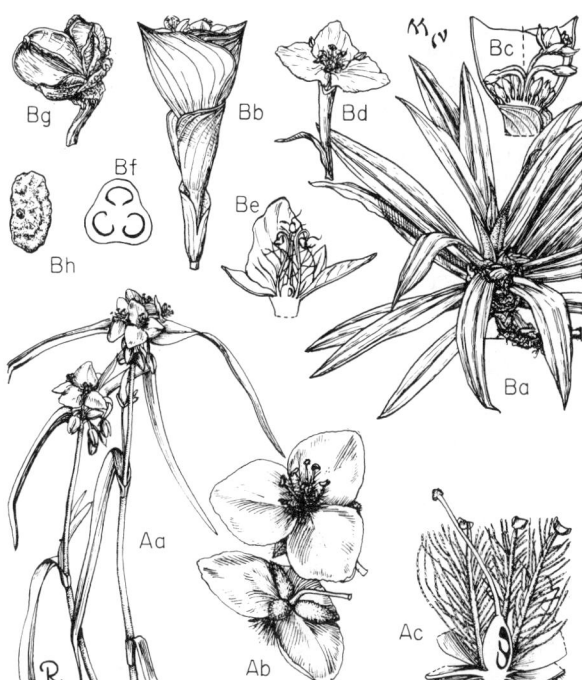

COMMELINACEAE. **A,** *Tradescantia* ×*Andersoniana:* **Aa,** flowering stems, × ⅛; **Ab,** flower, two views, × ½; **Ac,** flower, vertical section, × 2. **B,** *Rhoeo spathacea:* **Ba,** flowering plant, × ⅛; **Bb,** inflorescence subtended by bracts, × ½; **Bc,** inflorescence, upper bracts partly cut away, × ½; **Bd,** flower, × 1; **Be,** flower, vertical section, × 1½; **Bf,** ovary, cross section, × 5; **Bg,** capsule, × 3; **Bh,** seed, × 3.

COMMELINACEAE R. Br. SPIDERWORT FAMILY. Monocot; about 40 genera of herbs, widely distributed, particularly in the tropics; lvs. simple, alt., parallel-veined, entire, sheathing; infl. of sessile or peduncled, solitary or paired cincinni or bostryces, which are terminal, terminal and axillary, or axillary on the st., and often subtended by leafy bracts or arranged in thyrses; fls. usually bisexual, sepals 3, separate or united, petals 3, separate or united basally, stamens 1–3 or mostly 6, ovary superior, 2–3-celled; fr. a caps. or berry. The cult. genera are: *Callisia, Campelia, Cochliostema, Commelina, Commelinantia, Cuthbertia, Cyanotis, Dichorisandra, Geogenanthus, Gibasis, Hadrodemas, Palisota, Rhoeo, Setcreasea, Siderasis, Tinantia, Tradescantia, Tripogandra, Weldenia,* and *Zebrina.*

The family provides many ornamentals, most of which are grown under glass in the North or as ground covers in frost-free areas. A few species are annuals or hardy perennials useful even in northern gardens.

COMMELINANTIA Tharp. *Commelinaceae.* Two spp. of succulent herbs, native to s. Tex. and Mex.; sts. erect to decumbent, branched, brs. breaking through the lf. sheaths at the nodes; lvs. linear-spatulate to lanceolate, cordate-clasping; fls. 3–6 in a terminal unpaired cincinnus subtended by a single broad, flat, erect, cordate, clasping lf., outer 3 perianth segms. similar, inner 3 unequal, stamens 6, unequal, anthers oblong to orbicular, unequal, filaments bearded, ovary 3-celled, each cell with 2 ovules.

anomala (Torr.) Tharp [*Tinantia anomala* (Torr.) C. B. Clarke]. To 2 ft.; lower lvs. to 1 ft. long, upper lvs. to 8 in. long; inner perianth segms. very unequal, 2 of these showy, lavender-blue, 1 small, white. S. Tex.

COMPARETTIA Poepp. & Endl. *Orchidaceae.* About 7 spp. of epiphytes, native to trop. Amer.; pseudobulbs 1-lvd.; infl. lateral, pendent, racemose; petals and upper sepal spreading, lateral sepals united basally, forming a distinct spur, lip much larger than other perianth segms., united to column, the base prolonged into a forked appendage enclosed by the spur, column footless. For structure of fl. see *Orchidaceae.*

For culture see *Orchids.*

coccinea Lindl. To 10 in.; lvs. fleshy, narrow; raceme slender, loosely several-fld.; fls. to ½ in. across, vermilion, sepals and petals light orange inside, spur ¾–1 in. long, lip fan-shaped, somewhat 2-lobed at apex. Late summer. Brazil.

falcata Poepp. & Endl. Pseudobulbs oblong, clustered, smooth; lvs. elliptic-lanceolate, to 6 in. long or less, acute; scape arising from base of lf., to 28 in. long, filiform, raceme loosely 2–15-fld.; petals and upper sepal rose, to ½ in. long, spur slender, to ½ in. long, lip semiorbicular, 2-lobed, rose or rose-purple. W. Indies, Cent. Amer., S. Amer.

macroplectron Rchb.f. To 20 in.; raceme loosely many-fld.; fls. large, to 2 in. across, sepals and petals white or pale rose, with purple dots or spots, spur to 2 in. long, lip semiorbicular, 2-lobed, white with purple dots. Early spring. Colombia. Var. **punctatissima** Cogn. Fls. very densely covered with small rose dots throughout.

COMPOSITAE Giseke or, alternatively, **Asteraceae** Dumort. COMPOSITE FAMILY, SUNFLOWER FAMILY. Dicot.; about 950 genera and 20,000 spp. of cosmopolitan distribution, but mostly in temp. regions, herbs, sometimes shrubs, or occasionally trees in tropics, sometimes with milky or colored sap; lvs. opp. or alt., rarely whorled, basal or borne on the sts., entire to pinnatifid or compound; fls. in involucrate heads, the heads solitary or arranged in spikes, racemes, cymes, corymbs, thyrses, or panicles, involucral bracts (phyllaries) in 1 to several rows, of various shapes, textures, and colors, glabrous to variously hairy or glandular, the fl.-bearing surface of the head (receptacle) flat, convex, conical, or columnar, naked or with various scales (paleae) or bristles subtending the fls. (and then termed chaffy); fls. small, bisexual, unisexual, or neutral, of various colors, corolla either regular, tubular, and 4–5-lobed, or irregular and then strap-shaped (ligulate) or 2-lipped (bilabiate), stamens 5, rarely 3 or 4, borne on corolla tube, anthers usually united into a tube (syngenesious) around the style, sometimes tailed at base, ovary inferior, 2-carpelled, 1-celled, 1-ovuled, style usually 2-branched; fr. usually an achene, usually bearing at its apex a persistent or deciduous pappus consisting of bristles or scales or a combination of these, or sometimes a low ring or crown.

Many manuals use special terms descriptive of the head according to the type of fls. present: a ligulate head has only ligulate fls.; a discoid head has only tubular fls.; and a radiate head has tubular fls. (disc fls.) in the central area (the disc) and ligulate fls. (ray fls.) along the margin or circumference.

The *Compositae* are a huge family and have been divided by taxonomists into 12 or 13 tribes on the basis of such characteristics as presence or absence of milky or colored sap, corolla type, morphology of anthers, morphology of styles, and presence or absence of scales, chaff, or bristles on the receptacle. These tribes are described below.

Anthemis Tribe (Anthemideae Cass.). About 50 genera and 1,000 spp. of aromatic ann. or per. herbs or rarely subshrubs or shrubs, mostly native to the Old World, most numerous in Medit. region; lvs. alt., usually pinnatifid or pinnately parted or dissected, rarely simple; involucral bracts usually scarious or with scarious margins or tips, imbricate in several rows, receptacle naked or scaly; heads discoid or radiate; fls. bisexual or the outer ones female or neutral, disc fls. and ray fls. yellow, white, or greenish, anthers not tailed; pappus usually lacking, or present as a scarious cup or crown.

Arctotis Tribe (Arctoteae Cass.). About 20 genera and 200 spp. of per. herbs or rarely shrubs, native to the Old World, mostly S. Afr.; lvs. alt. or in rosettes, usually lobed or divided, sometimes more or less spiny; involucral bracts sometimes scarious, often spiny-tipped, imbricate in several rows, receptacle usually naked, rarely scaly or pitted; heads usually radiate; fls. bisexual or sometimes female or neutral, disc fls. usually yellow, ray fls. yellow, reddish, or purple, anthers not tailed; pappus of scales or a crown, or lacking.

Aster Tribe (Astereae). Over 100 genera and 2,000 spp. of mostly per. or sometimes ann. herbs, or shrubs, rarely trees, of cosmopolitan distribution, but mostly in temp. and montane regions; lvs. alt., entire to toothed or sometimes divided; involucral bracts usually imbricate in several rows, recepta-

COMPOSITAE. **A,** *Helianthella quinquenervis:* **Aa,** plant, × ⅛; **Ab,** heads, underside and upper side, × ¼; **Ac,** head, vertical section, × ½; **Ad,** base of ray corolla, × 2; **Ae,** disc flower with receptacular bract, × 2; **Af,** two anthers, × 6; **Ag,** stigmas, × 4; **Ah,** achene, × 1½. **B,** *Eupatorium maculatum:* **Ba,** plant, × ½₀; **Bb,** branch of inflorescence, × ½; **Bc,** head, × 1½; **Bd,** head, vertical section, × 2; **Be,** flower, × 2; **Bf,** two anthers, × 12; **Bg,** achene (with pappus), × 2; **Bh,** achene, × 4. **C,** *Gerbera Jamesonii:* **Cá,** plant, × ½₁₂; **Cb,** head, upper side, × ¼; **Cc,** head, underside (ligules cut short), × ½; **Cd,** head, vertical section, × ½; **Ce,** base of ray flower, × 1½; **Cf,** disc flower, × 2; **Cg,** two anthers, × 6; **Ch,** stigmas, × 10; **Ci,** achene, × 1½. **D,** *Lactuca perennis:* **Da,** plant, × ⅙; **Db,** head, upper side, × ¾; **Dc,** head, side view, × ¾; **Dd,** head, vertical section, × 1; **De,** flower, × 2; **Df,** two stamens, × 6; **Dg,** upper part of style and stigmas, × 5; **Dh,** achene, × 1½. **E,** *Jurinea mollis:* **Ea,** plant, × ½₁₀; **Eb,** head, × ½; **Ec,** head, vertical section, × ½; **Ed,** flower with receptacular bristles, × 1½; **Ee,** two stamens, × 3; **Ef,** stigmas, × 5; **Eg,** achene, × 2. **F,** *Helenium autumnale:* **Fa,** plant, × ½₀; **Fb,** head, upper side, × ½; **Fc,** head, underside, × ½; **Fd,** head, vertical section, × 1; **Fe,** base of ray flower, × 5; **Ff,** disc flower, × 6; **Fg,** two stamens, × 12; **Fh,** achene with withered disc flower, × 5.

cle naked; heads usually radiate; disc fls. usually bisexual, usually yellow or white, ray fls. bluish, reddish, whitish, or less frequently yellow, anthers not tailed; pappus usually of awns or bristles, rarely of scales or lacking.

Calendula Tribe (Calenduleae Cass.). About 10 genera and 160 spp. of herbs or shrubs, native to the Old World, chiefly Afr. and Medit. region; lvs. alt. or occasionally opp., entire to toothed or lobed, rarely divided; involucral bracts often with a scarious margin, nearly equal, in 1–3 rows, receptacle naked or rarely with a few bristles; heads radiate; disc fls. bisexual, male, or neutral, orange or yellow, ray fls. in 1 row, female or neutral, orange or yellow, anthers not tailed; achenes of various, usually irregular shapes, pappus lacking.

Cardus [*Cynara*] Tribe (Cardueae Cass. [*Cynareae* Less.]). About 50 genera and 1,500 spp. of thistles or thistlelike herbs, native chiefly to the N. Hemisphere of the Old World, a few in N. and S. Amer.; lvs. alt., sinuate to divided, rarely entire, usually spiny or prickly; involucral bracts in many rows, tips often spiny or bristly, receptacle bristly or hairy, seldom naked; heads discoid; fls. tubular, the marginal ones sometimes enlarged, 2-lipped or deeply 5-cleft, commonly female or neutral, disc fls. bisexual, deeply 5-lobed, anthers tailed; achenes mostly narrow or flat, sometimes beaked, pappus bristly or plumose, rarely of scales or lacking.

Cichorium Tribe (Cichorieae Dumort.). About 75 genera and 1,000 spp. of herbs, sometimes shrubs, rarely small trees, with milky sap, mostly native to the N. Temp. Zone, particularly numerous in the Old World; lvs. alt. or basal, entire to pinnatifid or rarely divided; involucral bracts nearly equal and imbricate in several rows, or equal and in 1 row; fls. all ligulate, bisexual, white, yellow, orange, red, purple, or sometimes blue, anthers not tailed; achenes often beaked, pappus of 1 or more rows of simple or plumose bristles, sometimes of awns or scales, or even lacking.

Eupatorium Tribe (Eupatorieae Cass.). About 50 genera and 2,050 spp. of per. herbs or shrubs, or rarely ann. herbs, native mostly to N. and S. Amer., chiefly in the tropics; lvs. mostly opp., sometimes whorled or alt., usually not divided; involucral bracts imbricate in several rows, or slightly unequal and in 1–2 rows, receptacle naked; heads discoid; disc fls. purple, reddish, or white, never truly yellow, ray fls. always lacking, anthers not tailed; pappus usually of rigid bristles, rarely plumose or of scales or lacking.

Helenium Tribe (Helenieae Benth. & Hook.f.). About 60 genera and 600 spp. of herbs or subshrubs, native mostly to N. Amer., chiefly sw. U.S. and Mex.; lvs. alt. or opp., entire to divided, sometimes gland-dotted; involucral bracts in 1–3 rows, receptacle usually naked, sometimes with bristles or hairs; heads usually radiate; disc fls. usually yellow, ray fls. usually fertile, usually yellow, anthers not tailed; pappus of scales, awns, or bristles, or sometimes lacking. An artificial assemblage of genera, sometimes included in the Helianthus Tribe, or a few genera in other tribes.

Helianthus Tribe (Heliantheae Cass.). Over 150 genera and more than 2,000 spp. of coarse herbs, subshrubs, or shrubs, native mostly to the New World; lvs. opp. (at least the lower ones) or alt., often glandular, entire or divided; involucral bracts imbricate in several rows, or nearly equal and in 2 rows, receptacle scaly; heads usually radiate; disc fls. and ray fls. usually yellow, anthers not tailed; pappus of scales or awns or lacking.

Inula Tribe (Inuleae Cass.). About 300 genera and 2,000 spp. of cosmopolitan distribution, but particularly numerous in S. Afr. and Australia; lvs. alt., opp., or basal, entire or less frequently toothed, often woolly or glandular; involucral bracts usually white or scarious, frequently very hairy, imbricate in several rows, receptacle naked or scaly; heads discoid or radiate; disc fls. usually light yellow or white, ray fls. present or lacking, anthers tailed; pappus of hairs, rarely of scales or lacking.

Mutisia Tribe (Mutisieae Cass.). About 55 genera and more than 500 spp. of herbs or shrubs, more rarely vines or trees of N. Amer., Afr., Asia, and chiefly S. Amer.; lvs. alt. or basal, entire to pinnatifid, rarely divided or prickly; involucral bracts usually imbricate in several rows, rarely equal and in 1 row, receptacle usually naked; disc fls. and ray fls. all 2-lipped, all the same color, anthers tailed; pappus of simple or plumose bristles, or narrow scales, or lacking.

Senecio Tribe (Senecioneae Cass.). About 50 genera and over 2,000 spp. of herbs or shrubs or sometimes trees of cosmopolitan distribution; lvs. usually alt. or basal, rarely opp., entire to toothed or divided; involucral bracts usually in 1 row, sometimes with an additional, differentiated outer calyxlike row, but rarely imbricate in several rows, receptacle usually naked; heads discoid or radiate; disc fls. bisexual, ray fls. female, neutral, or lacking, anthers not tailed; pappus of many hairlike bristles, rarely almost scaly or lacking.

Vernonia Tribe (Vernonieae Cass.). About 50 genera and 1,400 spp. of per. or rarely ann. herbs, or shrubs, rarely trees, native to N. and S. Amer. and Afr.; lvs. usually alt., occasionally opp., entire to toothed; involucral bracts nearly always imbricate in several rows, receptacle usually naked, rarely hairy, sometimes pitted; heads discoid; disc fls. bisexual, reddish-purple to white, never yellow, ray fls. lacking, anthers not tailed; pappus of many bristlelike hairs, rarely of scales or lacking.

The cultivated genera are: *Achillea, Ageratum, Agoseris, Amberboa, Amellus, Ammobium, Anacyclus, Anaphalis, Antennaria, Anthemis, Aphanostephus, Arctium, Arctotis, Arnica, Artemisia, Aster, Asteriscus, Athanasia, Baccharis, Baileya, Balsamorhiza, Bellis, Bellium, Berlandiera, Bidens, Boltonia, Brachycome, Brachyglottis, Brickellia, Buphthalmum, Calendula, Callistephus, Calocephalus, Carduus, Carlina, Carthamus, Cassinia, Castalis, Catananche, Celmisia, Centaurea, Chamaemelum, Chaenactis, Charieis, Chrysanthemum, Chrysocoma, Chrysogonum, Chrysopsis, Chrysothamnus, Cichorium, Cirsium, Cladanthus, Cnicus, Coreopsis, Corethrogyne, Cosmos, Cotula, Craspedia, Crepis, Crupina, Cynara, Dahlia, Dimorphotheca, Doronicum, Dracopis, Dyssodia, Echinacea, Echinops, Emilia, Encelia, Enceliopsis, Engelmannia, Erigeron, Eriocephalus, Eriophyllum, Eupatorium, Euryops, Felicia, Gaillardia, Galactites, Gamolepis, Gazania, Geraea, Gerbera, Gnaphalium, Grindelia, Guizotia, Gutierrezia, Gynura, Haastia, Haplopappus, Helenium, Helianthella, Helianthus, Helichrysum, Heliopsis, Helipterum, Heteropappus, Hieracium, Homogyne, Hulsea, Humea, Hymenopappus, Hymenoxys, Hypochaeris, Inula, Jurinea, Krigia, Kuhnia, Lactuca, Lasthenia, Layia, Leibnitzia, Leontopodium, Lessingia, Leucogenes, Leuzea, Liatris, Ligularia, Lindheimera, Lonas, Luina, Machaeranthera, Madia, Malacothrix, Marshallia, Matricaria, Melampodium, Mikania, Monolopia, Montanoa, Moscharia, Mutisia, Nothocalais, Olearia, Onopordum, Osteospermum, Otanthus, Othonna, Pachystegia, Palafoxia, Parthenium, Perezia, Petasites, Picris, Piqueria, Pityopsis, Podachaenium, Podolepis, Prenanthes, Raoulia, Ratibida, Reichardia, Rudbeckia, Santolina, Sanvitalia, Saussurea, Scolymus, Scorzonera, Senecio, Serratula, Silphium, Silybum, Simsia, Solidago, ×Solidaster, Spilanthes, Stevia, Stokesia, Tagetes, Tanacetum, Taraxacum, Telekia, Thelesperma, Tithonia, Tolpis, Townsendia, Tragopogon, Tridax, Tripleurospermum, Tussilago, Ursinia, Venidium, Verbesina, Vernonia, Viguiera, Vittadinia, Wedelia, Wyethia, Xanthisma, Xeranthemum,* and *Zinnia.*

Most composites need full sun and have simple cultural requirements; most are summer- or autumn-flowering. The family includes many ornamentals, and some species are grown for their oils.

COMPTONIA L'Hér. *Myricaceae.* One sp., a deciduous, usually monoecious shrub of e. N. Amer.; lvs. alt., narrow, pinnatifid, fragrant; male fls. in short catkins, stamens 4, female fls. in heads, ovary 1-celled, subtended by 8 narrowly linear, persistent bracts; fr. an ovoid nutlet subtended by bracts, in clusters.

Adapted for covering banks, doing well in peaty or dry sandy soil. Propagated by seeds, layering, or division of clumps.

asplenifolia: *C. peregrina* var.

peregrina (L.) J. Coult. SWEET FERN. To 5 ft., branchlets and lvs. pubescent; lvs. linear-oblong, deeply pinnately notched, to 4½ in. long and ½ in. wide; fr. catkins to 1 in. in diam., nutlets glabrous, brown, ³⁄₁₆ in. long. Nov. Sc. to N.C., Ind., and Mich. Var. **asplenifolia** (L.) Fern. [*C. asplenifolia* L.; *Myrica asplenifolia* (L.) Ait.]. Less pubescent; lvs. and catkins smaller. Pinelands, N.Y. to Va.

CONANDRON Siebold & Zucc. *Gesneriaceae.* One sp., a per. herb of Japan; lvs. in a basal rosette, deciduous; fls. 6–25 on a scape, calyx 5-parted, lobes narrow, corolla rotate, 5-lobed, stamens 5, anthers appendaged, united in a beaked cone, disc ringlike, ovary superior; fr. a loculicidal caps.

For cultivation see *Gesneriaceae.*

ramondioides Siebold & Zucc. Lf. blades ovate or oblong to elliptic, to 15 in. long, 4 in. wide, narrowed to a winglike base, sharply toothed, thin, rugose; scapes to 8 in. high; calyx lobes ¼ in. long, corolla ivory-white to pink or lilac, with orange lines or spots between lobes at the throat, to 1 in. wide, tube ¼ in. long, lobes triangular, anthers purplish; caps. about twice as long as calyx.

CONDALIA Cav. *Rhamnaceae.* Not cult. **C. lycioides:** *Ziziphus obtusifolia.* **C. Parryi:** *Ziziphus Parryi.*

CONGEA Roxb. *Verbenaceae.* About 7 spp. of climbing shrubs, native to se. Asia; lvs. opp., simple, entire; fls. white, pink or rose, in few-fld., capitate cymes arranged in panicles, the cymes subtended by 3 or 4 leaflike involucral bracts, calyx 5-toothed, corolla 2-lipped, the upper 2-lobed, the lower 3-lobed, stamens 4, exserted; fr. a drupe.

Sometimes grown out of doors in southern Calif. and other mild climates. Zone 10.

tomentosa Roxb. SHOWER ORCHID. Lvs. ovate to elliptic-ovate, to 8 in. long, tomentose beneath; bracts elliptic, to 1 in. long, white to lilac, tomentose; fls. white. Burma, Thailand.

CONICOSIA N. E. Br. *Aizoaceae.* About 10 spp. of ann., bien., or mostly per. succulents, native to S. Afr., root tuberous, fleshy, or some spp. with fibrous roots, sts. erect, decumbent to prostrate; lvs. opp. or sometimes alt., in terminal tufts, 3-angled to nearly cylindrical, persisting after withering; fls. solitary, long-pedicelled, borne on lateral brs. from the rosettes, which die after fr. ripens, calyx unequally or subequally 5-lobed, petals yellow, many, in several series, stamens many, filaments bearded basally, staminodes many, ovary inferior or partly superior, 10–20-celled, stigmas 10–20; fr. a caps., with a conical apex, separating into many, separate valves, expanding keels absent.

Growth occurs from late summer to early winter. Plants need a sandy soil and a sunny location, and in winter a relatively cool temperature of about 55° F. Propagated by seeds. See also *Succulents.*

communis N. E. Br. Roots fibrous, sts. to 1 ft., erect or bent down, fl. brs. deciduous; lvs. green, more or less glaucous, purplish at base, to 6 in. long on main st., shorter on brs., to ⅜ in. thick, 3-angled in section, linear in general outline; fls. solitary, to 2½ in. across, on pedicels to 5 in. long, calyx lobes longer than petals, petals yellow, the outer tinted red at tip and bronzy-yellow on back. Cape Prov.

pugioniformis (L.) N. E. Br. Roots fibrous, sts. to 3 ft. high, 1 in. in diam., erect, fl. brs. to 1 ft. long or more; lvs. glaucous-green, purplish at base, to 9 in. long, ½ in. wide at center on main st., shorter on fl. brs., 3-angled in section, upper side or all sides concave, tip acuminate; fls. 1–3 from fl. brs., to nearly 3 in. or perhaps 4 in. across, on pedicels to 5 in. long or more, calyx lobes shorter than petals, petals pale yellow, reddish on outside. S. Afr.

CONIFERS. A general term from the Latin, meaning cone-bearing, employed for cone-bearing trees such as cypresses *(Cupressus),* pines *(Pinus),* spruces *(Picea),* and the like, which belong to the families Araucariaceae, Cephalotaxaceae, Cupressaceae, Pinaceae, Podocarpaceae, Taxaceae, and Taxodiaceae.

The conifers are the most important class of the gymnosperms, ancient types of plants with ovules naked rather than enclosed in an ovary as in the angiosperms; other living gymnosperms are the cycads, of about ten genera, and *Ginkgo.* The conifers number about 550 species in about 50 genera, widely distributed but most prominent in temperate regions. They are all woody plants, many of them shrubs, others

majestic trees that give character to extensive areas. They are well represented in the native flora of North America. Some of the kinds bear berrylike cones rather than cones with evident scales, but the characters of foliage and of woody structure and the balsamic odors reveal their affinity, even to uncritical observers. A few genera include deciduous trees, such as the bald cypress *(Taxodium distichum),* dawn redwood *(Metasequoia),* and larches *(Larix),* but the group as a whole is classed among the evergreens and it has a horticultural unity.

Conifers are grown for ornament as single specimens, for shelter belts, the smaller ones for foundation plantings about buildings and in private grounds, some for Christmas trees, and the arboreous species for groves and forests. The timber trees among the conifers constitute the main large forestry stands in this country. All the kinds abound in interest, because of their evergreen character and their strong individuality. Although lacking showy flowers, the striking habit, interesting cones, details of foliage, and color of new growths give them an ornamental quality quite their own. The hardy genera are particularly striking in the winter landscape. These qualities vary widely among the different genera. Most of the genera are known in cultivation somewhere in the United States and Canada (see species recommended for specific hardiness zones, below).

The conifers are mostly plants of high land. Many of them do well on rather thin soil, yet in private grounds the best results are to be expected when the soil is good or well enriched, for much of their beauty depends on verdant growth. For low grounds, *Chamaecyparis, Larix, Metasequoia,* or *Taxodium* may be chosen. The common arborvitae *(Thuja)* and bald cypress *(Taxodium distichum)* are particularly valuable in low and even swampy places. When large trees are wanted, *Abies, Picea,* and *Pinus* are generally most adaptable, particularly in cold climates, but *Araucaria, Cryptomeria, Podocarpus, Pseudotsuga,* and *Sequoia* are majestic in milder climates. Of the smaller and shrubby kinds, selections may be made among *Chamaecyparis,* the true cypresses *(Cupressus), Juniperus, Taxus,* and *Thuja;* the retinosporas are juvenile states of *Chamaecyparis* and *Thuja.* Inasmuch as so many species of conifers are available for cultivation from so many parts of the world and of such varied characteristics, it follows that the successful planter of them is the one who notes with much care the requirements of each as to climate, soil, and exposure.

Seedlings of many conifers vary widely, as in *Chamaecyparis, Juniperus, Thuja,* and even in some species of *Picea.* The so-called dwarf conifers, which often originate in this way, are propagated by cuttings and layers. They are especially interesting for small places and for rock gardens, and they have the charm of special form and variety of color. Naturally or artificially dwarfed conifers are among many kinds of woody plants grown as bonsai (see *Bonsai).* Species favored by the Japanese include several of their native pines (especially *Pinus parviflora),* the Sargent juniper, *Juniperus chinensis* var. *Sargentii, Picea jezoensis,* and *Cryptomeria.*

Transplanting of conifers is best performed, as a rule, in spring just before the active new growth begins or about when the buds begin to swell. Early autumn planting is satisfactory in mild climates and with small potted or pruned stock if the soil is moist and in good condition and the exposure protected so that the plants do not dry out seriously before making a roothold. August planting, after the main growth is completed, is often successful if the rainfall is adequate or sufficient water can be supplied. The younger the tree the greater is the likelihood of success in transplanting; but the usual height for the arboreous species is 2–3 feet; any additional height is likely to entail greater care in the transplanting. Very large conifers should be moved only by those skilled in the work. Experience shows that moving large conifers with a frozen ball of earth large enough to include all the roots is usually successful.

The top is not pruned, as a rule, at transplanting. Therefore, the roots should be kept intact as much as possible, especial care being exercised in the digging, and they should not be allowed to dry out. Plants from shady positions should not be transplanted to the open sun. If the hemlock, for example, is wanted in a sunny, exposed place, young trees occupying such positions in the wild should be found. Better results with all conifers, however, are to be expected from well-handled nursery-grown plants. Newly planted trees may be mulched the first year with straw or similar material to retain the moisture. All the conifers, and especially the hemlocks *(Tsuga)*, should be well guyed after transplanting, for loss is certain if the newly planted tree is racked by the wind.

The aftercare of conifers requires no peculiar attention except to meet the attacks of the special insects and fungi, and for this work the most recent authoritative books or bulletins should be consulted. Probably the most serious of the diseases at present, since it involves natural forests, is the white-pine blister rust, due to an imported fungus. It attacks the five-leaved or white pines, appearing on the twigs and extending into the trunk. Thorough removal of the blistered or cankered twigs from valuable trees as soon as the injury appears may save the specimen, but the main procedure is to destroy the alternate hosts on which the fungus lives. These other hosts are species of *Ribes*, and none of these plants should be allowed to stand within 200 to 300 yards of white pines; the cultivated black currant is particularly susceptible to the disease. For aphis and scale insects, thorough spraying is the proper safeguard. The five-needle pines also suffer from the white pine weevil, which attacks the leading shoots.

Conifers require the minimum of pruning inasmuch as most of them are symmetrical growers. Pines seldom give satisfactory results when clipped. To keep spruces, firs, and some of the smaller kinds within bounds or to make them compact and to delay the death of the lower limbs, the tips of the shoots may be pinched back in spring or early summer.

Propagation of conifers is accomplished by means of seeds, cuttings, or grafting on other stocks. Seeds are the usual means for the raising of forest stock and for the propagation of the species in general. The horticultural cultivars, however, must be increased by cuttings, for seedlings may not come true. Species of which seed is not available, and also certain of the named cultivars, are grafted on other stocks.

Seeds are gathered as soon as ripe and kept in bags or boxes in a dry place until the following spring or else stratified over winter. The seeds are planted in rows in a mellow, well-prepared seed bed, and covered ½ inch or less depending on the size. Small seeds may be broadcast. Rows are usually as close together as 6 inches, and the bed is strewn with pine needles or other mulch. The young seedlings require protection under lath screens or brush and plenty of moisture, although the seeds themselves may be kept fairly free from water until germination takes place; seed beds therefore should be in well-drained soil. If mice, squirrels, or birds are likely to be troublesome, the beds may be covered with wire netting; the beds may be protected from washing by a border of boards. Care must be taken to avoid damping off under the screens. The plants will need protection the first winter. Care should be taken to keep the young seedlings constantly lightly mulched to prevent rain from spattering them with soil, which adheres to the young plants and causes considerable loss. In 18 months or more, when making the first set of rough leaves, the seedlings may be transplanted; and the subsequent process will determine itself for each species. Conifer seeds may also be stratified the first autumn in boxes or flats, and the seedlings allowed to grow in these boxes the first year; this is a good method for small quantities or for garden practice, and for tender species. Seedlings of some of the rarer species, as of *Abies*, are so small that it is inadvisable to transplant them until the end of the second year.

Cuttings are made from firm tip shoots late in the season, representing one-year and a two-year base, the bottom third or half being trimmed of leaves. These are set in clean sand or peat in flats or a greenhouse bench, close together in rows, and the soil firmed tightly about them. Mild bottom heat should be given at first, and raised to perhaps 70° F later. In four to eight months, depending on the kind of conifer and the conditions, the cuttings should be rooted and ready for transplanting. *Cedrus, Chamaecyparis, Juniperus, Taxus, Thuja*, and the like are the kinds most commonly grown from cuttings, although *Picea* and others are amenable. *Picea* and others that contain a large amount of resin are the most difficult to root, and removal of the resin by dipping the lower end in hot water has been recommended.

Cuttings may also be rooted in outdoor summer frames, with bottom heat provided by a little fermenting manure or other means; a fair percentage of some kinds will root without other bottom heat than that supplied by the sun.

Grafting of conifers is performed on stocks of the same genus, usually in spring when the roots begin to start. The stocks may be grown from seeds or cuttings, usually the former. The stock in any case represents the most abundant or most easily propagated or most seedful species of the genus, as *Juniperus virginiana* for the other junipers, *Thuja occidentalis* for the other arborvitaes, *Picea Abies* for the other spruces, *Pinus Strobus* for related species, and so on. When large enough for grafting, the stocks are potted and the scion is sideworked near the root and firmly tied. The grafted plants are kept in frames or a propagating house, and in four to six weeks union should have taken place. See the article *Propagation*.

Select species of conifers suitable for appropriate sites in specific plant hardiness zones of continental North America include the following, the zones listed from north to south. Zone 3: *Abies balsamea, Picea Abies, P. pungens, Pinus contorta, P. flexilis, P. nigra, P. ponderosa, P. sylvestris, Pseudotsuga Menziesii*. Zone 4: *Abies concolor, Juniperus chinensis, J. horizontalis, J. Sabina, J. scopulorum, J. virginiana, Larix decidua, Picea glauca, P. Omorika, P. pungens, Pinus nigra, Pseudotsuga Menziesii, Taxus cuspidata, Thuja occidentalis*. Zone 5 (except for Great Plains area): *Abies concolor, A. homolepis, Chamaecyparis obtusa, C. pisifera, Juniperus chinensis, Larix decidua, Metasequoia glyptostroboides, Picea Abies, P. pungens, Pinus Armandii, P. Bungeana, P. nigra, P. parviflora, P. Strobus, P. sylvestris, P. Wallichiana, Pseudotsuga Menziesii, Taxus baccata, T. cuspidata, Thuja occidentalis, Tsuga canadensis*. Zone 6 (in the eastern half of the zone): *Abies concolor, A. lasiocarpa, Chamaecyparis obtusa, Juniperus virginiana, Larix Kaempferi, Picea Omorika, P. orientalis, Pinus Bungeana, P. nigra, P. Strobus, Pseudolarix Kaempferi, Pseudotsuga Menziesii, Sciadopitys verticillata, Taxus cuspidata, Tsuga canadensis*. Zone 7 (excluding southwestern parts of the zone): *Abies concolor, A. homolepis, A. Nordmanniana, Calocedrus decurrens, Cedrus atlantica, C. Deodara, Chamaecyparis obtusa, C. pisifera, × Cupressocyparis Leylandii, Cupressus glabra, Juniperus chinensis, J. conferta, J. virginiana, Metasequoia glyptostroboides, Picea Abies, P. Omorika, P. orientalis, Pinus Bungeana, P. Cembra, P. nigra, P. parviflora, P. Strobus, P. Thunbergiana, P. Wallichiana, Pseudolarix Kaempferi, Sciadopitys verticillata, Taxodium distichum, Taxus cuspidata, Thuja occidentalis, Tsuga canadensis, T. caroliniana*. Zone 8 (in the East): *Calocedrus decurrens, Cedrus atlantica, C. Deodara, C. libani, Cryptomeria japonica, Cunninghamia lanceolata, Juniperus chinensis, J. virginiana, Picea pungens, Pinus palustris, P. Strobus, P. Taeda, P. Thunbergiana, Sciadopitys verticillata, Sequoia sempervirens, Taxodium distichum, Tsuga canadensis;* and in the Pacific Northwest, additionally the following: *Abies lasiocarpa, A. procera, Araucaria araucana, Chamaecyparis nootkatensis, Pinus contorta, P. densiflora, P. ponderosa, P. sylvestris, Pseudotsuga Menziesii, Thuja plicata, Tsuga heterophylla, Sequoiadendron giganteum*, and many others. Zone 9 (primarily in the South): *Cedrus Deodara, Cunninghamia lanceolata, Cupressus chinensis, C. glabra, Juniperus virginiana, Metasequoia glyptostroboides, Pinus echinata, P. glabra, P. palustris, P. Taeda, Platycladus orientalis, Podocarpus macrophyllus, P. Nagi, Taxodium distichum*. Zone 10 (West Coast in southern California): *Calocedrus decurrens, Cedrus atlantica, C. Deodara, Cupressus sem-*

pervirens, Juniperus chinensis, Pinus canariensis, P. Pinea, P. Thunbergiana, Platycladus orientalis, Podocarpus macrophyllus; and in the cooler San Francisco Bay area can be added *Abies concolor, Chamaecyparis Lawsoniana,* ×*Cupressocyparis Leylandii, Picea pungens, P. Smithiana, Pseudotsuga Menziesii, Tsuga heterophylla,* and others.

CONIOGRAMME Fée. *Polypodiaceae.* About 20 spp. of strong-growing ferns, mainly native to the Old World tropics from Afr. to Japan and Polynesia, with one sp. in Mex.; lvs. 1–2-pinnate; sori linear, following the veins, naked. By some authors considered a single polymorphic sp.

One species sometimes cultivated under glass, requiring a rather cool or moderate atmosphere and a well-drained soil; useful as a specimen plant. See also *Ferns.*

japonica (Thunb.) Diels. BAMBOO FERN. Lvs. mostly 1-pinnate, to 2 ft. long, pinnae to 1 ft. long and 1 in. wide, finely toothed; sori extending to the margin or nearly so. Temp. e. Asia.

CONIUM L. *Umbelliferae.* Two spp. of poisonous herbs of Eurasia; lvs. pinnately decompound; fls. small, white, in compound umbels, the bracts of involucre and bractlets of involucels numerous, lanceolate, inconspicuous; fr. ovate, somewhat flattened, with prominent undulate ribs.

One species grown for medicinal purposes; propagated by seeds.

maculatum L. HEMLOCK, POISON H., SPOTTED H., CALIFORNIA FERN, NEBRASKA F., WINTER F. Bien., to 10 ft.; lvs. finely cut into ovate, toothed segms., dark green. Eur.; naturalized in N. and S. Amer. Plant very poisonous in all its parts, and sometimes fatally so, if eaten by animals or man.

CONOBEA Aubl. *Scrophulariaceae.* Not in cult. **C. multifida:** *Leucospora multifida.*

CONOCARPUS L. BUTTON MANGROVE. *Combretaceae.* Two spp. of shrubs or trees of mangrove swamps of trop. N. and S. Amer. and Afr.; lvs. alt., simple, leathery, with pair of glands at base; fl. heads small, conelike, in terminal panicles; fls. minute, 5-merous, petals 0, stamens exserted; fr. small, angular, obcordate, 1-seeded, imbricate.

erectus L. BUTTONWOOD. Prostrate shrub to erect tree, to 60 ft.; lvs. typically glabrous, obovate to elliptic or ovate, to 4 in. long; fls. greenish, in heads to ½ in. across; fr. cluster conelike, purplish-green. Seashores, trop. Amer. and W. Afr. Produces a tanbark. Var. **sericeus** Fors ex DC. SILVER B., SILVER TREE. Lvs. densely silky-hairy, acuminate at each end.

CONOCLINIUM: *EUPATORIUM.*

CONOPHARYNGIA: *TABERNAEMONTANA.*

CONOPHYTUM N. E. Br. CONE PLANT. *Aizoaceae.* About 290 spp. of dwarf, nearly stemless, clump-forming succulents, native to S. Afr.; lvs. opp., fused into a fleshy, globose, obconical, ovoid, nearly cylindrical or oblong body (growth), apex flat, rounded, notched, or lobed, with a mouthlike orifice at the center, sometimes with translucent window spots, new growth developing within the old which dries to a thin shell protecting the new growth through the dry period; fls. solitary, on pedicels rising from the interior of the growth through the fissure, calyx 4–6-lobed, with a tube, petals usually many, in 1 to several series, fused basally into a slender tube, stamens few to many, ovary 4–6-celled, stigmas 4–6, usually united into a definite style; fr. a caps., expanding keels present, placental tubercles absent.

Growth occurs in spring or early summer when the new growth increases in size and bursts through the protective shell of the old growth. Soil should be sandy and loamy with a good supply of humus. As growth begins, the soil should be kept rather moist, and then watering entirely stopped. When grown indoors, light shading is necessary, and winter temperature should be relatively cool, about 60° F. Propagation easy by seeds or cuttings. See also *Succulents.*

advenum N. E. Br. Growths gray-green, often suffused with purple on the sides and with dark green or purplish-brown dots in lines transverse to orifice or scattered, to 5⁄16 in. high and nearly as wide, 3⁄16 in. thick, obconically obovoid and slightly notched at convex tip, the orifice outlined with confluent dots; fls. 3⁄16 in. across, petals yellowish-pink. Cape Prov.

aequale L. Bolus. Sts. to nearly 3 in., brs. with old lvs. persistent; growths pale green, glossy, sparsely green-dotted, to 1½ in. high and in diam., 1 side rounded, the other nearly flat, 2-lobed, fissure to ⅝ in. long, ¼ in. wide, lobes to ½ in. long, reddish-keeled, truncate; fls. ⅝ in. long, petals yellow. Cape Prov.

ampliatum L. Bolus. Growths smooth, dark green, dotted, to 1 3⁄16 in. long and in diam., obovoid to nearly globose or reniform in side view, 2-lobed, lobes 3⁄16 in. long, acute in top view, rounded in side view, margins and keel lined with dirty purple, translucent area nearly square; fls. ¾ in. long, petals golden-yellow. Cape Prov.

amplum L. Bolus. Growths pale glaucous-green, neither dotted nor with translucent area, to 2 in. long, 1 in. wide, 1 5⁄16 in. in diam., obcordate or oblong-obovate in side view, sides rounded, lobes with prominent pustule; corolla ¾ in. long, yellow. Cape Prov.

apiatum (N. E. Br.) N. E. Br. Growths whitish-green or light glaucous-green, dotted with dark green, to 2½ in. long, 1 in. wide, ¾ in. thick, 2-lobed, lobes to ⅝ in. long, often reddish on margins and keels; fls. 1 in. across, petals yellow, spreading. Cape Prov.

aureum: a listed name of no botanical standing.

Batesii N. E. Br. Growths gray-green, faintly lined with dark green dots, or dots scattered, or in 3–5 radiating lines on each side of orifice, to ⅝ in. high, ½ in. wide and nearly as thick, obconical, nearly circular to elliptic at convex tip, orifice ⅛ in. long; fls. to ½ in. across, nocturnal, petals pale creamy-yellowish. Cape Prov.

Braunsii: *C. Pearsonii.*

brevisectum L. Bolus. Brs. to 2⅝ in. long with persistent, pale brown, darker-dotted lf. sheaths; growths to 1 3⁄16 in. long, ⅝ in. in diam., obovate or oblong-obovate in side view, 2-lobed, lobes to ⅜ in. long, obtuse in top view, rounded in side view, with nearly square translucent zone; fls. several, corolla to ¾ in. long, golden-yellow. Cape Prov.

calculus (A. Berger) N. E. Br. Growths light glaucous- or chalky-green, not dotted, glabrous, globose, to ¾ in. in diam., orifice to 3⁄16 in. long; fls. ⅝ in. across, nocturnal, petals yellow. Cape Prov. Var. **calculus.** The typical var.; sides of orifice not turned up or red. Var. **protrusum** L. Bolus. Sides of orifice turned up and red.

citrinum L. Bolus. Growths glaucous, with scattered red dots, minutely velvety-papillate, to 1 in. long, ¾ in. wide, rounded-ovoid to elongate-ovoid, rounded beneath, compressed toward apex, lobes to ¼ in. long with red-edged keel; fls. about ⅝ in. across, petals lemon-yellow. Cape Prov.

Elishae (N. E. Br.) N. E. Br. Growths slightly bluish-green, irregularly dotted with darker green, to 1 in. long or more, ¾ in. wide, ⅝ in. thick, ovoid or oblong-ovoid, 2-lobed, keels of lobes often purplish; fls. to 1 in. across, diurnal, petals bright yellow. Cape Prov.

Ernianum Loesch & Tisch. Growths whitish gray-green, to 1 in. high, ¾ in. wide, ⅝ in. thick, somewhat compressed above, notched, lobes flat on inside, keeled at tip, keel reddish, margins and keel with crowded, large, dark green dots, edge of fissure zoned; fls to 1 in. across, petals pink to lilac. S.-W. Afr.

fenestratum Schwant. Mat-forming; growths dark olive-green to brown-green, to ⅝ in. high, ⅜ in. wide, 5⁄16 in. thick, short-cylindrical, terminal area divided into 2 rounded to flattened lobes with cream- to ocher-colored markings, often light and transparent; fls. to ⅜ in. across, petals white. S. Afr.

flavum N. E. Br. Cespitose; growths smooth, dark green, often reddish on the sides, to ¾ in. high and ½ in. wide, obconical, flat above or slightly convex, fissure bordered with a dark green line, surface with several dark green dots; fls. to ⅝ in. across, petals yellow. Cape Prov.

frutescens Schwant. Sts. to 4 in. high; growths dark green with light dots, to 1 3⁄16 in. long, 1 in. wide, ⅜ in. thick at base, deeply lobed, lobes 5⁄16 in. long, flat inside, keeled on back; fls. 1 in. across, petals deep orange-yellow. Cape Prov.

giftbergense Tisch. Cushion-forming; growths light gray-green, with unequal, irregularly placed, often slightly elevated, dark green to carmine dots, to ¾ in. high, ⅝ in. wide, ½ in. thick, broadly ellipsoid, 2-lobed, lobes slightly unequal, fissure to ¼ in. long, surrounded by a dark row of dots, sides purplish-tinted; fls. to 1 in. across, fragrant, nocturnal, petals light yellow. Cape Prov.

gratum (N. E. Br.) N. E. Br. Growths pale bluish-green, dotted with darker green, to 1 in. high and in diam., top-shaped in side view, globose in top view, orifice outlined in dark green when young, dotted pink on each side in age; fls. to 9⁄16 in. across, diurnal, petals magenta, recurved. Cape Prov.

hians N. E. Br. Growths minutely puberulous and somewhat velvety, light green, to ⅜ in. high, 5⁄16 in. wide, ¼ in. thick, obovoid or obconical, slightly compressed, shallowly 2-lobed, lobes slightly reddish, keeled at tip, rounded at back, notch 1/16 in. deep, outlined with a darker green or reddish line; fls. 3/16 in. across, petals reddish-yellow or white. Cape Prov.

Johannis-Winkleri (Dinter & Schwant.) N. E. Br. Growths light blue to gray-green, to 3/4 in. high, 7/8 in. across at circular, truncate, flat or only slightly convex top; petals yellow. S.-W. Afr.

Luisae Schwant. Mat-forming; bodies indistinctly dotted, to 5/8 in. long, 3/8 in. wide, 5/16 in. thick, cordate in outline in side view, 2-lobed, inner faces of lobes shortly hairy, fissure to 1/8 in. long, edges of lobes with darker borders and a dark spot on each side; fls. 3/4 in. across, on pedicels to 1/4 in. long, petals yellow. Cape Prov.

Meyerae Schwant. Growths dark gray-green, dotted with small dark spots, marked with a line of confluent dots on inner faces and back of lobes, to 2 in. long, 13/16 in. wide, deeply notched with tapered lobes to 1 in. long, flat on inner side, rounded on outer side; petals yellow. Cape Prov. Forma **apiculatum** (N. E. Br.) Tisch. Lobes slightly arched upward at tip.

Meyeri N. E. Br. Growths harshly velvety-puberulous to the touch, opaque green, to 1/2 in. high, about 1/4 in. thick, nearly globose, orifice very small and not depressed in the rounded apex; fls. about 5/8 in. across, petals yellow. Cape Prov.

minusculum (N. E. Br.) N. E. Br. Growths bright green, becoming dull green and often suffused with purple, minutely and densely dotted with white, to 3/8 in. long, 3/8 in. wide, 1/4 in. thick, obovoid, top elliptic and often slightly notched, orifice surrounded by a more or less diamond-shaped dark green or dark purple ring with dark green or dark purple lines outside; fls. to 13/16 in. across, diurnal, outer petals spreading, bright magenta above yellow base, inner petals 5–6, magenta or orange-yellow, tipped with purple. Cape Prov.

minutum (Haw.) N. E. Br. Growths light bluish-green or glaucous-green, sometimes with darker dots, to 1/2 in. long, 3/8 in. wide at the slightly convex top, obconical or subglobose-obconical; fls. to 7/8 in. across, diurnal, outer petals rose-magenta, spreading or recurved, inner petals yellow or sometimes magenta-tipped, ascending or spreading. Cape Prov.

multipunctatum Tisch. Cespitose; growths pale gray-green, minutely dark-dotted in upper part, to 3/4 in. high, 5/8 in. wide, pear-shaped in side view, top with crowded, irregular lines and impressed ends bordered with many minute dots, fissure to 3/16 in. long; fls. nocturnal, petals white. Cape Prov.

mundum N. E. Br. Growths dull grayish-green or glaucous-green, tinged purple and marked with prominent blackish-green or blackish-purple, mostly confluent, raised dots, to 1/2 in. long, 3/4 in. wide, broadly obconical, shallowly notched across the top, top elliptic or circular, flat or concave with raised rim; fls. to 1/2 in. across, petals white, pale straw-colored, or pale pink, recurved. Cape Prov.

muscosipapillatum Lavis. To 3 in., brs. erect, covered with old lf. sheaths; growths partly enclosed by light brown lf. sheaths with darker brown dots, gray-green to whitish, indistinctly green-dotted, finely velvety hairy, to 13/4 in. long, 11/4 in. wide, elongate or cordate in side view, laterally compressed with 1 side flat to concave, the other rounded, lobes unequal, truncate, to 3/8 in. long and wide, margins more or less recurved; fls. to 11/2 in. across, petals golden-yellow. Cape Prov.

obcordellum (Haw.) N. E. Br. Growths green or glaucous-green, usually tinged purple, with raised, often confluent, dark purplish or green dots on top, to 3/8 in. long or more, 1/2 in. wide, or more, obcordately obconical, notched across the top; fls. to 3/4 in. across, expanding in late afternoon, petals white to pale yellow, sometimes pink-tinged at tip. Cape Prov. Var. **multicolor**: forma *multicolor*. Forma **multicolor** (Tisch.) Tisch. [var. *multicolor* Hort.]. Top and sides metallic gray-green dotted with carmine.

obscurum N. E. Br. Growths dark green or dull brownish, with a few even darker dots and many tiny, pale, sunken dots, to 5/8 in. high, 5/16 in. wide, obconical, top circular or elliptic in outline, flattish; petals red. Cape Prov.

Pearsonii N. E. Br. [*C. Braunsii* Schwant.; *C. Pearsonii* var. *minor* N. E. Br.]. Growths light bluish- or nearly glaucous-green, not dotted, to 3/4 in. high, 1 in. wide, broadly obconical, top flat, circular, usually extending beyond the sides; fls. to 7/8 in. across, diurnal, petals spreading, bright magenta, fading to white at base. Cape Prov. Var. **minor**: *C. Pearsonii*.

Peersii Lavis. Mat-forming; growths enclosed in white, papery sheaths, pale yellow-green, distinctly dotted, to 7/8 in. high, 5/8 in. wide or more, pear-shaped in side view, almost flat at top with fissure 1/16 in. long; fls. 1 in. across, nocturnal, petals creamy-white. Cape Prov.

pictum (N. E. Br.) N. E. Br. Growths dull green, sometimes purplish on sides, marked with chocolate or purple-brown dots and branching

lines on top, to 3/4 in. long, 3/8 in. wide, obconical, notched across the elliptic or oblong top; fls. to 5/8 in. across, petals whitish. Cape Prov.

Pillansii Lavis ex L. Bolus. Growths in groups of 1–3, light yellow-green, reddish on sides, with translucent green dots on upper part, to 7/8 in. high and wide, 3/4 in. across, fissure 1/4 in. long, deepened, dots sometimes confluent into a window; fls. 1 in. across, petals purple. Cape Prov.

piriforme L. Bolus. Growths often 2–3, enclosed in persistent lf. sheath, olive-green, reddish-dotted, rough or minutely velvety to the touch, to 11/8 in. high, 5/8 in. across at center, 3/8 in. across at apex, pear-shaped to obcordate in side view, compressed, lobes 1/8 in. long, more or less acute, margins keeled, reddish; fls. 5/8 in. long, petals dark yellow. Cape Prov.

pisinnum (N. E. Br.) N. E. Br. Growths slightly velvety-papillate, gray-green, or tinged purple on the sides, inconspicuously dotted on top, to 3/8 in. high, 5/16 in. wide, obconical to nearly globose, top slightly convex; fls. 5/16 in. across, petals yellowish. Cape Prov.

Purpusii (Schwant.) N. E. Br. Growths bluish gray-green, with darker dots more or less in lines, minutely papillate on upper side, to 5/8 in. high, 1/2 in. wide, obconical, top nearly flat or slightly rounded, circular or nearly so in outline; fls. to 13/16 in. across, petals pale yellow. Cape Prov.

saxetanum (N. E. Br.) N. E. Br. Growths green, more or less purple-tinged and sometimes dotted with darker green, to 1/2 in. long, 3/16 in. thick at very convex apex, cylindrical or cylindric-club-shaped, orifice minute; petals white. S.-W. Afr.

springbokense N. E. Br. Growths smooth, gray-green with darker green dots, to 1 in. high, 3/4 in. wide, 5/8 in. thick, cylindrical, 2-lobed, lobes to 5/8 in. long, compressed, flat on inner faces, sharply keeled outside, margins sharp, keels purple; fls. 3/4 in. across, petals golden-yellow. Cape Prov.

turrigerum (N. E. Br.) N. E. Br. Growths light grayish-green or glaucous-green, with dark green raised lines and tinged purplish and dotted with dark green basally, to 1/2 in. long and wide, 1/4 in. thick, prominently 2-lobed, lobes nearly cylindrical, angularly convex, 1/4 in. in diam.; fls. 9/16 in. across, petals long-exserted, pink. Cape Prov.

Wettsteinii (A. Berger) N. E. Br. Growths glaucous-green, with faint and minute dots of darker green, to 11/16 in. high, 13/16 in. wide, 1 in. thick, broadly obconical, top circular or elliptic, often overhanging sides, orifice outlined with darker green; fls. to 13/16 in. across, diurnal, petals rose-magenta. Cape Prov.

Wiggetiae N. E. Br. Mat-forming; growths reddish to purple on sides, gray-green with conspicuous dark green dots on upper side, to 5/8 in. long, 3/8 in. wide, obconical in side view, slightly rounded and circular in top view, fissure slightly deepened, to 1/4 in. long; fls. 3/4 in. across, petals whitish. Cape Prov.

CONOSTEGIA D. Don. *Melastomataceae*. About 50 spp. of shrubs or small trees of trop. Amer.; lvs. 3–5-nerved; fls. in terminal panicles, small, white, stamens all similar, 2–5 times as many as the petals, not appendaged, ovary inferior; fr. berrylike, juicy, many-seeded.

xalapensis (Bonpl.) D. Don. SIRIN. Shrub, to 20 ft., often rounded to spreading, stellate-tomentose; lvs. ovate to lanceolate, 3–8 in. long, denticulate, 5- to many-nerved, stellate-puberulent to glabrescent, whitish to pale brown beneath; infl. many-fld., to 8 in. long; fls. pink or white, petals 5, to 1/4 in. long; fr. edible, delicious, like a blueberry in form and flavor. S. Mex., Cent. Amer. to Colombia, Cuba.

CONOSTYLIS R. Br. *Haemodoraceae*. About 40 spp. of per. herbs, native to Australia; fls. with perianth tube short, segms. uniseriate and equal, stamens 6, ovary inferior or nearly so, style conical at base.

candicans Endl. Lvs. arranged in 2 ranks or in crowded tufts on a short rhizome; fls. white or yellowish, 10–20 in terminal heads or dichotomous cymes. Usually grown in the greenhouse.

CONRADINA A. Gray. *Labiatae*. Four spp. of low shrubs of se. U.S.; sts. mostly square in cross section; lvs. in stiff clusters, needlelike, entire, revolute; fls. in axillary, 2–7-fld. verticillasters, calyx tubular, 13-nerved, 2-lipped, upper lip 3-toothed, lower lip 2-parted, teeth subulate, corolla white, lavender, purple, tube longer than calyx, swollen at base, limb 2-lipped, upper lip erect, retuse, lower lip 3-lobed, middle lobe emarginate, stamens 4, in 2 pairs; fr. of 4 nutlets.

canescens (Torr. & A. Gray) A. Gray. Much-branched, 1–3 ft.; lvs. linear-spatulate, mostly 1/4 in. long, obtuse, gray-pubescent; verticillasters 2–3-fld., in upper lf. axils; fls. pale purple. Sandy coastal pinelands, Fla. to Ala.

CONSOLEA: *OPUNTIA* subgenus *Consolea.*

CONSOLIDA (DC.) S. F. Gray. LARKSPUR. *Ranunculaceae.* About 40 spp. of ann. herbs, native from Medit. region to cent. Asia; lvs. palmately laciniate; infl. racemose to paniculate, pedicels subtended by bracts and bearing 2 bracteoles; fls. irregular, sepals 5, petaloid, the uppermost spurred, petal seemingly 1, nearly entire to 3–5-lobed, spurred, the spur nectariferous and extending into the sepal spur, stamens 5, pistil 1; fr. a follicle. Corolla differs from that of *Delphinium* in having the 2 upper petals united into 1, and in lacking the lower 2 petals.

Culture as for annual species of *Delphinium.*

Ajacis: see *C. ambigua.*

ambigua (L.) P. W. Ball & Heyw. [*C. Ajacis* of auth., not (L.) Schur; *Delphinium Ajacis* of auth., not L.]. ROCKET L. Pubescent ann., 1–2 ft., brs. few, almost horizontal; basal and lower lvs. long-petioled, the blades 3-cleft, the divisions dissected into linear segms., upper lvs. sessile; bracteoles inserted below the middle of peduncle; fls. 4–16, bright blue, rarely white or pink, sepals about ⅝ in. long, spur slender, ⅝ in. long; follicles pubescent, ⅝–1 in. long, gradually tapering, seeds with continuous transverse ridges. Medit. region; naturalized in Asia. Some material grown as *Delphinium Consolida* belongs here.

orientalis (J. Gay) Schrödinger [*Delphinium orientale* J. Gay]. Like *C. ambigua,* but brs. suberect, bracteoles inserted above the middle of the pedicel and reaching the base of the fr.; follicle abruptly beaked. N. Afr., s. Eur., w. Asia. Most garden material called *Delphinium Ajacis* belongs here.

regalis S. F. Gray [*Delphinium Consolida* L.]. To 4 ft., mostly divaricately branched; lvs. 2–3-ternate, lobes linear; infl. paniculate, pedicels slender, bracts linear, entire; fls. deep blue to pink or white; follicle glabrous or pubescent. Eur., w. Asia. Subsp. **regalis.** The typical subsp.; sts. mostly little-branched; sepals ½–⅝ in. long, usually light violet-blue; follicle glabrous, usually twice as long as wide. Cent. Eur. to Turkey. Subsp. **paniculata** (Host) Soó [*Delphinium paniculatum* Host]. Sts. much-branched; sepals about ⅜ in. long, usually dark violet-blue; follicle glabrous, usually 3 times as long as wide. Se. Eur. to Turkey.

sulphurea (Boiss. & Hausskn.) P. H. Davis [*Delphinium sulphureum* Boiss. & Hausskn.]. Low strigose plant; racemes 3–5-fld.; spur twice as long as the yellow sepals. Syria. Material cult. as *Delphinium sulphureum* is probably *D. Zalil.*

CONVALLARIA L. LILY-OF-THE-VALLEY. *Liliaceae.* One to three spp. of per. rhizomatous herbs, native to temp. regions of N. Hemisphere; rhizomes horizontal, the upright buds called "pips"; lvs. basal; fls. white to pink, in terminal, bracted, 1-sided racemes, perianth globose-campanulate, the lobes recurved, stamens 6; fr. a many-seeded red berry.

Lily-of-the-valley is hardy outdoors and is often used in beds or as a groundcover in shady places; it persists for many years without needing to be disturbed. It is often forced from pips planted in pots or in benches of sand in the greenhouse and kept at a temperature of about 65° F.

Keiskei Miq. [*C. majalis* var. *Keiskei* (Miq.) Mak.]. Smaller than *C. majalis;* lvs. 2 or 3, elliptic-oblong, to 6 in. long, cuspidate; fls. in short racemes, about as high as base of lf. blades, bracts lanceolate, half as long as pedicels. Japan. Some authors do not consider this sp. distinct from *C. majalis.*

majalis L. To 8 in. high, forming dense carpets; lvs. 2 or 3, lanceolate-ovate to elliptic, to 8 in. long, glabrous; fls. white, nodding, fragrant, bracts lanceolate, shorter than pedicels; seeds nearly globose. Eur.; naturalized in e. N. Amer. In Eur., sometimes cult. as a perfumery plant; the dried rhizomes also have medicinal properties. Cvs. include: 'Aureo-variegata', lvs. variegated with yellow; 'Fortunei', fls. and foliage larger; 'Rosea', fls. pink; 'Prolificans', fls. double. Var. **Keiskei:** *C. Keiskei.*

montana Raf. To 8 in., not forming carpets; lvs. to 1 ft. long and 4¾ in. broad; bracts linear, as long as or longer than pedicels; seeds lenticular or depressed-globose. Mts., W. Va. and Va. to e. Tenn. and n. Ga. Some authors do not consider this distinct from *C. majalis.*

CONVOLVULACEAE Juss. MORNING-GLORY FAMILY. Dicot; about 50 genera and 1,200 spp. of twining herbs, but often shrubs or even trees, often with milky juice, mostly trop. and subtrop. regions, but extending into temp. regions, particularly abundant in trop. Amer. and trop. Asia; lvs. alt., simple or compound; fls. often large and brightly colored,

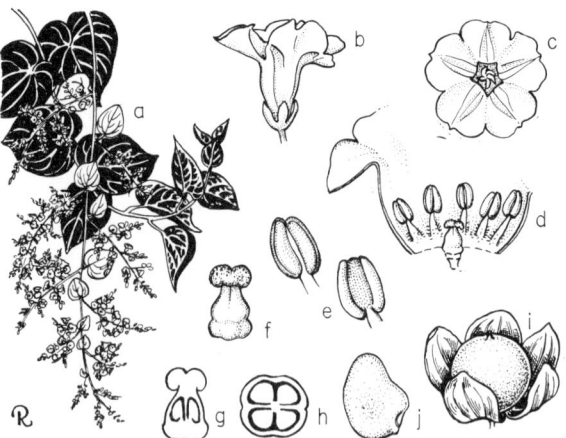

CONVOLVULACEAE. *Porana paniculata:* **a,** leafy branch and inflorescence, × ⅙; **b,** flower, side view, × 3; **c,** flower, face view, × 3; **d,** flower, with corolla expanded, × 5; **e,** anthers, two views, × 15; **f,** pistil, × 10; **g,** pistil, vertical section, × 10; **h,** ovary, cross section, × 15; **i,** fruit, × 1½; **j,** seed, × 3.

regular, bisexual, calyx 5-parted, corolla funnelform, pleated or often twisted in bud, stamens 5, ovary superior, prevailingly 2-celled; fr. a caps. or berry. One sp. is an important food plant, several spp. are used medicinally or as hallucinogens, and others are grown as ornamentals. Treated here are: *Argyreia, Astripomoea, Calystegia, Convolvulus, Dichondra, Evolvulus, Ipomoea, Jacquemontia, Merremia, Mina, Porana, Stictocardia,* and *Turbina.*

CONVOLVULUS L. [*Rhodorrhiza* Webb]. BINDWEED. *Convolvulaceae.* About 225 spp. of herbs, mostly twining or trailing, native mostly to temp. regions; lvs. simple or lobed, cordate, sagittate, or hastate at base; corolla campanulate or funnelform, limb 5-angled, pleated, stigmas 2, filiform or subulate; fr. a caps. Related to *Calystegia,* but having bracts small, not closely enclosing calyx, infl. many-fld., style brs. linear and slender, and fr. completely 2-celled.

Bindweeds are of easy cultivation but should be planted with care as they are likely to become troublesome weeds. They are grown out of doors as covering for fences and banks, and the tender kinds in the greenhouse. One species is the source of a cathartic drug. Propagated by seeds, cuttings of young wood, and by division.

arvensis L. FIELD B. Per., with deep persisting roots, glabrous or nearly so; lvs. oblong to ovate, to 2 in. long, sagittate or hastate at base; corolla pink or whitish, to 1 in. across. Eur. and Asia; naturalized and now widespread in temp. areas throughout the world, often a troublesome weed. In some places has been used in hanging baskets.

Cantabrica L. Per., to 2 ft., sts. erect or prostrate; lvs. oblong or lanceolate; fls. in clusters, corolla rose or pink, about ½ in. long. Medit. region.

Cneorum L. SILVERBUSH. Subshrub, to 4 ft., sts. erect or ascending; lvs. persistent, lanceolate or oblong, silvery-silky pubescent; fls. 1–6 in heads on short peduncles, corolla pink or white, hairy on outside. S. Eur.

cyclostegius: *Calystegia macrostegia* subsp.

elegantissimus Mill. Grayish-pubescent per., sts. twining; lvs. divided into 5–7 narrow lobes; fls. usually 2, corolla pink with dark red stripes. S. Eur. Attractive plant, but may become naturalized and rampant.

floridus L.f. [*Rhodorrhiza florida* (L.f.) Webb & Berth.]. To 6 ft., woody; lvs. linear-lanceolate; fls. in many-fld., terminal clusters, white or pale pink, small. Canary Is.

gharbensis Batt. & Pitard. Sts. decumbent; fls. violet, grouped together into a cluster surrounded by uppermost lvs. Morocco. Some plants cult. as *C. tricolor* belong here.

imperialis: a listed name of no botanical standing.

incanus Vahl. Finely pubescent, usually gray per., sts. trailing or decumbent, to 3 ft.; lvs. ovate, lanceolate, linear, with diverging lobes at base, to 2 in. long; fls. rose to white. Nebr. to Okla.

japonicus: *Calystegia hederacea.*

lineatus L. Cushion-forming per., sts. erect or decumbent, to 8 in. long; lvs. lanceolate, silky-pubescent; fls. few in terminal cymes, corolla pale reddish-purple, hairy on outside. S. Eur.

major: a listed name of no botanical standing.

mauritanicus Boiss. Per., sts. prostrate, woody at base; lvs. round-ovate, small; fls. 1–6 in a cluster, corolla blue or violet-purple with pale throat, to 2 in. across. N. Afr. Useful in baskets.

minor: a listed name of no botanical standing.

occidentalis: *Calystegia occidentalis.*

ocellatus Hook. [*C. Randii* Rendle]. Brownish- or silvery-tomentose per., sts. erect or prostrate; lvs. linear-oblong, to 2 in. long, sometimes palmately 5-parted; fls. usually solitary, axillary, corolla white with reddish-purple central spot, or pink to mauve. S. Afr.

pellitus forma **anestius:** *Calystegia hederacea* cv. 'Flore Pleno'.

pentapetaloides L. Ann., sts. prostrate; lvs. oblong or linear-lanceolate; fls. solitary, blue. S. Eur., w. Asia.

Randii: *C. ocellatus.*

Scammonia L. SCAMMONY. Per., sts. angular; lvs. cordate-sagittate; fls. white to pink, calyx without membranous bracts at base. Asia Minor. The dried roots are the source of scammony, a drug long used as a purgative.

sepium: *Calystegia sepium.*

Soldanella: *Calystegia Soldanella.*

spithamaeus: *Calystegia spithamaea.*

tricolor L. DWARF MORNING-GLORY. Ann., sts. erect or ascending, to 1 ft., often much-branched; lvs. linear-oblong; fls. 3 together, corolla blue with yellow throat, margined white, to 1½ in. across. S. Eur. An old flower garden plant. Some plants cult. under this name may be *C. gharbensis.*

undulatus Cav. Ann., sts. ascending; lvs. ovate-oblong, undulate; fls. in nearly sessile clusters, blue. Medit. region.

× **COOPERANTHES:** a listed name of no botanical standing, sometimes applied to hybrids between spp. formerly placed in *Cooperia* and spp. of *Zephyranthes.*

COOPERIA: *ZEPHYRANTHES.* **C. Drummondii:** *Z. brazosensis.* **C. pedunculata:** *Z. Drummondii.*

COPAIFERA L. *Leguminosae* (subfamily *Caesalpinioideae*). About 25 spp. of trees of trop. Amer. and Afr.; lvs. even-pinnate, lfts. opp. or alt., leathery, often with transparent dots; fls. small, almost regular, sessile in panicled spikes, sepals 4, petals 0, stamens 10; fr. an ovoid, scarcely flattened, dehiscent legume, usually 1-seeded.

The genus is important as a source of certain hard resins (copals) and oleoresins used in industry.

officinalis (Jacq.) L. To 80 ft.; lfts. 1–5, usually 3, the terminal 2 opp. and to 3 in. long; fls. white; fr. ovoid-globose. Tropics, S. Amer. Heartwood yields copaiba, an industrial oleoresin.

COPERNICIA Mart. *Palmae.* About 29 spp. of tall or medium palms with bisexual fls. in savannah of the W. Indies and S. Amer.; lvs. palmate, petiole elongate or rarely lacking, usually armed with stout spinose teeth, blade variously flabellate, orbicular, or wedge-shaped, shallowly divided into 1-ribbed segs.; infl. interfoliar, little or much exceeding the lvs., with tubular bracts on peduncle, subtending primary brs., and sometimes the rachillae; fls. solitary or in clusters of 2–4, sepals united in a 3-lobed calyx, petals united in a 3-lobed corolla, stamens 6, filaments joined basally to the corolla, carpels 3, more or less separate except united styles; fr. ovoid to globose, abortive carpels and stigmatic residue apical.

The leaves of copernicias are often used locally for thatching, and those of one species supply carnauba wax, most important of all vegetable waxes. Copernicias are handsome ornamentals suitable for tropical and subtropical plantings. Most species listed are suitable for the warmest parts of Zone 9b in Fla. For culture see *Palms.*

alba Morong. To about 100 ft.; lf. bases persistent on young trees, petiole to 2 ft. long or more, toothed basally, blades orbicular, 2 ft. long or more, densely waxy; infl. with bracts subtending rachillae; fls. paired; fr. ovoid, ¾ in. long. Brazil to Argentina.

Baileyana León. To 45 ft. or more, trunk to 2 ft. in diam., straight or somewhat swollen; lvs with petiole more than 3 ft. long, blade

orbicular, to 5 ft. long or more, segms. 110–130, moderately to densely waxy; infl. to 9 ft. long or more, rachillae to about 3 in. long, each subtended by a tubular bract; fls. to ¼ in. long, in clusters of 2–3 or solitary, pilose; fr. ¾ in. in diam. Cuba.

Berteroana Becc. To 15 ft. or more, trunk to 8 in. in diam.; lvs. with toothed petiole to 3 ft. long, blade orbicular, to 3 ft. long or more, segms. 88–100, green; infl. to 6 ft. long or more, rachillae to 5 in. long, not subtended by tubular bracts; fls. ⅛ in. long, in clusters of 2–4, pilose; fr. ¾ in. in diam. Hispaniola.

cerifera: *C. prunifera.*

glabrescens H. Wendl. ex Becc. To 20 ft., occasionally suckering; petiole to 3 ft. long, irregularly toothed, blade orbicular, to 3 ft. long, lightly to moderately waxy; infl. to 9 ft., rachillae short, to ⅝ in. long, subtended by bracts; fls. solitary or paired, to about ⅛ in. long; fr. to ⅝ in. long. W. Cuba.

hospita Mart. To 25 ft. or more; lf. bases not long-persistent, petiole to more than 3 ft. long, coarsely toothed, blade orbicular, to more than 3 ft. long, moderately to densely waxy; infl. to 8 ft. long, rachillae to ¾ in. long; fls. solitary or paired, to ³⁄₁₆ in. long; fr. to ¾ in. long. Cent. Cuba.

macroglossa H. Wendl. ex Becc. [*C. Torreana* León]. PETTICOAT PALM. To 20 ft. or more, trunk usually with a skirt of persistent dead lvs.; petiole absent, blade wedge-shaped, stiff, with spiny outer segms., to nearly 5 ft. long, green; infl. longer than lvs., rachillae thick, subtended by bracts, to 3 ft. long; fls. solitary, to ⁵⁄₁₆ in. long; fr. to ¾ in. long. Cent. Cuba.

occidentalis León. To 25 ft. or more; petiole to more than 3 ft. long, coarsely toothed, blade orbicular, to 4 ft. long, not usually waxy; infl. to more than 10 ft. long, rachillae yellowish-pilose, to ⁹⁄₁₆ in. long. W. Cuba. Of limited distribution and possibly of hybrid origin.

prunifera (Mill.) H. E. Moore [*C. cerifera* (Arr. Cam.) Mart.]. CARNAUBA PALM. To 45 ft. or more, trunk covered with persistent lf. bases when young and at base when old; lvs. usually densely waxy on both surfaces, petiole to more than 3 ft. long, coarsely toothed, blade orbicular, to 3 ft. long; infl. to 9 ft. long, brs. but not rachillae subtended by tubular bracts, rachillae to 6 in. long; fls. in clusters of 2–4; fr. ovoid, to 1 in. long or more. Ne. Brazil. Source of commercial carnauba wax.

tectorum (HBK) Mart. To 30 ft. or more, trunk to 1 ft. in diam., often with persistent lf. bases when young; lvs. with petiole more than 3 ft. long, blade orbicular, to 3 ft. long, segms. about 40, green; infl. about 3 ft. long, rachillae to 7 in. long, pilose, not subtended by tubular bracts; fls. ⅛ in. long, solitary, pilose; fr. ovoid, to 1⅛ in. long, ¾ in. in diam. Colombia, Venezuela.

Torreana: *C. macroglossa.*

Yarey Burret. To 25 ft., trunk to 10 in. in diam.; lvs. with petiole more than 3 ft. long, blade orbicular, to nearly 4 ft. long, segms. 58–80, moderately to densely waxy; infl. nearly 6 ft. long, rachillae to 1½ in. long, each subtended by a tubular bract; fls. in clusters of 2, to about ⅛ in. long, pilose; fr. to about ⅝ in. in diam. Cuba.

COPIAPOA Britt. & Rose. *Cactaceae.* About 15 spp. of globose to oblong, ribbed cacti, native to Chile; sts. simple or cespitose, ribs 8–30; fls. from woolly apex, campanulate to funnelform, mostly yellow, scales persistent in fr., ovary top-shaped, naked; fr. small, seeds large, glossy black, with large depressed hilum. Distinguished from *Wigginsia* by naked fr. crowned by persistent scales.

For culture see *Cacti.*

cinerea (Phil.) Britt. & Rose. Sts. simple, to 4 ft. high and 8 in. thick, ribs 18–30, obtuse, cross-furrowed; spines amber, becoming black, awl-shaped, deciduous, radial spines 1–4, central spine 1, to 1¼ in. long; fls. yellow, to 1¼ in. long; fr. red, ¾ in. long.

coquimbana (Karw.) Britt. & Rose. Sts. cespitose, to 5 in. thick, forming mounds to 3 ft. wide, ribs 10–17, obtuse; radial spines 5–10, slender, dark, ⅜ in. long, central spines 0–2, to 1 in. long; fls. yellow, 1¼ in. long.

COPROSMA J. R. Forst. & G. Forst. *Rubiaceae.* About 90 spp. of dioecious, evergreen shrubs or small trees, native to Australia, New Zeal., and the Pacific Is.; lvs. opp., stipules interpetiolar; fls. small, white or greenish, in clusters or solitary, corolla campanulate or funnelform, 4–5-lobed, stamens and styles usually much exserted; fr. a fleshy, variously colored drupe. Many spp. are extremely variable and hybrids are common, making it difficult sometimes to identify individual plants.

Coprosmas are grown as ornamentals in the open ground in Calif. and other warm regions, for the attractive foliage and fruit, and some of them for hedges. Propagated by cuttings of ripe wood. Dyes have been extracted from a few species.

areolata Cheesem. Shrub, to 15 ft., branchlets finely pubescent; lvs. orbicular-spatulate, to ⅝ in. long, acute, membranous, glabrous above, pilose beneath; fr. globose, ³⁄₁₆ in. across, black. New Zeal.

australis (A. Rich.) B. L. Robinson [*C. grandifolia* Hook.f.]. Shrub or small tree, to 18 ft., branchlets rather stout, glabrous; lvs. elliptic to obovate, to 8 in. long, glabrous, membranous to nearly leathery, somewhat glossy green above, paler beneath; fr. oblong, to ⅜ in. long, reddish-orange. New Zeal.

Baueri: *C. repens.*

brunnea (T. Kirk) Cockayne ex Cheesem. Prostrate or trailing shrub, brs. and branchlets slender, flexible, interlacing; lvs. narrowly oblong to obovate, to ⅜ in. long, leathery; fr. globose, to ¼ in. long, pale blue. New Zeal.

cuneata Hook.f. Shrub, to 6 ft., brs. rigid, divaricate, branchlets slender, pubescent, interlacing; lvs. usually clustered, linear- or cuneate-oblong, to ¾ in. long, stiff and leathery; fr. globose, ³⁄₁₆ in. across, red. New Zeal.

×**Cunninghamii** Hook.f.: *C. propinqua* × *C. robusta.* Intermediate between the two parents; lvs. frequently lanceolate or oblanceolate, to 1 in. long; fr. globose or oblong, to ¼ in. long, pale and translucent.

depressa Colenso ex Hook.f. [*C. ramulosa* Petrie]. Prostrate shrub, brs. long, slender, rooting, branchlets finely pubescent; lvs. broad-ovate, to ⅜ in. long, leathery; fls. solitary; fr. globose, to ¼ in. across, red. New Zeal.

grandiflora: a listed name of no botanical standing; may be an error for *C. grandifolia.*

grandifolia: *C. australis.*

×**Kirkii** Cheesem.: *C. acerosa* A. Cunn. × *C. repens.* Scrambling or suberect shrub, to 18 in. or more, densely branched, brs. straight and stiff; lvs. mostly linear-lanceolate, to 1½ in. long; fr. oblong, to ¼ in. long, speckled with red, translucent. Used as a ground cover.

lucida J. R. Forst. & G. Forst. Robust shrub or slender tree, to 18 ft., branchlets stout, glabrous; lvs. obovate, to 5 in. long, obtuse or acute, leathery, glossy; fr. oblong, ½ in. long, reddish-orange. New Zeal.

macrocarpa Cheesem. Shrub or slender tree, to 30 ft., branchlets stout, glabrous; lvs. broad- to elliptic-ovate, to 5 in. long, obtuse or acute, nearly leathery; fr. oblong, to 1 in. long, orange-red. New Zeal.

microcarpa Hook.f. Slender shrub, to 12 ft., branchlets pubescent; lvs. linear-oblong, to ½ in. long, membranous, dark green above, paler beneath; fr. globose, ⅛ in. long, white, translucent. New Zeal.

microphylla: see *C. quadrifidum.*

nitida Hook.f. Shrub, to 6 ft., brs. stiff, puberulous; lvs. linear-oblong to narrowly lanceolate, to 1½ in. long, leathery, glossy; fr. oblong, to ¼ in. long, pale orange-red. Se. Australia.

parviflora Hook.f. Low, densely branched shrub or small tree, to 15 ft., brs. divaricate, branchlets densely pubescent, at least when young; lvs. usually clustered, oblong to obovate, to ¾ in. long, leathery, glabrous; fr. globose, to ¼ in. across, dark purple or white, translucent. New Zeal.

Petriei Cheesem. Creeping, mat-forming shrub, branchlets slender, pubescent; lvs. linear-elliptic or oblong, to ¼ in. long, leathery, hairy at least when young; fls. solitary; fr. globose, to ⅜ in. across, purplish-red or pale blue, translucent. New Zeal. Useful in the rock garden.

propinqua A. Cunn. Shrub or tree, to 20 ft., brs. divaricate, interlacing, branchlets pubescent or glabrous; lvs. linear to broad-oblong, to ½ in. long, leathery, paler beneath; fr. globose, to ¼ in. across, pale blue, flecked with darker blue, translucent. New Zeal.

pumila Hook.f. [*C. repens* Hook.f., not A. Rich.]. Prostrate shrub, sts. to 2 ft. long, creeping and rooting, branchlets and lvs. glabrous; lvs. often in clusters, nearly sessile, elliptic to obovate-elliptic, to ⅜ in. long, leathery, somewhat fleshy; fls. solitary; fr. globose, to ⅜ in. across, red. New Zeal. Similar to *C. Petriei,* but glabrous and having red frs.

quadrifida (Labill.) B. L. Robinson [?*C. microphylla* A. Cunn. ex Hook.f.]. Shrub, to 6 ft., brs. slender, divaricate, frequently ending in needlelike spines, branchlets finely pubescent, with short side branchlets bearing clusters of lvs.; lvs. variable in size and shape, usually narrow-ovate or obovate, to ¾ in. long, nearly leathery; fr. oblong, to ¼ in. long, red. Se. Australia.

ramulosa: *C. depressa.*

repens A. Rich. [*C. Baueri* T. Kirk, not Endl.; *C. Stockii* B. S. Williams]. MIRROR PLANT, LOOKING-GLASS PLANT. Prostrate shrub or small tree, to 25 ft., branchlets stout, glabrous or pubescent; lvs. ovate to broadly oblong, to 3 in. long, obtuse or notched, recurved at margin, dark green and glossy above, paler and duller beneath, thick, almost fleshy; fr. in clusters of 3–6, obovoid, flattened laterally, to ⅜ in. long, orange-red. New Zeal.; escaped on Calif. Coast. The commonest sp. in cult. Withstands much clipping, useful in hedges; old gnarled trees are picturesque. Cvs. are: 'Argentea', lvs. silver-variegated; 'Marginata', lvs. margined yellow; 'Picturata': 'Variegata'; 'Variegata' [cv. 'Picturata'], lvs. blotched with yellowish-green. See also *C. pumila.*

rhamnoides A. Cunn. Shrub, to 6 ft., densely branched, brs. divaricate, with pubescent branchlets; lvs. orbicular to broadly ovate, to ½ in. long, leathery or nearly so, glabrous; fr. globose, to ⅛ in. long, dark red to almost black. New Zeal.

rigida Cheesem. Shrub, to 15 ft., brs. stiff, divaricate, branchlets wiry, somewhat glossy; lvs. obovate to oblong, to ¾ in. long, thick, leathery, glabrous; fr. oblong, to ¼ in. long, yellow or orange. New Zeal.

robusta Raoul. Robust shrub, to 15 ft., branchlets stout, glabrous; lvs. elliptic or ovate, to 5 in. long, leathery, dark green and glossy above, paler beneath; fr. oblong, to ⅜ in. long, dark orange-red. New Zeal. Similar to *C. australis,* but with lvs. more leathery; and to *C. macrocarpa,* but with lvs. narrower and fr. smaller.

rotundifolia A. Cunn. Shrub or small tree, to 15 ft., brs. slender, wide-spreading, branchlets hairy; lvs. orbicular or ovate-oblong, to 1 in. long, membranous, more or less hairy, especially on margins, dull green; fr. globose, to ⅛ in. across, red. New Zeal.

rugosa Cheesem. Shrub, to 10 ft., brs. stiff, divaricate, interlacing branchlets slender, hairy, somewhat 4-sided; lvs. linear, to ½ in. long, leathery, dark green above, paler beneath; fr. oblong or nearly globose, to ¼ in. across, marked with pale blue, translucent. New Zeal.

spathulata A. Cunn. Shrub, to 6 ft., brs. slender, clustered, branchlets pubescent; lvs. orbicular to broad-oblong, to ¾ in. long, thick, leathery, glabrous, glossy, petiole somewhat winged; fr. globose or oblong, to ¼ in. long, dark orange, red, or almost black. New Zeal.

Stockii: *C. repens.*

tenuicaulis Hook.f. Shrub, to 9 ft., brs. slender, somewhat divaricate and interlacing, branchlets slender, pubescent; lvs. orbicular-ovate or spatulate, to ½ in. long, nearly leathery, glabrous, petioles more or less winged, pubescent; fr. globose, ⅛ in. across, black. New Zeal. Similar to *C. areolata,* but having lvs. glabrous and more leathery.

tenuifolia Cheesem. Slender shrub or small tree, to 15 ft., brs. and branchlets stout, glabrous, ascending; lvs. ovate to oblong, to 4 in. long, membranous, pubescent above on midrib; fr. ovoid, to ⅜ in. long, orange. New Zeal.

COPTIS Salisb. GOLDTHREAD. *Ranunculaceae.* About 10 spp. of small, per. herbs of the N. Temp. Zone, with slender rhizomes; lvs. basal, evergreen, often ternately divided; fls. small, white or yellow, on scapes, sepals 5–7, petaloid, deciduous, petals 5–7, small, fleshy, tubular at apex, stamens 15–25, pistils 3–9, on slender stalks; fr. of follicles.

Rhizomes yield a yellow dye and have medicinal properties. A few species sometimes planted in the border or rock garden. The plants thrive in shady, damp places in peaty soil. Propagated by seeds and division of clumps.

asplenifolia Salisb. About 1 ft.; lvs. with 5 lfts., lfts. somewhat pinnatifid, sharply toothed; fls. 2, whitish, sepals and petals filiform. Alaska to B.C.

groenlandica (Oed.) Fern. CANKERROOT. Scape slender, 3–6 in.; lfts. 3, petioluled, cuneate-obovate, shining, coarsely toothed; fls. usually solitary, white, about ½ in. across, sepals not clawed, petals broader than long. Ne. N. Amer.

laciniata A. Gray. Much like *C. occidentalis;* lfts. narrower, 3-parted nearly to the base, with more acute teeth. Wash. to n. Calif.

occidentalis (Nutt.) Torr. & A. Gray. Scape 4–6 in.; lvs. with petioles 2–6 in. long, lfts. petioluled, 1–2 in. broad, 3-lobed almost to the middle, serrate, the teeth mucronulate; fls. 2–3, peduncles 1–3 in. long, sepals yellowish, ¼–½ in. long. B.C. to Mont.

quinquefolia Miq. Like *C. groenlandica,* but lfts. 5, rhombic. Japan.

trifolia (L.) Salisb. About 4–6 in.; lfts. 3, subsessile, rhombic, as long as broad; fls. solitary, white with yellow basal spots, sepals elliptic to elliptic-lanceolate, ³⁄₁₆ in. long, abruptly clawed at base; body of follicles less than ³⁄₁₆ in. long. Ne. Asia, Alaska. Used medicinally.

CORALLODISCUS Batal. *Gesneriaceae.* About 18 spp. of per. herbs in Asia; lvs. from a rhizome, in a basal rosette, with deeply impressed veins; fls. on scape, calyx 5-parted, corolla tubular, bearded inside in 2 lines from the throat, limb 2-lipped, with 2 smaller upper and 3 larger lower lobes, stamens 4, borne in pairs on the tube, filaments coiling spirally after pollen is shed, anthers coherent in pairs, disc ringlike, ovary superior, style short, stigma 2-lobed; fr. a loculicidal caps.

For cultivation see *Gesneriaceae.*

lanuginosus (Wallich ex A. DC.) B. L. Burtt [*Didymocarpus lanuginosus* Wallich ex A. DC.]. Lvs. obovate, to nearly 2½ in. long, 1¼ in. wide, obtuse, coarsely crenate, densely hairy when young, smoother with age; scape to 4 in.; fls. several, corolla to ½ in. long, pale blue or purplish; caps. ¾ in. long. Himalayas.

CORALLORHIZA (Haller) Chatel. CORALROOT. *Orchidaceae.* Twelve spp., native to temp. Eurasia and N. Amer.; saprophytic terrestrial herbs without chlorophyll, with masses of much-branched coral-like rhizomes; lvs. scale-like; fls. small, in terminal racemes, sepals and petals spreading, lip movable, attached to column-foot. For structure of fl. see *Orchidaceae.*

For culture see *Orchids.*

Bigelovii: *C. striata.*

maculata Raf. [*C. multiflora* Nutt.]. SPOTTED CORALROOT, LARGE C. To 8 in.; scape usually pinkish, racemes to 7½ in. long; sepals and petals brownish-purple, to about ⁵⁄₁₆ in. long, lip 3-lobed, white, or occasionally yellow, with purple spots. Nfld. to N.C., w. to Wash., Ore., Calif.

Mertensiana Bong. WESTERN CORALROOT. Plants very similar in color and size to *C. maculata,* but base of column produced into a prominent mentum. Summer. Alaska, B.C., nw. Calif., e. to Mont. and Wyo.

multiflora: *C. maculata.*

odontorhiza Nutt. LATE CORALROOT, AUTUMN C., SMALL C., CRAWLEY-ROOT, CHICKEN-TOES, DRAGON'S-CLAW. To 16 in., leafless; scape brown to madder-purple, few- to many-fld.; fls. small, commonly cleistogamous, purple or purplish-green, less than ¼ in. long, not 3-lobed. Early summer–autumn. Temp. e. N. Amer.; temp. Mex. and Guatemala.

striata Lindl. [*C. Bigelovii* S. Wats.]. STRIPED CORALROOT. To 1½ ft.; scapes often brownish-purple; fls. purplish, or occasionally yellow, striped with dark purple, about ½ in. long, lip tongue-shaped, not 3-lobed. Que. to B.C., s. to Mich., New Mex., and Calif.

CORCHOROPSIS Siebold & Zucc. *Byttneriaceae.* Perhaps 3 spp. of ann. herbs, native to e. Asia and Japan; lvs. alt., ovate to oblong-ovate, acute, coarsely crenate-dentate; fls. small, solitary, axillary, subtended by 3 filiform bracts, sepals 5, petals 5, yellow, fertile stamens 10–15, separate or united at base, staminodes 5, longer than stamens; fr. a 3-celled, 3-valved, cylindrical caps., seeds many.

crenata: *C. tomentosa.*

tomentosa (Thunb.) Mak. [*C. crenata* Siebold & Zucc.]. To 4 ft., sts. much-branched, stellate-pubescent; lvs. mostly 1½–3 in. long; sepals about ¼ in. long, recurved, petals obovate, slightly longer than sepals, staminodes to ⅜ in. long; caps. to 1½ in. long, less than ⅛ in. in diam., stellate-pilose. Japan, Korea, China.

CORCHORUS L. *Tiliaceae.* About 40 spp. of herbs or subshrubs, widely distributed in the tropics; lvs. alt., simple, toothed or rarely lobed, basal teeth often setose-pointed; fls. small, yellow, solitary or in few-fld. cymes, sepals and petals (4–)5, stamens 7 to many, on a short androgynophore; fr. a caps., 2–5-celled and -valved, elongate or globose, loculicidally dehiscent, 2- to many-seeded.

Jute is grown for the fiber obtained from the inner bark and for the young shoots, which are eaten as greens. It requires a warm, moist climate, and loamy soil. Seeds may be sown broadcast in spring, and the crop will be ready to harvest in about 3 months. The plant is grown for fiber from Egypt to Japan, most importantly in India and Bangladesh.

capsularis L. JUTE, WHITE J. Erect, often much-branched ann., to 12 ft.; lvs. ovate-oblong to lanceolate, 2–6 in. long, acute or acuminate; petals less than ¼ in. long; fr. globose, about ½ in. across, wrinkled,

seeds copper-colored. China; but widely cult. elsewhere. The main source of jute.

japonicus: *Kerria japonica.*

olitorius L. JEW'S MALLOW, TOSSA JUTE. Differs from *C. capsularis* in being a taller plant with larger, deeper yellow fls., and having caps. cylindrical, elongate, beaked, 1–3 in. long, seeds gray-green to blue-black, India, cult. in trop. Asia.; widely naturalized. A secondary source of jute, generally planted on better-drained soils.

CORDIA L. *Boraginaceae.* About 300 spp. of deciduous or evergreen shrubs, trees, or rarely lianas of tropics of Old and New Worlds; lvs. simple, alt., glabrous or hairy; fls. white, yellow, orange, or red, small or showy, in bractless clusters or coiled cymes, bisexual or sometimes unisexual, calyx and corolla mostly 5-lobed, stamens 5, style single, with 4 brs., stigmas 4; fr. a 1–4-seeded drupe or nut.

Grown in the greenhouse, and outdoors in warm regions, as an ornamental, and in the tropics for timber. Propagated by seeds and cuttings.

abyssinica R. Br. Medium-sized tree, to 30 ft. and more; lvs. ovate to suborbicular, 3–7 in. long, petiole 1–3 in. long; fls. white, in terminal, paniculate cymes, calyx strongly ribbed; drupe yellow, ⁵⁄₁₆–½ in. in diam. Trop. Afr.

alba: *C. dentata.*

alliodora (Ruiz & Pav.) Oken. LAUREL, LAUREL NEGRO. Large or medium-sized, evergreen tree, to 60 ft.; lvs. elliptic-oblong, to 8 in. long, entire, with stellate pubescence, short-petioled; fls. white, to ½ in. long, fragrant, many, in panicles, calyx conspicuously 10-ribbed. Trop. Amer. Wood is important commercially.

angiocarpa A. Rich. Deciduous tree, to 30 ft.; lvs. elliptic to orbicular-ovate, to 3½ in. long, undulate, with rough upper surface; fls. orange, to 2 in. long, in corymbose cymes, corolla 10–15-lobed, calyx not ribbed; drupe ovoid, to 1 in. long. Cuba.

Boissieri A. DC. ANACAHUITA. Evergreen shrub or tree, to 25 ft.; lvs. ovate or oblong-ovate, to 5 in. long, velvety-tomentose, margin entire to crenulate; fls. white with yellow center, 1½ in. long, in terminal clusters; drupe ovoid, ½ in. long, bright red-brown. S. New Mex., Tex. to Mex.

dentata Poir. [*C. alba* (Jacq.) Roem. & Schult.]. JACKWOOD. Large shrub or small to medium-sized, evergreen tree, to 30 ft.; lvs. elliptic to broad-ovate or suborbicular, rough, to 4 in. long, margin toothed to almost entire; fls. yellow or white, to ½ in. long, in large open cymes, corolla lobes emarginate; drupe white, oblong, to ½ in. long. Trop. Amer. Wood used for utilitarian purposes.

dodecandra DC. Tree, to 100 ft.; lvs. oblong, ovate, or suborbicular, to 5 in. long, rough; fls. orange, to 2 in. long, in small cymes; drupe yellowish, to 2 in. long. Mex., Guatemala. Used as a furniture wood.

leucosebestena Griseb. Shrub, to 3 ft.; lvs. elliptic to elliptic-ovate, to 2 in. long, entire, upper surface rough, short-petioled; fls. white, to 1¼ in. long, in few-fld., corymbose cymes, calyx not ribbed; drupe ovoid, to ¾ in. long. Cuba.

lutea Lam. Shrub or small tree, 5–10 ft.; lvs. elliptic-ovate to nearly orbicular, to 4 in. long, upper surface rough; fls. yellow, to 1½ in., corolla with more than 5 lobes, calyx strongly ribbed; drupe white. Marquesas Is., Galapagos Is., arid w. portion of Peru and Ecuador.

Myxa L. ASSYRIAN PLUM, SELU. Deciduous, polygamous shrub or tree, to 40 ft.; lvs. broad-ovate to suborbicular, 3–5 in. long, glabrous, margin entire to undulate; fls. white, to ½ in. long, in large clusters; drupe ovoid, tan to nearly black, ¾ in. in diam., mucilaginous and used in medicine. India to Australia; planted in Calif. and Amer. tropics.

nitida Vahl. RED MANJACK, WEST INDIAN CHERRY. Small or medium-sized tree, 20–60 ft.; lvs. elliptic to elliptic-obovate, to 6 in. long, entire, glabrous, shining on the upper surface; fls. white, many, ¼ in. long, in corymbose cymes; drupe red, globose, ¼ in. in diam. W. Indies.

obliqua Willd. Medium-sized, deciduous tree, to 50 ft.; lvs. ovate, 2–5 in. long, base rounded to nearly cordate; fls. white, small, in cymes; drupe pink or yellow, ovoid, to ½ in. long. Taiwan, Philippine Is., s. China, India, s. to trop. Australia.

Sebestena L. GEIGER TREE. Evergreen shrub or tree, to 30 ft.; lvs. ovate, to 8 in. long, rough-hairy, margins entire or undulate; fls. orange or scarlet, to 2 in. long, in large terminal clusters; drupe white, to ¾ in. long. Fla. Keys, W. Indies to Venezuela; widely cult. in tropics.

superba Cham. [*C. superba* var. *elliptica* Cham.]. Evergreen shrub or small to medium-sized tree, to 15 or 25 ft.; lvs. oblong-lanceolate to elliptic-obovate, 6–8 in. long, entire or serrate; fls. white, to 2 in. long, many, calyx not ribbed; drupe ovoid, 1½ in. long. E. Brazil.

thyrsiflora: *Ehretia acuminata.*

CORDULA: *PAPHIOPEDILUM.*

CORDYLINE Comm. ex Juss. DRACAENA. *Agavaceae.* About 20 spp. of shrubby or treelike plants in India and Australia and 1 in trop. Amer.; lvs. narrow, leathery or stiff, usually crowded at top of brs., often variegated; infl. a panicle; fls. greenish or yellowish, pedicelled, perianth segms. 6, united basally, stamens 6, ovary superior, 3-celled, each cell 6–15-ovuled; fr. a berry. See also *Dracaena.*

Grown under glass and out of doors in warm climates for the foliage. Propagated by seeds, cuttings, and root layering. The leaves may be removed from ripened stems, these stems cut into 2–4 in. lengths and laid in sand in a propagating bed with bottom heat. When the eyes have developed into shoots with about six leaves, the shoots should be cut off with an eye and put in propagating bed until rooted, then transplanted into pots.

australis (G. Forst.) Hook.f. [*Dracaena australis* G. Forst.]. GIANT D., FOUNTAIN D., CABBAGE TREE, PALM LILY, GRASS PALM. To 40 ft.; lvs. sword-shaped, to 3 ft. long, 2½ in. wide; panicles large, terminal; fls. white, fragrant, segms. nearly equal. New Zeal. Cvs. include: 'Atropurpurea', base of lf. and midrib beneath purple; 'Doucetii', lvs. edged and striped with white; 'Veitchii', midrib and base of lf. bright crimson.

Banksii Hook.f. To 10 ft.; lvs. petioled, to 6 ft. long or more, 3½ in. wide; panicles drooping, much branched, to 5 ft. long; fls. white, segms. nearly equal. New Zeal.

congesta: *C. stricta.*

Haageana C. Koch. To 3 ft.; lvs. to 6 in. long, 2½ in. wide, abruptly contracted into a long petiole; panicles few-branched, to 1 ft. long or less; fls. white to reddish-purple, to ⅜ in. long, segms. equal; fr. about ⅛ in. in diam. Australia. Plants listed as *Dracaena Haageana* or *D. Haagei* probably belong here.

indivisa (G. Forst.) Steud. [*Dracaena indivisa* G. Forst.]. BLUE D. To 25 ft.; lvs. sword-shaped, to 6 ft. long, 6 in. wide; panicle drooping, to 4 ft. long; fls. white, segms. nearly equal. New Zeal.

rubra Hügel ex Kunth [*Dracaena rubra* Hort., not Noronha]. To 15 ft.; lvs. to 15 in. long, 2 in. wide; panicles lateral; fls. lilac. Nativity unknown. Cv. 'Bruantii', Is listed.

stricta Endl. [*C. congesta* Endl.; *Dracaena stricta* Hort.]. To 12 ft.; lvs. sword-shaped, to 2 ft. long, 1⅜ in. wide; panicles terminal or lateral; fls. lilac, inner segms. longer than outer. Australia. Cv. 'Grandis'. Large, highly colored form.

terminalis (L.) Kunth [*Dracaena terminalis* L.]. TI, GOOD-LUCK PLANT, HAWAIIAN G.-L. P., TREE-OF-KINGS. To 10 ft.; lvs. petioled, to 2½ ft. long, 5 in. wide; panicles to 1 ft. long; fls. yellowish, white, or reddish, segms. nearly equal; fr. ⁵⁄₁₆ in. wide. E. Asia. There are many foliage forms, most of which have been grown under hort. names in *Dracaena.* Cvs. include: 'Amabilis' [*Dracaena amabilis* Hort.], lvs. glossy deep green, becoming spotted with rose and white; 'Baptisii' [*Dracaena Baptisii* Hort.], lvs. deep green, striped with pink and yellow; 'Hybrida' [*Dracaena hybrida* Hort. Veitch]', lvs. deep green with rose margin; 'Imperialis', lvs. deep metallic-green, marked with crimson or pink; 'Tricolor', lvs. 3-colored; 'Youngii', lvs. bright green, streaked with red-bronze in age.

COREMA D. Don. BROOM CROWBERRY. *Empetraceae.* Two spp. of dioecious, evergreen, heathlike shrubs, native to e. N. Amer., sw. Eur., the Azores, and Canary Is.; lvs. linear, alt. or whorled, crowded; fls. purplish in terminal, bracted heads, sepals 3–4, petals 0, stamens 3–4, ovary 2–5-celled; fr. drupaceous.

Propagated by cuttings.

Conradii (Torr.) Torr. ex Loud. POVERTY GRASS. To 2 ft.; lvs. linear, to ¼ in. long; male fls. with long purple stamens. Spring. Rocky and sandy places, Nfld. to N.J. Useful as a ground a cover.

COREOPSIS L. [*Calliopsis* Rchb.; *Leptosyne* DC.]. TICKSEED. *Compositae* (Helianthus Tribe). Over 100 spp. of ann. and per. herbs, seldom shrubby, in N. and S. Amer. and Afr.; lvs. opp. or alt., entire or variously pinnately lobed or cut; fl. heads radiate, solitary or loosely corymbosely panicled, longpeduncled, involucral bracts in 2 rows, the inner separate or only basally united; disc fls. yellow or purplish, ray fls. yellow, brownish, rose, or bicolored; achenes compressed, usually winged, pappus of smooth or barbed awns, or short scales or teeth, or lacking.

Coreopsises grow well in any garden soil and bloom in summer and autumn. The annuals are started from seeds sown indoors in early spring or in the open when the ground is warm; the perennials from seeds, or by cuttings of growing stems in summer, or by division.

Atkinsoniana Dougl. ex Lindl. [*Calliopsis Atkinsoniana* (Dougl. ex Lindl.) Hook.]. Ann. or per., to 4 ft.; lvs. 1–2-pinnate, segms. linear; heads 1½–2 in. across, outer involucral bracts ¼ as long as the inner; disc fls. brown-purple, ray fls. sterile, yellow with brown-purple base; achenes narrowly winged or margined. B.C. and Sask., s. to Ariz.

atrosanguinea: a hort. name for a fl. garden ann., perhaps *Thelesperma Burridgeanum,* but may be used for reddish-fld. cvs. of *C. tinctoria.*

auriculata L. Stoloniferous per., to 2 ft.; lvs. ovate to lanceolate, simple or with 1 or 2 small basal lobes; heads 1½ in. across; disc fls. yellow, ray fls. sterile, yellow; achenes with thick incurved wings. Va. to Fla. and Miss. Cv. 'Nana'. Dwarf, to 1 ft. Cv. 'Superba' is listed, but material grown under this name is often *C. basalis.*

basalis (Otto & A. Dietr.) S. F. Blake [*Coreopsis Drummondii* (D. Don) Torr. & A. Gray; *Calliopsis basalis* Otto & A. Dietr.; *Calliopsis Drummondii* D. Don]. Ann., to 16 in., glabrous to hispid; lvs. opp., mostly 1–3-pinnate, lfts. linear-lanceolate to orbicular; heads to 2 in. across, outer involucral bracts ½ to as long as the inner; disc fls. yellow, ray fls. sterile, yellow with small basal red-brown blotch; achenes black, with thick, cartilaginous, incurved margins, pappus lacking. Tex.

bicolor: *C. tinctoria.*

Bigelovii (A. Gray) Voss [*Leptosyne Bigelovii* A. Gray]. Ann., to 16 in.; lvs. mostly basal (sometimes also on the sts. in cult. plants), alt., 1–2-pinnate, lfts. linear, to ³⁄₃₂ in. wide; heads solitary, ½–1¾ in. across, outer involucral bracts linear or linear-lanceolate; disc fls. yellow, ray fls. fertile, yellow; disc achenes white-villous, pappus of 2 linear scales, ray achenes narrow-winged, glabrous, without pappus. Deserts and mts., s. Calif. Usually cult. mistakenly as *C. Stillmanii.*

california (Nutt.) H. K. Sharsm. [*Leptosyne californica* Nutt.]. Ann., to 16 in.; lvs. mostly basal, alt., linear-filiform, 4–6 in. long, entire or with 1–2 filiform lobes; heads to 1¼ in. across; disc fls. yellow, ray fls. fertile, yellow, often paler at apex; achenes all alike, dull tan, with tan, red-streaked wings, finely pubescent on faces. S. Ariz., s. Calif., n. Baja Calif. Commonly but mistakenly cult. as *C. Douglasii.*

calliopsidea (DC.) A. Gray [*Leptosyne calliopsidea* (DC.) A. Gray]. Closely related to *C. Bigelovii,* but usually leafy to the middle of st. or above, and with outer involucral bracts broadly ovate or triangular, not linear. S. Calif.

cardaminifolia (DC.) Nutt. [*Calliopsis cardaminifolia* DC.]. Ann., to 20 in., branched; lvs. opp., the lower 1–2-pinnate with linear lfts., the upper simple; heads many, to 1¼ in. across, outer involucral bracts ¼ as long as the inner; disc fls. dark purple, ray fls. sterile, yellow with brown-red basal spot; achenes winged, minutely 2-toothed or entire at apex. Kans. and La. to Ariz. and Mex.

Douglasii (DC.) H. M. Hall [*Leptosyne Douglasii* DC.]. Rarely cult.; material so named is usually *C. californica,* from which it differs chiefly in having achenes dark, glossy brown and glabrous on faces, with pale, unmarked wings. W.-cent. Calif.

Drummondii: *C. basalis*

gigantea (Kellogg) H. M. Hall [*Leptosyne gigantea* Kellogg]. Shortlived per., sts. thick, fleshy, to 1–4 ft., rarely to 10 ft., branching, leafy at ends of brs.; lvs. mostly alt., 2–3-pinnate, to 8 in. long, lfts. linearfiliform; heads to 2–3 in. across, usually 8 or more together, corymbose, peduncles 4–8 in. long; disc fls. yellow, ray fls. fertile, yellow; achenes flat, winged. Coastal, sw. Calif., n. Baja Calif. Not hardy north.

grandiflora Hogg ex Sweet. Per., to 2 ft. or more, sts. leafy almost to top; lvs. opp., petioled, the lowermost simple, the rest pinnate, lfts. linear to lanceolate; heads mostly solitary, to 2½ in. across; disc fls. orange-yellow, ray fls. sterile, yellow; achenes orbicular, convex, with entire wings and thick callus at top and bottom of inner face. Mo. and Kans., s. to Fla. and New Mex. This name is apparently often misused for large-headed forms of *C. lanceolata.* Var. **saxicola** (Alexand.) E. B. Sm. [*C. saxicola* Alexand.]. Wings of achenes pectinate or lacerate. N. Ga., Ala., Kans.

lanceolata L. Per., to 2 ft. or more, sts. erect or ascending, leafy mostly toward base, elongated and nearly naked above; lvs. opp., petioled, mostly simple, sometimes pinnately lobed, blades or lobes linear to oblanceolate; heads to 2½ in. across, very long-peduncled; disc fls. yellow, ray fls. sterile, yellow; achenes similar to those of *C. grandiflora.* Mich., s. to Fla. and New Mex. Cv. 'Grandiflora'. Applied to forms with especially broad heads.

maritima (Nutt.) Hook.f. [*Leptosyne maritima* (Nutt.) A. Gray]. SEA DAHLIA. Per., sts. to 3 ft., thick, fleshy, branching; lvs. alt. or opp., 2–3-pinnate, to 6 in. long, lfts. linear; heads 2½–5 in. across, mostly solitary or 2–3 together, on peduncles to 16 in. long; disc fls. yellow, ray fls. fertile, yellow; achenes flat, winged. Sw. Calif., n. Baja Calif. Not hardy north, but may usually be treated as an ann., flowering the first year from seed.

nana: a listed name for *C. tinctoria* cv.

rosea Nutt. Erect per., to 2 ft., stoloniferous; lvs. opp., entire to 2- or 3-parted, blades or segms. linear; heads 1 in. across; disc fls. yellow, ray fls. sterile, rose-colored; achenes wingless, black. Moist ground, Nov. Sc., to Del. and perhaps Ga. Forma **leucantha** Fern. Ray fls. white.

saxicola: *C. grandiflora* var.

Stillmanii (A. Gray) S. F. Blake [*Leptosyne Stillmanii* A. Gray]. Perhaps not in cult.; material so named is usually if not always *C. Bigelovii*, from which it differs chiefly in having achenes all alike, glabrous or nearly so, with thick wings, and pappus minute, cuplike. Cent. Calif.

tinctoria Nutt. [*Coreopsis bicolor* Hort.; *Calliopsis bicolor* Rchb.; *Calliopsis tinctoria* (Nutt.) DC.]. CALLIOPSIS. Ann., to 4 ft., much-branched; lvs. opp., mostly 1–2-pinnate, lfts. linear or linear-lanceolate; heads many, corymbose, to 1¼ in. across, outer involucral bracts ¼ as long as the inner; disc fls. dark red or purple, ray fls. sterile, bicolored yellow with brown base or, in garden forms, entirely yellow, brown, or purple-red; achenes slender, wingless, black, without pappus. Minn. and Sask., w. to Wash., s. to La. and Calif. The most common ann. sp. in cult. Cv. 'Nana' [var. *nana* Hort.]. Compact, low-growing.

tripteris L. Per., 3–9 ft., branched above; lvs. opp., mostly petioled, 3-parted, the central segm. sometimes again 3-parted, segms. linear to oblong-lanceolate, to 1 in. wide; heads to 2 in. across; disc fls. yellow, becoming purplish, ray fls. sterile, yellow; achenes narrowly winged, minutely setose at apex. Mass., w. to s. Ont. and Wisc., s. to Ga., La., and Kans.

verticillata L. Erect per., to 3 ft., corymbosely branched above; lvs. opp., sessile, palmately 3-parted, the divisions 1–2-pinnate, ultimate segms. linear-filiform; heads to 2 in. across, slenderly peduncled; disc fls. yellow, ray fls. sterile, yellow; achenes flat, narrowly winged, sometimes minutely 2-toothed at apex. Md. to Fla., w. to Ark.

CORETHROGYNE DC. *Compositae* (Aster Tribe). Three spp. of white tomentose per. herbs of Calif.; somewhat like *Aster* but style brs. with dense tufts of yellow hairs and ray fls. neutral; lvs. entire or serrate; heads radiate; disc fls. yellow, ray fls. violet to pink; pappus of reddish bristles.

californica DC. To 1½ ft., sts. prostrate or decumbent from a woody base, then ascending; lvs. narrowly oblanceolate, entire or toothed, the lower pedicelled, the upper sessile; heads to 1¼ in. across, 1 or a few at ends of sts., involucre hemispherical.

filaginifolia (Hook. & Arn.) Nutt. Sts. to 2½ ft., erect or ascending; lvs. lanceolate to oblanceolate, sometimes toothed, the upper ones sessile; heads about 1 in. across, in panicles, involucre turbinate or campanulate. Very variable. Var. **glomerata** H. M. Hall [var. *brevicula* (Greene) M. Canby]. To 1½ ft.; infl. glandular, heads smallish. Var. **linifolia:** *C. linifolia.*

linifolia (H. M. Hall) Ferris [*C. filaginifolia* var. *linifolia* H. M. Hall]. To 20 in., erect; lvs. linear, entire; involucre broadly turbinate, tomentose.

CORIANDRUM L. *Umbelliferae.* Two spp. of ann. herbs of s. Eur. and Asia Minor; lvs. pinnate; fls. small, white, rose, or lavender, in compound umbels; fr. ovoid.

One species grown for the fruits or seeds, which are used as seasoning. It is of easy culture in any garden soil. Propagated by seeds sown in autumn or spring, in the North preferably in spring.

sativum L. CORIANDER, CHINESE PARSLEY. To 3 ft., strong-smelling; lvs. decompound, upper lvs. divided into narrowly linear segms., lower lvs. with ovate, deeply cut segms. S. Eur. Foliage abundantly used in Chinese cooking.

CORIARIA L. *Coriariaceae.* Between 10 and 30 spp. of subshrubs, shrubs, or small trees, native to cent. and S. Amer., s. Eur., e. Asia, New Zeal., and the Pacific Is.; lvs. opp. or whorled; fls. small, greenish, in axillary or rarely terminal racemes, sepals 5, petals 5, stamens 10; fr. an achene surrounded by the fleshy, persistent petals.

Grown in the southern U.S. and Calif. Propagated by seeds, greenwood cuttings, suckers, and layers. The fruits of all species seem to be more or less poisonous.

japonica A. Gray. Shrub, 3–6 ft. or more; lvs. ovate to lanceolate-ovate, to 4 in. long, acute to long-acuminate, 3-nerved; racemes axillary; fls. greenish to reddish; fr. bright red, becoming violet-black. Japan. Zone 8.

microphylla Poir. [*C. thymifolia* Humb. & Bonpl. ex Willd.]. Subshrub, to 4 ft., brs. spreading-recurved; lvs. sessile or subsessile, oblong, to ¾ in. long, acute; fr. dark purple. Mex. to Peru. Fr. yields a black ink.

nepalensis Wallich. TANNER'S TREE. Large shrub, brs. arching, bark red; lvs. ovate, to 3 in. long, acuminate, 3–7-nerved; racemes axillary; fls. greenish; fr. black. N. India.

ruscifolia L. DEU. Shrub or small tree, to 25 ft.; lvs. ovate, to 3 in. long; racemes to 1 ft. long, drooping; fr. purple-black. S. Amer.

terminalis Hemsl. Subshrub, to 4 ft.; lvs. ovate, to 3 in. long, 5–9-nerved; racemes terminal, to 6 in. long; fr. black. China. Var. **xanthocarpa** Rehd. & E. H. Wils. Fr. translucent-yellow. India.

thymifolia: *C. microphylla.*

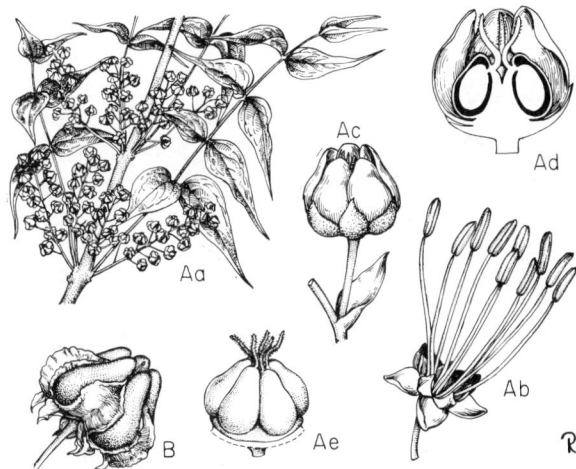

CORIARIACEAE. *Coriaria japonica:* **Aa,** fruiting branch, × ¼; **Ab,** male flower, × 5; **Ac,** female flower, × 4; **Ad,** female flower, vertical section, × 5; **Ae,** pistils, × 5. **B,** *C. myrtifolia:* fruit, × 3. (From Lawrence, *Taxonomy of Vascular Plants.*)

CORIARIACEAE DC. CORIARIA FAMILY. Dicot.; 1 genus, *Coriaria,* of up to 30 spp. of subshrubs, shrubs, or small trees, native to both hemispheres; lvs. opp., sometimes ternate; fls. in axillary or terminal racemes, bisexual or unisexual, sepals 5, petals 5, enlarging in fr., stamens 10, pistils 5–10, ovary superior; fr. an achene, but appearing drupaceous.

CORN. In North America, the word corn refers specifically to maize or Indian corn, *Zea Mays,* not to other cereal grains. Corn as a horticultural subject implies sweet corn or sugar maize (var. *rugosa*) as distinguished from the field or agricultural corns, and also certain kinds grown for the striped ornamental foliage.

Both commercial and home-garden culture of sweet corn rely on special hybrid strains. Sweet corn, grown for the edible immature ear, is a tender annual, requiring warm, well-prepared soil and full-sun exposure. The first planting should be made in the home garden as soon as frost is past. It is well to plant early, intermediate, and late cultivars at the same time, then at intervals of two weeks until early summer, thus having a succession from the first crop until autumn frosts. For the late crop, corn may be started in pots and transplanted when peas and other crops are finished. The soil for corn should be well fertilized. Corn for the garden is better planted in drills, the drills 3–4 feet apart, the seeds 10–12 inches apart in the drills. Some gardeners prefer to plant in hills 2–3 feet apart, each with 3–5 stalks.

Pop corn (var. *praecox*) is grown in the same manner as sweet corn.

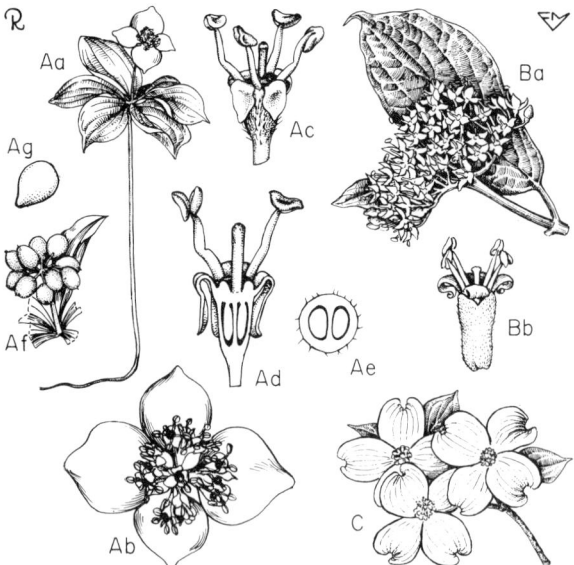

CORNACEAE. **A,** *Cornus canadensis:* **Aa,** plant, × ¹⁄₆; **Ab,** inflorescence subtended by involucre, × ¹⁄₂; **Ac,** flower, × 4; **Ad,** flower, vertical section, × 6; **Ae,** ovary, cross section, × 10; **Af,** fruit, × ¹⁄₂; **Ag,** seed, × 3. **B,** *C. sericea:* **Ba,** inflorescence and leaf, × ¹⁄₂; **Bb,** flower, × 2. **C,** *C. florida:* flowering branch. (Ba, Bb, C from Bailey, *Manual of Cultivated Plants,* ed. 2.)

CORNACEAE Dumort. DOGWOOD FAMILY. Dicot.; about 10 genera and 90 spp. of trees and shrubs, rarely herbs, widely distributed but native chiefly to temp. parts of N. Amer. and Asia; lvs. usually opp., simple; fls. bisexual or unisexual, regular, sometimes subtended by a showy corollalike involucre, in cymes or panicles, rarely in racemes, umbels, or heads, sepals 4–5, petals and stamens mostly 4–5, pistil 1, 2–4-carpelled, ovary inferior; fr. a drupe or berry. *Aucuba, Cornus, Corokia, Curtisia, Griselinia,* and *Helwingia* are grown as ornamentals.

CORNUS L. [*Chamaepericlymenum* J. Hill; *Cynoxylon* Raf.; *Swida (Svida)* Opiz; *Thelycrania* (Dumort.) Fourr.]. DOGWOOD, CORNEL. *Cornaceae.* About 45 spp. of mostly shrubs and small trees, native to N. Amer., Eur., and Asia, rare in S. Amer. and Afr.; lvs. simple, entire, usually opp., mostly deciduous; infl. of terminal cymes, panicles, umbels, or heads; fls. white, greenish-white, or yellow, bisexual or rarely unisexual, 4-merous, small, sometimes with an involucre of showy bracts; fr. a 2-celled, 2-seeded drupe.

Dogwoods are useful for shrub borders and sometimes as single specimens. They are of easy cultivation in any good soil. Propagated by cuttings of mature wood, layers, or the cultivars by budding and grafting on common stocks. The species listed below are hardy in the North unless otherwise stated.

alba L. TARTARIAN D., TATARIAN D. Shrub, to 10 ft.; brs. blood-red; lvs. ovate to elliptic, to 5 in. long, glaucous underneath; cymes to 2 in. across; fr. white or bluish-white. Late spring. Siberia, n. China, n. Korea. Zone 3. Cvs. are: **'Argenteo-marginata'** [cvs. 'Elegantissima Variegata', 'Sibirica Variegata', 'Variegata'], lvs. edged with white; **'Atrosanguinea'**, dwarf form, sts. brilliant crimson; **'Aurea'**: 'Spaethii'; **'Elegantissima Variegata'**: 'Argenteo-marginata'; **'Gouchaultii'**, lvs. variegated with yellowish-white and pink; **'Kesselringii'**, brs. purple; **'Rosenthalii'**, lvs. with broad yellow or gold margins; **'Sibirica'** [cv. 'Splendens'; var. *sibirica* (Lodd.) Loud.; *C. sibirica* Lodd.], SIBERIAN DOGWOOD, brs. bright coral-red; **'Sibirica Variegata'**: 'Argenteo-marginata'; **'Spaethii'** [cv. 'Aurea'], lvs. broadly edged with yellow; **'Splendens'**: 'Sibirica'; **'Variegata'**: 'Argenteo-marginata'.

alternifolia L.f. [*Swida alternifolia* (L.f.) Small]. PAGODA D., GREEN OSIER. Tree, to 25 ft.; lvs. alt., mostly crowded toward ends of brs., ovate to elliptic, to 5 in. long, with 5–6 pairs of lateral veins, pale beneath; cymes about 2½ in. across; fr. dark blue, rarely yellow. Late spring. Nov. Sc. to Minn., s. to Ala., Ga., Mo. Zone 5. Cvs. are: **'Argen-**

tea' [cv. 'Variegata'], lvs. marked with white; **'Arguta'**, a listed name; **'Variegata'**: 'Argentea'.

Amomum Mill. [*Swida Amomum* (Mill.) Small]. SILKY D., RED WILLOW. Shrub, 10 ft., brs. purple, pith brown; lvs. ovate, to 5 in. long, usually silky-pubescent beneath; cymes to 2½ in. across; fr. pale blue. Early summer. Nfld. to Fla. and Tex. Zone 5. Cvs. **'Grandiflorum'** and **'Xanthocarpum'** are listed.

asperifolia Michx. [*Swida microcarpa* (Nash) Small]. Shrub, to 12 ft., pith white; lvs. elliptic, to 3 in. long, rough above and beneath, not papillose beneath, petiole to ¹⁄₈ in. long; cymes to 2 in. across; stamens and fr. blue. Late spring. Coastal plain, S.C., Ga., Fla. Zone 9. Material offered as this sp. is probably *C. Drummondii.*

australis C. A. Mey. Shrub, brs. purplish or greenish; lvs. ovate, to 3 in. long, rough and hairy beneath; cymes small, dense; fr. purplish-black. Late spring. W. Asia.

Baileyi: *C. sericea* forma.

brachypoda: *C. macrophylla.*

×**californica** C. A. Mey.: *C. occidentalis* × *C. stolonifera.* CREEK D. Shrub, to 15 ft., sts. glabrous, purplish-red; lvs. ovate to elliptic, to 4 in. long, acute, somewhat puberulent; fr. white. Late spring–early summer. S. B.C. to s. Calif. Zone 8.

canadensis L. [*Chamaepericlymenum canadense* (L.) Asch. & Graebn.]. BUNCHBERRY, DWARF CORNEL, CRACKERBERRY, PUDDINGBERRY. Per. herb, to 9 in., with woody rhizomes; lvs. whorled, ovate to elliptic or obovate, to 3 in. long; infl. a dense head, subtended by involucre of 4–6 large, white, petal-like bracts; fr. bright red. Late spring–early summer. Greenland and Lab. to Alaska and e. Asia, s. to W. Va., New Mex., Calif. Zone 2.

capitata Wallich. Tree, to 40 ft.; partly evergreen; lvs. ovate-lanceolate to elliptic, to 4 in. long, leathery; infl. a dense head subtended by 4–6 petal-like bracts, these large, creamy-white, obovate, abruptly pointed; fr. scarlet, fleshy, strawberrylike. Early summer. Himalayas. Zone 9.

circinata: *C. rugosa.*

controversa Hemsl. GIANT D. Tree, to 60 ft.; lvs. alt., ovate, to 5 in. long, with 6–9 pairs of lateral veins, whitish beneath; cymes to 5 in. across; fr. blue-black. Late spring. China and Japan. Zone 5. Cv. **'Variegata'**. Lvs. narrow, edged with yellowish-white.

Drummondii C. A. Mey. Shrub, to 15 ft., brs. gray, pith usually brown; lvs. lanceolate to ovate, to 5 in. long, rough above, petiole to ³⁄₄ in. long; cymes to 2¾ in. across; fr. white. Late spring. S. Ont., w. to Kans. and Nebr., s. to Miss., La., and Tex. Zone 5.

×**dubia** Rehd.: *C. Amomum* × *C. paucinervis.* Shrub; lvs. with 3–4 pairs of lateral veins. Fr. almost black. Summer.

elegantissima: probably *C. alba* cv. 'Argenteo-marginata'.

florida L. [*Cynoxylon floridum* (L.) Small]. FLOWERING D. Tree, to 40 ft.; lvs. ovate, to 6 in. long; infl. a dense head, subtended by 4 petal-like bracts, these large, white, obovate, notched; fr. scarlet. Spring. Me. to Fla., w. to e. Kans. and Tex. Zone 5. Wood used for engravers' blocks, tool handles, and turnery. Cvs. are: **'Alba'**, a listed name; **'Alba Plena'**: 'Pluribracteata'; **'Fastigiata'**, with upright branching habit; **'Gigantea'**, infl. and bracts to 6 in. across; **'Magnifica'**, bracts larger; **'Multibracteata'**: 'Pluribracteata'; **'Nana'**, to 5–6 ft.; **'Pendula'**, brs. drooping; **'Pluribracteata'** [cvs. 'Alba Plena', 'Multibracteata', 'Plena'], infl. with 6–8 large and several smaller bracts; **'Plena'**: 'Pluribracteata'; **'Rubra'**, bracts pink or rose; **'Salicifolia'**, small tree with "willowy" growth; **'Starkii'**, a listed name; **'Welchii'**, lvs. variegated with red and yellow; **'Xanthocarpa'**, fr. yellow.

foemina: *C. stricta.*

glabrata Benth. BROWN D. Shrub, to 20 ft., brs. glabrous, sometimes pendulous, pith white; lvs. lanceolate to elliptic, to 2 in. long, gray-green, with 3–4 pairs of lateral veins; cymes to 1¾ in. across; fr. white or bluish. Late spring. Mts., s. Ore. to s. Calif.

Kousa Hance. KOUSA. Shrub or small tree, to 20 ft.; lvs. elliptic-ovate, to 4 in. long, abruptly long-acuminate, glaucous beneath; infl. a dense head, subtended by 4 petal-like bracts, these creamy-white, 1–2 in. long, ovate to lanceolate, acute to acuminate; fr. growing together into a fleshy, globose head, pinkish-red. Late spring–early summer. Japan and Korea. Zone 5b. Var. **Chinensis** Osborn. CHINESE D. Lvs. larger, often more pubescent; bracts about 2¼ in. long. China.—Cvs. are: **'Rubra'**, bracts pink; **'Speciosa'**, a listed name; **'Variegata'**, foliage variegated; **'Xanthocarpa'**, fr. yellow.

lutea: *C. sericea* cv. 'Flaviramea'.

macrophylla Wallich [*C. brachypoda* C. A. Mey.]. Tree, to 50 ft.; lvs. elliptic-ovate, to 6 in. long, abruptly acuminate, glaucous beneath; cymes paniclelike, to 6 in. across; fr. bluish-black. Summer. Himalayas, China, Japan.

mas L. [*C. mascula* L.]. CORNELIAN CHERRY, SORBET. Small tree or shrub, to 20 ft.; lvs. ovate, to 4½ in. long, lustrous above, with tufts of ashy hairs in axils of veins below; umbels ¾ in. across; fls. yellow, appearing before the lvs.; fr. dark red, ellipsoid, to ¾ in. long, edible. Early spring. Cent. and s. Eur., w. Asia. Zone 5. Cvs. are: 'Alba', fr. white; 'Aurea', lvs. yellow; 'Aureo-elegantissima' [cv. 'Elegantissima'], lvs. edged in gold, flushed with carmine at maturity; 'Elegantissima': 'Aureo-elegantissima'; 'Flava' [cv. 'Macrocarpa'], fr. yellow; 'Lanceolata', lvs. narrow, with narrow, white border; 'Macrocarpa': 'Flava'; 'Nana', a spherical bush; 'Variegata', lvs. bordered with white; 'Violacea', lvs. violet-blue.

mascula: *C. mas.*

Nuttallii Audub. MOUNTAIN D. Tree, to 75 ft.; lvs. ovate to obovate, to 5 in. long, glaucous beneath; infl. a dense head, subtended by 4–7, petal-like bracts, these white or pinkish, obovate, acute; fr. red or orange. Early spring–summer, frequently blooming again in autumn. B.C. to s. Calif. Zone 9. Wood used for mauls, tool handles, and turnery. Cv. 'Eddiei'. Foliage variegated.

obliqua: *C. Purpusii.*

occidentalis (Torr. & A. Gray) Cov. [*C. pubescens* Nutt.]. Shrub to 18 ft., brs. hairy, purple; lvs. lanceolate or ovate to elliptic, to 4 in. long, tomentose and glaucous beneath; cymes 2 in. across; fr. white. Spring–summer. B.C. to s. Calif. Zone 9.

officinalis Siebold & Zucc. JAPANESE CORNELIAN CHERRY, JAPANESE CORNEL. Small tree or shrub, to 15 ft.; lvs. elliptic, to 4¾ in. long, pale and with tufts of brown hairs in axils of veins beneath; umbels to about ¾ in. across; fls. yellow, appearing before the lvs.; fr. oblong, red. Early spring. Japan and Korea.

paniculata: *C. racemosa.*

paucinervis Hance. Shrub, to 10 ft.; lvs. elliptic-lanceolate to narrowly ovate, to 4 in. long, more or less persistent; cymes to 3½ in. across; fr. black. Summer. China. Zone 5.

pubescens: *C. occidentalis.*

Purpusii Koehne [*C. obliqua* Raf.]. SILKY D. Shrub, to 10 ft., brs. purple or yellowish-red, pith brown; lvs. ovate to oblong, to 3 in. long and about ¼–⅓ as wide, glaucous, papillose and with appressed hairs beneath; cymes to 2 in. across; fr. blue to nearly white. Spring–summer. Que. to Kans. Zone 5.

racemosa Lam. [*C. paniculata* L'Hér.]. PANICLED D. Shrub, to 15 ft.; lvs. lanceolate to ovate-lanceolate, to 4 in. long, papillose and with appressed hairs beneath; fls. in cymose panicles; fr. white, on red pedicels. Spring–summer. Me. to Minn., s. to N.C. and Okla.

rugosa Lam. [*C. circinata* L'Hér.]. ROUND-LEAVED D. Shrub, to 10 ft., young brs. green, blotched with purple, pith white; lvs. broadly ovate to orbicular, to 6 in. long, with 7–8 pairs of lateral veins, pale and pubescent beneath; cymes dense, to 2½ in. across; fls. white; fr. light blue. Late spring–summer. Nov. Sc., s. to Va. and N. Dak.

sanguinea L. BLOOD-TWIG D., PEGWOOD, DOGBERRY. Shrub, to 12 ft., brs. purple or red; lvs. ovate, to 3 in. long, abruptly short-acuminate; cymes to 2 in. across; fr. black. Late spring. Eur. Cvs. are: 'Mietzschii', lvs. marbled with streaks of white, gray, and green; 'Variegata', lvs. variegated with yellowish-white; 'Viridissima', brs. and fr. green.

sericea L. [*C. stolonifera* Michx.; *C. stolonifera* var. *coloradense* (Koehne) C. K. Schneid.]. RED-OSIER D., AMERICAN D. Shrub, to 10 ft., sts. often rooting at tips, brs. dark red, pith white, ⅓–½ diam. of the br.; lvs. oblong-lanceolate to ovate, to 5 in. long, with 4–7 pairs of lateral veins, papillose beneath; cymes to 2 in. across; fr. white or bluish. Spring–summer. N. Amer. Forma **Baileyi** (J. Coult. & W. H. Evans) Fosb. [*C. Baileyi* J. Coult. & W. H. Evans; *C. stolonifera* var. *Baileyi* (J. Coult. & W. H. Evans) Drescher, and forma *Baileyi* (J. Coult. & W. H. Evans) Rickett]. Lvs. with curling hairs on lower surface.—Cvs. are: 'Aurea': 'Flaviramea'; 'Flaviramea' [cvs. 'Aurea', 'Lutea'], GOLDEN-TWIG D., brs. yellow; 'Kelseyi' [cv. 'Nana'], low-growing, foliage dense; 'Lutea': 'Flaviramea'; 'Nana': 'Kelseyi'.

sibirica: *C. alba* cv.

Spaethii: *C. alba* cv.

stolonifera: *C. sericea.*

stricta Lam. [*C. foemina* Mill.; *Swida stricta* (Lam.) Small]. STIFF D. Shrub, to 15 ft., young brs. reddish, pith white; lvs. lanceolate, elliptic to oblanceolate, to 3½ in. long, with 4–5 pairs of lateral veins, glabrous or nearly so, papillose beneath; cymes to 2½ in. across; anthers and fr. blue. Va. to Fla. and Tex. Zone 8.

×**unalaschkensis** Ledeb.: *C. canadensis* × *C. suecica* L. Intermediate between parents; lvs. in a whorl of 6 at top of st. and an opp. pair below. Greenland, w. Nfld., Alaska.

variegata: a listed name; probably a cv. of *C. alba* or *C. sanguinea.*

CORNUTIA L. *Verbenaceae.* About 15 spp. of deciduous, odoriferous shrubs and trees, native to W. Indies, Mex. through Cent. Amer. to Brazil and Peru; lvs. opp., simple; fls. blue, violet, or purple, cymose, the cymes axillary or mostly panicled; calyx 4- or 5-toothed, or entire, corolla 2-lipped, the upper 3-lobed, the lower 1-lobed, stamens 4, ovary 4-celled; fr. a drupe.

grandifolia (Schlechtend. & Cham.) Schauer. Shrub or tree, to 25 ft., twigs 4-angled, densely hairy; lvs. elliptic or elliptic-ovate, to 13 in. long, acuminate, entire or toothed above the middle, hairy; fls. blue to purple. Mex., Cent. Amer.

COROKIA A. Cunn. *Cornaceae.* About 4 spp. of evergreen shrubs, native to New Zeal., silvery-white-tomentose on young brs., under side of lvs., and in infl.; lvs. alt. or fascicled, simple, entire; fls. bisexual, yellow, 5-merous, in axillary or terminal racemes, panicles, or fascicles; fr. a drupe.

Grown outdoors in Zone 9 on the Pacific Coast.

×**Cheesemanii** Carse: *C. buddleioides* A. Cunn. × *C. Cotoneaster.* To 12 ft.; lvs. oblanceolate to oblong-lanceolate, to 1½ in. long; fls. usually 4–5, in axillary fascicles or terminal panicles; fr. red.

Cotoneaster Raoul. To 10 ft., brs. many and interlaced; lvs. ovate, obovate, or orbicular, to 1 in. long, glossy above; fls. solitary or in groups of 2–4, axillary and terminal; fr. red.

macrocarpa T. Kirk. To 20 ft.; lvs. oblong-lanceolate to elliptic-oblong, to 4 in. long; fls. in axillary racemes shorter than lvs.; fr. dark red.

virgata Turrill. Shrub, to 10 ft., brs. wandlike; lvs. oblanceolate, to 1¾ in. long, glossy green above, white-tomentose beneath; fls. in clusters of 3; fr. orange-yellow. Probably a hybrid between *C. buddleioides* A. Cunn. and *C. Cotoneaster.*

CORONARIA: *LYCHNIS.* **C. coriacea:** *Lychnis Coronaria.*

CORONILLA L. CROWN VETCH. *Leguminosae* (subfamily *Faboideae*). About 20 spp. of mostly hardy shrubs and herbs of the Old World; lvs. odd-pinnate; fls. umbellate on long, axillary peduncles, papilionaceous, yellow or sometimes purple to white, standard orbicular, reflexed, stamens 10, 9 united and 1 free; fr. a slender legume, constricted between seeds and separating into 1-seeded segms.

Grown as ornamentals, as ground covers or for erosion control in full sun. Propagated by seeds and division, or by cuttings.

cappadocica Willd. Per., to 1 ft., glaucous; lfts. in 4–5 pairs, obovate, to ¾ in. long, retuse; fls. yellow, ½ in. long; fr. 4-angled, beaked. Asia Minor.

Emerus L. SCORPION SENNA. Shrub to 9 ft.; lfts. in 2–4 pairs, obovate, 1 in. long or more; fls. to ¾ in. long, yellow, standard marked with red, its long claw much longer than calyx; fr. cylindrical, 2–4 in. long. S. Eur. Zone 5.

glauca: *C. valentina* subsp.

minima L. Procumbent subshrub, to 4 in., gray-green; lfts. in 3–6 pairs, obovate, stipules minute; fls. fragrant, upper lip of calyx entire-truncate, petals golden-yellow; fr. pendent, to 1 in. long. Eur.

vaginalis Lam. Differs from *C. minima* in having large stipules about ¼ in. long, upper lip of calyx 2-toothed, and fr. slightly winged on angles. Eur.

valentina L. Shrub, to 4 ft.; lfts. in 2–6 pairs, obovate, to ¾ in. long, emarginate; fls. yellow, to ½ in. long, claws of petals almost as long as calyx; fr. pendent, to 2 in. long. Medit. region. Subsp. **valentina.** The typical subsp.; lfts. in 3–6 pairs; fr. with 3–7 segms. Se. France to Albania. Subsp. **glauca** (L.) Batt. [*C. glauca* L.]. Lfts. in 2–3 pairs; fr. with mostly 1–4 segms. Medit. region.

varia L. CROWN VETCH. Straggling herb, to 2 ft.; lfts. in 5–12 pairs, oblong; fls. ½ in. long, pink and white, claws of petals almost as long as calyx; fr. erect, long-beaked. Eur.; naturalized in ne. U.S. Useful as ground cover for holding banks.

COROZO: *ELAEIS.*

CORREA Andr. *Rutaceae.* Eleven spp. of shrubs or trees, endemic to Australia; lvs. opp., simple, usually stellate-pubescent; fls. white, green, or red, in cymose clusters, calyx cup-shaped, entire to 4-lobed, corolla usually appearing gamopetalous and 4-lobed, stamens 8; fr. splitting into 4, 1–2-seeded sections.

Grown under glass or in the open in warm regions. Hybridization is common among most species. Propagated by cuttings, or some species by grafting on *C. alba*. Shoots should be pinched back to induce bushy growth.

alba Andr. Prostrate to erect shrub, to 5 ft.; lvs. ovate, orbicular, or obovate, to 1¼ in. long or more, white-tomentose beneath; corolla white or pink, campanulate, petals soon spreading, ½ in. long.

Backhousiana Hook. Shrub, to 15 ft.; lvs. ovate to elliptic, to 1¼ in. long, cuneate or rounded at base; fls. cream-colored to pale green, corolla tubular to slightly funnelform, to about 1¼ in. long. Sometimes offered as *C.* × *magnifica*.

×**bicolor** Paxt.: probably *C. alba* × *C. pulchella*. Corolla tubular, with crimson tube and white lobes, white inside, to about 1 in. long.

×**Harrisii** Paxt.: *C. pulchella* × *C. reflexa*. Corolla tubular, scarlet, to about 1½ in. long.

×**magnifica** Paxt.: hybrid of unknown origin; lvs. ovate-cordate; corolla tubular, greenish, to about 1½ in. long. Material offered under this name may be *C. Backhousiana*.

neglecta: *C. pulchella.*

pulchella Mackay ex Sweet [*C. neglecta* Ashby]. Erect shrub, to 2 ft.; lvs. oblong, elliptic, or ovate, to about 1 in. long, glabrous; corolla tubular, pinkish-red, to about 1 in. long.

reflexa (Labill.) Venten. [*C. speciosa* J. Donn ex Andr.]. Shrub, 2–4 ft.; lvs. ovate, to 2 in. long; corolla tubular, green, or red with green tips, to 1⅜ in. long.

speciosa: *C. reflexa.*

ventricosa Nichols. Perhaps of hybrid origin; corolla bright crimson, with green lobes.

CORRYOCACTUS Britt. & Rose. *Cactaceae.* About 11 spp. of columnar cacti of s. Peru and n. Chile; sts. erect, branching from the base, strongly 6–8-ribbed; fls. diurnal, red or yellow, campanulate with rotate limb, perianth falling, scales of tube and ovary with axillary wool; fr. globose, with large areoles bearing deciduous spines.

For culture see *Cacti.*

brachypetalus (Vaup.) Britt. & Rose. Sts. to 13 ft. high and about 4 in. thick, ribs 7–8; spines about 20, at first black with brown base, unequal, mostly short, some to 6 in. long; fls. orange, to 2½ in. across, scales of ovary with black and white wool. S. Peru and n. Chile.

brevistylus (K. Schum. ex Vaup.) Britt. & Rose. Sts. to 10 ft. high and about 1 ft. thick, ribs 6–7; spines about 15, at first brownish, unequal, some to 10 in. long; fls. yellow, about 4 in. long and wide, scales of ovary with brown wool and white bristles. S. Peru.

melanotrichus (K. Schum.) Britt. & Rose [*Erdisia melanotricha* (K. Schum.) Backeb.]. Sts. branching from base, to 6 ft. high and 1½ in. thick, ribs 7–8; areoles ½ in. apart, spines awl-shaped, light yellow, radial spines 6–12, to ⅝ in. long, central spines 1–3, to 3 in. long; fls. yellow, drying reddish, to 3 in. long and wide, areoles with black bristles; fr. to 2½ in. in diam., with needle-shaped spines. Bolivia.

tristis: a listed name of no botanical standing.

CORTADERIA Stapf. PAMPAS GRASS. *Gramineae.* About 24 spp. of large, per., gynodioecious grasses in S. Amer. and New Zeal.; sts. forming clumps; lvs. crowded at the base of st., blades elongate, narrow, attenuate, usually serrulate; infl. a large, plumelike panicle; spikelets several-fld., rachilla internodes jointed, the lower part glabrous, the upper bearded and forming a stalk to the floret, glumes longer than lower florets, lemma of female spikelet clothed with long hairs. For terminology see *Gramineae.*

argentea: *C. Selloana.*

conspicua (G. Forst.) Stapf: *Chionochloa conspicua* (G. Forst.) Zotov. Material cult. as *Cortaderia conspicua* is *C. Richardii.*

jubata (Lem.) Stapf. Distinguished from *C. Selloana* by the looser, yellowish or purplish panicle and somewhat smaller spikelets ½–⅝ in. long, callus to ⅟₁₆ in. long, with white hairs to ⁵⁄₃₂ in. long, lemma with hairs to ⁵⁄₁₆ in. long appearing above level of top of palea. Ecuador and Peru to Argentina. Only female plants are known. Occasionally cult. for ornament, usually under the name *C. Quila* (Mol.) Stapf, a name of doubtful application, probably belonging to an undetermined sp. of *Chusquea.*

Quila: see *C. jubata.*

Richardii (Endl.) Zotov [*C. conspicua* of auth., not (G. Forst.) Stapf; *Arundo conspicua* of auth., not G. Forst.]. Sts. to 10 ft., unbranched; lf. blades linear; infl. to 20 in. long, light brown, glossy; spikelets 1–3-fld., to ⅝ in. long, glumes 1-nerved, light brown, lemma 3-nerved,

hairy at base, to nearly ⅜ in. long, palea more than half as long as lemma. New Zeal.

rosea: a listed name of no botanical standing.

rubra: a listed name of no botanical standing.

rudiuscula Stapf. Differs from *C. jubata* in having longer, narrower fls., shorter, less hairy callus, and no lemma hairs above level of top of palea. Peru, Chile. Material cult. under this name is probably *C. jubata.*

Selloana (Schult. & Schult.f.) Asch. & Graebn. [*C. argentea* (Nees) Stapf; *Gynerium argenteum* Nees]. Sts. in large clumps, to 10 ft. or more; panicle silvery-white to pink, 1–2 ft. long, 4–6 in. wide; spikelets 4–7-fld., ⅝–¾ in. long, the female silky with long hairs, the male not hairy, glumes white, papery, elongate, lemma long-awned, palea less than half as long as lemma. Brazil, Argentina, Chile. Cult. as a lawn ornamental in the South, also grown commercially for the plumes in s. Calif., and occasionally as a source of paper in S. Amer.

CORTUSA L. *Primulaceae.* About 8 spp. of per., hairy herbs, native from cent. Eur. to n. Asia; lvs. simple, basal, orbicular-cordate, lobed, long-petioled; fls. rose or yellow, in umbels on scapes longer than lvs., calyx 5-lobed, corolla campanulate, 5-lobed, stamens 5, attached at base of corolla tube, apex of anthers apiculate; fr. a 5-valved caps.

Cortusas do well in any good soil, but require winter protection in the North. Propagated by division of roots. A few species are planted in rock gardens.

Matthioli L. To 1 ft.; fls. rosy-purple, nodding. Forma **pekinensis** Al. Richt. Lvs. with deeply incised lobes, each lobe pinnately divided, densely hirsute. Japan, n. China. Forma **pubens** (Schott, Nym., & Kotschy) Schur [*C. pubens* Schott, Nym., & Kotschy]. Lvs. deeply lobed, lobes broad, with coarse teeth. Transylvania.

pubens: *C. Matthioli* forma.

CORYANTHES Hook. HELMET ORCHID. *Orchidaceae.* About 15 spp. of epiphytes, native to trop. Cent. and S. Amer.; similar to *Stanhopea* vegetatively, but pseudobulbs 2-lvd.; infl. lateral at base of pseudobulb, pendent, 1–3-fld.; fls. fleshy, short-lived, lateral sepals larger than the upper sepal and the petals, midlobe of lip much enlarged, bucket-shaped, column enclosed in lip, bent at apex. For structure of fl. see *Orchidaceae.*

Warmhouse culture as for *Stanhopea;* for further culture see *Orchids.*

Bungerothii Rolfe. Pseudobulbs ovoid-oblong, 2½ in. long; scape 1½ ft. long, 1-fld.; sepals and petals whitish-green, speckled with reddish-purple, upper sepal to 2½ in. long, lateral sepals to 6 in. long and 2 in. wide, petals very narrow, about 3 in. long, midlobe of lip yellow, spotted with brown inside. Venezuela.

macrantha Hook. MONKEY ORCHID. Pseudobulbs narrowly conical, to 6 in. long; usually strongly 8-ribbed; lvs. elliptic-lanceolate, to 1 ft. long, acuminate; scape to 6 in. long, usually 2-fld.; sepals and petals membranous, pale yellow or flesh-colored, dotted with red or purple, upper sepal oblong-lanceolate, lateral sepals lunate, 3–5 in. long, twisted, petals narrow, to 2½ in. long, undulate, lip fleshy, with a narrow claw about 1 in. long abruptly passing into a subglobose cup from which rises the helmet-shaped, 3-lobed, orange-yellow, red-spotted terminal lobe. Spring–summer. Trinidad, Venezuela, Guyana.

maculata Hook. Pseudobulbs ovoid and somewhat conical, slender, to 6 in. long; lvs. lanceolate, often broadly so, to about 15 in. long; scapes to 1½ ft. long; sepals and petals pale ochre-yellow, midlobe of lip lemon-yellow, spotted with purple inside. Late spring–summer, early winter. Guyana, Venezuela. Cv. 'Punctata'. Sepals, petals, and lip bright yellow, speckled with red.

speciosa (Hook.) Hook. [*Gongora speciosa* Hook.] BAT ORCHID. Pseudobulbs oblong-conical, to 5½ in. long, tapering slightly upward, deeply striate; lvs. linear-lanceolate, to 16 in. long, tapering at each end; scape to about 20 in. long, 2–5-fld.; fls. about 2½ in. across, fragrant, sepals and petals clear yellow, upper sepal ovate-lanceolate, about 1¼ in. long, lateral sepals lunate, to about 2½ in. long, twisted or undulate, midlobe of lip reddish to tawny-yellow. Cent. Amer., Trinidad and Tobago, Brazil.

CORYDALIS Venten. *Fumariaceae.* About 300 spp. of herbs, native to N. Temp. Zone and S. Afr., per. spp. with rhizomes or tubers; lvs. basal and on sts., pinnately decompound; fls. racemose, irregular, bisexual, perianth deciduous, sepals 2 or 0, petals 4, one of the outer pair with a basal spur, stamens 6, in two bundles of 3; fr. a slender, dehiscent caps.

Of easy cultivation in any garden soil. Propagated by division or seeds; seeds of *C. bulbosa, C. cava*, and *C. nobilis* cannot tolerate long dry storage, but must be planted soon after ripening.

angustifolia (Bieb.) DC. Differs from *C. bulbosa* in having racemes loosely 4–8-fld., fls. yellowish or white, fl. bracts trifid or upper ones entire. Caucasus.

aurea (Muhlenb. ex Willd.) Willd. Ann. or bien., 6–24 in., prostrate-ascending, many-stemmed, glaucous; lvs. 3-pinnate; racemes terminal, scarcely longer than lvs.; fls. yellow, to ¾ in. long, spur to half as long as rest of petal, fl. bracts toothed; caps. spreading or pendulous, to 1 in. long or more. Late spring–early summer. N. Amer.

bulbosa (L.) DC. [*C. Halleri* (Willd.) Willd.; *C. solida* (L.) Swartz]. FUMEWORT. Per., to 8 in., 1-stemmed, from solid, cormlike tuber about 1 in. in diam., st. with a conspicuous bract near base; lvs. generally 2–3, ultimate lobes usually lanceolate-oblong; racemes erect, usually 10–20-fld., lower pedicels more than ⁵⁄₁₆ in. long; fls. deep rose to purple, or white, sepals absent, spur usually longer than rest of corolla, fl. bracts broadly wedge-shaped, palmately lobed, shorter than pedicels in fr. Eur., Asia. The name *C. bulbosa* has been used for *C. cava*. May be offered as *C. decipiens*. Subsp. **bulbosa**. The typical subsp.; lvs. with secondary divisions only incised; fls. rose to purple, spur stout, fl. bracts divided into simple lobes. Subsp. **densiflora** (J. Presl & K. Presl) Hayek [*C. densiflora* J. Presl & K. Presl]. Lvs. with secondary divisions divided into separate lobes; fls. rose or white, spurs slender and elongate, fl. bracts much more dissected.

cashmeriana Royle. Per., to 6 in., 1-stemmed, with small, scaly tuber; st. lvs. nearly sessile, pinnatisect into linear, entire segms. ½–1 in. long; racemes terminal, densely 3–8-fld.; fls. ½–1 in. long, bright blue, tipped with dark blue, spur curved, about as long as rest of corolla, lower fl. bracts deeply trifid, upper ones 3-toothed. Kashmir to Sikkim.

cava (L.) Schweigg. & Körte. Differs from *C. bulbosa*, with which it has been confused, in lacking the bract near base of st., and in having tuber much larger, to 2 in. in diam., hollow, with a depression on under side, lvs. with ultimate lobes broader, sepals small but evident, corolla violet or white, spur more sharply curved downward near tip, fl. bracts large, entire. Cent. Eur. Cv. 'Albiflora'. Fls. white.

chaerophylla DC. Per., to 30 in., several-stemmed, with taproot; basal lvs. distinctly deltoid in outline, long-petioled, st. lvs. more or less sessile; fls. bright yellow, about ⅝ in. long, spur as long as rest of corolla, fl. bracts entire, small; caps. ovate-obovate. Cent. Himalayas.

cheilanthifolia Hemsl. Per., to 8 in. or more, nearly stemless; lvs. in dense rosette, with about 10 pairs of primary divisions, the divisions again pinnate; peduncles terminal, not longer than lvs., sometimes branched; fls. bright yellow, about ½ in. long, spur straight, shorter than rest of petal, fl. bracts entire; caps. long, linear. Cent. China.

cornuta Royle [*C. thalictrifolia* W. Jameson ex Regel]. Differs from *C. vaginans* in having sts. erect, inner petals purple-tipped, and seeds punctate, not glossy. Himalayas. Doubtfully in cult.

decipiens: *C. pumila;* but material offered as *C. decipiens* may be *C. bulbosa*.

densiflora: *C. bulbosa* subsp.

diphylla: *C. rutifolia*.

glauca: *C. sempervirens*.

Gortschakovii Schrenk. Similar to *C. rupestris*, but ultimate lobes of lvs. 3 times as large, and fl. bracts many-lobed. Himalayas to nw. China.

Halleri: *C. bulbosa*.

lutea (L.) DC. Per., to 15 in., many-stemmed, without tuber; lvs. green above, glaucous beneath; racemes axillary, long-peduncled, densely 6–16-fld.; fls. golden-yellow, darker at tip, about ¾ in. long, inner petals broadly winged toward apex, spur straight and about ⅛ in. long, fl. bracts small, entire; fr. pendent, pedicels more than half as long as pods, seeds glossy. Eur.

nobilis (L.) Pers. Per., to 30 in., robust, several-stemmed, roots and rhizomes fleshy, becoming hollow and sometimes latticed, sts. furrowed; lvs. usually 2–3, short-petioled, glaucous; racemes short, dense, headlike, 20–30-fld.; fls. whitish-yellow, tipped brown and dark purple, to 1 in. long, spur short and downcurved, lower fl. bracts dissected, upper ones nearly entire; caps. tapered at both ends. Cent. Asia. One of the most ornamental sp. of the genus.

ochotensis Turcz. Ann. or bien., to 2 ft., many-stemmed, without tuber, sts. thick, deeply furrowed, rather distinctly winged; racemes loose, to 10-fld.; corolla yellow, tipped with brown-purple, to ¾ in. long, spur as long as rest of petal, downcurved, lowermost fl. bracts unevenly deeply divided, others entire and ovate; caps. explosively dehiscent. N. China, Manchuria, Korea, Japan.

ochroleuca W. D. J. Koch. Per., to 15 in., many-stemmed, without tuber; lvs. glaucous on both surfaces, petioles narrowly winged; racemes axillary, dense; fls. to ⅝ in. long, yellowish-white, with short gibbous spur, fl. bracts entire; caps. erect, seeds not glossy. Italy, Yugoslavia, Albania, Greece; naturalized in cent. and w. Eur.

ophiocarpa Hook.f. & T. Thoms. Per., to 3 ft., many-stemmed, without tuber, gray-green; lvs. in dense rosette in young plants, petioles flattened, decurrent on sts. as wings; racemes many-fld.; fls. whitish, to ½ in. long, inner petals tipped with black-red or green, spur short and straight, fl. bracts entire; caps. very narrowly linear, about ¾ in. long or more, very curved and strongly knobby. E. Himalayas.

pallida (Thunb.) Pers. Per., to 18 in., many-stemmed, without tuber; racemes many-fld., 1–5 in. long; fls. golden-yellow, with brown patch toward tip, to nearly 1 in. long, spur short, fl. bracts entire, or lower ones toothed; caps. nearly 1 in. long, strongly knobby. N. and e. China, e. to Korea, Taiwan, Japan.

pumila (Host) Rchb. [*C. decipiens* Schott, Nym. & Kotschy]. Differs from *C. bulbosa* in having smaller, more delicate habit, and loose, 1–5-fld. infl., lower pedicels less than ³⁄₁₆ in. long. Eur.

ramosa: *C. vaginans*.

rosea Maxim. Per., to 2 ft., st. branched, leafy; racemes terminal, loose, to 10-fld.; fls. rose, 1 in. long, spur as long as rest of petal, lower fl. bracts pinnately parted, upper ones entire. China.

rupestris Kotschy ex Boiss. Per., to 8 in., many-stemmed, with thick rhizome, without tuber; lvs. with ultimate lobes less than ¼ in. long; racemes terminal, short, dense; fls. yellow, outer petals wide-winged apically, spur short, swollen, fl. bracts linear-lanceolate, entire; caps. ellipsoid, about ½ in. long, flattened, not knobby. Iran.

rutifolia Sibth. & Sm. [*C. diphylla* Wallich]. Per., to 8 in., 1-stemmed, from slender rhizome; lvs. 2–3, opp. or whorled; racemes 6–12-fld.; fls. to 1 in. long, bright purple, with darker tips, spur inflated, as long as or longer than rest of corolla, fl. bracts entire and veiny; caps. ovate-oblong, ⁵⁄₁₆ in. long. Mts., w. Asia to nw. China and Himalayas.

saxicola Bunt. [*C. thalictrifolia* Franch., not W. Jameson ex Regel]. Per., more or less decumbent, to 1 ft. long, many-stemmed, from long, woody rhizomes; lvs. to 15 in. long, with 5–7 long-stalked, irregularly lobed primary divisions 1–3 in. long; racemes many-fld., produced almost continually; fls. yellow, to 1 in. long, spur short, fl. bracts entire; caps. linear, 1½ in. long. In limestone crevices, cent. China. Not hardy north.

Scouleri Hook. Per., to 4 ft., many-stemmed, with thick rhizome; racemes to 25-fld.; fls. rose or white, to 1 in. long, spur very long and slender, ⅔ of total length of corolla, fl. bracts entire; caps. obovate-clavate. Vancouver Is., Wash., Ore.

sempervirens (L.) Pers. [*C. glauca* (Curtis) Pursh]. ROMAN WORMWOOD, ROCK-HARLEQUIN. Ann. or bien., to 4 ft., much-branched, very glaucous; racemes loosely paniculate, few-fld.; fls. pale pink to nearly purple, with yellow tips, to ¾ in. long, spur very short, blunt, fl. bracts very small, entire; caps. erect, narrowly linear, 1–2 in. long. Nfld. to Ga., w. to Minn., B.C., Alaska. Cv. 'Alba'. Fls. white. Cv. 'Rosea'. Fls. rose.

solida: *C. bulbosa*.

thalictrifolia: *C. cornuta;* but material offered as *C. thalictrifolia* is *C. saxicola*.

vaginans Royle [*C. ramosa* Wallich]. Ann. or bien., often decumbent, with thick taproot, glaucous, st. much-branched; racemes loosely fld.; fls. to ¾ in. long, yellow with brown veins, a little darker at tips, spur downcurved, as long as rest of petal, outer petal with conspicuous crest, fl. bracts divided, the lowermost leaflike; caps. elliptic-obovate, eventually reflexed, explosively dehiscent, seeds glossy and smooth. Nw. Himalayas.

Wilsonii N. E. Br. Per., to 1 ft., forming clumps, with taproot, st. short, reclining; lvs. usually glaucous, primary divisions about 7–9, pinnately lobed, to 3 in. long; racemes several; fls. bright yellow, about ¾ in. long, spur downcurved, ⅓ the length of corolla, fl. bracts entire; caps. linear, 4-angled. Cent. China. Not hardy north.

CORYLACEAE: *BETULACEAE*.

CORYLOPSIS Siebold & Zucc. WINTER HAZEL. *Hamamelidaceae*. About 10 spp. of deciduous shrubs or small trees, native to e. Asia and the Himalayas; lvs. alt., simple, toothed, strongly veined, usually cordate; racemes on leafless shoots in spring, pendent, with basal bracts; fls. fragrant, yellow, sepals, petals, and stamens 5, ovary half-inferior, 2-celled; fr. a 2-beaked caps., each cell with 2 glossy black seeds.

Planted as ornamentals, the attractive flowers appearing before the leaves in early spring. They thrive in a moist soil of peat and sand, and require protection in the North. Propagated by seeds, by greenwood cuttings under glass, by layers and by division; easily transplanted. Zone 7.

glabrescens Franch. & Sav. Large shrub, to 20 ft.; lvs. ovate-orbicular, to 4 in. long, with short, prominently awned teeth, glabrous above, sparingly stellate-pubescent beneath when young; racemes several-fld.; fls. about ½ in. long, stamens half as long as petals. Japan.

Gotoana Mak. Similar to *C. glabrescens*, but lvs. obovate, with short-awned teeth, fls. shorter, and stamens nearly as long as petals. Japan.

pauciflora Siebold & Zucc. BUTTERCUP W. H. Much-branched shrub, to 6 ft.; lvs. ovate, to 2 in. long, glabrous above, appressed-pilose beneath along veins, with 5–7 pairs of lateral veins; fls. 1–3 together, to ½ in. long. Japan.

platypetala Rehd. & E. H. Wils. Shrub, to 9 ft., shoots and petioles glandular; lvs. ovate, to 4 in. long, toothed, glabrous; racemes to 3 in. long; fls. pale yellow, to ½ in. long. Cent. China. Var. **laevis** Rehd. & E. H. Wils. Petioles glabrous.

sinensis Hemsl. To 15 ft.; lvs. to 4 in. long, obovate to oblong, with fine teeth, pubescent on veins, grayish-green beneath; racemes to 2 in. long, bracts silky outside; fls. to ¾ in. long, calyx pubescent. Cent. China.

spicata Siebold & Zucc. SPIKE W. H. To 6 ft.; brs. rather stout, young brs., petioles, and infl. yellowish-pubescent; lvs. ovate-orbicular, to 4 in. long, glabrous above, glaucous and pubescent beneath, with 6–7 pairs of lateral veins; racemes to 3 in. long; fls. to ⅜ in. long. Japan.

Veitchiana Bean. To 6 ft.; lvs. ovate to elliptic, to 4 in. long, glabrous above, sparingly pubescent beneath when young, with 6–7 pairs of lateral veins; racemes 10–15-fld., to 2 in. long; calyx hairy, anthers reddish-brown, exserted. W. China.

Willmottiae Rehd. & E. H. Wils. To 12 ft.; lvs. ovate to roundish, to 3½ in. long, glaucous and at first pubescent beneath, with 7–10 pairs of lateral veins; racemes 20-fld., to 3 in. long; fls. pale yellow, calyx glabrous, anthers yellow, not exserted. W. China. Similar to *C. Veitchiana*, but with calyx glabrous, stamens yellow and less prominent.

CORYLUS L. FILBERT, HAZEL, HAZELNUT. *Betulaceae*. About 10 spp. of deciduous, monoecious, small to large shrubs and some trees, native to the N. Temp. Zone; lvs. alt., generally ovate, doubly toothed; fls. unisexual, developing before lvs., male fls. in drooping catkins; fr. a nut with a leafy involucre, borne in clusters at ends of brs.

Grown for the edible nuts and as ornamentals. See *Filbert*.

americana Marsh. AMERICAN F., AMERICAN H. Shrub, to 10 ft.; lvs. to 5 in. long, pubescent beneath; fr. in clusters of 2–6, involucre about twice as long as nut, with deep irregular lobes. E. N. Amer.

Avellana L. EUROPEAN F., EUROPEAN H. Shrub, to 25 ft.; lvs. to 4 in. long, pubescent beneath; fr. in clusters of 1–8, involucre usually shorter than nut or only slightly longer, with deep irregular lobes. Eur. Produces large nuts much used in commerce. The seed oil is sometimes extracted, and the wood has many uses. Cvs. include: 'Atropurpurea': 'Fusco-rubra'; 'Aurea', lvs. and shoots yellow; 'Contorta', brs. and catkins curled and twisted; 'Fusco-rubra' [cv. 'Atropurpurea'; 'Purpurea'], lvs. dull purple or brownish-red; 'Grandis', COBNUT, nuts large; 'Heterophylla' [cvs. 'Laciniata', 'Quercifolia'], lvs. pinnately dissected; 'Laciniata': 'Heterophylla'; 'Pendula', brs. drooping; 'Purpurea': 'Fusco-rubra'; 'Quercifolia': 'Heterophylla'.

californica: *C. cornuta* var.

chinensis Franch. CHINESE F., CHINESE H. Tree to 120 ft.; lvs. to 7 in. long, pubescent; fr. in clusters of 3–6, involucre contracted above the nut into a tube, divided into linear lobes apically. China. Considered a var. of *C. Colurna* by some botanists.

Colurna L. TURKISH F., TURKISH H., TREE H. Tree to 80 ft.; lvs. to 5 in. long, pubescent on veins beneath; fr. in clusters of 3–6, involucre much longer than nut, divided into linear lobes ½–1 in. long. Se. Eur. and w. Asia.

cornuta Marsh. [*C. rostrata* Ait.]. BEAKED F., BEAKED H. Shrub, to 10 ft.; lvs. elliptic, ovate, or obovate, sometimes cordate at base, to 4 in. long, pubescent on nerves beneath; fr. 1–2, involucre tubular, bristly, much contracted above the nut into a cylindrical beak to 1¼ in. long. N. Amer. A widespread sp. with considerable local and regional variation. Var. **cornuta**. The typical var.; involucral tube at least twice as long as the nut. E. N. Amer. Var. **californica** (A. DC.) Sharp [*C. californica* (A. DC.) Rose]. Twigs more hirsute, involucral tube less than twice as long as the nut. B.C. to Calif.

ferox Wallich. Tree, to 40 ft.; lvs. obovate, to 4½ in. long, irregularly doubly serrate; fr. several together, involucre spiny-pubescent, resembling the bur of chestnut. Nepal and Sikkim.

heterophylla Fisch. & Trautv. Tree or shrub, to 25 ft.; lvs. elliptic to obovate, to 4 in. long, acuminate to nearly mucronate, obtuse to cordate at base, somewhat serrate or partly lobed, smooth above, pubescent along veins beneath; petiole to ¾ in. long, glandular-hairy; fr. 1–3, involucre longer than nut, campanulate, hairy at base, lobes entire or dentate. Ne. Asia. Var. **japonica** is listed. Var. **sutchuenensis** Franch. Lvs. truncate at apex, glabrous or nearly so.

mandshurica: *C. Sieboldiana* var.

maxima Mill. GIANT F. Shrub or small tree, to 30 ft.; lvs. to 5½ in. long; fr. 1–3, involucre tubular, lobed at top and about twice as long as nut. Se. Eur. Produces large nuts much used in commerce. Cv. 'Purpurea'. Lvs. dark purple.

×**mildredensis** C. A. Reed: *C. americana* × *C. Avellana*. MILDRED F. Invalid name used for a hybrid between these two spp.

occidentalis: a listed name of no botanical standing.

rostrata: *C. cornuta*.

Sieboldiana Blume. JAPANESE H. Shrub, to 15 ft.; lvs. elliptic to obovate, to 4 in. long, hairy on veins beneath; fr. 1–6, involucre tubular, constricted above nut, ⅝–1⅝ in. long, bristly. E. Asia. Var. **mandshurica** (Maxim. & Rupr.) C. K. Schneid. [*C. mandshurica* Maxim. & Rupr.]. Involucre only slightly constricted above nut, to 2 in. long.

CORYNABUTILON (K. Schum.) Kearn. *Malvaceae*. Three spp. of shrubs or small trees in cent., coastal Chile; distinguished from *Abutilon* in having style brs. at the apex laterally flattened, club-shaped, and stigmatic along each edge.

Propagated by seeds or softwood cuttings.

vitifolium (Cav.) Kearn. [*Abutilon vitifolium* (Cav.) K. Presl]. Soft-woody shrubs or small trees, 10–25 ft., the new growth white-tomentose; lvs. to 6 in. long or more, about as broad, palmately 3-, 5-, or 7-lobed, cordate at base, margins toothed; fls. solitary, or to about 6 in long-peduncled, naked cymes clustered in the upper lf. axils, calyx about ⅜ in. long, corolla white to bluish, 2–3½ in. across. Hardy in sheltered places to Long Is., although generally cult. as a winter-flowering, greenhouse shrub. Cv. 'Album'. Fls. white.

CORYNEPHYLLUM: *SEDUM*. C. viride: *S. Corynephyllum*.

CORYNOCARPACEAE Engl. CORYNOCARPUS FAMILY. Dicot.; 1 genus, *Corynocarpus*, of 4 spp. of evergreen trees, native to New Hebrides, New Caledonia, and New Zeal.; lvs. alt., simple, entire, without stipules; fls. bisexual, regular, in terminal panicles, sepals 5, petals 5, stamens 5, alternating with 5 staminodes, pistil 1, ovary superior, 1–2-celled, styles 1 or 2; fr. a drupe. *Corynocarpus* is sometimes planted as an ornamental.

CORYNOCARPUS J. R. Forst. & G. Forst. *Corynocarpaceae*. Four spp. of evergreen trees, native to New Hebrides, New Caledonia, and New Zeal.; lvs. alt., simple; fls. in terminal panicles, sepals, petals, stamens, and staminodes 5; fr. a drupe.

laevigata J. R. Forst. & G. Forst. To 50 ft.; lvs. elliptic-oblong to oblong-obovate, to 8 in. long, dark green, leathery, glossy; fls. greenish-yellow; drupe 1½ in. long, orange. New Zeal. Cult. in Calif., Zone 10a. The fleshy part of the fr. is edible, but the seed is poisonous.

CORYNOPUNTIA: *OPUNTIA* section *Corynopuntia*.

CORYPHA L. *Palmae*. About 8 spp. of very large monocarpic palms with bisexual fls., in trop. Asia to Australia; lvs. palmate, very large, petiole elongate, armed with stout spinose teeth on margins, blade stiff and heavy, deeply divided into many 1-ribbed segms. 2-cleft at apex; infls. few to many with tubular bracts on peduncles and brs. aggregated above the lvs. into a terminal compound structure, the plant dying after flowering and fruiting; fls. mostly in clusters along the rachillae, small, sepals 3, united, petals 3, separate, stamens 6, pistil 3-celled, 3-ovuled; fr. usually globose with stigmatic residue and abortive carpels basal, seed with homogeneous endosperm.

Planted as ornamentals in the tropics and occasionally the subtropics; hardy in Zone 10 in Fla. For culture see *Palms*.

australis: *Livistona australis*.

elata Roxb. [*C. Gembanga* (Blume) Blume]. GEBANG PALM. To 60 ft. or more, trunk to nearly 2½ ft. in diam., with rings and a spiral furrow; lf. blades to more than 6 ft. wide, divided into 80–100 segms.; petiole to 9 ft. long or more, margins black with stout teeth at least centrally; compound infl. conical, to 10 ft. long or more but not as wide as the lvs., the individual infls. emerging from the mouths of bracts on the trunk; fr. globose, 1 in. in diam. or less. Bengal and Burma, where perhaps not native, Philippine Is., e. Indies, perhaps to Australia.

Gembanga: *C. elata.*

umbraculifera L. TALIPOT PALM. To 80 ft. trunk to 3 ft. in diam., ringed but not spirally furrowed; lf. blades to 16 ft. in diam., petiole to 10 ft. long, margins with short dark teeth; compound infl. to 20 ft., the individual infls. piercing bracts on the trunk; fr. 1⅜ in. in diam. Ceylon, Malabar coast (India). Occasionally grown as specimen plants in the tropics. The giant infl. is the largest in the plant kingdom.

CORYPHANTHA (Engelm.) Lem. *Cactaceae.* About 60 spp. of low, tubercled cacti of Mex., Cuba, and the U.S.; sts. simple or cespitose, globose to oblong, with watery juice, tubercles succulent, cylindrical or angled, grooved on the upper surface from the terminal spine cluster usually down to the axil; fls. diurnal, from grooves usually of young tubercles and so nearly apical, mostly large for the plant, ovary naked or rarely almost scaly; fr. globose or ovoid to oblong, seeds light brown to black, smooth or pitted. Resembling *Mammillaria* but with areoles of only one kind, whose flower- and spine-bearing areas are connected by a usually woolly groove.

The genus has been divided into 3 subgenera, often treated as genera, and 5 sections. The species of a section possess the characteristics of that section and of the subgenus to which the section belongs. These characteristics are not repeated in the brief descriptions of the species; instead, the following symbols are used to indicate the subgenus and section to which each species belongs; Cc, *Coryphantha;* Cg, *Glanduligerae;* Cl, *Lepidocoryphantha;* Ee, *Escobaria;* Ep, *Pseudocoryphantha;* N, *Neobesseya.*

The distinguishing characters of the subgenera and sections follow:

Subgenus *Coryphantha* (C). Seeds light brown, smooth, hilum lateral, small, perisperm present; outer perianth segms. mostly entire; fr. ovoid to oblong, red.

Section **Coryphantha** (Cc). Tubercles grooved to base, glandspines absent; perianth segms. entire.

Section **Glanduligerae** (Salm-Dyck) Bravo (Cg). Tubercles grooved to base; glandspines present.

Section **Lepidocoryphantha** (Backeb.) Moran [*Lepidocoryphantha* Backeb.] (Cl). Tubercles grooved to middle; glandspines absent; perianth segms. ciliate, ovary sometimes with a few scales hairy in the axils.

Subgenus **Escobaria** (Britt. & Rose) A. Berger [*Escobaria* Britt. & Rose] (E). Seeds dark brown to black, with honeycombed surface, foveolate, hilum lateral or nearly basal, elliptic, small, perisperm present; outer perianth segms. usually ciliate; fr. globose to oblong; tubercles many, short, persisting as woody knobs after fall of spines.

Section **Escobaria** (Britt. & Rose) H. E. Moore (Ee). Fr. red; fls. less than 1 in. across.

Section **Pseudocoryphantha** (Buxb.) Moran (Ep). Fr. green; fls. 1–3 in. across.

Subgenus **Neobesseya** (Britt. & Rose) A. Berger [*Neobesseya* Britt. & Rose] (N). Seeds black, subglobose, pitted, hilum nearly basal, elongate, perisperm absent; outer perianth segms. mostly ciliate; fr. globose, red; tubercles few, long, not persisting as woody knobs.

For culture see *Cacti.*

aggregata: *Echinocereus triglochidiatus* var. *melanacanthus;* however, the name *C. aggregata* is commonly applied to *C. vivipara* var. *bisbeeana.*

Alversonii: *C. vivipara* var.

Andreae (J. Purpus & Böd.) A. Berger. Cc; sts. simple, globose, to 3½ in. thick, crown and axils woolly, tubercles in 5 and 8 spirals, rounded, to ¾ in. high and 1 in. wide; spines yellow-gray, radial spines about 10, needle-shaped, stellate or recurved, to ½ in. long, central spines 5–7, awl-shaped, recurved, to 1 in. long; fls. yellow, to 1½ in. long and 2½ in. wide, segms. ⅛ in. wide. E. Mex. Differs from *C. bumamma* in having narrow, acuminate perianth segms. and needle-shaped radial spines.

arizonica: *C. vivipara* var.

asperispina Böd. [*Neobesseya asperispina* (Böd.) Böd.]. N; sts. simple, globose, to 2½ in. thick, tubercles in 8 and 13 spirals, conoid, about ¾ in. long and ½ in. wide; spines needle-shaped, woolly-roughened, grayish-white, radial spines 9–10, stellate, to ⅜ in. long, central spine 0–1, shorter; fls. yellow-green, to 1 in. long. N. Mex.

asterias (J. F. Cels) Hübner. Cg; sts. solitary, to 5 in. high and 3 in. thick, tubercles thick; spines stiff, bulbous at base, yellowish, radial spines 9, stellate, central spines 1–2, the lower hooked, glandspine red, axillary; fls. white to pink. Mex.

bella (Britt. & Rose) Fosb. [*Escobaria bella* Britt. & Rose]. Ee; cespitose, sts. oblong, to 3 in. high, tubercles nearly cylindrical; radial spines about 15, almost stellate, needle-shaped, white, to ⅜ in. long, central spines 3–5, spreading, stouter, brown, unequal, to ¾ in. long, glandspine near center of groove, narrow, brown; fls. pink, ¾ in. wide. Tex. Probably the same as *C. strobiliformis.*

Bergerana Böd. Cg; sts solitary, to 5 in. high and 2½ in. thick, tubercles in 8 and 13 spirals, conoid, to ⅝ in. long and ⅜ in. wide; radial spines 18–20, stellate, needle-shaped, grayish, about ½ in. long, central spines 4, awl-shaped, bulbous at base, yellowish, tipped with brown, the upper 3 ascending, ½ in. long, the lower directed outward, to ¾ in. long, glandspines 1–2, axillary, red; fls. yellow, 1½ in. long, 3 in. wide. N. Mex.

bumamma (C. A. Ehrenb.) Britt. & Rose. Cc; similar to *C. elephantidens* and perhaps a var., but fls. yellow, to 2½ in. wide. Cent. Mex.

Chaffeyi (Britt. & Rose) Fosb. [*Escobaria Chaffeyi* Britt. & Rose]. Ee; sts. to 5 in. high and 2½ in. thick, tubercles short; radial spines many, setose, central spines several, shorter, dark-tipped; fls. cream or purplish, ⅝ in. long, inner segms. obtuse. Cent. Mex.

chihuahuensis (Britt. & Rose) A. Berger [*Escobaria chihuahuensis* Britt. & Rose]. Ee; sts. often solitary, globose to oblong, spiny, tubercles short; radial spines many, central spines several, longer, dark-tipped; fls. purple, to ⅝ in. long, inner segms. acute. N. Mex.

chlorantha: *C. vivipara* var. *deserti.*

clava (Pfeiff.) Lem. Cg; cespitose, sts. to 1 ft. high and 4 in. thick, tubercles somewhat 4-sided, to 1 in. long and ½ in. wide; radial spines 6–11, yellowish, about ½ in. long, central spines 1–4, stouter, to 1 in. long, glandspines 1–2, red or yellow, axillary; fls. pale yellow, to 3½ in. wide. Summer. Cent. Mex. Probably a var. or form of *C. octacantha.*

clavata (Scheidw.) W. T. Marsh. Cg; sts. simple, oblong, to 6 in. high, tubercles in 5 and 8 or 8 and 13 spirals; spines needle-shaped, radial spines 6–12, central spine 1, sometimes curved or hooked, glandspines 1 to several, in grooves, large, red; fls. creamy, ¾ in. long. Cent. Mex.

compacta (Engelm.) Britt. & Rose. Cc; sts. simple, to 2½ in. high and 3 in. thick, tubercles in 13 and 21 spirals, ⁵⁄₁₆ in. long; radial spines 14–16, awl-shaped, recurved, appressed, whitish, interlacing, to ¾ in. long, central spines usually 0; fls. yellow, ¾ in. long. Summer. N. Mex. Perhaps a form of *C. cornifera.*

cornifera (DC.) Britt. & Rose. Cd; sts. mostly simple, globose, to 5 in. high, tubercles in 5 and 8 spirals, nearly rhombic, to 1 in. long and wide; spines yellowish, becoming gray; fls. yellow, to 2½ in. long. Var. **cornifera** [*C. radians* (DC.) Britt. & Rose]. The typical var.; radial spines 7–17, needle-shaped, stellate, to ½ in. long, central spine 1, stout and often longer, directed outward or decurved. Cent. Mex. Var. **Echinus** (Engelm.) L. Bens. [*C. Echinus* (Engelm.) Britt. & Rose; *C. pectinata* (Engelm.) Britt. & Rose]. Radial spines 16–26, central spines 3–4, the lower larger, straight or curved, to ⅞ in. long. Tex. and n. Mex. Var. **scolymoides** (Scheidw.) Borg [*C. scolymoides* (Scheidw.) A. Berger]. Tubercles closer-set, ascending; radial spines more numerous, 4 of them darker.

daimonoceras Lem. Perhaps only a var. of *C. cornifera;* upper radial spines clustered, central spines 3–4.

dasyacantha (Engelm.) A. Berger [*Escobaria dasyacantha* (Engelm.) Britt. & Rose]. Ee; sts. simple or few-branched, to 3 in. thick and rarely 8 in. high, tubercles in 8 and 13 spirals, ⁵⁄₁₆ in. long; radial spines 25–35, capillary, white, ¼–¾ in. long, central spines 7–13, bristlelike, dark-tipped, longer; fls. pink, ¾ in. long. W. Tex., s. New Mex., n. Mex.

Delaetina: *C. Salm-Dyckiana.*

deserti: *C. vivipara* var.

difficilis (Quehl) A. Berger. Cc; sts. simple, nearly globose, to 3 in. thick, tubercles in 5 and 8 spirals, rhombic, to 1 in. wide; spines bulbous at base, radial spines 12–14, stellate, slender-awl-shaped, the upper to 3/4 in. long, central spines 4, in form of a cross, awl-shaped, curved, dark-tipped, about 3/4 in. long; fls. yellow. Mex.

durangensis (Runge) Britt. & Rose. Cc; sts. simple or cespitose, to 6 in. high and 2½ in. thick, tubercles in 5 and 8 spirals, rhombic, dorsally oblique, about 3/8 in. long; radial spines 6–8, needle-shaped, gray, to 3/8 in. long, central spine 1, black, often erect; fls. pale yellow, 3/4 in. long, the outer segms. purplish. N. Mex.

echinoidea (Quehl) Britt. & Rose. Cg; sts. simple, globose, to 2½ in. thick, tubercles at first conical, 5/8 in. long, ½ in. wide, later lower and wider; radial spines 20–25, needle-shaped, stellate, white, dark-tipped, to 5/8 in. long, interlocking, central spines 1–3, stouter, brown, the lower directed outward, glandspines 1–3, in groove, red; fls. rose, to 3 in. across. N. Mex. Perhaps a var. of *C. exsudans.*

Echinus: *C. cornifera* var.

elephantidens Lem. Cc; sts. cespitose, to 6 in. high and 8 in. thick, tubercles in 6 and 8 spirals, rounded, to 2 in. wide; spines 6–10, awl-shaped, recurved, brownish, to 1 in. long; fls. rose, to 4 in. long and across. Cent. Mex.

erecta Lem. Cg; sts. cespitose, to 1 ft. high and 3 in. thick, tubercles in 5 and 8 spirals, conical, to 5/16 in. long; spines needle-shaped, yellow, becoming brown, radial spines 8–14, stellate or somewhat spreading, to ½ in. long, central spines 2–4, the lowest directed outward or deflexed, the others erect, glandspine axillary; fls. yellow, to 2½ in. long. Cent. Mex.

exsudans (Zucc.) Britt. & Rose. Cg; sts. simple, oblong, to 1½ in. thick, tubercles ovoid, 5/16 in. long, ½ in. wide; spines yellow, slender, radial spines 6–7, to 3/8 in., central spine 1, erect, brown-tipped, glandspines axillary, pale yellow; fls. yellow. Cent. Mex.

Georgii Böd. Cg; perhaps only a var. of *C. unicornis,* but tubercles in 13 spirals, spines more slender; fls. white, 1 in. long. N. Mex.

gladiispina (Böd.) A. Berger. Cc; sts. simple, to 4 in. high and 2½ in. thick, tubercles in 8 and 13 spirals, conical, ½ in. long; radial spines 17–20, needle-shaped, grayish, the lower 10–12 to 5/8 in. long, the upper 7–8 somewhat angled, to 3/4 in., central spines 4, the lowest directed outward or deflexed, to 1 in. long, the others ascending; fls. yellow, nearly 2 in. across. N. Mex.

Lloydii (Britt. & Rose) Fosb. [*Escobaria Lloydii* Britt. & Rose]. Ee; sts. cespitose, oblong; radial spines about 20, slender, white, central spines several, stout, dark-tipped, to 3/4 in. long; fls. greenish, 1 in. long, segms. not ciliate. Cent. Mex.

macromeris (Engelm.) Lem. Cl; sts. cespitose, to 5 in. high and 3 in. thick, tubercles in 8 and 13 spirals, loose, soft, to 1¼ in. long; radial spines 10–17, needle-shaped, white, to 1½ in. long, central spines about 4, stouter, dark, to 2½ in. long; fls. purple, to 3 in. across. Summer. Var. **macromeris.** The typical var.; sts. green, to 6 in. high and 2 in. thick, tubercles mostly protruding 1 in. W. Tex., s. New Mex., n. Mex. Var. **Runyoni** (Britt. & Rose) L. Bens. [*C. Runyoni* Britt. & Rose; *Mammillaria Runyoni* (Britt. & Rose) V. L. Cory, not (Britt. & Rose) Böd.]. Sts. gray-green, to 3 in. high, 1½ in. thick, tubercles mostly protruding ½ in. Tex.

minima Baird [*C. Nelieae* Croiz.]. Cc; sts. simple or few-branched, to 2 in. high, tubercles in 8–14 rows, less than 1/8 in. long; radial spines 13–18, needle-shaped, white, 2–4 stouter, to nearly 3/16 in. long; fls. purple, to 5/8 in. long. W. Tex.

missouriensis (Sweet) Britt. & Rose [*Mammillaria missouriensis* Sweet, *Neobesseya missouriensis* (Sweet) Britt. & Rose]. N; sts. simple or cespitose, to 2½ in. high and 3 in. thick, tubercles in 8 and 13 spirals, conoid, to ½ in. long; radial spines 10–20, stellate, needle-shaped, gray, pubescent, to 3/8 in. long, central spine 0–1, directed outwards, slightly longer; fls. yellow-green, fragrant; fr. to ½ in. long, maturing next spring. N. Dak. and Mont. to n. Tex. Var. **missouriensis.** The typical var.; radial spines 8–20; fls. 1–2 3/16 in. across, sepaloid segms. ciliate. Var. **caespitosa** (Engelm.) L. Bens. [*C. similis* (Engelm.) Britt. & Rose; *Neobesseya similis* (Engelm.) Britt. & Rose]. Radial spines usually 12–15; fls. 2–2½ in. across, sepaloid segms. ciliate. Kans., Tex., nw. La. Var. **Marstonii** (Clover) L. Bens. Radial spines 10–19; fls. 1½–2 in. across, sepaloid segms. fringed. Utah, Ariz. Var. **robustior** (Engelm.) L. Bens. [*C. Wissmannii* (Hildm.) A. Berger; *Neobesseya Wissmannii* (Hildm.) Britt. & Rose]. Radial spines 12–15; fls. 1 5/8–2 in. across, sepaloid segms. not fringed. Tex.

Muehlenpfordtii: *C. Scheeri* var. *Scheeri.*

Nelieae: *C. minima.*

neomexicana: *C. vivipara* var. *radiosa.*

Nickelsiae: *C. sulcata* var.

octacantha (DC.) Britt. & Rose. Cg; sts. simple, to 20 in. high and 6 in. thick, tubercles in 5 and 8 spirals, 4-angled, to 1 in. long; radial spines 8, spreading, needle-shaped, horn-colored, to ½ in. long, central spines 1–2, stouter, to 1 in. long, glandspines 1–2, red, in groove; fls. pale yellow, 2½ in. wide. Cent. Mex.

Ottonis (Pfeiff.) Lem. Cg; sts. simple, to 5 in. high and 3 in. thick, tubercles in 5 and 8 spirals, conoid; radial spines 8–12, needle-shaped, yellowish, becoming gray, to 3/8 in. long, central spines 3–4, to 3/4 in. long; fls. white, 1½ in. long. Cent. Mex.

pallida Britt. & Rose. Cc; sts. solitary or cespitose, globose, to 5 in. thick, tubercles in 5 and 8 spirals, thick; radial spines 20 or more, stellate, needle-shaped, white, curved, 5/16 in. long, central spines mostly 3, awl-shaped, curved, 2 ascending, the lower directed outward or decurved, black-tipped or black, to ½ in. long; fls. yellow, to 3 in. long. S. Mex.

Palmeri Britt. & Rose. Cc; sts. simple, globose, tubercles in 13 irregular rows; radial spines 11–14, stellate, stout, yellowish, central spine 1, stout, hooked; fls. pale yellow, 1¼ in. long. N. Mex.

pectinata: a name applied originally to juvenile plants of *C. cornifera* var. *Echinus.*

Poselgerana (A. Dietr.) Britt. & Rose. Cg; sts. simple, to 9 in. high and 6 in. thick, tubercles in 5 and 8 spirals, rhombic, about 3/4 in. long and 1½ in. wide; upper spines 5–14, fascicled, erect, needle-shaped, yellowish, lower radial spines 4–6, awl-shaped, red to black, becoming gray, to 1½ in. long, central spine 1, directed outward, awl-shaped, to 1½ in. long, glandspines 1–4, red, in groove; fls. pink, to 2½ in. long. N. Mex.

pseudechinus Böd. Cg; sts. cespitose, to 3½ in. high and 2 in. thick, tubercles in 8 or 13 spirals, conoid, 3/8 in. long, radial spines 18–25, stellate, needle-shaped, white to dark, ½ in. long, interlacing, 1 of the central spines directed outward or ascending, awl-shaped, and 2–3 of them erect, needle-shaped, glandspines 2–3, yellow, in a groove; fls. violet, 3/4 in. long. N. Mex.

radians: a name applied originally to juvenile plants of *C. cornifera.*

radiosa: *C. vivipara* var.

ramillosa Cutak. Cc; sts. simple, globose to obovoid, to 3 in. high and 2½ in. thick, tubercles prominent, 5/16 in. long; radial spines 9–20, white, central spines 4, with 1–3 accessory ones above, upper 3 nearly white, lower dark brown, directed outward, to 1 5/8 in. long. S. Tex.

recurvata (Engelm.) Britt. & Rose. Cg; sts. cespitose, to 10 in. long and 6 in. thick, tubercles in 8 and 13 spirals, cylindrical, 3/8 in. long, ¼ in. in diam.; radial spines 12–30, needle-shaped, gray, recurved, appressed, interlacing, to 3/4 in. long, central spines 1–2, similar, decurved; fls. lateral, greenish-yellow, to 1½ in. long. Summer. Ariz., n. Mex.

retusa (Pfeiff.) Britt. & Rose. Cc; sts. simple, globose, to 4 in. wide, tubercles ovoid, large; spines 6–12, radial, yellowish, awl-shaped, and recurved-appressed except 2–3 needle-shaped upper ones; fls. yellow, 1¼ in. long. S. Mex.

Robertii A. Berger [*Escobaria Runyonii* Britt. & Rose]. Ee; sts. cespitose, globose to ovoid, tubercles 3/16 in. long; radial spines many, white, needle-shaped, to 3/16 in. long, central spines 5–7, stouter, brown, to 5/16 in. long; fls. pale purple, 5/8 in. long. S. Tex. and n. Mex.

robustispina: *C. Scheeri* var.

Roseana (Böd.) Moran [*Thelocactus Roseanus* (Böd.) Bravo]. Ee; sts. simple or few-branched, ovoid, to 2 in. high, tubercles in 8 and 13 spirals, conical, 1/8 in. long and thick; spines needle-shaped, yellow, becoming brown, radial spines about 15, the upper longer, to 5/8 in. long, central spines 4–6, similar; fls. pink. N. Mex.

Runyonii: *C. macromeris* var.

Salm-Dyckiana (Scheer) Britt. & Rose [*C. Delaetiana* (Quehl) A. Berger]. Cc; sts. solitary or cespitose, globose or club-shaped, to 6 in. thick, tubercles rhombic, 3/8 in. long, groove glabrous; radial spines 7–15, stellate, needle-shaped, grayish or whitish, to 3/8 in. long, the upper clustered, central spines 1–2, reddish to black, awl-shaped, directed outward or decurved, to 1 in. long; fls. pale yellow, to 1½ in. long. N. Mex.

Scheeri (O. Kuntze) L. Bens. Cg; sts. simple or cespitose, ellipsoid, to 7 in. high and 4 in. thick, tubercles elongate, 1–1½ in. long; radial spines 6–16, central spines 1–5, straw-colored with dark red tips or pink, nearly directed outward, needle-shaped, to 1½ in. long; fls. yellow, yellow with red streaks, salmon, or rarely white, to 3 in. across. Var. **Scheeri** [*C. Muehlenpfordtii* (Poselg.) Britt. & Rose]. The typical var.; sts. simple; areoles not woolly when young, radial spines 8–11, to 3/4 in. long, central spines not hooked at apex; fls. yellow, with red streaks. Tex., New Mex., n. Mex. Var. **robustispina** (Schott) L. Bens. [*C. robustispina* (Schott) Britt. & Rose]. Sts. cespitose; areoles woolly when young, radial spines usually 10–15, to 7/8 in. long, central spines usually curved or hooked at apex; fls. yellow, salmon, or sometimes white. Ariz. and n. Mex. Var. **uncinata** L. Bens. Areoles densely woolly when young, radial spines about 16, to 1 in. long, central spines hooked at apex. Tex. Var. **valida** (Engelm.) L. Bens. Sts. simple; areoles densely woolly when young, radial spines 9–16, to 1 3/16 in. long, central spines 1–5, to 1½ in. long, not hooked at apex. Tex. and Ariz., s. to n. Mex.

Schwartziana Böd. Cg; sts. simple, ovoid, tubercles short-conical, ⁵⁄₁₆ in. thick; radial spines to 20, grayish, somewhat curved, ⁵⁄₁₆ in. long, central spine 1, straight, slender, horn-colored, dark-tipped, not much longer. Cent. Mex.

scolymoides: *C. cornifera* var.

similis: *C. missouriensis* var. *caespitosa.*

Sneedii (Britt. & Rose) A. Berger [*Escobaria Sneedii* Britt. & Rose]. Ee; sts. cespitose; to 2½ in. high and 1 in. thick, tubercles to ⅛ in. long; spines 20 or more, stellate-appressed, white, the longer brown-tipped, to ¼ in. long; fls. pink, ⅜ in. long. W. Tex.

strobiliformis (Poselg.) Orcutt [*Escobaria tuberculosa* (Engelm.) Britt. & Rose]. Ee; sts. simple or few-branched, to 8 in. high and 2½ in. thick, tubercles in 8 and 13 or 23 and 21 rows, conoid, to ⁵⁄₁₆ in. long; radial spines 20–30, needle-shaped, white, to ⁵⁄₁₆ in. or the upper to ½ in. long, central spines 5–9; fls. pink or purplish, to 1 in. long; seeds brown, hilum lateral. Var. **strobiliformis.** The typical var.; sts. to 5 in. high and 2 in. thick; central spines 6–8, the most central longest, to ⅝ in. long. W. Tex. and se. Ariz., s. to n. Mex. Var. **durispina** (Quehl) L. Bens. Sts. to 8 in. high and 2 in. thick; the most central 1–2 spines surrounded by 4–6 other central spines, some of these smaller, radial spines reddish-tipped. Tex. Var. **Orcuttii** (Böd.) L. Bens. The most central 2–4 spines shorter than the remaining 4–6. New Mex. and Ariz.

sulcata (Engelm.) Britt. & Rose. Cc; sts. cespitose, to 5 in. thick, tubercles in 13 rows, conoid, to ¾ in. long; radial spines 8–15, needle-shaped, white, to ⅝ in. long, the upper fascicled, central spine 0–1, stouter, directed outward or decurved; fls. yellow- or red-centered, to 2½ in. long; seeds dark brown. Var. **sulcata.** The typical var.; sts. nearly globose, to 6 in. long and thick; spines yellow and pink or pink, becoming overlaid with gray or white; fls. to 2½ in. across. S. Tex. Var. **Nickelsiae** (K. Brandeg.) L. Bens. [*C. Nickelsiae* (K. Brandeg.) Britt. & Rose]. Sts. obovoid, to 2 in. high and thick; spines pink, overlaid with gray or white; fls. 1⅝ in. across. S. Tex. and n. Mex.

sulcolanata (Lem.) Lem. Cc; sts. cespitose, to 2 in. high and 5 in. wide, tubercles in 8 and 13 spirals, conoid, 5-angled at base; spines 9–10, radial spines needle-shaped, yellowish, becoming brown, dark-tipped, unequal, to ⅝ in. long; fls. yellow, to 2 in. long. Cent. Mex.

uncinata: a listed name of no botanical standing, probably for *C. Scheeri* var.

unicornis Böd. Cg; sts. cespitose, globose, to 3 in. thick, tubercles in 5 and 8 spirals, conoid, ⅝ in. long; radial spines 7–9, stellate, slenderly awl-shaped, yellowish, to ⅝ in. long, central spine 1, directed outward, stouter, to ¾ in. long, glandspines red, 1 axillary and sometimes 1 at spine cluster. N. Mex.

valida: a listed name of no botanical standing for *G. Scheeri* var.

Vaupeliana Böd. Cg; sts. simple, globose, to 3 in. thick, tubercles in 8 and 13 spirals, triangular-conoid, ¾ in. long, ½ in. wide; radial spines about 15, the lower slenderly awl-shaped, recurved, yellowish, to ½ in. long, the upper needle-shaped, clustered, whitish, central spines 4, in the form of a cross, awl-shaped, recurved, to ¾ in. long; fls. yellow. N. Mex.

vivipara (Nutt.) Britt. & Rose. Ep; sts. solitary or cespitose, depressed-globose to cylindrical, to 6 in. high and 3½ in. thick, tubercles to ½ in. long; radial spines 12–40, needle-shaped, to ⅝ in. long, central spines 1–8, with one directed outward or deflexed and the others ascending, usually white basally but tipped brown, reddish, or black, to ¾ in. long; fls. pink to purple or sometimes yellow-green, to 2 in. across. Var. **vivipara** [*Mammillaria vivipara* Nutt.]. The typical var.; sts. depressed-globose to ovoid, to 1 in. high and 2 in. thick; radial spines 12–20, white, to ½ in. long, central spines 4, the lower red and dark-colored, or white at base. Ore. to Minn., s. to New Mex., Tex. Var. **aggregata:** *Echinocereus triglochidiatus* var. *melanacanthus,* but most material cult. as var. *aggregata* is var. *bisbeeana.* Var. **Alversonii** (J. Coult.) L. Bens. [*C. Alversonii* (J. Coult.) Orcutt]. Sts. cylindrical, to 6 in. high and 3 in. thick, branching by rhizomes; radial spines 12–18, white, to ¾ in. long, central spines 8–10, white, with red or black tips, to ⅝ in. long; fls. magenta to pink, to 1¼ in. across. Calif. and Ariz. Var. **arizonica** (Engelm.) W. T. Marsh. [*C. arizonica* (Engelm.) Britt. & Rose; *Mammillaria vivipara* var. *arizonica* (Engelm.) L. Bens.]. Sts. ovoid, simple or branched, to 4 in. high and 2½ in. thick, sometimes forming mounds; radial spines 20–30, white, to ⅝ in. long, central spines 5–7, red with white base, to ¾ in. long; fls. deep pink, to 2 in. across. New Mex., Ariz., Nev., Utah. Var. **bisbeeana** (Orcutt) L. Bens. GOLF-BALL CACTUS. Sts. ovoid, simple or branched, to 3 in. high and 2¾ in. thick, sometimes forming mounds; radial spines 20–30, white to brown, to ½ in. long, central spines 5–6, brown or gray, tipped pink or brown, to ⅝ in. long; fls. pink, to 2 in. across. Ariz. and

n. Mex. Var. **deserti** (Engelm.) W. T. Marsh. [*C. chlorantha* (Engelm.) Britt. & Rose; *C. deserti* (Engelm.) Britt. & Rose; *Mammillaria vivipara* var. *chlorantha* (Engelm.) L. Bens.; *M. vivipara* var. *deserti* (Engelm.) L. Bens.]. Sts. cylindrical, simple, to 6 in. high and 3½ in. thick; radial spines 12–20, white, to ½ in. long, central spines 4–6, white with red tips, to ¾ in. long; fls. yellow-green to pink, to 1¾ in. across. Calif., Ariz., Nev., Utah. Var. **radiosa** (Engelm.) Backeb. [*C. neomexicana* (Engelm.) Britt. & Rose; *C. radiosa* (Englm.) Rydb.]. Sts. ovoid to cylindrical, to 3 in. high and about 2 in. thick; radial spines 20–40, white to pink, to ¾ in. long, central spines 3–4, lower one pink to red. New Mex. to Okla.

Werdermanii Böd. Cc; sts. solitary or cespitose, the juvenile stage to 2 in. high and 2½ in. thick, tubercles in 34 rows, pyramidal, 4-angled, to ³⁄₁₆ in. long; radial spines 15–20, stellate, needle-shaped, to ¼ in. long, central spine 0; adult stage beginning suddenly, to 3 in. high, tubercles in 13 rows, to ⅝ in. long, white-dotted; radial spines 25–30, to ¾ in. long, central spines 4, awl-shaped, to 1 in. long, 3 ascending, 1 directed outward. N. Mex.

Wissmannii: *C. missouriensis* var. *robustior.*

CORYTHOLOMA: *SINNINGIA.*

COSMIDIUM: *THELESPERMA.*

COSMOS Cav. *Compositae* (Helianthus Tribe). About 25 spp. of showy, late-flowering ann. or per. herbs, native from sw. U.S. to trop. Amer.; lvs. opp., usually pinnately cut; fl. heads radiate, solitary or in panicles; ray fls. white, rose, purple, or rarely yellow; achenes usually narrowed upward into a beak, pappus of barbed awns. Closely allied to *Dahlia.*

Cultivated in the flower garden, flowering late. Easily grown from seeds, but in the North may be sown indoors in early spring if flowers are desired in late summer; early forms should be chosen. Sandy soil is preferable, as the plants do not bloom well in rich soil in short-season climates.

atrosanguineus (Hook.) Ortg. [*Bidens atrosanguinea* (Hook.) Ortg.]. BLACK C. Differs from *C. diversifolius* in its smaller heads, about 1½ in. across, with dark red disc and ray fls. Mex.

bipinnatus Cav. Ann., to 10 ft.; lvs. 2-pinnate into linear segms.; heads to 4 in. across or more; disc fls. yellow, ray fls. white, pink, or crimson; achenes beaked, pappus usually lacking in cult. forms. Mex. In the anemone- and double-fld. forms, the disc is replaced by a compact mass of petal-like parts the same color as the ray fls. Early-flowering cvs. of the various forms are available.

diversifolius Otto. Per., to 2½ ft., with tuberous roots; lvs. entire or pinnately parted into 5–7 ovate or lanceolate segms.; heads to 3 in. across, long-peduncled; disc fls. yellow, ray fls. lilac to rose; achenes beaked or not. Mex. Usually grown as an ann.

sulphureus Cav. YELLOW C., ORANGE C. Ann., to 7 ft.; lvs. 2–3-pinnate, lfts. lanceolate; heads to 3 in. across, disc fls. yellow, ray fls. pale or golden-yellow or orange; achenes long-beaked. Mex. There are orange-red-fld., double-fld., and early-flowering cvs.

COSTUS L. SPIRAL FLAG. *Zingiberaceae.* About 140 spp. of stout, per., rhizomatous herbs, in tropics of both hemispheres; sts. often spirally twisted; lvs. spirally arranged, with tubular, closed sheaths; infl. terminal on the leafy st. or on a separate st., conelike, with imbricate bracts; fls. yellow, red, or white, calyx tubular, 3-lobed, corolla tube shorter or longer than calyx tube, staminodial lip large, petal-like, fertile stamen 1, with broad, petal-like filament, ovary 3-celled; fr. a caps., seeds arillate.

Plants require tropical temperatures, humidity, and rich moist soil. Propagated by cutting the stalks into 1 in. lengths and planting in sand and sifted moss or peat; also by division of the rhizomes. The plants are not often seen under glass as they require too much room. Grown outdoors in southern Fla. and on Gulf Coast.

afer Ker-Gawl. SPIRAL GINGER. To 9 ft. or more; lvs. broadly lanceolate, to 6 in. long, 1½ in. wide, glabrous; spike terminating the leafy st., surrounded by involucrelike lvs., bracts ovate to elliptic with obtuse somewhat turned-in apex; fls. white, lip deep yellow at base and middle. Afr.

cylindricus: *C. spicatus.*

elegans: *C. Malortieanus.*

igneus N. E. Br. To 3 ft.; lvs. oblong-lanceolate, to 6 in. long; spikes few-fld., terminating the leafy st.; fls. orange-red. Brazil.

Malortieanus H. Wendl. [*C. elegans* Hort.; *C. zebrinus* Hort.]. SPIRAL FLAG, SPIRAL GINGER, STEPLADDER PLANT. To 3 ft.; lvs. to 14 in. long and 7 in. wide, obscurely striped with darker green above; fl.

spikes to 2½ in. long, terminating the leafy st., bracts lacking a thickened callus at the tip; fls. yellow, lip marked with red. Cent. Amer.

melacaulis: a listed name of no botanical standing.

pulverulentus K. Presl [*C. sanguineus* J. D. Sm.]. To about 10 ft.; lvs. narrowly elliptic to narrowly obovate, to 1 ft. long, 5 in. wide, upper side glabrous or rarely villous; spike spindle-shaped, terminating the leafy st., to nearly 3 in. long and 2 in. wide, bracts red to orange-red where exposed, red where covered, with a callus below the tip; fls. red, lip red to yellow, to 1½ in. long. Mex. to cent. and w. S. Amer.

sanguineus: *C. pulverulentus*

speciosus (J. König) Sm. CREPE GINGER, WILD G. To 10 ft.; lvs. to 8 in. long and 2½ in. wide, glabrous or hairy; fl. spikes to 5 in. long, bracts green, flushed with red, tipped with a sharp, thickened point; fls. white, with yellow center. E. Indies.

spicatus (Jacq.) Swartz [*C. cylindricus* Jacq.]. To 8 ft.; lvs. narrowly elliptic, to about 1 ft. long and 4 in. wide, glabrescent on both sides; spike ovoid to cylindrical, terminating the leafy st., 2–11 in. long, to 4 in. wide, bracts greenish or reddish where exposed, red where covered, with a yellow callus below the tip; fls. yellow to pink, lip yellow, to 2 in. long and wide. Hispaniola.

zebrinus: *C. Malortieanus.*

COTINUS Mill. *Anacardiaceae.* SMOKE TREE, SMOKEBUSH. Three spp. of woody, deciduous, polygamous, shrubs or small trees, 1 native to N. Amer., 1 to Eurasia, and 1 to sw. China; lvs. simple; fls. small, in large, loose, terminal panicles, pedicels of sterile fls. lengthening after flowering and clothed with spreading hairs, stamens 5; fr. a small, compressed drupe.

Cotinus requires well-drained and not too rich soil. Propagated by seeds, root cuttings, and layers.

americanus: *C. obovatus.*

cotinoides: *C. obovatus.*

Coggygria Scop. [*Rhus Cotinus* L.]. SMOKE TREE, SMOKEBUSH, SMOKE PLANT, VENETIAN SUMAC, WIG TREE. Bushy shrub, to 15 ft.; lvs. elliptic, to 3 in. long; panicles much-branched, to 8 in. long, usually purplish, the hairy, pedicels producing a "smoky" effect. Early summer. S. Eur. to Asia. Zone 5. The lvs. and bark yield a tannin, and the wood a yellow dye called young fustic. Cy. 'Pendulus' [var. *pendulus* (Burv.) Dipp.]. Brs. drooping. Cv. 'Purpureus' [var. *purpureus* (Dup.-Jam.) Rehd.; var. *rubrifolius* Boom]. Lvs. purplish; panicles with dark purple hairs.

obovatus Raf. [*C. americanus* Nutt.; *C. cotinoides* (Nutt. ex Chapm.) Britt.; *Rhus cotinoides* Nutt. ex Chapm.; *R. Cotinus* Torr. & A. Gray, not L.]. AMERICAN S.T., CHITTAMWOOD. Small tree, to 30 ft. or more; lvs. mostly obovate, to 6 in. long, cuneate or tapering at base; panicles not showy, but lvs. brightly colored in autumn. Spring. Tenn., s. to Ala., and Mo., w. to Tex.

pendulus: a listed name of no botanical standing for *C. Coggygria* cv.

purpureus: a listed name of no botanical standing for *C. Coggygria* cv.

rubrifolius: a listed name of no botanical standing for *C. Coggygria* cv. 'Purpureus.'

COTONEASTER Medic. *Rosaceae.* About 50 spp. of woody plants of Old World temp. regions; lvs. alt., entire, deciduous or evergreen; fls. white or pink, solitary or in cymose clusters terminating lateral spurs; fr. a small red to black pome with 2–5 nutlets, mostly long-persistent and attractive in autumn and winter.

The genus includes many ornamentals; widely grown, and important in landscape work for their attractive habit, interesting bloom, and showy, often persistent fruits. Many of them are hardy in the North, but more kinds are grown in the South or on the West Coast. Cotoneasters prefer sunny locations in well-drained soil. Propagated by seeds sown when ripe or stratified, by layers in autumn, by cuttings of young wood under glass, and rare kinds by grafting on stock of *C. integerrimus*, or the common quince or hawthorn.

acuminatus Lindl. Deciduous, to 1 ft. or more, young twigs woolly; lvs. lanceolate-ovate, 1–2½ in. long, pubescent, acuminate; fls. pink, 2–5 in a cluster, ⅜ in. across; fr. red, ovoid, ⁵⁄₁₆ in. long, pubescent at apex. Himalayas. Zone 6.

acutifolius Turcz. Deciduous, to 10 ft., with pubescent twigs; lvs. ovate to elliptic, 1–2 in. long, pubescent on both sides when young; fls. 2–5, pink; fr. ellipsoid, black, ⅜ in. long. N. China. Zone 3. Var. **villosulus** Rehd. & E. H. Wils. Lvs. densely pubescent beneath, larger; fr. somewhat pubescent. China. Zone 6.

adpressus Bois. Deciduous, prostrate, to 10 in. high, spreading widely; lvs. broadly ovate, ³⁄₁₆–⅝ in. long, wavy at margins; fls. 1–2, pinkish, nearly sessile; fr. subglobose, red, ¼ in. in diam. W. China. Zone 5. Var. **praecox** Bois. & Berthault [*C. praecox* (Bois. & Berthault) Hort. Vilm.-Andr. ex Meuniss.]. To 2 ft. high; lvs. rounded, to 1 in. long. China. Cv. 'Conglomeratus' is listed.

affinis Lindl. Deciduous, to 16 ft., brs. erect to spreading, at first pubescent, later glabrous; lvs. obovate, to 3½ in. long; fls. 15–30, white; fr. subglobose, dark red-brown to almost black, ¼–⁵⁄₁₆ in. thick. Himalayas. Zone 7. Var. **bacillaris** (Wallich ex Lindl.) C. K. Schneid. [*C. bacillaris* Wallich ex Lindl.]. Lvs. broader, 1–2½ in. long; fr. to ¼ in. in diam.

×**aldenhamensis** (V. Gibbs) Marchant ex Grootend.: probably *C. frigidus* × *C. salicifolius*. Robust, to 10 ft., twigs pendulous; lvs. lanceolate, 1½–3 in. long; fls. in small clusters; fr. purple-red.

alpinus: a listed name of no botanical standing.

ambiguus Rehd. & E. H. Wils. Like *C. acutifolius*, to 6 ft.; lvs. densely hairy beneath; fls. 5–10, white, tinged red; fr. black, globose, to ½ in. in diam. China. Zone 6.

amoenus E. H. Wils. Like *C. Franchetii*, but more erect, bushier, with shorter internodes; lvs. ovate, ⅜–¾ in. long; fls. 4–14, white to pinkish; fr. bright red, ¼ in. in diam. Cent. China. Zone 7?

apiculatus Rehd. & E. H. Wils. CRANBERRY C. Like *C. horizontalis*, but more irregularly branched; lvs. nearly ovate, thin, ⅜–⅝ in. wide, pointed; fls. mostly solitary, pink; fr. scarlet, round, ⅜ in. in diam. China. Zone 5.

applanatus: *C. Dielsianus.*

bacillaris: *C. affinis* var.

bullatus Bois. Deciduous, to 10 ft., pubescent on young growth; lvs. oblong to lanceolate-ovate, 1–3 in. long, dark green above, gray-hairy beneath; fls. 3–7, pink; fr. bright red, globose, ⁵⁄₁₆ in. in diam. W. China. Zone 6. Forma **floribundus** (Stapf) Rehd. & E. H. Wils. Fls. many in cymes to 2³⁄₁₆ in. across. Var. **macrophyllus** Rehd. & E. H. Wils. Lvs. 2–6 in. long, to 3 in. wide; fls. many. W. China.

buxifolius Wallich ex Lindl. Evergreen, much-branched, erect, to 6 ft.; lvs. elliptic to obovate, ³⁄₁₆–⅝ in. long, pubescent above when young, woolly underneath, somewhat revolute; fls. 2–6, white; fr. red, obovoid, ¼ in. long, somewhat hairy. India. Zone 7? Material cult. under this name is often *C. rotundifolius*. Forma **vellaeus** Franch. Lvs. smaller; fls. often solitary. Cv. 'Bellus' is listed.

congestus Bak. [*C. microphyllus* var. *glacialis* Hook.]. Like *C. microphyllus*, but more dwarf and congested; lvs. more ovate, glabrous underneath at maturity; fls. pinkish, ¼ in. across. Himalayas. Zone 7.

conspicuus Marq. Evergreen, 3–6 ft., erect to spreading and arched; lvs. elongate-elliptic, to ⅜ in. long or more, strigose underneath; fls. solitary, white, ½ in. across, anthers red-purple; fr. round to obovoid, ⅜ in. in diam. Tibet. Zone 7. Most cult. material is var. *decorus*. Var. **decorus** P. G. Russell. Prostrate, matted. Se. Tibet.

Cooperi Marq. Deciduous, vigorous, 10–20 ft., soon quite glabrous; lvs. lanceolate, acuminate, 1½–4 in. long, glaucous beneath; fls. white, many, ½ in. across; fr. obovoid, ⁵⁄₁₆ in. long, black-red. Bhutan. Zone 7?

Cornubius: a listed name of no botanical standing for *Cotoneaster* cv. 'Cornubius'. Probably of hybrid origin from *C. frigidus*; shrub or small tree, brs. long, slender; lvs. elliptic or lanceolate, to 4½ in. long, pale and sparsely hairy beneath; frs. vermilion, 50 or more in a cluster.

Dammeri C. K. Schneid. [*C. humifusus* Duthie ex Veitch]. Prostrate, rooting, evergreen; lvs. leathery, obovate to round-ovate, about 1 in. long, dark and shining above, pale underneath; fls. solitary, sometimes 2, short-pedicelled, white, anthers reddish; fr. bright red, globose, ¼ in. in diam. China. Zone 6? Var. **radicans** C. K. Schneid. Lvs. ovate or elliptic to obovate; fls. 1–2, on pedicels to ⅝ in. long.

decorus: a listed name of no botanical standing for *C. conspicuus* var.

Dielsianus E. Pritz ex Diels [*C. applanatus* Duthie]. Deciduous or semievergreen, to 7 ft., hairy on young growth; lvs. elliptic to ovate, to 1 in.; tomentose beneath; fls. 3–7, pink or white, tinged red; fr. bright red, ¼ in. in diam. China. Zone 6. Var. **elegans** Rehd. & E. H. Wils. More or less evergreen; lvs. to ⅝ in. long; fr. somewhat hairy. China. Var. **major** Rehd. & E. H. Wils. Lvs. to 1½ in. long, thinner. W. China.

distichus: *C. nitidus.*

divaricatus Rehd. & E. H. Wils. Deciduous, upright, to 6 ft., with spreading brs.; lvs. elliptic, ⅜–¾ in. long, acute at both ends, shining dark green and glabrate above, lighter and usually pubescent beneath; fls. 2–4, pink; fr. bright red, ellipsoid, ⁵⁄₁₆ in. long. China. Zone 5.

floribundus: a listed name of no botanical standing, perhaps for *C. bullatus* forma.

foveolatus Rehd. & E. H. Wils. Deciduous, erect, to 10 ft., with spreading brs., yellowish-pubescent when young; lvs. elliptic to lanceolate, 1½–3 in. long, pubescent beneath; fls. 3–6, in hairy clusters, petals white and pink; fr. black, globose, ⁵⁄₁₆ in. in diam. China. Zone 5.

Franchetii Bois. Evergreen, to 10 ft., with arched brs., tomentose when young; lvs. mostly in 2 ranks, elliptic to broadly lanceolate, ¾–1⅜ in. long, shining above, yellow-felty beneath; fls. 5–15, petals erect, white to pink; fr. orange-red, ovoid, to ⁵⁄₁₆ in. long. China, Burma. Zone 7. Var. **cinerascens** Rehd. To 13 ft.; lvs. grayer beneath; fls. as many as 30. W. China.

frigidus Wallich ex Lindl. Deciduous or semievergreen shrub or small tree to 20 ft., branchlets soon glabrous; lvs. elliptic to oblong-obovate, 2½–5 in. long, dull and glabrous, tomentose beneath when young; fls. 20–40, white, in tomentose clusters; fr. bright red, sub-globose, ¼ in. in diam. Himalayas. Zone 7.

glabratus Rehd. & E. H. Wils. Evergreen, erect, 10–16 ft., with broadly spreading brs., young twigs lightly pubescent, soon glabrous; lvs. leathery, lanceolate to oblanceolate, 2–4 in. long, slightly pubescent beneath; fls. many, white; fr. bright red, globose, ³⁄₁₆ in. in diam. W. China. Zone 7?

glacialis: a listed name of no botanical standing for *C. congestus.*

glaucophyllus Franch. Evergreen, to 6 ft. or more, with arched brs.; lvs. ovate, acute at both ends, 1³⁄₁₆ in. long, glabrous above, glaucous beneath; fls. 6–20, in dense clusters, white; fr. ovoid, orange, ¼ in. in diam. China. Zone 7. Forma **serotinus** (Hutch.) Stapf [*C. serotinus* Hutch.]. Fls. about 40. China.

gracilis Rehd. & E. H. Wils. To 10 ft., deciduous, with spreading brs.; lvs. 1 in. long, white-tomentose beneath, ovate; fls. 3–6, rose, in tomentose clusters; fr. red, obovoid, ¼ in. in diam. China.

Harrovianus E. H. Wils. Evergreen, of loose spreading habit, to 10 or 12 ft. high; lvs. elliptic to obovate, 1–2½ in. long, leathery, densely tomentose beneath when young; fls. many, white, in dense clusters; fr. dark red, round, ⁵⁄₁₆ in. long. W. China.

hebephyllus Diels. Deciduous, to 8 ft., sometimes arborescent; lvs. elliptic to orbicular, ¾–1⅜ in. long, glabrous above, glaucous beneath; fls. 7–20, white, almost ½ in. across, anthers violet; fr. dark red, ovoid, ⁵⁄₁₆ in. in diam. W. China. Zone 7?

Henryanus (C. K. Schneid.) Rehd. & E. H. Wils. Evergreen in mild climates, to 10 or 12 ft., with pendulous brs. and downy twigs; lvs. leathery, narrow-obovate to lanceolate, 1½–4½ in. long, acute at both ends; fls. many, white, in clusters 1–2 in. across; fr. dark red, ovoid, ¼ in. in diam. China. Zone 7? Much material cult. under this name is *C. salicifolius.*

heterophyllus: a listed name of no botanical standing.

himalaicus: probably in error for *C. hymalaicus.*

horizontalis Decne. ROCK C. Semievergreen, low, to 3 ft., brs. spreading horizontally near the ground; lvs. roundish to broadly elliptic, ¼–½ in. long, dark glossy green above; fls. 1 or 2, pinkish to white; fr. bright red, ³⁄₁₆ in. long. W. China. Zone 6. Var. **perpusillus** C. K. Schneid. More compact; lvs. ¼–⁵⁄₁₆ in. long; fr. ellipsoid. Cent. China. Cvs. include: 'Minor', smaller and with smaller lvs. and frs.; 'Praecox', 'Prostratus', 'Robustus', listed names; 'Variegatus', lvs. edged with white; 'Wilsonii' [*C. Wilsonii* Hort., not Nakai], to 5 ft. tall; lvs. larger, pale and pubescent beneath.

humifusus: *C. Dammeri.*

hupehensis Rehd. & E. H. Wils. Deciduous shrub, to 6 ft., with arched brs., young twigs hairy; lvs. elliptic, 1–1½ in. long, green and glabrous above, thinly tomentose beneath; fls. 6–12, white, ⁵⁄₁₆ in. across; fr. bright red, globose, ⁵⁄₁₆–½ in. in diam. China.

hybridus: a listed name of no botanical standing.

hymalaicus Carrière. Large vigorous shrub, deciduous; lvs. oblong-elliptic, cuneate at base, obtuse, entire, to 4 in. long, villous when young, becoming glabrous; fls. rose; fr. globose, purplish-black. Of doubtful origin, possibly hybrid.

ignavus E. Wolf. Deciduous, spreading, to 7 ft. high, twigs pubescent when young; lvs. ovate, 1–2 in. long, pubescent, paler beneath; fls. 8–13, pinkish; fr. dark purple, ellipsoid, to ⁵⁄₁₆ in. long. Turkestan. Zone 6.

integerrimus Medic. [*C. vulgaris* Lindl.]. Deciduous shrub, 4–7 ft., twigs tomentose, later glabrous; lvs. nearly orbicular to elliptic, 1–2 in. long, tomentose beneath; fls. pinkish, in nodding, 2–4-fld. clusters; fr. red, round, ¼ in. in diam. Eur., n. Asia. Zone 6.

lacteus W. W. Sm. Evergreen, to 12 ft., broadly arched, at first tomentose; lvs. lanceolate to broad-elliptic, 1–3 in. long, tomentose

beneath; fls. white, many, in clusters 2–2½ in. across; fr. red, ovoid, ¼ in. long. W. China. Zone 6? Material cult. under the name *C. Parneyi* Hort. is probably a form of this sp., differing in having lvs. broadly ovate, rounded at tip, and fr. almost globose, larger, to nearly ⅜ in. in diam.

laxiflorus: *C. melanocarpus* var.

Lindleyi Steud. Resembling *C. racemiflorus*, but with lvs. longer, 1–2 in., gray-felty beneath; fr. purple-black, globose, ⅜ in. in diam. Himalayas. Zone 7.

lucidus Schlechtend. Deciduous, erect, to 10 ft., young brs. hairy; lvs. mostly in 2 ranks, ovate, shining green and glabrous above, whitish and pubescent beneath, to 2 in. long; fls. 3–12, white with pink tinge; fr. black, ovoid. N. Asia. Zone 5.

melanocarpus Lodd. Deciduous, erect and spreading, 3–6 ft., often arched, at first gray-pubescent, later glabrous; lvs. mostly 2-ranked, broadly ovate to ovate-oblong, 1–2 in. long, gray-downy beneath; fls. 2–12, in nodding clusters, pinkish-white; fr. black-red, ovoid, ⁵⁄₁₆ in. long. E. Eur. to Asia. Zone 5. Var. **laxiflorus** (Jacq. ex Lindl.) C. K. Schneid. [*C. laxiflorus* Jacq. ex Lindl.]. Lvs. larger; fls. 20–40.

Meyeri Pozhark. Deciduous, to 6 ft., spreading; lvs. oblong-elliptic, ½–1½ in. long, glabrous above, paler and at first thinly pilose beneath; fls. 7–12, corymbose, white; fr. obovate, globose, ³⁄₁₆–⁵⁄₁₆ in. long, glabrous, blackish-purple. Caucasus. Not known to be cult.; material offered under this name may be *C. Franchetii* or *C. racemiflorus.*

microphyllus Wallich ex Lindl. Low, evergreen, sometimes to 3 ft. high and 10 ft. across, densely branched; lvs. ovate, to ⁵⁄₁₆ in. long, obtuse, dark green and shining above, gray-pubescent beneath; fls. white, solitary, or 2–3, at ends of short side brs.; fr. bright red, ¼ in. in diam. Himalayas, w. China. Zone 7. Cv. 'Cochleatus'. Dwarf, creeping; lvs. somewhat spatulate. Var. **glacialis:** *C. congestus.* Var. **thymifolius** Koehne [*C. thymifolius* Hort. ex Lindl.]. Very compact; fls. 2–4, pink. Himalayas.

moupinensis Franch. Like *C. bullatus*, but fr. black, subglobose to ovoid, ¼–⁵⁄₁₆ in. in diam. China. Zone 7. Needs protection in the North.

multiflorus Bunge [*C. reflexus* Carrière]. Deciduous, 6 ft. to arborescent and 12 ft., with arched or pendulous brs., glabrescent; lvs. broadly ovate to elliptic, 1–2 in. long, gray-green beneath, glabrate; fls. white, 6–20; fr. red, obovoid, ¼–⁵⁄₁₆ in. long. Caucasus to e. Asia. Zone 6. Var. **calocarpus** Rehd. & E. H. Wils. Lvs. narrower; fls. more numerous; fr. to ½ in. in diam. W. China.

nitens Rehd. & E. H. Wils. Very leafy, deciduous, to 6 ft., dense, the young shoots tawny-hairy, glabrate; lvs. elliptic to ovate, ½–⅞ in. long, dark glossy green, glabrate beneath; fls. 2–6, pink; fr. ovoid-globose, ¼–⁵⁄₁₆ in. long, purplish-black. China. Zone 5.

nitidus Jacques [*C. distichus* J. Lange; *C. rotundifolius* Bak., not Wallich ex Lindl.]. Deciduous or semievergreen, erect, to 8 ft.; lvs. roundish to broadly obovate, ⁵⁄₁₆–½ in. long, scattered-pubescent when young; fl. usually 1, white with pink center; fr. bright red, broad-obovoid, ⅜ in. long. Himalayas, China. Zone 6.

obscurus Rehd. & E. H. Wils. Deciduous, to 10 ft., brs. arching, hairy, glabrate; lvs. elliptic to obovate, 1–1½ in. long, gray beneath; fls. mostly 3–7, in hairy clusters, white or pink; fr. subglobose, dark red, ⁵⁄₁₆ in. long. China. Zone 6. Var. **cornifolius** Rehd. & E. H. Wils. Lvs. 1½–2½ in. long, with impressed veins; fr. black-red, ⅜ in. long. W. China.

pannosus Franch. Evergreen or semievergreen, brs. arching, at first densely woolly; lvs. ovate to elliptic, ½–1¼ in. long, dull green, white-felted beneath; fls. white, ⁵⁄₁₆ in. across, about 6–20 in dense clusters; fr. red, subglobose, ¼ in. in diam. China. Zone 7. Cv. 'Nanus' is listed as a dwarf form.

Parneyi: a listed name of no botanical standing; see *C. lacteus.*

pendulus: a listed name of no botanical standing.

praecox: *C. adpressus* var.

procumbens G. Klotz. Evergreen, brs. prostrate, rooting; lvs. broad-elliptic, rarely orbicular, to ½ in. long, somewhat leathery, gray-green and lightly hairy beneath; fls. and fr. not described. Of garden origin. Some material cult. as *C. prostratus* and *C. repens* belongs here.

prostratus: *C. rotundifolius*, but see also *C. procumbens.*

racemiflorus (Desf.) J. R. Booth ex Bosse. Deciduous shrub, to 8 ft., brs. arching, at first gray-pubescent; lvs. elliptic, ⅝–1³⁄₁₆ in. long, glossy green above, gray or whitish beneath; fls. white, ⁵⁄₁₆ in. across, 3–12 in a cluster; fr. bright red, globose, ⁵⁄₁₆ in. in diam. N. Afr., w. Asia to Turkestan. Zone 5. Var. **nummularius** (Fisch. & C. A. Mey.) Dipp. Lvs. broader, obtuse; fls. 2–7. Asia Minor to w. Himalayas. Var. **Royleanus** Dipp. A low form with roundish lvs. Himalayas. Var. **soongoricus** (Regel & Herder) C. K. Schneid [*C. soongoricus* (Regel & Herder) Popov]. Lvs. more glabrate; fr. more persistent. W. China. Zone 4. Var. **Veitchii** Rehd. & E. H. Wils. Lvs. acute at both ends, elliptic. China.

repens: a listed name of no botanical standing for plants close to *C. buxifolius* or for *C. procumbens*.

roseus Edgew. Deciduous, to 6 or 8 ft., brs. slender, arched, white-hairy when young; lvs. mostly in 2 ranks, thin, elliptic to ovate, 1–2½ in. long, gray-green beneath; fls. pinkish, 3–9; fr. red, round, ⁵⁄₁₆ in. in diam. Nw. Himalayas. Zone 6.

rotundifolius Wallich ex Lindl. [*C. prostratus* Bak.]. Deciduous or semievergreen, stiff, spreading, 5–8 ft. or higher; lvs. ovate to rounded, mucronate, ⁵⁄₁₆–¾ in. long, dark, lustrous green above, glaucous beneath; fls. white, 1–3 in a cluster; fr. scarlet, round-obovoid, ½ in. long. Himalayas. Zone 7. Often cult. under the name of *C. buxifolius.* Cv. 'Lanatus' [cv. 'Wheeleri']. Lvs. tomentose beneath. *C. rotundifolius* Bak. is *C. nitidus.*

rubens W. W. Sm. Deciduous or semievergreen, to 7 ft., young twigs glabrous; lvs. in 2 ranks, round to broadly elliptic, to ¾ in. long, rounded at ends, yellowish, or whitish beneath; fl. solitary, red, calyx villous; fr. obovoid, ⁵⁄₁₆ in. long. China. Zone 7. Material cult. under this name is largely *C. microphyllus.*

rugosus E. Pritz. ex Diels. Evergreen or semievergreen, with widely arched brs., yellow-floccose when young; lvs. largely in 2 ranks, elliptic-lanceolate, 1½–3 in. long, acute at ends, green above, at first yellowish-hairy beneath; fls. white, 5–6; fr. red, ¼ in. long. China.

salicifolius Franch. Evergreen or partly so, to 15 ft., with arched brs.; lvs. narrowly lanceolate, 1½–3 in. long, rugose, tomentose beneath; fls. white, many, in tomentose clusters to 2 in. across; fr. bright red, to ¼ in. in diam. W. China. Zone 6. Some material cult. as *C. Henryanus* belongs here. Var. **floccosus** Rehd. & E. H. Wils. Lvs. shining above, at first tufted-woolly beneath. China. Var. **rugosus** (E. Pritz.) Rehd. & E. H. Wils. Lvs. dull green above, densely tomentose beneath. Cent. China.

serotinus: *C. glaucophyllus* forma.

Simonsii Bak. Semievergreen, to 10 ft., sparingly branched, yellow-hairy when young; lvs. elliptic to obovate, ¼–½ in. long, deep green above, lighter beneath; fls. 2–5, white with reddish tinge; fr. ellipsoid, coral-red, ⁵⁄₁₆ in. long. Himalayas. Zone 6.

soongoricus: *C. racemiflorus* var.

tenuipes Rehd. & E. H. Wils. Differing from *C. racemiflorus* in the acute or short-acuminate lvs., and mostly solitary, black frs. with narrower nutlets. W. China. Zone 6.

thymifolius: *C. microphyllus* var.

tomentosus (Ait.) Lindl. Resembling *C. integerrimus*, but larger in all parts, more hairy; lvs. broadly elliptic to ovate, 1–2½ in. long, gray-tomentose beneath; fls. 3–12. S. Eur. Zone 5.

turbinatus Craib. Semievergreen, to 10 ft., with arching brs.; lvs. leathery, elliptic-lanceolate, 1–2½ in. long, acute or obtuse, permanently white-tomentose beneath; fls. many, in clusters about 2 in. across, white, anthers pink; fr. bright red, ³⁄₁₆ in. in diam., hairy. China.

verruculosus Diels. Habit of *C. horizontalis,* but with verruculose branchlets, more persistent stipules, more orbicular lvs., and fr. 3 times as large. W. China.

vulgaris: *C. integerrimus.*

Wardii W. W. Sm. Differing from *C. Franchetii* in lvs. ovate, 1–2 in. long, silvery-white beneath. Cent. Asia. Zone 7?

×**Watereri** Exell: *C. frigidus* × *C. Henryanus.* Evergreen or partly evergreen, to 18 ft. or more, intermediate between parents.

Wilsonii Nakai. Not cult.; material grown under this name is *C. horizontalis* cv.

Zabelii C. K. Schneid. Deciduous, to 6 ft. or more, brs. slender; lvs. elliptic-ovate, obtuse, ⅝–1³⁄₁₆ in. long, gray-tomentose beneath; fls. pinkish, 3–10, in hairy nodding clusters; fr. bright red, hairy, ⁵⁄₁₆ in. in diam. China. Zone 6. Var. **miniatus** Rehd. & E. H. Wils. Fr. orange-red, smaller. China.

COTULA L. *Compositae* (Anthemis Tribe). About 60 spp. of aromatic, ann., bien., or per. herbs, mostly native to the S. Hemisphere, some naturalized as weeds in N. Hemisphere; lvs. alt. or in clusters at nodes of st., simple and entire to dissected, often sheathing; fl. heads solitary on scapose brs., discoid, involucral bracts imbricate in several rows, often scarious-margined, receptacle flat to convex or conical, naked; disc fls. bisexual or female or male, tubular, 4-toothed, white, yellow, brown, dark purple or black, or corolla sometimes absent, ray fls. absent; achenes flat, or curved, sometimes strongly ribbed or winged, the outer ones sometimes stalked, pappus absent.

atrata Hook.f. Creeping per., sts. ascending, about 8 in. long and 6 in. high; lvs. fleshy, narrowly oblong to narrowly obovate in outline, pinnatifid to pinnately dissected, to 1½ in. long, glandular-pubescent;

heads to ¾ in. across, on peduncles to 2⅜ in. long; fls. black to dark purple. New Zeal. Var. **Dendyi** (Cockayne) Cockayne ex Cheesem. [*C. Dendyi* Cockayne]. Fls. pale yellow to brown. New Zeal.

barbata DC. Tufted ann., sts. villous with silky hairs; lvs. mostly basal, pinnately parted, with linear, simple or forked segms., villous; heads to about ⁵⁄₁₆ in. across, on peduncles 5–6 in. long; fls. yellow. S. Afr.

coronopifolia L. BRASS-BUTTONS. Glabrous per., sts. somewhat decumbent, to 1 ft. long, fleshy; lvs. linear-obovate, to 3¼ in. long, entire or toothed, glabrous; heads to ⅜ in. across; fls. bright yellow; achenes winged. S. Afr.; naturalized widely around the world. Prefers moist or wet habitats along stream banks.

Dendyi: *C. atrata* var.

dioica (Hook.f.) Hook.f. Much-branched per., sts. creeping, to 1 ft. long, glabrous or sparsely hairy; lvs. alt. or in tufts at nodes, spatulate to obovate, serrate to pinnately dissected, to 2 in. long, essentially glabrous; heads unisexual, about ⁵⁄₁₆ in. across; fls. yellow; achenes curved, rounded on back. New Zeal.

pyrethrifolia Hook.f. Coarse, much-branched per., aromatic, glabrous, sts. creeping and rooting, ascending at tip; lvs. clustered on branchlets, broadly oblong in outline, pinnate to pinnately dissected, to 1½ in. long; heads unisexual, about ¾ in. across; fls. yellow; achenes compressed, obovoid, ribbed. New Zeal.

squalida (Hook.f.) Hook.f. Slender per., sts. creeping and rooting, wiry, hairy; lvs. in clusters at nodes, narrowly obovate in outline, deeply pinnatifid to pinnately dissected and fernlike, to 2 in. long, more or less pilose; heads unisexual, to ⁵⁄₁₆ in. across; achenes curved, rounded on back, almost 3-angled. New Zeal.

COTYLEDON L. *Crassulaceae.* About 35 spp. of succulent shrubs or subshrubs in S. Afr., 1 in E. Afr. and Arabia; lvs. opp. or alt., mostly persistent; fls. 5-merous, erect or pendent, in terminal cymes, corolla campanulate, tube commonly much longer than the calyx, lobes shorter to longer than tube, mostly recurved, stamens 10.

For culture see *Succulents.*

ausana: *C. orbiculata.*

Barbeyi G. Schweinf. Much-branched shrub; lvs. opp., obovate, 2½–6 in. long; fl. st. 2 ft.; fls. pendent, corolla yellow-green to orange, glandular, not inflated, tube ½ in. long, lobes as long or longer. E. Afr., Arabia.

Buchholziana Schuldt & P. Steph. Much-branched, low, glabrous shrub, often bare, brs. thick, with buds in spirally arranged conical depressions; lvs. mostly scalelike, a few linear-lanceolate, nearly circular in cross section, to ⅝ in. long and ³⁄₁₆ in. wide; fl. st. to 5 in., 1-fld.; corolla tube ½ in. long, lobes ⅛ in. long, with scattered papillae. Namaqualand.

cacaloides L.f. NENTA. Shrub, sts. to 20 in., branched from the base, ½ in. in diam. at apex, sts. and brs. rough with spiralled lf. bases; lvs. crowded, falling before flowering, cylindrical, 2–4 in. long, ¼ in. thick, acute, glabrous; fl. st. 1–2 ft.; fls. erect, corolla amber-yellow, tube 1 in. long, lobes spreading, as long as tube. Cape Prov. Poisonous to goats.

caespitosa: *Dudleya caespitosa.*

californica: *Dudleya caespitosa.*

chrysantha: *Rosularia pallida.*

Cooperi: *Adromischus Cooperi.*

decussata Sims [*C. Flanaganii* Schönl.]. Closely allied to *C. orbiculata,* with which it intergrades, but lvs. narrow and cylindrical or nearly so. Cape Prov. Cv. 'Walkeri'. Lvs. red-margined.

Dinteri Bak.f. Sts. 1 in. in diam. or more, bearing persistent lf. bases ⅜ in. long; lvs. alt., cylindrical, 1–4 in. long, falling before flowering; infl. glabrous; fls. pendent, corolla yellow-green, papillose, tube less than ⁵⁄₁₆ in. long, lobes shorter than tube. Namaqualand.

Flanaganii: *C. decussata.*

Galpinii Schönl. & Bak.f. Shrubby with prostrate sts.; lvs. opp., oblong-obovate, to 2½ in. long and 1 in. wide, glaucous, with red margin; fl. st. 4–10 in.; fls. pendent, corolla pale yellow with red, tube nearly 1 in. long, lobes oblong, ½ in. long. Cape Prov. Possibly a hybrid of *C. decussata* and *C. orbiculata.*

gracilis: see *C. Jacobseniana.*

grandiflora Burm.f Sts. to 1 ft. high or decumbent, rough with lf. bases; lvs. alt., falling before flowering, oblanceolate, 2–3 in. long, ½ in. wide, acute, channelled above, glabrous; fl. st. 6–20 in.; fls. 4–16, erect or spreading, pubescent, corolla red or yellow with red, tube often curved, 1¼–1½ in. long, lobes to ¾ in. long. Cape Prov.

Jacobseniana Poelln. [*C. gracilis* A. Berger, not Harv.]. Sts. slender, decumbent, to 8 in. long; lvs. opp., elliptic, 1–2 in. long, ¼ as wide, round in cross section, glabrous; fl. st. to 5 in.; fls. pendent, corolla greenish, glandular, tube ¼–⁵⁄₁₆ in. long, lobes slightly longer than tube. Namaqualand.

ladysmithiensis Poelln. Bushy, to 1 ft., tomentose; lvs. opp., oblong, to 2½ in. long and ¾ in. wide, turgid, obtuse, nearly petioled, lower lvs. with 2 blunt teeth near apex; fl. st. to 6 in.; fls. to 10, mostly pendent, pubescent, corolla reddish, tube ½ in. long, lobes half as long as tube. Cape Prov.

macrantha De Smet. Similar to *C. orbiculata,* but lvs. green, corolla lobes ⅔–¾ as long as tube. Probably e. Cape Prov.

oophylla: a listed name of no botanical standing; probably for *C. orbiculata* var. *oophylla.*

oppositifolia: *Chiastophyllum oppositifolium.*

orbiculata L. [*C. ausana* Dinter]. Shrub, to 4 ft.; lvs. opp., obovate-cuneate, 1½–5 in. long, mealy, often red-margined; fl. st. to 2 ft.; fls. pendent, corolla red or orangish, tube ⅜–1 in. long, lobes half as long as tube or less. Cape Prov., S.-W. Afr. Var. **Higginsiae** Jacobsen. Lvs. 1¼ in. long, ⅝ in. wide, ⅜ in. thick, with rounded margins. Var. **oophylla** Dinter. Sts. very short; lvs. long-ovate, 1½–2 in. long, rather thick. Material offered as *C. oophylla* probably belongs here. Cvs. 'Compacta', 'Major', 'Minor', and 'Variegata' are listed. The only sp. widely cult.

paniculata L.f. BOTTERBOOM. Shrub, to 6 ft., trunk with papery bark; lvs. alt., mostly falling before flowering, obovate to oblanceolate, 2–4 in. long, 1–2 in. wide, obtuse, pubescent or glabrous; fl. st. 1–2 ft.; fls. pendent, pubescent, corolla red, tube to ¾ in. long, lobes ⅔ to as long as tube. Cape Prov., S.-W. Afr.

papillaris L.f. Sts. slender, decumbent, to 6 in. long; lvs. opp., oblong-obovate, ½–2 in. long, ¼–½ in. wide, flattened; fl. st. 2–10 in., glandular; fls. pendent, papillose, corolla greenish-yellow or reddish, tube ¼ in. long, lobes mostly slightly longer than tube. Cape Prov.

Pearsonii Schönl. Much-branched subshrub, brs. ⅜ in. in diam., rough with lf. bases; lvs. small, linear, falling before flowering; fl. st. 3 in., glandular, woody-persistent; fls. pendent, glandular, corolla whitish, red-flecked, tube ⅜ in. long, lobes ¼ in. long. Namaqualand.

Pillansii Schönl. Shrub, to 1 ft.; lvs. opp., ovate-oblong, to 5 in. long, rough-hairy to nearly glabrous; corolla yellow-green, glandular, tube ¼–½ in. long, lobes mostly twice as long as tube. Cape Prov.

pygmaea W. F. Barker. To 2 in., glistening-papillose, sts. few-branched, to ⅜ in. in diam., smooth; lvs. alt., few, obovate, ¾ in. long, obtuse, channelled above, falling before flowering; fls. erect, corolla greenish-yellow, tube ³⁄₁₆ in. long, lobes as long as tube. Namaqualand.

racemosa E. H. Mey. Subshrub, to 1 ft., sts. to 1¼ in. in diam., bark peeling; lvs. alt., crowded, linear to spatulate, 1–2 in. long, ³⁄₁₆–⅝ in. wide, ⅛ in. thick, obtuse, glabrous or pubescent, pitted, with scattered glands; fl. st. 2–5 in.; fls. erect, glabrous, corolla greenish or whitish, tube to ⅝ in. long, lobes ¼ in. long. Namaqualand.

reticulata Thunb. Subshrub, to 1 ft., sts. thick, bark papery; lvs. alt. on fingerlike brs., elliptic-lanceolate, 1–3 in. long, nearly round in cross section, glabrous or glandular, falling mostly before flowering; fl. st. to 5 in., much-branched, glandular, wiry-persistent; fls. erect, corolla pubescent, yellowish marked with brown, tube ⁵⁄₁₆ in. long, lobes half as long as tube. Cape Prov., S.-W. Afr.

Schaeferana Dinter [*Adromischus Schaeferanus* (Dinter) A. Berger]. Rhizome fleshy, ½ in. in diam., sts. little-branching, to 1½ in. long and ³⁄₁₆ in. in diam.; lvs. alt., 1 or few, obovate-cuneate to nearly globose, at first glandular-puberulent, falling before flowering; fl. st. to 1½ in., mostly pubescent; fls. 1–3, erect, corolla tube ½ in. long, lobes obovate, pink, ⅛ in. long. S.-W. Afr.

simplicifolia: *Chiastophyllum oppositifolium.*

sinus-alexandri Poelln. Dwarf, glabrous subshrub, sts. 1 in. high, ³⁄₁₆ in. in diam.; lvs. alt., round or ovate, to ⅜ in. long and ³⁄₁₆ in. thick, purple-dotted, falling before flowering; fl. st. 1 in.; fls. 1–2, erect, corolla tube ½ in. long, lobes ¼ in. long. Namaqualand.

smithiensis: a listed name of no botanical standing, possibly an error for *C. ladysmithiensis.*

spinosa: *Orostachys spinosa.*

striata P. C. Hutchison. St. tuberlike, 2 in. in diam., brs. erect, to 6 in. long, ½ in. in diam., grayish-white, striped purplish-black, rough with lf. bases; lvs. alt., nearly cylindrical, 1–2½ in. long, ³⁄₁₆ in. in diam., acute, glandular, withering at flowering time; fl. st. to 2 ft., with elongate ascending brs.; fls. 10–40, erect, corolla whitish, strongly veined with red, glandular, tube ¾ in. long, lobes ¼ in. long. Namaqualand.

teretifolia Thunb. Hairy shrub; lvs. opp., nearly cylindrical, 1–5 in. long, ¼–½ in. in diam., green; fl. st. 1–1½ ft.; fls. pendent, yellow, corolla tube ¼–½ in. long, lobes 1–2 times as long as tube. Spring. Cape Prov.

Umbilicus: *Umbilicus rupestris.*

undulata Haw. SILVER-CROWN, SILVER-RUFFLES. Similar to *C. orbiculata,* in which it is sometimes included, but lvs. strongly undulate on the margin. Summer. Probably e. Cape Prov.

Van-der-Heydenii: a listed name of no botanical standing for *Adromischus clavifolius.*

viscida: *Dudleya viscida.* Var. **insularis:** *Dudleya virens.*

Walkeri: a listed name of no botanical standing, probably for *C. decussata* Cv. 'Walkeri'.

Wallichii Harv. NENTA. Sts. to 1 in. in diam., bearing persistent lf. bases; lvs. alt., linear, 2–3 in. long, glabrous, deciduous before flowering; fl. st. 1–2 ft., infl. glandular; fls. pendent, yellow-green, glandular, tube ½ in. long, lobes shorter than tube. Cape Prov.

Wickensii Schönl. Shrub, to 6 ft.; lvs. opp., ovate-lanceolate to oblanceolate, 3–4 in. long, 1–2 in. wide, acute to rounded, glaucous; fl. st. 1 ft.; fls. nodding, glandular, corolla red, tube ½ in. long, inflated at base, lobes longer than tube. N. Transvaal.

COUMAROUNA: *DIPTERYX.*

COURANTIA: *ECHEVERIA.*

COUROUPITA Aubl. *Lecythidaceae.* About 20 spp. of trees in trop. Amer. and the W. Indies; lvs. alt., simple, without stipules; fls. large, showy, in panicles or racemes, calyx 6-lobed, petals 6, very unequal, stamens many, borne centrally on an androphore and also at the apex of the flattened, overarching appendage of the androphore, ovary inferior, 6-celled; fr. a large, globose, woody caps. enclosing many seeds embedded in soft pulp.

guianensis Aubl. CANNONBALL TREE. To 50 ft.; lvs. oblong-obovate, 6–12 in. long, entire or obscurely serrate, pubescent on the veins beneath; infl. of racemes to 3 ft. long, arising from the trunk or large brs.; fls. with fruity fragrance, to 4 in. across, reddish or tinged yellowish on the outside, androphore rose; fr. reddish-brown, to 8 in. in diam., the inner pulp ill-smelling. Guianas; planted as a curiosity in trop. gardens and in Zone 10b in Fla.

COUTAREA Aubl. *Rubiaceae.* About 7 spp. of trees and shrubs, native to W. Indies and Mex., s. to S. Amer.; lvs. opp., petioled, membranous, stipules interpetiolar, short; fls. mostly in few-fld. cymes, large, 2–4 in. long, white or yellow, 5–8-merous, pedicelled, corolla funnelform-campanulate, tube often curved and inflated on one side; fr. an ovoid or obovoid caps., seeds many, winged.

hexandra (Jacq.) K. Schum. To 15 ft. or more; lvs. ovate to elliptic, to about 5 in. long, sharp-pointed, entire; fls. mostly in 3's, corolla white or yellowish, tinged purple toward base; caps. ¾ in. long. Mex. to Argentina. The bitter and astringent bark has properties similar to *Cinchona,* though less effective, and was formerly used in medicine.

COVER CROP. A cover crop is a crop grown primarily for the covering and protecting of land, particularly in orchards or cultivated fields, after the final tillage in summer until the following spring when tillage recurs. It may be a green crop not killed by the winter, as crimson clover, or a one-season crop that is killed by frost but remains on the land till spring, as peas. The crop is turned under in spring and then acts as an amendment to the soil. Many kinds of plants may be employed as cover crops, including: rape (*Brassica Napus*), crotalaria (*Crotalaria mucronata*), beggarweed (*Desmodium tortuosum*), buckwheat (*Fagopyrum esculentum*), soybean (*Glycine Max*), barley (*Hordeum vulgare*), pea (*Pisum sativum*), millet (*Setaria italica*), crimson clover (*Trifolium incarnatum*), wheat (*Triticum aestivum*), vetch (*Vicia sativa* and *V. villosa*), and cowpea (*Vigna unguiculata*).

COVILLEA: *LARREA.*

COWANIA D. Don. *Rosaceae.* About 5 or 6 spp. of shrubs or small trees of sw. U.S. and n. Mex.; lvs. leathery, gland-dotted, pinnatifid; fls. solitary, terminal, sepals 5, petals 5, pistils 4–12; frs. achenes with long plumose styles, several in a persistent, funnelform calyx tube.

Sometimes planted in native regions or regions of similar climate.

mexicana D. Don. Shrub, to 7 ft., with brownish bark and stiffly ascending brs., herbage usually viscid; lvs. cuneate-obovate, pinnately veined, deeply 3-cleft into entire lobes, glandular-punctate, ³⁄₁₆–⅜ in.

long; petals cream-colored, $\frac{5}{16}$ in. long. Mex. Var. **Stansburiana** (Torr.) Jeps. Bark grayish; lf. blades toothed. E. Calif. to Colo. and New Mex. Zone 6.

COXELLA: *ACIPHYLLA.*

CRABAPPLE: see *Apple.*

CRAIBIA Harms & S. T. Dunn. *Leguminosae* (subfamily *Faboideae*). About 10 spp. of trees and shrubs of trop. Afr.; lvs. alt., odd-pinnate or with 1 lft., the lfts. alt.; fls. racemose or panicled, often white, upper 2 calyx lobes united, stamens 10, 9 united and 1 free; fr. an ovate to oblong-obovate, flat legume, early dehiscent, seeds 1–2.

Brownii S. T. Dunn [*C. Elliotii* S. T. Dunn]. Slow-growing tree, to 40 ft., with large spreading crown; lfts. 3–7, elliptic, to 4 in. long, acuminate; fls. very fragrant, white or tinged pink, in terminal racemes to 3 in. long; fr. obovate, to 2¾ in. long, narrowed at each end, 1-seeded. Kenya.

Elliotii: *C. Brownii.*

CRAMBE L. *Cruciferae.* About 20 spp. of ann. to per. herbs, mostly from Canary Is. to w. Asia, sometimes woody at base, glabrous or with unbranched hairs; lvs. mostly thick or fleshy, glaucous, often very large, lobed, cut, lyrate, or pinnatifid; fls. small, many, in racemes or panicles, sepals 4, petals 4, white, with a short claw or wedge-shaped basally; fr. a 2-jointed indehiscent silicle, the upper joint 1-seeded and globular.

cordifolia Steven. COLEWORT. Stout per., to 7 ft.; basal lvs. cordate, to 2 ft. across and more, somewhat lobed and coarsely toothed, more or less hispid-hairy, long-petioled; fls. $\frac{5}{16}$ in. across, in a great, terminal, leafless panicle. Caucasus. Grown as an ornamental because of its striking appearance.

maritima L. SEA KALE, SCURVY GRASS. Stout, stocky per., to 3 ft.; lvs. large, glaucous-blue, fleshy, brittle, basal lvs. to 2 ft. long or more and nearly as broad, notched and shallowly lobed, stout-petioled; fls. in panicles. Seacoasts, w. Eur. to Asia Minor. Grown for succulent spring shoots, which are blanched. See *Sea Kale.*

hispanica L. Slender ann., to 3 ft., usually densely hispid; lvs. with elliptic to nearly orbicular terminal segm., lobed or lyrate below, to 3 in. across, sinuate; fls. in long open racemes. Medit. region. Cult. as a commercial oilseed crop.

CRANBERRY. Native to North America, the cranberry, *Vaccinium macrocarpon*, is cultivated entirely in the United States and Canada. Leading states producing cranberries in developed bogs or swamps are Massachusetts, Wisconsin, New Jersey, Washington, and Oregon. Canada has a limited acreage in British Columbia, Quebec, and parts of Nova Scotia. The small or European cranberry, *Vaccinium Oxycoccos,* native in the northern parts of America, is not cultivated. The fruits of the mountain cranberry or lingenberry, *Vaccinium Vitis-idaea,* are often collected from the wild and marketed, especially in Europe.

The cranberry plant is a low-growing vine with persistent leaves and a shallow, fine, fibrous root system. In late summer flower buds are initiated near the end of shoots (uprights) that arise from the main runners and on which the fruit are borne the subsequent year. Adequate pollination is essential and bee colonies are generally brought into bogs during the flowering period.

The cranberry is restricted to acid soils of pH 3.2 to 4.5; alkaline peat and ordinary garden and farm soils are not suitable for its culture. A large supply of water is needed near the bogs for irrigation, as well as for flooding as a means of protection against winter injury, untimely frosts, and insects. All except the West Coast bogs need to be flooded in winter to prevent "winter killing," a grower's term for winter dessication, a killing of the plants caused by moisture loss from the leaves at a time when roots are in frozen ground. It is unnecessary and undesirable to flood higher than the tallest cranberry vines.

Because cranberry bogs are situated in the lower elevations of the landscape, they are more susceptible than most crops to frosts in spring and autumn, when, on clear, still nights, the heavier, cold air from surrounding uplands drains onto

the bogs and stratifies, with the coldest layers at the base and warmer air above. Formerly it was customary to flood the bogs in anticipation of hazardous low temperatures, but since the mid-1960's some two-thirds of the cranberry acreage have been provided with low-gallonage sprinkler systems which provide almost instantaneous frost protection. Despite the development of sophisticated frost-warning systems, flooding the bogs is at best slow, requiring about 300,000 gallons per acre, and the onset of low temperatures frequently outpaced the protecting flood. With sprinklers, protection is assured with completion of the first rotation of the sprinkler heads, and protection continues as long as they are in operation.

Sprinklers are much more economical of water, most being designed to use about 50 gallons per acre per minute, an acre-inch being needed for all-night frost protection. They are infinitely more useful for summer irrigation than flooding and they have proved themselves efficient in the distribution of fungicides and insecticides.

New commercial bogs are developed in a series of beds about two acres in size and serviced by a single reservoir of water. The preparation and planting of a cranberry bog is an expensive and time-consuming operation. Existing vegetation and tree stumps must be removed and the peat leveled. Ditches must be dug around the swamp and at intervals through the bog to facilitate flooding and drainage. In most areas a few inches of sand is spread on the peat before spreading newly mown cuttings 3–4 inches long over the surface and "discing-in" with a simple machine looking like a disc harrow but with flat, blunt blades.

Rooted cuttings may also be planted at 12-inch spacings in and between rows. Then follows three or four years in which weed and insect control must be achieved before the first commercial harvest can be made. Every three to five years bogs are sanded with ½ inch of sand in the autumn after harvest to provide a suitable medium for root growth and insect control. During the growing season the water table is maintained at 9–12 inches below the surface. With careful management, a cranberry bog may continue to produce an annual crop thereafter for a century or more.

Because of high labor costs and a short harvesting season, cranberries are now largely harvested with special machines. Water harvesting, where the bog is flooded to a depth of 6–8 inches, is preferred over dry harvesting. The harvester rakes or beats the berries from the vines. These berries float to the surface and are gathered. Dry harvesting by mechanical means is less efficient because up to 30 percent of the crop is lost by berries dropping to the surface of the bog. Cranberries are now seldom harvested with hand scoops or by hand except occasionally for finishing up the margins of the bogs where it is difficult for machines to operate.

The average yield of an acre of cranberries is 100 barrels and occasional bogs will produce double that. Over half of all cranberries grown for processing are used in cranberry juices; the balance is made into sauces, relishes, and pie fillings. Only 20 percent of the cranberry crop is sold as fresh fruit.

Most of the annual crop is derived from named cultivars representing selections from wild cranberry vines. 'Early Black' and 'Howes' predominate in Massachusetts and New Jersey, 'Searless Jumbo' in Wisconsin, and 'McFarlin' in the Pacific Northwest. Hybrids derived from crosses of named selections are slowly being introduced, 'Stevens' being notable, particularly in Wisconsin.

The raising of cranberries is a highly specialized form of agriculture requiring heavy capital investment, daily surveillance of weather, insects, and other hazards, and in recent years the margin of profit has been narrow.

CRASPEDIA G. Forst. *Compositae* (Inula Tribe). About 7 spp. of ann. or per. herbs, native to Australia, New Zeal., and Tasmania; lvs. in a basal rosette or alt. on sts., entire; infl. a compound head composed of many 3–10-fld. individual heads crowded together in an ovoid or globose terminal cluster on a common convex, oblong, or cylindrical receptacle subtended by a common involucre of scarious bracts shorter than the fls.; fls. all tubular, bisexual; achenes usually compressed, silky-hairy, pappus of 1 row of plumose hairs.

alpina Backh. [*C. lanata* Hook.f.) Allan; *C. uniflora* var. *lanata* (Hook.f.) Cheesm.]. Per., to 1 ft.; rosette lvs. obovate, to 4 in. long, with dense, appressed, grayish-white hairs; compound heads ¾ in. across; fls. yellow or white; achenes nearly ovoid to oblong, densely silky-hairy. New Zeal.

incana Allan. Per., to 1 ft.; lvs. densely white-floccose, obovate-spatulate, to 4 in. long, st. lvs. successively reduced upward, the uppermost bractlike; compound heads to 1¼ in. across; fls. yellow; achenes obovoid, papillose-pubescent. New Zeal.

lanata: *C. alpina.*

uniflora G. Forst. Per., to 1½ ft.; rosette lvs. broadly ovate to elliptic-spatulate, hairy, the margins with white, tangled, cottony hairs, upper lvs. ovate to narrowly lanceolate or elliptic; compound heads to 1¼ in. across; fls. yellow or white; achenes silky-hairy. New Zeal., Tasmania, temp. Australia. Var. **lanata:** *C. alpina.*

CRASSINA: *ZINNIA.*

CRASSULA L. *Crassulaceae.* About 300 spp. of succulent, mostly per. herbs and shrubs, native mostly to Afr., especially S. Afr.; lvs. opp., usually united, sessile or petioled; fls. mostly 5-merous, white to red or yellowish, mostly small, variously arranged but commonly in corymbose cymes or in a thyrsoid infl., sepals separate, nearly erect, petals mostly nearly separate at base, stamens as many as and opp. sepals.

The genus has been divided into 6 sections. The species of a section possess the characteristics of that section. These characteristics are not repeated in the brief description of the species; instead, the following symbols are used to indicate the section to which each species belongs: C, *Crassula;* G, *Globulea;* P, *Pyramidella;* Sp, *Sphaeritis;* S, *Stellatae;* T, *Tuberosae.* The distinguishing characters of the sections follow:

Crassula [*Campanulatae* Schönl.] (C). Lvs. sessile; infl. various, often corymbose or paniculate; petals erect or spreading above, mostly with small mucro, nectar glands small.

Globulea (Haw.) Harv. (G). Lvs. sessile; infl. of dense cymules variously arranged on a terminal peduncle; sepals thick, nearly equalling corolla, petals white or yellowish, erect, ovate or panduriform, the base contracted, apex with large, nearly globose dorsal mucro, nectar glands ¼–½ as long as ovaries.

Pyramidella Harv. (P). Lvs. sessile, close-set, often forming a dense column or pyramid; infl. a sessile dense head or spike, sometimes with lateral fls. also; petals white or reddish, erect, united below into a distinct tube, nearly lanceolate or nearly spatulate, without mucro, nectar glands stipitate.

Sphaeritis (Eckl. & Zeyh.) Harv. (Sp). Lvs. sessile; infl. usually peduncled; petals white or yellowish, erect, apex longitudinally folded or thickened, often narrowed, the folded halves sometimes fused, rarely with mucro, nectar glands large.

Stellatae Schönl. (S). Lvs. ovate to spatulate, often petioled, mostly glabrous; infl. mostly terminal, thyrsoid to nearly umbellate; petals spreading from base, lanceolate, without mucro, white or pink, nectar glands minute.

Tuberosae Schönl. (T). Sts. herbaceous from tuberous rhizome; lvs. sessile or petioled; infl. nearly umbellate or thyrsoid; petals stellate or ascending, without mucro, anthers with distinct connective, nectar glands minute.

Grown in greenhouses and windows in the North and outdoors in warm regions. For culture see *Succulents.*

acutifolia Lam. C; glabrous subshrub; sts. decumbent or erect, to 1 ft.; lf. pairs scattered, lvs. mostly spreading, awl-shaped, to ¾ in. long; infl. peduncled, loosely umbellate; fls. white, ⅛ in. long. Var. **densifolia** (Harv.) Schönl. [*C. densifolia* Harv.]. Lf. pairs close-set.

albiflora Sims. C; sts. woody at base, to 2 ft., scabrous above; lf. pairs scattered, lvs. ovate to oblong, 1–1½ in. long, acute to obtuse, ciliate; infl. corymbose, 2–5 in. wide; fls. white, 5⁄16 in. long.

Alstonii Maloth. C; plant body nearly globose to cylindrical, few-branched from base; lvs. obliquely nearly 2-ranked, crowded, nearly

orbicular, ½–¾ in. long, slightly wider, rounded beneath, densely white-papillose; fl. st. scapose, 2–3 in.; fls. white, 3⁄16 in. long, in an open cyme.

arborea: a listed name of no botanical standing, probably a synonym of *C. arborescens.*

arborescens (Mill.) Willd. SILVER JADE PLANT, SILVER-DOLLAR, CHINESE JADE. S; glabrous shrub, to 10 ft.; lvs. obovate, 1½–2½ in. long, gray-glaucous, often with red margins, conspicuously dotted, nearly petioled. Slow-growing and rarely flowering in cult. Cv. 'Variegata' is listed.

Archeri Compt. P; similar to *C. pyramidalis,* but larger and with lateral branching, sts. to 8 in.; lvs. ¼ in. long and wide; fl. heads 1 in. wide.

argentea Thunb. [*C. portulacea* Lam.]. JADE TREE, BABY JADE, JADE PLANT, DOLLAR PLANT, CAULIFLOWER EARS, CHINESE RUBBER PLANT, DWARF R.P., JAPANESE R.P. S; glabrous shrub to 10 ft.; lvs. obovate, 1–2 in. long, green often with red margins, obscurely punctate, nearly petioled; fls. white or pink. Flowering freely outdoors in s. Calif. but seldom in the North, where it is a common pot plant. Cvs. 'Pacifica', 'Tricolor', and 'Variegata' are listed.

argyrophylla Diels. C; lvs. few, nearly basal, obovate, ¾–1¼ in. long, obtuse, sometimes somewhat oblique, turgid but flattened, finely pubescent; fl. st. scapose, about 4 in.; fls. ⅛ in. long, cymules corymbose. Plants that seem to belong here are grown as *C. namaquensis,* which has the petals narrowed and channelled at apex.

barbata Thunb. C; lvs. in a rosette, cuneate, 1–2 in. long, truncate, fringed with long white hairs; fl. st. 12–18 in., with reduced lvs., cymules in a spike; fls. white, 3⁄16 in. long.

brevisetosa: a listed name of no botanical standing.

cephalophora Thunb. G; lvs. nearly in a rosette, obovate to oblanceolate, 1–3 in. long, obtuse to nearly acute, gray-pubescent; fl. st. scapose, 1–2 ft.; fls. in scattered dense cymules ¼–½ in. wide.

ciliaris: a listed name of no botanical standing; plants grown under this name are probably *C. obvallata.*

clavifolia (E. H. Mey.) Harv. Sp; subshrub; lvs. oblong-spatulate, obtuse, glabrous or nearly so, sometimes ciliate; infl. peduncled, terminal, capitate.

coccinea: *Rochea coccinea.*

Collinberi: a listed name of no botanical standing; see *C. corymbulosa.*

columnaris Thunb. P; plant body ovoid, 2–4 in. high, ¾–1½ in. in diam., of about 5–12 densely crowded lf. pairs; lvs. orbicular, thick-rimmed apically and thus basin-shaped, uniformly dark green.

congesta N. E. Br. [*C. pachyphylla* Schönl.]. P; sts. erect, to 4 in., with 8–15 separated lf. pairs; lvs. ovate to lanceolate, 1–1½ in. long, ½–¾ in. wide, acute to obtusish, ascending to reflexed.

Cooperi Regel. C; tufted herb, 3–5 in.; lvs. elliptic-lanceolate, diminishing gradually upward, the lower 1 in. long, acute, convex above and rounded beneath, light green, punctate and black-blotched, ciliate; infl. somewhat corymbose; fls. pinkish.

corallina Thunb. C; to 1 in. high, brs. decumbent, rooting at the nodes; lvs. crowded, nearly globose or ellipsoid, 3⁄16 in. long, mealy and green-punctate above; infl. corymbose, sessile; fls. 1⁄16 in. long.

cordata Thunb. S; slender, glabrous subshrub, 1–3 in.; lvs. cordate, ½–1 in. long, obtuse to nearly acute, very glaucous beneath, punctate, petioled; infl. with bulbils; fls. 5-merous. Some material grown under this name may be *C. spathulata.*

cornuta Schönl. & Bak.f. C; plant body columnar, about 2 in. high and 1 in. in diam., of 5–8 densely crowded lf. pairs; lvs. triangular-ovate, ½ in. long, slightly wider, nearly as thick at the apex, obtuse, white-papillose; fl. st. scapose, 2–3 in., infl. a paniculate cyme, petals white, 1⁄16 in. long, twice as long as sepals.

corymbulosa Link & Otto. C; herbaceous; lvs. ovate to lanceolate, 1–7 in. long, acute, strongly flattened, punctate, often ciliate, on young shoots crowded in 4 sometimes nearly spiralled rows, on old shoots more scattered; fl. st. 6–30 in., infl. an elongate thyrse, cymules in small corymbs; fls. white, 1⁄16 in. long. Plants that seem referable here are grown under the names *C. Collinberi* and *C. elata.*

cultrata L. PROPELLER PLANT, AIRPLANE-PROPELLER PLANT. G; subshrub, 2–3 ft.; lvs. obovate or oblong-obovate, mostly ¾–1¼ in. long, flattish, obtuse to acutish, curved, sometimes minutely ciliate; fl. st. scapose, 1½–2½ in. or more, infl. a panicle of cymules; calyx half as long as the corolla, petals entire, erect.

deceptrix Schönl. & Bak.f. C; similar to *C. cornuta,* but lvs. more triangular, tessellate; fl. st. 1–1½ in.; calyx more than ⅔ as long as the corolla, petals slightly recurved.

decipiens: *C. tecta.*

dejecta Jacq. Apparently not cult.; *C. obvallata* is said to be grown under this name.

deltoidea Thunb. [*C. rhomboidea* N. E. Br.]. SILVER-BEADS. C; subshrub, to 4 in.; lvs. rhombic-ovate, ¾–1 in. long, ⅜–¾ in. wide, to ½ in. thick at the middle, where thickest, turgid, bluntly keeled, mealy, punctate; infl. a few-fld., flat-topped cyme; fls. pinkish, ³⁄₁₆ in. long.

densifolia: *C. acutifolia* var.

dentata Thunb. T; sts. 3–6 in.; lvs. several, blades thin, reniform, ½–1 in. wide, repand-crenate, petioles filiform, 1–3 in. long.

Dexteri: a listed name of no botanical standing.

Dregeana Harv. Apparently not cult.; *C. rubicunda* may be grown under this name.

elata N. E. Br. C; herbaceous, about 2 ft.; lvs. oblong or lanceolate, 1½ in. long or probably longer, nearly acute, white-pubescent; infl. an interrupted spike of dense verticillasters; fls. brownish, ⅛ in. long. Perhaps not in cult.; some plants grown under this name appear to be *C. corymbulosa*. Cv. 'Rosea' is listed.

erecta (Hook. & Arn.) A. Berger. A very small ann. not in cult. Material listed under this name is similar to *C. Justi-Corderoyi*.

ericoides Haw. C; much-branched, woody subshrub, about 1 ft.; lvs. crowded, ovate-lanceolate, ⅜ in. long, thin, nearly acute; infl. sessile, few-fld.; fls. white, ³⁄₁₆ in. long.

falcata H. Wendl. [*Rochea falcata* (H. Wendl.) DC.]. AIRPLANE PLANT, SICKLE PLANT, AIRPLANE-PROPELLERS, SCARLET-PAINT-BRUSH, PROPELLER PLANT. C; shrub, to 2½ ft., nearly simple; lvs. oblong-sickle-shaped, 3–4 in. long, obtuse, gray-papillose, not 4-ranked, the pairs obliquely alt.; infl. a dense corymbose cyme 3–4 in. wide; fls. bright red, ⁵⁄₁₆ in. long.

hemisphaerica Thunb. ARAB'S-TURBAN. C; plant body hemispherical, 1–2 in. in diam., of about 10–16 densely overlapping lf. pairs; lvs. nearly orbicular, retuse to nearly mucronate, punctate, ciliate, the margins curved downward against the lvs. beneath, the lower ½–1 in. long, the upper gradually smaller; fl. st. scapose, 4–8 in., infl. paniculate; fls. white, ⅛ in. long.

imperialis: a listed name of no botanical standing; said to apply to a hybrid intermediate in appearance between *C. lycopodioides* and *C. pyramidella*; called GIANT'S WATCH-CHAIN.

impressa: *C. Schmidtii.*

Justi-Corderoyi Jacobsen & Poelln. C; herbaceous, to 6 in.; lvs. elliptic-oblanceolate, acute, flattish ventrally, rounded dorsally, densely white-papillose, the crowded lower ones, to 2 in. long and ¼ in. wide, the upper ones more scattered and gradually smaller; fls. pink, ³⁄₁₆ in. long, nearly corymbose. Formerly grown under the name *C. namaquensis* var. *brevifolia*.

klinghardtensis Schönl. C; plant body columnar, 1 in.; lvs. nearly globose to ovate, about ⅜ in. long and wide, over half as thick, nearly acute, finely pubescent; fl. st. scapose, 2 in.; fls. white, ³⁄₁₆ in. long, in capitate cymules.

lactea Ait. FLOWERING C., TAILOR'S-PATCH. S; glabrous shrub, to 2 ft.; lvs. ovate-cuneate, 1–2½ in. long, acute to acuminate, punctate near the margin; fls. white or pink.

lineolata Ait. S; prostrate herb; lf. pairs remote, lvs. cordate-ovate, ⅝ in. long, entire, sessile or petioled, white-margined, lineolate, pilose at base.

longifolia: a listed name of no botanical standing, sometimes used for *C. perfoliata*.

lycopodioides Lam. MOSS C., RATTAIL C., TOY CYPRESS, WATCH-CHAIN. C; sts. slender, decumbent or ascending, woody at base, ½–2 ft., tetragonal, with 4-ranked, long-persistent, scalelike lvs.; lvs. green, ovate or broadly lanceolate, ⅛ in. long, obtuse to nearly acuminate; fls. greenish, minute, 1 or few, axillary. Var. **pseudolycopodioides** (Dinter & Schinz) Walth. [*C. pseudolycopodioides* Dinter & Schinz]. SKINNY-FINGERS, PRINCESS PINE. Sts. thicker; lvs. more obtuse, gray-green; axillary shoots more numerous; material cult. as var. *pseudolycopodioides* may not be this var.

marginalis Ait. TRAILING C., PINK-BUTTONS. S; prostrate, glabrous herb; lf. pairs remote, lvs. orbicular-cordate, ¼–¾ in. long, entire, united, often red-margined, punctate along the margin. Sometimes grown under the name *C. marginata*.

marginata: *C. pellucida;* but plants grown under this name are often *C. marginalis*.

mesembrianthemopsis Dinter. P; plant buried except lf. apices and fls., sts. short, with 4–8 close-set but upwardly diverging lf. pairs; lvs. oblong-cuneate, to 1¼ in. long and ½ in. wide, rounded beneath, obliquely truncate, pale green beneath, reddish-gray-papillose toward apex; infl. a head about ⅝ in. wide; fls. white.

monticola: *C. rupestris.*

montis-draconis Dinter. C; woody subshrub, to 16 in.; lvs. nearly cylindrical, 1–1¼ in. long, ½ in. wide, ⅜ in. thick, obtuse, glabrous; infl. cymose; fls. yellow, ⅛ in. long.

multicava Lem. [*C. quadrifida* Bak.]. S; sts. erect or somewhat decumbent, to 1 ft. long, lower internodes about 1 in. long; lvs. obovate, 1–3 in. long, ¾–1½ in. wide, obtuse to retuse, conspicuously punctate, narrowed to petioles; infl. with bulbils; fls. 4-merous.

namaquensis Schönl & Bak.f. Sp; lvs. nearly in a rosette, oblong-lanceolate, about 1 in. long and ⅜ in. in diam., semicylindrical, acute, densely covered with short thick papillae; fl. st. scapose, 2–3 in., infl. of 1 to several few-fld., capitate cymes; petals narrowed and channelled at apex. Some plants grown as *C. namaquensis* may be *C. argyrophylla*. Var. **brevifolia:** a listed name of no botanical standing for *C. Justi-Corderoyi*.

nudicaulis L. G; lvs. basal, awl-shaped, 2–6 in. long, ¼–½ in. in diam., semicircular in cross section, acute, somewhat pubescent; fl. st. scapose, 1–2 ft., infl. paniculate or thyrsoid.

obliqua Soland. S; shrub, to nearly 10 ft., sts. branched, brown; lvs. obliquely ovate, to 1⅝ in. long, 1³⁄₁₆ in. wide, blunt or tapered at apex, fleshy, silvery-green with dark markings; fls. pale pink, ¾ in. across. Material in cult. under this name may be a form of *C. portulacea*.

obvallata L. G; lvs. crowded at base, oblong-lanceolate or obliquely knife-shaped, 2–2½ in. long, ½–¾ in. wide, obtuse or nearly acute, glabrous, ciliate; fl. st. scapose, less than 1 ft., cymules hemispherical. Said to be sometimes mislabelled as *C. dejecta*.

orbicularis L. C; stolons frequent; lvs. in a rosette, spatulate-obovate to oblong, to 2 in. long, obtuse, glabrous, ciliate; fl. st. scapose, 6–8 in., infl. an interrupted thyrse of dense cymules; petals white or reddish above, curved outward from below the middle.

pachyphylla: *C. congesta.*

Peglerae Schönl. C; closely related to the extremely variable *C. ramuliflora*, of which it is perhaps a var., but lvs. ovate to lanceolate, the cilia short, blunt.

pellucida L. [*C. marginata* Thunb.]. S; glabrous, prostrate herb, rooting at the nodes; lvs. ovate-spatulate, ½–1½ in. long, acute to obtuse, often crenulate or denticulate, not punctate, sessile or petioled.

perfoliata L. C; shrub, to 2½ ft., nearly simple; lvs. lanceolate, 4–6 in. long, acute to acuminate, concave above, powdery; infl. a corymbiform cyme; fls. red or white. Close to *C. falcata* but lvs. 4-ranked, not oblique. Sometimes grown under the name *C. longifolia*.

perforata L. STRING-OF-BUTTONS. C; shrubby, to 2 ft.; lf. pairs more or less distant, lvs. connate-perfoliate, ovate, scarcely 1 in. long, acute to acuminate, spreading and flattened above, mostly ciliate; infl. a spicate panicle; fls. yellowish, small. Allied to *C. rupestris*, which has ascending, thicker, non-ciliate, more obtuse lvs. Cv. 'Gigantea', HEAVENLY TWINS, is listed.

perfossa: *C. rupestris.*

portulacea: *C. argentea.*

pseudolycopodioides: *C. lycopodioides* var.

pubescens Thunb. C; sts. erect, branching, glabrous; lvs. ovate, acute, thick, villous; fls. small, white, corymbose.

pulvinata: a listed name of no botanical standing.

Purcellii Schönl. Sp; shrub, to 1½ ft.; lf. pairs more or less distant, lvs. nearly cylindrical but flattened above, pubescent, the lower 1½ in. long, ¼ in. wide, the upper gradually smaller; cymules corymbose; petals channelled at apex.

pyramidalis Thunb. PYRAMID C. P; to 4 in., sts. branching dichotomously, densely leafy, the plant body 4-angled, compact; lvs. many and close-set, united, triangular or triangular-ovate, ⅛ in. long and wide, acute, flat and thin, ciliate toward base; fl. head ½ in. wide. Usually dies after seed is produced.

quadrifida: *C. multicava.*

radicans (Haw.) Harv. G; shrubby, lateral brs. spreading and rooting; lvs. more or less distant, oblong-lanceolate, about 1 in. long and ¼ in. wide, knife-shaped, acute, glabrous and smooth-edged; fl. st. scapose, cymules corymbose.

ramuliflora Link & Otto. C; leafy sts. ann. from rhizome, erect, 2–12 in., simple, pubescent; lf. pairs more or less distant, lvs. broadly ovate to oblong, ⅜–1 in. long, acute to obtuse, short-ciliate; infl. thyrsoid to subcapitate; petals white or reddish, ¼ in. long. A variable sp., perhaps including *C. Peglerae* and *C. reversisetosa*.

Reseda: a listed name of no botanical standing.

reversisetosa Bitter. C; similar to *C. ramuliflora* and perhaps not distinct; sts. decumbent, to 8 in. high; lvs. rhomboid-orbicular; fls. 3–7.

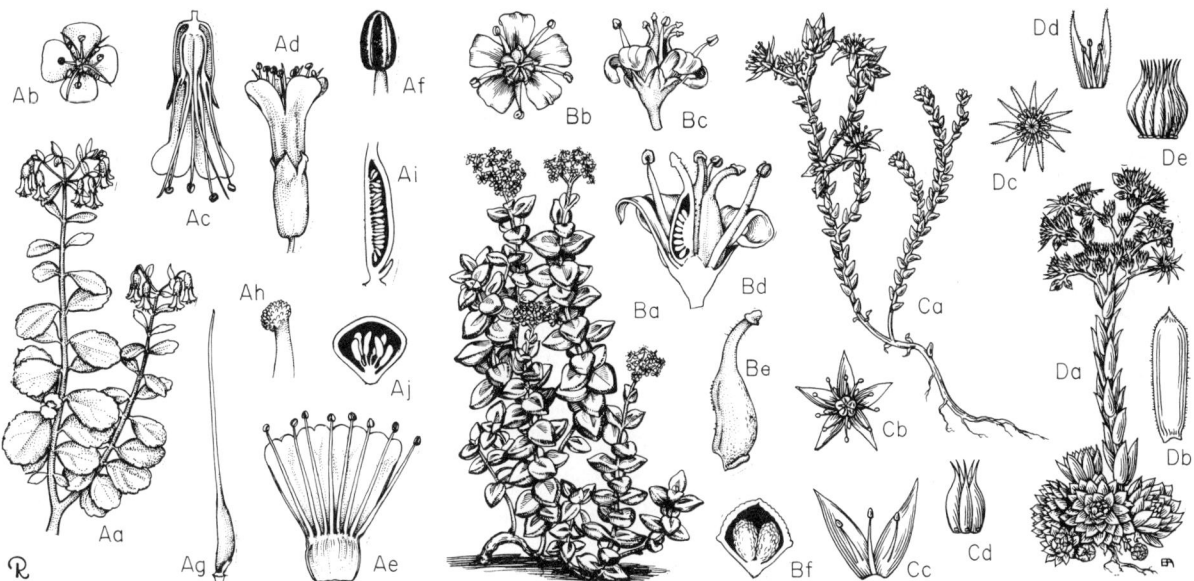

CRASSULACEAE. **A,** *Kalanchoe Fedtschenkoi:* **Aa,** flowering branch, × ⅕; **Ab,** flower, face view, × 1; **Ac,** flower, vertical section, × 1; **Ad,** flower, side view, × 1; **Ae,** corolla, expanded, × 1; **Af,** anther, × 4; **Ag,** carpel, × 1½; **Ah,** stigma, × 20; **Ai,** ovary, vertical section, × 3; **Aj,** ovary, cross section, × 8. **B,** *Crassula rupestris:* **Ba,** plant, × ½; **Bb,** flower, face view, × 3; **Bc,** flower, side view, × 3; **Bd,** flower, vertical section, × 5; **Be,** carpel, × 8; **Bf,** ovary, cross section, × 16. **C,** *Sedum acre:* **Ca,** plant, × ½; **Cb,** flower, face view, × 1; **Cc,** two petals with stamens, × 2; **Cd,** carpels, × 2. **D,** *Sempervivum tectorum:* **Da,** plant, × ¼; **Db,** cauline bract, × 1; **Dc,** flower, face view, × ½; **Dd,** two petals with stamens, × 1; **De,** carpels, × 2. (Ca–Cd, Da–De from Bailey, *Manual of Cultivated Plants,* ed. 2.)

rhomboidea: *C. deltoidea.*

rosularis Haw. C; lvs. in a rosette, oblong to spatulate, 3–5 in. long, acute, glabrous, ciliate; fl. st. scapose, infl. paniculate or thyrsoid; petals erect, white. Closely related to *C. orbicularis* but larger and usually without stolons.

rubicunda E. H. Mey. C; sts. herbaceous, 1–3 ft., mostly setose; lvs. linear-lanceolate to ovate, acute, glabrous to setose, ciliate, diminishing gradually upward, the lower 2–8 in. long; infl. corymbose, subsessile, 2–6 in. wide; fls. red, ⅛–¼ in. long. Plants seemingly of this sp., with lvs. densely covered by hyaline papillalike hairs, are grown as *C. Dregeana* Harv., but that is a much smaller plant, with white fls.

rubricaulis Eckl. & Zeyh. C; glabrous subshrub, diffusely branching, to 1 ft.; lvs. obovate to ovate, to 1 in. long and ½ in. wide, obtuse, minutely ciliate; infl. corymbose-paniculate; fls. 3/16 in. long.

rupestris Thunb. [*C. monticola* N. E. Br.; *C. perfossa* Lam.]. BUTTONS-ON-A-STRING, BEAD VINE, NECKLACE VINE, ROSARY VINE, ROSARY PLANT. C; slender, spreading, glabrous subshrub; lvs. connate-perfoliate, roundish or ovate, ½–1 in. long, nearly acute, ascending, somewhat concave above, thick, glaucous; infl. corymbose to thyrsoid.

sarcocaulis Eckl. & Zeyh. C; fleshy subshrub, to 8 in., nearly dichotomously branched; lvs. crowded, 3-angled and awl-shaped or nearly cylindrical, to ½ in. long, glabrous or scabrous; infl. a small corymb, nearly sessile; fls. white to pink, to ¼ in. long.

sarmentosa Harv. S; glabrous, climbing herb; lf. pairs remote, lvs. ovate, ½–1½ in. long, acute to acuminate, abruptly short-petioled, crenate-serrate.

Schmidtii Regel [*C. impressa* N. E. Br.]. C; cespitose herb, 2–6 in.; lvs. linear to lanceolate, acute, semicylindrical, ciliate, impressed-punctate, the lowest 1–2 in. long, ⅛ in. wide, the upper gradually shorter; infl. corymbose to thyrsoid; fls. pink, ⅛ in. long.

spathulata Thunb. MINIATURE TRAILING C. S; glabrous, trailing herb; lf. pairs remote, lvs. ovate, ½–1¼ in. long, ¼–⅝ in. wide, obtuse to nearly acute, crenate, tapered to the slender petiole or somewhat cordate; cyme loose. Sometimes grown under the name *C. cordata.*

tecta Thunb. [*C. decipiens* N. E. Br.]. C; lf. pairs 3–4, nearly basal, lvs. ovate, about 1¼ in. long, ¾ in. wide, and ½ in. thick, obtuse, flat above, densely covered with short, thick, white-tipped papillae; fl. st. scapose, to 6 in.; cymules 1 to several, dense. Usually included in section *Sphaeritis,* and close to *C. namaquensis* of that section, but petals not narrowed or channelled above.

teres Marloth. RATTLESNAKE C. P; plant body cylindrical, to 3 in. high and ¾ in. in diam., of 12–20 closely compacted lf. pairs; lvs. orbicular, cupped upward, pale green, punctate, margin hyaline, ciliate.

tetragona L. MINIATURE PINE TREE, BABY-PINE-OF-CHINA, CHINESE PINE. C; glabrous shrub, to 2 ft.; lf. pairs remote, lvs. spreading, awl-shaped or nearly 4-angled, ¾–1½ in. long, acute; infl. peduncled, corymbose-paniculate, loose; fls. white, ⅛ in. long.

tomentosa Thunb. Sp; densely bristly-hairy; lvs. mostly basal, obovate, obtuse; fl. st. 1–2 ft., with a few remote pairs of oblong acutish lvs., infl. an interrupted spike of dense, sessile cymules.

trachysantha (Eckl. & Zeyh.) Harv. Sp; densely retrorse-hispid subshrub, 1–1½ ft.; lvs. awl-shaped, ½–¾ in. long, acute; infl. corymbose; petal apex thick, glandlike.

Triebneri: a listed name of no botanical standing.

turrita Thunb. C; lvs. mostly nearly in a rosette, oblong or lanceolate, 2–3 in. long, ¾ in. wide, acute, glabrous, ciliate; fl. st. simple, ½–2 ft., leafy below, infl. a spike of cymules; fls. 1/16 in. long.

CRASSULACEAE DC. ORPINE FAMILY. Dicot.; about 30 genera and 1,500 spp. of ann. to mostly per., succulent herbs and shrubs, widely distributed in both hemispheres, especially in temp. regions; fls. mostly in cymes, spikes, racemes, or panicles, or occasionally solitary, 4–30-merous, but commonly 5-merous, sepals separate or united, petals as many, separate or united, stamens as many or twice as many, ovary superior, of as many carpels that are usually separate to or nearly to the base, usually with nectar gland at base of each carpel, ovules usually many. Several genera are grown in the greenhouse or rock garden or regularly in the open, as: *Adromischus, Aeonium, Aichryson, Chiastophyllum, Cotyledon, Crassula,* × *Cremneria, Cremnophila, Dudleya, Echeveria, Graptopetalum, Greenovia, Kalanchoe, Lenophyllum, Monanthes, Orostachys, Pachyphytum,* × *Pachyveria, Rochea, Rosularia, Sedum, Sempervivum, Tacitus, Umbilicus,* and *Villadia.*

CRATAEGUS L. HAWTHORN, THORN, THORN APPLE, RED HAW. *Rosaceae.* Mostly thorny, deciduous shrubs or small trees, native to N. Temp. Zone, often horizontally branched; lvs. alt., toothed or lobed; fls. white or rarely red, in corymbs, blooming in spring and early summer; fr. a small pome with 5 or fewer 1-seeded nutlets. About 1,000 spp. have been proposed, but the actual number is far below that, since many of them are apomicts.

Hawthorns are likely to be transplanted from the wild, being attractive in habit, in bloom, and in fruit. Most are hardy north. They prefer sunny locations and limestone or rich loamy soils. Propagated by seeds sown when ripe or stratified; seeds should be separated from the pulp by allowing the fruit to decay or by soaking the fruit in water. They will take two years or more to germinate, and should be sown in flats and kept in a cool cellar. Rare sorts may be budded or grafted on stock of *C. oxyacanthoides* or other species.

altaica (Loud.) J. Lange. Small tree, thorns few, about 2 in. long; lvs. ovate, deeply lobed and sharply serrate, bright green, to about 2 in. long; fr. yellow, spherical, 5/16 in. in diam. Cent. Asia. Zone 4.

ambigua C. A. Mey. Young branchlets more or less hairy, later glabrous and more or less purplish, thorns few, about 3/8 in. long; lvs. to 2½ in. long, deeply and narrowly 4–7-lobed, lobes with few apical, sharp teeth, glabrate; fls. 5/8 in. in diam., 12–18, pedicels and calyx glabrous, anthers red. Se. Russia. Zone 6.

apiifolia: *C. Marshallii.*

aprica Beadle. Shrubby or arborescent, to 20 ft., branchlets at first tinged red, villous, later ashy-gray and glabrous, thorns thin, 1–1½ in. long; lvs. broadly obovate to ovate, often somewhat lobed at apex, 1–1¼ in. long, serrate mostly above the middle; fls. 3–6, about ¾ in. across, sepals glabrous, glandular-serrulate, stamens 10; fr. orange-red, ½ in. in diam. Va. and Tenn., s. to Ga., Ala. Zone 6.

arkansana Sarg. To 20 ft., unarmed or with few thorns to ½ in. long; lvs. oblong-ovate to ovate, shallow-lobed, 2–3 in. long; fls. 1 in. across, pedicels pubescent, stamens 20; fr. subglobose, bright red, ¾–1 in. in diam. Ark.

arnoldiana Sarg. To 20 ft., with zigzag brs., thorns abundant, 2–3 in. long; lvs. broadly ovate, 1½–2 in. long, with 3–5, pointed, small, sharply toothed lobes on each side, pubescent beneath; fls. ¾ in. wide, many, in hairy corymbs, stamens 10; fr. round, bright red, 5/8 in. in diam. Conn., e. Mass.

Azarolus L. AZAROLE. Tree, to 30 ft., thorns none or few; lvs. 1½–3 in. long, deeply 3–5-lobed, pubescent and grayish beneath; fls. few, ½ in. across, stamens 20, anthers purple; fr. edible, orange-red to yellow, ¾ in. long. E. Medit. region. Zone 7.

biltmoreana Beadle [*C. coccinea* of auth. in part, not L.]. Like *C. Boyntonii,* but more pubescent; lvs. sharply serrate; fr. full orange or red. Vt., N.C., w. to Mo., Ark.

Boyntonii Beadle. Stout shrub or tree, to 25 ft. with nearly thornless brs. or with stout thorns to 1½ in. long; lvs. ovate or elliptic, simply or double serrate nearly to the base, usually with 3–4 pairs of shallow lateral lobes; fls. mostly 3–10, ½–¾ in. across; fr. 5/16–½ in. in diam., red or blotched red. S. N.Y. to Ala.

Calpodendron (J. F. Ehrh.) Medic. [*C. tomentosa* of auth., not L.]. BLACKTHORN, PEAR T. To 20 ft., thorns, if present, to 1½ in.; lvs. mostly ovate, to 5 in. long, usually with 3–5 pairs of shallow, often asymmetric lateral lobes, pubescent beneath; fls. about ½ in. wide, stamens about 20, anthers mostly pink; fr. oblong or obovoid, dull orange-red, ½ in. long. Ont. and Minn., s. to Ga., Mo. Zone 5.

Canbyi Sarg. Shrub or small tree, to 20 ft., thorns 1 in. long or more; lvs. oblong-obovate or elliptic, to 2½ in. long, sharply serrate, often slightly lobed, glabrous; fls. 5/8 in. wide, several, in glabrous corymbs, stamens 10–20, anthers pink; fr. bright red, 5/16 in. in diam. Penn., Del., Md.

×**Carrierei:** *C.* ×*Lavallei.*

cerronis: *C. erythropoda.*

chlorosarca Maxim. Small tree of pyramidal habit, mostly unarmed, thorns, if present, to ½ in. long; lvs. triangular to broadly ovate, 2–4 in. long, with 3–5 pairs of short, broad, serrate lobes, at first pubescent above and beneath, later glabrous above; fls. 3/8 in. across, in corymbs 1½–3 in. across, stamens 20; fr. black. E. Asia. Zone 2.

chrysocarpa Ashe. Intricately branched, to 20 ft., thorns many, to 1½ in. long; lvs. 1–2 in. long, ovate or elliptic to nearly orbicular, serrate except near base, with 3–4 pairs of small, triangular, lateral lobes; fls. ½ in. across or more, in villous corymbs, sepals serrate, stamens about 10, anthers pale; fr. yellow to red. Nfld. to Man., s. to N.Y. and New Mex. Zone 4. Var. **phoenicea** Palmer [*C. rotundifolia* Moench, not Lam.]. Fr. dark red or purplish-red. Nov. Sc. and N.Y., w. to Wisc.

coccinea: see *C. biltmoreana* and *C. pedicellata.*

coccinoides Ashe. Tree, to 20 ft., usually very thorny; lvs. broadly ovate, glabrous, shallowly lobed, often crisped on margins; fls. ½–5/8 in. across, 4–7, in glabrous corymbs, stamens 20, anthers pink; fr. often angular, ½–5/8 in. in diam. Ill., w. to Kans., Ark. Zone 6. Some material offered under this name may be *C. Putnamiana.*

collina Chapm. Tree, to 25 ft., thorns long; lvs. mostly obovate, usually not lobed, serrate except near the base, 1–3 in. long; fls. 5/8–

¾ in. across, few, stamens 10–15, anthers pale; fr. subglobose, 5/16 in. in diam., dull red. Va. to S.C., w. to Kans., Okla. Zone 6.

coloradensis: *C. succulenta.*

colorata: *C. macrosperma.*

columbiana T. J. Howell. Shrub or small tree, to 16 ft., thorns stout, 1–2 in. long; lvs. cuneate-obovate, 1–2 in. long, usually 5–9-lobed, irregularly serrate above the more or less entire, cuneate base, sparingly pubescent; corymb subglabrous, many-fld.; fr. purple or red. B.C. to n. Calif.

compta Sarg. Shrub or tree, to 20 ft., thorns slender; lvs. broadly ovate, slightly lobed, doubly serrate, with 3–5 pairs of acute, spreading, lateral lobes, glaucous beneath, to 3 in. long; fls. ¾ in. across, stamens 10, anthers red; fr. crimson, pale-dotted, obovoid, ½ in. long. S. Ont., s. to Mich. and Penn.

cordata: *C. Phaenopyrum.*

crus-galli L. COCKSPUR, COCKSPUR THORN. To 30 ft., broad-crowned, thorns to 3 in. long; lvs. obovate, cuneate at base, rounded apically, 1–3 in. long, glabrous, leathery, toothed; fls. to 5/8 in. across, stamens 10 or fewer; fr. dull red, ½ in. long. Que. to Mich., s. to N.C. Zone 5. Cv. 'Splendens': *C.* ×*prunifolia.*

cuneata Siebold. Shrubby, to 5 ft., densely branched, thorns slender, ¼ in. long; lvs. obovate to oblong, cuneate at base, cut and irregularly serrate, often 3-lobed at apex, pubescent beneath; fls. ½ in. across, few; fr. round to pear-shaped, red, small. Japan, China. Zone 6.

diffusa Sarg. To 30 ft., thorns to 1½ in. long; lvs. shallowly lobed, pale beneath, to 2 in. long; fls. ½ in. across; fr. dull red, about ½ in. in diam. New Hamp. to N.Y.

Douglasii Lindl. Spreading underground, to 35 ft. high, thorns few, to 1 in. long; lvs. broadly ovate, 1–3 in. long, serrate and slightly lobed, pubescent beneath on midrib; fls. 3/8 in. across, 10–20, in glabrous corymbs, stamens 20; fr. short-ellipsoid, deep red, then darker, ½ in. long. B.C. to Calif. and Minn. Zone 5. Fr. useful for jellies.

Dunbarii Sarg. Stout shrub, to 12 ft., usually thorny; lvs. ovate to rounded, with 3–4 pairs of shallow, lateral lobes, almost glabrous; fls. 5/8 in. across, in small compact glabrous corymbs, anthers about 10, red; fr. 3/8–5/8 in. in diam. crimson. W. N.Y.

Eganii: *C. macrosperma.*

Ellwangerana: *C. pedicellata* var.

erythropoda Ashe [*C. cerronis* A. Nels.]. Arborescent, to 16 ft., branchlets glabrous, thorns 1–1½ in. long; lvs. ovate to elliptic-ovate, 1–3 in. long, cuneate at base, irregularly serrate; corymbs glabrous; anthers few, pink to purple; fr. red to blackish, 5/16 in. in diam. Wyo., s. to New Mex. and Ariz.

flabellata (Spach) Kirchn. To 25 ft., branchlets slender, thorny; glabrous; lvs. ovate to rhombic, sharply serrate, with 4–6 pairs of small, acuminate lateral lobes; fls. ¾ in. across, in pubescent corymbs, anthers pink, 10 or fewer; fr. crimson, oblong or rounded. Que. Zone 4.

flava Ait. SUMMER HAW, YELLOW-FRUITED THORN. To 20 ft., brs. flexuous, thorny, more or less villous when young; lvs. ovate to elliptic, glandular-serrate, often trilobate or with 2–3 pairs of lateral lobes; fls. 5/8 in. across, mostly 5–7 in number, stamens mostly 10, anthers red; fr. oblong or pear-shaped, green or yellow, ½ in. in diam. Va. to Fla. Fr. useful for jellies.

Fontanesiana (Spach) Steud. Like *C. crus-galli,* but thorns fewer and to 1½ in. long; lvs. thinner, elliptic-lanceolate; stamens 16–18; fr. red, or green with red. Penn. Zone 6.

×**grignonensis** Mouill.: *C. pubescens* ×? Lvs. with 2–4 pairs of slightly wavy-toothed lobes; fr. nearly globose, 5/8 in. in diam., red.

hupehensis Sarg. To 16 ft., thorns 5/8 in. long; lvs. to 4 in. long, ovate to oblong-ovate, acuminate, serrate with glandular, incurved teeth, 3–4-lobed toward apex; fls. to ½ in. across, many, glabrous, anthers 20, red; fr. dark red, to 1 in. in diam. W. China. Fr. edible.

intricata J. Lange. Shrub, 3–10 ft., thorns curved, 1–1½ in. long; lvs. oblong-ovate to ovate, shallowly and sharply lobed, to 3 in. long; fls. 5/8 in. across, in glabrous corymbs, sepals gland-toothed, anthers whitish, 10; fr. dull red-brown, to ½ in. in diam. Mass. to Mich., s. to N.C. and Ind.

Jackii Sarg. Arborescent, very thorny; lvs. oblong-obovate or ovate, serrate nearly to the base, slightly lobed near the middle; fls. 5/8 in. across, in slightly villous corymbs, sepals glandular-serrate, anthers 5–10, pale yellow; fr. dull, dark red, 3/8 in. in diam. Que.

laevigata (Poir.) DC. [*C. oxyacantha* of auth., not L.; *C. oxyacanthoides* Thuill.]. ENGLISH H., QUICK-SET T. WHITE T. To 25 ft., largely glabrous, thorny; lvs. obovate in outline, to 2 in. long, 3–5-lobed, lobes rarely reaching halfway to the midrib, usually rounded in outline, serrate; fls. few, to about 10, ½ in. across, anthers pink or purple; fr. to ½ in. in diam., deep red. Eur., N. Afr., w. Asia. Zone 5. Cvs. include:

'Alba', fls. white; 'Coccinea Plena': 'Paulii'; 'Masekii', fls. delicate pink on a white ground; 'Paulii' [cvs. 'Splendens'; 'Coccinea Plena'], fls. bright scarlet, double; 'Plena', fls. double, white; 'Punicea', fls. single, carmine with white center; 'Rosea', fls. single, bright pink, white in center; 'Splendens': 'Paulii'.

×Lavallei Herincq [*C.* × *Carrierei* Vauv.; *C. crus-galli* × *C. pubescens*]. To 20 ft., thorns to 2 in. long; lvs. narrow-elliptic, acute at both ends, 2–4 in. long, irregularly serrate, dark green and finally glabrous above, pubescent beneath; fls. ¾ in. across, anthers pink; fr. ellipsoid, ⅝ in. long, orange-red. Zone 5.

Mackenzii Sarg. To 20 ft., thorny; lvs. ovate to triangular, sharply and deeply serrate, with 3–4 pairs of acute, triangular, lateral lobes; fls. to ¾ in. in diam., few, in glabrous corymbs, anthers about 20, pink; fr. dull red, pruinose, ½ in. in diam. Ky., w. to Iowa and Okla.

macracantha: *C. succulenta* var.

macrantha: a listed name of no botanical standing; perhaps meant for *C. macracantha.*

macrosperma Ashe [*C. colorata* Sarg.; *C. Eganii* Ashe]. To 25 ft., thorns to 1½ in. long; lvs. ovate to elliptic, sharply serrate, with about 5 pairs of broad, triangular, lateral lobes; fls. ⅝ in. across, mostly 5–12, in glabrous corymbs, anthers red, 10 or fewer; fr. obovoid to oblong, ⁵⁄₁₆–⅝ in. long, bright red. S. Canada and Wisc., s. to N.C., Tenn., Ill.

Marshallii Eggl. [*C. apiifolia* (Marsh.) Michx., not Medic.]. To 25 ft., thorny to scarcely so; lvs. to 1½ in. long, broadly ovate to triangular-ovate, deeply incised into 2–3 pairs of coarsely toothed lobes; fls. many, in pubescent corymbs, anthers about 10, red; fr. oblong to obovoid, ⁵⁄₁₆ in. long, bright red. Va. to Fla. and Tex., w. to Mo. Zone 6.

mercerensis Sarg. To 15 ft.; lvs. oblong-obovate to elliptic, undivided or rarely with 2–4 pairs of shallow lateral lobes above the middle, glabrous; fls. few, ½ in. across, in glabrous corymbs, anthers about 10, white; fr. orange-red, round, ½ in. in diam. W. Va., Md., Tenn. Cv. 'Sargentii' is listed.

mollis (Torr. & A. Gray) Scheele. To 35 ft., with or without thorns; lvs. to 4 in. long, mostly ovate or triangular, sharply or coarsely serrate, usually with 4–5 pairs of lateral lobes, pubescent beneath; fls. to 1 in. across, in tomentose corymbs, anthers about 20; fr. subglobose, ½–¾ in. in diam., red, pubescent toward the ends. Ont. and Minn., s. to Ala., Ark., and Miss. Zone 5. Fr. useful for jellies.

monogyna Jacq. ENGLISH H. To 30 ft., thorns to 1 in. long; lvs. ovate to obovate, deeply 3–7-lobed, lobes more or less entire; fls. to ½ in. across, many, in glabrous corymbs, anthers red, about 20; fr. bright red, ⁵⁄₁₆ in. in diam. Eur., N. Afr., Asia. Zone 5. Cvs. include: 'Alba', fls. white; 'Biflora' [cv. 'Praecox'], GLASTONBURY T., blooming in midwinter in mild seasons or climates, and also in spring, lvs. gray-felty beneath; 'Compacta', thornless, dense, compact; 'Filicifolia': 'Pteridifolia'; 'Pendula', branchlets pendulous; 'Praecox': 'Biflora'; 'Pteridifolia' [cv. 'Filicifolia'], lvs. deeply lobed; 'Rosea', fls. pink; 'Stricta', fastigiate.

nitida (Engelm.) Sarg. To 25 ft., often almost thornless; lvs. elliptic-lanceolate, 1–3 in. long, coarsely serrate to weakly lobed; fls. ¾ in. across; fr. dull red, ½ in. in diam. Ohio to Mo. and Ark. Zone 5.

Oxyacantha: see *C. laevigata.*

pedicellata Sarg. [*C. coccinea* of auth., in part, not L.]. Tree, to 25 ft., thorny, mature shoots glabrous; lvs. oblong-ovate to elliptic, sharply serrate nearly to the base, with 4–5 pairs of acute, shallow, lateral lobes; fls. ¾ in. across, many, in somewhat villous corymbs, stamens about 10, with reddish anthers; fr. bright red, oblong to obovoid, to ⅜ in. in diam. New Eng., Ont., w. to Ind., Ill. Zone 5. Var. **Ellwangerana** (Sarg.) Eggl. [*C. Ellwangerana* Sarg.]. Lvs. more pubescent; fls. many; fr. somewhat pubescent at ends. Ont. and Mich. to Penn. Zone 5.

peregrina Sarg. Tree, to 16 ft.; lvs. broadly ovate, to about 5 in. long, with 4–6 pairs of narrow lobes, pubescent beneath; fls. rather many, ¾ in. across, in villous corymbs; fr. dull purple, ½–1 in. long. Probably w. Asia, but possible a hybrid of *C. mollis.*

persistens Sarg. Like *C. crus-galli* and possible a hybrid of it, tree, to 12 ft.; lvs. elliptic to obovate, to 3 in. long, serrate, remaining green into winter; fls. ¾ in. across, stamens 15–20; fr. persistent, crimson, dotted, ⅝ in. in diam. Origin unknown. Zone 5.

Phaenopyrum (L.f.) Medic. [*C. cordata* Ait.]. WASHINGTON T. Tree, to 25 ft.; lvs. mostly ovate, irregularly serrate, often trilobate or with 2–3 pairs of spreading lateral lobes, the lowest enlarged; fls. ½ in. across, anthers pale yellow, about 20; fr. subglobose, ¼ in. in diam. bright red, lustrous. Penn. to Fla., w. to Mo. and Ark. Zone 5. Cv. 'Fastigiata'. Fastigiate.

pinnatifida Bunge. To 20 ft., thorns few or short; lvs. triangular-ovate, 2–4 in. long, pinnately 5–9-lobed, dark green above, shining on

both sides; fls. few, ⅝ in. across; fr. light red, finely dotted, to ¾ in. long. Ne. Asia. Zone 6.

pruinosa (H. L. Wendl.) C. Koch. To 25 ft., thorny, intricately branched; lvs. ovate, rounded or abruptly narrowed at base, sharply serrate, usually with 3–5 pairs of shallow lobes, glabrous, bluish-green; fls. 5–10, glabrous, to ¾ in. across, anthers usually pink, about 20; fr. often slightly angled, ½ in. in diam., dull crimson or green and dark-dotted, pruinose, with a prominent, elevated calyx. Nfld. to Wisc., s. to N.C. and Ark. Zone 5.

×**prunifolia** (Lam.) Pers. [*C. crus-galli* cv. 'Splendens']: ? *C. crus-galli* × *C. macracantha*. Shrub or small tree; lvs. broadly elliptic, to 3 in. long, sharply serrate, shining, dark green; fls. in dense, hairy, many-fld. corymbs, anthers pink; fr. red. Known in cult. only. Zone 6.

pubescens (HBK) Steud. forma **stipulacea** (Loud.) Stapf. To 30 ft., with little pubescence and few thorns; lvs. nearly elliptic to obovate, cuneate at base, serrate-crenate, 1½–3¼ in. long, stipules usually leafy; fls. ¾ in. across, 6–15, in mostly villous corymbs, stamens 15–20; fr. short-pear-shaped to globose, to 1 in. in diam., yellow, shading into orange, edible. Mex. Zone 7?

punctata Jacq. To 30 ft., with stout, usually thorny branchlets; lvs. mostly obovate, serrate above the middle, slightly lobed toward apex, 2–4 in. long, pubescent beneath; fls. ½ in. across, many, in pubescent corymbs, anthers red or yellow, about 20; fr. round, dull red, to ¾ in. in diam. E. Canada to Ky., w. to Ind., and Iowa. Zone 5.

punicea: a listed name of no botanical standing, probably for *C. laevigata* cv. 'Punicea'.

Putnamiana Sarg. To 30 ft., with slender, thorny, glabrous branchlets; lvs. triangular or broadly ovate, sharply serrate, with 3–4 pairs of shallow, lateral lobes, glabrous when mature; fls. to ¾ in. across, few, anthers red; fr. bright red, often slightly angular, ½ in. in diam., with a broad, nearly sessile calyx. Ohio, Ky., Ind., Ill. Some material offered as *C. coccinoides* may be this sp.

Pyracantha: *Pyracantha coccinea.*

rivularis Nutt. To 12 ft., glabrous; lvs. mostly 1½–3 in. long, elliptic to lanceolate, scarcely if at all lobed, doubly serrate, pale beneath; fls. ½ in. across, anthers about 10, whitish to rose or purple; fr. crimson to blackish, ⅜ in. in diam. Wyo. to Idaho, New Mex., Ariz., Nev.

rotundifolia: see *C. chrysocarpa* var. *phoenicea.*

sanguinea Pall. To 22 ft., branchlets purple-brown, mostly unarmed; lvs. rhombic-ovate to broadly ovate, 2–3 in. long, with 2–3 pairs of short, sharply serrate lobes, pubescent; fls. ⅝ in. across, in small, dense clusters, anthers purple, 20; fr. bright red, globose, ⅜ in. in diam. E. Siberia. Zone 4.

Smithiana: a listed name of no botanical standing; possibly *C. uniflora.*

spathulata Michx. To 25 ft., branchlets usually thorny, stoutish; lvs. narrowly obovate, mostly less than 1 in. long, with rounded teeth or small lobes above the middle, glabrous at maturity; fls. ½ in. across, many, in compact, glabrous corymbs, anthers pale yellow, about 20; fr. subglobose, ¼ in. in diam., red. Va. to Fla., w. to Mo. and Tex. Zone 6.

submollis Sarg. To 30 ft., branchlets flexuous, thorny, villous when young; lvs. ovate to elliptic, coarsely serrate, with 4–5 pairs of shallow lobes, tomentose beneath when young, later glabrous; fls. to 1 in. across, many, in loose, tomentose corymbs, anthers 10 or fewer, white or pale yellow; fr. pear-shaped, ½ in. in diam., bright red. E. Canada to N.Y. Zone 5.

succulenta Link [*C. coloradensis* A. Nels.]. To 25 ft., branchlets usually thorny, soon glabrous; lvs. elliptic to ovate, sharply serrate, leathery, glabrous, lustrous, with impressed veins, to 3 in. long, with 4–5 pairs of shallow lobes; fls. ½–¾ in. across, many, anthers mostly pink, about 20; fr. bright red, subglobose, to ½ in. in diam. Se. Canada to Penn., w. to Colo. and Ariz. Zone 4. Var. **macracantha** (Lodd.) Eggl. [*C. macracantha* Lodd.]. Stamens about 10; fr. hard and dry until late in the season. Se. Canada to New Engl., w. to Minn.

tanacetifolia (Lam.) Pers. Shrub or small tree, to 40 ft., branchlets tomentose when young; lvs. rhombic-ovate, 1 in. long, with 5–7 narrow lobes, glandular-serrate, villous-pubescent on both sides; fls. usually 5–8, to 1 in. across; fr. orange-yellow, 1 in. in diam. W. Asia. Zone 6.

tomentosa: see *C. Calpodendron.*

uniflora Muenchh. Slender shrub, to 5 ft., branchlets flexuous, thorny, villous when young; lvs. obovate to oblong or elliptic, serrate, sometimes obscurely lobed above the middle; fl. solitary or rarely more, to ½ in. across, anthers 20 or more, pale; fr. ½ in. in diam., red to greenish-yellow. N.Y. to Fla., w. to Ark. and Tex. Zone 7.

viridis L. Tree, to 40 ft., thorns to 1½ in. long; lvs. ovate to lanceolate-elliptic, to 2½ in. long, often asymmetrical, thin, glabrous at maturity except for tufts of tomentum in the axils of veins beneath;

fls. to nearly ½ in. across, many, in glabrous corymbs, stamens about 20, anthers yellowish to red; fr. red to orange-red, to ⁵⁄₁₆ in. in diam. Va. to Fla., w. to Ill., Mo., Tex. Zone 5.

Wattiana Hemsl. & Lace. Like *C. sanguinea*, the young branchlets reddish-brown, with or without short thorns; lvs. ovate, 2–3½ in. long, glabrous, 3–5-lobed on each side; anthers whitish, 15–20; fr. ⅜ in. in diam., orange-yellow. N. China to Baluchistan. Zone 6.

CRATEVA L. GARLIC PEAR. *Capparaceae*. About 15 spp. of trop. shrubs or trees; lvs. 3-foliolate, palmately compound; fls. large, yellowish, in bractless corymbs, stamens 8–50; fr. a large, round berry with fleshy pulp, seeds many.

Adansonii: *C. religiosa.*

religiosa G. Forst. [*C. Adansonii* DC.]. SACRED G. P. Small tree, brs. with striking white spots; lvs. at ends of brs., compound, glabrous, lfts. 3, lanceolate, 3–5 in. long; fls. 2 in. across, yellow to purplish, stamens many, pistil slender-stalked; fr. a large spotted berry with yellow pulp, 1½–2½ in. in diam., on long, thick stipe, seeds ¼ in. long. Old World tropics, where commonly cult. Not hardy north; prop. by cuttings in sand.

CRATOXYLUM Blume. *Hypericaceae*. About 10–12 spp. of trees or shrubs, native to trop. Asia; lvs. entire, usually papery; fls. white or pink, in axillary or terminal cymes, sepals and petals 5, stamens usually in 3 bundles; fr. a caps., seeds many, winged. Related to *Hypericum*, but caps. dehiscing loculicidally and seeds winged.

polyanthum Korth. [*Hypericum pulchellum* Wallich]. Aromatic shrub, branchlets flattened; lvs. elliptic-oblong, to 4 in. long but usually less, translucent-dotted and black-dotted beneath; cymes axillary, 1–3-fld.; fls. pink, to ½ in. across; seeds 1-winged, about ¼ in. long. China to Borneo.

CRAWFURDIA Wallich. *Gentianaceae*. About 10 spp. of per. herbs of e. Asia, with sts. climbing, spirally twisted; lvs. opp.; fls. 1–3, 4–5-merous, calyx tubular, corolla campanulate or funnelform, stamens straight, filaments of equal length, the free part thickened toward base; fr. a caps., seeds compressed, winged.

Blumei: see *Tripterospermum japonicum.*

japonica: *Tripterospermum japonicum.*

speciosa Wallich. [*Gentiana speciosa* (Wallich) Marq.]. Lvs. elliptic, to 3 in. long, acuminate, 3-nerved; fls. 1–3 in cymes, on slender pedicels, calyx tube to ½ in. long, teeth about ⅛ in. long, corolla to 1½ in. long, pleated. Himalayas.

trinervis: *Tripterospermum japonicum.*

✕CREMNERIA Moran. *Cremnophila✕ Echeveria. Crassulaceae*

expatriata (Rose) Moran [*Echeveria ✕expatriata* Rose]: *C. linguifolia ✕ E. microcalyx*. Glabrous, sts. to 6 in.; lvs. 30–50, oblanceolate-spatulate, 1–1½ in. long, to ½ in. wide, broadly acute, turgid, glaucous; fl. sts. horizontal to ascending, 6–12 in., the lvs. easily detached and rooting, infl. of 5–9 cincinni, each 1–6-fld., pedicels to ⁵⁄₁₆ in. long; sepals ascending, nearly equal, ³⁄₁₆ in. long, corolla pink, ⁵⁄₁₆ in. long. Autumn to spring.

mutabilis (Deleuil ex E. Morr.) Moran [*Echeveria ✕ mutabilis* Deleuil ex E. Morr.]: *C. linguifolia ✕ E. ?carnicolor*. Glabrous, sts. to 1 ft.; lvs. 25–40, obovate-spatulate, 2–5 in. long, mucronate, green to violet, low-papillose; fl. st. trailing, to 30 in., with several short cincinni of 1–5 fls., pedicels ¼ in. long; sepals erect, nearly equal, ⁵⁄₁₆ in. long, corolla light yellow to rose, ⅜ in. long.

scaphylla (Deleuil ex E. Morr.) Moran [*Echeveria ✕scaphophylla* Hort. ex A. Berger; *E. ✕ scaphylla* Deleuil ex E. Morr.]: *C. linguifolia ✕ E. agavoides*. Glabrous, sts. short, decumbent in age; rosettes dense, lvs. 60–100, oblong-lanceolate, about 3 in. long and 1¼ in. wide, acute, green, turgid but concave above; fl. st. pendent, cincinni 8–12, each 5–8-fld.; sepals appressed, unequal, ³⁄₁₆ in. long, corolla pale yellow, ⅜ in. long.

CREMNOPHILA Rose. *Crassulaceae*. Two spp. of glabrous, succulent, per. herbs of Mex., sts. trailing; lvs. in a rosette, turgid, with rounded margins; fl. st. axillary, deciduous, single fls. and short cincinni jointed to backward-pointing projections at nodes of flexuous infl. axis; fls. 5-merous, sepals appressed to corolla, unequal, stamens 10. Allied to *Echeveria* but infl. a narrow, spreading to nodding thyrse and petals thin, either induplicate-valvate or separate and rotate.

For culture see *Succulents.*

linguifolia (Lem.) Moran [*Echeveria linguifolia* Lem.]. Lvs. 15–40, crowded or separated, obovate to oblong-spatulate, 1½–4 in. long, ¾–2 in. wide, ½ in. thick, obtuse to rounded, green; infl. pendent, open; petals greenish-white, erect, ⅜ in. long, induplicate-valvate below. Winter, spring.

nutans Rose [*Sedum Cremnophila* R. T. Clausen; *S. nutans* Rose, not Haw.]. Lvs. 20-25, crowded, grayish, much as in *C. linguifolia* or more rhombic; infl. stiffly ascending to declined, dense; petals yellow, rotate, ¼ in. long, overlapping in bud. Winter.

CREPIS Vaill. *Compositae* (Cichorium Tribe). About 200 spp. of ann., bien., and per. herbs with milky sap, widely distributed in the N. Hemisphere; lvs. often in a basal rosette, entire, toothed, or pinnately lobed; fl. heads solitary to panicled, involucral bracts in 2 rows, the outer shorter than the inner; fls. all ligulate, bisexual, yellow, orange, pink, or white; achenes mostly cylindrical, beaked or beakless, pappus of simple capillary bristles.

A few grown in the flower garden; propagated by seeds.

aurea (L.) Cass. Rhizomatous per., to 12 in.; lvs. all basal, obovate to oblanceolate, dentate to pinnatifid, glabrous; heads solitary or rarely 2–3 on leafless, scapelike sts.; fls. yellow, orange, or reddish. Mts., s. Eur., Asia Minor.

barbata: *Tolpis barbata.*

blattarioides (L.) Vill. Per., to 20 in., with a woody taproot; basal lvs. oblanceolate, to 6 in. long, dentate, petioled, disappearing early, the upper st. lvs. lanceolate, clasping, auriculate; heads 1–5 in a cyme, the outer and the hairy inner involucral bracts nearly equal; fls. golden-yellow, the tube glabrous. Mts., Eur.

conyzifolia (Gouan) Dalla Torre. Differs from *C. blattarioides* chiefly in its persistent, often pinnatifid basal lvs., the outer involucral bracts half as long as the inner, and the tube of the fl. pubescent. Mts., s. Eur., e. Asia.

hokkaidoensis Babc. Dandelionlike, rhizomatous per., to 8 in.; basal lvs. lanceolate, pinnately lobed, to 5 in. long, pubescent, petioled, st. lvs. only 1–2, sessile; heads solitary or 2 on a st.; fls. yellow, the tube pubescent. Mts., Japan.

incana Sibth. & Sm. Per., to 6 in., with woody taproot; basal lvs. oblanceolate, pinnately divided and toothed, to 5 in. long, pubescent, the st. lvs. few, reduced, sessile; sts. several, simple or divaricately branched, 1–4-headed; involucre tomentose, outer bracts half as long as the inner; fls. magenta-pink. Mts., s. Greece.

Jacquinii Tausch. Rhizomatous per., to 10 in.; basal lvs. oblanceolate to linear, pinnately parted, to 6 in. long, glabrous except for puberulent midrib, st. lvs. several, similar but smaller; sts. scapelike or branched, 1–6-headed, tomentose; fls. yellow, the tube glabrous. European Alps.

occidentalis Nutt. Gray-tomentose per., to 10 in. or more, taprooted; basal lvs. elliptic, sinuately dentate to deeply pinnatifid, to 1 ft. long, st. lvs. similar, smaller, sessile; sts. branched, with 1–20 cymose heads; fls. yellow, the tube pubescent. Sw. Canada, w. U.S.

paludosa (L.) Moench. Rhizomatous per., to 40 in.; basal lvs. few, soon disappearing, oblanceolate, to 10 in. long, petioled, dentate, glabrous, st. lvs. several, remote, the upper lanceolate, clasping, auriculate; st. erect, branched above in a few-headed cyme; heads long-peduncled; fls. yellow, the tube glabrous. Eur., w. Siberia.

pannonica (Jacq.) C. Koch. Per., to 4 ft., taprooted; basal lvs. oblanceolate to elliptic, to 12 in. long, dentate, minutely setose and glandular-puberulent, petioled, st. lvs. many, the upper lanceolate, sessile; st. erect, leafy, paniled above, many-headed; fls. yellow, the tube pubescent. Cent. and w. Eur. to e. Asia.

rubra L. Ann., to 10–16 in., taprooted; basal lvs. oblanceolate, dentate to pinnatifid, to 6 in. long, pubescent, st. lvs. few, mostly small and bractlike; sts. scapelike or with 1–2 brs. from the base, with 1 or few heads 1½ in. across; fls. pink or white, the tube sparsely pubescent. E. Eur. Frequently cult., and blooming quickly from seed. Cv. 'Alba'. Fls. white. Cv. 'Rosea'. Fls. pink.

sibirica L. Per., to 5 ft., with woody rhizome; basal lvs. spatulate, to 16 in. long, dentate, puberulent to glabrescent, wing-petioled, mostly disappearing early, st. lvs. several, successively reduced in size upward along the st., the upper sessile; st. erect, branched, at summit, few-headed; fls. yellow, the tube pubescent. E. Eur.

CRESCENTIA L. *Bignoniaceae*. One sp., a native to trop. Amer.; lvs. alt. or clustered at the nodes, simple; fls. in clusters or solitary, borne on trunk and main brs., calyx 2-parted or deeply 5-lobed, corolla tubular, 5-lobed, stamens 4; fr. hard-shelled, globose.

Grown in the tropics as an ornamental and for the fruits which are widely used for utensils.

alata: *Parmentiera alata.*

Cujete L. CALABASH TREE, CALABASH. To 40 ft., with spreading brs. and broad head; lvs. nearly sessile, clustered at nodes, oblanceolate, to 6 in. long; fls. to 2 in. long, corolla yellowish with red or purple veins, lobes lacerate; fr. to 1 ft. across or more, smooth, resembling a gourd. Trop. Amer.

latifolia: *Enallagma latifolia.*

ovata: *Enallagma latifolia.*

CRESS. Several plants of the mustard family, Cruciferae, are known as cress, the piquant basal leaves used as salad, seasoning, or garnishing, but the usual kinds are of three very unlike genera and they should not be confused. See also *Cardamine* for bitter cress.

The usual or common garden cress is a pepper grass, *Lepidium sativum.* It is a quick-growing, hardy, upright annual, native to western Asia but now sometimes escaped as a weed. Seeds may be sown in the open as soon as the ground can be made ready, usually in drills about 1 foot apart; leaves may be had in five to eight weeks, and new ones arise if the cutting is not too close. New sowings. may be made every two or three weeks for succession, although the product is not so much prized in midsummer, and the plants quickly run to seed in hot weather. In August, sowings may be begun for autumn use in the North, while in mild regions plantings may be made at intervals during autumn and winter. The curled variety is most prized for garnishing, like parsley. Cress thrives in any good garden soil, one retentive of moisture being preferable.

Upland cress, sometimes called winter cress, is a hardy biennial, *Barbarea verna,* native to Europe and sometimes run wild in this country. Seeds of it may be sown in very early spring in the open, and considerable tufts of leaves are formed by midsummer or a little later; if left in the ground, the plant persists through the winter even in the northern states and in the spring goes to seed. A closely related plant is the common weedy yellow rocket or winter cress, *B. vulgaris,* which is conspicuous in spring in fields with its light yellow flowers. Upland cress is a rather coarse plant, and is not largely grown.

Watercress, *Nasturtium officinale,* is a prostrate or trailing plant whose brittle soft shoots root in the water and mud. It is native to Europe and is extensively naturalized in this country and elsewhere. The plant thrives in ditches, pools, and stream margins, but it can be grown readily in frames or other places where the ground can be kept wet. It is usually propagated by planting pieces of the stems, although it is readily grown from seeds. It is perennial, hardy nearly everywhere, and takes care of itself when once established. It may be colonized in a clear, clean pool or stream.

×**CRINDONNA:** ×*AMARCRINUM.*

CRINODENDRON Mol. [*Tricuspidaria* Ruiz & Pav.]. *Elaeocarpaceae.* Three spp. of trees, native to Chile and Argentina; lvs. alt. or subopp., simple, toothed; fls. solitary, axillary, sepals united into a short, toothed, deciduous ring, petals 5, valvate in bud, 3–5-toothed at apex, stamens 15–20, disc large, hairy, ovary 3–5-celled, with many ovules; fr. a leathery caps., each cell 1–4-seeded.

Grown as ornamentals in southern Calif. and sometimes under glass. Propagated by cuttings of half-ripe wood in summer or autumn. Do best with shade, ample moisture, and acid humus. The cultivated species have been confused and may be expected under erroneous names, but are readily distinguished by the leaves and flowers.

dependens: *C. Patagua.*

Hookeranum C. Gay [*C. lanceolata* Miq.]. To 25 ft.; lvs. lanceolate, to 3 in. long, ⅝ in. wide, generally acute, coarsely toothed; fls. red, to 1 in. long, petals 3-toothed, ovary white-tomentose. Chile.

lanceolata: *C. Hookeranum.*

Patagua Mol. [*C. dependens* (Ruiz & Pav.) O. Kuntze; *Tricuspidaria dependens* Ruiz & Pav.]. To 45 ft. or more; lvs. oblong or ovate-oblong, to 2 in. long, 1 in. wide, generally obtuse, shallowly and closely

toothed; fls. white, waxy, to ¾ in. long, petals 3-toothed, ovary sparsely hairy. Chile.

×**CRINODONNA:** ×*AMARCRINUM.* ×**C. Corsii:** ×*A. memoria-Corsii.*

CRINUM L. CRINUM LILY, SPIDER L. *Amaryllidaceae.* About 130 spp. of per. herbs with tunicate bulbs, native to trop. and warm-temp. regions of both hemispheres; lvs. sword-shaped to strap-shaped, mostly spirally arranged; fls. few to many, in an umbel terminal on a solid scape and subtended by 2 separate spathe valves, perianth salverform or funnelform, with long, straight or curved tube, lobes nearly equal, linear to lanceolate, ovary inferior, cells with many ovules; fr. nearly spherical, irregularly dehiscent or indehescent, seeds globose, green.

Grown for the showy lilylike, white, pink, or red flowers; mostly spring and summer bloomers, seldom grown indoors in the North because they require much space, but popular outdoors in the southernmost states, and 2 or 3 of them are hardy in protected ground as far north as New York City. The large, showy flowers appear with the leaves or after the foliage is well grown.

Crinums are of simple culture. Some species are evergreen; in others the leaves die away in summer or autumn. If taken up for the winter, the plants are treated as dormant bulbs, or the evergreen species kept semidormant in pots or boxes. In the early part of the growing season the soil should be kept moist and well fertilized. In the South, crinums are generally planted outdoors and allowed to remain undisturbed, often forming large clumps.

Propagation is by natural offsets from the bulbs. Sometimes the plants fruit, and seeds may then be sown, although good flowering plants are not to be expected before 2 or 3 years.

amabile J. Donn. Plant stout, bulb rather small, with neck about 1 ft. long; lvs. many, 3–4 in. wide, 3–4 ft. long; scape 2–3 ft. high, 20–30-fld.; fls. very fragrant, salverform, bright red outside and lighter within, tube 3–4 in. long, straight, lobes nearly linear, ½ in. or so wide. Sumatra.

americanum L. SOUTHERN SWAMP C. Lvs. few, very narrow, 2 in. wide or less; scape 18–24 in., usually appearing before the lvs., 2–6-fld.; fls. white, showy, fragrant, sessile, salverform, tube straight, 4–5 in. long, lobes linear. Winter and spring. Wet places, Fla. to Tex.

amoenum Roxb. Bulb globose, to 3 in. in diam., with very short neck; lvs. 10–12, linear, nearly erect, to 2 ft. long, 2 in. wide, bright green; scape to 2 ft., 6–12-fld.; fls. sessile, tube greenish, 3–4 in. long, lobes lanceolate, spreading, 2–3 in. long, to ½ in. wide, filaments red. Himalayas.

asiaticum L. [*C. floridanum*]. Fraser ex Steud.?]. POISON BULB. Lvs. many, 3–4 in. wide, forming a large clump; umbel 20–50-fld.; fls. on very short pedicels, salverform, white with greenish tube, fragrant, lobes very narrow, drooping. Trop. Asia. Frequently cult. in Fla., Gulf Coast region, and Calif.

augustum Roxb. Plant sturdy, bulb sometimes 6 in. thick, with neck 1 ft. long; lvs. many, 3–4 in. wide; scape 2–3 ft., many-fld.; fls. similar to those of *C. amabile,* but deeper wine-red color outside, milder fragrance, and broader, lanceolate lobes. Mauritius and Seychelles.

bulbispermum (Burm.f.) Milne-Redh. & Schweick. [*C. capense* of auth., not Herb.; *C. longifolium* Thunb.; *Amaryllis bulbisperma* Burm.f.]. Lvs. usually less than 3 in. wide, scabrous or denticulate on the margin; umbel 6–12-fld.; fls. on pedicels 1–2 in. long, funnelform, tube 3–4 in. long, curved, lobes about as long, and to 1 in. wide, white flushed with red on exterior. S. Afr. Cv. 'Album'. Fls. white. Cv. 'Roseum'. Fls. pink. Probably the hardiest and most commonly cult. sp. in the U.S.; hardy in parts of the West, and much planted in the South.

campanulatum Herb. Lvs. linear, channelled, 3–4 ft.; umbels few-fld.; fls. on pedicels ½–1 in. long, funnelform, light red, tube curved, 2 in. long or less, limb bell-shaped, as long as tube, lobes coming together, obtuse. S. Afr.

capense: see *C. bulbispermum.*

caribaeum Bak. [*C. floridanum* Griseb.]. Lvs. strap-shaped, 9–10 in. long, 3–4 in. wide at middle; umbel 3–4-fld.; fls. on pedicels as long as ovary, salverform, tube straight, 3–4 in. long, lobes linear, spreading, nearly as long as tube. Jamaica, W. Indies.

erubescens Ait. Lvs. many, thin, strap-shaped, slightly scabrous on margin; umbel up to 12-fld.; fls. salverform, white inside and purplish outside, tube erect, 5–6 in. long, lobes half as long, recurving. Trop. Amer.

fimbriatulum Bak. Lvs. rather narrow, 2–3 ft. long, 2 in. wide, ciliate on margin; umbel few-fld.; fls. sessile, funnelform, greenish-white, with red stripe in center of the broad lobes, tube 4–5 in. long. Angola.

fimbriatum: a catalogue name, probably in error for *C. fimbriatulum.*

floridanum: see *C. asiaticum* and *C. caribaeum.*

giganteum: *C. Jagus.*

haarlemense: a listed name of no botanical standing; may be *C.* × *Powellii* cv.

insigne: *C. latifolium.*

Jagus (J. Thomps.) Dandy [*C. giganteum* Andr.]. Lvs. lanceolate, 3–4 in. wide at middle, 2–3 ft. long; umbel mostly 4–6-fld.; fls. pure white, funnelform, tube slender, curved, to 7 in. long. Trop. Afr.

jemenicum, jemense: *C. yemense.*

Kirkii Bak. Lvs. strap-shaped, 3–4 ft. long, 4–4½ in. wide; umbel about 12-fld.; fls. funnelform, tube somewhat curved, greenish, about 4 in. long, lobes longer, keeled, bright red. Zanzibar.

Krelagei: a listed name of no botanical standing, possibly for *C.* × *Powellii* cv. 'Krelagii'.

Kunthianum Roem. Lvs. strap-shaped, 2–3 ft. long; umbel few-fld.; fls. white, salverform, tube 7–8 in. long, slender, straight, lobes lanceolate, about 2½ in. long. Trop. Amer.

latifolium L. [*C. insigne* (Ker-Gawl.) Herb. ex Sweet; *C. speciosum* Herb.]. To 2 ft.; bulb large, elongate, to 6 in. in diam., with stout neck; lvs. numerous, strap-shaped, to 2¾ ft. long, 3–4 in. wide, scabrous on margins; umbel 10–20-fld.; fls. on very short pedicels, tube curved, cylindrical, green, 3–4 in. long, limb funnelform, lobes white keeled with red, to 4 in. long, 1 in. wide. Trop. Asia and Afr. Var. **zeylanicum** (L.) Hook.f. ex Trimen [*C. zeylanicum* L.]. MILK-AND-WINE LILY. Bulb to 8 in. in diam., short-necked; lvs. fewer, shorter, undulate; perianth lobes with dark purple keel. Trop. Asia.

Laurentii T. Durand & DeWild. Lvs. about 20, lanceolate, to 16 in. long, 3 in. wide, reflexed from base; peduncle to 1 ft., umbel 2–4-fld.; fls. nearly or quite sessile, tube greenish, to 6 in. long, curved at apex, lobes to 4 in. long, spreading. W. Afr.

longifolium: *C. bulbispermum.*

Moorei Hook.f. Plant larger than in *C. bulbispermum,* with lvs. much broader, smooth on margins; fls. 4 in. or more across, funnelform, rose-red. S. Afr. Cv. 'Album'. Fls. white. Cv. 'Roseum'. Fls. pink.

natans Bak. Aquatic; bulbs submersed; lvs. about 20, floating, strap-shaped, to 3 ft. long and 1½ in. wide, undulate; scape shorter than lvs., borne above the water, umbel 4–6-fld.; fls. nearly sessile, white tinged with purple, tube 5–6 in. long, twice as long as lobes, filaments purple. Sierra Leone to Cameroon.

parvum Bak.: not cult. in N. Amer.; *Ammocharis heterostyla* has been offered under this name.

pedunculatum R. Br. To 3 ft.; lvs. to 4 ft. long and 4–5 in. broad, glaucous, thick; umbel about 25-fld.; fls. on pedicels 1–1½ in. long, salverform, tube green, to 4 in. long, segms. linear, greenish-white, 2½ in. long. Australia.

podophyllum Bak. To 1 ft.; lvs. usually 5–6, oblanceolate, to 1 ft. long and 2 in. wide; fls. sessile or on very short pedicels, white, funnelform, tube curved, to 6 in. long. Trop. Afr.

×**Powellii** Hort. ex Bak.: *C. bulbispermum* × *C. Moorei.* To 2 ft. or more; lvs. about 20, 3–4 ft. long, 3–4 in. wide near base, smooth on margins; umbel about 8-fld.; fls. pedicelled, tube curved, greenish, 3 in. long, lobes reddish, 4 in. long, 1 in. wide. Cvs. 'Album', 'Haarlemense', 'Krelagii', and 'Roseum' are listed.

purpurascens Herb. Plant amphibious, stoloniferous; lvs. nearly erect, strap-shaped, to 2 ft. long and 1 in. wide, undulate; scape less than 1 ft. long; umbel 6–10-fld.; fls. white, tinged with purple, tube 5–6 in. long, twice as long as lobes, filaments red. W. Trop. Afr.

Rattrayi Hort. To 4 ft.; umbel 6–7-fld.; fls. white, fragrant, to 7 in. across, lobes broad, longer than tube. Lake Albert, Afr. Related to and perhaps not distinct from *C. Jagus.*

Sanderanum Bak. Lvs. thin, 2 ft. long or less, 1–1½ in. wide, crisped and denticulate on margins; umbel few-fld.; fls. funnelform, white with red keels, tube curved, 5–6 in. long, lobes less than 1 in. broad and 3–4 in. long, not spreading. Trop. Afr.

scabrum Herb. Lvs. narrow, 2 in. wide or less, rough on margins; umbel few-fld.; fls. funnelform, white with crimson keels, tube greenish, curved, 3–5 in. long, limb shorter. Trop. Afr.

speciosum: *C. latifolium.*

virginicum: a listed name of no botanical standing.

yemense Deflers. Lvs. narrow, to 2½ in. wide; umbel 10-20-fld.; fls. sessile or nearly so, funnelform, white, 8–9½ in. long, tube curved. Arabia. A poorly known sp., sometimes listed as *C. jemense* or *C. jemenicum.*

zeylanicum: *C. latifolium* var.

CRITHMUM L. *Umbelliferae.* One sp., native to seashores of Eur., sparingly grown as a salad plant or as an ornamental.

maritimum L. SAMPHIRE. Per., 1–2 ft.; lvs. biternately or triternately compound, lfts. linear, fleshy, glaucous, ½ in. long; fls. in compound umbels, very small, white or yellowish; fr. ovoid, ribbed, ¼ in. long. Does best in sandy or gravelly soil. Prop. by seeds sown as soon as ripe, and by division.

CROCANTHEMUM: *HELIANTHEMUM.*

CROCOSMIA Planch. MONTEBRETIA. *Iridaceae.* Five spp. of cormous herbs of S. Afr., formerly included in *Tritonia,* but differing in having spathe valves brown, entire or bifid, and fr. a globose, 3-lobed caps., each cell with 3 or more seeds.

For culture see *Gladiolus.* Propagated by offsets or seeds.

×**crocosmiiflora** (V. Lemoine ex E. Morr.) N. E. Br. [*Montebretia crocosmiiflora* V. Lemoine ex E. Morr.; *Tritonia crocosmiiflora* (V. Lemoine ex E. Morr.) Nichols.]: *C. aurea* (Pappe) Planch. × *C. Pottsii.* Sts. 3–4 ft., branched; lvs. ¼–1 in. wide; fl. sts. slightly longer than lvs., perianth orange-crimson to crimson, 1½–2 in. across, tube curved, lobes spreading, longer than tube. Of garden origin. Cv. 'Aurantiaca'. Fls. deep orange.

Masoniorum (L. Bolus) N.E. Br. [*Tritonia Masoniorum* L. Bolus]. Differs from *C. Pottsii* in having infl. many-fld., unbranched, one-sided; perianth larger, orange-scarlet, segms. longer, narrower, much longer than stamens.

Pottsii (Bak.) N. E. Br. [*Montebretia Pottsii* (Bak.) Bak.]. Corms stoloniferous, sts. 2½–4 ft., forking; lvs. 4–6, mostly 12–18 in. long, to ¾ in. wide; infl. few-fld., forking, 6–9 in. long; perianth bright orange-yellow, tinged red, about 1¼ in. long, tube broadly funnelform, lobes oblong, half as long as tube. Natal, Transvaal.

CROCUS L. *Iridaceae.* About 75–80 spp. of cormous herbs, native from Spain and N. Afr. to Afghanistan, but chiefly to the Medit. region, corm tunicate; lvs. linear, grasslike, keeled; peduncle and ovary subterranean, the peduncle sometimes subtended at the base by a tubular spathe, the ovary immediately subtended by 1 or 2 membranous, colorless spathes (the "proper spathes"), the outer one tubular, the inner strap-shaped; fls. white, yellow, or lilac to deep purple, perianth tube long, slender, perianth segms. 6, essentially equal, stamens 3, not united, arising from the perianth tube, included in the tube, style brs. 3, sometimes exceeding the stamens, stigmas wedge-shaped, lacerate, or with linear, forked brs.; fr. a 3-valved caps., maturing below or at ground level. The spp. are distinguished by characters of the tunic of the corm, proper spathes, the stamens, and brs. of the style.

Mainly ornamental, but saffron, the dried stigmas of *Crocus sativus,* is an important yellow food colorant and flavoring.

In some species the flowers appear several weeks or months before the leaves and the species have been grouped as spring- or autumn-blooming, a distinction of less validity in warm temp. areas where the blooming period may extend from Sept. to May. For convenience, the cultivated species assigned to each group are as listed below:

Spring-flowering: *C. aerius, C. ancyrensis, C. angustifolius, C. Balansae, C. biflorus, C. Cambessedesii, C. candidus, C. chrysanthus, C. corsicus, C. dalmaticus, C. etruscus, C. flavus, C. Fleischeri, C. Imperatii, C. Korolkowii, C. minimus, C. Olivieri, C. Sieberi, C. stellaris, C. Tomasinianus, C. vernus, C. versicolor.*

Autumn-flowering: *C. asturicus, C. Boryi, C. byzantinus, C. cancellatus, C. Cartwrightianus, C. caspius, C. hadriaticus, C. karduchorum, C. Kotschyanus, C. laevigatus, C. longiflorus, C. medius, C. niveus, C. nudiflorus, C. ochroleucus, C. pulchellus, C. Salzmannii, C. sativus, C. speciosus, C. Tournefortii, C. vitellinus.*

Crocuses should be planted 3–4 in. deep in well-drained soil. New corms are formed each year above the old ones and so eventually push the plants out of the soil after several years; therefore it is well to dig the corms every 3-4 years after the leaves die down, dry them off and replant in Sept., earlier for autumn-flowering kinds. Most species withstand temperatures to −10° F. but some are much less resistant; all spring-flowering sorts may be mulched. Some species are especially sought by rodents.

aerius Herb. Tunic annulate, reticulate, bristly at apex; lvs. 3–6; proper spathes 2; fls. lilac, cup-shaped to globose, throat yellow, perianth segms. about 1 in. long, outer segms. heavily veined rich crimson to purple outside, style brs. not divided, dilated and crenate at apex, orange-scarlet, not exceeding the anthers. Early spring. Mt. Olympus (Greece). Hybridizes freely with *C. biflorus* and *C. chrysanthus*.

albiflorus: *C. vernus* var. *vernus*.

ancyrensis (Herb.) Maw. Tunic strongly reticulate apically, with parallel fibers basally; lvs. 3–6; proper spathes 2; fls. golden-yellow, perianth segms. about ¾ in. long, style brs. not divided, or the apex bifid. Late winter. Cent. Asia Minor.

angustifolius Weston [*C. susianus* Ker-Gawl.; *C. vernus* Mill., not J. Hill or All.]. CLOTH-OF-GOLD C. Tunic finely reticulate; lvs 4–8; proper spathes 2; fls. bright yellow, starlike, perianth segms. 1–1½ in. long, acute, outer segms. usually brown outside, style brs. not divided, finely toothed at apex, orange-red, exceeding the anthers. Late winter. Mts. of Crimea (sw. Russia). Cv. '**Minor**' is listed.

asturicus Herb. Tunic of matted, parallel fibers; lvs. 3; proper spathe 1; fls. appearing with or after the lvs., mauve to lilac, rarely white, throat hairy, perianth segms. 1½ in. long, acute, filaments white, style brs. much divided, scarlet. Autumn. Asturias Mts. (Spain). Cv. '**Atropurpureus**'. Fls. dark mauve.

aureus: *C. flavus*. Var. **luteus:** *C. flavus*.

Balansae J. Gay ex Maw. Tunic reticulate; lvs. 2–4; proper spathes 2; fls. bright orange-yellow, fragrant, perianth segms. expanding widely, to ¾ in. long, rounded, outer segms. variously marked or flushed brown to purple outside, style brs. 12 or more, slender, exceeding the anthers. Early spring. Asia Minor. Cv. '**Zwanenburg**'. Fls. deep orange, feathered bronze outside.

biflorus Mill. SCOTCH C. Tunic annulate, thick, hard; lvs. 4–6, overtopping the fls.; proper spathes 2; fls. white to pale purple, style brs. not divided. Late winter. S.-cent. Eur. to Asia Minor. The typical var. is reported to be sterile, but the other vars. produce seed. Var. **biflorus**. The typical var.; fls. larger than other striped vars., corolla white with yellow throat, perianth segms. about 1½ in. long, outer segms. with 5 feathery, purple stripes outside. Cv. '**Pusillus**'. Fls. white, suffused with pale buff inside, outer perianth segms. with 3–5 purple lines outside. Probably a clone. Var. **Adamicus** Herb. [var. *Adamii* (J. Gay) Bak.]. Fls. pale purple, outer perianth segms. only faintly striped purple. Caucasus and Crimea. Var. **albus** Herb. [var. *Weldenii* (Hoppe) Bak.]. Fls. white, with slight flecking of purple outside. Hungary, Bulgaria, Greece. Var. **argenteus** (Sab.) Bak. Lvs. 3–4, fls. earlier and smaller than in typical var., silvery, more starry, suffused with purple inside, outer perianth segms. boldly striped, dark purple outside. Italy. Var. **Parkinsonii** Sab. Fls. smaller than in the typical var., more globose, pure white inside, outer perianth segms. pale buff-colored, with 3 purple stripes. Var. **pusillus:** see var. *biflorus* cv. '**Pusillus**'. Var. **Weldenii:** var. *albus*.

Boryi J. Gay. Tunic of matted, parallel fibers; lvs. 3–6, appearing with the fls.; basal spathe absent, proper spathes 2; fls. white, flushed pale yellow, throat bright yellow, perianth segms. 1–1½ in. long, obtuse, anthers white, style brs. finely divided, scarlet, exceeding the anthers. Autumn. Greek Is. One of the least hardy spp.

byzantinus Ker-Gawl. [*C. iridiflorus* Heuff.]. IRIS-FLOWERED C. Tunic membranous, of fine parallel fibers; lvs. 2–4, appearing in spring; proper spathe 1; inner perianth segms. erect, white, suffused with lilac, about 1 in. long, outer segms. spreading, deep purple, about 2 in. long, anthers orange, style brs. much divided, lilac, exceeding the anthers. Autumn. Woodlands, Hungary. Thrives in shaded location and in soil high in organic matter.

caeruleus: *C. vernus* var. *vernus*.

Cambessedesii J. Gay. Tunic membranous, dark brown; lvs. 3–4; proper spathes 2; fls. white, suffused with very pale lilac, perianth segms. to ¾ in. long, obtuse, outer segms. buff-colored outside with purplish-gray veins, filaments white, style brs. not divided or shortly bifid, scarlet, exceeding the anthers. Winter, spring. Open woodlands, Balearic Is. Very dainty; does best in sun with good drainage; not hardy at ground temperatures below 25° F. Flowers from early Nov. to Mar., where native; therefore sometimes classed as autumn-flowering.

cancellatus Herb. Tunic of coarsely reticulate fibers, bristly at apex; lvs. appearing after the fls.; proper spathes 2; fls. globose, white to deep lilac, variously veined or striped purple, throat yellow, perianth segms. 1–1½ in. long, filaments white, style brs. much divided, scarlet, exceeding the anthers. Early autumn. Greece to Iran.

candidus E. D. Clarke. Tunic of pale tan, matted, parallel fibers forming a firm apical cap; lvs. about 6; proper spathes 2; fls. white, very pale yellow to deep orange in some vars., throat white, perianth segms. 1–1¼ in. long, outer segms. sometimes feathered brown-purple on outside, style brs. 12 or more, pale cream-colored, scarcely exceeding anthers. Spring. Region of Mt. Ida (nw. Turkey). Cv. '**Subflavus**'. Fls. pale yellow, outer perianth segms. stippled bronze-purple, style brs. yellow.

Cartwrightianus Herb. Differs from *C. sativus* in having fls. smaller, perianth segms. narrower, acute, purple-striped, and style brs. exceeding the anthers but not long-exserted or drooping. Autumn. Greece.

caspius Fisch. & C. A. Mey. Tunic smooth-membranous, rosy-brown; lvs. 4–5, short, appearing with the fls.; proper spathes 2; fls. white, throat yellow, perianth segms. 1¼ in. long, not veined outside, style brs. not divided, yellow, much exceeding the anthers. Autumn. W. and s. shores of Caspian Sea, Azerbaijan (U.S.S.R.).

chrysanthus (Herb.) Herb. Tunic annulate, smooth, with short stiff fibers at apex; lvs. 4–6; proper spathes 2, very long; fls. typically globose and yellow, but extremely variable in color and form, yellow or white to deep lilac, perianth segms. 1¼ in. long, outer segms. usually flecked and veined in shades of brown to red-purple, anthers with black basal barbs, style brs. not divided, reddish-orange. Winter. Bulgaria to Asia Minor. Var. **chrysanthus**. The typical var.; anther sacs yellow to orange. The many named variants, mostly clones, include: '**Bullfinch**', fls. globose, creamy-yellow, feathered crimson-purple, perianth segms. pure white inside except for yellow throat; '**E. A. Bowles**', fls. large, pale sulphur-yellow, perianth segms. expanding fully; '**Golden Pheasant**', similar to 'E. A. Bowles', but fls. larger, perianth segms. with darker, bolder veining; '**John Hoog**', fls. sulphur-yellow, perianth segms. spreading, outer segms. with rich purple stripes; '**Moonlight**', perianth segms. spreading, pale yellow, fading to pale cream at apex, '**Snow Bunting**', fls. white, outer perianth segms. spreading, with blue feathering or stripes on the outside, very early; '**Yellow Hammer**', fls. 3–4, globose, yellow, perianth segms. feathered brownish-purple outside; '**Zwanenburg Bronze**', fls. globose, golden-yellow, outer perianth segms. shaded bronzy-brown, but lacking dark stripes of cv. 'John Hoog'. Var. **fusco-tinctus** Bak. Anther sacs brownish-black.

corsicus Maw. Tunic finely reticulate; lvs. 4–6; proper spathe 1; fls. pale lilac, perianth segms. slightly spreading, 1¼ in. long, outer segms. buff-colored, with 3 purple stripes, filaments white, anthers orange, style brs. fimbriate, bright scarlet, exceeding the anthers. Late winter, spring. High elevations, mts. of Corsica. Often confused with *C. minimus*.

dalmaticus Vis. Tunic coarsely reticulate; lvs. 3–4; proper spathes 2; fls. rose-lilac to grayish-lavender, throat yellow or white, perianth segms. spreading, about 1½ in. long, acute, outer segms. dark-striped or buff-colored on outside, style brs. not divided, orange-yellow, exceeding the anthers. Winter. Shores, Adriatic, sw. Yugoslavia, Albania.

etruscus Parl. Tunic coarsely reticulate above, with a separate, star-shaped basal tunic, proper spathe 1; fls. lilac, throat yellow, perianth segms. somewhat spreading, to 1½ in. long, outer segms. buff-colored, inner segms. lightly veined purple outside, style brs. not divided, orange, exceeding the anthers. Late winter, early spring. Tuscany (Italy).

flavus Weston [*C. aureus* J. G. Sm.; *C. aureus* var. *luteus* Bergmans; *C. maesiacus* Ker-Gawl.]. Tunic reddish-brown, splitting into parallel fibers; lvs. 6–8, overtopping the fls.; proper spathes usually 2; fls. golden-yellow to orange, cup-shaped, perianth segms. 1¼–1½ in. long, not striped or darker colored outside except in some vars., style brs. not divided, not exceeding the anthers. Late winter, spring. Yugoslavia to Turkey. Long cult., and much garden material is sterile.

Fleischeri J. Gay. Tunic very finely reticulate with silky fibers, appearing as if pleated, corm bright yellow; lvs. 4–6, filiform; proper spathes 2; fls. glossy-white inside, starlike throat yellow, perianth segms. to 1¼ in. long, very narrow, all narrowly striped purple outside, style brs. divided, scarlet, exceeding the anthers. Winter. Asia Minor.

hadriaticus Herb. Tunic finely reticulate; lvs. many, appearing before or with the fls.; proper spathes 2; fls. white, throat yellow, bearded, perianth segms. to 1½ in. long, usually stained or streaked reddish-purple outside, filaments white, style brs. not divided, red, exceeding the anthers. Autumn. W. Greece and Albania. Closely related to *C. sativus*. Var. **chrysobelonicus** Herb. Perianth segms. marked with reddish-purple lines. Autumn. Greece.

Imperati Ten. Tunic of parallel fibers; lvs. 4–6; proper spathes 2; fls. very large, lilac, outer perianth segms. buff to yellow, sometimes with 3 purple veins outside, style brs. not divided but apically fringed, orange-yellow, exceeding the anthers. Winter. S. Italy.

iridiflorus: *C. byzantinus*.

karduchorum Kotschy ex Maw. Differs from *C. Kotschyanus* in having fls. smaller, perianth segms. bluish-tinted inside, and inner segms. with 2 small, orange spots basally inside. Autumn. Kurdistan. Not known to be cult.; material offered as *C. karduchorum* is *C. Kotschyanus* var. *leucopharynx*.

Korolkowii Maw & Regel. CELANDINE C. Tunic of fine parallel fibers, corm flattened, large; lvs. 8–12; proper spathes usually 2; fls. greenish-yellow, starlike, glossy, perianth segms. ¾–1 in. long, outer segs. densely brown-speckled and often veined outside, style brs. not divided, orange-yellow, exceeded by the anthers; caps. ripening below ground. Winter. Turkestan. Cv. 'Vinosus'. Perianth segms. stained and veined purple outside.

Kotschyanus C. Koch. [*C. zonatus* J. Gay ex Klatt]. Tunic thin, membranous, corm wide, flattened; lvs. appearing after the fls.; proper spathes 2; fls. pale rose-lilac, closely forming a ring at the mouth, anthers pale cream-colored to white, style brs. nearly entire, yellow, exceeding the anthers. Autumn. Mts. of s. Turkey to Lebanon. Var. **leucopharynx** B. L. Burtt [*C. karduchorum* Hort., not Maw]. Perianth segms. pale bluish-lavender, throat cream-white, without orange dots. S. Turkey.

laevigatus Bory & Chaub. Tunic hard, woody, glossy, split basally; lvs. 3–4, appearing with or before the fls.; proper spathes 2, very short; fls. white, very fragrant, throat orange-yellow, perianth segms. 1 in. long, obtuse, outer segms. veined crimson-purple outside, filaments yellow-papillose, style brs. much divided, scarlet, exceeding the anthers. Autumn. Greece. Cv. 'Fontenayi'. Fls. larger, bright rosy-lilac inside, buff-colored outside, throat yellow, outer perianth segms. richly feathered crimson-purple outside. Early winter.

longiflorus Raf. Tunic coarsely reticulate; lvs. 3–4, appearing before the fls.; proper spathe 1, green; fls. very pale to usually bright lilac, fragrant, throat orange, perianth segms. expanding widely, 1¼–1½ in. long, obtuse, outer segms. with or without darker veining outside, style brs. divided, scarlet. Autumn. S. Italy, Sicily, Malta. Var. **melitensis** Herb. Perianth segms. many-veined, feathered and blotched purple on outside. Malta.

maesiacus: *C. flavus.*

medius Balb. Tunic coarsely reticulate, with apical ring of bristles; lvs. 3–4, appearing after the fls.; proper spathe 1; fls. bright lilac, perianth segms. expanding widely, 1½–2 in. long, acute, with short, radiating, purple lines on inner surface at base, producing a starlike effect, style brs. much divided, fringed, bright scarlet, exceeding the anthers. Autumn. Maritime Alps (s. France to n. Italy). Very floriferous and hardy, increases abundantly.

minimus DC. Tunic of matted, parallel fibers; lvs. 4–5, longer than fls.; proper spathes 2; fls. lilac, small, perianth segms. about 1 in. long, obtuse, outer segms. buff to yellowish outside and mostly purple-feathered, filaments white, style brs. not divided, yellow. Early spring. Corsica, Sardinia.

napolitanus, neapolitanus: *C. vernus* var. *neapolitanus.*

niveus Bowles. Tunic of parallel fibers basally, the upper half finely reticulate, forming a cap about ¾ in. high; lvs. 4–6, appearing with the fls.; basal spathe present, proper spathes 2; fls. white, with a few very pale green veins, not fragrant, throat golden-orange, anthers yellow, style brs. divided, orange, exceeding the anthers. Late autumn. Mt. Taygetus (Greece). A hardy, robust plant.

nudiflorus Sm. Corms small, globose, producing vermiform stolons ½–2 in. long; lvs. appearing after the fls.; proper spathe 1, very long; fls. clear mauve-purple, with many slightly darker veins on both sides, perianth segms. about 2¼ in. long, obtuse, filaments white, style brs. divided, papillose at apex, orange, exceeding the anthers. Early autumn. Pyrenees (sw. France and Spain).

ochroleucus Boiss. & Gaillardot. Tunic membranous at base, with parallel fibers above; lvs. 4–5, well-developed at flowering time; proper spathes usually 2; fls. white, flushed with cream, throat tinged yellow to pale orange, perianth segms. 1 in. long, narrow, not striped or veined, filaments yellow, anthers cream-colored to white, style brs. not divided, scarcely exceeding the anthers. Late autumn. Syria.

Olivieri J. Gay. Tunic membranous, fibrous basally; lvs. mostly 2–3, about ⅜ in. wide; proper spathes 2; fls. brilliant orange, perianth segms. 1¼ in. long, acute, not darker-veined or -colored outside, filaments papillose, style brs. divided into 6 capillary strands, not reaching apex of anthers. Winter. Romania, Bulgaria, Greece. Easily prop. from seeds.

pulchellus Herb. Tunic thick, membranous-leathery; lvs. several, appearing after the fls.; proper spathes 2, very short; fls. large, pale lavender to bright lilac or rarely white, throat orange-yellow, perianth segms. to 1½ in. long, with 5 fine, bluish-lilac veins on both sides, filaments yellow and hairy, anthers white, style brs. much divided, yellow-orange, exceeding the anthers. Autumn. Greece, Turkey. Hybridizes freely with *C. speciosus.*

purpureus: *C. vernus* var. *neapolitanus;* perhaps sometimes used for *C. Sieberi* cv.

Salzmannii J. Gay. Tunic membranous, of soft parallel fibers, corms subglobose, to 2 in. in diam.; lvs. 5–6, appearing with the fls.; proper spathe 1, broad; fls. clear pale lilac, throat yellowish, not veined, perianth segms. about 1¾ in. long, style brs. shortly divided, orange, ex-

ceeding the anthers. Autumn. S. Spain and Tangiers. Vigorous, moderately hardy. Cv. 'Erectophyllus'. More robust; fls. darker colored.

sativus L. SAFFRON C. Tunic of parallel fibers, attenuating to a crown apically, corm globose; lvs. many; proper spathes 2; fls. large, fragrant, perianth segms. spreading, 1½–2 in. long, broad, obtuse, filaments white, anthers yellow, style brs. flattened and toothed at apex, brilliant blood-red, exserted and drooping over the anthers and the perianth segms. Autumn. Known only in cult. Grown commercially in several Old World countries for saffron, the dried stigmas used to color and flavor foods. Corms should be lifted and divided every 2–3 years. Cv. 'Cashmirianus'. Fls. white, style brs. bright scarlet, shorter than anthers.

Sieberi J. Gay. Tunic coarsely reticulate; lvs. 4–6; proper spathes 2; fls. becoming starlike, dark purple to white, throat orange, perianth segms. spreading, 1½ in. long, oblong, darker-streaked or -feathered outside, style brs. orange-red, nearly entire. Winter. Greece, Crete. Cv. 'Purpureus'. Fls. dark-colored.

speciosus Bieb. Tunic papery-membranous; lvs. 4–5, appearing after the fls.; proper spathes 2, very long; fls. bluish-lilac, veined blue inside, speckled blue outside, perianth segms. 1½–2 in. long, acute, filaments white, anthers yellowish-orange, style brs. much divided, brilliant scarlet, exceeding the anthers. Autumn. Se. Eur., w. to Iran, Turkey. Cv. 'Globosus'. Fls. globose, nearly pure blue. Var. **Aitchisonii** M. Foster. Fls. almost white in bud, opening to pale lavender with blue veins, perianth segms. nearly 3 in. long.

×**stellaris** Haw. Generally presumed to be a garden hybrid of *C. angustifolius* × *C. aureus;* tunic reticulate; fls. pale yellow, sterile, perianth segms. 1½ in. long, outer segms. with 5 feathered purple stripes outside. Winter. Cv. 'Pallidus'. Fls. cream-colored, with paler markings.

susianus: *C. angustifolius.*

Tomasinianus Herb. Tunic finely reticulate; lvs. 4–6, appearing shortly after the fls.; proper spathe 1; fls. lavender, starlike, throat white-bearded, perianth segms. to 1¾ in. long, narrow, acute, usually pale gray outside, filaments white, style brs. not divided, almost reaching apex of anthers. Winter. Cent. Yugoslavia. Cv. 'Barr's Purple'. Fls. large, lilac, darker than the sp., but not purple. Cv. 'Whitewell Purple'. Fls. reddish-purple, perianth segms. wide-expanded.

Tournefortii J. Gay. Tunic soft, of matted, parallel fibers; lvs. 3–4, appearing before or with the fls.; proper spathes 2; fls. warm rosy-lilac, throat bright yellow, perianth segms. to 1½ in. long, bluntly acute, with a dull purple line outside, anthers white, style brs. finely branched, scarlet, much exceeding the anthers. Autumn. Greek Is. Not considered hardy in ground temperatures below 20° F.; requires well-drained soil.

vernus (L.) J. Hill. DUTCH C. Tunic reticulate; lvs. several, widest at the middle; proper spathe 1; fls. white to lilac, purple, often feathered or striped darker purple outside, starlike, throat white, bearded, filaments white, anthers lemon-yellow, style brs. not divided or only fringed at apex, orange-scarlet, exceeding the anthers or not. Early spring. Cent. and s. Eur. *C. vernus* Mill. is *C. angustifolius.* Var. **vernus** [*C. albiflorus* Kit. ex Schult.; *C. caeruleus* Weston; *C. vernus* All., not Mill.]. The typical var.; fls. usually white or perianth segms. narrow, striped purple. Switzerland, France, Austria. Cv. 'Harlem Gem'. Fls. lilac-blue; said to be a hybrid of this sp. and *C. Tomasinianus.* Var. **neapolitanus** Ker-Gawl. [*C. napolitanus* Loisel.; *C. neapolitanus* Asch. ex Bergmans; *C. purpureus* Weston]. Fls. larger than in the typical var., purple, throat white. S. Italy.

versicolor Ker-Gawl. Tunic coarsely reticulate; lvs. 4–5; proper spathe mostly 1; fls. white, suffused with lilac, starlike, throat white to pale yellow, perianth segms. to 1½ in. long, inner segms. feathered purple outside, outer segms. purple outside, filaments white, style brs. undivided, orange-yellow. Late winter. S. France. Cv. 'Cloth-of-Silver'. Inner perianth segms. not feathered outside, outer segms. only blotched purple. Cv. 'Picturatus'. Fls. pure white inside and outside, perianth segms. feathered outside.

vitellinus Wahlenb. Tunic smooth, membranous, but very thick and polished; lvs. appearing with the fls.; proper spathes 2; fls. bright orange, fragrant, perianth segms. about ¾ in. long, narrow, acute, often bronze-striped outside, filaments papillose, style brs. much divided, orange-red. Early winter. Syria, Lebanon, Israel. Not very hardy.

zonatus: *C. Kotschyanus.*

CROSSANDRA Salisb. FIRECRACKER FLOWER. *Acanthaceae.* About 50 spp. of glabrous or pubescent shrubs or herbs of Afr., Madagascar, and Arabia; lvs. ovate; fls. showy, in 4-sided, terminal spikes, often long-peduncled, bracts large, ovate, imbricate, bractlets linear, calyx 5-lobed, irregular, corolla with slender tube, limb usually split to base making a single, 5-lobed lip, lobes rounded, stamens 4, borne in upper half of tube, included, filaments shorter than anthers, anther sac 1, disc not evident, ovary 2-celled, each cell with 2 ovules, style included, stigma cylindrical, thicker than style, obscurely 2-lobed; fr. an oblong caps., seeds ovate, flattened, covered with hairs or fringed scales.

Grown under glass or outdoors in warm countries and the tropics. Propagated by cuttings over heat.

infundibuliformis (L.) Nees [*C. undulifolia* Salisb.]. To 3 ft.; lvs. narrowly ovate to lanceolate, 2–5 in. long, undulate, narrowed to petiole ½–1 in. long; infl. pubescent, to 6 in. long, peduncle about 1 in. long; corolla bright orange or salmon-pink, tube slender, nearly 1 in. long, lip 1–1¼ in. across; fr. ½ in. long, seeds bearing fringed scales. S. India and Ceylon.

nilotica D. Oliver. Differs from *C. infundibuliformis* in having entire plant pubescent, lvs. not undulate, spike about 1 in. long, peduncle longer than spike. Trop. Afr.

pungens Lindau. Differs from the above 2 spp. in having extremely dense spikes, and bracts broadly ovate, with spinose tip. Trop. Afr.

undulifolia: *C. infundibuliformis.*

CROSSOSOMA Nutt. *Crossosomataceae.* Three or 4 spp. of glabrous, deciduous or partly deciduous shrubs, native to sw. N. Amer.; lvs. alt., narrow, entire, thickish, smooth and somewhat glaucous; fls. solitary, calyx tubular, 5-lobed, petals 5, white, deciduous, stamens 15–20, carpels 2–9, separate; fr. several-seeded follicles.

Occasionally grown as ornamentals in dry regions.

californicum Nutt. Shrub to 6 ft.; lvs. scattered, usually oblong, to 3½ in. long, pale green; fls. to 1½ in. across, petals rounded, to ¾ in. long; follicles 2–9. Santa Catalina and San Clemente Is. (Calif.) and Guadalupe Is. (Baja Calif.).

Bigelovii S. Wats. Differs from preceding in having lvs. often fascicled, smaller, to ¾ in. long, gray-green, and fls. smaller, to ¾ in. across, petals oblong, to ⅜ in. long. Desert regions, s. Calif., Ariz., and adjacent Sonora (Mex.).

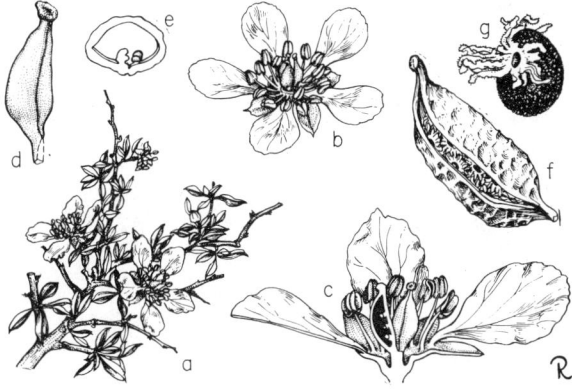

CROSSOSOMATACEAE. *Crossosoma Bigelovii:* **a,** flowering branch, × ½; **b,** flower, × 1; **c,** flower, vertical section, × 2; **d,** carpel, × 3; **e,** ovary, cross section, × 6; **f,** follicle, × 2; **g,** seed, × 5. (From Lawrence, *Taxonomy of Vascular Plants.*)

CROSSOSOMATACEAE Engl. CROSSOSOMA FAMILY. Dicot.; 1 genus, *Crossosoma,* of glabrous shrubs, native to sw. N. Amer.; lvs. alt., simple, entire; fls. solitary, somewhat showy; fr. a follicle.

CROTALARIA L. RATTLEBOX. *Leguminosae* (subfamily *Faboideae*). More than 500 spp. of herbs and shrubs of warm regions of the world; lvs. alt., of 3–7 or 1 lft.; fls. usually racemose, papilionaceous, standard orbicular, 2-auricled at base, keel petals curved, beaked, stamens 10, filaments alternately long with globose anthers and short with linear anthers; fr. an elongate, inflated, dehiscent legume.

One species, *C. juncea* L., SUNN, produces sunn hemp, an important fiber of Asia; a few species are grown as cover or green-manure crops in warm regions, and others are useful as ornamentals. Propagated by seeds soaked in warm water before planting, and the shrubby species also by cuttings.

africana Buscal. & Muschl. Much-branched shrub, branchlets densely pubescent; lvs. long-petioled, lfts. 3, about ½ in. long, pilose

on both surfaces when young; racemes elongate, many-fld.; petals yellow, slightly longer than calyx; fr. hairy. Kenya.

agatiflora G. Schweinf. CANARY-BIRD BUSH. Shrub or small tree; lfts. 3, to 3 in. long and 1 in. wide; racemes terminal, to 14 in. long; fls. large, bright green-yellow, keel tip brown-purple, keel to 1½ in. long; fr. glabrous, to 3 in. long. Kenya and Uganda, s. to Rhodesia.

anagyroides HBK. Shrub, to 8 ft.; lfts. 3, ovate-lanceolate or ovate, to 3 in. long or more; racemes terminal; fls. yellow, with darker lines, ¾ in. across; fr. oblong, 1½ in. long. Trop. n. S. Amer. Planted in the Old World tropics as a green manure.

brevidens Benth. Erect or decumbent ann. or per., to 6 ft. or more; lfts. 3, linear or lanceolate to elliptic, to 4 in. long or more; racemes terminal, opp. a lf., to 16 in. long or more; fls. with truncate, glabrous or puberulous calyx, standard cream to yellow, veined red-brown; fr. narrowly cylindrical, to 2 in. long. Afr. Var. **brevidens.** The typical var.; calyx glabrous. Sudan, Ethiopia. Var. **intermedia** (Kotschy) Polhill [*C. intermedia* Kotschy]. Calyx puberulous, to ⁵⁄₁₆ in. long, keel to 1 in. long. Tropics, e. Afr.

capensis Jacq. Much-branched shrub, to 5 ft.; lfts. obovate, 3, to 1 in. long, obtuse; racemes terminal or lateral; fls. large, bright yellow, 1 in. long or more. S. Afr., Mozambique.

Goetzei Harms [*C. rotundicarinata* Bak.f.]. Tall shrub; lfts. 3, oblanceolate, to 1½ in. long and ½ in. wide, petioles to ⁵⁄₁₆ in. long; fls. solitary or few together, keel less than ½ in. long, rounded beneath; fr. oblong, dark-villous. Nyasaland.

intermedia: *C. brevidens* var.; but material cult. as *C. intermedia* is probably *C. ochroleuca.*

macrocarpa E. H. Mey. Shrubby; lfts. 3, obovate, to more than 1 in. long, petioles longer; racemes terminal, loosely several- to many-fld.; fls. large; fr. oblong, to 3½ in. long, on stalk longer than calyx. S. Afr.

Mitchellii Benth. Per., to 3 ft., from a thick rhizome; differing from *C. retusa* in having lvs. broader, less cuneate, mostly ovate-elliptic to -lanceolate, racemes dense, to 6 in. long, standard ½ in. across, and fr. less than 1 in. long. Ne. Australia.

mucronata Desv. Coarse herb, to 8 ft.; lfts. 3, elliptic to elliptic-obovate, to 4 in. long, obtuse; racemes terminal, to 12 in. long; fls. yellow, striped with brown-purple outside, ½ in. long; fr. 1½ in. long. Tropics. Much planted in Fla. for green manure. Material cult. as *C. striata* probably belongs here.

ochroleuca G. Don. Slender ann., to 3 ft.; lfts. 3, linear, to 6 in. long, ½ in. wide; racemes terminal, very loose, to 12 in. long; fls. bright yellow, standard ⅝ in. long, conspicuously veined with purple; fr. 2 in. long. Tropics, Afr.

retusa L. Stout, slender ann., to 4 ft., pubescent; lvs. with 1 lft., oblanceolate, obtuse, to 3 in. long; racemes loose, terminal; fls. yellow, with standard streaked red, to 1 in. across; fr. glabrous, to 1½ in. long. Tropics, Asia. Sometimes planted in tropics and subtropics as an ornamental. Zone 10b.

rhodesiae Bak.f. Subshrub, brs. diffuse, zigzag, to 14 in. long; lfts. 3, elliptic or obovate, to ⅞ in. long, glaucous-green, with short petiolule; racemes axillary, short, mostly 2-fld.; fr. oblong-ovoid, ⅞ in. long, finally glabrescent. Rhodesia.

rotundicarinata: *C. Goetzei.*

spectabilis Roth. RATTLEBOX. Subshrub, to 4 ft., branchlets stout; lvs. with 1 lft., oblanceolate, to 6 in. long; racemes usually terminal, 20–50-fld., to 1 ft. long; fls. showy, to ¾ in. long, yellow, standard streaked purplish; fr. stalked, to 2 in. long. India, Malay Pen.

striata: a confused name of various application. Material cult. under this name is probably *C. mucronata.*

usaramoensis: *C. zanzibarica.*

zanzibarica Benth. [*C. usaramoensis* Bak.f.]. Erect herb, sts. streaked, pubescent; lfts. 3, elliptic, to 2¼ in. long; racemes loose, many-fld., to 10 in. long; calyx glabrous, petals yellow, standard streaked; fr. oblong-cylindrical, pubescent. Tanzania. Sometimes cult. in warm areas for green manure.

CROTON L. *Euphorbiaceae.* Over 700 spp. of monoecious or dioecious, often strong-scented herbs, shrubs, and trees, mostly of trop. and subtrop. regions in both hemispheres; lvs. alt. or rarely nearly opp., simple, entire or rarely 3–5-lobed, often toothed, usually with stellate hairs; fls. mostly in terminal spikes or spikelike racemes, with or without petals, ovary 3-(rarely 2–4-) celled; fr. a caps.

Infrequently grown as ornamentals but several species are important economically: the seeds of *C. Tiglium* L. yield croton oil, a powerful purgative; *C. lacciferus* L. is host plant to lac-producing insects and so important in the varnish industry. The widely cultivated "crotons"

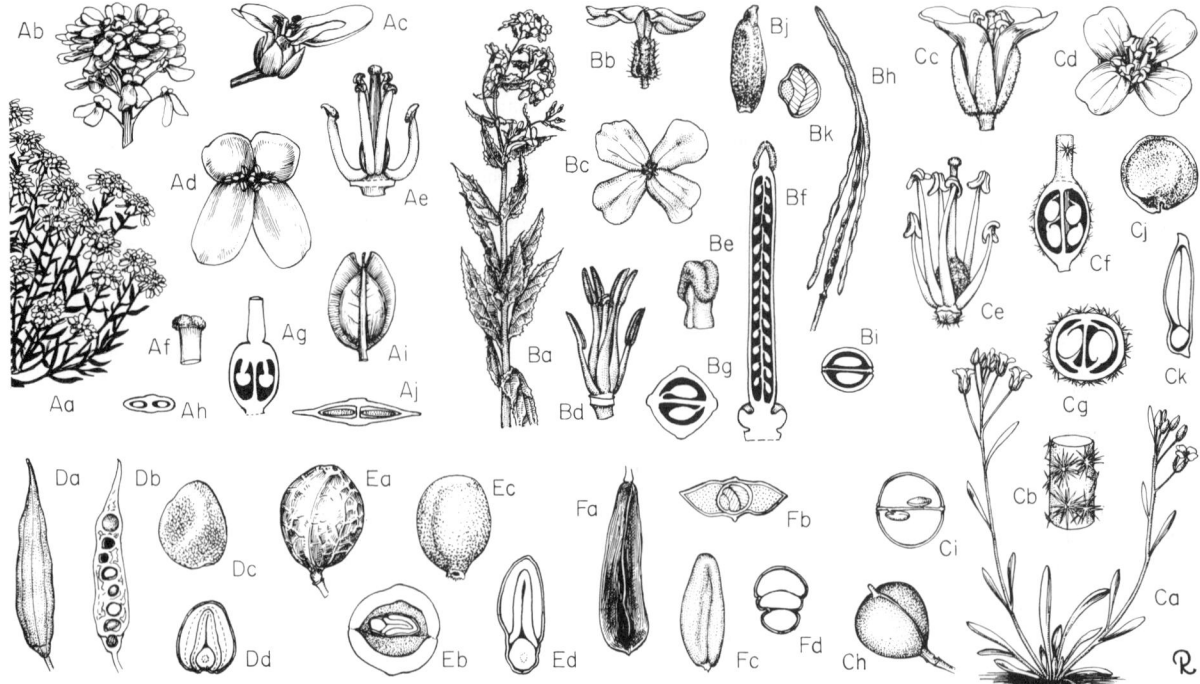

CRUCIFERAE. **A,** *Iberis sempervirens:* **Aa,** flowering plant, × ⅙; **Ab,** raceme, × ½; **Ac,** flower, side view, × 2; **Ad,** flower, face view, × 2; **Ae,** stamens and pistil, × 4; **Af,** stigma, × 6; **Ag,** base of pistil, vertical section, × 6; **Ah,** ovary, cross section, × 6; **Ai,** fruit (a silicle), × 1; **Aj,** fruit, cross section, × 2. **B,** *Hesperis matronalis:* **Ba,** flowering stem, × ⅛; **Bb,** flower, side view, × ¾; **Bc,** flower, face view, × ¾; **Bd,** stamens and pistil, × 1½; **Be,** stigma, × 10; **Bf,** pistil, vertical section, × 5; **Bg,** ovary, cross section, × 15; **Bh,** fruit (a silique), × ½; **Bi,** fruit, cross section, × 2; **Bj,** seed, × 5; **Bk,** seed, cross section (cotyledons incumbent), × 6. **C,** *Lesquerella alpina:* **Ca,** flowering plant, × ½; **Cb,** segment of stem with stellate hairs, × 10; **Cc,** flower, side view, × 2; **Cd,** flower, face view, × 2; **Ce,** stamens and pistil, × 3; **Cf,** base of pistil, ovary in vertical section, × 6; **Cg,** ovary, cross section, × 10; **Ch,** fruit, × 1½; **Ci,** fruit, cross section, × 1½; **Cj,** seed, × 5; **Ck,** seed, cross section (cotyledons accumbent), × 8. **D,** *Raphanus sativus:* **Da,** fruit, × ½; **Db,** fruit, vertical section, × ½; **Dc,** seed, × 3; **Dd,** seed, cross section (cotyledons conduplicate), × 3. **E,** *Crambe maritima:* **Ea,** fruit, × 1½; **Eb,** fruit, cross section, × 1½; **Ec,** seed, × 2; **Ed,** seed, cross section (cotyledons conduplicate), × 3. **F,** *Isatis tinctoria:* **Fa,** fruit, × 1½; **Fb,** fruit, cross section, × 4; **Fc,** seed, × 5; **Fd,** seed, cross section (cotyledons incumbent), × 8.

of horticulture with variegated foliage belong to the genus *Codiaeum.* The following epithets sometimes, but incorrectly, used in *Croton* are properly treated as cultivars of *Codiaeum variegatum* var. *pictum,* and are listed under that name: *Andreanum, angustissimum, anietumense, aucubifolium, bogoriense, bruxellense, Craigii, delicatissimum, edmontonense, gloriosum, graciosum, Grusonii, interruptum, linearis nigrescens, montefontainense, pictum, punctatum, punctatum aureum, Reidii, Sanderi, Schattii, spirale, Warrenii, Weismanii.*

macrostachys Hochst. ex A. Rich. Monoecious tree, to 30 ft. or more; lvs. ovate, 1½–4 in. long, cordate, crenulate; racemes usually unisexual, male to 10 in. long, many-fld., female to 4 in. long; female fls. without petals, male fls. with petals, stamens 15. S.-cent., se. and e. Afr.

megalobotrys Müll. Arg. Large, dioecious tree, 20–30 ft.; lvs. ovate to ovate-lanceolate, 1½–3 in. long, long-acuminate, rounded or truncate, serrate to dentate; male fls. with petals, many, in 1–3 in. racemes on short lateral branchlets, stamens 20–25. Se. and s.-cent. Afr.

megalocarpus Hutch. Monoecious tree, 70–80 ft.; lvs. oblong-lanceolate or elliptic-oblong, to 5 in. long, entire, densely scaly below; fls. with petals, in racemes, to 10 in. long, female fls. below, male fls. above, stamens 25. Trop. Afr.

monanthogynus Michx. PRAIRIE TEA. Monoecious, glandular ann. to 2 ft., sts. often umbellately 3–4-forked in lower part; lvs. oblong to ovate, entire; male fls. with petals, stamens 3–8, female fls. without petals, ovary often with only 1 or 2 cells. Va. to Kans., s. to Ga., Tex., and Mex.

pictum: *Codiaeum variegatum* var.

CRUCIANELLA L. CROSSWORT. *Rubiaceae.* About 30 or more spp. of ann. or per. herbs or half-shrubs, with slender 4-angled sts., from Medit. region, w. to Iran and cent. Asia; upper lvs. opp., lacking stipules, lower lvs. whorled; fls. in spikes or clusters subtended by bracts, small, white, rosy or blue, 4–5-merous, corolla funnelform, tube long; fr. dry, dehiscent into 2 halves.

Grown in rock gardens, where they thrive in partial shade. Propagated by division and by seeds.

angustifolia L. Ann., to 1½ ft.; lvs. in whorls of 4–6, all linear-subulate, very scabrous, margins recurved; fls. white, minute. Cent. and s. Eur.

herbacea Forssk. Ann., to 1 ft. or more; lvs. ovate-oblong or the upper linear; fls. in dense, linear spikes to 2 in. long. Egypt.

latifolia L. Ann., to 1½ ft.; lower lvs. obovate to oblong, upper lvs. linear-lanceolate; fls. whitish, in slender, linear spikes. S. Eur.

stylosa Trin. Prostrate ann., sts. to 9 in. long; lvs. in whorls of 8–9, lanceolate, to ¾ in. long; fls. deep rose, in globose heads ½ in. across, styles long-exserted. Iran. Cv. 'Carminea' is listed.

CRUCIFERAE Juss. or, alternatively, **BRASSICACEAE** Burnett. MUSTARD FAMILY. Dicot.; about 350 genera and 3,200 spp. of pungent or acrid herbs of various habit; lvs. alt., without stipules; fls. in terminal racemes or corymbs, usually bisexual, regular, sepals 4, deciduous, petals 4, their spreading limbs forming a cross, stamens 6, 2 of these shorter and inserted lower than the others, pistil of 2 carpels, ovary superior; fr. a 2-celled caps., varying in form (known as a silique when elongated or a silicle when short and broad) but usually opening by 2 valves from below, seeds without endosperm, filled by a large embryo curved or folded in various ways, yielding (along with the fr.) the important taxonomic characters of the family.

The cultivated genera are: *Aethionema, Alyssoides, Alyssum, Anastatica, Arabidopsis, Arabis, Armoracia, Aubrieta, Aurinia, Barbarea, Berteroa, Biscutella, Brassica, Bunias, Cardamine, Cheiranthus, Cochlearia, Crambe, Dentaria, Diplotaxis, Dithyrea, Draba, Eruca, Erysimum, Fibigia, Heliophila, Hesperis, Hugueninia, Hutchinsia, Iberis, Ionopsidium, Isatis, Kernera, Lepidium, Lesquerella, Lobularia,*

Lunaria, Malcolmia, Matthiola, Morisia, Nasturtium, Peltaria, Petrocallis, Phoenicaulis, Physaria, Raphanus, Rorippa, Schivereckia, Schizopetalon, Sisymbrium, Smelowskia, Stanleya, Stenodraba, Subularia, Thelypodium, Thlaspi, and *Thysanocarpus.*

The mustard family includes many ornamental species. It is also the source of important vegetables, particularly in the genera *Brassica* (broccoli, Brussels sprouts, cabbage, Chinese cabbage, kale, kohlrabi, rutabaga, turnip), *Lepidium* (cress), *Nasturtium* (watercress), and *Raphanus* (radish); of condiment-producing plants, such as the common horseradish *(Armoracia),* Japanese horseradish *(Wasabia japonica),* and mustard *(Brassica);* and of important oilseed plants *(Brassica, Crambe).*

CRUPINA Cass. *Compositae* (Carduus Tribe). Two or 3 spp. of ann. herbs, native to s. Eur. and w. Asia; lvs. pinnately dissected; fl. heads long-peduncled, involucral bracts acuminate, not spiny; fls. light purple, all tubular, few; pappus blackish-brown, in 2 rows, the outer of graduated bristles, the inner of scales.

vulgaris Cass. [*Centaurea Crupina* L.]. To 2 ft.; lowermost lvs. oblanceolate, to 6 in. long, entire or lobed, the rest smaller, cut into denticulate, linear segms.; heads ¾ in. long, 3–5-fld.; fls. not much longer than involucre. S. Eur.

CRUSEA Schlechtend. & Cham. *Rubiaceae.* About 13 spp. of usually low ann. or per. herbs, native to s. Ariz. and New Mex., s. to Mex. and Cent. Amer., with sts. cylindrical or sometimes more or less 4-angled; lvs. 4-ranked, ovate or lanceolate, conspicuously nerved, stipules united with petioles to form a sheath; fls. in heads surrounded by leaflike bracts, usually pink or violet, 4-merous, corolla funnelform, tube slender, lobes spreading; fr. longitudinally dehiscent into 2 dry, 1-seeded sections.

calocephala DC. [*C. violacea* Brongn. ex J. Neumann]. Per. or rarely ann., sts. usually decumbent, often rooting, cylindrical, hairy, erect sts. 4–10 in. or more; lvs. sessile, ovate, ¾–3½ in. long, with 6 veins parallel to midvein, stipules awned; fls. violet. Mex. and Cent. Amer.

violacea: *C. calocephala.*

CRYOPHYTUM: *MESEMBRYANTHEMUM.*

CRYOSOPHILA Blume [*Acanthorrhiza* H. Wendl.]. Palmae. A few spp. of small or medium palms with bisexual fls., in Mex., Cent. Amer. and n. S. Amer., root-spines closely covering the trunk at least towards the base; lvs. palmate, divided nearly to base at center and then into 1- to several-ribbed, acute segms. on each side, petiole with smooth margins; infl. among lvs., arched, with tomentose loosely sheathing bracts on peduncle, rachillae many; fls. solitary, creamy-white to purplish, sepals 3, briefly united basally, petals 3, imbricate, stamens 6, filaments united to the middle or above, carpels 3, with subulate styles; fr. yellowish to white, globose to pear-shaped or oblong, seed globose with homogeneous endosperm and no intrusion of the seed coat.

Several species planted as ornamentals. For culture see *Palms.*

argentea Bartlett. To nearly 20 ft.; lvs. to 3 ft. long, ribs about 44, blade divided to middle and into about 9 segms. on each side, lacking conspicuous cross-veinlets when dry; fr. about ½ in. in diam. Brit. Honduras, Guatemala.

nana (HBK) Blume ex Salomon [*Acanthorrhiza aculeata* (Liebm.) H. Wendl.]. Small tree to 15 ft., trunk gray with short spines to 1 in. long; lvs. green above, silvery beneath, lacking conspicuous cross-veinlets when dry, ribs to 50, segms. to 2 ft. long, 1 in. wide; infl. short, to 1 ft. long in fr., lower bracts to 6 in. long; stamens united nearly to apex; fr. globose, to 9/16 in. long. Calcareous mts., w. Mex. Warmest parts of Zone 9b in Fla. Sometimes confused with *C. Warscewiczii.*

Warscewiczii (H. Wendl.) Bartlett. To 20 ft. or more, trunk gray with long root-spines at base, becoming nearly smooth above in age; lvs. green above, silvery beneath, with conspicuous cross-veinlets when dry, segms. 50–60, to 3 ft. long, 1½ in. wide, 2–4-ribbed; infl. to 2 ft. long or more, lower bracts 8–10 in. long; stamens united about half their length; fr. globose to pear-shaped, to 1 in. long, white. Costa Rica to Panama. Cult. in s. Fla., often under the name *Acanthorrhiza aculeata.*

CRYPTANTHA Lehm. ex Fisch. & C. A. Mey. WHITE FORGET-ME-NOT. *Boraginaceae.* About 100 spp. of hispid or setose, ann. and per. herbs, mostly of w. N. Amer., but some native to w. and s. S. Amer.; lvs. simple, alt., entire; fls. white or rarely yellow, small, many, in bractless or bracted scorpioid spikes or racemes, rarely somewhat cymose-paniculate, calyx 5-lobed or -cleft, corolla 5-lobed, funnelform, corolla throat with scales, stamens 5, included; fr. of 1–4, erect, rough or smooth nutlets.

Rarely sown in the wild garden in the region where they grow.

intermedia (A. Gray) Greene. Much-branched, hispid ann., 1–1½ ft.; lvs. linear to lanceolate, to 1 in. long; infl. bractless; fls. white, to 3/16 in. across; nutlets usually 4, rough. N. Calif. to Baja Calif.

Sheldonii (Brand) Payson. Hairy per. with 1 or more ascending sts., to 10 in.; basal lvs. spatulate to oblanceolate, to 1½ in. long; infl. bracted, with many yellow hairs; fls. white, to ⅜ in. wide; nutlets 4, somewhat glossy, rough. E. Wash. and Ore. to Montana.

CRYPTANTHUS Klotzsch. EARTH-STAR. *Bromeliaceae.* About 20 spp. of terrestrial stoloniferous herbs, native to Brazil, usually with flattened rosettes of lvs., rarely with leafy sts.; lvs. stiff, prickly-margined; fls. white or greenish-white, borne in small heads among the foliage, inner fls. often sterile, sepals united into a tube, petals not appendaged, united into a tube, the lobes spreading, ovary inferior; fr. a berry, seeds without appendages.

Grown as foliage plants under glass, in the home, or outdoors in warm climates. Propagated by offsets; thrive in bright sun or filtered shade. For culture see *Bromeliaceae.*

Hybrids of several spp. are listed, the most common parents being *C. bahianus, C. Beuckeri,* and *C. zonatus. Cryptanthus Beuckeri* and *C. bahianus* have been crossed with spp. of *Billbergia* and the resulting hybrids are listed as × *Cryptbergia* or sometimes as × *Biltanthus.*

acaulis (Lindl.) Beer. STARFISH PLANT. Nearly stemless; lvs. elliptic-lanceolate, to 6 in. long, 1½ in. wide, with undulate, prickly margins, green, white-scurfy beneath; fls. 1⅝ in. long, tube of calyx much longer than the lobes, the lobes entire or nearly so. Small foliage plant with many cvs.: 'Roseo-pictus' is listed; 'Roseus', lvs. tinged rose-pink; 'Ruber' [var. *ruber* Hort. ex Beer], lvs. tinged red. Var. **bromelioides:** *C. bromelioides.* Var. **diversifolius:** *C. diversifolius.*

bahianus L. B. Sm. St. long and leafy; lvs. narrowly triangular, to 10 in. long, ⅝ in. wide, with spines to 3/16 in. long, green and smooth above, becoming red-tinged, white-scurfy beneath; fls. to 1 in. long, petals white. Withstands full sun.

Bankeri: a listed name, probably in error for *C. Beuckeri.*

Beuckeri E. Morr. Lvs. to 5 in. long, 2 in. wide, narrowed to a petiole about 2 in. long, or the inner sessile and triangular, brownish-green or rosy-spotted, or striped with light green.

bivittatus (Hook.) Regel. Stemless or nearly so; lvs. strongly acuminate, arching, spiny, greenish-brown above, with 2 reddish or pink longitudinal stripes; fls. white. Cv. 'Luddemanii', of larger size. Cv. 'Minor', is listed.

bromelioides Otto & A. Dietr. [*C. acaulis* var. *bromelioides* (Otto & A. Dietr.) Mez]. PINK C. Lvs. all alike, not petioled, to 7 in. long, 1⅜ in. wide, spiny-margined, green above, silvery beneath; infl. on a scape 6 in. high; fls. many, in clusters of 4–6 in axils of keeled fl. bracts, milky-white, 1⅝ in. long, tube of calyx longer than the lobes. Sometimes grown under the name *C. terminalis.* Var. **tricolor** M. B. Foster. RAINBOW-STAR. Lvs. striped with ivory-white and green, overlaid with carmine-rose.

diversifolius Beer [*C. acaulis* var. *diversifolius* (Beer) Mez]. Lvs. dimorphic, gradually narrowed at the base, to 1 ft. long, 1¾ in. wide, uniformly colored above and beneath; fl. bracts to ⅝ in. long; sepals acuminate.

Fosteranus L. B. Sm. Lvs. constricted at base, all alike, thick and fleshy, marked with irregular dark brown crossbands above; calyx 5/16 in. long.

Lacerdae Ant. SILVER-STAR. Small, stemless; lvs. all alike, not petioled, scarcely more than 2 in. long, ashy-white-scurfy but with 2 longitudinal, glabrous, green stripes; infl. few-fld.; fls. milky-white, ⅝ in. long.

×**Osyanus:** hort. name for the hybrid, *C. Beuckeri* E. Morr. × *C. Lacerdae* Ant.

Racinae: a listed name of no botanical standing.

roseo-pictus: a listed name of no botanical standing; probably *C. acaulis* cv. or *C. bivittatus.*

roseus: a listed name of no botanical standing; probably *C. acaulis* cv.

rubescens: a listed name of no botanical standing.

sinuosus L. B. Sm. [*C. undulatus* Otto & A. Dietr., in part]. Similar to *C. acaulis*, but plants smaller; fls. ⅞ in. long, tube of calyx shorter than lobes, the lobes strongly serrulate.

terminalis: a listed name for *C. bromelioides.*

undulatus: see *C. sinuosus.*

zonatus (Vis.) Beer. ZEBRA PLANT. Lvs. to 9 in. long, 1½ in. wide, crinkly, light green, with transverse bands of white, green, or brown above, and white-scurfy beneath. Cvs. are: **'Argyraeus'**, a listed name; **'Viridis'**, lvs. green beneath; **'Zebrinus'**, lvs. larger, reddish-brown, with very distinct silver bands.

×**CRYPTBERGIA** Hort.: *Billbergia* × *Cryptanthus. Bromeliaceae.* A hort. name used for intergeneric hybrids sometimes also listed as × *Biltanthus.*

Meadii Hort.: *Billbergia nutans* × *Cryptanthus Beuckeri.* Lvs. upright, mottled green and pink.

rubra Hort.: *Billbergia nutans* × *Cryptanthus bahianus.* Lvs. in an open, reflexed rosette, deep bronzy-red; fls. white.

CRYPTOCARYA R. Br. *Lauraceae.* About 200 spp. of evergreen trees and shrubs, native mostly to s. tropics and subtropics; lvs. alt. or opp., leathery; fls. small, in panicles, bisexual, perianth persistent, fertile stamens 9, anthers 2-celled; fr. small, dry, entirely enclosed by enlarged calyx tube.

Sometimes planted as a street tree or in parks in Calif.

chinensis (Hance) Hemsl. Medium-sized tree; lvs. elliptic, to 4 in. long, acuminate, glossy above, glaucous beneath; panicles axillary and terminal, to 1¼ in. long; fr. depressed-globose. Se. China. Taiwan, s. Japan.

Miersii: a listed name of no botanical standing, used for *Beilschmiedia Miersii.*

rubra (Mol.) Skeels. Tree, 50–60 ft.; lvs. nearly opp. or alt., ovate, 1–2 in., rarely 3 in. long, glabrous, glaucous beneath. Chile.

CRYPTOCEREUS Alexand. *Cactaceae.* Two spp. of epiphytic cacti, native to Mex. and Costa Rica; sts. of elongate joints, flattened, deeply lobed; areoles short-spined, in the axils of the lobes; fls. nocturnal, funnelform, perianth segms. many, longer than the tube, ovary spiny, style thick. Sts. as in some spp. of *Epiphyllum,* but spiny and with fls. intermediate between those of *Heliocereus* and *Hylocereus.*

For culture see *Cacti.*

Anthonyanus Alexand. Joints to 3 ft. long or more, 3–6 in. wide, lobes 1–1¾ in. long; spines 3; fls. creamy, fragrant, 5 in. long, 4–6 in. across, tube straight, scales of the ovary close-set and prominent but short, their axils with wool, bristles, and stout translucent spines to ⅛ in. long, style ¼ in. thick above. Mex.

CRYPTOCORYNE Fisch. ex Wydl. WATER-TRUMPET. *Araceae.* About 50 spp. of small, rhizomatous and often stoloniferous aquatic herbs of se. Asia and Indonesia; lvs. simple, petioles usually long; peduncle short, spathe slender, the length determined by depth of water, tube long, inflated at base, blades expanded and often tail-like and spiralled; fls. unisexual, spadix slender, much shorter than spathe, naked between zones of female and male fls.

Popular foliage plants for aquaria, thriving in a soil with some organic matter, relatively low light intensities, and temperatures about 68° F.

affinis N. E. Br. ex Hook.f. [*C. Haerteliana* Milkuhn]. Lf. blades elliptic-oblong to lanceolate, 2⅝–4 in. long and 1 in. wide, or larger, basally obtuse or emarginate, puckered dark green above with much paler midrib and veins, deep wine-red beneath; petioles slender, as long as blade or longer; spathes to 5–8 in. long or more, pale green outside, the blade spiralled and black-purple inside. Malay Pen.

Balansae Gagnep. Lf. blades linear, to 1½ ft. long and 1½ in. wide, wavy-margined, corrugated, bright glossy-green, petioles stout, to 2 in. long; spathe about 6 in. long, blade to 1½ in. long, spirally twisted, brownish. Thailand, Vietnam.

Beckettii Thwaites ex Trimen. Differs from *C. Nevillii* in having lf. blades broader, 3–6 in. long and to 1½ in. wide, basally obtuse-truncate to subcordate, olive-green, with purple midribs and streaks along transverse veinlets; spathes larger, to 5 in. long, blade erect and twisted, 1 in. long, yellowish, purple-brown in throat. Ceylon. Material offered under this name may be *C. Nevillii.*

Blassii De Wit. Lf. blades ovate, to 3 in. long and 1¾ in. wide, obtuse at apex, brownish-red above, wine-red beneath, petioles to 6 in. long; spathe to 2¾ in. long, with transverse corrugations, yellow. Thailand.

ciliata (Roxb.) Fisch. ex Schott. Rhizome to ¾ in. in diam.; lvs. often aerial, blades lanceolate or linear-oblong, 6–20 in. long and ¾–3½ in. wide, weakly undulate, light green, without purple markings, petioles stout, to 12(18) in. long, glabrous or minutely papillate; spathe 6–15 in. long, greenish outside, blade purple, 2–3 in. long with fimbriate margin, yellow in throat. India to Malay Pen. and Indonesia. Cvs. **'Major'** and **'Minor'** are listed.

cordata Griff. Lf. blades broadly to narrowly ovate-elliptic, 3–4 in. long and 1½ in. wide, cordate to emarginate, obtuse, red-purple beneath, petioles as long as blades to twice as long; spathe 9 in. long or more, tube pale rose, blade 1½ in. long, caudate, smooth, purple, yellowish in throat. Malay Pen. The juvenile phase commonly seen has lf. blades oblong-lanceolate, basally obtuse-subtruncate, and shortly decurrent on petiole.

elongata: a listed name of no botanical standing.

Griffithii Schott. Differs from *C. cordata* in having its spathe with tube shorter, about 1½ in. long, blade narrower, 1 in. long, and warty. Malay Pen.

Haerteliana: *C. affinis.*

johorensis Engl. Lf. blades ovate, to 7 in. long and 4 in. wide, cordate, with 5 pairs of prominent lateral veins, pale green, petioles to 7½ in. long; spathe to 9 in. long including the 6 in. tail, blade ovate, to 1¼ in. long, wine-red inside. Malay Pen. and Indonesia.

longicauda Becc. ex Engl. Lf. blades ovate, to 6 in. long and 4 in. wide, cordate, crenate or crisped, midrib very broad, petioles stout, longer than blades; spathe with tube 4 in. long or more, whitish basally, suffused with purple above, mouth deep red-purple, blade attenuate into a 6 in. tail, purplish. N. Borneo.

lutea Alston. Lf. blades elliptic to ovate, to 4½ in. long and 1½ in. wide, obtuse, mucronate, with 3–4 pairs of lateral veins, pale green beneath, petioles to 6 in. long; spathe to 2½ in. long, blade lanceolate, yellow or greenish-yellow inside, tip scarcely twisted. Ceylon.

Nevillii Trimen ex Hook.f. [*C. Beckettii* Hort., not Thwaites]. Lf. blades oblong-lanceolate, to 2¾ in. long and ¾ in. wide, basally attenuate to the petiole, dark green, midrib broad beneath, petioles to 5½ in. long; peduncle very short, spathe 2–3 in. long, tube purple-spotted basally, blade papillose, dark red-purple. Ceylon.

purpurea Ridl. Lf. blades ovate or elliptic-ovate, to 3½ in. long and 2 in. wide, obtuse, mucronate, reddish-purple, spotted above, reddish to dark green beneath, petioles to 9 in. long; spathe to 7 in. long, blade ovate, somewhat caudate, warty and purple-red to red inside, with yellow to purple throat. Malay Pen.

retrospiralis (Roxb.) Kunth. Rhizome to ⅜ in. in diam.; lf. blades lanceolate to linear, to 12 in. long and ¾ in. wide; narrowed toward each end, petioles stout, to 2 in. long, sheathing nearly to the blade; spathe to 8 in. long, tightly spiralled, green, streaked purple. India to Burma.

ribbonii: a listed name of no botanical standing.

spiralis (Retz.) Fisch. ex Wydl. Lf. blades linear-lanceolate, to 6 in. long and ⅜ in. wide, bright green, petioles to 3½ in. long; spathe to 9½ in. long, blade spirally twisted, to 7 in. long, wrinkled and purple inside. India, Ceylon.

Thwaitesii Schott. Lf. blades narrowly to broadly ovate, to 2½ in. long and 1¼ in. wide, bluntly toothed, olive-green, sometimes reddish beneath, spotted above, petioles to 3 in. long; spathe to 2½ in. long, blade linear, spotted reddish-purple inside. Ceylon.

Versteegii Engl. Lf. blades triangular-ovate, to 2¼ in. long and 1¼ in. wide, with 5–8 pairs of lateral veins, rather fleshy, deep green, petioles to 2 in. long; spathe to 3½ in. long, blade lanceolate, dark purple and with yellow throat inside. New Guinea.

Wendtii De Wit. Lf. blades oblong-lanceolate, to 4½ in. long and 1¼ in. wide, cordate to rounded, wavy-margined, dark green above, paler to reddish beneath, petioles to 6 in. long; spathes to 3 in. long, blade lanceolate, to 1¼ in. long, brownish-green, twisted toward tip, throat violet, edged with purple. Se. Asia.

Willisii Engl. ex H. Baum. Submerged lf. blades narrowly lanceolate, to 6 in. long and 1 in. wide, basally attenuate, wavy-margined, red-brown becoming light green in age, with darker veins, aerial lvs. darker green and basally obtuse to rounded; spathe to about 4 in. long, blade green-yellow or pale brown, throat bordered by a white and a green line. Ceylon.

CRYPTOGRAMMA R. Br. ROCK BRAKE. *Polypodiaceae.* Probably 4 spp. of small alpine and boreal ferns of both hemispheres; lvs. compound, dimorphic, the pinnules of the fertile lvs. podlike due to the folding back of the margins over the sori.

Sometimes grown in rock gardens. For culture see *Ferns.*

acrostichoides: *C. crispa* var.

crispa (L.) R. Br. [*Blechnum crispum* (L.) Hartm.]. EUROPEAN PARSLEY FERN, MOUNTAIN P.F. Lvs. many, clustered, 2–4-pinnate, fertile lvs. with inrolled linear pinnules, sterile lvs. with pinnules mostly cuneate at base and deeply cleft, petioles straw-colored, to 6 in. long, with basal scales uniformly tan to brown. Eur. and adjacent Asia. Var. **acrostichoides** (R. Br.) C. B. Clarke [*C. acrostichoides* R. Br.]. PARSLEY FERN, AMERICAN P.F. Fertile lvs. mostly 2–3-pinnate, sterile lvs. with pinnules mostly obtuse basally, crenate to incised, petioles with basal scales mostly with a darker median zone. Lake Huron, se. to mts. of New Mex., w. to Kamchatka and s. Calif.

densa: *Cheilanthes siliquosa.*

Stelleri (S. G. Gmel.) Prantl [*Pellaea gracilis* Hook.]. SLENDER CLIFF BRAKE, FRAGILE C.B. Differs from *C. crispa* var. *acrostichoides* in having creeping rhizomes, scattered lvs., and fertile lvs. with broader pinnules. N. N. Amer., Asia.

CRYPTOMERIA D. Don. *Taxodiaceae.*

One sp., a fast-growing, tall, evergreen, coniferous, monoecious tree of pyramidal habit, native to to temp. e. Asia; lvs. spirally arranged, awl-shaped, clasping at base, pointed forward and curved inward; male cones spicate, female cones globose, scales 20–30, ascending, subpeltate, tipped by 2–3 straight or curved appendages; seeds irregularly triangular, with rudimentary wings.

Much grown for timber in Japan and as an ornamental in mild temperate climates. Thrives best in fertile moist soils and clean air. Propagated by seeds and cuttings; transplants easily when young. For culture see *Conifers.*

japonica (L.f.) D. Don. JAPANESE CEDAR. To 150 ft. or more; lvs. to ½ in. long, keeled on both sides, bluish-green; male cones yellow, female cones globose, to 1 in. across, the scales wedge-shaped. Zone 8 and locally in Zone 7, but there the foliage usually browning in winter and recovering the following season. Var. **japonica.** The typical var.; of pyramidal habit, brs. spreading; lvs. small; cone scales usually 5-seeded. Japan. Var. **sinensis** Siebold & Zucc. Habit looser, branchlets slender, drooping; cone scales rarely more than 20, usually 2-seeded. S. China.—Cvs. are: 'Albovariegata': 'Nana Albispica'; 'Araucarioides', branchlets drooping, lvs. small, bright green; 'Compacta', compact, conical; 'Compressa', dwarf, flat-topped shrub; 'Cristata', large shrub, brs. fasciated, cockscomblike; 'Dacrydioides', compact, brs. short, lvs. small, brownish, closely set; 'Elegans', shrubby with dense, drooping branchlets, lvs. to 1 in. long; 'Globosa', globose shrub, slow-growing; 'Gracilis', upright; 'Knaptonensis', dwarf, lvs. white-variegated; 'Lobbii', compact, conical tree, brs. short, dense, lvs. lighter green; 'Monstrosa', columnar, to 6 ft., with irregularly spreading brs. and many short shoots with crisped needles; 'Nana', dwarf, spreading or procumbent; 'Nana Albispica' [cv. 'Albovariegata'], dwarf, with whitish br. tips; 'Pendulata', brs. long, slender, pendent; 'Pungens', compact, lvs. stiff, sharp-pointed, dark green; 'Pygmaea', dwarf; 'Selaginoides', large shrub, brs. with short-tufted branchlets near tips; 'Spiralis', shrub, lvs. twisted spirally; 'Variegata', lvs. variegated yellow; 'Vilmoriniana', dwarf, globose, lvs. light green; 'Viminalis', large shrub, brs. slender with short-tufted branchlets near tips.

CRYPTOSTEGIA R. Br. RUBBER VINE. *Asclepiadaceae.*

Probably 3 spp. of woody vines with milky juice, native to trop. Afr. and Madagascar; lvs. opp., simple; fls. in terminal cymes, calyx glandular at base, corolla funnelform, tube short, corona of 5 entire or 2-parted lobes, anthers with sharp appendages; fr. an angled or winged follicle.

Cryptostegias may be grown under glass in loamy soil, or in the open in warm areas such as southern Fla. Propagated by cuttings over bottom heat. Rubber can be manufactured from the latex.

grandiflora R. Br. RUBBER VINE, PURPLE ALLAMANDA. Woody, strong-growing vine; lvs. oblong, 3–4 in. long, glabrous and shining, fls. lilac-purple, 2–3 in. across, calyx leafy, about ½ in. long; corona lobes deeply forked into 2 filiform segms.; follicles to 4 in. long, sharply angled. Afr.

madagascariensis Bojer. Similar to *C. grandiflora*, but differs in having fls. reddish-purple, calyx to 1¼ in. long, and corona lobes entire. Madagascar.

CRYPTOTAENIA DC. *Umbelliferae.*

About 5 spp. of glabrous, branched, ann. or per. herbs, native to Afr., Eur., Asia, and e. N. Amer.; basal lvs. ternately compound, upper lvs. simple and toothed or lobed; fls. small, in compound umbels, involucre usually absent, involucels minute or absent; fr. linear-oblong, compressed.

canadensis (L.) DC. HONEWORT, WHITE CHERVIL. Per., to 3 ft.; lfts. oblong-lanceolate to obovate; fls. white. Woods, New Bruns., Que., to Ga., w. to Man., Nebr., and Tex.; also e. Asia.

CTENANTHE Eichl. *Marantaceae.*

Nine spp. of per. herbs, native to Brazil; basal lvs. long-petioled, lvs. on flowering shoots short-petioled; fls. hidden by persistent green bracts, in mostly dense terminal spikes or racemes, sepals 3, separate, corolla 3-lobed, with short tube, fertile stamen 1, staminodes 4, the outer 2 petal-like, ovary inferior, 1-celled.

Culture as for *Calathea.*

compressa (A. Dietr.) Eichl. To about 2 ft.; lf. blades linear-oblong or ovate-oblong, to 16 in. long and 4 in. wide just above base, green on both sides, petioles villous at apex; racemes solitary or paired, to 2 in. long, bracts marginally pubescent; fls. whitish. Se. Brazil.

glabra (Körn.) Eichl. [*Calathea glabra* Hort.]. To 4 ft., stoloniferous; lf. blades oblong-lanceolate, to 16 in. long and 4 in. wide; racemes short, commonly 3 together, congested, sessile, bracts glabrous. E. Brazil.

Kummerana (E. Morr.) Eichl. To 1½ ft., stoloniferous; lf. blades ovate to oblong, to 6 in. long and 2½ in. wide, green and with midrib and main lateral veins whitish above, purple beneath; peduncles red-hairy, racemes villous. Se. Brazil.

Lubbersiana (E. Morr.) Eichl. ex Petersen. To 2 ft.; lvs. linear-oblong, to 9 in. long, 2½ in. wide, green and heavily variegated with yellow above, pale green beneath; racemes glabrous; fls. white. Brazil. Cv. 'Variegata' is listed.

Oppenheimiana (E. Morr.) K. Schum. [*Maranta Oppenheimiana* Hort.]. To 3 ft.; lvs. lanceolate, to 18 in. long and 5 in. wide, dark green and with gray bands between main lateral veins above, purple beneath; peduncles 4 in. long, racemes in pairs, to 2¾ in. long. E. Brazil. Cv. 'Tricolor' [*Maranta Oppenheimiana tricolor* Hort.]. NEVER-NEVER PLANT. Lvs. with cream-colored blotches.

setosa (Roscoe) Eichl. [*Calathea setosa* Hort.]. To 3 ft., stoloniferous; lvs. linear-oblong to oblong-lanceolate, to 18 in. long and 4 in. wide, green on both sides, petioles villous; racemes to 8 in a panicle, 1 in. long, bracts villous; fls. white with yellow throat. Se. Brazil.

CTENITIS C. Chr. *Polypodiaceae.*

About 150 spp. of medium to large ferns of pantrop. distribution; lvs. 2-pinnatifid to decompound, broad at the base, veins separate; sori on veins, indusia reniform, or sometimes lacking. Formerly included in *Dryopteris*, but differing mainly in lvs. broad rather than narrow, and in soft, woolly, jointed hairs.

For culture see *Ferns.*

decomposita (R. Br.) E. Copel. [*Dryopteris decomposita* (R. Br.) O. Kuntze]. Lvs. to 2½ ft. long, the pinnules acute at apex. Australia. Material offered in the trade under this name is referable to *C. pentangularis.*

pentangularis (Colenso) Alston. Lvs. to 2 ft., the ultimate segm. obtuse at apex; also differs from *C. decomposita* in having more teeth on the sides of pinnules. New Zeal. Material offered in the trade as *C. decomposita* belongs here.

CUCUBALUS L. BERRY CATCHFLY. *Caryophyllaceae.*

One sp., a per. of Eurasia, to 3 ft.; lvs. opp.; infl. a terminal cyme; fls. bisexual, sepals united at base, 5-toothed, petals 5, clawed, with coronal scales at juncture of claw and limb, stamens 10, ovary 3-celled, styles 3; fr. berrylike, dry at maturity, seeds reniform, black.

baccifer L. Large per., to 40 in., diffusely branched, pubescent; lvs. ovate, acuminate, entire to sinuate, sparsely hairy; fls. to ¾ in. long, drooping, calyx campanulate, to ½ in. long, petals greenish-white, blades bifid, with 2 coronal scales; fr. ⁵⁄₁₆ in., black, globular. Nw. Afr., Portugal to the Netherlands, across Asia to Japan.

CUCUMBER.

The fruit of an annual, tendril-bearing vine, the cucumber, *Cucumis sativus*, is used while immature for pickles, for eating raw as a salad, and in some countries from the hand without dressing. The cucumber is characteristically a frost-tender, warm-weather plant. Cucumbers are grown directly from seeds and commonly planted in the field as soon as the soil is warm and the weather reliable. Plants may be started in the greenhouse and transplanted to the field for an early crop, provided they are grown in pots, bands, or blocks to avoid disturbance of roots in transplanting. Rows are usually 5–6 feet apart with spacing of single plants 6–12 inches apart in the rows, or, if hill plantings are used, two to three plants at a distance of about 2 feet. As soon as plants emerge or are set in the field, they should be treated with a recommended insecticide to avoid damage from beetles, damage which can be extremely sudden and severe if plants are unprotected. Later in the season cucumbers are subject to a number of diseases and insects, and local recommendations should be followed for controlling them.

Under favorable conditions, cucumbers should be ready to eat in 50 to 60 days from planting. They should be harvested while the fruits are young and picked every other day. Overmature or cull fruits should be removed from the vines if continued production is desired.

Shape of fruit, disease resistance, and flowering habit are all considerations in the choice of cultivars. The pickling kinds of commerce have a length-to-diameter ratio of about three to one, while the fresh market or slicing kinds have a ratio of about four to one. However, these two types can be used interchangeably in the home garden. Cultivars chosen for cooler areas should have resistance to both cucumber-mosaic virus and to scab, since these are prevalent diseases that are difficult to control by other means. Cultivars 'Marketmore' and 'Tablegreen' carry this combination of resistance. For warmer, humid areas, it is desirable to have multiple-disease resistance such as is found in 'Poinsett', namely to anthracnose, downy mildew, and powdery mildew. Numerous hybrid cucumbers are available that not only carry multiple-disease resistance but also have the gynoecious or all-female flowering habit. These are widely used for commercial plantings for pickles because of their high and concentrated yielding ability. For the home garden, however, the gynoecious hybrids may not be so satisfactory as the monoecious types, which have male and female flowers on the same plant and produce over a longer period of time with less concentrated production.

Still another type of cucumber is the parthenocarpic, or seedless, cucumber, which produces fruit without pollination or seed setting. Fruits of this type are usually considerably longer and grown mostly in the greenhouses of Europe. Cultivars have been developed which combine the gynoecious and parthenocarpic features so that seedless cucumbers can be grown outdoors, provided the field is sufficiently isolated from standard cucumbers to eliminate pollen being carried in by bees.

Greenhouse cucumbers have traditionally been trained to grow upright on string or wires so that the fruit hangs. A similar practice can be followed in growing outdoor cucumbers to get higher yields of fancy fruit from limited space.

The smallest pickling cucumbers are sometimes called gherkins, but the West India or bur gherkin is another species, *Cucumis Anguria*, which is more often grown in the United States for ornament or novelty than for pickles.

CUCUMIS L. *Cucurbitaceae.* About 23 spp. of ann., tender, running herbs, in Afr. and s. Asia, monoecious or with both bisexual and male fls.; lvs. angled, lobed or divided, tendrils simple; fls. yellow, ½–1 in. across, rotate, with short tube, male fls. in clusters or rarely solitary, axillary on spurs, with stamens 3, free, borne on fl. tube, anthers flexuous, and a central nectary cup, female fls. solitary or rarely clustered on spurs, with nectary ring at base of style; fr. indehiscent, with many horizontal seeds.

Grown for edible or interesting fruits.

Anguria L. [*C. erinaceus* Hort.; *C. grossulariiformis* Hort.]. WEST INDIAN GHERKIN, BUR G., GOOSEBERRY GOURD, GOAREBERRY G., BUR C. Sts. slender, angled, rough; lvs. to 3½ in. long, with 3 main rounded lobes and open sinuses; fr. ovoid or oblong, about 2 in. long, prickly, on long sts. Of cult. origin; probably derived from an Afr. sp. (*C. longipes* Hook.). Fr. grown for pickles and as curiosity. The common "gherkins" used for pickles are immature cucumbers. See *C. sativus.*

Chito: *C. Melo,* Chito Group.

Conomon: *C. Melo,* Conomon Group.

dipsaceus C. G. Ehrenb. ex Spach. HEDGEHOG GOURD, TEASEL G. Slender, sts. prickly; lvs. broad-ovate to reniform-ovate, not lobed; fr. a firm, bristly bur, 1–2 in. long, on a short stalk. Arabia. Grown as a curiosity and ornamental.

Dudaim: *C. Melo,* Dudaim Group.

erinaceus: *C. Anguria.*

flexuosus: *C. Melo,* Flexuosus Group.

grossulariiformis: *C. Anguria.*

Melo L. MELON. Sts. trailing, soft, hairy; lvs. round-ovate to nearly reniform, obtuse, angled or more rarely lobed; fls. about 1 in. across; fr. globose to oblong, or slender and curved or coiled, pubescent or becoming glabrous, often musky-scented and -flavored. Probably W. Afr. in origin. Widely cult. in many forms. For cult. see *Melon.* The sp. is very variable, being divided into two (or, by some, more) principal subdivisions: subsp. **agrestis (Naud.)** Greb., including all the wild forms with small fls. and inedible fr. the size of a plum; and subsp. **Melo** [var. *cultus* Kurz], with about 7 long-recognized cult. races or groups, all apparently interfertile, and many named cvs. of hybrids. In the latter subsp., the following groups (also variously treated as convarieties or subspp.) are cult. in the U.S., with the Inodorus and Reticulatus Groups and their many hybrids and cvs. an important home and commercial crop:

Cantalupensis Group [var. *cantalupensis* Naud.; var. *Cantalupo* Ser.]. CANTALOUPE. Fr. medium-sized, rind hard, rough-warty or scaly but not netted. Little grown in U.S., not at all commercially, the so-called cantaloupes of this country being referable to the Reticulatus Group.

Chito Group [var. *Chito* (E. Morr.) Naud.; *C. Chito* E. Morr.]. MANGO M., ORANGE M., GARDEN LEMON, MELON APPLE, VEGETABLE ORANGE, VINE PEACH. Lvs. mostly small; fr. yellow or orange, the size and shape of a lemon or orange, flesh white and firm, not fragrant. Used to make preserves and pickles, but grown mostly as an ornamental and perhaps properly referable to one of the prickly fruited spp.

Conomon Group [var. *Conomon* (Thunb.) Mak.; *C. Conomon* Thunb.]. ORIENTAL PICKLING M. Lvs. tending to be oblong and somewhat lobed and sharply toothed; fr. smooth, globose or oblong-cylindrical to club-shaped or constricted, flesh white or green, crisp, not musky. Used in preserving and pickling in the U.S.

Dudaim Group [var. *Dudaim* (L.) Naud.; *C. Dudaim* L.; *C. odoratissimus* Moench]. DUDAIM M., POMEGRANATE M., QUEEN ANNE'S POCKET M., STINK M. Plant small; fr. the size of an orange or smaller, more or less flattened at ends, marbled, highly fragrant and sometimes grown for this reason.

Flexuosus Group [var. *flexuosus* (L.) Naud.; *C. flexuous* L.]. SNAKE M., SERPENT M. Fr. 1½–3 ft. long or more, 3 in. thick or less, mostly curved or coiled. Grown as a curiosity and sometimes for preserves.

Inodorus Group [var. *inodorus* Naud.]. WINTER M., HONEYDEW M., CASABA M. Vine strong; lvs. large, sometimes prominently lobed; fr. large, only mildly scented, flesh white or green, crisp, rind smooth (in HONEYDEW) or wrinkled (in CASABA).

Reticulatus Group [var. *reticulatus* Ser.]. MUSKMELON, NETTED MELON, NUTMEG M., PERSIAN M. Fr. of medium size or large (PERSIAN), rind more or less strongly netted, flesh generally orange and musky. Probably the most important commercial melon.

metuliferus E. H. Mey. ex Schrad. AFRICAN HORNED CUCUMBER. Ann.; sts. hispid-hairy; lvs. broadly cordate-ovate, more or less 3-lobed, toothed; fls. much like those of *C. Melo;* fr. 3–5 in. long, oblong, spiny, red when ripe. Trop. and S. Afr.

odoratissimus: *C. Melo,* Dudaim Group.

sativus L. CUCUMBER. Rough-hairy, trailing vine; lvs. triangular-ovate, pointed, often somewhat 3-lobed; fls. similar to those of *C. MELO* but short-stalked and clustered in axils on main st.; fr. clustered, globular to oblong to short-cylindrical, prickly when immature, flesh white, firm, not sweet. S. Asia. Many cvs. are cult.; fr. eaten raw or in pickles. Immature cucumbers are known as "gherkins"; see *C. Anguria.* For cult. see *Cucumber.*

CUCURBITA L. SQUASH, PUMPKIN, GOURD. *Cucurbitaceae.* Over 20 spp. of monoecious, tendril-bearing, herbaceous plants, probably all originally from the W. Hemisphere, running and commonly rooting except in certain "bush" cvs., with per. or ann. roots; lvs. large, simple but variously angled or lobed; fls. mostly 5–6 in. across, yellow, solitary, or the male fls. perhaps in clusters, corolla campanulate, male fls. with 3 stamens, filaments separate, anthers flexuous, more or less united, female fls. with inferior ovary; fr. an indehiscent, fleshy or corky berry with hard rind (a pepo), seeds many, horizontal.

There are native gourds in Tex. and Mex. that may have some relation to prehistoric stocks, but the history of cultivated pumpkins and squashes is not fully known. Grown mostly for the large edible fruits, but some of them as ornamentals and for curiosity. See *Pumpkin and Squash.*

argyrosperma: *C. mixta.*

ficifolia Bouché [*C. melanosperma* A. Braun]. MALABAR GOURD, FIG-LEAF G. Long-running, per., in warm countries; lvs. orbicular-ovate to nearly reniform, lobed, with obtuse sinuses or merely sinuate; corolla lobes large, spreading; fr. oblong to nearly spherical, to 12 in.

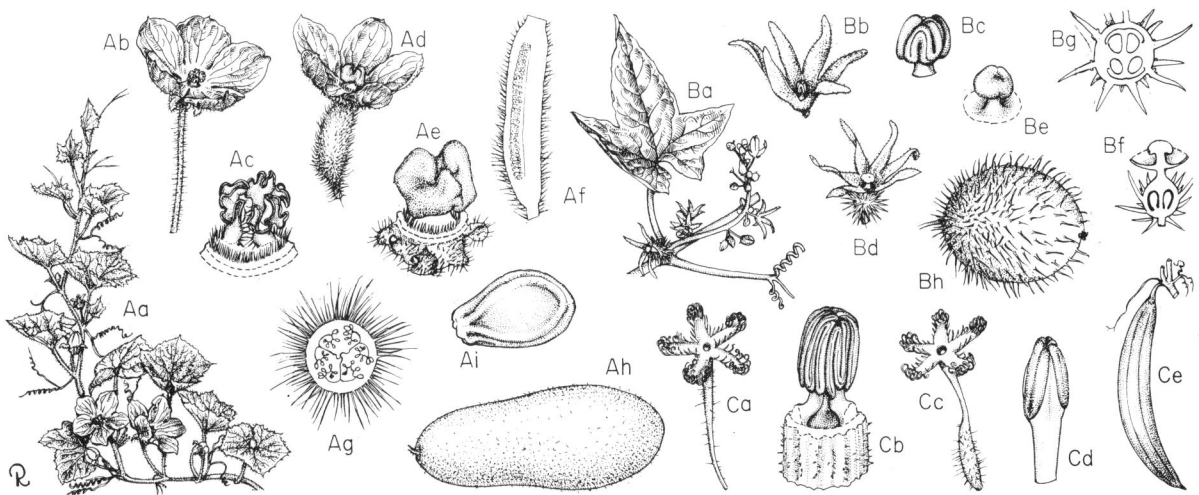

CUCURBITACEAE. **A,** *Benincasa hispida:* **Aa,** flowering stem, × ¹⁄₁₀; **Ab,** male flower, × ¼; **Ac,** anthers, × 1; **Ad,** female flower, × ¼; **Ae** stigma, × 1; **Af,** ovary, vertical section, × ½; **Ag,** ovary, cross section, × 1; **Ah,** fruit, × ¹⁄₁₀; **Ai,** seed, × 1. **B,** *Echinocystis lobata:* **Ba,** flowering node, × ½; **Bb,** male flower, × 2; **Bc,** anthers, × 6; **Bd,** female flower, × 1; **Be,** style and stigma, × 3; **Bf,** pistil, vertical section, × 2; **Bg,** ovary, cross section, × 3; **Bh,** fruit, × ½. **C,** *Trichosanthes Anguina:* **Ca,** male flower, × ½; **Cb,** anthers, × 4; **Cc,** female flower, × ½; **Cd,** stigma, × 3; **Ce,** fruit, × ⅛.

long, green with white stripes, flesh white, seeds often dark-colored, with smooth, obtuse margin. Trop. Amer.; but cult. in Old and New World; grown as an ornamental in U.S.

foetidissima HBK [*C. perennis* (James) A. Gray]. CALABAZILLA, FETID WILD PUMPKIN, MISSOURI GOURD. Per., long-running; lvs. cordate-triangular, stiff, grayish, crenate; fls. large; fr. striped green and yellow, of the size and shape of an orange, not edible. Nebr. to Calif. and Mex.

maxima Duchesne. AUTUMN and WINTER SQUASH and PUMPKIN. Ann. vine, only slightly prickly; lvs. orbicular or reniform, very obtuse, mostly not lobed; corolla lobes soft, spreading or drooping, mostly obtuse; fr. spherical to oblong or turban-shaped, often very large, long-keeping, peduncle spongy, not ridged, or prominently enlarged at apex. Of cult. origin, probably in S. Amer. Among many cvs. are: 'Banana', fr. gray, becoming creamy-pink, nearly cylindrical, to 20 in. long and 6 in. in diam., flesh orange-yellow, moderately dry; 'Blue Hubbard', fr. blue-gray, curved-obovoid, to 15 in. long and 12 in. in diam., flesh dull orange, medium dry; 'Boston Marrow', fr. orange, obovoid, to 14 in. long and 11 in. in diam., flesh orange-yellow, moderately moist; 'Buttercup', fr. dull dark green, spotted with gray, somewhat drum-shaped, broadly ribbed, to 5 in. long and 8 in. in diam., flesh orange, dry; 'Delicious', fr. dull green, spotted and streaked with gray, top-shaped, to 9 in. long and 8 in. in diam., flesh orange, dry; 'Hubbard', fr. deep dull green, often with pale green stripes from apex, curved-obovoid, to 15 in. long and 10 in. in diam., flesh yellow to orange, dry, suitable for baking; 'Mammoth', fr. orange, with paler stripes from apex, nearly globose, to 18 in. long and flesh light yellow to deep orange, moist, suitable for stock feed; 'Queensland Blue', vines to 25 ft., fr. dull green, mottled with gray, drum-shaped, to 6 in. long and 9 in. in diam., flesh orange, dry; 'Turbaniformis', TURBAN SQUASH, fr. orange with green turbanlike apex, grown for the ornamental fr.

melanosperma: *C. ficifolia.*

Melopepo: *C. Pepo* var.

mixta Pang. [*C. argyrosperma* Hort. ex L. H. Bailey]. WINTER SQUASH, PUMPKIN, CUSHAW, SILVER-SEED GOURD. Ann., long-running, sts. hard, angular, pubescent, lacking prickles; lvs. cordate, shallowly 5-lobed, white-spotted, male fls. with long, slender staminal column; fr. globose to ovoid, or variously constricted, flesh coarse-grained, peduncle hard, angled, enlarged by hard cork, seeds long, white tinged gray or bluish, with acute, scarcely scalloped margin. Mex. and Guatemala. Some cvs. are: 'Green-striped Cushaw', fr. pale yellow, striped with dark green, curved-obovoid, to 20 in. long and 10 in. in diam., flesh pale yellow, moist; 'Japanese Pie', fr. dark green with lighter stripes, curved-cylindrical, to 18 in. long and 9 in. in diam., flesh yellow, moderately coarse; 'Tennessee Sweet Potato', fr. pale yellow, pear-shaped, to 15 in. long and 10 in. in diam., flesh light yellow, moist; 'White Cushaw', fr. nearly white, curved-obovoid, to 20 in. long and 9 in. in diam., flesh pale yellow, insipid.

moschata (Duchesne) Poir. PUMPKIN, CANADA P., CROOKNECK SQUASH, WINTER C.S., CANADA C.S., WINTER SQUASH. Ann. vine, rather soft-hairy; lvs. broad-ovate to nearly orbicular-ovate, mostly not

lobed, often with whitish marks; calyx lobes often very large and leafy, corolla lobes wide-spreading, crinkly, mostly acute; fr. of many shapes, commonly oblong or crookneck, ripening in autumn and winter, peduncle angled, much expanded at apex. Of cult. origin, in Amer. Cvs. include: 'Butternut', fr. dull orange, nearly cylindrical to cylindric-obovoid, to 12 in. long and 6 in. in diam., flesh dark orange, moist; 'Cheese', fr. dark cream-colored, depressed-globose, ribbed, to 6 in. long and 14 in. in diam., flesh deep orange, juicy, suitable for canning or stock feed; 'Quaker Pie', similar to 'Cheese' but pear-shaped; 'Virginia Mammoth', fr. dark buff with lighter mesh, blunt-cylindrical, to 16 in. long and 12 in. in diam., flesh pale orange to amber, moist.

ovifera: *C. Pepo* var.

Pepo L. SUMMER and AUTUMN PUMPKIN and SQUASH, GOURD, MARROW. Harsh ann., sts. and petioles prickly; lvs. triangular or ovate-triangular, often prominently lobed; corolla lobes erect, sharp-pointed; fr. of many shapes, usually orange, furrowed, mostly not long-keeping, peduncle strongly angled and enlarging toward apex. Of cult. origin, probably in N. Amer. Var. **Pepo.** FIELD PUMPKIN, VEGETABLE MARROW, ACORN SQUASH. The typical var.; sts. running; fr. maturing in late summer or autumn. Among cvs. are: 'Acorn': cv. 'Table Queen'; 'Connecticut Field', fr. orange, nearly globose to ovoid, to 18 in. long and 14 in. in diam., flesh coarse, pale yellow, moist; 'Small Sugar', fr. orange, nearly globose but flattened at base and apex, narrowly ribbed, to 6 in. long and 8 in. in diam. or larger, flesh orange, moderately dry, suitable for pie; 'Table Queen' [cv. 'Acorn'], fr. dark green, ellipsoid-top-shaped, to about 6 in. long and 4 in. in diam., flesh pale orange, moderately dry, suitable for baking. Var. **Melopepo** (L.) Alef. [var. *condensa* L. H. Bailey; *C. Melopepo* L.]. BUSH PUMPKIN, BUSH SQUASH. Mostly summer kinds, not running. Cvs. include 'Cocozelle', COCOZELLE SQUASH, fr. dark green, striped pale greenish-yellow when edible, nearly cylindrical, to 18 in. long and 5 in. in diam., flesh light yellow; 'Summer Crookneck', SUMMER CROOKNECK SQUASH, fr. golden-yellow, more or less warty, club-shaped with curved neck, to 9 in. long and 3 in. in diam. or more, flesh light yellow, soft; 'Summer Straightneck', similar to 'Summer Crookneck' but not curved and essentially smooth; 'White Bush Scallop', PATTYPAN SQUASH, SCALLOP S., fr. white, disc-shaped, ribbed, to 3½ in. high and 9 in. in diam., flesh creamy-white; 'Zucchini', ZUCCHINI SQUASH, fr. dark green marked with very dark green when edible, maturing buff-colored, nearly cylindrical, to 12 in. long and 3 in. in diam. or more, flesh greenish-white. Var. **ovifera** (L.) Alef. YELLOW-FLOWERED GOURDS (as distinguished from the white-fld. gourds, *Lagenaria*). Running vines, producing many forms and colors of small, hard-shelled, ornamental, durable frs. Tex.

CUCURBITACEAE Juss. GOURD FAMILY. *Cucurbits.* Dicot.; about 114 genera and 500 spp. of monoecious or dioecious herbs and erect shrubs, mostly of trop. or subtrop. regions; the hort. kinds are herbaceous, mostly tender ann., and all but one (*Ecballium*) tendril-bearing vines; lvs. alt., palmately veined, lobed or dissected; corolla mostly yellow or greenish, sometimes large and showy, but ephemeral, petals

5, separate or united, male fls. with 1–5, but mostly 3 stamens, female fls. with usually 3-carpelled inferior ovary with 3 parietal placentas; fr. a fleshy berry or a pepo, indehiscent or irregularly bursting, often large and edible, seeds 1 to many. The cult. genera are: *Abobra, Benincasa, Bryonia, Citrullus, Coccinia, Cucumis, Cucurbita, Cyclanthera, Diplocyclos, Ecballium, Echinocystis, Ibervillea, Lagenaria, Luffa, Marah, Melothria, Momordica, Sechium, Sicana, Sicyos, Thladiantha,* and *Trichosanthes.*

An important horticultural family, including plants grown for edible fruits and as ornamental vines, as pumpkins, squashes, gourds, melons, watermelon, cucumbers, gherkins, and chayote. Grown from seeds and easily cultivated, but pumpkins, gourds, melons, and cucumbers require a warm quick soil, because they are frost-tender and in the northern parts of the country must make their growth rapidly. See *Cucumber, Gourd, Melon, Pumpkin and squash,* and *Watermelon.*

CUDRANIA Trécul. *Moraceae.* About 5 spp. of dioecious, often spiny trees, shrubs, or climbers, native from China to Australia; lvs. alt., simple; fls. unisexual, in axillary heads; fr. a fleshy syncarp.

Sometimes cultivated for ornament or hedges. The leaves are fed to silkworms in China. Propagated by cuttings of young wood under glass in summer.

tricuspidata (Carrière) Bur. ex Lavallée. Small tree, to 25 ft. or more, armed with slender thorns; lvs. ovate, to 3 in. long, sometimes 3-lobed at tip, glabrous to slightly pubescent beneath; fr. orange-red, edible, nearly globose, to 1 in. in diam. China, Korea. Zone 5. A good hedge plant.

CULCASIA Beauvois. *Araceae.* About 20 spp. of erect or scandent herbs of Afr.; lvs. lanceolate to elliptic, petioles long-sheathing, geniculate; peduncle slender, spathe convolute, finally deciduous; fls. unisexual, perianth absent.

Mannii (Hook.f) Engl. Erect, to 2 ft.; lf. blades elliptic, to 8 in. long, petioles 4 in. long, sheathed up to geniculum; peduncle 2 in. long, spathe expanded, white inside, 2 in. long and half as wide, spadix shorter, stalked, cylindrical, the zone of male fls. white, ovaries scarlet. Cameroon.

CULTIGEN. A cultigen is a plant or group of apparent specific rank, known only in cultivation, with no determined nativity, presumably having originated, in the form in which we know it, under domestication. Compare *Indigen.* Examples are *Cucurbita maxima, Phaseolus vulgaris, Zea Mays.* The term is not synonymous with cultivar.

CULTIVAR. A cultivar is a horticultural variety or race that has originated and persisted under cultivation, not necessarily referable to a botanical species, and of botanical or horticultural importance, requiring a name. Cultivar names are now formed from not more than three words in a modern language and are usually distinguished typographically by the use of single quotation marks, as *Vaccinium macrocarpon* cultivar (cv.) 'Early Black'.

CUMINUM L. *Umbelliferae.* One sp., an ann. herb, native to Medit. region.

Cyminum L. [*C. odorum* Salisb.]. CUMIN. To 6 in.; lvs. cut into threadlike divisions; umbels compound, bractlets of involucels long, narrow; fls. small, white or rose; fr. narrowly oblong, hairy or short-bristly. The frs. are used as flavoring. Prop. by seeds sown in spring.

CUNILA Royen ex L. DITTANY. *Labiatae.* Fifteen spp. of aromatic per. herbs of the New World, from e. N. Amer. to Uruguay; sts. mostly square in cross section; lvs. opp.; infl. a corymb of terminal and axillary cymes; fls. small, calyx tubular, 5-toothed, tube very hairy inside throat, corolla white to purple, 2-lipped, upper lip erect, flat, notched, lower lip spreading, 3-lobed, stamens 2, erect, exserted, staminodes 2, short; fr. of 4 nutlets. Related to *Origanum* and *Monardella* but having 2 fertile stamens.

Sometimes grown as a culinary herb; easily propagated by seeds.

origanoides (L.) Britt. AMERICAN D., COMMON D., STONE MINT, SWEET HORSEMINT. Sts. corymbosely branched, 8–16 in.; lvs. ovate to lanceolate, ⅝–2½ in. long, acuminate, rounded or cordate, weakly serrate, glabrous, gland-dotted, nearly sessile; cymes peduncled; calyx striate, corolla pinkish-purple, about ³⁄₁₆ in. long. E. N. Amer.

CUNNINGHAMIA R. Br. CHINA FIR. *Taxodiaceae.* Three spp. of coniferous, evergreen, monoecious trees, native to e. Asia, allied to *Cryptomeria;* lvs. spirally arranged, spreading in 2 ranks, stiff, linear-lanceolate, sharp-pointed, with broad white bands beneath; male cones in terminal clusters, female cones globose, scales thin, spine-tipped, seeds 3 to each scale, narrowly winged.

Grown as an ornamental in milder parts of the U.S. Propagated by seeds or cuttings. For culture see *Conifers.*

Konishii Hayata. To 100 ft.; lvs. to 1⅜ in. long, curved; female cones ovoid, to 1 in. long. Mts., Taiwan. Zone 8.

lanceolata (Lamb.) Hook. [*C. sinensis* R. Br.]. To 120 ft. or more; lvs. to 2½ in. long; female cones 1½–2 in. long. China. Zone 7. Wood widely used by Chinese. Somewhat hardier than *C. Konishii* and more commonly cult. Cv. 'Glauca'. Foliage blue-green.

sinensis: *C. lanceolata.*

CUNONIA L. *Cunoniaceae.* About 17 spp. of trees or shrubs, native mostly to New Caledonia, 1 to S. Afr.; lvs. opp., odd-pinnate, lfts. nearly sessile, serrate, leathery, stipules large, early deciduous; fls. small, in many-fld., spike-like racemes, sepals and petals 5, stamens 10, ovary superior, styles 2; fr. a 2-celled caps.

capensis L. Large shrub or small tree, to 15 ft. or more; lfts. 5–7, lateral lfts. paired, terminal lft. broadly lanceolate, to 4 in. long, somewhat narrower and longer than lateral lfts.; fls. white. S. Afr.

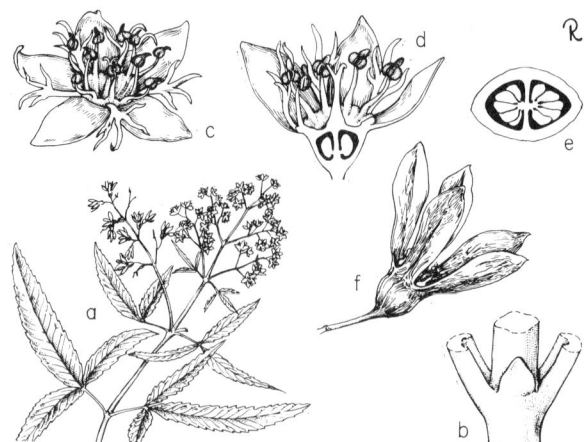

CUNONIACEAE. *Ceratopetalum gummiferum:* **a,** flowering branch, × × ⅓; **b,** node with stipule, × 5; **c,** flower, × 3; **d,** flower, vertical section, × 3; **e,** ovary, cross section, × 10; **f,** fruit, × 1½. (From Lawrence, *Taxonomy of Vascular Plants.*)

CUNONIACEAE R. Br. CUNONIA FAMILY. Dicot.; 26 genera and about 240 spp. of trees and shrubs, native almost exclusively to the S. Hemisphere; lvs. opp. or whorled, entire or pinnate; fls. small, bisexual or sometimes unisexual, the plants then dioecious, sepals 4–5, petals 4–5 or 0, stamens 4 or more, ovary usually superior, 2-celled; fr. usually a caps. *Ackama, Callicoma, Ceratopetalum, Cunonia, Geissois,* and *Weinmannia* are occasionally planted in Zone 10, principally in Calif., as ornamentals.

CUPANIA L. *Sapindaceae.* Not in cult. C. **anacardioides**: *Cupaniopsis anacardioides.* C. **sapida**: *Blighia sapida.*

CUPANIOPSIS Radlk. *Sapindaceae.* About 55 spp. of polygamous trees or shrubs, native to Oceania, but mostly to Australia and New Caledonia; lvs. alt., pinnate; fls. in axillary panicles or thyrses, regular, sepals and petals 5, stamens usually 6–8; fr. a 3-lobed caps.

anacardiopsis (A. Rich.) Radlk. [*Cupania anacardiopsis* A. Rich.]. Slender tree, to 40 ft.; lfts. 5–10, obovate or obovate-oblong, to 6 in. long, retuse at apex, leathery, glabrous; fls. white; caps. about ⅝ in. in diam. Australia.

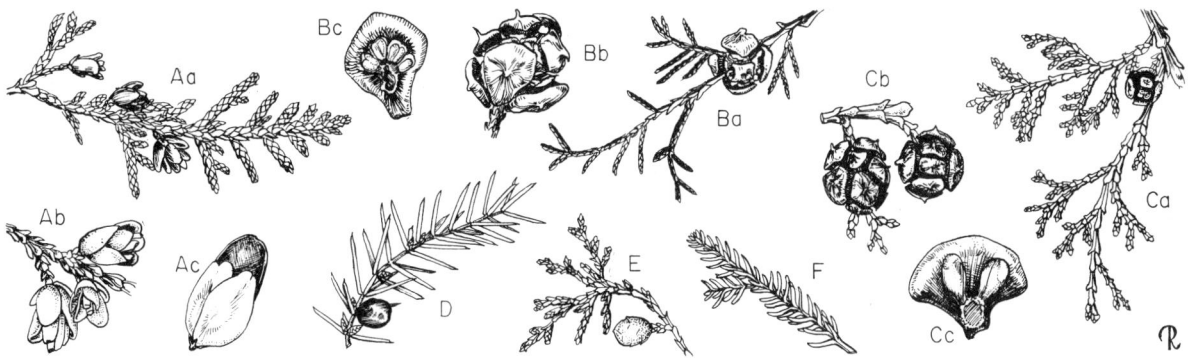

CUPRESSACEAE. **A,** *Thuja occidentalis:* **Aa,** coning branch, × ½; **Ab,** cones, × 1; **Ac,** cone scale with two seeds, × 2. **B,** *Cupressus macrocarpa:* **Ba,** coning branch, × ½; **Bb,** cone, × 1; **Bc,** cone scale with four seeds, × 2. **C,** *Chamaecyparis pisifera:* **Ca,** coning branch, × ½; **Cb,** cones, × 1; **Cc,** cone scale with two seeds, × 2. **D,** *Juniperus rigida:* coning branch, × ½. **E,** *Juniperus virginiana:* coning branch, × ½. **F,** *Juniperus communis:* juvenile foliage, × ½. (From Bailey, *Manual of Cultivated Plants*, ed. 2.)

CUPHEA P. Br. [*Parsonia* P. Br.]. *Lythraceae.* About 250 spp. of herbs or shrubs, native to W. Hemisphere; lvs. mostly opp. or whorled; fls. irregular, solitary, or in axillary clusters or terminal racemes, calyx tube often swollen on one side or spurred at base, calyx lobes 6, the upper or lower sometimes larger than the others, appendages usually present between calyx lobes inside, petals 6, rarely 4, 2, or 0, stamens mostly 11; fr. a papery caps., the caps. and calyx tube splitting together.

Cupheas are grown in the greenhouse or as tender annuals outside in the South. Easily cultivated; propagated by seeds, or the shrubs by cuttings.

aequipetala Cav. Coarsely hairy subshrub, to 3 ft.; lvs. opp., ovate, to 1 in. long; calyx tube purple and green, petals 6, 2 dark purple, reflexed, and 4 rose-purple, spreading, opp. the other 2. Mex.

cyanea Moç. & Sessé ex DC. Shrubby, to 6 ft. or more; lvs. ovate; fls. in racemose or branched terminal infl., calyx tube yellow, pink, and red, to 1 in. long, with 2 small, winglike appendages, petals violet, 2, minute. Mex. *C. lanceolata* has been grown under this name.

Hookerana [*C. Roezlii* Carrière]. Shrubby, to 2 ft. or more; lvs. lanceolate; fls. in racemose or branched terminal infl., calyx tube green and red, to ⅞ in. long, with 2 small, winglike appendages, petals violet or red, 2, large, sometimes with 4 very small additional ones. Mex. and Cent. Amer.

hyssopifolia HBK. FALSE HEATHER, ELFIN HERB. Small, branched shrub, to 2 ft.; lvs. crowded, linear to lanceolate, to ¾ in. long; fls. axillary, calyx tube green, about ¼ in. long, petals purple, pink, or white, 6, equal. Mex. and Guatemala. Cv. **'Alba'** is listed.

ignea A. DC. [*C. platycentra* Lem., not Benth.]. CIGAR FLOWER, FIRECRACKER PLANT, RED-WHITE-AND-BLUE FLOWER. Shrubby, to 3 ft.; lvs. oblong or lanceolate, to 3 in. long, but mostly smaller; fls. axillary, calyx tube bright red, with violet and white tip, to 1 in. long, glabrous, without appendages, lower calyx lobe longest, petals 0, ovules 14–20. Mex. and Jamaica. Material grown as *C. platycentra* is sometimes *C. micropetala.*

jorullensis HBK. To 2 ft. or more; lvs. opp., ovate to lanceolate, to 2⅜ in. long; fls. in leafy racemes, calyx tube red, green apically, to 1⅛ in. long, puberulent, without appendages, upper calyx lobe not elongate, petals white, 6, ovules 10–18. Mex. Apparently not in cult.; plants grown under this name are usually *C. micropetala.*

lanceolata Ait.f. To 4 ft., sts. sticky-hairy; lvs. opp., lanceolate, to 3 in. long, prominently veined beneath; calyx tube with purplish lines, slender, to 1 in. long, without winged appendages, petals deep violet, 6, the 2 upper largest, longest stamens densely bearded with rose-purple hairs. Mex. Var. **silenoides** (Nees) Regel [*C. silenoides* Nees; *C. zimapanii* E. Morr.]. Shorter; lvs. smaller, not prominently nerved; calyx tube shorter, upper petals white or pale-margined. Mex. Has been grown as *C. cyanea.*

Llavea Llave & Lex. Shrubby, to 3 ft.; lvs. opp., ovate to lanceolate, to 3 in. long; fls. in terminal racemes, calyx tube green and violet, to 1½ in. long, hirsute, without appendages, upper calyx lobe elongate, petals bright red, 2, 2 longest stamens bearded with violet hairs. Mex. Var. **miniata** (Brongn.) Koehne [*C. miniata* Brongn.]. Smaller, sts. hirsute; calyx tube to 1⅛ in. long. Most material cult. as var. *miniata* is *C. × purpurea.*

micropetala HBK. Subshrub, to 3 ft. or more; lvs. opp., lanceolate, to 6 in. long or more; fls. in terminal leafy racemes, calyx tube red,

shading to yellow-green, 1¼ in. long, without appendages, pubescent, inflated in fr., lowest calyx lobe longest, petals red, white, or yellow, 6, minute, ovules 60 or more. Mex. Sometimes grown under the names, *C. jorullensis* or *C. platycentra.*

miniata: *C. Llavea* var.; but material cult. as *C. miniata* is usually *C. × purpurea.*

×**Neubertii** Hort. ex Biedenf.: *C. ignea* × *C. Llavea.* Resembles *C. ignea*, but calyx tube crimson, pubescent, petals violet-black, 2. Plants of this parentage are apparently grown in s. Calif.

petiolata: *C. viscosissima.*

platycentra: see *C. ignea;* but material cult. as *C. platycentra* may be *C. micropetala.*

procumbens Cav. Herbaceous, to 1½ ft.; sts. often sticky; lvs. lanceolate, to 3 in. long; calyx tube with purplish lines, to ⅞ in. long, without winged appendages inside, somewhat inflated, petals rose-purple, 6, the 2 upper largest, longest stamens densely bearded with brownish or yellowish hairs. Mex. A parent of *C. × purpurea* and perhaps also crossed with *C. lanceolata.*

×**purpurea** Lem.: *C. Llavea* × *C. procumbens.* More or less intermediate between the parents; with stiff hairs, sts. herbaceous, to 1½ ft.; lvs. ovate-lanceolate; calyx tube colored toward apex, petals bright rose, tinged with violet. Many hort. forms listed as cvs. 'Avalon' or 'Firefly', or as *C. miniata* are of this alliance, varying in fl. color from deep to bright red and purple. Those having fls. verging on violet may represent an unnamed cross between *C. lanceolata* and *C. procumbens.*

Roezlii: *C. Hookerana.*

silenoides: *C. lanceolata* var.

viscosissima Jacq. [*C. petiolata* (L.) Koehne 1881, not Koehne 1877]. CLAMMY C., BLUE WAXWEED, TARWEED. Herbaceous, to 18 in.; lvs. opp., ovate-lanceolate, to 2 in. long; fls. solitary, calyx tube green, with purplish hairs, to ½ in. long, without appendages, upper calyx lobe elongate, petals purple, 6, the upper 2 longest, longest stamens bearded. Mass. to Ala., w. to Kans.

zimapanii: *C. lanceolata* var. *silenoides.*

CUPRESSACEAE Bartl. CYPRESS FAMILY. Gymnosperms; about 21 genera of resinous, coniferous, usually evergreen, monoecious or dioecious trees and shrubs of wide distribution; distinguished from the Pinaceae and Taxodiaceae by having lvs. opp. or whorled, usually flattened and scalelike, or sometimes, as in *Juniperus*, needle-shaped; cones woody, leathery or berrylike, cone scales few, ovules mostly several on each cone scale, erect and not inverted; seedlings usually with 2 cotyledons. The family includes a number of valuable timber trees, spp. that supply resins and flavorings, and many ornamentals. The cult. genera are: *Actinostrobus, Austrocedrus, Callitris, Calocedrus, Chamaecyparis,* ×*Cupressocyparis, Cupressus, Juniperus, Libocedrus, Platycladys, Tetraclinis, Thuja, Thujopsis,* and *Widdringtonia.*

×**CUPRESSOCYPARIS** Dallim. [*Chamaecyparis* × *Cupressus*]. *Cupressaceae.*

Leylandii (A. B. Jacks. & Dallim.) Dallim. & A. B. Jacks. A fertile hybrid of *Chamaecyparis nootkatensis* and *Cupressus macrocarpa,* resembling the former in habit and foliage, but differing in having female cones ⅝–¾ in. across, scales 8, and tubercled seeds usually 5 to each scale. Cvs. are: **'Leighton Green'**, brs. and branchlets upturned at ends, lvs. gray-green when young, becoming darker with age, paler beneath; **'Haggerston Gray'**, brs. loose, upturned at ends, sage-green above, pale gray-green beneath; **'Naylor's Blue'**, columnar, shoots and lvs. grayish-blue above, pale gray-green beneath.

CUPRESSUS L. CYPRESS. *Cupressaceae.* About 22 spp. of mostly tender, monoecious, coniferous, evergreen trees or shrubs, native to N. Amer., Eur., and Asia; lvs. small, scalelike in adult plants, linear in young plants; male cones small, female cones globose, scales woody, peltate, seeds many to each scale, maturing in 2 years. These are the true cypresses, to which *Chamaecyparis* is closely related.

Except for *C. arizonica, C. Bakeri,* and *C. glabra,* the species can be grown satisfactorily only in mild climates. Most easily propagated by seeds. For culture see *Conifers.*

Abramsiana C. Wolf. SANTA CRUZ C. Tree, to about 30 ft., pyramidal in outline, bark gray, fibrous; lvs. rich light green with only an inconspicuous closed pit on the back; female cones usually more than ⅝ in. long. Santa Cruz Co. (Calif.). Zone 8.

arizonica Greene [*C. arizonica* var. *bonita* Lemm.; *C. glabra* of auth., not Sudw.]. ARIZONA C. ROUGH-BARKED A.C. Tree, to 40 ft. and more; lvs. pale or glaucous-green, acute; female cones to 1 in. across, glaucous, S. Ariz., New Mex., Tex., Mex. Zone 6. Much planted in the sw. U.S. Cvs. include: **'Compacta'**, low, conical; **'Gareei'**, a listed name; **'Glauca'**, juvenile, lvs. silvery-gray; **'Oblonga'**, brs. markedly horizontal, producing an oblong effect, lvs. gray-green; **'Pyramidalis'**, a listed name; **'Verhalenii'**, lvs. bright glaucous-blue, softer and more graceful than wild forms; **'Watersii'**, narrowly pyramidal, compact.

Bakeri Jeps. MODOC C. Slender, 30–90 ft., with narrow crown, bark red-brown, becoming grayish in age, branchlets more or less regularly arranged around brs.; lvs. about $\frac{1}{16}$ in. long, gray-green, with dorsal gland on back; female cones to ⅞ in. in diam. N. Calif. Zone 5. Subsp. **Bakeri.** The typical subsp.; to 45 ft., branchlets mostly less than ½ in. long, female cones gray, slightly less than ½ in. in diam. Subsp. **Mathewsii** C. Wolf. SISKIYOU C. Rarely to 90 ft., branchlets mostly more than ½ in. long, female cones light gray-brown, to 1 in. in diam., warty.

Benthamii: *C. lusitanica* cv.

cashmeriana Royle ex Carrière. Tree, to 60 ft., with drooping branchlets; lvs. blue-gray; female cones ½ in. across. Kashmir or Tibet. Zone 9.

Duclouxiana Hickel [*C. torulosa* Rehd. & E. H. Wils., not D. Don]. Pyramidal tree, to 150 ft.; bark brown, branchlets drooping; lvs. obtuse, somewhat glaucous; female cones ½–¾ in. in diam. Sw. China. Zone 9.

Forbesii Jeps. [*C. guadalupensis* of auth., not S. Wats.]. TECATE C. Slender tree, to 30 ft., bark smooth, reddish, exfoliating; lvs. bright green; female cones to 1¼ in. long. S. Calif., Baja Calif. Zone 7.

funebris: *Chamaecyparis funebris.*

glabra Sudw. [*C. arizonica* of auth., not Greene]. SMOOTH-BARKED ARIZONA C. To 70 ft., long confused with and closely allied to *C. arizonica,* but differing in having the outer bark shedding annually, revealing the thin, very smooth, cherry-red inner bark. Cent. Ariz. Zone 7. Some cvs. listed under *C. arizonica* may belong to this sp.

Goveniana Gord. GOWEN C. Shrub or small tree, to 20 ft., or rarely to 50 ft., bark gray, becoming rough and fibrous; lvs. acute, bright green; female cones ½–⅝ in. long. Monterey Co. (Calif.). Zone 9. The name has also been used for *C. pygmaea.*

guadalupensis S. Wats. GUADALUPE C. To 40 ft. or more, branchlets bright red; lvs. acute, light bluish-green; female cones to 1¼ in. in diam. Guadalupe Is. (Baja Calif.). Cv. **'Glauca'.** Foliage deeper blue. Material offered under this name may be *C. Forbesii.*

Knightiana: *C. lusitanica* cv.

Lawsoniana: *Chamaecyparis Lawsoniana.*

Lindleyi: *C. lusitanica.*

lusitanica Mill. [*C. Lindleyi* Klotzsch; *C. sinensis* Lee ex Gord.; *C. thurifera* of auth., not HBK]. PORTUGUESE C., MEXICAN C., CEDAR-OF GOA. To 75 ft., with somewhat drooping branchlets; lvs. acute, glaucous-green; female cones ½ in. across; glaucous. Mex., Guatemala, Costa Rica. Cvs. are: **'Benthamii'** [*C. Benthamii* Endl.], branchlets pinnately and regularly arranged in 1 plane; **'Glauca'**, lvs. glaucous; **'Knightiana'** [*C. Knightiana* J. Knight & T. A. Perry], more regularly branched. The names Portuguese c. and Cedar-of-Goa were applied to this sp. by Eur. authors before it was generally known to be of Mex. origin.

Macnabiana A. Murr. MACNAB C. Shrub or tree, to 20 ft.; lvs. obtuse, fragrant, dark green or glaucous; female cones 1 in. across. Calif. Zone 7.

macrocarpa Hartweg. MONTEREY C. Tree, to 40 ft. and more; lvs. obtuse, dark or bright green; female cones to 1½ in. across. Monterey Co. (Calif.). Zone 8. Cvs. are: **'Glauca'**, a listed name; **'Golden Pillar'** and **'Lutea'**, shoots and lvs. yellow; **'Stricta'**, very slender, columnar.

nevadensis Abrams. PIUTE C. Conical tree, to 30 ft., bark of upper brs. sometimes exfoliating, lvs. less than ⅛ in. long, acute, gray-green; female cones clustered, ⅞–1¼ in. long. Piute Mts. (Calif.). Zone 7.

obtusa: *Chamaecyparis obtusa.*

pisifera: *Chamaecyparis pisifera.*

plumosa: *Chamaecyparis pisifera* cv.

pygmaea (Lemm.) Sarg. [*C. Goveniana* of auth., not Gord.]. MENDOCINO C. Tree, from 4 ft. on poor soils, to 100 ft. or more on good soils, bark gray, shredding; lvs. very dark, dull blackish-green, acute; female cones about ⅝ in. in diam., many-seeded, often remaining on tree unopened for several years. Mendocino Co. (Calif.). Zone 8.

pyramidalis: *C. sempervirens* cv. 'Stricta'.

Sargentii Jeps. SARGENT C. Slender, bushy tree, to 45 ft.; bark dark gray, thick and fibrous; lvs. acute, gray-green, fragrant; female cones to 1 in. in diam. Calif. Zone 8.

sempervirens L. ITALIAN C. Tree, to 80 ft., lvs. obtuse, dark green; female cones to 1½ in. across. S. Eur., w. Asia. Zone 8. Cvs. are: **'Glauca'**, a listed name; **'Horizontalis'**, brs. spreading horizontally; **'Indica'** [cv. 'Roylei'], columnar, female cones globose; **'Pyramidalis'**: 'Stricta'; **'Roylei'**: 'Indica'; **'Stricta'** [cv. 'Pyramidalis'], narrow-columnar; **'Worthiana'**, a listed name.

sinensis: *C. lusitanica.*

Stephensonii C. Wolf. CUYAMACA C. Tree, to 50 ft., bark thin, cherry-red, smooth, exfoliating, branchlets thick and stiff; lvs. blue-gray or gray-green, usually with a gland on back; female cones nearly spherical, about 1 in. in diam., seeds with broad wing. San Diego Co. (Calif.). Zone 8.

Stewartii: a listed name of no botanical standing; perhaps for *Chamaecyparis Lawsoniana* cv.

thurifera: material cult. under this name is *C. lusitanica,* but the true *C. thurifera* is *Juniperus flaccida* Schlechtend. var. *poblana* Martinez and is not cult.

thyoides: *Chamaecyparis thyoides.*

torulosa D. Don, not Rehd. & E. H. Wils. BHUTAN C. Tree, to 150 ft., branchlets drooping; lvs. somewhat acute, bright to bluish-green; female cones to ½ in. in diam. Himalayas. Zone 8. Cv. **'Majestica'** is listed. Commonly misidentified as *C. Duclouxiana.*

CURCAS: *JATROPHA.*

CURCULIGO Gaertn. *Hypoxidaceae.* About 14 or 15 spp. of stemless herbs, native to the tropics of the S. Hemisphere; rhizome short, thick; lvs. long, plicate; fls. small, borne near the ground in dense heads or spikes, concealed by lvs.; perianth of 6 segms., yellow, often hairy, stamens 6, ovary inferior, sometimes tapering to a long neck below the perianth; fr. berrylike, seeds small, globose, black.

Greenhouse foliage plants, or grown outdoors in the South. They require abundant moisture and high temperatures. Propagated by division.

capitata: probably misspelling for *C. capitulata.*

capitulata (Lour.) O. Kuntze [*C. recurvata* Dryand. ex Ait.]. PALM GRASS. Lvs. to 3 ft. long and 6 in. wide, recurving; heads scapose, the scapes brown-hairy, recurved at end; fls. yellow, ¾ in. across. Trop. Asia, Australia.

latifolia Dryand. ex Ait. Lvs. to 2 ft. long and 5 in. wide, curving; heads on short, erect scapes; fls. bright yellow, ovary neck ½ in. long.

recurvata: *C. capitulata.*

CURCUMA Roxb. HIDDEN LILY. *Zingiberaceae.* More than 65 spp. of robust, rhizomatous, per. herbs in trop. Asia; sts. short, leafy; infl. terminal on the leafy st. or on leafless peduncles from rhizome or from base of leafy shoot, a dense spike with many bracts united basally or halfway with adjacent bracts and usually topped by a tuft of sterile, colored bracts; fls. 2–7, bracteoled, in axils of bracts, calyx short, unequally toothed, corolla tube united with staminodial tube at base, corolla lobes thin, the upper one hooded, staminodial lip and lateral staminodes petal-like, anther versatile, the connective sometimes crested, ovary 3-celled; fr. an ellipsoid, thin-walled caps.

Grown in a warm greenhouse in rich moist soil but rested during the winter; planted in the open in warm countries; sometimes seen in collections of economic plants, as the tuberous rhizomes of several species yield dyes and spices. Propagated by division of the rhizomes in spring.

domestica Val. TURMERIC. Rhizomes short, tuberous, with yellow flesh; lvs. to 1½ ft. long and 8 in. wide; fl. spikes terminating the leafy st., to 7 in. long, with terminal tuft of white bracts; fls. pale yellow. India. Widely cult. in tropics; turmeric, used as a spice and dye, is obtained from the dried and ground rhizomes.

elata Roxb. To 4 ft. or more; lvs. oblong, to 4 ft. long, 1 ft. wide, narrowed toward base, acute, green throughout, finely hairy beneath; fl. spike on a separate st., to 8 in. long or more, bracts nearly 2 in. long, green, the terminal tuft violet; fls. pale yellow, shorter than bracts. Burma.

gigantea: a listed name of no botanical standing; plants so named are probably *C. elata.*

latifolia Roscoe. Similar to *C. elata,* but up to 12 ft. or more; lvs. with purplish midrib, finely pubescent beneath; bracts of infl. green with red-streaked tips, the terminal tuft red; fls. white. India.

longa L. A doubtful name that cannot be applied clearly, but which has been used for *C. domestica.*

pallida: *C. Zedoaria.*

petiolata Roxb. QUEEN LILY. Lvs. to 10 in. long, 6 in. wide, rounded or cordate at base, on petioles 4–6 in. long; fl. spikes terminating the leafy st., to 6 in. long, bracts green with recurved rose-pink or purplish margins, the terminal tuft deep rose-purple; fls. yellowish-white. Burma.

Roscoeana Wallich. To 3 ft.; lvs. oblong, 12–18 in. long, acuminate; fl. spike terminating the leafy st., 8 in. long or more, bracts deep scarlet or orange-red, the terminal ones with fls. in their axils, not sterile; fls. bright yellow, scarcely longer than bracts. India. Whether this sp. should be placed in *Curcuma* is open to question.

Zedoaria (Christm.) Roscoe [*C. pallida* Lour.]. ZEDOARY. Rhizomes large, tuberous; lvs. to 2 ft. long, 6 in. wide, with very long sheaths, green with purplish or chocolate midrib, glabrous beneath; fl. spike lateral, to 6 in. long or more, bracts green, the terminal tuft purple; fls. yellow, calyx whitish. Ne. India. Cult. in Ceylon and s. China for the rhizomes, rich in arrowrootlike starch.

CURRANT and **GOOSEBERRY.** These fruits, belonging to the same genus, *Ribes,* are so similar in cultural requirements that they may be considered together. The red and white currants are *Ribes sativum,* the black currant *R. nigrum,* the flowering current *R. odoratum;* the gooseberries of American origin are forms of the native *R. hirtellum* or hybrids from it; and the European gooseberries, which are much subject to mildew in this country, are *R. uva-crispa.* In localities where white pines are important, the growing of these fruits is restricted by law because they are an alternate host for the white-pine blister rust.

Currants and gooseberries are fruits of exceptional hardiness, their culture extending nearly to the Arctic circle. They reach their best development in a cool, somewhat humid climate and, therefore, are not well adapted to the warmer or drier parts of the United States. Cool, moist clay loams or silt loams of high fertility are more satisfactory for these fruits than the lighter soil types, but the soil must be well drained. Because they are among the hardiest and most productive of fruits and able to withstand neglect, they are often allowed to shift for themselves; yet no fruits respond more readily to good care and sufficient fertilizing.

Propagation of currants and some gooseberries is by means of stem cuttings. Vigorous shoots of the season's growth are cut from the bushes late in autumn and either planted in the nursery row immediately or stored in moist sand and planted in the spring. Gooseberries are usually propagated by mound layering. Soil is heaped about the bases of the stems, which send out roots. The rooted shoots thus formed are removed and set in the nursery row. For best success with this method, the plant should have been cut back to the ground so that all the shoots are but one season old.

Planting may be either in early spring or late autumn ex-

cept in the colder climates, where spring planting is advisable. Gooseberries and currants may be planted in hills 5 × 5 or 6 × 6 feet apart, or in rows 6–7 feet apart, with plants 4 feet apart in the row.

Clean tillage followed by cover crops late in the season is advisable for these fruits. A thick mulch of straw or coarse manure is very valuable, especially in the home planting, provided that mice do not cause serious damage. Stable manure is the best fertilizer, but when it is not available a complete commercial fertilizer may be applied. The partial shade afforded by a young orchard suits the currant well, and if the ground is in good condition no bad results will follow to the orchard provided that the currants are removed before the trees need the entire feeding space. A currant or gooseberry patch should continue in good bearing for ten to 20 years, if properly handled.

The red and white currants and the gooseberry produce fruit at the base of one-year-old wood, with the greatest production on the spurs of two- and three-year-old wood. Once older branches start to produce less fruit they should be gradually pruned out to permit development of the younger shoots.

The black currant makes a large and stronger plant. It bears mostly on wood of the previous year, and therefore it is important to have new wood constantly coming on. After a few years, in neglected plantations that make little new growth, the yield becomes small and poor.

Following are some of the popular cultivars: currants, 'Cherry', 'Fay', 'Perfection', 'Red Lake', 'Wilder' — 'White Imperial' is the best white-fruited currant; gooseberries, 'Oregon Champion', 'Poorman'. 'Poorman', a vigorous, productive red gooseberry, is highly recommended.

Pests and diseases should receive prompt attention. Both currants and gooseberries should have a dormant spray of lime-sulfur 1–15 for the control of scale and mildew. Currant aphids may be controlled by malathion, nicotine sulfate, or Diazinon applied to the undersides of young developing leaves and again directly after blooming. When the fruit is well formed, rotenone sprays should be used to control the imported currant worm, which occasionally defoliates currants.

CURTISIA Ait. *Cornaceae.* One sp., a tree, native to S. Afr.; lvs. opp., simple; fls. bisexual, white, 4-merous, in terminal panicles; fr. a drupe.

dentata (Burm.f.) C. A. Sm. [*C. faginea* Ait.]. To 30 ft. or more; lvs. ovate, to 6 in. long, strongly toothed, glossy above, tomentose and with prominent veins underneath; infl. covered with white or yellow hairs; fls. white. Zone 10 in Calif.

faginea: *C. dentata.*

CURTONUS N. E. Br. *Iridaceae.* One sp., a cormous herb endemic to S. Afr.; corm tunicate; lvs. basal, sword-shaped or lanceolate; infl. a stout, many-fld., terminal panicle, with a zigzag axis; perianth tube curved, narrowly constricted below the middle, the limb 2-lipped, the upper lip 1-lobed, concave, the lower lip 5-lobed, shorter, stamens 3, style brs. 3; fr. a 3-valved caps.

paniculatus (Klatt) N. E. Br. [*Antholyza paniculata* Klatt]. Corm subglobose, sts. to 4 ft.; lvs. to 2 ft. long, to 3 in. wide, rigid but thin; fls. red and yellow, to 2 in. long. Natal, Transvaal.

CUSSONIA Thunb. *Araliaceae.* About 25 spp. of armed or unarmed, shrubs or trees of S. Afr. and adjacent Is. of the Indian Ocean; sts. thick, somewhat succulent; lvs. mostly crowded at the ends of the brs., long-petioled, pinnate or palmately compound, rarely simple, mostly glabrous and glossy; fls. in dense spikes, racemes, or compound umbels, petals 5, valvate, ovary 2-celled, styles 2, scarcely united; fr. a drupe.

Some grown as greenhouse plants in the North, or outdoors in Zone 10.

paniculata Eckl. & Zeyh. CABBAGE TREE, LITTLE C.T. Evergreen shrub or tree, to 15 ft.; lvs. palmately compound, lfts. about 8–12, pinnatifid; fls. white or yellow-tinged, in dense spicate clusters to 3 in.

long, forming a panicle to 1 ft. long. S. Afr. Possibly the hardiest sp. of the genus.

spicata Thunb. CABBAGE TREE. Evergreen tree, to 15 ft.; lvs. palmately compound, lfts. 5–9, 3–5 in. long, those of juvenile stage simple, lanceolate, those of intermediate stage 3-parted, those of mature stage 3-parted or pinnate; fls. sessile, in spikes, these in umbellate clusters of 8–12. S. Afr. to Zambia.

thyrsiflora Thunb. Evergreen shrub or small tree, to 12 ft.; lvs. palmately compound, lfts. 6–8, sessile, leathery, obovate, 1–2 in. long, usually simple, rarely lobed or ternate at tips; fls. white, pedicelled, in racemes to 4 in. long, these in umbellate clusters. S. Afr.

CUTHBERTIA Small. *Commelinaceae.* Three spp. of per. herbs, native to se. U.S.; roots thickened, sts. often cespitose, erect or ascending; lvs. alt., sheathing; fls. pedicelled, bracted, in paired, sessile cincinni in axils of small bracts at the end of terminal or both terminal and axillary peduncles, sepals 3, separate, petals 3, separate, fertile stamens 6, in 2 nearly equal series, filaments bearded, anthers with broad connectives, ovary 3-celled, each cell with 2 ovules, style longer than stamens; fr. a caps.

graminea Small [*Tradescantia rosea* Venten. var. *graminea* (Small) E. Anderson & Woodson]. Similar to *C. rosea*, sts. cespitose; lf. blades linear, much narrower than the sheath; infl. borne above foliage, bracts subtending cincinni prominent, to ¼ in. long. Sand hill regions of coastal plain, N.C. to n. Fla. Diploid (N.C.), tetraploid (widely distributed), and hexaploid (n. Fla.) forms occur.

rosea (Venten.) Small [*Tradescantia rosea* Venten.; *Tripogandra rosea* (Venten.) Woodson]. Sts. to 16 in.; lvs. linear-lanceolate, to 8 in. long, ½ in. wide, blades about as broad as the sheath or broader; peduncles mostly longer than lvs., bracts subtending cincinni reduced, to ⅛ in. long; fls. bright rose or pink, to 1¾ in. across. Sandy coastal regions, N.C. to ne. Fla.

CUTTINGS: see *Propagation.*

CYAMOPSIS DC. *Leguminosae* (subfamily *Faboideae*). Three spp. of herbs of the Old World; lvs. alt., pinnate or with only 1 lft., pubescent, the hairs attached at their middle; racemes axillary; fls. small, purplish, papilionaceous, stamens 10, united; fr. a flat, beaked legume, with 3 ridges on each side.

Propagated by seeds. One species occasionally planted in the U.S.

psoraloides: *C. tetragonolobus.*

tetragonolobus (L.) Taub. [*C. psoraloides* (Lam.) DC.]. GUAR, CLUSTER BEAN. To 3 ft., appressed-hairy; lfts. 3, ovate, terminal lft. largest, to 4 in. long, rather distantly serrate; racemes to 5 in. long, bracts slender, longer than fls.; fr. thick, to 2 in. long. Nativity unknown, but probably India. Cult. in warm regions, especially India, as a vegetable (for young pods), as a forage crop, and for the seed, from which industrial guar gum is obtained.

CYANANTHUS Wallich ex Benth. TRAILING BELLFLOWER. *Campanulaceae.* About 30 spp. of low, mat-forming or tufted, per. herbs, native to the Himalayan region; lvs. alt., small, lobed or entire; fls. terminal on sts., calyx 5-lobed, corolla blue or white, open-campanulate to tubular, 5-lobed, stamens separate from the corolla, ovary superior, 3–5-celled; fr. a caps.

Propagated by seeds or from cuttings of soft growth in the autumn; carried over winter in frames or cool greenhouse.

integer Wallich ex Benth. Similar to *C. microphyllus,* but lvs. more or less cuneate at base, densely pubescent on both surfaces, and corolla funneliform with scant pubescence in throat. W. Himalayas. Material offered under this name has been *C. microphyllus.*

lobatus Wallich ex Benth. Tufted, sts. decumbent, to 1 ft. long or more; lvs. more or less obtriangular, to 1 in. long, coarsely lobed or toothed in upper half; calyx inflated, densely brown-purple-pubescent, nearly as long as the corolla tube, corolla gentian-blue, funnelform to salverform, to 1½ in. across. High Himalayas, India to Sikkim.

microphyllus Edgew. Mat-forming, sts. trailing, to 12 in. long, from a woody root; lvs. short-petioled, elliptic to lanceolate or oblong, to ½ in. long, cordate or obtuse basally, white-hirsute beneath, margins entire, revolute; calyx campanulate, about ½ in. long, densely hirsute with dark brown hairs, corolla violet-blue, white-pubescent in the throat, salverform, tube cylindrical, to about ⅝ in. long, lobes ¾–1¼ in. across. Nepal, n. India.

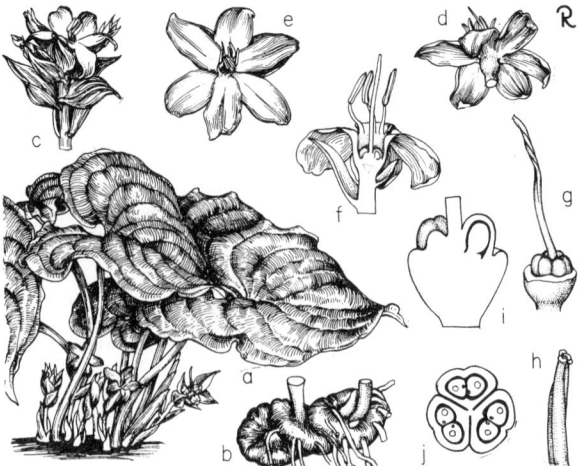

CYANASTRACEAE. *Cyanastrum cordifolium* var. *compactum:* **a,** plant, × ¼; **b,** tubers, × ½; **c,** inflorescence, × ½; **d,** flower, view from below, × ¾; **e,** flower, face view, × ¾; **f,** flower, vertical section, × 1; **g,** pistil, × 2; **h,** apex of style and stigma, × 6; **i,** base of pistil, vertical section, × 5; **j,** ovary, cross section, × 5.

CYANASTRACEAE Engl. CYNASTRUM FAMILY. Monocot.; allied to *Pontederiaceae,* but differing in its terrestrial habit, and in having tuberous rhizomes and regular fls. with a very short perianth tube and an inferior ovary. The only genus, *Cyanastrum,* is native to trop. Afr.

CYANASTRUM D. Oliver. *Cyanastraceae.* Seven spp. of per. herbs, native to trop. Afr., with corms or tubers and thick fleshy roots; lvs. on fl. st. 1 to few, oblong-lanceolate to ovate-cordate; infl. racemose or paniculate; fls. with perianth parts 6, similar, stamens 6, dehiscing apically, ovary inferior, 3-celled; fr. a 1-seeded caps.

Grown under glass or in the open in frost-free regions; needs partial shade.

cordifolium D. Oliver. Scapose, cormous per., to 1 ft.; lvs. ovate, blade 2–8 in. long, cordate, petiole 2–12 in. long; raceme spikelike, stout, 2–7 in. long; fls. blue-violet, nearly 1 in. long, fragrant, perianth parts elliptic to obovate, each fl. subtended by a large, lanceolate to orbicular, violet-tinged bract, the lowermost bracts sterile. Nigeria. Congo region. Var. **compactum** R.T. Clausen. Infl. much shorter than lvs., bracts broad-ovate to orbicular, peduncle to 1 in. long.

CYANELLA L. *Tecophilaeaceae.* About 8 spp. of per. herbs, native to Afr.; lvs. cylindrical or flat, in a basal rosette, from a fibrous-coated corm; infl. a simple or branched, bracted raceme; perianth deeply 6-parted, segms. petal-like, stamens 6, 3–5 arching and the other(s) declinate, ovary half-inferior, 3-celled, ovules many, in 2 rows in each cell; fr. a loculicidal caps., seeds many.

Cultivated in the greenhouse.

capensis L. To 1½ ft.; lvs. 6–8, flat, linear, 6 in. to 1 ft. long; infl. often branched; fls. bright blue or less frequently pale or reddish, perianth segms. acute, ¼–⅜ in. long, 5 stamens arching, with short anthers, 1 declinate, with longer anther.

lutea L.f. To 1½ ft.; lvs. flat, to 6 in. long, ½ in. wide; infl. often branched; fls. yellow, more rarely milky-white to reddish, perianth segms. acute, ½–¾ in. long; 5 stamens arching, with short anthers, 1 declinate, with longer anther.

orchidiformis Jacq. To 1 ft.; lvs. 3–4, flat, to 6 in. long, 1½ in. wide; infl. often branched; fls. nodding, bright red, perianth segms. obtuse, ½ in. long, 3 stamens arching, with long filaments and short anthers, 3 declinate, with short filaments and long anthers.

CYANOCOCCUS: *VACCINIUM.*

CYANOTIS D. Don. *Commelinaceae.* About 40–50 spp. of per. herbs, native to trop. Asia and Afr.; sts. creeping or weak; lvs. sheathing; fls. blue or reddish, in terminal and axillary unpaired cincinni, rarely solitary, petals 3, separate at very base but united above in a short or long tube, or rarely entirely separate, stamens 6, equal; fr. a caps.

Grown in greenhouses. Propagated by seeds or cuttings.

cristata (L.) Schult. & Schult.f. To 18 in., sts. slender, branched, brs. erect or ascending; lvs. ovate-oblong, to 4 in. long, hairy above or glabrous; cincinni enclosed by overlapping lf. sheaths; fls. blue. Malay Arch. to trop. Afr.

fasciculata (B. Heyne ex Roth) Schult. & Schult.f. Ann., with fibrous roots, sts. branched at base, to 8 in., arachnoid-woolly to nearly glabrous; lvs. very narrowly lanceolate, to 1½ in. long, woolly to glabrous; infl. mostly on peduncles to 1¼ in. long; fls. congested, blue or rose-purple. India.

kewensis (Hassk.) C. B. Clarke. TEDDY-BEAR VINE, TEDDY-BEAR PLANT. Sts. procumbent, reddish-villous; lvs. overlapping and 2-ranked, fleshy, lanceolate, 1–1½ in. long, green above with recurved red tips, red beneath; fls. 1–2 in axils of uppermost lvs., red, filaments blue-bearded. India. Plants so named are sometimes *C. somaliensis.*

moluccana (Roxb.) Merrill. Sts. creeping, glabrous; lvs. oblong, to 1¼ in. long, green, sometimes with bronzy pattern; fls. solitary, blue, scarcely emerging from sheath at ends of brs. Trop. Asia. Has been offered under the erroneous name *Tradescantia moluccana.*

naviformis: a listed name of no botanical standing.

somaliensis C. B. Clarke. PUSSY-EARS, FUZZY-EARS. Flowering sts. to 9 in. long; lvs. narrow-triangular, 1½ in. long, hairy; fls. blue, in dense cincinni not longer than lf. sheaths. Trop. Afr. Sometimes cult. erroneously as *C. kewensis.*

veldthoutiana: a listed name for *Tradescantia sillamontana.*

CYATHEA Sm. [*Hemitelia* R. Br.]. TREE FERN. *Cyatheaceae.* About 110 spp. of slender, evergreen tree ferns of the tropics and subtropics, trunks sometimes 50 ft. or more; lvs. very large, usually 2–3-pinnate; sori on lower surface of segms. midway between margin and midrib at forks of veinlets, indusia globose, bursting and persistent as a fringe.

Two species are cultivated as ornamentals in tropical or subtropical gardens or under glass, often in tubs. Propagated by spores. For culture see *Ferns.*

arborea (L.) Sm. WEST INDIAN T. F. Trunk to 24 ft.; petioles prickly, yellowish-green, the scales lanceolate-attenuate, to 1½ in. long, dirty-white, lvs. deciduous, 3-pinnate, pinnules serrate, ribs with 1–2 puffy, white scales. Trop. Amer., where frequently grown as a garden plant.

australis: *Alsophila australis.*

Cooperi: *Sphaeropteris Cooperi.*

Cunninghamii: *Alsophila Cunninghamii.*

dealbata: *Alsophila tricolor.*

Dregei: *Alsophila Dregei.*

incana: *Nephelea incana.*

insignis: *Sphaeropteris insignis.*

medullaris: *Sphaeropteris medullaris.*

meridensis Karst. Lvs. 3-pinnate, pinnules narrow-lanceolate, scales on ribs beneath, veins with 8–9 veinlets. Colombia.

mexicana: *Nephelea mexicana.*

Smithii: *Alsophila Smithii.*

tricolor: *Alsophila tricolor.*

Walkerae: *Alsophila Walkerae.*

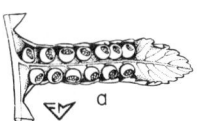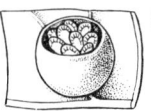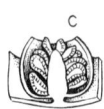

CYATHEACEAE. *Sphaeropteris Cooperi:* **a,** pinnule, lower surface, × 2; **b,** sorus, × 10; **c,** sorus, vertical section, × 10; **d,** sporangium, × 25. (From Bailey, *Manual of Cultivated Plants,* ed. 2.)

CYATHEACEAE Kaulf. TREE FERN FAMILY. Ferns; 8 genera and 650 spp. of ferns with distinct trunks or erect sts., native to tropics and subtropics; lvs. large, 2–3-pinnate; sori on lower surface or margins, sporangia stalked, annulus oblique. Differs from the Polypodiaceae in having sporangia with a complete rather than incomplete annulus, and from the Dicksoniaceae in having the sori on the lower surface of pinnules in forks of veins, rather than at the margins on vein tips, the indusia saucer-shaped to globose, or lacking, but not 2-valved. *Alsophila, Cyathea, Nephelea,* and *Sphaeropteris* are grown as ornamentals in trop. gardens or under glass in

the U.S. in Zone 10 where they thrive under humid conditions, sheltered from strong winds.

CYATHODES Labill. *Epacridaceae.* Perhaps 175 spp. of shrubs, native from se. Asia to Australia, New Zeal., and other Pacific Is.; lvs. alt., small, often crowded; fls. small, solitary or in spikes or racemes, peduncles sheathed by few to several persistent bracts, 5-merous, corolla tubular, lobes hairy to glabrous inside, stamens inserted near top of tube, but not exserted, ovary mostly 3–5-celled, 1-ovuled; fr. drupelike, rather dry, stone several-celled.

Cultivation as for *Erica,* in those parts of Zone 9 having cool summers.

Colensoi (Hook.f.) Hook.f. Prostrate to decumbent, to 6 ft. across; lvs. narrowly oblong, to about ⅜ in. long, obtuse and mucronulate, ciliate, with 3 or 5 distinct veins, glaucous beneath; racemes terminal, short, 3–5-fld.; fls. very small, corolla lobes hairy inside, tube hairy in upper part; fr. white to pink to dark red, globose, ³⁄₁₆ in. in diam., 5-celled. New Zeal.

empetrifolia Hook.f. Prostrate, to 2 ft. across; lvs. leathery, linear, to ³⁄₁₆ in. long, glaucous beneath, margins ciliate, recurved; fls. less than ⅛ in. long, solitary or in 2–4-fld. clusters; fr. reddish, ovoid, about ⅛ in. long, 3–5-celled. New Zeal.

Fraseri: *Leucopogon Fraseri.*

parviflora (Andr.) Allan. Erect, to 6 ft.; lvs. leathery, lanceolate to oblanceolate or elliptic-oblong, to about ¾ in. long, slightly glaucous beneath, margins recurved; fls. about ⅛ in. long, in dense spikes; fr. drying black, nearly orbicular to broadly ovoid, to ⅛ in. long, 3–5-celled. New Zeal.

CYBISTAX Mart. ex Meissn. *Bignoniaceae.* Perhaps 5 or 7 spp. of trees, native to trop. Amer.; lvs. opp., palmately compound; fls. in terminal corymbose cymes, calyx 2- or 5-lobed, corolla tubular, slightly 2-lipped, stamens 4; fr. a ribbed, linear caps.

Trees showy in flower.

antisyphilitica Mart. ex DC. Lfts. 5, elliptic, to 9 in. long, acuminate; fls. yellowish-green, to 2½ in. long. Brazil.

chrysea (S. F. Blake) Seib. [*Tabebuia chrysea* S. F. Blake]. To 60 ft., brs. stellate-pubescent; lfts. 5, elliptic-ovate to lanceolate-ovate, to 9 in. long, with stellate hairs; fls. yellow, to 2¾ in. long; fr. to 20 in. long, ribbed. Venezuela, Colombia.

Donnell-Smithii (Rose) Seib. [*Tabebuia Donnell-Smithii* Rose]. PRIMAVERA. To 75 ft. or more; lfts. 5–7, oblong to ovate, to 10 in. long; fls. yellow, tubular-campanulate, to 2⅜ in. long, with capitate hairs; fr. to 1½ ft. long, smooth or tuberculate. Mex., Guatemala. An important trop. timber.

CYBISTETES Milne-Redh. & Schweick. *Amaryllidaceae.* One sp., a S. Afr. herb with tunicate bulb; lvs. curved, strap-shaped, 2-ranked; scape lateral, compressed, erect, umbel 13–24-fld., subtended by 2 persistent spathe valves; fls. borne at an angle on the pedicels, perianth irregular, tube nearly cylindrical, lobes spreading at tip, stamens 6, unequal, declinate, exserted from the tube, ovary inferior, cells 8–18-ovuled; fr. on an elongated pedicel, indehiscent, seeds nearly globose. Often confused with *Ammocharis.*

longifolia (L.) Milne-Redh. & Schweick. [*Amaryllis longifolia* L.; *Ammocharis falcata* (Jacq.) Herb.]. Bulb ovoid, to 4 in. in diam., 7 in. long; lvs. 9–13, ½–⅝ in. wide, 2–16 in. long, mostly truncate at apex, glaucous, margins papery, erose to entire; scape to 8 in., pedicels to 4 in., infl. elongate and rigid in fr.; fls. pale to dark pink, shiny, fragrant, perianth tube to ⁹⁄₁₆ in. long, lobes oblanceolate, obtuse, to 2⅜ in. long. Infrequently cult. May be grown in pots in the greenhouse, or planted out and the bulbs stored in winter. It blooms in spring under glass and requires rich loamy soil.

CYCADACEAE L. Rich. CYCAD or CYCAS FAMILY. Gymnosperms; 1 genus, *Cycas,* of stiff, evergreen, dioecious, palm-like plants of slow growth, native to the Old World from Madagascar to Japan; trunk mostly unbranched, at least when young; lvs. in a crown, pinnate, the pinnae with a prominent midrib but lacking lateral veins; sporophylls spirally arranged, the male scalelike, in cones, the female leafy, pinnatifid, pectinate, or toothed, bearing large, naked seeds, clustered in a terminal head. Other genera formerly included in this family are now treated as composing the families Stangeriaceae and Zamiaceae.

Planted as ornamentals, but the trunks of several species yield a starchy, edible sago. For culture see *Cycads.*

CYCADACEAE. *Cycas revoluta:* **a,** plant, much reduced; **b,** male strobilus, × ¹/₂₅; **c,** male sporophyll, lower side, × ³/₈; **d,** male sporocarps, × 6; **e,** fruiting crown, much reduced; **f,** female sporophyll bearing seeds, ⅙. (From Bailey, *Manual of Cultivated Plants,* ed. 2.)

CYCADS. Cycads belong to ten genera of gymnosperms of the tropics, subtropics, and warm temperate regions, and to three plant families separated principally by differences in the type of leaf venation: *Cycadaceae* (with a midvein and no laterals), *Stangeriaceae* (with a midvein and lateral veins), and *Zamiaceae* (with a number of parallel or wavy, simple or forked veins running longitudinally). Modern cycads are among the most primitive of living seed plants and as such are disappearing remnants of an ancient cycad flora, which was very extensive in early Mesozoic times.

The cycads are very ornamental evergreen foliage plants of slow growth and mostly with an unbranched aerial trunk, at least when young, and stiff pinnate or bipinnate whorled leaves in a basal rosette or in a crown at the top of the stem, the latter habit similar to that of palms or tree ferns. Plants are either male or female, the reproductive structures borne on modified, usually scalelike leaves, which are usually densely grouped to form large, erect, conelike structures, the female cones being much larger than the male cones. In the wild or under cultivation, viable seed can be produced only when plants of both sexes are growing together and forming cones that mature sexually at the same time so that successful wind or insect pollination can be effected. Under cultivation, artificial pollination of exotic cycads is mandatory because the natural pollination is usually too capricious. Months after pollination the female plants mature their cones, which open from the top down, the ripe seeds being released as the cone disintegrates. Even without pollination female plants in the genera *Ceratozamia, Macrozamia,* and *Encephalartos* often mature cones with full-sized but nonviable seeds, which lack the important, tiny, coiled, threadlike embryos. The viability of seeds in these genera may be checked by splitting open a seed lengthwise and checking for the presence or absence of a developing embryo. Seeds without embryos will, of course, not grow.

Although slow-growing, cycads are of easy culture and are usually maintained as specimen plants outdoors in warm regions (Zone 10) or in the North in the conservatory. *Cycas revoluta* may be grown as a potted house plant, and in Japan this species is a popular bonsai subject. Some cycads are natives of wet forests and require shade and adequate moisture, but the majority in nature inhabit open sites, often in semiarid regions, and thrive in full sun.

Propagation is by suckers (basal or from the trunk), which

are taken when dormant and the leaves removed; also, when they are available, by viable seeds, sown in shallow boxes or benches in shade, and barely covered with sand. They are potted up after germination. Slanting sections of the trunk 2–3 inches thick may be used for propagation; they should be dried a few days, then planted, and when new plants form they should be repotted separately.

All the genera of cycads are represented in cultivation and include *Bowenia, Ceratozamia, Cycas, Dioon, Encephalartos, Lepidozamia, Macrozamia, Microcycas, Stangeria,* and *Zamia.*

CYCAS L. BREAD PALM, CONEHEAD, FUNERAL PALM, SAGO C. *Cycadaceae.* About 20 palmlike spp. of cycads, native principally to the Old World tropics, with characters of the family.

Cycas circinalis and *C. revoluta* are widely cultivated as ornamentals and the glossy foliage is often cut for decorative greens or wreaths. A starchy, edible sago is extracted from the trunks of several species, but this is now known to be carcinogenic. Usually propagated by seeds. For culture see *Cycads.*

circinalis L. SAGO PALM, FERN P., QUEEN SAGO. Trunk to about 20 ft.; lvs. to 8 ft. long, lfts. to 1 ft. long, margins flat; seed about size of walnut. Old World tropics. Zone 10b. Yields sago.

media R. Br. NUT PALM, AUSTRALIAN N.P. Trunk to 18 ft.; lvs. to 4 ft. long, lfts. many, to 8 in. long, straight or somewhat curved, obtuse or pointed, keeled beneath, margins flat; scales of male cones tapering into long spines. Australia.

Normanbyana F. J. Muell. Trunk to 10 ft. or more; lvs. oblong-obovate, lfts. to 8 in. long, linear, margins flat. Australia.

revoluta Thunb. SAGO PALM, JAPANESE S.P., JAPANESE FERN P. Trunk to 10 ft.; lfts. many, pungent-tipped, margins revolute; seed about 1½ in. long, somewhat flattened, vermilion-red. S. Japan. Ryukyu Is. Zone 9. Much planted in Japan where a frequent bonsai subject.

Rumphii Miq. Trunk to 20 ft.; lvs. similar to *C. media,* but shorter and with fewer lfts.; scales of male cones truncate or short-acuminate. N. Australia, Malay Arch. Differs from *C. circinalis* in having lfts. paler, thinner, and lanceolate. Rarely attains maximum height in cult.

CYCHNOCHES Lindl. SWAN ORCHID. *Orchidaceae.* About 12 spp. of epiphytes, native to trop. Cent. and S. Amer.; pseudo-bulbs elongated, several-lvd.; lvs. plicate; infls. lateral; fls. unisexual, more or less dimorphic, not resupinate, the female less frequently produced, sepals and petals similar, lip entire, divided, or fringed, usually with calluses, column curved, elongate and slender in male fls., short and fleshy in female fls. For structure of fl. see *Orchidaceae.*

Grown in the warm greenhouse; for culture see *Orchids.*

Amparoanum: *C. Egertonianum.*

aureum: *C. Egertonianum* var.

chlorochilon: *C. ventricosum* var.

Dianae: *C. Egertonianum* var.

Egertonianum Batem. [*C. Amparoanum* Schlechter]. Fls. markedly dimorphic, male racemes pendent, to 2½ ft. long, to 20-fld., the fls. membranous, to 2 in. across, sepals and petals spreading or recurved, lanceolate or narrower, purple to green, sometimes spotted, lip obovate, to ⅝ in. long, green to white, narrow-clawed, blade concave, fringed with several elongate, club-shaped marginal teeth; female racemes short, erect, 1- to several-fld., the fls. fleshy, larger than the male, 3–4 in. across, greenish-white, lip ovate-lanceolate, to 1½ in. long, convex, broad-clawed. Mex., s. to Peru and Brazil. Var. **aureum** (Lindl.) P. Allen [*C. aureum* Lindl.]. GOLDEN S.O. Male fls. 2½–3 in. across, sepals and petals spreading, yellow-green to nearly white, dotted with rose, sometimes veined with green, lip ovate, to 1 in. long, white with green stripes, marginal teeth slender, usually forked; female fls. like those of typical var. but larger, sepals and petals yellow-green, lip greenish-yellow, green at apex. Costa Rica and Panama. Var. **Dianae** (Rchb.f.) P. Allen [*C. Dianae* Rchb.f.]. Similar to typical var., but male fls. with sepals and petals rose-pink, lip white, marginal teeth very short, rounded or somewhat club-shaped. Costa Rica, Panama.

pentadactylon Lindl. Fls. markedly dimorphic, male racemes pendent, to 1 ft. long or more, many-fld., the fls. fragrant, membranous, to about 4 in. across, sepals and petals spreading, oblong-lanceolate, yellow-green, blotched with chocolate-brown, lip fleshy, linear-lanceolate, 1¼ in. long, green basally, white in the middle, yellowish apically, undulate, with a single arching fingerlike appendage on the dorsal surface of claw, lateral margins of the blade with 2 curved, fleshy teeth; female racemes short, erect, 1–3-fld., the fls. fleshy, to about 3 in. across, yellowish-white, spotted with purplish-red, lip ovate-oblong, about 1¼ in. long, white, entire, broad-clawed. Brazil.

ventricosum Batem. Fls. only slightly dimorphic, racemes nodding, to 1 ft. long, few-fld.; sepals and petals membranous, spreading or reflexed, elliptic-lanceolate, green to greenish-yellow, lip white, with an elongate basal claw, fleshy, ovate, convex, to 2 in. long, with a blackish-green, broadly rounded, not projecting callus at base, male fls. 3–4 in. across, female smaller, with shorter, stouter column. Summer–late autumn. Mex. to Panama. Var. **chlorochilon** (Klotzsch) P. Allen [*C. chlorochilon* Klotzsch]. Fls. large, about 5–6 in. across, sepals and petals yellow-green, lip not clawed, to 2½ in. long, green or whitish with projecting, dark green, triangular callus at base. Most material grown as *C. chlorachilon* is *C. ventricosum* var. *Warscewiczii.* Cent. Amer., Colombia, Venezuela, Guyana. Var. **Warscewiczii** (Rchb.f.) P. Allen [*C. Warscewiczii* Rchb.f.]. GREEN S.O. Fls. to 5 in. across, sepals and petals green to greenish-yellow, lip with a short claw, to 1¾ in. long, white, with projecting, dark green, triangular callus at base. Costa Rica, Panama.

Warscewiczii: *C. ventricosum* var.

CYCLAMEN L. PERSIAN VIOLET, ALPINE V., SOWBREAD. *Primulaceae.* About 15 spp. of tuberous herbs, native from cent. Eur. and Medit. region to Iran; lvs. basal, long-petioled, ovate, orbicular, or reniform, usually cordate, sometimes lobed, usually blotched or marbled above, margins often toothed; fls. pink, carmine, magenta, or white, nodding, solitary on scapes that usually coil downward bringing the mature fr. to the ground, calyx 5-lobed, corolla tube short, lobes 5, blotched at base, usually reflexed and twisted, sometimes with eared appendages at base, stamens 5; fr. a 5-valved caps., seeds sticky.

One species, *C. persicum,* is a popular florist's plant, and the others are grown outdoors where climate permits, or the tender ones in pots. Cyclamens grow best in a soil composed of 2 parts leaf mold, 1 part sand, and 1 part loam. They are sensitive to moisture conditions and require good drainage. Most of them grow best in shady locations, and some will grow in full sun in locations with little moisture where they go dormant in the summer and begin growing again with the autumn rains.

Tubers large enough to flower the first year may be purchased from seedsmen. Seeds may be sown in Sept., wintered in a cool house, repotted in May, and in July the hardy species may be planted outdoors, and the nonhardy ones transferred to pots in a shaded frame. Before frost, the nonhardy sorts should be taken indoors and grown in a cool house. *C. coum, C. purpurascens,* and *C. hederifolium* are the hardiest species; *C. africanum, C. persicum, C. cyprium,* and *C. Rohlfsianum* are the least hardy.

africanum Boiss. & Reut. Tuber to 8 in. in diam., flattened and somewhat concave above, with grayish-brown, corky and flaking surface, rooting all over; lvs. not fully mature until after flowering, orbicular to reniform, cordate, glossy and little marbled above, light green beneath, margins with coarse, horny teeth; fls. to 1¼ in. long, with a faint odor of violets, corolla lobes ovate-lanceolate to lanceolate, dark rose-pink or pale pink, with a basal crimson blotch, eared at base. Autumn. Algeria. Not hardy; should be dried off during summer and watered only sparingly after the first fl. buds are well developed.

alpinum Sprenger [*C. coum* subsp. *alpinum* (Sprenger) O. Schwarz]. Tuber to 1¼ in. in diam., flattened, bearing tufts of hairs, rooting on lower surface; lf. blades reniform to broadly ovate, to 2 in. long and wide, cordate, dark green and marbled above, deep glossy red beneath, margins wavy and with obscure teeth; fls. about ½ in. long, fragrant, corolla lobes slightly reflexed, twisted and standing horizontally to axis of fl., broadly ovate, rose-pink to deep carmine, with a crimson, basal, semicircular blotch. Winter and early spring. Mts., sw. Asia Minor.

×**Atkinsii** T. Moore: said to be a hybrid between *C. coum* and *C. persicum.* Lvs. blotched, crenate; fls. white, large, petals pointed; material now in cult. under this name probably represents selected forms of *C. coum.* Winter to early spring.

balearicum Willk. Tuber to 1 in. in diam., globose and slightly flattened, hairy, rooting on lower surface; lf. blades broadly ovate, to 3½ in. long, bluish-gray and marbled with silver above, crimson beneath, margins usually toothed or wavy; fls. about ¾ in. long, fragrant, corolla lobes lanceolate, white with pink veins, not eared. Spring. Balearic Is. and S. France.

caucasicum: *C. coum* subsp.

cilicium Boiss. & Heldr. Tuber flattened, hairy, rooting on lower surface; lf. blades suborbicular, irregularly marbled above, beet-red beneath, margins wavy and usually toothed; fls. fragrant, corolla lobes obovate, deep rose-pink to white, with a basal crimson blotch. Autumn. S. Asia Minor. Cv. **'Album'.** Fls. white. Var. **alpinum:** a listed name of no botanical standing; probably for *C. alpinum.*

coum Mill. Tuber to 1½ in. in diam., depressed-globose, hairy, rooting on lower surface; lf. blades reniform to suborbicular, sometimes broadly ovate, to 2¾ in. long, marbled or not above, red-purple beneath, margins entire to slightly wavy-toothed, petioles to 4 in. long; fls. to ¾ in. long, corolla lobes elliptic to ovate-elliptic, white to pink or carmine, with a basal violet blotch, tube with a white or pink rim. Winter to early spring. Subsp. **coum** [*C. hiemale* Hildebrand; *C. hyemale* Salisb.; *C. orbiculatum* Mill.]. The typical subsp.; lvs. reniform to suborbicular; corolla tube with a white rim. Se. Eur., Asia Minor. Cv. **'Album'.** Corolla lobes white with purple spot. Cv. **'Roseum'.** Corolla lobes pink with purple spot. Subsp. **alpinum:** *C. alpinum.* Subsp. **caucasicum** (C. Koch) O. Schwarz [*C. caucasicum* Willd. ex Steven; *C. ibericum* Lem.; *C. vernum* Sweet]. Lvs. cordate; corolla tube with pink or pale purple rim. Caucasus, n. Iran.

cyprium Schott & Kotschy. Tuber flattened, with corky surface; lf. blades broadly cordate or ovate-lanceolate, to 1½ in. long, olive-green with light green blotches above, bright carmine beneath, apex acute or tapering to long point, margins cut into shallow lobes; fls. about 1 in. long, very fragrant, corolla lobes lanceolate, white or shell-pink, with a basal V-shaped, pinkish-purple blotch, eared at base. Autumn. Cyprus. Not hardy.

europaeum: see *C. purpurascens.*

giganteum: a listed name of no botanical standing for *C. persicum* cv.

graecum Link [*C. pseudograecum* Hildebrand]. Tuber to 4 in. in diam., globose to subglobose, with corky surface, rooting from lower surface; lf. blades cordate, rarely somewhat angled, to 5½ in. long, dark green, with gray-green marbling above, dark violet-purple or pale gray-green beneath, margins dentate, slightly cartilaginous; fls. about 1 in. long, corolla lobes oblong-obovate, pale pink with magenta streaks toward the base, eared at base. Autumn to early winter. S. Greece, Aegean Is., s. Asia Minor.

hederifolium Ait. [*C. neapolitanum* Ten.]. BABY C. Tuber to 6 in. in diam., depressed-globose, with corky surface, rooting mostly on upper surface; lf. blades cordate, often angled or lobed, to 5½ in. long, marbled above, green or rarely beet-red beneath, margins obscurely toothed; fls. about 1 in. long, corolla lobes ovate-lanceolate, rose-pink to white, with basal crimson blotch, acute at apex, eared at base. Late summer to autumn. S. Eur. to w. Asia Minor. Cvs. **'Album'** and **'Roseum'** are listed.

hiemale, hyemale: *C. coum* subsp. *coum.*

ibericum: *C. coum* subsp. *caucasicum.*

indicum: see *C. persicum.*

libanoticum Hildebrand. Tuber to 1¼ in. in diam., subglobose, rooting mostly on lower surface, older tubers with rather corky surface; lf. blades cordate to depressed-cordate, 1½–2½ in. long and 1¼–2⅝ in. wide, dark green with paler blotches above, beet-red beneath, margins not cartilaginous; fls. about 1⅜ in. long, corolla lobes ovate, pink at apex and changing to white in lower part above the basal purple blotch. Late winter to early spring. Syria, Lebanon. Tender; suitable for pot culture.

mirabile Hildebrand. Tuber to 2¼ in. in diam., rooting from lower half of tuber, surface corky; lf. blades reniform to suborbicular, to about 1¼ in. long and wide, dull green with a central zone of pink or silvery-gray marbling above, violet-purple beneath, apex obtuse, base cordate, margins repand-dentate; fls. about ¾ in. long, corolla lobes oblong or somewhat obovate, pale pink, with a basal blotch, apex irregularly toothed. Autumn. Sw. Asia Minor.

neapolitanum: *C. hederifolium.*

orbiculatum: *C. coum* subsp. *coum.* Var. **Schlosseranum:** a listed name of no botanical standing.

persicum Mill. [*C. indicum* of auth., not L.; *C. vernale* Mill.]. FLORIST'S C. Tuber to 6 in. in diam., flattened-globose to subglobose, with corky surface, rooting from lower surface; lf. blades usually cordate, to 5½ in. long and wide, extremely variable in color above, usually green beneath, margins with closely set cartilaginous teeth; fls. about 2 in. long, very fragrant, on scapes 6–8 in. high, corolla lobes oblong-lanceolate, twisted, rose-pink to pale lilac-white or white, with a basal purple blotch; fr. scapes not coiled. Winter to spring. E. Medit. region. Many named cvs. are in the trade; these have large, odorless fls. varying in color from flame-red to almost black. Cv. **'Giganteum'.** Fls. very large.

pseudibericum Hildebrand. Tuber to 1⅜ in. in diam., flattened, hairy, rooting from lower surface; lf. blades ovate, to 2⅜ in. long and

2½ in. wide, dark green and marbled with silver above, purple beneath, hairy on both surfaces, base cordate, margins crenate with small teeth; fls. about 1 in. long, fragrant, corolla lobes elliptic, crimson-carmine or purplish, with basal reddish-purple blotch bordered by white. Winter to spring. S. Asia Minor. Tender; suitable for pot culture.

pseudograecum: *C. graecum.*

purpurascens Mill. [*C. europaeum* of auth., doubtfully L.]. Tuber to 1¼ in. in diam., globose or somewhat flattened, rooting all over; lf. blades reniform to cordate, to 3⅛ in. long and 2⅜ in. wide, green or sometimes marbled above, green to dark red beneath, margins obscurely toothed to almost entire; fls. about ¾ in. long, very fragrant, corolla lobes oblong or ovate, rose-pink or carmine to slate-magenta, with basal crimson blotch. Late summer and autumn. Cent. and s. Eur. Should never be dried off.

repandum Sibth. & Sm. Tuber to 1⅜(–2⅜) in. in diam., globose to somewhat flattened, rooting from lower surface; lf. blades broadly cordate, to 5 in. long and wide, acute, marbled or not above, bright reddish-purple beneath, basal lobes not overlapping, margins sharply toothed and shallowly lobed; fls. to about 1¼ in. long, sometimes slightly fragrant, corolla lobes oblong to linear-oblong, carmine-red, pink, or white, with a darker basal zone. Spring. Cent. and e. Medit. region.

Rohlfsianum Asch. Tuber to 1⅜ in. in diam., flattened, with corky surface, rooting mostly from sides and lower surface; lf. blades mostly reniform to depressed-globose, at flowering time 2½ in. long and 2⅜ in. wide, when mature 3⅜ in. long and 4⅜ in. wide, bright green and marbled above, beet-red beneath, margins toothed, somewhat angularly lobed, these lobes also shallowly lobed; fls. about ¾ in. long, sometimes fragrant, corolla lobes narrowly elliptic-oblong, rose-pink, with basal crimson blotch, stamens exserted. Autumn. Cyrenaica.

vernale: *C. persicum.*

vernum: *C. coum* subsp. *caucasicum.*

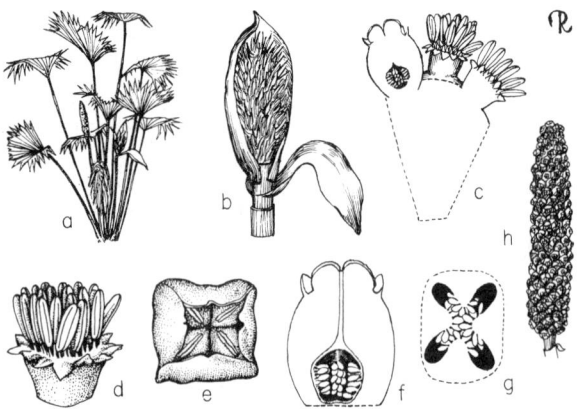

CYCLANTHACEAE. *Carludovica palmata:* **a,** flowering plant, greatly reduced; **b,** inflorescence partially enclosed in spathes, × ⅙; **c,** segment of flowering spadix, showing a female flower (in vertical section) and two male flowers (one in vertical section), × 2; **d,** male flower, × 5; **e,** female flower, top view, × 5; **f,** female flower, vertical section, × 4; **g,** ovary, cross section, × 10; **h,** fruiting spadix, × ⅙. (From Bailey, *Manual of Cultivated Plants,* ed. 2.)

CYCLANTHACEAE Dumort. CYCLANTHUS FAMILY. Monocot.; 11 genera of monoecious, palmlike, more or less herbaceous per., native to trop. Amer.; plants stemless, short-stemmed, or climbing; lvs. long-petioled, sheathing at base; fls. unisexual, male and female fls. alternating spirally, or in alt. whorls, or in spiraled units of a female fl. surrounded by male fls., in dense, unbranched spadices subtended by 2–11 foliaceous or petaloid spathes; perianth cup-shaped and toothed or lobed, or lacking, male fls. with many stamens, female fls. coalescent in whorls or discrete, with sepals 4, pistil 4-carpelled, 1-celled, stigmas 4; fr. of cohering fleshy carpels, seeds many. *Carludovica, Cyclanthus,* and *Dicranopygium* are cult. in trop. gardens and sometimes grown in greenhouses in the North.

CYCLANTHERA Schrad. *Cucurbitaceae.* Over 30 spp. of monoecious, ann. or per. herbaceous vines, native to warm parts of Amer. and extending n. as far as Kans.; lvs. lobed or compound; fls. very small, yellow, white or greenish, male fls.

racemose or panicled, stamen solitary, anther annular, female fls. solitary in axils, ovary inferior, usually 3-celled, ovules 1 or few in each cell; fr. small, scarcely fleshy, mostly spiny or setose.

Grown as annuals from seeds, as ornamentals, and as screens.

brachystachya (Ser.) Cogn. [*C. explodens* Naud.]. To 10 ft. or so, nearly glabrous; lvs. ovate-triangular to broad-oblong, 2–3 in. long, 3-angled or -lobed; fr. 1 in. long or more, usually curved, stout-spiny on one side, bursting forcibly. N. S. Amer.

explodens: *C. brachystachya.*

pedata (L.) Schrad. Glabrous, to 10 ft. and more; lvs. pedately parted, segms. 5–7, narrow, crenate-dentate; fr. about 2 in. long, with scattered prickles. Mex. to S. Amer. Used for food in Peru and Bolivia.

CYCLANTHUS Poit. *Cyclanthaceae.* One variable sp., native to trop. Amer.; stemless, clump-forming, milky-juiced, palmlike, monoecious herb; lvs. deeply 2-parted; fls. unisexual, fragrant, male and female fls. arranged in alt. whorls on spadices subtended by 4(–5) spathes.

Sometimes cultivated as an ornamental in tropical gardens. Culture as for *Carludovica.*

bipartitus Poit. Lvs. of mature stage 2-parted to base, those of young plants often undivided, petioles to 6 ft. long; spathes yellow. Trop. Amer.

CYCLOBOTHRA: *CALOCHORTUS.* C. flava, C. lutea: *Calochortus barbatus.*

CYCLOPHORUS: *PYRROSIA.*

CYCLOSORUS: *THELYPTERIS.*

CYDISTA Miers. *Bignoniaceae.* About 5 spp. of climbing shrubs, native to trop. Amer.; lvs. opp., with 2 lfts., often with a terminal, simple tendril; fls. in axillary or terminal racemes, calyx truncate or irregularly lobed, corolla white to lavender, often variegated or streaked, funnelform, stamens 4; fr. a long, linear caps.

Grown in subtropical regions.

aequinoctialis (L.) Miers [*Bignonia aequinoctialis* L.]. GARLIC VINE. Lfts. ovate to oblong or elliptic, to 6 in. long, shiny; corolla lavender to rose, often white with lavender lines. W. Indies and Cent. Amer., s. to Brazil.

CYDONIA Mill. QUINCE. *Rosaceae.* Two spp. of thornless, deciduous shrubs or small trees from Asia; lvs. entire, stipules linear; fls. solitary, white to rose-pink, sepals 5, glandular-serrate, petals 5, stamens 20 or more, in 1 row, carpels fused along the inner side only, styles 5, separate or coalescent by the pubescence only; fr. a pome.

Grown for the fruits, which are used stewed, or for marmalade or jelly. For culture see *Quince.*

oblonga Mill. [*C. vulgaris* Pers.]. COMMON Q. To 20 ft.; lvs. ovate to oblong, to 4 in. long, tomentose beneath; fls. white or pale pink, to 2 in. across, solitary at the ends of leafy shoots of the season; fr. pear-shaped or apple-shaped, yellow, to 3 in. in diam. or more, fragrant, flesh yellow, hard, rather unpalatable. W. Asia. Zone 5. Cult. widely since ancient times.

sinensis Thouin [*Chaenomeles sinensis* (Thouin) Koehne]. To 20 ft.; lvs. lanceolate, 3–4 in. long, gland-toothed; fls. about 1½ in. across, sepals ¼–⁵⁄₁₆ in. long, woolly above, petals pink, with white base; fr. dark yellow, oblong-ovoid, 4–6 in. long. China. Zone 6.

vulgaris: *C. oblonga.*

CYLINDROPHYLLUM Schwant. *Aizoaceae.* Five spp. of low, branched per. succulents, native to S. Afr.; lvs. 4-ranked, thick, cylindrical or 3-angled with rounded edges; fls. solitary, terminal, bractless, calyx 5-lobed, petals many, stamens many, staminodes present, ovary inferior, 7–8-celled, stigmas 6–8; fr. a caps., expanding keels present, placental tubercles small, seeds not fertile unless two different clones available for cross-pollination.

Propagation easy from cuttings. See also *Succulents.*

calamiforme (L.) Schwant. Sts. to 2 in. high, mat-forming; lvs. 6–8, gray-green, finely dotted, arched-ascending, to ¾ in. long, ⅜ in. wide, nearly cylindrical with flat upper side, slightly narrowed and curved toward the blunt tip; fls. to 2¾ in. across, on pedicels to ¾ in. long, opening in afternoon, petals pale pink shading to yellowish-white at base. Cape Prov.

Comptonii L. Bolus. Sts. in dense cushions to 10 in. across and 5 in. high; lvs. erect or spreading, to 3½ in. long, ⅜ in. wide, cylindrical or upper side slightly flattened, rough-margined, often rounded-keeled on lower side, tip acute or acuminate; fls. to 3 in. across, on pedicels ⅝ in. long, petals silvery-white. Cape Prov.

Tugwelliae L. Bolus. Mat-forming; lvs. 2 on a br., erect, glaucous, to 3$^{3}/_{16}$ in. long, ⅜ in. wide, ½ in. thick, nearly cylindrical with tapered tip;
fls. solitary, to 2 in. across, on pedicels to ¾ in. long, petals pale flesh-colored. Cape Prov.

CYLINDROPUNTIA: *OPUNTIA* subgenus *Cylindropuntia.*

CYMBALARIA J. Hill. *Scrophulariaceae.* About 10 spp. of creeping per. herbs, native to the Old World; often united with *Linaria,* but having lvs. palmately veined, and fls. solitary, axillary.

A few species are grown as ground covers in the greenhouse or in the open, or in vases or hanging baskets. They are tender in the North, but seed themselves freely, and thrive in moist and partly shaded locations, as in greenhouses and about yards. Propagated by division of the long stems, and by seeds.

aequitriloba (Viv.) A. Cheval. [*Linaria aequitriloba* (Viv.) K. Spreng.]. Pubescent; lvs. mostly opp., entire or slightly 3–5-lobed; corolla pale mauve, with reddish-purple throat. S. Eur.

hepaticifolia (Poir.) Wettst. [*Linaria hepaticifolia* (Poir.) Steud.]. Glabrous; lvs. mostly opp., with 3–5 short or indistinct lobes; corolla about ½ in. long, lilac-blue with yellowish throat; caps. shorter than sepals. Corsica.

muralis P. Gaertn., B. Mey., & Scherb. [*Linaria Cymbalaria* (L.) Mill.]. KENILWORTH IVY, COLISEUM I., PENNYWORT. Sts. glabrous, trailing and rooting at nodes; lvs. mostly alt., irregularly 3–7-lobed, glabrous; corolla ⅜ in. long, lilac-blue, with yellowish throat; caps. longer than sepals. Eur.; naturalized from Ont. to Penn., w. to Mo., and Pacific coast. Cv. **'Maxima'.** Fls. large. Var. *pallida* Hort. May be the same as *C. pallida.*

pallida (Ten.) Wettst. [*Linaria pallida* (Ten.) Ten. ex Guss.]. Pubescent, sts. trailing, or erect only at first, to 4 in.; lvs. opp., reniform or orbicular, to ⅝ in. across, entire or palmately, shallowly 3–5-lobed, short-pilose beneath and on petioles; corolla about ½ in. long, blue-violet, with golden-yellow throat; caps. as short as or shorter than calyx. Italy.

pilosa (Jacq.) L. H. Bailey [*Linaria pilosa* (Jacq.) Lam. & DC.]. Pubescent; lvs. opp. and alt., 3–11-lobed; corolla lavender, with yellow throat; caps. longer than sepals. Italy.

CYMBIDIUM Swartz [*Cyperorchis* Blume]. *Orchidaceae.* About 40 spp. of epiphytes, native to trop. Asia and Australia; sts. pseudobulbous, short, several-lvd.; lvs. leathery, long and narrow, rarely short, persistent; fls. in lateral racemes, sepals and petals similar, lip entire or 3-lobed, commonly with 2 ridges. For structure of fl. see *Orchidaceae.*

Cool greenhouse, sometimes planted out in southern Calif.; for culture see *Orchids.*

affine: *C. Mastersii.*

×**Alexanderi** Hort.: *C.* × *Veitchii* × *C. insigne.* A hybrid which, when used as a parent, has given many colorful progeny whose fls. have good keeping qualities. Fls. to 4 in. across, white, cream, or blush-pink. Cv. **'Album'.** Fls. white, with a little yellow on lip.

aloifolium Swartz. Lvs. linear, broadly obtuse, to 1½ ft. long; racemes pendent, to 2 ft. long, many-fld.; sepals and petals brownish-yellow, with purple median stripe, lip 3-lobed, brownish-red with yellow center. Summer. India, Indochina, Malay Pen.

atropurpureum (Lindl.) Rolfe [*C. Finlaysonianum* var. *atropurpureum* (Lindl.) Hort. Veitch]. Lvs. 2–3 ft. long; racemes pendent, loosely many-fld., 2 ft. long; fls. to 1½ in. across, sepals and petals dull yellow-green on the exterior, dark purple on the interior, with green edges at tips, lip recurved, shorter than sepals, lateral lobes pale purple, midlobe white, tinged with rose, with a few purple spots, the disc yellow, with 2 parallel ridges, column dark purple. Philippine Is.

cochleare Lindl. To 3½ ft.; lvs. fleshy, linear, with overlapping bases; infl. shorter than lvs., pendent, many-fld.; fls. fleshy, campanulate, to 2 in. long, sepals and petals olive-brown, suffused with green, lip 2-lobed, ochre-yellow, with red dots. Autumn. Sikkim, Assam.

×**Coningsbyanum** Hort.: *C. grandiflorum* × *C. insigne.* Fls. to 4 in. across, greenish-yellow, lip cream-white, with many red spots.

×**Cooperi** Rolfe: *C. insigne* × *C. Schroederi.* A natural hybrid, similar to *C. insigne* in habit; racemes erect, to 4 ft. long, many-fld.; fls. light brownish-pink with darker striations, lip pale yellow with red-brown spots. Annam (Vietnam).

cyperifolium Wallich. Lvs. very narrowly linear-lanceolate, to 2½ ft. long or more, ⅜–½ in. wide, acute, somewhat channelled; racemes shorter than lvs., 3–7-fld.; fls. to 1½ in. across, fragrant, sepals and petals spreading, lanceolate, green, becoming yellow, lip green, streaked and blotched with reddish-purple. Early spring. Sikkim, Himalayas.

Dayanum: *C. eburneum* var.

Devonianum Paxt. Pseudobulbs 2–5-lvd.; lvs. long-petioled, oblanceolate, acute, the blade to 14 in. long; racemes about as long as lvs., pendent, many-fld.; sepals oblong-lanceolate, to nearly 1 in. long, green or buff-yellow, streaked with brownish-purple, petals shorter, lanceolate-elliptic, similarly colored, lip obscurely 3-lobed, deep or light rose-purple, with a pair of darker spots near each margin. Early spring–summer. Himalayas.

eburneo-Lowianum: *C. Veitchii.*

eburneum Lindl. Lvs. linear, to 2 ft. long and ¾ in. wide; racemes to 8 in. long, 1–3-fld.; fls. to 4 or 5 in. across, ivory-white, fragrant, lip with yellow center and 3–4 hairy keels. Early spring–early summer. Himalayas, Indochina. Var. **Dayanum** (Rchb.f.) Hook.f. [*C. Dayanum* Rchb.f.; *C. Simonsianum* King & Pantl.]. Lvs. longer, narrower; fls. to 2 in. across, yellow-white, sepals and petals with port-wine-colored midline, lip white, with a row of purple spots on each side of disc. Var. **Parishii** (Rchb.f.) Hook.f. [*C. Parishii* Rchb.f.]. Pseudobulbs spindle-shaped, to 4 in. long; lvs. strap-shaped-linear, to 2 ft. long; racemes 3–7-fld.; fls. to 3 in. across, ivory-white, fragrant, lip with orange disc and crimson-purple spots.

elegans (Blume) Lindl. [*Cyperorchis elegans* Blume]. Pseudobulbs stout, clustered; lvs. many, narrow, to 2 ft. long or more; racemes pendent, densely fld.; fls. not fully expanding, 1½ in. long, tawny-yellow, sepals and petals connivent, lip 3-lobed, marked with deep red dots. Autumn. N. India.

ensifolium Swartz [*C. Munroianum* King & Pantl.]. Lvs. linear, acute, to almost 3 ft. long; racemes to 20 in. long, 3–12-fld.; fls. greenish-yellow, rarely whitish, veined with red-brown lines, lip with red-brown spots. Autumn–winter, late spring, late summer. India and se. Asia to China and Japan.

erythrostylum Rolfe. Pseudobulbs ovate-oblong, about 1 in. long, several-lvd.; lvs. arching, linear, acute, to 15 in. long; racemes nearly erect, to 1½ ft. long, 4–7-fld.; sepals white, about 1¾ in. long, petals a little shorter, white, lip yellowish-white, with red-purple lines or dots, column about 1 in. long, crimson. Late autumn. Annam (Vietnam).

Finlaysonianum Lindl. Lvs. strap-shaped, obtuse, to 3½ ft. long and almost 2 in. wide; racemes pendent, to 3½ ft. long, many-fld.; sepals and petals brownish-yellow, sometimes with a red median stripe, lip 3-lobed, spotted and marked with brownish-red and with white and yellow on the disc. Early spring–early summer, autumn. Se. Asia, Philippine Is. Var. **atropurpureum:** *C. atropurpureum.*

×**Gammieanum** King & Pantl.: *C. elegans* × *C. giganteum.* A natural hybrid; lvs. linear, to 3 ft. long; racemes loose or dense, to 20-fld.; fls. to 3 in. across, yellow, flushed with brown, and with brown lines, lip brighter yellow, with brown lines. Autumn. Himalayas.

×**gattonense** Hort.: *C. Lowianum* × *C. Tracyanum.* Resembling *C. Tracyanum* more than *C. Lowianum;* sepals and petals yellowish-green, with close purple lines, lip cream-white, spotted with red, the disc very hairy.

giganteum Wallich. Lvs. linear, acute, to 2½ ft. long; racemes somewhat longer than lvs., arching, 7–13-fld.; fls. to 4 in. across, fragrant, sepals and petals green or brownish-yellow, with dark red-brown lines, lip 3-lobed, yellow, marked with red, midlobe wavy-margined. Autumn, winter. Himalayas, China, Indochina.

×**Gottianum** Hort.: *C. eburneum* × *C. insigne.* Sepals and petals flushed with pink, lip spotted with purple.

grandiflorum Griff. [*C. Hookeranum* Rchb.f.]. Lvs. strap-shaped, acute, to 2 ft. long; racemes 2–4 ft. long; fls. to 5 in. across, sepals and petals olive-green, lip 3-lobed, bright yellow, dotted with purple-brown. Early autumn–early winter. Himalayas, China.

×**Hanburyanum** Hort.: *C. erythrostylum* × *C. Tracyanum.* Fls. honey-yellow, with red-brown lines, lip with darker markings.

Hookeranum: *C. grandiflorum.*

insigne Rolfe [*C. Sanderi* Hort.]. Lvs. oblong-linear, acute, to 3½ ft. long, ¾ in. wide; racemes to 5 ft. long, 10–15-fld.; fls. to 3½ in. across, sepals and petals pale rose, lip 3-lobed, light rose, spotted with purple-red, with 2 yellow, thickened lines. Winter. Indochina. Cv. **'Album'.** Fls. ivory-white, lip with greenish-yellow markings.

lancifolium Hook. Lvs. lanceolate, to 1 ft. long; racemes 4–5-fld.; sepals and petals white, to 1 in. long, petals with rose-colored median line, lip 3-lobed, white, purplish on exterior with occasional reddish-purple spots. Indonesia, Japan.

longifolium D. Don. Lvs. linear; racemes nearly erect, to 12-fld.; fls. to 3 in. across, sepals and petals green, striped brownish-purple, lip with purple lines. Autumn. Himalayas.

Lowianum Rchb.f. Lvs. linear, acuminate, to 2 ft. long; racemes arching, 10–25-fld.; fls. about 4 in. across, sepals and petals greenish-yellow with red-brown lines, lip 3-lobed, yellow, midlobe with crimson blotch edged with pale yellow. Winter–summer. Burma. Cv. 'Concolor' [var. *concolor* Rolfe]. Crimson blotch on lip absent, replaced by clear yellow area. Cv. 'Mandaianum' [var. *Mandaianum* Gower]. Fls. larger, clear yellow, front of lip light orange.

Mastersii Griff. ex Lindl. [*C. affine* Griff.; *Cyperorchis Mastersii* (Griff.) Benth.]. Lvs. linear, to 2 ft. long; racemes 4–6-fld.; fls. to 2½ in. long, snow-white, fragrant, lip yellowish, minutely pubescent. Autumn. Himalayas.

Munroianum: *C. ensifolium.*

Parishii: *C. eburneum* var.

×**Pauwelsii** Hort.: *C. insigne* × *C. Lowianum* var. *concolor.* Fls. large, yellow-green, suffused with red.

pendulum Swartz. Lvs. linear, to 2½ ft. long; racemes many-fld.; fls. to 1¼ in. across, dark purplish-brown with yellow margins. Late spring. Sikkim, s. India, Burma, Perak.

pumilum Rolfe. Dwarf; lvs. to 1 ft. long; racemes shorter than lvs., densely fld.; fls. small, to 1 in. across, sepals and petals reddish-brown, margined with yellow, lip 3-lobed, white to pinkish, dotted with reddish-brown. Spring. Yunnan (China).

roseum J. J. Sm. With habit of *C. insigne;* lvs. strap-shaped, to 16 in. long; fls. to 2 in. across, sepals and petals white, dotted with soft rose in longitudinal lines, lip 3-lobed, white with violet streaks and spots, to 1 in. long, blunt and tomentose. Early spring. Java.

Sanderi: *C. insigne.*

Sandersonii: *Ansellia gigantea.*

×**Schlegelii** Hort.: *C. insigne* × *C. Wiganianum.* Fls. large, of fine form, tinged with blush-pink, lip with many reddish-purple spots.

Schroederi Rolfe [*Cyperorchis Schroederi* (Rolfe) Schlechter]. Allied to *C. giganteum* and *C. Lowianum,* but fls. smaller, petals narrower, sepals and petals light green, with red-brown lines and minute dots, lip light yellow, lateral lobes with 5–6 red-brown stripes, midlobe with zone of red-brown. Annam (Vietnam).

Simonsianum: *C. eburneum* var. *Dayanum.*

tigrinum C. Parish ex Hook. Lvs. elliptic-lanceolate, acute, to 6 in. long and ¾ in. wide; racemes longer than lvs., 3–6-fld.; sepals and petals olive-green, lip 3-lobed, lateral lobes yellow, marked with red, midlobe white, spotted with red. Burma, Indochina.

Tracyanum Hort. ex O'Brien. Very similar to *C. giganteum* and *C. grandiflorum,* but fls. to about 6 in. across and darker colored. Autumn. Burma, Indochina.

×**Veitchii** Hort. [*C. eburneo-Lowianum* Hort.]: *C. eburneum* × *C. Lowianum.* Fls. fragrant, to about 5 in. across, sepals, petals, and lip white, tinted yellow, midlobe of lip with large V-shaped purple-crimson spot.

virescens Lindl. Small; lvs. linear, to 1 ft. long; scapes shorter than lvs., 1-fld.; sepals and petals spreading, to 1¼ in. long, greenish, with some purple at base of petals, lip white or greenish-white with purple blotches. Early spring. China, Japan.

Whiteae King & Pantl. Lvs. linear, to 3 ft. long; racemes to 18 in. long, 10–12-fld.; sepals and petals to 2 in. long, pale yellowish-green, spotted with dull red, lip white or pale pink, spotted with pale red. Late autumn. Sikkim.

CYMBOPETALUM Benth. *Annonaceae.* Nine spp. of small trees and shrubs, native to trop. Amer.; lvs. alt., large; fls. solitary, large, bisexual, petals 6, valvate, in 2 series, stamens and pistils many; fr. stalked, oblong-cylindric, tardily dehiscent.

penduliflorum (Dunal) Baill. Tree, to 60 ft. or more, branchlets softly hairy; lvs. oblong, nearly sessile, to 10 in. long, short-acuminate, obtuse to subcordate at base; fls. very fragrant, pendulous, pedicels 4 in. long, petals greenish-yellow, very thick and fleshy, inner ones with strongly involute margins; fr. short-stalked, red-brown, very hard, to 3 in. long and 1 in. thick. S. Mex., Guatemala, Brit. Honduras.

CYMBOPOGON K. Spreng. OIL GRASS. *Gramineae.* About 30 spp. of per., trop., mostly aromatic grasses in Old World; related to *Andropogon* but pairs of racemes included in an inflated spathe and the spathes in a large compound

infl., the well-developed sessile and pedicelled spikelets of lower pair alike but male or neuter. For terminology see *Gramineae.*

Several species are grown in the tropics for essential oil distilled from the leaves and used in perfumery, flavoring, and medicine. Propagated by division.

citratus (DC. ex Nees) Stapf. LEMONGRASS, WEST INDIAN L., FEVER GRASS. Forming dense clumps to 6 ft. high; lvs. to 3 ft. long, to ½ in. wide, tapered to both ends, margins scabrous; panicle large, usually very compound, loose, brs. slender, the ultimate ones somewhat nodding, joints of the racemes bearded or villous along the sides, spathe bracts long and narrow; first glume of the sessile spikelets concave on the back, linear to linear-lanceolate. S. India and Ceylon. Widely cult. in tropics. A cultigen which seldom flowers. Has been cult. in Fla. for the aromatic lemongrass oil.

Nardus (L.) Rendle. CITRONELLA GRASS, NARD G. Like *C. citratus* but panicle much congested, often interrupted, finally drooping; first glume of the sessile spikelets flat on the back, lanceolate or broader. Ceylon. Widely cult. in tropics, also in s. Fla. and s. Calif. Source of commercial citronella oil.

CYMOPHYLLUS Mackenz. *Cyperaceae.* One sp., a sedge of s. Appalachian Mts., differing from *Carex* in having st. (culm) bractless, with only 1 blade-bearing lf. lacking sheath, ligule, and midrib.

Fraseri (Andr.) Mackenz. [*Carex Fraseri* Andr.]. FRASER'S SEDGE. Per., with stout branching rhizomes, each terminating in a st. with 4–6 overlapping, closed, basal sheaths and a solitary lf. appearing after flowering, sts. smooth, stiff; lvs. evergreen, leathery, longitudinally striated, 8–24 in. long, 1–2 in. wide, with narrow, cartilaginous, undulating margin; spikes solitary on a st., the upper part male, brush-like, stamens 3, conspicuous in the axil of each scale, anthers white, lower part female, globose-ovoid, nearly ½ in. in diam., with 20–30 white perigynia in the axils of white scales. Mt. woods and along streams, Penn. to S.C. Easily grown in a moist, shaded location.

CYNANCHUM L. [*Vincetoxicum* N. M. Wolf, not Walt.]. *Asclepiadaceae.* Over 100 spp. of per. herbs, native to temp. and trop. regions; sts. erect or climbing with twining tips; lvs. opp. or sometimes whorled; fls. in cymes, 5-merous, corolla mostly rotate, deeply lobed, white to deep purple, corona mostly small, usually as high as stigma, anthers with apical membranous appendages; fr. a slender or thick follicle.

Weedy herbs flowering in late spring and summer. Propagated by division in the spring.

acuminatifolium: *C. ascyrifolium.*

ascyrifolium (Franch. & Sav.) Matsum. [*C. acuminatifolium* Hemsl.]. CRUEL PLANT, MOSQUITO PLANT. Erect, crisped-hairy herb, to 3 ft.; lvs. to 6 in. long, ovate or elliptic, acuminate; cymes axillary, panicled, corolla white, to ½ in. across, corona lobes slightly shorter than stigma; follicles to 2½ in. long, broadly lanceolate. Japan, ne. Asia.

laeve (Michx.) Pers., not K. Schum. [*Ampelamus albidus* (Nutt.) Britt.; *Gonolobus laevis* Michx.]. HONEY VINE, BLUE V., SAND V. Twining herb, to 6 ft.; lvs. triangular, mostly about 3 in. long, deeply cordate with a broad sinus; cymes axillary, racemelike, shorter than lvs., corolla white, lobes more or less erect, about ¼ in. long, corona lobes deeply bifid, much longer than stigma; follicles lanceolate, smooth, to 6 in. long. Penn. to Mo., s. to Ga. and Tex.

medium R. Br. Similar to *C. nigrum,* but having lvs. broader, acute, and corolla white, glabrous. E. Eur.

nigrum (L.) Pers. BLACK SWALLOWWORT. Erect or scrambling; lvs. ovate to lanceolate, to 5 in. long, acuminate; cymes open, axillary; corolla purple-black, about ⅜ in. across, pubescent inside. S. Eur.; naturalized in ne. U.S.

Vincetoxicum (L.) Pers. [*Vincetoxicum officinale* Moench]. Differs from *C. nigrum* chiefly in having lvs. narrower, corolla greenish-white, glabrous. Eur.

CYNARA L. *Compositae* (Carduus Tribe). Eleven spp. of coarse, thistlelike per. herbs, native to Medit. region and Canary Is.; lvs. mostly pinnately lobed or divided; fl. heads large, terminal, involucral bracts leathery, in many rows, receptacle fleshy, bristly; fls. all tubular, blue, violet, or white; achenes more or less compressed and 4-angled, glabrous, pappus of plumose bristles.

Two species are grown as garden vegetables. They need rich soil and abundant moisture. The cardoon is blanched in much the same way as celery or endive. It is propagated by seeds and by suckers. The artichoke is propagated also by division in early spring. Seeds give more variable results; if sown early enough, edible heads may be obtained the same year, but usually not until the second year.

cardunculus L. CARDOON. To 6 or 8 ft. or more; lvs. gray-green above, whitish-tomentose beneath, spiny, the lower to 3 ft. long or more; involucral bracts acute or acuminate, spine-tipped; fls. purplish-blue. S. Eur. Cult. for its edible root and thickened lf. stalks, occasionally also as an ornamental.

Scolymus L. ARTICHOKE, GLOBE A. To 5 ft.; lvs. similar to those of *C. cardunculus,* but essentially spineless; heads larger, involucral bracts ovate, thickened at base, slightly emarginate and sometimes tipped with a much-reduced spine apically, receptacle enlarged and fleshy; fls. purplish-blue. Probably derived from *C. cardunculus.* The immature fl. heads are cooked as a vegetable, the receptacle and fleshy bases of the involucral bracts being edible.

CYNODON L. BERMUDA GRASS, SCUTCH G. *Gramineae.* About 10 spp. of per. grasses with creeping stolons or rhizomes in Old World; lf. blades short; infl. of several slender spikes like fingers at the apex of the erect sts.; spikelets 1-fld., awnless, sessile, appressed and overlapping in 2 rows along one side of each spike, rachilla disarticulating above the glumes, glumes narrow, acuminate, 1-nerved, about equal, shorter than the floret, lemma firm, strongly compressed, 3-nerved, keel pubescent. For terminology see *Gramineae.*

Dactylon (L.) Pers. BERMUDA GRASS. Sts. creeping by scaly rhizomes or by stolons, flowering sts. to 16 in., flattened, usually erect; lf. blades flat, glabrous or pilose on the upper surface, those on basal shoots often 2-ranked; spikes usually 4–7, 1–2 in. long; spikelets imbricate, less than ⅛ in. long, lemma boat-shaped, acute. Warm regions of both hemispheres; introd. and naturalized from Md. to Okla., s. to Fla. and Tex., w. to Calif., occasional from Mass. to Mich., Ore. Important for pastures and lawns in s. states.

transvaalensis Davy. TRANSVAAL DOGTOOTH GRASS, AFRICAN B. G. Distinguished from *C. Dactylon* in having finer foliage, the lf. blades rarely more than ¹⁄₁₆ in. wide, mostly 2–3 spikes to ⅝ in. long, narrower spikelets, and shorter glumes. S. Afr.; introd. and escaped in Iowa and Calif. Cult. as a lawn grass.

CYNOGLOSSUM L. HOUND'S TONGUE, BEGGAR'S-LICE. *Boraginaceae.* About 80 to 90 spp. of ann., bien., or per. herbs, mostly in the temp. zones of all continents; sts. usually hairy; lvs. simple, alt., basal and cauline; fls. blue, purple, pink, or white, in terminal scorpioid cymes, calyx 5-cleft or -lobed, corolla funnelform to salverform, 5-lobed, throat with 5 scales, stamens 5, included; fr. of 4 nutlets, nutlets with shortly barbed prickles, forming a burr or "stick-tight," the surface convex.

Sometimes grown in the flower garden. Propagated by seeds; often rather weedy.

amabile Stapf & J. R. Drumm. CHINESE FORGET-ME-NOT. Hoary bien., to 2 ft.; basal lvs. lanceolate to oblong-lanceolate, 2–8 in. long, petioled, cauline lvs. smaller, sessile; fls. blue, white, or pink, ¼ in. long. E. Asia.

coelestinum: *Adelocaryum coelestinum.*

creticum Mill. Hairy bien., 1–2 ft.; lvs. oblong or oblong-lanceolate to elliptic, to 6 in. long, upper lvs. sessile, cordate, clasping; fls. blue, with red, purple, or dark blue veins, ¼ in. long; nutlets convex on the back. Medit. region.

grande Dougl. Glabrous per., 1–3 ft.; lvs. mostly basal, ovate or elliptic, glabrous or sparsely hairy, petioled; fls. blue or purple with white center, ½ in. long. Wash. to cent. Calif.

linifolium: *Omphalodes linifolia.*

nervosum Benth. ex Hook.f. Hairy bien. or per., to 3 ft.; lvs. lanceolate to oblong, distinctly veined, upper lvs. sessile; fls. blue, ½ in. long, ⅝ in. wide, corolla much longer than calyx. Himalayas.

officinale L. Hairy bien., to 2 ft. or more; lvs. oblong to lanceolate, to 1 in. wide, lower ones petioled, upper ones sessile to clasping; fls. dull purple, ¼ in. long, corolla lobes glabrous; nutlets flat or concave on the back. Eur.

CYNOSURUS L. DOGTAIL. *Gramineae.* Fewer than 6 spp. of ann. or per. grasses in the Old World; lf. blades narrow, flat; infl. dense, spikelike or nearly capitate; sterile and fertile spikelets paired, disarticulating above the glumes, the fertile sessile, nearly concealed by the short-pedicelled sterile one, the pairs imbricate on one side of the axis, sterile spikelets with 2 glumes and several narrow, acuminate, 1-nerved lemmas on a continuous rachilla, fertile spikelets 1–5-fld. with narrow glumes, lemmas broader, rounded on the back and awn-tipped. For terminology see *Gramineae.*

cristatus L. CRESTED D. Per., sts. to 2 ft., clustered or geniculate at base, erect; panicle spikelike, linear, more or less curved, 1⅜–5⅜ in. long, green or purplish; pairs of spikelets ¼ in. long, awns of lemma less than ¹⁄₁₆ in. long. Eur.; introd. from Nfld. to Mich. and N.C., Idaho, Wash. to Calif. Cult. for pasture and hay grass.

CYNOXYLON: *CORNUS.*

CYPELLA Herb. *Iridaceae.* About 20 spp. of trop., cormous herbs of S. Amer., allied to *Neomarica;* lvs. pleated; scape cylindrical; fls. cymose, perianth segms. 6, not united, the outer 3 obovate, spreading, showy, the inner 3 much narrower, erect, strongly recurved at apex; fr. a caps.

Cultivation as for gladiolus, preferably in light sandy soil. Propagated by cormlets, or from seeds, flowering the second year; the flowering season in N. Temp. Zone extends from mid-July to frost.

Herbertii (Lindl.) Herb. Corm to ¾ in. in diam., tunic membranous; lvs. linear, tapering at both ends, about ¼ in. wide; scapes 15–20 in. high, branched from below the middle; outer perianth segms. orange-yellow, with concave claw, inner segms. darker chrome-yellow, convolute, style brs. purplish. Paraguay, n. Argentina, s. Brazil, Uruguay. Cv. 'Pulchella'. Fls. predominantly lavender-purple, style brs. pinkish.

plattensis: a listed name of no botanical standing.

plumbea Lindl. Corm to 1¼ in. in diam.; lvs. linear, 12–18 in. long, nearly cylindrical to pleated, constricted basally into a long, channelled petiole; scapes 1½–3 ft. high, cymes 1–4; fls. few, to 3 in. across, segms. dull blue, yellow at base and apex, 1 in. long. Paraguay, s. Brazil, n. Argentina.

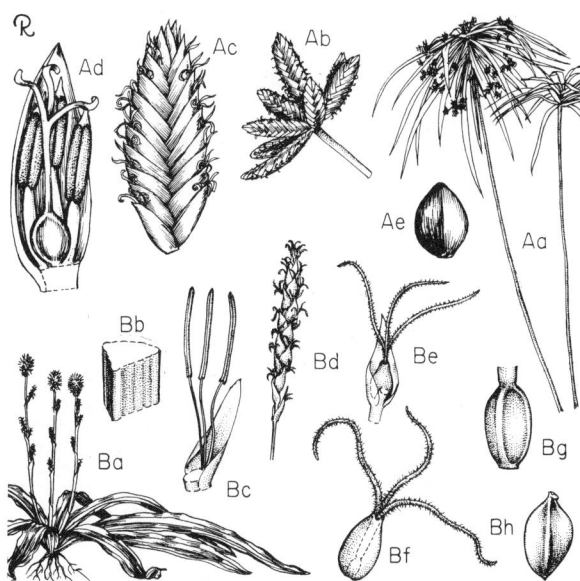

CYPERACEAE. **A,** *Cyperus alternifolius:* **Aa,** flowering and sterile stems, × ¹⁄₁₀; **Ab,** branch of inflorescence, × 1½; **Ac,** spikelet, × 4; **Ad,** flower subtended by scale, × 12; **Ae,** achene, × 12. **B,** *Carex plantaginea:* **Ba,** flowering plant, × ⅙; **Bb,** peduncle, cross section, × 4; **Bc,** male flower with subtending scale, × 2; **Bd,** female spike, × 1; **Be,** female flower with subtending brace, × 3; **Bf,** female flower with enclosing perigynium, × 4; **Bg,** ovary, × 15; **Bh,** achene, × 4.

CYPERACEAE Juss. SEDGE FAMILY. Monocot.; about 80 genera of grasslike or rushlike, mostly per. herbs, of worldwide distribution, often found in wet places; sts. (culms) solid, mostly 3-angled; lvs. 3-ranked, narrow, grasslike, with closed sheaths; infl. of 1 or more spikelets subtended by 1 or more involucral bracts; fls. small, subtended by a scale (sometimes called a glume or bract), perianth none or of bristles or scales, stamens 1–3, ovary superior, 1-celled, ovule 1, style simple or 2–3-parted; fr. an achene, 3-angled, flattened-convex or lens-shaped.

A few species of *Carex, Cymophyllus, Cyperus,* and *Eleocharis* are cultivated, mainly as ornamentals; many other species, and other genera, such as *Dichromena* Michx. have potential ornamental value. The greatest value of the family is in stabilizing soils in extensive wet areas of the world.

CYPERORCHIS: *CYMBIDIUM*.

CYPERUS L. [*Mariscus* Vahl]. GALINGALE, UMBRELLA SEDGE. *Cyperaceae*. About 600 spp. of ann. herbs with fibrous roots or per. herbs with rhizomes, native chiefly in the tropics and subtropics; lvs. at base of sts. (culms) or reduced to sheaths; involucral bracts 1 to many at base of umbellate or headlike infl., spikelets 1- to many-fld., the scales 2-ranked and enclosing a single bisexual fl.; perianth none, stamens 1–3, style 3-parted or simple, not enlarged at base and usually falling early; fr. a lens-shaped or 3-angled achene.

Includes papyrus of the ancients, a few species cultivated in pools and aquaria, some species (especially *C. corymbosus* Rottb.) used in India and elsewhere for making mats, and a few that are problem weeds. Propagated by division, by tubers (chufas), or by seeds sown in spring or early autumn. In *C. alternifolius* and *C. flabelliformis* the inflorescence with bracts trimmed back half their length, may be cut off and set in sand, and new plants will form from the leaf axils. The species in cultivation are perennial.

albostriatus Schrad. [*C. diffusus* Hort., not Vahl; *C. elegans* Hort., not L.]. Per., rhizome woody, sts. 8–20 in., slender, firm; basal lvs. many, some as long as st., sheaths purple, blades ⁵⁄₁₆–¾ in. wide with 3 rather prominent pale nerves; involucral bracts similar to lf. blades, overtopping infl.; infl. a compound umbel, rays 8–24, slender, 1–4 in. long, spikes 2–4, clustered, 8–24-fld., pale brown. Damp shady places at edges of forests, S. Afr. Zone 10, or as tender pot plant.

alternifolius L. UMBRELLA PLANT, UMBRELLA PALM, UMBRELLA SEDGE. Per., sts. cespitose, robust, 1½–3 ft., obtusely triangular to rounded, finely striate; basal lvs. reduced to sheaths, reddish-brown; involucral bracts 12–20, 4–12 in. long, ½–⅝ in. wide, drooping; infl. a compound umbel, primary rays as many as bracts and arising from their axils, very slender, ¾–4 in. long with a few very short raylets; spikes 3–12, clustered, ½–⁵⁄₁₆ in. long, dull brown; achenes black. Marshes, Madagascar, Reunion Is., Mauritius; widely naturalized in the tropics and subtropics. Cult. for over 200 years in water gardens and as pot plant. Tender. Scarcely separable from *C. flabelliformis.* The cv. 'Gracilis', DWARF UMBRELLA PLANT, may belong here; it is smaller and more slender, and rarely flowers.

diffusus: see *C. albostriatus*. Cv. 'Elegans': see *C. albostriatus.*

elegans: see *C. albostriatus.*

esculentus L. NUT SEDGE, YELLOW N. S., NUT GRASS, YELLOW N. G. Per., rhizomes slender, with terminal brown tubers, sts. 6–24 in., 3-angled, not striate; lvs. many, as long as st., ⅜–⁵⁄₁₆ in. wide, sheaths brownish; involucral bracts 2–6; infl. a simple or compound umbel, rays 5–10, spikelets distant, 5–24 in spikes, spreading, linear, pale brown. Late summer, early autumn. Damp soils, w. Asia and Afr.; now widespread in the New World. Often a troublesome weed in cult. ground. Var. **sativus** Boeck. CHUFA, EARTH ALMOND, ZULU NUT, RUSH N., TIGER N. Tubers crowded on short stolons, to ¾ in. long; rarely flowering. Cult. abroad for the edible, nutty-flavored tubers, which are rich in starch, sugar, and fat; eaten cooked or roasted or made into flour. Prop. by tubers. Not weedy. Sometimes grown in collections of economic plants.

flabelliformis Rottb. Per., rhizome stoloniferous, sts. 2–4 ft., stout, spongy at the base, obtusely triangular to rounded, striate to furrowed at the top; basal lvs. reduced to sheaths; involucral bracts 15–25, 8–20 in. long, ½–⅝ in. wide, spreading to scarcely drooping; infl. umbellate, primary rays as many as the bracts and arising from their axils, 2–4 in. long, rather thick, spikelets 5–15, clustered, lustrous brown. Swampy places, lakes, and streams in the forests and steppes of Afr. Grown in water gardens and as a pot plant. Tender.

isocladus Kunth [*C. Papyrus* cv. 'Nanus']. DWARF PAPYRUS, MINIATURE P. Rhizome creeping, sts. 12–28 in., triangular; basal lvs. reduced to sheaths; involucral bracts to 1 in. long; infl. an umbel, rays 50–100, nearly equal, 1–4 in. long, slender, spikes 1–5, clustered, dusky brown. Marshes and marshy shores, Zanzibar, Mozambique, S. Afr., S.-W. Afr. Tender. Useful for small pools and aquaria and as a pot plant.

natalensis: see *C. Owanii.*

Owanii Boeck. [*C. natalensis* of auth., not Hochst. ex C. F. Krauss; *Mariscus umbilensis* C. B. Clarke ex W. Wats.]. Per., sts. to 3 ft., 3-angled; lvs. to 2 ft. long; involucral bracts usually 8, leaflike, to 18 in. long; infl. a compound umbel, spikes in clusters of 2 or more, cylindrical, to 1 in. long, brown, peduncles to 2 in. long. S. Afr.; occasionally naturalized in Calif.

Papyrus L. PAPYRUS, BULRUSH (of the Bible), PAPER PLANT. Per., rhizome short, thick, woody sts. 4–8(–15) ft., bluntly triangular; basal lvs. reduced to sheaths, brown; involucral bracts 4–10, lanceolate-

acuminate, 8 to 3½ in. long, ½ in. wide, brownish; infl. umbellate, primary rays often over 100, 4–12 in. long, slender, drooping, each enclosed at base by a brown sheath 1 in. long and topped by 3–5 threadlike bracts subtending 3–5 spikes, each spike with 20–30 spikelets, each spikelet spreading, slender, 6–16-fld., brown. Banks and shores in quietly flowing water up to 3 ft. deep, N. and trop. Afr. Cv. 'Nanus': *C. isocladus.* Papyrus, the ancient writing paper of Egypt, Palestine, Syria, and s. Eur., was made from thin strips of pith from the sts. pressed together while still wet. The sp. is now used principally as a tender aquatic ornamental plant.

CYPHOMANDRA Mart. ex Sendtn. *Solanaceae.* About 30 spp. of erect, spineless herbs, shrubs, and trees of trop. Amer.; lvs. alt., large, either entire or pinnately dissected; infl. of racemes or scorpioid cymes; calyx campanulate, 5-lobed, corolla campanulate or rotate, 5-lobed, stamens 4 or 5, with conspicuously thickened connectives between anther cells, anthers opening either by apical pores or longitudinal slits; fr. a 2-celled berry, seeds many.

One species is grown in the tropics and subtropics and occasionally in the warm greenhouse for its edible fruit. A rapid grower, thriving best in deep fertile soil. Easily propagated by seeds or cuttings. Bears fruit after 1½–2 years. Culture as for *Eggplant.*

betacea (Cav.) Sendtn. TREE TOMATO, TOMATO TREE. Treelike shrub, to 10 ft. or more, pubescent; lvs. ovate, to 10 in. long and 5 in. wide, acuminate, entire; fls. few in axillary cymes, corolla pinkish-white, twice as long as calyx, about ½ in. across; fr. orange-red, ovate, about 2 in. long. Peru. Zone 10b. The pectin-rich fr. may be eaten fresh but is usually stewed and made into jelly.

CYPRIPEDIUM L. [*Fissipes* Small]. LADY'S-SLIPPER, LADY-SLIPPER, MOCCASIN FLOWER. *Orchidaceae.* About 50 spp. of terrestrial herbs, native to Eurasia, N. Amer.; lvs. broad, plicate; fls. solitary or in few-fld. terminal racemes, lip inflated, saclike, column with 2 fertile anthers flanking a glandlike staminode. For structure of fl. see *Orchidaceae.* The greenhouse "cypripediums" belong to the genera *Paphiopedilum* and *Phragmipedium.*

Grown in wild gardens or moist borders. For culture see *Orchids.*

acaule Ait. [*Fissipes acaulis* (Ait.) Small]. PINK L.-S., TWO-LEAVED L.-S., MOCCASIN FLOWER, NERVEROOT. Scape to 10 (rarely to 17) in. high; lvs. 2, basal, to 8 in. long and 3 in. wide, rarely to 11 in. long and 4½ in. wide; fls. solitary on a scape, to 5 in. across, sepals and petals greenish-brown, lip rose, veined with darker crimson. Late spring–summer. Dry acid woodlands or bogs, Nfld. to N.C. and Minn. Difficult to cult. Var. **albiflorum** E. L. Rand & Redf. Petals usually greenish-yellow, lip pure white or faintly tinged or marked with pink or green.

× **Andrewsii** Fuller: *C. Calceolus* var. *parviflorum* × *C. candidum.* Sts. leafy, to 8 in. high; fls. 1–2, sepals and petals greenish, suffused with madder-purple, lip cream-white, staminode orange-yellow, triangular. Late spring. U.S. and Canada.

arietinum R. Br. RAM'S-HEAD L.-S. Sts. leafy, to 1 ft. high; lvs. 3–5, to 3½ in. long and 1¼ in. wide; fls. small, solitary, sepals and petals madder-purple, streaked with green, lateral sepals separate, lip white, heavily veined with madder-purple. Ne. U.S. and adjacent Canada, w. to Minn. and Man.

Calceolus L. Sts. leafy, to about 2 ft. high; lvs. ovate to elliptic-lanceolate, to 8 in. long; fls. 1 or 2, sepals and petals greenish-yellow to purplish-brown, upper sepal lanceolate to lanceolate-ovate, lateral sepals usually united and behind the lip, petals lanceolate-linear, flat to spirally twisted, lip light to deep yellow, usually veined or spotted with purple inside. Spring–summer. Var. **Calceolus.** The typical var.; fls. fragrant, sepals and petals purplish-brown, petals wide-spreading, flat or only slightly twisted. Woodlands, Eurasia; rarely cult. in Amer. Var. **parviflorum** (Salisb.) Fern. [*C. parviflorum* Salisb.]. SMALL YELLOW L.-S., SMALL YELLOW M. F., SMALL GOLDEN-SLIPPER. Plant relatively slender; fls. fragrant, sepals and petals purplish-brown, petals somewhat drooping, several times strongly spirally twisted, lip somewhat laterally flattened, about 1 in. long, deep yellow. Mostly swamplands, N. Amer., from Nfld. to n. B.C., s. to N.J., Ill., Tex., Wash., and in the mts. to Ga. Var. **pubescens** (Willd.) Correll [*C. parviflorum* var. *pubescens* (Willd.) Knight; *C. pubescens* Willd.]. LARGE YELLOW L.-S., LARGE YELLOW M.F., GOLDEN-SLIPPER, WHIPPOORWILL-SHOE, AMERICAN VALERIAN, UMBILROOT, NERVEROOT, YELLOW INDIAN-SHOE, VENUS'-SHOE, NOAH'S-ARK. More robust, lvs. broader, and fls. generally larger than in var. *parviflorum;* fls. faintly scented, sepals and petals greenish-yellow, sometimes streaked with purple, petals less strongly twisted than in var. *parviflorum,* lip somewhat vertically flattened, 1½–2 in. long or more, usually less intense yellow. Woodlands and swamps, N. Amer., from Nfld. and Que. to Yukon Terr., s.

to Ga., La., Ariz., Ore. The Amer. vars. are very variable, and many plants intermediate in various characteristics are to be found in the wild; as a consequence, the two Amer. vars. are sometimes united as var. *pubescens*.

californicum A. Gray. Sts. leafy, to 2½ ft. high; lvs. elliptic-ovate to ovate-lanceolate, to 6 in. long; fls. 3–7 in axils of leaflike bracts, to 1¼ in. across, sepals and petals brownish-yellow, lip white or rose, spotted with brown. Late spring–summer. Ore., Calif.

candidum Muhlenb. ex Willd. SMALL WHITE L.-S. Sts leafy, to 1 ft. high; lvs. 3 or 4, to 5¼ in. long, 1½ in. wide; fls. solitary, sepals and petals greenish, veined with brown-purple, lip white, with purple spots around the mouth and inside. Late spring. N.Y. to Ky., w. to Minn. and Mo.

caudatum: *Phragmipedium caudatum.*

cordigerum D. Don. To 2 ft., sts. leafy; lvs. sessile, elliptic, sparingly pubescent; fls. solitary, sepals and petals spreading, pale yellow, white or pale green, lip white, with purple spots, staminode yellow, with brown or orange spots. Summer. Himalayas.

fasciculatum Kellogg ex S. Wats. Sts. 2–lvd., to 16 in. high; lvs. membranous, oblong-elliptic; fls. 2–4 in a short, corymbose raceme, occasionally solitary, dark purple or light yellow, veined with brownish-purple, lip small, globose, greenish-yellow. Spring–late summer. W. U.S.

hirsutum: *C. reginae.*

japonicum Thunb. Sts. erect, 2-lvd., to 18 in.; lvs. horizontal, fan-shaped, to 6 in. long, wavy-margined; fls. 1 or 2, 2½ in. across, drooping, sepals and petals pale yellowish-green, spotted with red at base, lip whitish to pinkish, with carmine spots and veins. Spring–early summer. Japan, China.

macranthum Swartz. Sts. 3–4-lvd., to 16 in. high; lvs. elliptic; fls. solitary, upper sepal, petals, and lip pink to purple, lateral sepals united, greenish-brown. Late spring–summer. Siberia, China, Japan, Taiwan.

montanum Dougl. ex Lindl. MOUNTAIN L.-S. Sts. leafy, to nearly 2 ft. high; lvs. to 6½ in. long, 3 in. wide; fls. in 1–3-fld. racemes, 4 in. across, sepals and petals reddish-brown, lip white, veined with purple. Late spring–summer. W. N. Amer.

parviflorum: *C. Calceolus* var. *parviflorum.* Var **pubescens:** *C. Calceolus* var. *pubescens.*

passerinum Richardson. SMALL WHITE L-S. Sts. leafy, hairy, 4–6-lvd., to 16 in. high; lvs. lanceolate-elliptic, to 6 in. long, sticky-hairy; fls. solitary, sepals greenish, lip longer than sepals, white, spotted with purple inside, about ½ in. long. Early summer. Canada, Alaska.

pubescens: *C. Calceolus* var. *pubescens.*

reginae Walt. [*C. hirsutum* Mill.; *C. spectabile* Salisb.]. SHOWY L.-S. Densely hairy, sts. leafy, to about 2½ ft. high; lvs. to 8¾ in. long and 4¾ in. wide; fls. 1–2 together, to 3 in. across, sepals and petals white, lip white, striped with rose, or purplish. Early summer, rarely late summer. E. N. Amer., w. to Minn. and Mo.

speciosum Rolfe. To 16 in.; lvs. about 4–6 in. long, 2–3 in. wide, pubescent; sepals and petals whitish or pink, veined with rose, 1¾–2¼ in. long, lip pink. Japan.

spectabile: *C. reginae.*

CYRILLA Gard. ex L. *Cyrillaceae.* One sp., a shrub or small tree, native along the coastal plain from se. Va. to Tex., also in W. Indies and n. S. Amer.; lvs. alt., simple, entire; fls. small, white, in clustered racemes borne at the end of preceding year's growth, sepals, petals, and stamens 5; fr. yellow, dry, indehiscent.

Planted in the South as an ornamental; propagated by seeds or by cuttings under glass.

parviflora: *C. racemiflora.*

racemiflora L. [*C. parviflora* Raf.]. LEATHERWOOD, TITI, BLACK T., RED T., WHITE T., HE HUCKLEBERRY, IRONWOOD, MYRTLE. To 30 ft. or more; lvs. elliptic to oblanceolate or obovate, to 4 in. long, glossy above, leathery; racemes to 6 in. long. A bee plant.

CYRILLACEAE Endl. CYRILLA FAMILY. Dicot.; 3 genera and about 14 spp. of deciduous or evergreen shrubs or trees, native from N. Amer. to S. Amer. and the W. Indies; lvs. alt., simple, entire; fls. bisexual, in terminal and axillary racemes, sepals 5, petals 5, stamens 5 or 10, ovary superior, 2–4-carpelled, style 1, stigmas 2; fr. drupaceous or dry, sometimes winged. *Cliftonia* and *Cyrilla* are occasionally planted.

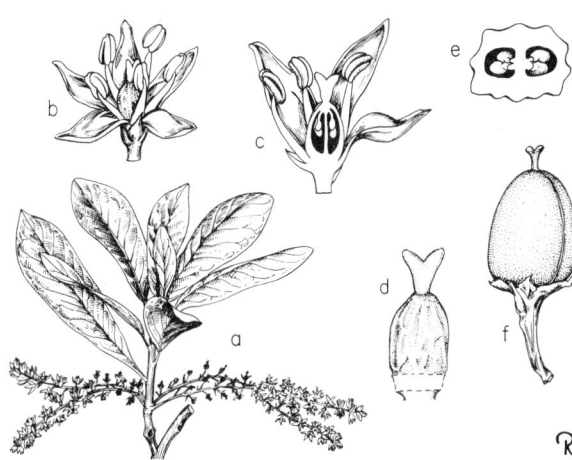

CYRILLACEAE. *Cyrilla racemiflora:* **a,** flowering branch, × ½; **b,** flower, × 5; **c,** flower, vertical section, × 6; **d,** pistil, × 8; **e,** ovary, cross section, × 15; **f,** fruit, × 5. (From Lawrence, *Taxonomy of Vascular Plants.*)

CYRTANTHERA: *JUSTICIA.* C. **magnifica:** *J. carnea;* C. **Pohliana** var. **obtusior:** *J. carnea.*

CYRTANTHUS Ait. FIRE LILY. *Amaryllidaceae.* About 45 spp. of S. Afr. bulbous herbs; fls. in an umbel terminal on a scape and subtended by 2–4 separate spathe valves, perianth red or white, tube 2–3 times as long as lobes, without corona, anthers dorsifixed, stigma headlike or 3-lobed, ovary inferior, ovules many; fr. a caps., seeds flat, black, somewhat winged.

May be grown outdoors in the southern U.S.

angustifolius (L.f.) Ait. To 1½ ft.; lvs. to 1½ ft. long, ¾ in. wide; umbel 4–10-fld.; fls. nodding, red, to 2 in. long, tube dilated upward, lobes obtuse-ovate, spreading.

lutescens: *C. ochroleucus.* Var. **Cooperi:** *C. Mackenii* var.

Mackenii Hook.f. IFAFA LILY. To 1 ft.; lvs. to 1 ft. long and ⁵⁄₁₆ in. wide; umbel 4–10-fld.; fls. almost erect, pure white, 2 in. long. Var. **Cooperi** (Bak.) R. A. Dyer [*C. lutescens* Herb. var. *Cooperi* Bak.]. Fls. yellow or cream-colored.

Obrienii Bak. Lvs. to 1 ft. long and ⁵⁄₁₆ in. wide; scape longer than lvs., umbel 7–8-fld.; fls. nodding, bright scarlet, 1½ in. long, tube curved, lobes ovate, spreading, to ³⁄₁₆ in. long.

ochroleucus (Herb.) Burchell ex Steud. [*C. lutescens* Herb.]. IFAFA LILY. To 1 ft.; lvs. linear or filiform, to 1 ft. long and ⅛ in. wide; umbel 2–3-fld., pedicels to ¾ in. long; fls. yellow, to 2 in. long.

parviflorus Bak. To 1 ft.; lvs. 1 ft. long, linear; umbel 6–12-fld.; fls. bright red, to 1¼ in. long, tube slightly curved, lobes oblong, not spreading, to ¼ in. long.

roseus: a listed name of uncertain reference, perhaps a color form of *C. Mackenii.*

sanguineus (Lindl.) Hook. To 1 ft.; lvs. to 16 in. long, ¾ in. wide; umbel 1–2-, rarely 3-fld.; fls. nearly erect, bright red, to 2 in. long.

CYRTOMIUM K. Presl. *Polypodiaceae.* About 10 spp. of ferns with densely scaly rhizomes, native to the Old World; lvs. usually persistent, mostly leathery, 1-pinnate or only pinnatifid toward apex, segms. with netted veins, petiole densely scaly at base; sori large, scattered, round, indusia peltate. Sometimes united with the Amer. genus *Phanerophlebia.*

Easily cultivated, mostly as greenhouse ferns or in the open in moderate temperate areas. See also *Ferns.*

caryotideum K. Presl. Pinnae 3–6 pairs, large, to 6 in. long, 2 in. wide, terminal pinna as large as or larger than the lateral ones, margins finely serrate-dentate to apex. India, China, Hawaii.

falcatum (L.f.) K. Presl [*Aspidium falcatum* (L.f.) Swartz; *Polystichum falcatum* (L.f.) Diels]. HOLLY FERN, JAPANESE H.F. Lvs. stiff, erect, to 2½ ft. long, glossy dark green above, pinnae ovate to elliptic, to 4 in. long, entire or weakly wavy. Asia, S. Afr., Polynesia. Cvs. include: 'Butterfieldii', margins deeply serrate; 'Compactum', dwarf; 'Mandaianum', segms. triangular, fimbriate; 'Mayi', segms. crested, often forked at apex; 'Rochfordianum', margins coarsely fringed.

Fortunei John Sm. [*Aspidium falcatum* var. *Fortunei* (John Sm.) Nichols.]. Similar to *C. falcatum,* but lvs. dull above, pinnae lanceolate-falcate, narrower, with sharply pointed teeth at apex. Japan.

CYRTOPERA Lindl. *Orchidaceae.* Not in general cult. **C. Woodfordii:** *Eulophia alta.*

CYRTOPODIUM R. Br. *Orchidaceae.* About 12 spp. of epiphtyic or terrestrial herbs, native to trop. Amer.; pseudobulbs large, fusiform, with several nodes; lvs. large, mostly narrow, plicate; infl. lateral, racemose or paniculate, with large bracts; sepals and petals spreading, mostly undulate, lip 3-lobed, with tubercled callus on disc, column with a distinct foot. For structure of fl. see *Orchidaceae.*

For culture see *Orchids.*

Andersonii R. Br. Infl. paniculate, to 5 ft. long; fls. large, yellow, to 1¼ in. across, sepals and petals orbicular, very lightly wavy, lip 3-lobed, lateral lobes smaller, erect, midlobe large, tubercled on disc, slightly ruffled in front. Venezuela to Brazil.

punctatum (L.) Lindl. COW-HORN ORCHID, BEE-SWARM O., CIGAR O. Epiphytic, pseudobulbs to 3 ft. long; lvs. to 2 ft. long, 2 in. wide; sepals and petals greenish-yellow or bright yellow, very wavy, irregularly spotted with madder-brown, to 1 in. long, lip with narrow claw, yellow, edged with red- or madder-purple. Late winter-late spring. Fla.; trop. Amer. Var. **Saintlegeranum** (Rchb.f.) Stein. Bracts greenish-brown, fls. darker yellow, with deeper brown spots.

Saintlegeranum: *C. punctatum* var.

Woodfordii: *Eulophia alta.*

CYRTOSIA Blume. *Orchidaceae.* Not in general cult. **C. Lindleyana:** *Galeola Lindleyana.*

CYRTOSPERMA Griff. *Araceae.* About 15 spp. of robust, tufted herbs, native to tropics of Old and New World; lvs. arising from a very short st. or tuber, entire or pinnately parted, sagittate or hastate, petioles long; petioles and peduncles verruculose to prickly, spathe expanded, persistent, spadix shorter than spathe; fls. unisexual, perianth 4–6-parted, ovaries 1-celled; seeds few.

Of easy culture in shaded locations, in soil high in organic matter, with abundant water during periods of active growth.

Johnstonii (Bull) N. E. Br. [*Alocasia Johnstonii* Bull]. To 3 ft. or more; lf. blades to 24 in. long and 18 in. wide, green with rose veins on upper surface, blackish-coppery underneath, petioles and peduncles mottled dark violet and rose; spathe hooded, to 6 in. long, dark violet outside, spadix stalked, becoming pale violet. Solomon Is.

CYROSTACHYS Blume. *Palmae.* About 12 spp. of cespitose, unarmed, monoecious palms from Malay Pen. to New Guinea and Solomon Is.; lvs. pinnate, sheaths forming a crownshaft, pinnae acute; infl. below the lvs., short-peduncled, paniculate, with 2 deciduous, equal bracts, rachillae with fls. in prominent, deep, open pits, near the base in triads (2 male and 1 female), above with paired or solitary male fls.; male fls. with sepals 3, separate, rounded, imbricate, petals 3, valvate, stamens 6–12(–15), filaments inflexed at the apex in bud, pistillode columnar or 3-cleft, female fls. with sepals and petals imbricate, ovary 1-celled; fr. ovoid to ellipsoid with apical stigmatic residue, endocarp thin, not operculate, seed with homogeneous endosperm and basal embryo.

Handsome ornamental palms suitable for culture only in the tropics; not hardy in the continental U.S.

Lakka Becc. SEALING-WAX PALM. To 15 ft. or more, slender; lvs. 4–5 ft. long, sheath, petiole, and rachis orange-red, pinnae about 50 on each side, grayish or glaucescent beneath, to 1½ ft. long, 1½ in. wide; fr. narrowly ovoid-conical, black, about ⅜ in. long. Malay Pen., Borneo.

Renda Blume. SEALING-WAX PALM. Similar to *C. Lakka* but to 30 ft.; fr. ovoid, abruptly constricted. Sumatra. Cv. **'Duvivieriana'.** Sheath, petiole, and rachis bright red.

CYSTOPTERIS Bernh. (*Filix* Adans., not Séguier). BLADDER FERN. *Polypodiaceae.* Perhaps 18 spp. of mostly n. temp. rock ferns; lvs. delicate, 2–4-pinnate, sori on veins, indusia hood-shaped, reflexed or withering early.

Useful for shaded exposures in rock gardens and protected damp rocky banks. For culture see *Ferns.*

bulbifera (L.) Bernh. BERRY B.F., BULBLET B.F., BULBLET F. Lvs. to 2½ ft. long and 5 in. wide, linear-lanceolate, long-tapering, 2–3-pinnate, bearing green bulblets on lower surface, which soon drop off to form new plants, petioles shorter than blade. Mainly on limestone, Nfld. to Ga. and Ariz.

fragilis (L.) Bernh. BRITTLE FERN, FRAGILE F. Lvs. to 1 ft. long, ovate-oblong, short-pointed, 2–3-pinnate, petioles shorter than blade. Cosmopolitan and very variable, temp. N. Hemisphere, s. to Chile.

montana (Lam.) Bernh. MOUNTAIN B.F. Lvs. to 1½ ft. long, triangular-ovate, accuminate, 1–2-pinnate, pinnules 1–2-pinnatifid, petioles twice as long as blade. Circumboreal.

CYTHEREA: *CALYPSO.*

CYTISUS L. BROOM. *Leguminosae* (subfamily *Faboideae*). About 50 spp. of unarmed shrubs, mostly of the Medit. region and Canary Is.; lvs. alt., with 3 lfts. or rarely with 1 lft., deciduous or persistent, or plants nearly leafless; fls. papilionaceous, mostly yellow, axillary or in terminal racemes or clusters, stamens united in a tube, anthers alternately attached at base or at back; fr. a small, flat legume. Differs from *Genista* in having an appendage or slight protuberance on one side of the hilum of the seeds, and petals all separate.

Many brooms are very showy; they are grown outdoors where hardy, and some are forced in the greenhouse for early spring bloom. They succeed in sunny positions in not too rich soil. In the greenhouse they should be kept cool until ready for forcing in Jan. Propagated by seeds, green wood cuttings, layering, or grafting.

albus Hacq. PORTUGUESE B. To 1 ft.; lfts. to ¾ in. long; fls. yellowish-white to white, in terminal heads. Summer. Se. Eur. Zone 6. Some material offered under this name may be *C. multiflorus* or *C. praecox.* Var. **pallidus** (DC.) Rehd. Fls. pale yellow.

alpinus: *Laburnum alpinum.*

Andreanus: a listed name of no botanical standing for *C. scoparius* cv.

Ardoini E. Fourn. Prostrate, to 8 in. high; lfts. linear-oblong, villous, blade to ⅜ in. long, petioles about ¼ in. long; fls. golden-yellow, to ½ in. long, 1–3 at ends of lateral branchlets; fr. to ¾ in. long, villous. S. France. Zone 6.

austriacus L. Differs from *C. supinus* in having petioles, lvs., and fr. appressed-silky-pubescent. Summer. Se. Eur. Var. **Heuffelii** (Wierzb. ex Griseb. & Schenk) C. K. Schneid. More slender, lfts. smaller, and fr. more silky. Hungary, Romania, Balkan Pen. Zone 5.

Battandieri Maire. To 15 ft., deciduous, branchlets appressed-silvery-pilose, becoming glabrate; lfts. broadly obovate, to 3½ in. long, obtuse, white-silky-pubescent on both surfaces, petioles to 2½ in. long, densely silvery-hairy; fls. ⅝ in. long, in dense racemes to 5 in. long; fr. erect, to 2 in. long, silvery-villous. Morocco. Zone 9.

×**Beanii** Nichols.: *C. Ardoini* × *C. purgans.* Semiprostrate and spreading, to 1½ ft. high; lvs. of 1 lft., linear, to ½ in. long, hairy when young; fls. deep golden-yellow, 1–3 at nodes of previous year's growth, forming sprays to 1 ft. long. Zone 6.

×**Burkwoodii:** a listed name of no botanical standing for *Cytisus* cv. 'Burkwoodii'. A complex garden hybrid, to 1½ ft.; fls. in long sprays, garnet-red with wing petals narrowly margined with gold.

canariensis (L.) O. Kuntze [*Genista canariensis* L.]. GENISTA (of florists). To 6 ft., evergreen, much-branched and very leafy, herbage white-villous; lfts. obovate to elliptic, to ½ in. long and ¼ in. wide but usually smaller, villous, nearly sessile or petioles less than half as long as lfts.; fls. bright yellow, ⅝ in. long, fragrant, in loose, 5–12-fld. racemes terminal on short lateral shoots, calyx villous, standard reflexed, hairy outside; fr. erect, 1 in. long, ³⁄₁₆ in. wide, hairy. Canary Is. Zone 10. Var. **ramosissimus** (Poir.) Briq. Lfts. very small; racemes shorter, more numerous.

×**Dallimorei** Rolfe: *C. multiflorus* × *C. scoparius* cv. 'Andreanus'. Slender, to 8 ft.; lvs. of 3 lfts. or of 1 lft., lfts. to ¾ in. long, petioles flat, winged; fls. axillary along sts., pink-purplish with crimson wing petals, or pure yellow, or in combinations of pink and yellow. The original cv. of the hybrid has pink-purplish fls. with crimson wing petals. Zone 6.

decumbens (Durande) Spach [*C. humifusus* Nym.; *Genista decumbens* (Durande) Willd.; *G. prostrata* Lam.]. Prostrate, to 8 in. high; lvs. deciduous, of 1 lft., oblong to obovate, to ¾ in. long; fls. 1–3 in axils, fr. to 1 in. long, 3–4-seeded. Late spring. S. Eur. Zone 6.

demissus: *C. hirsutus* var.

elongatus: *C. glaber.*

emeriflorus Rchb. [*C. glabrescens* Sartorelli, not Schrank]. To 2 ft. or more; lfts. elliptic-oblong, to ⅝ in. long; fls. golden-yellow; fr. to 1¾ in. long. Switzerland, n. Italy. Zone 6.

filipes (Webb & Berth.) Masf. Branchlets threadlike, sometimes leafless; lfts. narrowly oblanceolate to elliptic, nearly glabrous, petioles slightly shorter, very slender; fls. white, fragrant, axillary. Canary Is. Zone 10.

fragrans: *C. supranubius;* but the florist's plant offered as *C. fragrans* or *Genistra fragrans* may be *C. stenopetalus* or a hybrid. See under *C. racemosus.*

glaber L.f. [*C. elongatus* Waldst. & Kit.]. To 5 ft.; lfts. to 1 in. long; fls. yellow with standard marked with reddish-brown, 2–5 together in axils. Cent. and se. Eur. Zone 6.

glabrescens: material cult. under this name is *C. emeriflorus.* The older *C. glabrescens* Schrank is considered a confused name.

hirsutus L. [*Genista hirsuta* Hort., not Vahl]. To 2 ft., branchlets villous; lfts. to ¾ in. long, villous beneath; fls. yellow with brown keel, about 1 in. long, 2–4 together in axils; fr. more than 1 in. long, villous. Late spring. Se. Eur. Zone 6. Var. **demissus** (Boiss.) Halácsy [*C. demissus* Boiss.]. To only 8 in. high, brs. prostrate; lfts. to ⅜ in. long, hirsute; fr. 1 in. long, softly hirsute. Greece.

hispanicus: see *Genista hispanica.*

humifusus: *C. decumbens.*

×**kewensis** Bean [*Genista kewensis* Hort.]: *C. Ardoini* × *C. multiflorus.* Procumbent, to 1 ft. high; lvs. sometimes of 1 lft. but usually with 3 lfts., lfts. linear-oblong, soft-pubescent; fls. creamy-white or pale yellow, ½ in. long, on slender brs. Late spring. Zone 6.

maderensis (Webb) Masf. To 20 ft.; young flowering shoots, including calyx, tawny-villous, herbage at other seasons silvery-pubescent; lvs. to ½ in. long, half as broad, acute, dark green, nearly smooth on upper surface; fls. in axillary, 6–12-fld. racemes to 4 in. long that often terminate abruptly. Madeira. Zone 10. Var. **magnifoliosus** (O. Kuntze) Briq. Lfts. and racemes larger.

monspessulanus L. To 10 ft., evergreen; lfts. obovate, pointed, to ¾ in. long, hairy beneath, petioles short; fls. bright yellow, fragrant, in short racemes at tips of lateral branchlets. Spring. S. Eur. Zone 9.

multiflorus (L'Hér. ex Ait.) Sweet [*C. albus* (Lam.) Link, not Hacq.]. WHITE SPANISH B. To 10 ft., with erect, grooved branchlets; lower lvs. with 3 lfts., upper lvs. of 1 lft., lfts. to ⅜ in. long, somewhat silky-pubescent, petioles short; fls. white, sometimes tinged rosy, 1–3 in axils; fr. 1 in. long, appressed-pubescent. Spain, Portugal. Cv. 'Albus' is listed. Zone 6.

newryensis: a listed name of no botanical standing for *Cytisus* cv. 'Newryensis'. Fls. creamy-yellow and mahogany-red.

nigricans L. To 6 ft., branchlets cylindrical; lfts. obovate, to 1 in. long, nearly acute, slightly pubescent beneath; fls. yellow, ⅜ in. long, in slender, terminal recemes to 1 ft. long; fr. pubescent, more than 1 in. long. Summer. Cent. and se. Eur. Zone 5. Var. **elongatus** Willd. Blooming again in autumn at tips of the fruiting brs.

×**praecox** Bean [*Genista praecox* Hort.]: *C. multiflorus* × *C. purgans.* WARMINSTER B. To 10 ft., dense; lvs. usually of 1 lft., to ¾ in. long, silky-pubescent; fls. many, small, pale yellowish, with unpleasant odor, solitary or paired in axils. Late spring. Zone 6. Cv. 'Albus' [var. *albus* T. Sm.]. Smaller and brs. more pendent; fls. white. Cv. 'Luteus' [var. *luteus* T. Sm.]. Dwarf; fls. yellow.

procumbens (Waldst. & Kit.) Sprenger. Differs from *C. decumbens* in growing to 30 in. high, with pedicels and lower surface of lvs. appressed-pubescent. Se. Eur. Zone 6.

purgans (L.) Spach [*Genista purgans* L.]. To 3 ft., much-branched; lvs. mostly of 1 lft., oblanceolate, to ½ in. long, silky-pubescent, soon withering, sessile; fls. fragrant, solitary or paired in axils. Late spring. S. Eur., n. Afr. Zone 6.

purpureus Scop. [*Genista purpurea* (Scop.) E. H. L. Krause]. To 2 ft. high, sts. procumbent, nearly glabrous; lfts. obovate, to 1 in. long; fls. purple, white, or pink, in axils; fr. to 1⅜ in. long, glabrous. Late spring. S. Austria. Zone 6. Cv. 'Albus' [forma *albus* Kirchn.]. Fls. white. Cv. 'Roseus' [forma *albo-carneus* Kirchn.]. Fls. pale pink.

racemosus Hort. ex Marnock [*Genista racemosa* Hort.]. Shrub, to 3 ft. or more; lfts. ovate-lanceolate, somewhat silvery-pubescent; fls. bright yellow, in terminal racemes about 6 in. long. Late spring. Canary Is. Zone 10. Perhaps conspecific with *C. stenopetalus.* Material cult. as *C.* × *racemosus* Hort. as used by L. H. Bailey or *C. fragrans* Hort., with rather long-petioled, oblong-obovate lfts. and 1-sided infl. 2–4 in. long, may be *C. stenopetalus,* or hybrid perhaps between *C. canariensis* and *C. maderensis* var. *magnifoliosus.*

ratisbonensis Schaeff. To 6 ft.; lfts. to 1½ in. long, glabrous above; fls. bright yellow, 1 in. long, in clusters of 2–4 in axils. Late spring. Eur., w. Asia. Zone 6.

scoparius (L.) Link [*Genista scoparia* (L.) Lam.]. SCOTCH B. To 10 ft., branchlets slender, green; lfts. obovate to oblanceolate, to ½ in. long; fls. mostly solitary or paired in axils; fr. narrow, oblong, to 2 in. long, glabrescent but margin villous. Spring and summer. Eur.; naturalized in N. Amer. Zone 6. Cv. 'Andreanus' [var. *Andreanus* (Puiss.) Dipp.; *Genista Andreana* Puiss.]. NORMANDY B. Fls. yellow, wing petals dark crimson. Normandy. Cv. 'Fulgens'. Fls. bright copper-orange.

sessilifolius L. To 6 ft.; lfts. to ¾ in. long; fls. in short racemes at tips of lateral branchlets. Early summer. S. Eur., n. Afr. Zone 6.

stenopetalus (Webb) Christ. To 10 ft., branchlets whitish-silky-hairy; lfts. narrowly elliptic to oblanceolate, to 1½ in. long, silky, petioles to ⅝ in. long; fls. bright yellow, in axillary or terminal, more or less 1-sided, many-fld., silky-hairy racemes to 4¼ in. long, standard glabrous, ⅜ in. across; fr. about 1 in. long, appressed-pilose. Spring. Canary Is. Zone 10.

supinus L. To 3 ft., erect or procumbent, branchlets villous; lfts. obovate to elliptic, to 1 in. long, villous beneath; fls. to 1 in. long, fading brownish, in terminal heads. Summer. Eur. Zone 6.

supranubius (L.f.) O. Kuntze [*C. fragrans* Lam.; *Genista fragrans* (Lam.) Spach]. Bushy, to 6 ft.; lfts. narrowly lanceolate to oblanceolate, densely pubescent, almost as long as petioles; fls. white or flushed rose, ⁵⁄₁₆ in. long, very fragrant, in dense axillary clusters; fr. over 1 in. long, glabrous. Canary Is. Zone 10.

×**versicolor** (Kirchn.) Dipp. [*Genista versicolor* Hort., not Wallich ex Royle]: *C. hisutus* × *C. purpureus.* To 3 ft.; lfts. obovate, to 1 in. long; fls. solitary to 3 together in axils, with whitish standard, yellowish wing petals, and light purple keel; fr. appressed-silky-pubescent. Zone 6.

DABOECIA D. Don. *Ericaceae.* Two spp. of evergreen, heathlike, small shrubs, native from Ireland to Spain, and the Azores; young sts. glandular-hairy; lvs. alt., simple, entire; fls. rose, pink, purple, or white, nodding, in terminal racemes, calyx 4-parted, corolla urceolate, 4-lobed, stamens 8, ovary superior; fr. a 4-celled caps.

Daboecias do best in a peaty soil. They are suitable for rock gardens, but require protection in the North. Propagated by seeds and by cuttings of half-ripened wood under glass.

azorica Tutin & E. F. Warb. [*Menziesia azorica* Hort.]. To 10 in., sts. procumbent, forming a mound; lvs. ovate-lanceolate or broadly elliptic, to ¼ in. long, bright deep green above, white-hairy beneath; fls. bright rose. Summer. Azores.

cantabrica (Huds.) C. Koch [*D. poliifolia* (Juss.) D. Don; *Menziesia poliifolia* Juss.]. IRISH HEATH. To 2 ft.; lvs. elliptic, to ½ in. long, revolute, shining above, white-tomentose beneath; fls. purple, ½ in. long. Summer, autumn. W. Eur. Zone 7. Cvs. are: '**Alba**', fls. white; '**Atropurpurea**', fls. deep purple; '**Bicolor**' [cv. 'Versicolor'], fls. striped white and purple; '**Multiflora**', fls. pale pink; '**Nana**', dwarf, lvs. smaller; '**Pallida**' [var. *rosea* Hort.], fls. rose-pink; '**Praegerae**', fls. large, deep rose; '**Rubra**', fls. rosy-purple; '**Versicolor**': 'Bicolor'.

poliifolia: *D. cantabrica.*

DACRYDIUM Lamb. *Podocarpaceae.* About 22 spp. of usually dioecious, evergreen, coniferous trees or shrubs, native to the S. Hemisphere; lvs. mostly scalelike, or on young specimens, subulate or linear; male cones spikelike, female cones of a few scales surrounded by a cuplike, membranous to thickened aril, each scale, or only 1, bearing 1 ovule; seeds nutlike.

The genus includes valuable timber trees. Grown in cool frost-free areas on the Pacific Coast, Zone 10. For culture see *Conifers.*

cupressinum Soland. ex Lamb. RIMU, IMOU PINE, RED P. To 100 ft., with long, graceful, drooping brs. when young; juvenile lvs. subulate, ¼ in. long or less, decurrent, lvs. on mature parts about ⅛ in. long; female cones about ⅛ in. long. New Zeal. Yields a valuable wood.

Franklinii Hook.f. HUON PINE. To 100 ft., with short horizontal brs. and drooping branchlets; lvs. scalelike, imbricate, about ¹⁄₁₆ in. long; cones very small, with 4–8 scales. Tasmania. Yields timber and Huon pine wood oil.

laxifolium Hook.f. MOUNTAIN RIMU. Prostrate or somewhat erect shrub, brs. 2–3 ft. long; juvenile lvs. spreading, narrow-linear, to ½ in. long, lvs. on mature parts less than ⅛ in. long, spreading or imbricate; cones about ⅛ in. long, pointed at apex. New Zeal.

DACTYLIS L. *Gramineae.* About 1–3 spp. of per. grasses in Eurasia; lf. blades flat; spikelets few-fld., compressed, finally disarticulating between the florets, nearly sessile in dense, 1-sided fascicles, these borne at the ends of the few brs. of a panicle; glumes unequal, shorter than first floret, keeled, acute, keel hispid-ciliate, lemma compressed-keeled, mucronate, 5-nerved, keel ciliate. For terminology see *Gramineae.*

glomerata L. ORCHARD GRASS, COCK'S-FOOT. Sts. to 4 ft., in large clumps; lf. blades elongate, to ⁵⁄₁₆ in. wide; panicles to 8 in. long, brs. few, distant, stiff, solitary, ascending or spreading in flowering, appressed to the axis at maturity, the lowermost to 4 in. long; lemma about ⁵⁄₁₆ in. long, mucronate or short-awned. Eurasia; naturalized from Nfld. to se. Alaska, s. to Fla. and cent. Calif. Commonly cult. as a meadow and pasture grass, and sometimes for ornament.

DAEDALACANTHUS: *ERANTHEMUM.*

DAEMONOROPS Blume. *Palmae.* Nearly 100 spp. of usually spiny, climbing or cespitose and shrublike, dioecious palms, in trop. Asia, Malay Arch., and the Philippine Is., sts. slender; lvs. pinnate, sheath tubular, often armed with solitary to clustered or whorled spines, often with a ligule at apex, petiole and blade usually spiny or clawed, pinnae acute, rachis usually terminating in a clawed climbing organ (cirrus); infl. short or elongate, joined to sheath of lf. above, sheaths tubular, deciduous, leaving a scar at base of each primary br., primary brs. again branched into slender rachillae with sheathing bractlets; male fls. smaller than female, calyx tubular, truncate to 3-toothed, petals 3, stamens 6, female fls. with calyx tubular, truncate to 3-toothed, petals 3, staminodes in a ring, pistil 3-celled; fr. covered with imbricate scales, seed with ruminate endosperm.

Species of the genus are a source of rattan and of Sumatran dragon's blood, a resin used in special varnishes. Sometimes grown for interest in tropical gardens. For culture see *Palms.*

grandis (Griff.) Griff. ex Mart. Climbing; lvs. to 10 ft. long or more, sheath with unequal, separated spines, pinnae about 36 on each side, equidistant, more than ¾ in. wide; infl. sessile, short, outer bract enclosing inner bracts in bud; fr. globose, ¾ in. in diam. Malay Pen.

Margaritae (Hance) Hance ex Becc. [*Calamus Margaritae* Hance]. Climbing; lvs. to 6 ft. long or more, sheath with large and small spines in series, pinnae 50–75 on each side, equidistant, less than ¾ in. wide; infl. sessile, short, outer bract enclosing inner bracts in bud; fr. globose, to ⅞ in. in diam. Hongkong, Philippine Is.

ochrolepis Becc. Climbing; lvs. large, sheath with spines in series, pinnae many, equidistant; infl. elongate, outer bract not enclosing inner bracts in bud; fr. globose, ¾ in. in diam. Philippine Is.

periacantha Miq. Climbing; sheath with few large spines and larger ones at mouth, pinnae many, in groups of 2–5; infl. elongate, outer bract not enclosing inner bracts in bud; fr. globose, about ⅝ in. in diam. Malay Pen., Indonesia.

pseudosepal Becc. Climbing; sheath with more or less confluent large spines, lvs. with many equidistant pinnae; infl. peduncled, short, outer bract enclosing inner bracts in bud; fr. ¾ in. in diam. Malay Pen.

DAHLIA Cav. *Compositae* (Helianthus Tribe). About 27 spp. of tender, tuberous-rooted per. herbs, native to mts. of Mex., Cent. Amer., and Colombia, sts. to 20 ft., mostly unbranched, woody at the base, or sometimes scandent and epiphytic, internodes often hollow; lvs. opp. or whorled, 1–3-odd-pinnate; fl. heads radiate, long-peduncled, involucral bracts in 2 rows, the inner membranous, somewhat united basally, enlarging in fr., the outer somewhat fleshy, receptacle flat or curved, scaly; disc fls. bisexual (in many cvs. replaced by ligulate fls.), ray fls. neutral or female, white, yellow, orange, scarlet, or purple; achenes oblong or obovate, compressed, pappus of 2 obscure teeth or absent.

Dahlias require a full season's growth, and if the soil is very rich they may not give much bloom before frost in northern regions; rather open "quick" soil, as a light loam suitable for corn or general garden purposes, produces good results, and any fertilizer that may be used should be quickly available. Water must be supplied freely.

The customary propagation by the home gardener is by planting separately each tuberous root in the cluster. Care must be taken not to injure the crown at the point where the root joins the previous year's stem base. Only one stem should be allowed to grow after danger from cutworms and early accidents is past. The cluster of roots is carefully lifted in autumn as soon as flowering is past, dried in the sun after the tops are removed, and stored in the cellar as are potatoes. The roots are laid on the side when planted and covered about 6 in. deep. Plants are commonly set about 3 or 4 ft. apart. Tall individuals may need staking, as they are likely to be tipped over and broken by wind, but if the tip or center of the plant is pinched out after 2 or 3 joints have grown, it may stand alone.

Some dahlias are grown readily from seeds, which, in the North, may well be started under glass. The single and the low-growing dahlias come well by this method and flower well the same year in late summer and autumn. These plants produce tuberous roots, and these may be used for further propagation, or plants may be grown each year from seeds.

For more rapid propagation and particularly for the perpetuation of cultivars, cuttings may be used. These cuttings may be made of strong stems, cut just below a joint, or by the sprouting of roots; in either method, the work should be carried on under glass and the young plants kept growing until time for setting out in spring. If roots are used, they may be placed whole in a warm, light place, and the shoots taken off and treated like stem cuttings.

The species of *Dahlia* are infrequently cultivated; those dahlias which are in cultivation mostly represent the innumerable cultivars derived from hybridization or from selection of individuals grown from seeds. The original parents of present-day cultivars are probably *D. pinnata* and *D. coccinea.*

The American Dahlia Society recognizes 12 groups of cultivars based on the morphology of the head and the flowers.

1. SINGLE DAHLIAS. Heads with fewer than 2 complete rows of ray fls., the central area bearing small disc fls.; ligules of ray fls. flat or nearly so.

2. ANEMONE DAHLIAS. Heads with 1 or more rows of ray fls., the central area bearing tubular disc fls. longer than those in the single dahlias.

3. COLARETTE DAHLIAS. Heads with fewer than 2 complete rows of ray fls., 1 or more rows of small ray fls. of a different color, and disc fls. in the center; ligules of ray fls. flat.

4. PEONY DAHLIAS. Heads with 2 or more rows of ray fls., and with disc fls. in the center; ligules of ray fls. usually flat, sometimes the inner row next to the disc smaller and twisted or curled.

5. FORMAL DECORATIVE DAHLIAS. Heads with ray fls. only; ligules of ray fls. generally regularly arranged, their tips pointed or rounded and their margins not or only slightly revolute, the outer ligules tending to be recurved and the central ones tending to be cupped.

6. INFORMAL DECORATIVE DAHLIAS. Heads with ray fls. only; ligules of ray fls. irregularly arranged, generally long and twisted or pointed, their margins slightly or not revolute.

7. BALL DAHLIAS. Heads globose or slightly flattened, with ray fls. only, ligules of ray fls. with round or blunt tips, their margins involute more than half their length.

8. POMPON DAHLIAS. Heads globose and of miniature size, with ray fls. only, ligules of ray fls. involute their entire length.

9. INCURVED CACTUS DAHLIAS. Heads with ray fls. only, ligules of ray fls. with pointed tips incurving toward center of head, their margins revolute for half or more of their length.

10. STRAIGHT CACTUS DAHLIAS. Heads with ray fls. only, ligules of ray fls. with pointed tips which are straight or only slightly incurved or recurved, margins of most of the ligules revolute for most of their length.

11. SEMICACTUS DAHLIAS. Heads with ray fls. only; ligules of ray fls. with pointed tips, their bases broader than in the cactus dahlias, their margins revolute less than half their length.

12. MISCELLANEOUS DAHLIAS. This group accommodates any dahlia not fitting into any of the groups 1–11.

arborea: *D. imperialis.*

coccinea Cav. Rather slender herb, to 10 ft., sts. usually branched, sometimes glaucous or variously green to purple; lvs. opp. or in whorls of 3, simple to 3-pinnate, to 14 in. long including petiole; heads usually in 2's or 3's, on peduncles to 1 ft. long; disc fls. yellow or yellow tipped with scarlet, ray fls. typically 8, yellow, orange, scarlet-orange, or deep scarlet. Mex. This sp. and *D. pinnata* are probably the original parents of the modern hybrid garden dahlias.

imperialis Roezl. ex Ortg. [*D. arborea* Hort. ex Regel]. BELL TREE D., CANDELABRA D., TREE D. Herbaceous to woody per., to 20 ft., st. unbranched except in flowering part, obscurely 6-angled, younger sts. glaucous, green or reddish-green, older sts. tan or brown; lvs. 2–3-pinnate, to 3 ft. long including petiole, primary lfts. 9–15; heads up to 300 per plant, to 6 in. across, slightly campanulate; disc fls. yellow or yellow with reddish tips, ray fls. white to pale lavender or rose-purple. S. Mex., Guatemala, San Salvador, Costa Rica, Colombia.

Merckii Lehm. BEDDING D. Freely branching herb, to 6 ft.; lvs. 1–2-pinnate, to 15 in. long including petiole, the lfts. pinnately dissected; heads 1–2 in. across, 2–19 on peduncles to 1 ft. long; disc fls. yellow, purple, or yellow with purple tips, ray fls. whitish to pale lavender or purple. Mex.

pinnata Cav. [*D. variabilis* (Willd.) Desf.]. Herb, to 6 ft., st. unbranched except in flowering part, scabrous; lvs. simple to pinnately dissected or 2-pinnate, to 10 in. long including petiole; heads 2–4 in. across, in 2's or 3's but only 2–8 on a st.; disc fls. yellow, sometimes veined with light purple, ray fls. light purple or lavender-purple, often with a basal rosy or yellow spot. Mex. The names *D. pinnata* or *D. variabilis* have usually, but mistakenly, been used to include the highly developed COMMON or GARDEN DAHLIA. This, with its many cvs., however, is apparently the product of hybridization between *D. coccinea* and *D. pinnata.*

variabilis: *D. pinnata.*

DAIS L. *Thymelaeaceae.* Two spp. or more of deciduous shrubs or small trees, native to S. Afr. and Madagascar; lvs.

opp. or scattered, simple; infl. a peduncled, many-fld. terminal head, subtended by 2 or more bracts; fls. pink, calyx tubular, corollalike.

One species is grown outdoors in southern Calif. and southern Fla. Propagated by cuttings of half-ripened wood.

cotinifolia L. Shrub or small tree, to 18 ft.; lvs. obovate or oblong, to 3 in. long; heads to 3 in. across, peduncle to 2 in. long. S. Afr. The bark is said to yield a strong fiber used by natives of Natal as thread.

DALBERGIA L.f. *Leguminosae* (subfamily *Faboideae*). More than 200 spp. of trop. trees, shrubs, or lianas; lvs. alt., pinnate, with alt. lfts.; fls. abundant, small, white or purplish, papilionaceous, stamens 9–10, united in a tube split on 1 or 2 sides or sometimes 1 separate; fr. an elongate, very flat, indehiscent legume, seeds few.

Propagated by seeds or cuttings.

assamica Benth. Twiner; lvs. 6–10 in. long, lfts. 5–21, oblong-elliptic, obtuse; panicles axillary, 3–4 in. long, with slender silky rachises; petals less than ¼ in. long; fr. glabrous, to 4 in. long, 1–2-seeded. Himalayas.

brasiliensis Vogel. Small tree with pubescent branchlets; lfts. in 10–12 pairs, linear-oblong, 1½ in. long, ¼ in. wide, midrib hirsute beneath, petioles and infl. golden-rusty-pubescent; racemes bracted, sometimes panicled; fls. small; fr. 1-seeded. Trop. Brazil.

lanceolaria L.f. Tall, deciduous tree with slender brs.; lvs. 3–6 in. long, lfts. 11–15, elliptic, 1–2 in. long, emarginate, narrow at base; panicles wide, terminal and axillary; fls. mauve, stamens in 2 bundles of 5 each; fr. brown, to 4 in. long, ¾ in. wide. W. India, Ceylon.

latifolia Roxb. Deciduous tree; lvs. 4–6 in. long, lfts. 3–7, broadly elliptic or nearly orbicular, to 3 in. long, obtuse to emarginate; panicles axillary; fls. small, whitish, stamens 9; fr. 1–4-seeded. India. Yields a valuable lumber, the rosewood of s. India.

Sissoo Roxb. ex DC. SISSOO. Deciduous tree, to 80 ft.; lfts. 3–5, ovate or nearly orbicular, to 3 in. long, abruptly acuminate; panicles short, axillary; fls. yellowish-white, stamens 9; fr. to 4 in. long. India, where an important timber tree.

DALEA L. [*Parosela* Cav.]. INDIGO BUSH. *Leguminosae* (subfamily *Faboideae*). Perhaps 200 spp. or more of herbs and shrubs, native to the W. Hemisphere, mostly of dry or desert areas; lvs. odd-pinnate, rarely with 1 lft., glandular-dotted; infl. spicate or racemose; fls. papilionaceous, stamens 10 or 9, united; fr. a small, obovoid or nearly reniform, indehiscent legume, mostly 1-seeded.

Propagated by seeds.

aurea Nutt. [*Parosela aurea* (Nutt.) Britt.]. Per., to 30 in., silky-pubescent; lfts. 5–7, to ¾ in. long, silvery, the upper ones reduced; fls. yellow, in dense spikes to 3 in. long. S. Dak. to Tex. and Ariz.; Mex.

enneandra Nutt. Per., to 3½ ft.; lfts. 5–9, linear to oblong, 5/16 in. long, glabrous; spikes open, to 4 in. long; fls. white. N. Dak. to Colo., s. to Miss. and Tex.

Grayi (Vail) L. O. Williams. Per. herb, from woody rootcrown; lvs. to 1½ in. long, lfts. in 17–20 pairs, oblong to ovate, ⅛ in. long, mucronate; spikes dense, 1 in. long; fls. whitish. New Mex., Ariz., nw. Mex.

Schottii Torr. To 10 ft., shrubby, somewhat spiny; lfts. solitary, linear, to 1¼ in. long, glandular-dotted along margins; racemes to 4 in. long; fls. dark blue to purplish. Deserts, s. Calif., w. Ariz., Baja Calif. Var. **puberula** (S. Parish) Munz. Branchlets, young lvs., and calyces gray-pubescent.

spinosa A. Gray. SMOKE TREE. Spiny shrub, or small tree to 30 ft.; lvs. few, with 1 lft., linear-lanceolate, about ½ in. long, white-strigose, falling early; racemes 2 in. long, spinescent; fls. violet-purple; fr. canescent. Deserts, s. Calif., Ariz., nw. Mex.

DALIBARDA L. FALSE VIOLET, ROBIN-RUN-AWAY. *Rosaceae.* One sp., a low, unarmed per. of N. Amer., with creeping and densely tufted sts.; lvs. roundish-cordate, crenate, petioles slender; fls. of 2 kinds, a few upright, usually sterile, and white-petalled, and many on short curved pedicels, fertile, and apetalous.

repens L. ROBIN-RUN-AWAY. Downy; fls. white, to ½ in. across. Woods, Que. and Ont., s. to Conn., N.C., Ohio, Mich.

DAMASONIUM Mill. *Alismataceae.* Not in cult. **D. californicum:** *Machaerocarpus californicus.*

DAMNACANTHUS C. F. Gaertn. *Rubiaceae.* About 6 spp. of rigid, much-branched, usually spinose shrubs, native to

Asia; lvs. opp., leathery; fls. axillary, solitary or paired, white; corolla funnelform, 4–5-lobed; fr. a drupe, 1–4-seeded.

indicus C. F. Gaertn. To 5 ft., brs. hairy; lvs. ovate, to 1 in. long, acuminate, lustrous, obscurely veined; corolla to ⅜ in. long, 4-lobed; fr. globose, to ⅛ in. across. E. Asia.

DANAE Medic. *Liliaceae.* One sp., an evergreen shrub, native to sw. Asia; lvs. alt., scalelike, the apparent lvs. (cladophylls) being modified brs.; fls. bisexual, white, in short, terminal racemes, perianth segms. 6, united up to above the middle, stamens 6, exserted; fr. a many-seeded, 1-celled berry. The name has three syllables.

Sometimes planted as an ornamental for its attractive red berries and evergreen foliage, excellent for cutting. Propagated by division or seeds.

racemosa (L.) Moench [*Ruscus racemosus* L.]. ALEXANDRIAN LAUREL. Erect, to 3 ft.; cladophylls obliquely oblong-lanceolate, tapering to apex, to 4 in. long and 1½ in. wide; fls. white; fr. red.

DANDELION. The common dandelion, *Taraxacum officinale,* is often gathered for greens. Improved large-leaved horticultural forms are grown as an autumn and spring vegetable, the plants attaining a large size and the leaves being more tender. The seed may be selected from the best field-growing plants, but it is better to purchase seed of seedsmen. Sow in spring in well-manured soil, either in drills or in hills 1 foot apart. A cutting of leaves may be had in September or October, and some of the stools may stand until spring. The delicacy of the leaves may be improved by blanching them, either by the use of boards or earth. The plant is usually not left the second year.

DANIELLIA J. Benn. *Leguminosae* (subfamily *Caesalpinioideae*). Perhaps 12 spp. of large, resin-bearing trees of trop. Afr.; lvs. alt., even-pinnate, lfts. with petiolules, mostly opp., inequilateral at base, translucent-dotted; fls. in panicled racemes, sepals 4, deciduous, petals 5, 4 of them minute, stamens 10, separate; fr. a flat, stalked, leathery, dehiscent legume, usually 1-seeded.

The genus is the source of oleoresins used by industry. Propagated by seeds sown where plants are to grow.

Oliveri Hutch. & Dalz. Fast-growing tree, to 100 ft.; lfts. in 4–11 pairs, ovate to oblong, to 6 in. long, acuminate, young lvs. pink; fls. fragrant, creamy-white, in flat panicles 1 ft. long, stamens showy, to 1½ in. long; fr. elliptic, 3⁵⁄₁₆ in. long. Humid forests, Nigeria. Produces an oleoresin, a "wood oil."

DANTHONIA Lam. & DC. OAT GRASS, WILD O. G. *Gramineae.* Over 100 spp. of per. grasses in temp. regions, but mostly in S. Hemisphere; sts. clustered; panicles few-fld., open or spikelike; spikelets rather large, often of 2 kinds, cleistogamous spikelets 1–2-fld., in the lower sheaths, normal spikelets several-fld., rachilla disarticulating above the glumes and between the florets, glumes about equal, as long as the lowest floret or longer, broad, papery, acute, lemma rounded on the back, obscurely several-nerved, apex bifid, awned between the acute lobes, awn stout, flat, twisted, geniculate. For terminology see *Gramineae.*

purpurea (Thunb.) Beauvois ex Roem. & Schult. Sts. tufted, forming mats, very slender, to 8¾ in. high; lf. blades few, to 1⅝ in. long, folded, curved, pilose; panicles somewhat capitate with few to several spikelets on short, slender pedicels; spikelets ⁵⁄₁₆ in. long, glumes dark purple, fading to brown, florets ⅛ in. long, lemma pilose at base, with small tufts of white hairs across the middle of the back, awn to ⅛ in. long. S. Afr.

semiannularis (Labill.) R. Br. AUSTRALIAN D. Sts. to 3 ft., clustered; lf. blades very narrow, flat or convolute; panicle sometimes loose and spreading, more often narrow and compact; outer glumes acute, ½–1 in. long, lemmas 4–8, not exceeding the glumes, pilose at base and with tufted hairs at middle, lobes acute or tapering into a point or rather short fine awn, central awn twisted, to 1 in. long, palea often 2-pointed. Australia, Tasmania.

setacea R. Br. WALLABY GRASS. Confused with *D. semiannularis,* from which it differs in its more slender sts., frequently less than 1 ft. high, setaceous lf. blades, dense panicle, glumes much exceeding the spikelet, lemmas rarely more than 6, very short with long, very narrow lobes, tapering into fine awns, palea more obtuse. Australia.

DAPHNE L. *Thymelaeaceae.* About 50 spp. of deciduous or evergreen shrubs, native to Eur. and Asia; lvs. alt., rarely opp., simple, entire; fls. white, purple, or lilac, sometimes yellow or yellowish-green, in short, terminal or axillary heads or racemes, usually fragrant, calyx tube cylindrical, with 4 spreading lobes, forming the conspicuous part of the fl.; fr. leathery or fleshy, drupelike.

Grown outdoors or under glass, although most species are hardy to N.Y. and New Eng. Some are very low and good for borders or rock gardens. A well-drained light soil is best; for forced plants, a compost of peat and loam. Propagated by seeds sown at once or stratified; by soft wood cuttings, or the evergreen species by hard wood cuttings taken in autumn and carried till spring in a cool greenhouse; or by grafting in winter on seedling stocks or roots. Layering may also be used; compost should be used in place of soil for 2 or 3 in. about the plant, removed the following spring, and the small white buds planted in pots of fine soil.

acutiloba Rehd. Evergreen, to 6 ft., young shoots covered with more or less erect hairs; lvs. lanceolate or oblanceolate, to 4 in. long and 1 in. wide, tapered at both ends, leathery; fls. white, almost or entirely scentless, 6 or more in peduncled clusters at or nearly at ends of shoots; fr. red, showy. Early summer. W. China. Zone 7.

alpina L. Deciduous, low, to 1½ ft.; lvs. lanceolate to oblanceolate, to 2 in. long and ½ in. wide, pubescent, appearing before fls.; fls. white, fragrant, 4–10 in terminal heads; fr. reddish. Late spring. Limestone areas in mts., cent. and s. Eur. Zone 5.

altaica Pall. Deciduous, erect shrub, to 4 ft.; lvs. oblanceolate to oblong, to 2½ in. long, glabrous, dull green above, more or less glaucous beneath; fls. white, little scented, few in terminal and lateral clusters. Late spring. Siberia. Zone 6.

arbuscula Čelak. Evergreen, dwarf shrub, to 6 in., related to *D. petraea,* but having lvs. linear-lanceolate, to 1 in. long, revolute, dark, glossy; fls. rose-pink. Spring. Hungary. Zone 6.

Bholua Buch.-Ham. ex D. Don [*D. cannabina* Lour.]. Evergreen, usually erect shrub, to 7 ft.; lvs. oblanceolate or elliptic-lanceolate, to 4 in. long and 1 in. wide, undulate and obscurely glandular-denticulate; fls. reddish-purple outside, creamy-white inside, fragrant, several in terminal or axillary clusters. Winter. W. Himalayas. Bark fibrous, used for making paper and string in Nepal.

Blagayana Freyer. Evergreen, straggling, prostrate, to 1 ft., sts. rooting along ground; lvs. oblong or obovate, to 1¾ in. long and ¾ in. wide; fls. cream-white, fragrant, 20 or more in dense terminal heads. Late winter to spring. Mts., se. Eur. Zone 6.

×**Burkwoodii** Turrill. *D. caucasica* × *D. Cneorum.* Partly evergreen, upright shrub, to 4 ft.; lvs. linear-oblanceolate or narrowly elliptic-oblanceolate, to 1¼ in. long and ¼ in. wide; fls. white, flushed pink, fragrant, 6–16 in terminal heads surrounded by foliage lvs. Best known through cv. '**Somerset**'.

cannabina: *D. Bholua.*

caucasica Pall. Deciduous shrub, to 5 ft. or more; lvs. oblanceolate to lanceolate, to nearly 2 in. long; fls. white, pubescent outside, fragrant, in terminal heads. Late spring. Caucasus. Zone 7.

Cneorum L. GARLAND FLOWER. Evergreen, procumbent shrub, to 1 ft.; lvs. narrow-oblong to oblanceolate, to 1 in. long and ¼ in. wide; fls. pink to rose-red or white, fragrant, in dense terminal heads. Early spring, also in autumn. Mts., Eur. Zone 5. One of the most popular of the daphnes, with several cvs.: '**Albo-marginata**', lvs. variegated; '**Eximia**', fls. large, deep pink; '**Major**', lvs. large; '**Variegata**', lvs. variegated. Var. **pygmaea** Stoker [*D. pygmaea* Hort.]. Prostrate, compact, to 3 in.; lvs. small, to ⅜ in. long. Alps, n. Italy. Cv. '**Alba**'. Fls. white.

collina Sm. Evergreen, erect shrub, to 3½ ft.; lvs. obovate to oblanceolate, to nearly 2 in. long, smooth above, pubescent beneath; fls. deep rose, to ⅜ in. across, fragrant, in 10–15-fld. heads. Spring to late spring. Italy, Sicily, Crete, Asia Minor. Zone 7. Var. **neapolitana** (Lodd.) Lindl. [*D. neapolitana* Lodd.]. Lvs. glaucous beneath; fls. fragrant. It has been suggested that this var. is actually a hybrid, but this has not been verified.

Dauphinii: *D.* × *hybrida.*

Fioniana: *D.* × *hybrida.*

Fortunei: *D. Genkwa.*

Genkwa Siebold & Zucc. [*D. Fortunei* Lindl.]. Deciduous, to 3 ft.; lvs. opp., lanceolate, to 2 in. long; fls. lilac, 2–5 in clusters along brs. of previous year, appearing before the lvs.; fr. white and attractive. Spring. China. Zone 5. The few lilac fls. in lateral clusters are distinctive.

Giraldii Nitsche. Deciduous, glabrous, erect shrub, to 2½ ft.; lvs. oblanceolate, to 2½ in. long, glaucescent beneath; fls. yellow, slightly fragrant, 3–8 in terminal heads. Nw. China. Zone 6.

glandulosa: *D. oleoides.*

Gnidium L. Evergreen, erect shrub, to 4 ft.; lvs. narrowly lanceolate, to 1½ in. long, thick, glabrous; fls. creamy-white, few in terminal clusters; fr. ovoid, red or black. Medit. region.

×**Houtteana** Lindl. & Paxt.: *D. Laureola* × *D. Mezereum.* PURPLE-LEAVED D. Semievergreen shrub, to 4 ft., brs. stout, erect; lvs. oblanceolate, glabrous, purplish; fls. lilac-violet, 2–5 in short, peduncled, lateral clusters. Early spring.

×**hybrida** J. Cov. ex Sweet [*D. Dauphinii* Loud.; *D. Fioniana* Dipp.]: *D. collina* × *D. odora.* Vigorous, evergreen shrub, to 6 ft., much-branched; lvs. spreading horizontally from st., elliptic-oblong, to 3½ in. long, usually glabrous; fls. dark pink, fragrant, usually 6 in terminal clusters. Zone 7.

involucrata Wallich. Tall shrub or small tree, to 20 ft. in its native habitat; lvs. oblong-lanceolate, to 6 in. long; fls. white, flushed with pink, fragrant, few to many in terminal heads enclosed in bud by 2 colored involucral bracts; fr. black. E. Himalayas.

jasminea Sibth. & Sm. [*D. microphylla* Meissn.]. Evergreen, low shrub, to 15 in.; lvs. oblong-obovate; fls. purple, fragrant. Greece.

Laureola L. SPURGE-LAUREL. Evergreen, glabrous shrub, to 3 ft. or rarely to 5 ft.; lvs. oblanceolate, to 3 in. or rarely 5 in. long, 1½ in. wide; fls. yellowish-green, fragrant, in almost sessile racemes. Early spring. Eur., w. Asia. Zone 7. Useful for its evergreen foliage rather than its fls. Var. **Philippi** (Gren. & Godr.) Meissn. [*D. Philippi* Gren. & Godr.]. Semiprostrate, to 16 in.; lvs. obovate, to 2 in. long; fls. violet on outside. Pyrenees.

×**Mantensiana** Manten ex T. Taylor & Vrugtm.: *D.* × *Burkwoodii* × *D. retusa.* Evergreen shrub, to 2½ ft.; lvs. oblong to narrowly obovate-oblong, to 1¼ in. long; fls. orchid-purple, 13 or more in terminal clusters. Spring to summer, and autumn. Best known through the cv. 'Manten'.

Mezereum L. FEBRUARY D., MEZEREON, MEZEREUM. Deciduous, more or less erect, rounded shrub, to 4–5 ft.; lvs. usually elliptic, to 3½ in. long and ¾ in. wide; fls. lilac-purple or white, fragrant, in clusters along brs. of previous year, appearing before the lvs.; fr. scarlet or yellow. Early spring. Eur., w. Asia. Zone 5. One of the finest and most easily cult. of the daphnes. All parts of the plant are poisonous. Cvs. are: 'Alba', fls. white, fr. yellow; 'Grandiflora', fls. larger; 'Rubra', fls. reddish-purple.

microphylla: *D. jasminea.*

neapolitana: *D. collina* var.

odora Thunb. WINTER D. Evergreen shrub, to 4 ft. or sometimes 6 ft.; lvs. narrowly elliptic or oblong, to 3 in. long and ⅜ in. wide, smooth and glossy; fls. white to purple, very fragrant, in crowded terminal heads. Late winter to early spring. China. Zone 7. Often grown under glass, and also used as cut fls. Cvs. include: 'Alba', fls. white; 'Marginata', lvs. bordered with yellow; 'Rubra', fls. wine-red; 'Variegata', lvs. bordered with yellow, fls. pale pink.

oleoides Schreb. [*D. glandulosa* Bertol.]. Evergreen, erect shrub, to 3 ft., young shoots gray-pubescent; lvs. elliptic, obovate to lanceolate, to 1½ in. long, glabrous above, pubescent beneath at least at first, later more or less pitted with glands; fls. white or pale lilac, in terminal clusters of 3–6. Late spring. Medit. region. Sometimes said to extend e. through Afghanistan to the Himalayas, but this is questionable since the Afghanistan plant has recently been referred to *D. mucronata* Royle [*D. oleoides* Aitch., not Schreb.]. Zone 7. Cvs. 'Alba' and 'Rubra' are listed.

petraea Leyb. Evergreen, spreading, much-branched shrub, to 6 in.; lvs. crowded, oblong, to ½ in. long, leathery; fls. rose-pink, fragrant, 3–6 in terminal clusters. Late spring. N. Italy. Zone 6. Cv. 'Grandiflora'. Fls. larger.

Philippi: *D. Laureola* var.

pontica L. TWIN-FLOWERED D. Evergreen, spreading shrub, to 5 ft.; lvs. obovate or obovate-oblong, to 3 in. long and 1½ in. wide, glossy above; fls. yellowish-white or yellowish-green, fragrant, generally in pairs at ends of slender peduncles arising at the base of young shoots. Se. Eur., Asia Minor. Zone 7.

pygmaea: *D. Cneorum* var.

retusa Hemsl. Evergreen shrub, to 3 ft.; lvs. oblanceolate, to 3 in. long, obtuse or more often emarginate, glabrous; fls. white, tinged rose or violet, to ¾ in. long, fragrant, in many-fld. terminal heads; fr. red. W. China. Zone 7.

sericea Vahl. Evergreen shrub, to 2 ft.; lvs. crowded at ends of branchlets, lanceolate to oblanceolate, to ¾ in. long, glabrous above, usually pubescent beneath; fls. rose, to ¾ in. long, in 3–8-fld. heads. Sicily, Crete, Asia Minor. Zone 7. Plants offered under this name are usually *D. collina*, from which *D. sericea* differs in having shorter lvs. and few fls. in the head.

striata Tratt. Evergreen, prostrate shrub, to 9 in.; lvs. at ends of branchlets, oblanceolate; fls. rose-pink, usually 8–12 in terminal heads. Cent. Eur. Zone 6. Related to *D. Cneorum*, but differing in having weak, loosely branched, low sts. Difficult to grow.

Sureil W. W. Sm. & Cave. To 9 ft. or more, sts. ascending, twigs white-tomentose, becoming glabrous; lvs. lanceolate to oblong-lanceolate, to 5 in. long, acute, wedge-shaped at base, somewhat wavy-margined, petioles nearly ½ in. long; fls. ivory-white, to 1 in. long, usually 12–20 in loose heads, calyx lobes triangular, with revolute margins; fr. orange-red, to ⅝ in. long. E. Himalayas, where the tough bark is used for making paper and string.

tangutica Maxim. Evergreen, erect, rounded shrub, to 5 ft.; lvs. elliptic, oblong, or oblanceolate, to 3 in. long and ¾ in. wide, smooth, glossy above; fls. rose-purple, fragrant, in dense terminal heads; fr. a red fleshy berry. Early spring. Nw. China. Zone 7.

DAPHNIPHYLLACEAE Müll. Arg. DAPHNIPHYLLUM FAMILY. Dicot.; 1 genus, *Daphniphyllum*, of evergreen shrubs or trees, native to e. and se. Asia; lvs. simple, leathery; fls. in axillary racemes, calyx of 3–6, more or less united, imbricate segms., or obsolete, petals 0, stamens 6–12, filaments separate, ovary superior, imperfectly 2-celled; fr. a 1-seeded drupe.

DAPHNIPHYLLUM Blume. *Daphniphyllaceae.* About 25 spp. of dioecious, evergreen shrubs and trees, native from Japan and Korea s. to Australia; lvs. alt. or more or less whorled, simple, entire, leathery, resembling those of *Laurus;* fls. in axillary racemes, petals 0; fr. a 1-seeded drupe.

The species planted most commonly in this country, *D. macropodum*, withstands several degrees of frost, but requires winter protection; it is useful in the southern and Pacific coast states. Propagated by cuttings, or by seeds if procurable.

glaucescens Blume. Small tree; lvs. elliptic, to 6 in. long, sometimes glaucous beneath; racemes to 1½ in. long; fr. ellipsoidal, with a rough skin. S. India, Ceylon, Java.

humile Maxim. [*D. macropodum* var. *humile* (Maxim.) K. Rosenth.]. Small shrub, 2–3 ft. high; lvs. elliptic to oblong, to 5 in. long; fr. dark blue. N. Japan, Korea. Zone 7.

macropodum Miq. Shrub to small tree, to 30 ft. or more, twigs red; lvs. oblong to elliptic, 3–8 in. long, bluish-white underneath; racemes to 4 in. long; fr. black, with a bloom. Cent. and s. Japan, s. Korea. Zone 8. Var. **humile:** *D. humile.*

viridipes: a listed name of no botanical standing.

DARLINGTONIA Torr. [*Chrysamphora* Greene]. *Sarraceniaceae.* One sp., a per., carnivorous herb, native to wet swampy sites in n. Calif., and sw. Ore., differs from *Sarracenia* in having hood of lf. appendaged, scape bracted, and style 5-branched at the apex.

Culture as for *Sarracenia;* hardy through Zone 9 or in colder regions with protection. Propagated by seeds or by division.

californica Torr. [*Chrysamphora californica* (Torr.) Greene]. PITCHER PLANT, CALIFORNIA P. P., COBRA PLANT, COBRA ORCHID, COBRA LILY. Lvs. yellowish-green, in basal rosettes, erect, tubular, to 30 in. high, enlarged upward to an inflated, translucent, spotted hood having a 2-forked appendage and opening on the underside; scapes erect, exceeding the lvs., bracted; fl. solitary, nodding, sepals yellowish-green, lined with purple, 1½–2½ in. long, petals dark purple, shorter than sepals; caps. ovoid, to nearly 2 in. in diam.

DARWINIA Rudge. SCENT MYRTLE. *Myrtaceae.* About 23 spp. of evergreen, glabrous, heathlike shrubs, endemic in Australia; lvs. opp., linear, with oil glands; fls. subsessile, subtended by 2 bracts, calyx tube cylindrical, ribbed, calyx lobes 5, petal-like, petals 5, stamens 10, anthers opening by pores, style bearded towards apex; fr. 1-celled, nutlike, indehiscent, formed from the slightly enlarged and somewhat hardened calyx tube and ovary.

Propagated by lateral cuttings in spring or autumn. Requires a warm, well-drained location.

citriodora (Endl.) Benth. Shrub, 2–4 ft., young brs. with 2 prominent ridges under the lvs.; lvs. oblong to ovate-lanceolate, to ¾ in. long, margins recurved; fls. usually 4 in small terminal heads. W. Australia.

homoranthoides (F. J. Muell.) Black [*D. Schuermannii* (F. J. Muell.) Benth.]. Much-branched prostrate shrub; lvs. 2-ranked, linear, ⅜ in. long, 3-angled; fls. white with red anthers, drooping, solitary in lf. axils of branchlets. S. Australia.

Schuermannii: *D. homoranthoides.*

thymoides (Lindl.) Benth. Diffuse and much-branched low shrub; lvs. linear or lanceolate, to $\frac{3}{8}$ in. long, margins revolute; fls. white, sessile, in terminal heads. W. Australia.

DASHEEN: see *Taro.*

DASYLIRION Zucc. SOTOL, BEAR GRASS. *Agavaceae.* About 15 spp. of stemless or treelike, dioecious plants of dry areas from Tex. to Ariz. and Mex.; lvs. linear, usually spiny-margined, not ribbed, congested at end of trunk; infl. a narrow panicle of racemes; fls. unisexual, perianth segms. 6, small, whitish, denticulate, stamens 6, ovary superior, 1-celled, 2–3-ovuled; fr. dry, indehiscent, 3-winged, with a single seed.

The leaves are used for thatching and baskets; the fiber is used for cordage; and an alcoholic beverage, sotol, is extracted from the trunks. Cultivation as for *Yucca.*

acrotriche (Schiede) Zucc. Trunk 3 ft. or more; lvs. to 3 ft. long, $\frac{3}{8}$ in. wide or less, brush-tipped; infl. to 15 ft.; fr. $\frac{1}{4}$–$\frac{5}{16}$ in. wide, style as long as notch at apex. Mex.

glaucophyllum Hook. Trunk short; lvs. 3 ft. long or more, $\frac{1}{2}$ in. wide, glaucous, not brush-tipped; infl. to 18 ft.; fr. $\frac{1}{4}$–$\frac{5}{16}$ in. wide, with style half as long as notch at apex. Mex.

gracile: *Beaucarnea gracilis.*

leiophyllum Engelm. Trunk short; lvs. about 40 in. long, to $1\frac{1}{4}$ in. wide, green or glaucescent, smooth, margins with prickles directed toward base of lvs.; infl. to 12 ft.; fr. $\frac{3}{16}$–$\frac{1}{4}$ in. wide, with deep notch at apex, style not longer than notch. W. Tex., New Mex., n. Mex.

longifolium: *Nolina longifolia.*

serratifolium (Schult.) Zucc. Stemless or nearly so; lvs. to 3 ft. long, $1\frac{1}{2}$ in. wide, glaucous, rough, brush-tipped, margins prickly; fr. $\frac{1}{4}$–$\frac{5}{16}$ in. wide, truncate, with a narrow notch at apex, style as long as notch. Oaxaca (Mex.).

texanum Scheele. Trunk short or underground; lvs. 2–3 ft. long, $\frac{3}{8}$–$\frac{5}{8}$ in. wide, green, marginal prickles yellow turning brown; infl. to 15 ft.; fr. small, to $\frac{5}{16}$ in. wide, with a shallow notch at apex, style about as long as notch. Tex. and n. Mex. Cv. **'Glaucum'.** Lvs. glaucous.

Wheeleri S. Wats. SPOON FLOWER. Trunk to 3 ft.; lvs. to 3 ft. long, 1 in. wide, brush-tipped, margins with prickles directed toward apex; infl. to 15 ft.; fr. $\frac{1}{4}$–$\frac{5}{16}$ in. wide, wings rounded or obtuse, apex with a broad notch, style about as long as notch. W. Tex. to Ariz., n. Mex.

DATE. The fruit of a palm, *Phoenix dactylifera,* of very ancient cultivation in the arid regions of the Old World, principally northern Africa, where moisture is supplied by spring or underground water or by irrigation. High temperatures are required in the growing and ripening season and rain at harvest time is a decided detriment. The date of commerce is the naturally dried drupe of the palm, borne in heavy clusters. Dates are now grown in considerable plantations in the low desert valleys of southern California and Arizona, and are possibly suited to some parts of Texas and other regions. The date palm is also widely planted as an ornamental tree in the semiarid tropics and subtropics. When well established, the tree withstands several degrees of frost.

The date palm is dioecious; the male flowers are on one tree and the females on another. Seedless dates may be produced without pollination but they are inferior. Although adapted to wind pollination by nature, hand pollination has been practiced for centuries. One male tree to about 100 females is sufficient. This process consists in tying a piece of the male inflorescence a few inches long, bearing 30 or more flowers, to the female cluster; as not all the female flowers in a cluster open at the same time, this operation needs to be repeated. The time of ripening and characteristics of the fruit can be considerably influenced by the choice of pollen varieties.

Propagation is by seeds and offshoots, the latter being the prevailing method for the multiplication of particular or named cultivars; without as careful attention to cultivars as with oranges or apples, the rewards of date culture are small or negligible. The offshoots arise about the base of the tree mostly before it reaches full bearing age. The sex of the offshoot will, of course, be that of the tree from which it arises. The offshoots are moved when three to six years old, mostly in spring when the ground is warm, the tops being headed back. Experience is required to assure uniformly successful results. The cutting of offshoots extends through the first five to ten years of the mother palm's life. If many offshoots are removed at one time, it may require two years for the parent to recover, with consequent loss of fruit; leaving the offshoots on the tree also retards fruiting.

Trees grown from offshoots should bear first crops in five or six years, depending on soil, location, and treatment. At ten to 15 years the tree should be in full bearing and continue indefinitely, yielding 100 to 200 pounds of fruit annually. Trees may be planted about 30 feet apart.

Certain dates under good conditions ripen naturally on the tree, but the fruits are likely to cure unevenly and for the most part the bunches are cut intact and matured in a warm place, not unlike the handling of bananas. Special ripening processes have been developed for superior results.

Many kinds of dates, mostly of foreign origin, are grown, but, based on the texture of the fruit at maturity, cultivars are classified as soft, semidry, and dry types. In the United States the most commonly planted are the Iraqi soft-type cultivars 'Halawy' ['Hillawi'], 'Khadrawy', and 'Saidy'; and the semidry cultivars 'Dayeri' (from Iraq) and 'Deglet Noor' (from Algeria), the latter the most important commercial date in this country.

DATISCA L. *Datiscaceae.* Two spp. of stout, dioecious, per. herbs, 1 native to w. N. Amer., the other to s. Asia; lvs. pinnately incised to compound; fls. in racemes or the male sometimes in heads, petals 0, male fls. with sepals 4–9, stamens 8 to many, female fls. with calyx 3-toothed, styles 3, filiform, 2-branched, sometimes also with 2–4 stamens.

Propagated by seeds or division.

cannabina L. Bushy, to 7 ft.; lvs. odd-pinnate, lfts. 7–13, to 4 in. long, lanceolate-acuminate, serrate to more or less lacerate; fls. in racemes, anthers nearly sessile, to $\frac{1}{8}$ in. long, longer than calyx; fr. a cylindrical caps., to $\frac{3}{8}$ in. long. Midsummer. Asia Minor to India. Yields a yellow dye.

DATISCACEAE. *Datisca cannabina:* **a,** upper part of female plant, × $\frac{1}{6}$; **b,** male inflorescence, × $1\frac{1}{2}$; **c,** male flower, × 3; **d,** female inflorescence, × $\frac{1}{2}$; **e,** female flower, × 3; **f,** pistil, vertical section, × 4; **g,** ovary, cross section, × 8; **h,** fruit, × 2; **i,** seed, × 10.

DATISCACEAE Lindl. DATISCA FAMILY. Dicot.; 3 genera of mostly dioecious, per. herbs or trees, native to s. and se. Asia and w. N. Amer.; lvs. alt., simple to pinnate, without stipules; fls. in bracted racemes or spikes, rarely in heads, male fls. with sepals 3–9, free or united, petals 0 or 8, stamens 4 to many, female fls. with calyx 3–8-toothed, petals 0, ovary inferior, 1-celled, many-ovuled; fr. an apically dehiscent caps. *Datisca* is occasionally cult.

DATURA L. THORN APPLE. *Solanaceae.* Eight spp. of ann. or short-lived per. herbs, native to trop. and warm temp.

regions, mainly in the New World; lvs. alt., entire to sinuately dentate, strong-smelling; fls. solitary in the axils of brs., pedicelled, erect, 2–10 in. long, often fragrant, generally nocturnal and lasting only 1 day, calyx tubular, spathelike or with 2–5 acute to acuminate teeth, circumscissile above the base and falling with the corolla after flowering, the persistent base then expanding to form a cup, reflexed frill, or membranous disc, corolla funnelform, plicate in bud, sometimes double, white or white with purple markings, yellow, or purple to violet, stamens 5, equal, borne on the corolla, anthers long-linear, stigma often capitate; fr. a regularly or irregularly dehiscent caps., on a short pedicel, usually prickly or spiny, 2-carpelled, 4-celled because of a false septum, seeds small, hard and usually with a well-developed funicular caruncle.

The leaves and seeds of the species yield alkaloidal drugs with narcotic properties and have been used since ancient times. Some species are grown for the alkaloids or as showy ornamentals. Propagated by seeds, usually sown indoors in the spring when planted in cool regions.

arborea: *Brugmansia arborea*, but most material cult. as *D. arborea* is *B.* ×*candida*.

×**candida:** *Brugmansia* ×*candida*.

cearis: a listed name of no botanical standing.

ceratocaula Ort. Semiaquatic ann. herb, to 3 ft., fleshy, hollow-stemmed; lvs. ovate to lanceolate, pinnately lobed to sinuate, glabrous above, white or silvery-tomentose beneath; calyx spathelike, terminating in a point that is sometimes weakly divided unequally into 2 or more small teeth, corolla white, with reddish-purple markings in throat, 4–7 in. long, 5-toothed, the margin between the teeth forming an obtuse angle and the corolla appearing 10-angled; caps. pendent, fleshy, smooth. Mex. Seldom cult.

chlorantha: *D. Metel*.

cornigera: *Brugmansia arborea*.

cornucopia: *D. Metel* cv.

fastuosa: *D. Metel*.

ferox L. Probably not distinct from *D. Stramonium* from which it differs in having the fr. with 4 large spines at the apex and smaller ones below. Eur., Asia.

Gardneri: *Brugmansia suaveolens*.

grandiflora: a listed name of no botanical standing.

inermis: *D. Stramonium* forma.

inoxia Mill. DOWNY T. A., INDIAN APPLE, ANGEL'S-TRUMPET, SACRED D., TOLGUACHA. Ann. or per. herb, to 3 ft. or more, spreading, pubescent; lvs. ovate, to 10 in. long, entire to irregularly sinuate-dentate; fls. to 8 in. long, pink or lavender; calyx 5-toothed, circumscissile and leaving an appressed or reflexed frill subtending the caps.; caps. nodding, subglobose, irregularly dehiscent, covered with narrow, stiff spines to ⅜ in. long, the surface of the fr. and the spines pubescent. Subsp. **inoxia** [*D. meteloides* DC. ex Dunal]. The typical subsp.; ann. or short-lived per., villous-pubescent; corolla white to pink, 5-toothed but the margin between each 2 teeth with 2 sinuses and a central, small, obtuse lobe, giving the corolla the appearance of being 10-angled or -toothed. Sw. U.S. and Mex.; introd. into the Old World. Subsp. **quinquecuspida** (Torr.) A. S. Barcl. [*D. metel* var. *quinquecuspida* Torr.; *D. meteloides* of auth., not DC. ex Dunal; *D. Wrightii* Regel]. Differs from subsp. *inoxia* in being always per., more spreading in habit, finely gray-pubescent, and having corolla white to pale lavender, only 5-toothed. Sw. U.S., n. Mex. This subsp. is widely cult. as an ornamental; in many floras it is incorrectly given the name *D. meteloides*, which is actually a synonym of subsp. *inoxia*.

Metel L. [*D. chlorantha* Hook.; *D. fastuosa* L.]. DOWNY T. A., HORN-OF-PLENTY. Glabrous or glabrescent ann. herb, to 5 ft. or more; lvs. ovate, to 8 in. long, entire to irregularly sinuate-dentate; fls. erect, to 7 in. long, calyx tube 5-toothed at apex, circumscissile, the base forming an appressed, membranous, cuplike structure subtending the fr., corolla typically white, but with yellow and purple forms, single or double, 5-toothed; caps. nodding, subglobose, irregularly dehiscent, tubercled or covered with short spines, surface of the fr. and spines densely short-strigose-pubescent. Sw. China; widely cult. and naturalized in both hemispheres. A source of the alkaloidal drug scopolamine. Cvs. include: 'Alba', fls. white; 'Aurea', fls. yellow; 'Caerulea', fls. blue; 'Cornucopaea' [*D. Cornucopia* Hort.], fls. double; 'Huberana', fls. blue, yellow, and red.

meteloides: *D. inoxia* subsp. *inoxia;* the name *D. meteloides*, however, has in most floras been incorrectly applied to *D. inoxia* subsp. *quinquecuspida*.

mollis: *Brugmansia versicolor*.

quercifolia HBK. Probably not distinct from *D. Stramonium* from

which it differs in having lvs. mostly pinnately lobed, corolla purplish, not more than 2½ in. long, and fr. with relatively few, unequal spines, some of which are longer than ⅜ in. Tex. to New Mex. and n. Mex.

sanguinea: *Brugmansia sanguinea*.

serrata: a listed name of no botanical standing.

Stramonium L. [*D. Tatula* L.]. COMMON T. A., STRAMONIUM T. A., JIMSONWEED, JAMESTOWN WEED. Ann. herb, to 5 ft., generally glabrous, rank-smelling; lvs. ovate, to 8 in. long, coarsely and irregularly toothed or lobed; fls. 2–5 in. long, calyx 5-toothed, prismatic and keeled along the angles, circumscissile, the base forming a short, abruptly reflexed frill subtending the caps., corolla white or violet-purple, 5-toothed, about twice as long as calyx; caps. erect, dehiscing regularly by 4 valves, spiny, the spines more or less equal, seeds small, hard, lacking a caruncle. N. Amer.; widely naturalized throughout the world and sometimes grown as a source of the alkaloidal drug hyoscyamine. Forma *inermis* (Juss.) Hupka. Lacks spines on the caps.

suaveolens: *Brugmansia suaveolens*.

Tatula: *D. Stramonium;* the name *D. Tatula* was applied to purple-fld. forms.

Wrightii: *D. inoxia* subsp. *quinquecuspida*.

DAUBENTONIA: *SESBANIA*.

DAUCOPHYLLUM: *MUSINEON*.

DAUCUS L. *Umbelliferae*. About 25 spp. of cosmopolitan herbs; lvs. pinnately decompound; fls. small, white or yellowish, in compound umbels, involucre and involucels of many toothed or entire bracts, rarely absent; fr. ovate or oblong, flattened, prickly-winged, bristly.

One species grown for the edible root.

Carota L. Ann. or bien., to 3 ft., often branched, roots fusiform or fleshy-thickened; lvs. finely cut into many narrow segms.; umbels flat or rounded at flowering, becoming nestlike in fr., subtended by leaf-like bracts pinnately cut into fine divisions. Var. **Carota**. WILD CARROT, QUEEN-ANNE'S-LACE, QUEEN'S-LACE, DEVIL'S-PLAGUE. The typical var.; roots fusiform, white; st. lvs. ovate in outline. Eurasia; widely naturalized. Var. **sativus** Hoffm. CARROT. Roots fleshy-thickened, orange; middle and upper lvs. triangular in outline. Of cult. origin. For cult. see *Carrot*.

muricatus L. Ann., to 2 ft.; lvs. 2–3-pinnate, with narrow segms.; fls. white, in umbels, involucral bracts pinnately dissected, bractlets of involucels entire or trifid; fr. oblong, with spiny wings. Medit. region.

DAVALLIA Sm. *Polypodiaceae*. About 35 spp. of mostly epiphytic trop. and subtrop. ferns of the Old World, rhizomes chaffy, creeping; lvs. mostly evergreen, finely divided; sori at or near margins of pinnules, indusia attached at sides and base.

Davallias are often grown in hanging baskets or as fern balls. Old plants may be divided. Ordinarily grown in shallow pans at 60°–65° F.; it is often necessary to fasten down the rhizomes. See also *Ferns*.

affinis Hook. Not known to be cult.; the plant grown in gardens under this name is *D. trichomanoides*.

brasiliense: *Saccoloma inaequale*.

bullata: *D. trichomanoides* forma *barbata*, see also *D. Mariesii*.

canariensis Sm. DEER'S-FOOT FERN. Rhizomes to ¾ in. thick, covered with white-margined brown scales bearing long hairs; lvs. to 1½ ft. long and 1 ft. wide, 4-pinnate, pinnules not sharp-toothed at apex, those of fertile lvs. to ⅛ in. wide, narrowly cuneate; indusia nearly cylindrical, almost as long as broad, one on each pinnule. Canary Is. to Spain and N. Afr. Most of the material offered under this name refers to *D. trichomanoides*.

denticulata (Burm.f.) Kuhn. Rhizomes slender, covered with cinnamon-brown, toothed scales; lvs. leathery, to 2½ ft. long and 18 in. wide, 3-pinnate, glossy above, the lf. tissue with false veins between true veins, petioles pale brown, glabrous. Malay Arch., Australia, Madagascar.

dissecta: *D. trichomanoides*.

divaricata Blume. Rhizomes scaly, the scales broad-caudate, chestnut-brown, not peltate; lvs. leathery, 2–3 ft. long, to 2 ft. wide, 3-pinnate, pinnules caudate-acuminate; indusia about as wide as long. Malay Arch. to s. China.

fejeensis Hook. RABBIT'S-FOOT FERN. Rhizomes ½ in. thick or more, bearing scales with long marginal hairs; lvs. 1–2½ ft. long, triangular, 4-pinnate into linear pinnules with one nerve; indusia cylindrical, filling the fertile pinnule. Fiji Is. Cv. 'Plumosa'. Feathery, more gracefully drooping.

Griffithiana Hook. Rhizomes creeping, covered with white or yellowish scales; lvs. leathery, to 1 ft. long, 8 in. wide, 3–4-pinnate, pinnules toothed or cut; indusia broadly cup-shaped. India, s. China. Material offered under this name is probably *Humata Tyermannii*.

Mariesii T. Moore. SQUIRREL'S-FOOT FERN, BALL F. Like *D. trichomanoides*, but rhizome scales brown, lvs. smaller, 4–8 in. long and as wide. Temp. e. Asia. In Japan, where the sp. is much cult., the rhizomes are often fashioned into balls, boats, monkeys, and other figures. The sp. is sometimes listed by Japanese authors as a var. of *D. bullata*.

Mooreana: *D. pallida*.

pallida Kuhn [*D. Mooreana* T. Moore]. Rhizomes to ¾ in. thick; lvs. to 3 ft. long, 4-pinnate, pinnules triangular, petioles to 1½ ft. long, straw-colored; indusia nearly cylindrical, obtuse to semicircular at apex. Borneo, Aneityum (New Hebrides). Plants offered under this name may be *D. divaricata*.

pentaphylla Blume. Rhizomes to ⅜ in. thick; lvs. with terminal pinnae 4–6 in. long and ½ in. wide, and 2–3 pairs of lateral pinnae; sori in rows along the slightly toothed margin. Java, Polynesia.

pyxidata Cav. Rhizomes to ⅜ in. thick, densely covered with rusty-red, subulate scales with long marginal hairs; lvs. leathery, about 1 ft. long, 9 in. wide, 3-pinnate-pinnatifid, bullate, glossy above; sori several on each pinnule, indusia short-cylindrical, about as broad as long. Australia. Plants offered under this name are probably *D. trichomanoides*.

solida (G. Forst.) Swartz. Rhizomes ½ in. thick or more, densely covered with brown scales bearing fine hairs along the light margin; lvs. leathery, to 2 ft. long, 1½ ft. wide, 3–4-pinnate, pinnules acuminate; indusia twice as long as broad, usually winged laterally by margin of the fertile pinnule. Malay Arch.

tenuifolia: *Sphenomeris chinensis*.

trichomanoides Blume [*D. dissecta* John Sm.]. SQUIRREL-FOOT FERN, SQUIRREL'S-FOOT F., BALL F. Rhizomes to ⅜ in. thick, densely covered with whitish to tan-brown, toothed scales; lvs. to 1½ ft. long, 1 ft. wide, 3–4-pinnate, pinnules acutely serrulate to entire; indusia cylindrical, seemingly terminal on dilated pinnules or their lobes, which may project on one or both sides beyond the indusia as horns. Malay Arch. Material of this sp. may be offered as *D. pyxidata*. A form in cult. is larger and more finely divided. Of easy cult. outdoors in Calif., where grown as a ground cover or basket plant. Zone 10. Forma **barbata** (Alderw.) Backer & Posth. [*D. bullata* Wallich]. Rhizome scales red-brown, pinnules not as incised as the typical form, fertile lobes slightly or not at all dilated.

DAVIDIA Baill. *Nyssaceae*. One sp., sometimes placed in the Cornaceae or Davidiaceae, a deciduous tree, native to w. China; lvs. alt., simple; fls. small, unisexual, in axillary, dense, globose heads, subtended by 2 large bracts, petals lacking, stamens 1–7; fr. a drupe.

Propagated by seeds, cuttings of half-ripened wood, and by layers.

involucrata Baill. DOVE TREE, HANDKERCHIEF TREE. To 50 or 60 ft.; lvs. broad-ovate, to 6 in. long, acuminate, toothed, silky-pubescent beneath; infl. drooping, bracts creamy-white, unequal, to 6 in. long. Late spring. Zone 6. Var. **Vilmoriniana** (Dode) Wanger. Lvs. glabrous beneath.

DAVIESIA Sm. *Leguminosae* (subfamily *Faboideae*). About 60 spp. of shrubs of Australia; lvs. alt., simple, commonly rigid; fls. papilionaceous, in short lateral racemes or umbels with bracts at base, standard yellow with dark center, keel crimson, stamens 10, separate; fr. a flat, triangular, 1-seeded legume.

corymbosa Sm. Shrub, to 6 ft.; lvs. broadly linear, not rigid, to 4 in. long and ⅜ in. wide; racemes dense; standard ¼ in. across; fr. ¼ in. long. Se. Australia.

DEAMIA Britt. & Rose. *Cactaceae*. One sp., an epiphytic cactus, native to Cent. Amer.; sts. growing flat against tree trunks by means of aerial roots, with 3–8 unequally developed ribs or wings, those underneath suppressed; fls. nocturnal, large, white, with a slender tube; fr. spiny. Perhaps not distinct from *Selenicereus*.

For culture see *Cacti*.

testudo (Karw.) Britt. & Rose. TORTOISE CACTUS. Sts. 1½–4 in. wide; spines 10 or more, needle-shaped, brownish, to ¾ in. long; fls. to 11 in. long, tube 4 in. long, scales of tube and ovary with brown axillary hairs. Mex. to Colombia.

DEBREGEASIA Gaud.-Beaup. *Urticaceae*. Five spp. of monoecious or dioecious shrubs or small trees, native to trop. Asia and ne. Afr.; lvs. alt., serrate, 3-nerved from the base, stipules united, bifid at apex; fls. in globose clusters in axillary cymes, male fls. 4-merous, female fls. with urceolate, 4-toothed calyx; achenes enclosed in their fleshy calyces and aggregated into globose syncarps.

Tender, one species sometimes grown for its attractive foliage and its orange-yellow or red fruits produced beneath the leaves on the previous year's wood. Propagated by seeds or soft wood cuttings under glass.

longifolia (Burm.f.) Wedd. Shrub or small tree, to 20 ft.; lvs. oblong-lanceolate, to 6 in. long, acuminate, green and rugose above, white-tomentose beneath; syncarps to ¼ in. across, 2 or more on forking peduncles. Se. Asia.

DECACHAENA: *GAYLUSSACIA*.

DECAISNEA Hook.f. & T. Thoms. *Lardizabalaceae*. Two spp. of polygamous upright shrubs, native to Asia; lvs. alt., odd-pinnate, lfts. entire; fls. in panicled racemes terminal on lateral brs., sepals 6, petaloid, long-acuminate, male fls. with 6 stamens united into a column, female fls. with 3 pistils, staminodes not united; fr. an oblong, fleshy follicle, seeds many.

Fargesii Franch. To 16 ft.; lfts. ovate, in 6–12 pairs, glaucous beneath; fls. inconspicuous, greenish, 1 in. long, drooping; fr. blue, with a bloom, to 4 in. long. W. China. Zone 5.

DECKENIA H. Wendl. ex Seem. *Palmae*. One sp. of solitary, monoecious palms, native in the Seychelles Is.; lvs. pinnate, sheath and petiole spiny on young plants, only setose on mature plants, pinnae acute, regularly arranged; infls. below the lvs., short-peduncled, once- to twice-branched, with 2 deciduous bracts, the outer densely spiny, enclosing the less spiny inner, rachilla with fls. in triads (2 male and 1 female) at least basally and above these with paired or solitary male fls.; male fls. with sepals small, acute, petals ovate, asymmetrical, stamens 6–9, filaments erect, pistillode 3-angled, columnar, longer than petals, briefly 3-lobed at tip, female fls. with imbricate sepals and petals; fr. conic-oblong with basal stigmatic residue, endocarp operculate, seed with homogeneous endosperm.

Occasionally planted in the tropics for ornament. Zone 10b. For culture see *Palms*.

nobilis H. Wendl. ex Seem. To 100 ft. or more, trunk to 16 in. in diam.; lvs. to 15 ft. long, petiole short and setose, rachis with about 50–60 pinnae on each side; outer bract of infl. about 16 in. long, rachillae to 20 in. long; fr. black at maturity, ⅜ in. long. Prized for palm cabbage (edible, terminal bud); it may be endangered in its native land.

DECODON J. F. Gmel. *Lythraceae*. One sp., a per. herb of swamps and pools, native to the U.S.; sts. somewhat woody or corky, arched, rooting at apex; lvs. opp. or whorled; fls. purple, in axillary clusters, calyx tube campanulate, with 4–5(–7) teeth and as many horned appendages, petals 4–5(–7), stamens 8–10; fr. a caps.

verticillatus (L.) Elliott [*Nesaea verticillata* (L.) HBK]. SWAMP LOOSESTRIFE, WATER WILLOW, WATER OLEANDER. To 8 ft. or more; lvs. lanceolate, to 5 in. long; petals to ½ in. long. Cent. Me. to Fla., w. to s. Ill. and La. Sometimes planted in wet locations and pond margins.

DECUMARIA L. *Saxifragaceae*. Two sp. of deciduous or half-evergreen woody vines, climbing by aerial rootlets, 1 of w. China, 1 of se. U.S.; lvs. opp., petioled, mostly entire; infl. terminal, corymbose; fls. small, white, all fertile, calyx tube united to ovary, sepals and petals 7–10, stamens 20–30, ovary inferior, style short, stigma headlike; fr. a top-shaped, ribbed caps. dehiscing between the ribs.

Requires protection in the North; propagated by cuttings of young wood under glass or rarely by seeds.

barbara L. CLIMBING HYDRANGEA, WOOD-VAMP. Climbing to 30 ft.; lvs. elliptic, to 4 in. long, glabrous and glossy above, lightly pubescent beneath; infl. round-topped, to 4 in. across. Se. U.S. Zone 6.

DEINANTHE Maxim. *Saxifragaceae.* Two spp. of coarse per. herbs of e. Asia; rhizomes creeping, sts. erect; lvs. opp.; infl. of terminal corymbs; marginal fls. sterile, consisting of 2–3 enlarged calyx lobes, central fls. fertile, larger than the sterile fls. and showy, calyx tube short, partly united to ovary, calyx lobes 5, large, petals 5, large, stamens many, ovary partly inferior, style prominent; fr. a subglobose caps.

caerulea Stapf. St. solitary, to 1½ ft.; lvs. ovate, to 10 in. long, coarsely toothed, the larger ones usually bifid at apex; fls. bluish, sterile fls. to ½ in. across, fertile fls. to 1¼ in. across. China.

DELONIX Raf. POINCIANA. *Leguminosae* (subfamily *Caesalpinioideae*). Three spp. of unarmed trees, native to tropics of Old World; lvs. alt., 2-pinnate; fls. in corymbose racemes, showy, calyx lobes valvate, petals clawed, stamens 10, separate; fr. a large, flat, woody legume.

One species much planted in the tropics and subtropics as a very showy flowering tree. Culture as for *Caesalpinia;* requires a frost-free climate.

elata (L.) Gamble [*Poinciana elata* L.]. Differs from *D. regia* in having larger lfts., to ½ in. long, smaller fls., yellow-white, becoming orange, petals scarcely longer than calyx, filaments 2–4 in. long, exserted, bright red, and fr. to 8 in. long and 1 in. wide. Ethiopia to Egypt, Arabia, and India.

regia (Bojer) Raf. [*Poinciana regia* Bojer]. ROYAL P., FLAMBOYANT, PEACOCK FLOWER. Wide-branching tree, to 40 ft. or more; pinnae to 20 pairs, lfts. many, to ¼ in. long; fls. bright scarlet, 3–4 in. across, stamens not longer than petals; fr. to 2½ ft. long and 2 in. wide or more. Madagascar. Zone 10b.

DELOSPERMA N. E. Br. [*Schonlandia* L. Bolus]. *Aizoaceae.* About 140 spp. of dwarf, densely branched, bushy, succulent shrubs or shrublets, or sometimes bien. or per. succulent herbs, native to S. Afr., brs. prostrate to spreading, more or less ascending, papillate or scaly; lvs. opp., frequently crowded and obscuring the internodes, 3-angled to cylindrical or nearly flat, sometimes papillate, often ciliate, sometimes hooked at tip; fls. solitary, in 2's or 3's, or even in racemose cymes, calyx 4–8-lobed, petals many, stamens many, staminodes present, disc divided into 4–5 separate glands, ovary inferior, 4–5-celled, stigmas 4 or 5; fr. a caps., without a roof, tubercles absent.

Growth occurs in summer, but plants flower nearly all year. Plants grow best in a rich, porous soil in a sunny, not too damp spot outdoors, but require a drier soil and a relatively cool temperature of about 50° F during winter. Propagated by seeds or cuttings. See also *Succulents.*

aberdeenense (L. Bolus) L. Bolus. Shrub, finely papillate, herbaceous parts hairy, brs. often prostrate; lvs. spreading, to ¾ in. long, ¼ in. wide, flat above, rounded below; fls. ⅝ in. across, on pedicels to ⅜ in. long, petals purple. Cape Prov.

algoense L. Bolus. Brs. to 10 in. long, reddish becoming gray; lvs. gray-green, gray, or reddish, to 1 in. long, ⅝ in. wide and thick, 3-angled, upper surface flat, sides rounded, tip very obtuse; fls. less than 1½ in. across, petals snowy-white. Cape Prov.

Brunnthaleri (A. Berger) Schwant. To 16 in.; lvs. spreading or recurved, green, minutely papillate, to 1⅝ in. long, flat above, keeled toward tip beneath, ciliate; fls. several, to ¾ in. across, on short pedicels, petals violet-pink. Natal.

Cooperi (Hook.f.) L. Bolus. Sts. prostrate, papillate; lvs. spreading or incurved or recurved, striped with lines of gray-green papillae, to 2³⁄₁₆ in. long, ¼ in. wide, ³⁄₁₆ in. thick, nearly cylindrical but flattened on upper side and narrowed to tip; fls. to 2 in. across, solitary or 3–7, terminal, petals purple. Orange Free State.

echinatum: *D. pruinosum.*

macellum (N. E. Br.) N. E. Br. Sts. several, erect, to 2½ in. or more, from a fleshy rhizome; lvs. spreading, bluish- or gray-green, to 1 in. long, ⅛ in. wide, ¹⁄₁₆ in. thick, united at base, narrowed toward tip; fls. to ¾ in. across, on pedicels to ⅜ in. long, petals light purplish or magenta. Transvaal.

pruinosum (Thunb.) J. Ingram [*D. echinatum* (Ait.) Schwant.]. Shrub, to 1 ft., sts. forking, to ⅛ in. thick, gray or light brown, white-papillate, at least when young; lvs. light green, with large, bristly, acuminate papillae, thick, slightly united at base, to ½ in. long, ¼ in. wide, ovoid-hemispherical with flat upper side; fls. to ⅝ in. across, solitary, nearly sessile, petals whitish or yellowish. Cape Prov.

DELOSTOMA D. Don. *Bignoniaceae.* About 7 spp. of trees or shrubs, native to Colombia, Ecuador, and Peru; lvs. simple, alt., leathery, entire or dentate; fls. in terminal racemes or panicles, calyx 3–5-lobed, corolla funnelform, stamens 4; fr. an oblong woody caps.

One species is sometimes grown in southern Calif.

roseum (Karst. & Triana) K. Schum. Lvs. ovate or orbicular, to 6 in. long, tomentose beneath; fls. rose or pink, 1½ in. long, in panicles to 8 in. long; fr. dark purple, about 2 in. long. Colombia, Ecuador.

DELPHINIUM L. LARKSPUR. *Ranunculaceae.* Probably 300 or more spp. of ann., bien., or per. herbs, mostly of the N. Temp. Zone; lvs. palmate, variously cut and divided; fls. in racemes, mostly blue, but in garden races varying to pink, bluish, and white, a few spp. scarlet, red, or yellow, some garden strains double-fld., calyx showy, of 5 sepals, one of which is spurred, petals 2 or 4, smaller, often crowded in the throat and sometimes called the "bee," the upper pair with spurs that project into the calyx spur, stamens many, pistils 2–5; fr. of follicles.

Some of the species are poisonous to cattle. The Latin names are much confused in *Delphinium*, particularly in horticultural material.

Many *Delphinium* species are grown as perennials in the border or wild garden, not having been developed into modified or striking horticultural forms; they are sometimes referred to as "botanical" larkspurs. These are often spring and early summer bloomers that become dormant after flowering and usually have fleshy or tuberous roots; other species are continuous growers, and bloom in summer and autumn.

Most delphiniums are hardy north and require no very special attention as to soil and position, but thrive best in an open exposure. They generally grow readily from seeds, the perennials mostly blooming the year following the sowing. Of the perennial kinds, the clumps may be divided in autumn or spring, or cuttings may be made of young shoots in spring or from second growth in summer after the flower stems have been cut off. Asexual propagation of these kinds is essential in named garden varieties, but otherwise it is well to have fresh stock from seeds. As soon as the flowers fade, the flower stems should be cut off unless seeds are desired for sowing; frequently new flower stems then arise and give a second, but usually inferior bloom in late summer or autumn. Sand or sifted coal ashes may be put around the crowns for winter protection, particularly on moist or heavy soils. The stately delphiniums of the *D. elatum* type, with their long erect spikelike racemes, are suitable for massing and for back borders, while the lower and loosely branching bouquet and garland delphiniums are adaptable for beds and front border.

Delphiniums are subject to diseases and insect attack. They should be planted in uninfected soil, and care should be taken not to import diseases in soil that comes with the plants, nor to propagate from infected stock.

Ajacis: see *Consolida ambigua* and *C. orientalis.*

alpinum: *D. elatum.*

Andersonii A. Gray. Per., roots branched, woody-fibrous, sts. simple, to 2 ft., glabrous; lvs. basal, orbicular, to 1 in. wide, green at flowering, primary divisions with oblong segms.; infl. 5–12-fld.; sepals rich blue to purplish, ½ in. long, spur thick, ½ in. long, upper petals whitish; follicles ½–1 in. long, pubescent. Idaho and Nev., to e. Calif.

azureum: *D. carolinianum.*

×**Belladonna** Hort. ex Bergmans [*D. Bellamosum* Hort.; *D. formosum* Hort., not Boiss. & Huet]: *D. elatum* × *D. grandiflorum.* Like *D. elatum*, but lacking a pronounced central raceme; sepals rich blue, spur over 1 in. long, petals yellowish. Material offered as *D. formosum* belongs here.

Bellamosum: *D.* ×*Belladonna.*

bicolor Nutt. Per., roots deep, fascicled, stout, sts. stout, to 1½ ft., subglabrous; lvs. orbicular, 1–2 in. wide, rather thick, subglabrous, 5-parted and ultimately divided into narrow segms.; infl. 2–12-fld.; sepals dark violet-purple, ½ in. long, spur stout, about as long as sepals, upper petals yellow, purple-veined; follicles ⁵⁄₁₆ in. long, viscid-pubescent. Ore. and e. Wash., to Utah, Wyo., Sask.

Brownii: *D. glaucum.*

Brunonianum Royle. Per., sts. to 12 in., leafy, puberulent; lvs. cordate, 5-parted, upper lvs. 3-parted; infl. few-fld.; fls. light blue, balloon-shaped, large, somewhat hairy, sepals 1 in. long, spur very short; follicles 3–4. Himalayas.

Bulleyanum Forr. ex Diels. Per., sts. to 4 ft., leafy, more or less glaucous, glabrous except in infl.; lvs. 3–4 in. long, sparingly pilose, deeply 3-parted into lobed and notched divisions; infl. open-paniculate; fls. deep blue, to 1 in. long, spur curved back on itself; follicles 3, sparingly pilose. China.

californicum Torr. & A. Gray. Per., roots thick, woody, sts. simple, stout, to 7 ft., hollow, leafy; lvs. 2–5 in. wide, thin, 5–7-palmatifid, divisions cuneate, incisely lobed and toothed; racemes dense, 1–2 ft. long; fls. dull bluish or purplish inside, whitish with lavender or green tinge outside; follicles ½ in. long. Cent. Calif.

cardinale Hook. Per., roots deep, thick, woody, sts. erect, simple or branched above, to 6 ft., hollow, puberulent; basal lvs. 2–8 in. wide, withered at flowering, 5-parted, primary divisions cuneate, 3-lobed, st. lvs. 5–7-parted, then divided; infl. of open racemes or panicles; sepals mostly scarlet, about ½ in. long, spur stout, slightly longer, upper petals yellow with scarlet tips; follicles erect, ½ in. long. Baja Calif. to cent. Calif.

carolinianum Walt. [*D. azureum* Michx.]. Per., roots woody-fibrous, deep-seated, sts. simple or few-branched, to 3 ft., hirtellous below, glandular-hispid above; lower lvs. several, 3–5-parted, divisions cleft into linear lobes, upper lvs. scattered, less dissected; racemes slender, virgate; fls. about 1 in. long, deep blue or violet, spur 1½ times the limb of its sepal; seeds winged, rugose. Va. to Fla., w. to Mo., Okla., Tex. Var. **Nortonianum** (Mackenz. & Bush) L. M. Perry. Pubescence longer, almost floccose. Ark., s. Mo., Okla.

cashmerianum Royle. Low per., to 1½ ft., leafy; lvs. mostly basal, long-petioled, almost round, 2–4 in. wide, usually 5–7-lobed about to the middle, then cut-toothed; infl. corymblike, 10–12-fld., peduncles pubescent; fls. 1½ in. long, azure-blue, pubescent, sepals broad, obtuse, not expanding widely, spur broad, somewhat curved, shorter than sepals, upper petals black-purple, lower greenish; follicles hairy. Himalayas. Material cult. under this name is more likely *D. elatum* or one of its derivatives.

chinense: *D. grandiflorum.*

Consolida: *Consolida regalis,* but some material may be *C. ambigua.*

×**cultorum** Voss [*D. hybridum* Hort., not Steph. ex Willd.]. Name used for various garden plants of hybrid origin.

cuyamacae: *D. hesperium* subsp.

decorum Fisch. & C. A. Mey. Per., roots fleshy, sts. 1 to several, simple or few-branched, to 1 ft., pubescent; lvs. mostly basal, 1–1½ in. wide, 3-parted, center division entire or trifid, lateral divisions 1–2-bifid; infl. 2–5(–8)-fld.; fls. villous, sepals blue-purple, ½ in. long, with median pubescent band, upper petals whitish, lower bluish; follicles ⅜ in. long, glabrous. Calif. The name has been applied to garden material of *D. elatum.*

depauperatum Nutt. Per., crown slender, sts. to 1 ft., slender, weak, subscapose, glabrous; lvs. few, angular-orbicular, 1–2 in. wide, nearly glabrous, palmatifid into 3 or 5 simple or lobed divisions; infl. few-fld.; sepals bright dark blue, 5/16 in. long, spur slender, straight, 5/16–⅜ in. long; follicles ovoid, 5/16–½ in. long, glabrous. B.C. to Alta. and Calif.

Duhmbergii Huth. Per., sts. erect, to 2 ft., hairy below, glabrous above; lvs. 5–7-parted, divisions cuneate, laciniate, incised-serrate; infl. many-fld.; fls. blue or white, spur straight, ½ in. long, slightly shorter than sepals, glabrous, petals black, follicles 3, subreticulate. Russia, Siberia.

elatum L. [*D. alpinum* Waldst. & Kit.; *D. intermedium* Ait.]. Per., crown knotty, sts. spicate, to 6 ft.; lvs. large, palmately 5–7-parted to near base, or the upper 3-parted, ultimate segms. over ¼ in. wide; racemes dense, erect, bracts entire; fls. to 1 in. long, sepals blue, blunt, glabrous, ½ in. long, petals dark or dull purple, the 2 lower petals yellow-bearded; follicles 3, glabrous, seeds wrinkled, not scaly. S. and cent. Eur. to Siberia. Most plants cult. as *D. decorum* belong here. The sp. has been in cult. since 1578 and, with *D. cheilanthum* Fisch. ex DC. and others, has been the basis for garden forms such as *D. cashmerianum* Hort., not Royle, and for *D. hybridum* Hort., not L. or Steph. ex Willd.; see also *D.* ×*Belladonna.*

exaltatum Ait. TALL L. Per., roots fibrous, sts. slender, glabrous except at summit; lvs. many, rather uniformly distributed along st., deeply 3–5-cleft, then much divided, ultimate segms. lanceolate; racemes long, virgate, commonly branched at base; fls. blue, or purple, ½–1 in. long, grayish puberulent, spur about ½ in. long; follicles pubescent. Penn. and Ohio to Ala.

fissum Waldst. & Kit. Per., roots tuberous, sts. slender, 2–3 ft., leafy, pubescent; lvs. orbicular, lower lvs. 3–5 in. across, cut to base into many linear segms.; infl. simple, dense, spicate; fls. azure, spur straight, as long as sepals; follicles 3. Se. Eur.

formosum Boiss. & Huet. Per., sts. thick, tall, branched; lvs. 5–7-parted, glabrous; infl. branched, many-fld.; fls. intense violet-blue, sepals about 1 in. long, lower petals yellow-bearded; seeds scaly. Caucasus and Asia Minor. Probably not in cult., material offered under this name being *D.* ×*Belladonna.*

Geyeri Greene. Per., crown woody, vertical, sts. to 2½ ft., ashy-puberulent, especially below; lvs. several, mostly basal, repeatedly dissected into narrow segms.; racemes narrow, dense, strict; sepals ½ in. long, rich blue, spur 1½ times the limit of its sepal, upper petals yellow; follicles ½ in. long, finely hirsutulous. Wyo. to Nebr. and Utah. Little planted; one of the sp. poisonous to cattle.

glareosum Greene. Close to *D. bicolor,* but with a thick crown; sts. 3–8 in.; follicles 3–5, ½ in. long, glabrous or nearly so. Olympic Mts. (Wash.).

glaucum S. Wats. [*D. Brownii* Rydb.; *D. scopulorum* var. *glaucum* (S. Wats.) A. Gray]. Per., crown stout, woody, sts. 3–8 ft., coarse, hollow, leafy, glaucous, glabrous; lvs. 3–7 in. wide, palmatifid, segms. broad, cuneate, acutely incised and toothed; racemes 4–16 in. long, many-fld.; sepals violet-purple, to ½ in. long; follicles erect, ⅜–¾ in. long, glabrous or puberulent. Rocky Mts., Alaska to Calif.

grandiflorum L. [var. *chinense* (Fisch.) Fisch. ex DC.; *D. chinense* Fisch.]. Per., sts. rather slender, usually diffuse, 1–3½ ft., finely pubescent; lower lvs. petioled, base of the petiole not expanded or clasping, uppermost lvs. sessile, blades pinnatifid into many linear segms.; pedicels spreading or arched away from the axis, mostly 2–3 in. long; fls. 1–1½ in. across, sepals blue or violet, broad, obtusish, ½–1 in. long, spur usually longer than the sepals, upper petals yellowish or bluish, lower petals bluish, bearded; follicles 3, ½–1 in. long, pubescent. Siberia, China. This sp. is one of the most common garden larkspurs. Cvs. include: **'Album'**, fls. white; **'Azureum'**; **'Minor'**; **'Nanum'**; and **'Pumilum'**, habit dwarf. Var. **chinense:** *D. grandiflorum.*

Hansenii (Greene) Greene. Per., taproot slender, short, sts. to 3 ft., strigose; lvs. largely basal, 2–3½ in. wide, withering early, shallowly palmatifid, the upper smaller and palmatisect into narrow divisions, petioles with long spreading hairs; racemes rather compact, many-fld., sepals dark purple to bluish, or reddish, or white, ¼–5/16 in. long, generally cupped, spur slender, curving, ¼–5/16 in. long; follicles ½ in. long, hairy, seeds scaly-echinate. Calif.

hesperium A. Gray. Similar to *D. Hansenii,* but with hairs of petioles and lvs. short and curled; veins very prominent on under surface of lvs.; seeds with narrow, white, winglike margin. N. and cent. Calif. Subsp. **cuyamacae** (Abrams) F. H. Lewis & Epl. [*D. cuyamacae* Abrams]. Fls. dark purple-blue. S. Calif.

hybridum Steph. ex Willd., not Hort. Per., to 2 ft.; petioles much broadened at base, lvs. 3–4-parted, ultimate segms. linear; racemes dense; fls. blue, spur straight. Hungary, Caucasus. Probably not in cult.; plants cult. as *D. hybridum* probably vary in origin; see *D.* ×*cultorum* and *D. elatum.*

incanum: *D. Roylei.*

intermedium: *D. elatum.*

Leroyi Franch. ex Huth [*D. Wellbyi* Hemsl.]. Per., st. solitary, to 5 ft., retrorsely pubescent; lvs. reniform-orbicular, 5-parted, segms. cuneate-obovate, 3-lobed; infl. paniculate; fls. fragrant, white to deep blue, sepals with brown spot, to 1⅝ in. long, spur horizontal, curved upward, to 1¾ in. long, petals clawed; follicles 3, pubescent. Mts., E. Afr.

likiangense Franch. Sts. scapose, to 8 in., nearly glabrous; lvs. long-petioled, many-parted, segms. oblong and pointed; fls. 2–5, nearly bell-shaped, sepals rich blue to lilac, somewhat pubescent, spur straight, not longer than sepals, 1 in. long, petals lilac; follicles hirsute. W. China.

luteum A. Heller. Like *D. nudicaule,* but fls. cream or yellowish; follicles erect. Coast, cent. Calif.

Maackianum Regel. Per., sts. branched, to 3 ft., leafy; lvs. to 8 in. wide, 5-parted, segms. ovate, cuneate, incised or toothed, nearly glabrous to strigose, petiole dilated at base; infl. a panicle, with fls. subtended by broad, colored bracts; fls. blue, spur straight or curved; follicles 3. E. Siberia.

macrocentron D. Oliver. Hairy per., sts. nearly 7 ft., leafy below, branched only near top; lvs. 5–7-parted, segms. 3- to many-cut; racemes loose, few-fld.; fls. blue and green, drooping, hairy, sepals broad, spurs whitish, 2 in. long, petals oblong; follicles 3, hairy. Mts., E. Afr.

Menziesii DC. Per., tubers shallow, in small clusters, sts. 1–2 ft., soft-pubescent; basal lvs. round-pentagonal, 1–2 in. wide, palmatifid into cuneate, lobed divisions, st. lvs. bractlike; infl. 3–10-fld.; sepals deep rich blue, ½ in. long, hairy, upper petals pale, lower dark; follicles ½ in. long, white-hairy. B.C. to n. Calif.

Nelsonii Greene. Per., sts. breaking easily at roots, to 1½ ft., more or less puberulent; lvs. few, 1–2 in. wide, deeply parted, then divided into narrow segms.; infl. 6–10-fld., fls. blue-purple to pale blue, sepals

½–¾ in. long, spur slender, about ½ in. long; follicles often hairy. S. Dak. and Idaho to Ariz. and Nev.

nudicaule Torr. & A. Gray. Per., crown elongate, sts. erect or ascending, to 2 ft., glabrous; lvs. basal to cauline, 1–4 in. wide, 3–5-cut, center division broadly cuneate-obovate, ultimate lobes shallow; infl. few-fld.; fls. cornucopia-shaped, sepals orange-red or dull red, sometimes yellow, ½ in. long; follicles divergent, ⅝–¾ in. long. Calif., s. Ore.

Nuttallianum G. Pritz. Per., slender, to 14 in., from tuberous roots or short rhizome; lvs. mostly on st., orbicular, to 2 in. wide, 3–5-parted, segms. narrow, nearly undivided or palmately cleft; racemes 3–8-fld., sparsely hairy to hirsute; fls. nodding, dark blue or purplish-blue, sepals ½–⅝ in. long, spur straight, ½ in. long, upper petals whitish. B.C. to Mont., s. to Utah and Calif.

oxysepalum Borb. & Pax. Per., to 20 in., nearly glabrous to pubescent; lvs. 3–5-parted, segms. coarsely toothed; fls. deep blue or bluish-violet, sepals to 1¼ in. long, spur curved, petals ciliate; follicles glabrous. W. Carpathian Mts., Czechoslavakia and Poland.

paniculatum: *Consolida regalis* subsp.

Parishii A. Gray. Per., crown with several, woody shoots, sts. ½–2 ft., more or less glaucous, glabrous or pubescent; lvs. broadly cordate or roundish, 1–4 in. wide, primary divisions 3, cuneate, then with oblong lobes, upper lvs. parted to midrib, divisions narrow; racemes about 5–25-fld.; sepals azure-blue to lavender, ⁵⁄₁₆–½ in. long, spur to ½ in., hairy, lower petals bluish to violet, hairy; follicles to ½ in. long. Deserts, Calif.

Parryi A. Gray. Per., crown with woody, deep-seated roots, sts. slender, to 3 ft., puberulent; lvs. chiefly cauline, 1–3 in. wide, 3–5-parted, then divided into linear lobes; racemes 3–8 in. long; sepals deep purplish-blue, about ½ in. long, spur nearly straight, about ½ in. long, lower petals purplish-blue, floccose; follicles ½ in. long, puberulent. S. Calif.

Przewalskii Huth. Per., glabrous, to 10 in.; lvs. deeply 3–5-parted, lobes obtuse; fls. usually terminal, sepals blue, spur straightish, as long as sepals, ¾ in. long, petals dark brownish, glabrous; follicles 3, hairy. W. Mongolia.

Pylzowii Maxim. ex Regel. Per., root long, woody, sts. to 10 in., leafy, silky-pubescent; lvs. orbicular to reniform, divided, lobes obtusish; infl. 1–3-fld.; sepals deep purple, 2½ in. long, spur straight or curved at end; follicles 5. High mts., w. China. Probably not cult. in the U.S.

Roylei Munz [*D. incanum* Royle, not E. D. Clarke]. Per., sts. 2–4 ft., simple below, leafy, hoary; basal lvs. 2 in. wide, soon withering, lobes subpinnatifid into linear segms.; racemes simple or compound, dense; fls. bright blue, pubescent outside, to 1½ in. long, spur about as long as sepals; follicles 3, puberulous. Himalayas.

scopulorum A. Gray. Like *D. glaucum;* sts. 3–5 ft., not glaucous; lvs. 5–7-parted, 2–3 in. wide, segms. cuneate to laciniate, sepals and spurs ⅜ in. long. New Mex., Ariz. Var. **glaucum:** *D. glaucum.*

semibarbatum Bienert ex Boiss. [*D. Zalil* Aitch. & Hemsl.]. Per., roots tuberous, sts. simple or little-branched, 1–2 ft., becoming glabrous; lvs. palmatifid, ultimate divisions stiffish, linear; racemes loose; fls. bright yellow, sepals broad-elliptic, obtuse, glabrous outside, less than ½ in. long, spur straight, somewhat longer, lower petals bifid, lightly hairy; follicles 3, ribbed, glabrous. Iran. Material offered as *D. sulphureum* probably belongs here. Fls. yield a yellow or orange-red dye used for dyeing cottons and silks.

speciosum Bieb. Much like *D. elatum,* but seeds scaly; st. solitary, pubescent, to 2½ ft.; lvs. 5-parted, divisions broad, with large, coarse teeth; fls. 1¼ in. long or more, sepals violet, spur bent or hooked, petals black. Se. Asia.

sulphureum: *Consolida sulphurea,* but material offered as *D. sulphureum* is probably *D. semibarbatum.*

tatsienense Franch. Much like *D. grandiflorum,* but lvs. ternate at base, not palmately divided; infl. more diffuse; fls. violet-blue, 1¼ in. long, sepals violet-blue, with a spot near the apex, broad, obtuse, ½ in. long; spur ¾–1 in. long, upper petals dull yellow, lower petals blue, with yellow beard; follicles 3, ½ in. long or more, hirsute. W. China. Cv. '**Album**'. Fls. white.

tricorne Michx. DWARF L. Per., roots tuberous, sts. simple, to 3 ft., succulent; lvs. mostly basal, pedately 5-parted, then cleft into narrow lobes; racemes open, loose, with long, ascending pedicels; fls. blue or violet or variegated with white, 1–1½ in. long, spur straightish, ascending, ½–¾ in. long. Penn. to Minn. and Nebr., s. to Ga., Ala., Ark., Okla.

trolliifolium A. Gray. Per., crown deep, vertical, woody, sts. stout, to 5 ft., leafy throughout; lower lvs. 4–6 in. wide, orbicular, 5–7-parted, divisions 3-cleft, cuneate-obovate, upper lvs. reduced; infl. 15–30-fld., sepals violet-purple, appressed-villous on exterior, ⅝–1 in. long; follicles usually arcuate, to 1 in. long. Ore., n. Calif.

variegatum Torr. & A. Gray. Per., roots clustered, thick, sts. simple, to 2 ft., subglabrous to hairy; lvs. subbasal to mostly cauline, ½–2 in. wide, 3-parted, ultimate segms. linear to short and rounded; infl. few-fld.; sepals light blue to rich blue-purple, hirsutulous, ½–¾ in. long, spur straightish, about ½ in. long, upper petals yellow or whitish; follicles ½ in. long, puberulent. Cent. Calif.

vestitum Wallich ex Royle. Per., sts. simple, to 3 ft., spreading-hairy; lvs. pilose, 5–7-parted to middle into large cuneate, crenate lobes; racemes strict, many-fld.; sepals pale blue, broadly lanceolate, densely hairy, spur somewhat curved, petals deep blue; follicles 3, hirsute. Himalayas.

virescens Nutt. Similar to *D. carolinianum,* but taller, to 5 ft., crisp-pubescent at base, glandular-pubescent in upper parts; fls. less scattered, white or whitish, rarely pale blue, spur 1½–2 times as long as the limb of its sepal; seeds wingless, corrugate-prickly. Wisc. to Man., s. to Mo., Okla., Tex.

Wellbyi: *D. Leroyi.*

Zalil: *D. semibarbatum.*

DENDRIOPOTERIUM Svent. *Rosaceae.* One sp., a monoecious shrub, native to Canary Is.; lvs. odd-pinnate; infl. axillary, paniculate; fls. apetalous, small, 4-merous, crowded, stamens 40, style usually 1, exserted; fr. dry, usually 1-celled, 1-seeded, glabrous.

Menendezii Svent. To 5–6 ft., brs. brown, with remains of petiole bases; lvs. glabrous, lfts. 9–13, oblong-ovate, asymmetrical at base, crenulate; sepals whitish with purplish veins, those of male fls. ⅛ in. long, those of female fls. shorter; fr. ¹⁄₁₆ in. long, brown. Grand Canary Is.

virescens: a listed name of no botanical standing.

DENDROBIUM Swartz. *Orchidaceae.* About 900 spp. of epiphytes, native to trop. and subtrop. Asia, Australia, and Pacific Is.; sts. few- to many-jointed, erect or pendent, leafy; infl. a cluster, raceme, or panicle, 1- to many-fld.; fls. variable in size, sepals and petals spreading or erect, lateral sepals forming a distinct mentum with column foot, lip united to column foot, entire or lobed, column fleshy, with large stigmatic orifice. For structure of fl. see *Orchidaceae.*

For culture see *Orchids.*

aduncum Wallich ex Lindl. Sts. to 2 ft. long, slender, pendent, internodes to 1½ in. long; lvs. to 3 in. long, sessile, elliptic-lanceolate, lf. sheath nearly as long as internodes; fls. drooping, solitary or in few-fld. racemes, to 1¼ in. across, pale rose, lip smaller than petals, white, clawed, with short hooked tip. Summer. Himalayas.

aggregatum Roxb. [*D. Jenkinsii* Wallich]. Sts. pseudobulbous, about 2 in. long, with 1 lf. to 3 in. long; fls. in 3–12-fld. racemes, to 1½ in. across, golden- or orange-yellow, lip with deeper colored base. Spring. Himalayas, Burma, Indochina, Malay Pen.

×**Ainsworthii** Hort.: *D. aureum* × *D. nobile.* Similar to *D. nobile;* fls. to 3 in. across, white to yellow, suffused with pink, lip with large maroon blotch.

album: *D. aqueum.*

amoenum Wallich ex Lindl. Sts. pendent, to 2 ft. long, clothed with appressed lf. sheaths, internodes to 2½ in. long; lvs. to 4 in. long, linear-lanceolate; fls. 1–3 at each node, to 2¼ in. across, sepals and petals white with purple blotch at tips, lip with violet-purple blotch at tip and with yellow throat, mentum ½ in. long. Early summer. Nepal and Sikkim.

amplum: *Epigenium amplum.*

anosmum: *D. superbum* cv.

Aphrodite Rchb.f. [*D. nodatum* Lindl.]. Sts. to 1 ft. long, slender, branched, nodes swollen; lvs. to 3 in. long, oblong, obtuse, deciduous; fls. to 2½ in. across, on leafless st., yellow, spreading, lip yellow, 3-lobed, clawed, lateral lobes with deep maroon-purple spot at base, midlobe hairy, deep orange. Summer. Burma.

aqueum Lindl. [*D. album* Wight]. Sts. stout, compressed, to 20 in. long; lvs. to 5 in. long, ovate to lanceolate; fls. solitary or 2 together, creamy-white, to 2¼ in. across, lip recurved, 3-lobed, with deep yellow blotch in throat. Late summer. S. India.

atroviolaceum Rolfe. Sts. club-shaped, to 1 ft. long; lvs. 2, apical, to about 5 in. long; fls. about 2–3 in. across, in 2–8-fld. racemes, sepals and petals whitish-yellow with violet spots, lip dark violet, streaked with white and green on outer surface. Early winter–summer. New Guinea.

aureum Lindl. [*D. heterocarpum* Wallich ex Lindl.; *D. rhombeum* Lindl.]. Sts. stout, to about 20 in. long; lvs. to over 5 in. long; fls. to

2½ in. across, in clusters of 2 or 3, sepals and petals cream-colored, lip yellow, marked with red or reddish-purple. Blooming all year. Himalayas and Ceylon, e. to Java and Philippine Is.

barbatulum: *D. Fytchianum.*

bicameratum Lindl. [*D. breviflorum* Lindl.; *D. callibotrys* Ridl.]. Sts. spindle-shaped, to 16 in. long; lvs. linear-lanceolate, to 2 in. long; fls. 1–4, in racemes, dull yellow, spotted and streaked with purple, lip yellow, to ¾ in. across. Late summer. Trop. Himalayas.

bigibbum Lindl. COOKTOWN ORCHID. Sts. to 1½ ft. long; lvs. leathery, to 5 in. long; fls. purple-red, to 2 in. across, in 2–12-fld. racemes to 1 ft. long, lip 3-lobed, of deeper color, with double gibbosity at base just above mentum. Autumn. N. Australia. Cv. **'Candidum'.** Fls. white with purple blotch on each side of crest of lip. Var. **Phalaenopsis:** *D. Phalaenopsis.*

Boxallii: *D. gratiosissimum.*

breviflorum: *D. bicameratum.*

Brymeranum Rchb.f. Sts. to 2 ft. long; lvs. to 5 in. long; fls. golden-yellow, about 2½ in. across, in few-fld. lateral racemes, lip deeply fringed. Autumn–late spring. Burma, Indochina.

Bullenianum Rchb.f. [*D. erythroxanthum* Rchb.f.; *D. salaccense* Hort. ex Rchb.f.]. Sts. to 16 in. long; lvs. ovate-oblong, to 2½ in. long; fls. small, pinkish-yellow with purplish stripes, to ½ in. across.

Bulleranum: *D. gratiosissimum.*

Calceolaria: *D. moschatum* var.

callibotrys: *D. bicameratum.*

cambridgeanum: *D. ochreatum.*

canaliculatum R. Br. Sts. pseudobulbous, pear-shaped, 2–3 in. long; lvs. 3–5, fleshy, linear-acute, almost semicylindrical, twice as long as sts.; fls. 12–20, fragrant, in loose racemes, sepals and petals white with yellow tips, lip 3-lobed, white with mauve-purple disc. N. Australia.

candidum Wallich ex Lindl. Similar in habit to *D. nobile,* sts. to 1 ft. long; lvs. ovate-lanceolate, deciduous; fls. 1 or 2 at a node, white, fragrant, to 1½ in. across. Himalayas, India, Tibet.

capillipes Rchb.f. Sts. to 6 in. long, club-shaped, with 3 or 4 joints; lvs. lanceolate, to 6 in. long; fls. 1–2, about 1 in. across, yellow, sepals and petals spreading, lip about as large as rest of perianth, yellow with orange blotch at base and few red streaks on sides. Early spring. Burma. Cv. **'Elegans'.** Plants taller; fls. yellow with dark orange at base of lip.

capituliflorum Rolfe. Sts. to 8 in. long; lvs. lanceolate-oblong, to 3½ in. long; racemes many-fld., in dense axillary heads; fls. greenish-white, ½ in. across, lip with column and disc bright green. Late spring. New Guinea.

cariniferum Rchb.f. Pseudobulbs to 10 in. long; lvs. narrowly oblong, to 5 in. long; fls. in apical 1–4-fld. clusters, 1½ in. across, sepals and petals white, lip red-orange, tipped with white or pale orange, long-spurred. Spring. Himalayas, Burma.

×chlorostele Rchb.f. [*D. ×xanthocentron* Hort.]: *D. Linawianum* Rchb.f. × *D. pendulum.* Sepals white with purple margins, petals white in lower half, purple in upper half, lip amaranth-purple and yellow, similar to that of *D. pendulum.*

chrysanthum Wallich [*D. Paxtonii* Lindl.]. Sts. to 7 ft. long, leafy; lvs. to 6 in. long; fls. 1–6 at a node, golden-yellow, 1–2 in. across, waxy, lip fringed, with 2 dark maroon blotches on throat. Early spring–summer, early autumn–early winter. Himalayas, Burma, Indochina, China. Cv. **'Anophthalmum'.** Fls. yellow, lip without blotches. Cv. **'Microphthalmum'.** Petals serrate and blunt, fringe of lip short, the 2 blotches at base pale brown.

chrysocrepis C. Parish & Rchb.f. ex Hook.f. Sts. slender, to 10 in. long, dilated above into a flattened, leafy pseudobulb; lvs. 3 or more, elliptic-lanceolate, to 3 in. long; fls. golden-yellow with deeper lip, to 1½ in. across, solitary on old leafless sts., inner surface of lip covered with reddish hairs. Summer. Burma.

chrysotis: *D. Hookeranum.*

chrysotoxum Lindl. FRIED-EGG ORCHID. Sts. club-shaped or spindle-shaped, to 15 in. long; lvs. 3–8 at the summit, linear to oblong-elliptic, about 6 in. long; racemes pendent, loosely 8- or more-fld., about 6–9 in. long; fls. golden-yellow, about 2 in. across, lip orange in throat, fringed. Early spring–summer. Burma, Indochina, China. Var. **suavissimum** (Rchb.f.) Hook.f. [*D. suavissimum* Rchb.f.]. Fls. with large chestnut spot on lip.

ciliatum C. Parish ex Hook. Sts. to 1½ ft. long; lvs. sessile, to nearly 3 in. long, to 1 in. across, in 5–17-fld. racemes to 10 in. long, sepals and petals greenish-yellow, lip 3-lobed, yellow, veined with red, mid-lobe fringed. Autumn. Burma, Indochina.

clavatum Wallich. Sts. to 2 ft. long; lvs. ovate-lanceolate, to 4½ in. long; racemes few-fld.; fls. to 2½ in. across, orange-yellow, lip bright

yellow with transverse maroon blotch, pubescent on upper surface, denticulate at margin. Late spring. Trop. Himalayas.

Coelogyne: *Epigenium Coelogyne.*

crassinode: *D. pendulum.*

crepidatum Lindl. & Paxt. Sts. cylindrical, to 1½ ft. long; lvs. linear-lanceolate, to 6 in. long; racemes 2–3-fld.; fls. about 1–1½ in. across, white, suffused with rose or lilac, center of lip golden-yellow. Late winter–late spring. Himalayas, Burma, Indochina. Cv. **'Album'.** Fls. white. Cv. **'Roseum'.** Fls. darker than in typical form.

cretaceum Lindl. Sts. thickened, to almost 15 in. long, pendent; lvs. oblong-lanceolate, to 3 in. long, deciduous; fls. solitary, to 1½ in. across, cream-white, lip with disc yellowish, streaked with orange-red or purplish. Late spring–summer. Burma, Himalayas, Indochina.

cruentum Rchb.f. Sts. erect, cylindrical, to 1 ft. long; lvs. elliptic-oblong, deciduous; fls. solitary or in pairs, to 2 in. across, pale green, lip 3-lobed, lateral lobes crimson-scarlet, midlobe pale green bordered with scarlet, and with a large warty red crest. Early winter–late winter. Malay Pen.

crumenatum Swartz. PIGEON ORCHID. Sts. to 3 ft. long or more, with basal spindle-shaped pseudobulbous thickening to 6 in long; lvs. about 4 in. long; fls. 1½ in. across, solitary at the nodes on the leafless upper part of sts., white or suffused with pale rose, with yellow patch on lip. Winter–early autumn. Indochina, Burma, Malay Pen., Philippine Is.

crystallinum Rchb.f. Sts. to about 1½ ft. long, leafless when flowering; lvs. to 6 in. long, deciduous; fls. 1–3 in a cluster, about 2 in. across, sepals and petals white, tipped with rose, lip golden-yellow at base, bordered with white, amethyst-purple near front margin. Spring–early summer. Himalayas, Burma, Indochina. Cv. **'Albens'.** Sepals and petals pure white, lip rich yellow, tipped with white.

cucullatum: *D. Pierardii.*

cumulatum Lindl. Sts. pendent, to 2 ft. long; lvs. oblong, to 4 in. long; fls. to 1½ in. across, rosy-purple suffused with white, crowded into subglobose corymbs. Early autumn. Malay Pen., Burma, Java, Borneo, Sikkim.

cupreum: *D. moschatum* cv.

cymbidioides: *Epigenium cymbidioides.*

Dalhousieanum: *D. pulchellum.*

Dartoisianum: *D. tortile* cv.

Dearei Rchb.f. Sts. to 3 ft. long; lvs. to 3 in. long; racemes 3–8-fld.; fls. 2½ in. across, white, center of lip yellowish-green. Early winter–late spring, summer. Philippine Is.

densiflorum Wallich [*D. thyrsiflorum* Rchb.f.]. Sts. club-shaped, to 20 in. long; lvs. 3–5 at apex of sts., leathery, about 6 in. long; racemes dense, many-fld., pendent, to about 9 in. long; fls. about 2 in. across, pale or golden-yellow, with orange-yellow lip. Spring. Himalayas, Burma, Indochina. Cv. **'Bronckartii'.** Pseudobulbs more slender; racemes rather loose, to 12 in. long; sepals and petals rose-tinted, lip rhombic, rose-tinted with orange-yellow disc.

Devonianum Paxt. Sts. to 3½ ft. long; lvs. to 4 in. long; fls. about 2 in. across, usually solitary, or 2, on leafless sts., white tipped with rose, lip fringed, with 2 large orange-yellow spots. Late spring–late summer. Himalayas, Burma, Indochina.

dixanthum Rchb.f. Sts. somewhat club-shaped, to about 3 ft. long; lvs. linear-lanceolate, to 5 in. long; racemes 1–5-fld.; fls. to 1½ in. across, yellow, lip with orange spot, margin minutely serrate. Early summer. Burma, Indochina.

draconis Rchb.f. Sts. to 1½ ft. long; lvs. to about 3 in. long; racemes axillary on upper part of st., 2–5-fld.; fls. about 1½ in. across, ivory-white, lip with 3 golden-yellow or orange-red ridges. Late spring–summer. Burma, Indochina.

erythroxanthum: *D. Bullenianum.*

Falconeri Hook. Sts. much-branched, swollen at nodes, to 3 ft. long; lvs. to 6 in. long; fls. 2–3 in. across, solitary, white or pale rose, tipped with violet, lip with dark purple throat surrounded by orange-red. Late spring–summer. Burma, Himalayas. Cv. **'Giganteum'.** Sts. longer and stouter; lvs. larger and more numerous; fls. nearly twice as large as those of typical form.

Farmeri Paxt. Sts. club-shaped, to 1½ ft. long; lvs. 2–4 at apex of sts., elliptic-oblong, to 6 in. long, persistent; racemes many-fld., pendent; fls. about 2 in. across, sepals and petals white, yellowish-white, or pale rose, lip golden-yellow, tipped with rose. Spring–early summer. Himalayas, Burma. Cv. **'Albiflorum'.** Fls. white, lip with orange-yellow disc. Cv. **'Aureoflavum'.** Fls. golden-yellow, lip with deep yellow disc.

fimbriatum Hook. Sts. canelike, to about 5 ft. long; lvs. to 6 in. long; racemes pendent, to about 6 in. long, 6–12-fld.; fls. to almost 3 in. across, deep yellow, lip orange-yellow, fringed. Early spring. Himalayas, Burma. Var. **oculatum** Hook. Lip with large dark maroon-red or purple blotch in throat.

Findlayanum C. Parish. & Rchb.f. Sts. to 2 ft. long, with club-shaped internodes; lvs. 3 in. long; fls. 1 or 2 together on leafless sts., about 2–3 in. across, sepals and petals white, tinged with rose, lip deep yellow in throat, fading to white near edges. Winter–late spring. Burma.

formosum Roxb. Sts. to 1½ ft. long; lvs. to about 5 in. long; racemes 2–4-fld., near apex of sts.; fls. snow-white with center of lip orange-yellow, to 4 in. across. Winter–late spring. Himalayas, Burma. Cv. 'Giganteum'. Of larger growth; fls. to 5 in. across.

Friedricksianum Rchb.f. Sts. thick, much-furrowed; racemes 3–4-fld., slender, arching; fls. to 1 in. across, sepals and petals light yellow, lip bright yellow with purplish blotch, tomentose at base. Thailand.

fuscatum: *D. Gibsonii.*

fusiforme: *D. speciosum* var.

Fytchianum Batem. [*D. barbatulum* Batem.]. Sts. slender, erect, to 1½ ft. long; lvs. oblong-lanceolate, to 4 in. long, deciduous; racemes 10–15-fld.; fls. to 2 in. across, white, side lobes of lip rosy-purple, midlobe with tufts of yellowish hairs at base. Spring. Burma.

Gibsonii Lindl. [*D. fuscatum* Lindl.]. Sts. slender, to 2½ ft. long; lvs. lanceolate, to 6 in. long; racemes from upper nodes only, fls. 5–7 or more; fls. to 2 in. across, golden-yellow, lip with 2 maroon spots on disc. Summer. Trop. Himalayas.

×**Goldiei**: *D.* ×*superbiens.*

gratiosissimum Rchb.f. [*D. Boxallii* Rchb.f.; *D. Bulleranum* Batem.]. Sts. slender, pendent, to about 3 ft. long; lvs. linear-lanceolate, to 4 in. long, deciduous; fls. to 2½ in. across, usually in pairs, white, margined and tipped with mauve-purple, lip tawny-yellow, bordered with white and with a mauve-purple blotch at front margin. Late winter. Burma.

Griffithianum Lindl. Sts. spindle-shaped, to 1½ ft. long, furrowed; lvs. 3–5; racemes many-fld., pendent, to 10 in. long; fls. bright yellow, to nearly 2 in. across, sepals oblong, petals nearly orbicular, lip orange, orbicular, fringed. Late spring. Burma. Cv. 'Guibertii' [*D. Guibertii* Carrière]. Sts. less densely tufted; lvs. more leathery; racemes longer; fls. larger, brighter.

Guibertii: *D. Griffithianum* cv.

Hanburyanum: *D. lituiflorum.*

hercoglossum: *D. linguella.*

heterocarpum: *D. aureum.*

Hildebrandii Rolfe. Sts. slender below, thickened above, to 2 ft. long; lvs. elliptic-oblong, to 5 in. long; racemes axillary, 3–4-fld.; fls. to 2 in. across, sepals and petals somewhat twisted, pale green, whitish-yellow, or creamy-pink, lip yellow, sometimes with 2 brown blotches in throat. Early spring. Burma.

Hillii: *D. speciosum.*

Hookeranum Lindl. [*D. chrysotis* Rchb.f.]. Sts. rodlike, to 8 ft. long, swollen at base into small pseudobulbs; lvs. oblong-lanceolate, to 6 in. long; racemes pendent, 9–12-fld.; fls. 3–4 in. across, bright golden-yellow, lip with 2 maroon spots at base, fringed at margin. Flowering throughout the year. Sikkim, Assam.

infundibulum Lindl. Sts. cylindrical, to 2 ft. long; lvs. ovate-lanceolate, to 3 in. long; fls. about 3–4 in. across, snow-white, lip with orange-yellow spot, lateral sepals extended into a spurlike mentum. Late spring–late summer. Burma. Cv. 'Jamesianum' [*D. Jamesianum* Rchb.f.]. Sts. stouter; lip rough on inner surface, disc cinnabar-red.

Jamesianum: *D. infundibulum* cv.

Jenkinsii: *D. aggregatum.*

japonicum: *D. monile.*

Johannis Rchb.f. Sts. clustered, spindle-shaped, to 1 ft. long; racemes erect, many-fld.; fls. to 1½ in. across, sepals and petals twisted, brown, lip yellow. Late summer. N. Australia.

Johnsoniae F. J. Muell. [*D. Macfarlanei* Rchb.f.]. Sts. erect, to 8 in. long; lvs. usually 2, rarely 3, leathery, to 4 in. long; racemes ascending, 9- to many-fld.; fls. to 5 in. across, white, lip with large purple spot at front margin. New Guinea.

Kingianum Bidw. ex Lindl. Sts. pseudobulbous, to 6 in. long; lvs. 2–5, to about 4 in. long; racemes 3–12-fld.; fls. less than 1 in. across, rose or whitish striped with violet, lip 3-lobed, marked with a greenish-yellow callus. Early spring. Australia.

lasioglossum Rchb.f. Sts. slender, to 20 in. long; lvs. lanceolate, to 5 in. long; fls. to 1½ in. across, in clusters of 2 and 3 from uppermost nodes, white, lip 3-lobed, streaked red on lateral lobes, with tuft of orange hairs on disc, spur 2-lobed. Late winter. Burma, Timor.

leucolophotum Rchb.f. St. stoutish, erect, to 1¼ ft. long, pale brown; lvs. to 6 in. long; racemes 1-sided, to 18 in. long, many-fld.; fls. white, to 1 in. across, lip white and pale green. Late autumn. Malay Arch.

linguella Rchb.f. [*D. hercoglossum* Rchb.f.]. Sts. slender, to 2 ft. long, pendent; lvs. sessile, to 3 in. long; racemes slender, few-fld.; fls. to 1¼ in. across, pale rose, lip smaller than petals, white, clawed, front part yellow, with double crest at base. Malay Arch.

Linawianum Rchb.f. [*D. moniliforme* Lindl., not (L.) Swartz]. Sts. club-shaped, greatly thickened at nodes, deeply furrowed, to 1 ft. long or more; lvs. oblong, persistent; fls. in pairs at nodes of 2-year-old leafless sts., 2½ in. across, segms. rose-purple, white at base, lip crimson-purple at apex, toothed, with crimson spot on each side of disc. Winter. China.

lituiflorum Lindl. [*D. Hanburyanum* Rchb.f.]. Sts. thickened, to 2 ft. long; lvs. to 4 in. long; fls. 2–2½ in. across, in groups of 1–5 on leafless sts., sepals and petals amethyst-purple, lip curved like a trumpet, with maroon-purple or violet blotch in throat surrounded by a broad white zone. Early spring–early summer. Cv. 'Candidum'. Fls. larger, sepals and petals pure white, lip pale sulphur-yellow. Cv. 'Freemanii'. Sts. short, stiff, erect; sepals and petals deep purple, lip sulphur-yellow.

Loddigesii Rolfe [*D. pulchellum* Lodd., not Roxb. ex Lindl.; *D. Seidelanum* Rchb.f.]. Dwarf, dense, sts. to 4 in. long, on creeping rhizome; lvs. to 2 in. long; fls. solitary, to 1½ in. across, on pedicels as long as lvs., pale rosy-lilac, lip with large orange-yellow disc, margin fringed. China.

longicornu Lindl. Sts. slender, to 1 ft. long; lvs. to 2½ in. long, deciduous; fls. 1–3, to 1½ in. across, not fully expanding, translucent white, lip funnel-shaped, yellow, with broad orange-red central band. Autumn. India, Burma, China.

×**Louisae** Hort.: *D. Phalaenopsis* × *D. veratrifolium* Lindl. Petals and lip deep magenta, sepals paler.

Lowii Lindl. Sts. slender, to 1 ft. long or more, covered with blackish lf. sheaths; lvs. ovate-oblong, to 3 in. long; fls. to 2 in. across, yellow, lip with 6 red lines, disc crimson-fringed. Summer and late autumn. Borneo.

luteolum Batem. Sts. to 1½ ft. long, grayish-white, furrowed; lvs. linear-lanceolate, to 4 in. long; racemes lateral, 2–4-fld.; fls. to 2 in. across, primrose-yellow, lip with tomentose disc marked with a few reddish streaks, spur beaklike. Spring. Moulmein (Burma). Cv. 'Chlorocentrum'. Lip with tuft of greenish hairs.

Lyonii: *Epigenium Lyonii.*

Maccarthiae Thwaites. Sts. to 2 ft. long, pendent, with swollen blackish nodes; lvs. few, linear-lanceolate, to 4 in. long; racemes pendent, 2–3-fld.; fls. flattened vertically, to 4 in. across, pale rosy-mauve suffused with white, lip delicate mauve-purple, striped with deep purple and with maroon-purple disc, spur nearly as long as pedicel. Late spring. Ceylon.

Macfarlanei: *D. Johnsoniae.*

macrophyllum: *D. superbum.*

monile (Thunb.) Kränzl. [*D. japonicum* Lindl.; *D. moniliforme* (L.) Swartz]. Sts. clumped, to 1 ft. long, pendent; lvs. to 2 in. long, linear-lanceolate; fls. borne on leafless sts., solitary or in pairs, to 1½ in. across, white, lip speckled with purple at base. Late spring. Japan, Korea, China.

moniliforme: see *D. Linawianum* and *D. monile.*

moschatum Swartz. Sts. cylindrical, leafy throughout, to 6 ft. long; lvs. to 6 in. long; racemes to 12 in. long, pendent, 8–15-fld.; fls. to 4 in. across, reddish-yellow, lip pouchlike, with a pair of red-brown spots near the base. Late spring–late summer. Himalayas, Burma. Var. **Calceolaria** (W. Carey) Hort. Veitch [*D. Calceolaria* W. Carey]. Fls. smaller, sepals and petals bright orange-yellow, with deeper colored veins and reticulation, lip deeper orange-yellow, with 2 maroon spots near base. Var. **cupreum** Rchb.f. [*D. cupreum* Herb. ex Lindl.]. Fls. smaller, to 3 in. across, bright apricot-yellow, lip darker, with dark coppery-orange blotch on each side near base.

nobile Lindl. Sts. cylindrical, thickened at the nodes, to nearly 2 ft. long; lvs. to about 4 in. long; fls. to about 3 in. across, in 2's rarely in 3's, sepals and petals white, tipped with rosy-purple, lip white, tipped with rose, with dark purple throat. Winter–early summer. Himalayas, Burma, China. Cv. 'Albiflorum'. Fls. white, lip with black-purple spot. Cv. 'Album'. Fls. white, lip yellowish-white, with crimson-purple blotch in throat. Cv. 'Amesiae'. Fls. similar to preceding, but larger. Cv. 'Armstrongiae'. Sepals and petals white, lip very dark maroon-purple. Cv. 'Ashworthianum'. Fls. white, lip with green mouth. Cv. 'Ballianum'. Sepals and petals white, lip yellowish-white with 2 crimson spots. Cv. 'Caerulescens'. Fls. smaller, more deeply colored, lip with more ovate blade. Cv. 'Colmanianum'. Fls. large, white, lip with sulphur-yellow disc. Cv. 'Cooksonianum'. Petals concave, approaching lip in form, erect, lip and petals with large basal maroon blotch at base. Cv. **'Elegans'**. Fls. larger and more symmetrical, petals broader and white at base, lip with pale sulphur-yellow area around a maroon disc, apical margin rose-purple. Cv. **'Formosanum'**. Pseudobulbs longer, pendent; only tips of petals and of lip purple, mouth and mentum green. Cv. **'Jaspidium'**. Apex of fl. segms. red, variegated with purple. Cv. **'Murrhiniacum'**. Similar to cv. 'Ballianum' but finer; sepals and petals tinged with violet, disc rich violet, finely veined with rose-violet. Cv. **'Nobilius'**. Fls. larger, deep amethyst-purple, paler at base, lip with maroon disc surrounded by milk-white zone. Cv. **'Rajah'**. Like cv. 'Albiflorum', but sepals and petals broader and flushed with delicate pink. Cv. **'Sanderanum'**. Fls. dazzling purple, midline of mentum green, lip with large dark blotch encircled with rosy-purple, with white area in front. Cv. **'Schneideranum.'** Lip suffused with yellow, and with a deep purple spot. Cv. **'Schroederanum'**. Fls. larger, with broader segms., sepals and petals white, sometimes with pale amethyst-purple apical blotch, disc of lip rich maroon-purple, almost black, bordered with pale yellow and fading to white at margin. Cv. **'Tollianum'**. A monstrous form, with twisted pedicels; fls. never fully expanding and appearing inverted. Cv. **'Virginale'**. Fls. pure white except for pale yellow tinge on lip.

nodatum: *D. Aphrodite.*

ochreatum Lindl. [*D. cambridgeanum* Paxt.]. Sts. cylindrical, with thickened nodes, to 1 ft. long; lvs. ovate-lanceolate, to 3 in. long, deciduous; racemes short, 1–3-fld.; fls. 2–3 in. across, lip golden-yellow, with chestnut or purple throat. Spring. Himalayas, Burma.

palpebrae Lindl. Sts. club-shaped, 4-angled, to 9 in. long; lvs. 3–5, oblong-lanceolate; racemes loose, 6–10-fld., from nodes below lvs.; fls. fragrant, to 1½ in. across, white, lip with orange-yellow disc marked with 5 lines of long reddish hairs near base. Late summer. Burma, Thailand, China.

Parishii Rchb.f. Sts. thickened, to 1 ft. long; lvs. to 5 in. long, deciduous; racemes 1–3-fld.; fls. to 2 in. across, rose to lilac-purple, lip with pair of dark purple blotches in throat. Late spring–summer.

Paxtonii: *D. chrysanthum.*

pendulum Roxb. [*D. crassinode* R. Bens. & Rchb.f.; *D. Wardianum* Warner]. Sts. cylindrical, thickened at nodes, to 2 ft. long; lvs. to about 5 in. long; racemes short, 1–3-fld.; fls. to 2½ in. across, white, tipped with purple, lip with a yellow throat surrounded by a white zone and tipped with purple. Winter–early spring. Burma.

Phalaenopsis R. Fitzg. [*D. bigibbum* var. *Phalaenopsis* (R. Fitzg.) F. M. Bailey]. Sts. 2 ft. long or more; lvs. to 7 in. long; racemes to 2 ft. long, 4–18-fld.; fls. to over 3 in. across, rose, purple, or whitish-rose, lip with dark purple throat. Late spring–late autumn. Australia to New Guinea and Timor. Cvs. include: **'Album'**, fls. white, to 4 in. across; **'Hololeucum'**, fls. white; **'Lindeniae'**, fls. large creamy-white; **'Rothschildianum'**, fls. 4 in. across, sepals and petals white suffused with rose, lip rose, intensely veined; **'Rubescens'**, fls. exceptionally dark; **'Schroederanum'**, sepals white, petals and lip deep violet; **'Splendens'**, fls. bright magenta-rose, segms. white at base; **'Statteranum'**, fls. deep violet; **'Thundersleyense'**, fls. dark in color.

Pierardii Roxb. [*D. cucullatum* R. Br.]. Sts. cylindrical, to 3 ft. long; lvs. to 5 in. long; racemes 2–3-fld.; fls. to 2 in. across, sepals and petals pale rose or lavender, lip white-yellow, with carmine or purplish lines at base. Late winter–late spring. Himalayas, Burma, China. Cv. **'Latifolium'**. Sts. more robust; lvs. broader.

primulinum Lindl. Sts. cylindrical, to 1½ ft. long; lvs. to 4 in. long; racemes 1–2-fld., on leafless sts.; fls. to 3 in. across, sepals and petals pale rose or pale lilac, lip primrose-yellow, with purple-striped throat. Late winter–late spring. Himalayas, Burma, China. Cv. **'Giganteum'**. Sts. longer and more slender, pendent; fls. nearly twice as large, lip to 2 in. across.

pulchellum Roxb. ex Lindl. [*D. Dalhousieanum* Wallich ex Paxt.]. Sts. cylindrical, to 4 ft. long; lvs. to 6 in. long, deciduous; racemes pendent, 6–12-fld.; fls. about 3–5 in. across, pale yellow, veined and tinted with rose, lip 3-lobed, fringed and hairy at front, with pair of large dark purple spots in throat. Spring. Himalayas, Burma, Indochina. Cv. **'Luteum'**. Fls. straw-colored except for 2 basal blotches. *D. pulchellum* Lodd. is *D. Loddigesii.*

ramosum Lindl. [*D. Ruckeri* Lindl.]. Sts. to 20 in. long; lvs. lanceolate; fls. solitary or in pairs, rich yellow inside, white outside, to 1¾ in. across, lip 3-lobed, deep orange, margined with white, pale pink outside, midlobe with hairy ridge. Spring. Trop. Himalayas.

rhodopterygium Rchb.f. Sts. cylindrical, erect, to 20 in. long; lvs. to 3 in. long; fls. to 2½ in. across, rosy-purple mottled with white, lip deep purple, striated, bordered with white. Burma.

rhombeum: *D. aureum.*

rigidum R. Br. Straggly, sts. jointed, yellow; lvs. fleshy, blunt, to 1½ in. long; racemes short, loosely 3–5-fld.; fls. to ½ in. long, segms. fleshy, sepals and petals cream-colored, with purple dots or suffusion,

lip 3-lobed, lateral lobes white with purple veins, midlobe round, yellow with red blotches. Winter. N. Australia.

rotundatum: *Epigenium rotundatum.*

Ruckeri: *D. ramosum.*

Ruppianum: *D. speciosum* var. *fusiforme.*

salaccense: *D. Bullenianum.*

×**Sanderae** Rolfe: *D. aureum* × *D. nobile.* Very similar to *D. Dearei*, but fls. larger, lip with purplish, striped throat. Late spring–late summer. Philippine Is.

scabrilingue Lindl. Sts. erect, to 1 ft. long; lvs. oblong; fls. to 1½ in. across, in clusters of 2 and 3 from uppermost nodes, ivory-white, lip 3-lobed, yellow, with 5–7 orange-yellow lines on disc. Early spring. Burma.

secundum (Blume) Lindl. Sts. cylindrical, to about 3 ft. long; lvs. to almost 5 in. long; racemes densely many-fld.; fls. rose, lip with orange-yellow disc. Blooming all year. Burma, Indochina, Pacific Is. Cv. **'Niveum'**. Sts. shorter; fls. white, lip orange at apex.

Seidelanum: *D. Loddigesii.*

speciosum Sm. [*D. Hillii* Hook.f.]. ROCK LILY. Sts. club-shaped, to 14 in. long; lvs. 3–4, to 10 in. long; racemes many-fld., to 30 in. long; fls. never fully expanded, to 1 in. long, straw-colored or yellow, lip light yellow, spotted red or violet. Late winter. Australia. Var. *fusiforme* F. M. Bailey [*D. fusiforme* F. M. Bailey; *D. Ruppianum* Hawkes]. Sts. spindle-shaped.

spectabile (Blume) Miq. Sts. erect, club- or spindle-shaped, to about 2 ft. long; lvs. 2–5, to 8 in. long; racemes terminal, with up to 12 fls.; fls. to 3½ in. across, sepals and petals greenish-yellow, veined with deep reddish-brown or violet, lip whitish-yellow, with more intense purplish veining. Winter–spring. New Guinea, Solomon Is.

suavissimum: *D. chrysotoxum* var.

sulcatum Lindl. Sts. club-shaped, to 10 in. long, furrowed; lvs. apical, 2–3, ovate-oblong, to 4 in. long; racemes short, 10–15-fld.; fls. orange-yellow, crowded, to 1 in. across. Spring. Trop. Himalayas.

×**superbiens** Rchb.f. [*D.* × *Goldiei* Rchb.f.]: *D. discolor* Lindl. × *D. Phalaenopsis.* A natural hybrid, similar to *D. Phalaenopsis;* sts. to 5 ft. long, usually less; racemes to 20-fld., to 3 ft. long; fls. 2–3 in. across, sepals and petals crimson-purple with paler margins, petals slightly twisted, lip darker, with white crests. Flowering time variable. N. Australia.

superbum Rchb.f. [*D. macrophyllum* Lindl.]. Sts. cylindrical, to 4 ft. long; lvs. to 6 in. long, deciduous; fls. solitary or in 2's, rarely in 3's, rose-purple, to 4 in. across, lip with 2 large dark purple spots in throat. Winter–spring, autumn. Borneo, Celebes to Philippine Is. Cvs. include: **'Album'**, fls. white, lip pale purple; **'Dearei'**, fls. pure white, lip with faint yellow flush; **'Anosmum'** [*D. anosmum* Lindl.], sepals and petals white, lip pale purple at base; **'Giganteum'**, fls. larger than in typical form; **'Huttonii'**, fls. pure white, lip with 2 purplish blotches on disc.

tetragonum A. Cunn. Sts. slender, club-shaped, pendent, 4-sided, to 16 in. long; lvs. usually 2 at summit of sts., elliptic-lanceolate, acute, to 4 in. long; racemes 1–3-fld.; fls. to 4 in. across, sepals and petals yellowish, spotted or suffused with reddish-brown, lip cream-white, transversely barred with red, strongly recurved. Late autumn. Australia.

×**Thwaitesiae** Hort.: *D.* ×*Ainsworthii* × *D.* × *Wiganiae* Hort. A popular hybrid; fls. yellow, lip with large chestnut-brown blotch.

thyrsiflorum: *D. densiflorum.*

Tofftii F. M. Bailey. Very large, sts. spindle-shaped, with purple ribs, to 5 ft. long; lvs. ovate; racemes at apex of pseudobulb, to 18 in. long; fls. to 2 in. across, sepals white, petals faintly lined with violet, frequently twisted, lip white, stained with violet and marked with forked veins, with 3 violet plates on disc. Late autumn–spring. Australia.

tortile Lindl. Sts. club-shaped, to 1 ft. long, 2–3-lvd.; lvs. lanceolate-oblong, obtuse, to about 4 in. long; fls. in 2's or 3's at the nodes, to 3½ in. across, sepals and petals white, tinged with rose, lip lemon-yellow, with purple streaks at base. Early summer. Burma. Cv. **'Dartoisianum'** [*D. Dartoisianum* De Wild.]. Sepals and petals yellow or with yellowish suffusion. Cv. **'Roseum'**. Sepals and petals rose.

transparens Wallich. Sts. slender, to 1½ ft. long; lvs. linear-lanceolate, to 4 in. long, deciduous; fls. 2–3 at a node, 1½ in. across, on purplish pedicels, sepals and petals white, tinted with rose and mauve toward tips, lip white with purple stains on disc, pale mauve-purple at apex. Early spring. Trop. Himalayas. Cv. **'Album'**. Fls. glistening white.

undulatum R. Br. Sts. erect, spindle-shaped, to 4 ft. long; lvs. to 4 in. long; racemes to over 1½ ft. long, many-fld.; fls. about 2 in. across, yellowish-brown, lip with reddish-brown or violet lines, sepals and petals twisted. Early summer, autumn. Australia.

Victoriae-reginae Loher. Sts. slender, many-noded, to 1 ft. long, leafy above; lvs. deciduous, 2-cleft, to 3 in. long; racemes lateral, 2–5-fld.; fls. to 2 in. across; sepals and petals spreading, white with bluish-purple suffusion toward apex, lip pointed, bluish-purple, with paler veins. Early spring–late autumn. Philippine Is.

Wardianum: *D. pendulum.*

Williamsonii Day & Rchb.f. Sts. erect, clothed with black hairs, to 1 ft. long; lvs. many, to 4 in. long, lanceolate, hairy, 2-lobed; infl. 2-fld.; fls. to 3 in. across, ivory-white, tinged with yellow towards tips, sepals and petals lanceolate, lip hairy, undulate, disc bright orange-red. Trop. Himalayas.

×xanthocentron: *D.* ×*chlorostele.*

DENDROCALAMUS Nees. GIANT BAMBOO. *Gramineae.* About 20 spp. of woody, treelike, clump-forming grasses in s. and se. Asia; infl. of spikelets in globose heads in long panicles; spikelets elliptic to oblong, few-fld. to many-fld., lower florets imperfect, upper bisexual or female, glumes 2–3, upper keeled, lemma often spinescent-mucronate, stamens 6, filaments separate; fr. small, with a thick, hard wall and free seed. For terminology see *Gramineae.*

Propagated by seeds and division. See *Bamboos.*

latiflorus: see *Bambusa Oldhamii.*

strictus (Roxb.) Nees. MALE BAMBOO, CALCUTTA B. Sts. to 50 ft. high or more and 5 in. in diam., forming dense clumps, nearly or quite solid, glaucous-green when young, becoming yellowish with age, the brs. long and slender; lf. blades to 1 ft. long, about 1 in. wide, with prominent midrib and strong nerves on each side, pubescent on both surfaces; panicle large, with dense heads to 2 in. across; spikelets usually hairy. A variable sp. India, Java. Cult. in Hawaii, Puerto Rico, Fla., and s. Calif. Zone 10. Best known Indian bamboo and important there as source of paper pulp. Very drought resistant.

DENDROCHILUM Blume [*Platyclinis* Benth.]. CHAIN ORCHID. *Orchidaceae.* About 100 spp. of epiphytes, native to se. Asia and Malay Arch.; pseudobulbs small, 1-lvd.; lvs. narrow, evergreen; fls. small, in long, often pendent, apical racemes, sepals and petals similar, lip 3-lobed, column with teeth. For structure of fl. see *Orchidaceae.*

Warm greenhouse; for culture see *Orchids.*

Cobbianum Rchb.f. [*Platyclinis Cobbiana* (Rchb.f.) Hemsl.]. To about 20 in., pseudobulbs ovoid; racemes long-stalked, to 20 in., arching, many-fld.; fls. whitish or yellowish, about ½ in. across, lip orange-yellow. Spring–late autumn. Philippine Is.

cucumerinum Rchb.f. Pseudobulbs spindle-shaped, furrowed; lvs. to 5 in. long and ½ in. wide; fls. 2-ranked, many, small, golden-yellow, translucent, lip with toothed brown auricle at base, midlobe retuse, disc with 2 brown stripes. Philippine Is.

filiforme Lindl. [*Platyclinis filiformis* (Lindl.) Benth.]. GOLDEN C.O. Pseudobulbs to 1 in. long, spindle-shaped; lvs. to 6 in. long; racemes to 15 in. long, pendent, many-fld.; fls. minute, less than ¼ in. across, greenish-yellow, fragrant. Early spring–summer. Philippine Is.

glumaceum Lindl. [*Platyclinis glumacea* (Lindl.) Benth.]. HAY-SCENTED ORCHID. Pseudobulbs spindle-shaped; lvs. to 20 in. long; racemes long-stalked, pendent, many-fld., bracts dry and chaffy; fls. white to yellow, about ½ in. across, column with basal arms. Late summer–early summer. Philippine Is.

latifolium Lindl. [*Platyclinis latifolia* (Lindl.) Hemsl.]. Pseudobulbs spindle-shaped, to 2 in. long; lvs. to about 17 in. long including petiole; racemes long-stalked; fls. many, whitish, greenish-yellow, or orange, about ½ in. across. Late winter–summer. Philippine Is.

uncatum Rchb.f. [*Platyclinis uncata* (Rchb.f.) N. E. Br.]. Similar to *D. glumaceum,* but of somewhat smaller habit and having arms of column near the middle, not basal. Early autumn–winter, late spring–summer. Philippine Is.

DENDROMECON Benth. TREE POPPY, BUSH P. *Papaveraceae.* Probably a single variable sp., native to Calif., including offshore islands, and n. Baja Calif., glabrous, much-branched, evergreen shrub; lvs. alt., simple, entire, leathery; fls. solitary, sepals 2, petals 4, yellow, stamens many; fr. a slender-cylindrical caps.

Planted as an ornamental in warm climates. Propagated by seeds, which are very slow in germinating.

Harfordii: *D. rigida* subsp.

rhamnoides: *D. rigida.*

rigida Benth. [*D. rhamnoides* Greene]. Stiff rounded shrub; lvs. mostly lanceolate, 3–8 times as long as wide, 1–4 in. long, acuminate, minutely denticulate; peduncles usually longer than lvs.; petals ¾–1½ in. long. Cent. Calif., s. to n. Baja Calif., San Clemente Is. Subsp. **Harfordii** (Kellogg) Raven [*D. Harfordii* Kellogg]. ISLAND T.P. More or less rounded, erect shrub, or small tree to 18 ft., brs. spreading to drooping; lvs. oblong-ovate to elliptic or rounded-oblong, 1½–3 times as long as wide, 1¼–3 in. long, entire; peduncles not longer than lvs.; petals ¾–1½ in. long. Santa Cruz and Santa Rosa Is. (Calif.).

DENDROPANAX Decne. & Planch. [*Gilibertia* Ruiz & Pav., not J. F. Gmel.]. *Araliaceae.* About 30 spp. of unarmed, glabrous shrubs or trees of Amer. and e. Asia; lvs. simple, entire or rarely palmately 3–5-lobed; infl. a solitary or compound umbel or of umbels arranged in racemes; calyx irregularly toothed, stamens 5–8, petals 4–6, valvate, ovary 5–8-celled, styles separate or variously united; fr. a drupe, 5–6-angled.

arboreus (L.) Decne. & Planch. [*Gilbertia arborea* (L.) Marchal]. Shrub or small tree, 15–35 ft.; juvenile lvs. ovate-elliptic, 4–8 in. long, often lobed, mature lvs. shorter-petioled, ovate to oblong, entire or slightly crenulate; infl. a terminal, compact raceme of several umbels. S. Mex., s. to S. Amer. and W. Indies. Zone 10. Wood used for general carpentry.

Chevalieri (Vig.) Merrill [*Gilbertia Chevalieri* Vig.]. Small tree, to 18 ft.; lvs. elliptic, to 6 in. long, narrowed at both ends, entire; infl. terminal, of clustered umbels; fls. small, 5-merous; fr. black, oblong. Vietnam. Zone 10.

japonica: *D. trifidus.*

trifidus (Thunb.) Mak. ex Hara [*D. japonicus* (Jungh.) Seem.; *Gilibertia japonica* (Jungh.) Harms]. Small tree with gray-brown brs., green branchlets; lvs. broadly rhombic-ovate to ovate, 3–5 in. long, entire, or especially in juvenile stages 2–3-lobed or -parted; umbels usually solitary, terminal; fls. yellowish-green; fr. black, ellipsoid. Japan. Zone 8.

DENDROPHYLAX Rchb.f. *Orchidaceae.* Four spp. of epiphytes, native to W. Indies; roots copious, flexuous, filiform, green, sts. leafless, short; fl. usually solitary on a short scape, sepals and petals similar, reflexed, lip 3-lobed, with long spur, midlobe large, cuneate, 2-lobed apically. For structure of fl. see *Orchidaceae.*

For culture see *Orchids.*

funalis (Lindl.) Fawc. [*Polyrrhiza funalis* (Lindl.) Pfitz.]. Fls. pale green, large, sepals and petals ¾ in. long, reflexed, lip white, midlobe, to 1 in. across, spur long, filiform. Spring. W. Indies.

DENMOZA Britt. & Rose. *Cactaceae.* Two spp., native to Argentina; sts. globose to oblong, erect, many-ribbed, spiny; fls. nearly apical, tubular, curved, red, scales of tube and ovary appressed, with axillary silky hairs, perianth segms. similar, small, not spreading, stamens in 2 series, exserted; fr. globose, umbilicate, with persistent style base, dry, splitting, seeds dull black, pitted. Differs from *Cleistocactus* in the thicker sts. and in having a woolly ring below the stamens as in some spp. of *Borzicactus.*

For culture see *Cacti.*

erythrocephalus (K. Schum.) Backeb. & F. M. Knuth. Sts. to 5 ft. high and 1 ft. thick, ribs 20–30; spines to 30 or more, slender-awl-shaped, often curved, red, to 2½ in. long, in mature plants some bristlelike, white; fls. 3 in. long.

rhodacantha (Salm-Dyck) Britt. & Rose. Similar but having sts. to 6 in. thick, ribs about 15; radial spines 8–10, to 1¼ in., central spine stronger or 0.

DENNSTAEDTIA Bernh. CUP FERN. *Polypodiaceae.* About 70 spp. of large or medium-sized ferns, native in the tropics and subtropics, 1 in e. N. Amer.; rhizomes creeping, hairy; lvs. 1–3-pinnate; sori marginal, indusia cup-shaped, open-topped.

Of easy culture. See also *Ferns.*

adiantoides: *D. bipinnata.*

bipinnata (Cav.) Maxon [*D. adiantoides* (Willd.) T. Moore]. GLOSSY C. F., CUPLET F. Rhizome creeping, with short brs.; lvs. triangular, to 3 ft. long, 3-pinnate, smooth and glossy above; axes of tertiary pinnae with an herbaceous, pleatlike wing on both sides. Trop. Amer. to s. Fla.

cicutaria T. Moore. COMMON C. F. Rhizome about ½ in. thick, wide-creeping mostly on surface of soil; lvs. triangular, to 5 ft. long, 3-pinnate, dullish green, with whitish or reddish-brown hairs above. Trop. Amer.

davallioides (R. Br.) T. Moore. LACY GROUND FERN. Rhizome slender, wide-creeping beneath the soil; lvs. thin, herbaceous, triangular, to about 3 ft. long, 3-pinnate, delicately cut, medium green. Australia, Tasmania.

punctilobula (Michx.) T. Moore [*Dicksonia punctilobula* (Michx.) A. Gray]. HAY-SCENTED FERN, BOULDER F. Rhizome slender; lvs. narrowly triangular to lanceolate, to 2½ ft. long, 2-pinnate-pinnatifid, the rachises with gland-tipped hairs. E. N. Amer. Forming large clumps, usually in rather poor soils. Hardy; sometimes planted in the wild garden. Forms with crested or incised lvs. are known.

DENTARIA L. TOOTHWORT, PEPPERROOT. *Cruciferae.* More than 10 spp. of per. herbs of damp woods in N. Hemisphere, with long fleshy rhizomes; lvs. arising directly from rhizome, 2–3, compound or deeply cleft, petioled, differing from st. lvs., lower part of st. usually leafless; fls. varying from white to rose-purple or bluish-purple, in a terminal corymb or raceme; fr. a linear, flat, erect silique. Closely related to *Cardamine* but fleshy rhizome with characteristic rhizomal lvs.

Useful in the wild garden, rock garden, or for colonizing.

californica Nutt. [*D. integrifolia* Nutt. var. *californica* Jeps.]. MILK-MAIDS. To 20 in., glabrous; rhizomal lvs. of 3–5 lfts. or simple, st. lvs. with 3–5 lfts. or lobes; fls. white to purple, in many-fld. racemes. Sw. Ore., Calif. Var. **integrifolia** (Nutt.) Detl. Rhizomal lvs. simple or of 3 lfts.

diphylla Michx. Erect, 6–12 in., with a long continuous rhizome; st. lvs. usually 2, opp., with 3 ovate, toothed, or shallowly lobed divisions or lfts.; fls. white, in a glabrous cluster. Nov. Sc. to Minn., s. to S.C.

integrifolia: *D. californica* var.

laciniata Muhlenb. To 1 ft. or so, from a jointed rhizome; st. lvs. commonly 3, more or less whorled, with very narrow divisions; fls. white or purplish, in a somewhat pubescent cluster. Que. to Minn., s. to Fla.

DEPLANCHEA Vieill. *Bignoniaceae.* About 8 spp. of trees, native from Malay Arch. to Australia; lvs. simple, opp. or whorled; fls. yellow, in dense panicles, calyx 2–5-lobed, corolla tubular-ventricose, slightly 2-lipped, stamens 4, exserted; fr. an oblong-fusiform, woody caps.

tetraphylla (R. Br.) F. J. Muell. Lvs. in whorls of 4, sometimes opp. on young sts., ovate, to 2 ft. long, entire. N. Queensland.

DERRIS Lour. JEWEL VINE, FLAME TREE. *Leguminosae* (subfamily *Faboideae*). Perhaps 70–80 spp. of woody lianas and trees, native to Old World; lvs. alt., odd-pinnate; fls. in racemes or panicles, papilionaceous, white, yellowish, or purplish, stamens united or 1 sometimes separate; fr. a flat, indehiscent legume, with a narrow wing along one or both margins.

Derris root of commerce, one of the sources of the insecticide rotenone, is obtained from *D. elliptica, D. uliginosa* Benth., and *D. malaccensis* Prain. Cultivated mainly in Malay Pen. and Indonesia. Propagated by seeds, or the commercially important kinds by cuttings. *Lonchocarpus* and *Tephrosia* are also sources of rotenone.

dalbergioides: *D. microphylla.*

elliptica (Wallich) Benth. DERRIS, TUBA ROOT. Large climber, brs. densely brown-pubescent; lfts. in 4–6 pairs, obovate-oblong, to 6 in. long, brown-silky-hairy beneath; racemes to 1 ft. long; petals bright red, standard ⅝ in. across; fr. to 3 in. long, narrow-winged along one margin. India to Indonesia. Cult. in tropics; a major source of rotenone.

microphylla (Miq.) B. D. Jacks. [*D. dalbergioides* Bak.]. Tree, to 20 ft.; branchlets, pedicels, and calyces brown-silky; lfts. in 12–20 pairs, elliptic-oblong, 1 in. long, emarginate, whitish beneath; racemes many, axillary, to 5 in. long, shorter than lvs.; fls. red-violet; fr. thin, to 2½ in. long, ⅝ in. wide, winged on one margin, 1-seeded. India, Malay Pen., Indonesia.

robusta Benth. Tree, to 40 ft., branchlets and lvs. grayish-silky-hairy beneath; lfts. in 3–9 pairs, 1–2 in. long, usually acute; fls. whitish, in dense clusters on elongate racemes; fr. to 2½ in. long, narrowly winged on one margin, wing to ³⁄₃₂ in. wide. India, Ceylon.

scandens Benth. MALAY J. V. Large scandent shrub; lfts. in 4–9 pairs, oblong, to 2 in. long; fls. pale rose, racemes many, axillary, to twice

as long as lvs.; fr. to 3 in. long, very narrowly winged on one margin, wing about ¹⁄₃₂ in. wide. E. India to China, Malay Pen., n. Australia.

DESCHAMPSIA Beauvois. HAIR GRASS. *Gramineae.* About 50 spp. of ann. or usually per. grasses in temp. and cool regions, chiefly in N. Hemisphere; infl. of spikelets in narrow or open panicles; spikelets 2-fld., shining pale green or purplish, disarticulating above the glumes and between the florets, rachilla prolonged, glumes 1–3-nerved, longer than lowest floret, membranous, lemma thin, convex, 2–4-toothed at apex, awned at or below the middle, awn slender, usually twisted and bent. For terminology see *Gramineae.*

caespitosa (L.) Beauvois [*Aira caespitosa* L.]. TUFTED H. G. Per., sts. to 4 ft., in dense clumps, leafy at base; lf. blades to ⅛ in. wide, often elongate, flat or folded, scabrous above; panicle open, drooping or nodding, to 10 in. long, the brs. and branchlets bearing spikelets toward the ends; spikelets to ¼ in. long, pale green or purple-tinged, florets distant, glumes not exceeding the upper floret, 1-nerved or the second obscurely 3-nerved, acute, lemma smooth, awn from near the base, straight to weakly geniculate, twice as long as the spikelet. Greenland to Alaska, s. to N.C. and Calif.; Eurasia. Grown for ornament.

flexuosa (L.) Trin. CRINKLED H. G., COMMON H. G. Resembles *D. caespitosa*, but sts. only 1–3 ft. high, lvs. mostly in a basal tuft, blades involute, filiform, flexuous, panicle to 5 in. long, spikelets purplish or bronze, florets close, lemma scabrous, awn geniculate, twisted. Greenland to Alaska, s. to Ga., Okla.; Eurasia.

DESFONTAINEA Ruiz & Pav. *Loganiaceae.* One sp., an evergreen shrub, native to the Andes of Peru and Chile; lvs. opp.; fls. solitary in axils, 5-merous, corolla tubular; fr. a berry.

spinosa Ruiz & Pav. To 3 ft.; lvs. elliptic-oblong, to 2½ in. long, spiny-toothed; fls. scarlet and yellow, 1½ in. long. Cult. on the Pacific Coast in Zone 9. The hollylike lvs. and red fls. make it an attractive small shrub.

DESMANTHUS Willd. *Leguminosae* (subfamily *Mimosoideae*). More than 20 spp. of trees, shrubs, or herbs of W. Hemisphere and Madagascar; lvs. alt., 2-pinnate, with many small lfts.; fls. in solitary, axillary heads, small, 5-merous, stamens 10 or 5, exserted; fr. a flat legume, opening along both margins.

illinoensis (Michx.) MacMill. [*Mimosa illinoensis* Michx.]. PRAIRIE MIMOSA, PRICKLEWEED. Per., to 3 ft.; lvs. with 6–15 pairs of pinnae, lfts. in 20–30 pairs, narrow, to ¼ in. long, heads on peduncles to 3 in. long; fls. whitish, stamens 5; fr. in dense heads, oblong, curved, to 1 in. long. Ohio to Fla. and New Mex.

DESMAZERIA Dumort. [*Brizopyrum* Link]. *Gramineae.* About 4 spp. of ann. or per. grasses in w. Eur. and Medit. Afr., e. to Afghanistan; spikelets many-fld., flattened, borne separately on a simple axis, glumes papery, 1–3-nerved, lemma firm, keeled, 3–5-nerved, awnless. For terminology see *Gramineae.*

sicula (Jacq.) Dumort. [*Brizopyrum siculum* (Jacq.) Link]. SPIKE GRASS. Ann., sts. about 1 ft. high, spreading to geniculate; lf. blades 3–6 in. long, narrow, thin, glabrous; infl. a simple panicle, 1¼–2 in. long; spikelets about 12, flat, 2-ranked, awnless, about ½ in. long. Medit. region. Cult. for ornament.

DESMODIUM Desv. TICK TREFOIL, TICK CLOVER, BEGGAR'S-TICKS. *Leguminosae* (subfamily *Faboideae*). More than 300 spp. of herbs of world-wide distribution, often woody at base; lvs. mostly of 3 lfts.; fls. in racemes or panicles, small, papilionaceous, mostly pink or purple, stamens 10, united in a tube or 1 separate at base only; fr. a flat, jointed legume, pubescent with hooked hairs and separating readily into 1-seeded sections.

Several species are useful as fodder plants. Some of the species, native to dry woods and fields, are occasionally transferred to the perennial border and the wild flower garden. Propagated by seeds.

bicolor: a listed name of no botanical standing for *Lespedeza bicolor.*

canadense (L.) DC. Per., to 8 ft.; lfts. oblong or oblong-lanceolate, to 4 in. long; fls. purple, to ¾ in. long; fr. 1 in. long, 3–5-jointed. Nov. Sc., s. to N.C. and Okla.

gyrans: *D. motorium.*

motorium (Houtt.) Merrill [*D. gyrans* (L.f.) DC.]. TELEGRAPH PLANT. Per., to 4 ft.; terminal lft. oblong, to 4 in. long, lateral lfts. very small and moving by jerks under the influence of warmth and sunshine; fls. purple or violet, ¼ in. long; fr. to 1½ in. long, 6–10-jointed. Trop. Asia. Grown as a curiosity in greenhouses; treated as an ann.

penduliflorum: *Lespedeza Thunbergii.*

purpureum: see *D. tortuosum.*

Sieboldii: a listed name of no botanical standing for *Lespedeza Thunbergii.*

tortuosum (Swartz) DC. [*D. purpureum* (Mill.) Fawc. & Rendle, not Hook. & Arn.]. BEGGARWEED. Per., to 8 ft.; lfts. ovate or oblong, to 4 in. long; fls. blue or purple, 5/32 in. long; fr. twisted, to 1 in. long, 2–6-jointed. Trop. Amer. Grown as an ann. forage and cover crop in s. U.S. Seeds should be sown on rather moist land, in spring. No care is needed after first year as it reseeds itself.

DESMONCUS Mart. *Palmae.* Sixty or more spp. of slender, usually cespitose, climbing, monoecious palms of trop. Amer., spiny in some or all parts; lvs. pinnate, pinnae acute, the terminal ones modified into straight or reflexed hooks; infl. among lvs., simply branched, bracts 2, the upper inserted high on the peduncle, enclosing infl. in bud, rachillae with fls. in triads (2 male and 1 female); male fls. with calyx small, 3-cleft or 3-lobed, petals valvate, stamens 6, female fls. with calyx cupular, corolla tubular or urceolate, ovary 3-celled; fr. fleshy, with apical stigmatic residue, endocarp bony, with 3 pores near the middle, seed with homogeneous endosperm.

Sometimes planted in tropical gardens, Zone 10a. For culture see *Palms.*

horridus: *D. orthacanthos.*

major: *D. orthacanthos.*

orthacanthos Mart. [*D. horridus* Splitg. ex Mart.; *D. major* Crüger ex Griseb.]. Sts. to 60 ft.; lvs. to more than 6 ft. long, tipped with 5–8 pairs of straight hooks, sheaths with unequal straight spines, pinnae 15–23 on each side, lanceolate, acuminate, often in groups of 2–3; upper bract of infl. to 20 in. long, densely spiny, rachillae 25–30; fr. orange-red, ⅜ in. in diam. Trinidad, Tobago, e. S. Amer.

oxyacanthos: *D. polyacanthos.*

polyacanthos Mart. [*D. oxyacanthos* Mart.]. Sts. to 45 ft.; lvs. to 4½ ft. long, tipped with 4–6 pairs of slender reflexed hooks, sheaths densely spiny to nearly smooth, pinnae 8–12 on each side, lanceolate, acuminate; upper bract of infl. to 6½ in. long, with recurved bulbous spines, rachillae 10–15; fr. red, to ⅝ in. in diam. Trinidad, e. S. Amer.

quasillarius Bartlett. Sts. elongate; lvs. to more than 6 ft. long, tipped with about 9 pairs of recurved hooks, sheaths armed with black spines, pinnae about 22 on each side, acuminate, to 1 ft. long, 1¼ in. wide; upper bract of infl. nearly 1 ft. long, with short spines; fr. not described. Brit. Honduras, Guatemala.

DESMOTHAMNUS: *LYONIA.*

DETARIUM Juss. *Leguminosae* (subfamily *Caesalpinioideae*). Three spp. of trees of trop. Afr.; lvs. alt., pinnate, with translucent-dotted lfts.; fls. in panicles, small, fragrant, cream-colored, sepals 4, petals 0, stamens 10, separate, of 2 lengths; fr. a round, indehiscent, 1-seeded legume, resembling a drupe.

senegalense S. G. Gmel. TALLOW TREE, DATTOCK TREE. To 100 ft. or more; lvs. to 9 in. long, lfts. alt., 6–12, ovate to oblong, to 3 in. long, apically rounded or retuse; panicles to 6 in. long; fr. to 2½ in. in diam. Senegal to Congo region.

DEUTEROCOHNIA Mez. *Bromeliaceae.* Seven spp. of terrestrial shrubs, native to Andean S. Amer.; lvs. in basal rosettes, thick, spiny; infl. pinnately paniculate, on a tall, woody scape; fls. bisexual, petals separate, with large scale at base, ovary superior; fr. a caps., seeds many, winged.

Probably among the most hardy of the bromeliads. Grown in full sun. For culture see *Bromeliaceae.*

longipetala (Bak.) Mez. Lvs. to 1 ft., spiny-margined except at slender tip; infl. many-fld., brs. loosely arranged; fls. to 1 in. long, yellow, with green spot at tip. Argentina. Sometimes cult. under the name *D. Schreiteri.*

Schreiteri Castell. Lvs. with spines 3/32 in. long; infl. densely fld., brs. conelike; fls. yellow, to ½ in. long. Argentina. At least some plants so named in cult. have proved to be *D. longipetala.*

DEUTZIA Thunb. *Saxifragaceae.* About 40 spp. of shrubs of temp. Asia and mts. of Cent. Amer.; lvs. opp., usually deciduous, serrate; fls. white, pink, or lavender, mostly in panicles or racemes, calyx tube united to ovary, calyx lobes 5, petals 5, stamens usually 10, filaments flattened, ovary inferior, styles 3 or 4, long and filiform; fr. a caps., seeds many, small.

Deutzias thrive in any well-drained soil. Propagated by both greenwood and hardwood cuttings, also by division and layers, and by seeds sown in spring.

×**candelabrum** (Hort. Lemoine) Rehd.: *D. gracilis* × *D. scabra.* Lvs. ovate-lanceolate, serrulate, scabrid above; fls. in panicles. Cv. **'Fastuosa'** is listed.

×**candida** (Hort. Lemoine) Rehd.: *D.* ×*Lemoinei* × *D. scabra.* Lvs. ovate, to 2 in. long, slightly scabrid above; fls. in loose paniclelike corymbs.

candidissima: *D. scabra* cv.

×**carnea** (Hort. Lemoine) Rehd.: *D.* × *rosea* × *D. scabra.* Lvs. ovate to oblong-ovate, to 2 in. long, sharply serrulate; fls. pink, in loose upright panicles. Cv. **'Erecta'** is listed.

Chunii H. H. Hu. Lvs. oblong-lanceolate, remotely and minutely serrulate; fls. in panicles to about 3 in. long. E. China.

corymbiflora: *D. setchuenensis.*

corymbosa R. Br. To 9 ft.; lvs. ovate, to 5 in. long, usually rounded at base, stellate-hairy beneath with 8–12-rayed hairs; fls. white, in a many-fld. corymb or panicle 2–3 in. across. Himalayas. Zone 7.

crenata Siebold & Zucc. Lvs. ovate to broadly lanceolate, to 2¼ in. long, short-petioled, stellate-pubescent with 4–6-rayed hairs above and with 10–15-rayed hairs beneath; fls. in a simple raceme sometimes branched at base. Japan. A variable sp., closely related to *D. scabra.*

discolor Hemsl. To 6 ft.; lvs. oblong-lanceolate, to 4 in. long, rough and dull green above, gray and densely stellate-hairy beneath; fls. white, in many-fld. corymbs to 3 in. across. China. Zone 6. Cv. **'Candidissima'.** Fls. pure white. Cv. **'Major'.** Fls. rosy outside. Other cvs. listed are: **'Arcuata', 'Candida', 'Conspicua', 'Floribunda'.** Var. **elegantissima:** *D.* ×*elegantissima.* Var. **excellens:** *D.* ×*excellens.*

×**elegantissima** (Hort. Lemoine) Rehd. [*D. discolor* var. *elegantissima* Hort. Lemoine]: *D. purpurascens* × *D. scabra.* Lvs. ovate to oblong-ovate, irregularly and sharply serrulate, stellate-pubescent with 4–6-rayed hairs; fls. rose-colored, in many-fld., loose corymbs. Zone 6.

×**excellens** (Hort. Lemoine) Rehd. [*D. discolor* var. *excellens* Hort. Lemoine]: *D.* × *rosea* cv. 'Grandiflora' × *D. Vilmoriniae.* Lvs. ovate-oblong, to 4 in. long, gray-pubescent beneath; fls. ¾ in. across, in loose corymbs.

Fortunei: *D. scabra.*

globosa Duthie. Resembling *D. discolor,* but lvs. smaller and fls. creamy-white. Cent. China. Zone 6.

gracilis Siebold & Zucc. To 6 ft., brs. slender, wide-spreading or arching; lvs. lanceolate, to 2½ in. long, nearly glabrous beneath; fls. pure white, ¾ in. long, in open, simple or compound racemes. Japan. Zone 5. Cv. **'Alba'** is listed. Cv. **'Aurea'.** Fls. yellow. Var. **campanulata:** *D.* ×*rosea* cv. Var. **carminea:** *D.* ×*rosea* cv. Var. **Lemoinei:** *D.* ×*Lemoinei.* Var. **rosea:** *D.* ×*rosea.*

grandiflora Bunge. To 6 ft.; lvs. ovate, to 2 in. long, white-tomentose beneath; fls. white, 1 in. across or more, 1–3 together. N. China. Zone 6.

Hookerana (C. K. Schneid.) Airy-Shaw. Closely related to *D. corymbosa,* but stellate hairs of lower surface dense, small, 5–9-rayed, and of upper surface 3–5-rayed. Yunnan (China) and e. Himalayas.

hypoglauca Rehd. To 6 ft.; lvs. ovate-oblong to oblong-lanceolate, to 3½ in. long, glabrous and glaucous beneath; fls. white, to ¾ in. across, in many-fld. corymbs. Cent. China. Zone 6.

×**kalmiiflora** Hort. Lemoine: *D. parviflora* × *D. purpurascens.* Lvs. ovate-oblong, to 2 in. long, slightly hairy beneath; fls. white, carmine outside, ¾ in. across, in loose corymbs. Zone 6.

Kosterana: a listed name, probably a hort. form of *D. gracilis.*

laxiflora: *D. Schneiderana* var.

×**Lemoinei** Hort. Lemoine ex Bois: *D. gracilis* × *D. parviflora.* Lvs. elliptic-lanceolate, to 4 in. long; fls. pure white, ¾ in. across, in large corymbs or broad panicles. Zone 4. Cv. **'Compacta'.** Dwarf; fls. smaller.

longifolia Franch. [*D. Veitchii* E. H. Wils.]. To 6 ft.; lvs. lanceolate, to 5 in. long, pale and densely hairy beneath; fls. light purple, to 1 in. across, in many-fld. corymbs. W. China. Zone 7.

×**magnifica** (Hort. Lemoine) Rehd.: *D. scabra* × *D. Vilmoriniae.* Lvs. ovate-oblong, to 3 in. long, tomentose and grayish-green beneath; fls. double, white, in short panicles. Zone 6. Cv. **'Eburnea'.** Fls. campanulate, in rather loose panicles. Cv. **'Formosa'** is also listed.

×**maliflora** Rehd.: *D.* × *Lemoinei* × *D. purpurascens.* Lvs. ovate-oblong, to 1½ in. long, acuminate, serrulate; fls. purplish outside, whitish inside, to ¾ in. across, in corymbs to 2½ in. across. Cv. '**Avalanche**' is listed.

Monbeigii W. W. Sm. To 6 ft.; lvs. ovate-lanceolate, to 1¾ in. long, serrate, scabrid with 5–8-rayed hairs above and with dense, 15-rayed hairs beneath; fls. white, in 7–15-fld. corymbs. W. China. Zone 7.

×**myriantha** Hort. Lemoine: *D. parviflora* × *D. setchuenensis.* Lvs. oblong-ovate to -lanceolate, to 3½ in. long, hairy beneath; fls. white, ¾ in. across, in loose corymbs. Zone 7.

ningpoensis Rehd. To 7 ft.; lvs. ovate-oblong, broadly cuneate, entire or slightly toothed; fls. white, in panicles to 4 in. long, petals oblong, to ⁵⁄₁₆ in. long. E. China.

parviflora Bunge. To 6 ft.; lvs. ovate to ovate-lanceolate, to 4 in. long, somewhat hairy; fls. white, about ½ in. across, in many-fld. corymbs. N. China. Zone 5.

pulchra S. Vidal. To 8 ft. or more; lvs. ovate-oblong, to 4½ in. long, serrate, leathery, sparsely stellate-pubescent above, almost glabrous beneath; fls. white, pendulous, in few-fld. panicles usually to 4 in. long. Taiwan and Philippines.

purpurascens (L. Henry) Rehd. To 6 ft., brs. slender, curving; lvs. oblong-ovate to -lanceolate, to 2½ in. long, pubescent beneath; fls. white inside, purplish outside, ¾ in. across, in 4–10-fld. corymbs. W. China. Zone 7.

reflexa Duthie. To 3 ft. or more; lvs. elliptic-lanceolate, to 4 in. long, with simple hairs along midrib and veins; fls. white, densely clustered in corymbose panicles 2½ in. across, petal margins reflexed. China. Zone 6.

×**rosea** (Hort. Lemoine) Rehd.: *D. gracilis* × *D. purpurascens.* Lvs. ovate-oblong to -lanceolate, slightly hairy; fls. pinkish outside, ¾ in. across, in short panicles. Zone 5. Cvs. include: '**Campanulata**' [*D. gracilis* var. *campanulata* Hort. Lemoine], fls. white, about 1 in. across; '**Carminea**', fls. purplish outside; '**Eximia**', fls. only slightly pinkish outside; '**Floribunda**', infl. dense; '**Grandiflora**', infl. less dense; '**multiflora**' and '**Venusta**', fls. white.

scabra Thunb. [*D. Fortunei* Carrière; *D. Sieboldiana* Maxim.; *D. Sieboldiana* var. *Dippeliana* C. K. Schneid.]. To 7 ft.; lvs. ovate to oblong, to 3 in. long, stellate-pubescent with 3–4-rayed hairs above and with 4–6-rayed hairs beneath, those lvs. immediately below the infl. sessile, the others short-petioled; fls. in many-fld. panicles. Japan. Zone 6. Closely related to *D. crenata,* in which all lvs. are petioled. Cvs. offered are: '**Azaleiflora**', a listed name; '**Candidissima**' [cv. 'Wellsii'; *D. Wellsii* Hort.], fls. pure white; '**Excelsa**', a listed name; '**Fortunei**', fls. large; '**Mirabilis**', vigorous form, with large panicles; '**Plena**', fls. double, white, tinged with rose outside; '**Rosea**', fls. rose; '**Staphyleoides**', fls. very large, in drooping panicles; '**Suspensa**', a listed name; '**Thunbergii**', fls. white, with orange center; '**Watereri**', fls. white, tinged with carmine outside; '**Wellsii**': 'Candidissima'.

Schneiderana Rehd. To 6 ft.; lvs. elliptic-ovate, to 2½ in. long, grayish-tomentose beneath; fls. white, in broad, loose panicles. Cent. China. Zone 6. Var. **laxiflora** Rehd. Lvs. narrower; panicles broader.

setchuenensis Franch. [*D. corymbiflora* V. Lemoine]. To 6 ft.; lvs. lanceolate, to 4 in. long, densely pubescent beneath; fls. white, ½ in. or less across, in loose corymbs. China. Zone 7.

Sieboldiana: *D. scabra.* Var. **Dippeliana:** *D. scabra.*

staminea R. Br. ex Wallich. Lvs. ovate, to 2½ in. long, unequally serrate, densely stellate-pubescent beneath; fls. in corymbs to 2 in. across. Himalayas. Zone 7. Closely related to *D. setchuenensis,* but lvs. smaller, less acuminate, and brs. less spreading.

taiwanensis (Maxim.) C. K. Schneid. Lvs. lanceolate to elliptic, to 3 in. long, stellate-tomentose on both surfaces, scabrid above, paler beneath; fls. few, in a terminal panicle to 2½ in. long. Taiwan.

Veitchii: *D. longifolia.*

Vilmoriniae Hort. Lemoine. To 6 ft.; lvs. oblong-lanceolate to 3½ in. long, densely pubescent beneath; fls. white, to 1 in. across, in loose corymbs. China. Zone 6.

Watereri: *D. scabra* cv.

Wellsii: *D. scabra* cv. 'Candidissima'

Wilsonii Duthie. To 6 ft.; lvs. elliptic to oblong-lanceolate, to 5 in. long, pubescent; fls. white, ¾ in. across, in loose corymbs. W. China. Zone 7. A handsome shrub resembling *D. discolor.*

DEWBERRY. Trailing blackberries of the genus *Rubus* are frequently called dewberries, ground blackberries, or running blackberries. They are characterized by canes that trail on the ground and in cultivation are not self-supporting but must be tied to poles or a trellis, and whose fruit clusters ripen earlier and are smaller or more open than those of the erect blackberry types. Dewberries belong to such species as *Rubus flagellaris, R. macropetalus, R. mirus, R. ursinus,* and *R. vitifolius.*

The culture is like that of the blackberry. The canes are very vigorous and slender, requiring a wire trellis or tall stakes. The fruits are large, generally dark red to black, variable in flavor, and with large seeds. The torus separates from the pedicel with the attached drupelets.

Few new cultivars of dewberries have been developed. 'Lucretia' is widely grown in the United States except in the Gulf states; 'Mayes' is grown in Texas, while 'Cascade', 'Chehalem', 'Pacific', and 'Marion' are planted in the Pacific Northwest.

In cold climates, the trailing canes are mulched for protection. In spring they are tied to a stake or trellis. After fruiting, the old canes should be cut and removed as for blackberries, being replaced by the young canes, which will produce the next year's crop. It may be necessary to tie or train young canes to grow alongside the older ones to facilitate cultivation and picking. Dewberries are propagated by tip layers.

×**DIACATTLEYA:** × *CAULOCATTLEYA.*

DIACRIUM: *CAULARTHRON.* **D. indivisum:** *C. bilamellatum.*

DIALIUM L. *Leguminosae* (subfamily *Caesalpinioideae*). Perhaps 35–40 spp. of unarmed trees, mostly of the Old World tropics, 1 sp. in S. Amer.; lvs. alt., odd-pinnate, lfts. mostly 3–7, alt.; fls. in axillary or terminal panicles, small, calyx lobes 5, deciduous, petals 1–2 or 0, stamens 2 (–3), separate; fr. a nearly globose, indehiscent, 1–2-seeded legume.

guineense Willd. VELVET TAMARIND, SIERRA LEONE T. Tree, to 60 ft., branchlets rusty-puberulous; lfts. elliptic to lanceolate, to 5 in. long; panicles short, flat; fl. buds rusty-hairy, petals small, solitary, white; fr. flat, obovoid, to 1 in. across, velvety, with orange-red, edible pulp. Senegal to Congo region.

DIANELLA Lam. FLAX LILY. *Liliaceae.* About 25 spp. of rhizomatous, per. herbs, native from E. Trop. Afr. and Madagascar to China, Australia, Polynesia, and n. and w. S. Amer.; with or without a st., roots fibrous; lvs. 2-ranked, grasslike, sheathing; fls. blue or white, often nodding, in loose panicles, perianth segms. 6, mostly 3–8-nerved, separate, spreading or reflexed, stamens 6, anthers basifixed, opening by a pore; fr. a blue berry.

Plants succeed in a cool greenhouse, or outdoors in mild climates. Propagated by division or by seeds sown in spring with heat.

caerulea Sims. Sts. to 2 ft., leafy in lower part, sometimes branched; lvs. to 1½ ft. long and ½ in. wide, rough on midrib and margins; fls. blue, ⁵⁄₁₆ in. long, in panicles 1 ft. long, anthers pale yellow. New S. Wales.

ensifolia (L.) DC. [*Dracaena ensifolia* L.]. UMBRELLA DRACAENA. St. to 6 ft., leafy in lower part; lvs. to 1 ft. long and 1 in. wide; fls. blue or whitish, to ⁵⁄₁₆ in. long, anthers yellow. E. Trop. Afr., Madagascar, Asia, Australia, Hawaii.

intermedia Endl. Stemless, from creeping rhizomes; lvs. many, linear-ensiform, to 3 ft. long and ¾ in. wide, margins minutely roughened; fls. greenish-white or purplish-white, to ⁵⁄₁₆ in. across, in panicles to 2 ft., anthers yellow. New Zeal.

laevis R. Br. [*D. longifolia* R. Br.]. Stemless; lvs. few, crowded at base of st., to 1½ ft. long, flat, bright green, glabrous; fls. blue, peduncles to 3 ft., anthers yellow. New S. Wales.

longifolia: *D. laevis.*

revoluta R. Br. Stemless; lvs. crowded at base, linear, to 3 ft. long, revolute or flat, glaucous, sheath keeled; fls. deep blue, ⁵⁄₁₆ in. long, panicle to 2 ft. long, anthers yellow, brown, or black. New S. Wales and Tasmania.

tasmanica Hook.f. Stemless; lvs. widely ensiform, 3–4 ft. long and 1 in. wide, rigid, margins revolute, armed with short, sharp teeth; fls. pale blue, to ¾ in. across, in a large, much-branched panicle, peduncle to 5 ft., perianth segms. reflexed at maturity, anthers brown. Tasmania.

DIANTHUS L. PINK. *Caryophyllaceae.* About 300 spp., of ann., bien., or per. herbs chiefly Eurasian, extending to S. Afr.; lvs. opp., the pairs often united at the base and forming a sheath about the st., the nodes usually swollen; fls. solitary or panicled, or in heads surrounded by bracts, calyx tubular, 5-toothed, many-nerved, subtended by an epicalyx (1 or more pairs of scales), petals usually 5, limb often abruptly attenuated into an elongated claw, entire to many-toothed to fimbriate, sometimes spotted, stamens 10, ovary 1-celled, styles 2; fr. usually a 4-valved caps., cylindrical, oblong-ovoid, seeds usually many.

Pinks are well-suited to rock gardens and rock walls, since many species come from alpine habitats. The showy, often fragrant flowers are mostly pink or rose; some are red, purple, white, or yellow. Cultivation of pinks is generally easy. The perennial species may be kept vigorous by division and may be propagated by cuttings, or layers, or by seeds; cultivars should be propagated by cuttings, or layers, or division. Two-year plants usually give the best bloom.

acaulis: a listed name of no botanical standing.

×**Allwoodii** Hort. Allw.: *D. Caryophyllus* × *D. plumarius.* Tufted per.; lvs. mostly firm, broad, rather glaucous; fls. in many colors, petals variously fringed or entire. Hardy.

alpestris: *D. furcatus.*

alpinus L. Cespitose per., to 8 in., glabrous; lvs. oblanceolate, to ³⁄₁₆ in. wide; epicalyx scales 2–4, calyx to ¾ in. long, petals to ¾ in. long, bearded, red-purple, speckled white, rarely all white. E. Alps. Cv. 'Albus'. Fls. white. Cv. 'Allwoodii': *D.* ×*Allwoodii.*

anatolicus Boiss. Per., to 12 in.; lvs. linear; infl. 1–3-fld., pedicels more than ¼ in. long, epicalyx scales 4–6, ovate; calyx to ½ in. long, teeth acute, blade of petal linear, ⅛ in. long, often toothed, white. Turkey.

arboreus L. Per., to 20 in., woody at base; lvs. linear, to ⅛ in. wide, glaucous; fls. many, fragrant, pedicels short, epicalyx scales 10–20, petals ⁵⁄₁₆ in. long, dentate, bearded, pink. S. Greece and Crete.

arenarius L. Cespitose per., to 18 in.; sts. simple or branched; lvs. linear, extremely narrow; fls. fragrant, epicalyx scales 2–4, calyx to 1 in. long, blades of petals to ½ in. long, deeply dissected, bearded at base, white, spotted green, often margined purple. Sweden to Czechoslavakia to Russia.

Armeria L. DEPTFORD P. Pubescent ann. or bien., to 16 in.; lvs. oblong to linear; fls. clustered in heads, bracts resembling lvs., epicalyx scales as long as calyx, to ¾ in. long, petals to ¼ in. long, toothed, bearded, reddish. Cent. and s. Eur. to n. Iran; naturalized in e. N. Amer.

×**arvernensis** Rouy & Foucaud: *D. monspessulanus* × *D. Seguieri.* Per., 12–20 in.; lvs. narrow, basally attenuate, sheaths long; petals ½ in. long, toothed, purplish. Mts. e.-cent. France. Material cult. under this name is often misidentified.

atrococcineus: a listed name of no botanical standing; see *D. barbatus* cv. and *D. latifolius* cv.

atropurpureus: a listed name used in various senses, but most hort. material is probably *D. latifolius* cv.

atrorubens: *D. carthusianorum;* see also *D. carthusianorum* cv.

atrosanguineus: a listed name of no botanical standing, used for *D. barbatus* cv.

banaticus: *D. giganteus* subsp.

barbatus L. SWEET WILLIAM. Ann., bien., or per., but short-lived, nearly glabrous, to 2 ft., usually less; lvs. often short-petioled, lanceolate, midrib conspicuous; infl. many-fld., flat-topped cymes, pedicels short, epicalyx scales aristate; fls. sometimes double, petals bearded inside, varying from white to pink, rose, red, purple, violet, and bicolored. Pyrenees, Carpathian Mts., Balkan Pen.; naturalized in China and N. Amer. as an escape from gardens. A familiar ornamental. Cvs. are: 'Albus', fls. white; 'Atrococcineus', fls. deep red; 'Atrosanguineus', fls. dark blood-red; 'Auriculiflorus', petal blades auricled; 'Dunnettii', a listed name; 'Nanus', a dwarf form; 'Nigricans', fls. dark violet-purple.

bicolor: *D. Seguieri.*

biflorus Sibth. & Sm. [*D. cinnabarinus* Sprun. ex Boiss.]. Cespitose per., to 16 in.; st. lvs. in 3–4 pairs, sheaths very long; infl. 1- to few-fld., epicalyx scales 6, aristate; calyx to 1 in. long, petals ½ in. long, toothed, glandular-hairy above. Mts., cent. and s. Greece.

blandus: *D. plumarius.*

Boydii: a listed name of no botanical standing, probably for a hybrid strain.

brachyanthus: *D. subacaulis.*

brevicaulis Fenzl. Cushion-forming per., to 2 in.; lvs. to ¾ in. long, flat, toothed, very short-pointed; fls. solitary, often sessile, epicalyx scales 4–6, aristate, purplish, calyx ¾ in. long, cuspidate, purple, petals

¼ in. long, toothed, rose or carmine, yellowish beneath. Turkey. A good rock garden plant.

caerulens: a listed name of no botanical standing.

caesius: *D. gratianopolitanus.*

callizonus Schott & Kotschy. Per., to 8 in., glabrous; lvs. linear-lanceolate; fl. solitary, epicalyx scales 2–4, ovate, subulate at apex, calyx to ⅝ in. long, teeth acuminate, petals ½ in. long, carmine. Mts., Romania.

calocephalus Boiss. Per., to 2½ ft.; lvs. linear, 2–3 in. long, long-acuminate; infl. capitate, bracts ovate-oblong, cordate, leathery, epicalyx scales 4, ovate, less than half as long as calyx, aristate; calyx to ¾ in. long, teeth linear, to ¼ in. long, petals bearded, red. Balkans, Transcaucasia.

campestris Bieb. Per., 8–16 in., puberulent; lvs. extremely narrow, sheaths ⅛ in. long; fls. solitary or paired, terminal, epicalyx scales 4–6, calyx to ¾ in. long, petals toothed, bearded, pink or purplish above, yellowish-green beneath. Ne. Romania, Ukraine, e. Russia to w. Siberia.

capitatus Balb. ex DC. Glaucous per., to 2 ft.; lvs. linear, ⅛ in. wide, sheaths very long; infl. capitate, many-fld., bracts ovate, as long as calyx, epicalyx scales ovate, shorter than calyx, margin scarious; calyx to ¾ in. long, teeth ovate, petals ¼ in. long, bearded to subglabrous, purple. Se. Eur., Turkey, Caucasus to Siberia.

carthusianorum L. [*D. atrorubens* All.; *D. vaginatus* Chaix]. CLUSTER-HEAD P. Per., to 2 ft., glabrous; lvs. linear, sheaths long; fls. few to many, in heads, bracts lanceolate, epicalyx scales obcordate, aristate, usually dark purple, calyx ¾ in. long, petals ½ in. long, toothed, bearded, deep pink to purple, rarely white. S., w., and cent. Eur. Cvs. are: 'Atrorubens', fls. dark red; 'Giganteus', fls. bright pink; 'Nanus', sts. to 4 in., heads small; fls. purple; 'Saxigenus', infl. 6-fld., petals purple to dark purple; 'Vaginatus', fls. purple, heads in 3's.

Caryophyllus L. CARNATION, CLOVE P., DIVINE FLOWER. Cespitose per., glaucous, short-lived, sts. 1–3 ft., stiffly erect; lvs. 3–6 in. long, channelled, acuminate, bluish-glaucous, sheaths conspicuous; infl. 2–5-fld.; fls. long-stalked, 1–4 in. across, often double, white, pink, red, purple, yellow, apricot-orange, white spotted red, often very fragrant. Perhaps native in Medit. region; widely cult. elsewhere. Commonly cult. by florists, also grown in Eur. for use in perfumes. For cult. see *Carnation.*

caucasicus: *D. Seguieri.*

chinensis L. RAINBOW P. Ann., bien., or short-lived per., sts. 6–30 in., erect, internodes shorter than lvs.; basal lvs. withering early, st. lvs. 1–3 in. long, rarely to ¼ in. wide, ciliate, sheath ¼ in. long; infl. few- to 15-fld., loosely clustered, epicalyx scales 4, abruptly contracted into a long point; fls. ½–1 in. across, not fragrant, rosy-lilac with purplish eye, petals obovate. Cent. and e. China. Cv. 'Heddewigii'. A strain blooming first year from seed. Cv. 'Laciniatus' [*D. Heddewigii laciniatus* Hort.]. Petals laciniate. Cv. 'Splendens'. A listed name.

cibrarius Clementi. Per., sts. 10–24 in.; lvs. linear, extremely narrow, acuminate; infl. capitate, 7-fld., bracts ovate, leathery, epicalyx scales 4, narrowly ovate; calyx ¾–1 in. long, teeth mucronate, petals to ¼ in. long, toothed, red. W. Turkey. Closely related to *D. pinifolius.*

cinnabarinus: *D. biflorus.*

cognobilis Timb.-Lag. Cespitose per., glabrous, sts. 6 in., woody at base; lvs. linear, acute, keeled; infl. capitate, bracts obovate-lanceolate, mucronate, about ⅓ the length of the calyx; calyx leathery, teeth purplish, petals dentate, rose. Pyrenees.

collinus Waldst. & Kit. Per., 8–30 in., glabrous to pubescent; lvs. linear-lanceolate, to ⁵⁄₁₆ in. wide, basal lvs. few, st. lvs. many, 7–15 pairs, 3–5-veined; infl. capitate, heads usually paired, 2–8-fld., bracts shorter than fls.; calyx to ¾ in. long, petals to ½ in. long, bearded, pink or purplish. Austria, e. to Poland and Romania.

corsicus: a listed name of no botanical standing.

crinitus Sm. Robust per., sts. to 1 ft., erect; lvs. linear, 1–5 in. long, ½ in. wide, st. lvs. shorter than internodes; pedicels ¾ in. or longer, epicalyx scales 4–6–8, ovate, aristate; calyx 1–1½ in. long, teeth aristate, ciliate, petals ½–¾ in. long, fimbriate, white to pale pink. Nw. Afr., Turkey to Turkestan.

croaticus: *D. giganteus* subsp.

cruentus Griseb. Glaucescent per., to 3 ft.; lvs. linear, to ⅛ in. wide, sheaths long; infl. capitate, bracts ovate, awned, puberulent, epicalyx scales reddish-brown; calyx ¾ in. long, reddish-purple, puberulent, petals to ⁵⁄₁₆ in. long, dentate, bearded. Balkan Pen.

Cyri Fisch. & C. A. Mey. Ann., to 16 in.; lower lvs. linear, ⅛ in. wide; infl. much-branched, pedicels ¾ in. or longer, epicalyx scales 4, cuspidate; calyx warty, ½ in. long, teeth mucronate, petals ¼ in. long, dentate, pink. Arabia, Syria, Turkey, to Afghanistan.

deltoides L. MAIDEN P. Cespitose per., 6–18 in., green or glaucous, sts. puberulent; lvs. linear-oblanceolate to linear, margins pubescent; epicalyx scales 2(–4), ovate, pubescent; calyx ¾ in. long, pubescent, petals deep pink, rarely white, with dark, pale-spotted band at base of blade. Eur. Cvs. are: 'Albus', fls. white; 'Coccineus', fls. scarlet; 'Compactus' [*D. glaucus compactus* Hort.], compact; 'Erectus', of upright habit; 'Glaucus'. [*D. glaucus* L.], lvs. glaucous; 'Nanus' [*D. glaucus nanus* Hort.], dwarf; 'Roseus', fls. rose; 'Ruber', fls. red; 'Splendens', a listed name; 'Serpyllifolius', mat-forming, lvs. only ½ in. long. A vigorous sp. for the rock garden.

erythrocoleus Boiss. Per., to 8 in.; lvs. linear, ½ in. long, less than ⅛ in. wide, uppermost pair inflated, purplish at base; infl. often with solitary fl., epicalyx scales 4, cuspidate-aristate, purple-brown; calyx ¾ in. long, purple, teeth ciliate, petals ¼ in. long, fimbriate, pink or white. Ne. Turkey, nw. Iran.

Farreri: a listed name of no botanical standing.

fimbriatus: *D. orientalis.*

fragrans Adams. Cespitose per., glaucous, glabrous, sts. to 2 ft.; lvs. 1–3 in. long, acuminate; fls. 1–3, terminal, fragrant, 1 in. across; epicalyx scales 6–8, awned, as long as calyx, petals fimbriate, not bearded, rose to white, often spotted. Caucasus. Similar to *D. plumarius.*

fragrantissimus: a listed name of no botanical standing.

Freynii Vandas. Densely cespitose per., to 4 in.; lvs. blue-green to grayish; fls. solitary, ¾ in. across, borne above lvs., epicalyx scales 2–4, ovate-oblong, petals ⁵⁄₁₆ in. long, dentate, bright pink. Alpine regions, Balkan Pen.

frigidus: *D. sylvestris* var.

furcatus Balb. [*D. alpestris* Balb.]. Cespitose per., glaucous, sts. simple or forked, to 12 in.; lvs. mostly basal; fls. solitary, fragrant, about ½ in. across, epicalyx scales about half as long as calyx, calyx ¾ in. long, petals dentate, rose, rarely white. Mts., sw. Eur.

gelidus: *D. glacialis* subsp.

giganteiformis: *D. Pontederae* subsp.

giganteus D'Urv. Robust per., 8–40 in.; lvs. linear, ⅛ in. wide, acuminate; sheaths long; infl. capitate, subtended by 2 lvs., epicalyx scales half as long as calyx; calyx ¾ in. long, petals to ⁵⁄₁₆ in. long, dentate, purple. Turkey, Greece, Romania, to Italy. Subsp. **giganteus.** The typical subsp.; epicalyx scales glabrous, acute to acuminate; calyx to about ¾ in. long. Romania, Bulgaria, Turkey. Subsp. **banaticus** (Heuff.) Tutin [*D. banaticus* (Heuff.) Borb.]. Epicalyx scales puberulent, awned, awn less than ⅛ in. long; calyx ½ in. long. Sw. Romania. Subsp. **croaticus** (Borb.) Tutin [*D. croaticus* Borb.]. Epicalyx scales puberulent, awned, awn to ³⁄₁₆ in. long, calyx to ⅝ in. long. Bulgaria, Greece, Yugoslavia.

glacialis Haenke. Cespitose per., glabrous, sts. 3–4 in., 4-angled; lvs. obtuse, ¹⁄₁₆ in. wide; fls. solitary, ½ in. across or more, epicalyx scales 2–4, ovate, pointed, about as long as calyx, calyx ⁵⁄₁₆ in. long, ⅛–¼ in. wide, petals reddish-purple above, yellowish beneath. E. Alps and Carpathians. Subsp. **glacialis.** The typical subsp.; lf. margin nearly glabrous; calyx less than ¼ in. wide, petals about ¼ in. long. E. Alps and Carpathians. Subsp. **gelidus** (Schott, Nym. & Kotschy) Tutin [*D. gelidus* Schott, Nym. & Kotschy]. Lvs. ciliate at base; calyx ¼ in. wide, petals ½ in. long. Carpathians.

glaucus: *D. deltoides* cv. **D. glaucus** [var.] **compactus:** a hort. name of no standing, used for *D. deltoides* cv. 'Compactus'. **D. glaucus** [var.] **nanus:** a listed name of no standing, used for *D. deltoides* cv. 'Nanus'.

gracilis Sibth. & Sm. Glabrous per., to 16 in.; basal lvs. less than ¹⁄₁₆ in. wide, frequently lacking at flowering time, st. lvs. shorter than internodes, acuminate; fls. usually solitary, epicalyx scales 4–6, obovate, to ⅓ as long as calyx, petals dentate, bearded, pink above, yellow or purplish beneath. E. Greece.

graniticus Jord. Cespitose per., sts. to 8 in., 4-angled, puberulent at base; lvs. linear, acute, glabrous; fls. often solitary, epicalyx scales less than half as long as calyx, calyx ½ in. long, often purplish, petals purple above, paler beneath. S.-cent. France.

gratianopolitanus Vill. [*D. caesius* Sm.; *D. suavis* Willd.]. CHEDDAR P. Cespitose per., glabrous, sts. 3–10 in., often glaucous; lvs. linear-lanceolate, ¹⁄₁₆ in. wide, acute; fls. solitary or few, fragrant, epicalyx scales ovate to obovate, ¼–⅓ as long as calyx, petals bearded, toothed, rosy-pink. Gr. Brit., France, e. to Poland and Ukraine. Cvs. are: 'Albus', fls. white; 'Carmineus', fls. carmine; 'Compactus', habit dense; 'Grandiflorus', fls. large; 'Nanus Compactus', dwarf compact; 'Splendens' and 'Superbus Grandiflorus', listed names.

graveolens: a listed name of no botanical standing.

haematocalyx Boiss. & Heldr. Cespitose per., 1–12 in., glabrous; lvs. linear, green to glaucous; epicalyx scales 4–6; calyx ¾ in. long, petals bearded, ½ in. long, purple above, yellow beneath. Balkan Pen. Subsp. **haematocalyx.** The typical subsp.; to 1 ft., not glaucous; epicalyx scales gradually tapered, about as long as calyx. Yugoslavia, Greece. Subsp.

pindicola (Vierh.) Hayek [*D. pindicola* Vierh.]. Not glaucous, sts. 2 in.; lvs. linear-lanceolate; calyx not inflated. Albania, Greece. Subsp. **Sibthorpii** (Vierh.) Hayek [var. *alpinus* (Sibth. & Sm.) Boiss.]. Glaucescent, sts. to 4 in.; lvs. linear; calyx inflated at base. Albania, Greece. Var. alpinus: subsp. *Sibthorpii.*

×**heddensis:** a listed name of no botanical standing, used for plants with sts. long, as in *D. chinensis;* and fls. large and open, as in *D. chinensis* cv. 'Heddewigii'.

Heddewigii: a listed name of no botanical standing, used for *D. chinensis* cv. Var. **laciniatus:** a listed name of no botanical standing, used for *D. chinensis* cv.

Henkii: a listed name of no botanical standing.

Henteri Heuff. ex Griseb. & Schenk. Cespitose per., 6–12 in.; lvs. rigid, linear, extremely narrow, sheaths long; infl. capitate, 2–3-fld., bracts short, narrow, epicalyx scales aristate; calyx ½ in. long, green or purplish, teeth brown, petals ½ in. long, dentate. S. Carpathians of Romania.

Heutrei: probably a misspelling for *D. Henteri.*

Hoppei: *D. plumarius.*

hybridus: a listed name of no botanical standing.

hyssopifolius: see *D. monspessulanus.*

inodorus: *D. sylvestris.*

integer: *D. petraeus* subsp.

japonicus Thunb. [*D. nipponicus* Mak.]. Per., glabrous, sts. 8–20 in., erect; lvs. oblanceolate, margin papillose, basal lvs. petioled, st. lvs. sessile, to 3 in. long, to 1 in. wide, lustrous above; infl. capitate, manyfld., flat-topped, epicalyx scales caudate; calyx ¾ in. long, petals ¼ in. long, triangular, toothed, rose or rosy-purple. Japan, Ryukyu Is.

Kitaibelii: *D. petraeus.*

Knappii (Pant.) Asch. & Kanitz ex Borb. Per., to 16 in., pubescent; lvs. linear-lanceolate, 5–7-veined, sheaths short; infls. usually 2, manyfld. heads, bracts leaflike, epicalyx scales ovate, awned; calyx ⅝ in. long, petals sulphur-yellow. W. Yugoslavia.

laciniatus: a listed name of no botanical standing, used for *D. chinensis* cv.

laricifolius Boiss. & Reut. Cespitose per., sts. to 12 in.; basal lvs. rigid, linear-subulate, to ¾ in. long; fls. in pairs, epicalyx scales 4–8, calyx ¾ in. long, petals ¼ in. long, glabrous, bright magenta. Portugal and Spain.

×**latifolius** Willd. BUTTON P. Parentage uncertain; sts. 10–16 in., stiffly erect; lvs. 2–3 in. long, to ⅝ in. wide, basal lvs. petioled; infl. 1–6-fld., epicalyx scales about 6, of different lengths; fls. single or double, petals toothed, rose to dark red. A garden hybrid. Cv. 'Atrococcineus'. Fls. dark red. Cv. 'Atropurpureus'. Fls. dark purple.

longicalycinus: a listed name of no botanical standing, used for *D. superbus* cv.

Lumnitzeri: *D. plumarius* var.

lusitanicus: *D. lusitanus.*

lusitanus Brot. [*D. lusitanicus* of auth.]. Per., to 1½ ft., glaucous, sts. woody at base; lvs. linear, about ⅜ in. long, somewhat fleshy; infl. a cyme, epicalyx scales 4, ovate, about ⅓ as long as calyx, acuminate; calyx to ⅞ in. long, petals deeply toothed, bearded, pink to rose-purple. Spain, Portugal, N. Afr.

meliticus: a listed name of no botanical standing.

microlepis Boiss. Cespitose per., sts. to 4 in.; basal lvs. to ¾ in. long, st. lvs. scalelike; epicalyx scales 2; calyx ⅜ in. long, petals ¼ in. long, purple. Mts., Bulgaria. Cv. 'Albus'. Fls. white. Var. **Musalae** Velen. [*D. Musalae* (Velen.) Velen.]. Sts. longer, more slender; bracts herbaceous.

monspessulanus L. [*D. hyssopifolius* L., in part]. Loosely cespitose per., to 20 in.; lvs. linear, to ⅛ in. wide, sheaths short; infl. 1–7-fld., pedicels brief, epicalyx scales 4, subulate at apex; calyx to 1 in. long, petals to ¾ in. long, lobed, white or pink. S. and cent. Eur., n. Portugal to Yugoslavia. Subsp. **monspessulanus.** The typical subsp.; to 2 ft.; fls. 2–5. S. Eur. Subsp. **Sternbergii** (Sieber) Parl. ex Hegi [*D. Sternbergii* Sieber]. Sts. under 8 in., glaucous; fls. solitary, epicalyx brief, petals ⅝ in. E. Alps.

Musalae: *D. microlepis* var.

myrtinervius Griseb. Related to *D. deltoides;* tufted, leafy, to 2 in.; lvs. elliptic, ¹⁄₁₆–³⁄₁₆ in. wide, longer than internodes; fls. often solitary, epicalyx scales 2–4, calyx to ⁵⁄₁₆ in. long, petals ³⁄₁₆ in. long, bearded, pink. N. Greece and s. Yugoslavia.

nardiformis Janka. Cespitose per., to 4 in.; basal lvs. ⅜ in. long, setaceous, st. lvs. in 6–10-pairs; fls. solitary, epicalyx scales 4–6, aristate, calyx to ¾ in. long, petals ¼ in. long, dentate, bearded, pink. Lower Danube Valley.

neglectus: see *D. pavonius.*

nipponicus: *D. japonicus.*

nitidus Waldst. & Kit. Related to *D. alpinus;* loosely tufted, sts. to 12 in.; lvs. linear, obtuse; infl. 2–5-fld., epicalyx scales 2–4, ovate, subulate; calyx ½ in. long, petals ⅜ in. long, rose, spotted. Nw. Carpathians, s. Poland, Czechoslovakia. Thrives in limestone soil.

Noeanus: *D. petraeus* subsp.

orientalis Adams [*D. fimbriatus* Bieb.]. Per., to 16 in.; lvs. linear, to 3 in. long, ⅛ in. wide; fls. usually solitary, pedicels at least ¾ in., epicalyx scales 4–14, cuspidate to aristate, calyx to 1 in. long, petals fimbriate, finely bearded, pink. Nw. Afr., e. to Iran and Turkestan.

pallens Sibth. & Sm. Per., to 18 in.; lower lvs. linear, to 2 in. long; pedicels at least ¾ in. long, epicalyx scales 4–6, subulate at apex; calyx to ¾ in. long, petals ⅜ in. long, pink. Romania and Balkan Pen. to n. Iran.

Pancicii: *D. tristis.*

pavonius Tausch. [*D. neglectus* Loisel., in part]. Cespitose per., to 4 in.; lvs. linear, to 1½ in. long, acuminate; fls. usually solitary, epicalyx scales ovate, subulate at apex, calyx to ⅝ in. long, teeth scarious, petals bearded, purplish-red. Sw. and e. Alps.

Peristeri: a listed name of no botanical standing, used for *D. myrtinervius.*

petraeus Waldst. & Kit. [*D. Kitaibelii* Janka; *D. Suendermannii* Bornm.]. Mat-forming per., sts. to 12 in.; lvs. acuminate, 3-nerved, sheaths long; fls. solitary or in clusters, epicalyx scales 2–8, cuspidate, calyx to 1 in. long, petals to ⅜ in. long, laciniate, white or pink. Balkan Pen., Romania. Subsp. **petraeus.** The typical subsp.; epicalyx scales acute or acuminate, herbaceous; calyx about 1 in. long, petals dentate to laciniate. Balkan Pen. Subsp. **integer** (Vis.) Tutin [*D. integer* Vis.]. Calyx ½–¾ in. long, petals entire. Albania and Yugoslavia. Subsp. **Noeanus** (Boiss.) Tutin [*D. Noeanus* Boiss.]. Apex of epicalyx scales cuspidate; calyx over 1 in. long, petals laciniate. Bulgaria.

pindicola: *D. haematocalyx* subsp.

pinifolius Sibth. & Sm. Densely cespitose per., to 16 in.; lvs. rigid, linear, extremely narrow, sheaths short; infl. capitate, bracts ovate, aristate, epicalyx scales 6, aristate; calyx ¾ in. long, petals to ⅜ in. long, toothed, purple or lilac. Balkan Pen., sw. Romania.

plumarius L. [*D. blandus* (Rchb.) Hayek; *D. Hoppei* Portenschl.]. COTTAGE P., GRASS P. Mat-forming per., to 16 in., glabrous, glaucous; lvs. extremely narrow; infl. 1–3-fld., epicalyx scales usually 4, obovate, about ¼ as long as the calyx; fls. fragrant, calyx to 1 in. long, purplish, petals to ¾ in. long, often fringed, rose, purple, white, parti-colored. E.-cent. Eur. Cvs. are: 'Nanus', dwarf; 'Roseus', fls. rose; 'Scoticus' a listed name; 'Semperflorens', fls. double. Var. **albiflorus** Schur [*D. tatrae* Borb.]. Fls. white. Carpathians. Var. **Lumnitzeri** (Wiesb.) Novák [*D. Lumnitzeri* Wiesb.]. Calyx narrowly attenuate. E. Austria to ne. Hungary. Var. **praecox** (Kit. ex Willd.) Hayek [*D. praecox* Kit. ex Willd.]. Lvs. green; fls. pale pink or white. Bulgaria.

Pontederae A. Kern. Related to *D. giganteus;* smaller, more slender, to 8 in.; lvs. linear, ⅛ in. wide; epicalyx scales obovate, short-aristate; calyx ½ in. long, petals ³⁄₁₆ in. long, purplish. E.-cent. Eur. to n. Italy and Bulgaria. Subsp. **Pontederae.** The typical subsp.; calyx about ⅜ in. long; outer epicalyx scales brown, abruptly awned. Subsp. **giganteiformis** (Borb.) Soó [*D. giganteiformis* Borb.]. Calyx ⅝ in. long; outer epicalyx scales straw-yellow, acuminate. Hungary, Yugoslavia, Romania.

praecox: *D. plumarius* subsp.

prolifer: *Petrorhagia prolifera.*

pungens L. Cespitose per., 2–8 in., woody at base; lvs. rigid, ¾ in. long, acuminate; epicalyx scales 4, ovate, acuminate; calyx ⅝ in. long, petals ³⁄₁₆ in. long, glabrous, pink. E. Pyrenees.

pyrenaicus Pourr. Loosely cespitose per., to 18 in., sts. slender, woody; lvs. rigid, pungent; infl. branched, epicalyx scales 4–8, ovate, acuminate; calyx to 1 in. long, petals ⁵⁄₁₆ in. long, toothed, glabrous, pink. Portugal to Pyrenees.

pyridicola: a listed name of no botanical standing.

repens Willd. Mat-forming per., to 8 in., glabrous; lvs. linear, obtuse; epicalyx scales 4, lanceolate, subulate at apex; calyx ½ in. long, petals ½ in. long, bearded, pink to purplish. Arctic regions, Russia, Siberia, Alaska.

×**Roysii** Hort.: *D. callizonus* × *D. gratianopolitanus.* Fls. large, deep rose. Cv. 'Roseus'. Fls. rose-pink.

Ruprechtii: a listed name of no botanical standing.

saxigenus: a listed name of no botanical standing, used for *D. carthusianorum* cv.

scardicus Wettst. Nearly cespitose, sts. to 4 in.; lvs. to ⅝ in. long; fls. usually solitary, epicalyx scales 2, about half as long as calyx, calyx about ½ in. long, petals pink. Yugoslavia.

scoticus: a listed name of no botanical standing, probably for *D. plumarius* cv.

Seguieri Vill. [*D. bicolor* Adams; *D. caucasicus* Sm.]. Related to *D. chinensis;* cespitose per., green, sts. 1–2 ft., simple or forked; lvs. linear-lanceolate, ⅛ in. wide, sheaths short; infl. 1- to few-fld., epicalyx scales 2–6; calyx ¾ in. long, petals ⁵⁄₁₆–¾ in. long, toothed, bearded, reddish-pink, spotted white at base. Ne. Spain to s. Germany and Czechoslovakia.

semperflorens: a hort. name once used for a variant of *D. carthusianorum* and for *D. plumarius* cv.

serpyllifolius: a listed name of no botanical standing, used for *D. deltoides* cv.

shinanensis (Yatabe) Mak. Per., sts. 8–16 in., erect, nodes papillose; lvs. short-petioled, linear-lanceolate, 1–2½ in. long, to ⁵⁄₁₆ in. wide, dark green, glabrous, margin papillose; infl. dense, flat-topped, epicalyx scales long, linear to subulate; calyx ¾ in. long, petals ⁵⁄₁₆ in. long, bearded at base, rose-purple. Mt. valleys, cent. Japan.

speciosus: *D. superbus* subsp.

spectabilis: a listed name of no botanical standing.

spiculifolius Schur. Related to *D. petraeus;* per., green, sts. to 12 in.; lvs. linear, long, acute, green; fls. usually solitary, petals rose or white, laciniate, bearded. Romania, w. Ukraine. Thrives in limestone soil.

splendens: a listed name of no botanical standing.

squarrosus Bieb. Cespitose per., to 12 in.; lvs. linear, to ¾ in. long, acuminate; infl. branched, epicalyx scales 4, cuspidate; calyx 1 in. long, petals ⁵⁄₁₆ in. long, deeply laciniate, bearded. Ukraine to Kazakhstan. Cv. 'Nanus'. Dwarf form.

stenopetalus Griseb. Mat-forming per., to 16 in.; lvs. extremely narrow, convolute, sheaths long; infl. capitate, bracts ovate, awned, epicalyx scales ovate, awned, pale; fls. few to many, calyx ¼ in. long, somewhat inflated, purple. Balkan Pen.

Sternbergii: *D. monspessulanus* subsp.

strictus Banks & Soland. Cespitose per., 12–20 in., glabrous; basal lvs. withering before flowering, st. lvs. in 6–12 pairs, as long as internodes, to ⅛ in. wide, acuminate; epicalyx scales ovate, cuspidate, calyx ⅝ in., conical, warty, with purple lines, petals ⅜ in. long, dentate, bearded, pink, darker-veined. Crete, Turkey, w. Syria. Cvs. are: 'Brigantiacus', a listed name; 'Grandiflorus', large-fld.; 'Integer', repent or creeping, bracts ½ as long as calyx, fls. small, petals entire.

suavis: *D. gratianopolitanus.*

subacaulis Vill. [*D. brachyanthus* Boiss.]. Densely cespitose per., to 8 in., woody at base, sts. usually simple; lvs. linear-lanceolate, ⁵⁄₁₆ in. long; epicalyx scales 4, very short-pointed; calyx to ½ in. long, somewhat inflated, petals ⁵⁄₁₆ in. long, glabrous, pale pink. Mts., sw. Eur.

Suendermannii: *D. petraeus.*

superbus L. Per., to 3 ft., sts. decumbent basally, branched above; lvs. linear-lanceolate; epicalyx scales 2–4, ovate, awned; fls. fragrant, calyx to 1 in. long, petals to 1 in. long, deeply laciniate, bearded, pink, purplish, or white. Italy and Romania, n. to Scandinavia, e. to Russia and Japan. Subsp. **superbus.** The typical subsp.; scarcely glaucous; petals about ¾ in. long. Lowlands. Subsp. **speciosus** (Rchb.) Pawl. [*D. speciosus* Rchb.]. Glaucous; petals more than 1 in. long. Mts.—Cvs. are: 'Albus', fls. white; 'Alpester' and 'Amoenus', listed names; 'Longicalycinus', calyx elongated; 'Monticolus', 'Oreadus', and 'Speciosus', listed names.

sylvestris Wulfen [*D. inodorus* (L.) Gaertn.]. Densely cespitose per., to 16 in., glabrous; basal lvs. many, narrow, green, wiry; epicalyx scales 2–8, leathery; calyx ½–1 in. long, petals dentate or entire, usually pink. Spain to Jura and Greece. Var. **frigidus** (Kit.) F. N. Williams [*D. frigidus* Kit.]. Sts. 3–5 in.; fls. ½–¾ in. across.

tatrae: *D. plumarius* var. *albiflorus.*

tenuifolius Schur. Similar to *D. carthusianorum*, and perhaps only a subsp. of it; differs in having sts. to 20 in.; lvs. narrower, usually setaceous; fls. usually 1–4 in a head, epicalyx scales usually green. Carpathians.

trifasciculatus Kit. Per., to 30 in.; lvs. linear-lanceolate, to ⅜ in. wide, basal lvs. few, st. lvs. 10–20 pairs, veins 7–9, sheaths long; infl. capitate, many-fld., bracts 4, green, equalling fls., epicalyx scales lanceolate to ovate, about as long as calyx, subulate at apex; calyx ½ in. long, petals bearded, to ⅜ in. long. Se. Eur.

trifidus: a listed name of no botanical standing.

tristis Velen. [*D. Pancicii* Velen.]. Related to *D. cruentus;* smaller; st. lvs. ¹⁄₁₆ in. wide; infl. capitate, bracts and epicalyx glabrous, dark brown, epicalyx awns as long as scales; calyx ⅜ in. long, dark purple, petals pink, nearly glabrous. Balkan Pen.

uralensis Korsh. Per., 8–20 in., sts. woody at base, rigid, much-branched; lvs. linear, 3-veined, sparse at base of sts.; fls. solitary, epicalyx scales 4, obovate or oblong, mucronate, calyx ½ in. long, ⅛ in. across, petals pink above, yellowish-green beneath. S. Ural Mts.

vaginatus: *D. carthusianorum;* see also *D. carthusianorum* cv.

versicolor Fisch. ex Link. Per., 6–24 in., puberulent, woody at base; lvs. linear-lanceolate, 1–3 in. long, ⅛ in. wide, puberulent; fls. solitary, epicalyx scales subulate at apex, petals pinkish-purple above, greenish beneath. Russia and Siberia.

Waldsteinii Sternb. Sts. to 20 in.; lvs. flaccid, linear, to 2 in. long; infl. capitate, bracts 4, ovate, acuminate; fls. fragrant, calyx teeth lanceolate, petals laciniate, rose, anthers blue. Pyrenees, Alps, mts. of Yugoslavia.

Welleri: a listed name of no botanical standing.

Winteri: a listed name of no botanical standing, apparently for apricot- to yellow-fld. forms of *D. plumarius.*

zonatus Fenzl. Per., 3–12 in.; lvs. linear, 1–3 in. long, ¹⁄₁₆ in. wide, acuminate; infl. branched, pedicels 2 in., epicalyx scales 4–8, to ¾ as long as calyx; calyx to ¾ in. long, ³⁄₁₆ in. across, light green, tinged purplish, teeth mucronate, petals to ½ in. long, bearded, deep pink above, yellowish beneath. Turkey, w. Syria.

DIAPENSIA L. *Diapensiaceae.* Four spp. of evergreen, tufted, per. herbs, native to N. Amer., n. Eur., and Asia; lvs. alt. to opp., simple, entire; fls. white, yellow, pink to purple, solitary on terminal peduncles, calyx 5-lobed, corolla campanulate, 5-lobed, stamens 5; fr. a caps., enclosed within calyx.

Suitable for the rock garden, but of difficult culture at low elevations.

lapponica L. Forming dense cushion, to 4 in. high, glabrous; lvs. narrowly spatulate or linear-oblong, to ½ in. long, obtuse, thick, leathery; fls. erect, white, to ¾ in. across. Early summer. Circumpolar, extending s. to mts. of N.Y. and New Eng. Var. **obovata** Friedr.-Schmidt [subsp. *obovata* (Friedr. Schmidt) Hult.; *D. obovata* (Friedr. Schmidt) Nakai]. Lvs. obovate. Alaska, n. and ne. Asia, Japan.

obovata: *D. lapponica* var.

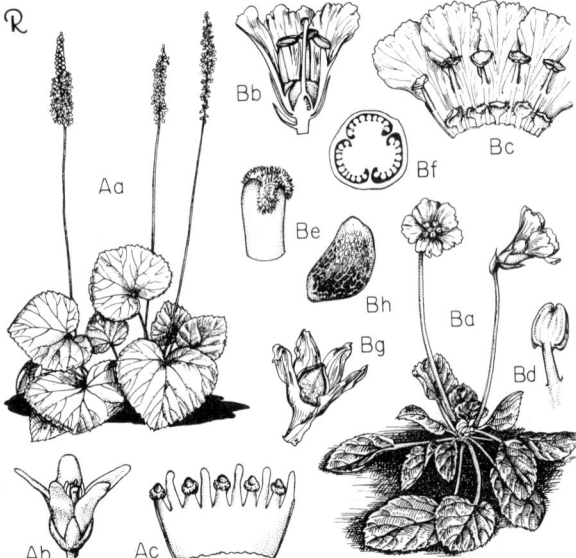

DIAPENSIACEAE. **A,** *Galax urceolata:* **Aa,** flowering plant, × ⅙; **Ab,** flower, × 3; **Ac,** staminal tube, expanded, × 4. **B,** *Shortia galacifolia:* **Ba,** flowering plant, × ¼; **Bb,** flower, vertical section, × 1; **Bc,** corolla, expanded, × 1; **Bd,** stamen, × 2; **Be,** stigma, × 6; **Bf,** ovary, cross section, × 4; **Bg,** fruit, × 1; **Bh,** seed, × 20.

DIAPENSIACEAE Lindl. DIAPENSIA FAMILY. Dicot.; about 6 genera and 10 spp. of evergreen shrublets or stemless, per. herbs, native to N. Temp. and Arctic Zones of Eurasia, and N. Amer.; lvs. alt. or basal, simple; fls. solitary or in racemes, bisexual, regular, calyx 5-lobed, corolla 5-lobed, stamens 5, inserted on corolla, sometimes alternating with 5 staminodes, ovary superior, 3-celled; fr. a 3-valved caps. *Diapensia, Galax, Pyxidanthera,* and *Shortia* are used as ground covers or cult. in rock gardens and wild gardens.

DIASCIA Link & Otto. *Scrophulariaceae.* About 50 spp. of low, slender, ann. or per. herbs of S. Afr.; lvs. mostly opp.; fls. violet or rose, in axillary or terminal racemes, calyx 5-parted, corolla 2-lipped, lower lip 2-spurred, corolla tube almost absent, stamens 4; fr. a caps., seeds many.

One species is grown in flower gardens and also as a pot plant. The cultural requirements are simple; easily propagated by seeds.

Barberae Hook.f. TWINSPUR. Erect ann., to 1 ft.; lvs. ovate, to 1½ in. long, toothed; fls. in terminal racemes to 6 in. long, corolla rosy-pink, with yellow spot in throat, ½ in. across.

DIASTEMA Benth. *Gesneriaceae.* Nearly 40 spp. of per. herbs in trop. Amer., with scaly underground rhizomes; lvs. opp.; fls. axillary or in terminal racemes, calyx 5-lobed, corolla cylindrical or more or less funnelform, limb 5-lobed, nearly regular, lobes rounded, small, stamens 4, borne at base of corolla tube, anthers united in pairs by their tips, disc of 2–5 glands, ovary half-inferior; fr. a caps.

Propagated by scaly underground rhizomes. For cultivation see *Gesneriaceae.*

maculatum (Poepp.) Benth. ex Walp. Lvs. ovate, to 3½ in. long, 1¾ in. wide, toothed, bullate, dark green, strigose; fls. in short racemes, to ⅞ in. long, tube yellowish with violet lines, limb spreading, lobes rounded, ⅛ in. long, with violet center and lilac (on upper 2) or white (on lower 3) margin, throat with violet lines. Peru.

pictum: see *D. vexans.*

quinquevulnerum Planch. & Linden. To 6 in.; lvs. of a pair slightly unequal, ovate-elliptic, to 3 in. long, 2 in. wide, sharply toothed, pale green, embossed with impressed veins; fls. 2–12 in terminal racemes, to ¾ in. long, tube white or creamy outside, yellow inside, hairy, with 3 grooves on lower side, limb of 2 erect lobes and 3 lobes directed forward, the lower 3 or all with violet spot. Venezuela.

rupestre Brandeg. To 6 in.; lvs. of a pair usually unequal, to 3½ in. long, 2 in. wide, coarsely toothed, thin, pale green; fls. up to 12 in terminal racemes, to ½ in. long, corolla tube somewhat flattened, yellowish, with 2 pale lilac grooves on lower side, lobes short, rounded, white. Mex.

vexans H. E. Moore [*D. pictum* Regel, not Benth.]. To 4 in.; lvs. ovate to lanceolate, to 3 in. long, 1½ in. wide, toothed, hairy; fls. 1 or several in axils, on pedicels to 1¼ in. long, calyx lobes oblong-elliptic, corolla funnelform, about 3 times as long as calyx, tube to ⅝ in. long, white, spotted with purple-brown, lobes ⅛ in. long, with purple-brown spot at base. Colombia.

DICENTRA Bernh. *Fumariaceae.* About 19 spp. of per. herbs, native to N. Amer. and Asia, sometimes stemless, often with rhizomes, or tubers; lvs. alt. or basal, mostly ternately compound or dissected; fls. racemose, usually nodding, irregular, corolla laterally flattened, cordate or 2-spurred at base, closed at top, composed of an outer and an inner pair of petals, stamens 6, united in 2 bundles, pistil with stigma 2–4-crested or -horned; fr. an oblong or linear caps.

Plants thrive in fertile light soil. Propagated by division of crowns or roots, or by seeds.

canadensis (J. Goldie) Walp. SQUIRREL CORN. To 1 ft., rhizome filiform, with many small yellow tubers; lvs. all basal, finely cut; fls. greenish-white, tinged with purple, fragrant, corolla cordate, inner petals conspicuously crested. Spring. Que. and Nov. Sc. to Minn., s. to N.C. and Mo.

chrysantha (Hook. & Arn.) Walp. GOLDEN-EARDROPS. To 5 ft., glaucous; lvs. 2-pinnate, to 1 ft. long; fls. erect, in large panicled racemes, bright yellow, oblong, to ⅝ in. long, outer petals saccate basally, spreading from about the middle, crests of inner petals crisped. S. Calif., Baja Calif.

Cucullaria (L.) Bernh. DUTCHMAN'S-BREECHES. To 10 in., from a cluster of small tubers; lvs. all basal, ultimate segms. linear; fls. nodding, in simple racemes, white, tipped with cream-yellow, spurs prolonged, widely divergent. Nov. Sc. to N.C., w. to Kans.

eximia (Ker-Gawl.) Torr. TURKEY CORN, STAGGERWEED, WILD BLEEDING-HEART. To 2 ft., from short, fleshy rhizome; lvs. all basal; fls. nodding in a panicle, produced almost continuously, pinkish to purple, cordate basally, narrowed above into a long neck, tips of outer petals spreading. Mts., N.Y. to Ga.

formosa (Andr.) Walp. WESTERN BLEEDING-HEART. To 18 in., from fleshy rhizome; lvs. all basal, long-petioled, glaucous beneath and often above, lf. segms. oblong; fls. in compound racemes, rose-purple to white, to ⅝ in. long, spurs short and rounded, tips of outer petals spreading and ovate. B.C. to Calif. Subsp. **formosa.** The typical subsp.;

lvs. usually glaucous only beneath; corolla rose-purple to pink or rarely white. Cv. **'Alba'.** Fls. white. Subsp. **nevadensis:** *D. nevadensis.* Subsp. **oregana** (Eastw.) Munz [*D. oregana* Eastw.]. To 10 in.; lvs. distinctly glaucous on both surfaces, corolla very shallowly cordate, outer petals cream, inner ones rose-tipped. Calif., Ore. Cv. **'Rosea'** is listed.

glauca: a listed name of no botanical standing, used for *D. formosa* subsp. *oregana.*

nevadensis Eastw. [*D. formosa* subsp. *nevadensis* (Eastw.) Munz]. Differs from *D. formosa* in having lf. segms. finer and more nearly linear, fls. distinctly smaller, outer petals cream to pinkish and less saccate basally, inner petals white with yellowish tips. Mts., cent. Calif.

ochroleuca Engelm. Similar to *D. chrysantha,* but fls. larger, to 1 in. long, straw-yellow to cream, outer petals spreading only near the apex. Dry places, Calif.

oregana: *D. formosa* subsp.

pauciflora S. Wats. Similar to *D. uniflora,* but ultimate lf. segms. linear and more acute, scapes 1–3-fld., fls. slightly larger, deeply cordate, sepals broader, and only the tips of outer petals recurved. Calif.

peregrina (J. H. Rudolph) Mak. [*D. peregrina* var. pusilla (Siebold & Zucc.) Mak.; *D. pusilla* Siebold & Zucc.]. To 6 in., from short, erect rhizome; lvs. all basal, glaucous, deeply cut, ultimate segms. linear; scapes longer than lvs., 2–3-fld.; fls. white to purple, basally cordate, outer petals strongly reflexed, inner ones purple-tipped. Summer. E. Siberia, e. to Kamchatka and Japan.

plumosa: a listed name of no botanical standing, used for *D. formosa* cv. 'Alba'.

pusilla: *D. peregrina.*

scandens (D. Don) Walp. [*D. thalictrifolia* (Wallich) Hook.f. & T. Thoms.]. Climbing, to 15 ft.; lvs. 2-ternately compound, lateral primary lfts. with 3 entire, ovate to lanceolate secondary lfts. about 1 in. long, median primary lft. modified into a tendril; racemes axillary, simple, 7–10-fld.; fls. yellow to white, tipped with pink or purplish, cordate basally and flaring toward apex, to ¾ in. long; caps. red at maturity, ovoid, to 1 in. long. Nepal to Assam, Yunnan, se. China.

spectabilis (L.) Lem. BLEEDING-HEART. To 2 ft., sts. leafy; lf. segms. broad, obovate to cuneate; racemes simple, to 9 in. long; fls. pendent, to 1$\frac{5}{16}$ in. long, basally cordate, outer petals rosy-red with tips reflexed, inner ones white and exserted. Japan. An old garden favorite. Cv. **'Alba'.** Fls. white.

thalictrifolia: *D. scandens.*

uniflora Kellogg. STEER'S-HEAD. To 3 in., from a cluster of tubers; lvs. all basal, ultimate lobes oblong; fls. solitary, white to pink, about ⅝ in. long, basally cordate, sepals lanceolate-oblong, outer petals narrow, strongly recurved from below their middle, inner petals purple-tipped. Wash. and Idaho, s. to Calif.

DICHANTHIUM Willem. *Gramineae.* About 30 spp. of per. grasses in Old World tropics; distinguished from *Andropogon* in having the lowest 1–3 pairs of spikelets male or sterile, otherwise the sessile spikelet bisexual, pedicelled spikelets male or sterile, about as long as the sessile one, upper lemma of the sessile spikelet not cleft, often stipitate and passing into the translucent base of an awn. For terminology see *Gramineae.*

annulatum (Forssk.) Stapf [*Andropogon annulatus* Forssk.]. DIAZ BLUESTEM, RINGED BEARD GRASS, BRAHMAN G., KLEBERG G. Has been confused with *D. aristatum,* from which it differs in having st. nodes with a collar of long hairs, ligule longish, racemes usually more than one, to 2⅜ in. long, and peduncle glabrous. India, China; naturalized in Tex.

aristatum (Poir.) C. E. Hubb. [*Andropogon nodosus* (Willem.) Nash]. ANGLETON GRASS, ANGLETON BLUESTEM. Sts. ascending from a decumbent base, leafy, branching, nodes glabrous or with band of short hairs; peduncle villous below the infl., racemes 1–4, approximate; sterile spikelets as conspicuous as the fertile, giving the appearance of a flat, 2-ranked, scaly spike, first glume broad, obtuse, many-nerved, awns slender, twisted and bent, to 1 in. long. Old World tropics; naturalized in Tex. Confused with *D. annulatum.*

caricosum (L.) A. Camus [*Andropogon caricosus* L.]. Distinguished from *D. annulatum* in having sheaths compressed, ligule a short, ciliate membrane, lower glume of the sessile spikelet obovate or oblong-truncate, without a median nerve. India.

DICHELOSTEMMA Kunth [*Brevoortia* A. Wood; *Stropholirion* Torr.]. *Amaryllidaceae.* About 6 spp. of low per. herbs, native to w. N. Amer.; corm dark brown, fibrous-coated; lvs. 2–5, flattened, long-linear, keeled beneath, grooved above; umbel on a slender scape, subtended by several usually colored spathe valves; fls. jointed to pedicel, bracted, perianth tube inflated or campanulate, as long as or longer than the lobes, fertile stamens usually 3 (6 in *D. pulchellum*), anthers basifixed, inserted on inner perianth lobes, staminodes 3, inserted on outer lobes, sometimes with reduced anthers, ovary superior, style enlarged apically and narrowly 3-winged, stigmas terminating the wings; fr. a loculicidal caps., seeds much longer than thick, longitudinally striate, sharply 3-angled, with ridges of equal prominence on all angles.

Culture as for *Brodiaea.*

californicum: *D. volubile.*

capitatum: *D. pulchellum.*

congestum (Sm.) Kunth [*Brodiaea congesta* Sm.]. OOKOW. Scape 1–3 ft.; lvs. to $\frac{5}{16}$ in. wide; spathe valves light purple, umbel compact, pedicels short, erect in fl. and fr., joined at base in a short pedunclelike projection above the spathe; fls. blue-violet, tube 6-angled, slightly constricted at throat. Wash. to cent. Calif. Has been confused with *D. pulchellum.*

Ida-Maia (A. Wood) Greene [*Brevoortia Ida-Maia* A. Wood; *Brodiaea coccinea* A. Gray; *Brodiaea Ida-Maia* (A. Wood) Greene]. FIRECRACKER FLOWER, FLORAL FIRECRACKER. Scape to 3 ft.; lvs. to $\frac{5}{16}$ in. wide, shorter than scape; spathe valves red-tinged, pedicels longer than valves, flexuous and somewhat pendulous in fl., turning upward in fr.; perianth tube bright red, rarely yellow, lobes light green, recurved in fl., staminodes white. Ore., n. Calif.

multiflorum (Benth.) A. Heller [*Brodiaea multiflora* Benth.]. WILD HYACINTH. Scape to 2½ ft.; spathe valves purple-tinged, umbels compact, pedicels erect, mostly shorter than spathe valves; perianth violet to lilac, to ¾ in. long, tube about as long as lobes, inflated, not angled, constricted at throat, staminodes white or violet-tinged. Ore., Calif. Sometimes offered as *Brodiaea grandiflora.*

pulchellum (Salisb.) A. Heller [*D. capitatum* (Benth.) A. Wood; *Brodiaea capitata* Benth.; *B. pulchella* (Salisb.) Greene; *Hookera pulchella* Salisb.]. BLUE-DICKS, WILD HYACINTH. Scape to 2 ft.; lvs. often as long as scape, to ½ in. wide; spathe valves tinged with purple to deep purple throughout, pedicels erect, usually shorter than spathe valves; perianth violet or rarely white, to ¾ in. long, tube not angled or constricted at throat, fertile stamens 6, those opp. the inner perianth lobes with sessile anthers and 2 lateral filament appendages, the others with smaller anthers and triangular-dilated filaments. Ore. to Baja Calif., e. to sw. Utah. Has been confused with *D. congestum.*

volubile (Kellogg) A. Heller [*D. californicum* (Torr.) A. Wood; *Brodiaea volubilis* (Kellogg) Bak.; *Stropholirion californicum* Torr.]. SNAKE LILY, TWINING BRODIAEA. Scape to 5 ft., flexuous and twining; spathe valves pink-tinged, pedicels slender, flexuous and spreading or drooping in fl., turning up in fr.; perianth light pink to rose pink, to ½ in. long, tube 6-angled, staminodes white. Calif.

DICHONDRA J. R. Forst. & G. Forst. *Convolvulaceae.* Nine spp. of small, creeping or prostrate, per. herbs, in s. U.S., Mex., W. Indies, S. Amer., Australia, New Zeal., e. Asia; lvs. cordate-orbicular to reniform, entire; fls. peduncled, solitary in the axils, minute, sometimes cleistogamous, corolla very small, greenish-yellow, open, calyx lobes hairy; fr. a 1–2-seeded caps. The spp. are sometimes difficult to distinguish.

One species is used as a substitute for lawn grass.

carolinensis Michx. LAWN LEAF. Lvs. suborbicular-reniform, to ¾ in. across, sparsely pubescent beneath, glabrous above, petioles usually to 2 in. long, weak and curved; peduncles to ¾ in. long, erect; calyx lobes usually more than twice as long as broad, longer than fr. Se. U.S., and Bermuda. May occur as a lawn weed, but probably not cult. Plants cult. under this name may be *D. micrantha.*

micrantha Urb. Lvs. suborbicular-reniform, to ½ in. across, sparsely appressed-pubescent beneath, nearly glabrous above, petioles usually less than 1½ in. long, weak and curved; peduncles to ½ in. long, erect in lower part, but sharply recurved in upper part just below fls., calyx lobes less than twice as long as broad, shorter than fr. Tex., n. Mex., W. Indies, China, s. Japan, Ryukyu Is. Zone 10. The commercial dichondra cult. as a substitute for lawn grass belongs here.

repens J. R. Forst. & G. Forst. Plants cult. under this name are probably *D. micrantha.*

DICHORISANDRA Mikan.f. *Commelinaceae.* About 30 spp. of per. herbs, native to trop. Amer.; lvs. alt., sheathing; fls. nearly regular, blue or purple, in racemes or thyrses on erect or ascending, simple or branched sts., stamens 5–6, anthers dehiscent by terminal pores; fr. a caps., seeds with an aril.

Grown under glass, in the home, or outdoors in warm regions. They require abundant water during the growing season. Propagated by seeds, cuttings, or division.

albomarginata: see *Campelia Zanonia* cv. 'Mexican Flag'.

caerulea: a listed name of no botanical standing.

musaica C. Koch & Linden. Sts. spotted; lvs. dark green above, with many dark crossbands and often purplish midrib, purple beneath; fls. blue and white, in a terminal raceme, stamens 6. Peru. Cv. 'Gigantea'. Fls. large. Var. **undata:** *Geogenanthus undatus.*

reginae (L. Linden & Rodig.). H. E. Moore [*Tradescantia reginae* L. Linden & Rodig.]. QUEEN'S SPIDERWORT. To 2 ft. or more, sts. red-purple, with green flecks and lines when young, becoming green in age; lvs. in 2 ranks, lanceolate-acuminate, often purple beneath, with silver stripes above on new growth, green with whitish flecking toward edges on old growth; fls. in compact terminal thyrses, petals blue with white base, the upper 2 overlapping, the lower deflexed, stamens 6; fr. ⁹⁄₁₆ in. long, green, mottled black before dehiscence, seeds with orange aril. Peru. Some material so labelled has proved to be *Campelia Zanonia* cv. 'Mexican Flag'.

thyrsiflora Mikan.f. To 3 ft. or more, st. simple or rarely branched; lvs. spirally arranged, glossy green, not variegated; fls. deep blue-violet. Brazil.

vittata: a listed name of no botanical standing, perhaps referable to *Rhoeo spathacea* cv. 'Variegata'.

DICHROSTACHYS (DC.) Wight & Arn. [*Cailliea* Guillem., Perrottet & A. Rich.]. *Leguminosae* (subfamily *Mimosoideae*). Several spp. of shrubs or small trees, native to tropics of Old World; lvs. alt., deciduous, 2-pinnate; fls. in spikes, petals 0, basal fls. sterile, with 10 long, slender staminodes, terminal fls. bisexual, with 10 short stamens; fr. a flat legume.

cinerea (L.) Wight & Arn. [*D. glomerata* (Forssk.) Chiov.; *Cailliea glomerata* (Forssk.) Macbr.]. Spiny, hard-wooded shrub or small tree; lvs. with 4–18 pairs of pinnae, lfts. many; infl. nodding, shorter than lvs.; sterile fls. pink or lilac, fertile ones yellow; fr. in heads, contorted, to 4 in. long. Trop. Afr., India. A serious pest in Cuba, where it is known as AROMA. Subsp. **cinerea.** The typical subsp.; lfts. linear, less than ⅛ in. wide. Arabia, Egypt to Rhodesia. Subsp. **nyassana** (Taub.) Brenan [*D. nyassana* Taub.; *Cailliea nyassana* Hort.]. Lfts. linear-oblong, broader, to more than ⅛ in. wide. Tropics, s. Afr.

glomerata: *D. cinerea.*

nyassana: *D. cinerea* subsp.

DICKSONIA L'Hér. *Dicksoniaceae.* Thirty spp. of tree ferns mostly of the mountainous tropics and warm temp. parts of the S. Hemisphere; trunk distinct, usually several ft. high; lvs. large, 2–3-pinnate; sori marginal at the tips of veins, indusia 2-valved, the outer valve seemingly formed of an incurved tooth of the pinnule.

Several species are cultivated in mild, temperate regions and in Calif. (Zone 10) and also under glass. Suitable for moist, shady sites protected from the wind. Propagated by spores. See also *Ferns.*

antarctica Labill. TASMANIAN TREE FERN. Trunk to 50 ft.; petioles greenish or mottled brown; lvs. to 6 ft. long, 3-pinnate, the central pinnae 3–4 times as long as wide, pinnules to 2 in. long, long-acute to acuminate, with 5–7 simple teeth at sides. Australia, Tasmania. Zone 10. Confused with the closely allied *D. fibrosa.* A frequent greenhouse fern.

-cicutaria: *Dennstaedtia cicutaria.*

fibrosa Colenso. WOOLLY TREE FERN, GOLDEN T. F. Trunk to 20 ft.; like *D. antarctica,* but the central pinnae 5–6 times as long as wide, the lvs. shorter, pinnules short-acute, with 2–3 simple teeth at sides. New Zeal. Zone 10.

punctilobula: *Dennstaedtia punctilobula.*

squarrosa (G. Forst.) Swartz. Trunk to 20 ft., slender, black; lvs. stiff, leathery, 3-pinnate, petioles and lower surface of rachis dark reddish to purple. New Zeal. Zone 10.

DICKSONIACEAE Bower. Ferns; 9 genera and about 155 spp., mostly tree ferns of trop. and temp. regions, with woolly hairs but without scales covering sts. and lvs., trunks erect, rarely decumbent; lvs. in a crown, usually leathery, repeatedly pinnate, often very large; sori marginal or terminal on veins, indusia 2-valved. Compare with Cyatheaceae. *Cibotium* and *Dicksonia* are cult. as ornamentals.

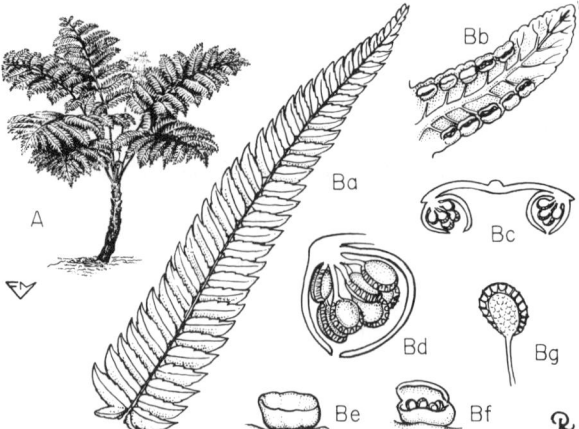

DICKSONIACEAE. **A,** *Cibotium Schiedei:* young plant, much reduced. **B,** *C. glaucum:* **Ba,** segment of leaf, × ½; **Bb,** pinnule, lower surface, × 2; **Bc,** pinnule, cross section, × 5; **Bd,** sorus and indusium, cross section, × 15; **Be,** sorus with indusium closed, × 5; **Bf,** sorus with indusium opened, × 5; **Bg,** sporangium, × 20. (A from Bailey, *Manual of Cultivated Plants,* ed. 2.)

DICLIPTERA Juss. *Acanthaceae.* Perhaps more than 150 spp. of shrubs or herbs, native to trop. and temp. parts of the world; sts. more or less hexagonal in cross section; lvs. mostly ovate, entire or undulate, petioled; fls. 1 to several in a cyme, each subtended by 2–4 conspicuous but not showy bracts, calyx 5-parted, corolla variously colored, 2-lipped, tube narrow, broadened upward, stamens 2, anther sacs often unequal, staminodes none; fr. an ovoid or suborbicular caps., seeds 2 or 4.

suberecta (André) Bremek. [*Jacobinia suberecta* André]. Per. herb, gray-velvety-tomentose, sts. weak and arching; lvs. ovate, to 2½ in. long, short-petioled; corolla brick-red, about 1¾ in. long. Uruguay. Useful as a hanging basket plant for the greenhouse or warm areas.

DICOTYLEDON (*Dicotyledoneae,* one of the two primary divisions of the angiosperms). A dicotyledon is a plant bearing two (rarely more, or sometimes only one evident) cotyledons or seed leaves, in contrast to those (monocotyledons) that have one seed leaf in the embryo; the cotyledons usually become apparent in germination. The dicotyledons (sometimes shortened to dicots) include most familiar seed plants and most of the entries in *Hortus Third.* Generally the venation of leaves is branched or reticulate (netlike). A cambium tissue is common, and hence, unlike the monocotyledons, the dicotyledons include many woody species, including the majority of trees. The floral parts occur usually in fours or fives. Dicotyledonous, pertaining to dicotyledons, is the adjectival form.

DICRANOPYGIUM Harling. *Cyclanthaceae.* About 44 spp. native from s. Mex. to Peru; plants small to medium, stemless or short-stemmed; lvs. scattered, 2-parted, petioles to twice as long as blade; fls. unisexual, male and female fls. alternating spirally on a spadix, subtended by 2–3(–4) crowded spathes, the lower ones triangular; male fls. with receptacle flat or shallowly concave, stamens exposed, female fls. united, perianth lobes reduced.

Culture as for *Carludovica.*

atrovirens (H. Wendl.) Harling [*Carludovica atrovirens* H. Wendl.]. Stemless; lvs. 2-parted to below middle, glabrous, very dark green above, segms. to 3 in. wide; male fls. with 50–60(–70) stamens. Nativity unknown; perhaps Colombia.

DICRANOSTIGMA Hook.f. & T. Thoms. *Papaveraceae.* Four spp. of herbs with woody roots, native to the Himalayas, and w. and cent. China; basal lvs. in a rosette, pinnately lobed, st. lvs. alt.; fls. yellow, petals 4, more or less at right angles to the peduncle; fr. a 2-celled caps., less than 4 in. long. Closely related to and resembling *Glaucium,* but differing in angle of attachment of petals, and in having fr. shorter, and seeds not embedded in spongy material.

Useful as rock garden plants.

Franchetianum (Prain) Fedde [*Chelidonium Franchetianum* Prain; *Glaucium vitellinum* Hort., not Boiss. & Buhse]. Glaucous ann., variable in size from low, compact plants with basal lvs. about 3 in. long, to much-branched plants to 5–6 ft. high with basal lvs. to 12 in. long; st. lvs. coarsely toothed, clasping, to 1½ in. long; fls. somewhat nodding, clear yellow, to 2 in. across, petals widely spreading; caps. oblong, tapering toward apex, to 3 in. long, glabrous or somewhat tubercled. W. China. Material offered under this name is sometimes *D. leptopodum.*

lactucoides Hook.f. & T. Thoms. To 2 ft.; basal lvs. 5–10 in. long, st. lvs. 2 in. long or more; fls. yellow, 2 in. across; caps. to 2¼ in. long, pubescent. Himalayas. Distinguished from *D. Franchetianum* and *D. leptopodum* by having buds rounded at apex and caps. velvety-hairy.

leptopodum (Maxim.) Fedde. Similar to *D. Franchetianum*, but having fls. smaller, to 1¼ in. across, and caps. linear, not tapering toward the apex. China. Sometimes offered as *D. Franchetianum.*

DICTAMNUS L. *Rutaceae.* One sp., an extremely variable per. herb, from s. Eur., to n. China; lvs. alt., pinnate, glandular-dotted; fls. white to rose, in terminal racemes, irregular, sepals and petals 5, stamens 10, curved upward; fr. a deeply 5-lobed caps.

albus L. [*D. Fraxinella* Pers.]. DITTANY, FRAXINELLA, GAS PLANT, BURNING BUSH. Strong-smelling, long-enduring, hardy per., to 3 ft.; lfts. 9–11, to 3 in. long, ovate, serrulate; fls. about 1 in. long. Foliage emits an ethereal inflammable oil. Cv. 'Purpureus'. Fls. dark. Cv. 'Ruber'. Fls. rosy-purple. Var. **caucasicus** (Fisch. & C. A. Mey.) Rouy [*D. caucasicus* (Fisch. & C. A. Mey.) Grossh.]. Large form, racemes longer, petals ovate.

caucasicus: *D. albus* var.

Fraxinella: *D. albus.*

DICTYOSPERMA H. Wendl. & Drude. PRINCESS PALM. *Palmae.* Two spp. of unarmed, monoecious palms in the Mascarene Is.; lvs. pinnate, sheaths forming a crownshaft, pinnae acute to acuminate; infls. infrafoliar, short-peduncled, with 2 deciduous bracts, the upper enclosed by the lower, brs. simple or the lower once-branched, rachillae with fls. in triads (2 male and 1 female) at least in lower half and above these with paired or solitary male fls.; male fls. asymmetrical, sepals imbricate, petals valvate, about 3 times as long as sepals, stamens 6, filaments inflexed at the apex in bud, pistillode slender, shorter than stamens, female fls. globose, sepals and petals imbricate, staminodes very small, pistil 1-celled, 1-ovuled; fr. ovoid or ellipsoid with apical stigmatic residue, endocarp thin, operculate, seed with deeply ruminate endosperm and basal ovule.

Elegant feather palms of fairly rapid growth. Grown for ornament in humid tropical and subtropical gardens, and in Zone 10 in southern Fla. For culture see *Palms.*

album (Bory) H. Wendl. & Drude ex Scheff. [*D. rubrum* Nichols.]. COMMON P. P. To 45 ft. or more; trunk closely ringed, dark gray or blackish; lvs. to 12 ft. long, with 50 or more regularly arranged pinnae on each side, pinnae to 2 ft. long, 1³⁄₁₆ in. wide, with strong secondary veins, acuminate; infl. spreading to drooping, to 16 in. long; male fls. to ⁵⁄₁₆ in. long, reddish-yellow; fr. about ½ in. long. Sometimes offered under the name *Areca rubra.* Nearly extinct where native, now found mostly as a cult. ornamental in trop. gardens.

aureum (Balf.f.) Nichols. [*D. album* var. *aureum* Balf.f.] YELLOW P. P. To 25 ft.; lvs. to 3 ft. long, pinnae without prominent secondary veins, acute; infl. erect or ascending; male fls. white or yellow, to ¼ in. long.

fibrosum: *Vonitra fibrosa.*

rubrum: *D. album.*

DIDIPLIS: *PEPLIS.*

DIDISCUS: *TRACHYMENE.* **D. pusillus:** *T. pilosa.*

DIDYMAOTUS N. E. Br. *Aizoaceae.* One sp. of stemless, succulent, per. herbs, native to S. Afr.; lvs. 2 or rarely more, opp., very fleshy, composing a thick, rather ellipsoid plant body (growth); fls. solitary, bracted, on both sides at base of growth, calyx nearly equally 6-lobed, petals many, stamens many, erect, disc glandular, entire, ovary inferior, 6-celled,

stigmas 6, plumose on inner face; fr. a caps. only partly covered by cell lids, placental tubercles absent.

Resting period occurs in early summer. Culture difficult, the plants requiring very dry soil with maximum sunlight in the greenhouse. Propagated by seeds. See also *Succulents.*

lapidiformis (Marloth) N. E. Br. Growths to 2 in. long; lvs. whitish gray-green, rough, to ¾ in. long, 1¼ in. across, triangular in top view and flat or somewhat convex with somewhat hooded margins, keeled beneath; fls. about 1⅝ in. across, petals pink, the tips sometimes darker, filaments violet. Cape Prov.

DIDYMOCARPUS Wallich ex D. Don. *Gesneriaceae.* Asiatic per. herbs similar to *Chirita*, but differing in having stigma capitate instead of oblique and often 2-lobed.

For cultivation see *Gesneriaceae.*

aurantiacus C. B. Clarke. Sts. short, villous; lvs. 2–4, ovate, to 6 in. long, toothed, villous; peduncles to 4 in. long, pedicels 1 in. long; calyx to ⅛ in. long, purplish, corolla elongate-funnelform, 1⅜ in. long, orange-red. Himalayas.

lanuginosus: *Corallodiscus lanuginosus.*

Mortonii C. B. Clarke. Sts. to 6 in., hairy; lvs. in 1–3 pairs, hairy above, the lowest largest, blades ovate, to 6 in. long, 4 in. wide, toothed; peduncles several, axillary, branched, 2–3 in. long; fls. pedicelled, calyx often concealed by bractlets, calyx lobes slender, less than ³⁄₁₆ in. long, corolla tube narrow, nearly ½ in. long, limb flat, purple, to ½ in. across; caps. nearly 1 in. long. Himalayas. Much of the material grown under this name proves to be *Streptocarpus Rexii.*

podocarpus C. B. Clarke. Sts. to 8 in., pale-hairy; lvs. in 2 pairs, ovate or elliptic, to 6 in. long, 4 in. wide, coarsely crenate, minutely hairy; peduncles 2–4 in axils, to 2½ in. long, pedicels subtended by broad, rounded, colored bracts; calyx campanulate, ¼ in. long, corolla purple, 1 in. long; caps. stalked, to twice as long as calyx. Himalayas.

pulcher C. B. Clarke. Sts. to 1 ft.; lvs. oblong or elliptic, unequal, to 4⅜ in. long, 2 in. wide, entire to toothed, minutely hairy above; peduncles terminal and axillary, to 3¼ in. long, with colored bracts; calyx campanulate, ¼ in. long, rose-purple, corolla to 1¼ in. long, dark purple, hairy outside; caps. to 1⅝ in. long. Himalayas.

DIDYMOPANAX Decne. & Planch. *Araliaceae.* Twenty or more spp. of spineless, tomentose shrubs or trees of trop. Amer.; lvs. palmately compound, lfts. whorled at the end of the petiole; infl. of umbels arranged in terminal or lateral panicles or racemes; fls. 5-merous, ovary 2–3-celled, styles 2–3, separate; fr. a somewhat flattened drupe, pyrenes 2.

Morototoni (Aubl.) Decne. & Planch. Tree with slender trunk, to 45 ft.; lvs. clustered at apex, lfts. 10–12, leathery, to 10 in. long, acuminate, those of mature plants entire, glabrous above, gray-pubescent beneath, those of juvenile plants conspicuously serrate-margined, hispid above and only slightly hairy beneath; umbels in panicles; fr. leathery, mostly ¼ in. long and nearly ½ in. broad. W. Indies, trop. N. and S. Amer. Zone 10b. Wood used for general carpentry and pulp.

DIDYMOSPERMA: *ARENGA.* **D. distichum:** *Wallichia disticha.*

DIEFFENBACHIA Schott. DUMB CANE, DUMB PLANT, MOTHER-IN-LAW'S TONGUE PLANT, TUFTROOT. *Araceae.* About 30 spp. of erect herbs, native to trop. Amer., sts. stout, unbranched, bearing lvs. toward the top; lvs. entire, petioles sheathing, often variegated; peduncle short, spathe greenish, convolute, spadix with lower (female) part united to spathe on one side; fls. unisexual, female fls. with conspicuous staminodes. With skunklike odor when bruised.

Through hybridization and natural mutation, many fancy-leaved dieffenbachias have arisen in cultivation. Cultivars considered to have originated from *D. Seguine* and *D. maculata* [*D. picta*] are listed under these species.

Favorite plants for greenhouses and interior decoration. Of easy culture in peaty loam with constant moisture and protection from drafts and temperatures below 60° F. Propagated by terminal cuttings, or 2–3 in. stem pieces laid in rooting medium. For large specimens, pot several plants of different heights together in one container. Tall plants may be topped and the tips rooted, or the tip may be air layered before it is cut off.

amoena Bull. Not in cult.; but name applied to a plant of huge size, to 6 ft. or more, and having lf. blades elliptic-oblong, to 20 in. long, obtuse-subtruncate basally, dark green with irregular zones of creamy-white along primary lateral veins, petioles to 12 in. long, sheathing and very broadly winged to about half their length, and spathe about 5 in. long.

Baraquiniana: *D. maculata* cv.

×**Bausei** Hort. ex M. T. Mast. & T. Moore: *D. maculata* × *D. Weirii* Berk. Lf. blades broadly lanceolate, to 12 in. long and half as wide, subtruncate basally, yellow-green, marked with few irregular, large, dark green spots or blotches and smaller white spots, dark green marginally, petioles to 8 in. long, green, broad-sheathing to half their length, whitish at base; spathe 12 in. long.

Bowmannii Hort. Veitch. Lf. blades narrowly ovate-elliptic, inequilateral, to 2 ft. long or more, truncate basally, with intermingled light and dark green elongate blotches oriented nearly parallel to primary lateral veins, midrib and margins green, petioles to 12 in. long, broad-sheathing in lower half, very pale toward base; spathe to 7 in. long, mottled. E. Brazil.

brasiliense: *D. maculata.*

chelsoni Bull. Lf. blades oblong, truncate basally, dark green with satiny luster, with many, irregular, greenish-yellow blotches and leathery-margined gray stripe along midrib, petioles shorter than blades, sheathing and winged to half their length; infl. unknown. Colombia.

daguensis Engl. To 4 ft. or more, sts. 2 in. in diam.; lf. blades obovate, 16 in. long, basally obtuse, bright green, with many wide-spreading lateral veins, petioles very short, long-sheathing; spathe 10 in. long. Colombia.

delecta Nichols. Sts. mottled green; lf. blades elliptic-lanceolate, 8–10 in. long, with a satiny luster and white variegation. Colombia. Material cult. under this name has lvs. pendent, narrow, with irregular yellow zone along midrib.

eburnea: probably *D. maculata* cv. 'Lancifolium'.

exotica: a listed name of no botanical standing; applied to a plant of compact habit; with lf. blades ovate, to 10 in. long and 4¾ in. wide, subcordate basally, dark green, heavily variegated with white or greenish-white, occasionally with some areas of pure green, midrib variegated green and white, petioles green, sheathing to well above half their length. Costa Rica.

Fosteri: a listed name of no botanical standing; applied to a plant similar to *D. Oerstedii*, but smaller and having lvs. with a satiny sheen. Costa Rica.

Fournieri Hort. Makoy ex M. T. Mast. Vigorous; lf. blades broadly oblong-lanceolate, to 15 in. long, basally truncate, dark green with small ivory spots and blotches parallel with lateral veins, midrib variegated pale green and ivory, petioles sheathing and broadly winged about half their length; spathe pale green, 5½ in. long. Colombia.

Hoffmannii: a listed name of no botanical standing; applied to a plant similar to *D. exotica* but having lf. blades broadly oblong-lanceolate, to 15 in. long and 6 in. wide, truncate at base, dark green with a satiny luster, midrib white, variegated green only near base, and petioles variegated white longitudinally. Costa Rica.

imperialis Linden & André. Lf. blades elliptic-ovate, to 2 ft. long, basally obtuse or subcordate, leathery, dark green, irregularly spotted yellow, midrib silvery, petioles as long as blades. Peru.

Jenmannii: *D. maculata* cv.

latimaculata Linden & André. Lf. blades lanceolate-oblong, to 16 in. long and 6 in. wide, basally obtuse, dark green, marked with few, irregular, large yellow spots, petioles to 5 in. long, sheathing and broadly winged nearly to apex; spathe 6 in. long. Colombia. Probably not in cult.; material offered under this name is *D. Bowmannii.*

Leonii: a listed name of no botanical standing; applied to a plant having lf. blades elliptic-oblong, to 10 in. long and 3½ in. wide, basally truncate, dark green with a satiny sheen and heavily variegated with large, irregular, yellow-green spots and blotches, whitish along green midrib, petioles slender, not much shorter than blades. Colombia.

Leopoldii Bull. Lf. blades broadly elliptic to ovate, to 14 in. long and 8 in. wide, basally truncate to subcordate, dark green, with a velvety sheen, midrib ivory, petioles shorter than blades, sheathing to half their length; spathe white, 6½ in. long. Costa Rica.

longispatha Engl. & Kurt Krause. Lf. blades elongate-oblong-lanceolate, to 22 in. long and 8–9 in. wide, basally obtuse, leathery, petioles to 16 in. long, very broadly sheathing ¾ their length; spathe to 17 in. long; female fls. large and sparse. Panama, Colombia.

maculata (Lodd.) G. Don [*D. brasiliense* Hort. Veitch; *D. picta* Schott]. SPOTTED D. C. Distinguished from *D. Seguine* in having lf. blades generally oblong or lanceolate, narrower, apically acuminate, often irregularly heavily white-spotted, with many pairs of primary lateral veins. Cent. Amer., n. S. Amer. Cv. 'Baraquiniana' [*D. Baraquiniana* Versch. & Lem.; *D. picta* var. *Baraquiniana* (Versch. & Lem.) Engl.]. Lf. blades oblong-lanceolate, basally obtuse, light

green, sparsely white-splotched, midribs white, especially beneath, petioles white. Cv. 'Jenmannii' [*D. Jenmannii* Hort. Veitch; *D. picta* var. *Jenmannii* Hort.]. Slender; lf. blades oblong, to 10 in. long and 2½ in. wide, nearly truncate or obtuse basally, green with irregular ivory markings along primary lateral veins, petioles 5–6 in. long. Guyana. Cv. 'Lancifolium' [*D. eburnea* Bull?; apparently not *D. lancifolium* Linden & André]. Differs in having lf. blades very narrowly lanceolate-oblong, to 10 in. long and 2 in. wide, attenuate at each end, closely white-spotted, petioles nearly as long as blades, reddish. Acre (Brazil). Cv. 'Rudolph Roehrs' [*D. Roehrsii* Hort.]. YELLOW-LEAF D. C. Mutant; newer lvs. ovate-elliptic, nearly cordate basally, mostly cream-white or chartreuse finely splotched white, midrib and margins green. Cv. 'Shuttleworthii' [*D. Shuttleworthiana* Bull]. Lf. blades narrowly elliptic-lanceolate, obtuse or truncate basally, green, midrib white, with a broad silvery-white band, petioles sheathing in basal ¼. Colombia. Cv. 'Superba'. Mutant; lf. blades very heavily splotched cream-white, midrib and margins green. Cv. 'Viridis'. Lf. blades oblong, nearly cordate basally, green. N. Brazil.

×**memoria-Corsii** Fenzi [*D. picta* var. *memoria* Hort.]: *D. maculata* × *D. Wallisii* Linden. Lf. blades elliptic-oblong, green, irregularly marked with gray-silver, especially along midrib, and with a few scattered white spots, petioles about 3 in. long, broadly sheathing nearly to base of blade in lvs. of adult phase, the sheaths apically auriculate; spathe 5 in. long.

nervosum: a listed name of no botanical standing.

Oerstedii Schott. To 3 ft.; lf. blades lanceolate-oblong to ovate, conspicuously inequilateral, to 10 in. long, truncate to emarginate basally, green, petioles shorter than blades, sheathing to about half their length; spathe 6–9 in. long; berries red. Mex. to Costa Rica. Cv. 'Variegata'. Midribs of lvs. and bases of petioles white.

Parlatorei Linden & André. To 3 ft.; lf. blades broadly oblanceolate, to 2 ft. long and 1 ft. wide, green or spotted yellowish-green, leathery, petioles very short, sheathing and broadly winged nearly to blades, sheaths apically auriculate; spathe to 7 in. long. Colombia. Cv. 'Marmorea'. Lf. blades with large, irregular blotches of white dotted with green, midribs white-streaked.

picta: *D. maculata.* Var. **Baraquiniana:** *D. maculata* cv. Var. **Jenmannii:** *D. maculata* cv. Var. **memoria:** *D. memoria-Corsii.*

Pittieri Engl. & Kurt Krause. Lf. blades oblique-oblong, to 9 in. long and 3 in. wide, basally obtuse to subacute, petioles to 5 in. long, sheathing and broadly winged up to blade; spathe to 8 in. long. Panama. Some material offered under this name differs in having lvs. elliptic-oblong, larger, basally emarginate-auriculate, dull dark green, irregularly marked with few to many pale green or white blotches. Panama.

pseudobractea: a listed name of no botanical standing.

Roehrsii: *D. maculata* cv. 'Rodolph Roehrs'.

Seguine (Jacq.) Schott. MOTHER-IN-LAW PLANT. Variable, huge, to 10 ft.; lf. blades oblong-elliptic to lanceolate or ovate, to 15 in. long or more, short-cuspidate, truncate, subcordate, or acute basally, glossy and dark green above or variously variegated, with a broad midrib and 9–15 pairs of primary lateral veins, petioles green or striate-spotted, somewhat shorter than blades, often sheathing more than half their length; spathe to 10 in. long. Trop. Amer. Cv. 'Liturata' [var. *liturata* (Schott) Engl.]. Lf. blades elliptic-oblong, obtuse-subtruncate basally, dark green, midrib with narrow yellowish-white zone on each side. Cv. 'Nobilis' [var. *nobilis* Versch. ex Engl., not *D. nobilis* Bull]. Differs in having lf. blades elliptic, dark green, marked with emerald-green spots. Para (Brazil).

Shuttleworthiana: *D. maculata* cv. 'Shuttleworthii'.

×**splendens** Bull: *D. Leopoldii* × *D. maculata.* Lf. blades elliptic, to 12 in. long and 5½ in. wide, abruptly long-acuminate, truncate basally, finely undulate, dark green with a velvety sheen, with many small, irregular, lime-green spots widely dispersed, midrib broad, creamy, petioles to 6 in. long, sheathing and broadly winged more than half their length; spathe to 5 in. long.

DIERAMA C. Koch. WANDFLOWER. *Iridaceae.* About 25 spp. of summer-blooming, cormous herbs, native to trop. and S. Afr.; sts. often tall, arching, branched; fls. in spikes, nodding or rarely erect, perianth tube funnelform, short, segms. spreading broadly, style brs. 3, club-shaped; fr. a small, membranous caps.

Cultivated in the open in Calif. and under glass in cold climates. Corms started in wire baskets under glass may be planted in open beds in colder climate.

gracile N. E. Br. to 20 in.; lvs. 3–4, to 9 (–12) in. long, ⅛ in. wide; spikes 2–4, to 1⅜ in. long, 3–7-fld., bracts membranous, light brown, to ½ in. long; fls. pendulous, corolla funnelform, mauve, to ⁹⁄₁₆ in. long, tube to ³⁄₁₆ in. long, segms. to ⅜ in. long, some with a dark purple spot at base. Transvaal.

intermedium: a listed name of no botanical standing.

pendulum (L.f.) Bak. [*Sparaxis pendula* (L.f.) Ker-Gawl.]. GRASSY-BELL, ANGELS'-FISHING-RODS. Sts. to 5½ ft.; basal lvs. 5–8, rigid, linear, to 3 ft. long, ¼ in. wide; bracts membranous, whitish, speckled with small brown lines, 1 in. long or less; fls. pendulous, pink, to 1⁹⁄₁₆ in. long, tube to ⅜ in. long; seeds many, globose, brownish-black. S. Afr.

pulcherrimum (Hook.f.) Bak. [*Sparaxis pulcherrima* Hook.f.]. Differs from *D. pendulum* in having bracts 1–1⅛ in. long, perianth dark violet-purple, 1⅜–1⅝ in. long, tube to ½ in. long, and lobes to 1³⁄₁₆ in. long. S. Afr.

DIERVILLA Mill. BUSH HONEYSUCKLE. *Caprifoliaceae.* Three spp. of small, deciduous shrubs of e. N. Amer., spreading by means of underground sts. and forming colonies; lvs. opp., simple; fls. yellow, in small, leafless, axillary clusters sometimes aggregated into terminal cymes, calyx 5-lobed, corolla 2-lipped, 5-lobed, stamens 5, exserted, ovary inferior, 2-celled; fr. a slender 2-valved caps., seeds many, minute.

Useful for holding banks, for background plantings, and as tall ground cover. Propagated readily by suckers.

Dropmoreana: a listed name of no botanical standing.

Lonicera Mill. [*D. lutea* Pursh; *D. trifida* Moench]. To 4 ft., spreading, branchlets cylindrical, glabrous or essentially so; lvs. ovate to elliptic, to 4 in. long, acuminate, distinctly petioled; corolla yellow, darkening with age, about 1 in. long. Banks and rocky places, Nfld. to Sask., s. to N.C. and Mich. Zone 4.

lutea: *D. Lonicera.*

rivularis Gatt. To 6 ft., branchlets cylindrical, densely pubescent; lvs. ovate to oblong-lanceolate, to 3 in. long, acuminate, nearly sessile; corolla lemon-yellow. Mts. and highlands, N.C., Tenn., Ga., Ala. Zone 6.

sessilifolia Buckl. To 5 ft., branchlets quadrangular, nearly glabrous; lvs. ovate-lanceolate, to 6 in. long, gradually acuminate, sessile; corolla sulphur-yellow. Va. and Tenn., s. to Ga. and Ala. Zone 5.

×**splendens** (Carrière) Kirchn. [*Weigela splendens* Carrière]: *D. Lonicera* × *D. sessilifolia.* Very similar to *D. sessilifolia,* but lvs. short-petioled.

trifida: *D. Lonicera.*

DIETES Salisb. ex Klatt. *Iridaceae.* About 5 spp. of herbs with creeping, stout rhizomes, native to trop. and s. Afr., 1 sp. to Lord Howe Is.; lvs. 2-ranked, linear to sword-shaped; fls. fugacious, perianth tube none, perianth segms. 6, inner segms. smaller than outer, stamens 3, filaments separate, style brs. 3, petaloid; fr. a 3-valved caps.

Cultivation as for *Iris.*

bicolor Sweet [*Moraea bicolor* (Sweet) Spae]. Sts. to 2 ft.; lvs. to 2½ ft. long; fls. to 2 in. across, lemon-yellow, outer perianth segms. with a blackish-brown basal spot. S. Afr.

catenulata: *D. vegeta.*

grandiflora N. E. Br. Sts. to 4 ft.; lvs. not 2-ranked, to 4 ft. long, erect; fls. to 4½ in. across, with orange-yellow and brownish basal spots, outer perianth segms. with yellow-bearded keel, style brs. banded with violet. S. Afr.

iridoides: *D. vegeta.*

Robinsoniana (F. J. Muell.) Klatt [*Moraea Robinsoniana* (F. J. Muell.) Benth.]. Sts. to 6 ft.; lvs. to 6 ft. long, firm; infl. branched; fls. to 4 in. across, white. Lord Howe Is. (Australia).

Saundersiae: a listed name of no botanical standing.

vegeta (L.) N. E. Br. [*D. catenulata* (Lindl.) Sweet; *D. iridoides* (L.) Sweet; *Moraea catenulata* Lindl.; *M. iridoides* L.; *M. vegeta* L.]. AFRICAN IRIS. Sts. to 2 ft.; lvs. 2-ranked, spreading like a fan; fls. to 2½ in. across, white, outer perianth segms. with yellow or brown spots, crests of style marked with blue. S. Afr. Cv. 'Johnsonii'. Lvs. longer, erect; fls. 4 in. across.

DIGITALIS L. FOXGLOVE. *Scrophulariaceae.* About 19 spp. of summer-flowering per. or bien. herbs, rarely shrubby, native from Eur. and nw. Afr. to cent. Asia; lvs. alt., simple, in basal rosettes in young plants, lower lvs. often very long; fls. showy, in terminal, often one-sided racemes, calyx 5-parted, corolla purple, yellow, brownish, or white, often spotted or streaked inside, somewhat 2-lipped, tube inflated or campanulate, stamens 4; fr. a septicidal caps.

The important cardiac drug, digitalis, is obtained from *D. purpurea* and *D. lanata.* Foxgloves are easily grown. The perennial species are propagated by seeds or by division. The common species and cultivars are usually treated as biennials, the seeds sown in the spring or summer, and producing flowering plants the following season.

alba: *D. purpurea* subsp. *purpurea* cv.

alpina: a listed name of no botanical standing.

Amandiana: *D. purpurea* subsp. *purpurea* var.

ambigua: *D. grandiflora.*

campanulata: *D. purpurea* subsp. *purpurea* cv.

canariensis: *Isoplexis canariensis,* but material grown as *D. canariensis* is sometimes *D. grandiflora.*

cariensis Boiss. ex Jaub. & Spach. Per., to 3 ft., sts. white-glandular-pubescent; fls. in dense to loose, interrupted racemes, calyx about half as long to nearly as long as corolla tube, lobes elliptic, corolla whitish-cream, all but lower lip finely striped red outside. E. Medit. Subsp. **cariensis.** The typical subsp.; racemes dense; calyx nearly as long as corolla tube. Subsp. **Lamarckii** (Ivanina) Werner [*D. orientalis* Lam., not Mill.]. Racemes very loose; calyx about half as long as corolla tube.

dubia Rodr. Dwarf per., to 1½ ft.; lvs. lanceolate, often more or less covered with white hairs; fls. in few-fld. racemes, corolla pink or purplish, spotted inside. Balearic Is.

ferruginea L. RUSTY F. Bien. or per., to 6 ft.; lvs. linear to oblong-lanceolate, glabrous or ciliate, sessile; calyx lobes ovate, scarious-margined, corolla to 1½ in. long, yellowish, marked with rusty-red, pubescent, middle lobe of lower lip longer than others. S. Eur. and w. Asia.

fulva Lindl. To 3 ft.; lvs. lanceolate, ciliate; corolla to 1⅜ in. long, yellow with rusty reticulations, funnelform, ventricose, hairy, middle lobe of lower lip longer than others. Nativity unknown; thought to be a hybrid between *D. grandiflora* and *D. purpurea.*

gloxiniiflora, gloxinioides: *D. purpurea* subsp. *purpurea* cv.

grandiflora Mill. [*D. ambigua* J. Murr.; *D. orientalis* Mill.]. YELLOW F. Hairy per. or bien., to 3 ft.; lvs. ovate-lanceolate, to 8 in. long, serrate, becoming smaller and sessile or clasping up the st.; calyx lobes linear, corolla to 2 in. long, yellowish, marked with brown. Eur. and w. Asia.

isabellina: *D. purpurea* subsp. *purpurea* cv.

laciniata: *D. obscura* subsp.

laevigata Waldst. & Kit. Glabrous per., to 3 ft.; lvs. obovate to linear-lanceolate; calyx lobes oblong, corolla to 1¼ in. long, yellow marked brown-purple, middle lobe of lower lip longer than others. S. Eur.

lanata J. F. Ehrh. GRECIAN F. Per. or bien., to 3 ft., sts. glabrous in lower part, white-hairy above; lvs. lanceolate, glabrous; fls. in dense racemes, calyx shorter than bracts, corolla as long as or shorter than bracts, 1 in. long, nearly white, with fine veins, middle lobe of lower lip longer than others. Danube region and Greece; naturalized in ne. N. Amer. Dried lvs. a source of the drug, digitalis.

lutea L. Glabrous or somewhat pubescent per., to 3 ft.; lvs. oblong or lanceolate; calyx lobes lanceolate, corolla to 1 in. long, yellow to white, upper lip 2-parted. Sw. and cent. Eur. and nw. Afr. Subsp. **lutea.** The typical subsp.; racemes one-sided, corolla ⅝–1 in. long, with recurved lateral lobes. Subsp. **australis** (Ten.) Arcang. [*D. micrantha* Schrad. ex Elmig.]. Racemes not one-sided; corolla ⅜–⅝ in. long, lateral lobes not recurved. Cent. and s. Italy, Corsica. Var. **grandiflora** Hort. is listed.

Lutzii Hort. A group of hybrids with fls. in shades of salmon.

maculata: *D. purpurea* subsp. *purpurea* cv.

mariana: *D. purpurea* subsp.

×**mertonensis** Buxt. & Darl.: *D. grandiflora* × *D. purpurea.* Very large, true-breeding tetraploid hybrid; fls. to 2¼ in. long.

micrantha: *D. lutea* subsp. *australis.*

monstrosa: *D. purpurea* subsp. *purpurea* cv.

nervosa Steud. & Hochst. ex Benth. Per., to 3 ft.; lower lvs. oblanceolate, upper lvs. sessile; racemes long, dense, corolla yellowish, small. Cent. Asia.

nevadensis: *D. purpurea* subsp. *purpurea* var.

obscura L. WILLOW-LEAVED F. Glabrous, woody-based per., to 2 ft.; lvs. narrowly linear-lanceolate, entire or deeply toothed, glabrous; corolla yellow, with bright red veins inside, tube very short. Spain. Subsp. **obscura.** The typical subsp.; lvs. entire. Subsp. **laciniata** (Lindl.) Maire [*D. laciniata* Lindl.]. Lvs. usually deeply toothed.

orientalis: *D. grandiflora,* but material cult. as *D. orientalis* is *D. cariensis* subsp. *Lamarckii.*

parviflora Jacq. Per., to 3 ft.; lvs. obovate or oblong-lanceolate; fls. in dense racemes, corolla to ½ in. long, brownish-purple. Mts., n. Spain.

purpurea L. COMMON F. Bien. or per., to 4 ft.; basal lvs. lanceolate to ovate or broadly ovate, long-petioled, st. lvs. sessile or short-petioled; fls. drooping, in one-sided racemes to 2 ft. long, calyx lobes ovate, corolla to 3 in. long, purple or sometimes pink or white, rarely yellowish, more or less spotted inside. A polymorphic sp. centered in w. Medit. region. Dried lvs. are principal source of the drug digitalis. Subsp. **purpurea**. The typical subsp.; lower lvs. lanceolate to ovate, greenish to whitish, glabrous to tomentose, gradually tapered to petiole; corolla purple or sometimes pink or white, rarely yellowish. Var. **purpurea**. The typical var.; variable. Cvs. are: 'Alba' [*D. alba* Schrank], fls. white; 'Campanulata' [*D. campanulata* Hort.], upper fls. united into large bell-shaped blooms; 'Gloxiniiflora' [*D. gloxiniiflora* Hort.; *D. gloxinioides* Carrière], more robust in habit, infl. longer, fls. wide-open; 'Isabellina' [*D. isabellina* Hort.], fls. yellowish; 'Maculata' [*D. maculata* Hort.], fls. spotted; 'Monstrosa' [*D. monstrosa* Hort.], form in which the terminal fl. is regular; 'Rosea', fls. rose. Var. **Amandiana** (Samp.) Werner [*D. Amandiana* Samp.]. Sts. glabrous, shining; lvs. mostly glabrous. Portugal. Var. **nevadensis** (Kunze) Amo [*D. nevadensis* Kunze]. Fls. pubescent outside. Mts. of Spain. Var. **tomentosa** (Link & Hoffmanns.) Webb [*D. tomentosa* Link & Hoffmanns.]. Taller, white-tomentose. Iberian Pen. Subsp. **mariana** (Boiss.) Riv.-God. [*D. mariana* Boiss.]. Lower lvs. broadly ovate, white-tomentose, more or less shortly contracted at base; corolla purple. Portugal, Spain.

×**sibirica** Lindl. A hybrid with *D. grandiflora* as one parent; hairy per., to 3 ft.; lvs. ovate-lanceolate; calyx lobes linear, corolla yellowish, middle lobe of lip much longer than others. Most material now cult. under this name is *D. grandiflora*.

thapsi L. Similar to *D. purpurea*, but plants covered with yellow, glandular hairs. Portugal, Spain.

tomentosa: *D. purpurea* subsp. *purpurea* var.

DIGITARIA Heist. ex Fabr. [*Syntherisma* Walt.]. CRAB-GRASS, FINGER GRASS. *Gramineae*. Over 100 spp. of ann. or per., often weedy cosmopolitan, grasses; infl. of slender racemes digitate or approximate on a short axis; spikelets lanceolate or elliptic, rounded on one side, nearly flat on the other, paired or in 3's, rarely solitary, subsessile or short-pedicelled, alt. in 2 rows on one side of a 3-angled winged or wingless rachis, first glume minute or absent, second glume equal to or shorter than the sterile lemma, fertile lemma cartilaginous, margins thin, pale. For terminology see *Gramineae*.

decumbens Stent. PANGOLA GRASS. Distinguished from *D. Pentzii* in having less densely clustered and more leafy sts., nearly glabrous sheaths, racemes spreading at maturity, usually slightly shorter spikelets, glabrous or sparingly silky between the nerves. S. Afr.; introd. as a pasture grass in Fla., Ga., and s. Calif.

didactyla Willd. BLUE COUCH GRASS, BLUE F.G. Ann., sts. to 16 in. long, slender, clustered, geniculate at base, then erect; lf. blades linear, acute, sheaths 1–2 in. long, glabrous; spikes 2–3, ascending, to 1½ in. long, the rachis flexuous, glabrous, flattened; spikelets oblong, acute, glossy, less than 1/16 in. long, glumes ciliate at the margins. Mauritius, Madagascar. Cult. in Fla. for pasture and putting greens.

Pentzii Stent. PENTZ F.G. Per., stoloniferous, sts. densely clustered, erect, with conspicuously hairy sheaths; racemes 3–12, ascending to spreading, approximate on a short axis; spikelets about 1/8 in. long, villous, first glume reduced, upper glume 2/3 as long as spikelet. S. Afr.; introd. for pasture in the s. states. Must be planted by cuttings.

sanguinalis (L.) Scop. HAIRY C. Ann., sts. to 3 ft. long, branching and spreading, often purplish, rooting at the decumbent base, flowering shoots ascending; lf. sheaths papillose-pilose, at least on the lower nodes, blades to 3/8 in. wide, glabrous to scaberulous; racemes few to several, to 6 in. long, digitate with usually 1–2 whorls a short distance below, rachis glabrous, winged or flat-margined, pedicels angled, scabrous; spikelets about 1/8 in. long, second glume about half as long as the spikelet or less, sterile lemma with spicules. Eur. used for forage and hay in Calif. A noxious weed in e. and s. states.

serotina (Walt.) Michx. [*Syntherisma serotinum* Walt.]. Creeping ann., sometimes forming extensive mats, flowering sts. ascending or erect, to 1 ft. high; lf. blades to 3¼ in. long, to ¼ in. wide, the sheaths villous; racemes usually 3–5, slender, often arching, to 4 in. long, rachis glabrous, with thin wings wider than the midrib; spikelets pale, less than 1/8 in. long, pedicels short, rounded, glabrous, first glume absent, second glume finely pubescent, scarcely half as long as the pale fertile lemma. Coastal plain, Penn. to Fla. and La.; Cuba.

DILLENIA L. [*Wormia* Rottb.]. *Dilleniaceae*. About 60 spp. of usually evergreen trees or shrubs of Asia and Madagascar, with 1 sp. in Australia; lvs. alt., simple, large, pinnately veined, petiole sometimes broadly winged, the wing clasping and enclosing the axillary bud; fls. usually terminal and solitary, or in racemes or panicles, sepals 5 or in multiples of 5, petals 5, stamens many, carpels several, coherent along a central conical receptacle; fr. dehiscent, fleshy, spreading starlike, or indehiscent and enclosed by the enlarged and fleshy sepals, seeds sometimes with an aril.

Burbidgei: *D. suffruticosa*.

indica L. [*D. speciosa* Thunb.]. Tree; lvs. oblong, to 14 in. long, 25–50-nerved; fls. white, showy, to 8 in. across, stamens many, yellow, carpels 15–20; fr. indehiscent, the mass globose, to 4 in. in diam., each carpel with 5 or more black seeds in colorless pulp. The most widespread sp., from India to Borneo and Java. Warmer parts of Zone 10, in Fla. The acid fr. is edible when fresh and is used in curries and jellies; called CHULTA in India.

ovata Wallich ex Hook.f. & T. Thoms. Tree; lvs. ovate or elliptic, to 10 in. long, 18–25-nerved; fls. to 6 in. across, yellow, carpels usually 10; fr. indehiscent, the mass to 2 in. in diam., each carpel with several black seeds in a glutinous pulp. Se. Asia. The fr. is sometimes used in jellies.

philippinensis Rolfe. Tree; lvs. elliptic to lanceolate, to 10 in. long; racemes few-fld.; fls. to 6 in. across, white, stamens many, yellow, carpels 10–12; fr. indehiscent, fleshy, slightly twisted, the mass to 2 in. across, each carpel with 1–4 seeds, each seed enclosed in a membranous aril. Philippine Is. to Sulu Arch. Fr. edible, made into a sauce or jam.

speciosa: *D. indica*.

suffruticosa (Griff.) Martelli [*D. Burbidgei* (Hook.f.) Gilg; *Wormia Burbidgie* Hook.f.; *W. suffruticosa* Griff.]. Large shrub, to 30 ft.; lvs. elliptic to obovate, to 10 in. long, 12–20-nerved; racemes 5–12-fld.; fls. about 4 in. across, yellow, with small staminodes surrounding many stamens, innermost stamens longer than outermost, carpels usually 7; fr. dehiscent, seeds brown or black, with a membranous scarlet aril. Malay Arch.

DILLENIACEAE. *Dillenia indica*: **a,** flowering twig, × 1/6; **b,** flower bud, × 1/3; **c,** flower, × 3/8; **d,** flower, vertical section (perianth partly cut away), × ½; **e,** stamens and carpels, × ½; **f,** one-quarter of cluster of carpels, cross section, × 1½; **g,** seed, × 1½. (a–d from Lawrence, *Taxonomy of Vascular Plants*.)

DILLENIACEAE Salisb. DILLENIA FAMILY. Dicot.; 11 genera and 275 spp. of trees, shrubs, or rarely herbs, native mostly to Australasia and trop. Amer.; lvs. alt.; fls. yellow, white, or rarely red, usually bisexual, sepals and petals 5, stamens many, separate or in bundles, carpels several, rarely only 1, 1-celled; fr. a follicle or berrylike. Some spp. yield timber and tannin and *Dillenia* and *Hibbertia* are sometimes planted as ornamentals in warm areas.

DILLWYNIA Sm. *Leguminosae* (subfamily *Faboideae*). About 10–15 spp. of small, heathlike shrubs, native to Australia; lvs. alt., simple, linear or cylindrical; fls. papilionaceous, standard reniform, usually yellow and red, the other petals crimson, stamens 10, separate; fr. a legume, ovate or broader.

Ornamentals adapted to mild parts of the Pacific Coast.

cinerascens R. Br. Erect, silky on young parts; lvs. spreading, cylindrical, to ½ in. long, obtuse, often recurved near apex; fls. 3–8 in terminal clusters, calyx usually canescent. Victoria.

ericifolia Sm. To several ft.; lvs. many, cylindrical or nearly so, slender, pointed; fls. in very short racemes or clusters at tips of sts., standard yellow with red spot at base; fr. small, ovate or nearly globose. E. Australia. Var. **glaberrima** (Sm.) Benth. [*D. glaberrima* Sm.]. Glabrous; lvs. to ½ in. long or more, mostly recurved at st. apex; fls. rather large, in dense terminal clusters. Tasmania and s. Victoria.

glaberrima: *D. ericifolia* var.

DIMORPHOTHECA Moench. CAPE MARIGOLD. *Compositae* (Calendula Tribe). About 7 spp. of ann. or somewhat shrubby per. herbs, native to S. Afr.; lvs. alt., simple to pinnatifid, coarsely sinuately toothed or lobed; fl. heads solitary on terminal peduncles, radiate, involucral bracts in 1 row, linear or linear-lanceolate, acuminate, receptacle naked; disc fls. tubular, the outer ones usually bisexual, the inner often abortive, ray fls. ligulate, female; disc achenes straight, compressed, with 2 thick wings, smooth, ray achenes incurved, 3-angled to nearly cylindrical, usually sharply tubercled or wrinkled, papus absent.

Cape marigolds are grown in the flower garden, and sometimes in the greenhouse or bedded out. They make a good display in warm, sunny locations, requiring a long season for best results. Propagated by seeds, and the perennial species also by cuttings.

annua: *D. pluvialis.*

aurantiaca: see *D. sinuata* and *Castalis Tragus.*

Barberae: *Osteospermum Barberae.*

calendulacea: *D. sinuata.*

Ecklonis: *Osteospermum Ecklonis.*

jucunda: *Osteospermum jucundum.*

nudicaulis: *Castalis nudicaulis.*

pluvialis (L.) Moench [*D. annua* Less.]. Glandular-hairy ann., to 16 in.; lvs. oblong or oblanceolate to obovate, to 3½ in. long, coarsely sinuate-dentate, upper lvs. lanceolate; heads to 2½ in. across; disc fls. yellow, often tipped with violet, ray fls. white above, violet to purple beneath. Var. **ringens** Hort. Watkins & Simpson [*D. ringens* Hort.]. Ray fls. white, with blue-violet base.

ringens: *D. pluvialis* var.

sinuata DC. [*D. aurantiaca* Hort., not DC.; *D. calendulacea* Harv.]. Glandular-pubescent ann., to 1 ft.; lvs. oblong to oblanceolate, to about 3 in. long, coarsely sinuate-dentate, upper lvs. oblanceolate; heads to 1½ in. across; disc fls. yellow, ray fls. orange-yellow, sometimes deep violet at base.

spectabilis: *Castalis spectabilis.*

DINEMA: *EPIDENDRUM.*

DINTERANTHUS Schwant. FLOWERING-STONE. *Aizoaceae.* Six spp. of stemless, mat-forming, per. succulents, native to S. Afr.; lvs. opp., very thick, united ⅓–⅔ their length making a rather globose body (growth), each member of lf. pair keeled toward apex, surface smooth or minutely granular, whitish, sometimes dotted; fls. solitary, bractless, expanding in late afternoon, calyx subequally 6–8-lobed, petals yellow, many, spreading, stamens many, erect, filaments bearded basally, ovary inferior, 6–9-celled, stigmas 6–9; fr. a 6–9-valved caps., with uncovered cells, expanding keels with broad, membranous margins, placental tubercles absent, seeds very minute.

Growth occurs in summer when plants require a small amount of moisture as excessive moisture causes bursting of the growths during the growing period; in winter they must be quite dry. Propagation easy by seeds. See also *Succulents.*

inexpectatus Jacobsen. Growth compact; lvs. smooth, gray, with more or less translucent greenish dots, smaller and rounder than in *D. microspermus,* distinctly keeled; fls. 1 in. across, golden-yellow. S.-W. Afr.

microspermus (Dinter & Derenb.) Schwant. ex N. E. Br. Brs. to 2 in. long, with old lvs. persistent; lvs. 2–4 in a growth, finely granular, white- to gray-olive-green or reddish-gray-violet, to 1¼ in. long, 1¼ in. wide, ¾ in. thick, united about half their length, upper side hemispherical in outline, lower side rounded, slightly keeled; fls. to 1¾ in. across, on pedicels to ⅝ in. long, petals golden-yellow with reddish tips above, pale yellow beneath. Cape Prov.

Pole-Evansii (N. E. Br.) Schwant. Growths mostly single, ellipsoid in side view, gray or tinged with yellow or red, not dotted, to 1¾ in. long, 1⅝ in. wide, 1 in. thick, united half their length and not much separated at apex, upper side flat, rugose, lower side rounded, keeled; fls. about 1⅝ in. across, yellow. Cape Prov.

puberulus N. E. Br. Lvs. 2–4, erect, scarcely spreading, finely granular-hairy, velvety to the touch, brownish gray-green, with many dark green dots, to 1⅛ in. long, ⅝ in. wide, ½ in. thick, united ⅓–½ their length, upper side flat or somewhat rounded, lower side round, slightly keeled toward apex; fls. 1⅛ in. across, golden-yellow. Cape Prov.

Vanzylii (L. Bolus) Schwant. [*Lithops Vanzylii* L. Bolus]. Growths to 1½ in. high; lvs. gray-green, rarely partly covered with inconspicuous red dots and lines, united high up, flattened, and each lf. semicircular in outline at tip; fls. ⅝ in. across, petals orange-yellow. Cape Prov.

Wilmotianus L. Bolus. Lvs. 2, smooth, gray, tinged with pink and minutely dotted with dark violet, to 2⅛ in. long, 2¼ in. wide, sheath to 1⅜ in. long, ⅞ in. wide, ⅝ in. thick, upper side of lf. tapered, lower side rounded, with 1–2 keels; fls. 1¼ in. across, on pedicels ⅝ in. long, petals golden-yellow. Cape Prov.

DIONAEA Ellis. *Droseraceae.* One sp., a low, carnivorous, per. herb of restricted range in bogs of coastal N.C. and S.C.; lvs. in a basal rosette; fls. in umbel-like cymes on scapes, sepals and petals 5, stamens usually 15; fr. a caps., seeds many.

Sometimes grown as a curiosity or for botanical demonstration. Thrives in sunshine in a humid atmosphere (as in a terrarium), and should be potted in sphagnum or in silver-sand and acid black silt, the pots set in about 1 in. of water; best given cooler conditions and allowed to become semidormant in winter. Propagated by seeds under a bell jar. Zone 8.

muscipula Ellis. VENUS'S-FLYTRAP. Lvs. to 5 in. long, petioles flat, winged, spatulate, blade reniform-orbicular, 2-lobed, usually reddish, the lobes hinged, fringed with stiffish cilia, and having on the upper surface 3 sensitive hairs, which, when stimulated in succession by insects or otherwise, cause the lobes to close together quickly; scape 3–15 in. high; fls. white, ¾ in. across.

DIOON Lindl. *Zamiaceae.* Four or 5 spp. of palmlike plants, native to Mex. and Cent. Amer.; lvs. stiff, pinnate, borne in a crown; male and female sporophylls (cone scales) in cones, scales of female cones with ends erect, flat, ovate-cordate, woolly.

Cycads grown as ornamentals, under glass or outdoors in Zone 10. Rather difficult to hand pollinate. Female cones require a year or more to ripen seeds. For culture see *Cycads.*

Dohenii: a listed name of no botanical standing; applied to a plant of sw. Mex. having lvs. smaller than other spp. and lfts. more closely arranged on the rachis.

edule Lindl. CHESTNUT D. Trunk to 6 ft., very stocky; lvs. 3–6 ft. long, pinnae entire in adult plants, but toothed at tip in young ones, veins 12 or less, sharp-pointed. Requires partial shade and rich soil. Seeds are edible.

Purpusii Rose. Trunk short; lvs. stiff, ascending, to 3 ft. long, pinnae spreading, somewhat recurved, linear, to 4 in. long, lower margin entire, upper usually with 1–3 spiny teeth; male cones 6–8 in. long, female cones ovoid, to 18 in. long.

spinulosum Dyer. Trunk to 20 ft., or said to reach 50 ft., more slender than *D. edule;* lvs. 4–6 ft. long, pinnae long, with separate, slender, spiny teeth on each margin, veins 18 or more, parallel. Wet forests.

DIOSCOREA L. YAM. *Dioscoreaceae.* Over 500 spp. of herbaceous or sometimes woody, tuberous-rooted twining vines, mostly of warm regions in both hemispheres; lvs. opp. or alt., often cordate, sometimes with bulbils in their axils; fls. in spikes or racemes, small, mostly unisexual; fr. a 3-angled or 3-winged caps., seeds winged.

Several species are cultivated for the edible, sturdy, tuberous roots, which are the true yams, important food plants in the tropics. Sometimes also grown for stockfood in the South (Zone 9). The inedible tubers of several Mexican species are rich in saponins and are widely collected in the wild for the manufacture of drug hormones. A few are also grown as ornamental vines. Yams need deep soil and require good drainage; they may be planted at any time of the year where hardy. Propagated by seeds, cut pieces of the roots, bulbils, or cuttings;

usually planted in hills. The word "yam" is sometimes applied in the United States to certain soft-fleshy varieties of sweet potato, *Ipomoea Batatas.* See also *Yam.*

alata L. WHITE Y., WATER Y. Tuberous roots to 8 ft. long, sts. 2–4-winged or -angled, twining clockwise, often with small axillary tubers; lvs. opp., ovate to oblong, deeply cordate; fr. broader than long, seeds encircled by wing. India to Malay Pen. Widely cult. in tropics for food with many cvs.; not hardy north.

Batatas Decne. CHINESE Y., CINNAMON VINE. Tuberous roots to 3 ft. long, cylindrical or flabellate, deep in ground, sts. long, climbing, twining clockwise, slightly angled, bearing small axillary tubers late in season; lvs. opp., ovate, broadened into 2 lobes at base; fr. broader than long, seeds encircled by wing. Temp. e. Asia; where much cult. for food. Grown in the U.S. primarily as an ornamental. Root hardy in Zone 5, persisting for years.

bulbifera L. AIR POTATO. Tuberous roots depressed-globose, small or none, sts. cylindrical, twining counterclockwise, bearing axillary, angled tubers; lvs. alt., ovate, cordate, to 6 in. wide or more; seeds with a long terminal wing. Trop. and warm temp. e. Asia. Zone 7. Edible and inedible forms exist; the former are cult. in the Orient.

caucasica Lipskii. Sts. cylindrical or slightly angled, twining counterclockwise; lvs. alt., more or less opp., or whorled, elliptic-ovate, slightly cordate, longer than broad, with 9–13 prominent nerves, pubescent underneath; fr. as broad as long, 1 in. wide or more, seeds encircled by wing. Caucasus.

×**cayenensis** Lam. YELLOW Y., ATTOTO Y., NEGRO Y. Tubers superficial, sts. annual, cylindrical or angled, twining counterclockwise; lvs. often alt. at base, opp. above, ovate to nearly triangular, to nearly 5 in. long and 4 in. wide, 7–9-nerved. Of hybrid origin, one parent perhaps *D. abyssinica* Hochst. ex Kunth.

discolor Kunth. Sts. somewhat angled, twining counterclockwise; lvs. alt., ovate, cordate, red underneath; fr. broader than long, seeds encircled by wing. Ecuador. May be only a form of *D. dodecaneura* Vell., native from Guyana to Paraguay. Grown as a greenhouse foliage plant.

divaricata: a name applied to 2 plants, neither placed with certainty.

elephantipes (L'Hér.) Engl. [*Testudinaria elephantipes* (L'Hér.) Burchell]. ELEPHANT'S-FOOT, HOTTENTOT-BREAD. Tuber half or more above ground, to 3 ft. in diam., covered with woody, faceted protuberances on the exterior, sts. to 10 ft., twining, somewhat woody; lvs. orbicular to reniform, to 2 in. wide, abruptly pointed; fr. a little longer than broad, seeds with short terminal wing. In semiarid bush, S. Afr. Grown as a curiosity in the desert garden (Zone 10) or in the greenhouse; tuber contains saponins, originally cooked and eaten by Hottentots as a famine food.

glauca: *D. quaternata.*

hirticaulis Bartlett. WILD Y. Sts. twining counterclockwise, finely hairy; lvs. mostly alt., ovate, to 4 in. long, about as broad as long, cordate, velvety-hairy underneath; fr. as broad as long, seeds with narrow wing. Wet places; N.J. to Ga.

quaternata (Walt.) J. G. Gmel. [*D. glauca* Muhlenb.]. WILD Y. Sts. erect in lower part, twining counterclockwise above; lvs. in whorls of 4–7, or opp. in the lower part, alt. in the upper; fr. to 1$\frac{3}{16}$ inn. long, seeds encircled by wing. Woods and slopes, Penn. to Fla., w. to Mo. and Okla.

trifida L.f. CUSH-CUSH, YAMPEE. Tubers small, sts. sharply angled or narrowly winged, twining clockwise; lvs. variable, to 10 in. long and wide, cordate, 3–5-lobed, middle lobe 3–5-nerved, minutely hairy above, pilose on nerves beneath; male fls. in racemes, female fls. in spikes; caps. oblong in outline, about 1 in. long, seeds winged on margin. S. Amer., W. Indies.

villosa L. WILD Y. Similar to *D. hirticaulis,* but sts. glabrous; lvs. glabrous or only lightly hairy beneath; seeds with wing broader than corky body. Wet woods and swamps, New Eng. to Minn., s. to Va. and Tex.

DIOSCOREACEAE R. Br. YAM FAMILY. Monocot.; 9–10 genera of widely distributed trop. or warm temp., twining, herbaceous or somewhat woody, monoecious or dioecious vines with rhizomes or tuberous roots; lvs. alt., net-veined; infl. racemose; fls. small, regular, perianth segms. 6, in 2 series, stamens 6 or 3, ovary typically 3-celled, with 3 styles; fr. a caps. or berrylike. Only *Dioscorea* is cult., primarily in the tropics for its edible tubers.

DIOSMA L. *Rutaceae.* Between 12 and 15 spp. of heathlike shrubs, endemic to S. Afr.; lvs. alt. or opp., simple, glandular-dotted; fls. white or red, in terminal cymose clusters, calyx 5-parted, petals 5, sessile, stamens 5; fr. a 5-carpelled caps., each carpel horned.

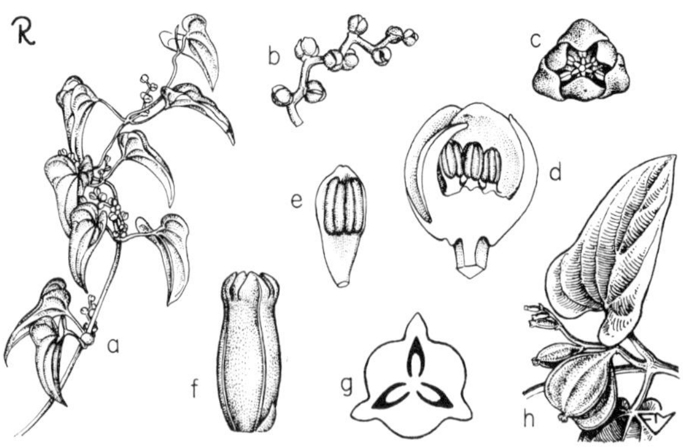

DIOSCOREACEAE. *Dioscorea Batatas:* **a,** part of flowering branch of male plant, × ¼; **b,** part of a male inflorescence, × 1; **c,** male flower, × 5; **d,** male flower, vertical section, × 8; **e,** stamen, × 15; **f,** female flower, × 5; **g,** ovary, cross section, × 20; **h,** fruit, × ½. (c, f, g, h from Bailey, *Manual of Cultivated Plants,* ed. 2.)

Diosmas are cultivated outdoors in the South and under glass as ornamentals and for floral decorations. Soil for diosmas should be similar to that for heaths; fibrous loam and leaf mold with sharp sand added. Plants should be cut back after flowering to induce bushy growth. Propagated by cuttings of young wood.

alba: *Coleonema album.*

ericoides L. BUCHU, BREATH-OF-HEAVEN. Glabrous, much-branched shrub, 1–2 ft.; lvs. crowded, erect, oblong, to ¼ in. long, obtuse and recurved at apex; fls. white, fragrant. Sometimes offered as *Coleonema ericoides.*

pulchella: *Agathosma pulchella.*

pulchra: a listed name of no botanical standing, used for *Coleonema pulchrum.*

purpurea: *Agathosma corymbosa.*

Reevesii: a listed name of no botanical standing.

DIOSPHAERA: *Trachelium.* **D. dubia:** *T. rumelianum.*

DIOSPYROS L. [*Brayodendron* Small]. PERSIMMON. *Ebenaceae.* Nearly 200 spp. of widely distributed, polygamodioecious trees and shrubs; lvs. alt., simple; fls. mostly 4–5-merous, female fls. solitary, with 4 to many staminodes, the other fls. in cymes or clusters, with 4 to many stamens; fr. a juicy, 1–10-seeded berry, with enlarged, persistent calyx at base.

D. Kaki and *D. virginiana* are grown for their edible fruit, and other species as ornamentals, or for their wood. Only *D. virginiana* is hardy as far north as New Eng., although *D. Lotus* is hardy perhaps to north-central regions; other species are tender. They succeed in most soils and are propagated by seeds, cuttings, and layers. The black sapote, *D. digyna,* thrives only in the tropics, but may tolerate 2 or 3 degrees of frost; it is propagated by seeds and by shield budding. See *Persimmon.*

chinensis: *D. Kaki.*

Chloroxylon Roxb. Tree, brs. sometimes spiny; lvs. elliptic to obovate-oblong, to 1¾ in. long, hairy underneath, petioles $\frac{3}{16}$ in. long; fls. 4-merous, male fls. in 4–10-fld. clusters, stamens 16, female fls. solitary, with 7–9 staminodes; fr. globose, ⅜ in. in diam. India.

cordifolia: *D. montana.*

digyna Jacq. [*D. Ebenaster* of auth., not Retz.; *D. nigra* in the sense of Bakh.]. BLACK SAPOTE. To 60 ft.; lvs. oblong-elliptic to elliptic-ovate, to 8 in. long, obtuse, glabrous, short-petioled; fls. small, fragrant, whitish; fr. about 4 in. in diam., olive-green, becoming nearly black, flesh very soft, chocolate-brown, edible. Mex., Cent. Amer.; naturalized in trop. Asia. Zone 10b. A popular fr. in Mex.

discolor Willd. [*D. Mabola* Roxb.; *D. utilis* Hemsl.]. To 45 ft.; lvs. oblong, to 10 in. long, leathery, pubescent underneath; fls. 4-merous, male fls. in 7-fld. cymes, petals whitish, stamens 24, glabrous, female fls. solitary, with 4 staminodes; fr. globose, to 4 in. in diam., brown-pubescent, edible. Philippine Is.

Ebenaster: a confused name, now recognized as a synonym of *D. Ebenum,* but previously erroneously applied to *D. digyna.*

Ebenum J. König ex Retz. [*D. Ebenaster* Retz.]. EBONY, EAST IN-DIAN E., MACASSAR E. Large tree, wood black with brown stripes, very hard; lvs. elliptic, to 4 in. long, obtuse, leathery, petioles less than ¼ in. long; fls. fragrant, mostly 4-merous, male fls. in clusters, stamens about 16, female fls. solitary; fr. globose, ¾ in. in diam. India, Ceylon. Source of the best ebony of commerce.

Embryopteris: *D. malabarica.*

eriantha Champ. ex Benth. Small tree, young brs. and underside of young lvs. rusty-strigose; lvs. subsessile, oblong-lanceolate, acuminate; fls. 4-merous, calyx very hairy, corolla white, hairy outside, male fls. 2–3 together, female fls. solitary; fr. oblong, more than ½ in. long, 1-seeded. Hong Kong.

japonica: *D. Lotus.*

Kaki L.f. [*D. chinensis* Blume]. KAKI, JAPANESE P., KEG FIG, DATE PLUM. To 40 ft.; branchlets brown-pubescent; lvs. ovate to obovate, to 7 in. long, acuminate, pubescent underneath; fls. yellowish-white, about ¾ in. long, male fls. with 16–24 stamens, female fls. with 8 staminodes; fr. variable in shape, to 3 in. in diam., orange to reddish, with orange flesh. The favorite fr. in Japan and China, where much cult. Many cvs. are listed.

Lotus L. [*D. japonica* Siebold & Zucc.]. DATE PLUM. To 45 ft.; lvs. elliptic to oblong, to 5 in. long, acuminate, broad-cuneate at base, somewhat pubescent underneath; fls. reddish or greenish, to ⁵⁄₁₆ in. long, 4-merous, male fls. with 16 stamens; fr. globose, ½ in. in diam., yellow, turning blackish. W. Asia to Japan. Much used in the Orient as grafting rootstocks for *D. Kaki.*

Mabola: *D. discolor.*

malabarica (Desr.) Kostel. [*D. Embryopteris* Pers.]. Dense tree; lvs. leathery, oblong, to 5½ in. long, petioles to ⅜ in. long; male fls. cymose, calyx pubescent, stamens 24–64, pilose, female fls. 1–5 together, with 1–12 staminodes; fr. mostly solitary, subglobose, 1–2 in. in diam. India to Indonesia.

mespiliformis Hochst. ex A. DC. To 70 ft.; lvs. oblong to oblong-elliptic, to 6 in. long; fls. yellowish-white, fragrant, 5-merous; fr. globose, about 1 in. in diam., 4–5-seeded. Trop. Afr.

montana Roxb. [*D. cordifolia* Roxb.]. Similar to *D. Lotus,* but lvs. smaller, to only 2½ in. long, obtuse to cordate at base; fr. ½–1½ in. in diam. India to Indonesia. Fr. is reportedly poisonous.

Morrisiana Hance. Shrub, sometimes a tree; lvs. oblong, or lower ones ovate, to 4 in. long, glossy above, petioles to ⅜ in. long; fls. white, 4-merous, male fls. 2–3 together, nodding, with 15–20 hairy stamens; fr. oblong or subglobose, about ⅝ in. in diam., yellow. Hong Kong.

nigra: *D. digyna.*

texana Scheele [*Brayodendron texanum* (Scheele) Small]. BLACK P. To 40 ft.; lvs. oblong-elliptic to obovate, to 1½ in. long, revolute, obtuse or retuse at apex, cuneate at base, pubescent on both sides when young, nearly sessile; fls. 5-merous; fr. globose, to 1 in. in diam., black with dark flesh. S. Tex., ne. Mex.

utilis: *D. discolor.*

vaccinioides Lindl. Low shrub, much-branched, young growth rusty-pubescent; lvs. ovate, ½ in. long, acute, leathery, glabrous; fls. 4-merous, nodding, calyx lobes hairy, ovary 3-celled; fr. globose. Hong Kong and Malay Pen.

virginiana L. COMMON P., POSSUMWOOD, POSSUM APPLE, DATE PLUM. Shrub or tree, to 40 ft. or more; lvs. elliptic to ovate, to 6 in. long, dark green and glossy above; fls. greenish-yellow, male fls. ½ in. long, with 16 stamens, female fls. larger, with 8 staminodes; fr. subglobose, 1–2 in. in diam., yellow to orange. Woods and fields, Conn. to Fla. and Tex. The fr. is edible when fully mature. Several cvs. are offered.

DIOSTEA Miers. *Verbenaceae.* Three spp. of shrubs or small trees, native to temp. and desert areas of Argentina and Chile; lvs. opp., simple; fls. in spikes, calyx tubular, 5-toothed, corolla tubular, 5-lobed, slightly 2-lipped, tube curved, stamens 4; fr. dry, 2-lobed, 2-celled, enclosed by persistent calyx.

Cultivated under glass and out of doors through Zone 8.

juncea (Gillies & Hook.) Miers [*Baillonia juncea* (Gillies & Hook.) Benth.]. Small tree or shrub, to 20 ft.; brs. rushlike; lvs. in remote pairs, oblong or ovate-oblong, to 1 in. long, dentate; fls. lilac or white, ¼–⁵⁄₁₆ in. long. Chile, Argentina.

DIOTIS: see *OTANTHUS.*

DIPELTA Maxim. *Caprifoliaceae.* Four spp. of deciduous shrubs resembling *Diervilla* and *Weigela,* native to cent. and w. China; lvs. opp., simple; fls. large, pinkish or purple, solitary or in racemes, calyx lobes narrow, corolla tubular-cam-

panulate, slightly 2-lipped, stamens 4, ovary inferior, 4-celled; fr. a caps., enclosed by large showy bracts.

Hardy in the North, dipeltas thrive in any good soil. Propagated by seeds in spring and by cuttings of green and hard wood.

floribunda Maxim. To 16 ft.; lvs. ovate to elliptic-lanceolate, to 4 in. long, entire; fls. pink with orange-yellow throat, fragrant, corolla slender at base, 1 in. long; fr. bract shieldlike, to 1 in. across. Zone 6.

ventricosa Hemsl. To 20 ft.; lvs. elliptic or narrower, to 5 in. long, mostly finely denticulate; fls. rose with orange throat, drooping, corolla swollen at base; fr. bract cordate, attached at base. Zone 7.

yunnanensis Franch. To 12 ft.; lvs. oblong-ovate to lanceolate-ovate, to 2 in. long, entire, usually slightly pubescent above and pubescent on veins beneath; fls. creamy-white, flushed pink, corolla campanulate, narrowed at base, to 1 in. long; fr. bract cordate, attached at base. Zone 7.

DIPHYLLEIA Michx. *Berberidaceae.* Two or 3 spp. of per., glabrous herbs, native to e. N. Amer. and Japan; lvs. on non-flowering plants solitary, radical, large and peltate, lvs. on flowering plants 2, cauline, smaller; fls. white, in terminal cyme, sepals 6, deciduous, petals 6, stamens 6, ovary ellipsoid, with 5–6 ovules; fr. a berry.

Suited to shaded rock garden or wild garden.

cymosa Michx. UMBRELLA LEAF. To 3 ft.; radical leaf to 2 ft. across, 2-lobed, with many-toothed secondary lobes, cauline lvs. more deeply 2-lobed, smaller; berry blue, about ½ in. long. Wet places in mts., Va. to Ga. and Tenn.

DIPLACUS: *MIMULUS.* **D. calycinus:** *M. longiflorus* var. *calycinus:* **D. glutinosus:** *M. aurantiacus;* **D. glutinosus** var. *grandiflorus:* *M. bifidus;* **D. grandiflorus:** *M. bifidus;* **D. parviflorus:** *M. Flemingii;* **D. rutilis:** *M. longiflorus* var. *rutilis.*

DIPLADENIA: *MANDEVILLA.* **D.** ×amoena: see *M.* ×amabilis.

DIPLARRHENA Labill. *Iridaceae.* Two spp. of tender herbs with short rhizomes, native to Australia and Tasmania; lvs. mostly basal, 2-ranked, narrow, stiff; fls. irislike, fugacious, 2 or more, in stiff terminal spathe, perianth tube none, outer perianth segms. longer than the inner, fertile stamens 2, style short, style brs. 3, flattened; fr. a caps.

Propagated by seeds or division.

Moraea Labill. Sts. 2–3 ft., leafy; lvs. shorter than sts., ¼–½ in. wide; spathe 2–3-fld., 2 in. long; fls. white, flushed lilac, about 1½ in. across, fragrant. When the plant is established, a clump produces a long succession of fls.

DIPLAZIUM Swartz. *Polypodiaceae.* Over 300 spp., mainly of trop. or warm temp. regions; lvs. simple or pinnate; sori and indusia elongate, often double and extending along both sides of the separate veins. Closely allied to and sometimes combined with *Athyrium.*

In the U.S. mostly grown under glass, but several species hardy in Zone 8. They grow best in high humidity and moist soil. See also *Ferns.*

acrostichoides (Swartz) Butters [*Asplenium acrostichoides* Swartz; *A. thelypteroides* Michx.; *Athyrium acrostichoides* Diels; *A. thelypterioides* (Michx.) Desv.]. Lvs. to 3 ft. long, deeply 2-pinnatifid, pinnae toothed, petioles long, straw-colored. N.C. to Ga. and Mo.; e. Asia.

australe (R. Br.) Wakef. [*D. thelypteroides* K. Presl; *Asplenium australe* (R. Br.) Brackenr., not Swartz; *Athyrium australe* (R. Br.) K. Presl; *A. umbrosum* (Ait.) K. Presl]. Lvs. deciduous, in tufts, to 5 ft. long, very broad, 2–3-pinnate, pinnules divided almost to the broadly winged midrib into oblong toothed segms., petioles thick, smooth; sori in 2 rows, very short and close to the midvein. Australia, New Zeal.

bantamense Blume. Lvs. of young plants simple, deeply cordate, lvs. of older plants 1-pinnate, to 24 in. long, 10 in. wide, with about 8 pairs of pinnae, the pinnae 5 in. long, 2 in. wide, terminal pinnae similar to others. Trop. Asia.

esculentum (Retz.) Swartz. VEGETABLE FERN. Rhizome erect, trunklike; lvs. 4–6 ft. long, triangular, those of young plants 1-pinnate, those of older plants 2-pinnate, veins netted. Trop. e. and s. Asia, Polynesia; naturalized in Fla. Zone 9.

japonicum (Thunb.) Beddome [*Athyrium japonicum* (Thunb.) E. Copel.]. JAPANESE LADY FERN. Lvs. to 2 ft. long, triangular, 1-pinnate at base, pinnae lanceolate, deeply cut into slightly toothed lobes; sori short, oblong. Temp. e. Asia, Australia, New Zeal.; naturalized in Fla. Zone 8.

lanceum (Thunb.) K. Presl [*D. subsinuatum* (Wallich) Tagawa]. Lvs. simple, lanceolate, to 9 in. long and 1 in. wide, usually entire. E. Asia, India, Ceylon. Zone 8.

proliferum (Lam.) Thouars. To 2 ft.; petioles stout and black-muricate-scaly, lvs. arching, leathery, pinnate, the pinnae many, sessile, usually 6–12 in. long, entire or slightly lobed, undulate, proliferous, forming plantlets in axils; sori linear, extending along veins in pinnate groups. Old World tropics.

pycnocarpon (K. Spreng.) Broun [*Asplenium angustifolium* Michx., not Jacq.; *A. pycnocarpon* K. Spreng.; *Athyrium angustifolium* Milde; *A. pycnocarpon* (K. Spreng.) Tidestr.]. SILVERY SPLEENWORT, NARROW-LEAVED S., GLADE FERN. Lvs. to 2½ ft. long, 1-pinnate, pinnae to 5 in. long, nearly entire. Que. to Kans., s. to Ga. and La.

subsinuatum: *D. lanceum.*

thelypteroides: *D. acrostichoides.*

DIPLOCYATHA N. E. Br. *Asclepiadaceae.* One sp., a leafless, dwarf, succulent per. herb, native to S. Afr., distinguished from *Stapelia* and other succulent asclepiads in having an annulus on the corolla, raised on an inner elongate tube up to the mouth of the corolla tube, and the lobes of the outer whorl of the corona united at base.

For culture see *Succulents.*

ciliata (Thunb.) N. E. Br. Sts. decumbent to ascending, to 3 in. long, 4-angled, the angles sharply toothed; fls. basal, mostly solitary, corolla to 3 in. across, campanulate, with spreading, white-ciliate lobes, yellow except for a grayish ring around the mouth, minutely spotted with red throughout, corona similarly colored.

DIPLOCYCLOS (Endl.) Von Post & O. Kuntze. *Cucurbitaceae.* Five spp. of ann., climbing, tendril-bearing, monoecious herbs, native to Afr., Asia, and Pacific Is.; fls. small, greenish, in clusters, mostly in lf. axils, calyx and corolla broadly campanulate, calyx 5-lobed, corolla 5-parted, male fls. with 3 separate stamens borne on perianth tube, anthers flexuous, pistillode lacking, female fls. with inferior ovary; fr. a berry, seeds horizontal.

palmatus (L.) C. Jeffr. [*Bryonopsis laciniosa* of auth., not (L.) Naud.]. Sts. slender, glabrous, tall-climbing; lvs. deeply 3–5-lobed, with obtuse sinuses, to nearly ¾ in. in diam., green or red, striped with white. Trop. Asia, Pacific Is. Grown as an ornamental and arbor vine. Long cult., but incorrectly, as *Bryonopsis laciniosa.*

DIPLOTAXIS DC. ROCKET. *Cruciferae.* About 35 spp. of ann. to per. herbs of cent. Eur., Medit. region, e. to nw. India; lvs. entire to pinnatifid or lobed; fls. yellow, white, rose, or lilac, in terminal racemes, sepals 4, petals 4, clawed; fr. a linear, elongated silique, erect or spreading, beak short, valves compressed, with a prominent midvein.

acris (Forssk.) Boiss. [*Moricandia hesperidiflora* DC.]. To 2½ ft.; lvs. oblong to obovate, obtuse, dentate to lobed; fls. lilac-pink to white, on ascending pedicels; siliques erect. Egypt, Israel, Arabia, Iran, nw. India.

erucoides (L.) DC. To 18 in., branching from base; lower lvs. lyrate; petals white, veined rose or lilac. Sw. Eur. Comes into fl. quickly from seed.

DIPLOTHEMIUM: *ALLAGOPTERA.* **D. caudescens:** *Polyandrococos caudescens.*

DIPORIDIUM: *OCHNA.*

DIPSACACEAE Juss. TEASEL FAMILY. Dicot.; 9 genera and about 160 spp. of mostly ann., bien., or per. herbs, rarely shrubs, native to Eur., Asia and Afr.; lvs. opp., rarely whorled; fls. small, irregular, bisexual, in dense involucrate heads or interrupted spikes, calyx cup-shaped, tubular, or divided into 5–10 segms. and then resembling a pappus enveloped by an involucel (epicalyx), corolla 4–5-lobed, stamens not united, usually 4, sometimes 2 or 3, arising from base of corolla tube, ovary inferior, 1-celled; fr. an achene, frequently crowned by the persistent calyx. *Dipsacus* has been of some economic importance, and *Cephalaria, Knautia, Morina, Pterocephalus, Scabiosa,* and *Succisa* are cult. as ornamentals.

DIPSACUS L. TEASEL. *Dipsacaceae.* About 15 spp. of coarse bien. or per. herbs, native to Eur., w. Asia, and N. Afr.

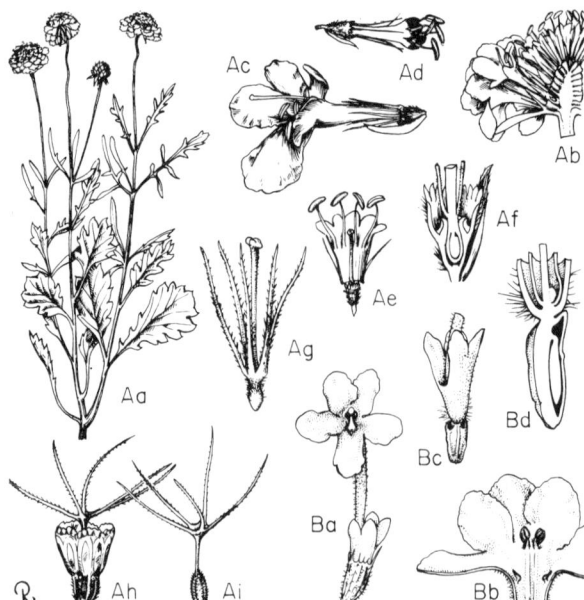

DIPSACACEAE. **A,** *Scabiosa atropurpurea:* **Aa,** plant, × ⅛; **Ab,** flower head, vertical section, × ½; **Ac,** marginal flower with bract, × 1; **Ad,** inner flower with bract, × 1; **Ae,** inner flower, corolla expanded, × 1; **Af,** bract, involucel, and base of flower, vertical section, × 3; **Ag,** ovary and style, × 3; **Ah,** achene enclosed in involucel, × 1½; **Ai,** achene, × 1½. **B,** *Morina longifolia:* **Ba,** flower with involucel, × ¾; **Bb,** upper part of corolla, expanded, showing two stamens and two staminodes, × 3; **Bc,** ovary, calyx, and base of style, × 1; **Bd,** base of flower, vertical section, × 3.

sts. usually prickly or spiny; lvs. basal or opp. on st. and often united at their bases, simple to pinnately cut; fls. in terminal, stalked heads subtended by spiny involucral bracts, each fl. subtended by spiny receptacular bracts, calyx cup-shaped, 4-angled, enveloped by a 4-lobed, cup-shaped involucel, corolla unequally 4-lobed, stamens 4; fr. an achene.

The heads of *D. sativus* are used for raising the nap on woolen cloth, and few species may be grown in the garden or used in dried arrangements.

azureus Schrenk. Bien., sts. to 4 ft., angled, without prickles; basal lvs. linear-lanceolate, entire or dentate at base; heads ovate-subglobose, involucral bracts rigid, spiny; fls. blue. Siberia.

fullonum L. [*D. sylvestris* Huds.]. COMMON T., WILD T. Bien., sts. to 6 ft., prickly on angles; basal lvs. oblanceolate, crenate, st. lvs. lanceolate, the upper ones entire, usually united at base; heads ovoid to subcylindrical, involucral bracts unequal, as long as the head or longer, curved upward, receptacular bracts with straight awns; fls. pale purple. Eur. Asia; weedy, extensively naturalized in N. Amer.

inermis Wallich. Bien., sts. to 6 ft., prickly, or unarmed toward the top; basal lvs. pinnatifid, terminal segm. largest, upper lvs. 3-parted to simple, toothed; heads nearly globose, the involucral bracts straight; fls. white or yellowish. Himalayas.

laciniatus L. Bien., sts. to 6 ft., prickly on angles; lvs. pinnatifid to 2-pinnatifid, ciliate, the bases of each pair forming a cup; heads ovoid, to 3 in. long, involucral bracts shorter or only slightly longer than heads; fls. white or pale pink. Eur., w. Asia; occasionally adventive in e. U.S.

pilosus L. Bien., sts. to 5 ft.; lvs. ovate to elliptic, sometimes prickly beneath on midrib, upper lvs. not united at base; heads globose, to 1 in. across, involucral bracts spiny, ciliate with silky hairs; fls. whitish, with dark violet anthers. Eur., w. Asia.

sativus (L.) Honck. [*D. fullonum* of auth., not L.]. FULLER'S T. Bien., sts. to 6 ft.; lvs. elliptic-oblanceolate to oblong, to 1 ft. long, entire, with scattered prickles beneath on midrib; heads cylindrical, to 4 in. long, involucral bracts shorter than head, becoming reflexed, bracts of receptacle with hooked tips; fls. pale lilac. Eur., N. Afr., Middle East; adventive locally in U.S.

Sylvestris: *D. fullonum.*

DIPTERYX Schreb. [*Coumarouna* Aubl.]. *Leguminosae* (subfamily *Faboideae*). About 10 spp. of trees of lowland trop. Amer.; lvs. alt., pinnate, often dotted, with alt. or nearly opp. lfts., rachises flattened; fls. in terminal panicles, papilionaceous, calyx 5-lobed, with the 2 upper lobes larger, oblong, stamens 10, united; fr. an ovoid, indehiscent, drupelike, 1-seeded legume.

The genus includes one species that supplies tonka beans, important in flavorings, and species used as ornamentals in the wet tropics. Propagated by seeds removed from their pods and planted where they are to grow.

odorata (Aubl.) Willd. [*Coumarouna odorata* Aubl.]. TONKA BEAN. To 100 ft. or more; lfts. 4–6, leathery, oblong, to 7 in. long, acuminate, rachis winged, tomentose, long-extended beyond lfts.; panicles short; fls. fragrant, calyx densely rusty-tomentose, petals bristle-tipped, nearly ½ in. long, standard white, other petals purplish-pink; fr. 2 in. long. Tropics, S. Amer. Principal source of tonka beans.

DIRCA L. LEATHERWOOD. *Thymelaeaceae*. Two spp., one in e. U.S., the other in Calif.; erect, deciduous shrubs with fibrous bark and tough flexible brs.; lvs. alt., entire; fls. yellow, 2–4 in nearly sessile clusters subtended by hairy bud scales, at the nodes of brs. of the previous season, appearing before the lvs.; fr. a small red or greenish drupe.

canadensis: a listed name of no botanical standing, probably referring to *D. palustris*.

occidentalis A. Gray. Shrub, to 6 ft.; lvs. obovate to elliptic, to 2¼ in. long, bud scales densely grayish-hairy. Calif.

palustris L. WICOPY, ROPEBARK, MOOSEWOOD. Shrub closely resembling *D. occidentalis*, but having lvs. somewhat larger, to 3 in. long, bud scales sparsely hairy, the hairs gray or sometimes black. Rich woods, New Bruns. to Minn., s. to Fla. Zone 5.

DISA Bergius. *Orchidaceae*. About 130 spp. of terrestrial herbs, native to S. Afr. and Madagascar; habit like that of *Habenaria*, roots tuberous, undivided, sts. leafy; fls. 1 to many in a raceme, upper sepal helmet-shaped, spurred, lateral sepals flat, petals separate, mostly held within upper sepal, lip narrow, tongue-shaped, column with horizontal or reflexed anther. For structure of fl. see *Orchidaceae*.

Require moist situations in the greenhouse. For culture see *Orchids*.

grandiflora: *D. uniflora*.

uniflora Bergius [*D. grandiflora* L.]. To 2 ft.; racemes 1–3-fld.; fls. the largest of the genus, to about 4 in. across, upper sepal red outside, paler inside, with deeper colored lines, spur short, straight, lateral sepals scarlet or carmine. Winter–early spring. S. Afr.

DISANTHUS Maxim. *Hamamelidaceae*. One sp., a deciduous glabrous shrub of Japan; lvs. long-petioled, palmately veined; fls. axillary, in pairs at apex of short peduncles, bisexual, sepals, petals, and stamens 5, ovary superior, 2-celled; fr. a caps., each cell with several seeds.

cercidifolius Maxim. Shrub, to 24 ft.; lvs. alt., orbicular-ovate, to 4 in. across, glabrous, entire, palmately 5–7-nerved; fls. dark purple, to ⅝ in. across, calyx pubescent, with recurved lobes. Grown for its autumn color, the lvs. becoming deep red with orange tints; fls. not showy, but with a faint odor. Zone 8.

DISCARIA Hook. *Rhamnaceae*. About 15 spp. of spiny shrubs in S. Amer., Australia, and New Zeal., with brs. usually rigid; lvs. deciduous, opp.; fls. small, axillary, calyx urceolate, petals often 0; fr. a leathery drupe, or dry and nutlike and separating into 3 parts. Related to *Colletia* but differing in technical characters of the fls.

crenata (Clos) Regel [*D. serratifolia* M. T. Mast., not Clos]. To 12 ft., brs. pendulous, spines to 1 in. long; lvs. narrow-oblong, to 1 in. long; fls. ⅛ in. across, many, greenish-white, fragrant. Chile and adjacent Argentina. Zone 7.

serratifolia: see *D. crenata*.

DISCHIDIA R. Br. *Asclepiadaceae*. About 80 spp. of mostly fleshy, epiphytic herbs, native to se. Asia, Polynesia, and Australia; sts. twining or climbing, rooting at the nodes, sap milky; lvs. opp. or more or less whorled, evergreen, waxy, sometimes inflated and hollow; fls. small, in axillary or terminal, often umbellate racemes, 5-merous, corolla urceolate-ovoid with a narrow mouth, fleshy, white, red, or violet,

corona of 1 whorl, 5-lobed, lobes erect, membranous, clawed, usually 2-lobed; fr. a follicle.

Culture as for *Hoya*.

bengalensis Colebr. Succulent, glaucous climber; lvs. elliptic to obovate, to about 1½ in. long; fls. in subsessile, axillary umbels, corolla white, less than ¼ in. long. India.

minima: a listed name of no botanical standing; plants offered under this name may be *Hoya serpens*.

platyphylla Schlechter. Slender-stemmed, white-mealy, clinging vine; lvs. orbicular to subreniform, to 2 in. broad, borne in sessile pairs appressed to the surface to which the vine is attached; corolla yellowish, tinged purple at the throat, to ³⁄₁₆ in. long. Philippine Is.

Rafflesiana Wall. Sts. climbing-twining, often hanging; lvs. dimorphic, either ovate-orbicular, to 1 in. long, or modified into inflated "pitchers" 2–5 in. long, often filled with roots arising from the same node, greenish or yellowish outside, purplish inside; corolla yellowish-white, purplish at throat, to ¼ in. long. India to Australia.

DISCOCACTUS Pfeiff. *Cactaceae*. About 9 spp. of nearly globose cacti of e. S. Amer.; sts. solitary, usually with small, sometimes bristly, apical woolly mass (cephalium), ribs 8–16, often tubercled, mostly spiny; fls. nocturnal, white or pinkish, fragrant, tube slender, scales spreading, petaloid, with naked axils; fr. small, naked, white or red, seeds globose, black, roughened. Differs from *Cactus* in smaller cephalium, larger and nocturnal fls.

Little grown. For culture see *Cacti*.

alteolens Lem. [*D. tricornis* Monv.]. Sts. to 2 in. high and 5 in. wide, cephalium with bristles, ribs 9–10, broad, low, each with 3–4 sterile areoles; spines 5–6, recurved, the upper slender, the lower stout, almost angular, black, becoming gray; fls. white, 2 in. long, perianth segms. obtuse. S. Brazil.

placentiformis (Lehm.) K. Schum. Sts. to 4 in. high and 7 in. wide, ribs 8–12, each with 6–7 sterile areoles; spines 3–8, recurved, often flattened, the lower to 1¼ in. long, those of upper areoles more numerous and smaller; fls. 2½ in. long, inner perianth segms. acute. S. Brazil.

tricornis: *D. alteolens*.

DISEASES AND PESTS. Under this heading may be included the full range of organisms which attack plants or which hinder their development as horticultural subjects. Diseases are caused primarily by a wide range of parasitic fungi (including those producing blights, mildews, rots, rusts, smuts, and wilts), which may attack any organ of the plant body; pests are generally insects but include other invertebrate animals such as mites and slugs. Species of vertebrates may also be pests on occasion, including birds in the home orchard or berry patch, and mammals, either large (deer) or small (rabbits and other rodents), in gardens. In addition, there are omnipresent weeds, which are simply unwanted plants. A species like Hall's Japanese honeysuckle (*Lonicera japonica* cv. 'Halliana'), for example, may be desirable in the North, where it is controlled by the colder climate, but becomes a weed and overly aggressive in the more favorable environment of the South.

Diseases and pests, as well as their methods of control, are so varied that it is impossible to treat them here in detail. Literature on the subject is abundant, and the gardener, when a real need arises, can depend on advice from agricultural extension offices at state and federal levels. Prevention is the first rule of control. Prevention also serves ecology better. Consistent cleanliness at all times is good insurance. This includes such practices as the elimination of plant refuse at the end of the garden season and of normal debris such as faded foliage and flowers, the use of sterilized soils and disinfected pots in home or greenhouse plantings, the regular syringing of house plants, the pulling of garden weeds before they seed or multiply, and the appropriate further action at the first sign of a disease or pest. Rotation of vegetable crops, when recommended, may avoid infection by disease.

Most diseases and pests can be controlled provided the correct control technique and/or pesticide is used in the recommended fashion. A number of kinds of fungicides control disease-producing fungi; various insecticides control insects and mites; and herbicides of several types control weeds. Pesticides are usually not all-purpose compounds but rather are specific. One that kills an insect that chews foliage will not always kill an insect like an aphid that sucks juices from within the plant.

DISOCACTUS Lindl. [*Chiapasia* Britt. & Rose.; *Pseudorhipsalis* Britt. & Rose]. *Cactaceae.* Seven spp. of erect or pendent, epiphytic cacti, native to W. Indies, Mex., Cent. and n. S. Amer.; primary sts. cylindrical, flattened at tip, brs. elongate, flat, crenate or serrate, with spineless marginal areoles; fls. diurnal, tube straight or curved at base, perianth segms. about 10–11, slender, spreading to ascending or recurved, stamens 10–65, ovary cylindrical, with a few naked scales; fr. globose or ovoid, smooth. Allied to *Epiphyllum.*

For culture see *Cacti.*

alatus (Swartz) Kimnach [*Pseudorhipsalis alata* (Swartz) Britt. & Rose]. Pendent, to 16 ft., brs. 8–16 in. long, 1–2 in. wide, serrate; fls. yellowish-white, 5/8 in. long and across, perianth tube less than 3/16 in. long; fr. ovoid, yellowish-green, 3/8 in. long. Jamaica.

biformis (Lindl.) Lindl. Sts. to 6 ft. or more, brs. 2–4 in. long, to 3/4 in. wide, serrate; fls. magenta, 2–2½ in. long, stamens slightly exserted. Honduras.

Eichlamii (Weing.) Britt. & Rose. Brs. 8–12 in. long, 1–2 in. wide, obliquely crenate; fls. red, 1½ in. long, tube curved at base, perianth segms. erect, stamens 13–20, exserted, ovary pubescent. Guatemala.

himantocladus (Rol.-Goss.) Kimnach [*Pseudorhipsalis himantoclada* (Rol.-Goss.) Britt. & Rose. Brs. erect or arching, 16–20 in. long, 3/8–1 in. wide, obtusely serrate; fls. white, purplish outside, 1 in. long. Costa Rica.

macranthus (Alexand.) Kimnach & P. C. Hutchison [*Pseudorhipsalis macrantha* Alexand.]. Brs. arching or pendent, to 3 ft. long and 1¾ in. wide, obtusely serrate; fls. yellow, 2 in. long, 3 in. across, perianth tube 1 in. long; fr. globose, red, 5/16 in. long. Autumn, winter. S. Mex.

Nelsonii (Vaup.) Lindinger [*Chiapasia Nelsonii* (Vaup.) Britt. & Rose]. Sts. 2–4 ft. long, brs. 4–10 in. long, 1–1½ in. wide; fls. to 4 in. long and 2½ in. across, perianth segms. in 2 whorls, purplish-pink, ascending, with tips recurved, the 5–6 inner to 3/4 in. wide. S. Mex. and Guatemala.

quetzaltecus (Standl. & Steyerm.) Kimnach. Sts. to 14 in. long, brs. oblong-linear to ovate-lanceolate, to 6¾ in. long and 2 in. wide, crenate; fls. light purplish, to 3⅝ in. long, tube curved at base, perianth segms. erect or incurved, stamens 35–45, exserted, ovary glabrous. Guatemala.

ramulosus (Salm-Dyck) Kimnach. Sts. to 28 in., brs. in 4 or 5 rows, lanceolate or linear, to 6 in. long or more, crenate or obtusely serrate; fls. pinkish to greenish-cream, salverform, to ½ in. long, tube straight, 8–9 inner perianth segms. rotate to recurved, stamens 12–30, exserted. W. Indies, Mex. to Brazil and Bolivia.

DISPORUM Salisb. ex D. Don. FAIRY-BELLS. *Liliaceae.* About 15 spp. of rhizomatous, per., woodland herbs, native to N. Amer. and Asia; st. branched, leafy; lvs. alt., sessile or clasping; fls. white or greenish-yellow, usually nodding, solitary or in few-fld. umbels, perianth segms. 6, stamens 6; fr. a berry.

Sometimes planted in the wild garden.

Hookeri (Torr.) Nichols. FAIRY-BELLS. To 2½ ft.; lvs. ovate to oblong-ovate, to 4 in. long, acute, at least the lower ones cordate-clasping; fls. creamy-white to greenish-white, ½ in. long, anthers usually included, ovary and style usually glabrous, stigma not lobed; fr. scarlet. Coast Ranges, cent. Calif. to s. Ore. Var. **oreganum** (S. Wats.) Q. Jones [*D. oreganum* (S. Wats.) W. Mill.]. Lvs. long-acuminate, anthers exserted, ovary and style usually pubescent. Ore. to B.C., e. to sw. Alta. and w. Mont.

lanuginosum (Michx.) Nichols. YELLOW MANDARIN. St. to 2½ ft., forked above; lvs. ovate to lanceolate-ovate, to 4¾ in. long, hairy beneath; fls. yellowish-green, ¼ in. long, stigma 3-lobed; fr. red, glabrous. W. N.Y. and s. Ont., s. to Ala. and Ga.

maculatum (Buckl.) Britt. NODDING MANDARIN. St. to 2 ft.; lvs. oblong or oblong-ovate, to 4 in. long, with stiff, spreading hairs beneath; fls. white, spotted with purple, ¾ in. long, stigma 3-lobed; fr. yellow, densely hairy. Ohio and s. Mich., s. to Ga. and Ala.

oreganum: *D. Hookeri* var.

sessile (Thunb.) D. Don. St. to 2 ft.; lvs. oblong or oblong-lanceolate, to 4 in. long, glabrous; fls. white, to 1 in. long, usually solitary or sometimes in 2's or 3's. Japan, China. Cv. **'Variegatum'.** Foliage variegated.

smilacinum A. Gray. St. flexuous, to 2 ft.; lvs. oblong, to 4 in. long, acute, glabrous; fls. white, about ½ in. long, solitary, erect. Japan.

Smithii (Hook.) Piper. FAIRY-LANTERN. St. to 3 ft.; lvs. ovate to lanceolate-ovate, to 4¾ in. long, rounded to subcordate at base; fls. whitish, to 1 in. long, 1–5 in umbels, stigma 3-lobed; fr. orange to red. Coastal shady woods, B.C. to cent. Calif.

trachycarpum (S. Wats.) Benth. To 2½ ft.; lvs. ovate, to 4 in. long, usually somewhat oblique at base; fls. creamy-white, 5/8 in. long, solitary or 2 or 3 together; fr. orange to bright red. N. Dak. and New Mex. and w. in U.S. and Canada, except Calif. and Nev.

DISSOTIS Benth. *Melastomataceae.* About 100 spp. of usually pubescent herbs or shrubs, native to trop. and S. Afr.; lvs. opp., short-petioled, simple, entire, 3–7-nerved; fls. solitary or in terminal, panicled cymes, calyx lobes alt. with hairy appendages, petals 4–5, stamens 8–10, strongly unequal, ovary 4–5-celled, adherent to calyx; fr. a caps.

canescens (R. C. Grah.) Hook. f. [*D. incana* (E. H. Mey. ex Hochst.) Triana]. Subshrub, to 3 ft., sts. 4-angled, coarsely hairy; lvs. ovate to oblong-lanceolate, 1–3 in. long, bluntly acute, gray-green, stellate-pubescent; cymes in the upper lf. axils; fls. ¾ in. across, deep crimson. Trop. Afr.

incana: *D. canescens.*

DISTICTIS Mart. ex Meissn. [*Phaedranthus* Miers]. *Bignoniaceae.* Perhaps 9 spp. of woody vines, native to W. Indies and trop. Amer.; lvs. with 3 lfts. or with 2 lfts. and a terminal tendril, lfts. entire; fls. purple, pink, red, or white, in terminal racemes or panicles, calyx truncate at apex to 5-lobed or unequally shortly 5-toothed, corolla funnelform or tubular-funnelform, slightly 2-lipped, stamens 4; fr. a caps., seeds thin, winged.

Grown in southern Calif.

buccinatoria (DC.) A. Gentry [*Bignonia Cherere* Lindl.; Phaedranthus buccinatorius (DC.) Miers]. BLOOD-TRUMPET. Brs. 4-angled; lfts. elliptic to obovate-oblong, to 4 in. long, tendrils filiform; fls. in few-fld. racemes, pendulous, corolla blood- or purple-red with yellow base; caps. narrowly elliptic in outline, obtusely tapered at each end, to 6 in. long, about 2 in. wide, 1⅜ in. thick, wrinkled, with scattered hairs. Mex.

cinerea: *D. laxiflora.*

lactiflora (Vahl) DC. Lfts. leathery, ovate or elliptic, to 2⅜ in. long, strongly reticulate-veined, minutely scaly beneath; corolla white with yellow throat, to 1⅝ in. long, puberulous to nearly glabrous. W. Indies. Material grown under this name is probably *D. laxiflora.*

laxiflora (DC.) Greenm. [*D. cinerea* Greenm.]. Lfts. ovate to oblong-elliptic, to 2⅜ in. long, not prominently reticulate-veined, pubescent, minutely scaly on both surfaces; corolla opening purple with yellow throat, aging lilac to nearly white, with reddish lines in throat, densely and minutely hairy outside, to 3⅜ in. long, limb to 2½ in. across; fr. to 3½ in. long. Mex.

×**Riversii:** a listed name of no botanical standing for *Distictis* cv. 'Rivers', a hybrid between *D. buccinatoria* and *D. laxiflora,* with fls. like those of *D. laxiflora* but almost twice as large.

DISTYLIUM Siebold & Zucc. *Hamamelidaceae.* About 8–10 spp. of evergreen, polygamous or dioecious trees and shrubs, native to Japan, China, and the Himalayas; lvs. alt.; fls. in axillary racemes, subtended by small bracts, calyx lobes 3–5, petals none, stamens 2–8, with short filaments, ovary superior; fr. a somewhat woody, hairy caps., seeds 1 in each cell.

Propagated by seeds, by layers or cuttings.

racemosum Siebold & Zucc. ISU TREE. To 80 ft., but shrubby in cult.; lvs. elliptic, to 3 in. long, entire, dark green and glossy above, sometimes with irregular margins; fls. in racemes 2–3 in. long, anthers red. Sw. Japan. Zone 8. Fine-grained wood used in Japan for furniture and art objects. Cv. **'Variegatum'.** Lvs. bordered or splashed with yellowish-white. There are also narrow-leaved and pendulous cvs.

DITHYREA Harv. SPECTACLE POD. *Cruciferae.* Three spp. of stellate-gray-pubescent, ann. herbs of sw. U.S. and adjacent Mex., sts. erect or decumbent, leafy; lvs. sinuate-dentate to nearly entire; fls. white or yellowish, in terminal racemes, sepals and petals 4; fr. divided into 2 equal rounded halves side by side, spectaclelike.

Wislizenii Engelm. Sts. erect, grayish, to 18 in.; lvs. linear-lanceolate to ovate-lanceolate, deeply sinuate-dentate to nearly entire; petals white, about ¼ in. long; pedicels elongating in fr. to ½ in. or more, each half of fr. ¼ in. across or more. W. Okla., w. Tex., to s. Utah and Nev., s. to Ariz. and ne. Mex.

DIVISION: see *Propagation.*

DIZYGOTHECA N. E. Br. FALSE ARALIA. *Araliaceae.* About 15 spp. of unarmed shrubs or small trees, native to New Caledonia and Polynesia; lvs. palmately compound, lfts. whorled at the end of the petiole; fls. small, in large, terminal umbels, petals 5, valvate, stamens 5, ovary 10-celled, styles separate; fr. a drupe.

The juvenile plants often grown for foliage in pots of sandy loam enriched with leaf mold or compost. Zone 10. Propagated mainly by cuttings of mature wood.

elegantissima (Hort. Veitch) R. Vig. & Guillaum. [*Aralia elegantissima* Hort. Veitch]. Juvenile plant straight-stemmed, sts., petioles, and lfts. mottled creamy-white; lfts. mostly 6–10, undulate, serrately lobed, pendent, red-brown. New Caledonia, Polynesia. Plants of this sp. may be offered under the name *Aralia laciniata.*

Kerchoveana (Hort. Veitch) N. Tayl. [*Aralia Kerchoveana* Hort. Veitch]. Juvenile plant slender-stemmed; lfts. 7–11, mostly ½ in. wide or more, margins prominently notched, midrib pale, petioles mottled. Polynesia.

Veitchii (T. Moore) N. Tayl. Juvenile plant with slender, erect sts.; lfts. 7–11, margins toothed or wavy, to 5 in. long, ¼ in. wide, green above, coppery-red beneath. New Caledonia. Cv. **'Gracilina'.** Lvs. narrower.

DOBROWSKA: *MONOPSIS.* **D. tenella:** *M. unidentata.*

DOCYNIA Decne. *Rosaceae.* A few spp. of small trees of e. Asia; lvs. simple, sometimes shallowly lobed; fls. before the lvs. or with them, white, in small umbels, calyx and pedicels tomentose, petals 5, clawed, stamens 30–50, ovary 5-celled. The genus is allied to *Malus* and *Pyrus* and is more closely related to *Cydonia,* the quince, in having several to many seeds in each cell of the fr.

Occasionally planted as an ornamental in the warmer parts of the U.S.; the fruits sometimes used in other countries for cooking.

indica Decne. To 15 ft.; lvs. lobed or toothed in young plants, ovate or oblong-lanceolate and acuminate in old plants, to 4 in. long, entire or serrulate, densely woolly to glabrate beneath; fls. to 1½ in. across, densely woolly; fr. 1–1½ in. in diam. Himalayas, Burma.

DODECATHEON L. SHOOTING-STAR, AMERICAN COWSLIP. *Primulaceae.* About 14 spp. of scapose, per. herbs, native mostly to N. Amer., 1 sp. in e. Siberia, sometimes with rice-grain bulblets among roots; lvs. simple, in a basal rosette; fls. white, magenta, lavender, or purple, nodding, in umbels, calyx and corolla 4- or 5-parted, corolla tube usually maroon with a yellow band at throat, lobes reflexed, stamens 4 or 5, filaments free or united into a tube, anthers slender, connivent into a cone; fr. a caps., valvate or dehiscing by a cap.

Grown in well-drained soil in a shady place; useful in the wild garden and some species in the rock garden. Propagated by division and seeds.

alpinum (A. Gray) Greene. ALPINE S.-S. Glabrous; lvs. linear to linear-oblanceolate, to 2⅜ in. long, entire; umbels 1-3-fld., on scapes 1½–5½ in. high; fls. 4-merous, magenta to lavender, filaments, connectives, and pollen sacs dark, stigma twice the diam. of the style. Mts., Ore., Calif., Nev.

amethystinum: *D. pulchellum.*

Clevelandii Greene. Glandular-pubescent, without rice-grain bulblets; lvs. oblanceolate to spatulate, to 4⅜ in. long, dentate, crisped; umbels 5–16-fld., on scapes 7–16 in. high; fls. 5-merous, magenta to white, filament tube dark maroon to black, connectives rugose, dark, pollen sacs yellow. S. Calif., n. Baja Calif. Subsp. **patulum** (Greene) H. J. Thomps. [*D. patulum* Greene]. LOWLAND S.-S. Umbels 1–6-fld., filament tube dark, with a white or yellow spot below each anther, pollen sacs dark, anthers bending back from the style at flowering. Mts., cent. Calif. Subsp. **sanctarum** (Greene) Abrams [*D. macrocarpum* (A. Gray) R. Knuth]. Umbels 3–7-fld.; filament tube with a white or yellow spot below each anther, pollen sacs usually yellow. Coast, between San Francisco Co. and Los Angeles Co., Calif.

Colrigo: a listed name of no botanical standing.

conjugens Greene. Glabrous, without rice-grain bulblets; lvs. linear-oblanceolate or obovate to oblanceolate, to 5½ in. long; umbels 1–7-fld., on scapes 3–10 ⅜ in. high; fls. 5-merous, magenta to white, filaments yellow, connectives rugose, dark, pollen sacs usually maroon to black. Wash. to Mont., s. to ne. Calif. and Wyo. Subsp. **viscidum** (Piper) H. J. Thomps. [*D. viscidum* Piper]. Lvs. glandular-pubescent, with long-stalked glands. Wash., Idaho, Mont., adjacent Canada.

Cusickii Greene. Heavily glandular-pubescent, without rice-grain bulblets; lvs. ovate to oblanceolate, to 6¾ in. long, entire or rarely dentate; umbels 2–17-fld., on scapes 5–10 in. high; fls. 5-merous, magenta or lavender to white, filament tube usually yellow, connectives smooth, dark, pollen sacs yellow, sometimes red to maroon. S. B. C. to Mont., s. to ne. Ore. and Idaho.

dentatum Hook. [*D. latilobum* (A. Gray) Elmer ex R. Knuth]. Glabrous, without rice-grain bulblets; lvs. ovate to elliptic, to 10 in. long, blade abruptly narrowed to petiole; umbels 1–7-fld., on scapes 4–14 in. high; fls. 5-merous, always white, filaments short, dark, connectives dark, smooth, pollen sacs maroon or black. Wash., and n. Ore. to cent. Idaho.

frigidum Cham. & Schlechtend. Glandular-pubescent, without rice-grain bulblets; lvs. ovate to elliptic, 2–6 in. long, blade abruptly narrowed to petiole, crenate-dentate; umbels 2–7-fld., on scapes 3½–10 in. high; fls. 5-merous, magenta to lavender, filaments short, dark, connectives black, smooth, pollen sacs maroon to black, style dark purple. Ne. Asia, Alaska, nw. Canada.

Hendersonii A. Gray [*D. latifolium* (Hook.) Piper]. SAILOR-CAPS, MOSQUITO-BILLS. Rice-grain bulblets present at flowering; lvs. spatulate to elliptic, to 6 in. long, blade abruptly narrowed to petiole, entire to slightly toothed; umbels 3–17-fld., on scapes 4¾–18 in. high, glandular-pubescent to glabrous; fls. 5-merous, white to magenta, filament tube dark, connectives rugose to smooth, dark, pollen sacs mostly dark red to black. S. Vancouver Is. to Calif.

Hugeri: *D. Meadia.*

Jeffreyi Van Houtte [*D. tetrandrum* Suksd. ex Greene]. SIERRA S.-S. Glandular-pubescent to glabrous; lvs. oblanceolate, to 20 in. long, entire or crenate; umbels 3–18-fld., on scapes 6–24 in. high; fls. 4- or 5-merous, magenta to lavender or white, filaments short, dark, connectives rugose, usually dark, pollen sacs maroon to yellow, stigma twice the diam. of the style. Alaska, s. to Calif., Idaho, Mont. Var. **redolens:** *D. redolens.*

latifolium: *D. Hendersonii.*

latilobum: *D. dentatum.*

macrocarpum: *D. Clevelandii* subsp. *sanctarum,* but material offered as *D. macrocarpum* is probably *D. pulchellum.*

Meadia L. [*D. Hugeri* Small; *D. pauciflorum* (E. Durand) Greene]. SHOOTING-STAR. Glabrous, or infl. glandular-pubescent, without rice-grain bulblets; lvs. ovate to spatulate, to 1 ft. long; umbels 4–125-fld., on scapes 6¾–20 in. high; fls. 5-merous, magenta or lavender to white, filaments free or united, yellow, connectives smooth, dark, pollen sacs yellow. Penn. to s. Wisc., s. to Ala. and e. Tex. Cv. **'Album'.** Fls. white. Cv. **'Splendidum'.** Fls. crimson.

patulum: *D. Clevelandii* subsp.

pauciflorum: *D. Meadia,* but material offered as *D. pauciflorum* is *D. pulchellum.*

poeticum L. F. Henders. Heavily glandular-pubescent, without rice-grain bulblets; lvs. oblanceolate, to 6 in. long; umbels 2–10-fld., on scapes 5–14 in. high; fls. 5-merous, magenta to lavender, filament tube dark, connectives smooth to slightly rugose, dark, pollen sacs dark. S. Wash., n. Ore.

puberulum: *D. pulchellum.*

pulchellum (Raf.) Merrill [*D. amethystinum* (Fassett) Fassett; *D. puberulum* (Nutt.) Piper; *D. radicatum* Greene; *D. vulgare* (Hook.) Piper]. Glabrous to glandular-pubescent, without rice-grain bulblets; lvs. oblanceolate, ovate-spatulate, to 10 in. long, entire, crenate or sinuate; umbels 3–25-fld., on scapes 2¼–20 in. high; fls. 5-merous, magenta to lavender, filaments united or nearly separate yellow, connectives smooth, usually dark, pollen sacs usually yellow. S. Alaska and w. Canada to Mex., localized in areas in e. U.S. Cv. **'Album'.** Fls. white. Subsp. **monanthum** (Greene) H. J. Thomps. ex Munz. Filament tube dark maroon to black. Ne. Calif., Ore., Utah. Subsp. **Watsonii** (Tidestr.) H. J. Thomps. [*D. uniflorum* Rydb.]. Small; lvs. to 1½ in. long; umbels 1–3-fld., on scapes to 2¼ in. high. S. Vancouver Is. and Ore. to w. Mont. and Wyo.

radicatum: *D. pulchellum.*

redolens (H. M. Hall) H. J. Thomps. [*D. Jeffreyi* var. *redolens* H. M. Hall]. Heavily glandular-pubescent; lvs. oblanceolate, to 16 in. long; umbels 5–10-fld., on scapes 10–24 in. high; fls. 5-merous, magenta to lavender, corolla tube entirely yellow, covering the bases of anthers, filaments short, black, connectives rugose, dark, pollen sacs dark, stigma twice the diam. of style. Cent. and s. Calif., Nev., w. Utah.

tetrandrum: *D. Jeffreyi.*

uniflorum: *D. pulchellum* subsp. *Watsonii.*

viscidum: *D. conjugens* subsp.

vulgare: *D. pulchellum.*

DODONAEA (L.) Jacq. *Sapindaceae.* About 50 spp. of polygamous, usually viscid shrubs and small trees, native to tropics and subtropics of both hemispheres, but mostly to Australia; lvs. alt., simple or pinnate; fls. small, usually in racemes or panicles, unisexual and bisexual, sepals 2–5, petals 0, stamens usually 8; fr. a 3–6-celled caps., winged, often purple or red.

Some species have medicinal properties, and most of them have resinous, sticky excretions.

attenuata A. Cunn. Viscid shrub, to 6 ft.; lvs. simple, narrowly oblanceolate to linear, to 2½ in. long; fls. in short, simple racemes. Australia.

cuneata Rudge. HOPBUSH. Shrub, usually viscid; lvs. obovate or cuneate, to 1 in. long; fls. in terminal racemes or axillary clusters. Australia.

truncatialis F. J. Muell. Glabrous, scarcely viscid shrub, to 18 ft.; lvs. narrowly lanceolate to linear, 2–5 in. long; fls. in axillary or terminal racemes to 2 in. long. Australia.

viscosa (L.) Jacq. Viscid shrub or slender tree, to 15 ft.; lvs. obovate-oblong to lanceolate, to 4¾ in. long; fls. in short racemes. Ariz. to S. Amer., W. Indies, and widely distributed in Old World tropics. Cv. 'Purpurea' [var. *purpurea* Hort.]. Foliage and seeds purplish-red.

DOLICHANDRA Cham. *Bignoniaceae.* One sp., a climbing shrub, native to Brazil, Uruguay, and Argentina; lvs. opp., with 2 lfts. and often a terminal 3-branched tendril; fls. in 2–3-fld. axillary cymes, calyx spathelike, corolla tubular, 5-lobed, 2-lipped, stamens 4, exserted, anthers scarcely diverging; fr. a linear caps.

cynanchoides Cham. [*Macfadyena cynanchoides* (Cham.) Morong]. Lfts. oblong to ovate, to 2 in. long, entire; fls. red, to 2½ in. long; fr. to 4 in. long.

DOLICHANDRONE (Fenzl) Seem. *Bignoniaceae.* About 9 spp. of trees, native from se. Afr., India, and Burma to Malay Arch., Philippine Is., n. Australia, and New Caledonia; lvs. opp., whorled, or alt., pinnate or with 1 lft.; fls. pure white, night-blooming, very fragrant, in terminal racemes or panicles, calyx spathelike, corolla long-funnelform, 5-lobed, essentially regular, much longer than calyx, stamens 4; fr. a caps.

alba (T. R. Sim) T. Sprague. Small tree; lvs. opp., lfts. 8, ovate, obovate, or elliptic, to 4 in. long, wavy, glabrous; fls. to 3 in. long; fr. linear, to 2 ft. long. Mozambique.

arcuata (Wight) C. B. Clarke [*D. crispa* (Buch.-Ham.) Seem.]. To 60 ft.; lvs. opp., to 1 ft. long, lfts. 9–11, elliptic, 2–3 in. long, pubescent; fls. to 3 in. long; fr. linear, to 1½ ft. long. India.

crispa: *D. arcuata.*

heterophylla F. J. Muell. Scrubby, glabrous tree to 15 ft.; lvs. mostly in whorls of 3, with 1 or 3–7 lfts., lfts. oblong-lanceolate to linear; fls. to 2 in. long. Queensland and N. Territory (Australia).

spathacea (L. f.) K. Schum. [*Bignonia spathacea* L. f.]. To 60 ft.; lvs. opp., to 1 ft. long, lfts. 7–9, ovate-lanceolate, to 6½ in. long; fls. in 2–6-fld. terminal racemes, to 7 in. long and 5 in. across; fr. to 2 ft. long. Se. Asia, Malay Arch., to New Caledonia.

DOLICHOS L. *Leguminosae* (subfamily *Faboideae*). About 60 spp. of mostly twining herbs of Afr. to India and e. Asia; lvs. of 3 lfts.; fls. in long-peduncled, sometimes nearly capitate racemes, or rarely solitary in lf. axils, papilionaceous, calyx 4-parted, stamens 10, 9 united and 1 separate; fr. a flat, beaked legume.

Grown as ornamentals, or in the tropics for the edible pods and seeds and as forage and green manure crops. Propagated by seeds sown where plants are to grow, or some species by cuttings.

chinensis: a listed name of no botanical standing.

Hosei Craib. SARAWAK BEAN. Forming mats to 6 in.; lfts. to 1½ in. long and ¾ in. wide; fr. ³⁄₁₆ in. across. Borneo. Grown far south as a cover crop; prop. by cuttings.

Lablab L. [*D. soudanensis* Hort.]. HYACINTH BEAN, LABLAB, LABLAB B., BONAVISTA B., LUBIA B., BOVANIST B., SEIM B., INDIAN B.,

EGYPTIAN B. Woody per. climber, 10–30 ft.; lfts. ovate-triangular or -rhombic, to 6 in. long, often as wide; fls. purple or white; fr. to 2½ in. long, seeds black or white. Probably Old World. Now widespread, and an important legume in the tropics. Sometimes grown as an ann. Many cvs. are known. Cv. 'Giganteus'. Large form with white fls. Cv. 'Enormis' is offered.

lignosus L. AUSTRALIAN PEA. Per., evergreen; lfts. to 1½ in. long, triangular-ovate; fls. rose-purple or white, less than ½ in. long; fr. to 1 in. long, seeds black. Probably Asia.

soudanensis: a listed name of no botanical standing for *D. Lablab.*

DOLICHOTHELE: *MAMMILLARIA.* Often, and perhaps correctly, maintained as a distinct genus. **D. Ludwigii:** a listed name of no botanical standing. **D. sphaerica:** *M. longimamma* var. **D. uberiformis:** *M. longimamma* var.

DOMBEYA Cav. [*Assonia* Cav.]. *Byttneriaceae.* Perhaps 200 spp. of shrubs or small trees, native to Afr., Madagascar, and Mascarene Is.; lvs. alt., simple, palmately veined and usually palmately lobed; fls. in mostly bracted, axillary or terminal cymes, the cymes sometimes umbellate, calyx 5-lobed, the lobes usually reflexed in mature fls., petals 5, persistent, becoming dry, brownish, and papery, staminal tube short, with 5 staminodes alternating with groups of 2–3 fertile stamens; fr. a 3–5-celled, ovoid, dehiscent caps., each cell 1- to several-seeded.

Grown as ornamentals in the tropics and subtropics (including Zone 10 in Fla. and southern Calif.) and sometimes in the greenhouse. Their appearance is somewhat marred after flowering by the persistent corollas. Propagated by seeds or cuttings over heat.

Burgessiae Gerr. ex Harv. [*D. Mastersii* Hook.f.; *D. nairobensis* Engl.]. Shrubs, 6–12 ft., branching from near the base, young sts. and peduncles reddish-stellate or simple-hispid-pubescent; lvs. to 8 in. long, about as broad, usually acutely 3-angled or 3-lobed in the upper half; cymes mostly many-fld., corymbose or umbellate; petals white with rose veins, or pink, up to 1 in. long; caps. about ⅜ in. in diam., cells 5, up to 4-seeded. Kenya to S. Afr.

calantha K. Schum. Shrub, to 12 ft., sts. brown-tomentose; lvs. often thickish, 3–5-lobed, to 12 in. long and broad; cymes mostly 10–20-fld., corymbose; fls. pink, to 1½ in. across; caps. to ½ in. in diam., cells 5, up to 8-seeded. Malawi.

×**Cayeuxii** André: *D. Burgessiae* × *D. Wallichii.* A variable hybrid including many forms, but in general similar to *D. Wallichii,* with large lvs. and pink fls. in drooping, many-fld., umbellate cymes, but differing in having smaller bracts subtending the umbel, to 1 in. long and ½ in. wide.

Dawei T. Sprague. Shrub, to 10 ft.; sts. brown-pilose, soon glabrescent; lvs. broadly ovate, to 6 in. long, acute, cordate, often more or less 3-lobed; fls. about ¾ in. long. Uganda. Probably not specifically distinct from *D. Burgessiae.*

Dregeana: *D. tiliacea.*

elegans Cordem., not K. Schum. Slender-branched, glabrous shrub; lvs. less than 5 in. long, unlobed or cuspidately 3-lobed, cordate, dentate; cymes axillary; fls. white or rose. Réunion.

Goetzenii K. Schum. Tree, to nearly 60 ft.; lvs. ovate to broadly ovate, 3–15 in. long, sometimes 3-lobed, cordate, pubescent above and beneath; cymes many-fld.; petals to about ¾ in. long, filaments nearly as long; cells of caps. 5, up to 4-seeded. Congo region and Uganda.

Mastersii: *D. Burgessiae.*

mollis Hook. Tree, to 30 ft., new growth with densely downy-stellate pubescence; lvs. cordate-ovate, up to 12 in. long, acuminately 3-lobed, serrate; peduncles to 8 in. long, 3–4-branched at apex, each br. with a many-fld. umbellate cyme; petals rose, to ⅜ in. long. Madagascar.

nairobensis: *D. Burgessiae.*

natalensis: see *D. tiliacea.*

nyassica Exell. Probably not specifically distinct from *D. Burgessiae,* from which it is distinguished in having sts. and lower surface of the lvs. at first gray- or white-tomentose, but soon glabrous. Malawi and Mozambique.

rotundifolia: *D. spectabilis.*

spectabilis Bojer [*D. rotundifolia* (Hochst.) Planch.]. Shrubs or small trees, to 45 ft., with reddish stellate pubescence; lvs. ovate to suborbicular, to 7 in. long, cordate, rounded to truncate-mucronate at apex, entire or dentate; cymes paniculate; fls. to ¾ in. across, white or pink, appearing before the lvs., ovary 2–3-celled, stigmas 2–4. Kenya to S. Afr. and Madagascar.

tiliacea (Endl.) Planch. [*D. Dregeana* Sond.; *D. natalensis* Sond.]. Small tree, to 25 ft., bark gray-brown; lvs. cordate-ovate, to 3½ in. long, acuminate, irregularly toothed; cymes (1–)2–6-fld., sometimes more, subtended by lanceolate to broadly ovate involucral bracts; fls. white, to 1¼ in. across; cells of caps. 5, 2–4-seeded. S. Afr. The plant offered in s. Calif. as *D. natalensis*, with pink fls. and larger, acutely 3-lobed lvs., is probably a hybrid, of which one parent may be *D. tiliacea.*

Wallichii (Lindl.) Benth. Shrub or small tree, to 30 ft.; lvs. very broadly cordate-ovate, to 12 in. long or more, toothed, sometimes acuminately 3-angled; umbels dense, many-fld., pendent, subtended by densely pubescent bracts up to 2½ in. long; fls. deep pink or red, to 1½ in. across. Winter. E. Afr. and Madagascar.

DOODIA R. Br. *Polypodiaceae.* Eleven spp. of trop. to temp. dwarf ferns, native from Ceylon to Australia, New Zeal., and Polynesia; lvs. stiff, pinnate or pinnatifid; sori in 2 separate rows parallel to midrib, indusia opening on side toward midrib.

Suitable for window boxes and protected ferneries; they should be protected from strong sunlight and the temperate species require an intermediate or cool atmosphere. Propagated by spores and sometimes by division. Mostly grown under glass, often under benches. See also *Ferns.*

aspera R. Br. HACKSAW FERN. Lvs. pinnatifid throughout, to 1½ ft. long and 4 in. wide, very rough, pinnae to 3 in. long, serrulate, sessile. Australia. Most material cult. under this name is *D. media.*

caudata (Cav.) R. Br. Lvs. pinnatifid or pinnate at base, to 1 ft. long and 2 in. wide, slightly rough, pinnae to 1½ in. long, the terminal one caudate. Australia, New Zeal.

maxima John Sm. Similar to *D. caudata,* but lvs. to 1½ ft. long and 3 in. wide, pinnae becoming much smaller basally and finally auricled, erose to apiculately serrulate, terminal segm. lanceolate, but not caudate. New S. Wales.

media R. Br. Lvs. to 2 ft. long, to 5 in. wide, pinnatifid in upper half, pinnate in lower half, pinnae stalked. Var. **Brackenridgei** Cav. Larger; sori in 2 irregular rows on each side of midrib. Australia, New Zeal., Polynesia.

× **DORITAENOPSIS** Guillaum. & Lami: *Dorites* × *Phalaenopsis. Orchidaceae.* A group of bigeneric hybrids generally intermediate in character between the parents.

For culture see *Orchids.*

DORITIS Lindl. *Orchidaceae.* Two spp. of epiphytes, native to se. Asia and Malay Arch.; plants similar to *Phalaenopsis;* sepals and petals spreading, column narrowly winged, the foot of column and base of sepals forming a spurlike mentum, lateral lobes of lip reduced to a pair of small linear appendages. For structure of fl. see *Orchidaceae.*

For culture see *Orchids.*

pulcherrima Lindl. [*Phalaenopsis Esmeralda* Rchb.f.]. To 2 ft.; lvs. to 8 in. long; infl. racemose, rarely paniculate, loosely 3- to many-fld.; fls. to 1¼ in. across, from amethyst-purple to almost white, upper sepals and petals separate, lateral sepals united to column foot, lip 3-lobed, with long claw, the midlobe fleshy, deep purple to orange-red. Autumn–winter, summer. Burma, Cambodia, Malay Pen.

DORMANCY: see *Propagation.*

DORONICUM L. LEOPARD'S-BANE. *Compositae* (Senecio Tribe). About 30 spp. or more of per. herbs of Eur. and temp. Asia, sts. simple or somewhat branched; basal lvs. long-petioled, st. lvs. alt., often clasping; fl. heads radiate, long-peduncled, involucral bracts in 2–3 rows, nearly equal; disc and ray fls. yellow; achenes 10-ribbed, pappus of simple hairs.

Doronicums thrive under average garden conditions, and are frequently cultivated in borders for their showy spring and summer flowers. Propagated by seeds or division.

austriacum Jacq. Hairy, to 4 ft., sts. few-branched; lvs. toothed, basal lvs. cordate, long-petioled, upper st. lvs. oblong-lanceolate, cordate and clasping; heads usually several, about 2 in. across. Eur.

calcareum: *D. glaciale.*

caucasicum: *D. cordatum.*

Clusii (All.) Tausch [*Arnica Clusii* All.]. To 2 ft.; lvs. softly hairy, basal lvs. mostly oblong, toothed or entire, narrowed to petiole, st. lvs. lanceolate, toothed, clasping; heads solitary, to 2 in. across. Mts., cent. Eur.

Columnae: *D. cordatum.*

cordatum (Wulfen) Schultz-Bip. [*D. caucasicum* Rochel; *D. Columnae* Ten.; *D. cordifolium* Sternb.]. Rhizome fibrous, sts. 10–30 in. high; lvs. cordate-ovate to ovate-lanceolate, toothed or lobed, clasping; heads solitary, to 2 in. across. Se. Eur., w. Asia. Cv. '**Magnificum**'. Heads larger.

cordifolium: *D. cordatum.*

excelsum: a listed name, used for a robust form of *D. plantagineum.*

glaciale (Wulfen) Nym. [*D. calcareum* Vierh.]. Sts. hairy, erect, about 6 in., simple, leafy; basal lvs. oblong-ovate, toothed, narrowed to broad petiole, st. lvs. lanceolate, clasping; heads solitary, to 2 in. across. Mts., cent. Eur.

grandiflorum Lam. To 12 in.; lvs. toothed, basal lvs. broadly ovate, long-petioled, st. lvs. lanceolate, clasping; heads 2 in. across. Cent. and s. Eur.

magnificum: a listed name of no botanical standing for *D. cordatum* cv.

Pardalianches L. Sts. hairy, to 3 ft. or more; lvs. cordate, toothed, basal lvs. with long, winged petioles, st. lvs. few, the uppermost clasping; heads 3–5 on a st., to 2½ in. across. Eur. Said to be poisonous. Formerly cult. as a medicinal plant.

plantagineum L. Sts. to 2 ft. or more, somewhat hairy, glandular-pubescent above; basal lvs. ovate-elliptic, narrowed gradually to a long petiole, uppermost lvs. sessile, slightly decurrent; heads solitary, to 3 in. across. Eur.

DOROTHEANTHUS Schwant. *Aizoaceae.* Ten spp. of dwarf, succulent, ann. herbs with short brs., native to S. Afr.; lvs. forming rosettes, opp. or alt. on brs., not much thickened, linear or spatulate, papillose; fls. solitary, calyx 5-lobed, petals few to many, in 1–2 series, stamens few to many, ovary inferior, 5-celled, stigmas 5; fr. a caps., cell lids stiff, expanding keels with membranous wings, placental tubercles absent.

Recommended as a pot plant, but can be grown in a cold frame or sown directly in the flower bed in spring. Seedlings may be overwintered in a cool room free from frost. See also *Succulents.*

bellidiformis (Burm.f.) N. E. Br. [*D. criniflorus* (L.f.) Schwant.; *Mesembryanthemum bellidiforme* Burm.f.; *M. criniflorum* L.f.]. LIVINGSTONE DAISY. Lvs. rough, papillate, to 2¾ in. long, ⅜ in. wide, obovate, narrowed toward base; fls. to 1¾ in. across, pedicelled, petals obtuse, bright rose-pink with darker margins or variously white, pale pink, red, orange, or white with red tips. Cape Prov.

criniflorus: *D. bellidiformis.*

gramineus (Haw.) Schwant. To 4 in., brs. reddish-papillate; lvs. medium green, to 2 in. long, linear-elongate, upper side flat, lower side rounded and papillate; fls. to 1 in. across, terminal, on pedicels to 2½ in. long, petals white in lower half, rose or cerise in upper half. Cape Prov.

tricolor (Willd.) L. Bolus [*Mesembryanthemum tricolor* Willd.]. Lvs. obtuse to subacute, to ½ in. wide; fls. solitary, on long pedicels, petals acute or acuminate, white in lower half, purplish in upper half, filaments and anthers black-purple. Cape Prov.

DORSTENIA L. *Moraceae.* About 170 spp. of monoecious herbs and shrubs, native to trop. Afr. and Amer., a few in Asia; lvs. basal or cauline, very variable, angled to pinnately lobed, entire or toothed, mostly long-petioled; fls. minute, crowded on saucerlike, long-peduncled, axillary receptacles, stamens usually 2, rarely 1 or 3; fr. small, fleshy, seeds bony.

Sometimes grown for curiosity. Propagated by seeds or division.

Contrajerva L. CONTRA HIERBA, TORUS HERB. Lvs. to 8 in. long and wide, deeply pinnately lobed, except palmately lobed at base, scabrous to puberulent, rough to the touch, petioles to 10 in. long; receptacles more or less 4-angled to irregularly lobed, enlarging with age, to 2 in. across, scabrous beneath, peltate, long-peduncled. Caribbean tropics.

DORYALIS: *DOVYALIS.*

DORYANTHES Corrêa. SPEAR LILY. *Agavaceae.* Two spp. of large, succulent plants of e. Australia; lvs. sword-shaped, in basal rosettes; infl. an elongate or globose cluster of 3–4-fld. spikes on st. with short lvs.; fls. large, red, perianth segms. 6, nearly distinct and spreading, stamens 6, shorter than perianth, anthers erect, ovary inferior, 3-celled; fr. a caps., each cell with 2 rows of flat seeds.

Occasionally cultivated in the South and Calif. for bold garden effect. Multiplied slowly by suckers.

excelsa Corrêa. GLOBE S.L. To 18 ft.; lvs. many, curved, to 4 ft. long, not ribbed; infl. to 12 ft., spikes in a globose head to 1 ft. across, with bright red bracts; fls. to 4 in. long. New S. Wales, Queensland.

Palmeri W. Hill. PALMER S.L. To 10 ft.; lvs. to 6 ft. long, 4 in. wide, slightly ribbed; spikes separated in an elongate infl. to 3 ft. long, with colored bracts. Queensland.

DORYCNIUM Mill. *Leguminosae* (subfamily *Faboideae*). About 10–15 spp. of herbs of the Medit. region and Canary Is., somewhat like *Trifolium;* lvs. of 5 lfts., the lower 2 stipule-like; fls. papilionaceous, in heads, the standard often nearly fiddle-shaped, stamens 10, 9 united and 1 separate, all or 5 suddenly dilated toward apex; fr. a small, cylindrical legume.

Cultivated as ornamentals. Of easy cultivation; propagated by seeds or division.

germanicum: *D. pentaphyllum* subsp.

hirsutum (L.) Ser. ex DC. To 2 ft., shrubby, white-hairy; lfts. cuneate-obovate, about $\frac{1}{2}$ in. long; fls. in heads to $1\frac{1}{2}$ in. across, white with rose lines and purple keel. Summer, early autumn. S. Eur.

pentaphyllum Scop. [*D. suffruticosum* Vill.]. Per. herb or shrubby, to $2\frac{1}{2}$ ft., much-branched; lvs. without rachis, lfts. linear, to obovate-oblong; fls. in 5–25-fld. heads, calyx teeth unequal, petals white, the keel tipped dark blue or purple; fr. ovoid-globose, to $\frac{3}{16}$ in. long. Cent. and s. Eur. Subsp. **pentaphyllum.** The typical subsp.; lfts. of upper lvs. to $\frac{1}{2}$ in. long, $\frac{1}{8}$ in. wide; fl. heads 5–15-fld.; standard very briefly pointed. Sw. Eur. Subsp. **germanicum** (Gremli) Gams [*D. suffruticosum* var. *sericeum* (Kováts ex Neilr.) G. Beck]. Lfts. of upper lvs. to $\frac{3}{4}$ in. long, $\frac{5}{32}$ in. wide; fl. heads 5–15-fld.; standard scarcely pointed. Cent. Eur., Balkan Pen.

suffruticosum: *D. pentaphyllum.* Var. **sericeum:** *D. pentaphyllum* subsp. *germanicum.*

DORYOPTERIS John Sm. *Polypodiaceae.* About 25 spp. of small ferns of tropics; lvs. sometimes moderately to strongly dimorphic, entire or palmately lobed or divided, sometimes pinnate or deeply pinnatifid, petioles black, glossy; sori confluent in a marginal line, indusia continuous.

Culture as for *Pteris.* See also *Ferns.*

concolor (Langsd. & Fisch.) Kuhn. Lvs. to 15 in. long, triangular, to 6 in. wide, 2–3-pinnatifid, the lowest pinnae larger than other pinnae and with lobes on lower side larger than the others. Tropics.

cordifolia (Bak.) Diels [*Pteris cordifolia* Bak.]. Lvs. dimorphic, sterile lvs. with blades simple, ovate, to nearly 8 in. long, cordate at base, fertile lvs. hastate to 3-parted, petioles dark purple. Madagascar.

palmata: *D. pedata* var.

pedata (L.) Fée. HAND FERN. Lvs. moderately dimorphic, to 16 in. long, long-petioled, fertile blade pentagonal, 3-parted, triangular in apical part, but wedge-shaped at base, coarsely pinnatifid-lobed to 2-pinnatifid, the lateral segms. coarsely lobed. Trop. Amer. Var. **palmata** (Willd.) Hicken [*D. palmata* (Willd.) John Sm.]. Segms. broader, less lobed. Mex.

DOUGLASIA Lindl. [*Gregoria* Duby]. *Primulaceae.* Six spp. of tufted per. herbs, from mts. of N. Amer., 1 sp. from the Alps and Pyrenees; lvs. in rosettes; fls. yellow or red to purple, in 1–7-fld. scapose umbels, calyx 5-lobed, corolla funnelform, crested in the throat, stamens 5, borne on the corolla; fr. a 5-valved caps.

Grown in the rock garden; culture as for *Androsace.*

biflora: *D. montana* var.

dentata: *D. nivalis.*

laevigata A. Gray [*Gregoria laevigata* (A. Gray) House]. Loosely tufted; lvs. oblong, oblong-lanceolate to spatulate, to $\frac{5}{8}$ in. long, fleshy, glabrous; fls. rose-pink, 2–6 in involucrate umbels. Wash., Ore. Var. **ciliolata** Const. Lvs. thin, ciliate on margins. Var. **olympica** is listed.

montana A. Gray [*Gregoria montana* (A. Gray) House]. Lvs. linear to linear-oblong, to $\frac{3}{8}$ in. long, ciliate on margins; fls. purple or lilac, usually solitary, if 2, the pedicels essentially of equal length. Mont., Wyo., Idaho. Var. **biflora** (A. Nels.) R. Knuth [*D. biflora* A. Nels.]. Infl. of 2 fls., with pedicels of unequal length.

nivalis Lindl. [*D. dentata* S. Wats.]. Loosely tufted; lvs. linear-oblong, oblanceolate, or spatulate, to $\frac{3}{4}$ in. long, stellate-hairy; fls. rose-violet, in 2–10-fld. involucrate umbels. Ne. Wash., Alta., B.C.

Praetutiana: a listed name of no botanical standing for *D. Vitaliana* cv.

Vitaliana (L.) Hook.f. [*Androsace Vitaliana* (L.) Lapeyr.; *Gregoria Vitaliana* (L.) Duby]. Sts. prostrate; lvs. in rosettes, linear-oblong, to $\frac{3}{8}$ in. long, stellate-hairy; fls. yellow, long-tubed, solitary or in pairs. Alps, Pyrenees. Cv. **'Praetutiana'.** Lvs. lime-incrusted.

DOVYALIS E. H. Mey. ex Arn. (sometimes but not originally spelled *Doryalis*) [*Aberia* Hochst.]. *Flacourtiaceae.* About 22 spp. of dioecious shrubs or small trees, with or without axillary spines, native mostly to Afr., with 1 sp. in Ceylon and 1 in New Guinea; lvs. alt., simple, usually entire; fls. unisexual, small and inconspicuous, petals none, stamens 10 to many; fr. an edible berry.

The plants are suitable for subtropical climates, the umkokolo withstanding drought and lower temperatures than the kitembilla. To ensure fruit both male and female plants must be provided. Propagated by seeds, layering, and shield-budding.

abyssinica (A. Rich.) Warb. Tree, to 30 ft.; spines robust, to $1\frac{1}{2}$ in. long; lvs. ovate, to $3\frac{1}{2}$ in. long; fls. green; berry apricot-colored, $\frac{1}{2}$ in. in diam. Trop. Afr. Fr. edible but very acid, excellent for jelly.

caffra (Hook.f. & Harv.) Warb. [*Aberia caffra* Hook.f. & Harv.]. KEI APPLE, KAI A., KAU A., UMKOKOLO. To 20 ft., spines stiff, sharp; lvs. obovate, to 2 in. long, usually in clusters at base of spines; berry yellow, smooth, about 1 in. in diam. with yellow, juicy, acid pulp. S. Afr. Useful for pickles and jelly.

hebecarpa (G. Gardn.) Warb. [*Aberia Gardneri* Clos.]. KITEMBILLA, CEYLON GOOSEBERRY. To 20 ft., spines sharp, long; lvs. lanceolate or ovate, to 4 in. long; berry maroon-purple, velvety, with purplish, edible, sweet pulp. Ceylon. Useful for preserves and jelly.

DOWNINGIA Torr. *Lobeliaceae.* Eleven spp. of small, ann. herbs, native to w. N. Amer., 1 sp. to Chile; lvs. sessile, alt., filiform to elliptic, mostly entire; fls. solitary in lf. axils, appearing pedicelled because of elongate, twisted ovary, corolla mostly blue, 2-lipped, the lower, larger lip usually spotted, tube entire, not split, anther tube usually exserted, lower 2 anthers tufted-pubescent at apex, and often with hornlike appendage, ovary inferior, 1–2-celled; fr. a fusiform caps., opening by longitudinal slits, seeds many.

Sometimes grown in the flower garden; propagated by seeds.

cuspidata (Greene) Greene ex Jeps. [*D. immaculata* Munz & I. M. Johnst.]. To about 10 in.; lvs. nearly linear, to $\frac{1}{2}$ in. long; corolla $\frac{3}{8}$–$\frac{5}{8}$ in. long, blue or white, lower lip reflexed, white-spotted, anther tube not incurved or only slightly so; caps. 2-celled, $\frac{3}{4}$–$1\frac{1}{2}$ in. long, seeds many, shiny, appearing twisted by the sculpturing of the walls. Calif.

elegans (Dougl.) Torr. To 16 in.; lvs. linear or narrow-elliptic, to 1 in. long; corolla $\frac{1}{2}$–$\frac{5}{8}$ in. long, blue or rarely white, lower lip concave, not reflexed, usually with a white spot marked with yellow, anther tube long-exserted, strongly incurved; caps. 1–$1\frac{3}{4}$ in. long, 1-celled, with papery, easily ruptured walls. Wash., s. to Idaho, Nev., n. Calif.

immaculata: *D. cuspidata.*

pulchella (Lindl.) Torr. To 10 in.; lvs. oblong-ovate, to $\frac{1}{2}$ in. long, but the upper ones sometimes to 1 in. long; corolla about $\frac{1}{2}$ in. long, deep blue, lower lip strongly reflexed, spotted white with purple and yellow markings, anther tube slightly or not incurved; caps. 1–$2\frac{3}{4}$ in. long, 2-celled, walls tough. Calif.

DOXANTHA: *MACFADYENA.*

DRABA L. *Cruciferae.* About 250 spp. of ann. to per., often deeply taprooted herbs, mostly in N. Temp. and boreal regions and in mts., growing in open, rocky, or gravelly locations; lvs. simple, entire, dentate, basal lvs. commonly forming a rosette, the sts. sometimes leafless; fls. small, dainty, white, yellow, rose, or purplish, in terminal racemes, sepals and petals 4; fr. a small silicle, often globular or orbicular.

The species are variable and difficult to identify. Many are ornamental, adaptable to alpine and rock gardens.

acaulis Boiss. Per., cushion-forming, sts. clothed with dead lvs. basally; lvs. overlapping, linear-obovate, soft, grayish-pubescent; fls. 1–3 on a short scape, yellow. Taurus Mts. (Turkey).

Adamsii: *D. alpina* var.

aizoides L. Tufted per., to 4 in.; lvs. in basal rosettes, linear, to $\frac{1}{2}$ in. long, acute, ciliate; fls. yellowish, in many-fld. racemes on glabrous scapes, stamens as long as petals; silicles elliptic, flat. Mts., cent. and s. Eur.

aizoon: *D. lasiocarpa.*

alpina L. Cespitose per.; lvs. basal, lanceolate-elliptic, entire or essentially so, pubescent, thin, not fleshy; fls. in close clusters on simple, erect, hairy scapes (1–8 in. tall in fr.), petals yellow, 2–3 times as long as sepals; silicles flat. Subarctic regions, circumpolar. A variable and complex sp. Var. **Adamsii** (Ledeb.) O. E. Schulz [*D. Adamsii* Ledeb.]. Plants pilose, densely hispid. Var. **glacialis** (Adams) Th. Fries [*D. glacialis* Adams]. Lvs. oblong-lanceolate, slightly fleshy, keeled; sepals hispid.

altaica (C. A. Mey.) Bunge. Cespitose per., to 3 in., much-branched; basal lvs. in rosettes, linear-lanceolate, to nearly ½ in. long, with acute, 1-2-toothed apex, pilose, ciliate, st. lvs. entire, sessile; fls. white, in compact, headlike racemes on hirsute, leafy scapes, silicles ovate, acute. Cent. Asia.

andina: see *D. oligosperma* and *Stenodraba colchaguensis.*

androsacea: *D. lactea.*

arabisans Michx. Diffuse per., 8–20 in., sts. many, erect; lvs. narrow, basal lvs. in a cluster, to 1½ in. long, st. lvs. scattered, smaller, toothed; fls. white, in corymbose racemes on glabrous to minutely stellate-pilose scapes; silicles long-acuminate. Nfld., s. to Ont. and N.Y.

armata: *D. aspera.*

aspera Bertol. [*D. armata* Schott, Nym. & Kotschy; *D. Bertolonii* Nym.; *D. longirostra* Schott, Nym. & Kotschy; *D. longirostra* var. *erioscapa* (Caruel) O. E. Schulz]. Similar to *D. aizoides,* but lvs. narrower, $\frac{1}{16}$ in. wide, and silicles inflated. Mts., s. Eur.

athoa (Griseb.) Boiss. Rather robust per., to 5 in.; lvs. broad-linear, to ¾ in. long, obtuse, ciliate; fls. yellow, rather large, in 8–20-fld. loose racemes; silicles elliptic, to ½ in. across, flat, usually glabrous. Mts., cent. and s. Eur.

aurea Vahl. Bien. or short-lived per., pubescent, sts. 1 to several from a basal rosette, to 20 in.; lvs. oblanceolate to lanceolate, to 2 in. long, entire or sparingly serrate; fls. yellow to nearly white, in 15–30-fld. racemes. Alaska, s. along Rocky Mts. to New Mex. and Ariz.

austriaca: *D. stellata.*

Bertolonii: *D. aspera.*

borealis DC. Cespitose per., to 12 in., unbranched or somewhat branched; lvs. ovate to oblong-ovate, to 1 in. long, with 1 or 2 teeth, stellate-pubescent; fls. white, in dense, corymbose racemes on densely pilose scapes, the hairs not stellate. Arctic regions, Canada and Siberia.

bruniifolia Steven [*D. diversifolia* Boiss.]. Tufted per., to 4 in.; lvs. in rosettes, linear, about ¼ in. long, obtuse; fls. orange, in loose racemes on short-pilose, leafless scapes, stamens shorter than petals, ovary with 4–10 ovules. Mts., Medit. region. A variable sp. Subsp. **olympica** (Sibth. ex DC.) Coode & Cullen [*D. olympica* Sibth. ex DC.]. Lvs. with simple hairs only along margins; infl. on villous scape, 3–8-fld.

bryoides: *D. rigida.*

carinthiaca Hoppe [*D. Johannis* Host]. Cespitose per., to 6 in., forming many rosettes; basal lvs. lanceolate, to ⅜ in. long, acute and usually entire or 1-toothed at apex, pilose, ciliate, st. lvs. shorter, ovate to oblong; fls. white, in loose, corymbose racemes on scapes glabrescent above and short-pilose toward base, petals to ⅛ in. long; silicles oblong-elliptic. Mts., s. and cent. Eur.

cuspidata Bieb. Densely tufted per., to 4 in.; lvs. linear, to ½ in. long, obtusish; fls. purplish, in loose racemes; silicles somewhat inflated. Crimea.

daurica DC. [*D. hirta* of auth., not L.]. Per., sts. flexuous, often unbranched, to 10 in., stellate-hairy at least below; basal lvs. narrowly lanceolate, to ¾ in. long, sometimes toothed at apex, minutely stellate-pubescent, remotely ciliate; fls. cream-white, 8–20 in a corymb; silicles ovate-lanceolate, to ½ in. across, flat. Arctic Eur. and mts. of Scandinavia.

Dedeana Boiss. & Reut. Densely cespitose per., to 2 in.; lvs. in rosettes, oblong-linear, about ¼ in. long, obtuse, ciliate; fls. white, rarely pale sulphur-yellow, 3–10 in a raceme. Spain.

densiflora Nutt. [*D. globosa* Payson; *D. globosa* var. *sphaerula* (Macbr. & Payson) O. E. Schulz; *D. Nelsonii* Macbr. & Payson; probably *D. Paysonii* Macbr.; *D. sphaerula* Macbr. & Payson]. Tufted per., to 2½ in.; lvs. in dense basal rosette, linear to narrowly spatulate, to ⅜ in. long or less, obtuse, margin pectinate-ciliate with long hairs; fls. yellow, in loose racemes on villous scapes. Utah to Calif., n. to Mont. and B.C.

dicranioides: *D. rigida.*

diversifolia: *D. bruniifolia.*

Doerfleri: *Schivereckia Doerfleri.*

dubia Suter. Many-stemmed, small, cespitose per., to 4 in.; basal lvs. in tight rosettes, obovate or oblong; fls. white, in loose racemes; silicles oblong-elliptic, to ⅝ in. long, glabrous or nearly so. Mts., cent. and s. Eur.

fladnizensis Wulfen. Cespitose, cushionlike per., 2–3 in.; basal lvs. oblong, to ⅜ in. long or more, obtusish, mostly entire, st. lvs. entire or remotely dentate; fls. greenish-white. Arctic region and mts. of cent. and s. Eur.; also in N. Amer. from Alaska s. to the Rocky Mts. Plants grown under this name may be *Arabis carduchorum.*

gigas: *Arabis carduchorum.*

glacialis: *D. alpina* var.

globosa: *D. densiflora.*

Haynaldii Stur. Very dwarf per., to 2½ in.; lvs. in basal rosettes, narrowly linear, about ¼ in. long, acute, briefly and finely ciliate but not pectinate-ciliate; fls. yellow, in corymbose racemes on glabrous scapes; silicles inflated at base. Mts., e. Eur.

hirta: see *D. daurica.*

incana L. Robust bien., sometimes per., to 1 ft., gray-pubescent; lvs. lanceolate, to 1 in. long, obtusish, entire, or sparsely dentate, the basal ones in rosettes; fls. white, sepals often purplish. Far north, N. Amer. and Eurasia.

incerta Payson [*D. oligosperma* var. *pilosa* (Regel) O. E. Schulz]. Cespitose per., to 5 in.; lvs. all basal, linear-oblanceolate, to ½ in. long, stellate-hairy, ciliate; fls. yellow, to ½ in. across, 3–14 on stout pedicels in loose racemes; silicles broadly lanceolate, to $\frac{5}{16}$ in. long, flat, with small but distinct beak. Mts., B.C., s. to Wyo. and Ore. Related to *D. oligosperma,* but generally a looser, taller plant.

Johannis: *D. carinthiaca.*

Kotschyi Stur. Similar to *D. dubia;* to 4 in., sts. decumbent, rooting; basal lvs. oblanceolate or elliptic, to ½ in. long, entire or with few teeth, hairy, sts. lvs. 1–3, incised-dentate; fls. white. Mts., cent. Eur.

lactea Adams [*D. androsacea* Wahlenb.]. Related to *D. fladnizensis,* but lacking st. lvs., and having basal lvs. with some branched hairs or occasionally with a few stellate hairs. Arctic regions.

lasiocarpa Rochel [*D. aizoon* Wahlenb.]. Robust, usually densely cespitose per., to 8 in.; lvs. broadly linear, to ¾ in. long; fls. deep yellow, in many-fld. racemes on glabrous scapes; silicles oblong-elliptic, to ⅜ in. long, flat, hairy. Mts., e. Eur.

laxa: *D. norvegica.*

longirostra: *D. aspera.*

mollissima Steven. Cushion-forming per., to 2 in.; lvs. all basal, imbricate, in rosettes, oblong, to ¼ in. long, entire; fls. yellow, in 6–18-fld. corymbose racemes on erect scapes to 2 in. high; silicles oblong-elliptic, to ¼ in. long, flat. Caucasus.

Nelsonii: *D. densiflora.*

nivalis Liljeblad. Many-stemmed, densely cespitose per., to 3 in.; lvs. narrow-obovate to ligulate, ¼ in. long or less, entire or with 1 or 2 teeth; fls. white, in dense racemes on short-pilose scapes; silicles oblong to elliptic, the persistent style less than $\frac{1}{16}$ in. long. Arctic and subarctic regions of Eur. and N. Amer., s. (in Amer.) to mts. in Utah.

norvegica Gunnerus [*D. laxa* Lindbl.; *D. rupestris* R. Br.]. Per., variable in habit, sts. 8 in., slender, often flexuous, somewhat hairy; lower lvs. oblong-lanceolate, to 2 in. long, acute, entire or few-toothed at apex, pilose, not stellate-hairy, ciliate; fls. white, infl. elongating in fr. Arctic and subarctic Eur.

oligosperma Hook. [*D. andina* (Nutt.) A. Nels., not Phil.; *D. oligosperma* var. *andina* Nutt.]. Loosely cespitose, matted per., to 4 in.; basal lvs. rigid, linear, to ⅜ in. long and $\frac{1}{16}$ in. wide, acute, short-pilose, ciliate but not pectinate-ciliate; fls. yellow, in loose racemes on short-pilose scapes, petals scarcely longer than sepals. Alaska to high mts. of n. Calif., e. to Rocky Mts. Var. **pilosa:** *D. incerta.*

olympica: *D. bruniifolia* subsp.

Paysonii: *D. densiflora.*

polytricha Ledeb. Cushion-forming per., to 2 in., rosettes dense, many, hairy; lvs. densely imbricated, linear-lanceolate, to ½ in. long, white-hairy; fls. yellow, in 4–10-fld. racemes; silicles ovate, to $\frac{3}{16}$ in. long, inflated, on pedicels to ¼ in. long. Caucasus.

pyrenaica: *Petrocallis pyrenaica.*

repens: *D. sibirica.*

rigida Willd. [*D. bryoides* DC.; *D. dicranioides* Boiss. & Huet]. Cespitose per. with many densely leafy brs.; lvs. rigid, broad-linear or elliptic, about ¼ in. long, obtuse, glossy, stiffly ciliate; fls. yellow, in few-fld. leafless scapes to 3 in.; silicles elliptic, to ¼ in. long. Asia Minor. Differs from *D. bruniifolia* in having 32–36 ovules in ovary.

ruaxes: *D. ventosa.*

rupestris: *D. norvegica.*

sibirica (Pall.) Thell. [*D. repens* Bieb.]. Plant soft green, sts. slender, more or less prostrate, sometimes 12 in. long; lvs. scarcely in rosettes, oblong-lanceolate, acute, entire, somewhat hairy; fls. yellow, on ascending sts. Siberia, Caucasus, e. Greenland.

sphaerula: *D. densiflora.*

stellata Jacq. [*D. austriaca* Crantz]. Cespitose per., to 4 in.; basal lvs. oblanceolate, to ⅜ in. long, stellate-pubescent, st. lvs. often toothed; fls. white, in 3–12-fld. terminal corymbs. Alps, Eur.

tomentosa Clairv. Loosely cespitose per., sts. loose, to 3½ in., pilose; lvs. mostly basal and crowded, elliptic or obovate, ¼ in. long, obtuse, entire, densely tomentose; fls. white or nearly so, in racemes on sparsely leafy sts.; silicles distinctly hairy, slightly inflated when ripe. Mts., cent. and s. Eur. Like *D. dubia*, but silicles hairy, slightly inflated.

ussuriensis Pohle. Loosely cespitose per., to 8 in.; lower lvs. obovate-oblong or spatulate, to ⅝ in. long, upper st. lvs. ovate-lanceolate, sessile; fls. white, in few-fld., loose racemes; silicles elliptic or oblong-ovate, to ⅜ in. long. Ne. Asia.

ventosa A. Gray [*D. ruaxes* Payson & St. John]. Cespitose, gray-pubescent per., from a branched caudex usually covered with remains of old lvs.; lvs. all basal, oblanceolate to suborbicular, about ¼ in. long, thick; fls. yellow, in 3–20-fld. racemes on leafless scapes. Alpine regions, nw. N. Amer.

vesicaria Desv. Densely tufted, grayish-pubescent per., tufts about 3½ in. across, the base clothed with remains of old lvs.; lvs. all basal, obovate, to ¼ in. long; fls. yellowish, in few-fld. racemes on leafless scapes; silicles ovoid, to ¼ in. long, inflated, hairy. Lebanon.

DRACAENA L. [*Pleomele* Salisb.]. *Agavaceae*. About 40 spp. of shrubby or treelike plants in tropics of the Old World, 1 in Amer.; sts. slender to very stout; lvs. narrow to broad; infl. a panicle; fls. similar to *Cordyline* but ovule solitary in each cell.

Stem resin of some species of *Dracaena* is one source of dragon's blood, used in the varnish industry and in photoengraving. DRACAENA is also the common name of *Cordyline*. For cultivation see *Cordyline.*

amabilis: *Cordyline terminalis* cv.

americana J. D. Sm. Sts. to more than 36 ft., 1 ft. in diam., but mostly smaller, brs. few; lvs. linear-sword-shaped, to 14 in. long, 1 in. wide, bright green, rather soft; panicle dense, ovoid, to 1 ft. long; fls. white or creamy-white, ¼ in. long; berry yellowish-green, to ¾ in. in diam. Mex. to Costa Rica.

arborea (Willd.) Link. TREE D. To 45 ft.; lvs. strap-shaped, to 40 in. long, 2¾ in. wide, green; panicle pendulous, to 4 ft. long; fls. creamy-white, about ⁹⁄₁₆ in. long, on conspicuous pedicels; fr. nearly ¾ in. in diam. W. Trop. Afr.

australis: *Cordyline australis.*

Baptisii: *Cordyline terminalis* cv.

Bausei: a listed name of no botanical standing for *D. deremensis* cv.

Bruantii: a listed name of no botanical standing for *Cordyline rubra* cv.

cincta Bak. [*D. gracilis* Hort., not Salisb. nor Wallich; *Pleomele gracilis* Hort.]. Trunk slender, short, unbranched; lvs. loosely spreading, sword-shaped, to 15 in. long, ½ in. wide, margins reddish-brown. An imperfectly known sp., to which material cult. as *D. gracilis* or *Pleomele gracilis* may belong. Some hort. material listed as *D. marginata* may also belong here.

concinna Kunth. To 6 ft.; lvs. oblanceolate, 2–3 ft. long, 2½–3 in. wide, the margins purple. Mauritius. Some hort. material listed as *D. marginata* may belong here.

deremensis Engl. To 15 ft.; lvs. to 2 ft. long, 2 in. wide; fls. dark red outside, white inside. Trop. Afr. Cvs. include: '**Bausei**', lvs. with central white stripe, margined dark green; '**Longii**', lvs. with central white stripe; '**Warneckii**', STRIPED D., lvs. with two white stripes; the cv. most frequently cult.

Doucetii: a listed name of no botanical standing for *Cordyline australis* cv.

Draco L. DRAGON TREE. To 70 ft.; lvs. to 2 ft. long, 1¾ in. wide, glaucous; fls. greenish; berries bright orange. Canary Is.

ensifolia: *Dianella ensifolia.*

fragrans (L.) Ker-Gawl. To 20 ft.; lvs. to 3 ft. long, 4 in. wide; fls. yellowish, fragrant. Upper Guinea. Cvs. include: '**Knerkii**', lvs. glossy light green; '**Lindenii**' [*D. Lindenii* Hort. Linden ex André], lvs. with broad, creamy-white marginal stripes; '**Massangeana**', CORN PLANT, lvs. with broad yellow central stripe; '**Rothiana**' [*D. Rothiana* Hort. Haage & Schmidt ex Carrière], lvs. leathery with whitish margins; '**Victoria**', resembling cv. 'Lindenii' but lvs. with broad, glossy, golden, marginal stripes.

Godseffiana: *D. surculosa.*

Goldieana Hort. ex Bak. Sts. slender, to 1 ft.; lvs. distinctly petioled, to 9 in. long, 5 in. wide, with gray and bright green, cross bands; fls. white, in dense heads; fr. red, ½–¾ in. in diam. Upper Guinea.

gracilis: see *D. cincta.*

Haageana, Haagei: listed names of no botanical standing; probably for *Cordyline Haageana.*

Hookerana C. Koch. To 6 ft. or more; lvs. sword-shaped, to 2½ ft. long, 2 in. across, somewhat ribbed beneath, margins white-pellucid; fls. greenish, to 1 in. long; berries orange. S. Afr. Cv. '**Latifolia**'. Lvs. to 3½ in. across. Cv. '**Variegata**'. Lvs. more or less white-striped.

hybrida: *Cordyline terminalis* cv.

imperialis: a listed name of no botanical standing for *Cordyline terminalis* cv.

indivisa: *Cordyline indivisa.*

Kelleri, Kellerana: listed names of no botanical standing, probably referable to *D. surculosa* cv. 'Kelleri'.

Knerkii: a listed name of no botanical standing for *D. fragrans* cv.

Lindenii: *D. fragrans* cv.

Longii: a listed name of no botanical standing for *D. deremensis* cv.

marginata Lam. Sts. slender, to 12 ft.; lvs. sessile, narrowly sword-shaped, to 2 ft. long, flat or somewhat concave toward base, sharp-pointed at apex, gray-green, margins purple; panicles elongate. Madagascar. The sp. is probably not cult. Material under this name may also be *D. cincta* or *D. concinna.*

Massangeana: a listed name of no botanical standing for *D. fragrans* cv.

Masseffana: a hort. name of no botanical standing, used for a hybrid between *D. fragrans* cv. 'Massangeana' and *D. surculosa;* also known as *Dracaena* cv. 'Pennock'. St. low, unbranched; lvs. petioled, ovate-lanceolate, spotted with yellow.

reflexa Lam. [*Pleomele reflexa* (Lam.) N. E. Br.]. Branched shrubs or small trees, to 30 ft.; lvs. loosely tufted at tips of brs., generally linear or lanceolate, much longer than wide; infl. simple or branched, often reflexed; fls. white, to ¾ in. long, lobes 4 times as long as tube. Madagascar, Mauritius. An extremely variable sp., with some 14 cvs.

Rothiana: *D. fragrans* cv.

rubra: see *Cordyline rubra.*

Sanderana Hort. Sander ex M. T. Mast. BELGIAN EVERGREEN. Lvs. to 9 in. long, 1¼ in. wide, with broad white marginal stripes. Cameroons.

stricta: *Cordyline stricta.*

surculosa Lindl. [*D. Godseffiana* Hort. ex Bak.]. GOLD-DUST D., SPOTTED D. Shrubby, to 3 or rarely 6 ft.; lvs. elliptic, more or less abruptly narrowed at each end, irregularly spotted with white; infl. racemose or capitate; fls. about ¾ in. long, greenish-yellow; fr. less than ⅜ in. in diam. W. Trop. Afr. Var. **surculosa.** The typical var.; fls. in a racemose infl. Cv. '**Kelleri**' [*D. Godseffiana* cv. 'Kelleri']. Lvs. thicker, more spotted and marbled with ivory-white. Var. **capitata** Hepper. Fls. in a capitate infl.

terminalis: *Cordyline terminalis.*

thalioides Hort. Makoy ex E. Morr. [*Pleomele thalioides* (Hort. Makoy ex E. Morr.) N. E. Br.]. Low shrub; lvs. long-petioled, lanceolate; infl. branched, with short lateral spikes; fls. white, flushed with red outside, to 1½ in. long, the lobes equalling the tube. Trop. Afr.

tricolor: a listed name of no botanical standing for *Cordyline terminalis* cv.

Veitchii: a listed name of no botanical standing for *Cordyline australis* cv.

Victoria: a listed name of no botanical standing for *D. fragrans* cv.

Warneckii: a listed name of no botanical standing for *D. deremensis* cv.

Youngii: a listed name of no botanical standing for *Cordyline terminalis* cv.

DRACOCEPHALUM L. DRAGONHEAD. *Labiatae*. About 45 spp., of ann. and per. herbs, sometimes subshrubs, chiefly of temp. Eur. and Asia, also N. Afr. and N. Amer.; sts. mostly square in cross section; lvs. opp., simple, dentate, entire, or incised; fls. in verticillasters arranged in axillary or terminal spikes or racemes, bracts often large; calyx tubular, 13–15-nerved, 5-toothed, upper tooth larger than other 4, corolla 2-lipped, upper lip 2-lobed, emarginate, lower lip 3-lobed, middle lobe largest, stamens 4, in 2 pairs, anthers 2-celled, style 2-lobed, ovary 4-parted; fr. of 4 glabrous nutlets. Differs from *Nepeta* in having calyx 2-lipped and 15-nerved, and upper stamen pair longer than lower.

Dragonheads thrive in a rather moist, partially shady location and moderately rich sandy loam. Propagated by seeds or division.

argunense Fisch. ex Link [*D. Ruyschiana* var. *japonicum* A. Gray]. Per., to 2½ ft.; lvs. lanceolate, to 2 in. long, entire, upper lvs. nearly sessile, bristly toothed; spikes leafy; corolla 2–3 times as long as calyx, about 1 in. long, blue or white, anthers hairy. Ne. Asia. Probably not distinct from *D. Ruyschiana*, differing in being a generally larger plant.

austriacum L. Per. herb or dwarf shrub, sts. erect, to 24 in.; lvs. to 1½ in. long, glabrous above, pilose beneath, pinnately cut into 3–7 segms., segms. linear, revolute; spikes dense, verticillasters 2–4-fld.; corolla funnelform, 1½–2 in. long, blue-violet, anthers and filaments glabrous. Se. France to Caucasus.

botryoides Steven. Evergreen per., 4–6 in., decumbent and ascending, villous, sts. woody at base; lvs. ovate, ¼–¾ in. long, pinnatisect, pilose above, densely woolly beneath, segms. usually 3–5, oblong; infl. a dense, headlike spike of verticillasters; fls. about ½ in. long, lavender-pink. Early summer. Caucasus. This sp. fls. infrequently under cult. in ne. U.S.

calophyllum Hand.-Mazz. Per. herb, closely allied to *D. Forrestii*, but sturdier, internodes longer; lvs. 1–1¾ in. long, broad, segms. 5–7, flat or weakly revolute; infl. glabrescent to short-pilose, not woolly; calyx tube longer, ¾ in. long, the margin longer-toothed. Kansu, sw. China to se. Tibet. Var. **Smithianum** Keenan. Lf. segms. mostly 7–11; infl. woolly. Most material cult. as *D. Forrestii* is this var.

Forrestii W. W. Sm. Not in cult.; material so listed is usually *D. calophyllum* var. *Smithianum*.

fruticulosum Steph. ex Willd. Not in cult.; plants so listed may be *Nepeta Stewartiana*.

grandiflorum L. Not in cult.; material so listed is usually *D. rupestre*.

Hemsleyanum (D. Oliver ex Prain) Prain ex Marq. & Airy-Shaw [*Nepeta Hemsleyana* D. Oliver ex Prain]. Allied to *D. Ruyschiana*, but differs in having anthers glabrous. Se. Tibet.

Moldavica L. Ann., 1–2 ft., branching, fragrant; lvs. lanceolate, ¾–1¾ in. long, incised-crenate, sometimes bristle-toothed; fls. in terminal racemes, corolla 2–3 times as long as calyx, ¾–1½ in. long, purple. Eur., cent. Asia, Siberia; naturalized in cent. Eur. and e. N. Amer. Cv. **'Album'**. Fls. white.

nutans L. Bien. or per., 8–24 in., appressed-pubescent; lvs. ovate to oblong, ¾–2 in. long, coarsely crenate-serrate, petioled; fls. in leafy, terminal, spicate racemes 1–6 in. long, corolla ½–¾ in. long, deep bright blue. Early summer. E. Russia to Siberia.

Nuttallii: *Physostegia parviflora*.

parviflorum Nutt. Ann. or bien., 4–36 in.; lvs. lanceolate to lanceolate-ovate, 1–3 in. long, sharply serrate, the teeth spinescent; fls. in spikes with spine-tipped, imbricate bracts, corolla slightly longer than calyx, ½–¾ in. long, light blue to violet. Ne. N. Amer. to New Mex. and Ariz.

peregrinum L. Per., sts. erect to ascending, to 2½ ft.; basal lvs. to 1½ in. long and ½ in. wide, incised, with 2–4 large teeth on both margins, petioled, upper lvs. linear-lanceolate, to ¾ in. long and ⅛ in. wide, glabrescent, nearly sessile; infl. 2–6 in. long, with fls. often on lateral brs.; calyx to ½ in. long, showy, red-purple, spinescent, corolla to 1½ in. long, bright dark blue-purple to dark blue-gray, or rose-red, or white. Summer. Cent. Asia.

Prattii (Lév.) Hand.-Mazz. Erect per., to 3 ft.; lvs. ovate-lanceolate, 1½–2 in. long, crenate, the lowermost petioled, the upper sessile; fls. in dense verticillasters, calyx to 5/16 in. long, toothed, corolla to 1 in. long, bluish-violet. Summer. W. China.

Purdomii W. W. Sm. Erect per., 6–8 in.; basal lvs. ovate, to 1½ in. long, to ½ in. wide, truncate to cordate at base, crenate, pilose, upper lvs. sessile; infl. terminal, dense, nearly globose, to 1¼ in. across; calyx to ½ in. long, glabrescent, corolla to 1 in. long, densely white-villous, intense blue. Summer. Nw. China. Related to *D. rupestre*.

Renatii Emberger. Low per., to 10 in., sts. ascending; lvs. ovate-oblong, about 1 in. long, entire, petioled; spikes long-hairy; calyx lobes nearly as long as tube, corolla about 1 5/16 in. long, cream-white, tube reddish, hairy outside. Morocco.

rupestre Hance. Small per. herb, forming dense clumps, 8–24 in.; lvs. ovate, mostly 1–2 in. long, cordate, sparsely hairy, petioled, basal lvs. broadest, 1½–2 in. wide, obtuse, crenate; spikes short, dense, rough-hairy; calyx half as long as corolla, reddish, teeth spinose, corolla 1½–2 in. long, dark bluish-violet, tube narrow at base, with pouch near mouth. W. China. Material cult. as *D. grandiflorum* is usually this sp.

Ruprechtii Regel. Not in cult.; material offered under this name may be *Hyssopus officinalis*.

Ruyschiana L. Per., to 2 ft., sts. erect or ascending, often short-hairy; lvs. linear-lanceolate, 2–3 in. long, obtuse, entire, revolute, glabrous, upper lvs. sessile; spikes with dense, 2–6-fld. verticillasters, bracts ovate-cuspidate, ciliate; calyx pubescent, teeth cuspidate, corolla to 1 in. long, bluish, rarely pink or white, hairy, tube not longer than calyx, anthers hairy. Eur. Var. **japonicum:** *D. argunense*.

tanguticum Maxim. Not in cult.; material so listed may be *D. calophyllum* var. *Smithianum* or *D. argunense*.

DRACOPHYLLUM Labill. *Epacridaceae*. About 48 spp. of shrubs or small trees, native to Australia and New Caledonia, but chiefly to New Zeal.; sts. marked by lf. scars; lvs. alt., imbricate or crowded toward ends of brs., with sheathing base and resembling lvs. of monocots; fls. solitary or in spikes, racemes, or panicles, sepals 5, corolla tubular or campanulate, white, pink, or red, stamens 5, ovary 5-celled; fr. a caps., seeds many.

Grown on Pacific Coast in those parts of zones 9 and 10 having cool summers.

longifolium (J. R. Forst. & G. Forst.) R. Br. Shrub or tree, to 36 ft.; lvs. erect, leathery, linear-subulate, to 10 in. long, acuminate, entire to serrulate; fls. in a terminal, 6–15-fld. raceme, corolla almost campanulate, white. New Zeal.

secundum (Poir.) R. Br. Shrub, to 10 ft., sts. procumbent to erect; lvs. linear-lanceolate, to 4 in. long; fls. in a loose raceme or panicle, corolla tubular, white, or pink. Australia.

DRACOPIS Cass. *Compositae* (Helianthus Tribe). One sp., an ann. herb of N. Amer.; lvs. alt., simple, clasping, glaucous, glabrous; fl. heads radiate, receptacle globose or ovoid, becoming broadly columnar in age; disc fls. brownish, ray fls. short, broad, somewhat drooping, yellow; achenes cylindrical, wrinkled, pappus lacking.

amplexicaulis (Vahl) Cass. [*Rudbeckia amplexicaulis* Vahl]. CONEFLOWER. St. simple in lower part, branched above, to 3 ft.; lvs. shallowly toothed or entire, the lower oblanceolate, the upper ovate or broadly lanceolate; ligules of ray fls. ½–1¼ in. long, often purplish-brown basally. Kans. to Tex., se. to Ga.

DRACUNCULUS Adans. *Araceae*. Two spp. of tuberous, per. herbs, native to Old World; lvs. pedate, petioles long-sheathing; infl. developing with the lvs., spathe convolute below, expanded above; fls. unisexual, spadix with the zones of female and male fls. contiguous, terminated by a long, exserted, malodorous sterile appendage; perianth present.

For culture see *Arisaema*.

canariensis Kunth. Differs from *D. vulgaris* in having spathe smaller, pale green, to 13 in. long, blade narrow, to 2 in. wide, and spadix with sterile appendage slender, yellow. Madeira Is. and Canary Is.

vulgaris Schott [*Arum Dracunculus* L.]. To 3 ft.; lf. blades fan-shaped in outline, segms. 13–15, lanceolate, entire, often white-spotted, the middle one largest, to 8 in. long and 2 in. wide, the lateral ones progressively smaller; spathe to 20 in. long, crisped-margined, greenish outside, reddish-purple within, spadix with sterile appendage clavate, purple. Medit. Eur. and Asia Minor. Zone 8.

DREJERELLA: *JUSTICIA*. **D. comosa:** *J. fulvicoma;* **D. guttata:** *J. Brandegeana*.

DRIED ARRANGEMENTS: see *Everlastings*.

DRIMYS J. R. Forst. & G. Forst. *Winteraceae*. About 40 spp. of aromatic, glabrous, evergreen trees and shrubs, native to Malay Pen., New Guinea, Australia, and from Mex. to S. Amer.; lvs. alt., with pellucid dots; fls. small in the cult. spp., solitary or clustered, sometimes unisexual, calyx enclosing petals in bud, splitting irregularly, petals 2 or more, spreading, stamens many, carpels separate; fr. of 1 or more indehiscent berries.

aromatica: *D. lanceolata*.

axillaris: *Pseudowintera axillaris*.

lanceolata (Poir.) Baill. [*D. aromatica* F. J. Muell.]. PEPPER TREE. Shrub or small tree of conical habit, to 10 ft., rarely to 30 ft., branchlets somewhat angled, reddish-brown or purplish; lvs. linear-lanceolate to lanceolate, to 2 in. long, almost leathery; fls. pale brownish, inconspicuous, often unisexual, in terminal umbels. Se. Australia and Tasmania.

Winteri J. R. Forst. & G. Forst. WINTER'S-BARK. To 50 ft.; lvs. elliptic or lanceolate, to 6 in. long, acuminate, entire, leathery, aromatic; fls. cream-colored, 1 in. across or more, fragrant. Winter and spring. Chile, Argentina. The aromatic bark is medicinal.

DROSANTHEMUM Schwant. *Aizoaceae.* About 95 spp. of succulent shrubs, native to S. Afr., brs. decumbent to creeping, widely spreading, bristly-papillate; lvs. 4-ranked, cylindrical to 3-angled, compressed, densely furnished with bright papillae; fls. solitary or in 3's, on short, lateral shoots, opening at noon or in the afternoon, calyx 5-lobed, papillate, petals in 1–2 series, stamens many, staminodes present or absent, nectary glands 5, distinct, ovary inferior, 5-celled, stigmas 4–6, almost threadlike; fr. a caps., cell lids stiff, expanding keels awned, placental tubercles sometimes present.

Free-flowering plants for outdoors in summer, or may be kept in a sunny, fairly warm room in winter or over-wintered in the cold house. Easily propagated by either seeds or cuttings; seedlings generally flower during the first year. See also *Succulents.*

bicolor L. Bolus. Stiffly branched shrub, to 1 ft., brs. dark in age; lvs. erect or ascending, green to yellow-green, obscurely papillate, to ¾ in. long, ⅛ in. thick, rounded in section, narrowing into a short-acuminate, recurved apex; fls. 1¼ in. across, solitary, on pedicels to ½ in. long, petals purple, golden-yellow at base. Cape Prov.

hispidum (L.) Schwant. Shrub, to 2 ft., 3 ft. across or more, brs. sometimes rooting; lvs. spreading or incurved, light green or reddish, with large watery papillae, to 1 in. long, ⅛ in. thick, cylindrical, tips obtuse; fls. to 1³⁄₁₆ in. across, 1–3, petals deep purple, glossy. S.-W. Afr., Cape Prov.

micans (L.) Schwant. Much-branched shrub, to 1 ft., brs. erect, slender, rough, yellow-brown, dotted with white in age; lvs. shorter than internodes, green, with glossy, crystalline papillae, to 1 in. long, ⅛ in. thick, somewhat united at base, nearly cylindrical but somewhat flattened on upper side; fls. to ⅝ in. across, on pedicels to ⅜ in. long, petals purple to yellowish. Cape Prov.

speciosum (Haw.) Schwant. DEWFLOWER, SHOWY D. Branched shrub to 2 ft., brs. slender, gray and rough-dotted in age, internodes prominent; lvs. curved upward, green, with crystalline papillae, to ⅝ in. long, ¼ in. thick, nearly cylindrical, tip blunt; fls. to 2 in. across, solitary, terminal, on pedicels to ⅜ in. long, petals bright orange-red, greenish at base. Cape Prov.

Stokoei L. Bolus. Shrub, brs. rough-hairy, spreading; lvs. papillose above, ⅛ in. thick, semicylindrical with upper side grooved at first, tip obtuse; fls. to ⅝ in. across, sessile or on short pedicels, petals pink. Cape Prov.

DROSERA L. SUNDEW, DAILY-DEW. *Droseraceae.* About 90–100 spp. of mostly per. herbs of wet places, of world-wide distribution, especially abundant in S. Hemisphere; sts. very short to elongate and climbing; lvs. alt. or rarely seemingly whorled, frequently in basal rosettes, covered and fringed (especially the blades) with sensitive, gland-tipped green to reddish hairs capable of slowly changing direction when irritated, and of holding and digesting insects; fls. small, white, pink, or purple, solitary or several in simple or branched 1-sided infl., sepals and petals usually 5, sometimes 4 or 8, stamens as many as petals, styles usually 3, often several-times divided; fr. a caps., seeds many.

Occasionally grown in the bog garden, or as curiosities under glass; culture as for *Dionaea;* susceptible to damage from aerosol sprays. Propagated by seeds, division, or cuttings of the rhizome.

Aliciae Hamet. St. short; lvs. in a basal rosette, about ⅝ in. long, petiole very short, ¹⁄₁₆ in. long, blade cuneate; scape ½ in. high, glandular-pubescent in upper part, 4–6-fld.; petals 5, ¼ in. long. N. Amer.

anglica Huds. [*D. longifolia* L., in part, and of some auth.]. St. short; lvs. all basal, erect, stipuled, petiole glabrous or sparsely glandular-hairy, 2–4 in. long, blade linear-oblanceolate, ⅝–1¼ in. long; scape 4–10 in. high, glabrous, 1–12-fld.; petals 5, white, ¼ in. long. N. Eurasia, and in N. Amer., s. to Que., Wisc., and Calif.

arcturi Hook. St. short or elongate; lvs. sessile, sheathing at base, without stipules, broadly linear, to 4 in. long or more, glandular-ciliate in upper half; scape to 7 in. high, glabrous, 1-fld.; petals 5, white, to ⁵⁄₁₆ in. long. Se. Australia and New Zeal.

auriculata Backh. ex Planch. St. erect, to 12 in. or more, slender, glabrous, from a small underground tuber; lvs. without stipules, basal lvs. reduced or in a rosette, petiole flat, to ⅜ in. long, blade orbicular, ⅛ in. across, st. lvs. alt., petiole slender, to ⅝ in. long, blade peltate,

orbicular, but with 2 tails on 1 side; scape to 4 in. high, 5–10-fld.; petals 5, pink, about ¼ in. long. Se. Australia and New Zeal.

binata Labill. [*D. dichotoma* Banks & Soland. ex Sm.; *D. intermedia* R. Cunn. ex A. Cunn., not Hayne]. St. short; lvs. basal, erect, stipuled, petiole to 14 in. long, glabrous, blade forked into 2 or 4 segms., segms. linear, to 6 in. long; scape to 20 in. high or more, glabrous, branched in upper part, many-fld.; petals 5, white, to ½ in. long. Se. Australia and New Zeal.

brevifolia Pursh. [*D. leucantha* Shinn.]. DWARF S. Ann., st. short; lvs. in a dense basal rosette, appressed to ground, stipules none or minute, petiole pubescent, to ⅜ in. long, blade broadly cuneate-obovate, to ⅜ in. long, usually longer than petiole; scape 3–6 in. high, glandular-pubescent, 2–6-fld.; petals 5, white or pink, ⅜–½ in. long. Coastal plain, se. Va. to Fla., w. to e. Tex.; also Mex., s. to Brazil, Uruguay, Paraguay, and ne. Argentina.

Burkeana Planch. St. short; lvs. in a basal rosette, stipuled, petiole slender or somewhat flattened, to 1 in. long, blade broadly spatulate or orbicular, ¼–⅜ in. long; scape 4–10 in. high, short-glandular-pubescent, 4–6-fld.; petals 5, pink or purple, ⅛–¼ in. long. S. Afr. and Madagascar.

Burmannii Vahl. St. short; lvs. in a tight rosette, appressed to the ground, stipuled, petiole none or very short, blade broadly cuneate-obovate, to ⅜ in. long, often retuse apically; scape 3–6 in. high, viscid in upper part, 3–10-fld.; petals 5, white, ⅛ in. long, styles 5. India to Japan, s. to n. Australia.

capensis L. St. short to elongate; lvs. crowded, stipuled, petiole dilated at base, glabrous or sparsely pubescent, 1½–4 in. long, blade linear to spatulate-linear, 1½–2¼ in. long; scape 8–14 in. high, hairy, glandular in upper part, 6–20-fld.; petals 5, purple, to ⅜ in. long. S. Afr.

capillaris Poir. PINK S. St. short; lvs. in a basal rosette, stipuled, the lower ones spreading, the upper erect, petiole pubescent but becoming glabrous, ⅜–1 in. long, blade broadly spatulate to almost orbicular, ⅛–¼ in. long; scape 2–16 in. high, nearly glabrous, 4–10-fld.; petals 5, pink, ¼ in. long. Coastal Plain, se. Va. to Fla., w. to e. Tex., also W. Indies, Mex. to n. S. Amer.

×**capulata:** a listed name of no botanical standing, applied to a hybrid between *D. capensis* and *D. spathulata,* said to have the foliage of the latter and fls. of the former.

cuneifolia L.f. St. short; lvs. in a basal rosette, stipuled, petiole indistinct, blade cuneate-obovate, blades of inner lvs. longer than the outer, ½–1¼ in. long, fringed with nonglandular cilia; scape 2½–10 in. high, glandular-pubescent, 4–16-fld.; petals 5, purple, ⅜–½ in. long. S. Afr.

dichotoma: *D. binata.*

elliptica: a listed name of no botanical standing, used for a sp. of the ne. U.S.

filiformis Raf. DEW-THREAD, THREAD-LEAVED S. St. short; lvs. basal, crowded, erect, stipuled, linear-filiform, 4–10 in. long, covered with purple glandular hairs, petiole not differentiated from blade; scape 3–9 in. high, glabrous, 4–16-fld.; petals 5, purple, to ⅝ in. long. Coastal, Mass. to Del. Var. **Tracyi** Diels [*D. Tracyi* Macfarl.]. Larger in all its parts; lvs. with green glandular hairs. Coastal Plain, S.C. to n. Fla. and La.

intermedia Hayne [*D. longifolia* L. in part, and of some auth.]. St. short or to 6 in. long; lvs. in a basal rosette or alt. and scattered, stipuled, ascending or spreading, petiole slender, glabrous, to 1½ in. long, blade obovate, ⅜ in. long; scape 1–10 in. high, glabrous or minutely glandular, 3–20-fld.; petals 5, white, ³⁄₁₆ in. long. N. Eurasia, e. N. Amer., W. Indies, and n. S. Amer. *D. intermedia* R. Cunn. ex A. Cunn., an Australian plant, is *D. binata.*

leucantha: *D. brevifolia.*

linearis Goldie. St. short; lvs. basal, crowded, erect, stipuled, petiole flat, glabrous, 1–2½ in. long, blade linear, 1–2 in. long; scape to 6 in. high, glabrous, 1–8-fld.; petals 5, white, ¼ in. long. Ne. N. Amer., s. to Me., n. Mich., Wisc., and Minn.

longifolia: a confused name, which has been used for both *D. anglica* and *D. intermedia.*

×**obovata** Mert. & W. D. J. Koch: *D. anglica* × *D. rotundifolia.* Intermediate between the parents; lvs. nearly erect, blade cuneate-obovate. Sterile hybrid, occurring frequently where the parents grow together.

peltata Sm. St. erect, 4–10 in., slender, glabrous, from an underground tuber; lvs. without stipules, lower lvs. in a rosette or reduced, often withered by flowering time, st. lvs. with petiole to ⅝ in. long, blade peltate, orbicular but with 2 tails on 1 side, ¹⁄₁₆ in. long, scape simple, 5–10-fld.; petals 5, white, ³⁄₁₆ in. long. India to Japan, s. to Australia.

pulchella Lehm. St. short; lvs. in a basal rosette, appressed to the ground, stipuled, petiole flat, winged, ¼ in. long, blade orbicular, about ⅛ in. across; scape ¾–1½ in. high, sparsely glandular, 1–4-fld.; petals 5, pink, ⅛ in. long, styles 5. Sw. Australia.

pygmaea DC. St. short; lvs. in a dense basal rosette, stipuled, petiole flat, narrowed upward, glabrous, to ¼ in. long, blade peltate, dish-shaped, about ¹⁄₁₆ in. across; scape to 1 in. high, capillary, glabrous, 1-fld.; petals 4, white, ⅛ in. long, styles 4. Se. Australia and New Zeal.

rotundifolia L. ROUND-LEAVED S. St. short; lvs. in a basal rosette, stipuled, petiole flat, glabrous to glandular-hairy, ½–2 in. long, blade orbicular to transversely elliptic, ³⁄₁₆–⅜ in. long, usually wider than long; scape 2–12 in. high, slender, glabrous, 1–25-fld.; petals 5, white to pink, ¼ in. long. Circumboreal, s. in N. Amer. to n. Fla., Ill., Minn., Mont., and Calif.

spathulata Labill. St. short; lvs. in a basal rosette, stipuled, petiole broad, glabrous basally, fringed above, to ⅜ in. long, blade spatulate to obovate, ³⁄₁₆ in. long; scape to 8 in. high, glandular-pubescent in upper part, 1–15-fld.; petals 5, white or pink, ⅛–¼ in. long. S. Japan, e. China, s. to New Zeal.

Tracyi: *D. filiformis* var.

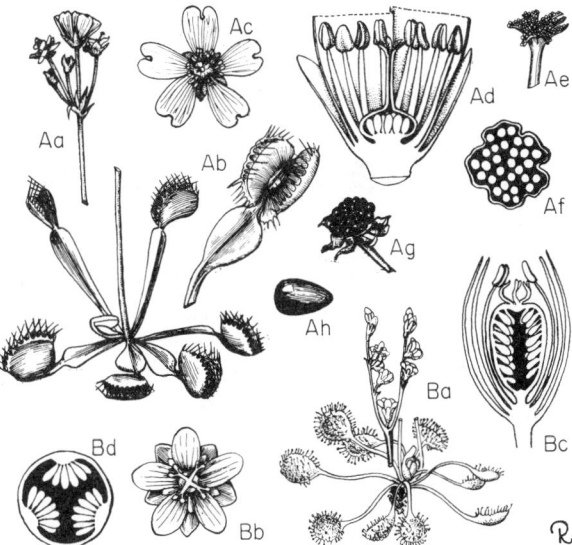

DROSERACEAE. **A,** *Dionaea muscipula:* **Aa,** plant in flower, × ¼; **Ab,** leaf, × ½; **Ac,** flower, × ¾; **Ad,** flower, vertical section, × 3; **Ae,** stigma, × 6; **Af,** ovary, cross section, × 4; **Ag,** capsule, dehisced, × 1; **Ah,** seed, × 5. **B,** *Drosera rotundifolia:* **Ba,** plant in flower, × ½; **Bb,** flower, × 2; **Bc,** flower, vertical section, × 12; **Bd,** ovary, cross section, × 15. (Ab, Ba–Bd from Bailey, *Manual of Cultivated Plants,* ed. 2.)

DROSERACEAE Salisb. SUNDEW FAMILY. Dicot.; 4 genera and 90–100 spp. of carnivorous herbs or subshrubs of cosmopolitan distribution, usually in bogs; lvs. mostly in basal rosettes, circinate, usually with sensitive, glandular hairs; fls. in cincinni or racemes or solitary, bisexual, sepals and petals 5, stamens 5–20, ovary superior, with parietal placentation, styles several; fr. a caps. *Aldrovanda, Dionaea, Drosera,* and *Drosophyllum* are sometimes cult. as curiosities.

DROSOPHYLLUM Link. *Droseraceae.* One sp., a carnivorous, small subshrub, native to sw. Eur. and nw. Afr.; lvs. in a rosette, alt., revolutely circinate in bud; fls. in loose, branched cymes, sepals and petals 5, stamens 10–20; fr. a caps., seeds many.

Grown infrequently, under glass, as a curiosity. May be grown in sphagnum or light, sandy loam, with sunshine and warmth, and with general growing conditions about the same as those for pelargoniums. Very susceptible to damage from aerosol sprays. Propagated by seeds.

lusitanicum (L.) Link. PORTUGUESE SUNDEW. About 1 ft. high, viscid-glandular-hairy throughout, st. short, woody at base in old plants, sometimes branching; lvs. many, crowded, 6–8 in. long, narrowly linear, with filiform tips, the older, dead lvs. persistent around st.; fls. sulphur-yellow, 1½ in. across. Upland heaths, where the spring growing season is wet but the summer long and dry; Portugal, sw. Spain, n. Morocco.

DRYANDRA R. Br. *Proteaceae.* About 50 spp. of shrubs, native to nontrop. W. Australia; lvs. alt., mostly sinuate or pinnatifid, sometimes pinnate, often prickly-toothed; infl. a dense head, in an involucre of scalelike bracts subtended by foliage lvs.; fls. mostly yellow; fr. a caps., usually hairy.

Two or more species introduced in southern Calif. Zone 10.

floribunda R. Br. Shrub, to 8 ft.; lvs. nearly or quite sessile, cuneate or obovate, mostly less than 1–2 in. long, undulate, prickly; fl. heads small, terminal, involucre to ½ in. long; fls. nearly 1 in. to 1½ in. long, more or less silky.

formosa R. Br. Erect shrub, to 15 ft.; lvs. divided to midrib, to 8 in. long; fl. heads large, terminal, involucre to 1½ in. in diam.; fls. to 1½ in. long, more or less silky.

DRYAS L. *Rosaceae.* A small genus of evergreen, creeping plants, native in the high latitudes and on mts. of the N. Hemisphere; somewhat woody at the base; lvs. alt.; fls. white or yellowish, solitary, sepals and petals 7–10, the sepals shorter than petals; fr. an achene with feathery style.

Suitable for rock gardens, making a rather close ground cover and sending up naked peduncles a few in. high. Propagated by cuttings, division or seeds.

alaskensis: *D. octopetala* subsp.

chamaedrifolia: *D. octopetala* subsp. *octopetala* var.

Drummondii Richardson ex Hook. Lvs. elliptic to obovate, to 1½ in. long, cuneate at the base, rounded at apex, white-tomentose beneath; pedicel 2–8 in. high; fls. yellow, nodding, not opening fully, sepals ovate, with black, gland-tipped hairs, petals to about ½ in. long, styles to 1½ in. long in fr. Alaska, s. to Ore., Mont., Que. Zone 1.

Hookerana: *D. octopetala* subsp.

integrifolia Vahl [*D. tenella* Pursh]. Lvs. lanceolate-ovate to almost linear, to 1 in. long, rounded to cordate at base, revolute, crenate in lower half, woolly underneath, shining green above; pedicels to 4 in. long; fls. white, open, to about 1 in. across, styles to 1½ in. in fr. Asia; Alaska to Greenland, s. to Mont., New Hamp., Nfld.

japonica: a listed name of no botanical standing.

lanata: *D. octopetala* var. *argentea.*

octopetala L. MOUNTAIN AVENS. Lvs. ovate-elliptic to oblong, toothed, white-tomentose beneath; fl. stalks 2–8 in. high, more or less black-hairy; fls. open, 1 in. across, sepals with black hairs, petals white, styles to 1⁵⁄₁₆ in. long. Alaska to Greenland; Eurasia. Zone 1. Cv. 'Minor' is listed as a very dwarf form. Subsp. **octopetala** [subsp. *chamaedryfolia* (Crantz) Hegi; *D. chamaedrifolia* S. F. Gray]. The typical subsp.; lvs. with narrow scales and many lateral white hairs on lower surface of midvein. Eur. Var. **argentea** Blytt [*D. lanata* Stein ex Correv.; *D. vestita* Hort.]. Lvs. more or less tomentose on both sides. E. Alps. Subsp. **alaskensis** (Porsild) Hult. [*D. alaskensis* Porsild]. Lvs. broadest toward apex, deeply toothed, without scales but with stalked capitate glands on lower surface of midvein. Alaska. Subsp. **chamaedryfolia:** subsp. *octopetala.* Subsp. **Hookerana** (Juz.) Hult. [*D. Hookerana* Juz.]. Lvs. broadest at middle, tapered toward apex, shallowly toothed, without scales but with stalked capitate glands on lower surface of midvein. B.C., s. to Colo.

×**Suendermannii** Kellerer ex Sünderm.: *D. Drummondii* × *D. octopetala.* Like *D. octopetala,* but fls. yellow in the bud, white on opening, nodding.

tenella: *D. integrifolia.*

vestita: a listed name of no botanical standing for *D. octopetala* subsp. *octopetala* var. *argentea.*

DRYMOCALLIS: *POTENTILLA.*

DRYMONIA Mart. *Gesneriaceae.* Thirty or more spp. of terrestrial or epiphytic shrubs or vines in trop. Amer.; lvs. opp., those of a pair equal or unequal; fls. solitary or clustered in lf. axils, sepals 5, large, often colored, unequal, the uppermost shortest, corolla funnelform, oblique in the calyx, spurred at base, limb of rounded lobes, the upper 2 lobes usually shorter than the lower 3, stamens 4, borne at base of corolla tube, anthers broadest at tip, narrowed basally to 2 separate spurs, united (before pollen is shed) by sides and faces with spurred bases uppermost, dehiscent by 2–4 pores, disc a solitary gland at the back of the ovary, ovary superior; fr. a fleshy caps., dehiscing and exposing pulpy placentas and seeds.

For cultivation see *Gesneriaceae.*

macrophylla (Ørst.) H. E. Moore. Sts. to nearly 6 ft.; lvs. elliptic, to 1 ft. long or more, 5 in. wide; sepals ½ in. long, ¼–⁵⁄₁₆ in. wide, minutely hairy, pectinately toothed, corolla pale yellow, to 1¼ in. long, tube waxy, with 2 red-purple lines inside, lobes ¼ in. long. Costa Rica, Guatemala.

mollis Ørst. Epiphytic vine; lvs. oblong, to 5 in. long, 2 in. wide, finely hairy; fls. solitary, sepals 1 in. long or more, hairy, finely toothed, corolla longer than calyx, yellowish-white, lobes fringed. Costa Rica. *Episcia punctata* has been offered erroneously as this sp.

parviflora Hanst. Epiphytic shrub; sts. 4-angled, pubescent; lvs. elongate-elliptic to obovate, to 12 in. long, 4 in. wide, narrowed to a decurrent base, minutely toothed; fls. clustered, sepals oblong-lanceolate, to ½ in. long, acuminate, sharply toothed, reddish, corolla to 1¼ in. long, yellow, puberulous outside. Costa Rica.

serrulata (Jacq.) Mart. [*D. spectabilis* (HBK) Mart.]. Vine; lvs. oblong, to 6 in. long, 1¾ in. wide, narrowed to base, slightly toothed, short-hairy; fls. solitary, sepals ovate-lanceolate, to 2 in. long, toothed, corolla to 2½ in. long, white, striped with red or purple, pubescent, lower lip fringed. Mex. to Brazil.

spectabilis: *D. serrulata.*

stenophylla (J. D. Sm.) H. E. Moore. Epiphytic; lvs. unequal, the smaller almost stipulelike, the larger narrowly elliptic to linear, to 10 in. long, 1¾ in. wide, glabrous; fls. 1–2, axillary, sepals lanceolate, unequal, to ⅝ in. long, corolla 1 in. long, pale yellow, rose in throat or tube, lobes fringed. Costa Rica.

strigosa (Ørst.) Wiehl. [*Alloplectus strigosus* Ørst.]. Terrestrial; lvs. unequal, blades obliquely oblong-elliptic, more or less rhomboidal, to 9 in. long, 3 in. wide, acuminate, nearly entire, puberulous; fls. solitary, pedicels angle-winged and thickened at tip, calyx red, puberulous, sepals cordate-ovate, remotely toothed, corolla tubular, swollen basally, S-curved above, to 1¼ in. long. S. Mex.

DRYMOPHLOEUS Zipp. [*Coleospadix* Becc.]. *Palmae.* About 15 spp. of small, solitary, monoecious palms, native from the Moluccas to the Solomon Is.; lvs. pinnate, sheaths tubular, forming a slender crownshaft, pinnae cuneate, toothed at the broad apex; infl. once- to twice-branched, peduncle prominent, bracts 2, the upper persistent and longer than the lower, rachillae with fls. in triads (2 male and 1 female); male fls. symmetrical, sepals imbricate, petals valvate, stamens many, anthers attached by back, pistillode shorter or longer than stamens, female fls. with sepals and petals imbricate, staminodes inconspicuous, pistil ovoid, 1-celled, 1-ovuled; fr. ovoid to ellipsoid with terminal stigmatic residue, seed with homogeneous or ruminate endosperm.

Graceful ornamental palms grown in shady tropical or subtropical gardens and in Zone 10 in southern Fla. For culture see *Palms.*

Beguinii (Burret) H. E. Moore. To 15 ft.; lvs. dark green, to 6 ft. long, pinnae 11–13 on each side, to 16 in. long, 6 in. wide, upper margin generally longest, apical pair not united beyond end of rachis; infl. twice-branched; male fls. to ³⁄₁₆ in. long, stamens about 24, pistillode shorter than stamens; fr. yellowish, to ⁹⁄₁₆ in. long, seed with ruminate endosperm. Molucca Is.

oliviformis (Giseke) Mart. To 20 ft. or more; lvs. dark green, to 8 ft. long, pinnae 10–11 on each side, to 18 in. long, 7½ in. wide, generally longest at the midrib, apical pair united in a briefly 2-cleft flabellum; infl. once-branched or lower brs. forked; male fls. to ⅜ in. long, stamens 50–60, pistillode longer than stamens; fr. lacquer-red, to ¾ in. long, seed with homogeneous endosperm. Amboina (Molucca Is.).

DRYNARIA John Sm. *Polypodiaceae.* About 20 spp. of epiphytic ferns, native to the Old World tropics; lvs. dimorphic, sterile lvs. erect, short, broad, sessile, soon turning brown and humus-collecting, fertile lvs. long, deeply lobed or pinnate, green, petioled; sori round, small or of moderate size, indusia absent. Sometimes included in *Polypodium.*

Usually grown as an epiphyte. For culture see *Ferns.*

quercifolia (L.) John Sm. [*Polypodium quercifolium* L.]. OAK-LEAVED FERN. Lvs. leathery, fertile lvs. long-petioled, to 3 ft. long, deeply lobed into oblong, entire pinnae to 9 in. long, sterile lvs. sessile, shaped like an oak lf., to 1 ft. long and 8 in. wide, lobed; sori in 2 regular rows between main veins. India, Malay Pen. to Australia.

rigidula (Swartz) Beddome [*Polypodium rigidulum* Swartz]. Fertile lvs. to 6 ft. long, 1-pinnate, pinnae jointed to rachis, to 6 in. long, ½ in. wide or more, acuminate, shallowly bluntly toothed. Sumatra, Australia, Polynesia.

DRYOPTERIS Adans. [*Aspidium* of auth., not Swartz; *Filix* Séguier, not Adans.]. WOOD FERN, SHIELD F. *Polypodiaceae.* About 150 spp. of temp. and trop., terrestrial ferns; lvs. 1-pinnate-pinnatifid to compound, lacking hairs; sori round, indusia reniform. Subdivided into several genera by some authors.

Many are woodsy plants native in the U.S. and Canada and are sometimes transferred to the woodland garden. The greenhouse species require no special treatment. For culture see *Ferns.*

acrostichoides: *Polystichum acrostichoides.*

acuminata: *Thelypteris acuminata.*

arguta (Kaulf.) D. Watt. COASTAL W. F. Lvs. 1–3 ft. long or more, 2-pinnate, pinnae sessile, oblong-lanceolate, pinnules spinulose-toothed; indusia firm, strongly convex, with deep narrow sinuses and glandular margins. Wash. to s. Calif.

atrata (Wallich) Ching. Lvs. 1-pinnate, pinnae lanceolate, truncate at base, coarsely serrate. China.

austriaca (Jacq.) Woyn. [*D. campyloptera* (Kunze) E. Clarkson; *D. spinulosa* vars. *americana* (Fisch.) Fern. and *dilatata* (Britt. & A. Br.) Rydb.]. Lvs. to 3 ft. long, 2–3-pinnate-pinnatifid, abruptly acuminate, pinnae 10–15 pairs, the lowest broadest, pinnules oblong, obtuse, spinulose-toothed, pinnules on lower pinnae strongly alt.; indusia glandular. N. Amer., Eur., Asia. Var. **intermedia** (Muhlenb.) C. V. Mort. [*D. intermedia* (Muhlenb.) A. Gray; *D. spinulosa* var. *intermedia* (Muhlenb.) Underw.]. Like var. *spinulosa,* but glandular on petioles and indusia; basal pinnules as long as or shorter than one next to it. E. N. Amer. Var. **spinulosa** (O. F. Müll.) Fiori [*D. spinulosa* (O. F. Müll.) D. Watt; *Aspidium spinulosum* A. Gray]. SPINULOSE W. F., FANCY F., FLORIST'S F. Lvs. glandless, 2-pinnate-pinnatifid, pinnules of lowest pinnae opp. or within ¼ in. apart, basal pinnule of lower side of lowest pinnae longer than one next to it; indusia glandless. N. Amer., Eur., Asia.

×Boottii (Tuckerm.) Underw. [*Aspidium Boottii* Tuckerm.]: *D. cristata* × *D. spinulosa* var. *intermedia.* BOOTT'S W. F. Lvs. to 2½ ft. long and 5 in. wide, 2–3-pinnate, pinnules finely toothed. Ne. N. Amer.

campyloptera: *D. austriaca.*

chrysoloba (Kaulf.) O. Kuntze. Not cult., but some material cult. under this name is *D. erythrosora.*

Clintoniana: *D. cristata* var.

cristata (L.) A. Gray [*Aspidium cristatum* Swartz]. CRESTED W. F., CRESTED F. Lvs. to 2½ ft. long and 6 in. wide, 2-pinnatifid, segms. finely toothed. Ne. N. Amer., to Va. and Ark.; Eur., Asia. Var. **Clintoniana** (D. C. Eat.) Underw. [*D. Clintoniana* (D. C. Eat.) Dowell]. CLINTON'S W. F. Lvs. broader.

decomposita: *Ctenitis decomposita.*

decursive-pinnata: *Thelypteris decursive-pinnata.*

dentata: *Thelypteris dentata.*

disjuncta: *Gymnocarpium Dryopteris.*

erythrosora (D. C. Eat.) O. Kuntze. JAPANESE S. F. Lvs. to 1½ ft. long and half as wide, 2-pinnate, pinnules pinnatifid, toothed; sori red when young. China, Japan. Some of the material cult. as *D. chrysoloba* belongs here.

Filix-mas (L.) Schott [*Aspidium Filix-mas* (L.) Swartz]. MALE FERN. Lvs. nearly evergreen, forming crowns, to 4 ft. long and 1 ft. wide, 2-pinnate, pinnules toothed or cut. N. Amer., Eur. There are crisped, crested, forked, and dwarf variants.

fragrans (L.) Schott. FRAGRANT FERN, FRAGRANT CLIFF F. Lvs. ¼–1 ft. long, glandular-aromatic, narrowly lanceolate, pinnae 1-pinnate, nearly covered beneath with large, thin, imbricate indusia. Circumboreal.

Goldiana (Hook.) A. Gray [*Aspidium Goldianum* Hook.]. GOLDIE'S W. F., GOLDIE'S F. Lvs. in large crowns, to 4 ft. long and 1½ ft. wide, pinnate-pinnatifid, pinnae toothed, dark green above. Ne. N. Amer.

hexagonoptera: *Thelypteris hexagonoptera.*

hirtipes (Blume) O. Kuntze. Lvs. stiff, to 3 ft. long and 16 in. wide, 1-pinnate, pinnae cut ⅓ to midrib, petioles black-scaly. India. Most material offered under this name is the very similar *D. atrata.*

intermedia: *D. austriaca* var.

Linnaeana: *Gymnocarpium Dryopteris.*

marginalis (L.) A. Gray [*Aspidium marginale* (L.) Swartz]. MARGINAL S. F., LEATHER W. F. Lvs. in crowns, to 2½ ft. long, 2-pinnate, pinnules entire or lobed; sori borne close to the margin. E. N. Amer.

mollis: *Thelypteris dentata.*

nevadensis: *Thelypteris nevadensis.*

normalis: *Thelypteris normalis.*

noveboracensis: *Thelypteris noveboracensis.*

octhodes: *Thelypteris octhodes.*

oregana: *Thelypteris nevadensis.*

Oreopteris: *Thelypteris Oreopteris.*

parallelogramma (Kunze) Alston. Lvs. in a crown, to 4 ft. long, 2-pinnatifid, segms. rectangular, petioles and rachis densely covered with dark brown, chaffy scales. Mex., Peru, Hawaii.

parasitica: *Thelypteris parasitica.*

patens: *Thelypteris patens.*

pennigera: *Thelypteris pennigera.*

Phegopteris: *Thelypteris Phegopteris.*

reticulata: *Thelypteris reticulata.*

Robertiana: *Gymnocarpium Robertianum.*

setigera: *Thelypteris setigera.*

spinulosa: *D. austriaca* var. Var. **americana:** *D. austriaca;* Var. **dilatata:** *D. austriaca.* Var. **intermedia:** *D. austriaca* var.

Thelypteris: *Thelypteris palustris.*

uliginosa: *Thelypteris uliginosa.*

varia (L.) O. Kuntze [*Polystichum varium* (L.) K. Presl]. JAPANESE HOLLY FERN. Lvs. to 2 ft. long, 1 ft. wide, lanceolate-triangular, abruptly acuminate at apex, 2–3-pinnate at base, lower pinnae largest, nearly triangular, unequal at base, with the lower downward-directed pinnules very long; indusium reniform or peltate, and thus approaching *Polystichum.* China, Japan.

DRYPIS L. *Caryophyllaceae.* One sp., a per. herb, native to s. Eur., sts. 4-sided; lvs. opp., spiny; infl. a compound dichasial cyme composed of nearly capitate clusters of fls., bracts spiny; calyx 5-toothed, petals 5, clawed, limb bifid, coronal scales at juncture of claw and limb, stamens 5, stigmas 3; fr. a 1–2-seeded caps., dehiscing irregularly.

Propagated by seeds or cuttings.

spinosa L. Glabrous, tufted per., to 1 ft., sts. stiff, many, much-branched; lvs. linear-subulate, to ½ in. long, spiny-acuminate, bright green and glossy; fls. white or pink, about ½ in. across, anthers bluish. Mts., cent. Italy to Greece.

DUCHESNEA Sm. INDIAN STRAWBERRY, MOCK S. *Rosaceae.* Two spp. of small, per. herbs with runners, native to s. Asia; like *Fragaria,* but fls. yellow, calyx bractlets leafy and toothed, and receptacle dry.

One species used as a ground cover and for hanging baskets.

indica (Andr.) Focke [*Fragaria indica* Andr.]. Lvs. ovate, coarsely toothed, silky-hairy at least underneath; fls. ½–1 in. across; "fr." red, surrounded by the large persistent calyx. Looks like a yellow-fld. strawberry. India; naturalized in N. Amer., where often weedy.

DUDLEYA Britt. & Rose [*Stylophyllum* Britt. & Rose]. *Crassulaceae.* About 40 spp. of glabrous succulents of w. Amer.; fl. st. axillary from mostly per. lf. rosettes; lvs. clasping, several-veined to base, withering-persistent; infl. of 1 to several cincinni; fls. 5-merous, petals united mostly ⅕ or less, erect in subgenus *Dudleya* or spreading above in subgenus *Stylophyllum* (Britt. & Rose) Moran, stamens 10. Included by some authors in *Echeveria* or formerly in *Cotyledon;* differs from *Echeveria* in having calyx disc wider than corolla base and petals convolute.

Grown occasionally in Calif. but not much in the trade. For culture see *Succulents.*

Abramsii Rose. Cespitose; lvs. 10–20, oblong-lanceolate or tapering, 1–3 in. long, 3/16 in. wide, acute, gray; fl. st. 2–8 in.; petals erect, pale yellow, flecked with red, 5/16–½ in. long. Spring. S. Calif., Baja Calif.

albiflora Rose. Cespitose; lvs. 10–25, tapering from base or slightly broadened at middle, cylindrical above, 1–2¼ in. long, ½–⅝ in. wide, slender-acute or acuminate, green or glaucous, fl. st. 2–18 in.; petals erect, white, ⅜–⅝ in. long. Spring. S. Baja Calif.

aloides: *D. saxosa* subsp.

arizonica Rose. Rosettes solitary, sessile, to 8 in. wide; lvs. 10–35, oblong, 2–6 in. long, ½–2 in. wide, acuminate, mealy; fl. st. ½–2 ft.; petals erect, yellow to mostly red, 5/16–⅝ in. long, united to the middle. Spring. S. Nev., w. Ariz., se. Calif., nw. Mex.

attenuata (S. Wats.) Moran. Cespitose; lvs. 5–20, cylindrical, 1–4 in. long, 3/16 in. wide or less, glaucous; fl. st. 4–10 in., infl. of 2–3 cincinni; petals yellow, spreading, 3/16–⅜ in. long. Late spring. Baja Calif. Subsp. **Orcuttii** (Rose) Moran [*Stylophyllum Orcuttii* Rose]. Petals white, flushed with rose. S. Calif., Baja Calif.

Brittonii Johans. [*D. grandis* Hort.; *D. ingens* Hort., not Rose]. Rosettes mostly solitary, to 1½ ft. across; lvs. 50–120, oblong, 3–10 in. long, 1–3 in. wide, acuminate, powdery white; fl. st. 1–3 ft.; sepals triangular-acuminate, petals erect, pale yellow, 5/16–½ in. long. Spring. Baja Calif. A green form is little cult.

caespitosa (Haw.) Britt. & Rose [*Cotyledon caespitosa* Haw.; *C. californica* Bak.; *Echeveria Cotyledon* (Jacq.) A. Nels. & Macbr.; *E. laxa* Lindl.]. Root crown usually elongate, branched; lvs. 15–30, oblong, 2–8 in. long, ½–2 in. wide, acute, green or glaucous; fl. st. 1–2 ft.; petals erect, white to yellow or red, 5/16–½ in. long. Late spring, early summer. Coast, cent. Calif. A variable and taxonomically difficult polyploid complex intergrading with *D. cymosa, D. farinosa,* and *D. lanceolata.*

candelabrum Rose. Rosette solitary, ½–1 ft. wide; lvs. 20–45, obovate to oblong-oblanceolate, 3–7 in. long, 1–2¾ in. wide, acuminate, green; fl. st. 1 ft.; petals erect, pale yellow, 5/16–½ in. long. Spring, early summer. Calif. Is.

candida Britt. Closely allied to *D. Brittonii,* from which it differs in smaller and clustered rosettes, lvs. 2–4 in. long, ⅜–1 in. wide or narrower in cult. Spring. Coronado Is. (Baja Calif.).

Collomiae: *D. saxosa* subsp.

cultrata Rose. Rosettes solitary or few, 1–3 in. wide; lvs. 20–30, oblong, 2–5 in. long, ⅜–⅝ in. wide, acute, green; fl. st. 8–16 in.; petals erect, pale yellow, ⅜–½ in. long. Spring. Baja Calif.

cymosa (Lem.) Britt. & Rose [*D. nevadensis* (S. Wats.) Britt. & Rose; *D. Plattiana* (Jeps.) Britt. & Rose; *D. Sheldonii* Rose; *Echeveria laxa* of auth., not Lindl.; *E. Purpusii* (K. Schum.) Wittm.]. Rosettes solitary or few, sessile; lvs. 10–25, oblanceolate, 1–6 in. long, ½–2 in. wide, acute to cuspidate, green to mealy; fl. st. 4–12 in.; petals erect, slender-pointed, yellow to red, 5/16–⅜ in. long. Spring, early summer. Calif. Subsp. **minor** (Rose) Moran [*D. minor* Rose]. Generally smaller; lvs. more rhombic. Var. **densiflora:** a listed name of no botanical standing.

densiflora (Rose) Moran [*Echeveria nudicaulis* (Abrams) A. Berger; *Stylophyllum densiflorum* Rose]. Cespitose; lvs. 20–40, nearly cylindrical, 3–6 in. long, 3/16–½ in. in diam., mealy; fl. st. 6–12 in., infl. a dense, many-branched cyme; petals spreading, white or pink, 3/16–⅜ in. long. Early summer. S. Calif.

edulis (Nutt.) Moran [*Echeveria edulis* (Nutt.) A. Berger; *Stylophyllum edule* (Nutt.) Britt. & Rose]. Cespitose; lvs. 15–25, cylindrical, 3–8 in. long, 3/16–⅜ in. in diam., pale green; fl. st. 1–1½ ft., infl. an open, several-branched cyme; petals spreading, white, 5/16–⅜ in. long. Late spring, early summer. S. Calif., Baja Calif.

farinosa (Lindl.) Britt. & Rose [*D. septentrionalis* Rose; *Echeveria Cotyledon* of auth., not (Jacq.) A. Nels. & Macbr.]. Root crown elongate, branching, decumbent; lvs. 15–30, 1–2 in. long, ⅜–1 in. wide, ovate-oblong, acute, green or mealy; fl. st. 6–12 in.; petals erect, pale yellow, ⅜–⅝ in. long. Summer. Coastal, cent. Calif. to s. Ore.

grandis: a listed name of no botanical standing for *D. Brittonii.*

ingens: see *D. Brittonii.*

lanceolata (Nutt.) Britt. & Rose [*D. lurida* Rose; *Echeveria lanceolata* Nutt.]. Rosettes solitary or few, short-stemmed; lvs. 10–25, oblong-lanceolate, 2–8 in. long, ½–1⅜ in. wide, acute, green or glaucous; fl. st. 1–3 ft.; petals erect, red to yellow, ⅜–⅝ in. long. Spring. S. Calif., Baja Calif. Var. **aloides:** a listed name of no botanical standing for *D. saxosa* subsp.

laxa: *D. caespitosa;* see also *D. cymosa.*

linearis (Greene) Britt. & Rose. Cespitose; lvs. 20–40, oblong-lanceolate, 1–2½ in. long, 3/16–⅜ in. wide, acuminate or narrowly acute, green; fl. st. 3–7 in.; petals erect, yellow, 5/16–½ in. long. Spring. Baja Calif. Is.

lurida: *D. lanceolata.*

minor: *D. cymosa* subsp.

nevadensis: *D. cymosa.*

Plattiana: *D. cymosa.*

pulverulenta (Nutt.) Britt. & Rose [*Echeveria pulverulenta* Nutt.]. CHALK LETTUCE. Rosettes solitary, to 2 ft. wide, powdery white; lvs. 30–80, oblong, 3–12 in. long, 1–5 in. wide, acuminate to cuspidate; fl. st. 1–3 ft., with several elongate brs.; fls. spreading to pendent, petals erect, united to middle, red, ½–¾ in. long. Late spring, summer. S. Calif., Baja Calif.

saxosa (M. E. Jones) Britt. & Rose. Sts. short; rosettes solitary or few; lvs. 10–25, oblong-lanceolate, 2–6 in. long, ¼–¾ in. wide, acute, glaucous; infl. of 2–3 brs.; petals yellow. Subsp. **saxosa.** The typical subsp.; fl. st. to 8 in.; petals yellow, marked with red, ⅜–½ in. long. Panamint Mts. (Calif.). Subsp. **aloides** (Rose) Moran [*D. aloides* Rose; *D. lanceolata* var. *aloides* Hort.]. Fl. st. 6–14 in.; petals erect, 5/16–⅝ in. long.

Spring. S. Calif. Subsp. **Collomiae** (Rose) Moran [*D. Collomiae* Rose]. Fl. st. to 16 in.; petals 1/4–3/4 in. long. Ariz.

septentrionalis: *D. farinosa.*

Sheldonii: *D. cymosa.*

stolonifera Moran. Stoloniferous, rosettes 2–5 in. wide; lvs. 15–25, oblong-obovate, 1–3 in. long, 5/8–1 1/4 in. wide, short-acuminate, green, becoming maroon-marked; fl. st. 3–10 in.; sepals wider than long, petals erect, with outcurved tips, yellow, 3/8 in. long. Late spring. S. Calif.

virens (Rose) Moran [*Cotyledon viscida* S. Wats. var. *insularis* (Rose) Jeps.; *Echeveria albida* (Rose) A. Berger; *Stylophyllum virens* Rose]. ALABASTER PLANT. Root crown short or elongate, branching; lvs. 20–45, oblong, 2–10 in. long, 3/8–1 in. wide, acute, green or glaucous; fl. st. 6–24 in.; petals spreading, white, 5/16–3/8 in. long. Spring. Coastal, s. Calif. and Is.

viscida (S. Wats.) Moran [*Cotyledon viscida* S. Wats.]. Herbage dark green, viscid, with resinous odor; lvs. 15–40, 2 1/2–6 in. long, 1/4–1/2 in. wide; fl. st. 8–16 in.; petals spreading, pink, 1/4–5/16 in. long. Late spring. S. Calif.

DUGGENA West. *Rubiaceae.* Twenty-two spp. of shrubs or small trees, native to S. Amer. and W. Indies; lvs. opp., stipules interpetiolar; fls. in terminal spikes, racemes, or panicles, small, usually 4-merous, corolla salverform or funnelform, tube short; fr. globose, berrylike, seeds many.

hirsuta: *D. spicata.*

spicata (Lam.) Standl. [*D. hirsuta* (Jacq.) Britt.]. To 10 ft.; lvs. ovate to lanceolate, to 7 in. long, pubescent or becoming glabrous; fls. white, 1/2 in. long, in spikelike panicles to 16 in. long; fr. white or blue. W. Indies, n. S. Amer.

DURANTA L. *Verbenaceae.* About 30 spp. of glabrous or woolly, sometimes spiny shrubs and trees, native to Key West, W. Indies, S. Amer., and Mex.; lvs. opp. or whorled, simple; fls. white, lilac, or purple, in racemes often arranged in panicles, calyx 5-toothed, corolla salverform, 5-lobed, stamens 4; fr. a drupe, enclosed by persistent calyx.

Planted in warm regions and under glass. Propagated by seeds and cuttings in spring.

Ellisia: *D. repens.*

grandiflora: *D. repens* var.

Lorentzii Griseb. Shrub, to 10 ft., brs. drooping; lvs. ovate or elliptic, small-toothed toward apex, leathery; fls. white. Argentina.

Plumieri: *D. repens.*

repens L. [*D. Ellisia* Jacq.; *D. Plumieri* Jacq.]. GOLDEN-DEWDROP, PIGEON BERRY, SKYFLOWER, BRAZILIAN S. Shrub or tree, to 18 ft., sometimes spiny, brs. often drooping or trailing; lvs. ovate to obovate, to 4 in. long, entire or coarsely toothed above the middle; fls. lilac, to 1/2 in. across; fr. yellow, to 1/2 in. across. Fla. to Brazil; naturalized in s. Tex. Zone 9. Cvs. are: **'Alba'** [var. *alba* (M. T. Mast.) L. H. Bailey], fls. white; **'Grandiflora'** [var. *grandiflora* Moldenke], fls. 3/4 in. across; **'Variegata'** [var. *variegata* L. H. Bailey], lvs. variegated.

stenostachya Tod. Spineless shrub, to 15 ft.; lvs. oblong-lanceolate, to 8 in. long, entire or toothed; fls. lilac, 1/2 in. across; fr. yellow, 5/16 in. across. Brazil. Zone 10.

DURIO Adans. *Bombacaceae.* About 30 spp. of evergreen trees, with center of distribution in Malay Pen., Borneo, and Sumatra; lvs. 2-ranked, simple, entire, pinnately veined, leathery; fls. in cymose clusters from leafless nodes along the larger brs., each fl. enclosed by an involucre in bud, calyx mostly deeply 5-lobed, petals 4–6 or more, involucre, calyx and petals deciduous after flowering, stamens many, separate or in 5 bundles, ovary 3–6-celled, ovules 2 to many in each cell; fr. a woody, spiny caps., seeds almost completely enveloped by fleshy aril.

The durian is widely cultivated as a fruit tree in Asian tropics, sparingly so in New World tropics, the delicate flavor of the malodorous aril of the seeds being highly esteemed by some. It thrives only under strictly tropical conditions. Propagated by seeds, or superior cultivars by budding on seedling stock.

zibethinus J. Murr. DURIAN. Large trees with buttresses; lvs. elliptic to oblong, to about 7 in. long; cymes 3–30-fld.; calyx 4–6-lobed, about 1 in. long, petals yellowish to greenish-white, to 2 1/2 in. long, stamens in 5 bundles; fr. ellipsoid to globose, about 10 in. long, spiny, pale green, several pounds in weight, seeds about 1 1/2 in. long, with white or yellowish, malodorous aril. W. Malay Arch. Occasionally planted in Hawaii and Puerto Rico.

DUVALIA Haw. *Asclepiadaceae.* About 17 spp. of very dwarf, succulent, leafless, per. herbs, mostly native to S. Afr., but 1 in trop. Afr. and 1 in Arabia; sts. 4–6-angled, the angles with spreading teeth; fls. mostly in clusters near base of sts., corolla rotate, 5-lobed, with a central cushionlike annulus, corona of 2 whorls, arising near the apex of staminal column, outer whorl a flat, more or less 5- or 10-angled disc with its margin resting on the rim or inner wall of the annulus, inner whorl of 5 separate, more or less horizontal, ovoid lobes; fr. an erect, smooth follicle.

For culture see *Succulents.*

compacta Haw. Sts. about 1 in. long, 4–5-angled, teeth rounded and apiculate; fls. 1–5 at the middle of the st., corolla 5/8–3/4 in. across, entirely dark chocolate, lobes narrow, ciliate only at base, outer corona brownish-red, inner with dull orange-red lobes. S. Afr.

concolor (Salm-Dyck) Schlechter. An imperfectly known sp., with fls. uniformly blackish-purple, similar to those of *D. reclinata,* but slightly larger. Probably not actually in cult.

Corderoyi (Hook.f.) N. E. Br. Sts. to 1 1/4 in. long, 6-angled, the angles tubercled; fls. long-pedicelled, at the middle or base of st., corolla 1 1/4–2 in. across, light or dull olive-green, reddish-brown toward apex, lobes often folded, annulus covered with long, soft, purple hairs, outer corona 5-angled, brick-red, inner corona with buff-colored lobes. S. Afr.

elegans (Masson) Haw. Sts. to 2 in. long, 4–5-angled, the angles tubercled-denticulate; fls. 1–3, basal, corolla 1/2–3/4 in. across, dark purple-brown, pilose over the inner face with soft, purple hairs, outer corona nearly circular, almost covering the annulus, dark red-brown, inner corona with brownish-yellow lobes. S. Afr. Var. **namaquana** N. E. Br. Annulus more prominent, corolla lobes 1/4–1/2 in. long.

maculata N. E. Br. Sts. tufted, decumbent, to 1 1/4 in. long, 4–5-angled, angles with conical, acute teeth; fls. mostly 4–8 together near base of st., corolla to 7/8 in. across, olive-brown or purple-brown, lobes strongly folded, annulus large, whitish, spotted purple-brown, corona yellowish. S. Afr. Var. **immaculata** Lückh. Annulus a deep purple-brown, not spotted.

obscura: a listed name of no botanical standing.

pallida: a listed name of no botanical standing.

polita N. E. Br. Sts. rather loose, elongated, to 2 1/2 in. long, 6-angled, the angles toothed; fls. in clusters of 3–4, corolla to 1 1/4 in. across, purplish-chocolate, the basal 5/8 of the lobes shining, annulus yellowish, irregularly marked with purple-brown lines, outer corona 5-sided, chocolate-red, inner corona with orange-red lobes. S. Afr. to Mozambique.

radiata (Sims) Haw. Sts. to 2 in. long, 4–5-angled, with stout, conical teeth; fls. mostly 2 together, corolla about 1 1/8 in. across, dark chocolate-brown, lobes strongly folded, outer corona nearly circular, reddish-brown, inner corona with yellowish lobes, sometimes tinged with red. S. Afr. Var. **obscura** (N. E. Br.) A. C. White & Sloane. Corolla more deeply colored.

reclinata (Masson) Haw. Sts. up to 3 in. long or more, slender, 4–5-angled, the angles tubercled; fls. 1–3 near the middle of st., corolla to 1 1/4 in. across, dark chocolate-brown lobes strongly folded, rim of annulus around the corona greenish, rather shiny, outer corona orange-brown, inner corona more orange. S. Afr. Var. **angulata** N. E. Br. Outer corona 10-angled.

DUVERNOIA E. H. Mey. ex Nees (commonly misspelled *Duvernoya*). *Acanthaceae.* Three or 4 spp. of shrubs of trop. Afr. and S. Afr.; lvs. opp., entire; fls. in terminal spikes with small bracts and bracteoles, calyx with campanulate tube, lobes shorter than tube, corolla with short tube and 2 long lips, upper lip entire, arched, lower lip 3-lobed, large, longer than upper, pendent, stamens 2, borne on corolla tube, anther sacs 2, one slightly higher, one or both with conical fleshy projection at base, filaments cylindrical, ovary on a disc, style entire; fr. a caps.

adhatodoides E. H. Mey. ex Nees [*Adhatoda Duvernoia* C. B. Clarke]. To 10 ft.; lvs. elliptic, to 7 in. long; calyx about 1/4 in. long, corolla 1 in. long, white, with purple markings on throat and lower lip, fls. fragrant. S. Afr.

DYCKIA Schult.f *Bromeliaceae.* About 103 spp. of stemless, succulent or tough, terrestrial or rock-inhabiting herbs, native chiefly to Brazil, Paraguay, and Argentina; lvs. in basal rosettes, stiff, spiny-margined; fls. yellow, orange, or red, in lateral scapose spikes, racemes, or panicles, petals united along their inner median line to the tube formed by united bases of filaments, separate at margins, ovary superior; fr. a caps., seeds with entire wings.

Dyckias usually form large clumps making them suitable as bedding plants in the tropical or subtropical garden. Grown in full sun. For culture see *Bromeliaceae*.

altissima Lindl. To 3 ft. or more; lvs. 1½ ft. long, pale beneath; infl. paniculate; fls. saffron, longer than fl. bracts, filaments united above their union with petals. Argentina.

brevifolia Bak. [*D. sulphurea* C. Koch]. PINEAPPLE D. To 1½ ft.; lvs. to 8 in. long, ¾ in. wide, pale beneath; infl. simple, racemose; fls. sulphur-orange, to ½ in. long, shorter than lower fl. bracts, stamens shorter than petals, filaments separate above their union with petals. Brazil.

corsica: a listed name of no botanical standing.

Fosterana L. B. Sm. To 4 in.; lvs. to 3¾ in. long, ⅜ in. wide, recurved; infl. unbranched, scape bracts longer than internodes; fls. short-pedicelled, orange, filaments united above their union with petals. Brazil. A number of foliage color variants exist.

frigida (Linden) Hook.f. Lvs. to 3 ft. long, 2 in. wide, pale or glaucescent beneath; infl. paniculate; fls. orange, longer than fl. bracts, filaments separate above their union with petals. Brazil.

leptostachya Bak. To 2 ft. or more; lvs. to 7 in. long, ½ in. wide, green to red above, pale beneath; infl. unbranched or rarely few-branched at base, spicate; fls. orange, stamens longer than petals, filaments separate above their union with petals. Brazil.

rariflora Schult.f. Not cult.; material under this name is *D. remotiflora*.

remotiflora Otto & A. Dietr. To 3 ft. or less; lvs. to 10 in. long, palish beneath; infl. simple, racemose; fls. orange or flame-colored, to 1 in. long, about as long as or longer than the lower fl. bracts, stamens shorter than petals, filaments separate above their union with petals. Argentina, Uruguay.

sulphurea: *D. brevifolia*.

DYPSIS Noronha ex Mart. A genus of small palms in Madagascar, not or only infrequently cult. **D. decipiens:** a listed name of no botanical standing; plants grown under this name are *Chrysalidocarpus madagascariensis*. **D. madagascariensis:** *Chrysalidocarpus madagascariensis*.

DYSCHORISTE Nees [*Calophanes* D. Don]. *Acanthaceae*. About 65 spp. of shrubs or herbs, in N. and S. Amer., Afr. and se. Asia; fls. in terminal or axillary spikes or cymes, bracts leafy, calyx deeply 5-lobed, corolla purple, obscurely or distinctly 2-lipped, stamens 4, didynamous, anther sacs 2, unequal; fr. a caps., solid at base, seeds 4, flat, round, covered with hygroscopic hairs.

linearis (Torr. & A. Gray) O. Kuntze. To 1½ ft.; lvs. linear to spatulate, 2½ in. long; corolla violet, spotted with purple, 1 in. long. Tex., w. to New Mex. and n. Mex.

thunbergiiflora (S. L. Moore) Lindau. Shrub, to 10 ft., differing from *D. linearis* in having lvs. obovate, corolla to 2 in. long. E. Trop. Afr.

DYSSODIA Cav. [*Thymophylla* Lag.]. DOGWEED, FETID MARIGOLD. *Compositae* (Helenium Tribe). About 32 spp. of strongly scented ann. or per. herbs or subshrubs, native to sw. U.S. and n. Mex.; lvs. opp. or alt., simple to pinnatifid or pinnate, glandular; fl. heads usually radiate, solitary or sometimes in cymose clusters, involucre hemispherical to narrowly turbinate or cylindrical, subtended by short calyxlike bracts, involucral bracts in 2 rows, separate or variously united, usually glandular, receptacle flat to conical, naked to minutely fringed; disc fls. bisexual, dull yellow, ray fls. usually present, female, red, orange, yellow, rarely white; achenes stout, obpyramidal or cylindrical, pappus of 1–2 rows of scales or bristles.

tenuiloba (DC.) B. L. Robinson [*Thymophylla tenuiloba* (DC.) Small]. DAHLBERG DAISY, GOLDEN-FLEECE. Erect to spreading, bushy ann. or short-lived per., to 1 ft.; lvs. opp. in lower part, alt. above, to ¾ in. long, pinnately parted into 7–11 linear-filiform, bristle-tipped segms., margins glandular; heads to ½ in. across, involucre turbinate-campanulate, involucral bracts united ¾ their length, glandular; disc fls. yellow, ray fls. golden-yellow-orange. S.-cent. Tex. and adjacent Mex.; naturalized in warmer parts of world. An excellent bedder, having a flowering period of several months. Blooming from seed in 4 months, preferring a well-drained sandy soil in full sun.

EBENACEAE Gürke. EBONY FAMILY. Dicot.; 6 genera of trees and shrubs with very hard wood, native to warm and temp. regions of both hemispheres; lvs. alt., entire; fls. regular, unisexual or bisexual, calyx and corolla prominently 3–7-lobed, stamens 2–3 times as many as corolla lobes, ovary superior, styles 2–8; fr. a berry. Some spp. of *Diospyros* are grown for the edible fr., others as ornamentals; and several are sources of commercial ebony wood. *Maba* and *Royena* are occasionally cult. as ornamentals.

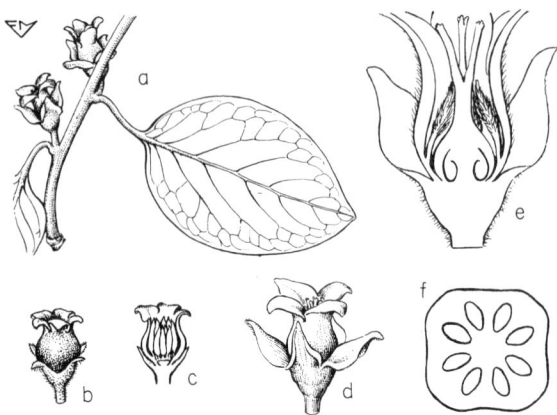

EBENACEAE. *Diospyros virginiana:* **a,** part of branch of female plant, × ½; **b,** male flower, × 1; **c,** male flower, vertical section, × 1; **d,** female flower, × 1; **e,** lower part of female flower, vertical section, × 2; **f,** ovary, cross section, × 4. (From Bailey, *Manual of Cultivated Plants,* ed. 2.)

EBENOPSIS: *PITHECELLOBIUM.*

EBRACTEOLA Dinter & Schwant. *Aizoaceae.* Not in cult. E. Derenbergiana: *Mesembryanthemum Derenbergianum.*

ECBALLIUM A. Rich. *Cucurbitaceae.* One sp., a monoecious, more or less trailing or prostrate per. herb of Medit. region, without tendrils; fls. yellow, rotate, male fls. racemose, stamens 3, separate, anthers flexuous, female fls. solitary, ovary inferior, with 3 parietal placentas; fr. a berry, seeds many, horizontal.

Elaterium (L.) A. Rich. [*Momordica Elaterium* L.]. SQUIRTING CUCUMBER. Hairy-pubescent and grayish; lvs. triangular-ovate, to 4 in. long, angled or obscurely lobed; fr. green, oblong, to 2 in. long, rough-hairy, becoming detached from the pedicel at maturity and squirting the seeds explosively from the basal opening. Grown as a curiosity; not hardy north, but flowering and fruiting the first year from seed. Fr. has been used medicinally.

ECCREMOCACTUS Britt. & Rose. *Cactaceae.* Three spp. of epiphytic cacti, native to Costa Rica and Ecuador; sts. branched basally, brs. flat, thickish, crenate or with long ovate lobes; areoles marginal, spines short or in cult. sometimes 0; fls. nocturnal, funnelform, whitish or greenish, perianth segms. many, obtuse, longer than the tube, the outer appressed, stamens many, in 2 zones, ovary scaly; fr. ovoid, red, spines few or many, seeds black, minutely pitted. Allied to *Epiphyllum,* but with spiny sts. and a short floral tube.

For culture see *Cacti.*

Bradei Britt. & Rose. Brs. 6–12 in. long, 2–4 in. wide, lobes short, semicircular; spines 1–3, brown, ¼ in. long; fls. 2½ in. long, tube with scales few, prominent, long-decurrent at base. Spring, autumn. Costa Rica.

imitans (Kimnach & P. C. Hutchison) Kimnach. Sts. to 3 ft., brs. 4–6 in. long, ¾–1¼ in. wide, lobes long, ovate; areoles white-woolly, spines usually 0, sometimes 1–3, reddish-brown, needle-shaped, less than ³⁄₁₆ in. long; fls. to 2¾ in. long, light cream-colored, tube and ovary with 1–10, mostly 5 spines at each areole. Costa Rica.

Rosei Kimnach. Sts. to 3 ft. long, 3¼ in. wide, brs. with lobes short, semicircular; areoles inconspicuously woolly, spines mostly 3, white to dark brown, needle-shaped, mostly ⅛ in. long or less; fls. to 2¾ in. long, greenish-cream, tube and ovary with many scales short-decurrent at base. Ecuador.

ECCREMOCARPUS Ruiz & Pav. [*Calampelis* D. Don]. GLORY FLOWER. *Bignoniaceae.* Three or 4 spp. of climbing shrubs, native to Peru and Chile; lvs. opp., 2-parted or 2-pinnate, with terminal branched tendril; fls. yellow, orange, or scarlet, in terminal racemes, calyx 5-parted, corolla tubular, more or less 2-lipped, stamens 4; fr. an ovoid or ellipsoid caps.

Grown as an annual in the North and as a perennial where it is hardy.

scaber (D. Don) Ruiz & Pav. [*Calampelis scaber* D. Don]. Woody, climbing to 12 ft., but sometimes treated as an herb and blooming first year from seed; lvs. 2-pinnate, lfts. to 1¼ in. long, ovate, entire, or toothed; fls. orange-red, 1 in. long, with small lobes, in racemes to 6 in. long; fr. 1½ in. long. Chile. Cv. 'Aureus'. Fls. golden-yellow. Cv. 'Carmineus'. Fls. carmine-red.

ECHEVERIA DC. [*Courantia* Lem.; *Oliveranthus* Rose; *Urbinia* Rose]. HEN-AND-CHICKENS. *Crassulaceae.* Perhaps 100 spp. of succulent per. herbs and shrubs, native from Tex. to Argentina, but especially in Mex.; lvs. alt., mostly in rosettes; fl. st. axillary, infl. of 1 or more cincinni, or a spike, raceme, or thyrse; fls. 5-merous, calyx deeply divided, disc narrower than corolla base, lobes erect to reflexed, often unequal, corolla yellow to red or pale, mostly 5-angled, often swollen between the sepals, petals thick, erect, mostly overlapping, united at base, stamens 10. Various of the supposedly local spp. could perhaps better be combined as subspp. or vars.

The genus has been divided into 3 somewhat intergrading sections. The species of a section possess the characteristics of that section. These characteristics are not repeated in the brief descriptions of the species; instead, the following symbols are used to indicate the section to which each species belongs: E, *Echeveria;* R, *Racemosae;* S, *Secundae.*

The distinguishing characters of the sections follow:

Echeveria (E). Plants, including fls., pubescent.

Racemosae (Bak.) Moran (R). Plants glabrous, at most papillose; infl. equilateral, a raceme or spike, sometimes subthyrsoid, some lower brs. with more than 1 fl.

Secundae (Bak.) Moran (S). Plants glabrous or rarely lvs. puberulent but fls. glabrous; infl. of 1 to several cincinni.

Grown as pot plants or in warm regions in rock gardens and for bedding. For culture see *Succulents.*

acutifolia Lindl. S; glabrous, st. to 1 ft. or more; lvs. about 15, rhombic-spatulate, 4–7½ in. long, 2–3½ in. wide, acute, concave, green, tinged with scarlet; fl. st. to 3 ft., cincinni several, 3–4-fld., pedicels ³⁄₁₆ in. long; sepals erect or ascending, unequal, ¼ in. long, corolla red, tinged with yellow, ½ in. long. Late autumn, early winter. S. Mex.

affinis Walth. S; glabrous, sts. to 4 in.; lvs. 30–60, oblong-oblanceolate, 2–3 in. long, ¾–1 in. wide, ³⁄₁₆–⅜ in. thick, acute, minutely pointed, bright green to greenish-black; fl. st. 8–15 in., with 2–5 close-set, simple or forked brs., cincinni 4–10-fld., pedicels ⅛–½ in. long; sepals erect, equal, ³⁄₁₆–⁵⁄₁₆ in. long, corolla red, ⁵⁄₁₆–½ in. long, petals thin. Late summer, autumn. W. Mex.

agavoides Lem. [*Urbinia agavoides* (Lem.) Rose]. MOULDED-WAX. S; glabrous, sts. short; lvs. 25–75, ovate, 1½–5 in. long, tip spinelike, stiff, green or tipped with dark red; fl. st. slender, 8–20 in.; fls. few, long-pedicelled, in 1-2 or more cincinni, sepals ascending-spreading, unequal, to 3/16 in. long, corolla reddish with yellow tips, to 1/2 in. long. Mex. A distinct but variable sp., of which several garden forms have been named. Var. **Corderoyi** (Bak.) Poelln. [*E. Corderoyi* (Bak.) E. Morr.]. A form with many (60–70) lvs. and 15–20 fls.

alba: a listed name of no botanical standing.

albida: *Dudleya virens.*

alpina: see *E. secunda.*

amoena De Smet. BABY E. S; glabrous, sts. to 6 in.; lvs. 20–30, oblong-spatulate, to 1 in. long, turgid, glaucous; fl. st. slender, 3–8 in., the lvs. easily detached and rooting; fls. few, long-pedicelled, in 2–3 cincinni, sepals roundish, appressed, corolla coral-red, cylindrical, 3/8 in. long. Late spring. Mex. *E. microcalyx* Britt. & Rose [*E. Purpusii* Britt., not (K. Schum.) Wittm.]. Scarcely different unless in having lvs. slightly larger.

angusta: *E. subrigida.*

angustata: a listed name of no botanical standing, possibly a misspelling for *E. angusta.*

atropurpurea Bak. [*E. sanguinea* E. Morr.]. R; glabrous, sts. to 8 in.; lvs. about 20, obovate-spatulate, 4–6 in. long, 1–2 in. wide, acute, dark purple, glaucous; fl. st. 1–2 ft., raceme to 6 in. long, 20–35-fld., pedicels to 1/2 in. long; sepals spreading or reflexed, nearly equal, 3/16 in. long, corolla red, to 1/2 in. long. Mex.

atrosanguinea: a listed name of no botanical standing; said to be a hybrid.

australis Rose. R; glabrous, sts. to 1 ft.; lvs. 15–20, spatulate to obovate, 1 1/2–3 in. long, glaucous; fl. st. 1–1 1/2 ft., raceme to 10 in., mostly nearly thyrsoid, pedicels to 3/16 in. long; sepals ascending, nearly equal, to 1/2 in. long, corolla red, about 1/2 in. long. Early spring. Costa Rica, Panama.

Batesii: a listed name of no botanical standing, possibly referring to *Villadia Batesii.*

bella Alexand. R; glabrous, sts. short, much-branched; lvs. 20–30, linear-oblanceolate, 1/2–1 in. long, 3/16 in. wide, acute, green; fl. st. 4–10 in., raceme 4–10-fld., pedicels to 3/8 in. long; sepals spreading, nearly equal, to 1/4 in. long, corolla red below, yellow above, 3/8 in. long. Spring, early summer. S. Mex.

bicolor (HBK) Walth. R; glabrous, sts. to 2 ft.; lvs. 15–30, cuneate-spatulate, 2–3 1/2 in. long, 1–2 1/2 in. wide, mucronate, green; fl. st. 1/2–2 ft., raceme 10–25-fld., pedicels to 1/2 in. long; sepals ascending to spreading, nearly equal, to 1/2 in. long, corolla red with yellow tips, to 1/2 in. long. Winter. Venezuela, Colombia.

bifida Schlechtend. S; glabrous, st. short, unbranched; lvs. 12–25, rhombic-oblanceolate, 1 1/2–4 in. long, 1/2–1 in. wide, acute, minutely pointed, glaucous, often reddish; fl. st. mostly 10–20 in., cincinni 2, pedicels to 5/16 in. long; sepals spreading, unequal, to 3/8 in. long, corolla glaucous-pink, often yellow at edges, 1/2 in. long. Summer, early autumn. E. Mex.

Bradburyana: a listed name of no botanical standing to be treated as *Echeveria* cv. 'Bradburyana'; said to be a spontaneous hybrid, probably of *E. elegans,* with lvs. red-edged, silvery-gray.

Byrnesii: *E. secunda* var.

carnicolor (Bak.) E. Morr. CORAL E. R; glabrous but papillose, sts. short; lvs. 20–30, oblanceolate-spatulate, 1–2 in. long, 1/2–3/4 in. wide, green or bluish with metallic sheen; fl. st. 6–10 in., raceme 6–20-fld., pedicels to 1/2 in. long; sepals spreading, nearly equal, 1/4 in. long, corolla flesh-colored, salmon above, 1/2 in. long. Winter. E. Mex.

chilonensis (O. Kuntze) Walth. R; glabrous, sts. short; lvs. 15–20, oblanceolate to linear, 2–3 in. long, 1/2 in. wide; fl. st. 1–2 ft., raceme 10–25-fld., nearly thyrsoid below, pedicels to 3/8 in. long; sepals ascending, nearly equal, to 5/16 in. long, corolla yellowish-white, 1/2 in. long. Early summer. Bolivia.

coccinea (Cav.) DC. [*E. pubescens* Schlechtend.]. E; gray-velvety pubescent, sts. to 3 ft.; lvs. 8–15, spatulate to obovate-cuneate, 2 1/2–4 1/2 in. long, 3/4–1 1/4 in. wide; fl. st. 1–3 ft., spike dense, 20–50-fld.; sepals spreading, nearly equal, to 5/8 in. long, corolla red, to 1/2 in. long. Autumn, early winter. Mex. Cv. **'Recurvata'** [*E. pubescens* cv. 'Recurvata' or cv. 'Tortuosa']. MEXICAN PALM. Lvs. short, broad, recurved, twisted.

Corderoyi: *E. agavoides* var.

Cotyledon: *Dudleya caespitosa;* see also *D. farinosa.*

Craigii Walth. S; glabrous, sts. short, few-branched; lvs. 30–50, elliptic-lanceolate, 3–4 1/2 in. long, 1/2–3/4 in. wide, acute, minutely pointed, glaucous, often purplish; fl. st. 12–20 in., with 5–18 mostly scattered, simple or forked brs., cincinni few-fld., pedicels to 3/4 in. long; sepals erect or ascending, nearly equal, to 5/16 in. long, corolla red, 3/8 in. long, petals thin. Late summer, autumn. W. Mex.

crenulata Rose [?*E. Hoffmanii* Hort.]. S; similar to *E. gibbiflora,* but lvs. green, with mostly wavy red margins. Late autumn, winter. Mex.

crispa: a listed name of no botanical standing; said to be similar to *E. crenulata* but larger, lf. margins strongly wavy.

cristata: a listed name of no botanical standing.

cuspidata Rose [*E. parrasensis* Walth.]. S; glabrous, sts. short; lvs. 40–100, oblong-obovate, 2–4 in. long, 1–2 in. wide, mucronate, glaucous; fl. st. 8–16 in., cincinni 1–2, 8–15-fld., pedicels to 1/2 in. long; sepals ascending, unequal, to 5/16 in. long, corolla deep pink, about 1/2 in. long. Winter to early summer. N. Mex.

dactylifera Walth. S; glabrous, sts. to 1 ft.; lvs. 25–60, elliptic-oblong, 15–20 in. long, 4–6 in. wide, acute, channelled above, often reddish or red-margined; fl. st. to 4 ft., with 5–12 ascending, 2–6-fld. cincinni to 4 in. long, pedicels to 1 in. long; sepals spreading, unequal, to 1 in. long, corolla deep pink, 1–1 1/4 in. long, petals with a pair of scales at base of filaments. Autumn. W. Mex.

Derenbergii J. Purpus. PAINTED-LADY, BABY E. S; glabrous, sts. short, forming offsets among lvs.; lvs. 40–70, cuneate-spatulate, 1–1 3/4 in. long, to 1 1/4 in. wide, mucronate, blue-glaucous, often red-tipped; fl. st. to 4 in., cincinnus solitary, 4–6-fld., pedicels to 1/2 in. long; sepals spreading to ascending, unequal, to 3/8 in. long, corolla yellow, red above, about 1/2 in. long, nearly as wide. Late winter, spring. S. Mex.

Desmetiana: *E. Peacockii.*

edulis: *Dudleya edulis.*

elegans Rose. PEARL E., MEXICAN-GEM, MEXICAN SNOWBALL, WHITE MEXICAN ROSE. S; glabrous, sts. short, forming offsets; lvs. 30–70, oblong-spatulate, 1 1/2–2 1/2 in. long, to 1 in. wide, mucronate, glaucous-green, turgid, margins translucent; fl. st. 4–7 in., cincinnus solitary, 5–12-fld., pedicels to 1/2 in. long; sepals ascending, unequal, to 3/8 in. long, corolla rose with yellow tips, 1/2 in. long. Late winter to early summer. Mex. Sometimes grown as *E. simulans.* Var. **simulans:** *E. simulans.*

×**expatriata:** × *Cremneria expatriata.*

fallax: a listed name of no botanical standing to be treated as *Echeveria* cv. 'Fallax' for the hybrid *E. Derenbergii* × *E. elegans.* S; glabrous, sts. short; lvs. about 40, obovate, to 2 in. long, rounded and mucronate, bluish-glaucous; fl. st. to 3 in., 4–7-fld.; sepals ascending, equal, 1/4 in. long, corolla orange-red, 5/8 in. long. Spring.

fimbriata C. H. Thomps. S; glabrous, sts. to 1 1/2 ft.; lvs. 12–20, obovate-spatulate, to 8 in. long and 3 1/2 in. wide, obtuse, short-mucronate, with margin thin and fimbriate, green or brownish; fl. st. 1–2 ft., cincinni 2–5, each 8–14-fld., pedicels to 5/8 in. long; sepals spreading, unequal, to 3/8 in. long, corolla rose-pink, 5/8 in. long. Late autumn, early winter. Mex.

flammea: a listed name of no botanical standing for *E. gibbiflora* cv.

fulgens Lem. [*E. retusa* Lindl.]. S; glabrous, sts. to 12 in.; lvs. 8–20, obovate-spatulate, 4–6 in. long, 2–3 in. wide, rounded or somewhat mucronate, glaucous, often red-margined; fl. st. 1–3 ft., cincinni 1–3, each about 12-fld., pedicels to 1/2 in. long; sepals spreading, unequal, to 3/8 in. long, corolla red outside, yellow inside, 3/8–5/8 in. long. Late autumn, early winter. Mex.

Funkii: a listed name of no botanical standing, apparently for an old garden hybrid.

gibbiflora DC. S; glabrous, sts. erect, to 3 ft.; lvs. 12–25, obovate to spatulate, 6–14 in. long, 4–10 in. wide, mucronate, gray-green or purplish; fl. st. to 5 ft., with 4–12 cincinni, each 5–15-fld., pedicels to 5/16 in. long; sepals spreading, unequal, to 3/8 in. long, corolla red, to 3/4 in. long. Autumn, early winter. Mex. Cvs. are: **'Carunculata'**, lf. with warty excrescence on upper side near base; **'Crispata'**, lf. margins finely wavy; **'Metallica'** [*E. metallica* Lem.], lvs. purplish-lilac becoming brownish-bronzy-green; **'Pallida'** [*E. pallida* Walth.], a Mexican garden form with pale green lvs. and broad sepals. Cvs. **'Flammea'** and **'Viride'** are also listed.

gigantea Rose. S; closely allied to *E. gibbiflora,* of which it is perhaps a var., but lvs. green, commonly red-margined. Late autumn, winter. S. Mex.

×**gilva** Walth.: *E. agavoides* × *E. elegans.* GREEN MEXICAN ROSE, WAX-ROSETTE. S; glabrous, sts. short, branching; lvs. 40–50, oblong-obovate, to 3 in. long, mucronate, yellowish-green or glaucous; fl. st. 10 in., cincinnus solitary, pedicels 1/2 in. long; sepals spreading, unequal, to 3/16 in. long, corolla pink, yellow-tipped, 3/8 in. long. Spring. Formerly grown as *E. simulans.*

giorgis: a listed name of no botanical standing.

glauca: *E. secunda* var.

×**glaucometallica:** *E.* × *imbricata.*

globosa: a listed name of no botanical standing; probably a form or hybrid of *E. secunda;* cvs. 'Cristata' and 'Gigantea' are also listed.

Goldmanii Rose. R; glabrous, sts. to 8 in., erect or decumbent; lvs. scattered, narrow-oblong, 1¼–2 in. long, pale green with red margins; fl. st. 10 in., raceme 10–15-fld., pedicels to ⅛ in. long; sepals ascending, unequal, to ³⁄₁₆ in. long, corolla red, ⅜ in. long. Mex.

gracilis Walth. R; glabrous, sts. to 8 in.; lvs. 20–25, scattered to nearly in a rosette, cuneate-spatulate, to 1¼ in. long and ½ in. wide, mucronate, green, turgid; fl. st. to 10 in., raceme 5–20-fld., pedicels to ⅜ in. long; sepals spreading, nearly equal, to ⅜ in. long, corolla red, orange above, ⅜ in. long. Early summer. Mex.

×**Graessneri** Van Keppel: *E. Derenbergii* × *E. pulvinata.* Glabrous, sts. to 6 in.; lvs. 30–50, crowded, obovate-spatulate, to 2¼ in. long and 1¼ in. wide, mucronate, glaucous, red-edged, low-papillose; fl. st. to 5 in., with 1–5 brs., each 1–2-fld., pedicels ½ in. long; sepals ascending, unequal, to ⅝ in. long, corolla salmon-orange, red on keel and edges, ¾ in. long. Sometimes grown under the name *E.* × *Haageana* Hort. Cv. 'Eric Walther'. Said to fl. thrice yearly, starting in early winter.

Haageana: a listed name of no botanical standing to be treated as *Echeveria* cv. 'Haageana' for the hybrid *E. agavoides* × *E. Derenbergii.* Material grown under this name, however, is probably *E.* × *Graessneri.*

Halbingeri Walth. S; glabrous, sts. short, much-branched; lvs. 30–40, obovate-cuneate, 1 in. long, obtuse and minutely pointed, glaucous; fl. st. 3–5 in., cincinnus solitary, pedicels to ⅜ in. long; sepals spreading, unequal, to ¼ in. long, corolla orange-yellow, ½ in. long. Spring, early summer. E. Mex.

Harmsii Macbr. [*Oliveranthus elegans* Rose]. RED E. E; puberulent, sts. branching to 20 in.; lvs. 12–20, oblanceolate, ¾–1½ in. long, acute; fl. st. to 8 in., 1–3-fld., pedicels 1 in. long; sepals spreading, equal, to ¾ in. long, corolla red outside, yellow inside, 1–1¼ in. long. Early summer. Mex.

heterosepala Rose [*Pachyphytum heterosepalum* (Rose) Walth.]. S; glabrous, sts. short, unbranched; lvs. 40–70, rhombic-oblanceolate, 1–1½ in. long, ⅜–⅝ in. wide, acuminate, glaucous; fl. st. to 18 in., cincinnus solitary, pedicels stout, to ¼ in. long; sepals ascending to spreading, unequal, to ⅜ in. long, corolla glaucous-green, ⅜ in. long and nearly as wide. Late spring, early summer. S. Mex.

Hoffmanii: a listed name of no botanical standing, perhaps for *E. crenulata.*

Hoveyi Rose. Treated as *Echeveria* cv. 'Hoveyi'. Lvs. 25–35, oblong-spatulate, truncate to rounded, erose, pale bluish-green with irregular longitudinal white or pinkish stripes. Said to revert rarely to the very different normal form treated as *Echeveria* cv. 'Zahnii'.

Howardii: a listed name of no botanical standing.

×**imbricata** Deleuil [*E.* × *glaucometallica* Hort.]: *E. gibbiflora* cv. 'Metallica' × *E. secunda* var. *glauca.* S; glabrous, sts. short, much-branched; lvs. about 50, obovate-cuneate, 2–3 in. long, 1–2 in. wide, mucronate, bluish-glaucous; fl. st. to 10 in., cincinni 1–2, pedicels to ⅝ in. long; sepals ascending, unequal, to ½ in. long, corolla deep pink, yellow-tipped, ⅝ in. long. Spring. The echeveria most widely grown in Calif.

Johnsonii Walth. S; glabrous, sts. weakly erect, branching; lvs. 40–50, oblong-oblanceolate, 1½ in. long, acute to obtuse, nearly round in cross section, or flattened; fl. st. 6 in., infl. nearly spicate; sepals ascending to spreading, nearly equal, ⁵⁄₁₆ in. long, corolla orange-yellow, ⅜ in. long, nearly as wide. Ecuador.

kewensis: a listed name of no botanical standing.

lanceolata: *Dudleya lanceolata;* but the name *E. lanceolata* is also applied to a hybrid of *E. agavoides.* Var. **aloides:** *Dudleya saxosa* subsp.

laxa: *Dudleya caespitosa;* see also *D. cymosa.*

leucotricha J. Purpus. CHENILLE PLANT, WHITE-PLUSH PLANT. E; densely hairy, sts. to 6 in., red-brown-hairy; lvs. about 25, in a loose rosette, oblong-oblanceolate, 2–4 in. long, to 1 in. wide, mucronate, thick, white-hairy; fl. st. 12–16 in., spike 12–15-fld., somewhat thyrsoid below; sepals erect, nearly equal, to ⅜ in. long, corolla cinnabar-red, ¾ in. long. Late winter. S. Mex.

Lindsayana Walth. S; glabrous, sts. short, branching in age; lvs. many, obovate to oblong, to 2½ in. long and 1½ in. wide, mucronate, glaucous-white; fl. st. to 20 in., cincinni 1–2, pedicels to ½ in. long; sepals nearly equal, to ⅛ in. long, corolla grenadine-pink, with light orange-yellow tips, ⅜ in. long. Late winter, early spring. Probably Mex.

linguifolia: *Cremnophila linguifolia.*

Lozanii Rose. S; glabrous, rosettes sessile, dense; lvs. oblong-oblanceolate, 4–8 in. long, ¾–2 in. wide, acute, glaucous; fl. st. 8–20 in., with 3–7 brs., each 2–4-fld., pedicels ⅜ in. long; sepals spreading, unequal,

to ½ in. long, corolla copper-colored, about ½ in. long. Autumn. W. Mex.

lurida: *E. racemosa.*

lutea Rose. S; glabrous, sts. very short, mostly unbranched; lvs. 20–50, linear to oblong, 2–6 in. long, to ¾ in. wide at the middle, where widest, acuminate, channelled above, green or purplish-tinged; fl. st. 1–2 ft., cincinni 1–2; fls. sessile, sepals spreading, nearly equal to unequal, ¼–1 in. long, corolla dandelion-yellow, ½–¾ in. long. Summer. E. Mex.

Macdougallii Walth. [*E. sedoides* Walth.]. R; glabrous shrub, to 1 ft.; lvs. 20–40, often scattered, obovate to oblong-oblanceolate, ¾–1¼ in. long, to ½ in. wide, acute to obtuse, turgid, with very obtuse margins, glaucous, often red-marked; fl. st. erect or spreading, 4–10 in., raceme 3–10-fld., pedicels ½–¾ in. long; sepals spreading, nearly equal, to ⁵⁄₁₆ in. long, corolla red, yellow at upper edges, ½–¾ in. long. Summer, autumn. S. Mex.

macrantha Standl. & Steyerm. E; pubescent, sts. erect, branched; lvs. orbicular-cuneate, 1¼ in. long; fls. about 3, to ¾ in. long. Guatemala. Probably not in cult., the plant commonly so named being apparently a hybrid allied to *E. secunda.*

macrophylla: a listed name of no botanical standing for a probable hybrid; said to be the largest of the echeverias and beautifully colored.

maculata Rose. S; glabrous, sts. very short, unbranched, roots thick; lvs. 12–20, narrowly oblanceolate or somewhat rhombic, 3–6 in. long, ¾–1¼ in. wide, acute to acuminate, green or slightly glaucous; fl. st. 1–3 ft., with 8–15 ascending, often elongate cincinni of 2–5 nearly sessile fls. or some reduced to 1 pedicelled fl.; sepals ascending-spreading, unequal, the longest ⁵⁄₁₆–⅝ in. long, corolla yellow or with red toward base, ½–⅝ in. long. Spring, summer. Mex. *Sedum indicum* has sometimes been grown under this name.

Maxonii Rose. R; glabrous, sts. to 2½ ft., branching; lvs. 10–15, oblanceolate or spatulate, 1–4 in. long, acute, channelled above, green with purplish margins; fl. st. to 2 ft., raceme somewhat thyrsoid below, pedicels to ³⁄₁₆ in. long; sepals spreading, nearly equal, to ³⁄₁₆ in. long, corolla salmon-pink, ⅜ in. long. Winter. Guatemala.

megacalyx Walth. R; glabrous, sts. short, branching; lvs. 15–40, oblong-spatulate, 2–4 in. long, 1–1½ in. wide, mucronate, green to bluish-glaucous, margins narrowly hyaline; fl. st. 8–30 in., infl. subspicate; fls. 20–50; sepals erect or ascending, nearly equal, ⅜ in. long, corolla yellow or with lower half red. Summer, autumn. S. Mex.

metallica: *E. gibbiflora* cv. 'Metallica'.

microcalyx: see *E. amoena.*

montana Rose [*E. nuda* var. *montana* (Rose) Poelln.]. R; glabrous, sts. to 4 ft.; lvs. 15–25, obovate-spatulate, 2–5 in. long, 1–2 in. wide, mucronate, glossy green; fl. st. 1–2 ft., raceme 15–25-fld., mostly papillose, pedicels to ½ in. long; sepals spreading, equal, ½ in. long, corolla red below, yellow above, ½ in. long. Early summer. S. Mex., Guatemala.

Moranii Walth. [*E. proxima* Walth.]. R; glabrous, sts. to 5 in., forming offsets in age; lvs. 15–40, obovate-cuneate, 1–2 in. long, ¾–1½ in. wide, to ⅜ in. thick, mucronate, grayish, margins purplish-red, papillose; fl. st. mostly inclined, 8–15 in., raceme 10–25-fld., pedicels to ½ in. long; sepals appressed, nearly equal, to ³⁄₁₆ in. long, corolla red, ⅜–⅝ in. long. Summer. S. Mex.

multicaulis Rose. COPPER ROSES, COPPER-LEAF E. R; glabrous, sts. to 4 ft., the surface subdivided by acute, nearly crenate ridges; lvs. 20–30, somewhat scattered, obovate to spatulate, 1–2 in. long, mucronate, glossy green, margins reddish; fl. st. 10–20 in., ridged like sts., raceme often somewhat thyrsoid below, pedicels to ⅜ in.; sepals ascending, nearly equal, to ⁵⁄₁₆ in. long, corolla red, yellow inside, ½ in. long. Winter. S. Mex.

×**mutabilis:** × *Cremneria mutabilis.*

nivalis: a listed name of no botanical standing for plants said to have lvs. semicylindrical, white. Perhaps a × *Pachyveria.*

nobilis: a listed name of no botanical standing for × *Pachyveria Clevelandii.*

nodulosa (Bak.) Otto. R; glabrous but papillose, sts. to 20 in.; lvs. 10–25, obovate-spatulate, 2–3 in. long, ¾ in. wide, acute, margins green and otherwise marked with purplish-red; fl. st. ½–2 ft., raceme 4–22-fld., pedicels becoming erect, ⅛–⅜ in. long; sepals spreading, nearly equal, to ½ in. long, corolla straw-yellow, tinged with red, ½–¾ in. long. Summer. S. Mex.

nuda Lindl. R; glabrous, sts. to 2 ft.; lvs. 12–20, scattered, obovate-spatulate, 1¾–3 in. long, 1 in. wide, mucronate, slightly glaucous; fl. st. 6–18 in., raceme 15–30-fld., often somewhat thyrsoid below, pedicels to ³⁄₁₆ in. long; sepals ascending to spreading, the longest as long as the corolla, corolla red below, yellow above, ½ in. long. Early summer. Mex. Var. **montana:** *E. montana.*

nudicaulis: *Dudleya densiflora.*

obtusifolia Rose [*E. scopulorum* Rose]. S; glabrous, sts. short; lvs. 10–20, oblanceolate to spatulate, rounded at apex, 3–4 in. long, 1–1½ in. wide, green, red-edged; fl. st. 8–14 in., cincinni 2–3, pedicels to ½ in.; sepals spreading, unequal, to ¼ in. long, corolla orange, to ½ in. long. Autumn. Mex.

Orpettii: a listed name of no botanical standing; to be treated as *Echeveria* cv. 'Orpettii'; said to be a hybrid of *E. grandifolia* Haw., with rosettes large, the outer lvs. rosy, the inner green.

ovalifolia: a listed name of no botanical standing.

oviformis: a listed name of no botanical standing.

pallida: *E. gibbiflora* cv.

Palmeri: *E. subrigida.*

paniculata A. Gray. S; glabrous, rosettes sessile; lvs. 15–40, oblanceolate, 2–4 in. long, to 1 in. wide, acute; fl. st. 15–20 in., with several short brs., each with 2–4 nearly sessile fls.; sepals spreading, unequal, to ⅜ in. long, corolla yellow, ⅝ in. long. Summer. Nw. Mex.

parrasensis: *E. cuspidata.*

Peacockii (Bak.) Britt. & Rose [*E. Desmetiana* E. Morr.]. PEACOCK E. S; glabrous, sts. short; lvs. 40–70, oblong-obovate, 1½–2½ in. long, to 1¼ in. wide, short-acuminate, white-mealy; fl. st. 6–14 in., cincinnus solitary, with 15–50 nearly sessile fls.; sepals ascending, markedly unequal, to ⅜ in. long, corolla red, to ½ in. long. Early summer. S. Mex.

perbella: a hort. name of no botanical standing for hybrids said to form a dense rosette; lvs. about 40, elliptic, minutely pointed, concave, waxy-green, tinted copper and red-edged.

pilosa J. Purpus. HAIRY E. E; white-hairy, sts. to 6 in.; lvs. 25–40, rhombic-spatulate, to 3 in. long and 1 in. wide, acute, concave above; fl. st. to 1 ft., cincinni several, 1–4-fld., pedicels to ¼ in. long; sepals spreading, nearly equal, to ⅝ in. long, corolla orange, to ½ in. long. S. Mex.

pinetorum Rose. R; glabrous, roots thick, sts. very short, unbranched; lvs. 10–15, oblanceolate, 1–2 in. long, to ¾ in. wide, acute, minutely pointed, green, margins narrowly hyaline, often minutely toothed; fl. st. 8–20 in., infl. spicate, 10–25-fld.; sepals ascending, unequal, ¼ in. long, corolla red, yellow at apex, ⅜ in. long. Summer, autumn. S. Mex.

Pittieri Rose. R; glabrous, sts. erect, branching; lvs. about 20, oblanceolate, 2–4 in. long, to ¾ in. wide, acute, green or slightly glaucous; fl. st. 4–8 in., spike dense; sepals erect, equal, green or purplish, 5/16 in. long, corolla pink, ½ in. long. Early winter. Guatemala, Nicaragua, Costa Rica.

plumosa: a listed name of no botanical standing, probably *E. pulvinata.*

potosina Walth. S; glabrous, sts. short; lvs. 40–60, obovate-cuneate, to 2¼ in. long and 1¼ in. wide, mucronate, blue-glaucous, often purplish, cupped above; fl. st. 10–16 in., cincinnus solitary, pedicels to 5/16 in. long; sepals appressed, unequal, to 3/16 in. long, corolla pink with yellow-green above, ½ in. long. Early spring, early summer. Presumably Mex. Cv. **'Alba'** is listed.

Pringlei (S. Wats.) Rose. E; puberulent, sts. decumbent, to 1 ft.; lvs. about 15, oblanceolate, 2–4 in. long, acute; fl. st. to 8 in., infl. a raceme, pedicels to 5/16 in. long; sepals spreading to ascending, nearly equal, to ⅝ in. long, corolla red, ½–⅝ in. long. Late autumn. W. Mex.

proxima: *E. Moranii.*

pubescens: *E. coccinea.*

Pulidonis Walth. S; glabrous, sts. short, branching; lvs. 25–60, obovate-oblong, 1¼–2 in. long, ¾ in. wide, ¼ in. thick, mucronate, light green, red-edged; fl. st. 7 in., cincinnus solitary, pedicels to 5/16 in. long; sepals spreading, unequal, to ¼ in. long, corolla yellow, ⅜ in. long, with recurved tips. Winter, spring. E. Mex.

pulverulenta: *Dudleya pulverulenta.*

pulvicarn: a listed name of no botanical standing to be treated as *Echeveria* cv. 'Pulvi-carn' for the hybrid *E. carnicolor* × *E. pulvinata.* E; finely hairy, sts. short; lvs. about 30, oblanceolate, to 3 in. long and 1 in. wide, acute; fl. st. to 2 ft., raceme 25–30-fld., pedicels to ⅜ in. long; sepals ascending, unequal, to ⅜ in. long, corolla peach-red, to ⅝ in. long. Early winter.

pulvinata Rose [?*E. plumosa* Hort.]. PLUSH PLANT, CHENILLE PLANT, ROSY HEN-AND-CHICKS. E; densely pubescent, silvery, becoming brownish, sts. to 8 in.; lvs. 15–20, separated, obovate-spatulate, 1–2½ in. long, ¾–1¼ in. wide, minutely pointed; fl. st. 8–12 in., raceme somewhat thyrsoid below, pedicels ⅛–½ in. long; sepals appressed, nearly equal, to ½ in. long, corolla yellow with red keels, ½–¾ in. long. Winter, spring. S. Mex. Cv. **'Ruby'.** Hairs many, bright red. A hybrid derivative is *Echeveria* cv. **'Doris Taylor':** *E. pulvinata* × *E. setosa.* WOOLLY ROSE. Resembles *E. setosa,* but differs in rosettes looser, lvs. to 3½ in. long and 1 in. wide, infl. more branched, and fls. to ¾ in.

pulvoliver: a listed name of no botanical standing to be treated as *Echeveria* cv. 'Pulv-Oliver' for the hybrid *E. Harmsii* × *E. pulvinata.* E; densely hairy, sts. to 4 in.; lvs. about 20, rhomboid-oblanceolate, 2 in. long, ¾ in. wide, acute; fl. st. 6–8 in., raceme 6–8-fld., pedicels to 1¼ in. long; sepals appressed to ascending, nearly equal, to ⅝ in. long, corolla coral-red, 1 in. long.

pumila: *E. secunda* var.

Purpusii: see *E. amoena;* see also *Dudleya cymosa.*

Purpusiorum A. Berger [*Urbinia Purpusii* Rose]. S; glabrous, rosettes sessile, dense; lvs. 30–60, obovate, 1½–2¼ in. long, to 1 in. wide, acuminate, gray-green, brown-mottled; fl. st. slender, 12–20 in., cincinnus 6–12-fld., pedicels 5/16–¾ in. long; sepals appressed, nearly equal, about 1/16 in. long, corolla ovoid, deep pink, yellow in upper ⅓, ½ in. long. Spring. S. Mex.

quitensis (HBK) Lindl. R; glabrous, sts. to 3 ft.; lvs. 20–30, in a loose rosette, oblanceolate to oblong, 1–2½ in. long, ⅜–¾ in. wide, mucronate, mostly green; fl. st. 4–10 in., raceme 4–20-fld., pedicels to ⅜ in. long; sepals ascending to spreading, nearly equal, to ½ in. long, corolla scarlet to yellow below, about ½ in. long. Colombia to Bolivia. Var. **Sprucei** (Bak.) Poelln. [*E. Sprucei* (Bak.) A. Berger]. Lvs. to ¼ in. wide; sepals reflexed. Ecuador.

racemosa Schlechtend. & Cham. [*E. lurida* Haw.]. R; glabrous, rosettes sessile; lvs. 15–20, oblong-oblanceolate, 2–4 in. long, 1 in. wide, acute, glaucous-green, becoming deeply purple-tinged, somewhat channelled above, margins somewhat cartilaginous; fl. st. 8–20 in., raceme 12–40-fld., pedicels to ½ in. long; sepals spreading, nearly equal, to ¼ in. long, corolla red or orange-red, about ½ in. long. Summer, autumn. Mex.

recurvata: a listed name of no botanical standing, perhaps referring to *E. coccinea* cv. 'Recurvata'.

Reinwardtii: a listed name of no botanical standing.

retusa: *E. fulgens.*

rosea Lindl. [*Courantia rosea* (Lindl.) Lem.]. DESERT ROSE. R; glabrous, sts. elongate; lvs. 15–30, often scattered, oblanceolate-spatulate, 1½–3½ in. long, ⅜–1 in. wide, cylindrical at base, often red; fl. st. 6–15 in., raceme dense, 20–70-fld., bracts red, about equalling fls., pedicels to ¼ in. long, often very short; sepals erect, red, as long as corolla, corolla light yellow, ½ in. long. Late autumn to late spring. E. Mex. Cv. **'Cristata'** is listed.

rosea-grandis: a listed name of no botanical standing; said to be a large plant with broad, copper-tinged, red-margined lvs.; probably a hybrid of *E. gibbiflora.*

Rosei: *E. subrigida.*

rubella: a listed name of no botanical standing for the hybrid *E. agavoides* × *E. cuspidata.*

rubromarginata Rose. S; glabrous, sts. to 1 ft.; lvs. 12–20, oblanceolate to obovate, 4–7 in. long, 3–4 in. wide, mucronate, glaucous, margins red; fl. st. 1½–4 ft., with several 5–15-fld. cincinni, pedicels to ⅛ in. long; sepals ascending, unequal, to ½ in. long, corolla rose, ½ in. long. Autumn. Mex.

Runyonii Rose ex Walth. S; glabrous, rosettes sessile; lvs. about 30, spatulate-cuneate, 2–3 in. long, 1½ in. wide, truncate or retuse, glaucous; fl. st. 6–8 in., cincinni 2, pedicels to 3/16 in. long; sepals spreading, unequal, to ⅝ in. long, corolla red, to ¾ in. long. N. Mex. Var. **Macabeana** Walth. Lvs. mucronate to acute.

Rusbyi: *Graptopetalum Rusbyi.*

sanguinea: *E. atropurpurea.*

×scaphophylla: × *Cremneria scaphylla.*

×scaphylla: × *Cremneria scaphylla.*

Scheeri Lindl. S; glabrous, sts. erect; lvs. oblong-spatulate, to 7 in. long and 2 in. wide, acute, glaucous; fl. st. 20 in., cincinni 3, each 10–12-fld., pedicels to ¼ in. long; sepals spreading, unequal, to ½ in. long, corolla red and yellow, to ⅞ in. long. Late spring to autumn. S. Mex.

×Scheideckeri: × *Pachyveria Scheideckeri.*

Schickendantzii: a listed name of no botanical standing.

scopulorum: *E. obtusifolia.*

secunda W. B. Booth. S; glabrous, sts. short, decumbent, forming offsets freely; lvs. 25–60, cuneate-spatulate, 1–3 in. long, ½–1½ in. wide, 3/16 in. thick, obtuse to truncate, mucronate, glaucous, sometimes red-edged; fl. st. 4–12 in., cincinnus solitary, 5–15-fld., pedicels 3/16–¾ in. long; sepals spreading, unequal, to 5/16 in. long, corolla red with yellow tip, 5/16–½ in. long. Spring, early summer. Mex. Var. **Byrnesii** (Rose) Poelln. [*E. Byrnesii* Rose]. A minor form with lvs. bright green or flushed with red, not glaucous. Var. **glauca** (Bak.) Otto [*E. glauca* Bak.]. Said to have lvs. thinner. Var. **pumila** (Schlechtend.)

Otto [*E. pumila* Schlechtend.]. A cult. form with lvs. narrower, to ⅝ in. wide, and sepals nearly equal. Cvs. **'Minima'** and **'Major'** are listed. Probably also to be referred here as vars. are *E. alpina* Walth., with lvs. thinnish, fls. ⅝ in. long; and *E. tolucensis* Rose, with lvs. thinnish, more acute, and fls. ⅝ in. long.

sedoides: *E. Macdougallii.*

semivestita Moran. S; sts. erect, to 1 ft. or more; lvs. 15–20, oblanceolate, 2–5 in. long, ½–1 in. wide, acute, green, purplish-edged, puberulent, channelled above; fl. st. 1–2 ft., puberulent below, glabrous above, infl. glabrous, bluish- or purplish-glaucous, cincinni 3–9, pedicels to ¼ in. long; sepals ascending, unequal, to ⅝ in. long, corolla deep pink, ½ in. long. Summer, E. Mex. Var. **semivestita.** The typical var.; plants puberulous. Var. **Floresiana** Walth. Glabrous throughout, sts. perhaps shorter.

setoliver; a listed name of no botanical standing to be treated as *Echeveria* cv. 'Set-Oliver' for the hybrid *E. Harmsii.* × *E. setosa.* E; hairy, sts. erect; lvs. about 25, oblanceolate, about 2¼ in. long and ½ in. wide, acute; fl. st. to 16 in., cincinni 2 or more, each 3–10-fld., pedicels to ¾ in. long; sepals ascending-spreading, nearly equal, ½ in. long, corolla red with yellow tip, nearly 1 in. long. Late autumn, early winter.

setosa Rose & J. Purpus. MEXICAN-FIRECRACKER, FIRECRACKER PLANT. E; bristly-hairy, sts. to 4 in., forming offsets; lvs. 80–175, oblanceolate-spatulate, 2–3 in. long, to ¾ in. wide, obtuse, minutely pointed; fl. st. 8–12 in., cincinni 1–2, each 7–10-fld., pedicels to 1 in. long; sepals spreading or ascending, nearly equal, to ⅜ in. long, corolla red, tipped with yellow, ½ in. long. Late spring, early summer. S. Mex. For a hybrid derivative, see *E. pulvinata.*

Shaviana Walth. S; glabrous, sts. short; lvs. 30–60, obovate-spatulate, 2–4 in. long, ¾–1½ in. wide, ⅛ in. thick, mucronate, bluish-glaucous, margins thin, white or pinkish, often crisped; fl. st. to 1 ft., cincinni 1–2, each 20–35-fld., pedicels to about 1/16 in. long; sepals ascending, unequal, the largest ⅜–¾ in. long, corolla deep pink, to ⅝ in. long. Summer. E. Mex.

simulans Rose [*E. elegans* var. *simulans* (Rose) Poelln.]. S; glabrous, sts. short; lvs. 30–45, cuneate-obovate, 2–3 in. long, ¾–1½ in. wide, ⅜–5/16 in. thick, mucronate, margins thin, hyaline, sometimes crisped; fl. st. 6–12 in., cincinnus solitary, pedicels ¼–¾ in. long; sepals ascending, markedly unequal, to ¼ in. long, corolla deep pink, yellow in upper ¼, to ⅝ in. long. Winter, spring. Ne. Mex. *E. elegans* and *E.* ×*gilva* have sometimes been grown under this name.

spectabilis Alexand. R; glabrous but papillose, sts. erect, branching, to 2 ft.; lvs. 15–25, obovate-spatulate, 2–3 in. long, ¾–1¼ in. wide, ⅛ in. thick, mucronate; dull green, red-edged; fl. st. 1–2 ft., raceme 5–12-fld., pedicels ½–1¼ in. long; sepals spreading, nearly equal, to ¾ in. long, corolla orange-red, 1 in. long. Summer. S. Mex.

Sprucei: *E. quitensis* var.

stolonifera (Bak.) Otto. S; glabrous, sts. short, stoloniferous; lvs. 30–40, obovate-spatulate, to 2½ in. long, half as wide, mucronate, slightly glaucous; fl. st. 6–8 in., cincinni 1–2, each 4–6-fld., pedicels to 3/16 in. long; sepals ascending, unequal, to ⅜ in. long, corolla red with yellow tip, ½ in. long. Early summer. Probably a garden hybrid.

strictiflora A. Gray. S; glabrous; rosettes sessile, lvs. 12–25, rhombic-oblanceolate, 2½–4 in. long, ½–1 in. wide, acuminate, glaucous; fl. st. 6–16 in., cincinni 1–2, each with 10–20 nearly sessile fls.; sepals ascending, unequal, to ½ in. long, corolla red, ½–⅝ in. long. Summer, autumn. W. Tex., n. Mex.

subrigida (B. L. Robinson & Seat.) Rose [*E. angusta* Poelln.; *E. Palmeri* Rose; *E. Rosei* A. Nels. & Macbr.]. S; glabrous, sts. to 4 in.; lvs. 15–30, obovate or rhombic to oblong-oblanceolate, 5–12 in. long, 2–5 in. wide, acute, green to strongly mealy, often narrowly red-edged, channelled above; fl. st. 2–3 ft., cincinni 6–15, each 1–10-fld., pedicels to 3/16 in. long; sepals ascending, nearly equal, to ½ in. long, corolla light orange to scarlet but with pink bloom, ¾–1 in. long. Summer. Mex.

tectorum: a listed name of no botanical standing; perhaps *Sempervivum tectorum* is meant.

teretifolia (Moç. & Sessé) DC. S; known only from the original plate, showing part of an infl. Mex.

tolucensis: see *E. secunda.*

tomentosa: a listed name of no botanical standing.

turgida Rose. S; glabrous, sts. short, forming offsets; lvs. 30–60, oblong-cuneate, 1–2 in. long, mucronate, thickish, somewhat glaucous; fl. st. 4–10 in., cincinnus solitary, 4–11-fld., pedicels ¼–1 in. long; sepals spreading, unequal, to ¼ in. long, corolla deep pink to orange, about ½ in. long. Spring. N. Mex.

venezuelensis Rose. R; glabrous, sts. elongate; lvs. 12–18, obovate-cuneate, to 3 in. long and 1½ in. wide, mucronate, glaucous; fl. st. to 16 in., raceme to 1 ft., pedicels ¼ in. long; sepals spreading, nearly equal, to 5/16 in. long, corolla pinkish, ⅜ in. long. Venezuela.

Walpoleana Rose. S; glabrous, sts. short; lvs. 15–30, oblong to oblanceolate, 2–5 in. long, ¾–1½ in. wide, acuminate, green or red-marked, often red-edged, channelled above; fl. st. 1–3 ft., cincinni 2–3, each of 6–15 nearly sessile fls.; sepals spreading, unequal, to ½ in. long, corolla orange-red below, yellow above, ½–¾ in. long. Summer, early autumn. Ne. Mex.

Waltheri Moran & Meyrán. R; glabrous but minutely papillose, sts. erect or sprawling, to 3 ft., little-branched; lvs. 12–25, spatulate or rhombic, 1–3 in. long, ½-1 in. wide, ⅛ in. thick, apiculate, light green, often red-edged; fl. st. 1–2 ft. including spike of 10–45 fls.; sepals erect, nearly equal, to ⅜ in. long, corolla white with red above, to ⅝ in. long. Late autumn, early winter. Mex.

Weinbergii: *Graptopetalum paraguayense.*

Weingartii: a listed name of no botanical standing to be treated as *Echeveria* cv. 'Weingartii' for the hybrid *E. Purpusiorum* × ?. FAIRY-LANTERNS. S; glabrous, rosettes dense, sessile; lvs. many, oblong, to 2 in. long, short-acuminate, dark green; fl. st. 1 ft., cincinni 1–2, loose; corolla nearly urceolate, red with yellow tip.

Whitei Rose. R; glabrous, sts. short, forming offsets near base; lvs. about 35, spatulate, 1½–2 in. long, ½ in. wide, mucronate, glaucous-green or brownish; fl. st. 1 ft., raceme 10-fld., often 1-sided, pedicels to ¾ in. long; sepals erect or ascending, unequal, ¼ in. long, corolla red, ½ in. long. Winter, spring. Bolivia.

Zahnii: a listed name of no botanical standing to be treated as *Echeveria* cv. 'Zahnii'. S; glabrous, sts. short; lvs. oblong-spatulate, 2–3 in. long, to 1½ in. wide, minutely pointed, pale green, broadly margined with white or pink; fl. st. to 2 ft., cincinni 1–2, each 12–20-fld., pedicels to ½ in. long; corolla pinkish, to ½ in. long. Summer. Supposedly a hybrid of *E. secunda.*

ECHIDNOPSIS Hook.f. *Asclepiadaceae.* Twenty or more spp. of leafless, succulent, per. herbs, native to s. Arabia, trop. and S. Afr., distinctive in their cylindrical, angled sts. divided into obtuse, apiculate tubercles; fls. in clusters, mostly apical, corolla rotate to rotate-campanulate, 5-lobed, fleshy, corona of 1 or 2 whorls, outer whorl, when present, cup-shaped or with 5 or 10 lobes or pouches, inner whorl of 5 inflexed lobes; fr. a follicle.

For culture see *Succulents.*

cereiformis Hook.f. Sts. elongate, 8-angled; corolla bright yellow, rotate-campanulate, about 5/16 in. across, outer corona absent, inner yellow. Saudi Arabia to Ethiopia. Var. **obscura** A. Berger. Corolla yellowish-brown.

Dammanniana Sprenger. Similar to *E. cereiformis,* but having corolla lobes dark purple-brown, disc yellowish with purple-brown dots, outer corona 5-lobed, purple-brown. E. Ethiopia.

Framesii A. C. White & Sloane. Sts. to 5 in., longitudinally and horizontally furrowed into 4–6-sided areas; fls. in 2–5-fld. fascicles near the apex of st., corolla purple, papillate, about ⅜ in. across, corona yellow. S. Afr.

repens R. A. Dyer & Verd. Sts prostrate or arching, 8–10-angled, tubercled; fls. solitary, corolla wine-red, ⅜ in. across, lobes minutely papillate, sparsely hairy toward margins, outer corona white at the base. Tanzania.

serpens: a listed name of no botanical standing.

serpentina (Nel) A. C. White & Sloane. Sts. trailing, to 5 in. long, 8-angled; corolla about ⅜ in. across, rose-purple with a whitish-yellow ring around corona, outer corona 10-lobed, sulphur-yellow. S. Afr.

ECHINACEA Moench [*Brauneria* Neck.]. PURPLE CONE-FLOWER. *Compositae* (Helianthus Tribe). Three spp. of coarse, rough-hairy, per. herbs in N. Amer.; lvs. alt., simple, large; fl. heads radiate, solitary or few, long-peduncled, receptacle conical, scales of receptacle stiff, spinescent, conspicuously longer than disc fls.; disc fls. purple-brown, ray fls. purple to whitish; achenes 4-angled, pappus a short crown.

The coneflowers are easily cultivated in the border or wild garden; they flower in mid- to late summer. Propagated by division, but this should not be practiced too frequently; also by seeds.

angustifolia DC. [*E. pallida* var. *angustifolia* (DC.) Cronq.; *Brauneria angustifolia* (DC.) A. Heller]. To 2 ft.; lvs. oblong-lanceolate to linear-lanceolate, entire, with 3–5-parallel nerves, lower lvs. long-petioled, upper lvs. sessile; ray fls. 1–1¾ in. long, rose-purple or whitish. Sask. to Minn., s. to Tex.; also in Tenn.

pallida (Nutt.) Nutt. [*Brauneria pallida* (Nutt.) Britt.; *Rudbeckia pallida* Nutt.]. Similar to *E. angustifolia,* but stouter, taller, to 3 ft., ray fls. 1½–3½ in. long and reflexing. Midwestern U.S., se. to La., Ala., Ga.; naturalized elsewhere. Var. **angustifolia:** *E. angustifolia.*

purpurea (L.) Moench [*Brauneria purpurea* (L.) Britt.; *Rudbeckia purpurea* L.]. To 3, rarely 6 ft.; lowermost lvs. ovate to broadly lanceolate, coarsely toothed, long-petioled, upper st. lvs. narrower, nearly entire, sessile; heads to 6 in. across; ray fls. rose-purple. Ohio to Iowa, s. to La. and Ga. There are cvs. of improved form or fl. color, and several, including **'Alba'**, with greenish disc fls. and white ray fls.

ECHINOCACTUS Link & Otto [*Homalocephala* Britt. & Rose]. VISNAGA. *Cactaceae.* About 16 spp. of ribbed, often large cacti of Mex. and the sw. U.S.; sts. solitary or cespitose, hemispherical to short-cylindrical, strongly ribbed, the crown woolly; areoles sometimes confluent on old plants and the ribs then grooved, principal spines annulate, not hooked, gland-spines absent; fls. solitary, at the upper side of young areoles, campanulate, mostly yellow, tube with scales entire, narrow, long-acuminate, mostly pungent, outer perianth segms. often pungent, stamens many to very many, borne on the funnelform tube, included; fr. woolly, persistent, usually dehiscing by a basal pore, seeds black, smooth or rarely papillose, with a small, nearly basal hilum. *Echinocactus* of early authors was a large and heterogeneous group, with more than 1,000 supposed kinds named; most are now referred to other genera.

Various kinds of echinocacti and of closely related genera are favorites for pot and tub culture and for plunging in the open in summer. They are propagated by seeds, as they do not branch nor readily produce offsets. Seeds are sown in late spring or early summer. Under glass they may require hand pollination to produce seeds. In winter, the plants may be placed in a light, dry greenhouse and kept fairly dormant; in spring and summer water may be supplied liberally to establish plants. For culture see *Cacti.*

acanthodes: *Ferocactus acanthodes.*

asterias: *Astrophytum asterias.*

cylindraceus: *Ferocactus acanthodes.*

electracanthus: *Ferocactus histrix.*

glaucescens: *Ferocactus glaucescens.*

grandis Rose. Sts. simple, globose to short-cylindrical, to 6 ft. high and 3 ft. thick, ribs about 30–50; areoles confluent on old plants, spines straight, yellowish, becoming brown, radial spines 5–6, to 1½ in., central spine 1, to 2 in. long; fls. yellow, to 2 in. long; fr. to 2 in. long. S. Mex.

Grusonii Hildm. BARREL CACTUS, GOLDEN B. C., GOLDEN BALL C., GOLDEN-BALL. Sts. simple or in small clusters, globose, to 3 ft. thick, ribs 21-37; spines golden-yellow, becoming pale and eventually brown, radial spines 8–10, to 1¼ in. long, central spines mostly 4, to 2 in. long; fls. yellow, to 2½ in. long; fr. to ¾ in. long. Cent. Mex.

horizonthalonius Lem. EAGLE-CLAWS, MULE-CRIPPLER CACTUS. Sts. simple, globose to short-cylindrical, to 1 ft. high and 6 in. thick, ribs mostly 8, low and rounded; spines straight or recurved, to 1½ in. long, often stout and flattened, radial spines 5–8, central spine 1, deflexed; fls. pink, 2½ in. long, perianth segms. obtuse, erose-dentate; fr. red, 1¼ in. long, soon drying and breaking transversely near the bottom. Spring, summer. W. Tex., s. New Mex., n. Mex.

ingens Zucc. LARGE BARREL CACTUS, MEXICAN GIANT BARREL, BLUE BARREL. Sts. solitary or in small clusters, globose, to 4 ft. thick, ribs 40–50; spines brown, straight, to 1¼ in. long, radial spines 8, central spine 1; fls. yellow, inner perianth segms. obtuse, entire, stigma lobes red; fr. 1¼ in. long. Early summer. Cent. Mex. Cv. **'Helephorus'.** Heavily banded with purple when young.

latispinus: *Ferocactus latispinus.*

Pfeifferi: *Ferocactus glaucescens.*

pilosus: *Ferocactus pilosus.*

polyancistrus: *Sclerocactus polyancistrus.*

polycephalus Engelm. & Bigel. Cespitose, sts. often 20–30, globose to ovoid, to 2 ft. high and 1 ft. thick, ribs 10–20; spines somewhat flattened, curved, densely puberulent, red to gray, radial spines 4–8, to 2 in. long, central spines 3–4, stouter, to 3½ in. long; fls. yellow, to 2½ in. long, scales very short; fr. to 1¼ in. long, seeds papillose. Spring. S. Nev., s. Utah, w. Ariz., se. Calif., n. Mex. Var. **xeranthemoides** J. Coult. [*E. xeranthemoides* (J. Coult.) Rydb.]. Sts. rarely more than 12; spines 10–15 glabrate, straight or nearly so; scales to 1¼ in. long; seeds checkered. S. Utah, n. Ariz.

Pringlei: *Ferocactus pilosus.*

saglionis: *Gymnocalycium saglione.*

texensis Hopffer [*Homalocephala texensis* (Hopffer) Britt. & Rose]. Sts. mostly simple, globose or usually depressed, to 1 ft. high and thick, ribs 13–27; spines reddish, more or less flattened, radial spines 6–7, spreading or recurved, to 2 in. long, central spine 1, decurved, to 2½ in. long and ⁵⁄₁₆ in. wide; fls. pink, with reddish center, to 2½ in. long; fr. globose, red, to 1½ in. in diam., becoming naked, apparently splitting open at maturity. Spring. Tex., s. New Mex., n. Mex. The monotypic genus *Homalocephala* was separated mostly because of the supposedly bursting fr. It is close to *E. horizonthalonius.*

viridescens: *Ferocactus viridescens.*

Visnaga Hook. Sts. short-cylindrical, to 10 ft. high and 3 ft. thick, ribs 15–40, acute; areoles in old plants confluent, spines 4, stout, awl-shaped, brown, the upper to 2 in. long, the lower 3 shorter; fls. yellow, 3 in. across; fr. to 4 in. long. Cent. Mex.

Wislizenii: *Ferocactus Wislizenii.*

xeranthemoides: *E. polycephalus* var.

ECHINOCEREUS Engelm. HEDGEHOG CACTUS, HEDGEHOG CEREUS, PITAYA. *Cactaceae.* About 35 spp. of low, ribbed cacti of Mex. and the sw. U.S.; sts. simple or commonly cespitose, globose to mostly cylindrical, erect to prostrate, usually spiny; fls. solitary, lateral, bursting through the epidermis above mature areoles, mostly opening several days and closing nights, campanulate to funnelform, red, purple, yellow, or white, ovary and tube spiny, stigma lobes green; fr. fleshy, the spine clusters easily removed, seeds black, tubercled.

Species of *Echinocereus* are more or less grown in collections but are not generally useful for greenhouse culture although the bloom is showy. The plants are not likely to last many years, and they may be renewed from the wild or from the stock of regular dealers. For culture see *Cacti.*

adustus Engelm. Sts. to 4 in. high and 2 in. thick, ribs 11–15; radial spines 16–20, needle-shaped, comblike-appressed, white to brown or red-tipped, to ¾ in. long, central spine 0 or 1, stout, white or brown, about 1 in. long; fls. purple, tube narrow, to 2 in. long, segms. narrow. New Mex. and n. Mex. Allied to the *E. pectinatus* complex, but smaller, with a strong central spine and more tubular fls.

aggregatus: *E. triglochidiatus* var. *melanacanthus.*

albispinus: *E. Reichenbachii* var.

amoenus: *E. pulchellus* var.

angusticeps: *E. Berlandieri* var.

arizonicus: *E. triglochidiatus* var.

australis: a listed name of no botanical standing.

Baileyi: *E. Reichenbachii* var. *albispinus.*

Barthelowanus Britt. & Rose. Cespitose, sts. to 8 in. high and 2 in. thick, ribs 8–12; spines 20–30, needle-shaped, swollen at base, white with brown tips. becoming gray, radiating in all directions, ¼–2½ in. long; fls. ½ in. long. S. Baja Calif.

Berlandieri (Engelm.) Rümpler [*E. Blanckii* of auth., not (Poselg.) Rümpler; *E. Blankii* F. Palmer; ?*E. leonensis* Mathss.; *E. Poselgeranus* Linke]. Sts. cespitose, erect to procumbent, to 12 in. long and 1½ in. thick, flabby, branching from underground rhizomes, ribs 5–8, tubercled; radial spines 6–8, needle-shaped, yellowish, to ½ in. long, central spine 1, brownish or black, to 2 in. long; fls. purple or reddish or yellow with red base, to 3 in. across. Spring. Var. **Berlandieri.** The typical var.; sts. many; fls. rose-purple or lighter. Tex. and ne. Mex. Var. **angusticeps** (Clover) L. Bens. [*E. angusticeps* Clover; *E. papillosus* Linke]. Sts. 1–10; fls. yellow, with red at base. Tex.

Blanckii (Poselg.) Rümpler. Not in cult, but the name has been used for *E. Berlandieri.*

Blankii: *E. Berlandieri.*

Bonkerae: *E. fasciculatus* var.

Boyce-Thompsonii: *E. fasciculatus* var.

Brandegeei (J. Coult.) K. Schum. Cespitose, sts. erect to prostrate, to 3 ft. long and 2 in. thick, narrowed at base, ribs 7–8, strongly tubercled; spines light yellow, tinged with red, becoming gray, radial spines about 12, needle-shaped, central spines mostly 4, in form of a cross, stout, flattened, to 3 in. long; fls. pink or purplish, 2–3 in. long, scales with axillary long white wool; fr. globose, 1¼ in. in diam. S. Baja Calif. Variable, probably including several vars.

Bristolii: *E. pectinatus* var. *minor.*

caespitosus: *E. Reichenbachii* var. *Reichenbachii.*

chisoensis: *E. Reichenbachii* var.

chloranthus (Engelm.) Rümpler. Sts. simple, to 10 in. high and 2½ in. thick, ribs 13–18; areoles ovate, radial spines 12–20, white, to ½ in. long, the upper bristlelike, central spines 3–5, the longest to 1¼ in.; fls. low on st., greenish-yellow, to 1 in. long; fr. purplish-red, to ⅝ in. long, seeds tubercled-pitted. Spring. W. Tex., s. New Mex., n. Mex. In juvenile plants the spines are sometimes hairlike.

cinerascens (DC.) Rümpler [*E. glycimorphus* Rümpler]. Sts. cespitose, to 1 ft. long and 2 in. thick, ribs 6–8; areoles remote, spines needle-shaped, white, to ¾ in. long, the radial spines 7–10, central spines 1–4; fls. rose to purple, 3 in. long. Spring. Cent. Mex. Cv. **'Cristata'.** Crested.

coccineus: *E. triglochidiatus* var. *melanacanthus.*

conglomeratus: *E. enneacanthus* var.

conoideus: *E. triglochidiatus* var. *melanacanthus.*

ctenoides: *E. pectinatus* var. *pectinatus.*

dasyacanthus: *E. pectinatus* var. *neomexicanus.*

Davisii: *E. viridiflorus* var.

Delaetii Gürke. LESSER OLD-MAN. Sts. cespitose, hidden by long flowing white hairs, to 1 ft. high and 3 in. thick, ribs 17–24, low; radial spines 20–30, needle-shaped, swollen at base, yellowish-white, to ⅜ in. long, the upper shorter, 2–5 of the central spines reddish, to 1 in. long, and 4–6 of them slender, white, curled, to 4 in. long; fls. pink, 2½ in. long. N. Mex.

dubius: *E. enneacanthus* var.

Ehrenbergii (Pfeiff.) Rümpler. Sts. cespitose, erect or procumbent, to 8 in. high and 1 in. thick, ribs 6; areoles remote, spines needle-shaped, pale yellow, radial spines 8–10, to 1½ in. long, central spines 3–4, to 2 in. long; fls. purple, 2½ in. long. Cent. Mex. Closely allied to *E. pentalophus* and perhaps a var. of it.

Engelmannii (Parry ex Englem.) Rümpler [*Cereus Engelmannii* Parry ex Englem.]. Sts. cespitose, to 2 ft. long and 3 in. thick, ribs 10–13; radial spines 6–15, almost angled, to ¾ in. long, central spines 2–6, stout, angled or somewhat flattened, the lower one deflexed and flattened; fls. purple or lavender, to 3 in. across; fr. red, 1¼ in. long. Spring. Sw. U.S. and n. Mex. Var. **Engelmannii.** The typical var.; sts. 5–15, to 8 in. long and 2 in. thick; spines yellowish, pink or gray, lower central spine to 1¾ in. long; fls. magenta, to 2½ in. across. Ariz. and Baja Calif. Var. **chrysocentrus** (Engelm. & Bigel.) Engelm. ex Rümpler. Sts. 3–10, to 13 in. long and 2½ in. thick; spine reddish to reddish-brown, or yellow, lower central spines white, to 2½ in. long; fls. purplish to magenta, to 3 in. across. Var. **decumbens** (Clover & Jotter) L. Bens. Poorly understood, of doubtful disposition, possibly belonging to *E. triglochidiatus.* Var. **Nicholii** L. Bens. Sts. 20–30, to 2 ft. long and 3 in. thick; spines yellow or straw-colored to nearly white, aging black or gray, lower central spine to 2½ in. long; fls. lavender, to 2½ in. across. Ariz. and n. Mex. Var. **variegatus** (Engelm. & Bigel.) Engelm. ex Rümpler. Sts. 3–6, to 6 in. long and 2 in. thick; radial spines nearly white, central spines dark red to nearly black, lower one white, to 1½ in. long. Ariz.

enneacanthus Engelm. STRAWBERRY CACTUS. Sts. cespitose, to 1 ft. high and 4 in. thick, flabby, ribs 7–13; areoles remote, spines needle-shaped, bulbous at base, radial spines 7–15, often 8, transparent-white, to 1 in. long, the upper shorter, central spines 1–4, variable, cylindrical or flattened, brownish, becoming gray, to 2 in. long; fls. purplish-red, 2–3 in. long and across, petaloid segms. 12–15, spreading; fr. nearly globose, green or purplish, to 1 in. long, edible. Spring. S. Tex., s. New Mex., n. Mex. Var. **enneacanthus.** The typical var.; sts. to 2 in. thick, ribs 7–10; spines not obscuring st., gray to straw-colored, central spine usually 1, to 2 in. long; fls. 2–3½ in across. Tex. and n. Mex. Var. **conglomeratus** (Först. ex K. Schum.) L. Bens. [*E. conglomeratus* Först. ex K. Schum.]. Spines as in var. *stramineus* but more slender, to 4½ in. long; fls. to 3 in. across. N. Mex. Var. **dubius** (Engelm.) L. Bens. [*E. dubius* (Engelm.) Rümpler]. Sts. to 4 in. thick, ribs 7–10; spines not obscuring st., gray to straw-colored, central spine usually 1; fls. 3–4 in. across. Tex. Var. **stramineus** (Engelm.) L. Bens. [*E. stramineus* (Engelm.) Rümpler]. Sts. to 350, forming mounds, to 3 in. thick, ribs mostly 10–12; spines dense, obscuring st., straw-colored, central spines 2–4, to 3½ in. long; fls. 4–5 in. across. W. Tex., se. New Mex., n. Mex.

fasciculatus (Engelm.) L. Bens. [*Mammillaria fasciculata* Engelm.]. Sts. cespitose, 3–20, elongate-cylindrical, to 18 in. long, 3 in. thick, ribs 8–18, not markedly tubercled; areoles circular, radial spines 12–13, white, gray, or yellow, needle-shaped, to ¾ in. long, central spines 2–4, straw-colored, gray, light brown or reddish-brown to tan or white, the largest spreading or turned downward, straight, to 4 in. long; fls. magenta to reddish-purple, to 2½ in. across. Var. **fasciculatus.** The typical var.; sts. 5–20, to 18 in. long, ribs 8–10; central spines pale gray, tipped with brown or black, spreading or deflexed, to 3 in. long. New Mex., Ariz. Var. **Bonkerae** (Thornber & Bonker) L. Bens. [*E. Bonkerae* Thornber & Bonker]. Sts. usually 5–15, to 8 in. long, ribs 11–16; central spines white or gray, tipped with brown, spreading, to 5/16 in. long. Ariz. Var. **Boyce-Thompsonii** (Orcutt) L. Bens. [*E. Boyce-Thompsonii* Orcutt]. Sts. 4–12, to 10 in. long, ribs 12–18; principal central spines light-colored, deflexed, to 4 in. long. Ariz.

Fendleri (Engelm.) Rümpler. Sts. solitary or few, to 18 in. high and 3 in. thick, ribs 9–12; spines bulbous at base, radial spines 7–10, white or gray, to 1 in. long, central spine 1, cylindrical, black becoming gray, curved upward, to 2 in. long; fls. purple to 3½ in. long; fr. 1¼ in. long. Var. **Fendleri.** The typical var.; sts. ovoid to cylindrical, to 10 in. high; central spine dark, becoming gray in age, curved upward, to 1¼ in. long. S. Utah to n. Mex. Var. **rectispinus** (Peebles) L. Bens. [*E. rectispinus* Peebles]. Sts. 1–5, not flabby, to 10 in. high, ribs 8–10; central spine directed outward, straight, gray, tipped with brown, to 1 in. long. Se. Ariz. Var. **robustus** (Peebles) L. Bens. Sts. 5–20, not flabby, to 18 in. high, ribs 8–10; central spine directed outward, gray, tipped with brown or black, to 3 in. long. Se. Ariz.

Ferreirianus H. E. Gates. Sts. cespitose, to 12 in. high and 3 in. thick, ribs 9–14; spines gray to brown, needle-shaped, radial spines 9–13, to ⅜ in. long, central spines 4, black-tipped, to 2 in. long; fls. 2½ in. long, segms. pink, throat orange, stigma pale; fr. 1½ in. Late summer. Baja Calif.

Fereirrae: a listed name of no botanical standing; evidently intended for *E. Ferreirianus.*

Fitchii: *E. Reichenbachii* var.

glycimorphus: *E. cinerascens.*

gonacanthus: *E. triglochidiatus* var.

grandis Britt. & Rose. Sts. solitary or few, to 16 in. high and 5 in. thick, ribs 21–25, low; spines needle-shaped, whitish, to ⅜ in. long, radial spines 15–25, spreading, central spines 8–12; fls. white, 2½ in. long, segms. erect. Spring. Is. (Gulf of Calif.). Belonging to the *E. pectinatus* complex and perhaps a var. of *E. pectinatus.*

horizonthalonius: a listed name of no botanical standing, probably intended for *Echinocactus horizonthalonius.*

Knippelianus Liebn. Sts. simple, to 8 in. high and 3 in. thick, flabby, dark green, ribs 5–7, prominent above; spines 1–3, weak, yellow, to ⅝ in. long; fls. pink, to 1½ in. long. Mex.

Ledingii Peebles. Sts. cespitose, 6–20 in. high, 2½–4 in. thick, ribs 12–16; spines cylindrical, yellow or straw-colored, radial spines 10–12, straight, ⅜ in. long, central spines 1–3, the lower decurved, 1 in. long; fls. rose-purple, about 2½ in. long. Spring. Mts., s. Ariz.

leonensis: see *E. Berlandieri.*

longisetus (Engelm.) Rümpler. Sts. several, to 10 in. high and 3 in. thick, ribs 11–14, tubercled; spines needle-shaped, white, radial spines 18–20, the lower to ⅝ in. long, central spines 5–7, unequal, the lower deflexed, to 2 in. long; fls. red. Ne. Mex.

longispinus: a listed name of no botanical standing for *E. Reichenbachii* var. *albispinus.*

maritimus (M. E. Jones) K. Schum. Sts. cespitose, many, to 6 in. high and 2 in. thick, ribs 8–10; radial spines about 10, spreading, central spines about 4, stout and angled, to 1½ in. long; fls. yellow, 1½ in. long. Spring. Baja Calif.

Marlinii: a listed name of no botanical standing.

melanocentrus: a listed name of no botanical standing; apparently for a var. of *E. pectinatus.*

Merkeri Hildm. Sts. cespitose, eventually decumbent, to 6 ft. long and 6 in. thick, ribs 8–9; areoles remote, spines white, vitreous, red on bulbous base, radial spines 6–9, the upper longest, to 1¼ in. long, central spines 1–2, often yellow, stouter, to 2 in.; fls. purple, 2½ in. long. N. Mex.

mojavensis: *E. triglochidiatus* var.

octacanthus: *E. triglochidiatus* var. *melanacanthus.*

oklahomensis: a listed name of no botanical standing for *E. Reichenbachii* var. *albispinus.*

pacificus: *E. triglochidiatus* var.

papillosus: *E. Berlandieri* var. *angusticeps.*

pectinatus (Scheidw.) Engelm. Sts. simple or few-branched, to 1 ft. high and 4 in. thick, ribs 15–22, low; areoles elongate, spines white to red, radial spines 12–22, flattened, comblike and appressed or spreading, to ⅜ in. long, central spines 0–9, mostly 3, in 1–3 vertical rows, to ⅛ in. long; fls. magenta or yellow, to 5 in. across; fr. globose, 1 in. in diam. Summer. Sw. U.S. and n. Mex. A difficult complex of different-looking but intergrading forms. Var. **pectinatus** [*E. ctenoides* (Engelm.) Rümpler]. The typical var.; radial spines 12–16, pink or pink and gray, spreading, to 5/16 in. long, central spines 3–5 in 1 or 2 vertical rows, to ⅛ in. long; fls. magenta, to 3½ in. across. Tex., Ariz., n. Mex. Var. **minor** (Engelm.) L. Bens. [*E. Bristolii* W. T. Marsh.; *E. Roetteri* (Engelm.) Rümpler; *E. scopulorum* Britt. & Rose]. Radial spines 7–15, pink or pink and gray, spreading, to ¾ in. long; fls. magenta, to 3 in. across. Tex., New Mex., n. Mex. Var. **neomexicanus** (J. Coult.) L. Bens. [*E. dasyacanthus* Engelm.]. RAINBOW CACTUS. Sts. to 1 ft. high and 4 in. thick, hidden by spines; radial spines 18–22, pale brown or pink, spreading, not appressed, to ½ in. long, central spines 3–9, usually in 2–3 vertical rows, to 5/16 in.; fls. mostly yellow. E. Ariz. to w. Tex., n. Mex. Var. **rigidissimus** (Engelm.) Engelm. ex Rümpler [*E. rigidissimus*

(Engelm.) Rose]. RAINBOW CACTUS. Sts. to 14 in. high and 4 in. thick, hidden by spines which form variously colored horizontal bands around the st.; radial spines 18–22, strongly appressed, flattened, to 5/16 in. long, central spines 0; fls. magenta, to 3½ in. across. S. Ariz. and n. Mex. *E. grandis, E. sciurus,* and *E. Websteranus* are probably also vars. of this sp. Cv. **'Castaneus'** is listed.

pensilis: *Morangaya pensilis.*

pentalophus (DC.) Rümpler [*E. procumbens* (Engelm.) Rümpler]. Sts. cespitose, erect or procumbent, to 4 in. long and ⅝ in. thick, ribs 4–6, almost tubercled; radial spines 4–6, rigid, white, less than 3/16 in. long, central spine 0–1, darker, to 5/16 in. long; fls. purple, 3 in. long or more, segms. commonly erose-toothed; fr. ovoid, green, to ¾ in. long. Spring. S. Tex.

perbellus: *E. Reichenbachii* var.

polyacanthus: *E. triglochidiatus* var. *neomexicanus.*

Poselgeranus: *E. Berlandieri.*

procumbens: *E. pentalophus.*

pulchellus (Mart.) K. Schum. Sts. simple or cespitose, to 4 in. high and 2 in. thick, ribs 12–13, rounded, somewhat tubercled; spines 3–5, flattened, yellowish-white, becoming gray, to ½ in. long, deciduous; fls. rosy-white, 1½ in. long, Cent. Mex. Var. **amoenus** (A. Dietr.) K. Schum. [*E. amoenus* (A. Dietr.) K. Schum.]. Spines 6–8; fls. magenta. Cent. Mex.

purpureus: *E. Reichenbachii.*

rectispinus: *E. Fendleri* var.

Reichenbachii (Tersch.) Britt. & Rose. LACE CACTUS. Sts. cespitose or often simple, to 8 in. high and 3½ in. thick, ribs 12–19; areoles vertically elongate, radial spines 12–32, needle-shaped, comblike-appressed to irregularly spreading, white to brown, to 1 in. long, central spines 0–7, similar; fls. pink to purple, 2–3 in. across, spines on tube slender, somewhat flexible, associated hairs short. Kans. to New Mex. Var. **Reichenbachii** [*E. caespitosus* Engelm.; *E. purpureus* Lahm.]. The typical var.; areoles very narrow, ⅛ in. long, radial spines 22–32, straw-colored to gray, pink-tipped, to ¼ in. long, central spines 0. Kans., Okla., Tex. Var. **albispinus** (Lahm.) L. Bens. [*E. albispinus* Lahm.; *E. Baileyi* Rose]. Areoles narrowly elliptic, 3/32 in. long, radial spines 12–14, pink at base, red, white, yellow, or brown at apex, to 1 in. long, central spines 1–3, to ⅛ in. long. S. Okla., Tex. Var. **chisoensis** (W. T. Marsh.) L. Bens. [*E. chisoensis* W. T. Marsh.]. Areoles elliptic, 3/32 in. long, radial spines 12–14, white or ashy, the upper rudimentary, central spines 1–4, to ½ in. long. Sw. Tex. Var. **Fitchii** (Britt. & Rose) L. Bens. [*E. Fitchii* Britt. & Rose]. FRILLED LACE CACTUS. Areoles elliptic, 3/32 in. long, radial spines 18–22, white or straw-colored, tan or brownish at apex, to nearly 5/16 in. long, central spines 4–7, to ¼ in. long. S. Tex. Var. **perbellus** (Britt. & Rose) L. Bens. [*E. perbellus* Britt. & Rose]. Areoles elliptic, 3/32 in. long, radial spines 12–20, straw-colored to pink, to ¼ in. long. W. Tex., e. New Mex., se. Colo.

rigidissimus: *E. pectinatus* var.

Roetteri: *E. pectinatus* var. *minor.*

Rosei: *E. triglochidiatus* var. *neomexicanus.*

Salm-Dyckianus: see *E. Salmianus.*

Salmianus Rümpler [*E. Salm-Dyckianus* of auth., not Scheer]. Sts. cespitose, often decumbent, to 4 in. long and 1¼ in. thick, ribs 7–9; spines needle-shaped, radial spines 8–10, to 5/16 in. long, central spine 1, to ½ in. long; fls. nocturnal, orange, to 4 in. long, tube slender. Spring. N. Mex. Allied to *E. Scheeri* and perhaps a var. of it.

sarissophorus Britt. & Rose. PURPLE HEDGEHOG CEREUS. Sts. cespitose, short, to 4 in. thick, ribs about 9; radial spines 7–10, needle-shaped, central spines several, angled, often bluish, 2–3 in. long; fls. purplish, 3 in. long; fr. globose, about 1 in. in diam. Ne. Mex.

Scheeri (Salm-Dyck) Rümpler. Sts. cespitose, often procumbent, to 9 in. long and 1 in. thick, ribs 8–10, low; spines needle-shaped, radial spines 10–12, to ⅛ in. long, central spine 1, stouter, to ½ in. long; fls. nocturnal, rose-red, to 5 in. long, tube slender. N. Mex.

sciurus (K. Brandeg.) Britt. & Rose. Sts. cespitose, to 8 in. high and 2 in. thick, ribs 12–17; spines needle-shaped, pale, brown-tipped, to ⅝ in. long, radial spines 15–18, spreading, central spines 1–6; fls. magenta, to 3 in. long. Spring. S. Baja Calif. Belonging to the *E. pectinatus* complex and perhaps a var. of that sp.

scopulorum: *E. pectinatus* var. *minor.*

stoloniferus W. T. Marsh. Sts. cespitose, branching underground, to 7 in. high and 2 in. thick, ribs 14–16; spines slender, black or red, becoming white, to ¼ in. long, radial spines 10–12, central spines 3–5; fls. yellow, to 2½ in. long, segms. spreading. Nw. Mex.

stramineus: *E. enneacanthus* var.

subinermis Salm-Dyck. Sts. simple or few, to 13 in. high and 4 in. thick, ribs 5–9, prominent; spines needle-shaped, to ¾ in. long, or often conical, to 3/32 in. long, sometimes 0, radial spines 3–8, central spine 1; fls. yellow, to 3 in. long; fr. obovoid, green, splitting. Nw. Mex.

subterraneus: a listed name of no botanical standing, said to be applied to *E. stoloniferus.*

triglochidiatus Engelm. Sts. cespitose, to 1 ft. high and 10 in. thick, ribs 5–12, somewhat tubercled; areoles remaining white-woolly, spines needle-shaped to awl-shaped, angled or ribbed, somewhat curved, radial spines 3–10, central spines 0–6, to 1¼ in. long; fls. scarlet or crimson, not closing at night, to 3 in. long, scales stiff, rounded at apex; fr. oblong, red, about 1 in. long. Spring. S. Colo. to w. Tex. and Ariz. Var. **triglochidiatus.** The typical var.; sts. few, to 1 ft. high and 3 in. thick, ribs 5–8; spines gray, to 1 in. long, angled, radial spines 3–6, central spines 0 or 1 and like radial spines; fls. 2 in. across. Sw. U.S., n. Mex. Var. **arizonicus** (Rose ex Orcutt) L. Bens. [*E. arizonicus* Rose ex Orcutt]. Sts. few, to 9 in. high and 10 in. thick, ribs about 10; spines dark gray, to 1½ in. long, radial spines 5–11, pinkish-tan, central spines 1–3; fls. to 2 in. across. Ariz. Var. **gonacanthus** (Engelm. & Bigel.) W. T. Marsh. [*E. gonacanthus* Engelm. & Bigel.]. Sts. few, to 5 in. high and 3 in. thick, ribs about 8; radial spines 5–8, stout, twisted, to 2½ in. long; fls. to 2¾ in. across. E. Ariz. and w. New Mex. Var. **melanacanthus** (Engelm.) L. Bens. [var. *octacanthus* (Mühlenpf.) W. T. Marsh.; *E. aggregatus* (Engelm.) Rydb.; *E. coccineus* Engelm.; *E. conoideus* (Engelm. & Bigel.) Rümpler; *E. octacanthus* (Mühlenpf.) Britt. & Rose; *Coryphantha aggregata* (Engelm.) Britt. & Rose; *C. vivipara* var. aggregata (Engelm.) W. T. Marsh.]. Sts. to 500, to 6 in. high and 2½ in. thick, ribs 9–10; spines gray, black, or pink to straw-colored, to 2½ in. long, radial spines 5–11, central spines 1–3, light or dark, spreading or the longest deflexed; fls. to 1½ in. across. Utah and Colo. s. to Ariz., Tex., n. Mex. Var. **mojavensis** (Engelm. & Bigel.) L. Bens. [*E. mojavensis* Engelm. & Bigel.]. Sts. to 500, to 6 in. high and 2½ in. thick, ribs 9–10; spines gray, pink or straw-colored, to 2¾ in. long, radial spines 5–8, central spines 1–2, light, usually twisting; fls. to 2 in. across. Utah, Nev., Ariz., Calif. Var. **neomexicanus** (Standl.) Standl. ex W. T. Marsh. [var. *polyacanthus* (Engelm.) L. Bens.; *E. polyacanthus* Engelm.; *E. Rosei* Woot. & Standl.]. Sts. mostly 5–45, to 1 ft. high and 4 in. thick, ribs 8–12; spines tan or pink, aging gray, to 1½ in. long, radial spines 9–12, central spines 2–4, gray, spreading; fls. to 1½ in. across. Tex. to Ariz., n. Mex. Var. **octacanthus:** var. *melanacanthus.* Var. **pacificus** (Engelm.) W. T. Marsh. [*E. pacificus* (Engelm.) J. Coult.]. Ribs 10–13; spines needle-shaped, red to gray, radial spines 10–14, about ¼ in. long, central spines 4–7, to 1½ in. long. N. Baja Calif. Var. **polyacanthus:** var. *neomexicanus.*

viridiflorus Engelm. Sts. simple or few-branched, globose or short-cylindrical, 1–6 in. high, ribs 13–14; spines needle-shaped, purplish, becoming gray, radial spines 12–18, appressed, to ½ in. long, central spines 0 or rarely 1–2; fls. yellowish-green, 1 in. long; fr. ½ in. long. Spring. S. Dak. and Wyo. to New Mex. and Tex. Var. **viridiflorus.** The typical var.; sts. to 3 in. long and 1½ in. thick, ribs 10–14; spines reddish to pale gray or white; petaloid segms. green. S. Dak. to Wyo., s. to New Mex. and Tex. Var. **Davisii** (Houghton) W. T. Marsh. [*E. Davisii* Houghton]. Dwarf, sts. to 1 in. high and ¾ in. thick, ribs 6–9; spines about 14, comblike, needle-shaped; petaloid segms. yellow-green. Tex.

Websteranus G. Lindsay. Sts. cespitose, to 2 ft. high and 3 in. thick, ribs 18–24; spines needle-shaped, yellow, becoming brown, to ½ in. long, radial spines 14–18, spreading, central spines 6–8; fls. lavender-pink, 2½ in. long. Nolasco Is. (Mex.). Belonging to the *E. pectinatus* complex and probably a var. of that sp.

ECHINOCHLOA Beauvois. *Gramineae.* About 20 spp. of ann. or per. grasses in warm countries; lf. sheaths inrolled, blades linear, flat; panicles compact, of short, densely fld. racemes along a main axis; spikelets rounded on one side, flat on the other, often stiffly hispid, subsessile, solitary or irregularly clustered on one side of the panicle brs., first glume pointed, about half as long as the spikelet, second glume and sterile lemma equal, pointed, mucronate, or the glume short-awned and the lemma long-awned, enclosing a membranous palea and sometimes a male fl., fertile lemma firm, smooth and glossy, acuminate. For terminology see *Gramineae.*

crus-galli (L.) Beauvois [*Panicum crus-galli* L.]. BARNYARD GRASS, BARN G., BARNYARD MILLET. Ann., sts. to 5 ft., erect to decumbent, stout, often branching at base; lf. sheaths glabrous, blades elongate, to ⅝ in. wide; panicle to 8 in. long, erect and stiff or slightly nodding when heavy, purple-tinged, racemes spreading, ascending or appressed, the lower somewhat distant, to 4 in. long, sometimes branched, the uppermost approximate; spikelets about ⅛ in. long, excluding the awns, crowded, hispidulous between the strongly tuberculate-hispid nerves, awn variable, mostly to ⅜ in. but sometimes to 1¼ in. long. E. Hemisphere; a troublesome weed from New Bruns. to Wash., s. to Fla, and Calif. Var. **frumentacea** (Roxb.) W. F. Wight.

JAPANESE MILLET, SANWA M., JAPANESE BARNYARD M., BILLION-DOL-LAR GRASS. Racemes incurved, thick, erect-appressed or only slightly spreading; spikelets thicker, awnless, mostly purple, with hispid nerves not or only slightly tubercled. A food plant in the Orient; occasionally cult. in the U.S. as a forage grass and escaped.

ECHINOCYSTIS Torr. & A. Gray. *Cucurbitaceae.* One sp., an ann., tendril-bearing, monoecious vine, native to U.S. and s. Canada; lvs. palmately 3–5-lobed; male fls. profuse in peduncled, axillary panicles, calyx with 6 bristlelike lobes, corolla with 6 slender lobes, stamens 3, filaments and anthers more or less united, female fls. solitary or paired, in same axils as male infls., ovary 2-celled; fr. a papery, inflated, spiny pod, bursting irregularly at apex.

fabacea: *Marah fabaceus.*

lobata (Michx.) Torr. & A. Gray. WILD CUCUMBER, MOCK C., PRICKLY C., BALSAM APPLE, WILD B.A. Sts. to 20 ft. or more; fls. greenish-white, corolla lobes to ¼ in. long; fr. ellipsoid or globose, to 2 in. long. New Bruns. to Sask., s. to Fla. and Tex. Frequently planted for covering arbors and fences.

macrocarpa: *Marah macrocarpus.*

oregana: *Marah oreganus.*

ECHINODORUS L. Rich. BURHEAD. *Alismataceae.* About 30 spp. of aquatic, ann. or per. herbs, often spreading by runners, native to N. and S. Amer. and Afr.; lvs. emersed or submersed, long-petioled, often with pellucid markings, linear-lanceolate to elliptic or cordate; fls. in globose heads arranged in branched or unbranched infls., unisexual or bisexual, sepals 3, sometimes enlarging in fr., petals 3, stamens 6–30, carpels several, spirally arranged on a hemispherical receptacle; fr. a head of ribbed, usually beaked, achenes.

Propagated by division or seeds.

Andrieuxii (Hook. & Arn.) Small. Lvs. erect, blades narrowly elliptic to ovate, to 8 in. long or rarely longer, base truncate, petioles winged; achenes 4–7-ribbed. W. Mex. to El Salvador and Brit. Honduras.

Berteroi (K. Spreng.) Fassett [*E. rostratus* (Nutt.) Engelm.]. Submersed lvs., when present, membranous and ribbonlike, emersed lvs. with blades broadly elliptic to broadly ovate, 6 in. long, base cordate to truncate, pellucid lines obvious; achenes beaked, ribs 5. Calif. to Kans., s. to Yucatan and W. Indies.

bracteatus P. Micheli. Lf. blades ovate, to 14 in. long or rarely longer, base cordate; scape to 9 ft.; achenes short-beaked, ribs about 5. Panama to Ecuador.

brevipedicellatus (O. Kuntze) Buchenau. Lf. blades lanceolate, to 11 in. long, 1¼ in. wide, acuminate at both ends, petioles to 6 in. long; scape to 3 ft.; achenes curved, ribs 8, narrowly winged. Brazil.

cordifolius (L.) Griseb. [*E. radicans* (Nutt.) Engelm.]. TEXAS MUD-BABY. Lf. blades broadly ovate, to 7½ in. long, 6 in. wide, base cordate to truncate, petioles to 7½ in. long; scapes becoming prostrate, to 4 ft. long, pedicels to 2⅜ in. long; achenes incurved near apex, ribs 3–4. Md. to Ill., s. to w. Fla. and s. Tex.

Grisebachii Small. Lf. blades lanceolate to oblong-ovate, to 4 in. long, with many pellucid dots; infl. simple or with few brs.; fls. nearly sessile; achenes short-beaked, ribs few, outermost winglike. Cuba, Costa Rica, Brazil. Often confused with *E. intermedius.*

intermedius (Mart.) Griseb. [*E. Martii* P. Micheli]. PYGMY CHAIN SWORD PLANT. Lf. blades linear, to 4¾ in. long and ⅝ in. wide, membranous, margins crisped, stamens 9; achenes 2–4-ribbed. Brazil.

longistylis Buchenau. Lf. blades oblong to elliptic, to 10 in. long and about 4 in. wide, petioles stout, to 20 in. long; scape to 3 ft., pedicels to ⅜ in. long; achenes beaked, ribs 6–8. Brazil.

magdalenensis Fassett. DWARF AMAZON SWORD PLANT. With many runners; lf. blades lanceolate to narrowly ovate, to 3⅛ in. long or sometimes longer, 1½ in. wide, petioles to 4 in. long or sometimes longer; scape to 1 ft.; achenes short-beaked, ribs faint or none. Colombia.

Martii: *E. intermedius.*

muricatus Griseb. Lf. blades oblong-ovate to broadly ovate, to 15 in. long, 9 in. wide, cordate at base, with stellate hairs particularly near base of blade and top of petiole, these often falling and leaving a bumpy surface; scape to 3 ft.; achenes short-beaked, ribs 4–5, weakly winged. Colombia, Venezuela, Guiana.

nymphaeifolius (Griseb.) Buchenau. Submersed lvs. ribbonlike, thin; emersed lvs. with blades ovate, to 4¾ in. long and 3½ in. wide, cordate at base; floating lvs. produced eventually; scape to 20 in.;

stamens 6; achenes short-beaked, ribs 6, crested. Yucatan, Brit. Honduras, Cuba.

paniculatus P. Micheli. AMAZON SWORD PLANT. Lf. blades variable, linear-lanceolate to elliptic or ovate, sometimes curved, to 1½ ft. long, base cuneate to truncate, petioles to 1 ft. long, winged; scape to 6 ft., pedicels long; stamens 10–24; achenes nearly flat, beaked, ribs 6–8. Brazil and Venezuela to Paraguay.

quadricostatus Fassett. Lf. blades lanceolate, to 2 in. long and ¼ in. wide; achenes long-beaked, ribs 8–9. N. Peru.

radicans: *E. cordifolius.*

ranunculoides (L.) Engelm. Submersed lvs. linear, grasslike, to 3 ft. long and ³⁄₁₆ in. wide, emersed lvs. wider, with a transition to ovate, to 4 in. long, ¾ in. wide; fls. on pedicels to 4 in. long, stamens 6; achenes curved, ribs 3. Eur., N. Afr.

rostratus: *A. Berteroi.*

tenellus (Mart.) Buchenau. AMAZON SWORD PLANT. Mat-forming, stoloniferous; submersed lvs. linear, to 4 in. long, emersed lvs. linear-lanceolate to oblong, to 1¼ in. long, dark green and slightly fleshy; scapes to 4 in. long, pedicels to 1 in. long; ribs 6–7. S. Amer.

ECHINOFOSSULOCACTUS G. Lawr. [*Stenocactus* (K. Schum.) A. Berger]. BRAIN CACTUS. *Cactaceae.* Perhaps 20 spp. of small, subglobose, many-ribbed cacti, native to Mex.; sts. solitary or rarely clustered, depressed-globose to oblong, ribs usually many and thin, often wavy; areoles remote, sometimes only 2–3 on each rib, larger spines often flattened, glandspines said to be absent; fls. nearly apical, opening several days, campanulate, scales of tube and ovary naked in their axils, perianth segms. often white-margined; fr. thin-walled, said to split longitudinally, seeds black. Probably many of the "species" are geographical vars. or forms.

For culture see *Cacti.*

albatus (A. Dietr.) Britt. & Rose [*Stenocactus albatus* (A. Dietr.) F. M. Knuth]. Sts. depressed-globose, to 5 in. wide, ribs about 35; spines yellowish-white, radial spines about 10, bristlelike, to ½ in. long, central spines 4, the upper erect, flat, to 1¾ in. long, the middle 2 similar, half as long, the lower cylindrical, to 1 in. long; fls. white, ¾ in. long. Mex.

anfractuosus (Mart.) G. Lawr. [*Stenocactus anfractuosus* (Mart.) A. Berger]. Sts. to 5 in. high and 2½ in. thick, dull green, ribs about 30; radial spines about 7, the upper 3 flat, to 1 in. long, central spine 1, flat, shorter; fls. purplish. Cent. Mex.

arrigens (Link) Britt. & Rose [*Stenocactus arrigens* (Link) A. Berger]. Sts. globose, to 3 in. thick, ribs about 24; radial spines 7–11, yellow, the upper flat, to 1½ in. long, central spines 0–3, slender, spreading; fls. 1 in. long, scales purple, with white margins. Mex.

caespitosus Backeb. Cespitose, sts. to 2 in. thick, ribs about 27; radial spines 4, needle-shaped, to ¼ in. long, central spines 4, flattened, yellowish, ¾ in. long, the upper erect, ³⁄₃₂ in. wide; fls. greenish-white, ½ in. long. Mex.

coptonogonus (Lem.) G. Lawr. [*Stenocactus coptonogonus* (Lem.) A. Berger]. Sts. simple or cespitose, globose, to 4 in. thick, ribs 10–14, stout; areoles ¾ in. apart, spines 3–5, stout, gray, the upper one flat, longest to 1 in. long, the lateral ones 4-angled, ascending; fls. purplish, 1¼ in. long. Cent. Mex.

crispatus (DC.) G. Lawr. [*Stenocactus crispatus* (DC.) A. Berger]. Sts. obovoid, ribs about 25; spines 10–11, rigid, unequal; fls. purplish, small. Cent. Mex.

hastatus (Hopffer) Britt. & Rose [*Stenocactus hastatus* (Hopffer) A. Berger]. Sts. to 4 in. high and 5 in. thick, ribs about 35, thick; radial spines 5–6, yellow, the upper flattened, to 1¼ in. long, central spine 1, directed outward, to 1½ in. long; fls. yellowish, large. Cent. Mex.

heteracanthus (Mühlenpf.) Britt. & Rose [*Stenocactus heteracanthus* (Mühlenpf.) A. Berger]. Sts. globose, to 3 in. wide, ribs 30–50; radial spines 10–13, stellate, ¼ in. long, central spines 4, the upper erect, flat, ⅝ in. long, the others angled or nearly cylindrical, shorter. Cent. Mex.

lamellosus (A. Dietr.) Britt. & Rose [*Stenocactus lamellosus* (A. Dietr.) A. Berger]. Sts. to 4 in. high and 3 in. thick, ribs 30–35; spines flat, white, radial spines 5, flat, to 1 in. long, central spine 1, directed outward, to 1½ in. long; fls. red, 1½ in. long. Cent. Mex.

lancifer (A. Dietr.) Britt. & Rose [*Stenocactus lancifer* (A. Dietr.) A. Berger]. Sts. subglobose, ribs many; areoles few to a rib, spines 8, white, brown-tipped, the 3 ascending and the 1 deflexed large and flat, the 4 lateral spines small, needle-shaped; fls. rose, large. Mex.

Lloydii Britt. & Rose [*Stenocactus Lloydii* (Britt. & Rose) A. Berger]. Sts. subglobose, 5 in. thick or more, ribs about 60; radial spines 10–15, needle-shaped, white, to ⁵⁄₁₆ in. long, central spines 3, brown, the upper flat, thin, erect, to 3½ in. long, the lateral spines shorter and narrower; fls. white, small. Cent. Mex.

multicostatus (Hildm.) Britt. & Rose [*Stenocactus multicostatus* (Hildm.) A. Berger]. Sts. subglobose, to 4 in. thick, ribs 100 or more, wavy, each with few areoles; spines 6–9, the upper 3 erect or ascending, flat, thin, to 3 in. long, the lower weakly awl-shaped, to ⅝ in. long; fls. purplish, 1 in. long. E. Mex.

obvallatus (DC.) G. Lawr. [*Stenocactus obvallatus* (DC.) A. Berger]. Sts. globose to obovoid, ribs about 25; spines about 8, the lower 4 to ⁵⁄₁₆ in. long, the upper ascending or spreading, narrow but flattened, much longer; fls. large. Cent. Mex.

Ochoterenaus (Tiegel) Oehme [*Stenocactus Ochoterenaus* (Tiegel) Bravo]. Sts. to 3 in. high and 4 in. thick, ribs about 30; radial spines about 20, needle-shaped, white, stellate, ½ in. long, central spines 4, yellow, becoming pale, flattened, the upper ascending, to 2½ in. long, the others spreading, shorter and narrower; fls. whitish. Cent. Mex.

pentacanthus (Lem.) Britt. & Rose [*Stenocactus pentacanthus* (Lem.) A.Berger]. Sts. globose to oblong, ribs 30 or more, each with few areoles; spines about 5, flattened, the upper broad, to 1½ in. long, the middle 2 narrower, the lower 2 to ⁵⁄₁₆ in. long; fls. purplish, ¾ in. long. Cent. Mex.

phyllacanthus (Mart.) G. Lawr. [*Stenocactus phyllacanthus* (Mart.) A.Berger]. Sts to 6 in. high and 4 in. thick, ribs 30–35, each with few areoles; spines 5–9, the upper one erect, flat, thin, annulate, to 1½ in. long, the others slender, much shorter; fls. yellowish, ¾ in. long. Cent. Mex.

Vaupelianus (Werderm.) Tiegel & Oehme [*Stenocactus Vaupelianus* (Werderm.) F.M.Knuth]. Sts. to 2½ in. high and 3½ in. thick, ribs 30–40; radial spines 15–25, needle-shaped, white, to ⅝ in. long, central spines 1–2, awl-shaped, directed outward or one ascending, to 3 in. long; fls. yellowish, ¾ in. long. Mex.

violaciflorus (Quehl) Britt. & Rose [*Stenocactus violaciflorus* (Quehl) A.Berger]. Sts. globose to oblong, to 4 in. thick, ribs about 35; spines 7–9, the lower 3–4 decurved, awl-shaped, to ½ in. long, the uppermost broad, flat, annulate, ascending or appressed, to 2½ in. long, the upper lateral spines narrower and thicker; fls. purplish, 1 in. long. Cent. Mex.

zacatecasensis Britt. & Rose [*Stenocactus zacatecasensis* (Britt. & Rose) A.Berger]. Sts. simple, globose, to 4 in. thick, ribs about 55; radial spines 10–12, needle-shaped, stellate, white, to ⅜ in. long, central spines 3, brown, the upper broad, flat, erect or incurved, to 1½ in. long; fls. white, tinged lavender, 1½ in. wide, stigma lobes bifid. Cent. Mex.

ECHINOMASTUS: *NEOLLOYDIA.*

ECHINOPANAX: *OPLOPANAX.*

ECHINOPS L. GLOBE THISTLE. *Compositae* (Carduus Tribe). About 100 spp. of bien. and per. herbs, native from the w. Medit. region to cent. Asia; lvs. in rosettes or alt. on the sts., mostly pinnatifid or 2–3-pinnately dissected, margins prickly; fl. heads of 1 fl. within its own involucre, the outer involucral bracts bristlelike, the inner bracts linear or lanceolate, separate or united, the individual heads aggregated into a dense globose compound head subtended by a small, common, reflexed involucre; fls. all tubular, blue or white; achenes 4-angled to nearly cylindrical, usually hairy, pappus of many inconspicuous scales.

Globe thistles are bold plants good for striking effects in the border or in colonized clumps. The prominent, stiff bracts of the individual heads are metallic-blue in the cultivated kinds, contributing to the color of the compound head; the flowers themselves may be blue or white. The plants are of simple culture, in open places. Propagation is by seeds, which gives blooming plants the following summer, but perennial kinds may be increased also by division and by root cuttings. They are mostly hardy north.

chantavicus Trautv. Per., to 3 ft., sts. almost glabrous in lower part, white-tomentose above, not glandular; lvs. oblong, 12–16 in. long, deeply pinnatifid, green and scabrous above, densely white-tomentose beneath, not glandular, margins spinose-ciliate; compound heads to 1½ in. across; fls. blue. Cent. Asia.

exaltatus Schrad. Per., to 5 ft., sts. white-tomentose, not glandular; lvs. pinnatifid, deep green, rough, and minutely setose above, white-tomentose beneath, margins spiny-toothed; compound heads to 2⅜ in. across; fls. blue. Russia.

humilis Bieb. Per., to 6–12 in., sts. simple; lower lvs. lyrate-sinuate, st. lvs. oblong-linear, spiny-toothed, all villous-cobwebby above, white-tomentose beneath; compound heads to 1½ in. across; fls. steel-blue. W. Asia.

niveus Wallich ex Royle. Per., sts. very leafy; lvs. lanceolate to ovate-lanceolate in outline, 3–8 in. long, deeply pinnatifid into linear to linear-lanceolate segms., cottony beneath, margins revolute, spiny; compound heads to 3 in. across. Nw. Himalayas.

Ritro L. [*E. Ritro* var. *tenuifolius* DC.]. SMALL G.T. Per., to 2 ft., sts. white-woolly, not glandular; lvs. oblong in outline, to 8 in. long, pinnately dissected into lanceolate, spiny-toothed segms., green and glossy above, densely white-woolly beneath; compound heads to about 1½ in. across; fls. bright blue. E. Eur., w. Asia.

sphaerocephalus L. GREAT G. T. Bushy per., to 7 ft., sts. gray-woolly, glandular-hairy above; lvs. ovate-oblong, to about 14 in. long, sinuate-pinnatifid, green, glandular and roughish above, white-tomentose beneath, margins spiny-toothed; compound heads to 2⅜ in. across; fls. pale blue to whitish. Cent. and s. Eur., w. Asia; naturalized here and there in N. Amer.

tschimganicus B.Fedtsch. Per., to 1 ft., sts. densely leafy, glandular, white-tomentose above; lvs. oblong-linear, deeply pinnately parted, spiny at apex, densely glandular above, white-tomentose beneath, margins revolute, nearly entire; compound heads about 1¼ in. across. Mts., Turkestan.

ECHINOPSIS Zucc. [*Pseudolobivia* (Backeb.) Backeb.]. SEA-URCHIN CACTUS. *Cactaceae*. About 30 spp. of globose to oblong, ribbed cacti, native to S. Amer.; sts. solitary or cespitose, ribs 8–24, straight or scarcely tubercled; fls. lateral, nocturnal or lasting longer, large, funnelform, white or pink, tube longer than the segms., scales of tube and ovary with axillary hairs, stamens declined, a distinct upper series at the throat; fr. globose to oblong, splitting. S. S. Amer. e of the Andes. Intergrades with *Lobivia* and with *Trichocereus*.

The kinds of echinopsis are often showy because of the long flowers, and although not much grown they are capable of becoming good window garden and conservatory plants. For culture see *Cacti*.

albispinosa K.Schum. Sts. simple or proliferating, grayish, to 6 in. high and 4 in thick, ribs 10–11; spines 11–14, stoutly needle-shaped, curved, dark brown, becoming white, to 1 in. long, central spines about 2; fls. white, 8 in. long. N. Argentina.

ancistrophora Speg. [*Pseudolobivia ancistrophora* (Speg.) Backeb.]. Sts. simple, globose, to 3 in. thick, ribs 15–16; radial spines 3–7, needle-shaped, recurved, to ⅝ in. long, central spine 1, curved or hooked, to ¾ in. long; fls. white, to 6 ½ in. long. N. Argentina.

arizonica: a listed name of no botanical standing, for a hybrid.

aurea Britt. & Rose [*Lobivia aurea* (Britt. & Rose) Backeb.]. Sts. simple, to 4 in. high, ribs 14–15, acute, entire; radial spines 8–10, needle-shaped, ⅜ in. long, central spines mostly 4, stouter, often flattened, to 1¼ in. long; fls. yellow, to 4 in. long. Argentina.

Backebergii: *Lobivia Backebergii.*

Bridgesii Salm-Dyck. Sts. subcespitose, to 1 ft. high and 3 in. thick, ribs 11–14; radial spines 8–13, awl-shaped, to ½ in. long, central spines 4, the upper longest, to ¾ in. long; fls. to 7 in. long. Bolivia.

calochlora K.Schum. Sts. globose, to 3½ in. thick, ribs 13, crenate; radial spines 10–14, needle-shaped, yellow, to ⁵⁄₁₆ in. long, central spines 3–4, similar; fls. white, 6½ in. long, inner segms. broad, acute. Brazil.

campylacantha: *E. leucantha.*

cordobensis Speg. Sts. simple, to 20 in. high and 14 in. thick, ribs 13, straight, acute; spines straight, black, becoming gray, radial spines 8–10, to ¾ in. long, central spines 1–3, bulbous at base, to 2 in. long; fls. to 9 in. long. fr. subglobose, 1 in. in diam. N. Argentina.

Eyriesii (Turp.) Zucc. Sts. cespitose, to 1 ft. high and 6 in. thick, ribs 11–18; spines conical, dark brown, to ³⁄₁₆ in. long, radial spines about 10, central spines 4–8; fls. white, to 10 in. long. S. Brazil, Uruguay, N. Argentina.

ferox (Britt. & Rose) Backeb. [*Lobivia ferox* Britt. & Rose; *Pseudolobivia ferox* (Britt. & Rose) Backeb.]. Sts. globose, to 1 ft. thick, ribs about 29, divided into thin, elongate tubercles; radial spines 10–12, slender, curved, to 2½ in. long, central spines 3–4, upcurved, to 6 in. long; fls. rose, 4 in. long, opening for only one morning. Bolivia.

Fiebrigii Gürke. Sts. simple, to 3½ in. high and 6 in. thick, ribs 18–24, crenate; spines awl-shaped, yellow, becoming gray, radial spines 8–10, recurved, to 1 in. long, central spine 1, upcurved, to 1½ in. long; fls. white, to 8 in. long. Bolivia.

Huottii (J.F.Cels) Labour. Sts. simple, to 14 in. high, slender, ribs 9–11, crenate; spines brown, black-tipped, radial spines 9–11, needle-shaped, unequal, about ¾ in. long, central spines 4, awl-shaped, twice as long; fls. white, to 8 in. long. Bolivia.

Kratochviliana Backeb. [*Pseudolobivia Kratochviliana* (Backeb.) Backeb.]. Sts. simple, to 1½ in. high and 2½ in. thick, ribs to 18; spines slenderly awl-shaped, brown, radial spines 8–12, curved, to ⅜ in. long, central spines mostly 1, hooked, to 1 in. long; fls. white or yellowish, to 2½ in. long. Argentina.

leucantha (Gillies) Walp. [*E. campylacantha* Pfeiff.]. Sts. simple, to 14 in. high and 5 in. thick, ribs 12–14; radial spines 7–10, somewhat recurved, brown, to 1 in. long, central spine 1, stouter, curved, to 4 in. long; fls. white, to 6 in. long or more. W. Argentina.

leucorhodantha Backeb. [*Pseudolobivia leucorhodantha* (Backeb.) Backeb.]. Sts. to 1½ in. high and 3 in. thick, ribs 18–20, acute; spines about 14, irregular, curved, to ⅜ in. long, several central, one long, curved at tip; fls. white with rose, 4 in. long. Argentina.

longispina (Britt. & Rose) Backeb. [*Lobivia longispina* Britt. & Rose]. Sts. to 10 in. high and 4 in. thick, ribs 25–50, deeply undulate; spines 10–15, stoutly needle-shaped, yellowish to brown, to 3 in. long; fls. slender, 1½ in. long, limb short. Argentina.

mirabilis: *Setiechinopsis mirabilis.*

multiplex (Pfeiff.) Zucc. BARREL CACTUS, EASTER-LILY C., PINK EASTER LILY. Sts. proliferous, to 8 in. high and 6 in. thick, ribs 12–15; spines needle-shaped, radial spines 9–10, yellowish, to 1 in. long, central spines mostly 4, stouter, darker, the lowermost longest, to 1½ in. long; fls. rose-red, to 10 in. long. S. Brazil.

nigra Backeb. [*Pseudolobivia nigra* (Backeb.) Backeb.]. Sts. sub-globose, to 6 in. thick, ribs about 20, divided into oblong, acute tubercles 1½ in. long; spines stoutly needle-shaped, curved, dark, becoming gray, radial spines 12–14, to 1½ in. long, central spines 2, the lower sometimes hooked, to 3 in. long; fls. white, 4 in. long. N. Argentina.

obrepanda (Salm-Dyck) K.Schum. [*Pseudolobivia obrepanda* (Salm-Dyck) Backeb.]. Sts. simple, to 6 in. high and 7 in. thick, ribs 17–18, acute, crenate; spines needle-shaped, dark, curved, radial spines 9–11, to 1¼ in. long, central spines 1–3, to 1½ in. long; fls. white to purplish, to 8 in. long. Bolivia. Cv. 'Amoena' is listed.

oxygona (Link) Zucc. Sts. cespitose, subglobose, to 6 in. thick or more, ribs 13–15; radial spines 5–15, unequal, to ⅝ in. long, central spines 2–5, longer; fls. rose, to 1 ft. long. S. Brazil.

paraguayensis: a listed name of no botanical standing; probably not the same as *E. tubiflora* var.

pelecyrhachis Backeb. [*Pseudolobivia pelecyrhachis* (Backeb.) Backeb.]. Sts. depressed-globose, ribs divided into oblong, acute tubercles; spines 10, radial, ⁵⁄₁₆ in. long; fls. white, 4 in. long. N. Argentina.

polyancistra Backeb. [*Pseudolobivia polyancistra* (Backeb.) Backeb.]. Sts. depressed, rarely 2½ in. wide, ribs 17–30, low, rounded, almost tubercled; spines many, bristlelike, to ½ in. long, central spines often curved or hooked; fls. very slender, white, to 4 in. long, fragrant. N. Argentina.

rhodotricha K.Schum. Sts. cespitose, to 2½ ft. high and 5 in. thick, ribs 8–13, weakly crenate; spines slenderly awl-shaped, curved, yellow-brown, radial spines 4–5, to ¾ in. long, central spines 0–1, to 1½ in. long; fls. white, 6 in. long; fr. 1¾ in. long, 1 in. in diam., with red hairs. Paraguay and n. Argentina. Var. **argentinensis** R. Mey. Sts. shorter, darker; radial spines 6–7. Var. **robusta** R. Mey. Radial spines 9–10.

Ritteri Böd. Sts. mostly simple, to 1 ft. high and 10 in. thick, ribs 21–32, obtuse; spines awl-shaped, yellowish, to ⁵⁄₁₆ in. long, radial spines 10–12, central spines 3–4; fls. white, to 6 in. long. Bolivia.

Silvestrii Speg. Sts. simple or clustered, to 4 in. high and 3 in. thick, ribs 12–14, obtuse, lightly crenate; spines slenderly awl-shaped, gray, to ½ in. long, radial spines 5–9, recurved, central spine 1, erect; fls. white, 8 in. long. N. Argentina.

Smrziana Backeb. Sts. cespitose, to 16 in. high and 8 in. thick, ribs 10–15; spines about 14, needle-shaped, white to yellow-brown, to ¾ in. long. N. Argentina.

Spegazziniana Britt. & Rose. Sts. simple, to 1 ft. high and 3½ in. thick, ribs 12–14, low; spines slenderly awl-shaped, brown, radial spines 7–8, straight, central spine 1, longer, to ¾ in. long; fls. white, to 7 in. long. N. Argentina.

spiniflora: *Acanthocalycium spiniflorum.*

tubiflora (Pfeiff.) Zucc. Sts. simple or clustered, globose, to 5 in. thick, ribs 10–12; areoles 1 in. apart, spines slender, straight, radial spines 7–9, central spines 1–3, stouter and longer, black-tipped, about 1 in. long; fls. white, to 4 in. wide, tube 8 in. long, 1½ in. across in upper part. Summer. N. Argentina. Var. **paraguayensis** R. Mey. Sts. to 1 ft. high and 7 in. thick; fls. smaller. Paraguay. Cv. 'Cristata' is listed.

turbinata (Pfeiff.) Zucc. Sts. becoming club-shaped, to 6 in. high, ribs 15–18; areoles less than ³⁄₁₆ in. apart, radial spines 10–12, slender, white, to ¼ in. long, central spines 6, black, ⅛ in. long; fls. white,

fragrant, 3 in. across, tube 6 in. long, 2 in. across in upper part. N. Argentina.

ECHINUS: *BRAUNSIA.* **E. Mathewsii:** *B. geminata.*

ECHIOIDES Ort. *Boraginaceae.* One sp., an erect, per. herb, native to the Near East; lvs. basal and cauline; fls. yellow, in terminal scorpioid cymes, calyx 5-parted, corolla 5-lobed, throat glabrous, tube hairy inside, stamens 5, borne at several levels, styles of different lengths; fr. of 4 nutlets, tawny and spotted with purple, the surface smooth or rough.

Of easy cultivation. Propagated by seeds, division or cuttings. Sometimes grown in the border or rock garden.

longiflorum (C. Koch) I. M. Johnst. [*Arnebia Echioides* (L.) DC.]. PROPHET FLOWER. To 1 ft.; lvs. oblanceolate to obovate-oblong; fls. yellow, with a purple spot at the base of each sinus between the lobes, changing to pure yellow, to 1¼ in. long, in simple or forked cymes. Armenia, Caucasus, n. Iran.

ECHITES P. Br. *Apocynaceae.* Not in cult. **E. rubro-venosa:** *Prestonia quinquangularis.*

ECHIUM L. VIPER'S BUGLOSS. *Boraginaceae.* About 35 spp. of mostly scabrous, hispid, or canescent, ann., bien., or per. herbs, or shrubs, native to the Canary Is., Azores, Madeira, Eur. particularly Medit. region, and w. Asia; lvs. simple, alt.; fls. blue, purple, red, pink, or white, in bracted, simple or forked scorpioid cymes aggregated into a thyrse or a panicle, calyx 5-lobed, corolla of 5 unequal, somewhat spreading or erect lobes, throat without scales, stamens 5, unequal, often exserted, inserted below the middle of corolla tube; fr. of 4, wrinkled, erect, nutlets.

Some of the large species from the Canary Is. are much planted in Calif., and other kinds are grown elsewhere in warm regions and sometimes under glass; all of them thrive in open sunny places. Propagated by seeds or the shrubby kinds by cuttings and layers.

Bourgaeanum: *E. Wildpretii.*

candicans L.f. Shrubby and branching, to 6 ft.; lvs. lanceolate, white-hairy, distinctly veined; fls. white, or blue with white lines, nearly sessile, in a dense, long thyrse. Madeira, Canary Is.

creticum L. Erect bien., to 3 ft.; basal lvs. narrowly oblanceolate, to 7 in. long, with spreading hairs, st. lvs. narrowly elliptic to oblong; fls. always reddish-purple or pale red turning blue or bluish-purple, stamens 1–2, exserted. Medit. region.

fastuosum Jacq. Shrubby and branching, to 6 ft.; lvs. lanceolate, gray-hairy with soft hairs, distinctly veined; fls. purple or dark blue, in a cylindrical thyrsoid panicle, stamens red, long-exserted. Canary Is.

Lycopsis L. [*E. plantagineum* L.]. Erect bien., to 2 ft. or more, with stiff white hairs; lvs. ovate to oblong or lanceolate, with appressed hairs but not rough, basal lvs. distinctly veined; fls. red changing to purple-blue, in a panicle, 2 stamens long-exserted, 3 included. Eng., Canary Is., Medit. region, Caucasus.

plantagineum: *E. Lycopsis.*

pomponium Boiss. Slender, mostly unbranched bien., to 6 ft. or more; basal lvs. linear or linear-lanceolate, to 16 in. long, white-hispid; fls. rose-pink, about ¾ in. long, in a dense, short thyrse, anthers blue. S. Spain, nw. Afr.

roseum: a listed name of no botanical standing.

rubrum: *E. russicum.*

russicum J. F. Gmel. [*E. rubrum* Jacq., not Forssk.]. Unbranched bien., to 3 ft.; lvs. linear-lanceolate, white-hairy; fls. red, in a dense narrow thyrse, corolla 4 times longer than calyx, stamens long-exserted. Eur., w. Asia.

vulgare L. BLUEWEED, BLUE-DEVIL. Bien., 1–3 ft., with stiff white hairs; lvs. oblong to linear-lanceolate, to 6 in. long, with prominent midrib; fls. blue, rarely pink or white, at first in a thyrse, but becoming paniculate in age, 4 stamens long-exserted, 1 included. Eur., Asia; naturalized in e. N. Amer., often a pernicious pasture weed.

Wildpretii H. Pearson ex Hook.f. [*E. Bourgaeanum* Webb]. Soft-hairy, much-branched shrub, to 10 ft.; lvs. linear-lanceolate, 6–8 in. long, sessile; fls. pale red, in a thick, pyramidal, paniculate thyrse, bracts longer than individual cymes, stamens equally long-exserted. Canary Is.

ECONOMIC PLANTS. Plants that directly or indirectly are major sources of man's food, clothing, and shelter, and of raw materials for industry and medicine, are termed economic plants. In a broader sense, the term sometimes also includes ornamentals that are sold in commerce.

Besides the many ornamentals, food plants, and timber species that constitute the major listings in this volume, there are numerous entries for plants that provide man with a variety of other economic products. Examples of such products (with some of the representative source genera) include: beverages *(Coffea, Cola, Thea, Theobroma, Vitis);* drugs *(Aloe, Atropa, Cinchona, Digitalis, Dioscorea, Papaver);* dyes *(Bixa, Crocus, Haematoxylon, Indigofera, Rubia);* fibers *(Agave, Cannabis, Ceiba, Corchorus, Gossypium, Linum, Musa, Pinus);* gums *(Acacia, Astragalus, Commiphora, Liquidambar);* narcotics *(Cannabis, Datura, Erythroxylon, Lophophora, Papaver);* essential and fatty oils *(Aleurites, Carthamnus, Citrus, Cocos, Elaeis, Gossypium, Lavandula, Linum, Olea, Rosa, Zea);* pesticides *(Chrysanthemum, Derris, Lonchocarpus, Urginea);* pulp for papermaking *(Broussonetia, Edgeworthia, Picea, Pinus, Phyllostachys, Populus);* rubber or other latices *(Ficus, Hevea, Manilkara, Palaquium);* smokes and masticatories *(Areca, Cola, Nicotiana, Piper);* spices *(Brassica, Capsicum, Cinnamomum, Mentha, Myristica, Pimenta, Piper, Syzygium, Vanilla, Zingiber);* sugars *(Acer, Arenga, Beta, Saccharum, Sorghum);* tannins *(Quercus, Rhizophora, Rhus, Tsuga);* and waxes *(Copernicia, Euphorbia, Myrica, Simmondsia).*

EDGEWORTHIA Meissn. *Thymelaeaceae.* Two or 3 spp. of deciduous or evergreen shrubs, native to Himalayas and China; lvs. alt., simple, crowded at ends of brs.; fls. yellow, fragrant, many, in dense axillary heads, calyx cylindrical, 4-lobed, corollalike, corolla absent; fr. dry, drupelike.

chrysantha: *E. papyrifera.*

Gardneri (Wallich) Meissn. Similar to *E. papyrifera,* but evergreen and having somewhat smaller lvs. Nepal and Sikkim.

papyrifera Siebold & Zucc. [*E. chrysantha* Lindl.; *E. tomentosa* Nakai]. PAPERBUSH, MITSUMATA. Deciduous shrub, to 6 ft., young brs. ternately branched, supple and tough; lvs. lanceolate-oblong, to 5 in. long and 2 in. wide; fls. appearing before the lvs., yellow, rarely orange, calyx tube to ½ in. long, silky on outside. China. Long cult. in s. Japan, where it is used as a source of soft, tough, handcrafted paper. Zone 8.

tomentosa: *E. papyrifera.*

EDITHCOLEA N. E. Br. *Asclepiadaceae.* Two spp. of succulent, leafless, per. herbs, native to ne. Afr.; sts. angled, the angles toothed; fls. apical, mostly solitary, corolla rotate, 5-lobed, with a very small hemispherical tube, corona of 2 whorls, the outer of 5 pouchlike lobes, the inner of 5 lobes, these erect, fleshy, conspicuously dilated and inflexed over the anthers at the apex; fr. a follicle.

For culture see *succulents.*

grandis N. E. Br. Sts. to 1 ft., 5-angled, the angles spiny-toothed; corolla 4-5 in. across, lobes to about the middle, inner surface rugose with concentric ridges, whitish or pale yellowish, marked with dark purple-brown spots, which are larger and confluent in an arc across middle of the lobes, tips of lobes purple-brown without markings, corolla tube about ¼ in. across, slightly raised at mouth. Somaliland to Tanzania.

EDRAIANTHUS A. DC. (sometimes, but not originally spelled *Hedraeanthus*). GRASSY-BELLS. *Campanulaceae.* About 12 spp. of tufted, per. herbs, native from Italy to the Caucasus, particularly in the Dalmatian-Balkan region, distinguished from *Wahlenbergia* by the irregular dehiscence of the caps., the generally solitary or clustered fls. immediately subtended by calyxlike involucral bracts, and the elongate, linear lvs.

The species are good spring- and summer-flowering rock garden plants, showy when in full bloom. The flower stems lop on the ground, making a clump 6–12 in. across or more, and rise at the end with clusters of purplish or violet flowers that may stand 1–6 in. above the ground. They grow readily from seeds.

bosniacus: a listed name of no botanical standing.

caricinus: *E. graminifolius.*

caudatus: *E. dalmaticus.*

croaticus: *E. graminifolius.*

dalmaticus (A. DC.) A. DC. [*E. caudatus* (Vis.) Rchb.f.; *Wahlenbergia dalmatica* A. DC.]. Tufted, sts. pilose; lvs. linear, more or less ciliate basally; fls. 6–10 in terminal heads, bracts long, attenuate, longer than heads, corolla violet-blue, tubular-campanulate, to ¾ in. long. Yugoslavia.

dinaricus (A. Kern.) Wettst. Tufted per., basal lvs. grasslike, st. lvs. to 2 in. long, hirsute above; fls. solitary at ends of brs., subtended by awl-shaped bracts about as long as the calyx, corolla violet-blue, about ¾ in. long, with spreading, acute lobes. Balkan Pen.

graminifolius (L.) A. DC. [*E. caricinus* Schott, Nym., & Kotschy; *E. croticus* (A. Kern.) A. Kern.; *E. intermedius* Degen; *E. Kitaibelii* (A. DC.) A. DC.; *Wahlenbergia Kitaibelii* A. DC.]. Tufted, condensed per., 2–4 in.; lvs. linear, usually less than 2 in. long, mucronate, green, glabrous or ciliate; fls. few, clustered on ends of sts., radiating from the base or on scapes projecting above the lvs., calyx lobes erect, usually appendaged at base of each sinus, corolla purple or white, campanulate or tubular, lobed about halfway to base, to about ¾ in. long. Italy, Hungary, s. to Bulgaria and Greece. A polymorphic sp. representing many named and unnamed forms, few of which are cult. Cv. **'Alba'.** Fls. white. Forma **Baldaccii** Janch. Involucral bracts broad at base and then abruptly attenuate, usually densely hairy; corolla smaller and narrower than usual.

intermedius: *E. graminifolius.*

Kitaibelii: *E. graminifolius.*

parnassicus (Boiss. & Sprun.) Halácsy. Spreading, cespitose per., sts. ascending to erect; lower lvs. petioled, spatulate, nearly crenate, upper lvs. sessile, lanceolate, pilose, not ciliate; fls. congested in terminal, glomerate heads, involucral bracts ovate-cuspidate, calyx lobes narrow-lanceolate, lacking appendages in sinuses, corolla violet. Macedonia, cent. Greece.

pumilio (Portenschl.) A. DC. [*Wahlenbergia pumilio* (Portenschl.) A. DC.]. Small, more or less hairy, cushion per.; lvs. linear, rarely more than 1 in. long; fls. erect, solitary, just above foliage, corolla amethyst-violet, narrow-campanulate with flaring lobes, to 1 in. long. Yugoslavia.

serbicus (A. Kern.) Petrovic. Differs from *E. dalmaticus* in having involucral bracts nearly orbicular, the outer ones short-acuminate, shorter than the fls. or mostly so; corolla ¾–1¼ in. long. Yugoslavia, e. Bulgaria.

serpyllifolius (Vis.) A. DC. [*Wahlenbergia serpyllifolius* (Vis.) G.Beck]. Compact, mat-forming per.; lower lvs. more or less in rosettes, linear-spatulate, mostly about 1 in. long, ciliate, otherwise glabrous; fls. erect, solitary at ends of brs. around the outside of mat, corolla rich violet or white, to 2 in. across. Yugoslavia. Cv. **'Albus'.** Fls. white. Cv. **'Major'.** Fls. large.

tasmanicus: a listed name of no botanical standing; material offered under this name is probably *Wahlenbergia albomarginata.*

tenuifolius (Waldst. & Kit.) A. DC. [*Wahlenbergia tenuifolia* (Waldst. & Kit.) A. DC.]. Compact, 4–6 in. high, in a mat, with more or less prostrate sts.; lvs. linear to narrow-lanceolate, to 4 in. long; fls. 6–15 in dense heads subtended by long, leaflike bracts often longer than heads, calyx lobes ovate, about as long as corolla tube, corolla violet-blue, about 1 in. long. Yugoslavia.

EGERIA: *ELODEA.*

EGGPLANT. The eggplant, *Solanum Melongena,* is a tender, branching, large-leaved herb, grown for its edible fruits, which are cooked in various ways. The fruits are usually purple, but may also be white, yellow, or striped.

The eggplant is most at home in the southern states, the long season suiting it. There the seeds may be sown in a plant bed and the young plants moved directly to the field. In the North, the plants must be started in the greenhouse and should be grown without check, the seed being sown about six weeks before tender crops can be set in the field. Plants should not be set in the field until danger of frost is past and soil is warm. The plants are usually set 18–24 inches apart in rows 3–4 feet apart. From three to six plants will usually provide enough fruit for an average family. Eggplants, especially when young, should be watched for flea beetles, which can cause sudden and serious damage. These can be controlled rather easily by application of a general-purpose garden insecticide. *Verticillium* wilt is the principal disease of eggplant. The organism causing it survives in the soil and also attacks tomatoes, potatoes, and strawberries. If these crops have shown *Verticillium* wilt in preceding years, eggplant should not be planted in the areas where they were grown. 'Black Beauty' has long been a standard cultivar, but some of the newer cultivars should be considered since a number of them are earlier in maturity and some may have *Verticillium* resistance. The fruit is usable over a wide range of size, but the quality is best before the seeds have turned brown.

EHRETIA P. Br. *Boraginaceae.* About 50 spp. of evergreen or deciduous shrubs and trees of trop. and subtrop. New and Old World; lvs. simple, alt. or fascicled on short brs., entire, undulate or serrate; fls. white or blue to mauve, in axillary or terminal corymbs or panicles, calyx 5-lobed, corolla mostly 5-lobed, funnelform to rotate, without scales in the throat, stamens 5, exserted, ovary, 2- or 4-celled, style bifid; fr. usually a small globose drupe.

Sometimes planted as an ornamental in the extreme southern U.S. Propagated by seeds and cuttings.

acuminata R. Br. [*Cordia thyrsiflora* Siebold & Zucc.]. Deciduous tree, to 50 ft. (to 90 ft. in Queensland); lvs. ovate or elliptic to obovate, to 7 in. long, serrate, apex acuminate, glabrous except on the veins; fls. white, in panicles to 8 in. long; fr. first orange then black. India, Japan, China, Philippine Is., Taiwan to e. Australia; fairly hardy North. A very variable sp. of several botanical vars.

Anacua (Terán & Berland.) I. M. Johnst. ANAQUA, KNACKAWAY. Deciduous shrub or tree, to 50 ft.; lvs. elliptic, oblong to oblong-ovate, to 2 in., undulate to serrate, apex sharp-pointed, upper surface rough; fls. white, fragrant, in panicles 2–3 in. long; fr. yellow. Se. Tex. to Mex.

buxifolia: *E. microphylla.*

Dicksonii Hance. Deciduous tree, 10–30 ft.; lvs. elliptic, broadly ovate to suborbicular, 3–8 in. long, serrate, apex short-acuminate, upper surface rough-hairy; fls. white, fragrant, in corymbose panicles 2–4 in. long; fr. yellow. China, Taiwan, Ryukyu Is.

hottentotica Burchell. Divaricately branched, evergreen shrub, to 10 ft.; lvs. obovate, to 1 in. long, entire, glabrous or slightly hairy when young, mostly fascicled on short brs.; fls. blue to mauve, in corymbose cymes to 1¼ in. long. S. Afr.

laevis Roxb. Deciduous tree or shrub, to 40 ft.; lvs. elliptic-ovate to ovate, to 5 in. long, serrate, apex short-acuminate, upper surface glossy, glabrous at maturity; fls. white, in corymbs 3 in. across; fr. red at maturity. India.

microphylla Lam. [*E. buxifolia* Roxb.]. PHILIPPINE TEA. Evergreen shrub, to 12 ft.; lvs. obovate or cuneate, to 2¼ in. long, fascicled on short shoots, entire, or toothed toward the apex, rough; fls. solitary or 2–4 together; fr. scarlet. India to Malay Pen. and Philippine Is.

tinifolia L. BASTARD CHERRY. Evergreen shrub or tree, to 35 ft. and more; lvs. oblong to ovate, to 4½ in. long, entire, glabrous, lustrous, apex rounded or acute; fls. white, in panicles to 6 in. long; fr. red or purple. Mex., W. Indies.

EHRHARTA Thunb. *Gramineae.* About 27 spp. of erect or decumbent, spreading, ann. or per. grasses in Afr., Mascarene Is., and New Zeal.; lf. blades flat; panicles narrow; spikelets compressed laterally, glumes ovate, rather obscurely keeled, rachilla disarticulating above the glumes, fertile floret enclosed by 2 large sterile lemmas, all falling together, sterile lemmas hard, compressed, 3–5-nerved, fertile lemma hard, ovate, 5-nerved, obtuse. For terminology see *Gramineae.*

calycina Sm. PERENNIAL VELT (or VELDT) GRASS. Per., sts. to 2½ ft., erect, leafy; panicles narrow, to 10 in. long, branchlets and pedicels nearly capillary; spikelets to ⁵⁄₁₆ in. long, purplish, glumes nearly as long as the lemmas, sterile lemmas thinly silky-villous, unequal, the second longer than the first, fertile lemma silky on the nerves. S. Afr. Cult in cent. and coastal Calif.

EICHHORNIA Kunth. *Pontederiaceae.* About 6 or 7 spp. of rhizomatous, aquatic herbs, native to trop. Amer.; lvs. floating or submerged; fls. showy, mostly in terminal spikes, ovary 3-celled; fr. a dehiscent caps., seeds many.

Grown in ponds and pools but can be a serious weed in warm areas. The water should not be more than about 1 ft. deep, and good soil should be provided. Propagated by division.

azurea (Swartz) Kunth. PEACOCK HYACINTH. Lf. blades broadly ovate to orbicular, petioles not inflated; fls. lavender-blue with purple center, perianth segms. erose-margined. Brazil.

crassipes (Mart.) Solms-Laub. WATER HYACINTH. Floating, with feathery roots; lf. blades ovate to orbicular, petioles much-inflated at base; fls. large and showy, perianth segms. entire, violet, upper lobe

with yellow-centered blue patch. Trop. Amer.; naturalized in se. U.S., and elsewhere where it often chokes waterways. Cv. 'Major'. Fls. rosy-lilac.

Martiana: *E. paniculata.*

paniculata (K. Spreng) Solms-Laub. [*E. Martiana* Seub.]. To 1 ft., rhizomes short and fleshy; basal lvs. with blades cordate-ovate, acuminate, to 4 in. long, longer than petiole, st. lvs. smaller; fls. pale violet to blue, 5–15, in panicles to 4 in. long. Brazil.

EKEBERGIA Sparrm. *Meliaceae.* About 15 spp. of trees or shrubs, sometimes dwarf shrubs, native to trop. and S. Afr., Madagascar; lvs. alt., odd-pinnate, lfts. mostly opp.; fls. in axillary panicles, calyx 4–5-lobed, petals 4 or 5, stamens 10 (rarely 9), filaments united in a campanulate tube, ovary 2–5-celled; fr. a berry.

africana: a listed name of no botanical standing.

capensis Sparrm. Large tree, wood hard, white; lvs. crowded toward tips of brs., lfts. 7–11, oblong, 2–3 in. long, paler beneath; seeds 1 or 2. S. Afr. Zone 10.

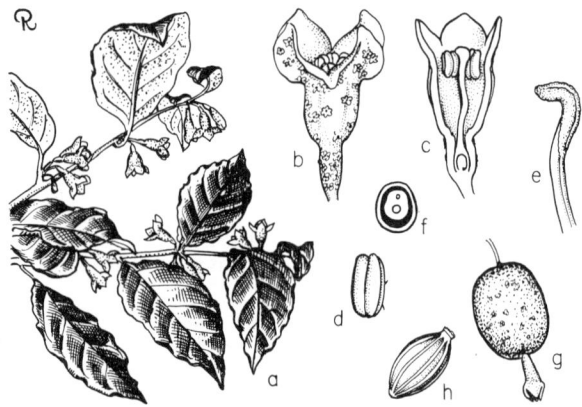

ELAEAGNACEAE. *Elaeagnus angustifolia:* **a,** flowering branches, × ³⁄₈; **b,** flower, × 2; **c,** flower, vertical section, × 2; **d,** anther, × 5; **e,** apex of style and stigma, × 5; **f,** ovary, cross section, × 10; **g,** fruit, × 1; **h,** achene, × 1.

ELAEAGNACEAE Juss. OLEASTER FAMILY. Dicot.; 3 genera and about 45 spp. of shrubs or trees, covered with silvery or brown scales, native to N. Hemisphere; lvs. alt., opp., or whorled, simple, entire; fls. solitary or in clusters or racemes, bisexual, or unisexual and plants then dioecious, perianth forming a saucer-shaped or tubular calyx tube, usually 4-lobed, stamens as many as the lobes or twice as many, borne on inner wall of calyx tube, ovary superior, 1-celled; fr. drupaceous, the achene enclosed by the fleshy fl. tube. *Elaeagnus, Hippophae,* and *Shepherdia* are cult. as ornamentals and sometimes for the edible fr.

ELAEAGNUS L. *Elaeagnaceae.* About 40 spp. of shrubs or small trees, sometimes evergreen, native to s. Eur. and Asia, with 1 in N. Amer.; lvs. alt., covered with minute silvery or brown scales; fls. inconspicuous, bisexual; fr. drupelike.

The species are grown in well-drained soil and sunny locations. Propagated by hardwood and root cuttings, layers, and grafting; also by seeds, preferably stratified, germination often not taking place until the second spring.

angustifolia L. [*E. argentea* Moench; *E. hortensis* Bieb.]. OLEASTER, WILD OLIVE, RUSSIAN O., SILVER BERRY. To 20 ft., deciduous, sometimes spiny, branchlets and underside of lvs. silvery; fls. fragrant, 1–3 in lf. axils; fr. yellow, silvery, on very short stalks. Summer. Eur., w. Asia. Zone 3. Var. **orientalis** (L.) O. Kuntze. Often spineless; lvs. broad; fr. large. Var. **spinosa** (L.) O.Kuntze. Usually spiny; lvs. broad, densely scaly; fr. small.

argentea: see *E. angustifolia* and *E. commutata;* material offered as *E. argentea* is *E. commutata.*

borealis: a listed name of no botanical standing.

Brevardii: a listed name of no botanical standing.

commutata Bernh. [*E. argentea* Pursh, not Moench]. SILVERBERRY. To 12 ft., deciduous; lvs. silvery on both sides; fls. fragrant, 1–3 in lf.

axils; fr. silvery, on very short stalks. Late spring. E. Canada, s. to Minn. and Utah. Zone 2. Very hardy.

×**Ebbingei** Boom: *E. macrophylla* × *E. pungens*. Shrub, to 9 ft., evergreen in mild climates; lvs. elliptic, to 4½ in. long, shining green above, silvery-scaly beneath; fls. white, 3–6 in lf. axils. Originated in Holland.

edulis: *E. multiflora.*

Fruitlandii: a listed name of no botanical standing for *E. pungens* cv.

glabra Thunb. To 20 ft., evergreen, climbing or running; lvs. with brown scales beneath; fls. fragrant; fr. gray or rusty. Autumn. Japan, China.

hortensis: *E. angustifolia.*

japonica: a listed name of no botanical standing.

latifolia L. OLEASTER, WILD OLIVE. Variable, either erect or climbing, sometimes treelike; lvs. ovate to elliptic or broader, obtuse or acute, to 5 in. long, silvery or rusty beneath; fls. many, clustered; fr. red, to 1½ in. long. India to China.

longipes: *E. multiflora.*

Loureirii Champ. Shrub, without thorns; lvs. ovate or elliptic-oblong, to 3 in. long, glabrous above, with rusty-brown scurfy scales beneath; fls. ½ in. long, 2 or 3 together in lateral clusters or short racemes. Hong Kong.

macrophylla Thunb. To 12 ft., evergreen; lvs. broad-ovate, to 5½ in. long, silvery beneath, becoming dark glossy green above; fls. fragrant, 4–6 in lf. axils; fr. red, to ⅝ in. long. Autumn. Japan.

multiflora Thunb. [*E. edulis* Carrière; *E. longipes* A. Gray]. CHERRY E., GUMI. To 6 ft., deciduous; lvs. silvery and with brown scales beneath; fls. fragrant, 1–2 in lf. axils; fr. scarlet, on slender stalks to 1 in. long, edible. Spring. Japan, China. Zone 5. Lvs. Variable in shape; some forms have been named as cvs.: 'Crispa', 'Ovata', 'Rotundifolia'.

parvifolia: *E. umbellata* var.

philippinensis Perrottet. To 9 ft., brs. drooping; lvs. silvery beneath, slightly toothed; fls. axillary, often solitary; fr. red. Philippine Is.

pungens Thunb. THORNY E. To 15 ft., evergreen, usually spiny; lvs. wavy-margined, silvery beneath, dotted with brown scales; fls. fragrant, in axillary clusters; fr. red, silvery and brown when young, short-stalked, edible. Autumn. China, Japan. Zone 7. Cvs. are: 'Aurea', lvs. yellow-margined; 'Compacta', listed; 'Fredrici' [cv. 'Fredrici Variegata'], lvs. with yellow center; 'Fruitlandii', listed; 'Maculata' [cv. 'Aureo-maculata'], lvs. with large yellow blotch in middle; 'Marginata', lvs. silver-edged; 'Nana', a dwarf form; 'Reflexa' [*E. reflexa* E. Morr. & Decne.], lvs. very brown-scaly beneath, not wavy-margined; 'Rotundifolia', listed; 'Simonii', [*E. Simonii* Carrière], lvs. silvery beneath, sometimes variegated yellow and pinkish-white; 'Variegata', lf. margins yellowish-white.

reflexa: *E. pungens* cv.

Simonii: *E. pungens* cv.

umbellata Thunb. To 18 ft., deciduous, branchlets silvery or covered with brown scales; lvs. silvery beneath; fls. fragrant, 1–3 in axils; fr. scarlet, silvery when young, short-stalked. Late spring. Himalayas, China, Japan. Var. **parvifolia** (Royle) C. K. Schneid. [*E. parvifolia* Royle]. Branchlets silvery; fr. silvery, becoming pink. Himalayas.

utilis: *Shepherdia argentea.*

ELAEIS Jacq. [*Corozo* Jacq. ex Giseke]. *Palmae.* Two spp. of solitary, monoecious palms of trop. Afr. and Amer. with erect or procumbent sts.; lvs. pinnate, petioles with spinelike fibrous processes along lower margin, pinnae acute, 1-ribbed; infls. short-peduncled, massive, dense, among lvs., bracts 2, the upper splitting into fibers, rachillae many, simple, with spinose tips; fls. dissimilar, on separate infls. on same plant or rarely mixed in same infl., male fls. paired or solitary, surrounded by united bractlets which form a honeycomblike pattern, sepals separate, petals valvate, stamens 6, female fls. solitary or with 2 lateral abortive male, more or less sunken in rachillae, sepals and petals imbricate, pistil 3-celled; fr. often irregular, red, oily-fleshy, endocarp bony, with 3 pores near apex, seed with homogeneous endosperm.

The two species are reported to hybridize in cultivation. One of the two most important palm genera economically, together with *Cocos*, and a major source of commercial palm oil. Also grown as ornamentals in the tropics and subtropics and occasionally in Zone 10b. For culture see *Palms.*

guineensis Jacq. [*E. melanococca* Gaertn.]. OIL PALM, AFRICAN O.P., MACAW-FAT. To 60 ft. or more; st. erect, roughened by lf. scars; lvs.

10–15 ft. long, pinnae many, more or less grouped and in several planes; infl. 1 ft. long or more, rachillae to 6 in. long, with stout spinose tip, bractlets of female rachillae longer than fls. and spinose; fr. ovoid or conic-ovoid, about 1 in. long. W. Trop. Afr. Cult. extensively in plantations in the tropics, especially Malay Pen., for palm oil and palm kernel oil.

melanococca: *E. guineensis,* but the name has long been applied in error to *E. oleifera.*

oleifera (HBK) Cortés [*Corozo oleifera* (HBK) L.H.Bailey]. AMERICAN OIL PALM. St. usually procumbent basally with erect apex; lvs. to 10 ft. long or more, pinnae many, regularly arranged in 1 plane; infl. to 1 ft. long or more, rachillae with short, thick, spinose tip, bractlets of female infl. sharp, shorter than fls.; fr. about 1 in. long. Cent. Amer., ne. S. Amer. Sometimes grown under the name *E. melanococca.*

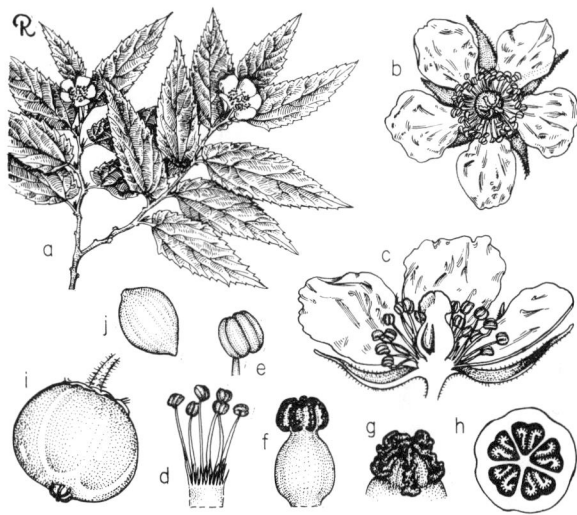

ELAEOCARPACEAE. *Muntingia Calabura:* **a,** flowering branch, × ¼; **b,** flower, × 1; **c,** flower, vertical section, × 2; **d,** stamens, × 3; **e,** anther, × 5; **f,** pistil, × 2½; **g,** stigma, × 3; **h,** ovary, cross section, × 4; **i,** fruit, × 1½; **j,** seed, × 10. (a from Lawrence, *Taxonomy of Vascular Plants.*)

ELAEOCARPACEAE DC. ELAEOCARPUS FAMILY. Dicot.; 8–12 genera and 350–400 spp. of trop. and subtrop. trees and shrubs, allied to the Tiliaceae; lvs. alt. or opp., simple; fls. often showy, in racemes or panicles, unisexual or bisexual, sepals and petals 4–5, petals sometimes 0, stamens many, inserted on or outside a disc, ovary superior, with 1–2 to several cells; fr. a caps., berry, or drupe. *Aristotelia, Crinodendron, Elaeocarpus,* and *Muntingia* are grown in the warmer parts of the U.S.

ELAEOCARPUS L. *Elaeocarpaceae.* More than 60 spp. of trees, native to the tropics and warm parts of the Old World; lvs. alt., simple; fls. in axillary racemes, mostly bisexual, sepals 5, petals 5, valvate in bud, fringed at apex, disc mostly 5-lobed, ovary 2–5-celled; fr. small, drupaceous, 1–5-seeded.

Sometimes grown as ornamentals in southern U. S., and in Calif. Propagated by cuttings, and by seeds when obtainable.

cyaneus: *E. reticulatus.*

dentatus (J. R. Forst. & G. Forst.) Vahl. To 60 ft., foliage mostly at ends of branchlets, which are silky; lvs. linear-oblong to narrowly obovate, to 4 in. long, finely wavy-toothed, leathery, margins recurved; fls. white, ½ in. across, drooping; fr. purplish-gray, ½ in. long. New Zeal.

Ganitrus: *E. sphaericus.*

reticulatus Sm. [*E. cyaneus* Ait. ex Sims]. Tree, to 60 ft., mostly glabrous; lvs. oblong or elliptic to nearly lanceolate, to 4 in. or more, acuminate, serrate; fls. white, in loose racemes; fr. blue, to ½ in. long, 1-seeded. Queensland, New S. Wales, Victoria (Australia).

sphaericus (Gaertn.) K. Schum. [*E. Ganitrus* Roxb.]. Tree; lvs. elliptic, 5–6 in. long, 2 in. wide, serrulate; fls. white, ½ in. across, in drooping racemes from old wood; fr. globose, purple, 5-seeded, to 1 in. in diam. India. Seeds made into buttons and beads.

ELAEODENDRON: *Cassine.* **E. capense**: *C. papillosa.*

ELAEPHORBIA Stapf. *Euphorbiaceae.* About 4 spp. of monoecious, woody or semisucculent trees, with milky juice, native to Afr.; lvs. alt., simple, fleshy, entire; fls. in cyathia (see *Euphorbiaceae*), on axillary peduncles, involucre of cyathium with 5 inner lobes alternating with 5 glands, ovary 3-celled; fr. a drupe. Like *Euphorbia* except for fr.

For culture see *Succulents.*

drupifera (Thonn.) Stapf. Tree, to 50 ft.; young brs. obscurely 4–6-angled, becoming cylindrical in age, spines in pairs on the angles; lvs. cuneate-oblong to obovate, to 8¼ in. long, deciduous. Trop. Afr.

ELAPHOGLOSSUM Schott. *Polypodiaceae.* More than 400 spp. of trop., epiphytic ferns primarily of the New World, rhizomes creeping; lvs. dimorphic, simple, rather thick, more or less tongue-shaped; sori covering the under surface of the fertile lvs., indusia lacking.

Treated as warm-house epiphytes, requiring abundant moisture and good drainage. See also *Ferns.*

crinitum (L.) Christ [*Acrostichum crinitum* L.]. ELEPHANT-EAR FERN, ELEPHANT'S-EAR F. Lvs. to 2 ft. long and 10 in. wide, petioles 1 ft. long, shaggy-haired. W. Indies, Mex., Cent. Amer. A striking plant, not much cult.

ELAPHRIUM: *BURSERA.*

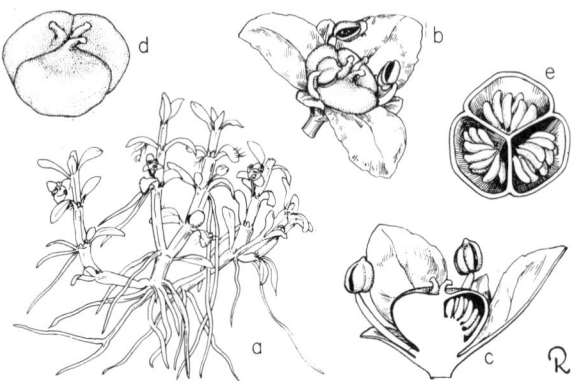

ELATINACEAE. *Elatine americana* (Pursh) Arn.: **a,** flowering plant, × 1½; **b,** flower, × 12; **c,** flower, vertical section, × 12; **d,** pistil, × 15; **e,** ovary, cross-sectioned, view into basal half, × 15. (Species representative, but not in general cultivation; from Lawrence, *Taxonomy of Vascular Plants.*)

ELATINACEAE Dumort. WATERWORT FAMILY. Dicot.; 2 genera and perhaps 40–50 spp. of herbs or subshrubs of cosmopolitan distribution in wet areas; lvs. opp. or whorled, stipuled; fls. regular, bisexual, axillary, solitary or in cymes, sepals and petals 3–5, separate, stamens 2–8, ovary superior, 3–5-celled; fr. a septicidal caps., seeds many. *Elatine* is cult.

ELATINE L. WATERWORT. *Elatinaceae.* Ten to 20 spp. of widely distributed herbs growing in wet places; sts. prostrate to erect, often rooting at nodes, rather succulent; lvs. opp. or whorled, often sessile; fls. axillary, usually solitary or in pairs, sepals and petals 2–4, stamens 2–8; fr. a many-seeded, membranous, 3–4-celled, septicidal caps.

Sometimes grown in aquaria.

Alsinastrum L. Plant robust, sts. to 1½ ft., hollow; lvs. in whorls of 4, sessile, linear to ovate; fls. greenish, sepals and petals 4, stamens 8. N. Afr., Eurasia.

hexandra (Lapierre) DC. Sts. prostrate to decumbent, to 4 in.; lvs. opp., spatulate, petiole shorter than blade; fls. pedicelled, sepals and petals 3, stamens 6. Norway, n. to Italy, Spain, and the Azores.

Hydropiper L. Slender ann.; lvs. opp., oblong-ovate, to ¾ in. long, petiole often longer than blade; fls. sessile, sepals and petals 4, stamens 8. N. Afr., Eurasia.

macropoda Guss. Ann., sts. to 4 in.; lvs. opp., oblong, to ¾ in. long, lower lvs. petioled, upper lvs. sessile, bright green; fls. pink, pedicelled, sepals and petals 4, stamens 8. Medit. region.

triandra Schkuhr. Ann., sts. decumbent, to 4 in.; lvs. opp., lanceolate

to ovate, to ⅜ in. long, short-petioled; fls. nearly sessile, rose, sepals and petals 3, stamens 3. Eurasia, S. Amer.

ELDERBERRY. The elderberry of culinary interest is the purplish-black fruit of the common American elder, *Sambucus canadensis,* native to the eastern half of the United States. Elderberries, often collected from the wild, are increasingly available from improved selections grown in the home or commercial garden. The fruit has a characteristic flavor not favored by all but is widely made into jelly (often mixed with grape or other tart fruit), pies (used alone or in combination with apples), and homemade wine. The common elder is a tall, stoloniferous shrub forming large clumps in favorable moist soil. Its flat clusters of white flowers make it a showy ornamental, and the abundant fruits that follow are of value not only for home consumption but for attracting birds to the garden. The fruit clusters are harvested entire, after which the berries are stripped for immediate culinary use, or they may be preserved for later use either by canning or by drying on trays in sun or oven.

The species is easy to grow and is attacked by few diseases or insects. Plants may be propagated by seeds but preferably by cuttings or division when select cultivars are to be increased. Several of the latter are recommended as being vigorous and productive, with both cluster and berry size much larger than in wild plants. Superior cultivars include 'Adams No. 2', 'Nova', and 'York'. Since the elder is not fruitful except when cross-pollinated, home plantings should consist of two or more different cultivars.

Sambucus caerulea, the arborescent blue elder of the Pacific Coast states, also produces an edible fruit, but it has not been improved horticulturally.

ELEIODOXA (Becc.) Burret. *Palmae.* One or a few spp. of dioecious, spiny, cespitose palms, with creeping sts., native in Malay Pen., Borneo, Sumatra, and the Bangka Is.; lvs. pinnate, pinnae 1-ribbed, acute; infl. terminal on st., nearly concealed among the lvs., bracts fibrous, brs. few, each br. with 2–4 or perhaps to 6 thick rachillae subtended by fibrous bracts; fls. in pairs of a female and a neuter, a bisexual and a neuter, or 2 male in axils of prominent bracts overlapping at margins, calyx 3-lobed, petals 3, valvate, stamens or staminodes 6, ovary 3-celled; fr. 1-seeded, covered with overlapping, appressed scales without a prolonged tip, seed discoid with very acid fleshy seed coat.

Occasionally cultivated in the tropics. For culture see *Palms.*

conferta (Griff.) Burret [*Salacca conferta* Griff.]. Lvs. few, erect, short or sometimes to 18 ft., petiole spiny, pinnae about 20 on each side, regularly arranged, green on both sides; infl. to about 1 ft. long; frs. crowded, to nearly 2 in. in diam. Malay Pen., Borneo.

ELEOCHARIS R. Br. SPIKE RUSH. *Cyperaceae.* About 160 spp. of cosmopolitan herbs, chiefly per. from creeping or matted rhizomes or cespitose ann., sts. (culms) simple, upright or ascending, cylindrical, 3- or 4-angled, or compressed; lvs. reduced to bladeless basal sheaths; spikelets terminal, solitary, erect, with few to many fls. in the axils of scales usually spirally imbricate; fls. bisexual, perianth of (3–)6–8 retrorsely barbed bristles, sometimes none, stamens 2–3, styles 2–3-cleft, style base bulbous and jointed, persisting in fr. as a tubercle on the apex of the lens-shaped or 3-angled achene.

acicularis (L.) Roem. & Schult. HAIR GRASS, LEAST S.R., SLENDER S.R. Per., rhizomes and stolons capillary, forming tufted mats, sts. capillary, 2–12 in. long (longer in deep water); spikelet flattened, rarely over ¼ in. long, 3–15-fld. Summer to autumn. Wet ground or under water, N. Amer., Eurasia. Used commonly in aquaria.

dulcis (Burm.f.) Trin. ex Henschel. CHINESE WATER CHESTNUT, MA-TAI. Per., densely tufted, stolons elongate, terminating in rounded tubers or corms about 1 in. long and 1½ in. in diam., sts. 1–3 ft., nearly cylindrical; sheaths red-brown; spikelet 1–2 in. long, about 50-fld., straw-colored, often lacking. Trop. e. Asia, Pacific Is., Madagascar, w. Afr. The tubers or corms are eaten fresh or cooked in e. Asia and are recognizable as the white, crunchy vegetable in Chinese foods. Prop. by offsets from tubers. Grown like rice in flooded fields, which are drained before harvest. Much cult. in China and occasionally as a specialty crop elsewhere, including the U.S. Zone 9.

ELETTARIA Maton. *Zingiberaceae.* Perhaps 6 spp. of per. herbs with stout rhizomes, native to India, Ceylon, Malay Pen., and Sumatra; sts. leafy, tall; lvs. 2-ranked, sheaths open opp. the blade; infl. on a separate, prostrate st. with scale lvs. subtending cincinni of several fls. with tubular bracts; calyx tubular, shortly 3-toothed, partly split on one side, corolla tube about as long as calyx, corolla lobes nearly equal, staminodial lip oblong-ovate, narrowed at base, emarginate at tip, sometimes hoodlike, lateral staminodes not petal-like, fertile stamen 1, filament shorter than anther, the connective crested, ovary inferior, 3-celled; fr. a thin-walled, smooth or ridged caps.

Plants succeed in moist, shady places in warm climates. Propagated by division of rhizomes and by seeds.

Cardamomum (L.) Maton [*Amomum Cardamomum* L.]. CARDAMOM, MALABAR C., CEYLON C. To 10 ft.; lvs. to 2½ ft. long and 3½ in. wide; infl. to 2 ft. long; lip white, striped pink; caps. to ¾ in. long, seeds aromatic. India. Cult. widely in se. Asia; the spicy seeds are used for culinary purposes, for medicine, and in India as a masticatory.

ELEUSINE Gaertn. GOOSE GRASS, YARD G. *Gramineae.* About 9 spp. of ann. or per. grasses, 8 native to Afr., 1 to S. Amer.; spikes 1 or mostly 2 to several, stout, digitate at the summit of the sts., sometimes with 1–2 a short distance below; spikelets few- to several-fld., flattened, awnless, sessile, closely imbricate, in 2 rows along one side of a rather wide rachis, rachilla disarticulating above the glumes and between the florets, glumes unequal, shorter than the first lemma, lemmas acute with 3–5 strong green nerves forming a keel; seed dark brown, roughened by fine ridges, loosely enclosed. For terminology see *Gramineae.*

coracana (L.) Gaertn. FINGER MILLET, AFRICAN M., RAGI, KORAKAN. Tufted ann., to 6 ft.; lvs. to 2 ft. long, ½ in. wide; spikes 4–7, to 3³⁄₁₆ in. long, ⅜ in. wide, at length curved inward. Similar to *E. indica,* but more robust. Old World tropics. An important food grain of India and Afr.; in N. Amer. sometimes grown at experiment stations.

indica (L.) Gaertn. WIREGRASS, GOOSE G. Tufted ann., to 3 ft., branching at base, ascending to prostrate, very smooth; lf. blades flat or folded, to 9 in. long and ¼ in. wide; spikes mostly 2–6, flat, to 6 in. long, ³⁄₁₆ in. wide, erect; spikelets about ³⁄₁₆ in. long. Old World tropics, now a pantrop. weed; introd. and naturalized from Mass. to S. Dak. and Kans., s. to Fla. and Tex., occasional elsewhere.

ELEUTHEROPETALUM: *CHAMAEDOREA.*

ELISENA: *HYMENOCALLIS.*

ELISMA: *LURONIUM.*

ELLIOTTIA Muhlenb. ex Elliott. *Ericaceae.* One sp., a deciduous shrub of sandy lands and pine woods, native to e. Ga. and s. S.C.; lvs. alt., simple; fls. white, many, in terminal racemes, calyx 4-lobed, petals 4, separate, stamens 8; ovary superior; fr. a caps.

racemosa Muhlenb. ex Elliott. To 20 ft.; lvs. elliptic to elliptic-oblanceolate, to 5 in. long, pointed, entire, glabrous above; fls. to ½ in. long. Zone 7?

ELMERA Rydb. *Saxifragaceae.* One sp., a low, pubescent, per. herb of the mts. of Wash.; lvs. mostly basal, reniform, long-petioled; fls. white, in terminal racemes on unbranched leafy sts., calyx tube cup-shaped, united to ovary only at base, petals 3–7-cleft, stamens 5, ovary with 2 short styles; fr. an ovoid caps., dehiscent along inner suture of styles, seeds many. Closely related to *Tellima,* but with petals less distinctly fringed and stamens 5; and to *Heuchera,* but with petals cleft and fl. sts. leafy.

racemosa (S. Wats.) Rydb. [*Heuchera racemosa* S. Wats.]. Sts. to 10 in.; fls. about 10–35, loosely arranged in racemes, calyx tube to ¼ in. long, yellowish-green, petals white, slightly longer than calyx lobes, not conspicuous; caps. to ³⁄₁₆ in. long.

ELODEA Michx. [*Anacharis* L. Rich.; *Egeria* Planch.; *Philotria* Raf.]. WATERWEED, WATER THYME, DITCH MOSS. *Hydrocharitaceae.* About 12 spp. of submersed aquatic herbs, native to the New World; lvs. whorled or opp., thin, 1-nerved; fls. unisexual or bisexual, 1–3 in axillary spathes, sepals and petals 3, stamens 3–9, filaments united into a short column, styles 3; fr. indehiscent, leathery, seeds few.

Grown in aquaria and ponds, and becoming weedy in some places. The flowers are water-pollinated, pollen floating onto the surface of the exposed stigmas. Propagated by cuttings and winter buds.

callitrichoides (L. Rich.) Casp. [*Anacharis callitrichoides* L. Rich.]. Sts. much-branched, to several ft. long; lvs. opp. or in whorls of 3, linear to ovate, to ¾ in. long, finely serrulate; fls. unisexual, female fls. solitary, the perianth tube elongating to 9 in. S. Uruguay, ne. Argentina.

canadensis Michx. [*Anacharis canadensis* (Michx.) Planch.]. WATERWEED. Dioecious, sts. to 3½ ft. long, rather fragile; lvs. mostly in whorls of 3, narrowly oblong-ovate, to ⅝ in. long, dark green, margin finely denticulate; male fls. not becoming detached, female fls. with perianth tube elongating to 11 in. Widespread in temp. N. Amer.; naturalized and noxious weed in much of Eur. Var. **gigantea:** *E. densa.*

densa (Planch.) Casp. [*E. canadensis* var. *gigantea* Hort. ex L. H. Bailey; *Anacharis densa* (Planch.) Vict.; *Egeria densa* Planch.]. BRAZILIAN W. Dioecious, sts. stout, several ft. long; lvs. crowded, in whorls of 4–5, linear-lanceolate, to 1½ in. long and ³⁄₁₆ in. wide; filaments club-shaped, female fls. with petals to ⁵⁄₁₆ in. long; fr. ⁵⁄₁₆ in. long. S. Amer.; naturalized in N. Amer.

Naias (Planch.) Casp. [*Egeria Naias* Planch.]. Sts. slender; upper lvs. in whorls of 4–8, linear, to 1 in. long and ¹⁄₁₆ in. wide, thin, sharply serrate; filaments strap-shaped, female fls. with petals to ¼ in. long. Brazil, Paraguay, Uruguay, n. Argentina.

Nuttallii (Planch.) St. John [*E. occidentalis* St. John; *Anacharis Nuttallii* Planch.]. Sts. slender, to 40 in. long; upper lvs. mostly in whorls of 3, linear-oblong, to ⅝ in. long and ¹⁄₁₆ in. wide, pale green, finely serrulate; male fls. becoming detached and floating, female fls. with perianth tube elongating to 3½ in. long; fr. ¼ in. long. Widespread in N. Amer.; naturalized in Eur.

occidentalis: *E. Nuttallii.*

ELSHOLTZIA Willd. *Labiatae.* About 30 spp. of ann. herbs or subshrubs of Eur., Asia, and Ethiopia, usually aromatic; sts. mostly square in cross section; lvs. opp., serrate, often glandular-punctate, petioles short; fls. in 2-fld. verticillasters arranged in crowded spikes, calyx campanulate, 5-nerved, 5-toothed, corolla 2-lipped, upper lip hooded, lower lip 3-lobed, stamens 4, usually slightly exserted; fr. of 4 nutlets. Distinguished by the nearly rotate calyx and corolla.

Propagated by seeds, or the woody species from softwood cuttings. Attractive late-blooming plants.

ciliata (Thunb.) Hyl. [*E. cristata* Willd.; *E. Patrinii* (Lepech.) Garcke]. Ann., to 2 ft.; lvs. elliptic-ovate, to 3½ in. long, 1 in. wide, dentate; spikes narrow, to 4 in. long, bracts round to reniform, ciliate; calyx urceolate, to ⅛ in. long, villous at throat, teeth lanceolate-acuminate, corolla tubular, slightly 2-lipped, ¼ in. long, purple. Late summer. Cent. and e. Asia; naturalized in Eur. and e. U.S.

cristata: *E. ciliata.*

Patrinii: *E. ciliata.*

Stauntonii Benth. MINT SHRUB. Subshrub, 3–5 ft.; lvs. ovate-elliptic, to 5 in. long, 1½ in. wide, acuminate, dentate; spikes narrow, bracts small, inconspicuous, linear; calyx white-pubescent, teeth deltoid-apiculate, corolla tubular, 2-lipped, purplish. Autumn. N. China.

ELYMUS L. WILD RYE, LYME GRASS. *Gramineae.* About 50 spp. of erect, ann. or per. grasses in the temp. N. Hemisphere; lf. blades flat or rarely convolute; spikes slender or bristly; spikelets usually crowded, 2–6-fld., usually paired or more rarely in 3's or 4's at each node of a continuous rachis, or placed flatwise at each joint, rachilla disarticulating above the glumes, glumes equal, somewhat asymmetrical, usually rigid, narrow to subulate, 1- to several-nerved, acute to aristate, lemma convex, obscurely 5-nerved, acute or usually awned from the tip. For terminology see *Gramineae.*

angustus Trin. ALTAI W.R. Sts. to 40 in., clustered, rhizomes present; lf. blades flat, about ¼ in. wide, inrolled, scabrous above; spike to 10 in. long; spikelets paired, 2–3-fld., glumes to ¾ in. long, lanceolate, lemmas to more than ½ in. long, 5–7-nerved, awn pointed, lower palea with obsolete nerves. Russia; introd., aggressive.

aralensis Regel. ARAL W.R. Distinguished from *E. arenarius* by shorter rhizomes, more erect lvs., poorer seed habit. Russia; introd. for sand dune control.

arenarius L. EUROPEAN DUNE GRASS, RANCHERIA G., LYME G., SEA L.G. Sts. to 4 ft., glaucous, with long rhizomes; lf. blades to ½ in. wide, flat, or involute during drought, the ligule very short, truncate; spike compact, to 16 in. long; spikelets sessile, paired or in 3's, 4-fld., with 3 bisexual florets and a rudimentary one, glumes lanceolate, awnless, ciliate on the keel, lemma long-ovate, acute, 7-nerved, short-pubescent, awnless. Eurasia.

canadensis L. CANADA W.R. Sts. to 5 ft., green or often glaucous, erect, clustered; lf. blades flat, hard, scabrous or sparsely hispid on the upper surface, mostly ⅜–¾ in. wide; spike dense, stiff, bristly, erect or rarely nodding or drooping, to 10 in. long; spikelets 2–5-fld., slightly spreading, glumes narrow, mostly 2–4-nerved, scabrous, the awn about as long as the body, lemma villous to glabrous, strongly nerved above, awn divergently curved when dry, to 1¼ in. long. Que. to s. Alaska, s. to N.C. and n. Calif.

chinensis (Trin.) Keng [*Agropyron pseudoagropyron* (Griseb.) Franch.]. CHINESE W.R., FALSE WHEATGRASS. Sts. coarse, to 1½ ft., rhizome to 12 ft. long; spike to 7¼ in. long, rachilla joint smooth; lemma acuminate or awned, the callus glabrous. China. Used in wind-eroded areas.

condensatus J. Presl & K. Presl. GIANT W.R. Sts. usually to 10 ft., robust, in large clumps, with short thick rhizomes; lf. blades firm, strongly nerved, flat, to 1¼ in. wide; spike erect, dense, to 20 in. long, usually more or less compound, with erect brs. to 2¾ in. long; spikelets often in 3's or 5's, commonly distorted by pressure, glumes subulate, awn-pointed, lemma awnless or only mucronate, glabrous to sparsely strigose, with a thin margin. Calif.

giganteus: *E. racemosus.*

glaucus Buckl. BLUE W.R. Sts. to 4 ft., clustered, erect, often bent at base, without rhizome; lf. blades flat, usually lax, to ⅝ in. wide, usually scabrous on both surfaces, sometimes narrow and nearly involute; spike slender, usually dense, to 8 in. long; spikelets 3–6-fld., appressed, glumes lanceolate at base, to ⅝ in. long, 3–5-nerved, acuminate or awn-pointed, lemma awned, awn 1–2 times as long as the body, erect to spreading. Ont. to s. Alaska, s. to Calif. and Ark.

junceus Fisch. RUSSIAN W.R. Sts. to about 2½ ft., erect, clustered, leafy, without rhizomes; lf. blades glaucous, short, linear, involute; spike narrow; spikelets 2–3-fld., in 2's or 3's, the internodes long, lower glume linear, setaceous, faintly 1-nerved, lemma twice as long as the glume, oblong-lanceolate, acute to acuminate, 5-nerved, pubescent. Eurasia.

racemosus Lam. [*E. giganteus* Vahl]. VOLGA W.R. Sts. robust, to 3 ft. or more, with stout rhizomes; lf. blades many at base, elongate, scabrous above; spike dense, 6–8 in. long, about ¾ in. thick; glumes and lemma sharp-pointed, glumes glabrous, lemma awnless, pointed, pubescent below. Siberia. Occasionally cult. for ornament, or for stabilizing sand dunes.

sibiricus L. SIBERIAN W.R. Sts. to about 2½ ft., forming clumps; spike loose, nodding, drooping or flexuous, to 10 in. long; spikelets sessile, usually paired, glumes linear-lanceolate to linear, tipped with an awn usually as long as or longer than the body, lemma usually scabrous, tapering into a more or less bent awn, usually ½–⅞ in. long. Russia to Japan. Cult. for forage in the n. Great Plains and intermountain region.

virginicus L. VIRGINIA W.R. Sts. to 4 ft., clustered, erect; lf. sheaths glabrous, blades flat, scabrous, mostly ¼–⅝ in. long; spike usually erect, often partly included, to 6 in. long; spikelets 2–4-fld., glumes to about 1½ in. long, indurate, yellowish at base, green above, hirsute to glabrous, the apex somewhat curved, tapering into a straight awn about as long as the body or shorter, lemma glabrous and nerveless below, scabrous and nerved above, tapering into a straight awn usually ⅜ in. long. Nfld. to Alta., s. to Fla. and Ariz.

EMBOTHRIUM J. R. Forst. & G. Forst. *Proteaceae.* Eight spp. of evergreen trees of the central and southern Andes; lvs. alt., entire, leathery; fls. bisexual, showy, in racemes; fr. a follicle, seeds many, winged.

coccineum J. R. Forst. & G. Forst. CHILEAN FIRE TREE, CHILEAN FIREBRUSH. Small tree, or to 40–50 ft.; lvs. ovate-lanceolate, to 2 in. long; fls. scarlet, to 2 in. long, style much exserted. Chile and Argentina. Zone 9 on Pacific Coast.

Wickhamii var. **pinnata**: *Orecallis pinnata.*

EMILIA Cass. *Compositae* (Senecio Tribe). About 20 spp. of slender ann. and per. herbs, mostly in tropics of Old World, occasionally in New World tropics; lvs. alt.; fl. heads discoid, rather small, solitary or clustered, involucre cylindrical or cup-shaped, involucral bracts in 1 row; fls. all tubular; achenes with 5 acute, ciliate angles, pappus of soft, white bristles.

coccinea: *E. javanica.*

flammea: *E. javanica.*

javanica (Burm.f.) C. B. Robinson [*E. coccinea* (Sims) G. Don; *E. flammea* Cass.; *E. sagittata* (Vahl) DC.; *Cacalia coccinea* Sims; *C. sagittata* Vahl]. TASSEL FLOWER, FLORA'S-PAINTBRUSH. Erect ann., to 2 ft. or more, glabrous or sparsely hairy; lvs. elliptic, ovate, or ovate-lanceolate, the lower ones narrowly wing-petioled, the upper with broad sagittate-clasping base; heads ½ in. across, in loose corymbs; fls. red or yellow. Tropics of both hemispheres; naturalized in s. Fla. The usual sp. in gardens. Cv. 'Lutea' [*Cacalia aurea* Hort.]. A name used to distinguish the yellow-fld. form.

sagittata: *E. javanica.*

sonchifolia (L.) DC. [*Cacalia sonchifolia* L.]. Ann., to 2 ft.; lower lvs. obovate, toothed or lyrate-pinnatifid; heads ½ in. across, in loose corymbs; fls. rose or purple, rarely white. Old World tropics; naturalized in s. Fla.

EMMENANTHE Benth. *Hydrophyllaceae.* One sp., an erect, glandular-viscid, ann. herb, native to w. N. Amer.; lvs. alt.; fls. pale yellow or light pink, many, in branched, loose, scorpioid cymes, calyx 5-parted, corolla campanulate, 5-lobed, persistent, stamens 5, style shortly 2-cleft; fr. a caps.

Seeds may be sown in open sunny exposure where the plants are to grow, or indoors if early bloom is desired.

penduliflora Benth. YELLOWBELLS, GOLDEN-BELLS, WHISPERING-BELLS. Sts. simple or much-branched, to 1½ ft., but often only a few in.; lvs. sessile or nearly so, oblong, pinnatifid, to 3 in. long; fls. drooping, about ½ in. long, on pedicels ½ in. long. Summer. Cent. Calif. to Baja Calif., e. to s. Utah and Ariz.

EMMENOPTERYS D. Oliver. *Rubiaceae.* Two spp. of deciduous trees, native to e. Asia; lvs. opp., leathery, stipules falling early; fls. in terminal corymbs, white or yellow, 5-merous, calyx with one lobe enlarged into a persistent leaflike limb, corolla funnelform; fr. a woody caps., seeds many, winged.

One species cultivated in mild regions; propagated by seeds and cuttings of soft wood under glass.

Henryi D. Oliver. To 75 ft.; lvs. elliptic, to 6 in. long; fls. about 1 in. long; fr. on a stalk nearly 2 in. long, ellipsoid, to 1¾ in. long, persistent calyx lobe to 2 in. long and half as broad. Cent. and s. China.

EMMENOSPERMA F. J. Muell. *Rhamnaceae.* Three spp. of trees and shrubs in Australia and New Caledonia; lvs. alt. or opp., mostly entire; fls. small, in short axillary panicles, calyx tube cup-shaped, petals shorter than calyx lobes; fr. a caps. Related to *Alphitonia* but having fr. dehiscent.

Pancheranum Baill. Much-branched shrub, to 6 ft.; lvs. obovate or obovate-elliptic, to 1¼ in. long, rounded or retuse at apex, leathery, glabrous; panicles shorter than lvs. New Caledonia.

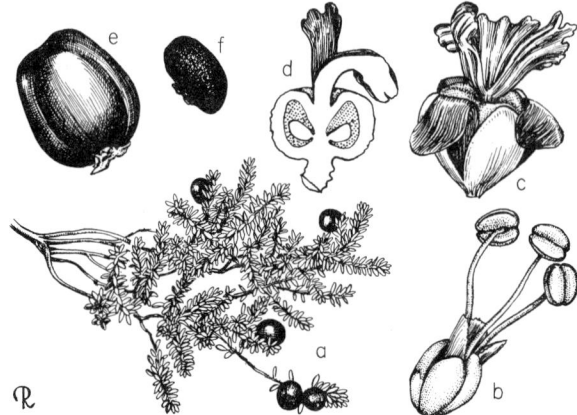

EMPETRACEAE. *Empetrum nigrum:* **a,** plant in fruit, × ½; **b,** male flower, × 4; **c,** female flower, × 8; **d,** pistil, vertical section, × 8; **e,** fruit, × 2; **f,** seed, × 6. (b-d from Bailey, *Manual of Cultivated Plants,* ed. 2.)

EMPETRACEAE S. F. Gray. CROWBERRY FAMILY. Dicot.; 3 genera and 6 or 7 spp. of monoecious, dioecious, or polygamous, small, heathlike, evergreen shrubs, native to arctic and temp. regions of N. Amer., Eurasia, and S. Amer.; lvs. small, simple, alt. to whorled, crowded, revolute; fls. axillary or in bracted heads, sepals 2–4, petals 0, stamens 2–4, ovary superior, 2–9-celled, style 1; fr. drupaceous. *Ceratiola, Corema,* and *Empetrum* are sometimes grown as ornamentals.

EMPETRUM L. CROWBERRY. *Empetraceae.* Three or 4 spp. of procumbent or low, evergreen shrublets, native to n. Eurasia, n. N. Amer., and s. S. Amer.; lvs. narrow, whorled; fls. axillary, unisexual or bisexual, small, greenish or purplish, sepals 3, petals 0, stamens 3, ovary 6–9-celled; fr. a berrylike drupe.

Eamesii Fern. & Wieg. ROCKBERRY. Prostrate, branchlets white-tomentose; lvs. elliptic-oblong to oblong-linear, to 3/16 in. long, ascending; fls. bisexual, or both bisexual and female fls. on same plant; fr. glossy, pink or red, to 3/16 in. in diam. Nfld. and adjacent mainland. Subsp. **hermaphroditum** (Hagerup) D. Löve [*E. hermaphroditum* Hagerup]. Branchlets glabrous but sometimes with brown fuzz; fr. black. N. N. Amer., n. Eurasia.

hermaphroditum: *E. Eamesii* subsp.

nigrum L. BLACK C., CRAKEBERRY, CURLEW BERRY, MONOX. Spreading, branchlets glandular when young; lvs. oblong to oblong-linear, to 3/8 in. long; fls. unisexual; fr. black, edible. N. N. Amer., s. to New Eng., Minn., and n. Calif.; Eurasia. Var. **purpureum** (Raf.) DC. A name of doubtful application; material offered under this name is probably a variant of *E. Eamesii* subsp. *hermaphroditum.*

ENALLAGMA Baill. *Bignoniaceae.* About 3 spp. of small trees or shrubs, native to trop. Amer.; lvs. alt., simple, entire; fls. mostly large, axillary or terminal, on young wood, usually solitary or in clusters of 2 or 3, calyx 2-parted, corolla tubular-campanulate, stamens 4; fr. hard-shelled, gourdlike.

Fruits used for utensils.

latifolia (Mill.) Small [*Crescentia latifolia* Mill.; *C. ovata* Burm.f.]. BLACK CALABASH. To 50 ft.; lvs. elliptic or obovate, to 8 in. long; fls. greenish or somewhat purplish, to 2 3/8 in. long; fr. to 3 in. across. S. Fla., W. Indies, s. Mex. to Venezuela.

ENCELIA Adans. *Compositae* (Helianthus Tribe). About 14 spp. of low, branching shrubs or per. herbs, native to sw. U.S. and Mex., also Chile, Peru, and Galapagos Is.; lvs. alt., entire or toothed; fl. heads medium-sized, radiate or discoid; disc fls. yellow or purple, ray fls. yellow; achenes flat, notched at apex, with ciliate white margin, pappus of 1–2 weak awns.

Actonii: *E. virginensis* var.

californica Nutt. Per., woody at base, to 5 ft. or more; lvs ovate to broad-lanceolate, to 2½ in. long, green; heads solitary, to 2½ in. across, long-peduncled, involucre white-hairy; disc fls. purple, ray fls. golden-yellow. Coastal, s. Calif. and nw. Baja Calif.

calva: *Simsia calva.*

farinosa A. Gray. BRITTLEBUSH, INCIENSO. Rounded shrub, to 4–5 ft.; lvs. ovate, to 2½ in. long, silvery-tomentose; heads about 1 in. across, in cymes, involucre slightly pubescent; disc fls. and ray fls. yellow. S. Calif., sw. Utah, Ariz., n. Mex. The clumps are conspicuous in early spring on deserts; the fragrant resin exuded by the sts. was used as incense by the Spanish padres.

frutescens (A. Gray) A. Gray. Rounded shrub, 4–5 ft.; lvs. ovate, to ¾ in. long, scabrous, green; heads 1 in. across, solitary on long peduncles; fls. yellow, ray fls. usually absent. Deserts, s. Calif., Ariz. Var. **Actonii:** *E. virginensis* var. Var. **virginensis:** *E. virginensis.*

scaposa A. Gray. Herbaceous per., to 14 in.; lvs. in basal tufts, linear, to 3 in. long; heads 1½ in. across, on long scapes. New Mex.

virginensis A. Nels. [*E. frutescens* var. *virginensis* (A. Nels.) S. F. Blake]. Differs from *E. frutescens* in its slightly larger, gray-green, appressed-pubescent lvs. and heads with ray fls. ½ in. long. Sw. Utah to s. Calif. and Ariz. Var. **Actonii** (Elmer) Keck [*E. Actonii* Elmer; *E. frutescens* var. *Actonii* (Elmer) S. F. Blake]. Lvs. larger, to 1½ in. long, white-puberulent; heads larger; ray fls. to 1 in. long. S. Calif., Nev.

ENCELIOPSIS (A. Gray) A. Nels. SUNRAY. *Compositae* (Helianthus Tribe). Four spp. of scapose, per. herbs, in dry areas of w. U.S.; lvs. in basal rosettes, petioled, rhombic to oblanceolate, entire, gray-pubescent; fl. heads discoid or radiate, long-peduncled; fls. yellow; achenes flat, black with white margin, pappus of a short crown and 2 awns.

argophylla (D. C. Eat.) A. Nels. To 2½ ft., often with many scapes; lf. blades orbicular to rhombic, cuneate to a shorter, broadly winged petiole; heads large; ray fls. many, ¾ in. long; achenes silky-villous. S. Utah, Nev., nw. Ariz. Var. **grandiflora:** *E. Covillei.*

Covillei (A. Nels.) S. F. Blake [*E. argophylla* var. *grandiflora* (A. Nels.) Jeps.; *E. grandiflora* A. Nels.]. PANAMINT DAISY, PANAMINT S. Differs from *E. argophylla* in its larger heads to 5 in. across, with ray fls. to 2 in. long, and puberulent or glabrate achenes. Panamint Mts. (s. Calif.).

grandiflora: *E. Covillei.*

nudicaulis (A. Gray) A. Nels. Less robust, to 18 in.; lf. blades orbicular to oblanceolate, usually longer than the slender petiole; heads 2½–3 in. across; ray fls. about 1 in. long; achenes silky-villous. Idaho to s. Calif.

ENCEPHALARTOS Lehm. *Zamiaceae.* About 20 spp. of dioecious palmlike plants, tuberous or with stout trunks, native to Afr.; lvs. stiff, pinnate, borne in a crown; sporophylls (cone scales) in a cone, female cones with scales thickened, truncate, and recurved at the ends.

A few species are grown under glass or outdoors in Zone 10, for the ornamental foliage. Seeds produced are often not viable. For culture see *Cycads.*

Altensteinii Lehm. [*Zamia Altensteinii* (Lehm.) Heynh.]. PRICKLY CYCAD, BREAD TREE. Trunks branched or unbranched, to 12 ft. or more and then often reclining; lvs. 1½–9 ft. long, straight or recurved, pinnae oblong, 4–6 in. long, rigid, margins with few teeth or entire; cones mostly in clusters of 2–5, yellowish-green, the male more or less cylindrical, to 20 in. long, the female broadly ovoid, to 22 in. long. S. Afr. Trunk is a source of starchy sago.

Barteri Carruth. ex Miq. Trunk to 50 ft. high, 10 in. in diam.; lvs. 3–5 ft. long, pinnae linear-lanceolate, to 7 in. long, apex spinescent, margins entire or with few spiny teeth, lower pinnae reduced to spines; male cones more or less cylindrical, 3–9 in. long, female cones more ellipsoid, 4–12 in. long. Cent. Afr.

brachyphyllus: *E. caffer.*

caffer (Thunb.) Lehm. [*E. brachyphyllus* Lehm.]. Sts. underground; lvs. to 3 ft. long, pinnae linear-lanceolate, to 4 in. long, in different planes, mostly entire, lower pinnae reduced to spines; male cones oblong-cylindrical, to 10 in. long, female cones broadly oblong-lanceolate, 8–12 in. long. S. Afr.

cycadifolius (Jacq.) Lehm. Trunk usually branched from the base, to 4 ft.; lvs. to 2½ ft. long, sometimes twisted, grayish or slightly silvery, pinnae ovate, to 5 in. long, margin entire, thickened, recurved; cones 1 or 2 together, whitish, woolly, the male cylindrical, to 8 in. long, the female broadly ovoid, to 12 in. long. S. Afr.

ferox Bertol. Trunk mostly unbranched, 3–6 ft.; lvs. 3–6 ft. long, straight, pinnae oblong-ovate, to 6 in. long, with 2–4 teeth on both margins, apex spiny, lower pinnae reduced to spines; cones 1–3 together, the male subcylindrical, to 16 in. long, the female ovoid, 10–20 in. long, salmon-pink or bright red in color. S. Afr.

gratus Prain. Trunk globose or more elongate, to 4 ft.; lvs. 3–6 ft. long, pinnae 60–140, lanceolate, 6–10 in. long, rigid, leathery, margins usually with few spiny teeth, lower pinnae grading into spines; male cones cylindrical to narrowly ovoid, 4–16 in. long, female cones cylindrical to subconical, 20–25 in. long. Nyasaland.

Hildebrandtii A. Braun & Bouché. Trunk to 20 ft. high and 1 ft. in diam.; lvs. 6–9 ft. long, pinnae linear-lanceolate, 6–15 in. long, leathery, woolly, becoming glabrous, margins with 1–4 teeth on each side, apex spiny; male cones cylindrical or conical, to 20 in. long, female cones similar but larger. Trop. Afr.

horridus (Jacq.) Lehm. Sts. underground or to about 1 ft. high, rarely more; lvs. to 2 ft. long, glaucous, pinnae to 4 in. long, curled, deeply cut along the lower margin into 1–3 spine-tipped lobes, lower pinnae reduced to spines; male cones cylindrical, to 3½ in. long, female cones oblong-ellipsoid, to 16 in. long. S. Afr.

Laurentianus De Wild. Trunk to 30 ft. high and 2½ ft. in diam.; lvs. to more than 20 ft. long, pinnae 12–20 in. long, leathery, margins with 6–10 teeth on each side, apex spiny; male cones clustered, ellipsoid, 6–14 in. long, female cones somewhat broader, to 16 in. long. W. Afr.

lebomboensis Verd. Smaller than *E. Altensteinii,* trunk to about 12 ft. high, 1 ft. in diam.; lvs. to 6 ft. long, pinnae to 7 in. long, 3/8–7/8 in. wide, reduced to prickles toward base of lf.; cones apricot-yellow, to about 18 in. long. S. Afr.

Lehmannii Lehm. Unbranched or more commonly branched from the base, 3–6 ft.; lvs. to 5 ft. long, stiff, straight or sometimes recurved, with a persistent, bluish or silvery bloom, pinnae in V-shaped ranks, linear, 5–8 in. long, entire or with 1–2 small teeth on lower margin; cones solitary, the male subcylindrical, 10–14 in. long, the female ovoid, to 16 in. long. S. Afr.

longifolius (Jacq.) Lehm. Trunk branched or unbranched, to 9 ft.; lvs. blue-green, to 5 ft. long, pinnae in V-shaped ranks, broadly to narrowly ovate to linear, to 8 in. long, entire or with few teeth, apex sometimes abruptly hooked; male cones cylindrical, to 20 in. long, female cones ellipsoid, to 24 in. long. S. Afr.

transvenosus Stapf & Davy. MODJADJI CYCAD. Trunk branched or unbranched, to 30 ft. or more, with brown woolly hairs at the crown; lvs. 3–8 ft. long, straight, pinnae spreading, more or less recurved, ovate, 4–8 in. long, toothed on both margins, lower pinnae reduced to spines; cones 2–4 together, the male subcylindrical, 12–16 in. long, the female ellipsoid, 20–30 in. long. Transvaal.

villosus (Gaertn.) Lem. [*Zamia villosa* Gaertn.]. Trunk entirely underground, woolly; lvs. 4–7 ft. long, glossy green, pinnae linear, to 10 in. long, teeth and apex spiny; cones solitary or clustered, subcylindrical, the male to 24 in. long, the female to 16 in. long. S. Afr.

ENCEPHALOCARPUS: *PELECYPHORA.*

ENCYCLIA: *EPIDENDRUM.* Encyclia macrochila: *Epidendrum atropurpureum.* Encyclia osmantha: *Epidendrum advenum.* Encyclia virens: *Epidendrum diurnum.*

ENDIVE. *Cichorium Endiva,* or endive, is a hardy annual or biennial grown for its rosette of leaves, which are used as salad and for greens. It is grown mostly as a late summer, autumn, and early winter product, more or less extending the season of lettuce.

Seedings should be started so that the plants will mature after the hot weather is past. The plants need protection from severe frosts and so should be carefully lifted and removed to a frame, where sash or cloth may cover them in freezing weather. The leaves, which constitute practically the whole plant, are blanched before being used; this is done either by tying them together or by standing boards on each side of the row, allowing the top of the boards to meet over the center of the row; in two to four weeks the interior leaves will be sufficiently blanched. If the foliage keeps wet inside, it is likely to decay; the leaves should be tied together only when dry, and it may be necessary to untie and open them after a rain. A similar precaution is necessary in other methods of blanching. The rows should be 1½ or 2 feet apart, the plants 1 foot apart in the rows.

ENDYMION Dumort. WOOD HYACINTH. *Liliaceae.* Three or four spp. of bulbous, scapose, per. herbs, native to w. Eur. and nw. Afr.; bulbs tunicate, renewed yearly, scales tubular; lvs. 6–9, all basal; fls. campanulate to rotate, blue, pink, or white, subtended by 2 bracts, in a raceme, perianth segms. 6, united at base, anthers 6, arising from perianth segms., versatile; fr. a 3-valved, loculicidal caps., seeds black, shining.

Culture as for *Scilla.*

hispanicus (Mill.) Chouard [*Scilla campanulata* Ait.; *S. hispanica* Mill.]. SPANISH BLUEBELL, SPANISH JACINTH, BELL-FLOWERED SQUILL. To about 20 in.; lvs. 5–9, strap-shaped, to 2 ft. long or more and 1½ in. wide or more; fls. campanulate, blue to rose-purple, to ¾ in. across, in an erect, cylindrical, 10–30-fld. raceme, anthers blue. Portugal, Spain, adjacent nw. Afr. Cvs. 'Alba', 'Alba Maxima', and 'Alba Major', are white-fld.; cvs. 'Caerulea' and 'Excelsior' are blue-fld.; cv. 'Rosea' is pink-fld.

italicus (L.) Chouard [*Scilla italica* L.]. ITALIAN SQUILL. To about 1 ft.; lvs. 4–6, strap-shaped, to 8 in. long and ½ in. wide, strongly keeled; fls. rotate, fragrant, lilac-blue, to ¼ in. long, hairy at tips, in a dense, conical, 6–30-fld. raceme, anthers dark blue. Italy and s. France.

non-scriptus (L.) Garcke [*Scilla non-scripta* (L.) Hoffmanns. & Link; *S. nutans* Sm.]. ENGLISH BLUEBELL, HAREBELL. To about 1½ ft.; lvs. linear, to 1½ ft. long and ½ in. wide; fls. campanulate, violet-blue, to ½ in. across, in a stout, 4–16-fld., 1-sided raceme drooping at tip, anthers cream-colored. W. Eur. Cvs. include: 'Alba', fls. white; 'Caerulea', fls. blue; 'Rosea', fls. pink.

ENGELHARDTIA Lesch. ex Blume. *Juglandaceae.* About 10 spp. of large, deciduous, monoecious trees with solid pith, native to trop. and subtrop. regions of se. Asia, Mex., and Cent. Amer.; lvs. usually alt., evenly pinnate, lfts. 6–14, opp. or nearly so; male fls. in long catkins, female fls. in bracted, pendulous spikes; fr. a small, globose, leathery, 1-seeded nut, winged through fusion to the enlarged, scarious, 3-lobed bract.

chrysolepis Hance. To 60 ft.; lfts. oblanceolate, to 1¼ in. long and ½ in. wide, entire, somewhat leathery. Sw. China.

sinensis: a listed name of no botanical standing.

spicata Blume. To 50 ft.; lfts. oblanceolate, to 4 in. long and 1¼ in. wide, undulate, more or less membranous. E. Himalayas, s. to Malay Arch.

ENGELMANNIA Torr. & A. Gray. *Compositae* (Helianthus Tribe). One sp., a hirsute, per. herb, in N. Amer.; lvs. alt., deeply pinnatifid; fl. heads radiate, receptacle scaly; disc fls. sterile, ray fls. fertile; each ray achene basally fused to its subtending involucral bract and adjacent receptacular scales, falling away with them.

pinnatifida Torr. & A. Gray. ENGELMANN DAISY. To 3 ft.; lvs. to 6 in. long; heads 1 in. across; fls. yellow, corymbose. Dry soils, Kans. to Colo., s. to La. and n. Mex.

ENKIANTHUS Lour. *Ericaceae.* About 10 spp. of deciduous shrubs of China, Japan, and the Himalayas; lvs. alt., simple, crowded toward ends of brs., brightly colored in autumn; fls. in drooping, terminal racemes or umbels, calyx 5-lobed, corolla campanulate or urceolate, stamens 10, anthers awned, ovary superior; fr. a 5-valved caps.

The plants thrive in well-drained, peaty soil, like many other members of the heath family, and are fairly hardy north. Propagated by seeds, cuttings, or layers.

campanulatus (Miq.) Nichols. To 30 ft.; lvs. elliptic to obovate, to 3 in. long, serrate; fls. in racemes, yellow to pale orange, with dark red veins, corolla campanulate, to ½ in. long, ovary glabrous. Japan. Zone 5. Cv. 'Albiflorus'. Fls. white. Var. **longilobus** (Nakai) Mak. [*E. longilobus* (Nakai) Ohwi]. Corolla lobes longer. Var. **Palibinii** (Craib) Bean. Lvs. rusty-hairy beneath; fls. red.

cernuus (Siebold & Zucc.) Mak. To 15 ft.; lvs. elliptic to obovate or oblong-obovate, to 2 in. long, serrate; fls. in racemes, white, corolla campanulate, with irregularly cut limb, to 5⁄16 in. long, ovary glabrous. Late spring. Japan. Zone 6. Var. **rubens** (Maxim.) Mak. [*E. Matsudai* Komatsu]. Fls. deep red.

chinensis Franch. [*E. sinohimalaicus* Craib]. To 12 ft., young sts. red-brown; lvs. elliptic to elliptic-oblong, to 3⅜ in. long, glabrous, margins wavy-toothed; fls. in glabrous racemes, salmon-red, corolla campanulate, filaments and ovary pubescent. W. China.

deflexus (Griff.) C. K. Schneid. [*E. himalaicus* Hook.f. & T. Thoms.]. Shrub or small tree, to 30 ft.; branchlets bright red; lvs. elliptic-obovate to oblong-lanceolate, to 3 in. long; fls. in racemes, yellowish-red, corolla broadly campanulate, to ⅝ in. long, ovary and style pubescent. W. China. Zone 7?

himalaicus: *E. deflexus.*

japonicus: *E. perulatus.*

longilobus: *E. campanulatus* var.

Matsudai: *E. cernuus* var. *rubens.*

perulatus (Miq.) C. K. Schneid. [*E. japonicus* Hook.f.]. To 6 ft.; lvs. obovate to elliptic-ovate, to 2 in. long, serrulate; fls. appearing before the lvs., in drooping umbels, corolla urceolate, 5⁄16 in. long, gibbous at base. Late spring. Japan. Zone 5.

sinohimalaicus: *E. chinensis.*

subsessilis (Miq.) Mak. To 10 ft.; lvs. elliptic to rhombic-obovate, to 2 in. long, serrulate; fls. appearing after the lvs., in racemes, white, corolla urceolate, 3⁄16 in. long, gibbous at base. Late spring. Japan. Zone 6.

Tobira: a listed name of no botanical standing.

ENSETE Horan. *Musaceae.* About 7 spp. of mostly large herbs in trop. Afr. and Asia, flowering once and dying; pseudostem solitary, dilated at base when developed; lvs. spirally arranged, bananalike; infl. terminal, pendulous, with usually persistent bracts; fls. many, in 2 rows in each bract, those of lower bracts bisexual or female, those of upper bracts male; fr. leathery, dry, or with scant pulp, containing a few rather large, globose or irregular, mostly smooth seeds with T-shaped embryo.

For culture see *Musa* and *Banana.*

Gilletii (De Wild.) E. E. Cheesm. [*Musa religiosa* Dyb.]. Smaller than *E. ventricosum* and cannalike, with lvs. along st.; seeds 5⁄16–⅜ in. across. Afr.

superbum (Roxb.) E. E. Cheesm. [*Musa superba* Roxb.]. To 12 ft., pseudostem to 8 ft. in circumference at base; lvs. bright green, to 5 ft. long, 1½ ft. wide; bracts orbicular, dull claret-brown, to 1 ft. long; fr. 3 in. long, seeds brown, to ½ in. broad. India.

ventricosum (Welw.) E. E. Cheesm. [*Musa Arnoldiana* De Wild.; *M. Ensete* J. F. Gmel.]. ABYSSINIAN BANANA. To nearly 40 ft., pseudostem often stained purple or purplish-brown; lvs. in a distinct crown, to 16 ft. long, 4½ ft. wide, green or glaucous; bracts red, purple, or green; fr. to 6 in. long, seeds black, ½–1 in. broad. Ethiopia, where the cooked fl. heads and seeds are commonly eaten. Zone 10.

ENTADA Adans. *Leguminosae* (subfamily *Mimosoideae*). About 30 spp. of unarmed, woody vines or small trees of trop. Amer. and Afr.; lvs. alt., 2-pinnate; fls. in spikes, 5-merous, stamens 10, separate; fr. an elongate legume, often huge, jointed between seeds, the segms. falling away separately leaving thick margins.

abyssinica Steud. ex A. Rich. Deciduous, small tree, to 30 ft.; pinnae to 16 pairs, lfts. many, small, linear; fls. yellowish-white, in clustered racemes to 5 in. long; fr. oblong, to 15 in. long, embossed over the seeds, margins scalloped. Trop. Afr.

gigas (L.) Fawc. & Rendle [*E. scandens* (L.) Benth.]. SWORD BEAN, NICKER B. Climbing, to 100 ft. or more; lvs. with terminal pinnae reduced to tendrils, and 2 pairs of pinnae, lfts. in 4–5 pairs, oblong-elliptic, to 3 in. long, obtuse or emarginate; spikes dense, lateral, almost as long as lvs.; fr. 3–6 ft. long, 4 in. broad or more. Pantrop. Provides food, fiber, and saponin.

scandens: *E. gigas.*

ENTANDROPHRAGMA C. DC. *Meliaceae.* About 10 spp. of trees, native to trop. and subtrop. Afr.; lvs. alt., pinnate; fls. greenish-yellow or whitish, in axillary panicles, calyx 5-toothed, petals 5, separate, stamens 10–12, filaments united in an urceolate or funnelform tube, disc stalklike, ovary 5-celled; fr. a woody caps., separating basally or apically into 5 valves.

Delevoyi DeWild. Over 100 ft.; lfts. 8–14, ovate- or lanceolate-oblong, asymmetrical at base, glabrous, on slender petiolules to 1⅜ in. long; fr. to 6 in. long, dehiscing from base. Cent. Afr.

caudatum (T. Sprague) T. Sprague. To 30 ft.; lfts. 8–12, ovate, to about 5 in. long, asymmetrical at base; fr. to 7½ in. long, pendulous, dehiscing from apex downward. S. Afr. Zone 10.

ENTELEA R. Br. *Tiliaceae.* One sp., a shrub or small tree, endemic to New Zeal.; lvs. cordate-ovate, acuminate, not lobed or shallowly palmately lobed, doubly toothed; fls. 4-merous, in subumbellate cymes, sepals separate, stamens many, fertile, style simple, stigma fringed or toothed; fr. a caps., globose, 4–7-celled, long-bristly, many-seeded.

arborescens R. Br. To 18 ft., young growth white-pubescent; lvs. 3–10 in. long or longer; fls. white, to 1 in. across; caps about ¾ in. in diam. Suitable for cult. in s. Calif.

ENTEROLOBIUM Mart. *Leguminosae* (subfamily *Mimosoideae*). Five or more spp. of unarmed trees of trop. Amer.; lvs. alt., 2-pinnate; fl. heads solitary, clustered, or racemose; fls. whitish, 5-merous, stamens many, exserted, united basally; fr. a flat, broad, curved, indehiscent legume.

Used as ornamental trees in the tropics, for the durable wood, and the pods for stock food.

contortisiliquum (Vell.) Morong [*E. Timbouva* Mart.]. Differs from *E. cyclocarpum* in having commonly 3–14 pairs of pinnae, the lfts. in 10–15 pairs, larger, to ¾ in. long, and fr. narrower, to 3 in. wide, glaucescent. Brazil.

cyclocarpum Griseb. ELEPHANT'S-EAR. To 100 ft. or more, with broad spreading crown; lvs. commonly with 7–10 pairs of pinnae, lfts. 20–30 pairs, oblique, linear-oblong, to ½ in. long; fl. heads about ½ in. in diam.; fr. to 4 in. wide. Trop. Amer.

inerme: a listed name of no botanical standing.

Timbouva: *E. contortisiliquum.*

EOMECON Hance. SNOW POPPY. *Papaveraceae.* One sp., a per. herb, native to e. China, with spreading rhizome, branched st. and reddish-orange sap; lvs. basal, tufted, long-petioled; fls. short-lived, white, in few-fld., terminal panicles, sepals 2, petals 4, stamens 70 or more.

Cultivated for the attractive white flowers in spring.

chionantha Hance. To 1 ft. or more; lvs. cordate, 3–6 in. long, palmately veined, petioles 6–8 in. long; fls. 2 in. across. Zone 7.

EPACRIDACEAE R. Br. EPACRIS FAMILY. Dicot.; about 30 genera of shrubs and small trees, native mostly to Australia

and New Zeal. in heaths and boggy ground; lvs. mostly alt., simple, without stipules; fls. bracted, regular, usually bisexual, 4–5-merous, calyx persistent, corolla tubular, stamens separate or inserted on the corolla, anthers commonly 1-celled, dehiscing longitudinally, ovary superior, 1–10-celled; fr. a caps. or drupe. *Astroloma, Cyathodes, Dracophyllum, Leucopogon, Pentachondra,* and *Styphelia* are cult.

EPERUA Aubl. *Leguminosae* (subfamily *Caesalpinioideae*). About 10 spp. of lowland trop. trees of n. S. Amer.; lvs. alt., even-pinnate, lfts. of each sp. very variable in shape, size, and number; sepals 4, petal 1, large, longer than wide, stamens 10, separate or briefly united basally; fr. a flat, oblong, dehiscent legume.

Jenmannii D. Oliver. Tree, to 100 ft. or more; lfts. ovate to oblong, in 3–5 pairs, 4 in. long or more, pitted, stipules to 1 in. long, ¾ in. wide; infl. very short, erect; petals mauve, to 3 in. long, filaments very unequal. Guyana. Perhaps not specifically distinct from *E. grandiflora* (Aubl.) Baill.

EPHEDRA L. JOINT FIR. *Ephedraceae.* Perhaps 40 spp. of the N. Hemisphere and S. Amer., with characters of the family.

Occasionally planted in this country in dry locations as ground cover or for the green-stemmed clumps. The drug ephedrine is obtained from Asiatic species. Propagated by division of clumps, and by seeds, suckers, and layering.

distachya L. To 3 ft., often lower or procumbent; lvs. opp.; female cones peduncled; seeds subglobose. S. Eur., n. Asia. Zone 6. A source of ephedrine.

minima Hao. To 5 in. high, erect or scandent; lvs. opp., linear; seeds scarcely ¼ in. in diam. China.

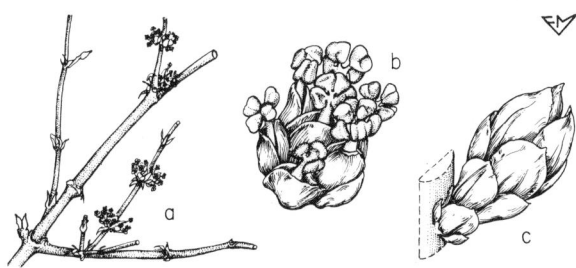

EPHEDRACEAE. *Ephedra Torreyana:* **a,** branch of male plant with cones, × ¼; **b,** male cone, × 4; **c,** female cone, × 3. (Species representative, but not in general cultivation; from Lawrence, *Taxonomy of Vascular Plants.*)

EPHEDRACEAE Wettst. EPHEDRA FAMILY. Gymnosperms; 1 genus, *Ephedra*, of much-branched, scraggly shrubs with slender green sts., typically dioecious, native to dry or desert regions of N. Hemisphere and S. Amer.; lvs. dry and scalelike, 2 or 3 at each node, cones small, borne at the nodes, the male cones with several stamenlike structures, the female cones with a terminal ovule; seeds with fleshy, red, outer coat.

×EPICATTLEYA Rolfe: *Epidendrum × Cattleya.* Orchidaceae. A small group of bigeneric hybrids generally intermediate between the parents. Most are known in the trade by grex names.

guatemalensis: *Cattleya × Deckeri.*

EPIDENDRUM L. [*Auliza* Salisb.; *Barkeria* Knowles & Westc.; *Dinema* Lindl.; *Encyclia* Hook.]. BUTTONHOLE ORCHID. *Orchidaceae.* Over 1,000 spp., commonly epiphytes or lithophytes, native to trop. and subtrop. Amer.; sts. either elongate and leafy or pseudobulbous; fls. 1- to many, in a terminal raceme or panicle, sepals and petals often similar, lip entire or lobed, clawed, claw free or partly to fully united to column, column cylindrical, often winged. For structure of fl. see *Orchidaceae.*

They are plants of various habit, and require mostly intermediate greenhouse temperature as for cattleyas. For culture see *Orchids.*

aciculare: *E. bractescens.*

advena Rchb.f. [*E. Capartianum* Linden; *E. Godseffianum* Rolfe; *E. osmanthum* Rodr.; *Encyclia osmantha* (Rodr.) Schlechter]. Pseudobulbs narrowly obovoid, 1–2-lvd.; lvs. to about 10 in. long; infl. simple or branched, to 2 ft. long; fls. to 1½ in. across, sepals and petals yellow or yellow-green, streaked with red or purple, ovate or elliptic, lip white, marked with crimson lines, 3-lobed, lateral lobes nearly quadrangular, midlobe orbicular, emarginate at apex. Autumn. Brazil.

alatum Batem. Pseudobulbs pear-shaped, to 5 in. long, 2–3-lvd.; lvs. leathery, to 15 in. long; peduncles erect, longer than lvs., many-fld.; fls. fragrant, 2 in. across, sepals and petals linear-spatulate, with revolute margin, basal half pale greenish-yellow, apical half brownish-purple, lip 3-lobed, shorter than sepals and petals, pale yellow, midlobe rugose, with a few red streaks. Early summer. Mex., Cent. Amer.

Allemanii Rodr. Pseudobulbs ovoid, 2-lvd.; infl. short, few-fld.; fls. fleshy, 1½ in across, sepals and petals similar, lanceolate, white with rose suffusion, lip partly fused to column, orbicular, apiculate, white with purple stripes at base. Late summer. Brazil.

altissimum Batem. ex Lindl. Robust, to 2–3 ft., pseudobulbs 2–3-lvd.; lvs. linear, fleshy, over 1 ft. long; infl. paniculate, many-fld.; fls. fleshy, to 1½ in. across, honey-scented, sepals and petals similar, lanceolate, pale green, lip 3-lobed, lateral lobes oblong-strap-shaped, midlobe orbicular, waxy, disc corrugated, yellow with red stripes. Winter. Bahama Is.

anceps Jacq. To 3 ft., sts. not pseudobulbous; lvs. oblong-elliptic, obtuse, sessile, to 8 in. long; infl. racemose, compressed, fls. crowded into a head at apex; fls. fleshy, light brown, greenish-brown, or tawny-yellow, sepals and petals to ½ in. long, lip 3-lobed, fleshy. Early spring–late autumn. Fla.; Mex., Cent. Amer., W. Indies, n. S. Amer.

aromaticum Batem. [*Encyclia aromatica* (Batem.) Schlechter]. Pseudobulbs pear-shaped, 2-lvd.; lvs. leathery, linear, to 1 ft. long; scape 2–3 times as long as lvs., much-branched, many-fld.; sepals and petals delicate in texture, light yellowish-green, to ¾ in. long, lip 3-lobed, white, veined with deep reddish-violet. Spring and summer. Mex., Guatemala.

atropurpureum Willd. [*E. macrochilum* Hook.; *Encyclia atropurpurea* (Willd.) Schlechter; *E. macrochila* (Hook.) Schlechter]. SPICE ORCHID. Pseudobulbs ovoid-pear-shaped, to 4 in. long, 2–30-lvd.; lvs. to about 16 in. long; racemes rarely branching, about 4-13-fld.; fls. 2–3 in. across, sepals and petals greenish-brown, often tinged with purple, lip white to deep purple, with purplish stripes, 3-lobed. Early winter–early spring. Mex. to Panama, W. Indies, n. S. Amer. Var. **Randianum** Linden & Rodig. Lvs. deep purplish, longer and narrower; fls. larger, sepals and petals russet-brown, bordered with light yellow-green, lip white, with red-purple blotch. Var. **roseum** Rchb.f. Fls. smaller than in var. *Randianum*, sepals and petals deep purplish-brown, lip rose, with purple blotch near base.

aurantiacum: *Cattleya aurantiaca.*

auritum: *E. Boothii.*

bahamense: *E. rufum.*

Barbeyanum Kränzl. Habit similar to that of *E. difforme;* lvs. leathery, to 2½ in. long; fls. in terminal, subumbellate clusters on short racemes, pea-green with darker markings, translucent, sepals 1¼ in. long, lip prominent, 1¼ in. across, ¾ in. long, 3-lobed. Autumn. Costa Rica, Panama.

bicornutum: *Caularthron bicornutum.*

bifidum Aubl. [*E. papilionaceum* Vahl]. Pseudobulbs oblong-ellipsoid, 2–3-lvd. at apex; lvs. narrowly oblong, to 14 in. long; scape to about 4 ft., simple or branched above, few- to many-fld.; sepals spatulate-oblong, greenish or pale purple, petals narrower, lip 2-lobed, purple or white with purple streaks. Autumn–late spring, late summer. W. Indies.

Boothianum Lindl. [*E. erythronioides* Sm.]. DOLLAR ORCHID, BOOTH'S E. To 10 in., pseudobulbs clustered, ovoid to pear-shaped, 2-lvd.; lvs. to 7 in. long, oblong-spatulate; fls. few, in loose racemes, sepals and petals yellow, spotted with dark brown to magenta-purple, lip yellow or white, 3-lobed. Summer–late autumn. S. Fla., W. Indies, Brit. Honduras, Mex.

Boothii (Lindl.) L. O. Williams [*E. auritum* Lindl.; *E. paleaceum* (Lindl.) Rchb.f.]. To 1 ft., pseudobulbs ellipsoid on creeping rhizome, 1-lvd.; lvs. narrow, to about 9 in. long, erect; infl. short, loosely several-fld.; fls. white to yellow, fragrant, sepals and petals to ¾ in. long. Blooms all year. Cent. Amer.

brachyphyllum: *E. secundum.*

bractescens Lindl. [*E. aciculare* Batem.]. Pseudobulbs oblong, 2-lvd.; lvs. long, narrow; racemes slender, erect, 6–7-fld.; fls. to 2 in. across, sepals and petals dull purple, lip 3-lobed, lateral lobes needle-shaped, midlobe round, white with rose venation. Spring. Mex. to Costa Rica.

brassavolae Rchb.f. Pseudobulbs ovoid to cylindric-pear-shaped, to 7 in. long, 2-lvd.; lvs. leathery, to 9 in. long and 1¾ in. wide; fls. to 4 in. across, in 3–12-fld. loose racemes, sepals and petals narrow, yellow or greenish-yellow, lip white or pale yellow tipped with violet-red. Spring–early autumn. Cent. Amer.

brevifolium: *E. pyriforme.*

campylostalix Rchb.f. Pseudobulbs clustered, ovoid, to 2¾ in. long, 1-lvd.; lvs. oblong or elliptic, to 12 in. long; infl. terminal, racemose or paniculate, branched, to 12 in. long; fls. to 1 in. across, semipendent, spreading, dull wine-colored, with whitish veins on outside, lip 3-lobed, ivory-white, column reddish-purple. Early summer. Cent. Amer.

Capartianum: *E. advena.*

catillus Rchb.f. & Warsz. [*E. imperator* Hort.]. Sts. not pseudobulbous; lvs. 2-ranked, oblong; racemes erect, terminal; fls. many, to 1 in. across, orange-red, lip 3-lobed, vermilion with yellow callus, disc keeled, midlobe 2-lobed, lobes toothed at ends. Summer. Colombia.

chocaoense Rchb.f. [*E. ionophlebium* Rchb.f.]. Pseudobulbs globose or ovoid, 2-lvd.; lvs. fleshy, to 10 in. long; infl. few-fld., shorter than lvs.; fls. fleshy, to ¾ in. across, campanulate, sepals and petals ovate-elliptic, greenish-white, lip shell-shaped, nearly orbicular, white with violet stripes, disc with a cushionlike callus at base. Winter–early summer. Cent. Amer., n. S. Amer.

chlorops Rchb.f. Sts. erect, leafy, to 2 ft.; lvs. fleshy, 2-ranked; infl. racemose, short, pendent, several-fld.; fls. fleshy, small, to ½ in. across, greenish-yellow, sepals ovate, petals filiform-lanceolate, lip 3-lobed, with 3 keels on disc. Late autumn–winter. Mex., Guatemala.

ciliare L. [*E. luteum* Hort.]. Pseudobulbs to about 7 in. long, 1–2-lvd.; lvs. leathery, rarely to 11 in. long; fls. several in a loose raceme, sepals and petals very narrow, yellowish-green, lip 3-lobed, white, with 2 yellow spots at base, lateral lobes deeply fringed, midlobe very narrow, longer than lateral lobes. Blooming all year. Trop. Amer. Var. **cuspidatum** (Lodd.) Lindl. [*E. cuspidatum* Lodd.]. Fls. larger and yellower, midlobe of lip not much longer than lateral lobes.

cinnabarinum Salzm. ex Lindl. Sts. leafy, to 4 ft. high; lvs. 2-ranked, oblong; infl. a terminal, corymbiform raceme; fls. bright scarlet, lip orange-yellow, spotted with red, 3-lobed, keeled, with paired calluses at base, lateral lobes deeply incised, front lobe contracted in middle, the apical half abruptly wedge-shaped with angles prolonged into 1 or 2 fine teeth. Late spring–summer. Brazil. Venezuela.

clavatum: *E. purpurascens.*

cnemidophorum Lindl. [*E. Pfavii* Rolfe]. Clump-forming, sts. stout, leafy; lvs. lanceolate, to 12 in. long; infl. many-fld.; fls. fleshy, sepals and petals rosy-purple, to ¾ in. long, lip creamy-white with rosy suffusion. Late spring–late summer. Cent. Amer.

cochleatum L. COCKLE-SHELL ORCHID, CLAM-SHELL O. Pseudobulbs to 10 in. long, 2-lvd. or rarely 3-lvd.; lvs. to 14 in. long; scapes commonly simple, loosely fld.; sepals and petals narrowly linear, twisted, whitish-green, lip uppermost, shell-shaped, dark purple with yellow radiating veins. Blooming all year. Trop. Amer.

conopseum R. Br. GREEN-FLY ORCHID. Forming dense mats, to 16 in. high, sts. leafy; infl. a loose raceme on elongated peduncle; fls. to ½ in. across, grayish-green, tinged with purple, sepals and petals narrow, with revolute margins, lip 3-lobed, fused to column, disc with 2 calluses at base. Winter–late summer. Mex. and se. U.S.

Cooperanum Batem. Sts. cylindrical, 2 ft. high, leafy in upper part; lvs. lanceolate; racemes drooping, many-fld.; fls. about 1½ in. across, sepals and petals narrow, yellowish-brown, lip rose, kidney-shaped, 2-lobed at apex, with 2 calluses at base. Late autumn–late spring, late summer. Brazil, Guyana.

coriifolium Lindl. Plants in dense clumps, sts. stout, leafy in upper part; lvs. erect, oblong-elliptic, leathery, to 10 in. long; racemes spicate, to 10 in. long; fls. fleshy, green, tinged with red or purple, enclosed by large, triangular, 2-ranked bracts, sepals to ¾ in. long, ovate, petals filiform, lip reniform, margin revolute, apex thickened. Blooming all year. Cent. Amer., nw. S. Amer.

coronatum Ruiz & Pav. [*E. moyobambae* Kränzl.; *E. subpatens* Schlechter]. To 2 ft., sts. concealed by lf. sheaths; lvs. 2-ranked, oblong-elliptic, leathery, to 6 in. long; racemes terminal, to 16 in. long, pendent, loosely 10–35-fld.; fls. fleshy, brownish-green and white, to 2 in. across, sepals pale rosy-brown, lip 3-lobed, waxy-white suffused with green. Spring–early summer. Trop. Amer.

crassifolium: *E. secundum.*

cuspidatum: *E. ciliare* var.

dichromum Lindl. Pseudobulbs ovate-spindle-shaped, to 4 in. long, 2-lvd.; lvs. 9–12 in. long, leathery; infl. a panicle on scape 3 ft. high; fls. to 2 in. across, pale rose, sepals and petals spatulate, lip 3-lobed, dark rose, midlobe yellow, margined with white. Brazil.

difforme Jacq. [*E. latilabre* Lindl]. Sts. cylindrical, to 16 in. high; lvs. strap-shaped to elliptic, to 4 in. long; fls. few to many in terminal, umbellate racemes, to about 2 in. across, green, lip much broader than long. Spring–late summer. Fla., Trop. Amer.

diffusum Swartz. Sts. flexous, concealed by lf. sheaths; lvs. on upper part of st., broadly elliptic, leathery, to 3 in. long; infl. a many-branched panicle; fls. small, many, translucent, greenish-yellow or reddish-yellow, sepals and petals spreading, to ⅜ in. long, lip triangular, cordate, united with column, forming a cup. Early summer–late autumn. Trop. Amer.

diurnum (Jacq.) Cogn. [*E. virens* Lindl. & Paxt; *Encyclia diurna* (Jacq.) Schlechter; *E. virens* (Lindl. & Paxt.) Schlechter]. Pseudobulbs ovoid-oblong, 2–3-lvd.; lvs. to 1½ ft. long; infl. to almost 3 ft. long, paniculate; fls. about 1–1½ in. across, sepals and petals green or greenish-yellow, lip white, with purple streaks. Blooming throughout the year. W. Indies, Venezuela, Colombia.

eburneum Rchb.f. Sts. tufted, to 2 ft. high; lvs. alt., to 4½ in. long, leathery; racemes terminal, 1–2-fld.; sepals and petals narrow, pale citron-green, 1¾ in. long, lip ivory-white, sessile on apex of column, orbicular-cordate, 1¼ in. across. Summer–late autumn. Panama.

elegans (Knowles & Westc.) Rchb.f. [*Barkeria elegans* Knowles & Westc.]. Sts. spindle-shaped, to 1 ft. high; lvs. linear-lanceolate, to 4 in. long; peduncles as long as sts., racemes loose, 5–7-fld., nodding; fls. lilac-purple suffused with white, to 1½ in. across, lip obovate-obtuse, white, with large rosy-purple blotch near apex. Winter. Mex.

ellipticum: *E. secundum.*

elongatum: *E. secundum.*

Endresii Rchb.f. Sts. leafy, to 9 in. high; lvs. ovate-cordate, to 1 in. long; racemes erect, 2–10-fld.; fls. white, with a few violet spots, to 1 in. across, sepals and petals spreading, lip 4-lobed, disc with 2 calluses above base. Early winter–early spring. Costa Rica.

equitantifolium Ames. Sts. to 9 in. high; lvs. 2-ranked, forming a fan, lanceolate-acuminate, to 10 in. long; fls. solitary on a terminal, leaflike peduncle, campanulate, dull chocolate-brown, to ½ in. long, sepals and petals narrow, lip united to column, rhombic or almost 3-lobed. Summer. Mex. to Panama.

erythronioides: *E. Boothianum.*

evectum Hook. Sts. slender, cylindrical, fleshy, brittle, to 5 ft., branched, leafy in upper part; lvs. 2-ranked, to 6 in. long, oblong-lanceolate, fleshy, brittle; peduncle long, with a short, dense, terminal raceme; fls. rose-purple, sepals and petals narrowly obovate, lip 3-lobed, fringed. Summer. Colombia, Ecuador.

falcatum: *E. Parkinsonianum* var.

floribundum: *E. paniculatum.*

fragrans Swartz. Pseudobulbs spindle-shaped, to 6 in. long, 1-lvd.; lvs. lanceolate, to 6 in. long; scape short, few-fld.; fls. fragrant, creamy-white, sepals and petals narrow-lanceolate, lip uppermost, concave, white, lined with violet. Winter and spring. Mex. and W. Indies to S. Amer.

fucatum Lindl. Pseudobulbs ovoid, clustered, 2-lvd.; lvs. fleshy, linear-oblong, to 1 ft. long; infl. paniculate, many-fld.; fls. small, to 1 in. across, sepals and petals oblanceolate, greenish-yellow, lip 3-lobed, lateral lobes ovate, midlobe elliptic, pointed, whitish with magenta markings, column without auricles. Spring–late summer. Cuba.

Ghiesbreghtianum A. Rich. & Galeotti. Pseudobulbs narrowly ovoid, 2-lvd.; lvs. linear, to 6 in. long; infl. 1–2-fld., shorter than lvs.; fls. large, to 1½ in. across, sepals and petals ovate-lanceolate, pointed, reflexed, greenish, with maroon markings, lip suborbicular, large, white with purple or violet markings at base. Early spring. Mex.

Godseffianum: *E. advenum.*

gracile Lindl. Pseudobulbs ovoid, completely enclosed by papery bracts, 2–30-lvd.; lvs. oblong-strap-shaped, to 10 in. long; infl. paniculate, many-fld.; fls. fleshy, large, to 1½ in. across, sepals and petals alike, green suffused with bronze, oblanceolate, lip 3-lobed, yellow with purple lines, midlobe cuneate, 2-lobed at apex. Summer–early autumn. Bahama Is.

graniticum: *E. oncidioides.*

Grisebachianum: *E. ochranthum.*

Hanburii Lindl. Pseudobulbs ovoid, to 3 in. long, 2-lvd.; lvs. narrowly sword-shaped, leathery, to 1 ft. long; racemes as long as lvs., many-fld.; fls. to 1½ in. across, sepals and petals spreading, spatulate, brown-purple, lip 3-lobed, claret-purple. Cent. Amer.

hastatum Lindl. Pseudobulbs to 1½ in. long, ovate, 1-lvd.; lvs. to 8 in. long; racemes terminal, few-fld.; fls. to 1 in. across, sepals and petals reddish-brown, lip orbicular, white, striped with brown. Late spring. Mex.

Howardii Ames & Correll. To 6 ft., pseudobulbs ovoid, tapering to the 2-lvd. apex; lvs. 2, leathery, to 16 in. long; infl. a sparsely branched panicle, loosely fld.; fls. brown, mottled with chocolate-brown, sepals oblanceolate, to ¾ in. long, petals spatulate, to ¾ in. long, lip magenta, united to column, deeply 3-lobed, midlobe nearly orbicular, apiculate at apex, ⅜ in. wide. Summer. Cuba.

ibaguense HBK [*E. radicans* Pav. ex Lindl.]. Sts. slender and tall, leafy in upper part; lvs. leathery, to 4 in. long; infl. racemose, at summit of a long, naked peduncle, densely fld.; fls. orange-red and yellow, to 1½ in. across, sepals and petals spreading, lip 3-lobed, toothed or fringed. Blooming all year. Cent. and S. Amer.

imperator: *E. catillus.*

indivisum: *Caularthron bilamellatum.*

inversum Lindl. Pseudobulbs spindle-shaped, to 6 in. long, 2-lvd. at apex; lvs. 6 in. long; fls. in 7–12-fld. racemes, pale straw-color or white, streaked with rose, lip with a rose spot. Autumn. Brazil.

ionophlebium: *E. chacaoense.*

lanipes Lindl. Sts. thick-cylindrical, to 2½ ft. high, leafy in upper part; lvs. 2-ranked, oblong-lanceolate, to 9 in. long; panicles to 1 ft. long; fls. small, brownish-yellow to yellow, sepals oblong-lanceolate, to ⅜ in. long, petals filiform, lip 3-lobed. Winter–spring. Andes, from Ecuador to Bolivia.

latilabre: *E. difforme.*

leucochilum Klotzsch. Sts. to 2 ft. high; lvs. 2-ranked, recurved, leathery; racemes terminal, drooping, 5–9-fld.; fls. greenish-yellow, to 3 in. across, sepals and petals lanceolate, with recurved margins, lip 3-lobed, lateral lobes nearly orbicular, midlobe lanceolate, longer, white. Summer. Colombia, Nicaragua.

Lindleyanum (Batem. ex Lindl.) Rchb.f. [*E. spectabile* (Batem. ex Lindl.) Rchb.f.; *Barkeria Lindleyana* Batem. ex Lindl.; *B. spectabilis* Batem. ex Lindl.]. Sts. cylindrical or spindle-shaped, to 1 ft. high; fls. racemose, rose-purple, to 2 in. across, lip rich purple at tip, with white disc. Autumn. Cent. Amer.

luteum: *E. ciliare.*

macrochilum: *E. atropurpureum.*

maculatum: *E. prismatocarpum.*

Mariae Ames. Pseudobulbs slenderly pear-shaped, to 1½ in. long, 2-lvd.; lvs. to 4 in. long, from sheathing bract; peduncles 5–7-fld.; fls. yellowish-green, to 3 in. long, sepals and petals narrow, lanceolate, lip large, 2-lobed at apex. Early summer–early autumn. Mex.

moyobambae: *E. coronatum.*

myrianthum: *E. verrucosum* var.

nemorale Lindl. [*Encyclia nemoralis* (Lindl.) Schlechter]. Pseudobulbs nearly globular to pear-shaped, to 4 in. long, 2–3-lvd.; lvs. to 13 in. long; infl. drooping, racemose or paniculate, to about 40 in. high, loosely 8- or more-fld.; fls. large, to 4 in. across, sepals and petals lilac or violet, lip with deeper colored lateral lobes and whitish midlobe with violet lines. Spring–summer. Mex.

nocturnum Jacq. Sts. cylindrical, erect, to 3 ft.; lvs. elliptic to oblong, to 6 in. long, obtuse, leathery; racemes very short, terminal, 2–3-fld.; fls. very fragrant, sepals and petals linear, greenish-yellow, lip white, 3-lobed. Blooming all year. Trop. Amer.

×**Obrienianum** Rolfe: *E. evectum* × *E. ibaguense.* SCARLET ORCHID, BUTTERFLY O., BABY O. Habit similar to that of *E. ibaguense;* fls. of same general shape as those of *E. evectum,* brilliant orange-scarlet, with a trace of orange. Spring and summer.

ochraceum Lindl. Pseudobulbs to 1½ in. long, pear-shaped, 1–3-lvd.; lvs. oblong-lanceolate, to 5 in. long; racemes simple, as long as lvs., few-fld.; fls. small, sepals and petals dingy-brown with greenish tips, lip 3-lobed, white, midlobe triangular. Summer. Mex., Guatemala.

ochranthum A. Rich. [*E. Grisebachianum* Cogn.]. Pseudobulbs clustered on distinct rhizome, ovoid, 2–3-lvd.; lvs. fleshy, to 8 in. long; infl. paniculate, few-branched, few-fld.; fls. fleshy, to 1½ in. across, sepals and petals lanceolate, yellowish, lip 3-lobed, lateral lobes ovate-palmate, midlobe orbicular, with purplish suffusion. Early winter. Cuba.

odoratissimum Lindl. [*Encyclia odoratissima* (Lindl.) Schlechter]. Pseudobulbs ovoid, 2–3-lvd.; lvs. to 16 in. long; infl. commonly paniculate, to 2 ft. long, loosely many-fld.; fls. about 1 in. across, greenish, often marked with purplish, sepals and petals oblanceolate, spatulate, lip 3-lobed, midlobe roundish. Winter–early spring, late spring–autumn. Brazil, Guyana.

oncidioides Lindl. [*E. graniticum* Lindl.; *Encyclia oncidioides* (Lindl.) Schlechter]. Pseudobulbs slender, pear-shaped or spindle-shaped, to 8 in. long, 2–3-lvd.; lvs. oblong-strap-shaped, to 2 ft. long; panicles to 6 ft. high, many-fld.; fls. 1–1½ in. across, fragrant, sepals and petals green or yellow, with large red-brown blotch, narrowly lanceolate, lip white or yellow, with red veins, 3-lobed, lateral lobes strap-shaped, midlobe obovate or elliptic. Autumn–late summer. Continental trop. Amer.

osmanthum: *E. advena.*

paleaceum: *E. Boothii.*

paniculatum Ruiz & Pav. [*E. floribundum* HBK]. To about 3½ ft. including infl., sts. erect, concealed by lf. sheaths; lvs. elliptic-ovate, to 9 in. long; infl. terminal, usually longer than lvs., a few-fld. raceme to compound panicle; fls. very variable, to 1 in. across, green to white to rose-purple, lip 3-lobed, very variable in degree of lobing. Summer. Trop. Amer.

papilionaceum: *E. bifidum.*

Parkinsonianum Hook. [*E. falcatum* Lindl.]. Large, sts. pendent, to 6 ft. long, pseudobulbs 1-lvd.; lvs. to 20 in. long; fls. fragrant, 1–3, pale yellowish-green, often mauve or purplish-brown on outer surface, sepals and petals to 3 in. long, linear, lip 3-lobed, white or yellowish-orange, midlobe lanceolate, Cent. Amer. Var. **falcatum** (Lindl.) Ames, F. T. Hubb., & C. Schweinf. Fls. smaller.

pentotis Rchb.f. Pseudobulbs slenderly spindle-shaped, to 14 in. long, 2-lvd.; lvs. linear-elliptic to lanceolate, to 10 in. long, leathery; spike short, terminal, few-fld.; fls. yellowish- or creamy-white, to about 3 in. across, fragrant, sepals and petals lanceolate, lip ovate-lanceolate, with a callus at base, white, striped with purple. Early spring–summer. Cent. Amer., Brazil.

Pfavii: *E. cnemidophorum.*

phoeniceum Lindl. CHOCOLATE ORCHID. Pseudobulbs ovate, 2-lvd.; lvs. linear-oblong, leathery, to 9 in. long; infl. paniculate, to 3 ft. long; fls. to 2 in. across, sepals and petals elliptic, deep bronze-purple shaded with brown and pale green, lip 3-lobed, rose-purple veined with deep crimson-purple, lateral lobes triangular, midlobe nearly orbicular, 2-lobed at apex. Summer–winter. Cuba.

polybulbon Swartz [*Dinema polybulbon* (Swartz) Lindl.]. Pseudobulbs on long creeping and branching rhizome, ovoid, erect or ascending, 2-lvd.; lvs. rarely to 2¾ in. long; fls. solitary, sepals and petals yellowish or brownish, lanceolate, spreading, lip snow-white with yellow markings, nearly orbicular. Early autumn–spring, early summer. Cent. Amer., W. Indies.

prismatocarpum Rchb.f. [*E. maculatum* Hort.]. RAINBOW ORCHID. Pseudobulbs pear-shaped to cylindrical, to 1 ft. long, 2–3-lvd.; lvs. to 15 in. long; fls. many, in racemes to 14 in. long, sepals and petals yellow-green, spotted with black-purple, lanceolate, lip 3-lobed, yellow-green at base, violet at apex, midlobe lanceolate, lateral lobes earlike. Early winter–late winter, late spring–late summer. Costa Rica, Panama.

purpurascens Focke [*E. clavatum* Lindl.]. Pseudobulbs ovate, stalked, 1-lvd.; infl. lateral, racemose, few-fld., peduncle completely enclosed by overlapping sheaths; fls. fleshy, to 1½ in. across, sepals and petals pale green, lanceolate, margin revolute, lip white, 3-lobed, claw united to column, lateral lobes squarish, midlobe trowel-shaped. Costa Rica to Brazil.

pygmaeum Hook. Pseudobulbs on creeping, branched rhizome, ellipsoid, erect, 2-lvd.; lvs. elliptic, to 4 in. long; fls. small, 1- to several, brownish-green or greenish, often tinged with lavender, lip white, with purple blotch at base of midlobe. Blooming throughout the year. Trop. Amer.

pyriforme Lindl. [*E. brevifolium* Jennings]. Pseudobulbs ovoid, clustered, 2-lvd.; lvs. fleshy, oblong-elliptic, blunt, to 6 in. long; infl. racemose or somewhat paniculate, few-fld.; fls. large, fleshy, to 2 in. across, sepals and petals oblanceolate, dark red, lip 3-lobed, lateral lobes oblong-strap-shaped, midlobe nearly orbicular, 2-lobed, white with purple lines toward base. Winter–summer. Cuba.

radiatum Lindl. Rhizome creeping, pseudobulbs spindle-shaped, 3–5 in. long, 2–3-lvd.; lvs. linear-strap-shaped, to 15 in. long; racemes 1- to many-fld.; fls. 1½ in. across, cream-colored, sepals and petals ovate, fleshy, spreading, lip round, shell-shaped, white, with bright purple radial lines. Cent. Amer., Mex.

radicans: *E. ibaguense.*

ramosum Jacq. Upright or pendent, simple to much-branched, in dense colonies, sts. flexuous, to 3 ft. long; lvs. linear-strap-shaped, to 5 in. long; infl. terminal, 20- to several-fld.; floral bracts conspicuous, fls. creamy-white or yellow-green, often tinged with dark red or bronze, variable in size and texture, sepals and petals to ½ in. long, linear-lanceolate, lip green, triangular-cordate. Blooming all year. Trop. Amer.

replicatum Lindl. Robust, pseudobulbs ovoid, 2–3-lvd.; panicle to 2–3 ft., many-fld.; fls, fleshy, to 1½ in. across, sepals and petals oblanceolate or spatulate, pointed, yellowish-green suffused with brown, lip 3-lobed, lateral lobes broadly ovate, midlobe broad, somewhat rhombic with a sharp point, white with purple stripes. Early summer. Cuba.

rigidum Jacq. Sts. cylindrical, from a creeping rhizome, to 1 ft. high; lvs. elliptic-oblong, to 3¾ in. long; racemes to 6 in. long; fls. small, green, sepals ovate, petals linear, lip nearly orbicular, disc with 2 calluses at base. Blooming all year. Trop. Amer.

Rousseauae Schlechter. To 6 in., pseudobulbs cylindrical, 1-lvd.; lvs. oblong-elliptic, blunt, to 4 in. long; infl. a lateral, few-fld. raceme; fls. green, small, to ¾ in. across, sepals ovate-elliptic, petals linear, lip 3-lobed, lateral lobes divided, midlobe lanceolate. Early summer. Panama.

rufum Lindl. [*E. bahamense* Griseb.]. Pseudobulbs pear-shaped, 2–3-lvd.; lvs. linear-oblong, to 1 ft. long; infl. paniculate, many-fld.; fls. fleshy, to 1½ in. across, sepals and petals alike, oblong-lanceolate, ochre-yellow, lip 3-lobed, lateral lobes oblong-strap-shaped, midlobe squarish, with revolute margins, yellow. Late spring. Bahama Is., Cuba.

Schlechteranum Ames. To 3–4 in., sts. concealed by densely overlapping fleshy lvs.; infl. terminal, sessile, 1–2-fld.; fls. fleshy, to ¾ in. across, greenish, sepals and petals linear-lanceolate, lip greenish or bluish, united to column, simple, ovate-cordate. Cent. and S. Amer.

Schumannianum Schlechter. Sts. erect, leafy, to 3 ft.; lvs. 2-ranked, large, ovate, leathery; infl. terminal, paniculate, many-fld.; fls. fleshy, to 1½ in. across, showy, sepals and petals yellowish-green, ovate to obovate, blunt, spreading, lip 3-lobed, the apical lobe 2-cleft, deep lavender, disc with a pair of calluses at base. Winter–spring. Costa Rica, Panama.

secundum Jacq. [*E. brachyphyllum* Lindl.; *E. crassifolium* Lindl.; *E. ellipticum* R. C. Grah.; *E. elongatum* Jacq.; *E. xanthinum* Lindl.]. Sts. cylindrical, wiry, leafy, to 5 ft. high; lvs. leathery, ovate-lanceolate to elliptic-oblong, to 4½ in. long; peduncle long, slender, densely many-fld. at apex; fls. variable in color, from white through yellow, orange, rose, and magenta, sepals and petals oblanceolate, acute, more or less reflexed, lip 3-lobed, coarsely toothed. Blooming all year. Trop. Amer.

selligerum Batem. ex Lindl. To 4 ft., pseudobulbs ovoid, to 4 in. long, 1–2-lvd.; lvs. linear-strap-shaped, to 15 in. long; infl. a loosely fld. panicle, to 3 ft. long; fls. showy, fragrant, green-brown or yellow, suffused with brown, sepals and petals to ¾ in. long, obovate or spatulate, lip deeply 3-lobed, white or yellowish, with purple veins, lateral lobes obtuse, midlobe orbicular. Winter–early summer. Cent. Amer.

Skinneri Batem. ex Lindl. [*Barkeria Skinneri* (Batem. ex Lindl.) A. Rich. & Galeotti]. Sts. slenderly spindle-shaped, erect, to 20 in., several-lvd.; lvs. elliptic, fleshy, to 6 in. long; racemes few- to many-fld.; fls. about 1–1½ in. across, dark rose or purple, sepals and petals spreading, broad, lip entire, with yellow ridges. Autumn–winter. Guatemala.

spectabile: *E. Lindleyanum.*

Stamfordianum Batem. Pseudobulbs spindle- to club-shaped, to 1 ft. long, 3–4-lvd.; lvs. to 10 in. long; fls. fragrant, in leafless, loose, lateral panicles to about 2 ft. long; sepals and petals yellow, spotted with purple, spreading, lanceolate, lip white, midlobe yellow, toothed, lateral lobes denticulate. Late autumn–early summer. Cent. Amer., Venezuela, Colombia.

stenopetalum Hook. Sts. in tufts, cylindrical, to 2 ft. high; lvs. linear-oblong, to 4 in. long, leathery; infl. a terminal, few-fld., corymbose raceme; fls. to 1½ in. across, rosy-mauve, sepals and petals broad-elliptic, lip entire, with square white blotch at base. Blooming all year. W. Indies, Cent. Amer., n. S. Amer.

strobiliferum Rchb.f. To 8 in., sts. slender, leafy, simple or branched; lvs. leathery, elliptic, 2-lobed, to 1½ in. long; infl. a terminal, few-fld. raceme; fls. small, to ¼ in. long, from 2-ranked, stiff bracts, sepals and petals fleshy, meeting at tips, greenish, lip triangular-hastate, with 2 calluses at base. Trop. Amer.

subpatens: *E. coronatum.*

tampense Lindl. BUTTERFLY ORCHID, FLORIDA B.O. To about 2½ ft., pseudobulbs pear-shaped, 1–2-lvd.; lvs. narrowly linear-oblong, to 9½ in. long; fls. loosely panicled, sepals yellowish-green, tinged with brown, petals similar but browner, lip 3-lobed, white with magenta-purple lines, midlobe nearly orbicular, sometimes white or magenta. Spring–summer, autumn–early winter. Fla., Bahama Is.

venosum Lindl. Rhizomes prominent, pseudobulbs widely-spaced, ovoid, 2-lvd.; lvs. fleshy, oblong-strap-shaped, to 6 in. long; racemes few-fld., as long as or shorter than lvs.; sepals and petals green, lanceolate, reflexed, lip 3-lobed, white with violet stripes, lateral lobes triangular, earlike, midlobe broadly ovate-cordate. Early summer. Mex.

verrucosum Swartz. Sts. stout, to 5 ft. high; lvs. oblong-lanceolate, to 9 in. long; infl. a compound panicle to a simple raceme, many-fld.; fls. to ½ in. across, white, lip deeply 3-lobed, with a callus 3-lobed apically. Blooming all year. Jamaica, Cent. Amer., Colombia. Var. **myrianthum** (Lindl.) Ames & Correll [*E. myrianthum* Lindl.]. Fls. deep ruby-red or purplish-red, lip 3-lobed, with 2-lobed callus.

virens: *E. diurnum.*

virgatum Lindl. [*Encyclia virgata* Schlechter]. Pseudobulbs ovoid to pear-shaped, 2–3-lvd.; lvs. to 2 ft. long or more; infl. paniculate, to 7 ft. long; fls. to 1¼ in. across, sepals and petals greenish, stained with brown, lip whitish-yellow. Autumn–summer. Mex. to Honduras.

vitellinum Lindl. Pseudobulbs to 2 in. long, 2–3-lvd.; lvs. to 1 ft. long; infl. loosely racemose or paniculate, several- to many-fld., to 1½ ft. long; fls. cinnabar-red, to 1½ in. across, all segms. entire, ovate-lanceolate. Late spring–autumn. Mex., Guatemala. Cv. 'Majus'. Fls. larger, brighter.

xanthinum: *E. secundum.*

EPIGAEA L. GROUND LAUREL. *Ericaceae.* Two spp. of evergreen, creeping shrubs, native to Japan and e. N. Amer.; lvs. alt., simple, entire, leathery; fls. white to rose, fragrant, bisexual or unisexual, clustered toward ends of brs., sepals 5, corolla urceolate or salverform, hairy inside, stamens 10, ovary superior; fr. a many-seeded caps.

Plants can be grown in the garden if given acid soil and shade, and their natural conditions imitated. Propagation by seeds is much more satisfactory than by division; sow as soon as seed is ripe.

asiatica Maxim. Sts. hairy; lvs. oblong to elliptic, to 3–4 in., cordate, acuminate; fls. rose, corolla urceolate or nearly so, the lobes recurved. Japan. Zone 6.

repens L. TRAILING ARBUTUS, MAYFLOWER. Sts. hairy; lvs. oblong-ovate, ovate, to suborbicular, to 3 in. long, cordate, rounded at apex, bright green; fls. white to pink, corolla salverform, lobes spreading. Spring. Nfld. to Fla. and Ky. Zone 2. Cv. 'Rosea'. Fls. rose.

EPIGENIUM Gagnep. [*Sarcopodium* Lindl. & Paxt.]. *Orchidaceae.* About 35 spp. of epiphytes, native to trop. Asia; pseudobulbs on a prominent, creeping rhizome, 1-lvd.; infl. terminal, 1-fld.; fls. dark colored, upper sepal enveloping column, lateral sepals united to the long column foot, petals united to and running along the column foot, lip fiddle-shaped, column short, without arms. For structure of fl. see *Orchidaceae.*

For culture see *Orchids.*

amplum (Lindl.) Summerh. [*Dendrobium amplum* Lindl.; *Sarcopodium amplum* (Lindl.) Lindl.]. Pseudobulbs to 2 in. long; lvs. to 6 in. long and 2 in. wide; fls. in few-fld. racemes, to 2½ in. across, white to greenish-brown, spotted with darker brown, midlobe of lip dark purple. Autumn. Trop. Himalayas.

Coelogyne (Rchb.f.) Summerh. [*Dendrobium Coelogyne* Rchb.f.; *Sarcopodium Coelogyne* (Rchb.f.) Kränzl.]. Pseudobulbs 2 in. long, 2-lvd.; lvs. leathery, to 6 in. long; fls. solitary, large, 2 in. across or more, sepals and petals yellowish-green, densely spotted with purple, lip dark purple. Autumn–early winter. Burma.

cymbidioides (Lindl.) Summerh. [*Dendrobium cymbidioides* Lindl.]. Pseudobulbs ovate, to 1½ in. long, 2-lvd.; lvs. leathery, oblong, longer than pseudobulbs; infl. a terminal, 5-fld. raceme; fls. spreading, to 1½ in. across, pale yellow, lip 3-lobed, white with dark purple lines near base. Late winter–late summer. Sumatra, Java, Philippine Is.

Lyonii (Ames) Summerh. [*Dendrobium Lyonii* Ames; *Sarcopodium Lyonii* (Ames) Rolfe]. Pseudobulbs ovoid, 2-lvd.; lvs. oblong-elliptic, rigid; infl. an arching, 10–15-fld. raceme; fls. to 5 in. across, rose-carmine, sepals and petals lanceolate, lip 3-lobed, wine-red. Late spring. Philippine Is.

rotundatum (Lindl.) Summerh.[*Dendrobium rotundatum* Lindl.]. Pseudobulbs ovoid, 2-lvd.; fls. nearly sessile, fleshy, to 1½ in. across, sepals and petals lanceolate, yellow-brown, lip 3-lobed, brown-purple, lateral lobes semiovate, midlobe nearly orbicular, the disc with a pair of ridges. Spring. Himalayas, Burma.

EPILOBIUM L. [*Chamaenerion* Séguier]. FIREWEED, WILLOW HERB. *Onagraceae.* Probably 200 spp. of ann. to per. herbs, or sometimes subshrubs, native to most temp. regions; lvs. alt. or opp., sometimes whorled, simple, entire to toothed; fls. solitary in axils, or in terminal racemes or panicles, 4-merous, regular or irregular, bisexual, sepals separate, petals entire or usually deeply emarginate, stamens 8, those on the sepals longer, ovary inferior; fr. an elongate caps., seeds many, each with a tuft of silky hairs.

Suitable for planting in wild gardens, in a border, or the smaller species useful in rock gardens. Propagated by seeds or division. Some species, especially those of New Zeal., not hardy in colder climates, but often seed themselves.

alpinum L. To 20 in., sts. tufted or mat-forming; lvs. ovate to oblong-elliptic, to 2⅜ in. long, to ¾ in. wide; fls. to ¼ in. long, petals milk-white, sometimes pink-tipped. Arctic, s. to alpine regions of New Hamp., Colo., Calif.

angustifolium L. [*Chamaenerion augustifolium* (L.) Scop.]. FIREWEED, GREAT W.H., WICKUP. Per., with underground rhizomes, sts. commonly 3–5 ft., leafy; lvs. alt., 2-6 in. long, acute, scarcely toothed; fls. many, in long, terminal, spikelike racemes, ⁵⁄₁₆–¾ in. long, rose to purple or white, style pubescent at base. N. Amer., Eurasia, especially in newly cleared land and burned areas.

brevipes Hook.f. Sts. to 14 in., stout, woody at base, straggling, red to purple; lvs. opp., crowded, petioled, leathery, blades elliptic-lanceolate to ovate-oblong, to 1 in. long; petals ⁵⁄₁₆ in. long, white or pink. New Zeal.

chloriifolium Hausskn. Sts. somewhat woody at base, 6–18 in., pubescent, rather stout; lvs. opp., ovate, ¼–¾ in. long, coarsely and remotely toothed, green to brownish; petals ⁵⁄₁₆ in. long, white or rose. New Zeal.

coloratum Biehler. Per. with basal rosettes, sts. to 3 ft., intricately branched above; lvs. mostly opp., elongate-lanceolate, 2–6 in. long, serrulate; petals pink, less than ³⁄₁₆ in. long. E. N. Amer.

crassum Hook.f. Sts. woody at base, creeping, to 6 in. high; lvs. opp., obovate to spatulate-oblong, to 1⅜ in. long, ½ in. wide, fleshy; fls. rose or white, about ⅜ in. long. New Zeal.

Dodonaei Vill. [*E. rosmarinifolium* Haenke]. Erect per., ½–3 ft., with underground fleshy rhizomes; lvs. alt., linear, 1–2½ in. long, scarcely toothed, minutely strigose; fls. crowded near ends of brs., petals narrow-elliptic, about ½ in. long, purplish-red, style hairy ⅓ its length. Eur., w. Asia.

Fleischeri Hochst. Close to *E. Dodonaei*, but shorter, sts. decumbent; lvs. more lanceolate; petals narrower, style hairy half its length. Alps.

glabellum G. Forst. Sts. many, to 12 in., woody at base, often colored and with 2–4 lines of pubescence; lvs. largely opp., about ½ in. long, remotely toothed; petals ¼–⁵⁄₁₆ in. long, white to pink. New Zeal.

Hectori Hausskn. Decumbent and rooting, but becoming 6 in. high; lvs. mostly opp., crowded, oblong or linear-oblong, ¼–½ in. long; fls. in upper axils, petals ¼ in. across, white. New Zeal. Much material cult. under this name is said to be *E. purpuratum*.

hirsutum L. Rhizomatous per., 2–6 ft., soft-hairy; lvs. opp., clasping at base, lanceolate, 2–4 in. long; fls. mostly in short racemes, petals ½–¾ in. long, purplish-red. Eurasia, N. Afr.; naturalized in U.S.

kaikoense: a listed name of no botanical standing.

latifolium L. [*Chamaenerion latifolium* (L.) Sweet]. RIVER-BEAUTY. Differing from *E. angustifolium* in being shorter, to 1½ ft.; lvs. alt., lanceolate to ovate, glaucous; fls. fewer, ½–¾ in. long, style glabrous at base. N. Amer., Eurasia.

luteum Pursh. Per., with creeping underground rhizome, sts. simple, erect, 6–15 in.; lvs. opp., ovate, 1–2½ in. long, sinuate-toothed, glabrous; fls. few, petals ½–¾ in. long, yellow. N. Calif. to Alaska.

nummularifolium A. Cunn. Prostrate, rooting at nodes, forming patches to 6 in. across, branchlets reddish-green; lvs. opp., roundish, to ½ in. long, pale beneath; fls. less than ³⁄₁₆ in. across, petals white or pale pink. New Zeal.

obcordatum A. Gray. ROCK-FRINGE. Decumbent or prostrate per., much-branched, sts. 2–6 in. long; lvs. opp., elliptic to ovate, ¼–1 in. long, glabrous; fls. 1 to few, solitary in upper axils, petals ½–¾ in. long, rose-purple. W. U.S.

purpuratum Hook.f. Sts. stiff, prostrate and rooting, purplish-black; lvs. opp., crowded, broadly oblong to nearly orbicular, to ½ in. long, thick, leathery; fls. few. New Zeal. May be cult. as *E. Hectori*.

rosmarinifolium: *E. Dodonaei.*

EPIMEDIUM L. [*Aceranthus* C. Morr. & Decne.]. *Berberidaceae.* About 21 spp. of low, rhizomatous per. herbs of temp. Eur. and Asia; lvs. small, pinnately or ternately divided; infl. simple or compound, fls. small, sepals 8, the outer 4 unequal, in 2 pairs, soon falling, the inner 4 petaloid, spreading or reflexed at flowering time, petals 4, flat and petal-like or extended into pouches or spurs, stamens 4, ovary with several ovules. The spp. have been frequently confused in cult.

Well suited to rock gardens and half-shady locations. Zone 7. In sheltered spots under trees, the foliage often remains all winter and leaves persist when dead. Any good woodland soil is satisfactory. Propagated by division of rhizomes.

album: a listed name of no botanical standing, used for plants perhaps referable to *E.* × *Youngianum* cv. 'Niveum'.

alpinum L. To 1 ft.; lvs. biternate; fls. to ½ in. across, sepals red, petals yellow, slipperlike, spurs short. S. Eur. Var. **rubrum:** *E.* × *rubrum.* Cv. **'Luteum'** is listed.

bicolorum: a listed name of no botanical standing, used for *E.* × *Youngianum.*

×**coccineum:** *E.* × *rubrum.*

colchicum: *E. pinnatum* subsp.

diphyllum Lodd. [*Aceranthus diphyllus* (Lodd.) C. Morr. & Decne.]. To 8 in.; lvs. basal and cauline, lfts. 2, ovate-cordate, oblique, to 2 in. long; fls. white, drooping, small, petals spurless. Japan.

elegans: a hort. name of no botanical standing, used for *E. pinnatum* subsp. *colchicum.*

grandiflorum C. Morr. [*E. macranthum* C. Morr. & Decne.]. To 1 ft.; lvs. basal and cauline, biternate or triternate; fls. 1–2 in. across, outer sepals red, inner sepals violet, petals white, spurs deflexed, prominently projecting, to 1 in. long. Japan, Korea, Manchuria. Cv. **'Violaceum'** [forma *violaceum* (C. Morr.) Stearn; *E. violaceum* C. Morr.]. Inner sepals and petals light violet, the petals not much longer than inner sepals.

hexandrum: *Vancouveria hexandra.*

lilacinum Donck. ex C. Morr. A name for an old hybrid, but plants so called in cult. today are *E.* × *Youngianum* cv. 'Roseum'.

luteum: a a listed name of no botanical standing for *E.* × *versicolor* cv. 'Sulphureum'.

macranthum *E. grandiflorum.*

Musschianum C. Morr. & Decne. A name of uncertain botanical application, but plants cult. under this name are usually *E.* × *Youngianum* cv. 'Niveum'.

ochroleucum: *E.* ×versicolor cv. 'Sulphureum'.

Perralderanum Coss. Differs from *E. pinnatum* in having lvs. only once ternate and lfts. more spiny-toothed; lvs. marked with bronze when young. Algeria.

pinnatum Fisch. To 1 ft.; lvs. all basal, usually biternate; fls. to ⅝ in. across, inner sepals bright yellow, spurs red, short. N. Iran, Caucasus. Subsp. **colchicum** (Boiss.) Stearn [*E. colchicum* (Boiss.) Hort. ex Trautv.; *E. elegans* Hort.; *E. pinnatum* var. *elegans* Hort. ex W. Mill.]. Lfts. fewer, usually 3 or 5. Var. **elegans:** subsp. *colchicum.*

roseum: a listed name of no botanical standing for *E.* × *Youngianum* cv.

×**rubrum** C. Morr. [*E. alpinum* var. *rubrum* (C. Morr.) Hook.f.; *E.* ×*coccineum* Silva-Tar.]: *E. alpinum* × *E. grandiflorum.* Fls. to 1 in. across, inner sepals bright crimson, petals pale yellow or white tinged with red, slipperlike, spurs slightly upcurved.

sulphureum: *E.* × *versicolor* cv.

×**versicolor** C. Morr.: *E. grandiflorum* × *E. pinnatum.* Lvs. mottled or red when young, later green; fls. nearly 1 in. across, inner sepals old rose, petals yellow, spurs tinged red. Cv. 'Neo-sulphureum', st. lvs. usually of 3 lfts., inner sepals creamy-yellow, petals lemon-yellow, spurs short, tinged brown. Cv. 'Sulphureum' [*E. luteum* Hort.; *E. ochroleucum* Farrer; *E. sulphureum* C. Morr.]. St. lvs. of 9 lfts., usually not mottled; inner sepals pale yellow, petals brighter yellow.

violaceum: *E. grandiflorum* forma.

×**Youngianum** Fisch. & C. A. Mey.: *E. diphyllum* × *E. grandiflorum.* To 1 ft.; fls. white or rose, to ¾ in. across, pendulous. Cvs. are: **'Album'**: probably 'Niveum'; **'Niveum'** [*E. Musschianum* Hort., not C. Morr. & Decne.], fls. pure white; **'Roseum'** [*E. lilacinum* Hort., not Donck. ex C. Morr; *E. roseum* Hort.], fls. rose-lilac.

EPIPACTIS Zinn [*Amesia* A. Nels. & Macbr.]. HELLEBORINE. *Orchidaceae.* About 24 spp. of terrestrial herbs with short rhizomes, native to temp. Eurasia, N. Amer., and N. Afr.; sts. erect, leafy; fls. in loose terminal racemes with conspicuous bracts, sepals and petals alike, greenish to purplish to variously colored, lip 3-lobed, sessile on base of column, fleshy, saccate at its base, column without a rostellum. For structure of fl. see *Orchidaceae.*

For culture see *Orchids.*

atrorubens: *E. rubiginosa.*

decipiens: *Goodyera oblongifolia.*

gigantea Dougl. ex Hook. [*Amesia gigantea* (Dougl. ex Hook.) A. Nels. & Macbr.; *Serapias gigantea* (Dougl. ex Hook.) A. A. Eat.]. GIANT H., GIANT ORCHID, STREAM O., CHATTERBOX. To 3 ft.; lvs. ovate to lanceolate, to 8 in. long; racemes loosely 2- to many-fld.; fls. about 1 in. across, sepals greenish to rose, with purplish veins, petals pale

pink to rose with red or purple veins, lip strongly veined and marked with red or purple. Summer. W. N. Amer., Mex.

Helleborine (L.) Crantz [*E. latifolia* (L.) All.]. BROADLEAVED H., BASTARD H. Erect, to 4 ft.; lvs. variable, clasping st.; racemes loosely or densely few- to many-fld., fl. bracts leafy, usually longer than fls.; fls. small, greenish, tinged with purple or rose-red, sepals and petals to ½ in. long, lip greenish and purplish, dark purple on basal half. Early summer–early autumn. Eurasia; naturalized, and sometimes weedy, from Que. and n. New Eng. to Mo.

latifolia: *E. Helleborine.*

pubescens: *Goodyera pubescens.*

repens: *Goodyera repens.*

rubiginosa Guad.-Beaup. ex W. D. J. Koch [*E. atrorubens* Schult.]. Sts. short, erect; lvs. 5–7, near base of st., clasping, ovate-lanceolate, red beneath; racemes stiff, spikelike, 8–18-fld., fl. bracts short; fls. small, wine-red, lip shorter than sepals, green, with red margins. Summer. Iran, Eur., Gr. Brit., Caucasus.

tesselata: *Goodyera tesselata.*

×**EPIPHRONITIS** Rolfe: *Epidendrum* × *Sophronitis. Orchidaceae.* A group of bigeneric hybrids generally intermediate between the parents.

For culture see *Orchids.*

Veitchii Hort.: *Epidendrum ibaguense* × *Sophronitis grandiflora.* Similar in growth habit to *Epidendrum ibaguense;* fls. about 1 in. across, orange-red, lip 3-lobed, with orange central disc in front of 2 calluses.

EPIPHYLLANTHUS A. Berger. *Cactaceae.* Three spp. of small epiphytic or terrestrial cacti, native to Brazil; sts. of short, cylindrical or somewhat flattened but not 2-winged joints, which branch and flower near the apex; areoles scattered over the surface, with bristlelike spines; fls. much as in *Schlumbergera truncata,* inner perianth segms. united into a tube oblique at the mouth, tube with a deflexed membranous appendage near the base, stamens on perianth tube, the lower ones united into a short tube, stigma lobes erect, connivent, ovary angled; fr. umbilicate.

For culture see *Cacti.*

obovatus: *E. opuntioides.*

obtusangulus (K. Schum.) A. Berger. Sts. erect to pendent, to 16 in. long, joints globose to cylindrical or club-shaped, ½–2½ in. long; areoles sometimes on low, elongate tubercles, bristles absent or 1–20, gray, to ¼ in. long; fls. purple to rose, 1½ in. long.

opuntioides (Löfgr. & Dusén) Moran [*E. obovatus* Britt. & Rose]. Sts. erect to decumbent, to 16 in. long, joints of trunk cylindrical, 1–2½ in. long, to 1 in. thick, ultimate joints flattened, obovate, 2–2½ in. long, about 1 in. wide and ¼ in. thick; bristles to ¼ in. long; fls. 2 in. long, rose.

EPIPHYLLUM Haw. [*Phyllocactus* Link]. ORCHID CACTUS, POND-LILY C. *Cactaceae.* About 16 spp. of mostly epiphytic cacti with often large and fragrant fls., native to trop. Amer.; sts. often cylindrical and woody, brs. elongate, flat, 2- or sometimes 3-winged, crenate or lobed; areoles marginal, in the indentations, spines bristlelike or mostly absent on mature plants; fls. diurnal or nocturnal, white, perianth tube longer than the segms., stamens many, inserted in the throat or tube, sometimes with a distinct series at the mouth, tube and ovary somewhat scaly; fr. with low ridges or tubercles, splitting at maturity. *Disocactus, Eccremocactus,* and *Nopalxochia,* sometimes included in *Epiphyllum,* are here treated separately, although they are very closely allied. Many hybrids of *Heliocereus, Hylocereus, Nyctocereus,* and *Selenicereus* with *Epiphyllum* and its segregates are grown under the common name epiphyllum or orchid cactus. *Epiphyllum crenatum* is said to be the only true *Epiphyllum* sp. used in any of these hybrids.

The epiphyllums are very useful as greenhouse and window garden plants and are frequently seen in summer on porches. They propagate readily by cuttings and have simple requirements. For culture see *Cacti.*

Ackermannii: *Nopalxochia Ackermannii.*

anguliger (Lem.) G. Don. FISHBONE CACTUS. Brs. oblanceolate, obtuse, to 4½ in. wide, lobed nearly to the midrib, lobes oblong and rounded to triangular and acute or obtuse, alt. on the 2 sides at midrib, the upper edge about perpendicular to midrib; fls. fragrant, lasting 2 days, 6 in. long, 5–6 in. wide, outer perianth segms. reddish-yellow, perianth tube with few scales, stamens in 2 series, style white; fr. green inside and out. S. Mex.

Anthonyanum: a listed name of no botanical standing, perhaps for *Cryptocereus Anthonyanus*.

caudatum Britt. & Rose. Sts. slender, cylindrical, brs. elongate-lanceolate, cuneate, long-acuminate, crenate, to 8 in. long and 1⅝ in. wide; fls. white, to 6 in. long, perianth tube slender, ovary naked. S. Mex.

chrysocardium Alexand. Brs. flattened, lobed to midrib, lobes to 6 in. long and 1⅝ in. wide, upcurved to acuminate apex; areoles notch-like at base of lobe, bristles 0–3; fls. 1 ft. long, 8 in. across, stamen filaments yellow, anthers slate-brown, ovary tubercled, scales with 2–4 bristles in axils. S. Mex.

Cooperi: a listed name of no botanical standing.

crenatum (Lindl.) G. Don. Brs. thick, obtuse, 2–3½ in. wide, coarsely obliquely crenate; fls. fragrant, lasting several days, 8 in. long, 4–6 in. across, perianth tube and ovary with linear scales 1 in. long, stamens yellow, in 2 series, style white; fr. red. Honduras and Guatemala. Much used in hybridizing.

Darrahii (K. Schum.) Britt. & Rose. Brs. lanceolate, acute or rounded, 8–12 in. long, 1½–2 in. wide, deeply toothed; fls. diurnal, fragrant, 5–7 in. long, about 4 in. across, outer perianth segms. yellow, style white; fr. green inside and out. S. Mex. Closely allied to *E. anguliger* and perhaps not distinct.

Gertrudianum: a listed name of no botanical standing.

guatemalense Britt. & Rose. Brs. 1½–3 in. wide, obtuse, coarsely obliquely crenate; fls. nocturnal, to 1 ft. long, tube with few scales, pilose inside, style orange. Guatemala.

hermosissimum: a listed name of no botanical standing.

Hookeri (Link & Otto) Haw. Climbing, to 30 ft. or more, brs. 2–4 in. wide, thin, obtusely serrate; fls. nocturnal, faintly fragrant, about 8 in. long, filaments white, in 1 series, ovary with few scales; fr. red, 3 in. long. Trinidad and ne. S. Amer.

Kermesianum: a listed name of no botanical standing.

lepidocarpum (A. Web.) Britt. & Rose. Brs. flat or sometimes 3-winged, 8–10 in. long, 1 in. wide; fls. nocturnal, 8 in. long, stamens in 2 series, ovary with many thick, narrow scales, style white; fr. violet-red, scaly, 3½ in. long, 1½ in. in diam., the pulp white. Costa Rica.

Loebneri: a listed name of no botanical standing.

Londonii: a listed name of no botanical standing.

macropterum (Lem.) Britt. & Rose. To 6 ft., brs. oblong, obtuse, thin, to 16 in. long, 2–5 in. wide, broadly and shallowly crenate, crenations not or scarcely oblique, margins horny; areoles with hairs; fls. lasting 2 or 3 days, to 1 ft. long and 8 in. across, perianth tube scaly, stamens yellow, in 2 series, scales of ovary with long axillary hairs, style white. Costa Rica.

mexicanum: a listed name of no botanical standing.

oxypetalum (DC.) Haw. DUTCHMAN'S-PIPE, DUTCHMAN'S-PIPE CACTUS. To 20 ft. or more, brs. lanceolate, acuminate, to 3 ft. long, 4-5 in. wide, obliquely crenate; fls. nocturnal, fragrant, to 11 in. long and 5 in. across, perianth tube with scattered scales, stamens in 2 series, style white or red; fr. red. Mex. to Brazil. Much cult.

Peacockii: a listed name of no botanical standing.

phyllanthoides: *Nopalxochia phyllanthoides.*

Phyllanthus (L.) Haw. To 10 ft., brs. oblong to linear, obtuse, to 2 ft. long, 1½–3 in. wide, obliquely crenate; fls. nocturnal, fragrant, 8–12 in. long, limb about 2 in. across, stamens in 1 series, style white or pinkish; fr. red, 2–3½ in. long, 1½ in. in diam. Panama to Peru and Brazil.

Pittieri (A. Web.) Britt. & Rose. To 10 ft., brs. thin, oblong, obtuse, 12–16 in. long, 1–2 in. wide, obtusely serrate; fls. nocturnal but lasting the next day, fragrant, 4–5 in. long, to 3½ in. across, perianth tube slender, with few scales, stamens in 1 series, style white or pink; fr. red, to 1 in. long. Costa Rica.

pumilum Britt. & Rose. To 18 ft., brs. thin, acute to acuminate, to 2 ft. long, 1–3½ in. wide, weakly obliquely crenate; fls. nocturnal, fragrant, 4–5 in. long, 2 in. across, perianth tube with few scales, stamens in 2 series, style white; fr. purple, pulp white. Guatemala.

roseum: a listed name of no botanical standing.

rugosum: a listed name of no botanical standing.

speciosum: a listed name of no botanical standing.

stenopetalum (C. F. Först.) Britt. & Rose [*Phyllocactus stenopetalus* C. F. Först.]. To 10 ft., brs. linear to lanceolate, acute to obtuse, to 3 ft. long and 5 in. wide, obliquely crenate; fls. nocturnal, fragrant, to 10 in. long, perianth tube with few scales, stamens in 2 series, style white or pink. S. Mex.

strictum (Lem.) Britt. & Rose. To 10 ft., brs. thick and stiff, linear, obtuse, 2–3 in. wide, obliquely crenate; fls. nocturnal, 9–10 in. long, 4–7 in. across, perianth tube with few scales, stamens in 1 series, style pink or red; fr. globose, 2 in. in diam. Summer. S. Mex. to Panama.

Thomasianum (K. Schum.) Britt. & Rose. Similar to *E. macropterum,* but having perianth tube 8 in. long, sepaloid segms. red, scales of ovary brown, lacking hairs in axils, stamens gray-brown. Nativity unknown.

truncatum: *Schlumbergera truncata.*

EPIPHYTE. This is a botanical term used to describe a plant which grows naturally on another plant, gaining only support from its host. Often mistakenly called parasites, epiphytes actually obtain all their water needs from rain or air moisture and essential nutrients from the organic material that naturally accumulates around or on them where they grow above the ground. For this reason they are often called air plants. Such root or rhizome systems as may be developed by epiphytes are used to secure them to the host plant or, when cultivated, to the artificial substrate, such as treefern block, cork bark, etc., supplied by the grower. In most temperate regions, mainly because of the harshness of winter, epiphytes are few and limited mainly to groups of lower plants such as lichens and mosses. Epiphytes have evolved in greatest numbers in the warm and humid tropics because growing conditions there are ideal throughout the year. Many highly specialized growth forms have been developed in epiphytes and aid in successfully maintaining their specialized existence. Such forms are exemplified by the water-holding tanks of certain Bromeliaceae, the humus-gathering nest habit of some of the large epiphytic ferns, and the succulence for water conservation seen in many Cactaceae, Gesneriaceae, Orchidaceae, and *Peperomia* (Piperaceae). In the tropics, epiphytes occupy all niches from the full sun of the highest tree tops to deep shade. Many epiphytes are grown as ornamentals because of their attractive plant form, showy foliage, or colorful or bizarre flowers. A knowledge of how epiphytes live in nature is essential for their successful culture. The families especially important as sources of ornamental epiphytes are the Araceae, Bromeliaceae, Cactaceae, Gesneriaceae, Orchidaceae, Piperaceae, Polypodiaceae, and Rubiaceae.

EPIPREMNOPSIS Engl. *Araceae.* One sp., a scandent vine of Philippine Is. to Molucca Is. and Malay Pen.; lvs. pinnatifid, perforate, petioles short-sheathing, geniculate; spathe reflexed in age, spadix covered with bisexual fls.; perianth absent, ovaries 1-celled, 2-ovuled. Sometimes included in *Epipremnum.*

Strictly tropical; for culture see *Philodendron.*

media (Zoll. & Moritzi) Engl. Climber, to 40 ft. or more; adult lvs. to 10 in. long, ovate in outline, pinnatifid into 3–4 segms. on each side, perforate especially near midrib, veinlets very conspicuous, dark green and bullate above, juvenile lvs. ovate, cordate, entire, but with many elliptic holes to ½ in. long; peduncle to 4 in. long, spathe ovate, yellowish, to 2 in. long.

EPIPREMNUM Schott. *Araceae.* Perhaps 10 spp. of scandent vines, native to se. Asia; lvs. entire or pinnatifid, petioles long, geniculate; spathe fugacious, spadix stout, covered with bisexual fls.; perianth absent, ovaries 1-celled, with a partial partition, ovules 2 to several, basal.

Strictly tropical; for culture see *Philodendron.*

aureum (Linden & André) Bunt. [*Pothos aureus* Linden & André; *Raphidophora aurea* (Linden & André) Birdsey; *Scindapsus aureus* (Linden & André) Engl.]. POTHOS, GOLDEN P., POTHOS VINE, TARO VINE, DEVIL'S IVY, SOLOMON ISLAND I., HUNTER'S-ROBE, GOLDEN H., VARIEGATED PHILODENDRON, GOLDEN CEYLON CREEPER, IVY ARUM. Juvenile growth with slender sts. and ovate-cordate lvs. to 12 in. long, glossy bright green, irregularly splotched or marbled yellow or white; mature shoots with sts. green or striped with yellow or white, climbing to 40 ft. or more; lf. blades to 30 in. or longer, ovate or ovate-oblong, basally cordate, irregularly pinnatifid ½–⅔ of way to midrib into few to many oblong, truncate segms., green to heavily variegated yellowish or white, on shorter stout petioles; spathe and spadix about 6 in. long, peduncle little shorter. Solomon Is. Cvs. are: '**Marble Queen**', lvs. white to creamy, irregularly flecked and blotched with green and gray-green, petioles ivory, and sts. striped with green; '**Tricolor**' [*Pothos tricolor* Hort.], lvs. medium green, marbled and spotted with deep yellow, cream, and pale green; '**Wilcoxii**' [*Pothos Wilcoxii* Hort.], variegations sharply defined from the green portions of lf. blades, petioles and sts. often ivory-white.

falcifolia Engl. Lf. blades elongate-lanceolate, to 2 ft. long and 5 in. wide, acute at each end, entire, petioles shorter than blade, sheathing nearly to the geniculum; spathe to 10 in. long. Indonesia?

Merrillii Engl. & Kurt Krause. Similar to *E. pinnatum*, but having sts. not clothed in fibrous remains of old bractlike lvs.; lf. blades regularly pinnatifid, sometimes quite to the midrib, slightly emarginate at base, segms. slightly contracted at their bases and truncate apically. Philippine Is.

pinnatum (L.) Engl. [*Monstera Nechodomii* Hort.; *Raphidophora pinnata* Schott]. High climber, st. and petiole bases clothed in fibrous remains of old bractlike lvs.; lf. blades of adult shoots elliptic-oblong, to 3 ft. long and 18 in. wide, basally truncate, somewhat irregularly pinnatifid to within ½ in. of the midrib, segms. oblong, 8–14 on each side, 1-nerved, curved-acuminate, with or without many small holes and translucent dots toward the midrib, lvs. of juvenile shoots oblong-lanceolate, entire or occasionally pinnatifid, with or without perforations; spathe to 9 in. long, greenish. Philippine Is. to Malay Pen. and Queensland.

EPISCIA Mart. CARPET PLANT, LOVEJOY. *Gesneriaceae.* About 10 spp. of stoloniferous, terrestrial, hairy herbs in trop. Amer.; lvs. opp., elliptic to ovate; fls. solitary or 2–6 on short peduncles in lf. axils, sepals linear to lanceolate, corolla nearly salverform to tubular-campanulate, spurred at the base, oblique in the calyx, limb oblique, 5-lobed, the lobes spreading, rounded, entire or fringed, stamens 4, borne on corolla tube, filaments depressed or coiled downward after pollen is shed, anthers united in a square, disc a single gland at the back of ovary, ovary superior, style elongating after pollen is shed, stigma mouth-shaped or 2-lobed; fr. a fleshy caps. Many foliage variants and some hybrids have been given cv. names.

For cultivation see *Gesneriaceae.*

chontalensis: *E. lilacina*, but most plants named *E. chontalensis* in cult. are *E. lilacina* cv. 'Panama'.

coccinea: a confused name; most material cult. under this name is *E. reptans*, or less frequently *E. cupreata*.

cupreata (Hook.) Hanst. FLAME VIOLET. Lvs. short-petioled, blades elliptic, 2–5 in. long, 1–3 in. wide, slightly to heavily embossed, appressed- to erect-hairy, coppery- or reddish-green to clear green or variegated with silver; fls. 3–4 on pedicels to 1¾ in. long from a short peduncle, sepals linear, ⅜ in. long, green or red-flushed, corolla tube reddish on upper side, yellowish with red markings on lower side, or very rarely entirely yellow, yellow and spotted with red inside, densely papillose at throat, limb orange-red, lobes to ⅜ in. long, the upper 2 bent backward, the lower 3 longer and spreading. Colombia, Venezuela. Var. **cupreata**. The typical var.; lvs. dark green or coppery. Cv. '**Metallica**' [*C. metallica* Hort.]. Lvs. banded centrally with pale green, margins metallic pink. Var. **viridifolia** (Hook.) Nichols. [*E. splendens* (Linden) Hanst.; *E. viridifolia* Hort.]. Lvs. light green, smoother. Cv. '**Tropical Topaz**'. CANAL ZONE YELLOW E. Fls. yellow. Cv. '**Variegata**'. Lvs. with silver central pattern.

decurrens: *Paradrymonia decurrens.*

dianthiflora H. E. Moore & R. G. Wils. LACE-FLOWER VINE. Stolons with tiny lvs. between the nodes and normal, nodal lvs., normal blades elliptic to ovate, to 1½ in. long, rounded, toothed, often veined red above; fls. solitary, sepals linear, ⅜ in. long, toothed, green, corolla glistening white, tube 1¼ in. long, spotted with purple at base and on inside of spur, throat rounded, lobes spreading, ½ in. long, deeply fringed; caps. green, ½ in. long. Mex.

fimbriata Fritsch. Sts. and stolons hairy; lvs. broadly elliptic to ovate, to 4 in. long, 2¼ in. wide, crenate, upper surface hairy and bullate, green with emerald-silver veins or bronzy-green with pale veins, lower surface pale or reddish with prominent veins; fls. solitary on villous pedicels, sepals linear-oblong, ½ in. long, minutely toothed, green, villous, corolla prominently spurred, to 1¼ in. long, white, hairy outside, throat open and sometimes yellowish, lobes to ⅜ in. long, fringed. Peru, Brazil.

fulgida: *E. reptans.*

lilacina Hanst. [*E. chontalensis* (Seem.) Hook.f.]. Sts. and stolons hairy; lvs. elliptic to ovate, to 4 in. long, 2½ in. wide, hairy, green to dark reddish-green, often rose-purple beneath; fls. solitary or 2–6 on pedicels to 1¼ in. long from a short peduncle, sepals oblong, to ⅜ in. long, minutely toothed or entire, green or reddish, corolla tube to 1⅜ in. long, prominently spurred, narrowed laterally at throat, white, short-hairy, with pale lavender limb and a pale yellow patch in throat, lobes to ¾ in. long, minutely toothed. Cvs. include: '**Cuprea**', lvs. bronzy; '**Mrs. Fanny Haage**', lvs. with pale nerves; '**Panama**', lvs. narrow, appressed-hairy; '**Viridis**', lvs. broad, softly hairy.

melittifolia: *Nautilocalyx melittifolius.*

metallica: a listed name of no botanical standing for *E. cupreata* cv.

punctata (Lindl.) Hanst. Sts. to 6 in., with brown stolons; lvs. ovate to ovate-elliptic, to 3 in. long, 2 in. wide, coarsely toothed, appressed-hairy, green, or the margins red-flushed; fls. solitary, short-pedicelled, sepals ½ in. long, remotely toothed, green or reddish, corolla tube to 1¼ in. long, pale yellowish-white, purple-spotted, hairy, throat broad, lobes spreading, to ⅜ in. long, toothed or fringed, heavily spotted with purple or violet; caps. brown, ¾ in. long. Mex., Guatemala.

reptans Mart. [*E. fulgida* (Linden) Hook.f.]. FLAME VIOLET, RED V., SCARLET V. Stolons brownish; lvs. broadly elliptic, to 5 in. long, 2½ in. wide, heavily embossed, erect-hairy, dark green with pale green or silvery pattern along midrib and lateral nerves; fls. 3–4 on pedicels to 1 in. long from a short peduncle, sepals oblong, ½ in. long, recurved at apex, toothed, red-flushed, corolla tube 1½ in. long, hairy, pale red outside, pink with obscure lines inside, lobes to ½ in. long, pale red outside, blood-red inside. Guyana to Peru.

splendens: *E. cupreata* var. *viridifolia.*

tessellata: *Nautilocalyx bullatus.*

variegata: a listed name of no botanical standing; probably *E. cupreata* var. *viridifolia.*

viridifolia: a listed name of no botanical standing; probably *E. cupreata* var.

EPITHELANTHA A. Web. ex Britt. & Rose. BUTTON CACTUS. *Cactaceae.* A few spp. of very small, tubercled cacti of w. Tex. and n. Mex.; sts. simple or cespitose, subglobose to club-shaped, apex woolly, with a conical tuft of young spines, tubercles small, close-set; spines many, slender; fls. from young areoles, diurnal, pink, small, perianth segms. and stamens few, ovary naked; fr. club-shaped, red, seeds few, black, finely tubercled, hilum elongate. Resembling *Mammillaria* but allied to *Ariocarpus.*

For culture see *Cacti.*

micromeris (Engelm.) A. Web. ex Britt. & Rose [*Mammillaria micromeris* Engelm.]. BUTTON CACTUS. Sts. globose, depressed at apex, to 1½ in. thick; spines in 2 series of about 20, white, mostly less than ⅛ in. long, in mature plant upper spines 6–8, linear-club-shaped, secretory, to 5⁄16 in. long, the tips later breaking off; fls. to ½ in. long; fr. ½ in. long. Tex., n. Mex. Var. **densispina** (Bravo) Backeb. Spines 20–24, dense, woolly, white, golden at base. N. Mex. Var. **fungifera** is listed. Var. **Greggii** (Engelm.) Borg. To 2½ in. wide, N. Mex. Var. **rufispina** (Bravo) Backeb. Spines 18-22, the upper ones red-brown, central spines 5. N. Mex.

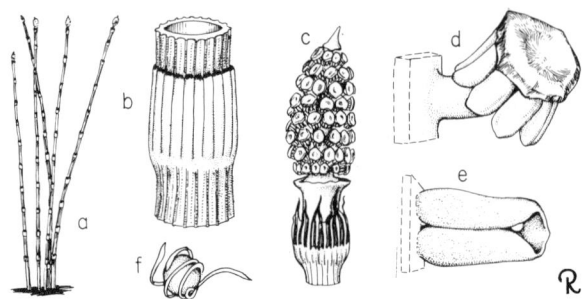

EQUISETACEAE. *Equisetum hyemale*: **a**, plant, × ⅛; **b**, stem section at node, × 3; **c**, strobilus, × 1½; **d**, sporophyll, × 10; **e**, sporangium, × 20; **f**, spore with elaters, × 80. (From Lawrence, *Taxonomy of Vascular Plants*.)

EQUISETACEAE L. Rich. ex DC. HORSETAIL FAMILY. Fern allies; 1 genus, *Equisetum*, of about 35 spp. of primitive, spore-bearing, vascular, ann. or per., rhizomatous herbs of nearly cosmopolitan distribution; sts. hollow, jointed, impregnated with silica, brs. whorled; lvs. scalelike, marginally united into a sheath around each node; sporophylls in a terminal, spikelike cone (strobilus) composed of peltate sporangia-bearing structures, spores all alike.

EQUISETUM L. HORSETAIL, SCOURING RUSH *Equisetaceae*. Perhaps 35 spp. of per. herbs, mostly of wet places, widely distributed except in Australia and New Zeal.; characters those of the family.

The siliceous stems are sometimes used in polishing. Occasionally used as an ornamental in moist places including pool margins. Easily propagated by division. See also *Ferns*.

hyemale L. COMMON SCOURING RUSH, COMMON H. Evergreen, to 4 ft., sts. slender, mostly simple, with central cavity, furrowed with 14–40 ridges, rough; strobilus pointed. Eurasia, Pacific N. Amer. Often grown in Japanese-style gardens and beside pools. Var. **affine** (Engelm.) A. A. Eat. [*E. prealtum* Raf.]. Sts. ¾–3 ft., sheaths with teeth mostly early deciduous. E. N. Amer. Var. **robustum** (A. Br.) A. A. Eat. [*E. robustum* A. Br.]. Sts. 1½–10 ft., sheaths with teeth tardily deciduous. E. N. Amer.

prealtum: *E. hyemale* var. *affine*.

robustum: *E. hyemale* var.

scirpoides Michx. DWARF SCOURING RUSH. Low and diffuse in habit, sts. lacking central cavity. N. Amer.

variegatum Schleich. VARIEGATED H., VARIEGATED SCOURING RUSH. Evergreen, sts. to 2 ft., tufted, slender, with central cavity, furrowed with 5–10 ridges, sheaths black above, with persistent teeth; strobilus about ³⁄₁₆ in. long. Eurasia, n. N. Amer.

ERAGROSTIS N. M. Wolf. LOVE GRASS. *Gramineae*. About 250 spp. of ann. or per. grasses in temp. and trop. regions; panicle open or contracted; spikelets few- to many-fld., rachilla disarticulated above the glumes and between the florets, or continuous, florets usually closely imbricate, glumes keeled, shorter than spikelet, lemma 3-nerved, acute or acuminate, keeled or rounded on the back, deciduous, palea persistent. For terminology see *Gramineae*.

abyssinica: *E. Tef*.

amabilis (L.) Wight & Arn. ex Nees [*E. tenella* (L.) Beauvois var. *plumosa* Stapf]. FEATHER L. G., JAPANESE L. G. Ann., sts. to 1 ft., branching, erect to spreading, slender, wiry; lf. blades flat to nearly involute, mostly less than 4 in. long, ¼ in. wide; panicle oblong or oblong-lanceolate, rather open, to 1½ in. wide; spikelets 4–8-fld., ⅛ in. long, glumes very short, lemma ovate, obtuse, keels of palea long-ciliate. Se. Asia; introd. and escaped in Ga., Fla., and Tex.

capillaris (L.) Nees. LACE GRASS. Ann., sts. to 20 in., erect soft, branched from base, brs. erect; lf. sheaths pilose, to nearly glabrous, blades flat, erect, pilose on upper surface near the base, elongate, to ⅛ in. wide; spikelets 1–5-fld., lead-colored, glumes acute, very short, lemma acute, obscurely 3-nerved, minutely scabrous toward the apex; grain somewhat grooved. Me. to Wisc., s. to Ga. and e. Tex.

chloromelas Steud. BOER L. G., BLUE L. G. Per., sts. to 3 ft., branching, erect, forming dense clumps; lf. blades elongate, somewhat involute; panicle to 8 in. long, loose; spikelets dark olive. S. Afr.; introd. for erosion control in sw. U.S.

curvula (Schrad.) Nees. WEEPING L. G. Sts. to 4 ft., erect, densely clustered, simple or sometimes branching at lower nodes; lf. sheaths narrow, glabrous, or sparsely hispid or the lower ones densely hairy toward the base, blades elongate, tapering to a fine point, involute, scabrous; panicle to 1 ft., brs. ascending, solitary or paired; spikelets 7–11-fld., to ⅜ in. long, gray-green, lemma prominently nerved. S. Afr.; introd. for ornament and erosion control, naturalized in Fla., Tex., and Ariz.

elegans Nees [*E. interrupta* (Lam.) Döll]. Sts. erect, geniculate at base; lvs. smooth, glabrous, blades linear, pointed; panicle elongate, dense, scabrous, brs. many, capillary; spikelets imbricate, small, 2–9-fld., the terminal with a short pedicel, the lateral subsessile, glumes hyaline, oblong-lanceolate, lemma hyaline, 1–3-nerved. Brazil.

interrupta: *E. elegans*.

Lehmanniana Nees. LEHMANN L. G. Per.; sts. prostrate, 1 to nearly 3 ft. long, the nodes rooting and producing tufts of brs.; panicle 4–6 in. long, open; spikelets linear, to ½ in. long. S. Afr.; introd. into the Southwest for erosion control, naturalized in Ariz.

suaveolens A. Becker ex Claus. Confused with *A. amabilis*, from which it differs in having sts. to 3 ft. high, diffuse panicle, comprising half or more the height of the plant, 7–11-fld. spikelets mostly more than ¼ in. long, and short-pointed lemma. W. Asia. Grown for bouquets.

Tef (Zuccagni) Trott. [*E. abyssinica* (Jacq.) Link]. TEFF. Ann., sts. to 3 ft. or more, branching and spreading, slender, glabrous; lf. blades long and narrow; panicle open, very loose, to 15 in. long; spikelets 5–9-fld., to ⁵⁄₁₆ in. long, lemma roughened on nerves and apex. Ne. Afr., where the seed is used for food. Occasionally cult. for ornament.

tenella var. **plumosa:** *E. amabilis*.

trichodes (Nutt.) A. Wood. SAND L. G. Per., sts. to 4 ft., erect, clustered; lf. sheaths pilose at the summit, blades flat to nearly involute, elongate, ⅛–¼ in. wide, tapering to a slender point, scabrous on the upper surface; panicle open, longer than broad, 3–4 times branched, brs. capillary; spikelets long-pedicelled, mostly 4–6-fld., purplish, to ¼ in. long, glumes acuminate, about ⅛ in. long, lemma to ⅛ in., acute, keel and lateral nerves strong. Ill. to Colo. and Tex.

ERANTHEMUM L. [*Daedalacanthus* T. Anderson]. *Acanthaceae*. About 30 spp. of herbs or shrubs of trop. Asia; lvs. opp.; infl. terminal or axillary, bracts large, longer than calyces; calyx deeply and equally 5-parted, corolla tube long, narrow, lobes 5, nearly equal, suborbicular, stamens 2, anther sacs 2, staminodes 2, small, ovary with 2 ovules in each cell; fr. a caps.

Eranthemums thrive in light rich soil with ample sunlight and water. Propagated by cuttings of young wood.

atropurpureum: see *Pseuderanthemum atropurpureum* and *P. kewense*.

bicolor: *Pseuderanthemum bicolor*.

elegans: *Lankesteria elegans*.

igneum: *Xantheranthemum igneum*.

indicum (Nees) C. B. Clarke. Shrub, to 4 ft.; lvs. lanceolate-elliptic, to 3 in. long; fls. in terminal racemes to 5 in. long, bracts small, shorter than calyx, corolla white, with purple lines, tubular in lower half, ventricose above. Himalayas.

nervosum: *E. pulchellum*.

pseudo-alatum: a listed name of no botanical standing.

pulchellum Andr. [*E. nervosum* (Vahl) R. Br.]. BLUE SAGE. Shrub, to 4 ft.; lvs. ovate, to 8 in. long, prominently veined; fls. in axillary and terminal spikes, bracts prominently nerved, corolla blue, 1 in. long, tubular, lobes spreading. India; escapes in trop. regions.

reticulatum: *Pseuderanthemum reticulatum*.

rubrovenosum: *Fittonia Verschaffeltii* var. *Verschaffeltii*.

tricolor Nichols. Straggling shrub; lvs. opp. or sometimes in 3's, oblong-ovate, irregularly blotched with purple and pink. Polynesia. Perhaps this sp. belongs in *Pseuderanthemum*.

tuberculatum: *Pseuderanthemum tuberculatum*.

Wattii (Beddome) Stapf. Differs from *E. pulchellum* in being herbaceous; lvs. ovate, to 4 in. long; corolla purple or violet, tubular, lobes spreading. N. India.

ERANTHIS Salisb. WINTER ACONITE. *Ranunculaceae*. About 7 spp. of low per. herbs with short tubers, native to Eur. and Asia; radical lvs. palmately dissected, involucral lvs. sessile; fls. solitary, yellow or white, sessile above involucre or pedicelled, sepals 5–8, petaloid, petals modified into small nectaries, stamens many, pistils few to many; fr. of many-seeded follicles.

Blooming in early spring; hardy and thriving in moist places; propagated by division.

cilicica Schott & Kotschy. Like *E. hyemalis*, but less robust, to 2½ in.; involucre more deeply and narrowly segmented; fls. larger, sepals almost ½ in. wide. Greece, Asia Minor.

hyemalis (L.) Salisb. Glabrous, sts. 2–6 in.; radical lvs. mostly solitary, orbicular, 3–5-lobed, then cut into segms.; involucre spreading horizontally; fls. sessile, yellow, about 1 in. across, sepals usually 6, narrowly ovate or oblong; follicles brown, to ⅝ in. long, stipitate. S. Eur.; naturalized farther north and in Amer.

pinnatifida Maxim. Sts. 4–6 in.; basal and involucral lvs. pinnatifid; fls. pedicelled, white; carpels scarcely stalked. Japan.

sibirica DC. Like *E. hyemalis*, but sepals 5, elliptic. E. Siberia.

×**Tubergenii** Bowles: *E. cilicica* × *E. hyemalis*. Erect, glabrous, 2–8 in.; involucre to 3 in. in diam., fls. 1–2¼ in. across, sepals mostly 6, yellow; follicles sterile.

ERDISIA Britt. & Rose. *Cactaceae*. About 6 spp. of low, ribbed cacti, native to Andean S. Amer.; sts. club-shaped and from underground rhizomes or slender and above ground, ribs 6–10; fls. diurnal, red, yellow, or purplish, perianth tube short, areoles spiny; fr. globose, spines deciduous. Perhaps not a natural group; some spp. perhaps too close to *Corryocactus*.

For culture see *Cacti*.

maxima Backeb. Loosely shrubby, sts. reclining, to 6 ft. long and 1¼ in. thick, ribs 6, narrow; areoles 1¼ in. apart, spines translucent, becoming yellowish, radial spines 10, to ¾ in. long, central spine 1, to 1¼ in. long; fls. 2 in. long and wide; fr. green. Cent. Peru.

melanotricha: *Corryocactus melanotrichus*.

Meyenii Britt. & Rose. Rhizomes present, joints club-shaped, to 8 in. long and 2 in. thick, ribs 5–8, to ½ in. high; spines awl-shaped, brown to blackish, to 2½ in. long, radial spines about 6–8, central spine 1; fls. yellow, 1½ in. long, areoles with felt and spines; fr. reddish, ¾ in. in diam. N. Chile, s. Peru.

Ruthae: a listed name of no botanical standing.

squarrosa (Vaup.) Britt. & Rose. Sts. prostrate or suberect, to 6 ft. long and 1 in. thick, ribs 7–9, ⁵⁄₁₆ in. high; areoles to 1 in. apart, spines stout, yellowish, swollen at base, radial spines 10–15, unequal, central spine 1, to 1½ in. long; fls. red, to 2 in. long and wide, spines bristlelike; fr. 1 in. long, seeds ³⁄₃₂ in. long. Peru.

EREMALCHE Greene. *Malvaceae*. Perhaps 4 spp. of small ann. herbs in sw. U.S., Calif., and n. Mex.; lvs. more or less orbicular, unlobed or palmately 3-, 5-, or 7-parted; fls. axillary, involucral bracts 3, corolla white or mauve, sometimes spotted basally, stamens united in a tubular column, style brs. as many as the mericarps, stigmas terminal; fr. a schizocarp, mericarps in a single whorl, each 1-seeded, indehiscent, with the dorsal wall united to the seed, and lateral walls sometimes absent.

rotundifolia (A. Gray) Greene [*Malvastrum rotundifolium* A. Gray]. DESERT FIVE-SPOT. Simple or branched, hispid herb, 1–2 ft.; lvs. reniform-orbicular, unlobed, coarsely dentate; corolla nearly globose, petals about 1 in. long, lilac to mauve-pink, spotted at base; mericarps 30–40, about ⅛ in. long, strongly compressed laterally, black, with faintly reticulate lateral walls. Spring. Deserts, Calif., Ariz., Nev., Mex.

EREMOCARPUS Benth. [*Piscaria* Piper]. *Euphorbiaceae*. One sp., a monoecious ann., with strong-scented herbage and stellate pubescence, native to w. N. Amer.; lvs. alt., entire, 3-nerved; fls. without petals, male fls. in axillary cymes, female fls. 1–3 in lower axils; ovary 1-celled, fr. a caps.

Suited to dry sites.

setigerus (Hook.) Benth. [*Piscaria setigera* (Hook.) Piper]. TURKEY MULLEIN, DOVEWEED. Sts. dichotomously branched, 5–8 in. high, forming rounded, prostrate mats 1–3 ft. wide; lvs. ovate to rhombic-ovate, ½–2½ in. long, petioles as long as blades; fls. small; caps. 1-seeded. Wash. to n. Baja Calif.

EREMOCHLOA Buse. *Gramineae*. About 10 spp. of creeping per. grasses in Asia; lvs. more or less equidistant and stiff; spikelets 1-fld., flat, 1-sided, awnless, solitary, sessile, glumes nearly flat, membranous, with pectinate margins. For terminology see *Gramineae*.

ophiuroides (Munro) Hack. CENTIPEDE GRASS, LAZY-MAN'S G. Creeping by thick, leafy stolons with short nodes, forming a dense clump, sts. decumbent or ascending, to 4 in. high; racemes spikelike, smooth, subcylindrical, terminal and axillary on slender peduncles, to 2⅜ in. long, rachis flat; spikelets sessile, first glume winged at apex. Se. Asia. Used as a lawn grass from S.C. to Fla., and the Gulf states.

EREMOCITRUS Swingle. AUSTRALIAN DESERT LIME, AUSTRALIAN DESERT KUMQUAT. *Rutaceae*. One sp., a spiny shrub or small tree, native to desert regions of subtrop. Australia; lvs. alt., simple, leathery; fls. small, white, solitary or 2 or 3 together in axils of lvs., sepals and petals 3–5, stamens 3 or 4 times as many as petals; fr. a leathery-skinned berry.

Remarkable for its resistance to cold and drought, and useful beyond the regular citrus belt. Can be grafted on *Citrus*, and vice-versa.

glauca (Lindl.) Swingle. To 15 ft.; lvs. linear, oblong, or cuneate, to 1½ in. long, gray-green, hairy, subtended by 1 spine; fls. fragrant; fr. light yellow, nearly globose or obovoid, about ½ in. in diam., thin-skinned, mildly acid and edible.

EREMOPHILA R. Br. *Myoporaceae*. Perhaps as many as 140 spp. of trees or shrubs, native to Australia; lvs. usually alt.,

entire; fls. axillary, usually showy, irregular, calyx and corolla 5-lobed, stamens 4; fr. a drupe.

maculata F. J. Muell. Evergreen shrub of varying height, brs. pubescent; lvs. linear-lanceolate to ovate-lanceolate, to 1¼ in. long, adult foliage glabrous; fls. solitary, peduncles curved but holding fls. upright, corolla red or pink, upper lip of 4 erect lobes, lower lip deeply cut and reflexed, stamens exserted. Ne. Australia, s. to New S. Wales.

EREMOSTACHYS Bunge. *Labiatae*. About 5 variable spp. of erect herbs of cent. and w. Asia which some consider to be 60 or more spp.; sts. mostly square in cross section, little branched; basal lvs. many, coarsely dentate to pinnatisect, st. lvs. small, often reduced to bracts; fls. sessile, in densely many-fld., glabrous to lanate-pilose verticillasters arranged in long spikes; calyx tubular, 5–10-nerved, 5-toothed, corolla yellow, tube pilose-ringed to glabrous inside, limb 2-lipped, upper lip erect, lower lip 3-lobed, stamens 4, in 2 pairs, style 2-lobed; fr. of 4 obovoid nutlets, densely pilose at apex.

Propagated by seeds or summer cuttings. Requires a very well-drained, sandy soil.

laciniata (L.) Bunge [*Phlomis laciniata* L.]. Hairy per., 3–6 ft., roots fleshy; lvs. 6–12 in. long, 2-pinnate or pinnatifid, segms. lobed or cut; calyx tubular, densely woolly, equally 5-toothed, teeth apiculate, corolla to 1 in. long, yellow or creamy-yellow, lower lip spreading, upper 2 stamens longer. Early summer. Mts., cent. and w. Asia.

EREMURUS Bieb. DESERT-CANDLE, KING'S-SPEAR. *Liliaceae*. Between 35 and 40 spp. of per. herbs, native to w. and cent. Asia; roots thick, fibrous or cordlike; lvs. mostly narrow, basal, forming tufts or rosettes; fls. white, pink, yellow, orange, or brown, in racemes terminating long scapes, perianth segms. 6, almost completely separate, 1- to several-nerved, stamens 6, anthers dorsifixed; fr. a 3-celled, loculicidal caps., seeds few to many.

Hardy in the North with winter protection. They do well in rich, well-drained soil, in sun. Propagated by division or slowly by seeds. They are seen to good advantage against background foliage.

altaicus (Pall.) Steven. To 4 ft.; lvs. strap-shaped, 6–9 in. long, to ½ in. wide, entire; fls. yellow, perianth segms. incurved, pedicels ½–¾ in. long, jointed at apex, erect in fr. Cent. Asia.

aurantiacus: *E. stenophyllus*.

bucharicus Regel. To about 3 ft.; lvs. 3-angled, glaucous, the keel and margins with retrorse teeth; fls. white, 1 in. across, in loose racemes. Bukhara.

Bungei: *E. stenophyllus*.

Elwesianus: *E. Elwesii*.

Elwesii M. Micheli [*E. Elwesianus* Hort.]. To 6–9 ft.; lvs. ovate-lanceolate, to 3 ft. long, glaucous, rather fleshy; fls. pink with darker midvein, many. Habitat unknown; once thought to be a hybrid between *E. himalaicus* and *E. robustus*. Cv. 'Albus'. Fls. white.

Hilariae M. Popov & Vved. To 3 ft.; lvs. linear, to 16 in. long, glaucous, gray-pubescent, scabrous on keel and margins; fls. white with yellow base, ⅝ in. long, subtending bracts hairy, as long as pedicels. Turkestan.

himalaicus Bak. To 3 ft.; lvs. strap-shaped, to 1½ ft. long, glabrous; fls. white, about 1 in. across, in dense racemes to 2 ft. long and 4 in. thick; caps. about ½ in. in diam., seeds not winged. Himalayas.

×isabellinus P. L. Vilm. [*E. × Shelfordii* Hort.; *E. × Warei* Hort. ex Mott.]: *E. Olgae × E. stenophyllus*. To 8 ft.; fls. in shades of orange, pale yellow, pink, white, and coppery-yellow.

lactiflorus O. Fedtsch. To 3 ft.; lvs. linear, to 1½ ft. long, glaucous, glabrous; fls. golden-yellow in bud, opening milk-white with yellow base, to 1½ in. across, perianth segms. revolute. Turkestan.

Olgae Regel. To 4½ ft.; lvs. linear, to 1 ft. long, rough on margins, recurved; fls. white to pink, 1 in. across, on ascending pedicels 1½–2¼ in. long, in a dense raceme. Turkestan.

Regelii Vved. [*E. spectabilis* var. *marginatus* O. Fedtsch.]. To 6 ft.; lvs. linear, glabrous; fls. brown with white margins, about 1 in. across, filaments longer than perianth segms. Turkestan.

robustus (Regel) Regel. To 8–10 ft.; lvs. strap-shaped, to 4 ft. long, glabrous; fls. bright pink, about ½ in. across, on jointed pedicels, in a dense raceme; caps. ¾ in. in diam., seeds broadly winged. Cent. Asia.

×Shelfordii: *E. × isabellinus*.

spectabilis Bieb. To 3 ft.; lvs. narrowly strap-shaped, to 16 in. long, glabrous, almost erect; fls. pale yellow, perianth segms. 3–5-nerved, filaments red, much longer than perianth segms. Crimea and Asia Minor to Turkmen S.S.R. and Afghanistan. Var. **marginatus:** *E. Regelii*.

stenophyllus (Boiss. & Buhse) Bak. [*E. aurantiacus* Bak.; *E. Bungei* Bak.]. To 2 ft. or more; lvs. linear, 1 ft. long, glabrous, ciliate on margins; fls. yellow, scarcely 1 in. across, on slender, spreading pedicels to about ¾ in. long. Sw. Asia.

×**Tubergenii** Hort. van Tuberg.: *E. himalaicus* × *E. stenophyllus*. To 8 ft.; fls. pale yellow.

×**Warei:** *E.* × *isabillinus*.

ERIA Lindl. [*Trichosma* Lindl.]. Orchidaceae. About 350 spp. of epiphytes of trop. Asia; sts. pseudobulbous and 1–3-lvd. at apex, or reedlike and leafy throughout; infl. lateral or axillary, racemose, few- to many-fld.; sepals and petals separate, lateral sepals and column foot forming a mentum, column fleshy, short, the foot prominent, often longer than the column itself. For structure of fl. see *Orchidaceae*.

Grown in the warm greenhouse. For culture see *Orchids*.

barbata: *Taeniopsis barbata*.

convallarioides: *E. spicata*.

coronaria (Lindl.) Rchb.f. [*Trichosma suavis* Lindl.]. Pseudobulbs cylindrical to 10 in. long, 2-lvd.; lvs. to 9¾ in. long; racemes loosely few-fld., a little shorter than lvs.; fls. fragrant, to 1½ in. across, white to greenish-yellow, lip 3-lobed, midlobe yellow, lateral lobes streaked with crimson-purple. Late summer–late winter. Himalayas, China.

elongata: *E. flava*.

Fitzalanii F. J. Muell. Pseudobulbs ovate, 1-lvd.; lvs. lanceolate, to 6 in. long; racemes to 8 in. long, densely many-fld.; fls. small, white to light cream, hairy outside, sepals to ½ in. long, broadly triangular, lip obscurely 3-lobed, finely crenate. Australia.

flava Lindl. [*E. elongata* Lindl.]. Pseudobulbs to 4 in. long, 2–5-lvd.; lvs. lanceolate, to 10 in. long; scapes white-tomentose, loosely fld.; fls. yellow, tomentose, lip marked with purple. Spring. Himalayas. Var. **lanata** (Griff.) Kränzl. [*E. lanata* Griff.]. Fls. smaller, midlobe purplish.

floribunda Lindl. Pseudobulbs cylindrical to spindle-shaped, to 1 ft. long, 3–7-lvd.; lvs. oblong-lanceolate, to 10 in. long; racemes pendent, to about 6½ in. long, dense, many-fld.; fls. to ⅜ in. across, rose-red to nearly white, sepals broadly ovate, petals lanceolate, lip 3-lobed, lateral lobes curved, midlobe cuneate-triangular, column dark purple. Blooming all year. Burma, Malay Pen., Philippine Is.

lanata: *E. flava* var.

Merrillii Ames. Pseudobulbs to 4 in. long, 2-lvd.; lvs. oblong-lanceolate, to 1 ft. long, dense; fls. fragrant, white suffused with purple, sepals to ¾ in. long, lip 3-lobed, lateral lobes curved, midlobe cuneate, rugose. Late autumn. Philippine Is.

spicata (D. Don) Hand.-Mazz. [*E. convallarioides* Lindl.]. Pseudobulbs to 9 in. long, 3–4-lvd.; lvs. to about 7 in. long; racemes pendent, to 4½ in. long, dense; fls. about ⁵⁄₁₆ in. across, whitish, sepals ovate, petals obovate, lip spatulate, long-clawed, yellow at the front. Late summer–autumn. Himalayas, Burma, Indochina.

ERIANTHUS Michx. PLUME GRASS, WOOLLY BEARD G. Gramineae. About 20 spp. of per. reedlike grasses in temp. and trop. regions; lf. blades elongate, flat; panicles terminal, oblong, usually dense, silky; spikelets in pairs, one bisexual, sessile, the other pedicelled, along a rachis which disarticulates below the spikelets, the rachis joint and pedicel falling attached to the sessile spikelet, glumes firm, nearly equal, usually with long, spreading, silky hairs, at the base, lemma and palea hyaline, the fertile lemmas usually with a slender awn. For terminology see *Gramineae*.

ravennae (L.) Beauvois. RAVENNA GRASS. Sts. stout, to 14 ft.; panicle to 2 ft. long, silvery; spikelets awnless or nearly so. S. Eur. Cult. for ornament, naturalized in Ariz. Zone 6.

ERIASTRUM Woot. & Standl. Polemoniaceae. Fourteen spp. of mostly ann. or rarely per. herbs or shrubs, native to w. N. Amer.; plants cobwebby-woolly; lvs. alt., entire to pinnately toothed or dissected; fls. blue, white, yellow, or pink, rarely solitary, usually in bracted heads covered by densely matted woolly hairs, calyx 5-parted, lobes unequal, corolla funnelform to almost salverform, 5-lobed, stamens 5, equal or unequal; fr. a 3-celled caps. Differs from *Gilia* in having calyx lobes unequal.

densifolium (Benth.) H. L. Mason [*Gilia densifolia* (Benth.) Benth.]. Shrub, subshrub, or woody-based per., to 2 ft. or more, woolly-tomentose when young; lvs. linear, often rigid, entire or lobed; corolla with blue lobes and white or yellow tube and throat. Late spring to autumn. Cent. Calif. to Baja Calif. Subsp. **austromontanum** (T. Craig) H. L.

Mason [*Gilia densifolia* var. *austromontana* T. Craig]. Smaller and less woolly. Subsp. **elongatum** (Benth.) H. L. Mason [*Gilia densifolia* var. *elongata* (Benth.) A. Gray ex Brand]. Less woody; lvs. more rigid, usually white-canescent.

ERICA L. HEATH. Ericaceae. About 500 spp. of much-branched, evergreen shrubs or small trees, native to Eur. and Medit. region, but chiefly to S. Afr.; lvs. usually whorled, needlelike, often revolute; fls. white, rose, purple, yellow, or green, solitary, or in axillary, or terminal panicles, racemes, or umbels, calyx 4-parted, corolla urceolate to campanulate or tubular, persistent, stamens 8, ovary superior; fr. a many-seeded, 4-valved caps.

Heaths are grown in rock gardens, although few of them are hardy in the North; also grown under glass for the profuse bloom. They are plants of compact habit and slow growth. *E. carnea* and *E. vagans* are perhaps the hardiest, surviving winters in N.Y. and central New Eng., but *E. cinerea* and *E. Tetralix* are nearly as hardy; *e. scoparia* is somewhat less hardy. Heaths of many kinds are popular in the open in Calif., where they bloom profusely in winter and early spring. They are particular as to soil in pot culture, preferring one of light peat and coarse sand. In the open, they are given a light or sandy soil; they do not grow well in limestone soils. Propagated by cuttings of young wood under glass, given good ventilation when rooted. New blooming wood may be produced by heading back after flowering.

arborea L. TREE H. Shrub or small tree, to 20 ft., sts. with long, stout ciliate hairs; lvs. in 3's, to ¼ in. long; fls. in large panicles, white, fragrant, ⅛ in. long, stigma white. Winter or spring. Medit. region. Zone 7. Source of briar root used for making smoking pipes. Var. **alpina** (Dieck) Bean. More erect, to 8 ft., foliage bright green.

australis L. To 8 ft., sts. with short hairs; lvs. in 4's, to ¼ in. long; fls. in terminal clusters, purplish-red, ⁵⁄₁₆ in. long. Spring. Spain, Portugal.

baccans L. BERRY H. Erect, glabrous, to 5 ft.; lvs. in 4's, slightly incurved, to ¼ in. long; fls. in 4's at ends of branchlets, rose-red, corolla urceolate, narrowed at throat, about ¼ in. long. S. Afr.

blanda: *E. doliiformis*.

canaliculata Andr. CHRISTMAS HEATHER. To 6 ft., branchlets densely hairy; lvs. in 3's, to ¼ in. long; fls. clustered toward ends of brs., white or pink, to ⅛ in. long, calyx deeply parted, stamens exserted, nearly black. S. Afr. Cvs. 'Purpurea' and 'Rubra' are listed. Cv. 'Rosea'. Fls. rosy-pink. Sometimes offered under the name *E. melanthera*.

capensis Salter. To 20 in., glabrous; lvs. in 4's; fls. in 4's or in umbels, red or white, to ³⁄₁₆ in. long, anthers included, ovary glabrous. S. Afr. Material so offered is probably not this sp.

carnea L. SPRING H., SNOW HEATHER. To 1 ft., brs. prostrate; lvs. in 4's, to ¼ in. long, glabrous; fls. in one-sided racemes, red, to ¼ in. long, anthers exserted, dark red. Spring. Eur. Zone 6. Cvs. are: 'Alba', fls. white; 'Coccinea', fls. bright red; 'Gracilis', slender, fls. pink; 'Praecox', early-blooming, fls. deep rose-red; 'Rubra', fls. crimson; 'Sherwoodii', fls. carmine-red; 'Vivellii', fls. light carmine-red.

Chamissonis Klotzsch ex Benth. To 2 ft., branchlets erect, leafy, hairy; lvs. crowded, in 3's, to ¼ in. long; fls. crowded toward ends of branchlets, rose, anthers included, black. S. Afr.

ciliaris L. FRINGED H., DORSET H. To 1 ft.; sts. prostrate; lvs. in 3's, ovate, to ⅛ in. long, ciliate; fls. in terminal racemes to 5 in. long, rosy-red, ⁵⁄₁₆ in. long. Summer, autumn. W. Eur. Zone 7? Cv. 'Alba'. Fls. white.

cinerea L. TWISTED H., SCOTCH H., BELL HEATHER. To 2 ft., finely pubescent when young; lvs. in 3's, to ¼ in. long, glabrous and shining above; fls. whorled, in terminal racemes or in umbels, purple changing to blue. Summer, early autumn. Eur.; naturalized locally on Nantucket Is. Zone 6. Cvs. are: 'Alba', fls. white; 'Atropurpurea', deep purple; 'Atrorubens', fls. dark red; 'Atrosanguinea', fls. scarlet; 'Atroviolacea', fls. deep violet; 'Coccinea': 'Fulgida'; 'Fulgida' [cv. 'Coccinea'], fls. ruby-red; 'Lilacina', fls. lilac; 'Rosea', fls. rose-pink; 'Rubra', fls. brilliant red; 'Splendens', fls. carmine; 'Violacea', fls. purple-blue.

codonodes: *E. lusitanica*.

concinna: *E. verticillata*.

cruenta Soland. Erect, to 3 ft.; lvs. in 3's, to ⁵⁄₁₆ in. long, pubescent when young; fls. blood-red, to 1 in. long, corolla more or less tubular. S. Afr.

×**darleyensis** Bean: *E. carnea* × *E. mediterranea*. To 2 ft.; lvs. in 4's, to ½ in. long; fls. in terminal, leafy racemes, pink, ¼ in. long. Zone 6.

decipiens K. Spreng. Erect, to 2 ft., sts. gray-pubescent; lvs. in 3's, linear, to ⁵⁄₁₆ in. long, glabrous; fls. in 3's, white to pale rose, less than ³⁄₁₆ in. long, ovary gray-pubescent. S. Afr.

diaphana K. Spreng. To 5 ft., brs. rigid; lvs. in 3's, to ¼ in. long, glabrous; fls. 1–3 toward ends of branchlets, purple shading through pink to white, corolla tubular, to 1 in. long, waxy transparent and viscid. S. Afr.

doliiformis Salisb. [*E. blanda* Andr.]. EVERBLOOMING FRENCH HEATHER. To 1 ft.; lvs. crowded, in 6's, to ½ in. long, glandular-ciliate, glabrous; fls. in umbels, rosy, corolla tubular, to ½ in. long. S. Afr.

exsurgens Andr. Erect, to 3 ft.; lvs. in 4's, to ¾ in. long; fls. crowded toward ends of branchlets, orange-yellow, corolla funnelform, to 1 in. long. S. Afr.

glandulosa Thunb. Erect, to 2 ft. or more; lvs. in 4's, to ½ in. long, glandular-hairy; fls. in 4's, white, corolla nearly tubular, to 1 in. long, usually pubescent or glandular. S. Afr.

glauca Andr. Stout, erect, glabrous plant, to 3 ft.; lvs. in 3's, to ½ in. long, glaucous; fls. in 4–7-fld. umbels, subtended by petaloid, colored bracts, corolla dull red to vivid purple, usually green-tipped or greenish along throat, ½ in. long. S. Afr.

globosa Andr. Erect, to 1½ ft., brs. pubescent or glandular-setose; lvs. in 3's, oblong or lanceolate, to ½ in. long, finely hairy or glabrous; fls. terminal and axillary, toward ends of branchlets, pink, corolla globose-urceolate, ¼ in. long, style exserted. S. Afr.

gracilis J. C. Wendl. Slender, branched, erect shrub, to 1 ft.; lvs. imbricate, in 4's, less than 3/16 in. long, glabrous; fls. in 4's at ends of branchlets, rosy, less than 3/16 in. long. S. Afr.

hibernica: *E. mediterranea.*

Hieliana: a listed name of no botanical standing for *E. hyemalis.*

hirtiflora Curtis. Bushy shrub, to 2 ft., sts. hairy; lvs. in 4's, linear, to 3/16 in. long; fls. in 4's at ends of branchlets, pale purple or pink, corolla tubular-ovoid, less than 3/16 in. long, rough-hairy. S. Afr. Plants offered as *E. regerminans* are usually this sp.

hyalina: a listed name of no botanical standing, probably for *E. hyemalis.*

hyemalis Nichols. WHITE WINTER HEATHER, FRENCH H. To 2 ft.; lvs. in 4's, to ⅜ in. long, ciliate; fls. borne along branchlets, forming leafy raceme, pink, tipped with white, to 1 in. long. Autumn, winter. Nativity unknown.

lateralis Willd. Erect, to 1½ ft.; lvs. in 4's, linear, to 5/16 in. long, glossy, glabrous or nearly so; fls. in 4's or in umbels, rosy, ¼ in. long. S. Afr.

lusitanica K. Rudolphi [*E. codonodes* Lindl.]. SPANISH H. Erect, dense shrub, to 12 ft.; lvs. 3–5 in a whorl or irregularly arranged, to ¼ in. long, glabrous; fls. borne profusely along brs., white, less than 3/16 in. long, stamens and stigma pink. Winter, spring. W. Eur. Zone 8. Var. **Veitchii**: a listed name for *E. × Veitchii.*

Mackaiana Bab. [*E. Mackaii* Hook.]. To 2 ft.; lvs. in 4's, oblong-lanceolate, dark green and glabrous above, white beneath; fls. red, ¼ in. long. England, nw. Spain.

Mackaii: *E. Mackaiana.*

mammosa L. Robust, erect shrub, to 4 ft.; lvs. in 4's or scattered, to ⅜ in. long; fls. pendulous, in dense, spicate clusters, dark red to orange or pink, corolla tubular, to 1 in. long. S. Afr.

Maxwellii: a listed name of no botanical standing.

mediterranea L. [*E. hibernica* (Hook. & Arn.) Syme]. IRISH H., MEDITERRANEAN HEATHER. To 10 ft., glabrous; lvs. in 4's, linear, to ¼ in. long, dark green, glabrous; fls. in short, dense, leafy racemes, deep red, corolla ovoid-urceolate, to ¼ in. long, stamens exserted, deep purple. Spring. W. Eur. Zone 7. Cvs. are: 'Alba', fls. white; 'Maxima', to 3 ft., fls. purplish; 'Superba', fls. large, pink.

melanthera L. To 2 ft.; lvs. in 3's, less than 3/16 in. long, becoming glossy; fls. red, less than 3/16 in. long, calyx with distinct tube, calyx lobes with a well-marked keel produced into a sharp point, corolla lobes spreading, stamens exserted, black. S. Afr. Zone 8. Probably not in cult.; material so offered is usually *E. canaliculata.*

multiflora L. To 1½ ft., or more in the wild; lvs. in 4's or 5's, linear, to ⅜ in. long; fls. in dense racemes, pink, 3/16 in. long, stamens exserted. S. Eur. Zone 7.

persoluta L. To 3 ft., branchlets downy; lvs. in 4's, linear, to ¼ in. long, glabrous to slightly downy; fls. in 4's toward ends of branchlets, forming a leafy raceme, rosy-red, corolla cup-shaped, less than 3/16 in. long. S. Afr.

Peziza Lodd. To 1½ ft., branchlets downy; lvs. in 3's, linear, less than 3/16 in. long, mostly shining, glabrous; fls. white, corolla cup-shaped, ⅛ in. long, hairy, anthers included, brown. S. Afr.

×**Praegeri**: *E. × Stuartii.*

pygmaea: *E. sicifolia.*

regerminans L. To 2 ft., glabrous; lvs. in 6's or sometimes in 3's or 4's, to ½ in. long; fls. in dense racemes or spikes, pink to bright red,

less than 3/16 in. long. S. Afr. Cvs. 'Rosea' and 'Rubra' are listed. Plants usually cult. under this name are *E. hirtiflora.*

scoparia L. BESOM H. To 10 ft.; lvs. in 3's or 4's, linear, to ¼ in. long, shining, glabrous; fls. in long, leafy racemes, greenish, less than ⅛ in. long. S. Eur. Zone 7?

Sherwoodii: a listed name of no botanical standing for *E. carnea* cv.

sicifolia Salisb. [*E. pygmaea* Andr.]. Suberect, straggling plant, to 8 in., sts. ascending; lvs. in 3's, to ½ in. long, glossy, glabrous; fls. in 3's, dark purple, to less than 3/16 in. long, viscid-pubescent. S. Afr.

sitiens Klotzsch. To 2 ft.; lvs. in 4's, to 5/16 in. long, glabrous but sometimes ciliate; fls. mostly in 4's, white to red, 3/16 in. long. S. Afr.

stricta: *E. terminalis.*

×**Stuartii** Linton [*E. × Praegeri* Ostenf; *E. Tetralix* var. *Praegeri* Hort.]: *E. Mackaiana* × *E. Tetralix.* To 1 ft.; fls. pink.

terminalis Salisb. [*E. stricta* Andr.]. CORSICAN HEATHER. To 4 ft., brs. stiff; lvs. mostly in 4's, to ¼ in. long, glabrous; fls. in terminal umbels, rosy-purple, ¼ in. long. Summer, early autumn. S. Eur. Zone 7?

Tetralix L. CROSS-LEAVED H., BOG HEATHER. To 2 ft., brs. prostrate; lvs. in 4's, to ⅛ in. long, glandular-ciliate, whitish beneath; fls. in dense terminal clusters, rose, ¼ in. long. Summer, autumn. Eur.; naturalized in e. N. Amer. Zone 4. Yields a yellow dye used by Scots. Var. **Praegeri**: *E. × Stuartii.* Cvs. are: 'Alba', fls. white; 'Mollis', dwarf, lvs. grayish, fls. white; 'Rubra', fls. red.

umbellata L. To 3 ft., sts. erect or ascending; lvs. imbricate, in 3's, linear, less than 3/16 in. long, glossy; fls. in 3–6-fld., terminal umbels, flesh-colored to rose-pink, less than 3/16 in. long, stamens exserted. W. Medit. region.

vagans L. CORNISH H. Low, spreading, glabrous shrub, to 1 ft.; lvs. in 4's or 5's, to ⅜ in. long, bright green, glabrous; fls. in leafy racemes to 6 in. long, purplish-pink, ⅛ in. long, stamens exserted. W. Eur.; naturalized locally on Nantucket Is. Zone 7. Cvs. are: 'Alba', fls. white; 'Nana', dwarf, fls. white; 'Rosea', fls. rose; 'Rubra', fls. deeper red.

×**Veitchii** Bean: *E. arborea* × *E. lusitanica.* To 6 ft.; fls. many, white, stamens and stigma pink.

ventricosa Thunb. To 6 ft., brs. stout, rigid; lvs. crowded, in 4's to ⅝ in. long, ciliate; fls. in dense umbels, white, pink, or red, ⅝ in. long. Spring and summer. S. Afr. Cv. 'Grandiflora'. Fls. larger, rosy-purple.

versicolor J. C. Wendl. To 4 ft.; lvs. imbricate or spreading, in 3's, to 5/16 in. long; fls. in 3's, corolla tubular, red with greenish-yellow lobes, to 1 in. long, anthers not awned, but sharply pointed at base. S. Afr.

verticillata Bergius [*E. concinna* Soland.]. To 5 ft.; lvs. mostly in 4's to 6's, to ¼ in. long, glabrous; fls. forming dense, leafy racemes, rosy, corolla tubular, to ¾ in. long, anthers awnless. S. Afr. Zone 6.

viridipurpurea L. Erect, to 2 ft.; lvs. in 4's, less than 3/16 in. long, glabrous, sometimes ciliate; fls. in 4's or clustered, many, red, ⅛ in. long. S. Afr.

vulgaris: *Calluna vulgaris.*

×**Watsonii** Benth.: *E. ciliaris* × *E. Tetralix.* Lvs. in 4's; fls. in short racemes, corolla urceolate, rosy, stamens included. Eur.

×**Williamsii** Druce: *E. Tetralix* × *E. vagans.* To 20 in.; lvs. in 4's, to 5/16 in. long, margins glandular; fls. in terminal umbels, rose-pink, corolla urceolate, stamens included. Cornwall (England).

×**Wilmorei** Knowles & Westc. Hybrid of unknown parentage; to 2 ft.; lvs. in 3's, to ¼ in. long; fls. rosy, tipped with white, corolla tubular, 1 in. long.

ERICACEAE Juss. HEATH FAMILY. Dicot.; about 70 genera and 1,900 spp., of mostly shrubs, or occasionally woody-based per. herbs or small trees, rarely vines, widely distributed on acid soils, mostly in temp. climates, rarer in subarctic and at higher elevations in the tropics; lvs. alt., sometimes opp. or whorled, simple; fls. solitary or in various axillary or terminal infls., regular or sometimes slightly irregular, bisexual, calyx 4–7-lobed, rarely of separate sepals, corolla often urceolate, 4–7-lobed, stamens commonly twice as many as corolla lobes, anthers often appendaged, frequently opening by a terminal pore, pistil 1, ovary superior or inferior, carpels typically 5, style 1; fr. a caps. or berry. Genera cult. are: *Agapetes, Agauria, Andromeda, Arbutus, Arctostaphylos, Befaria, Bruckenthalia, Calluna, Cassiope, Chamaedaphne, Cladothamnus, Comarostaphylos, Daboecia, Elliottia, Enkianthus, Epigaea, Erica, Gaultheria, Gaylussacia, Kalmia, Kalmiopsis, Ledum, Leiophyllum, Leucothoe, Loiseleuria, Lyonia, Macleania, Menziesia, Orphanidesia, Ox-*

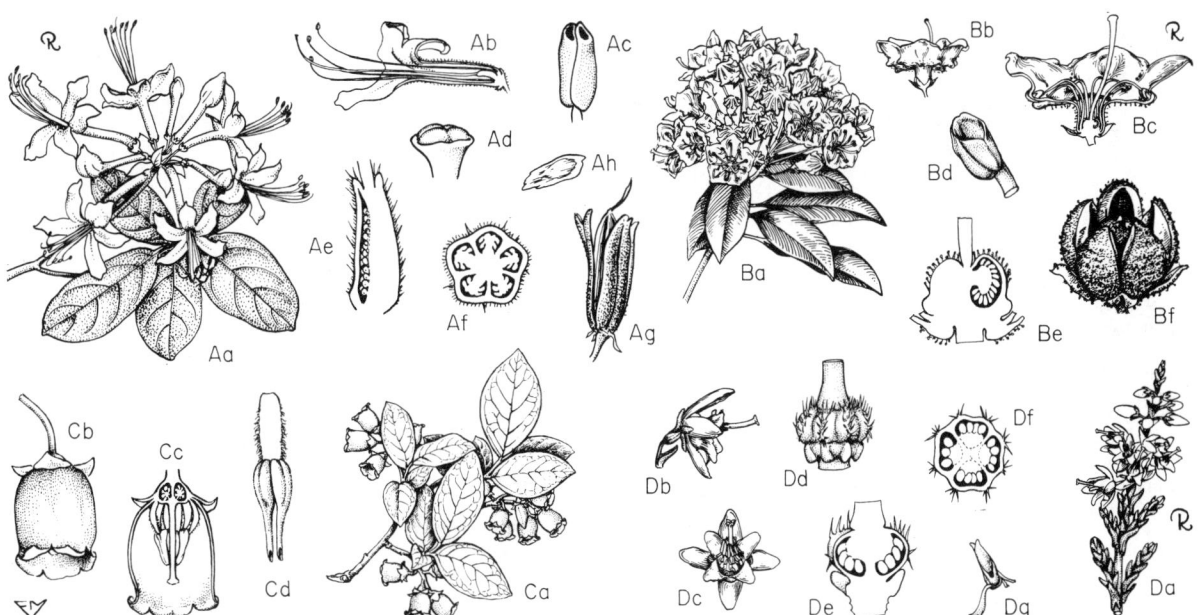

ERICACEAE. **A,** *Rhododendron canescens:* **Aa,** flowering branch, × ⅜; **Ab,** flower, vertical section, × ½; **Ac,** anther, × 5; **Ad,** stigma, × 8; **Ae,** ovary, vertical section, × 4; **Af,** ovary, cross section, × 6; **Ag,** capsule, × ¾; **Ah,** seed, × 5. **B,** *Kalmia latifolia:* **Ba,** flowering branch, × ¼; **Bb,** flower, side view, × ½; **Bc,** flower, vertical section, × 1; **Bd,** anther, × 5; **Be,** ovary, vertical section, × 5; **Bf,** capsule, × 3. **C,** *Vaccinium vacillans:* **Ca,** flowering branch, × ½; **Cb,** flower, × 2; **Cc,** flower, vertical section, × 2; **Cd,** stamen, × 5. **D,** *Calluna vulgaris:* **Da,** flowering branch, × 1; **Db,** flower, side view, × 2; **Dc,** flower, face view, × 2; **Dd,** base of pistil, × 8; **De,** ovary, vertical section, × 8; **Df,** ovary, cross section, × 8; **Dg,** stamen, × 5. (Ca-Cd from Bailey, *Manual of Cultivated Plants,* ed. 2.)

ydendrum, Pernettya, Phyllodoce, Pieris, Rhododendron, Rhodothamnus, Tripetaleia, Tsusiophyllum, Vaccinium, Xylococcus, and *Zenobia.*

The family has many ornamental species and some are the choicest broad-leaved evergreens. Some, such as the blueberry and cranberries, are grown for the edible fruits.

ERICAMERIA: *HAPLOPAPPUS.*

ERIGENIA Nutt. *Umbelliferae.* One sp., a tuberous, nearly stemless, per. herb of N. Amer.

bulbosa (Michx.) Nutt. HARBINGER-OF-SPRING, PEPPER-AND-SALT. To 9 in.; lvs. ternately decompound, segms. oblong, obtuse; fls. white, in small, usually compound umbels, involucre absent or leafy, involucels of few entire bractlets or absent; fr. compressed. Among the first plants to bloom in spring. S. Ont., w. N.Y. to Minn. and Kans., s. to D.C. and Ala.

ERIGERON L. FLEABANE. *Compositae* (Aster Tribe). About 200 spp. of ann., bien., or mostly per. herbs, mostly native to N. Amer. but nearly cosmopolitan; lvs. alt., rarely all basal, frequently sessile; fl. heads mostly radiate, solitary or few, or sometimes many and corymbose to paniculate, involucre campanulate to hemispherical, involucral bracts in 2–3 rows, narrow, from nearly equal and herbaceous to imbricate and scarcely herbaceous, receptacle flat, naked; disc fls. bisexual, yellow, ray fls. in about 2 rows, female, fertile, narrow, white to pink, blue, or purple, rarely orange or yellow; achenes compressed, usually 2-nerved, sometimes 4–14-nerved, usually pubescent, pappus of few to many nearly equal, soft, often fragile, capillary bristles, sometimes also with an outer row of short scales or bristles, or rarely only a crown of short scales, or even essentially absent.

Erigerons bloom mostly in spring or early summer. They are of easy culture in the border or wild garden or when colonized, and the low kinds are used in rock gardens. Propagated by seeds, division or cuttings, the tufted perennial species best by division.

acris L. [*E. elongatus* Ledeb.]. Ann., bien., or per., to 2½ ft., sts. usually branched in upper part, with long hairs; basal lvs. obovate-lanceolate, to 3 in. long, petioled, st. lvs. linear-lanceolate, semiclasp-

ing; heads solitary or in corymbose panicles, to ¾ in. across; outer disc fls. filiform, female, ray fls. erect, pale purple, scarcely longer than disc fls. Circumpolar, but the typical var. does not occur in N. Amer.

alpinus L. Coarsely hairy per., to 1 ft., sometimes taller; lvs. hairy, basal lvs. spatulate to linear-oblanceolate, to 2 in. long including the petiole, st. lvs. successively reduced upward, linear, semiclasping; heads usually solitary, sometimes 2–6, to 1½ in. across; outer disc fls. female, ray fls. spreading, pink to violet, much longer than disc fls. Eur. Cv. 'Roseus'. Heads to 1 in. across; ray fls. bright pink.

annuus (L.) Pers. DAISY F., SWEET SCABIOUS, WHITE-TOP. Coarse, leafy ann. or short-lived per., to 5 ft., sts. with long spreading hairs; basal lvs. ovate to nearly orbicular, to 4 in. long including petiole, coarsely toothed, st. lvs. broadly lanceolate, toothed, or upper lvs. nearly entire; heads several to many in a leafy corymbose panicle, to about ¾ in. across; ray fls. white, rarely bluish or pinkish. U.S. and s. Canada; naturalized in Eur.

aphanactis (A. Gray) Greene. Cespitose per., to 1 ft., from a taproot, with dense, short, spreading hairs; basal lvs. oblanceolate to spatulate, to 3 in. long including petiole, st. lvs. many, successively reduced upward; heads solitary or several; disc fls. yellow, often turning brownish with age, ray fls. lacking. Sw. Colo. to s. Calif., w. to sw. Idaho, se. Ore., and n. Calif.

arenarius: *E. Bellidiastrum.*

asper: *E. glabellus.*

asperugineus (D. C. Eat.) A. Gray. Per. herb, to 8 in., from a slender taproot, sts. spreading to almost erect, foliage with short, spreading hairs; basal lvs. to 3 in. long, elliptic to obovate or nearly orbicular, abruptly narrowed to a long petiole, st. lvs. successively reduced upward, linear; heads solitary or sometimes 2, to ⅝ in. across; ray fls. deep blue or violet, sometimes bright red-purple. Cent. Idaho and ne. Nev.

atticus Vill. Erect per., to 2 ft., with abundant glandular hairs; basal lvs. oblong-oblanceolate, narrowed to a petiole, hispid, glandular-hairy, st. lvs. successively reduced upward, oblong-lanceolate, semiclasping; heads mostly 3–8, sometimes more, in corymbose panicles; ray fls. purple. Mts., cent. Eur.

aurantiacus Regel. DOUBLE ORANGE DAISY. More or less velvety per., to 10 in.; basal lvs. spatulate-oblong, to 3¾ in. long including petiole, st. lvs. lanceolate, sessile or clasping; heads usually solitary, to about 1¾ in. across; ray fls. bright orange. Turkestan.

aureus Greene. Per. herb, to 6 in., with fibrous roots or weak taproot and a branching root crown, hairy; basal lvs. elliptic to obovate or nearly orbicular, to 3 in. long including petiole, st. lvs. reduced, few; heads solitary, to ¾ in. across; ray fls. yellow. High mts., s. Alta., s. B.C., Wash.

barbellatus Greene. Rather loosely cespitose per. herb, to 6 in., with much-branched root crown, finely strigose; lvs. mostly basal, oblanceolate, to 1½ in. long, petioles and bases of lowest lvs. glabrous, hard, glossy, purplish, otherwise finely strigose; heads solitary, to ¾ in. across; ray fls. blue to purple or white. Mts., cent. Calif.

basalticus Hoover. Sprawling or pendulous per., sts. leafy, particularly near their ends, foliage with spreading, finely glandular hairs; lvs. cuneate to obovate, to 1½ in. long, irregularly and more or less deeply 3–5-lobed toward apex; heads terminal on brs., about ½ in. across; ray fls. pink to pink-purple. S.-cent. Wash.

Bellidiastrum Nutt. [*E. arenarius* Greene]. WESTERN F. Ann., to 20 in., finely hirsute with incurved hairs, sts. branched above; basal lvs. oblanceolate, soon withering, blade to 1½ in. long, tapering to a 1½ in. petiole, entire, st. lvs. becoming successively more linear upward; heads rather numerous but not crowded, terminal on brs., to about 5/16 in. across; ray fls. white or pink. S. Dak. to Tex., w. to Wyo., Utah, and New Mex.

Bloomeri A. Gray. Cespitose per., to 6 in., with a taproot and a much-branched root crown, foliage with fine, white-strigose hairs; lvs. nearly all in a basal cluster, linear, to 2¾ in. long; heads solitary, to ¾ in. across; ray fls. absent. Idaho to cent. Nev., w. to cent. Wash., Ore., and n. Calif.

caespitosus Nutt. [*E. hyperboreus* Greene]. Cespitose per., to 1 ft., with a taproot and a stout, mostly branched root crown, foliage with dense, short, spreading hairs; basal lvs. oblanceolate or spatulate, to 4¾ in. long, 3-nerved, st. lvs. linear to ovate-oblong; heads 1–10, to 1 in. across; ray fls. white, pink, or blue. Alaska and Yukon, s. through e. Wash. and w. N. Dak. to Ariz., cent. New Mex., and w. Nebr.

compositus Pursh. Per., to 10 in., with a taproot and a stout, branching root crown, foliage glandular and with spreading hirsute hairs; basal lvs. from ternately dissected to 3–4-times ternate, st. lvs. few, reduced, mostly linear; heads solitary, to ¾ in. across; ray fls. white, pink, or blue, sometimes absent. W. Idaho and adjacent Wash. and Ore. Var. **discoideus** A. Gray [var. *pedatus* Hort.; var. *trifidus* (Hook.) A. Gray; *E. trifidus* Hook.]. Plant cespitose; lvs. usually only ternate. Alaska to Greenland, s. to s. Calif., and s. in the Rockies to n. Ariz. Var. **glabratus** J. Macoun [var. *nudus* (Rydb.) A. Nels.]. Lvs. 2–3-times ternate, segms. short. Alaska to Greenland, s. to n. Calif., n. Ariz., Colo. and S. Dak. Var. **nudus**: var. *glabratus*. Var. **pedatus**: var. *discoideus*. Var. **trifidus**: var. *discoideus*.

concinnus: *E. pumilus* subsp. *concinnoides*.

Coulteri T. C. Porter. Fibrous-rooted per., to 2 ft., with a slender rhizome, sts. very leafy, with spreading hirsute hairs; lvs. broadly oblanceolate to elliptic, to 3½ in. long, the lower petioled and toothed, the upper sessile and clasping; heads 1–4, to 1½ in. across; ray fls. white. Mts., nw. Mont. and adjacent Idaho, s. to cent. Calif., Utah, and New Mex.

divaricatus: see *E. divergens*.

divergens Torr. & A. Gray [*E. divaricatus* Nutt., not Michx.]. Ann. to short-lived per., to 20 in., divaricately and diffusely branched, with dense, short, spreading hairs, sts. decumbent to erect; basal lvs. oblanceolate to spatulate, to 2½ in. long, petioled, soon deciduous, st. lvs. many, linear to oblanceolate; heads many, to ¾ in. across; ray fls. light blue or pink to lavender or white. W. S. Dak. to B.C., s. to Okla., Ariz., Calif., and n. Mex.

Eatonii A. Gray. Per., to 1 ft., sts. decumbent, rarely erect, with reddish-purple base, foliage strigose or hirsute-strigose, the hairs appressed or ascending; basal lvs. linear, to 6 in. long, 3-nerved, tapering gradually to petiole, st. lvs. reduced; heads usually solitary, sometimes 2–7, to about ¾ in. across; ray fls. white, sometimes pink or blue. N. Ariz. to s. Idaho, Wyo., and Colo.

elongatus: *E. acris*.

eucephaloides: *E. speciosus* var. *macranthus*.

filifolius Nutt. Per., to 20 in., with a branched, woody root crown, more or less white-strigose; lvs. filiform to linear-oblanceolate, basal lvs. to 3 in. long, st. lvs. less crowded, shorter; heads 1 to several, to ½ in. across; ray fls. white, pink, or blue. S. B.C. and nw. Mont., s. to cent. Calif., w.-cent. Nev., and n. Utah.

flagellaris A. Gray. RUNNING F. Bien. or short-lived per., flowering sts. erect, to 16 in., sparsely leafy, some sts. trailing and apparently rooting at tip, foliage with mostly appressed hirsute or strigose hairs; basal lvs. oblanceolate, to 2 in. long, persistent, st. lvs. linear to linear-oblanceolate, to 1¼ in. long; heads solitary, to ¾ in. across; ray fls. white, pink, or blue. S. B.C., w. S. Dak., and Wyo., s. to Tex., Nev., and Ariz.

Flettii G. N. Jones. Per. herb, to 6 in., with a stout, branched root crown, sts. pilose or villous, the hairs spreading, often somewhat viscid-glandular; basal lvs. oblanceolate or spatulate, to 2 in. long, glabrous to somewhat hirsute, ciliate, st. lvs. reduced, inconspicuous; heads solitary, to 1¼ in. across; ray fls. white. Wash.

glabellus Nutt. [*E. asper* Nutt.]. Fibrous-rooted bien. or per., to 20 in., with appressed hirsute or strigose hairs; basal and lower st. lvs. oblanceolate, to 6 in. long, persistent, st. lvs. much-reduced, linear to lanceolate; heads 1–15, to 2 in. across; ray fls. blue, pink, or white. Alaska and n. Canada, s. to Utah, Colo., S. Dak., and Wisc. Subsp. **pubescens** (Hook.) Cronq. [*E. Turneri* Greene]. Sts. with spreading, often long and coarse hairs. Alaska, s. to Mont., Colo., N. Dak., and Wisc.

glaucus Ker-Gawl. [*E. hispidus* Nutt.]. BEACH ASTER, SEASIDE DAISY. Sprawling, rather succulent, cespitose per., to 20 in., with a short, thick rhizome, sts. villous-hirsute with spreading hairs, to glandular or even essentially glabrous; basal lvs. broadly spatulate to obovate, to 6 in. long, tapering to a winged petiole; heads 1–15, to 2 in. across; ray fls. lilac to violet. Coastal s. Calif. to n. Ore. Cv. **'Albus'**. Ray fls. white. Cv. **'Roseus'**. Ray fls. rose-pink.

hispidus: *E. glaucus*.

Howellii (A. Gray) A. Gray. Fibrous-rooted per., to 20 in., with a short, brittle rhizome, glabrous except for short-villous hairs below the heads; basal lvs. elliptic to nearly orbicular, to 3 in. long, abruptly contracted to the 4½ in. petiole, st. lvs. ovate to cordate, successively reduced upward, clasping; heads solitary, to ¾ in. across; ray fls. white. S. side of Columbia R. gorge (Ore.).

humilis R. C. Grah. Per. herb, to 10 in., sts. with spreading-villous, often dark hairs; basal lvs. oblanceolate to spatulate, to 3 in. long, villous to villous-hirsute when young, lower lvs. becoming glabrous, st. lvs. linear to linear-lanceolate, reduced; heads solitary, to ¾ in. across; ray fls. white, aging bluish-violet. Circumpolar; in N. Amer., Greenland to Alaska, s. to B.C. and nw. Mont.

hybridus Hieron. Cespitose per., to 1 ft.; basal lvs. linear-lanceolate, to 3½ in. long, leathery, glabrous above, densely white-tomentose beneath, entire; heads solitary, to ⅝ in. across; ray fls. bluish-white. Colombia. This sp. is not in cult.; the name *E. hybridus* has been applied in hort. incorrectly to a hybrid and a hybrid group. *E.* × *hybridus* Hort. [and *E. hybridus roseus* Hort.] has been used for the hybrid *E. atticus* × *E. aurantiacus*, a per. herb to 1 ft.; heads to 1 in. across; ray fls. violet-rose. More recently, the name *E.* × *hybridus* Bergmans has been used for a group of hybrids said to involve *E. elatior* (A. Gray) Greene, *E. Coulteri*, *E. peregrinus* subsp. *callianthemus*, *E. speciosus* var. *macranthus*, and other Amer. spp.; these hybrids are leafy-stemmed per. herbs, to 1½–2½ ft.; heads large, many; ray fls. light blue to lilac. Included here are cvs. **'Antwerp'**, **'Quakeress'**, **'Lasur'**, **'Ronsdorf'**, and **'Wuppertal'**.

hyperboreus: *A. caespitosus*.

Karvinskianus DC. [*E. mucronatus* DC.]. Per. herb or subshrub, to 1½ ft. high, sts. much-branched, decumbent and more or less trailing, to 3 ft. long; lvs. elliptic-lanceolate or obovate-cuneate, to 1¼ in. long, thinly pubescent, entire or with 3–5 coarse, obtuse and mucronate, apical teeth; heads solitary, to ¾ in. across; ray fls. white, fading pink and finally reddish-purple. Mex. to Venezuela. Blooms first year from seed, and for most of the year in warm climates.

leiomerus A. Gray. Tufted per., to 4 in., with a taproot and branched root crown, sts. glabrous or finely strigose; basal lvs. oblanceolate to obovate, to 2¾ in. long including petiole, essentially glabrous, lower st. lvs. oblanceolate, the upper reduced, linear; heads solitary, to 1 in. across; ray fls. deep blue to nearly white. Rocky Mts., ne. Nev. and s. Idaho, to n. New Mex., Colo., Wyo.

linearis (Hook.) Piper. Cespitose per., to 8 in., with taproot and branched root crown, gray-strigose; lvs. mostly basal, linear to linear-oblanceolate, to 3½ in. long; heads solitary or 2–3, to about ¾ in. across; ray fls. yellow. S. B.C. to Calif., s. Nev., w. Wyo., and Mont.

macranthus: *E. speciosus* var.

Mairei Br.-Bl. Cespitose per., to 3 in., hairy; lvs. mostly basal, linear-oblong, to 2 in. long, narrowed to petiole; heads solitary, to about ⅝ in. across; ray fls. lilac, not over ⅛ in. long. Mts., N. Afr.

Miyabeanus (Tatew. & Kit.) Tatew. & Kit. Per., to 6 in., densely pubescent; basal lvs. elliptic, to 1⅜ in. long, long-petioled, st. lvs. reduced; heads solitary, to 1⅜ in. across; ray fls. blue-purple. Japan.

montanensis: *E. ochroleucus*.

mucronatus: *E. Karvinskianus*.

multiradiatus (Lindl. ex DC.) Benth. [*Aster tibeticus* Hook.f., in part]. HIMALAYAN F. Per. herb, to 2 ft., pubescent; basal lvs. oblanceolate, to 8 in. long, narrowed to petiole, st. lvs. sessile, semiclasping, ovate-lanceolate, to 1½ in. long; heads solitary, to 2 in. across; ray fls.

pinkish or purplish. Himalayas. Cv. 'Roseus'. St. to 1 ft.; heads to 3 in. across; ray fls. rose.

nanus Nutt. Cespitose per., to about 3 in., with a taproot and branched root crown, sts. with spreading hairs; lvs. essentially all basal, tufted, erect, linear-lanceolate, to 1¼ in. long, hirsute to nearly glabrous; heads solitary, turbinate, ½ in. across; ray fls. violet or purple. Se. Idaho, sw. Wyo., n. Utah.

nudicaulis: *E. vernus.*

ochroleucus Nutt. [*E. montanensis* Rydb.]. Per. herb, to 16 in., with a taproot and root crown, sts. hairy; basal lvs. linear to linear-oblanceolate, to about 4¾ in. long, strigose to villous-strigose, or even nearly glabrous, st. lvs. linear, successively reduced upward; heads solitary or occasionally more, about 1 in. across; ray fls. blue, purple, or white. S. Alta. to se. Wyo., e. to Sask., w. S. Dak., and nw. Nebr. Var. **Scribneri** (W. Canby ex Rydb.) Cronq. [*E. Scribneri* W. Canby ex Rydb.]. Plant usually to 4 in.; st. lvs. few, not over 1⅛ in. long. S. Alta. to se. Wyo., e. to Sask., w. S. Dak., and nw. Nebr.

oreganus A. Gray. Per., to 6 in., with a stout taproot, simple root crown, and lax sts., glandular and loosely viscid-villous; basal lvs. tufted, spatulate to obovate, to 3½ in. long, toothed to incised, st. lvs. lanceolate to elliptic or ovate, to 1½ in. long; heads 1 to several, to about 1 in. across; ray fls. pink, white, or bluish. Columbia R. gorge (Ore. and Wash.).

peregrinus (Pursh) Greene. Fibrous-rooted per., to about 2½ ft., sts. usually leafy and sparsely villous; basal and lower st. lvs. petioled, linear-oblanceolate to oblanceolate or spatulate, to 8 in. long, entire to more or less dentate, margins usually long-ciliate, upper st. lvs. linear to ovate, to 3⅛ in. long; heads solitary or few, to about 2 in. across, involucral bracts villous on the back but not glandular; ray fls. white to purple. Alaska to B.C. Subsp. **callianthemus** (Greene) Cronq. [*E. salsuginosus* of auth., not (Richardson) A. Gray]. Sts. robust, leafy; lvs. usually entire; involucral bracts glandular on back; ray fls. rose-purple. Alaska to Calif., Alta., Colo., and New Mex.

pinnatisectus (A. Gray) A. Nels. Tufted per., to 4 in., with a short root crown; lvs. mostly basal, pinnatifid, essentially glabrous except for bristly-ciliate petioles, st. lvs. reduced to 1 or 2, linear; heads solitary, ½ in. across; ray fls. blue or purplish. Mts., s. Wyo., Colo., n. New Mex.

poliospermus A. Gray. Per., to 1 ft., but seldom over 6 in., variously hispid-hirsute, often glandular; basal lvs. linear-oblanceolate to spatulate, to about 3 in. long, st. lvs. few, linear, much-reduced; heads usually solitary, ½ in. across; ray fls. pink or purple to deep violet. S. B.C. to e.-cent. Ore. and w. Idaho.

pulchellus Michx. ROBIN'S PLANTAIN, POOR R. P. Fibrous-rooted bien. or short-lived per., to 2 ft., with slender, stoloniferous rhizomes, hirsute with long, spreading hairs; basal lvs. oblanceolate to nearly orbicular, to 5 in. long, entire or toothed, st. lvs. lanceolate-oblong or ovate, to 2¾ in. long; heads 1–6 in a corymb, to 1½ in. across; ray fls. blue, sometimes pink or even white. S. Me. to cent. Minn., s. to Ga., Miss., and e. Tex.

pumilus Nutt. Per. herb, to 20 in., with a taproot and root crown, sts. usually more or less leafy, hirsute with spreading hairs, sometimes finely glandular; lower lvs. tufted, oblanceolate to linear-oblanceolate, to 3 in. long; heads 1 to many, to 1¼ in. across; ray fls. usually white; outer pappus of inconspicuous bristles. Sask. to Colo. and Kans.; ne. Ariz. Subsp. **concinnoides** Cronq. [*E. concinnus* (Hook. & Arn.) Torr. & A. Gray]. Ray fls. usually pink or blue; outer pappus of coarse bristles or narrow scales. S. Calif. to s. Idaho, e. to w. Wyo. and n. New Mex.

purpuratus Greene. Per., to 4 in., with a root crown, st. glandular, villous with spreading hairs; basal lvs. oblanceolate or spatulate, to 1⅛ in. long, entire or the older lvs. 3-toothed or -lobed; heads solitary, to ¾ in. across; ray fls. white, aging purplish; pappus reddish-purple. Alaska, Yukon, B.C.

Roylei DC. A name of uncertain application; probably for a form of *E. alpinum.*

salsuginosus: *Aster sibiricus;* but material cult. as *E. salsuginosus* is *E. peregrinus* subsp. *callianthemus.*

Scribneri: *E. ochroleucus* var.

simplex Greene. Fibrous-rooted per., to 8 in., with a root crown, sts. solitary or few, more or less viscid-villous with spreading hairs; basal lvs. tufted, oblanceolate or spatulate, to about 3 in. long, glabrous or somewhat hirsute, margins ciliate, st. lvs. few, reduced; heads solitary, ½ in. across; ray fls. blue, pink, rarely white. High mts., ne. Ore. to Mont., s. to ne. Nev., n. Ariz., and New Mex.

speciosus (Lindl.) DC. More or less fibrous-rooted per., to 2½ ft., sts. several, leafy, with a woody root crown, foliage glabrous except for the ciliate lf. margins; lower lvs. oblanceolate to spatulate, narrowed to winged petioles, mostly deciduous, entire, uppermost lvs. mostly lanceolate, sessile; heads 1–13, to 1½ in. across, involucral bracts commonly hairy; ray fls. 65–150, blue or white. S. B.C. and Alta., s. to Ore.,

Ariz., New Mex., and e. to Mont. and w. S. Dak.; local in Baja Calif. Var. **macranthus** (Nutt.) Cronq. [var. *grandiflorus* Hort.; *E. eucephaloides* Greene; *E. macranthus* Nutt.]. Uppermost lvs. ovate; involucral bracts glabrous. Range that of the sp., but common from Idaho and Mont. southward.

subtrinervis Rydb. Per. herb, to 3 ft., with a woody root crown, sts. pubescent with spreading hairs; lower lvs. oblanceolate, to 5 in. long, more or less 3-nerved, pubescent particularly on the veins, narrowed to petiole, margins ciliate, upper lvs. sessile, oblong, lanceolate, or ovate, to 3 in. long; heads 1–4, to 1½ in. across; ray fls. blue or rose-purple. Mts., s. B.C. and Alta., e. to w. S. Dak. and Nebr., s. to Utah and New Mex.

Thunbergii A. Gray [*Aster japonicus* Less., not (Miq.) Franch. & Sav.]. Per. herb, to 15 in., with a short, slender rhizome, sts. solitary or tufted, densely pubescent; basal lvs. spatulate-oblong, to 3⅛ in. long, nearly glabrous, margins ciliate, st. lvs. fewer, to 1¼ in. long, densely pubescent; heads solitary, to 1⅜ in. across; ray fls. blue-purple. Japan. Var. **angustifolius** (Tatew.) Hara. Basal lvs. to ½ in. long, narrower; ray fls. often white.

trifidus: *E. compositus* var. *discoideus.*

Turneri: *E. glabellus* subsp. *pubescens.*

Tweedyi W. Canby. Per. herb, to 8 in., sts. lax or spreading, strigose; basal lvs. elliptic, obovate, or nearly orbicular, to 1 in. long, abruptly contracted to the 1½ in.-long petiole, gray with dense, silky-strigose hairs, st. lvs. reduced; heads 1–4, to ¾ in. across; ray fls. blue to purple, sometimes white. Dry areas in mts., nw. Wyo., sw. Mont., and adjacent Idaho.

uniflorus L. Per. alpine herb, to 6 in., sts. hairy; basal lvs. narrowly spatulate, to 1½ in. long, thick, nearly glabrous, ciliate, st. lvs. fewer, smaller, scarcely ciliate; heads solitary, to ⅝ in. across; ray fls. whitish, turning purple-blue with age. Mts., n. and cent. Eur.

ursinus D. C. Eat. Fibrous-rooted per., to 10 in., with a root crown of several slender, rhizomelike brs., sts. with appressed or rarely spreading hairs, purplish at base; basal lvs. oblanceolate, to 4¾ in. long including the tapering petiole, mostly glabrous, margins ciliate, st. lvs. linear or lanceolate, reduced; heads solitary, 1 in. across; ray fls. usually blue, sometimes pink-purple. S. Mont. to e. Nev., n. Ariz., and cent. Colo.

vagus Payson. Per. herb, with a root crown of several rhizomelike brs., foliage more or less spreading-hirsute and glandular; lvs. crowded in a basal rosette, mostly 3-lobed, to ¾ in. long including petiole; heads solitary, about 1 in. across; ray fls. pink or white. High mts., ne. Ore., cent. Calif., to sw. Colo.

vernus (L.) Torr. & A. Gray [*E. nudicaulis* Michx.]. Bien. or short-lived per., to 20 in., forming offset rosettes, sts. glabrous or sparsely hairy with appressed hairs; basal lvs. oblanceolate to nearly orbicular, to 4 in. long including short petiole, essentially glabrous, denticulate, st. lvs. very few, greatly reduced; heads to about ¾ in. across, solitary or 2–12 in a loose, nearly scapose corymb; ray fls. white. Coastal plain, Va. to La.

ERINACEA Adans. *Leguminosae* (subfamily *Faboideae*). One sp., a compact, dwarf, armed, shrub of the Medit. region; lvs. with 1 lft.; fls. papilionaceous, calyx 5-toothed, inflated, wings and keel petals united to the stamen tube; fr. a narrow legume.

Propagated by seeds or softwood cuttings.

pungens Boiss. To 1 ft., densely branched, sts. rigid, erect or ascending, green, spine-tipped; lvs. falling early, spatulate to linear-lanceolate, white-silky-hairy, to ½ in. long; fls. blue or violet, 1 in. long, in axillary clusters of 2–4; fr. to ¾ in. long, silky-hairy. S. France, Spain, Algeria, Tunisia. Zone 9.

ERINUS L. *Scrophulariaceae.* Two spp. of per. herbs, native to w. and cent. Eur. and N. Afr.; lvs. alt.; fls. in simple racemes, calyx 5-parted, corolla 5-lobed, stamens 4; fr. a caps.

Erinus is suitable for the steeper parts of a rock garden and for margins, but should be planted in partial shade and where there is very good drainage. Propagated by seeds or by division.

alpinus L. Tufted alpine per., to 6 in.; lvs. spatulate, to ½ in. long, coarsely toothed; fls. in racemes to 2½ in. long, corolla purple, to ½ in. across, lobes notched. Mts.; w. and cent. Eur. Var. **hispanicus** is listed. Cvs. 'Albus', 'Carmineus', 'Lilacinus', and 'Roseus' are color forms.

ERIOBOTRYA Lindl. *Rosaceae.* Several spp. of evergreen shrubs and small trees of e. Asia; lvs. large, alt., short-petioled or subsessile, simple, with strong pinnate veins; fls. whitish, in terminal panicles, sepals 5, petals 5, stamens about 20, pistil 1; fr. a small pome with 1 to few large seeds.

A few grown in warmer areas as ornamentals and for the edible fruit; propagated by seeds or selected cultivars by grafting.

buisanensis: *E. deflexa* var.

deflexa (Hemsl.) Nakai [*Photinia deflexa* Hemsl.]. Branchlets at first densely rusty-tomentose; lvs. oblong-obovate to elliptic, 5–10 in. long, 2 in. wide, coarsely serrate, obtuse at apex, cuneate at base, with 13–15 pairs of veins; infl. 4–5 in. long, rusty-tomentose when young, glabrate in age; fls. white, about ⅝ in. across; fr. subglobose, about ¾ in. in diam. Taiwan. Var. **buisanensis** (Hayata) Kaneh. & Sasaki [*E. buisanensis* (Hayata) Mak. & Nemoto]. Lvs. oblong to lanceolate, 4–6 in. long, ⅝–1 in. wide, acute at both ends. Taiwan. Var. **grandiflora** (Rehd. & E. H. Wils.) Nakai [*E. grandiflora* Rehd. & E. H. Wils.]. Lvs. oblong, rounded at apex, cuneate at base, 4–6 in. long, 1½–2 in. wide, crenate-serrate; fr. 1 in. in diam. Taiwan. Var. **koshunensis** Kaneh. & Sasaki. Lvs. obovate-oblong, 3–6 in. long, 1–2½ in. wide, obtuse at apex, acute at base. Taiwan.

grandiflora: *E. deflexa* var.

Hookeri: a listed name of no botanical standing; possibly a misspelling of *E. Hookerana*.

Hookerana Decne. Small tree; lvs. 8–12 in. long and 2–4½ in. wide, rusty-tomentose when young, glabrate, serrated nearly to the truncate, rounded or subacute base, veins 20–30 pairs; fls. ¼ in. across, white; fr. ¾ in. long, ellipsoid, yellow. E. Himalayas.

japonica (Thunb.) Lindl. Loquat, Japanese medlar, Japanese plum. To 25 ft.; lvs. 6–10 in. long and 1½–3 in. wide, densely soft-woolly, more or less rusty underneath, somewhat less so in age, veins 12–15 pairs; fls. ⅜–¾ in. across; fr. 1–1½ in. long, yellow. China, cent. and s. Japan, where much cult. for fr. Zone 7. Widely cult. as a subtrop. ornamental and for the edible fr., which is produced only under warm conditions. See also *Loquat*.

koshunensis: a listed name of no botanical standing for *C. deflexa* var.

ERIOCACTUS: *NOTOCACTUS.*

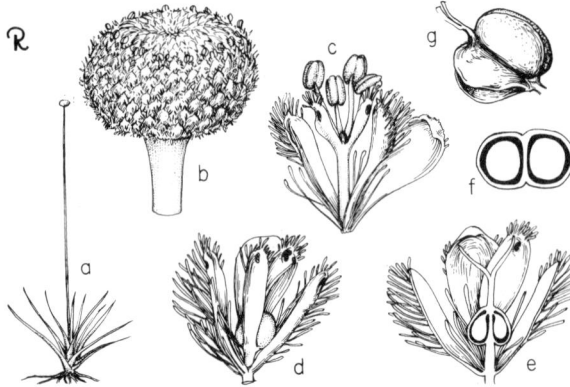

ERIOCAULACEAE. *Eriocaulon compressum* Lam.: **a,** flowering plant, × ⅛; **b,** inflorescence, × 2; **c,** male flower, × 6; **d,** female flower, × 6; **e,** female flower, vertical section, × 6; **f,** ovary, cross section, × 15; **g,** fruit, × 15. (Species representative, but not in general cultivation; from Lawrence, *Taxonomy of Vascular Plants.*)

ERIOCAULACEAE Desv. Pipewort family. Monocot.;

13 genera and over 1,000 spp. of mostly trop. monoecious plants growing in water, bogs, or wet ground; lvs. tufted, rushlike; fls. in compact, involucrate heads, small, not distinguishable in the head without dissection, unisexual, perianth of 2 series; fr. a 2–3-celled caps. The genus *Eriocaulon* is infrequently cult.

ERIOCAULON L. Pipewort. *Eriocaulaceae.* About 400

spp. of monoecious, per. herbs, of the tropics and subtropics, with a few in Japan and N. Amer.; lvs. basal, rushlike; fls. in solitary, woolly heads borne on slender scapes, small, unisexual, stamens twice as many as inner perianth segms.

One native N. Amer. species is offered for the bog garden.

decangulare L. Lvs. to 1½ ft. long and ½ in. across, longer than sheaths; heads about ½ in. across, white. Swamps, N.J. to Fla. and Tex.

ERIOCEPHALUS L. *Compositae* (Anthemis Tribe). About 30 spp. of aromatic, usually silvery or silky shrubs, native to S. Afr.; lvs. alt., opp., or clustered, mostly linear, entire or 3-parted; fl. heads solitary or in umbels or racemes, radiate, involucral bracts in 2 rows, those of the outer row separate, those of the inner united and woolly outside; fls. white, yellow or purple, disc fls. male, 5-lobed, subtended by bracts, ray fls. female, in 1 row; achenes flattened, not winged.

africanus L. Much-branched shrub, to 3 ft.; lvs. opp. or in clusters, linear, to 1 in. long, entire or lobed, channelled, silky; heads about ½ in. across, in terminal umbels; disc fls. purple, ray fls. white.

ERIOCEREUS: *HARRISIA.* E. tephracanthus: *Trichocereus tephracanthus.* E. Wislizenii: a listed name of no botanical standing.

ERIOCHLOA HBK. Cup grass. *Gramineae.* About 25 spp. of ann. or per., often branching grasses of cosmopolitan distribution; panicles terminal, of several to many spreading or appressed racemes; spikelets more or less pubescent, solitary or sometimes paired, borne in 2 rows on one side of a narrow rachis, with a terminal bisexual floret above a sterile one and 2 glumes, the back of the fertile lemma turned from the rachis, first glume reduced to a minute sheath united to the thickened lower rachilla joint, these forming a more or less ringlike, usually dark callus below the second glume, second glume and sterile lemma about equal, fertile lemma hardened, minutely papillose-rugose, mucronate or awned, the margins slightly inrolled. For terminology see *Gramineae.*

aristata Vasey. Branched c. g., Mexican everlasting g. Ann., sts. to nearly 3 ft., erect or spreading at base; lf. blades flat, mostly ⅜–½ in. wide, glabrous or scabrous; racemes several, ascending, overlapping, to ⅝ in. long, rachis pilose, pedicels stiffly hairy; spikelets ¼–⅜ in. long including awns, glume and sterile lemma awned, appressed-villous below, scaberulous above. Ariz., Calif., n. Mex. Cult. for hay in the southernmost states.

polystachya HBK. Carib grass, malojilla g., malogilla, malojillo. Per., stoloniferous, sts. to 7 ft., erect, nodes bearded; panicles terminal, with several to many loosely ascending or spreading brs.; spikelets usually paired, first glume developed as a minute, broad, loose membrane. W. Indies. Cult. from Fla. to Tex. Does not withstand cold or drought.

villosa (Thunb.) Kunth. Hairy c. g. Tall ann.; with few to several racemes, the rachis and pedicels very woolly; spikelets rather blunt, turgid, pubescent, about ¼ in. long. Asia. Occasionally cult. and adventive in Ore. and Colo.

ERIODENDRON: *CEIBA.* E. anfractuosum: *C. pentandra.*

ERIODICTYON Benth. Yerba santa. *Hydrophyllaceae.* About 8 spp. of glabrous and sticky to tomentose evergreen shrubs, native to w. N. Amer. and adjacent Mex.; lvs. alt., simple; fls. purple to white, in open to subcapitate, scorpioid cymes, calyx 5-parted, corolla mostly funnelform, 5-lobed, stamens 5, style divided to base; fr. dehiscent into 4 valves.

californicum (Hook. & Arn.) Torr. Sticky shrub, to 8 ft.; lvs. linear-lanceolate to ovate-lanceolate, to 6 in. long, entire to serrate or undulate, glabrous and sticky-resinous above, white-tomentose beneath between veins; fls. lavender to white, ½ in. long. Late spring and summer. Calif., Ore. The dried lvs. are used medicinally.

crassifolium Benth. Tomentose shrub, 3–10 ft.; lvs. lanceolate to elliptic, to 6 in. long, crenate to coarsely dentate, densely tomentose; fls. lavender, calyx lobes not glandular. Spring. S. Calif. Var. **niveum:** *E. tomentosum.*

lanatum (Brand) Abrams [*E. trichocalyx* var. *lanatum* (Brand) Jeps.]. Similar to *E. trichocalyx* but twigs pubescent, lvs. white-tomentose, hirsute, calyx lobes somewhat glandular-sticky. S. Calif., s. to n. Baja Calif., and Mex.

niveum: *E. tomentosum.*

Parryi: *Turricula Parryi.*

tomentosum Benth. [*E. crassifolium* var. *niveum* (Eastw.) Brand; *E. niveum* Eastw.]. Tomentose shrub, to 6 ft.; lvs. oblanceolate to elliptic, to 2½ in. long, entire to dentate, densely tomentose; fls. lavender to white, calyx lobes glandular. Early summer. Calif.

trichocalyx A. Heller. Sparsely hairy to almost glabrous, sticky shrub to 5 ft.; lvs. linear-lanceolate to ovate-lanceolate, to 4 in. long, serrate, glabrous and sticky above, sparsely hairy beneath; fls. purplish or white, calyx lobes densely hairy, but not glandular. Late spring–summer. S. Calif. to Baja Calif. Var. **lanatum:** *E. lanatum.*

ERIOGLOSSUM Blume. *Sapindaceae.* One sp., a polygamous shrub or tree, native from trop. Asia to n. Australia; lvs. alt., pinnate; fls. white, in erect, terminal panicles, irregular, sepals 5, petals 4, stamens 8, filaments pubescent; fr. drupaceous, 1–3-lobed.

rubiginosum (Roxb.) Blume. Shrub to 15 ft. or tree to 30 ft.; lvs. to 2 ft. long, lfts. 4–16, oblong-lanceolate to elliptic, to 7 in. long; infl. to 1 ft. long; fr. red, becoming black.

ERIOGONUM Michx. WILD BUCKWHEAT, UMBRELLA PLANT. *Polygonaceae.* About 150 spp. of ann. or per. herbs, shrubs, or cushion-forming plants, native to w. and se. U.S. and Mex.; lvs. in basal rosettes, st. lvs. alt., opp., or whorled; fls. borne in involucres in heads or umbels, or solitary, sepals 6, petal-like, white to yellow or red, enlarging in fr., stamens 9, styles 3; fr. an achene, 3-angled.

Mostly requiring sun and well-drained soil.

Allenii S. Wats. UMBRELLA PLANT. Per., to 1½ ft., white-woolly; basal lvs. long-petioled, upper st. lvs. reduced; fls. many, bright yellow, in flat-topped infl. Va. and W.Va.

annuum Nutt. Ann., to 3 ft., white-woolly; lvs. oblong, to 2 in. long; fls. white, in flat-topped cymes. S.Dak. to Tex.

arborescens Greene. Shrub, to 3½ ft.; lvs. linear or oblong, to 1¼ in. long, revolute, white-tomentose beneath; fls. rose, white-hairy at base, in heads in compound cymes. Santa Cruz Is., s. Calif.

cinereum Benth. Branching shrub, to 3 or 4 ft., sts. white-woolly, leafy below infl.; lvs. short-petioled, to 1½ in. long, crisped-margined; fls. white to pink, in open-branched infl., with scattered fl. heads. Coast, s. Calif.

compositum Dougl. ex Benth. Per., with woody root and short, branching, matlike rootcrown; lvs. basal, old lvs. 1½–4 in. long, shorter than petiole, woolly, thickly so beneath, persistent; fl. sts. 1–1½ ft. high, fls. creamy-white to yellow, in heads, in leafless to branching infl. Rocky places, Idaho and Wash., s. to n. Calif.

crocatum A. Davids. SAFFRON BUCKWHEAT. Low per., with woody, branching rootcrown, sts. 8–10 in., leafy below infl.; lvs. 1–1½ in. long, persistent; fls. yellow, in a dense cyme. Local, Ventura Co. of coastal s. Calif.

depauperatum Small. Low, branching, dwarf per., forming leafy cushions; lvs. narrow, woolly; fl. sts. short, slender, fls. pink, in a capitate infl. S. Dak.

depressum: *E. ovalifolium* var.

Douglassii Benth. Much-branched subshrub, with loosely branching, depressed sts.; lvs. clustered at ends of brs., narrow, woolly; fl. sts. to 4 in. long, bearing whorl of lvs. remote from infl.; fls. lemon, cream, or pink, in solitary fl. head. Wash. to Calif.

elatum Dougl. ex Benth. Per., with woody root and branched or unbranched rootcrown, sts. stout, leafless, to 2–3 ft.; lvs. basal, broadly lanceolate, 3–8 in. long, greenish above, loosely woolly; fls. white, to pinkish in age, in open-branching infl. with scattered fl. heads. Ne. Wash. to n. Calif., e. to w. Nev.

fasciculatum Benth. CALIFORNIA BUCKWHEAT. Rounded shrub, brs. spreading, to 3 ft.; lvs. heathlike, in clusters on branchlets, completely inrolled concealing the white-woolly undersurface; flowering branchlets leafless; fls. white to pinkish, in heads in cymose infl. Baja Calif., cent. and s. Calif., e. through sw. deserts. Subsp. **fasciculatum.** The typical subsp.; sts. glabrous, lvs. glabrate above, fls. glabrous. Calif. and Baja Calif. Subsp. **foliolosum** (Nutt.) S. Stokes. Sts., lvs., and fls. more or less hairy. Calif., Baja Calif. Subsp. **poliifolium** (Benth.) S. Stokes [*E. poliifolium* Benth.]. Sts. and lvs. cinereous; infl. reduced to solitary head; fls. pubescent. Limited to desert regions, s. and cent. Calif. to Utah and Nev.

flavum Nutt. Depressed per., to 8 in., with woody root and branched rootcrown; lvs. oblanceolate, to 2 in. long; fl. sts. scapelike, fls. yellow, in umbels. Man. to Colo. Subsp. **Piperi** (Greene) S. Stokes [*E. Piperi* Greene]. To 1 ft., sts. slender, depressed, bearing rosettes of lvs. forming mats; lvs. lanceolate to spatulate, to 4 in. long, white-tomentose beneath, pale green above; fls. yellow, often tipped red, pubescent. Mts., e. Wash. and Mont.

giganteum S. Wats. ST.-CATHERINE'S-LACE. Shrub, to 8 ft.; lvs. ovate, to 2½ in. long, white-woolly; fls. white-woolly, in heads in dense compound cymes. Santa Barbara Is., s. Calif.

grande Greene. Shrubby, to 3 ft.; sts. leafy, to 12 in. or more; lvs. 1½–3 in. long, green above, white-hairy beneath, margin wavy, revolute; fl. sts. naked, fl. heads white, scattered. Channel Is., s. Calif. Var. **rubescens** (Greene) Munz [*E. rubescens* Greene]. RED E. More or less depressed; fl. heads red, clustered.

heracleoides Nutt. Per., loosely branching, leafy in lower part, hairy throughout; lvs. oblanceolate; fl. sts. to 2 ft., with leaf whorl well below infl., fls. white or rose-tinged, in a compound umbel. Pacific Northwest.

incanum: *E. marifolium* var.

Jamesii Benth. Per., with branched, more or less leafy rootcrown; lvs. spatulate, woolly; fl. sts. decumbent to more or less erect, fls. white to cream, or yellow, in heads subtended by leafy bracts. Sw. U.S. and adjacent Mex.

latifolium Sm. Per., to about 2 ft., from a woody rootcrown, sts. leafy in lower part; lvs. about 2½ in. long, woolly beneath, sometimes slightly so above, drying and persistent; fl. sts. simple or forked, with 1 to few dense heads, fls. white or pinkish. Coastal cliffs and dunes, Ore. to s. Calif. Subsp. **grande:** *E. grande.*

Lobbii Torr. & A. Gray. Per., with stout rootcrown and short brs.; lvs. clustered in dense rosettes, elliptic, about 1½ in. long, on longer petioles, white-woolly; fl. sts. scapelike, 6–8 in. high, fls. pinkish, rose-colored in age, in heads in terminal clusters with leafy bracts. Sierra Nevada of Calif., and w. Nev.

marifolium Torr. & A. Gray. Per., with loosely branched rootcrown; brs. tufted, depressed, leafy; lvs. mostly elliptic, ½ in. long, grayish-woolly beneath; fl. sts. scapelike, 4–8 in. high, fls. yellow, in heads in terminal umbel. Mts., cent. Ore. to e. Calif. Var. **incanum** (Torr. & A. Gray) M. E. Jones [*E. incanum* Torr. & A. Gray]. Per., with branched rootcrown, forming a condensed mat; lvs. woolly on both surfaces; infl. subumbellate to nearly capitate. Sierra Nevada of Calif.

microthecum Nutt. Openly branched subshrub, to over 1 ft., lower brs. slender, woody, the upper leafy below infl.; lvs. short-petioled, varying from linear to narrow-obovate, broadest at tip, ½–1 in. long, woolly beneath; fls. in branched, flat-topped infl., among the named variations, fl. color may be yellow, white, or pink. Arid locations, nw. U.S. and adjacent Canada.

niveum Dougl. ex Benth. Per., to about 1 ft., with woody taproot and branched rootcrown; lvs. tufted, ovate, 1–2 in. long, with petioles as long as blades, white-woolly, reduced in upper part to bracts subtending small fl. heads; fls. cream or pink, in cymose infl. E. Ore. and w. Idaho, n. to B.C.

nudum Dougl. ex Benth. Habit and infl. like *E. elatum;* sts. glabrous; lvs. green above, woolly beneath; fls. white with rose-colored veins, occasionally yellow. Common, w. Wash. to s. Calif.

ochrocephalum S. Wats. Per., to 6 in., cespitose from depressed, branched rootcrown; lvs. oblanceolate or ovate, to 1¼ in. long, silvery-tomentose; fls. sts. scapelike, fls. yellow, in heads. Ore., Calif., Nev.

ovalifolium Nutt. Per., with closely branched rootcrown, usually forming dense mats; lvs. petioled, nearly elliptic, less than ½ in. long, woolly on both sides; fl. sts. scapelike, to 3 in. high; fls. pinkish to yellow. Alpine and subalpine, Ariz. and Great Basin, n. to Canada. Subsp. **vineum** (Small) S. Stokes [*E. vineum* Small]. Lvs. orbicular; fls. deep rose. Ore., e. and s. Calif., e. to Nev. Var. **depressum** Blankinship [*E. depressum* (Blankinship) Rydb.]. Plants dwarfed; lvs. mostly ⅝ in. long or less, pale silvery or greenish; infl. to 4 in.; sepals whitish, often with a dark or rose midvein. Alpine regions, Mont., Idaho, Ore., Canada.

parvifolium J. E. Sm. Habit like *E. fasciculatum;* lvs. ovate to oblong, to ½ in. long, woolly beneath; fls. pink or white, in heads or umbels. Coast, Calif. Subsp. **Paynei** C. Wolf ex Munz. Lvs. lanceolate, to 1 in. long; infl. very broad. S. Calif.

Piperi: *E. flavum* subsp.

poliifolium: *E. fasciculatum* subsp.

pyrolifolium Hook. Per., with woody root, and simple or branched rootcrown; lvs. tufted, basal, elliptic, to 1 in. long, leathery; fl. sts. scapelike, to 3½ in.; fls. white or pinkish, in small umbels. Wash. to Calif.

rubescens: *E. grande* var.

saxatile S. Wats. Per., to 1½ ft., with woody, little-branched rootcrown; lvs. dense, elliptic, white-woolly, persistent; fl. sts. several, leafless, openly branched, fls. white to rose in heads in the forks and ends of brs. Rocky places, cent. and s. Calif.

sphaerocephalum Dougl. ex Benth. Per., with loosely branched, depressed rootcrown, brs. to 8 in.; lvs. elliptic, 1¼ in. long, hairy beneath, in whorls on upper sts.; fl. heads hairy, 1–3 on each st.; fls. yellow or cream-colored. Nw. U.S. to n. Calif.

subalpinum: *E. umbellatum* var.

ternatum T. J. Howell. Loosely cespitose per., with woody, much-branched rootcrown; lvs. obovate or spatulate, to 1½ in. long including petiole, woolly; fl. sts. 4–12 in., naked except for lf. whorl subtending rays of umbels; fls. sulphur-yellow. Local, nw. Calif., sw. Ore.

thymoides Benth. Much-branched shrub, to 1 ft.; lvs. linear to spatulate, to ½ in. long, revolute, white-woolly; fl. sts. like *E. Douglassii,* fls. white to pink, very hairy. E. Wash. and e. Ore., to adjacent Idaho.

tomentosum Michx. Per., to 3½ ft., st. not much-branched; basal lvs. petioled, persistent, st. lvs. sessile, in whorls; fls. white to reddish, large for the genus, in fl. heads in lf. axils. S.C. to Fla.

umbellatum Torr. SULPHUR FLOWER. Per., with woody branched rootcrown, brs. spreading, leafy-tipped, forming loose mats to 1 ft. high or less (more condensed and matted in alpine forms); lvs. petioled, obovate or spatulate, green above, more or less woolly beneath; fls. bright yellow or paler and cream in some forms, in leafy-bracted umbel, or compound umbel. Highly variable and widespread, with many named forms. E. side Rocky Mts., n. through mts. of sw. and nw. U.S. Var. **stellatum** (Benth.) M. E. Jones. Umbels compound. Var. **subalpinum** (Greene) M. E. Jones [*E. subalpinum* Greene]. Fls. cream-colored.

vimineum Dougl. ex Benth. Ann., to 2 ft., sts. leafless; lvs. basal; fls. white or pinkish in heads, set closely along erect brs. Wash., Ore., Calif. Of little hort. value.

vineum: *E. ovalifolium* subsp.

Wrightii Torr. ex Benth. subsp. **subscaposum** (S. Wats.) S. Stokes. Per., woody, rootcrown branched, forming mats; lvs. dense, narrow, ¼–⅜ in. long, woolly; fl. sts. leafless, 3–6 in. long, fls. white in infl. of several semierect, spikelike brs., closely set with heads. Sierra Nevada of Calif. to mts. of s. Calif.

ERIOPHYLLUM Lag. *Compositae* (Helenium Tribe). Thirteen spp. of ann. or per. herbs or subshrubs, native to w. N. Amer.; lvs. alt., entire, toothed, or divided, white-tomentose; fl. heads of yellow disc and ray fls.; pappus of scales, sometimes absent.

Sometimes grown in gardens in dry regions.

artemisiifolium: *E. staechadifolium.*

caespitosum: *E. lanatum.*

confertiflorum (DC.) A. Gray. Somewhat woody per., to 2 ft.; lvs. to 1½ in. long, divided into linear segms., usually glabrate and green above, tomentose beneath; heads ¼–½ in. across, involucral bracts 4–7; ray fls. 4–6. Calif.

integrifolium: *E. lanatum* var.

lanatum (Pursh) J. Forbes [*E. caespitosum* Dougl. ex Lindl.; *E. pedunculatum* Heller]. Per., to 2 ft.; lvs. variable, to 2 in. long, pinnatifid, lobed, or nearly entire, usually glabrate and green above, white-woolly beneath; heads ¾–1½ in. across, long-peduncled, solitary or loosely corymbose; ray fls. 8–12. S. B.C. to Ore., e. to Mont. Var. **arachnoideum** (Fisch. & Avé-Lall.) Jeps. Sts. very leafy, often decumbent; lvs. 3–5-lobed, floccose-woolly; ray fls. 8–15. Coastal, n. Calif. Var. **integrifolium** (Hook.) Smiley [*E. integrifolium* (Hook.) Greene; *E. leucophyllum* Rydb.; *E. monoense* Rydb.; *E. multiflorum* (Nutt.) Rydb.]. Lower, mostly less than 8 in.; lvs. entire or 3–5-toothed at apex, usually permanently tomentose on both surfaces; ray fls. 5–8, rarely 10. Wash. and Calif., e. to Wyo. Var. **lanceolatum** (T. J. Howell) Jeps. [*E. lanceolatum* T. J. Howell]. Sts. to 16 in.; lvs. entire to serrate, woolly on both surfaces; ray fls. 10–15. N. Calif. and sw. Ore.

lanceolatum: *E. lanatum* var.

leucophyllum: *E. lanatum* var. *integrifolium.*

monoense: *E. lanatum* var. *integrifolium.*

multiflorum: *E. lanatum* var. *integrifolium.*

Nevinii A. Gray. Shrubby per., to 3 ft.; lvs. to 8 in. long, 2–pinnatifid, equally white-tomentose on both sides; heads ¼ in. across, many, in dense, compound, flat-topped corymbs; ray fls. 6–8, inconspicuous. San Clemente, Santa Barbara, and Santa Catalina Is. of Calif.

pedunculatum: *E. lanatum.*

rubellum: *E. Wallacei* var.

staechadifolium Lag. [*E. artemisiifolium* (Less.) O. Kuntze]. LIZARD-TAIL. Shrubby per., 1–4 ft.; lvs. thickish, to 2½ in. long, pinnatifid, glabrate and green above, white-tomentose beneath; heads ¼ in. across, several to many in dense corymbs; ray fls. 6–9, ⅛ in. long. Coastal, s. Ore. to s. Calif.

Wallacei A. Gray. Tiny ann., branched at base, ½–6 in.; lvs. spatulate, to ¾ in. long, mostly entire, white-tomentose; heads ½ in. across, solitary, terminal, peduncled; ray fls. 5–10. Deserts, s. Utah to Calif.,

Ariz., Mex. Var. **rubellum** (A. Gray) A. Gray. Ray fls. tinged with purple.

ERIOPSIS Lindl. *Orchidaceae.* Six spp. of trop. epiphytes of Cent. and S. Amer.; sts. pseudobulbous, conical to cylindrical, 2–4-lvd.; lvs. plicate, lanceolate; infl. from base of pseudobulb, racemose, loosely several- to many-fld.; fls. yellow to brown, sepals and petals nearly alike, spreading, lip 3-lobed. For structure of fl. see *Orchidaceae.*

For culture see *Orchids.*

rutidobulbon Hook. Pseudobulbs ovate-oblong, 2–3 in. long, 2–3-lvd. near apex; scape to 1½ ft. long; fls. to 1½ in. across, sepals and petals orange-yellow, with red-purple margins, midlobe of lip kidney-shaped, white with violet spots, disc 2-ridged, lateral lobes semiorbicular, orange-red. Late winter–late summer, autumn. Colombia, Venezuela.

ERIOSYCE Phil. *Cactaceae.* One sp., a large, spiny, ovoid, many-ribbed cactus, native to Chile; crown woolly; fls. almost lateral, diurnal, campanulate, tube thick-walled, scales pungent, stamens many, included, ovary densely woolly; fr. dry, with basal pore, seeds black, pitted. Perhaps referable to *Echinocactus* but with axillary spines at top of fr.

For culture see *Cacti.*

ceratistes (Otto) Britt. & Rose [*E. Sandillon* (Rémy) Phil.]. Sts. globose to oblong, to 3 ft. high and thick, ribs 21–35; areoles ¾ in. long, spines 11–20, awl-shaped, straight or curved, at first yellow, to 1½ in. long; fls. yellow or reddish, to 2 in. long; fr. to 1½ in. long, seeds ⅛ in. long.

Sandillon: *E. ceratistes.*

ERITRICHIUM Schrad. ALPINE FORGET-ME-NOT. *Boraginaceae.* About 30 spp. of low, depressed, hairy, per. herbs in boreal and temp. regions of N. Amer., Eur. and Asia; lvs. simple, alt.; fls. blue, in terminal racemose cymes, calyx deeply 5-lobed, corolla 5-lobed, throat with crests, stamens 5, included; fr. of 4 nutlets.

Sometimes planted in rock gardens.

argenteum: *E. elongatum* var.

elongatum (Rydb.) W. F. Wight. Plants densely cespitose, forming a mat, fl. sts. to 2½ in.; lvs. oblanceolate, ¼ in. long, with woolly hairs; fls. blue, with yellow crests, to ¼ in. across; nutlets smooth. Idaho to Wash., Ore., s. to Utah and New Mex. Var. **argenteum** (W. F. Wight) I. M. Johnst. [*E. argenteum* W. F. Wight]. Margins of nutlets toothed. Colo.

Howardii (A. Gray) Rydb. Matted, densely strigose per., fl. sts. to 5 in.; lvs. linear-oblanceolate, brownish-strigose, to ½ in. long; fls. dark blue, to ⅜ in. across. Mont., Wyo.

nanum (L.) Schrad. ex Gaudin. Densely white-woolly, tufted per., fl. sts. to 3 in.; lvs. elliptic to oblanceolate or linear, to ⅜ in. long; fls. sky-blue, with yellow crests, ¼ in. across. Alps.

strictum Decne. Appressed-silky, tufted per., fl. sts. to 10 in.; lvs. linear, to 1½ in. long, sessile; fls. blue, to ¼ in. across; nutlets with toothed margins. W. Himalayas.

ERODIUM L'Hér. HERON'S-BILL, STORKSBILL. *Geraniaceae.* Over 60 spp. of ann. or per. herbs of wide distribution; lvs. toothed and lobed or pinnately dissected; fls. in axillary umbels, sepals and petals 5, stamens 10, 5 fertile and 5 sterile, ovary 5-celled, carpels at maturity long-beaked, separating elastically from the base and twisting spirally.

Erodiums thrive in dry sunny locations in loamy soil in the border or rock garden; propagated by seeds and division. *Erodium Botrys, E. cicutarium,* and *E. moschatum* are forage plants in Calif. Some species have become weeds.

absinthoides Willd. [*E. olympicum* Clementi]. Per., to 8 in., hispid to villous; lvs. 2-pinnate, rachis toothed between lfts.; peduncles 2–8-fld., pedicels usually glandular; fls. violet, rarely rose or white, petals to ⅜ in. long; fr. to 1¾ in. long. Asia Minor. Var. **amanum** (Boiss. & Kotschy) Brumh. [*E. amanum* Boiss. & Kotschy]. Foliage gray-pubescent; fls. pale.

alpinum (Burm.f.) L'Hér. Per., to 6 in., hairy and sparsely glandular, st. very short; lvs. pinnate, to 2 in. wide, lfts. pinnately divided, the segms. broad, more or less acuminate, 3–7-toothed; peduncles 2–9-fld.; fls. violet, to ⅝ in. across; fr. to 2⅜ in. long. Italy.

amanum: *E. absinthoides* var.

chamaedryoides (Cav.) L'Hér. ALPINE GERANIUM. Per., to 3 in.; lvs. on long petioles, round-ovate, ⅜ in. long, more or less cordate, crenate but not lobed; peduncles 1-fld.; fls. white, with rose veins; fr. to ⅝ in. long. Balearic Is. and Corsica. Cv. **'Album'**. Fls. white. Cv. **'Roseum'** is listed, but most material so named appears to be *E. corsicum.*

cheilanthifolium Boiss. Per., to 4 in.; lvs. all basal, densely white-hispidulous with erect hairs, 2-pinnate, segms. of lfts. short, finely cut; peduncles 3–4-fld.; fls. to ¾ in. across, petals white, veined with rose, the two upper larger and red-splotched at base. Mts. of s. Spain and Morocco.

chrysanthum L'Hér. Tufted per., to 5 in., silvery; lvs. mostly basal, 2-pinnate; peduncles 2–5-fld.; fls. yellow, ½ in. across. Greece.

cicutarium (L.) L'Hér. ALFILARIA, RED-STEMMED FILAREE, WILD MUSK, PIN CLOVER, PIN GRASS. Ann., to 1½ ft.; lvs. pinnate, lfts. pinnatifid, rachis not toothed between lfts.; peduncles 5–10-fld., bracts united; fls. purple or pink, about ¼ in. across. Medit. region; naturalized in N. And S. Amer. A weedy plant, valuable for forage.

corsicum Léman. Per., to 6 in., st. short; lvs. ovate, toothed, sometimes more or less lobed; peduncles 1–3-fld.; fls. ¾ in. across, pink, veined with rose. Corsica and Sardinia. A compact, desirable rock-garden plant; prop. by cuttings or division. Sometimes grown under the name *E. chamaedryoides* cv. 'Roseum'.

gruinum (L.) L'Hér. Ann. or bien., to 1½ ft.; basal lvs. more or less deeply pinnately cut, st. lvs. 3-parted, the segms. toothed; peduncles 3–5-fld.; fls. violet-blue, about ⅝ in. across; fr. to 4 in. long. Sicily and N. Afr. to Iran.

Guicciardii Heldr. Tufted per., to 8 in., appressed-silvery-silky; lvs. 2-pinnate, rachis toothed between lfts.; peduncles 5–7-fld., pedicels glandless; fls. to ⅝ in. across, petals rose-pink, rounded at apex; fr. to 2⅜ in. long. Greece.

guttatum (Desf.) Willd. Shrubby per., to 6 in.; lvs. on long petioles, simple, blade elliptic, to ½ in. long, slightly lobed, silky; peduncle 2–3-fld., pedicels reflexed in fr.; fls. pink; fr. to 4 in. long. Sw. Medit. region.

×**Kolbianum** Sünderm. ex R. Knuth: *E. macradenum* × *E. supracanum.* A sterile hybrid; lvs. looser than in *E. supracanum;* fl. color variable.

leucanthum Boiss. Per., to 6 in., hairy and densely glandular; lvs. 2–3-times pinnately divided, segms. very slender; peduncles 2–5-fld.; fls. white, to ⅜ in. across. Asia Minor.

macradenum L'Hér. Per., to 1 ft.; lvs. all basal, 2-pinnate, subglabrous to villous, with soft, often glandular hairs on veins; peduncles up to 5-fld.; fls. about ½ in. across, petals light purple, upper 2 dark-spotted at base. Pyrenees. Cv. **'Roseum'.** Fls. rose-pink.

Manescavii Coss. Per., to 1½ ft.; lvs. all basal, pinnate, lobes of lfts. toothed; peduncles 5–7-fld., with large bracts united nearly to apex beneath pedicels; fls. rose-purple, to 1½ in. across. Pyrenees.

moschatum (L.) L'Hér. WHITE-STEMMED FILAREE, MUSK CLOVER. Ann. or bien., to 1½ ft.; lvs. pinnate, sparsely pubescent, lfts. usually shallowly toothed; peduncles 6–13-fld., with separate bracts; fls. rose-purple; fr. to 1⅝ in. long. Eur.; naturalized in N. and S. Amer.

olympicum: *E. absinthoides.*

pelargoniflorum Boiss. & Heldr. Shrubby per., to 1 ft.; lvs. simple, ovate-cordate, remotely lobed, obtusely dentate, pubescent above; peduncles 4–10-fld., pedicels 2–3½ times as long as calyx; petals white, the upper 2 pink-spotted at base; fr. to 1³⁄₁₆ in. long. Asia Minor.

petraeum (Gouan) Willd. Per., to 6 in.; lvs. all basal, long-petioled, 2-pinnate, often villous, rachis toothed between lfts.; peduncles 2–7-fld., pedicels villous, often glandular; petals all alike, veined with red; fr. to 1³⁄₁₆ in. long. Pyrenees.

romanum (Burm.f.) Ait. Per., to 8 in.; lvs. all basal, pinnate, white-hairy, lfts. serrate, rachis not toothed between lfts.; peduncles 4–9-fld.; fls. purplish, ½ in. across; fr. to 2 in. long. Medit. region.

roseum: a listed name of no botanical standing; see *E. chamaedryoides* and *E. corsicum.*

supracanum L'Hér. Per., to 4 in.; lvs. all basal, 2-pinnate, silvery-canescent above, green and nearly glabrous beneath, lfts. pinnatifid, rachis toothed between lfts.; peduncles 2–4-fld.; petals pink, veined with rose; fr. to ¾ in. long. Pyrenees.

trichomanifolium L'Hér. ex DC. Per., to 5 in.; lvs. all basal, 2-pinnate, densely glandular-hairy; peduncles 2–7-fld.; fls. ⁵⁄₁₆ in. across, petals violet, veined with rose. Syria.

×**Willkommianum** Sünderm. ex R. Knuth: *E. cheilanthifolium* × *E. macradenum.* A hybrid intermediate between the parents.

ERPETION: *VIOLA.* E. reniforme: *V. hederacea.*

ERUCA Mill. *Cruciferae.* Five spp. of ann. to per., erect herbs in Medit. region; lvs. large-toothed or pinnatifid; fls. whitish, yellow, or purplish, in long terminal racemes, sepals and petals 4; fr. an oblong silique, with 2 rows of seeds in each half and a broad, flat, seedless beak. Similar to *Brassica,* differing chiefly in technical characters of the silique.

sativa: *E. vesicaria* subsp.

vesicaria (L.) Cav. Half-hardy ann., branching, to 2½ ft., with scattered hairs; fls. to 1 in. long, whitish or creamy-yellow, with purplish veins; siliques 1 in. long or more, erect and appressed. Medit. region. Subsp. **sativa** (Mill.) Thell. [*E. sativa* Mill.]. ROCKET, ROCKET-SALAD, ROQUETTE, RUGULA. Sepals early-deciduous. This subsp. is the one usually cult. in the vegetable garden as a salad plant. The foliage is strong-tasting, and therefore it should be kept tender by continuous growth and frequent cutting. Best results are obtained in spring and autumn, since in summer the plant runs quickly to seed. Seeds are sown in open ground as soon as weather is settled, and usable lvs. should be ready in 2 months or less.

ERVATAMIA: *TABERNAEMONTANA.* E. coronaria: *T. divaricata.*

ERYNGIUM L. ERYNGO. *Umbelliferae.* About 200 spp. of cosmopolitan per. herbs; lvs. spiny-toothed, simple and variously lobed, or divided; fls. small, white or blue, sessile in dense, bracted heads; fr. ovoid, without ribs, but usually scaly; calyx prominent, persistent.

Planted in borders and rock gardens. They thrive in sunny locations in light, rich soil. Propagated by seeds sown as soon as ripe, and by division.

agavifolium Griseb. To 5 ft.; lvs. sword-shaped, coarsely spiny-toothed; heads 2 in. long, bracts entire to somewhat spiny-toothed, ovate, about 1 in. long. Argentina. Often offered under the name *E. bromeliifolium.*

alpinum L. To 2 ft.; lower lvs. triangular-cordate, spinose-serrate, upper lvs. round, often 3-lobed or palmately cut, tinged with blue; heads 1¼ in. long, bracts long, 2-pinnately dissected, finely divided; fls. blue or white. Eur. Cvs. **'Grandiflorum'** and **'Superbum'** are listed.

amethystinum L. To 1½ ft.; lvs. obovate, 2-pinnate; heads ½ in. long, bracts long, lanceolate; fls. blue. Eur. Plants grown under this name may be *E. planum.*

aquaticum L. To 4 ft.; lvs. linear to oblong-lanceolate, entire or remotely toothed, upper lvs. sometimes spiny-toothed to laciniate; heads ½ in. long, bracts long, reflexed; fls. white. N.J. to Ga. Most material cult. under this name is *E. yuccifolium.*

Bourgatii Gouan. To 1½ ft.; lvs. nearly orbicular, palmately 3–5-parted or -lobed, stiff, spiny-toothed; heads ¾ in. long, bracts long, spiny-tipped; fls. blue. Medit. region.

bromeliifolium F. Delar. Not known to be in cult.; see *E. agavifolium.*

coeruleum Bieb. To 3 ft.; lvs. ovate or oblong, cordate, undivided or 3-lobed or -parted; heads hemispherical, less than ½ in. long, bracts very long, stiff; fls. blue. Caucasus to cent. Asia.

eburneum Decne. To 10 ft.; lvs. linear, to 3 ft. long, very spiny, parallel-veined; heads about 1 in. long, bracts triangular to linear; entire infl. becoming ivory-colored. Brazil to Argentina.

elegans Cham. & Schlechtend. To 4 ft.; lvs. linear to spatulate-lanceolate, spiny; heads globose, about ½ in. long, bracts small, scarcely spiny-toothed, bractlets 3-toothed apically. Bolivia and s. Brazil to Argentina.

giganteum Bieb. To 6 ft.; lvs. ovate or triangular, cordate, st. lvs. 3-lobed; heads to 4 in. long, bracts long, rigid, long-toothed; fls. blue or pale green. Caucasus.

Heldreichii Boiss. To 1½ ft.; basal lvs. biternately compound, to 12 in. long, segms. prickly, overlapping, pale beneath and bluish-green above; heads subglobose, about ½ in. long, bracts mostly entire. Syria.

Leavenworthii Torr. & A. Gray. To 3 ft.; lvs. oblanceolate or palmately parted, very spiny; heads to 2 in. long, subtended by long, spiny, green or amethystine bracts, bearing an apical tuft of spiny bractlets; fls. purple. Kans. to Tex.

maritimum L. SEA HOLLY, SEA HOLM, SEA E. To 1 ft., glaucous-blue; lvs. fleshy and stiff, broadly ovate, 3-lobed, with coarse, spiny teeth; heads to 1 in. long, bracts similar to lvs. but much smaller; fls. pale blue. Eur.; naturalized on Atlantic coast of U.S.

×**Oliveranum** F. Delar. Hybrid of uncertain parentage; to 3 ft.; lvs. broadly ovate, cordate at base, upper st. lvs. palmately 4–5-parted; heads 1½ in. long, bracts stiff, linear, spinulose or spinose-serrate; fls. blue.

pandanifolium Cham. & Schlechtend. To 7½ ft.; lvs. linear, to 4½ ft. long, to 2½ in. wide, parallel-veined, spines weak, small, appressed;

heads usually maroon, in a panicle, to ⅜ in. long, longer than the small bracts. Brazil to Argentina.

paniculatum Cav. To 10 ft.; lvs. linear, spiny; heads globose, ½ in. long, bracts short, ovate to linear; fls. white. A very variable sp. Widespread in Chile and n. Patagonia.

planum L. To 3 ft.; lvs. elliptic to oblong, cordate, st. lvs. 3–5-lobed or -parted; heads ovoid, ½ in. long, bracts narrow, rigid; fls. blue. Eur., Asia. Cvs. **'Azureum'** and **'Roseum'** are color forms.

prostratum Nutt. Sts. prostrate, slender, 4–24 in. long, rooting at nodes, much-branched; lvs. elliptic or oblong, entire or few-toothed, st. lvs. sometimes 3-parted; heads axillary, ¼ in. long, dense, on thread-like peduncles, bracts narrow, entire, reflexed; fls. blue. Damp places, Ky. to Fla. and Tex.

Serra Cham. & Schlechtend. To 4 ft. or more; lvs. sword-shaped, spiny-toothed; heads globose, ⅜ in. across, bracts lanceolate, bractlets entire; fls. whitish. Brazil and Argentina.

Spinalba Vill. To 16 in., whitish-green; lvs. leathery and stiff, broadly ovate, 4–5-parted, with coarse, spiny teeth; heads 2 in. long, bracts stiff, spiny-pointed, pinnatifid; fls. blue. Alps.

yuccifolium Michx. RATTLESNAKE-MASTER, BUTTON SNAKE-ROOT. To more than 3 ft.; lvs. rigid, broadly linear, bristly, parallel-veined; heads to 1 in. long, involucre not as wide as head; fls. whitish. Conn. to Fla., w. to Minn., Kans., Tex.

×**Zabelii** Christ ex Bergmans: *E. alpinum* × *E. Bourgatii.* To 1½ ft.; heads about 1 in. long, bracts long, spinose-serrate.

ERYSIMUM L. WALLFLOWER, BLISTER CRESS, TREACLE MUSTARD. *Cruciferae.* About 80 spp. of ann. to per. herbs in Eur., Asia, and N. Amer., with branched hairs; lvs. entire to sinuate-dentate; fls. showy, lemon-yellow to golden or orange, or reddish to purplish, in usually crowded racemes, sepals and petals 4; fr. an elongate, linear silique. Related to *Cheiranthus*, differing chiefly in technical characters of the ovary and fr.

Plants are hardy and of simple requirements in cultivation. Annuals are usually sown where plants are to stand, for summer bloom. They should have a sunny exposure.

Allionii (DC.) O. Kuntze. Not cult.; the plant in cult. known by this name or as *Cheiranthus Allionii* may belong to *E. hieraciifolium;* it is often erroneously known as *E. Perofskianum.*

arkansanum: *E. asperum.*

asperum (Nutt.) DC. [*E. arkansanum* Nutt. ex Torr. & A. Gray; *Cheiranthus asper* Nutt.; *Cheirinia aspera* (Nutt.) Rydb.]. WESTERN W., PRAIRIE ROCKET. Per., to 3 ft., erect, pubescent; lvs. lanceolate or narrower, to 4 in. long, entire or lower lvs. remotely dentate; fls. orange to yellow; mature siliques spreading, slender, 2–4 in. long. W. and cent. N. Amer. Var. **perenne:** *E. perenne.*

aurantiacum Leyb. Sts. usually simple; lvs. linear-lanceolate; petals with white claw and orange-yellow limb. Se. Eur.

capitatum (Dougl.) Greene. COAST W. Bien., to 1½ ft., erect, leafy, simple or branching, lightly pubescent; lvs. linear to narrow-oblong, to 3 in. long, entire or dentate; fls. cream-colored, yellowish, or white. B.C. to Calif., e. to Idaho.

cheiranthoides L. WORMSEED MUSTARD. Ann., rarely bien., to 3 ft.; lower lvs. oblong-lanceolate, acute, entire to sinuate-dentate, green; petals yellow, to ¼ in. long, pedicels to ⅜ in. long in fl., elongating to ¾ in. in fr. Eur.; naturalized in N. Amer.

concinnum: *E. suffrutescens.*

decumbens (Schleich. ex Willd.) Dennst. [*E. ochroleucum* DC.]. Per., to 16 in., with creeping sts.; lvs. oblong or linear-lanceolate; petals yellow, ¾–1 in. long, pedicels to 3/16 in. long in fl., elongating to ⅜ in. in fr. Mts., s. and cent. Eur.

helveticum (Jacq.) DC. Cespitose per.; lower lvs. linear or linear-lanceolate, green or gray-green; petals yellow, ½–¾ in. long, pedicels 3/16 in. long in fl., elongating to ½ in. in fr. Mts., s., cent., and e. Eur.

hieraciifolium L. [*E. Marschallianum* Andrz. ex Bieb.]. Bien. or per., to 3½ ft.; lvs. linear or oblong, sinuate-dentate, gray or green; outer sepals not or scarcely saccate at base, petals mostly to ⅜ in. long, pedicels to 3/16 in. long in fl., elongating to ½ in. in fr.; siliques 1½–2¼ in. long. N., cent., and e. Eur.

Kotschyanum J. Gay. Cespitose per., sts. to 6 in.; lvs. narrow-linear to awl-like; petals bright yellow to ½ in. long. High mts., Asia Minor.

linifolium (Pers.) J. Gay [*Cheiranthus linifolius* Pers.]. Cespitose per., to 18 in.; lower lvs. filiform to linear, green or white; petals purple or violet, to ¾ in. long, pedicels to ⅛ in. long in fl., elongating to ¼ in. in fr. Spain, Portugal. Cv. **'Bicolor'**. With both white and pink fls. on the same plant.

Marschallianum: *E. hieraciifolium.*

murale: *E. suffruticosum.*

nanum: a listed name of no botanical standing.

ochroleucum: *E. decumbens.*

pachycarpum Hook.f. & T. Thoms. Robust per., to 2 ft., with appressed hairs, branched, sts. angled; lvs. lanceolate, sinuate-dentate, petioled; fls. orange-yellow. Himalayas.

perenne (S. Wats. ex Cov.) Abrams [*E. asperum* var. *perenne* S. Wats. ex Cov.]. Short-lived per., sts. mostly to 12 in., sometimes more, root crown clothed with remains of old lvs.; lower lvs. oblanceolate to spatulate, to 2 in. long, short-petioled, upper lvs. narrower and shorter; fls. yellow. Mts., n. and cent. Calif.

Perofskianum Fisch. & C. A. Mey. Ann., to 2 ft., erect, simple or little-branched, grayish-pubescent; lvs. lanceolate or narrower, to 3 in. long, entire or remotely toothed; fls. showy, yellow or orange. Afghanistan and Pakistan. See also *E. Allionii.*

pulchellum (Willd.) J. Gay [*E. rupestre* (Sibth. & Sm.) Sibth. & Sm.]. Per., cespitose or many-headed, from a few in. to 1 ft., green, sts. simple; lvs. oblong-spatulate, toothed or lyrate, upper lvs. narrow, deeply toothed; fls. deep orange; siliques erect-spreading, slender. Greece and Asia Minor.

pumilum: a name used in several senses; plants sold under this name are likely to be *E. helveticum.*

purpureum Auch. Per., to 12 in., sts. procumbent, woody, fl. sts. to 6 in.; lvs. narrow-linear, the lower pinnate, the upper toothed or entire; fls. purple. Asia Minor.

rupestre: *E. pulchellum.*

suffrutescens (Abrams) G. Rossb. [*E. concinnum* Eastw.]. BEACH W. Per., to 2 ft., woody, much-branched; lvs. narrowly linear; fls. yellow. Coastal, Calif.

suffruticosum K. Spreng. [*E. murale* Desf.]. Bien. or per., but may be grown as an ann., woody at base, sts. to 20 in. high, erect, usually branched, leafy; lvs. oblong-lanceolate, little if at all toothed; fls. golden-yellow, about ½ in. long, in compact racemes that lengthen in fr.; siliques erect, short, thick, to 1½ in. long. Nativity uncertain, perhaps Medit. region; long in cult.

torulosum Piper. Dwarf bien., usually not more than 8 in. high, usually unbranched; lvs. mostly basal, spatulate, to 3½ in. long, coarsely dentate to nearly entire; fls. yellow, to ⅝ in. across; siliques to 3½ in. long. W. N. Amer.

Wahlenbergii (Asch. & Engl.) Borb. Similar to *E. hieraciifolium* but inner sepals saccate at base, and siliques longer, to 3¾ in. long. Czechoslavakia.

Witmannii Zawadzski. Bien., to 10 in.; basal lvs. persistent, linear to linear-oblanceolate, entire to sinuate-pinnatisect, st. lvs. usually sinuate-dentate, the lower petioled; fls. yellow or greenish-yellow; siliques 2½–4½ in. long. Mts., Hungary, nw. Bulgaria.

ERYTHEA: *BRAHEA.* **E. Roezlii:** *B. armata.*

ERYTHRAEA: *CENTAURIUM.* **E. Centaurium:** see *C. Erythraea.* **E. ramosissima:** *C. pulchellum.*

ERYTHRINA L. CORAL TREE. *Leguminosae* (subfamily *Faboideae*). Perhaps 100 spp. of mostly deciduous, trop., armed trees, shrubs, or rarely herbs with stout branchlets; lvs. alt., of 3 broad lfts., the terminal usually largest; fls. papilionaceous, in mostly dense racemes, showy, red or orange, standard large, folded and enclosing other fl. parts, or spreading and reflexed, exposing other fl. parts, the keel and wing petals usually much shorter, stamens 10, 9 united and 1 separate; fr. an elongate, flat or nearly cylindrical legume, more or less constricted between seeds.

Grown as ornamentals in warm countries, usually thriving and flowering best where the climate is strongly seasonal; also grown under glass; often flowering without foliage in the wild. Some species have economic value: trees are planted as shade in coffee and cocoa plantations; flowers are cooked and eaten; seeds are made into necklaces; and some species have medicinal and poisonous properties. Easily propagated by woody cuttings, or seeds, or the herbaceous sorts by division. In cultivation, woody forms are sometimes treated as tender perennials. Mostly grown in Zone 10.

abyssinica Lam. ex DC. [*E. tomentosa* R. Br. ex A. Rich.]. Small tree, to 40 ft., flowering without lvs., rusty- or whitish-tomentose throughout, becoming glabrate, bark dark gray, fissured, corky; terminal lfts. transversely elliptic or nearly orbicular, to 7 in. long, 8 in. wide, obtuse to emarginate; fls. coral-red to scarlet, calyx bright red, at least when young, spathelike, cut into 5 slender lobes, standard to 1¾ in. long,

⅝ in. wide, glabrous, keel petals separate, to ¼ in. long; fr. woody, pubescent, segms. globose, seeds red, with black hilum. Savannas, Ethiopia, s. to Mozambique. Closely related to and often confused with *E. latissima.*

acanthocarpa E. H. Mey. Stiff shrub, to 6 ft., with large, succulent, underground root; lfts. transversely elliptic, to 1 in. long, 1½ in. wide, obtuse or short pointed, glaucous, especially beneath; peduncles very short; calyx campanulate, nearly truncate, tipped with green, folded, somewhat curved, to 2 in. long, 1½ in. wide; fr. woody, constricted, 4–10 in. long, prickly, seeds brown. Cape Prov. (S. Afr.). Zone 10.

americana Mill. Tree, spiny, flowering with lvs.; lfts. broadly ovate, acute or acuminate, to 4 in. long; fls. scattered in a raceme 3 in. long, rachis of raceme, pedicels, and calyx slightly pubescent, pedicels less than ¼ in. long, standard scarlet to light rose, to 2½ in. long, straight, folded, enclosing other fl. parts; fr. to 8 in. long, densely hairy at first, seeds red. Cent. Mex.

arborea: *E. herbacea.*

arborescens Roxb. Low tree, somewhat prickly, flowering without lvs.; lfts. membranous, to 1 ft. long and broad, pointed apically; racemes short, dense; calyx campanulate, standard folded, straight, to 1¾ in. long, 2–3 times longer than wide, keel petals to ½ in. long, united, about same length as wing petals; fr. flat, 6–9 in. long, 1 in. wide or more, seeds black, glossy. Himalayas.

Berteroana Urb. Tree, to 20 ft. or more, flowering with or without lvs.; lfts. rhombic-ovate, to 6 in. across, acute-acuminate waxy; racemes to 5 in., rarely to 18 in. long; calyx tubular, standard folded, straight, to 3¾ in. long, only ⅙ as broad, glabrous even in bud, keel petals united; fr. nearly woody, to 11 in. long, much twisted when mature, seeds scarlet, with very short black line from hilum. S. Mex. to Colombia; W. Indies. Zone 10b.

×**Bidwillii** Lindl.: *E. crista-galli* × *E. herbacea.* Garden hybrid, intermediate between parents, flowering with lvs.; fls in 3's in lf. axils and also forming terminal racemes, standard to 2 in. long, about ⅓ as broad, slightly open-reflexed away from other fl. parts.

caffra Thunb. [*E. Constantiana* P. Micheli; *E. insignis* Tod.]. Semi-evergreen tree, broadly spreading, to 60 ft., flowering with lvs.; terminal lfts. broadly ovate, about 7 in. across, nearly acute, racemes short; calyx papery, splitting irregularly; petals vermilion (rarely yellow-white), standard strongly reflexed, exposing other fl. parts, 2 in. long, ½ as broad, keel petals united, to 1 in. long; fr. nearly woody, to 4½ in. long, seeds red with black hilum. E. S. Afr. Zone 10.

Constantiana: *E. caffra.*

Corallodendrum L. Small tree; differs from *E. Berteroana* in having racemes to 12 in. long, calyx campanulate, standards red, shorter, broader, to 2⅛ in. long and ½ in. wide, keel petals separate, shorter than the wing petals. W. Indies. Zone 10. Material listed under this name may be misidentified.

coralloides DC. NAKED C.T. Tree, to 20 ft., somewhat prickly, flowering without lvs.; lfts. triangular, terminal lfts. to 4½ in. long; rachis of racemes, pedicels, and calyces densely brown-tomentose; standard to 3 in. long, less than ¼ as wide, folded, straight to slightly curved, keel petals united or separate, to ⅜ in. long, slightly longer than wing petals; fr. to 6 in. long, slightly constricted, seeds red. Ariz., ne. and cent. Mex. Zone 10.

crista-galli L. COCKSPUR C.T., CRY-BABY TREE. Large or medium-sized tree, flowering with the lvs., branchlets slender; terminal lfts. mostly elliptic, to 3 in. long or more; fls. solitary or 2–3 together, forming leafy, loose, terminal racemes, standard reflexed, nearly 2 in. long, 1 in. wide, stamens separate about ¼ in.; fr. woody, to 15 in. long, seeds blackish, with brownish markings. Uruguay, s. Brazil, Paraguay, n. Argentina. Zone 9. Often grown as a shrub, especially under glass.

falcata Benth. Differs from *E. crista-galli* in having infl. lateral, leafless, stamens separate to ⅝ in., fr. broader, to 1⅛ in. wide, and seeds flat at ends with a prominent funicle about ⅛ in. long, Brazil, Peru, Bolivia, Argentina. Zone 10.

flabelliformis Kearn. Shrub or small tree, flowering before or with young lvs.; lfts. papery, nearly orbicular to triangular, terminal lfts. broader than long, to 4¼ in. across, apically rounded or obtuse; racemes short, rachises and calyces densely ash-gray-pubescent, standard folded, to 3 in. long, less than ¼ as wide, gray-pubescent in bud, becoming glabrate, keel petals united; fr. to 1 ft. long. Ariz., New Mex., w. Mex.

fusca Lour. [*E. glauca* Willd.; *E. ovalifolia* Roxb.]. SWAMP IMMORTELLE. Often large tree; lfts. leathery, terminal lft. oblong-ovate to obovate, to 6 in. long, glaucous beneath; calyx brown-velvety, deeply 2-lobed, standard to 2 in. long and 1½ in. wide, keel petals shorter, united; fr. nearly woody, to 6 in. long. Tropics, Asia and Polynesia.

Gibbsae: *E. latissima.*

glauca: *E. fusca.*

herbacea L. [*E. herbacea* var. *arborea* Chapm.; *E. arborea* (Chapm.) Small]. CARDINAL-SPEAR, CHEROKEE BEAN, CORAL B. Per. herb, shrub, or small tree, brs. slender; lfts. thin, terminal lfts. hastately shallowly 3-lobed, to 5 in. long, long-acuminate; racemes to 2 ft. long; standard folded, narrow, straight, to 2 in. long; fr. nearly woody, to 8 in. long, seeds scarlet, with black line from hilum. S.C. to Fla., w. to Tex. and ne. Mex.

hondurensis Standl. Differs from *E. flabelliformis* in having terminal lfts. triangular or rhombic-ovate, usually slightly longer than broad, acuminate, pubescent with long, whitish, arachnoid hairs at maturity; keel petals hastate; seeds uniformly scarlet. Lowlands, Honduras and Nicaragua.

Humeana K. Spreng. Tree, to 20 ft.; terminal lfts. triangular or ovate, to 5 in. long, acute or acuminate, truncate at base; calyx tubular, shortly 5-toothed, standard 2 in. long, ¾ in. broad, folded, straight, keel petals very short, separate, uppermost stamen separate almost to base; fr. nearly woody, to 6 in. long, seeds red. Tropics, Afr. Zone 10. Var. **Raja** (Meissn.) Harv. Smaller, lfts. long-acuminate, more or less hastate basally, strongly recurved, uppermost stamen united to the others.

indica: *E. variegata.*

insignis: *E. caffra.*

latissima E. H. Mey. [*E. Gibbsae* Bak.f.]. Small tree, with thick corky bark, flowering with lvs.; lfts. woolly-pubescent when young, becoming thick, leathery, prominent-veined when mature, usually broader than long, terminal lft. to 8 in. wide, lateral lfts smaller; calyx brownish-pubescent, spathelike, divided into 5 linear lobes, standard to 2½ in. long, about half as broad, spreading but not reflexed, stamens only exserted, keel petals separate, ovate, to ½ in. long; fr. woody, pubescent, constricted, seeds red. Ne. and s. Afr.

lithosperma: *E. subumbrans.*

Livingstoniana Bak. Large tree; terminal lfts. hastately 3-lobed, 4 in. long and broad; peduncles long, glabrous, calyx spathaceous, standard to 1½ in. long and broad, wing petals orbicular, ⁵⁄₁₆ in. across; fr. 5–6 in. long, segms. globose. Mozambique.

lysistemon: *E. princeps.*

macrophylla A. DC. Differs from *E. americana* in having a raceme to 10 in. long, pedicels to ½ in. long, rachis of raceme, pedicels, and calyces densely brown-pubescent. Cent. Amer.

mitis Jacq. [*E. umbrosa* HBK]. Differs from *E. Berteroana* in having racemes 1½–4 in. long, calyx campanulate, markedly shorter on one side and convex at margin, standard broader, to 3 in. long and ¼ as wide, and keel petals separate. Venezuela.

monosperma: *E. tahitensis.*

Mulungu: *E. verna.*

Poeppigiana (Walp.) O. F. Cook. MOUNTAIN IMMORTELLE. Tree, to 60 ft., trunk with prickles; terminal lfts. rhombic-ovate to nearly orbicular, to 8 in. long; pedicels less than ½ in. long, calyx campanulate, no wider than long, standard orange, to 2½ in. long, only ⅓ as wide, keel petals united, nearly equal; fr. papery, not constricted, seeds brown, without markings. Wet tropics, S. Amer. Often planted as shade for cacao and coffee. Very showy in fl.

polianthes: *E. speciosa.*

princeps A. Dietr. [*E. lysistemon* Hutch.]. Differs from *E. caffra* in being smaller and having standard folded, narrower, enclosing other fl. parts. E. S. Afr., n. to s. Rhodesia. Zone 9b.

reticulata: *E. speciosa.*

sandwicensis: *E. tahitensis.*

senegalensis DC. To 15 ft. or more; lfts. leathery, ovate-oblong, terminal lfts. to 5 in. long; racemes lax, 6–9 in. long, rachis pubescent, lower fls. in clusters of 3; calyx campanulate, standard folded, ½ in. broad; fr. 4–5 in. long, segms. globose, seeds red. Savannas, Senegal to Cameroon.

speciosa Andr. [*E. polianthes* Brot.; *E. reticulata* K. Presl]. Small tree, flowering with lvs.; lfts. rhombic or nearly triangular, often wider than long, to 9 in. across, long-acuminate; calyx thin, campanulate, with apical spur, standard to 2¾ in. long, ½ in. wide, folded, straight to slightly curved, keel petals united; fr. nearly woody, to 12 in. long, scarcely constricted, seeds blackish, with tawny markings. S. Brazil.

subumbrans (Hassk.) Merrill [*E. lithosperma* Blume ex Miq.]. Tree, to 50 ft., flowering with lvs.; terminal lfts. rhombic-ovate, 4–6 in. long, acute-acuminate, nearly cordate at base; rachis of raceme mealy-pubescent; calyx deeply 2-lipped, velvety, standard open, ovate-oblong, to 1½ in. long; fr. 4–5 in. long, flat lower part sterile and indehiscent, upper part with 1–2 black seeds, 2-valved. Java, Philippine Is.

tahitensis Nadeau [*E. monosperma* Gaud.-Beaup.; *E. sandwicensis* Degener]. WILWILLI. Tree, to 30 ft., spiny, flowering without lvs.; lfts. ovate-triangular, to 3 in. long, leathery, tomentose beneath; fls. crowded near tips of racemes to 8 in. long, standard orange-red, rarely yellow or white, to 1½ in. long, nearly as broad, recurved, exposing stamens; fr. woody, tomentose, seeds red. Hawaii, Tahiti.

tomentosa: *E. abyssinica.*

umbrosa: *E. mitis.*

variegata L. [*E. indica* Lam.]. Broad tree, to 60 ft., flowering without lvs., stellate-pubescent; terminal lfts. orbicular to nearly reniform, to 6 in. long, cuspidate; racemes dense, 6 in. long; fls. to 2½ in. long, calyx spathelike, split to base, standard 1 in. across, keel petals separate; fr. to 12 in. long, seeds red-brown. Philippine Is., Indonesia. Cv. **'Alba'**. Fls. white. Var. **orientalis** (L.) Merrill. Lvs. variegated with yellow along the veins.

velutina Willd. Spreading tree, to 30 ft., related to *E. variegata*, but differing in flowering with lvs., and having terminal lfts. usually emarginate to obtuse, standard strongly reflexed, inequilateral, and seeds red, with a short broad black line from hilum. Trop. Amer. Much cult.

verna Vell. [*E. Mulungu* Mart. ex Benth.]. Differs from *E. Poeppigiana* in having pedicels ⅝–1⅝ in. long, calyx wider than long, and standard to 1¾ in. long and ⅔ as wide. Cent. and s. Brazil.

vespertilio Benth. Low tree, trunk to 3 ft. in diam.; lfts. very variable, broadly 3-lobed or fan-shaped, to 4 in. across, broadly cuneate at base, lateral lobes obtuse-spreading or recurved, median lobe, when present, shorter and attenuate-triangular, petiole slender; racemes erect; fls. pendent, calyx spathelike, standard recurved, ovate, salmon-red, 1½ in. long, keel petals separate; seeds red. Tropics, n. Australia and Queensland, where called GRAY CORKWOOD. Zone 10b.

Zeyheri Harv. Dwarf subshrub, ann. shoots to 1½ ft., from underground rhizome; lfts. ovate-rhomboid, to 10 in. long, acute or rounded, prickly beneath; rachis of raceme to 18 in. long, with fls. in upper ⅓ and pendent; standard to 1¼ in. long, curved, folded, enclosing other fl. parts, keel petals united; fr. constricted, 3 in. long or more, seeds red. E. S. Afr.

ERYTHRODES Blume. *Orchidaceae.* About 100 spp. of terrestrial herbs of subtropics and tropics of both hemispheres; sts. erect, ascending or prostrate; lvs. short-petioled, ovate to lanceolate, usually variegated; infl. a dense or loose spicate raceme; fls. small, nearly sessile, petals and upper sepals meeting at tips and forming a helmet, lip ascending from base of column, spurred at base. For structure of fl. see *Orchidaceae*

For culture see *Orchids.*

nobilis (Rchb.f.) Pabst. To 10 in.; lvs. oblong, dark green with silver venation; infl. densely many-fld.; fls. greenish-white, to ¼ in. long, lip 3-lobed, midlobe fringed. Brazil.

querceticola (Lindl.) Ames. Slender, leafy, glabrous, to 16 in., with underground stolons, sts. erect; lvs. to 3 in. long, lamina ovate-lanceolate, light green to yellowish- or brownish-green with white venation; racemes to 4 in. long, densely to loosely few- to many-fld.; fls. to ¼ in. long, nearly sessile, yellowish-green or white, lip 3-lobed, with a saccate spur. Blooming all year. Fla., La., Tex., W. Indies, Mex., to n. S. Amer.

ERYTHRONIUM L. ADDER'S-TONGUE, DOG-TOOTH VIOLET, TROUT LILY, FAWN L. *Liliaceae.* About 25 spp. of spring-blooming, per. herbs with membranous-coated corms, native mostly to temp. N. Amer., with one in Eur. and Asia; lvs. 2, basal or nearly so, nearly opp., often mottled; fls. white, yellow, pink, rose, or purple, nodding, solitary or several in a raceme, perianth segms. 6, separate, usually recurved, stamens 6, anthers basifixed, stigma 3-lobed to unlobed; fr. a 3-valved, loculicidal caps.

Planted in wild gardens or rock gardens. They do well in shady or partly shady places in well-drained soil rich in leaf mold; a winter mulch is beneficial. Propagated by seeds, or by offsets planted 3–5 in. deep.

albidum Nutt. WHITE DOG-TOOTH VIOLET, BLONDE LILIAN. To 1 ft., producing abundant offsets; lvs. elliptic, to 6 in. long, green, rarely mottled; fls. solitary, 1–2 in. long, bluish- to pinkish-white, yellow at base inside, anthers creamy-white, stigmas deeply lobed, lobes spreading. Ont. and w. N.Y. to Minn., s. to Ky., Ark., Tex. Var. **mesochoreum** (Knerr) Rickett [*E. mesochoreum* Knerr]. Does not produce offsets; lvs. narrower. Nebr. and Mo. to Tex.

americanum Ker-Gawl. YELLOW A.-T., TROUT LILY, AMBERBELL. To 1 ft., producing abundant offsets; lvs. elliptic, to 6 in. long, mottled with brown and whitish; fls. solitary, to 2 in. long, yellow, often spotted at base inside, anthers brown or yellow, stigma with very short lobes. Nov. Sc. to Minn., s. to Fla. and Ala.

californicum Purdy. FAWN LILY. To 4–14 in.; lvs. lanceolate-oblong or ovate-oblong to oblong, to 6 in. long, strongly mottled; fls. 1–3, to 1⅜ in. long, white to cream, with greenish-yellow base and transverse band of yellow, orange, or brown inside, anthers white, stigma with very short lobes. Coast Ranges, n. Calif. Var. **bicolor:** *E. helenae.*

citrinum S. Wats. To 1 ft.; lvs. lanceolate to oblong, to 6 in. long, mottled, with crisped margins; fls. 1–3, to 1½ in. long, creamy-white, greenish-yellow at base inside, inner segms. with saclike basal appendages on interior, anthers white, stigma not lobed. Nw. Calif. and sw. Ore.

Dens-canis L. DOG-TOOTH VIOLET. To 6–12 in.; lvs. oblong to elliptic, 4–6 in. long, mottled with reddish-brown and white; fls. solitary, 1 in. long, rose to purple, anthers blue, stigma deeply lobed. Eur., Asia. Cvs. include: **'Album'**, fls. white; **'Purpureum'**, fls. purple-violet. Cv. **'Robustum'** is also listed. Var. **japonicum** (Decne.) Bak. [*E. japonicum* Decne.]. Fls. violet-purple with black basal spot on inside of each segm. Japan.

giganteum: *E. grandiflorum,* but see also *E. oregonum.*

grandiflorum Pursh [*E. grandiflorum* var. *parviflorum* S. Wats.; *E. giganteum* Lindl.; *E. obtusatum* L. Goodd.]. AVALANCHE LILY. To 1–2 ft.; lvs. oblong-elliptic, to 6 in. long, not mottled; fls. 1 to several, bright golden-yellow, anthers dark red or maroon, stigma lobed. B.C. to Mont., s. to Ore. and Utah. Difficult to grow at low altitudes. Cv. **'Album'**. Fls. white, with yellow centers. Cv. **'Robustum'** [var. *robustum* Purdy]. Giant form; fls. large, golden. Subsp. **candidum** Piper [var. *idahoense* (St. John & G. N. Jones) R. J. Davis; *E. idahoense* St. John & G. N. Jones]. Lf. tips hooded, fls. greenish or creamy-white, yellow at base inside, anthers white. N. Idaho and adjacent Wash. Subsp. **chrysandrum** Appleg. [*E. parviflorum* L. Goodd.]. Anthers golden-yellow.

Hartwegii: *E. multiscapoideum.*

helenae Appleg. [*E. californicum* var. *bicolor* Purdy]. To 1 ft., producing offsets; lvs. ovate to lanceolate, to 6 in. long, strongly mottled; fls. 1 or more, 1½ in. long, white and chrome-yellow, fragrant, anthers golden-yellow, stigma lobes stout and short. Local in n. Calif.

Hendersonii S. Wats. To 1 ft.; lvs. lanceolate-oblong, 4–8 in. long, mottled, with crisped margins; fls. 1–4, to 1½ in. long, lavender, with purple base inside, surrounded by yellowish zone, filaments purple, anthers brownish, stigma almost entire. Nw. Calif. and sw. Ore.

Howellii S. Wats. To 8 in.; lvs. lanceolate to lanceolate-oblong, to 6 in. long, mottled; fls. 1–4, about 1 in. long, white, basally orange or barred with yellow inside, inner segms. lacking saclike basal appendages on interior, anthers white, stigma nearly entire. Nw. Calif. and s. Ore.

idahoense: *E. grandiflorum* subsp. *candidum.*

japonicum: *E. Dens-canis* var.

Johnsonii: *E. revolutum.*

mesochoreum: *E. albidum* var.

montanum S. Wats. To 1 ft. or more; lvs. ovate-lanceolate, to 6 in. long, not mottled; fls. 1 to several, 1½ in. long, white, orange at base inside, perianth segms. slightly recurved, anthers white, stigma deeply lobed. Alpine meadows, Ore., Wash., Vancouver Is., B.C.

multiscapoideum (Kellogg) A. Nels & Kennedy [*E. Hartwegii* S. Wats.; *E. Purdyi* Hort.]. To 8 in., producing offsets; lvs. oblanceolate, 1½–4 in. long, mottled; fls. usually solitary, 1–1½ in. long, white, pale greenish-yellow at base inside, perianth segms. spreading, recurved in age, anthers white, stigma lobes long and filiform. N. Calif.

obtusatum: *E. grandiflorum.*

oregonum Appleg. [*E. giganteum* of auth., not Lindl.]. To 1 ft.; lvs. lanceolate or oblong-lanceolate, to 6 in. long, mottled; fls. 1–6, to 2 in. long, white to pink, reddish or brown at base outside, yellow inside, tips of perianth segms. twisted, anthers golden-yellow, filaments broadly dilated, stigma lobes recurved. Ore. to B.C.

parviflorum: *E. grandiflorum* subsp. *chrysandrum.*

Purdyi: *E. multiscapoideum.*

revolutum Sm. [*E. revolutum* var. *Johnsonii* (Bolander) Purdy; *E. Johnsonii* Bolander; *E. Smithii* Orcutt]. To 16 in.; lvs. lanceolate-ovate, to 8 in. long, mottled, with crisped margins; fls. 1 to several, to 1¾ in. long, rose-pink, with basal yellow bands inside, anthers yellow, filaments strongly dilated basally, stigma lobed. N. Calif. to Vancouver Is., B.C.

Smithii: *E. revolutum.*

tuolumnense Appleg. To 1 ft.; lvs. lanceolate to broadly oblanceolate, to 1 ft. long, yellow-green, not mottled; fls. 1 to several, golden-yellow, stamens half as long as perianth, anthers yellow, stigma not lobed. Cent. Calif.

ERYTHROPHLEUM R. Br. *Leguminosae* (subfamily *Caesalpinioideae*). Perhaps 10 spp. of large trees of Afr., Madagascar, Asia, and Australia; lvs. alt., 2-pinnate, with 2–5 pairs of pinnae, lfts. alt.; racemes spikelike, dense; fls. small, regular, 5-merous, sepals united basally, petals oblanceolate, separate, stamens 10, separate; fr. a flat, oblong, dehiscent legume.

Propagated by seeds.

africanum (Welw. ex Benth.) Harms. To 50 ft.; young growth yellow-tomentose; lfts. elliptic-oblong, in 6–7 pairs on each pinna, 1½ in. long, obtuse; racemes 4–6 in. long; fls. honey-scented, green-yellow with orange-red anthers; fr. 5 in. long, 1 in. wide. Trop. Afr.

guineense: *E. suaveolens.*

suaveolens (Guillem. & Perrottet) Brenan [*E. guineense* G. Don]. RED-WATER TREE. To 100 ft.; branchlets rusty-pubescent; lfts. ovate-elliptic, in 4 pairs, acuminate; racemes to 3 in. long; fls. fragrant, cream or reddish; fr. a legume, to 4½ in. long, 2 in. wide, woody. Trop. Afr. Wood used for general construction, bark for arrow poison.

ERYTHROPSIS. Lindl. ex Schott & Endl. *Sterculiaceae.* Not in cult. E. Barteri: *Hildegardia Barteri.*

ERYTHRORHIPSALIS A. Berger. *Cactaceae.* One sp., an epiphytic cactus, native to Brazil; sts. cylindrical, jointed, branching apically; areoles evenly distributed, with bristles; fls. open for several days, rotate, fragrant; fr. umbilicate, red. Allied to *Rhipsalis,* in which it should perhaps be included, but fls. apical, perianth segms. slightly united, style exserted even in bud, and ovary scaly and bristly.

For culture see *Cacti.*

pilocarpa (Löfgr.) A. Berger. Sts. erect, becoming pendent, to 14 ft., cylindrical, brs. terminal, often whorled, to ¼ in. thick, often ribbed, the ultimate ones usually short; bristles 3–10; fls. white or rose, ¾ in. across; fr. globose, to ½ in. thick.

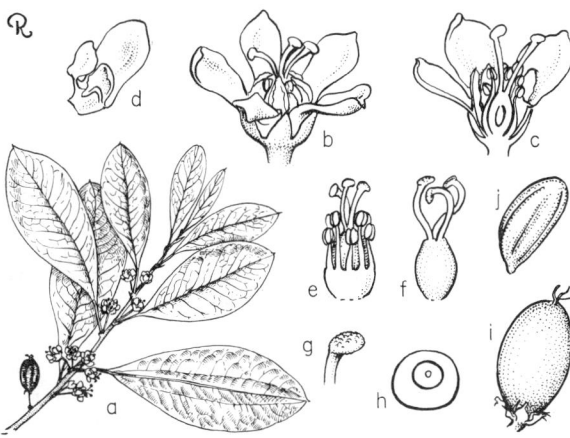

ERYTHROXYLACEAE. *Erythroxylum Coca:* **a,** flowering branch, × ½; **b,** flower, × 3; **c,** flower, vertical section, × 3; **d,** petal, inner face, × 3; **e,** stamens and pistil, × 4; **f,** pistil, × 5; **g,** stigma, × 8; **h,** ovary, cross section, × 8; **i,** fruit, × 1½; **j,** seed, × 1½. (a from Lawrence, *Taxonomy of Vascular Plants.*)

ERYTHROXYLACEAE Kunth. COCA FAMILY. Dicot.; 3 genera and about 205 spp. of glabrous shrubs and small trees, native mostly to trop. Amer., with a few spp. in Afr. and Asia; lvs. alt., simple; fls. solitary or fascicled, bisexual, regular, sepals 5, petals 5, with appendages on their inner faces, stamens 10, in 2 whorls, united basally into a tube, ovary superior, 3-celled, styles 3; fr. a berry, often drupaceous, usually 1-celled by abortion. Only *Erythroxylum* is cult.

ERYTHROXYLUM P. Br. *Erythroxylaceae.* About 200 spp. of glabrous shrubs and trees, mostly native to trop.

Amer., with a few spp. in Afr. and Asia; lvs. alt., simple, with stipules; fls. small, solitary or fascicled, sepals and petals 5, stamens 10, ovary 3-celled; fr. a drupaceous berry, usually 1-celled by abortion. Frequently, but not originally, spelled *Erythroxylon.*

Propagated by seeds or, under glass, by cuttings over bottom heat.

Coca Lam. COCA, COCAINE PLANT, SPADIC. Densely leafy shrub, to 12 ft.; lvs. to 2½ in. long, elliptic to obovate, mucronate; fls. yellowish, ¼ in. across, not showy; fr. about ⁵⁄₁₆ in. long, reddish. Probably e. Andes. Zone 10b (Fla.) Sometimes grown in the open in the far South, or as a greenhouse plant in the North. Cult. in the tropics as a drug plant or sometimes as an ornamental hedge plant. Coca, chewed daily by the Indians of w. S. Amer., is the dried lvs. (whole or powdered) of *E. Coca* mixed with lime. The center of production is in the Andes of e. Peru and Bolivia, where the crop is grown primarily for domestic use and partly as a source of the anesthetic drug, cocaine.

ESCALLONIA Mutis ex L.f. *Saxifragaceae.* About 39 spp. of evergreen shrubs or small trees of S. Amer., mostly in the Andean region; lvs. alt. or whorled, sessile or short-petioled, simple, entire or serrate, often resinous-dotted and glandular; fls. white, rose-red, or of intermediate shades, sometimes fragrant, mostly in terminal racemes or panicles, sepals, petals, and stamens 5, calyx tube united with ovary, petals separate, spreading, or erect with claws united, ovary inferior, 2–3-celled; fr. a many-seeded caps.

Several species are good ornamental shrubs. Specimens in cultivation, however, are difficult to identify because cultivated plants hybridize readily among themselves and produce fair amounts of viable seeds. Most garden plants are believed to be hybrids of mixed and sometimes unknown parentage, which tend to replace the species originally grown.

Escallonias thrive under the usual conditions of parks and yards, being rapid and free growers. They are sometimes trained as vines and on pillars. They are planted mostly in Calif., where they are prized for their general adaptability as well as for their habit of blooming in autumn and early winter, although several species bloom nearly continuously in proper climates. Propagated by cuttings placed in a cold frame in autumn and transplanted to the nursery in spring. Zone 8, for most species.

alba: a listed name of no botanical standing.

Balfourii: a listed name of no botanical standing for *E.* × *exoniensis* cv.

Berterana: *E. pulverulenta.*

bifida Link & Otto [*E. floribunda* Hook.f., not HBK; *E. montevidensis* (Cham. & Schlechtend.) DC.]. Shrub or small tree, to 12 ft., or more, branchlets glabrous but not viscid; lvs. narrowly elliptic, to 3 in. long, usually slightly emarginate at apex, very finely toothed; panicles to 6 in. long, often many, terminal on lateral brs., aggregated into large showy infl.; petals white, short-clawed, reflexed about midway, stamens and styles exserted, style headlike. Brazil, Paraguay, Uruguay, Argentina. Cv. 'Freytheyi': *E.* × *Rockii* cv.

donardensis: a listed name of no botanical standing; perhaps refers to one of the cvs. of *E.* × *langleyensis.*

×**edinensis:** *E.* × *langleyensis.*

×**exoniensis** Hort. Veitch: *E. rosea* × *E. rubra.* Shrub or small tree, to 15–20 ft., brs. and infl. axes more or less ribbed, pubescent and glandular; lvs. elliptic, to 1½ in. long, toothed, glabrous, glossy above, paler beneath; petals white, often rose-tinted, claws united, lobes spreading. Cvs. 'Balfourii' and 'Frades' belong here.

floribunda: *E. bifida.*

×**franciscana** Eastw.: presumably *E. illinita* × *E. rubra* var. *macrantha.* Shrub, more or less intermediate between the supposed parents, with the scent of *E. illinita* and the glandular-punctate lvs. of *E. rubra* var. *macrantha.* Cv. 'Eric Walther' belongs here.

Freytheyi: a listed name of no botanical standing for *E.* × *Rockii* cv.

glasneviensis: a listed name of no botanical standing.

glutinosa: *E. rubra* var.

Grahamiana: *E. illinita,* but plants grown as *E. Grahamiana* are hybrids between *E. illinita* and *E. rubra.*

illinita K. Presl [*E. Grahamiana* Hook. & Arn.; *E. viscosa* J. Forbes]. Shrub, to 10 ft. or more, young parts resinous and glandular, strongly scented; lvs. obovate or long-elliptic, to 2 in. long or more, obtuse or short-pointed, narrowed to base, serrate, glossy above; panicles bracted, to 4 in. long; petals white, claws long, united in a tube, the rounded tips of petals spreading, stamens and styles included in tube, style bifid. Chile. Cv. 'Eric Walther': *E.* × *franciscana* cv.

Ingramii: a listed name of no botanical standing, used for *E. rubra* var. *macrantha.*

×**Iveyi** Hort.: *Escallonia* cv. 'Iveyi'. A selection from a presumed hybrid between *E. bifida* and *E.* × *exoniensis;* large shrub, lvs. elliptic, to 2½ in. long, dark green; panicles terminal; petals white, claws united about ⅔ their length, lobes spreading, stamens and styles exserted.

laevis Vell. [*E. organensis* G. Gardn.]. Shrub, to 6 ft., very leafy, branchlets angled, glabrous but somewhat resinous or glandular; lvs. narrowly obovate to oblong, to 3 in. long, obtuse, dentate, often red-margined, firm; infl. of short, dense, broad, terminal clusters, scarcely standing above lvs.; petals rose-red, claws united in a tube, tips rounded, spreading, stamens and styles included. Brazil. Cv. **'Jubilee'** belongs to the (unnamed) hybrid between this sp. and *E. rubra.*

×**langleyensis** Hort. Veitch [*E.* × *edinensis* Hort.]: *E. rubra* × *E. virgata.* Shrub, usually said to be low-growing, but sometimes reaching 8 ft.; fls. usually solitary on short branchlets, large and showy, petals in shades of red and pink, spreading. Some cvs., all good garden plants, belonging here, are: **'Alice'**, **'Apple Blossom'**, **'Donard Brilliance'**, **'Donard Gem'**, **'Donard Scarlet'**, **'Donard Radiance'**, **'Donard Seedling'**, **'Glory of Donard'**, **'Gwendolyn'**, **'Pride of Donard'**, **'Slieve Donard'**.

leucantha Rémy. Large shrub or small tree, branchlets somewhat hairy; lvs. obovate to oblanceolate, to 1 in. long, finely toothed; racemes to 2 in. long, terminal on short lateral shoots, aggregated into large, showy panicles to 1 ft. long; petals white, oblanceolate, about ¼ in. long, not distinctly clawed. Chile, Argentina.

macrantha: *E. rubra* var.

microphylla: a listed name of no botanical standing.

montana: *E. rosea.*

montevidensis: *E. bifida.*

organensis: *E. laevis.*

Philippiana: *E. virgata.*

pterocladon: *E. rosea.*

pulverulenta (Ruiz & Pav.) Pers. [*E. Berterana* DC.]. Downy, viscid shrub, to 12 ft.; lvs. oblong, to 4 in. long, obtuse, tapering at base, fine-toothed, varnished above; fls. white, crowded in racemes to 9 in. long. Chile. Always recognizable by its long, slender cattail-like racemes.

punctata: *E. rubra.*

revoluta (Ruiz & Pav.) Pers. Shrub or small tree, to 25 ft. or more, white-pubescent; lvs. obovate, thick, to 2 in. long, obtuse or acutish, tapering basally, toothed, margins somewhat revolute; panicles terminal, dense, pyramidal; petals white, about ½ in. long, claws long, united in a tube, tips rounded, spreading, stamens and styles included, stigma headlike. Chile.

×**Rockii** Eastw.: *E. bifida* × *E. rubra* var. *macrantha.* More closely resembling *E. bifida,* in that it partly lacks the glandular hairs present in the infl. and lvs. of *E. rubra* var. *macrantha.* Cv. **'Freytheyi'** belongs here.

rosea Griseb. [*E. montana* Phil.; *E. pterocladon* Hook.]. Shrub, to 7 ft., branchlets more or less angled, reddish, glabrous or short-haired; lvs. sometimes 3–6 in a cluster, lanceolate, to 1½ in. long, toothed, glabrous; raceme loose, up to 18-fld.; petals white or red, less than ½ in. long, claws long, united in a tube, tips of petals spreading, stamens and styles included. Chile. Differs from *E. rubra* in its smaller stature, usually fewer-fld. infl., and somewhat smaller fls. Cvs. **'Balfourii'** and **'Frades'**: *E. exoniensis* cvs.

rubra (Ruiz & Pav.) Pers. [*E. punctata* DC.; *E. rubra* vars. *glabriuscula* Hook. & Arn. and *pygmaea* Bean]. Shrub, to 15 ft., branchlets shortly pubescent or hirsute, often more or less glandular and viscid; lvs. elliptic, lanceolate, or lanceolate-oblong, to 3 in. long, serrate, glabrous and smooth above, more or less resinous-glandular beneath; fls. few to about 30 in loose, terminal racemes or panicles to about 3 in. long or more; petals red or rose-red, usually ½–⅝ in. long, claws long, united in a tube, tips of petals rounded, spreading, stamens and styles included. Chile. A variable sp., with several intergrading vars., which are not always recognizable in cult. plants. In cult. it has hybridized with most of the other cult. spp. Cvs. **'C. F. Ball'**, **'Crimson Spire'**, **'Helene Strybing'**, **'William Watson'** belong here. Var. **glutinosa** (Phil.) Reiche [*E. glutinosa* Phil.]. Lvs. small, to 1 in. long; petals to ⅜ in. long. Perhaps not cult. Var. **macrantha** (Hook. & Arn.) Reiche [*E. macrantha* Hook. & Arn.; *E. sanguinea* Hort.]. Lvs. and infl. with prominent glands; lvs. to 3 in. long; fls. large, petals to ⅝ in. long. Var. **pygmaea:** *E. rubra.*

×**rubricalyx** Eastw.: *Escallonia* cv. 'Rubricalyx'. A selection of a supposed hybrid between *E. illinita* and *E. rubra.*

sanguinea: *E. rubra* var. *macrantha.*

tucumanensis Hosseus. Large erect shrub, to 12 ft.; lvs. mostly oblong, to 2 in. long, short-acuminate, cuneate, finely serrate; fls. in a loose panicle, sepal lobes subulate, petals white, claws long, united in a tube, tips rounded, spreading, stamens and styles scarcely exserted, stigma headlike. Argentina. Introd. in the early 1960's, readily recognized by its large white fls.

virgata (Ruiz & Pav.) Pers. [*E. Philippiana* (Engl.) M. T. Mast.; *E. virgata* var. *Philippiana* Engl.]. Shrub, to 6 ft., partially deciduous, branchlets reddish, finely pubescent; lvs. glabrous, lanceolate to obovate, to ¾ in. long, entire or sparsely serrate; raceme short, leafy, with up to 15 fls.; petals white or pale rose, suborbicular, to ¼ in. long, completely lacking a claw. Chile, Argentina. The hardiest sp. of *Escallonia.* Zone 7? Cv. **'Gwendolyn Anley'** belongs here.

viscosa: *E. illinita.*

ESCHSCHOLZIA Cham. CALIFORNIA POPPY. *Papaveraceae.* About 8–10 spp. of ann. or per. herbs with colorless sap, native to w. N. Amer.; lvs. alt., mostly glabrous, much-dissected; fls. solitary, showy, yellow to orange-red, sepals 2, coherent into a hoodlike cap and pushed off by the opening of the 4 petals, stamens 16 or more; fr. a slender, several-seeded, longitudinally ribbed caps.

Grown as annuals, the seeds sown where the plants are to stand in sunny exposure; in mild climates may be treated as winter annuals, and *E. californica* may live over winter after blooming.

alba: a listed name of no botanical standing for *E. californica* cv.

aurantiaca: a listed name of no botanical standing for *E. californica* cv.

caespitosa Benth. [*E. tenuifolia* Benth.]. Ann., sts. several, to 12 in., longer than basal tuft of lvs., sometimes leafy; lvs. dissected into many narrow segms. mostly less than ½ in. long; petals bright yellow, to 1 in. long; caps. to 3 in. long. Cent. to s. Calif.

californica Cham. [*E. cucullata* Greene; *E. glauca* Greene; *E. maritima* Greene]. CALIFORNIA POPPY. Ann. or per., flowering first year, sts. branched, more or less glaucous, usually glabrous, to 2 ft.; lvs. much dissected into narrow segms.; fls. from deep orange to pale yellow, petals ¾–2¼ in. long; caps. to 4 in. long. Widely distributed in Calif., where it is the state fl. The colorless juice is reported to be mildly narcotic and to have been used by Indians in Calif. in treatment of toothache. Variable in growth form and in color of fls.; some forms have received cv. names. Cvs. are: **'Alba'**, fls. cream-white; **'Aurantiaca'**, fls. orange; **'Compacta'**, of compact growth; **'Crocea'** [*E. crocea* Benth.], fls. deep orange; **'Rosea'**, fls. salmon-pink.

crocea: *E. californica* cv.

cucullata: *E. californica.*

glauca: *E. californica.*

hypecoides Benth. Ann., sts. branched and leafy, conspicuously glaucous, pubescent with short hairs or glabrous; lvs. much-dissected into narrow segms.; petals bright yellow, frequently orange-spotted at base or sometimes entirely orange. Cent. Calif. Rare in cult.

Lobbii Greene [*E. pulchella* Greene]. FRYING-PANS. Tufted, subglabrous ann., sts. scapose, to 12 in., standing above the lvs.; lvs. divided into relatively few linear segms.; fls. solitary, petals yellow, to ⅝ in. long; caps. to 2 in. long, seeds burlike. Foothills of Sierra Nevada, Cent. Calif.

maritima: *E. californica.*

mexicana Greene. Closely related to *E. californica;* distinguished with certainty only by a difference in cotyledons; tends to be a smaller scapose ann. with dark-orange fls. Ariz. to w. Tex., s. Utah, Sonora (n. Mex.).

pulchella: *E. Lobbii.*

tenuifolia: *E. caespitosa.*

ESCOBARIA: *CORYPHANTHA* subgenus *Escobaria.* **E. durispina:** a listed name of no botanical standing for *C. strobiliformis* var. **E. Runyonii:** *C. Robertii.* **E. tuberculosa:** *C. strobiliformis.*

ESCONTRIA Rose. *Cactaceae.* One sp., a treelike cactus, native to s. Mex.; fls. small, diurnal; fr. fleshy, with persistent papery scales naked in the axils, seeds many, black, rugose, hilum broad, basal.

For culture see *Cacti.*

Chiotilla (A. Web. ex K. Schum.) Rose. Trunk short, crown broad, of ascending brs., ribs 6–8; areoles close-set or confluent, radial spines 10–15, short, central spines several, the longest somewhat flattened, to 3 in. long; fls. yellow, 1¼ in. long; fr. globose, purple, edible, 2 in. in diam.

ESENBECKIA HBK. *Rutaceae.* About 18 spp. of spineless trees or shrubs, native to trop. Amer.; lvs. mostly alt., palmately compound, sometimes of 1 lft., glandular-dotted; fls. in axillary or terminal panicles, calyx 4–5-lobed or -parted, petals and stamens 4 or 5; fr. a caps., splitting into 4 or 5 carpels.

Runyonii C. V. Mort. Tree, to 15 ft.; lfts. 3, elliptic, 2–5 in. long, lustrous; fls. 5-merous, cream-white, in pubescent panicles, fragrant. Known only from Cameron Co. (Tex.).

ESMERALDA: *ARACHNIS.* E. Sanderana: *Vanda Sanderana.*

ESPALIER. An espalier is any shrub, tree, or vine trained in any formal or informal design in a flat vertical plane against a fence or wall; the word is also a verb, meaning to train a plant in such a manner. Espaliered plants were originally developed to introduce a kind of living architectural effect in gardens and particularly in the more formal gardens of Europe. Their use also permitted better employment of limited space for woody plants. Espaliered fruit trees, for example, can be introduced into small garden areas where there might not otherwise be space for fruit trees. Espaliered shrubs require more than usual care and training, primarily with the pruning shears, but the end effect is often worth the extra time and effort. For details on espaliering, the reader is referred to standard works on horticulture. Certain woody plants especially useful as espaliers in climates that are appropriate are to be found in the genera *Abelia, Abutilon, Agonis, Berberis, Buddleia, Camellia, Carissa, Ceanothus, Celastrus, Chaenomeles, Citrus, Cornus, Cotoneaster, Crataegus, Eriobotrya, Eucalyptus, Eugenia, Feijoa, Forsythia, Genista, Grewia, Hydrangea, Ilex, Jasminum, Kerria, Laburnum, Lonicera, Magnolia, Malus, Philadelphus, Podocarpus, Prunus, Psidium, Pyrus, Pyracantha, Rhododendron, Ribes, Rosa, Rosmarinus, Sorbaria, Tamarix, Taxus, Viburnum, Vitis, Weigela, Wisteria,* and *Xylosma.*

ESPOSTOA Britt. & Rose [*Binghamia* Britt. & Rose, not J. Agardh; *Facheiroa* Britt. & Rose; *Pseudoespostoa* Backeb.; *Thrixanthocereus* Backeb.]. *Cactaceae.* Four or more spp. of cacti, native to Peru and Brazil; sts. many-ribbed, cylindrical, erect, simple or branching above, flowering from a lateral cephalium; sterile areoles close-set, long-woolly; cephalium of several adjacent modified ribs, their areoles with more numerous hairs and bristles and fewer stout spines; the supra-areolar pedicellar zone with crowded axillary hairs; fls. nocturnal, white, funnelform, with spreading limb, scales of tube and ovary with axillary hairs, stamens included; fr. globose to obovoid, the perianth tardily falling off, seeds black. Differs from *Cephalocereus* in the scaly and hairy fls.

For culture see *Cacti.*

Blossfeldiorum (Werderm.) Buxb. [*Facheiroa Blossfeldiorum* (Werderm.) W. T. Marsh.; *Thrixanthocereus Blossfeldiorum* (Werderm.) Backeb.]. Sts. little-branched, to 3 ft. high and 3 in. thick, ribs 18–25, cross-furrowed; areoles white-floccose, soon glabrous, radial spines 20–25, needle-shaped, glassy, to ⁵⁄₁₆ in. long, central spine 1, awl-shaped, gray, black-tipped, to 1¼ in. long; cephalium 4–7 ribs wide, bristles to 2 in. long; fls. tubular-funnelform, white, 2 in. long, scales in lower part of perianth tube bristle-tipped. N. Peru.

huanucoensis: a listed name of no botanical standing.

lanata (HBK) Britt. & Rose. COTTON-BALL, PERUVIAN SNOWBALL, SNOWBALL CACTUS, NEW OLD-MAN C., PERUVIAN OLD-MAN. Sts. branched, 12–18 ft. high, 4 in. thick, ribs about 20–25, low; areoles with white wool, spines yellow or brownish, radial spines many, to ¼ in. long, central spines 1–2, to 2 in. long; cephalium sunken, ribs about 5, low; fr. red. N. Peru and s. Ecuador. Var. **sericata** (Backeb.) Backeb. [*E. sericata* (Backeb.) Backeb.]. Hair silkier, central spines 0–1, long.

melanostele (Vaup.) Borg [*Binghamia melanostele* (Vaup.) Britt. & Rose; *Pseudoespostoa melanostele* (Vaup.) Backeb.]. Sts. little-branched above base, to 6 ft. high and 4 in. thick, ribs about 25, cross-furrowed; areoles with brown wool, ⅜ in. long; spines black, radial spines many, bristlelike, to ³⁄₁₆ in. long, central spine 1, stouter,

mostly ascending, to 1½ in. long; cephalium not sunken, ribs about 8; fls. 2 in. long. W. Peru.

mocupensis: a listed name of no botanical standing.

sericata: *E. lanata.*

Ulei (Gürke) Buxb. [*Facheiroa Ulei* (Gürke) Werderm.]. Treelike, to 16 ft., trunk short, to 5 in. thick, brs. erect, to 3 in. thick, ribs 15–20; spines flexible, brown, radial spines 10–15, to ½ in. long, central spines 2–4, to ¾ in. long; cephalium to 8 in. long or more and 1½ in. wide; fls. 1¾ in. long, inner segms. ³⁄₁₆ in. long, half as wide; fr. globose to pear-shaped, 2½ in. long. Brazil.

EUANTHE: *VANDA.*

EUBOTRYS: *LEUCOTHOE.*

EUCALYPTUS L'Hér. EUCALYPT, AUSTRALIAN GUM, GUM TREE, IRONBARK, STRINGYBARK. *Myrtaceae.* Over 522 spp., 150 vars., and a few hybrids have been described from Australia and Tasmania, about 6 spp. extending n. to New Guinea, Philippine Is., Timor, and Java; evergreen trees, occasionally very tall, or sometimes shrubs, bark persistent or deciduous, plants in nearly all spp. passing through juvenile, intermediate, and mature stages, with differences in position, shape, and color of lvs.; fls. usually 3 or more together in axillary umbels or heads, rarely the umbels arranged in panicles, or fls. solitary, calyx tube united to inferior ovary, calyx lobes and petals united, forming a variously shaped deciduous bud cap (operculum or calyptra), stamens many, often showy, sometimes brightly colored; fr. a caps., sometimes hard and woody, valves of caps. exserted beyond or included within the rim of fr., seeds usually many, small.

Identification of species in so large a genus is difficult and has been based on a combination of characters of habit and size of plant, bark, leaves, flowers, and fruits. Leaves on immature plants are sometimes very different from those on mature plants; in the following descriptions of the species only leaves of mature plants are described.

It is the most important genus of Australian forest trees and the hard wood has been used for innumerable purposes. Some species furnish essential oils and tannins, and many more are useful as ornamentals. Some 200 species have been introduced into other temperate regions of the world for these several purposes. In the warmer regions of the U.S. the largest number have been introduced into Calif., where they now form part of the natural scene.

Common names listed are the Australian ones, and are useful because they often indicate the types of bark. These fall mostly into the following six main groups. In the first group the bark is deciduous; in the rest it is persistent.

GUMS, bark smooth and deciduous.
BLOODWOODS, bark rough but more scaly and flaky than in others.
BOXES, bark rough but fibrous.
PEPPERMINTS, bark finely fibrous.
STRINGYBARKS, bark long-fibrous.
IRONBARKS, bark hard, rough, fissured and dark colored.

acmenioides Schauer. WHITE MAHOGANY. Large tree, bark fibrous, persistent; lvs. alt., sickle-shaped, lanceolate, acuminate; umbels axillary or in terminal panicles, 3–10-fld., peduncles ⅝ in. long; buds pedicelled, ovate, ¼ in. long, bud cap conical to beaked, as long as or longer than calyx tube; fr. hemispherical, ¼ in. across, valves included. Queensland and New S. Wales. The name *E. triantha* has been misapplied to this sp.

agglomerata Maiden. BLUE-LEAVED S. Tree, to 100 ft., bark fibrous, deeply furrowed; lvs. alt., sickle-shaped, narrow-lanceolate, thick; umbels globular, 7–14-fld., peduncles to ½ in. long; buds sessile, elliptic, ⅜ in. long, bud cap narrow-conical, usually as long as calyx tube; fr. hemispherical, to ⁵⁄₁₆ in. across, valves included. New S. Wales and Victoria.

alba Reinw. ex Blume [*E. platyphylla* F. J. Muell.]. TIMOR WHITE GUM. Tree, to as much as 60 ft., bark smooth, white to salmon-pink; lvs. alt. or opp., ovate, acuminate, rather thin, conspicuously veined; umbels 3–7-fld., peduncles ¼ in. long or more; buds short-pedicelled, ovoid, ¼ in. long or more, bud cap hemispherical, slightly shorter than calyx tube; fr. hemispherical, to ⅜ in. across, valves included. Queensland and N. Territory of Australia, n. to Timor and New Guinea.

albens Benth. [*E. hemiphloia* var. *albens* F. J. Muell. ex Maiden]. WHITE BOX. Tree, with rounded crown, to 80 ft., bark persistent, finely fibrous, gray; lvs. alt., glaucous, broadly lanceolate; umbels 3–7-fld., axillary or in terminal panicles, peduncles to ¾ in. long; buds ¾ in. long, bud cap nearly angular, usually as long as slightly angular calyx tube; fr. short-pedicelled, cylindrical, to ⁵⁄₁₆ in. across, valves included. Queensland to Victoria, w. to S. Australia.

×**algeriensis** Trab. Medium-sized tree, bark smooth, peeling in small pieces; lvs. alt., sickle-shaped, lanceolate, glaucescent; umbels 7–9-fld.; fr. broadly top-shaped, to ⁵⁄₁₆ in. across. Reportedly a hybrid between *E. camaldulensis* and *E. rudis;* originated near Algiers, but does not appear to differ from *E. camaldulensis.*

alpina Lindl. GRAMPIAN S. Shrub or small tree, bark rough, fibrous; lvs. alt., oblong, asymmetrical, apiculate, thick; umbels sessile, 3–5-fld.; buds top-shaped, somewhat 4-sided, to ⅜ in. long, warty, irregular in shape, bud cap hemispherical, warty, shorter than calyx tube; fr. large, sessile, hemispherical, smooth or warty, to 1 in. across, closely appressed to st., valves exserted. Late autumn. Victoria.

amplifolia Naud. CABBAGE GUM. Medium-sized to large tree, bark smooth, deciduous; lvs. alt., broad-lanceolate; umbels axillary, 7–20-fld., peduncles flattened to angular, to ¾ in. long; buds to ⅝ in. long, bud cap horn-shaped, 3 times as long as calyx tube; fr. pedicelled, hemispherical, to ³⁄₁₆ in. across, valves exserted. Queensland and New S. Wales.

amygdalina Labill. [*E. salicifolia* Cav.]. BLACK PEPPERMINT. Slender tree, to 50 ft., bark fibrous, persistent except for sometimes smooth brs.; lvs. alt., narrow-lanceolate, aromatic; umbels, 5–12-fld., peduncles ⁵⁄₁₆ in. long; buds club-shaped, ¼ in. long; fr. sessile or nearly so, subglobose, to ¼ in. across, valves usually included. Tasmania. Zone 9.

Andreana: *E. elata.*

Andrewsii Maiden. To 50 ft. or more, bark rough, fibrous, dark gray to red-brown, persistent on trunk and large brs.; lvs. alt., sickle-shaped; umbels, 5–12-fld., peduncles to ¾ in. long; buds ¼ in. long, bud cap conical, shorter than calyx tube; fr. pedicelled, hemispherical, to ¼ in. across, valves included. New S. Wales.

angulosa: *E. incrassata.*

×**antipolitensis** Trab. Said to be a hybrid between *E. Globulus* and *E. viminalis;* tall tree, bark fissured; lvs. alt., narrow-lanceolate, thick, dark green; umbels, 3-fld.; fr. slightly ribbed, to ½ in. across. Originated in s. France.

argillacea W. Fitzg. [*E. leucophylla* Domin]. KIMBERLEY GRAY BOX. Shrub or small tree, bark short-fibrous, persistent, fissured on lower trunk, smooth and thin above; lvs. alt., sickle-shaped, broadly lanceolate, green and glossy to whitish and dull; umbels 4–6-fld., in short panicles, peduncles about ½ in. long; buds pedicelled, ovate, ⅜ in. long, glaucous, bud cap conical, shorter than calyx tube; fr. top-shaped, ¼ in. across, valves included. W. Australia and N. Territory of Australia.

astringens Maiden. BROWN MALLEE. To 60 ft., bark deciduous, trunk smooth; lvs. alt., lanceolate, leathery; umbels 3–7-fld., peduncles to ⅝ in. long; buds pedicelled, cylindrical, to 1 in. long, bud cap cylindrical, 2–3 times longer than calyx tube; fr. pedicelled, hemispherical to ovoid or campanulate, to ⁵⁄₁₆ in. across, valves exserted. W. Australia. Useful for tanning.

bicolor: see *E. largiflorens.*

Blakelyi Maiden. BLAKELY'S RED GUM. To 100 ft.; lvs. alt., lanceolate-sickle-shaped, rather conspicuously veined; umbels 4–8-fld., peduncles to ⅝ in. long; buds ½ in. long, bud cap conical, nearly twice as long as calyx tube; fr. pedicelled, hemispherical, to ¼ in. across, valves exserted. Queensland, s. to Victoria.

Blaxlandii Maiden & Cambage. BLAXLAND'S S. Medium-sized tree, bark reddish, deeply furrowed on trunk, smooth above; lvs. alt., narrow-lanceolate to slightly sickle-shaped; umbels 5–10-fld., peduncles to ⅜ in. long; buds sessile, to ¼ in. long, bud cap conical, slightly shorter than calyx tube; fr. in dense clusters, hemispherical, to ⅜ in. across, valves exserted. New S. Wales and Victoria.

Bosistoana F. J. Muell. BOSISTO'S BOX. Straight tree, to 180 ft., bark rough, persistent on lower trunk, deciduous above, smooth on upper trunk and brs.; lvs. alt., sickle-shaped, narrow-lanceolate, acuminate; umbels 3–7-fld., axillary or in short, terminal panicles, peduncles to ½ in. long; buds short-pedicelled, to ⅜ in. long, bud cap conical, as long as calyx tube; fr. hemispherical, to ¼ in. across, valves included. New S. Wales and Victoria.

botryoides Sm. To 40 ft. or more, bark nearly fibrous, persistent on trunk and main brs.; lvs. alt., broadly lanceolate, acuminate, finely veined; umbels 6–10-fld., peduncles flattened, to ½ in. long; buds sessile, angled, to ½ in. long, bud cap hemispherical, half as long as calyx tube; fr. barrel-shaped, to ⁵⁄₁₆ in. across, valves included. New S. Wales and Victoria. Wood important in ship building.

×**brevirostris** Blakely. Said to be a hybrid between *E. macrorhyncha* and *E. Mullerana.* Medium-sized tree, bark fibrous, persistent; lvs. alt., lanceolate to sickle-shaped-lanceolate; umbels 5–12-fld.; fr. ovoid to pear-shaped, to ¼ in. across.

Bridgesiana R. T. Bak. [*E. Stuartiana* of auth., not F. J. Muell.]. APPLE BOX. Large tree, bark soft, friable, light brown, persistent to the small brs.; lvs. alt., sickle-shaped, lanceolate, acuminate, pale green; umbels 4–7-fld., peduncles to ¼ in. long; buds ¼ in. long, bud cap conical, as long as calyx tube; fr. sessile or nearly so, top-shaped to hemispherical, ¼ in. across, valves exserted. Queensland, s. to Victoria.

Burdettiana Blakely & Steedm. Shrub, to 6 ft., branchlets yellowish, angular, bark smooth; lvs. alt., lanceolate, thick; umbels 3-5-fld., peduncle flattened, to 1 in. long; buds sessile, cylindrical, 2 in. long, bud cap cylindrical, somewhat longer than calyx tube, smooth in upper half, warty below; fr. hemispherical, to 1 in. across. W. Australia.

burracoppinensis Maiden & Blakely. BURRACOPPIN MALLEE. Shrub, to 15 ft., bark ragged and peeling on lower trunk, smooth and gray above; lvs. alt., lanceolate; umbels 3-fld., peduncles to 1 in. long; buds pear-shaped and beaked, to 1¼ in. long, bud cap hemispherical, beaked, faintly ribbed, slightly longer than calyx tube, stamens white; fr. top-shaped, to 1 in. across, valves scarcely exserted. W. Australia.

caesia Benth. Small tree, to 20 ft., bark peeling in strips leaving inner bark smooth, pale green; lvs. alt., lanceolate, glaucous; umbels 3-fld., peduncles recurved, to 1 in. long; buds slender-pedicelled, to ½ in. long, stamens pink; fr. campanulate-urceolate, striate, to ¾ in. across, valves included. W. Australia. Attractive small tree with branchlets, buds, fr., and lvs. powdery-gray.

calophylla R. Br. ex Lindl. MARRI, RED GUM. Small to large tree, bark rough, flaky; lvs. alt., broad-lanceolate, dark green above, paler beneath, with fine, sometimes obscure parallel lateral veins almost at right angles to midrib; umbels 3–7-fld., in panicles; buds greenish-white, stamens white or sometimes pink; fr. pedicelled, urceolate, thick-walled, to 1 in. long and 1¼ in. across, constricted below broad opening, seeds black, wingless. W. Australia.

calycogona Turcz. GOOSEBERRY MALLEE. Slender tree, to 25 ft., bark smooth, deciduous; lvs. alt., lanceolate; umbels 3–8-fld., peduncles ½ in. long; buds almost sessile, angular-club-shaped, ⁵⁄₁₆ in. long, bud cap conical, shorter than angular calyx tube; fr. 4-angled, urceolate, to ¼ in. across, valves included. Victoria, w. to W. Australia. The 4-angled frs. are distinctive.

camaldulensis Dehnh. [*E. camaldulensis* vars. *brevirostris* (F. J. Muell.) Blakely and *pendula* Blakely & M. Jacobs; *E. longirostris* F. J. Muell.; *E. rostrata* Schlechtend.]. MURRAY RED GUM. Medium-sized to large tree, bark smooth, ash-colored, deciduous; lvs. alt., lanceolate, acuminate, thin; umbels 5–10-fld., peduncles to ½ in. long; buds to ⅜ in. long, bud cap conical to beaked, somewhat longer than calyx tube; fr. pedicelled, hemispherical, to ⁵⁄₁₆ in. across, valves exserted. Australia. Compare with *E. rudis* and *E. tereticornis.*

camphora R. T. Bak. BROAD-LEAVED SALLY. Small tree, bark dark, hard, rough, flaky on lower trunk, smooth and deciduous above; lvs. alt., narrow- to broad-lanceolate; umbels 3–7-fld., peduncles to ⁵⁄₁₆ in. long; buds to ⅜ in. long, bud cap conical, longer than calyx tube; fr. pedicelled, hemispherical, to ⁵⁄₁₆ in. across, valves exserted. New S. Wales and Victoria.

capitellata Sm. BROWN S. Medium-sized tree; lvs. alt., oblong to obliquely lanceolate, dark green, glossy; umbels 5–9-fld., peduncles flattened, to ⅜ in. long; buds sessile, irregularly angular, to ½ in. long, bud cap conical, shorter than calyx tube; fr. crowded into dense heads, flattened-spheroid, to ⁵⁄₁₆ in. across, valves scarcely exserted. New S. Wales.

cephalocarpa Blakely [*E. cinerea* var. *multiflora* Maiden]. LONG-LEAVED ARGYLE APPLE. To 40 ft. or more, glaucous or subglaucous, bark fibrous, rough, persistent on trunk and large brs., deciduous on small brs.; lvs. alt., lanceolate-sickle-shaped, acuminate; umbels 3–10-fld., peduncles flattened, to ¾ in. long; buds sessile, to ⁵⁄₁₆ in. long, bud cap conical, shorter than calyx tube; fr. hemispherical, to ¼ in. across, valves exserted. New S. Wales and Victoria.

cinerea F. J. Muell. ex Benth. MEALY S., SILVER-DOLLAR TREE, SPIRAL E. Medium-sized, glaucous tree, bark reddish-brown, fibrous, persisting on trunk and main brs., peeling in slender ribbons from smaller brs.; lvs. alt. or opp., sessile, lanceolate; umbels 3-fld., peduncles to ⅜ in. long; buds sessile, to ⁵⁄₁₆ in. long, bud cap conical, shorter than calyx tube; fr. hemispherical, to ⁵⁄₁₆ in. across, glaucous, valves shortly exserted. New S. Wales and Victoria. Zone 9. Juvenile trees with lvs. opp., glaucous, ovate to orbicular, sometimes have fls. Var. **multiflora:** *E. cephalocarpa.*

citriodora Hook. LEMON-SCENTED GUM. Slender tree, to 50 ft., bark peeling irregularly, leaving a smooth, spotted trunk; lvs. alt., lanceolate, pendent, strongly lemon-scented; umbels 3–5-fld., in panicles, peduncles ¼ in. long; buds pedicelled, to ½ in. long, bud cap conical, shorter than calyx tube, stamens white; fr. urceolate, to ⁵⁄₁₆ in. across, valves included. Queensland. Yields an essential oil.

cladocalyx F. J. Muell. [*E. corynocalyx* F. J. Muell.]. SUGAR GUM. Slender tree, to 75 ft. or more, bark white or yellow-brown, flaking except on lower part of trunk; lvs. alt., narrow- to broad-lanceolate; umbels 5–16-fld., peduncles to ½ in. long; buds somewhat urceolate, to ⅜ in. long, bud cap rounded, much shorter than urceolate calyx tube, stamens white; fr. pedicelled, urceolate, ribbed, to ⁵⁄₁₆ in. across, valves included. S. Australia.

clavigera A. Cunn. ex Schauer. APPLE GUM, CABBAGE G. Widely spreading, densely leafy tree, to 20 ft. or more, bark checkered, flaky, thick, dark, persistent on most of trunk; lvs. opp., ovate, often broadly so, short-petioled, with about 15–25 pairs of lateral veins; umbels 3–7-fld. in panicles; buds pedicelled, club-shaped, ¼ in. long, bud cap rounded, shorter than calyx tube; fr. long-pedicelled, ovoid to urceolate, to ⅜ in. across, fragile, not persisting after seeds have shed. Queensland, w. to W. Australia.

Cloeziana F. J. Muell. QUEENSLAND-MESSMATE. Tree, to 50 ft., bark persistent on trunk and larger brs., soft, flaky-fibrous; lvs. alt., sickle-shaped, lanceolate, acuminate; umbels 4–6-fld., in broad panicles; buds globular-ovate, to ¼ in. long, bud cap hemispherical, half as long as calyx tube; fr. nearly sessile, hemispherical, to ⁵⁄₁₆ in. across, valves exserted. Queensland.

coccifera Hook.f. TASMANIAN SNOW GUM, MOUNT WELLINGTON PEPPERMINT. Small, glaucous tree, to 20 ft., bark peeling in long strips, leaving smooth white trunk; lvs. alt., lanceolate, with fine, hooked point, thick; umbels 3–6-fld., peduncles ⅜ in. long; buds sessile, somewhat angular, to ⁵⁄₁₆ in. long, bud cap depressed-concave, 2–3 times shorter than calyx tube; fr. broadly top-shaped, to ½ in. across, valves usually included. Tasmania. Zone 9.

Consideniana Maiden. YERTCHUK. Medium-sized tree, bark rough, flaky-fibrous; lvs. alt., sickle-shaped, narrow-lanceolate; umbels 5–10-fld., peduncles to ½ in. long; buds club-shaped, to ¼ in. long, bud cap hemispherical, much shorter than calyx tube; fr. pedicelled, pear-shaped, to ⁵⁄₁₆ in. across, valves included. New S. Wales and Victoria.

cordata Labill. HEART-LEAVED SILVER GUM. To 50 ft., bark smooth, white; lvs. opp., cordate-lanceolate, glaucous; umbels 3-fld., peduncles ⅜ in. long; buds sessile, ovate, to ¾ in. long, bud cap conical, shorter than calyx tube; fr. ovate to hemispherical, to ½ in. across, valves included. Tasmania.

cornuta Labill. YATE TREE. Medium-sized tree, bark on trunk dark, rough, furrowed; lvs. alt., narrow-lanceolate; umbels 5–15-fld., peduncles to 1½ in. long; buds sessile, horn-shaped to 1½ in. long, bud cap brownish, 2–3 times longer than green calyx tube, stamens greenish-yellow; fr. valves conspicuously exserted.

corymbosa: *E. gummifera.*

corynocalyx: *E. cladocalyx.*

cosmophylla F. J. Muell. CUP GUM. To 50 ft., bark smooth; lvs. alt., sickle-shaped, narrow- to broad-lanceolate, nearly glaucous; umbels 3–6-fld., peduncles stout, to ¼ in. long; buds ovoid, smooth or 2-ribbed, to ¾ in. long, bud cap conical, as long as calyx tube; fr. pedicelled, cup-shaped, to ¾ in. across, valves included or shortly exserted. S. Australia.

crebra F. J. Muell. [*E. racemosa* of auth., not Cav.]. NARROW-LEAVED I. Medium-sized tree, with slender, drooping branchlets, bark hard, furrowed, persistent, impregnated with reddish-brown gum; lvs. alt., sickle-shaped, narrow-lanceolate, gray-green; umbels 4–9-fld., in panicles, peduncles to ½ in. long; buds short-pedicelled, club-shaped, to ¼ in. long, bud cap conical, as long as calyx tube; fr. hemispherical, to ¼ in. long, thin-walled, valves included. Queensland and New S. Wales.

crucis Maiden. SOUTHERN-CROSS SILVER MALLEE. Glaucous shrub, to 25 ft., bark smooth, red, peeling; lvs. opp., oblong to acutely lanceolate, glaucous; umbels 3–7-fld., peduncles to ⅜ in. long; buds pedicelled, almost globose, ⁵⁄₁₆ in. long, bud cap hemispherical, about as long as calyx tube; fr. cup-shaped, to ½ in. across. W. Australia.

Dalrympleana Maiden. MOUNTAIN GUM. To 100 ft., bark smooth, white or pink-salmon, deciduous; lvs. alt., sickle-shaped, lanceolate, green and glossy; umbels 3-fld., peduncles to ¼ in. long; buds sessile, ovoid, ⅜ in. long, bud cap conical, as long as calyx tube; fr. ovoid, to ⁵⁄₁₆ in. across, valves exserted. New S. Wales and Victoria. Warmer parts of Zone 9.

dealbata A. Cunn. ex Schauer. TUMBLE-DOWN GUM. Small scraggy tree, bark rough and persistent on lower trunk, white and smooth above, branchlets glaucous; lvs. alt., narrow- to broad-lanceolate; umbels 5–8-fld., peduncles ½ in. long; buds ovoid, ⅜ in. long, glaucous, bud cap conical, as long as calyx tube; fr. sessile or nearly so, hemispherical, to ¼ in. across, valves shortly exserted. Queensland and New S. Wales.

Deanei Maiden. DEANE'S GUM. To 200 ft., bark usually smooth and deciduous except at base of trunk; lvs. alt., narrow-lanceolate, finely

veined; umbels 6–12-fld., peduncles ½ in. long; buds ovoid, to ⅜ in. long, bud cap conical, shorter than calyx tube; fr. sessile or nearly so, campanulate, ¼ in. across, valves included. Queensland and New S. Wales.

delegatensis R. T. Bak. [*E. gigantea* Hook.f., not Dehnh.]. ALPINE ASH. To 200 ft., dark brown, fibrous, becoming smooth and gray on brs.; lvs. alt., sickle-shaped, narrow- to broad-lanceolate, pleasantly aromatic; umbels 7–15-fld., peduncles to ¾ in. long; buds sessile or nearly so, club-shaped, to ⁵⁄₁₆ in. long, bud cap hemispherical, much shorter than calyx tube; fr. club-shaped to pear-shaped, to ⁵⁄₁₆ in. across, valves included. New S. Wales, s. to Tasmania. Warmer parts of Zone 9. Large tree and important source of commercial timber.

desmondensis Maiden & Blakely. DESMOND MALLEE. Shrub, to 15 ft., brs. flexuous, drooping, bark smooth and powdery; lvs. alt., oblong to lanceolate, glaucous; umbels 7–15-fld., peduncles flattened, to ¾ in. long; buds ovoid, to ⅝ in. long, bud cap conical, as long as calyx tube; fr. sessile, in dense clusters, hemispherical, valves included. W. Australia.

diptera C. Andr. TWO-WINGED GIMLET, BASTARD G. Small tree, to 30 ft., bark thin, brownish, smooth, deciduous; lvs. alt., narrow-lanceolate, thick; fls. in clusters of 3 or sometimes solitary, peduncles lacking, buds somewhat cordate, with 2 wings, ⅜ in. long, bud cap conical, beaked, as long as calyx tube; fr. hemispherical, distinctly 2-winged, to ¼ in. across, valves shortly exserted. W. Australia.

diversicolor F. J. Muell. KARRI GUM. Large tree; lvs. alt., not sickle-shaped, lanceolate, acute, paler beneath, bark smooth, gray to orange-yellow; umbels 3–6-fld., peduncles to 1 in. long; buds sessile or nearly so, club-shaped, to ¾ in. long, bud cap conical, usually shorter than calyx tube; fr. urceolate, to ½ in. across, valves included. W. Australia. Important timber tree.

dives Schauer. BROAD-LEAVED PEPPERMINT. Medium-sized tree, bark persistent on trunk and large brs., deciduous and smooth above; lvs. alt., broadly lanceolate, glossy, dark green, rather thick; umbels 7–15-fld., peduncles ⅝ in. long; buds club-shaped, ¼ in. long, bud cap conical, shorter than calyx tube; fr. sessile, hemispherical, to ⁵⁄₁₆ in. across, valves included. New S. Wales and Victoria. Lvs. with many oil glands yield an oil.

dumosa A. Cunn. ex Schauer. MALLEE, CONGOO M. Shrub or small tree, to 30 ft., bark rough, dark gray on lower part of trunk, smooth above; lvs. alt., lanceolate, hooked; umbels 4–7-fld., peduncles ½ in. long; buds short-pedicelled, club-shaped, to ½ in. long, bud cap conical, very much shorter than calyx tube, filaments pink or white; fr. sessile or nearly so, campanulate, faintly ribbed, to ⁵⁄₁₆ in. across, valves included or shortly exserted. New S. Wales and Victoria, w. to S. and W. Australia. Yields an essential oil.

elaeophora: *E. goniocalyx.*

elata Dehnh. [*E. Andreana* Naud.; *E. Lindleyana* DC.; *E. longifolia* Lindl., not Link & Otto; *E. numerosa* Maiden]. RIVER PEPPERMINT. Slender tree, to 150 ft., bark fibrous and persistent on lower several ft. of trunk, smooth and white above; lvs. opp., narrow-lanceolate; umbels 4–10-fld., peduncle ⅜ in. long; buds pedicelled, ¼ in. long, bud cap hemispherical, shorter than calyx tube; fr. pear-shaped, to ¼ in. across, valves included. New S. Wales and Victoria.

eremophila (Diels) Maiden. HORNED MALLEE. Shrub or small tree, bark smooth, except in summer when the outer bark is shed in strips; lvs. alt., narrow-lanceolate; umbels 3–7-fld., peduncles flattened, to 1¼ in. long, reflexed; buds short-pedicelled, to 1¼ in. long, bud cap glossy reddish-brown, horn-shaped, twice as long as green calyx tube, stamens yellowish; fr. urceolate, thick-walled, to ½ in. across, valves included. W. Australia.

erythrocorys F. J. Muell. ILLYARIE. Small tree, to 30 ft., bark more or less smooth, peeling in thin flakes; lvs. opp., sickle-shaped, lanceolate, acuminate; umbels 3-fld., peduncles flattened, to 1¼ in. long; buds sessile, top-shaped, strongly ribbed, 1¾ in. long, bud cap 4-angled, rather fleshy, warty, red, stamens yellow-green; fr. broadly campanulate, irregularly ribbed, to 2 in. across or more. W. Australia.

erythronema Turcz. RED-FLOWERED MALLEE. Small, crooked tree, bark smooth, powdery-gray; lvs. alt., narrow-lanceolate, pale green; umbels 3–8-fld., peduncles reflexed, ¾ in. long; buds pedicelled, ovoid and beaked, ⅞ in. long, bud cap red, conical, about twice as long as the calyx tube, stamens red; fr. top-shaped, ribbed, to ½ in. across, valves included. W. Australia.

eugenioides: see *E. globoidea.*

Ewartiana Maiden. EWART'S MALLEE. Slender shrub, to 20 ft., bark smooth, pinkish, peeling; lvs. alt., elliptic-lanceolate; umbels 3–7-fld., peduncles ¾ in. long; buds short-pedicelled, ovoid, to ⅜ in. long, bud cap conical, about as long as calyx tube; fr. conical-globular, to ½ in. across, valves exserted. S. and W. Australia.

eximia Schauer. YELLOW BLOODWOOD. Medium-sized tree, bark yellowish-brown, scaly; lvs. alt., sickle-shaped, lanceolate, nearly glaucous; umbels 4–7-fld., in panicles, peduncles stout, to 1 in. long; buds sessile, urceolate and beaked, ¾ in. long, bud cap conical and beaked, shorter than calyx tube; fr. urceolate, to ½ in. across or more, valves included. New S. Wales.

fastigiata H. Deane & Maiden. BROWN-BARREL, CUT-TAIL. Lofty tree, to as much as 150 ft., bark fibrous, gray-brown on trunk and lower brs., smooth and white above; lvs. alt., sickle-shaped, lanceolate, thin; umbels 7–12-fld., peduncles ⅜ in. long; buds club-shaped, to ¼ in. long, bud cap conical, as long as calyx tube; fr. sessile or nearly so, to ¼ in. across, valves usually slightly exserted. New S. Wales and Victoria.

fibrosa F. J. Muell. [*E. siderophloia* of auth., not Benth.]. BROAD-LEAVED RED I. To 120 ft., bark deeply furrowed, persistent; lvs. alt., sickle-shaped, ovate to broad-lanceolate, with a distinct intramarginal vein; umbels 4–8-fld., in panicles; buds cylindric-conical, ⅜ in. long, bud cap horn-shaped, twice as long as calyx tube; fr. pedicelled, pear-shaped, to ⁵⁄₁₆ in. across, valves shortly exserted. New S. Wales. Long known incorrectly as *E. siderophloia.*

ficifolia F. J. Muell. RED-FLOWERING GUM, SCARLET-FLOWERING G. Small tree, to 30 ft., bark rough, persistent; lvs. alt., broad-lanceolate; umbels 3–7-fld., in panicles, peduncles 1 in. long or more; buds pear-shaped, ¾ in. long, bud cap hemispherical, ⅓–½ as long as calyx tube, stamens scarlet; fr. pedicelled, ovoid-urceolate, to 1¼ in. across, valves included. W. Australia. Although called a gum this sp. has a rough bark. Well-known in cult. for its showy panicles of red fls. Closely related to *E. calophylla* and at least in cult. difficult to distinguish, but *E. ficifolia* is smaller, and has lvs. smaller, more rigid, deeper green, buds, calyx tube, and stamens scarlet, fr. without a neck at apical constricted rim, and seeds brown, winged. Hybrids with characters intermediate between these two spp. are known.

Flocktoniae Maiden. MERRIT. Shrub or tree, to 30–40 ft., bark smooth, gray or brown or mottled, older bark deciduous in patches; lvs. alt., sickle-shaped, lanceolate, dark green; umbels 3–7-fld., peduncles to ¾ in. long; buds short-pedicelled, urceolate and beaked, ¾ in. long, bud cap conical at base, abruptly elongated into beak up to twice as long as calyx tube; fr. urceolate, slightly furrowed, to ⁵⁄₁₆ in. across, valves included. S. and W. Australia.

foecunda Schauer. Shrub, to 15 ft., bark rough, dark gray and deciduous in strips at base of trunk, smooth and red-brown above; lvs. alt., narrow-lanceolate; umbels 3–7-fld., peduncles ⅜ in. long; buds short-pedicelled, ovoid, ⁵⁄₁₆ in. long, bud cap conical, longer than calyx tube; fr. subglobose, ¼ in. across, valves included. New S. Wales, w. to W. Australia.

Forrestiana Diels. FORREST'S MARLOCK, FUCHSIA GUM. Shrub, 10–15 ft., often forming low dense thickets; bark smooth, gray or brown; lvs. alt., narrow- to broad-lanceolate, thick; fls. axillary, solitary, peduncles reflexed, to 1½ in. long; buds scarlet, top-shaped and beaked, to 1½ in. long, bud cap beaked, ½ in. long, stamens red; fr. quadrangular-ovoid, truncate, to 1¼ in. across. W. Australia.

fraxinoides H. Deane & Maiden. WHITE ASH. To 120 ft., bark whitish, rough, fibrous; lvs. alt., sickle-shaped, narrow-lanceolate; umbels 5–8-fld., peduncles sometimes flattened, ⅝ in. long; buds pedicelled, ⅜ in. long, bud cap conical, shorter than calyx tube; fr. nearly urceolate, to ⁵⁄₁₆ in. across, valves included. New S. Wales.

gigantea: see *E. delegatensis.*

globoidea Blakely [*E. eugenioides* of Australian auth., not Sieber ex A. Spreng.]. WHITE S. Medium-sized tree, bark red-brown, fibrous on trunk, smooth on secondary brs.; lvs. alt., sickle-shaped-lanceolate; umbels 6–12-fld., peduncles ¼ in. long; bud cap conical, usually as long as calyx tube; fr. sessile, hemispherical, to ⁵⁄₁₆ in. across, valves included or shortly exserted. New S. Wales.

Globulus Labill. BLUE GUM, TASMANIAN B.G. Medium-sized to large tree, bark smooth, bluish, deciduous; lvs. alt., sickle-shaped, lanceolate, acuminate, aromatic; fls. solitary, buds large, bud cap warty, covered with a waxy bloom; fr. sessile, broad, top-shaped, ridged, to 1¼ in. across, with wide flat disc. Victoria and Tasmania; naturalized in Calif. Zone 9. One of the few spp. with solitary buds and frs. The most widely cult. of all spp. of *Eucalyptus* in Calif. and the world. Cv. 'Compacta'. Of very compact, dense habit. Originated in Calif. Wood used for tool handles, farm implements, ship building, and wood pulp; fresh lvs. yield an essential oil; dried lvs. used medicinally.

goniocalyx F. J. Muell. [*E. elaeophora* F. J. Muell.]. BUNDY. Usually a small tree, sometimes misshapen, bark soft, somewhat fibrous, irregularly cracked and ridged; lvs. alt., sickle-shaped, narrow-lanceolate, dull green; umbels 4–7-fld., peduncles to ¾ in. long; buds sessile, to ⅝ in. long, calyx tube cylindrical, 4-angled, 2–3 times as long as short, conical bud cap; fr. club-shaped or obovate, to ⁵⁄₁₆ in. across, valves included or only slightly exserted. Victoria and S. Australia.

Wood used in ship building as it is tough, durable, and resists water damage.

grandis W. Hill ex Maiden. ROSE GUM. Tall, straight tree, bark gray, fibrous on lower trunk, becoming smooth and deciduous above; lvs. alt., narrow-lanceolate, somewhat undulate; umbels 4–10-fld., peduncles flattened, to ½ in. long; buds sessile or nearly so, ⅜ in. long, usually glaucous, bud cap conical, equal to or shorter than calyx tube; fr. pear-shaped, glaucous, to ⁵⁄₁₆ in. across or less, valves included. Queensland and New S. Wales. Fast growing on favorable sites.

grossa F. J. Muell. COARSE-LEAVED MALLEE. Spreading shrub, to 15 ft., bark rough, longitudinally fissured, persistent; lvs. opp., broadly lanceolate to ovate, thick; umbels 3–8-fld., peduncles stout, ⅜ in. long; buds sessile, cylindric-conical, to ⁵⁄₁₆ in. long, bud cap conical, shorter than calyx tube, stamens bright yellow; fr. cylindrical, truncate, to ⁵⁄₁₆ in. across. W. Australia.

gummifera (Gaertn.) Hochr. [*E. corymbosa* Sm.]. RED BLOODWOOD. Medium-sized tree, bark dark brown, persistent, short-fibered, irregularly cracked; lvs. alt., narrow- to broad-lanceolate, finely veined; umbels 4–8-fld., in terminal corymbose infls., peduncles ½–¾ in. long; buds pedicelled, club-shaped, to ½ in. long, bud cap hemispherical, much shorter than calyx tube, stamens yellowish-white; fr. urceolate, to ¾ in. long, valves deeply included. Queensland, s. to Victoria.

Gunnii Hook.f. CIDER GUM, CIDER TREE. To 100 ft., bark green and white throughout, deciduous; lvs. alt., narrow- to broad-lanceolate; umbels 3-fld., peduncles ⅜ in. long; buds sessile or short-pedicelled, ⅜ in. long, bud cap conical, shorter than calyx tube; fr. hemispherical, to ⁵⁄₁₆ in. across, valves slightly exserted. Tasmania. Zone 9.

haemastoma Sm. SCRIBBLY GUM. Small to large tree, or shrubby with irregular crown, bark smooth, grayish, deciduous in small flakes, lvs. alt., sickle-shaped, lanceolate, thick; umbels 6–12-fld., in terminal panicles, peduncle ½–¾ in. long, buds pedicelled, club-shaped, ¼ in. long, bud cap hemispherical, shorter than pear-shaped calyx tube; fr. hemispherical-top-shaped, to ⁵⁄₁₆ in. across, valves included. New S. Wales and Victoria. Var. **capitata** Maiden. Low, bushy tree; lvs. narrow- to broad-lanceolate; umbels 15–20-fld. New S. Wales.

hemiphloia: *E. moluccana.* Var. **albens**: *E. albens.*

Huberana: see *E. viminalis.*

incrassata Labill. [*E. angulosa* Schauer; *E. incrassata* var. *angulosa* (Schauer) Benth.]. LERP MALLEE, RIDGE-FRUITED M. Shrub or small tree, bark smooth, whitish; lvs. alt., lanceolate to broad-lanceolate, thick; umbels 3–15-fld., peduncles flat, to 1 in. long; buds ovoid, smooth to ribbed, to ⅝ in. long, bud cap conical to beaked, as long as calyx tube; fr. sessile or nearly so, hemispherical to urceolate, smooth to coarsely ribbed, to ¾ in. across, valves included. Victoria, w. to S. and W. Australia.

Kirtoniana: *E.* × *patentinervis.*

Kruseana F. J. Muell. KRUSE'S MALLEE. Glaucous shrub, to 10 ft., bark smooth, deciduous; lvs. opp., sessile, cordate-orbicular to reniform; umbels 3–6-fld., peduncles ⅜ in. long; buds conical, ⅜ in. long, bud cap conical, as long as calyx tube; fr. short-pedicelled, hemispherical, ¼ in. across, valves deeply included. W. Australia. The rounded leaves are uncommon on mature trees in *Eucalyptus.*

Lane-Poolei Maiden. SALMON WHITE GUM. Tree, to 50 ft., bark smooth, white to pinkish, deciduous; lvs. alt., sickle-shaped, slender-lanceolate; umbels 3–6-fld., peduncles ½ in. long; buds pedicelled, ovoid, to ⅜ in. long, bud cap hemispherical, as long as calyx tube; fr. broadly top-shaped, to ½ in. across, valves exserted. W. Australia.

Lansdowneana F. J. Muell. & J. E. Br. CRIMSON MALLEE BOX. Shrub or small tree, to 17 ft., bark rough and flaky at base of trunk, smooth and gray above; lvs. alt., narrow- to broad-lanceolate; umbels 3–8-fld., peduncles ⅜ in. long; buds sessile, cylindric-club-shaped, bud cap conical, shorter than calyx tube, stamens pink or purple; fr. barrel-shaped, ⅜ in. across, with 2 or 4 faint longitudinal ridges. S. Australia.

largiflorens F. J. Muell. [*E. bicolor* of auth., not. A. Cunn. ex Hook.]. BLACK BOX. Small tree, to 30 ft. or sometimes more, bark hard, rugged, persistent; lvs. alt., slender-lanceolate, gray-green; umbels 3–7-fld., in panicles, peduncles ¼ in. long; buds pedicelled, club-shaped, ¼ in. long, bud cap hemispherical, shorter than calyx tube; fr. hemispherical, ³⁄₁₆ in. across, valves included. Queensland to Victoria, w. to S. Australia.

Lehmannii (Schauer) Benth. LEHMANN'S GUM, BUSHY YATE. Shrub, branching close to ground, to 30 ft., bark smooth, gray-brown, peeling irregularly; lvs. alt., oblong to lanceolate, short-petioled; umbels 7–15-fld., dense, peduncles thick, flat, to 2 in. long, reflexed; bud cap 3 times longer than the smooth, partly embedded calyx tube, stamens yellow-green, showy; fr. fused into a conglomerate, globular mass, valves long-exserted, cohering and forming a beak. W. Australia.

leucophylla: *E. argillacea.*

leucoxylon F. J. Muell. WHITE I. Medium-sized tree, bark mottled white and bluish, deciduous in irregular sheets; lvs. alt., narrow- to broad-lanceolate; umbels 3-fld., peduncles to ½ in. long; buds pedicelled, ovoid, ⅜ in. long, bud cap conical, usually as long as calyx tube; fr. ovoid-truncate, to ½ in. across, valves included. New S. Wales and Victoria. Yields an essential oil; wood used for piles, railroad ties, tool handles, and telephone poles. Cv. **'Rosea'**. Stamens pink. Cv. **'Purpurea'**. Stamens bright purple.

Lindleyana: *E. elata.*

linearis: *E. pulchella.*

longicornis F. J. Muell. RED MORELL. Small to medium-sized tree, bark rough and persistent on lower half of trunk, smooth and gray above; lvs. alt., narrow-lanceolate, dark green; umbels 5–10-fld., peduncles to 1 in. long; buds short-pedicelled, cylindrical to horn-shaped, ⅝ in. long, bud cap horn-shaped, twice as long as hemispherical calyx tube; fr. hemispherical to nearly globular, to ¼ in. across, valves exserted. New S. Wales.

longifolia Link & Otto, not Lindl. WOOLLYBUTT. Medium-sized to large tree, brs. pendulous, bark subfibrous and persistent on lower trunk, deciduous in irregular flakes on upper trunk and brs.; lvs. alt., sickle-shaped, lanceolate; umbels 3-fld., peduncles to 1 in. long, reflexed; buds 1¼ in. long, bud cap conical to beaked, about as long as 4-angled calyx tube, stamens cream-colored; fr. pedicelled, urceolate to campanulate, 4-angled, ½ in. across, valves included. New S. Wales and Victoria. See also *E. elata.*

longirostris: *E. camaldulensis.*

Luehmanniana F. J. Muell. YELLOW-TOPPED MALLEE ASH. Shrub, to 20 ft., bark smooth, glaucous, deciduous in strips; lvs. alt., narrow- to broad-lanceolate, glaucous, leathery; umbels 3–9-fld., peduncles to ¾ in. long; buds club-shaped, angular, to ½ in. long, bud cap conical, shorter than calyx tube; fr. short-pedicelled, hemispherical, to ½ in. across, valves included. New S. Wales. The name *E.* × *virgata* has been misapplied to this sp.

Macarthurii H. Deane & Maiden. CAMDEN WOOLLYBUTT. Spreading tree, to 80 ft., with dense canopy of lvs., bark rough, persistent; lvs. alt., narrow-lanceolate, dark green; umbels 3–7-fld., peduncles to ½ in. long; buds ovate, acute, $^3/_{16}$ in. long, bud cap conical, about as long as calyx tube; fr. globular-truncate, ¼ in. across. New S. Wales. Yields an essential oil.

macrandra F. J. Muell. ex Benth. LONG-FLOWERED MARLOCK. Shrub or small tree, to 25 ft., bark smooth; lvs. alt., narrow- to broad-lanceolate; umbels 8–16-fld., peduncles flattened, to ½ in. long; buds sessile, to 1½ in. long, bud cap reddish-tan, horn-shaped, about 3 times as long as calyx tube, stamens long, yellow; fr. campanulate, to ¼ in. across, valves included. W. Australia.

macrocarpa Hook. BLUEBUSH. Straggling, silvery-glaucous shrub, to 15 ft., bark smooth, gray; lvs. opp., oblong to broadly lanceolate, silver-gray; fls. large, solitary, or rarely in pairs, sessile, bud cap broadly conical, lightly striate, longer than calyx tube, stamens orange to crimson; fr. broadly top-shaped, woody, to 2 in. across. W. Australia.

macrorhyncha F. J. Muell. RED STRINGYBARK. Medium-sized tree, bark stringy, persistent; lvs. alt., sickle-shaped, lanceolate; umbels 6–12-fld., peduncles to ¾ in. long; buds short-pedicelled, $^3/_{16}$ in. long, bud cap conical or with beak, about as long as calyx tube; fr. globular, to ½ in. across, valves included or slightly exserted. New S. Wales and Victoria, w. to S. Australia.

maculata Hook. SPOTTED GUM. To 150 ft., bark smooth, white to glaucous, deciduous in large patches; lvs. alt., narrow- to broad-lanceolate, glossy; umbels 3–5-fld., in terminal panicles, buds short-pedicelled, ovoid, to ½ in. long, bud cap hemispherical, much shorter than calyx tube; fr. urceolate, to ½ in. across or more, valves included. Queensland, s. to Victoria. Wood used for shingles and in ship and bridge building.

maculosa: *E. mannifera* subsp.

Maidenii F. J. Muell. MAIDEN'S GUM. To 150 ft., bark deciduous, bluish-white, smooth; lvs. alt., sickle-shaped, narrow-lanceolate, dark glossy green; umbels 3–5-fld., peduncles to ½ in. long; bud cap broadly conical to almost flat, shorter than top-shaped calyx tube; fr. glaucous, top-shaped, 1–2-ribbed, to ½ in. across, valves exserted. New S. Wales and Victoria.

mannifera Mudie subsp. **maculosa** (R. T. Bak.) L. A. S. Johnson [*E. maculosa* R. T. Bak.]. RED-SPOTTED GUM. Medium-sized tree, brs. pendent, bark smooth, white, covered with white-powdery bloom, deciduous in sheets; lvs. alt., sickle-shaped, narrow-lanceolate, light green; umbels 3–7-fld., peduncles ¼ in. long; buds short-pedicelled, ovoid, ¼ in. long, bud cap conical, sometimes beaked, as long as calyx tube; fr. hemispherical, ¼ in. across, valves usually shortly exserted. New S. Wales and Victoria. Warmer parts of Zone 9.

marginata J. Donn ex Sm. JARRAH. To 150 ft., bark fibrous, stringy; lvs. alt., narrow- to broad-lanceolate, acuminate, with thickened margin; umbels 4–8-fld., peduncles to 1¼ in. long; buds short-pedicelled, ¾ in. long, bud cap narrow-conical, 2–3 times as long as calyx tube; fr. subglobose to pear-shaped, to ½ in. across or more, valves included. W. Australia. Principal timber tree in W. Australia.

megacarpa F. J. Muell. BULLICK. Erect tree, to 80 ft., bark yellowish-white, flaky; lvs. alt., sickle-shaped, lanceolate; umbels 3-fld., peduncles thick, somewhat flattened, to ½ in. long; buds almost sessile, ovoid to globular, ⅝ in. long, bud cap semiglobose, shorter than calyx tube; fr. hemispherical, somewhat ribbed, to 1¼ in. across, rim prominent. W. Australia.

megacornata C. Gardn. WARTED YATE. Small tree, to 20 ft., bark gray-brown, mottled, smooth; lvs. alt., oblong-lanceolate; umbels 2–3-fld., peduncles strap-shaped, reflexed; buds sessile, 3 in. long, bud cap cylindrical, warty, twice as long as calyx tube, stamens chartreuse; fr. campanulate, rugose-ribbed, to 1¼ in. across, valves slightly exserted. W. Australia.

melliodora A. Cunn. ex Schauer. YELLOW BOX. Medium-sized tree, brs. pendulous, bark scaly-flaky to subfibrous, persistent on trunk, smooth on brs.; lvs. alt., narrow- to broad-lanceolate; umbels 3–5-fld.; buds short-pedicelled, ¼ in. long, bud cap conical, usually slightly shorter than calyx tube; fr. hemispherical, ¼ in. across, valves included. Queensland, s. to Victoria.

micrantha: *E. racemosa.*

microcorys F. J. Muell. TALLOWWOOD. Large tree, to 100 ft., bark fibrous, persistent; lvs. alt., lanceolate, thin; umbels axillary or in terminal corymbose panicles, 4–8-fld., peduncles to ¾ in. long; buds short-pedicelled, pear-shaped, ¼ in. long, bud cap hemispherical, tiny, shorter than calyx tube; fr. cylindric-club-shaped, to $^5/_{16}$ in. across or less, valves included. Queensland and New S. Wales.

microtheca F. J. Muell. FLOODED BOX. Tree, to 40 ft., bark sordid-white, wrinkled, cracked, persistent on trunk, deciduous above; lvs. alt., sickle-shaped, lanceolate; umbels 3–5-fld., in lateral or terminal panicles, peduncles ⅜ in. long; buds almost sessile, ovoid, apiculate, ⅛ in. long, bud cap hemispherical, usually shorter than calyx tube; fr. ovoid-top-shaped, to $^3/_{16}$ in. across, valves exserted. N. Queensland, w. to W. Australia.

miniata A. Cunn. ex Schauer. DARWIN WOOLLYBUTT. Tree, to 40 ft., bark fibrous, persistent, with papery flakes interspersed among fibers; lvs. alt., broad-lanceolate, leathery, glaucous, paler beneath; umbels axillary or in terminal panicles, 3–7-fld., peduncles to ¾ in. long; buds sessile, club-shaped, to 1 in. long, glaucous; bud cap hemispherical, about half as long as calyx tube, stamens orange-scarlet; fr. barrel-shaped, ribbed, thick and woody, to 2 in. across, valves included. Queensland, w. to W. Australia.

moluccana Roxb. [*E. hemiphloia* F. J. Muell.]. GRAY BOX. Tree, to 100 ft., bark nearly fibrous, persistent on trunk, smooth and deciduous on brs.; lvs. alt., lanceolate, leathery; umbels 4–8-fld., in panicles, peduncles to ½ in. long; buds almost sessile, ovoid, ⅜ in. long, bud cap conical, about as long as calyx tube; fr. somewhat urceolate to pear-shaped, ¼ in. across, valves included. Queensland and New S. Wales.

×**Mortoniana** Kinney. Said to be a hybrid between *E. Maidenii* and *E. pseudoglobulus* Naudin; medium-sized tree, bark smooth, deciduous; lvs. alt., sickle-shaped, lanceolate; umbels 3–fld., peduncle to $^5/_{16}$ in. long; bud cap conical, as long as calyx tube; fr. campanulate to top-shaped, 1-ribbed, to ¾ in. across. Originated in Calif.

Muellerana Howitt. YELLOW S. Massive tree, to 150 ft., bark rough, fibrous, persistent; lvs. alt., narrow- to broad-lanceolate; umbels 7–12-fld., peduncles about ½ in. long; buds short-pedicelled, club-shaped, ⅜ in. long, bud cap conical, as long as calyx tube; fr. globose to pear-shaped, truncate, to ¾ in. across, valves included. Queensland, s. to Victoria, w. to S. Australia.

multiflora: *E. robusta.*

neglecta Maiden. OMEO ROUND-LEAVED GUM. Small tree, to 20 ft., bark rough and fibrous at base of trunk, smooth above and deciduous in long ribbons; lvs. opp., broadly lanceolate, often undulate, leathery; umbels sessile, 5–8-fld.; buds sessile, ovoid, $^3/_{16}$ in. long, bud cap conical, about as long as calyx tube; fr. hemispherical, to ¼ in. across. Victoria.

Nicholii Maiden & Blakely. NARROW-LEAVED BLACK PEPPERMINT, NICHOL'S WILLOW-LEAVED P. Tree, to 40 ft. or more, bark subfibrous, brown, persistent on trunk and brs.; lvs. alt., narrow-lanceolate, slightly gray-green; umbels 5–8-fld., peduncles to ⅜ in. long; buds short-pedicelled, ovoid, ¼ in. long, bud cap conical, about as long as calyx tube, stamens whitish; fr. hemispherical, $^3/_{16}$ in. across, valves shortly exserted. New S. Wales. Zone 9.

niphophila Maiden & Blakely. SNOW GUM. Shrub or small tree, to 20 ft., bark smooth, white, deciduous; lvs. alt., sickle-shaped, lanceolate, glaucous, thick, somewhat longitudinally veined; umbels 3–7-fld., peduncles thick, ¼ in. long; buds sessile or nearly so, club-shaped, ¼ in. long, glaucous; bud cap hemispherical, shorter than calyx tube; fr. globose to top-shaped, ⅜ in. across, usually glaucous. Restricted to alpine region of Mt. Kosciusko (New S. Wales). Zone 8. Perhaps the hardiest sp. of the genus. Closely related to and considered by some to be an alpine variant of *E. pauciflora*.

numerosa: *E. elata.*

nutans F. J. Muell. RED-FLOWERED MOORT. Shrub, to 8 ft., bark smooth, gray, sometimes mottled; lvs. alt., broadly lanceolate, thick; umbels 3–7-fld., peduncle flattened, to 1 in. long, somewhat reflexed; buds sessile, ovoid-oblong, ⅝ in. long, bud cap conical, shorter than the slightly ribbed calyx tube, stamens red; fr. broadly top-shaped, ribbed, to ½ in. across. W. Australia.

obliqua L'Hér. MESSMATE S. To 200 ft., bark fibrous, furrowed, persistent to small brs.; lvs. alt., sickle-shaped, obliquely lanceolate; umbels 7–16-fld., peduncles to ½ in. long; buds sessile or nearly so, club-shaped, ¼ in. long, bud cap hemispherical, apiculate, shorter than calyx tube; fr. pear-shaped, to ⁵⁄₁₆ in. across, valves deeply included. New S. Wales, s. to Tasmania, w. to S. Australia.

occidentalis Endl. FLAT-TOPPED YATE. Tree, to 80 ft., bark thick, rough and persistent on trunk and lower brs., smooth above, brs. widely spreading; lvs. alt., lanceolate, dark green, thick; umbels 3–7-fld., peduncles to 1 in. long, reflexed; buds short-pedicelled, to ¾ in. long, bud cap cylindric-conical, longer than calyx tube; fr. pedicelled, campanulate, to ½ in. across, valves exserted. W. Australia.

Oldfieldii F. J. Muell. OLDFIELD'S MALLEE. Shrub, to 10 ft., bark reddish-brown, peeling in loose flakes; lvs. alt., narrow- to broad-lanceolate; umbels 3-fld., peduncles thick, to ¼ in. long; buds sessile, globular to ovate and beaked, to ¾ in. long, bud cap hemispherical-beaked, slightly longer than cup-shaped calyx tube; fr. hemispherical, to ½ in. across, disc prominent, valves included. W. Australia. Closely related to *E. burracoppinensis*, but having buds and frs. sessile and bud caps smooth.

orbifolia F. J. Muell. ROUND-LEAVED MALLEE. Shrub, 20–25 ft., bark thin, reddish, peeling in persistent strips; lvs. opp., broadly obovate-orbicular, obtuse or retuse, gray-green; umbels 2–5-fld., peduncles to 1 in. long; buds pedicelled, bud cap conical-pointed, longitudinally striate, somewhat longer than calyx tube, stamens yellowish; fr. campanulate, woody, ¾ in. across, valves exserted. W. Australia.

Orpetii: a listed name for a plant grown in Calif. and said to a hybrid between *Eucalyptus caesia* and *E. macrocarpa*, though *E. orbifolia* is a more likely second parent. Plants so named strongly resemble *E. caesia*, but have lvs. ovate and more or less pointed.

ovata Labill. SWAMP GUM. Tall tree, bark scaly at base of trunk, smooth above and peeling in ribbons; lvs. alt., ovate to lanceolate; umbels 4–8-fld., peduncles to ½ in. long; buds short-pedicelled, ovoid, to ⅜ in. long, bud cap conical, about as long as funnel-shaped calyx tube; fr. sessile or nearly so, hemispherical, to ⁵⁄₁₆ in. across, valves included to shortly exserted. New S. Wales, s. to Tasmania, w. to S. Australia. Zone 9.

paniculata Sm. GRAY I. Large tree, bark hard, deeply furrowed, dark gray, persistent; lvs. alt., lanceolate; umbels 3–9-fld., in panicles; buds short-pedicelled, ovoid, ⅜ in. long, bud cap conical, as long as calyx tube; fr. nearly sessile, hemispherical to pear-shaped, to ⁵⁄₁₆ in. across, valves included. Queensland and New S. Wales.

parvifolia Cambage. SMALL-LEAVED GUM. Small tree, to 30 ft., bark smooth, dull gray; lvs. opp. and alt., linear-lanceolate to ovate-lanceolate; umbels 4–7-fld., peduncles to ¼ in. long; buds sessile, ellipsoid, ³⁄₁₆ in. long, bud cap conical, about as long as calyx tube; fr. to ³⁄₁₆ in. across, valves included. New S. Wales. Zone 9.

×**patentinervis** R. T. Bak. [*E. Kirtoniana* F. J. Muell.]: *E. robusta* × *E. tereticornis.* Medium-sized tree, bark scaly or somewhat fibrous, sometimes smooth on brs.; lvs. alt., sickle-shaped, narrow-lanceolate, acuminate, distinctly veined; umbels 5–10-fld., peduncles to 1 in. long; bud cap conical to beaked, longer than calyx tube; fr. campanulate, to ⁵⁄₁₆ in. across. New S. Wales.

pauciflora Sieber ex A. Spreng. CABBAGE GUM. Small to large tree, bark smooth, white or mottled, but rough and persistent at base; lvs. alt., sickle-shaped, broadly lanceolate, longitudinally veined; umbels 5–12-fld., peduncles to ½ in. long; buds sessile, club-shaped, bud cap conical, shorter than calyx tube; fr. to ⁵⁄₁₆ in. across, valves included. New S. Wales, s. to Tasmania, w. to S. Australia. Zone 9.

pendula: see *E. camaldulensis.*

Perriniana F. J. Muell. ex Rodw. ROUND-LEAVED SNOW GUM, SPINNING GUM. Small tree, to 20 ft., bark smooth, more or less blotched; lvs. alt., lanceolate, glaucous; umbels 3-fld., peduncles stout, to ¼ in. long; buds sessile, elliptic, ⅜ in. long, glaucous, bud cap conical, shorter than calyx tube; fr. hemispherical, to ⁵⁄₁₆ in. across, valves not exserted. New S. Wales to Tasmania. Zone 9.

phoenicia F. J. Muell. SCARLET GUM. Medium-sized tree, bark flaky, persistent; lvs. alt., narrow-lanceolate; umbels 5–20-fld., peduncles to ¾ in. long; buds short-pedicelled, club-shaped, ⅝ in. long, bud cap hemispherical, shorter than urceolate calyx tube, stamens scarlet, very showy; fr. sessile, ovoid to urceolate, ribbed, to ½ in. across. Queensland and N. Territory of Australia.

pilularis Sm. BLACKBUTT. Tall, straight tree, bark fibrous, persistent on lower trunk, smooth above; lvs. alt., sickle-shaped, lanceolate, glossy on both sides; umbels 6–12-fld., peduncles to ½ in. long; buds ovoid, ³⁄₁₆ in. long, bud cap conical to beaked, longer than calyx tube; fr. short-pedicelled, hemispherical, to ½ in. across, valves deeply included. Queensland to Victoria. Wood used for telephone poles and for building bridges and ships.

piperita Sm. SYDNEY PEPPERMINT. Medium-sized tree, with spreading brs., bark rough, fibrous, persistent; lvs. alt., narrow-lanceolate; umbels 7–15-fld., peduncles to ⅜ in. long; buds pedicelled, club-shaped, acute, ¼ in. long, bud cap conical, as long as calyx tube; fr. ovoid to urceolate, to ¼ in. across, valves included. New S. Wales and Victoria. Wood moisture resistant, used for posts and shingles and for building.

platyphylla: *E. alba.*

platypus Hook. ROUND-LEAVED MOORT. Tree, to 30 ft., bark smooth, gray, sometimes mottled; lvs. alt., orbicular to broadly lanceolate; umbels 4–9-fld., peduncles flattened, to 1 in. long; buds sessile, 1¼ in. long, bud cap cylindrical, longer than calyx tube, stamens dull red or yellow-green; fr. ovate-truncate, 2–3-ribbed, to ½ in. across, valves included. W. Australia.

podalyriifolia: a listed name of no botanical standing.

polyanthemos Schauer. SILVER-DOLLAR GUM, SILVER-DOLLAR TREE. Medium-sized tree, with low brs., bark short-fibrous, scaly, smooth above, sometimes shedding all of its bark like a gum; lvs. alt., orbicular to broadly lanceolate; umbels 6–8-fld., in panicles; buds pedicelled, club-shaped, ¼ in. long, bud cap conical, shorter than calyx tube; fr. hemispherical, to ¼ in. across, valves included. New S. Wales and Victoria. Valuable timber tree. The opp., orbicular, glaucous lvs. on juvenile trees are more decorative than the lvs. on mature trees, and are much used in fl. arrangements.

populifolia: *E. populnea.*

populnea F. J. Muell. [*E. populifolia* Hook.]. BIMBLE BOX. Small to medium, round-headed tree, bark nearly fibrous, persistent; lvs. alt., orbicular to ovate, glossy, dark green; umbels 4–7-fld., in panicles usually shorter than the lvs.; buds almost sessile, ovoid, ¼ in. long, bud cap broadly ovate, shorter than calyx tube; fr. nearly sessile, hemispherical, ³⁄₁₆ in. across, valves included. Queensland and New S. Wales.

Preissiana Schauer. BELL-FRUITED MALLEE. Straggly shrub, to 10 ft., bark smooth, mottled gray; lvs. opp., oblong to broadly lanceolate, thick; umbels 3-fld., peduncles angled or flattened; buds sessile, club-shaped, ¾ in. long, bud cap broadly conical-apiculate, stamens yellow; fr. woody, campanulate, to 1½ in. across, valves included. W. Australia.

ptychocarpa F. J. Muell. SWAMP BLOODWOOD, RED B. Medium-sized tree, bark fibrous, rough, persistent throughout; lvs. alt., broadly lanceolate; umbels 3–7-fld., in panicles; bud cap hemispherical, much shorter than the pear-shaped calyx tube, stamens pink to scarlet; fr. pedicelled, barrel-shaped, ribbed, to 1¼ in. across. N. Territory and W. Australia.

pulchella Desf. [*E. linearis* Dehnh.]. WHITE PEPPERMINT. Slender tree, to 50 ft., bark rough and scaly on lower trunk, smooth, white, and deciduous above; lvs. alt., linear to narrow-lanceolate, having pleasant peppermint smell; umbels 5–12-fld., peduncles to ⅜ in. long; buds short-pedicelled, club-shaped, ³⁄₁₆ in. long, bud cap hemispherical, shorter than calyx tube; fr. nearly sessile, to ¼ in. across. Tasmania.

pulverulenta Sims. SILVER-LEAVED MOUNTAIN GUM, MONEY TREE. Straggling tree, to 30 ft., bark smooth, white, peeling in small flakes; lvs. opp., sessile, cordate, silvery-gray; umbels glaucous, 3-fld., peduncles ⅜ in. long; bud cap conical, beaked, shorter than funnel-shaped calyx tube; fr. broadly top-shaped, to ¾ in. across. New S. Wales. Zone 9. The silvery, rounded, sessile to clasping lvs. on juvenile trees are often used in fl. arrangements.

punctata DC. GRAY GUM. Medium-sized tree with dark gray, deciduous bark; lvs. alt., lanceolate; umbels 6–10-fld., peduncles angled, to ¾ in. long; buds ¾ in. long, bud cap conical, acute, about as long as angled calyx tube; fr. sessile or nearly so, hemispherical, to ½ in. across, valves included. Queensland and New S. Wales.

pyriformis Turcz. PEAR-FRUITED MALLEE. Shrub, to 15 ft., bark smooth, light brown; lvs. alt., broadly lanceolate, nearly glaucous; umbels 3-fld., peduncles to ¾ in. long, reflexed; buds pear-shaped, bud cap large, conical, beaked, ribbed, about as long as equally ribbed calyx tube, stamens red; fr. depressed-globular, ribbed, to 2¾ in. across, valves included. S. and W. Australia.

racemosa Cav., not of auth. [*E. micrantha* DC.]. SNAPPY GUM. Medium-sized tree, with pendulous branchlets, bark smooth, mottled, deciduous; lvs. alt., sickle-shaped, lanceolate; umbels 6–20-fld., peduncles to ½ in. long; buds pear-shaped, to ¼ in. long, bud cap hemispherical, shorter than calyx tube; fr. short-pedicelled, hemispherical, ¼ in. across, valves shortly exserted or included. New S. Wales. See also *E. crebra.*

radiata Sieber ex DC. GRAY PEPPERMINT. Large, spreading tree, bark finely fibrous, persistent; lvs. opp., linear to lanceolate, thin; umbels 8–16-fld., peduncles ⅜ in. long; buds short-pedicelled, club-shaped, ¼ in. long, bud cap hemispherical, about as long as calyx tube; fr. hemispherical, to ¼ in. across, valves included. New S. Wales.

×**rariflora** F. M. Bailey: *E. crebra* × *E. populnea.* BLACK BOX. Medium-sized tree, bark dark colored, somewhat fibrous, persistent; lvs. alt., lanceolate, glossy, dark green; umbels 3–6-fld., in panicles; buds pedicelled, ovoid, ¼ in. long, bud cap conical, as long as calyx tube; fr. hemispherical, ³⁄₁₆ in. across, valves included. Queensland and New S. Wales.

regnans F. J. Muell. MOUNTAIN ASH, GIANT GUM. To 300 ft., bark rough and somewhat fibrous on trunk up to 25–50 ft., smooth, white, and deciduous above; lvs. alt., sickle-shaped, lanceolate; umbels 7–12-fld., peduncles to ⅝ in. long; buds pedicelled, to ⅜ in. long, bud cap hemispherical, shorter than calyx tube; fr. short-pedicelled, ovoid to campanulate, to ¼ in. across, valves included. Victoria and Tasmania. The tallest sp. of *Eucalyptus* and the tallest hardwood in the world; one of the important Australian hardwoods.

resinifera Sm. RED MAHOGANY. To 100 ft., bark reddish, fibrous, persistent; lvs. alt., lanceolate, pale beneath; umbels 5–10-fld., peduncles to ¾ in. long; buds ¾ in. long, bud cap acutely conical to beaked, 2–3 times longer than calyx tube; fr. short-pedicelled, hemispherical, to ⁵⁄₁₆ in. across, valves exserted. Queensland and New S. Wales. Wood used for posts, shingles, and general building.

×**rhodantha** Blakely & Steedm.: *E. macrocarpa* × *E. pyriformis.* ROSE MALLEE. Straggly shrub, to about 8 ft.; lvs. orbicular to acutely cordate, silvery; fls. red. Similar to *E. macrocarpa*, but having fls. on peduncles and fr. smaller. W. Australia.

Risdonii Hook.f. SILVER PEPPERMINT. Glaucous tree, to 20 ft., bark ash-gray, shedding in patches; lvs. opp., cordate-lanceolate, glaucous; umbels 3–9-fld., peduncles to ⅜ in. long; buds club-shaped, ¼ in. long, bud cap hemispherical, obtuse, shorter than calyx tube; fr. pedicelled, subglobose, to ⁵⁄₁₆ in. across, valves included. Tasmania.

Robertsonii Blakely. ROBERTSON'S PEPPERMINT. To 180 ft., bark dark gray, fibrous, persistent; lvs. alt., narrow- to broad-lanceolate, gray-green; umbels 9–12-fld., peduncles to ⅜ in. long; buds club-shaped, ¼ in. long, bud cap conical, about as long as top-shaped calyx tube; fr. club-shaped to pear-shaped, to ¼ in. across, valves included. New S. Wales and Victoria.

robusta Sm. [*E. multiflora* Poir.]. SWAMP MAHOGANY. Medium-sized tree, bark rough, fibrous, persistent; lvs. alt., broadly lanceolate, long-pointed, leathery; umbels 5–10-fld., peduncles to 1¼ in. long; bud cap conical to beaked, equal to or shorter than calyx tube; fr. urceolate, to ½ in. across, valves included. Queensland and New S. Wales. Wood used for shingles and for building ships.

rostrata: *E. camaldulensis.*

rubida H. Deane & Maiden. CANDLE-BARK GUM. To 100 ft., bark smooth, sometimes pale salmon, deciduous in strips; lvs. alt., lanceolate, gray-green; umbels 3-fld., peduncles to ⅜ in. long; bud cap conical, as long as calyx tube; fr. ovoid, glaucous, to ¼ in. across. Queensland, S. Australia, Tasmania. Zone 9.

rudis Endl. DESERT GUM. Tree, to 50 ft., bark rough, dark gray, persistent on trunk, smooth and deciduous above; lvs. alt., sickle-shaped, narrow- to broad-lanceolate, prominently veined; umbels 4–10-fld., peduncles to ⅝ in. long; bud cap conical, longer than shallow calyx tube; fr. campanulate, to ½ in. across, valves exserted. W. Australia. Compare with *E. camaldulensis.*

salicifolia: *E. amygdalina.*

saligna Sm. SYDNEY BLUE GUM. Tall tree, bark smooth and gray except at base of trunk; lvs. alt., lanceolate, with fine, almost parallel lateral veins; umbels 3–9-fld., peduncles to ½ in. long; bud cap conical, nearly as long as calyx tube; fr. sessile or nearly so, campanulate, to ¼ in. across, valves exserted. New S. Wales.

salmonophloia F. J. Muell. SALMON GUM. To 100 ft., bark smooth, salmon-colored, deciduous; lvs. alt., lanceolate; umbels 3–7-fld., peduncles ⅜ in. long; bud cap conical, as long as calyx tube; fr. pedicelled, globular-club-shaped, to ³⁄₁₆ in. across, valves slender, exserted. W. Australia.

salubris F. J. Muell. GIMLET GUM. To 80 ft., trunk often twisted, bark reddish-brown; lvs. alt., sickle-shaped, narrow-lanceolate, acuminate; umbels 3–8-fld., peduncles to ½ in. long; bud cap conical, longer than shallow calyx tube; fr. pedicelled, hemispherical, to ¼ in. across, valves exserted. W. Australia.

scabra Dum.-Cours. A dubious sp., described from unidentifiable cult. material. The name has been applied to *E. globoidea.*

sepulcralis F. J. Muell. BLUE WEEPING GUM. Willowlike tree, bark white, glaucous; lvs alt., lanceolate, acuminate; umbels 4–7-fld., peduncles slender, to 1½ in. long; bud cap conical, acute, shorter than calyx tube, stamens yellow; fr. pedicelled, cylindric-urceolate faintly ribbed, to 1 in. across or more, valves included. W. Australia.

siderophloia: see *E. fibrosa.*

sideroxylon A. Cunn. ex Woolls [*E. sideroxylon* var. *rosea* Ingham]. RED I. Medium-sized tree, bark black, hard, deeply furrowed, persistent; lvs. alt., lanceolate, nearly glaucous; umbels 3–7-fld., peduncles to ¾ in. long, reflexed; bud cap conical, shorter than calyx tube, stamens cream-white to deep rosy-red; fr. pedicelled, urceolate, to ⁵⁄₁₆ in. across, valves included. New S. Wales and Victoria.

Sieberana: see *E. Sieberi.*

Sieberi L. A. S. Johnson [*E. Sieberana* of auth., not F. J. Muell.]. BLACK MOUNTAIN ASH. Small to large tree, bark hard, deeply furrowed like an ironbark on the trunk, smooth and white above on brs.; lvs. alt., sickle-shaped, lanceolate; umbels 5–15-fld., peduncles ½ in. long; buds pedicelled, club-shaped, ¼ in. long, bud cap hemispherical, shorter than club-shaped calyx tube; fr. pear-shaped, to ⁵⁄₁₆ in. across, valves included. New S. Wales, s. to Tasmania.

Smithii R. T. Bak. GULLY GUM, BLACKBUTT PEPPERMINT. Large tree, bark dark, furrowed, persistent on lower trunk, smooth, brownish, and deciduous in strips from upper trunk and brs.; lvs. alt. sickle-shaped, narrow-lanceolate; umbels 5–9-fld., peduncles to ½ in. long; buds pedicelled, ovate, ¼ in. long, bud cap broadly conical, about as long as calyx tube; fr. top-shaped, to ¼ in. across, valves exserted. New S. Wales and Victoria.

spathulata Hook. SWAMP MALLEE. Shrub or slender tree, to 20 ft., bark smooth, reddish-brown; lvs. alt., linear-lanceolate, attenuate toward the base; umbels 3–7-fld., peduncles to ⅝ in. long; bud cap cylindrical, 2–3 times as long as calyx tube; fr. short-pedicelled, campanulate, to ⁵⁄₁₆ in. across, valves exserted. W. Australia.

Steedmanii C. Gardn. STEEDMAN'S GUM. Shrub or slender tree, to 25 ft., bark light brown, smooth, glossy, deciduous in thin flakes; lvs. alt., oblong-lanceolate, short-petioled, abundantly oil-dotted; umbels 1–4-fld., peduncles flattened, about ¾ in. long; bud cap ovoid, 4-angled, shorter than the prominently angled, pear-shaped calyx tube, stamens yellow; fr. top-shaped-obpyramidal, truncate, prominently 4-winged, to ½ in. across, valves exserted. W. Australia.

stellulata Sieber ex DC. BLACK SALLY. Small to medium-sized tree, bark dark, rough, flaky, and persistent on the lower part of the trunk, smooth, gray to olive-green above; lvs. alt., sometimes sickle-shaped, lanceolate, leathery; umbels dense, 7–16-fld., peduncles ³⁄₁₆ in. long; buds sessile, elliptic, ¼ in. long, bud cap conical to beaked, as long as calyx tube; fr. sessile, hemispherical, to ³⁄₁₆ in. across, valves included. New S. Wales and Victoria.

Stowardii Maiden. STOWARD'S MALLEE. Shrub, bark smooth, mottled, deciduous; lvs. alt., broadly lanceolate, thick; umbels 3–7-fld., peduncles to 1 in. long; buds to 1¼ in. long, bud cap cylindrical, ribbed, usually longer than the ribbed, pear-shaped calyx tube; fr. pear-shaped, 3–5-ribbed, to ½ in. across or more, valves slender, exserted. W. Australia.

Stricklandii Maiden. STRICKLAND'S GUM. Tree, to 40 ft., bark rough and dark on lower trunk, smooth, gray or red-brown above; lvs. alt., lanceolate, thick, glaucous; umbels 4–7-fld., peduncles stout, to ¾ in. long; buds ¾ in. long, bud cap cylindric-ovate, as long as angular calyx tube, stamens bright yellow, showy; fr. sessile, cylindric-angular, to ½ in. across, valves included. W. Australia.

stricta Sieber ex A. Spreng. BLUE MOUNTAIN MALLEE. Many-stemmed shrub to 12 ft., or small tree, bark smooth, deciduous in long strips; lvs. alt., acutely-lanceolate, rigid; umbels 3–7-fld., peduncles to ⅜ in. long; buds ¼ in. long, bud cap broadly conical, much shorter than calyx tube; fr. short-pedicelled, urceolate, to ½ in. across, valves included. New S. Wales and Victoria.

Stuartiana: see *E. Bridgesiana.*

tasmanica: *E. tenuiramis.*

tenuiramis Miq. [*E. tasmanica* Blakely]. SILVER PEPPERMINT. Tree, to 70 ft., usually glaucous, bark smooth, light gray, deciduous; lvs. alt., narrow-lanceolate, acuminate, abundantly oil-dotted; umbels 6–25-fld., peduncles stout, to ½ in. long; buds ¼ in. long, bud cap saucer-shaped, shorter than funnelform calyx tube; fr. short-pedicelled, hemispherical to pear-shaped, ⅜ in. across, valves usually included. Tasmania.

tereticornis Sm. FOREST RED GUM. Tall tree, bark smooth, irregularly blotched, deciduous; lvs. alt., narrow-lanceolate, thick, glossy; umbels 5–12-fld., peduncles to ½ in. long; buds to ⅝ in. long, bud cap conical to beaked, usually 2–3 times as long as cup-shaped calyx tube; fr. short-pedicelled, nearly pear-shaped, to ⅜ in. across, valves exserted. Queensland, s. to Victoria. Wood used for fences, poles, railroad ties, and general building. Closely related to *E. camaldulensis,* and not readily differentiated; in *E. tereticornis* lvs. usually broader, buds longer, pedicels somewhat stouter, and fr. larger. The name *E. umbellata* (Gaertn.) Domin has been misapplied to this sp.

tetragona (R. Br.) F. J. Muell. WHITE-LEAVED MARLOCK. Glaucous shrub or small tree, to 25 ft., bark smooth, glaucous; lvs. opp., ovate to broadly lanceolate; umbels 3-fld., peduncles flat, to ¾ in. long; buds to ½ in. long, bud cap hemispherical, much shorter than 4-ribbed calyx tube; fr. pedicelled, urceolate to almost globular, ribbed, ¾ in. across, valves included. W. Australia.

tetraptera Turcz. SQUARE-FRUITED MALLEE. Scrambling shrub, to 10 ft.; lvs. alt., broadly lanceolate, thick; fls. axillary, usually solitary, peduncles stout, flat, twisted, reflexed; buds red, 4-angled, to 3 in. long, bud cap conical, narrower and much shorter than calyx tube, stamens pink; fr. reflexed, 4-winged, to 1½ in. across, valves included. W. Australia.

torquata Luehm. CORAL GUM. Tree, to 25 ft. or more, bark dark, persistent and longitudinally fissured on trunk, smooth and gray above; lvs. alt., lanceolate, nearly glaucous; umbels 3–8-fld., peduncles slender, to 1 in. long; buds pedicelled, to ½ in. long, urceolate-beaked, ribbed, to 1 in. long, red, bud cap conical, beaked, basal part ribbed, smooth, as long as calyx tube, stamens red; fr. narrowly urceolate, much contracted at apex, to ½ in. across, valves included. W. Australia.

triantha Link. Not cult., but the name has been misapplied to *E. acmenioides.*

umbellata (Gaertn.) Domin. Not cult., but the name has been misapplied to *E. tereticornis.*

umbra R. T. Bak. WHITE MAHOGANY. Small to medium-sized tree, bark thick, fibrous, persistent; lvs. alt., sickle-shaped, lanceolate, thick, glossy; umbels axillary or in terminal panicles, 6–9-fld., peduncles to ¾ in. long; buds ⅜ in. long, bud cap conical to beaked, about as long as pear-shaped calyx tube; fr. short-pedicelled, hemispherical, to ⅜ in. across, valves small, usually included. New S. Wales.

urnigera Hook.f. URN-FRUITED GUM. Tree, to 50 ft., bark smooth, deciduous, mottled; lvs. alt., narrow- to broad-lanceolate; umbels 3-fld., peduncles to ¾ in. long; buds urceolate, to ½ in. long, bud cap broadly conical, about ⅓ as long as calyx tube; fr. pedicelled, urceolate, to ⅜ in. across, valves included. Tasmania. Zone 9.

viminalis Labill. MANNA GUM. Large tree, bark rough and persistent for a few ft. at base of trunk, white to yellowish-white and deciduous in long ribbons above; lvs. alt., sickle-shaped, lanceolate, acuminate; umbels 3-fld. or rarely more, peduncles to ¼ in. long; buds ovate, to ¼ in. long, bud cap thin, conical, about as long as calyx tube; fr. sessile or nearly so, hemispherical, to ¼ in. across, valves exserted. New S. Wales to Tasmania, w. to S. Australia. Zone 9. Bark yields a manna eaten by native peoples; wood used for shingles and rough carpentry. One of the most commonly cult. sp. The name *E. Huberana* Naudin has been applied to forms of this sp.

×virgata Sieber ex A. Spreng.: *E. Luehmanniana* × *E. obtusiflora* DC. The name has generally been misapplied to *E. Luehmanniana.*

Woodwardii Maiden. YELLOW-FLOWERED GUM, WOODWARD'S BLACKBUTT. Very glaucous tree, to 40 ft., bark smooth, light gray, deciduous except for a few ft. at base of trunk; lvs. alt., narrow- to broad-lanceolate, thick, rigid, glaucous; umbels 3–6-fld., peduncles stout, to ½ in. long; buds ovoid, beaked, to ½ in. long; bud cap conical, beaked, about as long as calyx tube, stamens lemon-yellow; fr. short-pedicelled, urceolate to campanulate, to ½ in. across, valves included. W. Australia. Has hybridized with *E. torquata,* the hybrid showing characters intermediate between the parents, with filaments orange to pink.

EUCHARIDIUM: *CLARKIA.* **E concinnum:** see *C. Breweri* and *C. concinna.* **E. grandiflorum:** *C. concinna.*

EUCHARIS Planch. *Amaryllidaceae.* Several spp. of herbs with tunicate bulbs, native to Cent. and S. Amer.; lvs. broad, basal, tapering to petioles; fls. in an umbel terminal on a scape and subtended by separate spathe valves; fls. large, pure white, perianth tube cylindrical, lobes spreading, stamens inserted at the throat, filaments with basal appendages forming a conspicuous cup, ovary inferior, ovules many; fr. a caps., seeds large, globose.

The Amazon lily is grown outdoors in warm countries, or in the greenhouse with the night temperature at about 65° F. It succeeds in coarse fibrous soil and should be liberally watered except in the resting period. Should be protected from the sun, except in the winter months. Propagated by offsets in spring or by seeds.

amazonica: *E. grandiflora.*

Bouchei Woodson & P. Allen. Lf. blades to 14 in. long, 6 in. wide, petioles to 1 ft. long; umbel 4–8-fld., scape to 20 in. high; fls. white, perianth tube to 2¾ in. long, 2 in. across, lobes spreading, stamen cup of 5 acutely tapered segms. without lateral teeth and united half their length. Panama.

grandiflora Planch. & Linden [*E. amazonica* Linden]. AMAZON LILY, EUCHARIST L., MADONNA L., LILY-OF-THE-AMAZON. Lf. blades about 1 ft. long and 6 in. wide, petiole 1 ft. long; umbel 3–6-fld., scape 2 ft. high; fls. fragrant, to 3 in. across. Andes of Colombia and Peru. Var. **Moorei** Bak. Lvs. smaller, thick; fls. smaller, with yellow lines on the white, sharply toothed stamen cup.

EUCHLAENA: *ZEA.*

EUCNIDE Zucc. *Loasaceae.* ROCK NETTLE. About 8 spp. of ann. or bien. herbs, native to sw. U.S. and Mex., allied to *Mentzelia,* but differing in having the petals united at the base and ovary with 4–5 placentas.

Propagated by seeds.

bartonioides Zucc. [*Mentzelia gronoviifolia* Fisch. & C. A. Mey.]. Bien., much-branched, usually spreading on the ground; lvs. ovate, laciniate or lobed; fls. bright yellow, opening only in full sun, on slender pedicels to 6 in. long; caps. opening at top by 5 valves. W. Tex. and Mex.

×EUCODONOPSIS: see ×*ACHIMENANTHA.* ×**E. achimenoides:** ×*A. naegelioides.*

EUCOMIS L'Hér. PINEAPPLE LILY. *Liliaceae.* About 10 spp. of per., bulbous herbs, native mostly to S. Afr., one in cent. Afr.; bulb tunicate; lvs. in basal rosettes; fls. greenish or whitish, in a terminal, bracted raceme crowned with a cluster (coma) of sterile leafy bracts, perianth segms. 6, 1-nerved, united basally into a cup, stamens 6, anthers versatile, filaments dilated and united basally; fr. a 3-valved, loculicidal caps.

Of easy culture in warm climates or in greenhouses in the North. Propagated by offsets or by seeds.

autumnalis (Mill.) Chitt. [*E. undulata* Ait.]. To 20 in.; lvs. strap-shaped, to 1½ ft. long and 3 in. wide, undulate; fls. green, to ¾ in. across, in a dense raceme, coma of 12–30 oblong bracts. S. Afr.

bicolor Bak. To 2½ ft.; lvs. oblong, to 1 ft. long and 3–4 in. wide, crisped on margin; fls. pale green with purple margins, 1 in. across, in a dense raceme, coma of 30–40 ovate bracts, filaments purple. S. Afr.

comosa (Houtt.) Wehrh. [*E. punctata* L'Hér.]. PINEAPPLE FLOWER. To 2 ft.; lvs. lanceolate, to 2 ft. long and 3 in. wide, spotted with purple beneath; fls. green, ½ in. long, in a loose raceme, coma of 12–20 oblong bracts. S. Afr.

pedunculata: a listed name of no botanical standing.

Pole-Evansii N. E. Br. To 3–6 ft.; lvs. broadly strap-shaped, to 2 ft. long and 6 in. wide, margins crisped and undulate; fls. greenish-white, becoming green at maturity, on pedicels 1¼ in. long, in a dense raceme, coma of 30 strap-shaped bracts with crisped margins. S. Afr.

punctata: *E. comosa.*

purpurea: a listed name of no botanical standing.

regia (L.) L'Hér. To 1 ft.; lvs. tongue-shaped, to 2½ ft. long and 3–4 in. wide, purple on back toward base; fls. green, ½ in. long, in a dense raceme on a purple-spotted, club-shaped scape, coma of 12–20 oblong, crisped bracts. S. Afr.

undulata: *E. autumnalis.*

EUCOMMIA D. Oliver. *Eucommiaceae.* One sp., a deciduous tree, native to China, flowering before or with lvs., with characters of the family.

Propagated by seeds, and cuttings of young wood; hardy in Zone 5.

ulmoides D. Oliver. To 60 ft.; lvs. elmlike, elliptic to oblong-ovate, to 3 in. long, serrate; anthers brownish-red; fr. to 1½ in. long. Cent. China. Yields rubber, and bark used medicinally.

EUCOMMIACEAE Engl. EUCOMMIA FAMILY. Dicot.; 1 genus, *Eucommia*, of dioecious trees with lamellate pith, native to China; lvs. alt., simple, petioled; fls. in lateral clusters, unisexual, without perianth, male fls. pedicelled, anthers 4–10, linear, on very short filaments, female fls. with ovary 1-celled, stigma bifid; fr. 1-seeded, flattened, oblong, winged.

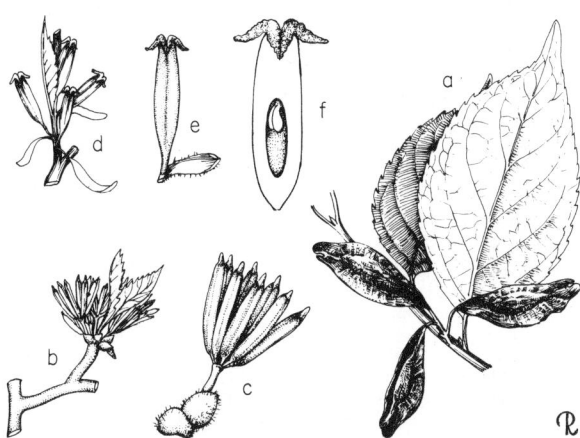

EUCOMMIACEAE. *Eucommia ulmoides:* **a,** fruiting branch, × ½; **b,** male inflorescence, × ½; **c,** male flower, × 1; **d,** female inflorescence, × ½; **e,** female flower, × 1; **f,** female flower, vertical section, × 2. (From Bailey, *Manual of Cultivated Plants,* ed. 2.)

EUCRYPHIA Cav. *Eucryphiaceae.* Four or 5 spp., native to se. Australia and Chile; evergreen trees or shrubs, with characters of the family.

Planted for their usually evergreen foliage and showy white flowers appearing in late summer and autumn, particularly on the West Coast, in those parts of Zones 9 and 10 where mild winters, cool and humid summers, and a lime-free soil meet their requirements; sometimes partly deciduous under cultivation. Propagated by seeds, layering, or, with difficulty, by cuttings.

Billardieri: *E. lucida.*

cordifolia Cav. Large shrub or tree, to 120 ft., but much less in cult.; lvs. simple, ovate-oblong or oblong, 1½–3 or even 5 in. long, cordate, crenulate to serrate, pubescent underneath; fls. 2 in. across, ovary glabrous. Chile. Said to be lime-tolerant; the least hardy sp.

glutinosa (Poepp. & Endl.) Baill. [*E. pinnatifolia* C. Gay]. Tree or shrub, 10–30 ft.; lvs. pinnately compound, lfts. 3–5, elliptic to oblong, 1½–2½ in. long, crenate-serrate, obscurely pubescent; fls. to 2½ in. across, ovary pubescent. Chile. Often partly deciduous in cult. Cv. **'Plena'.** Fls. double.

×**intermedia** Bausch: *E. glutinosa* × *E. lucida.* Small tree, intermediate between the parents; lvs. both simple and 3-foliolate, the simple lvs. and the lfts. elliptic-oblong, entire, or serrate in upper half, glaucescent underneath; fls. 2 in. across. Cv. 'Rostrevor' belongs here.

lucida (Labill.) Baill. [*E. Billardieri* Spach]. Tree, to 100 ft., but usually 20–45 ft. in cult.; lvs. simple, narrowly oblong, 1–2½ in. long, entire, glaucous underneath; fls. 1½ in. across, ovary pubescent. Tasmania.

Nymansay: see *E.* × *nymansensis.*

×**nymansensis** Bausch: *E. cordifolia* × *E. glutinosa.* Small tree, intermediate between the parents; lvs. both simple and pinnately 3-foliolate, the simple lvs. and the lfts. elliptic-oblong, serrate, paler and pubescent underneath; fls. to 2½ in. across. Also known as *Eucryphia* cv. 'Nymansay'. Said to be lime-tolerant.

pinnatifolia: *E. glutinosa.*

EUCRYPHIACEAE Endl. EUCRYPHIA FAMILY. Dicot.; 1 genus, *Eucryphia*, of evergreen trees or shrubs, native to se. Australia and Chile; lvs. opp., simple or pinnately compound, leathery, stipuled; fls. large, axillary, sepals 4, petals 4, white, stamens many, conspicuous; fr. a septicidally dehiscent caps.

EUCRYPHIACEAE. *Eucryphia cordifolia:* **a,** flowering branch, × ⅜; **b,** bud with caplike caducous calyx, × 1½; **c,** flower, × ¾; **d,** flower, vertical section, × 1; **e,** ovary, cross section, × 7; **f,** fruit, × 1½; **g,** seed, × 3. (From Lawrence, *Taxonomy of Vascular Plants.*)

EUGENIA L. [*Phyllocalyx* O. Berg; *Stenocalyx* O. Berg]. *Myrtaceae.* About 1,000 or more spp. of evergreen trees or shrubs, mostly in the Amer. tropics with a few in the Old World tropics; lvs. opp., simple, mostly firm and glossy; fls. in mostly lateral racemes, or rarely solitary, the racemes sometimes very short, calyx lobes 4, calyx tube not extending beyond summit of ovary, petals 4, white, spreading, stamens many, ovary inferior, 2-celled; fr. a berry, 1- or 2-seeded, crowned by the persistent calyx lobes, sometimes edible. Originally a large and heterogeneous group from both hemispheres. Recent workers, however, segregate many spp. from se. Asia into the large genus *Syzygium*, and some New World spp. in smaller segregate genera. Differs from *Syzygium* in having cotyledons usually united, seed coat smooth and free from the pericarp, and the infl. generally racemes of pedicelled fls.

Eugenias are grown in Calif., Fla., Hawaii and similar climates for the ornamental habit, foliage, flowers and berries, and some kinds for the edible fruits. They have simple requirements being propagated by seeds and by cuttings on a bench or in a frame.

aggregata (Vell.) Kiaersk. CHERRY-OF-THE-RIO-GRANDE. Shrub or small tree, to 15 ft., bark peeling in thin layers; lvs. short-petioled, narrow-elliptic, to 3 in. long, thick, glabrous, dark glossy green, veins obscure; fls. solitary, in opp. pairs, on peduncles 1 in. long, with 2 leafy, cordate bracts at base of each fl.; fr. an oblong or obovoid berry to 1 in. long, orange-red at first, later deep purple-red. Brazil. Fr. edible, with cherrylike flavor; can be used for pies. Cult. in Fla. and Calif. where it has been known erroneously as *Myrciaria edulis.*

alternifolia Benth. Small tree; lvs. obovate; fls. 7–15, in forked cymes. Colombia and Ecuador.

apiculata: *Luma apiculata.*

aromatica: *Syzygium aromaticum.*

atropunctata Steud. Shrub or small tree, to 18 ft.; lvs. oblong or lanceolate-oblong, 3–4½ in. long, acuminate, chartaceous, midrib impressed above, prominent beneath, petiole short; fls. white, in 6–12-fld. racemes; fr. round, ¼ in. across, black. Intro. into Fla. but not often seen.

australis: *Syzygium paniculatum.*

axillaris (Swartz) Willd. WHITE STOPPER. Shrub or small tree, bark scaly; lvs. elliptic-ovate to elliptic, to 2 in. long, paler beneath; fls. in cymelike clusters, on short, stout pedicels; fr. subglobose, to ¼ in. across, black. S. Fla. and W. Indies.

brasiliensis Lam. [*E. Dombeyi* (K. Spreng.) Skeels]. BRAZIL CHERRY, GRUMICHAMA, GRUMIXAMEIRA. Tree, to 50 ft.; lvs. elliptic to obovate-oblong, to 5 in. long, tapering at base, leathery; fls. white, solitary, on peduncles to 2 in. long; fr. about the size of a cherry, dark red, later black, edible. S. Brazil. Occasionally cult in tropics and subtropics. Zone 10b. Attractive as an ornamental. The fr. is pleasant to eat when fresh and also makes good jellies, jams, pies, and candied fr.

buxifolia: *E. foetida.*

caryophyllata: *Syzygium aromaticum.*

cauliflora: *Myrciaria cauliflora.*

confusa DC. [*E. Garberi* Sarg.]. RED STOPPER, IRONWOOD. Tree, with scaly bark; lvs. ovate or elliptic-ovate, to 2 in. long, slender-acuminate, leathery; fls. small, white, in axillary fascicles; fr. sub-globose, ⁵⁄₁₆ in. across. Fla. and W. Indies.

coronata Schumach. & Thonn. Shrub or small tree, to 20 ft.; lvs. elliptic or ovate-elliptic, to 3 in. long, leathery; fls. small, white in axillary and terminal fascicles, sweet-scented; fr. ovoid-ellipsoid, to 1 in. long, blue-black. Trop. W. Afr. Used in Fla. as a hedge plant.

cumini: *Syzygium cumini.*

Curranii C. B. Robinson. Tree, to 30 ft., young brs. 4-angled; lvs. oblong or obovate, 6 in., sometimes to 12 in. long, bluntly acuminate, cordate, sessile; fls. pinkish-white, many in short panicles; fr. globose, 1½ in. across, white, later red to dark purple, edible. Philippine Is.

cyanocarpa: *Syzygium Coolminianum.*

densiflora: *Syzygium pycnanthum.*

Dombeyi: *E. brasiliensis.*

edulis: *Myrciaria edulis.*

eucalyptoides F. J. Muell. Shrub or small tree, brs. pendulous; lvs. lanceolate, often sickle-shaped, to 6 in. long or more, narrowed to short petioles; fls. white, rather large, several in compact, terminal cymes; fr. globose, 1-seeded, edible. N. Territory of Australia. Cult. in Fla. The fr. is used for jam.

floribunda: *Myrciaria floribunda.*

foetida Pers. [*E. buxifolia* (Swartz) Willd.; *E. myrtoides* Poir.]. SPAN-ISH-STOPPER. Shrub or small tree, bark scaly; lvs. oblong, to 1½ in. long, cuneate at base, pale beneath; fls. white, in cymelike clusters, on short, stout pedicels; fr. ovoid, to ¼ in. long, black. Fla. and W. Indies.

Garberi: *E. confusa.*

grandis: *Syzygium grande.*

Hookeri, Hookerana: *Syzygium paniculatum.*

Jambolana: *Syzygium cumini.*

Jambos: *Syzygium Jambos.*

javanica: *Syzygium samarangense.*

Klotzschiana O. Berg. Shrub; lvs. oblong-lanceolate, to 2½ in. long, leathery, petiole short; fr. pear-shaped, to 1½ in. long, yellow. Brazil.

ligustrina (Swartz) Willd. Shrub or small tree; lvs. elliptic to elliptic-oblong, to 2 in. long, leathery, midrib impressed above, prominent beneath, lateral veins inconspicuous, petiole short; fls. white, solitary in axils of narrow bracts; fr. globose, ¼ in. across, black or scarlet, sweet, edible. W. Indies to Brazil.

longipes: *Psidium longipes.*

Luschnathiana Klotzsch ex O. Berg. PITOMBA. Shrub; lvs. oblong-lanceolate, to 2¼ in. long, leathery, pale beneath, petiole short; fls. solitary, axillary, long-pedicelled; fr. globose, 1 in. across, orange-yellow. Brazil. The soft juicy fr. is aromatic, mildly acid, and makes a good jelly.

malaccensis: see *Syzygium malaccense* and *S. Jambos.*

Mato: *Myrcianthes Mato.*

Michelii: *E. uniflora.*

microphylla: a listed name of no botanical standing.

monticola (Swartz) DC. Shrub or tree, to 35 ft.; lvs. ovate to narrowly lanceolate, to 1½ in. long; fls. white, small, in short racemes; fr. globose, ¼ in. across, black at maturity. W. Indies.

myriophylla: *Myrciaria myriophylla.*

myrtifolia: *Syzygium paniculatum.*

natalitia Sond. Much-branched shrub; lvs. ovate to elliptic, to 1½ in. long, glossy above, pale beneath; fls. in short racemes or cymes; fr. ellipsoid, about ½ in. long, purple. S. Afr.

oblanceolata C. B. Robinson. Tree, to 35 ft., branchlets 4-angled, often narrowly winged; lvs. oblanceolate sometimes broadly so, to 12 in. long, leathery, with 16–25 lateral veins, sessile or nearly so; fls. in terminal or axillary, cymose panicles, petals united, falling as a cap. Philippine Is.

oblata: *Syzygium oblatum.*

operculata: *Cleistocalyx operculatus.*

paniculata: *Syzygium paniculatum.* Var. *australis: S. paniculatum.*

Pitanga (O. Berg) Kiaersk. PITANGA. Low shrub, branchlets and young lvs. reddish-pubescent; lvs. elliptic-oblong, to 3 in. long, narrowed to an acute base; fls. solitary, axillary; fr. globose, about ½ in.

across, red, obscurely 8-nerved, edible. Brazil and Argentina. The fr. makes a good jelly.

polycephala: *Syzygium polycephalum.*

polycephaloides C. B. Robinson. Tree, to 60 ft., twigs 4-angled or slightly winged; lvs. oblanceolate to elliptic, to 8 in. long, with 14–18 pairs of lateral veins, petioles short; fls. sessile, usually in 3's subtended by 2 pairs of 2-ranked bracts. Philippine Is.

pungens O. Berg. Tree, to 40 ft.; lvs. elliptic-oblong, to 3 in. long, leathery, spine-tipped, petioles short; fls. white, solitary, on peduncles ¾ in. long; fr. ovoid-globose, about 1 in. across, black, with sweet yellow flesh. Brazil, Paraguay, Uruguay.

rubicunda Wight. Large shrub or small tree, branchlets 4-angled; lvs. narrow-oblong, to 3 in. long, attenuate at both ends, leathery, pellucid-punctate; fls. minute, in terminal cymes. S. India.

Simpsonii: *Myrcianthes Simpsonii.*

Smithii: *Acmena Smithii.*

supra-axillaris Spring. Tree, to 25 ft.; lvs. elliptic-oblong, to 5 in. long, glossy above, pale beneath; fls. about 9, in supra-axillary racemes; fr. globose to obovate, to 1 in. across. Brazil. Useful as a foliage plant.

tomentosa: *Myrcia tomentosa.*

Ugni: *Ugni Molinae.*

uniflora L. [*E. Michelii* Lam.]. SURINAM CHERRY, BRAZIL C., BARBADOS C., CAYENNE C., PITANGA. Shrub or small tree; lvs. ovate to elliptic, to 2½ in. long, pale beneath, veins impressed above, raised beneath, petioles short; fls. solitary, white, to ½ in. across, fragrant; fr. ovoid-globose, with 8 longitudinal grooves, to 1¼ in. across, yellow to red, edible. Trop. Amer. Zone 10b. The grooved fr. is distinctive. Widely cult. in trop. regions around the world as an ornamental, often used for hedges, and for the edible frs., used in jellies, jams, and sherbets.

Uvalha Camb. Small tree, branchlets pubescent; lvs. oblong, to 1¼ in. long; fls. solitary, axillary; fr. about size and shape of small pear, yellow, aromatic, edible. Brazil.

EULOPHIA R. Br. *Orchidaceae.* About 200 spp. of large, terrestrial herbs, rarely epiphytic, in both hemispheres, with thickened rhizomes or corms; lvs. several, leathery, plicate; infl. lateral, racemose, few- to many-fld.; sepals and petals meeting at tips, lip 3-lobed, saccate at base, lateral lobes erect, enfolding column, column with a foot. For structure of fl. see *Orchidaceae.*

For culture see *Orchids.*

alta (L.) Fawc. & Rendle [*Cyrtopera Woodfordii* Lindl.; *Cyrtopodium Woodfordii* (Lindl.) Sims]. WILD COCO, GROUND C. Erect, to 5 ft., corm to 2½ in. in diam., sts. short; lvs. 3–4 at apex of corm, lanceolate, plicate, to 4 ft. long; racemes to 3 ft. long, to 60-fld. or more; fls. to 1½ in. across, greenish or bronze, lip brownish-green, veined with purple. S. Fla., W. Indies, Mex. to n. S. Amer.; also Afr.

lurida: *Graphorkis lurida.*

maculata: *Eulophidium maculatum.*

scripta: *Graphorkis scripta.*

EULOPHIDUM Pfitz. *Orchidaceae.* About 30 spp. of terrestrial or epiphytic herbs, in both hemispheres; sts. pseudobulbous, 1-lvd. at apex; lvs. elongate, fleshy; infl. lateral, at base of pseudobulb, erect, longer than lf., simple, loosely racemose, few- to many-fld.; fls. small, sepals and petals nearly alike, lip 3-lobed, short-spurred at base, column dilated at base. For structure of fl. see *Orchidaceae.*

For culture see *Orchids.*

Ledienii: *E. maculatum.*

maculatum (Lindl.) Pfitz. [*E. Ledienii* (Stein ex N. E. Br.) De Wild.; *Eulophia maculata* (Lindl.) Rchb.f.]. Large, terrestrial or epiphytic, pseudobulbs ovoid, cylindrical, to 1½ in. long; lvs. to 1 ft. long, dark green with silvery-white transverse markings; racemes to 20 in. long; fls. small, pinkish-brown to wine-colored, commonly with white markings, lip short, pink to white, spur globose. Winter–early spring. Brazil, Paraguay.

EULOPHIOPSIS: *GRAPHORKIS.*

EULYCHNIA Phil. *Cactaceae.* Four or 5 spp. of decumbent to treelike, ribbed cacti, native to Chile; ribs 9–15, low; fls. small, open day and night, campanulate, white or pink, tube and ovary scaly, perianth short, scales with axillary wool or bristles; fr. globose, fleshy.

For culture see *Cacti.*

acida Phil. Low or treelike, to 25 ft., ribs 11–13; spines various, brown, becoming gray, radial spines 9–12, to 1 in. long, central spines 1–3, to 8 in. long; fls. rose, becoming white, 2 in. long, scales small, many, but scarcely overlapping, axils with short wool. Differs from *E. spinibarbis* in short wool of ovary and fr.

castanea Phil. Sts. spreading or decumbent, to 3 ft. high and 3 in. thick, ribs 9–11; areoles ⅜ in. apart, spines yellow, becoming gray, radial spines 8–10, unequal, to ¾ in. long, central spine 1, stout, directed outward, to 4 in. long; fls. white or pinkish, to 2 in. long, ovary tubercled, scales small, axils with short brown wool and slender brown bristles, ½ in. long; fr. 2 in. in diam., with persistent perianth.

iquiquensis (K. Schum.) Britt. & Rose. Treelike, to 25 ft., trunk short, ribs 12–15; areoles close-set, finally deciduous, spines at lower areoles 12–15, needle-shaped, mostly to ½ in. long, 1–2 stout, to 5 in. long, spines at flowering areoles bristlelike or hairlike; fls. white, to 3 in. long, axils with long silky hairs; fr. to 2½ in. in diam.

spinibarbis (Otto) Britt. & Rose. Sts. much-branched, to 15 ft. high and 3 in. thick, ribs 12–13; spines about 20, needle-shaped, mostly ¾ in. long, 1 to 6 in. long; fls. white to pinkish, to 2 in. long, axils with long brown wool.

EUONYMUS L. SPINDLE TREE. *Celastraceae.* About 170 spp. of deciduous or evergreen trees or shrubs, rarely creeping or climbing by rootlets, native mostly to Asia, rarely to Eur., N. Amer., Afr., and Australia, brs. usually 4-angled; lvs. opp., rarely alt. or whorled, simple; fls. small, greenish or purplish, in axillary cymes, bisexual or functionally unisexual, sepals, petals, and stamens 4 or 5; fr. a 3–5-valved caps., seeds enclosed in a scarlet to orange aril.

Many species, varieties, and cultivars are grown as ornamentals. Most are hardy north. Ordinary soil and location are satisfactory. Propagated by seeds stratified and sown in spring, hardwood cuttings, the evergreen species under glass, and layers. Cultivars, varieties, and less vigorous kinds are sometimes grafted on vigorous ones.

acuta: *E. Fortunei.*

alata (Thunb.) Siebold. WINGED S. T. Deciduous shrub, to 8 ft., brs. with 2–4 corky wings; lvs. elliptic to obovate, to 2 in. long, sharply and finely serrate; fls. 4-merous; caps. purplish, aril orange. Temp. e. Asia. Cv. 'Compacta'. Compact, dwarf form. Cv. 'Monstrosa' [*E. monstrosa* Hort.]. Very vigorous form. Cvs. 'Gracilis', 'Nana', and 'Striata' are listed.

americana L. STRAWBERRY BUSH, BURSTING-HEART. Erect or straggling shrub, to 8 ft.; lvs. ovate to oblong-lanceolate, to 3 in. long, acuminate, crenate to crenate-serrate; fls. 5-merous; caps. pink, warty, aril scarlet. N.Y., s. to Fla. and Tex.

atropurpurea Jacq. WAHOO, BURNING BUSH. Deciduous shrub or tree, to 25 ft.; lvs. elliptic, to 5 in. long, acuminate, finely serrate, pubescent beneath; fls. 4-merous, purple; caps. crimson, aril scarlet. Ont. to Fla., w. to Mont.

Bungeana Maxim. Deciduous shrub or small tree, to 15 ft.; lvs. elliptic-ovate or elliptic-lanceolate, to 4 in. long, long-acuminate, finely serrate, petioles to 1 in. long; fls. 4-merous, anthers purple; caps. yellowish to pinkish. China. Cv. 'Pendula'. Brs. drooping. Var. **semipersistens** (Rehd.) C. K. Schneid. Semievergreen.

Carrierei: *E. Fortunei* cv.

colorata: a listed name of no botanical standing for *E. Fortunei* cv.

Corlessii: a listed name of no botanical standing for *E. Fortunei* cv.

europaea L. EUROPEAN S.T. Deciduous shrub or small tree, to 20 ft.; lvs. ovate to oblong-lanceolate, to 3 in. long, acuminate, crenate-serrate, glabrous; fls. 4-merous, yellow-green; caps. red to pink, aril orange. Eur., w. Asia. Cvs. are: 'Aldenhamensis', fr. larger, bright pink, on long pedicels; 'Burtonii', compact form, fr. orange-red; 'Fructu Coccineo': 'Haematocarpa'; 'Haematocarpa' [cv. 'Fructu Coccineo'], fr. deep red. Var. **intermedia** Gaudin [*E. intermedia* Hort.]. Lvs. larger, rounder at base; fr. large, bright red.

fimbriata Wallich. Shrub or small tree; lvs. elliptic to oblong-obovate, to 4 in. long, abruptly acuminate, fimbriate-serrulate; fls. 4-merous; caps. orange, covered with long-pointed wings. Himalayas.

Fortunei (Turcz.) Hand.-Mazz. [*E. Fortunei* var. *acuta* Hort.; *E. radicans* Siebold ex Miq. var. *acuta* Rehd.]. Evergreen shrub, trailing or climbing by rootlets, to 20 ft.; lvs. elliptic, elliptic-ovate, or elliptic-obovate, to 2 in. long, crenate-serrate; fls. 4-merous, in long-peduncled cymes; caps. pinkish. Cent. and w. China.

Var. **acuta:** does not differ from typical *E. Fortunei*. Var. **radicans** (Siebold ex Miq.) Rehd. [*E. radicans* Siebold ex Miq.]. Differs from typical *E. Fortunei* in its smaller and less pointed lvs., which are distinctly and sharply serrate, of thicker texture, and have obsolete lat-

eral veins. Cent. Japan, s. Korea. Var. **vegeta** (Rehd.) Rehd. [*E. radicans* Siebold ex Miq. var. *vegeta* Rehd.]. Low, spreading shrub, to 5 ft. high or climbing by rootlets when supported; lvs. orbicular-ovate to elliptic, more coarsely crenate and leathery than in var. *radicans* and with larger infls.; caps. orange; perhaps more common in cult. than var. *radicans*.

Forma **Carrierei**: 'Carrierei'. Forma **colorata**: 'Colorata'. Forma **gracilis**: 'Gracilis'. Forma **kewensis**: 'Minima'. Forma **minima**: 'Minima'.

Cv. 'Albovariegata'. A listed name. Cv. 'Argenteo-marginata': 'Gracilis'. Cv. 'Carrierei' [*E. Fortunei* forma *Carrierei* (Vauv.) Rehd.; *E. Fortunei* cv. 'Erecta'; *E. Carrierei* Vauv.; *E. radicans* var. *Carrierei* Nicholas.]. More shrubby, habit distinctly nonclimbing; lvs. dark green and glossy above. Cv. 'Colorata' [*E. Fortunei* forma *colorata* (Rehd.) Rehd.; *E. colorata* Hort.; *E. radicans* forma *colorata* Rehd.]. Lvs. dark, deep purple above and paler beneath in autumn and winter. Cv. 'Corlessii' [*E. Corlessii* Hort.]. Upright shrub, to 4 or 5 ft. Cv. 'Erecta': 'Carrierei'. Cv. 'Gracilis' [*E. Fortunei* forma *gracilis* (Regel) Rehd.; *E. Fortunei* cv. 'Argenteo-marginata'; *E. Fortunei* cv. 'Roseo-marginata'; *E. Fortunei* cv. 'Variegata'; *E. radicans* var. *argenteomarginata* Hort.; *E. radicans* 'Argenteo-variegata'; *E. radicans* cv. 'Erecta'; *E. radicans* cv. 'Variegata']. Plant climbing; lvs. variously variegated with white, yellow, or pink, or combinations of these. Cv. 'Kewensis': 'Minima'. Cv. 'Minima' [*E. Fortunei* forma *minima* (Simon-Louis) Rehd.; *E. Fortunei* forma *kewensis* (Bean) Rehd.; *E. Fortunei* cv. 'Kewensis'; *E. radicans* Siebold ex Miq. var. *kewensis* Bean; *E. radicans* var. *minima* Simon-Louis; *E. kewensis* Hort. ex Hesse]. Plant sterile, creeping; lvs. only ⅝ in. long or less. Cv. 'Pyramidalis': 'Sarcoxie'. Cv. 'Robusta'. Upright; lvs. larger, light green. Cv. 'Roseo-marginata': 'Gracilis'. Cv. 'Sarcoxie' [*E. Fortunei* cv. 'Pyramidalis'; *E. radicans* cv. 'Pyramidalis']. Upright; lvs. about 1 in. long, glossy. Cv. 'Uncinata'. Lvs. gray-green with pale gray veins, margins serrate. Cv. 'Variegata': 'Gracilis'.

glabra Roxb. [*E. serrulata* Wallich]. Small tree; lvs. elliptic to ovate, to 6½ in. long, crenate-serrate toward tip; fls. 5-merous, white. E. Bengal.

grandiflora Wallich. Semievergreen shrub or small tree, to 25 ft.; lvs. obovate to obovate-oblong, to 4 in. long, crenate; fls. 4-merous, greenish or yellowish, ¾ in. across; caps. pale pink, aril scarlet. N. India to w. China.

Hamiltoniana Wallich [*E. Sieboldiana* Blume]. Shrub, or small, deciduous tree, to 40 ft.; lvs. elliptic, oblong, or ovate-elliptic, finely serrate, petioles to ½ in. long; fls. 4-merous, anthers purple; caps. deeply 4-lobed, aril scarlet or orange. Himalayas to Japan. Var. **Hamiltoniana**. The typical var.; caps. yellow. Himalayas. Var. **lanceifolia** (Loes.) Blakelock [*E. lanceifolia* Loes.]. Lvs. ovate; caps. pink to red, seeds rose-colored, aril orange. China. Var. **Maackii** (Rupr.) Kom. [*E. Maackii* Rupr.]. Lvs. lanceolate-acuminate; caps. pink to red, seeds red, aril orange. N. China to Korea. Var. **nikoensis** (Nakai) Blakelock [*E. nikoensis* Nakai]. Lvs. wider; caps. bright red, seeds green, aril orange. Japan. Var. **yedoensis** (Koehne) Blakelock [*E. yedoensis* Koehne]. Lvs. widely obovate; caps. pink to red, seeds enclosed in an orange aril, sometimes slightly exposed. China and Japan.

intermedia: a listed name of no botanical standing for *E. europaea* var.

japonica Thunb. SPINDLE TREE, JAPANESE S.T. Evergreen shrub or tree, to 10 or 15 ft., or sometimes taller; lvs. narrowly elliptic, ovate, or obovate, obtusely serrate, glossy above; fls. 4-merous, greenish-white; caps. pink, aril orange. Japan. Planted in the South.

Var. **albomarginata**: 'Albomarginata'. Var. **argenteovariegata**: 'Argenteo-variegata'. Var. **aurea**: 'Aurea'. Var. **aureomarginata**: 'Aureomarginata'. Var. **aureovariegata**: 'Aureo-variegata'. Var. **mediopicta**: 'Mediopicta'. Var. **microphylla**: 'Microphylla'. Var. **viridivariegata**: 'Viridi-variegata'.

Forma **albomarginata**: 'Albomarginata'. Forma **argenteovariegata**: 'Argenteo-variegata'. Forma **aureomarginata**: 'Aureo-marginata'. Forma **aureovariegata**: 'Aureo-variegata'. Forma **microphylla**: 'Microphylla'. Forma **viridivariegata**: 'Viridi-variegata'.

Cv. 'Albomarginata' [var. *albomarginata* T. Moore ex Rehd.; forma *albomarginata* (T. Moore ex Rehd.) Rehd.]. Lvs. with narrow white border. Cv. 'Albovariegata' is listed. Cv. 'Argenteo-variegata' [var. *argenteovariegata* Regel; forma *argenteovariegata* (Regel) Rehd.]. Lvs. edged and marked with white. Cv. 'Aurea' [var. *aurea* Carrière]. Lvs. yellow. Cv. 'Aureo-marginata' [var. *aureomarginata* Rehd.; forma *aureomarginata* (Rehd.) Rehd.]. Lvs. edged with yellow. Cv. 'Aureo-variegata' [var. *aureovariegata* Regel; forma *aureovariegata* (Regel) Rehd.]. Lvs. blotched with yellow. Cv. 'Duc d'Anjou': 'Viridi-variegata'; Cv. 'Gigantea' is listed as having large, glossy, deep green lvs., but may be the same as cv. 'Grandifolia'. Cv. 'Grandifolia'. Upright; lvs. large, deep green, glossy. Cv. 'Mediopicta' [var. *mediopicta* Hort.]. Lvs. with large yellow blotch in center. Cv. 'Microphylla' [var. *microphylla* H. Jaeg.; forma *microphylla* (H. Jaeg.) Beissn.; cv. 'Pulchella'; *E. microphylla* Hort. ex Carrière; *E. pulchella* Carrière]. Lvs. small. Cv. **'Picta'**. Dwarf; lvs. dark green. Cv. **'Pulchella'**: 'Microphylla'. Cv. **'Variegata'**. Dense; lvs. small, variegated with silver. Cv. **'Viridi-variegata'** [var. *viridivariegata* Rehd.; forma *viridivariegata* (Rehd.) Rehd.; cv. 'Duc d'Anjou']. Lvs. bright green, variegated with yellow and green.

kewensis: *E. Fortunei* cv. 'Minima'.

kiautschovica Loes. [*E. patens* Rehd.]. Partly evergreen, spreading shrub, to 10 ft.; lvs. ovate to obovate, to 3 in. long, crenate-serrate; fls. 4-merous; caps. pink, aril orange-red. E. and cent. China. Cv. **'Vincifolia'** [*E. vincifolia* Hort.]. Upright, spreading plant; lvs. *Vinca*-like.

Koopmannii: *E. nana.*

lanceifolia: *E. Hamiltoniana* var.

lanceolata Yatabe. Shrub; lvs. elliptic or oblong-lanceolate, to 4 in. long, acuminate, serrate, dark green above, paler beneath, petiole narrowly winged; fls. 5-merous, purple; caps. red. Japan.

latifolia (L.) Mill. Deciduous shrub or small tree, to 20 ft.; lvs. elliptic or obovate-oblong, to 5 in. long, acuminate, finely serrate; fls. 5-merous; caps. rosy-red, usually 5-winged, aril orange. Algeria and se. Eur. to n. Iran.

Maackii: *E. Hamiltoniana* var.

macroptera Rupr. Deciduous shrub or small tree; lvs. ovate to obovate, to 5 in. long, long-acuminate, cuneate, finely serrate; fls. 4-merous; caps. pink, 4-winged, aril deep red. Ne. Asia.

melanantha Franch. & Sav. Deciduous shrub, to 3 ft.; lvs. ovate or elliptic, to 2½ in. long, acuminate; fls. 5-merous, purple; caps. dark red, aril orange-red. Japan.

microphylla: *E. japonica* cv.

monstrosa: a listed name of no botanical standing for *E. alata* cv.

myriantha Hemsl. [*E. Sargentiana* Loes. & Rehd.]. Evergreen shrub or small tree, to 20 ft.; lvs. lanceolate or oblanceolate, to 6 in. long, acuminate, crenate-dentate; fls. 4-merous; caps. orange, 4-angled, aril orange-red. China.

nana Bieb. [*E. nana* var. *Koopmannii* (Lauche) Beissn. and var. *turkestanica* Dieck; *E. Koopmannii* Lauche]. Deciduous, often procumbent shrub, to 3 ft.; lvs. usually whorled, sometimes alt. or opp., linear to linear-oblong, to 1½ in. long, entire, often revolute; fls. 4-merous; caps. pink, aril orange. Caucasus to w. China.

nikoensis: *E. Hamiltoniana* var.

obovata Nutt. RUNNING STRAWBERRY BUSH. Deciduous, procumbent shrub, to 1 ft., brs. rooting; lvs. obovate or oblong, to 2 in. long, crenate-serrate; caps. crimson, warty, aril scarlet. Ont., s. to Tenn. and Mo. Cv. **'Variegata'**. Trailing plant; lvs. green and white.

occidentalis Nutt. ex Torr. WESTERN BURNING BUSH. Shrub or small tree, to 18 ft., branchlets greenish; lvs. ovate or elliptic, to 4 in. long, abruptly acuminate, finely serrate; fls. 5-merous, brownish to purple, to ½ in. across, petals scarious-margined; caps. reddish-purple, aril red. Puget Sound, s. to Calif. and w. Nev. Var. **Parishii** (Trel.) Jeps. [*E. Parishii* Trel.]. Branchlets whitish; lvs. usually somewhat obtuse. S. Calif.

oxyphylla Miq. Deciduous shrub or small tree, to 25 ft.; lvs. ovate to ovate-oblong, to 3½ in. long, serrate; fls. 5-merous, greenish-purple; caps. dark red, aril scarlet. Korea and Japan.

Parishii: *E. occidentalis* var.

patens: *E. kiautschovica.*

pendula Wallich. Small, evergreen tree, brs. drooping; lvs. oblong-lanceolate to ovate, to 5 in. long, acuminate, sharply spiny-serrulate; fls. 5-merous; caps. deeply 4-lobed, aril orange. Himalayas.

phellomana Loes. ex Diels. Deciduous shrub, to 15 ft., branchlets 4-angled, with corky wings; lvs. ovate or obovate, to 4½ in. long, acuminate, crenate-serrate; fls. 4-merous, anthers purple; caps. pink, aril red. N. and w. China.

planipes: *E. sachalinensis.*

pulchella: *E. japonica* cv. 'Microphylla'.

radicans: *E. Fortunei* var. Var. **acuta:** *E. Fortunei.* Var. **argenteomarginata:** *E. Fortunei* cv. 'Gracilis'. Var. **Carrierei:** *E. Fortunei* cv. 'Carrierei'. Var. **kewensis:** *E. Fortunei* cv. 'Minima'. Var. **minima:** *E. Fortunei* cv. 'Minima'. Var. **vegeta:** *E. Fortunei* var.
Forma **colorata:** *E. Fortunei.*
Cvs. **'Alexanderi'**, **'Albomarginata'**, **'Aureo-marginata'**, and **'Longwoodii'** are listed. Cv. **'Argenteo-variegata'**: *E. Fortunei* cv. 'Gracilis'; Cv. **'Erecta'**: *E. Fortunei* cv. Cv. **'Pyramidalis'**: *E. Fortunei* cv. 'Sarcoxie'. Cv. **'Variegata'**: *E. Fortunei* cv. 'Gracilis'.

sachalinensis (Friedr. Schmidt) Maxim. [*E. planipes* Koehne]. Shrub, to 12 ft.; lvs. obovate, to 5 in. long, acuminate, crenate-serrate; fls. 5-merous; caps. 5-angled, carmine-red, aril orange. Ne. Asia.

sanguinea Loes. ex Diels. Shrub or small tree, to 20 ft.; lvs. ovate or obovate, to 4½ in. long, fimbriate-serrulate; fls. 4–5-merous, purplish; caps. red, winged, aril orange. Cent. and w. China.

Sargentiana: *E. myriantha.*

Sargentii: a listed name of no botanical standing, perhaps in error for *E. Sargentiana,* a synonym of *E. myriantha.*

serrulata: *E. glabra.*

Sieboldiana: *E. Hamiltoniana;* however the plant usually cult. as *E. Sieboldiana* is *E. kiautschovica.*

vegeta: a listed name of no botanical standing for *E. Fortunei* var.

verrucosa Scop. Deciduous shrub, to 8 ft., branchlets densely warty; lvs. ovate, to 2½ in. long, acuminate, crenate-serrulate; fls. 4-merous, anthers yellow; caps. yellowish-red, deeply 4-lobed, aril red. S. Eur., w. Asia.

vincifolia: a listed name of no botanical standing for *E. kiautschovica* cv.

yedoensis: *E. Hamiltoniana* var.

EUPATORIUM L. [*Conoclinium* DC.; *Osmia* Schultz-Bip.]. BONESET, THOROUGHWORT. *Compositae* (Eupatorium Tribe). About 500 spp. of mostly per. herbs and shrubs, rarely ann., of almost cosmopolitan distribution, but chiefly of trop. Amer.; lvs. mostly opp., sometimes whorled or alt., usually petioled, filiform to orbicular, entire to dissected; fl. heads usually corymbose, rarely solitary or in panicles, discoid, involucral bracts more or less imbricate in 2 to many rows, receptacle flat to convex or conical, naked; fls. all tubular, bisexual, purple to rose-colored or white, never yellow; achenes usually 5-angled, pappus in a single row, but of many, capillary bristles.

Many tropical bonesets are very satisfactory in the greenhouse, and hardy species in the border or wild garden, flowering in late summer or autumn. Those grown under glass are treated like the florist's stevia (*Piqueria*), being propagated usually by cuttings in winter or early spring. The hardy herbaceous types require the treatment usual for perennials and are increased by division or by seeds.

ageratoides: *E. rugosum.*

altissimum L. Stout, hoary-pubescent per., to 8 ft.; lvs. in 20–30 pairs, lanceolate to elliptic-oblong, to 5 in. long, strongly 3-nerved, glandular-punctate, serrate above middle; heads about 5-fld., about ¼ in. across, corymbose; fls. white. Penn. to Nebr., s. to Ala. and Tex.

cannabinum L. HEMP AGRIMONY. Downy per., to 4 ft.; basal lvs. oblanceolate, st. lvs. 3–5-parted into coarsely toothed elliptic segms. to 4 in. long, uppermost lvs. ovate or lanceolate; heads 5–6-fld., about ¼ in. across, in dense corymbs; fls. reddish-mauve to whitish; achenes blackish. Eur., N. Afr., w. and cent. Asia.

coelestinum L. [*Conoclinium coelestinum* (L.) DC.]. MIST FLOWER, HARDY AGERATUM, BLUE B. Rhizomatous, puberulent per., to 3 ft.; lvs. triangular-ovate, to 3 in. long, coarsely toothed, sparsely hairy to nearly glabrous; heads 35–70-fld., about ½ in. across, in dense corymbs, receptacle conical; fls. bright blue to violet. N.J. to Kans., s. to Fla., Tex., W. Indies.

Fraseri, Frasieri: *E. rugosum.*

herbaceum (A. Gray) Greene [*E. occidentale* var. *arizonicum* A. Gray]. Per., to 1½ ft., sts. minutely scabrous, particularly above; lvs. triangular to ovate-triangular, to about 2¼ in. long including petiole, crenate, glabrous; heads 12–16-fld., to ¼ in. across, in dense corymbs; fls. white; achenes black. Se. Calif. to Utah and New Mex.

hirsutum Hook. & Arn. Per., to 2 ft., sts. hairy; lvs. nearly opp. or upper ones alt., triangular-ovate to ovate, to about 1½ in. long, acuminate, truncate at base, coarsely toothed, scabrous, particularly above; heads few-fld., to about ¼ in. across, in dense corymbs, involucral bracts imbricate, obtuse, with a dense apical tuft of pilose hairs; fls. bluish-purple. S. Brazil, Paraguay, Uruguay, n. Argentina.

hyssopifolium L. Per., to 3½ ft., sts. rough-hairy, particularly above; lvs. in whorls of 4, opp., or sometimes even alt., linear to linear-lanceolate or linear-oblong, to 4 in. long, entire to sparsely toothed, glandular-dotted; heads about 5-fld., about ¼ in. across, in dense corymbs; fls. white. Highly variable. E. U.S.

ianthinum: *L. sordidum.*

Lasseauxii (Carrière) Herter [*Ageratum Lasseauxii* Carrière]. Much-branched per., to 2 ft., sts. glandular-hairy; lvs., or at least the upper ones, alt., oblong-lanceolate, bluntly toothed; heads several-fld., in dense corymbs; fls. rose. Temp. S. Amer.

ligustrinum DC. Shrub, to 15 ft.; lvs. oblong, to 3½ in. long, acuminate, with few serrate teeth, glandular beneath; heads 4–8-fld., about

¼ in. across, involucral bracts linear, gland-dotted; fls. white; pappus often deep rose. Mex. to Cent. Amer.

maculatum L. JOE-PYE WEED, SMOKEWEED. Coarse per., 2–6 ft., sts. speckled or even blotched with purple, rarely glaucous; lvs. in whorls of 3–6, lanceolate, elliptic-lanceolate, or ovate-lanceolate, 2½–8 in. long, sharply serrate; heads 8–20-fld., to about ¼ in. across, in a flat-topped corymb, or the corymb divisions flat-topped, involucral bracts often purplish; fls. purple. Damp areas in calcareous soils, e. N. Amer., mostly e. of Mississippi River.

occidentale Hook. Many-stemmed per., to 2½ ft., from a woody root crown; lvs. mostly alt., triangular to triangular-ovate, usually ovate to truncate at base, serrate-dentate, gland-dotted beneath; heads 9–12-fld., to about ¼ in. across, in a cymose-panicle; fls. red or red-purple to white; achenes black. Wash. and n. Calif. to n. Idaho, and Utah. Var. **arizonicum:** *E. herbaceum.*

odoratum L. [*Osmia odorata* (L.) Schultz-Bip.]. Shrubby per., to 9 ft., sts. pubescent; lvs. ovate to lanceolate, to 6 in. long, dentate; heads 10–20-fld., to about ¼ in. across, in corymbs; fls. blue or pale lilac to white. S. Fla.; trop. Amer.

perfoliatum L. COMMON B., THOROUGHWORT. Rhizomatous, pubescent per., to 5 ft.; lvs. opp., lanceolate, to 8 in. long, acuminate, mostly connate-perfoliate, crenate-serrate, rugose; heads 10–40-fld., to about ¼ in. across, in flat-topped corymbs; fls. white. Moist or wet ground, e. N. Amer.

purpureum L. JOE-PYE WEED, SWEET J.-P.W., GREEN-STEMMED J.-P.w. Per., to 10 ft., sts. green or green with purple nodes, seldom glaucous; lvs. usually in whorls of 3–5, elliptic or lanceolate to ovate, to 1 ft. long, sharply serrate, vanilla-scented when bruised; heads 5–7-fld., in open, rounded, corymbose panicles; fls. pinkish to purplish, rarely white. E. N. Amer.

rugosum Houtt. [*E. ageratoides* L.f.; *E. Fraseri* Hort.; *E. Frasieri* Poir.; *E. urticifolium* Reichard]. WHITE SNAKEROOT, WHITE SANICLE. Glabrous to hairy per., to 5 ft.; lvs. opp., thin, ovate, to 7 in. long including petiole, acuminate, sharply and coarsely serrate, glabrous or hairy, particularly on veins beneath; heads 12–24-fld., to about ¼ in. across, in corymbs; fls. white. E. N. Amer.

sordidum Less. [*E. ianthinum* (E. Morr.) Hemsl.]. Shrub, to 6 ft. or more, sts. densely reddish-tomentose, at least when young; lvs. opp., ovate to oblong-ovate, blade to 4 in. long, coarsely toothed, petiole to 2 in. long; heads 50- to many-fld., to about ½ in. across; fls. violet, fragrant. Mex.

urticifolium: *E. rugosum.*

EUPHORBIA L. [*Chamaesyce* S. F. Gray; *Galarhoeus* Haw.; *Lepadena* Raf.; *Poinsettia* R. C. Grah.; *Tithymalopsis* Klotzsch & Garcke; *Tithymalus* Gaertn., not Mill.]. SPURGE. *Euphorbiaceae.* Over 1,600 spp. of monoecious or dioecious herbs, shrubs, or trees, with milky juice, of very variable habit, of cosmopolitan distribution; sts. often spiny and cactuslike; lvs. alt., opp., or whorled, simple, entire or toothed, petioled or sessile, sometimes rudimentary or absent; fls. in cyathia (see *Euphorbiaceae*), these solitary and terminal or axillary, or clustered in axils of lvs. or spines, or arranged in simple, umbel-like, paniculate, or whorled cymes; involucre of cyathium cup-shaped, with 5 inner lobes alternating with 1–5 (rarely more) glands, the glands separate, rarely united, entire, 2-lipped, or variously lobed, sometimes with petaloid appendages, ovary 3-celled; fr. a 3-valved caps.

The succulent cactuslike species are grown in the greenhouse, and for hedges and specimen plants in the South. For culture see *Succulents.* The hardy herbaceous species are suitable for the border or rock garden and thrive in any good garden soil. Seeds may be sown where the plants are to stand and then thinned to about 10 in.

The poinsettia, *E. pulcherrima,* is propagated by cuttings, usually taken in early summer from young growth of stock that has been kept over winter. These cuttings bloom about Christmas time. They should be kept in pots at a temperature of about 65° F. Where grown in the open, poinsettias may be propagated beginning in Apr. by canes about 3 ft. long stuck in the ground. Other shrubby euphorbias are similarly handled.

The milky juice of most euphorbias may produce a severe dermatitis in susceptible individuals, much like that of poison ivy. Succulent ones should not be planted along edges of stocked pools, since exudates from broken roots may be fatal to the fish. The juice of some species is used for arrow poisons and to stupefy fish.

abyssinica J. F. Gmel. Large tree, brs. leafless, succulent, and spiny, becoming woody, young brs. distinctly 8-angled, spines in groups of 5, to ½ in. long, weak, sharp; cyathia in cymes, crowded at ends of brs., glands 5, elliptic, yellow; caps. green, becoming deep crimson

streaked with white. Taranta Mt. (Ethiopia). Probably not in cult. Some of the plants listed under this name are *E. acrurensis* or *E. neglecta.* Var. **eritrea** is also listed.

acrurensis N. E. Br. Treelike, sts. spiny, woody, succulent, young brs. 7-angled, spines in pairs, to ½ in. long, gray with dark tips; cyathia in cymes, involucre golden-yellow, glands 5–8. Ethiopia. Has been distributed as *E. abyssinica.*

adenoptera Bertol. [*E. multiflora* Willd. ex Klotzsch & Garcke; *Chamaesyce adenoptera* (Bertol.) Small]. Prostrate, pubescent, herbaceous per., sts. several, from a thick root, to 1 ft.; lvs. opp., elliptic to ovate-elliptic, to ¼ in. long, strongly unequal at base; cyathia solitary, axillary, glands 4, with white petal-like appendages, 2 longer than the other 2. S. Fla., W. Indies, Mex.

aggregata A. Berger. Dioecious, succulent, spiny per., brs. forming tufted cushion, to 3 in. high, usually 8–9-angled, spines solitary, to ¼ in. long; lvs. minute, early deciduous; cyathia solitary, at the ends of brs., glands green or dark purplish-red. S. Afr. Var. **alternicolor** (N. E. Br.) A. C. White, R. A. Dyer & Sloane [*E. alternicolor* N. E. Br.]. Brs. variegated, horizontal green bands alternating with whitish-green ones.

alcicornis Bak. Erect, succulent, leafless shrub, main sts. cylindrical, ultimate brs. nearly so; cyathia unisexual, in small terminal heads, glands 5. Madagascar. Not in cult.; material offered under this name is *E. ramipressa.*

alternicolor: *E. aggregata* var.

Ammak G. Schweinf. Succulent, spiny tree, to 30 ft., brs. 4-angled, spines in pairs; lvs. oblanceolate, early deciduous; cyathia in cymes, glands 5, yellow. S. Arabia.

angularis Klotzsch [*E. Lemaireana* Boiss.]. Succulent, spiny, large shrub or tree, to 16 ft., brs. constricted into segms. to 8 in. long and 4½ in. thick, 3-angled, with broad, horny-margined wings, spines in pairs, to ⅜ in. long, gray; lvs. scalelike, rigid, the central part deciduous, leaving 2 rigid hooks between the bases of the spines; cyathia in cymes, glands 5. Trop. Afr.

antiquorum L. Succulent, spiny shrub, to 10 ft.; brs. constricted into segms., to 2 in. thick, erect, ridges somewhat dentate, spines in pairs, to ¼ in. long; lvs. minute, somewhat orbicular to ovate-spatulate. India. Occasionally used as a hedge plant, and confused in the trade with *E. lactea.*

antisyphilitica Zucc. CANDELILLA. Woody, spineless shrub, to 3 ft., brs. many, cylindrical, slender, erect, almost leafless, simple or branched; cyathia in clusters along sts. Desert, ne. Mex. to w. Tex. Sts. and brs. covered with a hard wax collected from wild plants for commercial use.

aphylla Brouss. Succulent, low, freely branching shrub, sts. cylindrical, gray-green, to ¼ in. thick and 30 in. high, forming a mound; lvs. few, linear; cyathia solitary or 2–3 at ends of brs., short-peduncled, glands 4. Canary Is.

atrispina: *E. stellaespina* var.

atropurpurea Brouss. Shrub, 3–6 ft., brs. fleshy, becoming woody; lvs. crowded at ends of brs., oblanceolate, to 4 in. long, glaucous-green; cyathia in umbel-like cymes, involucres surrounded by 2 semicircular, united, purple bracts, glands 4, transversely ovate. Tenerife (Canary Is.).

Barteri N. E. Br. Succulent, leafless, spiny tree, to 20 ft., sts. angled and constricted into segms., spines in pairs, diverging, minute, dark brown; cyathia in cymes, each cyme with 3 cyathia, glands 5, unequally 2-lipped. Nigeria.

Bergeri N. E. Br. Succulent, spineless, much-branched dwarf per. to 9 in., sts. cylindrical, tessellated, frequently curved; lvs. linear-spatulate, to ½ in. long, early deciduous; cyathia solitary, glands 5, green, with 3–7 linear appendages. Origin and distribution uncertain.

biglandulosa Desf. Glabrous per., to 2 ft., sts. many, from a rhizome, simple, erect, spreading to decumbent, forming a clump 3–5 ft. across; lvs. fleshy, in distinct spirals, lanceolate, to 2½ in. long, sometimes prickly pointed, glaucous; cyathia in umbel-like cymes, subtending bracts showy, yellow, glands 2, yellow. Asia Minor.

Bojeri: *E. Milii.*

bubalina Boiss. Succulent, spineless shrub, to 5 ft., brs. cylindrical, to ¾ in. thick, tubercled; lvs. scattered, lanceolate to oblanceolate, to 6 in. long, glabrous, sessile; cyathia in umbel-like cymes, on peduncles to 4¾ in. long, involucral bracts 2, sometimes 3, triangular, to ¾ in. long, green edged with crimson, often entirely crimson, glands 5, entire. S. Afr.

bupleurifolia Jacq. Succulent, spineless, dwarf per., sts. to 9 in. high and 3 in. thick, very rarely branched, tubercled; lvs. in a tuft at end of st., spatulate-lanceolate, to 6 in. long, early deciduous; cyathia solitary, on peduncles to 2 in. long, involucral bracts 2, suborbicular to reniform, green becoming red, glands 5. S. Afr.

Burmannii E. H. Mey. Dioecious, spineless shrub, 12–28 in. high, forming a large clump, young sts. succulent, becoming woody; lvs. opp., minute, early deciduous; cythia in cymes or racemes, glands 5, entire, greenish-yellow. S. Afr.

canariensis L. Succulent, spiny shrub or tree, to 20 ft. (to 50 ft. where native), brs. many, ascending, 4–6-angled, spines in pairs, to ³⁄₁₆ in. long, thin, black; lvs. minute, early deciduous; glands 5–7. Canary Is. Reported to be very poisonous.

candella: a listed name of no botanical standing for a succulent form of *Euphorbia*.

caput-Commelinii: a listed name of no botanical standing, probably referable to *E. caput-Medusae*.

caput-Medusae L. [*E. Commelinii* DC.]. MEDUSA'S-HEAD. Succulent, spineless, dwarf per. to 1 ft., brs. many, from a partly buried, globose st., forming a large clump to 30 in. across, tessellated, to 2 in. thick; lvs. minute, early deciduous; cythia solitary, on short peduncles, glands 5, with 3–6 linear, white appendages. S. Afr. Vars. **major** Ait. and **minor** Ait. are listed.

Carlsonii: a listed name of no botanical standing.

cereiformis L. [*E. Leviana* Croiz.]. MILK-BARREL. Dioecious, succulent, spiny shrub, st. to 3 ft. high, 2 in. thick, 9–15-angled, ridges tubercled, spines solitary, to ³⁄₈ in. long, reddish-brown, becoming gray with age; lvs. minute, early deciduous; cythia solitary, subtending bracts purple, glands 5, blackish-purple. Nativity unknown, perhaps S. Afr.

Characias L. Herbaceous, woody-based per., to 3 ft., sts. to ³⁄₈ in. thick, pithy; lvs. in close spirals, oblong-lanceolate, to 4 in. long, tapering gradually to a short petiole; cythia in axillary cymes and umbellate at ends of brs., involucral bracts 2, semicircular, glands 4, crescent-shaped, purple. S. Eur.

clandestina Jacq. Succulent, spineless per., to 2 ft., main st. usually unbranched, cylindrical, with spirally arranged tubercles; lvs. in a crown at end of st., somewhat fleshy, linear to linear-oblanceolate, to 1½ in. long; cythia sessile, solitary in axils of tubercles, subtending bracts 5–7, outer ones purple, inner ones green, glands 5–7, yellow. S. Afr.

clavarioides Boiss. Succulent, spineless, dwarf per., to 3 in., main st. obconic, thick and fleshy, mostly underground, brs. crowded at apex, forming a dense cushion, young brs. cylindrical, tesselately tubercled, dull green to purplish, with thickened rounded apex; lvs. minute, early deciduous; cythia bisexual, sessile, solitary at ends of brs., glands 5, greenish-yellow, ovary glabrous. S. Afr. Var. **truncata** (N. E. Br.) A. C. White, R. A. Dyer, & Sloane [*E. truncata* N. E. Br.]. Brs. simple, truncate at apex; cythia unisexual; ovary hairy.

coerulescens Haw. Succulent, spiny, rhizomatous, leafless shrub, to 5 ft., brs. many, constricted into oblong segms., 4–6-angled, bluish-glaucous, spines in pairs, diverging, stout, to ½ in. long, dark brown; cymes of 3 cythia, glands 5, bright yellow. S. Afr. Frequently confused with *E. Ledienii*.

Commelinii: *E. caput-medusae*.

Cooperi N. E. Br. Succulent, spiny tree, to 15 or 20 ft.; brs. constricted into segms., 5–6-angled, spines in pairs, to ¼ in. long, gray with blackish tips; lvs. scalelike, early deciduous; cymes in groups of 3, sessile, cythia 1–3, glands 5, yellow. S. Afr.

corollata L. [*Tithymalopsis corollata* (L.) Small]. FLOWERING S., TRAMP'S S., WILD HIPPO. Slender, herbaceous per., to 3 ft.; lvs. elliptic, ovate, oblong to linear, 1 or 2 in. long; cythia in umbel-like cymes, glands 5, with showy, white, petal-like appendages. Ont. to Fla. and Tex.

cotinifolia L. [*E. Scotana* (Schlechtend.) Boiss.]. Shrub or small tree, 9–18 ft.; lvs. usually 3 at a node, rounded-ovate to orbicular, 2–5 ½ in. long, long-petioled; cythia in dense terminal and axillary umbels, glands 5, transversely oblong, with semiorbicular, crenate appendages. Mex. to n. S. Amer.

cyathophora J. Murr. [*Poinsettia cyathophora* (J. Murr.) Klotzsch & Garcke.]. FIRE-ON-THE-MOUNTAIN, PAINTED LEAF, MEXICAN FIRE PLANT, FIDDLER'S S. Ann., 2–3 ft.; lvs. variable, ovate to linear, or sometimes fiddle-shaped, entire or toothed, glossy green, upper lvs. and bracts red or red-based; cythia in terminal clusters, glands 1 or 2, broad, more or less 2-lipped, opening between lips narrowly oblong, E. U.S., Mex.; often naturalized. Sometimes grown in fl. gardens. Usually cult. under the misapplied name, *E. heterophylla*.

Cyparissias L. [*Galarhoeus Cyparissias* (L.) Small; *Tithymalus Cyparissias* (L.) Scop.]. CYPRESS S. Herbaceous, glabrous per., to 1 ft., brs. many, from creeping rootstocks; lvs. many, linear, to 1½ in. long, entire; cythia in umbel-like cymes, subtending bracts ovate to triangular, yellowish when young, becoming purplish to reddish, glands crescent-shaped with 2 short horns, yellow. Eur.; naturalized in e. U.S.

on banks, along fence rows, roadsides, and cemeteries. A good ground cover, but may become a weed.

Deightonii Croiz. Succulent, spiny shrub or tree, to 15 ft., brs. 3–6-angled, ridges winged, spines in pairs, to ¾ in. long; lvs. scalelike, early deciduous; cymes 1–3 in a group, to ¾ in. long, glands 5. W. Trop. Afr.

echinus Hook.f. & Coss. Succulent, spiny, much-branched shrub, to 6 ft. or more, sts. 6-angled, lf. bases united into ribs, the ridges with continuous, horny gray margin, spines to ½ in. long, red or gray; cythia inconspicuous. Morocco.

edulis Lour. Succulent, spiny shrub, to 15 ft., brs. 3–4-angled, spines in pairs; lvs. oblong-cuneate, to 5½ in. long, petiole to ³⁄₈ in. long; cymes subsessile, glands pink to pale brown. Indochina, s. China. Widely cult. in tropics of both hemispheres.

encocephala: a listed name of no botanical standing, used erroneously for *E. leucocephala*.

enopla Boiss. Dioecious, succulent, spiny shrub, to 3 ft., sts. erect, leafless, to nearly 2 in. thick, 6–7-angled, grooves distinctly marked with irregular line along center, spines on ridges, solitary, to 1 in. long, purplish-brown to gray; cythia solitary, peduncled, involucres dark red, glands 5, entire. S. Afr.

epithymoides L. [*E. polychroma* A. Kern.]. Herbaceous per., to 1 ft., forming an attractive, hemispherical clump; lvs. oblong, dark green; cythia in umbel-like cymes, involucral bracts yellow, glands 2–4, entire. E. Eur. Showy in the border.

Esula L. LEAFY S., WOLF'S-MILK. Glabrous, herbaceous per., to 3 ft., sts. usually unbranched except at infl., from rhizomes bearing many buds; lvs. linear to linear-oblong, to ¼ in. wide, pale green; cythia in umbel-like cymes, involucral bracts reniform, sessile, entire, yellow-green, glands strongly 2-horned. Eur.; naturalized in ne. U.S., spreading westward to N. Dak., Colo., Wash., and n. Calif. A troublesome weed, particularly on well-drained soils. Not known in the trade, but seed is offered by botanic gardens.

fasciculata Thunb. Succulent, dwarf per., st. solitary, to 1 ft. high and 3 in. thick, cylindrical, tubercled, spines (here the remains of persistent peduncles) on tubercles, to 2 in. long, rigid; lvs. minute, early deciduous; cythia in umbel-like cymes toward apex of st., peduncled, from cavity near apex of tubercles, glands 4–5, nearly entire. S. Afr.

ferox Marloth. Dioecious, succulent, dwarf per., to 6 in. high, branched underground, forming clumps to 2 ft. across, brs. to 2 in. thick, 9–12-angled, spines along ridges, many, solitary, to 1¼ in. long, woody, persistent, brown to gray; lvs. minute, early deciduous; cythia solitary, peduncled, at apex of each br., involucre purple with small white dots, glands 5, green. S. Afr.

fimbriata Scop. Dioecious, succulent per., to 3 ft., spiny or sometimes with few or no spines, main st. erect and branched, or reduced, branching from the base, brs. few to many, erect to procumbent, to ½ in. thick, 7–15-angled, ridges with tubercles, spines (when present) solitary, between the tubercles, usually in whorls; lvs. minute, early deciduous; cythia solitary, peduncled, from axils of tubercles, glands 5, yellowish-green, green, or purple. S. Afr.

Franckiana A. Berger. Succulent, spiny shrub, to 3 ft., brs. constricted into segms., 3–4-angled, tubercled, 1 in. thick, gray-green, spines in pairs on tubercles along horny ridges; lvs. minute, early deciduous; cythia in cymes, borne on ridges between spines, glands 5. S. Afr.?

fruticosa Forssk. Succulent, spiny shrub, to 1 ft., branched from the base, brs. 10–13-angled, cylindrical to somewhat club-shaped, 2–3 in. thick, gray-green, spines in pairs, horizontally spreading, of unequal length, to about ¾ in. long, brownish at first, becoming black or gray; lvs. minute; cythia in cymes at ends of brs., involucre yellow, glands orbicular, with fringed appendages. S. Arabia.

fulgens Karw. ex Klotzsch [*E. jacquiniiflora* Hook.]. SCARLET-PLUME. Shrub, to 4 ft., brs. slender, drooping; lvs. lanceolate, 2–4 in. long, long-petioled; cythia in axillary cymes, glands 5, with scarlet, petal-like appendages. Mex. Grown under glass in the North.

geniculata Ort. [*Poinsettia geniculata* (Ort.) Klotzsch & Garcke.]. Ann. herb, to 3 ft.; lvs. 1½–3½ in. long, elliptic to ovate, upper lvs. sometimes fiddle-shaped; cymes crowded at ends of brs., involucre with 1 gland. Fla. Keys, W. Indies, Rio Grande region, Tex., Mex.

globosa (Haw.) Sims. Succulent, spineless, dwarf per., to 3 in., branching from the base, brs. forming a cushion, constricted into globose or club-shaped segms., about 1 in. thick; lvs. minute, early deciduous; cythia solitary, or 2 to several in cymes, long- or short-peduncled, glands 5, divided into 3–4 linear segms., with minute, white-margined pits. S. Afr.

Gorgonis A. Berger. Succulent, spineless, dwarf per., main st. globose, to 4 in. thick, brs. in a crown, radiating, cylindrical, 1–2 in. long, tubercled; lvs. minute, early deciduous; cythia solitary in axils of tubercles, glands 5, dark crimson to brownish-crimson, sometimes bright red. S. Afr. Lvs. and brs. often become elongated and less fleshy in cult, as more moisture is available.

grandicornis Goeb. COW'S-HORN. Succulent, spiny, much-branched shrub, to 6 ft., brs. constricted into segms., 3-angled, to 6 in. thick, ridges winglike with horny, grayish margins, spines in pairs, to 2½ in. long, grayish; lvs. scalelike; cymes between the spines, cyathia 3 in a cyme, the central one sessile, the outer 2 peduncled, glands 5, yellow. S. Afr.

grandidens Haw. BIG-TOOTH E. Succulent, spiny tree, to 30 or 40 ft., trunk 3 ft. in diam., primary brs. whorled, 3-angled, deeply toothed, ultimate brs. clustered at ends of brs., spines in pairs, divergent, small, gray; lvs. minute, early deciduous; cymes of 3 cyathia, solitary, glands 5, yellow-green. S. Afr.

Grantii D. Oliver. Robust shrub, 5–10 ft.; lvs. somewhat leathery, strap-shaped or linear-lanceolate, to 1 ft. long and 1 in. wide, sessile; cyathia in umbels to 15 in. across, glands 4. Trop. Afr.

griseola Pax. Succulent, spiny shrub, forming clumps to 2½ ft. high, sts. 4–6-angled, with sinuate-tubercled ridges, green, with lighter areas in grooves, spines in pairs, to ⅜ in. long, gray; lvs. minute, early deciduous; cymes solitary, with 1–3 cyathia, glands 5, yellow or greenish-yellow; caps. long-pedicelled. S. Afr.

hamata (Haw.) Sweet. Dioecious, succulent, spineless shrub, to 18 in., main st. elongated, thick, brs. many, often forming dense cushion, obscurely 3-angled, with recurved tubercles, gray in age; lvs. to ⅝ in. long, early deciduous; cyathia sessile, solitary at ends of brs., glands 5, red or yellow. S. Afr.

havanensis: see *E. lactea.*

heptagona L. [*E. Morinii* A. Berger]. MILK-BARREL. Dioecious, succulent, spiny shrub, 2–3 ft., branching from the base, brs. 5–10-angled, to 1¾ in. thick, spines (here modified sterile peduncles) solitary, to 1 in. long, brown; lvs. minute, early deciduous; cyathia solitary, at ends of brs., peduncled, glands 5, somewhat fleshy, entire, green. S. Afr.

Hermentiana: *E. trigona.*

heterochroma Pax. Succulent, spiny shrub, to 6 ft.; brs. slightly constricted at intervals, 4- or 5-angled, ridges more or less sinuate-tubercled, spines in pairs, to ¼ in. long, gray, sometimes obsolete; lvs. scalelike; cymes solitary, with 3 cyathia, glands 5, greenish-yellow; caps. on long recurved pedicels. S. Afr.

heterophylla L. [*Poinsettia heterophylla* (L.) Klotzsch & Garcke]. MEXICAN FIRE PLANT, JAPANESE POINSETTIA, ANNUAL P., MOLE PLANT, PAINTLEAF, PAINTED LEAF. Ann., 2–3 ft.; lvs. linear to ovate or obovate, or even fiddle-shaped, dull green, upper lvs. and bracts green or often purple-spotted, never red; cyathia in terminal clusters, glands 1 or 2, nearly stalked, funnelform, central opening circular. From Ariz. s. throughout trop. Amer.; naturalized in La. and Tex. Since this name has been universally misapplied to *E. cyathophora,* material cult. as *E. heterophylla* is probably exclusively *E. cyathophora.*

Hislopii: *E. Milii* var.

horrida Boiss. AFRICAN MILK-BARREL. Dioecious, succulent, spiny shrub, to 3 ft. or more, branching from the base, forming irregular clumps, brs. erect, cylindrical, 4–6 in. thick, many-angled (average about 14), ridges winglike, spines (here modified peduncles) many, on the ridges, solitary or 2–5 in groups, rigid, to 1½ in. long; lvs. minute, early deciduous; cyathia solitary, peduncled, glands 5, entire, green. S. Afr.

hottentota Marloth. Succulent, spiny shrub, to 6 ft., branching from the base, primary brs. many, erect, to 1¾ in. thick, 5-angled, ridges low, ultimate brs. 4-angled, spines in pairs, to $^{3}/_{16}$ in. long; cymes short-peduncled, with 3 cyathia, glands 5, crescent-shaped. S. Afr. and S.-W. Afr.

inermis Mill. [*E. viperina* A. Berger]. Resembling *E. caput-Medusae* but brs. ½ in. thick, and involucre with woolly, white hairs. S. Afr.

ingens E. H. Mey. [*E. similis* A. Berger]. Succulent, spiny tree, to 30 ft., branching into an obconic crown, brs. erect, leafless, flowering brs. constricted, 4-angled, the ridges winglike, spines absent or, if present, in pairs and minute; cymes peduncled, glands 5, green. Transvaal (S. Afr.). Var. **monstrosa** is listed.

ipecacuanhae L. [*Tithymalopsis ipecacuanhae* (L.) Small]. IPECAC S., WILD IPECAC, CAROLINA I. Herbaceous per., to 1 ft., brs. many, from a thick root, forking; lvs. elliptic, obovate, oblong, or linear, to 2¼ in. long, green to purple, entire; cyathia solitary, in the forks of brs., on long, slender peduncles, glands 5, with a narrow, yellow, green or purple appendage. Conn. to Fla. Used medicinally.

jacquiniiflora: *E. fulgens.*

jansenvillensis Nel. Dioecious, succulent, spineless, rhizomatous, dwarf per., to 1 ft., main st. underground, brs. erect, elongated, glaucous-green, 5-angled, ridges tubercled; lvs. at ends of brs., minute, early deciduous; cyathia solitary, on the ridges, toward the ends of brs., peduncled, glands 5, triangular, yellow-green. S. Afr.

Keysii: a listed name of no botanical standing; material offered under this name is *E. fulgens.*

lactea Haw. [*E. lactea* cv. 'Havanensis'; *E. havanensis* Hort., not Willd. ex Boiss.]. MOTTLED S., CANDELABRA CACTUS, FALSE C., HAT-RACK C., DRAGON-BONES. Succulent, spiny shrub or tree, of candelabra form, to 15 ft., brs. 3–4-angled, the sides with white band down the center, spines in pairs, on the ridges; lvs. between the spines, minute, suborbicular, early deciduous. Not known to flower. E. Indies. Cv. **'Cristata'.** CRESTED E., FRILLED-FAN, ELKHORN. Brs. crested. Planted under glass or in warm regions as an ornamental or for hedges. *E. antiquorum* is confused with this sp.

Lathyris L. [*Galarhoeus Lathyris* (L.) Haw.; *Tithymalus Lathyris* (L.) J. Hill]. CAPER S., MYRTLE S., MOLE PLANT. Ann. or bien., to 3 ft., sts. stout and unbranched; st. lvs. 4-ranked, oblong-linear to lanceolate, 2–6 in. long, often cordate, sessile; infl. lvs. ovate to ovate-lanceolate; cyathia in umbels, glands 4, crescent-shaped, 2-horned. Eur.; naturalized in N. Amer.

Ledienii A. Berger. Succulent, spiny shrub, 4–6 ft., branching from the base, brs. erect, to about 2 in. thick, constricted into segms., 4–7-angled, ridges tubercled, spines in pairs from the tubercles, diverging, to ¼ in. long, dark brown; lvs. minute, early deciduous; cymes usually in 3's, each with 3 cyathia, involucre campanulate, bright yellow, glands 5, oblong, entire. S. Afr. Var. **Dregei** N. E. Br. Differs only in having involucre obconic or funnelform. S. Afr. *E. coerulescens* is frequently confused with this sp.

Lemaireana: *E. angularis.*

leucocephala Lotsy. PASCUITA. Slender shrub to small tree, 5–12 ft.; lvs. mostly whorled, variable in shape, oblong to obovate, elliptic to oblong-lanceolate, to 3 in. long, long-petioled; cyathia in umbels, involucral bracts spatulate, white, glands 5, with white, petaloid appendages. S. Mex. to El Salvador. Extensively cult. in Jamaica.

Leviana: *E. cereiformis.*

lignosa Marloth. Dwarf, rigid per., to 1½ ft., main st. top-shaped, mostly underground, primary brs. many, forking repeatedly, forming a dense cushion to 3 ft. across, woody at maturity, spinelike; lvs. only on young branchlets, lanceolate, to ½ in. long; cymes terminal or axillary, long-peduncled, glands 5, funnelform, fringed. Namaqualand desert region and S.-W. Afr.

Livingstonia: a listed name of no botanical standing.

lophogona Lam. Erect shrub, to 1½ ft., succulent, but woody at base, brs. 5-angled, ridges spinescent, fringed; lvs. in tufts at ends of brs., ovate-spatulate to oblanceolate, 5–8 in. long, long-attenuate to a short petiole; cymes peduncled, involucral bracts 2, suborbicular, $^{5}/_{16}$ in. across, petaloid, white or pink, glands 5, yellow. Madagascar.

loricata Lam. Succulent, spiny shrub, to 3 ft., brs. cylindrical, tubercles more or less spirally arranged, spines (here modified peduncles) many, solitary, rigid, to 2 in. long, brown or gray; lvs. clustered toward ends of brs., well-developed, linear-lanceolate, to 3 in. long, obtuse; cyathia solitary, peduncled, involucral bracts broadly ovate, glands 5, entire, green. S. Afr.

Lyttoniana: *E. pseudocactus* var.

Lyttonii: used in error for *E. Lyttoniana.*

mammillaris L. CORKSCREW. Dioecious, succulent, spiny, dwarf per., to 8 in. or more, branching freely from a reduced main st., brs. clustered, cylindrical, to 2¼ in. thick, 7–17-angled, ridges tubercled, spines (here modified peduncles) in vertical rows, to ½ in. long, gray; lvs. scalelike; cyathia solitary, glands 5, purple to yellowish-green. S. Afr.

marginata Pursh [*E. variegata* Sims; *Lepadena marginata* (Pursh) Nieuwl.]. SNOW-ON-THE-MOUNTAIN, GHOSTWEED. Erect ann., to 2 ft., occasionally to 3 or 4 ft.; lvs. ovate to oblong, 1–3 in. long, upper lvs. white-margined; cyathia usually in a 3-rayed umbel, glands 4, with broad, white, petal-like appendages. Minn. to Colo. and Tex. Popular for fl. gardens. The latex is very corrosive to the skin, and may cause severe burns or dermatitis.

Marlothii: *E. Monteiroi.*

mauritanica L. Succulent, spineless shrub, to 4 ft., much-branched, forming a clump, brs. cylindrical, to ¼ in. thick; lvs. to 1 in. long, only on new growth, early deciduous; cyathia in terminal, sessile cymes or umbels, glands 5–8, entire, yellow. S. Afr., S.-W. Afr.

meloformis Ait. MELON S. Dioecious, succulent, globose, unbranched, dwarf per., st. to 4 in. high and 6 in. thick, 8-angled, usually spineless, except in some male plants, spines (here persistent peduncles) on the ridges; lvs. minute, early deciduous; cymes at end of st., glands 5, entire, green. S. Afr. Cv. **'Prolifera'.** Profusely branching in habit.

Milii Desmoul. [*E. Bojeri* Hook.]. CROWN-OF-THORNS, CHRIST PLANT, CHRIST THORN. Woody, spiny, climbing shrub, sts. to 4 ft. long, 3/16–3/8 in. thick, spines many, relatively slender, to 3/8 in. long and less than 1/8 in. wide at base; lvs. mostly on young growth, obovate, to 2½ in. long, wedge-shaped at base, truncate at apex, mucronate; cymes long-peduncled, cyathia subtended by 2 bright red or yellow, ovate bracts. Madagascar. Grown under glass. Var. **Hislopii** (N. E. Br.) Ursch & Leandri [*E. Hislopii* N. E. Br.]. To 6 ft., sts. 1¼–2⅜ in. thick, 8–10-angled; spines ½–1 in. long, with broad-conical bases; lvs. ovate-lanceolate, to ¾ in. long; bracts pink or red. Probably Madagascar. Var. **splendens** (Bojer ex Hook.) Ursch & Leandri [*E. splendens* Bojer ex Hook.]. To 6 ft., sts. 3/8 in. thick; spines numerous, ¾ in. long and 3/16 in. wide at base; lvs. oblong-ovate, to 2 in. long; cyathia in forked cymes, peduncles sticky, bracts brilliant red. Madagascar.

Monteiroi Hook.f. [*E. Marlothii* Pax]. Erect, succulent, usually 2–3 ft. in cult. (occasionally 10–13 ft. in Afr.), main st. to 2 in. thick, tubercled, fl. brs. erect and spreading, slender, not tubercled; lvs. spatulate, to 6 in. long, glaucous-green; cymes umbel-like on many-bracted peduncles 6–12 in. long, involucre chocolate-brown to dark reddish brown, glands 5, yellow-tipped, divided into 3–6 linear appendages. Trop. Afr., s. Afr.

Morinii: *E. heptagona.*

Muirii N. E. Br. Succulent, spineless, dwarf per., to 1½ ft., main st. underground, brs. 1 or few, slender, often with a crown of small branchlets at or near apex, tubercles many, large, usually tipped with persistent white lf. bases; lvs. fleshy, linear, to ½ in. long, erect, cyathia solitary, at ends of brs., glands 5, yellowish-green, with 4–6 linear appendages. S. Afr.

multiflora: *E. adenoptera.*

Myrsinites L. Herbaceous bien. or per., sts. to 10 in. long, ascending to erect, from a prostrate or decumbent woody base; lvs. fleshy, in close spirals, obovate to obovate-oblong, to 5/8 in. long, abruptly short-mucronate, sessile, lvs. of infl. reniform; cyathia in 5–10-rayed umbels, yellow, glands 4, 2-horned. Eur.

neglecta N. E. Br. Tree, to 20 ft. or more, brs. succulent, becoming woody with age, constricted into segms., usually 5–8-angled, ridges winglike, with conspicuous, swollen veins, spines in pairs, diverging, to 1½ in. long, gray; lvs. cuneately oblanceolate, to 3½ in. long, sessile. Described from cult. material; nativity uncertain. Often listed as *E. abyssinica.*

neriifolia L. HEDGE E., OLEANDER-LEAVED E. Succulent, spiny tree, 18–24 ft., brs. in whorls or slightly spiralled, 5-angled, bright green becoming gray; spines in pairs, short, black; lvs. leathery, fleshy, spatulate, 3–5 in. long; cymes in upper lf. axils, glands 5, yellow-green. E. India. Cv. 'Cristata'. Brs. crested. Cv. 'Variegata' is also listed.

nubica N. E. Br. Succulent, spineless shrub, to 6 ft., brs. cylindrical, slender, glabrous; lvs. early deciduous, lf. bases persistent; cyathia in terminal 3–7-rayed umbels, green, glands 4. Ne. Afr. Some of the material offered in the trade as *E. Schimperi* belongs here.

obesa Hook.f. LIVING-BASEBALL, GINGHAM GOLF-BALL. Dioecious, succulent, spineless, dwarf per., main st. unbranched, globose to cylindrical, to 8 in. high and 3½ in. thick, gray-green with transverse bands of fine purple lines, usually 8-(rarely 7–10-)angled, ridges minutely tubercled; lvs. minute, early deciduous; cymes or cyathia solitary, glands 5, red. S. Afr.

officinarum L. Succulent, spiny shrub, to 3 ft., sts. erect; brs. whorled, 9–13-(average 11-)angled, spines in pairs, spreading and often deflexed, unequal, to 5/8 in. long, whitish-gray; lvs. minute, early deciduous; involucral glands elliptic, yellow. N. Afr.

ornithopus Jacq. Succulent, spineless, dwarf per., 2–3 in. high, main st. obconical, with many rhizomes, brs. erect, cylindrical to club-shaped, constricted into long or short segms., tubercled; lvs. minute, early deciduous; cyathia solitary or in cymes, peduncles to 4 in. long, glands 4, rarely 5, with linear appendages bearing white-margined pits. S. Afr.

pendula Link. Name of doubtful application; material offered under this name is *Sarcostemma viminale.*

pentagona Haw. Dioecious or rarely monoecious, succulent, spiny, freely branching shrub, to 10 ft., brs. often whorled, acutely 5–6-angled, green to gray, with lighter line down each groove, spines (here modified peduncles) scattered, solitary, to ½ in. long, deciduous; lvs. minute, early deciduous; cyathia solitary or in cymes at ends of brs., peduncled, involucres purple, glands 5, entire. S. Afr.

Pfersdorfii: a listed name of no botanical standing for *E. submammillaris* cv.

platyphylla L. Erect ann., to about 30 in.; st. lvs. oblanceolate-spatulate to oblong-lanceolate, cordate, pubescent beneath, lvs. of infl. ovate; cyathia in 5-rayed umbels, glands 4, elliptic. Eur.; naturalized in se. Canada and Vt. to Mo.

polyacantha Boiss. FISHBONE. Succulent, spiny, leafless shrub, to 5 ft., brs. to 1½ in. thick, with slight constrictions, 4–5-angled, ridges crenately toothed, spines in pairs, diverging, to ¼ in. long, often up-curved, dark gray; cyathia in cymes between the spines, glands 5, entire. Ethiopia.

polycephala Marloth. Succulent, spineless, dwarf per., main st. compact, brs. many, closely packed, forming a cushion 1–2½ ft. in diam.; lvs. minute, early deciduous; cyathia solitary or in cymes, sessile or short-peduncled, glands 4, rarely 5, with linear appendages, green above, white-tomentose beneath. S. Afr.

polychroma: *E. epithymoides.*

polygona Haw. Dioecious, succulent, spiny or rarely spineless shrub, forming clumps rarely to 5 ft. high, young brs. 7-angled, becoming 12–20-angled in age, spines 1–3, rarely 5, in a group, to 3/8 in. long; lvs. minute, early deciduous; cyathia 1–3 in a group, near ends of older brs., glands 5, dark purple. S. Afr.

polygonifolia L. [*Chamaesyce polygonifolia* (L.) Small]. SEASIDE S. Glabrous ann., sts. prostrate to erect, to 10 in. long; lvs. opp., oblong-linear to oblong-lanceolate, to 5/8 in. long, strongly unequal; cyathia solitary in upper nodes, inconspicuous, glands 4, elliptic, appendages minute or absent. R.I. to Fla., sandy shores of Great Lakes.

pseudocactus A. Berger. Succulent, leafless, spiny shrub, to 6 ft., main st. reduced, brs. many, forming a large clump, constricted into segms., to 2 in. thick, gray-green, and often with yellow V-shaped markings, 4–5-angled, ridges with irregular tubercles, spines in pairs, on tubercles, ½ in. long, brown becoming gray; cymes in groups of 1–3, glands 5, oblong, entire, yellow. S. Afr. Var. **Lyttoniana** (Dexter) Frick [*E. Lyttoniana* Dexter]. A garden form, not known in the wild, which lacks spines.

pseudoglobosa Marloth. Dioecious, succulent, spineless, dwarf per., main st. underground, brs. several, compact, tubercled, 5–8-angled, dull green; lvs. minute, early deciduous; cyathia solitary, but clustered at ends of brs., glands 5, entire, green. S. Afr.

pteroneura A. Berger. Succulent, spineless, erect shrub, st. to 20 in., 5/16 in. thick, constricted at brs., 5–6-angled, ridges formed by decurrent lf. bases; lvs. to 1½ in. long, early deciduous; cymes umbel-like, at ends of sts., involucral bracts 2, subreniform, greenish-yellow, glands 4, elliptic. Mex.

pulcherrima Willd. ex Klotzsch [*Poinsettia pulcherrima* (Willd. ex Klotzsch) R. C. Grah.]. POINSETTIA, CHRISTMAS STAR, CHRISTMAS FLOWER, PAINTED LEAF, LOBSTER PLANT, MEXICAN FLAMELEAF. Winter-flowering shrub, to 10 ft.; lvs. ovate-elliptic to lanceolate, sometimes fiddle-shaped, 4–7 in. long, entire, toothed, or lobed, long-petioled; cymes umbel-like, terminal, cyathia subtended by many showy, vermilion bracts, involucre with 1 yellow gland. Cent. Amer., trop. Mex. Many cvs. have been developed, with bracts larger, and white, pink, or various shades of red.

pulvinata Marloth. Dioecious, succulent, spiny per., to 1 ft., brs. many, forming a compact cushion, 7–10-angled, ridges crenate-tubercled, with broad grooves between them, spines (here modified peduncles) solitary, scattered on ridges, red becoming brown or gray; lvs. minute, early deciduous; cyathia solitary but clustered at ends of brs., glands 5 or 6, entire, varying from purple or brownish-red to yellowish-green. S. Afr.

ramipressa Croiz. [*E. alcicornis* Hort. ex A. Berger, not Bak.]. Succulent, spiny shrub, or treelike when old, to 10 ft.; sts. usually 5-angled, fleshy, with elevated riblike lf. bases, brs. cylindrical, becoming 5-angled, then flat, spines short, slender, dark colored; bracts subtending cyathia not conspicuously colored. Nativity uncertain. Sometimes offered as *A. alcicornis.*

resinifera A. Berger. Succulent, spiny shrub, to 2 ft. (to 6 ft. in the wild), freely branching from the base, forming a dense cushion, brs. 4-angled, ridges shallowly notched, spines in pairs, to ¼ in. long, brown; lvs. minute, brownish; cymes with 3 cyathia, at ends of brs., glands 5. Morocco.

Royleana Boiss. Succulent, spiny tree, to 16 ft., brs. to 2¾ in. thick, 5-angled, ridges faintly undulate, spines in pairs, directed downward, to ¼ in. long, conical; cymes solitary, cyathia to 5/8 in. broad, yellow, glands 5. India.

Schimperi K. Presl. A confused name; material so listed may be *E. nubica* or *E. scoparia.*

scoparia N. E. Br. Succulent, spineless tree, 15–25 ft., ultimate brs. cylindrical, clustered at ends of larger brs.; lvs. present only on very young brs., linear, to 5/8 in. long, early deciduous; cyathia in dense, sessile clusters at ends of brs., glands 5, elliptic, entire. Ethiopia.

Scotana: *E. cotinifolia.*

sikkimensis Boiss. Herbaceous per., sts. 3–4 ft., from a woody base, branched in upper part; lvs. linear-oblong to linear-lanceolate, 2½–4 in. long, tapering to a short petiole; cyathia in terminal, several-rayed umbels, involucral bracts yellow, glands oblong. Sikkim Himalayas.

similis: *E. ingens.*

spinosa L. Glabrous, bushy subshrub, to 8 in., old sts. leafless, simulating long spines; st. lvs. lanceolate or linear-lanceolate, to ⅜ in. long, lvs. of infl. ovate or oblong; cyathia in 1–3-rayed umbels, each ray with 1 cyathium, glands 4, entire. S. Eur.

splendens: *E. Milii* var.

squarrosa Haw. Succulent, spiny, dwarf per., main st. mostly underground, tuberous, ovoid, to 4 in. thick, brs. many, trailing to erect, to 6 in. long, more or less twisted, 2–5-angled, with few tubercles, spines in pairs, from apex of tubercles, to ¼ in. long, reddish-green when young, grayish-brown when old; lvs. minute, early deciduous; cymes solitary, with 3 cyathia, glands 5, bright green, entire. S. Afr.

stellaespina Haw. Dioecious, succulent, spiny shrub, to 2 ft., sts. erect, branching from the base, in clumps, 10–16-angled, grooves to ¼ in. deep, green becoming brown in age, ridges toothed, spines (here modified peduncles) solitary, between the tubercles, to ½ in. long, starlike with a whorl of 3–5 brs. at tip, brown; lvs. minute, early deciduous; cyathia solitary, glands 5. S. Afr. Var. **atrispina** (N. E. Br.) A. C. White, R. A. Dyer, & Sloane [*E. atrispina* N. E. Br.]. Spines with 4–6 brs., on a very short stalk, or sessile. S. Afr.

stellata Willd. Succulent, leafless, spiny, dwarf per., main st. tuberous, to 6 in. thick, brs. several, prostrate, to 6 in. long, flattened, 2-angled, concave on upper side, tubercled, green with purple and gray mottling, spines in pairs, from apex of tubercles, minute, brown or gray; cymes solitary at ends of brs., glands 5, dull yellow. S. Afr.

submammillaris (A. Berger) A. Berger. Dioecious, succulent, spiny, much-branched per., to 1 ft., often forming a clump, brs. 7–10-angled, ridges toothed, spines (here modified peduncles) solitary, to ¾ in. long, pale brown; lvs. minute, early deciduous; cyathia solitary, peduncled, at ends of brs., involucre purple, glands 5, entire. Nativity uncertain, perhaps S. Afr. Cv. **'Pfersdorfii'.** Much more branched, brs. with few angles. Cv. **'Variegata'** is listed.

Susannae Marloth. Dioecious, succulent, spineless per., main st. mostly underground, brs. globose-cylindrical, to 3 in. long, 12–16-angled, ridges tubercled; lvs. only on young growth, minute, early deciduous; cyathia solitary or 2 in a cyme, sessile or on short peduncles, glands 5, entire, greenish-yellow. S. Afr.

Taphagoni: a listed name of no botanical standing.

tenuirama G. Schweinf. ex A. Berger. Succulent, spiny, irregularly branching, erect shrub, sts. 4–5-angled, brs. 3-angled, long, with slight

constrictions, 1 in. wide, with almost flat sides, bright green, spines in pairs, spreading, to ¼ in. long, slender, gray; cymes with 3 cyathia, many, along the ridges of the branchlets, glands entire. S. Arabia.

Tirucalli L. MILKBUSH, INDIAN TREE S., RUBBER E., FINGER TREE, PENCIL T. Dioecious, succulent, spineless tree, to 30 ft., brs. often clustered irregularly in a crown; lvs. minute, early deciduous; cyathia in clusters at ends of ultimate branchlets, sessile, glands 5, entire. Trop. and S. Afr. Grown in the open in s. Fla., under glass in the North.

tithymaloides: *Pedilanthus tithymaloides.*

triangularis Desf. Succulent, spiny tree, to 60 ft., sts. 1 or more, brs. whorled, in a rounded crown at ends of sts., constricted into segms., green, 3–5-angled, ridges winglike, with or without tubercles, spines in pairs, diverging, to ¼ in. long, brown turning gray; lvs. minute, early deciduous; cymes in pairs, peduncled, with 3 cyathia, glands 5, yellow. S. Afr.

tridentata Lam. Succulent, spiny, dwarf, rhizomatous per., brs. to 6 in. long, cylindrical or tapering, tessellate with hexagonal tubercles; lvs. minute, early deciduous; cyathia 3 or 4, at ends of brs., peduncled, glands 5, with 3 or 4 white, linear appendages. S. Afr.

trigona Haw. [*E. Hermentiana* Lam.]. ABYSSINIAN E., AFRICAN MILK TREE. Succulent, spiny shrub or small tree, brs. erect, straight, constricted into 6–8 in. segms., usually 3–4-angled, dark green, with wavy white band down each groove becoming obscure in age, ridges sinuately toothed, spines in pairs on ridges, to ⅜ in. long, reddish-brown; lvs. spatulate, to ¼ in. long. Trop. S.-W. Afr.

truncata: *E. clavarioides* var.

tubiglans Marloth ex R. A. Dyer. Dioecious, succulent, spineless, dwarf per., main st. tuberous, obconical, underground, brs. in clusters of 2–5, to 6 in. long, ¾ in. thick, 5-angled, ridges obscurely tubercled, lf. bases persistent; lvs. minute, early deciduous; cyathia solitary at ends of brs., peduncled, glands 5, reddish, with margins inrolled, forming a tube. S. Afr.

valida N. E. Br. Dioecious, succulent, dwarf per., to 1 ft., spineless, but often with persistent peduncles, main st. rarely branched, subglobose when young, becoming cylindrical in age, cylindrical at the base, to 5 in. thick, 8-angled above, dull to purplish-green with irregular transverse bands of light green; lvs. minute, early deciduous; cyathia in peduncled cymes, glands 5, olive-green. S. Afr.

variegata: *E. marginata.*

viperina: *E. inermis.*

virosa Willd. Succulent, spiny shrub, forming clumps to 6–8 ft., main st. almost wholly buried; brs. irregularly constricted, 5–8-angled,

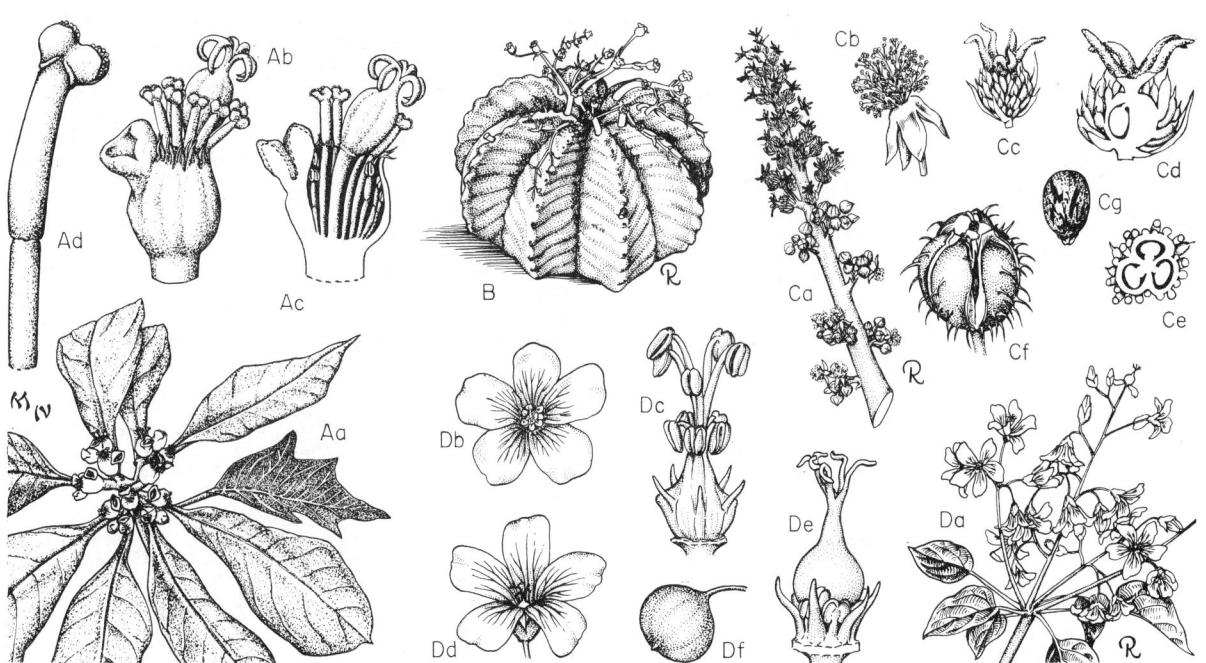

EUPHORBIACEAE. **A,** *Euphorbia pulcherrima:* **Aa,** colored bracts and inflorescence, × ½; **Ab,** a single cyathium, × 2½; **Ac,** cyathium, vertical section, × 2½; **Ad,** male flower, × 10. **B,** *Euphorbia valida:* flowering plant, × ½. **C.** *Ricinus communis:* **Ca,** inflorescence, × ¼; **Cb,** male flower, × 1; **Cc,** female flower, × 1; **Cd,** female flower, vertical section, × 2; **Ce,** ovary, cross section, × 2; **Cf,** capsule, × 1; **Cg,** seed, × ½. **D,** *Aleurites Fordii:* **Da,** flowering branch, × ¼; **Db,** male flower, × ½; **Dc,** stamens in male flower, × 2; **Dd,** female flower, × ½; **De,** pistil and staminodes in female flower, × 2; **Df,** fruit, × ¼.

ridges sinuate-tubercled, spines in pairs, to ⅜ in. long, glossy and dark red becoming dull and gray; lvs. minute, deciduous; cymes solitary, with 3 vertically disposed cyathia, glands 5, crescent-shaped. S. Afr.

Winkleri Pax. Succulent, spiny tree, 80–90 ft., crown small, regularly branched, brs. 3-angled, ridges winglike, much-compressed, sinuate, spines in pairs, minute, sometimes absent, dark brown; lvs. oblong to elliptic, 1–1½ in. long, entire; cymes in clusters of 2 or 3, sessile, glands 5, yellow. Tanzania.

Wulfenii Hoppe. Similar to *E. Characias* in habit, but glands thicker, yellow, and 2-horned. Dalmatia (Yugoslavia).

xylophylloides Brongn. ex Lem. Succulent, spineless, much-branched or treelike shrub, to 6 ft., sts. flat or 2-angled, ½ in. wide, ridges slightly crenate; lvs. minute, early deciduous. Madagascar.

EUPHORBIACEAE Juss. SPURGE FAMILY. Dicot.; about 283 genera and 7,300 spp. of monoecious or dioecious herbs, shrubs, trees, and even spiny, cactuslike succulents, often with milky juice, almost cosmopolitan in distribution, but the center of distribution in the tropics extending into the temp. zone; fls. usually in infls., sometimes solitary, unisexual, stamens 1 to several, separate or their filaments variously united, ovary superior, usually 3-celled; fr. usually a caps., splitting into 3, 1-seeded sections. *Euphorbia* and closely related genera have a compact infl., the cyathium, often simulating a complete fl., composed of 1 female fl. consisting of a single pistil, and of several male fls., each consisting of a single stamen on a jointed pedicel, all enclosed in an involucre, which is variously shaped and adorned with glands and appendages. The cyathia are usually bisexual, rarely unisexual, and may be solitary or in groups. In some genera, as *Euphorbia*, showy parts are colored bracts. The cult. genera are: *Acalypha, Aleurites, Andrachne, Antidesma, Bischofia, Breynia, Cleistanthus, Cnidoscolus, Codiaeum, Croton, Elaephorbia, Eremocarpus, Euphorbia, Garcia, Givotia, Hevea, Homalanthus, Hura, Jatropha, Joannesia, Macaranga, Manihot, Monadenium, Pedilanthus, Phyllanthus, Putranjiva, Ricinus, Sapium, Securinega, Stillingia, Synadenium,* and *Tetracoccus.*

In addition to many ornamentals, this family includes many plants of economic importance, which yield rubber, edible roots, and fruits, and have valuable medicinal and poisonous properties.

EUPHORIA Comm. ex Juss. *Sapindaceae.* About 15 spp. of polygamous trees, native to trop. Asia; lvs. alt., pinnate; fls. small, in axillary or terminal panicles, regular, calyx 5-parted, imbricate, petals 5, spatulate to lanceolate, stamens usually 8; fr. drupaceous, covered with flattened tubercles.

Longans are grown for the edible fruit. They withstand slight frost, but should be protected from the sun in summer; they thrive in protected places in Zone 10. Propagated by seeds, layers, and grafting.

Longan (Lour.) Steud. [*Nephelium Longan* Lour.]. LONGAN, LUN-GAN. Evergreen tree, to 40 ft.; lvs. to 1 ft. long, lfts. 4–10, elliptic to lanceolate, mostly 6½ in. long or longer, glossy; fls. yellowish-white; fr. yellow-brown, 1 in. in diam., with white, juicy, edible flesh. India. Cult. in Malay Arch. and s. China.

malaiensis (Griff.) Radlk. [*Nephelium malaiense* Griff.]. Evergreen tree, to 70 ft.; lvs. to 1½ ft. long, lfts. 6–10, elliptic or oblong, to 11 in. long, glossy; fls. fragrant; fr. to ¾ in. in diam. Malay Pen. and Indonesia.

EUPRITCHARDIA: *PRITCHARDIA.*

EUPTELEA Siebold & Zucc. *Eupteleaceae.* Three spp. of Asiatic trees and shrubs with characteristics of the family; flowering in early spring before or with the lvs.

These plants thrive in loamy well-drained soil in rather moist locations. The flowers are attractive because of the dark red color of the stamens. Propagated by seeds, and by grafting on their own roots. Hardy in Zone 7.

Franchetii: *E. pleiosperma.*

japonica: a listed name of no botanical standing.

pleiosperma Hook.f. & T. Thoms. [*E. Franchetii* Van Tiegh.]. Differs from *E. polyandra* in having lf. margins more regularly sinuate-dentate, with largest teeth to ³⁄₁₆ in. long, and lvs. more cuneate at base. China.

polyandra Siebold & Zucc. JAPANESE E. To 35 ft., slender; lvs. orbicular-ovate, to 5 in. long, broadly cuneate to truncate basally, coarsely and unequally dentate, with largest teeth to ⅝ in. long, pale beneath, red when unfolding, becoming red and yellow in autumn; fr. to ⅝ in. long. Japan.

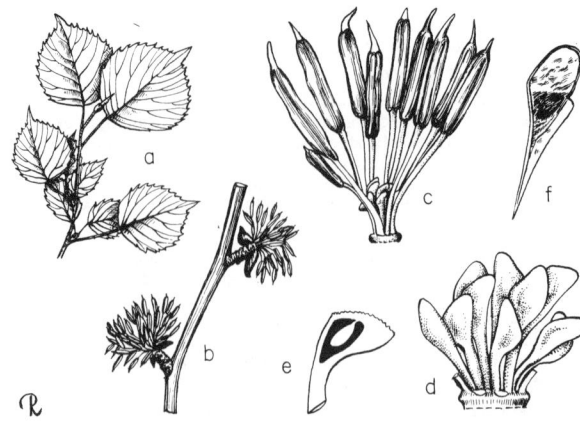

EUPTELEACEAE. *Euptelea polyandra:* **a,** leafy branch, × ⅙; **b,** part of flowering branch, × ½; **c,** flower, × 3; **d,** pistils, × 9; **e,** ovary, vertical section, × 10; **f,** fruit, × 2. (From Bailey, *Manual of Cultivated Plants,* ed. 2.)

EUPTELEACEAE Wilh. EUPTELEA FAMILY. Dicot.; 1 genus of hardy, deciduous, Asiatic trees and shrubs; lvs. alt., petioled, serrate; fls. in axillary clusters, bisexual, perianth lacking, stamens many, basifixed, pistils 8–18, separate, stipitate, 1-celled, with mostly 1–3 ovules attached parietally; fr. a samara. *Euptelea* is cult. as an ornamental.

EURYA Thunb. *Theaceae.* Perhaps 70 spp. of mostly dioecious, evergreen shrubs and small trees of trop. and subtrop. Asia and Pacific Is.; lvs. alt., mostly 2-ranked, simple, crenate-serrate, short-petioled; fls. small, axillary, solitary or in clusters, peduncles usually less than ³⁄₁₆ in. long, sepals 5, petals 5, connate about ⅓ their length, stamens 5–20 or more, in 1 series, anthers glabrous, basifixed, ovary superior, 2–5-celled; fr. indehiscent, berrylike, many-seeded.

Suitable for greenhouse culture or outside in moist half-shady sites in Zone 8. Propagated by cuttings. For culture see *Camellia.*

chinensis R. Br. Distinguished from *E. japonica* in having lvs. obovate, more finely toothed, usually smaller, and young branchlets and terminal buds pubescent; and from *E. emarginata* in having lvs. bluntly acuminate at apex, marginally flat, and sharply serrate. S. China, Taiwan.

emarginata (Thunb.) Mak. Shrub or small tree, young branchlets red-brown-tomentose; lvs. obovate to oblong-obovate, apically rounded and emarginate, cuneate, usually revolute, crenate-serrate, thick-leathery. Temp. e. Asia. Var. **microphylla** Mak. Lvs. obovate-orbicular, very small, to ¼(–⅜) in. long. Japan.

japonica Thunb. [*E. latifolia* Hort. ex C. Koch]. Small tree or shrub, completely glabrous in all parts; lvs. elliptic to oblanceolate, to 2½ in. long and 1 in. wide, narrowed toward each end, apically emarginate, undulate-serrate, never sharply toothed; fls. greenish-white, with strong unpleasant odor; fr. globose, ³⁄₁₆ in. across. Temp. e. Asia. Leafy brs. used in Shinto ceremonies in Japan. Not to be confused with *Cleyera japonica.* Var. **variegata:** *Cleyera japonica* cv. 'Tricolor'.

latifolia: *E. japonica.*

ochnacea: *Cleyera japonica.*

EURYALE Salisb. *Nymphaeaceae.* One Asian sp. of very prickly, aquatic herbs, suggestive of *Victoria,* but having lvs. marginally flat, and the fls. much smaller, with all stamens fertile; fls. day-blooming, with many petals and stamens; fr. a small, globose, many-seeded berry.

Cultivation as for *Victoria,* at 70–75° F. Hardy north to Philadelphia and St. Louis.

ferox Salisb. GORGON, PRICKLY WATER LILY. Lvs. 1–4 ft. across, circular, dark green and reticulate-rugose above, purple and spiny-ribbed beneath; sepals green and very prickly outside, reddish inside, petals shorter and purple; fr. 2–4 in. across. Japan, China to n. India.

EURYOPS Cass. *Compositae* (Senecio Tribe). About 50 spp. of evergreen shrubs, mostly in S. Afr.; lvs. alt., crowded, entire to pinnately lobed; fl. heads radiate, solitary, terminal, or axillary on erect peduncles, involucral bracts in 1 row, united at base and forming a cup; disc and ray fls. yellow; achenes somewhat compressed, wingless, and beakless, pappus of several rows of rough bristles, soon deciduous.

Suitable for planting in mild climates.

acraeus M. D. Henders. To 2 ft., branching to form a rounded shrub, brs. densely leafy at ends; lvs. oblong, to ¾ in. long, leathery, silvery-gray, becoming reflexed with age, margins revolute; heads about 1 in. across; ray fls. 11. S. Afr. Has been confused in hort. with *E. Evansii.*

Athanasiae Less. CLANWILLIAM DAISY. To 4 ft., resinous, glabrous; lvs. to 6 in. long, pinnately lobed, lobes in 4–7 pairs, filiform; heads to 3½ in. across, terminal on peduncles to 12 in. long; ray fls. many, to 1½ in. long. S. Afr.

Evansii Schlechter. Similar to *E. acraeus*, but taller and with longer lvs. S. Afr. Not known to be in cult.; material grown as *E. Evansii* is *E. acraeus.*

pectinatus Cass. GRAY-LEAVED E. To 3 ft., all parts soft-whitish-pubescent; lvs. to 3 in. long, deeply pinnatifid, lobes in usually 8–10 pairs, linear, obtuse; heads to 1½ in. across, terminal, peduncles to 6 in. long; ray fls. 12–14. S. Afr.

spathaceus DC. WAX-LEAF E. To 3 ft., glabrous, older brs. bare and scarred, younger brs. densely leafy; lvs. linear-spatulate or filiform, to 3 in. long, entire; peduncles to 3 in. long; ray fls. 6–8. S. Afr.

EUSCAPHIS Siebold & Zucc. *Staphyleaceae.* One sp., a small deciduous tree, native to temp. e. Asia; lvs. opp., odd-pinnate; fls. yellowish-green, in terminal panicles, bisexual, sepals, petals, and stamens 5; fr. of 1–3 reddish, leathery pods.

Occasionally planted; not fully hardy in the North. Propagated by seeds and cuttings of green wood under glass.

japonica (Thunb.) Kanitz. To 10 ft.; lfts. 7–11, lanceolate to lanceolate-ovate, to 3 in. long, serrulate, glabrous; panicles to 5 in. long; fr. ½ in. long. Zone 7.

EUSTEPHIA Cav. *Amaryllidaceae.* A few spp. of bulbous herbs, native to Peru and Argentina; fls. pedicelled, in umbels, scape compressed, perianth tube short, campanulate, lobes spreading, filaments separate, winged and toothed basally.

yuyuensis: a listed name of no botanical standing and of uncertain application.

EUSTOMA Salisb. *Gentianaceae.* Three spp. of glaucous herbs, from sw. U.S. to Fla., s. to Mex., W. Indies, n. S. Amer., with leafy sts.; lvs. opp.; fls. white or blue, in panicles or solitary, calyx keeled, corolla 5- or 6-lobed; fr. an ellipsoid, many-seeded caps.

Andrewsii: *E. grandiflorum.*

grandiflorum (Raf.) Shinn. [*E. Andrewsii* A. Nels.; *E. Russellianum* (Hook.) G. Don ex Sweet; *Lisianthus Russellianus* Hook.]. PRAIRIE GENTIAN. Ann. or bien., sts. erect, to 3 ft.; lvs. ovate to oblong, to 3 in. long; corolla pale purple, about 2 in. across and 2 in. long, erect or flaring. Colo. and Nebr., s. to Tex. and n. Mex. A showy plant, but not often cult.; sometimes treated as a bien., the well-established seedlings being carried over winter in a frame.

Russellianum: *E. grandiflorum.*

EUSTREPHUS R. Br. *Liliaceae.* One sp., a climbing, woody-based, per. herb, native to Australia; lvs. alt., glabrous; fls. white, light blue, pale pink, or purple, clustered in axils of upper lvs., perianth segms. 6, separate, the 3 inner fringed, the 3 outer hood-shaped at apex, stamens 6, filaments united into a tube; fr. a 3-celled, globular berry, seeds black.

Of easy culture under glass, or in the open in warm climates. Propagated by division or seeds.

latifolius R. Br. Much-branched, to several ft.; lvs. linear to ovate-lanceolate, to 4 in. long; fls. ¼ in. long; fr. orange, about ½ in. across. New S. Wales.

EUSTYLIS Engelm. & A. Gray. *Iridaceae.* Four spp. of per. herbs, native to s. U.S., Mex. and Guatemala; bulb tunicate, brown; lvs. linear, erect or nearly so, pleated; fls. 1 to several, spathe valves 2, with white, scarious margins; perianth regular, outer segms. spreading, broadly obovate, inner segms. slightly shorter and narrower, with rather narrow, pinched claws, stamens not united, appressed to style, anthers sessile, with broad thick connectives, style funnelform, style brs. 3, bifid; fr. an oblong caps.

Propagated by seeds or offsets.

purpurea (Herb.) Engelm. & A. Gray [*Nemastylis purpurea* Herb.]. PROPELLER FLOWER, PINEWOODS LILY, PURPLE PLEATLEAF. Bulb ovoid, about 1 in. long, sts. 6–18 in.; lvs. shorter than st.; fls. about 1½ in. across, outer perianth segms. red-purple to violet, basally flecked purple over brownish-yellow, inner segms. similar but darker, with bright yellow median blotch bordered with white; caps. about 1 in. long. Sandy pine woods, La. and Tex. Fls. in early summer; in cult. usually sends up another floral st. in Sept., producing about a dozen fls. over a few weeks.

EUTERPE Mart. *Palmae.* Perhaps 20 spp. of solitary or cespitose, unarmed, monoecious palms in trop. Amer.; lvs. pinnate, sheaths forming a prominent crownshaft, petiole short, pinnae 1-ribbed, acute, spreading or pendulous; infl. infrafoliar, short-peduncled, bracts 2, the upper enclosed by or little exceeding the lower, rachillae many, simple, with fls. in triads (2 male and 1 female) near the base and above these with paired or solitary male fls.; male fls. with sepals imbricate, petals 3, valvate, stamens 6, filaments not inflexed at the apex, pistillode small, 3-cleft, female fls. with sepals and petals imbricate, staminodes small, pistil 1-celled, 1-ovuled; fr. globose, with lateral stigmatic residue, seed with homogeneous or ruminate endosperm, embryo basal.

The genus is the major source of palm cabbage (terminal bud) eaten fresh or processed by commercial canneries as hearts of palm, principally in Brazil. Euterpes are attractive ornamental palms but are tender and thrive only in the tropics. For culture see *Palms.*

edulis Mart. ASSAI PALM. St. solitary, to 100 ft., 6 in. in diam. or more; crownshaft olive-green, to 5 ft. long, blade with 70–80 pinnae on each side; infl. whitish; male fls. with pale sepals and dark purple petals; fr. dark purple, seed with marginal ruminations. Brazil.

macrospadix: *E. precatoria.*

oleracea Mart. ASSAI PALM. Sts. usually cespitose, to 60 ft., 5 in. in diam.; crownshaft red-green, to 3 ft. long or more, petiole short, blade to 9 ft. long or more, pinnae spreading to pendulous, to 1⅝ in. wide, 50–80 on each side; infl. white; male fls. with white sepals and purple-red petals; fr. purple-black, to ⁹⁄₁₆ in. in diam., seed with ruminate endosperm. Brazil to Venezuela, Guyana.

panamensis: *E. precatoria.*

precatoria Mart. [*E. macrospadix* Ørst.; *E. panamensis* Burret]. St. solitary, to 70 ft. or more, 6 in. in diam., gray-brown; lvs. horizontal, crownshaft green, 4 ft. long or more, petiole short, blade to 9 ft. long, pinnae pendulous, narrow, to 1 in. wide, 60–75 on each side; infl. white; male fls. white with pinkish cast; mature fr. purplish, to ⅜ in. in diam., seed with homogeneous endosperm. Brit. Honduras to Peru.

EUTOCA: *PHACELIA.*

EVERGREENS. To many gardeners in cool-temperate climates this term connotes the evergreen conifers, mostly narrow-leaved evergreen plants, including the familiar pines, spruces, firs, junipers, or their counterparts from other lands. The term is far more inclusive however, for evergreens are properly any plants not seasonally deciduous—that is, that hold a full complement of leaves the year round. Most evergreens have broad rather than needlelike leaves, though there are evergreen conifers with needlelike leaves. *Buxus, Camellia, Eucalyptus, Hedera, Nerium, Rhododendron,* and the Palmae are familiar garden examples of broad-leaved evergreens. In wet tropical forests and many warm-temperate lands, most native plants are broad-leaved evergreens and few are conifers. Evergreens, both narrow-leaved and broad-leaved, are common plants in our gardens. For a sampling of recommended narrow-leaved evergreens for gardens see *Conifers.* Some of the most widely planted ornamental broad-leaved evergreens may be found within the genera *Arctostaphylos, Berberis, Buxus, Camellia, Daphne, Eleagnus, Euonymus, Hedera, Ilex, Kalmia, Leucothoe, Magnolia, Mahonia, Osmanthus, Paxistima, Pachysandra, Pieris, Pyracantha, Rhododendron, Skimmia, Viburnum,* and *Vinca;* to these, among others, may be added for the West Coast and especially the Pacific Northwest the genera *Arbutus, Carpenteria, Ceanothus, Choisya, Cistus, Cotoneaster, Eucryphia, Garrya, Gaultheria, Pernettya, Photinia, Sarcococca, Stranvaesia, Umbellularia,* and *Vaccinium;* additional genera popular in the Southeast or South are *Abelia, Aucuba, Bambusa, Callistemon, Ficus, Gardenia, Gelsemium, Jasminum, Michelia, Nandina, Nerium, Phyllostachys, Pseudosasa, Raphiolepis, Roystonea,* and *Sabal;* in the Mediterranean climate of southern California, *Acacia, Brahea, Callistemon, Chamaerops, Cinnamomum, Citrus, Dombeya, Eriobotrya, Escallonia, Eucalyptus, Eugenia, Ficus, Geijera, Hakea, Laurus, Melaleuca, Myrtus, Nandina, Nerium, Olea, Phoenix, Pittosporum, Schinus, Trachycarpus,* and *Washingtonia* are also popular.

EVERLASTINGS. Plants used for winter bouquets and dried arrangements, comprising various kinds that retain their form and color when dried, are called everlastings; usually the flowers have chaffy or papery parts.

Most of the common everlastings are members of the Compositae. The name strawflower is used for several kinds with everlasting heads (inflorescences), but usually for *Helichrysum bracteatum* cv. 'Monstrosum', with its brightly colored petaloid involucral bracts of red, orange, yellow, pink, purple, or white. The common immortelle is *Xeranthemum annuum,* an annual with persistent papery involucral bracts in a color range from white through pink to purple. Several valuable everlastings are found in the genus *Helipterum: H. Humboldtianum* has especially bright yellow heads; *H. roseum,* still sold under the former generic name *Acroclinium,* and *H. Manglesii* (formerly *Rhodanthe Manglesii*) have showy involucral bracts of white, pink, or red. The winged everlasting (*Ammobium alatum* cv. 'Grandiflora') is a perennial from Australia with bright yellow heads surrounded by snow-white involucral bracts.

Many common plants like goldenrod *(Solidago)* and yarrow *(Achillea)* have species with showy cultivars. The common white yarrow or milfoil *(Achillea Millefolium)* is an abundant naturalized species often dried for bouquets, but cultivars in shades of pink or red are easily grown in the garden. Cultivars of the yellow *A. filipendulina* and the white *A. ptarmicifolia* are popular. In many parts of North America, the native pearly everlasting *Anaphalis margaritacea)* may be gathered in open fields in summer, but cultivation makes it easier to time the harvest. The inflorescences are usually gathered in bud, but the flower heads are showier at a later stage with the seeds removed.

In the Plumbaginaceae, several species of *Limonium* are widely grown for their colorful papery calyces and are offered in seed catalogs as *Statice* or sea lavender. The foliage of the Amaranthaceae may be more colorful than the flowers, and leaves of some species are often dried for decoration. Globe amaranth *(Gomphrena globosa)* has cloverlike heads retaining colors of pink, rose, or purple, though one species, *G. Haageana,* turns a soft orange color when dried. *Celosia* is available in several colors and forms—plumed, feathered, or crested.

All of these everlastings are easily grown and dried. Inflorescences are cut before they are fully expanded and hung upside down in an airy, shady place. Flower heads like those of *Helichrysum* are best cut from the stems and wired before they harden.

Numerous ornamental grasses can also be used in dried arrangements. Popular annuals include cloud grass *(Agrostis nebulosa),* quaking grass *(Briza maxima),* and hare's-tail grass *(Lagurus ovatus).* Flowering stalks of wheat *(Triticum),* timothy *(Phleum),* oats *(Avena),* and other cereal or forage grasses are prized for decoration. The long silky plumes of pampas grass *(Cortaderia Selloana),* commonly cultivated in Zones 9 and 10, and the drooping panicles of native sea oats *(Uniola paniculata),* gathered or grown in the sandy coastal areas of the southeastern United States, are especially popular with flower arrangers. Grasses are collected at various stages of maturity to obtain the desired effect of color and

form. Some, like pampas grass, should be collected in bud to prevent shattering when dried.

With the development of new methods of flower preservation, almost any garden flower can qualify as an everlasting, but this requires fine sand, silica gel, or a similar dessicant and special techniques for retaining form and color.

A wide variety of other plant materials, including leaves, fruits, pods, woody spathes, cones, and nuts, may be gathered or grown to use with everlastings. Milkweed pods *(Asclepias),* the orange inflated fruits of the Chinese lantern plant *(Physalis Alkekengi),* and the papery septa of the pods of honesty *(Lunaria annua)* have long been popular in winter bouquets. More unusual material from plants cultivated or native in warmer parts of the South and West may be obtained from *Acacia, Agave, Eucalyptus, Ipomoea tuberosa* (wood roses), various Palmae, *Protea,* and *Yucca.* Many of these are available from commercial sources.

EVODIA J. R. Forst. & G. Forst. *Rutaceae.* Fifty or more spp. of deciduous or evergreen shrubs or trees, native to Madagascar, and from e. Asia to Australia and Polynesia; lvs. opp., simple or compound, glandular-dotted; fls. small, in axillary or terminal panicles or corymbs, unisexual, sepals, petals, and stamens 4 or 5; fr. splitting into 4 or 5, 2-valved, 1–2-seeded sections.

Some species are hardy in the North, and others are greenhouse plants. Propagated by seeds, cuttings of half-ripened wood, and root cuttings.

Danielii (J. Benn.) Hemsl. Small tree; lfts. 7–11, ovate to oblong-ovate, to 4 in. long; fls. white, in terminal corymbs to 6 in. across; fr. reddish. N. China and Korea.

fraxinifolia (D. Don) Hook.f. Tree, to 50 ft.; lfts. 5–11, oblong-lanceolate, to 9 in. long, smelling of caraway when bruised; fls. greenish-yellow, in rounded panicles; fr. red, ½ in. in diam. Himalayas.

Henryi Dode. Tree, to 30 ft.; lfts. 5–9, oblong-ovate to lanceolate-ovate, to 4 in. long, crenulate, slightly glaucous beneath; fls. pinkish, in corymbs to 3 in. across; fr. red-brown, ¼ in. across, sections with a beak. Cent. China.

hupehensis Dode. Tree, to 60 ft.; lfts. 5–9, ovate, to 5 in. long; fls. white, in corymbs to 6 in. across; fr. red-brown, sections with a hooked beak. Cent. China.

lepta (K. Spreng.) Merrill. Small tree, to 15 ft.; lfts. 3, ovate, to 5 in. long, acuminate; fls. white, in panicles about as long as petioles. Se. Asia.

meliifolia (Hance) Benth. Tree; lfts. mostly 5–7, oblong-lanceolate to ovate, 2–3 in. long, glossy above, glaucous beneath; fls. white, in cymose panicles 5–8 in. long. Se. Asia and Philippine Is.

EVOLVULUS L. *Convolvulaceae.* About 100 spp. of prostrate or erect herbs or sometimes shrubs, mostly in trop. Amer., from s. U.S., s. to Argentina, 2 spp. in trop. areas of the Old World; lvs. alt., small; fls. axillary, small, blue, rose, purple, or white, corolla 5-angled or -lobed; fr. a 1–4-seeded caps.

Nuttallianus Roem. & Schult. Per., woody in older parts, to 12 in., densely covered with spreading, villous, brownish or grayish hairs; lvs. linear-oblong, lanceolate, or oblong, to ¾ in. long; fls. solitary along sts., purple or blue. Mont., s. to Ariz., New Mex., Tex., e. to Ark. and Tenn.

EXACUM L. *Gentianaceae.* About 20–30 spp. of herbs of the Old World; lvs. opp., simple, entire, sessile; fls. blue or white, solitary or in forking cymes, calyx and corolla 4–5-lobed, corolla lobes spreading, stamens 4 or 5, filaments short, borne in throat of corolla; fr. a 2-valved caps.

Grown under glass or outdoors in warm regions. Propagated by seeds.

affine Balf.f. GERMAN VIOLET, PERSIAN V. Ann. or bien., to 2 ft., much-branched from base; lvs. ovate, to 1½ in. long, petioled; fls. bluish, to ½ in. across, anthers golden-yellow. Socotra. Cv. 'Atrocaeruleum' [var. *atrocaeruleum* Farringt.]. Fls. dark lavender.

macranthum Arn. Bien., to 2 ft., st. cylindrical; lvs. ovate, to 3 in. long, acuminate at apex, narrowed toward base, sessile; fls. terminal on slender peduncles, about 2 in. across, 5-merous, corolla purplish-blue, lobes pointed, anthers long, conspicuous, grouped into a cone-like cluster much as in some spp. of *Solanum.* Ceylon. The best of the genus, with showy, large, rich-blue fls.

teres Wallich. To 4 ft., st. scarcely branched, nearly 4-angled; lvs. lanceolate, to 3½ in. long, 3-nerved, sessile or the lowermost petioled; fls. blue, to 1 in. across, calyx and corolla lobes 4. Trop. foothills, Himalayas.

tetragonum Roxb. To 4 ft., st. 4-angled; lvs. broadly lanceolate, to 5 in. long, 5-nerved; fls. azure-blue. Trop. foothills of Himalayas to w. China. Not known to be in cult. but confused with *E. teres.*

zeylanicum Roxb. Ann., to 2 ft., st. 4-angled; lvs. elliptic-oblong or lanceolate, to 3 in. long; fls. blue, to 1½ in. across, in leafy corymbs, calyx and corolla lobes 5. Ceylon. Differs from *E. macranthum* in having corolla lobes obtuse.

EXBUCKLANDIA R. W. Br. [*Bucklandia* R. Br., not K. Presl ex Sternb.; *Symingtonia* Steenis]. *Hamamelidaceae.* Two spp. of evergreen trees in e. Himalayas, s. China, Malay Pen., and Sumatra; lvs. alt., stipules paired, folded against one another, protecting and enclosing the young axillary buds and infl.; fls. in heads, unisexual, sunken in the floral axis. Related to *Liquidambar* but has fewer fls. in the floral heads and can always be distinguished by its persistent lvs. with prominent stipules.

populnea (R. Br.) R. W. Br. [*Bucklandia populnea* R. Br.; *Symingtonia populnea* (R. Br.) Steenis]. Erect, evergreen tree; lvs. ovate-cordate, 4–6 in. long, palmately-nerved, leathery, glossy-green above, veins and lower surface reddish, petioles to 3 in. long, stipules paired, ovate-oblong to obovate, 1 in. long or more. E. Himalayas.

EXOCHORDA Lindl. PEARLBUSH. *Rosaceae.* A few spp. of spiraealike, deciduous shrubs, native to Asia; lvs. alt.; fls.

white, in terminal racemes, sepals 5, petals 5, spreading, obovate, stamens 15–30; fr. a 5-angled caps. separating into 5 bony sections, each with 1–2 winged seeds.

Pearlbushes are very ornamental and hardy north, prospering in sunny locations in well-drained soil. Propagated by seeds, layers, and cuttings of soft wood.

Albertii: *E. Korolkowii.*

Giraldii Hesse. To 15 ft. high, very broad; lvs. elliptic, entire, to 2½ in. long, petioles to 1 in. long, veins and petioles red; fls. 6–8, to 1 in. across, stamens 25–30. China. Var. **Wilsonii** Rehd. More erect, to 10 ft.; lvs. longer, more narrow, with green petioles and veins; stamens 20–25. Cent. China. Zone 5.

grandiflora: *E. racemosa.*

Korolkowii Lavall. [*E. Albertii* Regel]. To 12 ft., rather erect; lvs. oblong, glabrous, 1½–3 in. long, gray to yellow-green beneath, bright green above, petioles ½ in. long; fls. 5–8, to 1⅝ in. across, stamens about 25. Turkestan. Zone 6.

×**macrantha** (Hort. Lemoine) C. K. Schneid.: *E. Korolkowii* × *E. racemosa.* Vigorous, upright, with abundant white fls. and dense panicles, stamens about 20.

racemosa (Lindl.) Rehd. [*E. grandiflora* Hook.]. Ten to 12 ft., branchlets glabrous, red-brown; lvs. elliptic to oblong-obovate, to 2½ in. long, petioles to ½ in. long; fls. to 2 in. across, stamens 15. China. Zone 5.

serratifolia S. L. Moore. To 6 ft.; lvs. elliptic, 1–3 in. long, sharply serrate toward apex, sparsely hairy beneath; fls. 1½ in. across, stamens 25. Manchuria, Korea. Zone 5?

Wilsonii: a listed name of no botanical standing for *E. Giraldii* var.

FABACEAE: see *LEGUMINOSAE.*

FABIANA Ruiz & Pav. *Solanaceae.* About 25 spp. of erect, often viscid, heathlike shrubs of warm temp. S. Amer.; lvs. small, crowded, alt.; fls. small, white, usually many, terminal or opp. the lvs., calyx tubular-campanulate, shortly 5-toothed, corolla tube elongate, dilated or swollen on 1 side above, limb short, 5-lobed or scarcely lobed, stamens 5, unequal, borne on corolla, included, ovary 2-celled; fr. a caps., oblong, 2-valved.

One species cultivated as an ornamental on the West Coast or in cool greenhouses. Propagated readily from cuttings taken in late summer.

imbricata Ruiz & Pav. Tender, viscid-pubescent, evergreen shrub, to 8 ft.; lvs. imbricate, needlelike; fls. sessile or nearly so, borne singly but profusely on the ends of short branchlets, corolla about ½ in. long, lobes short, rounded, reflexed. Chile. Zone 9, where summers are cool. Cv. 'Violacea'. Fls. violet.

FACHEIROA: *ESPOSTOA.*

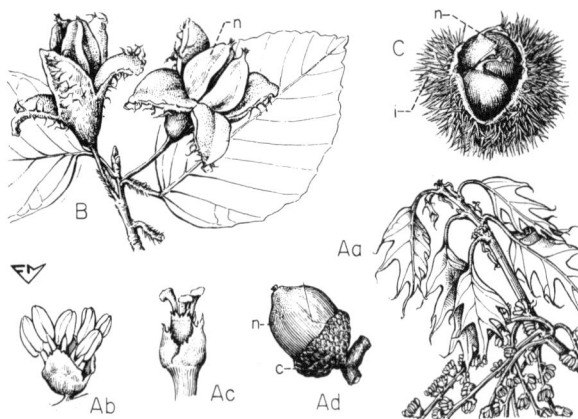

FAGACEAE. **A,** *Quercus rubra:* **Aa,** twig with male catkins below and female flowers above, × ½; **Ab,** male flower, × 3; **Ac,** female flower, × 3; **Ad,** acorn, × ½. **B,** *Fagus sylvatica:* fruiting twig, × ½. **C,** *Castanea mollissima:* fruit, × ½. (c cup, i involucre, n nut) (From Bailey, *Manual of Cultivated Plants,* ed. 2.)

FAGACEAE. Dumort. BEECH FAMILY. Dicot.; 6 genera and about 600 spp. of deciduous or evergreen, usually monoecious trees and shrubs, mostly native to temp. and subtrop. regions of the N. Hemisphere, *Nothofagus* in the S. Hemisphere; lvs. alt., simple, entire or variously cleft; fls. unisexual, male fls. in catkins or heads, female fls. solitary or clustered, perianth 4–7-lobed, stamens 4–20, ovary inferior, 3–7-celled; fr. a nut enclosed in a cup or bur. The cult. genera are: *Castanea, Castanopsis, Fagus, Lithocarpus, Nothofagus,* and *Quercus.*

The family furnishes valuable timber, edible nuts, tannins, medicinal products, cork, and numerous ornamentals. Most of the ornamentals are hardy in central or northern U.S., but some of them only far south; they comprise some of the desirable hardwood lawn and shade trees.

FAGARA: *ZANTHOXYLUM.* F. fruticosa: *Z. Clava-Herculis* var. *fruticosa.*

FAGOPYRUM Gaertn. BUCKWHEAT. *Polygonaceae.* About 6 spp. of soft herbs, native to Eur. and Asia; lvs. alt.; fls. small, white, in racemes or corymbs, sepals 5, not enlarg-

ing in fr., stamens 8, styles 3; fr. an achene, 3-angled, pointed, much longer than sepals.

Grown mostly for the fruits (seeds), from which flour is made, as a cover crop or catch crop and honey plant in orchards.

esculentum Moench [*F. sagittatum* Gilib.; *F. vulgare* Nees]. BUCK-WHEAT, NOTCH-SEEDED B., BRANK. To 3 ft.; lvs. triangular-ovate, to 3 in. long; fls. white, fragrant, in short dense racemes or clusters mostly near summit of plant. Cent. or n. Asia. A cultigen widely grown in cool temp. regions.

sagittatum: *F. esculentum.*

tataricum (L.) Gaertn. INDIA WHEAT, KANGRA B., TARTARIAN B. To 2 ft.; lvs. broadly arrow-shaped, to 2 in. long; fls. greenish or yellowish, in slender open racemes along st. India. Has been known as DUCK-WHEAT.

vulgare: *F. esculentum.*

FAGRAEA Thunb. *Loganiaceae.* Thirty-five spp. of trees and shrubs, native to se. Asia, Malay Arch., trop. Australia, and sw. Pacific Is.; lvs. opp., usually large, leathery, entire, stipuled; fls. showy, solitary or in a few- to many-fld. cymose infl., corolla tubular, 5-lobed; fr. a berry, seeds many, embedded in pulp.

Berterana A. Gray ex Benth. Tree, to 40 ft., or sometimes shrubby; lvs. ovate or obovate, to 6 in. long; fls. fragrant, large, to 3 in. long, few to many in widely branched infl. Pacific Is., Queensland. The fls. are used in leis and perfumes.

fragrans Roxb. Tree, to 75 ft., or sometimes shrubby; lvs. elliptic, to 6 in. long; fls. about 1 in. long, in few- to many-fld., branched infl., stamens and style exserted. India, Malay Arch. A beautiful tree planted for shade in trop. regions.

FAGUS L. BEECH. *Fagaceae.* About 10 spp. of large, deciduous, monoecious trees, with smooth, light gray bark, native to N. Temp. Zone; lvs. alt., toothed; male fls. in drooping heads; fr. of 1 or 2 brown, 3-angled nuts enclosed in a usually prickly involucre.

Beeches are excellent ornamental trees, and furnish nuts and valuable timber. They prosper on loamy limestone soil. Beeches are propagated readily by seeds sown in autumn or stratified and kept until spring. Seedlings should be transplanted to prevent formation of long taproots. Varieties are grafted on seedling stock under glass.

americana: *F. grandifolia.*

crenata Blume [*F. Sieboldii* Endl.]. JAPANESE B. To 90 ft., with rounded crown; lvs. ovate-rhomboid, to 3 in. long, broadest below middle; involucre bristly above, the lowermost appendages bractlike, spatulate, ½ in. long. Japan, where an important forest tree.

Cunninghamii: *Nothofagus Cunninghamii.*

Englerana Seemen. To 60–70 ft., with several trunks at base; lvs. elliptic, to 4 in. long, with 10–14 pairs of veins; involucre covered with downy, often linear bracts. China. Zone 6.

ferruginea: *F. grandifolia.*

grandifolia J. F. Ehrh. [*F. americana* Sweet; *F. ferruginea* Ait.]. AMERICAN B. Large tree; lvs. ovate-oblong, to 5 in. long, with 9–15 pairs of veins, glabrate, turning yellow in autumn. E. N. Amer. Zone 4. Wood has many uses. Differs from the frequently planted European beech in having lvs. longer, coarsely serrate, and with more veins.

longipetiolata Seemen [*F. sinensis* D. Oliver]. To 80 ft., twigs glabrous; lvs. ovate, to 5½ in. long, sparsely toothed or wavy, with 9–13 pairs of veins, pubescent beneath, petioles to 1 in. long; involucre with slender recurved bristles. China. Zone 6.

macrophylla: *F. orientalis.*

orientalis Lipsky [*F. macrophylla* (DC.) G. Koidz.]. To 100 ft., trunk very pale gray, twigs silky-hairy; lvs. obovate, to 6 in. long, with 7–10 pairs of veins, silky-hairy beneath; involucre bristly above, the lowermost appendages bractlike, spatulate. E. Eur. Zone 6. Wood has many uses.

Sieboldii: *F. crenata.*

sinensis: *F. longipetiolata.*

sylvatica L. EUROPEAN B. Tree, to 80 ft. or more; lvs. ovate, to 4 in. long, denticulate, with 5–9 pairs of veins, shining green above, turning reddish-brown in autumn. Eur. Zone 5. Wood has many uses and beechnuts important locally as stockfood in Eur. Some of the cvs. are: **'Albo-variegata'**, lvs. variegated with white; **'Asplenifolia'**, lvs. very narrow, deeply toothed or lobed; **'Atropunicea'** [cvs. 'Atropurpurea', 'Cuprea', 'Purpurea', 'Riversii'], COPPER B., PURPLE B., lvs. purple or coppery-red; **'Atropurpurea'**: 'Atropunicea'; **'Borneyensis'**, fountainlike, with trunk straight and upright, and brs. pendulous, hanging symmetrically; **'Cristata'**, slow-growing, lvs. small, clustered, deeply toothed and curved; **'Cuprea'**: 'Atropunicea'; **'Dawyckii'**: 'Fastigiata'; **'Fastigiata'** [cvs. 'Dawyckii', 'Pyramidalis'], columnar or fastigiate; **'Grandidentata'**, lvs. coarsely toothed; **'Heterophylla'**: 'Laciniata'; **'Incisa'**: 'Laciniata'; **'Laciniata'** [cvs. 'Heterophylla', 'Incisa'], FERN-LEAF B., CUT-LEAF B., lvs. variable, deeply toothed or lobed, or sometimes nearly entire and linear; **'Latifolia'**, lvs. to 6 in. long and 4 in. wide; **'Luteo-variegata'**, lvs. variegated with yellow; **'Miltonensis'**, trunk erect, brs. pendulous; **'Pendula'**, WEEPING B., larger limbs spreading horizontally from main st., brs. pendulous; **'Purpurea'**: 'Atropunicea'; **'Purpurea Pendula'**, brs. pendulous, lvs. purple; **'Pyramidalis'**: 'Fastigiata'; **'Quercoides'**, bark grooved, oaklike; **'Remillyensis'**: 'Pendula', 'Tortuosa'; **'Riversii'**: 'Atropúnicea'; **'Rohanii'**, lvs. purple, similar in shape to cv. 'Laciniata'; **'Roseo-marginata'**, lvs. purple, edged with pale pink; **'Rotundifolia'**, lvs. nearly orbicular, to 1 in. long; **'Spathiana'** may be cv. 'Zlatia'; **'Tortuosa'**, brs. twisted, drooping at tips, sometimes reaching to the ground; **'Tricolor'**, lvs. nearly white, spotted with green and edged with pink; **'Variegata'**, lvs. variegated with white or yellow; **'Zlatia'**, lvs. yellow, becoming pale green.

FALLUGIA Endl. APACHE-PLUME. *Rosaceae.* Small deciduous shrub with shredded bark, allied to *Cowania,* from which it differs in having no calyx bractlets and fewer pistils.

paradoxa (D. Don) Endl. To 7 ft., sts. whitish; lvs. rusty-scaly and pubescent, pinnately divided into 3–7 linear lobes to ½ in. long, margins revolute; fls. white, to 1½ in. across, usually solitary on long peduncles; achenes with purplish, feathery plumes to 1½ in. long. Utah, s. to Tex., Mex., Calif. Zone 6.

FAMILY. A family, in the botanical sense, is an assemblage of genera (see *Genus*) that rather closely or uniformly resemble one another in general appearance and technical characters. A few genera are individually so unlike all others that a family is constituted for each of them alone, as in the case of *Eucryphia, Eucommia, Cercidiphyllum, Casuarina, Punica,* and *Equisetum.* Other families are large associations of genera that are more like one another than they are similar to others, as the great Compositae or composite family, which comprises about 950 genera. Opinions differ as to the natural or practicable limits of families as well as genera and species; thus, the Leguminosae or legume family may be divided into three families, just as the maples may constitute the genus *Acer* or may be divided into *Acer* and *Negundo.* Nature sets no formal limits. More than 300 families of seed-bearing or flowering plants are commonly recognized. Further categories may be intercalated between family and genus, as subfamily (see, for example, *Leguminosae*). The family may also be divided directly into tribes, as in the Cactaceae or Compositae, or the subfamilies may be similarly divided. Tribes, in turn, are sometimes divided into subtribes, a category not distinguished in *Hortus Third.* See also *Classification.*

FARAMEA Aubl. *Rubiaceae.* Over 100 spp. of usually glabrous shrubs or small trees, native to Cent. and S. Amer., and W. Indies; lvs. opp., mostly leathery, stipules interpetiolar, long-aristate or short-triangular; fls. few to many, in often terminal panicles, 4-merous, calyx cup-shaped, corolla salverform; fr. berrylike or almost dry, 1-seeded.

eurycarpa J. D. Sm. To 10 ft.; lvs. oblong or oblanceolate-oblong, to 6 in. long; fls. blue, in small, but many-fld. panicles, corolla ⅜ in. long, lobes shorter than tube; fr. ⅜ in. across, blue. Costa Rica.

FARFUGIUM: *LIGULARIA.* **F. grande:** *L. tussilaginea.*

FARSETIA Turra. *Cruciferae.* Not in cult. **Farsetia clypeata:** *Fibigia clypeata.* **Farsetia eriocarpa:** *Fibigia eriocarpa.* **Farsetia lunarioides:** *Fibigia lunarioides.*

FASCICULARIA Mez. *Bromeliaceae.* Five spp. of mostly terrestrial herbs, native to Chile; lvs. in an open rosette, spiny, stiff; infl. sessile, unbranched to corymbose; petals distinctly fleshy, with 2 scales at the base, petals not united to inner series of filaments, pollen smooth, ovary inferior; fr. a dry berry, seeds without appendages.

Grown in full sun. For culture see *Bromeliaceae.*

bicolor (Ruiz & Pav.) Mez. Lvs. many, to 1½ ft. long, ⅝ in. wide, brownish beneath, green above, flushed with pink; infl. corymbose or headlike, 20–40-fld., outer bracts narrow, minutely toothed, longer than fls.; fls. pale blue, to 1⅝ in. long.

×**FATSHEDERA** Guillaum.: *Fatsia* × *Hedera.* ARALIA IVY, TREE I., BOTANICAL-WONDER, IVY TREE. *Araliaceae.* Evergreen shrub; lvs. palmately 3–5-lobed to near the middle, rarely entire; fls. sterile, in umbels arranged in terminal panicles, 5-merous, styles very short; fr. none.

Lizei (Cochet) Guillaum.: *Fatsia japonica* cv. 'Moseri' × *Hedera Helix* var. *hibernica.* Weak-stemmed, to 8 ft. or more, sts. rusty-pubescent when young, becoming glabrescent with age; lvs. to 8 in. long, 12 in. wide, glossy, leathery; panicles to about 6 in. long; fls. greenish-yellow, about ⅜ in. across, disc yellow. Originated in cult. in France. Zone 7. Cv. **'Variegata'**. Lvs. white-margined.

FATSIA Decne. & Planch. *Araliaceae.* One sp., an unarmed, evergreen shrub or tree, native to Japan; sts. thick, little-branched; lvs. large, palmately 7–11-lobed, leathery; infl. of umbels arranged in large, terminal panicles; petals 4–6, stamens as many as the petals, styles 5, divergent, ovary 2–6-celled; fr. a globose drupe, pyrenes 1–6.

Grown for bold foliage effect indoors in the North and outside in mild regions. Zone 8. Propagated by seeds or cuttings, and by root cuttings in spring.

japonica (Thunb.) Decne. & Planch. [*Aralia japonica* Thunb.; *A. Sieboldii* Hort. ex C. Koch]. JAPANESE F., FORMOSA RICE TREE, PAPER PLANT, GLOSSY-LEAVED P. P. To 20 ft., brs. with prominent, lunate lf. scars; lvs. to 16 in. across, glossy above, palmately cut beyond the middle into 7–11, toothed lobes; infl. of whitish, long-stalked umbels arranged in panicles to 18 in. long; fr. black. Cv. **'Moseri'** [*Aralia Moseri* Hort.]. Compact, but of vigorous growth. Cv. **'Variegata'**. Lvs. with creamy-white margins.

papyrifera: *Tetrapanax papyriferus.*

FAUCARIA Schwant. TIGER-JAWS. *Aizoaceae.* About 33 spp. of succulent per. herbs, native to S. Afr., sts. very short, lengthening somewhat with age and forming clumps; lvs. 4-ranked, 2–3 pairs on a shoot, short-rhomboidal or spatulate to lanceolate in general outline, more or less 3-angled in section, crowded, spreading, fleshy, united basally, more or less semicylindrical toward base, keeled toward apex, usually long-toothed, margins often curved over the upper surface toward tip, both sides often conspicuously spotted, margin and keel often cartilaginous; fls. solitary, sessile, opening in the afternoon, calyx 5-lobed, petals yellow or seldom white, linear, many, in 2–4 series, stamens many, ovary 4–5-celled, stigmas 4–5, threadlike; fr. a caps. forming a deep cup, 5-celled, the cell lids more or less perpendicular, the expanding keels bent wide apart, bearing stiff, flaglike valve wings supported and stiffened by a robust awn, seeds large, reddish-brown, with long, knobby projections at both ends.

Propagated readily by seeds, but less easily from cuttings, flowering usually the second year. Summer plants require only moderate watering, and less water in winter during the the resting season with a relatively cool temperature of about 58°F. See also *Succulents.*

acutipetala L. Bolus. Lvs. spreading, olive-green with white spots, short, scarcely 1 in. long, to ⅝ in. wide, ⁵⁄₁₆ in. thick, broadly ovate or triangular in outline in top view, apex rounded and somewhat laterally compressed in side view, margin white, with 3–5 white-awned teeth; petals in 2 series, acute, golden, to ¾ in. long. Cape Prov.

albidens N. E. Br. Lvs. 10–12 per shoot, bright green, smooth, glossy, covered with small, scattered, translucent dots, to about 1 in. long, lanceolate, convex beneath, keeled toward apex, margins with 2–4 white, horny teeth; fls. golden-yellow, 1½–2 in. across. Cape Prov.

arrabidae: a listed name of no botanical standing.

Bosscheana (A. Berger) Schwant. Lvs. 6–8 on a shoot, glossy, to 1¼ in. long and ⅜ in. wide, narrowly lanceolate to rhomboid, margins white-horny, with 4–6 irregular, recurved teeth to ⅛ in. long; fls. to 1½ in. across, petals golden-yellow. Cape Prov. Var. **Haagei** (Tisch.) Jacobsen [*F. Haagei* Tisch.]. Lvs. larger, often undulate; fls. 2–2⅜ in. across. Cape Prov.

Britteniae L. Bolus. Lvs. gray-green and dotted with gray, to 1⅜ in. long and ¾ in. wide, rhomboid-ovate in top view, upper side slightly concave, lower side rounded toward base, keeled toward base, margin with a white or reddish horny edge bearing several fine, recurved teeth; fls. about 2½ in. across, petals yellow above, purplish-pink beneath. Cape Prov.

cradockensis L. Bolus. Lvs. with many white tubercles, to 1¾ in. long and ⅝ in. wide, ovate to ovate-lanceolate in top view, acute, lower side rounded and keeled, the keel with 1–2 teeth, margin with 5–7 conical teeth, each terminating in a long bristle; fls. about 2½ in. across, petals yellow. Cape Prov.

Duncanii L. Bolus. Lvs. smooth, green, irregularly red-dotted toward tip, with dots arranged in a line or more or less confluent along keel and margin, to 1 in. long and ⅜ in. wide at base, boat-shaped, semicircular in section at base, upper side flat, lower side rounded toward base, sharply keeled toward tip, margin with 6–7 finely tipped, recurved teeth; fls. to about 2 in. across. Cape Prov.

felina (Weston) Schwant. ex Jacobsen. Lvs. bright green, often turning reddish with age, indistinctly white-dotted, to 1¾ in. long and ¾ in. wide, rhomboidal to triangular in top view, margin with 3–5 fleshy, recurved, finely pointed teeth, keel with white-horny margin; fls. to 2 in. across, 1–3, petals golden-yellow. Cape Prov. Var. **Jamesii** L. Bolus [*F. Jamesii* Hort.]. Lvs. smaller, glaucous, with crowded white dots, apex obtuse, margin whitish, with 4–6 teeth; fls. slightly smaller, petals golden-yellow inside, pink outside.

Haagei: *F. Bosscheana* var.

Hoodii: a listed name of no botanical standing.

Jamesii: *F. felina* var.

longidens L. Bolus. Lvs. spreading or ascending, glaucous-green, slightly roughened by dots, to 1¼ in. long and ⅝ in. wide, ovate or ovate-lanceolate in top view, sharply keeled toward apex, margin with 4–6 more or less recurved teeth to ⅛ in. long terminating in an awn to ⁵⁄₁₆ in. long; fls. to 2½ in. across, petals golden-yellow, white toward base, filaments white. Cape Prov.

longifolia L. Bolus. Lvs. suberect to nearly spreading, to 2¼ in. long and ⅝ in. wide, linear-lanceolate in top view toward apex, margin 1–4-toothed; fls. to 2¾ in. across, petals bright yellow. Cape Prov.

lupina (Haw.) Schwant. Lvs. spreading, somewhat recurved, to 1½ in. long and ⅝ in. wide, lanceolate in top view, 3-angled, upper side flat and smooth, lower side keeled, dotted, margin and keel with many long-ciliated, recurved teeth; fls. to 1½ in. across, solitary, subsessile, petals yellow. Cape Prov.

militaris Tisch. Clump-forming; lvs. 1–3 pairs, gray-green and with white dots beneath, to 1¼ in. long and ½ in. thick, boat-shaped, sharply keeled beneath, keel horny, pink, and with 2–4 short teeth toward apex, margin horny at base of lf., with 4–6, ciliated teeth; fls. to 2¾ in. across, petals glossy golden-yellow, tinged reddish-brown on margins, whitish toward base. S. Afr.

Peersii L. Bolus. Lvs. to 1⅝ in. long, 1 in. wide, ⅝ in. thick, half rhomboidal to rounded in top view, margins and keel white, margins entire or with 1–5 teeth usually lacking bristles; petals in 3–4 series, golden, the outside often suffused with pale rose, to 1 in. long. Cape Prov.

Ryneveldiae L. Bolus. Sts. crowded, forming clumps to 6 in. across; lvs. erect, dull green with many small white dots, to 2¾ in. long and ⅜ in. wide, linear-lanceolate in outline toward apex, upper side flat, lower side convex, keeled toward tip, margin entire or with 1–2 bristle-tipped teeth; fls. to 2½ in. across, petals golden-yellow, filaments white. Cape Prov.

subintegra L. Bolus. Lvs. green, smooth and glossy, with obscure white spots, very thick, to 1 in. long, ½ in. wide, ⅜ in. thick, upper part ovate in top view, obtuse or rarely nearly acute, apex rounded in side view, obtusely keeled, margin entire or with 1–3 unarmed or rarely bristle-bearing teeth; petals in 3–4 series, golden, ⅞ in. long. Cape Prov.

sulrueteria: a listed name of no botanical standing; plant described as having lvs. smooth, without prominent teeth, bluish, with slightly pink margin and base; petals yellow.

tigrina (Haw.) Schwant. [*F. tigrina* cv. 'Superba']. TIGER'S-JAW. Lvs. crowded, gray-green, with many white dots, to 2 in. long and 1 in. wide, rhomboidal-ovate in top view, upper side flat, lower side convex, keeled near tip, apex more or less chinlike, margins with 9–10 stout, recurved, ciliated teeth; fls. to 2 in. across, petals golden-yellow. Cape Prov. Lvs. become reddish on plants growing in a sunny location. Has

been offered as cv. 'Superba' to distinguish this sp. from the many less attractive hybrids of it often sold as *F. tigrina*.

tuberculosa (Rolfe) Schwant. Lvs. spreading, dark green, to 1 in. long and ¾ in. wide, ovate-triangular in top view, upper side convex, white-tubercled, lower side convex, white-dotted, margin with 3 stout teeth and few smaller teeth; fls. to 1½ in. across, petals yellow. Cape Prov.

FAURIA Franch. [*Nephrophyllidium* Gilg]. *Gentianaceae*. One sp., a per. of wet places, with stout creeping rhizomes, native to n. Japan, and from Alaska s. to Wash.; lvs. alt., simple, reniform, petioles mostly longer than blade; fls. in terminal cymes or corymbs, corolla deeply 5-lobed, stamens borne on corolla tube, style short, with 2-lobed stigma, ovary half-inferior.

Attractive and looking much like some of the large-leaved saxifrages. Adaptable to the bog garden or moist, mucky soil along pools or ponds.

crista-galli (Menz. ex Hook.) Mak. [*F. japonica* Franch.; *Nephrophyllidium crista-galli* (Menz. ex Hook.) Gilg]. DEER CABBAGE. To 1 ft.; lvs. to 5 in. wide, obtusely dentate, petiole 8–12 in. long, somewhat clasping the rhizome basally; fls. in fastigiate, terminal corymbs on erect peduncle, corolla white, about ½ in. across, lobes lanceolate, with a low crest along the midvein and crisped margin.

japonica: *F. crista-galli.*

FEDIA Gaertn. *Valerianaceae*. About 3 spp. of ann. herbs, native to Medit. region; lvs. opp., simple; fls. white to red, in small terminal cymes, calyx of 4 small teeth, corolla 2-lipped, stamens 2, ovary inferior, 3-celled; fr. dry, indehiscent, with 1 fertile and 2 sterile cells.

One species occasionally grown in the flower garden or as a salad plant.

cornucopiae (L.) Gaertn. AFRICAN VALERIAN, HORN-OF-PLENTY. Sts. to 1 ft., or sometimes taller, often purplish, glabrous; lvs. oblong to ovate or elliptic, to 4 in. long, entire or toothed; fls. red; fr. about ⅛ in. long.

FEIJOA O. Berg. *Myrtaceae*. Two spp. of evergreen shrubs in S. Amer.; lvs. opp.; fls. solitary in lf. axils, pedicelled, calyx lobes and petals 4, stamens many, in several series, long-exserted; fr. an oblong berry, crowned by persistent calyx lobes.

One species is planted in warm countries for its edible fruit and as an ornamental. It is adapted to subtropical dry climates but will withstand several degrees of frost. The best soil is sandy loam rich in humus. Propagated by seeds sown in pans or flats, a good soil being silver sand and well-rotted redwood sawdust; the seedlings should be shaded and transplanted permanently when about 4 in. high. Plants should be spaced 15–18 ft. apart. Also increased by layering, whip-grafting, and cuttings of young wood from ends of branches.

Coolidgei: a listed name of no botanical standing for *F. Sellowiana* cv.

Sellowiana O. Berg. PINEAPPLE GUAVA, FEIJOA. To 18 ft.; lvs. elliptic-oblong, to 3 in. long, green above, white-woolly beneath; fls. to 1½ in. across, petals fleshy, white-tomentose outside, purplish within, stamens dark red; fr. green, tinged with red, to 2–3 in. long. S. Brazil, Paraguay, Uruguay, n. Argentina. Zone 9. The edible fr. has a pleasant guavalike flavor, makes a good jelly. Cvs. include: 'Andre', 'Besson', 'Choiceana', 'Coolidgei', 'Hehre', 'Superba'.

FELICIA Cass. [*Agathaea* Cass.]. *Compositae* (Aster Tribe). About 83 spp. of ann. herbs, subshrubs, or rarely shrubs, native to trop. and S. Afr. and w. Arabia; lvs. alt., opp., or sometimes in rosettes, entire or toothed; fl. heads radiate, solitary, often long-peduncled, involucre hemispherical or campanulate, involucral bracts in 1 to several rows, receptacle flat, often pitted; disc fls. bisexual, usually fertile, yellow, ray fls. in 1–2 rows, female, fertile or sterile, blue, mauve, pink, or white; achenes flattened, sometimes with 1 or 2 faint ribs, usually hairy, pappus of 1 row of scabrous bristles, often early-deciduous.

Grown in greenhouses, and in the open in warm regions. Propagated by seeds and by cuttings.

adfinis: *F. dubia.*

aethiopica (Burm.) Grau [*Aster capensis* Less.]. Shrub, to 1½ ft.; lower lvs. opp., upper lvs. alt., elliptic to obovate, to ¾ in. long, glabrous to hispid or glandular; heads to about 1¼ in. across, solitary on glandular peduncles; ray fls. blue. S. Afr.

amelloides (L.) Voss [*Agathaea coelestis* Cass.]. BLUE DAISY, BLUE MARGUERITE. Straggling subshrub, to 3 ft., rough-hairy; lvs. opp., sessile to subsessile, oblong or obovate, to 1¼ in. long, entire or nearly so; heads to 1⅜ in. across, solitary on long, naked peduncles; ray fls. blue; achenes glabrous. S. Afr.

amoena (Schultz-Bip.) Levyns [*F. Pappei* (Harv.) Hutch.]. Ann. or per. herb, to 1½ ft., with soft hairs; lvs. mostly opp., linear or elliptic, to 1¼ in. long; heads to 1 in. across, solitary on long peduncles; ray fls. bright blue; achenes minutely hairy. S. Afr.

Bergerana (K. Spreng.) O. Hoffm. KINGFISHER DAISY. Bushy ann., 6–8 in., with long hairs, sts. wiry; lvs. alt. or opp., oblong-obovate, to 1½ in. long, entire to toothed; heads to 1 in. across, solitary on long peduncles; disc fls. not fertile, ray fls. blue; achenes densely hairy. S. Afr.

dubia Cass. [*F. adfinis* (Less.) Nees]. Ann., to 1 ft., hairy, sts. branching; lower lvs. opp., the others alt., obovate-oblong, to 1¼ in. long, cuneate basally, entire; heads usually solitary on long peduncles; ray fls. blue; achenes glabrous. S. Afr.

elongata (Thunb.) O. Hoffm. [*Aster elongatus* Thunb.]. Many-stemmed subshrub, to 2 ft.; lvs. opp., sessile, linear-lanceolate, to about 1 in. long, with silvery hairs, entire; heads to 2 in. across, solitary on leafless peduncles to 10 in. long; ray fls. white, with a reddish purple zone at base of the ligule; achenes hispidulous. S. Afr.

fruticosa (L.) Nichols. [*Aster fruticosus* L.]. Much-branched shrub, to 2½ ft.; lvs. alt., crowded, linear, to ½ in. long, entire, recurved; heads 1 in. across, solitary on slender peduncles 1–3 in. long; ray fls. usually purple, sometimes pink or white; achenes densely hairy. S. Afr.

hyssopifolia (Bergius) Nees. Much-branched, straggling subshrub, to 15 in., with dense soft hairs or nearly glabrous; lvs. alt., linear, to ½ in. long; heads solitary on long peduncles; ray fls. blue or mauve; achenes minutely hairy. S. Afr.

Pappei: *F. amoena*.

rosulata Yeo [*Aster natalensis* (Schultz-Bip.) Harv.]. Rhizomatous per. herb, to 1 ft.; lower lvs. in a rosette, elliptic to obovate, to 3½ in. long, densely hairy, entire to toothed, st. lvs. lanceolate, to 1¼ in. long; heads about 1¼ in. across, solitary on hairy peduncles; ray fls. blue. S. Afr.

FENDLERA Engelm. & A. Gray. *Saxifragaceae.* Two or 3 spp. of deciduous, intricately branched shrubs in sw. U.S. and adjacent Mex.; lvs. opp., entire; fls. mostly solitary, large and showy, calyx tube united at base to ovary, shorter than calyx lobes, the lobes 4, triangular, petals 4, clawed, stamens 8, ovary half-inferior, styles 4; fr. a 4-valved caps.

Fendleras do best in sunny places in well-drained sandy or peaty soil. Propagated by seeds or by greenwood cuttings struck under glass.

rupicola A. Gray. To 6 ft.; lvs. elliptic to oblong, to 1¼ in. long; fls. white, to 1½ in. across; caps. to ½ in. long. S. Colo., s. to w. Tex. and Ariz. Hardy as far north as New Eng.

FENESTRARIA N. E. Br. WINDOW PLANT. *Aizoaceae.* Two spp. of stemless, clump-forming, succulent per. herbs, native to S. Afr.; lvs. crowded, opp., erect, club-shaped, apex truncate, with transparent areas (windows); fls. solitary, calyx 5-lobed, petals linear, in 1 series, stamens many, staminodes absent, ovary almost superior, 10–11-celled, stigmas 10–11, spreading; fr. a caps. In the wild state, the lvs. become deeply covered by sand leaving only the windows visible.

Cultivate in soil ¾ sand with maximum illumination, moderate watering, and a relatively cool temperature of about 58° F. Growing period late winter to summer. Propagation best by seeds, although shoots will root; transplanting very difficult. See also *Succulents.*

aurantiaca N. E. Br. Forming cushions to 4 in. across; lvs. smooth, glaucous, to 1¼ in. long, broadest toward apex, apex convex, circular to nearly triangular in outline, with scattered transparent areas; fls. to 2¾ in. across, petals orange-yellow, stigmas plumose. Cape Prov.

rhopalophylla (Schlechter & Diels) N. E. Br. BABY-TOES, BABY'S-TOES. Lvs. glaucous-green, to 1½ in. long, broadest toward apex, apex convex, circular to nearly triangular in outline; fls. to 1¾ in. across, petals white, stigmas linear, not plumose. S.-W. Afr.

FERDINANDIA: see *FERNANDOA.*

FERETIA Delile. *Rubiaceae.* About 4 spp. of much-branched shrubs, native to trop. Afr.; lvs. opp., stipules ovate;

fls. axillary, few in clusters or solitary, corolla funnelform; fr. a globose berry, seeds few.

apodanthera Delile [*F. canthioides* Hiern]. Shrub, to 15 ft.; lvs. ovate-elliptic to obovate, to 2¼ in. long; fls. pink and white, to ¾ in. long; fr. to ⅜ in. across. W. Trop. Afr.

FERNANDOA Welw. ex Seem. (sometimes misspelled *Ferdinandia*). *Bignoniaceae.* Three spp. of shrubs or trees, native to trop. Afr.; lvs. opp., pinnate; fls. in axillary corymbose cymes, calyx unequally 3–4-lobed, corolla campanulate, slightly 2-lipped, stamens 4; fr. a spirally twisted caps.

magnifica Seem. Glabrous shrub or small tree; lvs. to 1 ft. long, lfts. 9–13, ovate or ovate-oblong, to 5 in. long, glabrous beneath; fls. orange, to 3 in. long.

FERNS and **FERN ALLIES.** These are all flowerless plants normally producing true roots from a rhizome, bearing leaves, and reproducing by spores produced in special sacs (sporangia), which, in the ferns, are often clustered into compact groups (sori or "fruit dots") on the lower surface of the mature leaves (fronds). The stems contain xylem and phloem tissues and so this whole group is treated among the vascular plants. For convenience to those of horticultural bent, these so-called flowerless plants continue to be combined here in the older familiar grouping of the pteridophytes, comprising the vascular plants that do not produce seeds. These are represented by many genera of ferns and by genera in such groups as the club mosses (*Lycopodium* and *Selaginella*), horsetails *(Equisetum)*, and whisk ferns *(Psilotum)*. Nowadays botanists do not consider the fern allies (except perhaps for *Psilotum*) to be close allies of the ferns. The ferns are believed to have closer affinity with the several groups of seed plants (conifers, cycads, and flowering plants).

However these plants are classified, they share a similar kind of life cycle and are consequently handled horticulturally in somewhat similar fashion. In all species of ferns and fern allies there are two distinctly different individuals that make up one full life cycle. The plant of the independent sexual generation, known commonly as a prothallium (gametophyte), is insignificant. In the ferns it is usually a small, green, fragile, heart-shaped structure. The prothallium is sometimes grown from the sowing of spores as the first step in the production of ferns and, more rarely, fern allies. Sex organs develop on the prothallium, and when the motile sperm unites with an egg there arises from the union the familiar spore-bearing plant (sporophyte), which is the fern, club moss, or horsetail grown for ornament. The life cycle is completed when one of the thousands of spores produced by such an individual is shed and falls into a moist spot favorable for the production of another prothallial individual. Thus there is what botanists call an alternation of generations—a plant producing sex cells alternating with a plant producing spores—in the continuing life cycle of these flowerless plants.

Some 10,000 species of ferns are presently known. They are perennial plants widely distributed over the earth, with the greatest species concentration and diversity in the humid parts of the tropics, especially in forested montane areas. There the majority of ferns are epiphytes, belonging primarily to the large family Polypodiaceae. The tree ferns (Cyatheaceae and Dicksoniaceae), delicate filmy ferns (Hymenophyllaceae), aquatic ferns (Marsileaceae, Parkeriaceae, and Salviniaceae), and various scandent ferns in several families are also characteristic primarily of the tropics and subtropics.

The cultivated ferns treated in *Hortus Third* will be found among genera listed in the families Cyatheaceae, Dicksoniaceae, Gleicheniaceae, Marattiaceae, Marsiliaceae, Ophioglossaceae, Osmundaceae, Parkeriaceae, Polypodiaceae, Salviniaceae, and Schizaeaceae. Botanical family groupings in the ferns are based on technical characters that are often obscure to anyone except a specialist. The most primitive of the cultivated ferns (the eusporangiate ferns) are the Marattiaceae and Ophioglossaceae, in which the spore-producing organs (sporangia) are not only of somewhat simpler structure but also produce many more spores than those of the more advanced leptosporangiate ferns of "true ferns," represented here by all other families listed. Of the latter, the Osmundaceae, including the native royal fern and similar kinds, and the Schizaeaceae appear to represent families that are intermediate between primitive families and highly evolved families such as the Polypodiaceae. Fern specialists increasingly tend to subdivide the Polypodiaceae, the largest fern family, and its largest genus, *Polypodium*, into many smaller families and genera, but such a treatment is not followed in this volume.

Gardeners in this country, especially in more temperate areas, usually recognize two groups of ferns: the hardier kinds, both native and exotic, largely cultivated outdoors; the tropical and warm-temperature kinds grown in the home, warm conservatory, or outdoors in the tropics and subtropics. Most ferns are shade plants, and, though they favor filtered sunlight, tolerate low levels of light intensity, so that the indoor kinds are suitable for north-, east-, and west-facing windows. Hardy ferns, especially the natives, are often transplanted from the wild to the garden, where the conditions of soil and light should be as near as possible to those in which the plants are naturally found. A number of tropical ferns are excellent for indoor culture and may be grown as pot plants, in hanging baskets, or, in some cases, on slabs of cork bark, cedar, cypress, or redwood. Ferns especially recommended for indoor planting include *Adiantum cuneatum, Aglaomorpha coronans, Asplenium bulbiferum, Cyrtomium falcatum, Davallia* species, *Lygodium japonicum,* cultivars of *Nephrolepis exalta, Pellaea viridis, Platycerium* species, *Polypodium aureum,* and *Stenochlaena palustris.* The specialized aquatic ferns of the genera *Azolla, Ceratopteris,* and *Salvinia* have value as floating plants in aquaria.

In culture of terrestrial and epiphytic ferns, standing water in the pot as also heavy clay soils and extremes in air temperature and in moisture should be avoided. Shade and protection from wind should be provided. For living room ferns, a night temperature of about 55° F is recommended, with a rise of 10°–20° by day in bright weather. Soils for pot ferns should be fibrous, spongy, and loose, and composed of osmunda fiber, sphagnum moss, a mixture of German peat moss and perlite, or a sand-peat combination. The important characteristics of any soil mix for ferns are the capacity to retain moisture and a porous structure which allows air to reach the roots. Ample drainage should be provided in the bottom. See that the pot does not dry out and that the atmosphere does not become very dry.

Ferns are propagated by division, by the buds or offsets that form on the leaves of some kinds, and by means of spores. The spores are usually borne on the underside of the leaf; when ripe they may be shaken off on paper, or parts of the frond may be cut and placed in dishes or paper bags in a dry, protected place until the spores shed. They may be sown on fine, sterilized, moist soil in well-drained pans or pots. Spores are sown on a well-prepared soil surface and not covered with earth or watered on top; the pans or pots may be kept in a closed propagating frame or terrarium, covered individually with sheets of clear glass, until germination takes place, when more air may be admitted. The temperature should be kept at about 65° F. The sporelings should be pricked out, usually at first in little clumps, and transplanted as soon as a deft person can handle them and the first regular foliage appears. Eight to 12 months are usually required to produce good ferns from spores.

Considerable success and faster development may be obtained by sowing fern spores on the surface of a liquid nutrient solution in a sterile jar plugged with cotton, with the glass top loosely in place during germination and early growth. Minute fern plants, at the stage where leaves and roots are differentiated and first evident, are transferred to small pots containing a sterilized mixture of equal parts of sand, peat, loam, and vermiculite. To prevent too-rapid drying, these pots are embedded in larger pots and pans fitted with peat and kept moist. The small pots are covered with glass to

retain moisture and watered weekly with dilute potassium permanaganate solution (pale purple in color) to inhibit fungus infections. The ferns are transplanted to ordinary soil mixtures when they are about 1 inch high.

Fern allies are to be found in the families Equisetaceae, Isoetaceae, Lycopodiaceae, Psilotaceae, and Selaginellaceae, but they are cultivated less frequently than ferns. Species of *Isoetes* are occasionally transferred from the wild to be used as aquarium subjects. Similarly, species of *Equisetum,* easily propagated by divisions, are transferred from moist sites. *Equisetum hyemale* is sometimes used in gardens of a Japanese type. *Selaginella* and *Lycopodium* are usually propagated by cuttings but otherwise are handled like ferns. Native terrestrial species of *Lycopodium* make good subjects for woodsy temperate gardens. The tropical epiphytic species of *Lycopodium* are best suited to hanging baskets potted with sphagnum; cuttings of young growth 1½–2½ inches long, taken in the spring, placed in fresh actively growing sphagnum, and kept at 70°F in high humidity are the usual means of propagating these.

The so-called asparagus fern, *Asparagus setaceus,* a common conservatory and windowsill plant, is not a fern but one of the Liliaceae.

The American Fern Society promotes interest in ferns through its journal and also provides its members with a source of living propagules of a large number of fern species through the society's annual spore list.

FEROCACTUS Britt. & Rose. BARREL CACTUS, FISHHOOK C., VISNAGA. *Cactaceae.* Perhaps 25 spp. of large, ribbed, ovoid cacti of Mex. and the sw. U.S.; sts. cespitose or mostly simple, globose to cylindrical, strongly ribbed, spiny; larger spines annulate, often flattened and hooked, glandspines functional in acropetal succession in the young areole; fls. solitary at upper side of young areoles, campanulate to funnelform, yellow to red, open several days, tube and ovary densely scaly, scales mostly fringed, naked, stamens very many, included, borne on the funnelform, thick-walled tube; fr. oblong, persistent, fleshy, indehiscent or opening by a basal pore, seeds black, pitted. Resembles *Echinocactus,* but perianth scales acute to rounded, with naked axils, and upper spines of areole usually modified into nectaries.

Candy is made from stems. For culture see *Cacti.*

acanthodes (Lem.) Britt. & Rose [*Echinocactus acanthodes* Lem.; *E. cylindraceus* Engelm.]. Sts. mostly solitary, cylindrical, to 6 or rarely 10 ft. high and 1 ft. thick, ribs 16–28; radial spines 5–7, stout, 3–7 bristlelike, central spines 1–4, pink or red, flattened, often twisted and hooked, to 6 in. long; fls. yellow to orange, to 2 in. long; fr. 1¼ in. long. Spring. S. Nev., se. Calif., w. Ariz., n. Baja Calif., n. Mex. Var. **acanthodes.** The typical var.; the inner 6–8 radial spines similar to central spines, to 2½ in. long and ¹⁄₁₆ in. wide, the outer 6–12 more slender, nearly white, flexible and curving, lower central spine red to gray, to 6 in. long and ⅛ in. wide, curved to nearly a right angle at apex. Ariz., Calif., n. Baja Calif. Var. **Lecontei** (Engelm.) G. Lindsay [*F. Lecontei* (Engelm.) Britt. & Rose]. Inner 6–8 radial spines similar to central spines, to 2 in. long and ³⁄₁₆ in. wide, outer 6–12 more slender, nearly white, flexible, curving, lower central spine red to gray, to 3 in. long and ⅛ in. wide, slightly curved at apex. Utah, Nev., Calif., Ariz. Var. **tortulospinus** (H. E. Gates) G. Lindsay [*F. tortulospinus* H. E. Gates]. Lower central spine grayish-red, to 4³⁄₁₆ in. long, twisted. N. Baja Calif.

alamosanus Britt. & Rose. Sts. solitary or cespitose, globose, to 1 ft. thick, ribs 18–23, narrow; spines straight, radial spines 8, to 1¼ in. long, central spine 1, to 3 in. long, flattened laterally; fls. yellow. Nw. Mex. Var. **platygonus** G. Lindsay. Sts. cylindrical, to 3 ft. high, ribs 11–14, broader; spines shorter, less flattened; fls. to nearly 2 in. long. The var. probably is more common in the trade.

chrysacanthus (Orcutt) Britt. & Rose. Sts. mostly solitary, cylindrical, to 4 ft. high and 1 ft. thick, ribs 13–22; spines yellow or red, radial spines bristlelike, central spines 4–10, curved, to 2 in. long; fls. yellow, rarely red; fr. yellow, 1¼ in. long. Cedros Is. (Baja Calif.).

coloratus: *F. gracilis* var.

corniger: a listed name of no botanical standing, perhaps for *F. latispinus.*

Covillei Britt. & Rose. Sts. simple, ovoid, to 5 ft. high and 1¾ ft. thick, ribs 22–32, thin; spines red to white, radial spines 5–8, awl-shaped, spreading, central spine 1, cylindrical or flattened, often hooked, to 5 in. long; fls. red to yellow, to 3 in. long; fr. yellow, to 2 in. long. Summer. Ariz. and nw. Mex.

crassihamatus: *Ancistrocactus crassihamatus.*

Diguetii (A. Web.) Britt. & Rose. Sts. simple, to 12 ft. high and 2½ ft. thick, ribs 25–35; spines 6–9, similar, curved, yellow, to 2 in. long; fls. 1½ in. long, segms. red, with yellow margins. Spring. Is. (Gulf of Calif.).

echidne (DC.) Britt. & Rose. Sts. simple or cespitose, depressed-globose, to 8 in. thick, ribs about 13, acute; areoles remote, spines nearly straight, yellow, radial spines about 7, central spine 1, to 1½ in. long; fls. yellow, 1¼ in. long, scales entire. E.-cent. Mex.

electracanthus: a listed name of no botanical standing; referable to *F. melocactiformis.*

Emoryi: *F. Wislizenii.*

flavovirens (Scheidw.) Britt. & Rose. Sts. cespitose, to 8 in. thick, ribs 11–13, acute; spines straight, stout, pale brown, becoming gray, central spines 4, to 3 in. long, radial spines about 8–14, shorter; fls. reddish-yellow, to 1½ in. long, outer segms. linear, long-ciliate. Cent. Mex.

Fordii (Orcutt) Britt. & Rose. Sts. simple, short-cylindrical, to 16 in. high, ribs about 21; radial spines about 15, needle-shaped, whitish, central spines usually 4, the longest flattened, hooked, to 1½ in. long; fls. rose, 1½ in. long, inner segms. linear. Cent. Baja Calif.

Gatesii G. Lindsay. Sts. simple, globose to nearly columnar, to nearly 5 ft. high and 1 ft. thick, ribs 30–32; spines pink, yellow, or horn-colored, radial spines about 16, central spines usually 4, in the form of a cross, flattened, to 2¾ in. long; fls. red, funnelform, to 2⅜ in. long and wide, scales of ovary maroon and yellow. Smith Is. (Baja Calif.).

glaucescens (DC.) Britt. & Rose [*Echinocactus glaucescens* DC.; *E. Pfeifferi* Zucc.]. BLUE B. C. Sts. solitary or cespitose, globose, to 16 in. thick, glaucous, ribs 11–15, acute; areoles connected, spines similar, straight, pale yellow, to 1½ in. long, radial spines 6, slightly spreading, central spine 1; fls. yellow, to 1 in. long. E. Mex.

gracilis H. E. Gates. Sts. simple, cylindrical, to 10 ft. high and 1 ft. thick, ribs about 24; radial spines 10–14, whitish, needle-shaped, to 1½ in. long, central spines 7–13, dark red, 2 flattened and sometimes hooked, the others awl-shaped; fls. 1½ in. long, perianth segms. straw-yellow with a maroon dorsal midstripe; fr. yellow. Cent. Baja Calif. Var. **gracilis**, The typical var.; upper and lower central spines ¼ in. wide or less, mostly twisted. Var. **coloratus** (H. E. Gates) G. Lindsay [*F. coloratus* H. E. Gates]. Upper and lower central spines to ⅜ in. wide, not twisted.

hamatacanthus (Mühlenpf.) Britt. & Rose [*Hamatocactus hamatacanthus* (Mühlenpf.) Borg.]. TURK'S-HEAD. Sts. mostly simple, oblong, to 2 ft. high, ribs 13–17, somewhat tubercled; spines brown to gray, radial spines 8–12, needle-shaped, to 3 in. long, central spines 4, angled, the lower hooked, to 5 in. long; fls. yellow, sometimes with red center, 3 in. long; fr. greenish. S. Tex., New Mex., n. Mex. Similar in seed characters to *Ferocactus,* not *Hamatocactus.*

Herrerae Ort. Sts. simple, cylindrical, to 6 ft. high, ribs 13–14; radial spines about 8 bristlelike and 8 stout, central spine hooked or straight; fls. 2½ in. long, segms. with yellow margins; fr. 1½ in. long. W. Mex.

histrix (DC.) G. Lindsay. ELECTRODE CACTUS. Sts. simple, cylindrical, to 2 ft. thick, ribs about 24; spines 10–12, yellow, becoming brown, 6–8 slender-awl-shaped, to 1¼ in. long, 3–4 more central and to 2½ in. long; fls. yellow, to 1½ in. long. E. Mex.

horridus: *F. peninsulae.*

Johnsonii: *Neolloydia Johnsonii.*

latispinus (Haw.) Britt. & Rose [*Echinocactus latispinus* (Haw.) Hemsl.]. DEVIL'S-TONGUE. Sts. simple, globose or depressed, to 16 in. thick, ribs 15–23; radial spines 6–18, yellowish, awl-shaped, 1–2 in. long, 4–6 of the central spines red, stout, 1 of them often deflexed, hooked, ¼ in. wide; fls. rose, to 1½ in. long; fr. 1½ in. long. Mex.

Lecontei: *F. acanthodes* var.

macrodiscus (Mart.) Britt. & Rose. Sts. simple, depressed-globose to short-cylindrical, to 1½ ft. wide, ribs 13–21; spines recurved, radial spines 6–8, awl-shaped, about 1 in. long, central spines 4, stouter and flatter, to 1½ in. long; fls. purple, 2 in. long. Mex.

melocactiformis (DC.) Britt. & Rose: a doubtful name based on a drawing not identified with any known sp.; but the name has been applied to *F. hystrix.*

nobilis: *F. recurvus.*

Orcuttii (Engelm.) Britt. & Rose [*Echinocactus Orcuttii* Engelm.]. Said to be a large phase of *F. viridescens,* with red fls. N. Baja Calif.

peninsulae (A. Web.) Britt. & Rose [*F. horridus* Britt. & Rose]. Sts. simple, cylindrical, to 8 ft. high and 1 ft. thick, ribs 12–20; radial spines about 11, nearly straight, some often white and bristlelike, central spines 4, the longest 3–6 in. long, often flattened and hooked; fls. yellow to red, 2½ in. long; fr. about 1 in. long. Baja Calif. Var. **viscainensis** (H. E. Gates) G. Lindsay [*F. viscaenensis* H. E. Gates]. Differs in having fls. shorter, stiffer, more tubular and spines shorter, less differentiated.

pilosus (Galeotti) Werderm. [*F. Pringlei* (J. Coult.) Britt. & Rose; *F. Stainesii* Britt. & Rose; *Echinocactus pilosus* Galeotti; *E. Pringlei* (J. Coult.) Rose]. Sts. simple or branched at base, to 4 ft. high, ribs 13–20; radial spines white, hairlike, central spines several, awl-shaped, purplish, becoming pale yellow; fls. yellow. Cent. Mex.

Pringlei: *F. pilosus.*

rafaelensis (J. Purpus) Borg. Sts. in clusters of 8–10, short-cylindrical, to 1 ft. high and 10 in. thick, ribs 13–20; radial spines 7–9, 1¼ in. long, central spine 1, to 2½ in. long. Cent. Mex.

rectispinus (Engelm.) Britt. & Rose. HATPIN CACTUS. Sts. globose to cylindrical, to 6 ft. high; radial spines 8–12, the 3 upper stouter and sometimes curved, central spine 1, to 3½ in. long, nearly straight; fls. yellowish, 2⅜ in. long. Baja Calif.

recurvus (Mill.) Y. Ito [*F. nobilis* (L.) Britt. & Rose]. Sts. simple, globose, to 10 in. high, ribs 13–15; spines reddish-brown, radial spines 8, ¾ in. long, central spine broad and flat, recurved at apex, to nearly 3 in. long; fls. red, 1½ in. long, perianth segms. narrow; fr. ¾ in. long. Mex.

robustus (Link & Otto) Britt. & Rose. Cespitose, clumps to 15 ft. wide, sts. globose, to 8 in. thick, ribs 8; radial spines 10–14, threadlike, central spines 4–6, awl-shaped, somewhat flattened, brown, to 2½ in. long; fls. yellow, 1½ in. long; fr. to 1 in. long. S. Mex. Glandspines apparently absent.

setispinus (Engelm.) L. Bens. [*Hamatocactus setispinus* (Engelm.) Britt. & Rose]. STRAWBERRY CACTUS. Sts. to 12 in. high and 5 in. thick, flabby, ribs thin, somewhat spiralled, undulate, deeply tubercled; spines cylindrical, radial spines 6–16, slender, white or brown, to 1½ in. long, central spines stouter, one hooked, to 1½ in. long; fls. yellow, with red center, to 3 in. long; fr. globose, red, ⁵⁄₁₆ in. in diam., pulp red. Spring to autumn. S. Tex. and n. Mex.

Stainesii: *F. pilosus.*

tortulospinus: *F. acanthodes* var.

Townsendianus Britt. & Rose. Sts. short-cylindrical, to 16 in. high or more, ribs about 16; radial spines 14–16, spreading, mostly threadlike, to 1⅝ in. long, central spines awl-shaped, straight except 1 curved or hooked at apex; fls. pink, to 2⅜ in. long. San Josef Is. (Gulf of Calif.).

uncinatus: *Ancistrocactus uncinatus.*

viridescens (Torr. & A. Gray) Britt. & Rose [*Echinocactus viridescens* Torr. & A. Gray]. Sts. cespitose or mostly simple, globose or depressed, to 1½ ft. high and 14 in. wide, ribs 13–21; spines awl-shaped, red, radial spines 9–20, to ¾ in. long, central spines 4, the lower stout, flattened, to 1½ in. long; fls. yellowish, 1½ in. long; fr. reddish, 1 in. long. S. Calif. and n. Baja Calif.

viscainensis: *F. peninsulae* var.

Visnaga: a listed name of no botanical standing, apparently referring to *Echinocactus Visnaga.*

Wislizenii (Engelm.) Britt. & Rose [*F. emoryi* (Engelm.) Orcutt; *Echinocactus Wislizenii* Engelm.]. FISHHOOK CACTUS. Sts. simple, columnar, to 10 ft. high and 2 ft. thick, ribs 20–30; radial spines about 12–24, white, threadlike to needle-shaped, to 2 in. long, central spines about 4, red, brown, or gray, the largest hooked, to 4 in. long; fls. orange-red to yellow, to 2½ in. long; fr. yellow, to 1¾ in. long. Summer. W. Tex. to Ariz., n. Mex.

FERONIA Corrêa. *Rutaceae.* One sp., a spiny, deciduous tree, native to se. Asia; lvs. alt., odd-pinnate, glandular-dotted; fls. in loose panicles, unisexual and bisexual, calyx 5-toothed, falling early, petals 5, stamens 10–12; fr. globose, hard-shelled, at first 4–6-celled, becoming 1-celled with seeds parietal and hairy.

elephantum: *F. Limonia.*

Limonia (L.) Swingle [*F. elephantum* Corrêa]. WOOD APPLE, INDIAN W. A., ELEPHANT A. Tree, to 30 ft.; lfts. 5–9, ovate or obovate, to 1½ in. long, rachis and petiole winged; fls. dull red; fr. to 3 in. in diam., with edible, pinkish, acid pulp. Pulp used in making jellies. *Citrus* spp. can be grafted on this sp.

FERRARIA Burm. ex. Mill. *Iridaceae.* About 17 spp. of tender, cormous herbs, native to S. Afr., 1 to Angola; allied to *Moraea,* but differing in having corms not tunicate, flat, tuberlike; fls. foetid, perianth segms. conspicuously crisp-wavy.

Although the flowers are malodorous and fugacious, they are very decorative and are produced in constant succession over a period of several weeks. Culture as for *Tigridia* or *Gladiolus.* Propagated by seeds or by offsets.

crispa Burm. [*F. undulata* L.]. Sts. to 18 in., stout, erect, branched; lvs. sword-shaped, about as high as sts.; fls. greenish-brown to plum-purple, blotched purple, 3–4 in. across, outer segms. spreading, twice as long as inner ones, filaments united nearly to the apex, anthers yellow. Late spring, early summer.

undulata: *F. crispa.*

FERTILIZERS. Of the numerous chemical elements required for plant growth, 12 are absorbed by plant roots normally from soil. Nitrogen, phosphorus, potassium, calcium, magnesium, and sulfur are needed in large quantities and are referred to as the major elements. Others, called trace elements, are needed in small quantities and include iron, manganese, boron, zinc, copper, and molybdenum; trace elements usually occur in most soils in sufficient quantity for good plant growth. Unfortunately, soil is often limited in its ability to supply plants with an adequate supply of some of the major elements, especially nitrogen, phosphorus, and potassium. This trio of nutrients is combined naturally by man in the many kinds of fertilizers used in agriculture.

Fertilizers are of two kinds, organic and inorganic. Organic fertilizers or manures are obtained from decomposing material of animal or plant origin, whereas inorganic or chemical fertilizers are produced industrially by chemical processes. Familiar examples of organic fertilizers are the excreta of animals (including birds), bone meal, green manures (crops grown specifically to be later ploughed into the ground as a soil fertilizer or conditioner), and compost. Inorganic fertilizers are the common commercial chemical preparations, either in powdered, granular, or liquid form, which are widely available in farm and garden stores throughout the country. Today the inorganic chemical fertilizers, convenient to manufacture, distribute, and utilize, are the principal ones used in modern agriculture.

The chemical elements found in organic and inorganic fertilizers are the same and there is no difference in the nature of crops, of whatever sort, produced with the aid of either one of these fertilizer types. However, most organic fertilizers provide to a degree, but in unknown proportions, all of the nutrient elements necessary for plant growth. In a sense they are therefore general purpose fertilizers. Inorganic fertilizers, on the other hand, are more versatile. They may be prepared for slow or quick action and for application to the soil or, in the form of absorptive liquid foliar sprays, directly to the leaves of the plant. They may be formulated to suit the needs of specific crops or types of crops, usually by varying the proportions of the major nutrient elements, nitrogen, phosphorus, and potash. The proportion of these is referred to (listed alphabetically by element) by the familiar three-digit numbers under which most chemical fertilizers are sold. Since nitrogen is used by plants mainly to produce vegetative growth (leaves, stems, and roots), phosphorus to promote reproductive structures (flowers and fruits), and potash to strengthen support tissues and in disease resistance, inorganic fertilizers may be prepared in varying mixes to suit the type of growth desired in a particular crop or garden ornamental. For example, lawn grasses are grown for their foliage, hence a fertilizer with a high proportion of nitrogen, such as 22–8–4, is preferred. Where the production of flowers (for ornament), or fruits (whether beans or raspberries) is the main objective, then the formulation usually combines a high proportion of phosphorus. A typical complete inorganic fertilizer for general all-around garden use has the designation 5–10–5.

Many organic fertilizers not only supply nutrients but also serve to improve the physical characters (humus level and tilth) of the soil. Most organic fertilizers must first decompose in the soil before their nutrients can become available to plant roots. Hence, such fertilizers are usually slower to act than chemical fertilizers but also act longer, their nutrients often being available to plants during a full growing cycle. Some organic fertilizers have special uses. Bone meal, for example, has a high phosphorus and calcium content, making it especially desirable for use with ornamentals like the spring-flowering bulbs, where large flower clusters have to be developed in a very short time. Unlike organic fertilizers, the inorganic kinds are already reduced to their primary nutrient elements and so are concentrated fertilizers with quick action. The home gardener must use them with special caution. Directions for using any fertilizer must be followed exactly. Too much fertilizer or too strong a mix can quickly kill plants by burning the leaves or roots. See also *Soils.*

FERULA L. *Umbelliferae.* Over 100 spp. of per., thick-rooted herbs, native from Medit. region to cent. Asia; lvs. pinnately decompound; fls. small, yellow or greenish, in compound umbels; fr. ovate, compressed.

Some species yield medicinal drugs and gums. Propagated by seeds sown in spring where plants are to grow.

communis L. COMMON GIANT FENNEL. To 12 ft.; lvs. very finely dissected into linear segms. S. Eur. to Syria. The edible fennel is *Foeniculum vulgare.*

tingitana L. To 6 ft., glabrous; lvs. glaucous-green, 4-pinnate, segms. oblong, divided; central umbel sessile or short-stalked; fr. to ⅜ in. long. Asia Minor and N. Afr.

FESTUCA L. [*Vulpia* C. C. Gmel.]. FESCUE. *Gramineae.* More than 100 spp. of ann. or per. grasses, worldwide but more abundant in temp. or cold regions; lf. blades sometimes auriculate; panicles narrow or open; spikelets 2- to several-fld., rachilla disarticulating above the glumes and between the florets, the uppermost floret reduced, glumes narrow, 1- or 3-nerved, acute or short-awned, lemma rounded or slightly keeled on the back, 5-nerved, with often obscure nerves, acute, obtuse, or awned from the tip or rarely from a minutely bifid apex. For terminology see *Gramineae.*

amethystina L. Per., sts. to 3 ft., slender, clustered; lf. blades filiform, soft, to 10 in. long; panicle to 4 in. long, rather narrow, much-branched, brs. mostly paired; spikelets purplish, 3–7-fld., 1⁵⁄₁₆ in. long, glumes short, unequal, lemma membranous toward the apex, acute. Cent. Eur.

arundinacea: *F. elatior.*

capillata: *F. tenuifolia.*

duriuscula: *F. ovina* var.

elatior L. [*F. arundinacea* Schreb.; *F. elatior* var. *arundinacea* (Schreb.) Wimm.]. REED F., ALTA F., TALL F. Distinguished from *F. pratensis* by taller, more robust sts., lack of rhizomes, longer lf. blades, panicles ½–1 ft. long with many brs. and spikelets; spikelets broader, looser, lemma to ⅜ in. long. Eur.; introd. and escaped from Me. to Wash., s. to N.Y. and Calif. Cult. as a meadow and forage grass. The name *F. elatior* has often been misapplied to *F. pratensis.*

geniculata (L.) Lag. [*F. stipoides* Mutel; *Vulpia geniculata* (L.) Link]. Ann., sts. slender, geniculate at the base, to 2 ft. high; panicle to 2½ in. long, rather compact; spikelets 3–5-fld., lemma awned. W. Medit. Sometimes cult. for ornament.

gigantea (L.) Vill. GIANT F. Per., sts. to nearly 7 ft.; lf. sheaths glabrous, blades glabrous, flat, to ⅝ in. wide, thin; panicles open, large, brs. branching above the middle, spreading or drooping, with several spikelets; spikelets 3–10-fld., lemma with flexuous awn 2–3 times as long as the lemma. Eurasia, N. Afr.; introd. in nw. states and escaped in N.Y.

glauca: *F. ovina* var.

glauca superba: a name of no botanical standing, probably for a form of *F. ovina* var. *glauca.*

heterophylla: *F. rubra* var.

nova-zelandiae: *F. ovina* var.

nutans: see *F. paradoxa.*

ovina L. SHEEP F. Per., sts. densely clustered, to 1 ft. or sometimes 16 in.; lf. blades slender, involute, from very scabrous to glabrous, not more than half as long as sts.; panicle narrow, often almost spikelike, few-fld., less than 4 in. long; spikelets mostly 4–5-fld., lemma to ⁵⁄₁₆ in. long, short-awned. N. Amer. from N. Dak. to Wash. and Alaska, s. to

Ariz. and New Mex., introd. eastward; Eurasia, N. Afr. Cult. as a meadow and forage grass. Var **duriuscula** (L.) W. D. J. Koch [*F. duriuscula* L.]. HARD F. Lf. blades smooth, wider and firmer. Eur. Var. **glauca** (Lam.) W. D. J. Koch [*F. glauca* Lam.]. BLUE F. Lf. blades elongate, glaucous. Eur.; introd. and cult. as a border plant. Var. **novae-zelandiae** Hack. [*F. novae-zelandiae* (Hack.) Cockayne]. Sts. 12–20 in.; lf. blades very narrow, cylindrical, as long as the sts.; spikelets 5–7-fld. New Zeal. Var. **vaginata** (Waldst. & Kit. ex Willd.) Hack. ex Nakai [*F. vaginata* Waldst. & Kit. ex Willd.]. Sts. to 2 ft.; lf. blades bluish, smooth, stiff; panicle loose, to 8 in. long; spikelets ¼ in. long. Hungary.

paradoxa Desv. [*F. nutans* Biehler, not Moench.]. Per., sts. few to several in a clump, to 4 ft.; lf. blades flat or nearly involute on drying, to 5/16 in. wide; panicle to 10 in. long, drooping, brs. not divergent, floriferous from near middle; spikelets 3–6-fld., lemma blunt. Penn. and Del. to S.C., Wisc., and e. Tex.

pratensis Huds. [*F. elatior* of many auth., not L.]. MEADOW F., ENGLISH BLUEGRASS. Per., sts. to 4 ft., clustered; lf. blades flat, to 2 ft. long, 5/16 in. wide, scabrous above, not tufted at base; panicle erect, to 1 ft. long, much-branched or nearly simple, contracted after flowering; spikelets usually 6–8-fld., to ½ in. long, glumes ⅛ in. long, lanceolate, lemma oblong-lanceolate, thick, about ¼ in. long, acute or rarely short-awned. Eurasia; introd. into the cooler parts of N. Amer.

rubra L. [*F. viridis* Panz. ex Schult.] RED F. Per., sts. usually loosely or occasionally densely clustered, bent or decumbent at the reddish or purplish base, erect to ascending, to 3 ft. high; lower lf. sheaths brown, thin, becoming fibrous, blades smooth, soft, very slender; panicle with mostly ascending brs.; spikelets 3–10-fld., pale green or glaucous, often purple-tinged, lemmas ¼ in. long, smooth or scabrous toward apex, bearing an awn about half as long. N. Amer., w. Canada to Mex., e. Canada to Ga.; Eurasia, N. Afr. Subsp. **rubra**. The typical subsp.; lf. blades folded, involute or rarely flat; panicle to 10 in. long; spikelets 4–6-fld. Cult. as meadow and forage grass. Var. **commutata** Gaud.-Beaup. [var. *fallax* (Thuill.) Hack.]. CHEWING F. Sts. more erect, producing a firmer sod. Eur. Var. **fallax**: var. *commutata*. Var. **heterophylla** (Lam.) Mutel [*F. heterophylla* Lam.]. SHADE F. Sts. densely clustered; basal lf. blades filiform, blades of st. leaves flat. Eur.; introd. for lawns in shady places. Var. **stolonifera**: a name of no botanical standing, see subsp. *pyrenaica*. Subsp. **pyrenaica** (Reut.) Hack. [*F. stolonifera* Miègev.]. Sts. to 10 in. high; lf. blades flat, those of st. often involute; panicle to 1½ in. long; spikelets few, 2–5-fld. France.

stipoides: *F. geniculata*.

stolonifera: *F. rubra* subsp. *pyrenaica*.

tenuifolia Sibth. [*F. capillata* Lam.]. HAIR F. Distinguished from *F. ovina* in having sts. lower, lf. blades capillary, flexuous, usually more than half as long as the sts., spikelets smaller and lemma about ⅛ in. long, awnless. Eur.; introd. and escaped from Nfld. and Me. to N.C. and Ore.

vaginata: *F. ovina* var.

viridis: *F. rubra*.

FIBIGIA Medic. *Cruciferae*. Several spp. of erect, per. herbs in Medit. region, with stellate-pubescence or sometimes with longer unbranched hairs; lvs. linear to spatulate, entire or dentate; fls. yellow or violet, sepals 4, petals 4, short-clawed; fr. a flattened silicle, seeds winged.

clypeata (L.) Medic. [*Farsetia clypeata* (L.) R. Br.]. Usually more than 12 in.; lower lvs. oblong, entire or repand-dentate, st. lvs. linear; petals yellow, to ½ in. long; silicles elliptic, to 1 in. long, grayish-stellate-pubescent. S. Eur., sw. Asia.

eriocarpa (DC.) Sibth. & Sm. [*Farsetia eriocarpa* DC.]. Lvs. linear-oblong, usually dentate; silicles with both stellate and long, simple or forked hairs; otherwise similar to *F. clypeata*. Greece.

lunarioides (Willd.) Sibth. & Sm. [*Farsetia lunarioides* R. Br.]. Per., usually less than 12 in., woody at base, much-branched; lvs. oblong-oblanceolate, entire, stellate-hairy; petals bright yellow, to ⅝ in. long; silicles elliptic to orbicular, to ⅞ in. long, grayish-stellate-pubescent. Greece.

FICOIDACEAE: *AIZOACEAE*.

FICUS L. FIG. *Moraceae*. About 800 spp. of monoecious or dioecious trees, shrubs, and woody root-clinging vines, with milky sap, native to tropics, but chiefly Old World; lvs. thick or stiff, mostly persistent, often large and showy; fls. minute, unisexual; seeds inside a globose, oblong, or pear-shaped fleshy receptacle or fig which has an ostiole (small opening) at its apex.

The genus includes edible figs and species yielding fodder, natural rubber, bark cloth, and host plants for the lac insect. Some figs are among the wonders of the plant kingdom, such as the banyan (*F. benghalensis*) which sends down aerial roots forming trunks to support the canopy, thus enabling the tree to extend over several acres; others, the strangler figs, begin as epiphytes, later strangling their host with their heavy inarching aerial roots and eventually becoming self-supporting, independent trees. The species listed have evergreen leaves, unless stated otherwise.

Many kinds of figs are widely planted for shade and ornament outdoors in the tropics and subtropics. A number of these also make satisfactory ornamentals for the home or conservatory. Propagation is easy, the ornamental, arboreal species usually by air-layering and the trailing species by division of the rooting stems.

Afzelii G. Don ex Loud. [*F. eriobotryoides* Kunth & Bouché ex Kunth]. Tree, to 40 ft. or more; lvs. leathery, oblanceolate, narrowly obovate to oblong-elliptic, to 1 ft. long and 4 in. wide, paler beneath; figs axillary, sessile, densely yellow- or red-hairy to glabrescent, to 1½ in. in diam. Trop. Afr.

altissima Blume. COUNCIL TREE. Large, spreading tree, to 75 ft.; lvs. thick, ovate to elliptic, to 6 in. long or more; figs ovoid, sessile, usually yellow, glabrous, to ¾ in. in diam. Assam to Malay Arch. and Philippine Is. Zone 10b.

aspera G. Forst. [*F. Parcellii* Veitch.]. CLOWN F. Shrub or small tree; lvs. thin, ovate or oblong, to 8 in. long, acuminate, hairy beneath, mottled ivory-white on dark green, very showy, often dotted and speckled white on green; figs peduncled, green, striped cream and pink, rusty-pubescent, to 1 in. in diam. S. Pacific Is.

aurea Nutt. GOLDEN F., STRANGLER F., FLORIDA S. F. Tree, to 60 ft., often starting as an epiphyte; lvs. elliptic, narrowed at both ends, to 4 in. long; figs sessile or nearly so, yellow, to 5/16 in. in diam. S. Fla., W. Indies.

auriculata Lour. [*F. Roxburghii* Wallich ex Miq.]. Tree or shrub, young twigs hollow; lvs. ovate, to 16 in. long, 13 in. wide, cordate, acute to acuminate or sometimes rounded; figs from brs. or trunk, pear-shaped to depressed-globose, white- or rusty-flecked, silky-hairy, to 2½ in. in diam. Himalayas.

australis: *F. rubiginosa*.

belgica: a listed name of no botanical standing for *F. elastica*.

benghalensis L. [*F. indica* L.]. BANYAN TREE, EAST INDIAN FIG TREE, INDIAN BANYAN. Very large tree, epiphytic when young, the top spreading by accessory trunks; lvs. leathery, broadly ovate to elliptic, to 8 in. long; figs in axillary pairs, globose, orange-red, puberulous, to ½ in. in diam. India, Pakistan, where considered sacred. Widely cult. in tropics. Zone 10b. Cv. 'Krishnae' [*F. Krishnae* C. DC.] KRISHNA-BOR, KRISHNA'S BUTTER-CUP. Lvs. curiously cup-shaped, unique.

benjamina L. [*F. nitida* Thunb.]. BENJAMIN TREE, WEEPING F., JAVA F., LAUREL, TROPIC L., WEEPING L., SMALL-LEAVED RUBBER PLANT. Tree or shrub, epiphytic when young, brs. drooping, poplarlike; lvs. thin, leathery, ovate-elliptic, to 5 in. long, cuspidate; figs in axillary pairs, red, globose, to ½ in. in diam or less. India, se. Asia, Malay Arch., n. trop. Australia. Var. **benjamina**. The typical var.; lvs. to 5½ in. long, 2½ in. wide; figs bright red, base not narrowed, twisted or bracted. Cv. 'Exotica' [*F. exotica* Hort.]. EXOTIC F. Tree, with slender, drooping brs. and long-tipped lvs. with twisted tips. Var. **nuda** (Miq.) Barrett [*F. comosa* Roxb.]. Lvs. narrower, longer, more acuminate; figs whitish or red-brown, with twisted, narrowed base and no bracts when mature.

brevifolia: *F. citrifolia*.

calophylloides: *F. subcordata*.

capensis Thunb. CAPE F., BUSH F. Tree, to 60 ft.; lvs. thin, leathery, ovate-elliptic to nearly orbicular, to 7 in. long, rounded or obtuse, entire to irregularly toothed, lf. scars with a fringe of hairs; figs globose, produced in simple or branched, grapelike clusters on the trunk and the lowest brs., to ¾ in. in diam. S. Afr., n. to trop. Afr. and Cape Verde Is.

carica L. COMMON F., FIG TREE. Broad, irregular, deciduous tree, to 30 ft., commonly a shrub in cult.; lvs. thick, usually deeply 3–5-lobed, scabrous above, pubescent beneath; figs variable, edible. Medit. region, Zone 8. Grown since earliest times for the fr. Many select cvs. exist. See *Fig*.

citrifolia Mill. [*F. brevifolia* Nutt.]. Tree, to 50 ft., or sometimes a shrub, epiphytic when young, twigs glabrous; lvs. lanceolate to oblong-ovate, to 8 in. long and 4¾ in. wide, acute to acuminate, base rounded to subcordate; figs among lvs., globose, glabrous, reddish to yellowish, to ⅝ in. in diam., peduncle to ¾ in. long. Fla. to Paraguay.

comosa: *F. benjamina* var. *nuda*.

cunia: *F. semicordata.*

decora: a listed name of no botanical standing for *F. elastica* cv.

deltoidea Jack [*F. diversifolia* Blume]. MISTLETOE F., MISTLETOE RUBBER PLANT. Shrub, to 6 ft.; lvs. mostly broadly obovate, 1–3 in. long, rusty-olive beneath; figs yellow, to 5/16 in. in diam., on long axillary peduncles. Malay Arch.

diversifolia: *F. deltoidea.*

Doescheri: a listed name of no botanical standing for *F. elastica* cv.

Dryepondtiana Gentil. CONGO F. Epiphyte, sts. mostly unbranched, slender; lvs. oblong-acuminate, 9–13 in. long, cordate, dark olive-green above, purple beneath, margins wavy; figs in clusters of 7–11 on older brs., globose, hairy, spotted greenish-white, about 1½ in. in diam. Cameroon, Congo, Gabon.

elastica Roxb. ex Hornem. [*F. belgica* Hort.; *F. rubra* Hort., not Roth]. INDIA RUBBER TREE, RUBBER PLANT, ASSAM RUBBER. Large, glabrous tree; lvs. thick, oblong or elliptic, to 12 in. long, glossy; figs sessile, usually in pairs, ovate-oblong, greenish-yellow, to ½ in. in diam. Nepal to Assam and Burma; widely cult. in tropics. Zone 10b. Much grown indoors in its juvenile state as a pot or tub plant. Formerly important and cult. as a source of an inferior natural rubber. Cv. **'Decora'** [*F. decora* Hort.]. BROAD-LEAVED INDIAN RUBBER PLANT. Lvs. dark glossy green with ivory midrib, red beneath. Cv. **'Doescheri'** [*F. Doescheri* Hort.]. Lvs. green at margins, marbled gray-green with creamy-yellow midrib, petioles pink. Cv. **'Variegata'.** Lvs. light green, margined white or yellow.

erecta Thunb. Shrub or small tree, to 15 ft.; lvs. ovate to obovate, to 3 in. long; figs solitary or in pairs, globose to pear-shaped, to ¼ in. in diam. Japan, Korea, Ryukyu Is. to Taiwan. Zone 9.

eriobotryoides: *F. Afzelii.*

exotica: a listed name of no botanical standing for *F. benjamina* cv.

glomerata: *F. racemosa.*

Henneana Miq.: *F. superba* var.

hispida L. f. Shrub or small tree, hispid; lvs. ovate-oblong, to 10 in. long, acute or cuspidate; figs fascicled, on trunk or leafy brs., ovoid to nearly pear-shaped, to 1 in. in diam., brown-pubescent, edible. Trop. Asia from India to n. Australia.

Hookeri: see *F. Hookerana.*

Hookerana Corner [*F. Hookeri* Miq., not Sweet]. Glabrous tree; lvs. thin, leathery, broadly elliptic, to 11 in. long, apex short, broad, long-petioled; figs in axillary pairs, sessile, ovoid, to 1 in. in diam. Sikkim, Assam, Yunnan.

indica: *F. benghalensis.*

infectoria: *F. virens.*

jacquiniifolia: *F. perforata.*

Krishnae: *F. benghalensis* cv.

lacor: *F. virens.*

lyrata Warb. [*F. pandurata* Hort. Sander, not Hance]. FIDDLE-LEAF F., FIDDLE-LEAF. Tree, to 40 ft.; lvs. fiddle-shaped, large, to 15 in. long, apex large, rounded; figs sessile, solitary or in pairs, globose, dotted white, to 1¼ in. in diam. Trop. Afr. Zone 10b. Juvenile stage popular indoors.

macrocarpa: see *F. macrophylla* and *F. punctata.*

macrophylla Desf. ex Pers. [*F. macrocarpa* Hügel ex Kunth & Bouché]. MORETON BAY F., AUSTRALIAN BANYAN. Large tree, to 50 ft. in cult., to 200 ft. in the wild; lvs. ovate to elliptic, 6–12 in. long, acute, glossy above, silvery to rusty-dotted beneath; figs axillary, globose, dark reddish-brown to purple with paler spots, to 1 in. in diam. E. Australia.

mallotocarpa Warb. Similar to *F. capensis,* differing in having lvs. elliptic to oblong or obovate, acuminate, mostly toothed, lf. scars without a fringe of hairs. Trop. Afr.

microphylla: a listed name of no botanical standing, probably for *F. rubiginosa.*

montana Burm.f. [*F. quercifolia* Roxb.]. OAK-LEAF F. Shrub, more or less prostrate; lvs. elliptic or ovate, to 6 in. long, lobed and notched on sides, scabrous; figs globose, peduncled, to ½ in. in diam. or less. Malay Arch., se. Asia. Grown indoors for its decorative foliage.

mysorensis B. Heyne ex Roth. MYSORE F. Tree, to 30 ft., twigs brown-tomentose, becoming glabrous; lvs. elliptic-ovate or obovate, to 8 in. long; figs ovoid, orange-red, sessile, axillary, in pairs, to 1 in. in diam. Trop. Asia. Fr. edible.

Nekbudu Warb. [*F. utilis* Sim]. KAFFIR F., ZULU FIG TREE. Epiphytic strangler or independent tree, to 70 ft.; lvs. oblong-elliptic, to 12 in. long; figs subglobose, hairy, dark red or sometimes tan. Trop. Afr. Some material so listed is *F. Vogelii.*

nemoralis: *F. neriifolia* var.

neriifolia Sm. Small tree, briefly deciduous in early spring; lvs. at first red, turning green, lanceolate to ovate, 3–6 in. long, 1–2 in. wide, narrowed to a long acumen, base cuneate, 3-nerved, otherwise with 7–14 pairs of pinnate nerves, entire, reticulations dark, conspicuous on lower surface, petiole to 1 in. long, reddish; figs axillary, solitary or paired, reddish, edible, 5/16 in. in diam. Himalayas. Var. **neriifolia.** The typical var.; figs sessile or nearly so. Nepal to Yunnan. Var. **nemoralis** (Wallich ex Miq.) Corner [*F. nemoralis* Wallich ex Miq.]. Peduncle of fig to ¼ in. long. Himalayas.

nitida: *F. benjamina.*

nota (Blanco) Merrill. Erect tree, to 25 ft., more or less pubescent; lvs. oblong to oblong-obovate, to 10 in. long or more, distantly and irregularly toothed, base unequal; figs borne in a large branched infl. arising directly from the trunk and the larger brs., subglobose, yellowish, to 1½ in. in diam. Philippine Is. to n. Borneo.

ovata Vahl. Large tree, often epiphytic at first; lvs. ovate to oblong-ovate, to 8 in. long; figs nearly sessile, axillary, paired, green with white spots, covered by a brown cap when young, to 1 in. in diam. Trop. Afr.

palmata Forssk. [*F. pseudocarica* Miq.]. Shrub or small tree; lvs. orbicular, sometimes 3–5-lobed, to 5 in. long, toothed or entire, nearly scabrous above, scabrid or shortly tomentose beneath; figs peduncled, subglobose to pear-shaped, to 1 in. in diam., the base constricted. Ne. Afr. to nw. India and Nepal. Frs. edible, resembling those of *F. Carica.*

pandurata Hance. Not cult. but the name has been misapplied to *F. lyrata* and *F. Willdemaniana.*

Parcellii: *F. aspera.*

perforata L. [*F. jacquiniifolia* A. Rich.]. WEST INDIAN LAUREL F. Shrub or tree; lvs. oblong, elliptic, or obovate, 1–2 in. long, about 1 in. wide or less, glabrous, apex rounded to nearly acute, base obtuse to nearly acute, petioles ⅛–¼ in. long; figs in pairs, globose, to ¼ in. in diam., glabrous. Cuba and Bahama Is. to Cent. Amer., n. S. Amer.

petiolaris HBK. Small to large tree; lvs. cordate-orbicular, to 3 in. wide, the apex broadly rounded, abruptly short-pointed; figs globose to depressed-globose, densely villous when young, becoming minutely puberulent to glabrescent, to ½ in. in diam., the ostiole (opening) prominent. Mex. Readily distinguished by tufts of long white hairs in the axils along the principal vein.

philippinensis Miq. Small, spreading, glabrous tree; lvs. oblong-elliptic, acuminate, to 4 in. long; figs subsessile, solitary or paired, globular, dark red, to 5/16 in. across. Philippine Is.

platyphylla Delile. Tree, often epiphytic at first; lvs. broadly oblong-elliptic, base cordate; figs in clusters of 2–5 toward tips of brs., subglobose, reddish, many, pilose to glabrous, often warty, to 1 in. in diam. Trop. Afr. Some material grown under this name is *F. umbellata.*

pseudocarica: *F. palmata.*

pseudopalma Blanco. PHILIPPINE F., DRACAENA F. Erect shrub, glabrous, unbranched; lvs. subsessile, crowded at tips of brs. and giving appearance of a small palm, blades oblanceolate, to 30 in. long, nearly cordate, acute to acuminate, coarsely sinuate-toothed, stipules persistent, lanceolate, 2–3 in. long; figs paired, ovoid, dark green, to 1½ in. long, short-peduncled. Philippine Is.

pumila L. [*F. repens* Hort., not Willd.; *F. stipulata* Thunb.]. CREEPING F., CLIMBING F., CREEPING RUBBER PLANT. Vine, clinging to walls by means of roots, fruiting brs. erect; lvs. of creeping sts. sessile or short-petioled, cordate-ovate, 1 in. long or less, base oblique, lvs. on fruiting brs. elliptic or oblong, 2–4 in. long; figs pear-shaped, yellowish, to 2 in. long. E. Asia from Japan to N. Vietnam. Common in greenhouses, conservatories, and in the open in Zone 9 under the name *"F. repens."* Cv. **'Minima'.** Lvs. slender, small (the juvenile stage). Cv. **'Quercifolia'.** Lvs. pinnately lobed. Cv. **'Variegata'.** Lvs. variegated green and white.

punctata Thunb. [*F. macrocarpa* Blume]. Sts. slender, creeping and rooting, lightly brown-hairy; lvs. linear-oblong or rhomboidal, to 1 in. long, somewhat narrowed to the more or less distinctly unequal to curved base; figs borne on the st., ovoid to pear-shaped, brown to orange, about ½ in. long. Se. Asia, Malay Arch. Sometimes grown under glass.

quercifolia: *F. montana.*

racemosa L. [*F. glomerata* Roxb.]. CLUSTER F. Tree, to 60 ft., not epiphytic when young; lvs. elliptic or ovate-lanceolate, to 6 in. long, entire, base rounded; figs borne from tubercles on the lower part of the trunk and the main brs., almost globose, green to red, to 1½ in. in diam. Trop. Asia from India to n. Australia. Often cult. in India for edible frs.

radicans: *F. sagittata.*

religiosa L. BO TREE, PEEPUL, SACRED F. Large, deciduous, fast-growing tree, usually starting as an epiphyte; lvs. round-ovate, with a distinct, narrow, terminal projection half as long as the main blade; figs sessile, dark purple, to ½ in. in diam. India to se. Asia, widely planted in tropics. Zone 10b. In India the tree is sacred to Hindus and Buddhists. The long, slender lf. tip distinguishes this from other spp.

repens: see *F. pumila.*

retusa L. INDIAN LAUREL, MALAY BANYAN, CHINESE B., GLOSSY-LEAF F. Glabrous shrub or tree, producing few aerial roots; lvs. broad-ovate or broad-elliptic, apex obtuse or barely elongated, base rounded or very slightly narrowed; figs sessile, axillary, in pairs, purplish, to ½ in. in diam. Malay Pen. to Borneo.

Roxburghii: *F. auriculata.*

rubiginosa Desf. ex Venten. [*F. australis* Willd.]. PORT JACKSON F., RUSTY F., LITTLE-LEAF F. Small tree, rusty-pubescent, especially on young twigs; lvs. leathery, ovate to elliptic-oblong, to 4 in. long or more, petioles and lower surface of blade rusty-pubescent to glabrescent; figs axillary, paired, globose, warty, rusty-pubescent to glabrescent, to ½ in. in diam. New S. Wales. Cv. **'Florida'**. A listed name. Cv. **'Variegata'**. Lvs. variegated, cream-yellow.

rubra: see *F. elastica.*

sagittata Vahl [*F. radicans* Desf.]. Sts. creeping, wiry; lvs. oblong-lanceolate, 2–4 in. long, acuminate, entire, glabrous. E. Himalayas to Philippine Is., and Caroline Is. Cv. **'Variegata'**. Lvs. gray-green, irregularly marked cream-white.

salicifolia: *F. subulata.*

semicordata Buch.-Ham. ex Sm. [*F. cunia* Buch.-Ham. ex Roxb.]. Small to medium-sized tree; lvs. elliptic to oblong-lanceolate, 6–15 in. long, entire to serrate, scabrous to glabrous above, usually pubescent beneath, the base auricled with 1 side overlapping petiole, petiole to ½ in. long; figs globose to pear-shaped, hispid, red-brown, ½ in. in diam. Trop. Asia.

stipulata: *F. pumila.*

subcordata Blume [*F. calophylloides* Elmer]. Epiphytic, becoming a powerful strangler; lvs. oblong-ovate, to 6 in. long, tip acuminate; figs ellipsoid to subglobose, pale yellow, about 1 in. in diam. Indonesia, s. Philippine Is., New Guinea.

subulata Blume [*F. salicifolia* Miq.]. Shrub, semiscandent, dioecious; lvs. elliptic-lanceolate, 4–10 in. long, glabrescent, pinnately nerved, nerves 7–10 pairs, petiole 5/16 in. long, stout, scabrous; figs axillary, nearly sessile, solitary or paired, orange-red, to ½ in. in diam. Ne. India, s. China, Malay Arch. to the Solomon Is.

superba Miq. SEA F. Large tree; lvs. elliptic, to 10 in. long and 5 in. wide, rounded or nearly cordate; figs bunched on twigs and brs., pear-shaped, dull purple, to ¾ in. in diam. Japan to Australia. Var. **superba.** The typical var.; twigs to ½ in. thick, stipules villous; lvs. to 5 in. wide; peduncles to 1⅜ in. long. Se. Asia, Malay Arch. Var. **Henneana** (Miq.) Corner [*F. Henneana* Miq.]. CEDAR F. Twigs to ¼ in. thick, stipules slightly hairy to glabrous; lvs. to 4 in. wide; peduncles to ½ in. long. N. Australia.

Sycomorus L. SYCAMORE F., EGYPTIAN SYCAMORE, MULBERRY F., SYCAMORE (of the Bible). Tree, to 60 ft.; lvs. ovate to nearly orbicular, to 6 in. long, nearly cordate; figs borne in panicles on leafless twigs from the trunk and brs., obovoid to globose, to 1 in. in diam. S. Afr. to Egypt and Lebanon in cult.

Thonningii Blume. Tree, to 60 ft., with many aerial roots, epiphytic when young; lvs. papery, obovate-elliptic, to 9 in. long, obtuse, dark green, glabrous; figs axillary, in pairs, globose, to 5/16 in. in diam. Trop. Afr., where commonly planted for shade.

ulmifolia Lam. Shrub or small tree, from 10 to 15 ft.; lvs. variable, oblong, subentire to coarsely toothed, sometimes deeply lobed, to 7 in. long, 1½–3 in. wide, scabrous; figs ovoid, orange-red to purplish, to ⅝ in. long, peduncle about ¼ in. long. Very variable. Philippine Is.

umbellata Vahl. Upright tree; lvs. ovate to 1 ft. long, 8 in. wide, broadly cordate, long-acuminate, entire but often wavy-margined; figs axillary, globose to obovoid, dark brown with lighter flecks, velvety, ¾ in. in diam. Trop. Afr.

utilis: *F. Nekbudu.*

virens Ait. [*F. infectoria* Willd.; *F. lacor* Buch.-Ham.]. SPOTTED F. Deciduous tree, to 50 ft.; lvs. elliptic to oblong-ovate, 3–7 in. long, nerves 5–7 pairs, inconspicuous, petioles 1–2 in. long, stipules to ½ in. long, broadly ovate, acute, pubescent; figs paired, whitish, flushed red and dotted, to ½ in. in diam. Trop. Asia from India to n. Australia. Commonly planted in India as an ornamental street tree.

Vogelii (Miq.) Miq. WEST AFRICAN RUBBER TREE. Epiphytic strangler or an independent tree; lvs. oblanceolate, to 8 in. long or more; figs axillary, paired, sessile, subglobose, yellow or red with lighter dots when mature, to ½ in. in diam. Trop. Afr.

Watkinsiana F. M. Bailey. Glabrous tree, to 60 ft. or to 150 ft. in the wild, trunk to 6 ft. in diam., buttressed, bark gray; lvs. elliptic, 4–8 in. long, 2–3 in. wide, glabrous; figs axillary, paired but often only one remaining, globose to ovoid, dark purple when ripe, to 1¾ in. long. E. Australia.

Willdemaniana Warb. Tree, or epiphytic when young, twigs sparsely pubescent to glabrous; lvs. leathery, oblong-lanceolate to fiddle-shaped, to 28 in. long and 10 in. wide, briefly rounded to cordate, acuminate, sparsely pubescent at base beneath; figs axillary, solitary or paired, nearly globose, green, spotted yellow, to 1⅝ in. in diam. Cameroon, Zaire.

FIG. The common cultivated fig, *Ficus carica,* originally native to the Mediterranean region, is but one of many species of the large, primarily tropical genus *Ficus.* It is a spreading tree (to 90 feet) or large shrub of the cooler subtropics, with soft wood, foliage that is deciduous in winter, and fruit maturing in summer and autumn. The pomological or commercial fig is not a fruit in the strict botanical sense but a hollow, fleshy receptacle with the many true fruits or "seeds" on the inside of it. Before ripening, there is an opening at the apex through which passes (in some cultivars) the special insect, a gall wasp, that pollinates the minute flowers and brings about development of the true fruits.

Propagation is by means of dormant hardwood cuttings 4–5 inches long, taken in winter or early spring, much after the way of grapes. For best results, the cuttings are made through a node and buried, leaving the tip even with the soil surface. Bearing plants may be expected in two to four years from rooted cuttings. The trees are usually planted about 18 to 25 feet apart and are fertilized like other deciduous fruits. Figs do best in Mediterranean climates but stand considerable frost, and some seedling or inferior kinds grow outdoors without protection in Zone 8. Many cultivars produce fruit on young sprouts, and as the roots endure some cold, these kinds may give a few figs even in Zone 5 if good winter protection is given. In such areas, the tree should be laid down in winter, particularly if the temperature is likely to go to below 10° F. For such treatment, the trees are trained to branch close to the ground, and the branches are then bent down and covered with earth and a mound is made over the central or trunk part. In the home garden in the North, figs may also be grown in tubs that can be moved to a cool, moist cellar to overwinter.

In Zone 9, especially in Louisiana, Texas, and California, the fig is grown in regular orchard plantations for commercial purposes. In the home garden no special pruning is required unless one wishes to keep the plant small. On sandy soils, figs may be seriously attacked by root knot nematode and should be heavily mulched to avoid such attack. In California which is the chief producer, cultivars are: 'Mission' (black-skinned), used fresh, dried, or for jams; 'Adriatic', usually dried; 'Turkey', used fresh; 'Calimyrna', with an autumn crop of large, lemon-yellow fruits with amber pulp; and 'Kadota', usually canned or dried. The 'Calimyrna' cultivar requires special provision for cross pollination by the gall wasp, but other cultivars need no pollination to produce fruit. In the southeastern states, 'Brown Turkey' (also sold under the name 'Everbearing'), 'Celeste', and 'Magnolia' are the cultivars usually grown. These and 'Kadota' are also grown in Texas. With winter protection, 'Brown Turkey' may be grown as far north as Zone 5.

FILBERT. Filberts are the fruit of species of *Corylus.* Two species, *C. Avellana,* the European filbert, and *C. maxima,* the giant filbert, represent the important cultivated filberts. These species have been crossed extensively to provide many of the commercial cultivars now in existence. *Corylus* species are widely distributed in the Northern Hemisphere, but commercial nut production is limited to four areas of the world, each with a climate moderated by a large body of water: Turkey, along the coast of the Black Sea, produces about 65 percent of the world production; Italy and Spain, in areas near the Mediterranean Sea, produce about 20 and 10 percent respectively; and the Willamette Valley of Oregon, where the climate is influenced by the Pacific Ocean, produces the remaining 5 percent. The European filbert is not satisfactory in the eastern United States, partly because of its lack of hardiness and partly because of its susceptibility to a fungus blight, *Cryptosporella anomala* (C. H. Peck) Sacc. The native species, *C. americana* and *C. cornuta*, often called hazelnuts, appear tolerant of this blight and have been crossed with *C. Avellana* in an effort to combine the nut size and quality of the latter with the hardiness and disease tolerance of the former. The cultivars 'Bixby', 'Buchanan', 'Potomac', and 'Reed' represent useful selections which are improvements over the native species and permit the home gardener to grow acceptable filberts in the East.

The climate of Oregon's Willamette Valley has proved ideally suited to the Old World filbert, and the industry there has been growing slowly but steadily since its introduction at the turn of the century. Crop production is completely mechanized, from time of tree planting to time of nut harvest. The eastern filbert blight has not been introduced to Oregon, but there is a bacterial filbert blight, *Xanthomonas corylina* (P. W. Mill. et al.) M. P. Starr & Burkholder, which can be a serious disease on young trees and fruiting branches. The only important insect pest is a gall-forming mite, *Phytocoptella avellanae* (Nalepa), for which there is no control other than the use of resistant cultivars. The industry is largely based on a single cultivar, 'Barcelona', which has a large, globe-shaped nut which falls free of its short husk. 'Du Chilly' is another important cultivar. 'Barcelona' and 'Du Chilly' are self-sterile, making cross pollination obligatory. The principal pollinizing cultivar is 'Daviana', a long nut.

Filberts thrive in deep, friable, well-drained soil. In the home garden, at least two different cultivars must be planted together a few yards apart to insure cross pollination. If trained as a tree, suckers should be kept pruned away from the base of the trunk.

FILIPENDULA Mill. MEADOWSWEET. *Rosaceae.* A small genus of hardy per. herbs, native to the N. Temp. Zone, once included in the genus *Spiraea;* lvs. alt., usually pinnate; fls. many, small, in terminal corymbose panicles on leafy sts., sepals and petals usually 5, stamens 20–40, pistils 5–15; frs. 5–15 achenes.

Flowering in late spring and summer; grown in the hardy border. Propagated by seeds and by division of old plants.

camtschatica (Pall.) Maxim. [*Spiraea camtschatica* Pall.]. Four to 10 ft.; terminal lft. several in. wide, glabrous beneath except on veins, 3–5-lobed, doubly serrate, lateral lfts. often absent; fls. white, fragrant, about ¼ in. across. Manchuria, Kamtchatka.

hexapetala: *F. vulgaris.*

multijuga Maxim. Sts. slender, to 2 ft., glabrous; basal lvs. of many pairs of lfts., the terminal lfts. cordate, 5-lobed, 2–5 in. across, acuminate, the lateral lfts. small, ovate, incised-serrate, stipules broad; fls. rose to white, to ¼ in. across. Japan.

palmata Maxim. [*Spiraea palmata* Pall., not J. Murr. or Thunb.]. To 3 ft.; lvs. with large, palmately 7–9-lobed terminal lft., 3–8 in. across, densely white-tomentose beneath, lateral lfts. frequently 2 pairs, lobed and incised, 1–3 in. long, stipules large, cordate; fls. pale pink, becoming white, small. Siberia, Kamtchatka. Plants offered under this name are usually referable to *F. purpurea*, but see also *F. rubra*. Cv. 'Nana' is offered.

purpurea Maxim. [*Spiraea palmata* Thunb., not J. Murr. or Pall.]. To 4 ft.; terminal lft. 5–7-lobed, doubly serrate, acuminate, 4–8 in. across, lateral lfts. few or none, stipules narrow; fls. carmine to pink, ⅜ in. across. Japan. Cvs. are: 'Alba', fls. white; 'Elegans', fls. white, stamens red; 'Nana' [*Spiraea digitata nana* Hort.], sts. only 6–10 in. high, flowering summer to autumn.

rubra (J. Hill) B. L. Robinson [*Spiraea lobata* Gronov. ex Jacq.; *S. palmata* J. Murr., not Pall. or Thunb.]. QUEEN-OF-THE-PRAIRIE. Glabrous, to 8 ft.; lvs. interruptedly pinnate, green and scarcely paler beneath, terminal lft. 4–8 in. across, 7–9-parted, the lobes lanceolate-oblong, incised, lateral lfts. also cut; petals deep peach-blossom pink. Penn. to Mich. and Iowa, s. to Ga., Ky., Ill.; escaped elsewhere from cult. Cv. 'Venusta' [*Spiraea venusta* Hort.]. Fls. deep rose or purplish-red.

Ulmaria (L.) Maxim. [*Spiraea Ulmaria* L.]. QUEEN-OF-THE-MEADOW. To 6 ft.; lvs. mostly 1–8 ft. long, including the long petiole, with 2–5 pairs of main lfts., these 1–3 in. long, ovate, sharply doubly serrate, usually white-tomentose beneath, terminal lft. longer, 3-lobed; fls. cream-white, petals ⅛ in. long. Eur., Asia; naturalized in e. N. Amer. Cv. 'Aureo-variegata'. Lvs. variegated with yellow. Cv. 'Plena'. Fls. double.

venusta: a listed name of no botanical standing; probably for *F. rubra* cv.

vulgaris Moench [*F. hexapetala* Gilib; *Spiraea Filipendula* L.]. DROPWORT. Rootstock tuberous, sts. to 3 ft.; lvs. glabrous, 4–10 in. long, fernlike, lfts. many, pinnatifid, about 1 in. long, stipules broad; fls. white, often tinged red outside, ¾ in. across. Eur., Asia. Cv. 'Flore Pleno.' Fls. double. Cv. 'Grandiflora'. Fls. cream-yellow, often somewhat larger.

FILIX: see *CYSTOPTERIS* and *DRYOPTERIS.*

FILLAEOPSIS Harms. *Leguminosae* (subfamily *Mimosoideae*). One sp., an unarmed tree of trop. Afr.; lvs. 2-pinnate, with large lfts.; fls. small, in panicled spikes, regular, 5-merous, calyx saucer-shaped, small, petals separate, stamens 10, separate, attached on thick disc; fr. a large, flat legume, with thickened margins, dehiscent, with transverse seeds.

discophora Harms. To 125 ft.; pinnae usually 1–2 pairs, opp., lfts. 4–8, alt., elliptic, to 3 in. long, acuminate; spikes to 8 in. long; fr. to 21 in. long and 7 in. wide. Nigeria to Angola. Roots, seeds, and young growth have onion odor. Wood used for general carpentry and construction.

FIRMIANA Marsili. *Sterculiaceae.* About 10 spp. of trees, native to e. and se. Asia, Malay Arch., and the Pacific Is.; lvs. alt., simple; fls. in axillary panicles, unisexual, petals none, calyx tubular, column elongating beyond the calyx at flowering, male fls. with knotlike cluster of about 10 stamens near apex and surrounding rudimentary carpels, female fls. with 5-carpelled ovary above large but sterile anthers; fr. of up to 5, separate, papery, leaflike follicles that open before maturity.

Grown as a street, shade, or lawn tree; propagated by seeds, easily transplanted.

colorata (Roxb.) R. Br. [*Sterculia colorata* Roxb.]. To 75 ft., with basal buttresses; lvs. variable, ovate or generally palmately 3–5-lobed, to 12 in. wide; calyx tubular, to 1 in. long, rusty- or tawny-tomentose outside, tube much longer than the 5 small lobes; follicles up to 3 in. long, glabrous, seeds 2–4, glossy black. India to Java.

platanifolia: *F. simplex.*

simplex (L.) W. F. Wight [*F. platanifolia* (L.f.) Marsili; *Sterculia platanifolia* L. f.]. CHINESE PARASOL TREE, CHINESE BOTTLE TREE, JAPANESE VARNISH TREE, PHOENIX TREE. To 60 ft., deciduous; lvs. palmately 3–5-lobed, to 12 in. across; calyx showy, lemon-yellow, to ½ in. across, lobes often reflexed, longer than calyx tube; follicles densely pilose, to 5 in. long. E. Asia, from Ryukyus to Vietnam. Much-planted in s. Japan. Zone 9. Cv. 'Variegata'. Lvs. mottled with white.

FISSIPES: *CYPRIPEDIUM.*

FITTONIA Coem. *Acanthaceae.* Two spp. of ornamental, hairy, low or creeping herbs, native to moist forests of Andean S. Amer.; lvs. opp., entire, with white or colored veins; fls. small, in axils of bracts in slender spikes, corolla tubular, 2-lipped.

Fittonias are grown as choice foliage plants in the greenhouse, often under benches. They should be kept shaded and the temperature never allowed to drop below 55° F. Propagated easily by stem cuttings.

argyroneura: *E. Verschaffeltii* var.

gigantea Linden ex André. To 1½ ft., erect; lvs. elliptic, short-pointed, dark green, veined with carmine; bracts orbicular, ⅜ in. across. Ecuador and Peru.

Pearcei: *F. Verschaffeltii* var.

rubrovenosa: *F. Verschaffeltii* var. *Verschaffeltii.*

Verschaffeltii (Lem.) Coem. MOSAIC PLANT, SILVER-NET PLANT, NERVE PLANT, SILVER F., WHITE-LEAF F., SILVER-NERVE, SILVER-THREADS. Creeping and rooting; lvs. ovate or elliptic, to 4 in. long, obtuse. Colombia to Peru. Var. **Verschaffeltii** [*F. rubrovenosa* Hort.; *Eranthemum rubrovenosum* Van Houtte]. The typical var.; lvs. dark green, veined with rosy-red. Var. **argyroneura** (Coem.) Nichols.

[*F. argyroneura* Coem.]. Lvs. light green, veins and midrib white. Var. **Pearcei** Nichols. [*F. Pearcei* Hort.]. Veins and midrib bright carmine, lower surface somewhat glaucous.

FLACOURTIA L'Hér. *Flacourtiaceae.* About 15 spp. of trees or shrubs, native to Old World tropics, with or without thorns; lvs. alt., simple; fls. mostly unisexual, petals none; fr. fleshy, berrylike.

Flacourtias are not particular as to soil but will not withstand frost. Planted in the tropics. Zone 10b. Propagated by seeds and budding.

indica (Burm.f.) Merrill [*F. Ramontchi* L'Hér.; *F. sepiaria* Roxb.]. MADAGASCAR PLUM, GOVERNOR'S P., BATOKO P., RAMONTCHI. Deciduous shrub or small tree, to 45 ft., with spines; lvs. variable in size, shape, texture, and pubescence, usually ovate, to ¾ in. long, rarely to 3 in. long, with 3–6 pairs of lateral veins, short-petioled; racemes short, few-fld., axillary or terminal on short, leafless shoots or woody thorns; fls. yellowish; frs. globose, to ½ in. in diam., blackish-red, translucent when ripe. Old World tropics. The rather astringent frs. are edible and are used medicinally.

Jangomans (Lour.) Räuschel. Small, deciduous tree, to 30 ft., with thorns; lvs. ovate-oblong to ovate-lanceolate, to 4 in. long, short-petioled; racemes axillary, few-fld.; frs. subglobose, to 1 in. in diam., dull brownish-red or purple, then blackish. Not known in wild state, but probably originally native to India. Tart juicy frs. make good marmalade; roots and lvs. used medicinally.

Ramontchi: *F. indica.*

Rukam Zoll. & Moritzi. Small tree, to 45 ft.; trunk and old brs. usually crooked and gnarled, with thorns except occasionally in cult.; lvs. usually elliptic-oblong, mostly coarsely but regularly crenate, with 5–7 pairs of lateral veins; racemes short, axillary, few-fld.; fls. greenish-yellow; fr. globose, 1 in. in diam., light green to pink, purplish-green, or dark red, crowned by 4–8 small, peglike styles in a circle. Malay Arch. The acid and astringent frs. are edible and used in jams and pies. Roots, frs., and lvs. are used medicinally.

sepiaria: *F. indica.*

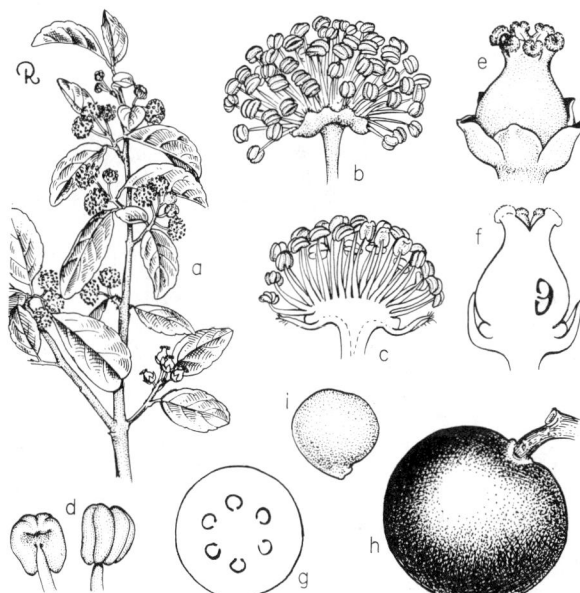

FLACOURTIACEAE. *Flacourtia indica:* **a,** flowering branch, reduced; **b,** male flower, × 4; **c,** male flower, vertical section, × 4; **d,** anthers, two views, × 10; **e,** female flower, × 5; **f,** female flower, vertical section, × 5; **g,** ovary, cross section, × 8; **h,** fruit, × 1; **i,** seed, × 2.

FLACOURTIACEAE DC. FLACOURTIA FAMILY. Dicot.; about 84 genera and 850 spp. of monoecious or dioecious trees or shrubs, native to trop. and subtrop. regions of both hemispheres; lvs. alt., simple, leathery, persistent; fls. regular, bisexual or unisexual, sepals and petals 4 or more, petals sometimes none, stamens many, ovary superior, 1-celled; fr. a caps., berry, or drupe. *Azara, Berberidopsis, Caloncoba, Carrierea, Idesia, Kiggelaria, Olmediella, Oncoba, Poliothyrsis, Scolopia,* and *Xylosma* are cult. as ornamentals; *Dovyalis*

and *Flacourtia* for the edible fr.; and *Hydnocarpus* for the medicinal oil.

FLAX. To gardeners the flaxes are annual and perennial species of *Linum* grown for their bright, showy flowers. The flax of commerce is *Linum usitatissimum,* an annual grown for the fiber of the bast in the stem, from which flax fiber and fine linen are derived, and for the seeds, from which linseed oil and linseed cake and meal are manufactured. These are not horticultural products. In North America, flax is raised mostly in Minnesota, North and South Dakota, and Canada. Seed is sown directly in the field when the weather is warm, as in May and June, and the crop should be ready in 100 days or less.

FLINDERSIA R. Br. *Rutaceae.* About 20 spp. of evergreen trees, native to e. Australia, Amboina, New Guinea, and New Caledonia; lvs. usually opp., mostly pinnate, glandular-dotted; fls. small, in terminal panicles, sepals 5-lobed, petals 5, stamens 5, alternating with staminodes; fr. a hard, tubercled, 5-valved caps., seeds winged.

australis R. Br. To 100 ft.; lvs. often crowded, alt. to opp., lfts. 3–13, lanceolate to oblong-elliptic, 2–4 in. long; fr. 2–3 in. long, seeds winged at upper end. Queensland and n. New S. Wales. Timber tree.

FLORA. This is a botanical term referring to all the plants of a particular area whether county, state, region, or country. The corresponding term for the animals is *fauna.* Published floras usually take the form of a technical descriptive and systematic listing of the plants by scientific name together with notes on ecology and geographical range. Floras are useful to horticulturists as sources of a variety of information pertinent to the cultivation or identification of specific plants or in the search for plants to cultivate. Many underdeveloped parts of the world, however, still lack adequate floras. Modern standard floras now cover most of the regions of the United States and are usually available in botanical, horticultural, or academic libraries. *Hortus Third* is a kind of specialized flora, arranged alphabetically rather than by relationship, treating the plants available for cultivation primarily in the gardens of North America.

FLORICULTURE: see *Horticulture.*

FOENICULUM Mill. *Umbelliferae.* Two or 3 spp. of herbs, native to the Old World; lvs. pinnately decompound; fls. small, yellow, in compound umbels without involucre or involucels; fr. narrow, prominently ribbed.

One species is grown for the leaves and aromatic seeds, which are used in flavoring; the leaves and leaf bases are sometimes eaten. Propagated by seeds sown in spring.

atrosanguineum: a listed name of no botanical standing.

consanguineum: a listed name of no botanical standing.

dulce: see *F. vulgare* var. *azoricum* and var. *dulce.*

officinale: *F. vulgare.*

vulgare Mill. [*F. officinale* All.]. FENNEL. Per., but grown as an ann., to 5 ft.; lvs. 3–4-pinnate into linear, threadlike segms. S. Eur. Subsp. **vulgare.** The typical subsp.; umbels 10–15-rayed; fr. ³⁄₁₆–⁵⁄₁₆ in. long. Represented in cult. by the following 2 vars. Var. **azoricum** (Mill.) Thell. [*F. dulce* DC., not Mill.]. FLORENCE F., FINOCCHIO, ANISE. Base of lvs. much thickened, edible when blanched; fr. to ¼ in. long. Var. **dulce** Batt. & Trab. [*F. dulce* Mill.]. Confused with var. *azoricum,* but lacks thickened lf. bases; fr. larger; cult. for essential oils in the fr.

FOLIAGE PLANTS. These are plants grown primarily for their attractive leaves rather than for flowers or fruits. Many ornamentals have both attractive flowers and foliage, as, for example, do numerous species of *Begonia, Pelargonium,* and the Gesneriaceae. Defined literally, foliage plants would have to include lawn species (grasses) and many ground covers, as well as certain shrubs (*Aucuba*) and trees (*Acer japonicum*) interesting primarily for their decorative foliage. In general horticultural practice, however, foliage plants are mostly those with attractive foliage grown in the home, patio, or conservatory. Familiar kinds will be found in such genera as

Aglaonema, Asparagus, Begonia, Caladium, Chamaedorea, Coleus, Dieffenbachia, Epipremnum, × *Fatshedera, Ficus, Fittonia, Dracaena, Hedera, Helxine, Monstera, Peperomia, Philodendron, Pilea, Podocarpus, Sansevieria, Schefflera, Scindapsis, Selaginella,* and *Syngonium,* and in the ferns. See *House Plants.*

FONTANESIA Labill. *Oleaceae.* Two spp. of deciduous, somewhat *Ligustrum*-like shrubs of Asia; lvs. opp., entire; fls. small, whitish, in narrow leafy panicles, petals 4, small, separate, stamens exserted; fr. a flat-winged nutlet. Late spring.

Fontanesias thrive in any good garden soil. Propagated by seeds, layers, and cuttings of green wood under glass.

californica: *F. Fortunei.*

Fortunei Carrière [*F. californica* Hort. ex Dipp.]. To 15 ft.; lvs. lanceolate or ovate-lanceolate, to 4 in. long, glossy; fls. about ⅛ in. long, in panicles to 2 in. long; fr. elliptic, ⁵⁄₁₆ in. long. China. Zone 5.

phillyreoides Labill. Closely related to *F. Fortunei,* but shorter, more densely branched and more spreading, and having lvs. somewhat smaller, minutely toothed, grayish-green. Asia Minor. Zone 7?

FONTINALACEAE W. Schimp. WATER MOSS FAMILY. Mosses; 7 genera and about 65 spp. of aquatic mosses, native mostly in temp. regions; plants anchored by rhizoids, brs. erect to ascending; leafy appendages arranged in 3 rows; sporophyte borne on lower part of axis, caps. sessile or on a short to long seta, annulus lacking, peristome double, with 16 free to partly united teeth. *Fontinalis* is cult.

FONTINALIS L. ex J. Hedw. WATER MOSS, FOUNTAIN M., SPRING M. *Fontinalaceae.* About 55 spp., predominantly of temp. regions; plants aquatic, or on exposed tree trunks in very humid situations, axis to 3 ft. long; leafy appendages plane to concave or nearly tubular, awl-shaped to spherical or rhomboidal, often keeled, not costate.

antipyretica L. ex J. Hedw. To 20 in. high, branched; leafy appendages to ⁵⁄₁₆ in. long and ⅛ in. wide, strongly keeled, dark olive-green. N. Amer., Eurasia, N. Afr. Sometimes grown in aquaria.

FORCING. Plants are said to be forced when made to grow or bloom outside their normal season, particularly in advance of the season, by some artificial means. The mere imitation of the natural conditions under which any plant grows may not constitute forcing. Growing in greenhouses is not necessarily forcing; it may be only protection. The word forcing has come to be associated with particular crops and sometimes quite independently of its proper, restricted meaning; thus we speak of the forcing of tomatoes, melons, cucumbers, and various bulbs. A forcing house is only a glasshouse; its use determines its title or designation.

The commonest example of true forcing is that often practiced in homes in temperate regions during the winter season of dormancy, wherein the branches of spring-flowering shrubs and trees are forced into bloom in advance of their normal flowering period. In such woody plants the flower buds are already fully formed in the autumn but require at least six weeks of cold temperature before dormancy can be broken. Thus, branches may be cut and brought indoors for forcing anytime after January 1. Branches for forcing should bear an abundance of flower buds on the younger shoots. Flower buds are usually larger and fatter and, in case of fruit trees such as *Malus, Prunus,* and *Pyrus,* are to be looked for on the short "spur" branches. After cutting, the stem ends are first pounded or mashed (to facilitate water intake during the period of forcing) and the stems then are completely submerged overnight in either a sink, bath, or laundry tub in water at room temperature. This necessary treatment moistens and loosens the tight bud scales, aiding in bud opening. Following this initial soaking, the branches are placed in a pail of water kept in a cool spot (60°–65°F) for the forcing period. Water should be changed on a weekly basis so that it will not sour. Warmer temperatures and dry rooms cause premature bud drop, so it is best to start forcing in a cool cellar or similar location, bringing the branches into light (but not sunlight) as soon as the buds become plump. A cool bed-room or partially heated sunporch is ideal for the later stages of forcing. When the buds show color, but before they open, the branches should be placed or arranged in display containers. Delaying until the flowers open often causes flower loss when taken from the pail. The blooming period of forced flowers can be prolonged if the forced material is kept in a cool place at night or when not on display.

Most trees and shrubs that flower in early spring, whether native or exotic, can be forced indoors, but the length of time required to bring cut branches into flower depends upon the kind of plant, the geographical location, and the time that it is cut and brought indoors. As spring approaches, the forcing time lessens, but with a little planning one can have continuous flowering material from mid-January to spring. The following genera include good subjects for forcing: *Acer, Aesculus, Amelanchier, Aucuba, Betula, Cercis, Chaenomeles, Chimonathus, Cornus, Corylopsis, Daphne, Forsythia, Hamamelis, Juglans, Larix, Lindera, Lonicera, Magnolia, Malus, Pieris, Populus, Prunus, Quercus, Rhododendron, Ribes, Salix,* and *Spiraea.*

FORESTIERA Poir. *Oleaceae.* Perhaps 20 spp. of deciduous, occasionally evergreen, dioecious or polygamodioecious trees or shrubs in N. Amer., W. Indies, and s. to Brazil; lvs. opp.; fls. small, yellowish, in clusters or racemes axillary on the brs. of the preceding year, petals 0; fr. a small black or dark purple drupe with scant flesh.

Only *F. acuminata* is hardy north without protection. They thrive best in moist locations. Propagated by seeds and layers.

acuminata (Michx.) Poir. SWAMP PRIVET. To 30 ft.; lvs. to 4 in. long, acuminate; fls. developing before lvs.; fr. ½ in. long. Spring. Ill., s. to Fla. and Tex. Zone 6. The wood is close-grained, hard, and suitable for turning.

ligustrina (Michx.) Poir. To 10 ft.; lvs. to 1½ in. long, obtuse; fls. developing after lvs.; fr. ⁵⁄₁₆ in. long. Tenn., s. to Fla. and Tex. Zone 7.

neomexicana A. Gray. DESERT OLIVE. To 10 ft.; lvs. to 1½ in. long, acute or obtuse; fls. developing before lvs.; fr. ⅜ in. long. Spring. Colo. and Tex., w. to Calif. Zone 5.

FORESTRY. Forestry is the growing and utilizing of forests, together with all the science, skills, and commerce related to these activities. The forest is a crop, making use of land, and its care is therefore agriculture in its broad sense. In its general relations it is also within the realm of political economy inasmuch as great permanent forests are almost necessarily public domains, and it is directly concerned in the conservation and utilization of natural resources as well as with governmental problems. These domains are to be kept and utilized in the interest of all the people, in consideration with all related questions. Silviculture is the science and practice of raising forests, one of the main department or components of forestry. Arboriculture is properly not within the realm of forestry, although popularly confused with it, but is rather a department of horticulture (see *Arboriculture*). Farm forestry is that smaller application having to do with the raising and using of wood lots. The American Forestry Association speaks for this applied science at the national level.

FORMA: see *Species.*

FORSTERA L. f. *Stylidiaceae.* Five spp. of per. herbs, native chiefly to New Zeal., 1 sp. in Tasmania; lvs. imbricate, entire, leathery; fls. solitary or rarely 2–5 on a terminal peduncle, calyx 5–6-lobed, corolla 5–9-lobed; fr. a 1-celled caps.

sedifolia L. f. Sts. to 1 ft., with few brs.; lvs. ovate to oblong-obovate, to ⅜ in. long, erect but becoming reflexed, sessile, semiclasping; fls. white, to ⅝ in. across, on peduncles to 4 in. long. New Zeal.

FORSYTHIA Vahl. GOLDEN-BELLS. *Oleaceae.* Six or 7 spp. of deciduous, erect or diffuse shrubs, in e. Asia, 1 in se. Eur.; lvs. opp., simple or 3-parted; fls. showy, yellow, appearing before the lvs., corolla deeply 4-parted, lobes oblong; fr. a woody caps., seeds winged.

Their habit of flowering early and profusely before the leaves appear makes forsythias some of the most useful of spring-flowering shrubs. They are hardy north and are not particular as to soil. Propagated by cuttings of young wood in summer, of ripe wood in autumn and winter, by seeds, and the drooping sorts by rooting at the tips.

Arnoldiana: a listed name of no botanical standing, probably used for one of the hybrid selections produced at the Arnold Arboretum; see *F.* × *intermedia*.

bronxensis: a listed name of no botanical standing, used for *F. viridissima* cv.

decipiens: a listed name of no botanical standing, used for *F. suspensa* cv.

europaea Degen & Bald. To 6 ft., brs. erect, with lamellate pith; lvs. to 3 in. long, entire or with few shallow teeth. Albania. Zone 6.

Fortunei: *F. suspensa* var.

Giraldiana Lingelsh. Upright shrub, to 12 ft., with lamellate pith; lvs. elliptic to oblong, to 5 in. long; fls. pale yellow, corolla lobes ¾ in. long. China.

×**intermedia** Zab.: *F. suspensa* × *F. viridissima*. To 10 ft., brs. arching or spreading, with pith solid at nodes, lamellate to hollow between nodes; lvs. to 5 in. long, sometimes 3-parted. Zone 5. Cvs. are: 'Arnold Dwarf', low growing, useful as a ground cover with brs. rooting where they touch the soil, fls. few, pale greenish-yellow; 'Arnold Giant', stiff plant, difficult to prop., lvs. thick, large; 'Beatrix Farrand', upright, with dense habit of growth, fls. many, large; 'Densiflora', fls. pale, profuse; 'Lynwood' [cv. 'Lynwood Gold'], fls. many, large, open; 'Nana', low, slow-growing, fls. late; 'Primulina', fls. pale yellow, crowded at base of brs.; 'Spectabilis', fls. bright yellow, more than 1 in. long; 'Spring Glory', resembles 'Primulina' but fls. larger, more profuse; 'Vitellina', fls. deep yellow, 1 in. long.

japonica Mak. Spreading shrub, with lamellate pith; lvs. ovate, sometimes broadly so, to 5 in. long, serrate, pubescent beneath; fls. solitary, to ¾ in. long. Japan. Var. **saxatilis** Nakai. Lvs. smaller; fls. pale yellow. Korea. Zone 6.

ovata Nakai. Spreading shrub, to 5 ft., with lamellate pith; lvs. ovate to broad-ovate, to 2½ in. long, not lobed, serrate; fls. solitary, amber-yellow, small, scarcely longer than ½ in. long. Korea. Zone 5. The earliest-flowering forsythia. Cv. 'Robusta'. A vigorous-growing form.

primulina: a listed name of no botanical standing, used for *F.* × *intermedia* cv.

Sieboldii: *F. suspensa*.

spectabilis: a listed name of no botanical standing, used for *F.* × *intermedia* cv.

suspensa (Thunb.) Vahl [*F. suspensa* var. *Sieboldii* (Dipp.) Zab.; *F. Sieboldii* Dipp.]. To 10 ft., brs. hollow, solid at nodes; lvs. to 4 in. long, often 3-parted, toothed; fls. golden-yellow. China. Zone 5. Commonly planted and very showy in spring. Cvs. include: 'Atrocarpa', branchlets dark purple; 'Aurea', lvs. yellow; 'Decipiens' [forma *decipiens* Koehne], fls. solitary, deep yellow, listed, but it may refer to *F.* × *intermedia* cv. 'Nana'; 'Variegata', lvs. variegated with yellow. Var. **Fortunei** (Lindl.) Rehd. [*F. Fortunei* Lindl.]. Upright habit, with arching or spreading brs.; lvs. often 3-parted or of 3 lfts.; fls. narrow, spreading, corolla lobes usually twisted.

viridissima Lindl. To 10 ft., brs. erect, with lamellate pith; lvs. to 6 in. long, toothed above middle; fls. greenish-yellow. China. Zone 6. Differs from *F.* × *intermedia* and *F. suspensa* in not having pith solid at nodes. Cv. 'Bronxensis'. Extremely dwarf in habit, flowering freely. Cv. 'Variegata'. Lvs. variegated with white. Var. **koreana** Rehd. Brs. more spreading; fls. larger. More showy. Korea. Zone 5.

FORTUNELLA Swingle. KUMQUAT. *Rutaceae.* Four or 5 spp. of evergreen shrubs or small trees, probably native to e. Asia and the Malay Pen.; lvs. alt., of 1 lft., thick, glandular-dotted, dark green above, paler beneath; fls. white, solitary or in few-fld. clusters, calyx 5-lobed, petals 5, stamens 16 or 20, stigma capitate, cavernous within; fr. a berry, ovoid or globose, fleshy, thick-skinned, each cell with 2 ovules.

Kumquats are grown in the orange belt as novelty citrus fruits, but are somewhat hardier than the sweet orange, particularly when grown on stock of *Poncirus trifoliata*. Species hybridize with other citrus species. The attractive, aromatic fruits are used for preserves and the whole fruit may be eaten raw. Kumquats are fine ornamentals either in the garden or as tub plants. For culture see *Citrus Fruits.*

japonica (Thunb.). Swingle [*Citrus japonica* Thunb.; *C. madurensis* Lour.]. ROUND K., MARUMI K. Much-branched, usually spiny shrub; lfts. elliptic, to 3 in. long, obtuse; style deciduous; fr. deep orange, round, to about 1¼ in. in diam., 5–6-celled, edible, the rind sweet. Origin unknown, probably s. China. Zone 9.

margarita (Lour.) Swingle. OVAL K., NAGAMI K. Shrub or small tree, to 15 ft., nearly thornless; lfts. lanceolate, to 4 in. long; style persistent; fr. orange-yellow, ovoid or oblong, to 1 in. in diam., 4–5-celled, edible, the rind sweet. Known only in cult., probably native to se. China. Zone 9.

FORTUNERIA Rehd. & E. H. Wils. *Hamamelidaceae.* One sp., a deciduous shrub, native to cent. and e. China; lvs. alt., simple, stipules early-deciduous; male fls. in catkinlike racemes, with rudimentary pistil, bisexual fls. in racemes with calyx 5-lobed, petals and stamens 5, and ovary partly superior; fr. a 2-valved caps., seeds 2.

sinensis Rehd. & E. H. Wils. To 25 ft.; lvs. oblong-obovate to obovate, to 6 in. long, short-acuminate, base truncate to rounded, margins toothed, glabrous above, hairy beneath on the veins; bisexual fls. to 2 in. long; caps. ½ in. long.

FOSTERELLA L. B. Sm. *Bromeliaceae.* Thirteen spp. of slender, terrestrial herbs, native to trop. Amer.; lvs. in basal rosettes, entire or remotely serrulate; fls. small, whitish or greenish, in a scapose, paniculate infl.; petals separate, without appendages, anthers basifixed, ovary superior; fr. a caps., seeds long-tailed. Many spp. of this genus were formerly placed in *Lindmania*.

Grown in filtered light. For culture see *Bromeliaceae.*

penduliflora (C. H. Wright) L. B. Sm. [*Lindmania penduliflora* (C. H. Wright) Stapf]. Lvs. to 10 in. long, and 1½ in. wide, green; infl. loose, to 8 in. long; fls. white or creamy, petals to ½ in. long. Peru.

FOSTERONIA G. F. Mey. *Apocynaceae.* Forty-eight spp. of woody or suffrutescent, twining vines with milky sap, native to trop. Amer.; lvs. opp. or whorled, entire, infls. terminal or lateral, dichasial or thyrsiform; fls. 5-merous, bisexual, corolla salverform, stamens borne on corolla, anthers exserted, ovary with 5 nectaries at base; fr. a pair of follicles, seeds many, with tuft of hairs at apex.

corymbosa (Jacq.) G. F. Mey. Woody vine, to 20 ft. or more; lvs. opp., obovate to broadly elliptic, to 3 in. long, obtuse to abruptly short-acuminate, leathery, petioles to ⅜ in. long; infls. mostly terminal, dense, compound; fls. small, red to flesh-colored, tube ⅛ in. long, lobes 3/16 in. long; follicles 4–6 in. long, relatively stout, blunt, sharply divergent. Cuba and Hispaniola. Planted in frost-free regions as an ornamental.

FOTHERGILLA L. *Hamamelidaceae.* Four to 5 spp. of deciduous shrubs, native to se. U.S.; lvs. alt., simple, coarsely toothed; fls. white, in terminal spikes or heads; fl. tube campanulate, calyx 4–7-lobed, petals none, stamens 15–24, filaments white, thickened near apex, ovary 2-celled; fr. a beaked caps. The white filaments are the conspicuous feature of the fls., which appear in spring, usually before the lvs.

Fothergillas are hardy (Zone 5) and thrive in moist soils. Propagated by seeds, by layers which will not root for 2 years, and *F. Gardenii* by suckers and root cuttings.

alnifolia: *F. Gardenii.*

carolina: *F. Gardenii.*

Gardenii J. Murr. [*F. alnifolia* L. f.; *F. carolina* (L.) Britt.]. WITCH ALDER. To 3 ft.; lvs. obovate to oblong, rounded or broadly cuneate at base, to 2 in. long, pale beneath; fls. before lvs. Va. to Ga.

major (Sims) Lodd. To 10 ft.; lvs. to 4 in. long, glaucous and stellate-pubescent beneath; fls. with the lvs. Ga. Differs from *F. monticola* in having more pyramidal and less spreading habit and fl. spikes shorter, 1–2 in. long.

monticola Ashe. To 6 ft., with spreading brs.; lvs. to 4 in. long, remotely dentate, light green and sparingly pubescent beneath; fls. with the lvs., spikes to 2½ in. long. N.C. to Ala.

parvifolia Kearn. To 2 ft.; lvs. suborbicular to ovate, often cordate at base, to 2¼ in. long, gray-pubescent beneath; fls. before lvs. N.C. to Fla.

FOUQUIERIA HBK. *Fouquieriaceae.* About 9 spp. of curious spiny shrubs or trees, native to Mex., 1 extending into the desert regions of sw. U.S.; lvs. simple, alt., the blades soon deciduous and petioles becoming spinose, secondary lvs. fascicled in axils of spines; fls. red, pale purple, or white, in racemes or panicles, sepals 5, corolla tubular or rarely campanulate, 5-lobed, stamens 10–17, exserted, basally hairy, styles 3-branched; fr. a caps.

Burragei Rose. Large shrub, to 20 ft.; fls. in racemes or panicles to 14 in. long, corolla pale purple to nearly white, to ½ in. long, the lobes orbicular. Baja Calif.

columnaris: *Idria columnaris.*

Diguetii (Van Tiegh.) I. M. Johnst. [*F. peninsularis* Nash]. Shrub, to 10 ft.; fls. in pyramidal panicles to 6 in long, corolla red, about ½ in. long, the lobes orbicular, erect. Baja Calif. and w. Sonora (Mex.).

formosa HBK. Shrub, to 10 ft.; fls. in racemes to 6 in. long, corolla red, to ¾ in. long, the lobes reflexed. S. Mex.

peninsularis: *F. Diguetii.*

splendens Engelm. OCOTILLO, COACH-WHIP, VINE CACTUS, JA-COB'S-STAFF. Shrub, to 20 ft.; lvs. to 1 in. long; fls. in panicles to 10 in. long, corolla red, tubular, to 1 in. long, the lobes recurved; fr. ¾ in. long. Spring–summer. New Mex. and Tex. to s. Calif., and Baja Calif. Sometimes planted as a hedge.

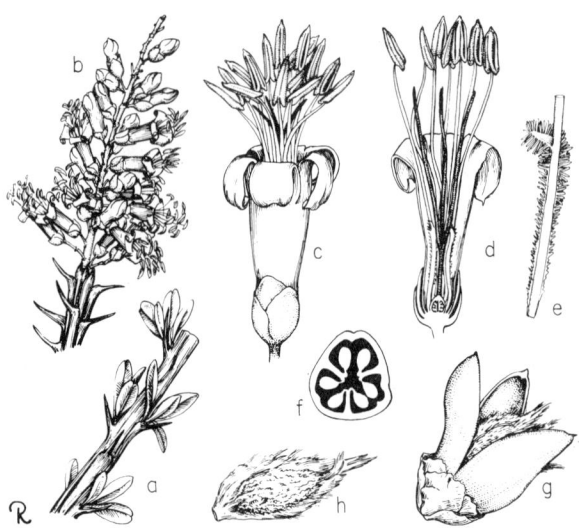

FOUQUIERIACEAE. *Fouquieria splendens:* **a,** section of stem, × ⅜; **b,** inflorescence, × ⅜; **c,** flower, × 1½; **d,** flower, vertical section, × 1½; **e,** base of filament, × 3; **f,** ovary, cross section, × 8; **g,** fruit, × 1; **h,** seed, × 1½. (From Lawrence, *Taxonomy of Vascular Plants.*)

FOUQUIERIACEAE DC. FOUQUIERIA or CANDLEWOOD FAMILY. Dicot.; 2 genera of spiny shrubs and trees, native to sw. N. Amer.; lvs. simple, alt., the blades soon deciduous and petioles becoming spinose, secondary lvs. fascicled in their axils; fls. bisexual, regular, in terminal racemes or panicles, sepals 5, corolla 5-lobed, stamens 10–17, in 1 or 2 whorls, exserted, ovary superior, 3-carpelled, 1-celled; fr. a 3-valved caps. *Fouquieria* and *Idria* are sometimes cult. in desert gardens or succulent collections.

FRAGARIA L. STRAWBERRY. *Rosaceae.* About 12 spp. of low per. herbs, with rooting runners, native to n. temp. regions; lvs. compound, lfts. 3, coarsely serrate, obovate-cuneate; fls. white or reddish, more or less cymose or racemose on scapes, sepals 5, with a bractlet at each sinus between sepals, petals 5, usually roundish, stamens few to many; "fr." not a true berry, but the fleshy, usually red receptacle bearing seedlike achenes on the surface.

In addition to the garden strawberry, a few species are grown as ornamentals, especially as ground covers, or for the edible fruit. Propagation by young plants formed at the ends of runners or stolons. For culture see *Strawberry.*

alpina: see *F. vesca* cv. 'Alpine'.

×**Ananassa** Duchesne: *F. chiloensis* × *F. virginiana.* GARDEN S., CULTIVATED S. Like *F. vesca,* but larger; lfts. glabrous above, hairy underneath, stalked; fr. to 1 in. long or more.

californica Cham. & Schlechtend. Rootstock short, not thick; lvs. rather few, stipules brownish, to ⅜ in. long, petioles slender, 1–5 in.

long, lfts. 1–2 in. long, glabrate above, silky beneath; petals ¼–⁵⁄₁₆ in. long; fr. to ½ in. in diam., achenes on the surface. Calif.

chiloensis (L.) Duchesne. BEACH S. Plants mostly dioecious, rootstock short, thick; lvs. many, stipules ⅜–¾ in. long, petioles stout, 2–8 in. long, lfts. 1–2 in. long, glabrous and shiny above in age, densely silky and tomentulose beneath; calyx silky, petals ⁵⁄₁₆–½ in. long; fr. rose, with white flesh. Coastal Alaska to Calif., S. Amer. One of the parents of the cult. or garden strawberry.

indica: *Duchesnea indica.*

vesca L. SOW-TEAT S., WOODLAND S. To 1 ft. high, rootstock thick, woody, runners long, arching; lfts. to 2½ in. long, glaucous underneath and silky; infl. subracemose; fls. ½–¾ in. across, bisexual; fr. ⅜–¾ in. in diam., mostly red, with achenes projecting from the surface. Eurasia; also in N. Amer., where both native and introd. from Eur. The cvs. known as '**Alpine**' (*F. alpina* Steud.?), '**Everbearing**', and '**Perpetual**' are said to have been derived from this sp. Forma **alba** (J. F. Ehrh.) Rydb. Fr. white, rather dry.

virginiana Duchesne. VIRGINIA S. Plants dioecious or polygamous, rhizome simple, thick; lfts. short-petiolulate, sharply toothed, 1–4 in. long, with 4–8 pairs of teeth; infl. umbelliform; fls. ¼–1 in. across; fr. ³⁄₁₆–¾ in. in diam., with reddish pulp, achenes in deep pits. Nfld. to Alta., s. to Ga., Tenn., Okla.

FRAILEA Britt. & Rose. *Cactaceae.* About 12 spp. of small, mostly subglobose cacti, native to S. Amer., with tubercled-ribs; sts. mostly cespitose, often umbilicate, ribs 10–20; fls. subapical, yellow, often cleistogamous, perianth tube short, scales with axillary wool and bristles, stamens in 1 series; seeds helmet-shaped, black or brown, pubescent or smooth, embryo straight. Perhaps referable to *Wigginsia* but supposedly has different seeds.

For culture see *Cacti.*

ancistrophora: a listed name of no botanical standing; said to have spines hooked and fls. large and yellow.

caespitosa (Speg.) Britt. & Rose [*Notocactus caespitosus* (Speg.) Backeb.]. Sts. cespitose, to 3 in. high and 2 in. thick, ribs 11–22, low; radial spines 9–11, bristlelike, yellowish, to ¼ in. long, central spines 1–4, the lower to ⅝ in. long; fls. yellow, 1½ in. long. Uruguay.

cataphracta (Dams) Britt. & Rose. Sts. globose, umbilicate, to 1½ in. thick, ribs 10–15, with purple, crescent-shaped band below areole; spines 5–9, radial, appressed, straight, yellow, becoming gray, to ³⁄₃₂ in. long; fls. yellow with red, to 1½ in. long; fr. to ⁵⁄₃₂ in. in diam. Paraguay.

columbiana (Werderm.) Backeb. Sts. subglobose, umbilicate, to 1½ in. thick, ribs 17–18, low; spines bristlelike, yellow, brown-tipped, radial spines 15–20, nearly comblike, to ⁵⁄₃₂ in. long, the upper shorter, central spines 2–5, to ¼ in. long; fls. 1 in. long. Colombia.

gracillima (Lem.) Britt. & Rose. Sts. to 4 in. high and 1 in. thick, ribs to 13, low, purple below areoles; spines bristlelike, white, radial spines to 16, appressed, to ³⁄₃₂ in. long, central spines 2–4, to ⁵⁄₁₆ in. long; fls. 1¼ in. long; seeds glossy. Paraguay.

Grahliana (F. A. Haage, jr.) Britt. & Rose. Sts. top-shaped, to 1½ in. thick, ribs about 13, low; spines 9–11, radial, curved, yellow, to ⁵⁄₃₂ in. long; fls. 1½ in. long; fr. globose, green, ¼ in. in diam., seeds prickly. Paraguay.

pseudopulcherrima: a listed name of no botanical standing.

pulcherrima (Arech.) Backeb. [*Malacocarpus pulcherrimus* (Arech.) Britt. & Rose]. Sts. to 2 in. high and 1 in. thick, ribs 19–21, low; spines 10–14, radial, needle-shaped, white, to ³⁄₃₂ in. long; fls. to 1 in. long; fr. top-shaped, ⅜ in. long. Uruguay.

pumila (Lem.) Britt. & Rose. Sts. globose, umbilicate, to 1¼ in. thick, ribs 13–15, strongly tubercled; spines bristlelike, brown, pubescent, radial spines 9–14, central spines 1–2; fls. ¾ in. long; seeds smooth. Paraguay.

pygmaea (Speg.) Britt. & Rose. Sts. often solitary, globose, to 1¼ in. thick, ribs 13–21, low; spines 6–9, bristlelike, white, appressed, to ⁵⁄₃₂ in. long; fls. to 1 in. long; seeds glossy. Uruguay and n. Argentina.

Schilinzkyana (F. A. Haage, jr.) Britt. & Rose. Sts. subglobose, umbilicate, to 1½ in. thick, ribs 10–13, very indistinct; radial spines 12–14, slender, appressed, black, to ⅛ in. long, central spine 1, stouter; fls. to 1½ in. long; fr. ³⁄₁₆ in. in diam. Paraguay and n. Argentina.

FRANCOA Cav. *Saxifragaceae.* Four or 5 spp. of per. herbs of Chile; lvs. basal, lyrate; fls. white or pink, in dense, terminal racemes, sepals and petals 4, petals oblong, stamens 8, ovary superior; fr. an oblong caps., seeds many, winged. A genus of 4–5 spp., by some reduced to a single very variable sp.

Suitable for planting in mild climates. Propagated by seeds sown in a cool house or frame, also by division.

appendiculata Cav. To 2½ ft.; fls. pale rose, sometimes spotted, in usually compact, very little-branched infl.

glabrata: *F. ramosa.*

ramosa D. Don [*F. glabrata* DC.]. BRIDAL-WREATH. To 3 ft.; fls. white, in a pubescent, much-branched infl.

sonchifolia Cav. To 2 ft.; petioles with broad wings at base; fls. pink, marked with darker color, in branched infl.

FRANKENIA L. *Frankeniaceae.* About 25 spp. of small, halophytic per. herbs or subshrubs, of wide distribution in warm, dry regions; sts. much-branched, wiry; foliage heath-like; fls. 4–6-merous, bisexual, calyx tubular and ribbed, petals free, stamens usually 6, sometimes 3–5, ovary 1-celled, with 3–5 parietal placentas; fr. a 3-angled caps.

thymifolia Desf. Evergreen, sts. creeping, woody at base; lvs. small, opp., close together, grayish, oblong, obtuse, revolute; fls. small, solitary or in small groups along brs., calyx glabrous, petals pale rose. Deserts, N. Afr.

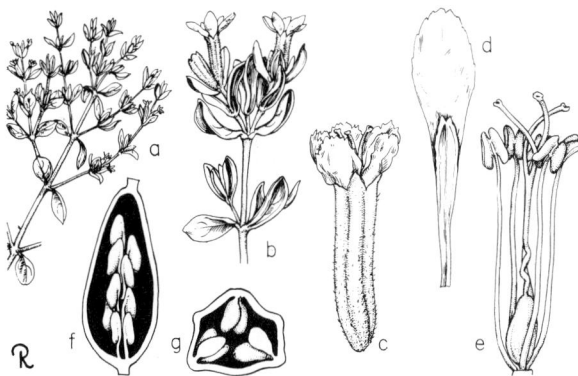

FRANKENIACEAE. *Frankenia grandifolia* Cham. & Schlechtend.: **a,** flowering branch, × ⅓; **b,** inflorescence, × 1; **c,** flower, × 3; **d,** petal, inner side, × 4; **e,** stamens and pistil, × 4; **f,** ovary, vertical section, × 10; **g,** ovary, cross section, × 15. (Species representative, but not in general cultivation; from Lawrence, *Taxonomy of Vascular Plants.*)

FRANKENIACEAE S. F. Gray. FRANKENIA FAMILY. Dicot.; 4 genera of herbs or subshrubs of warm regions, often halophytes; foliage often heathlike; stipules lacking; fls. small, mostly bisexual, regular, sepals 4–6, united, petals 4–6, usually not united, with scalelike appendages inside, stamens usually 6, not united, ovary superior, 1-celled, with parietal placentation; fr. a caps., enclosed in the calyx. *Frankenia* is sometimes cult.

FRANKLINIA Marsh. *Theaceae.* One sp., a deciduous shrub or small tree of N. Amer.; lvs. crowded toward tips of season's growth, alt., simple; fls. large, showy, axillary, subsessile, bisexual, sepals 5, deciduous, petals 5, stamens many, filaments separate, anthers versatile, ovary 5-celled, roundish; fr. a woody caps., subglobose, dehiscing from above and below alternately, seeds 6–8 in each cell, closely packed, wingless.

Hardy in Zone 6, thriving in well-drained acid soil of peat and loam with constant moisture. Propagated by softwood and hardwood cuttings, and by seeds.

Alatamaha Marsh. [*Gordonia Alatamaha* (Marsh.) Sarg.]. FRANKLIN TREE. To 30 ft.; lvs. oblanceolate to obovate, to 6 in. long, remotely serrulate, membranous, bright green and glossy above, turning scarlet in autumn; fls. solitary, white, 3 in. across, stamens golden; fr. maturing the following year. Summer until frost, se. Ga.; now known only in cult.

FRASERA Walt. GREEN GENTIAN, COLUMBO. *Gentianaceae.* About 15 spp. of large, stout, bien. or per., erect herbs, from bitter taproots, native to N. Amer.; lvs. mostly basal, opp. or whorled, simple, entire; fls. white, yellowish or bluish, in panicled clusters on tall, usually solitary sts., 4-mer-

ous, corolla rotate, with 1 or 2 more or less fringed glands at base of each lobe, stamens borne at base of corolla, style awl-shaped; fr. a caps. Closely related to *Swertia*, with which it has frequently been combined, but having slender awl-shaped style and fls. consistently 4-merous.

Sometimes transplanted from the wild. They need a moist but well-drained location. Increased by seeds or division.

albicaulis Dougl. ex Griseb. [*F. nitida* Benth.; *F. nitida* var. *albicaulis* (Dougl. ex Griseb.) Card; *Swertia albicaulis* (Dougl. ex Griseb.) O. Kuntze]. To 2 ft., fl. sts. usually several; lvs. linear-oblanceolate to narrowly spatulate, to 12 in. long, white-margined, 3-nerved; corolla bluish or greenish, to ¾ in. across, with deeply fringed glands. S. B.C., s. to Calif., e. to Idaho. and Mont.

caroliniensis Walt. To 7 ft.; lvs. to 6 in. long; fls. in panicles to 2 ft. long, corolla yellowish-white, spotted with brown-purple, 1 in. across, with fringed glands. Ont., s. to Ga. and Ark.

montana Mulf. To 3 ft.; lvs. narrowly white-margined, 3-nerved, basal lvs. linear-lanceolate, to 8 in. long, st. lvs. opp., reduced; fls. clear-white to cream, in a short congested thyrse. Idaho.

nitida: *F. albicaulis.*

Parryi Torr. [*Swertia Parryi* (Torr.) O. Kuntze]. St. usually 1, stout, to 4 ft.; basal lvs. to 8 in. long, white-margined; fls. in broad panicles to 1 ft. long, corolla greenish-white, lobes spotted with black around the yoke-shaped, fringed gland. S. Calif.

speciosa Dougl. ex Griseb. [*Swertia radiata* (Kellogg) O. Kuntze]. St. stout, to 6 ft.; basal lvs. oblanceolate to obovate, to 1 ft. long; fls. in narrow panicles to 2 ft. long, corolla greenish-white, spotted with purple, with fringed glands. Ore. to Mont. and Calif.

umpquaensis Peck & Appleg. [*Swertia umpquaensis* (Peck & Appleg.) St. John]. St. to 3 ft.; lvs. entirely green, basal lvs. oblanceolate, to 1 ft.; corolla greenish-white to pale yellowish, with fringed glands and hairs below the glands. S. Ore.

FRAXINUS L. ASH. *Oleaceae.* About 65 spp. of trees, mostly native in the N. Temp. Zone, but some of them extending to the tropics; lvs. opp., mostly pinnate, usually deciduous; fls. small, not showy, in panicles, appearing in early spring before the lvs. in some spp., bisexual or unisexual, calyx small, 4-lobed or irregularly dissected, or 0, petals 2–6, separate or united in pairs at base, or 0, stamens 2; fr. a 1-seeded, winged samara.

Ashes are valuable as timber, street, or lawn trees and succeed in good, fairly moist soil. They transplant readily. Propagated by seeds, which should be stratified and sown the following year. The named sorts are grafted in spring on seedling stocks or they are budded in summer.

alba: *F. americana.*

americana L. [*F. americana* var. *subcoriacea* Sarg.; *F. alba* Marsh.; *F. novae-angliae* J. F. Pott]. WHITE A. To 120 ft.; lfts. 5–9, to 6 in. long, glaucous beneath; fls. appearing before lvs., unisexual, petals 0; fr. with persistent calyx, linear-oblong, to 2 in. long. Nov. Sc. to Fla., w. to Tex. Zone 4. Valuable hardwood used for many purposes. Cv. 'Ascidiata'. Lfts. pitcher-shaped at base. Cv. 'Pendula'. Brs. drooping. Var. subcoriacea: *F. americana.*

angustifolia Vahl. To 75 ft.; lfts. to 7–13, lanceolate, to 3 in. long; fls. appearing before lvs., calyx and corolla 0; fr. elliptic-oblong, to 1½ in. long. S. Eur., N. Afr., w. Asia. Zone 7? Var. **lentiscifolia** (Desf.) A. Henry [*F. lentiscifolia* Desf.]. Lvs. to 10 in. long, lfts. remote. Var. **australis** (J. Gay ex Gren. & Godr.) C. K. Schneid. [*F. australis* J. Gay ex Gren. & Godr.]. Lfts. slightly pubescent beneath.

anomala Torr. ex S. Wats. SINGLE-LEAF A. To 20 ft., branchlets slightly winged; lvs. usually of 1 broad-ovate lft. to 2½ in. long; fls. appearing with lvs., petals 0; fr. with persistent calyx, oblong, ¾ in. long.. Colo. to Calif. Zone 6.

arbutifolia: *F. pennsylvanica.*

arizonica: *F. velutina* var. *glabra.*

atrovirens: *F. excelsior* cv. 'Crispa'.

aucubifolia: *F. pennsylvanica* cv.

australis: *F. angustifolia* var.

Berlandierana A. DC. To 40 ft.; lfts. 3–5, slender-stalked, lanceolate to obovate, to 4 in. long, glabrous or hairy beneath in the axils of veins; fr. oblong-obovate to spatulate, to 1¼ in. long, wing decurrent to near base. Tex. to ne. Mex. Related to *F. pennsylvanica.*

biltmoreana Beadle. To 50 ft.; lfts. 7–11, to 6 in. long, pubescent beneath; fls. appearing before lvs., unisexual, petals 0; fr. with persistent calyx, linear-oblong, to 1½ in. long, N.J., s. to Ga. and Ala. Zone

6. Related to *F. pennsylvanica,* but having lfts. papillose and usually very white beneath.

Bungeana A. DC. To 15 ft.; lfts. usually 5, broadly ovate, to 1½ in. long; fls. appearing with or after lvs., petals present; fr. oblong, 1 in. long. China. Zone 4.

californica: *F. latifolia.*

caroliniana Mill. [*F. platycarpa* Michx.]. WATER A., CAROLINA A., POP A. To 50 ft.; lfts. 5–7, to 5 in. long; fls. appearing before lvs., unisexual, petals 0; fr. with persistent calyx, elliptic to oblong, to 2 in. long, winged to base. Swamps, Va. to Fla. and Tex. Zone 7.

chinensis Roxb. To 50 ft.; lfts. 5–9, to 4 in. long; fls. with or after lvs., calyx present, petals 0; fr. lanceolate, to 2 in. long. China. Zone 6. Var. **rhynchophylla** (Hance) Hemsl. [*F. rhynchophylla* Hance]. Lfts. usually 5, to 6 in. long.

cuspidata Torr. [*F. mexicana* Sweet]. Shrub or small tree, to 20 ft.; lfts. 7, to 2½ in. long; fls. appearing with or after lvs., fragrant, petals 4, united in a tube; fr. oblong, 1 in. long. Tex. to Mex. Zone 8. To be planted only far south.

dipetala Hook. & Arn. FLOWERING A. To 15 ft., branchlets 4-sided; lfts. usually 5, to 1¾ in. long; fls. appearing with lvs., petals 2, white; fr. oblanceolate, 1 in. long. Calif., Utah, Ariz. Zone 8.

Elonza Kirchn. Small tree, branchlets with whitish warts; lfts. 9–13, to 3 in. long; fr. oblong. Origin uncertain.

excelsior L. EUROPEAN A. To 140 ft., with black buds; lfts. 7–11, to 5 in. long; fls. before lvs., calyx and corolla 0; fr. oblong, 1½ in. long. Eur., Asia Minor. Zone 4. Wood used for general carpentry. Some cvs. are: **'Asplenifolia'**, lfts. linear; **'Aurea'** [*F. jaspidea* Desf.], branchlets yellow; **'Aurea Pendula'**, branchlets yellow, pendulous; **'Aureo-variegata'**, lvs. variegated or edged with yellow; **'Crispa'** [cvs. 'Atrovirens' and 'Cucullata'; *F. atrovirens* Desf.], lfts. small, curled and twisted; **'Diversifolia'** [*F. heterophylla* Vahl; *F. monophylla* Desf.; *F. simplicifolia* Willd.], lvs. simple, sometimes 3-parted, usually incised-dentate; **'Erosa'**, lfts. very narrow, incised-serrate; **'Globosa'**: 'Nana'; **'Nana'** [cv. 'Globosa'; *F. polemoniifolia* Poir.], compact, slow-growing, dwarf form, lfts. small; **'Pendula'** [cv. 'Wendworthii'], brs. pendulous; **'Spectabilis'**, pyramidal; **'Verrucosa'**, brs. warty; **'Verticillata'** [*F. verticillata* Lodd. ex Dipp.], lvs. clustered; **'Wendworthii'**: 'Pendula'.

floribunda Wallich. To 120 ft.; lvs. with rachis slightly winged, lfts. 7–9, to 6 in. long; fls. appearing with or after lvs., in panicles to 1 ft. long, petals present; fr. linear, about 1 in. long. Himalayas. Zone 7.

formosana: *F. Griffithii.*

Greggii A. Gray. To 25 ft.; lfts. 3–7, to ¾ in. long, leathery; fls. appearing before lvs., calyx present, petals 0; fr. oblong, to ⅝ in. long. Tex. to Ariz. To be planted only far south.

Griffithii C. B. Clarke [*F. formosana* Hayata]. To 45 ft.; lfts. 5–11, ovate to elliptic-oblong, to 5 in. long, acuminate, entire; fls. in large panicles, petals present. China to Philippine Is. and Malay Arch.

heterophylla: *F. excelsior* cv. 'Diversifolia'.

holotricha Koehne. Small tree; lfts. 9–13, nearly sessile, ovate or oblong-lanceolate, to 1½ in. long, pubescent on both sides when young, only beneath when mature. E. Balkans. Zone 6.

integrifolia Moench. A name of uncertain application.

japonica Blume [*F. koshiensis* G. Koidz.]. Tree; lfts. 5–7, or 9, stalked, broadly ovate or lanceolate, 2–6 in. long, dentate, white-hairy along midrib beneath; fls. in panicles on young shoots, petals 0. Japan.

jaspidea: *F. excelsior* cv. 'Aurea'.

koshiensis: *F. japonica.*

lanceolata: *F. pennsylvanica.*

latifolia Benth. [*F. californica* Hort. ex C. Koch; *F. oregona* Nutt.]. To 75 ft.; lfts. 5–9, sessile, to 6 in. long, pubescent beneath; fls. appearing before lvs., unisexual, calyx present, petals 0; fr. 2 in. long, winged nearly to base. Wash. to Calif. Zone 7.

lentiscifolia: *F. angustifolia* var.

longicuspis Siebold & Zucc. [*F. pubinervis* Blume]. To 50 ft.; lfts. 5–7, long-acuminate to caudate, to 4 in. long, the lowest pair much smaller; fls. appearing with or after lvs., unisexual, calyx small, cup-shaped, minutely toothed, petals 0; fr. oblanceolate, 1½ in. long. Japan. Zone 6. Var. **Sieboldiana:** *F. Sieboldiana.*

mandshurica Rupr. MANCHURIAN A. To 100 ft.; lfts. 9–11, to 5 in. long, rusty-tomentose at base; fls. appearing before lvs., unisexual, calyx and petals 0; fr. oblong-lanceolate, to 1½ in. long. Ne. Asia. Zone 4.

Mariesii Hook.f. To 25 ft.; lfts. usually 3–5, close, to 3 in. long, pale beneath; fls. appearing with or after lvs., calyx and petals minute; fr. oblanceolate, to 1 in. long, purplish. China. Zone 7. The purplish frs. are attractive in summer.

mexicana: *F. cuspidata.*

monophylla: *F. excelsior* cv. 'Diversifolia'.

nigra Marsh. [*F. sambucifolia* Lam.]. BLACK A. To 75 ft.; lfts. 7–11, to 5 in. long, rusty-tomentose at base; fls. appearing before lvs., unisexual, calyx and petals 0; fr. oblong, to 1½ in. long, winged to base. Lowlands, Nfld. to W. Va., w. to Ark. Zone 3. Wood used for various purposes.

novae-angliae: *F. americana.*

oregona: *F. latifolia.*

Ornus L. FLOWERING A., MANNA A. To 60 ft.; lfts. usually 7, to 3 in. long; fls. fragrant, appearing with lvs., calyx present, petals white, linear; fr. linear or lanceolate, 1 in. long. S. Eur., w. Asia. Zone 6.

oxycanthifolia: *F. xanthoxyloides.*

oxycarpa Willd. Lfts. usually 7 or 9, ovate, to 2½ in. long, glabrous, but midrib and lower veins downy; fr. narrowly obovate to lanceolate, to 1½ in. long. S. Eur. to w. Asia. Zone 6.

parvifolia: *F. rotundifolia.*

Paxiana Lingelsh. To 60 ft.; lfts. 7–9, sessile, to 7 in. long; fls. appearing with or after lvs., calyx large, petals present; fr. linear, 1 in. long. Hupeh and Szechwan (China). Zone 6. A handsome tree with large lvs. and showy fls.

pennsylvanica Marsh. [*F. pennsylvanica* var. *lanceolata* (Borkh.) Sarg.; *F. arbutifolia* Hort. ex Dipp.; *F. lanceolata* Borkh.; *F. pubescens* Lam.; *F. Richardii* Bosc; *F. viridis* Michx.f.]. RED A., GREEN A. To 60 ft.; lfts. 5–9, to 6 in. long, pubescent beneath; fls. appearing before lvs., unisexual, calyx present, petals 0; fr. to 2½ in. long, winged nearly to base. Nov. Sc. to Ga. and Miss. Zone 3. Wood useful for many purposes. Var. **lanceolata:** *F. pennsylvanica.* Cv. **'Aucubifolia'** [*F. aucubifolia* Hort. ex Dipp.]. Lvs. mottled with yellow.

platycarpa: *F. caroliniana.*

platypoda D. Oliver. To 70 ft.; lfts. 7–11, sessile, to 4 in. long, petioles enlarged at base; fls. appearing before lvs., unisexual, calyx present, petals 0; fr. oblong, to 2 in. long, winged to base. China. Zone 6.

polemoniifolia: *A excelsior* cv. 'Nana'.

potamophila Herder. To 30 ft.; lfts. 9–11, to 2 in. long; fls. appearing before lvs., calyx and petals 0; fr. oblong, to 2 in. long. Turkestan. Zone 6.

pubescens: *F. pennsylvanica.*

pubinervis: *F. longicuspis.*

quadrangulata Michx. BLUE A. To 80 ft. or more, brs. 4-angled; lfts. 7–11, to 5 in. long; fls. appearing before lvs., bisexual, calyx and petals 0; fr. oblong, to 2 in. long, winged to base. Mich., s. to Ark. and Tenn. Zone 4. Lvs. turning pale yellow in autumn. A valuable hardwood timber tree.

retusa Champ. Tender shrub, allied to *F. Mariesii,* but having lfts. stalked, often dentate, reticulate beneath, fls. with a large calyx. E. China. Probably not cult.

rhynchophylla: *F. chinensis* var.

Richardii: *F. pennsylvanica.*

rotundifolia Mill. [*F. parvifolia* Lam.]. To 15 ft.; lfts. 7–13, sessile, to 1¼ in. long; fls. appearing before lvs., calyx and petals 0; fr. oblong, 1¼ in. long. S. Eur., w. Asia. Zone 7. Cv. **'Pendula'.** Brs. pendulous.

sambucifolia: *F. nigra.*

Sieboldiana Blume [*F. longicuspis* var. *Sieboldiana* (Blume) Lingelsh.]. Young brs., petioles, and infl. with minute, spreading hairs; lfts. 5, occasionally 7, ovate, to 4 in. long, long-acuminate, toothed or nearly entire, glabrous or with spreading, white hairs beneath; petals 4, white, separate, to ¼ in. long; fr. oblanceolate, 1 in. long. Japan, Korea. Zone 6. Wood much used in Japan.

simplicifolia: *F. excelsior* cv. 'Diversifolia'.

sogdiana Bunge. Small tree; lfts. 7–11, to 2½ in. long; fls. appearing before lvs., calyx and petals 0; fr. oblong, 1½ in. long. Turkestan. Zone 6.

Spaethiana Lingelsh. [*F. verecunda* G. Koidz.]. Tree of medium size; lfts. 5–9, variable in shape and size, terminal lfts. larger, ovate or oblong or obovate, 6–9 in. long; fls. in terminal panicles, petals 0; fr. broadly lanceolate, to 1½ in. long, pendulous. Japan. Zone 6.

syriaca Boiss. SYRIAN A. Small tree; lfts. 3–5, lanceolate, to 4 in. long; fls. appearing before lvs., calyx and petals 0; fr. obovate, to 1½ in. long. W. and cent. Asia. Zone 6.

texensis (A. Gray) Sarg. TEXAS A. To 50 ft.; lfts. usually 5, to 3 in. long; fls. appearing before lvs., unisexual, calyx present, petals 0; fr. oblong, to 1 in. long. Tex. Zone 7.

Toumeyi: *F. velutina.*

Uhdei (Wenz.) Lingelsh. SHAMEL A., EVERGREEN A. Evergreen or nearly so, to 50 ft.; lfts. 5–9, long-stalked, lanceolate or oblong-lanceolate, to 6 in. long, long-attenuate, serrate, glabrous except for white hairs along veins; fls. in large panicles, petals 0; fr. oblanceolate, to 1½ in. long, wing longer than body of fr. Mex. Much planted in Calif. as a street tree.

velutina Torr. [*F. velutina* var. *Toumeyi* (Britt.) Rehd.; *F. Toumeyi* Britt.]. VELVET A. To 50 ft.; lfts. 3–5, to 1½ in. long, pubescent beneath; fls. appearing before lvs., unisexual, calyx present, petals 0; fr. oblong, ½ in. long. Ariz., New Mex. Zone 6. The following vars. are not always distinguishable. Var. **coriacea** (S. Wats.) Rehd. MONTEBELLO A. Lfts. more leathery and reticulate, less pubescent. Var. **glabra** Rehd. [*F. arizonica* Hort.]. ARIZONA A., MODESTO A. Lfts. glabrous.

verecunda: *F. Spaethiana.*

verticillata: *F. excelsior* cv.

viridis: *F. pennsylvanica.*

xanthoxyloides (G. Don) DC. [*F. oxycanthifolia* Hort. ex Dipp.]. Small tree; lvs. with rachis winged, lfts. 5–9, to 1½ in. long; fls. appearing before lvs., calyx present, petals 0; fr. linear-oblong, to 2 in. long, winged to base. W. Asia. Zone 7.

FREESIA Eckl. ex Klatt. *Iridaceae.* About 19 spp. of cormous herbs, native to S. Afr.; corm tunicate, sts. unbranched or branched; lvs. few, 2-ranked, linear; fls. on the upper side of a spike, very fragrant, perianth tube funnelform, usually curved, abruptly expanded, 1–2 in. long, segms. 6, equal or not equal, stamens 3, filaments not united, arising from below the throat, style brs. 3, stigmas bifid; fr. a 3-celled caps.

Freesias are forced under glass for late winter and early spring bloom, but bulbs do not withstand the previous potting and cold treatment required by hyacinths and tulips. They should be kept cool and moist when growing, and the soil well drained. Flowers may be expected 10 or 12 weeks after planting if bulbs are strong. Several bulbs or corms are planted together in pots, pans, or boxes. Started in late winter or early spring, they are useful for porch and window boxes. After blooming and ripening, gradually dry off the plant, shake out the corms, and keep for subsequent planting.

alba M. Foster [*F. refracta* var. *alba* Hort. ex G. L. Mey.]. To 10 in.; lvs. ascending, linear, to 7 in. long, ⁵⁄₁₆ in. or rarely to 1 in. wide; sts. usually branched; fls. white, to 2½ in. long, perianth tube to 1⅜ in. long, yellow in slender lower part, segms. nearly equal, to ⁹⁄₁₆ in. long.

grandiflora: a listed name of no botanical standing.

×**hybrida** L. H. Bailey. A hort. group of unknown origin, but presumably of crosses between *F. Armstrongii* W. Wats., *F. refracta*, *F. Sparmannii* (Thunb.) N. E. Br., and *F. xanthospila* (DC.) Klatt var. *Leichtlinii* (Klatt) N. E. Br., including the large-fld. florist's types, with fls. single or double, from clear deep yellow to orange, brick-red, bronze, lavender-blue, purple, and combinations of these colors. Plants offered under the hort. names *F. Luzii*, *F. orchidea*, *F. Ragionieri*, *F. Regina-Maria*, *F. splendens*, and *F. Tubergenii* also belong here, each distinguishable by color characteristics, and probably to be treated as cvs.

Luzii: a listed name of no botanical standing; see *F.* × *hybrida.*

orchidea: a listed name of no botanical standing; see *F.* × *hybrida.*

Ragionieri: a listed name of no botanical standing; see *F.* × *hybrida.*

refracta (Jacq.) Klatt. Sts. slender, flexuous, simple or usually branched, 8–12 in. in the wild, but to 18 in. in cult.; basal lvs. linear, about 6 in. long, bright green; spikes loose, usually 5–8-fld., bracts obovate to oblong, ⅛–¼ in. long, whitish or tinted or veined with purple; fls. greenish-yellow, very fragrant, perianth tube about 1 in. long, basal fourth narrowly constricted, upper expanded part to ½ in. in diam., segms. spreading, overlapping, ovate, about ½ in. long, obtuse, upper segms. suffused with dull violet or purple outside, lower segms. marked with brownish-yellow and a central purple line. Var. **alba:** *F. alba.*

Regina-Maria: a listed name of no botanical standing; see *F.* × *hybrida.*

splendens: a listed name of no botanical standing; see *F.* × *hybrida.*

Tubergenii: a listed name of no botanical standing; see *F.* × *hybrida.*

FREMONTIA: see *FREMONTODENDRON.* Fremontia napensis: *Fremontodendron californicum* subsp.

FREMONTODENDRON Cov. [*Fremontia* Torr. 1854, not Torr. 1845]. *Bombacaceae.* FREMONTIA, FLANNEL BUSH. Two spp. of more or less evergreen shrubs or small trees, native

to Calif., Ariz., and Baja Calif.; lvs. alt., unlobed or palmately 3-, 5-, or 7-lobed; fls. solitary on short peduncles, showy, calyx petaloid, 5-lobed, glandular-pitted at base inside, usually subtended by 3 involucral bracts, petals 0, staminal tube divided into 5 divisions in upper half, each bearing 2 linear, 1-celled anthers; fr. a 4–5-valved, 4–5-celled caps., each cell 2–3-seeded.

Fremontias require well-drained soil. Propagated by seeds, or by softwood cuttings over heat.

californicum (Torr.) Cov. [*Fremontia californica* Torr.]. To 15, rarely 25 ft.; lvs. and fls. mostly on short spurlike brs.; lvs. nearly entire to 3-lobed, mostly less than 2 in. long, 1–3-veined from the base, densely tawny-tomentose beneath; calyx yellow, 1¼–2½ in. across, glands usually long-hairy; caps. ovoid, to 1¼ in. long, densely pubescent, seeds dull black. Calif., w. Ariz., and n. Baja Calif. Zone 9. Magnificent in fl., as the fls. tend to open at one time. Subsp. **napense** (Eastw.) Munz [*Fremontia californica* var. *napensis* (Eastw.) McMinn.; *Fremontia napensis* Eastw.]. Lvs. to only about 1 in. long; fls. smaller, to 1¼ in. across, often rose-tinged. Calif.

mexicanum A. Davids. [*Fremontia mexicana* (A. Davids.) Macbr.]. To 18 ft.; similar to *F. californicum*, but lvs. usually 5-lobed and 5-veined from the base; fls. more or less obscured by the foliage, calyx orange-yellow, to 3½ in. across, glands glabrous or glabrate; seeds glossy black. The flowering period extends over several weeks. S. Calif., and n. Baja Calif. Zone 9.

FREYCINETIA Gaud.-Beaup. *Pandanaceae.* About 65 spp. or more of dioecious, climbing or scrambling shrubs, native from se. Asia to Australia, New Zeal., and Pacific Is.; sts. with aerial prop roots and crowns of lvs. at ends of brs.; lvs. mostly lanceolate or linear, usually spinulose-serrate at margin and underneath on midrib; fls. in terminal spadices subtended by colored bracts, female fls. often with minute staminodes, ovaries separate or united in clusters, becoming woody or somewhat fleshy and berrylike in fr., forming an oblong, conelike, many-seeded, multiple fr. (syncarp).

Culture as for *Pandanus.*

Banksii A. Cunn. Climbing, to 100 ft. or more, much-branched; lvs. elongate-linear, to 3 ft. long and 1 in. wide, channelled; spadices in fascicles, cylindrical, to 6 in. long, bracts many, aromatic, innermost bracts with thick white or pale lilac bases; female fls. with 8–10 staminodes, ovaries densely crowded, ⁵⁄₁₆ in. long, fleshy at maturity. New Zeal. Bracts sweet and often eaten.

multiflora Merrill. Tall climber; lvs. narrowly lanceolate, 12 in. long, ¾ in. wide; syncarps 3–5 together, erect, nearly cylindrical, 3 in. long, peduncles brown-hispid, subtended by partly colored bracts, ovaries in fr. ³⁄₁₆ in. long, with usually 2 stigmas. Philippine Is.

FRITHA N. E. Br. FAIRY-ELEPHANT'S-FEET. *Aizoaceae.* One sp. of stemless, succulent per. herbs, native to S. Afr.; lvs. alt., in rosettes, club-shaped, round in section, apex truncate, with transparent areas (windows); fls. solitary, nearly sessile to sessile, calyx 5-lobed, fleshy, petals linear, many, in several series, joined basally into a tube, stamens many, arising from corolla tube, ovary inferior, 5-celled, stigmas 5; fr. a caps.

Cultivate in sandy soil, in a warm, well-illuminated area, with moderate winter watering, but dry in summer. Propagation easy by seeds. See also *Succulents.*

pulchra N. E. Br. Lvs. 6–9 in a tuft, erect, gray-green, ¾ in. long and to ¼ in. thick; fls. to ⅞ in. across, petals magenta with white base or sometimes white. Transvaal.

FRITILLARIA L. FRITILLARY. *Liliaceae.* About 100 spp. of spring-flowering, bulbous, per. herbs, native to w. N. Amer., Eur., Asia, and N. Afr.; bulb tunicate, or with 1 or more fleshy scales, sometimes with rice-grainlike bulblets; lvs. alt., opp., or whorled; fls. of various colors, sometimes checkered, nodding, funnelform to campanulate, solitary or in terminal racemes or umbels, perianth segms. 6, separate, at least the inner segms. bearing a nectar gland, stamens 6, anthers usually basifixed, style 1, entire to 3-parted; fr. a 3-valved, loculicidal caps., sometimes 6-winged or 6-angled, seeds many, flat.

Most species are hardy and of easy cultivation in good garden soil. Most kinds should be lifted and divided every 2 or 3 years. Propagated by offsets, rarely by seeds.

acmopetala Boiss. Bulb scales 2, very fleshy, st. to 1½ ft.; lvs. alt., linear to linear-lanceolate, 1–4 in. long; fls. 1–2, campanulate, green, streaked brown-purple, yellowish and shining inside, 1½ in. long, inner segms. subtruncate and contracted into a recurved tip, filaments papillose, style 3-parted. S. Asia Minor and w. Syria.

armena Boiss. Bulb scales 2, st. to 4 in.; lvs. alt., lanceolate to linear, to 4 in. long; fl. solitary, campanulate, brown-purple, glaucous outside, to 1 in. long, filaments papillose, style entire. Armenia.

atropurpurea Nutt. Bulb scales few, st. to 2 ft.; lvs. alt., or more or less whorled, linear to lanceolate, to 3½ in. long; fls. 1–4, sometimes up to 12, open-campanulate, dull purple-brown, spotted white and yellow, to ¾ in. long, filaments glabrous, style 3-parted. Ore. and n. Calif., e. to N. Dak. and New Mex.

camschatcensis (L.) Ker-Gawl. KAMCHATKA LILY. Bulbs consisting of many small bulblets, st. to 2 ft.; lvs. whorled, lanceolate, to 4 in. long; fls. 1–6, campanulate, uniformly purple-black, 1¼ in. long, filaments glabrous, style 3-parted. Japan to Kamtchatka, and coastal areas from Alaska to w. Wash.

cirrhosa D. Don. Bulb scales few, st. to 1½ ft. or more; lvs. opp. or whorled, elongate-oblong to linear-lanceolate, to 3 in. long, the upper with tendril-like tips; fls. 1–2, campanulate, yellowish-green, checkered with purple, to 2 in. long, filaments glabrous, style 3-parted. Himalayas.

citrina Bak. Bulb scales 2, st. to 10 in.; lvs. alt., oblanceolate or elliptic to linear-lanceolate, to 2½ in. long, glaucous; fls. 1–3, narrowly campanulate, pale yellow, greenish outside, 1 in. long, filaments finely hairy, style entire. S. Asia Minor.

Elwesii Boiss. Bulb scales few, st. to 1½ ft.; lvs. alt., linear, to 5 in. long, glaucous; fl. solitary, campanulate, green flushed purple on outside, 1 in. long, filaments pubescent, style 3-parted. Asia Minor.

gracilis (Ebel) Asch. & Graebn. Bulb scales 2, st. to 1½ ft.; lvs. alt., or lowest opp. or whorled, linear, to 3½ in. long, the upper often with tendril-like tips; fls. 1–3, widely campanulate, purple, checkered with brown and yellow, each segm. with a central green stripe, 1 in. long, filaments finely hairy, style 3-parted. Dalmatia.

graeca Boiss. & Sprun. Bulb scales 2, st. to 10 in.; lvs. alt., lanceolate to linear, to 4 in. long; fls. solitary, rarely 2, campanulate, to 1¼ in. long, chocolate-red, not checkered, but with central green line, filaments glabrous, style 3-parted. Greece.

Guicciardii Heldr. & Sartori. Much like *F. graeca* and perhaps not specifically distinct from it, but differing in its shorter sts., sturdier growth, and more glaucous foliage. Mt. Parnes, Greece.

imperialis L. CROWN-IMPERIAL. Bulb to 6 in. across, scales several, st. 2–4 ft., leafy, plant with skunklike odor; lvs. alt., lanceolate, to 6 in. long; fls. red-orange, to 2¼ in. long, pendent on curved pedicels, in a whorl below a tuft of lvs., at the end of a naked, terminal peduncle, filaments glabrous, style 3-parted. N. India, Afghanistan, Iran. Cvs. include: 'Aurea', fls. red-orange; 'Chitralensis', less vigorous, fls. butter-yellow; 'Lutea', fls. yellow; 'Maxima' [*F. maxima* Hort.], strong-growing form with orange-red fls.; 'Rubra', fls. very large, red; 'Sulphurea', fls. sulphur-yellow. An interesting, old-fashioned plant, persisting for years.

involucrata All. Bulb scales 2, st. to 15 in.; lvs. opp., the upper in a whorl of 3, linear, 2–4 in. long; fls. 1–2, rarely 3, campanulate, dull purple to brownish-yellow, sometimes checkered, nectary black, pitted, filaments papillose, style 3-parted. Maritime Alps.

karadaghensis Turrill. Bulb scales 2, st. 6–8 in.; lvs. alt., linear-lanceolate to linear-oblanceolate, to 3½ in. long, glaucous-green; fls. 1–3, broadly campanulate, greenish-yellow, flushed with purple, with a central greenish stripe, to 1¼ in. long, filaments papillosely hairy, style 3-parted. N. Iran.

lanceolata Pursh. CHECKER LILY, NARROW-LEAVED F. Bulb scales few, with many rice-grainlike bulblets, st. to 3 ft., sometimes to 4 ft.; lvs. whorled, linear-lanceolate to ovate-lanceolate, to 6½ in. long; fls. 1–4, sometimes as many as 12, bowl-shaped, dark purple-brown, mottled with greenish-yellow, to 1½ in. long, filaments glabrous, style 3-parted; caps. broadly winged. B.C. to s. Calif., e. to n. Idaho.

latifolia Willd. Bulb scales 2, st. to 1 ft.; lvs. alt. to opp., the upper whorled, oblong-lanceolate, lanceolate, or oblanceolate, to 4 in. long; fls. solitary, squarish-campanulate, purple, checkered yellowish or greenish, to 2 in. long, filaments glabrous, style 3-parted. Caucasus.

liliacea Lindl. WHITE F. Bulb scales few, round, st. to 1 ft., stout; lvs. alt., ovate to linear, to 4 in. long; fls. 1–5, campanulate, white, streaked with green, ¾ in. long, fragrant, filaments glabrous, style 3-parted; caps. stalked. Coastal Calif., from Sonoma Co. s. to Monterey Co.

lusitanica Wikstr. Bulb scales 2, st. to 1 ft.; lvs. on upper part of st., alt., linear, to 3½ in. long, glaucous; fls. solitary, campanulate, red-

maroon, glossy yellow inside, slightly checkered outside, to 1 in. long, style 3-parted. Portugal and sw. Spain.

maxima: *F. imperialis* cv.

Meleagris L. CHECKERED LILY, SNAKE'S-HEAD, GUINEA-HEN TULIP. Bulb scales 2, st. to 15 in.; lvs. alt., linear to oblanceolate, 3–6 in. long; fls. usually solitary, sometimes 2 or 3, campanulate, checkered and veined with shades of red-purple, 1½ in. long, filaments papillose, style 3-parted. Norway and England through middle Eur. to the Caucasus. Cv. 'Alba'. Fls. white. Cv. 'Purpurea'. Fls. purplish.

messanensis Raf. Bulb scales 2, st. to 2 ft.; lvs. opp. to alt., the upper usually whorled, linear, to 4 in. long, somewhat glaucous; fls. solitary, or rarely 2, campanulate, purplish with central green stripe on back, or purplish-brown with darker stripe, sometimes checkered, to 1¾ in. long, filaments papillose, style 3-parted. Greece, Crete, Sicily.

nigra Mill. [*F. tenella* Bieb.]. Bulb scales 2, white, st. to 1 ft.; lvs. alt., opp., or whorled, linear, to 4 in. long, rather grasslike, glaucous; fls. 1–3, narrowly campanulate, red-brown or greenish-yellow, flushed with purple, checkered and spotted outside, to ¾ in. long, filaments glabrous, style 3-parted. Italy to Caucasus.

Olivieri Bak. Bulb scales 2, producing bulblets freely, st. to 20 in.; lvs. alt., linear to lanceolate, to 4 in. long, bright green, slightly twisted; fl. solitary, campanulate, with recurved tips, green with purple-brown margin, about 1¼ in. long, filaments papillose, style 3-parted. W. Iran.

pallidiflora Schrenk. Bulb scales few, loosely joined, st. to 15 in.; lvs. alt., the lower opp., oblong to lanceolate, to 3 in. long, glaucous-green; fls. 1–12, squarish-campanulate, creamy-white to yellow-green, slightly flecked with brown, to 2 in. long, filaments glabrous, style 3-parted. S. Siberia.

persica L. Bulb scaly, to 2 in. thick, waxy, st. to 3 ft.; lvs. alt., oblong-lanceolate, to 5 in. long, glaucous; fls. 10–30, obconic-campanulate, violet-blue, ¾ in. long, slightly scented, filaments glabrous, style entire. Iran.

pluriflora Torr. ADOBE LILY, PINK F. Bulb scales several, yellowish, st. to 1½ ft.; lvs. alt., crowded toward base of st., elliptic to oblong-obovate, to 4¾ in. long; fls. 1–7, campanulate, pink-purple, to 1½ in. long, filaments glabrous, style 3-lobed. N. Calif.

pontica Wahlenb. Bulb scales 2, to 1½ ft.; lvs. alt. or opp. below, whorled above, lanceolate to oblong-lanceolate, to 3 in. long; fls. 1–3, campanulate, 1¾ in. long, filaments papillose-hairy, style 3-parted. Se. Eur. and Asia Minor.

pudica (Pursh) K. Spreng. YELLOW F. Bulb scales cream-colored, few, with many rice-grainlike bulblets, st. to 1 ft.; lvs. alt., linear to lanceolate, to 8 in. long; fls. 1–3, campanulate, yellow to orange, maturing brick-red, ¾ in. long, filaments glabrous, style entire. B.C. and Mont., s. to n. Calif. and Utah.

Purdyi Eastw. Scales few, fleshy, st. to 16 in.; lvs. alt., crowded just above the ground, ovate, to 2¼ in. long or longer; fls. 1–2, occasionally up to 7, campanulate, white, with purple spots and lines, to 1 in. long, filaments glabrous, style 3-parted. N. Calif.

pyrenaica L. Bulb scales 2, st. to 1½ ft.; lvs. alt., the upper linear, to 3 in. long, glaucous; fls. 1 or 2, occasionally 3, dark purple, spotted with green, checkered red-purple, recurved at tips, to 1¼ in. long, often ill-scented, filaments papillose, style 3-parted. Pyrenees.

recurva Benth. SCARLET F. Bulb scales several, thick, with rice-grainlike bulblets, st. to 3 ft.; lvs. usually in whorls toward middle of st., linear to linear-lanceolate, to 4 in. long; fls. 1–4, occasionally up to 9, campanulate-funnelform, with recurved tips, scarlet, checkered with yellow inside, tinged with purple outside, to 1½ in. long, filaments glabrous, style 3-parted. S. Ore., n. Calif., nw. Nev.

Roylei Hook. Bulb scales few, st. to 2 ft.; lvs. opp. or whorled, linear-lanceolate, to 4 in. long; fls. 1–3, campanulate, yellowish-green, checkered with purple, to 2 in. long, filaments papillose, style 3-lobed. Himalayas.

ruthenica Wikstr. Bulb scales 2, st. to 2 ft.; lvs. alt., the upper opp. or whorled and with tendril-like tips, narrowly linear, to 5 in. long; fls. 1–4, widely campanulate, dark purple, obscurely checkered, to 1¼ in. long, filaments papillose, style 3-parted; caps. 6-angled and 6-winged. Se. Eur., Caucasus, Turkestan.

Sewerzowii Regel. Bulb solid, to 2 in. thick, st. to 1½ ft.; lvs. opp., oblong, to 6 in. long, glaucous; fls. 4–12, funnelform, about 1 in. long, lurid-purple outside, greenish-yellow inside, filaments glabrous, style entire. Turkestan.

tenella: *F. nigra.*

Thomsoniana: *Notholirion Thomsonianum.*

Thunbergii: *F. verticillata* var.

Tuntasia Heldr. ex Halácsy. Bulb scales few, st. to 1 ft.; lvs. opp., alt. above, linear-lanceolate or linear, to 4 in. long, glaucous; fls. 1–2, obconic, black-purple, about 1 in. long, sweet-scented, filaments glabrous, style entire. Isle of Kythnos.

verticillata Willd. Bulb scales 2, st. to 2 ft.; lvs. opp. or whorled, linear-lanceolate, to 4 in. long, the upper ones with tendril-like tips; fls. 1–6, squarish-campanulate, white or yellow, flecked with green or purple, to 1¼ in. long, stamens half as long as filaments, filaments glabrous, style 3-parted, as long as ovary. Cent. Asia. Var. **Thunbergii** (Miq.) Bak. [*F. Thunbergii* Miq.]. Anthers longer, sometimes as long as filaments, styles 1½–2 times as long as ovary. China, Japan.

FROELICHIA Moench. COTTONWEED. *Amaranthaceae.* About 26 spp. of ann. or bien., woolly or silky herbs, native to N. and S. Amer.; lvs. opp.; fls. small, in dense spikes borne in panicles, bisexual, perianth tubular to the middle or higher, stamens 5, united, anthers 2-celled, ovule 1; fr. a utricle.

Drummondii Moq. Ann., to 3 ft.; lvs. narrowly oblong or lanceolate; spikes to 2⅜ in. long; wings of calyx tube erose. Okla. and Tex.

FUCHSIA L. LADY'S-EARDROPS, LADIES'-EARDROPS. *Onagraceae.* About 100 spp. of shrubs and trees, native from Mex. to Patagonia, also in New Zeal. and Tahiti; lvs. alt., opp. or whorled, simple; fls. usually showy, axillary or in terminal racemes or panicles, mostly pendulous, rather fleshy, in various shades of red to purple and white, calyx tube campanulate or tubular, sepals 4, petals 4, rarely 0, stamens 8, often exserted, ovary inferior, style long, exserted; fr. a berry.

Fuchsias thrive under cool growing conditions. They are grown outdoors in a mild climate and indoors in colder ones, where often bedded out in summer. They exhibit various forms, either naturally or with training, from semiscandent tall plants to smaller treelike or bush forms, or trailing or pendent plants useful in hanging baskets. Propagation is by cuttings of soft green wood. Flowering outdoors is largely in the summer. If plants are to be kept over winter, the branches should be cut back after blooming.

alpestris: *F. regia* var.

ampliata: *F. ayavacensis.*

arborescens Sims [*F. syringiflora* Carrière]. TREE F. Tall shrub or small tree, to 25 ft.; lvs. elliptic, 1–8 in. long, narrowed to both ends, entire; fls. many, in flat-topped panicles 2–10 in. across, sepals reddish to wine-purple, ⅛–5⁄16 in. long, petals lavender or lilac, shorter, spreading. Mex.

austromontana I. M. Johnst. [*F. serratifolia* of auth., not Ruiz & Pav.]. Bushy, to 10 ft.; lvs. in 2's, 3's, or 4's, narrow-oblong, 1–3 in. long, toothed; fls. in upper axils, calyx tube light red, 1–2 in. long, sepals red, ⅝ in. long, petals red, at least half as wide as long. Peru.

autumnalis: a listed name of no botanical standing.

ayavacensis HBK [*F. ampliata* Benth.]. To 10 ft.; lvs. in 3's or 4's, elliptic-lanceolate to -ovate, 2–3 in. long, pubescent; fls. in upper axils, calyx tube deep red, 1½–2 in. long, sepals and petals scarlet, ½ in. long. Peru.

bacillaris Lindl. To 6 ft.; lvs. more or less ovate, leathery; fls. solitary in axils, red, nearly cylindrical, 5⁄16–½ in. long. Mex.

Bohnstedtii: a listed name of no botanical standing.

boliviana Carrière. Bushy shrub or tree, to 20 ft., with spreading pubescence; lvs. mostly opp., elliptic-ovate, 2–7 in. long; fls. in profuse, drooping clusters, 2–3 in. long, calyx tube dark red, trumpet-shaped, 1–1½ in. long, sepals dark red, spreading-reflexed, ½–¾ in. long, petals red. Peru to Argentina. Var. **luxurians** I. M. Johnst. Calyx tube 2–2½ in. long. El Salvador to Ecuador.

carnea: a listed name of no botanical standing; used for dwarf plant with red and purple fls.

cinnabarina McClint. [*F. reflexa* Hort.]. Pubescent shrub, to 6 ft.; lvs. revolute, ovate, ½–1 in. long, inconspicuously serrate; fls. on pedicels ¼–½ in. long, calyx tube and sepals cinnabar, petals dull red, slightly reflexed, ¼ in. long. Origin unknown. Apparently close to *F. thymifolia.*

coccinea Soland. Bushy, to 3 ft., brs. slender, downy; lvs. ovate, ½–2 in. long, pointed, downy beneath; fls. solitary, in upper axils, calyx tube red, ¼ in. long, sepals scarlet, ¾ in. long, petals violet, 5⁄16 in. long. S. Brazil. Confused with *F. magellanica,* which has longer calyx tube and glabrous brs.

Colensoi Hook.f. Small shrub, brs., erect, with slender, puberulent twigs; lvs. oblong-ovate, ½–2 in. long, thin; fls. solitary, in axils, ½–1 in. long, sepals greenish to reddish, ½–⅝ in. long, petals purple, ⅛ in. long. New Zeal.

conica: *F. magellanica.*

corallina: a listed name of no botanical standing; said to be a synonym of *F. exoniensis.*

cordifolia Benth. Straggling shrub to small tree; lvs. opp., ovate to cordate-ovate, 1–4 in. long, toothed, almost glabrous; fls. solitary, in upper axils, calyx tube dull red, nearly cylindrical, 1½–2 in. long, sepals mostly green, ½ in. long, petals green. Mex.

corymbiflora Ruiz & Pav. Semiscandent shrub, to 12 or 15 ft.; lvs. opp., oblong-lanceolate, 3–5 in. long, soft-puberulent; fls. deep red, in long clusters, calyx tube 1½–2½ in. long, sepals erect-divergent, ½ in. long, petals narrow, slightly longer. Ecuador, Peru. Cv. **'Alba'.** Fls. white or nearly so.

denticulata Ruiz & Pav. [*F. serratifolia* Ruiz & Pav.]. Differs from *F. austromontana* in having sepals shorter, less than ⅝ in. long, and petals narrower, less than half as wide as long. Peru, Bolivia.

discolor: *F. magellanica.*

×**Dominiana:** a listed name of no botanical standing; used for a hybrid, supposedly between *F. austromontana [F. serratifolia]* and *F. macrostigma* var. *longiflora [F. spectabilis],* with long, drooping, red fls.

Encliandra Steud. [*F. parviflora* Zucc.]. Shrub, to 15 ft., brs. puberulent; lvs. thin, round-elliptic to lanceolate-ovate, 5⁄16–¾ in. long; fls. axillary, red, calyx tube cylindrical, 5⁄16 in. long. Mex.

erecta: a listed name of no botanical standing.

excorticata (J. R. Forst. & G. Forst.) L. f. TREE F. Shrub to small tree, bark loose, papery; lvs. alt., oblong-ovate to lanceolate-ovate, 1–4 in. long, thin, pale beneath; fls. axillary, solitary, ¾–1¼ in. long, green, then purplish-red, sepals about ½ in. long. New Zeal.

×**exoniensis** Paxt.: *F. cordifolia* × *F. magellanica* cv. *'Globosa'.* Fls. 2½–3 in. long, sepals scarlet, long-pointed, divergent, petals purple, blunt.

fulgens DC. Shrub, 4–6 ft.; lvs. opp., ovate-cordate, 2–5 in. long, acute, toothed, glabrous; fls. in short drooping racemes, calyx tube dull scarlet, cylindrical, 2–3 in. long, sepals yellowish to greenish at tips, ½ in. long, petals bright red, 5⁄16 in. long. Mex.

globosa: *F. magellanica* cv.

gracilis: *F. magellanica* var. *macrostema.*

Hemsleyana Woodson & Seib. Shrub, to 10 ft., minutely pubescent; lvs. mostly opp., nearly leathery, rhombic-elliptic to -obovate, to ¾ in. long, toothed; fls. solitary, axillary, rose, calyx tube cylindrical, ¼ in. long, sepals spreading, 3⁄16 in. long. Costa Rica, Panama.

Holstii: a listed name of no botanical standing.

×**hybrida** Hort. ex Vilm. Name applied to common cult. hybrid fuchsias, said to be derived probably from *F. fulgens* and *F. magellanica.*

integrifolia: *F. regia.*

leptopoda Kurt Krause. Scandent to erect shrub, to 10 ft.; lvs. in 2's or 3's, elliptic-lanceolate or -oblanceolate, 2–4 in. long, pointed, serrulate; fls. solitary, in upper axils, calyx tube dark red, cylindrical, 1½–2 in. long, sepals deep red, ¾ in. long, petals fiery red. Peru.

lycioides Andr. [*F. rosea* Ruiz & Pav.; *F. spinosa* K. Presl]. Shrub, to 10 ft., with stout older brs. and somewhat spinose lateral brs.; lvs. alt., lanceolate-ovate to ovate, ¼–1 in. long, nearly entire; fls. solitary, axillary, calyx tube red, ¼ in. long, sepals red, spreading-reflexed, ¼ in. long, petals purplish, shorter. Chile. Fairly hardy.

macrantha Hook. Trailing or straggling, downy; lvs. alt., elliptic-ovate, 2–4 in. long, nearly entire, largely deciduous at flowering; fls. crowded on short upper branchlets, pinkish-red, calyx tube 2½–4½ in. long, sepals 5⁄16–½ in. long, petals 0. Peru.

macrostema: *F. magellanica* var.

macrostigma Benth. Erect shrub, to 5 ft.; lvs. opp., elliptic, 2–7 in. long, nearly glabrous except on veins; fls. solitary, in upper axils, calyx tube reddish-purple, 2½–3 in. long, densely close-pubescent, sepals purplish-red or lighter, ⅝–1 in. long. Peru. Var. **longiflora** (Benth.) Munz [*F. spectabilis* Hook.]. Lvs. minutely puberulent, calyx more or less pilose-pubescent.

magellanica Lam. [*F. magellanica* var. *discolor* (Lindl.) L. H. Bailey; *F. conica* Lindl.; *F. discolor* Lindl.; *F. tenella* G. Don]. HARDY F. Shrubby or semiscandent, to 12 ft. or more, twigs slender, glabrous; lvs. in 2's or 3's, lanceolate-ovate, ½–1 in. long; fls. solitary, nodding, pedicels to 1½ in. long, calyx tube deep red, 5⁄16 in. long, sepals deep red, ¾ in. long, petals purplish. S. Chile, Argentina. Cv. **'Conica'.** Buds rounded. Cv. **'Globosa'** [*F. globosa* Lindl.]. Buds and fls. plump, roundish. Cv. **'Riccartonii':** see *F. Riccartonii.* Var. **alba:** var. *Molinae.* Var. **discolor:** typical *F. magellanica.* Var. **macrostema** (Ruiz & Pav.) Munz [*F. gracilis* Lindl.; *F. macrostema* Ruiz & Pav.]. Lvs. 1–2 in. long; pedicels about 2 in. long; sepals red, petals purple. S. Chile. Cv.

'Pumila'. A dwarf form of this var. Var. **Molinae** Espinosa [var. *alba* Hort.]. Sepals pink, petals lilac-pink. Chiloe (Chile).

microphylla HBK. Subshrub or shrub, to 6 ft., twigs puberulent; lvs. crowded, opp., leathery, ¼–¾ in. long, serrulate; fls. solitary, axillary, deep red, calyx tube ⁵⁄₁₆ in. long, sepals ⅛ in. long. Mex.

minima: a listed name of no botanical standing; possibly close to *F. thymifolia.*

minimiflora Hemsl. Shrub 3–12 ft., twigs reddish, crisp-puberulent; lvs. alt. or opp., to about 1 in. long; calyx tube obconical, extremely short, sepals whitish to reddish, ⅛ in. long, petals white to red. Mex.

minutiflora Hemsl. Close to *F. Hemsleyana,* but lvs. smaller, to ⅜ in. long, calyx tube ⅛ in. long. Mex.

monstrosa: a listed name of no botanical standing; used for plants with double red and white fls.

parviflora: *F. Encliandra.*

procumbens R. Cunn. Prostrate, slender; lvs. alt., roundish, ½–¾ in. long, serrulate; fls. erect, solitary, calyx tube dark red, ⁵⁄₁₆ in. long, sepals green, reflexed, ¼ in. long, petals 0; fr. bright red. New Zeal. Fairly hardy basket plant.

pumila: a listed name of no botanical standing for *E. magellanica* var. *macrostema* cv.

recurva: a listed name of no botanical standing.

reflexa: a listed name of no botanical standing; originally used for a plant with small lvs. and dark red fls.; more recently applied to *F. cinnabarina.*

regia (Vand. ex Vell.) Munz [*F. integrifolia* Camb.]. Semiscandent, to 20 ft., with slender, dark red, glabrous branchlets; lvs. in 2's or 3's, oblong-ovate, 2–4 in. long; fls. solitary, in upper axils, calyx tube deep red, ¼–⅝ in. long, sepals red, 1–1½ in. long, petals purplish. Brazil. Var. **affinis** (Camb.) Munz. Young growth puberulent. Brazil. Var. **alpestris** (G. Gardn.) Munz [*F. alpestris* G. Gardn.]. Young branchlets shaggy-pilose. Brazil.

Riccartonii: a listed name of no botanical standing; said to be a hybrid of *F. globosa* and a var. of *F. magellanica;* strong stiff grower, relatively very hardy.

rosea: *F. lycioides.*

sanctae-rosae O. Kuntze. More or less woody, 1–9 ft., young shoots purplish-red; lvs. in 3's and 4's, firm, elliptic-lanceolate or wider, 1–4 in. long, obscurely toothed; fls. in axils of upper, reduced lvs., calyx tube red, ½–¾ in. long, sepals and petals scarlet, ¼–⁵⁄₁₆ in. long. Peru, Bolivia.

serratifolia: *F. denticulata,* but frequently misapplied to *F. austromontana.*

simplicicaulis Ruiz & Pav. Shrub, to 12 ft., sts. slender, glabrous; lvs. in remote whorls of 4, lanceolate, 3–6 in. long; fls. in drooping clusters, bright red, calyx tube 2 in. long, sepals ⅝ in. long. Peru.

speciosa: a listed name of no botanical standing; often used to designate many different hybrid fuchsias of varied origin; to be referred to *F.* × *hybrida.*

spinosa: *F. lycioides.*

spectabilis: *F. macrostigma.*

splendens Zucc. Branched shrub to small tree, twigs more or less hairy; lvs. opp., ovate-cordate, 1–4 in. long, toothed; fls. in axils of reduced lvs., calyx tube red, ¾–1½ in. long, sepals scarlet, tipped green, ⁵⁄₁₆–⅝ in. long, petals green, ⁵⁄₁₆ in. long. Mex.

syringiflora: *F. arborescens.*

tenella: *F. magellanica.*

Thompsonii: a listed name of no botanical standing for a form of *F. magellanica.*

thymifolia HBK. Shrub, about 3 ft., openly branched, puberulent; lvs. opp. or alt., elliptic-ovate, ½–1 in. long, nearly entire; fls. white to pink, darker in age, calyx tube obconical, ¼ in. long, sepals ovate, reflexed, ³⁄₁₆ in. long. Mex.

triphylla L. HONEYSUCKLE F. Semishrub, 1–2 ft., downy; lvs. in 2's, 3's, or 4's, lanceolate to lanceolate-ovate, pointed, slightly toothed, purplish beneath; fls. in dense terminal racemes, calyx tube red, 1–1½ in. long, sepals red, ⁵⁄₁₆–½ in. long, petals red at apex. Haiti, Santo Domingo.

tuberosa Kurt Krause. Shrub, to 3 ft., tuberous-rooted; lvs. alt., lanceolate to ovate, 2–4 in. long, partly deciduous at flowering; fls. in upper axils, calyx tube red, 1½–3 in. long, sepals green, ½–¾ in. long, petals 0. Peru.

venusta HBK. Shrub or vinelike, downy; lvs. in 2's or 3's, elliptic, 2–4 in. long, entire; fls. in terminal, drooping clusters, calyx tube red, 1–1½ in. long, sepals red, ⅝ in. long, petals narrow-oblong. Colombia.

virgata: a listed name of no botanical standing; used for a plant with single, scarlet-purple fls.

FUMANA (Dunal) Spach. *Cistaceae.* About 9 spp. of low shrubs, native to Eur., differing from *Helianthemum* in having lvs. usually alt., and outer stamens sterile; fls. yellow, sepals scarious, prominently veined, outer 2 small, inner 3 large, style filiform, more or less bent at base; fr. a 3-valved caps., spreading apart at maturity.

ericoides (Cav.) Gand. [*Cistus coridifolius* Vill.; *Helianthemum coridifolium* (Vill.) Coutinho]. Erect or straggling-ascending, to 8 in.; lvs. linear, to ½ in. long; fls. 2–5, axillary or subterminal, scattered among lvs., pedicels longer than adjacent lvs., deflexed at apex in fr. Medit. region.

nudifolia: *F. procumbens.*

procumbens (Dunal) Gren. & Godr. [*F. nudifolia* Janchen; *Helianthemum procumbens* Dunal]. Sts. procumbent; lvs. linear, to 1½ in. long, mucronate; fls. 3–4, solitary in lf. axils; fr. pedicels as long as or shorter than adjacent lvs., recurved from base. Cent. and w. Eur.

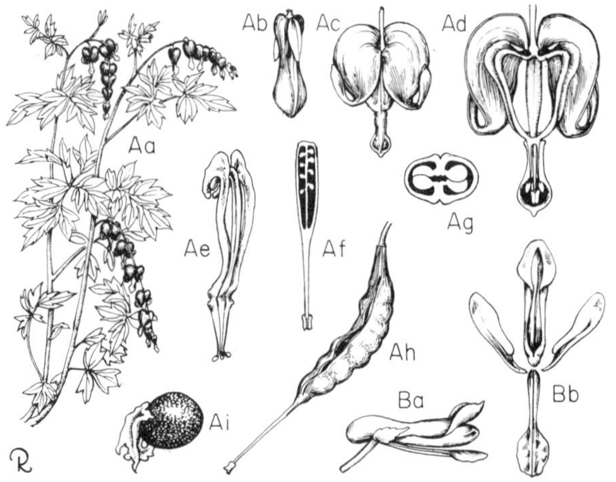

FUMARIACEAE. **A,** *Dicentra spectabilis:* **Aa,** flowering stems, × ¹⁄₁₂; **Ab,** flower bud, × 1; **Ac,** flower, × ½; **Ad,** flower, vertical section, × ¾; **Ae,** three connate stamens, × 1; **Af,** pistil, vertical section, × 1; **Ag,** ovary, cross section, × 5; **Ah,** fruit, × 1; **Ai,** seed, × 3. **B,** *Corydalis lutea:* **Ba,** flower, × 1; **Bb,** corolla, expanded, × 1.

FUMARIACEAE DC. FUMITORY FAMILY. (Sometimes included in *Papaveraceae.*) Dicot.; about 19 genera and 425 spp. of mostly per. herbs of N. Temp. Zone and S. Afr., some climbing; lvs. basal, or alt. to nearly opp., much dissected; fls. often irregular, bisexual, sepals 2, small, deciduous, petals 4, outer 2 often basally saccate or spurred, inner 2 narrower and crested, stamens 4, separate and opp. petals, or 6 united in 2 bundles, ovary superior, 1-celled; fr. a caps. or nutlet. *Adlumia, Corydalis, Dicentra,* and *Rupicapnos* are cult.

FUMIGATION: see *Propagation.*

FUNGI. The fungi are a diverse group of nonphotosynthetic (without chlorophyll) plants, including molds, mildews, yeasts, rusts, smuts, and mushrooms. They are important degraders of dead organic matter but many are serious parasites on other organisms, including the higher plants. Thus they are often very important to agriculture as plant disease organisms. A very few of the higher fungi are special horticultural subjects, of which the cultivated edible mushroom, *Agaricus bisporus,* is the best example. See *Mushrooms.*

FUNKIA: *HOSTA.* **F. lanceolata:** *H. lancifolia.*

FURCRAEA Venten. *Agavaceae.* About 20 spp. of succulent plants of trop. Amer.; sts. short to tall; lvs. sword-shaped, in basal rosettes or at tip of st.; infl. paniculate, scape very tall; fls. with perianth segms. 6, separate at base, stamens 6, filaments swollen basally, ovary inferior, 3-celled, with many ovules, style dilated and 3-angled at base; fr. a caps., seeds many.

Bulblets are commonly borne in the flower clusters. Plants usually flower only once and die. Several species are locally important as fiber plants. Cultivation as for *Agave*, but more moisture and heat are required.

Bedinghausii C. Koch. Trunk to 3 ft.; lvs. stiff, flat, glaucous, striate, to 2 ft. long, 3 in. wide, margins with closely set, minute teeth; infl. to 15 ft.; fls. 1⅝ in. long, ovary pubescent. Mex.

caribaea: a listed name of no botanical standing.

cubensis: *F. hexapetala*.

foetida (L.) Haw. [*F. gigantea* Venten.]. MAURITIUS HEMP, GREEN ALOE. Nearly trunkless; lvs. to 8 ft. long, 8 in. wide, with few, distant, curved prickles ⅛ in. long or more; infl. to 25 ft.; fls. 1½ in. long. N. S. Amer.; cult. widely in the tropics and commercially in Mauritius and St. Helena for its fiber. Cv. '**Mediopicta**' [*F. Watsoniana* Hort.]. Lvs. unarmed, variegated with cream color.

gigantea: *F. foetida*.

hexapetala (Jacq.) Urb. [*F. cubensis* (Jacq.) Haw.; *Agave cubensis* Jacq.]. CUBAN HEMP. Nearly trunkless; lvs. to 4 ft. long, 3–4 in. wide, with short, only slightly curved, spreading prickles up to ⅛ in. long; infl. to 15 ft. or more; fls. to 2 in. long. Cuba. Produces a useful fiber.

inermis: a listed name of no botanical standing.

Lindenii: *F. Selloa* var. *marginata*.

Macdougalii Matuda. St. unbranched, to nearly 30 ft., 8 in. in diam.; lvs. more or less persistent along the st., fleshy, linear-oblong, acuminate-subulate, to about 7 ft. long, 2¾ in. wide, dentate; infl. to about 25 ft.; fls. pendulous, nearly 1 in. long; fr. to 2¾ in. long. Oaxaca (Mex.).

Selloa C. Koch. Trunk to 5 ft.; lvs. to 4 ft. long, 3 in. wide, with curved prickles; infl. to 20 ft.; fls. 1½ in. long. Colombia. Var. **marginata** Trel. [*F. Lindenii* André]. Lvs. margined with white or yellow.

tuberosa (Willd.) Ait.f. Nearly trunkless; lvs. broadly lanceolate, to nearly 7 ft. long, 8 in. wide, with teeth to ³⁄₁₆ in. long; infl. to 25 ft., bearing many bulblets. W. Indies.

Watsoniana: *F. foetida* cv. 'Mediopicta'.

GAILLARDIA Foug. BLANKET FLOWER. *Compositae* (Helenium Tribe). About 14 spp. of ann., bien., and per. herbs in N. and S. Amer.; lvs. basal, entire, toothed, or pinnatifid, pubescent; fl. heads radiate or discoid, solitary, large, showy, receptacle hemispherical; disc fls. hairy, red-purple or sometimes yellow, ray fls. yellow or red, ligules 3-toothed; achenes obpyramidal, hairy, pappus of awned scales.

Gaillardias grow best in light, open, well-drained soil and full sunlight. They are summer-flowering and are favorites for cut flowers. The annuals are propagated by seeds sown in the open where the plants are to grow or started earlier under glass; the perennials by seeds, by cuttings in Aug. or Sept., or by division; sometimes root cuttings are used in early spring.

Amblyodon J. Gay. Ann., to 2 ft.; lvs. oblong-lanceolate, to 3 in. long, entire or nearly so, sessile and auriculate; heads to 2 in. across, involucral bracts papery, with green tips; lobes of disc fls. obtuse, ray fls. brown-red throughout. Tex.

aristata Pursh. Per., to 2½ ft.; lvs. oblanceolate to linear-lanceolate, lower lvs. often pinnately lobed, 8–10 in. long, petioled, upper lvs. entire, sessile; heads to 4 in. across; disc fls. yellow or purple, ray fls. yellow, sometimes purplish at base. N. Dak. to Colo., w. to Ore. and sw. Canada. Now seldom grown, having been replaced in cult. by the hybrid *G.* × *grandiflora*.

Drummondii: *G. pulchella*.

×**grandiflora** Van Houtte: *G. aristata* × *G. pulchella*. Per., similar to *G. aristata*, but more vigorous and easier to grow, and often flowering first year from seeds; tetraploid. Of garden origin; now naturalized in w. parts of U.S. Cvs. 'Aurea', 'Aurea Pura', 'Golden Goddess', 'Golden Goblin', 'Goldkobold', 'Sun God', 'Yellow Queen' have yellow ray fls.; 'Burgundy' has narrow, red ray fls.; 'Tangerine' has orange ray fls.; 'Attraction', 'Baby Cole', 'Bremer', 'Dazzler', 'Goblin', 'Sunset' have yellow, red-banded ray fls. The Monarch and Portola strains probably belong here.

lanceolata Michx. Ann. or per., to 2½ ft.; lvs. entire or nearly so, the lower oblanceolate, to 4 in. long, petioled, the upper linear to oblanceolate, sessile; heads about 2 in. across, long-peduncled; disc fls. purplish-brown, with long-acuminate lobes, ray fls. red or yellow. S.C. to Fla., w. to Tex.

Lorenziana: a listed name of no botanical standing for *G. pulchella* cv.

picta: *G. pulchella* var.

pinnatifida Torr. Per., to 20 in.; lvs. only on lower half of plant, deeply pinnatifid, lobed, or occasionally entire, the lower to 3 in. long, petioled, the upper sessile; heads 2 in. across, long-peduncled; disc fls. yellow, with purple tips, the lobes only acute, ray fls. yellow, veined with purple. Utah and Colo., s. to Ariz., Tex., n. Mex.

Portola: a listed name of no botanical standing; probably a strain of *G.* × *grandiflora*.

pulchella Foug. [*G. Drummondii* DC.]. Ann., to 2 ft.; lower lvs. oblanceolate to spatulate, to 5 or 6 in. long, toothed or pinnately lobed, sessile or short-petioled, upper lvs. oblong or oblanceolate, usually entire, sessile; heads 2 in. across, long-peduncled, involucral bracts green, with short papery base; disc fls. yellow or with red tips, the lobes long-acuminate, ray fls. red, tipped with yellow, or entirely yellow or red. Coastal Va. to Fla., w. to New Mex. and Mex., n. to Colo., Nebr., and Mo. Var. **picta** (Sweet) A. Gray [*G. picta* Sweet]. Somewhat succulent-lvd.; most of the cult. material of this sp. belongs to this var. Tex. Cvs. 'Indian Chief' and 'Red Giant' belong to this sp., as well as 'Lorenziana', the last with many or most of the disc fls. greatly enlarged and funnelform, red, yellow, or bicolored, the normal ray fls. lacking.

GALACTITES Moench. *Compositae* (Carduus Tribe). Three spp. of thistlelike herbs, native to Medit. region; fl. heads in corymbs; fls. tubular, purple, marginal fls. sterile, enlarged and raylike; pappus plumose, deciduous.

One species is sometimes grown as an ornamental. Propagated by seeds.

tomentosa Moench. Ann. or bien., to 2½ ft., sts. white-tomentose; lvs. pinnately lobed or parted into spiny, lanceolate lobes, green and white-marked above, white-tomentose beneath; heads to 1½ in. across, involucral bracts spine-tipped.

GALANTHUS L. SNOWDROP. *Amaryllidaceae*. About 12 spp. of mostly spring-blooming bulbous herbs, native to Eur. and Asia; bulb membranous-coated; lvs. 2 or 3, basal; fls. solitary, pendent, white, subtended by a papery spathe split on one side, perianth segms. separate, the 3 inner ones shorter, overlapping and appearing tubular (thus differing from *Leucojum*), ovary inferior; fr. a berry.

Hardy and of easy culture in usual garden soil. Bulbs should be planted in autumn 3–4 in. deep. Species other than the following are offered abroad.

byzantinus Bak. Lvs. 2, appearing with fls., to 5½ in. long, ¾ in. wide, somewhat glaucous, margins folded outward in bud; fls. with outer segms. white, about ⅞ in. long, inner segms. green at base and around sinus at apex. Asia Minor.

Elwesii Hook. GIANT S. Lvs. 2, appearing with fls., to nearly 4 in. long, 1³⁄₁₆ in. wide, erect, the outer ones folded around the inner in bud; fls. nearly 2 in. across, outer segms. white, inner segms. white with green markings at base and around sinus at apex. Asia Minor.

×**grandiflorus** Bak. [*G. nivalis* L. cv. 'Maximus']: *G. caucasicus* (Bak.) Grossh. × *G. plicatus*. Lvs. flat, with margins narrowly folded outward, to 10 in. long or more and ¾ in. wide at maturity; fls. white, inner segms. tipped with green.

ikariae Bak. Lvs. 2, appearing with fls., the outer folded around the inner in bud, deep green, to 5½ in. long, 1 in. wide, obtuse and recurved at apex; fls. about 1¾ in. across, outer segms. white, inner segms. white with green markings from sinus toward base. Subsp. **ikariae**. The typical subsp.; outer segms. about twice as long as broad. Is. of Nikaria. Subsp. **latifolius** F. C. Stern. Outer segms. about 3 times as long as wide. Asia Minor.

imperati Bertol. An incompletely known sp. Cv. 'Atkinsii': *G. nivalis* cv.

nivalis L. COMMON S. Lvs. 2, appearing with fls. (in cult. forms), narrow, to nearly 4 in. long, ¼ in. wide, pressed flat against each other in bud; fls. about 1 in. across, outer segms. white, inner segms. white with green markings around sinus at apex. Eur. Cvs. include: 'Atkinsii', blooming very early, fls. large; 'Flore Pleno', fls. double; 'Lutescens', inner segms. and ovary with yellow markings; 'Maximus': *G.* × *grandiflorus*; 'Simplex', fls. single; 'Scharlokii', spathes long, separate; 'Viridapicis', segms. tipped with green.

plicatus Bieb. Lvs. 2, flat, with margins folded outward in bud, green with glaucous center, to 4 in. long, ⅜ in. wide in fl., or to 1 ft. long and 1 in. wide at maturity; fls. nearly 1 in. long, outer segms. white, inner segms. white with large, deep green marks about sinus. Crimea.

GALARHOEUS: *EUPHORBIA*.

GALAX L. *Diapensiaceae*. One sp., an evergreen, stemless, per. herb, from matted, scaly rhizomes, native from Va. to Ga.; lvs. basal, simple; fls. white, small, in spikelike racemes on scapes, calyx 5-parted, corolla 5-lobed, stamens 5, filaments united in a 10-toothed tube; fr. a 3-celled caps.

The leaves of galax are extensively collected for use in floral decorations, and the plants make a good ground cover in acid humus, in shade. They are sometimes grown in rock gardens and for colonizing in woods. Propagated by division.

aphylla: see *G. urceolata*.

urceolata (Poir.) Brumm. [*G. aphylla* of auth., not L.]. WAND-FLOWER, WAND PLANT, BEETLEWEED, GALAXY, COLTSFOOT. Lvs. in rosettes, cordate to nearly orbicular, to 5 in. across, crenate-toothed, glossy and turning purple or bronze in autumn, petioles to 9 in. long; racemes scapose, to 2½ ft. long. Late spring–early summer. Hardy well north of its natural range.

GALEANDRA Lindl. *Orchidaceae.* About 20 spp. of terrestrial herbs or epiphytes, native to Cent. and S. Amer. and W. Indies; sts. elongate, spindle-shaped, or with short tuberlike pseudobulbs; lvs. narrow, elongate, plicate, more or less deciduous; infl. terminal, racemose or paniculate, loosely few- to many-fld.; fls. large, showy, segms. spreading, sepals and petals nearly alike, lip 3-lobed, with funnel-shaped to conical spur. For structure of fl. see *Orchidaceae.*

For culture see *Orchids.*

Baueri Lindl. Epiphyte, pseudobulbs pear-shaped; lvs. several, deciduous, lanceolate, to 7 in. long; infl. a 4–5-fld. raceme, shorter than lvs.; fls. 2½ in. long, sepals and petals reflexed, pale yellowish-olive to brownish-green, lip large, funnel-shaped, deep purple with white margin, yellow throat, and yellow spur. Summer. Mex., Guatemala, Fr. Guiana.

Descagnolleana: *G. lacustris.*

Devoniana Lindl. Sts. elongate, cylindrical, to 6 ft. high, 5–6-lvd.; lvs. linear-lanceolate; racemes few-fld.; sepals and petals reflexed, sepals to 1½ in. long, dark purple, green at margins and at base, lip to 2½ in. long, white, tipped and streaked with purple, obscurely 3-lobed, forming a loose tube around column. Summer. Venezuela, Brazil.

lacustris Barb.-Rodr. [*G. Descagnolleana* Rchb.f.]. HELMET ORCHID. To 1 ft., sts. spindle-shaped, 3–5-lvd.; lvs. deciduous, linear, to 6 in. long; racemes pendent, 2–6-fld.; sepals and petals whitish-green, suffused with wine-purple, lip white with purple spots at apex, spur yellow, to 1 in. long. Winter–early summer. Brazil, Peru.

nivalis Hort. Epiphyte, sts. erect, to 1 ft., pseudobulbs to 4 in. long; lvs. narrow, to 8 in. long; racemes nodding from apex of sts.; fls. to 2 in. long, sepals and petals reflexed, olive, lip to 1 in. long, white, with central violet blotch. Amazon basin.

GALEGA L. *Leguminosae* (subfamily *Faboideae*). Six to 8 spp. of erect, per. herbs of s. Eur., w. Asia, and e. trop. Afr.; lvs. odd-pinnate; racemes longer than lvs.; fls. blue to white, papilionaceous, stamens 10, 9 united and 1 separate to middle of staminal tube; fr. a linear, cylindrical legume, seeds many.

Grown as ornamentals. Seeds may be sown in spring where plants are to grow, or root crown may be divided.

bicolor Hausskn. Differs from *G. officinalis* in having more open racemes, fls. with deep blue standard and bluish-white wing and keel petals, and larger flat fr., to 2½ in. long. W. Asia. Var. **Hartlandii:** *G.* × *Hartlandii.*

× **Hartlandii** Hartland [*G. bicolor* var. *Hartlandii* Hort. ex K. Först.; *G. officinalis* var. *Hartlandii* Hort. ex N. Tayl.]. Natural garden hybrid, differing from *G. officinalis* in having fls. with bluish-lilac standard, and wing and keel petals white tinged with lilac.

officinalis L. GOAT'S RUE. To 5 ft.; lfts. in 5–8 pairs, oblong, mucronate, stipules large, lanceolate; fls. white, lilac, sometimes pinkish; fr. about 1 in. long. Cent. Eur. to Iran. Cv. 'Alba'. Fls. white. Used medicinally and also as food for livestock. Var. **Hartlandii:** *G.* × *Hartlandii.*

GALEOLA Lour. *Orchidaceae.* About 25 spp. of e. Himalayas to Australia, and Comoro Is.; the largest of saprophytic orchids; sts. dull brown, commonly vinelike, from a rhizome; infl. terminal and in axils of scalelike, upper lvs., producing a succession of yellowish or brownish fls.; sepals and petals equal, base of lip enclosing column. For structure of fl. see *Orchidaceae.*

For culture see *Orchids.*

Lindleyana Rchb.f. [*Cyrtosia Lindleyana* (Rchb.f.) Hook.f. & T. Thoms.]. Sts. stout, to 5 ft. high, brownish-purple; panicles short, loosely few-fld.; fls. bright yellow, lip with red blotch, cup-shaped, obscurely 3-lobed, papillose above. Late winter. Himalayas, Sumatra.

GALEOPSIS L. HEMP NETTLE. *Labiatae.* About 10 spp. of erect, ann., pilose herbs of temp. Eur. and Asia; sts. mostly square in cross section, divaricately branched, internodes swollen at upper end; lvs. opp., simple, often toothed; fls. sessile, in several- to many-fld. verticillasters arranged in spikes, red to yellow, calyx tubular, 5–10-nerved, 5-toothed, teeth subulate, corolla tube longer than calyx, limb 2-lipped, upper lip hooded, lower lip 3-lobed, middle lobe 2-lobed, gland-tipped, stamens 4, in 2 pairs, anthers 2-celled, styles

2-lobed; fr. of 4 ovoid, glabrous nutlets. Distinguished by the anther sacs opening by transverse slits bordered with hairs.

Species of disturbed ground and waste places, often weedy, a few adapted to the wild garden; propagated by seeds.

dubia: *G. segetum.*

ochroleuca: *G. segetum.*

segetum Neck. [*G. dubia* Leers; *G. ochroleuca* Lam.]. Sts. 12–18 in., silky-pubescent; lvs. ovate-lanceolate, to 2 in. long, ¾ in. wide, coarsely dentate, short-petioled; verticillasters in lf. axils; calyx to ⅜ in. long, unequally 5-toothed, teeth acuminate, corolla tubular, 2-lipped, somewhat dilated at throat, to 1¼ in. long, yellow. W. Eur.

speciosa Mill. Sts. to 3 ft. or more, hispid and glandular-hairy; lvs. ovate-lanceolate, 3–4 in. long, acuminate; verticillasters in the lf. axils; calyx ½ in. long, corolla ¾–1½ in. long, yellow with large purple blotch on lower lip.

GALEORCHIS: *ORCHIS.*

GALEOTTIA: *MENDONCELLA.*

GALIUM L. BEDSTRAW, CLEAVERS. *Rubiaceae.* About 300 spp. of slender, mostly weak herbs with usually square sts., native mostly to temp. regions; lvs. whorled, sessile, stipules lacking; fls. small, in axillary or terminal panicles, usually 4-merous, corolla rotate, deeply 4-parted; fr. 2-lobed, 2-seeded, dry, indehiscent, sometimes bristly or hairy.

A few species sometimes grown in rock gardens, and as cut flowers to give a filmy effect in bouquets. Propagated by seeds and division; of ordinary cultural requirements.

aetnicum: see *G. corrudifolium.*

aristatum L. FALSE BABY'S-BREATH. Strong per., to 3 ft. or more, making clumps, sts. 4-angled; lvs. whorled, to 1½ in. long, narrow, often glaucous beneath, fls. many, very small, white, on hairlike pedicels; fr. glabrous. Eur. See *G. Mollugo*, with which this sp. has been confused.

aureum: *G. firmum.*

baldense K. Spreng. Per., to 4 in., rarely more, sts. prostrate, or ascending to upright, 4-angled, glabrous; lvs. in whorls of 8–10, oblanceolate to linear; fls. usually in 3's or 5's. Cent. Eur.

boreale L. NORTHERN B. Per., to 3 ft., stoloniferous; lvs. in whorls of 4, lanceolate, to 1½ in. long; fls. white; fr. somewhat hispid. N. Amer.

corrudifolium Vill. [? *G. aetnicum* Biv.]. Sts. to 2 ft. long, 4-angled, upper internodes elongate; lvs. linear, to ½ in. long; fls. white, in loose panicles. S. Eur.

firmum Tausch [*G. aureum* Vis.]. Per., erect, to 3½ ft.; lvs. in whorls of 6 or 8, oblanceolate, mucronate; fls. deep yellow, in loose panicles, corolla lobes long-cuspidate; fr. glabrous. E. Eur.

humifusum Bieb. [*Asperula humifusa* (Bieb.) Bieb.]. Per., decumbent, much-branched; lvs. in whorls of 6, narrow-linear; fls. cream-colored, corolla tube about as long as lobes. Se. Eur.

longifolium (Sibth. & Sm.) Griseb. [*Asperula longifolia* Sibth. & Sm.]. Glabrous per., sts. cylindrical; lvs. in whorls of 6–8, linear-lanceolate, acute, mucronate, 1-nerved; fls. white, in loose panicles; fr. glabrous. Cent. Eur.

Mollugo L. WHITE B., FALSE BABY'S-BREATH. Per., to 3 ft., sts. many, weak, somewhat erect from a decumbent base; lvs. in whorls of 6 or 8, oblanceolate to linear, to 1 in. long, bristle-tipped; fls. white. Eur.; naturalized and weedy in N. Amer. Confused with *G. aristatum*, but having lvs. linear, shorter, not glaucous, and pedicels not slender. Also often confused with *Gypsophila paniculata*, although very different.

odoratum (L.) Scop. [*Asperula odorata* L.]. WOODRUFF, SWEET W., WOODROOF. Fragrant per., sts. erect or spreading, to 1 ft.; lvs. in whorls of 6–8, to 1½ in. long, bristle-tipped, roughish on margin; fls. white, to ¼ in. long, in loose, branching cymes. Eur., N. Afr., Asia.

purpureum L. Per., to 1½ ft.; lvs. in whorls of 8–10, linear, acute to mucronate, glabrous; fls. red. Eur.

verum L. YELLOW B., OUR-LADY'S B. Per., to 3 ft., base somewhat woody, sts. often decumbent; lvs. in whorls of 6–8, linear, to ½ in. long, bristle-tipped; fls. yellow, throughout summer; fr. smooth. Eur. to Iran; naturalized and weedy in N. Amer.

GALPHIMIA Cav. [*Thryallis* L., not Mart.]. *Malpighiaceae.* About 12 spp. of shrubs or small trees, native to trop. Amer.; lvs. opp., simple; fls. yellow, in racemes, corymbs, or panicles, sepals 5, without glands, petals 5, clawed, stamens

10, filaments alternately long and short, styles 3; fr. a caps., separating into 3 sections.

Grown under glass or outdoors in the South. Propagated by cuttings with heat.

glauca Cav. [*Thryallis glauca* (Cav.) O. Kuntze]. Glaucous shrub, to 6 ft., sts. with many reddish hairs; lvs. oblong, ovate, or elliptic, to 2 in. long, obtuse or rounded at base, short-petioled; fls. to ¾ in. across, in a dense, many-fld., terminal raceme, pedicels with 2 bracteoles at middle or below. Mex., Guatemala.

gracilis Bartl. Shrub or small tree, to 10 ft.; lvs. elliptic-oblong or elliptic-lanceolate, 2–3 in. long, cuneate, bearing 2 glands at base, short-petioled; fls. yellow, to ½ in. across, in a loose, many-fld., terminal raceme, pedicels with 2 bracteoles near apex. Mex. to Peru.

GALTONIA Decne. *Liliaceae.* Three spp. of bulbous, per. herbs, native to S. Afr.; bulb coat tunicate; lvs. basal, fleshy; fls. white or greenish-white, nodding, on jointed pedicels, terminating a large, bracted raceme on a long scape, perianth segms. 6, united into a tube, stamens 6, filaments inserted on perianth tube; fr. a loculicidal, 3-valved caps., seeds many, black, angled.

Galtonias succeed in rich, moist soil; in northern regions they should be lifted and stored overwinter. Propagated by offsets or by seeds.

candicans (Bak.) Decne. [*Hyacinthus candicans* Bak.]. SUMMER HYACINTH. Scape 2–4 ft., stout; lvs. strap-shaped, 2–3 ft. long, 2 in. wide; fls. pure white, fragrant, to 1½ in. long. Summer and autumn.

princeps (Bak.) Decne. [*Hyacinthus princeps* Bak.]. Similar to *G. candicans*, but with shorter scapes and fewer fls., fls. greenish-white, to 1½ in. long.

GALVEZIA Dombey ex Juss. *Scrophulariaceae.* About 8 spp. of shrubs of the islands off s. Calif., Baja Calif., Mex., and coastal Peru and Ecuador; lvs. opp. or in whorls of 3, entire; fls. red, in terminal racemes; sepals 5, corolla tubular, strongly 2-lipped, saccate, a palate more or less closing the throat, stamens 4; fr. a caps.

speciosa (Nutt.) A. Gray [*Antirrhinum speciosum* (Nutt.) A. Gray]. Evergreen shrub, to 7 ft., glabrous or pubescent, young growth herbaceous; lvs. elliptic to ovate, to 1½ in. long; fls. scarlet, 1 in. long. Is. off s. Calif. Planted in Calif.

GAMOLEPIS Less. [*Psilothonna* E. H. Mey. ex E. P. Phillips, an invalid name; *Steirodiscus* Less.]. *Compositae* (Senecio Tribe). About 15 spp. of small shrubs and herbs in S. Afr.; lvs. alt., entire to 3-lobed or pinnately divided; fl. heads radiate, sessile or peduncled, involucral bracts in 1 row, united basally ⅓–⅔ their length, receptacle without scales; fls. yellow to orange, disc fls. fertile or sterile, ray fls. fertile; achenes without pappus.

Propagated by seeds.

annua: *G. Tagetes.*

chrysanthemoides DC. Shrub, 2–3 ft., glabrous; lvs. crowded at ends of brs., to 2 in. long, pinnately parted, segms. oblong-linear; heads 1½–2 in. across, on peduncles 4–6 in. long, involucre campanulate, involucral bracts 10–12, united in basal ⅓; ray fls. yellow; achenes glabrous.

speciosa Pillans [*Psilothonna speciosa* (Pillans) E. P. Phillips]. Ann., to 1 ft.; sts. erect, zigzag, branched above middle; lvs. to 2½ in. long, pinnately parted, segms. narrow-linear; heads 1½ in. across, on peduncles to 2 in. long, involucre ovoid, involucral bracts 16–18, narrow, united to well above middle; ray fls. orange; achenes glabrous.

Tagetes (L.) DC. [*G. annua* Less.; *Psilothonna Tagetes* (L.) E. H. Mey. ex Phillips]. Slender, glabrous ann., to about 1 ft., sts. wiry, branching above; lvs. 1½–2 in. long, pinnately dissected, the segms. linear, sometimes lobed again; heads ¾ in. across, on peduncles 2–3 in. long, involucre ovoid-cylindrical, involucral bracts 12–14, united ⅔ their length or more; ray fls. bright yellow or orange; achenes glabrous.

GARCIA Vahl. *Euphorbiaceae.* Two spp. of monoecious shrubs or small trees, native to e. Mex.; lvs. alt., simple, entire, pinnately veined, petioled; fls. with petals, pink to maroon, stamens over 60, ovary 3-celled; fr. a caps.

nutans Vahl. Shrub or tree, to 50 ft.; lvs. oblong, elliptic or oblanceolate-elliptic, glabrous to hairy, paler beneath, 3–7 in. long; fls. in terminal cymes, ovary densely hairy; fr. 1½ in. in diam. Cult. in Colombia and W. Indies. The seeds of this sp. contain an oil similar to tung oil. See *Aleurites.*

GARCINIA L. *Guttiferae.* About 200 spp. of polygamous trop. trees or shrubs, native to the Old World; lvs. opp., simple, usually thick; fls. axillary or terminal, sepals and petals 4 or 5, stamens 8 to many, ovary 2–12-celled; fr. a leathery, indehiscent berry, seeds surrounded by pulpy, often edible aril.

One species, *G. Mangostana*, the mangosteen, grown for its edible fruit; the yellow gum resin of other Asiatic species, obtained from incisions made in the bark, yields commercial gamboge, used as an artist's pigment and medicinally as a cathartic.

Mangosteens require a moist, warm, lowland tropical climate with well-distributed rainfall and a moist well-drained soil, rich in organic matter. Because the seeds possess nucellar embryos, plants come true from seed, which is the usual method of propagation. Seeds are very short-lived after removal from the fruit. They should be sown in pots and the seedlings shaded and grown to about 2 ft. before transplanting. Young plants are difficult to transplant, hard to rear, and slow-growing, seldom bearing before 8 years. They are best suited for the tropical home garden.

dulcis (Roxb.) Kurz. Tree, to 20 ft.; lvs. oblong, 6 in. long or more, tapering apically to a slender point, entire, pale beneath; fls. cream-colored, globular; fr. yellow, smooth, about the size of an apple, seeds surrounded by yellow palatable aril. Molucca Is. The fr. is edible raw or cooked; it makes an excellent jam.

Livingstonei T. Anderson. To 35 ft., somewhat columnar, young brs. bearing whorls of short brs.; lvs. oblong, to 5 in. long, rounded or obtuse at apex, leathery; fls. white or pale yellow, small, about ¼ in. long; fr. orange-yellow to reddish, globose, about 1 in. in diam., edible. Trop. Afr. Zone 10b.

Mangostana L. MANGOSTEEN. Handsome evergreen tree, to 30 ft.; lvs. thick, leathery, elliptic-oblong, to 10 in. long, with many parallel lateral veins, dark green; fls. solitary, 2 in. across, rose-pink; fr. 2–3 in. in diam., rind smooth, thick, reddish-purple, enclosing 5–7 seeds, each in a snow-white, edible aril. Malay region. Cult. commonly as a dooryard tree in Indonesia, but rarely cult. elsewhere in the tropics. Not hardy and not productive outside the tropics. One of the best trop. frs.

spicata Hook.f. Medium-sized tree, with wide-spreading brs.; lvs. broadly elliptic, obtuse, to 8 in. long; fls. small, to 5/16 in. across; fr. globose, about the size of a walnut, smooth, deep green, 1–3-seeded. India and Ceylon.

tinctoria: *G. Xanthochymus.*

Xanthochymus Hook.f. ex T. Anderson [*G. tinctoria* (DC.) W. F. Wight]. To 40 ft.; lvs. oblong or elliptic-oblong, acute, to 18 in. long, thick and leathery, with many parallel lateral veins; fls. white, to ¾ in. across; fr. dark yellow, globose, 2–3 in. in diam. W. Himalayas, n. India.

GARDEN. In its historical significance a garden is a plant-growing area of small or limited dimensions, usually enclosed and connected with a residence. Ornamental subjects, fruits and vegetables for household use, and plantings constituting part of the setting for a home or building are the essential components of it, and gardening is the rearing, establishing, and maintenance of the plants and care of the area devoted to them. Gardens dealing with ornamentals may be formal or informal or sometimes reflect special area or plant-material interests such as are to be found in a rock garden, patio garden, Japanese garden, wild flower garden, or desert garden. In modern times, the word garden has taken on an expanded meaning, involving much larger areas and commercial undertakings, and the older, more restricted unit is often called the home garden. The kinds of plants or crops now constitute the main distinction between commercial gardening (including so-called truck and market gardens) and agriculture (with its introduction, test, or trial gardens) and there is no clear line of demarcation; yet one ordinarily and properly thinks of a home and a pleasure ground, personal satisfactions, and a particular kind of skilled training, when employing the words garden, gardener, gardening. See *Horticulture, Landscape Gardening.*

The home garden should be useful in the degree to which it expresses the sentiments of its maker or owner; a garden planned without regard to personality may not fulfill the requisite. To accomplish essential results, the garden maker must be well prepared to meet the requirements of the plants and to defend them against injury, insect, and disease; to this end he must be informed by the latest bulletins and books on the subject. See *Arboretum, Botanical Garden, Rock Gardening,* and *Vegetable Gardening.*

GARDENIA Ellis. *Rubiaceae.* About 200 spp. of shrubs or small trees, native to tropics and subtropics of Old World; lvs. opp. or in whorls of 3, stipules interpetiolar, sheathing, often truncate and secreting a resinous fluid; fls. solitary or paired, terminal or appearing axillary, white or yellow, usually large and fragrant, calyx tube well developed, corolla usually more or less funnelform, ovary 1-celled; fr. a berry.

Gardenias were formerly very popular greenhouse plants and are now grown indoors for cut flowers and outdoors in mild climates. They require a warm close house with a night temperature of about 65° F. Buds should be kept pinched off until late in Sept., then allowed to set, to produce flowers in midwinter. Propagated by cuttings with 3 or 4 buds kept over bottom heat and with frequent syringing.

carinata Wallich. Shrub or tree, to 20 ft. or more; lvs. obovate to oblanceolate, to 7 in. long, glossy above, paler and hairy beneath, lateral veins parallel, 16–18 pairs, straight, stout; fls. solitary or paired, axillary, fragrant, corolla creamy-white, becoming yellow, 3 in. across, lobes spreading, tube 1 in. long. Malay Pen.

citriodora: *Mitriostigma axillare.*

Coolidgei: a listed name of no botanical standing.

cornuta Hemsl. Shrub; lvs. obovate or oblanceolate, to 1½ in. long; fls. solitary, subterminal, calyx with a cleft, 2-lipped limb and 6 cylindrical appendages to ⅜ in. long, corolla salverform, to 2½ in. long, 6-lobed, the lobes broadly spreading, tube slender; fr. somewhat pear-shaped, to 2 in. long, golden-yellow, with persistent calyx appendages. S. Afr.

florida: *G. jasminoides.*

Fortunei: *G. jasminoides* var. *Fortuniana.*

Glazeri: a listed name of no botanical standing.

globosa: *Rothmannia globosa.*

grandiflora: *G. jasminoides.*

imperialis K. Schum. Tree, to 60 ft. with stout branchlets; lvs. obovate, to 8 in. long or more, glossy, lateral veins parallel, 13–29 pairs; fls. in pairs, terminal or sometimes appearing axillary, corolla white, 3 in. across, 5-lobed, tube to 8 in. long, flared toward top; fr. ellipsoid, to 2 in. long, red-brown. W. Trop. Afr.

jasminoides Ellis [*G. florida* L.; *G. grandiflora* Lour.; *G. radicans* Thunb.]. COMMON G., CAPE JASMINE. Evergreen shrub, to 6 ft.; lvs. lanceolate or obovate, to 4 in. long, thick; fls. often double, fragrant, calyx with 5 long teeth, corolla white, to 3 in. across, tube cylindrical, to 1½ in. long; fr. ovate, to 1½ in. long, orange, fleshy. China. Cv. **'Prostrata'**. A low form. Var. **Fortuniana** Lindl. [*G. Fortunei* Hort.; ?*G. Veitchii* Hort.]. Fls. large; double-fld. forms often cult.

Jovis-tonantis (Welw.) Hiern. Small tree, to 15 ft.; lvs. obovate, to 5 in. long; fls. fragrant, corolla creamy-white, to 3 in. across, 8–9-lobed, tube cylindrical, to 3 in. long; fr. ellipsoid, sometimes curved, to 4 in. long, somewhat woody. Trop. Afr.

lucida Roxb. Small deciduous tree, brs. resinous; lvs. elliptic-oblong, to 10 in. long, lateral veins parallel, 20–30 pairs; fls. solitary, axillary, fragrant, corolla white, turning yellow, to 3 in. across, salverform, 5-lobed, tube slender, to 2 in. long; fr. ovoid, calyx lobes persistent at apex. India.

palustris: a listed name of no botanical standing.

pseudopsidium (Blanco) Fern.-Vill. Shrub or small tree; lvs. 4 in. long or more, lateral veins parallel, 12–18 pairs; fls. fragrant, corolla white, to 2 in. across, 5-lobed or more, tube to 2½ in. long. Philippine Is.

radicans: *G. jasminoides.*

Rothmannia: *Rothmannia capensis.*

spathulifolia Stapf. & Hutch. Small tree, to 15 ft.; lvs. obovate or rhombic-obovate, to 2 in. long; fls. solitary, terminal, mildly fragrant, corolla white, tinged with green, turning yellow, to 2 in. across, 6–9-lobed, tube cylindrical, to 3 in. long; fr. ovoid, to 2¼ in. long, somewhat woody. S. Afr.

stricta-nana: a listed name of no botanical standing; used for a free-flowering form of *G. jasminoides.*

Thunbergia L.f. Shrub, to 10 ft., brs. stiff, rigid; lvs. elliptic, to 6 in. long; fls. solitary, terminal, fragrant, corolla 3 in. across, 8-lobed, tube slender, to 3 in. long; fr. ovoid, 2 in. long or more, woody. S. Afr. Similar to *G. spathulifolia,* but having fls. slightly larger.

tubifera Wallich. Small tree, brs. resinous; lvs. obovate-lanceolate, to 9 in. long, leathery, lateral veins parallel, 12–14 pairs; fls. solitary, axillary, corolla white, turning yellow, finally bright orange, to 1 in. across, lobes 6–9, short, tube slender, to 4½ in. long; fr. globose, to 1½ in. across, smooth or obscurely ribbed. Malay Pen., Sumatra, Borneo.

turgida Roxb. Small deciduous tree, to 25 ft., sometimes spiny, brs. rigid, robust; lvs. elliptic-obovate or orbicular, to 4 in. long; fls. solitary, axillary, fragrant, corolla white, lobes 5, about as long as tube, tube short, broad, to ½ in. long; fr. ovoid or globose, to 3 in. long. India.

urcelliformis: *Rothmannia urcelliformis.*

Veitchii: a listed name of no botanical standing; used for a form of *G. jasminoides.*

GARDOQUIA Ruiz & Pav. *Labiatae.* Not cult. **G. betonicoides:** *Agastache mexicana.*

GARLIC. *Allium sativum* or garlic is a rather small onion-like plant with flat leaves and thinly covered bulb that breaks up into separable parts or cloves. It is native in southern Europe. For relationships, see *Onion.*

The bulbs are used in cookery. The species is propagated by the cloves or bulblets, which are planted in early spring in any good garden land. Seed is not available, as it is rarely produced.

GARRYA Dougl. SILK-TASSEL, SILK-TASSEL BUSH. *Garryaceae.* About 15 spp., with characters of the family.

The garryas are ornamentals flowering in late winter and early spring. May be hardy as far north as N.Y. in protected, sunny locations; propagated by cuttings of half-ripened wood, by layers, or by seeds.

buxifolia A. Gray. Low shrub, mostly under 5 ft.; lvs. oblong-elliptic, to 1½ in. long, glossy and bright- or olive-green above, silver-gray-pubescent beneath with straight appressed hairs; male catkins 2–3 in. long, in clusters of 2–4, fruiting catkins 1–3½ in. long; fr. to ¼ in. in diam., nearly glabrous, bluish-black, with a pair of sepals usually evident at the apex. N. Calif. to sw. Ore. Zone 8.

Congdonii Eastw. Shrub, to 7 ft., yellow-green, young twigs silky-pubescent; lvs. narrowly ovate to elliptic, to 2½ in. long, densely tomentose beneath with long wavy hairs; male catkins to 3¼ in. long, female catkins to 2 in. long; fr. globose to ovoid, about ¼ in. in diam., densely pubescent. Dry canyons and ridges, largely on serpentine, Calif.

elliptica Dougl. Shrub or small tree, to 25 ft.; lvs. elliptic to ovate-lanceolate, mostly 2–4 in. long, rounded or obtuse, mostly undulate or crisped, green, nearly glabrous above, tomentose beneath, the hairs curly; male catkins loose, 3–8 in. long, fruiting catkins 2–4 in. long; fr. globose, ¼–½ in. in diam., tomentose but becoming glabrous with age. Coast, cent. Calif. to Ore. Zone 8. Bark and lvs. used medicinally.

flavescens S. Wats. Shrub, 3–10 ft.; lvs. lanceolate to elliptic, mostly 1–3 in. long, yellowish-green, glabrous above, pubescent with straight appressed hairs beneath; male and fruiting catkins stiff, to 2 in. long; fr. ovoid to obovoid, about ¼ in. in diam., silky-pubescent. S. Utah and New Mex., s. to n. Mex. and w. Tex. Var. **pallida** (Eastw.) Bacig. ex Ewan. Lvs. with whitish or bluish bloom above. Cent. Calif. to n. Baja Calif.

Fremontii Torr. Shrub, to 15 ft.; lvs. oblong-elliptic to oblong-ovate, to 2 in. long, mostly tapering at each end, glabrous above and nearly so beneath; male catkins loose, to 8 in. long, fruiting catkins to about 2 in. long; fr. globose, less than ¼ in. in diam., blackish, nearly glabrous. S. Wash. to s. Calif. Zone 8. Lvs. used medicinally.

Veatchii Kellogg. Shrub, to 6 ft.; branchlets white-tomentose; lvs. lanceolate to ovate-elliptic, to 3 in. long, acuminate, flat or nearly undulate along margin, tomentulose above, densely tomentose beneath; male catkins moderately stiff, 2–4 in. long, fruiting catkins about 2 in. long; fr. subglobose, slightly over ¼ in. in diam., buff to purple-brown, becoming glabrous with age. Cent. Calif. to n. Baja Calif. (Mex.).

Wrightii Torr. Shrub, to 10 ft.; lvs. elliptic-ovate to suborbicular, to 2 in. long, minutely denticulate, puberulent when young, then glabrous above and below; male catkins loose, to 5 in. long, fruiting catkins to 3 in. long; fr. about ¼ in. in diam., purplish or blackish, glabrous. Ariz., New Mex., w. Tex. Probably the hardiest sp. Zone 7.

GARRYACEAE Lindl. SILK TASSEL FAMILY. Dicot.; 1 genus, *Garrya,* of dioecious, evergreen shrubs or small trees,

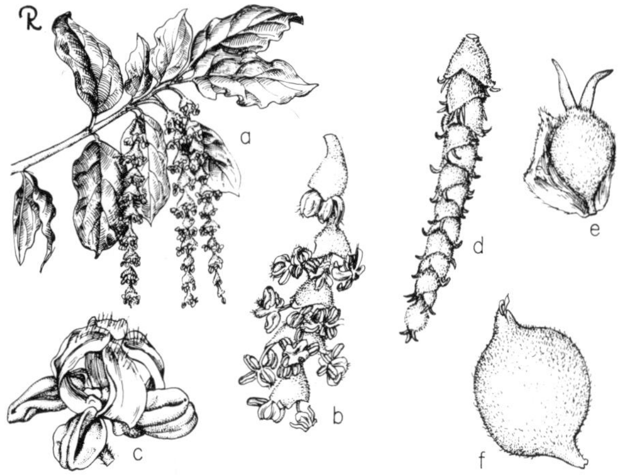

GARRYACEAE. *Garrya elliptica:* **a,** flowering branch of male plant, × ⅓; **b,** part of male inflorescence, × 1; **c,** male flower, × 5; **d,** female inflorescence, × 1; **e,** female flower, × 3; **f,** fruit, × 2. (From Lawrence, *Taxonomy of Vascular Plants.*)

with mostly ascending, somewhat quadrangular brs., native to w. N. Amer.; lvs. opp., simple, usually entire, leathery; fls. without petals, in pendulous, loose or stiff catkins, male fls. in 3's, in the axils of 4-ranked, united bracts, sepals 4, valvate, stamens 4, alternating with sepals, female fls. solitary in the axils of bracts, sepals 2, small or obsolete, ovary inferior, 1-celled, 2-ovuled, styles 2, stigmatic along inner surface; fr. berrylike, 1–2-seeded.

GARUGA Roxb. *Burseraceae.* About 7 spp. of deciduous, polygamous trees, native from se. Asia and Philippine Is., s. to E. Indies, Melanesia, and n. Australia; branchlets hairy; lvs. alt., odd-pinnate; fls. in much-branched axillary panicles, calyx lobes and petals 5, stamens 10; fr. a berry.

pinnata Roxb. Tree, 30–40 ft. or more, bark furrowed; lvs. 6–18 in. long, lfts. 11–21, lanceolate to ovate-lanceolate, 2–6 in. long; fls. yellow, the filaments, ovary, and style hairy. India, Burma.

GASTERIA H. Duval. COW-TONGUE CACTUS, LAWYER'S-TONGUE, MOTHER-IN-LAW'S-TONGUE, OX-TONGUE, DUTCH-WINGS. *Liliaceae.* Perhaps 50 spp. of per., succulent herbs, native to S. Afr.; plants mostly stemless, forming clumps; lvs. 2-ranked or in spiral rosettes, fleshy, flat or somewhat keeled, spotted or tubercled; fls. red or rose, often with green tips, in loose racemes or panicles, perianth tubular, with an inflated, curved tube, stamens 6, anthers versatile; fr. a 3-valved, loculicidal caps., seeds flattened and winged.

For culture see *Succulents.*

acinacifolia (Jacq.) Haw. Lvs. in many rows, ensiform, spreading, to 14 in. long and 2 in. wide, strongly acuminate, dark green with many small greenish-white spots in transverse bands, lower part with tubercles; fls. to 2 in. long, in racemes to 4 ft. long.

angulata (Willd.) Haw. Lvs. 2-ranked, to 10 in. long and 2 in. wide, green, marked with small white dots in transverse bands, margins with sharp edges; fls. 1 in. long, in infls. to 3 ft. long.

Armstrongii Schönl. St. short or lacking; young plants with lvs. 2-ranked, tongue-shaped, to 2 in. long and 1¼ in. wide, rounded but mucronate at apex, with white tubercles in transverse rows, the older lvs. nearly prostrate, plants several years old with lvs. in spiral rosettes, ovate-triangular, to 2¼ in. long and 1½ in. wide, acuminate, with tubercles becoming confluent into spots. Perhaps only a juvenile form of *G. Beckeri.*

Beckeri Schönl. Lvs. in a spiral rosette, to 4¾ in. long, with prominent greenish-white dots on both sides, tubercles elongated and marginal. Perhaps not distinct from *G. decipiens.*

brevifolia Haw. Lvs. more or less 2-ranked, tongue-shaped, to 6 in. long and 2 in. wide, thick, rounded and mucronate at apex, dark green, with confluent white spots in transverse bands, margin dentate and cartilaginous; fls. ¾ in. long, in racemes to 2 ft. long.

caespitosa Poelln. PENCIL-LEAF G. Sts. short; lvs. 2-ranked, triangular, to 5½ in. long and ¾ in. wide, glabrous, with stout tip at apex, spotted light green above, the spots confluent into indefinite transverse bands on underside of lf.

carinata (Mill.) Haw. Lvs. in spiral rosettes, lanceolate, 5–6 in. long, 3-angled, narrowed to horny spine at apex, dull green, rough, with many raised, white, scattered papillae, margin and keel strongly papillose; fls. 1 in. long, in infls. to 3 ft. long.

×**cheilophylla** Bak.: probably *G. pulchra* × *G. verrucosa.* Lvs. in spirally twisted rosettes, ensiform, to 1 ft. long and 1½ in. wide, with many confluent white spots, apex with white, horny margin.

colubrina N. E. Br. St. leafy, to 6 in.; lvs. 2-ranked or spirally 2-ranked in age, strap-shaped, or triangular-acuminate at apex, to 10 in. long and 1¼ in. wide, bright green or purple, with small whitish spots, fls. ¾ in. long, in infl. to 4 ft. long.

decipiens Haw. Lvs. in spiral rosettes, erect but recurving in age, triangular, tapering to a pungent apex, to 4 in. long, dark green, glossy, roughened by dirty-white, irregularly spaced dots, keeled on the back.

disticha (L.) Haw. [*G. lingua* (Thunb.) A. Berger]. Lvs. 2-ranked, tongue-shaped, to 10 in. long and 2 in. wide, with white spots in transverse lines; fls. about 1 in. long, in infl. to 3 ft. long.

excavata (Willd.) Haw. Lvs. 12–16, spirally 2-ranked in rosettes, elongate-lanceolate, 4–6 in. long and 1½ in. wide, pale dull green, with small, indistinct, whitish spots, margins tubercled, apex cuspidate; fls. 1 in. long, in infl. to 2 ft.

excelsa: *G. fuscopunctata.*

fuscopunctata Bak. [*G. excelsa* Bak.]. Rosette to 1½ ft. high, to 2½ ft. across; lvs. in many rows, lanceolate, to 1 ft. long and 3½ in. wide, triangular-mucronate at apex, spotted with brown, margin with cartilaginous teeth; fls. pink, 1 in. long, in panicles.

Gaucheri: a listed name of no botanical standing.

Herreana Poelln. St. short, leafy; lvs. 2-ranked, strap-shaped, to 5½ in. long and 1⅜ in. wide, 3-angled at apex, spotted on both sides, spots confluent, not in transverse bands; fls. about ⅝ in. long, in racemes to 2 ft. long.

Herrei: a listed name, perhaps in error for *G. Herreana.*

hybrida: a name applied to various hybrids of unknown parentage.

liliputana Poelln. St. short; lvs. in spirals, lanceolate, to 2⅜ in. long, dark green, shining, spotted with white; fls. ⅝ in. long, in racemes to 4 in. long.

lingua: *G. disticha.*

maculata (Thunb.) Haw. Sts. leafy, to 1 ft.; lvs. 2-ranked to spirally arranged, tongue-shaped, 6–8 in. long, to 2 in. wide, dark green, glossy, with white spots; fls. ¾ in. long, in infl. to 4 ft. long.

madagascariensis: a listed name of no botanical standing.

Marlothii: a listed name of no botanical standing.

marmorata Bak. St. leafy, to 10 in.; lvs. 2-ranked, lanceolate, to 6 in. long and 1½ in. wide, dark green, with confluent green spots; fls. ¾ in. long, in racemes 2½ ft. long.

minima: a listed name of no botanical standing.

nitida (Salm-Dyck) Haw. St. short; lvs. in many rows, broadly triangular-lanceolate, to 9 in. long and 2½ in. wide, glossy, with whitish spots, those on underside of lvs. confluent into irregular transverse bands; fls. 1 in. long, in racemes to 3 ft. long.

obscura: a listed name of no botanical standing.

obtusifolia (Salm-Dyck) Haw. Lvs. 2-ranked, tongue-shaped, to 6 in. long, to 2½ in. wide, rounded-truncate at apex, green, with greenish-white spots in transverse bands; fls. 1 in. long, in racemes to 2½ ft. long.

×**pethamensis:** see × *Gastrolea pethamensis.*

picta Haw. Becoming short-stemmed in age; lvs. spirally 2-ranked in rosettes, lorate-lanceolate, to 14 in. long and 2 in. wide, black-green, glossy, spotted with confluent white dots in transverse bands, margins thickened; fls. to ¾ in. long, in infl. to 3 ft. long.

planifolia Bak. Sts. leafy, to 10 in.; lvs. 2-ranked, elongate-ensiform, to 8 in. long and 1 in. wide, dark green, glossy, the confluent white spots not in transverse bands; fls. ¾ in. long, in racemes to 6 ft. long.

pulchra (Ait.) Haw. Sts. leafy, to 1 ft.; lvs. nearly 2-ranked, linear-ensiform, to 1 ft. long and 1 in. wide, dirty-green, shining, with confluent white spots in transverse bands; fls. ¾ in. long, in branched infl. to 3 ft. long.

scaberrima: *G. verrucosa* var. *asperrima.*

spiralis Bak. St. leafy, to 6 in.; lvs. spirally 2-ranked, tongue-shaped, to 6 in. long, stiff, dark green, glossy, triangular-cuspidate at apex, with many white spots; fls. ¾ in. long, in racemes to 2½ ft. long.

Stayneri Poelln. Lvs. ovate-oblong to tongue-shaped, dark green, younger lvs. 2-ranked and tubercled, older lvs. spirally arranged and smooth. Perhaps only a juvenile form of *G. decipiens.*

sulcata (Salm-Dyck) Haw. Lvs. 2-ranked, tongue-shaped, to 4 in. long and 1 in. wide, dark green, with small greenish dots; fls. to ¾ in. long, in racemes to 2½ ft. long.

trigona Haw. Lvs. spirally arranged in many rows, ensiform, 6–8 in. long, to 1½ in. wide, fresh green, very smooth, with many small white spots in band, all lvs. except the outer ones ascending; fls. almost 1 in. long, in simple or branched infl. to 2½ ft. long.

verrucosa (Mill.) H. Duval. WARTY ALOE, WART G., RICE G. Lvs. 2-ranked, lanceolate, 4–9 in. long, to 1½ in. wide, triangular-cuspidate at apex, dull green, the spots pure white and raised, forming roughened surface; fls. ¾–1 in. long, in racemes to 2 ft. long. Var. **asperrima** (Salm-Dyck) Poelln. [var. **scaberrima** (Salm-Dyck) Bak.; *G. scaberrima* Hort.]. Lvs. more strap-shaped, incurved, tubercles greenish-white, nearly same color as lf.

GASTROCOCOS Morales. *Palmae.* One sp., a monoecious palm in Cuba; trunk spiny when young, often nearly smooth when old except on new growth, much swollen toward top; lvs. pinnate, pinnae acute; infl. among lvs., simply branched, with 2 bracts, the upper enclosing the infl. in bud, prickly, rachillae with fls. in triads (2 male and 1 female) near the base and above these with paired male fls., bractlets neither prominent nor united; male fls. with calyx cupular, 3-lobed, petals valvate, stamens 6, female fls. with calyx cupular, 3-lobed, petals united half their length, staminodes in a tube united to petals basally, 6-lobed above, pistil 3-celled; fr. smooth, globose or depressed-globose, mesocarp thin, separating easily from pitted endocarp, pores at middle, seed with homogeneous endosperm.

Sometimes planted as ornamentals in the tropics and subtropics. Slow-growing when young but later fast-growing. For culture see *Palms.*

armentalis: *G. crispa.*

crispa (HBK) H. E. Moore [*Acrocomia armentalis* (Morales) L. H. Bailey; *A. crispa* (HBK) C. F. Bak. ex Becc.]. To 50 ft. or more; lvs. to 9 ft. long or more, pinnae usually in several planes, glaucous beneath, to 1 in. wide, often with pale prickles on midrib near base above and beneath; male fls. to 5/16 in. long, female fls. ⅜ in. long; fr. yellow, to 1¼ in. in diam. Warmer parts of Zone 10a in Fla.

×**GASTROLEA** Walth.: *Gasteria* × *Aloe.* SPOTTED-BEAUTY. *Liliaceae.* A hybrid genus, comprising about 20 "spp." of stemless, per. herbs, usually forming clumps of rosettes; lvs. in a spiral, variously spotted or tubercled, mostly 3-angled or keeled; fls. greenish, reddish at base, in lateral, simple or branched racemes, perianth tubular, scarcely inflated, segms. longer than tube, stamens 6, ovary superior, 3-celled.

For culture see *Succulents.*

almanzis: a listed name of no botanical standing, for a plant described as having rosettes of short, mottled lvs.

Beguinii (Radl) Walth. [*Aloe* × *Beguinii* Radl]: *Gasteria verrucosa* × *Aloe aristata.* LIZARD-TAIL, PEARL ALOE. Lvs. triangular-acuminate, 3–4 in. long, rarely over 1 in. wide at base, short-pointed, tubercles of lf. surface blunt, those of margins sharp-pointed; infl. to 2 ft. long. Var. **perfectior** (Radl) Rowley [× *Gastrolea perfectior* (Radl) Walth.; *Aloe* × *perfectior* (Radl) A. Berger]. Taller, lvs. longer, light green.

mortolensis (A. Berger) Walth. [*Aloe* × *mortolensis* A. Berger]: *Gasteria acinacifolia* × *Aloe variegata.* Basal offsets many; lvs. triangular-lanceolate, less than 2 in. wide at base, smooth, pale green with longitudinally confluent spots, with many marginal teeth; infl. to 2 ft. long.

perfectior: × *G. Beguinii* var.

pethamensis (Bak.) Walth. [*Aloe* × *pethamensis* Bak.]: parentage doubtful; *Aloe variegata* × either *Gasteria verrucosa* or *G. carinata.* Lvs. 8–12 in. long, to 2 in. wide at base, short-pointed, tubercles prominent. By some thought to be a hybrid between *Gasteria carinata* and *Gasteria verrucosa,* in which case its correct name would be *Gasteria* × *pethamensis* Bak.

GAUDICHAUDIA HBK. *Malpighiaceae.* About 10 spp. of scandent shrubs, native from Mex. to n. S. Amer.; lvs. opp., simple, with 2 glands at base of blade; fls. in corymbs or umbels, yellow, dimorphic, "normal" fls. with sepals 5, having 8–10 glands, petals 5, clawed, stamens 5, all or only 2–3 fertile, carpels 3, fr. of 3 samaras; "abnormal" fls. with calyx glandless, petals and stamens mostly rudimentary, carpels 2.

cynanchoides HBK. To about 10 ft.; lvs. oblong, to 2 in. long, narrowed at base, almost sessile; fertile stamens 3. Mex.

mucronata (Sessé & Moç. ex DC.) A. Juss. Lvs. oblong to oblong-ovate, to 3 in. long, rounded or subcordate and somewhat auriculate, petioled; fertile stamens 3. Mex., Cent. Amer.

GAULTHERIA L. [*Chiogenes* Salisb.]. *Ericaceae.* About 100 spp. of evergreen, erect or prostrate shrubs, or rarely small trees, native chiefly to the Andes of S. Amer., but also to N. Amer., and from Asia to Australia; lvs. alt. or rarely opp., simple; fls. pink or white, solitary or in racemes or panicles, calyx usually 5-parted, corolla urceolate or campanulate, rarely tubular, stamens 8–10, anthers awned, ovary superior; fr. a caps., usually enclosed by the fleshy bright-colored calyx.

An aromatic oil is derived from several species. Moist sandy or peaty soils and partial shade are desirable. Propagated by seeds, layers, suckers, division, and by cuttings of half-ripened wood.

adenothrix (Miq.) Maxim. Low shrub, sts. cylindrical, ascending; lvs. short-petioled, ovate to nearly orbicular, to 1¼ in. long, sharply serrulate; fls. 2–15 in axillary racemes, white, calyx tube long-setose, anthers spurred; fr. red. Japan. Zone 6.

adpressa: a listed name of no botanical standing for *G. antipoda* cv.

antipoda G. Forst. Shrub, to 5 ft., occasionally procumbent; lvs. oblong-lanceolate to obovate or orbicular, to ⅜ in. long, persistent; fls. solitary, fragrant, white or pink; fr. red. New Zeal., Tasmania. Fr. is edible. Cv. **'Adpressa'.** A procumbent form.

cuneata (Rehd. & E. H. Wils.) Bean. Compact, to 1½ ft.; lvs. narrowly ovate to obovate, to 1¼ in. long; fls. in terminal racemes, white, ovary hairy; fr. white. W. China. Zone 6.

depressa Hook.f. Depressed shrub, to 1 ft., sts. creeping and rooting, branchlets setose; lvs. broadly oblong to orbicular-obovate, to ⅜ in. long, crenate, often setose; fls. axillary, sometimes in leafy racemes; fr. white or red, to ⅝ in. in diam. New Zeal.

Forrestii Diels. Glabrous, to 5 ft.; lvs. elliptic or oblong to oblanceolate, to 3 in. long, bright green above, paler beneath; fls. in racemes, white, with white pedicels; fr. blue. W. China. Zone 7?

fragrantissima Wallich. Shrub or small tree; lvs. elliptic or ovate to obovate, to 4 in. long; fls. white to pink, fragrant; fr. violet-blue. Mts., India, Ceylon, Burma.

hispida R. Br. WAXBERRY. Erect, spreading shrub, to 6 ft., sts. pubescent; lvs. lanceolate to oblong, to 2 in. long, somewhat serrulate; fls. in dense racemes, white; fr. white. Tasmania. Zone 7?

hispidula (L.) Muhlenb. ex Bigel. [*Chiogenes hispidula* (L.) Torr. & A. Gray ex Torr.; *C. serpyllifolia* (Pursh) Salisb.]. CREEPING SNOWBERRY, MOXIE PLUM, MAIDENHAIR BERRY. Trailing, matted, semiherbaceous shrub; lvs. ovate, to ⅜ in. long, revolute, bristly beneath; fls. white, less than 3/16 in. long; fr. white. Late spring. N. Amer. Zone 4.

Hookeri C. B. Clarke. To 6 ft., branchlets hispid; lvs. almost sessile, elliptic-ovate, to 2 in. long; fls. in downy racemes, white, corolla tubular; fr. white, downy. Himalayas. Zone 7?

humifusa (R. C. Grah.) Rydb. [*G. Myrsinites* Hook.]. ALPINE WINTERGREEN. To 4 in., sts. matted, tufted; lvs. elliptic or orbicular, to ¾ in. long, subentire to crenate; fls. solitary, white, ⅛ in. long, calyx glabrous; fr. scarlet. Summer. B.C. to Colo. and Calif. Zone 6. Fr. edible, used in preserves.

Itoana Hayata. Erect or decumbent shrub, to 6 in.; lvs. oblong, to ⅜ in. long, toothed; fls. in few-fld. racemes, white, corolla globose-urceolate; fr. white. Taiwan.

laxiflora: *G. yunnanensis.*

macrostigma: a listed name of no botanical standing for *Pernettya macrostigma.*

Miqueliana Takeda. Woody evergreen, to 1 ft.; lvs. elliptic to obovate, to 1⅜ in. long, crenate-serrate; fls. nodding, in pubescent racemes, white or pinkish, less than ¼ in. long, anthers 4-awned; fr. white. Japan. Zone 6.

Myrsinites: *G. humifusa.*

nummularifolia: a listed name of no botanical standing for *G. nummularioides.*

nummularioides D. Don. Prostrate shrub, sts. bristly; lvs. 2-ranked, ovate to suborbicular, to ⅝ in. long, ciliate, pubescent beneath; fls. solitary, pale pinkish-white; fr. blue-black. Himalayas and w. China. Zone 7?

oppositifolia Hook.f. To 8 ft., much-branched; lvs. opp., almost sessile, ovate or oblong-ovate, to 2¼ in. long, cordate, leathery; fls. mostly in panicled racemes, white, less than 3/16 in. long. New Zeal.

ovatifolia A. Gray. To 8 in.; lvs. ovate, to 1½ in. long, toothed, rather thick; fls. solitary, white, less than ³⁄₁₆ in. long, calyx pubescent; fr. scarlet. Early summer. B.C. to n. Calif. and Idaho. Zone 6.

perplexa: *Pernettya macrostigma.*

procumbens L. [*G. repens* Raf.]. WINTERGREEN, CHECKERBERRY, TEABERRY, MOUNTAIN TEA, IVRY-LEAVES. Sts. creeping; lvs. elliptic to narrowly obovate, to 2 in. long, bristly serrate, shining above; fls. solitary and nodding, white, ¼ in. long; fr. scarlet. Summer, early autumn. Nfld. to Man. and Minn., s. to Ga. and Ala. Zone 4. Original source of oil of wintergreen, now obtained from *Betula lenta.*

pyrolifolia: *G. pyroloides.*

pyroloides Hook.f. & T. Thoms. ex Miq. [*G. pyrolifolia* Hook.f. & T. Thoms. ex C. B. Clarke]. Low shrub, to 1 ft.; lvs. ovate to nearly orbicular, to 1½ in. long; fls. in loose racemes to 2½ in. long, white, anthers 2-awned; fr. blue-black. Himalayas and w. China. Zone 7?

repens: *G. procumbens.*

rupestris (L.f.) G. Don. To 4 ft., much-branched, erect or rarely prostrate; lvs. variable, oblong to ovate or nearly orbicular, to 2 in. long, leathery; fls. in racemes, white. New Zeal. Zone 7?

semi-infera (C. B. Clarke) Airy-Shaw. To 6 ft., twigs bristly; lvs. elliptic, to 3 in. long, toothed, glabrous above, sparsely setose beneath; fls. in racemes, white, stamens 5; fr. blue. Himalayas and w. China.

Shallon Pursh. SALAL, SHALLON. To 6 ft., branchlets glandular-pubescent; lvs. oblong or ovate to nearly orbicular, to 4 in. long, finely serrate; fls. in racemes, white or pink, ⅜ in. long; fr. purple, becoming black. Spring, early summer. S. Alaska, B.C. to s. Calif. Zone 6. The foliage of this is the LEMONLEAF of florists.

sinensis Anth. Compact, matted shrub, to 1 ft.; lvs. oblong to ob-ovate, to ½ in. long, dark green, shining; fls. solitary, white, anthers 2-awned; fr. blue. Tibet, Yunnan, to upper Burma.

tetramera W. W. Sm. Low shrub, to 2 ft. or rarely more, twigs bristly; lvs. elliptic to obovate or suborbicular, to 2 in. long, toothed, glossy above; fls. in racemes, white, often 4-merous; fr. blue. W. China and Tibet. Zone 7?

trichophylla Royle. Spreading, prostrate shrub, to 6 in., sts. bristly; lvs. elliptic to oblong, to ½ in. long, ciliate, not pubescent; fls. solitary, white to pink, anthers 4-awned; fr. blue. Himalayas and w. China. Zone 7?

Veitchiana Craib. Shrub, to 3½ ft., sts. occasionally decumbent, branchlets bristly; lvs. elliptic to oblong-obovate, to 4 in. long, mucronate, dark green and glossy above, paler and often setose beneath; fls. nodding, in axillary and terminal racemes to 2 in. long, white, corolla urceolate; fr. bright blue, to ¼ in. in diam. W. China. Zone 7? Probably hardy as far north as Philadelphia.

Wardii Marq. & Airy-Shaw. To 3 ft. or more, densely covered with brown hairs; lvs. elliptic to lanceolate-oblong, to 2⅛ in. long, revolute, with long hairs beneath; fls. in short, dense racemes, white; fr. purplish-blue. Se. Tibet. Zone 7?

yunnanensis (Franch.) Rehd. [*G. laxiflora* Diels]. Straggly shrub, to 5 ft., brs. arching; lvs. oblong-lanceolate to ovate, to 4¾ in. long, cordate; fls. solitary or in racemes, white, externally blotched or banded with brown; fr. black. W. China.

GAURA L. *Onagraceae.* About 18 spp. of ann. to per. herbs of N. and S. Amer.; lvs. mostly alt., simple; fls. white to pink, yellow in 1 sp., in spicate racemes or panicles, 4- or sometimes 3-merous, ovary inferior; fr. a small, woody, caps., nutlike, indehiscent, 4- to 1-seeded.

Sometimes grown in the wild garden or hardy border. Propagated by seeds and division.

coccinea Nutt. ex Pursh. Low, bushy per., sts. several, to 2 ft.; lvs. many, oblong-lanceolate, about 1 in. long, mostly pubescent; fls. in crowded spikes, sepals to ⅜ in. long, petals ¼ in. long, whitish to pink, aging red; fr. obtusely 4-angled above, narrowed beneath, ¼ in. long. Alta. to Mex.

Lindheimeri Engelm. & A. Gray. Per., erect, to 4 ft.; lvs. lanceolate, 1–3½ in. long; fls. in open panicles, petals ½–1 in. long, white, aging rose; fr. 4-angled, ⁵⁄₁₆ in. long. La., Tex., adjacent Mex.

odorata Sessé ex Lag. Related to *G. coccinea,* but with sepals ⅜–½ in. long; petals ⁵⁄₁₆ in. long. Tex. to Mex.

parviflora Dougl. ex Hook. Winter ann. or bien., 1–5 ft., freely branched above, soft-villous and clammy; lvs. lanceolate-ovate, 1–4 in. long; fls. opening at night, minute, petals pink to rose; fr. ¼–⁵⁄₁₆ in. long, sessile. W. Amer.

sinuata Nutt. ex Ser. Per., 1–3 ft.; lvs. crowded, spatulate to lanceolate or linear, ½–2 in. long; fls. in open panicles, petals ⁵⁄₁₆ in. long, white, aging red; fr. 4-angled, to ⁵⁄₁₆ in. long. Okla. to n. Mex.

GAUSSIA H. Wendl. (*Aeria* O. F. Cook). *Palmae.* Two spp. of solitary, unarmed, monoecious palms, native to limestone hills of Cuba and Puerto Rico; lvs. pinnate, sheath not forming a conspicuous crownshaft, petiole short, pinnae acute; infl. interfoliar, long-peduncled, with 6–8 tubular bracts sheathing peduncle, brs. simple or the lower once-branched, rachillae slender, glabrous, with fls. borne in lines (acervuli) of 4–5, the lowest female, the remainder male; female fls. with sepals imbricate, petals valvate, stamens 6, female fls. with sepals imbricate, petals imbricate basally, subvalvate to valvate and spreading apically at flowering, staminodes 6, minute, pistil 3-celled, 3-ovuled; fr. obovoid, orange to red, fleshy, usually 1-seeded, seed with homogeneous endosperm and lateral embryo.

Sometimes grown as ornamentals in the tropics and subtropics; Zone 10b in Fla. For culture see *Palms.*

attenuata (O. F. Cook) Becc. Trunk to nearly 100 ft., 6 in. in diam. at base, increasing to 10 in. in diam. at about 9 ft., then very gradually tapered, not prominently ringed; lvs. with about 68 pinnae on each side, these regularly arranged but borne in several planes, the blade thus appearing ragged; infl. to 3 ft. long; male fls. yellow, sepals thin, lacking a dark margin; fr. about ⅝ in. long. Puerto Rico.

princeps H. Wendl. Similar to *G. attenuata* but the trunk usually conspicuously swollen; male fls. with thick, dark brown-margined sepals. Cuba.

GAYA Cav. *Malvaceae.* Not cult. **G. Lyallii:** *Hoheria Lyallii.*

GAYLUSSACIA HBK [*Buxella* Small; *Decachaena* Torr. & A. Gray; *Lasiococcus* Small]. HUCKLEBERRY. *Ericaceae.* About 40 spp. of shrubs, native to N. Amer., but chiefly S. Amer.; lvs. alt., simple; fls. white, pink, or red, in axillary racemes, calyx 5-lobed, corolla urceolate, campanulate, or tubular, stamens 10, anthers not awned, ovary inferior; fr. a berrylike drupe. Distinguished from *Vaccinium* in having ovary 10-celled.

Huckleberries should have a shady location in peaty or sandy soil. They do not thrive on limestone soils. Propagated by seeds, layers, division, and the evergreen sorts by cuttings of half-ripe wood under glass.

baccata (Wangenh.) C. Koch [*Decachaena baccata* (Wangenh.) Small]. BLACK H. Deciduous shrub, to 3 ft., brs. sticky when young; lvs. elliptic to oblong-lanceolate, to 2 in. long, entire, resinous on both surfaces; fls. reddish, in dense, drooping racemes to 1 in. long; fr. black, glossy, edible. Late spring. Nfld. to Ga., w. to Iowa.

brachycera (Michx.) A. Gray [*Buxella brachycera* (Michx.) Small]. BOX H. Creeping evergreen, to 1½ ft.; lvs. elliptic to ovate, to 1 in. long, finely crenate-toothed, glabrous; fls. white or pink, in short racemes, corolla cylindric-campanulate; fr. blue. Spring. Local, Del. to W. Va. and Tenn. Zone 6.

dumosa (Andr.) Torr. & A. Gray [*Lasiococcus dumosus* (Andr.) Small]. DWARF H. Deciduous shrub, to 1½ ft., sts. creeping, glandular-pubescent; lvs. elliptic to obovate, to 2 in. long, entire; fls. white, pink, or red, in loose, leafy-bracted racemes, corolla campanulate; fr. black, glandular-pubescent. Late spring. Nfld. to Fla. and La. Zone 2?

frondosa (L.) Torr. & A. Gray ex Torr. [*Decachaena frondosa* (L.) Small]. DWARF H., DANGLEBERRY, BLUE-TANGLE. Slender, deciduous shrub, to 6 ft.; lvs. oblong to elliptic-obovate, to 2¾ in. long, entire, resinous beneath; fls. white to greenish-purple, in loose racemes to 3 in. long, corolla campanulate; fr. dark blue, glaucous. Spring. New Hamp. to Fla. Zone 5.

GAZANIA Gaertn. *Compositae* (Arctotis Tribe). About 16 spp. of rhizomatous, per., rarely ann., herbs or subshrubs, with milky juice, native to S. Afr., one in trop. Afr.; lvs. mostly in basal rosettes, rarely on the sts., entire to lobed or pinnatifid; fl. heads solitary, on long peduncles, radiate, closing at night, involucral bracts in 2 to several rows, united basally into a cup, receptacle pitted; disc fls. tubular, bisexual, ray fls. ligulate, sterile, white, yellow, orange, or scarlet, sometimes with basal spots; achenes villous, pappus of 2 rows of delicate, scarious, toothed scales.

Gazanias are grown in the flower garden for edgings, or as a ground cover. Propagated by seeds, division, and also by cuttings taken in summer from shoots near the crown of the plants.

leucolaena: *G. ringens* var.

linearis (Thunb.) Druce [*G. longiscapa* DC.]. Rhizomatous per., brs. short; lvs. in rosettes, linear to linear-lanceolate or rarely pinnatifid, ciliate and somewhat revolute, nearly glabrous above, white-tomentose beneath; heads to 2¾ in. across, on scapes to about 14 in. long; ray fls. yellow or orange, occasionally with a dark brown basal spot.

longiscapa: *G. linearis.*

pinnata (Thunb.) Less. Per.; lvs. lanceolate, pinnately dissected, revolute, hirsute above, white-woolly beneath; heads to 3 in. across, on hairy peduncles; ray fls. orange-yellow, with a dark basal spot.

rigens (L.) Gaertn. [*G. splendens* Hort. ex E. G. Henders. & A. Henders.]. TREASURE FLOWER. Rhizomatous per., sts. decumbent, to 16 in. long, glabrous or hairy; lvs. lanceolate or obovate-lanceolate, to about 3¼ in. long, entire or sometimes pinnatifid, green and glabrous above, white-tomentose beneath; heads to about 3 in. across, on peduncles to 4–6 in. long; ray fls. yellow to orange, with a brown-black, white-eyed basal spot. Var. **leucolaena** (DC.) Roessler [*G. leucolaena* DC.]. More or less tomentose; heads about 1½ in. across; ray fls. entirely yellow.

splendens: *G. rigens.*

GEIJERA Schott. *Rutaceae.* About 5 spp. of small, evergreen trees or shrubs or e. Australia and New Caledonia; lvs. alt., simple, glandular-dotted; fls. small, yellowish-white, in short, terminal panicles, sepals 5, persistent, petals 5, deciduous, stamens 5; fr. dehiscing into separate, obtuse sections.

parviflora Lindl. Tree, to 30 ft., brs. often pendulous; lvs. linear, 3–6 in. long, glabrous.

GEISSOIS Labill. *Cunoniaceae.* About 9 spp. of shrubs or trees, native to the sw. Pacific, 2 in Queensland; lvs. opp., odd-pinnate, lfts. 3 or 5, serrate or entire, leathery; fls. small, in many-fld. racemes, sepals 4–5, petals 0, stamens 10–20, ovary superior; fr. a leathery, 2-celled caps.

Benthamii F. J. Muell. [*Weinmannia Benthamii* (F. J. Muell.) F. M. Bailey]. Tree; lfts. 3, to 4 in. long, repand-serrulate, leathery, glabrous, stipules almost circular, to 1 in. across; racemes spikelike; fls. yellow. Queensland.

GEISSORHIZA Ker-Gawl. *Iridaceae.* About 65 spp. of cormous herbs, native to S. Afr.; fls. of various colors, sessile, in open spikes or panicles; resembling *Ixia* in general appearance and closely allied to *Hesperantha*, but differing in having the undivided part of style longer than the perianth tube, style brs. short, recurved, and longer than the anthers.

Usually grown under glass, flowering in spring and early summer, or in the open in mild climates. Propagated by seeds or cormlets.

furva Ker-Gawl. Sts. about 4 in., tunics concentric, brown, hard; lvs. 2–3, filiform, to 4½ in. long, nearly quadrangular; fls. solitary, perianth reddish-purple, segms. obovate, about ⅝ in. long. Stony soil, S. Afr.

secunda (Bergius) Ker-Gawl. Sts. 10–16 in. long, much-branched, flexuous, hispid, tunics imbricate, hard; lvs. 8–12 in. long, glabrous; infl. a loose, 3–6-fld., 1-sided spike; perianth bluish-purple, segms. to ½ in. long, subacute. Sandy soil, S. Afr.

splendidissima Diels. Sts. 6–9 in., mostly unbranched, hirtellous, tunics imbricate, thickened; basal lvs. 2, contracted above the base, to 3/32 in. wide, hirtellous, margin thickened, st. lvs. wider, with many prominent veins; infl. a loose 1-sided, 4–5-fld. spike; perianth brilliant dark purple, with yellowish-green throat, segms. obovate, about 1 in. long, acute. Clay loam, S. Afr.

GELASINE Herb. *Iridaceae.* One sp., a cormous herb, native to Uruguay and s. Brazil; allied to *Cipura* and *Nemastylis;* lvs. pleated; fls. 2–3 in a terminal cluster, emerging from 2 green spathe valves, fugacious, perianth cup-shaped, perianth tube very short, segms. nearly equal, filaments united at base, style brs. 3, linear; fr. a caps.

azurea Herb. Tunics membranous, sts. 1½–2 ft.; basal lvs. to 2 ft. long and 1 in. wide at the middle; fls. bright blue, segms. with small white basal blotch, obovate, cuspidate, about ¾ in. long. Prop. by seeds or cormlets.

GELSEMIUM Juss. YELLOW JESSAMINE, CAROLINA Y. J., CAROLINA JASMINE. *Loganiaceae.* Three spp. of twining shrubs, 1 native to e. Asia, 2 to e. N. Amer.; lvs. opp., entire; fls. solitary or in small cymes, corolla funnelform; fr. a 2-valved caps.

Propagated by cuttings under glass and by seeds.

Rankinii Small. Differs from *G. sempervirens* in having lvs. rounded at base, pedicels scaly only on lower part, fls. odorless, calyx lobes narrow and acuminate, and fr. about ½ in. long, long-beaked. Rare, N.C., Fla., Ala.

sempervirens (L.) Ait. EVENING TRUMPET FLOWER. Evergreen; lvs. lanceolate, to 4 in. long, glossy above, narrowed at base; fls. fragrant, bright yellow, to 1½ in. long, borne on scaly pedicels, calyx lobes obtuse; fr. ¾ in. long or more, short-beaked. Va. to Fla., w. to Tex., and Cent. Amer. Grown in U.S. as a cover for porches and banks and sometimes under glass; valued for its fragrant yellow fls. produced throughout the season.

GENIOSTOMA G. Forst. & J. R. Forst. *Loganiaceae.* Thirty to 40 spp. of shrubs or small trees, native to Madagascar, Malay Pen., New Guinea, Polynesia, Australia, New Zeal.; lvs. opp., usually petioled; fls. small, in axillary clusters or cymes, 5-merous, ovary 2-celled; fr. a caps., seeds many.

ligustrifolium A. Cunn. Glabrous, bushy shrub, to 9 ft.; lvs. ovate, to 2½ in. long, pale beneath; fls. small, greenish-white, in few-fld. axillary cymes. New Zeal. Cult. in Calif. in Zone 10.

GENIPA L. GENIP. *Rubiaceae.* About 6 spp. of trees, native to trop. Amer.; lvs. opp., large, somewhat leathery, stipules interpetiolar, deciduous; fls. large, few in terminal cymes, 5–6-merous, corolla salverform, tube short; fr. a berry.

Genipas can be grown only in the tropics without protection or risk, and grow best in rich loam with abundant moisture. Propagated by seeds and by shield budding.

americana L. MARMALADE BOX, GENIPAP. To 50 ft.; lvs. obovate to oblong, to 1 ft. long; fls. white or pale yellow, 1 in. across, silky; fr. brown, to 3 in. across. Mex., s. to Peru and Brazil. The strong, resistant and flexible wood is used for many purposes. The edible fr. is dark colored and not particularly palatable; it yields an indelible dark blue dye much used as a body paint by uncivilized Indians of trop. Amer. It is used in preserves or drinks where native.

GENISTA L. BROOM. *Leguminosae* (subfamily *Faboideae*). About 75–90 spp. of sometimes armed shrubs of Eur., n. Afr., and w. Asia; lvs. usually alt., with 1 lft., or sometimes with 3 lfts.; fls. mostly yellow, papilionaceous, in terminal racemes or heads, calyx 2-lipped, claws of wing and keel petals united to staminal tube; fr. a flat legume. Differs from *Cytisus* in the absence of any appendage or small calluslike protuberance near the hilum of seed.

Several species are dye plants. Brooms have showy ornamental flowers and are adapted to sunny dry locations and mild, Medit. type of climate. Propagated by seeds, layering, or softwood cuttings.

aethnensis DC. MOUNT ETNA B. To 20 ft., brs. almost leafless, drooping; lvs. with 1 lft., lfts. linear; fls. axillary along the brs., golden-yellow, fragrant. Summer. Sicily, Sardinia. Zone 9b.

Andreana: *Cytisus scoparius* cv.

anglica L. To 3 ft., sometimes procumbent, spiny; lvs. with 1 lft., lfts. about 5/16 in. long, bluish-green, glabrous; fls. in terminal, leafy, few-fld. racemes. W. Eur. Frost-hardy.

canariensis: *Cytisus canariensis.*

cinerea (Vill.) DC. To 3 ft., unarmed; lvs. with 1 lft., lfts. to 5/16 in. long, acute, pubescent; fls. in racemes to 8 in. long, bright yellow, fragrant. Spring. S. Eur., n. Afr. Zone 9b.

dalmatica: *G. silvestris* var. *pungens.*

delphinensis: *G. sagittalis.*

decumbens: *Cytisus decumbens.*

falcata Brot. To 2 ft. or more, brs. erect, dense, spiny; lvs. mostly with 1 lft., lfts. ovate-oblong to lanceolate, to ⅛ in. long; fls. in loose, few-fld. racemes; fr. to 1 in. long, strongly curved, glabrous. Spain, Portugal. Zone 9b.

fragrans: *Cytisus supranubius,* but the florist's plant offered under the name *G. fragrans* may be *Cytisus stenolobus.* See also under *C. racemosus.*

germanica L. To 2 ft., armed with usually compound spines, branchlets hairy, the flowering ones not spiny; lvs. with 1 lft., lfts. elliptic-oblong, villous beneath; fls. small, in racemes to 2 in. long; fr. elliptic, villous. Summer. Eur. Frost-hardy.

hirsuta: see *Cytisus hirsutus.*

hispanica L. [*Cytisus hispanicus* Hort., not Lam.; *Ulex hispanicus* Hort., not Pourr. ex Willk. & J. Lange]. SPANISH B. To 2 ft., brs. with slender spines; lvs. with 1 lft., lfts. lanceolate to oblanceolate, to ½ in.

long, with spreading hairs; fls. golden-yellow, in terminal heads or clusters; fr. to ⅜ in. long, nearly glabrous. Late spring. Sw. Eur. Frost-hardy. Subsp. **hispanica.** The typical subsp.; lfts. with spreading hairs; standard ¼–5/16 in. across. E. Pyrenees and e. Spain. Cv. **'Compacta'.** Habit denser. Cv. **'Nana'.** Habit dwarf. Subsp. **occidentalis** Rouy [*G. occidentalis* (Rouy) Coste]. Lfts. with appressed hairs; standard 5/16 to nearly ½ in. across. W. Pyrenees and n. Spain.

horrida (Vahl) DC. To 18 in., densely branched, branchlets stiff, very spiny; lvs. of 3 lfts., opp. or whorled, lfts. linear; fls. few, in terminal heads; fr. more than 1 in. long. Summer. France, Spain. Frost-hardy.

×**hybrida:** a listed name of no botanical standing for +*Laburnocytisus Adamii*, but material offered as *G.* × *hybrida* is a group of hardy *Cytisus* hybrids with pink, scarlet, buff, or orange fls.

humifusa: a confused name used by several authors in various ways; identity of material cult. under this name is not certain.

juncea: *Spartium junceum.*

kewensis: a listed name of no botanical standing for *Cytisus* ×*kewensis.*

monosperma (L.) Lam. To 10 ft., nearly leafless; fls. in short, lateral racemes, fragrant, calyx purple, petals white; fr. broad, ½ in. long, 1–2-seeded. Early spring. Spain, n. Afr. Zone 10. Cv. **'Pendula'** is listed.

occidentalis: *G. hispanica* subsp.

pilosa L. Prostrate, with ascending branchlets to 20 in. high, unarmed; lvs. with 1 lft., lfts. obovate to oblong, to ⅝ in. long, obtuse, hairy; fls. yellow, in short racemes. Late spring. Eur. Frost-hardy.

praecox: a listed name of no botanical standing for *Cytisus* × *praecox.*

prostrata: *Cytisus decumbens.*

purgans: *Cytisus purgans.*

purpurea: *Cytisus purpureus.*

racemosa: a listed name of no botanical standing for *Cytisus racemosus.*

radiata (L.) Scop. To 2 ft., much-branched, unarmed; lvs. of 3 lfts., some lvs. opp. or whorled, lfts. linear-lanceolate, ½ in. long, silvery-hairy; fls. in 3–10-fld. heads; fr. elliptic, pubescent, 1–2-seeded. Early summer. S. Eur. Frost-hardy.

sagittalis L. [*G. delphinensis* J. Verl.]. Procumbent, fl. sts. to 20 in. high, sts. flat, broadly 2-winged, green, pubescent; lvs. with 1 lft., lfts. ovate to oblong, ¾ in. long, villous, especially when young; fls. yellow, in terminal racemes. Early summer. Eur., w. Asia. Zone 5.

scoparia: *Cytisus scoparius.*

sibirica: see *G. tinctoria.*

sylvestris Scop. To 6 in. high, spiny; lvs. with 1 lft., lfts. linear to narrowly lanceolate; fls. bright yellow, in terminal racemes to 4 in. long; fr. ovoid, usually 1-seeded. Se. Eur. Frost-hardy. Var. **pungens** Vis. [*G. dalmatica* Bartl.]. More spiny.

tinctoria L. [*G. ?sibirica* L.]. DYER'S GREENWEED, WOODWAXEN, WOADWAXEN, DYER'S B. To 3 ft., erect or procumbent, brs. striped; lvs. bright green, with 1 lft., lfts. mostly elliptic-oblong, to 1 in. long, ciliate, nearly glabrous; fls. in many-fld., leafy racemes panicled at ends of brs.; fr. narrowly oblong, 6–10-seeded. Summer. Eur., w. Asia; naturalized in e. N. Amer. Zone 5. Fls. yield a yellow dye.

versicolor: *Cytisus versicolor.*

Villarsii Clementi. Low, suffrutescent, unarmed per., young branchlets very hairy; lvs. with 1 lft., lfts. oblong-lanceolate, usually densely silky beneath; fls. 1–3 in axils, yellow, silky outside; fr. oblong, silky-villous, 2-seeded. S.-cent. Eur. Frost-hardy. Fls. yield a yellow dye.

virgata (Ait.) Lowe. To 12 ft. or more, broadly bushy, brs. slender, drooping, gray-silky; lvs. with 1 lft., lfts. nearly sessile, of variable size and shape, silky-pubescent especially beneath; fls. in small, terminal, nearly capitate racemes, lemon-yellow, becoming golden- to orange-brown as they wither; fr. hoary-pubescent. Summer, autumn. Madeira. Zone 10.

GENTIANA L. GENTIAN. *Gentianaceae.* About 200–350 spp. of per., rarely ann. or bien. herbs, often tufted, mostly of temp. and arctic regions, or montane regions in tropics, often in wet places; lvs. opp., sessile or petioled, sometimes clasping; fls. white to yellow or blue to purple, or red, often spotted, solitary to many in elongated or capitate clusters, 4–5-(rarely 6-)merous, calyx tubular to campanulate, variously lobed or cleft, corolla funnelform, campanulate or salverform, sometimes tubular or club-shaped, variously lobed, with pleats, teeth, or appendages between lobes, stamens united to corolla tube; fr. a caps., seeds many, flat, winged. Because of its large size and its variability, *Gentiana* has been divided into segregate genera; two recognized here are *Gentianella* and *Gentianopsis.*

The good blues of the flowers make gentians favorite garden plants. They are grown mostly in the rock garden, but also in other parts of the garden. They require good drainage with plenty of moisture and a cool temperature, as the cultivated ones are mostly mountain plants. Some species require special treatment, and are grown only by fanciers. Propagated by seeds sown as soon as ripe, by cuttings, and by root division. The bitter glucosides contained in gentian roots have been used medicinally.

acaulis L. [*G. excisa* K. Presl; *G. Kochiana* Perr. & Song.]. STEMLESS G. To 4 in.; lvs. in a basal rosette, elliptic or lanceolate to obovate, at least 1½ times as long as wide; fls. solitary, calyx funnelform, ½ in. long, lobes ovate, ¼ in. long, mostly less than ½ as long as tube, narrowed at base, corolla dark blue, spotted inside, more or less campanulate, 2 in. long, appendage between lobes shorter than lobes, stigma lobes rounded, fimbriate. Alps and Pyrenees. Cv. **'Alba'.** Fls. white. Cv. **'Gigantea'.** A large form.

affinis Griseb. ex. Hook. [*G. Bigelovii* A. Gray]. Sts. clustered, to 1 ft.; lvs. oblong to linear; fls. mostly many in terminal or axillary clusters, calyx lobes unequal, corolla blue, narrowly funnelform, to 1 in. long, the pleats or appendages of the sinuses lacerate into narrow segms. B.C., s. to Calif. and Ariz., e. to Rocky Mts., sporadically to Minn. and Ont.

alba Muhlenb. [*G. flavida* A. Gray]. Sts. erect, stout, unbranched, to 3 ft.; lvs. ovate-lanceolate, to 5 in. long, 3–7-nerved, light yellowish-green; fls. in terminal, often large clusters, corolla white, marked with greenish veins, tubular, to 2 in. long. Ne. N. Amer.

algida Pall. [*G. algida* var. *sibirica* Kuzn.; *G. Romanzovii* Ledeb. ex Bunge]. To 15 in.; basal lvs. oblanceolate, to 5 in. long, obtuse, 3-nerved, glossy, st. lvs. lanceolate, acutish, to 1½ in. long; corolla yellowish-white, often minutely dotted with blue-green, tubular-campanulate, to 2 in. long. E. Asia and w. N. Amer.

alpina Vill. Forming rosette, sts. erect, unbranched, to 5 in.; basal lvs., broadly elliptic, to ¾ in. long, scarcely longer than wide, leathery, st. lvs. smaller; fls. solitary, terminal, calyx campanulate, to ½ in. long, lobes ovate, ⅛ in. long, corolla deep blue, spotted green, funnelform, to 1¾ in. long, lobes rounded. Alps, Eur.

altaica Laxm. Tufted, to 4 in.; lvs. mostly basal, linear, acute; fls. solitary, terminal on very short sts., corolla blue, long-trumpet-shaped, to 2 in. long. Siberia.

Amarella: *Gentianella Amarella.*

Andrewsii Griseb. CLOSED G., BOTTLE G. To 2 ft.; lvs. ovate to lanceolate; fls. in terminal, sessile clusters or in upper axils, corolla blue, becoming purplish in age, completely closed, 1½ in. long. E. N. Amer. See also *G. clausa.* Forma **albiflora** Britt. Fls. white. Occurs in the wild and sometimes cult.

angulosa: *G. verna.*

angustifolia Vill. Similar to *G. acaulis,* but having lvs. linear-lanceolate to oblanceolate, and calyx lobes at right angles to the tube. Alps, Eur.

asclepiadea L. Sts. leafy, erect, to 2 ft.; lvs. ovate-lanceolate, to 3 in. long, prominently 3–5-veined from base; fls. 1–3 in axils, sessile, corolla dark blue, narrowly campanulate, 1½ in. long. Cent. and s. Eur., e. to Caucasus and Asia Minor. White-fld. forms commonly cult.

autumnalis L. [*G. Porphyrio* J. F. Gmel.]. PINE-BARREN G. Sts. 1, occasionally 2–3, erect, usually unbranched, to 20 in.; lvs. usually linear, 1-nerved; fls. generally solitary, corolla yellowish below, blue above, spotted within. Autumn to early winter. Sandy moist meadows and pine barrens, N.J. to S.C. Forma **albescens** (Fern.) Fern. Fls. white.

axillariflora: *G. triflora* var. *japonica.*

bavarica L. Forming mats, sts. erect, to 6 in.; basal lvs. obovate to spatulate, to ¼ in. long; fls. solitary, terminal, corolla deep blue, 1 in. long, lobes spreading, to ¾ in. across. Alpine regions, mts. of cent. Eur.

Bigelovii: *G. affinis.*

bisetaea T. J. Howell. Decumbent, sts. to 16 in. long, more or less ascending; lvs. elliptic to oblong, or upper lvs. lanceolate, all obtuse; fls. solitary, corolla blue, ½ in. long or more, with 2 setae in sinuses. Marshes, mts. of sw. Ore.

Burseri Lapeyr. Robust, sts. unbranched, to 3 ft.; basal lvs. elliptic-ovate, 8–10 in. long, 7-nerved; fls. in axillary whorls, calyx spathelike, corolla yellow, narrowly campanulate, to 1½ in. long. Pyrenees and w. Alps.

cachemirica Decne. Low, spreading, forming rosettes, sts. somewhat ascending, to 8 in. long; lvs. ovate, to ½ in. long, base clasping st.; calyx tubular, ½ in. long, corolla azure-blue, striped with yellowish-white and darker blue, campanulate, to 1¼ in. long. W. Himalayas.

calycosa Griseb. Cespitose, sts. leafy, procumbent or ascending, to 1 ft.; lvs. ovate, to 1 in. long; fls. usually solitary, terminal, calyx tubular, to ½ in. long, corolla dark blue, spotted with green, campanulate, 1½ in. long. Wet mt. meadows, B.C. to Calif., e. to Rocky Mts.

campestris: *Gentianella campestris.*

Catesbaei Walt. [*G. Elliottii* Chapm., not Raf.; *G. parvifolia* (Chapm.) Britt.]. CATESBY'S G., SAMPSON'S SNAKEROOT. To 2 ft.; lvs. ovate-lanceolate, to 2 in. long, 3-nerved, margins rough; fls. few in crowded terminal clusters, corolla blue, to 1 in. long. Del., s. to Fla. and Ala.

cerina Hook.f. Sts. several, trailing or prostrate, stout, to 14 in. long; basal lvs. obovate or oblong-spatulate, to 1½ in. long, 3-nerved, thick, glossy; fls. crowded in terminal corymbs, corolla white with red or purple veins, broadly rotate-campanulate, to ¾ in. long, deeply lobed. New Zeal.

clausa Raf. CLOSED G., BOTTLE G., BLIND G. Similar to *G. Andrewsii*, with which it has long been confused, but in *G. Andrewsii* the corolla lobes are narrower and shorter than the broad fimbriate pleats and in *G. clausa* the corolla lobes are about as wide and long as the 2–3-cleft pleats. E. N. Amer.

Clusii Perr. & Song. Related to *G. acaulis*, but having calyx lobes triangular with straight sides, not contracted at base, usually more than ½ as long as tube, and pressed against the corolla. Mts., cent. and s. Eur.

cordifolia: *G. septemfida.*

corymbifera T. Kirk. Sts. erect, stout, usually unbranched, sparsely leafy, to 18 in.; basal lvs. oblong or narrowly oblong-spatulate, to 4 in. long; fls. several in compact terminal corymb, corolla white, campanulate, to 1 in. long. Summer. New Zeal.

crinita: *Gentianopsis crinita.*

cruciata L. Forming rosettes, to 16 in.; basal lvs. ovate-lanceolate, to 5 in. long, 3-nerved; fls. in terminal and axillary clusters, corolla dark blue, ¾ in. long. Eur. and n. Asia. Subsp. **cruciata.** The typical subsp.; calyx lobes broadly triangular, usually shorter than tube, corolla 3 times as long as calyx. Subsp. **phlogifolia** (Schott & Kotschy) Tutin [*G. phlogifolia* Schott & Kotschy]. Calyx lobes narrower, linear to linear-lanceolate, about as long as tube, corolla 2 times as long as calyx. E. Eur.

dahurica Fisch. Sts. erect or procumbent, to 12 in.; basal lvs. lanceolate, to 8 in. long, obscurely 1–3-nerved, st. lvs. narrower, shorter; fls. solitary in upper lf. axils, corolla deep blue, with white spots, narrowly funnelform, to 1¼ in. long. Ne. Asia.

decumbens L.f. Forming rosettes, to 10 in.; basal lvs. linear-lanceolate, to 5 in. long, st. lvs. smaller; fls. 1–3 in terminal clusters; calyx spathelike, corolla deep blue, campanulate, to 1¼ in. long. Asia.

dendrologi Marq. Erect or ascending, to 14 in.; basal lvs. lanceolate to linear, to 10 in. long, st. lvs. broader, to 4 in. long; fls. in terminal or axillary clusters, calyx spathelike, to ⅝ in. long, corolla white, cylindrical, to 1½ in. long. W. China.

depressa D. Don. Tufted, stoloniferous, to 2 in.; lvs. overlapping, ovate, to ¾ in. long; fls. solitary, calyx tubular, ¼ in. long, corolla pale to greenish-blue, with white veins, campanulate, to 1¼ in. long. Himalayas.

detonsa: *Gentianopsis detonsa.*

dinarica G. Beck. Per., sts. tufted, erect, to 5 in.; basal lvs. broadly elliptic, to 1½ in. long, st. lvs. shorter, narrower; fls. solitary, terminal, calyx lobes about ½ as long as tube, narrowed at base, corolla deep blue, narrow-campanulate, lobes lanceolate, to ⅜ in. long, spreading. S. Eur.

elegans: *Gentianopsis thermalis.*

Elliottii: *G. Catesbaei.*

Elwesii C. B. Clarke. Ann. or per., forming rosettes, to 15 in.; basal lvs., elliptic to ovate, to 2 in. long, st. lvs. shorter and broader; fls. in terminal heads, calyx to ⅜ in. long, lobes unequal, corolla pale blue, tubular, closed at mouth, to 1¼ in. long. Autumn. Himalayas.

excisa: *G. acaulis.*

Farreri Balf.f. Prostrate, stoloniferous sts. ascending at tips; lvs. linear, the pairs united basally; fls. solitary, corolla blue, with white throat and yellowish-white stripes, to 2½ in. long. Late summer. China.

Fetisowii Regel & C. Winkl. Tall, erect; basal lvs. lanceolate, to 6 in. or more, st. lvs. smaller; fls. in terminal and axillary clusters, calyx spathelike, to ½ in. long, corolla deep blue, tubular-campanulate, to 1½ in. long. China.

flavida: *G. alba.*

Freyniana Bornm. ex Freyn. Sts. erect, leafy, to 12 in.; lvs. linear-lanceolate, to 1 in. long, 3-veined; fls. solitary or few at end of st.; calyx tubular, to ½ in. long, spathelike, corolla blue, campanulate, to 1¼ in. long. Autumn. Asia Minor.

frigida Haenke. Sts. tufted, ascending or erect, to 6 in.; basal lvs. spatulate-linear, to 3 in. long, st. lvs. linear, shorter; fls. solitary, terminal, sessile, corolla yellowish, spotted and streaked with blue, campanulate. Mts., w. Eur.

fulgens: a listed name of no botanical standing.

fulgida: a listed name of no botanical standing.

glauca Pall. Forming rosettes, to 6 in., with creeping rhizomes; lvs. elliptic, less than ½ in. long, glaucous; corolla blue, about ½ in. long. Alaska and Yukon, s. to B.C. and the Rocky Mts.; Asia.

gracilipes Turrill. Forming rosettes, to 10 in.; lvs. lanceolate, to 6 in. long, st. lvs. much smaller; fls. solitary, on pedicels to 2 in. long in axils of uppermost lvs., calyx spathelike, corolla tubular, to 1½ in. long, tube greenish outside, lobes spreading, blue-purple. Kansu (Nw. China). Often mistakenly grown as *G. Purdomii.*

Grombczewskii Kuzn. Loosely tufted, sts. ascending or erect, to 16 in.; basal lvs. oblong-lanceolate, to 12 in. long, 5-nerved, st. lvs. to 4 in.; fls. sessile, in terminal heads, corolla yellow, tubular-funnelform. Turkestan.

hascombensis: see *G. septemfida.*

hexa-Farreri: see *G. hexaphylla.*

hexaphylla Maxim. ex Kuzn. Sts. many, tufted, to 6 in., flowering sts. decumbent, sterile sts. erect; lvs. in whorls of 6, linear, to ½ in. long; fls. solitary, terminal, erect, corolla blue, spotted with green, funnelform, to 1¾ in. long, lobes 6. W. China and e. Tibet. A hybrid with *G. Farreri* is called *Gentiana* cv. **'Hexa-Farreri'.**

holopetala: *Gentianopsis holopetala.*

Kesselringii: *G. Walujewii.*

Kochiana: *G. acaulis.*

Kurroo Royle. Forming rosettes, sts. decumbent or ascending, to 10 in.; basal lvs. linear to lanceolate, to 4 in. long, st. lvs. smaller; fls. usually solitary, terminal, corolla blue, spotted with green and white, narrowly funnelform, to 1¼ in. long. Late summer. Himalayas.

lagodechiana (Kuzn.) Grossh. ex Möller [*G. septemfida* Pall. var. *lagodechiana* Kuzn.]. Prostrate, slender, to 15 in.; lvs. ovate to cordate, to 1 in. long; fls. solitary, terminal or axillary, calyx tube ¼ in. long, lobes ½ in. long, broadly lanceolate, contracted at base, corolla tubular-funnelform, to 1½ in. long. Late summer, early autumn. Caucasus.

linearis Froel. CLOSED G. To 2 ft.; lvs. linear or linear-lanceolate; fls. in terminal clusters, corolla blue, to 2 in. long. Late summer. Ne. N. Amer.

lutea L. YELLOW G. Sts. erect, leafy, to 6 ft.; lvs. ovate, to 12 in. long, 5–7-veined; fls. on long pedicels in axillary clusters, calyx spathelike, ½ in. long, corolla yellow, rotate, to 1 in. long, lobed nearly to base. Eur., Asia Minor. The chief commercial source of gentian root, used as a medicinal and for flavoring in vermouth.

Macaulayi: see *G. sino-ornata.*

macrophylla Pall. Sts. nearly erect, to 18 in.; basal lvs. lanceolate, to 1 ft. long, 3–5-veined, st. lvs. smaller; fls. in terminal clusters, calyx spathelike, corolla pale blue, tubular, to 1 in. long. Late summer. Siberia and n. China.

Makinoi Kuzn. Sts. erect, leafy, to 2 ft.; lvs. lanceolate to lanceolate-ovate, to 2 in. long, 3-nerved, upper lvs. largest; fls. usually in heads at ends of sts.; calyx ½ in. long, lobes unequal, variable in size and shape, corolla blue, variously spotted, tubular-campanulate, to 1½ in. long. Late summer. Mts., cent. Japan.

Menziesii: *G. sceptrum.*

Moneyi: a listed name of no botanical standing.

Moorcroftiana: *Gentianella Moorcroftiana.*

Newberryi A. Gray. ALPINE G. Alpine, 2–4 in.; lvs. mostly basal, broad-obovate to oblanceolate, to 1½ in. long; fls. solitary, terminal on leafy st.; calyx tubular, ½ in. long, corolla white inside, blue outside with brownish stripes, 1 in. long or more. Summer to autumn. Mts., Calif., s. Ore., w. Nev.

nipponica Maxim. Sts. straggling, branched, leafy, to 5 in.; lower lvs. ovate to ovate-lanceolate, ½ in. long; fls. usually 2–3, terminal, corolla purplish-blue, funnelform, to ¾ in. long. Late summer. Wet alpine areas, n. Japan.

nivalis L. Ann., sts. erect, slender, to 6 in.; basal lvs. ovate or obovate, to ¼ in. long; fls. solitary, corolla blue, ⅝ in. long. Summer. Eur., Asia Minor, arctic N. Amer.

ochroleuca: *G. villosa.*

Olivieri Griseb. Forming rosettes, sts. erect, to 9 in.; basal lvs. spatulate, to 4 in. long, st. lvs. more ovate, shorter; fls. in a terminal umbel, calyx tubular, to ¼ in. long, corolla deep blue, campanulate, to 1¼ in. long. Summer. Asia Minor.

oregana Engelm. ex A. Gray. Closely related to *G. affinis*, but having longer, nearly equal calyx lobes and longer, broadly funnelform corolla. N. Calif. to B.C.

Orfordii: *G. sceptrum.*

ornata Wallich ex Griseb. Semiprostrate, sts. leafy, to 4 in.; basal lvs. linear, to 1 in. long, st. lvs. shorter; fls. solitary, terminal, sessile, calyx campanulate, lobes linear, slightly shorter than tube, corolla pale blue, with dark spots, broadly campanulate, to 1½ in. long. Nepal. Confused in cult. with *G. Veitchiorum* and *G. sino-ornata.*

pannonica Scop. Sts. stout, erect, to 2 ft.; basal lvs. elliptic-cuneate, to 8 in. long, margins rough, st. lvs. ovate to lanceolate, upper lvs. sessile; fls. in terminal and axillary clusters, corolla brownish-purple, spotted darker, broadly campanulate, to 1½ in. long. Summer. Cent. and e. Eur.

Parryi Engelm. Similar to *G. affinis* and sometimes united with it, but having lvs. succulent, and seeds wingless. Mts., Wyo., Colo., Utah.

parvifolia: *G. Catesbaei.*

phlogifolia: *G. cruciata* subsp.

platypetala Griseb. Sts. stout, leafy, to 16 in.; lvs. elliptic, to 1½ in. long; corolla blue, to 1⅜ in. long. Alaska.

plebeja: *Gentianella Amarella.*

Pneumonanthe L. Sts. slender, to 1 ft.; lvs. oblong-lanceolate to linear; fls. terminal and axillary, forming a racemelike cyme, calyx campanulate, to ½ in. long, corolla deep blue, with green streaks outside, funnelform, to 2 in. long. Late summer. Eur., n. Asia.

Porphyrio: *G. autumnalis.*

procera: *Gentianopsis procera.*

propinqua: *Gentianella propinqua.*

prolata Balf.f. Prostrate, stoloniferous, to 6 in., the shoots turning upward at the end and terminated by fls.; lvs. thickish, about ½ in. long, lower ones elliptic, the others lanceolate to oblong; fls. purple-striate, to 1½ in. long, lobes blue. Summer. W. Himalayas. Sometimes grown as *G. ornata.*

Przewalskii Maxim. Sts. tufted, to 8 in., fertile and sterile; lower lvs. narrowly spatulate, to 3 in. long, st. lvs. somewhat smaller; fls. several in loose terminal heads, calyx cylindrical, to ¾ in. long, corolla blue and white, cylindrical, to 1½ in. long. Late summer. Nw. China and ne. Tibet.

pterocalyx Franch. ex F. Forbes & Hemsl. Ann., branched, 1 ft. or more; lvs. cordate-ovate, 1 in. long or less; fls. solitary, or few terminating sts., corolla deep azure varying to yellowish, 2 in. long or more. Yunnan (China).

puberula: *G. Saponaria;* see also *G. puberulenta.*

puberulenta Pringle [*G. puberula* of auth., not Michx.]. To 2 ft.; lvs. oblong-lanceolate or sometimes nearly linear, 1-nerved; fls. 1–6 in terminal clusters subtended by pair of involucral lvs., corolla colorless below, blue above, vase-shaped, opening fully, to 1¼ in. long. Summer to autumn. Prairie and grassland, Man. and Ont., s. to Kans., Ark., and Ky. This sp. has long been incorrectly known as *G. puberula.*

pumila Jacq. Sts. tufted, to 3 in.; lower lvs. lanceolate, to ½ in. long, upper lvs. smaller, all with rough margins; fls. solitary, terminal, calyx tubular, ¼ in. long, corolla deep blue, ½ in. long, lobes spreading. Alps.

punctata L. Sts. erect, unbranched, 1–2 ft., glabrous; lvs. ovate or narrower, 3 in. long or less, strongly ribbed; fls. in dense terminal or nearly terminal clusters, corolla light yellow, violet-spotted, campanulate, not opening widely, to 1½ in. long. Summer. Alps and east.

Purdomii Marq. Sts. erect, to 8 in., glabrous; lvs. linear-lanceolate, 6 in. long or less, st. lvs. few, 1 in. long, with prominent sheaths; fls. 6–8 in terminal, bracted clusters, pedicelled, corolla yellowish (when dried) with purple streaks, 1 in. long or more. High mts., Kansu (China). Probably not in cult.; the name has been applied to at least two other cult. gentians, *G. gracilipes* and *G. dahurica.*

purpurea L. Forming loose rosettes, sts. erect, hollow, unbranched, to 2 ft.; basal lvs., ovate-lanceolate, 5-nerved; fls. few, terminal and in upper axils, corolla red with yellowish throat, about 1½ in. long. Summer. Alps.

pyrenaica L. Sts. tufted, sterile and fertile, to 3 in.; lvs. close-set, lanceolate-linear, less than 1 in. long, pointed, margins rough; fls. solitary, terminal, corolla violet inside, green outside, funnelform, to 1½ in. long. Late spring. Pyrenees and Caucasus.

quadrifaria Blume. Small herb, with taproot; lvs. ovate to elliptic or obovate, to ⅜ in. long; fls. solitary, terminal, calyx to ¼ in. long, divided about halfway, corolla dark blue, tubular-campanulate, to ⅜ in. long. Java.

quinquefolia: *Gentianella quinquefolia.*

Rochelii A. Kern. Sts. 2 or 3 in.; lvs. clustered at base of st., lanceolate, about 1½ in. long, acute; fls. solitary, terminal, corolla blue, about 2 in. long. Hungary. Related to and perhaps only a variant of *G. Clusii.*

Romanzovii: *G. algida.*

rubricaulis Schweinitz. CLOSED G. To 28 in.; lvs. ovate, to 3 in. long; fls. several in terminal head, corolla pale violet to white, tubular, to 1½ in. long. Wet meadows; s. Man. to Ont., s. to Minn., Mich. and Wisc., rare in New Bruns. and Me.

Saponaria L. [*G. puberula* Michx.]. SOAPWORT G. To 2½ ft.; lvs. lanceolate or oblong; fls. in terminal and axillary clusters, calyx tubular, lobes linear-oblanceolate, to ½ in. long, about as long as tube, corolla blue, club-shaped, to 1½ in. long. Penn. to Ill., s. to Ala. and La.

saxosa G. Forst. Per., but sometimes cult. as ann., forming loose rosettes, sts. more or less erect, or decumbent, branched from base, to 6 in.; basal lvs. spatulate, to 1½ in. long, fleshy, dark green; fls. solitary or several in terminal cyme, pedicelled, corolla white, with brownish veins, broadly campanulate, to ½ in. long, lobes cut more than halfway. New Zeal.

scabra Bunge. Sts. more or less erect, leafy, to 1 ft.; lvs. ovate, margins and midrib rough; fls. several in terminal clusters, calyx tubular, to ½ in. long, corolla dark blue, campanulate, to 1¼ in. long. N. China. Var. **Buergeri** (Miq.) Maxim. To 3 ft. or more; lvs. 10–20 pairs; corolla blue, to 2⅜ in. long. Japan.

sceptrum Griseb. [*G. Menziesii* A. Gray; *G. Orfordii* T. J. Howell]. Cespitose, to 4 ft.; lvs. oblong-lanceolate; fls. in clusters, calyx from ½–⅔ as long as corolla, corolla dark blue, often greenish-dotted, tubular-campanulate, to 2 in. long. Wet, boggy places, B.C. to Calif.

septemfida Pall. [*G. cordifolia* C. Koch]. CRESTED G. Sts. several, erect or ascending, leafy, to 1 ft.; lvs. ovate, to 1½ in. long, 5–7-nerved; fls. few in terminal clusters, corolla dark blue with paler spots inside, laciniately cut and prominently pleated, campanulate, to 2 in. long. Summer. W. Asia. Variable, with many forms. Has been crossed with related spp. *Gentiana* cv. **'Hascombensis'** is a selection of the hybrid with *G. lagodechiana.* Var. **lagodechiana:** *G. lagodechiana.*

setigera A. Gray. MENDOCINO G. Sts. several, erect, decumbent at base, to 1 ft.; lvs. ovate to roundish, to 2½ in. long; fls. solitary or several in terminal clusters, corolla blue, broadly funnelform, to 1½ in. long. Coastal, n. Calif.

sikkimensis C. B. Clarke. Forming mats, to 6 in. high; lvs. oblong-cuneate, to 1 in. long; fls. in terminal clusters, calyx tubular, to ¼ in. long, spathelike, corolla blue, with white throat, tubular, to 1 in. long and 1 in. across. W. China and se. Tibet.

sikokiana Maxim. Sts. slender, erect, leafy, to 8 in. or more; lvs. elliptic-acute, to 3 in. long, undulate, 3-veined; fls. usually 3 together in uppermost lf. axils, calyx ½ in. long, corolla blue or purplish-blue, funnelform, to 2 in. long. Woods, Japan.

sino-ornata Balf.f. Stoloniferous, forming loose rosettes, sts. spreading or prostrate, to 7 in.; basal lvs. linear-lanceolate, to 1¼ in. long; fls. solitary, sessile, calyx lanceolate, ½ in. long, lobes twice as long as tube, stiff, corolla deep blue, broadly funnelform, to 2¼ in. long. Autumn. Wet places, w. China. Hybridized with *G. Veitchiorum*, it has produced *Gentiana* cv. **'Stevenagensis'** [*G. ×stevenagensis* Hort. ex F. Barker]; and with *G. Farreri* it has produced *Gentiana* cv. **'Macaulayi'.**

siphonantha Maxim. ex Kuzn. Sts. erect or ascending, to 1 ft.; basal lvs. linear-lanceolate, to 9 in. long, st. lvs. becoming shorter upward; fls. sessile, in terminal heads, calyx to ¼ in. long, with unequal lobes, sometimes spathelike, corolla purplish-blue, tubular-funnelform, to 1 in. long. W. China and se. Tibet.

speciosa: *Crawfurdia speciosa.*

×stevenagensis: see *G. sino-ornata.*

straminea Maxim. Robust, to 12 in.; basal lvs. linear-lanceolate to lanceolate, to 9 in. long, 5-nerved; fls. several in subterminal racemes, calyx to ¾ in. long, papery, spathelike, corolla greenish-white to pale yellow, campanulate, to 1¼ in. long. Early summer. Alpine meadows, nw. China and ne. Tibet.

stylophora C. B. Clarke. Tall, robust, to 6 ft. in fl.; basal lvs. elliptic, to 1 ft. long, st. lvs. to 6 in. long; fls. short-stalked, terminal or axillary, calyx broadly funnelform, to ¾ in. long, lobes ovate, corolla pale yellow, campanulate, to 2½ in. long. Late summer. Himalayas.

tenella: *Gentianella tenella.*

thermalis: *Gentianopsis thermalis.*

Thunbergii (G. Don) Griseb. Ann. or bien., forming rosettes, to 6 in.; basal lvs., ovate, to 1¼ in. long, margins translucent, st. lvs. narrower and shorter; fls. solitary, stalked, calyx half as long as corolla, corolla blue, to 1¼ in. long. Japan, Korea, Manchuria, China. Var. **minor** Maxim. Fls. smaller, pale blue. Japan.

tibetica King ex Hook.f. Forming rosettes, sts. stout, unbranched, to 2 ft.; basal lvs. lanceolate, to 1 ft. long, 5–7-nerved, st. lvs. to 6 in. long; fls. many, crowded toward top of st., calyx ½ in. long, papery, spathelike, corolla greenish-white, tubular-funnelform, to 1¼ in. long. Late summer. Himalayas.

tongolensis Franch. Ann.; basal lvs. obovate-oblong, st. lvs. oblong-lanceolate; fls. yellow, solitary, corolla narrowly tubular, to 2 in. long. W. China.

trichotoma Kuzn. Sts. erect, mostly 3-forked at apex, to 2 ft.; lvs. oblong-lanceolate to spatulate; fls. axillary and nearly terminal, usually in 3's, on long peduncles, calyx tubular, to ⅜ in. long, corolla blue, varying to whitish, tubular-funnelform, 1 in. long or more. W. China and Tibet. Cv. 'Alba' is listed.

triflora Pall. Sts. erect, to 32 in.; lower lvs. united in sheaths to ⅜ in. long, upper lvs. separate, linear-lanceolate to lanceolate, to 5 in. long, ⁵⁄₁₆ in. wide; fls. solitary or usually crowded in few-fld. clusters at top of st. and in upper lf. axils, 5–6-merous, calyx to ¾ in. long, unequally toothed, corolla twice as long as calyx, dark blue, tubular-clavate. Var. **triflora.** The typical var.; lvs. linear-lanceolate; fls. in clusters of 1–3–5. E. Siberia, Korea, Sakhalin. Var. **japonica** (Kuzn.) Hara [*G. axillariflora* Lév. & Vaniot]. Upper lvs. lanceolate or broader; fls. solitary or paired in upper lf. axils and at top of st. Late summer, early autumn. Japan.

trinervis: *Tripterospermum japonicum.*

Veitchiorum Hemsl. Decumbent, fl. sts. to 5 in.; basal lvs. linear-oblong, to 1½ in. long, st. lvs. shorter; fls. solitary, terminal, calyx to 1 in. long, lobes ovate-lanceolate, more than half as long as tube, corolla deep royal-blue, with broad green-yellow stripes on outside, funnelform, to 2 in. long. Late summer. W. China and e. Tibet.

verna L. [*G. angulosa* Bieb.]. Forming rosettes, sts. tufted, erect, unbranched, to 4 in.; basal lvs. ovate, to ¾ in. long, st. lvs. smaller; fls. solitary, terminal, calyx ½ in. long, lobes lanceolate, ½ as long as tube, corolla deep blue, salverform, to 1 in. long, lobes spreading, ¾ in. across. Late spring. Eur., Asia.

villosa L. [*G. ochroleuca* Froel.]. SAMPSON'S SNAKEROOT. Sts. erect, usually unbranched, to 18 in.; lvs. obovate, to 3 in. long; fls. in terminal clusters, calyx tube to ¾ in. long, lobes linear, to 1 in. long or more, corolla greenish-white, sometimes suffused with blue-violet, tubular, 1½ in. long. N.J. south.

Waltonii Burkill. Sts. several, nearly erect or decumbent, to 16 in.; basal lvs. linear-lanceolate, to 8 in. long, st. lvs. shorter; fls. solitary in upper axils or several in a loose, terminal raceme, calyx to ¾ in. long, spathelike, lobes unequal, corolla deep blue to purplish-blue, narrowly campanulate, to 1¾ in. long. Tibet.

Walujewii Regel & Schmalh. [*G. Kesselringii* Regel]. Forming rosettes, sts. coarse, erect or ascending, to 1 ft.; basal lvs. ovate-lanceolate, to 6 in. long; st. lvs. shorter and broader; fls. crowded in a terminal cluster, corolla whitish, dotted with pale blue. Turkestan. Of little garden value.

wutaiensis Marq. Decumbent, to 8 in.; basal lvs. strap-shaped, to 6 in. long, st. lvs. narrower, shorter; fls. densely clustered near end of st., calyx to ⅜ in. long, spathelike, corolla blue, tubular-campanulate, to 1 in. long. China.

Zollingeri Fawc. Ann. or bien., to 6 in.; lvs. ovate, to ½ in. long; fls. 1–3, terminal, calyx tubular, to ¼ in. long, corolla blue or purplish, to 1 in. long. Japan.

GENTIANACEAE Juss. (including *Menyanthaceae* Dumort.) GENTIAN FAMILY. Dicot., about 70 genera and 800 spp. of herbs, rarely shrubs, of worldwide distribution but most abundant in temp. regions; lvs. mostly opp., simple, entire; fls. regular, bisexual, sepals, petals and stamens 4–12, ovary superior, 1- or 2-celled; fr. a caps. A number of genera and spp. are cult. as ornamentals and among these are some of the best blues among fls. The genera cult. are: *Centaurium, Chironia, Crawfurdia, Eustoma, Exacum, Fauria, Frasera, Gentiana, Gentianella, Gentianopsis, Halenia, Lisianthus, Macrocarpaea, Menyanthes, Nymphoides, Orphium, Sabatia, Swertia,* and *Tripterospermum.*

GENTIANELLA Moench. GENTIAN. *Gentianaceae.* About 150–200 spp. of ann. or bien., rarely per., herbs, often with square sts., in n. Eur., Asia, and N. Amer., also in S. Amer. and New Zeal.; lvs. opp.; fls. blue or lavender to white, clus-

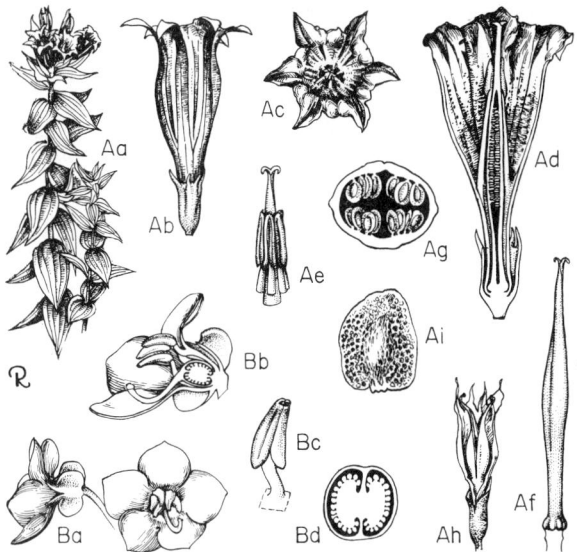

GENTIANACEAE. **A,** *Gentiana asclepiadea:* **Aa,** upper part of flowering stem, × ¹⁄₆; **Ab,** flower, side view, × ¾; **Ac,** flower, face view, × ¾; **Ad,** flower, vertical section, × 1; **Ae,** upper part of stamens and pistil, × 1½; **Af,** pistil, × 1; **Ag,** ovary, cross section, × 5; **Ah,** capsule (within withered corolla), × 1½; **Ai,** seed, × 8. **B,** *Exacum affine:* **Ba,** flower, side and face views, × 1; **Bb,** flower, vertical section, × 1½; **Bc,** stamen, × 3; **Bd,** ovary, cross section, × 5.

tered in 3–10-fld. cymes on short bracted pedicels, 5-merous, calyx tubular, sometimes spathelike, lobes with green margins, corolla tubular, funnelform or campanulate to rotate, without appendages between the lobes, lobes entire, stamens borne near middle of corolla tube, ovary sessile; seeds globose, smooth. *Gentianella* is a segregate of the larger genus, *Gentiana,* but differs from it in lacking small lobes or pleats between the larger lobes of the corolla, and in having ovary sessile and seeds rounded and wingless. Related to *Gentianopsis,* but has fls. 5-merous, clustered in cymes on short, bracted pedicels, corolla lobes with entire margins, ovary sessile, and seeds smooth.

Amarella (L.) Borner [*Gentiana Amarella* L.; *Gentiana plebeja* Cham. ex Bunge]. Erect ann., to 1 ft.; basal lvs. spatulate, to 1¼ in. long, st. lvs. more lanceolate, shorter; fls. pale lilac, to ½ in. long, axillary. N. regions of N. Amer., Eur., and Asia.

campestris (L.) Borner [*Gentiana campestris* L.]. Ann. or bien., to 14 in.; lvs. sessile, ovate-lanceolate, to 1½ in. long, entire; fls. terminal, 4-merous, calyx lobes with flat, green margin, 2 larger, enclosing 2 smaller ones in bud, corolla bright purple to white, salverform, to 1 in. long, lobes oblong-lanceolate, fringed at base. N. and cent. Eur., e. to w. Russia, s. to Spain and Italy.

Moorcroftiana (Wallich ex Griseb.) Airy-Shaw [*Gentiana Moorcroftiana* Wallich ex Griseb.]. Slender ann., to 1 ft. or more; lvs. oblong or elliptic, about 1 in. long; fls. pale blue, about 1 in. long, in leafy clusters. Summer. Himalayas.

propinqua (Richardson) J. M. Gillett [*Gentiana propinqua* Richardson]. Ann., forming rosettes, to 14 in.; basal lvs. elliptic to spatulate, to 1¼ in. long, st. lvs. smaller; fls. pale lilac or violet, solitary or in few-fld. terminal or axillary cymes, calyx to ½ in. long, lobes unequal, about twice as long as tube, corolla tubular to narrowly funnelform, to ¾ in. long. Alaska and Yukon, s. to B.C. and n. Mont., e. to Que. and Nfld.

quinquefolia (L.) Small [*Gentiana quinquefolia* L.]. Ann. or sometimes bien., to 2 ft., branched above; lvs. ovate-acuminate, entire, glabrous, the pairs united at the base; fls. pale lilac, to 1 in. long, erect, usually in terminal clusters of 3–5. E. N. Amer.

tenella (Rottb.) Börner [*Gentiana tenella* Rottb.]. Ann. forming a rosette, to 6 in., sts. slender; basal lvs. 2 in. long, elliptic or obovate to spatulate; fls. blue to white, to ⅜ in. long, solitary, terminal or axillary. Early summer. N. regions of Eur., Asia, and N. Amer.

GENTIANOPSIS Ma. FRINGED GENTIAN. *Gentianaceae.* About 15 spp. of ann. or bien. herbs of the N. Hemisphere;

lvs. opp.; fls. showy, blue or purplish, rarely white, solitary, on slender, bractless pedicels, 4-merous, calyx tubular, 4-angled, lobes in two unequal pairs, with thin hyaline margins, corolla funnelform to campanulate, lobes fringed, stamens borne in upper ⅓ of corolla tube, ovary on a stalk; seeds oblong or elliptic, covered with papillae. Originally placed in the large genus, *Gentiana*, later in *Gentianella*, but now considered a distinct genus. See *Gentianella*.

crinita (Froel.) Ma [*Gentiana crinita* Froel.]. Ann., to 3 ft.; lvs. ovate to lanceolate; fls. few to many, or solitary, corolla bright blue, 2 in. long, lobes delicately fringed all around. E. N. Amer., widespread and variable.

detonsa (Rottb.) Ma [*Gentiana detonsa* Rottb.]. Ann. or bien., to 2 ft., usually branched; basal lvs. sometimes in a dense rosette, obovate-elliptic to spatulate, to 1½ in. long, st. lvs. narrower; fls. solitary and terminal, long pedicelled, corolla pale to dark blue, narrowly funnelform, to 1½ in. long. Circumboreal.

holopetala (A. Gray) Iltis [*Gentiana holopetala* (A. Gray) T. Holm]. SIERRA GENTIAN. Erect ann., to 1 ft. or more; lvs. mostly toward base, obovate to linear, to 1½ in. long; fls. solitary, terminating the scape, corolla blue, narrow, 2 in. long, lobes entire or nearly so. Mts., Calif.

procera (T. Holm) Ma [*Gentiana procera* T. Holm]. Resembling *G. crinita* in habit, but having lvs. linear-lanceolate, and corolla lobes fringed only along their sides and with only small teeth at ends. Wet places, Ont. and s. N.Y., w. to Wisc., Ind., and Iowa.

thermalis (O. Kuntze) Iltis [*Gentiana elegans* A. Nels.; *Gentiana thermalis* O. Kuntze]. Slender ann., to 1 ft.; lvs. obovate; fls. solitary, corolla deep blue, streaked with lighter blue, 2 in. long. Colo. to Ariz.

GENUS (plural, genera). A more or less closely related and definable group of plants, including one or more species; the name of the genus becomes the first word of the binomial employed in horticultural and botanical literature. Thus, the oaks belong to the genus *Quercus*: the white oak is *Quercus alba*, the English oak *Q. Robur*, the cork oak *Q. Suber*. *Rosa* is the generic name of the roses, *Pinus* of the pines, *Lilium* of the lilies, *Delphinium* of the larkspurs, *Lycopersicon* of the tomatoes, *Mentha* of the mints, *Fragaria* of the strawberries. In some cases, the technical, generic name has become also the common vernacular name, as begonia, chrysanthemum, crinum, dahlia, gladiolus, grevillea, iris, magnolia, petunia, rhododendron, and verbena. By bearing in mind that the first of the two words in the Latin or botanical designation of a plant is the generic name, the gardener arrives at the first step in tracing plants in books and indices, just as he must know a person's surname to use a directory. See *Species* and *Family*. Approximately 10,000 or more genera are commonly recognized among seed-bearing or flowering plants. In the botanical hierarchy, a genus may be subdivided into subgenera, and these in turn into sections, as in *Coryphantha*. See also *Classification*.

GEOGENANTHUS Ule. *Commelinaceae*. Three spp. of per., rhizomatous, semisucculent herbs, native to Brazil and Peru; sts. erect or geniculate; lvs. 2–4, in a false whorl at end of st., lower nodes with tubular sheaths but no lvs.; fls. in unpaired cincinni breaking through base of sheaths at lower nodes of st. or appearing radical, sepals and petals 3, separate, stamens 5–6, the upper 3 shorter, often hairy, the lower 2–3 longer and glabrous, anthers lunate, dehiscing longitudinally, ovary 3-celled; fr. a loculicidal caps., each cell with 2–4 angular seeds.

Grown in the greenhouse or as foliage plants in the home where temperatures are not allowed to fall too low. They require well-drained soil, abundant water, and protection from strong sun. Propagated by seeds and division.

undatus (C. Koch & Linden) Mildbr. & Strauss [*Dichorisandra musaica* C. Koch & Linden var. *undata* (C. Koch & Linden) W. Mill. ex L. H. Bailey]. SEERSUCKER PLANT. Sts. one or several, to 10 in., unbranched; lvs. short-petioled, ovate, 3–5 in. long, 2–4 in. wide, somewhat leathery, with undulating surface, wine-red beneath, dark green and striped lengthwise with silvery-green above; fls. several in a short cyme, petals violet, fringed, about ⅜ in. long, withering by later afternoon, stamens 5, upper 3 hairy, lower 2 glabrous; caps. 5/16 in. long. Brazil, Peru.

GEONOMA Willd. *Palmae*. Seventy-five or more spp. of very small to moderate, unarmed, monoecious, forest palms in wet trop. Amer.; sts. solitary, clustered, or sometimes not apparent, without a crownshaft; lvs. pinnate or undivided, 2-cleft at apex and pinnately ribbed, pinnae acute, or sometimes toothed when several-ribbed; infl. among lvs., at least in flowering, spicate to paniculate, subtended by 2 basally inserted bracts, these about equal or the upper longer than the lower and sometimes tubular, peduncles short or long, rachis generally short, brs. simple or 2–3 times branched, rachillae with fls. in triads (2 male and 1 female) sunken in spirally arranged 4-ranked or whorled pits; male fls. with sepals imbricate, petals united basally, valvate above, stamens 6, filaments erect, united basally, anthers 2-cleft, pistillode short, female fls. with sepals imbricate, petals united basally, valvate above, staminodes united in a truncate or 6-toothed or 6-lobed tube, ovary 1-celled; fr. with basal stigmatic residue, endocarp not operculate, seed with homogeneous endosperm and basal embryo.

Handsome small to medium-sized shade-tolerant palms, difficult to grow and uncommon in cultivation. Mainly suitable for tropical gardens but some grown in protected places, mostly in Zone 10b in southern Fla., or under glass. See also *Palms*.

binervia: *G. interrupta*.

deversa (Poit.) Kunth [*G. longepetiolata* Ørst.]. Sts. cespitose, to 15 ft. or more; lvs. to 3 ft. long or more, pinnae 3–8 pairs, 1- to mostly several-ribbed; infl. paniculate, pits whorled, 2-lipped; fr. black, globose, ¼ in. in diam. Cent. and n. S. Amer.

interrupta (Ruiz & Pav.) Mart. [*G. binervia* Ørst.; *G. oxycarpa* Mart.]. Variable, mostly to 20 ft. or more, rarely nearly stemless, usually solitary; lvs. light green, to 9 ft. long, irregularly divided into 2–20 or more 1- to several-ribbed pinnae or rarely undivided except at apex; infl. prominently peduncled, mostly 2–3 times branched or rarely simply branched, minutely hairy, pits spirally arranged, lower lip entire, upper lip not developed; fr. globose, black or purple-black, about ¼ in. in diam. Lesser Antilles, Trinidad, Mex. to Peru. Lvs. used for thatching and the young infls. for food.

longepetiolata: *G. deversa*.

oxycarpa: *G. interrupta*.

Schottiana Mart. Sts. cespitose, to 10 ft.; lvs. to 3 ft. long or more, pinnae 25–40 pairs, 1-ribbed, linear, to 18 in. long, ¾ in. wide; infl. paniculate, pits 4-ranked, 2-lipped; fr. black, ovoid, 5/16 in. in diam. Brazil.

GERAEA Torr. & A. Gray. *Compositae* (Helianthus Tribe). Two spp. of ann. or short-lived per. herbs, in sw. U.S. and n. Mex.; lvs. alt., toothed; fl. heads radiate or discoid, large, in panicles; fls. yellow; achenes compressed, black with white margin, pappus of 2 awns united at base into a crown.

canescens Torr. & A. Gray. DESERT SUNFLOWER. To 2 ft., white-hairy; lvs. ovate to lanceolate, to 1–4 in. long; heads radiate, to 2 in. across, involucral bracts white-ciliate. Utah, s. Calif., Ariz., n. Mex.

viscida (A. Gray) S. F. Blake. Short-lived per.; heads discoid, 1 in. across, involucral bracts glandular. S. Calif.

GERANIACEAE Juss. GERANIUM FAMILY. Dicot; 11 genera of herbs or shrubs widely distributed over the world; fls. bisexual, mostly regular, usually 5-merous, sepals separate or partly united, petals separate, imbricate, rarely 0, stamens 5, 10, or 15, some sometimes lacking anthers, ovary superior, 3–5-lobed; fr. a caps. *Erodium, Geranium, Monsonia, Pelargonium,* and *Sarcocaulon* are cult. as ornamentals.

Some species of *Erodium* are forage plants, and the leaves of several species of *Pelargonium* yield an essential oil used in perfumery. Members of this family are of simple culture. The true geraniums and the erodiums are mostly hardy in Zone 5, but pelargoniums, hardy in Zone 9, are usually treated as annual bedding plants or house plants elsewhere.

GERANIUM L. CRANESBILL. *Geraniaceae*. Over 300 spp. of ann. or per. herbs or rarely shrubs, cosmopolitan in temp. regions or montane tropics; lvs. usually palmately parted or divided into usually toothed lobes; fls. solitary and axillary, or clustered and terminal, white, pink, or purplish, sepals and petals 5, stamens 10, ovary 5-celled, each cell 2-ovuled; fr. long-beaked, carpel bodies one-seeded, articulate with the

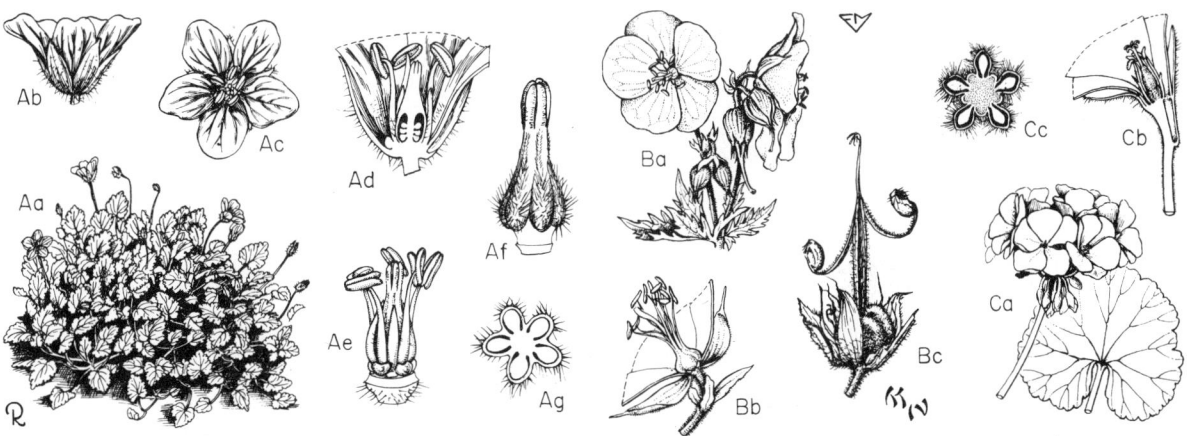

GERANIACEAE. **A,** *Erodium chamaedryoides:* **Aa,** plant, × ½; **Ab,** flower, side view, × 2; **Ac,** flower, face view, × 2; **Ad,** base of flower, vertical section, × 5; **Ae,** stamens and pistil, × 5; **Af,** pistil, × 8; **Ag,** ovary, cross section, × 10. **B,** *Geranium pratense:* **Ba,** branch of inflorescence, × ½; **Bb,** base of flower, part of perianth cut away, × 1; **Bc,** fruit, with two carpels dehisced, × 1. **C,** *Pelargonium × hortorum:* **Ca,** inflorescence and leaf, × ¼; **Cb,** base of flower, vertical section (except for pistil), × 1; **Cc,** ovary, cross section, × 5. (Ba, Bb, Ca-Cc from Bailey, *Manual of Cultivated Plants,* ed. 2.)

styles or more commonly coiling upward with them at maturity.

Grown in the hardy border or rock garden. Propagated by seeds and division of roots. Perennials should be transplanted from the seedbed in early spring. They are mostly hardy plants (Zone 5), and some of them are introduced weeds. See *Pelargonium,* to which the greenhouse and florist's geraniums belong.

albanum Bieb. [*G. cristatum* Steven]. Per., sts. decumbent to ascending; lvs. reniform-orbicular, to 2½ in. across, lobes 5–7, deeply toothed; peduncles and pedicels spreading-pilose; fls. rose-purple, to ¾ in. across; carpel bodies in fr. stiff-hairy, reticulate, with a toothed crest on the back. Asia Minor and Iran.

alpinum: *G. pratense;* but see also *G. Meeboldii* and *G. sanguineum.*

anemonifolium: *G. palmatum.*

argenteum L. SILVER-LEAVED G. Per. or bien., to 5 in.; lvs. hoary and silky, 5–7-lobed nearly to base, lobes divided into 3 lanceolate segms.; peduncles solitary, 2–fld.; fls. 1 in. across, petals pink with darker veins. N. Italy.

armenum: *G. psilostemon.*

balkanum Hort. ex N. Tayl. Insufficiently known, described from cult. as having fragrant foliage, fls. on sts. erect from rootcrown, dark magenta, 1 in. across.

caespitosum: a name used in various senses; the identity of plants so called in hort. is not known.

cataractarum Coss. Per., with woody rhizome, hirsute, sts. to 16 in. long; lvs. orbicular in outline, 5-lobed to base, lobes irregularly pinnatifid; peduncles axillary, several-fld.; petals bright pink, ⅝ in. long, stamens only slightly longer than sepals; carpel bodies in fr. separating from beak, glabrous. Shady damp places, mts. of se. Spain.

celticum: *G. Robertianum* cv. 'Album'.

cinereum Cav. Per., to 6 in.; lvs. 5–7-lobed nearly to base, lobes deeply toothed; peduncles axillary or from the root-crown; fls. about 1 in. across, petals pink, with dark stripes, filaments nearly glabrous. Pyrenees. Cvs. 'Album' and 'Splendens' are listed. Var. **subcaulescens** (L'Hér. ex DC.) R. Knuth [*G. subcaulescens* L'Hér. ex DC.]. Differs in having hairs on sepals spreading or divergent, not appressed. E. Eur.

collinum Steph. ex Willd. Per., somewhat decumbent, to 1½ ft.; lvs. deeply 5–7-lobed; peduncles axillary, 2-fld., pedicels glandular; fls. less than ½ in. across, petals purplish-violet with darker veins. Eurasia.

cristatum: *G. albanum.*

dalmaticum (G. Beck) Rech.f. Similar to *G. macrorrhizum,* but smaller, more slender, lvs. paler beneath, peduncles only 2–4-fld., petals rose. Dalmatia. The lvs. become red and yellow in autumn.

Donianum Sweet. Per., from rhizome, sts. ascending, branched, retrorsely hairy; lvs. reniform or orbicular in outline, to 1⅝ in. across, deeply 7-lobed nearly to base, lobes irregularly incised; peduncles 2-fld.; fls. purple, to ¾ in. long. Himalayas.

Endressii J. Gay. Per., to 1½ ft.; basal lvs. many, deeply 5-lobed,

petiole much longer than blade; peduncles axillary, 2-fld., pedicels retrorse-strigose, not glandular; fls. rose, ⁵⁄₁₆ in. across. Pyrenees.

erianthum DC. Per., sts. solitary, appressed-short-pubescent; lvs. deeply 5–7-lobed, lobes acutely toothed; infl. erect, terminal, branched, pedicels glandular or glandless, often villous; fls. ¾ in. long, petals bluish or rose-purple, entire, bearded and ciliate at base, filaments long-haired. B.C. to Alaska; n. Asia.

eriostemon Fisch. ex DC. Per., to 2 ft., sts. villous; lvs. paler beneath, 5-lobed, lobes somewhat obtusely toothed; infl. erect, terminal, branched, pedicels glandular; fls. violet-blue, 1 in. across, petals bearded and ciliate at base, filaments long-haired. Siberia to China. Var. **eriostemon.** The typical var.; calyx more or less silky, or pilose with more or less glandular hairs. E. Siberia, China, Korea. Var. **Reinii** (Franch. & Sav.) Maxim. [*G. japonicum* Franch. & Sav.]. Sts. very hairy, lvs. nearly villous on lower surface; calyx with long woolly hairs. Japan.

Farreri Stapf. Per. from short rhizome, with partly fleshy, cylindrical roots; sts. erect or decumbent, to 6 in. long, sparsely and finely hairy; lvs. opp., the lower long-petioled, the upper short-petioled, blades reniform, to 1 in. across, appressed-hairy, 3–5-lobed beyond the middle, lobes obovate-cuneate, coarsely crenate or 3-lobed; peduncles 2-fld., to 4 in. long, pedicels to 1⅝ in. long; sepals ⁵⁄₁₆ in. long, nearly glabrous, petals pale rose or lilac, to ¹¹⁄₁₆ in. long, ⁹⁄₁₆ in. wide, short-bearded at base; seeds minutely pitted. S. China. Material cult. under the misapplied name *G. napuligerum* belongs here.

Fremontii Torr. ex A. Gray. Per., 1 ft. or more high, sts. tufted, erect, becoming decumbent; lvs. 5–7-lobed; peduncles axillary, 2-fld.; fls. 1 in. across, petals rose-purple, pilose along basal ¼ of veins. Rocky Mts.

grandiflorum: see *G. himalayense.* Var. **alpinum:** *G. Regelii.*

Grevilleanum: *G. Lambertii.*

himalayense Klotzsch [*G. grandiflorum* Edgew., not L.]. Per., mostly 1 ft. or more, sts. ascending; lvs. deeply 5–7-parted, to nearly 3 in. or rarely 4 in. across, lobes broadly rhombic-obovate or obovate-spatulate, incised-toothed to pinnately parted; peduncles axillary, 2-fld., to 8 in. long, pedicels glandular; fls. to 1½ in. across, petals lilac with purple veins. Turkestan, s. to n. India and Tibet.

ibericum Cav. Per., to 1½ ft., sts. villous; lvs. 7-lobed nearly to base; infl. erect, branched, terminal, pedicels glandular-villous; petals purple, deeply obcordate, 1¼ in. long, bearded and ciliate at base; filaments short-ciliate, with few long hairs. Sw. Asia. Cv. 'Album'. Fls. white. Var. **platypetalum:** *G. platypetalum.*

japonicum: *G. eriostemon* var. *Reinii;* however, material in cult. under the name *G. japonicum* is usually *G. macrorrhizum.*

Lambertii Sweet [*G. Grevilleanum* Wallich]. Per., sts. prostrate; stipules large, linear-lanceolate, lvs. reniform, pubescent, 5-lobed, lobes deeply cut, but not to midrib; peduncles 2-fld., pedicels usually glandular-pubescent; fls. to 2 in. across, petals rose, often purple-spotted, filaments villous. Himalayas.

lancastrense: *G. sanguineum* var. *prostratum.*

macrorrhizum L. Per., to 1½ ft., with long, thick root; lvs. 5–7-lobed nearly to base; infl. terminal, branched, with reduced lvs.; fls. magenta, stamens 2½–3 times as long as sepals and longer than petals; beak of fr. abruptly narrowed to a slender point as long as enlarged portion, carpel bodies rugose. Eur. Has been cult. under the name *G. japonicum.*

maculatum L. WILD G., WILD C., SPOTTED C., ALUMROOT. Per., to 2 ft., sts. appressed-pubescent; lvs. deeply 3–5-parted; infl. erect, terminal, branched, pedicels glandless, strigose; fls. 1 in. across, petals rose-purple, entire, barbate-ciliate at base, filaments short-ciliate. N. Amer. Forma **albiflorum** (Raf.) House [var. **album** Lauman]. Fls. white.

molle L. DOVE'S-FOOT C. Ann., sts. prostrate to ascending, to 2 ft. long, branched; lvs. 5–7-lobed, lobes 3-toothed; peduncles 2-fld., in axils of reduced lvs. or lvs. lacking; petals purple, ³⁄₁₆–⁵⁄₁₆ in. long, not much longer than sepals; carpel bodies separating from beak in fr., glabrous, ridged or rarely smooth, seeds smooth. Eurasia; naturalized in e. U.S., and often a weed in lawns.

napuligerum: Franch. Apparently not in cult.; see *G. Farreri.*

nepalense Sweet. Per., sts. decumbent or ascending, to 1½ ft. long, basal and lower st. lvs. deeply 5-lobed, st. lvs. 3-lobed; peduncles axillary, longer than lvs., 2-fld., pedicels retrorse-strigose, sometimes glandular; fls. to ⅝ in. across, petals rose-purple to white with red veins. Mts. of Asia. Var. **Thunbergii** (Siebold & Zucc.) Kudo. Pedicels sometimes glandular, petals whitish with red veins; seeds finely reticulate. Often grown under the name *G. Wilfordii.*

palmatum Cav. [*G. anemonifolium* L'Hér.]. Per., to 1½ ft.; lvs. 5-lobed to base, lobes pinnately toothed or divided, petioles to 15 in. long; infl. terminal, branched; petals pale purple, stamens 2½–3 times as long as sepals and longer than petals; beak of fr. abruptly narrowed to a slender point as long as enlarged portion, carpel bodies rugose. Canary Is. Perhaps not hardy north.

Parryi (Engelm.) A. Heller. Per., to 2 ft., sts. tufted, becoming decumbent, glandular; lvs. to 2¼ in. across, 3–5-lobed, lobes usually incised; peduncles axillary, 2-fld.; fls. to 1¼ in. across, petals pinkish-purple, pilose along basal ½ of veins. Mts. of Wyo., Colo., Ariz.

patulum: *G. phaeum* var. *lividum.*

phaeum L. Erect per., to 2 ft.; lvs. deeply 5–7-lobed; infl. terminal, mostly much-branched, with reduced lvs.; petals dark blue or almost black, with white spot at base, spreading to reflexed. Eur. Var. **lividum** (L'Hér.) Pers. [*G. patulum* Vill.]. Petals sordid lilac above the base, often with lilac flecks.

platypetalum Fisch. & C. A. Mey. [*G. ibericum* var. *platypetalum* (Fisch. & C. A. Mey.) Boiss.]. Per., to 2 ft.; lvs. deeply 5–7-parted, lobes broadly rhombic to nearly cuneate, incised-dentate; infl. to 10-fld.; peduncles mostly to 4 in. long, pedicels often densely glandular-villous; petals purple, broadly obcordate, to ¾ in. long, ciliate at base, filaments pubescent. Caucasus to Armenia, Iran.

pratense L. [*G. alpinum* Kit.]. Per., to 3 ft.; lvs. deeply 7-lobed, much dissected; infl. erect, terminal, branched, pedicels glandular, mostly shorter than to equalling calyx, deflexed in fr.; fls. about ½ in. across, petals purple, entire, bearded and ciliate at base, filaments short-ciliate. Eurasia. Cv. 'Album' [var. *albiflorum* Griz.]. Fls. white. This sp. has been grown erroneously under many names, among them *G. anemonifolium, G. cinereum, G. Endressii, G. grandiflorum, G. platypetalum, G. sessiliflorum, G. sylvaticum.*

prostratum: *G. sanguineum* var. *haematodes.*

psilostemon Ledeb. [*G. armenum* Boiss.]. Per., to 2 ft.; lvs. deeply 5-lobed; infl. erect, terminal, branched, pedicels glandular; fls. about 1½ in. across, petals dark red, spotted with black at base, entire, bearded and ciliate at base, filaments nearly glabrous. Armenia.

pusillum Burm.f. Prostrate, much-branched ann.; lvs. deeply 5–9-lobed, lobes 3-toothed; peduncles 2-fld., shorter than petioles; fls. ¼ in. across, petals blue-purple, notched at apex, not much longer than sepals; carpel bodies separating from beak in fr., densely appressed-strigose, keeled, seeds smooth. Eur. to Himalayas. A weedy sp.

Pylzowianum Maxim. Per., to 1 ft.; sts. erect, from slender, tuber-bearing rhizomes; lvs. 5-lobed, nearly to base, lobes 3-toothed; peduncles axillary, 2-fld.; fls. purple, 1¼ in. across. China.

pyrenaicum Burm.f. Per., to 2 ft., soft-pubescent; lvs. 5–7-lobed; peduncles 2-fld., longer than petioles; fls. ½ in. across, petals blue-violet, twice as long as sepals, 2-lobed at apex; carpel bodies separating from beak in fr., densely appressed-strigose, keeled, seeds smooth. Eur. A weedy sp.

Regelii Nevskiĭ [*G. grandiflorum* Edgew. var. *alpinum* (Regel) R. Knuth]. Per., stemless or sts. to 8 in., rarely 1 ft.; lvs. deeply 5–7-parted, to 1⅝ in. across, lobes broadly cuneate, incised-dentate; peduncles axillary, to about 6 in. long, pedicels to 1³⁄₁₆ in. long, with hairs of 2 lengths and often glandular. Turkestan to Pakistan.

Renardii Trautv. Per., to 8 in.; lvs. silvery-silky beneath, palmately 5-lobed halfway to base, lobes shallowly toothed; infl. erect, terminal, branched; petals white with violet veins, obcordate, bearded and ciliate at base. Caucasus Mts.

Richardsonii Fisch. & Trautv. Per., to 3 ft.; lvs. deeply 3–5-lobed; infl. erect, terminal, branched; fls. 1 in. across, petals white, usually red-veined, entire, hairy along the veins at base. W. N. Amer.

Robertianum L. HERB ROBERT, RED ROBIN. Ann. or bien., to 1½ ft.; lvs. 3–5-parted, segms. deeply pinnatifid or 2-pinnatifid; peduncles 2-fld., solitary or clustered in a terminal infl.; fls. red-purple, about ¼ in. long, stamens shorter than sepals; carpel bodies separating from the beak in fr., transversely rugose. Mostly in woods or damp places, N. Amer., Eurasia, N. Afr. Cv. 'Album' [forma *albiflorum* (G. Don) House]. Fls. white; has been grown under the name *G. celticum* Hort.

Ruprechtii (Voronov) Voronov ex Grossh. Similar to *G. pratense* and perhaps only a subsp. of it, with fls. larger, more intensely colored, often deep violet, filaments deep blue or violet, more pilose at base. Caucasus.

sanguineum L. Per., to 1½ ft., sts. spreading, with spreading white hairs; lvs. 5–7-lobed nearly to base, lobes with long, lanceolate teeth; peduncles axillary, 1-fld.; fls. reddish-purple or paler. Eurasia. Cvs. are: 'Album', fls. white; 'Alpinum' and 'Nanum', of low compact habit. Var. **haematodes:** a name apparently without standing, for var. *prostratum.* Var. *prostratum* (Cav.) Pers. [*G. lancastrense* Mill.; *G. prostratum* Cav.]. Dwarf; fls. reddish-purple or rose-pink, with darker veins.

sessiliforum Cav. Per. to 4 in.; lvs. all basal, deeply 5–7-lobed; peduncles short, from the crown; fls. white, to ½ in. across. Andes. Cv. 'Nigrum' has been listed.

sibiricum L. Per., sts. ascending or procumbent, to 3 ft., hispidulous; lvs. reniform-cordate, deeply 5-lobed, lobes toothed; peduncles 1-fld., or fls. axillary, petals lilac to pale rose, with darker veins. E. Eur., e. to Korea and Himalayas.

striatum L. Per., to 18 in., sts. ascending; basal and lower st. lvs. reniform-orbicular, palmately 5-lobed, to 3 in. wide, pubescent, st. lvs. narrower, 3-lobed; peduncles axillary, 2-fld., these and pedicels spreading-pilose; fls. with sepals puberulent, awned, petals white, veined rose-red, emarginate, twice as long as sepals. Cent. Eur.

subcaulescens: *G. cinereum* var.

sylvaticum L. Per., to 2½ ft.; lvs. deeply 7-lobed; infl. erect, terminal, branched, pedicels usually glandular-hairy; fls. about 1 in. across, petals violet, entire or slightly emarginate, short-hairy along veins at base. Eur. and Asia. Cv. 'Album'. Fls. white. Var. **eglandulosum** Čelak. Pedicels without glands.

Traversii Hook.f. Per., to 1½ ft., spreading, gray-pubescent; lvs. 7-lobed to about the middle, lobes shallowly toothed; peduncles axillary, 1-fld.; fls. rose or white, 1 in. across. Chatham Is. (New. Zeal.)

tuberosum L. Erect per., to 15 in., with fleshy, ovoid tubers ⅝ in. thick; basal lvs. long-petioled, 5–7-lobed to the base, lobes pinnately incised, upper st. lvs. sessile; infl. terminal, branched, with reduced lvs., peduncles 1- to several-fld.; fls. large, deep rose-purple to violet, stamens shorter than petals; carpel bodies in fr. not rugose, but appressed-pilose. S. Eur.

viscosissimum Fisch. & C. A. Mey. Per., to 2 ft., sts. sticky; lvs. 3–5-lobed; infl. erect, terminal, branched, pedicels densely glandular; petals pinkish-purple, ¾ in. long, entire, hairy along the veins at base. S. Dak. to Calif.

Wallichianum D. Don ex Sweet. Prostrate per., sts. to 2 ft. long; lvs. 3–5-lobed, lobes deeply cut, stipules ovate, to ¾ in. long, ⅝ in. wide; peduncles axillary, 2-fld.; fls. purple, to 2 in. across. Himalayas.

Webbii: a listed name of no botanical standing.

Wilfordii Maxim. Procumbent; lvs. 3-lobed, lobes oblong-ovate, acuminate, deeply toothed; peduncles axillary, 2-fld., pedicels retrorse-strigose, longer than the calyx in fr.; fls. ½ in. across, petals white, striped with rose. Manchuria. Most material cult. under this name appears to be *G. nepalense* var. *Thunbergii.*

zonale: *Pelargonium zonale.*

GERARDIA: *AGALINIS.* G. flava: *Aureolaria flava.* G. virginica: *Aureolaria virginica.*

GERBERA L. *Compositae* (Mutisia Tribe). Perhaps 70 spp. of scapose per. herbs, native to Afr., Madagascar, Asia, and Indonesia; lvs. in a basal rosette, petioled; fl. heads solitary on scapes, involucral bracts in 2 to many rows, receptacle naked; fls. 2-lipped, disc fls. bisexual, ray fls. larger, mostly female, their outer (lower) lip long, strap-shaped; achenes flattened, ribbed, often beaked, pappus of 2 or more rows of bristles.

Gerberas are grown in a temperate greenhouse, or outdoors in mild or protected places. They may survive northern winters if given a protection of leaves and decomposed manure. Propagated by seeds or by cuttings of side shoots.

Anandria: *Leibnitzia Anandria.*

Jamesonii H. Bolus ex Hook.f. TRANSVAAL DAISY, BARBERTON D., AFRICAN D., VELDT D. To 1½ ft.; lvs. oblong-spatulate, deeply lobed to lyrate-pinnatifid, blade to 10 in. long, hairy, very woolly beneath, petioles to 6 in. long, pilose; heads to 4 in. across, solitary on pilose scapes, involucral bracts in 3 rows, woolly; ray fls. scarlet to orange-red, disc fls. paler. Transvaal. Not hardy in northernmost states, but commonly grown under glass for cut fls. Zone 8. Many color forms are known in the cult. strains, the ray fls. ranging through shades of yellow, salmon, pink, and red, and present in a single or several rows.

Kunzeana: *Leibnitzia Kunzeana.*

GESNERIA L. *Gesneriaceae.* About 60 spp. of per. herbs or shrubs in W. Indies and n. S. Amer.; roots fibrous, sts. often woody; lvs. alt., entire to lobed or toothed; fls. solitary or several on axillary peduncles, calyx 5-lobed, corolla tubular to funnelform, red to yellow or green, limb nearly regular to 2-lipped, stamens 4, borne at base of corolla tube, anthers touching at their tips in pairs, disc ringlike, ovary inferior; fr. a caps., dehiscing by 2 valves at top, seeds twisted, very small.

For cultivation see *Gesneriaceae.*

acaulis L. Subshrub, to 1 ft.; lvs. to 7 in. long, 1½ in. wide, crenate to irregularly lobed, bullate, pubescent to glabrous, not scabrous; peduncles not longer than lvs., usually with many fls. borne horizontally on green pedicels at flowering time; calyx lobes to ½ in. long, ⅛ in. wide, corolla tubular, bent at the middle, red to orange with darker limb. Jamaica.

albiflora: *G. pedunculosa.*

cardinalis: *Sinningia cardinalis.*

Christii: see *G. pedicellaris.*

citrina Urb. Pendent or decumbent subshrub; lvs. oblanceolate, to 1⅝ in. long, coarsely crenate, leathery, glabrescent; peduncles about as long as lvs., bearing 1–4 fls. on reddish pedicels; calyx lobes lanceolate, ¼ in. long, corolla tubular, yellow. Puerto Rico.

cuneifolia (Moç. & Sessé ex DC.) Fritsch. Subshrub to 1 ft.; lvs. oblanceolate-cuneate, to 6 in. long, bullate, glabrous above; peduncle about as long as lvs., bearing 1 fl. on a green or red pedicel; calyx lobes flat, triangular, as broad as long, corolla gradually curved, to 1¼ in. long, yellow to red, limb to ⅝ in. across, more or less spreading. Cuba, Hispaniola, Puerto Rico.

Lindenii: see *Kohleria Lindeniana.*

macrantha: see *Sinningia cardinalis.*

mornincola Urb. & Ekm. Not in cult.; see *G. saxatilis.*

pauciflora Urb. Subshrub, to 8 in.; lvs. to 4 in. long, flat, cuneate, serrate, not bullate, glabrescent; peduncles much longer than lvs., bearing 1 or a few fls.; calyx lobes lanceolate, to $^3/_{16}$ in. long, corolla tubular, not bent, yellow-orange. Puerto Rico.

pedicellaris Alain. Pendent or erect subshrub, to 30 in., sts. pubescent; lvs. to 5 in. long, 1¼ in. wide, irregularly crenate, bullate, scabrous; peduncles shorter than lvs., bearing 1–6 fls. on reddish pedicels; calyx lobes ⅜ in. long or less, corolla borne upright at flowering time, tubular, bent, red to yellow, with red lines. Dominican Republic. This sp. was misidentified as *G. Christii* Urb. when introd. to cult.

pedunculosa (DC.) Fritsch [*G. albiflora* (Decne.) O. Kuntze]. Glabrous and resinous shrub, to 6 ft. or more; lvs. elliptic to obovate, to 4 in. long, leathery; peduncle more than twice as long as lvs., bearing 2–4 fls.; calyx lobes linear-lanceolate, to ⅜ in. long, corolla more or less campanulate, yellow to greenish-white, limb often with purple spots, stamens exserted, twice as long as corolla. Puerto Rico.

saxatilis Alain. Shrub to 4½ ft., glabrous except for reddish hairs in lf. axils; lvs. obovate to elliptic-obovate, to ⅞ in. long, ⅜ in. wide, flat, cuneate at base, toothed near apex, leathery; peduncle 1-fld., shorter than pedicel, with 2 bracts at junction; corolla cylindrical, ½ in. long, red, stamens included. Dominican Republic. This sp. was misidentified as *G. mornincola* when introd. to cult.

GESNERIACEAE Dumort. GESNERIA FAMILY. Dicot.; about 120 genera of mostly trop., terrestrial or epiphytic, mostly hairy herbs or subshrubs, more rarely shrubs, vines, or small trees; roots fibrous, rhizomes, scaly rhizomes, tubers, or stolons sometimes present, sts. simple or branched; lvs. opp., or whorled in a basal rosette, or rarely alt. or lacking, then one cotyledon much enlarged and appearing and functioning as a lf. (in *Streptocarpus*), blades simple, sometimes unequal in each pair, usually toothed; fls. solitary or in cymes or racemes, sepals 4–5, separate or united, corolla with a short to long tube, the limb usually 2-lipped, flat or spreading to erect, 4–5-lobed, stamens 2–5, the filaments often retracting the anthers after pollen is shed and style then elongating, and stigma expanding, disc, when present, ringlike or of 1–5 glands, ovary superior to nearly inferior, 1-celled or very rarely 2-celled, with parietal placentas and many minute ovules; fr. a berry or caps. Genera in cult. are: ×*Achimenantha, Achimenes, Aeschynanthus, Agalmyla, Alloplectus, Asteranthera, Boea, Briggsia, Capanea, Chirita, Chrysothemis, Codonanthe, Columnea, Conandron, Corallodiscus, Diastema, Didymocarpus, Drymonia, Episcia, Gesneria,* ×*Gloxinantha, Gloxinia, Haberlea, Jankaea, Koellikeria,* ×*Koellikohleria, Kohleria, Loxostigma, Lysionotus, Mitraria, Nautilocalyx, Nematanthus, Niphaea, Opithandra, Paradrymonia, Petrocosmea, Phinaea, Ramonda, Rehmannia, Rhynchoglossum, Saintpaulia, Sarmienta, Seemannia, Sinningia, Smithiantha, Streptocarpus,* and *Titanotrichum.*

Gesneriaceae or gesneriads are grown in the home, often under lights, or in the greenhouse, and a few hardy species as rock garden plants out of doors. A light, well-drained soil and sufficient moisture are essential to good growth, and most require warm temperatures, protection from prolonged direct exposure to sunlight, and high humidity. A mixture of ⅓ good soil, ⅓ drainage material such as sand or chopped osmunda, and ⅓ moisture-retaining material such as peat moss or sphagnum is suggested for plants grown indoors.

The African violet *(Saintpaulia ionantha),* the gloxinia *Sinningia speciosa),* and some species and hybrids of *Streptocarpus* are popular pot plants. Many other species are suited to pot culture, but the epiphytic species of *Aeschynanthus, Agalmyla, Asteranthera, Codonanthe, Columnea, Mitraria, Nematanthus,* and *Sarmienta* are subshrubs or vines and are often grown in hanging baskets, as are some terrestrial kinds of *Achimenes* and *Episcia. Asteranthera* has been grown as a vine out of doors in cool mild climates, and *Rehmannia* may be cultivated as an annual. *Conandron, Corallodiscus, Haberlea, Jankaea,* and *Opithandra* are grown in the rock garden, where drainage should be excellent; they seem to do best in very narrow crevices between rocks, with a northern exposure.

Propagation is by the minute seeds sown on a moist substrate or on agar, by division, or most often by stem or leaf cuttings rooted in sand under mist or in a humid chamber. Some genera—*Achimenes, Diastema, Gloxinia, Koellikeria, Niphaea, Phinaea, Seemannia, Smithiantha*—normally produce scaly rhizomes, which may be planted entire or the scales sown individually on a moist substrate. Many of these genera undergo a dormant period in late autumn, when they may be dried off, put under the greenhouse bench, and repotted when signs of growth appear in the spring.

GESNOUINIA Gaud.-Beaup. *Urticaceae.* Two spp. of monoecious shrubs or small trees of the Canary Is.; lvs. alt., entire, 3-veined from just above the base; fls. in 3-fld. involucres, clustered in spikes or panicles, the outer 2 fls. male, 4-merous, soon deciduous, the middle fl. female, with filiform style; fr. an achene enclosed by the tube of the involucre and capped by its lobes.

May be grown in the open only in the South; propagated by cuttings.

arborea (L.f.) Gaud.-Beaup. Tree, to about 20 ft.; lvs. thin, lanceolate to elliptic, to 5 in. long, acute or acuminate, white-tomentulose beneath; panicles leafy, to 10 in. or more; fls. minute.

GEUM L. [*Acomastylis* Greene; *Sieversia* Willd.]. AVENS. *Rosaceae.* Over 50 spp. of per. herbs of temp. and cold regions; lvs. pinnate or lyrate, usually with large terminal lobes, mostly basal, those on the sts. smaller; fls. solitary or corymbose, bisexual, white, yellow, or red, calyx tube bell-shaped or flattish, sepals 5, usually with 5 bractlets in between, petals 5, often broad and showy, stamens many, pistils many; frs. achenes with persistent styles that may be jointed or plumose.

Grown as ornamentals in the open; propagated by seeds or division.

aleppicum Jacq. Somewhat hairy, to 5 ft.; lvs. with 5–9 cuneate-obovate to cuneate-oblanceolate incised lfts., or the terminal lft. enlarged; sepals to $^5/_{16}$ in., petals orange to deep yellow, rounded to obovate, $^3/_{16}$–⅜ in. long, pistils long-villous, the head rounded. Eurasia.

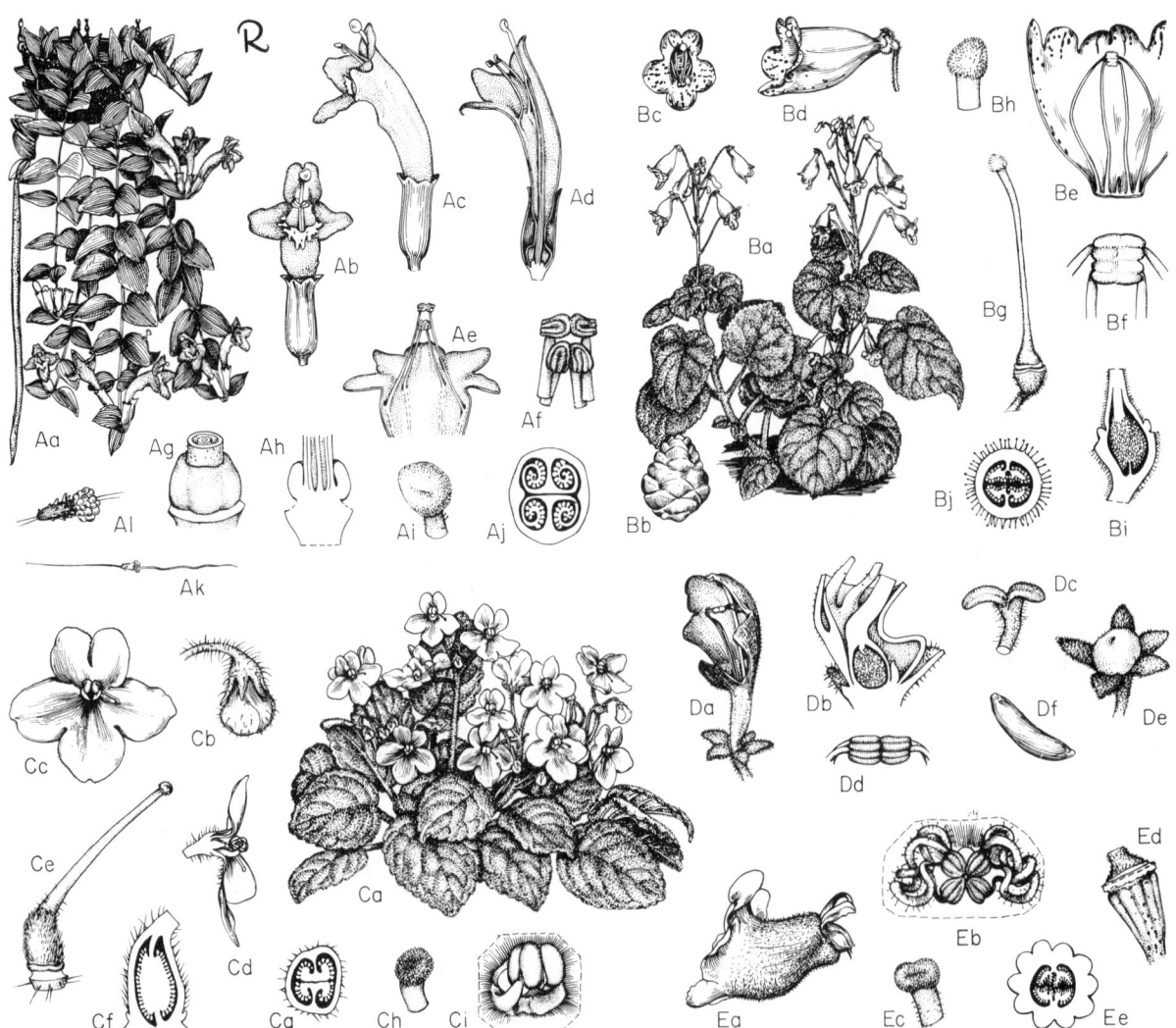

GESNERIACEAE. **A,** *Aeschynanthus pulcher:* **Aa,** flowering and fruiting plant (elongate capsule at left), × ⅙; **Ab,** flower, face view, × ½; **Ac,** flower, side view, × ½; **Ad,** flower, vertical section, × ½; **Ae,** upper part of corolla, expanded, × ½; **Af,** anthers, × 2; **Ag,** base of ovary surrounded by ringlike disc, × 3; **Ah,** disc and base of the elongate ovary, vertical section, × 3; **Ai,** stigma, × 3; **Aj,** ovary, cross section, × 8; **Ak,** seed, × 2; **Al,** seed, detail, × 8. **B,** *Smithiantha zebrina:* **Ba,** flowering plant, × ⅛; **Bb,** scaly rhizome, × ¾; **Bc,** flower, face view, × ½; **Bd,** flower, side view, × ½; **Be,** corolla, expanded, × ¾; **Bf,** anthers, × 3; **Bg,** pistil, with perianth removed, × 1; **Bh,** stigma, × 2; **Bi,** ovary, vertical section, × 2; **Bj,** ovary, cross section, × 3. **C,** *Saintpaulia ionantha:* **Ca,** flowering plant, × ¼; **Cb,** flower bud, × 1½; **Cc,** flower, face view, × ¾; **Cd,** flower, vertical section, × ¾; **Ce,** pistil, × 3; **Cf,** ovary, vertical section, × 5; **Cg,** ovary, cross section, × 5; **Ch,** stigma, × 8; **Ci,** stamens, × 3. **D,** *Columnea gloriosa:* **Da,** flower, × ⅜; **Db,** base of flower, vertical section, × 2; **Dc,** stigma, × 1; **Dd,** anthers, × 1½; **De,** fruit, × ½; **Df,** seed, × 8. **E,** *Gloxinia perennis:* **Ea,** flower, side view, × ½; **Eb,** stamens, × 2; **Ec,** stigma, × 2; **Ed,** ovary, with perianth removed, × 1½; **Ea,** ovary, cross section, × 3.

Var. **strictum** (Ait.) Fern. [*G. strictum* Ait.]. Body of achene glabrous to short-pilose. Que. to B.C., s. to W. Va., Nebr., Mex.

atrosanguineum: a listed name of no botanical standing for *G. Quellyon.*

×**Borisii** Kellerer ex Sünderm.: *G. bulgaricum* × *G. reptans.* With lf. form of *G. bulgaricum* and nodding yellow fls. Material grown under this name has orange-scarlet fls. and is nearer to *G. coccineum.*

bulgaricum Panč. Sts. pilose, with short, glandular hairs, to 2 ft.; lvs. with many, small, scattered, 3-toothed lateral lobes, terminal lft. very large, cordate-reniform, with jagged teeth; fls. 3–7, nodding, bright yellow or orange, petals ¾ in. long. Balkans. Material grown under this name has erect fls. and is closer to *G. coccineum* and *G.* ×*Heldreichii.*

calthifolium Sm. [*Acomastylis calthifolia* (Sm.) F. Bolle]. Low, leafy, to 1 ft., hairy; basal lvs. with large, terminal, rounded or reniform lft. and minute or no lateral lfts.; fls. 1 or a few, bright yellow, 1 in. across or more. B.C. to Alaska, e. Asia. Cv. **'Dilatatum'** is listed.

canadense Jacq. To 3 ft., slender, glabrous or nearly so; lvs. with 3–5 rhombic, serrate lfts., or simple and undivided, stipules ovate-oblong;

fls. white, about ½ in. across; achenes many. Nov. Sc. and Minn., s. to La. and Kans.

chilense: *G. Quellyon.*

chiloense: a listed name of no botanical standing for *G. Quellyon.*

ciliatum: *G. triflorum* var.

coccineum Sibth. & Sm. Resembling *G. Quellyon,* but terminal lft. about 3–4 times as long as the largest lateral lfts.; filaments yellow. S. Eur., Asia Minor. Plants cult. under this name are often *G. Quellyon.*

elatum Wallich. Sts. very slender, 1–6-fld.; lvs. 4–12 in. long, narrow, lfts. ½–1 in. long, terminal lft. orbicular; fls. ½–1½ in. across, sepals silky, petals golden-yellow. Himalayas.

×**Heldreichii:** a listed name of no botanical standing, used for plants with orange-red fls., said to be derived from *G. coccineum.*

macrophyllum Willd. Like *G. urbanum,* but more robust; lower lvs. with 5–7 pairs of lateral lfts. and a large, 3–7-lobed, roundish, terminal lft. 2–4 in. wide, stipules less toothed; fls. usually larger, petals yellow, to ⁵⁄₁₆ in. long; receptacle sparsely short-hairy, achenes bristly at apex. Lab. to Alaska, s. to N.Y., Mont., Calif.; Asia.

montanum L. [*Sieversia montana* (L.) K. Spreng.]. Soft-hairy, 6–12 in.; lvs. 1–4 in. long, terminal lft. larger than lateral lfts.; fls. erect, yellow, 1¼–1¾ in. across, styles feathery in fr. S. Eur. Cv. **'Maximum'** is listed.

Peckii Pursh. Sts. smoothish, to 15 in.; lowest lvs. with terminal lft. rounded-reniform, 2–5 in. wide, and with lateral lfts. minute; fls. 1–5, petals yellow to orange, about ½ in. long. Nov. Sc. to New Hamp.

pentapetalum (L.) Mak. [*Sieversia pentapetala* (L.) Greene]. Glabrous, to 6 in. high, with ascending or somewhat decumbent brs.; lfts. 5–7, obovate to oblanceolate, serrate; fls. white, about 1 in. across. Aleutian Is., Asia.

pyrenaicum Mill. Sts. hairy, erect, to 1½ ft., 1–4-fld.; lvs. as in *G. montanum,* but longer; fls. nodding, yellow. Pyrenees.

Quellyon Sweet [*G. atrosanguineum* Hort.; *G. chilense* Lindl.; *G. coccineum* Hort., not Sibth. & Sm.]. Hairy and glandular, 1–2 ft.; lvs. with large terminal lft. about twice as long as the largest of the unequal lateral lfts.; fls. erect, scarlet, about 1 in. across, filaments mostly red; achenes in a small, dense, hairy head. Chile. Cv. **'Plenum'**. Fls. double.

reptans L. [*Sieversia reptans* (L.) K. Spreng.]. Plants 6–8 in. high, with long runners; lfts. deeply toothed, terminal lfts. not greatly enlarged; fl. solitary, 1¼–1½ in. across, sepals lanceolate-linear, ½ in. long, petals 5–8, ⅝–¾ in. long, styles to 1¼ in. long in fr., feathery. Eur.

×rhaeticum Brügg.: *G. montanum* × *G. reptans.* Plant 6–8 in.; fls. golden-yellow, 1 in. wide.

rivale L. INDIAN CHOCOLATE, PURPLE AVENS, WATER A., CHOCOLATE ROOT. Pubescent, to 2 ft.; lvs. with 3–6 pairs of unequal lateral lfts. to ¾ in. long, and large terminal lft. 1–2 in. long, lfts. all dentate; fls. few, nodding, calyx purple, petals ⅜–⅝ in. long, dull orange-pink; fruiting head stalked, erect. Eurasia, N. Amer.

Rossii (R. Br.) Ser. [*Acomastylis Rossii* (R. Br.) Greene]. Plant glabrous or pilose, to 7 in.; lower lvs. pinnate and glabrous, lfts. 3-lobed, ciliate on margin; fl. solitary, yellow, 1½ in. across, style straight, not hairy. Alaska, Yukon, Asia.

sibiricum: a listed name of no botanical standing. Plant to 10 in.; fls. bright red, coppery.

strictum: *G. aleppicum* var.

sylvaticum Pourr. To 2 ft.; basal lvs. with few lateral lfts. and a large cordate, elongate-elliptic, terminal lft.; fls. 1–2, yellow, to 1 in. across. Iberian Pen., Morocco.

triflorum Pursh [*Sieversia triflora* (Pursh) K. Spreng.]. Soft-hairy, to 1½ ft.; lvs. with many, cuneate, almost uniform, shallowly cut lfts.; fls. nodding, sepals purple, shorter than the bractlets, petals purplish to straw-colored, styles not jointed, to 2 in. long, feathery in fr. Ont. to Alta., s. to Ill., Nebr., Mont. Var. **ciliatum** (Pursh) Fassett [*G. ciliatum* Pursh; *Sieversia ciliata* (Pursh) G. Don]. Lfts. dissected at least halfway; style tip deciduous. Alta. to B.C., s. to Wash. and New Mex.

turbinatum Rydb. More or less pubescent, to 1 ft.; lf. segms. 11–33, oblanceolate to obovate, 3–5-cleft or -toothed; fls. yellow, about ½ in. across, styles not much elongate in fr. Rocky Mts. Close to *G. Rossii.*

urbanum L. CLOVEROOT, HERB BENNET. To 2 ft., more or less pubescent, erect; lvs. with 2–3 pairs of unequal, lateral lfts. 3/16–⅜ in. long, and with large terminal lft. 2–3 in. wide, all crenate or toothed, stipules to 1 in. long, deeply toothed; fls. erect, few, calyx green, petals yellow, 3/16–5/16 in. long, spreading, pistils glabrous, forming a sessile head. Eur., w. Asia., N. Afr.

GEVUINA Mol. (Sometimes, but not originally, spelled *Guevina.*) *Proteaceae.* Three spp. of evergreen trees or shrubs, 1 in Chile and Argentina, 2 in Australia and New Guinea; lvs. alt., simple or odd-pinnate; fls. paired in axils of bracts in axillary racemes or panicles, bisexual, perianth tubular, cylindrical, lobes ovate, recurved; fr. a thick, elongate drupe.

Avellana Mol. CHILEAN NUT, CHILE HAZEL. To 40 ft.; lvs. glossy, lfts. toothed; fls. white; fr. coral-red, later black, about size of cherry, seed with edible kernel. Occasionally grown in s. Calif. Zone 10. Wood used for making furniture, picture frames, shingles and for turnery.

GIBASIS Raf. *Commelinaceae.* Ten or more spp. of caulescent, suberect or erect herbs, native to Amer. tropics; lvs. ovate to lanceolate, brs., when present, emerging through orifice of sheath; infl. of 1 to several, peduncled, solitary cincinni terminal and axillary on the st., or sometimes subumbellate; fls. white, pink, or purple, sepals 3, herbaceous, petals 3, stamens 6, nearly equal, filaments usually bearded, anthers with broad connectives, longitudinally dehiscent, ovary 3-celled, each cell with 2 ovules, 1 cell sometimes aborting, style filiform, stigma shortly 3-branched; fr. a caps.

Mostly grown under glass. Propagated by seeds and cuttings.

geniculata (Jacq.) Rohw. Sts. elongate, rooting at nodes; lvs. green, ovate-lanceolate; cincinni in a loose branched infl.; fls. white. Trop. Amer. Not offered in the trade, but sometimes cult. as a laboratory demonstration plant.

Karwinskyana (Schult. & Schult.f.) Rohw. Sts. to 1 ft., roots tuberous-thickened; lvs. glaucescent, lanceolate; cincinni often subumbellate; fls. pink. Ne. Mex.

GIBBAEUM Haw. ex N. E. Br. [*Argeta* N. E. Br.; *Mentocalyx* N. E. Br.; *Rimaria* N. E. Br.]. FLOWERING-QUARTZ. *Aizoaceae.* About 21 spp. of usually cespitose, succulent per. herbs, native to S. Afr., sts. short or prostrate; lvs. opp., basally united to form an oblong-ovoid or subcylindrical body (growth) with an oblique fissure resembling a mouth, dividing the growth into equal or unequal lobes, surface smooth, roughened, or hairy; fls. solitary, terminal, bractless, pedicelled, calyx 6-lobed, lobes keeled, 4 shorter than other 2, petals many, stamens many, ovary 6-celled, stigmas 6, more or less plumose; fr. a 6-celled caps., cell lids winged.

These plants need good illumination, a minimum temperature of about 60° F., moderate watering, but kept dry during their resting period. Propagation easy by seeds and cuttings; blooming usually at beginning of growth period. See also *Succulents.*

album N. E. Br. Growths finely and densely white-hairy, to 1 in. high and ⅝ in. thick, obliquely ovoid to nearly globose, keeled, fissure widening in age; fls. appearing lateral to new growth, to 1 in. across, petals white or rose. Cape Prov.

dispar N. E. Br. Growths single or in dense clumps, gray-green, flushed brownish, velvety with fine hairs, to ¾ in. high and 1 in. thick, subglobose-ovoid or subglobose, slightly keeled, fissure deep but closed; fls. to 1 in. across, petals violet-red. Cape Prov.

gibbosum (Haw.) N. E. Br. [*G. perviride* (Haw.) N. E. Br.]. Clumps to 6 in. across; growths smooth, green to yellowish-green, to 2½ in. long and ¾ in. thick, cylindrical; lvs. unequal, the larger 2-keeled on lower side toward tip, the smaller triangular in general outline, upper side flat, lower side rounded, fissure slight, widening in age; fls. to 1¼ in. across, petals pale pink, magenta, or purple. Cape Prov.

Heathii (N. E. Br.) L. Bolus [*Rimaria Heathii* (N. E. Br.) N. E. Br.; *R. Luckhoffii* (L. Bolus) L. Bolus]. Clumps compact, to 1 ft. across; growths smooth, light green to whitish-green, to 1¾ in. high, 1 3/16 in. thick, nearly globose, central fissure deep; lvs. 2, equal, to 1¼ in. long and ¾ in. thick; fls. to 1½ in. across, petals white to cream-colored, often fading pink. Cape Prov.

Nebrownii: *Imitaria Muirii.*

Nelii: *Antegibbaeum fissoides.*

perviride: *G. gibbosum.*

petrense (N. E. Br.) Tisch. [*Argeta petrensis* N. E. Br.]. Clump often 2–4 in. across, growths with 1–2 pairs of nearly equal lvs.; lvs. glabrous, gray-green or whitish-green, to ⅜ in. long and ¼ in. thick, triangular or triangular-ovate in outline, keeled, upper side flat or somewhat rounded, lower side rounded toward base, apex pointed; fls. to ⅝ in. across, petals reddish. Cape Prov.

pubescens (Haw.) N. E. Br. Growths silvery to grayish-white from minute, dense, appressed hairs, obliquely ovoid, cylindric-ovoid or oblong-ovoid; lvs. unequal, the larger to 1¼ in. long and ⅝ in. wide, obliquely keeled toward the hooklike tip, the smaller to ⅜ in. long; fls. to ⅝ in. across, petals violet-red. Cape Prov.

Schwantesii Tisch. Clumps compact, growths velvety to the touch, green to yellowish-green or brownish; lvs. very unequal, the larger to 2¾ in. long, 1 3/16 in. wide at base, more or less shaped like the prow of a canoe, upper side flat but curved, lower side strongly keeled and curved to tip, smaller lf. about half as large and fitting against larger; fls. in front of a new pair of lvs., to 2 in. across, petals light red. Cape Prov.

Shandii N. E. Br. Growth green, covered closely with stellate hairs, obliquely ovoid, cylindric-ovoid, or oblong-ovoid; lvs. unequal, the larger to 1¼ in. long, the shorter to ⅜ in. long; fls. to ⅞ in. across, petals reddish. Cape Prov.

velutinum (L. Bolus) Schwant. [*Mentocalyx velutinus* (L. Bolus) Schwant.]. Clumps 6–8 in. across; lvs. broadly spreading, light glaucous-gray, velvety with minute, whitish hairs, united basally, unequal, the longer lf. to 2⅜ in. long, upper side concave to slightly angled, lower side obtusely keeled, apex with a hooklike tip, the shorter lf.

to 1¼ in. long, upper side slightly convex, lower side strongly keeled; fls. to 2 in. across, petals pink, stamens white. Cape Prov.

GILIA Ruiz & Pav. *Polemoniaceae.* Between 20 and 30 spp. of ann., bien., or per. herbs, native to the New World, chiefly w. N. Amer.; lvs. alt., sometimes in a basal rosette, entire to dissected, usually variously hairy, often glandular; fls. blue, pink, red, yellow, or white, in heads or rarely solitary, in paniculately branched infls., calyx 5-parted, corolla funnelform to salverform, stamens 5; fr. a 3-celled caps., distending or rupturing the calyx, seeds few to many in a cell.

Seeds are sown where plants are to grow, in sunny open places.

abrotanifolia: *G. capitata* subsp.

achilleifolia Benth. Erect, glabrous, villous, or glandular ann., to 3 ft.; lower lvs. in basal rosette, mostly twice-pinnately dissected; fls. in dense, terminal, fan-shaped heads, corolla violet or blue-violet, ⅜–¾ in. long. S. Calif., Baja Calif. Subsp. **multicaulis** (Benth.) A. D. Grant & V. E. Grant [*G. multicaulis* Benth.]. Infl. more open; corolla smaller, ³⁄₁₆–⅜ in. long.

aggregata: *Ipomopsis aggregata.*

androsacea: *Linanthus androsaceus.*

aurea: *Linanthus aureus.*

californica: *Leptodactylon californicum.*

capitata Sims [*G. capitata* var. *alba* Orcutt]. Glabrous or glandular ann., to 3 ft.; lvs. to 4 in. long, 2–3 times pinnately dissected into linear segms.; fls. blue, violet, or white, 50–100 in terminal heads to about 1 in. across on naked peduncles. B.C. to cent. Calif., e. to w. Idaho. Subsp. **abrotanifolia** (Nutt. ex Greene) V. E. Grant [*G. abrotanifolia* Nutt. ex Greene]. Heads 25–50-fld. S. Calif., n. Baja Calif.

caruifolia Abrams. Glabrous, pubescent, or glandular ann., to 3 ft.; lower lvs. 2–3 times pinnate into slender, finely toothed or lobed segms.; fls. in panicles, corolla blue-violet, lavender, pink, or white, throat purple-dotted. S. Calif., Baja Calif.

cephaloidea: *Ipomopsis spicata.*

coronopifolia: *Ipomopsis rubra.*

densiflora: *Linanthus grandiflorus.*

densifolia: *Eriastrum densifolium.*

dianthoides: *Linanthus dianthiflorus.*

dichotoma: *Linanthus dichotomus.*

erecta: *G. laciniata* var.

floribunda: *Linanthus Nuttallii* subsp.

globularis: *Ipomopsis spicata* subsp. *capitata.*

incisa Benth. Weak, pubescent ann., to 1½ ft.; lvs. almost entire to incisely toothed or cleft; fls. blue or white, long-pedicelled, in open panicle. Tex.

laciniata Ruiz & Pav. Glandular-pubescent, erect ann., to 1 ft.; lvs. twice pinnately dissected into linear segms.; fls. rose, pale lilac to white, in few-fld. clusters. Peru, Chile, Argentina. Var. **erecta** (Hieron.) Brand [*G. erecta* Hieron.]. Lvs. somewhat fleshy.

latiflora (A. Gray) A. Gray. Erect ann., to 1 ft., glabrous and glaucous beneath, glandular above; basal lvs. in rosette, strap-shaped, to 2¾ in. long, toothed to pinnately lobed, lightly cobwebby-pubescent; fls. in a subcymose panicle, corolla blue or violet to pinkish with yellow throat. Mojave Desert (Calif.).

latifolia S. Wats. Erect, glandular ann., to 8 in.; lvs. simple or pinnately lobed, to 4¾ in. long and 2 in. wide; fls. pink inside, buff on exterior, in paniculate infl., opening in the evening. Deserts, s. Calif., e. to Nev. and Utah.

leptomeria A. Gray. Glandular-pubescent, erect ann., to 1 ft.; basal lvs. in rosette, strap-shaped, linear or oblanceolate, to 3¾ in. long, toothed or lobed; fls. in panicle, corolla white to pale rose, usually with a purple streak from throat to tip of each lobe. E. Wash. to Calif., e. to Idaho, Colo., Ariz.

liniflora: *Linanthus liniflorus.*

longiflora: *Ipomopsis longiflora.*

lutea: *Linanthus androsaceus* subsp.

micrantha: *Linanthus androsaceus* subsp.

multicaulis: *G. achilleifolia* subsp.

Nuttallii: *Linanthus Nuttallii.*

punctata: *Langloisia punctata.*

pungens: *Leptodactylon pungens.*

rubra: *Ipomopsis rubra.*

spicata: *Ipomopsis spicata.*

tricolor Benth. BIRD'S-EYES. Erect ann., to 2½ ft., more or less

glandular-pubescent; lvs. twice pinnately dissected into linear segms.; fls. in a few-fld., terminal cyme, corolla with lilac or violet lobes, yellow tube, and throat marked with purple. Calif.

valdiviensis Griseb. Glandular-hairy ann., with ascending brs.; lvs. pinnatisect into linear or lanceolate segms.; fls. in 3-fld. cymes, corolla with blue limb and pale tube. Chile.

GILIBERTIA: *DENDROPANAX.* **G. japonica:** *D. trifidus.*

GILLENIA Moench. *Rosaceae.* Two spp. of erect, branching per. herbs, native to N. Amer.; lvs. almost sessile, with 3 lfts.; fls. white or pinkish, long-stalked, in terminal panicles, calyx 5-toothed, petals 5, stamens 10–20; fr. of 5 follicles.

Grown in wild or rock gardens; of easy culture. Propagated by seeds and by division.

stipulata (Muhlenb.) Baill. AMERICAN IPECAC. To 4 ft.; lfts. lanceolate, deeply incised, stipules large and leaflike, doubly incised; fls. to ½ in. across. N.Y. to Ill., s. to Ga., Tex., Kans.

trifoliata (L.) Moench. INDIAN-PHYSIC, BOWMAN'S-ROOT. Lfts. oblong-ovate, cut-serrate, stipules small, subulate, entire or slightly incised. N.Y., Ont., Mich., s. to Ga. and Ala.

GINKGO L. [*Salisburia* Sm.]. *Ginkgoaceae.* One sp., a tree of se. China, but now evidently extinct in the wild, with characters of the family.

Mostly grown as a street or ornamental tree in temperate regions. The seeds yield oil which cause dermatitis in some people, but the kernels, called ginkgo nuts, are much eaten in the Orient. Hardy through Zone 5 and of easy culture in good soil. Propagated by stratified seeds, layers, cuttings, and the named cultivars by grafting and budding. The female tree is undesirable because of the unpleasant odor (butyric acid or rancid butter) of the mature, fallen seeds.

biloba L. [*Salisburia adiantifolia* Sm.]. MAIDENHAIR TREE. To 120 ft.; lvs. 2–3 in. long; seeds yellowish, drupelike, to 1 in. long, long-peduncled. Cvs. are: 'Aurea', lvs. bright yellow; 'Fastigiata', of pyramidal habit; 'Laciniata', lvs. deeply divided; 'Macrophylla', lvs. exceptionally large; 'Mascula', a listed name; 'Pendula', brs. pendulous; 'Pyramidalis', a listed name; 'Variegata', lvs. variegated yellow.

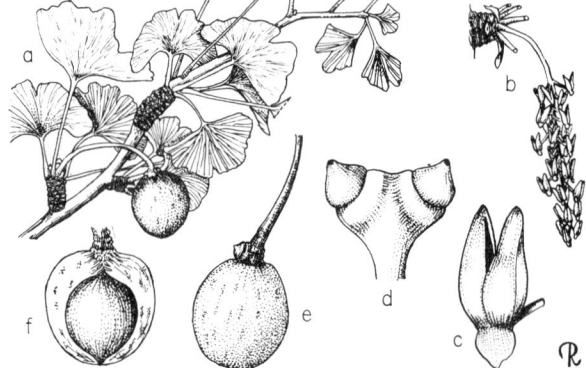

GINKGOACEAE. *Ginkgo biloba:* **a,** branch with mature seed, × ¼; **b,** male catkin, bearing microsporophylls, × 1; **c,** microsporophyll, × 8; **d,** pair of ovules, × 4; **e,** seed, × ½; **f,** seed, vertical section, × ½. (From Bailey, *Manual of Cultivated Plants,* ed. 2.)

GINKGOACEAE Engl. GINKGO FAMILY. Gymnosperms; 1 genus, *Ginkgo,* a deciduous, resinous, dioecious tree, native to se. China; brs. stiff, with both elongate and spur shoots; lvs. alt. or clustered, fan-shaped, cut or divided in middle, dichotomously veined, long-petioled; reproductive structures on spur shoots in axils of lvs. or bracts, the male catkinlike, the female consisting of 2 ovules, rarely more, on a long peduncle, usually only 1 maturing; seeds plumlike in appearance, outer coat fleshy, inner coat stony.

GINORIA Jacq. *Lythraceae.* About 14 spp. of mostly glabrous shrubs, native to Mex. and W. Indies, often spiny at the nodes; lvs. opp.; fls. purple to rose, or white, solitary or clustered in lf. axils, or in short racemes, calyx tube semiglobose or spreading, generally without appendages, calyx lobes 4–6, petals 4–6, stamens 10–23; fr. a globose caps., not or scarcely longer than calyx tube.

Rohrii (Vahl) Koehne. To 15 ft., sts. with 2–4 short, decurrent spines at nodes; lvs. obovate or elliptic-ovate, to 3⅜ in. long, 2⅜ in. wide, almost leathery; fls. 2–8, in axillary umbels, petals white, to ⅜ in. long, stamens 16–20. W. Indies.

GIVOTIA Griff. *Euphorbiaceae.* Two spp. of dioecious trees, with white, stellate hairs, native to India and Madagascar; lvs. alt., simple, palmately veined, broadly ovate to cordate; infl. racemose or paniculate cymes; fls. with petals, stamens 15–25, ovary 2–3-celled; fr. a drupe.

rottleriformis Griff. Small, much-branched tree; lvs. 4–7 in. wide, broadly ovate, cordate at base, dentate; ovary with stellate hairs; fr. about 1 in. long, hairy. India.

GLADIOLUS L. CORN FLAG, SWORD LILY. *Iridaceae.* Between 250 and 300 spp. of per. herbs with tunicate corms, native to Eur., Medit. region, the Near East, but chiefly to trop. and S. Afr.; sts. usually unbranched, leafy; lvs. basal and cauline, sword-shaped, less frequently linear or cylindrical; fls. showy, in 1-sided spikes, irregular, borne in 2 spathe valves, perianth segms. 6, united basally into a curved, funnelform tube, the upper 3 segms. larger than the lower 3, stamens 3, filaments not united, borne below the throat, style brs. 3, entire; fr. a 3-valved caps.

The names of many species have appeared in nursery catalogues and are described below. The common garden gladiolus does not represent a single species, but is the product of hybridization of a few species that were early introduced into cultivation or that have proved to be especially useful horticulturally. It is likely that *G. carneus, G. cardinalis* Curtis, *G. natalensis, G. oppositiflorus* Herb., *G. primulinus, G. purpureoauratus* Hook.f., and *G. Saundersii* Hook.f. have contributed most to the development of common garden gladioli. One of the early forms, a reputed hybrid, was *G.* × *gandavensis;* subsequently, as the garden gladiolus was modified and began to assume its present character, such names as *G.* × *Lemoinei* Hort. ex Bak., *G.* × *nanceianus* Hort., and *G.* × *Childsii* Hort. became current, but are of little interest to present-day growers. There are many excellent cultivars, their merit residing particularly in the number of flowers, their shape, size, color, markings, texture, keeping qualities, season, and the character of the inflorescence.

Gladioli are tender and should be grown between spring and autumn frosts, although the corms often persist even in northern states if well protected with ground covering. Open sunny exposure is best. Strong corms set in good earth the first of May yield plants that should begin to bloom by late July or the first of Aug. The ground should be well prepared and have good drainage. The use of stable manure the previous year should produce good results, but it should not be applied with the corms. Plant the corms as soon as the ground becomes warm, 3–6 in. deep, in succession for later bloom. The plants usually stand up better with the deeper planting, but the greater depth is advisable only on warm, open land, and with strong corms. For strong specimen spikes, plant 5–8 in. apart, but for mass effect plant them twice as thick. Planted 5 in. deep and 3–5 in. apart, the plants probably will not require staking. Before freezing weather, lift the plants, remove the tops, and store the corms in a cool dry place until spring. See that the corms are firm, clean, dry, and well cured before being put away, and protect from rodents.

Cultivars are propagated by means of the cormlets that form around the old corms. The cormlets are planted in drills in spring, then treated as the regular flowering corms. They should bloom in the second or third year. Gladioli can also be grown from seeds. Gladioli are well adapted to use as cut flowers. If grown in the herbaceous border, the smaller flowered cultivars are best.

alatus L. Sts. to 1 ft.; lvs. 4, linear to sword-shaped, rigid, ciliate on the veins; fls. 3–5, fragrant, dark red and pink, perianth segms. very unequal, with a narrow claw, the upper 3 to 1½ in. long, the lower 3 green and pink. S. Afr.

angustus L. Sts. 2–3 ft.; lvs. 3–4, linear, to 2 ft. long and ¼ in. wide or less, firm; fls. 2–6, white, the lower 3 perianth segms. marked with purple, tube 1½–2 in. long, much longer than segms. S. Afr.

blandus: *G. carneus.*

brevifolius Jacq. Sts. to 2 ft.; basal lf. 1, linear, to 2 ft. long, pilose, st. lvs. 2–4, sheathing, brown; fls. 6–13, pink, the lower 3 perianth segms. with a yellow blotch, tube ¾ in. long, about as long as the segms. S. Afr. Var. **robustus** G. J. Lewis. To 33 in.; fls. 12–20, pink and white or lilac and white.

byzantinus Mill. Sts. to 3 ft., robust; lvs. 3–5, sword-shaped, about

1 ft. long; spikes loose, many-fld.; fls. purple, perianth segms. 1–1¼ in. long, the upper 3 about ¾ in. wide, the lower 3 with central white line. Medit. region. Cv. 'Albus'. Fls. white. Cv. 'Ruber'. Fls. bright cerise-scarlet.

callistus: *G. carneus.*

carinatus Ait. Sts. to 2 ft., often flexuous; lvs. 3, linear, the upper usually longer than the st., the lower shorter; fls. 2–8, violet-scented, blue, mauve, or brownish-yellow, the lower 3 perianth segms. blotched yellow, tube to about ¾ in. long. S. Afr.

caryophyllaceus (Burm.f.) Poir. [*G. hirsutus* Jacq.]. Sts. to 2 ft., hairy; lvs. 4–6, sword-shaped, rigid, prominently ribbed, short-hairy; spikes loose, 6-fld.; fls. bright red, perianth segms. to 1½ in. long, tube to 1½ in. long. S. Afr.

carmineus C. H. Wright. Sts. to 1½ ft.; lvs. linear, about 8 in. long, midrib thick; fls. about 3 in. wide, carmine, the 2 inner, lower perianth segms. with a pale, dark-margined spot. S. Afr.

carneus D. Delar. [*G. blandus* Ait.; *G. callistus* F. Bolus.]. Sts. to 2 ft., sometimes branched; lvs. 4, to 1 ft. long and ¾ in. wide, firm, glabrous; spikes loose, 3–10-fld.; fls. pale pink or cream-colored, perianth segms. acute, the upper 3 to 1 in. wide, the lower 3 to ½ in. wide, with a red or purplish median mark, tube crimson or dark pink. S. Afr.

× **Colvillei** Sweet: *G. cardinalis* Curtis × *G. tristis.* Sts. to 1½ ft., robust, glaucous; lvs. about 4, linear to sword-shaped, prominently nerved; fls. nearly erect, scarlet, perianth segms. acute, the lower 3 with a bright yellow, lanceolate, basal blotch. One of the earliest known garden hybrids. Cvs. are 'Albus' [cv. 'The Bride'], fls. pure white; 'Roseus', fls. soft pink; 'Ruber', fls. carmine-red.

communis L. Sts. to 2½ ft.; lvs. 3–5, sword-shaped, to 1 ft. long; spikes loose, 4–8-fld.; fls. bright purple, perianth segms. about 1½ in. long, nearly equal in length, anthers shorter than filaments. France, Germany, Medit. region. Var. **carneus**: *G. pallidus.*

Cooperi: *G. natalensis.*

crassifolius Bak. Sts. to 3 ft.; lvs. 6–7, to 2 ft. long, rigid, prominently ribbed; fls. many, bright red, perianth segms. ½ in. long, about ¼ in. wide, obtuse, tube ⁵⁄₁₆ in. long. S. Afr.

cuspidatus: *G. undulatus.*

Dehnianus Merxm. Sts. to 2 ft.; lvs. about 4, sword-shaped, to 1 ft. long, rigid, prominently ribbed; spike flexuous, 20–30-fld.; fls. pale greenish-ocher, perianth segms. spotted with purple, and purple along midvein. S. Rhodesia.

dracocephalus: *G. natalensis.*

elegans Vaup. Sts. to about 1 ft.; lvs. narrowly lanceolate; fls. about 6, white, perianth segms. 1⅛ in. long, stamens half as long as segms. Nyassaland.

Elliotii Bak. Sts. to 1 ft.; basal lvs. about 4, sword-shaped, 6–9 in. long, rigid, prominently ribbed; spikes dense; perianth segms. claret-red, to 1 in. long, tube ¾–1 in. long, stamens shorter than segms. Transvaal.

× **gandavensis** Van Houtte: *G. cardinalis* Curtis × *G. natalensis* or *G. natalensis* × *G. oppositiflorus* Herb. Sts. to 4½ ft., robust; lvs. broadly sword-shaped; spikes dense, many-fld.; fls. bright red and reddish-yellow, perianth segms. variously streaked and lined, the upper 3 horizontal or hooded. Summer-flowering garden hybrid from which most modern gladioli have been developed.

gracilis Jacq. Sts. to 2½ ft., very slender; lvs. 3–4, cylindrical, to 2½ ft. long, rigid; fls. 2–6, fragrant, blue or pale pink, perianth segms. to 2 in. long, the lower 3 dark-streaked, cream-colored in lower half, tube to ⅝ in. long. S. Afr.

grandis: *G. liliaceus.*

× **harlemensis** Hort. van Tuberg. Name used for a group of hybrids derived from *G.* × *Colvillei* cv. 'Albus'; sts. wiry; fls. variable in color, white, cream, pink, rose, and violet, perianth segms. sometimes veined with darker shades in the throat, sometimes wavy.

hirsutus: *G. caryophyllaceus.*

Hookeri: *G. natalensis* cv.

× **hortulanus** L. H. Bailey. GARDEN G. An inclusive group, for the prevailing cult. kinds of gladiolus to which no recognized botanical specific name will now apply, and which cannot be included in any of the spp. Perhaps descendants more or less directly from *G. natalensis,* variously modified. Strong very floriferous plants of sturdy growth; spikes heavy; fls. often spread wide open, in many shades and markings, most of them with tints of lilac and violet, the upper perianth segms. sometimes hooded. There are hundreds of named cvs.

illyricus W. D. J. Koch. Sts. to 3 ft.; lvs. 2–3, linear, to 1 ft. long, glaucous; fls. 4–8, crimson-purple, perianth segms. long-clawed, tube ¼ in. long, anthers half as long as filaments. Eng. and Portugal, w. to Balkans and Caucasus.

imbricatus L. Sts. to 2 ft.; lvs. 2–3, linear, about 2 ft. long, to ½ in. wide; spikes dense, 4–10-fld.; fls. opening wide, purple-red, the lower 3 perianth segms. clawed, anthers shorter than filaments. E. Eur., w. Asia.

liliaceus Houtt. [*G. grandis* Thunb.]. Sts. to 2 ft.; lvs. 3–4, cylindrical or linear, to 2 ft. long, prominently ribbed; fls. 1–6, fragrant, cream-colored, yellowish, or red-brown, perianth segms. frequently mottled or streaked with pink or brown, to 2⅛ in. long, tapering or recurved at apex, tube to 2⅛ in. long. S. Afr.

Melleri Bak. Sts. to 1½ ft.; lvs. few, linear, to 1 ft. long, prominently ribbed; spikes loose, not 1-sided; fls. red, perianth segms. to 1½ in. long, tube ¾ in. long. E. Trop. Afr.

Meyeri: a listed name of no botanical standing.

nanus: *Babiana nana.*

natalensis (Eckl.) Reinw. ex Hook. [*G. Cooperi* Bak.; *G. dracocephalus* Hook.f.; *G. psittacinus* Hook.]. Sts. 3–4 ft.; lvs. about 4, sword-shaped, to 1½ ft. long and ¾ in. wide, rigid; fls. 10–12, the upper 3 perianth segms. dark crimson, hooded, ¾ in. wide, the lower 3 much smaller, yellow and red mixed, tube to 2 in. long, anthers ⅓ as long as filaments. *G. Quartinianus* may not be distinct from this sp. Se. Afr. Cv. **'Hookeri'** [*G. Hookeri* Hort.]. Fls. large, clear yellow; flowers late in the season.

nebulicola C. Ingram. Sts. to 3½ ft.; lvs. 6–9, sword-shaped, to 14 in. long and 1½ in. wide; fls. 3–5, chrome-yellow, the upper 3 perianth segms. hooded. S. Rhodesia.

odoratus L. Bolus. Sts. to about ½ ft.; lf. 1, developing after the fls., sword-shaped, to 9 in. long, spirally twisted, the margin yellow; fls. 7–13, fragrant, variable in color, perianth segms. dull violet-red with light yellow margins, to ¾ in. long, the uppermost center segm. hooded, tube about ¾ in. long. S. Afr.

orchidiflorus Andr. Sts. to 1½ ft.; basal lvs. 3–4, linear, to 1 ft. long, firm; spike flexuous, 3–4-fld.; fls. greenish-yellow, perianth segms. clawed, the upper 3 hooded, the lower 3 curved downward, tube ½ in. long. Cape Prov. (S. Afr.).

pallidus Bak. [*G. communis* var. *carneus* Ker-Gawl.]. Sts. to 2 ft.; basal lvs. many, linear, midrib thick; spike 6–20-fld.; fls. pale pink, perianth segms. to 1¼ in. long, the lower 3 reflexed, tube 1 in. long. Angola.

palustris Gaudin. Sts. to 1½ ft.; lvs. 2–3, linear, about as long as st., ribbed; fls. 3–8, purple-red, perianth segms. 1 in. long, the lower 3 clawed, tube ¼ in. long, anthers shorter than filaments. Cent. and se. Eur.

permeabilis D. Delar. Sts. to 2 ft., slender; lvs. 3–4, linear to nearly cylindrical, to 1 ft.; infl. simple or forked, 6–12-fld.; fls. pink or lilac, perianth segms. ¾ in. long, tube ½ in. long. S. Afr.

pilosus: *G. punctulatus.*

primulinus Bak. Sts. 2–4 ft., stout; basal lvs. 3, sword-shaped, to 1 ft. long, prominently ribbed; fls. 4–5, primrose-yellow, the upper 3 perianth segms. hooded, 2 in. long, more than 1 in. wide, the central segms. drooping, the lower 3 much smaller, reflexed. Se. trop. Afr. Thought by some to be a color form of *G. Quartinianus.*

psittacinus: *G. natalensis.*

purpureus: *Babiana purpurea.*

punctulatus Schrank [*G. pilosus* Eckl.; *G. villosus* Ker-Gawl.]. Sts. to 2½ ft., but usually not as high; lvs. 3, linear to lanceolate, to 6 in. long, but usually shorter, firm, with 2–5 prominent veins, margins cartilaginous; fls. 2–8, to 2 in. long, pink to mauve, lobes of lower perianth segms. with orange, reddish, or purple streaks in the lower half, and the outer lower segms. white or yellow in the lower half. S. Afr.

Quartinianus A. Rich. Sts. 2–3 ft.; lvs. 3 or 4, linear to sword-shaped, to 1½ ft. long and ¾ in. wide, rigid; fls. 6–9, blood-red to pale yellow, perianth segms. 3 in. or more long, the upper 3 hooded, the lower 3 much smaller, reflexed, tube 1½ in. long, anthers as long as filaments. Trop. Afr. Perhaps not distinct from *G. natalensis; G. primulinus* is thought by some to be a color form of this sp.

recurvus L. Sts. slender, to 2 ft.; lvs. 3, cylindrical, the lowest one about 1 ft. long, firm, prominently ribbed; fls. 3–6, fragrant, perianth segms. about 3 in. long, the upper 3 lilac, the lower 3 yellow, with mauve or lilac markings, tube 1½–2 in. long. S. Afr.

segetum Ker-Gawl. CORN FLAG. Sts. to 2 ft.; lvs. 3–4, sword-shaped, to 1½ ft. long; fls. 6–10, open or flaring, bright purple, perianth segms. to 1½ in. long, tube slightly curved, ¼–⁵⁄₁₆ in. long, anthers longer than filaments; caps. top-shaped, ½ in. long. Medit. region to Turkestan and Iran; occasionally naturalized in warmer parts of U.S.

tenellus Jacq. [*G. trichonemifolius* Ker-Gawl.]. Sts. to 1½ ft., cylindrical, slender; lvs. 3, rigid, nearly cylindrical, the lowest to 1 ft. long; fls. 2–5, yellowish or greenish-white, perianth segms. tinged with lilac, spotted with black around the throat, to 1 in. long, tube to 1 in. long. S. Afr.

trichonemifolius: *G. tenellus.*

tristis L. Sts. to 2 ft., slender; lvs. 3, cylindrical, to 1½ ft. long, prominently 3–5-ribbed; fls. 3–4, fragrant, yellowish-white, perianth segms. with purple on keels, to 1¼ in. long, tube to 2½ in. long. S. Afr. Cv. **'Ruber'.** Fls. red. Var. **concolor** (Salisb.) Bak. Fls. pale yellow to very white. S. Afr.

×Tubergenii: a listed name of no botanical standing for a hybrid of unknown origin resembling *G.* × *Colvillei,* but larger; sts. to 2½ ft.; lvs. narrow; fls. soft pink to bright purplish-rose.

turkmenorum Czerniak. Sts. ½–3 ft.; lvs. 3, lanceolate, about as long as st., long-acuminate; spikes dense, 8–12-fld.; fls. reclining, rose-purple, perianth segms. to 1½ in. long, tube ⅜ in. long; caps. elliptic-ovate, ¾ in. long. Turkmen.

undulatus L. [*G. cuspidatus* Jacq.]. Sts. to 3 ft.; lvs. 3–4, linear, to 2 ft. long, rigid; spikes loose, 4–8-fld.; fls. white or pale pink, perianth segms. 2½ in. long, ⁵⁄₁₆ in. wide, recurved and acuminate at apex, the lower 3 with small purple blotch, tube slightly curved, 2–3 in. long. S. Afr. Some material under this name may be *Ixia paniculata* var. *tenuiflora.*

villosus: *G. punctulatus.*

Watermeyeri L. Bolus. Sts. to 8 in.; lvs. 3–4, to about 1 ft. long; fls. 2, the upper 3 perianth segms. pale, flushed and lined with pinkish-purple, to about 1 in. long, the center segm. hooded, the lower 3 yellowish-green, tube very short, anthers dark blue. S. Afr.

GLANDULARIA: *VERBENA.*

GLAUCIDIUM Siebold & Zucc. *Ranunculaceae.* Two spp. of herbs, native to Japan and China; sts. 1–2, from a short horizontal rhizome; lvs. alt.; fls. solitary, sepals 4, petaloid, petals none, stamens many, carpels 2; fr. of follicles.

Sometimes grown in the rock garden.

palmatum Siebold & Zucc. Sts. 4–16 in., puberulous; lvs. mostly 2, reniform, 4–12 in. in diam., cordate, 4–7-lobed to middle, lobes rhombic-ovate, toothed, acuminate; sepals 1½–2 in. long, pale mauve. Japan.

GLAUCIUM Mill. HORNED POPPY, SEA P. *Papaveraceae.* About 20–25 spp. of ann., bien., or per., glaucous herbs with orange-colored sap, mostly native to the Medit. region and sw. and cent. Asia; lvs. in a basal rosette, pinnately lobed; fls. solitary, large, yellow or red, petals sometimes marked at base with brown or black blotch, held at an acute angle to the pedicel to form a funnelform corolla, sepals 2, petals 4, stamens many; fr. a cylindrical caps., over 4 in. long, 2-celled, seeds many, embedded in corky or spongy material. See also *Dicranostigma.*

Several species grown in the flower garden, usually as annuals. They thrive in any garden soil in sunny locations; propagated by seeds.

corniculatum (L.) J. H. Rudolph [*G. phoeniceum* Crantz; *G. tricolor* Bernh.]. Ann., to 1½ ft.; fls. red or orange, often with black spot at base of narrow petal, usually hidden among the lvs.; caps. bristly-hairy, linear. Eur., sw. Asia. Material offered under this name is often *G. grandiflorum,* a more ornamental sp.

flavum Crantz [*G. luteum* Scop.]. Ann. or bien., st. stout, stiff, to 3 ft.; fls. golden-yellow or orange, occasionally reddish or reddish-mauve, to 2 in. across, ovary tubercled most of its length; fr. to 12 in. long, smooth or with scattered tubercles. Eur., Canary Is., N. Afr., Turkey; naturalized in e. U.S. Seeds yield oil used as an illuminant and for making soap.

grandiflorum Boiss. & Huet. Similar to *G. corniculatum,* but fls. larger, usually red, on longer peduncles standing above the lvs. Turkey, Iraq, w. Iran. Often offered as *G. corniculatum.*

leiocarpum: *G. oxylobum.*

luteum: *G. flavum.*

oxylobum Boiss. & Buhse [*G. leiocarpum* Boiss.; *G. vitellinum* Boiss. & Buhse]. Related to *G. flavum,* but with straggling, untidy habit; fls. smaller, ovary tubercled only near apex; fr. usually smooth, slightly indented between seeds. Sw. Asia.

phoeniceum: *G. corniculatum.*

squamigera Kar. & Kir. Ann., to 1½ ft.; basal lvs. lyrate-pinnatifid, petioled, st. lvs. usually trifid, small, sessile; fls. yellow or orange, to 1½ in. across; fr. to 8 in. long, with scattered bristly hairs. Russia and cent. Asia.

tricolor: *G. corniculatum.*

vitellinum: *G. oxylobum;* but the name misapplied in cult. to *Dicranostigma Franchetianum.*

GLECHOMA L. *Labiatae.* About 10 spp. of low, diffuse, creeping herbs in Eur. and Asia; sts. mostly square in cross section; lvs. opp., nearly orbicular to reniform, crenate, long-petioled; fls. blue or violet, in axillary verticillasters, calyx tubular, oblique, 15-nerved, unequally 5-toothed, corolla limb 2-lipped, upper lip erect, emarginate, lower lip spreading, 3-lobed, middle lobe emarginate, lateral lobes small, stamens 4, in 2 pairs, upper pair longer, anther cells at right angles; fr. of 4 glabrous nutlets. Differs from *Nepeta* most obviously in having fls. all bisexual and in axils of regular foliage lvs.

hederacea L. [*Nepeta Glechoma* Benth.; *N. hederacea* (L.) Trevisan]. GROUND IVY, GILL-OVER-THE-GROUND, RUNAWAY ROBIN, FIELD BALM, ALEHOOF. Creeping or decumbent per.; lvs. to ½ in. long, ¾ in. wide, cordate at base; verticillasters few-fld., loose; calyx ¼ in., teeth acute to acuminate, corolla bluish, to ½ in. long. Eur.; widely naturalized in N. Amer. usually in damp soil. May be used as a ground cover, but in many places it is a serious lawn and garden weed.

GLEDITSIA L. HONEY LOCUST. *Leguminosae* (subfamily *Caesalpinioideae*). About 12 spp. of deciduous trees of wide distribution, usually armed with stout spines; lvs. alt., odd-pinnate, 1- or 2-pinnate, often both on same tree, lfts. crenulate; fls. small, greenish, mostly in spikelike racemes, unisexual or bisexual, sepals and petals 3–5, stamens 6–10; fr. a large, flat legume, tardily or not dehiscent.

Most species have a very durable timber, often used, where native, for posts, etc. Planted as specimens and for shade. Propagated by seeds soaked in hot water before planting, or cultivars budded on *G. triacanthos.*

amorphoides (Griseb.) Taub. To 40 ft., differing from *G. triacanthos* in having a smaller number of pinnae and lfts., and straight or curved fr. to 3 in. long and about 1 in. wide with few seeds. Warm-temp. S. Amer.

aquatica Marsh. WATER LOCUST, SWAMP L. To 60 ft., with simple, somewhat flattened spines to 5 in. long; lvs. simply pinnate, with lfts. in 6–9 pairs, ovate-oblong, 1 in. long, and also 2-pinnate, with 3–4 pairs of pinnae; racemes to 4 in. long; fr. thin, ovate, 1–2 in. long, 1–2-seeded. S.C. to Fla. and Tex.

caspica Desf. To 40 ft., very spiny, young branchlets green; fr. straight or curved, to 8 in. long. Azerbaijan, n. Iran.

japonica Miq. To 70 ft., with simple or branched, somewhat flattened spines to 4 in. long, young branchlets purplish; lfts. obtuse or emarginate, to 2¼ in. long; fr. flat, twisted, to 1 ft. long. Japan, China. Zone 8.

sinensis Lam. To 40 ft., with cylindrical, sometimes branched spines; lvs. very rarely 2-pinnate; fr. to 7 in. long, convex, not twisted. China. Zone 8.

triacanthos L. HONEY LOCUST, SWEET L., HONEYSHUCK. To 140 ft., spines somewhat flattened, simple or 3-branched, to 4 in. long, on trunks and brs.; pinnate lvs. with lfts. in 10–15 pairs, oblong-lanceolate, to 1⁵⁄₁₆ in. long, 2-pinnate lvs. with 4–7 pairs of pinnae and lfts. to ¾ in. long; racemes to 2¾ in. long; fr. flat, to 1½ in. long, finally twisted. E. U.S. Var. **elegantissima** (Grosd.) Rehd. Unarmed, of dense bushy habit; lfts. smaller. Var. **inermis** Willd. More or less unarmed. Var. **nana** (Loud.) A. Henry. Small shrub or tree of compact habit and rather small, broad lfts. Several cvs. offered produce no fr. or produce neither spines nor fr.

GLEICHENIA Sm. *Gleicheniaceae.* Ten spp. of thicket-forming, trop. ferns with long, creeping rhizomes; lvs. leathery, 2-pinnate or apparently dichotomous and then pinnate; sori on lower surface of pinnules, solitary, usually of 4 sporangia.

For culture see *Ferns.*

dichotoma: *G. linearis.*

flabellata R. Br. Lvs. "branched" dichotomously, then pinnatifid, pinnules linear. Australia, Tasmania, New Zeal., New Caledonia.

linearis (Burm.f.) C. B. Clarke [*G. dichotoma* Hook.]. SAVANNAH FERN. Rachis zigzag, repeatedly 2- or 3-"branched," ultimate "branches" bearing a pair of forked pinnae. Malay Pen. to Sumatra.

GLEICHENIACEAE (R. Br.) K. Presl. GLEICHENIA FAMILY. Ferns; 5 genera and about 150 spp. of rhizomatous,

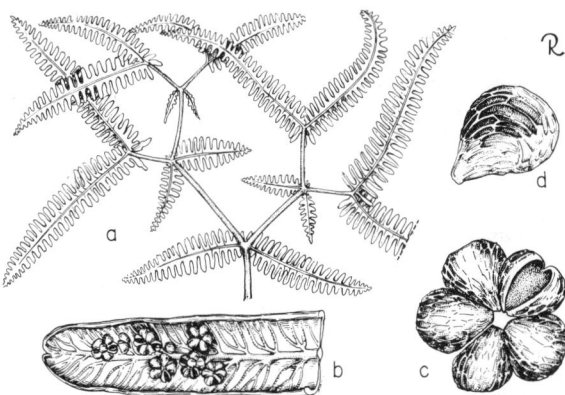

GLEICHENIACEAE. *Gleichenia flexuosa* (Schrad.) Mett.: **a,** portion of leaf, × ¼; **b,** pinnule, underside with sori, × 5; **c,** sorus, × 30; **d,** sporangium, × 40. (Species representative, but not in general cultivation; from Lawrence, *Taxonomy of Vascular Plants.*)

thicket-forming, sun-loving ferns of the tropics and subtropics; lvs. with continuous growth, pinnate or seemingly dichotomously forked by repeated abortion of the growing point, the pinnae pinnate; sori with 2–15 large sporangia, indusia absent, annulus obliquely horizontal. *Gleichenia* is cult.

GLIRICIDIA HBK. *Leguminosae* (subfamily *Faboideae*). About 6–10 spp. of small, unarmed trees and shrubs of trop. Amer.; lvs. alt., odd-pinnate; fls. mostly pink, papilionaceous, in axillary racemes, standard orbicular, reflexed, stamens 10, 9 united and 1 separate; fr. a narrow, flattened, dehiscent legume.

Showy in flower; one species much planted in warm countries for shade, living fences, etc. Easily propagated by cuttings or seeds.

maculata: *G. sepium.*

sepium (Jacq.) Kunth ex Walp. [*G. maculata* (HBK) Steud.]. MADRE, NICARAGUAN COCOA-SHADE. Deciduous tree, to 30 ft., young branchlets pubescent; lfts. in 4–7 pairs, to 2¾ in. long and 1 in. wide; racemes many-fld., to 4 in. long; petals to ¾ in. long, rose-pink to nearly white; fr. nearly woody, to 6 in. long, ½ in. wide. Trop. Amer., where widely planted as shade for coffee and cacao plants. Lvs., bark, and seeds are poisonous if eaten.

GLOBBA L. *Zingiberaceae.* Over 70 spp. of per., rhizomatous herbs in Asia; sts. leafy; infl. terminal, erect or decurved, often with a few sterile bracts at base, with few to many brs. in axils of small to prominent primary bracts, each br. with few to many fls. in a cincinnus; calyx 3-lobed, corolla tube slender, longer than calyx, 3-lobed, staminodes as long as corolla lobes or to twice as long, staminodial lip united with fertile stamen to form a tube above point of attachment of staminodes and corolla lobes, stamen filament long, slender, curved, anther often with 2–4 acute spurs, ovary 1-celled, with several ovules on each of 3 parietal placentas; fr. a caps., seeds arillate.

For culture see *Zingiberaceae.*

Winitti C. H. Wright. To 2 ft.; lvs. oblong-lanceolate, cordate at base, minutely hairy and glaucous beneath; infl. pendulous, bracts ovate, lilac-purple, to 1¼ in. long, cincinni 1- to several-fld., peduncled; corolla yellow, tube ⅜ in. long, lip and staminodes orange-yellow, stamen filament ¾ in. long, anther with 2 spurs, ovary glabrous. Thailand.

GLOBULARIA L. *Globulariaceae.* About 20 spp. of per. herbs and subshrubs, native to cent. Eur. and Medit. region; lvs. alt. or in basal rosettes, simple, glabrous; fls. sessile, in dense, involucrate heads, bisexual, irregular, calyx tubular, 5-lobed, corolla tubular, blue, with very short upper lip and deeply 3-lobed lower lip, stamens 4, in 2 pairs, inserted at mouth of corolla tube, ovary superior, 1-celled; fr. dry, 1-seeded, indehiscent, enclosed in the calyx.

Mostly rock garden plants, of easy culture in full sun; flowering in late spring or early summer. Propagated by seeds, the rhizomatous species also by division.

Aphyllanthes Crantz [*G. elongata* Crantz; *G. Willkommii* Nym.]. Differs from *G. vulgaris* in having more slender rootstock, lvs. apically entire to retuse or 3-toothed, the central tooth obtuse and smaller than the lateral ones, calyx lobes at least as long as tube, and central fls. with lower lip of corolla trifid nearly to base. Cent. and s. Eur., Caucasus. A white-fld. plant offered as *G. Willkommii alba* may belong here.

bellidifolia: illegitimate name of variable application; material cult. under this name may be *G. meridionalis* or a variant of *G. cordifolia.*

cordifolia L. Prostrate, evergreen subshrub, forming loose mats 2–6 in. high; lvs. rosulate, glossy, deep green, broadly obovate to spatulate, about 1 in. long and 1/4 in. wide, apically emarginate or more or less 3-toothed, long-petioled; peduncles essentially bractless, fl. heads solitary, terminal, about 3/8 in. across, involucral bracts pilose; calyx tube bristly on angles, at least as long as lobes, lower lip of corolla trifid to middle. S. Eur. Cv. **'Alba'.** Fls. white. Var. **nana:** *G. repens.*

dumulosa O. Schwarz. Low, bushy subshrub, to 30 in. across; lvs. congested toward tips of brs., blades nearly orbicular, to 5/8 in. across, apically acutish or rounded, abruptly narrowed below into a petiole as long as blade; fl. heads terminal, solitary, subsessile, to 1 in. across, involucral bracts aristate-acute, minutely villose; calyx tube very short, lobes hairy, upper lip of corolla deeply bifid, lower lip trifid nearly to throat. Turkey.

elongata: *G. Aphyllanthes.*

incanescens Viv. Shrubby, prostrate, 2–4 in. high, stoloniferous; lvs. blue-green, nearly orbicular, apically mostly retuse, rather thin, long-petioled; peduncles with many leafy acuminate bracts, fl. heads terminal, solitary, about 1/2 in. across; lower lip of corolla deeply trifid, upper lip undivided. N. Italy. One of the more desirable spp.

meridionalis (Podp.) O. Schwarz [*G. bellidifolia* Ten. (1811), not Ten. (1825)]. Differs from *G. repens* in being loosely cespitose, more vigorous, and having lvs. larger, widely lanceolate, to 3 1/2 in. long, fl. heads long-peduncled, outer involucral bracts hairy, calyx lobes about as long as tube. Italy. Cv. **'Alba'.** Fls. white.

nana: *G. repens.*

nudicaulis L. Herb, to 10 in., from nonrhizomatous rootstock; lvs. rosulate, to 8 in. long, blade obovate, apically obtuse, attenuate to petiole; peduncle finally much longer than lvs., fl. heads terminal, solitary, to 1 1/8 in. across, involucral bracts and calyx glabrous; calyx lobes shorter than tube, upper lip of corolla deeply trifid. Spain to Yugoslavia.

repens Lam. [*G. cordifolia* var. *nana* (Lam.) Camb.; *G. nana* Lam.]. Similar to *G. cordifolia,* but smaller and forming dense mats; lvs. narrowly lanceolate, mostly acuminate at apex; peduncles very short, scarcely longer than lvs., outer involucral bracts more or less glabrous on inner surface; calyx tube densely hairy, much shorter than lobes, lower lip of corolla divided only 1/3 its length. S. Eur.

stygia Orph. Subshrub, 1–2 in. high, forming open mats, rhizomes subterranean; lvs. congested, to about 3/8 in. long, nearly orbicular, apically mucronulate, truncate or rarely slightly retuse, basally abruptly attenuate into winged petiole; fl. heads terminal, solitary, 1/2 in. across, almost sessile at flowering, involucral bracts obtuse, glabrous on inner surface; calyx lobes at least 1 1/2 times as long as tube, marginally bristly with long white hairs. Greece.

trichosantha Fisch. & C. A. Mey. GLOBE DAISY. Cespitose herb, to 1 ft. across; lvs. rosulate, spatulate-obovate, obtusely 3-toothed apically; peduncles to about 6 in. long at flowering, elongating to 1 ft. in fr., bracts subsessile, broad- to linear-lanceolate, fl. heads terminal, solitary; corolla lobes very long and narrow, upper lip bifid. E. Bulgaria, Turkey, Crimea.

vulgaris L. To 1 ft., rootstock stout, nonrhizomatous; lvs. rosulate, obovate or elliptic, to 1 in. wide, apically rounded and usually with 3–5 spinescent teeth of equal size or the median longest, basally tapering to long petioles; peduncles with many leafy bracts, fl. heads terminal, solitary, to 3/4 in. across, involucral bracts aristate; calyx lobes acute, typically shorter than tube, lower lip of corolla trifid 2/3 its length. Spain, s. France, Balearic Is., s. Sweden.

Willkommii: *G. Aphyllanthes.*

GLOBULARIACEAE DC. GLOBULARIA FAMILY. Dicot.; 3 genera of herbs and shrubs, native to s. Eur. and sw. Asia; lvs. alt., simple; fls. in dense, bracted heads, bisexual, calyx 5-parted, corolla 2-lipped, stamens 4, inserted on the corolla, ovary superior, 1-celled; fr. a nutlet, enclosed in the calyx. Only *Globularia* is cult.

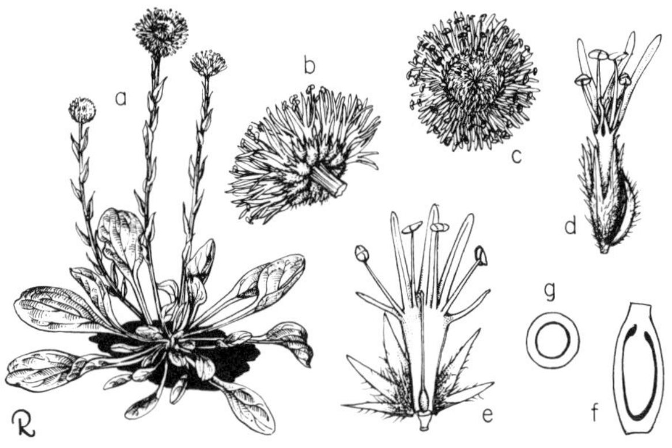

GLOBULARIACEAE. *Globularia Aphyllanthes:* **a,** flowering plant, × 1/6; **b,** flower head, lower side, × 1; **c,** flower head, face view, × 1; **d,** flower with bract, × 3; **e,** flower, with calyx and corolla expanded, × 3; **f,** ovary, vertical section, × 20; **g,** ovary, cross section, × 20.

GLORIOSA L. GLORIOSA LILY, GLORY L., CLIMBING L. *Liliaceae.* Five or 6 spp. of tuberous, climbing, per. herbs, native to Afr. and Asia; sts. weak, clambering; lvs. alt., opp., or whorled, usually with a coiled, tendril-like tip; fls. yellow to red or purple, showy, on long pedicels from upper lf. axils, perianth segms. 6, separate, spreading or reflexed, margins often wavy and crisped, stamens 6, anthers versatile, style bent at base at right angles to ovary; fr. a loculicidal, 3-valved caps., seeds bright red.

Gloriosa lilies are grown under glass, and outdoors in the South. Tubers should be potted from Jan. to Mar. for bloom in summer and autumn. Propagated by seeds, offsets, or division of tubers.

Carsonii Bak. To 3 ft.; lvs. oblong-lanceolate to ovate-lanceolate, to 5 in. long; fls. purple-red with yellow center, perianth segms. oblanceolate, to 2 1/2 in. long, strongly reflexed, wavy along margins. Cent. Afr.

Greeneae: a listed name of no botanical standing, applied to a yellow-fld. plant, perhaps only a color form of *G. Carsonii* or *G. Rothschildiana.*

Plantii: *G. simplex.*

Roehrsiana: a listed name of no botanical standing, for a plant of garden origin, probably a form of *G. Rothschildiana.*

Rothschildiana O'Brien. To 8 ft.; lvs. lanceolate to ovate-lanceolate, 5–7 in. long; fls. crimson, yellow and whitish on margins and at base, perianth segms. oblong-lanceolate to ovate-lanceolate, to 3 in. long, strongly reflexed and recurved, flat or wavy along margins. Trop. Afr.

simplex L. [*G. Plantii* Loud.; *G. virescens* Lindl. ex Sims]. To 4 ft.; lvs. ovate-lanceolate, to 6 in. long; fls. greenish, changing to yellow and red, perianth segms. broadly oblanceolate, to 2 in. long, flat or wavy but not crisped along margins. Trop. Afr.

superba L. To 5 ft. or more; lvs. oblong-lanceolate to ovate-lanceolate, 4–6 in. long; fls. yellow, changing to red, perianth segms. linear to narrowly lanceolate, to 3 in. long, usually reflexed, wavy and much crisped along margins. Trop. Afr. and Asia. Cv. **'Lutea'.** Fls. clear yellow.

Verschuurii T. Hoog. To 5 ft.; lvs. lanceolate to narrowly ovate, to 8 in. long; fls. crimson, yellow on margins and at base, perianth segms. oblanceolate, straight and reflexed, wavy along margins. Nativity unknown; perhaps E. Afr.

virescens: *G. simplex.*

GLOTTIPHYLLUM Haw. ex N. E. Br. TONGUELEAF. *Aizoaceae.* About 58 spp. of dwarf, succulent, per. herbs, native to S. Afr.; lvs. 2-ranked or obliquely 4-ranked, crowded, 4 or more on a shoot, subequal or unequal in each pair, obliquely tongue-shaped to nearly cylindrical, often with a swelling at base on upper side, pulpy and soft, brownish or glossy green, some spp. with translucent dots; fls. solitary, bractless, calyx 4-lobed or rarely 5-lobed, petals yellow or rarely white, many, stamens many, staminodes absent, ovary inferior, 8–20-celled, style absent, stigmas 8–20, radiating, plumose; fr. an 8–20-valved caps., each valve with awnlike tips, expanding keels wingless, brown, each cell roofed with rigid wings, placental tubercles present.

Free-flowering plants of easy propagation by seeds or cuttings, growing chiefly during late spring and early summer. Plant outside when soil temperature permits, in a sunny place; best kept in pots in mixture of heavy loam and sand; overwinter in a cool, frost-free location. See also *Succulents.*

depressum (Haw.) N. E. Br. FIG MARIGOLD. Lvs. 6–8 on a shoot, 2-ranked and lying nearly flat, very crowded, green, to 4 in. long, 1 in. wide, ½ in. thick, elongate, obliquely keeled, rounded-angled in section, curved upward at tip; fls. 2¼ in. across, on pedicels ¾ in. long, petals yellow. S. Afr.

linguiforme (L.) N. E. Br. Lvs. 2-ranked, glossy, green, to 2⅝ in. long, 1¾ in. wide, bluntly rounded at apex; fls. to 2¾ in. across, nearly sessile, petals golden-yellow. S. Afr. Most of the plants in cult. are hybrids.

Nelii Schwant. Brs. more or less prostrate; lvs. 2-ranked, light green, to 2 in. long, ¾ in. wide, ½ in. thick, the longer lf. with upper side flat, obliquely keeled, tip rounded and slightly hooklike, shorter lf. bent upward, tip and margins rounded; fls. 1½ in. across, sessile, petals golden-yellow. Cape Prov.

oligocarpum L. Bolus. Brs. prostrate or creeping; lvs. 4, 2-ranked, unequal, spreading, indistinctly fine-velvety, whitish to olive, with definite, slightly prominent dots crowded near apex, to 1¾ in. long, ⅞ in. wide and ⅜ in. thick at center, upper side flat, apex blunt, smaller lf. widely rounded; fls. to 2⅜ in. across, on pedicels ½ in. long, petals yellow. Cape Prov.

semicylindricum (Haw.) N. E. Br. Sts. small, brs. stiffly spreading in age; lvs. 4–6, 4-ranked, glossy, green, covered with slightly prominent dots, to 2 in. long and ¼ in. across, more or less prostrate and curved, slightly bent upward, united basally into a short sheath, semicylindrical, compressed laterally, keeled apically, tip prolonged, upper side flat or concave, margins with small toothlike projections at the center; fls. 1¾ in. across, on pedicels to 1 in. long, petals golden-yellow. Cape Prov.

Starkeae L. Bolus. Lvs. spreading, 2-ranked, unequal, green, turned with one edge lying on the ground, to 3 in. long, elongate, blunt at the end or truncate and obliquely tapering, obscurely bristle-tipped, upper margin flatly compressed at tip and impressed into the larger lf. when young, to ⅝ in. wide or rarely more, ¼ in. thick; fls. to 3¼ in. across, on pedicels 3/16 in. long, petals golden-yellow. Cape Prov.

×**GLOXINANTHA** R. E. Lee: *Gloxinia* × *Smithiantha. Gesneriaceae.* A hybrid genus with one or more cvs. but no named "spp."

×**GLOXINERA:** *SINNINGIA.*

GLOXINIA L'Hér. *Gesneriaceae.* A few spp. of per. herbs in Cent. and S. Amer., with scaly rhizomes; lvs. opp., toothed; fls. solitary in axils of lvs. or sometimes oppositely arranged in racemes with reduced lvs., calyx 5-lobed, corolla funnelform to campanulate, blue, lavender, white, or pink, stamens 4, borne at base of corolla tube, filaments recoiled when pollen is shed, anthers united in a starlike cluster, disc ringlike, ovary inferior; fr. a caps. The generic name has long been used in hort. for spp. and hybrids that properly belong to the genus *Sinningia.*

Propagated by the scaly rhizomes. For cultivation see *Gesneriaceae.*

crassifolia: *Sinningia speciosa,* Fyfiana Group.

fimbriata: *Achimenes glabrata.*

gymnostoma Griseb. [*Achimenes gymnostoma* (Griseb.) Fritsch]. To 2 ft., with slender, scaly stolons borne at base of st.; lvs. ovate, to 3 in. long, 1¾ in. wide, thin, hairy; fls. solitary in axils, long-pedicelled, calyx lobes very narrowly triangular, ½ in. long, corolla funnelform, 1⅜ in. long, rose-pink, limb spotted with darker red, 5-lobed, upper 2 lobes shorter than lower 3. Argentina.

×**hybrida:** *Sinningia speciosa,* Fyfiana Group.

macrophylla: *Sinningia speciosa,* Fyfiana Group.

perennis (L.) Druce. CANTERBURY-BELLS G. To 2½ ft., nearly glabrous; lvs. ovate, to 7 in. long, 6 in. wide, coarsely crenate, deep green above, paler or reddish beneath; fls. solitary in axils of normal or reduced lvs. in a terminal raceme, calyx with 10 grooves, lobes broad, corolla lavender, with dark violet spot in the strongly pouched base, filaments densely glandular-hairy. Colombia to Peru.

regina: a listed name for *Sinningia regina.*

tigrina: *Sinningia speciosa,* Fyfiana Group.

violacea: *Sinningia speciosa,* Fyfiana Group.

GLYCINE L. *Leguminosae* (subfamily *Faboideae*). Probably 9–10 spp. of scandent to suberect herbs of warmer parts of the Old World; lvs. of 3 or rarely 5 or 7 lfts.; fls. small, papilionaceous, in axillary racemes, purple or pink, calyx 5-toothed, with upper 2 lobes partly united; fr. a linear legume, constricted between seeds, valves spiral after dehiscence.

Includes the soybean, *G. Max,* one of the oldest and most important crops. Widely grown, mostly for its seeds, the most highly proteinaceous vegetable food known and the source of a valuable oil, raw material, and protein for industry; also valued as a forage, cover, and green-manure crop. Grown under a wide range of soil and moisture conditions, but seeds must be sown after all danger of frost is past. See *Soybean.*

Apios: *Apios americana.*

Max (L.) Merrill [*G. Soja* Hort., not Siebold & Zucc.]. SOYBEAN, SOJA BEAN, SOYA B. Hairy, erect ann., to 6 ft.; lfts. 3, ovate; fls. not conspicuous; fr. to 3 in. long, brown and hairy, pendent. Se. Asia. Widely cult. in the Orient and elsewhere and one of the major agricultural crops in the U.S. Many cvs. are grown.

Soja: see *G. Max.*

GLYCOSMIS Corrêa. *Rutaceae.* About 35 spp. of spineless, evergreen shrubs or trees, native from se. Asia and the Philippine Is. to n. Australia; lvs. usually alt., pinnate, glandular-dotted; fls. small, in axillary, cymose panicles, fragrant, sepals and petals 4 or 5, stamens 8 or 10; fr. a small berry with thin pulp.

Grown under glass or in the open in southern Fla.

citrifolia: *G. parviflora.*

parviflora (Sims) Little [*G. citrifolia* (Willd.) Lindl.]. Shrub or small tree; lfts. 1–5, elliptic or oblong-elliptic, to 8 in. long, lateral veins 12–15; infl. 1–2 in. long, rusty-tomentose when young; fr. white or pinkish, translucent, about 5/16 in. in diam., with 1 or 2 seeds. S. China, Thailand, Indochina.

pentaphylla (Retz.) Corrêa. JAMAICA MANDARIN ORANGE. Shrub or small tree; lfts. usually 5, elliptic to ovate, or obovate, to 4½ in. long, dark green above, pale beneath, lateral veins 5–7; infl. to 1½ in. long, rusty-tomentose; fr. white or pinkish. India and Philippines Is., s. to n. Australia.

GLYCYRRHIZA L. *Leguminosae* (subfamily *Faboideae*). About 12 spp. or more of temp. and subtrop. herbs of widespread distribution; lvs. alt., odd-pinnate; fls. in axillary racemes or spikes shorter than lvs., papilionaceous, stamens 10, 9 united and 1 separate, the alt. anthers smaller; fr. an oblong, flat legume, with 2–4 seeds.

The roots of one species, widely grown in southern Eur. and southwestern Asia, yield commercial licorice, which is used in medicine, in industry, and as a flavoring. The plant thrives in rich moist soil; propagated by division of rootstocks, as well as by seeds.

glabra L. LICORICE, LIQUORICE, SWEETWOOD. To 3 ft., stoloniferous; lfts. in 4–8 pairs, elliptic to oblong, obtuse, viscous beneath; fls. small, bluish or violet; fr. nearly glabrous. Medit. region and cent. and sw. Asia.

GLYPTOSTROBUS Endl. *Taxodiaceae.* One sp., a small, coniferous tree of se. China, differing from *Taxodium* chiefly in having lvs. trimorphic; female cone pear-shaped, scales thin, elongate rather than shield-shaped, coarsely toothed apically; seeds small-winged. In young trees, lvs. on deciduous twigs flat and linear; in older trees, lvs. on deciduous twigs needlelike, lvs. on persistent twigs scalelike.

Sometimes planted as an ornamental. For culture see *Conifers.*

heterophyllus: *G. lineatus.*

lineatus (Poir.) Druce [*G. heterophyllus* (Brongn.) Endl.; *G. pensilis* (D. Don) C. Koch]. CHINESE WATER PINE, CHINESE SWAMP CYPRESS. Lvs. deciduous, those on sterile brs. linear and flat, or needlelike, those on cone-bearing brs. imbricate and scalelike; cones ovoid, ¾ in. long. Zone 9. Some material grown as *Glyptostrobus* has proved to be *Taxodium distichum* var. *nutans.*

pensilis: *G. lineatus.*

GMELINA L. *Verbenaceae.* About 20 spp. of spiny or unarmed trees or shrubs, native to Philippine Is., and e. Asia to n. Australia; lvs. opp., simple, entire to lobed; fls. blue, pale purple, yellow, or brownish, in cymes or racemes often arranged in panicles, calyx 4–5-toothed or entire, corolla 2-lipped, stamens 4; fr. a drupe.

arborea Roxb. Deciduous tree, to 60 ft.; lvs. long-petioled, ovate, to 9 in. long, acuminate, entire, pubescent beneath; fls. brownish-yellow, to 1 in. across, in cymes arranged in a panicle to 1 ft. long; fr. $\frac{3}{4}$ in. long, yellow. India. Zone 10.

asiatica L. [*G. elliptica* Sm.]. Shrub, sometimes spiny; lvs. ovate or obovate, to 4 in. long, entire or coarsely lobed; fls. yellow, in racemes to 2 in. long. India, Ceylon. Zone 10.

elliptica: *G. asiatica.*

GNAPHALIUM L. CUDWEED, EVERLASTING. *Compositae* (Inula Tribe). About 120 spp. of ann. or per. herbs or small shrubs, of cosmopolitan distribution; lvs. alt., simple, entire; fl. heads discoid, in spikes, corymbs, or panicles, involucre ovoid or campanulate, involucral bracts imbricate in several rows, scarious, receptacle flat, naked; fls. all tubular, the inner bisexual, the outer female; achenes oblong, pappus of 1 row of capillary bristles.

californicum DC. Glandular, strongly scented bien., to $2\frac{1}{2}$ ft., often flowering first year; lower lvs. oblong-lanceolate, to 4 in. long, upper lvs. successively reduced upward; heads to $\frac{1}{4}$ in. across, in a corymbose panicle, involucre nearly globose, involucral bracts pearly-white aging to straw-colored; fls. yellowish. Ore. to s. Calif. and adjacent Baja Calif.

norvegicum Gunnerus. Per. herb, to 1 ft.; lvs. lanceolate, to 6 in. long, 3-nerved, reduced in size only above middle of st., green above, gray-felty beneath, acuminate; heads to $\frac{1}{4}$ in. long, in a compact spike, involucral bracts with scarious dark brown margins and central olive stripe; fls. pale brownish. Mts., Eur., Caucasus.

ramosissimum Nutt. Erect, slender, sweet-scented, glandular bien., to 4 ft.; lvs. linear-lanceolate, to $2\frac{3}{8}$ in. long, successively reduced upward; heads to $\frac{3}{16}$ in. long, clustered at ends of brs. of large, terminal panicle, involucre turbinate, involucral bracts pink; fls. yellow. Cent. and s. Calif.

supinum L. Dwarf, tufted per. herb, to 5 in., sometimes higher; lvs. to $\frac{3}{4}$ in. long, woolly, lower lvs. linear-oblanceolate, st. lvs. linear; heads to $\frac{5}{16}$ in. across, solitary or to 8 in a compact, terminal spike; involucre campanulate, involucral bracts with scarious brown margins and central olive stripe. Circumboreal, and mts. of cent. Eur. and w. Asia.

trinerve G. Forst. Per., sts. prostrate or decumbent, to 2 ft. long; lvs. obovate-lanceolate or spatulate, to 1 in. long, glabrous above, white-woolly beneath; heads $\frac{5}{16}$–$\frac{1}{2}$ in. across, in corymbs, involucral bracts white, spreading. New Zeal.

Traversii Hook.f. Dwarf, tufted per., to 4 in.; lvs. linear-spatulate or linear-obovate, to 2 in. long, woolly on both sides; heads to $\frac{1}{2}$ in. across, solitary, involucral bracts scarious, glossy, pale brownish-yellow. New Zeal. Var. **Mackayi** (J. Buchan.) T. Kirk. Plants making small loose mats; lvs. linear-oblong to obovate-spatulate, to $\frac{3}{4}$ in. long; heads to $\frac{3}{16}$ in. across. New Zeal.

GNIDIA L. *Thymelaeaceae.* About 100 spp. of evergreen, often heathlike shrubs, native chiefly to Afr., a few in Madagascar; lvs. usually small, opp. or alt.; fls. usually yellow or white, in terminal clusters, calyx tubular, corollalike.

polystachya Bergius. To 6 ft.; lvs. alt., closely set, linear, to $\frac{1}{4}$ in. long; fls. yellow, many, in rounded clusters to 1 in. across. S. Afr.

GODETIA: *CLARKIA.* **G. Goddardii:** *C. purpurea* subsp. *viminea.* **G. grandiflora** and **G. Lindleyana:** *C. amoena* subsp. *Lindleyi.* **G. quadrivulnera:** *C. purpurea* subsp. **G. viminea:** *C. purpurea* subsp. **G. vinosa:** *C. amoena.* **G. Whitneyi:** *C. amoena* subsp.

GODMANIA Hemsl. *Bignoniaceae.* Two spp. of trees, native to trop. Amer.; lvs. opp., long-petioled, palmately compound, lfts. 5–7; fls. small, many, in dense corymbs, calyx 5-toothed, corolla campanulate-ventricose, slightly 2-lipped, stamens 4; fr. a long, ribbed caps.

aesculifolia (HBK) Standl. To 30 ft.; lfts. ovate to ovate-oblong, to $6\frac{3}{4}$ in. long; fls. to $\frac{1}{2}$ in. long, hairy outside. Mts., s. Mex., s. to Panama and Venezuela.

GOETHEA Nees. *Malvaceae.* Two spp. of shrubs from Brazil; lvs. petioled, ovate to oblong-elliptic, unlobed, entire or sinuate-dentate, prominently stipuled; fls. in umbellate clusters on very short, naked, axillary branchlets, involucral bracts 4, leafy, red, longer than calyx and corolla, calyx 5-lobed, corolla more or less tubelike, petals white, reddish at base, stamens united in a tubular column, the column slightly exserted, with spreading filaments beneath the 5-toothed apex, style brs. 10, slender, stigmas discoid, ovary 5-celled, each cell with 1 ovule.

strictiflora Hook. Glabrate, leafy shrubs, to about 3 ft.; lvs. ovate to ovate-elliptic, to about 8 in. long, sinuate-dentate, especially in upper half, leathery; fls. more or less erect, peduncles to about $\frac{5}{8}$ in. long, involucral bracts erect, cordate to triangular or ovate, to 1 in. long, yellowish-white at the base, becoming reddish-striate then red at margin and apex, calyx and petals to about $\frac{1}{2}$ in. long, style brs. to $1\frac{1}{4}$ in. long.

GOLDFUSSIA: *STROBILANTHES.*

GOMESA R. Br. *Orchidaceae.* Twelve spp. of epiphytes of Brazil; sts. pseudobulbous, 1–3-lvd.; infl. lateral, arching or pendent, racemose, several-fld.; fls. small, upper sepal and petals nearly alike, lateral sepals united, lip geniculate, the basal part parallel with column. For structure of fl. see *Orchidaceae.*

For culture see *Orchids.*

planifolia Klotzsch. Pseudobulbs to about 2 in. long; racemes from base of pseudobulbs, pendent, to 10 in. long, many-fld.; fls. to $\frac{1}{2}$ in. across, greenish-yellow, fragrant, lateral sepals partly united, lip yellow, with 2 crests. Late summer, autumn–late winter. Brazil.

GOMPHOCARPUS R. Br. *Asclepiadaceae.* Not cult. **G. fruticosus:** *Asclepias fruticosa.* **G. physocarpus:** *Asclepias physocarpa.*

GOMPHRENA L. *Amaranthaceae.* More than 100 spp. of erect or prostrate per. and ann. herbs, native to trop. Amer., Australia, se. Asia; fls. in dense chaffy heads, bisexual, perianth 5-lobed or 5-parted, stamens 5, filaments united into a tube, anthers 2-celled, ovule 1; fr. a utricle.

Useful for bedding, for cut fls., and for winter decoration. Grown readily from seeds.

globosa L. GLOBE AMARANTH. Ann., to $1\frac{1}{2}$ ft., erect, branching, somewhat stiff; lvs. oblong to elliptic, to 4 in. long, ciliate; fl. heads subtended by 2 leafy bracts, purple, orange, rose, white, or variegated, about 1 in. across. Old World tropics. Cv. **'Rubra'** is listed.

Haageana Klotzsch. Per., but grown as ann., to $2\frac{1}{2}$ ft.; lvs. oblanceolate to oblong-linear, to 4 in. long; heads subtended by 2 bracts, light red with yellow florets, 1 in. across. Tex., Mex.

GONATANTHUS Klotzsch. *Araceae.* Two spp. of tender, tuberous, stemless herbs of Himalayas, with slender, stolonlike shoots bearing clusters of bulbils; lvs. few, peltate, notched at base; fls. unisexual, perianth absent, spathe convolute, the blade long, slender, bent away from the basal part, which is short, inflated, constricted between the zones of female and male fls. of spadix.

Tender; for culture see *Caladium.*

pumilus (D. Don) Engl. & Kurt Krause [*G. sarmentosus* Klotzsch]. To about 2 ft.; lf. blades ovate, to 10 in. long, petioles longer; spathes to 12 in. long, yellow, becoming greenish toward base. Se. Asia.

sarmentosus: *G. pumilus.*

GONGORA Ruiz & Pav. *Orchidaceae.* About 20 spp. of epiphytes of Cent. and S. Amer.; pseudobulbs ovoid, 2-lvd.; lvs. upright, plicate; scapes lateral, bearing pendent, several- to many-fld. racemes; upper sepal united to column, lateral sepals united to column foot, petals smaller than sepals, united to column, lip continuous with column foot, fleshy, 3-lobed, lateral lobes erect, with horns or bristles, midlobe often pointed, column slender, without wings. For structure of fl. see *Orchidaceae.*

Temperate greenhouse. For culture see *Orchids.*

armeniaca (Lindl.) Rchb.f. [*Acropera armeniaca* Lindl.]. Pseudobulbs to $2\frac{1}{2}$ in. long; lvs. lanceolate-elliptic; scapes to about 20-fld.; fls. fragrant, sepals reflexed, apricot-colored or salmon, with reddish-purple spots, petals very small, lip inflated, yellow and fleshy. Early summer–early autumn. Cent. Amer.

atropurpurea: *G. quinquenervis.*

galeata (Lindl.) Rchb.f. [*Acropera Loddigesii* Lindl.; *Maxillaria galeata* Lindl.]. Pseudobulbs about 1¾ in. long; lvs. to 1 ft. long and 1¾ in. wide; racemes to 8 in. long; fls. nearly globose, brownish-yellow or wine-colored, on arching pedicels. Early summer–early autumn. Mex.

maculata: *G. quinquenervis.*

quinquenervis Ruiz & Pav. [*G. atropurpurea* Hook.; *G. maculata* Lindl.; *G. tricolor* Rchb.f.]. Pseudobulbs ovoid-oblong, furrowed; lvs. elliptic-lanceolate; racemes to over 2 ft. long, loosely fld.; fls. variable in color, commonly yellow, spotted with dark red, sepals reflexed, petals arching, curved. Winter–early autumn, late autumn. Trop. Amer.

speciosa: *Coryanthes speciosa.*

tricolor: *G. quinquenervis.*

truncata Lindl. Similar to *G. galeata* in habit; fls. whitish or straw-colored, with brownish-purple transverse markings, lip clear, varnished yellow. Late autumn–late spring. Mex.

GONIOLIMON Boiss. *Plumbaginaceae.* About 20 spp. of per. herbs with woody root crown, mostly in the U.S.S.R., extending e. to Mongolia, also in N. Afr.; lvs. in basal rosettes; fls. in 2–6-fld. spikelets, these borne on terminal, sometimes more or less angled or winged brs. of compound panicles or corymbs on scapes; calyx narrowly or broadly funnelform, scarious, white, corolla violet-rose, usually slightly longer than calyx, united only at base, stamens 5, styles 5, separate, hairy below, stigmas capitate. Related to *Limonium*, but styles hairy and stigmas capitate.

callicomum (C. A. Mey.) Boiss. [*Limonium callicomum* (C. A. Mey.) O. Kuntze; *Statice callicoma* C. A. Mey.; *S. incana* Ledeb., not L. or Bieb.]. To 2 ft., caudex somewhat thickened by old lf. remnants; lvs. oblong-elliptic to lanceolate, to 2 in. long, mucronate; fl. scapes 2–6 or more, branched in upper ½–⅔, brs. angled or scarcely winged, spikes rather loose; calyx broadly funnelform. Siberia.

speciosum (L.) Boiss. [*Limonium speciosum* (L.) O. Kuntze; *Statice speciosa* L.]. To 2 ft., caudex strongly thickened by old lf. remnants; lvs. broadly lanceolate to rounded-obovate, to 3 in. long or more, apiculate-cuspidate, tapering to a broad, flat petiole; fl. scapes 1 or 2, erect, angled or winged, infl. corymbose-paniculate, with spikelets 2–3-fld., in short, dense spikes; calyx ⁵⁄₁₆ in. long, petals pink, longer than calyx. Ural Mts., (se. Russia), Soviet cent. Asia, Siberia.

tataricum (L.) Boiss. [*Limonium tataricum* (L.) Mill.; *Statice tatarica* L.]. To 18 in., caudex thickened by old lf. remnants; lvs. broadly lanceolate to oblong-obovate, to 6 in. long or more, gradually narrowed to a broad, flat petiole; fl. scapes 1 or 2, rarely more, infl. dichotomously branched, brs. angled, spikelets 2–3-fld., in 1-sided short spikes; calyx ⁵⁄₁₆ in. long, petals rose-pink, longer than calyx. N. Afr., s. Eur., Caucasus, Russia.

GONOLOBUS Michx. [*Vincetoxicum* Walt., not N. M. Wolf]. ANGLEPOD. *Asclepiadaceae.* Over 100 spp. of twining herbs, native to the Americas; lvs. opp., mostly cordate-ovate; fls. in axillary, peduncled, umbellate or corymbose cymes, 5-merous, corolla deeply divided, lobes longer than broad, corona disclike or cup-shaped, shorter than or about equalling stigma, anthers with spreading, more or less laminate, fleshy dorsal appendages; fr. an angled or winged follicle.

carolinensis: *Matelea carolinensis.*

gonocarpos (Walt.) L. M. Perry [*Vincetoxicum gonocarpos* Walt.]. Lvs. oblong-ovate to round, to 8 in. long; corolla about 1 in. across, brownish-purple to greenish-purple, lobes linear-lanceolate, about 3 times as long as calyx lobes; follicles to 5 in. long with prominent, scarcely winged angles. Autumn. Se. U.S.

laevis: *Cynanchum laeve.*

GOODENIACEAE R. Br. GOODENIA FAMILY. Dicot.; perhaps 13 genera of herbs and shrubs, mostly native to Australia, a few pantrop.; sap not milky; fls. irregular, bisexual, calyx and corolla 5-lobed, stamens many, ovary inferior or rarely superior, 1–2-celled, stigmas subtended by a small pollen-collecting cup; fr. a caps., drupe, or nut. Closely allied to the *Lobeliaceae*, but differing in having clear sap and a pollen-collecting cup around stigmas. *Scaevola* is occasionally cult.

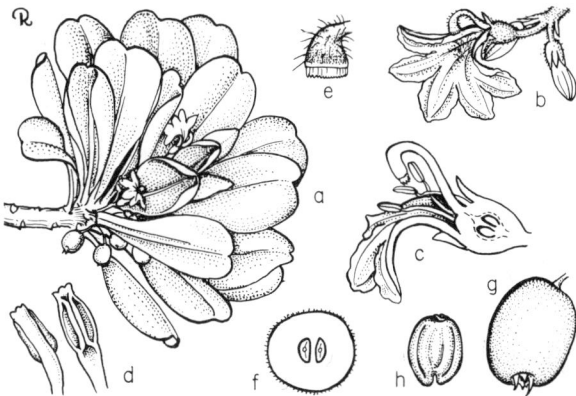

GOODENIACEAE. *Scaevola frutescens:* **a,** flowering and fruiting branch, × ½; **b,** flower and bud, × 1; **c,** flower, vertical section, × 2; **d,** anther, two views, × 5; **e,** stigma, × 3; **f,** ovary, cross section, × 3; **g,** fruit, × 1; **h,** seed, × 1.

GOODYERA R. Br. [*Peramium* Salisb.]. RATTLESNAKE PLANTAIN, LATTICELEAF. *Orchidaceae.* About 40 spp. of cosmopolitan, terrestrial, rhizomatous herbs; sts. leafy; lvs. often variegated; infl. terminal, racemose or spicate, many-fld.; sepals and petals meeting at tips, forming a helmet, lip distinctly saccate, column short. For structure of fl. see *Orchidaceae.*

Grown in shady places outdoors. For culture see *Orchids.*

Dawsonii: *Haemaria discolor* var. *Dawsoniana.*

decipiens: *G. oblongifolia.*

Menziesii: *G. oblongifolia.*

oblongifolia Raf. [*G. decipiens* (Hook.) F. T. Hubb.; *G. Menziesii* Lindl.; *Epipactis decipiens* (Hook.) Ames]. GIANT R. P., MENZIES' R. P. To 17 in.; lvs. in a basal rosette, to 4 in. long, dark green, veined with white; raceme strongly 1-sided or spiralled, to 6 in. long, densely fld.; fls. small, white, tinged with green. Summer. N. Amer.

pubescens (Willd.) R. Br. [*Epipactis pubescens* (Willd.) A. A. Eat.]. DOWNY R. P., SCROFULA WEED, DOWNY RATTLESNAKE ORCHID. To 16 in.; lvs. 3–8 in a basal rosette, to 3 in. long, dark green with white reticulations; raceme to 5 in. long, densely many-fld.; fls. globose, small, white, pubescent. Summer. E. N. Amer.

repens (L.) R. Br. [*Epipactis repens* (L.) Crantz]. DWARF R. P., NORTHERN R. P., LESSER R. P. To 1 ft.; lvs. to about 1¾ in. long, dark green, unicolored or with indistinct white veins; spikes 1-sided; fls. nearly globose, small, white. Summer. N. Eurasia, Japan, n. N. Amer. Var. **ophioides** Fern. WHITE-BLOTCHED R. P., NETLEAF, SQUIRREL-EAR. Lvs. distinctly white-veined. Nfld. to N.C., w. to Alaska and Minn.

Schlechtendaliana Rchb.f. Sts. to 10 in. long, from a rhizome; lvs. to 1½ in. long, green with white reticulations; infl. to 4 in. long, 7–12-fld., hairy; fls. half open, white to rose, lip nearly as long as sepals. Late summer. Japan, Korea, China.

tesselata Lodd. [*Epipactis tesselata* (Lodd.) A. A. Eat.]. CHECKERED R. P., SMOOTH R. P. To about 14 in.; lvs. to 2½ in. long, dark green, veined with lighter green; spikes somewhat loosely 1-sided or spiral; fls. ovoid, small, whitish. Summer–early autumn. E. N. Amer.

velutina Maxim. Sts. to 6 in. long; lvs. several, to 1½ in. long, deep green and purple, with white markings along midvein; infl. 4–10-fld.; fls. small, whitish, soft-hairy. Late summer. Korea, Japan.

GOOSEBERRY. See *Currant and Gooseberry.*

GORDONIA Ellis. *Theaceae.* About 30 spp. of evergreen trees and shrubs of warmer parts of Asia and s. U.S.; lvs. alt., simple, leathery; fls. solitary, axillary, on long peduncles, bisexual, sepals and petals 5, calyx persistent, at least in young fr., stamens many, filaments united at base, anthers versatile, ovary 3–5-celled; fr. a woody caps., seeds 2–8 in each cell, flat, winged at one end.

Hardy in the southern states; plants succeed in moist peaty or sandy soil. Propagated by seeds, layering, or greenwood cuttings under glass.

Alatamaha: *Franklinia Alatamaha.*

anomala: *G. axillaris.*

axillaris (Roxb. ex Ker-Gawl.) D. Dietr. [*G. anomala* K. Spreng.].

Large shrub or small tree; lvs. elliptic-oblong to oblanceolate, to 6 in. long and 1½ in. wide, apically blunt, remotely toothed in upper part, dark green above; fls. white, to 3 in. across, nearly sessile, stamens golden; fr. 1–1½ in. long. Taiwan to Vietnam. Zone 9.

Lasianthus (L.) Ellis. LOBLOLLY BAY, BAY, BLACK LAUREL. Tree, to 90 ft.; lvs. lanceolate to elliptic, to 6 in. long, acute, serrate in upper half, dark green and glossy above; fls. white, to 2½ in. across, peduncle 2–3 in. long; fr. to ¾ in. long. Summer. N.C., s. to Fla. and Miss. Zone 7b. Yields a cabinet wood.

GORMANIA: *SEDUM.* **G. Watsonii:** *S. oregonense.*

GOSSYPIUM L. [*Thurberia* A. Gray]. COTTON. *Malvaceae.* Thirty-two spp. of coarse ann. herbs, shrubs, or small trees in warm-temp. and trop. regions of the world; herbage irregularly dotted with black oil glands, lvs. simple, entire, sometimes unlobed but more generally palmately lobed or parted; fls. 1 or several, axillary, involucral bracts 3, usually leafy and persistent, lacerate or sometimes entire, calyx cup-shaped, truncate at apex to 5-lobed, petals white to yellow or purple-red, often spotted purple-red toward the base, longer than staminal column, ovary 3–5-celled, each cell 2- to many-ovuled, style unbranched, stigmas coherent or slightly spreading; fr. a woody to papery, loculicidally dehiscent caps., seeds usually covered with close tomentum (fuzz) and sometimes also with a loose, woolly tomentum (lint).

Cotton is grown commercially as an annual field crop from the southeastern U.S. westward to Calif. It requires a long hot growing season with abundant moisture, followed by dry weather for harvesting. It is not commonly grown as an ornamental plant nor does it thrive in northern regions under glass.

arboreum L. [*G. indicum* Tod.; *G. obtusifolium* Roxb.]. TREE C. Puberulent ann. or per. herb or shrub, to 10 ft. or more; lvs. deeply 3-, 5-, or 7-lobed, lobes ovate to linear; involucral bracts to about 1 in. long, ovate, entire or few-toothed, closely investing the bud, corolla pale yellow to deep red-purple, usually spotted purple-red at the base; caps. oblong-acute, profusely glandular-pitted, to 1 in. long, 3- or rarely 4-celled, each cell 6–17-seeded, seeds generally with both fuzz and lint. Wild and cult. throughout tropics and subtropics of Asia.

barbadense L. [*G. peruvianum* Cav.; *G. vitifolium* Lam.]. SEA ISLAND C., TREE C. Shrub or ann. subshrub, 3–9 ft., glabrous to rather densely pubescent; lvs. cut ⅔ into 3 or 5 slender, tapering lobes; involucral bracts about as broad as long, to about 2 in. long, lacerate with 10–15 teeth; corolla yellow, often tinged purple, spotted at the base, not widely expanded; caps. to 1½ in. long, gradually tapering to an acute tip, with rough, glandular-pitted surface, 3–4-celled, each cell 5–8-seeded, seeds with copious lint, with or without fuzz. Trop. Amer.; introd. into most cotton growing regions of the world. Var. **braziliense** (Raf.) Fryx. [var. *brasiliense* (Macfady.) Mauer; *G. brasiliense* Macfady.]. KIDNEY C. Caps. over 1½ in. long, lvs. and fl. parts generally larger, seeds usually united. E. trop. S. Amer.; introd. into Cent. Amer., the Antilles, Afr., and India.

brasiliense: *G. barbadense* var. *braziliense.*

herbaceum L. LEVANT C. Sparsely hairy ann. or per. herb, 1–5 ft.; lvs. broadly 3-, 5-, or 7-lobed to about the middle; involucral bracts broadly ovate to triangular, to 1 in. long, sharply 6–8-toothed, flaring from the fl. and fr., corolla yellow, with a purple center, to 2 in. long; caps. ovoid, beaked, mostly about 1 in. long, 3–4-celled, surface with few oil glands, seeds with both lint and fuzz, less than 11 in each cell. Afr., Asia Minor, India.

hirsutum L. [*G. mexicanum* Tod.]. UPLAND C. Ann. or per. herb or shrub, to about 5 ft. or more; lvs. broadly 3- or sometimes 5-lobed in the upper half, sometimes unlobed; involucral bracts ovate, mostly 1½–2½ in. long, lacerate with 7–13 slender teeth, corolla generally whitish to yellow, fading pinkish-purple, to 3 in. long; caps. about 1½ in. long, ovoid, beaked, smooth, with few oil glands, 3–5-celled, seeds 5–11 in each cell, with copious lint and fuzz. Cent. Amer.; introd. into most cotton-growing regions of the world. Var. **punctatum** (Schumach.) J. B. Hutch. [*G. punctatum* Schumach.; *G. religiosum* L.]. Sts. woody, to 9 ft.; fls. smaller, more or less tubelike beneath. Cent. Amer., Gulf Coast to Fla., s. to W. Indies.

indicum: *G. arboreum.*

mexicanum: *G. hirsutum.*

obtusifolium: *G. arboreum.*

peruvianum: *G. barbadense.*

punctatum: *G. hirsutum* var.

religiosum: *G. hirsutum* var. *punctatum.*

Sturtianum Willis [*G. Sturtii* F. J. Muell.]. STURT'S DESERT ROSE. Glaucous, glabrous shrub, sts. many, black-tubercled, 3–9 ft.; lvs. orbicular to ovate, unlobed or shallowly 3-lobed; involucral bracts ovate to triangular, about ⅝ in. long, entire or rarely somewhat lacerate, corolla mauve with purple center, about 3 in. across; caps. ovoid, acute, about ½ in. long, black-punctate, 3–4-celled, seeds 4–6 in each cell, with greenish fuzz, without lint. Australia.

Thurberi Tod. [*Thurberia thespesioides* A. Gray]. ARIZONA WILD C. Glabrate, branching shrub, 3–14 ft.; lvs. palmately 3-, 5-, or 7-lobed, the lobes lanceolate, acuminate, upper lvs. sometimes a simple, lanceolate blade; involucral bracts narrowly ovate, entire, to ⅜ in. long, corolla white or yellowish, purplish beneath, about 1 in. long; caps. ovoid, mucronate, about ⅝ in. long, 3–4-celled, seeds 8–10 in each cell, with fuzz. Ariz. and n. Mex.

vitifolium: *G. barbadense.*

GOURD. A general name applied to any of various fruits —usually those with hard and durable shells—of cucurbits, plants allied to the pumpkins, cucumbers, and melons. The yellow-flowered gourds of American gardens are *Cucurbita Pepo* var. *ovifera;* the white-flowered gourds are *Lagenaria siceraria.* The snake or serpent gourds are either *Lagenaria siceraria* or *Trichosanthes Anguina.* White or wax gourd is *Benincasa hispida.* Dishcloth gourds are *Luffa,* mostly *L. aegyptiaca.* The maté gourd of Paraguay, used as a utensil, is a small form of *Lagenaria siceraria.* Gooseberry gourd is *Cucumis Anguria,* hedgehog gourd *C. dipsaceus,* and ivy gourd *Coccinia grandis.* Calabash gourds are *Lagenaria siceraria,* but the calabash itself is not a gourd but the fruit of a tropical tree, *Crescentia Cujete.* Sometimes the word gourd is applied in a general way to all the cultivated species of *Cucurbita.* In North America, the word is employed for fruits grown as ornaments or curiosities rather than for food.

All the gourds denoted above are annual plants (or treated as such) of the simplest cultivation, requiring the treatment accorded pumpkins, cucumbers, and melons. Seeds are commonly sown where the plants are to stand, as soon as the weather is warm and settled. If wanted earlier, they may be started in pots or boxes, but they do not transplant readily if the roots are disturbed. All of them are frost-tender. The vines make good screens and covers if given support. See *Cucurbita, Pumpkin.*

GOURLIEA Gillies ex Hook. *Leguminosae* (subfamily *Faboideae*). One sp., a tender, spiny shrub of s. S. Amer.; lvs. even-pinnate; fls. showy, papilionaceous, stamens 10, separate; fr. a nearly drupaceous, ovoid-subglobose legume, 1-seeded.

chilensis: *G. decorticans.*

decorticans Gillies ex Hook. [*G. chilensis* Clos]. CHANAL, CHANAR. To 20 ft., with many spines to 5/16 in. long; lfts. in 3–5 pairs, oblong, ¼ in. long; fls. orange-yellow, streaked red, in loose racemes to ¾ in. long; fr. brownish, about 1 in. in diam., edible. Chile, Argentina, s. Peru.

GRAFTING. In horticulture, grafting is the practice of causing parts of plants to unite, usually a part of one plant with another of the same species or of a closely related species, although parts of the same individual may sometimes unite in nature or be united in cultivation. Grafting is used to propagate cultivars that are not easily propagated by other methods; to combine in one plant the desirable qualities of two or more, as fruit trees on dwarfing stocks, or wine grapes on disease-resistant stocks, or more than one cultivar on a single stock; or to repair damage. Most commonly, a detached part of one plant (the scion) is grafted to the rooted part of another (the stock), which may be a seedling or a clonal propagation. Less frequently, parts of adjacent plants are joined while both plants retain their identity until the union is formed. Approach grafting, as the latter method is called, is used when plants otherwise unite only slowly and with difficulty. Successful grafting requires that the cambium of the grafted plants grow together, the cambium being the new and growing tissue under the bark and outside the wood. (For this reason monocotyledons, which lack a cambium

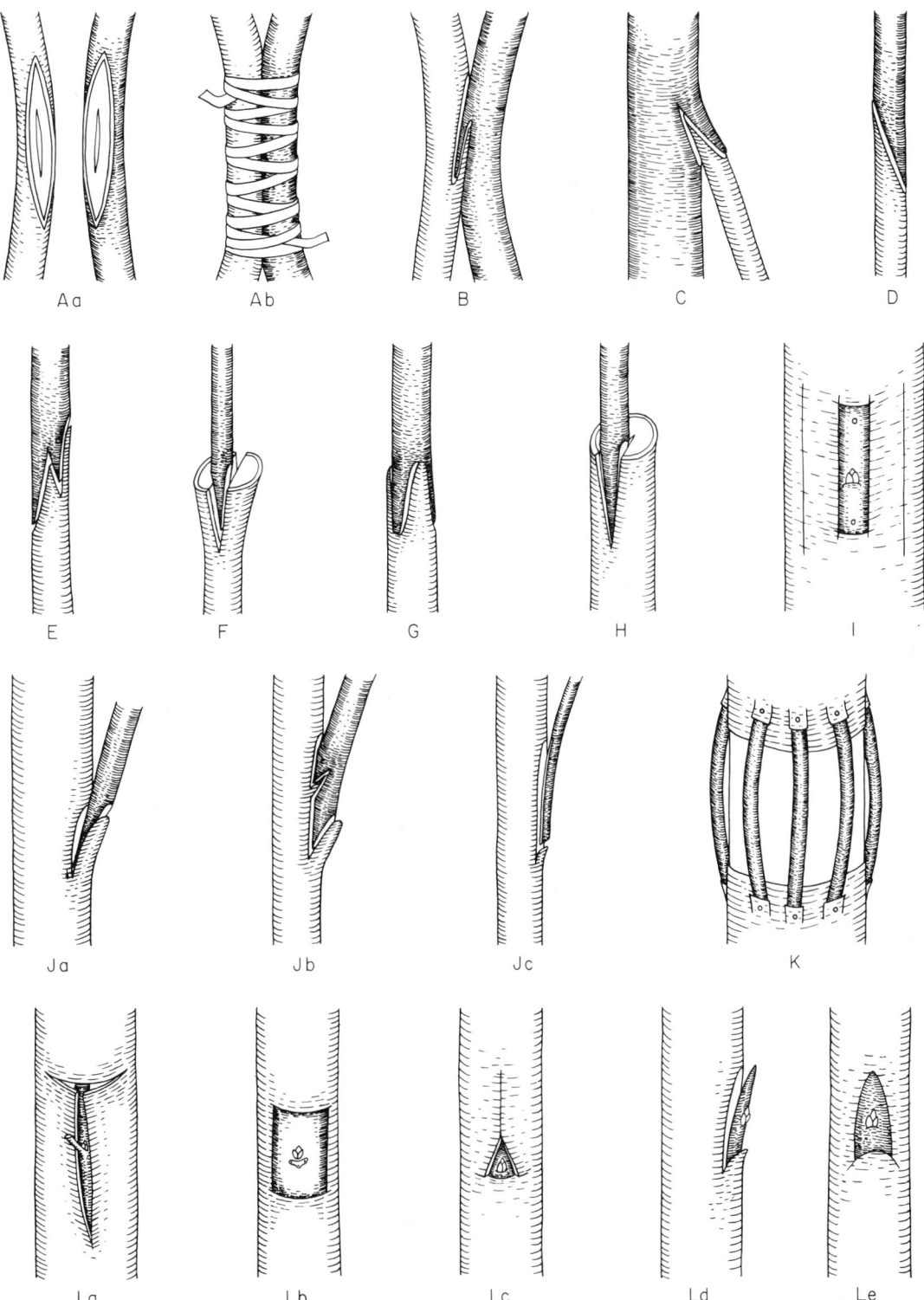

GRAFTING. **A,** Simple splice approach graft; **Aa,** stock and scion showing cut surfaces; **Ab,** cut surfaces of stock and scion joined and bound. **B,** Tongued approach graft, tongues of stock and scion interlocking. **C,** Inarching, stock cut and inserted into scion. **D,** Whip graft, a simple splice of stock and detached scion. **E,** Whip and tongue graft. **F,** Cleft graft. **G,** Saddle graft. **H,** Inlay graft. **I,** Veneer graft. **J,** Side grafts; **Ja,** side cleft graft; **Jb,** side tongue graft; **Jc,** side veneer graft. **K,** Bridge graft. **L,** Budding; **La,** shield bud; **Lb,** patch bud; **Lc,** microbud; **Ld, Le,** chip bud in side and face views. (Scion with dark shading; stock with light shading.)

layer, can seldom be grafted.) The line of demarcation between bark and wood on scion and stock should therefore coincide. Most grafting is done during the period of active growth, but sometimes during the period of dormancy. Scions are usually collected when dormant and stored at a low temperature. The joined parts are secured in place and protected from dessication and infection by a sealing material.

Many special tools have been developed for grafting, but for most operations a sharp knife (or a razor blade, for herbaceous materials), a pair of secateurs or pruning shears, a saw, and tying and sealing material will suffice. Tools should be kept sharp and clean. Sealing materials of various types are usually available at garden centers. The most commonly used are grafting waxes, bituminous sealants, rubber latex, nurserymen's adhesive tape or plastic tape, plastic and rubber sheeting, or even petroleum jelly. Waxed string, rubber strips, or raffia are the more common tying materials, but some grafts may be nailed, clipped, or splinted together. An illustrated handbook of grafting is a useful adjunct to other equipment.

In approach grafting, the scion is joined to the stock by a simple splice (Fig. A), in which two lateral surfaces are cut in an equal pattern, placed together, and secured, or by the tongue method (Fig. B), in which initial slices are removed from both stock and scion, a tongue is cut in each sliced portion, about halfway down on the stock and halfway up on the scion, and the tongues interlocked and secured. Inarching (Fig. C) is a modification of approach grafting. The top of the stock is removed at an angle and inserted into a cut in the scion and secured until the scion is united to the stock and can be separated from its own roots. Trees may be strengthened by inarching or splicing shoots from the same individual to form a brace between branches.

There are several ways of grafting detached scions. For deciduous trees, these are cut when dormant and stored in moist sphagnum or similar material in plastic bags in a refrigerator (but not a freezer) for short periods, or at 32° F for periods over a month, or buried below frost level in a well-drained situation on the north side of a protective building, wall, or hedge, until needed in late winter or early spring. One of the most common methods is whip-and-tongue grafting (Fig. E), which is used mostly when the stock and scion are an inch in diameter or less. In this, the whip graft (Fig. D), a simple splice in which both stock and scion are cut diagonally and joined, is modified by cutting into each surface matching tongues that interlock when the graft is tied and sealed. The cleft graft (Fig. F) is used for stocks up to three inches in diameter and for limbs; the scion may be of equal or smaller size. The scion is cut with a wedge-shaped lower end, which is inserted into a split in the stock so that the cambium of stock and scion are in contact and the graft is then tied and sealed. This mode of grafting is also used with herbaceous materials. The saddle graft (Fig. G) reverses the procedure, so that the split scion fits over the wedge-shaped apex of the stock.

When the scion is much smaller than the stock, inlay grafting and veneer grafting may be used. For an inlay graft (Fig. H), the lower end of the scion is cut on a long slant, the stock is cut across and grooved on one side to correspond with the cut edge of the scion, which is carefully fitted, tied or nailed, and sealed into the stock. The veneer graft (Fig. I) uses a scion with one or more buds, and may be used to fill out areas of a trunk that is destitute of branches. The scion is shaved to the pith opposite the bud, cut across about an inch below and an inch above the bud, and inserted into a corresponding space with parallel sides cut out of the bark on the stock, where it is tied or nailed in place and sealed. Side grafts (Figs. Ja, Jb, Jc) are similar in that scions are inserted in the side of the stock, but the top of the latter is not cut off until the union is complete. Side grafts may be of scions that are cut to a basal wedge as in the cleft graft, but inserted in the side of the stock, or that are spliced to the side with or without a tongue.

Bridge grafting (Fig. K) is not a method of propagation but only a means of healing or overcoming wounds. Most often it is employed when a tree is girdled by mice or some other injury. The wound is trimmed away on either edge to fresh, clean bark and wood, and long scions spanning the wound are nailed in exposed channels at either side. This is essentially the same as the veneer graft, except that both ends of the scion are inlaid. The grafts should be placed about two inches apart over the injured areas. The work is then sealed to protect wound and scions alike. Shoots should be prevented from growing from the scions. Eventually the wound should be completely covered by a new solid growth of wood from the ring of scions.

In the above grafts, scions usually have more than one bud. Another form of grafting, known as bud grafting or budding, consists of inserting a vegetative bud underneath the bark of the stock. Shield budding (Fig. La) is used when the stock is young or the bark not too thick, and is a common nursery practice. Twigs of current growth are cut from the plant that it is desired to propagate, and the buds are cut off with a sharp knife, leaving a shield-shaped bit of bark and perhaps a little wood with each. The bud is then inserted into a T-shaped slit made in the bark of the stock and is held in place by tying. In two or three weeks the bud will have grown fast to the stock and the tie should then be removed to prevent it from strangling the stock. For earlier budding, buds are taken from the previous season's growth. Patch budding (Fig. Lb) is performed in a similar fashion, except that a bud on a usually square or rectangular patch of bark replaces an equal, similarly shaped patch of bark on the stock. Microbudding (Fig. Lc) is a variation of shield budding in which the scion is very small, essentially restricted to the bud alone and a small piece of wood beneath it. This is inserted right side up in the bottom of an inverted-T-shaped cut and covered by plastic budding tape, which is removed in two to three weeks when the bud has united with the stock. This form of budding is most frequently used with citrus trees.

Chip budding (Fig. Ld, Le) is done when plants are not actively growing, usually before growth starts in the spring. A bud is removed by using a slanting cut from an inch or less above to a little below the bud, followed by a second slanting cut below the bud upward to the first cut. This chip is then fitted into a similarly shaped cut in the stock, tied, and sealed.

The bearing part of an orchard tree may be changed to another cultivar by grafting or budding in a practice known as top-working. Usually three to five principal branches not more than four inches in diameter are selected as scaffold branches, well distributed around the tree and up the main trunk. The other branches are removed when dormant or shortly after growth starts, and the scaffold branches themselves are cut back to a desired length. Scions are grafted or budded on the scaffold branches by one of the means described above. Often a few nurse branches are left, or whitewash is used to protect grafted branches from the sun. Nurse branches are removed or are themselves grafted after the second or third year.

Double-working interposes an intermediate stock between the primary stock and the scion to overcome incompatibility between the rooted stock and the top or to introduce a dwarfing effect, cold resistance, or other benefit from the intermediate stock.

GRAMINEAE Juss. or, alternatively, **POACEAE** Barnh. GRASS FAMILY. Monocot.; about 700 genera and 7,000 spp. of ann. or per. grasses of worldwide distribution; sts. (culms) solitary or clustered, creeping or erect, often stoloniferous or rhizomatous, rarely thickened basally into corms, herbaceous or more rarely (mostly in the bamboos) woody, very small to nearly 100 ft., hollow or solid but always with solid joints (nodes), simple, or branched at the base or above; lvs. solitary at the joints, borne in 2 ranks, the sheath surrounding the st. above the node, its margins overlapping (sheath open) or sometimes united partly or completely in a cylinder (sheath closed), a membranous appendage or sometimes a row of hairs (ligule) present on inner surface at junction of sheath

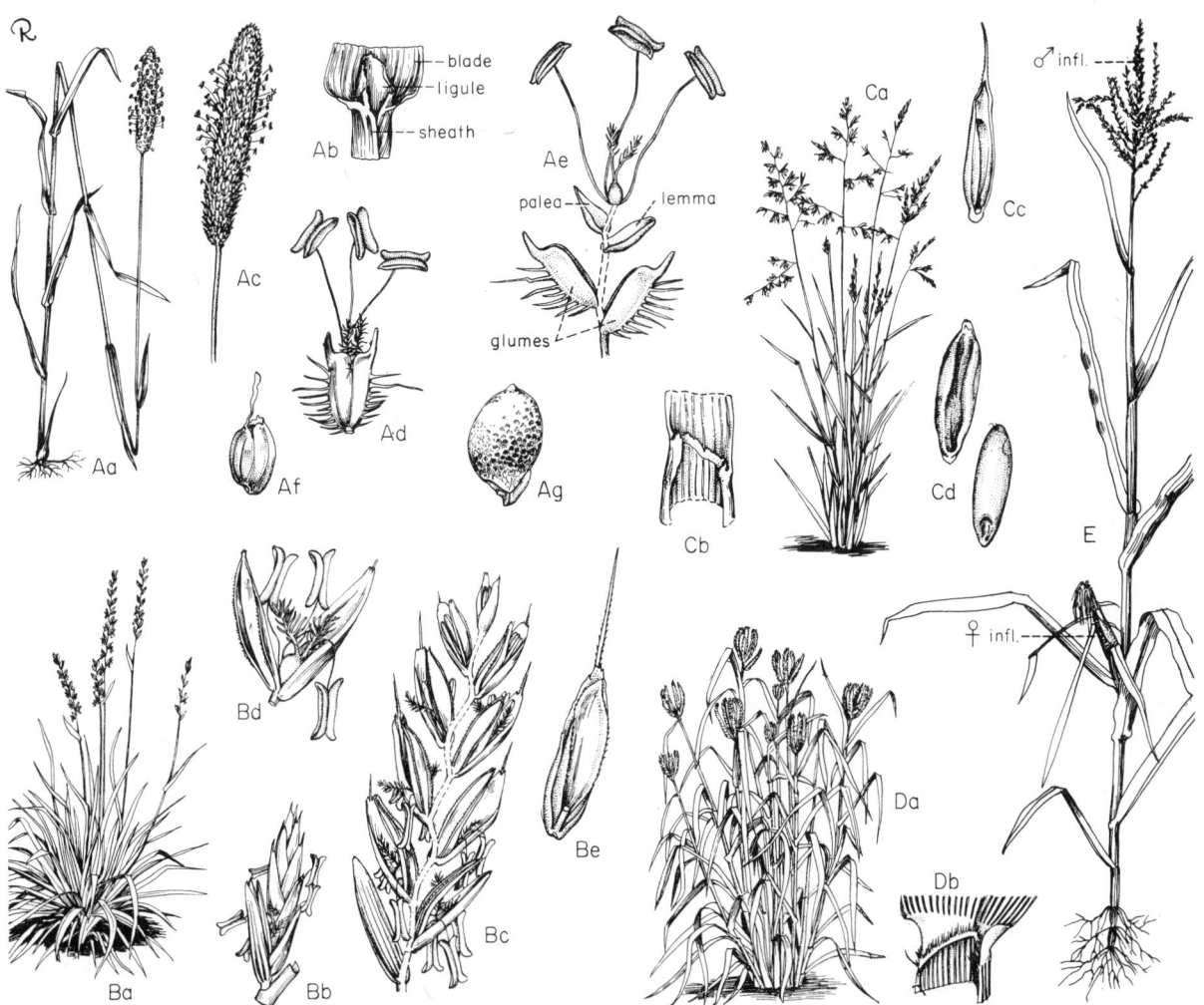

GRAMINEAE. **A,** *Phleum pratense;* **Aa,** flowering stem, $\times \frac{1}{4}$; **Ab,** segment of leaf at junction of sheath and blade, $\times$ 2; **Ac,** inflorescence, $\times \frac{1}{2}$; **Ad,** a single spikelet (one-flowered), $\times$ 4; **Ae,** spikelet diagrammatically "exploded" to show the parts, $\times$ 4; **Af,** fruit (caryopsis enclosed by lemma and palea), $\times$ 6; **Ag,** caryopsis, $\times$ 12. **B,** *Lolium multiflorum:* **Ba,** flowering plant, $\times \frac{1}{8}$; **Bb,** a single spikelet (several-flowered), $\times$ 2; **Bc,** spikelet diagrammatically "exploded," $\times$ 3; **Bd,** floret, $\times$ 4; **Be,** fruit (caryopsis enclosed by lemma and palea), $\times$ 4. **C,** *Festuca rubra:* **Ca,** flowering plant, $\times \frac{1}{10}$; **Cb,** segment of leaf at junction of sheath and blade, $\times$ 5; **Cc,** fruit (caryopsis enclosed by lemma and palea), $\times$ 3; **Cd,** caryopsis, two views, $\times$ 5. **D,** *Eleusine coracana:* **Da,** flowering plant, $\times \frac{1}{16}$; **Db,** segment of leaf at junction of sheath and blade, $\times 1\frac{1}{2}$. **E,** *Zea Mays:* flowering plant, $\times \frac{1}{16}$. (Ac, Ae from Lawrence, *An Introduction to Plant Taxonomy;* E from Bailey, *Manual of Cultivated Plants,* ed. 2.)

and blade, the blade usually flat and without petiole but often involute (rolled inward from the edge) or convolute (rolled longitudinally) in dry regions, broadened in the tropics, and in many bamboos narrowed to a short petiole, sometimes with earlike appendages (auricles) on either side at the base; infl. of complex, sessile or pedicelled spikelets borne along an axis (rachis) in racemose, spicate, or more often in paniculate arrangement, the spikelets sometimes separating (disarticulating) between the florets, each spikelet consisting of a short axis (rachilla) with small overlapping bracts in 2 ranks, sometimes with 1 or 2 nerves (keels) more prominent than others, the first 2 bracts (glumes) empty, followed by 1–50 bisexual or unisexual florets, each floret composed usually of an outer bract (lemma), an inner bract (palea), 2–3 minute rudiments of perianth (lodicules), 1–6 or rarely more, but mostly 3 stamens, and a 1-celled, 1-ovuled ovary with usually 2, rarely 1 or 3 styles and papillate or plumose stigmas; fr. rarely a nut or a berry, usually a specialized seedlike grain (caryopsis) consisting of the seed and adherent fr. wall, this sometimes also enclosed in the palea and lemma, rarely the seed not adherent, seed with abundant endosperm.

One of the largest families in number of genera and species, the most important economically, and, among the flowering plants, probably the largest in number of individuals and one of the most widely distributed. See *Bamboos, Grasses,* and *Lawns.* Genera represented in N. Amer. and Hawaii by spp. in cult. are: *Aeluropus, Agropyron, Agrostis, Alopecurus, Ammophila, Ampelodesmos, Andropogon, Anthoxanthum, Arrhenatherum, Arundinaria, Arundinella, Arundo, Avena, Axonopus, Bambusa, Bothriochloa, Bouteloua, Brachiaria, Briza, Bromus, Buchloe, Chasmanthium, Chimonobambusa, Chloris, Chrysopogon, Coix, Cortaderia, Cymbopogon, Cynodon, Cynosurus, Dactylis, Danthonia, Dendrocalamus, Deschampsia, Desmazeria, Dichanthium, Digitaria, Echinochloa, Ehrharta, Eleusine, Elymus, Eragrostis, Eremochloa, Erianthus, Eriochloa, Festuca, Gynerium, Helictotrichon, Hilaria, Holcus, Hordeum, Hyparrhenia, Koeleria, Lagurus, Lamarckia, Leersia, Lolium, Melica, Melinis, Mibora, Milium, Miscanthus, Molinia, Neyraudia, Oplismenus, Oryza, Oryzopsis, Panicum, Paspalum, Pennisetum, Phalaris, Phleum, Phragmites, Phyllostachys, Poa, Polypogon, Pseudosasa, Rhynchelytrum, Saccharum,*

Sasa, Schizachyrium, Secale, Semiarundinaria, Setaria, Shibataea, Sorghastrum, Sorghum, Spartina, Sporobolus, Stenotaphrum, Stipa, Stipagrostis, Themeda, Thysanolaena, Triticum, Uniola, Vetiveria, Zea, Zizania, and *Zoysia.*

GRAMMATOPHYLLUM Blume. *Orchidaceae.* About 10 spp. of epiphytes of Malay Arch., with either naked pseudobulbs with few lvs. toward top, or long, canelike, fleshy, leafy sts.; lvs. 2-ranked, leathery; infl. lateral, erect or pendent, many-fld., racemose; sepals and petals spreading, lip usually 3-lobed, fleshy, with 3 low ridges, column fleshy, hollowed basally. For structure of fl. see *Orchidaceae.*

For culture see *Orchids.*

Fenzlianum: *G. scriptum.*

Measuresianum: *G. scriptum.*

multiflorum: *G. scriptum.*

Rumphianum: *G. scriptum.*

Sanderanum: *G. speciosum.*

scriptum Blume [*G. Fenzlianum* Rc̀hb.f.; *G. Measuresianum* Weathers; *G. multiflorum* Lindl.; *G. Rumphianum* Miq.]. Pseudobulbs ovoid, 2–3-lvd.; lvs. to 1 ft. long; infl. arching, many-fld.; fls. 2–3 in. across, pale green, suffused or spotted with large brown blotches, sepals and petals nearly alike, lip sessile, 3-lobed, lateral lobes parallel with column, midlobe triangular. Philippine Is. Cv. **'Tigrinum'**. Fls. somewhat larger and more intensely spotted.

speciosum Blume [*G. Sanderanum* Hort.]. QUEEN-OF-ORCHIDS. Sts. stout, to 10 ft. long; lvs. many, 2-ranked, linear, to 18 in. long; scapes to 10 ft. long, bearing as many as 100 fls.; fls. to 4 in. across, yellow, finely spotted with brown, sepals and petals nearly alike, lip 3-lobed, midlobe hairy. Se. Asia, Philippine Is., Borneo, Java.

GRAPE. Grapes belong to the genus *Vitis.* In the form of various species, hybrids, and races, they are grown for their edible or ornamental berries over the greater part of North America except in regions of extreme cold, and are sometimes grown under glass. *Vitis Labrusca* is the most important of the native species involved in the hybrids that are termed American cultivars. These are the mainstay of grape-growing east of the Rocky Mountains, with the most extensive plantings near the southern shores of the Great Lakes. The cultivars of the Old World grape, *V. vinifera,* are extensively grown in California and Arizona, and are also grown elsewhere to a minor extent where there is no injury from either winter cold or excessive summer rains. California produces about 90 percent of the commercial grape crop. Cultivars that combine the qualities of *V. vinifera* and American species have been created by French grape breeders, and under the general designation of French hybrids are increasing in popularity where American cultivars are now prominent. The muscadine grape, *V. rotundifolia,* is grown in the cotton belt. Thus, there are in North America four cultural classes: American cultivars, *V. vinifera* cultivars, French hybrids, and muscadine cultivars.

Productive grapevines are grown on soils of various kinds, provided they are fairly deep and well drained. Sandy loams can be excellent if at least 3–4 feet deep and well drained. The site should afford a frost-free season of at least 150 days, although a season of 180 days is much better; a site from which cold air can drain to a lower area is effective in reducing the frequency of frosts in spring and autumn. Grapevines should not be in the shade of trees or structures.

Weed control is necessary. In the home garden this can be done by mulching or by shallow cultivation during the first three to four months of shoot growth, followed by mowing of weeds or seeding of a cover crop that will be killed by frost. Nitrogen fertilization is generally necessary to stimulate an adequate growth of shoots. Depending on the soil, there could be a need for fertilization with potassium, magnesium, boron, or manganese, or for application of zinc or iron. The indiscriminate application of them is unwise. Liming to raise the soil pH is not necessary.

American cultivars, cultivars of French hybrids, and cultivars of *V. vinifera* can be propagated by hardwood cuttings. These are made from cane prunings, about one foot in length, usually with three buds. They are taken in winter and are stored in moist sand or sawdust to callus. In early spring the cuttings are planted out in the nursery row, with the top bud level with the surface of the ground; they make usable vines at the end of the first or second season. New and rare cultivars are sometimes propagated by single-eye hardwood cuttings in a frame or under glass. Cultivars of muscadine grapes are propagated by layering or by softwood cuttings, methods which are also applicable to the other kinds of grapes. Cuttings or layers produce vines on their own roots. However, the roots of some cultivars of grapes (especially of *V. vinifera*) are susceptible to soil pests, including the root louse (Phylloxera) and certain nematodes. Where these are present—and *Phylloxera* is present in many grape-growing areas—the control is by grafting the susceptible cultivar to a virus-free rootstock that is resistant to the particular pest.

Planting distances vary with region and cultivar. Either one-year-old or two-year-old rooted cuttings or grafted vines may be planted, usually in early spring. In the northeastern United States, vines are commonly planted 8 feet apart in rows 9 feet apart. Muscadine vines are usually planted 15–20 feet apart in rows 9–10 feet apart. Row direction should be determined by the contour or by cross-slope to minimize water loss by runoff and soil loss by erosion.

At planting, the vine is cut back to two or three good buds. The hole in which the plant is to be set should be large enough to allow a full spreading of the roots. Fine soil should be worked around the roots and firmed with the feet, and a mulch of coarse litter may be spread around the vine. If all the buds start, the strongest two may be allowed to grow; the shoots should be staked or supported by a low wire. Any flower clusters produced the first year should be removed early.

Pruning of the vine is essential to success in grape growing. To understand the pruning of grapes, the grower must be aware that the fruit is borne on a shoot of the present season, which arises from wood of the previous season, called a cane. A shoot growing during one year has a compound bud in the axil of each leaf, and there is a leaf at each node. The shoot may grow to be 3–15 feet long. After leaf fall, the matured shoot is termed a cane. If pruned to a ten-node length in early spring of the following year and retained for fruiting that year, a new shoot will likely grow that year from each node. Near the base of each of these new shoots there will be one to four clusters of grapes. Generally, the canes which are darkest-colored, large, and are well exposed as actively growing shoots will be productive in the following year. The skilled grape pruner can tell by these characteristics which canes will have the most productive buds.

Training of the grapevine is the arranging or shaping of the vine with emphasis on the position and extent of the renewal area. Some definitions are necessary: *renewal area* is the location on the vine of the spurs or canes to be retained after pruning (*low* renewal area means one at a height of 2–4 feet from the ground; *high* renewal area means one at 5–6 feet from the ground for trellised grapevines, and at least 7 feet for arbored grapevines); *cane* and *spur* refer to the relative length—five to 12 nodes for a cane, and one to three nodes for a spur—of the retained portion of the previous year's shoot; *cordon* is a usually horizontal extension of the trunk, is two or more years old, and is a renewal area.

For cultivars of *V. vinifera* in California, the renewal area for spurs can be at the top of a low trunk, or it can be for canes at the top of a low trunk; or there can be cordons from a low trunk, with the cordons then the renewal areas for spurs. For cultivars of muscadine grapes, the usual training is with high cordons with spur pruning. For American cultivars and French hybrid cultivars, the renewal area without cordons is usually high (or there may be two renewal areas, one high and another low, as with the familiar four-arm Kniffin system described below), with cane pruning. Arbor training is high

(7 feet), and is with cordons meandering over the top of the arbor as renewal areas for cane pruning.

Grapevine pruning consists of: (1) selecting the appropriate number of the most mature and largest canes originating in the renewal area; (2) pruning these to the appropriate length; (3) for cane pruning, retaining one-node spurs at the rate of one per retained cane for renewal purposes the subsequent year; and (4) removing by pruning of all other canes. The appropriate number and appropriate length are based on the principle of retaining more nodes (there is a compound bud at each node) on large vines. For example, on four-arm Kniffin-trained vines (in which there is a trunk to a height of 5 feet to 6 feet, with two renewal areas, one at 2 feet to 3 feet and one at 5 feet to 6 feet, at each of which usually two canes are retained), four eight-node canes should be retained for average-sized vines, four six-node canes for smaller vines, and from four ten-node canes up to a maximum of six ten-node canes for larger than average vines.

Where the renewal area is high, as in grape culture in eastern North America, the vine is usually supported by a trellis whose top wire is nearly 6 feet high and whose second wire is about 3 feet lower. The trellis posts are about 8 feet long, driven or set 2 feet deep, and spaced at intervals of 21–24 feet. In our example of four-arm Kniffin, the usual four canes, two at each renewal area, are tied along the wire in each direction at each level. These four (or six) canes are renewed every year, using the new canes that arise from the renewal area near the trunk, or from a cane growing near the base of the cane retained at the previous pruning.

Grape yields vary greatly. During the first two years the flower clusters or fruit should be removed from the vine early in the season, in order to develop a large vine that can yield more in its third and subsequent years. The yield of a four- or five-year-old vine should be nearly that of mature vines. Vines spaced at 8 feet in rows 9 feet apart and whose leaves fill the trellis will usually produce 7–20 pounds of fruit per vine. Vines very widely spaced or on arbors will, of course, yield more per vine.

A grapevine with limited space in a vineyard should bear only a limited weight of fruit, not more than 2–3 pounds per foot of row. Overcropping leads to inferior quality fruit, to stunted grapevines, and to vines more subject to winter injury. It is avoided by proper pruning in the dormant season, and by removal of excess flower clusters before flowering or of excess clusters of fruit just after flowering.

Because of the great variation in winter hardiness and in susceptibility to certain devastating diseases, regionally adapted cultivars should be chosen. Cultivars are listed here in order of ripening, from early to late.

In the areas of New England and New York, northern Michigan, Wisconsin, and the north-central states, where winter lows of −20° F are common, only the very cold-hardy sorts like 'Beta', 'Blue Jay', and 'Red Amber' are recommended. These all inherit their cold-resistance from *Vitis riparia.*

Major American cultivars of the more temperate vineyard regions of the northeastern and central states are 'Delaware', 'Niagara', 'Concord', 'Catawba', and many more of lesser commercial importance like 'Ontario', 'Van Buren', 'Moore Early', 'Worden', 'Fredonia', 'Buffalo', and 'Steuben'.

The French hybrids are primarily wine grapes but include some that may serve as dessert grapes. Originally designated by the name of the hybridizer and a number, these interspecific hybrids are becoming established in the traditional vineyard areas of the East. Some of the more common and widespread are the red wine grapes: 'Baco Noir' (Bacol), 'Marechal Foch' (Kuhlmann 188–2), 'De Chaunac' (Seibel 9549), and 'Chancellor' (Seibel 7053). Leading whites include: 'Aurore' (Seibel 5279), 'Verdelet' (Seibel 9110), 'Seyval' (Seyve-Villard 5–276), and 'Villard Blanc' (Seyve-Villard 12–375).

American bunch grapes grown more successfully in the southern states include the older cultivars 'Champanel', 'Ellen Scott', 'Lenoir', and 'Ives'. 'Portland' and 'Fredonia' are later introductions, which appear on many state lists. For Florida, the recent introductions 'Blue Lake', 'Stover', and 'Lake Emerald' are reported to be adapted.

Muscadine cultivars grown commercially in the South are primarily 'Hunt', 'Thomas', and 'Scuppernong'. A long list of newer introductions is gradually replacing these old cultivars, including the bronze cultivars 'Carlos', 'Dearing', 'Fry', 'Higgins', 'Magnolia', and 'Welder', and the black cultivars 'Albemarle', 'Chief', 'Cowart', 'Creek', 'Jumbo', 'Magoon', 'Noble', 'Pride', 'Southland', and 'Tarheel'.

Cultivars of *V. vinifera* grown as table grapes on the Pacific Coast include 'Cardinal', 'Thompson Seedless', 'Emperor', 'Flame Tokay', and 'Ribier'.

For wine, the premium named *V. vinifera* cultivars are the reds, 'Pinot Noir' and 'Cabernet Sauvignon', and the whites, 'Chardonnay' and 'White Riesling'. Cultivars being used in larger quantity are 'Carignane', 'Grenache', and 'Zinfandel' for red wines, and 'French Colombard' and 'Muscat of Alexandria' for white wines.

Many diseases, such as black rot, downy mildew, powdery mildew, and dead-arm, injure both foliage and fruit of the grapevine. Similarly, insects such as grape leaf hoppers, grape berry moth, and red-banded leaf roller injure the vine or fruit. The severity of these and other pests varies by season, locality, and cultivar. They are not all serious in every year. These diseases and insects can be controlled. The grower is referred to his state agricultural extension service for current information on control procedures.

GRAPHORKIS Thouars [*Eulophiopsis* Pfitz.]. *Orchidaceae.* Four spp. of terrestrial herbs of Madagascar and Mascarene Is.; pseudobulbs several, jointed, completely enclosed in remnants of scarious sheaths; infl. paniculate, from new growth; sepals and petals similar, spreading, lip 3-lobed, column short, with small spur at base, pollinia 2, cleft, on a distinct stalk. For structure of fl. see *Orchidaceae.*

For culture see *Orchids.*

lurida (Swartz) O. Kuntze [*Eulophia lurida* (Swartz) Lindl.]. Lvs. fleshy, lanceolate; panicles to 18 in. long, many-fld.; fls. to ¼ in. across, sepals and petals blunt, purplish, lip yellow. Blooming throughout the year. Afr.

scripta (Thouars) O. Kuntze [*Eulophia scripta* (Thouars) Lindl.]. Pseudobulbs with up to 6 internodes, to 4½ in. long; lvs. to 16 in. long; panicles to 2 ft. long, to 200-fld.; fls. greenish-yellow with reddish-brown spots, lip yellow. Réunion.

GRAPTOPETALUM Rose [*Byrnesia* Rose]. *Crassulaceae.* About 12 spp. of glabrous, succulent, per. herbs and shrubs of Mex. and Ariz.; lvs. alt., mostly in rosettes; fl. st. axillary, the lvs. mostly reduced, infl. of 1 to several alt. cymes; fls. pedicelled, mostly 5-merous, sepals nearly equal, appressed to corolla, petals united below, imbricate in bud, stamens twice as many or rarely as many, outcurved in age, carpels erect, mostly abruptly short-styled. Allied to *Echeveria,* but petals spreading from middle, with red dots or blotches often more or less in transverse bands.

For culture see *Succulents.*

amethystinum (Rose) Walth. [*Pachyphytum amethystinum* Rose]. JEWEL-LEAF PLANT. Sts. decumbent, to 1 ft. long; lvs. 12–15, oblong-obovate, 1¼–2¾ in. long, 1–1½ in. wide, to ¾ in. thick, obtuse to rounded at apex, glaucous, lavender, turgid, margins rounded; fl. st. 6 in., with 3–10 brs., each 3–6-fld.; fls. to ⅝ in. wide, petals cross-banded. Spring, early summer. W. Mex.

filiferum (S. Wats.) Whitehead. Cespitose; lvs. 50–300, spatulate, ½–2 in. long, ³⁄₁₆–⅜ in. wide, ⅛ in. thick, narrowed to a filamentous tip to ½ in. long; fl. st. 2–4 in., with 2–5 brs., each 2–5-fld.; fls. ½–¾ in. wide, petals closely cross-banded. Spring. Nw. Mex.

filiforme: a listed name of no botanical standing; probably an error for *G. filiferum.*

grande Alexand. Shrub, to 6 ft.; lvs. 15–25, rounded to nearly truncate; 2–3¼ in. long, ¾–1¼ in. wide, ³⁄₁₆ in. thick, cuneate-spatulate, glaucous; fl. st. to 2 ft., with 8–15 brs.; fls. to 1 in. wide, petals cross-banded. Winter, spring. S. Mex.

Macdougallii Alexand. Stoloniferous, rosettes sessile; lvs. 25–50, oblong-cuneate, ¾–1¾ in. long, ½–⅝ in. wide, 3/16 in. thick, short-acuminate, glaucous; fl. st. weak, to 6 in., with lvs. like those of rosette, infl. of 1–3 brs., each 2–5-fld.; fls. to 1¼ in. wide, petals closely red-lineolate. Winter, early spring. S. Mex.

occidentale Rose. Not in cult.; the plant grown under this name appears to be a large form of *G. Rusbyi.*

pachyphyllum Rose. Sts. trailing, to 8 in., branching below; lvs. 20–50, nearly round in cross section, ⅜–¾ in. long, 3/16–⅜ in. in diam., clavate, blue-glaucous, often red-tipped; fl. st. 1–4 in., with lvs. similar to st. lvs., infl. of 1–4 brs., each 2–5-fld.; fls. ½–¾ in. wide, petals sparsely dotted or scarcely banded. Early summer. Mex.

paraguayense (N. E. Br.) Walth. [*G. Weinbergii* (Rose) Walth.; *Byrnesia Weinbergii* Rose; *Echeveria Weinbergii* Hort. ex Rose; *Sedum paraguayense* (N. E. Br.) Bullock; *S. Weinbergii* (Rose) A. Berger]. GHOST PLANT, MOTHER-OF-PEARL PLANT. Sts. decumbent, to 1 ft.; lvs. 15–25, obovate-spatulate, 1½–3 in. long, ½–1 in. wide, ⅜ in. thick, acute or short-acuminate, turgid, margins obtuse, glaucous, lavender, becoming gray; fl. st. 6 in., with 2–6 brs., each 3–14-fld.; fls. to ¾ in. wide, petals sparsely dotted. Late winter, early spring. Probably Mex. Widely grown; readily prop. by rooting detached lvs.

Rusbyi (Greene) Rose [*Echeveria Rusbyi* (Greene) Kearn. & Peebles]. Cespitose; lvs. 10–35, oblanceolate to spatulate, obtuse, ½–2 in. long, ⅛–⅝ in. wide, about 1/16–3/16 in. thick, minutely pointed, papillose; fl. st. to 5 in., with 2–3 brs., each 4–7-fld.; fls. 5–7-merous, to ⅝ in. wide, petals cross-banded. Spring. Ariz., n. Mex.

Weinbergii: *G. paraguayense.*

GRAPTOPHYLLUM Nees. *Acanthaceae.* About 10 spp. of evergreen shrubs in Australia and sw. Pacific; lvs. opp., entire, glabrous, often colored or spotted; fls. purple or red, in short terminal racemes or panicles, corolla tubular, 2-lipped, stamens 2; fr. a caps.

Propagated by cuttings.

hortense: *G. pictum.*

pictum (L.) Griff. [*G. hortense* Nees]. CARICATURE PLANT. To 8 ft.; lvs. elliptic, to 6 in. long, entire, purplish or green, marked with yellow; corolla purple or crimson, 1½ in. long, stamens exserted. Probably New Guinea. Widely cult. in warm regions as a foliage plant.

GRASSES. All true grasses are members of the family Gramineae. The horticultural grasses are the kinds grown as ornamentals, as distinct from the pasture and meadow grasses, the forage or fodder grasses, the timber grasses (bamboos), the cereal grains, and grasses grown for various specialty products. The ornamental grasses have three general uses: in the flower garden; in yard, landscape, or border plantings; and in lawns and ground covers.

Grasses used in the flower garden are mostly hardy annuals, prized for their feathery or otherwise ornamental sprays, which are employed as greenery in living bouquets or are dried and used in winter bouquets, being prepared as are the other everlastings. These annual grasses are grown readily from seed, usually sown where the plants are to stand in open sunny places. Sometimes the smaller kinds are grown to maturity in pots for table decoration, the little species of *Briza, Mibora,* and the delicate kinds of *Agrostis* being well adapted to the purpose. The leading annual grasses listed as ornamentals are in *Agrostis, Anthoxanthum, Avena, Briza, Bromus, Chloris, Coix, Deschampsia, Desmazeria, Digitaria, Echinochloa, Eleusine, Eragrostis, Festuca, Holcus, Hordeum, Koeleria, Lagurus, Lamarckia, Oryza, Oryzopsis, Panicum, Paspalum, Pennisetum, Phalaris, Polypogon, Secale, Setaria, Sorghum, Triticum, Zea,* and *Zizania.*

The grasses adapted to yard, landscape, or border planting are mostly tall-growing perennial species; some of them also yield excellent material for dry bouquets, as *Miscanthus, Cortaderia,* and *Gynerium.* In tropical and warm-temperate regions the bamboos are commanding examples, the following genera being cultivated in the United States: *Arundinaria, Bambusa, Chimonobambusa, Dendrocalamus, Phyllostachys, Pseudosasa, Sasa, Semiarundinaria,* and *Shibataea.* These genera are mostly Asian, but one species of *Arundinaria* is native in eastern North America. (See *Bamboos.*)

Important perennial horticultural grasses which are not bamboos are to be found in *Agropyron, Agrostis, Alopecurus, Ammophila, Ampelodesmos, Andropogon, Anthoxanthum, Arrhenatherum, Arundinaria, Arundo, Axonopus, Bothriochloa, Briza, Bromus, Chasmanthium, Chloris, Cortaderia, Cymbopogon, Cynodon, Cynosurus, Dactylis, Deschampsia, Dichanthium, Elymus, Eragrostis, Eremochloa, Festuca, Gynerium, Holcus, Hordeum, Koeleria, Lolium, Melica, Melinis, Miscanthus, Molinia, Neyraudia, Oplismenus, Oryzopsis, Panicum, Paspalum, Pennisetum, Phalaris, Phleum, Phragmites, Poa, Saccharum, Schizachyrium, Setaria, Sorghum, Stenotaphrum, Stipa, Stipagrostis, Thysolaena, Uniola, Vetiveria,* and *Zoysia.*

A third class of grasses comprises the sod-forming kinds employed in the making of lawns, but in this case the plants are not raised and treated separately and need not be separately listed here. In horticulture, a lawn may be defined as an area of the landscape carpeted with a greensward designed as a foundation setting for buildings, for border planting, or for pleasure grounds. The term is usually sufficiently broad to include both grasses and other plants that require regular mowing or clipping, but not other low-growing carpeters such as *Liriope, Pachysandra, Vinca,* and other genera used as ground covers. Generally speaking, the lawn is a permanent feature and as such is usually composed of perennial species of the grass genera *Agrostis, Axonopus, Buchloe, Cynodon, Festuca, Lolium, Poa, Stenotaphrum,* or *Zoysia.*

Agricultural grasses are of three main kinds, enumerated here, but not treated in detail.

(1) Food grasses. The most important food plants are the cereals and small grains, which belong to the following genera: *Avena, Coix, Echinochloa, Eleusine, Hordeum, Oryza, Panicum, Pennisetum, Secale, Sorghum, Setaria, Triticum, Zea,* and *Zizania,* to which can be added sugar cane *(Saccharum)* and those bamboos which provide sprouts used as vegetables *(Bambusa, Phyllostachys).*

(2) Forage grasses. They are grown for hay, pasturage, soiling, and silage: *Agropyron, Agrostis, Andropogon, Arrhenatherum, Axonopus, Bouteloua, Bromus, Chloris, Cynodon, Dactylis, Eragrostis, Festuca, Holcus, Panicum, Paspalum, Pennisetum, Phleum, Poa, Rhynchelytrum, Setaria, Sorghum, Spartina, Stipa,* and *Zea.*

(3) Soil-holding grasses. They are used as sand binders, or to fix steep banks by their strong creeping rhizomes: *Agropyron, Ammophila, Arundinaria, Bambusa, Dendrocalamus, Elymus, Phyllostachys, Semiarundinaria,* and *Spartina.*

Among those with other uses can be noted the genera of aromatic grasses, *Cymbopogon* and *Vetiveria,* furnishing essential oils used in perfumery; and a few grasses from which various objects and products are made: brooms *(Sorghum),* Leghorn hats *(Triticum),* matting or hats *(Arundo, Avena, Oryza, Phragmites),* reeds for woodwinds *(Arundo),* starch and alcohol *(Hordeum, Oryza, Secale, Triticum, Zea),* pipes for tobacco *(Zea),* fishing rods and diverse handcrafted products *(Arundinaria, Bambusa, Phyllostachys),* and paper pulp *(Bambusa, Dendrocalamus, Phyllostachys).*

GRAVISIA: *AECHMEA.* **G. exsudans:** *A. aquilega.*

GREENHOUSE. This is now a general term for a glasshouse or similar structure in which plants are maintained or grown. Originally, the word was applied to those houses in which plants are merely preserved or kept green in the winter, but this meaning is now little known in America. Special types of glasshouses include the conservatory, in which plants are kept or displayed; the stove or hothouse, in which plants are grown in a high temperature; the propagating pit, in which the multiplication of plants is carried forward; the forcing house, in which special plants are made to yield their products far out of their natural period or sequence; the orangery, devoted to the indoor culture of *Citrus;* and the houses of various temperatures, as cold, cool, and intermediate.

GREENOVIA Webb. *Crassulaceae.* Four spp. of succulent per. herbs of the Canary Is.; lvs. alt., in dense, sessile rosettes;

fl. st. terminal, infl. a glandular cyme of several crowded cincinni; fls. 16–32-merous, petals narrow, yellow, stamens twice as many, nectar glands none. Formerly included in *Sempervivum.*

For culture see *Succulents.*

aurea (C. A. Sm.) Webb & Berth. Rosettes 3–10 in. wide, half-closed and urceolate in resting condition, offsets few; lvs. spatulate or cuneate, 2–4 in. long, retuse to truncate and minutely pointed, glaucous, glabrous, with few or no cilia; fl. st. 1–1½ ft.; fls. about 30-merous, ¾–1 in. wide. Early spring.

diplocycla Webb. Resembling *G. aurea* but smaller, offsets none; lvs. 2–3 in. long, ciliate; fl. st. 4–8 in.; fls. about 20-merous, ⅝ in. wide. Late winter.

dodrentalis (Willd.) Webb [*G. gracilis* C. Bolle]. Rosettes loose, 1–2½ in. wide, offsets many, long-stemmed; lvs. green or glaucous, glabrous, finely ciliate; fl. st. 6–10 in.; fls. about 20-merous, ¾ in. wide. Late winter.

gracilis: *G. dodrentalis.*

GREENS. Potherbs are sometimes known as greens, particularly those that come in early spring when green food is specially welcome. Such greens may be *Brassica oleracea* Acephala Group, *Chenopodium, Portulaca, Rumex, Spinacia, Taraxacum,* and other plants grown or gathered that make acceptable eating when cooked in a pot. Accounts of the most important of these plants will be found under their appropriate generic entries.

Christmas greens are various kinds of plants that hold their foliage and color in winter and can be employed in holiday decoration. Some of these plants are grown for the purpose, but the larger part of the durable ones are gathered from the wild, including such kinds as various conifers, *Galax, Ilex, Kalmia, Lycopodium,* and *Smilax.* The indiscriminate and destructive gathering of such wildings is to be discouraged, and other means of Christmas decoration should be developed for large undertakings.

GREGORIA: *DOUGLASIA.*

GREVILLEA R. Br. SPIDER FLOWER. *Proteaceae.* About 250 spp. of evergreen trees and shrubs, native to Australia except for few spp. in Malay Arch.; lvs. alt.; fls. bisexual, in pairs in many-fld. racemes or panicles, perianth tubular, often brightly colored, styles long, filiform, showy; fr. a leathery follicle.

Some grown as ornamental and avenue trees in warm regions, some as garden shrubs, and sometimes in the juvenile stage as pot plants in the greenhouse. Propagated by seeds.

Aquifolium Lindl. HOLLY-LEAVED G. Spreading shrub, to 4 ft.; lvs. hollylike, to 3 in. long, veined, rigid, glabrous or pubescent; racemes terminal or on short axillary brs., to 2 in. long; fls. red. Victoria.

Banksii R. Br. Shrub or tree, to 20 ft.; lvs. pinnately cut, segms. 3–11, linear or lanceolate, to 4 in. long, silky-tomentose beneath, margins revolute; fls. red or sometimes white, in dense, terminal, 1-sided racemes to 6 in. long. Queensland. Cv. **'Alba'.** Fls. white. Plants with red fls. have been called var. *Fosteri* or var. *Forsteri,* but this designation has no botanical standing.

bipinnatifida R. Br. Shrub, to 4 ft., sometimes prostrate; lvs. acanthuslike, to 4 in. long, pinnately cut, segms. 9–21, oblong or pinnatifid; fls. red, in loose, 1-sided racemes to 6 in. long, sometimes panicled. W. Australia.

crithmifolia R. Br. Shrub, to 8 ft.; lvs. to 1 in. long, pinnately cut, segms. 3–5, narrow-linear; fls. creamy-white, in short, dense, sessile racemes, producing much nectar and having a somewhat foetid odor. W. Australia.

Endlicherana Meissn. Shrub, to 7 ft.; lvs. linear, to 4 in. long, silvery-pubescent on both sides; fls. pink or white, in dense racemes to ¾ in. long. W. Australia.

eriostachya Lindl. Shrub, to 9 ft.; lvs. narrow-linear, to 8 in. long, usually pinnately cut, segms. 3–5; fls. orange, in dense, terminal, 1-sided, tomentose, cone-shaped racemes to 6 in. long. W. Australia.

Hilliana F. J. Muell. Tree, to 60 ft.; lvs. entire, or deeply divided at end into 2 or 3 lobes, or pinnatifid into 5–7 segms., to 1 ft. long, silvery-pubescent beneath; fls. red to pink and white, in dense axillary, cylindrical racemes to 8 in. long. Queensland, New S. Wales.

juniperina R. Br. [*G. sulphurea* A. Cunn.]. Small shrub; lvs. spreading, linear, to 1 in. long, sharp-pointed, stiff, silky-pubescent beneath, margins revolute; fls. pale yellow or tinged with red, in very short, sessile racemes. New S. Wales.

lanigera A. Cunn. Shrub; lvs. linear, to ½ in. long, pubescent above, silky-tomentose beneath, margins revolute; fls. reddish, in dense terminal racemes. New S. Wales, Victoria.

lavandulacea Schlechtend. Shrub, prostrate, to 4 ft.; lvs. oblong-linear or lanceolate, to 1 in. long; fls. from pink, to light mauve to red, in terminal, short, almost umbel-like racemes. Victoria and S. Australia.

leucopteris Meissn. Shrub, to 8 ft.; foliage fernlike, lvs. 1 ft. long or more, pinnately divided, segms. narrow-linear, to 10 in. long, tomentose beneath; fls. white, in large showy panicles rising above the foliage. W. Australia. A shrub for dry areas; can be grown successfully on calcareous soils if the drainage is good.

mimosoides R. Br. Tree; lvs. lanceolate, falcate, to 10 in. long and 1 in. wide, entire, glaucous; fls. pinkish-white, in terminal, leafless panicles of slender, glabrous racemes to 4 in. long. N. Terr. of Australia.

obtusifolia Meissn. Shrub, spreading or procumbent, much-branched; lvs. oblong-linear, rusty-pubescent beneath, margins revolute; fls. in short, loose, 1-sided racemes. W. Australia.

oleoides Sieber. Shrub, to 4 ft.; lvs. linear or lanceolate, to 4 in. long, tomentose beneath, margins recurved; fls. bright red, in short, nearly sessile racemes. New S. Wales, Victoria.

ornithopoda Meissn. Glabrous shrub; lvs. to 4 in. long, divided into 3 lanceolate lobes; fls. white, small, in short, axillary racemes. W. Australia.

paniculata Meissn. Shrub, to 8 ft.; lvs. once- or twice-divided, segms. 3 or 2, cylindrical, sharp-pointed; fls. small, in axillary, short racemes. N. Australia.

polybotrya Meissn. Tall shrub; lvs. oblong or oblong-lanceolate, to 1½ in. long; fls. in panicle of dense, cylindrical racemes or spikes to 2 in. long. N. and w. Australia.

polystachya R. Br. Shrub or small tree, to 30 ft.; lvs. to 10 in. long, linear or linear-lanceolate, entire or broadening upwards and irregularly divided into 2–6 linear-lanceolate segms., tapering into the petiole, glabrous above, silky-pubescent beneath; fls. white, many in terminal racemes or panicles. N. Australia.

punicea R. Br. Shrub, to 5 ft.; lvs. oblong or nearly elliptic, to 2 in. long, tomentose beneath, margins recurved; fls. bright red or pink, in short, dense racemes. New S. Wales.

pyramidalis A. Cunn. Tall shrub or small tree; lvs. glabrous, glaucous, 1- or 2-pinnate, lfts. few, linear-cuneate or oblanceolate, 3–5 in. long; fls. small, many, in terminal racemes or panicles. N. Australia.

robusta A. Cunn. SILKY OAK, SILK O. Tree, to 150 ft.; lvs. fernlike, pinnate, lfts. lanceolate, entire or lobed, margins recurved; fls. orange, in 1-sided racemes to 4 in. long on short leafless brs. Queensland, New S. Wales. Zone 10. Valued timber tree. Formerly much grown from seeds as a decorative pot and florist's plant. Used as a decorative and street tree in Calif., Fla., and Hawaii.

rosmarinifolia A. Cunn. Shrub, to 6 ft. or sometimes lower and semiprostrate; lvs. linear, to 1½ in. long, silky-pubescent beneath, margins revolute; fls. reddish, in short, dense, sessile racemes. New S. Wales. Zone 9.

sulphurea: *G. juniperina.*

Thelemanniana Endl. Shrub, to 5 ft.; lvs. to 2 in. long, divided into many linear segms.; fls. pink tipped with green, in terminal, 1-sided racemes to 1½ in. long. S. and w. Australia.

triternata R. Br. Shrub, several ft. high; lvs. to 3 in. long and wide, 2–3-ternately divided, segms. narrow-linear, rigid, sharp-pointed, divaricate; fls. small, in terminal, cylindrical racemes. New. S. Wales.

Wilsonii A. Cunn. FIREWHEEL. Glabrous shrub, to 5 ft.; lvs. 2–3-ternately divided, segms. linear, to 1 in. long, sharp-pointed, stiff; fls. reddish, in loose racemes or panicles. W. Australia.

GREWIA L. *Tiliaceae.* Perhaps 150 spp. of shrubs, climbers, or trees, native to warm regions of Old World; lvs. alt., simple, serrate, mostly 3–7-nerved from the base; fls. axillary or terminal, in few-fld. cymes or panicles, rarely solitary, sepals 5, longer than petals, stellate-pubescent outside, often colored like petals inside, petals 5, with claws usually nectariferous, stamens many, on short or obsolete androgynophore, ovary 2–4-celled, cells 2–8(–many)-ovuled; fr. drupaceous, 1–4-lobed, cells 1–4, hard-walled, 1–2-seeded.

Sometimes grown as an ornamental far south and in Calif., but *G. biloba*, is hardy in Zone 7.

asiatica L. Shrub, to about 4 ft., with per. and subherbaceous, arching brs.; lvs. suborbicular, to 5 in. long, cordate, 5–7-nerved from the base, densely short-tomentose beneath; fls. axillary, about 5/8 in. across, peduncles as long as petioles or longer; fr. red, small. Described from cult.

biloba G. Don [*G. biloba* var. *parviflora* (Bunge) Hand.-Mazz.; *G. parviflora* Bunge; *G. parviflora* var. *glabrescens* (Benth.) Rehd. & E. H. Wils.]. Shrub, to 8 ft., brs. and lvs. glabrous or tomentose; lvs. ovate to rhombic-ovate, to 5 in. long, often doubly serrate, sometimes remotely 3-lobed, 3-nerved from the base; fls. yellow, about 3/8 in. across, in umbellate clusters at ends of brs. or opp. lvs.; fr. red or orange, mostly 2-lobed. China and Taiwan.

caffra Meissn. Climbing, many-stemmed shrub; lvs. oblong or lanceolate, to 3 in. long, acute or acuminate, glabrate; fls. axillary, sepals linear, less than 1/2 in. long, petals yellow; fr. globose, not lobed, glabrous or sparsely stellate-pubescent. E. and S. Afr. Plants offered under this name are usually *G. occidentalis*.

columnaris: *G. orientalis*.

Damine Gaertn. [*G. salviifolia* B. Heyne ex Roth, not L.f. or Roxb.]. Shrub or small tree, brs. leafy to apex; lvs. elliptic-oblong, to 3 in. long, obtuse or acute, serrulate, 3-nerved from the base, bicolored, densely gray-pubescent beneath; fls. in 2–3-fld. axillary cymes, peduncles up to 3/8 in. long; fr. 2-lobed, glabrous. India, Ceylon.

denticulata: a listed name of no botanical standing.

flavescens Juss. Shrub, to 15 ft., older sts. 4-angled; lvs. oblanceolate to suborbicular, to 4 in. long, acuminate, cordate, harshly pubescent; fls. yellow, few in axillary cymes, sepals to 3/4 in. long, petals 1/2 as long; fr. yellowish-brown, depressed-globose, mostly 2-lobed, stellate-pubescent. Afr., e. to Arabia and India.

occidentalis L. Shrub, or arborescent, to 9 ft., brs. slender; lvs. lanceolate to rhombic-ovate, to 3 in. long, acute or rounded, glabrous or pubescent; fls. 1–3 on slender, axillary peduncles, sepals linear to oblong, to 3/4 in. long, purple or pink inside, petals pink, mauve, rarely white; fr. red-purple, mostly 4-lobed, to 3/4 in. across, shiny-glabrescent. Afr.

orientalis L. [*G. columnaris* Sm.]. Straggling or erect shrub; lvs. ovate to oblong, to 3 in. long, short-acuminate, 3-nerved from the base, scabrous beneath; fls. few in terminal or axillary cymes, sepals yellow, about 5/16 in. long, petals white or yellow; fr. purplish, shallowly 4-lobed, to 1/2 in. in diam., villous. India.

parviflora: *G. biloba*.

retinervis Burret. Similar to *G. flavescens*, but shorter, up to 6 ft., sts. cylindrical; lvs. mostly glabrous; fr. shiny red-brown, not lobed, minutely and sparsely pubescent. E. Afr.

Rothii DC. [*G. salviifolia* Roxb., not L.f. or B. Heyne ex Roth]. Closely related to *G. Damine*, but having lvs. acuminate, remotely serrate, peduncles longer, and fr. not lobed, white-tomentose. India.

salviifolia: see *G. Damine* and *G. Rothii*.

similis K. Schum. Shrub, often climbing, 3–15 ft.; lvs. ovate to ovate-elliptic, to 4 in. long; fls. in 3–6-fld., axillary cymes, sepals oblong, to 3/4 in. long, mauve inside, petals mauve, less than 1/2 in. long; fr. deep orange, 4-lobed. Trop. Afr.

tiliifolia Vahl. Small tree; lvs. ovate to orbicular, to 4 in. long, 5–7-nerved from the base, stipules leafy, curved, auriculate; fls. in few-fld., axillary cymes, on peduncles shorter or longer than petioles, sepals 1/4–1/2 in. long; fr. blackish, 2-lobed or not lobed. India.

trifoliolatum: a listed name of no botanical standing.

GREYIA Hook. & Harv. NATAL BOTTLEBRUSH. *Melianthaceae*. Three spp. of small trees and shrubs, native to S. Afr.; lvs. alt., simple, without stipules, long-petioled; fls. in axillary racemes, showy, regular, 5-merous, stamens 10, exserted; fr. a 5-celled caps.

Grown in Zone 10, and sometimes under glass; propagated by seeds or by cuttings of half-ripened wood.

Radlkoferi Szysz. Larger than *G. Sutherlandii*, with young lvs. tomentose beneath and petals narrowed slightly to the base.

Sutherlandii Hook. & Harv. Large shrub or small tree, to 15 ft., flowering even when young; lvs. clustered near tips of brs., to 3 in. long, orbicular to oblong, cordate, coarsely toothed, glabrous; fls. in dense racemes to 10 in. long, scarlet, 1 1/2 in. long, petals oblong; fr. 5-lobed, seeds minute.

GRINDELIA Willd. GUM PLANT, GUMWEED, ROSINWEED, STICKY-HEADS, TARWEED. *Compositae* (Aster Tribe). Between 50 and 60 spp. of coarse ann., bien., or mostly per. herbs, mostly taprooted, native to w. N. Amer. and S. Amer., sts. simple to paniculately or corymbosely much-branched; lvs. alt., usually sessile, often clasping, glandular-dotted; fl. heads radiate or discoid, usually gummy, solitary, involucre hemispherical, involucral bracts imbricate in several rows, often spreading or revolute, receptacle flattish to slightly convex, pitted, naked; disc fls. bisexual, fertile, or the central ones sterile, ray fls. female, fertile, sometimes lacking; achenes glabrous, compressed to somewhat 4-angled, pappus of 2–10 stiff, deciduous awns.

Sometimes grown as ornamentals in the regions where they grow, succeeding on poor land. Propagated by division, cuttings, or seeds.

arenicola: *G. stricta* subsp. *venulosa*.

camporum Greene. Per., to 4 1/2 ft., sts. erect, branched above the middle; lvs. somewhat leathery, obovate to oblong, to 4 1/2 in. long, dentate to serrate, the upper clasping, reduced; heads to 1 1/2 in. across, involucral bracts spreading or reflexed apically. Calif.; naturalized elsewhere.

chiloensis (Cornelissen) Cabr. [*G. speciosa* Lindl. & Paxt.]. Glabrous, glutinous, shrubby per., to 2 ft.; lvs. variable in shape, narrowly oblanceolate to obovate, to 4 3/4 in. long, successively reduced upward, entire, serrate, or even runcinate-pinnatifid; heads to 3 in. across; disc fls. orange-yellow, ray fls. yellow. Argentina. Used medicinally.

humilis Hook. & Arn. Somewhat woody-based per., to 4 1/2 ft., sts. erect, branched above; lvs. sessile, linear to oblanceolate, to 3 in. long, acute or obtuse, leathery, crenate-serrulate or almost entire; heads 3/4 in. across, involucral bracts with ascending or reflexed tips. Salt marshes, cent. Calif.

integrifolia DC. Per., to 2 1/2 ft., glabrate to glandular-villous, sts. erect, branched above; lvs. sessile or clasping, to 3 in. long, thin, entire or denticulate, the lower oblanceolate, the upper ovate-lanceolate; heads 1–1 1/2 in. across, involucral bracts spreading. Wash., Ore. Var. **macrophylla**: *G. stricta*.

latifolia Kellogg. Succulent per. herb, to 2 ft.; lvs. mostly on the sts., lanceolate-ovate to broadly oblong, to about 3 in. long, somewhat cordate to clasping, serrate to sharply dentate, scabrous-ciliate; heads to 2 in. across, solitary or in a tight cluster of 2–3, often partly enclosed by subtending lvs.; ray fls. chrome-yellow to orange-yellow. Coastal, cent. Calif. Subsp. **platyphylla** (Greene) Keck [*G. robusta* var. *platyphylla* Greene]. Plants less succulent, less leafy; heads sometimes subtended by small leafy bracts, but not enclosed by them. Coastal, cent. Calif.

maritima (Greene) Steyerm. [*G. robusta* var. *maritima* (Greene) Jeps.]. Woody-based per., to 2 1/2 ft., sts. glabrous, rarely villous; basal lvs. tufted, narrowly oblanceolate, to 7 1/4 in. long, st. lvs. oblong to lanceolate, to 2 3/4 in. long, clasping, serrate; heads to 1 1/2 in. across, terminal on slender brs.; disc and ray fls. yellow. San Francisco (Calif.).

robusta Nutt. Glabrous per., to 4 ft., sts. few, erect, stout, usually corymbosely branched; basal lvs. oblanceolate, to 7 1/4 in. long, upper st. lvs. reduced, ovate-lanceolate to linear-oblong, clasping, all entire to sharply toothed; heads to 2 in. across; ray fls. yellow. Coastal, s. Calif. to n. Baja Calif. Occasionally used medicinally in home remedies. Var. **maritima**: *G. maritima*. Var. **platyphylla**: *G. latifolia* subsp. *platyphylla*.

speciosa: *G. chiloensis*.

squarrosa (Pursh) Dunal. CURLY-CUP GUMWEED. Erect ann., bien., or short-lived per., to 3 1/2 ft.; middle and upper lvs. mostly oblong or ovate, 2–4 times as long as wide, abundantly glandular-dotted, margins callose, sinuate, or even entire to sharply toothed; heads to 1 1/4 in. across; ray fls. lemon-yellow to bright yellow, sometimes absent. S. Minn., s. S. Dak., and Wyo., s. to Kans. and Tex.; introd. eastward and westward. Used medicinally. Var. **serrulata** (Rydb.) Steyerm. Middle and upper lvs. mostly linear-oblong, oblong, or oblanceolate, 5–8 times as long as wide. Se. Wyo. and n. Utah, s. to nw. New Mex. and ne. Ariz.; introd. eastward and westward.

stricta DC. [*G. integrifolia* var. *macrophylla* (Greene) Cronq.]. Per., to 3 in., sts. to 30 in. long, prostrate; lvs. firm, entire to serrulate, basal lvs. oblanceolate, attenuate, acute to rounded, st. lvs. oblong, to 4 in. long, clasping, acute to obtuse; heads 1 1/2-2 in. across, involucral bracts erect or spreading. Coast of w. N. Amer., Alaska to Ore. Subsp. **venulosa** (Jeps.) Keck [*G. arenicola* Steyerm.]. Sts. whitish or yellowish; lvs. broader, fleshier, more rounded; involucral bracts strongly reflexed. Coast, Ore. and n. Calif.

GRISELINIA G. Forst. *Cornaceae*. About 6 spp. of dioecious, evergreen shrubs or trees, native to New Zeal. and

Chile; lvs. alt., simple, leathery, glossy; fls. small, 5-merous, in panicles or racemes; fr. a berry.

Grown outdoors in Calif., Zone 10.

littoralis Raoul. Tree, to 50 ft.; lvs. ovate or oblong-ovate, to 4 in. long; panicles to 3 in. long; fls. with petals. New Zeal. Cv. **'Variegata'**. Lvs. variegated.

lucida G. Forst. Stout shrub or small tree, to 25 ft.; lvs. ovate or oblong, to 7 in. long, very unequal at base; panicles to 6 in. long, male fls. with petals, female fls. without petals. New Zeal. Cv. **'Variegata'**. Lvs. variegated. Var. **macrophylla** Hook.f. [*G. macrophylla* Hort.]. More robust, lvs. larger.

macrophylla: *G. lucida* var.

GRONOPHYLLUM Scheff. [*Kentia* Blume (1838), not Adans. or Blume (1830)]. *Palmae.* About 14 spp. of solitary, unarmed, monoecious palms in the Celebes, Molucca Is., New Guinea, and Australia; lvs. pinnate, sheaths forming a prominent crownshaft, pinnae 1- or several-ribbed, the apices obliquely toothed to 2-cleft, acuminate; infl. below lvs., with 2 deciduous, thin bracts, the upper enclosed in the lower, peduncle short, rachillae pendulous, with fls. in triads (2 male and 1 female) usually in 2–3 rows; male fls. with sepals small, acute, petals acute to acuminate, valvate, stamens erect, 6–12, female fls. with sepals rounded, imbricate, petals imbricate below, markedly valvate above, valvate portion as long as or longer than imbricate portion, pistil 1-celled, 1-ovuled; fr. mostly ellipsoid, with terminal stigmatic residue, seed with homogeneous or ruminate endosperm.

For culture see *Palms.*

Ramsayi (Becc.) H. E. Moore [*Kentia Ramsayi* (Becc.) Becc.]. Trunk to more than 100 ft. high, 8 in. in diam.; lvs. with glaucescent crownshaft over 30 in. long, blade about 5 ft. long with many equidistant pinnae to 30 in. long, nearly 2 in. wide; infl. twice-branched, rachillae to 2 ft. long; male fls. to 9/16 in. long, stamens 6; fr. about 5/8 in. long, 5/16 in. in diam. Ne. Australia.

GROSSULARIA: *RIBES.* **G. hesperia:** *R. californicum.* **G. reclinata:** *R. uva-crispa.*

GROUND COVERS. In horticulture, ground covers may be considered to be those perennial plants, usually requiring minimum maintenance, that may be substituted for lawn grasses on special sites where the latter normally do not thrive or where lawn maintenance becomes difficult, as in dense shade, on steep slopes or terraces, and on sandy or rocky soil where water is not available. Lawn grasses certainly are ground covers but are distinguished from the latter in *Hortus Third* on the basis of their needing to be regularly mowed. Furthermore, true lawns provide outdoor living and recreational space but most ground covers are neither suited nor planted for such use. An exception is *Dichondra,* widely used as a lawn subject in California and the Southwest. *Fragaria chiloensis* and several kinds of lily turf, *Liriope* and *Ophiopogon,* may be put to similar use mainly in the South and West, but like *Dichondra* these species will not bear heavy recreational traffic nor are they mowed, so they are best considered as ground covers. Bedding plants grown mainly for color, often on a large scale, are also not to be considered as true ground covers.

In the well-watered temperate United States, the familiar ground covers for shade are few but attractive and evergreen. All are easily propagated vegetatively. Among them are *Ajuga* and the trailing periwinkle or myrtle *(Vinca minor),* a hardy perennial (Zone 5) with glossy, dark green, persistent leaves and attractive lavender-blue, purple, or white flowers in spring; it spreads over the ground by runners. Japanese spurge *(Pachysandra terminalis),* equally hardy, is excellent when once established but should have loose, well-textured soil since it spreads by slender underground rhizomes. Plants are set at intervals of about 8 inches in soil best prepared by adding a liberal mixture of equal parts of leafmold, peat, and sand, plus 1 quart of bonemeal to every bushel of compost. This mixture should be incorporated into the soil to a depth of at least 10 inches. A mulch of peat may be used if the basic soil is very sandy. Also much used is the less hardy (Zone 6) English ivy *(Hedera Helix),* a vine with much more rampant growth covering an area quickly but requiring more upkeep by trimming, etc. It is available in a large assortment of leaf variants, and some cultivars are hardier than others. In its northern limits (Zone 6) it is best used in a northern exposure where not subject to burning from the winter sun. Like *Vinca,* but unlike *Pachysandra, Hedera* is satisfactory on poorer soils, steep slopes, or under shallow-rooted trees like certain of the large maples, where few plants can be grown. Not used as much as they should be, as ground covers for partial shade (in Zones 8 and 9), are the dwarf bamboos *Sasa Veitchii, Shibataea Kumasaca,* and several pygmy species of *Phyllostachys.* On very sandy and dry terraces in sun or partial shade, the bearberry *(Arctostaphylos Uva-ursi)* does very well, forming a dense, glossy, evergreen carpet about 4 inches deep; some of the prostrate junipers (*Juniperus* species) are also effective in such sites.

In certain milder parts of the country, especially those with a Mediterranean climate, like southern California, the range of ground covers is greater and they serve especially on open or sunny slopes that cannot be maintained in lawn. The species involved not only cover the ground but usually produce showy flowers as well. Important are *Ajuga reptans, Carpobrotus edulis, Delosperma, Dimorphotheca, Fragaria chiloensis, Convolvulus, Gazania, Lampranthus, Lantana montevidensis, Malephora crocea* var. *purpureocrocea, Osteospermum fruticosum, Pelargonium peltatum, Polygonum capitatum, Potentilla Crantzii,* and *Sedum.* See *Bedding* and *Lawn.*

GROWTH REGULATORS: see *Plant Hormones.*

GRUSONIA: *OPUNTIA* section *Grusonia.* **G. Hamiltonii:** a listed name of no botanical standing, probably referable to *O. rosarica.*

GUAIACUM L. LIGNUM-VITAE. *Zygophyllaceae.* About 6 spp. of evergreen trees and shrubs, native to drier sites of trop. and subtrop. Amer.; wood very heavy, hard, resinous, brs. articulate; lvs. opp., leathery, pinnate, lfts. 2–14, in pairs; fls. blue, purple, rarely white, long-pedicelled, solitary or in umbel-like clusters, sepals and petals 4 or 5, stamens 8–10, style 1; fr. 2–5-celled caps.

The species listed are sources of lignum-vitae, hardest of commercial woods, as well as sources of guaiacum, a hard resin with medicinal properties. Planted in the tropics as ornamentals, attractive for foliage and flowers and resistance to salt spray in seaside plantings; of interest in southern Calif. and southern Fla., Zone 10.

officinale L. Tree, 10–30 ft.; lvs. to 3½ in. long, lfts. 4–6, to 2 in. long, ovate to broadly obovate; fls. in few- to many-fld. terminal clusters, blue or rarely white, ½ in. long, petals slightly tomentose, at least at apex; caps. yellow, usually broadly obovoid, to ¾ in. long, seeds light to dark brown. Panama to n. S. Amer., W. Indies.

sanctum L. Large shrub or tree, sometimes to 30 ft.; lvs. to 4 in. long, lfts. 4–10, to 1½ in. long, oblong or obovate; fls. 1 to several, terminal, blue or purple, petals glabrous, less than ½ in. long; caps. greenish-yellow to bright orange, broadly obovoid, to ¾ in. long, seeds dark brown or black. S. Fla., W. Indies, Mex. to n. S. Amer.

GUAVA. Guavas are tropical American fruits of the myrtaceous genus *Psidium.* They have a very high vitamin C content (several times that of oranges) and are eaten fresh or more frequently are processed into jams or jellies. Two shrubby species are widely cultivated in the tropics and subtropics, the common guava, *P. Guajava,* and the purple strawberry guava, *P. littorale* var. *longipes.* The former is more tender and in the United States is more at home in Hawaii and subtropical Florida, while the latter is about as hardy as the lemon and so is frequently planted in the southern parts of California and Florida. In the tropics, wherever introduced, *P. Guajava* has become a weed tree or shrub, especially in pastures and clearings; much of the fruit in such areas is collected from wild or semiwild plants.

Fruits of the common guava vary greatly in size (some weigh over ½ pound), seediness (seeds few to many), and flesh color (white, yellowish, or salmon-red). Plants for the home garden should be select cultivars, if at all possible. Air layering now makes guava propagation easy for the home gardener. Guavas are rather free of insect pests and diseases, although in tropical America the fruits are often attacked by fruit flies. The strawberry guava is a medium-sized shrub with small, thick, glossy leaves. Its round, dark red fruits, up to 1½ inches in diameter, are considered by some more flavorsome than those of the common guava.

GUETTARDA L. *Rubiaceae.* About 60 or more spp. of trop., evergreen shrubs or small trees; lvs. opp. or whorled, stipules interpetiolar; fls. in axillary cymes, 4–9-merous, corolla salverform; fr. a few-seeded drupe.

uruguensis Cham. & Schlechtend. Small tree; lvs. elliptic-oblong, to 2 in. long, hairy on both surfaces; corolla tube to ¼ in. long, lobes 5, rounded. Brazil, Uruguay, Argentina. The fr., about the size of a cherry, is said to be edible. Sometimes cult. as an ornamental in mild regions.

GUIBOURTIA J. Benn. emended by J. Léonard. *Leguminosae* (subfamily *Caesalpinioideae*). About 15–17 spp. of trees and shrubs in trop. Amer. and Afr.; lvs. alt., lfts. 1 pair, curved, translucent-dotted; fls. small, in racemes or panicles, nearly regular, sepals 4, petals 0, stamens 10 (8–12), alternately of 2 lengths; fr. a nearly orbicular or obliquely elliptic legume, flat or inflated, mostly 1-seeded.

coleosperma (Benth.) J. Léonard. To 60 ft.; lfts. ovate, 2–4¾ in. long, strongly asymmetrical, glossy above; fls. pedicelled, to ½ in. across, sepals yellow; fr. a leathery, flat legume about 1 in. long, somewhat wider. Angola and S.-W. Afr. to Rhodesia.

GUILIELMA: *BACTRIS.* **G. utilis:** *B. Gasipaes.*

GUIZOTIA Cass. *Compositae* (Helianthus Tribe). About 12 spp. of herbs in trop. Afr.; lvs. mostly opp.; fl. heads radiate, peduncled, receptacle conical, scaly; disc and ray fls. yellow; achenes compressed, glabrous, pappus lacking.

abyssinica (L.f.) Cass. NIGER, RAMTIL, RAMTILLA. Leafy ann., to 3 ft. or more; lvs. lanceolate-oblong, to 6 in. long, serrate, sessile; heads ¾ in. across. Ethiopia; naturalized in Calif. Cult. in some countries for the seeds, which yield the edible niger oil and which are used in birdseed mixtures. May be grown as an ornamental.

GUNNERA L. *Gunneraceae.* About 35 spp. of terrestrial herbs, sometimes gigantic, of trop. and warm temp. regions, with characters of the family.

Plants of mostly cool, moist, frost-free climates, adapted to cooler parts of Zone 9 and 10. The larger kinds are grown for the striking effect of the clumps of enormous rhubarblike foliage, the smaller kinds, mostly in the rock garden, for their rosettes or cushions of decorative roundish leaves. The clusters of red fruits are also ornamental. Rich, moist soil is needed, and preferably a sunny location. Propagated by division or seeds.

chilensis Lam. [*G. scabra* Ruiz & Pav.; *G. tinctoria* Mirb.]. Large, to 6 ft.; lf. blades orbicular-reniform, palmately lobed, coarsely toothed, to 5 ft. across, scabrous, with fleshy prickles on veins beneath and on long petioles; infl. a dense, cylindrical panicle to 3 ft. high, the brs. spicate, 1–3 in. long, rigid, fleshy and contiguous in fr. Patagonia.

dentata T. Kirk. Low, stoloniferous; lf. blades leathery to rather thin, narrowly ovate, ¼–1 in. long, coarsely and irregularly toothed, gray-green, hairy, petioles broad, to 2 in. long; infl. spicate, 1–3 in. high. New Zeal.

Hamiltonii T. Kirk. ex W. S. Hamilt. Low, stoloniferous, forming cushions; lf. blades leathery, triangular-ovate, 4–6 in. long, finely and evenly crenate, glabrous or nearly so, dark gray-green, petioles stout, winged, 1–2 in. long; infl. to 2½ in. high. New Zeal.

magellanica Lam. Low, to about 5 in., stoloniferous; lf. blades orbicular or reniform, to about 2 in. across, crenate, glabrous to pilose, long-petioled; infl. a short panicle, the male longer than lvs., the female shorter than lvs. Patagonia, Falkland Is.

manicata Linden. Distinguished from *G. chilensis* by its even larger lvs., to 9 ft. across; infl. taller, less dense, to 1 ft. thick, brs. to 6 in. long, flexuous, separate in fr. Colombia.

prorepens Hook.f. Low, stoloniferous; lf. blades thin, ovate, ⅜–2 in. long, finely crenate to entire, brown- to purplish-green, glabrous or hairy, petioles slender, ¾–2 in. long; infl. spicate, on scape 1–8 in. long. New Zeal.

scabra: *G. chilensis.*
tinctoria: *G. chilensis.*

GUNNERACEAE Meissn. GUNNERA FAMILY. Dicot.; 1 genus of about 35 spp. of rhizomatous, per. herbs, native to trop. and warm temp. regions; lvs. in basal rosettes, orbicular to reniform, with stipules; infl. many-fld., scapose, spicate, or much-branched; fls. very small, bisexual or unisexual, calyx lobes 2, petals 2 or 0, stamens 1–2, styles 2, ovary inferior, 1-celled, 1-ovuled; fr. a red to purple drupelet. *Gunnera* is cult., chiefly for its foliage.

GUSTAVIA L. *Lecythidaceae.* About 45 spp. of large shrubs or trees in Cent. and trop. S. Amer.; lvs. alt., simple, without stipules, usually serrate; fls. in terminal or axillary corymbs or racemes, calyx 4–6-lobed, petals 6–8, slightly unequal, stamens many, borne on a cuplike androphore, ovary inferior, 4–6-celled; fr. fleshy, berrylike.

superba (Kunth) O. Berg. Tree, to 45 ft.; lvs. crowded at br. tips, narrowly oblanceolate, to 3 ft. long or more, acuminate, serrate, short-petioled; infl. of terminal or lateral racemes; fls. 3–5 in. across, rosy outside, white inside, stamens incurved, purple-tipped; fr. yellow-green, to 2½ in. in diam., edible. Panama, Colombia, Ecuador.

GUTIERREZIA Lag. MATCHWEED, MATCHBRUSH, SNAKEWEED, RESINWEED, BROOMWEED, TURPENTINE WEED. *Compositae* (Aster Tribe). About 25 spp. of sticky, per. herbs, often somewhat woody, in dry soils of w. N. and S. Amer.; lvs. alt., filiform to narrowly oblanceolate, entire; fl. heads radiate, small, many in cymes or panicles, involucral bracts imbricate, leathery; fls. all yellow; achenes oblong, hairy, pappus of 10–12 scales.

Sarothrae (Pursh) Britt. & Rusby. Subshrub, sts. many, slender, to 2 ft.; lvs. linear, to 2 in. long; infl. flat-topped, heads ¼ in. across, narrowly turbinate; disc and ray fls. each 3–8. Sw. Canada and w. U.S. to n. Mex.

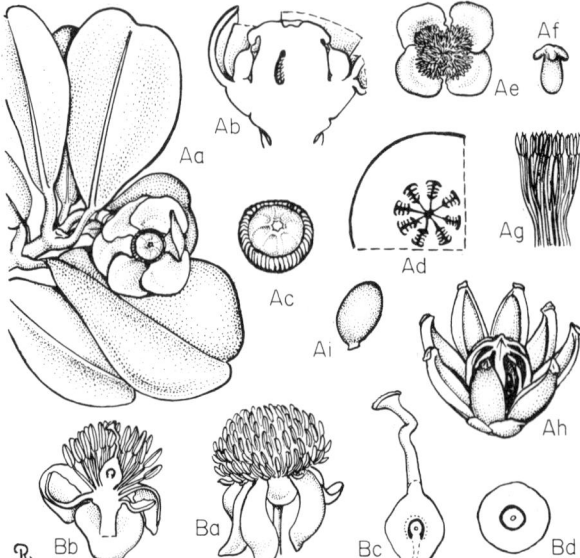

GUTTIFERAE. **A,** *Clusea rosea:* **Aa,** flowering twig of female tree, × ¼; **Ab,** female flower, vertical section (perianth partly cut away), × ¾; **Ac,** pistil surrounded by staminodes, × ½; **Ad,** ovary, cross section (partly cut away), × 1½; **Ae,** male flower, × ½; **Af,** pistillode, × 1; **Ag,** stamens, × 1; **Ah,** dehiscing capsule, × ¼; **Ai,** seed, × 3. **B,** *Calophyllum inophyllum:* **Ba,** bisexual flower, × 1; **Bb,** flower, vertical section, × 1; **Bc,** pistil, with ovary in vertical section, × 3; **Bd,** ovary, cross section, × 3.

GUTTIFERAE Juss. or, alternatively, **CLUSIACEAE** Lindl. GARCINIA FAMILY. Dicot.; about 40 genera and 1,000 spp. of trop., dioecious or polygamous trees or shrubs; lvs. mostly opp. or whorled, simple, often thick, and mostly evergreen; fls. solitary or cymose, regular, unisexual or sometimes bisexual, petals 4–12, stamens usually many and separate or somewhat united, styles more or less united; fr. drupelike, berrylike, or sometimes capsular, 1–2- or more-celled. The family includes genera of economic importance grown in the tropics for the edible frs., dyes, and cabinet wood. Among those cult. are: *Calophyllum, Clusia, Garcinia, Mammea, Mesua,* and *Rheedia.*

GUZMANIA Ruiz & Pav. *Bromeliaceae.* About 126 spp. of terrestrial or epiphytic herbs, native to trop. Amer.; lvs. usually in basal rosettes, stiff, entire; fls. yellow or white, in several vertical ranks, in terminal spikes or panicles, often showy-bracted, petals united in a tube about as long as the calyx, ovary superior; fr. a caps., seeds plumose.

Grown outdoors in warm climates or under glass. Requires filtered or subdued light. For culture see *Bromeliaceae.*

angustifolia (Bak.) Wittm. Sts. short, or to 8 in. and branched; lvs. dense, narrowly triangular, green above, purplish beneath; scape almost concealed by lvs., infl. to 2⅝ in. long, few-fld., fl. bracts slightly shorter than fls.; petals bright yellow. Costa Rica to Colombia and Ecuador.

Berteroniana (Schult.) Mez. Stemless, to 16 in.; lvs. many, to 10 in. long, 2 in. wide, pale green, glabrous; scape about as long as lvs., infl. spicate, elongate, bracts bright red, glabrous, imbricate, the lower acuminate, the upper sterile; fls. yellow, to 2⅜ in. long, longer than the bracts. Puerto Rico, Dominican Republic.

Danielii L. B. Sm. To 4½ ft.; lvs. to 2½ ft. long, reddish-green; scape erect, infl. 8 in. long, bracts elliptic, about as long as sepals; sepals united for ¾ in. Colombia.

dissitiflora (André) L. B. Sm. Usually stoloniferous, to 3 ft.; lvs. to 3 ft. long, pale green with fine longitudinal brown stripes; infl. erect, about as high as lvs.; fls. spreading, pedicelled, sepals to 1⅛ in. long, petals white. Costa Rica to Colombia.

Eduardii André ex Mez. St. to 28 in. long, longer than infl.; lvs. in a rosette; infl. dense, digitate, of about 10 spikes, fl. bracts pale green or yellow; petals yellow or white, 1⅝ in. long. Colombia.

gloriosa (André) André ex Mez. More than 28 in. high; lvs. to 2 ft. long, green with red tip; infl. dense, fl. bracts red, about as long as sepals; sepals red, petals yellow. Colombia, Ecuador.

Lindenii (André) Mez. To more than 3 ft.; lvs. to 28 in. long, dark green above, spotted with red-brown beneath; infl. longer than lvs., paniculate, with ovoid to ellipsoid brs., fl. bracts broad, as long as sepals; petals white. Peru.

lingulata (L.) Mez. Epiphytic, st. stout, to 1 ft.; lvs. to 1½ ft. long and more than 1 in. wide; infl. corymbose, outer bracts usually red or pink, larger than the reduced, hooded inner bracts; fls. to 1¾ in. long, white. A variable sp. of trop. Amer. with 5 vars. Var. **lingulata.** The typical var.; lvs. green, more than 1 in. wide; outer bracts of infl. erect, red or pink; fls. many. Var. **cardinalis** (André) André ex Mez. Lvs. more than 1 in. wide, spreading; bracts bright scarlet. Colombia, Ecuador. Var. ×**magnifica** Hort.: var. *cardinalis* × var. *minor.* Plant 20 in. across; lvs. delicate green; infl. 7 in. long, 6 in. across, with 20 scarlet bracts and white fls. Var. **minor** (Mez) L. B. Sm. [*G. minor* Mez]. Lvs. 1 in. wide or less, lf. sheath same color as blade; infl. bracts red; fls. few. Var. **splendens** (Planch.) Mez [cv. 'Peacockii']. Lvs. more than 1 in. wide, with red-purple longitudinal stripes; outer bracts of infl. erect, red or pink.

×**magnifica:** *G. lingulata* var.

minor: *G. lingulata* var.

monostachia (L.) Rusby [*G. tricolor* Ruiz & Pav.]. Stemless, to 16 in.; lvs. linear, to 16 in. long, ¾ in. wide, light green; scape shorter than to as long as lvs., infl. spicate, elongate, bracts white, tipped with orange; fls. white, about 1 in. long, scarcely longer than bracts. W. Indies, Fla., Cent. Amer., S. Amer. Var. **variegata** M. B. Foster. Lvs. variegated with white.

musaica (Linden) Mez. Terrestrial, rarely epiphytic, stemless; lvs. to 2½ ft. long, 3 in. wide, with dark green transverse lines above and purple lines beneath; infl. unbranched, headlike, fl. bracts golden-yellow striped with rose; fls. yellowish, to 2 in. long, sepals petal-like, longer than petals. Colombia.

nicaraguensis Mez & C. F. Bak. Lvs. 10–15, in a dense rosette, to 2 ft. long, pale, often with red lines; infl. unbranched, densely fusiform, few-fld., bracts red; fls. yellow, over 2⅜ in. long. Cent. Amer.

sanguinea (André) André ex Mez. Stemless, to 8 in.; lvs. to 1 ft. long, all or only the inner ones bright red; infl. sunken in lf. rosette; fls. yellow and white, 2¾ in. long, sepals united, to $^{9}/_{16}$ in. long. Costa Rica to Colombia and Ecuador.

tricolor: *G. monostachia.*

vittata (Mart. ex Schult.f.) Mez. Stemless, to 22 in.; lvs. to 2 ft. long, usually with broad, dark, transverse bands beneath; scape erect, with tightly imbricate bracts, infl. densely digitate or unbranched, fl. bracts enfolding bases of sepals; petals ¾ in. long, white. Brazil, Colombia.

Zahnii (Hook.f.) Mez. Stemless or nearly so, to 20 in.; lvs. in rosettes of 20–30, to 2 ft. long, spreading; scape red, erect, slightly shorter than lvs., infl. compound, yellow; petals bright yellow. Panama.

×**GUZVRIESEA** Dutrie ex M. B. Foster: *Guzmania* × *Vriesea. Bromeliaceae.*

magnifica (Carrière) M. B. Foster [*Vriesea* × *magnifica* (Carrière) Hort. Makoy]: *Guzmania Zahnii* × *Vriesea splendens.* PAINTED-FEATHER. To nearly 3 ft.; panicle 1½–2 ft., densely branched in several directions, fl. bracts red-yellow; petals yellow, longer than sepals.

GYMNADENIA: *HABENARIA.*

GYMNADENIOPSIS: *HABENARIA.*

GYMNOCACTUS: *NEOLLOYDIA.* **G. Gielsdorfianus:** *Thelocactus Gielsdorfianus.* **G. Knuthianus:** *Thelocactus Knuthianus.*

GYMNOCALYCIUM Pfeiff. [*Weingartia* Werderm.]. CHIN CACTUS. *Cactaceae.* Perhaps 40 spp. of globose cacti, native to S. Amer., with tubercled ribs; sts. simple or cespitose, mostly with a protrusion (chin) below each areole; fls. subapical to lateral, campanulate to short-funnelform, opening several days in succession, white to pink, rarely yellow, perianth tube glabrous, scales of tube and ovary mostly remote, broad, rounded, stamens in 1 series or with a separate basal series also, fr. oblong, red, seeds cap-shaped to dome-shaped, tubercled, hilum large. Bolivia and s. Brazil to Argentina.

For culture see *Cacti.*

Andreae (Böd.) Backeb. & F. M. Knuth. Sts. cespitose, to 2 in. thick, ribs 8, low, rounded; spines needle-shaped, curved, to $^{5}/_{16}$ in. long, radial spines 7, white, central spines 1–3, brownish; fls. yellow, 1½ in. long. N. Argentina. Perhaps a var. of *G. Leeanum.*

Anisitsii (K. Schum.) Britt. & Rose. Sts. simple, to 4 in. thick, ribs 11, strongly tubercled; spines 5–7, awl-shaped, angled, tortuous, to 2 in. long; fls. white, 1½ in. long. Paraguay.

Baldianum (Speg.) Speg. [*G. Venturianum* Frič ex Backeb.]. Sts. simple, depressed-globose, dark gray-green, to 1⅝ in. high and 2¾ in. thick, ribs 9–11; spines 3–7, mostly 5, radial, dirty pale ash-gray; fls. wine-red, to 1⅝ in. long. Argentina.

Bodenbenderanum (Hosseus) Backeb. & F. M. Knuth. Sts. depressed, to 3 in. thick, ribs 11–14, low, rounded; spines 3–5, awl-shaped, decurved, brown, to ⅜ in. long; fls. rose, to 1½ in. long. N. Argentina. Perhaps referable to *G. stellatum* Speg.

Bruchii (Speg.) Backeb. A sp. of uncertain identity; perhaps the same as *G. lafaldense.*

chubutense (Speg.) Backeb. Sts. simple, to 4 in. high and 6 in. thick, ribs about 15, low, wide; radial spines 6–7, stout, to 1½ in. long, central spine 0–1; fls. pink, to 2 in. long. S. Argentina. Perhaps a var. of *G. gibbosum.*

Cumingii: a listed name of no botanical standing, probably referring to *G. neocumingii.*

Damsii (K. Schum.) Britt. & Rose. Sts. simple, ribs about 10, low; spines 6–8, radial, needle-shaped, to ½ in. long; fls. white, 2½ in. long, stamens in 2 series. Paraguay. Perhaps a var. of *G. Schickendantzii.*

Delaetii: *G. Schickendantzii.*

denudatum (Link & Otto) Pfeiff. SPIDER CACTUS. Sts. simple, to 4 in. high and 6 in. thick, ribs 5–8, low, rounded, scarcely tubercled; spines 5–8, radial, appressed, needle-shaped, yellowish, ½ in. long; fls. white or pale rose, to nearly 3 in. across, scales acutish. S. Brazil to n. Argentina.

Fidaianum (Backeb.) P. C. Hutchison [*Weingartia Fidaiana* (Backeb.) Werderm.]. Root tuberous, sts. mostly solitary, to 8 in. high and 5 in. thick; spines needle-shaped, straw-yellow to dark purple, radial spines about 9, to 1¼ in. long, central spines 3–4, to 2 in. long; fls. yellow, to 1¼ in. long, open continuously, perianth segms. rounded; fr. small, opening below. Bolivia.

Fleischeranum Backeb. Sts. globose, to 2¾ in. high and 4 in. thick, ribs 8, rounded, not tubercled; radial spines about 20, bristlelike, brown, to 1 in. long, central spines similar; fls. white, with rose throat. Paraguay.

Friederickii: a listed name of no botanical standing, doubtless referring to *G. Mihanovichii* var.

gibbosum (Haw.) Pfeiff. Sts. solitary, to 10 in. high and 6 in. thick, ribs 12–14, strongly tubercled; spines 7–12, radial, needle-shaped to awl-shaped, spreading, mostly brown; fls. white, to 2½ in. long. Argentina. Cvs. are: **'Ferox'**, spines more numerous, flexible; **'Nigrum'**, spines very dark; **'Schlumbergii'**, spines more numerous, stiff, pinkish-red to amber-yellow.

Hossei (F. A. Haage, jr.) Backeb. & F. M. Knuth. Ribs 13; spines mostly 7, spreading and recurved, awl-shaped or flattened, brown, becoming gray, to ⅝ in. long; fls. rose. N. Argentina.

hyptiacanthum (Lem.) Britt. & Rose. Sts. simple, to 3 in. thick, ribs 9–12, broad, obtuse; radial spines 5–9, spreading or appressed, to ½ in. long, central spine 0–1; fls. white, 2 in. long. Uruguay.

Kurtzianum: *G. Mostii* var.

lafaldense Vaup. Sts. cespitose, to 2 in. thick, ribs 8–12; spines needle-shaped, radial spines 12–20, white to brown, to ¼ in. long, central spines 0–3; fls. violet-rose, to 2 in. long, stamens in 1 series. Argentina. Perhaps referable to *G. Bruchii* whose identity is uncertain.

Leeanum (Hook.) Britt. & Rose. Sts. about 3 in. thick, ribs about 16, irregular, strongly tubercled; radial spines about 7–10, needle-shaped, appressed, ½ in. long, central spine 1, directed outward; fls. pale yellow, to 2 in. long. Argentina, Uruguay. Var. **Netrelianum** (Monv.) Backeb. [*G. Netrelianum* (Monv.) Britt. & Rose]. Tubercles said to be broader than high, spines longer.

leptanthum (Speg.) Speg. Similar to *G. platense* and probably only a var. of it, with ribs 8–11, fls. to nearly 3 in. long.

loricatum: *G. Spegazzinii.*

mazanense Backeb. Sts. solitary, about 4 in. thick, ribs 10–11, low, rounded, almost tubercled; spines awl-shaped, often curved, gray, to 1½ in. long, radial spines 7–9, central spines 0–2; fls. white to rose, with red center, to 1½ in. long. N. Argentina.

megalothelos (Sencke ex K. Schum.) Britt. & Rose. Sts. cespitose, to 6 in. thick, ribs 10–12, strongly tubercled; spines needle-shaped, brownish, often curved, radial spines 7–8, to ⅝ in. long, central spine 1, to 1¼ in. long; fls. pinkish, 1½ in. long. Paraguay.

michoga Y. Ito. Sts. simple, globose, gray-green, ribs about 11, tubercled; spines about 7, radial, dark brown, becoming whitish-black, to ¾ in. long; fls. white, to 2 in. long. Argentina.

Mihanovichii (Frič & Gürke) Britt. & Rose. PLAIN CACTUS. Sts. simple, to 2½ in. thick, ribs 8, nearly acute, scarcely tubercled but prominently cross-ridged; spines needle-shaped, grayish, often curved, radial spines 5–9, to ½ in. long, central spine 0–1; fls. pale yellow, to 1¾ in. long, stamens in 2 series. Paraguay. Var. **Friedrichii** Werderm. Sts. reddish; spines deciduous; fls. pink.

Monvillei Pfeiff. Sts. to 9 in. thick, ribs 13–17, strongly tubercled; spines 11–13, slender-awl-shaped, curved, yellowish, to 2 in. long; fls. white, to 3 in. long. Paraguay.

Mostii (Gürke) Britt. & Rose. Sts. to 5 in. thick, ribs 11–14, strongly tubercled; spines slender-awl-shaped, angled, horn-colored, brown-tipped, radial spines 7–9, central spine 1; fls. pink, to 3 in. long. Paraguay. Var. **Kurtzianum** (Gürke) Backeb. [*G. Kurtzianum* (Gürke) Britt. & Rose]. Fls. white with red throat.

multiflorum (Hook.) Britt. & Rose. Sts. simple or cespitose, to 5 in. thick, ribs 10–15, irregular, rounded, strongly tubercled; spines 5–10, radial, slender-awl-shaped, often recurved, yellowish, to 1¼ in. long; fls. white or pinkish, 1½ in. long. Brazil to Argentina. Var. **albispinum** (K. Schum.) Backeb. Spines white, appressed.

neocumingii (Backeb.) P. C. Hutchison [*Weingartia neocumingii* Backeb.]. Sts. simple, globose, to 4 in. thick, tubercles $^3/_{16}$ in. high, projecting below the areole; radial spines 20 or more, white to yellow, to ⅜ in. long, central spines 2–8, stouter, darker; fls. orange-yellow, 1 in. long. Bolivia.

Netrelianum: *G. Leeanum* var.

Neumannianum (Backeb.) P. C. Hutchison [*Weingartia Neumanniana* (Backeb.) Werderm.]. Root tuberous, sts. to 3 in. high and 2 in. thick, tubercles low, united in about 14 ribs; spines dark brown to reddish, radial spines about 6, central spine 1, longer, to 1 in. long; fls. orange-yellow, 1 in. long, segms. acute. N. Argentina.

nidulans Backeb. Sts. to 4½ in. thick, ribs to 17, strongly tubercled; spines 6, radial, 1 erect, the others reflexed; fls. rosy. N. Argentina.

nigriareolatum Backeb. Sts. simple, to 6 in. thick, ribs about 18, scarcely tubercled; areoles ¼ in. long, becoming black, spines slender-awl-shaped, slightly curved, pale, radial spines about 7, central spine 1, to 1¼ in. long; fls. white, to 2 in. long. N. Argentina.

occultum: a listed name of no botanical standing; said to be similar to *G. Quehlianum.*

Ochoterenae Backeb. Sts. 2½ in. thick, ribs about 16, almost tubercled; spines about 3–5, radial, recurved, yellowish, dark-tipped, ½ in. long; fls. white, 1½ in. long. Argentina. Cv. **'Variispinum'** is listed.

oenanthemum Backeb. Sts. simple, about 4 in. thick, ribs about 11, divided into oblong tubercles; spines about 5, radial, recurved, awl-shaped, reddish, to ⅝ in. long; fls. pale claret, to 2 in. long. N. Argentina.

Ourselianum: a listed name of no botanical standing, probably applying to *G. multiflorum.*

Pflanzii (Vaup.) Werderm. Sts. cespitose, to 4 in. thick or perhaps much more, ribs about 8, low, rounded, almost tubercled; areoles remote, spines 6–10, spreading thick-needle-shaped, often curved, whitish, to 1 in. long; fls. white to pink, to 2 in. long. Bolivia. Perhaps not distinct from *G. saglione.*

platense (Speg.) Britt. & Rose. Sts. to 4 in. thick, ribs about 14, almost tubercled; spines 5–7, radial, appressed, needle-shaped, to ⅝ in. long; fls. white, 2 in. long. N. Argentina.

Quehlianum (F. A. Haage, jr.) Vaup. ex Hosseus. Sts. simple, globose, red-green, to 6 in. thick, ribs 8–13, tubercled; spines 5, radial, horn-colored, with red base; fls. white with red center. Argentina.

saglione (J. F. Cels) Britt. & Rose [*Echinocactus saglionis* J. F. Cels]. Sts. simple, to 1 ft. thick, ribs 13–32, low, rounded, somewhat tubercled; radial spines 8–10 or on older plants more, awl-shaped, recurved, dark, to 1½ in. long, central spines 1 to several; fls. white or pink, 1½ in. long. N. Argentina.

Schickendantzii (A. Web.) Britt. & Rose [*G. Delaetii* (K. Schum.) Hosseus]. WHITE CHIN CACTUS. Sts. simple, to 6 in. thick, ribs about 10–15, scarcely to strongly tubercled; spines 6–7, radial, recurved, flattened and grooved, reddish, becoming gray, to 1¼ in. long; fls. white to pink or yellowish, 2 in. long, stamens in 2 series. N. Argentina.

Sigelianum (Schick) A. Berger. Sts. to 3 in. thick, ribs 10, low, weakly tubercled; spines 3, stout, dark, at first scaly, ½ in. long, the lower 1 decurved, the others straight, spreading. Argentina.

Spegazzinii Britt. & Rose [*G. loricatum* (Speg.) F. M. Knuth]. Sts. to 6 in. thick, ribs 13, rounded, scarcely tubercled; spines 5–7, radial, appressed, recurved, semicylindrical, awl-shaped, brown, to 1 in. long; fls. rosy, to 3 in. long. N. Argentina.

Stuckertii (Speg.) Britt. & Rose. Sts. to 2½ in. thick, ribs 9–11, strongly tubercled; spines 7–9, radial, appressed, cylindrical or flattened, gray, covered with small scales, to 1 in. long; fls. white to pink, 1½ in. long. Argentina.

Sutteranum (Schick) A. Berger. Cespitose, ribs 10, of oblong tubercles; spines 5, slender, to ⅝ in. long, the lower decurved, the lateral spreading; fls. large, pinkish. Argentina.

Urselianum: a listed name of no botanical standing, perhaps referring to *G. multiflorum.*

Velenowskyi: a listed name of no botanical standing; ribs 20 or more, tubercled; radial spines 9–12, short, central spines 1–4, the longest decurved, to 1 in. long; fls. yellow. Argentina.

Venturianum: *G. Baldianum.*

Weissianum Backeb. Sts. to 5½ in. thick, ribs to 19, prominently tubercled; radial spines 8, slightly turned out at tips, to 1¼ in. long, interlacing, central spine 1, ascending; fls. pink. Argentina. Cv. **'Atroroseum'**. Spines longer; fls. darker.

GYMNOCARPIUM Newm. *Polypodiaceae.* Two or 3 spp. of delicate, boreal ferns, with slender, widely creeping rhizomes; lvs. triangular, 6–10 in. long, 2-pinnate-pinnatifid to 3-pinnate, with enlarged basal pinnae, veins few; sori submarginal, round or elongate, frequently confluent, without indusia.

Dryopteris (L.) Newm. [*Dryopteris disjuncta* (Ledeb.) C. V. Mort.; *D. Linnaeana* C. Chr.; *Polypodium disjunctum* Rupr.; *P. Dryopteris* (L.) Fée]. OAK FERN. Lvs. triangular, to 11 in. long and wide, 2-pinnate, pinnae entire or wavy-toothed. N. N. Amer., Eur., Asia.

Robertianum (Hoffm.) Newm. [*Dryopteris Robertiana* (Hoffm.) C. Chr.]. NORTHERN OAK FERN, SCENTED O. F., LIMESTONE O. F., LIMESTONE POLYPODY. Petioles and lvs. minutely glandular beneath, lvs. to 8 in. long and 7 in. wide, 2–3-pinnatifid. N. N. Amer., Eur.

GYMNOCLADUS Lam. *Leguminosae* (subfamily *Caesalpinioideae*). Three spp. of deciduous, unarmed dioecious or polygamous trees in e. U.S. and e. Asia, with stout brs.; lvs. 2-pinnate, lfts. entire; fls. in terminal, loose panicles, 5-merous, regular, greenish-white, stamens 3–10, separate; fr. oblong, thick, flat.

Yields a durable timber. Planted for ornament. Propagated by seeds and cuttings. Foliage appears later than most trees.

canadensis: *G. dioica.*

dioica (L.) C. Koch [*G. canadensis* Lam.]. KENTUCKY COFFEE TREE, NICKER TREE, CHICOT. To 100 ft.; pinnae in 3–7 pairs, larger terminal ones with 3–7 pairs of ovate, acute lfts. to 3 in. long, new lvs. pink; racemes with female fls. to 1 ft. long, those with male fls. denser, to 4 in. long; fr. a red-brown legume, to 10 in. long, persistent. Temp. e. U.S. Seeds have been used for a coffee substitute.

GYMNOGRAMMA: *PITYROGRAMMA.*

GYMNOLOMIA Kunth. Compositae. Not cult. **G. multiflora:** *Viguiera multiflora.*

GYMNOSPERM (Gymnospermae, one of the two main divisions of the seed plants). A gymnosperm is a plant lacking flowers and reproducing by seeds borne naked on a special bract or sporophyll, most often in a cone, in contrast to the angiosperms, which have flowers and have seeds enclosed in (mature) ovaries. See *Conifers, Cycads,* and *Ginkgo.*

GYMNOSPORIA: *MAYTENUS.*

GYNANDRIRIS Parl. *Iridaceae.* About 20 spp. of cormous, per. herbs, native mostly to Afr., 1 sp. from Medit. region to cent. Asia; corm tunicate, the fibers soft, parallel, at least the inner ones; lvs. linear; fls. in clusters, produced in succession, fugacious, spathe valves 2, thin, membranous, colorless, perianth tube none, perianth segms. 6, not united, the 3 outer (the falls) reflexed, the 3 inner (the standards) erect, stamens 3, filaments partly united, ovary elongated apically into a beak, style brs. 3, deeply 2-cleft, the divisions petal-like; fr. a 3-valved caps., enclosed within the spathe valves.

Sisyrinchium (L.) Parl. [*Iris Sisyrinchium* L.]. SPANISH NUT. Sts. to about 15 in.; lvs. mostly 2, longer than the sts.; infl. 1–6-fld., spathe valves inflated; fls. lavender or lilac to blue-purple, falls obovate-spatulate, to 1½ in. long, with a white blotch, bluish dots, and a yellow ridge on claw; standards oblanceolate. Portugal and Medit. region to cent. Asia.

GYNANDROPSIS: *CLEOME.*

GYNERIUM Humb. & Bonpl. *Gramineae.* One sp. of tall, dioecious, per. reeds in trop. Amer.; panicles plumelike; spikelets several-fld., glumes of female florets long-attenuate, lemma smaller, long-silky, glumes of male florets shorter, lemma glabrous. For terminology see *Gramineae.*

argenteum: *Cortaderia Selloana.*

sagittatum (Aubl.) Beauvois. UVA GRASS, WILD CANE, ARROW C. Sts. to more than 30 ft.; lf. blades sharply serrulate, to 6 ft. long or more and 2⅜ in. wide, forming a fan at summit of sterile sts., old sheaths persistent on st.; panicle pale, densely fld., 3 ft. long or more, main axis erect, brs. drooping. River banks, trop. Amer. Amerindians used sts. for arrow shafts. Occasionally cult. in trop. gardens or in greenhouses for ornament.

GYNURA Cass. *Compositae* (Senecio Tribe). About 100 spp. of herbs and subshrubs in Old World tropics, from Afr. to Malay Arch.; lvs. alt.; heads discoid, not very showy, solitary or in corymbs, involucre cylindrical, involucral bracts in 2 rows, the outer few, short, the inner longer, narrow, erect, coherent, receptacle flat, naked; fls. all tubular, bisexual, yellow, red, or purple, unpleasantly scented; achenes linear, 5–10-ribbed, pappus of many, white, capillary bristles.

Gynuras are grown under glass as foliage plants. They need plenty of light to bring out the color in the foliage; soil and moisture requirements are like those for coleus and geraniums. Easily propagated by cuttings.

aurantiaca (Blume) DC. VELVET PLANT, PURPLE V.P., ROYAL V.P. Per. herb, velvety-purple-hairy throughout, sts. erect when young, later clambering, to 9 ft.; lf. blades ovate to broadly elliptic, to 8 in. long, 4½ in. wide, coarsely dentate, narrowed to a petiole, often auriculate at base, upper lvs. sessile; heads ⅝–¾ in. long, few in an open corymb, involucral bracts purple-hairy; fls. longer than involucral bracts, orange-yellow, aging to purple. Java; naturalized in warm regions. Cv. **'Purple Passion'** [cv. 'Sarmentosa'; *G. procumbens* Hort., not (Lour.) Merrill; *G. sarmentosa* Hort., not (Blume) DC.]. PURPLE-PASSION VINE. Differs in having sts. decumbent or clambering, more slender, lf. blades narrower, oblong-lanceolate, to 4½ in. long, 2 in. wide, coarsely and distinctly dentate to pinnately lobed, surface green above, purple beneath; fls. about as long as involucral bracts. The exact origin and status of this cv. is uncertain. Cv. **'Sarmentosa':** cv. 'Purple Passion'.

bicolor DC. Per. herb, glabrous except for occasional scattered hairs, sts. erect, to 3 ft., dark purple below, green above; lf. blades ovate-lanceolate to oblanceolate, to 6 in. long or more, pinnately lobed and coarsely dentate, green or purplish above, deep purple beneath, slightly downy, short-petioled; heads to 1 in. long, several in open corymbs, involucral bracts glabrous, purple-tipped; fls. shorter than involucral bracts, orange-yellow. Moluccas.

procumbens (Lour.) Merrill [*G. sarmentosa* (Blume) DC.]. Nearly glabrous, sts., infl. brs., and involucres purple, sts. erect at first, later climbing, to 9 ft. or more; lf. blades ovate to lanceolate, to 5 in. long, 2¼ in. wide, entire to remotely dentate, green with purple midrib, sparsely short-hairy or glabrous, rounded to cuneate at base, lower lvs. petioled, uppermost lvs. sessile; heads in loose corymbs, involucral bracts glabrous; fls. shorter than involucral bracts, orange-yellow. Malay Arch., Philippine Is. Material offered under this name may be *G. aurantiaca* cv. 'Purple Passion'.

sarmentosa: *G. procumbens,* but material offered in the U.S. as *G. sarmentosa* is commonly *G. aurantiaca* cv. 'Purple Passion'.

scandens O. Hoffm. Somewhat shrubby, glandular-pubescent, sts. high-climbing; lf. blades ovate to broadly elliptic, entire to remotely denticulate to coarsely dentate, petioled; heads in dense, hemispherical corymbs; fls. longer than involucral bracts, orange-yellow. Trop. E. Afr.

GYPSOPHILA L. *Caryophyllaceae.* About 125 spp. of ann., bien., or per. herbs or rarely subshrubs, native mostly to Eurasia, 1 sp. in Egypt, 1 in Australia; herbage glaucous, glabrous or glandular-hairy; lvs. opp., linear-subulate, lanceolate, or spatulate, almost fleshy; fls. white or pink, small, many, in dichasial cymes, or panicles of heads or cymes, bracts usually scarious; calyx 5-toothed, or 5-cleft; petals 5, with little distinction between claw and limb, without coronal scales, stamens usually 10, styles mostly 2; fr. a 1-celled caps., dehiscent by 4 valves, seeds flat, nearly reniform, black, usually tubercled.

Florists commonly cultivate *G. paniculata* and *G. elegans.* Other species are cultivated for the misty effect in rock gardens and borders, and for bouquets. Propagated by seeds, division, and cuttings.

acutifolia Steven ex K. Spreng. Erect per., to 6 ft., much-branched, glabrous at base, glandular-pubescent toward apex; lvs. linear-lanceolate, 3 in. long, long-acuminate; infl. densely panicled, pedicels to nearly 3/16 in. long, calyx nearly 3/16 in. long, teeth acuminate, petals 5/16 in. long, white. Romania, s. Ukraine, Caucasus.

aretioides Boiss. Cespitose per., to 3 in.; lvs. linear, 3-angled, obtuse; infl. 1- to few-fld.; calyx obconic, lobes ovate, white-margined, petals oblong, longer than the calyx, entire, white; seeds minutely prickly. Alpine zone of Elburz Mts. (n. Iran).

bicolor: *G. paniculata* subsp.

Bungeana: *G. sericea.*

carminea: *G. elegans* cv.

cerastioides D. Don. Per., 4–10 in., much-branched, pubescent; lvs. obovate, ½–2 in. long, ¼–¾ in. wide, ciliate, basal lvs. petioled, st. lvs. sessile; cymes loose, bracts leafy; fls. either sessile or pedicelled, ⅛–½ in. across, calyx ¼ in. long, pubescent, lobes ciliate, petals spatulate, 3-nerved, lilac. Himalayas, Kashmir to Sikkim.

dubia: *G. repens.*

elegans Bieb. BABY'S-BREATH. Ann., 8–20 in., much-branched; lvs. linear-lanceolate, 1–2 in. long, 1–3-veined; infl. a panicle of cymes, bracts scarious, midrib dark, pedicels long; calyx 3/16 in. long, petals ¼–1 in. long, white, with purple veins. S. Ukraine, Caucasus, e. Turkey, n. Iran. Much planted, graceful. Cvs. include: **'Carminea'** [*G. carminea* Hort.], fls. carmine-rose; **'Grandiflora Alba'** [*G. grandiflora alba* Hort.], fls. large, white; **'Purpurea'**, fls. purplish; **'Rosea'**, fls. rose-pink.

flore-pleno: a listed name of no botanical standing, used for *G. paniculata* cv. 'Flore Pleno'.

Franzii: a listed name of no botanical standing.

fratensis: a listed name of no botanical standing; plant creeping, fls. pink.

glandulosa (Boiss.) Walp. Per., prostrate or ascending, to 8 in., glandular-pubescent; basal lvs. spatulate, upper st. lvs. elliptic, to ⅜ in.

long; infl. a cyme; calyx widely campanulate, to ⁵⁄₁₆ in. long, petals oblanceolate, 1½ times longer than calyx, purple-pink. Turkey, Caucasus, w. Transcaucasia.

grandiflora alba: *G. elegans* cv.

libanotica Boiss. Suffrutescent per., to 16 in., glabrous at the base, glandular-hairy above; lvs. linear-lanceolate, to 1 in. long, glaucous; cymes about 20-fld., bracts lanceolate, scarious, pedicels to ¾ in. long, glandular-hairy; calyx about ⅛ in. long, teeth apiculate, petals ¼ in. long, emarginate, white to pink. Lebanon, w. Syria, s.-cent. Turkey.

Manginii: a listed name of no botanical standing, used for per. plants with thick, fleshy roots; lvs. smooth, glaucous; fls. rather large, light rose, in small panicles.

muralis L. Ann. herb, to 8 in., sts. very slender, glabrous above, pubescent below; lvs. linear, to 1 in. long; infl. loose, panicled; calyx long-campanulate, to ⅛ in. long, petals cuneate, to ¼ in. long, pink to white. Eur., Caucasus, Siberia; naturalized locally in e. N. Amer.

nana Bory & Chaub. Cespitose per., to 6 in., viscid-pubescent; lvs. oblong, to ⅜ in. long, obtuse, the bases persistent on rootcrown; infl. to 10-fld., pedicels to ½ in. long; calyx ³⁄₁₆ in. long, petals ⅜ in. long, pale purplish. Mts., s. Greece and Crete.

Oldhamiana Miq. To 30 in.; lvs. lanceolate to linear, to 2½ in. long; cymes terminal, dense, headlike, to 1½ in. across; petals pink. Korea, Manchuria, China.

pacifica Kom. Per., to 3 ft., much-branched; lvs. sessile, fleshy, ovate-oblong, lower lvs. about twice as long as broad; fls. pale rose or purple. Manchuria, Siberia, cent. Asia.

paniculata L. BABY'S-BREATH. Per., with stout rhizome, sts. to 3 ft., diffusely branched, glaucous, glabrous, rarely pubescent; lvs. lanceolate, to 3 in. long, acute; infl. loose, diffusely panicled, pedicels to ¼ in. long, calyx less than ⅛ in. long, teeth ovate, petals linear-spatulate, about ⅛ in. long, white or pinkish to reddish. Cent. and e. Eur. to cent. Asia. Cvs. are: **'Alba'**, fls. white; **'Compacta'**, dense-growing; **'Flore Pleno'**, fls. double; **'Grandiflora'**, fls. large. Subsp. **bicolor** (Freyn & Sint.) Freyn ex Grossh. [*G. bicolor* Freyn & Sint.]. Lvs. to ¾ in. wide; calyx to ⅛ in. long, petals to ⅜ in. long. Caucasus to cent. Asia.

perfecta: a listed name of no botanical standing.

perfoliata L. Per., to 3 ft., yellow-green, glandular-pubescent below to glabrous above; lvs. clasping, ovate, lower lvs. to 3 in. long, 3–7-veined, pubescent; calyx under ⅛ in. long, teeth ovate, petals emarginate, white to purplish. E. Bulgaria and Romania to cent. Asia.

petraea (Baumg.) Rchb. Cespitose per., sts. many, to 8 in., woody at base, mostly glabrous, unbranched; lvs. linear, to 2 in. long, st. lvs. to 1 in. long, the pairs united basally; infl. dense, headlike, to ¾ in. across, bracts ovate, ciliate; calyx lobes ovate, petals longer than calyx, to ¼ in. long, emarginate, white or pale purplish. E. Hungary, Romania, Bulgaria. See also *G. sericea.*

pilosa Huds. [*G. porrigens* (L.) Boiss.]. Ann., to 2 ft., glabrous to villous or hispid, sts. stout; lvs. lanceolate, to 3 in. long, 3-veined; calyx ¼ in. long, petals ½ in. long, pink or pale purple. Turkey and Israel to Afghanistan; naturalized in Eur.

porrigens: *G. pilosa.*

repens L. [*G. dubia* Willd.]. Per., to 10 in., glabrous, rhizome much-branched, sts. many; lvs. curved, to 1 in. long; infl. 5–30-fld., nearly corymbose, bracts scarious, pedicels to ⁵⁄₁₆ in. long; calyx ⅛ in. long, petals ¼ in. long, white, lilac, or pale purplish. Mts., nw. Spain to Carpathians. Cvs. are: **'Alba'**, fls. white; **'Bodgeri'**, fls. double, pink; **'Rosea'**, fls. rose-pink.

rosea Barkhoud. Not cult. The name has been used in hort. for *G. viscosa.*

sericea (Ser.) Kryl. [*G. Bungeana* D. Dietr.; *G. petraea* (Bunge) Fenzl, not Rchb.]. Stoloniferous per., to 4 in., sts. many; lvs. sessile, linear-lanceolate, to ⅝ in. long, pedicels to ¾ in. long; fls. solitary, axillary, calyx ³⁄₁₆ in. long, glandular-hairy, petals ⅜ in. long, white or lilac. Altai Mts. of Mongolia.

silenoides Rupr. Tufted per., prostrate to ascending, to 10 in., glaucous, glabrous; lvs. linear-spatulate to linear-oblong, to 2⅜ in. long, glaucous; infl. a loose cyme; calyx campanulate, to ⅛ in. long, petals obcordate-cuneate to obovate, to ⁵⁄₁₆ in. long, white or pinkish, often purple-veined. Ne. Turkey, Caucasus, Transcaucasia.

tenuicaulis: a listed name of no botanical standing, perhaps intended for *G. tenuifolia.*

tenuifolia Bieb. Cespitose per., to 8 in., woody at base, glabrous, sts. many; lvs. imbricate at base of st., linear, to ⅜ in. long, pilose; infl. 3–15-fld., bracts lanceolate, scarious, pedicels to ⅝ in. long; calyx ³⁄₁₆ in. long, teeth short-pointed, petals to ⅜ in. long, emarginate, white or pink. Caucasus, ne. Turkey.

viscosa A. Murr. Erect ann., to 2 ft., glabrous, upper brs. viscid; lvs. oblanceolate to linear, to 2½ in. long; infl. a loose cyme, bracts triangular, scarious, pedicels to ⅝ in. long; calyx to ⅛ in. long, teeth ovate, petals about ³⁄₁₆ in. long, emarginate, white or pale pink. Turkey to Sinai and Arabia.

GYROTHECA: *LACHNANTHES.*

HAAGEOCEREUS Backeb. [*Peruvocereus* Akers]. *Cactaceae.* More than 40 spp. of slender-spined, ribbed, cylindrical cacti, native to Peru; sts. mostly erect, branching from the base, ribs 12–26, low; areoles close-set, with many bristlelike to needle-shaped spines and sometimes with silky hairs; fls. funnelform, nocturnal, white to red, perianth tube longer than the more or less spreading segms., scales of ovary and tube small, with hairs in the axils, stamens many, said to be in 1 series, not declined; fr. nearly globose, spineless, green to red, with white flesh, perianth persistent, seeds black, glossy, dotted. Probably not distinct from *Trichocereus.*

For culture see *Cacti.*

acranthus (Vaup.) Backeb. Sts. 3 ft. high and 2 in. thick, ribs 12–14; radial spines 20–30, yellow, unequal, to ⅜ in. long, the outer slender, central spines 2, awl-shaped, to ¾ in. long; fls. greenish-white, to 3½ in. long.

australis Backeb. Sts. prostrate or pendent, to 3 ft. long and 2½ in. thick, dark green, often club-shaped, ribs 14, low; spines gray, radial spines about 30, slender, to 5/16 in. long, central spines 1–2, awl-shaped, to 2 in. long; fls. white, to 3 in. long; fr. pink. S. Peru.

caespitosus: a listed name of no botanical standing.

chosicensis (Werderm. & Backeb.) Backeb. [*Binghamia chosicensis* (Werderm. & Backeb.) Werderm.]. Sts. 3–10 ft. high and 2½–4 in. thick, ribs 18–26, to about ⅛ in. high; areoles 5/16–½ in. apart, with white to yellowish hairs, radial spines many, bristlelike to finely needle-shaped, yellow or brown to white, to ⅜ in. long, central spines 1–4, mostly 1 deflexed, stout, ½–1½ in. long; fls. white to red, 3 in. long; fr. globose, 1½–2½ in. in diam. W.-cent. Peru. Var. **rubrispinus** (Akers) Backeb. [*Peruvocereus rubrispinus* Akers]. Central spines red.

decumbens (Vaup.) Backeb. Sts. procumbent, to 3 ft. long and 2 in. thick, ribs 20, low, cross-furrowed; radial spines about 30, thin, to 3/16 in. long, central spines 5, stouter, 2 of them dark and to ¾ in. long; fls. white, 2½ in. long. S. Peru.

laredensis Backeb. Sts. to 2½ in. thick, ribs about 18, low; spines 40–45, needle-shaped, yellow, to ½ in. long, central spine sometimes 1, longer; fls. white. N. Peru.

multangularis: a listed name of no botanical standing.

Olowinskianus Backeb. Sts. to 3 ft. high and 3 in. thick, ribs about 13, to ¼ in. high; areoles ⅜ in. apart, radial spines about 40, needle-shaped, brown, becoming gray, central spines 1–2, stouter, to 2½ in. long; fls. white, 3 in. long. Cent. Peru.

pacalaensis Backeb. Sts. to 5 ft. high and 3½ in. thick, ribs about 19, low; areoles ⅜ in. apart, radial spines about 40, yellow, ½ in. long, central spine 1, deflexed, to 2 in. long; fls. white; fr. green. N. Peru.

platinospinus (Werderm. & Backeb.) Backeb. Sts. creeping, 2 in. thick, ribs about 13, tubercled, ¼ in. high; spines white with brown tips to dark brown, radial spines 10–13, needle-shaped, to ⅝ in. long, central spines 2–4, awl-shaped, to 2½ in. long; fls. white, to 3 in. long; fr. green. S. Peru.

stellaspinus: a listed name of no botanical standing.

superbus: a listed name of no botanical standing.

versicolor (Werderm. & Backeb.) Backeb. Sts. to 5 ft. high and 3 in. thick, ribs to about 22, low; spines yellow to dark red, the color varying from zone to zone along the st., radial spines 25–30, needle-shaped, to 3/16 in. long, central spines 1–2, to 1½ in. long; fls. white, 4 in. long; fr. yellow, 1¼ in. in diam. N. Peru. Cvs. **'Aureospinus'**, **'Centrispinus'**, **'Echinatus'**, and **'Humifusus'** are listed.

viridiflorus (Akers) Backeb. [*Peruvocereus viridiflorus* Akers]. Sts. to 3 ft. high and 3 in. thick, ribs 19–20; radial spines about 60, very slender, to 3/16 in. long, central spine 1, to 1 in. long; fls. green, to 1⅝ in. across.

HAASTIA Hook.f. *Compositae* (Aster Tribe). Three spp. of tufted subshrubs, endemic to New Zeal.; sts. much-branched; lvs. persistent, imbricate, concealing the sts.; fl. heads discoid, solitary, terminal, sessile and sunk among the uppermost lvs., involucre hemispherical or broadly campanulate, involucral bracts in about 2 rows, with scarious margins and tips, receptacle flat, slightly pitted; disc fls. bisexual, funnelform, with short styles, fls. of the outer 2 to several rows female, tubular, very short, with long-exserted styles; achenes compressed or nearly cylindrical, glabrous, pappus of 1 row of rigid bristles.

pulvinaris Hook.f. VEGETABLE-SHEEP. Plants forming large cushions to 6 ft. across, brs. many, densely compacted; lvs. densely imbricate, broadly obcuneate, to ⅜ in. long, thickly covered with woolly hairs, crenulate; heads to 5/16 in. across.

recurva Hook.f. Plant tufts to 10 in. across, brs. procumbent, dense to loose; lvs. loosely imbricate, strongly recurved at the middle, obovate, to 1 in. long, covered with floccose hairs; heads to ¾ in. across.

Sinclairii Hook.f. Plant tufts loose, to 1 ft. across, brs. decumbent to nearly erect; lvs. loosely imbricate, spreading, oblong-obovate, to 1⅜ in. long, with appressed to subappressed hairs; heads to 1 in. across.

HABENARIA Willd. [*Blephariglottis* Raf.; *Coeloglossum* Hartm.; *Gymnadenia* R. Br.; *Gymnadeniopsis* Rydb.; *Limnorchis* Rydb.; *Lysias* Salisb.; *Platanthera* L. Rich.]. FRINGED ORCHID or ORCHIS, REIN ORCHID or ORCHIS. *Orchidaceae.* About 100 spp. of terrestrial herbs of temp. and trop. areas of both hemispheres; sts. erect, simple, leafy; lvs. linear to oblanceolate; racemes terminal, loosely or densely 1- to many-fld.; petals usually smaller than sepals, lip entire, lobed, or often fringed, spurred at base, anther firmly fused to column. For structure of fl. see *Orchidaceae.*

For culture see *Orchids.*

bifolia R. Br. LESSER BUTTERFLY ORCHID. St. to 1 ft.; lvs. 2, opp., basal, to 5 in. long, oblong-obovate; infl. loosely 7–15-fld., to 3½ in. long; fls. white or greenish-white, sweet-scented, dorsal sepal and petals forming a hood, lip strap-shaped, longer than sepals, white with greenish tip, spur to 1 in. long, greenish. Early spring–summer. Eur., N. Afr., Asia Minor, Siberia, China.

blephariglottis (Willd.) Hook. WHITE F.O., SNOWY O. St. to about 3 ft.; lvs. to 8 in. long and 1½ in. wide; raceme densely or loosely fld., to 8 in. long; fls. white, sepals to ½ in. long, lip coarsely fringed, spur as long as the pedicelled ovary. Summer–early autumn. Nfld. to Fla. and Miss.

Bonatea Rchb.f. St. to 18 in., leafy; lvs. to 4½ in. long, undulate, leathery; spike to 7 in. long, erect, many-fld.; fls. to 1 in. across, sepals and petals green, lip white, fleshy, 3-lobed, spur as long as ovary. Spring. Cape of Good Hope.

bracteata: *H. viridis* var.

carnea N. E. Br. St. short; lvs. to 3 in. long, lanceolate, dull green with white spots; spike to 20 in. long; fls. showy, 5–20, to 1 in. across, rose-pink to white, lip 3-lobed, spur pale brown, to 3 in. long. Thailand, n. Malay Arch.

ciliaris (L.) R. Br. [*Blephariglottis ciliaris* (L.) Rydb.; *Platanthera ciliaris* (L.) Lindl.]. YELLOW F.O., ORANGE-PLUME, ORANGE-FRINGE. St. to about 3½ ft., leafy; lvs. to 1 ft. long; raceme densely or loosely fld., to 8 in. long; fls. bright yellow or deep orange, lip to ½ in. long, copiously ciliate-fringed, spur slender, longer than the pedicelled ovary. Summer. E. U.S.

clavellata (Michx.) K. Spreng. [*H. tridentata* (Muhlenb. ex Willd.) Hook.; *Gymnadeniopsis clavellata* (Michx.) Rydb.]. GREEN WOODLAND ORCHID, GREEN R.O., SOUTHERN R.O., LITTLE CLUB-SPUR O., FROG-SPIKE. St. to 1 ft.; lvs. 1 or 2 at middle of st., to about 7 in. long; raceme few- to several-fld., to 3½ in. long; fls. greenish- or yellowish-white, sepals and petals similar, ovate, lip elongate-quadrangular, 3-toothed at apex, spur club-shaped. Early summer–early autumn. Nfld. to Fla. and Tex.

conopsea (Willd.) Benth. [*Gymnadenia conopsea* (Willd.) R. Br.]. St. to 16 in.; lvs. to 6 in. long, linear; raceme to 4 in. long, dense, many-fld.; fls rose or purple-violet, fragrant, spur longer than ovary, sepals and petals meeting at tips, lip 3-lobed, cuneate at base. Summer. Eurasia, Japan.

cristata (Michx.) R. Br. [*Blephariglottis cristata* (Michx.) Raf.; *Platanthera cristata* (Michx.) Lindl.]. GOLDEN F.O., CRESTED F.O.,

CRESTED YELLOW O., CRESTED R.O., ORANGE-CREST. St. to 3 ft., leafy; lvs. to 8 in. long, linear-lanceolate; raceme densely many-fld., to 6 in. long; fls. rather small, orange, to ½ in. across, dorsal sepal and petals meeting at tips, lateral sepals spreading, lip ovate, fringed along margins, spur shorter than ovary. Early summer–early autumn. Mass. to Fla. and La.

dilatata (Pursh) Hook. [*Limnorchis dilatata* (Pursh) Rydb.; *Platanthera dilatata* (Pursh) Lindl.]. LEAFY WHITE ORCHID, TALL WHITE BOG O., BOG-CANDLE, SCENT-BOTTLE. To 4 ft.; lvs. to 1 ft. long and 1½ in. wide; raceme loosely many-fld., to 16 in. long; fls. white, lip entire, spur about as long as the lip. Spring–early autumn. N. N. Amer. Var. **leucostachys** (Lindl.) Ames [*H. leucostachys* (Lindl.) S. Wats.]. WHITE-FLOWERED BOG ORCHID, SIERRA R.O. Spur 1½–2 times as long as lip. Spring–early autumn. Alaska to Calif. and Ariz.

elegans: *H. unalascensis* var. *elata.*

Elwesii Hook. St. erect, leafy; lvs. erect, ovate-lanceolate; raceme few- to many-fld.; fls. greenish, petals 2-lobed, filiform. Sw. India.

fimbriata: *H. psycodes* var. *grandiflora.*

gracilis: *H. saccata.*

grandiflora: *H. psycodes* var.

Hookeri Torr. ex A. Gray [*Lysias Hookerana* (Torr. ex A. Gray) Rydb.]. HOOKER'S ORCHID. St. to 16 in.; lvs. 2, basal, orbicular, to 7 in. long; raceme loosely few- to many-fld., to 10 in. long; fls. yellowish-green, lip lanceolate, spur about ¾ in. long. Early summer–early autumn. Nov. Sc. to Penn. and Iowa.

hyperborea (L.) R. Br. [*Limnorchis hyperborea* (L.) Rydb.]. NORTHERN GREEN ORCHID, LEAFY N. G. O. St. to over 3 ft., leafy; lvs. several, to 1 ft. long, variable in shape; raceme spicate, densely or loosely few- to many-fld., to 10 in. long; fls. small, green or yellowish-green, fragrant, rarely marked or suffused with brownish-purple, lip fleshy, lanceolate, to ⅜ in. long, spur somewhat club-shaped, shorter than lip. Nfld. to Alaska, s. to Penn., Utah, and Ore.; also Greenland, Iceland.

lacera (Michx.) Lodd. [*Blephariglottis lacera* (Michx.) Farw.]. RAGGED F. O., GREEN F. O., RAGGED O. St. to 2½ ft., somewhat ribbed, leafy below, bracted above; lvs. to 8½ in. long; raceme loosely or densely fld., to 10 in. long; fls. pale yellowish-green or whitish-green, lip 3-lobed, deeply fringed or lacerate, spur slender, as long as or longer than the pedicelled ovary. Late spring–late summer. E. N. Amer.

leucostachys: *H. dilatata* var.

Michaelii: *H. unalascensis* var. *elata.*

nivea (Nutt.) K. Spreng. [*Gymnadeniopsis nivea* (Nutt.) Rydb.]. SNOWY ORCHID, SAVANNAH O., WHITE R. O., SOUTHERN SMALL WHITE O., BOG-TORCH, FROG-SPEAR, WHITE FROG-ARROW. St. to 3 ft., slender; lvs. 2–3 near base, linear-lanceolate, to about 10 ¼ in. long, those toward the base longer; raceme many-fld., to 6 in. long; fls. white, rarely tinged with pink, lip uppermost, entire, shorter than spur. Late spring–early autumn. Pine barrens, N.J., s. to Fla., Ala., and Tex.

obusata (Banks ex Pursh) Richardson. BLUNT-LEAF ORCHID, ONE-LEAF R. O., NORTHERN SMALL BOG O. St. to 8 in., naked, or rarely with linear bract at middle; lf. solitary, oblanceolate, to 6 in. long; fls. greenish-white, lip fleshy, linear, pendent, with small grooved callus at base, lateral margins revolute, to ½ in. long, spur to ⅜ in. long, almost as long as lip. Early summer–early autumn. Lab. to Alaska, s. to n. U.S.

orbiculata (Pursh) Torr. [*Lysias orbiculata* (Pursh) Rydb.]. ROUND-LEAVED ORCHID, MOON-SET, HEAL-ALL. St. scapose, to 2 ft., with basal lvs. and several lanceolate bracts above; lvs. 2, orbicular, to 10 in. long, spreading flat on ground, silvery beneath; raceme loosely few- to many-fld., to 1 ft. long; fls. greenish-white, lip strap-shaped, pendent, to 1 in. long, spur club-shaped, to ¼ in. long. Early summer–early autumn. Lab. to Alaska, s. to N.C. and Ore.

peramoena A. Gray. PURPLE FRINGELESS ORCHID, PURPLE-SPIRE O., PURPLE FRET-LIP, PRIDE-OF-THE-PEAK. St. to 3½ ft.; lvs. linear to lanceolate, erect, to 5 in. long; raceme densely or loosely fld., to 6 in. long; fls. rich violet-purple, showy, lip 3-lobed, to ¾ in. long, midlobe entire, notched at apex, spur club-shaped, to 1 in. long. Early summer–autumn. W. N.Y., s. to Gulf States.

psycodes (L.) K. Spreng. [*Blephariglottis psycodes* (L.) Rydb.]. SMALL PURPLE F. O., LESSER P. F. O., BUTTERFLY O., FAIRY-FRINGE, SOLDIER'S-PLUME. St. to 3 ft., leafy; lvs. several, up to 9 in. long; infl. racemose, densely many-fld.; fls. showy, purple, lilac, or rarely white, fragrant, dorsal sepal and petals forming a hood, lateral sepals spreading, lip 3-lobed, with fringed margins, spur to ¾ in. long. Summer. Nfld. to N.C. and Tenn. Var. **grandiflora** (Bigel.) A. Gray [*H. fimbriata* (Willd.) R. Br.; *H. grandiflora* (Bigel.) Torr. ex L. Beck; *Blephariglottis grandiflora* (Bigel.) Rydb.; *Platanthera fimbriata* (Willd.) Lindl.]. LARGE PURPLE F. O., GREATER P. F. O., LARGE BUTTERFLY O., PLUME-

ROYAL. More robust; raceme larger, denser; fls. often twice as large as in the typical form. Throughout the range of the sp.

radiata: *Pecteilis radiata.*

saccata Greene [*H. gracilis* S. Wats.]. SLENDER BOG ORCHID. St. glabrous, light green, to 3 ft.; lvs. scattered, or occasionally clustered at base, to 5½ in. long; raceme loosely few- to many-fld.; fls. small, green, commonly tinged or marked with purplish-brown, lip linear, tapering at apex, entire, purplish, spur cylindric-clavate, often purplish, ½–⅔ length of lip. Late spring–early autumn. Alaska to Calif., e. to Alta. and Ariz.

tridentata: *H. clavellata.*

unalascensis (K. Spreng.) S. Wats. ALASKAN ORCHID, ALASKA PIPERIA. St. to 2 ft.; lvs. in a basal rosette; infl. erect, loosely many-fld.; fls. very small, green or greenish-purple, dorsal sepal and petals forming a hood, lateral sepals reflexed, lip trowel-shaped, fleshy, spur conical, arched. Ont. to Alaska, and w. and sw. U.S., Mex. Var. **elata** (Jeps.) Correll [*H. elegans* (Lindl.) Bolander; *H. Michaelii* Greene]. Differs from the typical var. in having sts. straw-colored, fls. white or greenish, suffused with purple, sepals and petals spreading, spur long, hooked, much longer than ovary. B.C., Idaho, Mont., s. to Calif.

HABERLEA Friv. *Gesneriaceae.* Two spp. of per. herbs of Bulgaria; lvs. obovate or ovate-oblong, coarsely crenate; fls. on brownish, 1–6-fld. scapes, nodding, pale lilac or rarely white, calyx lobes about as long as tube, brownish-purple-hairy, corolla tubular, lobes 5, rounded, stamens 4, borne at base of corolla tube, anthers united in pairs by tips, disc ring-like, low, ovary superior; fr. a septicidal caps.

For cultivation see *Gesneriaceae.*

Ferdinandi-Coburgii Urum. Differs from *H. rhodopensis* in being smaller and having lvs. smooth above and corolla tube only slightly longer than calyx.

rhodopensis Friv. Lvs. to 3 in. long, softly hairy above and beneath; scape to 6 in.; fls. ¾ in. long, corolla tube nearly twice as long as calyx. Cv. 'Virginalis' [*H. virginalis* Hort.]. Fls. white.

virginalis: *H. rhodopensis* cv.

HABRANTHUS Herb. *Amaryllidaceae.* About 10 spp. of bulbous herbs, native to N. and S. Amer.; lvs. linear; scape in most spp. 1-fld., in a few 2–4-fld., spathe tubular beneath, 1-sided and bifid above; fls. pink, yellow, or red, declinate, perianth tube short, lobes unequal, stamens declinate, of 4 lengths; fr. a caps., 3-lobed.

advena: *Hippeastrum advena.*

Andersonianus: an error for *Andersonii.*

Andersonii Herb. [*Zephyranthes Andersonii* (Herb.) Bak.]. To 6 in.; lvs. narrowly linear, to 6 in. long; fls. yellow, veined with red outside, 1½ in. long, tube nearly wanting. S. Amer. Var. **texanus:** *H. texanus.* Cv. 'Cupreus' is listed.

Bagnoldii: *Hippeastrum Bagnoldii.*

brachyandrus (Bak.) Sealy [*Hippeastrum brachyandrum* Bak.]. Lvs. few, to 12 in. long; scape to 12 in., tapered upward; fls. solitary, funnel-form, 3 in. across, orchid-pink above, shading to dark reddish-purple beneath. S. Amer.

cardinalis: *Zephyranthes bifolia.*

gracilifolius Herb. [*Zephyranthes gracilifolia* (Herb.) Nichols.]. Lvs. nearly cylindrical, to 1½ ft. long; scape 1–2-fld., to 8 in. high; fls. 1⅜ in. long, tube green, lobes pale purple, stigma trifid. Autumn. Uruguay.

juncifolius Traub & Hayw. Lvs. to 2½ ft. long, cylindrical, hollow, to ³⁄₁₆ in. wide; scape 2–4-fld.; fls. to 2⅜ in. long, white, flushed with pink, tube short, reddish-green. Argentina.

miniatus: *Hippeastrum advena.*

phycelloides: *Phycella phycelloides.*

pratensis: *Hippeastrum pratense.*

robustus: *H. tubispathus.*

roseus: *Hippeastrum roseum,* but plants listed as *Habranthus roseus* in the trade may be *Hippeastrum bifidum* var. *spathaceum.*

Sparkmannii: a listed name of no botanical standing and of uncertain application.

texanus (Herb.) Herb. ex Steud. [*H. Andersonii* var. *texanus* (Herb.) Herb.; *Hippeastrum texanum* Bak.; *Zephyranthes texana* Herb.]. To 8 in.; lvs. narrowly linear, to 4 in. long; fls. yellow, coppery and striped with purple outside, 1 in. long. Summer. Tex. Perhaps only a var. of *H. Andersonii.*

tubispathus (L'Hér.) Traub [*H. robustus* Herb. ex Sweet; *Zephyranthes robusta* (Herb. ex Sweet) Bak.]. To 9 in.; lvs. linear, recurved-spreading, appearing after fls.; fls. rose-red, to 3 in. long, tube short, greenish. Argentina.

HACKELIA Opiz. STICKSEED, BEGGAR'S-LICE. *Boraginaceae.* Between 35 and 40 spp. of hairy, bien. and per. herbs of Eur., Asia, N. and S. Amer.; lvs. simple, alt., entire, basal and cauline; fls. blue, pink, or white, pedicels reflexed in fr., in mostly nonbracted, scorpioid, racemose or paniculate cymes, calyx deeply 5-lobed, corolla 5-lobed, with crests in the throat, stamens 5, included, ovary 4-lobed, style shorter than nutlets; fr. of 4 nutlets armed with barbed bristles on the margins and angles.

Jessicae (McGreg.) Brand. Erect or ascending per., to 3 ft., with soft hairs; basal lvs. oblanceolate, to 6 in. long, st. lvs. lanceolate, smaller, sessile; fls. pale blue with yellow crests, to ¼ in. across. B.C. to Calif., Idaho and Nev.

HACQUETIA Neck. ex DC. *Umbelliferae.* One polygamous sp., a per. herb, native to Eur., sometimes grown in the rock garden and prop. by division.

Epipactis (Scop.) DC. To 8 in.; lvs. basal, deeply palmately lobed; fls. yellow, in short-stalked umbels subtended by large, leafy involucral bracts. Spring.

HADRODEMAS H. E. Moore. *Commelinaceae.* One sp., a per. herb, native to Guatemala; sts. thick, crowned with rosette of sessile lvs.; infl. terminal, elongate, branched, with lvs. reduced, cincinni 2–3 on short peduncles, in axils of sheaths and bracts; fls. short-pedicelled, bracted, sepals 3, herbaceous, separate, colored, persistent, petals 3, separate, stamens 6, equal, filaments glabrous or bearded, anthers with broad connectives, ovary 3-celled, each cell with 2 ovules, style longer than stamens, stigma slightly expanded; fr. a caps.

Cultivated in the greenhouse. Propagated by cuttings.

Warszewiczianum (Kunth & Bouché) H. E. Moore [*Spironema Warszewiczianum* (Kunth & Bouché) Brückn.; *Tradescantia Warszewicziana* Kunth & Bouché; *Tripogandra Warszewicziana* (Kunth & Bouché) Woodson]. Sts. often dichotomously branched, to 18 in.; lvs. narrowly oblong, to 8 in. long, 1½ in. wide; sepals lilac, petals purple.

HAEMANTHUS L. BLOOD LILY, AFRICAN B.L. *Amaryllidaceae.* About 60 spp. of low bulbous herbs, native to Afr.; lvs. broad, basal; fls. red or white, in dense umbellate heads terminal on a solid scape and subtended by more than 2 separate spathe valves, perianth tube short, lobes ascending or reflexed, ovary inferior, cells 2-ovuled; fr. a berry.

Grown for summer and autumn bloom and the colorful berries. Plants should have a night temperature of 50–55° F. Bulbs should be rested over winter and started into growth in spring. Propagated by offsets.

albiflos Jacq. To 1 ft.; lvs. thick and fleshy, to 8 in. long and 4 in. wide, ciliate; spathe valves ascending, white with green veins, fl. head 2 in. across; fls. white, ¾ in. long, lobes ascending. S. Afr. Cv. '**Brachyphyllus**' is listed.

amarylloides Jacq. Lvs. 2, thick, fleshy, to 12 in. long, 2 in. wide, bright green, glabrous, developing after fls.; scape to 1 ft., fl. head subtended by 1–6 spreading spathe valves about 1 in. long; fls. 50 or more, pinkish or white, to ½ in. long, lobes spreading. S. Afr.

carneus Ker-Gawl. To 1 ft.; lvs. 2, thick and fleshy, to 6 in. long, 5 in. wide, softly hairy; spathe valves 5–6, reflexed, reddish, fl. head 2–3 in. across; fls. pink to white, to ½ in. long, lobes spreading. S. Afr.

coccineus L. To 10 in.; lvs. thick and fleshy, to 2 ft. long and 8 in. wide; spathe valves ascending, bright red, fl. head to 3 in. across; fls. red, 1 in. long, lobes ascending. S. Afr.

Katharinae Bak. CATHERINE-WHEEL. To 1 ft.; lvs. thin, to 14 in. long and 6 in. wide; spathe valves reflexed, fl. head to 9 in. across; fls. bright red, 2½ in. long, lobes spreading. S. Afr.

magnificus Herb. GIANT STOVE-BRUSH. Similar to *H. natalensis*, but the 6–8 spathe valves bright green, fls. bright scarlet. S. Afr.

multiflorus Martyn. To 1½ ft.; lvs. 3–4, to 1 ft. long, short-petioled, bases forming a pseudostem; spathe valves reflexed, fl. head 3–6 in. across; fls. blood-red, to 1 in. long, lobes spreading; berry scarlet. Trop. Afr.

natalensis Pappe ex Hook. NATAL PAINTBRUSH. Lvs. 8–9, developing after fls., thin, light green, oblong, to 1 ft. long, 4–5 in. wide, narrowed to clasping bases forming a pseudostem 1 ft. long; scape flat on one side, spotted with maroon, spathe valves bronzy-green, ascending, fl. head 3–4 in. across; fls. flesh-colored or pale green, to 1¾ in. long, including the pink filaments. S. Afr.

puniceus L. To 15 in.; lvs. thin, to 1 ft. long and 4 in. wide; spathe valves ascending, imbricate, fl. head to 4 in. across; fls. pale scarlet to white, 1 in. long, lobes ascending. S. Afr.

HAEMARIA Lindl. GOLD-LACE ORCHID. *Orchidaceae.* One sp., a terrestrial herb of trop. Asia; lvs. near base of st., more or less purplish, with red or gold veins; fls. in terminal racemes, small, whitish, upper sepal and petals forming a hood, lateral sepals spreading, lip twisted, saccate at base with 2-lobed, sessile gland on each side, column twisted clockwise. For structure of fl. see *Orchidaceae.*

Warm greenhouse; grown for the attractive foliage. For culture see *Orchids.*

discolor (Ker-Gawl.) Lindl. St. short, 3–6-lvd.; lvs. black to dark purple or dark green with red or gold veins, or black-green with pale green veins; peduncle to 6 in. long, hairy, raceme many-fld., with pink bracts. Malay Arch. Var. **Dawsoniana** Rchb.f. [*Goodyera Dawsonii* Boxall ex Naves]. Lvs. beautifully veined with red.

HAEMATOXYLUM L. *Leguminosae* (subfamily *Caesalpinioideae*). Three spp. of spiny shrubs or trees of trop. Amer. and Afr.; lvs. even-pinnate; fls. in short, loose, axillary racemes, small, yellow, nearly regular, 5-merous, stamens 10, separate; fr. a flat, thin legume, dehiscing by splitting longitudinally along center of each valve.

Source of important dyes. Sometimes planted in warm countries as ornamentals. Propagated by seeds.

campechianum L. LOGWOOD, BLOODWOOD TREE. Fast-growing shrub or tree, to 25 ft. or more, with gnarled trunk, brs. often with spines ½ in. long; lfts. in 2–4 pairs, cuneate-obovate, to 1 in. long, apically obtuse to emarginate; racemes narrow, dense, to 4½ in. long; fr. lanceolate-oblong, to 2 in. long. Yucatan Pen. (Mex.) and W. Indies. Heartwood yields the purplish-red dye hematoxylin.

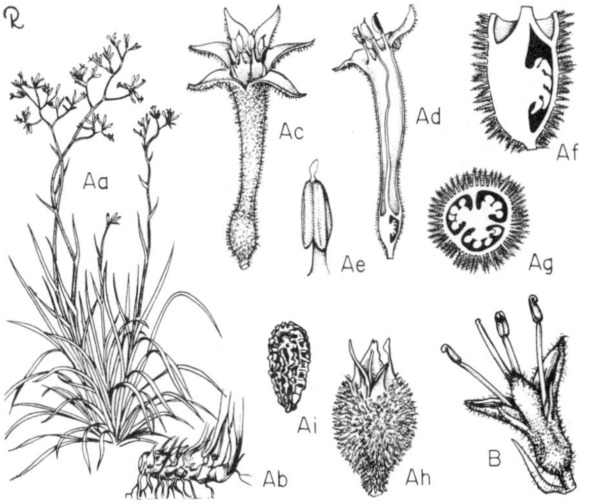

HAEMODORACEAE. **A,** *Anigozanthos flavidus:* **Aa,** flowering plant, × 1/16; **Ab,** rootstock, × ¼; **Ac,** flower, × ¾; **Ad,** flower, vertical section, × ¾; **Ae,** stamen, × 3; **Af,** ovary, vertical section, × 3; **Ag,** ovary, cross section, × 3; **Ah,** fruit, × 1½; **Ai,** seed, × 6. **B,** *Lachnanthes caroliana:* flower, × 1½.

HAEMODORACEAE R. Br. BLOODWORT FAMILY. Monocot.; about 16 genera of per. herbs with fibrous roots, tubers, or rhizomes, mostly native to the S. Hemisphere, but 2 in e. U.S.; lvs. mostly basal, linear or sword-shaped, parallel-veined; infl. racemose, paniculate, or cymose; fls. bisexual, mostly regular, often densely villous, perianth persistent, tube absent to long, segms. 6, in 1 or 2 series, stamens 6 or 3, ovary superior to inferior, 3-celled, ovules 1 to many; fr. a loculicidal caps. *Anigozanthos, Conostylis, Lachnanthes, Lophiola, Wachendorfia,* and *Xiphidium* are cult.

HAKEA Schrad. PINCUSHION TREE. *Proteaceae.* About 100 spp. of Australian, evergreen shrubs or low trees; lvs. alt.; fls. bisexual, in pairs in short axillary racemes or clusters; fr. a woody caps. Differs from *Grevillea* chiefly in having seeds with long terminal wings.

Hakeas are grown outdoors in southern and southwestern U.S. and withstand slight frost. They are drought-resistant and do best in light well-drained soil. Propagated by seeds in winter or early spring and the seedlings kept in boxes for the first year. As the capsules are very hard, they must be dried some time before discharging the seeds. Hakeas may also be propagated by cuttings. Well adapted to Calif., Zone 10.

acicularis R. Br. [*H. sericea* Schrad.]. Tall shrub or small tree, glabrous except for infl.; lvs. needlelike, to 2 or rarely 3 in. long; fls. in sessile axillary clusters; fr. usually 1 in. long, ½–¾ in. wide, thick and rugose, with short obtuse, smooth and straight beak. New S. Wales, Victoria, Tasmania.

arborescens R. Br. Tall shrub or small tree, young shoots silky; lvs. linear, lanceolate or broader, and falcate, 3–6 in. long, obscurely several-veined; fls. in short, dense, almost globular racemes, often on old wood; fr. to 2 in. long, 1 in. wide, nearly straight, very shortly beaked. N. Terr. of Australia, Queensland.

auriculata Meissn. Shrub, to 2 ft. or more; lvs. cuneate, to 3 in. long, auriculate at base, prickly-toothed or -lobed; fls. in axillary clusters. W. Australia.

cristata R. Br. Shrub, to 8 ft.; lvs. broad-obovate to oblong, to 3 in. long, prickly-toothed, stiff, glaucous; fls. white, in short racemes. W. Australia.

cucullata R. Br. Shrub, to 14 ft.; lvs. sessile, cordate-orbicular, to 4 in. across, entire or prickly-toothed, stiff; fls. pink, in sessile, umbel-like clusters in the axils of uppermost lvs., styles long-exserted. W. Australia.

cyclophora Lindl. Shrub, to 6 ft.; lvs. to 8 in. long, to 1½ in. wide, oblong-lanceolate, tapering from middle to short petiole, obscurely several-veined; fls. in axillary clusters or very short racemes; fr. 1½ in. long, 1 in. wide, curved, with a broad, rather long, closely inflexed beak. W. Australia.

dactyloides Cav. Tall shrub; lvs. linear- or oblong-lanceolate, to 4 in. long, prominently 3-nerved, stiff; fls. whitish, many in small, axillary clusters. New S. Wales.

elliptica R. Br. Shrub, to 10 ft.; lvs. elliptic, to 4 in. long and 2 in. wide, wavy-margined, parallel-veined, rusty-pubescent when young; fls. white, in sessile clusters. W. Australia.

erinacea Meissn. Shrub, to 3 ft.; lvs. to 1 in. long, divided, segms. 3–5, cylindrical, entire or divided, stiff; fls. in sessile clusters. W. Australia.

eucalyptoides: *H. laurina.*

gibbosa Cav. Shrub, to 10 ft.; lvs. needlelike, to 3 in. long, entire, spine-tipped, stiff; fls. white, in sessile clusters. New S. Wales, Victoria.

glabella R. Br. Shrub, to 15 ft.; lvs. obovate or oblong, to 3 in. long, auriculate at base, usually prickly-toothed; fls. white. W. Australia.

ilicifolia: *H. varia.*

incrassata R. Br. Shrub, to 4 ft.; lvs. linear-lanceolate or oblong-linear, to 2 in. long, entire, thick; fls. brown and cream-colored, in sessile clusters. W. Australia.

laurina R. Br. [*H. eucalyptoides* Meissn.]. SEA-URCHIN TREE. Shrub or tree, to 30 ft.; lvs. lanceolate or narrow-elliptic, to 6 in. long and 1 in. wide, entire, parallel-veined; fls. crimson, in sessile, globose clusters, styles long, yellow. W. Australia.

leucoptera R. Br. Shrub, to 9 ft.; brs. slender, wandlike, minutely pubescent; lvs. cylindrical, to 3½ in. long, stiff; fls. white, in short, axillary racemes. E. Australia.

marginata R. Br. Shrub, to 8 ft.; lvs. lanceolate, to 1½ in. long, with prominent midrib and margins, thick and stiff; fls. small, in axillary clusters. W. Australia.

multilineata Meissn. Tall shrub; lvs. linear-lanceolate to oblong, to 8 in. long, with many small nerves, pubescent, thick; fls. pink, in spikelike racemes to 8 in. long. S. and W. Australia.

pectinata: *H. suaveolens.*

petiolaris Meissn. Tall shrub, to 8 ft.; lvs. rounded or ovate, short-acuminate, entire, narrowed to a petiole; fls. purplish, many, in axillary, globose clusters, styles long, exserted, yellow, resembling those of *H. laurina.* W. Australia.

platysperma Hook. Lvs. cylindrical, to 5 in. long, thick and stiff; fls. in sessile clusters. W. Australia.

propinqua A. Cunn. Tall shrub; lvs. crowded, needlelike, to 1½ in. long, rather thick and smooth; fls. very small, clustered. New S. Wales.

pugioniformis Cav. Shrub, to 8 ft.; lvs. needlelike, to 1 in. long, stiff and spine-tipped; fls. white, in sessile clusters, styles long, differing from *H. gibbosa* in having perianth pubescent. New. S. Wales, Victoria, Tasmania.

purpurea Hook. Rigid shrub, to 6 ft.; lvs. cylindrical, to 2 in. long, once or twice bifid or trifid, smooth; fls. purple, in sessile or short-peduncled axillary umbels. New S. Wales, Victoria.

recurva Meissn. Stout, rigid shrub; lvs. cylindrical, to 4 in. long, sharp-pointed, rigid; fls. many in sessile, axillary clusters or dense racemes. W. Australia.

ruscifolia Labill. Shrub, to 8 ft.; lvs. ovate-oblong to lanceolate, to 1 in. long, entire and spine-tipped, rigid; fls. white, small, in dense clusters along upper part of sts. W. Australia.

saligna J. Knight. Shrub, to 8 ft.; lvs. oblong or lanceolate, to 6 in. long, entire, pale or grayish-green; fls. white, small, in dense clusters, styles long. Queensland, New S. Wales.

sericea: *H. acicularis.*

speciosa: a listed name of no botanical standing.

suaveolens R. Br. [*H. pectinata* Colla]. Shrub, to 10 ft.; lvs. cylindrical, to 4 in. long or more, usually pinnate but sometimes undivided, segms. stiff, spine-tipped; fls. white, in dense racemes, fragrant. W. Australia.

subsulcata Meissn. Shrub, to 7 ft.; lvs. cylindrical, to 4 in. long, mucronate. W. Australia.

tetraphylla: a listed name of no botanical standing.

trifurcata R. Br. Shrub, to 10 ft., much-branched; lvs. cylindrical, to 3 in. long, divided into 3 segms., stiff, sometimes with few flat, oblong lvs.; fls. in sessile clusters. W. Australia.

ulicina R. Br. Tall, erect shrub, to 9 ft.; lvs. linear, 2–8 in. long, sharp-pointed, tapering to both ends, rigid; fls. white, in short, dense, axillary clusters. Se. Australia, Tasmania.

varia R. Br. [*H. ilicifolia* R. Br.]. Shrub, to 8 ft.; lvs. to 2 in. long, prickly lobed or pinnatifid; fls. small, in clusters. W. Australia.

Victoriae J. Drumm. Perhaps not distinct from *H. cucullata*, but taller (to 12 ft. or more) and uppermost lvs. subtending fl. clusters variously colored from whitish-yellow to orange, and finally crimson. W. Australia.

vittata R. Br. Shrub, to 12 in.; lvs. cylindrical, slender, to 2½ in. long, sharp-pungent; fls. reddish, few in short, axillary umbels or clusters. S. Australia.

HALENIA Borkh. SPURRED GENTIAN. *Gentianaceae.* More than 70 spp. of ann., bien., or per. glabrous herbs in Eur., Asia, N. and S. Amer.; lvs. opp., entire, usually 3–5-nerved from base; fls. usually yellowish, in axillary or terminal cymes, calyx 4-parted, corolla campanulate, 4-lobed, lobes spurred near base; fr. a 2-valved caps.

corniculata (L.) Cornaz. Ann. or bien., sts. 24 in., often branched, 4-angled; lvs. oblong to narrowly ovate, to 4 in. long; fls. pale yellow, to ⅜ in. long. E. Eur. to e. Asia.

HALESIA L. [*Mohrodendron* Britt.]. SILVER-BELL, SILVER-BELL TREE, SNOWDROP TREE. *Styracaceae.* About 5 spp. of deciduous shrubs or trees, native to e. N. Amer. and e. China; lvs. alt., toothed; fls. white, drooping, in axillary clusters on branchlets of previous year, in spring, calyx tube 4-toothed, corolla campanulate, 4-lobed, open before reaching full size, stamens 8–16, ovary inferior, 2–4-celled; fr. dry, oblong, with 2 or 4 longitudinal wings.

Only *H. carolina* and *H. monticola* are hardy north. Halesias do well in rich, well-drained soil with some shelter; they transplant readily. Propagated by seeds sown as soon as ripe or stratified, and by layering, root cuttings, and greenwood cuttings from forced plants.

carolina L. [*H. tetraptera* Ellis]. WILD OLIVE, SHITTIMWOOD, OPPOSSUMWOOD. To 40 ft.; lvs. ovate to ovate-oblong, to 4 in. long; fls. to ¾ in. long, corolla shallowly lobed; fr. 4-winged, to 1½ in. long. W. Va., s. to Fla. and e. Tex. Zone 5.

diptera Ellis. To 30 ft.; lvs. elliptic to obovate, to 5 in. long; fls. 1 in. long, corolla deeply lobed; fr. broadly 2-winged, to 2 in. long. S.C. to Fla., Tenn., and Tex. Zone 8.

monticola (Rehd.) Sarg. To 100 ft.; lvs. elliptic to oblong-obovate, to 7 in. long; fls. to 1 in. long, corolla shallowly lobed; fr. 4-winged, 2 in. long. N.C. to Ga. and Tenn. Zone 5. Cv. 'Rosea' [forma *rosea* Sarg.]. Fls. pinkish. Forma **rosea:** cv. 'Rosea.' Var. **vestita** Sarg. Lvs.

mostly rounded at base, at first tomentose, especially on veins beneath.

tetraptera: *H. carolina.*

×**HALIMIOCISTUS** Janch.: *Cistus* × *Halimium*. *Cistaceae*. Occurring in cult. and in the wild; evergreen shrub showing characters intermediate between the two parent genera.

Sahucii (Coste & Soulié) Janch.: naturally occurring hybrid, *C. salviifolius* × *H. umbellatum*. To 1½ ft.; lvs. linear-lanceolate, to 1 in. long, white-pubescent; fls. in clusters of 2–5, white, 1¼ in. across. S. France.

wintonensis (Hort. Hillier) O. E. Warb. & E. F. Warb: garden hybrid, presumably *C. salviifolius* × *H. lasianthum*. To 2 ft., grayish-pubescent; lvs. elliptic-lanceolate, to 2 in. long, 3-nerved; fls. white, with purple-brown blotch at base, 2 in. across. Originated in Eng.

HALIMIUM (Dunal) Spach. *Cistaceae*. About 9 spp. of low, evergreen, variously hairy, shrubs, native to Medit. region; lvs. opp., 4-ranked; sepals 5 or 3, petals 5, yellow or white, soon deciduous, stamens many, style short and straight, or absent; fr. a 3-valved caps. Closely related to *Helianthemum*.

For culture see *Helianthemum*.

alyssoides (Lam.) C. Koch [*Helianthemum alyssoides* (Lam.) Venten.]. Shrub, to 2 ft., gray-tomentose; lvs. ovate-lanceolate, to 1½ in. long, sessile or petioled; fls. to 1½ in. across, sepals 3, petals bright yellow, without blotches. Sw. Eur.

atriplicifolium (Lam.) Spach [*Helianthemum atriplicifolium* (Lam.) Willd.]. Shrub, to 3 ft.; lvs. silvery-scaly, those of nonflowering shoots narrowly ovate, to 1¼ in. long, 3-nerved, short-petioled, those of fl. shoots oblong-cordate, sessile; fl. brs. rigid, to 8 in. long, peduncles and pedicels with purplish spreading hairs, sepals 3, petals yellow, with basal blotch, ⅝ in. long. S. Spain, Morocco. Var. **macrocalycinum** Pau. Larger, especially the calyx and caps. Morocco.

commutatum Pau [*Halimium Libanotis* (Willd.) J. Lange, in part; *H. rosmarinifolium* Spach; *Helianthemum Libanotis* Willd., in part]. Shrub, to 1½ ft., much branched; lvs. linear, to 1½ in. long, revolute, glabrous above, gray-tomentose beneath; fls. usually 1–3 in terminal cymes, sepals glabrous, petals yellow. Coastal Spain and Portugal.

formosum: *H. lasianthum* subsp. *formosum.*

halimifolium (L.) Willk. & J. Lange [*Cistus halimifolius* L.; *Helianthemum halimifolium* (L.) Willd.]. Shrub, 3–4 ft.; lvs. oblong to lanceolate, to 2 in. long, white-tomentose, becoming gray-green; fls. in paniculate cymes, to 1½ in. across, sepals 5, petals yellow, sometimes blotched at base. S. Eur., N. Afr. Cv. 'Multiflorum'. Fls. orange-pink.

lasianthum (Lam.) Spach [*Helianthemum formosum* (Curtis) Dunal; *Helianthemum lasianthum* (Lam.) Pers.]. Shrub, to 3 ft., resembling *H. alyssoides*, but pedicels and sepals with long silky hairs and sepals often with long purple bristles. S. Spain, s. Portugal. Cv. 'Concolor'. Fls. clear canary-yellow. Subsp. **formosum** (Curtis) Heyw. [*H. formosum* (Curtis) Willk.]. Fls. 2 in. across, petals spotted.

Libanotis: see *H. commutatum.*

ocymoides (Lam.) Willk. & J. Lange [*Cistus algarvensis* Sims; *C. ocymoides* Lam.; *Helianthemum ocymoides* (Lam.) Pers.]. Erect, pubescent shrub, to 3 ft.; lvs. of nonflowering shoots obovate, about ½ in. long, 1–3-veined, gray-tomentose, lvs. of fl. shoots green, sessile, to 1¼ in. long; fls. long-pedicelled, 1 in. across, sepals 3, petals yellow, with basal blotch. Spain, Portugal.

rosmarinifolium: *H. commutatum.*

umbellatum (L.) Spach [*Helianthemum umbellatum* (L.) Mill.]. Diffusely branched shrub, to 1 ft., whitish-pubescent; lvs. crowded at ends of brs., linear to linear-lanceolate, to 1 in. long, revolute, green above, white-downy beneath; fls. about ½ in. across, pedicelled, 3–6 in short terminal clusters, petals white. Spain, Portugal, France. Var. **verticillatum:** *H. verticillatum.*

verticillatum (Brot.) Sennen [*H. umbellatum* var. *verticillatum* (Brot.) Willk.; *Cistus verticillatus* Brot.]. Resembling *H. umbellatum*, but larger, to 2 ft., brs. short and straight; lvs. distributed along brs., margins revolute or not. Portugal.

HALIMODENDRON Fisch. SALT TREE. *Leguminosae* (subfamily *Faboideae*). One sp., hardy, deciduous, spiny shrub of saline plains of cent. Asia; lvs. even-pinnate; fls. papilionaceous, stamens 10, 9 united and 1 separate; fr. an inflated, obovoid to cylindrical, leathery legume.

Grown as an ornamental; propagated by seeds, layering, cuttings over bottom heat, or by grafting on *Laburnum* or *Caragana*.

argentium: *H. halodendron.*

halodendron (Pall.) Voss [*H. argenteum* DC.]. To 6 ft., gray-downy; lfts. in 1 or 2 pairs on a persistent, spine-tipped rachis, oblanceolate, to 1½ in. long; fls. pale purple, ⅝ in. long, in lateral, 2–3-fld. racemes; fr. to 1 in. long, short-beaked. Zone 5.

HALLERIA L. *Scrophulariaceae*. About 5 spp. of glabrous shrubs or trees, native to Afr.; lvs. simple, opp.; fls. red, in axillary clusters, or solitary, calyx 3–5-lobed, corolla tubular, 4–5-lobed, stamens 4; fr. a berry.

lucida L. Much-branched, evergreen shrub, to 6 ft., becoming trees to 30 ft. where native; lvs. ovate, to 3 in. long, acuminate, finely toothed; fls. scarlet, to 1 in. long, curved, drooping; fr. deep purple, almost black. Trop. and S. Afr.

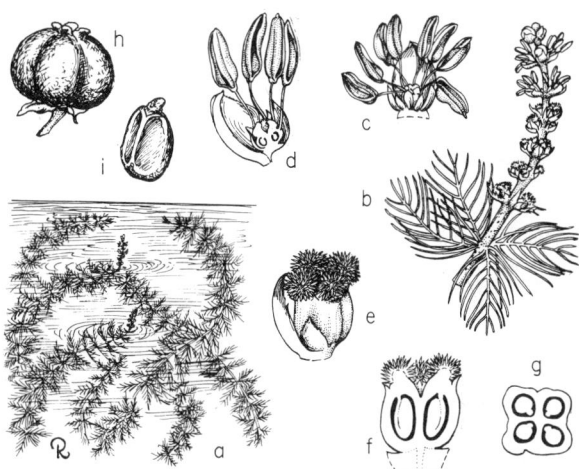

HALORAGACEAE. *Myriophyllum verticillatum:* **a,** flowering plants, much reduced; **b,** uppermost submersed leaves and inflorescence, × 1; **c,** bracts with male flower, × 4; **d,** bracts with male flower, vertical section, × 5; **e,** bracts with female flower, × 6; **f,** female flower, vertical section, × 8; **g,** ovary, cross section, × 8.

HALORAGACEAE R. Br. [sometimes incorrectly spelled *Haloragidaceae, Halorrhagaceae*]. WATER MILFOIL FAMILY. Dicot.; 6 genera, with about 125 spp. of ann. or per. herbs, mostly aquatic or marsh plants, of wide distribution; lvs. alt., opp., or whorled, without stipules, often pinnatifid to pinnate; fls. small, inconspicuous, bisexual or unisexual, calyx lobes and petals 2–4 or 0, stamens mostly 4 or 8, ovary inferior, 1–4-celled, each cell 1-ovuled; fr. a nutlet or drupelet. *Myriophyllum* and *Proserpinaca* are cult. in aquaria and pools.

HAMAMELIDACEAE R. Br. WITCH HAZEL FAMILY. Dicot.; 23 genera of deciduous or evergreen trees or shrubs,

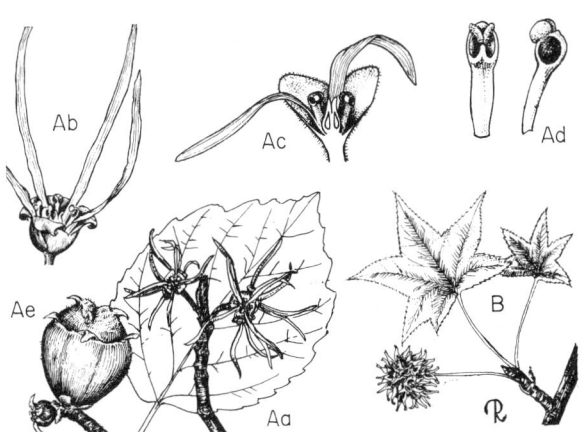

HAMAMELIDACEAE. **A,** *Hamamelis virginiana:* **Aa,** twig in flower, and leaf, × ½; **Ab,** flower, × 1; **Ac,** flower, vertical section, × 1; **Ad,** stamen, face and side view, × 6; **Ae,** fruit, × 1. **B,** *Liquidambar Styraciflua:* fruiting twig, × ¼. (From Bailey, *Manual of Cultivated Plants*, ed. 2.)

native mostly to warm temp. regions of Asia, a few to Afr., Australia, N. Amer., and Madagascar; lvs. alt., simple, toothed or sometimes palmately lobed, stipuled; fls. bisexual or unisexual, in heads or racemes, fl. tube with 4–5 sepals, 4–5 petals or none, stamens 4 or more, ovary 2-celled; fr. a 2-beaked, woody caps. The cult. genera are: *Corylopsis, Disanthus, Distylium, Exbucklandia, Fortuneria, Fothergilla, Hamamelis, Liquidambar, Loropetalum, Parrotia, Parrotiopsis, Rhodoleia, Sinowilsonia,* and *Sycopsis.*

Some genera are sources of commercial timber and resins. Many of the genera are ornamental and most of them are hardy north.

HAMAMELIS L. WITCH HAZEL. *Hamamelidaceae.* About 6 spp. of deciduous shrubs or small trees, native to temp. e. N. Amer. and temp. e. Asia; lvs. simple, toothed; fls. in axillary, more or less sessile clusters, appearing in autumn or early spring, calyx 4-parted, petals 4, strap-shaped, stamens 4, short, staminodes 4; fr. a caps.

Witch hazels thrive in rather moist soil. Propagated by seeds which require 2 years to germinate, by layers, or by grafting on stock of *H. virginiana.* Most hardy north (Zone 5).

arborea: *H. japonica.*

brevipetala: a listed name of no botanical standing.

×**intermedia** Rehd.: *H. japonica* × *mollis.* Intermediate between the 2 parents, but showing variation in amount of pubescence, size and shape of lvs., and color of fls.

japonica Siebold & Zucc. [*H. japonica* var. *arborea* (Hort. Ottol. ex M. T. Mast.) Gumbl., and var. *Zuccariniana* (Hort. Ottol. ex M. T. Mast.) Gumbl.; *H. arborea* Hort. Ottol. ex M. T. Mast.; *H. Zuccariniana* Hort. Ottol. ex M. T. Mast.]. JAPANESE W.H. Shrub or tree, to 30 ft., with spreading brs.; lvs. rhombic-orbicular, broadly ovate or obovate, to 5 in. long, stellate-pubescent when young; fls. yellow, calyx lobes usually purple within, petals ¾ in. long. Winter–early spring. Japan. Cv. 'Flavo-purpurascens'. Petals reddish at base.

macrophylla: *H. virginiana.*

mollis D. Oliver. CHINESE W.H. Shrub or small tree, to 30 ft.; lvs. orbicular-obovate, toothed, to 6 in. long, slightly roughened above, grayish-stellate-tomentose beneath, obliquely cordate at base; fls. golden-yellow, calyx lobes purplish-red inside, petals to ½ in. long. Winter–early spring. W. China. Foliage yellow in autumn. Cv. 'Brevipetala'. Fls. deep orange; lvs. longer.

obtusifolia: a listed name of no botanical standing.

populifolia: a listed name of no botanical standing.

purpurea: a listed name of no botanical standing.

vernalis Sarg. Shrub, to 6 ft., spreading by means of short stolons; lvs. obovate to elliptic, to 4 in. long, coarsely crenate, glabrous above or stellate-hairy along veins, somewhat glaucous and stellate-hairy along veins beneath; fls. dull yellow, calyx lobes dark red inside, petals to ½ in. long. Winter–early spring. Mo. to La. and Okla. Fls. more fragrant but less showy than in most other spp. Cv. 'Rubra'. Petals reddish, at least near base. Cv. 'Tomentella'. Lvs. more pubescent beneath.

virginiana L. [*H. macrophylla* Pursh]. Shrub or small tree, to 15 ft.; lvs. obovate, to 6 in. long, coarsely dentate, nearly glabrous or pubescent along veins beneath; fls. golden-yellow, calyx lobes dull brownish-yellow inside, petals to ¾ in. long. Late autumn; fr. ripening the following autumn. E. N. Amer. A coarse shrub, but attractive for its late fls., which appear as the lvs. become bright yellow before falling. The astringent bark and lvs. reputedly have medicinal properties.

Zuccariniana: *H. japonica.*

HAMATOCACTUS Britt. & Rose. *Cactaceae.* Spp. originally assigned to this genus are now referred to *Ancistrocactus* and *Ferocactus.* **H. setispinus:** *Ferocactus setispinus.* **H. uncinatus:** *Ancistrocactus uncinatus.*

HAMELIA Jacq. *Rubiaceae.* About 40 spp. of evergreen shrubs or small trees, native to Mex., Paraguay, and W. Indies; lvs. opp. or whorled, entire, stipules inconspicuous, interpetiolar, deciduous; fls. in terminal, often 1-sided, branching cymes, red or yellow, rather small, 5-merous, corolla tubular; fr. a small berry, seeds many.

Propagated by seeds and cuttings of half-ripe wood under glass.

erecta: *H. patens.*

patens Jacq. [*H. erecta* Jacq.; *H. sphaerocarpa* Ruiz & Pav.]. SCARLET BUSH, FIREBUSH. To 25 ft., gray-pubescent; lvs. elliptic or ovate,

to 6 in. long; fls. scarlet or orange, to ¾ in. long; fr. ovoid, ¼ in. long, dark red or purple. Fla. and W. Indies, s. to Bolivia and Paraguay. Confused in cult. with *Ixora.* Grown outdoors in Calif. and s. U.S.

sphaerocarpa: *H. patens.*

HAPLOPAPPUS Cass. (Originally spelled *Aplopappus,* but the spelling *Haplopappus* has been conserved.) [*Ericameria* Nutt.; *Sideranthus* Nutt.; *Stenotus* Nutt.]. *Compositae* (Aster Tribe). About 150 spp. of ann. or per. taprooted herbs and shrubs in s. and w. N. Amer., usually resinous or glandular; lvs. alt., entire to lobed or dissected; fl. heads radiate or discoid, variously disposed, involucral bracts nearly equal or imbricate; disc and ray fls. usually yellow; pappus of 1 or more rows of unequal capillary bristles.

acaulis (Nutt.) A. Gray. Cespitose per.; basal lvs. oblanceolate, 1–2 in. long, rigid, 3-nerved, entire; heads many, radiate, 1 in. across, solitary on scapelike sts. 2–6 in., involucral bracts acute or acuminate; pappus white or pale brown. Mts., from Sask. to Colo., w. to Calif. Var. **glabratus** D. C. Eat. Nearly glabrous except for lf. margins.

armerioides (Nutt.) A. Gray [*Stenotus armerioides* Nutt.]. Similar to *H. acaulis,* but slightly larger; involucral bracts obtuse or rounded; pappus white. Mont. to Nebr., s. to Ariz. and New Mex.

Clementis (Rydb.) S. F. Blake. Per., 4–16 in.; lvs. in a basal rosette, oblong-lanceolate, 2–6 in. long, entire or toothed, glabrous to puberulent; heads 1½ in. across, radiate, usually solitary on few-bracted villous sts., involucral bracts acute; pappus light brown. Rocky Mts., Wyo., Colo., Utah.

coronopifolius: *H. glutinosus.*

criniflorus: a listed name of no botanical standing.

croceus A. Gray. Per. herb, 4–24 in.; basal lvs. petioled, lanceolate, to 1 ft. long, entire, glabrous, st. lvs. smaller, the upper sessile; heads to 3 in. across, radiate, usually solitary, terminal, involucral bracts obtuse; fls. orange-yellow; pappus brownish. Rocky Mts., Wyo. to Ariz. and New Mex.

cuneatus A. Gray [*Ericameria cuneata* (A. Gray) McClat.]. Twiggy, dwarf shrub, to 2 ft. or more; lvs. cuneate-obovate or spatulate, to ¾ in. long, obtuse to retuse, entire or undulate, resin-pitted, sticky; heads small, ⁵⁄₁₆ in. across, cymose; ray fls. 1–5 or lacking; pappus pale brown. Sw. U.S. and Baja Calif. Var. **spathulatus** (A. Gray) S. F. Blake [*Ericameria cuneata* var. *spathulata* H. M. Hall]. The rayless form, not always considered worthy of nomenclatural distinction.

cuneifolius Nutt. Cespitose, short-stemmed plant, 4–6 in.; lvs. sessile, cuneate-obovate, ½ in. long, glabrous and sticky, obtusely few-toothed; heads radiate, terminal, solitary, 1 in. across, involucral bracts glabrous, linear, acute; ray fls. orange-yellow; pappus brown. Chile, Argentina.

ericoides (Less.) Hook. & Arn. [*Ericameria ericoides* (Less.) Jeps.]. Heathlike shrub, to 3 ft. or more; lvs. filiform, ¼–½ in. long, resin-pitted, with dense fascicles of lvs. in their axils; heads radiate, ½ in. across, cymose-panicled, involucre turbinate, outer bracts acute; ray fls. 2–6; pappus pale brown. Sand dunes, coastal Calif.

eximius H. M. Hall. Per., to 6 in., rhizomatous, forming loose mats; lvs. spatulate, 1–2 in. long, obtuse, dentate above the middle, glandular-puberulent; heads radiate, 1 in. across, solitary and terminal on erect, glandular, leafy sts., involucral bracts oblong to obovate, obtuse; pappus dirty-white. Mts., Calif., Nev.

glutinosus Cass. [*H. coronopifolius* DC.]. Loosely cespitose per., from woody basal brs., mat-forming, to 12 in. high; lvs. tufted, to ½ in. long, lobed or pinnatifid, attenuate, sticky; heads radiate, terminal and solitary on scapelike peduncles; pappus reddish. Chile, Argentina.

gracilis (Nutt.) A. Gray. Slender ann. herb, to 10 in., branching from the base; lvs. linear to lanceolate, ½–1 in. long, dentate or pinnatifid, the lobes bristle-tipped; heads radiate, ¾ in. across, involucral bracts imbricate in 5–6 rows, bristle-tipped, green-spotted; pappus brown to whitish. Dry plains, sw. U.S. and n. Mex.

lanuginosus A. Gray. Similar to *H. acaulis,* but lvs. to 4 in. long, soft, not rigid, glandular to tomentose. Mont. to Wash. and Ore.

Lyallii A. Gray. Related and similar to *H. eximius,* but lvs. entire or sparingly denticulate, involucral bracts lanceolate, acute or acuminate. High Mts., s. B.C. and Alta. to Nev., Colo.

Parishii (Greene) S. F. Blake. Arborescent shrub, to 15 ft.; lvs. crowded, ascending, linear to lanceolate-oblong, to 2 in. long, entire, thick, resin-pitted; heads discoid, many, ³⁄₁₆ in. across, densely cymose, involucre turbinate; ray fls. lacking; pappus dull white or brownish. S. Calif. and n. Baja Calif.

phyllocephalus DC. [*Sideranthus phyllocephalus* Small]. Stout ann. herb, to 3½ ft.; lvs. sessile, oblong, to 2 in. long, toothed or lobed, the lobes bristle-tipped; heads radiate, to 1¼ in. across, solitary or cymose on the brs., involucral bracts imbricate in 2–4 rows, bristle-tipped; ray fls. yellow or reddish; pappus brown. In various forms, from e. Mex., n. to Colo. and Kans., e. to w. Fla.

pulcherrimus: a listed name of no botanical standing.

pygmaeus (Torr. & A. Gray) A. Gray. Tufted per., to 2½ in., related to *H. eximius* but without rhizomes, not glandular, the lvs. entire, sparsely puberulent. High peaks in Rocky Mts., Wyo. to New Mex.

spinulosus (Pursh) DC. [*Sideranthus spinulosus* (Pursh) Sweet ex Rydb.]. Per. herb with woody base, to 2 ft.; lvs. oblong-spatulate, to 2 in. long, from nearly entire to 2-pinnatifid, with bristle-tipped teeth or lobes, variously pubescent; heads radiate, ¾ in. across, solitary on short brs.; pappus brown. Rather variable; Alta. and Sask. to Minn., s. to n. Mex.

HAPLOPHRAGMA Dop. *Bignoniaceae*. About 3 spp. of trees, native from ne. India to Malay Pen.; lvs. opp., pinnate, large, leathery; fls. in axillary or terminal, woolly panicles, calyx irregularly 3–5-lobed, corolla tubular-ventricose, stamens 4; fr. an elongate, twisted, 2-valved caps.

adenophyllum (Wallich ex G. Don) Dop [*Heterophragma adenophyllum* (Wallich ex G. Don) Seem. ex Benth. & Hook.f.]. Stout tree, to 50 ft.; lvs. to 2 ft. long, lfts. 5–7, elliptic, to 7 in. long; panicles to 8 in. long; fls. yellowish-brown, woolly-tomentose outside; caps. to 2 ft. long. Ne. India to Malay Pen.

HARDENBERGIA Benth. *Leguminosae* (subfamily *Faboideae*). Three spp. of vines and subshrubs of Australia; lvs. alt., odd-pinnate, with 3–5 lfts. of variable shape, or of 1 lft.; fls. small, papilionaceous, in long racemes, wings adherent to keel petals, stamens 10, 9 united and 1 separate; fr. a linear legume. Differs from *Kennedia* in having many and smaller fls. and keel petal obtuse, shorter than wing petals.

Grown as ornamentals outdoors in Zone 10, or in greenhouses, where they require peaty, well-drained soil. Propagated by seeds, and softwood cuttings in spring.

Comptoniana Benth. Evergreen, twining vine, to 8 ft.; lfts. 3 or 5, ovate to narrowly lanceolate, to 5 in. long and 2 in. wide, obtuse; fls. in racemes to 5 in. long or more, violet-blue, with green and white splotch at base of standard, less than ½ in. long; fr. to 2 in. long. W. Australia.

monophylla: *H. violacea.*

violacea (Schneev.) F. C. Stern [*H. monophylla* Benth.]. VINE LILAC, CORAL PEA. Evergreen shrub, with scandent brs., differing from *H. Comptoniana* in having solitary lfts. and violet to rose or white fls. with yellow splotch; fr. turgid, 1½ in. long. E. Australia, Tasmania. Cv. 'Rosea'. Fls. pink.

HARPEPHYLLUM Bernh. ex C. F. Krauss. *Anacardiaceae*. One sp., a dioecious tree, native to S. Afr.; lvs. pinnate, leathery; fls. in compact axillary panicles, stamens 10; fr. 4-celled, 2 of the cells small and sterile.

Planted in warm climates.

caffrum Bernh. ex C. F. Krauss. KAFFIR PLUM. Tree, to 30 ft.; lfts. lanceolate, to 2½ in. long, glossy; fls. white or greenish; fr. dark red, about 1 in. long and ½ in. in diam., edible. Summer. Grown in Zone 10 as an ornamental. Fr. used in jellies.

HARPULLIA Roxb. *Sapindaceae*. About 35 spp. of dioecious or polygamous trees, native from trop. Asia to Australia and Madagascar; lvs. alt., pinnate; fls. small, in axillary racemes or panicles, regular, sepals 5, petals 4–5, stamens 5–8; fr. a leathery, inflated, 2-valved caps.

arborea (Blanco) Radlk. To 35 ft. or more; lfts. 8–10, oblong-lanceolate, to 6 in. long, glossy; fls. in drooping panicles, greenish, about ½ in. long, sepals deciduous, petals clawed; fr. bright orange, broader than long, about 1½ in. in diam., seed large, smooth, black. India, Malay Pen., Philippine Is.

cupanioides Roxb. To 60 ft.; lfts. 6–12, oblong-lanceolate or elliptic, 3–8 in. long, glossy; sepals persistent, petals not clawed; fr. orange, about ¾ in. in diam. Se. Asia, Indonesia. Has been confused with *H. arborea.*

pendula Planch. To 50 ft.; lfts. 4–8, oblong to oblong-lanceolate, to 6 in. long; sepals deciduous; fr. orange, 1–1½ in. in diam. Australia. Wood used in cabinetry.

HARRIMANELLA: *CASSIOPE.*

HARRISIA Britt. [*Eriocereus* (A. Berger) Riccob.]. *Cactaceae*. About 20 spp. of slender, ribbed cacti of Fla., W. Indies, and S. Amer.; sts. prostrate, scrambling, or shrubby, ribs 4–12, mostly low, rounded, and somewhat knobby, sinuous, with sinuses acute; spines mostly needle-shaped; fls. funnelform, nocturnal, white, tube slender, scales with hairs in axils, ovary tubercled; fr. globose, spiny or not, red and splitting (*Eriocereus*, S. Amer.) or yellow to orange and not splitting (*Harrisia*, Fla., W. Indies), the perianth persistent, seeds many, small. Sometimes united with *Cereus.*

For culture see *Cacti.*

Bonplandii (Parm.) Britt. & Rose [*Eriocereus Bonplandii* (Parm.) Riccob.]. Sts. erect, to 10 ft. high, or clambering, 1¼ in. thick or more, ribs 4–6, low, obtuse; areoles ½–1¼ in. apart, radial spines 4–8, the upper longest, ½ in. long, central spine 1, to 1 in. long; fls. white, to 10 in. long; fr. red, spineless, to 2½ in. in diam., flesh white, seeds ⅛ in. long. Brazil.

Earlei Britt. & Rose. Sts. prostrate, to 10 ft. long, 1–2½ in. thick, 5–7-angled, becoming cylindrical; areoles ¾–1½ in. apart, spines 5–8, gray, the longer ascending, to 2 in. long; fls. white, 8 in. long, hairs in axils of scales short, white; fr. yellow, to 3 in. in diam. Cuba.

eriophora (Pfeiff.) Britt. Erect, to 12 ft., brs. ascending, 1½ in. thick, ribs 8–9, rounded; areoles ¾–1½ in. apart, spines 6–9, black-tipped, the longest to 1½ in. long; fls. white, 5–7 in. long, hairs in axils of scales long, white; fr. orange, to 2½ in. in diam., edible. Spring, summer. Cuba.

fragrans Small. Sts. clambering, to 18 ft.; ribs 10–12; areoles ¾ in. apart; spines 9–13, the longest to 1½ in.; fls. white, odorous, 5–8 in. long, hairs in axils of scales copious, long, white; fr. dull red, to 2½ in. in diam. S. Fla. Probably only a var. of *H. eriophora.*

gracilis (Mill.) Britt. Sts. much-branched, to 25 ft., slender, ribs 9–11, rounded; areoles to ¾ in. apart, spines 10–16, whitish, black-tipped, to 1 in. long; fls. white, to 8 in. long, hairs in axils of scales white, perianth segms. minutely toothed; fr. yellow, to 3 in. in diam. Cuba and Jamaica.

Guelichii (Speg.) Britt. & Rose [*Eriocereus Guelichii* (Speg.) Backeb. & F. M. Knuth]. Sts. climbing, to 80 ft. long, 1–2 in. thick, ribs 3–4, acute, undulate; areoles 1–2½ in. apart, radial spines 4–5, the upper to 1 in. long, central spine 1, to 1 in. long; fls. white, fragrant, to 10 in. long, axils of tube nearly naked; fr. red, spineless, edible, to 2 in. in diam., flesh white. Argentina.

Jusbertii (Rebut) Borg [*Eriocereus Jusbertii* (Rebut) Riccob.]. MOON CACTUS. Sts. clambering, dark green, to 2½ in. thick, ribs 6, sinuses broadly concave; areoles to ¾ in. apart, spines conical, brown, to ¼ in. long, radial spines 7, central spine 1; fls. white, fragrant, 7 in. long; fr. red, to 2½ in. in diam. Paraguay? Position doubtful, said to be a hybrid.

Martinii (Labour.) Britt. & Rose [*Eriocereus Martinii* (Labour.) Riccob.]. MOON CACTUS. Sts. clambering, much-branched, 1 in. thick, ribs 4–5, of nearly separate, long-elliptic tubercles; areoles to 1½ in. apart, radial spines about 5–7, central spine 1, to 1¼ in. long; fls. white, 8 in. long; fr. red, spiny, 1½ in. in diam. Argentina.

Nashii Britt. Erect, to 10 ft., brs. to 1½ in. thick, ribs 9–11; areoles to 1 in. apart, spines 3–6, gray, to ⅝ in. long; fls. to 8 in. long, acute in bud, hairs in axils of scales few, short, white, perianth segms. entire; fr. to 3 in. in diam. Hispaniola. Perhaps to be called *H. fimbriata* (Lam.) F. M. Knuth.

pomanensis (A. Web.) Britt. & Rose [*Eriocereus pomanensis* (A. Web.) Backeb. & F. M. Knuth]. Sts. prostrate or clambering, bluish, ribs 4–6, entire; areoles to ¾ in. apart, spines awl-shaped, white or gray, radial spines 6–8, to ⅜ in. long, central spine 1, to ¾ in. long; fls. white, 6 in. long. Argentina. Cv. 'Grossei'. Bright green, ribs 3–4.

portoricensis Britt. To 10 ft. high, brs. few, erect, to 1½ in. thick, ribs 11; areoles ¾ in. apart, spines 13–17, grayish to brown, dark-tipped, to 1¼ in. long; fls. white, obovoid and truncate in bud, 6 in. long, hairs in axils of scales deciduous; fr. yellow, to 2½ in. in diam. Puerto Rico.

robusta: a listed name of no botanical standing.

Simpsonii Small. Erect, to 20 ft., or spreading, ribs 8–10; areoles to ¾ in. apart, spines 7–14, gray, to 1 in. long; fls. white, 5–7 in. long, hairs in axils of scales few, white, perianth segms. erosely minutely toothed; fr. orange-red, to 2½ in. in diam. S. Fla. Probably only a var. of *H. gracilis.*

tortuosa (J. Forbes ex Otto & A. Dietr.) Britt. & Rose [*Eriocereus tortuosus* (J. Forbes ex Otto & A. Dietr.) Riccob.]. Sts. decumbent, to 1½ in. thick, ribs about 7; areoles ¾ in. apart, spines awl-shaped, reddish-brown, becoming gray or black, radial spines 5–8, to ¾ in.

long, central spine 1, to 1½ in. long; fls. white, to 6½ in. long; fr. red, short-spiny, to 2 in. in diam. Argentina.

HARTWEGIA: *NAGELIELLA*.

HATIORA Britt. & Rose. *Cactaceae*. Five spp. of epiphytic cacti, native to Brazil; sts. slender, cylindrical, jointed, branching apically, joints short, club-shaped to cylindrical, with areoles apical or at least mostly above the middle, spineless; perianth segms. separate, erect, white or yellow to orange, withering, persistent, ovary globose, smooth; fr. globose to obovoid, white, semitransparent. Atavistic brs. of rounded, bristly joints sometimes occur. Allied to *Rhipsalis*, but with fls. apical and joints with unlike ends.

For culture see *Cacti*.

bambusioides (A. Web.) Britt. & Rose. Erect, to 6 ft., joints club-shaped, 1–2 in. long, ⁵⁄₃₂ in. thick above, only slightly narrowed downward, apparently with 1 compound areole at apex; fls. orange; fr. obovoid.

clavata (A. Web.) Moran [*Rhipsalis clavata* A. Web.]. Soon pendent, to 3 ft., joints club-shaped, sometimes 4-angled when young, ½–2 in. long, to ⅛ in. thick, with 1 compound areole at apex; fls. white, ⅝ in. long; fr. globose, ¼ in. in diam.

cylindrica Britt. & Rose. Joints cylindrical, to 1¼ in. long, apparently with 1 compound areole at apex; fls. yellow or orangish, ½ in. long. Perhaps not distinct from *H. bambusioides*.

salicornioides (Haw.) Britt. & Rose. SPICE CACTUS, DANCING-BONES C., DRUNKARD'S-DREAM. Erect or eventually pendent, to 6 ft., joints to 1¼ in. long, club-shaped, to ¼ in. thick above, abruptly narrowed at the middle, much narrower below, areoles in the upper half; fls. yellow, ⅜ in. long; fr. obovoid.

HAUYA DC. *Onagraceae*. About 14 spp. of trees or shrubs, native from Mex. to Cent. Amer.; lvs. alt., simple, petioled, entire; fls. large, solitary in axils, white to pinkish, 4-merous, calyx tube cylindrical, elongate, sepals reflexed in age, stamens 8, ovary inferior; fr. a woody caps.

Rarely cultivated in Calif.

ruacophila J. D. Sm. & Rose. Six to 30 ft., with dense soft pubescence; lvs. round-cordate to oblong-ovate, blades 2–5 in. long; calyx tube 2–4 in. long, petals ovate, 1½–1¾ in. long, white. Summer. Guatemala.

HAWORTHIA H. Duval. WART PLANT, STAR CACTUS, CUSHION ALOE. *Liliaceae*. Perhaps as many as 160 spp. of succulent, per. herbs of S. Afr., with many vars. and forms; stemless or short-stemmed, often suckering and forming clumps; lvs. imbricate, mostly in many rows in dense rosettes, often tubercled, usually keeled underneath; fls. white with green or rosy stripes, in racemes or panicles, perianth tubular, 2-lipped, stamens 6, anthers dorsifixed; fr. a loculicidal, 3-valved caps.

For culture see *Succulents*.

adelaidensis: *H. Reinwardtii* var.

albicans: *H. marginata*.

altilinea Haw. Stemless; lvs. lanceolate-obovate, to 2¼ in. long, tipped with a long bristle, upper surface with longitudinal lines, margins and apex of keel toothed; fls. ⅝ in. long, in racemes. Var. **denticulata** (Haw.) Poelln. [*H. denticulata* Haw.]. Lvs. nearly oblanceolate, slightly narrower, with more numerous teeth. Var. **limpida**: *H. mucronata* var. Var. **Morrisiae**: *H. mucronata* var. Var. **mucronata**: *H. mucronata*.

angustifolia Haw. Stemless; lvs. lanceolate, to 2 in. long, tipped with a bristle, old lvs. recurved, marked with longitudinal lines, margins and keel with white translucent teeth; fls. to ¾ in. long, in racemes. Var. **albanensis** (Schönl.) Poelln. Rosettes smaller, lvs. darker green, to 1½ in. long. Var. **liliputana** Uitew. Lvs. to ¾ in. long. Var. **subfalcata** Poelln. Lvs. often somewhat laterally curved, with minute teeth, often tubercled on upper surface toward apex.

arachnoidea (L.) H. Duval. Stemless; lvs. oblong-lanceolate, to 2 in. long, tipped with a bristle, margins and keel with long translucent teeth; fls. ⅝ in. long, in a loose raceme.

Armstrongii Poelln. St. to 4 in. long, densely leafy; lvs. lanceolate, to 1½ in. long, erect, dark green, tubercled on keel and margins, young lvs. white-tipped.

asperiuscula Haw. Stemless; lvs. 3-ranked, triangular, about ½ in.

long, sharply keeled underneath near apex, somewhat sticky, very finely roughened; fls. ¾ in. long, in a very loose, few-fld. raceme.

asperula Haw. Stemless; lvs. triangular-ovate, to 1⅜ in. long, recurved, roughened with minute papillae; fls. ⅝ in. long, in a loose few-fld. raceme.

atrovirens: *H. herbacea*.

attenuata Haw. Stemless; lvs. 30–40, triangular-oblong, to 3 in. long, glossy, dark green, upper surface with central line of white tubercles, lower surface rounded and keeled, with many white tubercles. Var. **argyrostigma** (Bak.) A. Berger. St. to 6 in., leafy; lvs. erect, to 1¼ in. long, tubercles on upper surface colorless and tiny, those on lower surface white, often irregular, never confluent. Var. **Britteniana** (Poelln.) Poelln. [*H. Britteniana* Poelln.]. Lvs. to 2¾ in. long, lower surface with large white tubercles in irregular, loose, transverse rows, and smaller tubercles scattered irregularly. Var. **caespitosa** (A. Berger) R. Farden [*H. fasciata* (Willd.) Haw. var. *caespitosa* A. Berger]. Sts. to 1½ in., lvs. flat, to 2¾ in. long, turning purple-green, with white tubercles in transverse bands on lower surface. Var. **clariperla** (Haw.) Bak. [*H. clariperla* Haw.]. Lvs. to 2⅜ in. long, with pearly, prominently raised tubercles arranged mostly irregularly on lower surface. Var. **Odonoghueana** R. Farden. Lvs. flat, bright green, to 1½ in. long, with white tubercles in regular, very fine, transverse bands on lower surface. Var. **Uitewaaliana** R. Farden. Lvs. bright green, to 1½ in. long, with very prominent white tubercles in close transverse bands on lower surface, and fine white tubercles covering upper surface. Cv. 'Variegata'. Lvs. variegated.

Batesiana Uitew. Stemless, suckering and forming dense cushions; lvs. lanceolate-ovate or oblong, to 1 in. long, tipped with a long bristle, both sides with 4–5 longitudinal lines uniting at apex, margins and keel irregularly set with minute, translucent teeth.

Beecroftiana: a listed name of no botanical standing.

bicarinata: a listed name of no botanical standing.

bilineata Bak. Stemless; lvs. oblong-lanceolate, to 2 in. long, tipped with a bristle, dark green, with 1–2 longitudinal lines, upper surface rather translucent, keel and margins ciliate-toothed.

Britteniana: *H. attenuata* var.

caespitosa Poelln. Stemless, suckering and forming dense cushions; lvs. lanceolate, 1¼ in. long, tipped with a bristle, pale green, somewhat translucent and glossy, both surfaces with 3–4 obscure longitudinal lines, upper surface with few flat tubercles, margins and keel irregularly set with tiny teeth. Perhaps not distinct from *H. laetevirens*.

Cassytha Bak. St. to 4 in., leafy, suckering; lvs. all ascending, ovate, to 1¼ in. long and ¾ in. wide, dull green, somewhat tubercled on upper surface and whitish along margin, with strongly raised white tubercles on lower surface.

Chalwinii Marloth & A. Berger. ARISTOCRAT PLANT, COLUMN-OF-PEARLS. St. to 5 in., leafy; lvs. ovate-triangular, about 1 in. long, bronze-purple, tubercles pearly white, in definite transverse rows; fls. ⅝ in. long, in a raceme. By some authors considered to be a var. of *H. Reinwardtii*.

chloracantha Haw. Stemless; lvs. ovate-lanceolate, to 1½ in. long, erect to recurved-spreading, dark green or often purple, margins and keels fimbriate-serrate, with a few rigid teeth.

chlorantha: a listed name of no botanical standing.

clariperla: *H. attenuata* var.

coarctata (Salm-Dyck) Haw. St. to 8 in., leafy, suckering; lvs. triangular-lanceolate, to 2⅜ in. long, dark green, lower surface with greenish-white tubercles in longitudinal lines.

confusa: *H. tenera* var.

conspicua: a listed name of no botanical standing.

Cooperi Bak. Stemless; lvs. oblong-lanceolate, to 1¾ in., pale green, tipped with a translucent awn and with translucent spots on upper half, margins and keel finely toothed; fls. to ¾ in. long, in a simple raceme to 1½ ft. high.

Curtisii: a listed name of no botanical standing.

cuspidata Haw. Stemless; lvs. obovate-cuneate, to 1 in. long, pale green, translucent at apex, strongly recurved, awned, margins and keel with tiny teeth; fls. ⅝ in. long, in a loose raceme to 1½ ft.

cymbiformis (Haw.) H. Duval. WINDOW H., WINDOW PLANT. Stemless, suckering; lvs. obovate, to 1½ in. long, glabrous, gray-green, with darker longitudinal stripes toward apex, translucent at apex, upper surface concave, entire; fls. very pale pink, striped with green, in a raceme to 1 ft. high. Var. **obesa** Poelln. Lvs. 20–40 in a rosette, to ¾ in. long, with translucent teeth on margins and often on keel. Var. **obtusa**: *H. obtusa*.

decipiens Poelln. Stemless; lvs. oblong-lanceolate, to 1½ in. long, blue-green, with many dark green longitudinal stripes, apex translucent, ending in a long bristle, margins bearing white teeth.

deltoidea: a listed name of no botanical standing.

denticulata: *H. altilinea* var.

Dielsiana: *H. obtusa* var.

Eilyae Poelln. St. to 8 in., leafy, erect, suckering; lvs. lanceolate, to 2 in. long, apex tipped with brownish point, upper surface with greenish-white tubercles in a longitudinal line near the margins, lower surface with 8–12 longitudinal lines and irregularly scattered tubercles, margins and keel with tubercles and an interrupted horny edge. Cv. 'Robusta'. Rosettes wider.

Emelyae Poelln. Stemless; lvs. oblong, to 1½ in. long, upper surface obliquely truncate at apex, lower surface dark green at apex, with few glossy, translucent tubercles, keel and margins toothed toward apex.

Engleri: *H. tessellata* var.

fasciata (Willd.) Haw. ZEBRA H. Stemless; lvs. triangular-lanceolate, to 1½ in. long, incurved toward apex, slightly glossy, lower surface with large, white tubercles confluent into transverse lines. Var. **caespitosa:** *H. attenuata* var. Cv. 'Ovato-lanceolata' [forma *ovato-lanceolata* Poelln.]. Lvs. ovate-oblong, to 2 in. long, tubercles on lower surface in indistinct longitudinal lines, but rarely if ever in transverse lines. Cv. 'Sparsa' [forma *sparsa* Poelln.]. Lvs. to 2 in. long, with tubercles fewer, arranged in distinct longitudinal lines and only indistinct transverse bands. Cv. 'Subconfluens' [var. *subconfluens* Poelln.; forma *subconfluens* (Poelln.) Poelln.]. Lvs. to 2¼ in. long, with white tubercles scattered on lower surface or confluent into short transverse lines. Cv. 'Vanstaadensis'. Lvs. to 2 in. long, with few tubercles scattered on lower surface, or few tubercles in longitudinal lines, rarely in indistinct transverse bands. Var. **staadensis:** a listed name, perhaps in error for cv. 'Vanstaadensis'.

glabrata (Salm-Dyck) Haw. Rosettes to 4¾ in. high, suckering; lvs. lanceolate-triangular, to 6 in. long, bluish-green, upper surface smooth, lower surface with tubercles in remote rows, margins and keel with translucent tubercles. Var. **concolor** Salm-Dyck. Lvs. brilliant green, with many green tubercles on lower surface, margins and keel with small white tubercles. Var. **perviridis** Salm-Dyck. Rosettes higher; lvs. more numerous, green to bluish, with larger tubercles.

glauca Bak. St. to 3 in., leafy; lvs. oblong-lanceolate, to 1⅜ in. long, pale glaucous-green, tipped by a short bristle, tubercles lacking, lower surface with 5–7 prominent, longitudinal, dark green lines.

gracilis Poelln. Stemless; lvs. oblong to oblong-ovate, to 1½ in. long, bluish, incurved toward apex, tipped with a bristle, upper surface with 3–5 longitudinal lines, margins and keel with few teeth.

granata: *H. margaritifera* var. *minima*.

Greenii Bak. St. to 8 in., procumbent in age, suckering and forming clumps; lvs. lanceolate-triangular, to 1½ in. long, incurved, lower surface with 6–8 longitudinal lines, both surfaces with whitish tubercles.

Haageana Poelln. Stemless; lvs. ovate-lanceolate, to 1½ in. long, incurved toward apex, pale green to reddish, frequently mottled, often with indistinct longitudinal lines, the keel with tiny tubercles. Var. **subreticulata** Poelln. Lvs. with a terminal bristle, margins and keel often inconspicuously toothed.

Helmiae Poelln. Stemless; lvs. oblong-ovate or oblanceolate, to 1½ in. long, somewhat glossy, tipped with a bristle, translucent toward apex, lower surface with a longitudinal line of tubercles, margins and keel with whitish teeth.

herbacea (Mill.) Stearn [*H. atrovirens* (DC.) Haw.]. Stemless, suckering, forming a dense clump; lvs. upright, lanceolate, to ¾ in. long, tapering to point, translucently punctate, lower surface with white tubercles and longitudinal and transverse green lines, margins and keel with translucent teeth; fls. in a loose raceme. Var. **variegata** is listed.

Herrei Poelln. St. to 4 in., leafy, suckering and forming clumps; lvs. triangular-lanceolate to almost lanceolate-ovate, to 2 in. long, tapering to a point, gray-green, lower surface with 5–10 longitudinal lines irregularly beset with tubercles, tubercles solitary or confluent into ridges. Var. **depauperata** Poelln. Lower lf. surfaces with 1–5 longitudinal lines.

Hurlingii Poelln. Stemless; lvs. oblong-ovate to ovate, to ¾ in. long, pale green, both surfaces with 5–7 longitudinal lines, margins and keel with small teeth toward base. Var. **ambigua** Triebn. & Poelln. Suckers few; lvs. more spreading, with keel and longitudinal lines more distinct.

icosiphylla Bak. Stemless; lvs. triangular-lanceolate, to 1½ in. long, slightly recurved, lower surface roughened by tiny tubercles.

incurvula Poelln. Stemless, suckering; lvs. oblong-ovate, to ¾ in. long, soft, light green, translucent above, both surfaces with dark longitudinal lines.

integra Poelln. Stemless, forming clumps; lvs. oblong to oblong-ovate, to 1½ in. long, inflated near center, tipped with a long, white bristle, upper surface with longitudinal lines.

Janseana Uitew. Stemless, suckering and forming clumps; lvs. ovate-lanceolate, to 1 in. long, pale gray-green, tipped with a long bristle, both surfaces with many longitudinal lines, margins and keel with fine teeth with translucent tips.

Jonesiae Poelln. St. to 8 in., brs. forking above, leafy, suckering; lvs. lanceolate, to 1 in. long, tipped with a bristle, pruinose, lower surface with faint longitudinal lines and fine, irregularly scattered tubercles.

Kingiana: *H. subfasciata* var.

laetevirens Haw. Stemless, suckering; lvs. oblong-lanceolate, to 1½ in. long, tipped with a short bristle, pale green, becoming reddish with age, translucent toward apex, with darker horizontal and longitudinal lines, margins and keel denticulate; fls. ¾ in. long, in a loose raceme to 1 ft. long.

limifolia Marloth. FAIRY-WASHBOARD. Stemless; lvs. triangular, to 2 in. long, sharply tapering to apex, dark green-brown, both surfaces with 15–25 horizontal ribs. Var. **stolonifera** Resende. Forming large clumps by offsets, lvs. 3-angled, lanceolate, to 3 in. long. Var. **ubomboensis** (Verd.) G. G. Sm. Producing offsets by suckering; lvs. stiffer, spreading, ovate-lanceolate, to 2½ in. long, margins horny, tubercles in transverse lines.

Longiana Poelln. Stemless; lvs. triangular-lanceolate, to almost 1 ft. long, long-acuminate, lower surface with tubercles on lower half, margins sharp, entire.

magnifica Poelln. Stemless; lvs. to 1⅜ in. long, stiff, brownish-green, recurved and triangular at apex, translucent and somewhat inflated, apex finely tubercled, margins and keel toothed.

Maraisii Poelln. Stemless, suckering; lvs. ovate-lanceolate, to 1⅜ in. long, light green, apex roundish-triangular, horizontally truncated, translucent, upper surface with small, irregularly placed tubercles, margins toothed.

margaritifera (L.) Haw. PEARL PLANT. Stemless, suckering, forming rosettes about 6 in. across; lvs. triangular-ovate, to 3 in. long, erect, then spreading, dark green, both surfaces covered with pearly tubercles; fls. ⅝ in. long, in a dense raceme to nearly 2 ft. high. Var. **granata:** var. *minima*. Var. **maxima** Uitew. [var. *semimargaritifera* (Salm-Dyck) Bak.; *H. semimargaritifera* (Salm-Dyck) Haw.]. Lvs. oblong-ovate, to 4 in. long, tubercles on upper surface fewer and more or less confined to a faint central ridge. Var. **minima** (Ait.) Uitew. [var. *granata* (Willd.) Bak.; *H. granata* (Willd.) Haw.]. Forming a more closed rosette; lvs. to 1¼ in. long, with smaller, more crowded tubercles. Var. **semimargaritifera:** var. *maxima*. Var. **variegata** is listed.

marginata (Lam.) Stearn [*H. albicans* Haw.]. Stemless; lvs. ovate-lanceolate, to 3 in. long, tapering to a sharp point, rigid, greenish-white, lower surface sharply keeled, margins and keel white from confluent tubercles. Var. **virescens** (Haw.) Uitew. [*H. virescens* Haw.]. Lvs. more ovate, tapering, with fewer, scattered tubercles.

Marumiana Uitew. Stemless, suckering; lvs. lanceolate-ovate, ¾ in. long, tipped with a bristle, both surfaces with few tubercles, margins and keel with translucent teeth.

Maughanii Poelln. Stemless; lvs. in rosettes, almost cylindrical, to 1 in. long, gray-green to reddish-brown, translucent and truncate at apex.

metallica: a listed name of no botanical standing, for a plant having dark lvs. with iridescent spots.

minima: *H. tenera*.

mirabilis (Haw.) Haw. Stemless, suckering; lvs. to 1⅜ in. long, pale green, transparent toward apex, upper surface with 3–5 longitudinal lines, lower surface 3-angled, keeled, margins and keel toothed.

monticola Fourc. Stemless; lvs. usually partly buried in ground, erect, straight to incurved, without lines, dark green in upper part, translucent in lower half. Not certainly distinct from *H. angustifolia*.

mucronata Haw. [*H. altilinea* var. *mucronata* (Haw.) Poelln.]. Stemless; lvs. to 2¼ in. long, tipped with a bristle, pale green, usually translucent toward apex, margins toothed. Var. **limpida** (Haw.) Poelln. [*H. altilinea* var. *limpida* (Haw.) Poelln.]. Lvs. ovate-lanceolate or oblong-lanceolate, with 7–9 longitudinal lines on upper surface, and 11–13 longitudinal lines on lower surface. Var. **Morrisiae** (Poelln.) Poelln. [*H. altilinea* var. *Morrisiae* (Poelln.) Poelln.]. Lvs. ovate-lanceolate, to 2 in. long, with 8–14 longitudinal lines on upper surface.

nigra (Haw.) Bak. St. to 4¾ in., leafy; lvs. ovate, to 2 in. long, tipped with a bristle, spreading horizontally, black-green, margins and both surfaces tubercled. Var. **Schmidtiana** (Poelln.) Uitew. [*H. Schmidtiana* Poelln.]. Lvs. lanceolate to ovate-lanceolate, with dark green, rather sticky upper surface, and tubercles on both surfaces.

obtusa Haw. [*H. cymbiformis* var. *obtusa* (Haw.) Bak.]. Stemless; lvs. oblong to oblong-ovate, about 1 in. long, tipped with a bristle, dirty-green, translucent toward apex, with several dark longitudinal lines. Var. **columnaris** (Bak.) Uitew. [*H. pilifera* Bak. var *columnaris* (Bak.) Poelln.]. Lvs. darker, to 1⅜ in. long, with 4–6 longitudinal lines on upper surface, and a long, terminal bristle. Var. **Dielsiana** (Poelln.) Uitew. [*H. Dielsiana* Poelln.]. Lvs. to 1⅛ in. long, abruptly tapering to apex, with 12 translucent lines on upper surface, margins and keel set with translucent teeth. Var. **pilifera** (Bak.) Uitew. [*H. pilifera* Bak.]. Lvs. light green, oblong, to 1 in. long, tipped with a fine bristle, nearly translucent on both surfaces in upper ⅓, and marked with simple, continuous, longitudinal lines.

papillosa (Salm-Dyck) Haw. PEARLY-DOTS. Forming a vertically elongated rosette to 8–10 in. high at maturity; lvs. few, ovate-lanceolate, to 4 in. long, ascending, tipped with a bristle, upper surface with scattered tubercles, lower surface with many prominent tubercles often in transverse lines.

paradoxa Poelln. Stemless, suckering; lvs. ovate to oblong-ovate, to 1¼ in. long, with triangular translucent area at apex and tipped with a bristle, dark green, upper surface with 1–2 faint longitudinal lines, lower surface with translucent spots in longitudinal lines, margins and keel toothed.

Parksiana Poelln. Stemless; lvs. lanceolate to oblong-ovate, to ¾ in. long, light green, erect-spreading, recurved near apex, upper surface with a central line, finely tubercled, margins finely toothed toward apex.

pentagona: *Astroloba pentagona.*

pilifera: *H. obtusa* var. Var. **columnaris:** *H. obtusa* var.

planifolia Haw. Stemless, suckering; lvs. ovate to oblong-ovate, to 2 in. long, dull light green, upper surface flat, with 1 or 2 longitudinal furrows, margins and apex rather translucent. Var. **exultata** Poelln. Lvs. flatter, broader, with tiny, often indistinct teeth on keel. Var. **setulifera** Poelln. Lvs. lanceolate-obovate, to 2⅛ in. long, with a deciduous terminal bristle, and glabrous margins and keel.

pygmaea Poelln. Stemless; lvs. oblong-ovate, to 1¼ in. long, dark green and slightly granulate, upper surface angled below the apical ⅓, the terminal triangular area thus formed nearly translucent at its base, lower surface rounded and keeled.

radula (Jacq.) Haw. Stemless, cespitose; lvs. triangular-lanceolate, to 3 in. long, acuminate, both surfaces covered with tiny white tubercles.

ramosa G. G. Sm. St. to 2 in., leafy, branching and rooting, forming clumps; lvs. obovate, to 1⅜ in. long, abruptly acuminate, tipped with a bristle, upper surface with central translucent line and spots, lower surface with translucent spots toward apex and 20 indistinct lines, margins greenish-white below, translucent above.

Reinwardtii (Salm-Dyck) Haw. St. to 6 in., leafy; lvs. lanceolate to ovate-lanceolate, to 2 in. long, upper surface with few whitish or greenish tubercles in 1–3 series, lower surface with many white tubercles in transverse and longitudinal lines. A very variable sp., with many vars. Var. **adelaidensis** Poelln. [*H. adelaidensis* Hort.]. Lvs. to 1¼ in. long, with tubercles on lower surface confluent into transverse rows. Var. **Archibaldiae** Poelln. With many, large, white tubercles on upper surface of lvs. Var. **chalumnensis** G. G. Sm. Lvs. longer, more spreading, tubercles mostly confluent, forming transverse rows on lower surface. Var. **committeesensis** G. G. Sm. Lvs. smaller, lighter green when young, more red when old, with smaller, less prominent tubercles. Var. **conspicua** Poelln. Upper surface of lvs. with scattered, whitish tubercles, lower surface with tubercles in 10–12 longitudinal lines, mostly also confluent in transverse rows. Var. **fallax** Poelln. Lvs. pale green, more spreading at apex of plant, with nearly smooth upper surface, lower surface with small and large tubercles in 5–12 longitudinal rows and often forming confluent transverse rows. Var. **major** Bak. [var. *pulchra* Poelln.]. Sts. taller; tubercles larger, in transverse rows on lower lf. surfaces. Var. **peddiensis** G. G. Sm. Smaller; lvs. shorter, less acuminate, with tubercles on upper lf. surface in 3 longitudinal rows. Var. **pulchra:** var. *major.* Var. **riebeckensis** G. G. Sm. Plant smaller; tubercles in longitudinal rows on lower lf. surface. Var. **tenuis** G. G. Sm. Taller, with smaller, procumbent sts.; tubercles less white.

Resendeana Poelln. St. elongated, branching at base, procumbent; lvs. ovate to triangular-ovate, to ¾ in. long, upper lvs. incurved, dark green, upper surface smooth, lower surface green, with tubercles somewhat confluent, white-tipped, in longitudinal rows.

reticulata Haw. Stemless; lvs. oblong-lanceolate, to 1¼ in. long, very thick, tipped with a long bristle, pale green and transparent in upper ⅓, with few longitudinal lines, margins minutely scabrous. Var. **acuminata** Poelln. Lvs. longer, tapering.

retusa (L.) Haw. Stemless, suckering; lvs. triangular-ovate, to 2 in. long, spreading, pale green, upper part recurved, terminal area trian-

gular, translucent, with 5–8 pale longitudinal lines, lf. margins toothed.

rigida (Lam.) Haw. St. to 6 in., erect, leafy; lvs. ovate-lanceolate, to 2¼ in. long, 5-ranked, in crowded spirals, rigid, thick, recurved, dull green, rough, margins and keels with horny teeth. Var. **expansa** (Haw.) Bak. Smaller; lvs. shorter, more recurved-spreading, glossy.

rugosa (Salm-Dyck) Bak. Stemless, suckering; lvs. lanceolate, ending in triangular apex, to 4 in. long, older lvs. spreading, dark green, with whitish and translucent tubercles.

Ryderana Poelln. Stemless; lvs. ovate, to 1½ in. long, apex triangular-acuminate, tipped with a bristle, upper surface with few tubercles toward apex, but with 8–10 irregularly confluent, longitudinal, green lines, lower surface with translucent spots in longitudinal lines toward apex, margins and keel toothed, teeth bristle-tipped.

Schmidtiana: *H. nigra* var.

Schuldtiana Poelln. Stemless; lvs. oblong-lanceolate, to 1½ in. long, stiff, recurved near apex, green to brown-green or reddish-green, upper surface with few tubercles, lower surface with many small tubercles and several dark longitudinal lines, margins and keel with white teeth. Var. **Whitesloaneana** (Poelln.) Poelln. [*H. White-sloaneana* Poelln.]. Lvs. ovate-lanceolate, with translucent apices and large teeth on margins.

semiglabrata Haw. Stemless; lvs. triangular-lanceolate, to 3¼ in. long, apex horny, upper surface with few tubercles, lower surface with tubercles in indistinct transverse rows.

semimargaritifera: *H. margaritifera* var. *maxima.*

setata Haw. LACE H. Stemless; lvs. oblong-lanceolate, to 1 in. long, tipped with a translucent bristle, deep green, lower surface with 1 or 2 keels, margins and keels with snow-white teeth.

Skinneri: *Astroloba Skinneri.*

subattenuata (Salm-Dyck) Bak. Stemless, suckering; lvs. triangular-lanceolate, to 2¾ in. long, deep green, often somewhat reddish, upper surface with green tubercles in central line, lower surface with rows of white tubercles.

subfasciata (Salm-Dyck) Bak. Stemless; lvs. triangular-lanceolate, to 5 in. long, tapering and often recurved near apex, dirty-green, upper surface shining, lower surface with translucent tubercles in transverse rows, margins tubercled. Var. **Kingiana** (Poelln.) Poelln. [*H. Kingiana* Poelln.]. Lvs. green, glossy, ovate-tapering, with tubercles on both surfaces.

submaculata Poelln. Stemless; lvs. ovate-lanceolate, to 1½ in. long, apex slightly incurved, tipped with a bristle, dark gray-green, upper surface sometimes with indistinct tubercles in distinct central line, lower surface with many longitudinal lines, margins and keel with bristle-tipped teeth.

subrigida: *H. tortuosa* var. *pseudorigida.*

subulata (Salm-Dyck) Bak. Stemless, suckering; lvs. triangular-lanceolate, to 4¾ in. long, old lvs. with recurved-spreading apex, green, upper surface flat, with central line and uniformly colored tubercles, lower surface with pearly tubercles in more or less transverse rows, margin tubercled.

tenera (Bak.) Poelln. [*H. minima* Bak.]. Stemless; lvs. narrowly lanceolate to narrowly ovate, to ¾ in. long, tipped with a somewhat curved bristle, gray-green, lighter on upper surface or with light spots, lower surface with 4–8 longitudinal lines, with 1 or 2 keels toward apex, margins armed with teeth. Var. **confusa** (Poelln.) Uitew. [*H. confusa* Poelln.]. Lvs. light gray-green, to 1⅜ in. long, with several confluent longitudinal lines on both surfaces, and many teeth on margins and keel. Var. **major** (Poelln.) Uitew. Lvs. green, to 1⅜ in. long, with triangular teeth on the keels and margins.

tessellata (Salm-Dyck) Haw. Stemless; lvs. broadly triangular-ovate, to 2 in. long, recurved-spreading, pointed at apex, dark green, upper surface usually translucent, with 5–7 anastomosing pale green lines, lower surface irregularly roughened by small white tubercles, margins with fine, recurved, white teeth. Var. **Engleri** (Dinter) Poelln. [*H. Engleri* Dinter]. Lvs. fewer, their margins armed with blunt, horny teeth. Var. **inflexa** Bak. Lvs. dull purplish-green, with inflexed margins. Var. **parva** (Haw.) Bak. Lvs. shorter, in smaller rosettes.

Tisleyi Bak. Stemless; lvs. triangular-lanceolate, to 1⅛ in. long, upper surface flat, lower surface often reddish, somewhat roughened by fine tubercles.

tortuosa Haw. St. to 5 in. long, leafy, suckering; lvs. 3-ranked, ovate-lanceolate, to 1½ in. long, green, rough, upper surfaces concave, lower surface convex, margins and keel tubercled. Var. **major** (Salm-Dyck) A. Berger. Taller and stouter. Var. **pseudorigida** (Salm-Dyck) A. Berger [*H. subrigida* (Schult. & Schult.f.) Bak.]. Lvs. thicker, rougher, less grooved.

translucens Haw. Stemless, suckering; lvs. oblong-lanceolate, to 1¼ in. long, incurved near apex and tipped with a bristle, pale green, both surfaces with longitudinal lines and bristle-bearing translucent spots toward apex, margin and keels with fine, more or less translucent teeth.

truncata Schönl. Stemless; lvs. 2-ranked, linear, to ¾ in. long, incurved, with truncate and more or less translucent apex, dark greenish-brown, both surfaces rough-tubercled. In nature the plant is buried in the ground except for the translucent lf. tips.

tuberculata Poelln. St. very short; lvs. ovate-lanceolate, to 2¾ in. long, 3-angled, apex blunt, both surfaces of lvs. covered with many, large, dark brown-green tubercles.

turgida Haw. Stemless, suckering; lvs. oblong-lanceolate, to ¾ in. long, pale green, apex inflated, decurved, stiff, upper surface with 3–7 paler green, longitudinal lines, translucent toward apex, lower surface rounded, keeled. Var. **pallidifolia** G. G. Sm. Lvs. longer and larger, with more numerous translucent spots, more conspicuous lines, and a thicker terminal bristle. Var. **suberecta** Poelln. Lvs. more erect, 1¼–1½ in. long, terminal bristle nearly lacking. Var. **subregularis** is listed.

umbracticola Poelln. Stemless, suckering; lvs. oblong-obovate to obovate, to 1¼ in. long, light green, thickened below apex, apex blunt, tipped with a bristle, both surfaces with longitudinal lines, translucent toward apex, margins and keel toothed.

variegata L. Bolus. Stemless; lvs. linear-lanceolate, to 2⅛ in. long, deep brown with lighter spots, upper surface with central line, margins and keel bearing minute teeth.

virescens: *H. marginata* var.

viscosa (L.) Haw. St. to 8 in., leafy, suckering and forming clumps; lvs. 3-ranked, ovate, dirty-green, sticky, with sharp-pointed apex, both surfaces papillate. Var. **torquata** (Haw.) Bak. Lvs. lanceolate to 3-angled, with tubercles on both surfaces.

Whitesloaneana: *H. Schuldtiana* var.

HEBE Comm. ex Juss. *Scrophulariaceae.* Between 70 and 80 spp. of hairy or glabrous shrubs, trees, and shrublets of s. S. Amer., New Guinea, but mostly of New Zeal.; lvs. opp., simple, 4-ranked, often imbricate, entire or toothed, often leathery, leaving conspicuous scars when falling; fls. white, pink, blue, or purple, solitary or in axillary spikes or racemes, calyx and corolla usually 4-lobed, stamens 2, ovary superior; fr. a septicidally dehiscent, more or less flattened caps. Formerly united with *Veronica,* but differing in being mostly woody, having lvs. opp., and caps. dehiscent. With the exception of *H. elliptica,* which has a wider range, the names listed are of New Zeal. spp. or derivatives of them.

Hebes are extensively grown outdoors in mild climates, as in Calif., and sometimes under glass in the North. Several species are used as evergreen hedges. Propagated by seeds, and by cuttings, which if taken from mature plants in autumn will bloom the following summer.

albicans (Petrie) Cockayne [*Veronica albicans* Petrie]. Much-branched, spreading shrub, to 4 ft.; lvs. imbricate, oblong to broadly ovate, to 1 in. long, entire, glaucous; fls. white, in many-fld. racemes. Probably a hybrid.

Allionii: *Veronica Allionii.*

amplexicaulis (J. B. Armstr.) Cockayne & Allan [*Veronica amplexicaulis* J. B. Armstr.]. Usually decumbent shrub, to 3 ft.; lvs. imbricate, oblong to elliptic-oblong, to 1 in. long, entire, glaucous, very thick; fls. white, ¼ in. across, in spikes to 1½ in. long.

×**Andersonii** (Lindl. & Paxt.) Cockayne [*Veronica Andersonii* Lindl. & Paxt.]: *H. salicifolia* × *H. speciosa.* Shrub, to 6 ft.; lvs. narrower than in *H. speciosa,* but wider than in *H. salicifolia;* corolla white, tipped with violet. Cv. **'Variegata'.** Lvs. variegated with cream-yellow.

Astonii: *H. subsimilis* var.

Balfouriana (Hook.f.) Cockayne [*Veronica Balfouriana* Hook.f.]. Erect, glabrous shrub, to 3 ft.; lvs. elliptic-ovate, to ¾ in. long, entire, with narrow brown margin, leathery, glossy above; fls. pale blue, ½ in. across, in racemes to 3 in. long.

×**Bidwillii:** *Parahebe* ×*Bidwillii.*

Bollonsii (Cockayne) Cockayne & Allan [*Veronica Bollonsii* Cockayne]. Much-branched, erect shrub, to 6 ft.; lvs. obovate-oblong to elliptic-oblong, to 3 in. long, smooth and glossy, margin thickened, ciliate toward base; fls. lilac, ⅜ in. across, in racemes to 4 in. long.

buxifolia (Benth.) Cockayne & Allan [*Veronica buxifolia* Benth.]. Glabrous shrub, to 5 ft.; lvs. broadly oblong-obovate, to ⅜ in. long, truncate at base, entire, thick and stiff; fls. white, ⅜ in. across, in spikes to 1 in. long forming corymbose heads.

canescens: *Parahebe canescens.*

×**carnea** Hort. [*Veronica carnea* Hort. ex J. B. Armstr., not Vitm.]: *Hebe* cv. **'Carnea'.** Large spreading shrub; lvs. linear-oblong, to 2 in. long, pubescent beneath, margins pink, ciliate; fls. rose and white, to ⅜ in. across, in racemes to 3 in. long; caps. twice as long as calyx.

catarractae: *Parahebe catarractae.*

chathamica (J. Buchan.) Cockayne & Allan [*Veronica chathamica* J. Buchan.]. Much-branched shrub, to 1½ ft., sts. prostrate or trailing; lvs. elliptic to oblong, to 1 in. long; fls. purple, ¼ in. across, in racemes to 1 in. long.

cupressoides (Hook.f.) Cockayne & Allan [*Veronica cupressoides* Hook.f.]. Much-branched, round-topped shrub, to 6 ft.; lvs. scalelike, $^1/_{16}$ in. long or, on young plants, to ¼ in. long; fls. pale purple or rarely white, ⅛ in. across, in small, terminal heads. Cv. **'Nana'** is listed.

decumbens (J. B. Armstr.) Cockayne & Allan [*Veronica decumbens* J. B. Armstr.]. Small, much-branched, decumbent shrub, to 3 ft.; lvs. short-petioled, to ¾ in. long, margin bright red; fls. white, ¼ in. across, in racemes to 1 in. long.

decussata: *H. elliptica.*

elliptica (G. Forst.) Penn. [*H. decussata* Hort.; *Veronica decussata* Ait.; *V. elliptica* G. Forst.]. Much-branched shrub or small tree, to 20 ft.; lvs. to 1¼ in. long, apiculate; fls. in racemes to 1½ in. long, corolla white or veined with purple or pale blue, ⅝ in. across. New Zeal., Falkland Is., s. Chile. Cv. **'Variegata'** is listed.

epacridea (Hook.f.) Cockayne & Allan [*Veronica epacridea* Hook.f.]. Much-branched, prostrate or decumbent, rigid shrub; lvs. imbricate, broadly oblong to obovate-oblong, mostly obtuse, keeled, leathery, margin usually red, thickened, ciliate toward base; fls. white, small, in dense, terminal, ovate heads.

Gibbsii (T. Kirk) Cockayne & Allan. Shrub to 1 ft.; lvs. loosely imbricate, elliptic to ovate, to ¾ in. long, glaucous, margin more or less red; fls. white, in spikes; caps. longer than calyx, slightly hairy.

glaucophylla (Cockayne) Cockayne [*Veronica glaucophylla* Cockayne]. Low-growing round shrub; lvs. linear-oblong to linear-ovate, ⅝ in. long, entire, glaucous, midrib sunken on both surfaces; fls. white, closely set, in racemes to 2¼ in. long.

Hectorii (Hook.f.) Cockayne & Allan [*Veronica Hectorii* Hook.f.]. Rigid, tufted, erect shrub, to 2½ ft., brs. cylindrical; lvs. scalelike, closely imbricate, orbicular-oblong, to ⅛ in. long, very thick, pairs united to middle; fls. white or pink, ¼ in. across, in small, terminal heads.

Hulkeana (F. J. Muell.) Cockayne & Allan [*Veronica Hulkeana* F. J. Muell.]. Loosely branched shrub, to 3 ft.; lvs. ovate or oblong-ovate, to 2 in. long, toothed; fls. pale lilac, to ¼ in. across, in panicles to 1 ft. long.

imperialis: *H. speciosa* cv.

laevis: *H. venustula.*

Lavaudiana (Raoul) Cockayne & Allan [*Veronica Lavaudiana* Raoul]. Sparingly branched shrub, to 9 in.; lvs. broadly obovate or obovate-spatulate, crenate-serrate, leathery, margins usually red; fls. white, to ⅜ in. across, in spikes arranged in corymbs.

Lewisii (J. B. Armstr.) A. Wall [*Veronica Lewisii* J. B. Armstr.]. Erect, closely branched shrub, to 6 ft. or more, brs. gray-pubescent; lvs. oblong to elliptic-oblong, to 2½ in. long, margin entire, edged with white-pubescent line; fls. pale blue, ⅜ in. across, in racemes to 2½ in. long. Thought to be a hybrid, perhaps between *H. elliptica* and *H. salicifolia.*

linifolia: *Parahebe linifolia.*

Lyallii: *Parahebe Lyallii.*

lycopodioides (Hook.f.) Cockayne & Allan [*Veronica lycopodioides* Hook.f.]. Rigid, much-branched shrub, to 4 ft., adult brs. 4-angled; lvs. scalelike, densely imbricate, to ⅛ in. long, broadly ovate-deltoid, suddenly narrowed into a stout point, leathery, grooved on the back, pairs united to middle; fls. white, ⅜ in. across, crowded into small, terminal heads.

macrantha (Hook.f.) Cockayne & Allan [*Veronica macrantha* Hook.f.]. Stout, sparingly branched, erect shrub, to 2 ft.; lvs. obovate-lanceolate to obovate or oblong-ovate, to 1 in. long, toothed, thick, leathery and glossy; fls. white, to ¾ in. across, in 3–8-fld. racemes.

Menziesii (Benth.) Cockayne & Allan [*Veronica Menziesii* Benth.]. Compact, glabrous shrub, to 12 ft.; lvs. linear-oblong to lanceolate, to 1 in. long, rigid, leathery; fls. white or pale lilac, to ¼ in. across, in simple or corymbosely branched racemes to 2 in. long.

Pageana: a listed name of no botanical standing for *H. pinguifolia* cv. 'Pagei'.

Pagei: a listed name of no botanical standing for *H. pinguifolia* cv.

parviflora (Vahl) Cockayne & Allan [*Veronica parviflora* Vahl]. Much-branched shrub or tree, to 20 ft.; lvs. narrowly linear-lanceolate, to $2\frac{1}{2}$ in. long, entire, glabrous, sessile; fls. white, $\frac{1}{8}$ in. across, in densely-fld. racemes to 3 in. long.

pimeleoides (Hook.f.) Cockayne & Allan [*Veronica pimeleoides* Hook.f.]. Much-branched, prostrate to suberect per., to $1\frac{1}{2}$ ft.; lvs. obovate-oblong, ovate-oblong to elliptic-lanceolate, to $\frac{3}{8}$ in. long, glaucous, sessile; fls. dark purple-blue, $\frac{1}{4}$ in. across, in spikes to 1 in. long. Cv. **'Nana'** is listed.

pinguifolia (Hook.f.) Cockayne & Allan [*Veronica pinguifolia* Hook.f.]. Much-branched, erect or decumbent, glaucous shrub, to 4 ft.; lvs. imbricate, oblong, obovate-oblong to suborbicular, to $\frac{3}{4}$ in. long, leathery or almost fleshy; fls. white, $\frac{3}{8}$ in. across, in dense spikes longer than lvs. Cv. **'Pagei'** [*H. Pageana* Hort.; *H. Pagei* Hort.; *Veronica Pageana* Hort.]. Sts. purplish, glaucous at nodes; lvs. elliptic-obovate, very glaucous, margins purplish; fls. white, anthers purple, turning brown in age.

recurva Simps. & J. S. Thoms. Much-branched, glabrous shrub, to 3 ft.; lvs. deflexed, linear-oblong, to 2 in. long, entire, thin; fls. white, in racemes to $2\frac{3}{8}$ in. long.

rotundata (T. Kirk) Cockayne [*Veronica rotundata* T. Kirk]. Loosely branched shrub, to 6 ft.; lvs. oblong-lanceolate or elliptic-lanceolate, to 4 in. long; fls. purple or lilac, $\frac{1}{4}$ in. across, in racemes to 6 in. long. Probably a garden hybrid.

salicifolia (G. Forst.) Penn. [*Veronica salicifolia* G. Forst.]. Much-branched, erect shrub, to 12 ft.; lvs. linear-lanceolate to oblong-lanceolate, to 6 in. long, mostly entire; fls. white, tinged lilac, $\frac{1}{8}$ in. across, in racemes to 6 in. long or more. An extremely variable sp. with several vars., which hybridize among themselves and with other spp. of *Hebe*.

speciosa (R. Cunn. ex A. Cunn.) Cockayne & Allan [*Veronica speciosa* R. Cunn. ex A. Cunn.]. Stout, glabrous shrub, to 5 ft., with thick branchlets; lvs. obovate or obovate-oblong, to 4 in. long, entire, glossy, subsessile; fls. dark reddish or blue-purple, in racemes about 4 in. long. An extremely variable sp., running into vars. and cvs. and hybridizing freely. Cv. **'Imperialis'** [*H. imperialis* (Boucharlat ex Planch.) Cockayne]. Fls. purple-crimson.

subalpina (Cockayne) Cockayne & Allan [*Veronica subalpina* Cockayne]. Much-branched, erect shrub, to 6 ft.; lvs. lanceolate to oblong-lanceolate, to $1\frac{1}{2}$ in. long, entire, sessile; fls. white, in racemes to 2 in. long.

subsimilis (Colenso) Ashw. Bushy shrub, to 1 ft.; lvs. imbricate, deltoid to deltoid-oblong, to $\frac{3}{32}$ in. long, very thick, pairs united; fls. white, to $\frac{3}{16}$ in. across, in 4–8-fld. spikes; caps. longer than calyx. Var. **Astonii** (Petrie) Ashw. [*H. Astonii* (Petrie) Cockayne & Allan; *Veronica Astonii* Petrie]. Plant more slender.

Traversii (Hook.f.) Cockayne & Allan [*Veronica Traversii* Hook.f.]. Dense, glabrous, rounded shrub, to 5 ft. across; lvs. elliptic to linear-oblong, to 1 in. long, entire, thick; fls. white, $\frac{1}{4}$ in. across, in many-fld. racemes to 3 in. long.

venustula (Colenso) L. B. Moore [*H. laevis* (Benth.) Cockayne & Allan]. Bushy shrub, to 5 ft.; lvs. elliptic-oblong, to $\frac{3}{4}$ in. long, bright green above; infls. sometimes branched, fls. white; caps. erect, more than twice as long as calyx, glabrous.

HEBENSTRETIA L. *Scrophulariaceae.* About 30 spp. of ann. or per. herbs, subshrubs or shrubs, mostly of S. Afr.; lvs. alt., the lower sometimes opp., simple, usually narrow; fls. yellow or white, in dense terminal spikes, calyx spathelike, corolla 4-lobed, tube often split in the front, stamens 4; fr. indehiscent.

Seeds should be sown outside in Apr. or inside if earlier results are desired; treated as annuals.

comosa Hochst. Per., with woody sts., to 4 ft.; lvs. lanceolate or linear-lanceolate, to 2 in. long, toothed; fls. in spikes to 6 in. long, fragrant at night, corolla yellow or white with orange-red blotch on limb, $\frac{1}{2}$ in. long. S. Afr.

dentata L. Similar to *H. comosa*, but to 2 ft.; lvs. linear to linear-oblanceolate, toothed only above the middle. S. Afr.

HEBESTIGMA Urb. *Leguminosae* (subfamily *Faboideae*). One sp., a tree of Cuba; lvs. alt., odd-pinnate, with large lfts.; fls. in racemes, papilionaceous, with reflexed standard, stamens 10, 9 united and 1 separate; fr. a woody, dehiscent legume.

cubense (HBK) Urb. To 40 ft.; lvs. to 12 in. long, lfts. mostly in 3–4 pairs, ovate to oblong-lanceolate, terminal ones larger, to 6 in. long, pointed; racemes to 6 in. long; fls. rose, to $\frac{3}{4}$ in. long; fr. to 7 in. long, $1\frac{1}{4}$ in. wide. Cuba.

HECHTIA Klotzsch. *Bromeliaceae.* About 45 spp. of succulent, terrestrial, dioecious herbs, native from s. U.S. to Cent. Amer.; lvs. in dense rosettes, long, stiff, spiny-toothed; fls. small, in terminal panicles; petals separate, ovary slightly to wholly superior; fr. a caps., seeds mostly with entire wings.

Grown in full sun. For culture see *Bromeliaceae.*

argentea Bak. ex Hemsl. Fl. sts. to 3 ft.; lvs. to 2 ft. long, 1 in. wide, silvery; infl. a loose panicle of many sessile, spikelike brs., to $1\frac{1}{2}$ ft. long, fl. bracts strongly convex, longer than the pedicels; fls. $\frac{5}{16}$ in. long. Mex.

glomerata Zucc. Fl. sts. to 3 ft.; lvs. to 16 in. long, linear-triangular, glabrous and green above, densely white-scurfy beneath, with stout spines; infl. cylindrical, with dense, sessile, headlike brs., mostly less than 1 in. long; fls. white, to $\frac{3}{16}$ in. long. Tex., Mex.

Meziana L. B. Sm. To about 3 ft.; lvs. to 3 ft. long, $1\frac{1}{4}$ in. wide, with coarse, hooked teeth; infl. loosely branched and flowered, scape bracts shorter than internodes, fl. bracts and sepals uniformly rose; fls. pedicelled, rose-colored. Mex.

Purpusii: *H. tillandsioides.*

Roseana L. B. Sm. Fl. sts. to 3 ft.; lvs. to $1\frac{1}{2}$ ft. long, $1\frac{1}{2}$ in. wide, finely pale-scurfy; infl. pyramidal, fl. bracts flat, shorter than pedicels; fls. white, to $\frac{3}{16}$ in. long. Mex.

rubra: a listed name of no botanical standing.

scariosa L. B. Sm. Perhaps to 6 ft.; lvs. to 14 in. long, $\frac{3}{4}$ in. wide; infl. loosely pyramidal, fl. bracts and sepals deep rose with broad pale margin; fls. to $\frac{3}{8}$ in. long. Tex., Mex.

texensis S. Wats. Fl. sts. to 6 ft.; lvs. to $1\frac{1}{2}$ ft. long, 2 in. wide, glabrous and glossy above at maturity, pale beneath; infl. a loosely fld. panicle, brs. to 8 in. long, fl. bracts brownish; fls. $\frac{5}{16}$ in. long, solitary and sessile. Rio Grande region, Tex.

tillandsioides (André) L. B. Sm. [*H. Purpusii* Brandeg.]. Less than 3 ft.; lvs. to 1 ft. long, $\frac{3}{4}$ in. wide, pale, finely toothed; infl. loosely branched, fl. bracts membranous, pedicels $\frac{1}{8}$ in. long, longer than bracts; fls. white, $\frac{3}{16}$ in. long. E. Mex.

HEDEOMA Pers. *Labiatae.* About 30 spp. of ann. or per. herbs of N. and S. Amer., usually aromatic; sts. mostly square in cross section; lvs. opp., small, entire or sparsely toothed; fls. in axillary verticillasters, calyx tubular, 13-nerved, swollen at base, 2-lipped, upper lip 3-toothed, lower lip 2-toothed, shorter, tube hairy inside throat, corolla bluish or purple, 2-lipped, upper lip erect, entire or 2-lobed, lower lip spreading, 3-lobed, stamens 2, staminodes 2; fr. of 4 glabrous nutlets.

Plants of dry soil; drought tolerant.

camporum: *H. Drummondii.*

Drummondii Benth. [*H. camporum* Rydb.]. Sts. 6–12 in., pubescent; lvs. oblong-elliptic or spatulate, to $\frac{1}{2}$ in. long, $\frac{1}{8}$ in. wide, pubescent; calyx tubular, inflated below middle, to $\frac{1}{4}$ in. long, teeth 5, awned, corolla tubular, to $\frac{3}{8}$ in. long, bluish-purple. Spring. N.Dak. to Nev., Tex., and Mex.

pulegioides (L.) Pers. AMERICAN PENNYROYAL, MOCK P., PUDDING GRASS. Ann., sts. 12–15 in., pubescent; lvs. elliptic-rhombic, to 1 in. long, $\frac{3}{4}$ in. wide, entire or somewhat dentate, glabrous to glabrescent; calyx somewhat inflated, to $\frac{3}{16}$ in. long, upper teeth triangular, lower teeth 3, awned, corolla to $\frac{1}{4}$ in. long, bluish-purple. Summer. Nov. Sc. to S.Dak., s. to Fla. and Ark.

HEDERA L. IVY. *Araliaceae.* About 5 spp. of evergreen, woody vines, rarely shrublike, native to Eur., N. Afr., and w. Asia, with juvenile and adult foliage, the juvenile on flexuous, aerial, root-bearing sts. with lvs. usually palmately lobed, at least basally, the adult on stiff nonclimbing and rootless sts. with lvs. usually elliptic-lanceolate and not lobed; fls. small, greenish, in umbels arranged in panicles, produced only on brs. of the adult stage.

Ivies thrive in a rich moist soil having high organic content. Propagated by cuttings and layers, or by seeds which usually germinate the second year. Cuttings of the adult stage may be rooted and grown as an erect shrub. The juvenile stage is planted as a wall or ground cover, often in complete shade, or grown indoors as a pot subject for its foliage. The many foliage forms are unstable mutations, which frequently revert to the original form with age. They are clonal cultivars and are maintained only by constant repropagation from selected typical branches.

algeriensis: *H. canariensis.*

arborea: *H. Helix* cv. 'Arborescens'.

baltica: a listed name of no botanical standing for *H. Helix* cv.

canariensis Willd. [*H. algeriensis* Hibb.; *H. maderensis* C. Koch]. ALGERIAN I., CANARY I., MADEIRA I. Sts. and petioles burgundy-red; juvenile lvs. ovate, to 6 in. wide, entire or shallowly 3–7-lobed, cordate, adult lvs. ovate-lanceolate; fr. black. Canary Is., N. Afr. Much cult. outdoors in the subtropics; tender to heavy freezes. Zone 8. Cvs. are: **'Canary Cream'**, sts. and petioles green, lvs. heavily blotched or variegated ivory-white, sometimes almost wholly cream; **'Margine-maculata'**, sts. and petioles burgundy-red, lf. margins cream-colored and flecked or spattered green; **'Striata'**, twigs and petioles burgundy-red, lf. margins green, midvein section streaked light green to ivory; **'Variegata'**, VARIEGATED I., HAGENBURGER'S I., GLOIRE-DE-MARENGO I., lf. margins less flecked than 'Margine-maculata', midvein section blue- or gray-green; **'Variegata Arborescens'**, GHOST TREE I., SOLEDAD T.I., shrubby, not vining, with ovate, or slightly lobed lvs. variegated cream and green; prop. vegetatively from the adult flowering stage of cv. 'Variegata' and thus more or less stabilized in this stage; **'Viridis'**, twigs and petioles green, lvs. pale green with a darker network of veins, often with variegated areas.

Cavendishii: a listed name of no botanical standing for *H. Helix* cv.

cinerea: *H. nepalensis.*

colchica C. Koch [*H. cordifolia* Hibb.; *H. coriacea* Hibb.]. COLCHIS I., FRAGRANT I., PERSIAN I. Juvenile lvs. thick, leathery, heart-shaped, to 10 in. long, entire or slightly lobed, dark dull green; fr. black. Caucasus to n. Iran. Zone 7. Cv. **'Dentata'** [*H. dentata* Hort. ex Carrière]. Lvs. weakly and sparsely denticulate. Cv. **'Dentato-variegata'**. Lvs. as in 'Dentata' but marginally variegated cream.

conglomerata: *H. Helix* cv.

cordata: probably *H. colchica* is intended.

cordifolia: *H. colchica.*

coriacea: *H. colchica.*

dentata: *H. colchica* cv.

digitata: a listed name of no botanical standing for *H. Helix* cv.

Hahnii: a listed name of no botanical standing for *H. Helix* cv. 'Hahn's Self-branching'.

Helix L. ENGLISH I. Juvenile lvs. typically 5-lobed, 2–3 in. long, dark green, veins whitish above, adult lvs. elliptic to ovate; infl. produced when juvenile brs. reach top of support or heights of usually more than 15 ft.; fr. typically black. Eur., w. Asia, N. Afr.; naturalized in U.S. Var. **Helix.** The typical var.; juvenile lvs. 5-lobed, with terminal lobe largest, becoming ovate and unlobed in the adult stage. Var. **hibernica** (Kirchn.) H. Jaeg. [cvs. 'Hibernica' and 'Scotica'; *H. hibernica* Hort.]. IRISH I. Differs from var. *Helix* in being larger and more vigorous, with lvs. 3–5 in. long and uniformly glossy green; more common in cult. in Amer. than the typical var.

Many cvs. have arisen, since juvenile shoots mutate freely giving rise to various foliage forms and growth habits. Identification is difficult. Some of the common cvs. are listed here. The symbol "R" designates the "self-branching," or Ramosa type in which brs. are freely and spontaneously produced. **'Albany'**, R, twigs fasciated, lvs. sharply 5-lobed, purplish-green with paler veins, purplish beneath; **'Angularis'**: 'Sagittifolia'; **'Arborescens'** [*H. arborea* Carrière], shrubby, not vining, with ovate, unlobed lvs.; really only an adult, flowering stage of the sp., which can be prop. vegetatively and more or less stabilized in this stage; **'Argenteo-variegata'**, lvs. variegated white; **'Atropurpurea'**: 'Minima'; **'Aureo-variegata'**, lvs. variegated creamy-yellow; **'Baltica'**, hardy, from Latvia; **'Bechtoldii'**, lvs. glossy, crinkle-edged; **'Bulgaria'**, drought-resistant, hardy, from Bulgaria; **'Caenwoodiana'**, lvs. small, prominently 3-lobed, dark green with raised white veins; *'California Gold'*, R, lvs. rounded, light green, marbled with yellow; **'Cavendishii'** [cvs. 'Marginata' and 'Variegata'], lvs. pentagonal, with a gray-green center and creamy-white margin; **'Chryso-carpa'**: see cv. 'Poetica' and *H. nepalensis;* **'Compacta'**, compact, lvs. small; **'Conglomerata'** [*H. conglomerata* Hort. ex Carrière], JAPANESE I., sts. contorted, crowded, lvs. small, undulate, stiff, dark green; **'Conglomerata Erecta'** [cv. 'Erecta'], sts. erect, lvs. broadly triangular, pointed, 2-ranked; **'Conglomerata Minima'**, slow-growing, lvs. very small, closely set; **'Contracta'**: 'Sagittifolia'; **'Coriacea'**: probably *H. colchica* is intended; **'Crenata'** [cv. 'Fan'], FAN I., lvs. fan-shaped, pleated; **'Cristata'**: 'Parsley Crested'; **'Curlilocks'** [cv. 'Curly Locks'], R, bushy, young shoots at each lf. axil; **'Cuspidata'**: 'Triloba'; **'Deltoidea'** [cv. 'Sweetheart'], lvs. rounded to heart-shaped, basal lobes overlapping, probably includes cv. 'Heart'; **'Denticulata'**, lvs. somewhat cupped, rounded, with round basal lobes; **'Digitata'** [cv. 'Pal-

mata'; *H. palmata* Hort. ex Carrière], lvs. fan-shaped, veins white, lobes 5, equal triangles; **'Discolor'** [cv. 'Marmorata'], sts. wiry, lvs. small, mottled or spotted white on dark green; **'Elegantissima'**: 'Tricolor'; **'Emerald Jewel'**, sts. long, slender, lvs. glossy, 3-lobed, terminal lobe longest; **'Erecta'**: 'Conglomerata Erecta'; **'Fan'**: 'Crenata'; **'Fluffy Ruffles'**, R, lvs. roundish, margins undulate and crested; **'Glacier'**, lvs. small, triangular, variegated gray and green, margins pink and white; **'Glymii'**, sts. creeping, with aerial rootlets, lvs. ovate-cordate, glossy; **'Gold Dust'**, lvs. 3-lobed, mottled green and white; **'Gold Heart'**, sts. reddish, lvs. small, 3–5-lobed, green with yellow and cream center; **'Gracilis'**, spindly, with long internodes, sts. and petioles reddish, lvs. small, 3–5-lobed; **'Green Feather'**: 'Meagheri'; **'Green Ripples'**, lvs. often deformed, frilled, abundant, large and small; **'Green Spear'**, lvs. spear-shaped, long-pointed, laciniate, veins light green; **'Hahn's Self-branching'** [*H. Hahnii* Hort.], R, very bushy, making a dense mat of growth, sts. branching near the tips; **'Heart'**: probably 'Deltoidea'; **'Helvetica'**, sts. stiff, lvs. cordate to 3-lobed, shield-shaped, veins white; **'Hibernica'**: var. *hibernica;* **'Howardii'**, lvs. edged silvery-white; **'Irish Lace'**, lvs. finely cut, with a lacy appearance; **'Itsy Bitsy'**, compact, lvs. to ½ in. long, ⅛ in. wide; **'Ivalace'**, R, close growth, lvs. 5-lobed, margins curled, lacy; **'Jubilee'**, R, lvs. very small, variegated with white, gray, and light green; **'Lobata Major'**, related to var. *hibernica,* but lvs. with sinuses deep and narrow, not shallow and wide; **'Maculata'**, lvs. 5-lobed, variegated yellow-green, dark green, cream and white; **'Manda's Crested'**, sts. reddish, lvs. star-shaped, jade-green, with rose margins, lobes fluted and undulate; **'Maple Queen'**, R, compact, sts. reddish, lvs. small, with pale veins; **'Marginata'**: 'Cavendishii'; **'Marmorata'**: 'Discolor'; **'Meagheri'** [cv. 'Green Feather'], GREEN-FEATHER, R, lvs. narrowly laciniate, feathery, lateral lobes spoonlike; **'Merion Beauty'**, R, dense, lvs. small, variously shaped; **'Minima'** [cv. 'Atropurpurea'], lvs. small, 3–5-lobed, undulate, cordate; **'Needle-point'**, R, dwarf, brs. erect, lvs. small, 3-lobed, 2-ranked; **'Nepalensis'**: *H. nepalensis;* **'Palmata'**: 'Digitata'; **'Parsley Crested'** [cv. 'Cristata'], PARSLEY I., sts. long, slender, lvs. 5-lobed, rounded, margins frilled and crimped; **'Pedata'**, BIRD'S-FOOT I., sts. long, lvs. small, lobes laciniate, veins white; **'Peltata'**, lvs. very small, dark green; **'Pin Oak'**, R, sts. creeping, reddish, lvs. cut into narrow curved lobes; **'Pittsburgh'**, R, bushy, lvs. small to medium, long-pointed, very hardy; **'Pixie'**, growth stunted, compact, lvs. small, 3–7-lobed; **'Poetica'** [cv. 'Chryso-carpa'], ITALIAN I., fr. yellow; **'Purpurea'**, lvs. purplish, darker purple in winter; **'Ripples'**, brs. pendent, lvs. irregularly lobed, margins curled or crested; **'Rochester'**, lvs. small to medium; **'Sagittifolia'** [cvs. 'Angularis', 'Contracta', 'Taurica'], sts. purplish, prostrate, lvs. narrow-sagittate, small, grayish-green with whitish veins; **'Scotica'**: var. *hibernica:* **'Scutifolia'**, HEART-LEAF I., sts. reddish, lvs. small, heart-shaped, petioles reddish; **'Shamrock'**, twigs red, lvs. bright green, 3-lobed, lateral lobes folded towards center; **'Smithii'**, lvs. starlike, 5-lobed, lobes fluted with tips recurved; **'Star'**, R, bushy, lvs. 5-lobed, lobes slender, starlike; **'Stardust'**, lvs. edged creamy-white with central portion mottled silvery-green and darker green; **'Sweetheart'**: 'Deltoidea'; **'Sylvan Beauty'**: 'Sylvanian'; **'Sylvanian'** [cv. 'Sylvan Beauty'], R, compact, lvs. dense, like shingles on a roof; **'Taconic'**, lvs. larger than 'Baltica', hardy form; **'Taurica'**: 'Sagittifolia'; **'Telecurl'**, bushy, sts. red, lvs. 5–7-lobed, terminal lobe dissected to base, lateral lobes overlapping, ruffled; **'Thorndale'**, lvs. glossy green, veins creamy-white; **'Tricolor'** [cv. 'Elegantissima'], lvs. variegated cream, margins turning reddish in autumn, petioles purplish; **'Triloba'** [cv. 'Cuspidata'], dwarf, lvs. small, purplish-green, slightly 3-lobed, narrow, oblong, pointed; **'Variegata'**: 'Cavendishii'; **'Walthamensis'**, BABY I., lvs. very small, white-veined; **'Williamsiana'**, lvs. 3–5-lobed, the long tips recurved, margins wavy, greenish-white, center gray-green; **'Wilsonii'**, very compact plant, lvs. small, pointed, hardy.

hibernica: a listed name of no botanical standing for *H. Helix* var.

japonica: *H. rhombea.*

maderensis: *H. canariensis.*

minima: a listed name of no botanical standing for *H. Helix* cv.

nepalensis C. Koch [*H. Helix* cvs. 'Chrysocarpa' and 'Nepalensis'; *H. cinerea* (Hibb.) Bean]. NEPAL I. Juvenile lvs. elliptic-lanceolate, with 2–4 narrow lobes on each side, dull green mottled with gray-green between lateral veins; fr. golden-yellow. Himalayas, Afghanistan to w. China and n. Burma.

palmata: *H. Helix* cv. 'Digitata'.

rhombea (Miq.) Bean [*H. japonica* Paul, not Jungh.]. JAPANESE I. Differs from *H. nepalensis* in the broadly ovate, 3–5-lobed, juvenile lvs., from *H. colchica* in the lobed lvs. and absence of pungent odor when crushed, and from *H. Helix* in the scalelike, not stellate, hairs on young shoots and petioles. Japan and Ryukyu Is. Zone 8. Cv. **'Variegata'**. Lf. margins narrowly variegated with cream.

HEDGE. A hedge is a dense, permanent row or line of living plants, frequently trimmed into more or less formal shape, answering the purpose of a fence, a screen, or a windbreak. It is composed of durable woody plants that make a thick, intertangled or impenetrable growth and that withstand shearing. Plants tolerant of shade or poor soil are often particularly useful. Hedges proper are to be distinguished from edgings, which are low and sometimes temporary lines about walks, flower beds, and borders.

Both trees and shrubs may be used for hedges. Among the trees may be included *Acer campestre, A. Ginnala, Cedrus atlantica* cv. 'Fastigiata', *Cryptomeria japonica, Cupressus, Fagus sylvatica, Larix decidua, Pinus Mugo, Quercus imbricaria, Thuja,* and *Tsuga canadensis,* along with *Casuarina stricta, Melaleuca Leucadendron, Podocarpus,* and several species of palms such as *Chamaerops humilis, Chrysalidocarpus lutescens,* and *Phoenix reclinata* for mild climates.

Shrubs, clipped or unclipped, are more frequently used, since a great many make acceptable hedges. The following are only a sampling: *Abelia floribunda, Berberis, Buxus, Caragana pygmaea, Chaenomeles, Cornus mas, Elaeagnus commutata, Euonymus, Forsythia, Ilex, Lavandula angustifolia, Ligustrum, Lonicera, Mahonia, Pieris japonica, Rhamnus Frangula, Rhododendron, Rosa, Salix purpurea* cv. 'Nana', *Spiraea, Syringa* ×*chinensis, Taxus,* and *Teucrium Chamaedrys;* for mild climates may be added *Ardisia japonica, Brunfelsia pauciflora* var. *calycina, Choisya ternata, Coleonema pulchrum, Corokia Cotoneaster, Correa pulchella, Diosma, Hebe elliptica, Leptospermum laevigatum* cv. 'Reevesii', *Michelia Figo, Myrsine africana, Myrtus communis* cv. 'Compacta', *Nandina domestica, Nerium Oleander, Osmanthus, Pittosporum eugenioides, Poncirus trifoliata, Prunus ilicifolia, P. Laurocerasus, P. Lyonii, Rhaphiolepis, Rhapidophyllum hystrix, Rhapis excelsa, Serenoa repens, Ugni Molinae,* and *Viburnum suspensum.*

To obtain a good hedge, it is necessary to have a thoroughly well-prepared deep soil, to set the plants close, and to shear them at least twice every year. Arborvitaes may be set 1–2½ or 3 feet apart, and hemlocks and spruces much the same; these distances may be taken as a general guide for many other plants.

The hedge should be trimmed the year after it is set, although it should not be cut very closely until the plants reach the desired or permanent height. Thereafter it should be sheared into the desired form in late spring when most of the current season's growth is removed. Plants that grow rapidly may need to be trimmed three or more times a year if they are to be neat. If the plants are allowed to grow a year or two without trimming, they lose the lower leaves and become open and straggly. Clipped hedges should be kept narrower at the top than at the bottom so as to encourage dense growth close to the ground. A hedge 2 feet high should be up to 4 inches narrower at the top than at the bottom, and this basic shape should be started with the trimming of the first season after planting.

Hedges are much less used in North America than in Europe, and for several reasons. The climate is relatively dry, and most hedges do not thrive as well here as there; labor is high-priced, and the trimming is likely to be neglected; farms are so large that much fencing is required; timber and wire are usually cheaper than live hedges. However, they are grown with good effect about home grounds, where they will set off and ornament the garden from within as well as protect it from outside.

HEDYCARYA J. R. Forst. & G. Forst. *Monimiaceae.* Perhaps 20 spp. of dioecious trees and shrubs, native to Pacific Is., Australia, and New Zeal.; lvs. opp.; fls. in axillary cymes or racemes, inconspicuous, unisexual, perianth segms. 5–10, inflexed, stamens or carpels many; fr. drupaceous, several together.

arborea J. R. Forst. & G. Forst. To 40 ft.; lvs. leathery, lanceolate to elliptic-obovate, to 5 in. long, coarsely serrate; fls. to ½ in. across, in branched racemes; drupes bright red, ½ in. long, stipitate, up to 10 together. New Zeal. Grown in Calif. Zone 10.

HEDYCHIUM J. König. GINGER LILY, GARLAND L. *Zingiberaceae.* About 50 spp. of robust, per. herbs in trop. Asia and the Himalayas; sts. leafy, from stout rhizomes; infl. a terminal spike or panicle; fls. in axils of bracts, calyx tubular, unequally toothed, corolla tube slender, longer than calyx, corolla lobes reflexed, staminodial lip broad, petal-like, more or less deeply 2-lobed, lateral staminodes petal-like, stamen filament long, the connective narrow, without a crest, anther not spurred, ovary inferior, 3-celled; fr. a caps.

Grown in the greenhouse or frostless areas outdoors; prized for the showy flowers and fragrance. Ginger lilies require rich soil and plenty of water, or may even be immersed up to the crown. Propagated by division of the rhizomes.

acuminatum: *H. spicatum* var.

aurantiacum Wallich ex Roscoe. To 10 ft.; lvs. to 1½ ft. long and 1 in. wide; fl. spikes to 6 in. long; fls. orange, corolla tube ¾ in. long, corolla lobes 1 in. long, stamen filament bright red. India.

aureum C. B. Clarke & Mann ex Bak. Dwarf; lvs. lanceolate, to 8 in. long, acuminate, slightly pubescent beneath; spikes dense, to 2 in. long; fls. golden-yellow, to ¾ in. long, staminodes linear, about ½ in. long, stamen filament as long as lip. India.

chrysoleucum Hook. [*H. coronarium* var. *chrysoleucum* (Hook.) Bak.]. Differs from *H. flavescens* in having base of lip and lateral staminodes deep orange-yellow. India.

coccineum Buch.-Ham. RED GINGER LILY, SCARLET G.L. To 6 ft.; lvs. to 20 in. long and 2 in. wide; spikes dense, to 10 in. long; fls. red, corolla tube 1 in. long, corolla lobes 1 in. long, stamen filament pink. India. Var. **angustifolium** (Roxb.) Bak. Lvs. shorter; fls. brick- or salmon-red.

coronarium J. König. GARLAND FLOWER, BUTTERFLY GINGER, WHITE G., BUTTERFLY LILY, GINGER L., CINNAMON JASMINE. To 6 ft.; lvs. to 2 ft. long and 5 in. wide; spike somewhat ovate, to 1 ft. long, fl. bracts large, firm, closely imbricate, each with 4–6 white, very fragrant fls. in its axil; corolla tube 2–3 in. long, staminodial lip large, broad, nearly 2 in. long and 1½ in. wide, 2-lobed, sometimes with smaller lobes, sometimes tinged yellow in lower part, stamen filament with anther shorter than lip. Trop. Asia; naturalized extensively in trop. Amer. Zone 9. Cv. '**Angustifolium**' is listed. Var. **chrysoleucum:** *H. chrysoleucum.* Var. **flavescens:** *H. flavescens.* Var. **maximum:** *H. maximum.*

densiflorum Wallich. To 9 ft. or more; lvs. oblong-lanceolate or oblong, to 14 in. long, 4 in. wide, glabrous; spikes to 8 in. long; fls. orange-yellow. India.

elatum R. Br. To 12 ft. or more; lvs. to 2 ft. long and 2½ in. wide; spikes loose, to 1 ft. long; fls. yellowish-white, corolla tube 1 in. long, corolla lobes ¾ in. long, stamen filament pink. India.

ellipticum Buch.-Ham. ex Sm. To 5 ft.; lvs. to 14 in. long and 5 in. wide; spikes dense, 4 in. long; fls. yellowish-white, corolla tube to 3 in. long, corolla lobes 1 in. long, stamen filament purple. India.

flavescens W. Carey [*H. coronarium* var. *flavescens* (W. Carey) Bak.]. YELLOW GINGER. To 6 ft. or more; lvs. lanceolate; fls. to 5½ in. long, corolla yellowish, deeper colored in basal part, staminodial lip obcordate, narrower than long, narrowed to a claw, reddish-yellow at base. India.

flavum Roxb. To 5 ft.; lvs. oblong to lanceolate, to 14 in. long, slender-pointed; spikes oblong, bracts imbricate, oblong-ovate, acute or obtuse, 2½ in. long and 2 in. wide; fls. yellow, lip broadly obovate, about as broad as long, narrowed to a short claw. India.

Gardneranum Roscoe. KAHILI GINGER. Lvs. to 1½ ft. long and 6 in. wide; spikes to 1½ ft. long; fls. light yellow, corolla tube 2 in. long, corolla lobes 1½ in. long, stamen filament red, long-exserted. India.

glaucum Roscoe [*H. gracile* var. *glaucum* (Roscoe) Bak.]. To 5 ft.; lvs. to 10 in. long and 3 in. wide, glaucous beneath; spikes loose, to 8 in. long; fls. white, corolla tube 1 in. long, corolla lobes 1¼ in. long, stamen filament red. India.

gracile Roxb. To 2 ft.; lvs. to 5 in. long and 1½ in. wide, glaucous beneath; spikes to 4 in. long; fls. greenish-white, corolla tube 1 in. long, corolla lobes ¾ in. long, stamen filament red. India. Var. **glaucum:** *H. glaucum.*

Greenei W. W. Sm. To 6 ft.; lvs. to 10 in. long and 2 in. wide; spikes dense, to 5 in. long; corolla tube 1½ in. long, staminodial lip dark red, 1½ in. long, the linear lobes lighter red, stamen filament red. India.

maximum Roscoe [*H. coronarium* var. *maximum* (Roscoe) Bak.]. Differs from *H. coronarium* in having lvs. broader, fls. pure white, lateral staminodes frequently bearing a lobe or tongue from the center, stamen filament tinged pink, lip nearly 2¾ in. long and 1¾ in. wide. India.

spicatum Buch.-Ham. To 3 ft.; lvs. to 16 in. long and 4 in. wide; spikes loose, to 8 in. long; fls. yellow, corolla tube 3 in. long, corolla lobes 1 in. long, stamen filament reddish. India. Rhizome used for perfumery in Asia. Var. **acuminatum** (Roscoe) Wallich [*H. acuminatum* Roscoe]. Lvs. tomentose beneath; corolla lobes purple.

thyrsiforme Buch.-Ham. To 6 ft.; lvs. to 14 in. long and 5 in. wide; spikes dense, to 4½ in. long; fls. white, corolla tube 1 in. long, corolla lobes 1 in. long, stamen filament white. India.

villosum Wallich. To 8 ft.; lvs. to 14 in. long and 4 in. wide; spikes loose, to 10 in. long; corolla tube white, to 2½ in. long, corolla lobes yellow, 1¼ in. long, stamen filament purple. India.

HEDYOTIS L. [*Houstonia* L.]. *Rubiaceae*. About 400 spp. of trop., subtrop., and sometimes temp. regions, weak-stemmed shrubs or herbs, sometimes tufted, occasionally prostrate; lvs. opp., stipules interpetiolar; fls. solitary, sometimes in terminal or axillary cymes, sometimes small, usually 4-merous, corolla funnelform or salverform; fr. a caps., seeds several to many.

caerulea (L.) Hook. [*Houstonia caerulea* L.]. BLUETS, QUAKER-LADIES, INNOCENCE. Per., to 7 in., tufted; lvs. oblanceolate, ½ in. long; fls. solitary, corolla salverform, to ½ in. long, violet, blue, or white, with yellow eye; caps. ⅛ in. across, broader than long. Nov. Sc. to Que. and Wisc., s. to Ga. and Ark.

calycosa: *H. purpurea*, var.

lanceolata: *H. purpurea* var. *calycosa*.

longifolia: *H. purpurea* var.

Michauxii Fosb. [*H. serpyllifolia* (Michx.) Torr. & A. Gray, not Poir.; *Houstonia serpyllifolia* Michx.]. CREEPING BLUETS. Per., to 10 in., sts. prostrate, rooting at nodes; lvs. ovate to orbicular, to ⅜ in. long; fls. solitary, corolla salverform, to ½ in. long, deep blue or violet; caps. to ⅛ in. across, broader than long. Penn., s. to Ga. and Tenn.

nigricans (Lam.) Fosb. [*Houstonia angustifolia* Michx.; *H. nigricans* (Lam.) Fern.]. Per., to 2 ft., branched above; lvs. often clustered, sessile, linear, to 1¼ in. long; fls. in terminal cymes grouped into a panicle, corolla salverform, to ¼ in. long, white or purplish; caps. more or less oblong or cylindrical. Ind. to Iowa, s. to Fla., Tex., n. Mex. Var. **filifolia** (Chapm.) Shinn. [*Houstonia filifolia* (Chapm.) Small]. Lvs. narrow. Fla. to Tex.

purpurea (L.) Torr. & A. Gray [*Houstonia purpurea* L.]. Per., with usually several sts. from base, simple or branched above, to 18 in.; lvs. sessile, ovate or ovate-lanceolate, to 2 in. long; fls. in terminal cymes, corolla purple or lilac, funnelform, to ⅜ in. long; caps. to ⅛ in. long. S. New Eng. to Mich. and Mo., s. to Ala. and e. Tex. A variable sp. with several botanical vars. Var. **calycosa** (Shuttle. ex A. Gray) Fosb. [*H. calycosa* Shuttl. ex A. Gray; *H. lanceolata* Lam. ex Poir.; *Houstonia calycosa* (Shuttl. ex A. Gray) C. Mohr; *H. lanceolata* (Lam. ex Poir.) Britt.]. Lvs. oblong-lanceolate, to ½ in. long; calyx lobes linear-lanceolate, to ½ in. long. Var. **ciliolata** (Torr.) Fosb. [*Houstonia canadensis* Willd. ex Roem. & Schult.; *H. ciliolata* Torr.]. Basal lvs. in well-developed rosette, persistent, st. lvs. narrowly oblong to lanceolate or oblanceolate, to 1¼ in. long, all lvs. ciliate with more or less conspicuous hairs. Ont. to Sask., s. to N.Y., Tenn., Mo. Var. **floridana** (Standl.) Fosb. [*Houstonia floridana* Standl.]. Lvs. narrowly linear or filiform, to ¾ in. long; not to be confused with *H. nigricans* var. *filifolia*, which has caps. oblong to cylindrical. S. Fla. Var. **longifolia** (Gaertn.) Fosb. [*H. longifolia* (Gaertn.) Hook.; *Houstonia longifolia* Gaertn.]. Basal lvs. not in a rosette, lvs. broadly linear to narrowly oblong, to 1¼ in. long, Me., w. to Ont. and Sask., s. to S.C. and Ark. Var. **montana** (Small) Fosb. [*Houstonia montana* Small]. To 8 in., dwarf and compact, with short internodes; lvs. ovate, to 1¼ in. long. Mts., N.C. and Tenn. Var. **tenuifolia** (Nutt.) Fosb. [*Houstonia Nuttalliana* Fosb.; *H. tenuifolia* Nutt.]. Lvs. linear, to 1½ in. long; pedicels very slender; caps. to ⅛ in. long. Penn. to Mo. and Okla., s. to Va., Ga., Tex.

serpyllifolia: *H. Michauxii*.

HEDYSARUM L. *Leguminosae* (subfamily *Faboideae*). Perhaps 100–150 spp. of per. herbs and small shrubs of N. Temp. Zone; lvs. alt., odd-pinnate; fls. in axillary racemes, showy, papilionaceous, with wing petals shorter than keel, stamens 10, 9 united and 1 separate; fr. a flat legume, with scalloped margins, separating into 1-seeded segms.

Grown as ornamentals; of easy culture in sunny, well-drained soil. Propagated by seeds and division.

alpinum L. [*H. boreale* of auth., not Nutt.]. Sts. several, to 2 ft.; lfts. in 7–11 pairs, lanceolate to oblong, to 1 in. long and ⅜ in. wide, stipules

brown, conspicuous; fls. pink to purple, to ⅝ in. long, in elongate racemes, calyx teeth triangular, shorter than tube; fr. 3–5-jointed, wing-margined, with nearly regular reticulation. Circumboreal.

boreale Nutt. Differs from *H. alpinum* in having a calyx with lanceolate to subulate teeth longer than tube, 4–6 pairs of lfts. only weekly nerved, usually reddish fls., and joints of the fr. not wing-margined but strigose with laterally elongate reticulations. Sask. and N. Dak. to Utah and Okla. Cv. 'Rosea' is listed. Material offered as *H. boreale* may be *H. alpinum*.

coronarium L. FRENCH HONEYSUCKLE. Per. or bien., to 4 ft.; lfts. in 3–7 pairs, elliptic, to 1½ in. long; fls. fragrant, in crowded racemes on long peduncles, deep red, to ¾ in. long; fr. minutely roughened. Eur. Sometimes cult. as food for livestock.

hedysaroides (L.) Schinz & Thell. [*H. obscurum* L.]. To 20 in., glabrous, with horizontal rhizome; lfts. in 5–9 pairs, ovate or oblong; fls. violet or whitish, in loose racemes, standard shorter than wings; fr. pendent, glabrous, narrowly winged. Eur.

obscurum: *H. hedysaroides*.

ocidentale Greene. To 2 ft.; lvs. to 6 in. long, lfts. in 6–9 pairs, oblong or lanceolate, to 1 in. long; racemes longer than lvs.; fls. reddish-purple, ¾ in. long; fr. 2–5-jointed. Wash.

HEDYSCEPE H. Wendl. & Drude. *Palmae*. One sp., a solitary, unarmed, monoecious palm of moderate stature from Lord Howe Is. (Australia); trunk green, closely and prominently ringed; lvs. pinnate, sheaths forming a tubular crownshaft, pinnae regularly arranged, stiff, ascending from a curved rachis, acute, with 1–2 prominent veins each side of midrib; infl. below lvs., bracts 2, deciduous, inserted on short peduncle, lower brs. once-branched, rachillae glabrous, with fls. in triads (2 male and 1 female) nearly throughout and above these with paired or solitary male fls.; male fls. asymmetrical, sepals 3, acute, narrow, petals 3, angled, valvate, stamens 9 or perhaps to 12, pistillode about as long as stamens, attenuate from a broad base, female fls. with sepals 3, imbricate, petals 3, imbricate, briefly valvate apically, staminodes 3, pistil 1-celled, 1-ovuled; fr. broadly ellipsoid with nearly apical stigmatic residue, seed with homogeneous endosperm, embryo basal.

An attractive rather slow-growing palm hardy in the warmer parts of Zone 10a, especially in southern Calif.; also suitable for pot or tub culture in the home or greenhouse. For culture see *Palms*.

Canterburyana (C. Moore & F. J. Muell.) H. Wendl. & Drude [*Kentia Canterburyana* C. Moore & F. J. Muell.]. UMBRELLA PALM. To nearly 30 ft., trunk 4–5 in. in diam., green becoming gray; lf. sheath silvery-blue, 14 in. long, pinnae 40 or more on each side, to 21 in. long, 1 in. wide; infl. 18 in. long; fr. dull deep red when mature, to 1½ in. long, 1 in. in diam.

HEERIA: see *HETEROCENTRON*.

HEIMERLIODENDRON: *PISONIA*. H. **Brunonianum:** *P. umbellifera*.

HEIMIA Link. *Lythraceae*. Two spp. of glabrous shrubs, native to trop. N. and S. Amer.; lvs. small, opp. or whorled; fls. yellow, solitary, axillary, regular, calyx tube campanulate, calyx lobes alternating with hornlike appendages, petals 5–7, stamens 10–13, ovary 3–6-celled; fr. a caps.

myrtifolia Cham. & Schlechtend. To 3 ft.; lvs. linear to lanceolate, to 2½ in. long; calyx tube semiglobose in fr., calyx lobes connivent, petals less than ⅛ in. long, anthers orbicular. Brazil.

salicifolia (HBK) Link. To 10 ft.; lvs. linear-lanceolate, to 3½ in. long; calyx tube campanulate in fr., calyx lobes spreading, petals to ¾ in. long, anthers elliptic. Mex. to Argentina.

HELENIUM L. SNEEZEWEED. *Compositae* (Helenium Tribe). About 40 spp. of ann. or per. herbs, native to N. and S. Amer.; sts. branched or unbranched; lvs. alt., glandular-dotted, frequently decurrent; fl. heads radiate or discoid, solitary or cymose, peduncled, involucral bracts in 2 rows, deflexed or spreading with age, receptacle convex to ovoid or globose, naked; disc fls. bisexual, yellow, red-brown, or red-purple, ray fls. present or absent, female or sterile, mostly yellow; achenes turbinate or obpyramidal, 4–5-angled, pappus of 5–10 scarious, awn-tipped, often fringed scales.

Heleniums thrive in fairly rich soil and a sunny location; propagated by seeds, cuttings, and division. They are useful for the back of borders and in wild gardens.

amarum (Raf.) Rock [*H. tenuifolium* Nutt.]. BITTERWEED. Strong-smelling, bushy ann., to 2 ft., sts. very leafy, striate to ribbed but not winged; lowest lvs. oblanceolate, pinnately lobed, soon withering, upper lvs. mostly clustered, linear to linear-filiform, to 3⅛ in. long; heads to 1 in. across, receptacle globose; fls. yellow. Va. to Fla., w. to Kans. and Tex.; spreading northward as a weed.

autumnale L. Fibrous-rooted per., to 5 ft., sts. branched, winged by decurrent lf. bases; lvs. linear-lanceolate to elliptic or ovate-lanceolate, to 6 in. long, usually serrate, nearly glabrous, lower lvs. often deciduous; heads to 2 in. across, receptacle nearly globose to hemispherical; disc fls. yellow, ray fls. yellow to bright yellow. Que. to Fla., w. to B.C. and Ariz. Cv. 'Grandicephalum'. Sts. to 5 ft.; heads large; ray fls. clear yellow. Cv. 'Nanum Praecox'. Dwarf; disc fls. yellow. Cv. 'Peregrinum'. Ray fls. mahogany-red, faintly edged with yellow. Cv. 'Praecox'. Fls. yellow, brown, red. Cv. 'Pumilum'. To 2½ ft.; fls. yellow. Cv. 'Pumilum Magnificum'. To 3 ft.; fls. pale yellow. Cv. 'Rubrum'. Fls. deep red. Cv. 'Superbum'. To 5 ft.; ray fls. bright yellow with wavy margins.

Bigelovii A. Gray. Per., to 3 ft., sts. unbranched or sparingly branched, usually several from a woody root crown, forming a clump; lower lvs. oblanceolate to linear-lanceolate, to 10 in. long, glabrous or sparsely hairy, petioled, st. lvs. successively reduced upward, the uppermost sessile and decurrent; heads to 2½ in. across, solitary, long-peduncled, receptacle depressed-globose; disc fls. yellow or brownish, ray fls. yellow. Sw. Ore. to s. Calif. Cv. 'Aurantiacum'. Ray fls. golden-yellow.

flexuosum Raf. [*H. nudiflorum* Nutt.; *H. polyphyllum* Small]. Erect per., to 3 ft., producing a single, paniculately much-branched st. from the previous season's rosette; basal lvs. linear-lanceolate or elliptic-lanceolate to spatulate or oblanceolate, to 8½ in. long, entire to pinnatifid, densely hairy to glabrate, dotted, st. lvs. lanceolate to oblong, reduced, sessile and decurrent; heads to 1½ in. across, receptacle almost globose to ovoid-globose; disc fls. mostly 4-lobed, red-brown to red-purple, ray fls. yellow or brown-purple, or absent. Mass. to Fla., w. to Mo. and Tex.

grandicephalum: a listed name of no botanical standing for *H. autumnale* cv.

Hoopesii A. Gray. Stout per., to 3½ ft., from a root crown or rhizome, foliage yellow-green, becoming glabrate; basal lvs. oblanceolate, to 1 ft. long, entire, petioled, upper lvs. reduced, lanceolate, entire, sessile, not decurrent; heads to 3 in. across, 3–8 in a loose, terminal corymb, receptacle hemispherical; fls. orange or yellow, ray fls. very narrow. Mts., Wyo. to New Mex., w. to s. Ore. and cent. Calif.

nanum: a listed name for *H. autumnale* cv.

nudiflorum: *H. flexuosum.*

peregrinum: a listed name for *H. autumnale* cv.

polyphyllum: *H. flexuosum.*

praecox: a listed name for *H. autumnale* cv.

puberulum DC. ROSILLA. Coarse ann. or short-lived per., to 5 ft., sts. divaricately and paniculately branched; lower lvs. soon withering, st. lvs. lanceolate-oblong to linear, to 6 in. long, puberulent, sessile and decurrent; heads to ½ in. across, long-peduncled, receptacle globose; fls. yellow or reddish-brown, ray fls. inconspicuous, shorter than receptacle, reflexed. Ore. to Baja Calif.

pumilum: a listed name for *H. autumnale* cv.

rubrum: a listed name for *H. autumnale* cv.

tenuifolium: *H. amarum.*

HELIANTHELLA Torr. & A. Gray. *Compositae* (Helianthus Tribe). Eight spp. of rough-hairy, per. herbs in w. N. Amer., sts. leafy, erect; lvs. simple, entire, usually 3- to 5-nerved, the lower opp., the upper often alt.; fl. heads radiate, solitary or few and large, or many and smaller, receptacle scaly; fls. yellow; achenes strongly compressed, pappus lacking or of 2 awns, with or without additional scales.

Propagated by seeds or division.

Parryi A. Gray. To 20 in.; basal lvs. spatulate, large, long-petioled, st. lvs. oblanceolate, somewhat obtuse, nearly sessile; heads mostly 1–3, nodding, involucre ¾ in. across; ray fls. pale yellow. Mts., Colo., New Mex., e. Ariz.

quinquenervis (Hook.) A. Gray. Sts. 2–5 ft.; basal lvs. elliptic, large, long-petioled, st. lvs. ovate-lanceolate to elliptic, acuminate, petioled; heads 1–3, nodding, long-peduncled, involucre 1½–2 in. across; ray fls. bright yellow. Rocky Mts., Mont. to Ariz. and New Mex.

uniflora (Nutt.) Torr. & A. Gray [*Helianthus uniflorus* Nutt.]. To 4 ft., without enlarged basal lvs., st. lvs. lanceolate to elliptic, obtuse or acute, short-petioled or sessile; heads solitary or few, erect, involucre to ¾ in. across; ray fls. bright yellow. S. B.C. to Nev. and Colo.

HELIANTHEMUM Mill. [*Crocanthemum* Spach]. SUN ROSE, ROCK R. *Cistaceae.* About 110 spp. of herbs or sub-shrubs, native to Old World and N. and S. Amer.; usually pubescent with stellate hairs; lvs. opp. or alt., usually small and narrow; petals and sepals 5, stamens many, style short and straight, or filiform and bent, or lacking, stigma capitate; fr. an ovoid, 3-valved caps.

In the North winter protection is advisable. They thrive in a sunny exposure on dry limestone soil. Propagated by division, greenwood cuttings, and seeds. One of the sun roses *(H. nummularium)* is hardy and common in the North.

alpestre: *H. oelandicum* subsp.

alyssoides: *Halimium alyssoides.*

amabile: a cv., 'Amabile', with orange fls. tinged pink.

apenninum (L.) Mill. [*H. poliifolium* Pers.; *H. pulverulentum* of auth.; *H. velutinum* Jord.]. Shrub, much-branched from base, to 18 in.; lvs. oblong, to 1¼ in. long, more or less revolute, gray-tomentose beneath; fls. white, 1 in. across. Eur. and Asia Minor. Var. **roseum** (Jacq.) Willk. [*H. rhodanthum* Dunal]. Fls. reddish.

atriplicifolium: *Halimium atriplicifolium.*

astrosanguineum: a listed name; probably a *H. nummularium* cv.

aureum Pers. Probably *H. hirtum;* but material cult. as *H. aureum* is *H. nummularium* cv.

bicolor: see *H. croceum.*

californicum: a listed name of no botanical standing; perhaps referable to *H. scoparium.*

canadense (L.) Michx. [*Crocanthemum canadense* (L.) Britt. & A. Br.]. FROSTWEED. Per., to 20 in., stellate-hairy, sts. erect, wiry, sparingly branched; lvs. elliptic-lanceolate, to 1 in. long, densely pubescent beneath; fls. of two kinds, the cleistogamous (not opening) small, on short pedicels, terminal and in upper lf. axils, the chasmogamous (opening) not mixed with cleistogamous fls., on pedicels to ⅜ in. long, petals to ½ in. long. E. U.S.

carneum: a listed name; probably a *H. nummularium* cv.

Chamaecistus: *H. nummularium.*

cinereum (Cav.) Pers. [*H. rotundifolium* Dunal]. Dwarf shrub, usually with erect brs., but variable; lvs. ovate to lanceolate, rounded or cordate at base, gray-tomentose beneath and above, or green and glabrous above; fls. yellow, usually in a panicle, rarely a cyme. Medit. region.

citrinum: a listed name of no botanical standing for *H. nummularium* cv.

coccineum: a listed name; probably a *H. nummularium* cv.

coridifolium: *Fumana ericoides.*

corymbosum Michx. Suffrutescent per., roots with tuberous thickenings, sts. to 12 in., stellate-canescent; lvs. elliptic to oblanceolate, to 1¼ in. long; fls. of two kinds, the cleistogamous (not opening) small, on pedicels less than ¼ in. long, in compact terminal cymes, the chasmogamous (opening) larger, scattered among the cleistogamous fls., on pedicels to ¾ in. long, petals yellow, about ⅜ in. long. Coastal plain, se. U.S.

croceum (Desf.) Pers. [*H. glaucum* Pers.; *H. bicolor* K. Presl probably belongs here]. Low shrub, to 12 in., brs. erect or procumbent; lvs. suborbicular to linear-lanceolate, to ¾ in. long, fleshy, usually stellate-tomentose on both surfaces; fls. yellow or white, to ¾ in. across, in 3–15-fld. cymes. W. Medit. region. Variable in habit, lf. shape, pubescence, and fl. color.

Croftianum: a listed name of no botanical standing.

formosum: *Halimium lasianthum.*

glaucum: *H. croceum.*

grandiflorum: *H. nummularium* subsp.

guttatum: *Tuberaria guttata.*

halimifolium: *Halimium halimifolium.*

hirtum (L.) Mill. Tufted subshrub, to 1 ft., sts. erect, rarely procumbent; lvs. ovate to linear-lanceolate, to ½ in. long, somewhat fleshy; fls. white or yellow, to ½ in. across, in 5–17-fld. cymes. Sw. Eur. Forma **erectum** Willk. Sts. erect, fastigiate; lvs. strongly revolute; fls. usually yellow.

icelandicum: a listed name of no botanical standing; perhaps in error for *H. oelandicum.*

lasianthum: *Halimium lasianthum.*

latifolium: a listed name of no botanical standing.

Libanotis: see *Halimium commutatum.*

lunulatum (All.) DC. Low, dense subshrub, to 1 ft.; lvs. elliptic-oblong, to ½ in. long, green, slightly pubescent; fls. few, at ends of leafy brs., petals yellow, with basal orange blotch. Mts., cent. Eur.

luteum: a listed name; perhaps a *H. nummularium* cv.

mutabile: *H. nummularium* cv.

nummularium (L.) Mill. [*H. Chamaecistus* Mill.; *H. variabile* Spach.; *H. vulgare* Gaertn.]. To 18 in., brs. ascending or procumbent; lvs. ovate to lanceolate, to 2 in. long, gray-tomentose beneath, margins flat or slightly revolute; fls. yellow, rarely cream, pale yellow, white, or pink, 1 in. across, in 1–12-fld. 1-sided cymes. Eur. The commonly cult. sp. Subsp. **grandiflorum** (Scop.) Schinz & Thell. [*H. grandiflorum* Scop.]. Petals to ¾ in. long. Subsp. **obscurum** (Pers.) J. Holub [*H. obscurum* Pers.]. Lvs. green, but with long hairs on surfaces and margins; petals about ½ in. long. Some cvs. are listed: '**Albo-plenum**', fls. double, white; '**Aureum**', fls. deep yellow; '**Citrinum**', fls. golden-yellow; '**Cupreum**', fls. copper-colored, often variegated with yellow; '**Macranthum**', petals white with yellow blotches at base; '**Mutabile**' [*H. mutabile* (Jacq.) Moench], fls. changing to lilac or nearly white; '**Roseum**', fls. pale rose; '**Roseo-plenum**', fls. double, pale rose; '**Rubro-plenum**', fls. double, red; '**Speciosum**', fls. large; '**Stramineum**', lvs. whitish beneath, petals with dark yellow blotch at base.

obscurum: *H. nummularium* subsp.

ocymoides: *Halimium ocymoides.*

oelandicum (L.) DC. Low, tufted subshrub; lvs. oblong-lanceolate to lanceolate, ⅜ in. long, green on both surfaces; fls. yellow, ¼ in. across, petals about twice as long as sepals, style shorter than stamens, strongly bent at base. Eur. Subsp. **alpestre** (Jacq.) Breistr. [*H. alpestre* (Jacq.) DC.]. Compact shrub; lvs. pubescent; sepals long-pubescent, with hairs mostly appressed. Mts., cent. and s. Eur.

pilosum (L.) Pers. [*H. violaceum* Pers.]. Low subshrub; lvs. linear to oblong, to ¾ in. long; fls. 1 in. across, sepals yellowish or purplish, petals white with yellow blotch at base. Medit. region.

poliifolium: *H. apenninum.*

praecox: *Tuberaria praecox.*

procumbens: *Fumana procumbens.*

pulverulentum: *H. apenninum.*

rhodanthum: *H. apenninum* var. *roseum.*

roseum: a listed name; perhaps referable to *H. apenninum* var. *roseum,* or a *H. nummularium* cv.

rosmarinifolium Pursh [*Crocanthemum rosmarinifolium* (Pursh) Janch.]. Per., to 2 ft.; lvs. linear, to 1 in. long, white-pubescent beneath; fls. of 2 kinds, the cleistogamous (not opening) in dense clusters, small, on short pedicels, the chasmogamous (opening) few, with petals to ½ in. long, pedicels ½ in. long. Se. U.S.

rotundifolium: *H. cinereum.*

scoparium Nutt. [*Crocanthemum scoparium* (Nutt.) Millsp.]. RUSH ROSE. Suffrutescent, rushlike, to 3 ft.; lvs. linear, to 2 in. long, glabrous to sparsely stellate-pubescent, deciduous in summer; fls. to 1 in. across. Calif. Var. **scoparium.** The typical var.; low-growing and much-branched, to 12 in.; infl. leafy, few-fld. Var. *Aldersonii* (Greene) Munz. Taller, rushlike; fls. many, 1 in. across, in a sparsely leafy, open, spreading panicle. Var. *vulgare* Jeps. Similar to var. *Aldersonii,* but fls. about ½ in. across, in a narrow panicle.

×sulphureum Willd.: *H. apenninum* × *H. nummlarium.* Lvs. linear-lanceolate, to ¾ in. long, grayish-stellate-tomentose beneath; fls. sulphur-yellow.

tigrinum: a listed name of no botanical standing.

Tuberaria: *Tuberaria lignosa.*

umbellatum: *Halimium umbellatum.*

variabile: *H. nummularium.*

velutinum: *H. apenninum.*

violaceum: *H. pilosum.*

vulgare: *H. nummularium.*

HELIANTHOCEREUS: *TRICHOCEREUS.*

HELIANTHUS L. SUNFLOWER. *Compositae* (Helianthus Tribe). About 150 spp. of coarse ann. or per. herbs, native to the New World, often with fibrous or tuberous roots and rhizomes; lvs. opp. in lower part, usually alt. above, simple; fl. heads radiate, rarely discoid, usually solitary on long peduncles, or corymbose, involucre mostly saucer-shaped to

hemispherical, involucral bracts nearly equal to imbricate in 2–4 rows, receptacle flat to convex, scaly; disc fls. many, bisexual, fertile, ray fls. in 1 row, female, sterile, yellow; achenes laterally compressed but with thin edges, pappus early-deciduous, of 2 awns with scalelike bases, sometimes with additional smaller scales.

A few species of sunflowers are grown in borders and masses for the showy bloom, and one for the inulin-rich, edible tubers; the common annual sunflower is cultivated in many parts of the world for its edible seeds, which are used also as feed for poultry and birds, and are important as the source of a drying oil.

No special culture is required for sunflowers. Any ordinary soil in full sun suits them well. Seeds of annuals are sown where the plants are to stand as soon as the weather is settled, or they may be started under glass 2–4 weeks in advance if earlier results are desired. Perennials should bloom the year following seed sowing, or, often, the first year; they may also be divided, and some species are propagated by stolons or offsets.

angustifolius L. SWAMP S. Per., sts. to 6 ft., simple below but paniculately branched above, usually scabrous and hispid; lvs. mostly alt., linear to narrowly lanceolate, to 8 in. long, entire and revolute, scabrous above, pubescent beneath; heads to 3 in. across; disc fls. purple, ray fls. deep yellow. Swamps, N.Y. to Fla., w. to s. Mo., se. Okla., and e. Tex.

annuus L. COMMON S., MIRASOL. Coarse, rough-hairy ann., to 10 ft.; lvs. mostly alt., ovate, to 1 ft. long, truncate to cordate at base, dentate, scabrous-bristly above, hispid beneath, petioles to 1 ft. long; heads to 1 ft. across or more; disc fls. red or purple, ray fls. orange-yellow. Throughout U.S., s. Canada, and n. Mex. Grown commercially in many countries for its seed soil, as well as for the edible seeds themselves. Cv. 'Purpureus'. Heads small; ray fls. wine-red.

atrorubens L. DARK-EYE S. Per., sts. to 3 ft., rough-hairy; lvs. mostly opp., oblong-lanceolate to ovate, scabrous above, to 7 in. long and abruptly narrowed to a winged petiole to about 4 in. long; heads to 2 in. across; disc fls. purple. Dry woods, Va. to Ga., w. to Ky. and La.

cucumerifolius: *H. debilis* subsp.

debilis Nutt. Usually much-branched ann., to 6½ ft., upper brs. scabrous, usually mottled; lvs. mostly alt., triangular-lanceolate to triangular-ovate, to about 3 in. long, more or less cordate, serrate, petioles to about 3 in. long; heads to 3 in. across; disc fls. deep red-purple. Coast of Fla. Subsp. **cucumerifolius** (Torr. & A. Gray) Heiser [*H. cucumerifolius* Torr. & A. Gray]. CUCUMBER-LEAF S. Erect ann., to 3 ft., sts. hispid in lower part; lvs. lanceolate or triangular or triangular-ovate, to 3½ in. long, cuneate to truncate or cordate at base, often undulate, petioles to about 3 in. long. Se. Tex.

decapetalus L. THIN-LEAF S. Per., to 5 ft.; lvs. mostly opp., ovate-lanceolate to ovate, to 8 in. long, long-acuminate, serrate, scabrous to subglabrous, petioles to 2¼ in. long; heads to 3 in. across; disc fls. yellow. Me. to S.C. and Ga., w. to Wisc. and Iowa. Var. **multiflorus**: *H. × multiflorus.*

giganteus L. GIANT S. Rhizomatous per., roots often fleshy, sts. to 10 ft., much branched in upper part, rough-hairy; lvs. mostly alt. above, lanceolate, to 6 in. long, serrate to nearly entire, scabrous above, sessile or with a short petiole; heads to 3 in. across; disc fls. yellow. Moist sites, Me. to n. S.C. and n. Ga., w. to Ill. and Minn.

gracilentus A. Gray. Per., from a woody root crown, sts. tufted, to 5 ft.; lvs. mostly alt., sometimes clustered in. lf. axils, lanceolate to lanceolate-ovate, to 4¾ in. long, hispid, usually entire, nearly sessile to short-petioled; heads to 2 in. across; disc fls. yellow. Dry areas, n. Calif. to n. Baja Calif.

laetiflorus Pers. SHOWY S. Per., to about 7 ft., sts. nearly glabrous to rough-hairy; lvs. mostly opp., lanceolate to narrowly ovate, frequently rhombic-lanceolate, to 11 in. long, acute, firm, serrate, scabrous, sessile to short-petioled; heads to 4 in. across; disc fls. usually yellow, rarely brown to purple. Dry areas, Ind., w. to Minn., Mont. and New Mex. Considered by some authorities to be a hybrid, *H. rigidus* × *H. tuberosus.* Var. **rigidus**: *H. rigidus.*

Maximiliani Schrad. MAXIMILIAN S. Stout per., to about 10 ft., with a woody crown; lvs. mostly alt., lanceolate, to 1 ft. long, acuminate at both ends, entire to serrate, hairy, grayish-green, sessile; heads to 3 in. across, racemose or paniculate; disc fls. yellow. Across s. Canada, s. to N.C., Ky., and Tex.

mollis Lam. ASHY S. Densely and softly hairy per., to 3 ft.; lvs. mostly opp., ovate-lanceolate or ovate, to 3½ in. long, entire to serrulate, scabrous-hispid above, ashy-pubescent beneath, sessile and clasping; heads to 3 in. across; disc fls. yellow. Mass. to n. Ga., w. to Wisc., e. Kans., Okla., and Tex.

×multiflorus L.: *H. annuus* × *H. decapetalus.* Per., to 6 ft., sts.

slightly hispid; lvs. mostly alt., ovate, to 10 in. long, acute; heads to 5 in. across, "single" or "double"; disc fls. sometimes lacking, depending on how double the head is. Not known in the wild.

orgyalis: *H. salicifolius.*

rigidus (Cass.) Desf. [*H. laetiflorus* var. *rigidus* (Cass.) Fern.]. STIFF S. Erect per., to 6 ft., sts. usually red, sparingly to densely scabrous-hispid; lvs. opp. or the uppermost alt., usually oblong-lanceolate to lanceolate-ovate, to 10½ in. long, acuminate, very scabrous, subsessile or on petioles to ¾ in. long; heads to 4 in. across; disc fls. deep red to yellow. S. Man. to Wisc., s. to e. Tex.

salicifolius A. Dietr. [*H. orgyalis* DC.]. Per., to 3 ft., sometimes to 6 ft., sts. mostly glabrous; lvs. mostly alt., crowded, drooping, linear to linear-lanceolate, to 8 in. long, long-acuminate; heads many, to 2 in. across; disc fls. purple-brown. Dry areas and areas with limestone, w. Mo. and e. Kans., s. to Okla. and n. Tex.

tuberosus L. JERUSALEM ARTICHOKE, GIRASOLE. Stout per., to 12 ft., producing edible subterranean potatolike tubers; lvs. mostly alt., only those of the lower ⅓ or ¼ of st. opp., blade ovate-lanceolate or oblong-lanceolate to ovate, to 8 in. long, acuminate, serrate-dentate to dentate, scabrous above, on winged petioles to 3½ in. long; heads to 3½ in. across; disc fls. yellow. Nov. Sc. to Man., s. to n. Fla., La., and Tex. Often cult. here and abroad for the tubers, a commercial source of inulin and a good carbohydrate food for diabetics. Prop. by the tubers, planted in autumn or spring. On good ground the crop needs little attention and can become weedy.

uniflora: *Helianthella uniflora.*

×**HELIAPORUS** Rowley: *Aporocactus* × *Heliocereus. Cactaceae.*

Smithii (Pfeiff.) Rowley [*Aporocactus* ×*Mallisonii* (Pfeiff.) Hort. ex Borg]: *A. flagelliformis* × *H. speciosus.* Sts. creeping, mostly 6 angled, to 1½ in. thick; fls. crimson or variable, tube short or long.

HELICHRYSUM Mill. EVERLASTING, IMMORTELLE. *Compositae* (Inula Tribe). Between 300 and 500 spp. of ann. or per. herbs, subshrubs, or shrubs, native to warmer areas of the Old World, particularly abundant in S. Afr. and Australia; lvs. alt., rarely opp., often downy or woolly; fl. heads discoid, solitary or in terminal clusters, involucre hemispherical to cylindrical, involucral bracts imbricate in many rows, scarious, membranous, often enlarged and petal-like, frequently brightly colored, receptacle naked; fls. all tubular, yellow, bisexual, or the outer row sometimes female; achenes 5-angled to nearly cylindrical, pappus of simple bristles, or plumose only toward apex.

A few species are grown in the flower garden, in the rock garden, or as everlastings for use in winter bouquets. Propagated by seeds sown outdoors or started under glass for earlier bloom, and *H. thianschanicum* also by cuttings.

angustifolium (Lam.) DC. WHITE-LEAF E. Woody-based per., to 1 ft.; lvs. filiform, to 1½ in. long, revolute, white-tomentose; heads to ⅛ in. across, in terminal clusters to 2 in. across, involucral bracts yellow. Medit. region.

apiculatum (Labill.) DC. Silvery-white-tomentose per. herb, to 2 ft.; lvs. obovate-cuneate to oblanceolate or linear, to 2½ in. long; heads ⅛ in. across, in terminal clusters to about 1¾ in. across, involucral bracts golden-yellow, occasionally white to pinkish. Australia.

argyrosphaerum DC. Prostrate per. herb, sts. 6–10 in. long, cobwebby; lvs. linear-oblong or spatulate, to 1 in. long, cobwebby-villous, sessile; heads about ½ in. across, solitary, outer involucral bracts silvery-white, the inner pink. S. Afr.

baccharoides: *H. Hookeri.*

belloides Willd. Much-branched per., sts. to 1½ ft. long, trailing, with erect or ascending brs.; lvs. spatulate to obovate, to ½ in. long, green above, white-woolly beneath; heads to ½ in. across, solitary, involucral bracts spreading, silvery-white. New Zeal. Probably not hardy north of Philadelphia.

bracteatum (Venten.) Andr. STRAWFLOWER. Stout per., but grown as an ann., to 3 ft., sts. branched above, minutely roughened; lvs. oblong-lanceolate, to 5 in. long, green and glabrous or nearly so; heads to 2½ in. across, involucral bracts rigid, glossy, the outer short, the inner petal-like, elongated, yellow, orange, red, or white. Australia. Frequently grown as an everlasting. Cv. **'Monstrosum'** [*H. monstrosum* Hort.]. Heads larger, involucral bracts more numerous.

coralloides (Hook.f.) Benth. Stout, much-branched shrub, to 2 ft.; lvs. appressed, imbricate, oblong, to ¼ in. long, resembling glossy tubercles; heads to 5/16 in. across, solitary. New Zeal.

depressum (Hook.f.) Benth. Nearly erect to prostrate, much-branched shrub to 3 ft., foliage hoary; lvs. appressed, imbricate, linear, 3/32 in. long, silky to woolly on back; heads to ¼ in. across, solitary, involucral bracts few. New Zeal.

diosmifolium (DC.) Less. Erect shrub, to 20 ft.; lvs. linear, to ½ in. long, revolute; heads many in dense terminal corymbs, involucral bracts white tinged with pink. Australia.

Doerfleri Rech.f. Cespitose shrub, to 3¼ in.; rosette lvs. linear-spatulate, to ⅜ in. long, woolly-tomentose, st. lvs. oblanceolate-spatulate, to 1¼ in. long, the uppermost linear; heads to ⅝ in. across, in clusters of 2–3, involucral bracts white; fls. pale yellow. Crete.

frigidum (Labill.) Willd. Subshrub, sts. to 10 in. long, prostrate to ascending, white-tomentose; lvs. linear-oblong, to ¼ in. long, gray-hairy; heads ½–⅝ in. across, solitary, involucral bracts white. Corsica.

fulgidum (L.f.) Willd. Per. herb, to 3 ft., sts. erect, loosely woolly; lvs. oblong to lanceolate, to 8 in. long, scabrous and glandular, margins woolly, st. lvs. shorter; heads to 1½ in. across, in clusters, involucral bracts deep bright yellow. S. Afr. Var. **monocephalum** DC. Heads solitary. S. Afr.

Hookeri (Sond.) Druce [*H. baccharoides* F. J. Muell. ex Benth.]. Erect, much-branched shrub, to 5 ft.; lvs. scalelike, appressed, 3/32 in. long, margins reflexed and concealing lower surface; heads minute, in dense clusters in a leafy thyrsoid panicle, involucral bracts straw-colored. Victoria, Tasmania.

Leontopodium: *Leucogenes Leontopodium.*

marginatum DC. Per. herb, to 10 in., from a thick, woody root; lower lvs. oblong-ligulate, to 2 in. long, upper lvs. linear-oblong, older lvs. glabrous except for woolly margin; heads solitary, involucral bracts radiating, glossy, snowy-white. S. Afr.

microcephalum Camb. Woody-based per., to 3½ ft.; lvs. linear, to ⅜ in. long, tomentose, revolute; heads 3/32 in. across, in compact, terminal corymbs, involucre oblong-cylindrical, involucral bracts pale yellow. W. Medit. region.

Milfordiae Killick. Gray-woolly, cushion-forming per. herb, to 4¾ in.; basal lvs. obovate to spatulate, to ⅝ in. long, st. lvs. lanceolate, elliptic, or spatulate, slightly clasping; heads to 1⅛ in. across, solitary, involucral bracts glossy, white, often crimson, or occasionally brown at base and apex. Basutoland and Natal.

monstrosum: *H. bracteatum* cv.

obcordatum (DC.) F. J. Muell. ex Benth. Erect shrub, to 5 ft., brs. glabrous to downy; lvs. obovate, to ½ in. long, but frequently not over ¼ in. long, leathery, glossy, green above, pale or white beneath; heads ⅛ in. long, many in dense, hemispherical, terminal corymbs to 2 in. across, involucral bracts golden-yellow. Australia, Tasmania.

orientale (L.) DC. Woody-based per., to 16 in.; lvs. linear to oblanceolate-obovate, to 3 in. long, downy on both sides; heads to ½ in. across, in terminal clusters to 3 in. across, involucral bracts straw-colored. Se. Eur.

pachyrhizum Harv. Woody-based per., with many spreading or prostrate shrubby sts. giving rise to many tufted twigs to 2 in. long; lvs. linear-lanceolate to spatulate, to ¾ in. long, white-woolly, sessile; heads solitary or several in clusters, involucral bracts glossy, white or whitish. S. Afr.

petiolatum (L.) DC. LICORICE PLANT. Shrubby per., to 4 ft., sts. flexuous; lvs. ovate to cordate or nearly orbicular, to 1½ in. long including petiole, felty with white, woolly hairs; heads to about ¼ in. across, in terminal clusters of corymbose cymes to 2½ in. across, involucral bracts ivory- or creamy-white. S. Afr.

plicatum (Fisch. & C. A. Mey.) DC. Woody-based per., sts. ascending, to 1½ ft., grooved; lvs. linear or linear-spatulate to oblong, to 5 in. long, gray-pubescent; heads to 5/16 in. across, in terminal, congested, corymbose clusters to 2 in. across, involucral bracts golden-yellow. Se. Eur.

roseum (Lindl.) Druce. Erect, glabrous ann., to 1 ft.; lvs. often opp., linear, to 3 in. long; heads to ⅜ in. long, solitary, on peduncles to 8 in. long, involucre globose, involucral bracts pink. W. Australia.

scorpioides (Poir.) Labill. Erect., per. herb, to 1½ ft.; lvs. oblanceolate to linear, to 3½ in. long, with soft, white, woolly hairs; heads to 1 in. across, solitary, involucre hemispherical, outer involucral bracts brown, woolly, wrinkled, the inner yellow, wrinkled, with green, woolly claw. Se. Australia, Tasmania.

Selago (Hook.f.) Benth. Much-branched shrub, to 15 in., brs. usually crowded; mature lvs. closely appressed, imbricate, ovate-triangular, to ⅛ in. long, keeled on back, glossy outside, woolly inside; heads ¼ in. across, solitary, sessile, involucral bracts dull white. New Zeal. Var. **acutum** Cheesem. Sts. thicker; lvs. to 5/16 in. long, with acute, papery apex. New Zeal.

semipapposum (Labill.) DC. Per., to 1½ ft.; lvs. narrowly linear, to 2 in. long, nearly glabrous, aromatic; heads to ⅜ in. across, many, densely corymbose, involucral bracts golden-yellow. Australia.

Swynnertonii S. L. Moore. Woody-based, per. herb, to 3½ in., sts. gray-tomentose; lvs. oblong-lanceolate to oblong-ovate, gray-tomentose, sessile; heads about 1 in. across, solitary, involucre campanulate, involucral bracts pale whitish-yellow. Rhodesia.

thianschanicum Regel. Much-branched, woody-based, white-woolly, per. herb, to 2 ft.; lvs. linear-lanceolate, acute, entire; heads in corymbs, involucral bracts yellow to orange, somewhat woolly. Turkestan.

virgineum (Sibth. & Sm.) Griseb. White-hairy, cespitose per., to 3 in.; basal lvs. oblong to oblong-spatulate, crowded, to 1½ in. long, st. lvs. linear-spatulate or linear, reduced in size, white-tomentose; heads to ¾ in. across, solitary or in clusters of 2–3, involucral bracts white, glossy. Greece.

HELICODICEROS Schott. *Araceae.* One tuberous, stemless, per. herb of Medit. region; similar to *Dracunculus,* but having spadix with zone of sterile, rudimentary fls. separating the zones of female and male fls.

For culture see *Arisaema.*

muscivorus (L.f.) Engl. [*Arum crinitum* Ait.]. TWIST ARUM. To 2 ft.; lvs. pedate, the spreading central lobe 3-parted, to 10 in. long, lateral lobes 3–4-parted, erect and twisted; spathe bright green outside, spotted with dark olive or purplish, the lower part tubular and 5 in. long, constricted above and bent horizontally, the limb expanded, 10 in. long and 8 in. wide, pale purple, covered with purple hairs, spadix with exserted sterile appendage green, covered with long purple hairs, and malodorous. Corsica, Sardinia, Balearic Is.

HELICONIA L. LOBSTER-CLAW, FALSE BIRD-OF-PARADISE. *Heliconiaceae*(sometimes placed in *Musaceae*or *Strelitziaceae*) with characters of the family.

Heliconias are grown in the warm greenhouse or outdoors in warm regions, both for their decorative foliage and for the brilliant bracts of the inflorescence. Plants make large clumps if given room and thrive in rich loam with plenty of water. Propagation by division of the rhizomes, or by seeds when available.

amazonica: a listed name of no botanical standing.

angustifolia: H. bicolor.

aurantiaca Ghiesbr. ex Lem. Sts. to 5 ft.; lvs. borne along entire length of st., to 12 in. long and 2½ in. wide; infl. terminal, erect, compact, glabrous, bracts 2–5, orange, shading to green at tip, 2–3 in. long; fls. 5–8 in each bract, yellowish-white to orange. S. Mex. to Cent. Amer.

aureostriata: H. striata.

bicolor Benth. [*H. angustifolia* Hook.; *H. brasiliensis* cv. 'Flava']. Sts. 4–5 ft.; lvs. 3 ft. long, 10 in. wide, petioles with light brown tomentose patches; infl. erect, nearly sessile, bracts 6–10, 2-ranked, lanceolate, remote, red or yellow, glabrous; fls. 2–2½ in. long, white, to green at tip, ovary and peduncle red or yellow according to color of bract, ovaries exserted beyond edge of bract. Brazil.

Bihai L.f. [*H. distans* Griggs]. WILD PLANTAIN, FALSE P., BALISIER, FIREBIRD, MACAW FLOWER. Similar to *H. caribaea,* but shorter and with lf. tips gradually acute; infl. short-peduncled, bracts to 6, scarlet with yellow tips, margins and inner surface widely separated; fls. with white-tipped segms. Lesser Antilles, n. S. Amer. Probably not cult.; plants under this name are usually *H. caribaea, H. humilis,* or *H. Wagnerana.*

brasiliensis Hook. [*H. speciosa* Hort. ex Horan.]. Lvs. green above, paler beneath, to 2 ft. long, long-petioled; infl. erect, puberulous, bracts lanceolate, remote, scarlet, glabrous; fls. yellow or red. Brazil. Plants listed in the trade by this name are usually referable to *H. bicolor.* Cv. 'Flava': H. bicolor.

caribaea Lam. WILD PLANTAIN, BALISIER. Sts. to 6 ft.; lvs. 3–6 ft. long, 1 ft. wide, petioles 3–5 ft. long; infl. erect, sessile, rachis straight but hidden by the bracts, bracts 6–15, 2-ranked, broadly triangular, overlapping, solid red or sometimes yellow or green, lower bracts to 10 in. long, 2–3 in. high, becoming shorter toward the tip of the infl.; fls. white with green tip. W. Indies.

coccinea: a listed name of no botanical standing.

Collinsiana: H. pendula.

curtispatha Petersen. Sts. to 20 ft.; lvs. 6–9 ft. long, 18–24 in. wide, petioles 2–4 ft. long; infl. pendent, 4–8 ft. long, bracts 25–40, 2-ranked, reflexed, red, all nearly the same size, 4 in. long, 1½ in. high; fls. 18–24 in each bract, yellow. Panama and Costa Rica.

distans: H. Bihai.

Edwardus-Rex Hort. Sander. Sts. to 1 ft.; lvs. 1½ ft. long, to 6 in. wide, pale yellowish-green with red midrib and blotches on upper surface, rich crimson beneath; fls. unknown. New Guinea. A hort. form not placed botanically.

elongata: H. Wagnerana.

flava: a listed name of no botanical standing.

humilis Jacq. LOBSTER-CLAW. Sts. to 4 ft.; lvs. to 5 ft. long, 10 in. wide; infl. erect, short-peduncled, bracts 3–6, 2-ranked, not overlapping, red with green tip and edge, rachis slightly flexuous; fls. white with green tip. N. S. Amer. A dwarf form ascribed to this sp. is also in cult., the entire plant being less than 2 ft. high.

indica var. **aureostriata:** H. striata.

illustris Ball. ex M. T. Mast. Lvs. ovate-lanceolate, to 1 ft. long, 4 in. wide, midrib, marginal nerves, and petioles bright rose. A hort. form from S. Pacific not placed botanically. Cv. 'Rubricaulis'. Sts. redder.

Jacquinii: a listed name of no botanical standing.

latispatha Benth. Sts. to 10 ft.; lvs. 3–5 ft. long, 1 ft. wide; infl. upright, usually borne conspicuously above the lvs., 12–20 in. high, bracts 10–20, spirally arranged, remote, yellowish-green through bright orange to dark red in different populations; fls. yellow, fading to green at tips and edges of segms., 20–24 in each bract. S. Mex. to Cent. Amer.; one of the commonest and most conspicuous roadside spp.

Mariae Hook.f. BEEFSTEAK H. Sts. to 10 ft.; lvs. 10 ft. long, 24–30 in. wide, the entire plant often more than 24 ft. high; infl. pendent, 12–30 in. long, peduncle 12–30 in. long, bracts 40–70, 2-ranked, overlapping, dark crimson; fls. 12 in each bract, pink, shading to white at base. Honduras to n. S. Amer.

metallica Planch. & Linden ex Hook. [*Heliconia* cv. 'Frosty']. Sts. 4 ft.; lvs. 2–3 ft. long, 1 ft. wide, velvety green above with a silvery midrib blending into the blade, metallic-purple beneath; infl. erect, peduncle 1 ft. long, bracts 4–8, 2-ranked, linear-lanceolate, distant, green; fls. 3 in. long, deep pink with white tips, ovary green at apex blending into the white pedicel. Colombia.

osaensis Cuf. Sts. 6–10 ft.; lvs. nearly sessile, 3–4 ft. long, 8 in. wide; infl. terminal, erect, 1 ft. high, bracts 6–10, 2-ranked, red, remote, narrow; fls. 10–15 in each bract, orange, 2 in. long. Golfo Dulce area (Costa Rica).

pendula Wawra. [*H. Collinsiana* Griggs]. Sts. to 6 ft.; lvs. 2–3 ft. long, 10–12 in. wide; infl. pendulous, bracts 6–9, spirally arranged, reflexed, red, tapering in size from tip of infl., where 3 in. long, to base, where 12–18 in. long; fls. 15–20 in each bract, yellow. Guatemala to Peru. Any plants with pendulous, red-bracted infls. in cult. have usually been grown as *H. Collinsiana,* but it is probable that more than 1 sp. is actually involved.

platystachys Bak. Lvs. oblong, to 4 ft. long, 1 ft. wide, glabrous; infl. pendulous, short-peduncled, 1 ft. long, rachis brown-hairy, bracts few, lanceolate, remote, to 8 in. long; fls. few, pedicels hairy. Guatemala or Colombia.

psittacorum L.f. PARROT'S PLANTAIN, PARROT'S FLOWER, PARAKEET F. Sts. to more than 6 ft.; lvs. 12–18 in. long, 2–4 in. wide, borne along entire length of st.; infl. terminal, erect, peduncle 6–12 in. long, bracts 3–6, narrow, green or orange, shading to red at tip, glaucous; fls. orange with green tip. N. S. Amer. A dwarf form of this sp. which does not exceed 18 in. in total height is also in cult.

rostrata Ruiz & Pav. Sts. to 6 ft. (usually shorter in cult.); lvs. 2–4 ft. long, 6–12 in. wide; infl. pendulous, 1–2 ft. long, rachis red, bracts 15–20, 2-ranked, not overlapping, red at base, shading to yellow at tip with green edge, 4 in. long, nearly the same size along entire length of infl.; fls. greenish-yellow. Argentina to Peru.

rubra Sessé & Moç. A poorly understood sp. Cult. material under this name probably belongs to some other sp.

Schneeana Steyerm. Sts. to 6 ft.; lvs. 3–4 ft. long, 10–14 in. wide; infl. erect, long-peduncled, emergent from lvs., bracts red, narrow, reflexed on older infls.; fls. yellow. Venezuela.

Schiedeana Klotzsch. To 6 ft.; lvs. oblong, to 3½ ft. long, 9 in. wide, pubescent on midrib beneath; infl. erect, bracts red or orange-red, reflexed, rachis red; fls. yellow; fr. blue. Mex.

speciosa: H. brasiliensis.

spectabilis L. Linden & Rodig. Lvs. long-petioled, oblong-lanceolate, 18 in. long, 8 in. wide. A hort. form not placed botanically.

striata Hort. Veitch ex Guilm. [*H. aureostriata* Hort. ex Rodig.; *H. indica* Lam. var. *aureostriata* Hort.]. Sts. striped green and yellow; lvs. with transverse veins striped bright yellow; fls. unknown. Is. of w. Pacific.

stricta: H. Wagnerana.

velutina: a listed name of no botanical standing.

Wagnerana Petersen. [*H. elongata* Griggs; *H. stricta* J. Huber]. Sts. to 4 ft.; lvs. 4–6 ft. long, 1 ft. wide, undulate; infl. erect, sessile, bracts 12–20, 2-ranked, heavy, overlapping, deep pink to pale crimson, shading to cream at base with green edge; fls. white with dark green tip. Costa Rica and Panama.

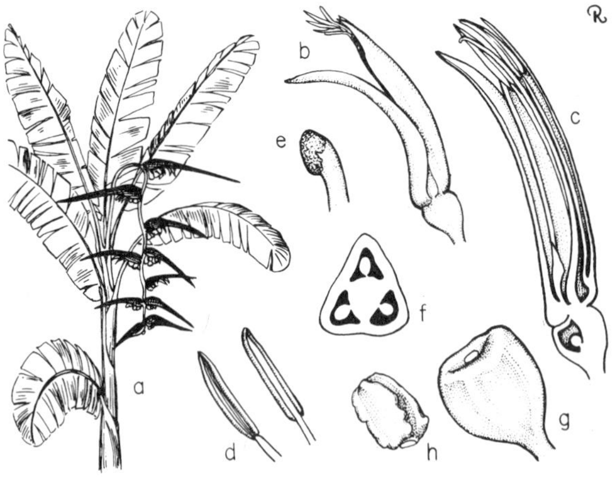

HELICONIACEAE. *Heliconia* aff. *pendula:* **a,** flowering plant, much reduced; **b,** flower, X ½; **c,** flower, vertical section, X ¾; **d,** anther, two views, X 1; **e,** stigma, X 5; **f,** ovary, cross section, X 1½; **g,** fruit, X 1; **h,** seed, X 1.

HELICONIACEAE. (Endl.) Nakai. HELICONIA FAMILY. Monocot.; 1 genus, *Heliconia,* and about 150 spp. of dwarf to large herbs, native to trop. Amer., a few spp. to islands of Pacific; lvs. 2-ranked, bananalike; fls. clustered in axils of stiff, showy, boat-shaped bracts in an erect or pendulous, terminal infl., bisexual, sepals and petals variously partly united, fertile stamens 5, staminode 1, ovary 3-celled, 3-ovuled; fr. a 1–3-seeded, berrylike caps.

HELICTERES L. *Byttneriaceae.* About 40 spp. of shrubs or small trees, native to trop. Amer. and Asia; lvs. alt., 2-ranked, simple; fls. axillary, solitary or in clusters, calyx tubular, 3–5-cleft, often 2-lipped, petals 5, clawed, equal or unequal in size, the smaller usually auriculate-appendaged, androgynophore present, often very long, staminal tube short, stamens 6, 8, or 10, in pairs alternating with obscure or conspicuous staminodes; fr. of 5 many-seeded, nearly cylindrical follicles, usually spirally twisted around one another.

Isora L. Shrubby, to 12 ft.; lvs. broadly obovate, 2–8 in. long, serrate, more or less lobed apically, rounded to cordate basally; fls. fascicled, in 2–3-fld. small cymes, calyx yellowish, to ¾ in. long, petals bluish, then bright red, 1–1½ in. long; fr. 1½–3 in. long, twisted, not bristly. Malay Arch.

HELICTOTRICHON Bess. ex Roem. & Schult. *Gramineae.* About 30–40 spp. of tufted per. grasses in Eurasia and N. Amer.; panicles rather narrow; spikelets glossy, 3- to several-fld., rachilla bearded, disarticulating above the glumes and between the florets, glumes about equal, 1–5-nerved, lemma convex, several-nerved, with twisted and geniculate awns much longer than spikelets. For terminology see *Gramineae.*

sempervirens (Vill.) Pilg. [*Avena sempervirens* Vill.]. Sts. to 5 ft.; lf. blades glaucous, involute; panicle to 6 in. long; spikelets to ½ in. long, bisexual florets 2, hairy at base, hairs as long as floret, rachilla not disarticulating, glumes 1–3-nerved, lemma irregularly toothed, slightly longer than the glumes, lemma of lower floret awned. Eur.

HELIOCARPUS L. *Tiliaceae.* About 22 spp. of trees and shrubs, native to trop. Amer.; lvs. simple, lobed or unlobed; fls. small, unisexual or bisexual, in cymose panicles, sepals 4–5, sometimes with apical appendages, petals 0 or 4–5, glandular at base, stamens to about 40, in female fls. often present as sterile filaments, ovary 2-celled; fr. a flattened caps., indehiscent, with a biseriate fringe of mostly plumose hairs around the margin, cells with 2 seeds separated by a septum.

popayanensis HBK [*H. trichopodus* Turcz.]. Large tree, young brs. often floccose-stellate; lvs. ovate to suborbicular, to 8 in. long, acuminate, truncate to cordate, unlobed or shallowly and acutely 3-lobed, serrate; sepals 4, without appendages, petals 4, about ⅛ in. long, stamens about 16; caps. short-stalked, less than ¼ in. long, plumose fringe about $^3/_{16}$ in. long. Panama, s. to trop. S. Amer.

trichopodus: *H. popayanensis.*

HELIOCEREUS (A. Berger) Britt. & Rose. *Cactaceae.* About 5 spp. of few-ribbed, slender cacti, native to Mex. and Cent. Amer.; sts. erect or procumbent, ribs 3–7; spines needle-shaped or bristlelike; fls. funnelform, diurnal, showy, mostly red, with short tube, stamens many, declined, ovary spiny. Differs from *Nopalxochia* in the spiny ovary and in sts. with more ribs and spines.

For culture see *Cacti.*

cinnabarinus (Eichlam) Britt. & Rose. Sts. to 1¼ in. thick, ribs 3–4, weakly sinuate; areoles to 1½ in. apart, spines 10–12, needle-shaped, brown, to ¼ in. long; fls. brick-red, 4 in. long, 2 in. across, inner perianth segms. minutely pointed. Guatemala.

coccineus Britt. & Rose [*H. elegantissimus* Britt. & Rose]. Sts. decumbent, light green, 1–2 in. thick, ribs 3–4, toothed; areoles about ¾ in. apart, spines 8–14, the upper needle-shaped, $^3/_{32}$ in. long, the lower bristlelike, ¼ in. long; fls. scarlet, to 6 in. across, inner perianth segms. acuminate, style red, not exceeding stamens. Mex.

elegantissimus: *H. coccineus.*

speciosus (Cav.) Britt. & Rose. SUN CACTUS. Sts. clambering, bright green, reddish when young, 1–2 in. thick, ribs 3–5, crenate; areoles to 1¼ in. apart, spines 8–11, needle-shaped, ½ in. long; fls. scarlet, to 6 in. across, inner perianth segms. minutely pointed or rounded; fr. ovoid, 2 in. long. Cent. Mex. Var. **amecamensis** (Heese) Backeb. & F. M. Knuth. Fls. white. Cent. Mex.

superbus (C. A. Ehrenb.) A. Berger. Ribs 7; perhaps a var. of *H. speciosus.*

HELIOPHILA E. P. Phillips. *Cruciferae.* More than 100 spp. of S. Afr., usually ann. herbs, or rarely shrubby; lvs. usually linear, entire, toothed, sinuate, or pinnatisect; fls. yellow, white, pink, or blue, in long leafless racemes, sepals and petals 4; fr. a flattened or cylindrical silique, often pendulous or deflexed, with edges straight or sinuate, valves flat, often membranous.

leptophylla Schlechter. Ann., to 1½ ft., blue-green and glaucous; lvs. filiform, to 2 in. long; fls. blue with yellow center, to ½ in. across, in loose, many-fld. racemes; siliques drooping, moniliform.

linearifolia Burchell ex DC. Subshrubby, sts. erect or decumbent, to 3 ft.; lvs. linear, to 1 in. long, entire; fls. blue, with yellow center, in 10–16-fld. loose racemes; siliques linear, to 2 in. long, 3-nerved, not constricted between seeds.

longifolia DC. Branched ann., to 15 in. or sometimes more, brs. wandlike; lvs. linear, to 2 in. long, entire or 3-lobed; fls. rich blue, about ½ in. across; siliques to 2 in. long, constricted between the seeds. The blue fls. and wandlike brs. make this sp. reminiscent of flax.

HELIOPSIS Pers. OXEYE. *Compositae* (Helianthus Tribe). Twelve spp. of per. or ann. herbs, native to the New World; lvs. opp., simple; fl. heads radiate, terminal and solitary on brs., involucral bracts in 1–2 rows, nearly equal, receptacle convex to conical, scaly, often hollow; disc fls. bisexual, yellow to brownish-yellow, purple, or red, ray fls. female, fertile, orange-yellow to yellow, or purple; achenes 4-sided, or triangular with the outer surface convex, pappus of a few teeth, or an irregular crown, or lacking.

Culture as for *Helianthus;* blooming in summer.

helianthoides (L.) Sweet [*H. laevis* Pers.]. Short-lived, nearly glabrous per., to 5 ft.; lf. blades lanceolate-ovate to oblong-ovate, to 4¾ in. long, serrate, petioles 1½ in. long; heads to 2½ in. across; disc fls. brownish-yellow, ray fls. pale yellow. N.Y. to Mich. and n. Ill., s. to Ga., Ala., and Miss. Cv. **'Pitcherana'** [*H. Pitcherana* Hort.]. Sts. to 3 ft., much-branched; fls. more numerous, ray fls. deeper yellow. Subsp. **scabra** (Dunal) T. R. Fisher [*H. scabra* Dunal]. Sts. slightly pubescent in upper part; lf. blades lanceolate to ovate-lanceolate, scabrous above, glabrous beneath, petioles to 1 in. long; ray fls. orange-yellow. Mo. and cent. Ill., s. to e. Tex. and w. La. Extremely variable; cvs. include: **'Excelsa',** heads nearly "double," ray fls. chrome-yellow; **'Gratissima',** ray fls. pale yellow; **'Incomparabilis'** [*H. incomparabilis* Hort.], heads "double," to 3 in. across, fls. golden-yellow; **'Patula'** [*H. patula* Hort.], to 2½ ft., ray fls. golden-yellow; **'Vitellina'**, heads "double," fls. golden-yellow; **'Zinniiflora'**, heads "double."

incomparabilis: *H. helianthoides* subsp. *scabra* cv.

laevis: *H. helianthoides.*

Lemoinei: a listed name for a plant described as a compact per., to 4 ft., with golden-yellow, semidouble heads to 4 in. across.

patula: *H. helianthoides* subsp. *scabra* cv.

Pitcherana: *H. helianthoides* cv.

scabra: *H. helianthoides* subsp.

HELIOSPERMA: *SILENE.* **H. albanicum:** *S. quadridentata.* **H. alpestre:** *S. quadrifida.* **H. monochorum:** *S. quadridentata.*

HELIOTROPIUM L. HELIOTROPE, TURNSOLE. *Boraginaceae.* About 250 spp. of mostly hairy, rarely glabrous herbs, subshrubs, and shrubs of temp. and trop. regions of all continents; lvs. simple, alt. or rarely nearly opp.; fls. blue, purple, pink, or white, in scorpioid cymes, or sometimes axillary, calyx deeply 5-lobed, corolla 5-lobed, without scales in the throat, stamens 5, included, ovary 4-celled, not lobed; fr. of 4 nutlets, which separate or cohere in pairs.

Some species are popular in greenhouse and borders, others are weedy plants; one species is used in perfumery. The greenhouse heliotropes are treated as annuals and require abundant heat and light rich soil. Propagated by cuttings and seeds; seeds may be sown indoors and the seedlings transplanted. Strong plants may be set out and the new growths pegged to the ground where they will form roots.

arborescens L. [*H. peruvianum* L.]. HELIOTROPE, CHERRY-PIE. Hairy per., to 4 ft.; lvs. elliptic or oblong-lanceolate, 1–3 in. long; fls. violet or purple, varying to white, fragrant, to ¼ in. long. Peru. Common under glass and sometimes planted out. In s. Eur. cult. for use in perfume.

convolvulaceum (Nutt.) A. Gray. Hispid ann., to 1 ft.; lvs. lanceolate to ovate, to 1½ in. long; fls. white, fragrant, ½ in. long, solitary in lf. axils. Calif. to Tex., adjacent Mex.

curassavicum L. SEASIDE H. Glabrous, fleshy ann. or short-lived per., to 2 ft.; lvs. linear to obovate or spatulate, succulent, to 1½ in. long; fls. white with a yellow eye, turning to violet-purple, 3/16 in. long. Frequent in alkaline or saline areas of the U.S.; widely distributed throughout the world.

hybridum: a listed name of no botanical standing, probably referable to *H. arborescens.*

peruvianum: *H. arborescens.*

regale: a listed name of no botanical standing.

tenellum (Nutt.) Torr. Strigose-canescent, erect ann., to 1½ ft.; lvs. linear, to 1½ in. long, with revolute margins; fls. white, to ⅛ in. long, solitary in lf. axils or terminal. Ala. to Tex., n. to Mo., e. to Ky. Some material cult. under this name may be *H. convolvulaceum.*

HELIPTERUM DC. [*Acroclinium* A. Gray; *Rhodanthe* Lindl.]. EVERLASTING, STRAWFLOWER. *Compositae* (Inula Tribe). Between 60 and 90 spp. of ann. or per. herbs, subshrubs, or shrubs, native to S. Afr., Australia, and Tasmania; lvs. alt., very rarely opp., entire; fl. heads discoid, solitary, clustered, or corymbose, involucre broadly hemispherical, narrow-ovoid, or cylindrical, involucral bracts many, imbricate in several rows, scarious, often petal-like and colored, receptacle flat, convex, or conical, naked; fls. all tubular, bisexual, or the outer row female; achenes usually nearly cylindrical, pappus of 1 row of plumose bristles.

Of simple culture. Seeds usually are sown where plants are to grow, but may be started indoors for earlier results. Flowers are often cut and dried for winter bouquets.

albicans (A. Cunn.) DC. [*H. incanum* (Hook.) DC.]. Gray-woolly ann. or perhaps even per., to 16 in.; lvs. alt., mostly near base of sts. or brs., obovate-oblong to oblanceolate or linear, to 5 in. long; heads to 1½ in. across, solitary, involucre hemispherical, outer involucral bracts silvery, the inner yellow or white, sometimes tinged with pink. Australia.

anthemoides (Sieber) DC. Per., to 1 ft., sts. simple, glabrous or with short, scattered hairs; lvs. often crowded and erect, linear, about ⅜ in. long; heads to 1 in. across, solitary, involucre hemispherical, outer involucral bracts white, tinged brown, the inner white. E. Australia, Tasmania.

corymbiflorum Schlechtend. Erect, white-woolly ann., to 1 ft.; lvs. linear to lanceolate, to 1½ in. long, semiclasping; heads about 1 in. across, in loose terminal corymbs, involucre turbinate, outer involucral bracts golden-brown, the inner white. Australia.

Humboldtianum (Gaud.-Beaup.) DC. [*H. Sandfordii* Hook.]. Erect, sparsely woolly ann., to 1½ ft.; lvs. linear to linear-lanceolate, to 1¼ in. long, white-tomentose; heads 5/16 in. across, in dense clusters arranged in corymbs to 4 in. across, involucre cylindrical, outer involucral bracts brown, the inner pale or bright yellow. W. Australia.

incanum: *H. albicans.*

Manglesii (Lindl.) F. J. Muell. ex Benth. [*Rhodanthe Manglesii* Lindl.]. SWAN RIVER E. Erect, glabrous ann., to 2 ft., corymbosely branched; lvs. oblong to ovate, to 4 in. long, cordate and clasping at base, glaucous; heads to 1½ in. across, solitary on long peduncles, involucral bracts radiating, light to bright pink. W. Australia. Cv. **'Maculatum'.** Sts. taller, more vigorous; involucral bracts bright pink, with blood-red spots.

roseum (Hook.) Benth. [*Acroclinium roseum* Hook.]. Stout, glabrous ann., to 2 ft.; lvs. linear to lanceolate, to 2½ in. long; heads to 2 in. across, solitary on long peduncles, involucre hemispherical, involucral bracts rose to white. W. Australia.

Sandfordii: *H. Humboldtianum.*

HELLEBORUS L. HELLEBORE. *Ranunculaceae.* About 20 spp. of per. herbs with stout rootstocks, native to limestone regions of Eur. and Asia; lvs. mostly basal, palmately divided; fls. in cymes, sepals 5, green or petaloid, petals forming inconspicuous nectaries, stamens many; fr. of 3–10 sessile follicles.

Hellebores have a burning taste and are very poisonous. They bloom in early spring in the North or in winter in mild climates, although the flowers of *H. niger* are very durable and cold-resistant. They thrive in partially shaded, moist situations in good soil, and are propagated by division, preferably in late summer or autumn; also by seeds; they may also be forced under glass.

abchasicus A. Braun. Evergreen, radical lvs. 2–4, about 1 ft. across, segms. 5–7, lanceolate-ovate, doubly serrate; scape to 1½ ft., 3–4-fld.; fls. drooping, maroon or red-purple, with small darker spots, 2½–3 in. across, sepals narrow, pointed. Caucasus.

antiquorum A. Braun. Evergreen, to 12 in.; lvs. 1–2, to 1 ft. long, segms. 5–7, elliptic, sharply toothed; fls. 2½ in. across, cup-shaped, red-purple. Olympus Mts. in Turkey. Plants cult. as *H. olympicus* or *H. orientalis* may belong here.

atropurpureus: *H. atrorubens.*

atrorubens Waldst. & Kit. [*H. atropurpureus* Schult.; *H. cupreus* Host]. Evergreen only in mild climates, lf. segms. mostly 9, broadly lanceolate, sharply serrate; fls. 2–9, deep maroon with violet tinge, becoming more violet in age, 1½–2 in. across. Hungary, Austria.

caucasicus: *H. orientalis;* however garden plants named *H. caucasicus* may be hybrids.

corsicus: *H. lividus* subsp.

cupreus: *H. atrorubens.*

cyclophyllus Boiss. Deciduous, radical lf. 1, large, segms. 7–9, broadly lanceolate, more or less divided; fls. 3–4, round, bright green, 2½ in. across, sepals broad, overlapping. Balkan Pen.

foetidus L. Evergreen, foetid per., sts. leafy, to 1½ ft., glandular in upper part; lower st. lvs. with segms. 3–9, dark green, narrow-lanceolate, middle st. lvs. passing into broadly ovate entire bracts; fls. many, drooping, bell-shaped or globular, pale green, ½–1¼ in. across. W. and s. Eur.

lividus Ait. Sts. leafy, to 1 ft.; lf. segms. 3, not or slightly toothed, marbled in paler green above, purplish underneath; fls. 2½ in. across, sepals pale green or suffused with purple. Subsp. **lividus.** The typical subsp.; lf. segms. entire or with small teeth. Balearic Is. Subsp. **corsicus** (Willd.) Tutin [*H. corsicus* Willd.]. Lf. segms. spinescent-dentate. Corsica, Sardinia.

niger L. CHRISTMAS ROSE. Evergreen, acaulescent; lf. segms. ovate-cuneate, slightly toothed toward apex; fls. usually borne singly on red-spotted peduncles, white, sometimes suffused with pink, 2–3 in. across or more. Eur. Has been used medicinally. Cvs. **'Angustifolius'** and **'Praecox'.** Fls. smaller. Cvs. **'Major'** and **'Multiflorus'** are listed. Subsp. **macranthus** (Freyn) Schiffn. [cv. 'Maximus']. Peduncle not spotted, more dwarf.

odorus Waldst. & Kit. Evergreen, caulescent, to 2 ft.; radical lf. usually 1, segms. 7–11, broadly lanceolate, finely toothed; scape to 1 ft., few-fld.; fls. round, yellowish-green, 2–3 in. across, sepals 5, ovate. Danube R. region. Cv. **'Atrosanguineus'** is listed.

olympicus Lindl. Evergreen; lf. segms. 5–7, linear-oblong, serrate;

fls. 2–3, white, green at base, pendent, not spotted, 2½–3 in. across. Greece. Plants cult. under this name may be *H. antiquorum.*

orientalis Lam. [*H. caucasicus* A. Braun.]. LENTEN ROSE. Evergreen; lvs. to 16 in. across, segms. 7–9, elliptic-oblong, sharply serrate; scapes to 15 in.; fls. cream on opening, fading to brown, to 3 in. across. Macedonia, Thrace, Asia Minor. Plants cult. under this name may be *H. antiquorum.* Cvs. **'Alba'** and **'Atropurpureus'** are listed.

purpurascens Waldst. & Kit. Deciduous, pilose; radical lvs. large, segms. mostly 5, broadly cuneate, deeply divided into 3–6 serrate parts; scape low, 3-fld.; fls. to 3 in. across, sepals spreading, broad, dull greenish inside, purple-violet outside with darker veins. Hungary and Poland to the Balkans.

rubra: a listed name of no botanical standing.

viridis L. Deciduous, sts. erect, to 16 in.; radical lvs. usually 2, segms. 7–11, narrow-elliptic, prominently serrate; st. lvs. smaller, similar; fls. 2–4, drooping, 1–2 in. across, sepals spreading, yellow-green. Eur.; naturalized in e. N. Amer.

HELONIAS L. *Liliaceae.* One sp., a spring-blooming, per. herb with tuberous rhizomes, native from N.J. to nw. Ga.; lvs. basal; fls. in a dense, bracted, spikelike raceme terminating a stout, hollow scape, perianth segms. 6, distinct, spreading, stamens 6, filaments longer than perianth, styles 3, separate to base; fr. a 3-lobed, 3-valved, loculicidal caps., seeds many, linear, with white appendage at each end.

Suitable for bog gardens. Easily propagated by division.

bullata L. SWAMP PINK. Glabrous, to 3 ft. when mature; lvs. oblong-spatulate, to 15 in. long and 2 in. wide; fls. fragrant, pink or purplish, ¼ in. long, anthers blue.

HELONIOPSIS A. Gray. *Liliaceae.* About 4 spp. of rhizomatous, per. herbs, native to Korea, Japan, and Taiwan; lvs. in basal rosette; fls. campanulate, drooping, few, in a loose raceme or somewhat umbellate, perianth segms. 6, separate, stamens 6, anthers versatile, purple-blue, filaments red, style longer than perianth, entire, red, tipped by purple stigma; fr. a 3-valved, loculicidal caps., seeds many, linear, with an appendage at each end.

Does best in a cool, moist but well-drained soil. Propagated by seeds or division.

breviscapa: *H. orientalis* var.

japonica: *H. orientalis.*

orientalis (Thunb.) T. Tanaka [*H. japonica* Maxim.]. To 10 in. or more; lvs. oblanceolate, to 4 in. long, acute, green, usually flushed reddish-purple beneath; fls. carmine-red, ½ in. long, usually 3–10 in a raceme, perianth segms. oblanceolate, spreading, as long as pedicels. Japan, Korea, Sakhalin. Var. **breviscapa** (Maxim.) Ohwi [*H. breviscapa* Maxim.]. Fls. bluish-white, to ⅝ in. long, in an umbellate raceme. Japan.

HELWINGIA Willd. *Cornaceae.* Three spp. of dioecious, deciduous shrubs, native to e. Asia; lvs. alt., simple, toothed; fls. small, borne in clusters on upper surface of lvs., sepals obsolete, petals and stamens 3–5; fr. a berrylike drupe.

One species is sometimes grown as a curiosity and ornamental. Propagated by cuttings of green wood under glass.

japonica (Thunb.) F. Dietr. To 5 ft.; lvs. ovate, to 3 in. long, glabrous; fls. greenish-white; fr. black, ¼ in. in diam. Early summer. China and Japan. Zone 5.

HELXINE: see *SOLEIROLIA.*

HEMEROCALLIS L. DAYLILY. *Liliaceae.* Perhaps 15 spp. of clump-forming, per. herbs, native from cent. Eur. to China and especially in Japan; roots fibrous or more or less tuberous; lvs. basal, linear, keeled, often rather grasslike; fls. ephemeral, yellow, orange, reddish, or purplish, in clusters on long scapes, perianth funnelform to campanulate, segms. 6, joined below into a tube, stamens 6, anthers versatile, filaments inserted in throat of perianth; fr. a 3-valved, loculicidal caps., seeds few.

An important group of hardy spring- and summer-blooming herbs with lilylike flowers; of simple cultural requirements in any good garden soil. Propagated by division, and sometimes by seeds if available. The species fall into two groups, as determined by the type of inflorescence: those in which the flowers are borne in a more or less open or branched cluster terminating the scape; and those including only *H. Dumortieri* and *H. Middendorffii* in which the flowers are close together and almost sessile in a headlike cluster subtended by broad, short bracts resembling an involucre. In recent years daylilies have been extensively hybridized and greatly improved, so that there are many new cultivars, and the original species, with 2 or 3 exceptions, less commonly planted.

altissima Stout. To 6 ft., main roots coarsely fibrous, a few enlarged; lvs. to about 5 ft. long and 1⅛ in. wide; fls. nocturnal, fragrant, pale yellow, 4 in. long and 4 in. across, perianth tube to 1½ in. long. Summer and autumn. China.

aurantiaca Bak. To 3 ft., with spreading rhizomes, main roots enlarged; lvs. 2–3 ft. long and 1 in. wide or more, sharply keeled, coarse, remaining green until winter; fls. nearly sessile, orange and often flushed with purple, to 4 in. across, not opening as widely as in some other spp., perianth tube to ¾ in. long. Summer. China. Var. **major** Bak. Less hardy, fls. larger, opening to 6 in. across.

Baronii: *H.* × *ochroleuca* cv.

citrina Baroni. To 4 ft., roots tapering, elongated, fleshy; lvs. to 3½ ft. long, over 1 in. wide, coarse; fls. many, nocturnal, fragrant, lemon-yellow, to 6 in. long, perianth tube to 1½ in. long, lobes to ⅝ in. wide. Midsummer. China. Cv. **'Baronii':** *H.* × *ochroleuca* cv.

Dumortieri E. Morr. [*H. graminea* Schlechtend.; *H. Sieboldii* Hort. ex Bak.]. To 1½ ft., main roots very fleshy; lvs. to 1½ ft. long and ½ in. wide; scape unbranched, spreading, shorter than lvs.; fls. 2–4, almost sessile, in close clusters subtended by broad, lanceolate bracts as long as pedicels, fragrant, pale orange, 2½ in. long, perianth tube to ¼ in. long. Spring. Japan.

earliana: a listed name, for *Hemerocallis* cv. 'Earliana', an old hybrid to 24 in. high, with large, wide-petalled, yellow-orange fls.

esculenta: *H. Middendorffii* var.

flava: *H. Lilioasphodelus.*

flavina: a listed name, for *Hemerocallis* cv. 'Flavina'; to 1 ft., fls. lemon-yellow. Summer.

Forrestii Diels. To 1½ ft., roots fleshy; lvs. to 1½ ft. long and ½ in. wide, ascending and recurving; scape slender, ascending, not longer than lvs., bracts of infl. conspicuous; fls. 4 or more, not fragrant, clear cadmium-yellow, to 3 in. long, perianth tube about ½ in. long. Spring. Sw. China.

fulva (L.) L. ORANGE D., TAWNY D., FULVOUS D. To 6 ft., forming clumps by spreading rhizomes, main roots fleshy; lvs. to 2 ft. long and 1⅜ in. wide; scapes erect; fls. not fragrant, fulvous- or rusty-orange-red, usually with darker zone and stripes, to 5 in. long and 3½ in. across when fully opened, perianth tube to 1 in. long. Summer. Eur., Asia; naturalized in e. U.S.; probably introd. very early into Eur. The old, well-known, commonly cult. form is a self-sterile triploid and does not ordinarily set seed; it has been distinguished as cv. 'Europa'. Cv. **'Cypriana'**. Lvs. glossy; fls. many, brownish, to 4½ in. across. Cv. **'Flore Pleno':** cv. 'Kwanso'. Cv. **'Kwanso'** [cv. 'Flore Pleno'; var. *Kwanso* Regel; *H. Kwanso* Hort.]. Stouter, later-flowering; lvs. coarser, green or striped with white; fls. double. Cv. **'Maculata'** [var. *maculata* Baroni; *H. maculata* (Baroni) Nakai]. Fls. larger, marked and banded inside with red-purple. Cv. **'Rosea'** [var. *rosea* Stout]. Fls. rose-red. Cv. **'Virginica'**. Fls. double, orange, overlaid with rose. Var. **longituba** (Miq.) Maxim. [*H. longituba* Miq.]. Lvs. narrower, to ½ in. wide; perianth tube relatively longer, to 1½ in. long, to ⅓ as long as lobes. Japan.

Goldenii: a listed name, for *Hemerocallis* cv. 'Goldenii', a hybrid to 3 ft., with fls. deep golden-orange.

gracilis: a listed name for *Hemerocallis* cv. 'Gracilis', a hybrid to 2 ft., with lvs. ½ in. wide or less, fls. lemon-yellow to golden-yellow.

graminea: *H. Dumortieri,* but plants offered as *H. graminea* are probably *H. minor.*

hybrida: a listed name of no botanical standing.

Kwanso: *H. fulva* cv.

Lilioasphodelus L. [*H. Lilioasphodelus* var. *flava* L.; *H. flava* (L.) L.]. YELLOW D., LEMON D., LEMON LILY. To 3 ft., rhizome spreading, roots enlarged; lvs. to 2 ft. long and ¾ in. wide; scape weak, more or less lopping; fls. fragrant, yellow, to 4 in. long, perianth tube to 1 in. long, pedicels 1–2 in. long. Spring. E. Siberia to Japan. Cv. **'Major'**. Taller; fls. larger, deep yellow. More than one cv., and even hybrid seedlings, however, have been distributed under this name. Cv. **'Rosea'**. Said to be 40 in. tall, with fls. deep pink.

longituba: *H. fulva* var.

×**luteola** Hort. ex Jenk.: *H. aurantiaca* var. *major* × *H. Thunbergii.* To 3 ft., forming dense clumps; lvs. to 30 in. long; fls. golden-yellow, to 5 in. across when fully expanded, perianth segms. broad. Cv. **'Major'**. Lvs. wider, shorter; scapes more widely branched, fls. larger. Cv. **'Pallens'**. Actually a hybrid, *H. citrina* × *H.* × *luteola;* correctly,

Hemerocallis cv. 'Pallens', fls. pale yellow, to 5 in. across when fully expanded.

maculata: *H. fulva* cv.

Middendorffii Trautv. & C. A. Mey. To 1 ft. or more, main roots cylindrical and fibrous; lvs. to 2 ft. long and 1 in. wide; scape unbranched, slightly longer than lvs.; fls. nearly sessile, subtended by broadly ovate bracts, tightly clustered, fragrant, orange, to 2¾ in. long, perianth tube to ⅝ in. long. Late spring. E. Siberia, n. China, Korea, Japan. Cv. **'Major'**. More robust, scapes more erect, longer. Var. **esculenta** (G. Koidz.) Ohwi [*H. esculenta* G. Koidz.]. Fls. short-pedicelled, subtended by narrowly ovate bracts, perianth tube ¾–1½ in. long. Japan. The fl. buds are eaten in Japan.

minor Mill. DWARF YELLOW D. To 18 in., roots slender, fibrous, crown compact; lvs. to 20 in. long and ¼ in. wide; scape forked or branched at top, fls. fragrant, yellow, to 4 in. long, perianth tube to 1 in. long. Spring. E. Siberia to Japan.

×Muelleri: *H. × ochroleuca.*

multiflora Stout. To 3 ft., roots fleshy, crown compact; lvs. to 15 in. long and ¾ in. wide, dark green, recurved; scape slender, much-branched and taller than foliage; fls. very numerous, golden-yellow inside, reddish-tinged outside, to 2½ in. long and 3 in. across, inner perianth segms. ¾ in. wide. Late summer and autumn. China.

nana W. W. Sm. & Forr. Dwarf, to 1½ ft., roots usually fleshy at some distance from crown; lvs. to 15 in. long and ½ in. wide, strongly recurving; scapes slender, erect or curved; fls. 1–3, usually 1, fragrant, orange within, often reddish-brown outside, to 3 in. across, perianth tube to ½ in. long. China.

nubiana: a listed name, for *Hemerocallis* cv. 'Nubiana'; fls. dark chocolate-red, with yellow stripe on inner perianth segms.

×ochroleuca Sprenger [*H. × Muelleri* Sprenger]: *H. citrina × H. Thunbergii.* Cvs. include: **'Baronii'**, fls. on slender, 3 ft. scapes, very large, fragrant, canary-yellow; **'Ochroleuca'**, lvs. dark green, scapes much-branched, slender, 2–3 ft., fls. large, fragrant, sulphur-yellow, with gold anthers; **'Muelleri'**, a vigorous form, lvs. dark green, fls. on scapes to 4 ft., to 4 in. across, canary-yellow.

plicata Stapf. To 1½ ft., roots fleshy; lvs. to 20 in. long and ¼ in. wide, somewhat folded lengthwise; scapes usually shorter than foliage or nearly so; fls. golden-yellow, rarely fulvous, solitary to few. China.

semperflorens: a listed name, for *Hemerocallis* cv. 'Semperflorens'. Lvs. erect, recurved, coarse, evergreen; scapes ascending, to 3½ ft.; fls. coarse, to 4½ in. across, cadmium-yellow.

serotina: *H. Thunbergii.*

Sieboldii: *H. Dumortieri.*

Thunbergii Hort. ex Bak. [*H. serotina* Focke]. To 3 ft., vigorous, roots mostly slender-cylindrical but somewhat fleshy; lvs. to 2½ ft. long and ¾ in. wide; scapes stiff, erect, branched near apex; fls. fragrant, lemon-yellow, 3 in. long, perianth tube about 1 in. long. Summer. Japan. In the past sometimes grown erroneously as *H. citrina.*

virginica: *H. fulva* cv.

washingtonia Traub. A name proposed to include all those hybrids that are allotetraploid and true-breeding.

HEMIANDRA R. Br. *Labiatae.* About 7 spp. of glabrous to white-pubescent or hispid subshrubs of sw. Australia; sts. usually square in cross section, often rigidly diffuse; lvs. opp., rigid, needle-shaped, narrow, entire; fls. in axillary, 2-fld. verticillasters, pedicelled, subtended by 2 bractlets, calyx campanulate, to 15-nerved, 2-lipped, upper lip entire to unequally 3-toothed, lower lip with 2–5 obtuse to needlelike teeth, corolla white to rose, tube longer than calyx, limb 2-lipped, upper lip erect, shortly 2-lobed, lower lip 3-lobed, middle lobe often 2-lobed, stamens 4, in 2 pairs, anthers 1-celled; fr. of 4 reticulate nutlets.

pungens R. Br. SNAKEBUSH. Evergreen, spreading or creeping, 2–3 ft.; lvs. linear-lanceolate, ½–1 in. long, sharp-pointed, sessile; corolla about ⅝ in. long, pink to white, dotted crimson, upper lip 4-lobed, lower lip 2–3-lobed. Summer. Sw. W. Australia. Grows in sand, so requires good drainage. Cult. in Calif., where grown in full sun. Prop. from softwood cuttings.

HEMIEVA: *SUKSDORFIA.*

HEMIGRAPHIS Nees. *Acanthaceae.* Over 60 spp. of trop. Asian herbs; lvs. opp.; fls. small, mostly in terminal heads and subtended by large bracts, corolla tubular, 5-lobed, stamens 4, included, didynamous; fr. a caps.

Grown in the tropics and in southern Fla. (Zone 10b) as basket plants or ground cover, but must be protected or kept in the greenhouse in winter. Propagated by cuttings.

alternata (Burm.f.) T. Anderson [*H. colorata* (Blume) H. G. Hallier]. RED IVY, RED-FLAME I. Prostrate, rooting per.; lvs. ovate-cordate, to 3 in. long, toothed, bullate, purplish beneath, gray above; corolla white, ½–¾ in. long, pollen apparently sterile; fr. never produced. Nativity uncertain, probably e. part of Malay Arch. Prop. vegetatively.

colorata: *H. alternata.*

repanda (L.) H. G. Hallier. Prostrate herb; lvs. linear, to 2½ in. long; fls. in terminal spikes, corolla white, ½–¾ in. long; sterile, like *H. alternata.* Nativity unknown.

HEMIONITIS L. *Polypodiaceae.* Seven spp. of small, terrestrial, trop. ferns, all but one in the New World; lvs. somewhat dimorphic, palmately or pinnately lobed, fertile lvs. stiff, long-petioled, sterile lvs. short-petioled; sporangia borne along all the reticulate veins, indusia absent.

Propagated by division, buds, and spores. See also *Ferns.*

arifolia (Burm.f.) T. Moore. Lvs. sagittate to hastately lobed or triangular, usually 2–5 in. long, essentially entire, glabrescent above, petioles black with cinnamon-brown scale hairs, fertile lvs. much longer petioled with areoles between veins beneath often wholly obscured. Trop. Asia.

palmata L. STRAWBERRY FERN. Sterile lvs. palmately lobed, to 6 in. long and wide, with 5 triangular divisions, irregularly crenate, pubescent, petioles brown, fertile lvs. with areoles between the veins beneath quite apparent. Trop. Amer.

HEMIPTELEA Planch. *Ulmaceae.* One sp., a deciduous tree, brs. often rigid and spinelike, native to ne. Asia; lvs. short-petioled, serrate, pinnately veined; fls. unisexual and bisexual, in 1–4-fld. axillary clusters; fr. a small, asymmetrical, winged nutlet.

Propagated by seeds, layers, and grafting on *Ulmus.*

Davidii (Hance) Planch. Small tree, spines ½–4 in. long, slender or stout, leafy, mostly on young plants; lvs. elliptic, to 2 in. long, lateral veins 8–12 pairs; fr. to ¼ in. long. Zone 6. Sometimes planted for hedges.

HEMITELIA: *CYATHEA.* **H. Smithii:** *Alsophila Smithii.* **H. Walkeri:** *A. Walkeri.*

HEPATICA Mill. LIVERLEAF. *Ranunculaceae.* About 10 spp. of small, hardy, mostly somewhat hairy, per. herbs of the N. Hemisphere, blooming in early spring; lvs. long-petioled, cordate, 3–5-lobed, thickish, evergreen; fls. white to purple or blue, solitary, terminal on scape; involucre calyxlike, of 3 small bracts, sepals petaloid, petals 0. Sometimes united with *Anemone.*

Hepaticas thrive in rich, well-drained soil. They are woodland plants, useful for naturalizing. Propagated by seeds and division of roots.

acutiloba DC. To 9 in., differing from *H. americana* chiefly in having lvs. less oblate, acute; involucral bracts narrower, acute; sepals bluish or white. Me. to Man., s. to Ga., Ala., Mo. Cv. **'Coerulea'** is listed.

americana (DC.) Ker-Gawl. [*H. triloba* of Amer. auth., not Gilib.; *Anemone Hepatica* of Amer. auth., not L.]. To 6 in.; lvs. oblate-reniform, lobes entire, rounded at apex; involucral bracts broadly elliptic or ovate, obtuse; fls. ½–1 in. across, sepals about 5–7, lavender-blue to white and rose-colored, elliptic to oblong. Nov. Sc. to Man., s. to n. Fla. and Mo.

angulosa: see *H. transsilvanica.*

nobilis Gars. [*H. triloba* Gilib.; *Anemone Hepatica* L., not Amer. auth.]. Rhizomes short, thick; lvs. cordate, 3-lobed, lobes ovate, usually entire, often purplish and silky to villous beneath; scape to 6 in., involucral bracts entire; fls. 1 in. across or more, with stouter styles and larger stigmas. Eurasia.

transsilvanica Fuss. [*H. angulosa* of auth., not (Lam.) DC.]. Like *H. nobilis,* but long and slender; lf. lobes crenate-dentate; involucral bracts 2–3-toothed near apex; fls. 1–1½ in. across. Romania.

triloba: see *H. americana* and *H. nobilis.*

HERACLEUM L. COW PARSNIP. *Umbelliferae.* About 60 spp. of coarse, bien. or per. herbs, native to Eurasia and N. Amer.; lvs. large, pinnately or ternately compound; fls. white or pinkish, greenish, or yellowish, in compound umbels, involucre deciduous or absent, involucels of small bractlets or absent; fr. flattened, the oil tubes clearly visible.

Planted in wild gardens for bold effects and sometimes as specimen plants. They thrive on rich, moist soil. Propagated by seeds and division. The foliage has been known to produce a skin rash in susceptible persons.

giganteum: *H. laciniatum.*

japonicum: a listed name of no botanical standing.

laciniatum Hornem. [*H. giganteum* Hort.; *H. villosum* (Hoffm.) Fisch. ex K. Spreng.]. To 12 ft.; lvs. simple, deeply cut and toothed, gray- or white-tomentose beneath; fls. white; fr. prickly margined. Caucasus.

lanatum: *H. Sphondylium* subsp. *montanum.*

Mantegazzianum Somm. & Levier. GIANT HOGWEED. To 9 ft., st. and petioles red-flecked; lvs. to 3 ft. long, ternately compound, lfts. very large, deeply cut, green beneath; umbels to 4 ft. across; fls. white. Caucasus; naturalized locally in N.Y.

maximum: *H. Sphondylium* subsp. *montanum.*

Sphondylium L. Bien. or per., to 9 ft. or sometimes more, sts. glabrous to hispid; lvs. simple and palmately lobed to pinnate, then with 5–9 toothed segms., nearly glabrous to hispid above, pubescent to hispid or white-tomentose beneath; umbels 15–45-rayed, to 8 in. across; fls. white to greenish, yellowish, or pinkish. N. Temp. Zone, Eur., Asia, N. Amer. A variable sp. with many subspp. Subsp. **montanum** (Schleich. ex Gaudin) Briq. [*H. lanatum* Michx.; *H. maximum* Bartr.]. MASTERWORT, AMERICAN C. P. To 9 ft.; lvs. ternately compound, lfts. broadly ovate, lobed and toothed, tomentose beneath; umbels 15–30-rayed, peduncles tomentose, but villous just below umbel; fls. white; fr. somewhat pubescent. Nfld. to Ga., w. to Alaska and Calif.; Eur.; Siberia.

villosum: *H. laciniatum.*

HERBERTIA: see *ALOPHIA.* **H. caerulea** and **H. Watsonii:** *A. Drummondii.*

HERBS. As defined in a horticultural rather than botanical sense, herbs are those garden plants employed in a secondary way in cooking for flavoring and seasoning, as garnishes for foods, and also as domestic remedies. They are mostly aromatic and sweet-smelling plants and are sometimes referred to as culinary herbs or sweet herbs. They are prevailingly of the mint and parsley families (Labiatae and Umbelliferae).

Herbs do not constitute a single cultural group, except that they are usually only incidents to the kitchen garden, and an area 2 or 4 feet square generally yields a sufficient supply for a family. Herbs also are decorative plants, and may be used as edging or in borders. Three classes of herbs may be specified. (1) Some are annual and are therefore grown each year from seeds sown usually directly in the garden, as anise (*Pimpinella Anisum*), coriander (*Coriandrum sativum*), false saffron (*Carthamnus tinctorius*), summer savory (*Satureja hortensis*), and sweet basil (*Ocimum Basilicum*). (2) Others are biennials or only short-lived perennials, as caraway (*Carum Carvi*), clary (*Salvia Sclarea*), dill (*Anethum graveolens*), fennel (*Foeniculum vulgare*), and sweet marjoram (*Origanum Majorana*). (3) The larger number are perennial, persisting for many years; they are grown from seeds or division and include lemon balm (*Melissa officinalis*), catnip (*Nepeta Cataria*), costmary (*Chrysanthemum Balsamita*), horehound (*Marrubium vulgare*), hyssop (*Hyssopus officinalis*), lavender (*Lavandula angustifolia*), lovage (*Levisticum officinale*), marjoram (*Origanum Majorana*), oregano (*Origanum vulgare*), pennyroyal (*Mentha Pulegium*), peppermint (*Mentha × piperita*), rosemary (*Rosmarinus officinalis*), sage (*Salvia officinalis*), tansy (*Tanacetum vulgare*), tarragon (*Artemisia Dracunculus*), thyme (*Thymus vulgaris*), winter savory (*Satureja montana*), and wormwood (*Artemisia*).

Interest in herbs in this country is centered in the Herb Society of America.

HEREROA (Schwant.) Dinter & Schwant. *Aizoaceae.* About 34 spp. of succulent, cespitose, per. herbs or small shrubs, native to S. Afr.; lvs. opp., 4-ranked, soft, semicylindrical to 3-angled, surface green, roughened with large dots; fls. solitary or in cymes, calyx 5-lobed, petals yellow, becoming pink, rarely white, many, in several series, stamens many, erect, ovary inferior, 5-celled, stigmas 5; fr. a caps., cell lids stiff, placental tubercles small, almost translucent.

Growth occurs in summer. In winter the plants require a fairly dry place with a relatively cool temperature of about 55° F. Free-flowering plants easily propagated by seeds and cuttings. See also *Succulents.*

dolabriformis: *Rhombophyllum dolabriforme.*

Dyeri L. Bolus. ELKHORN. Compact, 4 in. across, brs. short, covered with persistent lf. remains; lvs. 2–6 on a br., erect to inclined, unequal in length, often dimorphic, green, with prominent dots, to 2 in. long and ⅜ in. thick, semicylindrical at base, mostly widened, axe-shaped in side view, and 2-lobed at apex; fls. 1 in. across, opening in the afternoon, in 3's on pedicels to 2⅜ in. long, petals golden-yellow. Cape Prov.

granulata (N. E. Br.) Dinter & Schwant. Lvs. spreading, often prostrate, slightly recurved, dark green, roughened with many more or less transparent dots, to 5¼ in. long, ¼ in. wide, to ⅛ in. thick, semicylindrical basally but keeled toward apex on lower side, slightly expanded and pointed at tip. Cape Prov.

Nelii Schwant. Lvs. 2–6 on a growth, green, covered with many transparent tubercles, to 1¼ in. long, ¼ in. wide, ⅜ in. thick, curved, upper side flat, lower side rather rounded near the base and indistinctly keeled at apex; fls. 1–3, petals yellow. Cape Prov.

odorata (L. Bolus) L. Bolus. Small, glabrous shrub, brs. spreading to ascending, fl. branchlets erect; lvs. spreading to ascending, almost glaucous-green, older lvs. mostly to 1¼ in. long and ¼ in. thick, longer than internodes, mostly semicylindrical, obscurely keeled, obtuse at apex, younger lvs. flat on upper side, eccentrically keeled beneath; fls. in 2's, 3's or pairs of 2, nocturnal, fragrant, on pedicels to ⅜ in. long, petals yellow, with reddish tips. Cape Prov.

Rehneltiana (A. Berger) Dinter & Schwant. Sts. with short brs.; lvs. soft, erect, slightly recurved, light green, covered with many slightly prominent, transparent dots, to 4 in. long, ⅜ in. wide, ¼ in. thick, upper side flat or a little concave, compressed and keeled in the upper ⅓, margins rounded, bluntish above, with a small cartilaginous point; fls. to ⅞ in. across, 3–7 on a scape to 8 in. high, petals yellow. S. Afr.

Stanleyi (L. Bolus) L. Bolus. Shrub, to 3½ in., branchlets erect from ascending brs.; lvs. 6–8, ascending to spreading, erect when young, blue-green, to ½ in. long, ⅛ in. wide, flat above, keeled beneath, sides slightly convex, keel entire or with 1, rarely 2 teeth; fls. to 1 in. across, solitary, fragrant, petals golden-yellow, reddish outside at tip. Cape Prov.

HERITIERA Ait. [*Argyrodendron* F. J. Muell.; *Tarrieta* Blume]. *Sterculiaceae.* About 30 spp. of monoecious trees with buttresses, native to se. Asia, trop. Afr., and Australia; lvs. alt., simple or digitate-compound; fls. small, in axillary panicles; calyx campanulate or urceolate, 4–5-cleft, petals none, male fls. with 8–10 stamens in a whorl near the apex of a column, sometimes overtopped by vestigial carpels, female fls. with 3–5(–6) carpels in a whorl, each 1–2-ovuled, with sterile anthers at their base, mature carpels 1(–2)-seeded, with a dorsal ridge or wing.

trifoliolata (F. J. Muell.) Kosterm. [*Argyrodendron trifoliolatum* F. J. Muell.; *Tarrieta argyrodendron* Benth.; *T. trifoliolata* (F. J. Muell.) F. J. Muell.]. To about 100 ft.; lfts. (1–)3–5, lanceolate to suboblanceolate, 3–6 in. long, acuminate, leathery, glossy above; panicles loosely many-fld.; calyx rotate-campanulate, about ½ in. across, white with green base, mature carpels with wings to 1¾ in. long, ¾ in. wide. Celebes to New Guinea, trop. Queensland, and New S. Wales.

HERMANNIA L. [*Mahernia* L.]. *Byttneriaceae.* Over 100 spp. of herbs and small shrubs, mostly native to S. Afr.; lvs. alt., simple, often with leaflike stipules; fls. 1 to several, on axillary, usually bracted peduncles, calyx 5-lobed, petals 5, the margins often inrolled at base, stamens 5, opp. petals, filaments separate or united basally, obovate with membranous wings, or cruciform in the middle; fr. a 5-celled, loculicidally dehiscent caps.

One species is an ornamental of easy culture for greenhouse, hanging baskets, or outdoors in the South and southern Calif.; propagated by seeds.

verticillata (L.) K. Schum. [*Mahernia verticillata* L.]. HONEYBELLS. Decumbent subshrub, usually appearing herbaceous when grown in the greenhouse, brs. to about 1 ft. high; lvs. to 1½ in. long, pinnately cut into linear segms., stipules leafy; fls. fragrant, 1–2, on long, slender, bracted peduncles, petals yellow, to ½ in. long. Winter to spring. S. Afr.

HERMODACTYLUS Mill. *Iridaceae.* One sp., a tuberous, clump-forming per. herb, native to the Medit. region, similar to *Iris* in habit and fls.; lvs. 2-ranked, linear, 4-angled; fls. solitary, spathe valve usually 1, longer than fl., perianth tube short, segms. 6, the 3 outer (the falls) beardless, much longer than the 3 inner (the standards), stamens 3, style brs. 3, petal-like, 2-lobed; fr. a 1-celled caps.

Culture as for tuberous irises.

tuberosus (L.) Mill. [*Iris tuberosa* L.]. SNAKE'S-HEAD IRIS. Tubers 2–4, fingerlike, about 1 in. long, sts. to about 1½ ft.; lvs. 2–3, to 2 ft. long, glaucous; fls. 2 in. long, outer perianth segms. plum-purple, velvety, inner segms. pea-green, long-cuspidate, obscured by falls, stamens yellow, style brs. pea-green. S. France to e. Medit. region; naturalized locally in Eng. and Ireland.

HERNANDIA L. *Hernandiaceae.* About 14 spp. of monoecious trees of wide distribution in the tropics; lvs. alt., entire, long-petioled; fls. unisexual, in large panicles, ultimate brs. of infl. with 4-parted involucres subtending 3 fls., the central fl. female, with 8 perianth segms., a basal cuplike involucel, and inferior ovary, the lateral 2 male, with 6 perianth segms. and 3 stamens; fr. ellipsoid, enclosed in the enlarged involucel.

ovigera L. [*H. peltata* Meissn.]. To 40 ft.; lvs. broadly ovate, peltate, to 8 in. long, usually cordate; fls. greenish-yellow; fr. black, dry, about 1¼ in. in diam., involucel much inflated, whitish, pear-shaped, to 2½ in. long, with a large apical opening. Zone 10b.

peltata: *H. ovigera.*

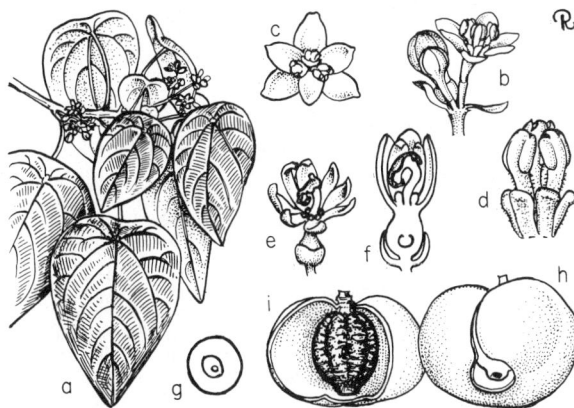

HERNANDIACEAE. *Hernandia ovigera:* **a,** flowering branch, × ¼; **b,** male flower (open), with female and another male flower in bud, × 1; **c,** male flower, face view, × 1; **d,** stamens and staminodes of male flower, × 3; **e,** female flower, × 1; **f,** female flower, vertical section, × 1½; **g,** ovary, cross section, × 3; **h,** fruit enclosed in involucel, × ½; **i,** same, part of involucel cut away, × ½.

HERNANDIACEAE Blume. HERNANDIA FAMILY. Dicot.; 4 genera of trop. trees and shrubs of wide distribution; allied to *Lauraceae,* but differing in having an inferior ovary, no true petals, and female fls. surrounded at base by a fleshy, cup-shaped involucel that ultimately envelopes the fr. *Hernandia* is cult. in this country.

HERNIARIA L. HERNIARY. *Caryophyllaceae.* About 35 spp. of ann. or per. herbs, native to Eur., Medit. region to Afghanistan, and S. Afr.; sts. much-branched; lvs. opp. or the upper alt.; fls. usually crowded in axillary clusters, bracts inconspicuous, sepals 4 or 5, petals rudimentary or absent, stamens 2–5, styles 2-branched; fr. an indehiscent nutlet, seed 1, black, glossy.

Well-suited to the rock garden or rock wall. Propagated by seeds or division.

alpina Chaix. Cespitose per., sts. densely leafy, with short internodes; lvs. elliptic-obovate, to ³⁄₁₆ in. long, ciliate, glabrescent; infl. few-fld., mostly terminal, loose, or fls. sometimes solitary, sepals hairy. E. Pyrenees, Alps, Apennines.

glabra L. RUPTUREWORT. Ann. to per., sts. hairy to glabrescent; lvs. alt. toward apex, ovate-lanceolate, ⅛–⅜ in. long, glabrous to ciliate;

infl. axillary, on short brs.; sepals ovate, ¼ in. long, usually glabrous, petals minute, white. Eur., nw. Afr., Turkey, to cent. Asia.

HERPESTIS: *BACOPA.* **H. amplexicaulis:** *B. caroliniana.*

HERPOTHAMNUS: *VACCINIUM.*

HERREANTHUS Schwant. *Aizoaceae.* One sp., a dwarf, cespitose, succulent, per. herb, native to S. Afr.; lvs. 4-ranked; fls. solitary, fragrant, bracted, calyx 6-lobed, with a short tube, petals white, in several series, united basally into a short tube, stamens many, disc entire, ovary inferior, 6-celled, stigmas 6, long and threadlike; fr. a caps., lid cells absent, expanding keels winged, placental tubercles absent.

Growth occurs chiefly in autumn in the window or the greenhouse, where proper light and warmth are required with moderate water during the growing period; in winter a sunny location is required with a relatively cool temperature of about 60° F. Propagated easily by seeds or cuttings. See also *Succulents.*

Meyeri Schwant. Lvs. light bluish-green, smooth, with slightly prominent dots, to 1½ in. long, ¾ in. wide, ⅝ in. thick, united for ⅜ in. at base, thick, 3-angled in section, upper side tapering-triangular in outline, flat, mucronate, lower side rounded at base, flatly keeled toward tip; fls. 1 in. across, fragrant, nearly sessile, petals white. Cape Prov. At first, fls. open in sunshine, eventually remain open day and night for almost 10 days.

HERTRICHOCEREUS: *LEMAIREOCEREUS.*

HESPERALOE Engelm. *Agavaceae.* Three spp. of stemless herbs, native to n. Mex. and adjacent U.S., with bulbous, fibrous bases, forming grasslike clumps; lvs. linear-elongate, fibrous, margins filiferous; infl. a raceme or panicle; fls. narrowly campanulate, segms. 6, connivent, inserted on fleshy receptacle, stamens 6, inserted on receptacle or at base of perianth segms., included, ovary superior, 3-celled; fr. a dehiscent caps., seeds many, large, thin, flat, black.

Cultivation as for *Yucca.*

Engelmannii: *H. parviflora* var.

funifera (C. Koch) Trel. Lvs. to nearly 6 ft. long, 2⅜ in. wide near base, nearly straight, marginal threads coarse; infl. to 8 ft.; fls. green, tinged with purple, about 1 in. long; fr. to 2 in. long. Ne. Mex.

nocturna Gentry. Tufted per., forming large clumps, like bear grass (*Nolina microcarpa*); lvs. linear, arching, to 5 ft. long, ½–⅝ in. wide above base, margins with few fine threads; infl. to 7 or 8 ft., simple or 1–3 branched; fls. in clusters, 1 in. long, greenish, tinged with pink or lavender, opening whitish inside at night; fr. globose, woody. Sonora (Mex.).

parviflora (Torr.) J. Coult. [*H. yuccifolia* Engelm.]. Lvs. to about 4 ft. long, 1¼ in. wide, arching-spreading, marginal threads very fine; infl. to about 4 ft.; fls. dark to light red, 1¼ in. long, nodding; fr. to 1¼ in. long or more. Tex. Var. **Engelmannii** (Krausk.) Trel. [*H. Engelmannii* Krausk.]. Fls. more bell-shaped, about 1 in. long.

yuccifolia: *H. parviflora.*

HESPERANTHA Ker-Gawl. *Iridaceae.* About 40 spp. of cormous herbs, native to S. Afr., allied to *Ixia;* lvs. grasslike; infl. a green-bracted spike; fls. opening in the evening, the undivided part of style as long as perianth tube, style brs. 3, exserted; fr. a caps.

Usually grown under glass, flowering in spring, or in the open in mild climate; propagated by seeds or cormlets.

Baurii Bak. Corms about ½ in. in diam., sts. to 2 ft.; basal lvs. 3, to 1 ft. long and ¼ in. wide, strongly ribbed; fls. bright rose-red, to 1¼ in. long, perianth tube cylindrical, straight, about ½ in. long and not longer than green spathes, segms. slightly reflexed or ascending, about as long as tube. Transvaal.

Buhrii L. Bolus. Corms about ⅝ in. across, tunics imbricate, sts. to 10 in., 2-branched, glabrous; basal lvs. 3, 6–9 in. long, ³⁄₁₆ in. wide; infl. a 6–7-fld., loose, 2-ranked spike; perianth segms. to ¾ in. long, white, outer segms. flushed pink outside. Cape Prov.

inflexa (D. Delar.) R. Foster. Tunics imbricate, sts. to 1 ft.; basal lvs. 2, to ⁵⁄₁₆ in. wide, curved; infl. loose, 2–3-fld.; perianth tube ³⁄₁₆ in. long, perianth segms. about 1¼ in. long, outer segms. larger, dull yellow, dark purple at base, inner ones golden-yellow, with spatulate purple blotch at apex. Cape Prov. Not known to be cult. in N. Amer. Var. **Stanfordiae** (L. Bolus) R. Foster [*H. Stanfordiae* L. Bolus]. Infl. 2-fld.; fls. clear yellow, fragrant, segms. about 1 in. long.

Stanfordiae: *H. inflexa* var.

HESPERIS L. ROCKET. *Cruciferae*. About 24 spp. of bien. to per., erect, branching herbs from Medit. region to cent. Asia; lvs. narrow, mostly undivided, entire or toothed; fls. white to rose or mauve-purple, often showy, in long, terminal, mostly paniculate racemes, sometimes fragrant, sepals 4, petals 4, long-clawed; fr. an elongated silique with 1 row of seeds in each half.

lutea: *Sisymbrium luteum.*

matronalis L. [*H. nivea* Baumg.]. DAME'S ROCKET, SWEET R., DAME'S VIOLET. Rather coarse, much-branched per. or sometimes bien., to 3 ft., hirsute or rarely glabrous; lvs. lanceolate to lanceolate-ovate, to 4 in. long, toothed; fls. large, ½ in. across and more, lilac or light purple, varying to white and to double forms, fragrant. Late spring, early summer. Cent. and s. Eur.; naturalized in N. Amer. A variable sp., long cult. as an ornamental. Prop. by seeds.

nivea: *H. matronalis.*

tristis L. Bien. or per., to 20 in.; lvs. ovate-lanceolate, to 2 in. long, acuminate, entire, glabrous or sparsely hairy; fls. yellowish-green with rose-violet veins, to 1 in. long or more; siliques erect or ascending, to 5 in. long. Cent. and e. Eur.

HESPEROCALLIS A. Gray. *Liliaceae*. One sp., a bulbous, leafy-stemmed herb, native to the deserts of s. Calif. and w. Ariz.; bulb deep-seated, tunicate; lvs. linear, strongly crisped, white-margined; fls. in a stout, scarious-bracted, terminal raceme; perianth segms. 6, united into a tube, stamens 6, anthers versatile, filaments inserted on perianth; fr. a deeply 3-lobed, loculicidal caps., seeds many, flattened, dull black.

undulata A. Gray. DESERT LILY. To 2 ft.; lvs. to 2 ft. long and ¾ in. wide; fls. fragrant, funnelform, to 2¾ in. long, perianth segms. about twice as long as tube, white, with broad green stripe on back.

HESPEROCHIRON S. Wats. *Hydrophyllaceae*. Two spp. of dwarf, stemless, per. herbs, native to w. N. Amer.; lvs. in a basal rosette, simple; fls. white or bluish, solitary, on long, slender, naked peduncles, calyx 5-parted, corolla funnelform or rotate, anthers 5, style 2-cleft; fr. a 1-celled caps.

Propagated by seeds.

californicus (Benth.) S. Wats. To 4 in.; lvs. many, narrowly oblong to elliptic, to 2 in. long, gray-pubescent; corolla funnelform to salverform, sometimes irregular, short-hairy or nearly glabrous inside, the lobes shorter than tube. Spring. E. Wash. to Baja Calif., e. to Mont. and Utah.

pumilus (Griseb.) T. C. Porter. To 5½ in.; lvs. linear-oblong to oblanceolate, sometimes elliptic, to 2⅜ in. long, mostly glabrous; corolla rotate, long-hairy inside, lobes longer than tube. Spring. E. Wash. to n. Calif., e. to Idaho, Nev., n. Ariz.

HESPEROXALIS: *OXALIS.*

HESPEROYUCCA: *YUCCA.*

HETERANTHERA Ruiz & Pav. MUD PLANTAIN. *Pontederiaceae*. About 10 spp. of aquatic herbs, native mostly to subtrop. and trop. Afr. and Amer., extending into temp. N. Amer.; lvs. submersed or floating; fls. regular, in a 1- to several-fld. spathe, perianth 6-parted, stamens 3, sometimes unequal, ovary 1–3-celled; fr. a caps., enclosed in the perianth tube.

Grown chiefly in aquaria.

dubia (Jacq.) MacMill. WATER STAR GRASS. Submersed, sts. flexuous, to 3½ ft. long; lvs. sessile, linear, to 6 in. long; fls. light yellow, 1 in each spathe, stamens all alike. Widespread in N. Amer., trop. Amer.

reniformis Ruiz & Pav. Lf. blades reniform to nearly orbicular, to 1¼ in. across, petioles to 6 in. long; fls. white to pale blue, 3–10 in each spathe, anthers dimorphic. Trop. Amer., n. to Tex. and Conn.

zosterifolia Mart. Sts. to 3 ft.; submersed lvs. sessile, linear, to 2 in. long and ¼ in. wide, blade of floating lvs. spoon-shaped, to 1½ in. long, petioles to 2¾ in. long; fls. light blue, usually 2 in each spathe, anthers 3. Brazil, Bolivia.

HETEROCENTRON Hook. & Arn. [*Heeria* Schlechtend., not Meissn.; *Schizocentron* Meissn.]. *Melastomataceae*. About 27 spp. of herbs or shrubs, native to s. Mex. and Cent. Amer.; lvs. small, entire, 3–15-nerved, petioled; fls. solitary or in

panicles, small, white, rose, or purple, 4-merous, stamens 8, dimorphic, ovary often setose; fr. a 4-valved caps.

Several species grown in warm climates outdoors or under glass for the pleasing flowers. Propagated by cuttings.

elegans (Schlechtend.) O. Kuntze [*Heeria elegans* Schlechtend.; *Schizocentron elegans* (Schlechtend.) Rose]. SPANISH-SHAWL. Trailing subshrub, sts. slender, round to slightly angled, sparsely to moderately pubescent; lvs. ovate to oblong-ovate, ¼–1 in. long, ⅛–½ in. wide, acute, crenate to entire, sparsely strigose to glabrous, petiole to ⅛ in. long, hairy; infl. of solitary fls., terminal on side brs.; calyx lobes acute, ciliate, petals purple, 1 in. across. Localized in highlands, s. Mex., Guatemala, and Honduras. Grown in the temp. greenhouse.

macrostachyum Naud. [*Heterocentron roseum* A. Braun & Bouché; *Heeria rosea* (A. Braun & Bouché) Triana]. Erect, suffrutescent herb, to 3 ft., very sparingly branched, densely pubescent; lvs. elliptic to ovate, to 1½ in. long, acute, densely pubescent; infl. few- to several-fld.; petals purple, about ¼ in. long, minutely glandular-ciliate, ovary with apical triangular scales, usually densely ciliate. Oaxaca (Mex.); naturalized in Hawaii, Jamaica, Java, and New Guinea. A very variable sp. Long cult.

roseum: *H. macrostachyum*, but sometimes misapplied to the pink-fld. form of *H. subtriplinervium* var. *subtriplinervium.*

subtriplinervium (Link & Otto) A. Braun & Bouché var. **subtriplinervium**. Erect, suffrutescent herb, to 6 ft., sparsely branched, sts. often green-winged, reddish-brown-hairy; lvs. elliptic to ovate, to 4 in. long, acute, 11–15-nerved, hairy, petiole very short; infl. cymose-paniculate, glabrous to often glandular-hairy; petals to ⅜ in. long, white, minutely glandular-ciliate, ovary with apical triangular scales, these glabrous or rarely sparsely ciliate. Vera Cruz (Mex.); naturalized in Hawaii, Colombia, and Jamaica. Widely cult. A pink-fld. form is commonly cult. but not known in the wild; it is sometimes known as *H. roseum*, a name which is properly a synonym of *H. macrostachyum.*

HETEROMELES M. J. Roem. TOYON, CHRISTMAS BERRY. *Rosaceae*. One sp., an evergreen, treelike, unarmed shrub, native to Calif.; lvs. simple, leathery, toothed; fls. white, small, in large corymbose panicles, sepals and petals 5, stamens 10; fr. a berrylike pome.

Hardy in mild temperate areas; propagated by seeds, cuttings, and by layers. In Calif., much planted as an ornamental and used in holiday decorations.

arbutifolia (Ait.) M. J. Roem. [*Photinia arbutifolia* (Ait.) Lindl.]. To 30 ft.; lvs. elliptic to oblong, to 4 in. long; petals less than ³⁄₁₆ in. long; fr. ¼ in. in diam., persistent. Calif., adjacent n. Baja Calif. Zone 8. Var. **cerina** Jeps. [cv. 'Chrysocarpa']. Fr. yellow. Var. **macrocarpa** (Munz) Munz. Fr. red, to ⅜ in. in diam., in larger clusters and less eaten by birds. Santa Catalina Is., San Clemente Is.

HETEROPAPPUS Less. *Compositae* (Aster Tribe). About 12 spp. of bien. herbs, native to e. Asia; sts. erect or decumbent; lvs. alt.; fl. heads radiate, in loose corymbs, involucre nearly globose, involucral bracts in 2 rows, nearly equal, receptacle slightly convex, pitted; disc fls. bisexual, fertile, yellow, ray fls. female, fertile, blue-purple or white; achenes compressed, densely pilose, pappus of the disc achenes of bristles, of the ray achenes a short crown.

altaicus (Willd.) Novopokr. [*Aster altaicus* Willd.]. Plant strigose-pubescent, the hairs often intermixed with glossy glands, sts. to 1½ ft.; basal lvs. absent at maturity, st. lvs. linear-lanceolate or spatulate, to 2 in. long, sometimes even to 4 in. long, reduced upward; heads to 2 in. across, solitary or in loose corymbs; ray fls. pale blue to mauve. Cent. Asia, nw. Himalayas, Afghanistan, Iran.

hispidus (Thunb.) Less. Sts. to 1 ft., densely leafy, coarsely hirsute; basal lvs. oblanceolate, to about 5 in. long, st. lvs. oblanceolate to linear, to 2¾ in. long, ciliate; heads to 2 in. across; ray fls. purple or white. E. Asia. Var. **arenarius** (Kitam.) Kitam. Basal lvs. spatulate; heads to 1⅜ in. across. Japan.

HETEROPHRAGMA DC. *Bignoniaceae*. Not in cult. **H. adenophyllum:** *Haplophragma adenophyllum.*

HETEROPTERIS Fée. *Polypodiaceae*. Not in cult. **H. argentea:** a listed name of no botanical standing; material so offered may be *Cheilanthes.*

HETEROSPATHE Scheff. [*Ptychandra* Scheff.]. *Palmae*. About 20 spp. of solitary or sometimes cespitose, small to moderate, unarmed, monoecious palms, native to the Philippine Is., Micronesia, Molucca Is. to New Guinea and Solomon Is.; lvs. pinnate, sheaths often not forming a prominent crownshaft, pinnae acute to acuminate, with prominent midrib; infl. among or below lvs., peduncle prominent, with 2 unequal bracts, the cylindrical, beaked, often deciduous upper bract exceeding the persistent, 2-edged lower bract, brs. simple or 1–3 times branched, rachillae with fls. in triads (2 male and 1 female); male fls. slightly asymmetrical, sepals 3, broadly imbricate, rounded, petals 3, valvate, stamens 6–36 or more, filaments strongly inflexed at apex in bud, pistillode small, conic or columnar, nearly as long as stamens, female fls. with sepals 3, broadly imbricate, rounded, petals 3, imbricate with briefly valvate apices, staminodes 3, pistil 1-celled, 1-ovuled; fr. globose to ellipsoid, with nearly apical to lateral stigmatic residue, endocarp thin, operculate, seed globose to ellipsoid, endosperm ruminate, embryo basal.

Tender feather palms grown mainly in tropical gardens but sometimes planted in warmer parts of Zone 10a. When young, suitable for pot or tub culture in home or greenhouse. For culture see *Palms.*

elata Scheff. SAGISI PALM. Solitary, to 50 ft., trunk to 8 in. in diam.; lvs. 8–13 ft. long, tip often curved at right angle to lower portion, sheath 18 in. long, margin fibrous, petiole 1½–5 ft. long, pinnae 60–70, regularly arranged in a single plane, yellowish-green, to 3 ft. long, 1½ in. wide; infl. to 3 ft. long or more, 1–4 times branched into slender rachillae; male fls. creamy-white, stamens 6, pistillode columnar; fr. globose, white maturing red, ¼ in. in diam., stigmatic residue nearly apical. Amboina (Molucca Is.) to Philippine Is.

glauca (Scheff.) H. E. Moore. To 30 ft. or more, trunk to 9 in. in diam.; lvs. to 12 ft. long, sheath tubular at first, to 2 ft. long or more, petiole to 2 ft. long, rachis to 10 ft. long, pinnae about 50 on each side, to 2½ ft. long, 1½ in. wide, glaucous beneath; infl. below lvs., 1–3 times branched into stout rachillae; male fls. with stamens 34; fr. red, ⅞ in. long, ¾ in. in diam., stigmatic residue nearly apical. Batjan Is. (Molucca Is.).

HETEROTHECA Cass. *Compositae* (Aster Tribe). Similar to *Chrysopsis,* but ray achenes without pappus. Not cult. **H. camporum:** *Chrysopsis camporum.* **H. falcata:** *Pityopsis falcata.* **H. foliosa:** *Chrysopsis villosa* var. **H. gossypina:** *Chrysopsis gossypina.* **H. graminifolia:** *Pityopsis graminifolia.* **H. mariana:** *Chrysopsis mariana.* **H. microcephala:** *Pityopsis graminifolia.* **H. nervosa:** *Pityopsis nervosa.* **H. pinifolia:** *Pityopsis pinifolia.* **H. Rutteri:** *Chrysopsis villosa* var. **H. villosa:** *Chrysopsis villosa.*

HEUCHERA L. ALUMROOT. *Saxifragaceae.* About 35–50 spp. of per. herbs of N. Amer., largely western; basal lvs. tufted, rounded-cordate or broadly 5–9-lobed, toothed, long-petioled; scapes several, slender, overtopping the foliage; fls. in narrow panicles or racemes, small, greenish, white, red, or purplish, calyx tube cup-shaped, urn-shaped, or saucer-shaped, united to ovary, calyx lobes, petals and stamens usually 5, ovary partly inferior, with 2 apical beaks; fr. a caps. dehiscent along inner side of beaks.

Native mostly on cliffs, hills, and mountains. One species, *H. sanguinea,* is planted commonly in the perennial border and a few others are sometimes grown in rock gardens and wild gardens. They thrive in the average garden soil, preferably in an open location. Propagated by division of the clumps in spring or in autumn, or by seeds.

alba: *H. pubescens* var. *brachyandra.*

americana L. ROCK GERANIUM. To 3 ft.; foliage mottled when young, becoming plain green; petals greenish-white, about as long as calyx lobes, stamens much exserted. Ont. to Ill. and Mich., s. to Ga., La., Mo. Var. **hirsuticaulis** (Wheelock) Rosend., Butters, & Lakela [*H. hirsuticaulis* (Wheelock) Rydb.]. Petioles densely hirsute; fls. about $\frac{3}{16}$ in. long, petals oblanceolate. Ind. to Mo.

bracteata (Torr.) Ser. Densely tufted, to 6 in.; infl. spikelike; petals very narrow, slightly longer than calyx lobes, stamens slightly exserted. S. Wyo. and Colo.

brevistaminea Wiggins. Stemless, tufted, to 12 in.; lvs. nearly orbicular, to 1 in. across, petioles densely white-tomentose; infl. a narrow, rather loose panicle; fls. strongly irregular, stamens shorter than calyx lobes. Mts., San Diego Co. (Calif.).

×**brizoides** Hort. Garden hybrids involving *H. micrantha, H. sanguinea,* and possibly *H. americana;* infl. a narrow, diffuse, long panicle; fls. about ⅛ in. long, pink to white. Sometimes confused with ×*Heucherella tiarelloides,* but differs in not being stoloniferous and in having 5 rather than 5–10 stamens.

chlorantha Piper. Tufted, to 3 ft.; lvs. and petioles with whitish hairs beneath; scapes coarsely villous, infl. spikelike, petals greenish, very small or none, stamens included. B.C. to Ore.

×**convallaria** Hort. A garden hybrid, probably *H. pubescens* × *H. sanguinea;* infl. a narrow panicle, scape and fls. with scattered glandular hairs; fls. small, greenish, tipped with pink.

cylindrica Dougl. ex Hook. To 2½ ft.; petioles densely hirsute; infl. spikelike, bracts ⅜ in. long or more; petals yellowish-green to cream-colored, minute or sometimes none. B.C. to n. Calif., e. to Alta., Mont., Wyo., Nev. Var. **glabella** (Torr. & A. Gray) Wheelock [*H. glabella* Torr. & A. Gray]. Petioles, lower part of st., and lvs. glabrous, lf. bases shallowly to deeply cordate. Var. **ovalifolia** (Nutt.) Wheelock [*H. ovalifolia* Nutt.]. Lf. bases cuneate, truncate, or subcordate.

flabellifolia: *H. parvifolia* var. *dissecta.*

glabella: *H. cylindrica* var.

glabra Willd. ex Roem. & Schult. To 20 in.; fl. sts. 1–3-lvd., glabrous; all lvs. cordate or round-cordate, deeply 5–7-lobed; infl. a panicle; petals white. Ore. and northward.

grandiflora Raf. A name of uncertain application.

Hallii A. Gray. Tufted, to 12 in.; infl. a narrow panicle, to nearly 3 in. long, cymules 2–4-fld.; fls. greenish-white, sometimes suffused with red, petals to twice as long as calyx lobes, stamens included. Colo.

himalayensis Decne. ex Jacques. A name of uncertain application.

hirsuticaulis: *H. americana* var.

hispida Pursh. To 4 ft., sts. white-hairy; infl. a narrow panicle; petals as long as or slightly shorter than calyx lobes. Mts., Va. and W. Va.

lithophila: *H. rubescens* var. *glandulosa.*

longiflora Rydb. Stemless, tufted plant, to 2½ ft.; infl. a wide panicle, becoming very open at maturity; fls. yellow, large, petals slightly longer than calyx lobes, both purple-tipped. Ky. to N.C. and Ala.

maxima Greene. St. from a heavy, long root crown; basal lvs. round-cordate, to 7 in. across, 7–9-lobed; fl. brs. stout, leafy, usually hirsute, bearing a narrowly cylindrical panicle; fls. to ⅜ in. long, petals white. Islands off coast of s. Calif.

micrantha Dougl. ex Lindl. To 2 ft., lower part of st. and petioles usually long-villous with whitish hairs that turn brownish when dried; lf. blades often longer than broad, with rounded, shallow lobes; infl. a loose panicle; fls. whitish, petals about 2–2½ times as long as calyx lobes. B.C., s. to cent. Calif.

ovalifolia: *H. cylindrica* var.

parvifolia Nutt. ex Torr. & A. Gray. Stemless, cespitose; lvs. small, reniform, with 7–9 shallow lobes; fl. sts. to 15 in., with elongating infl.; petals yellowish or white. Rocky Mts., from Alta. to New Mex., w. to Idaho, Nev., Ariz. Var. **dissecta** M. E. Jones [*H. flabellifolia* Rydb.]. Lvs. mostly to 1¼ in. across; fl. sts. mostly less than 8 in. Alta. to Mont. and cent. Idaho.

Pringlei Rydb. [*H. rubescens* var. *Pringlei* (Rydb.) Jeps.]. Closely related to *H. rubescens,* but lvs. narrower, somewhat truncate at base, petioles shorter, fls. hemispherical. Mts., Calif.

pubescens Pursh. To 3 ft.; infl. an open panicle; fls. purplish, petals slightly longer than calyx lobes, stamens included in calyx tube or exserted. Rich woods in mts., Penn. to N.C. Var. **brachyandra** Rosend., Butters, & Lakela [*H. alba* Rydb.]. Stamens about as long as calyx lobes, included or only slightly exserted.

racemosa: *Elmera racemosa.*

Richardsonii R. Br. Tufted, to 3 ft.; infl. a narrow panicle; fls. greenish, cylindrical-campanulate, petals spatulate, about as long as calyx lobes. E. side of Rocky Mts. to Sask. and Man., s. to Minn. and Ind.

rosea: a listed name of no botanical standing, possibly used for a form of *H. sanguinea.*

rubescens Torr. To 15 in.; lvs. round-cordate; infl. an open, 1-sided, panicle; sepals pinkish, green-tipped, petals about twice as long as calyx lobes. Mts., se. Ore. to s. Calif., e. to Idaho, Utah, Colo. Var. **glandulosa** Kellogg [*H. lithophila* A. Heller]. Infl. rarely 1-sided; fls. usually less than $\frac{3}{16}$ in. long. Var. **Pringlei:** *H. Pringlei.*

sanguinea Engelm. CORALBELLS. To 2 ft.; infl. open; fls. bright red, to ½ in. long, campanulate, petals shorter than calyx lobes. New Mex. and Ariz., s. to Mex. This is hardy north and is the most popular sp. for cult. Cvs. listed include: **'Alba'**, fls. white; **'Grandiflora'**, plant more robust, fls. larger; **'Maxima'**, fls. dark crimson; **'Oxfordii'**, fls. deep scarlet; **'Splendens'**, fls. dark crimson; **'Virginalis'**, fls. white.

splendens: *H. sanguinea* cv.

×**tiarelloides:** ×*Heucherella tiarelloides.*

×**undulata** Hort. A hybrid of uncertain parentage; to 30 in.; fls. greenish-white, in many-fld., loose, much-branched racemes.

villosa Michx. To 3 ft.; panicles open; fls. nearly white, petals twice as long as calyx. Va. to Ga. and Tenn.

virginalis: *H. sanguinea* cv.

×**HEUCHERELLA** Wehrh.: *Heuchera* × *Tiarella*. Hybrids known only from cult., intermediate in character between the parent genera; low, per. herbs; lvs. in basal tufts; fls. small, calyx lobes and petals 5, stamens 5–10, carpels 2, slightly unequal.

tiarelloides Wehrh. ex Stearn [*Heuchera* × *tiarelloides* Hort. Lemoine]: *Heuchera* × *brizoides* × *Tiarella cordifolia*. Stoloniferous; lvs. long-petioled, blades to 3½ in. long, suborbicular to broad-ovate, cordate, 7-lobed and crenate, hirsute, mottled with brown when young; infl. a narrow panicle, to 16 in., glandular-hirsute; fls. about ³⁄₁₆ in. long, calyx deep pink, petals paler, longer than calyx lobes, stamens exserted; seeds not produced.

HEVEA Aubl. [*Siphonia* L. Rich.]. *Euphorbiaceae*. Eight or 9 monoecious spp. of trop. trees, with milky juice, native to n. S. Amer., s. to Bolivia, and the Mato Grosso region of Brazil; lvs. trifoliolate; infl. a panicled cyme; fls. small, without petals, ovary 3-celled; fr. a large caps.

The best and most important source of natural rubber, much cultivated in Old World tropics; seeds used as food by aborigines in the northwestern part of the Amazon Valley; and the plant sometimes grown as an ornamental. It does best at low altitudes in hot wet climates. Propagated by seeds, by budding and grafting, and sometimes by cuttings when planted as an ornamental or when grown under glass.

brasiliensis (Willd. ex A. Juss.) Müll. Arg. [*Siphonia brasiliensis* Willd. ex A. Juss.]. PARA RUBBER TREE, CAOUTCHOUC TREE. To 60 ft., or to 130 ft. in native sites; lfts. elliptic, 2–24 in. long, thick and leathery; fls. white; seeds about 1 in. long. Flood plains in the watersheds of the Amazon and Orinoco Rivers. Cult. mainly in Ceylon and Malay Arch. Strictly trop.

HEXAGLOTTIS Venten. *Iridaceae*. Three or 4 spp. of per. herbs, with tunicate corms, native to S. Afr.; sts. branched; lvs. few, linear; fls. yellow, fugacious, produced in succession, in numerous sessile clusters along brs. of panicle, perianth tube none, perianth segms. 6, not united, stamens 3, filaments united basally around the style, style short, style brs. 6, filiform, spreading; fr. a cylindrical, 3-valved caps., seeds minute.

longifolia (Jacq.) Venten. Sts. flexible, to 1½ ft.; basal lvs. 5–6, flat, as long as sts.; fls. in loose but not imbricate clusters, perianth segms. about ⅝ in. long.

virgata (Jacq.) Sweet. Sts. rigid, to 1½ ft. or more; basal lvs. mostly 3, cylindrical, longer than st.; fls. in imbricate clusters, perianth segms. to ¾ in. long, with green midvein.

HEXASTYLIS: *ASARUM*.

HEXISEA Lindl. *Orchidaceae*. Five spp. of epiphytes of trop. Amer.; sts. cylindrical, several-jointed, with pairs of lvs. at apex or joints; lvs. linear; infl. terminal, short, racemose, few-fld.; fls. brightly colored, sepals and petals similar, spreading, lip entire, with a distinct claw fully united to front of column, and the blade deflexed at a right angle to column, column 2-auricled, without a foot. For structure of fl. see *Orchidaceae*.

For culture see *Orchids*.

bidentata Lindl. To 1 ft.; sts. spindle-shaped, grooved, purple; lvs. linear, to 4 in. long; fls. to 1 in. across, vermilion-red, sepals, petals, and lip similar, linear-oblong. Mex. to Venezuela and Peru.

HEYDERIA: *CALOCEDRUS*.

HIBBERTIA Andr. [*Candollea* Labill.]. BUTTON FLOWER, GUINEA GOLD VINE. *Dilleniaceae*. More than 100 spp. of erect or procumbent shrubs, mostly in Australia and Tasmania, also New Caledonia, Fiji, Malay Arch., and Madagascar; lvs. alt., simple; fls. solitary or in few-fld. racemes, usually yellow, sessile or short-pedicelled, sepals and petals 5, stamens usually many, carpels several or many, separate; fr. a follicle, 1- to several-seeded, seeds with an aril.

Grown outdoors in southern Calif., Zone 10.

cuneiformis (Labill.) Sm. [*Candollea cuneiformis* Labill.]. Erect shrub, to 6 ft.; lvs. oblong, to 1 in. long, toothed at apex, petiole narrowly winged; fls. solitary, yellow, 1½ in. across, sessile, carpels 5, glabrous. Australia.

dentata R. Br. Shrub, sts. trailing or twining; lvs. ovate-oblong, to 3 in. long, sparsely toothed; fls. solitary, to 1½ in. across, on short peduncles, carpels 3, glabrous. New S. Wales and Victoria.

perfoliata Endl. Shrub, erect or sometimes trailing; lvs. ovate, to 2½ in. long, sparsely toothed, perfoliate; fls. solitary, to 1½ in. across, on peduncle to 2 in. long. W. Australia. Distinguished by its perfoliate lvs.

scandens (Willd.) Dryand. [*H. volubilis* (Andr.) Venten.]. SNAKE VINE, GOLD GUINEA PLANT. Shrub, sts. trailing or twining; lvs. lanceolate or ovate, to 3 in. long, silky-pubescent beneath, especially on young lvs., petiole narrowly winged; fls. yellow, solitary, terminal on short, few-lvd., pubescent lateral shoots, sepals silky-hairy. Australia.

volubilis: *H. scandens*.

HIBISCUS L. [*Paritium* Juss.]. MALLOW, ROSE M., GIANT M. About 250 spp. of herbs, shrubs, and trees, in warm-temp. and trop. regions; lvs. usually simple, mostly palmately veined, lobed or parted; fls. mostly solitary in the lf. axils, but sometimes in racemes, corymbs, or panicles, involucral bracts 4–20, separate, sometimes basally united or united to the calyx, calyx mostly bell-shaped, 5-lobed, sometimes prominently 10-veined, the median vein to each lobe usually bearing a raised gland, petals 5, mostly longer than calyx, white to yellow, red, purplish or rarely bluish, generally with a basal maroon spot, stamens united in a tubular column, included or much longer than petals, style usually 5-branched at the apex, sometimes only 5-lobed; fr. a 5-celled caps., each cell with 3 or more seeds.

A few species yield food, fiber, or medicinal products, but in N. Amer. grown as ornamentals. The annuals or species treated as annuals may be grown from seeds sown where the plants are to stand. The herbaceous perennials are propagated by seeds or division; many of these are native to swampy regions and require ample moisture. The shrubby species may be grown from seeds, but the named cultivars of *H. Rosa-sinensis* and *H. syriacus* are propagated by cuttings, grafting, or layering, since they do not come true from seed.

Abelmoschus: *Abelmoschus moschatus*.

abutiloides: *H. tiliaceus*.

acerifolius: see *H. syriacus* and *H. platanifolius*.

Acetosella Welw. ex Hiern [*H. Eetveldeanus* De Wild. & T. Durand]. Glabrate or rarely stiff-pubescent ann. or per. herb, to about 5 ft., herbage green, suffused red, or red; lvs. various, unlobed to irregularly 3- or 5-lobed or -parted; fls. solitary, on jointed, axillary pedicels, involucral bracts 9–10, apically forked, calyx usually longer than bracts, to ¾ in. long, prominently 10-nerved, glands large, petals purple-red or yellow, with deep purple base; caps. about 1 in. long, setose. Cent.-e. Afr. The red-lvd. form is generally cult. in the U.S.

africanus: *H. Trionum*.

×**Archeri** W. Wats.: *H. Rosa-sinensis* × *H. schizopetalus*. Similar to *H. Rosa-sinensis*, but having branching more delicate; lvs. more coarsely serrate; and petals laciniate or crenate, though not as much as *H. schizopetalus*.

Arnottianus A. Gray. Shrub or small evergreen tree, to 30 ft.; lvs. to 6 in. long or more, ovate, short-acuminate, entire, not lobed, dark green, leathery; fls. solitary, on pedicels to 6 in. long, involucral bracts 5–7, mostly less than ½ in. long, calyx tubular, about 1 in. long, corolla to 4 in. across or more, petals white with pinkish veins or pure white, staminal column exserted, 3–6 in. long, the upper ⅓ with slender, spreading, red filaments. Hawaii. May be cult. in Calif. and along the s. border of the U.S. Plants offered under this name are sometimes *H. Rosa-sinensis*.

Brackenridgei A. Gray. Glabrate to pubescent, sometimes spinescent shrub or small tree, to 30 ft.; lvs. to about 6 in. across, mostly deeply 3-, 5-, or 7-lobed, coarsely serrate; fls. solitary or in racemes on axillary pedicels to ½ in. long, involucral bracts 7–10, ⁵⁄₁₆–1¼ in. long, sometimes channelled apically, calyx about 1 in. long, petals to 3½ in. long, yellow, sometimes with maroon base, staminal column included; caps. to ⅞ in. long, villous-hispid. Hawaii.

californicus: *H. lasiocarpus*.

calycinus: *H. calyphyllus*.

calyphyllus Cav. [*H. calycinus* Willd.]. Per. herb or shrub, reaching

9 ft. in the wild; lvs. to 5 in. long, about as broad, obscurely to distinctly 3- or 5-lobed; fls. solitary, on axillary pedicels, involucral bracts 5, about ¾ in. long, varying in shape but mostly broadest at the middle and caudate at apex; corolla 3–4 in. across, petals yellow, usually with brownish or reddish base, staminal column included; caps. about 1 in. long, valves aristate. Trop. and S. Afr., Madagascar and Mascarene Is.

Cameronii Knowles & Westc. Tall, little-branched per.; lvs. to about 4½ in. long, 3-, 5-, or 7-lobed half way to the base, rarely unlobed, lobes usually broadest above the middle, serrate; fls. solitary or in leafy racemes or corymbs, involucral bracts reduced to small teeth at base of calyx, calyx to 1⅜ in. long, prominently 10-nerved, membranous, petals to 3¼ in. long, flushed pink above, with deeper rose or reddish-purple base, staminal column exserted; caps. 1¼ in. long, hirsute. Madagascar. Cult. in Hawaii.

cannabinus L. KENAF, INDIAN HEMP, DECKANER H., DECCAN H., BASTARD JUTE, BIMLI J., BIMLIPATUM J. Prickly but otherwise mostly glabrous, simple or branched ann., to about 6 ft.; lower lvs. unlobed or nearly so, upper lvs. palmately 3-, 5-, or 7-parted, segms. linear to lanceolate, serrate; fls. axillary or in racemes, on pedicels to ½ in. long, involucral bracts 7–10, to ¾ in. long, not forked, calyx ½–1 in. long at flowering, white-woolly and setose, petals 1½–3 in. long, yellow or rarely purplish, with purple base, staminal column included. Probably Afr. Yields a good fiber, much like jute and used for the same purposes; seeds yield an oil that is used for burning in Afr.

chinensis: see *H. Rosa-sinensis* and *H. syriacus.* Plants offered under this name are usually cvs. of *H. Rosa-sinensis,* rarely *H. syriacus.*

cisplatinus St.-Hil. Coarse shrub, 3–8 ft., sts. with stout, yellowish spines; lvs. to about 6 in., lower lvs. hastately 3- or 5-lobed, upper lvs. unlobed, lanceolate; fls. solitary, in upper lf. axils, involucral bracts 10–12, to ¾ in. long, lanceolate-filiform, calyx tubular-bell-shaped, to 1 in. long, enlarging in fr., petals 2–3 in. long, rose above, grading to violet-purple basally. S. Brazil and Paraguay to Argentina. Apparently only cult. in Hawaii.

coccineus (Medic.) Walt. [*H. speciosus* Soland. in Ait.]. Glabrous, glaucous, per. herb, to 6 ft. or more; lvs. palmately 3-, 5-, or 7-parted or compound, the divisions linear-lanceolate, remotely toothed; fls. solitary, in upper lf. axils, involucral bracts 10 or more, to 1¼ in. long, curvilinear, calyx to 2 in. long, petals about 3 in. long, deep red, spreading in a flat whorl, staminal column exserted. Coastal swamps, Ga. and Fla. Not hardy much n. of Philadelphia.

collinus: *H. platanifolius.*

Cooperi: *H. Rosa-sinensis* cv.

diversifolius Jacq. Often arborescent in the wild, but cult. as an ann. or small shrub, brs. stiff, pubescent, generally stout-spiny; lvs. 6 in. long and broad or more, usually palmately angled or parted; fls. solitary or in naked racemes, involucral bracts usually fewer than 10, to ½ in. long, not forked, calyx to about ⅝ in. long, enlarging in fr., prominently 10-veined, petals 1½–2½ in. long, yellow or reddish-purple, with maroon base. Trop. Afr. and Asia; introd. into trop. regions of New World.

Eetveldeanus: *H. Acetosella.*

elatus Swartz [*Paritium elatum* (Swartz) G. Don]. CUBAN BAST, MAHOE. Tree, to about 80 ft., often confused with *H. tiliaceus* but differing in having calyx large, 1–2 in. long, deciduous with involucre after flowering, petals 3–5 in. long, not overlapping; caps. 1¼–1⅝ in. long, seeds villous-pubescent. Jamaica and Cuba. Wood used for cabinet work, gunstocks, and fishing rods.

esculentus: *Abelmoschus esculentus.*

Farragei F. J. Muell. DESERT R.M. Stoutly branched shrub, to about 3 ft.; lvs. to 4 in. wide, more or less orbicular, somewhat palmately angled, green above, whitish below; fls. usually in clusters of 2–3 on short, axillary peduncles, or racemose in upper part of plant, involucral bracts 8–10, oblanceolate, united at base, calyx about ½ in. long, petals about 2 in. long, purplish, staminal column included, stigma 5-lobed. W. Australia, New S. Wales, Victoria.

fulgens: *H. Rosa-sinensis.*

furcellatus Desr. [*H. Youngianus* Gaud.-Beaup. ex Hook. & Arn.]. Coarse per. herb or shrub, to 8 ft., usually setose-pubescent; lvs. mostly 2–5 in. long, ovate to orbicular, unlobed or sometimes deeply 3-, 5-, to 7-lobed; fls. solitary, on stout pedicels in upper axils, involucral bracts mostly 10–14, forked at the apex, calyx longer than bracts, ½–1 in. long, prominently 10-nerved, petals 2–3 in. long, pale magenta to rose-pink, with darker base, staminal column included. Fla., W. Indies, Cent. and S. Amer., Hawaii.

fuscus Garcke [*H. gossypinus* Harv., not Thunb. or Baill.]. Brownish-stellate-pubescent shrub, 3–8 ft.; lvs. to 3 in. long, ovate to orbicular, rarely lobed; fls. clustered near ends of brs., involucral bracts 6–10, less than ¼ in. long, calyx slightly longer than bracts, petals about 1 in. long, white to yellowish. Edge of forests and savannas, from Ethiopia to S. Afr., w. to Congo region.

gossypinus: see *H. fuscus* and *H. platanifolius.*

grande: a listed name of no botanical standing; plants so offered are apparently *H. tiliaceus.*

grandiflorus Michx., not Torr. GREAT R.M. Similar to *H. Moscheutos,* but having lvs. 4–12 in. across, broader than long, deeply 3-, or 5-lobed, truncate to cordate at base, calyx mostly 1½–2½ in. long, petals 5–6 in. long, whitish, pinkish or purplish-rose, sometimes with basal crimson spot. Coastal marshes, Ga., Fla., w. to Miss. Plants offered under this name have generally been selections from the hybrids between *H. Moscheutos* and the other per. herbs of N. Amer. or forms of *H. Moscheutos.* See also *H. lasiocarpus.*

Hamabo Siebold & Zucc. Branching shrub, to about 15 ft.; differing from *H. tiliaceus* in having lvs. to about 3 in. long, transversely elliptic to ovate, mucronate, serrulate. Japan and Korea. Plants offered as *H. Hamabo* are usually cvs. of *H. syriacus,* with corolla single, pinkish or pinkish-lavender, with basal crimson spot.

hastatus L.f. Shrub or small tree; differing from *H. tiliaceus* in having lvs. commonly and often unevenly 3-lobed, with terminal lobe generally twice as long as the basal lateral lobes or more, and petals generally apically lobed. Society Is.

hawaiiensis: a listed name of no botanical standing; probably refers to a cv. of *H. Rosa-sinensis.*

heterophyllus Venten. Erect, evergreen shrub or small tree, to 15 ft., brs. often spiny; lvs. to 8 in. long, from unlobed and linear-lanceolate to 3-lobed, the lateral lobes nearly parallel with the terminal lobe; fls. solitary, in the upper axils, involucral bracts about 10, to ⅞ in. long, linear, simple, calyx ⅞–1¼ in. long, prominently 10-nerved, petals to 3 in. long, white, with crimson base. New S. Wales and Queensland.

Huegelii: *Alyogyne Huegelii.*

incanus: *H. lasiocarpus.*

indicus (Burm.f.) Hochr. Similar to and often confused with *H. mutabilis,* but having involucral bracts 5–9, ovate, mostly ⅛–½ in. wide, caps. long-beaked, woody with inner valve margins glabrous, and seeds with appressed hairs. Probably e. Asia.

Kokio Hillebr. ex Wawra. Shrub or small tree, to 18 ft. or more; lvs. 1–5 in. long, oblong-elliptic to ovate, usually serrate apically, glossy-green, leathery; fls. 1 or few near the ends of brs., involucral bracts 6–8, lanceolate-linear to subulate, to ⅝ in. long, calyx tubular, to 1¼ in. long, petals 1½–2½ in. long, orange-red to red, reflexed, staminal column conspicuously exserted, style brs. 5, spreading, longer than staminal column. Hawaii.

lampas: *Thespesia lampas.*

lasiocarpus Cav. [*H. californicus* Kellogg; *H. grandiflorus* Torr., not Michx.; *H. incanus* J. C. Wendl.; *H. lasiocarpus* var. *californicus* (Kellogg) L. H. Bailey]. Generally densely pubescent, per. herb, 3–7 ft.; lvs. to about 6 in. long, ovate, acuminate, rarely and then only obscurely lobed, usually serrate; fls. solitary, axillary, pedicel often united to the petiole, involucral bracts 10–14, linear-lanceolate, ½–1½ in. long, calyx broadly tubular-campanulate, to 1½ in. long, enlarging slightly in fr., petals 2½–4 in. long, white, pinkish or rarely yellowish, with a basal maroon spot; caps. to 1¼ in. long, ovoid, usually hirsute as well as stellate-pubescent. Marshes, s. Ill. and Mo., s. to Fla., Tex., e. New Mex., also cent. Calif. Var. **californicus:** *H. lasiocarpus.*

Lindnegii: a listed name of no botanical standing.

Ludwigii Eckl. & Zeyh. Similar to *H. calyphyllus,* but having involucral bracts broadest at the base, linear-lanceolate to ovate, usually longer than calyx. Ethiopia to S. Afr.

macrophyllus Roxb. ex Hornem. Tree, to 80 ft., new growth, except the lvs., with coarse, yellowish-brown, stellate pubescence; lower lvs. to 2 ft. across, cordate-orbicular, upper lvs. smaller, more ovate, stipules to 6 in. long, surrounding the bud, early deciduous; fls. solitary or in cymes near ends of brs., involucral bracts 8–14, linear, to 1 in. long, calyx about as long as bracts, petals 2½–3 in. long, yellow, with purple-red base. India to Java; cult. and naturalized in Hawaii.

Manihot: *Abelmoschus Manihot.*

matensis: a listed name of no botanical standing; plants so offered have proven to be a cv. of *H. Rosa-sinensis.*

Meehanii: a listed name of no botanical standing; plants offered under this name may be cvs. of *H. syriacus* or hybrids of *H. Moscheutos* with other spp.; see *H. Moscheutos.*

militaris Cav. SOLDIER R.M., HALBERD-LEAVED R.M. Smooth, glabrous or nearly glabrous per. herb, 3–7 ft.; lower lvs. to about 6 in. long, mostly cordate-ovate, upper lvs. mostly triangular and hastately 3- or 5-lobed, terminal lobe much the longest; fls. solitary in upper lf. axils, involucral bracts 10–14, filiform to linear-lanceolate, ½–1 in.

long, calyx broadly tubular-campanulate, ¾–1¼ in. long, enlarging in fr., petals 2–3 in. long, pale pink or near white, with crimson base, staminal column included. Mostly in wet woods, Penn. to Minn., s. to Fla. and Tex.

Moscheutos L. COMMON R.M., SWAMP R.M., MALLOW ROSE, WILD COTTON. Per. herb, to 8 ft.; lvs. to 8 in. long, lanceolate to broadly ovate, unlobed or shallowly 3- or 5-lobed, green above, white-pubescent beneath; fls. solitary, axillary, pedicel long, often fused basally to petiole, involucral bracts mostly 10–14, lanceolate-linear, to 1 in. long, calyx ¾–1½ in. long, slightly enlarged in fr., petals 3–4¼ in. long, white, pink, or rose, usually with crimson base; caps. ovoid, short-beaked, glabrous. Marshes, e. U.S., from Mass. to Mich. and s. to Ala., Ga., and perhaps Fla. Subsp. **Moscheutos** [*H. oculiroseus* Britt.]. The typical subsp.; lvs. mostly narrowly ovate to lanceolate, unlobed, lower lvs. 3-lobed; pedicels usually fused over half their length with the petiole, petals white, style brs. usually glabrous. Va. to Ohio and south. Subsp. **palustris** (L.) R. T. Clausen [*H. palustris* L.]. MARSH M., SEA HOLLYHOCK. Lvs. mostly ovate to rounded, commonly 3-lobed; pedicels united only at the base of the petiole if at all, petals white, pink, or rose, style brs. mostly densely pubescent. Mass. to coastal N.C., w. to n. Ind. Many cvs., selections from progeny of crosses involving this sp. and *H. coccineus* and *H. militaris* are offered. Hybrids of this sort have been listed as *H. Meehanii. H. grandiflorus* Hort., not Michx. usually refers either to these hybrids or to either of the subspp.

mutabilis L. [*H. sinensis* Mill., not Hort.]. COTTON ROSE, CONFEDERATE R. Shrub or small tree, to 15 ft.; lvs. about as broad as long, shallowly and angularly 5- or 7-lobed, those just beneath the fls. about 6 in. long; fls. clustered near ends of brs., involucral bracts 8–12, separate, linear-lanceolate to lanceolate-ovate, to 1 in. long, mostly less than ⅛ in. across, calyx to 1¼ in. long, enlarging in fr., petals 2–3 in. long, flushed pink to reddish, with darker base, staminal column included; caps. subglobose, not beaked, thin-walled, inner valve margins pilose, seeds with a median line of pilose hairs. S. China.

oculiroseus: *H. Moscheutos* subsp. *Moscheutos.*

palustris: *H. Moscheutos* subsp. *palustris.*

paramutabilis L. H. Bailey. Shrub or small tree, to 12 ft. or more; similar vegetatively to *H. mutabilis,* but having 4–6 involucral bracts, more or less united at the base, ovate-elliptic, about 1 in. long, calyx to 1 in. long, scarcely enlarging in fr.; caps. woody, beaked, and valve margins glabrous inside. E.-cent. China.

pedunculatus L.f. Shrub, 3–6 ft.; lvs. dark green, to 3 in. long, mostly 3-lobed, lobes mostly oblong, rounded at the apex; fls. solitary, axillary, generally nodding, on elongate pedicels, involucral bracts 7–9, about ⅞ in. long, calyx usually shorter than bracts, petals to about 2 in. long, pale rose-purple, staminal column included; caps. ⅜–⅞ in. long, more or less cylindrical, thin-walled. Mozambique to S. Afr.

platanifolius (Willd.) Sweet [*H. acerifolius* (Link & Otto) DC., not Salisb.; *H. collinus* Roxb.; *H. gossypinus* Baill., not Thunb.]. Shrub or small tree; lvs. mostly 3–6 in. long, about as broad, mostly 3-lobed, lobes elliptic, acuminate, nearly entire; fls. solitary, in the upper lf. axils, involucral bracts 6–9, united at base, cordate-ovate, ½–1 in. long, usually with crisped margins, calyx ⅜–⅞ in. long, petals 1½–2½ in. long, white, with crimson base, staminal column included; caps. to ⅞ in. long. Trop. Asia.

radiatus Cav. Similar to *H. cannabinus,* but without median gland on each calyx lobe and with involucral bracts usually forked. Trop. Asia.

Rosa-sinensis L. [*H. chinensis* Hort. in part, not Roxb. or DC.; *H. fulgens* Hort.; *H. sinensis* Hort., not Mill.]. CHINESE H., HAWAIIAN H., ROSE-OF-CHINA, CHINA ROSE, BLACKING PLANT. Glabrate shrub, seldom over 8 ft. in cult., but treelike, to 15 ft. or more, in trop. regions; lvs. to 6 in. long, ovate, usually serrate, mostly glossy green; fls. solitary, in upper lf. axils, involucral bracts 6–9, linear-lanceolate, ¼–⅝ in. long, calyx tubular-campanulate, to 1¼ in. long, petals mostly 2–5 in. long, reddish or deep red, darker toward base, but in cvs. the corollas vary from single to double and from white to various shadings of red, yellow, and orange; staminal column exserted. Probably trop. Asia. Grown in all subtrop. and trop. regions of the world under many fancy and Latin cv. names. Cv. 'Cooperi' [*H. Cooperi* Hort. ex Van Houtte]. Foliage variegated.

Sabdariffa L. ROSELLE, JAMAICA SORREL, INDIAN S. Ann. or per. herb, to 6 ft. or more, sts. mostly glabrous, rarely somewhat spiny; lower lvs. ovate, undivided, grading in upper part of plant to palmately 3- or 5-lobed or -parted; fls. usually in terminal racemes with reduced lvs., involucral bracts about ⅝ in. long, channelled at apex, calyx becoming large, fleshy, and bright red in fr., petals to about 2 in. long, yellow, with brownish-red base, staminal column included. Probably trop. Afr., now widely cult. and naturalized throughout tropics. St. yields fiber for cordage; calyx used in drinks and for making jelly. See also *Roselle.*

schizopetalus (M. T. Mast.) Hook.f. JAPANESE H., JAPANESE-LANTERN. Shrub, to 9 ft., brs. slender, drooping; lvs. to 5 in. long, ovate, serrate; fls. delicate, pendent on long slender pedicels, petals to 2½ in. long, more or less streaked with pink or red, recurved and deeply laciniate, staminal column slender, long-exserted. Trop. e. Afr. Commonly grown as a basket plant under glass and outside through the same range as *H. Rosa-sinensis.*

sinensis: see *H. mutabilis* and *H. Rosa-sinensis.*

sinosyriacus L. H. Bailey. Similar to *H. syriacus,* but having lvs. larger, to 4 in. long and about as broad; involucral bracts mostly longer, ⅝–1 in. long, and broader, ⅛–⅜ in. wide. Cent. China.

speciosus: *H. coccineus.*

syriacus L. [*H. acerifolius* Salisb., not DC., *H. chinensis* Hort. in part, not Roxb. or DC.; *Althaea frutex* Hort. ex Mill.; *A. syriaca* Hort.]. ROSE-OF-SHARON, ALTHAEA, SHRUB A. Erect, nearly glabrous shrub or small tree, 6–10 ft. or more; lvs. mostly less than 3 in. long, triangular- to rhombic-ovate in outline, mostly deeply and narrowly 3-lobed, coarsely toothed; fls. on short pedicels, in upper lf. axils, involucral bracts 6–8, mostly lanceolate, less than ⅝ in. long and ⅛ in. wide, calyx slightly longer than bracts, corolla single or in some cvs. double, petals 1½–3 in. long, white, reddish, purplish or bluish-lavender, with generally crimson base, staminal column included. E. Asia. Commonly planted n. to Ontario; offered under many fancy and Latin cv. names, sometimes under the generic name *Althaea.*

tiliaceus L. [*H. abutiloides* Willd.; *Paritium tiliaceum* (L.) Juss.]. MAHOE. Spreading, evergreen shrub or small tree, to 20 ft. or more; lvs. mostly 3–8 in. long, ovate to orbicular, unlobed, leathery, green above, whitish beneath, stipules to about 2 in. long, clasping st.; fls. clustered near ends of brs., involucral bracts united in a 7–12-toothed cup to ½ in. long, calyx twice as long as bracts, petals 1¾–3 in. long, overlapping one another, yellow or whitish when fresh, usually with red or brownish-red base, fading through orange-yellow to deep red, staminal column included. Mostly littoral, Old and New World tropics. Yields fiber for cordage.

Trionum L. [*H. africanus* Mill.; *H. vesicarius* Cav.]. FLOWER OF-AN-HOUR. Erect or straggling, hispid herb, to 4 ft.; lvs. to about 3 in. long and wide, usually deeply 3- or 5-lobed or -parted, divisions pinnately incised; fls. solitary, axillary, involucral bracts 7–12, to ½ in. long, calyx to 1 in. long, scarious, with raised, purplish veins, inflated and enclosing the caps. in fr., petals to about 1½ in. long, white, cream, or yellow, with red base. Warm temp. and trop. regions of Old World; naturalized in similar regions of the New World.

vesicarius: *H. Trionum.*

Waimae A. Heller. Small, gray-barked tree, to about 30 ft.; similar to *H. Arnottianus,* but having lvs. broadly ovate to orbicular, crenate to crenate-serrate, velvety-tomentose beneath; calyx 1¼–1⅝ in. long. Hawaii.

Youngianus: *H. furcellatus.*

HICKORY NUT. This is the hard, husk-enclosed fruit of various species of the genus *Carya,* native to North America and including species much prized both as shade and as nut trees. Their fruits are gathered in the wild, and one species is much planted in its native South (see *Pecan*). Although slow in coming into bearing, all the hickories are readily raised from seeds (nuts), stratified and planted in spring, or sown directly in the ground in autumn if they can be protected from rodents. Because of the taproot, seedlings transplant with considerable loss if allowed to stand in the original nursery more than two years. A more branching root system can be produced by cutting the taproot of the seedling about 6 inches below the ground at least a year before transplanting.

Named cultivars of hickory may be propagated by budding and grafting. The principles involved are the same as with other fruit trees, but greater skill and accuracy in workmanship are required. With seedlings ½ inch in diameter, ring or annular budding is successful, either in the early spring as growth starts, using dormant scions, or preferably in July just as the current season's growth hardens. Somewhat larger stocks may be cleft-grafted or side-grafted. With young trees 1½–4 inches in diameter, the bark or inlay graft is suitable. Scions of vigorous one- or two-year shoots should be dormant. Grafting is done in the spring, from the time growth starts until trees are well leaved out. It is important that all cut surfaces of the stock and the entire surface of the scion, including the buds, be covered with wax.

Aside from the pecan, the most prized of the hickory nuts

is the shagbark, *Carya ovata;* crosses with the pecan have produced cultivars such as 'Burton', 'Gerardi', and 'Pixley'. The latter are excellent shade trees but produce minimal nut crops. The shellbark, *C. laciniosa,* is also a vigorous handsome shade tree but has nuts of poorer quality (with thick shells). Other species also produce edible nuts, although the pignut *(Carya glabra)* and the bitternut *(C. cordiformis)* produce bitter, inedible nuts.

HICKSBEACHIA F. J. Muell. *Proteaceae.* Two spp. of Australian trees; lvs. deeply lobed or pinnate, rigid, margin spiny-toothed; fls. bisexual, regular, corolla tube straight, lobes soon reflexed; fr. indehiscent, seed solitary.

pinnatifolia F. J. Muell. Lvs. about 2 ft. long; lfts. 18–20, 5–9 in. long; fls. in racemes 7–13 in. long; fr. an ellipsoid nut, 1½ in. long, reddish, seed edible.

HICORIA: *CARYA.* **H. microcarpa:** *C. glabra;* **H. Pecan:** *C. illinoinensis.*

HIERACIUM L. HAWKWEED. *Compositae* (Cichorium Tribe). Between 700 and 1,000 spp. (although thousands of forms, mostly apomictic, have been described as spp.), of per. herbs with milky sap, often stoloniferous, native mostly to the N. Hemisphere, some in s. India and Ceylon, S. Afr., and S. Amer.; lvs. in a basal rosette or alt. on the sts., entire to dentate, rarely deeply lobed; fl. heads corymbose to variously panicled, sometimes solitary, involucre cylindrical to campanulate, involucral bracts of unequal length, more or less imbricate, in 1–3 rows, receptacle flat, naked; fls. all ligulate, bisexual, usually yellow, sometimes white or orange; achenes cylindrical, truncate at apex, 10–15-ribbed, pappus of 1–2 rows of usually brownish or whitish, fragile, capillary bristles.

A few hawkweeds are sometimes cultivated, especially in rock gardens. They thrive in poor soil. Care must be exercised to keep them from spreading too much, as they may become weedy. Propagated by seeds, also by division of the stolons.

alpinum L. Sts. to 6 in.; lvs. in a basal rosette, obovate or obovate-lanceolate, nearly entire to slightly toothed, deep green, long-hairy and glandular; head to 1⅜ in. across, solitary; fls. bright yellow, styles yellow; achenes reddish-black. Mts., n. Eur., Scotland, cent. Asia, Greenland.

aurantiacum L. ORANGE H., DEVIL'S-PAINTBRUSH, KING-DEVIL. Stoloniferous per., to 20 in., hirsute with long, spreading hairs; lvs. mostly in a basal rosette, oblanceolate to elliptic-obovate, to 8 in. long, green; heads to 1 in. across, corymbose, involucral bracts with black-tipped, glandular hairs; fls. orange-red; achenes dark brown. Eur.; a troublesome weed in e. N. Amer. and on Pacific Coast.

bombycinum Boiss. & Reut. Sts. ascending, to about 1 ft.; lvs. in a basal rosette, blade elliptic to obovate, to 3 in. long, silvery-pubescent, petiole to 2½ in. long; heads ½–1½ in. across, solitary or in 2's or 3's, not crowded, involucral bracts densely silvery-hairy; fls. yellow; achenes dark brown. Cent. Spain.

faeroense Dahlst. Sts. to 2 ft., often rather flexuous, with pilose and stellate hairs, particularly toward the base, essentially glabrous toward the apex; lvs. in a basal rosette and also on the sts., the rosette lvs. often withering at flowering time, elliptic or lanceolate to oblong-lanceolate or linear-oblong, successively reduced upward along the st., remotely toothed, dark green, spotted dark purple and almost glabrous above, red-purple and more or less densely pilose beneath; heads in corymbose panicles, outer involucral bracts moderately pilose, inner ones glabrous or moderately pilose; fls. yellow. Faeroe Is.

glaucum All. Sts. to 20 in., glabrous; lvs. in a basal rosette, lanceolate to linear-lanceolate, sparsely dentate, rigid, glaucous, glabrous or hairy on the median veins beneath or on margins; heads to 1 in. across, 2–12 in a loose corymbose panicle, involucral bracts essentially glabrous; fls. yellow; achenes dark brown to black. S. Eur.

Gronovii L. Sts. to 5 ft., leafy mostly below the middle, with spreading hairs toward the base, obscurely stellate-pubescent or nearly glabrous toward the apex; lower lvs. obovate to elliptic or oblong, to 8 in. long, upper lvs. successively shorter, mostly setose above, finely stellate beneath; heads to ½ in. across, many in a panicle about 3 times longer than wide, involucral bracts glabrous or glandular below the middle; fls. yellow; achenes dark brown. Mass. to Kans., s. to Fla. and Tex.

Heldreichii Boiss. Sts. to 20 in., long-pilose; lvs. mostly in a basal rosette, obovate or oblong-obovate, long-silky or setose-pilose, entire or minutely toothed toward the base; heads 1–10, panicled, involucral bracts silky-villous; fls. yellow; achenes pale. Balkan region.

humile Jacq. Sts. to 1 ft., with spreading hairs; lvs. mostly in a basal rosette, elliptic to obovate, petioled, moderately pubescent with long hairs and shorter glandular hairs; heads 1–5, to 1¼ in. across, involucral bracts glandular-pilose; fls. yellow; achenes dark brown or black. S. and cent. Eur.

intybaceum Wulfen. Sts. to 1 ft., glandular-hairy, leafy; lvs. of basal rosette withering at flowering time, sessile, linear-lanceolate, dentate, glandular-hairy; heads to 1⅜ in. across, solitary on brs., involucral bracts glandular-hairy; fls. whitish-yellow; achenes dark brown. Alps.

japonicum Franch. & Sav. Sts. to about 1 ft.; lvs. mostly in a basal rosette, oblanceolate, about 2–4 in. long, sharply dentate, glandular-hairy and with long, spreading, coarse, brownish hairs; heads to ¾ in. across, few, racemose, involucral bracts blackish; fls. deep yellow; achenes brownish-black, pappus pale brown. Japan.

lanatum Vill. [*H. tomentosum* All.]. Sts. to 20 in., densely gray-tomentose; lvs. mostly on the sts., lanceolate, oblong, elliptic, or ovate, almost entire, densely gray-tomentose; heads to 1 in. across, clustered, involucral bracts densely hairy; fls. yellow; achenes dull black. S. Eur.

maculatum Sm. Sts. to about 20 in., reddish-hairy particularly toward base; lvs. on the sts. or a few in a basal rosette, oblong to elliptic-lanceolate, ciliate, often toothed, usually spotted with dark purple, with stiff hairs; heads in a loose panicle, involucral bracts moderately hairy, floccose, densely glandular; fls. yellow, styles dark; achenes blackish. Cent. Eur.; naturalized in Eng. and Ireland.

murorum L. GOLDEN LUNGWORT. Sts. to 2½ ft.; lvs. mostly in a basal rosette, elliptic, rounded to cordate or nearly truncate at base, shallowly to coarsely toothed, petioles villous; heads about 1 in. across, in a loose, corymbose panicle, involucral bracts densely covered with stalked glands; fls. yellow; achenes brown. Eur.; adventive in ne. N. Amer.

Pamphilii Arv.-Touv. Sts. to 16 in., white-hairy; lvs. mostly in a basal rosette, elliptic-lanceolate to ovate-lanceolate, white-hairy; heads to 1¾ in. across, solitary, involucral bracts densely villous; fls. yellow; achenes dark brown. Sw. Alps.

Pilosella L. MOUSE-EAR H. Very stoloniferous per., to 1 ft., hairy; lvs. mostly in a basal rosette, oblong or oblanceolate to spatulate, to about 5 in. long, entire, bristly, stellate-tomentose beneath when young; heads to 1 in. across, usually solitary, involucral bracts with various glandular and nonglandular hairs; fls. pale yellow; achenes purplish-black. Eur., w. Asia; naturalized as a troublesome weed in e. N. Amer. and Ore.

Scouleri Hook. Sts. to about 3 ft., long-setose and sometimes stellate-pubescent below; lvs. on the sts. and in a basal rosette, lanceolate to oblanceolate, to 10 in. long, essentially entire, setose, inconspicuously stellate; heads about ½ in. across, panicled, involucral bracts finely stellate-pubescent, sometimes setose and sometimes with gland-tipped bristles; fls. yellow; achenes dark brown. B.C. to Ore., e. to Mont. and w. Wyo.

staticifolium All. Sts. to about 1 ft., mostly glaucous and glabrous; lvs. in a basal rosette, linear to linear-oblanceolate, to 4 in. long, glabrous, remotely toothed; heads to 1¼ in. across, mostly solitary, involucral bracts mealy; fls. sulphur-yellow; achenes brown. Alps.

tomentosum: *H. lanatum.*

umbellatum L. NARROW-LEAVED H. Never stoloniferous, to 3 ft.; lvs. all on the sts., linear to linear-lanceolate, nearly entire or with 2–3 remote teeth, dark green, scabrous; heads to 1½ in. across, in an umbellate panicle, involucral bracts usually blackish-green; fls. golden-yellow; achenes brownish-black. Ont. to Alaska, s. to Mich., Wisc., Colo., Ore.; also Eur., Asia.

venosum L. RATTLESNAKE WEED, POOR ROBIN'S PLANTAIN. Sts. to about 3 ft., essentially glabrous; lvs. mostly in a basal rosette, elliptic to ovate or oblanceolate, to 6½ in. long, toothed, usually veined reddish-purple; heads to ½ in. across, in an open corymbose panicle, involucral bracts more or less glandular toward base; fls. yellow; achenes dark brown. Vt. and New Hamp., s. to Ala. and Ga.

villosum L. SHAGGY H. Sts. to 2 ft., soft-silky-pubescent; lvs. basal and on the sts., oblong, oblanceolate, or ovate, nearly entire, silky-pubescent; heads to 2 in. across, solitary or sometimes 2–4, involucral bracts densely pubescent; fls. yellow; achenes brown. S. Eur.

Waldsteinii Tausch. Sts. to 1½ ft.; lower lvs. in a false rosette, withering at flowering time, st. lvs. many, elliptic or obovate, densely finely plumose with white hairs; heads in a loose panicle, involucral bracts hairy, sometimes glandular; fls. yellow; achenes straw-colored to light yellow-brown. Balkan Pen.

Walteranum: a listed name of no botanical standing.

Welwitchii: a listed name of no botanical standing for a plant described as about 1 ft. tall, with gray-felty lvs. and yellow fls.

HILARIA HBK. *Gramineae.* About 7 spp. of per. grasses in N. Amer., sts. stiff, solid; lf. blades narrow; spikelets sessile, erect, in groups of 3 along a terminal spike, the groups falling entire from the axis, central spikelet bisexual, usually 1-fld., 2 lateral spikelets male, usually 2-fld., glumes leathery, those of the 3 spikelets forming a false involucre, usually awned, lemma and palea thinner than glumes, about equal. For terminology see *Gramineae.*

Belangeri (Steud.) Nash. CURLY MESQUITE. Sts. to 12 in., erect, slender, villous at nodes, forming clumps, sending out slender stolons, internodes of stolons wiry, to 8 in. long; lf. blades flat, to ⅛ in. wide, scabrous, more or less pilose, usually short, crowded at base; spike usually ¾–1¼ in. long, with mostly 4–8 fan-shaped groups of spikelets to ¼ in. long along flat axis, internodes alternately curved, glumes variable in a single spike, united basally, firm, scabrous, 2–3-nerved, sometimes awned or toothed. Tex. to Ariz. and n. Mex.

Jamesii (Torr.) Benth. GALLETA. Sts. to 1 ft., erect, nodes villous, base often decumbent or rhizomatous, bearing tough scaly rhizomes; lf. blades to 2 in. long, ⅛ in. wide, rigid, soon involute, the upper reduced; groups of spikelets not fan-shaped, to ⁵⁄₁₆ in. long, long-villous at base, glumes of lateral spikelets narrowed toward base, acute, usually with a single awn. Wyo. and Utah to Tex. and Calif.

mutica (Buckl.) Benth. TOBOSA GRASS. Sts. to 2 ft., clustered, glabrous, nodes pubescent; lf. blades flat or somewhat involute, to ⅛ in. wide; spikes to 2⅜ in. long; groups of spikelets fan-shaped, about ¼ in. long, bearded at base, glumes of lateral spikelets very unsymmetrical, widened toward the ciliate apex, glumes of fertile spikelet strongly keeled, with few to several narrow, ciliate lobes and slender awns. Tex. to Ariz. and n. Mex.

rigida (Thurb.) Benth. ex Scribn. BIG GALLETA. Sts. to 3 ft., many, rigid, felty-pubescent, glabrate and scabrous above, branching, brs. mostly erect or ascending; lvs. felty or glabrous, usually woolly at the top of the sheath, blades to 2 in. long or more on sterile shoots, to ⅛ in. wide, more or less involute, acuminate; groups of spikelets about ⁵⁄₁₆ in. long, densely bearded at base, glumes variable, those of the lateral spikelets thin, with 1–3 of 7 nerves excurrent into slender awns, lemma thin, ciliate, 2-lobed, short-awned. S. Utah and Nev. to Ariz., s. Calif., and n. Mex.

HILDEGARDIA Schott & Endl. *Sterculiaceae.* About 8 spp. of shrubs or trees, one in Cuba, the others in the Old World tropics; lvs. alt., cordate-ovate, entire; fls. unisexual, in axillary racemes or panicles, petals none, anthers about 10 in 2 whorls at the apex of a slender column, carpels 5, stipitate, coherent, 1–2-ovuled; mature carpels closed, membranous, sometimes winged, 1–2-seeded.

Barteri (M. T. Mast.) Kosterm. [*Erythropsis Barteri* (M. T. Mast.) Ridl.] Tree with buttresses, to about 100 ft.; fls. in slender panicles, appearing before the lvs.; calyx scarlet, ¾ in. long, constricted in the middle, stamens and carpels exserted; fr. reddish, submembranous, broadly and obliquely inflated, to 3 in. long, 1-seeded. Trop. Afr.

HIPPEASTRUM Herb. [*Amaryllis* of some Amer. auth., not L.; *Rhodophiala* K. Presl]. AMARYLLIS, BARBADOS LILY. *Amaryllidaceae.* About 75 spp. of herbs with tunicate bulbs, native mostly to trop. Amer., 1 in w. Afr.; lvs. linear to strap-shaped; umbel 1–10-fld., terminal on a hollow, leafless scape, and subtended by separate spathe valves; fls. usually declinate, perianth tube generally short, stamens declinate, unequal, of 4 different lengths, stigma declinate, ovary inferior; fr. a loculicidal caps., seeds few to many, either disc-shaped, winged and black, or rarely globose and black, or subglobose, angular, and brown.

Species and hybrids of *Hippeastrum* are grown in the North as house plants or outdoors, but then the bulbs must be lifted before winter. In the South they are commonly grown as garden plants. The best soil is composed of fibrous loam, leaf mold, and sand, with a neutral or slightly alkaline reaction. Plants propagated from seeds reach blooming size in about 2 years. The common cultivated kinds are largely hybrids or variants and often of complex parentage. Among the most common parent species are *H. aulicum, H. elegans, H. puniceum, H. reginae, H. reticulatum,* and *H. striatum.* Named hybrid cultivars are propagated from bulb divisions.

A group of narrow-leaved species is sometimes separated as the genus *Rhodophiala.* A number of these not listed for sale but grown by specialists are described as *Amaryllis* in H. P. Traub, *The Amaryllis Manual,* 1958.

×**Ackermannii:** a hort. name for hybrids derived from *H. aulicum.*

advena (Ker-Gawl.) Herb. [*Amaryllis advena* Ker-Gawl.; *Habranthus advena* (Ker-Gawl.) Herb.; *H. miniatus* D. Don ex Sweet; *Rhodophiala advena* (Ker-Gawl.) Traub]. To 1 ft.; lvs. linear, glaucous; umbel 2–6-fld.; fls. yellow or red, to 2 in. long, perianth tube very short, lobes oblong-acute, stigma trifid. Chile. Some material cult. under this name may be *H. bifidum.* Cv. 'Miniatum' is listed.

Albertii: *H. puniceum* cv. 'Semiplenum'.

ambiguum: *H. elegans* cv. 'Longiflorum'.

argentinum (Pax) Hunz. [*H. candidum* Stapf; *Amaryllis candida* (Stapf) Traub & Moldenke; *A. immaculata* Traub & Moldenke]. To 2½ ft.; lvs. about 1 in. wide, somewhat glaucous; umbel 6-fld.; fls. white, with greenish base, to 8 in. long, perianth tube about 4 in. long, lobes crisped, to 5 in. long, stigma trifid. Argentina.

aulicum (Ker-Gawl.) Herb. [*H. robustum* A. Dietr.; *Amaryllis aulica* Ker-Gawl.]. LILY-OF-THE-PALACE. To 2 ft.; lvs. to 2 in. wide, bright green, obtuse; umbel 1–2-fld.; fls. red with green throat, to 6 in. long, lobes obovate, the 2 upper wider than others, throat with a distinct incurved corona, filaments red, stigma trifid. Cent. Brazil to Paraguay.

Bagnoldii (Herb.) Bak. [*Amaryllis Bagnoldii* (Herb.) D. Dietr.; *Habranthus Bagnoldii* Herb.; *Rhodophiala Bagnoldii* (Herb.) Traub]. To 1 ft.; lvs. linear, glaucous; umbel 4–6-fld.; fls. erect, to 2 in. long, yellow tinged with red, stigma trifid. Chile.

barbatum Herb. [*Amaryllis Belladonna* var. *barbata* (Herb.) Traub & Moldenke]. Similar to *H. puniceum,* but summer-flowering and with fls. creamy-white. Surinam.

bifidum (Herb.) Bak. [*Amaryllis bifida* (Herb.) K. Spreng.; *Rhodophiala bifida* (Herb.) Traub]. To 1 ft.; lvs. linear, somewhat glaucous; umbel 3–6-fld.; fls. bright red, to 2 in. long, perianth tube very short, lobes oblanceolate, clawed at base, stigma trifid. Argentina, Uruguay. Sometimes cult., mistakenly, as *H. advena.* Var. **spathaceum** (Herb.) H. E. Moore [*Rhodophiala bifida* var. *spathacea* (Herb.) Traub]. Umbel 2–6-fld., spathe split to base on one side. Argentina. Has been offered as *Habranthus roseus* in the trade.

brachyandrum: *Habranthus brachyandrus.*

candidum: *H. argentinum.*

chilense (L'Hér.) Bak. [*Rhodophiala chilensis* (L'Hér.) Traub]. To 10 in.; lvs. narrow, to about 10 in. long, developing at same time as fls.; umbel 2-fld., pedicels to 1 in. long; fls. bright red or yellow, to 2 in. long, funnelform, stamens shorter than perianth, stigma trifid. Spring. S. Chile.

correiense (Bury) Worsl. [*H. organense* Hook. ex Herb.; *Amaryllis organensis* (Hook. ex Herb.) Traub & Uphof]. Lvs. broad, glaucous; umbel 2-fld.; fls. to 6 in. long, perianth tube short, with an incurved corona at throat, lobes bright crimson, with green keel in lower half, stigma deeply trifid. Brazil.

elegans (K. Spreng.) H. E. Moore [*H. solandriflorum* (Lindl.) Herb.; *Amaryllis elegans* K. Spreng.; *A. solandriflora* Lindl.]. To 2 ft.; lvs. 1 in. wide or more, developing at same time as fls.; umbel 2–4-fld.; fls. greenish-white, to 10 in. long, tube 4–5 in. long, stigma headlike. S. Amer. Cv. 'Longiflorum' [*H. ambiguum* Herb.; *Amaryllis ambigua* (Herb.) Sweet ex Steud.]. Perhaps of hybrid origin, not well known. Var. *divifrancisci* (Cardenas) H. E. Moore. Differs from the typical var. in having bulb neck longer, to 4 in. long, lvs. erect, pedicels longer, to 1¾ in. long, lobes more acute, and stigma clearly trifid. Bolivia.

equestre: *H. puniceum.*

Evansiae (Traub & I. S. Nels.) H. E. Moore [*Amaryllis Evansiae* Traub & I. S. Nels.]. Similar to *H. puniceum,* but fls. horizontal, perianth light chartreuse-green, aging to lighter green or very light yellow, tube shorter. Bolivia.

×**Garfieldii:** a listed name of no botanical standing, applied to a hybrid strain of undetermined origin.

×**hybridum:** a listed name of no botanical standing, applied to various hybrids.

×**Johnsonii** (Bury) Herb. [*Amaryllis* ×*Johnsonii* Bury]: *H. reginae* × *H. vittatum.* ST. JOSEPH'S LILY. An old hybrid, probably now represented by more recent crosses and variants.

Leopoldii Dombr. [*Amaryllis Leopoldii* Hort. Veitch ex T. Moore]. Lvs. strap-shaped; umbel 2-fld.; fls. to 5 in. long, perianth tube short, lobes nearly regular, white toward tip, red at middle with 2-parted white keel, throat greenish-white, stigma headlike. Peru.

miniatum (Ruiz & Pav.) Herb. [*Amaryllis miniata* Ruiz & Pav.]. To 18 in.; lvs. strap-shaped, about 1 in. wide; fls. to 4 in. long, bright red, stamens shorter than perianth, stigma headlike. Peru.

Morelianum Lem. [*Amaryllis Moreliana* (Lem.) Traub]. To 20 in.; lvs. to 18 in. long, 1⅝ in. wide; umbel 2-fld.; fls. bright ocher-red, netted with purple, with green star in throat, perianth tube with recurved scales, stigma slightly trifid. Brazil.

organense: *H. correiense.*

phycelloides: *Phycella phycelloides.*

pratense (Poepp.) Bak. [*Habranthus pratensis* (Poepp.) Herb.; *Rhodophiala pratensis* (Poepp.) Traub]. Lvs. linear, to ½ in. wide, developing at same time as fls.; umbel 2–5-fld.; fls. bright red or violet-purple, to 2½ in. long, stigma headlike. Chile.

procerum: *Worsleya Rayneri.*

psittacinum (Ker-Gawl.) Herb. [*Amaryllis psittacina* Ker-Gawl.]. Lvs. 1–1½ in. wide, glaucescent; umbel 2–4-fld.; fls. to 5 in. long, perianth tube short, with distinct incurved corona, lobes with crimson edge, green keel, and crimson stripes radiating from the keel. S. Brazil.

puniceum (Lam.) Voss [*H. equestre* (Ait.) Herb.; *Amaryllis Belladonna* of Amer. auth., not L.; *A. equestris* Ait.; *A. punicea* Lam.]. To 2 ft.; lvs. bright green, to 2 in. wide, developing after fls.; umbel 2–4-fld.; fls. bright red, with green base, to 5 in. long, perianth tube about 1 in. long, stamens shorter than lobes, stigma headlike. Spring. Trop. Amer. Cv. 'Semiplenum' [*Amaryllis Albertii* Lem.]. Fls. semidouble or double, scarlet. Var. **Haywardii** (Traub & Uphof) H. E. Moore. Fls. yellowish-white at base, clear pink toward apex. The name *Amaryllis Belladonna* has been applied to this sp. by some authors in recent years.

reginae (L.) Herb. [*Amaryllis reginae* L.]. Lvs. to 1½ in. wide; umbel 2–4-fld.; fls. to 5 in. long, bright red with greenish-white star in throat, perianth tube short, stamens as long as perianth, stigma headlike. Trop. Amer., w. cent. Afr.

reticulatum (L'Hér.) Herb. [*Amaryllis reticulata* L'Hér.]. To 1 ft.; lvs. 2 in. wide; umbel 3–5-fld.; fls. to 4 in. long, perianth tube to 1 in. long, lobes coming together below, bright mauve-red with deeper cross bars; seeds few, hard, round, and black. Brazil. Var. **striatifolium** (Herb.) Herb. Lvs. broader, with a prominent white rib, perianth lobes not noticeably barred.

robustum: *H. aulicum.*

roseum (Sweet) Bak. [*Amaryllis Barlowii* Traub & Moldenke; *Habranthus roseus* Sweet; *Rhodophiala rosea* (Sweet) Traub]. To 6 in.; lvs. linear, glaucous, developing at same time as fls.; umbel 1–2-fld.; fls. to 2 in. long, bright red, perianth tube greenish, very short, stigma trifid. Chile.

rutilum: *H. striatum.*

solandriflorum: *H. elegans.*

striatum (Lam.) H. E. Moore [*H. rutilum* (Ker-Gawl.) Herb.; *Amaryllis rutila* Ker-Gawl.; *A. striata* Lam.]. To 1 ft.; lvs. bright green, strap-shaped, 1 in. wide or more; umbel 2–4-fld.; fls. to 4 in. long, bright crimson with a green keel halfway up the lobes, stigma trifid. Brazil. Cv. 'Crocatum'. Fls. smaller, pastel-pink, perianth lobes undulate. Cv. 'Fulgidum'. Lvs. broader, fls. brilliant scarlet.

texanum: *Habranthus texanus.*

vittatum (L'Hér.) Herb. [*Amaryllis vittata* L'Hér.]. To 3 ft.; lvs. broad; umbel 2–4-fld.; fls. to 6 in. long, perianth tube short, lobes striped with red between white margins and keel, stigma trifid. Peru. Var. **costaricensis:** a listed name of no botanical standing.

HIPPOBROMA G. Don. *Lobeliaceae.* One sp., probably a per. herb, with poisonous milky sap, native to W. Indies; lvs. alt., basal and on sts., simple; fls. axillary, on pedicels with 2 bracts, corolla white, salverform, tube elongate, not split, narrowly cylindrical, lobes nearly equal, anther tube oblique, anthers white-bearded at tip, the shorter 2 densely tufted-hairy; fr. a caps.

longiflora (L.) G. Don [*Isotoma longiflora* (L.) K. Presl; *Laurentia longiflora* (L.) Endl.]. Mostly unbranched, to 2 ft.; lvs. nearly sessile, lanceolate to oblanceolate, to 8 in. long, pinnately dentate; corolla tube 2–3½ in. long, less than ¼ in. across, lobes to ¾ in. long; caps. to ⅝ in. long. W. Indies, trop. Amer.; Pacific Is., w. to Madagascar; now weedy in tropics.

HIPPOCASTANACEAE Torr. & A. Gray. HORSE CHESTNUT FAMILY. Dicot.; 2 genera and about 15 spp. of deciduous or evergreen polygamous trees, native from Eur., e. Asia and N. Amer., s. to n. S. Amer.; lvs. opp., palmately compound; fls. white, red, or yellow, in terminal panicles, irregular, calyx 5-lobed or of 5 sepals, petals 4–5, stamens 6–8, pistil 1, ovary

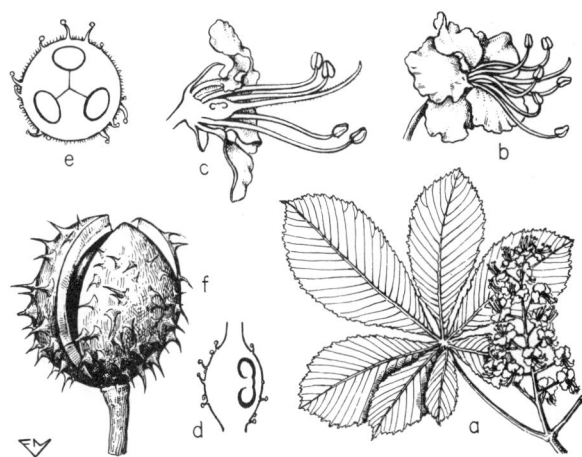

HIPPOCASTANACEAE. *Aesculus Hippocastanum:* **a,** twig with leaf and inflorescence, × ¹⁄₁₀; **b,** flower, × 1; **c,** flower, vertical section, × 1; **d,** ovary, vertical section, × 2; **e,** ovary, cross section, × 4; **f,** fruit, × ½. (From Bailey, *Manual of Cultivated Plants,* ed. 2.)

superior, 3-celled, style 1; fr. a leathery, warty, or smooth caps. Only *Aesculus* is cult.

HIPPOCREPIS L. HORSESHOE VETCH. *Leguminosae* (subfamily *Faboideae*). About 12 spp. of herbs and small shrubs of Medit. region; lvs. alt., odd-pinnate, with many, small lfts.; fls. in long-peduncled umbels or headlike racemes, or solitary, yellow, papilionaceous, alt. stamens dilated in upper part; fr. a flat legume, with horseshoe-shaped sinus opp. each curved seed.

Planted in rock gardens; propagated by seeds or division.

comosa L. Per., 1–2 ft.; lfts. in 4–7 pairs, oblong; peduncles longer than lvs.; frs. many, to 1 in. long, covered with reddish glands. Cent. and s. Eur.

HIPPOPHAE L. SEA BUCKTHORN. *Elaeagnaceae.* Two spp. of dioecious spiny shrubs or trees covered with silvery scales, native to Eur. and Asia; lvs. alt., deciduous, willowlike; fls. inconspicuous, yellow, appearing before lvs.; fr. drupelike. The name has four syllables.

Any soil is satisfactory. To ensure fruit, care must be taken to have a few male plants. Propagated by seeds sown in autumn or stratified, cuttings of ripened wood in spring, root cuttings, layers, and suckers.

rhamnoides L. [*H. rhamnoides* var. *angustifolia* Lodd. ex Loud.]. SALLOW THORN. To 30 ft.; fr. bright orange-yellow, ¼ in. long, persisting through the winter. Eur. to n. China. Very hardy. Fr. is edible; wood sometimes used for turning. Var. **procera** Rehd. To 55 ft. W. China.

salicifolia D. Don. To 50 ft., brs. drooping; lvs. stellate-tomentose beneath, dull green above; fr. yellow. Himalayas. Hardy only in the South.

HIPPURIDACEAE Link. HIPPURIS or MARE'S-TAIL FAMILY. Dicot.; 1 genus, *Hippuris,* a per., aquatic herb of wide distribution; lvs. whorled, simple, entire; fls. minute, sessile, axillary, perianth absent, stamen 1, carpel 1; fr. hard, nutlike, 1-seeded.

HIPPURIS L. *Hippuridaceae.* Generally treated as comprising 1 sp., with characters of the family.

vulgaris L. MARE'S-TAIL. Lvs. in whorls of 6–12, linear, entire, emersed lvs. firm, ¼–1½ in. long, submersed lvs. flaccid, to 4 in. long. N. Amer., Patagonia, Eur., Asia. In shallow water, simple, erect, aerial, fl. sts. ½–2 ft. high are produced; in deep or running water, sts. may be several ft. long, remaining submersed and sterile. Occasionally cult. in bog gardens or pools.

HIPTAGE Gaertn. *Malpighiaceae.* About 25 spp. of erect or climbing shrubs, native to trop. Asia; lvs. opp., simple, leathery, with 2 glands at base of blade; fls. in terminal or axillary racemes, rarely in congested panicles, irregular, sepals 5, with 2 smaller than the other 3, and with a large gland

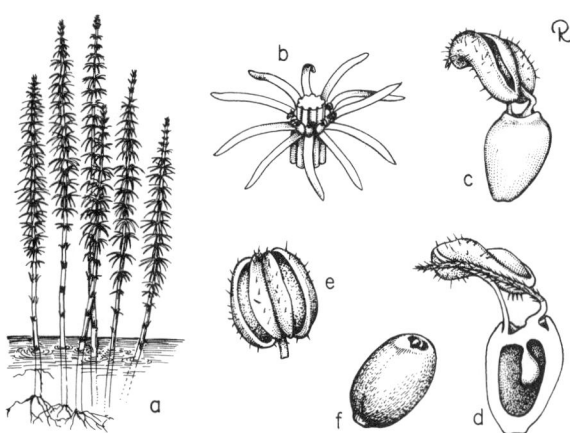

HIPPURIDACEAE. *Hippuris vulgaris:* **a,** plants, × ⅙; **b,** node of stem with axillary flowers, × 1½; **c,** flower, × 12; **d,** flower, vertical section, × 15; **e,** anther, × 12; **f,** fruit, × 8.

between them that is decurrent on the pedicel, petals 5, with 2 smaller than the other 3, clawed, toothed or fimbriate, usually hairy on exterior, stamens 10, the filament of one wider, longer, and recurved, style 1, recurved, slightly longer than the longest stamen; fr. a 3-winged samara.

benghalensis (L.) Kurz. Habit variable, high-climbing liana to large shrub, with white or yellowish hairs; lvs. lanceolate to ovate-lanceolate, to 8 in. long; fls. pink to white, with yellow marks, in 10–30-fld. racemes. Ceylon, se. Asia, Philippine Is., Taiwan. Cult. in the tropics for its fragrant fls.; used medicinally in India.

HISTIOPTERIS (J. Agardh) John Sm. *Polypodiaceae.* About 10 spp. of trop., terrestrial ferns with long, creeping rhizomes; lvs. firm to leathery, huge, glabrous, 1–2-pinnate, pinnae opp., veins netted; sori continuous along margins, indusia false, consisting of reflexed lf. margins. Like *Pteridium* in hairy rhizome, but lvs. glabrous and with netted veins.

For culture see *Ferns.*

incisa (Thunb.) John Sm. Lvs. usually 2–3-pinnate to 4-pinnatifid, the ultimate lobes triangular to oblong, clearly marked beneath with brownish veins that form narrow areoles along midvein. Tropics. In the wild the lvs. are scrambling or climbing and the lf. blades may reach 10 ft. long on petioles to 6 ft. long.

HOFFMANNIA Swartz. *Rubiaceae.* About 100 spp. of shrubs or herbs, native to Mex., s. to Argentina; lvs. opp. or whorled, usually colored, stipules interpetiolar; fls. in axillary cymes, small, white, yellow or red, 4-merous, corolla funnelform or almost rotate, tube elongate or short; fr. a small berry, seeds many, small.

Several species are grown as foliage plants in the greenhouse. Propagated by cuttings.

discolor (Lem.) Hemsl. Herbaceous or suffrutescent, about 6 in., hairy; lvs. obovate, to 6 in. long, satiny above, purple beneath; cymes long-stalked; fls. red. Probably Mex.

Ghiesbreghtii (Lem.) Hemsl. Shrub, sts. stout, 4-angled, to 4 ft., nearly glabrous; lvs. oblong-lanceolate, to 1 ft. long, dark velvety green above, purple-red beneath; cymes short-stalked; fls. yellow, with red spot. Guatemala, probably s. Mex. Cv. **'Variegata'.** Lvs. mottled above.

refulgens (Hook.) Hemsl. TAFFETA PLANT, QUILTED-TAFFETA PLANT. Herbaceous or suffrutescent, to 12 in., sts. stout, cylindrical, sometimes hairy; lvs. narrowly obovate, to 6 in. long, fleshy, dull green and somewhat iridescent above, wine-red beneath; fls. pale red, to 1 in. across; fr. red. Mex. to Cent. Amer. Cv. **'Vittata'.** Lvs. with prominent silver-gray veins and margins on upper surface.

regalis (Hook.) Hemsl. Subshrub, sts. stout, somewhat fleshy, cylindrical or obscurely 4-angled; lvs. round-ovate, somewhat leathery, glabrous, glossy, dark green above, purple-red beneath; cymes nearly sessile; fls. yellow. Probably Mex.

Roezlii Hort. ex Gentil. Similar to *H. refulgens* and perhaps only a form of it, but having sts. and lvs. almost glabrous, and fls. somewhat larger. Probably Mex.

vittata: a listed name of no botanical standing; see *H. refulgens* cv.

HOHENBERGIA Schult.f. *Bromeliaceae.* About 36 spp. of stemless epiphytes, native to trop. Amer.; lvs. in basal rosettes, spiny, strap-shaped; infl. scapose, bracted, paniculate, brs. with conelike spikes; fls. blue or white, petals separate, pollen sculptured, ovary inferior, ovules many, caudate or obtuse; fr. a berry.

Grown in nearly full sun. For culture see *Bromeliaceae.*

Blanchetii (Bak.) E. Morr. ex Mez. Lvs. broadly linear, to 4 in. wide or more, spiny; fl. bracts rounded at apex; sepals ⅛ in. long, petals blue, ¼ in. long, ovules caudate. Brazil.

catingae Ule. To 3 ft.; lvs. to 1½ ft. long, 1⅝ in. wide, spiny; infl. purplish, spikes sparsely woolly-tomentose, fl. bracts acuminate; petals to ½ in. long, ovules caudate. Brazil.

distans (Griseb.) Bak. Lvs. to 2½ ft. long, narrowly strap-shaped, entire or minutely toothed; scape curving downward, infl. to nearly 2 ft. long, drooping, brs. 10–20, loosely arranged, to 5 in. long, bearing 10-fld. stalked spikes, the spikes 2–10 times as long as their peduncles; fls. white or greenish-yellow, to ¾ in. long, ovules obtuse. Jamaica.

inermis Mez. Lvs. linear, to 3 ft. long, 2½ in. wide, nearly spineless; spikes sessile; fls. white, to ¾ in. long, ovules obtuse. Jamaica.

penduliflora (A. Rich.) Mez. Lvs. blue-green, broadly linear, minutely spiny, to 2 ft. long, 3⅜ in. wide; spikes with 15 or more fls., scarcely longer than their peduncles; fls. to ⅝ in. long, ovules obtuse. W. Indies.

Salzmanii (Bak.) E. Morr. ex Mez. Similar to *H. Blanchetii,* but with lvs. broader, sepals longer, petals violet, to ½ in. long. Brazil.

stellata Schult.f. Lvs. broadly linear, to 3 ft. long, 3 in. wide, spiny, light green; spikes glabrous, bracts acuminate, orange-red; fls. dark blue, to 1 in. long, ovules caudate. Trinidad to Brazil.

HOHERIA A. Cunn. LACEBARK. *Malvaceae.* Five or perhaps only 2 very variable spp. of small trees in New Zeal.; lvs. alt., simple, often lobed in juvenile stages and unlobed in adult stages, serrate to crenate, stipules falling early; fls. in axillary or terminal cymes, or solitary, involucral bracts 0, petals 5, white, stamens united in a tubular column, the column divided apically into 5 bundles of filaments, style brs. as many as the mericarps, stigmas capitate or slightly decurrent; fr. a schizocarp, mericarps 5–15, in a single whorl, each winged or ridged along the back, 1-seeded.

Hoherias are attractive, summer-flowering ornamentals suitable for outdoor cultivation in Calif. and in the southern U.S. where frost is not severe. They generally develop first as shrubs with often suborbicular, lobed leaves, and only with age do they become arborescent. Even then there may be a mixture of juvenile and adult leaves. They are best propagated by cuttings or by layering, for there is considerable variation in the plants grown from seeds.

angustifolia Raoul [*H. populnea* var. *angustifolia* (Raoul) Hook.f.]. Closely allied to *H. populnea,* but having lvs. often clustered, narrow, obovate to lanceolate, 1–2 in. long, about ½ in. wide, spinulose-dentate-serrate; fls. 5 or less in cymose clusters.

glabrata T. Sprague and Summerh. Similar to *H. Lyallii,* and perhaps only a var. of it; differing in having lvs. less densely pubescent, stigmas capitate or only slightly decurrent.

Holmannii: a listed name of no botanical standing.

Lyallii Hook.f. [*Gaya Lyallii* (Hook.f.) Bak.f.; *G. Lyallii* var. *ribifolia* T. Kirk; *Plagianthus Lyallii* (Hook.f.) A. Gray ex Hook.f.]. LACEBARK. Slender, deciduous tree, to 30 ft., young brs., lvs, and infls. densely pubescent; lvs. ovate, to 5 in. long, acuminate, rounded to truncate at the base, 2–3 times crenate or lacerate-crenate; fls. solitary or in cymes of 2–5, 1½ in. across, petals broadly obovate, overlapping, styles filiform with obliquely capitate to decurrent stigmas; mericarps 10–15, pubescent, not winged or obscurely winged. Plants listed under this name are usually *H. glabrata.* Var. **ribifolia:** *H. Lyallii.*

macrodonta: a listed name of no botanical standing.

populnea A. Cunn. LACEBARK. More or less evergreen tree, to 30 ft., glabrous or nearly so; lvs. ovate to ovate-elliptic, 2–6 in. long, usually acuminate, rounded to subcordate, deeply and coarsely serrate-dentate, somewhat leathery; fls. solitary or in (2–)5–10-fld. clusters, less than 1 in. across, petals narrow-obovate, scarcely overlapping; mericarps 5(–6), broadly winged. Wood used in cabinet making and the bark for ropes and cords. Cv. **'Osbornii'.** Lvs. darker, purplish-veined; filaments purple. Var. **angustifolia:** *H. angustifolia.* Var. **lanceolata:** *H. sexstylosa.*

sexstylosa Colenso [*H. populnea* var. *lanceolata* Hook.f.]. RIBBONWOOD. Closely allied to *H. populnea,* but having lvs. narrowly ovate to lanceolate, 2–4 in. long; cymes 2–5-fld.; mericarps (5–)6–8.

HOLACANTHA A. Gray. *Simaroubaceae.* Two spp. of dioecious shrubs of arid sw. U.S. and n. Mex.; brs. many, rigid, spine-tipped; lvs. scalelike, deciduous; fls. solitary or in dense panicles, sepals and petals 6–8, male fls. with 12–16 stamens, female fls. with sterile stamens, and 5–6 weakly cohering carpels, disc annular; fr. a drupe.

Emoryi A. Gray. CRUCIFIXION THORN. Thorny shrub, to 15 ft., brs. cylindrical; drupe red, obliquely ovoid. Early spring to summer. Calif., Ariz., n. Mex.

HOLARRHENA R. Br. *Apocynaceae.* About 7 spp. of deciduous trees and shrubs, native to trop. Afr. and Asia; lvs. opp., entire; fls. in terminal or subaxillary, many-fld. corymbose cymes, white, fragrant, 5-merous, corolla salverform, lobes oblong, tube slightly widened below middle, naked at throat, stamens borne near base of corolla tube, included, anthers not sagittate, forming a cone but free from stigma, pistil with 2 ovaries, style very short; fr. a pair of spreading, slender, terete, usually curved follicles, seeds with tuft of long, red-brown hairs.

antidysenterica (Roxb. ex Flem.) Wallich ex DC. Tree, to 15 ft.; lvs. elliptic-oblong to ovate, to 1 ft. long, bluntly acuminate, petioles very short; cymes 3–6 in. in diam.; corolla white, 1–2 in. across, tube very slender to ½ in. long, lobes oblong, rounded at apex; follicles to 16 in. long, nearly parallel, seeds with tuft of hairs 2 in. long. India to Malaya. Important medicinal plant where native.

Wulfsbergii Stapf. Medium-sized tree, brs. slender, somewhat pendulous, glabrous; lvs. elliptic to elliptic-oblong, to 5 in. long, membranous, sometimes with hairs in some vein axils beneath, petioles slender, 3/16 in. long; infls. at ends of very short branchlets, dense, 2½ in. in diam.; corolla white, fragrant, tube very slender, 5/16 in. long, lobes obovate-oblong, about 3/16 in. long; follicles to more than 1 ft. long. Ghana to Nigeria, where wood used for making tool handles, combs, and images.

HOLBOELLIA Wallich. *Lardizabalaceae.* About 10 spp. of monoecious, twining shrubs, native to the Himalayas and China; lvs. alt., palmately compound, long-petioled; infl. few-fld., axillary racemes or corymbs; fls. with sepals 6, petal-like, male fls. with 6 stamens, female fls. with 3 pistils; fr. a fleshy, indehiscent pod, seeds many, black.

coriacea Diels. Sts. to 20 ft. or more, glabrous; lfts. 3, elliptic, leathery, to 6 in. long, with the central one longest, dark glossy green; male and female fls. in separate infls., male fls. purplish, to ½ in. long, female fls. cream-colored, ⅝ in. long; fr. purple, to 2 in. long, seeds black. Cent. China.

grandiflora Reaub. Sts. to 18 ft.; lfts. 3–7, leathery, oblong to oblanceolate, to 5½ in. long, dark green above, reticulate and glaucous beneath; fls. white, to 1¼ in. long, fragrant; fr. purple, to 5 in. long, edible. W. China.

latifolia Wallich. Lfts. 3–7, leathery, oblong to obovate, to 6 in. long, glossy above, reticulate beneath; fls. to ⅝ in. long, fragrant, male and female fls. in the same infl., male fls. greenish-white, female fls. purplish; fr. purple, to 3 in. long, edible. Himalayas.

HOLCUS L. *Gramineae.* About 8 spp. of per. grasses in Eurasia; lf. blades flat; panicles contracted; spikelets 2-fld., articulated below the glumes, glumes about equal, longer than the florets, lower floret bisexual, awnless, second floret male, lemma bearing a short awn on the back. For terminology see *Gramineae.*

lanatus L. VELVET GRASS. Sts. to 3 ft., erect, clustered, grayish, velvety-pubescent; lf. blades to 5/16 in. wide; panicles to 6 in. long, contracted, purplish, soft; spikelets ⅛ in. long, glumes villous, hirsute on the nerves, the second broader than the first, 3-nerved, lemma smooth and glossy, the awn of the second hooklike. Eur.; introd. and occasionally cult. as a meadow grass on light or sandy soil, Me. to Ga. and Kans., and B.C. to Calif. and Ariz.

sudanensis: *Sorghum sudanense.*

HOLMSKIOLDIA Retz. *Verbenaceae.* About 10 spp. of spiny or unarmed shrubs of India, Madagascar, and trop. Afr.; lvs. opp., simple; fls. in axillary or terminal cymes or racemes, calyx obscurely 5-lobed, enlarging in fr.; corolla tubular, unequally 5-lobed, stamens 5; fr. a drupe.

Planted out of doors in warm climates and sometimes under glass, particularly for its large ornamental calyx.

sanguinea Retz. CHINESE-HAT PLANT, MANDARIN'S-HAT, CUP-AND-SAUCER PLANT. Straggling evergreen shrub, to 30 ft.; lvs. ovate, to 4 in. long; calyx spreading, brick-red or orange, to 1 in. across, corolla red, 1 in. long. Himalayas. Zone 10. Now a characteristic plant throughout the tropics.

HOLODISCUS Maxim. *Rosaceae.* A few spp. of deciduous shrubs or small trees, native to w. Amer.; lvs. simple, alt., toothed, without stipules; fls. whitish or pinkish, small, racemose or panicled, sepals 5, 3-nerved, petals 5, calyx tube saucer-shaped, stamens usually 20, pistils 5, separate; fr. 5 achenes.

Planted as ornamentals, thriving in sunny, well-drained locations. Propagated by seeds, by layers, and sometimes by greenwood cuttings under glass.

ariifolius: *H. discolor.*

discolor (Pursh) Maxim. [*H. ariifolius* (Sm.) Greene; *Spiraea ariifolia* Sm.]. CREAMBUSH, OCEAN-SPRAY. To 20 ft.; lvs. elliptic to ovate, to 3 in. long, not decurrent on petiole, 3–7-toothed on each margin, glabrous or scattered-pubescent above, villous to tomentose beneath; fls. cream-white, in panicles to 8 in. long. B.C. to Mont., s. Calif. Zone 6. Var. **franciscanus** (Rydb.) Jeps. Lf. blades to 2 in. long, 2–4-toothed on each margin; infl. to 5 in. long. S. Ore. to s. Calif.

dumosus (Nutt.) A. Heller. ROCK SPIRAEA. To 3 ft. or more; lf. blades decurrent on petioles, usually less than 1 in. long, coarsely toothed; panicles to 7 in. long. Wyo. to Utah and Ariz., some forms to n. Mex. Zone 6.

microphyllus Rydb. Like *H. dumosus,* but lf. blades toothed mostly at apex, not along the sides, obovate to spatulate, less than 1 in. long. Ore. to Baja Calif. Zone 6.

HOLOPTELEA Planch. *Ulmaceae.* Two spp. of deciduous trees, one native to India, one to Afr.; closely related to *Ulmus,* but differing in having lvs. entire and in technical characters of fl. and fr.

integrifolia (Roxb.) Planch. Large tree, twigs pubescent; lvs. elliptic or obovate-oblong, to 6 in. long, lateral veins 5–7 pairs; fr. a nearly round, notched samara, to 1 in. across, on a slender stalk. India. Not hardy in the North.

HOMALANTHUS A. Juss. [*Carumbium* Reinw.]. *Euphorbiaceae.* About 40 spp. of monoecious or dioecious shrubs and trees, with milky juice, native to trop. Asia and Australia; lvs. alt., simple, pinnately veined, entire, long-petioled; fls. without petals, in terminal racemes; fr. a caps.

Sometimes grown in southern U.S. as an ornamental or for curiosity.

populifolius R. C. Grah. [*Carumbium populifolium* (R. C. Grah.) Benth. & F. J. Muell.]. QUEENSLAND POPLAR. Glabrous, monoecious shrub or small tree; lvs. triangular-ovate, to 6 in. long; racemes 2–4½ in. long; female fls. on long pedicels, male fls. on very short pedicels; fr. about ⅜ in. in diam. Ceylon to Pacific Is. Bark and lvs. yield a black dye.

HOMALOCEPHALA: *ECHINOCACTUS.*

HOMALOCLADIUM (F. J. Muell.) L. H. Bailey. *Polygonaceae.* One sp., a shrub, native to Solomon Is.; sts. flat, articulated, striate, usually leafless in flowering stage; lvs. lanceolate, ½–2½ in. long, often lobed at base; fls. small, greenish, in little sessile clusters at alt. joints, calyx deeply 5-parted, stamens 8, stigmas 3; fr. an achene, triangular, smooth, enclosed by enlarged, deep red or purplish calyx.

platycladum (F. J. Muell.) L. H. Bailey [*Muehlenbeckia platyclada* (F. J. Muell.) Meissn.]. CENTIPEDE PLANT, TAPEWORM PLANT, RIBBONBUSH. In tropics with cylindrical canes to 12 ft., 2–4 ft. in cult.

HOMALOMENA Schott. *Araceae.* About 130 spp. of herbs, with mostly short, erect sts., of trop. Asia and Amer.; lvs. entire, petioles sheathing; peduncles many, short, spathe convolute, persistent, green to white or red; fls. unisexual, perianth absent, female fls. often with 1(–3) staminodes, ovaries nearly 2–3-celled, with many axile ovules.

Strictly tropical; for culture see *Anthurium.*

humilis (Jack) Hook.f. Small; lf. blades velvety dark green, broadly to narrowly elliptic or lanceolate-elliptic, to 4¾ in. long and 2 in. wide, margins irregularly notched, basally obtuse-subtruncate, with 5–10 ascending primary lateral veins, petioles purplish, 4–6 in. long; peduncle 1½ in. long, spathe ½ in. long. Malay Pen. Material offered under this name appears to be *H. pygmaea*.

Lindenii (Rodig.) Ridl. [*Alocasia? Lindenii* Rodig.; *H. singaporensis* Engl., not Regel]. Lf. blades spreading, triangular-ovate, very long-acuminate, cordate, to 16 in. long and 10 in. wide or larger, bright green, with golden midrib and veins above, petioles sheathing in basal half, longer than blades, nearly white. New Guinea. Probably the same as *H. alba* Hassk.

novoguineensis Engl. Lf. blades oblong or oblanceolate-oblong, 5 in. long and to 2 in. wide, very inequilateral, obtuse, with about 12 pairs of primary lateral veins, petioles as long as blades or a little shorter; peduncle slender, 2 in. long, spathe 1 in. long. New Guinea.

polyandra Alderw. Sts. stout, creeping, to 4 in. long; lf. blades lanceolate, to 8½ in. long and 2½ in. wide, dark emerald-green above, irregularly spotted pale green, rose-brownish when young; paler beneath with midrib and main lateral veins glandulose-puberulent, petioles 6 in. long; peduncle slightly shorter than petioles, both minutely roughened and rosy-brownish when young, becoming green and smooth, spathe to 1½ in. long, green or brownish-green. Origin unknown. Material offered under this name differs from the sp. in having grayish-green lvs. with wine-red petioles.

pygmaea (Hassk.) Engl. Small; to 12 in. or more; lf. blades elliptic, 2–4 in. long and ¾–1½ in. wide, inequilateral, acute at each end, undulate, with 3 or 4 pairs of ascending primary lateral veins, bright green or purplish beneath; peduncle to 1 in. long, spathe nearly as long, green or yellow-green. Philippine Is., Malay Pen., Indonesia.

Roezlii (M. T. Mast.) Regel. Differs from *H. Wallisii* in having lf. blades larger, 12–24 in. long and 8–16 in. wide, less abruptly acuminate, paler green above and spotted yellow-green or light green, petioles shorter-sheathing, as long as blades; spathe 5–6 in. long, brownish-olive basally becoming rose or green above. Costa Rica to Colombia.

rubescens (Roxb.) Kunth. To 2 ft. or more, sts. stout; lf. blades ovate-cordate, to 14 in. long and 9 in. wide, glossy green above, paler beneath with reddish veins, young lvs. rose-brownish, petioles 12–18 in. long, red-purple; peduncle 4–6 in. long, red-brown, spathe cylindrical, 3½ in. long, dark red. N. India, Burma.

singaporensis: see *H. Lindenii*.

sulcata Engl. Large; lf. blades subtriangular-ovate, to 8 in. long and 5 in. wide, basally emarginate-subcordate, green above, coppery beneath, petioles 2–3 times longer than blade; peduncle to 2½ in. long, spathe 1 in. long. Borneo.

Wallisii Regel. Aromatic when bruised, sts. short, erect; lf. blades ovate or obovate-oblong, 5–8 in. long and 2¼–2¾ in. wide, obtuse or nearly truncate, bright green, irregularly spotted golden, petioles sheathing well above middle, to 3 in. long; peduncle as long as petiole, spathe 3 in. long, reddish, spotted whitish. Venezuela.

HOMERIA Venten. *Iridaceae*. About 40 spp. of per. herbs with tunicate corms, endemic to S. Afr.; lvs. few, narrowly sword-shaped; fls. yellow, copper-colored, orange, or lilac, fugacious, produced in succession, in terminal clusters, perianth tube absent, perianth segms. 6, curved to form a cup, stamens 3, filaments united in a tube around the style, style brs. 3, stigmas minutely ciliate; fr. a 3-valved, loculicidal caps.

Cultivation as for *Ixia*.

Breyniana (L.) G. J. Lewis [*H. collina* (Thunb.) Venten; *Moraea grandiflora* Eckl.]. St. to about 1½ ft.; lvs. 2–4, to 2½ ft. long; fls. salmon-pink or yellow, very fragrant, to 1½ in. long, the cup about ⅜ in. across. Cv. 'Aurantiaca' [*H. ochroleuca* var. *aurantiaca* Hort.]. Fls. with yellow claw.

collina: *H. Breyniana*.

lilacina L. Bolus. St. to 9 in.; lvs. 3, linear, 1 ft. long, acuminate; fls. lilac, veined purple and with yellow-speckled purple basal blotch, the cup to 1⅜ in. across.

ochroleuca Salisb. [*Moraea collina* Thunb. var. *ochroleuca* Hort.]. St. to 2½ ft., branched; lvs. 3–4, to 3 ft. long; fls. to 1⅝ in. long, unpleasantly fragrant, golden-yellow or salmon-pink and yellow, the cup about ¾ in. across. Var. **aurantiaca:** *H. Breyniana* cv. 'Aurantiaca'.

HOMOGYNE Cass. *Compositae* (Senecio Tribe). Three spp. of rhizomatous per. herbs, native to mts. of cent. Eur. and Balkan Pen.; lvs. basal, petioled; fl. heads discoid, solitary, rarely more, on scapes bearing a few scales, involucre cylindrical, involucral bracts in 1 row, nearly equal, receptacle naked; fls. all tubular, fertile, the outer ones female, the inner ones bisexual; achenes cylindrical, slightly ribbed, pappus of simple hairs in several rows.

Occasionally grown in the rock garden. Propagated by division and seeds. Best suited to moist soil.

alpina (L.) Cass. Lvs. reniform to orbicular, to 1½ in. across, dark green above, purplish beneath, shallowly sinuate-toothed, petioles to 3½ in. long; heads ⅝ in. long, on scapes to 16 in. long; fls. pale violet.

HONCKENYA: *CLAPPERTONIA*.

HOODIA Sweet. *Asclepiadaceae*. About 16 spp. of succulent, leafless, per. herbs, native from Angola to S. Afr.; sts. many-angled, tubercled, each tubercle tipped by a bristle or spine; fls. borne above middle of sts., in clusters of 2–5 or sometimes solitary, corolla flat or cup-shaped, nearly entire, the lobes shallow, abruptly contracted to a subulate point, corona of 2 whorls united at base, each 5-lobed; fr. a follicle.

For culture see *Succulents*.

Bainii R. A. Dyer. To 15 in., bushy, sts. 12–15-angled; fls. 1–2 together, corolla cup-shaped, to 3 in. across, light yellow to pale buff, corona blackish, less than ¼ in. across. S. Afr.

HOODIOPSIS Lückh. *Asclepiadaceae*. One sp., a succulent, leafless, per. herb, native to Sw. Afr.; sts. 7–9-angled, the angles toothed; fls. solitary, arising from middle of sts., corolla nearly flat but with a broadly depressed, open tube, 5-lobed to beyond the middle, corona of 2 whorls, united at base, each 5-lobed; fr. a follicle.

For culture see *Succulents*.

Triebneri Lückh. Sts. to 8 in. or more, with prominent, spine-tipped teeth; corolla to 4 in. across, densely papillate, wine-red, unmarked, corona purple-black.

HOOKERA: *BRODIAEA*. **H. coronaria:** *B. coronaria*. **H. hyacinthina:** *Triteleia hyacinthina*. **H. pulchella:** *Dichelostemma pulchellum*.

HOPLOPHYTUM: *AECHMEA*.

HORDEUM L. BARLEY. *Gramineae*. About 25 spp. of ann. or per. grasses in the temp. N. Hemisphere; lf. blades flat; spikes dense, bristly; spikelets usually 1-fld., mostly 3 together at each joint of the articulate or continuous rachis, middle spikelet sessile and bisexual, lateral ones mostly unisexual, usually pedicelled and often reduced to awns, rachilla disarticulating above the glumes and prolonged behind the palea as a bristle in the central spikelet, sometimes bearing a rudimentary floret, glumes narrow, often subulate and awned, standing in front of the spikelet, lemma rounded on the back, 5-nerved, tapering into a usually long awn. For terminology see *Gramineae*.

brevisubulatum (Trin.) Link. SHORT-AWNED B. Per., sts. to 3 ft., clustered; lf. blades scabrous above; spikes to 3⅝ in. long, dark or greenish-purple, with the rachis very fragile and disarticulating at maturity; spikelets with lateral florets male, glumes scabrous, awns to ⅜ in. long, lemma of the central spikelet mucronate or with a very short awn, glabrous to scabrous at the apex. Se. Eur., Asia; introd. for wet sites, but undesirable because of weedy character and awned spikelets.

bulbosum L. BULBOUS B. Per., sts. to 4 ft., glaucous, smooth, with a bulbous swelling at the base, covered with brown or scarious scales or old sheaths; lf. blades scaberulous or white-hairy; spike dense, to 5½ in. long, ⅝ in. wide; spikelets in 3's, the 2 lateral pedicelled, the central sessile, glumes slender, scabrid, lemmas of the lateral spikelets awnless, that of the central with a slender awn. Medit., trop. Afr., w. Asia; introd. and cult. for forage on the Pacific coast. Not hardy.

jubatum L. SQUIRRELTAIL B., SQUIRRELTAIL GRASS. Per., tufted, to 2½ ft.; lvs. scabrous, to 5 in. long, 3/16 in. wide; spikes to 4 in. long, nodding; awns slender, to 3 in. long. N. temp. regions. Weedy, but sometimes grown for the abundant ornamental drooping spikes.

sativum: *H. vulgare*.

violaceum Boiss. & Hohen. Per., sts. to 3 ft., clustered, erect, leafy, swollen at base; lf. blades linear, flat, short; spike cylindrical, dense, dark purple, axis fragile; middle spikelet sessile, bisexual, lateral ones pedicelled, male, glumes setaceous, scabrous, longer than florets, lower lemma acuminate, the others awned, shorter to nearly as long as the floret. Armenia to Transcaucasus.

vulgare L. [*H. sativum* Pers.]. BARLEY, COMMON B., NEPAL B. Ann., sts. to 4 ft., erect; lf. blades flat, mostly ¼–⅝ in. wide; spike erect or nearly so, to 4 in. long excluding awns; spikelets 3, sessile, glumes divergent at base, narrow, nerveless, awned, awn of lemma straight, erect, mostly 4–6 in. long; fr. about ⅜ in. long, short-pointed, furrowed the length of the face, smooth, more or less tightly enclosed in the lemma and palea, but sometimes quite free. Temp. Old World. Now widely cult. for the grain, sometimes escaped, but not persistent. This, the hardiest of the cereal crops, is of great antiquity and is grown for food and as a source of malt. There are two main groups of barley cvs.: most commonly grown (for malt) are the 2-rowed barleys, whose probable ancestor is *H. spontaneum* C. Koch of Asia; barleys of this group have sterile lateral spikelets so only two of spikelets develop. All spikelets are fertile in the 6-rowed barleys (including so-called 4-rowed barley, or "bere," the hardiest of barley cvs.) which, with a higher protein content, are mainly used for food.

HORKELIA Cham. & Schlechtend. *Rosaceae.* About 17 spp. of per. herbs, native to w. N. Amer., related to *Potentilla;* lvs. pinnate, with several pairs of expanded lfts.; fls. white to cream or pinkish, in cymes, 5-merous, calyx tube cup-shaped or flattened, stamens 10, filaments dilated, pistils many or few; frs. achenes.

frondosa (Greene) Rydb. Stout, erect or decumbent, 1–2½ ft., aromatic, glandular, more or less pilose; lfts. 1–2½ in. long, ovate to oblong, serrate to almost cleft; calyx tube cup-shaped, petals less than ³⁄₁₆ in. long. Cent. Calif.

truncata Rydb. Erect, to 1½ ft., glandular-pubescent; lfts. to 1 in. long, rounded-truncate and toothed at apex; calyx tube saucer-shaped, shallow, petals ¼ in. long. S. Calif., adjacent Baja Calif.

HORMINUM L. *Labiatae.* One sp., a rhizomatous, per. herb of mts. of s. Eur.; sts. mostly square in cross section, usually leafless above; lvs. in basal rosettes; fls. in axillary, 2–6-fld. verticillasters, calyx tubular-campanulate, 13-nerved, 2-lipped, upper lip 3-toothed, lower lip 2-lobed, tube glabrous inside throat, corolla violet, hairy inside, limb nearly 2-lipped, upper lip emarginate, lower lip spreading, 3-lobed, middle lobe emarginate, stamens 4, in 2 pairs, anthers 1-celled, style 2-lobed; fr. of 4 glabrous nutlets.

A fine rock garden plant; thrives in limey soil.

pyrenaicum L. DRAGON-MOUTH. Sts. 4–12 in., woody at base, usually leafless; lvs. mostly basal, ovate, 1–3 in. long, cordate, crenate-serrate, petioled; fls. in several verticillasters along st., calyx to ⅜ in. long, teeth acuminate, corolla about ⅝ in. long, showy, bluish-violet. Early summer. Alps, Pyrenees. Cv. 'Album'. Fls. white.

HORMONES: see *Plant Hormones.*

HORRIDOCACTUS: *NEOPORTERIA.*

HORSERADISH. The comestible part of the horseradish, *Armoracia rusticana,* a deep-rooted perennial native to southeastern Europe and also run wild in this country, is the fleshy root, which is grated and employed as a relish or appetizer with meats, seafoods, and other foods. The plant blooms freely but does not mature seeds; it is therefore propagated by root cuttings, which are planted in spring. The roots are harvested in late autumn of the same year, or for home use are left in the ground until spring. By growing horseradish as an annual crop and thoroughly cleaning the land of roots at harvest time, the plant does not become established as persistent, docklike weed, and a more shapely, tender, easily managed product is obtained. The usual practice of keeping a few old plants near the house for home use produces tough, shapeless, stringy roots.

Side roots saved from the trimmings, from the size of a lead pencil to ¾ inch in diameter, are cut to 5–8 inches long; these cuttings are tied in bundles and stored in the cellar till spring, when they are set in a slanting position where the plants are to grow, in rows far enough apart to allow of good tillage and 10–18 inches in the row; the top of the cutting should be 3–5 inches below the surface of the ground.

HORTENSIA: *HYDRANGEA.*

HORTICULTURE. This is a broad, inclusive term covering the making and care of home gardens, market gardens, orchards, nurseries, and greenhouses, as well as the plant-raising phase of parks, estates, and botanical gardens. It com-prises whatever has to do with the growing of ornamentals, of vegetables, of fruits, of plants of all kinds prized for their general interest. It is not generally concerned with the so-called field crops, which pertain to agronomy, or with the management of trees (grown for pulp, timber, or cover), which belongs to forestry, but like these disciplines it is founded upon the principles of its mother science, botany.

The formal departments of horticulture, and defined by the plant subjects, are pomology or fruit growing, floriculture or flower growing, olericulture or vegetable growing, plant breeding, ornamental horticulture, and landscape practice.

To grow a great range of plants successfully and to defend them against insect and disease requires experience and definite knowledge. The plant resources of the earth are largely within the purview of the horticulturist, involving conceptions of plant geography, climate, and adaptations. These resources afford endless opportunities in plant breeding. It follows that the exact identification of the kinds of plants grown is an indispensable part of horticultural knowledge. Horticultural subjects have been put into pedagogical form and are now effective means of elementary, specialized, and higher education. Personal skill in cultivation and in technique is essential to success and real satisfaction; yet horticulture and gardening are much more than the growing of plants.

Horticulture is a growing avocation for many people and is represented formally by numerous general or specialized horticultural organizations and societies. At the national level all horticulture is represented by the American Society for Horticultural Science and by the American Horticultural Society. See also *Garden.*

HOSTA Tratt. [*Funkia* K. Spreng; *Niobe* Salisb.]. PLANTAIN LILY, DAYLILY. *Liliaceae.* Perhaps as many as 40 spp. of per. herbs, with short rhizomes, mostly native to Japan, a few spp. to China and Korea; plants forming large clumps; lvs. basal, tufted, petioled; fls. white, blue, lilac, or violet, in a terminal, scapose, bracted, 1-sided raceme, which is generally much taller than lvs., perianth segms. 6, united into a tube, stamens 6, curved, distinct or rarely united to perianth; fr. a 3-valved, loculicidal caps., seeds many, thin, winged.

Plantain lilies are hardy and of easy cultivation, doing well in moist, shady places, and making neat, attractive clumps of foliage. Propagated by division of the clumps, and only seldom by seeds; some do not produce capsules. *Hosta ventricosa* and *H. plantaginea* have shallow, clumpy rhizomes with large scars, other species have more fibrous but thick roots from the crown or from short rhizomes. The long, white, waxlike flowers of *H. plantaginea* are very fragrant, appearing in late summer and autumn; the others have short, lavender-purple ("blue") or lilac flowers, sometimes almost white, drooping or soon becoming so, and little if at all odorous. *H. ventricosa* differs from all others in having the flower suddenly enlarged or widened in its upper half; the other lilac- or blue-flowered kinds have gradually widening flower tube.

albomarginata: *H. Sieboldii.*

aurea: a listed name; may refer to *H. Fortunei* cv.

caerulea: *H. ventricosa.*

crispula F. Maek. To about 3 ft.; lf. blades ovate, to 8 in. long, with 7–9 nerves on each side of midrib, long-pointed, margin white, undulate; fls. funnelform, lavender, not striate, to 2 in. long, in a loose, many-fld. raceme; seeds freely produced. Japan, but known only in cult.

decorata L. H. Bailey [*H. decorata* var. *marginata* Hort.]. To 2 ft.; lf. blades ovate to elliptic, to 6 in. long, with 4 or 5 nerves on each side of midrib, blunt, or with only a very short and abrupt point, white-margined, petioles winged; fls. narrowly campanulate, dark violet, to 2 in. long or more; seeds produced freely. Summer. Origin unknown.

elata Hyl. [*H. Fortunei* var. *gigantea* L. H. Bailey]. Robust, to 3 ft. or more; lf. blades undulate, ovate, to 10 in. long, with 8–10 nerves on each side of midrib, dark green, glaucous beneath and often above, cordate, apex short or long-pointed; fls. funnelform, bluish-lavender, to 2¼ in. long, in a loose raceme, bracts spreading to recurving, anthers yellow; seeds produced freely. Japan.

erromena: *H. undulata* cv.

Fortunei (Bak.) L. H. Bailey. To 2 ft. and more, scapes much taller than lvs.; lf. blades ovate, to 5 in. long, with 8–10 nerves on each side of midrib, cordate, pruinose beneath; fls. funnelform, pale lilac to violet, to 1½ in. long, anthers purplish. Late spring, early summer. Japan. Cv. 'Albomarginata': cv. 'Marginato-alba'. Cv. 'Aurea' [*H. lancifolia* var. *aurea* Wehrh.]. Lvs. thinner, yellow at first, becoming light green by summer. Cv. 'Aureomaculata' [var. *albopicta* (Miq.) Hyl.; var. *viridis-marginata* Hort.]. Lvs. thinner, yellow, with a narrow green margin in spring. Cv. 'Marginato-alba' [cv. 'Albomarginata'; var. *marginato-alba* L. H. Bailey]. Plant robust; lf. blades to 11 in. long, green, with a broad white margin. Var. **gigantea**: *H. elata*. Var. **robusta**: probably *H. elata*.

glauca: *H. Sieboldiana*.

grandiflora: *H. plantaginea* cv.

japonica: see *H. lancifolia*.

lanceolata: a listed name; material so offered may be *H. lancifolia*.

lancifolia Engl. [*H. japonica* (Thunb. ex Houtt.) A. Voss, not Tratt.; *Funkia lanceolata* Siebold ex Miq.]. NARROW-LEAVED P.L. To 2 ft.; lf. blades ovate-lanceolate, to 5 in. long, with 5–6 nerves on each side of midrib, dark green, glossy, often long-pointed, petiole slender, not winged, purple-dotted; fls. funnelform, dark violet, fading with age, to 2 in. long, in a loose, 5–30-fld. raceme, anthers dark violet; seldom setting seed. Summer. Japan. Var. **albomarginata**: *H. Sieboldii*. Var. **aurea**: *H. Fortunei* cv. Var. **fortis**: *H. undulata* cv. 'Erromena'. Var. **tardiflora**: *H. tardiflora*. Var. **undulata**: *H. undulata*. Var. **variegata** is listed.

lilacina: a listed name of no botanical standing.

longissima Honda ex F. Maek. [*H. longissima* var. *brevifolia* F. Maek.]. To 20 in.; lf. blades spatulate to linear-lanceolate, to 7½ in. long, with 3–4 nerves on each side of midrib, tapering into winged petiole; fls. funnelform, pale rose-purple, about 1 in. long, in a 3–5-fld. raceme; fr. to 1¼ in. long. Japan.

marginata: a listed name of no botanical standing; perhaps material so offered is *H. crispula*, or one of the others kinds with white-margined lvs.

minor Nakai. Plant short; lf. blades broadly orbicular-ovate, base truncate to short-cordate; fls. campanulate-funnelform, to 2¼ in. long. Japan, Korea. Cv. 'Alba'. Fls. white; some material offered under this name may be *H. Sieboldii* cv. 'Alba'.

Nakaiana F. Maek. To 1½ ft.; lf. blades oblong-ovate, to 3 in. long, with 5–7 nerves on each side of midrib, thin, long-pointed, base cordate-truncate, margins slightly undulate; fls. campanulate, lilac to purple, to 2 in. long, in a capitate raceme, scape angled. Japan.

Okamii F. Maek. To 1½ ft.; lf. blades lanceolate to oblong-lanceolate, to 4 in. long, acute, tapering to petiole; fls. funnelform, pale purple, to 1½ in. long, in a rather loose 1-fld. raceme, anthers long-exserted. Autumn. Japan.

ovata: *H. ventricosa*.

plantaginea (Lam.) Asch. [*H. subcordata* (K. Spreng.) Hort.]. FRAGRANT P.L. To 2½ ft.; lf. blades ovate to cordate-ovate, to 10 in. long, with 7–9 nerves on each side of midrib, yellow-green, glossy; fls. funnelform, fragrant, white, to 5 in. long, in a capitate raceme, filaments united to perianth. Late summer and autumn. China, Japan. Cv. 'Grandiflora' [var. *grandiflora* (Siebold & Zucc. ex Lem.) Asch. & Graebn.; *H. grandiflora* Hort.]. Lvs. more elongate; fls. longer, narrower.

rectifolia Nakai. To about 3 ft.; lf. blades lanceolate or oblong-lanceolate to ovate, to 12 in. long, with 3–7 nerves on each side of midrib, semierect, sharp-pointed, petiole winged; fls. campanulate, cobalt-violet, to about 2 in. long, in a loose, 15–35-fld. raceme; seeds produced freely. Japan.

robusta: a name of variable application, sometimes used for *H. undulata*.

Sieboldiana (Lodd.) Engl. [*H. glauca* (Siebold ex Miq.) Stearn]. To 2½ ft.; lf. blades ovate, cordate, to 10–15 in. long, with about 12 nerves on each side of midrib, usually very glaucous, rigid and very thick, short-pointed; fls. funnelform, pale lilac, to 1½ in. long, in a short, dense, 6–10-fld. raceme on a scape usually shorter than lvs.; seeds freely produced. Spring and early summer. Japan. Cvs. 'Aurea Marginata', 'Gigantea', 'Robusta', 'Major', and 'Variegata' are listed.

Sieboldii (Paxt.) J. Ingram [*H. albomarginata* (Hook.) Ohwi; *H. lancifolia* var. *albomarginata* (Hook.) L. H. Bailey]. SEERSUCKER P.L. To 2½ ft. or perhaps taller, not densely cespitose; lf. blades elliptic or elliptic-lanceolate to elliptic-ovate, to 6 in. long, with 4–5 nerves on each side of midrib, short-pointed, flat, with a narrow white to yellowish-white margin, petiole winged; fls. funnelform, violet, striate, to 2 in. long, in an erect, 30-fld. raceme, anthers light yellow; seeds freely produced. Japan. Cv. 'Alba'. Lvs. green; fls. white.

sinensis: a listed name of no botanical standing.

subcordata: *H. plantaginea*.

tardiflora (W. Irving) Stearn [*H. lancifolia* var. *tardiflora* (W. Irving) L. H. Bailey]. To about 1 ft.; lf. blades lanceolate, to 6 in. long, with 4–5 nerves on each side of midrib, glossy, dark green, petiole purple-spotted; fls. funnelform, pale purple, to 1½ in. long, in a dense, 12–50-fld. raceme on a scape not much longer than lvs., anthers yellow. Autumn. Japan, but known only in cult.

undulata (Otto & A. Dietr.) L. H. Bailey [*H. lancifolia* var. *undulata* (Otto & A. Dietr.) L. H. Bailey]. To 3 ft.; lf. blades elliptic to ovate, to about 6 in. long, with about 10 nerves on each side of midrib, striped lengthwise with cream or white, sharp-pointed, strongly undulate, abruptly narrowed into winged petiole; fls. funnelform, pale lavender, to 2 in. long, in a many-fld. raceme, segms. recurved, anthers violet. Late spring. Japan, but known only in cult. Cv. 'Erromena' [var. *erromena* (Stearn) F. Maek.; *H. erromena* Stearn; *H. lancifolia* var. *fortis* (L. H. Bailey) Stearn]. MIDSUMMER P.L. More robust; lvs. larger, entirely green, slightly undulate. Cv. 'Univittata' [var. *univittata* (Miq.) Hyl.]. Robust; lvs. with a narrow, white, central stripe, less undulate. Several other cv. names occur in catalogues, including: 'Argentea', 'Aurea', 'Medio-picta', and Variegata', none of which may actually be distinct from the typical sp.

variegata: a listed name; material offered under this name may be *H. undulata* cv.

ventricosa Stearn [*H. caerulea* (Andr.) Tratt.; *H. caerulea* var. *lanceolata* Hort.; *H. ovata* Hort.]. BLUE P.L. To 3 ft.; lf. blades ovate-cordate, to 9 in. long, with 7–9 nerves on each side of midrib, dark green, petiole narrowly winged; fls. abruptly campanulate above tube, dark violet with darker veins, to 2 in. long, in a long, erect, loose, 10–15-fld. raceme, anthers dark violet; seeds produced freely. Summer. E. Asia.

venusta F. Maek. To 1 ft., often less; lf. blades ovate to elliptic-ovate, to 2 in. long, with 3–4 nerves on each side of midrib, base subcordate or cuneate, petiole winged above; fls. funnelform, pale purple, to 1½ in. long, in a few-fld. raceme, scape hollow. Japan and Cheju Is. (Korea).

HOTBED. A hotbed is a frame or box that has artificial heat and a transparent covering and in which plants are grown. It differs from a coldframe in having artificial bottom heat. This bottom heat is supplied by fermenting organic matter, hot water or steam in pipes underneath the bed, hot air conducted in horizontal flues, or electric heating cables. Formerly, fermenting manure was the heating material, but mechanical devices are now mostly employed. Information on the several hotbed heating devices may be obtained from dealers in gardening equipment or from federal or state extension services.

The hotbed is covered with sash (fitted with glass or sometimes plastic), of which the usual or standard size is 3 feet wide and 6 feet long. These sashes are laid crosswise on the box or frame. The standard size of frame is 6 feet wide and 12 feet long. A frame, therefore, accommodates four sashes. However, the frame may be of any length desired. This frame is ordinarily made of boards, and the back of it is 3 or 4 inches higher than the front, so that the sashes slope to the sun. It is customary to have the lower or front side of the sash about 6–10 inches above the ground. The location in which the frames are set should be protected from cold and prevailing winds by a rising slope, a high board fence, a building, a hedge, or other obstruction. If the frame yard is near the main buildings, it is much more accessible in rainy or snowy times, and the plants are likely to have better care. Water should also be at hand.

When to start a hotbed depends on the kinds of plants to be grown, the time one wishes to gain, and something, also, on the character of the heat. The hardier the plant, the earlier it can be started. In Zone 5, from the first to the middle of March is the usual time for starting a hotbed. In this bed are sown seeds of early flowers and such vegetables as cabbage, cauliflower, and tomato. It is essential that plants in the hotbed do not become leggy. To prevent this, they must be given plenty of room, thorough ventilation on all pleasant days, and not too great heat. It is well to transplant them once or twice before they are finally set in the field, particularly if they are started as early as the first or middle of March. When transplanted, they can be set in another hotbed or in a coldframe, but it is important that the succeeding frames in which they are set should not be very much colder than the one in which have been growing, or they may become stunted. It is well, however, to transplant them into a gradually cooler and freer atmosphere to harden them off, so that they may go into the open ground without danger.

On pleasant days, raise the sash at the upper end 1 or 2 inches, or, if the sun shines brightly and the wind does not blow, give even more air, and eventually strip off the sashes entirely. It is important that the atmosphere not be kept too close and the plants thereby grown too soft. It is usually advisable to sow cabbage, lettuce, and hardy plants in different frames from tomatoes and other tender things, in order that the proper requirements may be given to each. At night the hotbeds (at least early in the season) need more protection than is afforded by the sash covers. Straw matting or other material may be used to cover the sash. This is rolled out on the sashes at night in one or two thicknesses, and if the weather is sharp, board shutters, the size of the sash, may be laid on top.

One must not expect to gain as much time in the crop as one gains in the starting of the seeds; that is, if seeds are started two months ahead of the normal season, one will not gain two months in the ripening of the crop. Ordinarily, one cannot expect to gain much more than one-half the time, if the plants are transplanted to the field from the hotbed.

Some plants may be grown to maturity in the hotbed, as lettuce and radishes. After hotbeds have been emptied of their plants, the sashes may be stored away, and the frames employed for the growing of other crops, such as melons or cucumbers.

HOTEIA: *ASTILBE.*

HOTTONIA L. FEATHERFOIL, WATER VIOLET. *Primulaceae.* Two spp. of floating, aquatic herbs, native to Eurasia, and N. Amer.; lvs. pinnately dissected, whorled or scattered; fls. white or lilac, whorled, in racemes on hollow scapes, calyx 5-parted, corolla with 5-parted limb, stamens 5; fr. a caps.

Sometimes used as an aquarium plant.

palustris L. Per.; lvs. to 4 in. long; racemes to 16 in. high; fls. lilac with yellow throat, to 1 in. across. Eurasia.

HOULLETIA Brongn. *Orchidaceae.* About 10 spp. of epiphytes of Cent. and S. Amer.; pseudobulbs 1–lvd.; lvs. plicate, petioled; scape simple, erect or pendent, raceme 1- to many-fld.; fls. large, sepals and petals similar, spreading, lip divided into hypochil and epichil, column slender with a pronounced foot, pollinia 2, on a slender stalk. For structure of fl. see *Orchidaceae.*

For culture see *Orchids.*

Brocklehurstiana Lindl. Pseudobulbs conical, furrowed, to 3 in. long; lf. to 1 ft. long; raceme lateral, to 1 ft. long, 8–12-fld.; fls. nodding, fragrant, 3–4 in. across, orange-brown with dark purplish spots, lip shorter than other segms., yellow, spotted with brown, purple toward apex, hypochil short, hornlike. Early spring. Brazil.

odoratissima Linden ex Lindl. & Paxt. Variable, pseudobulbs ovoid, to 3 in. long; lvs. lanceolate-elliptic, to 2 ft. long; infl. lateral, to 3 ft. long, 5–16-fld.; fls. large, 1½ in. long, purple-green, reddish-flesh-colored, or brown outside and reddish inside, petals shorter and narrower than sepals, lip 3-lobed, narrow, nearly as long as petals, white, often marked with red or yellow, hypochil sickle-shaped, epichil sagittate. Early spring–early autumn. Andes, Venezuela to Peru. Var. **antioquensis** Linden. Fls. deep mahogany-red, lip white, faintly tinged with yellow, lateral lobes dark purple. Early spring–early summer. Colombia.

picta Linden & Rchb.f. Pseudobulbs ovate-lanceolate, to 3 in. long; lvs. elliptic-lanceolate; scape from base of pseudobulb, 6–10-fld.; fls. to 3½ in. across, cinnamon-brown, yellow-checkered on lower half, lip shorter than petals, pale yellow, mottled with short, transverse, red-

purple bars, hypochil sickle-shaped, epichil triangular-sagittate. Colombia.

Wallisii Linden & Rchb.f. Infl. pendent, few-fld.; fls. buff-yellow, with many red-brown blotches, sepals oblong, obtuse, lateral sepals united, petals cuneate-oblong, acute, lip 3-lobed, hypochil hatchet-shaped, epichil anchor-shaped, acute. Colombia.

HOUSE PLANTS. House plants are those plants that will thrive and grow in a house, decorating the rooms and giving pleasure to the occupants. They are grown for foliage (foliage plants) or for flower; most are more or less permanent acquisitions for the home, but some others, like certain holiday plants and many potted flowering bulbs, are grown only for temporary display indoors, usually in winter or early spring. The home conditions under which house plants are grown may too often be suitable for the human occupants but inhospitable to most plants, being usually too dark, too dry, and too warm.

Success in growing house plants lies in selecting kinds that best fit one's own particular home environment. All homes, whether separate dwellings or apartments, are not the same, especially with regard to the light that is available. Neither are available house plants all alike, and indeed their growing needs may vary greatly. All potential house plant subjects must therefore be considered with respect to their own particular needs as to light, temperature, soil, water, and humidity. Only with a properly equipped home conservatory, or one of the modern indoor planters or growth cabinets with adequate controls for artificial light and others factors, or a terrarium (see *Terrarium*) can most of these standard needs be brought under easy control. The gardener must therefore first analyze his own home environment especially with regard to the available daylight and temperature in locations intended for plant culture. These are essential factors over which he has little control. On the other hand, requirements related to soil, water, and humidity can be more readily managed. Only those plants should be selected that have a chance to thrive under the particular environmental conditions actually presented in the house. To become familiar with suitable plants will require some study of the extensive literature about house plants; their identities as well as some of their special cultural requirements may be found elsewhere in this volume. The grower should be aware that some house plants require cool night temperatures, and that in certain cases flowering may depend upon day length (see *Photoperiod*) or its artificial manipulation—or on light intensity itself. Once appropriate plants are selected, there comes the easier task of keeping them healthy and growing in an ideal soil mix, with appropriate and regular fertilization and proper watering. But even here one should be familiar with the individual needs of each kind, a task which becomes easier with practice and experience. Still, the grower needs to keep in mind that many house plants die by being grown in the wrong kind of soil, or because they are either over- or under-fertilized or over- or under-watered.

House plants will thrive in a variety of containers, including the familiar clay as well as modern plastic or ceramic pots; large specimens are usually tubbed. Whatever the container, it should have a drainage hole in the bottom. Chief cultural differences in containers have to do with the watering. Plants grown in porous clay pots require more frequent watering, for they dry out faster than those grown in other types. Watering (preferably with water at room temperature) of the house plant should be based on need rather than upon maintenance of fixed schedules. Normally it is time to water a potted plant when the soil is dry to the touch and then watering should be sufficient to have it run out the drainage hole. Pots should not stand in water for more than a few minutes after watering. However, humidity, beneficial to most plants, can be increased by placing pots on a layer of pebbles (as in a planter) in which water can usefully stand—though below pot level. Certain plants, like desert cacti, require water only during their normal growing season, and from November to March should be given a light watering only once or twice a month. Although the tap water normally available in most houses is usually satisfactory, there may be occasional species grown which are sensitive to chlorinated or hard water; in such instances rainwater or distilled water should be used.

Ordinary garden soil is usually inadequate for the culture of most potted house plants, which require a mix that not only supports the specimen but also administers properly to its water, nutrient, and oxygen requirements. Preferably all soil and sand should be sterile (they may be pasteurized in the oven for an hour at 200° F). For most house plants a mixture of two to three parts of good garden loam, two parts of peat moss (for better water and nutrient retention), and one part of builder's sand (for drainage and aeration) is adequate. Desert succulents require better drainage, so no peat but more sand plus crushed limestone and crushed brick are recommended. For ferns and epiphytes accustomed in nature to pure organic soils, a greater proportion of peat or equivalent material is needed. The wise gardener annually repots most of his house plants, using clean, sterile containers. This is best done in summer to permit plants to readjust during the growing season. For more details on soil mixes, see *Soils.*

Between annual repottings, house plants require fertilizing. Numerous commercial preparations are available and easy to use, though mixes applied in liquid form are the most convenient. Fertilizer may be given monthly during active growth or by weekly feeding (of a more dilute mix), the latter being preferable. A 7–6–19 fertilizer (medium in nitrogen and phosphorus and high in potash) is ideal.

Because house plants are normally isolated from their natural pests, the latter are usually less of a problem in the home than outdoors or in a greenhouse. Pests are usually introduced on new plants, so it is wise to keep such isolated from established house plants for a few weeks until they can be given a clean bill of health. Sanitation is insurance against future troubles, so fading flowers and foliage on house plants should be quickly removed and disposed of. Commonest pests of house plants are aphids, mealy bugs, mites, red spider, scale, and white fly. See *Diseases and Pests.*

Under good culture, house plants may thrive to the extent that they may require some pruning or trimming. Plants that get leggy and unattractive and that cannot be severely pruned back should be disposed of and replaced with younger specimens. Many house plants are easy to propagate; for some of the methods used, see *Propagation.*

Except where special artificial lighting is available (see below), plants in most homes must be grown near windows where the daylight conditions are most favorable. They may be grown individually or as a group to form a sort of house garden in a window area. A house garden may occupy an entire window or set of windows, or it may consist simply of a jardiniere, or a few choice pot plants on a stand. Small greenhouse windows are also now available permitting better control of heat, humidity, and light. Expensive arrangements of window plants are by no means necessary, nor is a large collection. The plants and flowers themselves are the main consideration, and a small collection well cared for is better than a large one that is not kept in good condition. A window box or planter in a room will be seen near at hand, so may be more or less ornamental in character. A neatly made and strong wooden box of ¾-inch plywood of a length corresponding to the width of the window, about 10 inches wide and 8 inches deep, answers quite as well as a costlier receptacle. A metal tray or liner of a size to fit into the wooden box may be specially ordered. It tends to keep the soil from drying out too rapidly. This may be provided with a false wooden bottom, with cracks for drainage, 2 inches above the real bottom of the tray, or the bottom of the tray may be covered to the same depth in pebbles. The plants will then have a vacant space below them into which drainage water may pass. Such a planting may be watered thoroughly as required, without danger of the water running on the floor. Of course, a petcock should be provided at some suitable point on a level with the bottom of the tray, to permit its

being drained as needed. Water needs to be changed occasionally and it should never rise to the false bottom or above the pebble layer, for then the soil in the pots might become too wet. Water standing below the pots is beneficial as it adds humidity to the air immediately around the plants.

Some persons attach the planter to the window, or support it on brackets below the windowsill, but a preferable arrangement is to support it on a low and light stand of suitable height provided with rollers. It may then be drawn back from the window, turned around from time to time to give the plants light on all sides, or turned with the attractive side inward as may be desired.

The window for winter plants should have a southern, southeastern, or eastern exposure. Plants need all the light they can get in the northern winter, especially those expected to bloom. The window should be tight-fitting. Double windows and a curtain are an advantage in cold weather. The plants should have a certain regularity in conditions. It is trying on them, and often fatal to success, to be snug and warm one night and in a temperature only a few degrees above freezing the next. Some plants live in spite of it, but they cannot be expected to prosper.

From time to time, the foliage will need cleansing to free it from dust. Pots can be carried to a sink or bathtub, turned on their sides, and the plants then freely syringed without danger of making the soil too wet. It is usually advisable not to wet the flowers, especially waxy kinds. The foliage of types like *Begonia × rex-cultorum* should be cleansed with a piece of dry or only slightly moist cotton or soft cloth, but if the leaves can be quickly dried off by placing them in the open air on mild days, the foliage may be syringed. In general, syringing of house plants for any purpose should only be done when weather is bright so that they may soon dry off. Plants should not go into the night with soaking leaves, for this invites attack by fungi.

Plants suitable for the winter window garden mostly belong to the groups that florists grow in their medium and cool houses. The former are given a night temperature of about 60°F., the latter about 50°F. In each case the temperature is 10 to 15° higher for the day time. A variation of five degrees below these temperatures is allowable without any injurious effects; even more may be borne, but not without more or less check to the plants. In bright sunny weather the day temperature may be higher than in cloudy and dark weather.

Gardening in the home under artificial light is a new method of growing house plants that is increasing in popularity, for it makes it possible for anyone with spare space of any kind, even in a basement, to grow a wide range of ornamentals or other plants, completely independent of window space and natural daylight. Plants of compact growth lend themselves best to such culture. Among the more popular plants grown in homes completely under artificial lights are *Begonia × tuberhybrida, Sinningia, Saintpaulia ionantha,* the Orchidaceae, and a wide variety of foliage plants. Additionally, artificial-light planters are much used in the North for starting seed and small plants for garden use in the summer. Various types of planters are used together with specially designed fluorescent growing lamps, which, by means of a standard timer, can automatically supply any photoperiod required. For example, flowering plants normally require 12 to 16 hours of light, whereas foliage plants need only four to six hours. There are numerous advantages to indoor gardening under artificial light. Among others, the plants produced grow more symmetrically, and those grown for flowers yield more of them and can be induced to come into flower as desired by being given their normal photoperiodic requirements rather than being dependent upon the slow seasonal changes of natural day length. Devotees of artificial-light gardening indoors have their own society, the Indoor Light Gardening Society of America, a recommended source of practical information on the general subject.

The range of subjects for use as house plants is great, largely because many perennial species of the wet and arid tropics and subtropics, not normally available for outdoor planting—at least not in the North—are suitable as indoor plants, assuming appropriate growing conditions are supplied. The gamut includes perennial herbs, shrubs, vines, and small trees, and among them will be found such collector's groups as Begoniaceae, Bromeliaceae, Cactaceae and other succulents, ferns, Gesneriaceae, and Palmae. Additional information may be found under some of those headings. There follow here separate listings of some house plants recommended for special situations in the home, grouped by light, temperature, and moisture requirements, and by growth form. See also *Bulbs, Cacti, Ferns and Fern Allies, Orchids, Palms,* and *Succulents.*

Light

High light intensity (full light or preferably 5,000–8,000 footcandles all day, dawn to dusk, with no obstruction to shade the window): *Abutilon pictum, Aloe, Asparagus densiflorus, Araucaria heterophylla, Aucuba, Beaucarnea, Begonia,* some Bromeliaceae, *Carissa, Caryota urens, Ceropegia Woodii, Chrysalidocarpus lutescens, Cissus quadrangula, Codiaeum, Cordyline terminalis, Crassula arborescens, Cyanotis kewensis, Dizygotheca, Dracaena, Euphorbia Milii* var. *splendens,* × *Fatshedera Lizei, Fatsia japonica, Ficus benjamina* cv. 'Exotica', *F. lyrata, Graptopetalum paraguayense, Gynura aurantiaca, Hedera Helix, Hibiscus, Homocladium platycladum, Hoya, Justicia Brandegeana, Kalanchoe, Licuala grandis, Livistona chinensis, Monstera, Pedilanthus tithymaloides, Pelargonium peltatum, P. zonale, Pilea, Pittosporum, Podocarpus, Rhoeo spathacea, Sansevieria, Schefflera,* and *Veitchia Merrillii.*

Medium light intensity (for lightly shaded windows, preferably with 1,000–4,000 footcandles all day): *Acanthus, Aechmea, Aglaonema modestum, Asparagus setaceus, A. densiflorus* cv. 'Sprengeri', Bromeliaceae, *Begonia foliosa, B. rex, B. cucullata* var. *Hookeri, Caladium bicolor, Chlorophytum comosum, Cissus antarctica, C. discolor, C. erosa, C. rhombifolia, Dieffenbachia, Dracaena surculosa, Epipremnum aureum, Ficus, Hoya carnosa, Ligularia tussilaginea, Pandanus, Peperomia griseoargentea, Philodendron, Piper ornatum, Polyscias, Saintpaulia ionantha,* and *Syngonium.*

Low light intensity (no strong direct light source but 100–500 footcandles per normal day): *Aglaonema, Aspidistra elatior, Asplenium Nidus, Chamaedorea, Cyrtomium falcatum, Epipremnum aureum, Ficus elastica, F. macrophylla, Howea, Nephrolepis exaltata, Philodendron, Ptychosperma Macarthurii, Rhapis excelsa, Rumohra adiantiformis,* and *Spathiphyllum.*

Temperature

Cool (average 60° F, with variations from 55° to 70° F): *Adiantum Raddianum, Araucaria heterophylla, Asparagus densiflorus, Asplenium Nidus, Aucuba, Camellia, Carissa, Chamaerops, Citrus, Crassula argentea, Cyclamen, Cyrtomium falcatum, Episcia cupreata,* × *Fatshedera, Fatsia, Hedera, Howea, Nephrolepis, Pelargonium, Philodendron Selloum, Pilea Cadierei, Pittosporum, Podocarpus macrophyllus, Primula, Rhapis excelsa, Rhododendron* (azaleas), *Rhoeo spathacea, Rumohra adiantiformis, Solanum Pseudocapsicum,* and most bulbs.

Warm (average 75° F, with variations from 65° to 85° F): *Aglaonema, Aspidistra, Begonia,* Bromeliaceae, *Caryota, Chamaedorea, Chrysalidocarpus lutescens, Codiaeum, Cordyline, Dieffenbachia, Dizygotheca, Dracaena reflexa, Epipremnum, Euphorbia pulcherrima, Ficus, Licuala grandis, Livistona chinensis, Monstera, Pandanus Veitchii, Philodendron, Phoenix Roebelenii, Polyscias, Ptychosperma Macarthurii, Sansevieria, Schefflera, Spathiphyllum, Syngonium,* and *Veitchia Merrillii.*

Hot, dry, and sunny: *Aeonium arboreum, Aloe, Cryptanthus zonatus, Echeveria gigantea, Gasteria, Haworthia planifolia, Kalanchoe, Mammillaria microcarpa, Notocactus Leninghausii, Sansevieria, Sempervivum, Senecio serpens,* and *Stapelia.*

Moisture

Moist (frequent watering required, the soil surface not being allowed to become dry): *Adiantum Raddianum, Aglaonema, Araucaria, Asparagus densiflorus, Aspidistra, Asplenium Nidus, Begonia, Carissa, Caryota, Chamaedorea, Chamaerops, Chrysalidocarpus, Chrysanthemum, Codiaeum, Cyclamen, Cyrtomium falcatum, Dieffenbachia, Dizygotheca, Euphorbia pulcherrima,* × *Fatshedera, Fatsia, Ficus, Hedera, Howea, Licuala, Livistona, Monstera, Nephrolepis, Philodendron Selloum, Pilea, Phoenix, Podocarpus, Polyscias, Polystichum, Primula, Ptychosperma, Rhapis, Spathiphyllum, Syngonium, Veitchia,* and most bulbous species.

Dry (soil surface being allowed to become dry before adding water): *Aucuba,* Bromeliaceae, *Cordyline, Crassula argentea, Dracaena, Epipremnum, Pandanus, Philodendron, Pittosporum, Rhoeo spathacea, Sansevieria,* and *Schefflera.*

High humidity (species requiring constant high humidity in the air such as is formed in terrarium or greenhouse): *Adiantum Raddianum, Ardisia crenata, Asparagus setaceus, Calathea ornata, Ficus pumila, F. sagittata, Fittonia Verschaffeltii, Pilea microphylla, Saxifraga stolonifera, Selaginella uncinata, Soleirolia Soleirolii,* and ferns of most kinds, as well as the smaller species of *Begonia.*

Special Growth Forms

Arborescent plants (tall plants suitable for large pots and tubs): *Araucaria heterophylla, Brassaia actinophylla, Chamaedorea, Chrysalidocarpus lutescens, Citrus, Coffea arabica, Cordyline, Cycas revoluta, Ficus elastica, F. lyrata, F. retusa, Grevillea robusta, Howea Belmoreana, H. Forsterana, Livistona chinensis, Podocarpus macrophyllus,* and *Rhapis excelsa.*

Vining plants: *Ceropegia, Cissus, Ficus pumila, F. sagittata, Hedera, Hoya, Passiflora, Philodendron* and other vining genera of Araceae, and *Thunbergia.*

Basket plants: *Abutilon megapotamicum, Achimenes, Aeschynanthus, Begonia, Ceropegia, Cissus, Chlorophytum, Codonanthe, Columnea, Episcia, Fuchsia, Hoya, Hypocyrta, Pelargonium* (ivy types), *Philodendron, Plumbago, Rhipsalis, Saxifraga stolonifera, Selaginella uncinata, Tradescantia,* and *Zygocactus.*

HOUSTONIA: *HEDYOTIS.* **H. angustifolia:** *Hedyotis nigricans.* **H. calycosa:** *Hedyotis purpurea* var. **H. canadensis** and **H. ciliolata:** *Hedyotis purpurea* var. ciliolata. **H. filifolia:** *Hedyotis nigricans* var. **H. floridana:** *Hedyotis purpurea* var. **H. lanceolata:** *Hedyotis purpurea* var. calycosa. **H. longifolia:** *Hedyotis purpurea* var. **H. montana:** *Hedyotis purpurea* var. **H. Nuttalliana:** *Hedyotis purpurea* var. tenuifolia. **H. serpyllifolia:** *Hedyotis Michauxii.* **H. tenuifolia:** *Hedyotis purpurea* var.

HOUTTUYNIA Thunb. *Saururaceae.* One sp., a per. herb, native to temp. e. Asia; lvs. alt., entire, stipules united to petioles; infl. a dense lateral spike subtended by 4 involucral bracts; fls. small, bracted, perianth none, stamens 3, united at base to 1-celled ovary, stigmas 3; fr. dry, opening at top.

Grown in moist locations; propagated by division and seeds.

cordata Thunb. To 15 in., rhizome creeping; lvs. ovate, 2–3 in. long, cordate, 5-nerved from base, gland-dotted; spike ¼–1 in. long, involucral bracts 4, white, to ½ in. long, each fl. subtended by a small bract; fr. spike to 2 in. long. Japan, s. to mts. of Java and Nepal.

HOVEA R. Br. ex Ait.f. *Leguminosae* (subfamily *Faboideae*). Ten to 12 spp. of shrubs of Australia; lvs. alt., simple, entire or prickly-toothed; fls. blue or purple, papilionaceous, mostly in axillary clusters or very short racemes, calyx 2-lipped, standard reflexed, the alt. stamens longer; fr. a turgid, ovoid to globose, dehiscent legume.

May be grown outdoors in mild climates; propagated by seeds.

longifolia Ait.f. [*H. purpurea* Sweet]. Stout shrub, to 10 ft.; lvs. rigid, oblong-lanceolate or linear, ¾–2 in. long, obtuse, with revolute margins, veins rusty-tomentose beneath; fr. sessile, to ½ in. across, softly rusty-pubescent. E. Australia. Zone 10. A variable sp.

purpurea: *H. longifolia.*

HOVENIA Thunb. *Rhamnaceae.* Two spp. or more of deciduous trees or shrubs in e. Asia; lvs. alt., long-petioled, 3-nerved from base; fls. small, purplish, in axillary and terminal cymes, bisexual, 5-merous; fr. indehiscent, on fleshy peduncles.

dulcis Thunb. [*H. dulcis* var. *glabra* Mak.]. JAPANESE RAISIN TREE. Tree, to 30 ft.; lvs. ovate, to 7 in. long, toothed; fls. greenish, in many-fld. racemes; fr. about ¼ in. across with peduncles fleshy, reddish, club-shaped. Japan. Zone 5. Peduncles of fr. sometimes eaten. Thrives in sandy loam. Prop. by seeds, root cuttings, and cuttings of mature wood under glass. It has been recommended as a fr. plant; hardy well north. Var. **glabra:** *H. dulcis.*

HOWEA Becc. SENTRY PALM. *Palmae.* Two spp. of solitary, slender, unarmed, monoecious palms without a crownshaft, from Lord Howe Is. (Australia); lvs. pinnate, pinnae 1-ribbed, acute; infl. of 1 or several long-peduncled spikes from a short common bract in lf. axil, in bud each spike surrounded by a thin cylindrical bract inserted at apex of peduncle; fls. in triads (2 male and 1 female) sunken in pits, male fls. with sepals imbricate, petals valvate, boat-shaped, stamens many, filaments erect, pistillode minute, female fls. with sepals and petals imbricate, ovary 1-celled; fr. about 1½ in. long, ellipsoid with apical stigmatic residue, endocarp not operculate, seed with homogeneous endosperm and basal embryo.

Handsome ornamental palms much grown for indoor use as pot or tub plants. Grown outdoors in the tropics and subtropics and in the U.S. in warmer parts of Zone 9b, especially in Calif. Formerly much used as greenhouse palms and in the trade erroneously called kentias. For culture see *Palms.*

Belmoreana (C. Moore & F. J. Muell.) Becc. [*Kentia Belmoreana* C. Moore & F. J. Muell.]. BELMORE S.P., CURLY P. Medium-sized palm; lvs. to 7 ft. long, strongly arching, petioles very short, pinnae crowded, directed upward from the rachis, about 1 in. wide; spikes solitary in lf. axils; male fls. with 30–40 stamens.

Forsterana (C. Moore & F. J. Muell.) Becc. [*Kentia Forsterana* C. Moore & F. J. Muell.]. SENTRY PALM, FORSTER S.P., KENTIA P., THATCH-LEAF P. Differs from *H. Belmoreana* in being a larger and stouter tree to 60 ft. or more and in having lvs. larger, at length horizontal, not strongly arched, petioles long, pinnae broader, mostly horizontal or somewhat pendulous; spikes 3–6 in a lf. axil; and stamens 80–100. Faster-growing and the more commonly cult. sp.

HOWITTIA F. J. Muell. *Malvaceae.* One sp., an Australian shrub; lvs. short-petioled, ovate to lanceolate-ovate, unlobed, acute or rounded at apex, truncate to cordate at base, entire, undulate, or serrate, stipules minute, early deciduous; fls. solitary or to 3 on slender, axillary peduncles, involucral bracts 0, stamens united in a tubular column, ovary 3-celled, each cell with 2 ovules, style unbranched, terminated by a 3-parted stigma; fr. a depressed-globose, loculicidally dehiscent caps., seeds reniform, glabrous.

Not hardy north; propagated by seeds or cuttings.

trilocularis F. J. Muell. Stellate-tomentose shrub; lvs. 1–3 in. long, green above, whitish beneath; fls. pale violet, petals ½–1 in. long, staminal column less than ¼ in. long, shorter than slender style; caps. densely pubescent with simple and stellate hairs.

HOYA R. Br. *Asclepiadaceae.* WAX VINE, PORCELAIN FLOWER. Perhaps 200 spp. of root-climbing, twining, or loose shrubs, native from India and s. China, to the Pacific Is. and Australia; lvs. opp., evergreen, simple, entire, fleshy or leathery; fls. in axillary, umbellate clusters, calyx small, corolla fleshy, often appearing waxy, rotate, lobes 5, mostly spreading or reflexed, corona of 5, mostly spreading, lobes; fr. a follicle.

Hoyas are plants for the moist, warm greenhouse preferring moderate temperatures, a little shade, and well-drained soil. Some, such as *H. bella* and *H. lacunosa,* are excellent basket plants, but most are climbing vines. The peduncles of the old inflorescences should not be removed, for new inflorescences form on these. Propagation is by cuttings from the previous year's wood or by layering; *H. bella* is sometimes grafted on a stronger-growing species. Hoyas should not be forced in winter.

angustifolia J. Traill, not Elmer. Slender climber, sts. and lvs. sparsely pubescent; lvs. linear-lanceolate, to 6 in. long; infl. few-fld.; corolla white, to ¾ in. across, corona purple at center. China.

australis R. Br. ex J. Traill [*H. Dalrympliana* F. J. Muell.]. Succulent, glabrous twiner; lvs. ovate, obovate, or nearly orbicular, to 3 in. long, obtuse or short-acuminate; peduncles rarely longer than petiole, infl. many-fld.; corolla about ½ in. across, white, corona white, with reddish markings at base. Australia.

bandaensis Schlechter. Glabrous, somewhat fleshy, branched twiner; lvs. elliptic, to 5 in. long, acute or short-acuminate; cymes umbellate, many-fld.; corolla to ⅝ in. across, the lobes triangular, papillate. Moluccas.

bella Hook. [*H. Paxtonii* Hort. ex Nichols.]. MINIATURE WAX PLANT. Delicate, diffusely branched dwarf shrubs; lvs. ovate-lanceolate, to 1¼ in. long, acuminate; cymes umbellate, axillary and terminal, 8–10-fld.; corolla white, to ⅝ in. across, corona deep crimson. India.

carnosa (L.f.) R. Br. [*H. Motoskei* Teysm. & Binnend.]. WAX PLANT, HONEY PLANT. Succulent, glabrous or puberulous shrub, with trailing or climbing sts; lvs. ovate to oblong-ovate or obovate, to 3 in. long, short-acuminate; cymes umbellate, many-fld.; corolla to ⅝ in. across, lobes white, spreading, corona red. S. China to Australia. Cvs. include: **'Alba'**, fls. white; **'Compacta'**, lvs. close together; **'Exotica'**, lvs. variegated with yellow and pink, margined with green; **'Krinkle Kurl'** ['Green Curls'], HINDU-ROPE, lvs. crowded, folded lengthwise, curled and contorted; **'Latifolia'**, lvs. broad; **'Variegata'** [*H. variegata* Siebold ex C. Morr.], lvs. white-margined.

cinnamomifolia Hook. Branched, glabrous twiner; lvs. on short, very thick petioles, blades ovate-acuminate, to 5 in. long, with 3 conspicuous major veins; umbels dense, spherical, many-fld.; corolla to ⅝ in. across, yellow-green, corona deep purple-red. Java.

coronaria Blume. Suffruticose climber, sts. thickish, puberulent; lvs. oblong, to nearly 6 in. long, short-acuminate, leathery, with prominent midrib; umbels many-fld.; corolla open-campanulate, to 1⅜ in. across, yellowish with reddish or violet spots toward base, corona yellowish. Java.

Dalrympliana: *H. australis.*

Darwinii Loher. Glabrous, clinging vine; lvs. oblong to oblong-ovate, to 3½ in. long, acuminate; umbels loosely few-fld.; corolla lobes strongly reflexed, to ½ in. long, whitish with a purple base, corona lobes to ¼ in. long, whitish. Philippine Is.

exotica: a listed name of no botanical standing; probably *H. carnosa* cv.

imperialis Lindl. Puberulent-stemmed climber, lvs. obovate to oblanceolate, to 9 in. long, leathery; peduncles longer than lvs., umbels pendulous, loosely few-fld.; corolla up to 3 in. across, lobes purplish but darker toward base, corona whitish. Borneo.

Kerrii Craib. Woody climber, young growth puberulent; lvs. orbicular-obcordate, 2–3½ in. long and broad, deeply emarginate; peduncles stout, to 3 in. long, umbels many-fld.; corolla revolute but flat, to ½ in. across, creamy-white fading brownish, papillate inside, corona lobes purple. Thailand and Laos.

Keysii F. M. Bailey. Similar to *H. australis* but downy-puberulent, young lvs. cordate-ovate but eventually ovate to nearly orbicular. Queensland.

Kirkii bogoriensis: a listed name of no botanical standing.

lacunosa Blume. Slender-stemmed climber; lvs. ovate, to 1¾ in. long, acuminate, fleshy; peduncles slender, often longer than lvs., umbels many-fld.; corolla rotate, to about ¼ in. across, white or greenish-yellow, with a circle of erect hairs on the tube, lobes eventually reflexed. Indonesia.

latifolia G. Don. Long-stemmed climber; lvs. ovate to oblong-ovate, to 10 in. long, thick, leathery; peduncles stout, to 3 in. long, several from a tubercled base at the nodes, cymes many-fld., but small; corolla pinkish, less than ⁵⁄₁₆ in. across. Malaya. Plants offered under this name may sometimes be *H. carnosa* cv. 'Latifolia'.

longifolia Wallich. Glabrous, stout-stemmed climber; lvs. oblanceolate, to 8 in. long, 1½ in. broad, very fleshy, obscurely nerved, bent downward abruptly at apex of petiole; peduncles stout, less than 2 in. long, umbels several-fld.; corolla white or flushed pink, ¾–1½ in. across, corona lobes spreading, reddish toward the center. Cent. Himalayas. Var. **Shepherdii** (Hook.) N. E. Br. [*H. Shepherdii* Hook.]. Lvs. to about 6 in. long, ½ in. wide, corolla ½–¾ in. across.

macrophylla Blume. Glabrate climber; lvs. oblong-lanceolate, 6–10 in. long, long-acuminate, leathery; peduncles violet, to 3 in. long, umbels many-fld.; corolla about ½ in. across, red outside, densely white-papillose inside, corona white or pink. Java.

Motoskei: *H. carnosa.*

obovata Decne. Sts. twining; lvs. elliptic or obovate, to 2½ in. long, obtuse or slightly emarginate, attenuate to petiole, glabrous; peduncles short; corolla about ⅝ in. across, papillate inside, color not known. Celebes. Material offered under this name is probably *H. Kerrii.*

Paxtonii: *H. bella.*

purpurea-fusca Hook. Similar to *H. cinnamomifolia,* but with corolla ash-brown, hirsute-puberulent, and corona deep purple-brown. Java. Often offered as *Hoya* cv. 'Silver Pink'.

serpens Hook.f. Sts. creeping and rooting, minutely roughened; lvs. nearly sessile, ovate to broadly elliptic, to ¾ in. wide, papillose on both surfaces; infl. an umbellate raceme longer than lvs.; corolla to ½ in. across, white, papillate-tomentose inside, corona white, perhaps with a red center. Sikkim. Has been offered as *Dischidia minima.*

Shepherdii: *H. longifolia* var.

variegata: *H. carnosa* cv.

HUDSONIA L. BEACH HEATHER. *Cistaceae.* Three spp. of small, evergreen, heathlike shrubs or subshrubs, native to e. N. Amer.; lvs. alt., sessile, scalelike or awl-like; fls. solitary at ends of short brs., sepals usually 3, petals 5, yellow, stamens 10–30, style elongate, stigma minute; fr. a 3-valved caps.

Hudsonias may be colonized in dry places in sandy soil or along the seashore. They are difficult to grow and short-lived. Propagated by seeds and probably by cuttings.

ericoides L. GOLDEN HEATHER. To 7 in., soft-pubescent; lvs. awl-like, to ½ in. long; fls. ⁵⁄₁₆ in. across, on slender pedicels. Nov. Sc. to N.C.

montana Nutt. To 6 in., tufted, slightly hairy; lvs. awl-like, to ½ in. long; fls. ⁵⁄₁₆ in. across, on short pedicels. Mts., N.C.

tomentosa Nutt. POVERTY GRASS. To 8 in., tufted, hoary-pubescent; lvs. scalelike, densely imbricate, ⅛ in. long; fls. ⁵⁄₁₆ in. across, sessile. New Bruns. to Va., w. along Great Lakes to Minn.

HUERNIA R. Br. DRAGON FLOWER. *Asclepiadaceae.* About 60 spp. of dwarf, succulent, leafless, per. herbs, native to trop. and S. Afr., 1 in s. Arabia; sts. glabrous, angled, the angles toothed; fls. clustered near middle or base of sts., corolla campanulate or with a short, closed tube, 5-lobed, with 5 small teeth alternating with the lobes, corona of 2 whorls, the outer 5- or 10-lobed, more or less united to base of corolla tube, the inner of 5 simple lobes arising from upper part of staminal column; fr. a follicle.

For culture see *Succulents.*

aspera N. E. Br. Sts. procumbent or ascending, to 10 in., 5–6-angled; fls. 3–5 or more in sessile, basal clusters, corolla about 1 in. across, roughened with pointed papillae, blackish-purple, inner whorl of corona yellowish. Tanzania.

barbata (Masson) Haw. To 3 in., sts. glaucous-green; fls. basal, corolla 1¼–2 in. across, shallowly lobed, sulphur-yellow to buff, marked with blood-red spots, tube covered with purple, clavate hairs inside. S. Afr.

brevirostris N. E. Br. Sts. erect, to 2½ in., 4–5-angled; fls. 3–6 in a basal cluster, corolla 1–1¾ in. across, rotate, with a short tube, papillate, lobes pale yellow, tube pinkish inside, and evenly spotted crimson, entirely crimson at the base, outer whorl of corona nearly black, inner whorl dull yellow, spotted purple-brown. S. Afr. Var. **scabra** (N. E. Br.) A. C. White & Sloane [*H. scabra* N. E. Br.]. Corolla with an annulus. S. Afr.

clavigera (Jacq.) Haw. Sts. erect, to 4 in., 4–5-angled; fls. 1 to several, basal, corolla 1¼–1½ in. across, campanulate, with somewhat constricted tube, lobes spreading to suberect, pale ochre-yellow to dull greenish-yellow, spotted crimson, grading to entirely blood-red in the tube, inside of tube with purple, clavate hairs, corona purple-black. S. Afr.

confusa E. P. Phillips. Sts. erect, stout, to 3 in.; fls. basal, corolla 1¼ in. across, tube yellowish-crimson, overhung by an annulus, this glossy, prominent, yellowish-crimson, greenish-white-flecked, corolla lobes spreading, triangular, greenish-white, with irregular red markings, corona bright yellow. S. Afr.

distincta N. E. Br. Tufted, sts. to 3 in., 8–9-angled, less noticeably so with age; fls. basal, corolla about 1¼ in. across, with distinct tube and spreading lobes, dull yellow, crimson-papillate-pubescent, and with crimson spots that, at base of tube, fuse into irregular lines, corona purple-black. S. Afr.

flavicorona: *H. macrocarpa* var. *flavicoronata.*

guttata (Masson) R. Br. To 3 in.; fls. basal, corolla 1¼–1½ in. across, with a prominent annulus around mouth of tube, light yellow, dotted crimson, with pointed papillae in the tube, outer whorl of corona with pinkish or whitish lobes with purple margins and black basal spot, inner whorl of corona with yellow lobes. S. Afr.

Hislopii Turrill. Sts. slender, 5-angled, fluted; fls. solitary, corolla to 1¼ in. long, campanulate with ascending lobe tips, cream-colored, spotted with blood-red, but entirely blood-red in tube; outer whorl of corona nearly black, inner whorl of corona with lobes white, tipped red. Rhodesia.

hystrix (Hook.f.) N. E. Br. Sts. to 5 in., 5-angled; fls. basal, corolla to 1½ in. across, with short, open tube and reflexed lobes, ochreous-yellow marked with crimson spots and lines and covered, except for lower part of tube, with long, fleshy spinelike processes, outer whorl of corona yellow or black, inner whorl expanded at apex, yellow, red-dotted. S. Afr. to Mozambique.

insigniflora Maass. Sts. to 5 in., more or less square in cross section, tubercled-toothed; fls. mostly solitary, basal, corolla to 1¾ in. across, rotate, annulus and tube shiny, purple-brown, lobes pale rose, not marked, inner whorl of corona yellow, flecked purple. S. Afr.

keniensis R. E. Fries. KENYA D.F. Sts. decumbent to ascending, nearly cylindrical to 5-furrowed; fls. 1–3, basal, corolla about 1¼ in. long, campanulate, papillate, deep purple, corona obscure, blackish-purple. Kenya. Var. **nairobiensis** A. C. White & Sloane. Corolla more conical, conspicuously scabrid outside, more densely finely papillate inside. Kenya.

Kirkii N. E. Br. Sts. acutely 5-angled; fls. 1–5 together, basal, corolla up to 2 in. across, rotate, with a swollen, apically constricted tube, sulphur-yellow with maroon spots, tube covered with fleshy, often red-tipped spines about the mouth of tube. S. Afr. and s. Rhodesia.

Langii: a listed name of no botanical standing.

Levyi Oberm. Sts. erect, deeply 4–5-angled; fls. basal, corolla to 1½ in. long, tubular, with short, triangular-acuminate, yellowish, red-spotted lobes, scabrous and mottled reddish-purple outside, dark maroon inside, with a raised, papillate annulus at base of tube. Rhodesia.

longituba N. E. Br. Sts. tufted, erect, thick, 4–5-angled; fls. 1–3, basal, corolla up to 1½ in. long, campanulate to somewhat tubular, yellowish, smooth, prominently 20-nerved outside, creamy-yellow spotted with deep red inside, but nearly entirely purple-red in tube. S. Afr.

macrocarpa (A. Rich.) Sprenger. Sts. erect to procumbent, 4–7-angled, the angles spinescently toothed; fls. 1–4, basal, corolla to 1 in. across, campanulate, papillate or smooth, yellow, with crowded, concentric, purple lines, or entirely crimson to purple, outer whorl of corona 5-lobed, dark-colored, inner whorl variously purple and yellow. Ne. Afr., Arabia. Var. **cerasina** A. C. White & Sloane. Sts. 5–7-angled; corolla papillate inside and out, uniformly cherry-red. Var. **flavicoronata** A. C. White & Sloane [*H. flavicorona* Hort.]. Corolla minutely papillate outside, dark reddish-brown, lobes of inner whorl of corona maroon and bright yellow. Var. **Penzigii** (N. E. Br.) A. C. White & Sloane [*H. Penzigii* N. E. Br.]. Differs from var. *cerasina* in having corolla dark purple. Var. **Schweinfurthii** (Berger) A. C. White & Sloane. Distinguished from var. *flavicoronata* in having corona lobes entirely maroon.

namaquensis Pillans. Sts. erect, to 3 in.; fls. 2–4 in a basal cyme, corolla about 1 in. across, campanulate, with lobes more or less erect, bristly papillate above the throat, whitish-yellow, spotted purple, corona yellow, marked purple. S. Afr.

oculata Hook.f. Sts. to about 3 in., 5-angled, the angles strongly toothed; fls. basal, corolla to 1 in. across, campanulate, lobes and upper part of tube blackish-purple, lower part white, forming a conspicuous eye. Sw. Afr.

pendula Bruce. Sts. pendent, branched or simple, to 3 ft. or more long, to about ¼ in. in diam.; fls. in 3–4-fld. cymes near the ends of short, lateral, apically clustered branchlets; corolla about ⅝ in. across, deep maroon, tubercled inside, corona purplish-black; follicle 1–2 in. long. S. Afr.

Penzigii: *H. macrocarpa* var.

Pillansii N. E. Br. COCKLEBUR. Sts. tufted, short, densely covered with conical, recurved, bristle-pointed tubercles; fls. basal, corolla to 1¼ in. across, pale yellow, pinkish in the tube, crimson-spotted and densely papillate except in lower part of tube, lobes lanceolate-acuminate. S. Afr.

praestans N. E. Br. Sts. 1–2 in., 4-angled, the angles sharply toothed; fls. basal, corolla to 1½ in. across, rotate, lobes and annulus greenish-yellow, spotted and dusted purple, the tube more or less uniformly purple, annulus stoutly papillate. S. Afr.

primulina N. E. Br. Sts. to 2½ in., 4–5-angled, the angles with triangular, acute, recurved-tipped, dark-colored teeth; fls. 3–8 in a basal cluster, corolla with a closed tube and spreading lobes, about 1 in. across, entirely sulphur-yellow, corona lobes purple-black to purple-brown. S. Afr.

quinta (E. P. Phillips) A. C. White & Sloane. Sts. stout, to 3 in., 4-angled, teeth horny; fls. 4–7 in a basal cluster, corolla about 1¼ in. across, yellow with dark red bands about mouth of the open tube. S. Afr.

reticulata (Masson) Haw. Sts. 3–4 in., angled, the angles acute, with large triangular teeth; fls. 1–4 in a basal cluster, corolla to 1¾ in. across, yellowish, with large purple spots, annulus smooth, shining, tube blood-red and purple-hairy inside. S. Afr.

scabra: *H. brevirostris* var.

Schneiderana Berger. RED D.F. Sts. to 2 in., with minute, subulate teeth; fls. basal, corolla about 1 in. across, brownish with a deeper purple-black tube, papillose and black-hairy. Nyasaland to Mozambique.

somalica N. E. Br. Sts. to 3 in., 5-angled, the angles with large teeth; fls. basal, corolla to 1–1½ in. across, deep, dull purple, lobes short, yellowish, inner whorl of corona bright yellow, with dull purple margin. Ne. Afr.

stapelioides Schlechter. Sts. about 4 in., 4-angled, the angles acute, sharply toothed; fls. in basal clusters, corolla about 1½ in. across, yellow with transverse, maroon bands, densely papillate, outer whorl of corona maroon, inner whorl yellow, swollen and crested toward apex. S. Afr.

Thuretii J. F. Cels. Sts. about 4 in., 4–5-angled, the angles acute, stoutly toothed; fls. basal, corolla about 1 in. across, rotate, with a more or less constricted tube, buff with blood-red dots and bands, and blood-red tube, outer whorl of corona nearly black, inner whorl purple-brown. S. Afr.

transmutata A. C. White & Sloane. Sts. about 2 in., 4–5-angled, with prickly teeth; fls. basal, corolla about 1¼ in. across, rotate, deep maroon, with small scattered spots of cream, papillate, corona velvety purple-black. Known only in cult.

transvaalensis Stent. Sts. to 3 in., 4–5-angled, acutely toothed; fls. 1–3, basal, corolla up to 2 in. across, lobes mottled and banded with purple and yellow, annulus shiny, purple, tube purple-black, flecked with yellow, pubescent with purple hairs, outer whorl of corona yellowish, inner whorl purple. S. Afr.

Vansonii: a listed name of no botanical standing.

Whitesloaneana Nel. Sts. to 2 in., 4–5-angled, sharply toothed; fls. 4–5 in basal fascicle, corolla about ⅝ in. long, campanulate, mottled purple outside, inside purple at base of tube, then banded purple and yellow and in the upper part irregularly mottled, corona purplish. S. Afr.

zebrina N. E. Br. OWL-EYES, LITTLE O. Sts. to 3 in., 5-angled, with spreading, acute teeth; fls. basal, corolla to 1¾ in. or more across, yellow annulus thick, fleshy, spotted, lobes with broken bands of purple-brown, corona mostly yellowish. S. and e. S.-W. Afr.

HUERNIOPSIS N. E. Br. *Asclepiadaceae.* Four spp. of succulent, leafless, per. herbs, native to S. Afr.; differing from *Huernia* in lacking teeth in the sinuses between the corolla lobes; and from *Stapelia* in the absence of an outer corona whorl or its reduction to short, longitudinally channelled teeth between the bases of the inner corona lobes; fr. a follicle.

For culture see *Succulents.*

atrosanguinea (N. E. Br.) A. C. White & Sloane. Sts. 2–3 in., 4-angled, the angles sharply toothed; fls. 2–3 together, halfway up the young sts., corolla about 1¾ in. across, deep blackish-crimson, unmarked, lobes of outer whorl of corona dull orange-yellow, reddish in the channel, lobes of inner whorl yellowish, conspicuously exserted.

decipiens N. E. Br. Sts. more or less decumbent, to 3 in. long, 4-angled, the angles sharply toothed; fls. 2–4 together, above the middle of the sts., corolla about 1 in. across, brownish-red or -crimson, mottled yellow, corona yellow.

gibbosa Nel. Sts. cespitose, to 3 in., 4-angled, with sharp, triangular teeth, each tooth with 2 smaller teeth at its base; corolla about 1 in. across, dark purple, with lobes greenish-yellow, corona lobes yellowish, conspicuously exserted.

papillata Nel. Sts. decumbent, to 2 in. long, 4-angled, the angles tubercled, toothed, each tooth with 2 smaller teeth at its base; fls. in subterminal fascicles, corolla 1½ in. across, greenish-white, spotted reddish-purple, papillate, corona lobes whitish or purple-spotted.

HUGUENINIA Rchb. *Cruciferae.* Two spp. of per. herbs native to montane Eur., more or less stellate-hairy; lvs. pinnately divided; fls. small, yellow, sepals 4, petals 4, longer than sepals; fr. a silique, valves 1-veined, seeds not winged, mucilaginous when moistened. Closely related to *Sisymbrium,* but stellate-hairy.

tanacetifolia (L.) Rchb. To 2½ ft.; lower lvs. to 12 in. long, long-petioled, with 8–10 pairs of segms.; petals ⅛ in. long; siliques to ⅝ in. long. Mts., cent. and sw. Eur.

HULSEA Torr. & A. Gray ex A. Gray. *Compositae* (Helenium Tribe). About 8 or 9 spp. of ann., bien., or per., aromatic, glandular herbs in w. N. Amer.; lvs. alt., entire to pinnatifid; fl. heads radiate, many-fld., involucre hemispherical, involucral bracts green, in 2–3 rows, reflexing, receptacle flat, naked; fls. all bisexual, fertile, disc fls. yellow, ray fls. yellow or purplish; achenes slenderly club-shaped, villous, pappus of 4 translucent, fringed scales.

Adapted to alpine gardens.

nana A. Gray. Tufted per., 2–6 in.; lvs. basal, to 2½ in. long, fleshy, oblanceolate, pinnately lobed, green and glandular or woolly; heads scapose, 1 in. across; fls. yellow, ray fls. ½ in. long, narrow. Volcanic mts., Wash. to n. Calif.

HUMATA Cav. *Polypodiaceae.* About 50 spp. of small, rhizomatous, epiphytic ferns, native from Madagascar to Pacific Is.; lvs. uniform or dimorphic, leathery, triangular or oblong, entire to pinnatifid, sterile lvs. less cut than fertile; sori borne near the margins of segms., terminal on veins. Similar to *Davallia,* but differing in having sides of the indusia separate and forming a shallow, cupped flap.

For culture see *Davallia* and *Ferns.*

Tyermannii T. Moore. BEAR-FOOT FERN, BEAR'S-FOOT F. Rhizome creeping, white-scaly; lvs. to 12 in. long, 3–4-pinnate-pinnatifid. Much like *Davallia trichomanoides* in general appearance, except for white-scaly rhizomes. Grown outdoors in s. Calif. Zone 10. Material of this sp. has probably been offered as *Davallia Griffithiana.*

HUMEA Sm. *Compositae* (Inula Tribe). About 7 spp. of herbs and shrubs, native to Madagascar and S. Australia; lvs. alt., entire; fl. heads discoid, small, 1–4-fld., in panicles or corymbs, involucral bracts scarious, colored; fls. all tubular; achenes without pappus.

Humeas are heavy feeders and need plenty of moisture. The seeds may be sown from the first of July till Sept. In the North the young plants should be kept nearly dry and in a coolhouse in winter. They may be planted in the garden in June.

elegans Sm. Erect bien., to 6 ft.; lvs. ovate-lanceolate or oblong, the lower to 10 in. long, clasping at base, sweet-scented; heads cylindrical, in large, loose, graceful panicles; fls. purplish, brownish-red, rose, or pink. The foliage has been reported to cause a dermatitis in some persons.

HUMULUS L. HOP. *Cannabaceae.* Two spp. of rough-stemmed, tall-twining, dioecious, per. herbs in the temp. N. Hemisphere; lvs. opp., broad-toothed; fls. small, male fls. in loose, axillary panicles, sepals 5, stamens 5, female fls. in short, solitary, bracted spikes which appear conelike at maturity, each bract 2-fld.; fr. an achene.

Hardy plants grown as ornamentals, but primarily for "hops," the scaly mature female inflorescence, whose resinous and bitter properties are basic to the production of beer. Propagated by cuttings of underground stems.

americanus: *H. Lupulus.*

japonicus Siebold & Zucc. JAPANESE H. Lvs. deeply 5–7-lobed, strongly serrate; spikes scarcely enlarged in fr., the bracts ovate-orbicular in fr., to ¾ in. long, herbaceous, green, partly purplish-brown. Temp. e. Asia. Cv. **'Variegatus'.** Foliage streaked and splashed with white. Usually grown as an ann. from seeds, for porches and screens.

Lupulus L. [*H. americanus* Nutt.]. COMMON H., EUROPEAN H., BINE. Rhizomatous per.; lvs. mostly 3–5-lobed, lobes about as broad as long and short-pointed, coarsely toothed; spikes much enlarged in fr., the bracts round, to ¾ in. long, blunt or acute, papery-membranous. N. temp. regions, often naturalized elsewhere. Source of commercial hops. Cv. **'Aureus'.** Foliage yellow.

HUNNEMANNIA Sweet. *Papaveraceae.* One sp., a glabrous, glaucous, per. herb, native to Mex.; closely related to *Eschscholzia* but with 2 separate sepals.

fumariifolia Sweet. MEXICAN TULIP POPPY, GOLDEN-CUP. To 2 ft.; lvs. ternately dissected, glaucous; fls. yellow, to 3 in. across; fr. linear, to 4 in. long. Usually grown as an ann. Requires warm, sunny exposure. Prop. by seeds.

HUNTLEYA Batem. *Orchidaceae.* About 10 spp. of epiphytes without pseudobulbs, native to Cent. and S. Amer.; sts. short, completely enclosed by bases of overlapping lvs.; lvs. often forming a fan; infl. axillary, 1-fld.; fls. large, showy, fleshy, sepals and petals similar, lip clawed, with toothed or fimbriate callus, column fleshy, cylindrical, with a pronounced foot. For structure of fl. see *Orchidaceae.*

For culture see *Orchids.*

Burtii: *H. meleagris.*

meleagris Lindl. [*H. Burtii* (Endres & Rchb.f.) Pfitz.; *Batemannia Burtii* Endres & Rchb.f.]. Cushion-forming; lvs. few, to 15 in. long; fls. to 4 in. across, sepals and petals spreading, broadly ovate-triangular, red-brown, spotted with light yellow, often checkered, lighter toward base, lip white, clawed, with a semicircular, fringed callus, midlobe red-brown. Summer. Costa Rica to Brazil. Var. **Wallisii** (Rchb.f.) Rolfe. Fls. larger, perianth segms. broader, sepals and petals chestnut- or mahogany-brown, only slightly checkered, white at base. Colombia.

HURA L. *Euphorbiaceae.* Two spp. of monoecious trees with irritating milky juice, native to trop. N. and S. Amer.; lvs. alt., simple, pinnately veined, petioles about as long as blades; fls. without petals, male fls. sessile on long-peduncled spikes, female fls. axillary, solitary, ovary 5–20-celled; fr. a large caps., with explosive dehiscence.

Sometimes planted as an ornamental in tropical regions. It does best on a light loamy soil; propagated by cuttings and seeds. Juvenile specimens sometimes grown under glass.

crepitans L. SANDBOX TREE, MONKEY-PISTOL, JAVILLO, MONKEY'S-DINNER-BELL. Great tree, to 100 ft., brs. spiny; lvs. broadly ovate, cordate at base, to 2 ft. long, toothed; fls. red; fr. about 3–4 in. in diam., many-ribbed, splitting explosively into segms. when ripe. W. Indies, Costa Rica, S. Amer.

HUTCHINSIA R. Br. *Cruciferae.* Two or 3 spp. of small per. *Draba*-like herbs in mts. of cent. and s. Eur., glabrous or with simple hairs; lvs. pinnate or entire; fls. small, white, in close racemes, sepals 4, petals 4, clawed; fr. an elliptic to lanceolate silicle with 2 seeds in each half.

Planted in alpine and rock gardens.

alpina (L.) R. Br. Tufted per., to 4 in.; lvs. basal, pinnatisect into elliptic or oblong lobes, 1 in. long or less, petioled; fls. pure white. Spring and summer. Mts., cent. and s. Eur. A variable sp. Subsp. **alpina.** The typical subsp.; fl. sts. straight, more or less leafless, to 4 in.; fls. about ⅛ in. across, petals narrow. Subsp. **Auerswaldii** (Willk.) M. Laínz [*H. Auerswaldii* Willk.]. Like subsp. *alpina,* but fl. sts. more or less leafy, flexuous, to 6 in. Subsp. **brevicaulis** (Hoppe) Arcang. [*H. brevicaulis* Hoppe]. Fl. sts. straight, more or less leafless, to 2 in.; fls. to $^1/_{16}$ in. across, petals narrow.

Auerswaldii: *H. alpina* subsp.

brevicaulis: *H. alpina* subsp.

stylosa DC. [*Iberis stylosa* (DC.) Ten.]. Bien., tufted, to 3 in.; lvs. obovate-oblong or oblong, nearly entire, petioled; fls. white, in corymbs. Italy.

HYACINTHELLA Schur. *Liliaceae.* About 10 spp. of bulbous, scapose, per. herbs, native from se. Poland to Israel and n. Iran; bulbs tunicate; lvs. usually 2, rarely 1 or 3, basal, narrow, usually with raised veins; fls. blue, violet, or rarely white, erect to horizontal but never nodding, in cylindrical racemes terminating the scape, perianth campanulate, funnelform, or tubular, 6-parted to ⅓ its length, persistent, stamens 6, inserted in tube below base of perianth lobes; fr. a leathery, depressed-globose, 3-valved, loculicidal caps. with rounded carpels, seeds black, wrinkled, 1–2 in each cell.

azurea: *Muscari azureum.*

dalmatica (Bak.) Chouard [*Hyacinthus dalmaticus* Bak.]. To 4 in.; lvs. 2, linear-lanceolate, 2–3 in. long, thick and leathery; fls. tubular-campanulate, pale blue, to $^3/_{16}$ in. long. Dalmatia.

HYACINTHUS L. *Liliaceae.* One sp., a bulbous, per. herb, native to Medit. region, Asia Minor, and Syria; bulb tunicate; lvs. basal, narrow; fls. white, yellow, pink, red, or blue, in a bracted, cylindrical raceme terminating a scape; perianth funnelform, with cylindrical tube and 6 spreading to reflexed lobes, deciduous, stamens 6, filaments arising from perianth tube, anthers versatile; fr. a 3-valved, 3-angled, 3-celled, loculicidal caps., seeds carunculate, black, 8–12 in each cell.

The hyacinth is hardy in the U.S. and Canada, blooming in spring with the midseason tulips. Strong, carefully grown and selected bulbs must be used if best results are to be obtained. The bulbs may be planted in the North in Sept. and Oct., 5 or 6 in. apart, the bottom of the bulb being 5 or 6 in. below the surface in properly prepared well-drained ground. Mulch thoroughly for the winter.

For winter bloom, bulbs are set in pots in Oct., in a porous soil of loam and leaf mold, lightened with sand if necessary to keep it friable and open. The tip of the bulb is allowed to show at the surface of the soil or to be barely covered. A large bulb is sufficient for a 5 in. pot; specially-made hyacinth pots are deeper than the ordinary kind and preferable. The pots are placed in a coldframe or similar place to allow the bulbs to root, being covered a few in. deep with soil or sifted coal ashes. In 6–8 weeks the roots will have formed and the pots may be brought into a room with a temperature of about 50° F. Here they are allowed to remain till the shoots are vigorous, stocky, and dark green, when they may be brought to the living room, some of them perhaps being left in the intermediate temperature to provide succession. If the bulbs are not well rooted when brought in from the frame so that the roots fill the pot, the results will not be satisfactory. After the bloom is past, the bulbs are discarded or planted in the garden.

Hyacinths are sometimes forced in glasses that are made for the purpose and may be had of dealers in garden supplies. There is a flange at the top to hold the bulb; the glass is kept filled with water up to the bottom of the bulb. A few pieces of charcoal placed in the bottom of the glass will keep the water sweet. The glasses are set aside in a dark, cool place for the bulbs to form roots as in soil, although quicker results are usually obtained with water culture. When the roots have reached the bottom of the glass, the glasses are brought to an intermediate temperature and handled as for potted plants.

Propagation of hyacinths is by means of bulblets or offsets from the old bulbs, which should give blooming bulbs in 2 or 3 years. The production of bulblets is stimulated by variously cutting the bulb, but the home gardener might better depend on the commercial supply.

amethystinus: *Brimeura amethystina.*

azureus: *Muscari azureum.*

candicans: *Galtonia candicans.*

ciliatus: *Bellevalia ciliata.*

corymbosus: *Periboea corymbosa.*

dalmaticus: *Hyacinthella dalmatica.*

orientalis L. HYACINTH, DUTCH H., COMMON H., GARDEN H. Bulb tunics whitish or purplish, flowering plant to 1½ ft.; lvs. 4–6, strap-shaped, with upturned margins, to 1 ft. long or more and 1 in. wide, many-nerved; fls. intensely fragrant, in various colors, about 1 in. long, often double, nodding, in a dense raceme on a hollow scape. Early spring. N. Afr., Greece to Asia Minor and Syria. Cult. in s. France as source of perfume. Var. **albulus** Bak. ROMAN HYACINTH. Smaller and earlier; fls. white to bright blue, in more open racemes. S. France.

paucifolius: *Periboea paucifolia.*

plumosus: *Muscari comosum* cv.

princeps: *Galtonia princeps.*

romanus: *Bellevalia romana.*

Saviczii: *Bellevalia Saviczii.*

HYBOPHRYNIUM K. Schum. [*Bamburanta* L. Linden]. *Marantaceae.* One sp., a tall shrubby herb, native to trop. Afr.; lvs. alt., entire, petioles sheathing; fls. in pairs, in elongate, simple, bracted, terminal spikes, sepals 3, corolla tube much shorter than sepals, lobes 3, lanceolate, acuminate, fertile stamens 1, staminodes 3, the outermost as long as the petals, the innermost one with a long pendulous appendage, ovary papillose, 3-celled; caps. muricate.

Braunianum K. Schum. [*Bamburanta Arnoldiana* L. Linden]. Lvs. oblong to broad-lanceolate, to 6 in. wide, acuminate, glabrous; infl. to 5 in. long, bracts to 1 in. long; fls. whitish, 1 in. long; caps. 3-lobed, ½ in. in diam., yellow. Sierra Leone to Angola.

HYBRID. The term hybrid is used to designate the offspring that result from crosses between plants (or animals) belonging to different species or to distinct forms of the same species. In nature, naturally formed hybrids have played major roles in plant evolution by providing a means for genetic exchange between and within species or even for the creation of new species, especially when hybridization is accompanied by polyploidy (see *Ploidy*). In horticulture, hybridization is of equal importance. It has given the horticulturist, principally through the selection of offspring from controlled hybridization programs, the opportunity to create new cultivars and forms that combine desired traits of their parents or to select strains incorporating traits like early maturity, increased vigor or yield, disease resistance, and increased flower size.

The rules governing the names of hybrids are set forth in the International Code of Botanical Nomenclature. Hybrids between two species of the same genus, known as interspecific hybrids, may be designated by either a formula or by a name. Thus, the glossy abelia, which is a hybrid between *Abelia chinensis* and *A. uniflora,* may be known by the name *Abelia* × *grandiflora* or by the formulas *Abelia chinensis* × *A. uniflora* or *Abelia chinensis* × *uniflora.* The name *Abelia* × *grandiflora* is formed according to the same rules governing the formation of species names but is distinguished from the name of a true species by the multiplication sign placed directly before the "specific" epithet. The multiplication sign is not read but is a symbol indicating that the "species" is of hybrid origin. Intergeneric hybrids, that is hybrids between species of two or more genera, also are designated by a formula or by a name. The formula consists of the names of the parents connected by the multiplication sign, as, for example, *Amaryllis* × *Brunsvigia* or *Brassovola* × *Cattleya* × *Laelia.* The "generic" name of an intergeneric hybrid usually is a combination of parts of the names of the genera involved: × *Amarygia* for the bigeneric hybrid *Amaryllis* × *Brunsvigia,* for example, and × *Brassolaeliocattleya* for the trigeneric hybrid *Brassovola* × *Cattleya* × *Laelia.* In a sense these hybrid "generic" names may be considered condensed formulas. The multiplication sign directly precedes the name of an intergeneric hybrid and, again, is not read but indicates that the "genus" is of hybrid origin. In names of "species" of hybrid "genera," the multiplication sign precedes only the "generic" name and is not inserted or repeated before the "specific" epithet—as in, for example, × *Amarygia Bidwellii,* the hybrid between *Amaryllis Belladonna* and *Brunsvigia orientalis.*

In horticulture many cultivars of suspected or known hybrid origin are not given "specific" epithets or referred to by parental formulas. They are commonly recognized merely as cultivars of the particular genus to which they belong. For example, a cultivar of the cross *Ilex cornuta* × *I. Pernyi,* known by the fancy name 'Doctor Kassab', may be referred to simply as *Ilex* cv. 'Doctor Kassab' with or without designation of its parental formula.

HYDASTYLUS: *SISYRINCHIUM.*

HYDNOCARPUS Gaertn. [*Taraktogenos* Hassk.]. *Flacourtiaceae.* About 40 spp. of trees or sometimes shrubs, usually dioecious, native to trop. se. Asia; lvs. alt., entire; fls. axillary, in branched cymes or solitary; fr. indehiscent, globose, hard.

The fatty oil extracted from seeds of most species used in healing skin diseases.

Kurzii (King) Warb. [*Taraktogenos Kurzii* King]. Tree, to 60 ft.; lvs. lanceolate-oblong, to 9 in. long, somewhat leathery and glossy; cymes few-fld., short; sepals 4, petals 8, stamens many; fr. rugose, to 4 in. in diam. Burma and Thailand. Sometimes planted in collections of trop. economic trees. The seeds yield chaulmoogra oil, used in treatment of leprosy.

HYDRANGEA L. [*Hortensia* Comm. ex Juss.]. *Saxifragaceae.* About 23 spp. of erect or climbing, deciduous or evergreen shrubs of N. and S. Amer., and e. Asia; lvs. opp., entire or serrate, rarely pinnately lobed; fls. white, pink, lavender, or blue, in terminal or occasionally axillary, com-

pound, branched, rounded or pyramidal clusters; fertile fls. many, small, bisexual, calyx tube united to ovary, sepals and petals 4 or 5, stamens 8 or 10, rarely 20, ovary inferior or half-inferior, sterile fls. sometimes present also, showy, consisting of 3–5 enlarged conspicuous petal-like sepals, usually lacking other fl. parts., few and arranged along the periphery of the infl., or, in some cult. forms, numerous and making up almost the entire infl.; fr. a dehiscent caps., seeds many, small. Variation within the genus is not great and the spp. are distinguished mostly by small differences in the fls., the type of infl., and, to a lesser extent, the lf. characters.

Hydrangeas require a rich, porous, somewhat moist soil; they bloom most freely in full sun, but also do well in partial shade. They should be pruned rather severely in the autumn or early spring. The hardy species are propagated by green cuttings in summer under glass; the tender ones by cuttings taken at any time from vigorous young wood, usually in late winter. Suckers can be separated in some species, while layering is occasionally employed in others. *H. quercifolia* is increased by little suckers; *H. paniculata* easily from young wood taken in June and planted under glass. Seeds may be used when available.

acuminata: *H. macrophylla* subsp. *serrata.*

altissima: *H. anomala* subsp. *anomala.*

anomala D. Don. Deciduous climber, clinging by aerial rootlets, sparsely pubescent; lvs. ovate, to 5 in. long, glabrous or nearly so; fls. white, in a several-branched corymb, sterile fls. on margin of infl., long-pedicelled, with 3–4 enlarged calyx lobes, fertile fls. short-pedicelled, with petals united and falling as a cap, stamens 9–20, ovary inferior. United petals are not found in any other sp. of the genus. Subsp. **anomala** [*H. altissima* Wallich]. The typical subsp.; stamens 9–15. Himalayas and China. Zone 6. Subsp. **petiolaris** (Siebold & Zucc.) McClint. [*H. petiolaris* Siebold & Zucc.; *H. scandens* Maxim., not Poepp. or Rehd.; *H. volubilis* Hort., may belong here]. CLIMBING H. Stamens 15–20. Japan, Taiwan. Zone 5.

arborescens L. HILLS-OF-SNOW, WILD H., SEVENBARK. Much-branched shrub, to 4 ft., branchlets and infl. strigose-pubescent or puberulent; lvs. ovate, sometimes broadly so, to 6 in. long, variously pubescent beneath; infl. a rounded, much-branched cluster; sterile and fertile fls. present, ovary inferior. Zone 4. The dried root has been used medicinally as a diuretic and cathartic. Subsp. **arborescens** [var. *australis* Harb.; *H. cordata* Pursh]. The typical subsp.; lower surface of lvs. glabrous or nearly so, green. S. N.Y., s. to N.C. and Tenn., w. to Ark. Cv. '**Grandiflora**'. Fls. all sterile. Subsp. **discolor** (Ser.) McClint. [*H. cinerea* Small]. Lower surface of lvs. pubescent, grayish. Mts. of se. U.S., w. to Ark. Zone 5. Cv. '**Sterile**'. Fls. all sterile. Subsp. **radiata** (Walt.) McClint. [*H. nivea* Michx.; *H. radiata* Walt.]. Lower surface of lvs. white-tomentose. Mts., se. U.S. Zone 5.

aspera D. Don. To 6 ft., branchlets and infl. pubescent with stiff, upwardly appressed or curling hairs; lvs. lanceolate to broadly ovate, to 12 in. long, serrate; infl. a flat-topped, much-branched cluster; sterile fls. white, fertile fls. blue, ovary inferior. Zone 7. Subsp. **aspera** [*H. villosa* Rehd.]. The typical subsp.; lvs. lanceolate, strigose beneath. E. Asia. Subsp. **robusta** (Hook.f. & T. Thoms.) McClint. [*H. robusta* Hook.f. & T. Thoms.]. Lvs. ovate, often broadly so, strigose with straight, appressed hairs beneath. E. Asia. Subsp. **Sargentiana** (Rehd.) McClint. [*H. Sargentiana* Rehd.]. Lvs. broadly ovate, to 12 in. long, velvety beneath. W. China. Subsp. **strigosa** (Rehd.) McClint. [*H. strigosa* Rehd.]. Lvs. velvety with erect or somewhat curled hairs beneath. E. Asia.

Belzonii: *H. macrophylla* subsp. *macrophylla.*

Bretschneideri: *H. heteromalla.*

canescens: a listed name, perhaps referring to *H. arborescens.*

cinerea: *H. arborescens* subsp. *discolor.*

cordata: *H. arborescens* subsp. *arborescens.*

cuspidata: *H. macrophylla* subsp. *serrata.*

globosa: a listed name of no botanical standing.

heteromalla D. Don [*H. Bretschneideri* Dipp.; *H. pekinensis* Hort. ex Dipp.; *H. vestita* Wallich; *H. vestita* var. *pubescens* Maxim.; *H. xanthoneura* Diels; *H. xanthoneura* vars. *setchuenensis* Rehd. and *Wilsonii* Rehd.]. To 6 ft., branchlets and infl. pubescent with upwardly curled hairs; lvs. ovate, often broadly so, to 8 in. long, glabrous to sparsely or densely pubescent beneath; infl. a flat-topped cluster to 12 in. across; sterile and fertile fls. white, ovary half-inferior. Himalayas. Zone 5 or 6.

Hortensia: *H. macrophylla* subsp. *macrophylla.*

hortensis: *H. macrophylla* subsp. *macrophylla.*

involucrata Siebold. To 6 ft.; branchlets, infl., and lower lf. surface pubescent with appressed hairs; lvs. ovate, to 10 in. long; infl. a rounded, several-branched cluster, bracts broadly ovate, to 1 in. long, enveloping the unopened infl.; sterile and fertile fls. lavender, ovary inferior. Japan. Zone 7.

japonica: *H. macrophylla* subsp. *macrophylla.*

Lindleyana: *H. macrophylla* subsp. *macrophylla.*

macrophylla (Thunb.) Ser. FRENCH H., HORTENSIA. To 5 ft., or as much as 8 ft., deciduous, or evergreen in mild climates, glabrous, or pubescent with upwardly curled hairs; lvs. ovate, to 9 in. long, thin to thickish; infl. a flat-topped, several-branched cluster; sterile and fertile fls. white, pink, or blue, ovary inferior in fl., half-inferior in fr. Zone 6 or 7. Subsp. **macrophylla** [*H. Belzonii* Siebold & Zucc.; *H. hortensis* Sm.; *H. japonica* Siebold; *H. Lindleyana* Hort. ex Lavall.; *H. opuloides* (Lam.) C. Koch; *H. Otaksa* Siebold & Zucc.; *Hortensia* Siebold; *H. Hortensia opuloides* Lam.; *Hydrangea stellata* Siebold & Zucc. may also belong here]. The typical subsp.; glabrous shrub, to 8 ft.; lvs. ovate, to 9 in. long, coarsely serrate, thickish, more or less glossy above. Var. **macrophylla.** The garden HORTENSIA. The typical var.; infl. rounded; fls. almost all sterile. Of spontaneous origin in the wild in the same area as var. *normalis,* and in cult., through selection, giving rise to many cvs. Var. **normalis** E. H. Wils. Both fertile and sterile fls. present. S. coast of island of Honshu (Japan). Subsp. **serrata** (Thunb.) Mak. [*H. acuminata* Siebold & Zucc.; *H. cuspidata* (Thunb.) Miq.; *H. serrata* (Thunb.) Ser.; *H. Thunbergii* Siebold]. TEA-OF-HEAVEN. To 5 ft., branchlets, lvs., and infl. glabrous, or pubescent with appressed hairs; lvs. ovate, to 6 in. long, thin, closely serrate, dull above. Japan and Cheju Is. (Korea).

nivea: *H. arborescens* subsp. *radiata.*

opuloides: *H. macrophylla* subsp. *macrophylla.*

Otaksa: *H. macrophylla* subsp. *macrophylla.*

paniculata Siebold. Shrub or small tree, to as much as 30 ft., branchlets, infl., and lvs. with appressed pubescence; lvs. ovate, to 6 in. long; infl. a pyramidal cluster, to 10 in. long; sterile and fertile fls. white, ovary half-inferior. China and Japan. Zone 4. The only Asiatic sp. with a pyramidal infl., a character also found in the American *H. quercifolia.* Cv. 'Grandiflora'. PEEGEE H. The commonly grown form; infl. large, showy, consisting mostly of sterile fls., the fls. opening white and aging to pinkish, then bronze, long-persistent. Cv. 'Praecox'. Said to be early-flowering. Cv. 'Tardiva'. Late-flowering.

pekinensis: *H. heteromalla.*

petiolaris: *H. anomala* subsp.

quercifolia Bartr. Stoutly branched shrub, to 6 ft., young branchlets and petioles densely tomentose, brs. of infl. pilose with short, coarse hairs; lvs. nearly orbicular or elliptic in outline, to 12 in. long, mostly 5-lobed, lobes coarsely serrate; infl. a much-branched, pyramidal cluster to 10 in. long; sterile and fertile fls. white, ovary inferior. Se. U.S. Zone 5. Distinguished from *H. paniculata* by its lobed lvs.

radiata: *H. arborescens* subsp.

robusta: *H. aspera* subsp.

Sargentiana: *H. aspera* subsp.

scandens: *H. anomala* subsp. *petiolaris.*

serrata: *H. macrophylla* subsp.

stellata: *H. macrophylla* subsp. *macrophylla.*

strigosa: *H. aspera* subsp.

Thunbergii: *H. macrophylla* subsp. *serrata.*

vestita: *H. heteromalla.*

villosa: *H. aspera* subsp. *aspera.*

volubilis: see *H. anomala* subsp. *petiolaris.*

xanthoneura: *H. heteromalla.*

HYDRASTIS Ellis. ORANGEROOT, YELLOW PUCCOON. *Ranunculaceae.* Two spp. of low per. herbs, 1 native to Japan, 1 to e. N. Amer.; lvs. palmately lobed; fls. small, solitary, sepals 3, petaloid, petals 0, stamens many, clavate; fr. a berry, several in a cluster.

The Amer. species is grown or gathered for the roots, which have medicinal properties. Hydrastis does best in rich moist soil with plenty of leafmold. For commercial plantings, lath coverings or trees are often used to simulate natural conditions. Propagation is by seeds or by division.

canadensis L. GOLDENSEAL, ORANGEROOT, TURMERIC. To 1 ft., rhizome thick, yellow; basal lvs. to 8 in. across, cordate at base, 5–9-lobed, lobes doubly serrate, st. lvs. 2, the upper one sessile under the fl.; fls. greenish-white, ½ in. across. Vt. to Minn., s. to Ga., Ala., Ark.

HYDRIASTELE H. Wendl. & Drude. *Palmae.* About 9 spp. of mostly cespitose, slender, unarmed, monoecious palms in ne. Australia and New Guinea; lvs. pinnate, sheaths tubular, forming a slender crownshaft, pinnae 1-ribbed or several-ribbed, often oblique and toothed at apex; infl. below lvs., with 2 deciduous bracts, peduncle short, rachillae mostly simple, with fls. in triads (2 male and 1 female) borne in rows; male fls. asymmetrical, sepals 3, short, scarcely imbricate, petals 3, acute, stamens 6, filaments erect, pistillode lacking, female fls. with sepals 3, imbricate, petals 3, imbricate, with briefly valvate apices, staminodes lacking, pistil 1-celled, 1-ovuled; fr. small, ellipsoid, with apical stigmatic residue, seed with homogeneous or ruminate endosperm, embryo basal.

Tender palms for tropical plantings. For culture see *Palms.*

Wendlandiana (F. J. Muell.) H. Wendl. & Drude. Sts. tall; pinnae many, to 1½ ft. long, toothed at apex; infl. about 1 ft. long; fr. ovoid, ⁵⁄₁₆ in. long, endosperm homogeneous. Ne. Australia. Plants cult. under this name often are *Ptychosperma elegans.*

HYDRILLA L. Rich. *Hydrocharitaceae.* One sp., a submersed aquatic herb, native to the Old World; lvs. whorled; fls. unisexual, solitary, in axillary spathes, sepals, petals, and stamens 3, ovary beaked, styles 3, entire.

verticillata (L.f.) Royle. Sts. branched; lvs. 3–8 in a whorl, lanceolate, to 1½ in. long, green with red-brown dots and lines, sharply serrate-dentate; fr. roughened with short, sharp projections. Sometimes grown in aquaria.

HYDROCARYACEAE: *TRAPACEAE.*

HYDROCHARIS L. *Hydrocharitaceae.* Two spp. of floating aquatic herbs, native to Old World; lvs. long-petioled, cordate-orbicular; fls. white, unisexual, long-pedicelled, subtended by 1–2 spathe valves, petals broader and longer than sepals.

Grown in aquaria. Propagated by cuttings or long runners, and in the wild by winter buds that form in the autumn.

Morsus-ranae L. FROG'S-BIT. Roots fine and silky; lvs. 2 in. across, cordate at base; fls. nearly 1 in. across. Eur., e. Asia.

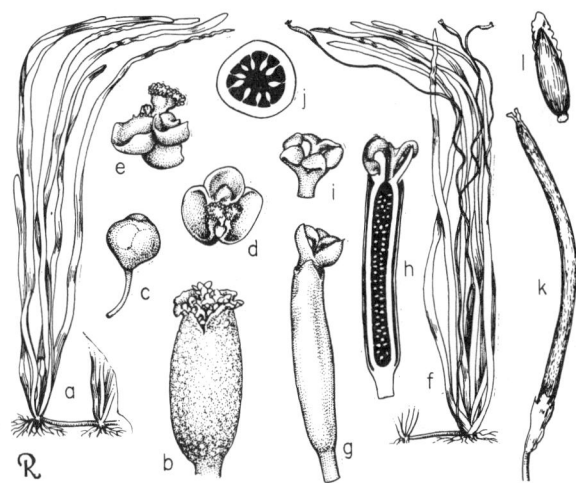

HYDROCHARITACEAE. *Vallisneria americana:* **a,** male plants, × ⅙; **b,** spathe enclosing male flowers, × 2; **c,** male flower bud, × 12; **d,** male flower, face view, × 12; **e,** male flower, side view, × 12; **f,** female plants, × ⅙; **g,** spathe enclosing female flower, × 1½; **h,** female flower, vertical section, × 1½; **i,** stigma, × 2; **j,** ovary, cross section, × 5; **k,** fruit, × ½; **l,** seed, × 5.

HYDROCHARITACEAE Juss. FROG'S-BIT FAMILY. Monocot.; 14 genera of aquatic herbs of worldwide distribution, some submersed, the fls. often coming to the surface on long, very slender stalks, others floating; fls. mostly unisexual, sometimes bisexual, regular, borne in a spathe, perianth of 3 calyxlike and 3 petal-like parts, stamens 3–12, ovary inferior, 1-celled; fr. berrylike, submersed. *Blyxa, Elodea, Hydrilla, Hydrocharis, Lagarosiphon, Limnobium, Ottelia, Stratiotes,* and *Vallisneria* are sometimes grown in ponds and aquaria.

HYDROCLEYS L. Rich. *Butomaceae.* About 4 spp. of aquatic herbs with milky sap, native to trop. Amer.; lvs. floating, with long, basally sheathing petioles; fls. large, bisexual, sepals 3, leathery, petals 3, yellow, withering early, stamens many, pistils 3–8, united at base, styles long, ovules many; fr. a caps., seeds many.

Of easy cultivation in ponds and aquaria. To grow in tubs, fill the lower ⅔ of container with soil and the upper ⅓ with water. Propagated by division of rooted stems.

nymphoides (Willd.) Buchenau [*Limnocharis Humboldtii* L. Rich]. WATER POPPY. Sts. prostrate, rooting; lvs. clustered, blades mostly floating, broadly ovate or elliptic, cordate, 2–3 in. across; fls. showy, 2 in. across, long-peduncled, in clusters. Trop. S. Amer. Tender.

HYDROCOTYLE L. WATER PENNYWORT, NAVELWORT. *Umbelliferae.* About 50–60 spp. of almost cosmopolitan, creeping, per. herbs; lvs. stipuled, nearly or quite orbicular, sometimes peltate, palmately lobed or veined, usually crenate; fls. small, white or greenish, in small, simple or proliferous (one above the other) umbels; fr. strongly compressed laterally.

Sometimes used as a ground cover in wet or moist locations. Propagated by seeds, cuttings, or layers.

dissecta Hook.f. Creeping and rooting at nodes; lvs. to ¾ in. across, hirsute, 5–7-parted ⅔ to the base, lobes finely and sharply toothed; peduncles slender, about as long as lvs., umbel 40–50-fld.; fr. sessile. New Zeal. Lvs. have odor of parsley when crushed.

peduncularis R. Br. Sts. creeping, densely matted, covered with imbricated stipules; lvs. orbicular-cordate or kidney-shaped, ³⁄₁₆ in. long, 5-lobed; peduncles filiform, usually longer than lvs.; fr. sessile. Probably not cult., material so listed being *H. sibthorpioides.* Tasmania.

rotundifolia: *H. sibthorpioides.*

sibthorpioides Lam. [*H. rotundifolia* Roxb.]. LAWN W.P. Creeping and rooting at nodes; lvs. suborbicular, ³⁄₁₆–⅜ in. across, glabrous, shallowly 7-lobed, lobes crenate; peduncles filiform, longer than lvs., umbel 3–10-fld.; fr. sessile. Asia; widely naturalized.

vulgaris L. Sts. creeping or floating; lvs. peltate, orbicular, to 2 in. across, crenate; umbels 2–5-fld., sometimes several, one above another; fls. purplish-green. N. Afr., Eur., w. to Caspian region.

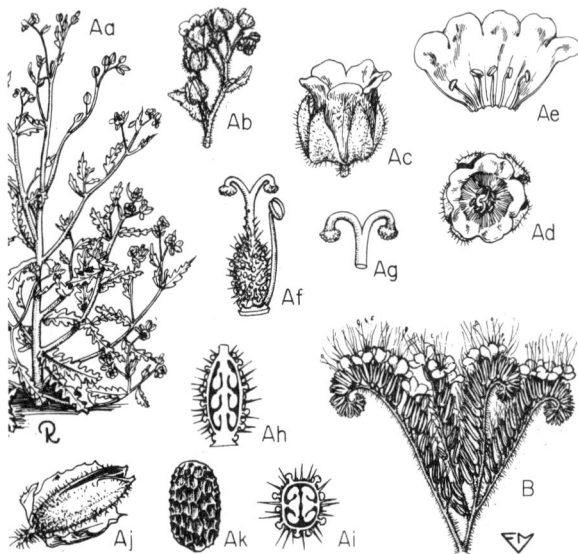

HYDROPHYLLACEAE. **A,** *Emmenanthe penduliflora:* **Aa,** flowering plant, × ¹⁄₁₀; **Ab,** branch of inflorescence, × ½; **Ac,** flower, side view, × 1½; **Ad,** flower, face view, × 1½; **Ae,** corolla, expanded, × 1½; **Af,** pistil and one stamen, × 4; **Ag,** stigmas, × 6; **Ah,** ovary, vertical section, × 6; **Ai,** ovary, cross section, × 6; **Aj,** capsule, × 1½; **Ak,** seed, × 5. **B,** *Phacelia tanacetifolia:* inflorescence (panicle of scorpioid cymes), × ½. (B from Bailey, *Manual of Cultivated Plants,* ed. 2.)

HYDROPHYLLACEAE R. Br. WATERLEAF FAMILY. Dicot.; about 25 genera and 250 to 300 spp. of mostly ann. or per. herbs, rarely shrubs, native chiefly to w. N. Amer., but on all continents except Australia; plants usually hairy, often glandular or bristly; lvs. alt. or opp., sometimes basal, entire, divided or compound; fls. solitary or in a cymose infl., regular, bisexual, calyx 5-lobed or -parted, corolla 5-lobed, stamens 5, exserted or included, pistil 1, ovary superior, typically 1-celled, styles 1 or 2, deeply 2-parted to undivided; fr. a loculicidal caps. dehiscing by 2 or rarely 4 valves. Similar to the *Polemoniaceae,* which have a single 3-lobed style and 3-celled ovary. Genera in cult. as ornamentals are: *Emmenanthe, Eriodictyon, Hesperochiron, Hydrophyllum, Nemophila, Phacelia, Pholistoma, Romanzoffia, Turricula,* and *Wigandia.*

HYDROPHYLLUM L. WATERLEAF. *Hydrophyllaceae.* About 8 spp. of bien. or per. herbs, native to e. and w. U.S., and adjacent Canada, the per. spp. with horizontal rhizomes; lvs. alt., basal and cauline, pinnatifid, lobed, or divided; fls. purple, violet, greenish, or white, in open or capitate terminal cymes, calyx 5-parted, corolla mostly campanulate, 5-lobed, stamens 5, exserted, style shortly 2-cleft; fr. a caps.

Sometimes transplanted to the wild garden.

capitatum Dougl. ex Benth. CAT'S BREECHES. Per., 8–18 in., grayish-puberulent; lvs. ovate to elliptic in outline, to 4¾ in. long, pinnately parted, the divisions 5–7, to 2 in. long, often 2–3-cleft and again lobed; fls. purplish-blue to white, in headlike cymes. Late spring–early summer. B.C. to Alta., s. to e. Ore., Utah, and Colo.

virginianum L. VIRGINIA W., SHAWNEE-SALAD, INDIAN-SALAD, JOHN'S CABBAGE. Per. to 3 ft.; lvs. ovate to elliptic in outline, to 10 in. long and more, pinnately divided, the segms. 5–7-toothed; fls. white or violet-purple, in loose cymes. Late spring–summer. Que. to Man., s. to Va., Kans. and n. Ark. The tender shoots were eaten by the Amer. Indians. Var. **atranthum** (Alexand.) Const. Lvs. with mostly 7–9 divisions; fls. dark violet. W.Va. to N.C.

HYDROPONICS. This is one of the terms applied to the growing of plants in aqueous nutrient solution without aid or support of soil. It is also called soilless gardening, tank farming, tray agriculture, or water culture. Hydroponics has long been practiced as a laboratory and experimental procedure at plant research centers and occasionally for production of special crops in areas, or under circumstances, where standard agricultural techniques cannot be undertaken. To be successful, hydroponics must be under the constant supervision of a trained technician familiar with the principles of plant growth. Because of this, it is not advised for use by the amateur or the average commercial horticulturist.

HYDROSME Schott. *Araceae.* Not in cult. **H. Rivieri:** *Amorphophallus Rivieri.*

HYDROTRIDA: *BACOPA.*

HYGROPHILA R. Br. [*Nomaphila* Blume; *Synnema* Benth.]. *Acanthaceae.* About 100 spp. of herbs, in wet places in trop. regions around the world; lvs. opp., sessile, uniform or often of 2 distinct forms; fls. in axillary cymes or clusters, forming racemes or panicles, bracts small, bracteoles linear, calyx lobes 5, linear, slightly unequal, corolla 2-lipped, the tube gradually widened above, stamens 4, didynamous; fr. a sessile, linear-oblong caps., seeds 4–18.

The species in cultivation are grown primarily in tropical aquaria, usually in the submerged state.

difformis (L.f.) Blume [*Synnema triflorum* (Roxb. ex Nees) O. Kuntze]. WATER WISTARIA. Sts. decumbent, rooting at base, to 2 ft. long; lvs. varying in shape, submerged lvs. pectinate to pinnately divided, to 4½ in. long, pale green, fragile in texture, aerial lvs. smaller, lanceolate to ovate, crenate, darker green, thicker in texture; fls. in clusters of 1–3 in the axils, corolla to ½ in. long, pale violet, streaked red-violet inside. Wet places, India to Thailand; often a weed of rice fields.

lacustris (Schlechtend. & Cham.) Nees. Per., aerial sts. hairy; lvs. lanceolate, to 3 in. long; corolla white, to ¼ in. long. Wet places, Amer. tropics

polysperma (Roxb.) T. Anderson. Ann., sts. branching, to 1½ ft.; lvs. narrowly oblong to ovate, to 1½ in. long; corolla white to pale blue, to 5/16 in. long, pubescent, stamens 2. India and Bhutan.

salicifolia (Vahl) Nees. Sts. to 3 ft.; lvs. nearly sessile, linear-lanceolate to lanceolate, to 5 in. long and ¾ in. wide; fls. in axillary whorls, corolla violet, to ¾ in. long, stamens 4. Se. Asia and Indonesia.

stricta (Vahl) Nees [*Nomaphila stricta* (Vahl) Nees]. Sts. usually much-branched, pubescent in upper part; lvs. linear-lanceolate to oblong-lanceolate, to 8¾ in. long and 2¾ in. wide; cymes glandular-hairy; corolla to ¼ in. long, pale blue, palate violet and white. India and Malay Pen. to Indonesia.

HYLOCEREUS (A. Berger) Britt. & Rose [*Wilmattea* Britt & Rose]. *Cactaceae.* About 18 spp. of cacti in trop. Amer.; sts. mostly 3-angled or -winged, with short spines, climbing by aerial roots; fls. nocturnal, white or sometimes red, often large, perianth tube and ovary with large, leafy, mostly naked scales persisting on the fr., style mostly thick, stigma lobes sometimes branched. Mex., W. Indies, Cent. Amer., n. S. Amer.

For culture see *Cacti.*

extensus (Salm-Dyck) Britt. & Rose. Sts. 3-angled, green, ⅝ in. thick; spines 2–4, stout, to 5/32 in. long; fls. rose-red. Trinidad.

guatemalensis (Eichlam) Britt. & Rose. Sts. 3-winged, glaucous, 1–3 in. wide, margins horny, low-undulate; areoles to ¾ in. apart, spines 2–4, conical, to ⅛ in. long; fls. white, 1 ft. long, outer segms. acuminate, as long as the inner; fr. to 3 in. in diam. Guatemala.

minutiflorus Britt. & Rose [*Wilmattea minutiflora* Britt. & Rose]. Sts. 3-angled or sometimes nearly cylindrical, green, to ½ in. thick, angles weakly undulate; areoles ¾–1½ in. apart, spines 1–3, small; fls. white, 2 in. long, fragrant, tube shorter than segms., scales of ovary with axillary felt and sometimes bristles. Guatemala and Honduras.

ocamponis (Salm-Dyck) Britt. & Rose. Sts. 3-angled, glaucous, about 1 in. thick, angles undulate, horny; areoles ¾–1½ in. apart, spines 5–8, needle-shaped, to ½ in. long; fls. white, 10–12 in. long and across, outer perianth segms. linear-lanceolate, acuminate, inner perianth segms. oblong, acuminate. Probably Mex.

peruvianus Backeb. Sts. 3-winged, glaucous, to 2 in. wide; spines few, short but robust; fls. not described. N. Peru.

polyrhizus (A. Web.) Britt. & Rose. Sts. mostly 3-angled, green or glaucous, about 1½ in. thick, angles nearly straight; spines 2–4, stout, to 5/32 in. long; fls. white, to 1 ft. long or more, fragrant; fr. red, 4 in. long. Panama and Colombia.

stenopterus (A. Web.) Britt. & Rose. Sts. 3-winged, green, about 1½ in. wide, margins somewhat undulate; spines 1–3, small; fls. red, 4–5 in. long. Costa Rica.

triangularis (L.) Britt. & Rose. Sts. 3-angled, green, about 1½ in. thick, angles somewhat undulate; areoles about ¾ in. apart, spines 6–8, needle-shaped, with swollen bases; fls. white, 8 in. long or more; fr. red. Jamaica. See *H. undatus.*

trigonus (Haw.) Saff. Sts. 3-angled, green, about 1 in. thick, angles strongly undulate; spines about 8, to ¼ in. long; fls. white, large; fr. red, 4 in. long. W. Indies.

undatus (Haw.) Britt. & Rose. NIGHT-BLOOMING CEREUS, QUEEN-OF-THE-NIGHT, HONOLULU-QUEEN. Sts. 3-winged, green, wings 1–2 in. wide, margins undulate, horny; areoles about 1½ in. apart, spines 1–5, to 5/32 in. long; fls. white, to 14 in. long, fragrant; fr. red, edible, 4–5 in. in diam. Widespread in trop. Amer., but origin unknown. Much grown and one of the plants best known as night-blooming cereus. Sometimes misidentified as *H. triangularis* but distinguished by the horny margins of the sts. and by the larger fls.

HYMENAEA L. [*Trachylobium* Hayne]. *Leguminosae* (subfamily *Caesalpinioideae*). About 20–30 spp. of unarmed trees of trop. Amer., 1 sp. in e. trop. Afr. and Madagascar; lvs. alt., with 2 lfts.; fls. in dense, corymblike, terminal panicles; fls. nearly regular, petals 5, stamens 10, separate; fr. a very thick, indehiscent, oblique-obovoid or oblong legume, with few seeds.

Propagated by seeds, or cuttings over heat.

Courbaril L. WEST INDIAN LOCUST, SOUTH AMERICAN L., LOCUST TREE. To 100 ft.; lfts. oblong to ovate, to 3½ in. long, inequilateral, basally very oblique; petals white, gland-dotted, stamens white, exserted; fr. woody, rough, nearly cylindrical, to 5 in. long, half as broad. Trop. Amer. Yields a valuable timber, and a copal, a hard resin used in varnishes.

verrucosa Gaertn. [*Trachylobium verrucosum* (Gaertn.) D. Oliver]. EAST AFRICAN COPAL, ZANZIBAR C. Evergreen, to 100 ft., with flat crown; lfts. obliquely oblong to elliptic, to 4 in. long, glossy; fls. white and pink; fr. oblong, warty, to 2 in. long, 1–2-seeded. Trop. e. Afr., Madagascar. Source of a commercial hard resin.

HYMENANTHERA R. Br. *Violaceae.* About 7 spp. or more of mostly dioecious, stiff shrubs or small trees, native mostly to New Zeal., also to Australia, Tasmania, and Norfolk Is., evergreen or partly so; lvs. small, alt., simple, often clustered; fls. small, regular, 5-merous, mostly unisexual, solitary or in clusters, mostly axillary; fr. a small, few-seeded berry.

Several grown outdoors in Calif. Propagated by seeds, cuttings, and layers.

alpina (T. Kirk) W. Oliver. Low shrub, to 2 ft., brs. rigid, branchlets spinous; lvs. oblong-obovate, less than ½ in. long, leathery; fls. on short, straight peduncles, petals recurved; berry white, flecked with purple. New Zeal.

chathamica (F. J. Muell.) T. Kirk. Dioecious shrub, to 9 ft.; lvs. lanceolate, to 5 in. long, more or less serrate, leathery; fls. in clusters along brs.; berry white. New Zeal.

crassifolia Hook.f. Dioecious shrub, to 5 ft., sometimes prostrate, much-branched; lvs. linear-obovate, to 1½ in. long, entire or margins wavy, leathery; fls. few in lf. axils; berry purplish. New Zeal.

dentata R. Br. Much-branched shrub, to 20 ft.; brs. often spine-tipped; lvs. oblong to linear, to 1½ in. long, remotely toothed, leathery; fls. solitary or in 2's; berry purplish. Se. Australia.

novae-zelandiae (A. Cunn.) Hemsl. Stout, dioecious shrub, to 10 ft.; lvs. ovate or obovate, to 4 in. long, usually wavy-toothed, leathery; fls. in clusters; berry purplish. New Zeal. Material grown under this name may be *H. chathamica.*

obovata T. Kirk. Erect to spreading, dioecious shrub, to 9 ft.; lvs. obovate to elliptic, mostly to 1½ in. long, entire or slightly toothed; fls. solitary or few; berry purplish. New Zeal.

HYMENOCALLIS Salisb. [*Elisena* Herb.; *Ismene* Salisb.]. SPIDER LILY, CROWN-BEAUTY, SEA DAFFODIL, BASKET FLOWER. *Amaryllidaceae.* About 25 or 30 spp. of summer-flowering bulbous herbs, native to N. and S. Amer.; lvs. basal, linear, strap-shaped, or more rarely oblanceolate-oblong, petioled; fls. white or yellow, mostly fragrant; umbel terminal on a solid scape, subtended by 2 or more separate spathe valves, perianth tube short to long, lobes narrow, stamens basally united into a cuplike crown or corona, ovary inferior, 3-celled, ovules mostly 2, rarely to 8, in each cell, basal; fr. a caps., seeds oblong to globose, with fleshy, green coat.

Of easy cultivation in warm climates, where the bulbs will bloom year after year if given good care. Propagated by seeds and offsets.

Amancaes (Ruiz & Pav.) Nichols. [*Ismene Amancaes* (Ruiz & Pav.) Herb.]. To 2 ft.; lvs. strap-shaped, bright green; fls. 3–6, bright yellow, tube to 3 in. long, lobes to 2½ in. long, corona to 2 in. long, filaments incurved, ½ in. long, cells of ovary 2-ovuled. Peru.

americana: *H. littoralis.*

calathina: *H. narcissiflora.*

caroliniana (L.) Herb. [*H. occidentalis* (LeConte) Kunth]. To 22 in.; lvs. 6–12, narrowly oblanceolate, to 17 in. long, 1⅝ in. wide; fls. 3–9, fragrant, tube to 4¾ in. long, lobes to 4 in. long, corona to 1⅝ in. long. Ga., w. to La. and Ind.

caribaea (L.) Herb. [*Pancratium caribaeum* L.]. Lvs. many, evergreen, to 1 ft. long or more and 3 in. wide, shining; fls. 8–10 or more, fragrant, tube to 2½ in. long, lobes linear, to 4 in. long or more, corona funnelform, with erect margins, about 1 in. high, filaments to 2 in. long. W. Indies. Much of the material in the trade under this name is *H. latifolia.*

×**festalis** Hort. ex Schmarse [*Ismene* ×*festalis* Hort.]: *H. longipetala* × *H. narcissiflora.* Resembling *H. narcissiflora,* but with filaments to 1 in. long, perianth tube to 2 in. long.

Harrisiana Herb. [*Ismene Harrisiana* Hort.]. To about 10 in.; lvs. oblanceolate, to 1 ft. long, 2 in. wide, somewhat erect, tapered to petiolelike base; fls. with greenish slender tube to 5¼ in. long, lobes to 3 in., whitish, corona funnelform, to ¾ in. long. Mex.

keyensis: *H. latifolia.*

lacera: see *H. rotata.*

latifolia (Mill.) M. J. Roem. [*H. keyensis* Small]. Similar to *H. caribaea,* but perianth lobes shorter than tube and lvs. distinctly arching. Fla., W. Indies. Frequently offered as *H. caribaea.*

littoralis (Jacq.) Salisb. [*H. americana* (Mill.) M. J. Roem.; *H. sene-*

gambica Kunth & Bouché, in part]. To 2½ ft.; lvs. numerous, evergreen, to 3 ft. long and 2½ in. wide; fls. 8–11, tube 4 to (usually) 6 in. long or more, lobes linear, spreading, to about 5 in. long, corona funnelform, margins spreading, filaments to 2 in. long. Trop. Amer.; naturalized in Afr.

longipetala (Lindl.) Macbr. [*Elisena longipetala* Lindl.]. To 3 ft.; lvs. linear, to 2 ft. long; fls. 5–10, tube very short, to ⅜ in. long and broadly funnelform, lobes linear, to 4 in. long, corona deflexed and horizontal, funnelform, about 1¾ in. long, margins reflexed, filaments declinate, to 3 in. long. Peru.

macrostephana Bak. Lvs. to 3 ft. long and 3 in. wide; fls. with tube 3 in. long, lobes linear-lanceolate, somewhat longer; corona large, 2 in. long, filaments 1 in. long. Probably a hybrid, perhaps *H. narcissiflora* × *H. speciosa.*

narcissiflora (Jacq.) Macbr. [*H. calathina* (Ker-Gawl.) Nichols.; *Ismene calathina* (Ker-Gawl.) Herb.]. BASKET FLOWER, PERUVIAN DAFFODIL. To 2 ft.; lvs. to 2 ft. long and 2 in. wide; fls. with tube to 4 in. long, lobes lanceolate, about as long as tube, corona funnelform, fringed, 2 in. long, filaments ½ in. long. Andes of Peru and Bolivia. Probably the most frequently cult. sp. Cv. 'Minor' is listed. Cv. 'Sulphurea'. Fls. pale yellow.

occidentalis: *H. caroliniana.*

Palmeri S. Wats. ALLIGATOR LILY. To 16 in.; lvs. linear, to 1 ft. long, ⅜ in. wide; fl. solitary, slightly fragrant, white, tube yellow-green, to 3 in. long, lobes to 3 in. long, corona 2 in. wide, with 1 short and 2 long teeth between filaments. Fla.

pedalis Herb. [*H. senegambica* Kunth & Bouché, in part]. Lvs. tapered to base and apex, to 50 in. long, 3 in. wide; fls. 5–14, sessile, tube to 9 in. long, lobes to 5½ in. long, corona to 1⅜ in. long, funnelform. E. S. Amer.; naturalized in Afr.

pedunculata (Herb.) Macbr. [*Ismene Macleana* Herb.]. Similar to *H. narcissiflora*, but the tube only to 2 in. long, lobes narrower, corona about 1½ in. long. Peru.

rotata (Ker-Gawl.) Herb. [*H. lacera* Salisb., in part]. Stoloniferous; lvs. to 1½ ft. long and 1 in. or less wide; fls. with tube to 4 in. long, lobes linear, about as long as tube, corona rotate, 1 in. long, filaments 1½ in. long. N.C. to Fla., w. to Mex.

senegambica: a name based on a mixture of material of *H. littoralis* and *H. pedalis.*

speciosa (Salisb.) Salisb. Lvs. petioled, blades broadly elliptic or oblong-elliptic, to 2 ft. long or more, acute; fls. 7–12, pedicelled, greenish, tube to 3⅜ in., lobes to 4½ in. long. W. Indies.

tenuiflora Herb. Lvs. many, sessile, sword-shaped, to 2½ ft. long, recurved; fls. with slender tube to nearly 6 in. long, lobes very narrow, to 4 in. long, corona funnelform, with erect margins, to ¾ in. high, filaments to 2 in. long. Guatemala.

HYMENOLEPIS: *ATHANASIA.*

HYMENOPAPPUS L'Hér. *Compositae* (Helenium Tribe). About 10 spp. of bien. or per. herbs, native to U.S. and Mex.; sts. leafy or nearly scapose; lvs. in basal rosettes and alt. on sts., usually pinnately dissected, rarely simple or only lobed; fl. heads usually discoid, in cymose panicles, involucral bracts in 2–3 rows, receptacle dome-shaped to nearly flat, usually naked; disc fls. bisexual, yellow, white, sometimes reddish-purple, ray fls., if present, female, fertile, white, often absent; achenes usually obpyramidal, 4-angled, pappus absent or of 12–22 translucent scales.

Adapted to the wild garden or hardy border, doing best in a loose, well-drained soil. Propagated by seeds or division.

carolinensis: *H. scabiosaeus.*

corymbosus: *H. scabiosaeus* var.

scabiosaeus L'Hér. [*H. carolinensis* (Lam.) T. C. Porter]. Bien., to 3 ft., sts. usually solitary, much-branched above, leafy to apex, hairy; lvs. 1–2-pinnatifid, to 10 in. long, green above, white-tomentose beneath; heads corymbose, involucral bracts thin, petal-like, white or white-margined; disc fls. white, ray fls. absent. Sporadic, S.C. and Fla., n. to Ill. and n. Ind., w. to e. Tex., Okla., Mo. Var. **corymbosus** (Torr. & A. Gray) B. L. Turner [*H. corymbosus* Torr. & A. Gray]. OLD-PLAINSMAN. Lvs. successively reduced upward; involucral bracts oblong to oblong-obovate, shorter than the fls., greenish. Se. Nebr., s. to Tex. and adjacent Mex.

HYMENOSPORUM R. Br. ex F. J. Muell. *Pittosporaceae.* One sp., an evergreen Australian shrub or tree.

Planted outdoors in southern U.S. Cultivation as for *Pittosporum.*

flavum (Hook.) F. L. Muell. To 50 ft.; lvs. obovate, entire, to 6 in. long; fls. large, yellow, fragrant, 1½ in. long, borne in loose terminal umbel-like panicles, petals united into a tomentose tube about 1 in. long; caps. 1 in. long, seeds winged.

HYMENOXYS Cass. [*Actinea* of auth., not Juss.; *Actinella* of auth., not Pers.; *Rydbergia* Greene; *Tetraneuris* Greene]. *Compositae* (Helenium Tribe). About 20 spp. of ann. or per., scapose or leafy-stemmed herbs, native to w. N. Amer. and S. Amer.; lvs. basal, or alt. on sts., entire, lobed, or pinnatifid, dotted with impressed glands; fl. heads usually radiate, solitary or corymbose, involucral bracts herbaceous, in 2–3 rows, similar and separate or those of the outer row different and partly united, receptacle naked; fls. yellow; achenes obpyramidal, 5-angled, hairy, pappus of 5–8 scales.

acaulis (Pursh) K. Parker [*Actinea simplex* (A. Nels.) A. Nels.; *Actinella acaulis* (Pursh) Nutt.]. Tufted, scapose per., 1–15 in.; lvs. basal, linear or linear-oblanceolate, entire, appressed-silky-pubescent, to 2 in. long; heads ½–1½ in. across, solitary, involucral bracts all alike. Plains, s.-cent. Canada to Tex. Var. **caespitosa** (A. Nels.) K. Parker [*Actinella lanata* Nutt.]. Lvs. woolly-villous, some lacking glandular dots. Mts. and plains, s. Idaho to s. Calif. and n. Ariz. Var. **glabra** (A. Gray) K. Parker [*Actinea herbacea* (Greene) B. L. Robinson]. Lvs. thinly villous, becoming nearly glabrous; heads to 1¾ in. across. S. Ont., Ohio, Ill.

biennis: *H. Cooperi.*

californica: *Lasthenia coronaria.*

Cooperi (A. Gray) Cockerell [*H. biennis* (A. Gray) H. M. Hall]. Bien. or short-lived per., sts. 1 to few, leafy, to 2 ft.; lvs. pinnate, to 4 in. long, pubescent; heads to 1½ in. across, corymbose, outer involucral bracts partly united. Idaho to Ariz. and e. Calif.

grandiflora (Torr. & A. Gray ex A. Gray) K. Parker [*Actinea grandiflora* (Torr. & A. Gray ex A. Gray) O. Kuntze; *Actinella grandiflora* Torr. & A. Gray ex A. Gray; *Rydbergia grandiflora* (Torr. & A. Gray ex A. Gray) Greene]. Woolly per., sts. to 15 in., simple or branched near base, stout, leafy; lower lvs. pinnatifid into linear lobes, upper lvs. linear, entire; heads to 3 in. across, solitary, involucral bracts all alike. Alpine, Idaho and Mont., s. to Utah and Colo.

linearifolia Hook. [*Actinea linearifolia* (Hook.) O. Kuntze; *Tetraneuris linearifolia* (Hook.) Greene]. Erect, branching ann., to 15 in., sparsely villous; basal lvs. spatulate, with a few short lobes, upper st. lvs. linear, entire; heads 1 in. across, on slender peduncles, involucral bracts all alike. Kans. and La., w. to New Mex.

scaposa (DC.) K. Parker [*Actinea angustifolia* (Rydb.) A. Nels.]. Tufted, scapose per., to 1 ft.; lvs. basal, linear, to 4 in. long, ¹⁄₁₆–¼ in. wide, entire, villous or glabrate; heads to 1½ in. across, solitary, involucral bracts all alike. Colo. to Kans., s. to New Mex., Tex. Mex. Var. **linearis** (Nutt.) K. Parker [*Actinella fastigiata* (Greene) A. Nels.; *Tetraneuris stenophylla* Rydb.]. Bushier and woodier, rhizome more branched; lvs. densely imbricate, to ¹⁄₁₆ in. wide. Range of the sp.

HYOPHORBE Gaertn. [*Mascarena* L. H. Bailey]. PIGNUT PALM. *Palmae.* Five spp. of solitary, unarmed, monoecious palms in the Mascarene Is.; trunks enlarged at base, spindle-shaped, or of uniform diam.; lvs. pinnate, sheaths forming a prominent crownshaft, pinnae acute; infl. below lvs., peduncle elongate, with several tubular, deciduous bracts, lower brs. twice-branched into slender rachillae with fls. in lines (acervuli) of usually a basal female and 3–6 male above; male fls. symmetrical, sepals 3, separate and imbricate or united in lower half in a cupule with lightly imbricate lobes, petals 3, united basally, valvate above, stamens 6, filaments united below in a tube as long as or longer than corolla tube and joined to it, separate, awl-shaped, and erect above, pistillode small, 3-lobed to conic-ovoid and nearly as long as stamens, female fls. with sepals 3, separate and imbricate or united in a low cupule with lightly imbricate lobes, petals 3, united basally, valvate above, staminodes 6, united and joined to corolla basally, separate and triangular above, pistil 3-celled, 3-ovuled; fr. purplish, 1-seeded, ellipsoid to obovoid, with basal stigmatic residue, mesocarp fleshy, endocarp thin; seed obovoid to ellipsoid, endosperm homogeneous, embryo lateral at middle or in upper ⅓.

Grown as ornamentals in the tropics and subtropics and the warmer parts of Zone 10a in Fla. For culture see *Palms.*

lagenicaulis (L. H. Bailey) H. E. Moore [*Mascarena lagenicaulis*

L. H. Bailey]. BOTTLE PALM. St. swollen basally, then narrowed to crownshaft above; pinnae 40–70 on each side, stiff, ascending, essentially continuous along rachis with overlapping edges, to 18 in. long, 2 in. wide, midrib and usually 4 lateral veins prominent and scaly below; male fls. yellow-green on green rachillae, sepals united in lower half, anthers attached by back near apex; fr. ellipsoid, about 1 in. long, ½–⅝ in. in diam., seed ellipsoid, embryo in upper ⅓. Round Is., Mauritius.

Verschaffeltii H. Wendl. [*Mascarena Verschaffeltii* (H. Wendl.) L. H. Bailey]. SPINDLE PALM. St. stout, somewhat enlarged upward but not prominently narrowed to crownshaft; pinnae 30–50 on each side, separated along the rachis, soft and more or less pendulous at tip, to 30 in. long, 1 in. wide, only the midrib prominent and scaly below; male fls. orange on white rachillae, sepals separate, imbricate, anthers attached by back at middle; fr. narrowly ellipsoid, to ¾ in. long, 5/16 in. in diam., seed narrowly ellipsoid, embryo at middle. Rodriques Is.

HYOSCYAMUS L. *Solanaceae.* About 15 spp. of ann. or per. herbs, native from s. Eur. and N. Afr., to sw. and cent. Asia; lvs. alt., coarsely toothed or pinnatifid, rarely entire; fls. axillary, the uppermost in a leafy cluster or spike, calyx tubular-campanulate, 5-toothed, enlarged in fr., corolla dull whitish or brownish-yellow, reticulate, funnelform, 5-lobed, sometimes unequally so, often splitting down 1 side, stamens 5, borne on the corolla, usually exserted; fr. a circumscissile caps.

Grown as a source of alkaloidal drugs, occasionally as ornamentals.

niger L. HENBANE, BLACK H., STINKING NIGHTSHADE. Viscid-pubescent ann. or bien., with fetid odor, from a stout root; lower lvs. to 8 in. long, ovate-lanceolate, deeply lacerate-lobed, with winged petioles, upper lvs. sessile, clasping; calyx to ¾ in. long, tube hairy, corolla to 1¼ in. long, greenish-yellow, purple-veined; caps. about ½ in. long, enclosed in enlarged calyx. Anns. bloom in late summer, biens. in late spring. Temp. Eurasia; naturalized in U.S. Grown as a source of drugs; all parts are poisonous. Dried henbane lvs., usually collected from wild plants in areas where native, are one of the sources of the alkaloidal drug hyoscyamine.

HYPARRHENIA Anderss. ex E. Fourn. *Gramineae.* About 70 spp. of tall, per. grasses in Afr.; infl. large, elongate, of paired, peduncled, more or less crowded racemes and their spathes; spikelets in pairs, those of the lower pairs alike, male and awnless, fertile spikelets 1 to a few in each raceme, cylindrical or flattened on the back, the lemma strongly and geniculately awned. For terminology see *Gramineae.*

hirta (L.) Stapf. Distinguished from *H. rufa* in having shorter sts., usually not over 3 ft. high, more or less involute, flexuous lf. blades, usually less than ⅛ in. wide, and whitish or grayish, silky-villous racemes. Cult. in the extreme South and Southwest, mostly for erosion control.

rufa (Nees) Stapf. Sts. erect, to 8 ft., rather stout; lf. blades flat, elongate, to 5/16 in. wide or more, very scabrous on the margins; infl. to 16 in. long, racemes about ¾ in. long, reddish-brown, on long, slender, flexuous peduncles; fertile spikelets mostly 5–7 in each raceme, ⅛ in. long, flattened on the back, pubescent with dark red hairs, pedicels and rachis joint ciliate with red hairs, awn to ¾ in. long, red-brown, hispidulous, bent twice and twisted. Sparingly cult. in Fla. for forage; escaped on Gulf Coast. Does not withstand frost.

HYPENANTHE: *MEDINILLA.*

HYPERICACEAE Juss. HYPERICUM FAMILY, ST.-JOHN'S-WORT FAMILY. (Sometimes included in *Guttiferae.*) Dicot.; about 8 genera and 350 spp. of shrubs or herbs, rarely trees, native to temp. and trop. regions; lvs. opp. or whorled, simple, mostly entire, usually translucent-dotted or black-dotted; fls. mainly yellow, cymose or solitary, regular, bisexual, petals separate, stamens many, commonly united into clusters, styles usually separate; fr. a caps. *Cratoxylon* and *Hypericum* are grown as ornamentals.

HYPERICUM L. [*Androsaemum* Duhamel; *Ascyrum* L.; *Sarothra* L.]. ST.-JOHN'S-WORT. *Hypericaceae.* About 300 spp. of herbs, shrubs or subshrubs, native to temp. regions, sts. sometimes winged or angled; lvs. evergreen or deciduous, opp., entire, often black-dotted or translucent-dotted; fls. in various shades of yellow, sepals and petals 5, stamens many,

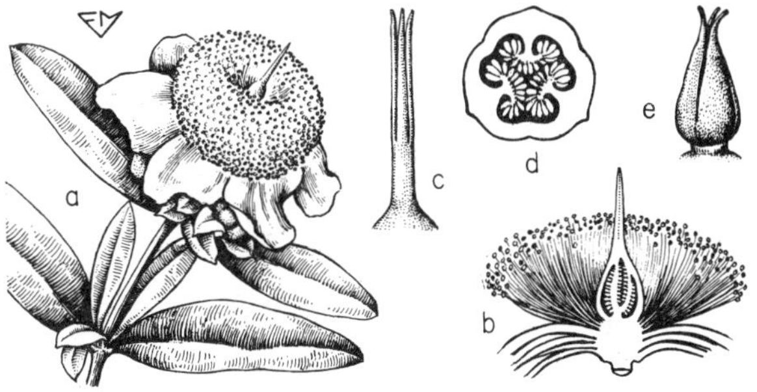

HYPERICACEAE. *Hypericum frondosum:* **a,** flowering branch, × ½; **b,** flower, vertical section, × 1; **c,** style and stigmas, × 2; **d,** ovary, cross section, × 3; **e,** capsule, × 1. (From Bailey, *Manual of Cultivated Plants,* ed. 2.)

separate or in 3 or 5 bundles; fr. a caps., dehiscing septicidally, rarely berrylike.

The genus furnishes many ornamentals for borders, the rock garden, shrub groupings, and less frequently ground covers. Hypericums are of easy cultivation, some of them growing in shady locations. Propagated by seeds, greenwood cuttings under glass in summer, and the low kinds by division and suckers. Most of the species are hardy in Zone 5 unless otherwise noted.

acutum: *H. tetrapterum.*

anagalloides Cham. & Schlechtend. Low, mat-forming per., brs. procumbent or ascending, to 1 ft. long; lvs. elliptic or ovate, to ½ in. long; fls. very small, in few-fld. cymes, styles 3. Moist places, B.C. to Baja Calif.

Andrewsii: a listed name of no botanical standing.

Androsaemum L. TUTSAN. Semievergreen shrub, to 3 ft.; lvs. ovate to ovate-oblong, to 4 in. long, whitish beneath; fls. 1 in. across, solitary or in cymes, sepals leaflike, nearly as long as petals, styles 3; caps. black, berrylike. Eur. w. Asia.

annulatum Moris [*H. intermedium* Steud. ex A. Rich.]. Per. herb, to 2½ ft., more or less pubescent; lvs. ovate or ovate-lanceolate, to 2 ¼ in. long, with black glandular dots above and sometimes beneath; fls. about 1 in. across, many in panicled cymes, sepal margins black-dotted. E. Trop. Afr.

×**Arnoldianum** Rehd.: *H. densiflorum* var. *lobocarpum* × *H. galioides.* Fls. in cylindrical panicle; fr. 3–5-celled.

Ascyron L. [*H. pyramidatum* Ait.]. Per. herb, 2–6 ft., sts. 4-angled; lvs. clasping st., ovate-oblong, to 5 in. long; fls. to 2 in. across, in few-fld. cymes. Ne. N. Amer.; e. and cent. Asia.

aspalathoides: *H. fasciculatum.*

aureum: *H. frondosum.*

balearicum L. Low shrub, to 1 ft. or more, twigs warty; lvs. ovate, to ⅜ in. long; fls. yellow, solitary, terminal, to 1½ in. across. Medit. region.

Beanii N. Robs. [*H. patulum* var. *Henryi* Bean]. Vigorous shrub, 5–6 ft., brs. 2-edged or 2–4-lined or sometimes cylindrical; lvs. ovate, to 3 in. long; fls. shallowly bowl-shaped, to 2 in. across, sepals ovate to elliptic or rarely lanceolate to narrowly oblong, usually twice as long as broad, acute to acuminate at apex, petals incurved, stamens about half as long as petals, spreading to form a ring at base of ovary, styles 5, separate. W. China.

boreale (Britt.) Bickn. Per., to 18 in., st. branched above middle; lvs. sessile, elliptic to ovate, to 1 in. long, 3–5-nerved; fls. small, in cymes, stamens few. Ne. N. Amer.

Buckleyi M. A. Curtis. Decumbent subshrub, to 1 ft., sts. prostrate, with many erect brs.; lvs. obovate, to ¾ in. long; fls. 2 in. across, 1–3 together, styles 3. Mts., N.C. and Ga. May be planted far south.

calycinum L. [*H. grandiflorum* Salisb.]. ROSE-OF-SHARON, AARON'S BEARD, CREEPING S.-J.-W., GOLDFLOWER. Vigorous, stoloniferous, evergreen subshrub; lvs. ovate-oblong to oblong, to 4 in. long, glaucous and conspicuously net-veined beneath; fls. to 2 in. across, solitary or in cymes, petals spreading, stamens erect and spreading, anthers reddish, styles 5. Se. Eur., w. Asia Minor. Hardy ground cover, growing best in shade. Distinguished by its net-veined lvs., spreading petals and stamens, and reddish anthers. A supposed parent of the spontaneously appearing cv. **'Hidcote'** (see *H. Forrestii*)

canariense L. [*H. floribundum* Ait.]. Shrub, to 15 ft.; lvs. oblong-lanceolate, to 3 in. long; fls. to 1¼ in. across, in panicles. Canary Is. Grown in far south and Calif.

cerastoides (Spach) N. Robs. [*H. rhodopeum* Friv.]. Per. herb, sts. decumbent or ascending, to 10 in. long; lvs. oblong or ovate, to 1¼ in. long; fls. to 1½ in. across, sepals unequal, leafy, petal margins black-dotted, styles 3. Se. Eur.

cernuum: *H. oblongifolium.*

chinense L. Semievergreen, spreading shrub, to 3 ft. or more; lvs. oblong, to 3 in. long, pale and conspicuously net-veined beneath; fls. 1½–2 in. across, petals and stamens irregularly spreading, styles united nearly to the shortly 5-parted apex. China.

cistifolium Lam. Stoloniferous subshrub, to 3 ft.; lvs. oblong to linear-lanceolate, to 3 in. long, revolute; fls. ½ in. across, in loose cymes, styles 3. Se. U.S.

concinnum Benth. GOLDWIRE. Low, spreading per., to 1 ft., sts. many, wiry; lvs. linear to lanceolate, to 1½ in. long, mostly folded; fls. to 1¼ in. across, sepal and petal margins black-dotted. Dry chaparral slopes, Sierra Nevada and n. Coast Ranges, Calif.

confertum Choisy. Herbaceous to subshrubby, procumbent, to 1 ft., papillose-puberulent; st. lvs. ovate-lanceolate, to ¾ in. long, lvs. of axillary twigs smaller and revolute; fls. ¾ in. across, sepals fringed with stalked glands. Asia Minor.

Coris L. Evergreen, nearly erect subshrub, to 1 ft. or more; lvs. in whorls of 3 or sometimes 4, linear, to 1 in. long, entire, revolute; fls. ¾ in. across, sepals fringed with black glands, stamens in 3 groups, styles 3. S. Eur. Grown in southern states.

corsicum: *H. tetrapterum* var.

densiflorum Pursh [*H. glomeratum* Small]. Evergreen shrub, to 6 ft.; lvs. linear-oblong to linear, to 2 in. long; fls. to ½ in. across, in dense cymes, styles 3; caps. 3-celled, shallowly lobed. N.J. to Fla., w. to Tex. Var. **lobocarpum** (Gatt.) Svens. [*H. lobocarpum* Gatt.]. Differs in caps. 4–5-celled, deeply lobed. N.C. to Okla. and La.

Dyeri Rehd. [*H. lysimachioides* Wallich ex Dyer]. Shrub, to 4 ft., branchlets angled; lvs. ovate, to 1½ in. long, glaucous and with marked venation beneath; fls. to 1½ in. across, in loose cymes, sepals acute to acuminate, spreading and even somewhat reflexed, petals lanceolate, usually about 3 times longer than wide, styles 5. Himalayas. For southern states and Calif.

elatum: *H. inodorum.*

elegans Steph. ex Willd. Upright per., to 16 in., sts. 2-angled; lvs. sessile, ovate-lanceolate, to 1½ in. long, obscurely reticulate-veined and with several large translucent dots; fls. to 1 in. across, in terminal panicles, petal margins black-dotted, styles 3. Cent. Eur. to Altai Mts.

ellipticum Hook. Per. herb, to 2½ ft., with prominent rhizomes, st. unbranched below infl.; lvs. elliptic, to 1¼ in. long; fls. about ½ in. across, in few- to many-fld. cymes. E. N. Amer.

empetrifolium Willd. Evergreen shrub, erect or sometimes prostrate, to 1 ft.; lvs. in 3's, linear, to ¾ in. long; fls. to ¾ in. across, in panicles, sepal margins with few sessile black glands, styles 3. Se. Eur. to Asia Minor. To be planted far south.

fasciculatum Lam. [*H. aspalathoides* Willd.]. SANDWEED. Evergreen shrub, to 1½ ft. or more, bark spongy-thickened, exfoliating in thin sheets, brs. 4-angled; lvs. linear-subulate, to ¾ in. long, fls. brilliant orange-yellow, sepals as long as petals or nearly so. N.C. to Miss.

floribundum: *H. canariense.*

formosum Kunth var. **Scouleri** (Hook.) J. Coult. [*H. Scouleri* Hook.]. Rhizomatous per., to 1½ ft.; lvs. ovate-oblong, 1 in. long; fls. in many-fld. corymbs, petals dotted at tip with dark violet glands, styles 3. W. N. Amer. from B.C. to cent. Mex.

Forrestii (Chitt.) N. Robs. [*H. patulum* var. *Forrestii* Chitt.]. Shrub, 3–4 ft. high and wide; lvs. lanceolate to ovate, to 3 in. long, apex obtuse to rounded, mucronate; fls. bowl-shaped, sepals broadly elliptic or ovate to subrotund, petals incurved, stamens about half as long as petals, spreading to form a ring around base of ovary, styles 5, about twice as long as stamens. W. China, Burma, Assam. This sp. and *H. calycinum* may be the parents of the vigorous *Hypericum* cv. **'Hidcote'**, which differs from *H. Forrestii* in having lvs. triangular-lanceolate, somewhat net-veined beneath, petals only slightly incurved, and anthers orange-colored.

fragile Boiss. & Heldr. Apparently not in cult.; resembles *H. nummularium* but plant smaller, lvs. smaller, neither lf. margins nor sepal margins black-dotted. Greece. The plant usually grown under this name is a form of the variable *H. olympicum.*

frondosum Michx. [*H. aureum* Bartr.; *H. splendens* Small]. Deciduous shrub, to 4 ft., sts. 2-winged; lvs. ovate-oblong to oblong, to 3 in. long, bluish-green; fls. to 2 in. across, solitary or few together, styles 3. S.C., w. to Tenn. and Tex.

galioides Lam. Shrub, to 3 ft.; lvs. linear, to ¾ in. long; fls. ½ in. across, solitary or in cymes, styles 3. Del., s. to Fla. and Tex.

Gebleri Ledeb. Related to *H. Ascyron,* from which it differs in having fls. solitary or in 3's. Siberia.

gentianoides (L.) BSP [*H. nudicaule* Walt.; *H. Sarothra* Michx.; *Sarothra gentianoides* L.]. ORANGE GRASS, PINEWEED. Ann., to 1½ ft.; sts. wiry, fastigiately branched; lvs. reduced to awl-shaped, appressed scales; fls. yellow, minute, scattered along brs. E. N. Amer.

glomeratum: *H. densiflorum.*

grandiflorum: *H. calycinum.*

grandifolium Choisy, [*H. elatum* Ait.; *H. Webbianum* Hort.; *Androsaemum Webbianum* Spach]. Half-evergreen shrub, to 5 ft., branchlets 2-edged; lvs. clasping st., ovate, to 3 in. long; fls. to 1½ in. across, several to many in terminal panicles, stamens in 5 bundles, styles 3 or 4. Canary Is. and Madeira.

Griffithii Hook.f. & T. Thoms. ex Dyer. Shrub; lvs. ovate, to 4½ in. long, younger lvs. more lanceolate and acute; styles 5. Bhutan. Doubtfully cult.

Henryi: *H. patulum.*

hircinum L. Round, compact, half-evergreen subshrub, to 3 ft., branchlets 2-edged; lvs. ovate-lanceolate, to 2½ in. long; fls. 1½ in. across, solitary or clustered, styles 3. Medit. region. Foliage with goat-like odor when crushed. Cv. **'Pumilum'** [var. *pumilum* P. Wats.]. Plant dwarf, compact, rounded, about 1 ft. high.

Hookeranum Wight & Arn. [*H. oblongifolium* Hort. in part, not Choisy]. Evergreen shrub, to 6 ft.; lvs. ovate to oblong, to 4 in. long; fls. bowl-shaped, to 2 in. across, sepals rounded, overlapping, petals incurved, stamens about ¼ as long as petals, in 5 bundles, 60–80 per bundle, spreading to form a ring around base of ovary, styles 5. Himalayas and w. China. A handsome sp., with attractive foliage and large, golden-yellow fls., to be grown far south and in Calif. This sp. and *H. Leschenaultii* may be the parent of *Hypericum* cv. **'Rowallane'** (sometimes called ROWALLANE HYBRID), a vigorous grower with fls. bowl-shaped, long-lasting, and appearing throughout the year. 'Rowallane' differs from *H. Hookeranum* in having sepals obovate, not overlapping. Var. **Leschenaultii:** *H. Leschenaultii.*

hypericoides (L.) Crantz [*Ascyrum hypericoides* L.]. ST.-ANDREW'S-CROSS. Evergreen subshrub, to 2½ ft., much-branched and often decumbent; lvs. oblong to linear, to 1½ in. long; fls. to 1½ in. across, in terminal or axillary, few-fld. cymes, sepals in 2 unequal pairs, petals 4, stamens separate, styles 2, short. E. N. Amer., s. to W. Indies and Cent. Amer.

hyssopifolium Vill. Subshrub, to 1 or 2 ft.; sepal and petal margins black-dotted; stamen bundles and styles 3. Sw. Eur.

inodorum Mill. [*H. elatum* Ait.]. Arching shrub, to 4½ ft., branchlets 2-edged; lvs. ovate or ovate-oblong, to 2 in. long; fls. 1 in. across, in dense, few-fld. cymes. Medit. region. Intermediate, and perhaps a hybrid, between *H. hircinum* and *H. Androsaemum;* lvs. lack goatlike odor when crushed.

intermedium: *H. annulatum.*

japonicum Thunb. Ann. or per., to 1½ ft., sts. 4-angled; lvs. ovate or elliptic, to ½ in. long; fls. ¼ in. across, in cymes. China and Japan, s. to India and Australia.

Kalmianum L. Evergreen shrub, to 3 ft.; lvs. oblong-linear or oblanceolate, to 2½ in. long; fls. 1 in. across, in few-fld. cymes, styles 5. Que. to Ill.

Kelleri Bald. Procumbent per.; lvs. oblong or elliptic, to ¼ in. long, petioled; sepals obtuse to subacute, black-dotted, stamen bundles and styles 3. Crete.

Kotschyanum Boiss. Herb, to about 8 in.; lvs. oblong; fls. in cymes or panicles. Asia Minor. Not hardy north.

kouytchense Lév. Irregularly branched, more or less deciduous shrub, to 3 ft. or more, branchlets with 4 lines; lvs. ovate or elliptic-ovate, to 3 in. long, glaucous beneath; fls. to 2½ in. across, sepals ovate-lanceolate, acute to acuminate, petals lemon-yellow, obovate-oblong, spreading, not cupped, stamens in 5 indistinct bundles, almost as long as petals, erect and spreading, styles 5, slightly shorter than stamens. W. China. *H. kouytchense* has been known in the trade as *H. penduliflorum* and *H. patulum* cv. 'Sungold'.

lanceolatum: *H. revolutum.*

lanuginosum Lam. Subshrub, to 2 ft., usually unbranched except for infl., gray-tomentose; lvs. sessile, nearly clasping st., ovate to oblong, woolly beneath; fls. yellow, to ¾ in. across, in terminal panicles, sepals glandular-ciliate, glands not black, stamen bundles and styles 3. Greece and Asia Minor.

Leschenaultii Choisy [*H. Hookeranum* var. *Leschenaultii* (Choisy) Dyer]. Shrub, usually not more than 3 ft., brs. slender, arching; lvs. ovate to lanceolate, blunt to acute at apex, rounded at base, to 2½ in. long, dark green above, glaucous beneath; fls. shallowly bowl-shaped.

to 3 in. across, sepals narrowly oblong or elliptic to oblanceolate, acute to subacute, petals incurved, stamens ¼–⅓ as long as petals, styles 5, free. Java, Sumatra. Related to *H. Hookeranum* but with fls. larger, and sepals narrowly oblong to elliptic. A supposed parent of *Hypericum* cv. 'Rowallane' (see *H. Hookeranum*).

linarifolium Vahl. Per., to 1½ ft.; lvs. linear, to ⅝ in. long; fls. in loose corymbs, sepals black-dotted, styles 3. W. Eur., Canary Is., Madeira.

linarioides Bosse [*H. repens* of auth., not L.]. Prostrate per., sts. creeping; lvs. oblong to linear-oblong, ⅜ in. long; infl. subspicate; fls. 1 in. across, sepal margins sometimes black-dotted, petals often red-ringed or red-veined, stamen bundles and styles 3. Se. Eur. and Asia Minor.

Lobbii N. Robs. [*H. oblongifolium* Hort. in part, not Choisy]. Evergreen shrub, to 4½ ft., sts. erect or spreading; lvs. ovate or ovate-triangular, to 2 in. long, short-petioled; fls. to 24 in a corymb, to 2 in. across, sepals rounded, mucronate, overlapping, petals incurved, denticulate on inner margin, stamens ⅓ as long as petals, stamen bundles and styles 5. Assam.

lobocarpum: *H. densiflorum* var.

lysimachioides: *H. Dyeri*.

maculatum: see *H. punctatum*.

Mitchellianum Rydb. BLUE RIDGE S.-J.-w. Sparingly branched per., to 2½ ft.; lvs. sessile, somewhat clasping sts., ovate-oblong, to 2¼ in. long; fls. to 1 in. across, sepals with dark lines, seldom dotted; styles 3. Blue Ridge Mts., from Va., s. to N.C. and Tenn.

montanum L. Per., to 3 ft.; lvs. somewhat clasping st., oblong to ovate, to 2 in. long, pale beneath, margins black-dotted; fls. to ¾ in. across, in cymes, sepals shortly dentate-glandular, about half as long as petals. Eur., N. Afr., ne. Asia Minor.

×**Moseranum** André: *H. calycinum* × *H. patulum*. GOLD FLOWER. Shrub, to 2 ft.; lvs. ovate, to 2 in. long, net-veined beneath; fls. shallowly bowl-shaped, to 2½ in. long, solitary or in cymes, petals somewhat incurved, stamens about half as long as petals, spreading to form ring around base of ovary, anthers reddish, styles 5. Cv. 'Tricolor' [var. *tricolor* Maumené]. Lvs. variegated with white and edged with red.

nudicaule: *H. gentianoides*.

nudiflorum Michx. Shrub, to 3 ft.; lvs. oblong to oblong-lanceolate, to 2¼ in. long; fls. pale yellow, to ¾ in. across, in loose cymes on leafless peduncles, styles 3. N.C., s. to Fla. and Ala.

nummularium L. Subshrub, to 12 in., sts. many, slender; lvs. round, ½ in. long; fls. ¾ in. across, in terminal cymes, sepals glandular-ciliate, petals 3–4 times as long as sepals. France, Spain, Italy. Probably not hardy north.

oblongifolium Choisy [*H. cernuum* Roxb. ex D. Don]. Shrub, sts. much-branched; lvs. narrowly elliptic to ovate-lanceolate, to 3 in. long, conspicuously net-veined beneath; fls. 2 in. across, long-stalked, nodding, petals obovate, stamens nearly as long as petals, styles 5, separate, slender, nearly as long as stamens. W. Himalayas. Some material cult. under this name is *H. Hookeranum* or *H. Lobbii*.

olympicum L. [*H. polyphyllum* Hort., not Boiss. & Bal.]. Upright or sometimes decumbent subshrub, to 1½ ft.; lvs. sessile, oblong-lanceolate to elliptic-oblong, to 1½ in. long, markedly translucent-dotted; fls. to 2½ in. across, in terminal cymes, sepals acuminate, not glandular, styles 3. Se. Eur., Asia Minor.

orientale L. Per., erect or decumbent, to 12 in.; lvs. clasping st., auriculate, obovate to linear-oblong, to 1 in. long, margins ciliate-glandular; fls. 1 in. across, in terminal cymes, stamen bundles and styles 3. Asia Minor.

patulum Thunb. [*H. Henryi* Lév. & Vaniot]. Evergreen shrub, 3–4 ft., brs. with 2–4 lines or 4-angled; lvs. ovate to ovate-oblong or lanceolate-oblong, to 2½ in. long, pale beneath; fls. bowl-shaped, to 2 in. across, solitary or in cymes, sepals broadly ovate to rounded, overlapping, denticulate, usually mucronate, petals incurved, stamens in 5 bundles, half as long as petals, spreading to form a ring at base of ovary, styles 5. China. Var. **Forrestii**: *H. Forrestii*. Var. **Henryi**: *H. Beanii*. Var. **uralum**: *H. uralum*. Cv. 'Sungold': *H. kouytchense*.

penduliflorum: a listed name of no botanical standing, used for *H. kouytchense*.

perforatum L. Per., to 2 ft., sts. many, upright; lvs. oblong to linear, to 1 in. long; fls. to 1 in. across, in terminal cymes, sepals and petals black-dotted, stamens in 3 clusters, styles 3. Eur.; naturalized in N. Amer.

polyphyllum Boiss. & Bal. Probably not cult.; garden plants of this name belong to *H. olympicum*.

prolificum L. BROOMBRUSH, SHRUBBY S.-J.-w. Shrub, to 5 ft.; lvs. narrowly oblong, to 3 in. long; fls. to ¾ in. across, in cymes, styles 3. Ont. to Ga., w. to Minn. and La.

pulchellum: *Cratoxylum polyanthum*.

pulchrum L. Per. herb, to 2 ft., sts. wiry, erect or ascending; lvs. ovate, ½ in. long; fls. to ¾ in. across, in panicles; sepal margins black-dotted, petals red-tinged, stamen bundles and styles 3, anthers orange to reddish-pink. Eur.

punctatum Lam. [*H. maculatum* Walt., not Crantz]. Per., to 3 ft.; lvs. ovate-lanceolate, to 3 in. long, black-dotted; fls. yellow, black-dotted. E. U.S.

pyramidatum: *H. Ascyron*.

repens: see *H. linarioides*.

reptans Hook.f. & T. Thoms. ex Dyer. Prostrate shrub, sts. 2-edged, rooting and mat-forming; lvs. elliptic-oblong, ½ in. long; fls. solitary, to 1¾ in. across, stamens in 5 clusters, styles 5. W. China and Himalayas. Planted far south.

revolutum Vahl [*H. lanceolatum* Lam.]. Large, spreading shrub, to 10 ft.; lvs. lanceolate, to 1 in. long, entire, acute, dotted, pale beneath; fls. to 2 in. across, terminal, petals oblong to obovate, becoming reddish-brown on outside, stamens in 5 bundles, style 5-branched at apex. Sw. Arabia and mts. of e. Afr., s. to Comoro Is., Madagascar, Réunion, and Cape Prov.

rhodopeum: *H. cerastoides*.

Richeri Vill. Per., to 2 ft.; lvs. ovate-lanceolate, glaucous beneath, only slightly dotted; fls. to 1½ in. across, in few-fld. cymes, sepals subentire or ciliate, black-streaked or -dotted, petals profusely black-dotted, stamen bundles and styles 3. S. and cent. Eur.

rumelicum Boiss. Per., to 1 ft., glabrous; lvs. narrowly oblong-linear, to ¾ in. long, not dotted, margins strongly revolute; fls. in corymbose cymes, sepal and petal margins black-dotted. Se. Eur.

Sarothra: *H. gentianoides*.

Scouleri: *H. formosum* var.

stans (Michx.) W. P. Adams & N. Robs. [*Ascyrum stans* Michx.]. ST.-PETER'S-WORT. Subshrub, to 2 ft., branchlets 2-edged, especially when young; lvs. somewhat clasping st., oblong or obovate, to 1½ in. long; fls. to 1 in. across, in terminal or axillary, few-fld. cymes, sepals 4, in 2 unequal pairs, petals 4, stamens separate, styles 3 or 4, short. N.J., s. to Fla. and Tex.

tetrapterum Fries [*H. acutum* Moench]. Per. herb, sts. erect or procumbent, 4-winged; lvs. sessile, ovate, orbicular, or broadly elliptic, to ½ in. long, minutely translucent-dotted; fls. about 1 in. across, in subcorymbose or pyramidal cymes, stamen bundles and styles 3, rarely 4. Eur. Var. **corsicum** (Steud.) Boiss. [*H. corsicum* Steud.]. Petals red-veined.

tomentosum L. More or less tomentose per., to 12 in., sts. ascending; lvs. ovate, to ¾ in. long, woolly; fls. to ¾ in. across, in corymbs, petal margins black-dotted, stamen bundles and styles 3. Sw. Eur.

tuberaria: a listed name of no botanical standing; perhaps refers to *Helianthemum Tuberaria*.

uralum Buch.-Ham. ex D. Don [*H. patulum* var. *uralum* (Buch.-Ham. ex D. Don) Koehne]. Shrub, to 3 ft., brs. arching, with 2–4 lines or angles; lvs. ovate to lanceolate, to 1½ in. long, glaucous beneath; fls. bowl-shaped, about 1 in. across, sepals oblong to elliptic or oblong-spatulate. W. China, Himalayas, Thailand, Sumatra. Related to *H. patulum*, but fls. smaller, to 1 in. across, and sepals entire, narrower, not mucronate.

Webbianum: *H. grandifolium*.

HYPHAENE Gaertn. GINGERBREAD PALM. *Palmae*. Fewer than 30 spp. of short to moderate, dioecious palms of Afr., Madagascar, and India; sts. solitary or clustered, sometimes forked or swollen; lvs. costapalmate, petiole elongate, with spinelike teeth along margins; infls. among lvs., peduncle elongate, sheathed by several bracts, primary brs. several, each sheathed by a tubular bract and few, digitately arranged, catkinlike flowering brs. covered with imbricate bractlets in the male infl., flowering brs. similar in the female infl. but only 1–2; fls. sunken in pits formed by bractlets, male fls. in clusters of 3, calyx 3-lobed, petals united in a solid base with 3 separate, imbricate lobes, stamens 6, pistillode minute, female fls. solitary, stalked, sepals and petals 3, similar, imbricate, staminodes united in a 6-lobed ring, pistil 3-celled, 3-ovuled; fr. stalked, variable in shape, usually 1-seeded, dryish-fibrous, endocarp thin, endosperm homogeneous. Differences among spp. are not always clear.

Grown in the tropics and subtropics for the unusual (for palms) branching habit. Seed usually planted where the palm is to stand. For culture see *Palms*.

crinita Gaertn. A poorly known sp. of an unknown origin, described only from the rounded, short-stalked fr. The identity of plants so listed is uncertain.

Schatan Bojer. More or less cespitose, trunk simple or becoming branched; lf. blades about 2 ft. long, segms. rigid, minutely scaled; fr. mostly obovoid with a truncate or slightly convex top, short-stalked, about 2 in. long. Madagascar.

thebaica (L.) Mart. DOUM or DOOM PALM, EGYPTIAN DOUM or DOOM P., GINGERBREAD P., GINGERBREAD TREE. To 20 ft. or more, commonly forked 1 or more times, but sometimes simple; lf. blades stiff, nearly orbicular, to 3 ft. long, cut to middle or deeper into 20 or more segms.; fr. mostly obliquely ovoid or oblong, longer than broad, to 3½ in. long. Nile region of N. Afr. Zone 10 in Fla.

HYPOCALYPTUS Thunb. *Leguminosae* (subfamily *Faboideae*). One sp., an evergreen shrub of S. Afr.; lvs. alt., petioled, of 3 lfts.; fls. in terminal racemes, showy, papilionaceous, standard reflexed, stamens 10, united; fr. a linear, flat, many-seeded legume, with thickened margins.

Propagated by cuttings of side shoots in sand.

sophoroides (Bergius) Druce. To 15 ft., very dense; lfts. obcuneate to obcordate, to 1½ in. long, emarginate or truncate and mucronate; racemes dense, many-fld., to 3 in. long; fls. rose to lilac, standard with yellow spot at base; fr. 1½ in. long. Cape Prov. Zone 10.

HYPOCHOERIS L. CAT'S-EAR. *Compositae* (Cichorium Tribe). Fifty to 70 spp. of ann. or per. herbs with milky sap, native to Asia, Eur., N. Afr., but chiefly S. Amer.; sts. mostly scapose, often enlarged beneath the fl. heads; lvs. mostly in a basal rosette; fl. heads solitary or somewhat corymbose, involucral bracts imbricate in many rows, receptacle flat, scaly; fls. all ligulate, bisexual, yellow or white; achenes 10-ribbed, at least the inner row beaked, pappus of plumose bristles, but sometimes the outer row of simple hairs.

Sometimes cultivated in the wild garden; propagated by seeds or division.

lanata Dusén. Per., to about 5 in.; lvs. in a basal rosette from a woody crown, linear-lanceolate, to 3⅛ in. long, pinnatifid, woolly; heads to ¾ in. across, solitary, involucral bracts blackish below apex, woolly except at apex and on the scarious margins; fls. white. Patagonia.

radicata L. SPOTTED C.-E. Per., to 2 ft.; lvs. in a basal rosette, oblanceolate, obovate, or oblong-lanceolate, to 5½ in. long, sometimes longer, toothed to pinnatifid, hispid; heads to 1½ in. across, usually several, involucral bracts bristly on midvein; fls. bright yellow. Eur., Asia, N. Afr.; naturalized and weedy in various parts of the world, including N. Amer.

uniflora Vill. Per., to 1½ ft., hairy, particularly just below the head; lvs. oblong-lanceolate to oblanceolate, toothed, hairy; heads to about 2¼ in. across, usually solitary, involucral bracts hairy; fls. yellow. Alps.

HYPOCYRTA: *NEMATANTHUS.* **H. Nummularia:** *Alloplectus Nummularia.* **H. radicans:** *N. gregarius.* **H. Selloana:** *N. fissus.* **H. Teuscheri:** *Alloplectus Teuscheri.*

HYPOESTES Soland. ex R. Br. *Acanthaceae.* More than 40 spp. of per. herbs or evergreen shrubs of S. Afr., Madagascar, and se. Asia; lvs. opp., entire; fls. in terminal and axillary cymes in uppermost pairs of lvs., calyx 5-parted, shorter than corolla tube, corolla 2-lipped, tube slender, upper lip 3-lobed, erect, lower lip entire, stamens 2, borne at mouth of tube, filaments slender, anther sac 1, style filiform, exserted with stamens, stigma 2-lobed, ovary 2-celled, each cell with 2 ovules; fr. a caps., seeds smooth, flat, round, with narrow, membranous wing.

aristata R. Br. Branched herb, to 3 ft.; lvs. 2–3 in. long, upper lvs. shorter; fl. heads axillary, of many 1-fld. spikelets, corolla rose-purple, 1 in. long, lower lip curled, upper erect. S. Afr.

foetida: a listed name of no botanical standing.

phyllostachya Bak. POLKA-DOT PLANT, PINK P.-D. PLANT, MEASLES PLANT, FLAMINGO PLANT, BABY'S-TEARS, FRECKLE-FACE, PINK-DOT. Per. herb with woody base, to 3 ft.; lvs. ovate, to 2½ in. long, thin, dark green, marked with lavender-pink spots, petioles slender, to 1½ in.; fls. solitary, axillary, corolla lavender. Madagascar. Erroneously known in cult. as *H. sanguinolenta.*

sanguinolenta (Van Houtte) Hook.f. Not in cult.; material grown under this name is *H. phyllostachya.*

HYPOLEPIS Bernh. *Polypodiaceae.* About 45 spp. of trop. and subtrop., terrestrial ferns of both hemispheres, with creeping rhizomes; lvs. 2–4-pinnate; sori in the sinuses of lvs., covered by the reflexed margins. Allied to *Cheilanthes,* but sori dorsal, not strictly marginal.

Sometimes grown under glass. See also *Ferns.*

tenuifolia (G. Forst.) Bernh. Lvs. to 3 ft. long and 2 ft. wide, 4-pinnate into wavy-toothed pinnules, petioles to 2 ft. long, brown. Possibly merely a var. of *H. punctata.* Java.

punctata (Thunb.) Mett. Lvs. large, to 8 ft. long, triangular, 4-pinnate, rachises and midveins with short, crisped hairs. Tropics.

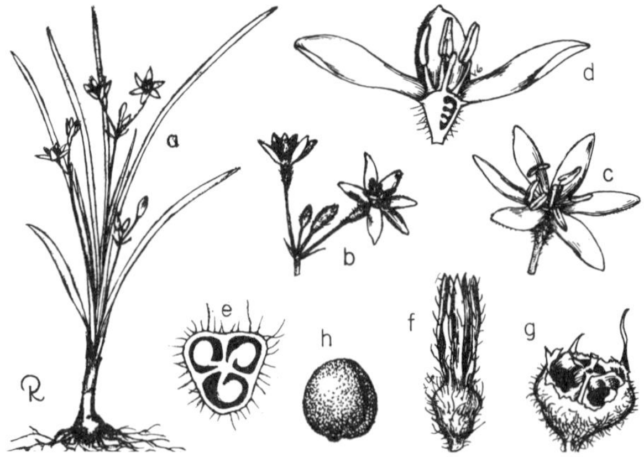

HYPOXIDACEAE. *Hypoxis hirsuta:* **a,** plant, × ⅓; **b,** inflorescence, × ½; **c,** flower, × 1; **d,** flower, vertical section, × 3; **e,** ovary, cross section, × 8; **f,** fruit with withered perianth, × 2; **g,** fruit, perianth removed, × 4; **h,** seed, × 6.

HYPOXIDACEAE R. Br. STAR GRASS FAMILY. Monocot.; 5 or 6 genera with tuberous rhizomes or fibrous-coated corms, native mainly to the S. Hemisphere and trop. Asia; lvs. mostly basal, parallel-veined, often hairy, grasslike to broad and plicate; infl. scapose and spicate, racemose, or nearly umbellate; fls. regular, 6-parted, bisexual, perianth segms. separate or sometimes united in a short tube, stamens 6 or rarely 3, ovary inferior, ovules many on axile placentas; fr. a caps. or berry, seeds small, globose, often black and muricate or irregular. *Curculigo, Hypoxis,* and *Rhodohypoxis* are cult.

HYPOXIS L. STAR GRASS. *Hypoxidaceae.* About 110 spp. of stemless herbs, mostly of the S. Hemisphere; rhizome short, cormlike; lvs. linear; scape 1- to several-fld.; fls. white or yellow, perianth of 6 separate segms., stamens 6, in 1 series, filaments slender, anthers erect or versatile, stigma not lobed; fr. a caps., seeds small, globose, with black, crustaceous seed coat.

Of simple culture in the wild garden or border in dry soil. Propagated by division.

erecta: *H. hirsuta.*

hirsuta (L.) Cov. [*H. erecta* L.]. To 12 in.; lvs. to 1 ft. long or more and $\frac{3}{16}$ in. wide, hairy; scapes 1–7-fld., fls. bright yellow, starlike, perianth segms. ½ in. long, anthers versatile, ovary pilose. Spring. Me., s. to Fla. and Tex.

hygrometrica Labill. GOLDEN WEATHERGLASS. To 6 in.; lvs. narrow-linear, to 1 ft. long, somewhat pilose; scape mostly 1–3-fld., fls. yellow, anthers versatile, ovary glabrous. Australia. Common name derived from fls. closing in cloudy weather.

leptocarpa Engelm. Similar to *H. hirsuta,* but lvs. soft, nearly glabrous, to ½ in. wide, scape 1–3-fld. Va. to Mo., s. to Fla. and Tex.

stellata L. Lvs. glabrous, to 12 in. long; fls. white on inside, green-striped outside, perianth segms. to 1 in. long, anthers erect, not versatile. S. Afr. Var. **elegans** (Andr.) Pers. Fls. white, banded basally with purplish-black.

HYPSELA K. Presl. *Lobeliaceae.* Four spp. of prostrate, per. herbs, native to S. Amer., New Zeal., and Australia. Allied to *Pratia* and *Centropogon* but differing from *Pratia* in not having corolla tube split and from *Centropogon* in its creeping habit, and in having lower 2 anthers 2-awned and pilose at apex.

Suitable for rock gardens.

longiflora: *H. reniformis.*

reniformis (HBK) K. Presl [*H. longiflora* (Hook.f.) Benth. & Hook.f.]. Sts. matted, to about 2 in.; lvs. sometimes clustered, blades to ½ in. long and nearly as broad, entire, generally folded along midrib, shorter than petioles; fls. solitary, pedicels to 2 in. long, corolla about ½ in. long, white or rose, purple- or carmine-veined, throat yellow-spotted; fr. a greenish berry. S. Amer. Hardy north, but needs protection from summer sun.

HYPTIS Jacq. *Labiatae*. About 400 spp. of herbs or shrubs of trop. Amer.; sts. mostly square in cross section; lvs. opp., often toothed; fls. in peduncled, axillary verticillasters arranged in terminal or axillary racemes, calyx 10-nerved, 5-toothed, corolla funnelform, limb 2-lipped, upper lip 2-lobed, lower lip 3-lobed, middle lobe concave, lateral lobes deflexed, stamens 4, in 2 pairs; fr. of 4 ovoid, glabrous nutlets.

Emoryi Torr. DESERT LAVENDER. Erect, aromatic shrub, 3–10 ft., brs. many, slender, densely white-scurfy-tomentose, the hairs stellate; lvs. ovate, to 1 in. long and wide, crenate-dentate, petioles about ¼ in. long; fls. in short-peduncled verticillasters, the racemes in panicles; calyx to ¼ in. long, stellate-woolly, teeth bristly, corolla to ¼ in. long,

violet. Winter–spring. Deserts, s. Ariz. and s. Calif. to Baja Calif. and Sonora (Mex.).

HYSSOPUS L. HYSSOP. *Labiatae*. About 5 spp. of per. herbs or subshrubs of s. Eur. and Medit. region to cent. Asia; sts. mostly square in cross section; lvs. opp., linear to lanceolate, entire; fls. in 4–16-fld. verticillasters arranged in terminal spikes, calyx tubular, 15-nerved, 5-toothed, corolla funnelform, 2-lipped, upper lip erect, emarginate, lower lip 3-lobed, middle lobe largest, emarginate, stamens 4, in 2 pairs, exserted, anthers 2-celled, style 2-lobed; fr. of 4 glabrous nutlets. Differs from *Origanum* in lacking bearded calyx.

Hyssop is grown as an ornamental or sweet herb; propagated easily by seeds, cuttings, or division.

aristata: *H. officinalis.*

asiatica: a listed name of no botanical standing.

officinalis L. [*H. aristata* Godr.; *H. vulgaris* Bubani]. HYSSOP. Subshrub or a suffrutescent per., aromatic, sts. 18–24 in., hairless to very hairy; lvs. linear-lanceolate to elliptic-lanceolate, ¾–1½ in. long, to ⅝ in wide, short-petioled; verticillasters 6- to many-fld.; calyx tubular, to ⁵⁄₁₆ in. long, corolla ½ in. long, deep bluish-violet, or in cvs., white, rose, or red. A variable sp. of s. and e. Eur. Easily grown, as a low edging plant or for medicinal use; does well in dry, rocky, limestone soils. Cvs. are: 'Alba', fls. white; 'Grandiflora', fls. large, to ¾ in. long; 'Rosea', fls. rose; 'Rubra', fls. red.

vulgaris: *H. officinalis.*

IBERIS L. CANDYTUFT. *Cruciferae.* About 30 spp. of small, usually glabrous, ann. or per. herbs, sometimes woody and durable at base and evergreen, usually growing in limy soils in cent. Eur. and Medit. region; lvs. narrow, entire or dentate, in some spp. pinnatifid; fls. white, pink, red, purple, in umbelliform clusters or in racemes that lengthen with age, sepals 4, petals 4, the 2 outer larger than the inner; fr. a broad, more or less orbicular silicle usually winged at apex, seeds solitary in each cell, often winged.

The candytufts of flower gardens and borders are of 2 classes—the half-hardy annuals and the evergreen perennials. They all thrive in ordinary garden soil and require no special treatment. The annuals are used for flower beds, edgings, and for cutting. Seeds are sown where the plants are to grow, the plants thinned eventually to 6–12 in. apart. Bloom may be expected in 2 months or less. In mild climates, seeds are sometimes sown in autumn for winter and spring bloom. The flowers are largely white, but run into flesh-colored, purple, and crimson; some kinds are fragrant. The ground should not be allowed to become very dry, and spent flowers should be cut off, or the plants will tend to run rapidly to seed. Perennial candytufts are low, compact plants, somewhat woody at base, with white flowers sometimes becoming lilac with age. They are propagated by division, by cuttings, or by seeds sown a year before bloom is wanted.

affinis: plants cult. under this name may belong to *I. odorata, I. crenata, I. pinnata,* or one of the other ann. spp.

amara L. [*I. coronaria* D. Don]. ROCKET C. Erect ann., to 1 ft., sparsely pubescent; lvs. oblanceolate to spatulate, to 3 or 4 in. long, coarsely few-toothed, thickish; fls. large, white, fragrant, the raceme soon elongating. Mainly w. Eur. A variable sp. This is the florist's candytuft. Much used in the flower garden, and has many name cvs., including: 'Hyacinthiflora', 'Giant Empress', and 'Miniature Gem'.

corifolia: *I. sempervirens* var. *correifolia.*

correifolia: *I. sempervirens* var.

coronaria: *I. amara.*

crenata Lam. [*I. pectinata* Boiss.; *I. panduriformis* Pourr. may also belong here]. Erect, hispid ann., to 12 in.; sts. branched above, brs. straight and leafless; lower lvs. linear-spatulate, pectinate-toothed, upper lvs. narrower, entire; fls. white, in a many-fld., dense, convex corymb. Spain.

Dunnettii: a listed name of no botanical standing; see *I. umbellata* cv.

Garrexiana: *I. sempervirens.*

gibraltarica L. GIBRALTAR C. Evergreen, cespitose per., essentially glabrous, with a woody caudex from which arise lf. rosettes and many ascending fl. sts. to 1 ft.; lvs. oblong-spatulate, to 1 in. long, more or less toothed; fls. lilac or light purple, the inner ones often white, in flattish clusters to 2 in. across, not elongating in fr. Gibraltar and Morocco. Much used as an ornamental, especially for edgings.

Jordanii: *I. Pruitii.*

jucunda: *Aethionema coridifolium.*

Lagascana: *I. Pruitii.*

odorata L. Diffusely branched, short-hispid ann., sts. flexuous, leafy, to 12 in.; lvs. linear-spatulate, pinnatifid, with 1–2 pairs of segms.; fls. white, in a flat, dense corymb surrounded by upper lvs. Se. Eur., N. Afr., sw. Asia.

panduriformis: see *I. crenata.*

pectinata: *I. crenata.*

pinnata L. Erect ann., to 12 in., rugose-papillose or scarcely pubescent; lvs. obovate-oblong, pinnatifid or pinnatisect, with 1–3 pairs of linear segms.; fls. white to lilac, fragrant, in short, usually dense, convex corymbs. S. Eur., Asia Minor.

Pruitii Tineo [*I. Jordanii* Boiss.; *I. Lagascana* DC.; *I. Tenoreana* DC.]. Low, cespitose per. or ann., sts. procumbent-ascending, to 15 in.; lvs. entire or with few teeth at apex, rather fleshy, the lower obovate-spatulate, the upper narrower; fls. white to lilac, in rather dense corymbs. Medit. region. Sometimes forming mats to as much as 7 ft. across.

pygmaea: a listed name of no botanical standing.

saxatilis L. Low, evergreen subshrub; lvs. linear, to ⅛ in. wide, those on nonflowering shoots semicylindrical, those on fl. sts. more or less flat; fls. white, in terminal corymbs elongating in fr. S. Eur. Often confused with *I. sempervirens,* but lvs. narrower and infl. terminal.

semperflorens L. Evergreen subshrub, to 2 ft., glabrous, branched in upper part; lvs. flat, entire, thickish, the lower spatulate, to 3 in. long, the upper oblong-spatulate, smaller; fls. white, in corymbs elongating in fr.; silicles ovate-rhombic, to ⅝ in. across, broader than long. Sicily, w. coast of Italy. The only winter-flowering sp.; distinguished by its broader-than-long silicles.

sempervirens L. [*I. Garrexiana* All.]. EDGING C. Evergreen subshrub, to 12 in., glabrous or nearly so; lvs. linear or narrow-oblong, to 1½ in. long, blunt, entire; fls. white, in lateral racemes elongating in fr. S. Eur. Useful for edgings. Cvs. include: 'Compacta', 'Nana', and 'Superba'. Var. **correifolia** (Nichols.) Boom [*I. corifolia* Hort.; *I. correifolia* Nichols.]. Plant compact, infl. at first very flat. Cvs. include: 'Camlaensis', 'Climax', 'Little Gem', 'Snowflake'.

stylosa: *Hutchinsia stylosa.*

taurica DC. Ann. or bien., to 8 in., branched from base, pubescent with short, white hairs; lvs. linear or linear-spatulate; fls. lilac to white, in loose racemes. Asia Minor.

Tenoreana: *I. Pruitii.*

umbellata L. GLOBE C. Ann., to 16 in., branching, glabrous or nearly so; lvs. lanceolate, to 3½ in. long, acuminate, entire or with 1 or 2 marginal angles, thin; fls. pink, violet, purple, red, not fragrant, in an umbel which remains dense even in fr. Medit. region; escaped and spontaneous in Calif. The common ann. candytuft of gardens, with several named cvs.: 'Atropurpurea', 'Cardinal', 'Lavender', 'Lilacea', 'Rosea'. Some cvs., such as 'Dunnettii', are actually hybrids between this sp. and *I. amara.*

IBERVILLEA Greene ex Small. *Cucurbitaceae.* Three spp. of dioecious vines in sw. U.S. and nw. Mex.; fls. small, with a tubular or bell-shaped corolla tube, sepals 5, petals 5, oblong, obovate, or linear, male fls. in axillary clusters or racemes, stamens 3, at the throat of fl. tube, separate, anthers oblong, straight, female fls. axillary, solitary, ovary with 3 parietal placentas, style without basal disc; fr. ovoid to nearly globose, 1–2 in. long, smooth, seeds many.

Lindheimeri (A. Gray) Greene ex Small. WILD BALSAM, HIERBA-DE-VIBORA. Per. herb, sts. to 12 ft.; lvs. broadly ovate, to 2¼ in. long, cordate or nearly reniform, often 3–5-lobed, white-dotted; fls. yellow or greenish; fr. orange or red when ripe, 1–2 in. in diam., seeds round, margined. Tex. to Calif. and n. Mex.

IBICELLA Van Eselt. *Martyniaceae.* Two spp. of viscid-pubescent herbs, native to S. Amer.; lvs. broadly ovate to nearly orbicular; infl. a dense, terminal raceme; fls. showy, yellow, sepals 5, separate, corolla campanulate, 5-lobed, fertile stamens 4; fr. cylindric-ovoid, woody caps. with a slender beak, longer than the spiny body.

Fruit may be used for pickles; see *Proboscidea* for culture.

lutea (Lindl.) Van Eselt. [*Proboscidea lutea* (Lindl.) Stapf] Spreading, to 1½ ft.; lvs. nearly orbicular, to 1 ft. across, dentate, usually 5-nerved; fls. greenish-yellow outside, deeper yellow to orange inside, sometimes red-blotched. N. Argentina, Paraguay, Uruguay, s. Brazil.

IBOZA N. E. Br. *Labiatae.* About 12 spp. of dioecious herbs or shrubs of trop. and S. Afr.; sts. mostly square in cross section; lvs. opp., often toothed, usually petioled, aromatic; infl. paniculate; fls. fragrant, calyx minute, 3–5-lobed, male fls. with corolla small, stamens 4, separate, exserted, nonfunctional ovaries often present, female fls. with corolla smaller, often with staminodes, ovary 4-lobed, stigmas linear, spreading; fr. of 4 nutlets.

riparia (Hochst.) N. E. Br. Stout herb, 3–6 ft., white-pubescent, aromatic; lvs. broadly ovate, 4–6 in. long, to 5 in. wide, slightly to deeply crenate, petioled; panicle mostly 8–15 in. long; calyx to $\frac{1}{16}$ in. long, corolla unequally 4–5-lobed, to $\frac{3}{16}$ in. long, white. Natal and Transvaal (S. Afr.). Grown under glass or outdoors in the South. Treated much like salvia or coleus; plants are cut back after blooming and cuttings can be used for prop.

ICACOREA: *ARDISIA.* **I. paniculata:** *A. escallonioides.*

ICHTHYOMETHIA: *PISCIDIA.*

IDESIA Maxim. *Flacourtiaceae.* One sp., a deciduous, dioecious or polygamous tree, native to Japan and China; fls. in large terminal panicles, sepals usually 5, petals none, stamens many; fr. a fleshy, many-seeded berry.

Propagated by seeds, root cuttings and cuttings of green wood; transplants easily. Used as shade tree for lawn, park, or street plantings. Zone 7.

polycarpa Maxim. IIGIRI TREE. To 50 ft.; lvs. alt., cordate-ovate, to 10 in. long, toothed, glaucous beneath, 5–6-nerved from base; berries orange-red, $\frac{5}{16}$ in. in diam.

IDRIA Kellogg. *Fouquieriaceae.* One sp., a bizarre tree, native to Baja Calif., Mex., with soft, often hollow trunk and spreading spiny brs.; lvs. simple, deciduous; fls. yellow, in large panicles, sepals 5, corolla campanulate, 5-lobed, stamens 10, exserted, style stout, 3-angled; fr. a caps.

columnaris Kellogg [*Fouquieria columnaris* (Kellogg) Kellogg ex Curran]. BOOJUM TREE. To 50 ft., trunk columnar, tapering to apex, brs. with spines to 1½ in. long; lvs oblanceolate to obovate, to ¾ in. long; fls. ½ in. long, in panicles to 16 in. long; fr. ¾ in. long. Sometimes planted in warmer parts of s. Calif. and Ariz.

ILEX L. HOLLY. *Aquifoliaceae.* About 400 spp. of dioecious or polygamodioecious, often evergreen shrubs or trees, native primarily in temp. and trop. regions of N. and S. Amer. and Asia; lvs. alt., short-petioled, blades often thick, leathery, margins entire to toothed or spinescent; fls. axillary, solitary or in fascicles or cymes, usually pedicelled, small, regular, calyx small, 4–6(–9)-parted, persistent, corolla rotate, white or greenish, petals separate or united at base, stamens as many as and alt. with petals, ovary superior, mostly 2–6-celled, capped by a lobed stigma; fr. drupaceous, usually globose, red or black, containing mostly 4–6, sometimes more, bony-covered seeds (pyrenes).

The dried leaves of some hollies yield tealike beverages, one, *I. paraquariensis,* supplying maté, a popular S. Amer. drink. Other species are among our important ornamental shrubs valued for their good habit, attractive foliage, and showy berries. Some evergreen kinds are variable and select cultivars are grown in commercial orchards to supply the florist industry with berried wreaths and sprays.

Evergreen hollies are cultivated in regions of moderate climate (mostly through Zone 7); deciduous hollies tolerate harsher situations (through Zone 5). Although some species occur in swampy sites, all hollies succeed in fertile, well-drained soils. In northern latitudes the evergreen hollies require a moist soil before the ground freezes and protection from winter winds and sunshine. Evergreen kinds are transplanted with a soil ball in spring or fall. Hollies are propagated by cuttings, either softwood or hardwood, by budding or grafting, or by stratified seeds. Due to immaturity of the embryo, germination requires 3 months to a year or more depending upon the species. The Holly Society of America is the best source of detailed information on all cultivated species of hollies. The *Handbook of Hollies* published cooperatively by the Society and The American Horticultural Society is available as is the first part of an *International Checklist of Cultivated Ilex* (Part 1, *Ilex opaca,* National Arboretum Contribution No. 3) being compiled in cooperation with the United States National Arboretum.

The hollies are nomenclaturally a complex group. Many cultivars are offered, particularly in *I. Aquifolium, I. crenata,* and *I. opaca.* In earlier times these were offered as Latin-named varieties or forms, but recently many fancy-named cultivars have been introduced. In this *Hortus,* Latin-named horticultural varieties and forms are listed as cultivars following appropriate species entries in order to recognize properly their cultivar status. A selected number of fancy-named cultivars are also listed to give a sample of the available range of offerings.

In addition to cultivars that may be assigned to individual species, many holly cultivars of hybrid origin exist. Being of mixed parentage, these are not easily accommodated in our standard format. A selection of the more desirable of these hybrid cultivars is listed below, al-

phabetically by parentage. Since hollies are dioecious, that is plants are either male or female, the sex of each cultivar is given. Unless otherwise noted all are hardy through Zone 7.

   I. × *altaclarensis* 'Wilsonii' × I. sikkimensis. **'San Jose'**, female.
   I. Aquifolium × *I. cornuta.* **'Hallowell'**, male; **'Edward J. Stevens'**, male; **'Maplehurst'**, male; and **'Nellie R. Stevens'**, female.
   I. ciliospinosa × *I. Pernyi.* **'Dr. Hu'**, female.
   I. ciliospinosa hybrid. **'Arnold Shine'**, female; **'Brooklyn Queen'**, female.
   I. cornuta × *I. ciliospinosa.* **'Albert Close'**, female; **'William Cowgill'**, female; **'Howard Dorset'**, male; **'Edward Goucher'**, female; and **'Harry Gunning'**, male.
   I. cornuta × *I. Pernyi.* **'Doctor Kassab'**, female.
   I. cornuta 'Burfordii' × *I. Pernyi.* **'Lydia Morris'**, female; **'John T. Morris'**, male; **'Moon Glow'**, female.
   I. integra × *I. Pernyi.* **'Accent'**, male; **'Elegance'**, female.
   I. myrtifolia × *I. opaca.* **'Monongahela'**, female; **'Oriole'**, female, Zone 7b; **'Tananger'**, female, Zone 7b.
   I. opaca × *I. Aquifolium.* **'Shin Nien'**, male, Zone 6.
   I. 'Nellie R. Stevens' × *I. leucoclada.* **'Clusterberry'**, female.
   I. Pernyi × *I. ciliospinosa.* **'Brian K. Stevens'**, male.
   I. Pernyi hybrid. **'Jermyn's Dwarf'**, male.
   I. serrata × *I. verticillata.* **'Autumn Glow'**, female, Zone 6; **'Harvest Red'**, female, Zone 6; **'Sparkleberry'**, female, Zone 6.

× altaclarensis (Dallim.) Rehd.: *I. Aquifolium* × *I. Perado.* Vigorous, evergreen tree; lvs. leathery, elliptic, 2½–4 in. long, margins slightly undulate, bearing few, spiny teeth. Zone 7. Many cvs. are available, of which the following is a sample; in the trade these are often listed under *I. Aquifolium.* '**Altaclarensis**', HIGHCLERE H., vigorous, dense, male; '**Atrovirens Variegata**', lvs. golden-blotched at center, male; '**Belgica**', DUTCH H., vigorous, lvs. large, spiny, female; '**Camelliifolia**', vigorous, dense foliage, fr. large, female; '**Colburn**', similar to the preceding but with more spinose lvs., female; '**Donning-tonensis**', lvs. variable but with a purplish cast, lanceolate with few or no spines, male; '**Eldridge**', lvs. large, flat, with strong spines, fr. large, female; '**Hendersonii**', compact, lvs. comparatively dull, entire or few-spined, fr. large, female; '**Hodginsii**', vigorous, sts. purplish, lvs. often boldly spiny, reported as both a male and a female clone; '**J. C. van Tol**' [cv. 'Polycarpa'], lvs. dark green, glossy, almost spineless, fr. large, female; '**Laurifolia**', SMOOTH-LEAVED H., lvs. dark green, very glossy, smooth, mostly entire, male; '**Lawsoniana**', lvs. mostly spineless, blotched yellow in the center, female; '**Maderensis**', vigorous, dark-stemmed, lvs. flat, regularly spined, male; '**Marnockii**', similar to 'Camelliifolia' but less dense, margins often spineless, female; '**Moorei**', sts. green, tinged reddish-purple, lvs. large, dark green, strongly spined, male; '**Mundyi**', sts. green, lvs. large, spiny, male; '**Nigrescens**' [*I. Perado* var. *platyphylla* cv. 'Nigrescens'], vigorous, sts. purple, lvs. mostly entire, male; '**Nobilis**', lvs. glossy, irregularly spined, male; '**Polycarpa**': 'J. C. van Tol'; '**Shepherdii**', sts. green, lvs. glossy, mostly spined, male; '**Wilsonii**', compact, sts. green, lvs. large, evenly spined, female.

ambigua (Michx.) Torr. Deciduous shrub or small tree, with glabrous to densely pubescent brs.; lvs. dull green, lanceolate to elliptic or obovate, 1½–7 in. long, acute or acuminate, finely to coarsely toothed, slightly rugose beneath; fls. 4-merous, the male fascicled, usually on short spurs, the female axillary, solitary; fr. red, translucent, globose, about ¼ in. in diam., pyrenes mostly 4. Var. **ambigua** [*I. montana* var. *Beadlei* (Ashe) Fern.]. The typical var.; lvs. to about 3 in. long, apex acute to short-acuminate. N.C. to Fla. and Ala. Zone 7. Var. **montana** (Torr. & A. Gray) Ahleš [*I. montana* Torr. & A. Gray; *I. monticola* A. Gray]. MOUNTAIN H., LARGE-LEAVED H., MOUNTAIN WINTER-BERRY. Lvs. mostly 2½–7 in. long. Mass. to Ala. and Ga. Zone 5.

Amelanchier M. A. Curtis. SARVIS H., SWAMP H. Deciduous shrub or small tree; lvs. thin, narrowly ovate to obovate, 2–4 in. long, entire or finely serrate, strongly rugose beneath; fls. 4-merous, the male in 3–5- or several-fld. cymes, the female solitary in axils of current year's brs.; fr. dull red, subglobose, to ⅜ in. in diam. Hills of coastal plain, se. Va. to Ga. Zone 6.

Aquifolium L. ENGLISH H., EUROPEAN H., OREGON H. Evergreen tree, to 50 ft., bark smooth, gray, brs. green or purplish, short, spreading, forming a dense, conical head; lvs. thick, leathery, mostly dark green, glossy, elliptic to oblong-ovate, 1–2 in. long, margins mostly thickened, undulate, with stiff, spiny, divaricate teeth, rarely entire; fls. white, fragrant, in fascicles on brs. of previous year; fr. bright red, globose or obovoid, to nearly ⅜ in. in diam. Eur., N. Afr., w. Asia. Zone 7. In Eur. wood used for veneers and inlays. Many cvs. are offered. A number of these are now referred to *I* × *altaclarensis,* which see. The following list is a selection of commonly offered Latin-named cvs. and their fancy-named synonyms. For more extensive lists of fancy-named cvs. consult the *Handbook of Hollies.* '**Albomarginata**', perhaps best considered a group name applying to cvs. with silver-white or cream-colored lf. margins; '**Alcicornis**', free growing, very spiny, lvs. bright green; **'Angustifolia'**, narrowly conical, lvs. lanceolate, small, flat, margins long-spined, both male and female clones; **'Argenteo-marginata'**, best considered a group name applying to clones with lvs. silver-variegated; **'Argenteo-marginata Pendula'** [cvs. 'Perry's Weeping', 'Silver Weeping'], brs. pendulous, lf. margins creamy-white; **'Argentea Regina'** [cvs. 'Silver King', 'Silver Queen'], sts. red, lvs. mottled gray, margins white; **'Aureo-marginata'**, best considered a group name for female clones with lvs. variegated, margins yellow; **'Aurea Medio-picta'** [cvs. 'Golden Butterfly', 'Golden Milkboy', 'Harlequin', 'Medio-picta'], best considered a group name for both male and female clones with lvs. blotched yellow in the center and green margins; **'Aurea Regina'** [cvs. 'Golden King', 'Golden Queen'], lvs. variegated with deep golden-yellow, male; **'Bacciflava'** [cv. 'Fructu Luteo'], fr. yellow; **'Balearica'**, lvs. thick, bright green, margins entire or with few to many spines; **'Bicolor'**: 'Muricata'; **'Calamistrata'**: 'Crispa'; **'Ciliata Major'**, vigorous, sts. purple, lf. margins with spines in 1 plane, female; **'Contorta'**: 'Crispa'; **'Crispa'** [cvs. 'Calamistrata', 'Contorta', 'Marginata', 'Revoluta', 'Tortuosa'], SCREW-LEAVED H., lvs. spirally twisted, margins much-thickened, undulate, mostly entire, male; **'Echinata'**: 'Ferox'; **'Elegantissima'**, sts. green, lvs. with spiny, creamy-white margins; **'Ferox'** [cv. 'Echinata'], HEDGEHOG H., PORCUPINE H., upper lf. surface prickly, margins revolute, male; **'Ferox Argentea'**, SILVER HEDGEHOG H., sts. purple, lvs. with white spines and margins, male; **'Ferox Aurea'**, GOLD HEDGEHOG H., lvs. blotched gold to yellow-green at center, male; **'Fisheri'**, free-growing, sts. green or purple, lvs. very dark green, mostly spiny, male; **'Flavescens'**, MOONLIGHT H., lvs. tinged soft yellow through season, best marked in sunny exposure, female; **'Foxii'**, sts. purple, lvs. bright green, margins spiny, male; **'Fructu Aurantiaca'** [cv. 'Orange Gem'], fr. orange-yellow; **'Fructu Luteo'**: 'Bacciflava'; **'Handsworthensis'**, compact, sts. green or brownish, lvs. small, spiny, male; **'Hastata'**, dwarf, lvs. small, spiny toward the base, male; **'Heterophylla'**, a group name for clones with both spiny and entire lvs. on same plant; **'Ingramii'**, lvs. small, central portion dark green, margins and spines grayish-white, male; **'Integrifolia'**, sts. purple, lvs. ovate, entire, sometimes slightly twisted; **'Latispina'**, free-growing, pyramidal, lvs. dark green, glossy, mostly few-spined; **'Lichtenthalii'**, lvs. bright green, oblong, large, pale beneath and at margins, spiny; **'Lutescens'**, similar to cv. 'Flavescens' and perhaps not distinct; **'Medio-picta'**: 'Aurea Medio-picta'; **'Monstrosa'**, dense, lvs. bright green, very spiny; **'Marginata'**, a name variously applied, may be applied to cv. 'Crispa', clones with yellow- or white-margined lvs., or to clones with lvs. strongly thickened at the margin; **'Muricata'** [cv. 'Bicolor'], sts. green, lvs. with gold margin, female; **'Ovata'**, lvs. ovate, margins slightly undulate with small, sinuate teeth, male; **'Pendula'**, brs. pendulous, lvs. dark green, spiny, female; **'Myrtifolia'**, small, sts. greenish or purplish, lvs. small, ovate-lanceolate, margin entire or spiny, female; **'Platyphylla'**: I. Perado var. platyphylla; **'Pyramidalis'**, similar to cv. 'Heterophylla', sts. and lvs. green, margins variously spined; **'Recurva'**, slow-growing, dense, sts. purplish, lvs. strongly spined, recurved, male; **'Revoluta'**: 'Crispa'; **'Robinsonana'** [cv. 'Robinson'], lvs. deep green, glossy, narrow, viciously spined, male; **'Scotia'**, erect, densely leafy, lvs. deep green, mostly slightly twisted and spineless, with a cuplike depression below the apex; **'Serratifolia'**, similar to 'Myrtifolia' but spines more divaricate, male; **'Smithana'**, dense, sts. purplish, lvs. narrow, spineless; **'Tortuosa'**: 'Crispa'; **'Watererana'**, of the 'Aureo-marginata' group, lvs. with irregular yellow margin, male; **'Whittingtonensis'** [cv. 'Whittington'], sts. purple, lvs. thin, glossy, dark green, spiny, male.

×**aquipernyi** Gable ex W. Clarke: *I. Aquifolium* × *I. Pernyi.* Small evergreen tree, densely branched; lvs. glossy, dark green, spiny-margined, similar to but larger than those of *I. Pernyi.* Zone 7. Cvs. include: **'Brilliant'**, fr. large, bright red; **'Edward Nosal'**; **'San Jose'**.

asprella (Hook. & Arn.) Champ. ex Benth. Deciduous shrub, to 10 ft., brs. slender and elongate, or spurlike and fruiting; lvs. thin, dull olive-green, usually pubescent above, ovate to ovate-elliptic, to 3 in. long, apex acute to mucronate, margins serrate; fls. white, 4–6-merous, solitary or in few-fld. fascicles; fr. on pedicels to 1 in. long or more; black, globose, to ¼ in. in diam., pyrenes 4–6. Se. China, Taiwan, Philippine Is. Zone 10.

×**attenuata** Ashe: *I. Cassine* × *I. opaca.* Loosely branched, evergreen tree, lvs. flat, light green, obovate to oblanceolate, occasionally toothed near apex; fr. on current year's brs., small, clustered, scarlet. Cvs. include: **'Fosteri'** [*I. opaca* var. *Fosteri* Hort.], best considered as the Foster Hybrid Group, including several numbered forms; **'East Palatka'**; **'Hume'**, in several numbered forms; **'Oriole'**; **'Savannah'**; **'Tanager'**; **'Topelii'**.

bioritensis Hayata [*I. Pernyi* var. *Veitchii* Bean ex Rehd.]. Evergreen shrub or small tree, to 30 ft., brs. glabrate or sparsely pubescent; lvs. crowded, thick-leathery, brownish to yellowish-green, glossy, ovate or quadrangular, 1–2½ in. long, apex acuminate, spine-tipped, margins with 3–4 spines on each side; fls. 2–4-merous, the male and

female in fascicles; fr. ellipsoid, to ⅜ in. long, pyrenes usually 2. China, Taiwan. Material offered as *I. Pernyi* var. *Veitchii* may be forms of *I.* ×*aquipernyi.*

Buergeri Miq. Evergreen tree, to 45 ft.; bark smooth, gray, brs. pubescent; lvs. leathery, glossy green, lanceolate to ovate or oblong, 2–3½ in. long, apex usually acuminate, margins irregularly serrate; fls. yellowish-green, in 4–10-fld. fascicles on previous year's brs.; fr. red, globose or subglobose, to ¼ in. in diam., pyrenes 4. Japan, e. China. Zone 7.

Burfordii: a listed name of no botanical standing for *I. cornuta.* cv.

canariensis Poir. Conical, evergreen shrub or small tree, 10–20 ft.; lvs. thin, leathery, oblong-ovate to lanceolate, 1½–2½ in. long, to 1 in. wide, entire; fr. solitary, black, globose to ellipsoid, to ⅜ in. long. Madeira and Canary Is. Zone 8. Probably not in cult., material offered as *I. canariensis* may be *I.* ×*altaclarensis* or *I. Perado.*

Cassine L. [*I. Dahoon* Walt.]. DAHOON, CASSINA, CASSINE, CASSENA, YAUPON. Evergreen, puberulent tree, to about 40 ft.; lvs. flat, leathery, dark green, lanceolate to elliptic, oblanceolate, or obovate, 1–4 in. long, to 1½ in. wide, margins somewhat revolute, entire to sparsely toothed; fls. 4-merous, yellowish-white, the male in compound, axillary cymes, the female solitary or in 3-fld. cymes in the lf. axils; fr. red or sometimes orange or yellow, to 5/16 in. in diam. Var. **Cassine** [*I. Cassine* var. *angustifolia* Ait.]. The typical var.; lvs. narrowly lanceolate to obovate, to 4 in. long; fr. less than ¼ in. in diam. N.C. to Fla. Zone 7b. A bitter tea, cassine, is prepared from the dried lvs. Cvs. include: **'Baldwin'**, **'Bryanii'**, **'Dodd's'**, **'Sebrings'**, **'Willow Leaf'**. Var. **myrtifolia** (Walt.) Sarg. [*I. myrtifolia* Walt.]. Lvs. linear to lanceolate, to 1½ in. long; fr. to 5/16 in. in diam., persisting through the winter. N.C. to Fla. and La. Zone 7b. Cv. **'Lowei'** [*I. myrtifolia* forma *Lowei* S. F. Blake]. Fr. yellow.

centrochinensis S. Y. Hu. Evergreen shrub, to 10 ft., brs. slender, angular, puberulent or nearly glabrous; lvs. leathery, brownish-green, glossy, elliptic-lanceolate to -ovate, 2–3 in. long, apex acuminate, margins with 4–10 spiny teeth on each side; fls. 4-merous, fascicled on previous year's brs., pedicels short; fr. purple-red, globose, about ¼ in. in diam., pyrenes 4. Cent. China. Zone 7. Material offered as *I. centrochinensis* is usually *I. ciliospinosa.*

chinensis Sims [*I. Oldhamii* Miq.; *I. purpurea* Hassk.; *I. purpurea* var. *Oldhamii* (Miq.) Loes.]. KASHI H. Glabrous, evergreen tree, to 40 ft., bark smooth, gray; lvs. drooping, thin, leathery, glossy green, elliptic-lanceolate to ovate, 1½–4 in. long, to 1½ in. wide, margins crenate or sometimes sharply toothed; fls. lavender or red, 4-merous, on current year's brs., the male in 7–15-fld. cymes, the female in 3–7-fld. cymes; fr. scarlet, glossy, ellipsoid, to ⅜ in. long, pyrenes 4–5. Japan, China. Zone 7. Widely cult. and used for decoration at the Chinese New Year; the young shoots are sometimes blanched for salads.

ciliospinosa Loes. Compact, evergreen shrub or small tree, to 20 ft., brs. densely pubescent; lvs. leathery, olive-green, elliptic to ovate-elliptic, 1–2 in. long, margins with 4–6 weak spines on each side; fls. greenish, 4-merous, fascicles on previous year's brs., pedicels short; fr. often in pairs, bright red, ellipsoid, to 5/16 in. long, pyrenes 1–3. W. China. Zone 7. Widely cult. under the name *I. centrochinensis.*

cinerea Champ. Evergreen shrub or small tree, 6–20 ft., brs. puberulent; lvs. subsessile, oblong-lanceolate, 4–6 in. long, to 1½ in. wide, rugose beneath, margins crenate or sharply blackish-toothed; fls. greenish-yellow, 4-merous, the male in few-fld. cymes, the female solitary, both in turn in fascicles on previous year's brs.; fr. red, globose, to ¼ in. in diam., pyrenes 4. Hong Kong. Zone 10.

collina Alexand. Deciduous small tree, 10–12 ft., bark gray, smooth, brs. spreading; lvs. elliptic to obovate, 2–3 in. long, margins finely serrate, teeth slightly appressed, abruptly tipped with large glands, pedicels ⅜–⅝ in. long; fr. ¼ in. in diam., bright red. Sw. Va. to W.Va. Zone 6. Considered by some to be a sp. of *Nemopanthus.*

convexa: a listed name of no botanical standing for *I. crenata* cv.

corallina Franch. Evergreen tree, to 25 ft., brs. slender, smooth, glabrous or sometimes puberulent; lvs. leathery, dark green, glossy, narrowly ovate to ovate-elliptic, 2–5 in. long, to 2 in. wide, margins crenate or undulate with short spiny teeth; fls. few, in fascicles on brs. of previous year, pedicels short; fr. bright red, subglobose, ⅛–3/16 in. in diam., pyrenes 4. W. China. Zone 8.

coriacea (Pursh) Chapm. [*I. lucida* (Ait.) Torr. & A. Gray]. LARGE GALLBERRY, SWEET G., BAY GALL BUSH. Evergreen shrub, to about 15 ft., brs. glabrous or puberulent; lvs. leathery, dark green, glossy, obovate to elliptic, to about 3 in. long, acute, spiny-toothed above the middle; fls. 5–9-merous, white, the male in dense fascicles on spurs, the female fewer; fr. black, glossy, globose or subglobose to ¼ in. long, to ⅜ in. in diam., juicy, ripening early, pyrenes up to 7. Coastal plain, se. Va. to Fla. and Tex. Zone 7.

cornuta Lindl. & Paxt. CHINESE H., HORNED H. Densely branched, evergreen shrub or small tree, brs. smooth, stout; lvs. thick, leathery, dark green, glossy, varying from cordate or oblong-entire to quadrangular and sinuately toothed with 1–3 teeth on each side, mostly about 2 in. long; fls. 4-merous, yellowish, fascicled on brs. of previous year, pedicels to about ⅜ in. long; fr. red, globose, to ⅜ in. in diam., pyrenes 4. E. China. Zone 7. A sampling of cvs. includes: 'Burfordii', vigorous, habit globose, brs. pendent, lvs. dark green, glossy, oblong, entire except for terminal spine, female; 'Burfordii Compacta' and 'Burfordii Nana': 'Dwarf Burford' or 'Rotunda'; 'D'or', lvs. entire, fr. yellow; 'Dwarf Burford' [cvs. 'Burfordii Compacta', 'Burfordii Nana', 'Compacta', in part], dense, compact habit; 'Hume', lvs. large, quadrangular, 5-spined, female; 'National', lvs. spineless except at apex, female; 'Pendula', brs. pendent; 'Rotunda' [cv. 'Compacta', in part], compact, spreading habit, lvs. small, spiny, male; 'Shangri-la', lvs. quadrangular, spiny, dark green, glossy, fr. vermilion, ½–¾ in. in diam.; 'Shiu-ying', slow-growing, compact, small tree, lvs. dark green, glossy, quadrangular, strongly spined, fr. large, in fascicles of 7–8.

crenata Thunb. JAPANESE H., BOX-LEAVED H. Densely branched, compact, evergreen shrub or small tree, to 15 ft., sts. puberulous; lvs. leathery, glabrous, lustrous, deep green above, paler and glandular beneath, elliptic, oblong, or narrowly obovate, to 1¼ in. long, margins crenate to serrate; fls. white, the male in few-fld. fascicles, the female solitary; fr. black, globose, about ¼ in. in diam. Japan. Zone 6b. In Japan much cult. as formally trained specimen plants, as hedge plants, or as bonsai subjects. Var. **paludosa** (Nakai) Hara [*I. radicans* Nakai]. Sts. low, creeping. Swampy, coastal regions, Japan, Sakhalin, Kurile Is. Many cvs. are offered. The principal Latin-named cvs. are listed below; for fancy-named cvs., consult the *Handbook of Hollies*. 'Bullata': 'Convexa'; 'Buxifolia': 'Convexa'; 'Compacta', compact, upright; 'Convexa' [cvs. 'Bullata', 'Buxifolia'], best considered a large group of clones, generally characterized by bullate, convex lvs.; 'Divaricata', spreading; 'Excelsa', upright, lvs. dark green; 'Fortunei': 'Latifolia'; 'Globosa', compact, dwarf; 'Hatfieldii', upright, brs. gray, male; 'Helleri', compact, dwarf, lvs. elliptic, ¼–¾ in. long, female; 'Hetzii', spreading, lvs. bullate, glossy, large; 'Horizontalis', spreading; 'Latifolia' [cv. 'Fortunei'], lvs. oblong to elliptic, ¾–1¼ in. long, to ⅝ in. wide, serrate; 'Longifolia', lvs. lanceolate to oblong-elliptic, to 1¼ in. long, ½ in. wide; 'Luteo-variegata' [cv. 'Variegata'], lvs. mottled yellow; 'Macrophylla', lvs. large; 'Major', lvs. dark green, glossy, obovate, to 1 in. long; 'Mariesii' [cv. 'Nummularia'], dwarf, lvs. crowded at the ends of brs., suborbicular, to ⅜ in. long, obscurely crenate, female; 'Maxwellii' [cv. 'Maxwell'], lvs. oblong to oblong-ovate to 1 in. long, with 5–6 teeth on each side; 'Microphylla', lvs. oblong, ⅜–¾ in. long, ¼ in. wide, margins serrate; 'Nana', dwarf, lvs. elliptic, small; 'Nigra', conical, lvs. large; 'Nummularia': 'Mariesii'; 'Prostrata', low, spreading, lvs. small; 'Pyramidalis', broadly conical, lvs. crowded, glossy, female; 'Repandens', spreading, lvs. closely spaced, thin, flat; 'Rotundifolia', upright, lvs. dark green, glossy, to 1¼ in. long, serrate; 'Stokesii' [cv. 'Stokes'], compact, lvs. small, male; 'Variegata': 'Luteo-variegata'; 'Vaseyi', a selection of 'Latifolia', lvs. loosely arranged, oblong-ovate, to ½ in. long, more or less convex.

cumulicola: *I. opaca* var. *arenicola*.

Dahoon: *I. Cassine*.

decidua Walt. POSSUM HAW. Deciduous shrub or small tree, to 30 ft.; lvs. dull green, thin or moderately thick, lanceolate to elliptic or obovate, to 3 in. long, apex mostly rounded, base cuneate, margins toothed, surface beneath glabrous or with midrib pilose; fls. 5-merous, both male and female solitary or in clusters of up to 3; fr. glossy, red or sometimes yellow, subglobose, ⅛–¼ in. in diam. Var. **decidua**. The typical var.; pedicels in fr. to ⅜ in. long. Ill. to Fla. and Tex. Zone 5. A number of cvs. are offered including: 'Byer's Golden'; 'Fraser's Improved'; 'Oklahoma'; 'Sundance'; 'Warren's Red'. Var. **longipes** (Chapm.) Ahles [*I. longipes* Chapm.]. GEORGIA H. Pedicels in fr. ⅜–1¼ in. long. W.Va. and Tenn. to Tex. and Fla. Zone 6.

Fargesii Franch. Evergreen tree, to 20 ft., bark gray, smooth, brs. green; lvs. thin, leathery, dull green, linear-lanceolate to oblanceolate, 2½–4½ in. long, to ¾ in. wide, toothed toward apex; fls. white, fragrant, fascicled on previous year's brs., pedicels to ³⁄₁₆ in. long; fr. in clusters of 3–4, red, less than ¼ in. in diam., early ripening. Cent. China, Burma. Zone 8.

Fortunei: *I. crenata* cv. 'Latifolia'.

Fosteri: a listed name of no botanical standing for *I. × attenuata* cv.

fragilis Hook.f. Deciduous, glabrous, shrub or small tree, to 30 ft., brs. elongate bearing conspicuous white lenticels; lvs. thin, bright green, ovate or elliptic, 2–5 in. long, to 2½ in. wide, margins with dark-colored, apiculate teeth; fls. 5-merous, fascicled or solitary on spurs or sometimes at basal portion of brs., pedicels short; fr. red, depressed-

globose, ⅛–³⁄₁₆ in. in diam., pyrenes 6 or more. E. Himalayas. Zone 10.

Franchetiana Loes. Evergreen, glabrous shrub or small tree, to 20 ft., brs. stout; lvs. thin, more or less leathery, brownish-green, oblanceolate to broadly elliptic, 2–4½ in. long, to 1½ in. wide, margins finely black-toothed in the upper ⅔, veins prominent beneath; fls. 4-merous, fascicled on previous year's brs., pedicels ¼ in. long; fr. abundant, red, globose, ¼ in. in diam., pyrenes 4. W. China. Zone 8. Perhaps not distinct from *I. Hookeri*.

fujisanensis: *I. pedunculosa*.

geniculata Maxim. FURIN H. Deciduous, glabrous shrub or small tree; lvs. thin, oblong to elliptic or obovate, 1½–4 in. long, to 2 in. wide, sharply serrate with dark-colored teeth, pubescent above and beneath; fls. white, solitary, rarely in 3's, pedicels 1–2 in. long; fr. solitary, red, about ⅛ in. in diam., nodding, pyrenes 5, rarely 6. Japan. Zone 6.

Georgei Comber. Evergreen, compact shrub, to 20 ft.; brs. pubescent; lvs. thick, leathery, glossy green, lanceolate, ovate-lanceolate, or ovate, ¾–1½ in. long, to ½ in. wide, margins thickened, recurved, with 4–7 spines on each side; fls. greenish, 4-merous, in fascicles on previous year's brs.; fr. usually in pairs, red, obovoid-ellipsoid, ³⁄₁₆–¼ in. long, about ¼ in. in diam., pyrenes 1–2. Sw. China and n. Burma. Zone 8.

glabra (L.) A. Gray. GALLBERRY, BITTER G., INKBERRY, WINTERBERRY, APPALACHIAN TEA. Stoloniferous, evergreen shrub, to 10 ft., brs. erect or ascending, pubescent; lvs. flat, leathery, glossy green above, obovate to elliptic, 1–2½ in. long, to ¾ in. wide, sparingly toothed toward apex, often punctate beneath; fls. white, 5–7-merous, the male in 3–7-fld. axillary cymes, the female solitary or in 2–3-fld. cymes; fr. black, rarely white, to ⅜ in. in diam., pyrenes 5–7. Coastal plain, Nov. Sc. to Fla. and Tex. Zone 5. A bee plant. A number of cvs. are offered including: 'Compacta'; 'Improved'; 'Ivory Queen'; 'Leucocarpa', fr. white; 'Nigra', lvs. purple in winter; 'Viridis', lvs. green through winter.

Hanceana Maxim. Compact, boxlike, evergreen shrub, brs. puberulent; lvs. thin, leathery, small, obovate, to 1¼ in. long, entire; fls. 4-merous, few in fascicles on brs. of previous year, pedicels puberulent, very short; fr. mostly in pairs, glossy brownish-red, globose, to ³⁄₁₆ in. in diam., late-ripening, pyrenes 4. Hong Kong. Zone 10.

Hatfieldii: a listed name of no botanical standing for *I. crenata* cv.

Helleri: a listed name of no botanical standing for *I. crenata* cv.

Hookeri King. Glabrous, evergreen tree, to 50 ft., brs. stout, smooth, light gray; lvs. thick, leathery, elliptic or obovate-elliptic, 2–4 in. long, to 1¾ in. wide, margins serrate with apiculate teeth, veins prominent beneath; fls. 4-merous, in fascicles on brs. of previous year, fr. red, globose, about ¼ in. in diam., pyrenes 4. Himalayas. Zone 8.

ilicifolia: a listed name of no botanical standing.

insignis Hook.f. Evergreen shrub or small tree, brs. stout, smooth; lvs. leathery, elliptic-lanceolate, 6–9 in. long, 1½–3 in. wide, obscurely toothed, prominently veined; fls. greenish, fascicled, pedicels very short; fr. to nearly ½ in. in diam., pyrene 1. E. Himalayas. Similar to *I. latifolia*.

integra Thunb. MOCHI TREE. Compactly branched, glabrous, evergreen shrub or small tree, 10–25 ft.; lvs. leathery, dark green, glossy, obovate to elliptic, 1–3 in. long, to 1¼ in. wide, petioles stout; fls. yellow-green, fascicled on previous year's brs.; fr. red, globose, to nearly ½ in. in diam., on pedicels of equal length, pyrenes 4. Japan. Zone 8. A birdlime is produced from the bark. Cvs. include: 'Ellipsoidea', fr. ellipsoid; 'Lanceolata', lvs. lanceolate; 'Oblanceolata', lvs. narrow; 'Xanthocarpa', fr. yellow.

× Koehneana Loes.: reputedly a hybrid between *I. Aquifolium* and *I. latifolia*. Evergreen shrub or small tree, young shoots sometimes flushed purple; lvs. elliptic to oblong-lanceolate, glossy green, margins somewhat undulate, spiny, fr. large, red. Cvs. include: 'Chestnut Leaf', lvs. thick, yellowish-green, strongly spined; 'Chieftain', lvs. light green, flat, male; 'Jade', lvs. very dark green, male; 'Lassie', lvs. flat, female; 'Ruby', lvs. very dark green, margins wavy, female; 'Wirt L. Winn', lvs. dark green, very large, female, tolerant of poorly drained soil.

laevigata (Pursh) A. Gray. SMOOTH WINTERBERRY. Deciduous shrub, to 12 ft.; brs. smooth, glabrous; lvs. thin, leathery, glossy green above, lanceolate-ovate to elliptic or obovate, to 3½ in. long, finely toothed, glabrous or with pubescent veins beneath; fls. white, the male 1–2 on pedicels to ¾ in. long, the female mostly solitary; fr. translucent, scarlet or yellow, to ⁵⁄₁₆ in. in diam.; pyrenes 6–8. S. Me. to Ga. Zone 5. Cv. 'Hervey Robinson'. Fr. yellow.

latifolia Thunb. LUSTER-LEAF H., TARAJO. Glabrous, evergreen tree, to 50 ft., with dense, round head, brs. stout; lvs. thick, leathery, dark green, glossy, oblong-elliptic, 3–7 in. long, to 3 in. wide, sharply serrate with black teeth; fls. yellowish, 4-merous, more or less in panicles in the lf. axils of previous year's brs.; fr. mostly clustered, red, ⁵⁄₁₆ in. in diam., pyrenes 4. E. China, Japan, where often planted in shrine and temple gardens. Zone 7b.

leucoclada (Maxim.) Mak. Small, glabrous, evergreen shrub, with gray brs.; lvs. somewhat leathery, flat, deep green, broadly lanceolate to oblong-ovate, 3–5 in. long, to 1¾ in. wide, entire or remotely toothed; fls. white, few in axillary fascicles of previous year's brs.; fr. red, globose, to ⅜ in. in diam. Japan. Zone 7.

liukiuensis Loes. Small, glabrous, evergreen tree, to 25 ft.; lvs. leathery, obovate to oblong-elliptic, 1½–3 in. long, to 1¼ in. wide, margins recurved, thickened, remotely crenulate, veins prominent and reticulate beneath; fls. fascicled on brs. of previous year; fr. red, globose, about ³⁄₁₆ in. in diam. Ryukyu Is. Zone 7b.

longipes: *I. decidua* var.

lucida: *I. coriacea.*

macrocarpa D. Oliver. Deciduous tree, to 30 ft., with both elongate and spurlike brs.; lvs. often crowded at the ends of the spurs, thin, dull green, glabrous or pubescent, ovate to ovate-elliptic or oblong-elliptic, 2–6 in. long, to nearly 3 in. wide, margins serrate, veins prominently reticulate; fls. 5–6-merous, solitary or few to many in axillary fascicles on current year's brs.; fr. solitary, black, to ⅝ in. in diam., pyrenes 5–9. China. Apparently rare in cult.

macropoda Miq. Deciduous tree, to 40 ft., with both elongate and spurlike, glabrous brs.; lvs. on elongate shoots and crowded on spurlike brs., thin, dull olive-green, ovate to broadly elliptic, 1½–3 in. long, to 2 in. wide, margins serrate; fls. 5–6-merous, solitary or in few-fld. fascicles; fr. red, globose, to about ¼ in. in diam., pyrenes 5. China, Japan. Zone 6. The Asiatic counterpart of the N. Amer. *I. ambigua.* In Japan the wood is used for turnery, utensils, and matches.

maderensis: *I. Perado* var. *Perado,* but plants offered as *I. maderensis* may be *I.* × *altaclarensis* cv. 'Maderensis'.

× **Makinoi** Hara: reputedly a hybrid between *I. leucoclada* and *I. rugosa.* Differing from *I. rugosa* in its larger parts and narrowly oblong, more or less acute lvs., 2–2½ in. long, with less prominent veins. Japan. Zone 7.

memecyllifolia Champ. ex Benth. Evergreen shrub, to about 6 ft., brs. slender, pubescent; lvs. thick, leathery, dull green, ovate-oblong or rarely obovate, to 3 in. long, nearly 1½ in. wide, margins entire; fls. white, fragrant, 4–6-merous, fascicled on previous year's brs.; fr. in clusters, red, globose, to ¼ in. in diam., pyrenes 4–5. Hong Kong. Zone 8.

× **Meserveae** S. Y. Hu.: *I. rugosa* × *I. Aquifolium.* Evergreen shrub, to 7 ft., brs. spreading or erect; lvs. leathery, ovate to elliptic, ¾–2 in. long, margins spiny-toothed; fls. 4-merous, in axillary fascicles; fr. red, globose, to ⁵⁄₁₆ in. in diam. Cvs. include: 'Blue Boy' and 'Blue Girl'.

micrococca Maxim. Glabrous, deciduous tree, to 60 ft., brs. stout, smooth, with conspicuous lenticels; lvs. thin, dull olive-green, oblong to oblong-ovate, 3–5 in. long, to 2 in. wide, apex acuminate, margins subentire to sharply serrate, veins prominent; fls. 5–8-merous, in compound, cymose, axillary fascicles; fr. many in clusters, red, to ⅛ in. in diam., pyrenes 6–8. Japan, e. and s. China, Vietnam, Taiwan. Zone 7.

mitis (Jacq.) Radlk. Tree, to 45 ft., bark smooth, white; lvs. elongate-ovate, acuminate, to 3 in. long, to 1¼ in. wide, petioles to ½ in. long; fr. red, globose, about ¼ in. in diam. Zone 8.

montana: *I. ambigua* var.

monticola: *I. ambigua* var. *montana.*

myrtifolia: *I. Cassine* var.

Nemotoi: *I. serrata,* but material offered as *I. Nemotoi* may be *I. nipponica.*

nipponica Mak. Deciduous shrub or small tree, brs. glabrous; lvs. thick, broadly oblanceolate to obovate, 1½–5 in. long, apex acuminate to rounded, margins with scattered, mucronulate teeth; fls. white, the female in clusters of 3–7 in the lf. axils; fr. red, globose, about ¼ in. in diam. Japan. Zone 6. Material of this sp. may be offered under the name *I. Nemotoi.*

nobilis: a listed name of no botanical standing for *I. insignis.*

nothofagacifolia F. K. Ward. Glabrous, evergreen tree, to 20 ft., brs. covered with longitudinal rows of corky warts; lvs. thin, rather dull olive-green, elliptic to rarely ovate or obovate, to about ½ in. long, sharply serrate with 4–7 teeth on each side; fls. apparently 4-merous, in few-fld. fascicles; fr. usually solitary, depressed-globose, pyrenes 4. S. China, n. Burma, Assam. Usually offered as *I. nothofagifolia.*

Oldhamii: *I. chinensis.*

opaca Ait. AMERICAN H. Conical to columnar, evergreen tree, to 50 ft.; brs. short, spreading; lvs. thick, leathery, flat or keeled, sometimes twisted, dull or glossy green above, oblong to elliptic, 1½–4 in.

long, to 1½ in. wide, margins sinuate, spinose or entire with an apical spine; spines in 1 plane or divaricate; fls. creamy-white, 4-merous, the male in compound, axillary cymes, the female solitary or in 2–3-fld. cymes; fr. scarlet to crimson, globose or ellipsoid, ⁵⁄₁₆–½ in. in diam., persisting through the winter. E. Mass. to Fla., Mo., and Tex. Zone 6. Berried sprays are much used as Christmas decorations and the wood is used for turnery, interior finishing, and cabinetry. Var. **arenicola** (Ashe) Ashe [*I. cumulicola* Small]. DUNE H. Brs. fastigiate, bark pale; lvs. to 1¾ in. long, margins revolute, shallowly sinuate, spinescent, spines pointed forward. Fla. More than 1,000 named cvs. of this sp. are listed in the *International Checklist of Cultivated Ilex,* Part 1, *Ilex opaca,* to which the reader is referred. Unlike *I. Aquifolium* and *I. crenata,* few cvs. are known by Latin names; the currently offered Latin-named cvs. are: 'Brilliantissima', together with 'Pyramidalis', best considered synonyms of the cv. 'George E. Hart', narrowly conical, lvs. dark green, small; 'Femina', a name used to designate female clones; 'Fosteri': *I* × *attenuata* cv.; 'Fructu Luteo', fr. yellow; 'Howardii', apparently equivalent to cv. 'Howard', compact, lvs. dense, glossy green, sparsely spined; 'Humei', a name of the numbered selections of cv. 'Hume', lvs. flat, sparsely spined; 'Mascula', a name used to designate male clones; 'Pyramidalis': see 'Brilliantissima'; 'Rotunda', upright, lvs. smooth, entire, dark glossy green, fr. many; 'Rotundifolia', lvs. suborbicular; 'Subintegra', lvs. with spineless margins; 'Xanthocarpa', fr. yellow.

paraguariensis St.-Hil. MATÉ, YERBA-DE-MATÉ, PARAGUAY TEA, YERBA MATÉ. Evergreen tree, to about 20 ft.; lvs. leathery, flat, dark green, elliptic to obovate, 1–5 in. long, to 2½ in. wide, margins coarsely crenate in the upper ⅔; fls. greenish-white, on current year's brs.; fr. deep red, globose, less than ¼ in. in diam. Paraguay and adjacent Argentina and Brazil, where cult. as a source of an important and widely used tea, maté, prepared from the dry lvs. Zone 10.

pedunculosa Miq. [*I. fujisanensis* Hort. Sakata]. Glabrous, evergreen shrub or small tree, to 15 ft., brs. slender, puberulent; lvs. thin, somewhat leathery, dull green, ovate to oblong-elliptic, 2–3 in. long, to 1¼ in. wide, apex acuminate, margins usually entire, petioles ¾ in. long; fls. 4–5-merous, solitary or in few-fld. fascicles on current year's brs., peduncles 1–2 in. long; fr. pendent, red or sometimes yellow, globose, to ⁵⁄₁₆ in. long, pyrenes 5. China, Japan. Zone 6.

Perado Ait. var. **Perado** [*I. maderensis* Lam.]. MADEIRA H. The typical var.; densely branched, well-foliaged, evergreen tree, to about 30 ft.; lvs. leathery, dark green, glossy, ovate to elliptic-oblong, 3–6 in. long, 2–3 in. wide, margins recurved, entire or toothed with short spines; fls. fascicled on brs. of previous year; fr. dark red, slightly ellipsoid, less than ⁵⁄₁₆ in. in diam. Canary and Madeira Is., Azores. Zone 7. Var. **platyphylla** (Webb & Berth.) Loes. [*I. platyphylla* Webb & Berth.]. CANARY ISLAND H. Evergreen tree, to 40 ft.; lvs. thick, leathery, flat, yellowish-green to dark green, ovate-oblong, 4–6 in. long, 2–4 in. wide, margins entire or with few to many small, spine-tipped teeth. Canary and Madeira Is. Cv. 'Nigrescens': *I.* × *altaclarensis* cv.

Pernyi Franch. Evergreen shrub or small tree, to 24 ft., brs. pubescent; lvs. close together, nearly sessile, leathery, olive-green, ovate to broadly lanceolate, usually about 1 in. long, apex triangular, spined, margins with 1–3 spines on each side; fls. 4-merous, yellowish, male and female in fascicles; fr. red, globose, to ⁵⁄₁₆ in. in diam., pyrenes 4. Cent. China. Zone 6. Var. **Veitchii:** *I. bioritensis.* Cv. 'Compacta' is offered.

platyphylla: *I. Perado* var.

pubescens Hook. & Arn. Hirsute, evergreen shrub or small tree, to 10 ft. or more, brs. more or less quadrangular, somewhat zigzag; lvs. thin, olive-green, elliptic to obovate-elliptic, 1–2 in. long, margins subentire to obscurely but sharply toothed in the upper half; fls. 6–8-merous, pinkish, in fascicles, or the female more or less paniculate; fr. red, globose, to ³⁄₁₆ in. in diam., pyrenes mostly 6 but sometimes 5 or 7. E. China, Taiwan. Zone 10.

purpurea: *I. chinensis.*

radicans: *I. crenata* var. *paludosa.*

rotunda Thunb. KUROGANE H. Glabrous, evergreen tree, to 60 ft. with trunk to 3 ft. in diam.; lvs. leathery, dark green, glossy, on current year's growth only, elliptic or obovate, 1½–3½ in. long, entire; fls. white, 4–7-merous, in mostly 4–6-fld., solitary, axillary, umbellate cymes; fr. red, globose to ellipsoid, to ⁵⁄₁₆ in. long, pyrenes 5–7. Japan, China, Korea, Taiwan, Vietnam. Zone 7. Cvs. include: 'Lord', conical, fr. abundant; 'Romal', spreading, male. Plants offered as *I. rotunda* may be *I. opaca* cvs. 'Rotunda' or 'Rotundifolia'.

rotundifolia: a listed name of no botanical standing for *I. opaca* cvs. 'Rotunda' or 'Rotundifolia'.

rugosa Friedr. Schmidt. TSURU H. Low, spreading or creeping, evergreen shrub with sparse brs.; lvs. crowded, leathery, deep green, glossy, lanceolate to oblong-ovate, to 1½ in. long, margins toothed; fls. white, solitary or few in fascicles on previous year's brs.; fr. red, globose, about ¼ in. in diam. Japan, Sakhalin, s. Kurile Is.

serrata Thunb. [*I. Nemotoi* Mak.]. JAPANESE WINTERBERRY. Much-branched, deciduous, dioecious shrub, 4–10 ft., brs. glabrous or pubescent; lvs. thin, puberulous, oblong to elliptic or obovate, 1½–3 in. long, apex acute to abruptly acuminate, margins sharply toothed; fls. lavender to white, the male in fascicles of up to about 15, the female solitary or in few-fld. fascicles; fr. red, globose, to 3/16 in. in diam. Japan, China. Zone 5. Cv. **'Leucocarpa'** [forma *leucocarpa* Beissn.]. Fr. white. Cv. **'Sieboldii'** [*I. Sieboldii* Miq.; *I. serrata* var. *Sieboldii* (Miq.) Rehd.]. Lvs. hirsute-pubescent. Cv. **'Xanthocarpa'** [forma *xanthocarpa* (Rehd.) Rehd.]. Fr. yellow.

Sieboldii: *I. serrata* cv.

sikkimensis Kurz. Tree, to 30 ft. or more, brs. stout; lvs. thin, leathery, 5–8 in. long, 1–2½ in. wide, margins often doubly toothed; fr. 3/16 in. in diam. Himalayas. Zone 7.

Sugerokii Maxim. Densely branched, evergreen shrub, to 15 ft., brs. brownish, pubescent; lvs. thin, leathery, olive-green, glossy, ovate to ovate-elliptic, to 1½ in. long, apex acute to acuminate, margins toothed in the upper half; fls. white, 4–6-merous, borne on current season's brs., the male in fascicles of up to 7, the female solitary; fr. red, globose, to ¼ in. in diam. Japan, China. Zone 7. Var. **Sugerokii** [subsp. *longipedunculata* (Maxim.) Mak.]. The typical var.; pedicels to 1½ in. long. Var. **brevipedunculata** (Maxim.) S. Y. Hu. Pedicels to ⅝ in. long.

Topelii: a listed name of no botanical standing for *I.* × *attenuata* cv.

triflora Blume. Evergreen shrub or small tree with zigzag, pubescent, often ridged brs.; lvs. somewhat leathery, brownish-olive, oblong-elliptic to ovate, 1–3½ in. long, to 1½ in. wide, minutely serrate, slightly undulate, punctate beneath; fls. solitary or in cymes, these in turn in axillary fascicles; fr. globose or ellipsoid, to 5/16 in. long, pyrenes 4. S. China, Taiwan, se. Asia. Zone 7. Often offered under the spelling *I. trifolia.*

verticillata (L.) A. Gray. WINTERBERRY, COMMON W., BLACK ALDER. Deciduous shrub or sometimes small tree, to 15 ft., brs. glabrous or pubescent; lvs. dull to moderately glossy above, lanceolate to obovate or elliptic, to 4 in. long, 2 in. wide, serrate, cuneate, rugose and glabrous or pubescent beneath; fls. 5–7-merous, sepals ciliate, the male in few to many-fld. cymes, the female solitary or sometimes few in lf. axils; fr. red, rarely yellow, globose, about 5/16 in. in diam. Nfld. to Minn., s. to Tex. and Ga. Zone 4. The most widespread of the N. Amer. hollies, a variable sp. with many intergrading forms. Cvs. include: **'Chrysocarpa'** [forma *chrysocarpa* B. L. Robinson], fr. yellow; **'Polycarpa'**, vigorous, fr. large; **'Xmas Cheer'**, upright, heavy-fruited. Other cvs. are: **'Bright Horizon'**, **'Cacapon'**, **'Christmas Gem'**, **'Fairfax'**, **'Jackson'**, **'Maryland Beauty'**, **'Nana'**, **'Shaver'**.

vomitoria Ait. YAUPON, CASSINA, CASSENA, CASSINE. Stiffly branched, evergreen shrub or small tree, to 24 ft., brs. pubescent; lvs. leathery, glossy above, ovate to oblong or elliptic, to 1½ in. long, toothed; fls. white, 4-merous, the male in fascicles, the female solitary or in 2–3-fld., sessile cymes; fr. red or sometimes yellow, lustrous, globose, to ¼ in. in diam., pyrenes 4. Se. Va. to Fla. and Tex. Zone 7b. A bitter tea, cassine or black drink, may be prepared from the dried lvs. Cvs. include: **'Aurea'**; **'Dewerth'**; **'Folsom Weeping'**; **'Grey's Littleleaf'**; **'Huber's Compact'**; **'Jewel'**; **'Nana'**; **'Otis Miley'**, lvs. small, fr. yellow; **'Pendula'** [forma *pendula* Foret & Solym.], brs. pendulous; **'Pride of Houston'**; **'Pyramidalis'**; **'Schellings Dwarf'**; **'Stokes Dwarf'**; **'Tricolor'**; **'Wiggins Yellow'**; **'Yawkeyii'**.

Wilsonii Loes. Evergreen, glabrous tree, to about 30 ft.; lvs. leathery, brownish-olive, glossy above, ovate to obovate-oblong, to about 2½ in. long; apex caudate, margins entire; fls. 4-merous, the male in fascicles of 3–5-fld. cymes, the female in fascicles of single-fld. peduncles; fr. red, globose, about 3/16 in. in diam., pyrenes 4. China, Taiwan. Zone 7b.

yunnanensis Franch. Evergreen shrub or small tree, 12–36 ft., brs. reddish-villous; lvs. closely spaced, leathery, brownish, glossy above, villous when young, ovate to ovate-lanceolate, to 1½ in. long, apex acute to mucronate, margins toothed with often aristate teeth; fls. white, sometimes pinkish or reddish, 4-merous, the male in few, 1–3-fld. cymes, the female mostly solitary; fr. red, globose, to ¼ in. in diam., pyrenes 4. China, n. Burma, Taiwan. Zone 6.

ILIAMNA Greene. *Malvaceae.* Seven spp. of per. herbs or subshrubs in N. Amer.; lvs. simple, palmately lobed; fls. axillary, sometimes solitary, but usually in clusters forming interrupted spikes or racemes, involucral bracts 3, persistent, petals 5, white, pink, or rosy-mauve, stamens united in a tubular staminal column, the column hirsute-pubescent, style brs. as many as the mericarps, terminated by obliquely truncate to more or less discoid stigmas; fr. a schizocarp, mericarps 10–15 in a single whorl, each 2–4-seeded, nearly completely dehiscent loculicidally, densely hirsute with erect, simple hairs on the back and apex.

Propagated by seeds or division.

acerifolia: *I. rivularis.*

remota Greene [*Sphaeralcea remota* (Greene) Fern.]. Per. herb, sts. 3–6 ft., many, erect, densely pubescent; lvs. cordate-orbicular, 2–8 in. long, deeply 3-, 5-, or 7-parted, segms. triangular, deeply serrate; involucral bracts linear-lanceolate, to ⅜ in. long, calyx to about ½ in. long, petals pale rose-mauve, broadly obcordate, to 1 in. long; mericarps about ⅜ in. long, seeds with long simple hairs. Early summer. Ill. Zone 5.

rivularis (Dougl.) Greene [*I. acerifolia* (Nutt. ex Torr. & A. Gray) Greene; *Sphaeralcea acerifolia* Nutt. ex Torr. & A. Gray; *S. rivularis* (Dougl.) Torr.]. Similar to *I. remota,* but smaller, sts. and lvs. glabrous or glabrate; calyx usually only about ¼ in. long; seeds closely puberulent with short, golden-brown hairs. Early–late summer. B.C., s. to n. Calif. and Ariz. Zone 6.

ILLECEBRACEAE: *CARYOPHYLLACEAE.*

ILLICIACEAE A. C. Sm. ILLICIUM FAMILY. Dicot.; 1 genus of evergreen, often aromatic woody plants, native to Asia and Amer.; lvs. mostly alt., thick, leathery, sometimes clustered or seemingly whorled, petioled and without stipules; fls. axillary, bisexual, perianth segms. many, in several series, stamens many, with short filaments and basifixed anthers, carpels many, separate in a circle, with superior, 1-celled ovary; fr. of many, separate, 1-seeded follicles. Related to *Magnoliaceae.* Some spp. of *Illicium* are cult. as ornamentals, and one for an important, commercial oil.

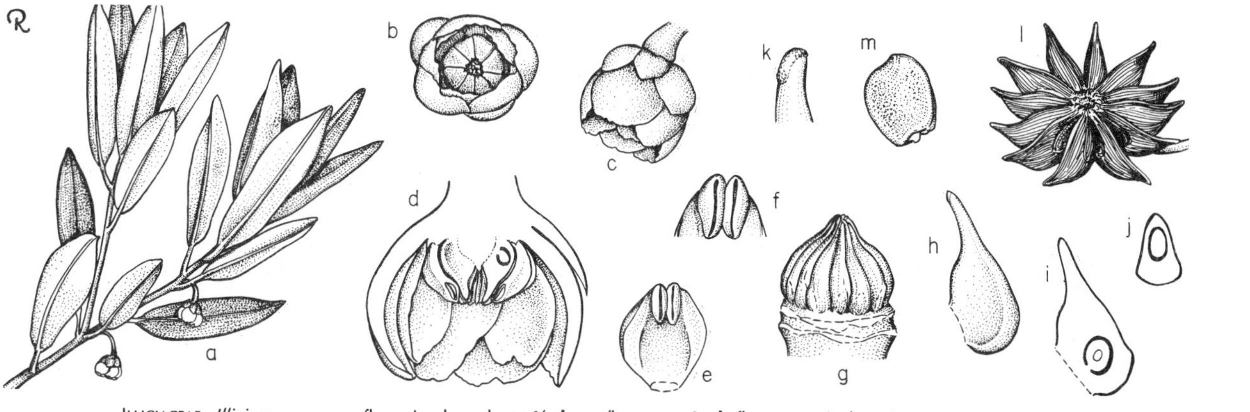

ILLICIACEAE. *Illicium verum:* **a,** flowering branch, × ½; **b, c,** flower, × 2; **d,** flower, vertical section, × 4; **e,** stamen, × 5; **f,** anther, × 8; **g,** carpels, × 5; **h,** single carpel, × 8; **i,** carpel, vertical section, × 8; **j,** carpel, cross section, × 8; **k,** stigma, × 12; **l,** fruit, × 1½; **m,** seed, × 3.

ILLICIUM L. ANISE TREE. *Illiciaceae* (previously included in *Magnoliaceae*). Forty-two spp. of glabrous, evergreen shrubs or small trees, native to Asia and Amer., with characters of the family; lvs. entire; fls. solitary or 2–3 together, rarely in clusters on trunks or old brs.

Grown as ornamentals in warm regions; may be propagated by seeds, but usually by cuttings of half-ripened wood.

anisatum L. [*I. religiosum* Siebold & Zucc.]. CHINESE ANISE, JAPANESE A. T. To 25 ft.; lvs. obovate to elliptic, to 4 in. long, with anise aroma when crushed; peduncles bracted; fls. white to yellow, fragrant, perianth segms. 17–24, spreading, to 7⁄8 in. long, stamens 17–25. Japan and s. Korea. Zone 8. Cut brs. are common Buddhist grave decorations in temple grounds in Japan.

floridanum Ellis. PURPLE ANISE. To 10 ft.; lvs. elliptic-lanceolate to ovate, to 6 in. long; peduncles to 2 in. long; fls. red-purple, to 2 in. across, nodding, petals 21–33, very narrow, stamens 30–38. Fla. to La. Zone 9.

religiosum: *I. anisatum*.

verum Hook.f. STAR ANISE. Slow-growing tree, to 60 ft.; lvs. usually obovate- to oblong-elliptic, to 6 in. long; peduncles short, nearly or quite bractless; fls. globose, perianth segms. 7–12, to 3⁄8 in. long, the largest often as broad as long, not spreading, at first whitish but changing to pink and then to purple, stamens 11–20. Se. China and ne. Vietnam. The unripe fr. is the source of a culinary spice and a distilled oil used in medicine and in industry for flavoring.

IMANTOPHYLLUM: *CLIVIA*.

IMITARIA N. E. Br. *Aizoaceae*. One sp., a clump-forming, succulent, per. herb, native to S. Afr.; lvs. united to form an obconical body (growth) divided equally at apex by a transverse fissure, apex with transparent areas (windows); fls. solitary, from fissure, calyx 6-lobed, petals in several series, united basally into a tube, staminodes many, stamens many, arising from the corolla tube, ovary inferior, 6-celled, style 1; fr. a 6-valved caps., with cell lids, expanding keels with membranous wings, placental tubercles lacking.

Culture as for *Gibbaeum*. See also *Succulents*.

Muirii N. E. Br. [*Gibbaeum Nebrownii* Tisch.]. Growths nearly spherical, often 2–8 in a clump; lvs. soft, fleshy, minutely hairy, gray-green or brownish, light green in cult., to 5⁄8 in. high, 7⁄8 in. wide, 5⁄8 in. thick, apex with window of transparent tissue; fls. 3⁄4 in. across, petals pink. Cape Prov.

IMPATIENS L. BALSAM, JEWELWEED, SNAPWEED, TOUCH-ME-NOT. *Balsaminaceae*. About 500 spp. of ann. or per. herbs or subshrubs, widely distributed, particularly in the tropics and subtropics of Asia and Afr.; sts. mostly succulent; lvs. simple, alt. or opp. or whorled, generally without stipules; fls. solitary or variously clustered, sepals 3, rarely 5, the upper 2 small and generally green, the lowest one petaloid, asymmetrically funnelform, usually with a long nectariferous spur, petals 5, the uppermost one (the standard) flat or helmet-shaped, the 4 lower ones usually united in lateral pairs (the wings), stamens 5, united in a short tube toward the top, ovary superior, 5-celled; fr. a 5-valved caps., explosively dehiscent into 5 coiled valves.

Tender plants grown in the flower garden or under glass for the showy flowers. The common garden balsam, *I. Balsamina*, requires fertile, sandy soil. Seeds should be sown in Apr., and the plants set out when danger of frost is past. The greenhouse species may be increased by seeds or cuttings and may be grown in the open if treated like tender annuals.

Balfourii Hook.f. Glabrous, per. herb, 2–3 ft.; lvs. alt., 3–5 in. long, lanceolate-ovate, long-acuminate, serrate; fls. clustered in loose, terminal racemes, lowest sepal or lip about 1¼ in. long, with spur incurved and thickened at the tip, standard orbicular, reflexed, white suffused with rose, wings 1¼ in. long, with a yellowish lower lobe and a larger, bright rose upper lobe; caps. erect, linear, to 1½ in. long. W. Himalayas.

Balsamina L. GARDEN B., ROSE B. Glabrate or pubescent, branching ann., to 2½ ft.; lvs. alt., to 6 in. long, narrowly to broadly lanceolate, acuminate, deeply serrate; fls. axillary, short-pedicelled, overtopped by leafy shoots, 1–2 in. across, white to yellow or dark red, often spotted, spur of variable length, incurved; caps. asymmetrically elliptic, hairy, ½–¾ in. long. India, China, and Malay Pen. Many forms, chiefly double-fld., are offered.

biflora: *I. capensis*.

capensis Meerb., not Thunb. [*I. biflora* Walt.]. JEWELWEED, SPOTTED T., LADY'S-EARRINGS. Glabrous ann., to 5 ft.; lvs. ovate to elliptic, to about 3½ in. long, coarsely toothed; fls. drooping on slender pedicels, in few-fld. axillary racemes, commonly orange-yellow, spotted with reddish-brown, but various color forms occur, spur to 1 in. long, strongly incurved. Moist places, Nfld. to Sask., s. to Ala. and Okla. *I. capensis* Thunb. is a synonym of *I. Duthieae*.

celebensis: a listed name of no botanical standing.

Duthieae L. Bolus [*I. capensis* Thunb., not Meerb.]. Per. herb, to about 2 ft., erect or straggling, usually glabrous; lvs. alt., lanceolate-ovate to elliptic, to 4 in. long, acuminate, cuneate, crenulate-denticulate; fls. axillary, solitary or in few-fld. clusters, pale pink, with two spots at base of lower sepal, spur slender, about 1 in. long, slightly incurved, petals about 5⁄16 in. long; caps. spindle-shaped, less than ½ in. long. Angola to Malaivi (Nyasaland), s. to the Transvaal.

glandulifera Royle [*I. Roylei* Walp.]. Coarse garden ann., to 6(–10) ft.; lower lvs. opp., upper lvs. mostly in whorls of 3, all ovate to ovate-lanceolate, 2–6 in. long, sharply serrate; fls. in 3- or more-fld. axillary racemes, about 1¼ in. long, deep purple to bluish or white, spur very short. Himalayas; naturalized in ne. U.S.

Hawkeri Bull. Herb, to 2 ft., sts. stout, spreading, dull red; lower lvs. opp., upper lvs. in whorls of 3, all ovate-oblong, 4–6 in. long, sharply serrate; fls. on long, slender pedicels, solitary or in axillary corymbs, 2¼–3 in. across, bright- to brownish-red, but with claws white with bluish markings, spur nearly 3 in. long. New Guinea.

Holstii: *I. Wallerana*. Var. **Liegnitzia**: *I. Wallerana* cv.

kilimanjari D. Oliver. Sprawling, glabrous herb; lvs. alt., broadly ovate, mostly less than 1 in. long, acute, crenate; fls. axillary, on pedicels generally longer than lvs., about 1 in. long, scarlet, lower sepal strongly dilated, spur short, yellowish, green-tipped. Mt. Kilimanjaro, Tanzania.

linearifolia Warb. Small, glabrous herb; lvs. whorled, linear, of different sizes at the same node, to 3 in. long, remotely serrate; fls. axillary, solitary, about 1 in. across, purple-red, spur slender, up to 1½ in. long. New Guinea.

Marianae Rchb.f. ex Hook.f. Stout-stemmed ann.; lvs. cuneate-oblong, 2–4 in. long, acute, deep green, paler between the veins; fls. in axillary cymes, light purple, standard with a projection below the tip, spur long, slender, hooked. Assam.

niamniamensis Gilg. Herb, glabrous in lower part, yellowish-pubescent above; lvs. alt., congested, oblong-ovate, to 7 in. long, subacuminate, decurrent on the petiole; fls. 1–2 in the axils, on pedicels to 2 in. long, lower sepal pendulous, purple or purple-red, about ¾–1 in. long, spur about ½ as long, strongly upturned, standard whitish to greenish-yellow, about ½ in. high. E. Trop. Afr.

Noli-tangere L. TOUCH-ME-NOT. Erect, glabrous ann., to about 1½ ft.; lvs. alt., ovate-oblong, 2–5 in. long, coarsely and remotely toothed; fls. in few-fld. axillary cymes, bright yellow with red-brown spots, about 1½ in. long, including the spur. Summer, late summer. Gr. Brit. and Eur.

Oliveri C. H. Wright ex W. Wats. Glabrous, erect, shrubby per., 4–8(–10) ft., sts. pale green; lvs. in whorls of 4–8, oblanceolate, to 8 in. long, acute or acuminate, ciliate-toothed; fls. axillary, solitary, up to 2½ in. across, on pedicels to 3 in. long, pale lilac or rose, almost white on exterior, spur to 1¾ in. long, curved downward. E. Trop. Afr.

oppositifolia L. Erect, diffusely branched, floriferous ann.; lvs. opp., the upper linear-lanceolate, the lower broader, all remotely serrate; fls. axillary, solitary, on glabrous pedicels shorter than lvs., about 1 in. across, rose-red, purplish, or pink, lower sepal conical, spur short and straight; caps. glabrous, ellipsoid. India and Ceylon.

pallida Nutt. JEWELWEED, PALE T., PALE S. Similar to *I. capensis*, but sts. more glaucous, fls. canary-yellow, unspotted or sparingly reddish-brown-spotted, lower sepal broader than long, spur short and bent at right angles. Summer to late summer. Nfld. to Sask., s. to Ga. and Kans.

platypetala Lindl. Ann. or per., 1½ ft. or more, sts. stout, succulent, branched, usually reddish-purple; lvs. in whorls, lanceolate to ovate, acute or acuminate, hairy underneath; fls. axillary, on pedicels shorter than lvs., 1½ in. or more across, purple, rose, pink, or white, spur long, slender, sickle-shaped. Java. Cv. **'Tangerine'**: subsp. *aurantiaca*. Subsp. **aurantiaca** (Teysm. ex Koord.) Steenis [cvs. 'Aurantiaca' and 'Tangerine']. Fls. salmon-orange, with deep crimson eye. Celebes.

repens Moon. Straggling, procumbent ann. or per., rooting at nodes; lvs. small, broadly cordate-ovate to subreniform, acute, obscurely serrate, glabrous; fls. solitary, on axillary pedicels much longer than lvs., about 1½ in. long, yellow, hairy on exterior, spur very broad, clavate, straight. India and Ceylon.

Roylei: *I. glandulifera.*

Sultanii: *I. Wallerana.*

Wallerana Hook.f. [*I. Holstii* Engl. & Warb.; *I. Sultanii* Hook.f.]. ZANZIBAR B., BUSY LIZZY, PATIENT LUCY, PATIENCE PLANT, SULTANA. Succulent per. herb, less than 3 ft., the brs. usually forming a flat top; lvs. alt. or the upper sometimes opp., lanceolate-ovate to elliptic-oblong, mostly 1½–4 in. long, acute to cuspidate, crenate-denticulate, mostly cuneate and decurrent on petiole, green or reddish-green on both surfaces; fls. solitary or in axillary or terminal racemes, 1–2 in. across, carmine, pink, reddish-orange, purple, white, or variegated, lower sepal to 2 in. long, with a slightly curved spur; caps. oblique-fusiform, ¾ in. long, glabrous. Tanzania to Mozambique. Many races and cvs. are offered. Cvs. **'Liegnitzia'** [*I. Holstii* var. *Liegnitzia* Grign.], and **'Nana'** are of low, compact form. Cv. **'Variegata'**. Lvs. white-margined.

IMPERATA Cyr. *Gramineae.* Not cult. **I. saccharifera:** a name of no botanical standing used for *Miscanthus sacchariflorus.*

INCARVILLEA Juss. [*Amphicome* Royle]. *Bignoniaceae.* Fourteen spp. of ann. or per., caulescent or acaulescent herbs with woody or tuberous roots, native to Asia; lvs. basal or alt., rarely opp., pinnate or pinnatifid; fls. red, rose, pink, white, yellow, or purple, solitary or in terminal racemes or panicles, calyx 5-toothed or 5-lobed, corolla funnelform, stamens 4, inserted on petals, in 2 series of unequal length; fr. a caps., often winged, seeds winged, or with a tuft of hairs at each end.

Propagated by seeds or division; grown in rock gardens and greenhouses.

brevipes: *I. Mairei* var. *Mairei.*

compacta Maxim. Acaulescent per. herb; lvs. pinnate, to 8 in. long, lateral lfts. in 4–9 pairs, ovate, to 1½ in. long, entire, terminal lft. elliptic to orbicular, to 1½ in. long; fls. in racemes to about 1 ft. long, purple, 2½ in. long, 1½ in. across. China, Tibet.

Delavayi Bur. & Franch. Acaulescent per. herb; lvs. pinnate, to 10 in. long, lateral lfts. in 6–11 pairs, lanceolate to narrow-ovate, to 2 in. long, crenate or cut, terminal lft. elliptic or obovate, to 1⅜ in. long; fls. in racemes to 2 ft. or longer in fr., to 3 in. long and wide, corolla with purple lobes and yellow and purple tube. China.

emodi (Lindl.) Chatterj. [*Amphicome emodi* Lindl.]. Caulescent per. herb, to 3 ft.; lvs. pinnate, to 10 in. long, lateral lfts. in 4–5 pairs, ovate, to 1½ in. long, dentate or cut, terminal lft. ovate, sometimes united with upper lfts.; fls. to 2½ in. long, corolla purple with orange throat. Afghanistan, w. Pakistan, India, Nepal.

Farreri: *I. sinensis* subsp. *variabilis* forma *Przewalskii.*

grandiflora: *I. Mairei* var.

Mairei (Lév.) Grierson. Acaulescent per. herb; lvs. pinnate, usually to about 6½ in. long, lateral lfts. to 4 pairs, ovate or oblong, to 1½ in. long, crenate or serrulate, terminal lft. ovate or oblong, usually to 2½ in. long, crenate or serrulate, veiny; fls. to about 4 in. across, corolla crimson, tube yellow, white, or gray inside, peduncles to 10 in. long, or longer in fr. China. Var. **Mairei** [*I. brevipes* Hort.; *I. grandiflora* var. *brevipes* T. Sprague]. The typical var.; lfts. mostly in 2–4 pairs, peduncles branching above the middle. Var. **grandiflora** (Wehrh.) Grierson [*I. grandiflora* Bur. & Franch.]. Lfts. mostly in 2 pairs, peduncles branching at or below the middle.

Olgae Regel. Caulescent per. herb, to 3 ft.; lvs. opp., pinnate, to 6 in. long, lateral lfts. in 3–4 pairs, narrowly elliptic, to 2¼ in. long, entire or with 1–3 teeth, terminal lft. elliptic, to 2 in. long, separate or united with upper lfts.; fls. in panicles, rose, to 1½ in. long, 1 in. across. Cent. Asia.

sinensis Lam. Caulescent ann. or per. herb, to 2 ft. or more; lvs. opp. in lower part., alt. in upper part of plant, usually 2-pinnately parted, to about 5 in. long; fls. red or reddish-purple to rose, to 1 in. across, in racemes. Subsp. **sinensis.** The typical subsp.; ann. herb; calyx teeth ³⁄₁₆–⅜ in. long, corolla red or reddish-purple. China. Subsp. **variabilis** (Batal.) Grierson [*I. variabilis* Batal.]. Per. herb; calyx teeth to ¼ in., corolla rose to rose-pink. China, Manchuria, Siberia. Forma **Przewalskii** (Batal.) Grierson [*I. Farreri* Hort.; *I. variabilis* var. *Farreri* W. W. Sm.]. Fls. yellow.

variabilis: *I. sinensis* subsp.; var. **Farreri:** *I. sinensis* subsp. *variabilis* forma *Przewalskii.*

Younghusbandii T. Sprague. Acaulescent per. herb; lvs. pinnate, to 1 in. long, lfts. crisped-crenate, bullate above, lateral lfts. in 3–7 pairs, ovate or oblong, to ⅜ in. long, terminal lft. ovate to orbicular, to about ⅝ in. long; fls. solitary, on peduncles to 1¾ in. long, corolla purplish-pink with white lines in throat, 1½ in. across. Tibet, Nepal.

INDIGOFERA L. INDIGO. *Leguminosae* (subfamily *Faboideae*). Perhaps 700–800 spp. of shrubs and per. herbs of warmer parts of the world, pubescence of hairs attached at the middle; lvs. odd-pinnate, sometimes with only 1 lft.; fls. in axillary racemes, papilionaceous, usually red or purple, stamens 10, 9 united and 1 separate; fr. a legume, cylindrical to 3–4-sided or compressed.

Grown as ornamentals in borders and shrubberies, and some species formerly as a source of indigo and now escaped. Most species are not hardy in the North. Propagated by seeds and cuttings.

amblyantha Craib. Shrub, to 6 ft.; lfts. in 3–5 pairs, to 1½ in. long; fls. pink, ¼ in. long, in racemes shorter than lvs. China. Hardy north.

australis Willd. Shrub, to 4 ft., variable; lfts. blunt, in 4–8 pairs, ovate to nearly linear, to ¾ in. long; fls. showy, red, about ¼ in. long, in racemes about as long as lvs.; fr. cylindrical, to 1½ in. long. Australia.

cylindrica DC. Similar to *I. frutescens,* but much more slender and only half-woody; fls. smaller, to ¼ in. long, in dense, many-fld. racemes. S. Afr.

decora: *I. incarnata.*

Dosua Buch.-Ham. ex D. Don. Low shrub; lfts. in 10–15 pairs, to ½ in. long; fls. red, to ½ in. long, in racemes about as long as lvs. India. Plants cult. under this name may be *I. Gerardiana.*

frutescens L.f. Shrubby, robust; lfts. obovate, in 2–4 distant pairs, glaucous, to ¾ in. long; racemes erect, loose, about as long as lvs.; calyx almost truncate, very spreading; fr. nearly cylindrical, corrugated, glabrous. S. Afr.

Gerardiana R. C. Grah. Shrub, to 6 ft., much-branched; lfts. in 6–10 pairs, to ½ in. long, pale green, glaucous beneath; fls. rosy-purple, ½ in. long, in racemes about as long as lvs. India.

hebepetala Benth. ex Bak. Tall shrub; lvs. to 6 in. long, lfts. in 3–5 pairs, ovate-oblong, to 1½ in. long, obtuse; fls. pale pink to deep red, to ⅜ in. long, in loose, tapering racemes 2–4 in. long. Himalayas.

hirsuta L. Ann., to 2 ft., sometimes decumbent, brs., petioles, infl., and calyces clothed with spreading hairs; lfts. obovate to oblong, to 1 in. long, appressed-pubescent; racemes dense, to 4 in. long; petals scarcely exceeding sepals; fr. 4-angled, ½ in. long, hirsute. E. Australia.

incarnata (Willd.) Nakai [*I. decora* Lindl.]. To 2 ft.; lfts. in 3–6 pairs, elliptic, to 2½ in. long; racemes to 8 in. long, longer than lvs.; fls. rosy with paler standard, to ¾ in. long. Japan, China.

Kirilowii Maxim. ex Palib. Shrub, to 4 ft.; lfts. in 3–5 pairs, to 1½ in. long; fls. bright rose, ¾ in. long, in racemes longer than lvs. N. China, Korea. Hardy north.

Potaninii Craib. Shrub, to 5 ft.; lfts. in 2–4 pairs, to 1½ in. long; fls. lilac-pink, ⁵⁄₁₆ in. long, in racemes longer than lvs. China. Hardy north.

pseudotinctoria Matsum. Shrub, to 3 ft.; lfts. in 4–5 pairs, to about ¾ in. long, blunt; fls. red, in racemes longer than lvs. Asia.

INDOOR-LIGHT GARDENING: see *House Plants* and *Photoperiod.*

INGA Mill. *Leguminosae* (subfamily *Mimosoideae*). About 250 spp. or more of trop., unarmed trees or shrubs, native to the New World; lvs. alt., even-pinnate, with few large lfts.; fls. in heads or spikes, regular, 5-merous, mostly white, stamens many, long-exserted, united basally; fr. a flat to nearly cylindrical, linear legume, seeds often embedded in white, edible pulp.

Native in tropical Amer., where some of the species are planted for shade in coffee plantations and as windbreaks; the fleshy pulp around the seeds is edible. Some species may be planted as ornamentals in Zone 10, especially in Fla.

affinis DC. Tree, to 30 ft.; brs., petioles, and infl. rusty-pubescent; lf. rachis winged between lfts., lfts. in 4–6 pairs, lanceolate to elliptic, 3–6 in. long, pubescent beneath; peduncles axillary, solitary or paired, spikes to 2 in. long; stamens 2 in. long; fr. to 6 in. long, velvety, margins very dilated. Brazil, Argentina, Bolivia. Doubtfully in cult. in U.S.

dulcis: *Pithecellobium dulce.*

guadalupensis: *Pithecellobium guadalupense.*

pulcherrima: *Calliandra Tweedii.*

INSECTIVOROUS PLANTS: see *Carnivorous Plants.*

INULA L. *Compositae* (Inula Tribe). Over 100 spp. of ann. or per. herbs, native to temp. and subtrop. regions of the Old

World, sts. often glandular or hairy; lvs. basal or alt.; fl. heads radiate or discoid, solitary or in racemes, corymbs, or panicles, involucre hemispherical or campanulate, involucral bracts imbricate in several rows, the outer often herbaceous, the inner usually narrow and scarious, receptacle flat or convex, naked; disc fls. tubular, bisexual, yellow, anthers sagittate-tailed, ray fls. female, yellow or orange-yellow; achenes nearly cylindrical to 4–5-ribbed or -angled, pappus of 1 row of few to many capillary bristles.

The species grow well in the average garden soil but require a sunny location. Propagated by division and by seeds. Useful in the border, and mostly hardy north.

acaulis Schott & Kotschy ex Boiss. Stemless per., to about 4 in.; lvs. all basal, oblong-spatulate, to 1½ in. long, entire, ciliate-pectinate; heads to 2 in. across, solitary; fls. yellow. Asia Minor.

ensifolia L. Erect, clump-forming per., to 2 ft., sts. nearly glabrous; lvs. linear to linear-lanceolate, to 4 in. long, glabrous, sessile; heads to 1½ in. across, solitary; fls. yellow. Eur.

glandulosa: *I. orientalis.*

grandiflora Willd. Hairy per., to 2 ft.; lvs. oblong to elliptic-lanceolate, to 4 in. long, glandular-serrate and fringed with long hairs, sessile; heads to 5 in. across, solitary; fls. orange-yellow. Caucasus to w. Himalayas.

Helenium L. ELECAMPANE. Robust per., to 6 ft., sts. furrowed, with spreading hairs; lvs. irregularly toothed, nearly glabrous above, velvety-tomentose beneath, basal lvs. elliptic, to 16 in. long on petioles to 1 ft. long, st. lvs. ovate-cordate, successively reduced upward, sessile, clasping; heads to 3⅛ in. across, solitary or 2–3 in a cluster; fls. yellow. Probably native to cent. Asia; naturalized in Eur., W. Asia, Japan, N. Amer. The root is used medicinally.

hirta L. Per., to 1½ ft.; lvs. lanceolate or ovate-oblong, to about 3 in. long, reticulate, nearly entire; heads to 2¾ in. across, solitary; fls. yellow. Eur., w. Asia.

magnifica Lipskii. Robust per., to 6 ft.; lower lvs. elliptic-ovate to ovate, to 12 in. long, on long petioles, upper lvs. reduced, glabrous above, hairy beneath, sessile; heads to 6 in. across, in corymbs; disc corollas yellow with orange tips, ray fls. golden-yellow. Caucasus.

montana L. Per., to 14 in.; basal lvs. lanceolate or oblanceolate, to 3½ in. long, narrowed to petiole, upper lvs. reduced, all hairy, entire or slightly toothed; heads to 2 in. across, solitary; fls. yellow. N. Afr. and Spain to Switzerland and Italy.

Oculus-Christi L. Downy per., to 2 ft., sts. simple or corymbosely branched above; basal lvs. elliptic to oblanceolate, to 8 in. long, entire, petioled, st. lvs. elliptic, oblong, or lanceolate, to 3 in. long, entire to slightly toothed, sessile, cordate-amplexicaul; heads to 2 in. across; fls. bright golden-yellow. E. Eur.

orientalis Lam. [*I. glandulosa* Willd.]. CAUCASIAN I. Hairy per., to 2 ft.; basal lvs. petioled, st. lvs. sessile, oblong, to 6 in. long, nearly cordate, semiclasping, entire or with marginal glands; heads to 2¾ in. across, solitary; fls. orange-yellow. Caucasus.

rhizocephala Schrenk. Stemless bien. or per., forming a clump 2–14 in. across; lvs. in a basal rosette, oblong, to 3 in. long, ciliate; heads congested, to 1¼ in. across. Afghanistan, Iran.

Royleana DC. Stout per. herb, to 3 ft.; basal lvs. ovate to oblong, tomentose beneath, on winged petioles, st. lvs. ovate, serrate, auriculate at base; heads to 4 in. across, solitary; fl. buds black, fls. orange-yellow. Himalayas.

salicina L. Stiffly erect per., to 1½ ft., sts. simple or corymbosely branched above, brittle, very leafy; lower lvs. oblanceolate, to 2¾ in. long, st. lvs. sessile, elliptic, cordate basally, semiclasping, all glabrous or hairy beneath, entire to remotely serrate, ciliate; heads to 1¼ in. across, solitary or in clusters of 2–5; fls. golden-yellow. Eur., w. Asia.

thapsoides (Willd.) DC. Silky-tomentose per., to 2½ ft., sts. corymbosely branched; lower lvs. oblong, to 9 in. long, short-petioled, upper lvs. sessile, decurrent, entire or serrulate; heads to ⅝ in. across, in congested corymbs, involucre cylindrical; fls. orange-yellow. Caucasus, n. Iran.

viscosa (L.) Ait. Erect, aromatic per., to 3 ft., sts. woody in lower part, glandular-viscid; lvs. lanceolate, to 3 in. long, glandular, entire to remotely toothed, st. lvs. sessile, semiclasping; heads about ⅝ in. across, in long racemes; fls. yellow. Medit. region.

IOCHROMA Benth. *Solanaceae.* About 20 spp. of shrubs or small trees of trop. S. Amer.; lvs. alt., entire, often large; fls. in pairs or clusters, calyx tubular to campanulate, 5-toothed, corolla purple, blue, white, yellow, or scarlet, long-tubular or narrow-trumpet-shaped, 5-lobed, the throat more or less closed by appendages or folds, stamens 5, borne on the corolla; fr. a pulpy, globose or ovoid berry, enclosed by the enlarged calyx.

Grown as ornamentals in warm regions or under glass. Propagated by cuttings in late winter or by seeds when available.

cyaneum (Lindl.) M. L. Green [*I. lanceolatum* (Miers) Miers; *I. tubulosum* Benth.]. Shrub, to 10 ft., pubescent; lvs. ovate-lanceolate, 3–8 in. long, acute to acuminate; fls. in supra-axillary or terminal umbellate clusters, long-pedicelled, calyx tubular, 5-toothed, about ¼ in. long, corolla tubular, about 1½ in. long, typically deep blue, varying to purplish-blue. Nw. S. Amer.

lanceolatum: *I. cyaneum.*

tubulosum: *I. cyaneum.*

IONOPSIDIUM Rchb. DIAMOND FLOWER. *Cruciferae.* About 5 spp. of slender, glabrous, ann. herbs of s. Eur. and n. Afr.; basal lvs. in rosettes; infl. leafy or bracteate at base; fls. white, purple, or pink, sepals and petals 4; fr. a laterally compressed silicle with keeled valves, seeds 2–6 in each half.

acaule (Desf.) Rchb. Cespitose, usually stemless; lvs. nearly orbicular, to ½ in. across, long-petioled; fls. white, lilac, or purple, usually solitary on slender pedicels 3–4 in. long in the axils of basal lvs. Portugal. A dainty miniature plant useful especially in the cool, shaded rock garden and adaptable to pots in the cool greenhouse. Seeds may be sown in early spring for bloom before midsummer; or in summer for autumn bloom; or in autumn for spring bloom, the transplants being carried over in pots under glass. Protect plant from drying winds and burning sun.

IONOPSIS HBK. *Orchidaceae.* Twelve spp. of epiphytes of trop. Amer.; pseudobulbs small, few-lvd.; lvs. 2-ranked, leathery; infls. 1–3, lateral, racemose or paniculate; fls. small to rather large, sepals and petals similar, meeting at tips, lateral sepals united at base forming a sac, lip united to base of column, longer than other perianth segms., cuneate basally, 2-lobed apically, column slender, auricled. For structure of fl. see *Orchidaceae.*

Cultivation as for *Oncidium.* For general culture see *Orchids.*

paniculata: *I. utricularioides.*

satyrioides (Swartz) Rchb.f. [*I. testiculata* Lindl.]. To 5 in.; lvs. cylindrical, to 5 in. long; infl. shorter than lvs., racemose or paniculate; fls. about ¼ in. long, cream-white, often with purple lines, lip scarcely longer than sepals, entire, callus 2-lobed at base. Early spring–late autumn. W. Indies, Honduras, Costa Rica, Colombia, Venezuela.

testiculata: *I. satyrioides.*

utricularioides (Swartz) Lindl. [*I. paniculata* Lindl.]. To 2½ ft., sts. very short, thickened; lvs. congested, lanceolate, to 7 in. long; infl. to 3 ft. long, simple or spreading-paniculate, few- to many-fld.; fls. white to lavender to rose-purple, petals as long as upper sepal, lip twice as long as sepals, to ¾ in. long, deeply 2-lobed. Winter–summer. S. Fla., W. Indies, Cent. Amer. to Paraguay.

IONOXALIS: *OXALIS.* **I. Martiana:** *O. corymbosa.*

IPHEION Raf. *Amaryllidaceae.* A few spp. of S. Amer., scapose, per., onion-scented herbs with membranous tunicate bulbs; lvs. basal, linear, not keeled; fl. solitary on a scape, subtended by a spathe of 2 valves, basally united, perianth tubular to about the middle, lobes spreading, stamens 6, in 2 series, 3 inserted near base of tube and 3 near the middle, all shorter than tube and not exserted, ovary superior, stigma headlike and obscurely 3-lobed; fr. a caps.

uniflorum (R. C. Grah.) Raf. [*Brodiaea uniflora* (Lindl.) Engl.; *Leucocoryne uniflora* (Lindl.) Greene; *Milla uniflora* R. C. Grah.]. SPRING STARFLOWER. Lvs. nearly flat, slightly glaucous, to ⅜ in. wide, mostly longer than scape; scape 6–8 in. high; fl. to 1½ in. across, salverform, white with bluish tinge to blue, lobes often with deeper midvein, stamens bright orange. Argentina, Uruguay.

IPOMOEA L. [*Calonyction* Choisy; *Quamoclit* Moench]. MORNING-GLORY. *Convolvulaceae.* About 500 spp. of twining, prostrate or erect, ann. or per. herbs, sometimes becoming shrubby, native to trop. and warm-temp. regions; lvs. alt., entire, lobed or divided; fls. axillary, solitary or in few- to many-fld. clusters, corolla funnelform or campanulate, 5-lobed, with 5 stripes, stamens and styles included or exserted, style solitary, stigma entire or 2–3-lobed; fr. a 4–6-valved caps. Divided into 8 sections on the basis of habit, infl., and characters of fl., fr., and seed. Some of these sections have been recognized as separate genera, such as *Quamoclit* and *Calonyction. Ipomoea* is distinguished from *Convolvulus* in having stigma capitate or lobed, not linearly divided, and from *Turbina* and *Argyreia* in having dehiscent caps.

Ipomoeas include many ornamentals, some species with hallucinogenic properties, and the sweet potato, one of the most important root crops. They are of easy cultivation in any good soil. In the North the tuberous roots of the perennial kinds should be dug up and kept indoors over winter. They are useful for covering fences, trellises, and banks, and may also be grown in pots. Propagated by seeds which germinate more readily if the hard seed coat is notched with a file. The perennial species are increased by cuttings under glass, and rarely by division or grafting on common stocks.

acuminata (Vahl) Roem. & Schult. [*I. Learii* Paxt.]. BLUE DAWN FLOWER. Per., sts. twining or prostrate, pubescent; lvs. broadly ovate to orbicular, to 8 in. long, cordate, entire or 3-lobed, finely pubescent beneath; corolla to 5 in. across, limb blue turning pink, tube white. Trop. Amer. Cult. in tropics and subtropics around the world for its large showy fls.

alba L. [*I. Bona-Nox* L.; *I. grandiflora* Roxb., not (Jacq.) H. G. Hallier; *I. noctiflora* Griff.; *Calonyction aculeatum* (L.) House]. MOON-FLOWER. Robust, per. climber with milky juice, sts. more or less prickly; lvs. broad-ovate, to 8 in. long, sometimes 3-lobed; corolla white, often banded with green, tube to 6 in. long, limb 6 in. across. Probably trop. Amer.; escaped in tropics of both hemispheres. Cult. for its large, fragrant, nocturnal fls.

Batatas (L.) Lam. SWEET POTATO, SWEET-POTATO VINE, YAM. Per. with tuberous edible roots, sts. trailing, rooting; lvs. varying from ovate and entire to palmately lobed, to 6 in. long; corolla rose-violet or pale pink, 2 in. long. An ancient root crop; perhaps native to trop. Amer.; now pantrop. and widely cult. as an ann. with many cvs. Two types of sweet potatoes are grown, one with dry, mealy, yellowish flesh, and the other softer and sweeter, with a moist, orange, gelatinous flesh. In the South the latter are called yams, a name more appropriately reserved for the true yams *(Dioscorea).* See also *Sweet Potato.*

beraviensis: *Stictocardia beraviensis.*

Bona-Nox: *I. alba.*

bonariensis Hook. Branching twiner, with tuberous roots, sts. purplish; lvs. palmately 3–5-lobed, cordate; corolla purplish-lilac, funnelform, to 2½ in. long. S. Amer.

cairica (L.) Sweet. Per. twiner; lvs. palmately divided, segms. 5, elliptic, to 2 in. long; corolla pale pink, to 2½ in. long. Trop. Old World.

cardinalis: a listed name of no botanical standing, used for *I. × multifida.*

coccinea L. [*Quamoclit coccinea* (L.) Moench]. STAR I., RED M.-G. Ann., glabrous twiner, to 10 ft.; lvs. ovate-ovate, to 6 in. long, entire or coarsely dentate; corolla scarlet, with yellow throat, to 1½ in. long; fr. pedicels reflexed. Penn., s. to Ga., w. to Ark. and Okla. Var. **hederifolia:** see *I. cristulata* and *I. hederifolia.*

crassicaulis: *I. fistulosa.*

cristulata H. G. Hallier [*I. coccinea* var. *hederifolia* of auth., not (L.) A. Gray]. Related to *I. coccinea,* but having lvs. entire to 3–7-lobed, fr. pedicels erect or reflexed. W. Tex., New Mex., Ariz., s. to Mex.

dissecta: *Merremia dissecta.*

fistulosa Mart. ex Choisy [*I. crassicaulis* (Benth.) B. L. Robinson]. Sts. prostrate or ascending, fleshy, becoming woody; lvs. cordate, to 6 in. long, acuminate, glabrous above, soft-hairy beneath, petiole hairy, 1–2 in. long; fls. solitary or in pairs, sepals imbricate, rounded at apex, corolla purplish, to 3 in. long; caps. globose, glabrous. Fla., trop. Amer.

grandiflora: see *I. alba* and *I. tuba.*

hederacea Jacq. Ann. twiner, hairy; lvs. cordate-ovate, to 3½ in. long, usually 3-lobed; corolla blue or pale purple, usually less than 2 in. long. Trop. Amer. Differs from related spp. in having sepals contracted into linear, recurved or spreading tips. Improved forms are listed as cvs. 'Grandiflora' and 'Superba'. Becomes weedy on roadsides and waste places.

hederifolia L. [*I. coccinea* L. var. *hederifolia* (L.) A. Gray; *Quamoclit hederifolia* (L.) G. Don]. Ann. twiner; lvs. 3–5-lobed, middle lobe ovate-lanceolate, lateral lobes narrower; corolla scarlet, tubular. Se. U.S., s. to n. Argentina. Often confused with *I. coccinea,* but having lvs. always lobed.

Horsfalliae Hook. Large, glabrous, woody twiner; lvs. palmately divided, segms. 5–7, obovate, entire, thick, to 4 in. long; corolla rose

or pale purple, to 2½ in. long, limb becoming revolute. W. Indies. Commonly cult. in tropics and greenhouses around the world. Cv. 'Briggsii'. Rooting easily, fls. many, magenta-crimson.

imperialis: a listed name of no botanical standing for *I. Nil.*

Learii: *I. acuminata.*

leptophylla Torr. BUSH M.-G., BUSH MOONFLOWER, MANROOT, MAN-OF-THE-EARTH. Per., with large tuberous roots, sts. erect or ascending, to 4 ft.; lvs. linear, to 5 in. long, entire; corolla purple or pink, 3 in. across. Dry plains, Nebr. and Wyo., s. to Tex. and New Mex. Adapted to dry regions because of the large tuberous roots.

Lindheimeri A. Gray. Twiner, finely pubescent, hoary when young; lvs. deeply 3–5-cleft; fls. 1–2 on a peduncle, corolla blue, funnelform, to 3½ in. long. Tex. to New Mex., s. to n. Mex.

mexicana: see *I. purpurea* var. *diversifolia.*

×**multifida** (Raf.) Shinn. [*I. × Sloteri* (House ex L. H. Bailey) Van Ooststr.; *Quamoclit × Sloteri* House ex L. H. Bailey]: *I. coccinea* × *I. Quamoclit.* CARDINAL CLIMBER, HEARTS-AND-HONEY VINE. Ann. glabrous twiner; lvs. broadly deltoid-ovate, to 4½ in. across, divided nearly to base, segms. 7–15, long-acuminate, to ½ in. wide; corolla crimson with a white eye, salverform, to 2 in. long.

muricata (L.) Jacq. Twiner, glabrous or nearly so, sap milky; lvs. broadly ovate to orbicular, to 8 in. long, cordate at base; corolla purplish, tube to 2½ in. long, limb spreading, to 3 in. across. Probably native to Amer. tropics; now escaped from cult. in the tropics of both hemispheres. Related to *I. alba* but having smaller fls. Seeds said to be purgative.

Nil (L.) Roth. Ann. or per., twining or trailing, hairy; lvs. broadly cordate-ovate, to 6 in. across, usually shallowly 3-lobed; fls. showy, corolla to 2 in. long, violet, purple, rose, blue, sometimes fringed, fluted, and double. Circumtrop. The seeds are said to be purgative. Many named cvs. are offered, such as 'Scarlett O'Hara' and 'Limbata', the latter with corolla violet-purple, margined white. The often highly developed IMPERIAL JAPANESE MORNING-GLORIES [*I. imperialis* Hort.] belong here. Related to *I. purpurea* but having outer sepals lanceolate, up to 1 in. long, attenuate toward apex. Sometimes confused with *I. hederacea* but that sp. distinguished by the shape of the sepals.

noctiflora: *I. alba.*

pandurata (L.) G. F. Mey. WILD SWEET-POTATO VINE, WILD POTATO V., MAN-OF-THE-EARTH. Per., with large tuberous root, trailing or twining; lvs. broadly cordate-ovate or fiddle-shaped, to 6 in. long; corolla white, with purple throat, to 4 in. across. Conn., s. to Fla. and Tex.

Pes-caprae (L.) R. Br. BEACH M.-G., RAILROAD VINE. Creeping, to 60 ft., roots to 2 in. thick and 10 ft. long; lvs. orbicular to elliptic, to 4 in. across, sometimes emarginate, fleshy; corolla rose-purple, campanulate, to 2 in. long. Sandy beaches, pantrop. Useful as a sand-binding plant.

purpurea (L.) Roth. COMMON M.-G. Ann. twiner, sts. hairy; lvs. broadly cordate-ovate, to 5 in. long, entire; outer sepals oblong, acute, not more than 1 in. long, corolla purple, blue, or pink, with pale tube, to 3 in. long, sometimes double. Trop. Amer.; naturalized in N. Amer. Popular garden plant. Cvs. are: 'Alba', fls. white; 'Huberi', lvs. marked silver-white; fls. pink to purple, margined white; 'Violacea', fls. violet-purple, double. Var. *diversifolia* (Lindl.) O'Don. [*I. mexicana* A. Gray]. Lvs. entire and 3–5-lobed on the same plant.

Quamoclit L. [*Quamoclit pennata* (Desr.) Bojer]. CYPRESS VINE, CARDINAL CLIMBER, STAR-GLORY. Ann., to 20 ft.; lvs. pinnately cut into threadlike segms.; fls. scarlet, to 1½ in. long. Amer. tropics; widely naturalized.

rubrocaerulea: *I. tricolor.*

setosa Ker.-Gawl. BRAZILIAN M.-G. Per. twiner, sts. with stiff purplish hairs; lvs. cordate-ovate, to 10 in. across, 3-lobed and grapelike, sinuately toothed; calyx nearly smooth, corolla rose-purple, to 3 in. long. Trop. Amer.

sidifolia: *Turbina corymbosa.*

×**Sloteri:** *I. × multifida.*

tricolor Cav. [*I. rubrocaerulea* Hook.]. Stout per. twiner, glabrous; lvs. orbicular or ovate, to 10 in. across, cordate at base, thickish; corolla funnelform, to 4 in. long, purplish-blue, tube white, limb red before opening, but variable in cult. Trop. Amer. Used by the Aztecs in Mex. as a hallucinogen in religious ceremonials and in medicine. See also *Turbina corymbosa.* Cvs. include: 'Blue Star', fls. light sky-blue, with dark blue stripes; 'Flying Saucers', fls. striped-patterned with dark sky-blue and white; 'Heavenly Blue', fls. dark sky-blue; 'Pearly Gates', fls. white; 'Summer Skies', fls. light sky-blue; 'Wedding Bells', fls. rose-lavender.

Tuba (Schlechtend.) G. Don [*I. grandiflora* (Jacq.) H. G. Hallier, not Roxb.; *Calonyction grandiflorum* (Jacq.) Choisy; *C. Tuba* (Schlechtend.) Colla]. Per. twiner; lvs. ovate to reniform, to about 6 in. long, fleshy; fls. white, calyx lobes to 1 in. long, obtuse, corolla tube slender, to 4 in. long or more, limb to 4 in. across, style and stamens exserted; caps. ovoid, longer than calyx. Coastal, pantrop.

tuberosa: *Merremia tuberosa.*

violacea L. A name of disputed application, used by some for plants here called *I. tricolor,* by others for *I. Tuba.*

IPOMOPSIS Michx. *Polemoniaceae.* About 24 spp. of mostly per. or bien., or a few ann. herbs, native to N. Amer., one sp. in Argentina and Patagonia; sts. leafy; lvs. alt., entire to pinnately dissected, with sharp-tipped segms., variously hairy; fls. of various colors, in cymose infl., sometimes congested, each subtended by a bract; calyx 5-lobed, corolla salverform or tubular, stamens 5, often unequal in length and insertion; fr. a caps., seeds usually long, slender, curved. Differs from *Gilia* in having sts. with well-developed lvs., fls. with individual bracts, and long, curved seeds.

aggregata (Pursh) V. E. Grant [*Gilia aggregata* (Pursh) K. Spreng.]. SCARLET GILIA, SKYROCKET. Glandular-puberulent to pilose bien., to 2 ft.; lvs. to 2 in. long, pinnately dissected into linear segms.; fls. red, golden-yellow, pink, or nearly white, in a long thyrselike panicle. Mts., B.C. to Calif., e. to Rocky Mts. Subsp. **aggregata.** The typical subsp.; corolla tube stout, expanded upward, deep red with yellow mottling. Subsp. **attenuata** (A. Gray) A. D. Grant & V. E. Grant [*Gilia aggregata* var. *attenuata* A. Gray]. Corolla tube narrower, not much expanded upward, pink, white, or yellow. Calif.

longiflora (Torr.) V. E. Grant [*Gilia longiflora* (Torr.) G. Don]. Ann. or perhaps bien., to 20 in.; lvs. entire to pinnatifid with filiform lobes; fls. white to somewhat bluish, to 2 in. long, in open, flat-topped panicle. Nebr. to Utah, s. to Ariz. and Tex.

rubra (L.) Wherry [*Gilia coronopifolia* Pers.; *G. rubra* (L.) A. Heller]. STANDING CYPRESS. Unbranched, bien. or per., to 6 ft., glabrous or nearly so; lvs. pinnately parted into filiform segms. about 1 in. long; fls. scarlet outside, yellow and dotted red inside, in a narrow, terminal, thyrselike panicle. S.C. to Fla., w. to Tex.

spicata (Nutt.) V. E. Grant [*Gilia cephaloidea* Rydb.; *G. spicata* Nutt.]. Bien. or per., to 14 in.; lvs. entire and linear, or pinnately parted into linear, short-mucronate lobes; fls. white or cream-colored, in heads arranged in spikes, calyx glandular. S. Dak. and Wyo., s. to Kans., Utah, New Mex. Subsp. **capitata** (A. Gray) V. E. Grant [*G. globularis* Brand; *G. spicata* Nutt. var. *capitata* A. Gray]. Fls. in globose heads, calyx with long silky hairs. High mts., cent. Colo.

IRESINE P. Br. BLOODLEAF. *Amaranthaceae.* About 70 spp. of herbs and subshrubs, sometimes climbing, with ornamental foliage, native to many trop. and temp. regions; lvs. opp.; fls. small, in paniculately arranged heads or spikes, bisexual or unisexual, stamens 5, united basally, anthers 2-celled, ovule 1.

A few species are cultivated as house plants and bedding plants. They are handled in the same way as coleus. Propagated by cuttings taken in late summer for house plants and in Feb. or Mar. for summer bedding purposes in the North. The stock plants for these are easily over-wintered.

Herbstii Hook. [*I. reticulata* Hort.; *Achyranthes Herbstii* Hort.]. BEEF PLANT, BEEFSTEAK PLANT, CHICKEN-GIZZARD. To 6 ft.; lvs. broad-ovate, to 5 in. long, notched at tip, purplish-red or green, with yellowish veins. S. Amer. Cv. 'Aureo-reticulata'. Lvs. green or greenish-red, with yellow veins.

Lindenii Van Houtte. Lvs. usually deep blood-red, narrow, sharp-pointed. Ecuador. Cv. 'Formosa' is listed.

reticulata: a listed name of no botanical standing for plants referable to *I. Herbstii.*

IRIDACEAE Juss. IRIS FAMILY, IRIDS. Monocot.; about 60 genera and 800 or more spp. of bulbous, cormous, or rhizomatous per. herbs with fibrous roots, fairly cosmopolitan in distribution; lvs. mostly basal, usually 2-ranked, linear to sword-shaped; fls. bisexual, regular or irregular, solitary, in clusters in 2 spathelike bracts (spathe valves), or in racemose or paniculate infl., perianth segms. 6, separate or basally united into a short or long tube, stamens 3, filaments separate or united, ovary inferior, usually 3-celled, with axile placentation, rarely 1-celled with parietal placentation; fr. a 3-valved,

loculicidal caps., seeds sometimes with an aril. Genera in cult. in N. Amer. are: *Acidanthera, Alophia, Aristea, Babiana, Belamcanda, Chasmanthe, Crocosmia, Crocus, Curtonus, Cypella, Dierama, Dietes, Diplarrhena, Eustylis, Ferraria, Freesia, Geissorhiza, Gelasine, Gladiolus, Gynandriris, Hermodactylus, Hesperantha, Hexaglottis, Homeria, Iris, Ixia, Lapeirousia, Libertia, Melasphaerula, Moraea, Nemastylis, Neomarica, Orthrosanthus, Patersonia, Romulea, Schizostylis, Sisyrinchium, Solenomelus, Sparaxis, Sphenostigma, Streptanthera, Synnotia, Tigridia, Trimezia, Tritonia,* and *Watsonia.*

The family includes many ornamental plants, yields some medicinal products, and includes other plants with minor economic uses. They are hardy perennials for the open garden, summer "bulbs," and a few nonhardy species are glasshouse subjects. There are no special difficulties in their cultivation except, perhaps, that some of the bulbous and stoloniferous species of *Iris* may require careful attention to soil conditions and temperature.

IRIS L. FLAG, FLEUR-DE-LIS. *Iridaceae.* About 200 or more spp. of rhizomatous or bulbous per. herbs, native mostly to the N. Temp. Zone; lvs. mostly basal, 2-ranked, linear to sword-shaped; infl. branched or unbranched; fls. in groups of 1 or more, borne in 2 spathe valves (often called a "head"), showy, in many colors, perianth tube of varying length, perianth segms. 6, the outer 3 segms. (falls) narrowed basally in a "haft," sometimes bearded, the inner 3 segms. (standards) narrowed into a claw, usually erect and arching, sometimes spreading or reflexed, stamens 3, filaments not united, borne at base of falls, style brs. 3, bifid or crested beyond the stigma, petal-like, colored, covering the stamens; fr. a caps., 3- or 6-angled, mostly leathery, seeds many, sometimes with an aril.

Most irises are grown as ornamentals, but several Old World species produce orris, the dried powdered rhizomes with the odor of violets and used in perfumery.

The color of the flowers in iris covers a wide range of tints and shades of pink, blue, lilac and purple to white, brown, yellow, orange, and almost black; true reds are unknown, and are not likely to be developed. The color pattern often consists of complex markings and the shading of one tint into another, and the tints and shades are so numerous that it is practically impossible to differentiate among them accurately in words.

Classification of Irises

The genus *Iris* can be separated rather naturally into 2 divisions: species with a rhizome [subgenus *Iris* (Mill.)] and species with a bulb [subgenera *Xiphium* (Mill.) Spach and *Scorpiris* Spach]. A single anomalous species, *I. nepalensis,* neither bulbous nor strictly rhizomatous but having a minute rhizome terminating a cluster of fleshy roots, forms a third division [subgenus *Nepalenses* (Dykes) G. H. M. Lawr.].

The rhizomatous division includes 3 main groups: the bearded or pogon irises, the crested or evansia irises, and the beardless or apogon irises.

The bearded irises have a "beard" or pattern of hairs on the basal half of the falls. In this general bearded group are subgroups of various habit and floral characteristics (the names used here for these subgroups are horticultural rather than strictly botanical ones). One subgroup, the "true" pogon irises, has seeds without an evident or conspicuous aril, rhizomes stout and more or less regular, and hairs in a dense line on the falls; they are native from Portugal and Morocco through southern and central Eur. to Asia Minor, Manchuria, and western China. It is this subgroup that is usually meant when horticulturists refer to "bearded" irises. The other subgroups (regelia, pseudoregelia, oncocyclus, crested) have seeds with prominent cream-colored arils, and beards of different character; they are often referred to as "aril" irises. The regelia irises have stolons arising from the main rhizome, 2 or 3 flowers in a spathe, and hairs in a line on both standards and falls; they are native to the Afghanistan and Turkestan region north of the great mountains. The pseudoregelia irises have a compact rhizome without stolons, hairs in lines on the falls, and the capsule pointed; they are native east of the Pamirs on the southern side of the Himalayas. The oncocyclus irises have reddish, crowded rhizomes producing stolons, 1 flower to a spathe or stem, and hairs scattered on the falls; this is a small subgroup, native from southwestern Asia to Egypt.

The crested or evansia irises have, instead of a beard or hairs, a central serrated ridge or cockscomblike crest along the basal half of

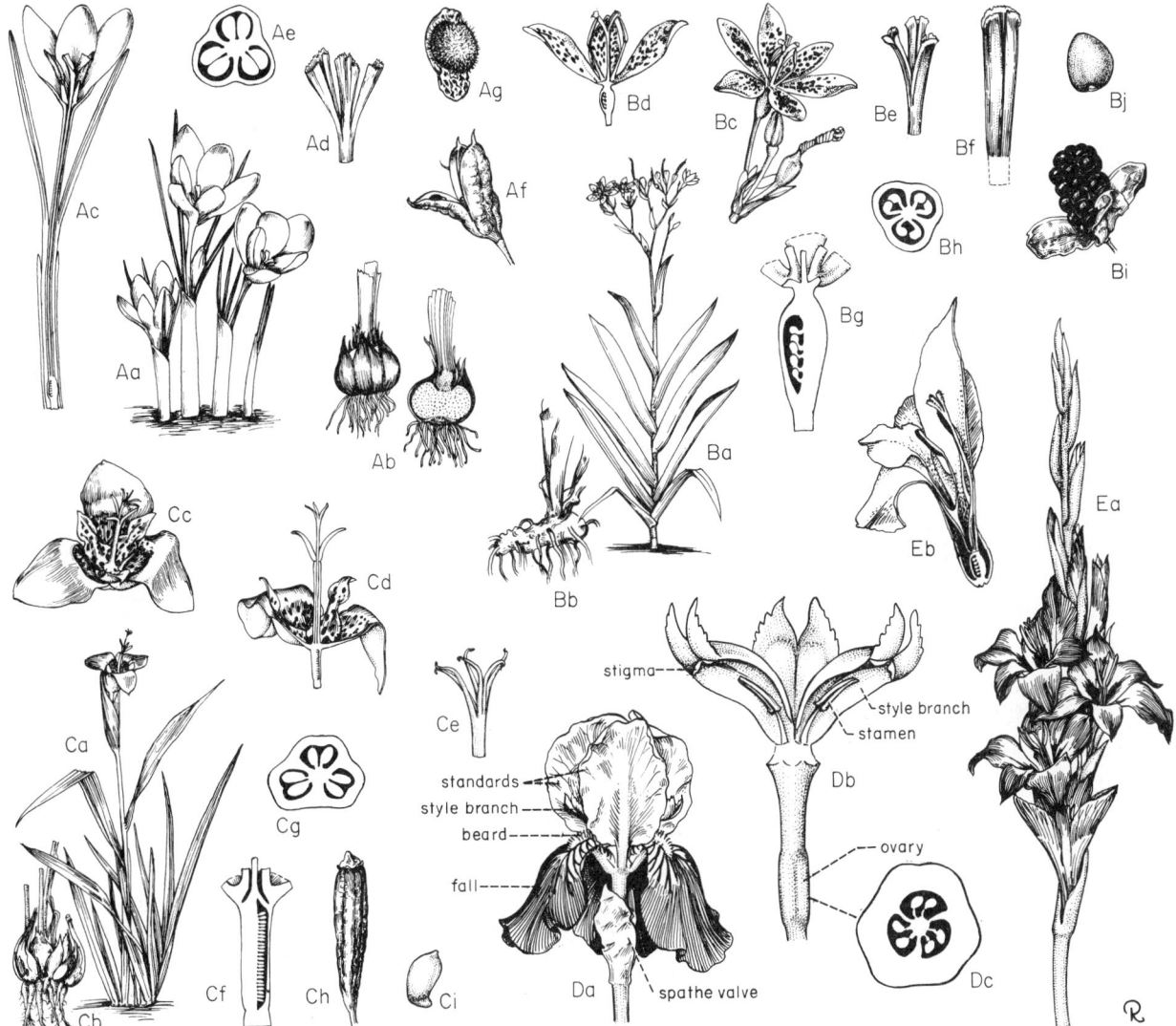

IRIDACEAE. **A,** *Crocus flavus:* **Aa,** flowering plants, ½; **Ab,** corm (left) and corm in vertical section (right), × ½; **Ac,** spathe, leaves, and flower, vertical section, × ½; **Ad,** stigmas, × 2; **Ae,** ovary, cross section, × 5; **Af,** capsule, × ½; **Ag,** seed, × 2½. **B,** *Belamcanda chinensis:* **Ba,** flowering plant, × ⅛; **Bb,** rhizome, × ¼; **Bc,** flower, bud, and withered flower subtended by spathes, × ½; **Bd,** flower, vertical section, × ½; **Be,** style branches and stigmas, × 1½; **Bf,** style branch viewed from inner side, × 3; **Bg,** ovary and base of flower, vertical section, × 2; **Bh,** ovary, cross section, × 3; **Bi,** capsule dehisced, exposing seeds, × ½; **Bj,** seed, × 2. **C,** *Tigridia Pavonia:* **Ca,** flowering plant, × ⅛; **Cb,** bulbs, × ⅙; **Cc,** flower, × ¼; **Cd,** flower, vertical section, × ¼; **Ce,** stigmas, × 1; **Cf,** ovary, vertical section, × 1; **Cg,** ovary, cross section, × 3; **Ch,** capsule, × ½; **Ci,** seed, × 2. **D,** *Iris × germanica:* **Da,** flower, × ¼; **Db,** flower with perianth removed, × ½; **Dc,** ovary, cross section, × 2. **E,** *Gladiolus × hortulanus:* **Ea,** inflorescence, × ¼; **Eb,** flower, vertical section, × ½. (Da-Dc from Lawrence, *An Introduction to Plant Taxonomy*.)

the falls. They are a small group, native to eastern N. Amer. and eastern Asia.

The beardless irises have smooth falls, without either hairs or crest, and leaves that are prevailingly relatively long and narrow. They are the group most numerous in species and most widely distributed. Except for 2 species of crested irises, they are the only irises native to N. Amer., but they occur also in the temperate regions of Asia and Eur.

The bulbous group comprises the subgenera *Xiphium* and *Scorpiris*. The subgenus *Xiphium* includes the xiphion irises and the reticulata irises. The xiphion, or so-called English, Dutch, and Spanish irises, have large, erect standards and smooth bulbs without roots in the resting stage; they are native to southwestern Eur. and northwestern Afr. The reticulata irises differ from the xiphion irises particularly in the netted, fibrous covering of the bulbs; they are native to the Caucasus, Asia Minor, and southern Israel. The subgenus *Scorpiris* includes the juno irises, with small or even minute spreading or deflexed standards and bulbs with thick, fleshy roots in the resting stage; they are native from the Medit. region to Asia Minor, Turkestan, and the frontiers of India and Pakistan.

The "flags" of old gardens are irises, mostly of the "true" pogon iris or bearded subgroup. The horticultural kinds have been greatly improved in recent years, and there are many named cultivars that cannot be definitely referred to botanical species, since most are hybrids of complicated and sometimes obscure parentage.

Named cultivars of bearded irises are particularly numerous and constitute most of the currently listed types, aside from the very different Japanese irises; they have been known under the collective name of German iris, but this designation is inexact and is now largely abandoned. The bearded horticultural irises are commonly classified as to stature into miniature dwarfs, standard dwarfs, intermediates, miniature talls (table iris), border iris, and standard tall beardeds. To a lesser degree there have been additions of cultivars in the oncocyclus group, in the beardless rhizomatous irises such as the spurias (a series of species and hybrids related to *I. spuria*), and in the bulbous irises. Certain native American irises have found their way into the trade, *Iris cristata* being one of the more popular species. The irises known as the Louisiana irises have produced natural hybrids and color forms in the wild, mainly through the interbreeding of *I. fulva, I. giganticaerulea,* and to a lesser degree *I. brevicaulis;* these species and hybrids have been collected, and additional cultivars have been bred from them.

Descriptions and lists of cultivars of the various groups may be found in books and the reports and journals of societies such as the American Iris Society.

Bearded irises are divided and planted just after the flowering period, in July or Aug. (in the North) and should bloom the following year, if given proper soil and care. The rhizome is thick and grows near the surface of the ground, and will withstand considerable drying and exposure. These irises require an open, sunny exposure and well-drained ground, and should be shallowly planted. It is well to take up the plants every fourth or fifth year after blooming, remove the old and weak rhizomes, and replant in newly worked ground. Strong clumps of iris should produce 8 or 10 flowering stalks, and in new plantings the plants should be spaced for this result, say 1½–2 ft. apart. Irises are durable perennials, but plantings only a few years old are likely to flower best. A little chemical fertilizer should give good returns, but stable manure is not advised.

Horticultural beardless types include several subgroups, of which the Japanese and Siberian irises are the most prominent. They may be planted in the spring or autumn. The rhizome is mostly rather slender and fibrous-rooted and will not withstand much exposure. Most of these irises grow best in moist places; they usually do not thrive in limy soils. The Japanese irises comprise 2 groups, 1 derived from *I. Kaempferi* and the other from *I. laevigata,* the commonly grown cultivars probably being from the former. *Iris Kaempferi* is not a real bog plant and should be kept comparatively dry except when in active growth, at which time the spaces between plants may be filled with water. *Iris laevigata,* however, is a bog plant and thrives where continuously wet. Some growers recommend application of liquid manure to Japanese irises just before blooming if especially good flowers are desired.

Regelias and pseudoregelias are rather difficult to grow except in mild climates, as in southern Calif., where there are dry and moist seasons, the rains coming so late that the plants do not start into autumn growth. They may be hardy in the East and North, but are dormant in summer and are likely to start growth in the autumn and be injured. If lifted when the foliage is about ripe, the roots may be kept dry and then planted so late that they will not start till spring. The oncocyclus irises require similar treatment, although *I. susiana,* the commonest oncocyclus iris in cultivation, is rather difficult to grow permanently.

There are about half a dozen species of crested or evansia irises, none of which has been greatly modified by cultivation. There are no general rules for culture, as they are of various requirements and degrees of hardiness. *Iris japonica* does well in Calif., and *I. tectorum* where winters do not destroy the evergreen foliage; *I. gracilipes* of Japan and *I. cristata* and *I. lacustris* of N. Amer. are hardy in the North.

Bulbous irises are planted in autumn. Some kinds tend to start into growth before winter unless planted very late, and may need protection in cold regions. As garden plants, they are excellent where they can be given good conditions and care, because of their showy, often orchidlike early blooms. They do well in Calif. and can be raised successfully also in the northeastern states. They are sometimes forced indoors like tulips, and good results are obtained if the bulbs have been properly ripened. For this purpose, the bulbs are planted in autumn in deep pans or boxes, then either set outside and brought in as required like other hardy bulbs, or placed in a cool house and then grown slowly at a temperature of 50° to 55° F., for bloom in later winter or early spring.

Irises are commonly propagated by dividing the rhizomes, or by using the offsets or bulblets in the bulbous species. Each piece of rhizome should have at least one strong bud. Bearded irises are commonly divided just after flowering, so that flowering buds may be formed before autumn. Beardless and crested species may be handled similarly, but preferably, as a rule, by division when growth begins in spring.

Seeds commonly germinate readily in spring if sown immediately on ripening the previous year. Transplant into permanent position as soon as the seedlings are large enough to handle. The bearded irises usually bloom the year following germination, but other kinds mostly in the third year.

Species of Iris Cultivated or Offered in North America

To economize space in the following brief diagnoses of the species, symbols are used at the beginning of each species to distinguish the subgenus and the group or association into which the species falls: R, rhizomatous; B, bulbous; I, subgenus *Iris;* N, subgenus *Nepalenses* (Dykes) G. H. M. Lawr.; S, subgenus *Scorpiris* Spach; X, subgenus *Xiphium* (Mill.) Spach; a, apogon or beardless; c, crested or evansia; j, juno; o, oncocyclus; p, pogon or bearded; ps, pseudoregelia; r, regelia; ret, reticulata. It is understood that the characteristics of the various groups (as described in *Classification of Irises*) indicated by these symbols apply to the species so marked.

acutifolia: a listed name of no botanical standing.

acutiloba C. A. Mey. R, I, o; sts. to 8 in.; lvs. linear, curved, 3–4 in. long, to ¼ in. wide; spathes 1-fld.; perianth tube about 1 in. long, green, mottled with purple, segms. creamy-white, prominently veined brown to purple-brown, falls lanceolate, signal patch and beard brown. Caucasus.

alata: *I. planifolia.*

alba: *I. albicans,* but plants offered as *I. alba* may be white-fld. variants of many spp.

Albertii Regel. R, I, p; sts. branched; lvs. sword-shaped, shorter than sts., to 2 ft. long and 2 in. wide, glaucous; spathes 1–3-fld.; perianth tube ½ in. long, falls obovate, to 2 in. long, lavender-purple, or occasionally yellow, haft veined reddish-brown, beard white, tipped with yellow, standards lavender-purple, veined reddish-brown toward claw. Turkestan. Does best in a hot, dry location.

×**albicans** J. Lange [*I. alba* Savi]. R, I, p; sts. to 1½ ft.; lvs. sword-shaped, often twisted at maturity; spathes 2–3-fld., spathe valves scarcely scarious except in upper ⅓; perianth tube about ¾ in. long, falls white, haft veined greenish-yellow, beard yellow and white. A natural sterile hybrid. Often confused with *I.* ×*germanica* var. *florentina.* Yemen. Used in Mohammedan graveyards.

albomarginata R. Foster [*I. coerulea* B. Fedtsch., not Spach]. B, S, j; sts. to 15 in.; lvs. erect, lanceolate, to 8 in. long, with a white, horny margin; fls. 1–5, axillary, perianth tube to 1½ in. long, segms. azure-blue, falls oblong-lanceolate, to 1⅜ in. long, standards about ⅝ in. long. Turkestan.

anglica: *I. xiphioides.*

aphylla L. R, I, p; sts. to 1 ft. or more, branched mostly near the base; lvs. sword-shaped, usually as long as st., curved, glaucous-green, withering in autumn; spathes 1–2-fld.; fls. 3–4 in. across, perianth tube to 1 in. long, falls reflexed, obovate, purple, beard white, tipped blue, becoming yellow toward haft, standards purple. E. Eur. to Caucasus.

arenaria Waldst. & Kit. R, I, r; sts. to 6 in.; lvs. linear, 3–4 in. long; spathes 1–2-fld.; perianth tube ½ in. long, segms. to 1¼ in. long, yellow, all with yellow beard. Hungary to U.S.S.R.

atrofusca Bak. [*I. Haynei* Bak.]. R, I, o; sts. to 1 ft.; lvs. sheathing and obscuring st., sword-shaped, about 1 ft. long; spathes 1-fld.; perianth segms. dark brown, prominently veined and dotted red-black, perianth tube to 2½ in. long, falls 3 in. long, signal patch velvety-black, beard yellow, tipped brown, standards longer than falls. Israel. Var. **Eggeri:** *I. atropurpurea.*

atropurpurea Bak. [*I. atrofusca* var. *Eggeri* Dinsm.; *I. Eggeri* Hort.]. R, I, o; sts. to 8 in.; lvs. linear, curved, about 6 in. long, somewhat glaucous; spathes 1-fld.; perianth tube 1¼ in. long, green, with dark streaks, falls to 2 in. long and 1½ in. wide, almost black, veined greenish-yellow, haft veined red-purple, signal patch velvety-black, beard yellowish, tipped purplish-black, standards to 3 in. long and 2 in. wide, reddish-purple, with inconspicuous, black veins. Syria.

attica: *I. pumila.*

Aucheri (Bak.) Sealy [*I. sindjarensis* Boiss. & Hausskn.]. B, S, j; sts. to 9 in.; lvs. lanceolate, to 10 in. long and 2 in. wide, glossy above; fls. 3 or more, axillary, sessile, perianth tube to 2½ in. long, segms. pale blue, falls oblong-cuneate, to 2 in. long, with central yellow ridge, haft winged, standards horizontal or reflexed, oblanceolate to obovate, 1 in. long, clawed. Ne. Syria, n. Iraq, s. Asia Minor.

auranitica Dinsm. R, I, o; sts. to about 2 ft.; lvs. nearly erect, linear, to 10 in. long; spathes 1-fld.; perianth tube 1 in. long, segms. bronze-yellow, dotted and veined reddish-brown, falls to 3 in. long, signal patch maroon, beard yellow, tipped purple, standards erect, to 4 in. wide. Israel.

aurea: *I. crocea.*

Bakerana M. Foster. B, X, ret; sts. very short or none; lvs. cylindrical, hollow, becoming 1 ft. long or more, 8-nerved; spathes 1-fld.; fls. violet-scented, perianth tube 3–6 in. long, falls 3 in. long, violet, the center yellow, spotted violet, standards 3 in. long, deep lilac. Asia Minor, Iraq.

balkana: *I. Reichenbachii.*

Barnumiae Bak. & M. Foster. R, I, o; sts. 3–6 in.; lvs. 5–6, linear, to 6 in. long, pale glaucous-green, conspicuously nerved; spathes 1-fld.; perianth tube ½ in. long, segms. red-purple, with darker veins, falls obovate-cuneate, 2 in. long, beard yellow, tipped purple, standards orbicular, 3¼ in. long, clawed. Egypt to Israel. Var. **Mariae:** *I. Helenae.*

basaltica: *I. susiana.*

Bastardii: *I. Pseudacorus.*

benacensis A. Kern. ex Stapf. R, I, p; sts. to 1 ft.; lvs. sword-shaped, to 1 ft. long; spathe valves tinged purple, scarious at tip at maturity; perianth segms. violet, haft veined brown-violet, beard yellow-white. S. Tyrol.

Benjaminii: a listed name of no botanical standing for plants having white fls., with black veins and signal patch.

biflora: see *I. subbiflora.*

×**binata** Schur. R, I, p; probably a natural hybrid between *I. aphylla* and *I. pumila;* sts. to 3 in.; lvs. narrow, somewhat curved; spathes 2–4-fld.; fls. sordid-yellow, fragrant. Transylvania.

Bismarkiana Hort. Dammann. R, I, o; sts. to 1 ft. or more, stout; lvs. sheathing st., sword-shaped, to 9 in. long, glaucous; spathes 1-fld.; perianth tube about 1 in. long, falls orbicular, to 2 in. long, creamy-yellow, dotted and veined black-purple, yellowish under beard, signal patch and beard purple-black, standards sky-blue, with dark veins and dots. Lebanon.

Bloudowii Ledeb. R, I, r; sts. 4–6 in.; lvs. basal, to 8 in. long and ½ in. wide; spathes 2–6-fld.; falls rounded, yellow, haft with brownish veins, beard yellow, standards bright yellow, beard yellow. Turkestan to China.

bracteata S. Wats. R, I, a; sts. 4–12 in., bracted; lvs. few, stiff, linear, longer than st., spathes 2-fld.; perianth tube ⅜ in. long, segms. yellow, with brown-purple veins, falls broadly oblanceolate, to 3 in. long, standards oblanceolate, to 2⅞ in. long. Sw. Ore., nw. Calif.

brevicaulis Raf. [*I. foliosa* Mackenz. & Bush]. LAMANCE I. R, I, a; sts. to 1½ ft. long, flexuous, weak and reclining; lvs. to 2 ft. long and 1⅛ in. wide; spathes 2–3-fld.; perianth tube ¾ in. long, segms. to 4 in. long, deep blue or blue-purple, falls ovate, with greenish-white blotch, standards oblanceolate, ovary 6-angled. Moist areas, Ala. to Tex., n. to Ohio, w. to Kans. Cvs. are: 'Brevipes' [*I. brevipes* Alexand.], falls ovate, rosy-lavender, veined smoky-lilac, standards light violet to light blue-violet, s. La.; 'Flexicaulis' [*I. flexicaulis* Small], sts. strongly zigzag, falls obovate, smaller, deep violet, standards narrowly spatulate, violet, e. Tex.; 'Mississippiensis' [*I. mississippiensis* Alexand.], falls suborbicular, lavender to lavender-violet, with brownish-olive veins, standards lavender or lavender-violet, white basally. S.-cent. La.

brevipes: probably best treated as a color variant or cv. of *I. brevicaulis.*

bucharica M. Foster. B, S, j; sts. to 1½ ft.; lvs. 7–11, lanceolate, to 1 ft. long, glossy above, glaucous beneath; fls. 5–7, axillary, perianth tube to 2 in. long, falls suborbicular, 2 in. long or more, golden-yellow, haft white, standards much smaller than falls, white, 3-lobed, middle lobe mucronate. Uzbek (S.S.R.) and Turkestan.

Bulleyana Dykes. R, I, a; sts. to 1½ ft., hollow; lvs. linear, to 1½ ft. long, glossy above, glaucous beneath; spathes 1–2-fld.; perianth tube ½ in. long, falls obovate, cream-colored, veined and blotched blue-purple, standards oblanceolate, pale blue-purple. W. China.

californica: *I. macrosiphon.*

caroliniana: *I. virginica.*

carthaliniae Fomin [*I. violacea* Klatt, not Savi, or (Ker-Gawl.) Sweet]. R, I, a; sts. to 3 ft., leafy; basal lvs. sword-shaped, longer than st.; spathes 1-fld.; falls spreading horizontally, linear to linear-lanceolate, sky-blue, with dark blue veins and central yellowish stripe, standards erect, oblanceolate, emarginate. Caucasus.

caucasica Hoffmanns. B, S, j; sts. to 8 in.; lvs. 4–6, lanceolate, curved, to 6 in. long, bright glossy green above, glaucous beneath; fls. 1–3, perianth tube about 1½ in. long, segms. pale yellow, falls obovate, to 1½ in. long, standards reflexed, oblanceolate, toothed. E. Asia Minor and Caucasus to Iran.

Cengialtii Ambrosi. R, I, p; sts. to 1 ft.; lvs. sword-shaped, about 6 in. long; spathes 1–3-fld.; perianth tube about ⅜ in. long, falls broadly obovate, blue-purple, haft gray-white, veined brown-purple, standards obovate, lighter than falls, claw white, veined red-purple. S. Tyrol, n. Italy. Var. **illyrica** (Tomm.) Pamp. [*I. illyrica* Tomm.]. Lvs. glaucous.

Chamaeiris Bertol. [*I. italica* Parl.; *I. lutescens* Lam.]. R, I, p; sts. to 10 in.; lvs. 4–6, sword-shaped, 3–6 in. long, ½ in. wide, slightly glaucous; spathes 1–2-fld.; perianth tube about 1 in. long, falls obovate, blue-purple, yellow, or white, beard white, tipped orange, standards oblong, crisped. S. Eur.

chrysographes Dykes. R, I, a; sts. to 1½ ft., hollow; lvs. linear, to 1½ ft. long; spathes 2-fld.; perianth tube ⅜ in. long, falls oblong, to 2¼ in. long, deep velvety-violet, with variable golden veining, haft golden, standards oblanceolate, deep violet, anthers ½ in. long. W. China. Cv. 'Rubella'. Fls. wine red.

chrysophoenicia: probably best treated as a color variant or cv. of *I.* ×*vinicolor.*

chrysophylla T. J. Howell. R, I, a; sts. to 8 in.; lvs. longer than sts., light green, pink to red at base; spathes usually 2-fld.; perianth tube to 3½ in. long, segms. pale creamy-yellow to nearly white, sometimes with a bluish tinge, the veins darker, falls oblanceolate, to 2⅝ in. long, standards lanceolate, to 2⅛ in. long, crests of stigma lanceolate, to ¾ in. long. W. Ore., nw. Calif. Cv. 'Alba'. Fls. white.

Clarkei Bak. R, I, a; sts. to 3 ft., often branched, not hollow; lvs. linear, to 2 ft. long, glossy above, glaucous beneath; spathes 1–2-fld., spathe valves herbaceous, green; perianth tube ½ in. long, falls obovate, to 1⅜ in. long, purple-violet, with a central white area and basal yellow blotch, standards erect, oblanceolate, to 1¾ in. long, violet. Himalayas.

coerulea: see *I. albomarginata* and *I. pumila.*

confusa Sealy. R, I, c; sts. branched, to 3 ft.; lvs. in apical tuft, sword-shaped, slightly curved, to 2 ft. long; infl. branched; fls. 1½–2 in. across, perianth segms. white, faintly tinged with mauve, with yellow blotch and orange spots, falls and standards undulate-crenate, crests ciliate-fimbriate. W. China.

cretensis: *I. unguicularis.*

cretica: *I. unguicularis.*

cristata Ait. DWARF CRESTED I., CRESTED I., CRESTED DWARF I. R, I, c; sts. 1–3 in.; lvs. about 6, sword-shaped, to 9 in. long and ¾ in. wide; spathes 1–2-fld.; perianth tube longer than spathe, falls obovate, to 1½ in. long, crest white and yellow, more or less dotted lilac-purple, standards oblanceolate. Md. to Ga., w. to Mo. Cv. 'Alba'. Fls. white. Cv. 'Caerulea'. Fls. blue.

crocea Jacquem. ex R. Foster [*I. aurea* Lindl.; *I. spuria* var. *aurea* Hort.]. R, I, a; sts. to 3½ ft., stout; lvs. sword-shaped, to 2 ft. long; spathes 2–3-fld.; perianth tube ½ in. long, segms. bright golden-yellow, falls oblong, to 3½ in. long, crisped, standards oblanceolate. Kashmir.

cypriana Bak. & M. Foster. R, I, p; sts. to 3 ft., weak; lvs. sword-shaped, slightly glaucous, blue-green; spathes 2–3-fld.; fls. 6–7 in. across, fragrant, perianth tube to 1 in. long, segms. bright blue, falls wedge-shaped, beard white, tipped yellow, standards obovate. Cyprus.

Danfordiae (Bak.) Boiss. B, X, ret; sts. 2–4 in.; lvs. 2, linear, hollow, to 1 ft. long, bluish-green; spathes 1-fld.; perianth tube 1½ in. long, falls ovate-lanceolate, 1¼ in. long, yellow, spotted with olive-green, with a conspicuous orange ridge, standards reduced to erect bristles, less than ¾ in. long. E. Asia Minor.

darwasica Regel [*I. Suworowii* Regel]. R, I, r; sts. to 1 ft.; lvs. linear, to 15 in. long and 1 in. wide, glaucous; spathes 2-fld.; perianth tube about 1 in. long, falls oblong or linear-lanceolate, to 2½ in. long, green-brown, veined brown-purple, beard white, tipped blue, standards oblong. Uzbek (S.S.R.) and Turkestan.

Delavayi M. Micheli. R, I, a; sts. 3–4 ft., hollow; lvs. linear, to 2½ ft. long, glaucescent, conspicuously nerved; spathes 2-fld.; fls. 2½ in. across, perianth tube ½ in. long, falls orbicular, notched at apex, violet-purple, with white blotch and markings, standards oblong-lanceolate, paler. Marshes, Yunnan (China).

Demetrii Akhv. & Mirz. R, I, a; sts. to 3 ft.; lvs. linear to sword-shaped, to 1¾ ft. long; spathes 4–5-fld., spathe valves with narrow membranous margin; falls rounded-elliptic to nearly orbicular, emarginate, deep blue, with broad, central yellow stripe, standards erect, obovate, emarginate, deep blue. Armenia.

desertorum: *I. spuria* var. *halophila.*

dichotoma Pall. R, I, a; sts. to 3 ft., branched; lvs. 6–8, sword-shaped, to 1 ft. long; spathes 5–6-fld., spathe valves scarious; fls. many, fugacious and successive, opening in the afternoon, perianth tube obsolete, segms. greenish-white, spotted brown-purple, or reddish-purple with white blotches, falls oblanceolate-spatulate, to ¾ in. long, standards oblanceolate, emarginate. Siberia to n. China.

Douglasiana Herb. [*I. Douglasiana* var. *Watsoniana* Hort.; *I. Watsoniana* Purdy]. R, I, a; sts. to 2½ ft., sometimes branched; lvs. often longer than st., pinkish or reddish at base, conspicuously nerved; spathes 2–3-fld.; perianth tube about 1 in. long, segms. variable in color from red-purple and lilac-purple to cream or white, falls oblanceolate to obovate, to 3½ in. long, standards oblanceolate, to 2¾ in. long. S. Calif. to Ore. Cv. 'Alba'. Fls. white. Cv. 'Amabilis'. Listed name.

Dykesii Stapf. R, I, a; sts. to 1½ ft.; lvs. linear, to 2½ ft. long, tapering, acute, dull dark green; spathes 2-fld.; perianth tube 1¼ in. long, falls elliptic, to 3½ in. long, brilliant violet, with a yellow median stripe, standards erect, spatulate-oblong, to 2 in. long, dark violet, anthers 1 in. long. Nativity uncertain, perhaps China.

Eggeri: *I. atropurpurea.*

elongata: *I. scariosa.*

ensata Thunb. SWORD-LEAVED I. R, I, a; sts. to 16 in., flattened; lvs. tufted, linear, longer than sts., to 2 ft. at maturity, glaucous; spathes 1–3-fld.; perianth tube very short, falls oblanceolate, white with greenish veins, to dark red-purple, standards oblanceolate, usually darker than falls. Japan, Korea, China, cent. Asia. Var. **spontanea** (Mak.) Nakai. More robust; lvs. linear-lanceolate; fls. 4 in. wide, red-purple. Japan.

excelsa: a listed name of no botanical standing.

Farreri Dykes. R, I, a; sts. to 8 in.; lvs. linear, to 2 ft., finely nerved; spathes 2-fld.; falls fiddle-shaped, about 1¾ in. long, gray-white, veined and dotted blue-purple, standards oblanceolate, about as long as falls, red-purple. W. China.

Fernaldii R. Foster. R, I, a; sts. to 16 in.; lvs. linear, to 16 in. long, gray-green, red at base, glaucous; spathes 2-fld.; perianth tube to 2⅜ in. long, segms. creamy-yellow, often variously veined, falls oblanceolate to spatulate, to 2¾ in. long, standards narrowly oblanceolate, 2⅜ in. long. Cent. Calif.

filifolia Boiss. B, X; sts. to 2 ft., slender; lvs. filiform, to 1 ft. or more; spathes 2-fld.; perianth tube to 1 in. long, falls orbicular, to 2½ in. long, reddish-purple, with darker veins, signal patch orange, standards obovate, reddish-purple. S. Spain, nw. Afr.

flavescens Delile. R, I, p; sts. 2–2½ ft.; lvs. sword-shaped, to 15 in. long, glaucous; spathes 2–3-fld.; perianth tube ¾–1 in. long, falls obovate-cuneate, 2½ in. long, pale yellow to almost white, with brownish veins, beard yellow, standards obovate, pale lemon-yellow. Probably a garden hybrid.

flavissima Pall. R, I, p; sts. to 4½ in.; lvs. 3–4 in a tuft, very narrowly sword-shaped, to 4 in. long; spathes 2–3-fld.; perianth tube funnelform, ¼ in. long, falls oblong to 1½ in. long, bright yellow, haft veined brown-purple, beard orange, standards oblong, yellow, veined brown-purple on margin. Hungary to ne. Asia.

flexicaulis: probably best treated as a color variant or cv. of *I. brevicaulis.*

florentina: *I.* × *germanica* var.

foetidissima L. SCARLET-SEEDED I., STINKING I., GLADWIN, STINKING G. R, I, a; sts. 2–3 ft., flattened; lvs. evergreen, sword-shaped, to 2½ ft. or more, slightly glaucous, ill-smelling when bruised; spathes 2–3-fld.; perianth tube about ½ in. long, segms. purplish-gray or yellow, falls obovate to nearly orbicular, to 2 in. long, slightly emarginate, standards oblanceolate to spatulate; seeds scarlet, globular, remaining attached to caps. Eng., w. Eur. to Greece, N. Afr.

foliosa: *I. brevicaulis.*

Forrestii Dykes. R, I, a; sts. to 1½ ft., hollow; lvs. narrowly linear, to 1¼ ft. long, glossy; spathes 1–2-fld.; perianth segms. yellow, falls oblong-ovate, 2 in. long, haft veined brown-purple, standards nearly erect, oblanceolate. High elevations, sw. China.

Fosterana Aitch. & Bak. B, S, j; sts. 6–8 in., to 1 ft. long after flowering; lvs. 4–6, sheathing and obscuring st., lanceolate, curved, to 10 in. long, acuminate; spathes 1-fld.; perianth tube 1⅜ in. long, falls orbicular, to 2 in. long, pale yellow, standards obovate, 1½ in. long, bright purple. Afghanistan and adjacent U.S.S.R.

fulva Ker-Gawl. COPPER I., RED I. R, I, a; sts. to 4 ft.; lvs. sword-shaped, to 3 ft. long, bright green; spathes 2–3-fld.; perianth tube to 1 in. long, segms. reddish-brown or copper-colored, rarely yellow, falls oblanceolate, to 2½ in. long, standards 2 in. long, emarginate; caps. 6-angled, to 2 in. long. Swamps, Ga., w. to Ill., Mo., Tex.

× **fulvala** Dykes: *I. brevicaulis* × *I. fulva;* R, I, a; sts. intermediate in height between parents; similar to *I. fulva* in texture, but more sturdy; perianth segms. red-purple, falls rounded-ovate, standards oblanceolate.

Gatesii M. Foster. R, I, o; sts. to 1½ ft.; lvs. very narrowly sword-shaped, to 1 ft. long, glaucous; spathes 1-fld.; perianth tube to 2 in. long, falls orbicular, to 4 in. wide, pale greenish or grayish-white, veined and dotted purple, beard of groups of gray, greenish, or brownish hairs, standards orbicular, 4–5 in. wide, flecked with purple; caps. to 5 in. long. Asia Minor.

× **germanica** L. [*I. violacea* Savi, not (Ker-Gawl.) Sweet, or Klatt]. FLAG, FLEUR-DE-LIS. R, I, p; sts. to 2½ ft., branched; lvs. sword-shaped, to 1½ ft. long and 1½ in. wide, glaucous; spathes 2–3-fld.; perianth tube 1 in. long, falls obovate, to 3 in. long, deep violet, haft veined with brown, yellow, and white, beard white, tipped yellow, standards arching, obovate, to 3 in. long, light violet. Nativity unknown, perhaps Medit. region; escaped from cult. and naturalized in various parts of the world. Var. **florentina** (L.) Dykes [*I. florentina* L.]. ORRIS. Perianth segms. nearly white, with traces of blue or purple. The major source of orris, the powdered dried rhizome, used in perfumery. *I. albicans* is confused with this var.

giganticaerulea Small. R, I, a; sts. to 5 ft., erect, stout; lvs. linear, to

1½ in. wide, attenuate, glaucous; spathes 1–2-fld.; fls. musk-scented, falls elliptic, about 4 in. long, violet-blue, haft greenish, with yellow blotch, standards broad-spatulate, slightly shorter than falls, violet-blue, claw white or greenish-white. S. La. Cv. 'Miraculosa' [*I. miraculosa* Small]. Fls. white.

goniocarpa Bak. [*I. gracilis* Maxim., not Bigel., or E. Berg.]. R, I, p; sts. to ¼ ft. long; lvs. linear, 6–10 in. long; spathes 1-fld.; perianth tube to ¾ in. long, falls obovate-cuneate, to 1 in. long, mottled blue-purple, beard white, tipped yellow, standards oblong. At high elevations, Sikkim to w. and cent. China.

Gormanii: *I. tenax.*

gracilipes A. Gray. R, I, c; sts. forked, to 1 ft., slender; lvs. sword-shaped, to 16 in. long; spathes 1-fld.; perianth tube funnelform, ½ in. long, falls obovate, 1 in. long, notched, lilac, with deeper veins and central white area, crest yellow, standards spatulate-oblong, pink-lilac. Japan. Cv. 'Alba'. Fls. white.

gracilis: see *I. goniocarpa, I. prismatica,* and *I. pumila.*

Graeberana Sealy. B, S, j; sts. about 1 ft. long at flowering, elongating to 16 in.; lvs. 8, lanceolate, about 5½ in. long at flowering, elongating to 7 in. long, glossy and bluish-green above; spathes 1-fld.; fls. 4–6, axillary except for terminal one, perianth tube to 2¼ in. long, falls oblong, about 1 in. long, blue with darker veins over white areas, deeper blue toward apex, standards spreading, spatulate, about 1 in. long, pale blue-mauve. Turkestan.

graeca: a listed name of no botanical standing.

graminea L. R, I, a; sts. to 9 in., 2-edged; lvs. linear, to 3 ft. long; spathes 1–2-fld., spathe valves usually very unequal in length; fls. hidden among lvs., with fragrance of ripe plums, perianth tube nearly obsolete, falls orbicular, ½ in. wide, yellowish-white, veined purple, standards broad-lanceolate, ¼ in. wide. Cent. and s. Eur. to Caucasus.

Grant-Duffii Bak. [*I. melanosticta* Bornm.]. R, I, a; sts. to ¼ ft.; lvs. linear, to 1½ ft., remains of lvs. forming a ring of sharp, rigid bristles on rhizome; spathes 1-fld.; perianth tube less than ½ in. long, falls obovate, 2½ in. long, yellow, with orange blotch, standards oblanceolate, yellow, claw lilac or purple. Israel and se. Asia Minor.

halophila: *I. spuria* var.

Hartwegii Bak. SIERRA I. R, I, a; sts. to 1 ft.; lvs. linear, to 1½ ft., the remains of lvs. covering rhizome; spathes 1–2-fld.; perianth tube to ⅜ in. long, falls obovate-cuneate, to 2¾ in. long, mostly creamy to pale yellow, sometimes deep yellow or lavender, standards oblanceolate, to 2⅜ in. long. Butte to Kern Co. (Calif.). Subsp. **australis** (S. Parish) Lenz [var. *australis* S. Parish]. Sts. to 16 in.; fls. lavender to purple. S. Calif.

Haynei: *I. atrofusca.*

Helenae Barb. [*I. Barnumiae* var. *Mariae* (Barb.) Dykes; *I. Mariae* Barb.]. R, I, o; sts. to ½ ft.; lvs. linear, curved, to 4 in. long, pale green; spathes 1-fld.; perianth tube ½ in. long, falls orbicular-cuneate, to 2½ in. long, lilac, veined red-brown, haft dark velvety-purple, standards orbicular, clawed, 2 in. wide. Egypt, Israel.

hexagona Walt. R, I, a; sts. to 4 ft., mostly unbranched, leafy; lvs. sword-shaped, 2–3 ft. long, 1½ in. wide; spathes 1–2-fld., terminal spathes, 2–3-fld.; perianth tube to 1½ in. long, falls obovate, to 4¼ in. long, lilac or sometimes white, standards erect, spatulate, lilac varying to white; fr. 6-sided. Swamps, S.C. to Fla., e. to La. and Tex.

hispanica: *I. Xiphium.*

Histrio Rchb.f. B, X, ret; sts. almost lacking; lvs. usually 2, linear, 4-angled, to 8 in. long, at flowering, elongating to about 1 ft.; spathes 1-fld., spathe valves membranous, white; fls. usually appearing after lvs., odorless, perianth tube 3–4 in. long, falls obliquely ascending, obovate-spatulate, to 2½ in. long, deep blue at margins, creamy-white with blue blotches in center, standards oblanceolate, blue. Israel. Var. **aintabensis** Hort. Listed as early flowering; fls. bright blue.

histrioides S. Arn. B, X, ret; sts. to 9 in.; lvs. rather stiff, linear, 4-angled, appearing with the fls.; spathes 1-fld.; perianth tube to 3½ in. long, falls nearly horizontal, ovate, to 2¼ in. long, bright blue-purple, with white central blotch and yellow ridge, standards erect, spatulate, 2¼ in. long, violet-blue. N. Asia Minor. Cv. 'Major'. Flowering very early; fls. bright blue.

hollandica: a name that has been used for a hort. strain of *I. Xiphium* hybrids, more often referred to as Dutch bulbous iris.

Hoogiana Dykes. R, I, r; sts. to 1¾ ft.; lvs. sword-shaped, slightly curved, to 1½ ft. long, glaucous-green; spathes 2–3-fld.; perianth tube about 1 in. long, segms. uniformly gray-blue or blue-purple, or sometimes white, falls rounded-obovate, to about 3 in. long, beard golden-yellow, thick, standards obovate, clawed, to 3 in. long, beard golden-yellow, thin. Turkestan. Cv. 'Purpurea'. Fls. purple.

Hookeri: *I. setosa* var. *canadensis.*

humilis Bieb. R, I, a; sts. to 1½ in.; lvs. firm, linear, to 1 ft., conspicuously nerved, glaucous; spathes 1-fld., appearing sessile between 2 lvs.; perianth tube to 1½ in. long, falls nearly orbicular, deep blue-purple, with darker veins, haft greenish-yellow to white, with reddish-brown veins, standards oblanceolate, blue-purple. Transylvania to Caucasus and perhaps beyond.

iberica Hoffmanns. R, I, o; sts. 3–6 in.; lvs. 5–6, crowded, linear, 4–6 in. long, glaucous; spathes 1-fld.; perianth tube 1 in. long, falls nearly orbicular, about 3 in. long, whitish-yellow, veined brown-purple, signal patch velvety, purple-black, standards orbicular, silvery-white, dotted and veined purplish or brownish. Caucasus to n. Iran.

illyrica: *I. Cengialtii* var.

imbricata Lindl. [*I. sulphurea* C. Koch]. R, I, p; sts. to 1½ ft.; lvs. sword-shaped, to 15 in. long, yellow-green; spathes 2–3-fld., spathe valves inflated, green; perianth tube about 1 in. long, segms. greenish-yellow tinged brown at back, falls obovate, 2¼ in. long, beard whitish, tipped orange, standards rounded-oblong. Sw. Asia.

innominata L. F. Henders. R, I, a; sts. to 8 in.; lvs. many, linear, to 14 in. long, glossy and dark green in upper part, pink to purplish-red basally; spathes 1–2-fld.; perianth tube to 1⅛ in. long, segms. golden-yellow and variously veined to clear yellow, or lavender to deep purple, falls lanceolate to oblanceolate, to 2½ in. long, standards to 2¼ in. long. Sw. Ore. and adjacent Calif. Cv. **'Lutea'**. Fls. yellow. Cv. **'Lilacina'**. Fls. lavender.

intermedia: a listed name of no botanical standing, used for bearded irises, 1¼–2¼ ft., chiefly clones of hybrid origin, blooming after the dwarfs and tall irises; fls. 4–5 in. across.

italica: *I. Chamaeiris.*

japonica Thunb. R, I, c; sts. to 2½ ft., branched; lvs. sword-shaped, to 1½ ft. long, green above, paler beneath; spathes 3–4-fld.; fls. 2–3 in. wide, perianth tube to ¾ in. long, falls oblong-spatulate, lavender-blue, with conspicuous yellow crests and orange markings, standards oblong, to 1¼ in. long, clawed, mauve, crests of styles fimbriate. Japan, China.

Kaempferi Siebold ex Lem. JAPANESE I. R, I, a; sts. to 2 ft., frequently branched; lvs. sword-shaped, to 2 ft. long or more, with prominent midrib; spathes 2-fld.; perianth tube to ¾ in. long, segms. red-purple, falls drooping, elliptic to obovate, to 3 in. long, haft yellow at center, standards narrowly oblanceolate, to 2 in. long. Japan. Cv. **'Azurea'**. Fls. blue. Also many fancy-named cvs., the fls. of various colors, sometimes double.

kashmeriana Bak. R, I, p; sts. 2–4 ft., branched; lvs. sword-shaped, to 2 ft. long, yellowish-green, glaucous; spathes 1–3-fld.; fls. fragrant, perianth tube 1 in. long, segms. white, falls obovate, to 3 in. long, beard white and yellow, standards oblong, to 3 in. long. Kashmir, Afghanistan, Baluchistan. Cv. **'Alba'**. Fls. white.

Kernerana Asch. ex Bak. R, I, a; sts. to 1 ft.; lvs. in clusters, sheathing, and obscuring sts., sword-shaped, about 1½ ft. long, yellowish-green; spathes 2–3-fld.; perianth tube to ½ in. long, segms. yellow, falls broadly lanceolate, about 2½ in. long, undulate, standards tending to twist, linear-lanceolate, notched, undulate. Asia Minor.

Kimballiae: probably best treated as color variant or cv. of *I. savannarum.*

×**Kochii** A. Kern. ex Stapf. R, I, p; sts. 1½–2 ft., branched; lvs. sword-shaped, ½–2 ft.; spathes 2–3-fld.; perianth segms. red-purple, falls obovate, haft veined brown, beard yellow. N. Italy. Perhaps only a variant of *I.* ×*germanica,* but shorter and differing in fl. color.

koreana Nakai. R, I, a; somewhat taller than *I. minutaurea;* lvs. longer than sts., to 14 in. long; spathes 2-fld.; perianth segms. yellow, falls obovate, standards erect, elliptic, emarginate. Korea.

Korolkowii Regel. R, I, r; sts. to about 1 ft.; lvs. narrowly sword-shaped, about 1 ft. long, glaucous; spathes 2-fld.; perianth tube 1 in. long, falls obovate, to 3 in. long, creamy-white, with veins and signal patch olive-green or brown, standards erect, obovate, whitish, veined brown, not bearded. Turkestan. Cv. **'Concolor'** [var. *concolor* M. Foster]. Fls. bright lilac-purple. Cv. **'Violacea'** [var. *violacea* M. Foster]. Perianth segms. creamy-white, veined red-violet.

kamaonensis Wallich ex D. Don (often misspelled *kumaonensis*). R, I, ps; plant compact, sts. usually less than 2–3 in.; lvs. erect, linear, about 6 in. long at flowering, elongating to 1½ ft., glaucous; spathes 1–2-fld.; perianth tube 1–2 in. long, falls oblong-ovate, blue-purple, veined and mottled with dark purple, haft white, veined purplish, beard white, occasionally tipped orange or brownish-yellow, standards papery, clawed. High elevations, cent. Himalayas.

lacustris Nutt. R, I, c; sts. 1–3 in.; lvs. broadly linear, to 2⅜ in. long at flowering, elongating to about 7 in.; spathes 1–2-fld.; fls. to about 2 in. wide; perianth tube scarcely longer than spathe valves, to 1 in. long, dull yellow, segms. blue, falls obovate, standards emarginate. Gravelly shores, Lakes Huron, Michigan, and Superior.

laevigata Fisch. R, I, a; sts. to about 2 ft.; lvs. ½–2 ft. long, glaucous, lacking a distinct midrib; spathes usually 3-fld.; perianth tube to ¾ in. long, segms. clear blue, falls obovate, to 2½ in. long, standards erect, oblanceolate, 2½ in. long; caps. obtuse. E. Asia, China, Japan. Cvs. are: **'Alba'**, fls. white; **'Albopurpurea'**, falls streaked, standards white; **'Atropurpurea'**, fls. white, with splashes of violet; **'Colchesterensis'**, fls. marine blue, segms. edged with white; **'Semperflorens'**, fls. cobalt-blue.

Leichtlinii: *I. stolonifera.*

lilacinaurea: probably best treated as color variant or cv. of *I.* ×*vinicolor.*

longipetala Herb. R, I, a; sts. to 2 ft., stout, usually branched; lvs. narrowly sword-shaped, to 2½ ft. long; spathes 3–6-fld.; perianth tube to ½ in. long, segms. white veined lilac, falls obovate, to 4 in. long, standards oblong, to 3½ in. long, emarginate. Coastal, cent. Calif.

Lortetii Barb. ex Boiss. R, I, o; sts. about 1 ft.; lvs. sword-shaped, curved, less than 1 ft. long at flowering, glaucous; spathes 1-fld.; perianth tube to 2 in. long, falls strongly reflexed, obovate, to 3 in. wide, pale lilac, veined and dotted crimson, signal patch crimson, beard yellow, standards erect, orbicular, 3–4 in. wide, pale lilac, with darker veins. Lebanon.

lurida Ait. R, I, p; sts. to 1½ ft.; lvs. sword-shaped, to 1 ft. long, conspicuously veined; spathes 2–3-fld.; perianth tube 1 in. long, falls oblong, to 2½ in. long, reddish-maroon, yellow and strongly veined with purple in lower half, beard orange, standards elliptic, emarginate, dull purple. Probably of garden origin.

lusitanica: *I. Xyphium.*

lutea: *I. Pseudacorus.*

lutescens: *I. Chamaeiris.*

macrosiphon Torr. [*I. californica* Leichtl.]. R, I, a; sts. to 10 in.; lvs. linear, longer than st., colorless at base; spathes mostly 2-fld.; perianth tube to 2⅝ in. long, segms. yellow, cream, or pale lavender to deep blue-purple, falls oblanceolate to obovate, to 2⅝ in. long. Cent. to n. Calif.

magnifica Vved. B, S, j; sts. to 16 in.; lvs. spaced apart, not obscuring st., curved, about 7 in. long; fls. 2–8, axillary, perianth tube to 2 in. long, falls to 2 in. long, light lilac to almost white, with darker central veins, haft winged, standards horizontal to reflexed, oblong-oblanceolate, almost 1 in. long, pale lilac, with darker veins. Cent. Asia.

mandshurica Maxim. R, I, p; sts. to 6 in., sometimes branched; lvs. sword-shaped, 6–8 in. long; spathes 2-fld.; perianth tube ½ in. long, segms. greenish-yellow, falls obovate-cuneate, to 2 in. long, beard yellow, standards shorter. S. Manchuria and Korea.

Mariae: *I. Helenae.*

melanosticta: *I. Grant-Duffii.*

mellita Janka [*I. rubromarginata* Bak.]. R, I, p; sts. to 10 in.; lvs. sword-shaped, 3–5 in. long, slightly glaucous; spathes 1–2-fld.; fls. delicate in texture, fragrant, perianth tube about 2 in. long, falls strongly reflexed, obovate, brown-purple varying to yellow, standards slightly larger than falls. Se. Eur., Asia Minor. Differs from *I. pumila* in having spathes herbaceous, keeled, more rigid.

mesopotamica Dykes. R, I, p; sts. 3–4 ft., branched; lvs. sword-shaped, to 2 ft. long; spathes 2–3-fld.; falls obovate, lavender-blue, haft white, veined purple-bronze, beard white and orange, standards obovate, lighter than falls. Probably Armenia.

Milesii M. Foster. R, I, c; sts. to 3 ft., 2–4-branched, leafy; lvs. sword-shaped, to 2 ft. long, pale green; spathes 2–4-fld.; fls. about 4 in. wide, perianth tube about ½ in. long, falls oblong, to 1¼ in. long, reddish-lilac, with darker veins and blotches, crests prominent, orange and yellow, finely lacerate, standards spreading. Nw. Himalayas.

minuta: *I. minutaurea.*

minutaurea Mak. [*I. minuta* Franch. & Sav.]. R, I, a; sts. to 2½ in., tufted; lvs. linear, 5–6 in. long in flower, elongating to 15 in.; spathes 1-fld.; perianth tube about ¾ in. long, falls obovate, ⅝ in. long, emarginate, yellow, spotted purple, standards shorter. Japan.

miraculosa: probably best treated as color variant or cv. of *I. giganticaerulea.*

mississippiensis: probably best treated as color variant or cv. of *I. brevicaulis.*

missouriensis Nutt. WESTERN BLUE F. R, I, a; sts. to 2 ft., often branched, lvs. to 1½ ft. long, glaucous, remains of lvs. covering rhizome; spathes 1–2-fld., spathe valves scarious except on the outside and at base; perianth tube ⅜ in. long, falls obovate, to 2⅜ in. long, light lilac or white, veined lilac-purple, standards oblanceolate to spatulate, ovary to 1⅛ in. long; caps. oblong, to 2 in. long. S. Dak. to B.C., s. to Calif., Ariz., and adjacent Mex. Cv. 'Alba'. Fls. white. Var. **pelogonus** (L. Goodd.) R. Foster [*I. montana* Nutt. ex Dykes]. Lvs. shorter, thicker; pedicels shorter, ovary not over ⅝ in. long.

Monnieri DC. R, I, a; sts. to 4 ft., stout; lvs. lanceolate, to about 2 ft. long; spathes 2-fld.; fls. fragrant, segms. soft lemon-yellow, falls orbicular, 1½ in. wide, emarginate, standards oblong-cuneate. Crete. Related to *I. spuria*.

montana: *I. missouriensis* var. *pelogonus*.

Munzii R. Foster. R, I, a; sts. to 2⅜ ft., unbranched, stout; lvs. to 2 ¾ ft. long, gray-green, glaucous, remains of lvs. borne on rhizomes; spathes usually 3-fld.; perianth tube to ⅜ in. long, segms. light lavender to blue-violet, falls oblong-ovate to oblanceolate, to 3½ in. long, standards oblanceolate to spatulate, to 3¾ in. long. Tulare Co. (Calif.).

musulmanica Fomin. R, I, a; sts. to about 2 ft.; lvs. linear, about as long as sts.; spathes 1-fld.; perianth tube about ⁵⁄₁₆ in. long, segms. bluish or yellowish-white, falls reflexed, elliptic-orbicular, yellowish at base, abruptly narrowed at haft, standards obovate, gradually narrowed to claw, retuse; caps. beaked, 6-angled. Azerbaijan.

nazarena Hort. Rivoire. R, I, o; sts. to 1½ ft.; lvs. sword-shaped, to 9 in. long; spathes 1-fld.; perianth tube, 2¾ in. long, falls orbicular-ovate, to 6 in. long, cream-colored, with red-brown embossed spots and purple or maroon veins, signal patch ringed dark brown, standards orbicular, to 4 in. long, white, veined blue, with purple dots toward margins, claw dark red-brown. Israel.

×**Nelsonii** Randolph: (?) *I. brevicaulis* × *I. fulva* × *I. giganticaerulea*. R, I, a; a naturally occurring, true-breeding hybrid; sts. to 3⅝ ft., branched; lvs. sword-shaped, to 3 ft. long; fls. drooping, to 4¾ in. across, perianth segms. bright red-purple, or very rarely yellow, falls oblanceolate-spatulate to 2¾ in. long and 1½ in. wide, standards oblanceolate-spatulate, to 2⅛ in. long and ¾ in. wide. Abbeville Swamp (La.).

nepalensis D. Don. N; roots dahlialike, flattened, white, fleshy, sts. to 1 ft.; lvs. very narrowly sword-shaped, about 1 ft. long at flowering, elongating to 2 ft., fibrous remains of old lvs. covering short rhizome; spathes usually 2-fld.; perianth tube 1½ in. long, falls oblong, to 1½ in. long, white, veined violet, haft yellow, standards oblanceolate, clawed, darker violet. Temp. regions of Himalayas.

nigricans Dinsm. R, I, o; sts. to about 1 ft.; lvs. curved, to 8¾ in. long; spathes 1-fld.; perianth tube 2⅜ in. long, falls obovate, about 2½ in. long, veined and dotted dark brown-purple, signal patch black, standards elliptic, white, veined dark purple-lilac. Israel.

notha Bieb. [*I. spuria* var. *notha* Hort.]. R, I, a; sts. to 2¾ ft., erect, leafy; lvs. linear to 1⅝ ft. long, long-acuminate; spathes 1-3-fld.; perianth tube ¾ in. long, falls reflexed, broadly elliptic, dark blue, haft with yellow band, standards erect, oblong. Wet areas, Caucasus.

ochroleuca: *I. orientalis*.

odoratissima: *I. pallida*.

orchidoides Carrière. ORCHID I. B, S, j; sts. to 1 ft., leafy; lvs. to 1 ft. long and 2 in. wide, glossy above, glaucous beneath; fls. 1, axillary, perianth tube to 2 in. long, segms. deep yellow, falls ovate, ½ in. wide, emarginate with greenish and darker color on each side of crest, standards commonly reflexed, lanceolate, to ¾ in. long. Turkestan.

orientalis Mill., not Thunb. [*I. ochroleuca* L.; *I. spuria* var. *ochroleuca* Hort.]. R, I, a; sts. to 3 ft.; lvs. sword-shaped, 2-3 ft. long, dark green; spathes 2-3-fld.; perianth tube less than ½ in. long, falls reflexed, orbicular, 1¾ in. wide, white with golden-yellow central blotch, standards rounded-cuneate, to 3½ in. long, lemon-yellow to whitish. W. Asia Minor. Perhaps not distinct from *I. spuria*, or only a var. of it. *I. orientalis* Thunb. is *I. sanguinea*.

pallida Lam. [*I. odoratissima* Jacq.]. ORRIS. R, I, p; sts. to 3 ft., stout, branched; lvs. to 2 ft. long, glaucous; spathes 2-3-fld., spathe valves silvery-white, scarious; fls. fragrant, perianth tube about ½ in. long, segms. lavender-blue, falls obovate, haft veined brown-purple, beard white, tipped yellow, standards obovate, paler than falls; seeds red-brown, compressed, angled. S. Tyrol. One of the irises grown for the production of orris, the powdered dry rhizome used in perfumery. Cv. 'Dalmatica'. Lvs. wider, lvs. lavender. Cv. 'Variegata'. Lvs. variegated.

paradoxa Steven. R, I, o; sts. to 6 in. long; lvs. 4-5, linear, curved, to 6 in. long, glaucous; spathes 1-fld.; fls. large, showy, perianth tube to ¾ in. long, falls horizontal, strap-shaped, 2 in. long, to ¾ in. wide, pale pinkish-crimson, beard of scattered purple-black hairs, standards orbicular, blue or white, with blue-purple veins and dots. Caucasus to n. Iran.

Pavonia: *Moraea neopavonia*.

persica L. PERSIAN I. B, S, j; sts. none or very short; lvs. 4-5, basal, linear, folded, to 3 in. long in flower; fls. 1-2, perianth tube 2-3 in. long, segms. white, tinged pale greenish-blue or sea-green, falls ob-

ovate-spatulate, to 2½ in. long, with orange ridge, purple lines and dots, and a dark purple blotch, standards twisted or turned downward, linear-spatulate, ¾ in. long, blue. E. Asia Minor to Iran.

planifolia (Mill.) T. Durand & Schinz [*I. alata* Poir.]. B, S, j; sts. very short; lvs. linear to linear-lanceolate, to 4 in. in flower, elongating to 1 ft.; fls. 1-3, perianth tube 4-6 in. long, falls oblong, 3-4 in. long, lilac-purple, ridge yellow, haft winged, standards horizontal, oblanceolate-spatulate, to 1 in. long. Spain to Sicily and N. Afr.

Polakii Stapf. R, I, o; sts. to 8 in.; lvs. linear, 3-4 in. long in flower; spathes 1-fld.; perianth tube ⅝ in. long, falls reflexed, obovate-cuneate, to 2 in. long, maroon, beard and pair of signal patches black-purple, standards obovate, to 3¼ in. long, purple, with darker veins. N. Iran.

prismatica Pursh [*I. gracilis* Bigel., not Maxim., or E. Berg]. SLENDER BLUE F. R, I, a; sts. to 2½ ft., branched, slender, wiry, solid; lvs. erect, linear, to 2½ ft. long; spathes 1-3-fld.; perianth tube to ⅛ in. long, segms. blue to blue-violet, falls ovate to obovate, about ¾ in. wide, with darker veins, haft greenish, veined purple, standards erect, obovate, to 1¾ in. long; caps. sharply 3-angled. Nov. Sc. to Ga.

Pseudacorus L. [*I. Bastardii* Spach; *I. lutea* Lam.]. YELLOW I., YELLOW F., WATER F. R, I, a; rhizomes pink inside, sts. to 5 ft., branched; lvs. sword-shaped, about as long as st., rather glaucous; spathes 3-5-fld.; perianth tube about ½ in. long, not constricted, segms. light yellow to almost orange, falls ovate to obovate, about 2 in. long, often veined violet, standards elliptic, to 1 in. long; caps. 6-angled. Widespread in wet areas, w. Eur., N. Afr.; naturalized in e. N. Amer. Cvs. are: 'Alba', fls. creamy-white; 'Gigantea', fls. larger, medium yellow; 'Mandshurica', fls. burnished yellow; 'Variegata' lvs. variegated yellow and green.

pseudopumila Tineo [*I. statellae* Tod.]. R, I, p; sts. to 7 in. long; lvs. sword-shaped, to 8 in. long, glaucescent; spathes 1-fld.; perianth tube 2-3 in. long, shorter than st., falls obovate, white, yellow, or purple, haft wedge-shaped, beard white, tipped yellow, standards oblong, lighter than falls. Sicily, s. Italy.

pumila L. [*I. attica* Boiss. & Heldr.; *I. coerulea* Spach, not B. Fedtsch.; *I. gracilis* E. Berg, not Maxim., or Bigel.; *I. violacea* (Ker-Gawl.) Sweet, not Savi, or Klatt]. R, I, p; sts. short to almost lacking; lvs. sword-shaped, to 4 in. long in flower, elongating to 8 in.; spathes 1-2-fld.; perianth tube 2-3 in. long, usually longer than st., segms. varying from yellow to bright or dark lilac, falls reflexed, oblong, about 2 in. long, beard bluish, white, or yellow, standards oblong, 2 in. long, Cent. Eur. to s. Russia and Asia Minor. Many color forms are offered, including the following cvs.: 'Alba', fls. cream-colored; 'Atropurpurea', fls. purple; 'Atroviolacea', fls. rich wine-red; 'Aurea', fls. clear, bright yellow; 'Azurea', fls. sky-blue, veined lilac; 'Caerulea', fls. soft blue; 'Cyanea', fls. deep blue; 'Excelsa', to 6 in. tall, fls. pale yellow; 'Lutea', fls. golden-yellow.

Purdyi Eastw. R, I, a; sts. to about 1 ft.; lvs. somewhat compressed, to 1½ ft. long and about ¼ in. wide, pinkish or reddish at base, upper lvs. reduced to inflated bracts; spathes usually 2-fld.; perianth tube to 1⅞ in. long, segms. pale creamy-yellow veined brown-purple, falls oblanceolate, 2¼-3¼ in. long, sometimes paler with a lavender tint, standards lanceolate, to 2¾ in. long. Coastal, n. Calif.

pyrenaica: *I. xiphioides*.

reginae I. Horvat & M. Horvat. R, I, p; sts. to 1¾ ft., branched; lvs. sword-shaped, curved, to about 14 in. long, glaucous-green, conspicuously nerved; spathes 2-3-fld.; perianth tube to 1¼ in. long, falls oblong-cuneate, to 2¼ in. long, upper surface pale violet to white, with dark violet veins merging toward apex and forming dark violet triangular spot, lower surface pale violet, beard yellow and white, standards erect, oblong-elliptic, to 2½ in. long and ¾ in. wide, emarginate, pale violet, with pale apical spot. Cent. Macedonia.

Reichenbachii Heuff. [*I. balkana* Janka]. R, I, p; sts. 3-12 in.; lvs. sword-shaped, 3-6 in. long in flower, elongating with age; spathes 1-2-fld., spathe valves sharply keeled; perianth tube funnelform, to 1½ in. long, segms. yellow with orange beard, or chocolate with bluish beard, falls obovate-cuneate, standards oblong-elliptic. S. Hungary, Balkans.

reticulata Bieb. B, X, ret; sts. very short; lvs. linear, 4-angled, 8-10 in. long in flower, elongating to 1½ ft.; spathes 1-fld.; fls. violet-scented, perianth tube 3-6 in. long, segms. deep violet-purple, falls ovate, ½ in. wide, crests yellow, standards erect, 2½ in. long, ¼ in. wide. Caucasus. Cv. 'Alba'. Fls. white.

rubromarginata: *I. mellita*.

ruthenica Ker-Gawl. R, I, a; sts. to 8 in.; lvs. linear, to 6 in. in flower, elongating to 1 ft.; spathes 1-2-fld.; fls. fragrant; perianth tube to 1 in. long, falls broadly elliptic, ½ in. wide, creamy-white, with blue-purple veins and dots, standards lanceolate, deep purple-violet. E. Eur., w. to n. China, Korea.

samariae Dinsm. R, I, o; sts. about 16 in., robust; lvs. sword-shaped, to about 16 in. long; spathes 1-fld.; perianth tube to 2 in. long, falls not reflexed, obovate, to 2 in. long, cream-colored, streaked and dotted with purple, signal patch dark brown, beard red-brown, standards orbicular, to 2½ in. long, streaked with dark brown. E. Medit.

sanguinea Hornem. [*I. orientalis* Thunb., not Mill.; *I. sibirica* var. *orientalis* (Thunb.) Bak.]. R, I, a; sts. to 1½ ft., hollow; lvs. linear, to 1½ ft. long and ½ in. wide; spathes 2–3-fld.; fls. to 3¼ in. across, falls suborbicular, white, usually veined blue-purple, haft veined faint yellow, standards broadly elliptic, slightly shorter than falls, blue-purple or white. Manchuria, Japan.

sari Schott ex Bak. R, I, o; sts. to 6 in.; lvs. linear, straight to slightly curved, to 1 ft. long; spathes 1-fld.; perianth tube 1½ in. long, falls obovate-cuneate, to 3 in. long, yellow or greenish, veined brownish-red, signal patch reddish-black, beard yellow with some marginal hairs brown-tipped, standards coherent, nearly orbicular, to 3¾ in. long, somewhat darker than falls. Asia Minor.

savannarum Small. R, I, a; sts. to 3 ft.; lvs. erect, linear, to 3 ft. long; spathes 1-fld.; perianth tube to ½ in. long, falls elliptic, to 3⅛ in. long, violet or violet-blue, flecked with white, standards nearly linear to spatulate, violet or bluish. Peninsular Fla. Cv. **'Kimballiae'** [*I. Kimballiae* Small]. Falls violet, standards blue, style brs. more sharply toothed. N. Fla.

scariosa Willd. ex Link [*I. elongata* Hort.]. R, I, p; sts. to 6 in.; lvs. to 1 ft. long and ¾ in. wide, very glaucous; spathes 1–2-fld., spathe valves to 2½ in. long, dry, more or less transparent; perianth tube to 1½ in. long, brown-purple, falls reflexed, obovate, to 1¾ in. long, red-purple, with darker veins, beard yellow on haft, tipped purple on blade, standards obovate, red-purple, to 1½ in. long. Turkestan.

setosa Pall. ex Link. R, I, a; sts. to 2 ft., stout, branched; lvs. sword-shaped, to 2 ft. long and 1 in. wide; spathes 2–3-fld.; perianth tube to ⅜ in. long, falls more or less orbicular, about 1 in. wide, dark blue-purple, with a white basal blotch and lighter streaks, standards oblanceolate, to ¾ in. long, setose at apex. blue-purple. Ne. Asia and Alaska. Var. **canadensis** R. Foster [*I. Hookeri* Penny]. BEACHHEAD I., BEACHHEAD F. Smaller; lvs. fewer and smaller; falls with basal white spot, larger, standards smaller. Coastal, n. Me. to Lab.

Shrevei: *I. virginica var.*

sibirica L. SIBERIAN I. R, I, a; sts. to 3¾ ft., branched toward the top, hollow; lvs. linear, to 2½ ft.; spathes 2–3-fld., spathe valves brown and scarious; perianth tube ½ in. long, falls reflexed, rounded-oblong, ¾ in. wide, lilac-blue or blue-purple, or even grayish, standards broadly lanceolate, shorter than falls. Cent. Eur., Russia. Cv. **'Alba'**. Fls. white. Cv. **'Caerulea'**. Fls. blue. Var. **orientalis**: *I. sanguinea.*

sikkimensis Dykes. R, I, p; sts. to 6 in.; lvs. sword-shaped, to 8 in. in flower, elongating to 1½ ft. long, ¾ in. wide; spathes 1–2-fld.; perianth tube to 2 in. long, deep purple, falls obovate, to 2½ in. long, purple-lilac, with darker mottling at end of beard, beard white, tipped orange, standards oblong, 2 in. long, deeply emarginate, pale mauve-lilac, faintly mottled. Sikkim.

sindjarensis: *I. Aucheri.*

×**sindpers** J. M. C. Hoog: *I. Aucheri* × *I. persica*. B, S, j; sts. to 9½ in.; lvs. curved, to about 7 in. long and 1½ in. wide; fls. essentially sessile, falls to 1⅝ in. long, mauve, paler toward apex, ridge yellow, standards horizontal or somewhat reflexed, to 1 in. long, mauve.

Sintenisii Janka [*I. Urumovii* Velen.]. R, I, a; rhizome wiry, sts. to 1 ft., cylindrical; lvs. linear, to 1½ ft. long and to ⅓ in. wide, acuminate; spathes 1-fld.; perianth tube short, falls elliptic, to 1¼ in. long, white veined blue-purple, standards erect, oblanceolate, to 1 in. long, emarginate, deep blue-purple. Se. Eur., Asia Minor.

Sisyrinchium: *Gynandriris Sisyrinchium.*

sogdiana: *I. spuria* var. *halophila.*

spuria L. BUTTERFLY I., SPURIA I. R, I, a; sts. to 2 ft., branched, stout, cylindrical; lvs. linear, to 1 ft. long, stiff, glaucous; spathes 1–3-fld.; perianth tube ½–¾ in. long, segms. blue-purple or lilac, orbicular, falls about 2 in. long, with a yellow ridge, standards oblanceolate, about ½ in. wide. Cent. and s. Eur., Algeria to Iran. Cv. **'Lilacina'**. Fls. orchid-colored. Var. **aurea**: *I. crocea*. Var. **halophila** (Pall.) Dykes [*I. desertorum* Ker-Gawl.; *I. halophila* Pall.; *I. sogdiana* Bunge]. Sts. shorter; fls. dull yellow or white and veined yellow, or grayish-lilac. Caucasus and s. Russia, e. to Iran, nw. Pakistan, cent. Asia, w. Siberia, Mongolia. Var. **notha**: *I. notha*. Var. **ochroleuca**: *I. orientalis.*

statellae: *I. pseudopumila.*

stolonifera Maxim. [*I. Leichtlinii* Regel; *I. vaga* M. Foster]. R, I, r; sts. to 2 ft., sheathed by lvs.; lvs. sword-shaped, to 2 ft. long, blue-green, conspicuously nerved; spathes 1–2-fld.; perianth tube funnelform, to 1 in. long, falls reflexed, obovate, to 3 in. long, wavy, blue-purple, strongly veined with brown, beard yellow, standards obovate, to 2½ in. long, blue-purple, brown toward margin, beard yellow. Uzbek (S.S.R.) Turkestan. Cv. **'Compacta'**. Fls. brown.

stylosa: *I. unguicularis.*

subbiflora Brot. [*I. biflora* L., in part]. R, I, p; sts. to 1 ft.; lvs. sword-shaped, to 8 in. long and 1 in. wide; spathes 1–2-fld.; perianth tube to 1 in. long, falls obovate, to 1½ in. long, deep blue-purple, haft whitish, veined brown-purple, beard bluish and white, tipped blue or some hairs tipped brownish-yellow, standards obovate, paler than falls. Portugal, Spain.

sulphurea: *I. imbricata.*

susiana L. [*I. basaltica* Dinsm.]. MOURNING I., PALESTINE I. R, I, o; sts. to 15 in.; lvs. few, reduced, basal lvs. linear, 1 ft. long, 1 in. wide, yellowish-green; spathes 1-fld.; fls. large, perianth tube 1–1⅓ in. long, segms. gray, veined and spotted purple-black, falls ovate, 3–4 in. long, signal patch velvety purple-black, beard broad, brownish, standards orbicular, somewhat lighter. Probably Asia Minor and Iran. An old garden plant.

Suworowii: *I. darwasica.*

tectorum Maxim. WALL I., ROOF I. R, I, c; sts. to 1 ft. or more, branched; lvs. sword-shaped, to 1 ft. long, thin, conspicuously nerved; spathes 2–3-fld.; perianth tube 1 in. long, segms. deep lilac to blue-purple, with darker veins, falls nearly orbicular, to 2 in. long, crest deeply cut, wavy-margined, white with brown-violet streaks, standards spreading, obovate, lilac. China. Cv. **'Alba'**. Fls. white.

tenax Dougl. ex Lindl. [*I. Gormanii* Piper]. R, I, a; sts. slender, to 14 in.; lvs. linear, to 20 in. long, tough and fibrous; spathes 1–2-fld., pedicels to 1½ in. long; perianth tube funnelform, to ⅜ in. long, segms. yellow, lavender to blue, purple, or rarely white, falls oblanceolate to obovate, to 2½ in. long, standards lanceolate. E. Ore., e. Wash. Subsp. **klamathensis** Lenz. Fls. larger, perianth segms. buff-yellow, falls to 3 in. long, pale buff-yellow, usually veined brown or maroon. Nw. Calif. Subsp. **Thompsonii** (R. Foster) Q. Clarkson [*I. Thompsonii* R. Foster]. Fls. purple.

tenuifolia Pall. R, I, a; rhizome very slender, wiry, sts. to 16 in., leafy; lvs. stiff, linear, to 1 ft. long and less than ¼ in. wide; spathes 2–fld.; perianth tube to 4 in. long, segms. blue-purple, falls with wedge-shaped haft, standards oblanceolate, anthers blue or purplish. Cent. Asia to China.

tenuis S. Wats. R, I, a; sts. to 1 ft.; lvs. sword-shaped, to 1 ft. long and ½ in. wide, thin; spathes 1-fld.; perianth tube very short, segms. white, blotched yellow, veined blue-purple, falls spreading, oblong-spatulate, sometimes over 1 in. long, standards erect, somewhat shorter, emarginate. Nw. Ore.

tenuissima Dykes. R, I, a; sts. to 1 ft.; lvs. linear, to 16 in. long, gray-green; spathes 2-fld.; perianth tube to 2¼ in. long, segms. pale cream-colored, veined brown, reddish-brown, or lavender, falls lanceolate or linear-lanceolate, to 3 in. long, standards to 2½ in. long, stigmas slender, triangular to ligulate. N. Calif. Subsp. **purdyformis** (R. Foster) Lenz. Spathe valves broadly lanceolate, inflated stigmas triangular to rounded. Plumas Co. (Calif.).

Thompsonii: *I. tenax* subsp.

tingitana Boiss. & Reut. B, X; sts. to 2 ft., stout, cylindrical; lvs. sheathing st., basal lvs. linear, to 1½ ft. long, conspicuously nerved; spathes 1–2-fld.; perianth tube 1½–2 in. long, falls obovate to nearly orbicular, to 3 in. long, light blue or lilac, ridge orange-yellow, standards linear-lanceolate, to 4 in. long, tapering, acute, blue-purple. Morocco.

tridentata Pursh [*I. tripetala* Walt.]. R, I, a; sts. to 16 in., slender, stiff, sometimes twisted; lvs. linear, to 15 in. long; spathes usually 1-fld.; fls. fragrant, perianth tube funnelform, less than 1 in. long, falls nearly orbicular, to 2 in. long, violet to white, yellow at base, standards erect, oblanceolate, to ½ in. long, often 3-toothed. N.C. to Fla.

tripetala: *I. tridentata.*

trojana A. Kern. ex Stapf. R, I, p; sts. to 3 ft., branched; lvs. sword-shaped, shorter than sts., somewhat glaucous; spathes 1–2-fld.; fls. fragrant, about 4 in. across, falls obovate, blue- or violet-purple, with a somewhat reddish tint, beard white tipped yellow, or yellow, standards obovate, rounded at apex, light blue-purple. Introd. from region of ancient Troy, Asia Minor, but nativity uncertain.

Tubergeniana M. Foster. B, S, j; sts. to 4 in.; lvs. lanceolate, to 3⅛ in. long, with cartilaginous, ciliate margins, conspicuously nerved, glaucous-green; fls. 1–3, axillary, sessile, perianth tube to 2 in. long, falls fiddle-shaped, to 2 in. long, yellow, haft sometimes marked olive-green at center, crest yellow, cut into conspicuous filaments, standards horizontal, minute, 3-toothed. Turkestan.

tuberosa: *Hermodactylus tuberosus.*

unguicularis Poir. [*I. cretensis* Janka; *I. cretica* Herb. ex Bak.; *I. stylosa* Desf.]. R, I, a; sts. short or almost none; lvs. firm, linear, to 2 ft. long and ½ in. wide; spathes 1-fld.; perianth tube 9 in. long, falls oblong-cuneate, to 3 in. long, bright lilac, central area cream-colored, veined deep lilac, standards oblong, to ¾ in. wide, upper part lilac or lavender. Algeria and Greece, e. to Syria and Asia Minor. Cvs. are: **'Alba'**, fls. white; **'Angustifolia'**, smaller, fls. smaller, lavender or purple; **'Marginata'**, fls. fragrant, segms. violet, with yellow and white markings; **'Speciosa'**, fls. deep blue; **'Violacea'**, fls. violet.

Urumovii: *I. Sintenisii.*

vaga: *I. stolonifera.*

variegata L. R, I, p; sts. to 15 in., branched; lvs. sword-shaped, to 1½ ft. long, conspicuously nerved; spathes 2–3-fld., inflated; perianth tube ¾ in. long, falls obovate, about ¾ in. wide, yellow, variegated chestnut or purple, beard yellow or orange, standards oblong, rounded at apex, bright yellow. Austria, Balkans. Considered to be the progenitor of the yellow-fld., tall bearded irises. The name *variegata* is also applied to cvs. of other spp. with striped lvs.

Vartanii M. Foster. B, X, ret; sts. none or almost none; lvs. 4-angled, to 9 in. long in flower, elongating to 1½ ft.; spathes 1-fld.; fls. almond-scented, perianth tube 2–3 in. long, bright greenish-yellow, segms. slaty-lilac, or grayish varying to white, falls lanceolate, 2 in. long, with darker veins, haft with yellow ridge, standards narrow-lanceolate, with faint veins. Israel. Cv. **'Alba'**. Fls. white.

verna L. DWARF I., VIOLET I. R, I, a; sts. to 6 in.; lvs. linear, to 6 in. long in flower, elongating with age; spathes 1–2-fld.; perianth tube to 1½ in. long, falls narrowly obovate, 1½ in. long, violet-blue to white, haft yellow or orange, pubescent, standards erect, obovate, violet-blue. Penn., s. to Ky. and Ga.

versicolor L. WILD I., BLUE F., POISON F. R, I, a; sts. to 3 ft., often branched; lvs. firm, linear to sword-shaped, 3 ft. long, 1 in. wide, somewhat glaucous; spathes 2–3-fld.; perianth tube funnelform, to ½ in. long, falls ovate to reniform-ovate, to 3 in. long, lavender, violet, blue-violet, or red-violet, rarely white, often with a greenish basal spot, standards erect, ½–⅔ as long as falls. E. Canada, s. to Penn. and Minn. Cv. **'Kermesina'**. To 2 ft.; fls. wine-magenta. Cv. **'Rosea'**. Fls. pink.

vicaria Vved. B, S, j; sts. to about 1½ ft.; lvs. curved, to 1½ in. wide, with scabrous margin, pale green; fls. 2–4, perianth tube to 1¾ in. long, falls oblong, to 2⅛ in. long, pale violet, veined dark violet, spotted dark yellow along the ridge, standards 3-lobed to rhomboid, or obovate, to 1 in. long, violet, with darker veins. Cent. Asia.

×vinicolor Small: *I. fulva* × *I. giganticaerulea*. R, I, a; sts. to 3 ft. or more, usually branched; lvs. linear, 1–3 ft. long, attenuate, bright green; spathes 1–2-fld.; perianth segms. wine-purple, falls elliptic, 2½–3 in. long, crest yellow, standards broadly spatulate, shorter than falls. S. La. Cv. **'Chrysophoenicia'** [*I. chrysophoenicia* Small]. Fls. dark violet-purple. S. La. Cv. **'Lilacinaurea'** [*I. lilacinaurea* Alexand.]. Fls. deep lilac. S. La.

violacea: see *I. carthaliniae*, *I.* ×*germanica*, or *I. pumila;* but in hort. *I. violacea* has been applied to cvs. of various spp. of irises.

virginica L. [*I. caroliniana* S. Wats.]. BLUE F., SOUTHERN B.F. R, I, a; sts. 2–3 ft., branched; lvs. arching to erect, broadly sword-shaped, as long as st. or longer, bright green; spathes 2–3-fld.; falls obovate or elliptic-obovate, 3 in. long, lavender or lilac, or sometimes violet or white, with a hairy, bright yellow area, standards obovate to obovate-spatulate, about 2 in. long; caps. ovoid to ellipsoid-ovoid, 1½–2¾ in. long, about as broad as long. Wet areas on coastal plain, se. Va. to Tex. Cv. **'Alba'**. Fls. white. Var. **Shrevei** (Small) E. Anderson [*I. Shrevei* Small]. Caps. long-cylindrical, 2¾–4 in. long, about half as broad as long. Marshes, cent. U.S.

warleyensis M. Foster. B, S, j; sts. to 16 in.; lvs. curved, to 6 in. long and 1½ in. wide, pale green; fls. 3–5, axillary, sessile, perianth tube to 2 in. long, falls obovate to oblong, about 2 in. long, velvety violet-purple, often edged white, ridge white, often surrounded by orange blotch, standards 3-lobed, to ¾ in. long, violet, with darker veins. Cent. Asia.

Watsoniana: *I. Douglasiana.*

Wattii Bak. ex Hook. f. R, I, c; sts. to 3 ft. or more in cult., branched, leafy; lvs. broadly sword-shaped, to 2–3 ft. long and 1½–3 in. wide, conspicuously ribbed; spathes 2–3-fld.; fls. 40–50, to 3½ in. across, perianth tube about ½ in. long, falls obovate to nearly orbicular, to 2 in. long, with crisped margins, lavender-blue, the centers and crest white with orange-yellow spots, surrounded by darker mauve spots, crest entire to fimbriate, standards oblong, to 2 in. long, undulate, lavender-blue. Assam (India) and Yunnan (China).

Willmottiana M. Foster. B, S, j; sts. to 8 in.; lvs. sheathing and obscuring st., lanceolate, curved, to 6 in. long, deep green; spathes 1-fld., spathe valves not inflated; fls. 4–6, sessile, perianth tube about 2 in. long, falls oblong, violet to blue or white, standards turned downward, rhomboidal to 3-lobed, to ⅝ in. long, violet. Turkestan. Cv. **'Alba'**. Fls. white.

Wilsonii C. H. Wright. R, I, a; sts. about 2 ft., hollow; lvs. very narrowly sword-shaped, about 2 ft. long, slightly glaucous; spathes 1–2-fld., pedicels 1–4 in. long; perianth tube to ⅜ in. long, falls ovate, to 2 in. long, pale yellow, the center bright yellow, veined reddish-brown, standards diverging at 45°, lanceolate, to 1¼ in. long, frilled, yellowish-white, veined faint purple. China.

Winogradowii Fomin. B, X, ret; sts. to 8 in.; lvs. linear, 4-angled, elongating to 16 in. long; spathes 1-fld.; perianth tube ¾ in. long, falls reflexed, broadly oblong to rounded-elliptic, 2 in. long, pale yellow, ridge orange, center dark-dotted, standards erect, oblanceolate-spatulate, to 2 in. long, pale yellow. Caucasus.

xiphioides J. F. Ehrh. [*I. anglica* Hort. ex Steud.; *I. pyrenaica* Bubani]. ENGLISH I. B, X; sts. to 1½ ft.; lvs. linear, to 1½ ft. long, channelled; spathes 2–3-fld., pedicels 1–3 in. long; perianth tube to ½ in. long, falls nearly orbicular, 2–3 in. long, deep blue-purple, varying in cult., with golden blotch, haft winged, standards almost orbicular. Pyrenees.

Xiphium L. [*I. hispanica* Hort. ex Steud.; *I. lusitanica* Ker-Gawl.]. SPANISH I. B, X; sts. to 2 ft.; lvs. nearly cylindrical, to 2 ft. long, channelled, glaucous; spathes 1–2-fld.; perianth tube almost obsolete, falls nearly orbicular, separated by a narrow neck from the broadly cuneate haft, to 2½ in. long, typically blue-purple or pale slaty-blue, with a yellow or orange blotch, but the color varying in cult. forms to white and yellow, standards erect, oblanceolate, to about 2½ in. long. S. France, Portugal, Spain, N. Afr. This is one of the parents of the bulbous Dutch irises, cvs. of which also involve, variously, *I. filifolia*, *I. Fontanesii*, or *I. tingitana.*

ISATIS L. WOAD. *Cruciferae.* About 30 spp. of ann. or per. herbs of cent. Eur. and Medit. region to cent. Asia, erect and branching, glabrous to tomentose; lvs. simple, often clasping; fls. small, yellow or yellowish, in bractless, often panicled racemes, in late spring and early summer, sepals and petals 4; fr. an indehiscent, flat, pendulous, black, 1-seeded silicle.

glauca Auch. ex Boiss. Per., to 3 ft., glabrous, glaucous; lvs. long-oblong, to 10 in. long, obtuse, entire, tapering to petiole, not clasping; fls. mustard-yellow, in very large terminal panicle. Turkey. Sometimes planted as an ornamental, from seeds planted the year before flowering. Distinguished from *I. tinctoria* in being per. and lvs. usually leathery, always entire, and very glaucous.

tinctoria L. DYER'S W., ASP-OF-JERUSALEM. Bien., to 3 ft., glabrous above; lvs. oblong to lanceolate, to 4 in. long, entire or toothed, st. lvs. clasping or auricled; fls. yellow, in terminal panicles. Eur. Formerly grown for the blue dye, obtained from the lvs.

ISERTIA Schreb. *Rubiaceae.* About 25 spp. of shrubs or trees, native to W. Indies and trop. Amer.; lvs. opp. or in 3's, large, leathery, stipules intrapetiolar; fls. many, in a terminal panicle or corymb, red or yellow, rarely white, 5–6-merous, corolla funnelform or salverform, leathery; fr. a small, globose berry, seeds many.

Haenkeana DC. Shrub, to 9 ft.; lvs. obovate to oblong-obovate, to 18 in. long, glabrate above, gray-pubescent beneath; fls. yellow or orange-red, in a panicle, corolla to 1½ in. long, hairy; fr. purple, to ¼ in. across. Cuba and Cent. Amer., s. to Venezuela and Colombia.

parviflora Vahl. Shrub or small tree; lvs. oblong, to 1 ft. long, glabrous above, sparsely pubescent beneath; fls. pink or white, corolla to ¾ in. long, glabrous. Venezuela and Trinidad to Brazil.

ISLAYA: *NEOPORTERIA.* **I. minor:** *N. islayensis* forma.

ISMENE: *HYMENOCALLIS.* **I. Macleana:** *H. pedunculata.* **I. calathina:** *H. narcissiflora.*

ISNARDIA: *LUDWIGIA.*

ISOCHILUS R. Br. *Orchidaceae.* Two spp. of epiphytes of Trop. Amer.; sts. slender, leafy throughout; lvs. 2-ranked, erect, linear, emarginate at apex; infl. a short, terminal raceme, loosely or densely 1- to many-fld.; fls. small, campanulate, white to reddish, rose-purple, or orange, sepals nearly equal, separate, lateral sepals somewhat saccate at base under lip, petals shorter than sepals, more or less clawed, lip about as long as petals, narrower, linear, commonly S-curved at base and often above, column slender, toothed at apex. For structure of fl. see *Orchidaceae.*

For culture see *Orchids.*

linearis (Jacq.) R. Br. To 2½ ft., sts. many, many-lvd.; lvs. to 2½ in. long; infl. loosely or densely 1- to many-fld.; fls. white to rose-purple, upper sepal elliptic-lanceolate, concave, to ⅓ in. long, lateral sepals lanceolate, united below middle, petals elliptic. Trop. and subtrop. Amer.

major Cham. & Schlechtend. Sts. simple; lvs. to 4 in. long, unequally 2-lobed at apex; infl. 1-sided, several- to many-fld.; fls. subtended by conspicuous papery bracts, upper sepal ½ in. long, oblanceolate, lip ½ in. long, elliptic-linear, entire or obscurely lobed, bent and fleshy at base. Cent. Amer., Jamaica.

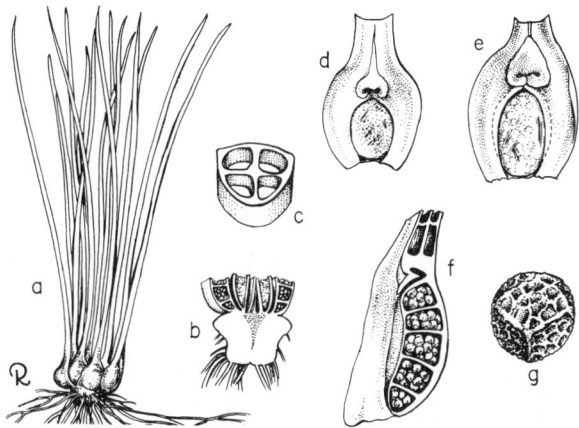

ISOETACEAE. *Isoetes Engelmannii:* **a,** plant, × ⅓; **b,** vertical section through rhizome and base of leaves, × 1; **c,** leaf, cross section, × 4; **d,** inner surface of leaf base with microsporangium, × 2; **e,** inner surface of leaf base with megasporangium, × 2; **f,** leaf base with megasporangium, vertical section, × 3; **g,** megaspore, × 20.

ISOETACEAE Dumort. QUILLWORT FAMILY. Fern allies; 2 genera with about 60 spp. of primitive, spore-bearing, vascular, per., aquatic herbs, without apparent sts., widely distributed in chiefly temp. regions; lvs. arising from cormlike subterranean rhizome, quill-like, cylindrical, tapering to apex, dialated and spoon-shaped at base; spores of 2 kinds embedded in the bases of the lvs., those of the outermost lvs. producing relatively few large spores (megaspores), those of the inner lvs. producing large numbers of small spores (microspores). *Isoetes* is cult.

ISOETES L. QUILLWORT. *Isoetaceae.* About 60 spp. of aquatic per. herbs, widely distributed in temp. regions, rare in tropics; characteristics those of the family.

Sometimes grown in aquaria. The identification of species is difficult and generally requires microscopic examination of the spores. See also *Ferns.*

echinospora Durieu. SPINY-SPORED Q. Aquatic, sometimes emersed later in the year; lvs. to 14 in. long, coarse but flaccid, pale green; megaspores white to yellowish, covered with fragile spines. Circumboreal.

Engelmannii A. Braun. ENGELMANN'S Q. Lvs. 10–40, usually 4–12 in. long, pale green, growing naturally emersed or submersed, although rarely in habitats where submersed at all seasons. Ne. N. Amer.

lacustris L. Plants submersed; lvs. stiff, to 8 in. long, occasionally longer, dark green; megaspores yellowish or rarely white, tubercled. Eur.

ISOLATOCEREUS: *LEMAIREOCEREUS.*

ISOLOMA: *KOHLERIA.* **I. Ceciliae:** *K. amabilis.* **I. hirsutum:** *K. eriantha.* **I. hybridum:** see *K. gigantea.* **I. multiflorum:** see *K. eriantha.* **I. pictum:** *K. bogotensis.*

ISOMERIS: *CLEOME.* **I. arborea:** *C. Isomeris.*

ISOPLEXIS Lindl. *Scrophulariaceae.* Three spp. of subshrubs, native to Canary Is. and Madeira; lvs. alt.; fls. yellow, in dense terminal racemes, calyx 5-parted, corolla incurved, equally 2-lipped or 5-lobed, stamens 4; fr. a caps. Differs from *Digitalis* chiefly in having corolla lips equal.

Grown in the open in Calif. Cultivation and propagation as for the shrubby forms of *Digitalis.*

canariensis (L.) Lindl. ex G. Don [*Digitalis canariensis* L.]. Stiff, to 4 ft.; lvs. lanceolate, to 6 in. long, sharp-toothed, glossy, thick; fls. in racemes to 1 ft. long, corolla yellow-brown, 1 in. long, strongly 2-lipped. The plant sometimes grown in the East as *Digitalis canariensis* is *D. grandiflora.*

ISOPOGON R. Br. *Proteaceae.* About 30 spp. of shrubs, native to Australia; lvs. stiff, rigid; fls. bisexual, regular, in dense conelike spikes, each fl. sessile in the axil of a deciduous bract or scale, perianth tube slender, upper part and 4 lobes deciduous, stamens 4, connectives with appendages; fr. small, hairy, nutlike.

Culture as for *Hakea.*

anemonifolius J. Knight. To 6 ft.; lvs. to 4 in. long, 2–3-pinnately divided, segms. linear, flat, entire or lobed; fls. yellow; cones nearly globose, to ¾ in. across. New S. Wales.

anethifolius J. Knight. To 4 ft.; lvs. 1–2-pinnately divided, segms. needlelike, cylindrical; fls. yellow; cones globose, to 1 in. across. New S. Wales.

roseus Lindl. To 4 ft.; lvs. to 3 in. long, 1–2-ternately divided, segms. linear or lobed; fls. pink; cones globose, to 1 in. across. W. Australia.

sphaerocephalus Lindl. Lvs. sessile, linear, to 4 in. long; fls. yellow-hairy; cones globose, to ¾ in. across. W. Australia.

ISOPYRUM L. *Ranunculaceae.* About 30 spp. of the N. Hemisphere, mostly small, delicate, per. herbs; lvs. basal, decompound, aquilegialike; fls. white, solitary, or in panicles or umbellate cymes, sepals 5–6, petaloid, deciduous, petals small or 0, stamens many, filaments clavellate; follicles 2–5.

Sometimes transferred to the wild garden or naturalized. Propagated by seeds or division.

biternatum (Raf.) Torr. & A. Gray. To 1 ft.; lvs. 2-ternate, lfts. glabrous beneath; fls. solitary, terminal or axillary, petals none; follicles commonly 4, divaricate. Ont. to Fla. and Tex.

fumarioides: *Leptopyrum fumarioides.*

Hallii A. Gray. Sts. 1–3 ft.; lfts. puberulent beneath; fls. 3–8, cymose-umbellate; follicles 4–5. S. Wash., n. Ore.

thalictroides L. Sts. 9–15 in.; lfts. glabrous; fls. small, nodding, ⅜–¾ in. across; follicles mostly 2. Eur.

ISOTOMA: *LAURENTIA.* **I. longiflora:** *Hippobroma longiflora.*

ISOTRIA Raf. WHORLED POGONIA, FIVE-LEAVED ORCHID. *Orchidaceae.* Two spp. of low, terrestrial herbs, native to N. Amer.; sts. erect, with 5–6 lvs. in a whorl at apex; fls. 1 or 2, sessile, sepals and petals spreading-erect, lip 3-lobed, column slender, pollen grains cohering in groups of 4. For structure of fl. see *Orchidaceae.*

For culture see *Orchids.*

verticillata (Muhlenb. ex Willd.) Raf. [*Pogonia verticillata* (Muhlenb. ex Willd.) Nutt.]. GREEN ADDERLING, PURPLE F.-L.O. To 14 in., sts. purplish; lvs. at right angles to st., oblong-lanceolate, to 3¾ in. long; sepals madder-purple, to 2¼ in. long, petals yellowish-green, to 1 in. long, lip to 1 in. long, yellowish-green, streaked with purple. Spring–late summer. New Eng. to Fla., w. to Mich. and Tex.

ITEA L. *Saxifragaceae.* Perhaps 10 spp. of deciduous or evergreen trees or shrubs, 1 in N. Amer., the rest in trop. and temp. Asia; lvs. alt., simple; fls. small, many, greenish-white, in terminal or axillary racemes, calyx lobes, petals, and stamens 5, petals narrowly oblong, ovary superior.

Propagated by cuttings and by division of the roots, also by seeds.

ilicifolia D. Oliver. Evergreen shrub, to 10 ft.; lvs. to 4 in. long, spiny-toothed, hollylike; fls. greenish-white, in drooping racemes to 1 ft. long. China. Zone 7?

virginica L. SWEETSPIRE, VIRGINIA WILLOW, TASSEL-WHITE. Deciduous shrub, to 10 ft.; lvs. to 4 in. long, finely toothed; fls. white, fragrant, in erect racemes to 6 in. long. N.J., s. to Fla. and La. Zone 6. Foliage colors brilliant red in autumn. Thrives in any soil and in both sun and shade.

yunnanensis Franch. Similar to *I. ilicifolia,* but lvs. narrower, toothed or nearly entire, and racemes usually shorter. Yunnan (sw. China).

IVESIA Torr. & A. Gray. *Rosaceae.* Over 20 spp. of w. N. Amer., close to *Horkelia,* but the lfts. usually very small, many, imbricate; fls. white or yellow, stamens 5 or 20, filaments filiform.

Gordonii (Hook.) Torr. & A. Gray [*Potentilla Gordonii* (Hook.) Greene]. Sts. subscapose, to 8 in., often viscid-glandular; lfts. 10–25 pairs, to ⁵⁄₁₆ in. long, divided to base into 2–5 segms.; petals yellow, less than ³⁄₁₆ in. long. High mts., Wash. and Mont., s. to Calif. and Colo.

IXIA L. [*Morphixia* Ker-Gawl.]. CORN LILY, AFRICAN C. L. About 30 spp. of cormous herbs, native to the Cape Prov., S. Afr.; lvs 2–6, mostly basal, grasslike; fls. in spikes or panicles, perianth tube straight, segms. nearly equal, spreading, style exserted, style brs. 3, short, linear; fr. a caps.

Ixias are not hardy in the North. They may be planted outdoors in late Nov. in some parts of the country, but should be well protected by mulch. Bulbs should be set about 2 to 3 in. deep in the open with a little sand sprinkled under them. They may also be planted in spring for summer bloom. After flowering, the bulbs should remain in the ground until July, when they should be lifted and stored in boxes without packing. In the North, ixias are usually grown under glass for winter and early spring bloom. The corms may be planted in Sept. or Oct., 5 or 6 of them in a 6-in. pot, about 1 in. deep. They should be retarded at first and then kept in a temperature of about 55° F. until after flowering.

aurantiaca: *I. leucantha* var. *lutea.*

azurea (Eckl.) Grey. Sts. to 18 in., unbranched, tunics reticulate; lvs. narrowly linear; infl. a many-fld., loose spike; fls. about 1½ in. across, perianth segms. pale Prussian-blue, with violet-black blotch, filaments dark purple, anthers yellow.

campanulata Houtt. [*I. crateroides* Ker-Gawl.]. Sts. to 1 ft., corms about ½ in. in diam., tunics fibrous; basal lvs. 4–6, linear, glabrous; infl. a dense, erect spike, perianth segms. dark purple-lilac to dark crimson, oblong, about ¾ in. long.

coelestina: *Sphenostigma coelestinum.*

columellaris Ker-Gawl. Sts. 1–2 ft., tunics closely reticulate; lvs. curved, short; infl. a corymb, usually 4–6-fld.; perianth lilac to mauve-purple, with darker eye, segms. ovate, to 1 in. long, acute, anthers black.

crateroides: *I. campanulata.*

incarnata Jacq. Differs from *I. scariosa* in having 1 basal lf. erect and the other curved. Known in S. Afr. as CLANWILLIAM BLUEBELL.

leucantha Jacq. Sts. to 2 ft., tunics of very fine parallel fibers; lvs. to 1 ft. long, glabrous; infl. a many-fld., dense, erect spike; perianth white, segms. about ¾ in. long, tube very short. Garden material under this name having pink to lavender fls. may be of hybrid origin. Var. **lutea** (Bak.) Grey [*I. aurantiaca* Klatt; *I. lutea* Bak.]. Fls. deep clear yellow.

longiflora: *I. paniculata.*

lutea: *I. leucantha* var.

maculata L. Sts. to 2 ft., tunics of parallel fibers; lvs. to 1 ft. long, ¼ in. wide, strongly ribbed; perianth yellow, varying to white, with purple to black blotch at throat, segms. oblong-elliptic, about 1 in. long, obtuse, tube mostly twice as long as spathe. In white-fld. forms, the blotch may be reduced to short purple lines. Var. **nigroalbida** (Klatt) Bak. Perianth white, with black blotch. Var. **ochroleuca** Ker-Gawl. Perianth sulphur-yellow, with brown blotch. Var. **ornata** Bak. Perianth segms. white, with deep red basal blotch, tinged purple outside.

micrandra Bak. Sts. to 10 in., simple, tunics of very fine fibers; lvs. about ⅛ in. wide; infl. a few-fld., short, erect spike; fls. pure white, perianth segms. ascending-spreading, ½ in. long, tube as long as spathe. Very early flowering.

monadelpha D. Delar. Sts. to 12 in., tunics fibrous; lvs. to ½ in. wide, somewhat twisted, midrib prominent; infl. a few-fld., short spike; perianth typically lilac with green basal blotch, but variable in color, limb starlike, becoming saucer-shaped, segms. ⅝–1 in. long, tube ½–¾ in. long, filaments united into a tube. Var. **columnaris** (Andr.) Bak. Perianth claret-red, with no blotch, segms. narrow. Var. **curta** Ker-Gawl. Perianth cup-shaped, cadmium-yellow, with reddish-brown basal blotch. Var. **grandiflora** (Pers.) Bak. Fls. large, perianth lilac, with dull blue throat. Var. **latifolia** (Klatt) Bak. Lvs. flat, broad; perianth lilac, with greenish-brown throat. Var. **purpurea** (Klatt) Bak. Perianth claret-red, segms. narrowly oblong.

paniculata D. Delar. [*I. longiflora* Berguis; *Morphixia paniculata* (D. Delar.) Bak.]. Sts. to 3 ft.; basal lvs. 6–15 in. long, ½–¾ in. wide, glabrous; infl. 6–12-fld., loosely spicate to paniculate; fls. 1–1½ in.

across, perianth segms. creamy-white, with purplish-black basal blotch, tube narrowly cylindrical, 1½–3 in. long. Var. **tenuiflora** (Ker-Gawl.) Bak. Perianth segms. shorter, with no basal blotch, tube usually less than 2 in. long. May be offered as *Gladiolus cuspidatus.*

patens Ait. Sts. 1–1½ ft.; basal lvs. 6–12 in. long, ½ in. wide; infl. a many-fld., dense spike; perianth pale red, with green throat, limb campanulate, about 1 in. long, tube less than ½ in. long, filaments red, anthers yellow. Material grown as *I. viridiflora* may be this sp. Var. **flavescens** Eckl. Perianth pale yellow, without a blotch.

polystachya L. Sts. to 2 ft.; basal lvs. linear, about ¼ in. wide, glabrous; infl. many-fld., dense, spicate to paniculate; fls. about ¾ in. across, perianth segms. white, tube about ¾ in. long, filaments and anthers yellow.

rosea: *Romulea rosea.*

Rossinii: a listed name of no botanical standing.

scariosa Thunb. Sts. 8–12 in., very slender, branched; basal lvs. sword-shaped, 4–8 in. long; infl. a 4–6-fld., loose spike; fls. about 1 in. across, perianth lilac to red-purple, tube funnelform, about ½ in. long.

speciosa Andr. Sts. 6–12 in., often somewhat arching; basal lvs. linear; infl. 3–6-fld., short, congested; perianth deep crimson, limb about 1 in. long, campanulate to funnelform, with paler stripe outside, tube cylindrical, ¼–½ in. long, filaments purple, anthers yellow. Does best in partial shade and moist location.

spectabilis: *I. viridiflora.*

viridiflora Lam. [*I. spectabilis* Salisb.]. Sts. 15–22 in., unbranched; basal lvs. narrowly linear, to 12 in. long; infl. 9–20-fld., unbranched, loose; perianth blue-green, with black throat, segms. oblong-lanceolate, 1 in. long, tube cylindrical, ¼ in. long, filaments black, anthers yellow. Material grown under this name may be *I. patens.*

IXIOLIRION Fisch. LILY-OF-THE-ALTAI. *Amaryllidaceae.* About 3 spp. of Asian herbs with tunicate bulbs; lvs. very narrow, basal; infl. more or less umbellate, borne on a leafy st.; fls. blue or violet, perianth segms. separate, ovary inferior; fr. a caps.

Not reliably hardy in the North, but bulbs may be stored over winter.

Ledebourii: *I. tataricum.*

montanum: *I. tataricum.*

Pallasii: *I. tataricum.*

tataricum (Pall.) Herb. [*I. Ledebourii* Fisch. & C. A. Mey.; *I. montanum* (Redouté) Herb.; *I. Pallasii* Fisch. & C. A. Mey.]. SIBERIAN LILY, TARTAR L. Bulb ovoid, to 1 in. in diam.; basal lvs. 3–8, persistent, linear; sts. to 16 in., with 2–3 smaller lvs.; umbel 2–18-fld., pedicels unequal; fls. light to dark blue, to 1½ in. long. Asia Minor to cent. Siberia.

IXORA L. *Rubiaceae.* About 400 spp. of shrubs or trees, native mostly to trop. Asia and Afr., extending to Australia, the Pacific Is., and Amer.; lvs. opp. or whorled, leathery stipules interpetiolar; fls. in compact corymbs, white, yellow, orange, pink, red, corolla long-tubular, lobes 4–5, spreading; fr. a hard, fleshy berry.

Ixoras are handsome plants in cultivation, with bright-colored flowers and attractive foliage. They are grown in the greenhouse, and in the open in warm climates as Fla. and the Gulf Coast. They should have a night temperature of about 65° F. Propagated by cuttings, preferably with 3 or 4 joints, in spring and kept over bottom heat; also by seeds when produced.

acuminata Roxb. Shrub, to 6 ft.; lvs. variable, elliptic to linear-oblong, to 9 in. long or more; fls. fragrant, in corymbs to 4 in. across, corolla white, tube to 1½ in. long, lobes ⅝ in. across. Himalayas.

alba: see *I. chinensis* cv.

amabilis: a listed name of no botanical standing; used for a plant with pinkish fls. suffused with orange.

amboinica: *I. longifolia.*

aurantiaca: a listed name of no botanical standing; used for a plant with orange-red fls.

Bandhuca: *I. coccinea.*

barbata Roxb. Large shrub; lvs. elliptic, to 8 in. long and nearly half as broad, more or less acute; fls. in short-stalked, large cymes to 12 in. across, broader than high, corolla white, tube slender, to 1½ in. long, with fringe of hairs at throat. Andaman and Nicobar Is.

chelsonii: a listed name of no botanical standing; used for a plant with brilliant, salmon-orange fls.

chinensis Lam. [*I. Colei* Hort. ex Gentil probably belongs here; *I. stricta* Roxb.]. Shrub, to 3 ft.; lvs. elliptic, lanceolate-elliptic, or narrowly obovate, to 6 in. long, acuminate; fls. in many-fld., much-branched, crowded cymes, corolla red to white, tube to 1 in. long. Malay Pen. and China. Cv. **'Alba'** [*I. alba* Hort., not L.]. Fls. white. Cv. **'Dixiana'** [*I. Dixiana* Hort. ex Gentil]. Fls. dark orange.

coccinea L. [*I. Bandhuca* Roxb.; *I. incarnata* DC.; *I. lutea* Hutch.]. FLAME-OF-THE-WOODS, JUNGLE-FLAME, JUNGLE GERANIUM. Shrub, to 4 ft.; lvs. oblong, to 4 in. long; fls. in large dense corymbs, corolla red, tube nearly 2 in. long. India. A variable sp., much cult. in warm regions. Cv. **'Fraseri'** [*I. Fraseri* Hort. ex Gentil]. Fls. brilliant reddish-salmon.

Colei: see *I. chinensis.*

congesta Roxb. Evergreen tree; lvs. elliptic to elliptic-oblong or -lanceolate, to 1 ft. long and 6 in. wide, acuminate, nerves 13–19 pairs; fls. in large corymbs with clustered, not spreading brs., corolla red, tube to 1½ in. long. Burma, Malay Pen.

Dixiana: *I. chinensis* cv.

Duffii T. Moore [*I. macrothyrsa* of auths., not (Teysm. & Binnend.) T. Moore]. Rigid shrub; lvs. linear-oblong to lanceolate-oblong, about 12 in. long, slender-pointed; fls. in very large corymbs, corolla deep red, tinged crimson in age, tube 1½ in. long. Caroline Is.

Finlaysoniana Wallich ex G. Don. Shrub or small tree, to 18 ft.; lvs. lanceolate-elliptic to obovate, to 6 in. long; fls. in corymbs to 4 in. across, scented, corolla white, tube to 1¼ in. long. Probably Thailand.

flore-lutea: a listed name of no botanical standing; used for a plant with yellow fls.

fragrans (Hook. & Arn.) A Gray. Shrub, to 12 ft.; lvs. variable, obovate to elliptic or ovate, to 5 in. long; fls. in 3-fld. infl. subtended by 2 leaflike bracts; corolla tube to ½ in. long. Se. Polynesia.

Fraseri: *I. coccinea* cv.

fulgens Roxb. Shrub, to 4 ft.; lvs. lanceolate, to 5 in. long, slender-pointed; fls. in dense terminal corymbs, corolla clear orange-scarlet or orange, becoming scarlet, tube slender, about 1 in. long. Nativity uncertain.

Griffithii Hook. [*I. congesta* Roxb. ex Hook.f.]. Shrub, to 9 ft.; lvs. oblong-elliptic, to 9 in. long, leathery, glabrous, petiole to ¾ in. long;

fls. many in a large, showy, nearly flat-topped, compound cyme, calyx tube to ¼ in. long, corolla with tube red, slender, to 1¼ in. long, lobes 4, red-orange, spreading. S. Burma, Malay Pen., Sumatra, n. Borneo.

incarnata: *I. coccinea.*

javanica (Blume) DC. Shrub or small tree, to 25 ft.; lvs. ovate-oblong, to 10 in. long; fls. in corymbs with coral-red brs., corolla orange-red, tube to 1½ in. long, slender. Se. Asia.

laxiflora Sm. Shrub or small tree, to 12 ft.; lvs. oblong-lanceolate, to 8 in. long, acuminate; fls. in large 3-forked panicles, fragrant, corolla white, tinged pink, tube to 1¼ in. long. W. Trop. Amer.

longifolia Sm. [*I. amboinica* (Blume) DC.]. Rigid shrub; lvs. lanceolate-oblong or lanceolate, to 10 in. long, slender-pointed; fls. in loose, many-fld. corymbs, deep red. Moluccas.

lutea: *I. coccinea.*

macrothyrsa: see *I. Duffii.*

odorata Hook. Small shrub; lvs. ovate to somewhat obovate, sometimes 12 in. long, acute or acuminate, firm; fls. very fragrant, in large purple-branched clusters to 1 ft. across or more; corolla white, pink-tinged, changing to brownish, tube 4–5 in. long, very slender. Madagascar.

parviflora Vahl. Tree; lvs. oblong or elliptic, to 6 in. long; fls. fragrant, in subglobose clusters to 6 in. across, corolla white, tube short, to ⁵⁄₁₆ in. long. India.

roseo-splendens: a listed name of no botanical standing.

stricta: *I chinensis.*

Thwaitesii Hook.f. Large shrub or small tree; lvs. oblong to broadly oblanceolate, to 5 in. long, more or less undulate but entire, somewhat leathery; fls. in compact terminal corymbs, fragrant, corolla white, tube to 1¼ in. long, slender. Ceylon.

×**Westii** J. Huds. A presumed hybrid of garden origin; fls. pale rose, becoming bright rose, in subglobose corymbs to 6 in. across.

Williamsii Sandw. Shrub, to 10 ft.; lvs. elliptic or ovate-elliptic, to 6 in. long, dark green and glossy above, paler beneath; fls. in dense, globose corymbs to 6 in. across, corolla deep red, tube slender, to 1¼ in. long. Nativity unknown. One of the best sp. for garden and greenhouse use.

JACARANDA Juss. GREEN EBONY. *Bignoniaceae.* About 50 spp. of shrubs and trees, native to trop. Amer.; lvs. opp., mostly 2-pinnate, lfts. many; fls. blue to violet, rarely white or pink, in axillary or terminal panicles, calyx 5-toothed or truncate, corolla funnelform to campanulate-funnelform, somewhat 2-lipped, stamens 4, staminode 1, about at long as the stamens; fr. a 2-celled caps.

Jacarandas are grown for their showy flowers and are much planted in tropical and subtropical regions as garden or street trees or under glass in the North. Propagated by cuttings of half-ripened wood when seeds are not available.

acutifolia Humb. & Bonpl. Tree, to 10 ft.; lvs. glabrous, fernlike, with 5–6 pairs of pinnae, lfts. linear-lanceolate; fls. blue; fr. ellipsoid, to 1¼ in. wide, shortly or obtusely cuspidate. Peru. Often confused with *J. mimosifolia.*

arborea Urb. [*J. Sagraeana* Griseb., not DC.]. Shrub or small tree, to 12 ft.; lvs. with 1–4 pairs of pinnae, lfts. sessile or nearly so, obovate or narrowly obovate, to ¾ in. long; fls. purple or rose, to 1¼ in. long, hairy outside; fr. ellipsoid to oblong-ellipsoid, to 1¾ in. long. Cuba.

caerulea (L.) Griseb. [*J. Sagraeana* DC., not Griseb.]. Small tree; lvs. with 4–13 pairs of pinnae, lfts. obliquely oblong, to 1 in. long, glabrous; fls. blue, lilac, or almost white, to 1½ in. long, glabrous; fr. ellipsoid, to 2⅜ in. long. Bahama Is.

Caroba (Vell.) DC. Small tree, to 12 ft.; lvs. to 8 in. long, with 4–6 pairs of pinnae, lfts. oblong-lanceolate or subrhombic, to 1½ in. long; fls. lilac to purple, to 2 in. long; fr. to 2 in. long. Brazil.

chelonia Griseb. To 90 ft.; lvs. with 15–20 pairs of pinnae, lfts. elliptic-oblong, ½–¾ in. long, mucronate, membranous; fls. in panicles to 1 ft. long, violet-blue, to 1½ in. long, glandular-pubescent; fr. to 3 in. long. Paraguay, Argentina.

cuspidifolia Mart. To 30 ft.; lvs. to 2 ft. long, with 8–10 pairs of pinnae, lfts. lanceolate, about 1 in. long, glabrous; fls. blue-violet, 1½ in. long; fr. to about 3 in. long. Brazil, Argentina.

filicifolia: *J. obtusifolia* var. *rhombifolia.*

mimosifolia D. Don [*J. ovalifolia* R. Br.]. To 50 ft. or more, deciduous only in early spring; lvs. fernlike, with 12 or more pinnae, lfts. oblong-rhomboid, to ⅜ in. long, pubescent, except for the uppermost ones; fls. blue, 2 in. long and 1½ in. across; fr. to 2¼ in. across, rounded at apex. Nw. Argentina. Wood used for general carpentry work.

obtusifolia Humb. & Bonpl. Tree, usually less than 60 ft.; lvs. to 1½ ft. long, with many pairs of pinnae, lfts. subrhombic-oblong, to ⅝ in. long, shining above, glaucous beneath; fls. often borne on old leafless branchlets, bluish-mauve to lilac, to 2 in. long, ovary with adpressed grayish-white hairs; fr. to 2¾ in. long, stoutly apiculate-cuspidate. Venezuela, Guiana. Var. **rhombifolia** (G. F. Mey.) Sandw. [*J. filicifolia* A. Anders. ex D. Don; *J. rhombifolia* G. F. Mey]. Ovary glabrous.

ovalifolia: *J. mimosifolia.*

rhombifolia: *J. obtusifolia* var.

Sagraeana: see *J. arborea* and *J. caerulea.*

JACOBAEA: *SENECIO.*

JACOBINIA: *JUSTICIA.* Jacobinia coccinea: *Pachystachys coccinea;* Jacobinia incana: *Justicia Leonardii;* Jacobinia magnifica: *Justicia carnea;* Jacobinia Mohintli: *Justicia spicigera;* Jacobinia obtusior: *Justicia carnea;* Jacobinia pauciflora: *Justicia Rizzinii;* Jacobinia ×penrhoziensis: see *Justicia Rizzinii;* Jacobinia Pohliana: *Justicia carnea;* Jacobinia suberecta: *Dicliptera suberecta;* Jacobinia velutina: see *Justicia carnea.*

JACQUEMONTIA Choisy. *Convolvulaceae.* About 120 spp. of herbaceous, twining vines, mostly in tropics and subtropics of Amer., a few spp. in the Old World; lvs. usually entire, fls. blue or white, in cymes or panicles, corolla campanulate, differs from *Ipomoea* in having fls. usually smaller and in closer clusters and stigmas 2, flattened.

Cultivated as for *Ipomoea.*

pentantha (Jacq.) G. Don. Lvs. cordate-ovate, to 2 in. long; cymes on peduncles as long as lvs. or longer; fls. blue, 1 in. across. Fla. to S. Amer.

JACQUINIA L. *Theophrastaceae.* About 25 spp. of shrubs and trees, native to drier sites in trop. Amer.; lvs. alt. or whorled, simple, leathery, sometimes spine-tipped; fls. small, red, yellow, or white, in racemes, corymbs, or panicles, calyx 5-parted, corolla 5-lobed, stamens 5, staminodes 5, petal-like; fr. a yellow, orange, or red berry.

Several species are sources of fish poisons; grown as ornamentals in Zone 10 in Fla.

aculeata (L.) Mez [*J. ruscifolia* Jacq.]. Shrub, to 10 ft.; lvs. lanceolate, to 1 in. long, whorled, spine-tipped, entire; fls. red, in terminal panicles; fr. red. Cuba.

armillaris: *J. Barbasco.*

Barbasco (Loefl.) Mez [*J. armillaris* Jacq.]. BARBASCO. Shrub or small tree, to 15 ft.; lvs. obovate or oblong-obovate, to 4 in. long, somewhat fleshy, mostly clustered; fls. white, fragrant, in terminal racemes; fr. orange, ½ in. in diam. W. Indies. Used as a fish poison.

pungens A. Gray. Shrub or small tree, to 12 ft.; lvs. alt. to whorled, linear-lanceolate to elliptic-oblong, to 2¼ in. long, spine-tipped; fls. reddish-yellow, in short racemes; fr. orange-yellow. Mex.

ruscifolia: *J. aculeata.*

JACQUINIELLA Schlechter. *Orchidaceae.* Two spp. of epiphytes of trop. Amer.; sts. straight or zigzag, leafy throughout; lvs. small, 2-ranked, linear; infl. terminal, scape 1-fld. or with a terminal cluster of fls.; sepals nearly equal, separate or united at base, petals similar but smaller, lip separate, meeting at tips with other segms., with short claw, sometimes bent, nearly orbicular, concave, simple or 3-lobed at apex, column short, not united to lip, pollinia 4, waxy, laterally compressed. For structure of fl. see *Orchidaceae.*

For culture see *Orchids.*

globosa (Jacq.) Schlechter. Sts. erect, to 6 in., concealed by closely appressed lf. sheaths; lvs. to 1 in. long, fleshy-leathery, usually marked with purple; fls. deflexed, yellowish, sepals fleshy-thickened and often red or dull rose at apex, concave, to 1 in. long, lateral sepals united at base and connivent with lower part of lip to form a large sac, lip fleshy at apex, abruptly bent, to ⅛ in. long, constricted below middle, orbicular-saccate below constriction. W. Indies, Cent. Amer., n. S. Amer.

JAMBOSA: *SYZYGIUM.* J. alba: *S. samarangense;* J. australis: *S. paniculatum;* J. Caryophyllus: *S. aromaticum;* J. densiflora: *S. pycnanthum;* J. Jambosa: *S. Jambos;* J. vulgaris: *S. Jambos.*

JAMESIA Torr. & A. Gray. *Saxifragaceae.* One sp., a deciduous shrub of w. N. Amer.; lvs. opp., toothed; fls. in terminal, cymose clusters, calyx tube campanulate, united to lower half of ovary, calyx lobes 5, triangular, petals 5, oblong-obovate, entire, stamens 10, ovary half-inferior, styles 3–7, separate.

Hardy north, succeeding in sunny locations in well-drained soil. Propagated by seeds and by cuttings of ripe wood.

americana Torr. & A. Gray. Shrub, to 6 ft., with flaking bark; lvs. ovate to roundish, to 2½ in. long, coarsely crenate-serrate, green and pubescent above, gray-tomentose or strigose beneath; fls. white or pink, petals ¼ in. long. Var. **californica** (Small) Jeps. Low shrub, to 18 in.; fls. deep rose-pink. Sierra Nevada of Calif. and mts. of sw. Nev. and New Mex. to s. Wyo. Zone 5.

JANKAEA Boiss. *Gesneriaceae.* One sp., a per. herb of Greece; lvs. in a basal rosette; fls. on 1–4-fld. scapes, calyx 4–5-lobed, tube a little longer than lobes, corolla campanulate, 4–5-lobed, lobes ovate, obtuse, stamens 4, borne on corolla tube, disc absent, ovary superior; fr. a septicidal caps.

For cultivation see *Gesneriaceae.*

Heldreichii (Boiss.) Boiss. [*Ramonda Heldreichii* (Boiss.) Benth. & Hook.f. ex C. B. Clarke]. Lvs. elliptic to ovate, to 1¼ in. long, ¾ in. wide, entire, rusty-woolly above, densely silvery-hairy beneath; scapes to 3 in.; calyx lobes ⅛ in. long, corolla lavender, tube ⅜ in. long, lobes 5/16 in. long; caps. 5/16 in. long.

JASIONE L. [*Jasionella* Stoĭanov & Stefanov]. *Campanulaceae.* Doubtfully more than 10 spp. of ann. or per. herbs, native to Eur. and Asia Minor; lvs. usually simple, clustered at base or along the lower half of st.; fls. clustered in dense terminal heads, borne on long, naked peduncles, and subtended by an involucre of bracts, corolla blue, sometimes white, parted to near the base, anthers, except in *J. bulgarica,* united at the base, ovary 2-celled; fr. a caps., dehiscing by 2 apical pores.

Thrives in full sun and in light, well-drained soil. Propagated by seeds and division.

bulgarica Stoĭanov & Stefanov [*Jasionella bulgarica* (Stoĭanov & Stefanov) Stoĭanov & Stefanov]. Glabrous per., sts. erect, to about 9 in., from a slender rhizome; lower lvs. in a rosette, oblong-spatulate, entire or remotely denticulate, st. lvs. lanceolate or oblong-lanceolate, fls. in heads less than 1 in. across, bracts ovate to lanceolate, remotely toothed, corolla blue. Bulgaria.

humilis Loisel. Per., sts. slender, 3–9 in., unbranched; lvs. linear-obovate, to ⅜ in. long, entire; fls. in short-peduncled heads to ½ in. across, bracts broadly ovate-elliptic, corolla blue. Pyrennees.

Jankae: *J. montana.*

montana L. [*J. Jankae* Neilr.]. Very variable, usually bien. herb, sts. few to many, erect, to 12 in. or more, simple or branched, glabrous or pubescent; lvs. linear to lanceolate, to 1¾ in. long, sinuate, toothed; fls. in long-stalked heads to 1 in. across or more, bracts ovate to lanceolate, to ⅜ in. long, corolla pale blue. Eur.

perennis Lam. [*J. pyrenaica* Sennen]. SHEPHERD'S SCABIOSA, SHEEP'S-BIT. Moderately hairy per., sts. erect, to 18 in., branched or unbranched; lower lvs. narrowly obovate to oblanceolate, to 4 in. long, upper lvs. shorter and linear, remotely denticulate; fls. in long-stalked, globose heads to 2 in. across, corolla blue. S. Eur.

pyrenaica: *J. perennis.*

Vialii: a listed name of no botanical standing.

JASIONELLA: *JASIONE.*

JASMINUM L. JASMINE, JESSAMINE. *Oleaceae.* About 200 spp. of trop. and subtrop., deciduous or evergreen shrubs, often clambering climbers, of e. and s. Asia, Malay Arch., Afr., and Australia; lvs. opp. or alt., pinnate, lfts. 3–7, or reduced to 1; fls. white, yellow, or pink in terminal or axillary cymes, rarely solitary, calyx mostly with 4–9 lobes of varying lengths, corolla salverform, with slender tube and 4–9 lobes; fr. usually a black berry, more or less 2-lobed.

Some have fragrant flowers and are used as the principal source of jasmine perfume. Jasmines are grown outdoors in warm regions and as greenhouse plants elsewhere. They are of easy cultivation. Propagated by cuttings of nearly ripe wood in summer, or ripe wood in autumn, by layers, and sometimes by seeds.

absimile: *J. Leratii.*

angulare Vahl. Evergreen shrub, usually scrambling or climbing; lvs. opp., lfts. 3, occasionally 5, ovate, to 1½ in. long, terminal lft. slightly longer than lateral ones; fls. white, in terminal compact cymes, calyx campanulate, tube to 3/16 in. long, calyx teeth 7, shorter than tube, corolla tube to 1¼ in. long, lobes 5, about half as long as tube. S. Afr. Some plants cult. as *J. azoricum* belong here.

angustifolium (L.) Willd. Not cult., but the name variously applied in hort.

azoricum L. Scandent shrub; lvs. opp., lfts. 3, ovate, acute, 1¼–2 in. long; fls. white, fragrant, pedicelled, in terminal panicles, calyx short, tubular-campanulate, calyx teeth 5, 1/16 in. long, corolla tube to ⅛ in. long, lobes 5–6, ½–⅝ in. long. Madeira. Most material cult. under this name is *J. fluminense.*

bahiense: *J. fluminense.*

Beesianum Forr. & Diels. To 3 ft. or more, somewhat clambering; lvs. opp., of 1 lft., lanceolate or ovate-lanceolate, to 2 in. long, sharp-pointed; fls. red or rose, in 1–3-fld. cymes, fragrant, calyx teeth ¼ in. long, longer than tube, corolla tube to ½ in. long, lobes 6, rounded, shorter than tube. W. China. Zone 7.

bignoniaceum Wallich ex G. Don. Shrub or small tree; lvs. alt.; lfts. 5–9, sometimes fewer (3 or 1) toward base of shoots, elliptic to obovate, terminal lfts. to ¾ in. long, lateral ones to ½ in. long; fls. yellow, more or less in an umbel terminal on side shoots, calyx teeth much shorter than tube, corolla lobes as broad as long, less than ⅓ as long as tube. India and Ceylon. Closely related to *J. humile,* but having lateral lfts. shorter, broader, and corolla tube wider, with lobes short and broad.

dichotomum Vahl. Scrambling shrub or woody climber, to 25 ft.; lvs. opp., of 1 lft., ovate or broadly lanceolate, to 4 in. long; fls. white, red on outside and in bud, many in more or less dense corymbs, calyx lobes small, mostly 1/16 in. long, corolla tube white, to 1 in. long, lobes 5–9, oblanceolate, about half as long as tube. Trop. Afr. Zone 10.

dispermum Wallich. Deciduous climber, glabrous except at nodes; lvs. opp., lfts. 5, terminal lft. to 4½ in. long, lateral lfts. usually in 2 pairs, lanceolate, to 1½ in. long; fls. white, often tinged with pink, in axillary or terminal cymes, fragrant, calyx to ½ in. long, teeth 5, short, triangular, corolla tube to ½ in. long, lobes 5, obovate, to 5/16 in. long, spreading. Himalayas and sw. China. Similar to *J. officinale,* but having short calyx teeth.

diversifolium: *J. subhumile.*

floridum Bunge. Erect, semievergreen; lvs. alt., lfts. 3 or rarely 5, elliptic to ovate-oblong, to 1½ in. long; fls. yellow, in many-fld. cymes, calyx teeth subulate, as long as tube, corolla tube to ¾ in. long, lobes ovate, acute, about half as long as tube. China, Japan. Zone 7.

fluminense Vell. [*J. bahiense* DC.]. Woody climber, shaggy-pubescent to thinly tomentose; lvs. opp., lfts. 3, pubescent on both surfaces, terminal lft. to 2 in. long, lateral ones smaller; fls. white, nearly sessile or short-pedicelled, in broad loose cymes, fragrant, calyx to 1/16 in. long, teeth 5–6, shorter than tube, corolla tube to 1 in. long, lobes 5–6, shorter than tube. Trop. Afr. Closely related to *J. angulare,* but having smaller calyx and broad infl.

fruticans L. Evergreen or partly so, 9 ft. or more, not climbing, brs. weak; lvs. alt., lfts. 3, oblong, to ¾ in. long, obtuse; fls. yellow, in 2–5-fld. cymes, calyx teeth subulate, as long as tube, corolla tube to ½ in. long, lobes 5, obtuse, about half as long as tube. S. Eur., N. Afr., sw. Asia. Zone 7.

gracile: *J. volubile.*

gracillimum Hook.f. PINWHEEL J., STAR J. Climbing, pubescent; lvs. opp., of 1 lft., ovate-lanceolate, to 1½ in. long; fls. white, in many-fld. cymes, fragrant, calyx teeth to ½ in. long, corolla tube to ¾ in. long, lobes 9, pointed, shorter than tube. N. Borneo. Scarcely distinct, specifically, from *J. multiflorum.*

grandiflorum L. CATALONIAN J., ROYAL J., SPANISH J. Straggling climber; lvs. opp., lfts. 5–7, ovate, to ¾ in. long, terminal lft. longer; fls. white, in terminal infl., with pedicels of central fls. shorter than lateral ones, fragrant, calyx teeth linear, to ⅜ in. long, corolla tube to ¾ in. long, lobes 5–6, oblong. Arabia? Fls. contain an essential oil used in perfumery. Frost-tender. The name, *J. grandiflorum,* has also been applied in hort. to *J. officinale* forma *affine.*

heterophyllum: *J. subhumile*

humile L. Evergreen or semievergreen, to 20 ft., erect and sometimes almost treelike, brs. weak; lvs. alt., lfts. 3–7, ovate to lanceolate, to 2 in. long; fls. yellow, in umbellate or nearly umbellate clusters, fragrant or inodorous, calyx teeth very short, corolla tube to ¾ in. long, lobes rounded, about half as long as tube. Himalayas of w. China. Zone 7. Var. **glabrum:** forma *Wallichianum.* Cv. **'Revolutum'** [*J. humile* var. *revolutum* (Sims) J. Stokes; *J. revolutum* Sims]. ITALIAN J. Large and fragrant-fld., but frost-tender clone, cult. for over a century. Forma **Wallichianum** (Lindl.) P. S. Green [*J. humile* var. *glabrum* (DC.) Kobuski; *J. Wallichianum* Lindl.]. Lfts. 7–11; fls. relatively few.

ilicifolium: a listed name of no botanical standing, often applied to *J. nitidum.*

Leratii Schlechter [*J. absimile* L. H. Bailey]. Evergreen climber; lvs. opp., of 1 lft., ovate to lanceolate, to 2 in. or sometimes 3 in. long; fls. white, in terminal or axillary, few- to many-fld. panicles, calyx teeth lanceolate, to 1/16 in. long, scarcely longer than tube, corolla tube to ¾ in. long, lobes 5–7, lanceolate, about half as long as tube. New Caledonia, Loyalty Is.

ligustrifolium Lam. Not cult., the name apparently incorrectly applied in hort. to *J. Leratii.*

magnificum Lingelsh. Not cult., but the name sometimes incorrectly used in cult. for *J. nitidum.*

Mesnyi Hance [*J. primulinum* Hemsl.]. JAPANESE J., PRIMROSE J., YELLOW J. Evergreen, to 10 ft., not climbing, branchlets long, 4-angled; lvs. opp., lfts. 3, oblong to lanceolate, to 3 in. long; fls. solitary, often double, calyx teeth leafy, longer than tube, corolla yellow with darker center, lobes 6, usually longer than tube. W. China. Zone 8. Showy; sometimes grown under glass.

multiflorum (Burm.f.) Andr. [*J. pubescens* Willd.]. STAR J. Evergreen, densely pubescent climber; lvs. opp., of 1 lft., ovate, to 2 in. long, rounded or cordate at base; fls. white, in few- to many-fld. clusters, calyx teeth to ½ in. long, covered with spreading yellow hairs, corolla lobes about half as long as tube. India.

nitidum Skan. ANGEL-WING J., WINDMILL J., STAR J., CONFEDERATE J. Partly climbing; lvs. opp., of 1 lft., elliptic-lanceolate, to 3 in. long; fls. white, often reddish on the outside in bud, fragrant, calyx teeth linear, spreading, to ⅜ in. long, corolla tube to ¾ in. long, lobes ½ in. long or more. Admiralty Is.

noumeense Schlechter. Climbing; lvs. opp., of 1 lft., rounded, to 2 in. long; fls. white, corolla tube long. New Caledonia. Recently introd.

nudiflorum Lindl. Deciduous, to 15 ft., diffuse but not climbing, branchlets 4-angled; lvs. opp., lfts. 3, oblong or ovate, to 1 in. long; fls. yellow, solitary, appearing before lvs., calyx teeth leafy, to ⅜ in. long, about as long as tube, corolla tube about ½ in. long, lobes 5–6, obovate, somewhat shorter than tube. China. Zone 6. Showy shrub in early spring.

odoratissimum L. Evergreen shrub, to 9 ft. or more, more or less erect; lvs. alt., lfts. 3 or 5, rarely 7, ovate-lanceolate, 1–2 in. long; fls. yellow, 10–20, in corymbose-paniculate infls., calyx teeth to ¹⁄₁₆ in. long, corolla tube to ⅝ in. long, lobes 4–6, to ⅜ in. long. Madeira and Canary Is. Fls. contain an essential oil used in perfumery.

officinale L. POET'S JESSAMINE. To 30 ft., climbing or with weak sts.; lvs. opp., lfts. 5–7, ovate, to 2½ in. long, terminal lft. larger; fls. white, in clusters, on nearly equal pedicels, fragrant, calyx teeth linear, to ½ in. long, corolla tube nearly 1 in. long, lobes 4–5, shorter. Himalayas of w. China. Fls. contain an essential oil used in perfumery. Cv. 'Aureovariegatum'. Lvs. variegated. Forma affine (Royle ex Lindl.) Rehd. [*J. grandiflorum* Hort., not L.]. Fls. somewhat larger.

Parkeri S. T. Dunn. Prostrate, to 1 ft.; lvs. alt., lfts. 3–5, ovate, to ¼ in. long; fls. yellow, solitary, calyx tube about ¹⁄₁₆ in. long, lobes shorter, corolla tube to ½ in. long, lobes about half as long. Himalayas. Zone 7.

polyanthum Franch. Deciduous or sometimes evergreen, vigorous scrambling shrub; lvs. opp., lfts. 5–7, lanceolate, rounded at base, attenuate at apex, 3-nerved, leathery, terminal lfts. to 3½ in. long, lateral ones shorter; fls. white on inside, pink outside, in few- to many-fld. axillary panicles, fragrant, calyx to ⅛ in. long, teeth subulate, as long as tube, corolla tube to ¾ in. long, lobes 5, elliptic-oblong, about half as long as tube. W. China.

primulinum: *J. Mesnyi*.

pubescens: *J. multiflorum*.

revolutum: *J. humile cv.*

rex S. T. Dunn. Glabrous climber; lvs. opp., of 1 lft., broadly ovate, to 8 in. long; fls. pure white, 2–3 in axillary cymes, scentless, calyx lobes 6, linear, to ¼ in. long, about twice as long as calyx tube, corolla tube to 1 in. long, lobes usually 8, obovate, as long as tube. Thailand.

rigidum Zenk. Not cult., but the name sometimes incorrectly applied in hort. to *J. Leratii* and *J. nitidum*.

Sambac (L.) Ait. ARABIAN J. Evergreen, climbing, sts. pubescent; lvs. opp., lfts. 1, sometimes in 3's, broad-ovate, to 3 in. long; fls. white, in clusters, fragrant, calyx teeth linear, to ⅜ in. long, corolla tube to ½ in. long, lobes oblong to orbicular, about as long as tube. Cv. 'Grand Duke of Tuscany'. Fls. double. In cult. so long that nativity uncertain, but probably Asiatic. Fls. used to flavor tea.

simplicifolium G. Forst. An Australian sp. rare in cult.; plants offered under this name may be *J. Leratii* or *J. volubile*, closely related spp.

×stephanense Hort. Lemoine: *J. Beesianum × J. officinale*. Lvs. opp., lfts. usually 1, sometimes 3 or incompletely divided; fls. pink, fragrant.

subhumile W. W. Sm. [*J. diversifolium* Kobuski; *J. heterophyllum* Roxb.]. Shrub or small tree; lvs. alt., lfts. 1 or 3, ovate-lanceolate, 3–5 in. long, thickish, glossy above; fls. yellow, in corymbs, calyx teeth minute, shorter than tube, corolla tube to ⅜ in. long, lobes rounded, about ¼ in. long. Himalayas of w. China.

tortuosum Willd. Climber; lvs. opp., lfts. 3, linear-lanceolate to linear-oblong, to 1½ in. long; fls. white, 3–5, terminal on brs. or lateral branchlets, calyx lobes 5–6, triangular, to ⅛ in. long, somewhat shorter than tube, corolla tube to 1 in. long, lobes usually 6, about half as long as tube. S. Afr.

volubile Jacq. [*J. gracile* Andr.]. Evergreen climber; lvs. opp., of 1 lft.; fls. white, corolla tube to ½ in. long. Australia. Closely related to

J. Leratii, but having minute calyx teeth, shorter corolla tube. Some cult. jasmines called *J. simplicifolium* belong here.

Wallichianum: *J. humile* forma.

JATROPHA L. [*Adenoropium* Pohl; *Curcas* Adans.]. *Euphorbiaceae*. About 125 spp. of monoecious or dioecious per. herbs, shrubs, or trees with milky or watery juice, native to trop. and subtrop. N. and S. Amer., Afr., and Asia; lvs. alt., simple, palmately or pinnately veined, sometimes palmately lobed or cut, sometimes peltate; infl. cymose; fls. with petals, yellow, purple, or scarlet to vermilion.

Propagated by seeds or cuttings. See *Cnidoscolus*.

Curcas L. [*Curcas Curcas* (L.) Britt. & Millsp.]. BARBADOS NUT, PHYSIC NUT. Tree, 8–15 ft.; lvs. ovate to slightly 3–5-lobed, palmately lobed and veined, 2½–7 in. wide, petioles about as long as the blades; fls. yellow. Trop. Amer. Yields oil used for candle or soap making, also a purgative.

hastata: *J. integerrima*.

integerrima Jacq. [*J. hastata* Jacq.; *Adenoropium hastatum* (Jacq.) Britt. & P. Wils.; *A. integerrimum* Pohl]. PEREGRINA, SPICY J. Shrub or small tree, 3–10 ft., glabrous or close-pubescent; lvs. oblong-obovate, frequently constricted below the middle and fiddle-shaped, sharp-acuminate; fls. scarlet to vermilion or rose, to 1 in. across. Cuba. The lf. shape in this sp. is very variable, and the venation may be pinnate or palmate.

Manihot: *Manihot utilissima*.

multifida L. [*Adenoropium multifidum* Pohl]. CORAL PLANT, PHYSIC NUT. Shrub or tree, to 20 ft.; lvs. nearly orbicular, to 1 ft. across, deeply parted into 7–11 entire or cut lobes, glaucous beneath; cymes compound; fls. scarlet. Trop. Amer.

podagrica Hook. TARTOGO, AUSTRALIAN BOTTLE PLANT. Shrub, to about 1½ ft., sts. swollen and knobby, with bristled scars; lvs. orbicular-ovate, peltate, long-petioled, to 12 in. across, deeply 3–5-lobed with obtuse sinuses; cymes terminal, long-peduncled, pedicels red; fls. small, coral-red. Cent. Amer. Planted in warm countries and sometimes under glass.

Standleyi Steyerm. Tree; lvs. simple, glabrous, entire, oblong-obovate, cuneate at base; fls. purple, urceolate. Mex.

texana: *Cnidoscolus texanus*.

urens: *Cnidoscolus urens;* var. *inermis*: *Cnidoscolus Chayamansa*.

JEFFERSONIA B. Barton. *Berberidaceae*. Two spp. of small per. herbs, native to e. N. Amer. and ne. Asia; lvs. basal, blades palmately veined or lobed; fls. white or blue, solitary, terminal on slender scapes, perianth usually of about 12 segms., the inner petaloid, stamens 6, ovary ovoid; fr. leathery.

diphylla (L.) Pers. TWINLEAF. To 1½ ft. when in fr.; lf. blades to 6 in. long and 5 in. across, divided into 2 kidney-shaped, entire or lobed divisions, glaucous beneath, petioles as long as scapes; fls. white, 1 in. across; fr. dehiscent by a terminal lid. Ont. to Iowa, s. to Ala.

dubia (Maxim.) Benth. & Hook.f. ex Bak. & S. L. Moore. To nearly 1 ft.; lf. blades orbicular to nearly reniform, with deep basal cleft, to 4 in. across, margin irregularly angled, petioles longer than scapes; fls. lavender-blue, to 1 in. across; fr. dehiscent by oblique longitudinal slit. Ne. Asia.

JEPSONIA Small. *Saxifragaceae*. One very variable sp. of Calif. and Baja Calif., a per. herb with cormlike rhizomes; lvs. mostly basal, round-cordate, petioles long, fl. sts. leafless; fls. in terminal cymes, calyx tube campanulate, united at base to ovary, calyx lobes 5, petals 5, stamens 10, ovary nearly superior, the 2 carpels separate above the middle; fr. of 2 follicles.

Parryi (Torr.) Small. Lvs. to 2 in. across, petioles to 2 in. long; fl. sts. to 12 in.; calyx tube purple-striate, to ¼ in. long, petals white, entire, to ¼ in. long, stamens shorter than petals; follicles to ¼ in. long, extending beyond calyx tube. Lvs. appearing in spring, then withering, fls. appearing in autumn.

JOANNESIA Vell. *Euphorbiaceae*. Two spp. of large monoecious trees, native to Brazil; lvs. alt., palmately compound, long-petioled; fls. in cymes, with petals, ovary 2-celled; fr. a drupe.

Rarely planted in southern U.S., but frequently cultivated in the tropics.

principes Vell. Lfts. 3–7, ovate, elliptic, or obovate, to 6 in. long; fls. yellow, petals longer than calyx; fr. to 4¾ in. long, warty. Seeds yield oil used medicinally as a purgative.

JOHANNESTEIJSMANNIA H. E. Moore [*Teysmannia* Rchb.f. & Zoll., not Miq.]. *Palmae.* Four spp. of small palms with bisexual fls., native to Malay Pen., Borneo, and Sumatra; sts. not evident or short; lvs. long-costapalmate and appearing pinnately veined, elongate-cuneate in outline, blade and petiole spinose-toothed along margins; infl. among the lvs., peduncle short, with several sterile bracts, rachis bearing few to many brs.; fls. mostly in clusters of 2–3, calyx cupular with 3 very short lobes, petals 3, briefly united basally, valvate above, stamens 6, filaments united basally in a cup, carpels 3, separate except united styles; fr. with corky-warty surface, seed with homogeneous endosperm deeply intruded by seed coat, embryo lateral.

Tender palms. Zone 10b in Fla. For culture see *Palms.*

altifrons (Rchb.f. & Zoll.) H. E. Moore. St. not normally evident; lvs. about 10, ascending from the crown, to 8 ft. long, petiole to 2½ ft. long; infl. short, bracts brown; fls. white, rank-smelling; fr. brown, about 1¼ in. in diam. Malay Pen., Borneo, Sumatra.

JOVELLANA Ruiz & Pav. *Scrophulariaceae.* About 6 spp. of herbs or subshrubs of Chile and New Zeal.; allied to *Calceolaria* but having the 2 corolla lobes of nearly equal size.

Sinclairii (Hook.) Kranzl. Glandular-pubescent herb, to 1½ ft.; lvs. simple, opp., ovate, to 3 in. long, coarsely toothed or lobed; fls. in terminal, paniculate cymes, corolla white or yellow, spotted with purple, ¼ in. across. New Zeal.

JOVIBARBA: *SEMPERVIVUM.*

JUANIA Drude. *Palmae.* One sp., a solitary, moderate, unarmed, dioecious palm of the Juan Fernandez Is. (Chile); lvs. pinnate, sheaths not forming a crownshaft, pinnae acute; infl. among lvs., long-peduncled, paniculate, bearing 4 bracts, rachillae with fls. not clustered; male fls. with sepals short, united, petals separate, imbricate basally, stamens 6, filaments erect, pistillode minute, female fls. with perianth similar, staminodes 6, ovary 3-celled; fr. globose, orange-red, with apical stigmatic residue, endocarp not operculate, seed with homogeneous endosperm and basal embryo.

Rarely cultivated. For culture see *Palms.*

australis (Mart.) Drude ex Hook.f. To 25 ft. or more, trunk green; lvs. to 6 ft. long, pinnae about 80 on each side, regularly arranged, green above, grayish beneath; infl. to nearly 3 ft. long; fls. white; fr. ⅝ in. in diam.

JUBAEA HBK. *Palmae.* One sp., a solitary, massive, unarmed, monoecious palm of coastal cent. Chile; lvs. pinnate, sheath fibrous, open, petiole not toothed along the margin, pinnae 2-dentate or becoming 2-cleft apically, stiff, midrib prominent; infl. among the lvs., long-peduncled, bracts 2, the lower concealed by lf. sheaths, the upper fusiform, beaked, not pleated externally, splitting abaxially, rachillae many, simple, with fls. in triads (2 male and 1 female) near the base and above these with paired or solitary male fls.; male fls. with calyx elongate, angled, and solid at base, lobes 3, acute, petals valvate, 3 or more times as long as calyx-lobes, stamens many, filaments slightly inflexed at apex in bud, anthers attached by back, pistillode minute, 3-cleft, female fls. with sepals 3, imbricate, equalling the 3 imbricate, valvate-tipped petals, staminodes united in a low cupule, pistil 3-celled, 3-ovuled; fr. 1-seeded, ovoid, mesocarp fleshy-fibrous, endocarp thick, with 3 pores near the base, seed with hollow, homogeneous endosperm, embryo near base.

Much grown worldwide in Medit. type of climate including southern Calif.; also sometimes grown under glass in the juvenile state and in tubs for planting out where hardy. Does not thrive in Fla. For culture see *Palms.*

chilensis (Mol.) Baill. [*J. spectabilis* HBK]. CHILEAN WINE P., HONEY P., SYRUP P., COQUITO P., LITTLE COKERNUT. To 30 ft. or more, trunk to 3 ft. in diam. or more; lvs. green or silvery-green, spreading to ascending and arcuately curved at tip, petiole short, rachis to 4½ ft. long, pinnae about 120 on each side, borne in 1 plane, regularly ar-

ranged or in groups of 2–5; infl. more than 3 ft. long, maroon; male fls. maroon with yellow center and stamens; fr. 1½ in. long, yellow. In Chile the massive trunks have long been felled as a source of sap yielding commercial palm honey, and few wild stands remain.

spectabilis: *J. chilensis.*

JUBAEOPSIS Becc. *Palmae.* One sp., an unarmed, monoecious palm in Transkei Prov., S. Afr.; lvs. pinnate, petiole not toothed along the margin, pinnae slender, unequally 2-cleft or 2-dentate at apex, midrib prominent; infl. among lvs., long-peduncled, bracts 2, the upper fusiform, woody, not pleated externally, rachillae many, simple, sinuate, with fls. in triads (2 male and 1 female) near the base and above these paired or solitary male fls.; male fls. with sepals 3, acute, basally imbricate, petals 3, angled, valvate, much longer than sepals, stamens 7–16, erect, pistillode small, 3-cleft apically, female fls. ovoid, sepals 3, broadly imbricate, petals 3, imbricate except briefly valvate apex, about twice as long as sepals, staminodes united in a low, lobed cupule, pistil 3-celled, 3-ovuled; fr. 1-seeded, subglobose, beaked, mesocarp thin, endocarp thick, with pores slightly below the middle, seed irregular, endosperm homogeneous, embryo below middle.

Occasionally cultivated, thriving best in regions with Medit. type of climate, including southern Calif. For culture see *Palms.*

caffra Becc. Sts. to 20 ft.; lvs. to 15 ft. long, pinnae regularly arranged, to 30 in. long, 1½ in. wide; infl. 3 ft. long or more, rachillae waxy, to 18 in. long; male fls. to ⅞ in. long; fr. 1¼ in. in diam. Zone 10a.

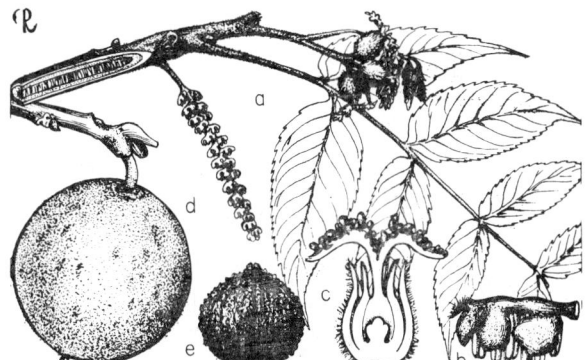

JUGLANDACEAE. *Juglans nigra:* **a,** flowering branch, stem sectioned to show chambered pith, × ½; **b,** male flower, × 2; **c,** female flower, vertical section, × 2; **d,** fruit, × ½; **e,** seed, × ½. (From Bailey, *Manual of Cultivated Plants,* ed. 2.)

JUGLANDACEAE A. Rich. ex Kunth. WALNUT FAMILY. Dicot.; 6 genera and about 60 spp. of deciduous, monoecious trees, native to N. and S. Amer., Asia, and Eur.; lvs. alt., pinnate; fls. unisexual, male fls. in drooping catkins, with or without perianth, stamens 3–many, female fls. a few together or in racemes, calyx 3–5-lobed, ovary inferior; fr. a winged nutlet, or drupe enclosing a stone or nut. *Carya, Engelhardtia, Juglans, Platycarya,* and *Pterocarya* are cult. as ornamentals, for shade, for the edible nuts, and some spp. for timber.

JUGLANS L. WALNUT. *Juglandaceae.* About 20 spp. of deciduous, monoecious trees, native to N. and S. Amer., and from se. Eur. to e. Asia; lvs. large, aromatic, odd-pinnate; male fls. in drooping catkins borne on the previous year's wood, female fls. on wood of current year; fr. a drupelike furrowed nut enclosed within a thick, indehiscent husk. Distinguished from *Carya* by having the pith in the twigs chambered or with minute cross-partitions.

Walnuts are grown as ornamentals, for the edible nuts, and for the fine-grained wood used for furniture and cabinet work. For culture see *Walnut.*

ailantifolia Carrière [*J. Sieboldiana* Maxim., not Göpp.]. JAPANESE W. To 60 ft.; lfts. 11–17, elliptic, to 6 in. long, pubescent beneath; fr. broadly ovoid to nearly globose, 1½ in. long, sticky-pubescent, nut ovoid, pointed, rugose, thick-shelled. Japan. Var. **cordiformis** (Maxim.) Rehd. [*J. cordiformis* Maxim., not Wangenh.]. HEART NUT. Nut cordate or cordate-ovoid, flattened, relatively thin-shelled, with shallow groove on each side. Japan.

californica S. Wats. CALIFORNIA W. Shrub or tree, to 30 ft., often with several trunks; lfts. 11–15, ovate-lanceolate, to 3 in. long; fr. globose, ¾ in. across, soft-pubescent, nut shallowly grooved, thick-shelled. S. Calif. Var. **Hindsii** *J. Hindsii.*

cathayensis Dode. CHINESE W., CHINESE BUTTERNUT. Shrub, or tree to 80 ft.; lfts. 9–17, ovate-oblong, to 6 in. long or more, pubescent beneath; fr. ovoid, to 2 in. long, pointed, sticky-pubescent, nut 6–8-angled, spiny-ridged, thick-shelled. W. China. Zone 6. Vigorous tree with large lvs. and edible nuts.

cinerea L. BUTTERNUT, WHITE W. To 100 ft.; lfts. 11–19, oblong-lanceolate, to 5 in. long, pubescent; fr. ovoid-oblong, to 3 in. long, sticky-pubescent, nut with 8 prominent and many broken ridges, thick-shelled. New Bruns. to Ark. Zone 3. Wood valued for furniture.

cordiformis: *J. ailanthifolia* var.

Hindsii (Jeps.) Jeps. [*J. californica* var. *Hindsii* Jeps.]. Closely related to *J. californica,* but taller, with single trunk, lfts. usually 15–19, to 4 in. long, and nuts somewhat larger. Cent. Calif. Zone 7? Used as a street tree in Calif. and as a stock for budding *J. regia,* English walnut.

Honorei: *J. neotropica.*

insularis: *J. jamaicensis.*

jamaicensis C. DC. [*J. insularis* Griseb.]. WEST INDIES W. To 70 ft., occasionally to 150 ft.; lfts. usually 16–20, ovate-lanceolate, to 4½ in. long, glabrate beneath; fr. nearly globose, to 1¼ in. long. W. Indies.

japonica: a listed name of no botanical standing.

major (Torr.) A. Heller. ARIZONA W. To 60 ft.; lfts. 9–13 or more, narrow-ovate to oblong-lanceolate, pubescent on rib and rachis underneath; fr. nearly globose, 1 in. long or more, finely pubescent, nut nearly globose, deeply grooved, thick-shelled. W. Tex., New Mex., Ariz., s. to n. Mex. Zone 7.

mandshurica Maxim. MANCHURIAN W. To 60 ft.; lfts. 9–17, oblong, to 8 in. long; fr. subglobose or ovoid, 2 in. long, sticky-pubescent, nut with 8 prominent ridges and many broken ridges. Manchuria. Zone 5.

microcarpa Berland. [*J. rupestris* Engelm. ex Torr.]. LITTLE W., RIVER W. Shrub or tree, rarely to 30 ft.; lfts. 15–23, lanceolate, to 3 in. long; fr. globose, ¾ in. in diam., nearly glabrous, nut with thick shell. W. Okla., Tex., New Mex., n. Mex. Zone 6.

neotropica Diels [*J. Honorei* Dode]. To 90 ft., bark on trunk somewhat thick, and furrowed or fissured; lfts. usually 15–19, ovate to ovate-oblong, thick and usually rugose above, densely fascicled-hairy beneath; fr. subglobose or broadly elliptic, to 2 in. long, conspicuously longitudinally ridged. W. Venezuela, Colombia, Ecuador, n. Peru. Nuts edible; wood valuable for cabinetry.

nigra L. BLACK W. To 150 ft.; lfts. 15–23, ovate-oblong, to 5 in. long, pubescent beneath; fr. globose, to 2 in. in diam., pubescent, nut sub-globose to ovoid, strongly ridged, thick-shelled. Mass. to s. Ont., s. to Fla. and e. Tex. Zone 5. Nuts edible, wood prized for fine furniture and gun stocks. Cv. 'Laciniata' [forma *laciniata* Rehd.]. Lfts. laciniate.

orientis: *J. regia* var.

regia L. [*J. regia* var. *sinensis* C. DC.]. ENGLISH W., PERSIAN W., MADEIRA NUT. To 100 ft., bark silvery gray; lfts. usually 7–9, oblong, to 5 in. long; fr. nearly globose, to 2 in. in diam., glabrous, nut somewhat wrinkled, thick- or thin-shelled. Se. Eur., w. Asia. Zone 7. Much planted as a nut tree in the warmer parts of the country, particularly in Calif. Produces a valuable cabinet wood. A recently introd. strain from the Carpathian Mts., which has withstood low temperatures is known as the CARPATHIAN W. This may prove useful in colder parts of the country. Cvs. listed are: 'Laciniata' [*J. regia* forma *laciniata* (Jacques) C. K. Schneid.], lfts. pinnately cut; 'Maxima' ['Macrocarpa'], nuts large; 'Monophylla' [*J. regia* forma *monophylla* (Dochn.) C. K. Schneid.], lvs. simple or with 3 lfts.; 'Pendula' [*J. regia* forma *pendula* (Pépin) C. K. Schneid.], brs. drooping; 'Praeparturiens' [*J. regia* forma *praeparturiens* (Pépin) Rehd.], shrubby, early-maturing form. Var. **orientis** (Dode) Kitam. [*J. orientis* Dode]. Branchlets and lvs. glabrous; lfts. 3–9, obtuse, entire except in young tree; nut somewhat thin-shelled. China.

rupestris: *J. microcarpa.*

Sieboldiana: *J. ailantifolia.*

JUJUBE. The species of jujube principally planted in the United States is *Zizyphus Jujuba,* a small, somewhat spiny tree of Eurasia. Cultivars in this country originated in China (hence the alternative name Chinese date), where the species has been grown and selected for several thousand years, with the result that the fruits of Chinese cultivars are far superior in size (to 2 inches long) to those grown elsewhere. Jujube drupes are elliptical to oblong in form, with a thin, dark brown skin and a crisp flesh that is mild and quite sweetish. The fruits are usually candied or glacéed, dried, or canned. Trees are very ornamental with their small, shiny, green leaves and zigzag branchlets and seem to be largely free of pests and diseases. The species is especially well adapted to the hot desert valleys of California and the Southwest but grows elsewhere in Zone 9, although not often as productively. Fruits seldom mature in the North because they require a long growing season. Select large-fruited cultivars ('Li', 'So', 'Tanku Vu', 'Yu') can be propagated by grafting or root cuttings.

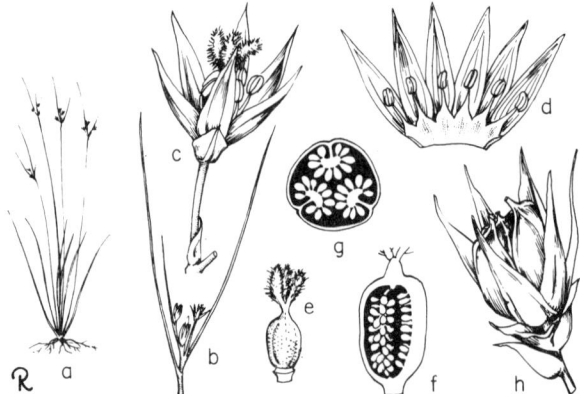

JUNCACEAE. *Juncus tenuis* Willd.: **a,** flowering plant, × ¹⁄₁₀; **b,** inflorescence, × ½; **c,** flower, × 5; **d,** perianth and stamens, expanded, × 4; **e,** pistil, × 4; **f,** ovary, vertical section, × 9; **g,** ovary, cross section, × 10; **h,** fruit with subtending bracts, × 6. (Species representative, but not in general cultivation; from Lawrence, *Taxonomy of Vascular Plants.*)

JUNCACEAE Juss. RUSH FAMILY. Monocot.; 8 or 9 genera of sedgelike herbs of wide distribution; fls. small, bisexual, greenish, sepals and petals 3, similar, scalelike, stamens 3 or 6, ovary superior, 3-celled with axile placentation, or 1-celled with parietal placentation, style short, stigmas 3, filiform, hairy; fr. a 3-celled caps. A few spp. of *Juncus* and *Luzula* are cult., mainly as ornamentals, but *Juncus effusus* as a source of matting.

JUNCAGINACEAE L. Rich. ARROW GRASS FAMILY. Monocot.; 4 genera and 17 spp. of ann. or per., rhizomatous, aquatic or marsh herbs of cosmopolitan distribution in cool-temp. regions; lvs. mostly basal, linear, sheathing, with a ligule between blade and sheath; fls. unisexual or bisexual, regular, in scapose, terminal spikes or racemes, perianth segms. 3 or 6, stamens 3, 4, or 6, ovary superior; carpels 3, 4, or 6, separating at maturity. *Triglochin* is sometimes cult.

JUNCUS L. RUSH, BOG R. *Juncaceae.* About 240 spp. of glabrous, stiffish herbs, native mostly to temp. regions; lvs. sometimes reduced to basal sheaths; infl. cymose; sepals and petals 3, scalelike, stamens 3 or 6, ovary 3-celled; fr. a caps., seeds several to many.

In moist, often shaded locations; one an important specialty crop in Japan, others occasionally grown as ground covers or curiosities; the cultivars of *J. effusus* sometimes grown in pots. Propagated by seeds and division.

balticus Willd. Per., sts. 1–3 ft., not striated, arising in clumps from a creeping, forked rhizome; cymes with brs. mostly openly forked, perianth segms. brownish, midrib green, margins pale whitish. Eur. and N. Amer. A very variable sp.

effusus L. [*J. polyanthemus* Buchenau]. SOFT R., JAPANESE-MAT R. Per., sts. 1–6 ft., arching, ascending, in dense tussocks, striated and ridged; cymes many-fld., open, the brs. many; fls. yellowish-green to pale brown. Eurasia, N. Amer., Australia, New Zeal., e. and s. Afr.

Intensively grown in sw. Japan for weaving tatami, the standard floor covering of Japanese homes. Many variants are recognized, including the cvs.: 'Aureus Striatus', sts. banded with yellow-green; 'Spiralis', sts. spirally twisted; 'Vittatus', sts. narrowly banded with white; 'Zebrinus', sts. broadly banded with white or greenish-white.

Lesueurii Bolander. SALT R. Per., sts. 1–3 ft., stout, smooth, arising at intervals from creeping rhizomes; cymes with 3–4 brs., each to 1½ in. long; fls. dark brown, perianth segms. with purple scarious margins. Salt marshes, Alaska to s. Calif.

pauciflorus R. Br. Per., sts. to 3 ft., leafless, from a horizontal, creeping rhizome; infl. an irregularly compound panicle. E. Australia and Tasmania.

polyanthemus: *J. effusus.*

JUNEBERRY. Shadbush, serviceberry, and sugarplum are a few other common names applied to about 25 species of *Amelanchier* indigenous to North America. Such species as *A. sanguinea, A. spicata,* and *A. stolonifera* produce edible fruit but ripen later than *A. alnifolia,* the species from which most domesticated clones have been obtained. However, the old cultivar *A. stolonifera* 'Success' is still one of the best known.

Juneberries are extremely winter hardy and are found growing wild in the Great Plains area northward into Saskatchewan, Canada, where temperatures and rainfall are low. They thrive on a wide range of soil types. They are propagated by seed and suckers. *Amelanchier alnifolia* is a small, attractive, shrubby tree which may attain a height of 25 feet. If suckers are not removed, a bush type of growth habit will develop. The trees are highly ornamental because of the many small white flowers which appear in late April and the highly colored foliage in autumn. Fruits vary in size from that of a pea to ¾ inch in diameter. They are mostly purplish-blue to black with a heavy bloom, resembling a blueberry. They are juicy, rather insipid, mild-flavored, and ripen in late June. Juneberries are often planted to attract wildlife, and attempts have been made to plant them near cherry orchards to lure the birds from the cherries, but with varied results.

Indians and early settlers gathered the berries and dried and stored them for winter use. In areas where few other fruits survive, they are used for pies and preserves. The flavor in cooking is enhanced by the addition of lemon juice.

Of *A. alnifolia* cultivars, 'Shannon' and 'Indian' are new, superior, and very productive, with larger fruits. 'Smoky' and 'Pembina' are also productive and of good quality, with medium-sized fruit. 'Forestburg' produces the largest fruit, which is, however, only of fair quality, while 'Altaglow' is excellent for ornamental purposes and its fruit is quite sweet.

JUNIPERUS L. JUNIPER. *Cupressaceae.* About 70 spp. of coniferous, evergreen, mostly small, monoecious or dioecious trees or shrubs, widely dispersed in the N. Hemisphere, some of them arctic; lvs. needlelike or scalelike, commonly appressed on old branchlets, spreading on new growth; male cones yellow, catkinlike; female cones berrylike, scales 3–8, fleshy, coalescing, seeds 1–12, not winged.

Many species are grown as ornamentals, some supply useful timber, and one a flavoring. Some, as *J. virginiana,* are known as cedars. For culture see *Conifers.*

Ashei Buchh. OZARK WHITE CEDAR, ASHE J. Dioecious shrub or small tree, to 20 ft., bark gray-brown, shredding, branchlets 4-angled; lvs. mostly opp., denticulate, keeled; female cones blue-black, to ⁵⁄₁₆ in. long, mostly 1-seeded. Limestone soils, Ark., Mo., Okla., Tex., to Mex.

Ashfordii: a listed name of no botanical standing for *J. communis* var. *communis* cv.

barbadensis: *J. bermudiana,* but material cult. as *J. barbadensis* is probably *J. silicicola.*

bermudiana L. [*J. barbadensis* L.]. BERMUDA CEDAR. To 40 ft.; lvs. 4-ranked, thick, grooved, mostly overlapping, spiny-pointed, pale bluish-green; female cones blue, glaucous. Bermuda. Zone 10.

californica Carrière. Shrub, to 12 ft., rarely a tree; lvs. in pairs, overlapping, scalelike, glandular on back, juvenile lvs. very glaucous; female cones reddish-brown, ½–¾ in. long. Calif. Zone 8.

canadensis: *J. communis* var. *depressa.*

Cedrus Webb & Berth. CANARY ISLANDS J. To 100 ft., branchlets drooping; lvs. pointed forward, linear; female cones orange-brown, about ½ in. in diam., 3-seeded. Canary Is. Cult. in the open in Zone 10 and under glass.

chinensis L. [*J. sphaerica* Lindl.]. Dioecious, to 60 ft. and more, or only a shrub; juvenile lvs. needlelike, mostly ternate, rigidly spinescent, adult lvs. scalelike, opp., obtuse, entire; female cones mostly subglobose, about ⁵⁄₁₆ in. in diam., mostly brown or purplish-brown, commonly glaucous, maturing in 2 years, usually 2–3-seeded. Temp. e. Asia. Zone 4. A variable sp. Subject to one's inclinations, 2 or more botanical vars. may be recognized. Cvs. belong principally to the typical var.

Var. **chinensis.** The typical var. Cvs. are: 'Alba' [cv. 'Squamata Variegata'], twig tips mostly creamy-white; 'Albispica', differs from 'Alba' in some twig tips golden-yellow; 'Albovariegata': probably 'Variegata'; 'Arbuscula' [cv. 'Smithii'], allied to 'Sheppardii' but smaller and more dense, lvs. bright green; 'Armstrongii', sport of 'Pfitzerana' with flatter profile, lvs. squamiform, yellow-green; 'Aurea', broadly pyramidal, branch tips exposed to sun becoming light golden-yellow, most lvs. juvenile; 'Aureo-globosa', plants male, globose, lvs. suffused golden-yellow; 'Aureo-Pfitzerana', differs from 'Pfitzerana' in having twigs and new lvs. bright yellow, lvs. later becoming green; 'Aureo-plumosa', a sport of 'Plumosa', having outer lvs. suffused yellow; 'Aureo-variegata', a yellow-variegated sport of 'Plumosa', plants male; 'Blaauw', dense, slow-growing, upright, vase-shaped, lvs. blue; 'Columnaris', a rapid-growing clone of 'Pyramidalis', but of narrower habit and with a definite trunk; 'Densa', a clone of 'Pyramidalis', but more slender and irregular; 'Densa Glauca', more glaucous and still more slender; 'Denserecta', a listed name; 'Douglasii': *J. horizontalis* cv.; 'Excelsa': 'Pyramidalis'; 'Expansa': 'Parsonii'; 'Fastigiata', a listed name; 'Foemina', a name for female plants of tall conical shape; 'Fortunei', apparently the same as 'Mas'; 'Fruitlandii', compact, dense like 'Pfitzerana'; 'Glauca', probably a trade name for typical *J. chinensis;* 'Globosa' [cv. 'Virginalis Globosa'], globose, male plant, lvs. dull green; 'Hetzii' [cv. 'Glauca Hetzii'], shrubby, low, lvs. blue-green; 'Jacobiana': 'Pyramidalis'; 'Japonica' [*J. japonica* Carrière], shrub to 5 ft., densely branched, lvs. needlelike, prickly; 'Kaizuka': 'Torulosa'; 'Keteleeri', lvs. longer, more sharply pointed than typical; 'Kosteriana', much like 'Pfitzerana' but more even, almost nestlike; 'Maneyi', brs. blue-green, spreading, ascending; 'Mas' [cvs. 'Fortunei', 'Mascula', 'Neaboriensis'], erect, broadly columnar male trees, to 30 ft.; 'Meyeri', allegedly a very glaucous plant; 'Nana', a listed name; 'Neaboriensis': 'Mas'; 'Oblonga' [cv. 'Sylvestris'], pyramidal tree, to 20 ft., once thought to be dwarf and subglobose, lvs. bright green; 'Parsonii' [cv. 'Expansa'], low shrub, to 2½ ft. high, branchlets cordlike as in 'Torulosa', gray-green; 'Pendula', a name applied to any variant with drooping branchlets; 'Pfitzerana', broad spreading shrub, to 6 ft. high and 9 ft. across, branchlets nodding—named clonal sports are numerous and include 'Armstrongii', 'Aureo-Pfitzerana', 'Compacta', 'Glauca', and 'Nana'; 'Plumosa', vase-shaped female shrub, becoming subglobose, brs. plumose, lvs. mostly scalelike, bright olive-green; 'Procumbens': var. *procumbens;* 'Pyramidalis' [cvs. 'Excelsa', ?'Jacobiana'], ovate-conical shrub, 9–20 ft. high, lvs. glaucous, harsh, ½ in. long; 'Reevesii', an unidentified name variously applied, usually to typical *J. chinensis;* 'Sargentii': var. *Sargentii;* 'Sheppardii', broadly pyramidal tree, to 18 ft., brs. ascending, with nodding tops, lvs. gray-green; 'Shimpaki', a listed name; 'Smithii': 'Arbuscula'; 'Spiralis': 'Torulosa'; 'Squamata Variegata': 'Alba'; 'Stricta', upright, narrow, brs. erect; 'Sylvestris': 'Oblonga'; 'Torulosa', [cv. 'Kaizuka', 'Spiralis'], shrub to 6 ft. without leader, or tree to 25 ft., densely tufted, with clusters of twisted, cordlike, irregular branchlets, lvs. all scalelike; 'Variegata', tips of branchlets cream-colored, otherwise resembling 'Pyramidalis' and 'Densa', or the name may be applied to variegated dwarf forms; 'Viridis': var. *Sargentii* cv.; 'Virginalis', semierect, lvs. bright green; 'Virginalis Globosa': 'Globosa'; 'Weaveri', a listed name; 'Wilsonii', broad, with dense brs., lvs. dark green.

Var. **procumbens** (Endl.). Miq. [*J. procumbens* Endl.]. Depressed shrub, lower brs. prostrate, others elongate-undulate or twisted and upcurving, branchlets glaucous, lvs. ⅜–½ in. long. Japan. Color and habit cvs. are: 'Albovariegata', 'Aureo-variegata', 'Conglomerata', 'Glauca', 'Nana', and 'Variegata'.

Var. **Sargentii** A. Henry [*J. Sargentii* (A. Henry) Nakai]. SARGENT J. Mound-forming shrub, juvenile lvs. needlelike, often opp., mostly less than ¼ in. long, green above, glaucous beneath. Kurile Is. to n. Japan. Cvs. are: 'Glauca', lvs. markedly blue-green when young; 'Maney', to nearly 4 ft., broader than high, lvs. blue-green, very distinct in winter; 'Viridis', lvs. grass-green when young.

communis L. COMMON J. Erect or prostrate shrub, or small tree, sometimes to 35 ft.; lvs. ternate, all linear, spreading, and sharp-pointed, concave, with a single white longitudinal band above, weakly keeled below; female cones blue or black, glaucous, ¼–½ in. in diam., mostly 3-seeded. N. Amer., Eurasia. Zone 3. The dried berrylike cones are the source of the characteristic flavoring of gin. A very variable sp. represented in cult. by a series of botanical vars. and cvs.

Var. **communis.** The typical var.; arborescent or shrubby, lvs. linear, acuminate-subulate, to 1 in. long, central glaucescent band on upper surface twice as broad as each green margin. N. Amer., Eurasia. Cvs. are: **'Alpina'**, a listed name, perhaps for var. *saxatilis* or *J. horizontalis* cv. 'Alpina'; **'Ashfordii'**, columnar, branchlets erect, dense, lvs. bluish-green; **'Aurea'** and **'Aureospica'**, new growth golden-yellow, becoming green by the second year, see also var. *depressa;* **'Canadensis'**: var. *depressa;* **'Columnaris'**, very slender, 4–5 ft. high, 4–5 in. across, lvs. ¼ in. long; **'Compacta'**, a listed name for dense forms; **'Compressa'**, dwarf, columnar to narrowly pyramidal, to 4 ft. high; **'Cracovia'**, POLISH J., columnar to conical tree, to 15 ft., tips of branchlets nodding, lvs. dull yellow-green; **'Depressa'**: var. *depressa;* **'Echiniformis'**, dwarf, bushy, with small, deep green, prickly lvs.; **'Effusa'**: var. *depressa* cv.; **'Erecta Glauca'**, BLUE-SPIRE J., very glaucous, a derivative of 'Hibernica'; **'Fastigiata'**: 'Suecica' or 'Hibernica'; **'Hemisphaerica'**: var. *hemisphaerica;* **'Hibernica'** [*J. hibernica* Lodd. ex Loud.; cvs. 'Fastigiata', 'Pyramidalis', and 'Stricta'], IRISH J., narrow-columnar, dense, to 15 ft., brs. fastigiate, branchlets erect, lvs. mostly ⅜–⅝ in. long, glossy green, becoming bronzy in winter; **'Horizontalis'**, a listed name for low forms, perhaps sometimes for *J. horizontalis;* **'Hornibrookii'** [cv. 'Pendula'], dwarf, creeping, brs. upturned; **'Jackii'**: var. *Jackii;* **'Montana'**: var. *saxatilis;* **'Nana'**: var. *saxatilis* or any of several dwarf forms; **'Nipponica'**: *J. rigida* subsp. *nipponica;* **'Oblonga Pendula'**, columnar, fastigiate, branchlets long, pendulous; **'Pendula'**, branchlets pendulous, lf. whorls somewhat remote; **Prostrata'**: 'Hornibrookii' or other low, creeping forms; **'Pyramidalis'**: 'Hibernica' or other pyramidal forms; **'Repanda'**, dwarf, semiprostrate, lvs. somewhat bronzy in winter; **'Saxatilis'**: var. *saxatilis;* **'Sibirica'**: var. *saxatilis;* **'Stricta'**: 'Hibernica'; **'Suecica'** [cv. 'Fastigiata'], shrub, similar to 'Hibernica' but with branchlets nodding.

Var. **depressa** Pursh [*J. canadensis* Lodd. ex Burgsd.]. GROUND J., PROSTRATE J. To 3 ft. high, main brs. horizontal, branchlets erect, forming an open-spreading shrub, lvs. to ⅜ in. long, with narrow, glaucous band above as broad as or narrower than green margins. Lab. to B.C., s. to N.Y. and Mont. Cvs. are: **'Aurea'** and **'Aureospica'**, new growth golden-yellow, becoming green the second year; **'Effusa'**, semiprostrate, wide-spreading, lvs. remaining green in winter; **'Plumosa'** and **'Prostrata'**, listed names.

Var. **hemisphaerica** (J. Presl & K. Presl) Parl. [var. *saxatilis* Willd., not auth.]. Shrub to 6 ft., bushy, lvs. densely set, glaucous. High mts., Medit. region.

Var. **Jackii** Rehd. Prostrate shrub with slender, trailing brs., nearly unbranched except for few clusters of short branchlets, lvs. incurved. Calif., Ore.

Var. **montana:** var. *saxatilis.*

Var. **nana:** var. *saxatilis.*

Var. **saxatilis** Pall. [*J. communis* var. *communis* cvs. 'Montana', 'Nana', 'Saxatilis', and 'Sibirica'; *J. communis* vars. *montana* Ait. and *nana* (Willd.) Baumg.; *J. sibirica* Burgsd.]. MOUNTAIN J. Prostrate shrub to 2 ft. high; lvs. dense, incurved, to ⅝ in. long, with whitish band above 2–3 times as wide as green margins. Arctic and high mts., Eur. and N. Amer.

conferta Parl. [*J. litoralis* Maxim.]. SHORE J. Procumbent spreading shrub, lvs. linear, spreading, spiny-pointed, yellowish or bluish-green, with white band above, tapering to a spiny tip; female cones black, glaucous, to ½ in. in diam., seeds 3. Sakhalin, Japan. Zone 6.

Coxii: *J. recurva* var.

cupressifolia: a listed name of no botanical standing for *J. Sabina* cv.

Deppeana Steud. Tree, to 35 ft., bark in quadrangular plates; lvs. denticulate, needlelike and scalelike; female cones light brown, about ½ in. in diam.; 3–4-seeded. Sw. U.S. and Mex. Var. **Deppeana.** The typical var.; not known to be cult. Var. **pachyphlaea** (Torr.) Martinez [*J. pachyphlaea* Torr.]. ALLIGATOR J., SWEET-FRUITED J. Lvs. glandular, mostly opp., thickened on back and obtusely keeled toward apex. Tex. to Ariz., s. into Mex. Zone 7–8, in the West. Cv. **'Silver'**. Said to be very glaucous.

drupacea Labill. SYRIAN J., PLUM J., HABBEL. To 60 ft., of pyramidal habit, or often narrowly columnar in cult.; lvs. linear-lanceolate, spreading, spiny-pointed, with 2 white lines above; female cones bluish or brown, glaucous, to 1 in. in diam., edible, seeds united into a 3-celled "stone." Greece, Asia Minor. Zone 7.

excelsa Bieb. GREEK J. To 60 ft., pyramidal; lvs. mostly scalelike, dark or bluish-green; female cones purplish-brown, glaucous, seeds 4–6. Se. Eur. to cent. Asia. Zone 6b. Fr. used medicinally. Cvs. are: **'Densa'**, compact; **'Stricta'**, narrowly pyramidal, juvenile form with glaucous lvs.; **'Variegata'**, lvs. variegated with yellowish-white.

Fargesii: *J. squamata* var.

formosana Hayata. To 45 ft., branchlets drooping; lvs. spreading, spiny-pointed, with 2 broad white bands above; female cones reddish- or orange-brown. Taiwan and China. Zone 5. Cult. material confused with *J. communis* cv. 'Oblonga Pendula', but easily distinguished from it by 2 white bands on lvs. and color of female cones.

Glauca Hetzii: a listed name of no botanical standing for *J. chinensis* var. *chinensis* cv. 'Hetzii'.

hibernica: *J. communis* var. *communis* cv.

horizontalis Moench [*J. hudsonica* J. Forbes; *J. prostrata* Pers.]. CREEPING J., CREEPING SAVIN J., CREEPING CEDAR. Procumbent shrub, with long trailing brs., twigs ascending, forming a mat about 1 ft. high; lvs. opp., scalelike, entire, acute to apiculate, typically bluish-green; female cones to 5/16 in. in diam., blue-black, glaucous, mostly 2–4-seeded. Nov. Sc. to Alaska, s. to N.J., Minn., and Mont. Zone 3. Distinguished from *J. Sabina* in lvs. lacking strong foetid odor when crushed. A variable sp. with a number of cvs.: **'Alpina'**, plants erect, to 1 ft. when young, the leader then becoming procumbent and ends of brs. turning upward to 2½ ft., lvs. almost all needlelike; **'Aurea'**, young growth golden-yellow; **'Bar Harbor'**, low, compact, lvs. steel-blue; **'Depressa'**: *J. communis* var.; **'Douglasii'** [*J. chinensis* cv. 'Douglasii'], WAUKEGAN J., lvs. varying from scalelike to all needlelike, very glaucous, steel-blue, becoming purplish-glaucous in winter; **'Glauca'** similar to or not distinct from 'Douglasii'; **'Glomerata'**, main brs. shorter and slower-growing than usual, lateral brs. erect or ascending, branchlets crowded in dense irregular clusters, lvs. nearly all scalelike; **'Lividus'** a listed name; **'Plumosa'**, brs. spreading horizontally, lvs. all needlelike, turning bright rose-violet in winter; **'Prostrata'**, not distinct from typical form; **'Repens'**, less strongly branched than typical form, lvs. gray-green or gray; **'Wiltonii'**, a dwarf form of 'Douglasii'.

hudsonica: *J. horizontalis.*

japonica: *J. chinensis* var. *chinensis* cv.

litoralis: *J. conferta.*

lucayana Britt. Not cult.; confused with *J. silicicola,* from which it differs in having lvs. smaller, 4-ranked, and female cones depressed, more or less laterally flattened. W. Indies.

lusitanica: *J. Sabina.*

macrocarpa: *J. Oxycedrus* subsp.

monosperma (Engelm.) Sarg. CHERRYSTONE J. To 50 ft., bark gray; lvs. mostly scalelike, grayish-green; female cones reddish, brown, or purplish, less than ½ in. in diam., glaucous, drying raisinlike, 1- or rarely 2-seeded. Colo. to Tex. and Mex. Zone 7.

nipponica: *J. rigida* subsp.

occidentalis Hook. SIERRA J., CALIFORNIA J. Shrub or tree, to 40 ft. or more, twigs cylindrical, cordlike; lvs. mostly scalelike, overlapping, grayish-green; female cones bluish-black, glaucous, seeds 2–3. Wash. to cent. Calif. Zone 6. Cv. **'Glauca'** is listed.

osteosperma (Torr.) Little [*J. utahensis* (Engelm.) Lemm.]. Bushy tree, to 20 ft.; trunk very short or absent, bark peeling in strips; lvs. mostly scalelike, in 3's, overlapping, light yellowish-green, not glandular; female cones subglobose, to ⅜ in. long, reddish-brown, glaucous. Mont. to New Mex. and Calif. Zone 5. Closely allied to *J. californica.*

Oxycedrus L. PRICKLY J. Shrub or tree, to 12 or rarely to 30 ft.; lvs. linear, tapering from the middle, ½–1 in. long, less than ⅛ in. wide, spreading, spiny-pointed; female cones reddish-brown to purple, about ½ in. in diam., seeds usually 3. Medit. region to Iran. Zone 8. Subsp. **Oxycedrus.** The typical subsp.; a small tree or erect shrub, female cones glossy, to ⅜ in. long. Subsp. **macrocarpa** (Sibth. & Sm.) J. Ball [*J. macrocarpa* Sibth. & Sm.]. Small tree or prostrate shrub, female cones dull, to ⅝ in. long.

pachyphlaea: *J. Deppeana* var.

phoenicea L. Shrub or tree, to 10 ft., usually monoecious, brs. ascending; lvs. mostly scalelike, dark or bluish-green; female cones yellow or reddish-brown. Medit. region. Zone 8.

Pinchotii Sudw. RED-BERRY J. Tree, to 20 ft.; lvs. mostly scalelike; female cones reddish-brown. Tex. Zone 8. Perhaps only a variant of *J. monosperma.*

procera Hochst. ex Endl. AFRICAN J. To 100 ft. or more, round-topped; lvs. lanceolate and spreading, or scalelike; female cones brown or purplish, fleshy, resinous, of strong odor. E. Afr. Zone 10b.

procumbens: *J. chinensis* var.

prostrata: *J. horizontalis.*

pseudosabina Fisch. & C. A. Mey. Low shrub, branchlets cylindrical, ascending; lvs. mostly scalelike, opp., rhombic; female cones black, to ⁵⁄₁₆ in. in diam., 1-seeded, stalk recurved. E. Asia. Zone 6. Closely allied to *J. Wallichiana.*

recurva Buch.-Ham. ex D. Don. HIMALAYAN J., DROOPING J. Monoecious shrub or tree, to 30 ft.; brs. curved, branchlets drooping; lvs. linear-lanceolate, sharply pointed, grayish- or bluish-green, with 2 white bands above; female cones brown or purple; 1-seeded. Himalayas. Zone 8. Differing from *J. squamata* in habit and the recurved or drooping br. tips. Var. **Coxii** (A. B. Jacks) Melv. Bark more orange than gray-brown; lvs. more widely spaced, to ½ in. long. Burma. Zone 8.

rigida Siebold & Zucc. NEEDLE J. Pyramidal shrub or tree, to 30 ft., with drooping branchlets, or low prostrate shrub; lvs. filiform, spiny-pointed, narrowly and deeply grooved and yellowish-green with white band above; female cones brownish-black, glaucous, to ⁵⁄₁₆ in. in diam. E. Asia. Zone 6, but needs protection from severe winter winds. Subsp. **rigida.** The typical subsp.; shrub or tree, lvs. long, spreading. Japan, Korea, n. China. Subsp. **nipponica** (Maxim.) Franco [*J. communis* var. *communis* cv. 'Niponica'; *J. communis* var. *nipponica* (Maxim.) E. H. Wils.; *J. nipponica* Maxim.]. Low, dwarf shrub; lvs. closely placed, almost imbricate, to ⅜ in. long. Japan.

Sabina L. [*J. lusitanica* Mill.]. SAVIN. Shrub, to 10 ft., usually spreading or procumbent; lvs. needle-shaped and spreading, or scalelike and overlapping, dark green; female cones brownish-blue, glaucous, usually 2-seeded. Eur., w. Asia. Zone 3. Young twigs used medicinally. The native plant once supposed to be this sp. is *J. horizontalis.* Some of the cvs. are: 'Cupressifolia', procumbent, lvs. scalelike, bluish-green; 'Fastigiata', slender-columnar; 'Foemina': *J. chinensis* cv.; 'Hicksii', to 4 ft., lvs. gray-blue; 'Horizontalis', a listed name; 'Prostrata': *J. horizontalis;* 'Pyramidalis', listed as more conical; 'Sanderi', foliage finer, blue; 'Tamariscifolia', low, spreading shrub, lvs. usually all needle-shaped, bright green; 'Variegata', branchlets variegated creamy-white.

Sargentii: *J. chinensis* var.

scopulorum Sarg. ROCKY MT. J., COLORADO RED CEDAR. Tree, to 30 ft. or more; lvs. scalelike, green, often glaucous, scarcely or not overlapping; female cones purplish-blue-black, glaucous, ¼ in. in diam., usually 2-seeded, maturing mostly in 2 years. B.C., s. to Ariz. and Tex. Zone 4. Closely allied to and perhaps only a subsp. of *J. virginiana.* Many named cvs. have been introd. in recent years: 'Alba', pyramidal, lvs. bluish; 'Argentea', narrow, conical, lvs. silvery-glaucous; 'Chandleri', pyramidal, compact, lvs. bluish-silver; 'Columnaris', columnar, moderately open; 'Cupressifolia', dense, pyramidal, brs. ascending, branchlets somewhat pendulous; 'Cupressifolia Glauca', similar but lvs. silvery-glaucous; 'Erecta', upright, loosely columnar, lvs. both needlelike and scalelike; 'Funalis', upright, brs. slender, lvs. bluish-green; 'Glauca', upright, compact, lvs. gray-green; 'Globosa', rounded shrub, lvs. feathery, silver-gray-green; 'Gracilis', upright, compact, lvs. silver-green; 'Horizontalis', upright, brs. horizontal, lvs. bluish-white; 'Kenyonii', slow-growing, compact, erect to 12 ft., lvs. steel-blue; 'Moffetii', pyramidal, foliage dense, silvery-green; 'Montana', slow-growing, more or less dwarf, lvs. dark green; 'Pendula', upright, brs. pendulous; 'Prostrata', low, spreading; 'Welchii', narrowly pyramidal to columnar, lvs. greenish-silver.

sibirica: *J. communis* var. *montana.*

silicicola (Small) L. H. Bailey. SOUTHERN RED CEDAR. To 50 ft., branchlets drooping; lvs. scalelike, overlapping, light green; female cones dark blue, glaucous, 1–2-seeded. N.C. to Fla. and e. La. Zone 8. Most material listed as *J. barbadensis* is this sp. Differs from *J. virginiana* in having more slender twigs, larger male cones, and smaller female cones.

sphaerica: *J. chinensis.*

squamata D. Don. Decumbent or erect shrub, brs. erect or ascending; lvs. all needlelike, ternate, linear-lanceolate, nearly ⁵⁄₁₆ in. long; female cones reddish-brown, becoming purplish-black, ovoid, 1-seeded. India and Tibet, e. to Taiwan. Zone 5. Many cvs. are offered, but few belong to this rarely cult. sp., most being cvs. of the several-seeded *J. chinensis.* Var. **squamata.** The typical var. Cvs. are: 'Loderi', small conical shrub, lvs. glaucous; 'Meyeri', irregularly branched shrub, to 10 ft., lvs. very glaucous, introd. from cult. in China; 'Parkmanii', a listed name; 'Prostrata', a dense mat of low horizontal brs.; 'Wilsonii', shrubby, lvs. bright green. Var. **Fargesii** Rehd. & E. H. Wils. [*J. Fargesii* (Rehd. & E. H. Wils.) Kom.]. Tree, 15–75 ft., often with several erect sts., branchlets pendulous.

stricta: a name used by several authors in various senses; material cult. under this name may be a cv. of *J. chinensis* var. *chinensis, J. communis* var. *communis,* or *J. excelsa.*

sylvestris: a listed name of no botanical standing, perhaps for *J. chinensis* var. *chinensis* cv. 'Oblonga'.

thurifera L. INCENSE J. Pyramidal tree, to 40 ft.; lvs. scalelike or needle-shaped; female cones dark blue, glaucous, fleshy, sweetly fragrant. S. Eur., N. Afr. Zone 9.

utahensis: *J. osteosperma.*

virginalis: a listed name of no botanical standing for *J. chinensis* var. *chinensis* cv. 'Globosa'.

virginiana L. RED CEDAR. To 75 ft.; juvenile lvs. linear-acicular, pungent, opp., or ternate, adult lvs. scalelike, strongly overlapping, acute, entire; female cones purplish-blue-black, glaucous, ¼ in. across, 1–3-seeded, maturing in 1 year. Ne. N. Amer. Zone 3. Wood very durable; the fragrant red heartwood is the red cedar used in chests and closets. The alternate host for the apple-rust fungus, therefore should not be planted where apples are important as a crop. Cvs. many, including: 'Albospica' [cv. 'Argentea'], some twig tips green, others completely white or cream-white; 'Ambigens', low, saucer-shaped shrub, brs. prostrate, spreading or subascendent; 'Argentea': 'Albospica'; 'Burkii', male plant, dense, narrowly pyramidal tree, to 30 ft., lvs. very glaucous, purplish in winter; 'Canaertii', female plant, compact, pyramidal tree, to 30 ft., branchlets cordlike, often clumped, yellow-green in spring, dark green in winter; 'Cinerascens', new growth ash-gray to silvery; 'Columnaris', erect, columnar; 'Cupressifolia', conical, loosely branched, lvs. yellow-green; 'Cupressiformis', conical shrub lacking trunk, brs. many, arising from ground, lvs. mostly scalelike, dark green, (the same plant trimmed may be sold as 'Globosa'); 'Elegantissima', bushy, conical tree, twigs or parts of them bright yellow; 'Fastigiata', narrowly columnar, branchlets erect, lvs. bluish-green; 'Glauca', columnar, narrow, branchlets very glaucous; 'Globosa', compact, globose shrub, to 4 ft.; 'Henryi', a listed name; 'Hillii' [cv. 'Pyramidiformis Hillii'], dense, columnar, 6–12 ft., brs. spreading, lvs. greenish-blue; 'Horizontalis', prostrate, mat-forming, branchlets slender, whiplike, lvs. glaucous, scalelike; 'Keteleeri': *J. chinensis* cv. Keteleeri; 'Kosteri', male plant, wide-spreading, mound-shaped shrub, to 4 ft., br. tips plumose, lvs. green, mostly scalelike; 'Lebretonii', offered but not well known, and some material so listed is *J. Deppeana* var. *pachyphlaea;* 'Nova', narrowly columnar, brs. erect, lvs. gray-green; 'Pendula', rather open tree, most branchlets pendulous; 'Pendula Viridis', female plant of similar habit, foliage bright green; 'Plumosa', pyramidal shrub or small tree, branchlets white or whitish, becoming greenish or green; 'Prostrata', prostrate, wide-spreading; 'Pseudocupressus', narrowly columnar, brs. erect, lvs. bluish-green; 'Pyramidalis', columnar or very narrowly pyramidal tree, to 35 ft., about 4 times as high as wide, branchlets bright green; 'Pyramidiformis', columnar, to 40 ft., lvs. dark green; 'Pyramidiformis Hillii': 'Hillii'; 'Reptans', flat prostrate shrub, branchlet tips nodding, lvs. green, believed to be no longer cult.; 'Schottii', female plant, dense, narrowly pyramidal tree, to 35 ft., nearly 3 times as tall as wide, differing from 'Canaertii' in having branchlets mostly yellowish-green in winter; 'Smithii', offered but not well known, some material so listed is *J. chinensis* cv. 'Arbuscula'; 'Tripartita', male plant, dense, spreading shrub, to 5 ft. high and 10–14 ft. across, lvs. mostly needle-shaped; 'Venusta', differs from 'Burkii' in having lvs. ash-gray, not glaucous-blue.

JURINEA Cass. *Compositae* (Carduus Tribe). Between 100 and 150 spp. of ann., bien., and per. herbs or subshrubs, native to nw. Afr. and cent. and s. Eur. to cent. Asia and China, sts. very short to well-developed and much-branched; lvs. in a rosette or alt. on the sts., simple to deeply pinnatifid, unarmed; fl. heads long-peduncled, solitary or corymbose, involucre nearly globose, ovoid, or cylindrical, involucral bracts imbricate in many rows, entire, mucronate or spine-tipped, receptacle densely bristly; fls. all tubular, bisexual, purple, anthers sagittate at base; achenes 4–5-angled, pappus persistent, of several rows of rough, unequal bristles.

Propagated by seeds or division, and planted in any ordinary garden soil.

alata (Desf.) Cass. Bien. or per., to 3 ft.; basal lvs. oblong in outline, to 6 in. long, lyrate-pinnatifid, glabrescent above, hairy beneath, st. lvs. lanceolate, dentate, decurrent; heads solitary, hemispherical, to 1 in. across; fls. purplish-blue. Caucasus.

arachnoidea Bunge. Per., to 3 ft.; basal lvs. pinnately parted, puberulous above, gray-tomentose beneath, st. lvs. linear, sessile, not decurrent; heads solitary, globose, to 1 in. across; fls. purple; achenes pitted, pubescent. Se. Eur. to w. Siberia.

cyanoides (L.) Rchb. Per., to 2 ft.; sts. wandlike, rarely branched, gray-pubescent; lvs. cobwebby above, glabrous beneath, lower lvs. pinnately dissected into linear segms. with revolute margins, upper lvs. entire, sessile; heads solitary, globose, about 1 in. across; fls. pale purple to pink; achenes glabrous, smooth or faintly pitted. Cent. Eur. to cent. Asia.

depressa (Steven) C. A. Mey. Per., to 6 in.; lvs. in a rosette, pale green above, gray-hairy beneath, lyrate, the lateral lobes ovate or triangular, terminal lobe larger than laterals, ovate or cordate, obtuse, margins entire or denticulate; heads hemispherical; fls. purple. Caucasus.

Dolomiaea Boiss. [*J. macrocephala* (DC.) Benth. ex Hook.f., not DC.]. Stemless per.; lvs. in a rosette, oblong-lanceolate in outline, to 1½ ft. long, pinnatifid to pinnate, gray-green above, white-tomentose beneath; heads 3–30, about 1 in. across; fls. pinkish-blue. W. Himalayas. Treated by some taxonomists as *Dolomiaea macrocephala* DC.

macrocephala DC., not Benth. ex Hook.f. Per., to 2–3 ft.; lvs. lanceolate, to 2 in. long, cordate and half-clasping at base, grayish-tomentose; heads solitary, about 2¾ in. across. Iran. *J. macrocephala* (DC.) Benth. ex Hook.f. is *J. Dolomiaea*.

macrocalathia C. Koch. Per., to 3 ft., sts. simple, flocculose-tomentose; lower lvs. in a rosette, oblong in outline, pinnatifid, st. lvs. oblong, entire, shortly decurrent, gray-tomentose beneath; heads solitary, globose, to about 2¼ in. across. Se. Eur.

mollis (L.) Rchb. Per., to 2½ ft., sts. erect, simple or little-branched; lvs. in a rosette, oblong in outline, to 6 in. long, pinnatifid into linear or lanceolate segms., undulate, white-tomentose beneath, st. lvs. few, reduced, linear; heads solitary, to 2½ in. across; fls. rose-purple. S. Eur.

JUSSIAEA: *LUDWIGIA.* **J. californica:** *L. peploides.* **J. grandiflora:** see *L. uruguayensis.* **J. natans:** *L. helminthorrhiza.* **J. repens** var. **glabrescens:** *L. peploides* subsp. **J. repens** var. **peploides:** *L. peploides.* **J. salicifolia:** *L. octovalvis* var. *linearifolia.* **J. suffruticosa:** see *L. octovalvis.*

JUSSIEUIA: *CNIDOSCOLUS.*

JUSTICIA L. [*Adhatoda* Medic.; *Beloperone* Nees; *Cyrtanthera* Nees; *Drejerella* Lindau; *Libonia* C. Koch; *Jacobinia* Nees ex Moric.; *Sericographis* Nees]. WATER WILLOW. Acanthaceae. About 300 spp. of per. herbs or shrubs, native to the tropics and subtropics of both hemispheres and extending into temp. N. Amer.; sts. erect or ascending, smooth or variously pubescent; lvs. opp., petioled, mostly lanceolate to ovate, entire, rarely otherwise; fls. in cymes, spikes, or panicles, bracts of various shapes, sizes, and colors, calyx mostly 5-parted, segms. various, corolla white to red or purple, sometimes marked in the throat, tube usually short, straight or incurved, limb 2-lipped, stamens 2, ovary 2-celled, style slender, stigma entire, capitate; fr. a caps., seeds 4 or 2. The largest genus in the family. It has been divided into a number of segregate genera by various workers. Characters used in making these segregations are tenuous and difficult to follow, and the treatment here follows that of recent workers who have chosen to recognize *Justicia* in the broad sense.

Grown in the greenhouses and in the open in warm regions. They are of easy cultivation but likely to become weedy unless properly restrained and cared for. Propagated by cuttings as well as by seeds.

Adhatoda L. [*Adhatoda Vasica* (L.) Nees]. Evergreen shrub, to 8 ft. or more; lvs. elliptic, to 8 in. long, secondary veins prominent; fls. in axillary peduncled spikes; corolla 1¼ in. long, white, lower lip with reddish markings, upper lip distinctly curved. India and Ceylon.

atramentaria: *J. spicigera.*

aurea Schlechtend. [*Justicia umbrosa* Benth.; *Jacobinia aurea* (Schlechtend.) Hemsl., not Hiern]. Shrub, to 12 ft., sts. more or less angled and puberulent; lvs. lanceolate-oblong or ovate, sometimes broadly so, to 12 in. long; fls. in dense, terminal spikes to 12 in. long, corolla about 2 in. long, yellow, 2-lipped to near middle, pubescent. Mex. and Cent. Amer.

Brandegeana Wassh. & L. B. Sm. [*Beloperone guttata* Brandeg., not *Justicia guttata* Wallich; *Drejerella guttata* (Brandegee) Bremek.]. SHRIMP PLANT, MEXICAN S. P., SHRIMP BUSH, FALSE HOP. Evergreen shrub, to 3 ft., sts. rather weak; lvs. ovate, to 3 in. long, softly hairy, narrowed to petiole; fls. in terminal, drooping spikes to 6 in. long or more, bracts cordate, bronze to rose to yellow-green, nearly 1 in. long, conspicuous and overlapping the fls., corolla deeply 2-lipped, white, with reddish spots on lower lip. Mex.; escaped and apparently naturalized in peninsular Fla. *Beloperone lutea,* a listed name, probably belongs here and probably is used for cv. 'Yellow Queen', with chartreuse-green bracts. *B. longispicua* Hort. and *B. tomentosa* Hort. are probably both forms of this sp.

brasiliana Roth [*Beloperone Amherstiae* Nees; *B. brasiliana* (Roth) Bremek.]. To 3 ft. or more, sts. somewhat 4-angled; lvs. ovate to lanceolate, to 6 in. long, acuminate, attenuate at base, glabrous or lightly pubescent, petiole to ⅜ in. long; fls. in dense, subsessile, axillary spikes to 1 in. long, bracts narrow, green, to ⅜ in. long, inconspicuous, corolla to 1½ in. long, red, erect, upper lip straight, lower lip reflexed, 3-lobed; caps. club-shaped, to ½ in. long. Brazil.

californica (Benth.) D. Gibs. [*Beloperone californica* Benth.]. CHUPAROSA, HONEYSUCKLE. Subshrub, often leafless, to 4 ft. or more, brs. greenish-canescent; lvs. ovate, to 3 in. long, pubescent, petioles short; fls. in short, axillary racemes, bracts linear-subulate, inconspicuous, calyx segms. lanceolate, corolla red, straight. Desert regions, s. Calif., Ariz., Baja Calif.

carnea Lindl. [*Cyrtanthera magnifica* Nees; *C. Pohliana* Nees var. *obtusior* Nees; *Jacobinia carnea* (Lindl.) Nichols.; *Jacobinia magnifica* (Nees) Lindau; *Jacobinia obtusior* (Nees) L. H. Bailey; *Jacobinia Pohliana* (Nees) Lindau; *Jacobinia velutina* (Nees) Voss, not Lindau]. BRAZILIAN-PLUME, PLUME FLOWER, PLUME PLANT, FLAMINGO PLANT, PARADISE PLANT, KING'S-CROWN. To 6 ft., sts. 4-angled or -grooved; lvs. oblong-ovate, to 10 in. long, sparingly pubescent, with prominent venation, decurrent on petioles about 2 in. long; fls. in dense, short, terminal panicles, bracts prominent, oblong-acuminate, to ¾ in. long, corolla to 2 in. long, rose-purple or pink, viscid-pubescent. N. S. Amer. An old favorite for conservatories and warm, protected sites.

carthaginensis Jacq. [*Beloperone violacea* Planch. & Lindl.]. Per. herb or subshrub, to 4 ft.; lvs. ovate or elliptic-ovate, to 4½ in. long, acuminate, glabrous or lightly pubescent, narrowed to slightly winged petiole; fls. in dense, terminal or axillary spikes 1–2½ in. long, bracts green, not conspicuous, calyx segms. linear-lanceolate, to ½ in. long, corolla to 1¼ in. long, purple; caps. clavate, ½ in. long. W. Indies, Cent. Amer., n. S. Amer.

coccinea: *Pachystachys coccinea;* but some material grown as *J. coccinea* is *Odontonema strictum.*

cydoniifolia (Nees) Lindau [*Adhatoda cydoniifolia* Nees]. Shrub, to 3 ft. or more, pubescent; lvs. ovate, to 6 in. long, petiole to 1 in. long; fls. 1–2 on short axillary peduncles, calyx to ¼ in. long, corolla tube short, about as long as calyx, upper lip arched and hoodlike, white with purple margin, lower lip purple, broadly expanded. Brazil. Material cult. under the name *Adhatoda cydoniifolia* may be *Megaskepasma erythrochlamys.*

extensa T. Anderson. Per. herb or subshrub, to 10 ft., sometimes climbing, young sts. densely pubescent; lvs. ovate, sometimes silvery-variegated; fls. in short-branched, tawny-pubescent, terminal panicles to 10 in. long, corolla about ¼ in. long, green, pink-spotted. W. Trop. Afr.

flava (Forssk.) Vahl. Per. herb, to 4 ft., erect or straggling, sts. grooved, pubescent; lvs. ovate-lanceolate, to 3 in. long, pubescent, decurrent to short-petioled; fls. in terminal, pubescent spikes to 6 in. long or more, corolla to ½ in. long, yellow, dark-streaked. W. Trop. Afr.

floribunda: *J. Rizzinii.*

fulvicoma Schlechtend. & Cham. [*Beloperone comosa* Nees, not *Justicia comosa* Vahl; *B. fulvicoma* (Schlechtend. & Cham.) A. W. Hill; *Drejerella comosa* (Nees) Lindau; *D. fulvicoma* (Schlechtend. & Cham.) Lindau]. Subshrub, similar to *J. Brandegeana* in vegetative characters, differing chiefly in having infl. shorter, erect, with bracts more leaflike, less colorful, green to red-purple, and being thus less ornamental. Mex.

Ghiesbreghtiana Lem. [*Cyrtanthera Ghiesbreghtiana* (Lem.) Decne.; *Jacobinia Ghiesbreghtiana* (Lem.) Hemsl.; *Sericographis Ghiesbreghtiana* (Lem.) Nees]. To 5 ft., glabrous or lightly pubescent; lvs. ovate-lanceolate, to 3 in. long, entire, short-petioled; fls. in few-fld. panicles, corolla orange or red, 2-lipped in upper ¼, lower lip coiled. Mex. Probably not in cult.; plants so named are *J. spicigera.*

Leonardii Wassh. [*Jacobinia incana* (Nees) Hemsl., not *Justicia incana* T. Anderson; *Serigraphis incana* Nees]. Shrub, to about 3 ft., sts. densely pubescent; lvs. oblong to ovate, to 6 in. long, densely pubescent beneath, petioled; fls. few in terminal and axillary cymes, corolla to 1½ in. long, red, glabrous, lower lip coiled. Mex. Known erroneously in Calif. as *Anisacanthus Thurberi.*

pauciflora: see *J. Rizzinii.*

Rizzinii Wassh. [*J. floribunda* Hort.; *J. pauciflora* (Nees) Griseb., not Vahl; *Jacobinia pauciflora* (Nees) Lindau; *Libonia floribunda* C. Koch; *Sericographis pauciflora* Nees]. Small, pubescent shrub, to 2 ft.; lvs. oblong to obovate, to ¾ in. long, lvs. of each pair slightly unequal in size; fls. on short, slender, axillary peduncles, usually nodding, corolla to ¾ in. long, lower part scarlet, upper ¼ yellow, lips less than ¼ in. long. Brazil. A hybrid between *J. Rizzinii* and *J. Ghiesbreghtiana* has been reported in Eur. and named *Jacobinia* × *penrhoziensis* (Carrière) L. H. Bailey [*Libonia* × *penrhoziensis* Carrière]; it is doubtful that this is in the Amer. trade; plants so named are probably *J. Rizzinii.*

rosea: a listed name of no botanical standing, may refer to *J. carnea.*

secunda Vahl. Suffrutescent, sts. 4-angled, glabrous or sparsely hairy; lvs. ovate to oblong-ovate, to 6 in. long, lightly pubescent; fls. crowded on 1-sided brs. of a panicle, corolla to 1½ in. long, red. W. Indies and Colombia.

spicigera Schlechtend. [*Justicia atramentaria* Benth.; *Jacobinia Mohintli* (Nees) Hemsl.; *Jacobinia spicigera* (Schlechtend.) L. H. Bailey; *Sericographis Mohintli* Nees]. Shrub, to 6 ft., sts. 4-angled, pubescent or glabrous; lvs. oblong-lanceolate to ovate, to 7 in. long; fls. in few-fld., axillary or terminal 1-sided racemes, corolla to 1½ in. long, orange or red, deeply 2-lipped, lower lip coiled. Mex., s. to Colombia. Called MOHINTLI (or variations of this name) in Mex., where the lvs. are placed in hot water to produce a bluing used in whitening clothes. Also yields a dye and has been used medicinally. Most plants in the trade called *J. Ghiesbreghtiana* belong here.

tomentosa: a listed name of no botanical standing, may refer to *J. Brandegeana.*

umbrosa: *J. aurea.*

Vasica: a listed name of no botanical standing, probably refers to *J. Adhatoda.*

JUTTADINTERIA Schwant. *Aizoaceae.* Twelve spp. of cespitose, succulent, per. herbs or subshrubs, native to S. Afr.; lvs. 4-ranked, thick, half-ovoid or boat-shaped, united at base in pairs, more or less triangular in section near apex, keel and edges sharp to rounded, edges and often keel and upper part of lower side with blunt or sharp teeth or protuberances; fls. solitary, short-pedicelled, without bracts, opening in afternoon, often scented, calyx unequally 4-lobed, petals white to dark red, in 1–3 series, stamens many, ovary inferior, 5–11-celled, disc annular, stigmas 5–11; caps. 5–11-celled, valve wings well-developed, cell lids rarely well-developed, tubercle lacking, seeds brownish, rough, globose to pear-shaped.

For culture see *Succulents.*

kori: a listed name of no botanical standing.

Simpsonii (Dinter) Schwant. Brs. ascending; lvs. dense, slightly roughened, light glaucous and inconspicuously dark-dotted, to 1⅜ in. long, ½ in. wide at base and ¾ in. wide at apex, ⅝ in. thick, semicircular in section, upper side nearly flat, lower side rounded, keeled toward apex, margins, keel, upper part of upper side and sides with reddish teeth; fl. about 1⅜ in. across, petals white. S.-W. Afr.

tetrasepala L. Bolus. To about 3 in., brs. prostrate; lvs. smooth, glaucous, with few dots, to ¾ in. long, ⅜ in. wide and thick, upper side flat, pustulate basally, sides rounded, keel scarcely evident in age, tip acute or obtuse; petals white, in 2 series, to ⁹⁄₁₆ in. long, stigmas 8. Cape Prov.

KADSURA Juss. *Schisandraceae* (previously included in *Magnoliaceae*). Twenty-two spp. of evergreen, twining shrubs, native to trop. and warm temp. se. and e. Asia; lvs. slender-petioled, without stipules; fls. unisexual, axillary, usually solitary, perianth segms. 7–24, white or pinkish, male fls. with stamens many, separate or united and forming a globose head, female fls. with many 1-celled pistils in a head, developing into globose heads of berries, the receptacle not elongate.

Propagated by cuttings or half-ripened wood, and by seeds.

japonica (L.) Dunal. To 12 ft., dioecious; lvs. elliptic to oblong-lanceolate, to 4 in. long, acuminate, sometimes remotely toothed; peduncles to 2 in. long; fls. cup-shaped, to ¾ in. across, stamens united in heads; fr. heads showy, red, about 1 in. in diam. Autumn. S. Korea, Japan, Taiwan.

KAEMPFERIA L. *Zingiberaceae*. Over 50 spp. of often nearly stemless, per. herbs in Asia and Afr., with thick, aromatic rhizomes and sometimes thickened roots; lvs. clustered at base or 2-ranked, sheaths open opp. the blade; infl. a 1- to many-fld. spike or head, from the base of the plant or on a leafy st.; fls. solitary in axils of bracts, white, yellow, violet, or purple, calyx tubular, often split on one side, corolla tube short to long, corolla lobes 3, lanceolate, staminodial lip large, usually 2-lobed, lateral staminodes petal-like, fertile stamen 1, filament short, the connective broad, usually crested, anther not spurred at base, ovary 3-celled.

Cultivated as pot plants in greenhouse, or outdoors in the South, in a well-drained mixture of loam and peat. Plants become dormant in the autumn and should be kept in a warm place, repotted in spring, and given ample water. Rhizomes of some species, notably *K. Galanga* and *K. rotunda*, are used medicinally and as flavoring in southeastern Asia.

atrovirens N. E. Br. PEACOCK PLANT. To 6 in.; lvs. 4–5, petioled, or the upper ones sessile, ovate, to 6 in. long, 3 in. wide, dark green and more or less iridescent; spike appearing with lvs., about 1 in. across, free-blooming; fls. white, lip lavender, pink, or violet, spotted yellow at base. Borneo.

Galanga L. Stemless, with odorless tuberous roots; lvs. 2, horizontal, to 5 in. long, 3½ in. wide, rounded; fls. white, fragrant, appearing with lvs., lip 1 in. long, spotted with lilac at base, anther crest 2-lobed. Se. Asia.

Gilbertii Bull. Stemless; lvs. ascending, short-petioled, oblong, to 4 in. long, 1⁵⁄₁₆ in. wide, dark green, sometimes white-striped in middle; fls. appearing with lvs., white, corolla tube 1 in. long, lip 1 in. long or more, striped violet. India.

ovalifolia Roxb. [*K. Parishii* Hook.f.]. St. leafy; lvs. long-petioled, oblong-acuminate, to 8 in. long, 3¼ in. wide; spike sessile; fls. sometimes appearing before lvs., corolla and staminodes white, lip violet, anther crest irregularly 3-lobed. Tenasserim and Malacca.

Parishii: *K. ovalifolia*.

pulchra Ridl. Stemless; lvs. 1–2, spreading horizontally, ovate, to 5 in. long, 3½ in. wide, dark green with pale bands; fls. many, in a short spike from the base, appearing with lvs., flat, lilac lip spotted with white and yellow at base, anther crest linear, elongate. Thailand and Langkawi Is., Malay Arch.

Roscoeana Wallich. DWARF GINGER LILY, PEACOCK L. Similar to *K. pulchra*, but fls. white, anther crest short, ovate, acute. Burma.

rotunda L. RESURRECTION LILY, TROPICAL CROCUS. Lvs. 2, erect, petioled, to 18 in. long, 4 in. wide, usually variegated above, purple beneath; spike appearing from leafless rhizome in spring, sheaths of infl. purple-tinged, to 3 in. long or more; fls. about 10, nearly 2 in. across, white with lilac lip, anther crest narrow, 2–4-lobed. Se. Asia.

KAGENECKIA Ruiz & Pav. *Rosaceae*. Small, evergreen, dioecious trees, native to Chile; lvs. leathery, sharp-toothed; female fls. solitary, male fls. in racemes or corymbs.

One species occasionally grown in southern Calif. Zone 10.

oblonga Ruiz & Pav. To 30 ft., glabrous; lvs. obovate to elliptic-lanceolate, 1–2½ in. long; fls. white, ¾ in. across, petals 5, roundish. Chile.

KALANCHOE Adans. [*Bryophyllum* Salisb.; *Kitchingia* Bak.]. PALM-BEACH-BELLS. *Crassulaceae*. About 125 spp. of succulent per. or monocarpic herbs or shrubs, mostly of Afr. and Madagascar, a few Asiatic or pantrop.; lvs. mostly opp., sessile or petioled, entire to lobed or rarely pinnate; infl. usually terminal and of opp. cymes; sepals separate or united into a tube, corolla tubular, lobes usually shorter than the tube, stamens 8, rarely 4. Differs from *Cotyledon* in fls. 4-merous. The name is pronounced with four syllables.

The kalanchoes are grown in greenhouses in the North and outdoors in the South, some for their foliage, some for their bright flowers. Those of section *Bryophyllum* are grown as curiosities because of the plantlets borne on leaf margins and inflorescence. Propagated by seeds, leaf- or stem-cuttings, or plantlets when present. See also *Succulents*.

The genus has been divided into 3 somewhat intergrading sections. The species of a section possess the characteristics of that section. These characteristics are not repeated in the brief descriptions of the species; instead, the following symbols are used to indicate the section to which each species belongs: B, *Bryophyllum*; K, *Kalanchoe*; Kit, *Kitchingia*.

The distinguishing characters of the sections follow:

Bryophyllum (Salisb.) Boiteau & O. Mannoni (B). Fls. pendent, calyx commonly more or less tubular and inflated, segms. shorter or longer than tube, corolla often contricted against the pistils, filaments borne mostly toward base of corolla, pistils erect, styles longer than ovary; plantlets often borne in infl. and in notches of lf. margins.

Kalanchoe (K). Fls. erect, sepals usually little united, corolla not constricted, often flask-shaped, filaments borne mostly toward top of corolla tube, pistils erect, styles often shorter than ovary.

Kitchingia (Bak.) Boiteau & O. Mannoni (Kit). Fls. pendent, calyx segms. mostly as long as or slightly longer than tube, corolla not constricted, filaments borne toward top of corolla tube, pistils more or less spreading, styles longer than ovary.

Adolphi-Engleri Hamet. B; similar to *K. Gastonis-Bonnieri*, but having lvs. sessile, clearly dilated in their lower part, and lacking a whitish, mealy covering. Se. Madagascar.

aleuroides Stearn. K; glabrous herb, to 2 ft.; lvs. sessile, oblong-spatulate, to 5 in. long, entire, mealy, the pairs remote; thyrse dense, interrupted; corolla urceolate, yellowish, tube to ½ in. long, lobes lanceolate, nectar glands wider than high, nearly entire. Rhodesia.

Aliciae: *K. pubescens*.

alternans: see under *K. flammea*.

aromatica Perr. K; glandular-viscid, aromatic, cespitose herb, to 2 ft.; lvs. lanceolate, 2–5 in. long, acute, irregularly serrate-toothed, petioles ½–1 in. long; thyrse loose, pedicels ¼ in. long; corolla cylindrical, yellowish, the tube to ⁵⁄₁₆ in. long, stamens exserted, nectar glands narrowly rectangular. Madagascar.

Beauverdii Hamet. B; glabrous, scrambling, to 10 ft., woody below; lf. pairs remote, lvs. reflexed, mostly linear-lanceolate, 2–3½ in. long, with 2–6 bulbiliferous teeth at apex, sessile; thyrse loose, many-fld., pedicels ½–1 in. long, corolla yellow-green or purplish, campanulate. Madagascar. Var. **Beauverdii**. The typical var.; corolla tube to ⅝ in. long. Var. **parviflora** Boiteau & O. Mannoni [*K. scandens* Perr.; *Bryophyllum scandens* (Perr.) A. Berger]. Corolla tube to ½ in. long, lobes slightly longer.

beharensis Drake. FELTBUSH, VELVETLEAF, VELVET ELEPHANT-EAR. K; shrub, to 12 ft.; felty with 3-branched hairs; lvs. crowded at tips of brs., peltate, triangular or nearly hastate, 4–15 in. long, 3–14, in. wide, nearly acute, irregularly toothed, concave above, petioles nearly cylindrical, 2–8 in. long; fl. st. axillary, 1–1½ ft., pedicels to ½ in. long; corolla somewhat urceolate, yellowish, the tube ⁵⁄₁₆ in. long, the lobes nearly as long, nectar glands wider than long, united. Madagascar. Cv. 'Viridis' is listed.

Beharottii: a listed name of no botanical standing, perhaps for a hybrid of *K. beharensis* with some other sp. such as *K. Millotii*.

behartosa: a listed name of no botanical standing; perhaps for a hybrid of *K. beharensis* and *K. tomentosa*.

Bentii C. H. Wright ex Hook.f. [*K. teretifolia* Deflers, not Haw.]. K; glabrous, unbranched, to 3 ft.; lvs. linear, 3–6 in. long, acute, half-cylindrical, grooved above, cyme compound, many-fld., pedicels to ½ in. long; sepals separate, ¼–½ in. long, corolla white, tube 1½ in. long, lobes spreading, ½ in. long, Arabia.

Blossfeldiana Poelln. [*K. globulifera* var. *coccinea* Perr.]. K; glabrous, branching herb, to 1 ft.; lf. blades elliptic-oblong, 1–3 in. long, obtuse or nearly acute, sinuate to crenate in upper half, glossy green, tapering to petioles to 1 in. long; infl. somewhat corymbose; fls. many, sepals lanceolate, corolla salverform, tube to ⁵⁄₁₆ in. long, lobes scarlet, ³⁄₁₆ in. long, anthers each with apical globular gland, nectar glands linear. Madagascar. Common pot plant valued for winter fls., remaining fresh 7–8 weeks. Many cvs. are listed.

brachyloba Welw. K; glabrous, tuberous herb, to 3 ft.; lf. blades lanceolate, 3–5 in. long, obtuse, entire or nearly so, glaucous; infl. corymbose; fls. yellow, sepals triangular-ovate, ⅛ in. long and nearly as wide, corolla tube funnelform, ½ in. long, lobes ³⁄₁₆ in. long, nectar glands linear. Trop. Afr.

brasiliensis: *K. integra* var. *verea.*

coccinea: *K. integra.*

crenata: *K. integra* var. *crenata.*

cruentum: a listed name of no botanical standing.

Daigremontiana Hamet & Perr. [*Bryophyllum Daigremontianum* (Hamet & Perr.) A. Berger]. DEVIL'S-BACKBONE. B; glabrous herb, 1–3 ft.; lf. blades oblong-lanceolate, 4–10 in. long, serrate, purple-blotched beneath, the lower nearly peltate, petioles 1–2 in. long, each notch of lf. margin with spoon-shaped bulbiliferous spur; infl. a compound cyme; corolla purplish, 1 in. long, lobes ⅓ as long, nectar glands wider than high. Madagascar. Of easy cult., the plantlets lavishly produced.

Dyeri: see *K. Quartiniana.*

Engleri: a listed name of no botanical standing; perhaps intended for *K. Adolphi-Engleri.*

eriophylla Hilsenb. & Bojer. K; low plant, cottony with 3-branched hairs, sts. spreading, to 1 ft.; lvs. a few crowded pairs, narrowly obovate or nearly cylindrical, to ¾ in. long, obtuse, entire, sessile; peduncle 3–6 in., cyme 2–7-fld.; corolla blue-violet, ½ in. wide, lobes about equalling tube. Madagascar.

Fedtschenkoi Hamet & Perr. [*Bryophyllum Fedtschenkoi* Hort.]. SOUTH AMERICAN AIR PLANT, LAVENDER-SCALLOPS. B; glabrous, erect, to 2 ft., the sterile shoots decumbent and rooting; lvs. rather crowded, obovate, 1–2 in. long, crenate-toothed mostly in upper half, glaucous, short-petioled; cyme loose; calyx tube ⁵⁄₁₆–½ in. long, the segms. shorter, corolla purple or yellow, ¾–1 in. long, lobes obtuse, ¼ as long as tube. Madagascar. Cv. '**Major**' is listed. Cv. '**Marginata**'. Lvs. margined with cream-white.

Figuereidoi Croiz. K; glabrous, sts. to 8 in.; lvs. a few close-set pairs, obovate, to 2½ in. long, rounded, crenate, irregularly purplish-spotted, sessile; fl. st. bare, to 1 ft., with broad loose cyme, pedicels ¼–½ in. long; corolla white or rose to red, ⁵⁄₁₆ in. long, tube longer than the erect lobes. Mozambique.

flammea Stapf. K; glabrous, or pubescent in infl., to 1½ ft.; lvs. obovate, 2–3½ in. long, obtuse, mostly entire, nearly sessile; cyme corymbose; sepals lanceolate, falling, corolla tube yellow, to ½ in. long, the limb bright red or pink, ¾ in. wide. Somali Republic. Possibly the correct name for this sp. is *K. alternans* (Vahl) Pers.

Gastonis-Bonnieri Hamet & Perr. B; herb, to 2½ ft.; lvs. lanceolate to spatulate, sinuate to coarsely crenate, glabrous, white-mealy, attenuate to a broad, indefinite petiole, the lower nearly in a rosette, 6–15 in. long; calyx nearly urceolate, strongly inflated, ¾–1 in. long, the lobes shorter than tube, corolla yellowish or reddish, somewhat glandular-pubescent, at least toward apex, 1½ in. long, lobes acute, shorter than tube, nectar glands about as wide as high. Madagascar. Similar to *K. pinnata* in fls., but corolla more glandular and lvs. always simple with wider indefinite petioles and sometimes larger. Cult. plants referred here differ from the type in their larger and more variable lvs., larger calyx, and less pubescent corolla.

glaucescens Britten. K; close to *K. flammea*, but lvs. petioled, nearly crenate or almost lobed, sepals more persistent, and corolla yellow or orange, with erect lobes. Winter, early spring. Arabia, trop. Afr.

globosa: a listed name of no botanical standing.

globulifera Perr. Not cult. Var. **coccinea**: *K. Blossfeldiana.*

grandiflora Wight & Arn. K; glabrous; lvs. sessile, obovate, 2–3 in. long, obtuse, crenate toward tip, glaucous; cyme corymbose, pedicels

½ in. long; sepals ½ in. long, corolla yellow, tube ½ in. long, lobes shorter, stamens somewhat exserted, nectar glands linear. India, E. Afr. See also *K. marmorata.*

Greyi: a listed name of no botanical standing.

gummifera: a listed name of no botanical standing.

Hildebrandtii Baill. K; shrub, to 15 ft., thinly covered with scalelike, 3-branched hairs; lf. blades nearly orbicular or obovate, ½–1½ in. long, entire, tapering to a somewhat shorter petiole; thyrse dense, pedicels to ³⁄₁₆ in. long; sepals triangular, to ⅛ in. long, corolla whitish, nearly urceolate, tube to ³⁄₁₆ in. long, lobes shorter, nectar glands nearly 4-angled. Madagascar.

hirta Harv. K; hispid; lvs. ovate or oblong, repand-crenate, petioled; cyme trichotomous, panicled, the subdivisions flat-topped; sepals ovate, acute, corolla golden-yellow. S. Afr.

Houghtonii: a listed name of no botanical standing to be treated as *Kalanchoe* cv. 'Houghtonii' for the hybrid *K. Daigremontiana × K. tubiflora.* COCONUT PLANT. Intermediate between the parents; lvs. in 3's, narrow-lanceolate, serrate, purple-blotched on both sides. Also known as *Kalanchoe* cv. 'Houghton's Hybrid'.

integra (Medic.) O. Kuntze [*K. coccinea* Welw.]. FLAME K. K; glandular-pubescent, 1–6 ft.; lvs. ovate or oblong, 2–6(–12) in. long, obtuse, crenate or doubly so, petioled; cymes nearly corymbose or panicled, pedicels to ⁵⁄₁₆ in. long; sepals oblong, ⅛–¼ in. long, corolla red or orange-red, tube inflated on 1 side below, ⁵⁄₁₆–½ in. long, limb ⁵⁄₁₆–⅝ in. wide, nectar glands linear. Yemen to cent. Afr. Var. **crenata** (Andr.) Cuf. [*K. crenata* (Andr.) Haw.; *K. Schumacheri* Koord.]. Glabrous; fls. yellow. E. Afr., Malay Arch. Var. **crenata-rubra** Cuf. Glabrous; fls. red. Tanzania to S. Afr. Var. **subsessilis** (Britten) Cuf. [*K. Kirkii* N. E. Br.]. Lvs. sessile or nearly so, pubescent; fls. red. Mozambique. Var. **verea** (Jacq.) Cuf. [*K. brasiliensis* Camb.]. Pubescent; fls. yellow. Cent. Afr., Malay Arch., Brazil.

×kewensis Dyer: *K. Bentii × K. flammea.* K; glabrous, sts. simple, erect, to 4 ft.; lvs. to 1 ft. long, linear-lanceolate or mostly pinnately dissected with 1–2 pairs of nearly cylindrical pinnae, grooved above; cyme corymbose, to 1 ft. wide; sepals spreading, corolla pink, tube ¾ in. long.

Kirkii: *K. integra* var. *subsessilis.*

laciniata (L.) DC. CHRISTMAS-TREE K., FIR-TREE K. K; glabrous, about 16 in.; lvs. 2–4 in. long, pinnatifid, with 3–5 crenate to entire, lanceolate segms.; upper lvs. entire, linear; cyme loose; sepals lanceolate, spreading, corolla yellow, tube ¾ in. long, limb 1 in. wide, upper stamens exserted. S. or se. Asia? Many spp. formerly placed in synonymy here are now distinguished; see *K. flammea, K. glaucescens, K. integra, K. longiflora.*

lanceolata (Forssk.) Pers. K; ann., 10–14 in., glandular-pubescent in upper half, sts. 4-angled or narrowly 4-winged below; lvs. obovate to oblong, 2–6 in. long, 1–2¼ in. wide, rounded and crenate above, sessile; cyme paniculate, pedicels ⅛ in. long; calyx tube much shorter than to longer than lobes, corolla tube ⁵⁄₁₆–½ in. long, limb orange, often flushed with red, ⁵⁄₁₆–½ in. wide, stamens mostly well included, styles very short. India to S.-W. Afr.

laxiflora Bak. [*Bryophyllum crenatum* Bak.]. B; glabrous herb, to 3 ft.; lf. pairs separated, blades ovate or elliptic-oblong, 1–2 in. long, obtuse, crenate, rounded to auriculate at base with auricles upturned, petioles to 1 in. long; cyme loose; calyx tube ¼–½ in. long, the lobes shorter, corolla red to yellow, ¾–1 in. long, lobes rounded. Madagascar. Subsp. **violacea** Boiteau & O. Mannoni. Lvs. generally reddish-spotted at edges; calyx violet, corolla less narrowed at base.

longiflora Schlechtend. K; glabrous shrub, to 2 ft., sts. 4-angled; lvs. obovate, 1½–3½ in. long, cuneate, crenate-serrate toward tip, nearly sessile; cyme corymbose; sepals triangular, to ⅛ in. long, corolla yellow, tube ⅝–¾ in. long, lobes less than ⅓ as long. Natal (S. Afr.). Cv. 'Coccinea' is listed.

Lugardii Bullock. K; glabrous shrub, to 7 ft.; lvs. spatulate and sessile to peltate and slender-petioled, to 8 in. long, toothed or crenate, often dark-spotted; fls. many, white or creamy, corolla tube ½–¾ in. long, lobes ¾ in. long, stamens exserted. Ethiopia to Congo region.

Manginii Hamet. & Perr. B; glandular-pubescent, much-branched at base, to 16 in.; lvs. obovate-cuneate, ½–1¼ in. long, to ½ in. wide and ⅜ in. thick, rounded, glabrescent, nearly petioled, the lower lvs. weakly crenate at apex; cyme loose, few-fld., with many plantlets, pedicels to ½ in. long; sepals nearly separate, ovate, to ⅜ in. long, corolla bright red, tube 1 in. long, lobes ³⁄₁₆ in. long. Madagascar.

marginata: a listed name of no botanical standing.

marmorata Bak. [*K. grandiflora* A. Rich., not Wight & Arn.; *K. somaliensis* Bak.]. PEN-WIPER. K; glabrous shrub; lvs. obovate, 4–10 in. long, obtuse, undulate or crenate, often spotted with purple, narrowed to a short petiole; cymes corymbose, pedicels to 2 in. long;

sepals ½–1½ in. long, corolla white above, the tube 4-angled, 3–4 in. long, nectar glands linear. Ethiopia, Somali Republic.

Marnierana Jacobsen. B; glabrous, to 1 ft.; lf. blades elliptic, to 1¼ in. long, rounded and weakly 3–5-crenate at apex, nearly cordate at base, petiole ¼ in. long; cyme loose, pedicels to ½ in. long; calyx tube to ½ in. long, lobes shorter, corolla rose, tube ¾–1¼ in. long, lobes rounded, to ¼ in. long. Madagascar.

Millotii Hamet & Perr. K; low, branching from base, closely tomentose with 3-branched hairs; lf. blades ovate, 1¼–2¼ in. long, obtuse, dentate, petiole ½ in. long; cyme compact, pedicels 3/16 in. long; calyx ovoid, 5/16 in. long, lobed nearly to the middle, corolla orange-yellow, tube ⅜ in. long, lobes ⅛ in. long, recurved. Madagascar.

miniata Hilsenb. & Bojer. B; glabrous, sts. erect or decumbent at base, sparsely leafy, 1–2 ft. long; lf. blades ovate, 1–3 in. long, nearly obtuse, crenate, often red-spotted at sinuses, petiole nearly cylindrical, broadened at base, to 1 in. long; cyme loose and broad, often with plantlets; calyx about ⅜ in. long, lobes slightly exceeding tube, corolla red, tube 1 in. long, lobes ⅕ as long and slightly wider, nectar glands slightly higher and wider. Madagascar.

Mortagei Hamet & Perr. B; glabrous, unbranched, 1–2 ft.; lf. blades ovate-lanceolate, 3–4 in. long, 1–1½ in. wide, obtuse, nearly cordate, crenate, petiole 1–2 in. long; cymes several, pedicels to ¾ in. long; calyx ovoid-inflated, purplish-red, 1 in. long, lobes 5/16 in. long, corolla tube 1¼ in. long, lobes acuminate, orange, ½ in. long. Madagascar.

oblonga: a listed name of no botanical standing.

obtusa Engl. K; low plant; lvs. 3–5 pairs, ovate, ½–1¼ in. long, rounded, entire to crenulate in upper ⅔, glabrous, petiole 3/16 in. long; cyme compact, pubescent, pedicels ⅛ in. long; sepals nearly separate, ¼ in. long, corolla red, tube 5/16 in. long, lobes spreading, 3/16 in. long. E. Afr.

orgyalis Bak. K; shrub, to 7 ft., upper parts and young lvs. reddish-brown, with scalelike 3-branched hairs; lf. blades ovate, 3–5 in. long, tapered basally, entire, petiole cylindrical, grooved above; sepals triangular, to ¼ in. long, corolla urceolate, yellow, ⅜ in. long, lobes ⅓ as long, nectar glands wider than high. Madagascar.

paniculata Harv. K; glabrous, 3–6 ft.; lf. blades oblong, to 8 in. long and 3 in. wide, obtuse or nearly acute, almost entire, often folded upward, tapering to a broad petiole; cyme loose, several times trichotomous, flat or rounded, to 16 in. wide, pedicels to ½ in. long; sepals triangular, to ⅛ in. long, corolla greenish-yellow, tube to ⅜ in. long, lobes to 3/16 in. long. S. Afr., Socotra Is.

peltata (Bak.) Baill. [*Kitchingia peltata* Bak.]. Kit; glabrous, woody at base, to 6 ft.; lvs. triangular-ovate, obtuse, almost entire to crenate, 1–4 in. long, peltate, petioles 1–4 in. long; cymes corymbose; calyx lobes about as long as tube, to 3/16 in. long, corolla pink, ¾–1 in. long, the lobes short, nectar glands wider than high. Madagascar.

pilosa Bak. Not cult.; material grown under this name is *K. tomentosa.*

pinnata (Lam.) Pers. [*Bryophyllum calycinum* Salisb.; *B. pinnatum* (Lam.) Kurz]. AIR PLANT, LIFE PLANT, FLOPPERS, MEXICAN LOVE PLANT, CURTAIN PLANT, MOTHER-IN-LAW, GOOD-LUCK LEAF, MIRACLE L., SPROUTING L. B; glabrous and more or less glaucous, sts. hollow, 1–6 ft., little-branched, suckering at base; lvs. pinnate with 3–5 short-stalked lfts. or the lower lvs. simple, blades of lvs. and lfts. elliptic or oblong, 2–8 in. long, crenate, petioles nearly cylindrical, channelled above; calyx papery, much-inflated, 1–1½ in. long, lobes shorter than tube, corolla sparsely glandular, reddish, to twice as long as calyx, lobes acute, shorter than tube, nectar glands longer than wide. Of uncertain nativity but now established in many trop. and subtrop. countries. Easily prop. by plantlets.

prolifera (Bowie) Hamet. B; glabrous, sts. often 4-angled, 3–12 ft., little-branched, often suckering at base; lvs. pinnate, to 1½ ft. long, lfts. 7–11, oblong-lanceolate, 3–6 in. long, oblique, nearly obtuse, crenate, sessile, petiole nearly cylindrical, channelled above; cymes paniculate, often with plantlets; calyx nearly campanulate, to 1 in. long, lobes shorter than tube, corolla tubular-urceolate, yellow, tipped with red, tube to 1 in. long, lobes much shorter, nectar glands nearly 4-angled. Madagascar.

pubescens Bak. [*K. Aliciae* Hamet]. B; hairy subshrub, to 4 ft.; lf. blades ovate to nearly orbicular, 2–5 in. long, obtuse, crenate to irregularly toothed, petioles about 1 in. long, broadened to triangular clasping base; calyx tube to 3/16 in. long, lobes nearly as long, corolla red, 1¼ in. long, lobes blunt, less than ⅓ as long as tube, nectar glands about as wide as high. Madagascar.

pumila Bak. K; glabrous, with a bloom, to 1 ft.; lvs. obovate-cuneate, to 1 in. long, rounded and strongly crenate in upper half, nearly sessile; cyme few-fld., pedicels to ⅜ in. long; sepals nearly separate, to 3/16 in. long, corolla tube to 5/16 in. long, lobes slightly longer, spreading or recurved, obovate, rose to violet. Madagascar.

Quartiniana A. Rich. K; glabrous, to 2½ ft.; lf. blades elliptic to obovate, 4–7½ in. long, obtuse, crenate, petioles 1½–3 in. long; cymes corymbose, pedicels ¾ in. long; sepals to ½ in. long, corolla white, tube 1¾ in. long, nectar glands linear, styles longer than ovary. Ethiopia, Nyasaland. *K. Dyeri* N. E. Br. has been considered synonymous but needs further study.

rhombopilosa O. Mannoni & Boiteau. K; erect, to 20 in.; lvs. alt., obovate-cuneate to fanlike, to 1 in. long, 5-toothed on margin toward tip, irregularly dark-streaked, with 4-branched hairs, short-petioled; fl. st. bare, slender, 10 in., cyme loose, compound, pedicels ⅛ in. long; calyx to about 1/16 in. long, corolla yellow-green lined with red-violet, tube 3/16 in. long, lobes shorter, reflexed. Madagascar.

rotundifolia Haw. K; glabrous herb, 1–3 ft.; lf. blades roundish-obovate to spatulate, 1–3 in. long, nearly entire or crenulate, tapering to short, indefinite petiole; cyme corymbose, often open, pedicels to ½ in. long; sepals awl-shaped, less than ⅛ in. long, corolla yellow to red, tube to ⅜ in. long, segms. about half as long, nectar glands linear. S. Afr., Socotra Is.

scandens: *K. Beauverdii* var. *parviflora.*

scapigera Welw. K; glabrous; lvs. rather crowded or nearly in a rosette, obovate to nearly orbicular, ¾–2 in. long, obtuse, entire, mealy, sessile or nearly so; fl. st. nearly scapose, cyme corymbose, pedicels to ¼ in. long; calyx tube and segms. to ⅛ in. long, corolla yellow or the lobes red, tube to ½ in. long, lobes about half as long, nectar glands linear. Cent. Afr., Socotra Is.

Schumacheri: *K. integra* var. *crenata.*

sexangularis N. E. Br. K; glabrous herb, to 3 ft., sts. simple, hexagonal; lvs. elliptic to nearly orbicular, to 5 in. long, obtuse, more or less crenate, petioled; cymes long-peduncled, in often corymbose clusters; sepals ovate, to ⅛ in. long, corolla yellow, tube ⅜ in. long, lobes ¼ as long, nectar glands linear. Transvaal? (S. Afr.).

somaliensis: *K. marmorata.*

suarezensis Perr. B; to 2 ft.; lvs. oblong, to 6 in. long, coarsely and irregularly serrate, gray-green, bearing plantlets at apex, petioled; corolla reddish-violet, tube ⅝ in. long, lobes spreading or recurved, ⅜ in. long. Madagascar.

synsepala Bak. K; sts. short, with a few-lvd. rosette, stolons bare, slender, to 1 ft.; lvs. spatulate, to 8 in. long, glabrous, broadly petioled; fl. st. axillary, scapose, to 1 ft., cyme dense, corymbose, glandular; calyx about ⅛ in. long, lobes shorter than tube, corolla pink, tube ¼–½ in. long, lobes shorter, nectar glands linear. Madagascar.

teretifolia: see *K. Bentii.*

thyrsiflora Harv. K; glabrous, glaucous herb, 1–4 ft.; lvs. obovate-spatulate, 3–4 in. long, obtuse, entire, sessile; thyrse dense-cylindrical or interrupted; sepals linear, 3/16 in. long, corolla nearly urceolate, tube ⅝ in. long, lobes yellow, ovate-orbicular, ⅓ as long, nectar glands slightly higher than wide, irregularly crenate. S. Afr.

tomentosa Bak. PUSSY-EARS, PLUSH PLANT, PANDA PLANT, PANDA-BEAR PLANT. K; densely felty with 3-branched hairs, sts. densely leafy above, to 10 in.; lvs. alt., thick, variable but mostly oblong-obovate, 1½–3 in. long, obtuse, crenate toward tip, silvery, crenations brown, sessile; fl. st. 1–2½ ft.; sepals 3/16 in. long, corolla tube yellowish, ½ in. long, lobes purplish, ⅛ in. long and somewhat wider, nectar glands wider than high. Madagascar. Sometimes grown under the misapplied name of *K. pilosa.*

triflora: a listed name of no botanical standing.

tubiflora (Harv.) Hamet [*K. verticillata* Scott-Ell.; *Bryophyllum tubiflorum* Harv.]. CHANDELIER PLANT. B; glabrous herb, to 3 ft., sts. simple, suckering at base; lvs. mostly in 3's, linear, 1–6 in. long, nearly cylindrical but channelled above, spotted with violet-brown, apex with 1–4 pairs of conical teeth between which are spoon-shaped bulbiliferous spurs; cymes in a corymbose cluster; calyx tube to 3/16 in. long, lobes mostly longer, corolla salmon to scarlet, tube about 1 in. long, lobes obovate, about ⅓ as long. S. Afr., Madagascar. Widely grown, prop. by the abundant plantlets; becoming a weed.

uniflora (Stapf) Hamet [*Bryophyllum uniflorum* (Stapf) A. Berger]. KITCHINGIA. B; prostrate herb, rooting at nodes; lvs. ovate to obovate, ½–1 in. long, obtuse, 3–5-crenate toward tip, glabrous; fls. 1–30, on slender pedicels, glabrous or glandular, calyx lobes to 3/16 in. long and somewhat wider, exceeding tube, corolla nearly urceolate, red or purplish, to 1 in. long, lobes about ⅓ as long or less, nectar glands linear. Madagascar. A handsome basket plant.

verticillata: *K. tubiflora.*

violacea: a listed name of no botanical standing; perhaps for *K. laxiflora* subsp. *violacea.*

Waldheimii Hamet & Perr. B; glabrous herb, to 1 ft., st. bases persistent and suckering; lf. blade obovate, 1½–4 in. long, obtuse, crenate toward tip, glaucous, narrowed to an indistinct, winged petiole; calyx tube to ⅝ in. long, lobes ⅓ as long, corolla pink, tube to ¾ in. long, lobes half as long or more, obtuse, nectar glands wider than high. Madagascar.

Welwitschii Britten. K; glabrous, glaucous, 3–5 ft.; lvs. ovate-lanceolate, obtuse, dentate, petioled, the lower lvs. 8–10 in. long; infl. diffusely corymbose; sepals lanceolate, ½–⅝ in. long, corolla sulphur-yellow, tube ¾ in. long, limb ¾–1 in. wide, nectar glands linear. Angola.

zimbabwensis Rendle. K; papillate-hairy, sts. to 2 in. in diam.; lvs. ovate, 2 in. long, rounded at apex, nearly sinuate, almost sessile; cyme rounded, few-fld.; fls. nearly sessile, yellow, 3¼ in. long. Rhodesia.

KALE. The kales, *Brassica oleracea* Acephala Group, *B. Napus* Pabularia Group, and others, are of many kinds; they are cool-season plants allied to the common cabbage and grown as greens or potherbs for their succulent, edible leaves, which are used either in autumn or spring. For an autumn crop, seeds are sown in late spring where the plants are to stand, or in some cases in seed beds and the young plants transplanted. In milder parts of the country, such as represented by Zone 8, kale is mostly a spring crop, seeds being sown in late summer or in autumn, the plants standing in the field over winter. In market kale, the entire plant is cut; in kitchen gardens, leaves are often taken as needed and the plants allowed to stand, in which case the distances between them may be 10–24 inches in the row depending on the cultivar. When the entire plant is to be removed in harvesting, the space need be only half as much or even less. The curled or crimped types (cultivars of *B. Napus* Pabularia Group) are usually most prized. The plant goes to seed the second year. The pests are those of cabbage. See *Collard;* also *Brassica.*

KALIMERIS: *BOLTONIA.*

KALMIA L. [*Kalmiella* Small]. LAUREL, AMERICAN L. *Ericaceae.* About 6 spp. of evergreen or rarely deciduous shrubs, native to N. Amer. and Cuba; lvs. alt., opp., or whorled, simple, entire, leathery; fls. white, pink to purple, in lateral or terminal corymbs or umbels, rarely solitary, calyx 5-lobed, corolla broadly campanulate to somewhat funnelform, with 10 pouches in which the anthers are held under tension until they discharge their pollen, stamens 10, ovary superior; fr. a 5-celled, many-seeded caps. Foliage is poisonous if eaten.

Most of the species are hardy north and very ornamental. They do well on sandy or peaty soils, which preferably are rather moist, but do not thrive on clay or limestone. Propagated by seeds sown in pans of sandy peat or sphagnum and set outdoors the following year; also by cuttings of half-ripened wood under glass, by layers, and cultivars by veneer grafting.

angustifolia L. SHEEP L., DWARF L., PIG L., LAMBKILL, WICKY. Slender shrub, to 3 ft.; lvs. usually opp. or in 3's, oblong to oblong-lanceolate, to 2½ in. long; fls. in lateral corymbs, purple to crimson, to ½ in. across, calyx glandular-hairy. Early summer. E. N. Amer. Zone 2. Cv. **'Candida'**. Fls. white. Cv. **'Ovata'**. Lvs. ovate to elliptic. Cv. **'Rubra'**. Fls. dark purple. Var. **carolina** (Small) Fern. [*K. carolina* Small]. Lvs. smaller, gray-pubescent beneath; calyx pubescent but not glandular. Va. to S.C.

carolina: *K. angustifolia* var.

cuneata Michx. WHITE WICKY. Semievergreen to deciduous shrub, to 2½ ft.; lvs. alt., obovate-cuneate, to 2 in. long; fls. in axillary clusters, pinkish-white, calyx glabrous. N.C. and S.C. Zone 7?

glauca: *K. poliifolia.*

hirsuta Walt. [*Kalmiella hirsuta* (Walt.) Small]. Shrub, to 2 ft.; lvs. alt., nearly sessile, elliptic to lanceolate, to ⅜ in. long, hirsute; fls. solitary, axillary, pink to rose-purple. S.C. to Fla. and Ala. Zone 7?

latifolia L. MOUNTAIN L., CALICO BUSH, IVY, IVYBUSH, SPOONWOOD. Shrub or small tree, to 10 ft. or more; lvs. alt., sometimes opp. or in 3's, elliptic, to 5 in. long; fls. in terminal, glandular-pubescent corymbs, rose-colored to white with purple markings inside. Late spring. E. N. Amer. Zone 5. Cvs. include: **'Alba'**, fls. white; **'Angustata'**, lvs. narrowly oblanceolate to linear; **'Fuscata'**, fls. with broad, chocolate-purple band inside; **'Myrtifolia'**, dwarf, lvs. to 1½ in. long; **'Obtusata'**, lvs. ovate, rounded at each end; **'Ostbo Red'**, fl. buds red; **'Polypetala'**, corolla deeply divided into 5 lobes; **'Rubra'**, fls. red.

microphylla (Hook.) A. Heller [*K. poliifolia* vars. *microphylla* (Hook.) Rehd. and *nana* Hort.]. WESTERN L., ALPINE L. Low alpine to straggling shrub, to 2 ft.; lvs. opp., nearly sessile, ovate to lanceolate, to 1½ in. long, not revolute, midrib without stalked glands; fls. to ½ in. across, in terminal, racemose clusters. Var. **microphylla.** The typical var.; low alpine, to 8 in. high, lvs. ovate to elliptic, less than ¾ in. long, Alaska to cent. Calif., Rocky Mts. Zone 2. Var. **occidentalis** (Small) Ebing. Lvs. lanceolate, more than 1 in. long. Lowlands, Alaska to B.C. and Ore.

poliifolia Wangenh. [*K. glauca* Ait.]. BOG K., BOG L., PALE L. Straggling shrub, to 2 ft.; lvs. opp. or in 3's, nearly sessile, lanceolate to linear, to 1½ in. long, revolute, glossy green above, glaucous-white beneath; fls. in glabrous, terminal corymbs, rose-purple, ½ in. across. Late spring, summer. N. Amer., e. of Rocky Mts. Zone 2. Cv. **'Leucantha'**. Fls. white. Vars. **microphylla** and **nana:** *K. microphylla.* Var. **rosmarinifolia** (Pursh) Rehd. Lvs. linear-oblong, strongly revolute.

KALMIELLA: *KALMIA.*

KALMIOPSIS Rehd. *Ericaceae.* One sp., an evergreen shrub, native to Ore.; lvs. alt., simple, leathery; fls. rose-purple, in terminal racemes, calyx 5-parted, corolla broadly campanulate, stamens 10, ovary superior; fr. a 5-valved caps.

Leachiana (L. F. Henders.) Rehd. [*Rhododendron Leachianum* L. F. Henders.]. Sts. erect, to 1 ft.; lvs. elliptic-obovate, to ¾ in. long, entire, glabrous above, gland-dotted beneath; calyx red, fleshy, glandular. Dry, rocky, exposed areas at 2,000–4,000 ft. elevation, Siskiyou Mts. (Ore.). Zone 7.

KALOPANAX Miq. *Araliaceae.* Two spp. of glabrous or hairy, sometimes prickly, deciduous trees, native to China, Manchuria, and Japan; lvs. palmately compound or lobed to the middle; fls. in umbels forming large, terminal panicles, petals 5, white, valvate, stamens 5, ovary 2-celled; fr. a laterally compressed drupe.

innovans: *Acanthopanax innovans.*

pictus (Thunb.) Nakai. [*K. ricinifolius* (Siebold & Zucc.) Miq.; *Acanthopanax ricinifolius* (Siebold & Zucc.) Seem.; *Acer pictum* Thunb.]. Round-headed tree, to 80 ft.; lvs. to 12 in. across, 5–7-lobed, lobes toothed, dark green above, light green beneath, usually glabrous but somewhat pubescent when young. Zone 5. Var. **Maximowiczii** (Van Houtte) Hara. Lf. lobes cut beyond the middle. Var. **magnificus** (Zab.) Nakai. Lvs. with shallow, ovate lobes, densely pubescent beneath.

ricinifolius: *K. pictus.*

KELSEYA Rydb. *Rosaceae.* One sp., native to w. N. Amer., allied to *Petrophytum,* but with lvs. densely imbricate, fls. solitary, nearly sessile at the ends of short dense brs., and stamens 10.

uniflora (S. Wats.) Rydb. Densely cespitose, semiprostrate undershrub; lvs. ⅛ in. long, entire, crowded; fls. bisexual, white, ¼ in. across; fr. a follicle. Mts., Mont., Idaho, Wyo. Adapted to rock gardens, and does best on limestone.

KENNEDIA Venten. CORAL PEA. *Leguminosae* (subfamily *Faboideae).* About 15 spp. of showy, scandent shrubs, native to Australia; lvs. alt., pinnate, lfts. mostly 3, rarely 5 or 1, entire or obscurely 3-lobed; fls. papilionaceous, red to nearly black, stamens 10, 9 united and 1 separate; fr. a linear legume. Similar to *Hardenbergia.*

Grown as ornamentals in greenhouses or outdoors in warm climates (Zone 10). Propagated by seeds and cuttings.

prostrata R. Br. ex Ait.f. Prostrate; lfts. 3, broadly obovate to orbicular, usually less than 1 in. long, pubescent, stipules prominent; fls. scarlet, 2–4 on a long peduncle, standard obovate-orbicular; fr. nearly cylindrical, to 2 in. long, pubescent. Australia.

rubicunda (Schneev.) Venten. Large twiner, pubescent; lfts. 3, ovate to orbicular, to 4 in. long or more; fls. dull red, to 1½ in. long, in drooping racemes, standard abruptly reflexed at middle; fr. flat, to 4 in. long. E. Australia.

KENSITIA Fedde [*Piquetia* N. E. Br., not H. G. Hallier]. *Aizoaceae.* One sp., a shrubby, per. succulent, native to S. Afr., sts. with distinct internodes; lvs. opp., only slightly united basally, 3-angled, each pair nearly equal; fls. solitary, calyx 5-lobed, petals united basally, staminodes and stamens many, arising from corolla tube, connivent with some petals to form a dome in the center of fl., ovary inferior, 8–10-celled, stigmas radiating; fr. an 8–10-valved caps., expanding keels with awnlike tips, without wings, placental tubercles present.

Culture as for *Lampranthus*. See also *Succulents*.

Pillansii (Kensit) Fedde [*Piquetia Pillansii* (Kensit) N. E. Br.]. Erect, to 2 ft., brs. many, glabrous, forked, reddish; lvs. spreading and slightly incurved, glaucous, dotted, to 1⅜ in. long, ¼ in. wide, and ⅜ in. thick, sharply 3-angled, tip acute; fls. terminal, to 2 in. across, petals rose-purple, white basally. Transvaal.

KENTIA: *GRONOPHYLLUM.* **K. Belmoreana:** *Howea Belmoreana.* **K. Canterburyana:** *Hedyscepe Canterburyana.* **K. Forsterana:** *Howea Forsterana.* **K. Macarthurii:** *Ptychosperma Macarthurii.* **K. Mooreana:** *Lepidorrhachis Mooreana.* **K. Ramsayi:** *Gronophyllum Ramsayi.*

KENTIOPSIS Brongn. *Palmae.* One sp., a solitary, unarmed, monoecious palm in New Caledonia; lvs. pinnate, sheaths forming a crownshaft, pinnae stiff, acuminate, midrib prominent above; infl. below lvs., much-branched, rachillae with fls. in triads (2 male and 1 female); male fls. slightly asymmetrical, sepals 3, imbricate, acute, petals valvate, acute, stamens 15–18, filaments erect, pistillode absent, female fls. with sepals 3, imbricate, petals 3, slightly longer than sepals, imbricate with briefly valvate apices, staminodes 3, pistil 1-celled, 1-ovuled; fr. ovoid-ellipsoid, with terminal stigmatic residue, seed with homogeneous endosperm and basal embryo.

A tropical species infrequently cultivated in U.S. For culture see *Palms.*

oliviformis (Brongn. & Gris) Brongn. To 90 ft. or more; lvs. large, pinnae stiff, to 3 ft. long, nearly 2 in. wide; rachillae to 16 in. long; male fls. ¼ in. long; fr. to about ⅝ in. long, ⅜ in. in diam.

KENTRANTHUS: *CENTRANTHUS.*

KENTROPHYLLUM: *CARTHAMUS.*

KERNERA Medic. *Cruciferae.* Four spp. of per. herbs of cent. and s. Eur.; like *Cochlearia*, differing chiefly in having stamens sharply curved.

saxatilis (L.) Rchb. [*Cochlearia saxatilis* L.]. To 12 in., usually less, glabrous or nearly so; basal lvs. in rosettes, oblong to spatulate, somewhat dentate, st. lvs. few, lanceolate; fls. white, in terminal many-fld. racemes. Summer. Mts., s. and cent. Eur. Sometimes grown in rock gardens.

KERRIA DC. JAPANESE ROSE. *Rosaceae.* One sp., an unarmed shrub, native to temp. e. Asia; lvs. alt., simple, stipules awl-like, deciduous; fls. solitary, terminating leafy shoots of the season, bisexual, sepals and petals 5, stamens many, pistils 5–8; frs. 5–8 achenes.

Commonly planted as an ornamental, does well in partial shade, and is hardy north. Propagated by cuttings, layers, and division.

japonica (L.) DC. [*Corchorus japonicus* Thunb.]. To 8 ft.; lvs. oblong-ovate, doubly toothed, to 2 in. long; fls. golden-yellow, to 2 in. across. China, Japan. Zone 5. Cvs. include: 'Argenteo-variegata': 'Picta'; 'Aureo-variegata', lvs. edged yellow; 'Aureo-vittata', branchlets striped green and yellow; 'Picta' [cv. 'Argenteo-variegata'], lvs. edged with white; 'Pleniflora', fls. double, the most commonly cult. form.

KETELEERIA Carrière. *Pinaceae.* Perhaps 9 spp. of very tall, evergreen, monoecious trees of s. China, se. Asia, and Taiwan; lvs. solitary, linear, glossy above, pale green beneath; cones large, erect, woody, with persistent scales; close to *Abies*, but differing in having cone scales persistent, and lvs. keeled, pale beneath but lacking glaucous bands.

Adapted only to mild climates, Zone 8. For culture see *Conifers.*

Davidiana (C. Bertrand) Beissn. To 100 ft. or more, branchlets short-pilose or glabrous; lvs. rounded or notched at apex on mature trees; cones to 8 in. long, green when young. China, Taiwan. Probably hardier than *K. Fortunei.*

Fortunei (A. Murr.) Carrière. To 100 ft.; young branchlets orange-red, glabrous or sparsely pubescent; lvs. spiny-pointed on young trees, becoming blunt on mature trees; cones to 7 in. long, purple when young. China.

KHAYA A. Juss. AFRICAN MAHOGANY. *Meliaceae.* About 10 spp. of tall trees, often with buttresses, native to trop. Afr.

and Madagascar; lvs. closely crowded at ends of brs., even-pinnate, glabrous, lfts. 4–14; fls. in axillary panicles, sepals and petals 4 or 5, stamens 8–10, filaments united in an urceolate tube, ovary 4- or 5-celled; fr. a woody caps., seeds many, winged.

nyasica Stapf ex Bak.f. NYASALAND MAHOGANY. Timber tree, to 150 ft., with red wood; lvs. 6–12 in. long, glossy, lfts. 6–10, ovate to oblong, strongly asymmetrical at base; fls. white, sepals and petals 4, stamens 8, ovary 4-celled. Cent. Afr.

senegalensis (Desr.) A. Juss. SENEGAL MAHOGANY. Tree, 6–90 ft.; lvs. 6–12 in. long, lfts. 4–10, oblong to oblong-elliptic, 2–5 in. long, symmetrical at base; panicles loose; fls. white; caps. 4-valved. N. Trop. Afr. A common substitute for mahogany, because of the rich color and beautiful figure of the wood.

KIGELIA DC. *Bignoniaceae.* About 10 spp. of trees, native to trop. Afr.; lvs. opp. or in 3's, pinnate; fls. orange to red, in loose, drooping, long-peduncled panicles, calyx irregularly 5-lobed, corolla campanulate above, narrowing to a cylindrical or constricted tube, 2-lipped, stamens 4; fr. cylindrical, 1-celled, hard, indehiscent.

Grown in U.S. tropical and subtropical gardens as an oddity.

pinnata (Jacq.) DC. SAUSAGE TREE. To 50 ft.; lvs. in 3's, lfts. 7–9, elliptic-oblong, to 6 in. long; fls. claret-colored, to 3 in. long; fr. somewhat gourdlike, to 1½ ft. long or more, pendent on cordlike stalks to several ft. long. Zone 10b, in Fla.

KIGGELARIA L. *Flacourtiaceae.* Four spp. of dioecious, unarmed shrubs or small trees, native to Afr.; female fls. solitary, male fls. in axillary cymes, sepals and petals 5, stamens 8–10; fr. a globose, leathery caps.

africana L. Shrub or small tree, to 15 ft.; lvs. elliptic, to 3 in. long, serrate, pale beneath, short-petioled; fr. about ½ in. in diam., seeds nearly globose, enclosed in bright red aril. S. Afr. Zone 10.

KIRENGESHOMA Yatabe. *Saxifragaceae.* One or 2 spp. of per. herbs of Japan and Korea; rhizome short, stout; lvs. opp., palmately lobed, petioled; fls. few, in terminal and axillary cymes, large, yellow, calyx tube cup-shaped, partly united at base to ovary, calyx lobes 5, petals 5, erect in lower half, recurved above middle, stamens 15, ovary partly inferior, styles 3, filiform; fr. a broadly ovate, dehiscent caps.

Propagated by division or by seeds.

palmata Yatabe. To 4½ ft.; lvs. lobed, coarsely toothed, to 8 in. long; fls. to 1½ in. long, showy. Wooded mts. of s. Japan.

KIRKIA D. Oliver. *Simaroubaceae.* About 8 spp. of Afr. trees, sometimes polygamous; lvs. somewhat clustered toward ends of brs., alt., pinnate; fls. in many peduncled, cymose corymbs forming a broad leafy panicle, calyx 4-lobed, petals and stamens 4, disc and ovary 5-lobed; fr. dry, 4-sided, separating into 4 one-seeded sections.

acuminata D. Oliver. Medium-sized tree; lvs. to 1 ft. long, lfts. 13–19, lanceolate to ovate-lanceolate, to 3 in. long; infl. no more than half as long as lvs. Trop. Afr.

Wilmsii Engl. Deciduous tree, 10–20 ft.; lvs. 4–5 in. long, lfts. 10–12, lanceolate, to ¾ in. long, rachis narrowly winged between lfts.; infl. about as long as lvs. S. Afr.

KITAIBELIA Willd. *Malvaceae.* One sp., a per. herb from Yugoslavia; lvs. simple, palmately lobed; fls. solitary or in few-fld. axillary cymes, involucral bracts 6–9, leafy, slightly united basally, petals 5, white to rose, stamens united in a tubular column, style brs. filiform, stigmas apically decurrent; fr. a schizocarp, mericarps many, at maturity appearing to be arranged in superposed whorls, each 1-seeded, eventually splitting into 2 valves to release the seed.

Propagated by seeds, cuttings, or division.

vitifolia Willd. Robust, sts. many, few-branched, to 5 ft. or more, new growth white-hispid; lvs. to 8 in. long, angularly 3-, 5-, or 7-lobed, coarsely toothed; involucral bracts cordate-ovate, long-acuminate, to about ¾ in. long, usually slightly longer than sepals, petals about 1 in. long; mericarps brownish-black, white-hairy, enclosed by the dry bracts and sepals.

KITCHINGIA: *KALANCHOE.*

KLEINHOVIA L. *Byttneriaceae.* One sp., a tree, native to trop. Asia and e. Afr.; lvs. alt., simple; fls. in loose, terminal, panicled cymes, calyx deeply divided with unequal lobes, early-deciduous, petals 5, the uppermost one long-clawed, hoodlike, the other 4 subequal, androgynophore present, slender, stamens in 5 groups of 3, the groups alternating with toothlike staminodes, all basally united into a short cup; fr. a loculicidally dehiscent caps., membranous, inflated, pear-shaped, 5-carpelled.

Sometimes grown as an ornamental in tropical gardens.

hospita L. To 60 ft.; lvs. broadly ovate, to 12 in. long, 9 in. wide; sepals reddish, to ½ in. long, petals red, the hoodlike upper one yellow-tipped; caps. about 1 in. long and broad.

KLEINIA: *SENECIO.* **K. tomentosa:** *S. Haworthii.* **K. gomphophylla:** *S. Herreianus.* **K. neriifolia:** *S. Kleinia.* **K. repens:** *S. serpens.* **K. Gregorii:** *S. stapeliiformis.*

KLUGIA: *RHYNCHOGLOSSUM.*

KNAUTIA L. *Dipsacaceae.* About 40 spp. of ann. or per. herbs, native to N. Afr. and Eur., to Caucasus and w. Siberia; lvs. opp., simple to pinnatifid; fls. in involucrate, long-stalked heads, without receptacular bracts, calyx cup-shaped, with many bristles or teeth, enveloped by an obscurely toothed, cup-shaped involucel, corolla 4–5-lobed, stamens 4; fr. an achene.

arvensis (L.) T. Coult. BLUE-BUTTONS. Per., to 4 ft., sts. glandular-pubescent to hirsute in lower part; basal lvs. oblanceolate, simple to lyrate-pinnatifid, st. lvs. pinnatifid, hairy; fls. lilac. N. Afr., Eur., Caucasus, w. Siberia; naturalized in ne. N. Amer. Very variable sp., particularly in lf. shape.

drymeia Heuff. Per., to 2½ ft., sts. ascending, softly hairy; st. lvs. lanceolate to ovate, acuminate, serrate, pubescent; heads to nearly 2 in. across; fls. reddish-violet to purple. Balkans.

lyrophylla (Panc.) Panč. [*Scabiosa lyrophylla* Hort.]. Per., to 2 ft., sts. slender, obscurely retrorse-hispid; lvs. lyrate to lyrate-pinnatifid, appressed-pubescent underneath, lower lvs. long-petioled; heads small; fls. dark purple. E. Yugoslavia. By some auths. considered only a variant of *K. macedonica.*

macedonica Griseb. [*Scabiosa macedonica* (Griseb.) Vis.]. Per., to 2½ ft., sts. slender, much-branched; basal lvs. lyrate, st. lvs. entire to pinnatifid, pubescent; fls. dark purple. Cent. Eur.

orientalis L. Ann., sts. to 2 ft., slender, somewhat sticky; lower lvs. oblong to oblong-linear, entire to pinnatisect, upper lvs. linear, acuminate; fls. purple, heads usually 5–10-fld. Se. Eur. and Caucasus.

sylvatica (L.) Duby [*Scabiosa sylvatica* L.]. Per., to 3 ft.; lvs. ovate, elliptic, or lanceolate, toothed, thin, pubescent; heads to 1½ in. across; fls. violet. Eur.

tatarica (L.) Szabó [*Cephalaria tatarica* (L.) Schrad.]. Bien., to 6 ft., lower part of st. hairy; lvs. pinnatifid, to 10 in. long, glabrous, lobes oblong-elliptic, toothed; heads to 1½ in. across; fls. bright yellow. E. Russia, Siberia.

KNIGHTIA R. Br. *Proteaceae.* Three spp. of trees and shrubs of New Zeal. and New Caledonia; lvs. alt., leathery, entire or toothed; fls. bisexual, in dense racemes, perianth cylindrical, lobes lanceolate, spirally recurved, stamens 4, anthers lanceolate, attached to perianth lobes, ovary superior, 1-celled, ovules 4, ascending; fr. a leathery follicle, seeds winged at apex.

excelsa R. Br. Tree, to 90 ft., resembling a Lombardy poplar in habit; lvs. oblong, to 6 in. long, very stiff; fls. to 1½ in. long, brown-tomentose, in racemes to 4 in. long. New Zeal. Excellent wood for cabinet making.

KNIPHOFIA Moench [*Tritoma* Ker-Gawl.]. TORCH LILY, POKER PLANT, RED-HOT-POKER, TRITOMA. *Liliaceae.* Perhaps 60–70 spp. of stout, rhizomatous, per. herbs, native to Madagascar, trop. and s. Afr.; usually stemless, roots cordlike, thick; lvs. basal, grasslike; fls. red or yellow, drooping, on short, articulate pedicels, in showy, pokerlike spikes or dense racemes terminating long scapes, perianth cylindrical to funnelform, tube much longer than the 6 lobes, stamens 6, the outer 3 shorter, anthers versatile; fr. a loculicidal caps.

Poker plants may be hardy in the North with a winter mulch, but where they are not, the roots may be lifted in autumn and stored in a cellar in boxes of dry earth. Propagated by root division, offsets if produced, and seeds.

alooides: *K. Uvaria.*

caulescens Bak. ex Hook.f. Rosette of lvs. on a woody st. to 1 ft. high; lvs. linear, to 3 ft. long and 3 in. wide, very glaucous; fls. red, or the older ones yellow, 1 in. long, in dense spikes to 6 in. long, on scapes 4–5 ft. high, stamens exserted. S. Afr.

×**corallina** (Hort. ex de Nob.) Bak.: *K. Macowanii* × *K. Uvaria.* To 2 ft.; fls. coral-red.

elegans: *K. Schimperi.*

foliosa Hochst. [*K. Quartiniana* A. Rich.]. To 3 ft.; lvs. ensiform, to 3 ft. long and 2 in. wide; fls. cylindrical, bright yellow, to 1 in. long, in dense, cylindrical racemes to 1 ft. long, stamens long-exserted. Ethiopia.

Galpinii Bak. To 3 ft.; lvs. linear, to 2½ ft. long and about ⅛ in. wide, margins smooth, not rough; fls. narrowly cylindrical, reddish-orange, to 1 in. long, in dense racemes to 3 in. long, stamens slightly exserted. S. Afr.

gracilis Harv. ex Bak. To 2 ft.; lvs. linear, to 2 ft. long and 3/16 in. wide; fls. pale yellow, to ⅝ in. long, with very slender perianth tube, in dense racemes to 3 in. long, the longer stamens exserted. S. Afr.

Macowanii Bak. To 2 ft.; lvs. linear-subulate, to 2 ft. long, 3/16 in. wide, strongly keeled, margins strongly serrulate; fls. yellowish or orange-red, in dense racemes to 4 in. long, stamens included. S. Afr.

mirabilis a listed name of no botanical standing; used for plants, perhaps of hybrid origin, described as being 3 ft. tall, with dense, cylindrical fls. in shades of yellow.

multiflora J. M. Wood & M. Evans. To 6 ft.; lvs. linear, 3–6 ft. long and 1 in. wide, strongly keeled, margins serrulate; fls. narrowly funnelform, white, erect, to ⅝ in. long, swollen basally, in dense spikes, stamens long-exserted, twice as long as fls. S. Afr.

Northiae Bak. Rosette of lvs. on a short st.; lvs. lanceolate, to 5 ft. long and 6 in. wide, glaucous, not keeled, margins denticulate; fls. red at first, becoming pale yellow, 1 in. long, in dense racemes to 1 ft. long on stout scapes shorter than lvs., stamens long-exserted. S. Afr.

×**Pfitzeri** Nichols.: *K. Uvaria* × ?. To 7 ft.; fls. red, anthers long-exserted.

pumila (Ait.) Kunth. To 2 ft.; lvs. linear, to 2 ft. long and ½ in. wide, glaucous, with rough margins; fls. narrowly funnelform, orange-red, ½ in. long, in dense racemes, stamens and style long-exserted. S. Afr.

Quartiniana: *K. foliosa.*

rufa Leichtl. ex Bak. To 1½ ft.; lvs. linear, to 1½ ft. long and ⅜ in. wide; fls. cylindrical, ¾ in. long, in loose racemes, primrose-yellow, upper fls. tinged red, stamens exserted. Natal.

Schimperi Bak. [*K. elegans* Engl.]. To 3 ft.; lvs. to 2 ft. long and ½ in. wide, many and limp; racemes loose, to 1 ft. long, on slender scapes to 2½ ft. high, fls. subcylindrical, curved, pale yellow, to 1¼ in. long, on short pedicels, stamens and style included. Trop. Afr.

semperflorens: a listed name of no botanical standing.

Tubergenii: a listed name of no botanical standing, for plants described as having creamy-yellow fls. on 2½ ft. scapes.

Tuckii Leichtl. ex Bak. To 5 ft.; lvs. ensiform, to 2 ft. long and 1 in. wide, margins serrulate and rough; fls. sulphur-yellow, tinged red when young, to ⅝ in. long, in dense racemes to 6 in. long, stamens slightly exserted. S. Afr.

Uvaria (L.) Oken [*K. alooides* Moench]. POKER PLANT, TORCH FLOWER, RED-HOT-POKER. To 4 ft.; lvs. linear-ensiform, to 3 ft. long and 1 in. wide, gray-green, strongly keeled, margins often rough; fls. scarlet, becoming yellow with age, to 2 in. long, in dense racemes to 10 in. long, stamens unequally exserted. S. Afr. Var. **grandis:** var. *maxima.* Var. **maxima** Bak. [var. *grandis* Hort.]. Plant taller, stouter; fls. larger, racemes longer. Var. **nobilis** (Guillon) Bak. To 6 ft. high; lvs. to 3 ft. long; fls. many, red, becoming orange with age.

zombensis Bak. To 5 ft.; lvs. ensiform, to 2 ft. long and ¾ in. wide, not strongly keeled; fls. cylindrical, red, becoming yellow-green, 1 in. long, in dense racemes 3–4 in. long, stamens included. Trop. Afr.

zululandi: a listed name of no botanical standing.

KOCHIA Roth. *Chenopodiaceae.* Perhaps 80 spp. of Eurasian herbs and subshrubs; lvs. alt., narrow, entire; fls. small, axillary, solitary or clustered, bisexual or female, calyx 5-lobed, corolla none, stamens 5, exserted, ovary 1-celled, stigmas mostly 2; fr. a utricle, enveloped by the calyx, which develops transverse wings in age.

One species grown as an ornamental. Propagated by seeds.

Childsii: *K. scoparia* forma *trichophylla* cv.

scoparia (L.) Schrad. SUMMER CYPRESS, BELVEDERE. Ann., to 5 ft., usually much-branched, of columnar or pyramidal to globular habit, more or less hairy; lvs. lanceolate to narrow-linear, to 3 in. long, ciliate; fls. inconspicuous. S. Eur. to Japan; now widely naturalized. Forma **trichophylla** (Schmeiss) Schinz & Thell. (often misspelled *trichophila*) [*K. scoparia* var. *culta* (Voss ex Farw.) L. H. Bailey]. BURNING BUSH, FIREBUSH, RED SUMMER CYPRESS. Of dense, globular or ellipsoidal habit; lvs. narrowly linear, turning purplish-red in autumn. Cv. 'Childsii'. An improved strain.

trichophylla: *K. scoparia* forma.

KOELERIA Pers. *Gramineae.* About 20 spp. of slender ann. or per. grasses in temp. regions of N. and S. Hemispheres; lf. blades narrow; panicles glossy, spikelike; spikelets 2–4-fld., compressed, rachilla disarticulating above the glumes and between the florets, prolonged, first glume 1-nerved, second 3–5-nerved, lemma scarious, obscurely 5-nerved, the awn, if present, borne just below the apex. For terminology see *Gramineae.*

brevifolia: see *K. Reuteri.*

glauca (Schkuhr) DC. Per., sts. to 2 ft., bulbous at base; lf. blades short, involute or flat, glaucous above, appressed-pubescent beneath; spikelets 2–3-fld., ⅛–¼ in. long, glumes glaucous, lemma glaucous or appressed-pubescent. Cent. Eur. to Siberia.

Reuteri Rouy [*K. brevifolia* Reut., not (Willd.) K. Spreng]. Per., sts. to 10 in.; lf. blades very narrow, to 1¼ in. long, convolute; panicle ovate-oblong, 1¼ in. long, whitish-green or purplish; spikelets ¼ in. long, glumes about equal, lemma larger than palea, ending in a very acute point. France.

KOELLIKERIA Regel. *Gesneriaceae.* One or a few spp. of per., terrestrial herbs with scaly rhizomes, native to Cent. and S. Amer.; lvs. congested at base; fls. in a raceme, in axils of small alt. bracts, calyx lobes about as long as tube, corolla tubular, 5-lobed, the upper 2 lobes short, the lower 3 lobes larger and more or less toothed or fimbriate, stamens 4, borne on corolla tube, anthers united by sides and tips, disc ringlike, ovary half-inferior; fr. a caps.

Propagated by the scaly rhizomes. For cultivation see *Gesneriaceae.*

erinoides (DC.) Mansf. Lvs. ovate to obovate, to 4 in. long, 2½ in. wide, toothed, hairy, spotted with velvety-green and often veined with deeper reddish-green; racemes to 1 ft.; corolla ⅜ in. long, white or creamy with deep pink or red flush on upper side, throat blotched yellow, with red lines, lower lobes to ⅛ in. long.

×KOELLIKOHLERIA Wiehl.: *Koellikeria × Kohleria. Gesneriaceae.* A hybrid genus with one "species."

For cultivation see *Gesneriaceae.*

rosea Wiehl.: *Koellikeria erinoides × Kohleria spicata.* Plants with scaly rhizomes, pilose, sts. to 1 ft.; lvs. congested, blades ovate to obovate, to 5½ in. long, 2 in. wide, crenate; fls. 1–4 in axils of opp. bracts in a terminal infl., corolla tubular, oblique in the calyx, ½ in. long, dark red above, dull white beneath and inside, lobes magenta-rose, the lower 3 with 2 white stripes, disc ringlike, ovary half-inferior, stigma slightly 2-lobed.

KOELREUTERIA Laxm. GOLDEN-RAIN TREE. *Sapindaceae.* Four spp. of deciduous trees, native to China, Korea, Taiwan, and Fiji; young brs. and twigs strongly lenticilled; lvs. alt., pinnate or 2-pinnate; infl. a large terminal panicle to 1–1½ ft. long; fls. bisexual, irregular, fragrant, calyx urn-shaped, 5-lobed; petals 4–5, yellow, each with 2 crimson appendages at base, stamens usually 8; fr. a bladdery, loculicidal, 3-valved caps., seeds usually 3, black, round, bony.

Koelreuterias are not particular as to soil, but thrive in sunny locations. Propagated by seeds or by root cuttings. All are desirable flowering trees with fragrant flowers attractive to bees.

bipinnata Franch. [*K. integrifoliola* Merrill]. To 60 ft.; lvs. 2-pinnate, to 18 in. long, lfts. 7–12, broadly ovate to oblong-ovate, to 5 in. long, 1¾ in. wide, usually slightly oblique, acute to acuminate, serrate to entire, lower surface usually with scattered hairs on veins and tufted hairs in axils; petals 4; caps. 2–2¼ in. long, separating into 3 rose-colored, ovate, papery segms. Summer. Sw. China. Warmer parts of Zone 7. Lfts. usually broader, less oblique, caps. larger and plants hardier than in *K. elegans.*

elegans (Seem.) A. C. Sm. [*K. formosana* Hayata; *K. Henryi* Dümmer; *K. vitiensis* A. C. Sm.]. FLAMEGOLD. To 60 ft.; lvs. 2-pinnate, to

1½ ft. long, lfts. 9–16, usually narrowly ovate, to 3½ in. long, 1¼ in. wide, nearly entire to unequally serrate, lustrous; petals 5; caps. about 1½ in. long, separating into 3 rose-colored, ovate, papery segms. Late summer. Taiwan and Fiji; naturalized in Fla. Zone 9.

formosana: *K. elegans.*

Henryi: *K. elegans.*

integrifoliola: *K. bipinnata.*

paniculata Laxm. [*K. paniculata* var. *apiculata* (Rehd. & E. H. Wils.) Rehd.]. VARNISH TREE. To 45 ft.; lvs. mostly pinnate, sometimes 2-pinnate, to 18 in. long, lfts. 12–18, ovate to oblong, to 3½(–6) in. long, 2¾ in. wide, shallowly lobed, irregularly crenate-serrate, often pinnatisect to pinnate at base; petals 4; caps. to 2 in. long, separating into 3 brownish, papery, lustrous, pointed segms. Early summer. China, Korea, naturalized in Japan. Fls. used medicinally by the Chinese, and necklaces made from the seeds. The hardiest and most widely cult. sp. Zone 5. Cv. '**Fastigiata**' [var. *fastigiata* Bean; forma *fastigiata* (Bean) Rehd.]. Columnar in habit. Cv. '**September**'. Fls. in late summer.

vitiensis: *K. elegans.*

KOHLERIA Regel [*Isoloma* Benth. ex Decne.; *Tydaea* Decne.]. TREE GLOXINIA. *Gesneriaceae.* More than 50 spp. of hairy, terrestrial herbs with scaly rhizomes, or shrubs, native from Mex. to n. S. Amer.; lvs. opp. or whorled; fls. solitary or a few together in lf. axils, or several clustered on a short peduncle in lf. axils or in a raceme, calyx lobes 5, erect to recurved, corolla cylindrical or swollen toward the throat, limb small, symmetrical or more or less 2-lipped, 5-lobed, the upper 2 lobes bent backward, stamens 4, borne at base of corolla tube, disc of 5 separate or partly united glands, ovary half-inferior; fr. a caps.

Propagated by the scaly rhizomes. For cultivation see *Gesneriaceae.* Several hybrids are known, sometimes erroneously under species names. The major groups of hybrids have been derived from *K. amabilis* (Amabilis Hybrids), *K. bogotensis* (Bogotensis Hybrids), *K. eriantha* (Eriantha Hybrids), and from *K. digitaliflora* and/or *K. Warszewiczii* (Regel) Hanst. (Sciadotydaea Hybrids). Within these groups, fancy-named cultivars are sometimes recognized.

amabilis (Planch. & Linden) Fritsch [*Isoloma amabile* (Planch. & Linden) Hort. ex Bellair & St.-Léger; *I. Ceciliae* (André) Hort. ex Bellair & St.-Léger]. Herbaceous, sts. white-hairy; lvs. ovate, to 4 in. long, 3 in. wide, crenate, stiff, dark green with purplish-brown veins and sometimes marked with silver above, paler green and often flushed with red beneath; fls. nodding on pedicels to 3 in. long, calyx lobes spreading, corolla deep rose, barred and spotted with brick-red inside, tube swollen beneath throat, to 1 in. long, lobes spreading, rose, barred and dotted with purple-red. Colombia. Erroneously introd. to cult. under the name *K. Seemannii* (Hook.) Hanst.

bella C. V. Mort. Sts. to 16 in., brown-hairy; lvs. ovate or ovate-elliptic, to 5½ in. long, 3 in. wide, unequal-sided at base, crenate-serrate, green; fls. several from a leafy-bracted peduncle to 1⅝ in. long, calyx lobes erect, triangular, green, corolla slightly swollen at middle, narrowed at throat, hairy, red, but yellowish on lower side, lobes yellow, spotted with purple, the longer ⅛ in. long. Costa Rica.

bogotensis (Nichols.) Fritsch [*Isoloma pictum* Hort.; *K. picta* Hort., not *K. picta* (Hook.) Hanst.]. Sts. to 2 ft.; lf. blades ovate, to 3 in. long, 1½ in. wide, closely toothed, densely hairy, velvety dark green marked with paler green or white and sometimes brown-flushed above, green or suffused with red beneath; fls. solitary or paired, pedicels to 2 in. long, calyx lobes spreading, oblong-ovate, corolla swollen beneath throat, 1 in. long, red, shading to yellow basally, yellow dotted with red inside, lower lobes about ¼ in. long, yellow, dotted red, upper lobes smaller, red. Colombia. Has been grown erroneously under the name *K. tubiflora.*

digitaliflora (Linden & André) Fritsch. Robust, sts. densely white-hairy; lf. blades elliptic-lanceolate to elliptic-ovate, to 8 in. long, 4¾ in. wide, crenate, dark green and hairy; fls. few to several on an axillary peduncle, calyx lobes spreading outward and downward, ovate, ¼ in. long, woolly, corolla slightly swollen on upper side, narrowed at throat, to 1¼ in. long, densely woolly outside, white with a rose flush on upper side, lobes spreading, ¼ in. long, green, finely spotted with purple. Colombia. A parent of many hybrids.

eriantha (Benth.) Hanst. [*Isoloma erianthum* (Benth.) Benth. ex Decne.; *I. hirsutum* Hort.; *K. hirsuta* Hort., not *K. hirsuta* (HBK) Regel]. Shrub, sts. to 4 ft., densely reddish- or whitish-hairy; lvs. ovate, to 5 in. long, 2½ in. wide, crenate, short-hairy above, densely woolly beneath, red-hairy on margin; fls. solitary or 3–4 together, pedicels to 4 in. long, from a short peduncle, calyx lobes erect, lanceolate, ¼ in.

long, reddish-hairy, corolla expanded upward, to 2 in. long, orange-red, hairy, lobes ¼ in. long, the lower 3 yellow-spotted. Colombia. *Isoloma multiflorum* Hort. probably belongs here.

×**gigantea** (Planch.) Fritsch: *K. bogotensis* × *K. Warszewiczii* (Regel) Hanst. To 3 ft.; lvs. similar to those of *K. bogotensis;* fls. 9–12 in axils, calyx lobes spreading, broad, corolla similar to that of *K. bogotensis,* but tube longer, less swollen. Plants probably belonging here have been offered under such hort. names as *Isoloma hybridum, Tydaea hybrida,* and *T. grandiflora.*

hirsuta (HBK) Regel. Suffruticose, to 3 ft., densely hairy; lvs. opp. or in 3's, obliquely ovate-oblong, to 6 in. long, 2½ in. wide, shallowly toothed, softly hairy above, long-hairy and often reddish beneath; fls. solitary or several in axils, on red-hairy pedicels to 1¼ in. long, calyx lobes erect, narrowly triangular, red-tipped, corolla tubular, 1¼ in. long, broadest near middle, orange-red outside, orange-yellow inside, long-hairy, lobes spreading, small, ⅛ in. long, yellow, with red crescent in center. Trinidad, Colombia to Guyana. *K. eriantha* has also been grown, erroneously, under this name.

lanata Lem. Herbaceous, sts. to 15 in., woolly; lvs. ovate or elliptic, to 5 in. long, 2 in. wide, toothed, green above, paler and with brown hairs beneath; fls. solitary in axils or in a raceme, calyx lobes triangular-ovate, ¼ in. long, woolly, corolla to 1⅝ in. long, orange-red, densely hairy, not narrowed at the oblique throat, limb more or less 2-lipped, lobes 3/16 in. long, purple-spotted, disc of 5 glands united halfway up in a ring. Mex.

Lindeniana (Regel) H. E. Moore. Herbaceous, to 1 ft., producing stolons and scaly rhizomes; lvs. ovate, to 3 in. long, 2 in. wide, crenate, deep green, velvety-hairy, silver-veined above, pale or red-flushed beneath; fls. solitary or few in axils, pedicels to 2½ in. long, calyx lobes spreading, ¼ in. long, corolla tube more or less campanulate, swollen on lower side, ½ in. long, white, flushed with yellow above, with lavender-violet patch at throat and on lower 3 lobes, lobes nearly as long as tube, upper 2 banded with lavender-violet. Ecuador. Has been grown under the erroneous name *Gesneria Lindenii.*

ocellata (Hook.) Fritsch [*Tydaea ocellata* (Hook.) Regel]. Shrubby, sts. to 2 ft., purplish-hairy; lvs. elliptic-ovate, to 5 in. long, 2½ in. wide, sharply toothed, with short, stiff, appressed hairs and wrinkled surface above, purplish beneath; fls. 1 or few in axils, calyx lobes erect, lanceolate, ¼ in. long, corolla ¾ in. long, bright red, lobes spreading, the upper 2 smaller, red with black spots, the lower 3 to ⅛ in. long, red with purplish-black dots and white or pale yellow patterning. Colombia.

picta: see *K. bogotensis.*

sciadotydaea: see Sciadotydaea Hybrids under *Kohleria.*

Seemannii: see *K. amabilis.*

spicata (HBK) Ørst. Sts. to 4½ ft., densely red-hairy; lvs. opp. or in 3's, blades slightly curved, elliptic or elliptic-lanceolate, to 6 in. long, 2 in. wide, toothed, velvety above, red-silky beneath; fls. 1–3 in axils of the lvs. or of bracts in a raceme, calyx lobes ovate to triangular, ⅛ in. long, corolla tube swollen below throat, ¾ in. long, orange-red, lobes short, the upper 2 uniformly colored, the 3 lower 3/16 in. long, spotted paler orange-yellow. Mex. to n. S. Amer. Has been offered erroneously as *K. strigosa.*

strigosa C. V. Mort. Not in cult., see *K. spicata.*

tubiflora (Cav.) Hanst. To 2 ft., densely hairy; lvs. ovate, to 3½ in. long, 2 in. wide, sharply toothed, densely short-hairy and dark green above, green with red veins beneath; fls. 1–3 in axils of upper lvs., calyx lobes triangular-ovate, ⅛ in. long, corolla cylindrical, slightly swollen near middle but narrowed to throat, to 1⅛ in. long, reddish-orange, greenish-yellow toward apex, lobes erect, 1/16 in. long, green, spotted dark red. *K. bogotensis* has been grown erroneously under this name.

KOHLRABI. Kohlrabi is the common name of *Brassica oleracea* Gongylodes Group, called also stem turnip because of the turniplike enlargement of the stem 1–3 inches above the ground. It is a low biennial plant of the Old World but of unknown nativity, producing seeds the second year from old stocks left over or planted out. The tuberous stem is used the same as turnips, both for the table and for stock feed. For the table, the tubers should be taken when 2 or 3 inches in diameter, before they become hard and bitter. Kohlrabi is grown the same as turnips. Seeds are usually sown where plants are to stand, in rows far enough apart for tillage (say 18–20 inches), and thinned to 5–10 inches in the row; sow from early spring to early summer if succession is desired, as for table turnips. Keep the plants growing rapidly for a tender product. Pests are those of the cabbage, a close relative. There are green and purplish cultivars.

KOKIA Lewt. *Malvaceae.* Four spp. of small trees from Hawaiian Is.; lvs. simple, palmately 5-, 7-, or 9-lobed, leathery, black-dotted; fls. showy, slightly irregular, solitary, axillary, on jointed peduncles, with 1 early deciduous bract at the joint, involucral bracts 3, foliar, entire or 3–5-lobed, longer than calyx, calyx shallowly 5-lobed, the upper part usually deciduous by a transverse suture, petals red or orange-red, reflexed, stamens united in a tubular curved column; fr. a woody caps., 5-celled, each cell 1-seeded, seeds reddish-tomentose.

Propagated by seeds. Flowering early to late spring; suitable for cultivation only in essentially frost-free areas.

Cookei Degener [*K. drynarioides* as misapplied by Lewt.]. To 15 ft.; lvs. reddish when young, up to 5 in. wide, glabrous except for reddish-brown tufts on the lower surface at the basal angles of the veins; peduncles 2–4 in. long, the bract about ½ in. long, involucral bracts ovate to oblong, 1–1½ in. long, about 1 in. wide, petals reddish-orange, about 3 in. long, longer than staminal column. Molokai Is., but now extinct in the wild.

drynarioides (Seem.) Lewt. [*K. Rockii* Lewt.]. KOKIO. To 13 ft., trunk grayish, to 1 ft. in diam.; similar to *K. Cookei* but having greater development of brownish pubescence on lower surface of lf.; peduncles generally longer, involucral bracts obovate to suborbicular, 1½–2½ in. long, petals red, about 4 in. long, staminal column nearly as long as petals. Hawaii.

Rockii: *K. drynarioides.*

KOLKWITZIA Graebn. *Caprifoliaceae.* One sp., native to cent. China, a showy, deciduous shrub resembling *Abelia;* lvs. opp., simple; fls. in pairs in terminal corymbs, the pair united at their bases, one inserted above the other, sepals 5, corolla campanulate, 5-lobed, stamens 4, ovary 3-celled; fr. dry, bristly.

Propagated by cuttings of green wood late in summer.

amabilis Graebn. BEAUTYBUSH. To 15 ft.; lvs. ovate, to 3 in. long; pedicels and sepals bristly, corolla pink with yellow throat, ½ in. long; fr. bristly, ¼ in. long. Late spring. Zone 6.

KOPSIA Blume. *Apocynaceae.* About 30 spp. of trees and shrubs with milky sap, native to trop. se. Asia; lvs. opp., entire, acuminate at each end, glabrous; fls. in cymes, 5-merous, bisexual, corolla salverform, tube long and inflated in upper part, pilose in throat, stamens borne on corolla, included, anthers lanceolate, acuminate, connivent about the stigma, ovaries 2, distinct, each with 2 ovules; fr. a leathery, 1-seeded drupelet.

arborea Blume. To 30 ft.; lvs. oblong-lanceolate to elliptic, to 7–9 in. long, thin, yellow-green above; cymes axillary and terminal, branched; corolla white, fragrant, 1 in. long, lobes lanceolate, nearly as long as tube; fr. ellipsoid, 1 in. long, purple-violet. Indonesia. Some material listed under this name is *Ochrosia elliptica.*

flavida Blume. Shrub or small tree; lvs. elliptic to oblong-lanceolate, to 9 in. long and 3½ in. wide, thin, intensely green above, yellower beneath; cymes few-fld.; corolla white, yellowish in throat, 2 in. across, tube 1½ in. long, lobes oblong and obtuse, about half as long as tube. New Guinea.

fruticosa A. DC. Shrub, to 20 ft.; lvs. elliptic to elliptic-lanceolate, to 8 in. long, caudate, thin, glossy above; cymes flat-topped; corolla pink with red throat, about 2 in. across, tube 1½ in. long; fr. usually solitary, to more than 1 in. long, urn-shaped, truncate at apex, greenish-purple. Malay Pen.

KOSTELETZKYA K. Presl. SEASHORE MALLOW. *Malvaceae.* About 25 spp. of herbs and subshrubs in N. and S. Amer., Afr., Madagascar, and Malay Arch.; lvs. unlobed or palmately lobed, often hastate; fls. solitary or in terminal racemes or panicles, involucral bracts 5–10(–13), rarely obsolete, petals white to yellowish, pink, or purplish, stamens united in a tubular column, the column mostly exserted, 5-toothed at apex, ovary 5-celled, each cell with 1 ovule, style brs. 5, stigmas capitate, expanded; fr. a depressed-globose, prominently 5-angled, loculicidally dehiscent caps.

Propagated by seeds or cuttings.

hastata: *K. pentasperma.*

pentasperma (Bertero ex DC.) Griseb. [*K. hastata* K. Presl]. Erect herb or subshrub, to 10 ft., more or less pubescent with simple and minutely stellate hairs; lvs. variable, uppermost lvs. often unlobed, hastate, lower lvs. often 3-, 5-, or 7-parted; fls. usually in panicles, involucral bracts and calyx less than $\frac{3}{16}$ in. long, petals $\frac{1}{2}$–$\frac{3}{4}$ in. long, white, yellowish, or purplish; caps. discoid, to $\frac{3}{8}$ in. across, hispid on angles. W. Indies to Mex. and n. S. Amer.

virginica (L.) K. Presl ex A. Gray. Rather scabrous, erect, per. herb to $4\frac{1}{2}$ ft.; lower lvs. 3- or 5-lobed, to 6 in. long, upper lvs. smaller, triangular-hastate; fls. solitary or in leafy panicles, involucral bracts linear, to $\frac{3}{8}$ in. long, usually slightly shorter than the calyx, petals to $1\frac{1}{2}$ in. long, pink, spreading; caps. about $\frac{3}{8}$ in. across, villous-hirsute. Summer. Coastal marshes, N.Y. to Fla., w. to La.

KRAINZIA: *MAMMILLARIA.*

KRAUSSIA Harv. *Rubiaceae.* Three or 4 spp. of shrubs, native to trop. and S. Afr.; lvs. opp.; fls. in axillary, few-branched panicles, corolla top-shaped to campanulate, tube short; fr. a 2-seeded berry.

floribunda Harv. [*Tricalysia floribunda* (Harv.) Stuntz; *T. Kraussiana* (C. Hochst.) Schinz]. Shrub or small tree, to 20 ft.; lvs. obovate-oblong or lanceolate, to 3 in. long; corolla white, tube $\frac{1}{4}$ in. long, lobes oblong, somewhat longer than tube; fr. globose, black, to $\frac{1}{4}$ in. across. Natal. Sometimes cult. in warm regions.

KRIGIA Schreb. DWARF DANDELION. *Compositae* (Cichorium Tribe). Seven or 8 spp. of ann. or per. herbs with milky sap, native to N. Amer.; lvs. mostly in a basal rosette, sometimes alt. or nearly opp. on the sts., entire to pinnatifid; fl. heads solitary or several, involucral bracts of equal length, in 1–2 rows, receptacle flat, naked; fls. all ligulate, bisexual, yellow or orange; achenes not beaked, pappus lacking or of 1 or 2 rows of scales or bristles.

biflora (Walt.) S. F. Blake. Per., to $2\frac{1}{2}$ ft.; lvs. chiefly basal, lanceolate to elliptic or oblanceolate, to 10 in. long, entire, toothed or runcinate- or lyrate-pinnatifid, sts. branched, with 1–3 clasping lvs.; heads several, to about $1\frac{1}{4}$ in. across; fls. orange-yellow. Mass. to Minn., s. to Ga. and Ark., sporadic in Colo. and New Mex.

bulbosa: a listed name of no botanical standing; perhaps for *K. Dandelion.*

Dandelion (L.) Nutt. Per., to 20 in.; lvs. all basal, linear-lanceolate, to 8 in. long, entire or few-lobed; scapes simple, leafless; heads solitary, to $1\frac{3}{8}$ in. across; fls. orange-yellow. N.J. to Mo., s. to Fla. and Tex.

montana (Michx.) Nutt. Per., to 16 in., sts. simple or branched, leafy; lvs. chiefly basal, linear to linear-spatulate, elongate, entire or pinnately lobed; heads 1–3, about $\frac{3}{4}$ in. across; fls. orange-yellow. Mts., N.C. and Tenn. to Ga.

KUHNIA L. *Compositae* (Eupatorium Tribe). Six spp. of per. herbs of the U.S. and Mex.; lvs. alt. to opp., resinous-dotted; fl. heads in terminal corymbs or solitary on long peduncles, discoid; fls. tubular, white, yellowish, or purple; achenes cylindrical, pappus of plumose, brownish bristles.

eupatorioides L. [*K. glutinosa* Ell.]. Sts. erect, to 4 ft., minutely pubescent; lvs. lanceolate, the lower petioled, dentate, the upper sessile, entire; heads $\frac{1}{2}$ in. long, 7–14-fld., corymbosely clustered; fls. cream or yellowish. Late summer. N.J., s. to Fla. and e. Tex. Var. **corymbulosa** Torr. & A. Gray [*K. Hitchcockii* A. Nels.]. Heads $\frac{5}{8}$ in. long, 14–30-fld. Ohio and Mont., s. to New Mex. and Tex.

glutinosa: *K. eupatorioides.*

Hitchcockii: *K. eupatorioides* var. *corymbulosa.*

KUNZEA Rchb. *Myrtaceae.* About 25–30 spp. of evergreen heathlike shrubs in Australia; lvs. alt., rarely opp., small, entire; fls. usually sessile, in terminal heads, calyx tube adnate to ovary at base, calyx lobes 5, small, petals 5, small, stamens many, longer than petals, separate, ovary inferior, 2–5-celled; fr. a caps. or rarely fleshy, crowned with persistent calyx lobes. Differs from *Leptospermum* in having stamens longer than the petals, from *Melaleuca* in having stamens separate and from *Callistemon* in having the calyx persistent.

ambigua (Sm.) Druce [*K. corifolia* (Venten.) Rchb.]. To 15 ft., shoots pubescent; lvs. crowded, linear to linear-lanceolate, $\frac{1}{4}$–$\frac{1}{2}$ in. long; fls. white, sessile, solitary in lf. axils of short brs., forming loose or dense spikes; caps. globose, about $\frac{1}{8}$ in. across. Se. Australia, Tasmania.

Baxteri (Klotzsch) Schauer. To 4 ft., stiff, shoots silky-hairy; lvs. linear-oblong, to $\frac{3}{4}$ in. long; fls. red, in bottlebrush infl. to 2 in. long, stamens red, to 1 in. long. W. Australia. Resembles *Callistemon* in showy red fls.

corifolia: *K. ambigua.*

ericifolia Rchb. To 15 ft., shoots pubescent; lvs. linear, to $\frac{1}{4}$ in. long; fls. yellow, in dense globular heads. W. Australia.

micrantha Schauer. To 10 ft.; lvs. rigid, linear or linear-cuneate, to $\frac{3}{8}$ in. long; fls. blue or purple, many in dense globular heads. W. Australia.

pomifera F. J. Muell. Small shrub, sts. prostrate, sometimes rooting; lvs. ovate or rounded, to $\frac{1}{4}$ in. long, mucronate; fls. white, few in dense globose heads, calyx tube becoming enlarged and somewhat fleshy in fr.; fr. berrylike, to $\frac{3}{8}$ in. across, purplish when mature. The frs. called muntries, are used for preserves and tarts. Se. Australia.

recurva Schauer. To 6 ft., many-stemmed and spreading to 8 ft. across; lvs. flexible, ovate, to $\frac{1}{4}$ in. long, slightly recurved; fls. pink, many in globular heads at the ends of most brs. W. Australia.

rosea: a listed name of no botanical standing.

sericea (Labill.) Turcz. To 12 ft.; lvs. stiff, obovate, acute, to $\frac{1}{2}$ in. long, gray-green, silvery when young; fls. rose-red, polygamous, the bisexual solitary, the male in terminal clusters with red stamens $\frac{1}{2}$–$\frac{3}{4}$ in. long. W. Australia.

KYDIA Roxb. *Bombacaceae.* One variable sp. or perhaps up to 5 spp. of stellate-pubescent, monoecious trees, native from Sikkim to Indochina; lvs. simple, palmately nerved, usually palmately lobed; fls. in panicles or rarely solitary, involucral bracts 4–6, united basally, becoming larger, leaflike, and spreading in fr., male fls. with a short staminal tube with 5–6 slender divisions at the apex, each with 2–5 sessile, reniform anthers, the rudimentary pistil included in the tube, female fls. with 3-branched style longer than the sterile staminal column, each style br. with a fringed, peltate stigma, ovary with 2 ovules in each cell, usually only one maturing; fr. a 3-celled caps.

Propagated by seeds or cuttings.

calycina Roxb. Arborescent shrub, or tree to 50 ft.; lvs. nearly circular, up to 6 in. long, cordate, shallowly palmately lobed; fls. in panicles, involucral bracts about $\frac{1}{4}$ in. long at flowering, to nearly 1 in. long in fr., petals white or pink, obcordate, fringed, less than $\frac{1}{2}$ in. long; caps. $\frac{1}{4}$ in. in diam. Sometimes grown in Fla.; flowering in autumn and often again in spring.

LABIATAE Juss. or, alternatively, **LAMIACEAE** Barnh. MINT FAMILY. Dicot.; about 180 genera and 3,500 spp. of herbs and shrubs, of worldwide distribution, but chiefly of the Medit. region; sts. mostly square in cross section; lvs. 4-ranked, simple, without stipules, mostly with glands secreting pungent, volatile oils; fls. irregular, in cymes in the axils of opp. bracts or lvs., forming false whorls (verticillasters), arranged in a simple or compound infl., sometimes subtended by bractlets, calyx 4–5-lobed, 2-lipped, persistent, corolla 4–6-lobed, usually 2-lipped, stamens 4, rarely 2, inserted on corolla, ovary superior, carpels 2, deeply lobed, style 1, from central depression of lobes, stigma nearly 2-lobed; fr. of 4 one-seeded nutlets. The cult. genera, grown chiefly as ornamentals or as sweet herbs, are: *Acinos, Acrocephalus, Agastache, Ajuga, Amethystea, Ballota, Blephilia, Calamintha, Cedronella, Clinopodium, Coleus, Collinsonia, Colquhounia, Conradina, Cunila, Dracocephalum,*

Elsholtzia, Eremostachys, Galeopsis, Glechoma, Hedeoma, Hemiandra, Horminum, Hyptis, Hyssopus, Iboza, Lallemantia, Lamiastrum, Lamium, Lavandula, Leonotis, Leonurus, Lepechinia, Lycopus, Marrubium, Meehania, Melissa, Mentha, Micromeria, Moluccella, Monarda, Monardella, Nepeta, Ocimum, Origanum, Perilla, Perovskia, Phlomis, Physostegia, Plectranthus, Prostanthera, Prunella, Pycnanthemum, Pycnostachys, Rosmarinus, Salazaria, Salvia, Satureja, Scutellaria, Sideritis, Solenostemon, Stachys, Teucrium, Thymbra, Thymus, Tinnea, Trichostema, and *Westringia.*

The volatile oils of certain species are of economic importance: distilled oils and perfumes for industry are obtained from *Lavandula, Mentha, Pogostemon* Desf., *Rosmarinus,* etc.; and *Perilla, Ocimum, Origanum, Salvia, Thymus,* and others are used as sweet herbs. Tubers of *Stachys* are edible.

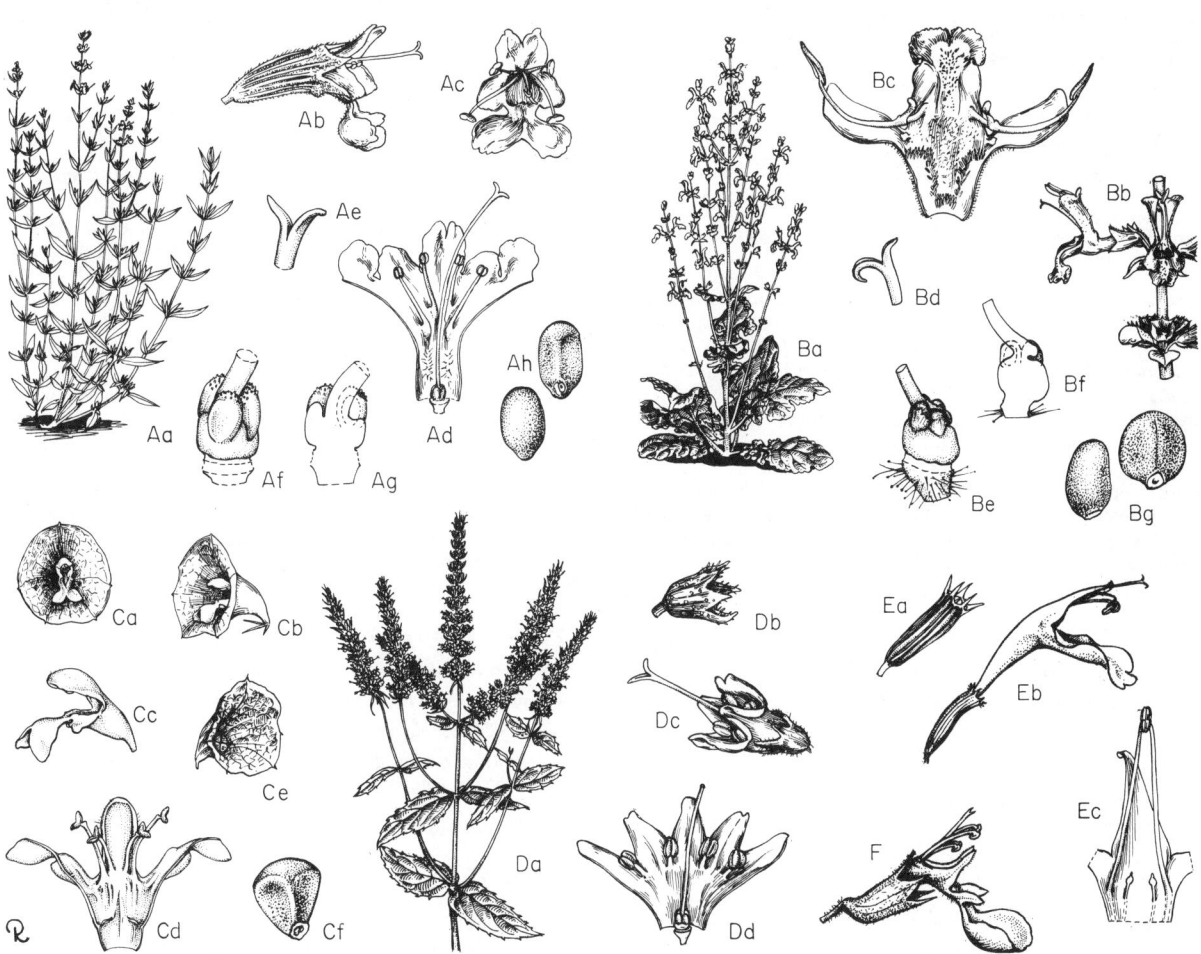

LABIATAE. **A,** *Hyssopus officinalis:* **Aa,** plant, × ⅛; **Ab,** flower, side view, × 3; **Ac,** flower, face view, × 3; **Ad,** flower, corolla expanded, × 3; **Ae,** stigma, × 10; **Af,** base of pistil, × 10; **Ag,** base of pistil, vertical section, × 10; **Ah,** nutlets, two views, × 5. **B,** *Salvia Forskaohlei:* **Ba,** plant, × ¹⁄₁₆; **Bb,** two verticillasters, × ½; **Bc,** corolla, expanded, × 1; **Bd,** stigma, × 6; **Be,** base of pistil, × 5; **Bf,** base of pistil, vertical section, × 5; **Bg,** nutlets, two views, × 5. **C,** *Molucella laevis:* **Ca,** flower, face view, × ½; **Cb,** flower, three-quarter side view, × ½; **Cc,** corolla, × 1; **Cd,** corolla, expanded, × 1; **Ce,** fruit within calyx, × ½; **Cf,** nutlet, × 3. **D,** *Mentha spicata:* **Da,** inflorescence, × ½; **Db,** calyx, × 8; **Dc,** flower, × 5; **Dd,** flower, corolla expanded, × 5. **E,** *Monarda didyma:* **Ea,** calyx, × 1½; **Eb,** flower, × 1; **Ec,** segment of corolla, expanded to show stamens and staminodes, × 1. **F,** *Teucrium Chamaedrys:* flower, × 2. (B, species representative of *Salvia,* but not in general cultivation; Eb, F from Bailey, *Manual of Cultivated Plants,* ed. 2.)

+LABURNOCYTISUS C. K. Schneid.: *Cytisus* + *Laburnum. Leguminosae* (subfamily *Faboideae*). One sort of graft chimera produced by grafting *Cytisus* on *Laburnum;* prop. by grafting on *Laburnum anagyroides.*

Adamii (Poit.) C. K. Schneid. [*Laburnum* + *Adamii* (Poit.) Lavall.]: *Cytisus purpureus* + *Laburnum anagyroides.* Small tree, often producing brs. of *Laburnum anagyroides* with yellow fls., more rarely of *Cytisus purpureus;* similar to *Laburnum anagyroides,* but lfts. smaller, nearly glabrous, racemes smaller, nodding, and fls. usually dull purplish.

LABURNUM Medic. BEAN TREE. *Leguminosae* (subfamily *Faboideae*). Four spp. of ornamental trees and shrubs of the Old World; lvs. alt., of 3 lfts.; fls. in terminal racemes, yellow, papilionaceous, petals all separate, stamens 10, united; fr. a flat legume.

Laburnums are mostly hardy north. Propagated by seeds and layering, and cultivars by grafting and budding on seedling stocks.

Adamii: +*Laburnocytisus Adamii.*

alpinum (Mill.) Bercht. & J. Presl [*Cytisus alpinus* Mill.]. SCOTCH L. To 30 ft.; racemes to 15 in. long, pendent; fr. with thin wing on one margin. Early summer. S. Eur. Forma **pendulum** (Loud.) Kirchn. Brs. pendent.

anagyroides Medic. [*L. vulgare* Bercht. & J. Presl]. GOLDEN-CHAIN. To 30 ft.; lfts. elliptic-obovate to -oblong, to 3 in. long; racemes pendent, 4–8 in. long; fls. ¾ in. long; fr. 2 in. long, thickened on one margin, pubescent. Late spring. Cent. and s. Eur. All parts of plant poisonous, particularly the seeds. Cv. **'Pendulum'** [var. *pendulum* (Bosse) Rehd.]. Brs. pendent.

×**Vossii:** a listed name of no botanical standing for *L.* ×*Watereri* cv.

vulgare: *L. anagyroides.*

×**Watereri** (Kirchn.) Dipp.: *L. alpinum* × *L. anagyroides.* GOLDEN-CHAIN TREE. Intermediate between parents; lower surface of lfts., racemes, and fr. sparingly pubescent; racemes long, slender, to 10 in. long; fr. rarely developed, with narrow wing, few-seeded. Cv. **'Vossii'** [*L.* × *Vosii* Hort.] is listed.

LACCOSPADIX Drude & H. Wendl. *Palmae.* One sp., a cespitose, unarmed, monoecious palm in trop. e. Australia; lvs. pinnate, sheaths not forming a crownshaft, pinnae 1-ribbed, acuminate; infl. solitary, among lvs., long-peduncled, spicate, bearing 2 thin bracts, the upper cylindrical, inserted at apex of peduncle, the lower short, basal, rachillae with fls. in triads (2 male and 1 female) sunken in pits; male fls. with sepals imbricate, petals valvate, stamens 9–12, filaments erect, pistillode minute, female fls. with sepals and petals imbricate, ovary 1-celled; fr. red, ellipsoid, stigmatic residue apical, endocarp not operculate, seed with ruminate endosperm and basal embryo.

For culture see *Palms.*

australasica H. Wendl. & Drude. To 12 ft., in dense clumps; lvs. long-petioled with dark green, regularly arranged pinnae; infl. pendulous; male fls. dirty yellow.

LACHENALIA Jacq.f. ex J. Murr. CAPE COWSLIP. *Liliaceae.* About 50 spp. of small, scapose, bulbous, per. herbs, native to S. Afr.; bulbs tunicate; lvs. basal, usually 2, often spotted; fls. mostly white, yellow, or red, in terminal spikes or racemes, perianth cylindrical to campanulate, segms. 6, united basally, stamens 6, attached to perianth tube, anthers versatile; fr. a 3-angled, loculicidal caps.

Lachenalias should be potted in rich loam in Aug. and kept in coldframe until the last of Nov., when they should be removed to a greenhouse with a night temperature of 50° F. After flowering they should be placed in a light place and watered until the foliage has ripened, after which they should be kept dry and dark until repotted. Propagated by offsets and seeds.

aloides (L.f.) Hort. ex Asch. & Graebn. [*L. tricolor* Jacq.f.]. To 1 ft.; lvs. usually 2, lanceolate-strap-shaped, to 1 in. wide, often spotted; fls. 3–12, to 1 in. long, drooping, yellow, tipped with red, outer segms. much shorter than inner. Cvs. are: **'Aurea'** [*L. aurea* Lindl.], fls. bright orange-yellow; **'Conspicua'**, fls. orange, with purple margins and yellow-red tips; **'Luteola'** [*L. luteola* Jacq.], fls. lemon-yellow, tipped with green; **'Nelsonii'** [*L. Nelsonii* Hort.], fls. bright yellow, tinged green; **'Quadricolor'** [*L. quadricolor* Jacq.], fls. red at base, greenish-yellow in middle, outer segms. tipped with green, inner with red-purple.

aurea: *L. aloides* cv.

Bachmannii Bak. To 10 in.; lvs. usually only 2, linear, 4–8 in. long, folded lengthwise; fls. campanulate, to ¼ in. long, in dense, more or less spicate raceme to 2 in. long, segms. oblong, white with red keel.

bulbiferum (Cyr.) Hort. ex Asch. & Graebn. [*L. pendula* Ait.]. To 1 ft., robust; lvs. 2, linear-lanceolate, to 1 ft. long and 2 in. wide, occasionally spotted; fls. cylindrical, to 1½ in. long, drooping, in a few- to many-fld. raceme, outer segms. yellow, red toward apex, slightly shorter than the red-purple inner segms. Cv. **'Superba'** [*L. pendula* Ait. var. *superba* Hort.]. An improved form.

contaminata Ait. To 8 in.; lvs. 6–10, channelled, cylindrical in the terminal half, to 9 in. long, nearly erect; fls. many, white, broadly campanulate, to ¼ in. long, in dense racemes, inner segms. tipped greenish-brown, outer segms. often flushed red, with apical swellings, shorter than inner segms.

glaucina Jacq. To 16 in.; lvs. usually 2, lanceolate, to 11 in. long and 1 in. wide, frequently spotted; fls. many, white, tinged with iridescent blue, red, yellow, or green, to ¾ in. long, sessile, spreading, inner segms. spreading at apex, slightly longer than outer segms.

juncifolia Bak. To 6 in.; lvs. 2, channelled, nearly cylindrical, to 8 in. long and 3/16 in. in diam.; fls. 6–12, oblong-campanulate, white tinged red, 3/16 in. long, inner and outer segms. of equal length, stamens exserted.

liliflora Jacq. To 1 ft.; lvs. 2, lanceolate, curved, to 9 in. long and 1 in. wide, heavily pustulate on upper surface; fls. 12–20, white, oblong-cylindrical, to ¾ in. long, with spreading segms., in more or less spicate racemes.

luteola: *L. aloides* cv.

mediana Jacq. To 16 in.; lvs. 1 or 2, strap-shaped, to 1 ft. long, erect, channelled; fls. many, spreading, tubular, to 5/16 in. long, greenish-white, iridescent, outer segms. oblong, with pale blue basal blotch and a purple apical swelling, inner segms. wedge-shaped, with small reddish apical blotch, all obtuse.

mutabilis Lodd. To 1 ft.; lvs. usually 2, lanceolate, to 1¾ in. wide, bright green; fls. many, the upper ones abortive, in an elongated, loose raceme, sky-blue in bud, outer segms. pale blue, inner segms. greenish-yellow, aging crimson-brown, apex with purple blotch.

Nelsonii: *L. aloides* cv.

orchioides (L.) Ait. To 14 in.; lvs. 1 or 2, lanceolate, to ¾ in. wide, frequently spotted; fls. many, 5/16 in. long, pink, white, yellow, or blue-green, iridescent, almost sessile, outer segms. blue to blue-green, inner segms. cream-colored, tinged mauve, apex recurved.

orthopetala Jacq. To 10 in.; lvs. 4–5, linear-subulate, to 6 in. long, channelled; fls. many, oblong, ½ in. long, white or tinged red, in dense more or less spicate racemes, inner segms. slightly longer than outer, style exserted.

pallida Ait. To 10 in.; lvs. 2, lanceolate, to 9 in. long and 1¼ in. wide, pustulate or blistered; fls. campanulate, white, to ¼ in. long, in rather dense racemes, outer segms. green-tipped, slightly shorter than the inner.

Pearsonii: a listed name of no botanical standing.

pendula: *L. bulbiferum.*

Piersonii: a listed name of no botanical standing.

quadricolor: *L. aloides* cv.

reflexa Thunb. To 6 in., or rarely taller; lvs. 2, lanceolate or strap-shaped, to 6 in. long and 1¼ in. wide, bright green, spreading, reflexed; fls. few, 1 in. long, erect, yellowish-green, in a short spike, perianth tube swollen, oblique, inner segms. slightly longer than outer.

tricolor: *L. aloides.*

LACHNANTHES Elliott [*Gyrotheca* Salisb.]. *Haemodoraceae.* One sp., a stout, per. herb growing in swamps from Mass. to Fla. and Cuba; fls. in dense, white-woolly panicles to 5 in. across, stamens 3, exserted, ovary inferior.

Sometimes transplanted to wild gardens.

caroliana (Lam.) Dandy [*L. tinctoria* (Walt.) Elliott]. REDROOT, PAINT ROOT, DYE ROOT. To 2½ ft., rhizomes with red sap, roots red, fibrous; lvs. linear, upper lvs. reduced to bracts, lower lvs. shorter than sts.; fls. yellowish.

tinctoria: *L. caroliana.*

LACTUCA L. [*Cicerbita* Wallr.; *Mulgedium* Cass.]. LETTUCE. *Compositae* (Cichorium Tribe). Between 50 and 90 spp. of ann., bien., or per. herbs with milky sap, widely distributed, particularly in the N. Hemisphere; lvs. alt. on the sts., the early lvs. sometimes in a basal rosette, entire to pinnatifid; fl. heads small, in irregular panicles, involucral bracts imbricate in several rows, receptacle flat, pitted, naked; fls. all ligulate, yellow, pink, blue, or white; achenes compressed, ribbed, often beaked, pappus deciduous, of soft, white, capillary hairs.

A few species rather uncommonly cultivated in this country as ornamentals, but lettuce is a commonly cultivated garden vegetable. Propagated by seeds.

alpina (L.) A. Gray [*Mulgedium alpinum* (L.) Less.]. MOUNTAIN SOW THISTLE. Stout, erect per., to 6 ft., bristly below, with dense reddish-glandular hairs in upper part; lower lvs. lyrate- to runcinate-pinnatifid, with a broadly triangular terminal lobe and few smaller lobes, lvs. successively reduced upward, glabrous and more or less glaucous beneath; heads to ¾ in. across, involucral bracts in 2 rows, purplish-green, glandular-hairy; fls. pale blue; achenes not beaked. Arctic and alpine Eur.

Bourgaei (Boiss.) Irish & N. Tayl. [*Mulgedium Bourgaei* Boiss.]. Thick-stemmed per., to 6 ft.; lvs. oblong-lanceolate, lyrate, with terminal segm. largest, bristly; heads small, panicled, involucral bracts pinkish; fls. lilac. Asia Minor.

perennis L. Erect, glabrous per., to 2 ft.; lvs. oblanceolate, pinnatifid, with linear segms., st. lvs. clasping; heads to 1⅜ in. across, in corymbose panicles; fls. light blue or pale violet; achenes black with white beak. S. Eur.

Plumieri (L.) Gren. & Godr. Stout per., to 4 ft., glabrous throughout; lvs. lyrate-pinnatifid, to 16 in. long, glaucous beneath; heads to 1 in. across, in a loose corymb; fls. blue; achenes grayish. Mts., cent. Eur.

sativa L. GARDEN LETTUCE. Ann. or bien., to 3 ft.; lvs. in a basal rosette before flowering, to 10 in. long, entire or runcinate-pinnatifid, st. lvs. ovate to orbicular, entire, glabrous, sessile; heads less than ½ in. across, many in a dense corymbose panicle; fls. pale yellow; achenes straw-colored or black, with white beak. Not known in the wild. An old and widely grown salad plant, with many cvs., mostly in the groups known as the COS or ROMAINE LETTUCES, with upright, oblong to obovate lvs. to 1 ft. long, with very broad midribs; the CURLED LETTUCES, with a nonheading, loose rosette of fringed or crisped lvs.; and the HEAD or CABBAGE LETTUCES, with a dense rosette of lvs. forming a cabbagelike head. See *Lettuce*.

Scariola: *L. Serriola*.

Serriola L. [*L. Scariola* L.]. PRICKLY LETTUCE. Bien. or winter ann., to 5 ft., often prickly-bristly below, glabrous in upper part; lvs. oblong or oblong-oblanceolate, to 8 in. long, lobed or pinnatifid, saggitate-clasping, glabrous, margins spiny-ciliate, main veins prickly beneath; heads to ½ in. across, many in a pyramidal panicle, involucral bracts glaucous-green, with purple tips; fls. yellow; achenes olive-gray with white beak. Eur.; generally distributed as a weed in most parts of the world.

LAELIA Lindl. *Orchidaceae*. About 30 spp. of epiphytes, native to Cent. and S. Amer.; pseudobulbs 1–2-lvd.; lvs. folded lengthwise, fleshy; infl. terminal, 1- to few-fld.; fls. often showy, sepals and petals spreading, petals often wider than sepals, lip simple or 3-lobed, the lateral lobes enclosing the footless column, pollinia 8. For structure of fl. see *Orchidaceae*.

Intermediate greenhouse. For culture see *Orchids*.

acuminata: *L. rubescens*.

albida Batem. ex Lindl. Pseudobulbs ovoid, 2-lvd., to 2 in. long; lvs. to 7 in. long, lanceolate; raceme terminal, erect, 3–9-fld.; fls. to 2 in. across, fragrant, white, often tinged with rose, sepals ovate-lanceolate, petals ovate, lip 3-lobed, pale to deep rose-pink, with 3 yellow crests down center. Autumn–winter. Mex. Cv. **'Rosea'**. Differing from typical form in having the margins of petals and midlobe of lip flushed with rose, lateral lobes of lip red-dotted toward base.

anceps Lindl. Pseudobulbs oblong-compressed, to 5 in. long; lvs. 1–2, lanceolate, to 7 in. long; infl. racemose, 2–5-fld., to 3 ft. long; fls. to 4 in. across, long-lasting, sepals and petals spreading, ovate-lanceolate, petals broader, rose-lilac, lip 3-lobed, deep purple, lateral lobes broad, semiovate, yellow, marked with deep red lines, midlobe strap-shaped, emarginate in front. Late autumn–winter. Mex. Cvs. are: **'Alba'**, fls. pure white, except for pale yellow spot in throat; **'Amesiana'** [var. *Amesiana* O'Brien], fls. white with delicate pink blush on outer half of segms., sepals emerald-green at tips, petals with a crimson-feathered pattern toward tips; **'Ashworthiana'**, fls. white, lip with lilac venation in throat, midlobe pencilled sparingly with lilac; **'Ballantiniana'**, sepals and petals tipped with deep rose; **'Barkerana'** [var. *Barkerana* Lindl.], sepals and petals deep purplish-rose, lip shorter and narrower than in typical form, intense magenta-purple with yellow disc; **'Chamberlainiana'**, fls. larger than in typical form, lip deep crimson-purple; **'Dawsonii'** [var. *Dawsonii* J. Anderson], sepals and petals white, lip with radiating purple lines, and with yellow crest under column; **'Delicata'**, scapes 4–6-fld., sepals and petals white, stained with rosy-purple, lip white, suffused with reddish-purple, shaded with violet, throat orange-yellow; **'Grandiflora'** [var. *grandiflora* L. O. Williams], fls. to twice as large as in typical form; **'Hilliana'** [var. *Hilliana* Rchb.f.], sepals and petals white, lip yellowish, 3-lobed, lobes with pastel pink tips; **'Holochila'** [var. *holochila* Rolfe], lip entire, elliptic-lanceolate, to 2 in. long, ¾ in. wide, light purple, disc white with some yellow at base, sepals and petals pale lilac, almost identical; **'Percivaliana'** [var. *Percivaliana* Rchb.f.], lvs. narrower and more pointed than in typical form, fls. blush-pink, lip 3-lobed, midlobe truncate, apical ⅓ bright purple-magenta, basal ⅔ white, disc light orange; **'Rosea'** [var. *rosea* Rchb.f.], fls. pale rose, lip large, bright rosy-magenta, throat pale yellow, dark red lines lacking; **'Sanderana'** [var. *Sanderana* Rchb.f.], fls. white, petals not as broad as in typical form; **'Schroederana'** [var. *Schroederana* Rchb.f.], fls. large, white, lip broad, streaked on inside with forked purplish-crimson lines, midlobe with raised orange-colored disc; **'Scottiana'** [var. *Scottiana* Warner & B. S. Williams], the darkest-colored form, fls. to 5 in. across, sepals and petals deep violet-purple, lip deep purple with orange throat; **'Stella'** [var. *Stella* Rchb.f.], sepals, petals, and lip white outside, lateral lobes of lip pale yellow, diagonally veined with dull, pale purple, disc yellow; **'Veitchiana** [var. *Veitchiana'* Rchb.f.], fls. white, suffused with lilac, petals 1 in. across at center, lateral lobes of lip violet-purple; **'Williamsii'** [var. *Williamsii* Hort. Sander], fls. white, lip with yellow disc and yellow throat striped with crimson-purple.

autumnalis Lindl. [*L. Gouldiana* Rchb. f.]. Pseudobulbs to 6 in. long, 2–3-lvd.; lvs. leathery, to 7 in. long; infl. to 2½ ft. long, 4–9-fld.; fls. to 4 in. across, rose-purple, sepals lanceolate, petals lanceolate-elliptic, lip white basally, 3-lobed, lateral lobes ovate, midlobe elliptic, disc 2-keeled. Autumn–spring. Mex. Cvs. include: **'Alba'**, fls. pure white; **'Atrorubens'** [var. *atrorubens* Backh.], fls. deep rose or magenta; **'Fournieri'** [var. *Fournieri* André], fls. to 7 in. across, sepals and petals purple-red, lip white, midlobe purple-red; **'Venusta'**, in habit similar to cv. 'Atrorubens', fls. large, rosy-mauve. Var. **furfuracea** (Lindl.) Rolfe [*L. furfuracea* Lindl.]. Dwarf alpine; petals usually broad.

Boothiana: *L. lobata*.

cinnabarina Batem. Pseudobulbs cylindrical, to 10 in. long, 1–2-lvd.; lvs. leathery, to 10 in. long; infl. erect, to 20 in. high; fls. 4–5, reddish-orange, to 2½ in. across, sepals and petals similar, lanceolate, lip narrow, 3-lobed, lateral lobes enclosing column. Spring, late autumn. Brazil. Var. **crispilabia:** *L. crispilabia*.

×**Crawshayana** Rchb.f. A natural hybrid, possibly *L. anceps* × *L. autumnalis* or *L. albida* × *L. anceps;* pseudobulbs and lvs. as in *L. albida;* scape few-fld., as long as in *L. anceps*, with shorter, narrower sheaths; sepals and petals narrower than in *L. anceps*, of fine amethyst color, lip rich purple at apex, throat yellow, veined with purple, 3-keeled.

crispa (Lindl.) Rchb.f. Pseudobulbs to 10 in. long, l-lvd.; lf. to 1 ft. long; infl. to 1 ft. long, 4–7-fld.; fls. white, to 6 in. across, petals and lip crisped, sepals and petals lanceolate, petals broader, lip with purple margin and yellow throat, ovate-lanceolate, obscurely 3-lobed. Summer, early winter. Brazil.

crispilabia A. Rich. ex Rchb.f. [*L. cinnabarina* var. *crispilabia* (A. Rich ex Rchb.f.) Hort. Veitch]. Pseudobulbs cylindrical, dilated toward base, 1-lvd.; lvs. fleshy; infl. to 14 in. long, racemose, loosely fld.; fls. amethyst-purple, to 2 in. across, sepals and petals lanceolate, similar, lip 3-lobed, lateral lobes semiovate, midlobe ovate, white, with crisped amethyst margins, recurved. Late summer. Brazil.

Dayana: *L. pumila* var.

Digbyana: *Rhyncholaelia Digbyana*.

elegans: × *Laeliocattleya elegans*.

flava Lindl. Pseudobulbs to 8 in. long, 1-lvd.; lvs. to 5 in. long; infl. to 1½ ft., erect; fls. 4–8, bright yellow, to 2½ in. across, sepals and petals strap-shaped, lip 3-lobed, not longer than petals, midlobe recurved, crisped, disc 4-keeled. Late summer–late winter. Brazil.

furfuracea: *L. autumnalis* var.

glauca: *Rhyncholaelia glauca*.

Gouldiana: *L. autumnalis*.

grandiflora: *L. speciosa*.

grandis Lindl. & Paxt. Pseudobulbs to 1 ft. long, 1-lvd.; lvs. to 10 in. long; infl. to 7 in. high, 3–5-fld.; fls. 4–7 in. across, sepals and petals brownish-yellow, lip white, veined with rose-purple. Late spring–summer. Brazil. Var. **tenebrosa** Gower [*L. tenebrosa* (Gower) Rolfe]. Sepals and petals citron-yellow, lip trumpet-shaped, purple, margin white with purple venation.

×**harpophylla** Rchb.f. A natural hybrid; pseudobulbs to 1½ ft. long, 1-lvd.; lvs. to 8 in. long; infl. shorter than lvs., 3–7-fld.; fls. to 3 in. across, vermilion, sepals and petals similar, lanceolate, lip yellow edged with white at apex, 3-lobed, lateral lobes semiovate, acuminate, midlobe linear-lanceolate, crisped on margins.

Humboldtii: *Schomburgkia Humboldtii.*

Lindleyana: ×*Brassocattleya Lindleyana.*

lobata (Lindl.) Hort. Veitch [*L. Boothiana* Rchb.f.; *Cattleya lobata* Lindl.]. Pseudobulbs to 8 in. long, 1-lvd.; lvs. leathery, to 10 in. long; infl. to 20 in. long, 2–5-fld.; fls. about 5 in. across, rose-purple with deeper colored veins, sepals linear-lanceolate, petals ovate, with minutely crenate margins, lip ovate, somewhat 3-lobed, with prominent veins. Spring. Brazil.

longipes Rchb.f. Pseudobulbs short, ovoid, 1-lvd.; lvs. small, erect; infl. terminal, 2–4-fld., longer than lvs.; fls. to 2 in. across, sepals and petals similar, rose-magenta, lip 3-lobed, orange-yellow, margins undulate-crisped. Late summer–early winter. Brazil.

Lundii Rchb.f. & Warm. ex Rchb.f. [*L. Regnellii* Rodr.]. Pseudobulbs spaced on the rhizome, ovoid, 2-lvd.; lvs. fleshy, semicylindrical, pointed; infl. terminal from leafless new growth, short, few-fld., racemose; fls. delicate, to 1½ in. across, sepals and petals similar, linear-lanceolate, lavender or pale magenta, lip 3-lobed, pale yellow with dark purple veins and spot in throat, lateral lobes enfolding column, midlobe nearly orbicular, crisped. Early summer. Brazil.

Lyonsii: *Schomburgkia Lyonsii.*

majalis: *L. speciosa.*

monophylla: *Neocogniauxia monophylla.*

Perrinii (Lindl.) Lindl. Pseudobulbs to 1 ft. long, 1-lvd.; lvs. to 14 in. long; infl. to 5 in. long, few-fld.; fls. about 5 in. across, sepals and petals linear-oblong, rose-lilac, petals somewhat broader, lip purple-crimson in front, straw-yellow at throat, obscurely 3-lobed, lateral lobes enveloping column, midlobe elliptic, undulate. Autumn. Brazil.

praestans: *L. pumila* cv. 'Major'.

pumila (Hook.) Rchb.f. Pseudobulbs to 4 in. long, 1-lvd.; lvs. to 4 in. long; infl. to 3 in. long, 1-fld.; fls. drooping, rose-purple, to 4 in. across, sepals oblong-linear, recurved, petals narrowly ovate, lip tubular, deep purple with yellow throat. Autumn. Brazil. Cv. 'Alba'. Fls. white with yellow throat. Cv. 'Dayana' [var. *Dayana* (Rchb.f.) Burb. ex Dean; *L. Dayana* Rchb. f.]. Sepals and petals rose-purple, lip with deep purple margin. Cv. 'Major' [var. *major* Lem.; *L. praestans* Rchb. f.]. Fls. larger than in typical form, segms. broader, lip rich purple. Cv. 'Marginata'. Sepals and petals rose-crimson, lip with white border.

purpurata Lindl. Pseudobulbs to 18 in. long, 1-lvd.; lvs. to 16 in. long; infl. to 1 ft. long, 3–7-fld.; fls. fleshy, to 8 in. across, white to pale rose, sepals oblong-lanceolate, petals ovate-rhombic, undulate, with revolute margins, lip elliptic-ovate, purple in front, throat yellow with purple venation. Spring. Brazil. Cvs. include: 'Alba', fls. white; 'Ashworthiana' [var. *Ashworthiana* Andresen], petals wider than in typical form, to 2 in. wide, purplish-rose with darker stripes; 'Atropurpurea' [var. *atropurpurea* B. S. Williams], sepals and petals deep rose, lip large, purple-magenta, throat yellow with purple venation; 'Carnea', fls. white, lip with rose-carmine markings; 'Mandaiana', pseudobulbs narrower than in typical form, fls. white with tinge of pink on lip; 'Nelisii' [var. *Nelisii* Lem.], sepals and petals rose, midlobe of lip ovate, acute; 'Praetexta' [var. *praetexta* Rchb.f.], fls. white, lip purple, throat yellow with purple venation, midlobe white at apex; 'Purpurea', fls. red-purple; 'Rosea' [var. *rosea* Regel], sepals and petals white, suffused with rose along midrib, lip clear rose; 'Russelliana' [var. *Russelliana* B. S. Williams], fls. larger than in typical form, sepals suffused with lilac, petals broader, deeper lilac, lip rose-lilac, throat yellow with rose venation; 'Schroederi' [var. *Schroederi* Rchb.f.], fls. white, lip tinged with rose at center, throat pale yellow with fine purple venation; 'Werkhauseri', fls. white, lip with deep bluish-violet marking, throat yellowish with bluish venation.

Regnellii: *L. Lundii.*

rubescens Lindl. [*L. acuminata* Lindl.]. Pseudobulbs ovate, to 2½ in. long, usually 1-lvd.; lvs. to 5 in. long; infl. to 1 ft. long, racemose, 2–8-fld.; fls. fragrant, to 2 in. across, white to rose-purple, sepals linear-lanceolate, petals ovate-lanceolate, lip dark purple at base, obscurely 3-lobed, lateral lobes enveloping column, midlobe ovate. Mex. and Cent. Amer.

rupestris Lindl. Pseudobulbs to 4 in. long, 1-lvd.; lvs. 4–5 in. long; infl. to 10 in. long, 2–4-fld.; fls. fleshy, purplish-violet, to 1½ in. across, sepals and petals similar, oblong-ovate, lip nearly orbicular in outline, 3-lobed, lateral lobes semiovate, midlobe round, undulate-crisped. Winter–summer. Brazil.

speciosa (HBK) Schlechter [*L. grandiflora* Lindl.; *L. majalis* Lindl.]. Pseudobulbs to 2 in. long, 1-lvd.; lvs. to 6 in. long; infl. as long as lvs., 1- or rarely 2-fld.; fls. showy, rose-lilac, to 5 in. across, sepals obovate-lanceolate, petals ovate-rhombic, undulate, lip 3-lobed, lateral lobes small, white, streaked with lilac, midlobe round, large, white at center, shading to lilac at margins, spotted with dark lilac. Late spring. Mex. Cv. 'Alba'. Fls. pure white.

superbiens: *Schomburgkia superbiens.*

tenebrosa: *L. grandis* var.

Thomsoniana: *Schomburgkia Thomsoniana.*

tibicinis: *Schomburgkia tibicinis.*

undulata: *Schomburgkia undulata.*

virens: *L. xanthina.*

xanthina Lindl. [*L. virens* Lindl.]. Pseudobulbs elongate, 1-lvd.; lvs. fleshy, to 12 in. long; infl. erect, 3–5-fld.; fls. to 3 in. across, fleshy, ochre-yellow, sepals and petals similar, oblong-strap-shaped, spreading, lip white, streaked with crimson-purple on disc, ovate-elliptic, with sides upcurved and parallel with column. Summer. Brazil.

×**LAELIOCATTLEYA** Rolfe: *Cattleya* × *Laelia.* *Orchidaceae.* A group of mostly artificial bigeneric hybrids generally intermediate in character between the parents.

For culture see *Orchids.*

Canhamiana Rolfe: *Cattleya Mossiae* × *Laelia purpurata.* Infl. 1- to several-fld.; fls. to 4 in. across, sepals and petals lavender or pale lilac, lip of same color but with darker veins and markings.

Charlesworthii Hort.: *Cattleya Dowiana* × *Laelia cinnabarina.* Infl. several-fld.; fls. to 3 in. across, sepals and petals linear-oblong, of varying shades of orange-red or vermilion, lip 3-lobed, undulate, darker, with yellow markings on disc.

Dormaniana (Rchb.f.) Rolfe: *Cattleya bicolor* × *Laelia pumila.* Pseudobulbs stemlike, 2-lvd.; lvs. leathery, opp., to 5 in. long; infl. short, 1-fld.; fls. showy, to 4 in. across, sepals and petals similar, ovate-oblong, dark green with bronze suffusion along the margins, dotted with dark maroon, lip 3-lobed, rose with darker veins, midlobe kidney-shaped, dark magenta, disc with yellow spot.

elegans (C. Morr.) Rolfe [*Laelia elegans* (C. Morr.) Rchb.f.]: *Cattleya Leopoldii* × *Laelia purpurata.* Pseudobulbs stemlike, 1-lvd.; lvs. fleshy, to 10 in. long; infl. short, few-fld., racemose; fls. of good texture, to 5 in. across, sepals and petals spreading, with revolute margins, rose-magenta, lip 3-lobed, lateral lobes enfolding column, yellowish with pink suffusion, midlobe cuneate-rotund, undulate, dark crimson. Early spring. Brazil.

LAELIOPSIS Lindl. *Orchidaceae.* Two spp. of herbs of W. Indies; similar vegetatively to *Cattleyopsis;* pseudobulbs small, spindle-shaped, jointed; lvs. rigid, fleshy, sharply serrate; infl. terminal, racemose; sepals and petals spreading-erect, not united, lip sessile, funnel-shaped, column without a foot, pollinia 4. For structure of fl. see *Orchidaceae.*

For culture see *Orchids.*

domingensis Lindl. [*Broughtonia domingensis* (Lindl.) Rolfe; *B. lilacina* Henfr.]. Pseudobulbs 2-lvd.; lvs. oblong, leathery; infl. slender, to 8-fld.; fls. to 1½ in. across, sepals and petals similar, lilac, lip 2-lobed, rose-lavender with yellow veins, minutely toothed, disc bearded along central veins. Spring. Hispaniola.

LAFOENSIA Vand. *Lythraceae.* About 10 spp. of glabrous trees or shrubs, native to Amer. tropics; lvs. opp., leathery, glossy; infl. racemose or nearly paniculate; fls. 8–16-merous, calyx tube campanulate or subglobose, petals large, stamens 16–32; fr. a loculicidal, 2–4-valved caps., seeds winged.

punicifolia DC. To 50 ft., brs. often 4-angled or -winged; lvs. oblong-lanceolate, 2–4⅜ in. long, obtuse to retuse, sometimes with a very short central point, with prominent pore below apex; fls. 12–16-merous, petals pale yellow, turning red in age, 1–1½ in. long; caps. ovoid, 1 in. long or more. Mex. to n. S. Amer. Yields a yellow dye.

LAGAROSIPHON Harv. *Hydrocharitaceae.* About 15 spp. of submersed, aquatic herbs, native to trop. and S. Afr., Madagascar, and India; sts. branched; lvs. alt., in close spirals; fls. unisexual, in axillary, solitary spathes, male spathes many-fld., female spathes 1-fld., sepals, petals, and stamens 3, staminodes 2–3, ovary beaked, styles 3, notched.

muscoides Harv. Sts. few-branched, to 1 ft. or more; lvs. linear, to ¾ in. long, 1-nerved, serrulate; perianth tube to 1½ in. long, stamens arising from perianth tube, staminodes 3, twice as long as stamens. Angola. Var. **major** Ridl. Sts. stouter, to 5 ft.; lvs. dark green, recurved. S. Afr. Occasionally grown in aquaria.

LAGENANDRA Dalzell. *Araceae.* About 6 spp. of rhizomatous herbs of bogs, native to India and Ceylon, allied to *Cryptocoryne;* lvs. simple, petioles usually long; fls. unisexual, spadix shorter than spathe, naked between zones of female and male fls., the female fls. in superposed rows.

Occasionally grown in aquaria.

lancifolia (Schott) Thwaites. Lf. blades elliptic to lanceolate, to 4 in. long and ¾ in. wide, leathery, dark green above, paler and with white spots beneath, petiole to 6 in. long, subtended by linear scales to 2 in. long; spathe dark purple, 1–2 in. long. Ceylon.

ovata (L.) Thwaites. Lf. blades elliptic, to 18 in. long and 4¾ in. wide, dark green, leathery, petioles to 20 in. long, subtended by long-pointed scales; spathe purple, to 1 ft. long. Ceylon.

Thwaitesii Engl. Lf. bases oblong-lanceolate to linear-lanceolate, to 6 in. long and 1½ in. wide, dark green, margin slightly wavy, silvery-white, petioles to 6 in. long, subtended by scales to 1½ in. long; spathe to 2 in. long. Ceylon.

LAGENARIA Ser. *Cucurbitaceae.* Six sp. of long-running, tender, mostly monoecious ann. vines of the Old World tropics and S. Amer.; fls. solitary, white, male fls. long-peduncled, stamens 3, borne on the campanulate or funnel-shaped fl. tube, anthers flexuous, pistillode lacking, female fls. with inferior ovary, style short, thick, stigmas 3, 2-lobed; fr. indehiscent, woody, seeds obovate to triangular, blunt or toothed at tip, pale.

Widely cultivated as ornamentals, and naturalized in warm regions. The hard shells of the fruits are used for utensils, and young fruits are eaten in some countries. Readily grown from seeds.

leucantha: *L. siceraria.*

longissima; a hort. name sometimes used for the form of *L. siceraria* known as HERCULES' CLUB.

siceraria (Mol.) Standl. [*L. leucantha* (Duchesne) Rusby; *L. vulgaris* Ser.]. WHITE-FLD. GOURDS (as distinguished from the yellow-fld. gourds, *Cucurbita Pepo* var. *ovifera*), CALABASH G. To 30 ft. or more, viscid-pubescent; lvs. cordate-ovate or broader, usually not lobed, petiole with 2 glands at apex; fr. smooth, hard-shelled when ripe, in many sizes and shapes, from 3 in. to 3 ft. long, and from nearly globose to oblong, long-cylindric and bent, club-shaped, dumbbell-shaped, or crooknecked. Old World tropics. Includes the DIPPER, SUGAR-TROUGH, HERCULES'-CLUB, BOTTLE, KNOB-KERRIE, and TRUMPET GOURDS.

vulgaris: *L. siceraria.*

LAGERSTROEMIA L. *Lythraceae.* About 55 spp. of small to large trees, of warmer parts of Asia and Pacific Is.; lvs. mostly alt. or subopp., without apical pore; fls. showy, purple or red to white, 5–9-merous, mostly in terminal panicles, calyx tube semiglobose or top-shaped, smooth or ribbed, petals usually clawed, stamens 15–200; fr. a loculicidal caps., longer than calyx tube, seeds winged.

Showy ornamentals of easy cultivation, primarily tropical and subtropical but one species hardy in Zone 7. Sometimes grown as pot plants in the greenhouse. Propagation by seeds or cuttings.

×**amabilis** Mak.: *L. indica* × *L. subcostata.* Intermediate between parents.

calyculata Kurz. To 60 ft.; lvs. lanceolate, 4–8 in. long, ¾–3⁵⁄₁₆ in. wide, hairy beneath; panicle brown-tomentose; fls. nearly sessile, calyx tube ¼ in. long, obscurely 12-ribbed, brown-tomentose, petals obovate, ³⁄₁₆–⁵⁄₁₆ in. long, stamens many; caps. black. Burma to Indochina.

Duperreana Pierre ex Gagnep. [*L. Thorelii* Gagnep.]. Small tree; lvs. oblong-lanceolate, to 8 in. long, 2¼ in. wide, glabrous; panicles axillary; calyx tube rounded in bud, minutely appendaged, not ribbed, stellate-tomentose, petals ½ in. long, orbicular, crisped, purple or lilac, fading to white, stamens many, ovary glabrous. Indochina. Zone 10.

elegans: *L. indica.*

Fauriei Koehne. Deciduous tree, brs. glabrous; lvs. leathery, oblong to ovate, to 4 in. long, 2 in. wide, with 8–13 pairs of nerves and tufts of hairs in axils of veins beneath; infl. glabrous; calyx tube less than ³⁄₁₆ in. long, 12-ribbed, petals orbicular, clawed, ⁵⁄₃₂ in. long, stamens 30–36. Japan, Ryukyu Is.

floribunda Jack. Small tree; lvs. oblong-lanceolate, to 8 in. long, 2½ in. wide, subtomentose to glabrous; calyx tube broadly top-shaped in bud, depressed at apex, with short beak and winglike appendages, ribbed, tomentose, petals pale rose to white, stamens 48–70, ovary pubescent. Var. **floribunda.** The typical var.; fl. buds rusty-tomentose, to ⅜ in. long. Thailand, Malay Pen. Var. **brevifolia** Craib [*L. turbinata* Koehne]. Fl. buds smaller, golden or pale yellow. Thailand, Indochina, China.

Flos-Reginae: *L. speciosa.*

hirsuta (Lam.) Willd. [*L. reginae* Roxb.]. Evergreen tree, to 30 ft. or more; lvs. oblong, to nearly 10 in. long, 3⁵⁄₁₆ in. wide, glabrous; panicle grayish or brownish; fl. buds ashy, calyx tube 12-ribbed, lobes spreading in fr., petals nearly orbicular, about 1⁵⁄₁₆ in. long, stamens many, ovary glabrous; caps. 1 in. long. India, Burma, New Guinea.

indica L. [*L. elegans* Wallich ex Paxt.]. CRAPE MYRTLE. Deciduous shrub or small tree, to 20 ft. or more; lvs. oblong-elliptic to rounded, to 2¾ in. long, glabrous or pubescent on veins; calyx tube rounded in bud, not ribbed, glabrous, petals white, pink, or purple, to 1⅛ in. long, the blade cordate-orbicular, crisped, stamens 36–42, ovary glabrous. China. Zone 7. Widely cult. in warm temp. and subtrop. regions. Many cvs. are listed: **'Nana Caerulea'**, dwarf, fls. bluish; **'Prostrata'**, prostrate, fls. pink; **'Alba'**, **'Purpurea'**, **'Rosea'**, **'Rubra'**, color variants.

lanceolata: *L. microcarpa.*

Loudonii Teysm. & Binnend. Tree, to 18 ft.; lvs. elliptic to elliptic-lanceolate, 3½–8 in. long, 2–3½ in. wide, glabrous above in age, minutely tomentose beneath; panicles lateral, 4–8 in. long; fls. white to bluish, (7–)8-merous, calyx tube rounded in bud, not apiculate, ribbed, petals ciliate above the middle, about 1½ in. long, stamens about 64, ovary pubescent. Thailand. Zone 10.

microcarpa Wight [*L. lanceolata* Wallich]. Lvs. elliptic-lanceolate, about 3 in. long, narrowed at both ends, glabrous and often white beneath, petioles ¼–½ in. long; calyx tube not ribbed, petals white, ¼–⁵⁄₁₆ in. long, stamens 25–49, ovary glabrous. India. Zone 10.

parviflora Roxb. To 80 ft.; lvs. ovate to lanceolate, whitish or purplish-pubescent beneath; calyx tube rounded in bud, not ribbed, petals white, to ⁵⁄₁₆ in. long, blade ovate or oblong, not cordate or crisped, stamens 26–49, ovary glabrous. India. Wood used for general carpentry.

reginae: *L. hirsuta.*

speciosa (L.) Pers. [*L. Flos-Reginae* Retz.]. QUEEN'S CRAPE MYRTLE, PRIDE-OF-INDIA. To 80 ft.; lvs. oblong to elliptic-ovate, to 1 ft. long, 4 in. wide, glabrous, leathery; fls. preceding lvs., calyx tube rounded in bud, lightly 12-ribbed, grayish-pubescent, petals purple or white, 1 in. long or more, stamens 130–200, ovary glabrous. India to China, s. to New Guinea and Australia. Zone 10. Much planted in the tropics. Useful for railroad ties and for general construction.

subcostata Koehne. Deciduous, much-branched tree, bark deciduous; lvs. ovate-lanceolate, to 4 in. long, acuminate, glabrous or puberulous above; calyx tube about ⅛ in. long, lightly 12-ribbed, glabrous, petals white or rose, orbicular, crisped, about ⁵⁄₁₆ in. long, stamens 15–30, ovary glabrous. Taiwan, Ryukyu Is., se. China. Zone 9.

Thorelii: *L. Duperreana.*

tomentosa K. Presl. To 90 ft.; lvs. oblong-lanceolate or lanceolate, to 5½ in. long, 1¾ in. wide, glabrous at maturity, except for midvein beneath; panicles 4–8 in. long; fls. 5–6(–7)-merous, calyx tube rounded in bud, not apiculate, ribbed, tomentose, petals white to purple, to ⅞ in. long, not ciliate, stamens 24–70, ovary pubescent. India.

turbinata: *L. floribunda* var. *brevifolia.*

villosa Wallich ex Kurz. To 60 ft.; lvs. lanceolate to ovate, 1–4 in. long, ¾–1⅝ in. wide, greenish-gray, puberulous beneath, pilose on nerves above and beneath in age; calyx tube narrowed to a pedicel-like base, ¼ in. long, ribs as many as lobes, petals lanceolate to elliptic, clawed, to ¼ in. long, stamens many; fr. ellipsoid, to ⅞ in. long. Burma, Thailand, s. China.

LAGUNARIA (DC.) G. Don. *Malvaceae.* One sp., an evergreen tree in e. Australia, Lord Howe Is. and Norfolk Is.; lvs. unlobed, ovate to oblong-lanceolate, entire; fls. solitary in the upper lf. axils, involucral bracts 3–5, linear, early deciduous, calyx cup-shaped, shallowly 5-lobed, petals pale pink to rose-purple, stamens united in a tubular column, style terminated by 5 separate, radiating stigmas; fr. a 5-celled, loculicidally dehiscent caps., each cell several-seeded, seeds large, shiny red, somewhat fleshy.

Propagated by cuttings over heat or by seeds.

Patersonii (Andr.) G. Don. To 40 or 50 ft., new growth covered with scurfy scales; lvs. to 3 or 4 in. long, somewhat leathery, white beneath; fls. 1½–2½ in. across, staminal column included; caps. obovate to elliptic, about 1 in. long, tawny-pubescent.

LAGURUS L. *Gramineae.* One sp., an ann. grass in Medit. region; heads pale, dense, ovoid or oblong, feathery; spikelets 1-fld., woolly, rachilla disarticulating above the glumes, glumes subequal, 1-nerved, villous, gradually tapering into a plumose point, lemma shorter, glabrous, awned above the middle, awn slender, exserted, somewhat geniculate, palea narrow, the 2 keels ending in minute awns. For terminology see *Gramineae.*

ovatus L. HARE'S-TAIL, HARE'S-TAIL GRASS, RABBIT-TAIL G. Sts. to 1 ft., branching at the base, slender, pubescent; lf. sheaths somewhat inflated, pubescent, blades flat, lax, pubescent; panicle to 1¼ in. long, nearly as thick, pale and downy; glumes very narrow, ⅜ in. long, much exceeded by awns of the lemma. Cult. for ornament or dry bouquets and sparingly escaped in N.J., N.C., Calif.

LALLEMANTIA Fisch. & C. A. Mey. *Labiatae.* About 5 spp. of small ann. or bien., glabrous to gray-pubescent herbs of Asia; sts. mostly square in cross section; lvs. opp., toothed, long-petioled to nearly sessile; fls. in axillary, 6-fld. verticillasters, bractlets ciliate-dentate, calyx tubular, erect, 15-nerved, 5-toothed, corolla tube slender, as long as calyx or only slightly longer, limb 2-lipped, upper lip erect, nearly concave, emarginate, lower lip 3-lobed, middle lobe broad, stamens 4, in 2 pairs, anthers 2-celled; fr. of 4 glabrous nutlets.

canescens (L.) Fisch. & C. A. Mey. Bien., or short-lived per., to 18 in., pubescent; lvs. oblong-lanceolate, to 2 in. long, cuneate, more or less denticulate; infl. racemose, to 10 in. long; calyx 2-lipped, corolla longer than calyx, to 1 in. long, bluish-lavender. Sw. Asia. Late summer. Treated as an ann. or bien. in the flower or rock garden.

LAMARCKIA Moench. *Gramineae.* One sp., a low ann. grass of the Medit. region; lf. blades flat; panicles oblong, 1-sided, dense, of crowded, drooping fascicles which fall entire; spikelets of 2 kinds in each fascicle, the terminal one fertile and hidden, except the awns, by the many sterile ones, fertile spikelets with 1 bisexual awned floret, 1 rudimentary, glumes narrow, acuminate or short-awned, 1-nerved, lemma broader, awned, sterile spikelets 1–3 in each fascicle, linear. For terminology see *Gramineae.*

aurea (L.) Moench. GOLDENTOP. Sts. to 16 in., erect or decumbent at base; lf. blades soft, to ¼ in. wide; panicle to 2¾ in. long and ¾ in. wide, glossy, golden-yellow to purplish; fertile spikelets less than ⅛ in. long, awn of lemma about twice as long as spikelet, sterile spikelets to ⁵⁄₁₆ in. long. Sometimes cult. for ornament and escaped in Tex., Ariz., s. Calif., and n. Mex.

LAMBERTIA Sm. *Proteaceae.* Eleven spp. of Australian shrubs; lvs. commonly in whorls of 3; fls. bisexual, red or yellow, solitary or in clusters of 7 surrounded by an involucre of colored bracts, perianth regular, lobes 4, spirally revolute, anthers borne on lobes, ovary with 2 pendulous ovules; fr. a hard follicle.

ericifolia R. Br. To 10 ft.; lvs. linear, about ½ in. long, margins revolute; involucre 7-fld., inner bracts ½ in. long; fls. 1½ in. long.

formosa Sm. HONEY FLOWER, MOUNTAIN DEVIL. Tall shrub; lvs. linear, to 2 in. long, pale beneath, margins recurved; inner bracts of 7-fld. involucre to 2 in. long; fls. to 2 in. long.

multiflora Lindl. To 4 ft.; lvs. linear, to 2 in. long; involucre 7-fld., inner bracts ½ in. long; fls. 1½ in. long.

LAMIACEAE: see *LABIATAE.*

LAMIASTRUM Heist. ex Fabr. *Labiatae.* One sp., an herb, native from w. Eur. to Iran; like *Lamium,* but corolla yellow, lower lip with essentially equal lobes, middle lobe somewhat triangular, acute.

Galeobdolon (L.) Ehrend. & Polatsch. [*Lamium Galeobdolon* (L.) L.]. YELLOW ARCHANGEL. Variously hairy, erect per., to 2 ft., sometimes stoloniferous; lvs. ovate to ovate-orbicular, to 3 in. long, truncate

to barely cordate at base, coarsely toothed, rarely crenate; bracts similar to lvs.; calyx to ⅜ in. long, teeth ¼ as long as tube, corolla ½–1 in. long, bright yellow with brown marks, tube straight, with ring of hairs inside. A variable sp. Woods and shady sites. Cv. 'Florentinum'. A listed name. Cv. 'Variegatum'. Lvs. variegated.

LAMIUM L. DEAD NETTLE. *Labiatae.* About 40 spp. of decumbent ann. or per. herbs of n. Afr., Eur., and Asia; sts. square in cross section; lvs. opp., mostly toothed, basal lvs. small, long-petioled, middle lvs. cordate, doubly-toothed; verticillasters in upper lf. axils; calyx tubular, 5-nerved, 5-toothed, corolla dilated at throat, 2-lipped, upper lip hooded, lower lip 3-lobed, middle lobe notched, stamens 4; fr. of 4 nutlets.

Easily grown from seeds or division of perennial species. Some species are desirable for the rock garden, some tend to become invasive.

album L. SNOWFLAKE, DEAD NETTLE, WHITE D. N., DUMB NETTLE, ARCHANGEL. Decumbent per., 1–2 ft., generally unbranched, sparsely to densely hairy; lvs. ovate, to 3 in. long, acuminate, coarsely crenate-serrate; calyx teeth as long as tube, corolla about ¾ in. long, white, upper lip densely long-pubescent outside, lateral lobes of lower lip with 2–3 small teeth, anthers hairy. Summer. Eur. and Asia; naturalized in e. N. Amer.

Galeobdolon: *Lamiastrum Galeobdolon.*

maculatum L. SPOTTED D. N. Decumbent per., to 18 in., sparsely to densely hairy; st. lvs. ovate, crenate-dentate, often with whitish blotches bordering midrib, basal lvs. cordate, petioled; calyx to ⅝ in. long, teeth unequal, becoming divergent, corolla to 1 in. long, showy, pink, purple or brownish-purple, rarely white, lateral lobes of lower lip with 1 tooth. Spring and summer. Eur. and Asia; naturalized in N. Amer. Cvs. are: 'Album', fls. creamy-white; 'Aureum', lvs. with yellow blotches along midrib; 'Variegatum' [*L. variegatum* Hort.], lvs. mottled green and white.

marginatum: a listed name of no botanical standing.

variegatum: probably *L. maculatum* cv.; some material may be *Lamiastrum Galeobdolon* cv.

LAMPRANTHUS N. E. Br. *Aizoaceae.* About 160 spp. of glabrous, per. subshrubs, native to S. Afr., brs. creeping, decumbent to erect; lvs. opp., many, slightly united, cylindrical to 3-angled, more or less curved; fls. solitary or in cymes, calyx 5-lobed, petals white, pink, red, purple, or yellow to orange, in several series, stamens many, staminodes present or absent, glandular ring present, ovary inferior, 5-celled, stigmas 5; fr. a 5-valved caps., cell lids winged, expanding keels with marginal wings, placental tubercles absent.

Free-flowering plants for outdoor summer planting, or suitable for pots or baskets, requiring good ventilation, temperatures not exceeding 50° F., and a light, moderately dry location for overwintering. Propagated by seeds or cuttings. See also *Succulents.*

amoenus (Salm-Dyck) N. E. Br. Shrub, sts. ascending; lvs. somewhat reddish, to 1½ in. long, cylindrical to 3-angled, apex rather blunt, spiny; fls. to 1½ in. across, in 3's, petals purple. Cape Prov.

aureus (L.) N. E. Br. [*Mesembryanthemum aureum* L.]. Shrub, sts. erect, to 1½ ft., dark brown; lvs. green, smooth, slightly pruinose, with tiny, transparent dots, to 2 in. long, 3-angled, tip reddish, spiny; fls. to 2½ in. across, petals glossy, vivid orange. Cape Prov.

blandus (Haw.) Schwant. Shrubby, sts. to 2 ft., ascending to erect, bright red; lvs. gray-green, with translucent dots, 1¼–2 in. long, equally 3-sided; fls. in 3's, on pedicels to 2¾ in. long, petals pink. Cape Prov.

Brownii (Hook.f.) N. E. Br. [*Mesembryanthemum Brownii* Hook.f.]. Compact, erect subshrub, to 1 ft., sts. brown; lvs. glaucous-green, to ⅝ in. long, cylindrical, acute; fls. to ¾ in. across, solitary or in 3's, petals orange-red inside, yellow outside, both sides reddish in age. Cape Prov.

conspicuus (Haw.) N. E. Br. Shrub, to 1½ ft., brs. with many lf. scars; lvs. at tips of brs., erect or spreading, to 3 in. long, cylindrical to 3-angled, with reddish tip; fls. to 2 in. across, solitary or in 3's, on pedicels to 3½ in. long, petals purple. Cape Prov.

emarginatus (L.) N. E. Br. To 2 ft., brs. erect to spreading, brown; lvs. glaucous-green, slightly roughened with translucent dots, to ¾ in. long, nearly cylindrical, curved; fls. to 1¼ in. across, solitary or in 3's, petals violet-pink, filaments white. Cape Prov.

glaucus (L.) N. E. Br. Shrub, to 1 ft., with erect brs.; lvs. glaucous-green, to 1 in. long, flattened-3-angled; fls. to 2 in. across, solitary, on pedicels to about 1 in. long, petals lemon-yellow or light yellow. Cape Prov.

multiradiatus (Jacq.) N. E. Br. [*L. roseus* (Willd.) Schwant.; *Mesembryanthemum multiradiatum* Jacq.; *M. roseum* Willd.]. Subshrub to 2 ft., brs. erect to spreading; lvs. glaucous, incurved, to 1 in. long, somewhat 3-angled, apex spiny; fls. to 2 in. across, solitary or in 3's, on pedicels to 2 in. long, petals rose to purplish-rose, rarely white. Cape Prov.

roseus: *L. multiradiatus.*

spectabilis (Haw.) N. E. Br. Somewhat woody per., with prostrate brs.; lvs. crowded on short shoots, glaucous, incurved, to 3 in. long, 3-angled, ending in a reddish awn; fls. to 2¾ in. across, solitary, on pedicels 3–6 in. long, petals purple, filaments white. Cape Prov.

LANDSCAPE GARDENING. In its original definition, landscape gardening was the making of landscapes to please the imagination, by means of gardening designs, practices, and materials.

With the development of the profession of the high art of landscape subdivision and design, the term landscape architecture has come into use, the word architecture being taken in its larger sense of plan or undertaking, and the tendency is to restrict the term landscape gardening to the horticultural applications; some persons, however, prefer the latter, older term to landscape architecture, the word gardening being taken also in its larger sense as the art associated with buildings and the utilization of the personal or domestic property. In this meaning, landscape gardening is no more technical gardening than landscape architecture is technical or professional architecture.

In its restricted sense, landscape gardening is the growing and the adapting of plants in the making of grounds, the application of horticultural materials, forms, and methods to the development or improvement of landscapes. It may be practiced independently, complete in itself for certain limited areas or purposes, or may also be considered one of the practical means or subordinated in the interpretation of landscape architecture.

The landscape gardener, in whatever sense the term is taken, may or may not be a practiced propagator and grower of plants, but he must certainly know their artistic values and their adaptations to soils, climates, seasons, and settings, and the extent to which they may be associated for the making of pleasing and harmonious groupings throughout the year.

Every parcel of land under the control of man may derive character and dignity from the proper employment of plant materials. The utilization of such materials to these ends is much more than ornament or than the planting of flowers and showy colored foliage and the making of display; it must have close relation to the essential merits of the area and to the nature of the construction and the setting. The plants are grown not so much for their separate individual merits as for the ways in which they may be adjusted and combined. The landscape gardener is possessed of an artistic quality, and his appreciation of nature should be as pronounced as is his reaction to garden objects and forms.

The arrangement and design of landscapes constitutes one of the noblest of the arts, deserving keener recognition, and the utilization of plant materials is one of the essential factors in the execution of it.

LANGLOISIA Greene. *Polemoniaceae.* Five spp. of ann. herbs, native to deserts of w. N. Amer.; lvs. alt., linear to cuneate, pinnatifid with bristle-tipped teeth; fls. pink, blue, lilac, white, or yellowish, in terminal, few-fld., bracted heads, calyx 5-parted, lobes spine-tipped, corolla more or less 2-lipped, stamens 5, exserted; fr. a caps.

punctata (Cov.) L. Goodd. [*Gilia punctata* (Cov.) Munz]. LILAC-SUNBONNET. Tufted ann., to 8 in.; lvs. with 2–3 forked bristles on margins; fls. nearly regular, corolla lilac, lobes entire, purple-dotted. Early spring to summer. Se. Calif., e. to w. Nev. and w. Ariz.

LANGUAS: *ALPINIA.*

LANKESTERIA Lindl. *Acanthaceae.* Four spp. of shrubs of trop. Afr.; lvs. entire; fls. in heads, spikes, or panicles, bracts

long, calyx 5-lobed, lobes nearly equal, linear, corolla tube long, narrow, lobes 5, nearly equal, obovate, stamens 2, staminodes 2; fr. an ellipsoid caps., base contracted, solid, seeds 2, covered with hygroscopic hairs.

elegans (Beauvois) T. Anderson [*Eranthemum elegans* (Beauvois) R. Br. ex Roem. & Schult.]. Lvs. elliptic, 5–9 in. long, petioles short; fls. in terminal spikes, bracts conspicuous, to 1 in. long, loosely overlapping, corolla orange, withering to dull reddish, tube slender, to 1½ in. long, lobes nearly ½ in. long.

LANTANA L. SHRUB VERBENA. *Verbenaceae.* About 155 spp. of prickly or unarmed shrubs or per. herbs, native mostly to subtrop. and trop. N. and S. Amer., some in the Old World; lvs. opp. or whorled, often rugose; fls. of various and changeable colors, in axillary or terminal spikes or heads, calyx small, corolla almost equally 4–5-lobed, stamens 4, included; fr. a cluster of small drupes resembling a blackberry.

One species, *L. Camara,* is a common florist's subject. It and others may be grown in the South and Calif. Zone 9. Plant in a moderate greenhouse and out of doors in summer. Propagated by cuttings of soft wood, and also by seeds.

×**Calloviana:** a hort. name of no botanical standing for a patented hybrid between *L. Camara* and *L. montevidensis.* Sts. trailing or prostrate; fls. bright yellow.

Camara L. YELLOW SAGE. Hairy shrub, to 4 ft., sometimes prickly; lvs. ovate to oblong-ovate, to 5 in. long, crenate-dentate, rough above; fls. orange-yellow or orange changing to red or white, in flat-topped heads to 2 in. across, peduncles longer than the lvs.; fr. black. Trop. Amer.; naturalized Fla. to Tex. and a serious weed in Hawaii. Occasionally used medicinally in home remedies. Cvs. are: 'Aculeata', armed with stout, recurved prickles; 'Alba' and 'Nivea', fls. white; 'Flava', fls. sulphur-yellow, becoming saffron; 'Hybrida' [*L. hybrida* Neub.], dwarf garden form, fls. yellow; 'Mista' [*L. Craigii* Hort.], outer fls. yellowish, becoming saffron and brick-red, inner fls. yellow, becoming orange; 'Mutabilis', outer fls. opening white, changing through yellowish, lilac, rose, and blue, inner fls. opening yellow; 'Sanguinea', fls. deep red, 'Varia', fls. yellow, the outer becoming purple, the inner orange.

Craigii: a listed name of no botanical standing for *L. Camara* cv. 'Mista'.

delicata: a listed name of no botanical standing for *L. montevidensis.*

delicatissima: a listed name of no botanical standing for *L. montevidensis.*

hispida HBK. Shrub, to 6 ft.; lvs. ovate-oblong to ovate or elliptic, to 3½ in. long, crenate; fls. white, lilac, or purple, in involucrate heads, peduncles shorter than or as long as lvs.; fr. black. Mex., Cent. Amer.

horrida HBK. Shrub, to 3 ft., often prickly; lvs. broadly ovate, to 3 in. long, coarsely serrate-crenate; fls. orange or yellow, becoming red, in hemispherical heads; fr. black. S. Tex., Mex.

hybrida: *L. Camara* cv.

montevidensis (K. Spreng.) Briq. [*L. delicata* Hort.; *L. delicatissima* Hort.; *L. Sellowiana* Link & Otto]. WEEPING L., TRAILING L., POLE-CAT GERANIUM. Shrub, sts. weak, trailing, about 3 ft. long; lvs. ovate, to 1 in. long, coarsely toothed; fls. rosy-lilac, in heads 1 in. across or more, peduncles longer than lvs. S. Amer.; naturalized Fla. to Tex. Useful as a ground cover.

rugulosa HBK. Shrub; lvs. ovate, to 2½ in. long, crenate, rough above, hairy beneath; fls. lilac, in hemispherical heads, peduncles long; fr. red. Ecuador.

salviifolia Jacq. Erect, aromatic shrub, to 6 ft.; lvs. oblong-ovate, to 2 in. long, coarsely crenate, rough above, pubescent beneath; fls. white or lilac, in dense spikes becoming 1 in. long in fr., peduncles long; fr. purple. Trop. and S. Afr.

Sellowiana: *L. montevidensis.*

tiliifolia Cham. Shrub, coarsely and harshly hairy; lvs. elliptic to broadly ovate, to 4 in. long, crenate-dentate; fls. yellow or orange, becoming brick-red. S. Amer. Often cult. under the name *L. Camara.*

trifolia L. Little-branched shrub, to 6 ft.; lvs. mostly whorled, oblong-lanceolate to elliptic-lanceolate, to 5 in. long, crenate-serrate; fls. pink, lavender or purple, in dense spikes, peduncles shorter than or as long as lvs.; fr. purple or lavender. W. Indies, Mex., Cent. and S. Amer.

LANUGIA N. E. Br. *Apocynaceae.* Three spp. of trees, native to trop. e. Afr.; lvs. opp., entire; fls. in axillary cymes, 5-merous, bisexual, corolla salverform, tube constricted below stamens, lobes hairy on inner surface, stamens borne on corolla, included, anthers sagittate, connivent and adhering to stigma; fr. a pair of spreading, slender, cylindrical, somewhat woody follicles, seeds many, slender, with tuft of rusty hairs at apex.

latifolia N. E. Br. To 25 ft.; lvs. broadly oblanceolate to elliptic-oblong; fls. white, nearly 1 in. across, corolla tube ⅜ in. long, lobes ovate, recurved at apex; fr. to 4 in. long. Mozambique.

LAPAGERIA Ruiz & Pav. CHILEAN BELLFLOWER, CHILE-BELLS, COPIHUE. *Liliaceae.* One sp., a showy, evergreen, woody vine, native to s. Chile, where it is the national fl.; lvs. alt., leathery; fls. pendulous, solitary or in 2's or 3's, perianth segms. 6, separate, fleshy, the 3 outer smaller than the 3 inner, stamens 6; fr. an oblong-ovate berry, seeds many.

Sometimes grown in cool greenhouses, and in cool frost-free climates outdoors. Good drainage and loose soil are necessary, and protection from direct sun. Propagated by layering, cuttings, and seeds.

rosea Ruiz & Pav. Lvs. ovate-lanceolate, 2–3 in. long, with 3–5 main veins connected by smaller reticulations, glossy, long-pointed; fls. rose to rose-crimson, faintly spotted with rose, to 3 in. long and 2 in. wide. Var. **albiflora** Hook. Fls. white.

LAPEIROUSIA Pourr. (frequently but not originally spelled *Lapeyrousia*). [*Anomatheca* Ker-Gawl.]. *Iridaceae.* About 50 spp. of summer-blooming, cormous herbs, native to S. Afr.; allied to *Watsonia;* lvs. mostly basal, narrow, the lowest 1 or 2 usually curved, spreading or prostrate; fls. regular, perianth tube often long, stamens borne at the mouth.

Hardy in the North with winter protection and grown also under glass for spring bloom. Corms should be lifted and divided every few years. Plant in light sandy soil in full sun.

aculeata: a listed name; of no botanical standing; see *L. denticulata.*

anceps Ker-Gawl. [*L. Jacquinii* N. E. Br.]. Basal lvs. 2, erect or spreading, 6–10 in. long, to 5/16 in. wide, margins weakly crisped or flat; perianth dark purple or magenta, marked with white, tube 1¼ in. long, segms. about 5/16 in. long, the uppermost erect, the others spreading. Sometimes confused with *L. compressa* and *L. denticulata.* Var. **aculeata:** *L. denticulata.*

compressa Pourr. Differs from *L. anceps,* in having perianth pale bluish-white, segms. marked with dark blue, longitudinal streaks that do not reach the margin, and tube about as long as the outer spathe valve. Mauritius. Material cult. under this name may be *L. anceps* or *L. denticulata.*

corymbosa Ker-Gawl. Tunics terminated by ring of bristles, st. 8–12 in. with 1–2 lvs.; basal lf. 4–6 in. long; infl. a many-fld., dense corymb, spathe valves scarious at tips; fls. pale to deep violet, perianth tube about ⅜ in. long, segms. oblong, about ½ in. long or less, nearly acute, stamens as long as segms. Var. **purpureolutea** (Klatt) Grey [*L. purpureolutea* Klatt]. Spathe valves herbaceous; perianth segms. yellow, with bright violet basal spot.

cruenta: *L. laxa.*

denticulata (Lam.) G. H. M. Lawr. [*L. anceps* (L. f.) Bak., not Ker-Gawl.; *L. anceps* var. *aculeata* (Sweet) Bak.]. Basal lf. usually 1, linear, about 6 in. long, margins undulate or strongly crisped; infl. 6–12 in. high, brs. 2–5-fld., compressed and markedly finely toothed; perianth lilac to white, tube about 1½ in. long, segms. oblanceolate, about ½ in. long, stamens ¼ in. long or less, anthers yellow. Material offered as *L. aculeata* probably belongs here.

divaricata Bak. Sts. nearly cylindrical; basal lf. linear, 6–9 in. long; infl. 6–12 in. high, nearly cylindrical, paniculately branched from near base; perianth whitish, tube about ¼ in. long, segms. about twice as long, oblanceolate, stamens half as long as segms.

fissifolia (Jacq.) Ker-Gawl. Tunics thick, brownish-black, tipped by ring of bristles, st. 3–5 in.; basal lf. spreading, lanceolate, 1–4 in. long; st. lvs. spirally imbricate, congested, curved; infl. spicate, usually 3–10-fld.; fls. ivory-white flushed pink, becoming lilac-colored with age, perianth tube 1 in. long or more, segms. oblong-elliptic, about 5/16 in. long, usually with 1–2 purple blotches, stamens with purple anthers.

juncea (L.f.) Pourr. Sts. cylindrical; basal lvs. 4–8, horizontal to nearly erect, sword-shaped, usually 3–9 in. long; infl. 6–18 in. high, a loose 4–8-fld. spike, spathe valves obtuse; perianth pale pink to rose-red, tube about ¾ in. long or less, segms. oblanceolate-oblong, 5/16–½ in. long, the lower 3 with dark red basal blotch, stamens half as long as segms., anthers greenish-yellow.

laxa (Thunb.) N. E. Br. [*L. cruenta* (Lindl.) Bak.; *Anomatheca cruenta* Lindl.]. Sts. slender, cylindrical; basal lvs. mostly 6, erect, to 8 in. long; infl. 4–10 in. high, a dense 1-sided, spicate raceme, often

branched; perianth bright red, tube about 1 in. long, segms. oblong, half as long, the outer ones usually with dark red basal spot, anthers red. One of the most hardy of the genus. Cv. 'Alba'. Fls. pure white.

purpureolutea: *L. corymbosa* var.

Sandersonii Bak. Basal lvs. 2, erect, linear, 1–1½ ft. long; infl. many-fld., 1–1½ ft. high, paniculate, very much branched from near base, brs. acutely angled, each with 2–4 fls. at apex; perianth lilac-blue to whitish, tube ¼–5/16 in. long, segms. oblanceolate, tube and stamens as long as segms. Very showy.

LAPIDARIA (Dinter & Schwant.) Dinter & Schwant. ex N. E. Br. *Aizoaceae.* One sp., an essentially stemless, succulent, per. herb, native to S. Afr.; lvs. of 3–4 pairs, shortly united basally, each pair at first forming a spherical body (growth) which splits apart exposing the next spherical pair, upper side flat to slightly concave, lower side rounded, keeled, translucent dots absent; fls. solitary, terminal, calyx nearly equally 7-parted, petals in many series, stamens many, filaments bearded basally, ovary inferior, 6–7-celled, stigmas 6–7; fr. a 6–7-valved caps., cell lids winged, expanding keels winged, placental tubercles absent.

Culture as for *Dinteranthus.* Propagation easy by seeds. See also *Succulents.*

Margaretae (Schwant.) Schwant. ex N. E. Br. KAROO ROSE. Older plants cespitose, to 1¾ in.; lvs. firm, glabrous, to ¾ in. long, ⅜ in. wide, and ⅝ in. thick, upper side broadly ovate in outline; fls. to 2 in. across, petals golden-yellow above, whitish-yellow but fading reddish beneath. S.-W. Afr.

LAPPULA Moench. STICKSEED. *Boraginaceae.* About 14 spp. of hairy ann. herbs, native to all continents except Australia; lvs. simple, alt., basal and cauline; fls. blue or white, on erect pedicels, in bracted scorpioid cymes, calyx deeply 5-lobed, corolla 5-lobed, salverform, with scales in the throat, stamens 5, included; style longer than the nutlets; fr. of 4 erect or incurved nutlets armed with barbed prickles on the margins and angles.

occidentalis: *L. Redowskii.*

Redowskii (Hornem.) Greene [*L. occidentalis* Greene]. Erect or diffuse ann., 6–14 in.; lvs. linear to narrowly lanceolate or oblanceolate; fls. blue, to ⅛ in. long; nutlets with a single row of barbed prickles. Eurasia, Argentina, w. U.S. and Canada. This is an exceedingly variable sp. and is a weed of roadsides and waste places.

LARDIZABALA Ruiz & Pav. *Lardizabalaceae.* Two spp. of evergreen, woody, dioecious vines of Chile; lvs. alt., ternately compound; fls. purple, male fls. in drooping racemes, female fls. solitary, sepals 6, nectaries 6, stamens 6, united into a column; fr. an oblong berry.

Propagated by cuttings of half-ripened wood, and by seeds.

biternata Ruiz & Pav. Twining, to 40 ft. or more; lvs. glossy, dark green, 1–3-ternately compound, lfts. ovate-oblong, to 4 in. long, entire or sinuate-toothed; male racemes to 4 in. long, calyx purple-brown, male fls. about ¾ in. across, female fls. about 1 in. across, on peduncles 1 in. long, nectaries glandular, white; fr. sweet, pulpy, dark purple, to 3 in. long, edible. Zone 9.

LARDIZABALACEAE Decne. LARDIZABALA FAMILY. Dicot.; 7 genera of monoecious or dioecious, mostly twining

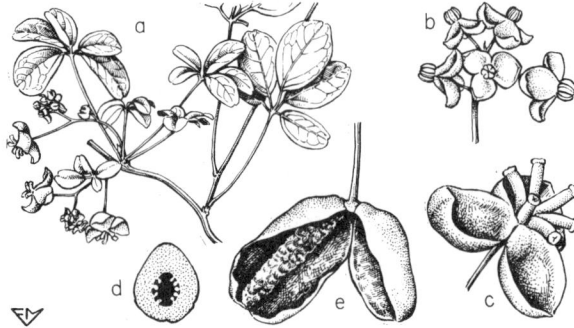

LARDIZABALACEAE. *Akebia quinata:* **a,** flowering branch, × ¼; **b,** male flowers, × 1; **c,** female flower, × 1; **d,** ovary, cross section, × 6; **e,** fruit, × ¼. (From Bailey, *Manual of Cultivated Plants,* ed. 2.)

woody plants, native to e. Asia and Chile; lvs. alt., compound; fls. unisexual, sepals 6 or 3, petaloid, petals 0, but nectaries often present, stamens 6, pistils 3–9, ovary superior; fr. berry-like. *Akebia, Decaisnea, Holboella, Lardizabala, Sinofranchetia,* and *Stauntonia* are cult.

LARIX Mill. LARCH. *Pinaceae.* About 10 spp. of tall, deciduous, coniferous trees with spreading brs., native to colder parts of N. Hemisphere; lvs. short, linear, needle-shaped, spirally arranged on the terminal shoots, clustered on the spurs; male cones solitary, female cones subglobose, woody, scales persistent, bracts narrow, often brightly colored; seeds 2 to each scale, 2-winged, maturing in 1 year.

Larix laricina and *L. Lyallii* become 50–60 ft. tall, the other spp. taller. The species yield strong and durable timber and *L. decidua* is the source of a valuable turpentine. All species are hardy at least through Zone 5. The leaves turn an attractive yellow in autumn. For culture see *Conifers.*

americana: *L. laricina.*

dahurica: *L. Gmelinii.*

decidua Mill. [*L. europaea* DC.]. EUROPEAN L. Lvs. to 1½ in. long, obtuse; cones to 1½ in. long, scales pubescent and straight. Eur. Zone 3. Important for timber and Venetian turpentine. Cv. **'Pendula'.** Branchlets drooping. Cv. **'Pyramidalis'.** Narrow-conical, brs. ascending.

×**eurolepis** A. Henry: *L. decidua* × *L. Kaempferi.* DUNKELD L. Differs from *L. Kaempferi* in having smaller lvs., fewer rows of stomata, and less glaucous brs.

europaea: *L. decidua.*

Gmelinii (Rupr.) Rupr. ex Kuzen. [*L. dahurica* Trautv.; *L. kurilensis* Mayr]. DAHURIAN L. Branchlets hairy; lvs. to 1½ in. long, bright green; cones 1½ in. long, scales about 20, shiny. E. Siberia. Zone 2. Var. **japonica** (Maxim ex Regel) Pilg. Young branchlets bluish-red. Sakhalin and Kurile Is.

Kaempferi (Lamb.) Carrière [*L. leptolepis* (Siebold & Zucc.) Gord.]. JAPANESE L. Lvs. to 1½ in. long, obtuse, light or bluish-green, with 2 conspicuous bands beneath; cones to 1½ in. long, scales recurved at apex. Japan. Zone 5. Cv. **'Minor'.** Dwarf. Cv. **'Pendula'.** A listed name.

kurilensis *L. Gmelinii.*

laricina (Du Roi) C. Koch [*L. americana* Michx.]. AMERICAN L., TAMARACK, HACKMATACK, BLACK L. Branchlets glabrous, often glaucous, reddish-yellow; lvs. to 1½ in. long, obtuse, light bluish-green; cones to ¾ in. long, scales shiny, glabrous. N. Amer. Zone 2.

leptolepis: *L. Kaempferi.*

Lyallii Parl. Branchlets brown-pubescent; lvs. to 1½ in. long, 4-angled, acute, stiff; cones to 2 in. long, scales pubescent, becoming reflexed, bracts exserted and erect. B.C. to Mont. Zone 5.

occidentalis Nutt. To 180 ft., branchlets becoming glabrous; lvs. to 1¾ in. long, sharp-pointed, stiff, rounded above, keeled beneath; cones to 1½ in. long, scales hairy at base, bracts exserted and erect. B.C. to Mont. Zone 5.

×**pendula** (Soland.) Salisb.: *L. decidua* × *L. laricina.* Differs from *L. laricina* in having branchlets mostly pink, rarely glaucous, and cones about 1 in. long, with scales pubescent below middle.

Potaninii Batal. CHINESE L. Branchlets glossy and glabrous, drooping; lvs. to 1¼ in. long, 4-angled, acute, grayish-green; cones to 1¾ in. long, bracts purple, exserted. W. China. Zone 5.

sibirica Ledeb. Lvs. to 1½ in. long, bright green, soft, keeled beneath; cones 1½ in. long, scales minutely hairy, incurved at apex. U.S.S.R. Zone 2.

sudetica: a listed name of no botanical standing.

LARREA Cav. [*Covillea* Vail]. CREOSOTE BUSH. *Zygophyllaceae.* Three or 4 spp. of evergreen, resinous shrubs of dry regions, native to sw. U.S., Mex., and S. Amer.; sts. jointed and swollen at nodes; lvs. opp., pinnate, lfts. 2–16; fls. yellow, solitary, terminal on short lateral twigs, sepals and petals 5, stamens 10, each with a laciniate appendage; fr. globose, hairy, finally splitting into 5 indehiscent, 1-seeded nutlets.

divaricata Cav. Shrub, to 10 ft., twigs and lvs. ashy; lfts. 2, to ⅝ in. long; petals to ¼ in. long. Peru to Argentina. Material offered under this name in the U.S. is *L. tridentata.*

mexicana: *L. tridentata.*

tridentata (DC.) Cov. [*L. mexicana* Moric.]. Strongly scented, olive-green bush, to 10 ft., brs. with black, glandular rings at nodes; lfts. 2, obliquely ovate, to ⅜ in. long; petals to ¼ in. long; fr. villose-tomentose. Calif. to Tex. and Mex. By some authors not considered distinct from *L. divaricata.* Fl. buds pickled and eaten like capers; plant has medicinal uses.

LASIOCOCCUS: *GAYLUSSACIA.*

LASTHENIA Cass. [*Baeria* Fisch. & C. A. Mey.]. *Compositae* (Helenium Tribe). Sixteen spp. of ann., bien., or short-lived per. herbs, native to w. N. Amer., chiefly Calif., 1 sp. in Chile; sts. sometimes slightly succulent, glabrous or hairy; lvs. opp., entire to pinnatifid; fl. heads radiate, terminal, peduncled, involucre cylindrical to hemispherical, involucral bracts separate to entirely united, receptacle subulate, conical, or hemispherical, naked or scaly; disc fls. bisexual, yellow, ray fls. female, greenish, yellow, or white; achenes nearly cylindrical or compressed, glabrous or hairy, pappus absent, or of awns or scales, or a mixture of both.

Sometimes grown in the flower garden.

chrysostoma (Fisch. & C. A. Mey.) Greene [*L. hirsutula* Greene; *Baeria chrysostoma* Fisch. & C. A. Mey.; *B. chrysostoma* subsp. *gracilis* (DC.) Ferris and subsp. *hirsutula* (Greene) Ferris; *B. gracilis* (DC.) A. Gray; *B. hirsutula* (Greene) Greene]. GOLDFIELDS. Erect to decumbent ann., to 16 in., simple to corymbosely much-branched; lvs. linear, to 2¼ in. long, sometimes serrate, hairy; heads to 1 in. across, involucral bracts separate; fls. bright yellow; pappus absent or of awns or awned scales. S. Ore. to s. Ariz. and n. Baja Calif.

coronaria (Nutt.) Ornd. [*Baeria aristata* (Nutt.) A. Gray; *B. californica* (Nutt.) Chamb.; *B. coronaria* (Nutt.) A. Gray; *Hymenoxys californica* Hook.]. Simple or much-branched ann., to 16 in., sts. pubescent, hairs often glandular; lvs. linear, to 2¼ in. long, entire or pinnately divided; heads ½–¾ in. across, involucre turbinate to hemispherical, involucral bracts separate, glandular; fls. yellow; achenes linear, pappus none or of fimbriate or awn-tipped scales. S. Calif. to n. Baja Calif.

glabrata Lindl. [*L. glabrata* var. *californica* Jeps.]. Simple or branched ann., to 2 ft.; lvs. fleshy, linear to subulate, to 6 in. long, united at base, entire to obscurely toothed, glabrous; heads to 1 in. across, involucre depressed-hemispherical, involucral bracts united, receptacle conical; fls. yellow; achenes obovoid or club-shaped, pappus absent. N. Calif.

gracilis: *L. chrysostoma.*

hirsutula: *L. chrysostoma.*

macrantha (A. Gray) Greene [*Baeria macrantha* (A. Gray) A. Gray]. Ann., bien., or short-lived per., to 16 in., sts. usually branched at base; lvs. linear to oblong, to 8½ in. long, glabrous to densely hirsute, entire or with few teeth, margin ciliate; heads to 1½ in. across, involucre campanulate to depressed-hemispherical, involucral bracts separate, receptacle broadly conical; fls. yellow; pappus absent or of a few subulate awns. Coastal, s. Ore. to cent. Calif.

LASTREA: *THELYPTERIS.*

LATANIA Comm. LATAN PALM. *Palmae.* Three spp. of tall, stout, solitary, dioecious palms of the Mascarene Is.; lvs. costapalmate, petioles elongate, margins sometimes armed basally with spinelike teeth; infls. among lvs., unlike, with elongate peduncles sheathed by several tubular bracts, the male with several primary brs. along an elongate axis, each sheathed basally by a tubular bract and each divided into several rachillae bearing imbricate bractlets, the female with brs. usually simple, bractlets sheathing; male fls. solitary, in pits formed by bractlets, sepals and petals 3, nearly alike, separate or only shortly united, stamens many, pistillode columnar, shorter than stamens, female fls. much larger than male, solitary, sessile; sepals and petals 3, similar, imbricate basally, staminodes in a 6-lobed ring, pistil 3-celled, 3-ovuled; fr. globose or obovoid, fleshy-fibrous, 1–3-seeded, seeds variously sculptured, endosperm homogeneous.

Ornamental fan palms often planted in the tropics and subtropics and in Zone 10a in Fla., but not thriving in southern Calif. For culture see *Palms.*

borbonica: *L. lontaroides.*

Commersonii: *L. lontaroides.*

Loddigesii Mart. BLUE LATAN. To 50 ft.; lf. blades to 5 ft. long or more, glaucous-blue; infls. to 5 ft. long, with 5–12 brs., male rachillae woolly, 10 in. long or less; fr. to 2⅜ in. long, seeds irregularly and coarsely ribbed at apex with a central ridge to base. Mauritius Is.

lontaroides (Gaertn.) H. E. Moore [*L. borbonica* Lam.; *L. Commersonii* J. F. Gmel.]. RED LATAN. To 50 ft. or more; lf. blades 5 ft. long or more, gray-green or slightly bluish, petiole and base of blade tinged red or violet or blades reddish when young; infls. to 5 ft. long or more, male rachillae to 1 ft. long or more, not woolly; fr. to 1¾ in. long, seeds with low, curved ribs on back joining at rounded apex. Réunion Is.

Verschaffeltii Lem. YELLOW LATAN. To 50 ft. or more; lf. blades to 4½ ft. long or more, pale green suffused or margined with yellow, yellow-green when young; infls. to more than 6 ft. long, male rachillae to 1 ft. long, not woolly; fr. to 2 in. long, seeds with nearly parallel sides, roughened, apex with 2 lateral lobes and a point formed by the strong central rib. Rodrigues Is.

LATHYRUS L. [*Orobus* L.]. VETCHLING, WILD PEA. *Leguminosae* (subfamily *Faboideae*). More than 100 spp. of herbs, some scandent, native to N. Temp. Zone and mts., Afr. and S. Amer.; sts. winged or angular; lvs. alt., even-pinnate, the vining spp. with usually branched tendrils; fls. showy, axillary, racemose or solitary, papilionaceous, differing from *Vicia* in having wing petals nearly or quite separate from keel petals and a flattened style bearded on the inner face; fr. a legume, usually flat and dehiscent.

Several species are cultivated in southern Eur. for fodder and for edible seeds. Grown mostly as an ornamental. Perennial species are propagated by seeds and cuttings, and are of easy culture in any soil; annual species thrive in a deep, moist soil and plenty of sunlight. In the North, they are propagated by seeds in spring; in the South and in greenhouses the seeds may be sown in autumn for late winter bloom. Ample support should be provided for scandent species, and the seed pods picked often to lengthen flowering season.

cyaneus C. Koch. Per., about 1 ft.; lfts. in 2–3 pairs, close together, oblong-linear to awl-shaped, stipules sagittate; peduncles exceeding lvs.; fls. blue, calyx teeth unequal. Caucasus.

grandiflorus Sibth. & Sm. TWO-FLOWERED PEA, EVERLASTING P. Per., to 6 ft., sts. climbing, 4-angled, not winged; lfts. in 1 pair, ovate; fls. large, rose-purple, 2–3 on a peduncle; fr. cylindrical. S. Eur.

hirsutus L. SINGLETARY PEA, CALEY P., ROUGH P., WINTER P., WILD W.P., AUSTRIAN W.P. Ann., to 4 ft., sts. scandent, narrowly winged; lfts. in 1 pair, linear-lanceolate; fls. red-violet, 2–3 on a peduncle; fr. linear, hairy. Medit. region.

incanus (J. G. Sm. & Rydb.) Rydb. Erect, to 1 ft., densely hairy; lfts. in 3–4 pairs, linear or linear-oblong, stipules smaller; fls. purple, 1 in. long, in 3–5-fld. racemes; fr. to 1½ in. long. Nebr., w. to Colo. and Wyo.

japonicus Willd. [*L. maritimus* Bigel.]. BEACH PEA, HEATH P., SEA-SIDE P. Per., sts. decumbent, wingless, to 2 ft. long, stipules broadly ovate; lfts. in 3–6 pairs, oblong or ovate, to 2 in. long; fls. purple, in 6–10-fld. racemes. Shores of seas and lakes, N. Amer., Eur., Asia. A variable sp. sometimes divided into subspp.

laetiflorus Greene. Per., to 9 ft., sts. scandent, not winged; lfts. in 4–6 pairs, linear to ovate, to 2 in. long; pedicels $^{3}/_{16}$ in. long, fls. nearly white, veined with purple, many on a peduncle; fr. to 3 in. long. S. Calif. Subsp. **Alefeldii** (T. G. White) R. Brads. [*L. strictus* Nutt., not Grauer]. Pedicels ⅜ in. long, fls. deep red, to 1 in. long, standard more strongly reflexed. Subsp. **barbarae** (T. G. White) C. L. Hitchc. Fls. pink to lavender.

latifolius L. PERENNIAL PEA, EVERLASTING P. Per., climbing to 9 ft., glabrous, sts. strongly winged; lfts. in 1 pair, ovate-lanceolate, to 4 in. long, stipules like lfts.; fls. large, rose-colored or white, several to many on elongate peduncles, standard 1 in. across or more; fr. 3–5 in. long. Eur.; widely naturalized in U.S. Cv. **'Albus'**. Fls. white. Cv. **'Splendens'**. Fls. dark purple and red.

littoralis (Nutt. ex Torr. & A. Gray) Endl. BEACH PEA. Per., densely hairy, sts. erect or decumbent, to 2 ft. long, stipules larger than lfts.; lfts. in 2–4 pairs, oblanceolate-oblong, silky; fls. 2–6 on a peduncle, purple, wing petals and keel white. Seashore, B.C. to Calif.

luteus (L.) Peterm. [*Orobus luteus* L.]. Per., to 3 ft.; lfts. in 3–5 pairs, oblong, glaucous beneath; fls. bright yellow, in 5–15-fld. racemes. Eur. Var. **aureus** (Stev.) G. Beck. Racemes loose; fls. fawn-colored. Turkey.

maritimus: *L. japonicus.*

odoratus L. SWEET PEA. Ann., climbing to 6 ft., lightly pubescent; lfts. in 1 pair, elliptic, to 2 in. long; fls. fragrant, in many colors, to nearly 2 in. across, 1–4 on a peduncle; fr. pubescent, 2 in. long. Italy. Var. **nanellus** L. H. Bailey. Not climbing, the plants very compact.

ornatus Nutt. ex Torr. & A. Gray. Erect per., to 1 ft. or more; lfts. in 4–7 pairs, linear; fls. purple, 1 in. long, in 3–5-fld. racemes. S. Dak. to Wyo. and Okla.

pannonicus (Jacq.) Garcke. Glabrous per., to 2 ft., sts. angular; lfts. in 2–4 pairs, linear-lanceolate; fls. 3–8 in a raceme, white or buff, often suffused rose or purple. S. Eur. Var. **varius** (C. Koch) Zenari. Sts. flattened and winged, to 20 in.; lvs. narrow, pointed; fls. yellow and rose, lowest tooth of calyx about as long as tube or longer.

pratensis L. YELLOW V. Per., to 3 ft., pubescent, scandent; lfts. in 1 pair, lanceolate, stipules almost sagittate, nearly as long as lfts.; fls. yellow, to ⅝ in. long, usually 4–9 in a raceme; fr. black at maturity. Eur., s. Asia, and n. Afr.

purpureus K. Presl [*Orobus purpureus* Hort.]. Erect, sts. 4-angled; lfts. in 1 pair, linear or lanceolate-linear, acuminate, stipules ovate, semisagittate, longer than the winged petioles, tendrils branched; fls. nodding, on 1-fld. peduncles, corolla pale purple or rose; fr. lanceolate, netted, glabrous. Sicily.

splendens Kellogg. PRIDE-OF-CALIFORNIA. Per., somewhat shrubby; lfts. in 3–5 pairs, ovate-oblong, 1 in. long; fls. rose, violet, or magenta-red, 6–12 on a stout peduncle; fr. to 3 in. long, beaked. S. Calif., Baja Calif.

strictus: see *L. laetiflorus* subsp. *Alefeldii.*

sylvestris L. FLAT PEA, EVERLASTING P., PERENNIAL P. Per., to 6 ft., climbing, glabrous; lfts. in 1 pair, lanceolate to linear-lanceolate; fls. rose, variegated with purple and green, ½ in. long, 4–10 on a peduncle as long as lvs.; fr. lanceolate, to 3 in. long. Eur., sw. Asia. Cv. **'Wagneri'**. Fls. dark red.

tuberosus L. EARTH-NUT PEA, DUTCH-MICE, TUBEROUS V. Per., climbing or trailing to 4 ft., tendril- and tuber-bearing; lfts. in 1 pair, oblong to broadly lanceolate, to 1½ in. long; fls. rose, 3–5 on a long peduncle; fr. nearly cylindrical, to 1½ in. long. Eur., w. Asia. Tubers edible.

venosus Muhlenb. ex Willd. Per., sts. stout, to 3 ft., strongly 4-angled, pubescent; lfts. in 4–6 pairs, oblong-ovate, to 2 in. long; peduncles crowded, 8–16-fld.; fls. purple, to ⅝ in. long; fr. smooth. Late summer. New Bruns. to Alta., s. to Ga. and Tex.

vernus (L.) Bernh. [*Orobus vernus* L.]. SPRING V. Nearly erect per., to 2 ft.; lfts. in 2–3 pairs, ovate, to 3 in. long; fls. blue-violet, 5–8 on a peduncle; fr. glabrous, 1½ in. long. Eur. Cv. **'Albus'**. Fls. white.

vestitus Nutt. ex Torr. & A. Gray. Per., usually whitish-pubescent, to 16 in.; lfts. in 5 pairs, narrow, to $1^{3}/_{16}$ in. long, stipules smaller; corolla whitish, with pink or purple lines, varying to pink or lavender or reddish-purple, usually fading yellowish; fr. pubescent, about 2 in. long. Ore., Calif. Subsp. **puberulus** (T. G. White ex Greene) C. L. Hitchc. Taller, usually scandent and pubescent; fls. pinkish to lilac. Calif.

LAURACEAE Juss. LAUREL FAMILY. Dicot.; about 47 genera and 2,000–2,500 spp. of trees and shrubs, often aromatic, native mainly to trop. and subtrop. regions; lvs. mostly evergreen, leathery, alt., rarely opp. or subopp., occasionally whorled, without stipules; infl. axillary or nearly terminal, usually paniculate, occasionally racemose; fls. small, usually inconspicuous, green or yellow, without surrounding involucre, usually bisexual, the perianth segms. usually 6, in 2 whorls of 3 each, equal or nearly equal in length (except in *Persea*), the fertile stamens usually 9, the 3 outer whorls of

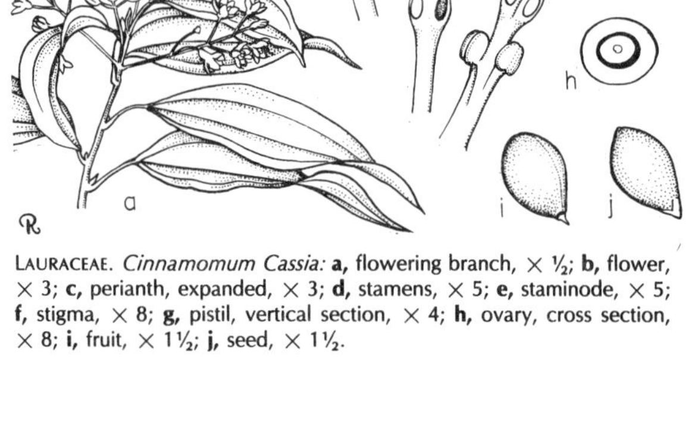

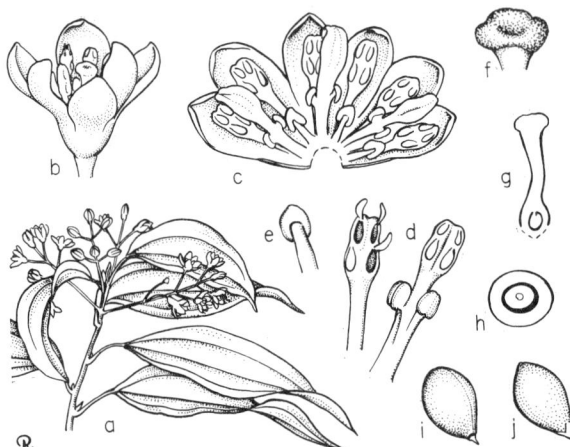

LAURACEAE. *Cinnamomum Cassia:* **a,** flowering branch, × ½; **b,** flower, × 3; **c,** perianth, expanded, × 3; **d,** stamens, × 5; **e,** staminode, × 5; **f,** stigma, × 8; **g,** pistil, vertical section, × 4; **h,** ovary, cross section, × 8; **i,** fruit, × 1½; **j,** seed, × 1½.

3 each, whorl 4, when present, consisting of 3 staminodes, varying in size and shape, smaller than fertile stamens, the anthers of fertile stamens basifixed, 2–4-celled, the ovary usually superior, 1-celled; fr. a green, yellow-green, or red berry, in a few related genera seated on naked pedicel (i.e. *Beilschmiedia, Cryptocarya,* etc.) without remnants of perianth, but usually more or less subtended by, or occasionally enclosed by, a fleshy cupule. Genera cult. as ornamentals are: *Actinodaphne, Beilschmiedia, Cinnamomum, Cryptocarya, Laurus, Lindera, Litsea, Neolitsea, Parabenzoin, Persea, Sassafras,* and *Umbellularia.*

Among other economic products, members of the family yield camphor *(Cinnamomum Camphora),* cassia *(C. Cassia),* cinnamon *(C. zeylanicum),* the avocado *(Persea americana),* and important timbers *(Aniba, Nectandra,* etc.).

LAURELIA Juss. *Monimiaceae.* Two spp. of tall, aromatic, dioecious or polygamous trees, native to Chile and New Zeal.; lvs. opp., leathery; fls. in axillary cymes or racemes, unisexual or bisexual, perianth 5–12-lobed, stamens 6–12, carpels several; fr. an achene.

novae-zealandiae A. Cunn. To 120 ft., buttressed at base; lvs. oblong or obovate, to 3 in. long, coarsely toothed, glossy above; racemes to 1 in. long; fls. ¼ in. across, styles silky-hairy, to ¾ in. long. New Zeal. Grown in Calif. Zone 10.

LAURENTIA Adans. [*Isotoma* (R. Br.) Lindl.]. *Lobeliaceae.* About 25 spp. of ann. or sometimes per. herbs, native to Medit. region, Afr., Australia, and the Americas; lvs. alt. or rarely whorled; fls. solitary or in racemes, corolla 2-lipped or nearly regular, tube not split, filaments inserted on petals or separate, anther tube slightly exserted, stigma 2-lobed; fr. a caps. Differs from *Lobelia* chiefly in corolla tube.

fluviatilis (R. Br.) F. E. Wimm. [*Isotoma fluviatilis* (R. Br.) F. J. Muell.]. Delicate, glabrate, prostrate per.; lvs. about ½ in. long, lower lvs. ovate or orbicular, upper ones linear; fls. longer than lvs., corolla to ⅝ in. long, blue, lobes nearly equal, acute-oblong, lower anthers awn-tipped and hispidulous. S. Australia, Tasmania, New Zeal.

longiflora: *Hippobroma longiflora.*

minuta (L.) A. DC. [*L. tenella* (Biv.) A. DC.]. Acaulescent herbs; lvs. in loose rosettes, spatulate to oblong; fls. on erect, bracted pedicels to 4 in. long, corolla pale violet, white or yellow-spotted inside. Medit. region, S. Afr.

petraea (F. J. Muell.) F. E. Wimm. [*Isotoma petraea* F. J. Muell.]. Glabrous, erect per., to 18 in.; lvs. oblong-ovate, to 2½ in. long, deeply and irregularly toothed; fls. on bractless pedicels to 6 in. long, corolla white or lilac, 1¼–1¾ in. long, lobes almost equal, lanceolate, tube slender, longer than lobes, lower anthers awn-tipped; caps. ½–¾ in. long. Australia.

tenella: *L. minuta.*

LAUROCERASUS: *PRUNUS.* **L. officinalis:** *P. Laurocerasus.* **L. rotundifolia:** *P. Laurocerasus* cv. **L. schipkaenis:** *P. Laurocerasus* cv. **L. Zabeliana:** a listed name of no botanical standing for *P. Laurocerasus* cv.

LAUROPHYLLUS Thunb. [*Botryceras* Willd.]. *Anacardiaceae.* One sp., an evergreen, dioecious, large shrub or small tree of S. Afr.; lvs. alt., simple; female infl. resembling much-branched antlers, male panicles loose and slender; fls. small, calyx 4–5-cleft, persistent, petals 4–5, triangular, ½–1 in. long, persistent, male fls. with stamens 4–5 on a fleshy disc, female fls. with ovary 1-celled, style 1, stigma 3-lobed; fr. a compressed, scarcely fleshy, winged drupe.

capensis Thunb. [*Botryoceras laurinum* Willd.]. Tree, to 20 ft.; lvs. persistent, elliptic-oblong to oblanceolate, 2–5 in. long, leathery, margins reflexed, serrate; fr. less than ³⁄₁₆ in. long. Cape of Good Hope.

LAURUS L. LAUREL, SWEET BAY. *Lauraceae.* Two spp. of aromatic, evergreen, medium-sized trees, 1 native to Medit. region, the other to Madeira and Canary Is.; lvs. alt., simple; fls. small, in axillary umbels, enclosed in bud by an involucre, bisexual or unisexual, perianth segms. 4, male fls. with fertile stamens 12 or more, anthers 2-celled; fr. a berry.

Includes the true laurel of antiquity, *L. nobilis,* whose branches in a garland symbolized victory or accomplishment. Laurel withstands several degrees of frost and neglect. It thrives in rich peaty soil with abundant moisture; propagated mostly by cuttings of ripened wood under glass, and sometimes by seed. Often grown as a tub plant.

Camphora: *Cinnamomum Camphora.*

glandulifera: *Cinnamomum glanduliferum.*

nobilis L. LAUREL, BAY, SWEET B. To 40 ft., often with suckers at base; lvs. lanceolate to elliptic, to 4 in. long, dark glossy green; fls. yellowish; fr. black or dark purple. Medit. region. Variable in stature and lf. shape; several cvs. are listed: **'Angustifolia'**, WILLOW-LEAF BAY, lvs. narrowly lanceolate; **'Aurea'**, lvs. yellowish; **'Salicifolia'**: 'Angustifolia'; **'Undulata'**, lf. margins wavy. The aromatic lvs. are used in cooking and yield an essential oil used in perfumery and medicine.

officinale: a listed name of no botanical standing; may refer to *L. nobilis.*

LAVANDULA L. LAVENDER. *Labiatae.* About 20 spp. of aromatic shrubs or herbs from the Atlantic Is., Medit. region to Somalia and India; sts. mostly square in cross section; lvs. opp., entire or dissected; fls. in verticillasters in loose or crowded spikes, bracts small, except for terminal ones in some spp., calyx ovoid-tubular, erect, nearly equally 13–15-nerved, slightly 5-toothed, corolla blue, violet, or purple, rarely white, tube longer than calyx, limb 2-lipped, upper lip 2-lobed, lower lip 3-lobed, lobes ovate, equal, stamens 4, in 2 pairs, anthers 1-celled, styles shortly 2-lobed; fr. of 4 glabrous nutlets.

Lavender is propagated by seeds or division, but preferably by autumn or spring cuttings. All species thrive in a sunny, well-drained location. Oil of lavender, used in perfumery, is distilled from the flowers of *L. angustifolia* and *L. Stoechas.*

abrotanoides: *L. multifida* subsp. *canariensis.*

alba: a listed name of no botanical standing for *L. angustifolia* cv.

angustifolia Mill. ENGLISH L. Shrub, 2–3 ft., tomentose; lvs. linear-lanceolate to linear-oblanceolate, to 2½ in long, to ¼ in. wide, white-tomentose when young, becoming green; spikes to 3¼ in. long, verticillasters 6–10-fld.; calyx ¼ in. long, 13-nerved, dense-pubescent, corolla twice as long as calyx, about ½ in. long, usually purple. Medit. region. Widely cult. as an ornamental and for perfumery. Subsp. **angustifolia** [*L. delphinensis* Jord. ex Billot; *L. officinalis* Chaix; *L. Spica* L. var. *angustifolia* L.f.; *L. vera* DC.]. The typical subsp.; bracts usually shorter than calyx; calyx about ³⁄₁₆ in. long, appendage on upper tooth obscure. Cvs. are: **'Alba'**, fls. white; **'Atropurpurea'**, fls. dark purple; **'Compacta'**, of compact habit; **'Dutch'**, fls. deep blue; **'Fragrance'**, fls. heavily scented; **'Hidcote'**, slow-growing, fls. deep purple; **'Munstead'**, fls. lavender-blue, early-blooming; **'Nana'**, dwarf; **'Rosea'**, fls. rose-pink; **'Twickel Purple'**, spikes long, fls. purple, in fanlike clusters; **'Waltham'**, fls. deep purple. Subsp. **pyrenaica** (DC.) Guinea [*L. pyrenaica* DC.]. Bracts usually longer than calyx; calyx about ¼ in. long, appendage on upper tooth distinct. Ne. Spain and e. Pyrenees.

atropurpurea: a listed name of no botanical standing for *L. angustifolia* cv.

Buchii: *L. pinnata.*

canariensis: *L. multifida* subsp.

delphinensis: see *L. angustifolia* subsp. *angustifolia* and *L. dentata.*

dentata L. [*L. delphinensis* Hort., not Jord. ex Billot]. FRENCH L. Shrub, 1–3 ft., densely gray-tomentose; lvs. linear-oblong, crenately toothed to pectinate-pinnatifid, obtuse, revolute, sessile; spikes to 1½ in. long, ½ in. in diam., verticillasters 6–10-fld., bracts obovate, to ⅜ in. long, acute, purplish, upper bracts sterile, lanceolate, to ½ in. long, purple; calyx 5-lobed, ¼ in. long, corolla slightly longer than calyx, 5-lobed, purple. S. and e. Spain, Balearic Is. Var. **candicans** Batt. Lvs. larger, densely white-tomentose when young.

lanata Boiss. Resembles *L. angustifolia* subsp. *angustifolia,* but sts. and lvs. densely white-woolly, and calyx 8-nerved and 8-toothed. Mts., s. Spain. Material offered under this name may be *L. angustifolia.*

latifolia Medic. Like *L. angustifolia* subsp. *angustifolia,* but lvs. gray-green and more densely tomentose, bracts linear to linear-lanceolate, and corolla about ⅜ in. long. Medit. region and Portugal.

multifida L. [*L. pubescens* Decne.]. Shrub or suffrutescent herb, to 2 ft., gray-tomentose; lvs. pinnately to 2-pinnately dissected, to 1½ in. long or more, segms. ¼–¾ in. long; spikes solitary or in 3's, 1–2½ in. long, compact, peduncles 6–20 in. long, verticillasters 2–fld., bracts cordate-ovate, about ³⁄₁₆ in. long; calyx about ³⁄₁₆ in. long, 15-nerved, upper tooth lacking appendage, corolla about ½ in. long, blue-violet. W. Medit. region, Portugal. Subsp. **canariensis** (Mill.) Pit. & Proust [*L. abrotanoides* Lam.; *L. canariensis* Mill.; *L. multifida* var. *canariensis*

(Mill.) O. Kuntze]. Lvs. less dissected, segms. narrower. Canary Is. Plants offered as *L. pinnata* var. *Buchii* may belong here.

nana: a listed name of no botanical standing for *L. angustifolia* subsp. *angustifolia* cv.

officinalis: *L. angustifolia* subsp. *angustifolia*.

pedemontana: a listed name of no botanical standing for *L. Stoechas*.

pedunculata: *L. Stoechas* subsp.

pinnata L.f. [*L. Buchii* Webb & Berth.; *L. pinnata* var. *Buchii* (Webb & Berth.) Benth.]. Shrub, to 3 ft.; lvs. pinnate, to 2½ in. long, segms. broad, to ⅛ in. wide or wider; spikes 2–3 in. long, simple or branched, peduncles 8–14 in. long, often shorter in cult. material, bracts 4-ranked, lanceolate; corolla lavender, mostly ¼–⅜ in. long. Madeira and Canary Is. Var. **Buchii:** *L. pinnata*, but plants offered as *L. pinnata* var. *Buchii* may also be *L. multifida* subsp. *canariensis*.

praecox: a listed name of no botanical standing for *L. angustifolia* subsp. *angustifolia*.

pubescens: *L. multifida*.

pyrenaica: *L. angustifolia* subsp.

serrata: a listed name of no botanical standing; probably intended for *L. dentata*.

Spica L. An ambiguous name, but as used in hort. referring to *L. angustifolia*.

Stoechas L. SPANISH L., FRENCH L. Shrub, to 3 ft., tomentose; lvs. linear to oblong-lanceolate, ¾–1 in. long, entire; spikes ¾–1¼ in. long, verticillasters 6–10-fld., upper bracts sterile, oblong-obovate, to 2 in. long, usually purple; calyx to ¼ in. long, 13-nerved, corolla dark purple, about ⅜ in. long. Cult. as an ornamental and for perfumery. Medit. region, Portugal. About 6 subspp. are recognized. Subsp. **pedunculata** (Mill.) Samp. ex Rozeira [*L. pedunculata* (Mill.) Cav.]. Peduncles 4–10 in. long; calyx shorter than lower bracts, appendage entire. Cent. Spain, mts. of ne. Portugal.

vera: *L. angustifolia* subsp. *angustifolia*.

LAVATERA L. TREE MALLOW. *Malvaceae*. Between 20 and 25 spp. of herbs or shrubs, mostly of the Medit. region, but also the Canary Is., Asia, Australia, and the Channel Is. off s. Calif. and Baja Calif.; lvs. usually long-petioled, palmately angled or lobed; fls. axillary or in terminal racemes, involucral bracts 3–6 or 9, united basally in a deep or shallow cup, petals 5, obcordate, white or rose-purple, style brs. filiform, stigmatic on inner edge, as many as the mericarps; fr. a schizocarp, mericarps 5 or more, in a whorl about the central conical or umbrellalike receptacle, each 1-seeded.

Lavateras are of easy cultivation; seeds are sown where the plants are to stand. The perennials come poorly from cuttings.

alba: *L. trimestris*.

arborea L. TREE MALLOW. Bien., but often flowering the first year, treelike, soft-downy-pubescent, 3–10 ft.; lvs. 3–9 in. long and wide, 5-, 7-, or 9-lobed; fls. clustered, axillary, shorter than the lvs., involucre 3-lobed, calyx shorter than involucre, enlarging and spreading in fr., petals purple-red with darker veins basally, about 1 in. long; mericarps 6–9, dorsally and laterally ridged, the edges sharp. Eur.; naturalized in coastal Calif. Cv. 'Variegata'. Lvs. mottled.

assurgentiflora Kellogg. MALVA ROSA. Mostly glabrous, coarse shrub, 6–15 ft.; lvs. 3–6 in. wide, with 5 or 7 coarsely toothed, triangular lobes, paler beneath than above; fls. solitary, axillary, on recurved-ascending pedicels, involucral bracts 3, ovate, united only at the base, petals rose-purple with darker veins, about 1½ in. long, mericarps woody, about ¼ in. long. Channel Is. off Calif.; naturalized in Calif. and Baja Calif.

cachemiriana Camb. Soft-pubescent herb, 4–8 ft.; lower lvs. cordate-orbicular, 5-lobed, shallowly crenate, upper lvs. more distinctly 3- or 5-lobed, the middle lobe acute and longest; fls. solitary in upper lf. axils, involucral bracts 3, ovate, united to about the middle, shorter than the calyx, petals pink, deeply bifid, about 1½ in. long. Kashmir.

cretica L. Sparsely pubescent, erect ann. or bien., 4–6 ft.; lower lvs. cordate-orbicular, the upper lvs. truncate, shallowly and broadly 5-lobed; fls. 2–8 in loose, axillary clusters, shorter than the lvs., involucre with 3 rounded lobes shorter than the calyx, petals lilac to purple, to ¾ in. long; mericarps mostly 7–9, smooth or slightly ridged, the edges rounded. S. Eur.; sparingly naturalized elsewhere.

maritima Gouan. Small shrub, to about 4 ft., new growth densely whitish-tomentose; lvs. suborbicular to reniform, obtusely 5-angled or -lobed, mostly about 2 in. long and wide; fls. 1 or 2, axillary, pedicelled, involucral bracts to about ¼ in. long, nearly separate to the base, shorter than the calyx, petals white or pink with a purple base, ⅝–

1¼ in. long; mericarps 9–13, strongly ridged, the edges sharp and denticulate. W. Medit.

Olbia L. TREE L. Hispid-stemmed shrub, to 6 ft. or more; lvs. tomentose, lower lvs. to 6 in. long, 5-lobed, upper lvs. smaller, 3-lobed and with the middle lobe longest, or scarcely lobed and oblong; fls. solitary and axillary, or in elongate, naked racemes, involucral bracts 3, united to the middle, ovate-acuminate, to ½ in. long, petals reddish-purple, to 1¼ in. long; mericarps mostly more than 15, the edges rounded. W. Medit.

rosea: *L. trimestris*.

splendens: *L. trimestris* cv.

thuringiaca L. Tomentose, per. herb, sts. erect, to 4 ft. or more; lvs. to about 3 in. long and wide, cordate-ovate, 3- or 5-lobed; fls. solitary in axils of upper lvs. or in loose terminal racemes, involucre 3-lobed, about ⅜ in. long, shorter than the calyx, petals purplish-pink, ⅝–1¾ in. long; mericarps about 20, slightly ridged, the edges rounded. Cent. and se. Eur.

trimestris L. [*L. alba* Medic.; *L. rosea* Medic.]. Branching, sparsely pubescent ann., to 3 ft. or more; lvs. suborbicular, mostly less than 2 in. long and wide, palmately angled; fls. solitary in axils of upper lvs., on elongate pedicels, involucral bracts 3, united for most of their length, broadly ovate, calyx enlarging markedly in fr., petals white, rose-pink or red, 1–1¾ in. long; mericarps mostly 10–15, overlain by the broad umbrellalike receptacle. Medit. region. Cv. 'Splendens'. Fls. large, rose-red or white.

LAVAUXIA: *OENOTHERA*.

LAWN. A lawn is a regularly mowed planting, typically of grasses, usually maintained for attractive landscaping adjacent to a habitation. Lawns provide useful outdoor living space, and do much to make the environment more pleasant. They protect and improve the soil, hold down dust, ameliorate temperatures, both summer and winter, and contribute to biological balance.

Grasses (Gramineae) are especially well adapted for lawns, growing as they do from a basal meristem that is not lost to mowing. Prostrate plants in many families could conceivably serve for a lawn, but most are not suited to mechanized mowing, fertilization, or pest control, and are better considered as ground covers managed as are flower beds (see *Ground Covers*). An exception is *Dichondra*, of the Convolvulaceae, which is widely used for lawns in California and the southwestern United States; clovers, especially species of *Trifolium*, of the Leguminosae, are grass companions in many turfs. Adventives such as ground ivy (*Glechoma hederacea*), knotweed (*Polygonum aviculare*), and milky spurge (*Euphorbia maculata*) contribute seasonally to lawn cover, but are commonly regarded as weeds along with more discordant genera such as dandelion (*Taraxacum*) and plantain (*Plantago*).

By and large, for the United States and portions of the rest of the world where formal lawns are maintained, the following are the chief species planted. Limited use is made of other grasses where they are locally better adapted (as on alkaline soils in the dry plains).

For northerly climates (e.g., areas in the United States roughly north of a line drawn from San Francisco, California, to northern Arizona, Tennessee, and Washington, D.C.: Kentucky bluegrass (*Poa pratensis*), best for most lawns, widely adaptable, and an excellent sod former; perennial ryegrass (*Lolium perenne*), quick-sprouting and attractive but not spreading by rhizomes, not mowing cleanly, and not holding up as well in extreme weather as bluegrass; fine fescue (*Festuca rubra* and its cultivars), good companion of bluegrass, adapted to poor soil, shade, and drought, and needing little fertilization; bent grasses (*Agrostis* species), trailing species requiring close, frequent clipping, doing best in moist climates.

For southerly climates (for those parts of the South and Southwest falling mainly in plant hardiness Zones 8, 9, and 10): Bermuda grass (*Cynodon Dactylon* and its hybrids); zoysia (*Zoysia* species); centipede grass (*Eremochloa ophiuroides*); Bahia grass (*Paspalum notatum*); St. Augustine grass (*Stenotaphrum secundatum*).

Occasionally coarser pasture grasses are utilized in difficult locations, such as tall fescue *(Festuca elatior)* in the border states, buffalo grass *(Buchloe dactyloides)* where lawns cannot be irrigated in the plains country, or carpet grass *(Axonopus affinis)* for poorly drained terrain in the southernmost states. On the whole, however, unselected pasture grasses are not recommended, for species such as tall fescue may become some of the worst weeds in otherwise fine-textured lawn plantings.

Not until the last two decades have selection and breeding of fine turf cultivars been undertaken in the same fashion as breeding of ornamentals and vegetables. 'Merion' Kentucky bluegrass was the first improved pure line, making its mark in the 1950's, and leading to many modern cultivars for cooler regions. Some of the most significant breeding of turfgrass cultivars for warmer regions has been at Tifton, Georgia, where common bermuda grass was crossed with a South African species to yield a series of sterile triploids highly esteemed for golf courses, lawns, and athletic fields.

Not only do cultivars change, but the complexion of their handling as well. For example, the nurse grass concept, in the sense of a temporary, quick cover that eventually will give way to the wanted grass, has become outdated for new seedings. A nurse grass competes with the desired turf for space and nutrients, and may interfere with the lawn's establishment. And it may persist, turning unsightly in time, as annual ryegrass *(Lolium multiflorum)* and redtop *(Agrostis gigantea)* often do. Instead, attractive cultivars having permanent value are suggested, such as those of perennial ryegrass (notably fast to germinate) or even fine fescue (moderately fast to germinate). Even so, skilled lawnsmen generally prefer to plant only those species and cultivars that they want to be represented permanently in the lawn.

The newer lawn grass cultivars, bred as they are especially for lawns, have characteristics that will influence lawn maintenance. Most have low, decumbent growth that retains more photosynthetic tissue below mowing height than do common grasses. This should provide greater density, hence fewer weeds, and greater vigor for better wear. New cultivars are selected for resistance to lawn diseases, and should do well without preventive spraying for disease. Many also have a longer season, a deeper color, and a finer texture, which make them more attractive than old-fashioned grass.

Lawns are planted both from seed and vegetatively by means of sod, sprigs, or plugs. Autumn is the preferred time to plant bluegrass or bent grass lawns (late August in northernmost states and by mid-September in border states). Seeding is normally the most economic way to start a lawn, and avoids possible importation of diseases, weed seeds, and insect pests that may be hidden in fresh sod. On the other hand, sodding gives instant cover, and sod that is professionally grown and laid, although more expensive than seeding, should yield an equally satisfying turf. Planting of sprigs (individual stems) or plugs (biscuits of sod) is an inexpensive means for starting grasses that do not come true from seed; it is practiced especially in the South. No matter whether the lawn is started from seed or vegetatively, soil-bed preparation should be equally thorough; sod needs a good rooting medium just as much as does seed.

The traditional, and most effective, method of seed bed preparation is to cultivate the soil at least 2 or 3 inches deep, raking out clumps of old vegetation or other debris that may surface. This is the time to mix in a phosphorus-containing fertilizer (phosphorus fixes on soil particles, will not work down into the root zone very quickly when applied after the grass is growing). Also, supply the soil with basic needs such as lime, if a soil test so indicates. Except when the soil has a very poor structure, it is not necessary to work organic matter into the soil bed. Grass builds up organic residues as its diffuse root system grows. The least amount of cultivation needed to make a seed bed loose is suggested, avoiding pulverizations that break down soil structure. Rolling is generally not recommended, for it recompacts the soil. Ordinarily a newly worked soil bed is best settled for final leveling by soaking the ground rather than by rolling it.

Almost all soils contain some viable weed seeds, which can be killed only by drastic measures such as soil sterilization (as with methyl bromide, under a tarpaulin). Most weeds disappear in time, decapitated by mowing, crowded out by the grass, or a victim of lawn herbicides. Fortunately, modern lawn grass seed is carefully grown and cleaned, so that it contains almost no troublesome weed seeds; however, "bargain" offerings may include off-types (noted as "crop" on the label) that can introduce unwanted pasture plants. When buying lawn seed, read the label carefully to be sure you are getting just the seeds you want, with a minimum of weeds or crop.

Lawn seed can be sown by hand, but is more quickly and accurately distributed with a mechanical spreader. Inaccuracy is minimized if half the seed is spread in one direction, the other half at right angles. With a loosened seed bed, the seed sifts into the crevices between soil chunks and is ideally situated for sprouting. If the surface is not crumbly, a light raking or dragging may be required after sowing. Only fluffy soils merit rolling after seeding, to reestablish capillarity. The surface of a rolled seed bed tends to become less pervious, rejects entry of water, and puddles quickly.

Most of the time a new lawn seeding is profitably mulched, as with a thin layer of straw, excelsior, or woven netting (obtainable at garden centers). Not only does this protect the soil from wash, but it keeps the seed bed from drying out rapidly and thus facilitates sprouting. Sprouting occurs within just a few days with perennial ryegrass, if the seed bed is kept moist and the weather is warm, but two or three weeks may be needed for much show with Kentucky bluegrass. Not much can be done about the weather (sprouting will always be slow during cool spells, as in early spring), but frequent light sprinklings enable the seedlings to prosper. Most mulches are left in place to decay, and are soon overtopped by seedling grass. The young grass should be mowed before it doubles its customary mowing height.

Established lawns can be renovated without so disruptive a procedure as soil cultivation, with at least a fair likelihood of success. Restrain the old vegetation as much as possible, and scarify the soil to provide lodging sites for the new seeds. An exceptionally low mowing (scalping), raking out thatch (powered machines are available for this), or chemical knockdown of the old vegetation (using materials that leave no residual toxicity in the soil), all serve to reduce competition for the new grass. Scarifying machines, variously termed thinners, spikers, power rakes, serve to scratch the soil surface enough so that seed is held for rooting. Watering should be frequent until the new grass is established, and gentle enough so that no runoff occurs. Essentially this same series of steps is undertaken when adding winter grass (any of the northern species, but especially ryegrass) to southern turf (particularly bermuda grass) when it goes dormant in late autumn.

Care of an established lawn varies from place to place, according to preference of the homeowner and the kind of grass. By definition, all lawns require mowing; most of them receive fertilization periodically, possibly irrigation, and occasionally pest control.

Height of mowing should match the kind of grass. Bent grasses in the North and Bermuda grasses in the South are typically clipped fairly low, often 1 inch or less. The common types of other northern grasses, and Bahia and St. Augustine grass in the South, are usually mowed tall, 2 inches or more. The improved northern grasses, common Bermuda grass, most zoysias, and centipede grass are usually mowed at intermediate heights. Low mowing is ordinarily best undertaken with a reel mower, while the more versatile and less expensive rotary mowers are well suited to cutting taller grass. Mowing should be undertaken any time the grass much exceeds half again its usual height, and may be required every second day with the very low-mowed creeping bent grasses and Bermuda grasses, about every five days (at the height of the season) with other grasses, and perhaps not for weeks on end during drought or other weather-induced dormancy.

Water requirements of lawns vary with climate, being greater in dry habitats and under high temperature than in humid locations or cooler climates. On the average, grass transpires about 1 inch of water per week in good growing weather. In the more humid regions, lawns ordinarily survive without supplementary irrigation, although they may turn off-color temporarily. In arid regions, irrigation is necessary even to have any lawn at all with conventional lawn grass. Lawns should be irrigated at a rate permitting water to soak into the soil without runoff; sandy soils absorb water rapidly, clay types and compacted soils only slowly.

Most of the new lawn grass cultivars were bred in expectation that the lawn would receive at least occasional fertilization, and even the older common grass is denser and of better color when fertilized. Kentucky bluegrass lawns should be fertilized generously in autumn, for this is the time of year when tillering occurs abundantly and food reserves build up (though the grass remains relatively low in response to the season, and mowing problems are not incurred). Southern grasses are best fertilized throughout the growing season. Fertilizers rich in nitrogen, which encourages leaf growth, are recommended for lawns. Typical analyses that are good are 22 (nitrogen)-8 (phosphorus)-4 (potash), 24–9–5, and 30–5–8. Types containing slow-release nitrogen have been developed specifically for turf. Much of their nitrogen is in polymerized form, and must be acted upon by the soil microorganisms before becoming available. Ureaform, a copolymer of urea and formaldehyde, is widely used. Gradual-release fertilizers typically do not burn lawns, unlike dusty products containing soluble salts that dessicate grass tissue. Fertilizer with weed killer, containing 2,4-D, offers an efficient weed-and-feed treatment at one time.

Experts suggest fertilization rates ranging from 1 or 2 pounds of elemental nitrogen per 1,000 square feet annually for grasses adapted to poor soils, like fescue and centipede grass, to as much as 8 pounds or more for heavy feeders like 'Merion' bluegrass and Bermuda grass cultivars. For a lawn to be attractive, dense, and able to maintain itself, it should be fertilized at least once or twice yearly, typically with a complete fertilizer (containing phosphorus and potassium as well as nitrogen), at a rate of 1–2 pounds of nitrogen per 1,000 square feet per application. Half-rate fertilization is appropriate for hot weather.

Weeding is perhaps the most practiced pest control activity with lawns. Disease control is complex and expensive, usually beyond the interest and capacity of a homeowner, although professionals (such as superintendents of golf courses) undertake preventive fungicidal sprayings regularly. As already noted, the newer lawn grass cultivars are for the most part tolerant of disease, and their use is the easiest way to prevent epidemics. Insects can be devastating, but fortunately attack lawns infrequently. Environmental laws restrict insecticide availability, and in general biodegradable products are required when spraying for chinchbug, sod webworm, or similar lawn pests. Chlordane, soaked into the ground at relatively high rates, has been the traditional preventive for soil insects (e.g., grubs of June beetles, Japanese beetles), but is has become restricted in some states, and no really long-lasting substitute is available.

Control of broadleaf dicotyledonous weeds such as dandelions and plantains is relatively simple, since such plants can be eliminated selectively in grass with phenoxy chemicals; 2, 4-D is often combined with other synergistic compounds such as MCPP and dicamba, a combination lethal to almost all broadleaf species but not injurious to grass when used as recommended. Only very light rates are needed, but even so such hormonal herbicides should be used with caution, and not near budding shrubbery or other ornamentals. Autumn is a good time to kill broadleaf weeds when danger of damage to ornamentals is less. Some southern lawn grasses, such as St. Augustine grass, are not tolerant of phenoxy chemicals, and for them special herbicides are offered, these often based upon triazine compounds.

Selective control of grass weeds in lawns is more difficult.

Crabgrass preventers kill annual grass seedlings as they germinate, or most annual grasses can be eliminated later with two or three arsenate sprays about a week apart. Elimination of coarse perennial grasses almost requires spot killing of all vegetation, or a drawn out attempt to outgrow the weed species by encouraging the lawn grass. Glyphosate, paraquat, and cacodylic acid kill living tissue contacted, but leave no residual toxicity in the soil (glyphosate is systemic, being carried into the underground parts, such as the rhizomes of quack grass, *Agropyron repens*). Chemicals such as these are suggested for quick knockdown before reseeding. Other compounds, such as amitrol and dalapon, are effective perennial grass killers, but they leave toxic residues in the soil that require a wait of a few weeks for dissipation. Limited selective success has been achieved through careful regulation of rates, so that a chemical sets back the unwanted grass before becoming injurous to the lawn cultivars, but this is a difficult judgment for the nonprofessional. Monocotyledonous pests other than grass can often be controlled selectively, however: nut grass or sedge (*Cyperus esculentus*), for example, with repeat sprays of arsenate or bentazon, rushes (*Juncus*) with combinations of the 2,4-D-MCPP-dicamba type.

LAWSONIA L. *Lythraceae.* One sp., a variable shrub, native to N. Afr., Asia, and Australia; lvs. opp.; fls. in many-fld., terminal panicles, 4-merous; fr. indehiscent, longer than calyx tube.

Planted as an ornamental in warm regions; the dried ground leaves yield henna, a very fast orange dye.

alba: *L. inermis.*

inermis L. [*L. alba* Lam.]. HENNA, MIGNONETTE TREE. To 20 ft.; lvs. elliptic or elliptic-lanceolate, ½–2 in. long; fls. white, rose, or cinnabar-red, ¼ in. across or less, fragrant. Cvs. 'Alba' and 'Rubra' are listed. Naturalized in trop. Amer.

rubra: a listed name of no botanical standing for *L. inermis* cv.

LAYERING: see *Propagation.*

LAYIA Hook. & Arn. ex DC. *Compositae* (Helianthus Tribe). About 15 spp. of low, ann. herbs in Calif.; lvs. entire, toothed or pinnately lobed; fl. heads radiate, solitary, terminal, involucral bracts in 1 row, their bases enclosing the ray achenes; disc fls. many, yellow, ray fls. yellow or white; disc achenes with pappus of scales or often basally plumose bristles, ray achenes without pappus.

Of easy cultivation in the flower garden. Propagated by seeds sown in the open or started indoors.

elegans: *L. platyglossa.*

platyglossa (Fisch. & C. A. Mey.) A. Gray [*L. elegans* Torr. & A. Gray]. TIDY-TIPS. Decumbent to erect, to 12 in., hirsute and glandular; lvs. linear to narrowly oblong, the lower toothed or pinnatifid, the upper entire; heads to 2 in. across; ray fls. yellow with cream-white tips, anthers black; pappus of rough or plumose bristles. One of the conspicuous early summer field fls. of Calif.

LEBECKIA Thunb. *Leguminosae* (subfamily *Faboideae*). About 45 spp. of suffrutescent herbs or small shrubs, often spiny, native to S. Afr.; lvs. alt., of 1–3 lfts.; fls. yellow, papilionaceous, in racemes, calyx oblique, 5-parted, with rounded sinuses between teeth, keel longer than the wing petals and often the standard, stamens 10, united; fr. a linear legume.

Simsiana Eckl. & Zeyh. Shrubby, sts. nearly simple, almost erect, to 18 in., glaucous; lvs. many, filiform, to 4 in. long, jointed above middle, ascending; racemes terminal, to 12 in. long, dense, many-fld.; fls. showy, nodding, ½ in. long; fr. cylindrical, pendent, 1½ in. long. Cape Prov. Zone 10.

LECYTHIDACEAE Poit. LECYTHIS FAMILY. Dicot.; 15 genera of trees in trop. Amer.; lvs. alt., simple, without stipules; fls. solitary or in spikes, racemes, or corymbs, bisexual, regular or corolla and stamens irregular, sepals mostly 4–6, valvate, petals mostly 4–6, separate or rarely somewhat united, stamens many in several whorls, borne on a disclike androphore and often arranged on 1 side of the fl.; ovary inferior, 2–6-celled; fr. a berry or woody caps., indehiscent or opening by a lid and known popularly as "monkey pot."

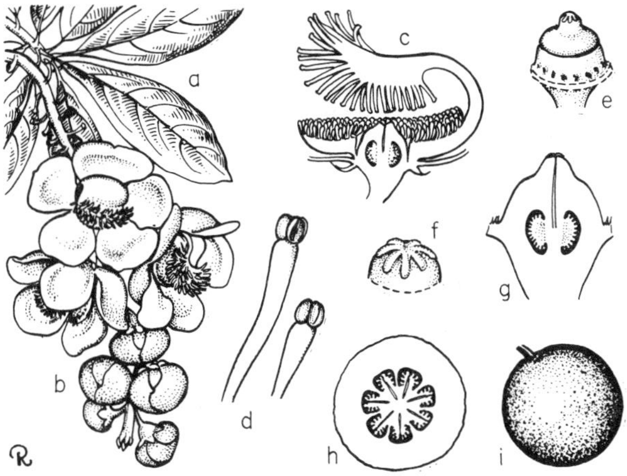

LECYTHIDACEAE. *Couroupita guianensis:* **a,** leafy twig, × ¼; **b,** inflorescence, × ¼; **c,** flower, vertical section, × ¾; **d,** stamens, × 5; **e,** pistil, × 1; **f,** stigma, × 4; **g,** pistil, vertical section, × 1½; **h,** ovary, cross section, × 2; **i,** fruit, × 1/12.

Cult. genera include: *Bertholletia, Couroupita, Gustavia,* and *Lecythis.*

LECYTHIS Loefl. *Lecythidaceae.* About 50 spp. of mostly large trees in trop. Amer.; lvs. alt., simple, leathery, without stipules; infl. of racemes or panicles; calyx 6-lobed, petals 6, unequal, stamens many, borne centrally on an androphore which is prolonged laterally into an overarching ligule bearing many sterile appendages apically on its inner surface, ovary inferior, 4-celled; fr. woody, opening by a lid, often known as "monkey pot."

The sapucia or paradise nuts of commerce are the seeds of trees of this genus, especially *L. usitata* Miers and *L. Zabucayo.* Suitable for cultivation in Zone 10b in Fla.

elliptica: *L. minor.*

minor Jacq. [*L. elliptica* HBK]. Tree; lvs. elliptic, 6–7 in. long, short-acuminate, dentate-crenate; fls. in strict racemes or panicles about 1 ft. long, petals white to rose, about 1¼ in. long; fr. subglobose, to 2½ in. long with a moderately lobed or unlobed rim at the middle or toward the base. Colombia.

Pisonis Camb. Lofty tree; lvs. lanceolate-oblong, to 6 in. long, abruptly acuminate, obscurely crenulate, dark green, glossy; fls. violet, about 2 in. across; fr. subglobose, to 8 in. long, and broad, with a ring of 6 prominent lobes near the middle. Brazil.

tuyrana Pitt. Tree, to 90 ft.; lvs. elongate-oblong, 8–15 in. long, to 4½ in. wide, abruptly acuminate, entire, brownish-olive; fls. many in panicles, sessile, sulphur-yellow, about 2 in. across; fr. brown, subglobose, to 6 in. long, obscurely 6-lobed above the middle. Panama.

Zabucayo Aubl. SAPUCIA NUT, PARADISE N., MONKEY N. Tree, to 70 ft., brs. spreading; lvs. oblong-lanceolate, to 6 in. long, acuminate, entire or obscurely serrate; fls. white, about 1 in. across, androphore rose; fr. subglobose, to 6 in. long, with unlobed rim about 1 in. below lid. French Guiana.

LEDEBOURIA Roth. *Liliaceae.* About 16 spp. of bulbous, scapose, per. herbs, native mostly to S. Afr., 1 sp. in India; bulbs tunicate, scales never fibrous toward apex; lvs. basal, often marked with green or red spots, particularly on upper surface; infl. an erect or flexuous, axillary raceme; fls. pink, dull red, green, or green and purple, perianth segms. reflexed or erect, stamens 6, filaments separate, ovary superior; fr. a loculicidal caps., seeds 2 in each cell.

socialis (Bak.) Jessop [*Scilla socialis* Bak.; *S. violacea* Hutch.]. To about 6 in., bulb produced above ground; lvs. 3–5, lanceolate to oblong-lanceolate, 2–4 in. long, somewhat fleshy, lower surface often pink or violet, upper surface with silvery sheen; fls. campanulate, perianth segms. recurved, green with white margins, filaments purple. S. Afr.

LEDENBERGIA Klotzsch ex Moq.: *FLUECKIGERA* O. Kuntze. *Phytolaccaceae.* Not in cult.; material offered as **L. roseo-aenea** is *Trichostigma peruvianum.*

LEDUM L. *Ericaceae.* Perhaps 3 or 4 spp. of evergreen shrubs, of sphagnum bogs and damp places, native to cold parts of N. Amer. and Eurasia; lvs. alt., simple, entire, leathery; fls. white, in dense, terminal, umbel-like clusters, calyx 5-toothed, petals 5, separate, stamens 5–10, ovary superior; fr. a 5-valved caps.

Ledums succeed in sandy, peaty, moist soil, and are suitable for evergreen borders. Propagated by seeds in spring, and by layers and division.

columbianum: *L. glandulosum* var.

decumbens: *L. palustre* var.

glandulosum Nutt. To 6 ft.; lvs. ovate to oblong or elliptic, to 2 in. long, about half as broad as long, glaucous and glandular-lepidote beneath, flat or slightly revolute; stamens 8–10. Summer. Nw. N. Amer. to Rocky Mts. Zone 6. Var. **columbianum** (Piper) C. L. Hitchc. [*L. columbianum* Piper]. Lvs. strongly revolute, narrower. Coastal, s. Wash. to n. Calif.

groenlandicum Oed. LABRADOR TEA. To 3 ft.; lvs. linear-oblong to oblong, to 2 in. long, rusty-tomentose beneath; stamens 5–7. Late spring. N. N. Amer., Greenland. Zone 2. Cv. **'Compacta'.** A dwarf form.

nipponicum: *L. palustre* var. *diversipilosum.*

palustre L. CRYSTAL TEA, WILD ROSEMARY. To 3 ft.; lvs. linear or linear-oblong, to 1½ in. long, rusty-tomentose beneath; pedicels glandular. N. Eur., n. Asia. Zone 2. Var. **decumbens** Ait. [*L. decumbens* (Ait.) Lodd. ex Steud.]. Decumbent; lvs. small, linear, to ⅛ in. wide. N. Amer., n. Asia. Var. **dilatatum** Wahlb. Lvs. broad. N. Scandinavia. Material offered as this var. may be broad-lvd. forms of other spp. Var. **diversipilosum** Nakai [var. *nipponicum* Nakai; *L. nipponicum* (Nakai) Tolm.]. Lvs. to ½ in. wide, glaucous beneath. Ne. Asia.

LEEA L. *Leeaceae.* About 70 spp. of evergreen shrubs or small trees, native to trop. Asia and Afr.; lvs. opp. or alt., simple or pinnately compound; fls. in terminal cymes, perianth segms. united basally into a tube, base of filaments forming a tube usually united to perianth, ovary 4–8-, usually 5-celled; fr. a berry.

Grown as foliage plants under glass or in the open in Zone 10. Propagated by cuttings.

aculeata Blume. Shrub or small tree, sts. and brs. spiny; lvs. with 3 lfts. to pinnately decompound, lfts. oblong-elliptic, 2–6 in. long, acuminate, dentate-serrate; fls. greenish-white; fr. yellowish-green, about ½ in. in diam. Malay Arch.

aequata L. [*L. hirta* Hornem.]. Shrub, to 14 ft.; lvs. 2–3-pinnate, lfts. lanceolate, hairy, with pearly glands beneath; infl. 2–4 in. across, setose. India to Philippine Is.

amabilis Hort. Veitch ex M. T. Mast. Lfts. 5–7, lanceolate, serrate, acuminate, upper surface deep velvety green with broad white stripe along midrib, lateral veins white toward base. Borneo. Cv. **'Splendens'.** Lfts. marked with red.

coccinea Planch. WEST INDIAN HOLLY. Glabrous shrub, to 8 ft.; lvs. mostly 2-pinnate, leathery; lfts. 2–4 in. long, elliptic to obovate, cuspidate, serrate; fls. in flat-topped infl. 3–5 in. across, buds red, rose-red to pink, staminal tube yellow. Burma. Plants begin to flower when only 1 ft. high. Material from trop. Afr. cult. under this name is probably *L. guineensis.*

guineensis G. Don [*L. coccinea* Bojer, not Planch.]. Shrub, to 6–8 ft.; lvs. mostly 1–2-pinnate, lfts. 4–8 in. long, elliptic, glabrous, distantly shallow-serrate; infl. a much-branched cyme; fls. bright orange-red outside, yellow to orange inside; fr. hard, to ⅜ in. in diam. Trop. Afr. Not known to be offered under this name, but some material cult. as *L. coccinea* may belong here.

hirta: *L. aequata.*

lutea: a listed name of no botanical standing.

manillensis Walp. [*L. sambucina* Blanco, not Willd.]. Glabrous shrub or small crooked tree, to 10–20 ft.; lvs. 3–4-pinnate, lfts. 2½–6 in. long, elliptic to oblong-ovate, acuminate, finely serrate; infl. 10–20 in. across; fls. with red pedicels and calyces, petals pink outside, yellow inside, with pinkish margins; fr. dark red, ⅛ in. in diam. Philippine Is. Cult. in s. Fla. Zone 10b. Sometimes offered as *L. sambucina.*

sambucina (L.) Willd., not Blanco. Shrub, to 5–12 ft.; lvs. 2–3-pinnate, glabrous or nearly so, lfts. broadly elliptic, 4 in. long, coarsely crenate, flushed with bronze, veins sometimes rose-tinged; fls. greenish-white. Trop. Asia, ne. Australia.

LEEACEAE Dumort. Dicot.; 1 genus of trees and shrubs, *Leea,* native to Old World tropics from New Guinea across

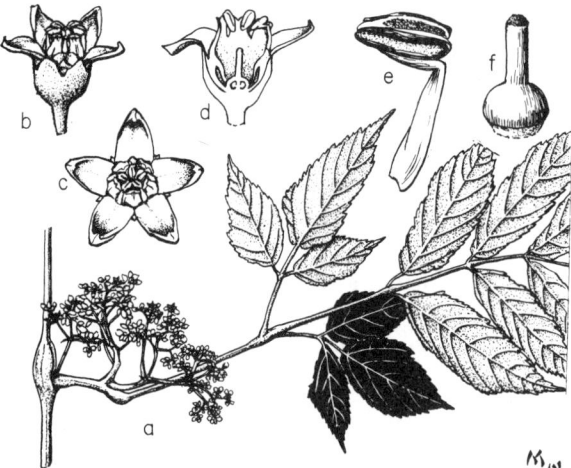

LEEACEAE. *Leea guineensis:* **a,** section of stem with leaf and inflorescence, × ⅙; **b,** flower, side view, × 2½; **c,** flower, face view, × 2½; **d,** flower, vertical section, × 3; **e,** stamen, × 12; **f,** pistil, × 8.

Malay Arch., India, to n. Madagascar, and cent. Afr.; long included in the *Vitaceae* but differing in having no tendrils, infls. terminal on lateral brs., fls. with segms. united basally into a tube, anthers dehiscing extrorsely, glandular disc below or around the pistil absent, and ovary 4–8-celled; fr. a berry.

LEEK. The leek is an onionlike plant, *Allium Ampeloprasum* Porrum Group, very hardy, grown in the vegetable garden for eating. The leek is used in cookery, the soft bulb and leaves being employed. It is milder than the onion, and the flavor is distinct. The plant is not known truly wild, and is supposed to be a development from another species of Europe and western Asia. For relationships, see *Allium* and *Onion.*

Leek is a long-season plant. Seeds sown in spring give edible plants for late autumn, winter, and spring. Usually the rows or drills are hilled up somewhat to blanch the lower part of the plant. Leeks may stand 4–6 inches apart in the row; for the best results, they should be transplanted to this distance from a seed bed. Plants may be lifted before hard weather and stored in the cellar, like celery, and in many parts of the country they are left in the ground all winter.

LEERSIA Swartz. CUTGRASS, WHITE GRASS. *Gramineae.* About 8 spp. of per. grasses in Amer. or Eurasia, usually with creeping rhizomes; lf. blades flat, scabrous; panicles mostly open; spikelets 1-fld., bisexual, laterally compressed, disarticulating from the pedicel, glumes absent, lemma boat-shaped, usually 5-nerved, palea as long as the lemma but narrower, usually 3-nerved. For terminology see *Gramineae.*

oryzoides (L.) Swartz. RICE C. Sts. to 5 ft., weak, often decumbent at base; lf. sheaths and blades strongly retrorse-scabrous, blades to ⅜ in. wide; panicles terminal and axillary, open, with spreading capillary brs., lower brs. fascicled, axillary panicles partly included in sheaths; spikelets elliptic, ¼ in. long, less than ⅛ in. wide, sparsely hispidulous, cleistogamous. Canada and U.S., except the extreme South. Cult. as forage.

LEGOUSIA Durande [*Specularia* A. DC.]. *Campanulaceae.* About 15 spp. of ann. herbs, native to Eur., w. Asia, and n. Afr.; lvs. alt., simple; fls. nearly sessile, clustered near ends of brs., mostly all opening, not cleistogamous as in *Triodanis,* 5-merous, corolla more or less rotate, divided to beyond the middle, filaments glabrous at the base; fr. a cylindrical caps., contracted and dehiscent at the apex.

Grown in the flower garden, rock garden, and for edgings. Propagated readily by seeds.

hybrida (L.) Delarbre [*Campanula hybrida* L.]. To about 6 in., glabrescent or puberulent, sts. simple or few-branched; lvs. sessile, obovate to oblong, to ¾ in. long, undulate-crenate; infl. few-fld.,

corymbose; calyx lobes awl-shaped, to ⅜ in. long, corolla blue, slightly longer than calyx; fr. mostly 1–1¼ in. long. Eur. and n. Afr.

pentagonia (L.) Thell. [*Campanula pentagonia* L.; *Specularia pentagonia* (L.) A. DC.]. Erect, 6–12 in., few-branched, slightly pubescent; lvs. spatulate to obovate or the upper lvs. ovate, to 1½ in. long, entire to remotely denticulate; calyx lobes linear-lanceolate to lanceolate, ⅜–¾ in. long, ½ to longer than the corolla, corolla blue; fr. ¾–1¼ in. long. E. Medit. region.

Speculum-Veneris (L.) Chaix [*Campanula Speculum-Veneris* L.; *Specularia Speculum-Veneris* (L.) A. DC.]. VENUS'S-LOOKING-GLASS. To 18 in., glabrous or nearly so, sts. diffusely branched; lvs. oblong to spatulate, to 1½ in. long, narrowed at the base or sessile, crenulate; fls. clustered in 3's in the upper lf. axils, calyx lobes longer than corolla tube, corolla blue or white, sometimes double, to 1 in. long; fr. ½–1 in. long. Cent. and s. Eur. Cv. 'Alba'. Fls. white. Cv. 'Grandiflora'. Fls. larger.

LEGUME. Technically and typically, a legume is the fruit or pod characteristic of the Leguminosae, well represented in the garden pea *(Pisum sativum).* It is a simple carpel dehiscent or splitting on both edges or sutures. Many of the pods in the Leguminosae do not conform in all ways to the ideal or pattern structure; some, like those of *Albizia* and *Arachis,* are indehiscent. As a general agricultural term, a legume is a plant of the Leguminosae, as clover *(Trifolium),* vetch *(Vicia),* bean *(Phaseolus),* pea *(Pisum),* and locust *(Robinia).* In French horticultural writing, a legume is a garden vegetable or pot herb.

LEGUMINOSAE Juss. or, alternatively, **FABACEAE** Lindl. PEA or PULSE FAMILY. Dicot.; about 600 genera and 12,000 spp. of sometimes spiny herbs, shrubs, trees, vines, or lianas of cosmopolitan distribution; lvs. mostly alt., usually compound, sometimes reduced to a single lft. or to a flattened, leaflike petiole (phyllode), stipules present, sometimes modified into thorns; fls. solitary or in racemes, panicles, spikes, heads, regular or irregular, calyx 5-lobed, petals usually 5, rarely 1 or 0, all separate or the lower 2 united, stamens 10 or fewer to many, all separate or 9 united in a tube and 1, the uppermost, usually separate, pistil 1-celled, ovules 2 to many; fr. a legume, splitting on both margins, or rarely indehiscent, sometimes constricted into 1-seeded sections and then termed a loment. The family is divided into 3 subfamilies, which by some authors have been treated as separate families. The most familiar representatives of the family in many regions of the U.S. are those of the subfamily Faboideae (or family Fabaceae), having papilionaceous or butterflylike (pealike) fls. with upper petal (standard) large and outermost, 2 lateral petals (wings) usually clawed, and 2 lower petals united basally forming a pouch (keel), usually enclosing the stamens and pistil. In the Caesalpinioideae (or family Caesalpiniaceae), the fls. are not papilionaceous or only imperfectly so, but are irregular, with the upper petal overlapped by the lateral petals, and usually separate stamens mostly 10 or fewer. The subfamily Mimosoideae (or family Mimosaceae) has mostly heads or dense racemes of small regular fls. with valvate petals and mostly many, separate or united stamens. Genera treated here are: *Abrus, Acacia, Acrocarpus, Adenanthera, Adenocarpus, Afzelia, Albizia, Alysicarpus, Amblygonocarpus, Amherstia, Amorpha, Amphicarpaea, Anadenanthera, Andira, Anthyllis, Apios, Apoplanesia, Arachis, Aspalathus, Astragalus, Baikiaea, Baphia, Baptisia, Barklya, Bauhinia, Bolusanthus, Brachysema, Brachystegia, Brownea, Butea, Caesalpinia, Cajanus, Calliandra, Calophaca, Calpurnia, Camoensia, Campylotropis, Canavalia, Caragana, Carmichaelia, Cassia, Castanospermum, Centrolobium, Centrosema, Ceratonia, Cercidium, Cercis, Chordospartium, Chorizema, Cicer, Cladrastis, Clianthus, Clitoria, Colutea, Colvillea, Copaifera, Coronilla, Craibia, Crotolaria, Cyamopsis, Cytisus, Dalbergia, Dalea, Daniellia, Daviesia, Delonix, Derris, Desmanthus, Desmodium, Detarium, Dialium, Dichrostachys, Dillwynia, Dipteryx, Dolichos, Dorycnium, Entada, Enterolobium, Eperua, Erinacea, Erythrina, Erythrophleum, Fillaeopsis, Galega, Genista, Gleditsia, Gliricidia, Glycine, Glycyrrhiza, Gourliea, Guibourtia, Gymnocladus, Haematoxylum, Halimodendron,*

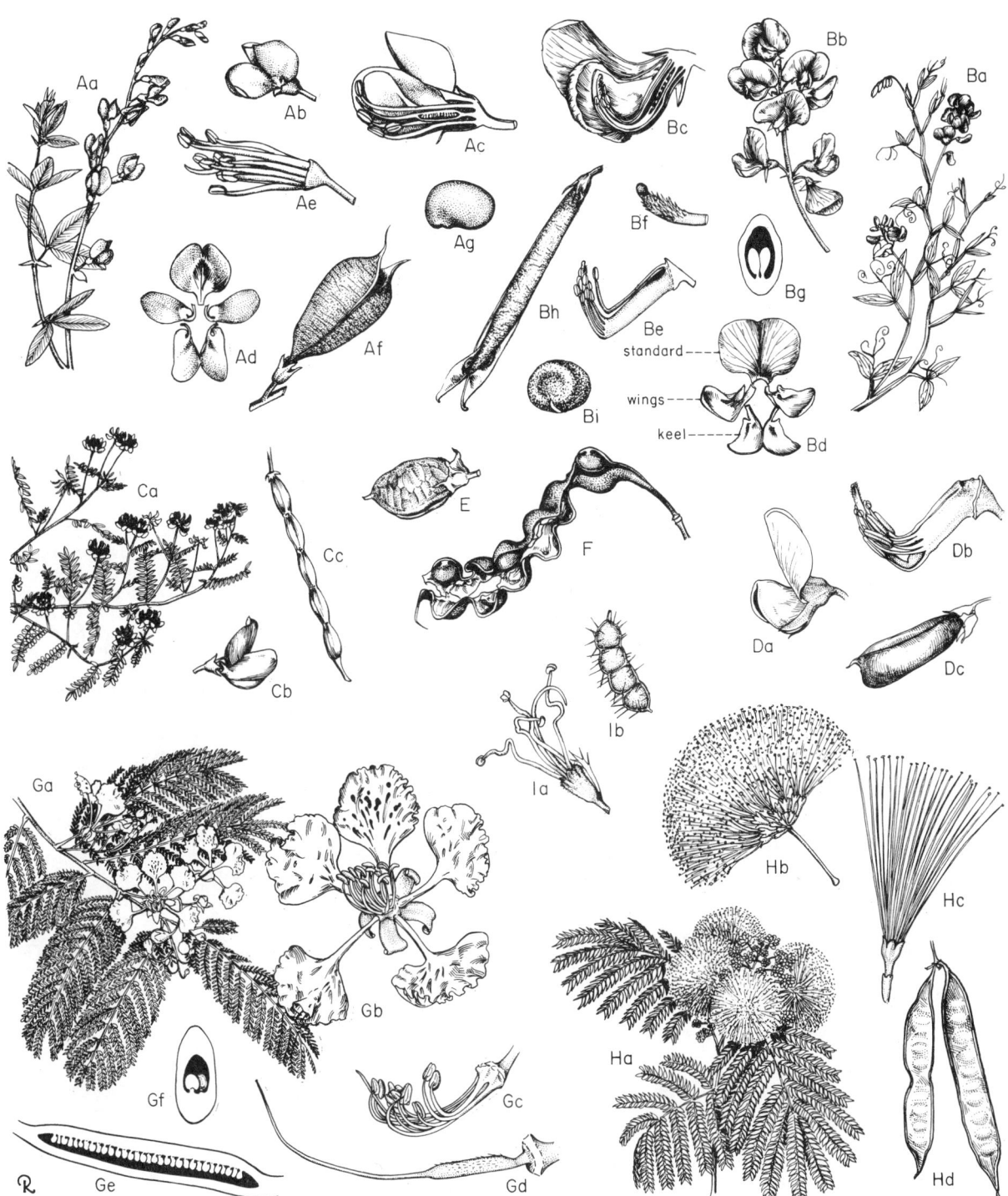

LEGUMINOSAE. Subfamily FABOIDEAE: **A,** *Baptisia australis:* **Aa,** part of flowering stem, × ¼; **Ab,** flower, × ½; **Ac,** flower, vertical section, × 1; **Ad,** corolla, expanded (keel partially split), × ½; **Ae,** stamens surrounding pistil, × 1; **Af,** fruit, × ½; **Ag,** seed, × 3. **B,** *Lathyrus latifolius:* **Ba,** flowering stem, × ⅛; **Bb,** raceme, × ¼; **Bc,** flower, vertical section, × 1; **Bd,** corolla, expanded (keel partially split), × ½; **Be,** stamens surrounding pistil, × 1; **Bf,** apex of style, × 2; **Bg,** ovary, cross section, × 8; **Bh,** fruit, × ½; **Bi,** seed, × 2. **C,** *Coronilla varia:* **Ca,** flowering stems, × ⅙; **Cb,** flower, × 1; **Cc,** fruit, × 1. **D,** *Crotalaria spectabilis:* **Da,** flower, × ¾; **Db,** stamens surrounding pistil, × 1½; **Dc,** fruit, × ½. **E,** *Melilotus alba:* fruit, × 4. **F,** *Erythrina herbacea:* fruit, × ½. Subfamily CAESALPINIOIDEAE: **G,** *Delonix regia:* **Ga,** flowering branch, × ⅙; **Gb,** flower, × ½; **Gc,** stamens and pistil, × ½; **Gd,** pistil, × 1; **Ge,** ovary, longitudinal section, × 3; **Gf,** ovary, cross section, × 6. Subfamily MIMOSOIDEAE: **H,** *Albizia Julibrissin:* **Ha,** flowering branch, × ⅙; **Hb,** umbel of flowers, × ½; **Hc,** flower, × 1; **Hd,** fruits, × ¼. **I,** *Mimosa pudica:* **Ia,** flower, × 3; **Ib,** fruit, × 1.

Hardenbergia, Hebestigma, Hedysarum, Hippocrepis, Hovea, Hymenaea, Hypocalyptus, Indigofera, Inga, Kennedia, + *Laburnocytisus, Laburnum, Lathyrus, Lebeckia, Lens, Lespedeza, Leucaena, Lonchocarpus, Lotononis, Lotus, Lupinus, Lysidice, Lysiloma, Maackia, Medicago, Melilotus, Millettia, Mimosa, Mucuna, Myroxylon, Neptunia, Notospartium, Olneya, Onobrychis, Ononis, Ormocarpum, Ormosia, Ougeinia, Oxytropis, Pachyrhizus, Paramacrolobium, Parkia, Parkinsonia, Parochetus, Peltophorum, Petalostemon, Petteria, Phaseolus, Phyllocarpus, Pickeringia, Piptanthus, Piscidia, Pisum, Pithecellobium, Platylobium, Platymiscium, Podalyria, Pongamia, Prosopis, Psophocarpus, Psoralea, Pterocarpus, Pterogyne, Pterolobium, Pueraria, Pultenaea, Robinia, Sabinea, Samanea, Saraca, Schizolobium, Schotia, Schrankia, Sesbania, Sophora, Spartium, Sphenostylis, Stahlia, Strongylodon, Sutherlandia, Swainsona, Swartzia, Tamarindus, Templetonia, Tephrosia, Tetrapleura, Thermopsis, Tipuana, Trifolium, Trigonella, Ulex, Vicia, Vigna, Viminaria, Virgilia, Voandzeia, Wallaceodendron, Whitfordiodendron, Willardia, Wisteria,* and *Xeroderris.*

There are many species of economic importance and the family is, after the Gramineae, the most import source of food for man, but also supplies field and forage plants, timber, fiber, dyes and tannins, gums and oleoresins, insecticides, flavorings, and many other products. It also includes a large number of ornamentals.

LEIBNITZIA Cass. *Compositae* (Mutisia Tribe). Five spp. of scapose per. herbs, native to Asia; lvs. in a basal rosette, pinnately lobed; plants producing normal fls. in spring and cleistogamous fls. in autumn; fl. heads solitary, involucral bracts imbricate in a few rows, receptacle flat, pitted; disc fls. tubular, 2-lipped, bisexual, anthers sagittate, ray fls. ligule-like, 2-lobed, fertile or sterile; achenes hairy, more or less flattened, pappus persistent, of many smooth or minutely scabrous bristles.

Anandria (L.) Nakai [*Gerbera Anandria* (L.) Schultz-Bip.]. Scapes to 8 in., from a short rhizome, cobwebby-woolly when young; lvs. broadly oblanceolate, sometimes ovate-cordate, pinnatifid or lobed, to about 6 in. long, cobwebby; heads to ½ in. across; fls. white inside, red-purple outside. China and Taiwan to Siberia and Japan.

Kunzeana (A. Braun & Asch.) Pobed. [*Gerbera Kunzeana* A. Braun & Asch.]. Scapes to 1 ft., bearing many threadlike bracts; lvs. lanceolate, to 6 in. long, entire, toothed, sinuately lobed, or pinnately lobed, densely woolly beneath; heads to ¾ in. across, involucral bracts glabrous; pappus chestnut-brown. Himalayas.

LEIOPHYLLUM (Pers.) R. Hedw. SAND MYRTLE. *Ericaceae.* One variable sp., an evergreen shrub, native to e. N. Amer.; lvs. alt. to opp., simple, entire, leathery; fls. white to pink, in terminal, umbel-like corymbs, calyx 5-parted, petals 5, separate, stamens 10, exserted, ovary superior; fr. a caps.

Suitable for borders and rock gardens, where they should be given a peaty or sandy, loamy soil. Propagated by seeds in a cold frame, and by layers.

buxifolium (Bergius) Elliott. BOX S.M. To 3 ft.; lvs. alt., oblong, ⁵⁄₁₆ in. long, shining above; pedicels glabrous. Late spring. N.J. Zone 6. Cv. 'Nanum'. Much-branched, dwarf; fls. pink. Var. **Hugeri** (Small) C. K. Schneid. [*L. Hugeri* (Small) K. Schum.]. Pedicels glandular. N.J., N.C., S.C., e. Ky. Var. **prostratum** (Loud.) A. Gray [*L. Lyonii* (Sweet) Sweet]. ALLEGHENY S.M. Prostrate; lvs. mostly opp., elliptic to orbicular, pubescent; pedicels glandular. Mts., Tenn., N.C., n. Ga.

Hugeri: *L. buxifolium* var.

Lyonii: *L. buxifolium* var. *prostratum.*

LEITNERIA Chapm. *Leitneriaceae.* One sp. of deciduous hardy shrubs or trees, with characters of the family.

floridana Chapm. CORKWOOD. To 25 ft., forming colonies; lvs. elliptic-oblong to lanceolate, crowded toward tips of brs., to 6 in. long, silky-hairy beneath; fls. before the lvs., male catkins erect, to 1½ in. long, female catkins woolly, smaller; drupes ellipsoidal, glabrous, to ⅝ in. long. Wet woods, s. Fla., w. to Mo. and Tex.

LEITNERIACEAE Benth. CORKWOOD FAMILY. Dicot.; 1 genus, *Leitneria*, with a single sp., a dioecious tree or shrub, native to temp. U.S.; lvs. alt., entire; fls. in axillary catkins, perianth none, stamens 8–12, ovary 1-celled, 1-ovuled; fr. a drupe.

LEITNERIACEAE. *Leitneria floridana:* **a,** twig with female catkins, × ¼; **b,** twig with male catkins, × ¼; **c,** male catkin, × 1½; **d,** bract with stamens, × 5; **e,** female catkin, × 1½; **f,** pistil, × 5; **g,** fruiting branch, × ¼. (From Lawrence, *Taxonomy of Vascular Plants.*)

LEMAIREOCEREUS Britt. & Rose [*Armatocereus* Backeb.; *Hertrichocereus* Backeb.; *Isolatocereus* (Backeb.) Backeb.; *Machaerocereus* Britt. & Rose; *Marginatocereus* (Backeb.) Backeb.; *Marshallocereus* Backeb.; *Polaskia* Backeb.; *Ritterocereus* Backeb.; *Stenocereus* (A. Berger) Riccob.]. *Cactaceae.* About 26 spp. of mostly large, ribbed, cylindrical cacti of N. and S. Amer.; sts. simple to treelike, ribs 3–20; fls. campanulate to tubular-funnelform, diurnal or nocturnal, perianth tardily shed from fr., ovary tubercled, with scales and felty areoles; fr. spiny, many-seeded, bursting irregularly. Ariz., Mex., and Cuba to Venezuela and Peru.

For culture see *Cacti.*

Beneckei (C. A. Ehrenb.) Britt. & Rose [*Hertrichocereus Beneckei* (C. A. Ehrenb.) Backeb.; *Stenocereus Beneckei* (C. A. Ehrenb.) A. Berger & Buxb.]. Much-branched, to 18 ft., sts. glaucous, to 3 in. thick, ribs 7–8, rounded, serrate-tubercled; areoles to 1½ in. apart, spines needle-shaped, brown to black, radial spines 2–6, to ½ in. long, central spine 1, ascending, to 2 in. long; fls. funnelform, to 3 in. long, limb rotate, white, ovary spiny; fr. red, 2 in. in diam., with basal pore. Cent. Mex.

candelabrum: a listed name of no botanical standing, probably for *L. Weberi.*

Cartwrightianus Britt. & Rose [*Armatocereus Cartwrightianus* (Britt. & Rose) Backeb.]. Much-branched, to 18 ft., with woody trunk, joints to 2 ft. long and 6 in. thick, ribs 7–8; areoles large, spines about 20, variegated, to ¾ in. long, or to 5 in. long on old brs.; fls. slender, white, 3 in. long; fr. to 3½ in. long, flesh white. Ecuador.

Chende (Rol.-Goss.) Britt. & Rose. Much-branched, to 25 ft., with a short trunk, sts. about 4 in. thick, ribs 7–9, sharp; areoles ¾ in. apart, radial spines 1–6, mostly 5, needle-shaped, to 1 in. long, central spine 1, longer; fls. white or rose, to 2 in. long; fr. globose, red, 1½ in. in diam., flesh red. S. Mex.

Chichipe (Rol.-Goss.) Britt. & Rose [*Polaskia Chichipe* (Rol.-Goss.) Backeb.]. Treelike, to 20 ft., with broad dense crown and short trunk, brs. about 4 in. thick, ribs 9–12, acutish, ¾ in. high; areoles about ½ in. apart, radial spines 6–7, to ⅜ in. long, central spine 1, to 6 in. long; fls. yellowish-green, 1¼ in. long; fr. globose, red, to 1 in. in diam., flesh red. S. Mex.

deficiens (Otto & Dietr.) Britt. & Rose [*Ritterocereus deficiens* (Otto & Dietr.) Backeb.]. Tall and treelike, with many ascending brs., ribs 7–8, broad at base; radial spines about 8, often appressed, grayish, black-tipped, about ½ in. long, central spine 0–1, somewhat flattened, 1¼ in. long; fls. 2½ in. long, ovary spineless; fr. spiny. Venezuela.

Dumortieri (Scheidw.) Britt. & Rose [*Isolatocereus Dumortieri* (Scheidw.) Backeb.]. Treelike, to 50 ft., brs. many, erect, bluish, ribs 5–9, mostly 6, prominent; areoles close-set or confluent, spines straw-yellow, becoming black, to 1½ in. long, radial spines 10–20, central spines 1 or more; fls. to 2 in. long and 1 in. across; fr. to 1½ in. long, with few bristlelike spines, flesh reddish. Cent. Mex.

Eruca (Brandeg.) Britt. & Rose [*Machaerocereus Eruca* (Brandeg.) Britt. & Rose]. CREEPING-DEVIL CACTUS. Sts. prostrate, ascending at apex, to 10 ft. long and 4 in. thick, dying behind, ribs about 12–15; areoles large, ¾ in. apart, spines about 20, unequal, gray, the outer cylindrical, the longest to 1¼ in.; fls. yellow, to 5 in. long; fr. 1½ in. long. S. Baja Calif.

euphorbioides (Haw.) Werderm. [*Cephalocereus euphorbioides* (Haw.) Britt. & Rose; *Cereus euphorbioides* Haw.]. Sts. erect, to 25 ft., mostly unbranched, 4–6 in. thick, ribs 7–10, mostly 8, to 1¼ in. high; areoles to ½ in. apart, radial spines 3–8, needle-shaped, short, central spine 1, awl-shaped, dark, to 1½ in. long; fls. nocturnal, funnelform, pink, with unpleasant odor, to 4 in. long; fr. yellow-green, splitting, the sections spreading, flesh white. N. Mex.

Godingianus Britt. & Rose [*Armatocereus Godingianus* (Britt. & Rose) Backeb.]. Treelike, to 35 ft., brs. ascending, annually constricted, ribs 7–11; spines needle-shaped, to 1½ in. long; fls. slender, white, to 4½ in. long, tube thick-walled, with yellow bristles; fr. yellow-spiny, 4 in. long. Ecuador.

griseus (Haw.) Britt. & Rose [*Ritterocereus griseus* (Haw.) Backeb.; *Stenocereus griseus* (Haw.) Buxb.]. To 25 ft., branching at base or forming a trunk, ribs 8–10, glaucous; spines needle-shaped, gray, to 1½ in. long; fls. pinkish, to 3 in. long, style exserted; fr. subglobose, 2 in. in diam., flesh red. Venezuela, Trinidad and nearby islands.

gummosus (Engelm.) Britt. & Rose [*Machaerocereus gummosus* (Engelm.) Britt. & Rose]. DAGGER CACTUS. Shrubby, to 15 ft., brs. erect or sprawling, to 2–3½ in. thick, ribs 8–9, obtuse; areoles about ¾ in. apart, spines awl-shaped, angled, thickened at base, gray, radial spines 8–12, to ½ in. long, central spines 3–6, the longest 1½ in.; fls. purplish, to 6 in. long; fr. globose, red, to 3 in. in diam., edible, flesh purple. W. Mex.

Hollianus (A. Web. ex J. Coult.) Britt. & Rose. Sts. simple or few-branched, to 20 ft. high and 5 in. thick, ribs 8–12, acute; spines red, becoming gray, radial spines about 12, unequal, to 1¼ in. long, central spines 3–5, swollen at base, the lower longer, deflexed, to 4 in. long; fls. white, 4 in. long; fr. purple, to 4 in. long. S. Mex. Cv. **'Cristatus'** is listed.

hystrix (Haw.) Britt. & Rose. Treelike, to 40 ft., with short trunk, brs. ascending, to 4 in. thick, ribs mostly 9–10; spines needle-shaped, gray, brown-tipped, radial spines about 10, central spines 3, the longest to 1½ in.; fls. white, to 3½ in. long, ovary spineless; fr. red, to 2½ in. long, bursting, flesh red. W. Indies.

laetus (HBK) Britt. & Rose [*Armatocereus laetus* (HBK) Backeb.]. Treelike, to 20 ft., with short trunk, brs. erect, gray, about 5 in. thick, annually constricted, ribs 4–8, prominent; areoles about 1 in. apart, spines awl-shaped, brown, becoming gray, to 1 or sometimes 3 in. long; fls. white, 3 in. long; fr. green, splitting, flesh white. Ecuador, N. Peru.

littoralis (K. Brandeg.) H. E. Gates. Branching from base, sts. ascending or sprawling, to 4 ft. high and 3 in. thick, ribs about 15, low; spines needle-shaped, reddish, soon gray, radial spines about 10, to 1 in. long, central spine 1, to 1½ in. long; fls. pink, 3 in. long, opening in afternoon. S. Baja Calif.

marginatus (DC.) Backeb. & F. M. Knuth [*Cereus marginatus* DC.; *Marginatocereus marginatus* (DC.) Backeb.; *Pachycereus marginatus* (DC.) Britt. & Rose; *Stenocereus marginatus* (DC.) A. Berger & Buxb.]. ORGAN-PIPE CACTUS. Simple, treelike, or branching at base, to 25 ft. high, sts. green, about 5 in. thick, ribs 5–7; areoles close-set or confluent, spines needle-shaped, to ⅜ in. long, radial spines 4–7, central spine 1, or in age more, upper areoles with many bristlelike spines ¾ in. long; fls. sometimes paired, tubular, 1½ in. long; fr. globose, 1½ in. in diam., flesh yellowish-red, seeds 5/32 in. long. Cent. Mex.

Martinezii Ort. Treelike, to 18 ft., with short trunk, ribs 9, prominent; spines black, radial spines 7–11, to ⅜ in. long, central spines 2–3, the longest deflexed, to 2 in. long. W. Mex.

matucanensis (Backeb.) W. T. Marsh. [*Armatocereus matucanensis* Backeb.]. Similar to *L. laetus*, but lower and with a broader perianth. Cent. Peru.

pruinosus (Otto) Britt. & Rose [*Ritterocereus pruinosus* (Otto) Backeb.]. POWDER-BLUE CEREUS. Treelike, to 25 ft., brs. ascending, glaucous, about 4 in. thick, ribs 5–6, high; areoles 1½ in. apart, spines needle-shaped, gray, dark-tipped, radial spines 7–9, central spine 1, longer, to 1¼ in. long; fls. white or rosy, to 3½ in. long; fr. ovoid, red, to 3 in. long. S. Mex.

queretaroensis (A. Web.) Saff. [*Ritterocereus queretaroensis* (A. Web.) Backeb.]. Treelike, to 30 ft., with short trunk, ribs 6–8, prominent; areoles large, brown, glandular, ⅜ in. apart, spines 6–10, needle-shaped, red, becoming gray, ½–2 in. long; fls. 3 in. long; fr. 2 ½ in. long, edible. Cent. Mex.

stellatus (Pfeiff.) Britt. & Rose [*Stenocereus stellatus* (Pfeiff.) Riccob.]. Branching at base, to 10 ft., ribs 8–12, low, obtuse; radial spines 8–12, to 1 in. long, central spines 4–6, the upper sometimes 2½ in. long; fls. red, 1½ in. long; fr. globose, red, 1¼ in. in diam. S. Mex.

Thurberi (Engelm.) Britt. & Rose [*Cereus Thurberi* Engelm.; *Marshallocereus Thurberi* (Engelm.) Backeb.]. ORGAN-PIPE CACTUS. Sts. erect, branching from the base or with short trunk, to 15 or sometimes 25 ft. high, to 8 in. thick, ribs 12–19, to ¾ in. high; areoles brown, glandular, mostly about ½ in. apart, spines 14–19, needle-shaped, brownish to black, rarely 2 in. long; fls. nocturnal, white to purplish, to 3 in. long; fr. globose, red, to 3 in. in diam., flesh red. Spring, summer. S. Ariz. and w. Mex.

Treleasei Britt. & Rose [*Stenocereus Treleasii* (Britt. & Rose) Backeb.]. Sts. simple or few-branched, to 25 ft., ribs about 20, serrately nearly tubercled; spines needle-shaped, yellowish, short, central spine 1, longer; fls. diurnal, pinkish, to 2 in. long; fr. red, 2 in. in diam. S. Mex.

Weberi (J. Coult.) Britt. & Rose [*Stenocereus Weberi* (J. Coult.) Buxb.]. CANDELABRA CACTUS. Treelike, to 35 ft., with short trunk and broad dense crown, brs. erect, bluish, to 8 in. thick, ribs about 10; areoles about 1 in. apart, radial spines 6–12, needle-shaped, to ¾ in. long, central spine 1, often deflexed, flattened, 3–4 in. long; fls. to 4 in. long, brown-hairy; fr. to 3 in. long, edible. S. Mex.

LEMNA L. DUCKWEED, DUCK'S-MEAT, FROG-BUTTONS. *Lemnaceae*. About 9 spp. of cosmopolitan, minute, floating, per. or over-wintering herbs; plant body with a single rootlet, proliferating, the offshoots remaining connected for a short time; fls. rarely produced, marginal, the 2 stamens or 1 pistil each usually considered to represent a fl.

gibba L. Plant bodies solitary, or 2–4 in a cluster, obovate to orbicular, ⅛–¼ in. long, asymmetrical at apex, flat to slightly convex, with 3–5, indistinct nerves, mottled yellow-green above, often marked with red-purple. Cosmopolitan.

minor L. COMMON DUCKWEED, LESSER D. Plant bodies solitary or few-clustered, orbicular to elliptic-obovate, 1/16–3/16 in. long. Cosmopolitan. Waterfowl feed on these plants.

paucicostata: *L. perpusilla.*

perpusilla Torr. [*L. paucicostata* Hegelm.]. Plant bodies solitary or 3–5 in a cluster, obovate to orbicular-obovate, to about ⅛ in. long, asymmetrical, convex above, with 1–3 nerves or none, light to medium green. Widespread in New and Old Worlds.

trisulca L. STAR DUCKWEED. Plant bodies remaining connected, often forming mats, oblong to oblong-lanceolate, narrowed at the base to a slender stipe, ¼–1 in. long, frequently lacking rootlets. Cosmopolitan.

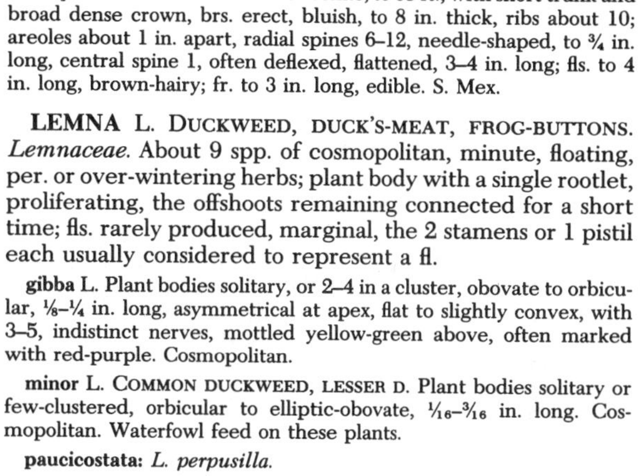

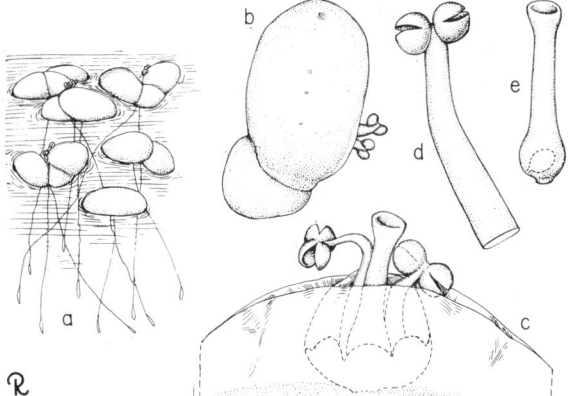

LEMNACEAE. *Lemna minor:* **a,** flowering plants floating on water, × 2; **b,** plant in flower, viewed from above, × 8; **c,** sheath with inflorescence of three flowers, × 25; **d,** male flower, × 40; **e,** female flower, × 40. (From Lawrence, *Taxonomy of Vascular Plants.*)

LEMNACEAE. S. F. Gray. DUCKWEED FAMILY. Monocot.; 6 genera and 30 spp. of minute floating per. herbs, nearly cosmopolitan in trop. and temp. regions, usually considered monoecious; plant body a green, leaflike or globose thallus, with or without rootlets, and prop. by proliferation from the base; fls. rarely produced, minute, unisexual, each of the 1 or 2 stamens then representing a male fl., the 1 pistil a female fl. *Lemna, Spirodela, Wolffia,* and *Wolffiella* sometimes grown on the surface of aquaria or pools as ornamentals or as food for fish or water fowl.

LENOPHYLLUM Rose. *Crassulaceae.* About 6 spp. of glabrous, succulent, per. herbs of s. Tex. and ne. Mex.; lower lvs. a few opp. pairs, often crowded, thick; fl. st. terminal, with scattered, smaller, often alt. lvs., infl. a cyme of few cincinni or a spike or narrow thyrse; fls. 5-merous, sepals erect, nearly equal, about as long as corolla, petals yellow, erect, with recurved tips, narrowed below and separated at base, stamens 10.

For culture see *Succulents.*

guttatum Rose. Lvs. elliptic-ovate or rhombic, ¾–1½ in. long, half as wide, obtuse, gray, flecked with purple-black; fl. st. to 8 in., cincinni 2–6, each 5–12-fld.; fls. nearly sessile, sepals club-shaped, ¼ in. long, obtuse. Late summer, autumn. Mex.

pusillum Rose. Lvs. acute, to ⅝ in. long; fl. st. 2 in., with solitary terminal fl.; sepals acute. Poorly known, perhaps described from a depauperate specimen. Late autumn. Probably Mex.

texanum (J. G. Sm.) Rose. Lvs. elliptic-ovate to lanceolate, ½–1½ in. long, acute to acuminate; fl. st. to 14 in., infl. a spike or narrow thyrse; sepals lanceolate to ovate, ⅛ in. long, acute. Late summer to winter. Tex., Mex. Weedy, the lvs. falling easily and rooting.

Weinbergii Britt. Lvs. obovate-cuneate, trough-shaped, ⅝ in. long and about as wide, nearly truncate and obtuse at apex; cyme few-fld.; sepals club-shaped, 3/16 in. long, obtuse. Mex.

LENS Mill. *Leguminosae* (subfamily *Faboideae*). About 6 spp. of herbs of Medit. region and w. Asia; lvs. alt., pinnate, ending in a tendril or short bristle; fls. small, white, or bluish, solitary or few in racemes, papilionaceous, wing petals adherent to keel, stamens 10, 9 united and 1 separate; fr. a short, flat legume, with 1–2 lens-shaped seeds.

One species is widely cultivated for its seeds, a highly nutritious source of food, and for forage. Propagated by seeds sown in early spring.

culinaris Medic. [*L. esculenta* Moench]. LENTIL. Ann., to 1½ ft.; lfts. in 4–7 pairs, ½ in. long, ending in a tendril; fr. to ¾ in. long and nearly as broad. Sw. Asia. One of the oldest of food plants.

esculenta: *L. culinaris.*

LENTIBULARIACEAE L. Rich. BLADDERWORT FAMILY. Dicot.; 5 or more genera of mostly carnivorous small herbs, of wide distribution in water or wet habitats; lvs. very diverse; fls. irregular, bisexual, calyx 2–5-lobed, corolla 2-lipped, often spurred, stamens 2, ovary superior, 1-celled; fr. a dehiscent caps. A few spp. of *Pinguicula* and *Utricularia* are cult. in wet places or water gardens, in aquaria, or under glass.

LEONOTIS (Pers.) R. Br. LION'S-EAR. *Labiatae.* About 30 spp. of ann. and per. herbs or shrubs of trop. and S. Afr.; sts. mostly square in cross section; lvs. opp., usually toothed; fls. in axillary, many-fld. verticillasters, bractlets many, linear-subulate; fls. large, showy, white, yellow, orange, or scarlet, calyx tubular, 10-nerved, 8–10-toothed, teeth needlelike, corolla tube longer than calyx, hairy inside, limb 2-lipped, upper lip erect, concave, lower lip 3-lobed, stamens 4, in 2 pairs, anthers 2-celled; fr. of 4 glabrous nutlets.

Propagated by seeds or cuttings. Cuttings are taken in spring and grown outdoors during summer, and pinched often to induce branching; in the autumn before frost they may be cut back and transplanted to the greenhouse where they may bloom in Nov. or Dec.

dysophylla Benth. ex E. H. Mey. Sts. to 2 ft., woody at base, robust, pubescent; lvs. ovate-lanceolate, to 3 in. long, to 1½ in. wide, crenate-serrate, densely yellowish-villous beneath; verticillasters dense, solitary or few; calyx spiny, teeth 8, corolla to 1½ in. long, deep orange-yellow. S. Afr.

laxifolia MacOwan. Tender herb, pubescent; lvs. ovate, 3–4 in. long, acuminate, incised-dentate, more or less pubescent beneath; corolla to 1 5/16 in. long, orange-yellow. S. Afr.

Leonurus (L.) R. Br. [*Phlomis Leonurus* L.]. LION'S-EAR. Tender shrub, 6–7 ft., short-pubescent; lvs. oblong-lanceolate to oblanceolate, to 4½ in. long, crenate-serrate, very short-pubescent; corolla to 2½ in. long, orange. S. Afr.

nepetifolia (L.) R. Br. Ann. herb, 1–5 ft., pubescent; lvs. ovate, 2–5 in. long, crenate; calyx to ¾ in. long, spiny, corolla to 1 in. long, orange-yellow or scarlet. Summer to autumn. Pantropic, but original nativity uncertain; naturalized in se. U.S.

LEONTODON L. *Compositae* (Cichorium Tribe). Not cult.
L. Taraxacum: *Taraxacum officinale.*

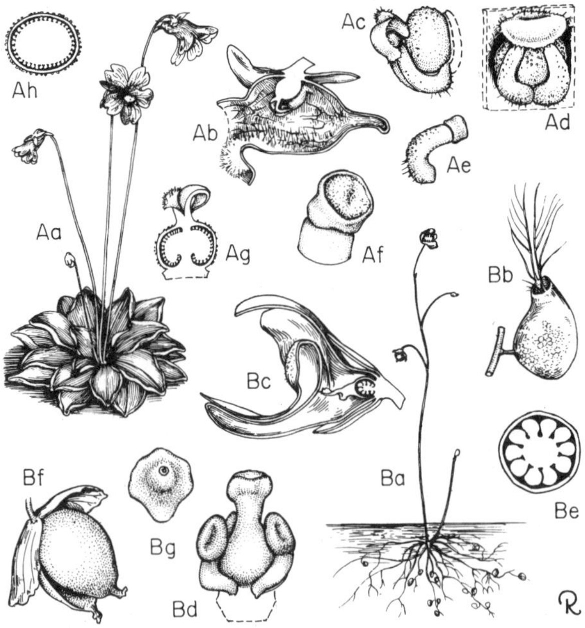

LENTIBULARIACEAE. **A,** *Pinguicula caerulea* Walt.: **Aa,** flowering plant, × ¼; **Ab,** flower, vertical section (corolla lobes cut away and pistil without detail), × 1; **Ac,** pistil and stamens, side view, × 2; **Ad,** pistil and stamens, face view, × 2; **Ae,** stamen, × 2; **Af,** anther, × 5; **Ag,** pistil, vertical section, × 2; **Ah,** ovary, cross section, × 3. **B,** *Utricularia biflora* Lam.: **Ba,** flowering plant in water, × ½; **Bb,** bladder-like leaf, × 5; **Bc,** flower, vertical section, × 4; **Bd,** pistil and stamens, × 8; **Be,** ovary, cross section, × 10; **Bf,** capsule, × 5; **Bg,** seed, × 8. (Both species representative, but not in general cultivation.)

LEONTOPODIUM R. Br. *Compositae* (Inula Tribe). Low, herbaceous, tufted and woolly per. herbs in mts. of Eur. and Asia; lvs. basal or alt., entire; fl. heads small, discoid, crowded into terminal dense cymes subtended by conspicuous bractlike lvs.; involucral bracts imbricate, woolly, scarious-margined; fls. all tubular, unisexual, the outer ones usually fertile, the inner sterile, or plants sometimes dioecious; achenes nearly cylindrical, pappus of bristles, deciduous. A difficult genus taxonomically, in which a superabundance of spp. have been segregated and named, and the names variously applied by different authors.

One species, the edelweiss, is grown as an alpine in the North in the rock garden or sometimes indoors in pots. It requires deep, gritty or sandy loam, since the roots travel far. Propagated by division of the old plants and by seeds. If seeds are sown about the first of Feb., by late spring the plants are large enough to be set in their permanent quarters.

albanicum: a listed name of no botanical standing.

aloysiodorum: a hort. name, used for plants of *L. haplophylloides.*

alpinum Cass. EDELWEISS. To 12 in. or more, creeping by rhizomes and loosely tufted; lvs. linear to oblong-lanceolate, white-tomentose above and beneath; bractlike lvs. ovate to linear-oblong, white-woolly, broader than upper lvs. and about as long, forming a star ½–4 in. across. Pyrenees, Alps, and Carpathian Mts., Eur. Var. **albanicum:** a listed name of no botanical standing. Var. **altaicum:** *L. ochroleucum* var. *campestre.* Var. **crasense:** see var. *krasense.* Var. **Fauriei:** *L. Fauriei.* Var. **himalayanum:** *L. calocephalum,* but may be used in hort. for *L. himalayanum.* Var. **krasense** (Derg.) Stoîanov & Stefanov [spelled *crasense* by Stoîanov & Stefanov; *L. crassense* Hort.]. Of slender habit; lvs. smaller, with pure white tomentum; involucral bracts narrower. Nw. Yugoslavia. One of many minor variations scarcely worthy of nomenclatural recognition. In hort. literature the name has been mistakenly applied to a choice form of *L. nivale.* Var. **rebunense:** a listed name of no botanical standing. Var. **Stracheyi:** *L. Stracheyi.*

altaicum: a listed name of no botanical standing; perhaps for *L. ochroleucum* var. *campestre.*

calocephalum (Franch.) Beauverd [*L. alpinum* var. *himalayanum* Franch.]. To 16 in., plant robust, not stoloniferous; lvs. many, the lower lanceolate or linear-lanceolate, withering by flowering time, the upper much shorter, ovate-lanceolate, glabrous to gray-silky above, gray- to white-tomentose beneath; bractlike lvs. triangular-acute, forming a dense star to 4 in. across. Tibet, China.

campestre: *L. ochroleucum* var.

chokoiyense: a listed name of no botanical standing.

crasense, crassense: see *L. alpinum* var. *krasense* and *L. nivale.*

discolor Beauverd [*L. tataricum* Kom.]. Sts. to 12 in., often procumbent basally, glabrescent below; lvs. lanceolate to linear-lanceolate, glabrous to cobwebby above, white-tomentose beneath, the lower lvs. still alive at flowering time; bractlike lvs. as long as the lvs., white-tomentose, forming a star to 2½ in. across. E. coast of Siberia, Japan, Korea.

Fauriei (Beauverd) Hand.-Mazz. [*L. alpinum* var. *Fauriei* Beauverd]. Sts. to 8 in.; st. lvs. linear to spatulate-lanceolate, all of about equal length, about ⅛ in. wide, white- to yellow-gray-tomentose, the lower lvs. still alive at flowering time; bractlike lvs. slightly shorter than upper lvs., linear, silvery-gray-pubescent, forming a star to 2 in. across; heads 4–10; achenes hirsute. Japan. Var. **angustifolia** Hara & Kitam. ex Takeda. Lvs. narrower, ⅟₁₆ in. wide.

haplophylloides Hand.-Mazz. [*L. aloysiodorum* Hort.]. Sts. to 14 in., densely leafy; lvs. linear-lanceolate, gray-tomentose, densely set with black glands beneath, lemon-scented; bractlike lvs. shorter and broader than lvs., white-tomentose, forming a star 1–2 in. across. Cent. China.

hayachinense (Takeda) Hara & Kitam. Differs from *L. discolor* in the broadly clasping lf. bases, larger achenes, and papillose fls. Mt. Hayachine (Japan).

himalayanum DC. To 10 in.; st. lvs. lanceolate, the upper broader, silvery-tomentose; bractlike lvs. as large as upper lvs., linear to slightly dilated at tips, silvery-woolly, forming a star to 2½ in. across. Himalayas.

Jacotianum Beauverd. Differs from *L. alpinum* in having many above ground stolons, basal lvs. quickly withering and subulate-tipped, lvs. white-tomentose beneath, glabrate above. Himalayas.

japonicum Miq. Sts. 10–22 in., leafy throughout, simple or branched above; lvs. lanceolate or narrowly oblong, ¼–½ in. wide, green and glabrate above, white-tomentose beneath, basal and lower st. lvs. smaller than middle and upper lvs., withering by flowering time; bractlike lvs. smaller than upper lvs., yellowish-tomentose, less showy than in most spp. China, Korea, Japan.

kamtschaticum: *L. kurilense.*

kurilense Takeda [*L. kamtschaticum* Kom.]. To 8 in.; lvs. linear-lanceolate, basal and lower lvs. smaller than the upper, upper lvs. and upper parts of sts. glandular under the tomentum; bractlike lvs. shorter and broader than upper lvs., forming a densely floccose star to 1½ in. across. Kurile Is., Sakhalin, e. Siberia.

leontopodioides (Willd.) Beauverd [*L. sibiricum* Cass.]. Sts. very slender, to 24 in., leafy but often naked for a few in. below infl.; lvs. erect, linear-lanceolate, gray-woolly, greener above than beneath; bractlike lvs. few, smaller than upper lvs., not forming a conspicuous star. Se. Siberia, Mongolia, Manchuria, ne. China.

leontopodinum: *L. ochroleucum.*

macrocephalum: a listed name of no botanical standing.

monocephalum Edgew. Sts. slender, to 5 in., purplish, loosely white-woolly; lvs. spatulate, often purplish at base, densely white- or yellowish-tomentose; bractlike lvs. larger than lvs., spatulate to obovate, white- to yellowish-woolly, forming a showy star to 1½ in. across. Himalayas.

nivale (Ten.) Huet [*L. crassense* Hort.]. Densely tufted, to 5 in.; lvs. spatulate to narrowly ovate-lanceolate, gray- to white-woolly; bractlike lvs. shorter and broader than upper lvs., often more densely and whitely woolly, forming a star to 2 in. across. Mts., cent. Italy, Yugoslavia, Bulgaria.

ochroleucum Beauverd [*L. leontopodinum* (DC.) Hand.-Mazz.]. To 4 in., forming dense tufts with many sterile rosettes; bractlike lvs. broadly lanceolate to elliptic, loosely yellowish-felty, forming a small compact star under 1 in. across. Mts., cent. Asia. Var. **campestre** (Ledeb.) Grubov [*L. alpinum* var. *altaicum* Beauverd; *L. campestre* (Ledeb.) Hand.-Mazz.]. Loosely tufted, 6–14 in.; bractlike lvs. linear to narrow-lanceolate, yellowish to nearly white, forming a loose, poorly defined star about 1 in. across. Steppes, cent. Asia.

Palibinianum Beauverd. To 16 in.; lvs. lanceolate to linear-lanceolate, gray-tomentose; bractlike lvs. as long as or smaller than upper lvs., narrowly ovate, densely white-tomentose above, greenish beneath, forming a star to 2½ in. across. N. Asia.

rebunense: a listed name of no botanical standing.

shinanense Kitam. Differs from *L. Fauriei* in its shorter sts., to 4 in., fewer heads (2–3), and glabrous achenes. Alpine, Japan.

sibiricum: *L. leontopodioides.*

sikkimense: a listed name of no botanical standing.

Souliei Beauverd. Differs from *L. calocephalum* chiefly in being stoloniferous, and having lvs. narrower, linear, and bractlike lvs. linear, forming an open star to 2 in. across. S. China.

Stracheyi (Hook.f.) C. B. Clarke [*L. alpinum* var. *Stracheyi* Hook.f.]. Sts. to 20 in., densely leafy; lvs. ovate-lanceolate, brownish-glandular-hairy and thinly tomentose above, white-tomentose beneath; bractlike lvs. ovate-lanceolate, white-tomentose, forming a dense star to 2½ in. across. Tibet, w. China.

tataricum: *L. discolor.*

Wilsonii Beauverd. Similar to *L. japonicum*, but lvs. narrower, revolute, bractlike lvs. white-tomentose, forming a showier star to 3½ in. across. W. China.

LEONURUS L. MOTHERWORT. *Labiatae.* About 4 spp. of bien. or per. herbs of temp. Eur. and Asia; often pubescent; sts. mostly square in cross section; lvs. opp., incised or coarsely toothed, sometimes palmately parted; fls. in many-fld. verticillasters, calyx campanulate, 5-nerved, 5-toothed, teeth spiny, corolla tube shorter than calyx, limb 2-lipped, upper lip erect, entire, lower lip spreading, 3-lobed, stamens 4, in 2 pairs, anther cells opp., opening by a common slit; fr. of 4 glabrous, 3-angled, nutlets.

For the flower border; propagated readily by seeds.

Cardiaca L. Per., to 5 ft., glabrous to villous; lower lvs. deeply and palmately 2–5-lobed, to 3 in. long, lobes deeply dentate; bracts half as long as calyx; calyx tube prominently 5-veined, teeth almost as long as tube, lower 2 teeth deflexed, corolla longer than calyx, white or pale pink, sometimes with purple spots, tube with ring of hairs inside, upper lip densely villous on back. Summer. Eur. and Medit. region.

sibiricus L. Bien., to 4–6 ft., gray-green, white-pubescent; basal lvs. ovate-cordate, toothed and incised, long-petioled, withering before fls. appear, st. lvs. 2–4 in. long, pinnately dissected, long-petioled, uppermost lvs. often entire, linear-lanceolate; fls. ⅝ in. long, bractlets shorter than calyx, calyx teeth spiny, corolla rose-pink. Ne. Asia, Japan, Taiwan.

LEPACHYS: *RATIBIDA.* **L. columnaris:** *R. columnifera.* **L. pulcherrima:** *R. columnifera* forma.

LEPADENA: *EUPHORBIA.*

LEPECHINIA Willd. *Labiatae.* About 40 spp. of aromatic, suffrutescent herbs or shrubs, native from Calif. to Argentina, and in Hawaii; sts. mostly square in cross section; lvs. opp., serrate to nearly entire; fls. showy, solitary and axillary in racemes, or in 2–6-fld. verticillasters arranged in spikes, calyx campanulate, 5-toothed, corolla tube hairy inside, limb 5-lobed, lobes rounded, stamens 4, in 2 pairs; fr. of 4 black, glabrous nutlets.

Propagated by seeds or by cuttings.

calycina (Benth.) Epl. [*Sphacele calycina* Benth.]. PITCHER SAGE. Shrub, to 4 ft., pubescent; lvs. ovate to oblong-lanceolate, to 3½ in. long, nearly entire to serrate; infl. racemose, bracts leaflike; calyx ⅝ in. long, enlarging to 1 in. in fr., corolla to 1¼ in. long, white or pink with purplish blotches and veins; nutlets about ⅛ in. across. Late spring. Chaparral of low mts., Calif.

LEPIDIUM L. PEPPERGRASS, PEPPERWORT, TONGUE-GRASS. *Cruciferae.* More than 100 spp. of ann. to per. herbs, some of them subshrubby, of widespread distribution, largely in temp. regions, erect, more or less branching, glabrous or pubescent; lvs. various, mostly long rather than broad, dentate to pinnatifid; fls. very small, white or greenish, in terminal, bractless racemes, sepals and petals 4; fr. a short, broad silicle, valves strongly keeled and winged.

cartilagineum (J. Mayer) Thell. Per., sts. flexuous, to 2 ft. or more, branched above; lvs. broadly elliptic to linear-lanceolate, leathery-succulent; petals white, to ⅛ in. long; silicle ovate, to ⅛ in. across. In saline places, cent. and e. Eur.

sativum L. GARDEN CRESS. Glabrous, more or less glaucous, to 2 ft.; basal lvs. pinnatifid, toothed, st. lvs. linear, entire. Egypt and w. Asia; escaped in N. Amer. Long known as a piquant salad plant. Some cult. forms have curled, crisped lvs. Sometimes called UPLAND CRESS.

LEPIDORRHACHIS (H. Wendl. & Drude) O. F. Cook. *Palmae.* One sp., a solitary, unarmed, monoecious palm of low stature, native to Lord Howe Is. (Australia); lvs. pinnate, sheath open nearly to the swollen base, petiole short, pinnae stiff, ascending, regularly arranged, with 2 prominent veins on each side of the midrib, acute; infl. among lvs. in bud, usually below lvs. in flowering, with 2 thin, deciduous bracts, the upper slightly exserted from the lower, peduncle very short, lower brs. twice-branched, rachillae short, stiff, with fls. in triads (2 male and 1 female); male fls. slightly asymmetrical, sepals 3, rounded, imbricate, petals 3, valvate, stamens 6, filaments inflexed at apex in bud, pistillode narrowly cylindrical with expanded apex, slightly longer than stamens in bud, female fls. symmetrical, sepals 3, rounded, imbricate, petals 3, imbricate with briefly valvate apices, staminodes 3, pistil 1-celled, 1-ovuled; fr. globose, with lateral stigmatic residue, endocarp thin, operculate, seed globose with elongate raphe, endosperm homogeneous, embryo basal.

Not widely cultivated. For culture see *Palms.*

Mooreana (F. J. Muell.) O. F. Cook [*Clinostigma Mooreanum* (F. J. Muell.) H. Wendl. & Drude; *Kentia Mooreana* F. J. Muell.]. To 8 ft., trunk 4 in. in diam., green; lf. sheaths brownish-scurfy, about 1 ft. long, pinnae 33–40 on each side of rachis, to about 21 in. long, 1¼ in. wide; infl. about 18 in. long; fr. red, ½ in. in diam. Zone 10b in Fla.

LEPIDOZAMIA Regel. *Zamiaceae.* Two spp. of palmlike dioecious trees of Australia, differing from *Macrozamia* in having pinnae inserted along upper midline of rachis and sessile or subsessile, lf. bases short-tomentose, cones not stalked, the ends of cone scales tomentose, produced into a spreading, obtuse to acute, but not spine-tipped wing.

Ornamentals for outdoor culture in Zone 10, or under glass. For culture see *Cycads.*

Peroffskyana Regel [*Macrozamia Denisonii* C. Moore & F. J. Muell.; *M. Peroffskyana* (Regel) Miq.]. Trunk to 20 ft. or more, clothed with persistent lf. bases; lvs. to 10 ft. long, pinnae 200 or more, 4–12 in. long, to ½ in. wide, glossy above, broadly linear, recurved; male cones subcylindrical and more or less twisted, to 2 ft. long, female cones ovoid, to 32 in. long, 12 in. in diam.; seeds red when ripe. E. Australia.

LEPISMIUM Pfeiff. *Cactaceae.* Not cult. **L. cruciforme:** *Rhipsalis cruciformis.*

LEPTANDRA: *VERONICASTRUM.*

LEPTARRHENA R. Br. *Saxifragaceae.* One sp., a rhizomatous, per. herb of w. N. Amer.; basal lvs. short-petioled, leathery, persistent, st. lvs. few, reduced; fls. small, many in compact, several-branched, terminal clusters; calyx tube saucer-shaped, united at base to ovary, calyx lobes erect, petals 5, small, persistent, stamens 10, longer than petals and calyx lobes, carpels 2, fused only at base, ovary partly inferior. Closely related to *Saxifraga,* but carpels separate from each other almost to base, but united basally to the calyx tube.

amplexifolia: *L. pyrolifolia.*

pyrolifolia (D. Don) R. Br. ex Ser. [*L. amplexifolia* (Sternb.) R. Br. ex Ser.]. Sts. to 15 in. or more; basal lvs. to 4 in. long, toothed; calyx lobes to ¹⁄₁₆ in. long, exceeded by petals and the stamens, petals spatulate to oblanceolate. Wet places, Alaska to Ore., e. to Rocky Mts. of sw. Alta., w. Mont., n. Idaho.

LEPTODACTYLON Hook. & Arn. *Polemoniaceae.* About 5 spp. of shrubs or subshrubs, native to w. N. Amer.; lvs. alt. or opp., palmately or pinnately parted into linear, spine-tipped segms.; fls. pink, lilac, yellow, cream, or white, usually congested in cymes, rarely solitary, calyx 5-lobed, corolla funnelform or salverform, stamens 5, included; fr. a 3–4-celled caps. Differs from *Gilia* in having shrubby habit and lvs. fascicled, spinose, pinnately or palmately parted.

californicum Hook. & Arn. [*Gilia californica* (Hook. & Arn.) Benth.]. PRICKLY PHLOX. Densely leafy shrub, to 3 ft. or more; lvs. palmately parted into 3–9 pungent lobes; fls. pink or rarely white, salverform, 1½ in. across. Late winter to summer. Calif.

Nuttallii: *Linanthus Nuttallii.*

pungens (Torr.) Rydb. [*Gilia pungens* (Torr.) Benth.]. GRANITE GILIA. Densely leafy shrub, to 3 ft.; lvs. palmately parted into 3–7 pungent lobes; fls. pink, lilac, yellow or white, narrowly funnelform, ¾ in. long. Late spring to summer. B.C. to n. Baja Calif., e. to Rocky Mts. and New Mex.

LEPTODERMIS Wallich. *Rubiaceae.* About 30 spp. of deciduous shrubs, native to the Himalayas and e. Asia; lvs. opp., entire, stipules interpetiolar, triangular; fls. in axillary, head-like clusters, 5-merous, corolla tubular-funnelform; fr. a caps.

Propagated by cuttings of green wood in summer and by seeds.

oblonga Bunge. To 4 ft.; lvs. elliptic to oblong, to ¾ in. long; fls. violet-purple, ½ in. long. Late summer–autumn. N. China. Fairly hardy in the North.

LEPTOPTERIS K. Presl. *Osmundaceae.* Seven spp. of ferns, native to New Guinea, Polynesia, and New Zeal.; lvs. clustered at top of stout rhizome, dark green, very thin (2 cells thick), 2–3-pinnate into small linear pinnules; sporangia on lower surface of lvs. along the veins and veinlets. Closely allied to *Todea,* differing in the absence of stomates.

Sometimes planted in Zone 10, or as greenhouse plants. Propagated by spores. For culture see *Ferns.*

hymenophylloides (A. Rich.) K. Presl [*Todea hymenophylloides* A. Rich.]. Lvs. to 2½ ft. long and 1 ft. wide, petioles to 1 ft. long. New Zeal.

superba (Colenso) K. Presl [*Todea superba* Colenso]. PRINCE-OF-WALES FERN, PRINCE-OF-WALES-PLUME. Lvs. plumelike, to 4 ft. long and 10 in. wide, lower pinnae gradually reduced in size, petioles to 4 in. long. New Zeal.

LEPTOPYRUM Rchb. *Ranunculaceae.* One sp., an ann. herb, native to cent. Asia; lvs. pinnately compound; fls. small, sepals 4–5, petal-like, nectaries many, stamens 8–10, pistils 8–20; fr. of follicles.

fumarioides (L.) Rchb. [*Isopyrum fumarioides* L.]. Erect or spreading, glabrous, to 6–8 in.; lvs. glaucous, radical lvs. long-petioled, st. lvs. whorled, lfts. small, lobed; fls. white, ⅛ in. across.

LEPTOSPERMUM J. R. Forst. & G. Forst. *Myrtaceae.* About 40 spp. of evergreen shrubs or small trees, mostly in Australia, 1–2 in Malay Arch., and 3 in New Zeal.; lvs. alt., entire, 1–3-nerved or nerveless; fls. white, pink, or red, solitary, or 2–3 together in the axils or at ends of short branchlets, sometimes crowded, sessile or nearly so, calyx lobes 5, petals 5, clawed, limb orbicular, stamens many, ovary with few to many ovules in each cell; fr. a hard, woody caps., long-persisting, 3–10-valved, the valves scarcely exserted beyond the rim of the calyx, to prominently exserted beyond the rim. Related to *Kunzea,* but having lvs. alt., fls. solitary, or when crowded not in heads, and stamens not longer than the petals.

Leptospermums are planted outdoors in mild climates or are grown in the greenhouse. *L. laevigatum* is extensively used for the reclamation of moving sands. Plants in the greenhouse should be kept cool until Feb. or Mar. and then given a temperature of 55–60° F. Propagated by seeds in spring, cuttings under glass in May, or hardwood cuttings in autumn. They make excellent shrubbery in regions where hardy.

bullatum: *L. scoparium* cv.

citratum: *L. Petersonii.*

citriodorum: *L. flavescens* var. *citriodorum;* see *L. Liversidgei.*

ericoides A. Rich. Tree, to 30 ft., or more, trunk with bark shredding in long flakes; lvs. lanceolate, sometimes narrowly so, to ¾ in. long, sessile; fls. white, to ¼ in. across, many, axillary in axils of uppermost lvs., calyx lobes persistent, petals orbicular, short-clawed. New Zeal.

flavescens Sm. Large shrub or small tree, to 25 ft.; lvs. linear to lanceolate, to ¾ in. long or more; fls. yellowish-white, to ½ in. across, solitary, axillary, nearly sessile. Var. **grandiflorum** (Lodd.) Benth. [*L. grandiflorum* Lodd.]. Lvs. and fls. large. Ne. Australia. Var. **citratum:** *L. Petersonii.* Var. **citriodorum:** perhaps *L. Liversidgei.*

floribundum: see *L. scoparium.*

grandiflorum: *L. flavescens* var.

juniperinum Sm. Shrub, to 6 ft.; lvs. linear-lanceolate, to ¾ in. long, stiff, pungent; fls. to ½ in. across, solitary, sessile; caps. 5-valved. E. Australia.

Keatleyi: a listed name of no botanical standing for *L. scoparium* cv.

laevigatum (Soland. ex Gaertn.) F. J. Muell. AUSTRALIAN TEA TREE. Large shrub or tree, to 20 ft., trunk often twisted, bark shredding in long flakes; lvs. broadly oblanceolate, to 1 in. long, mucronulate, leathery, with very inconspicuous veins; fls. white, to ¾ in. across, solitary, axillary, sessile or nearly so; caps. 8–10-valved. Se. Australia and Tasmania. Cv. **'Compactum'**. Of compact habit, to 3 ft. Cv. **'Reevesii'**: perhaps 'Compactum'.

lanigerum (Ait.) Sm. [*L. pubescens* Lam.]. TEA TREE, WOOLLY T. T. Tall shrub or tree, to 20 ft., young growth pubescent; lvs. oblanceolate to obovate, to ¾ in. long, acute or obtuse, silky-pubescent, particularly beneath; fls. white, to ¾ in. across, solitary, axillary, or terminal on short shoots; caps. 5-valved, valves exserted above rim. Se. Australia and Tasmania.

Liversidgei R. T. Bak. & H. G. Sm. Shrub, to 12 ft., brs. drooping; lvs. obovate to oblong, to ¼ in. long, with prominent oil glands, strongly lemon-scented when crushed; fls. white, to ⁵⁄₁₆ in. across, solitary, axillary, on short peduncles; caps. 5-valved. Ne. Australia. *L. flavescens* var. *citriodorum* F. M. Bailey may belong here.

Martinii: a listed name of no botanical standing for *L. scoparium* cv.

Nichollsii: a listed name of no botanical standing for *L. scoparium* cv.

persiciflorum: *L. squarrosum.*

Petersonii F. M. Bailey [*L. flavescens* var. *citratum* J. F. Bailey & C. T. White; *L. citratum* (J. F. Bailey & C. T. White) Chall., Cheel, & Penf.]. Shrub or tree, to 20 ft.; lvs. linear or linear-lanceolate, to 2 in. long; fls. white, to ⅝ in. across, solitary, axillary or terminal on lateral branchlets, sessile or nearly so; caps. 5-valved, valves slightly domed above rim. Ne. Australia. The lvs. yield a lemon-scented, aromatic, essential oil. Resembles *L. flavescens*, which lacks lemon-scented oil.

pubescens: *L. lanigerum.*

Reevesii: a listed name of no botanical standing for *L. laevigatum* cv.

rotundifolium (Maiden & Betche) Domin. Shrub, to 6 ft.; lvs. orbicular, to ¼ in. long, grooved, recurved at tips; fls. pale pink, to 1 in. across, solitary, petals crinkled. E. Australia.

scoparium J. R. Forst. & G. Forst. [*L. floribundum* Salisb. may belong here]. TEA TREE, NEW ZEALAND T. T., MANUKA. Large or small shrub, branchlets and young lvs. pubescent; lvs. narrowly lanceolate to ovate, to ½ in. long, rigid, pungent; fls. white or pink, to ½ in. across, solitary, usually axillary; caps. 5-valved, exserted above rim. New Zeal. and Tasmania. Zone 9. Var. **grandiflorum**: *L. squarrosum.* A variable sp. which has many cvs., including the following: **'Album Flore Pleno'**, fls. double, white; **'Bullatum'** [*L. bullatum* Hort. ex Loud.], lvs. large, fls. about ¾ in. across, light red; **'Chapmanii'**, lvs. brownish, fls. large, single, bright rose; **'Flore Plenum'**, fls. double, red; **'Keatleyi'**, fls. single, to ¾ in. across, pale pink, petal margins wavy; **'Martinii'**, fls. single, rose-red; **'Nichollsii'** [var. *Nichollsii* Turrill], lvs. bronze, fls. single, ⅝ in. across, rose-red; **'Roseum'**, lvs. gray-green, fls. nearly 1 in. across, rose-pink with dark center; **'Sandersii'**, has been spelled **'Saundersii'**, fls. single, petals pink, edged with white; **'Walkeri'**, fls. single, varying from red to pink and white on same plant. Var. **grandiflorum**: *L. squarrosum.*

sphaerocarpum Cheel. Shrub, to 8 ft.; lvs. linear to linear-lanceolate, to ⅜ in. long; fls. white, solitary, terminal on branchlets, calyx tube hairy, petals orbicular, ³⁄₁₆ in. across; caps. spherical, 3–4-valved, valves exserted above rim. Se. Australia.

spinescens Endl. Spiny shrub; lvs. obovate to cuneate-oblong or oblanceolate, to ½ in. long; fls. white, solitary, sessile. W. Australia.

squarrosum Soland. ex Gaertn. [*L. persiciflorum* Rchb.; *L. scoparium* var. *grandiflorum* Hook.]. Shrub, to 9 ft.; lvs. somewhat crowded, ovate, acuminate, to ½ in. long, somewhat recurved; fls. white with pink flush in age, solitary, mostly axillary, sessile or nearly so; caps. 5-valved, valves exserted above rim. Se. Australia.

LEPTOSYNE: *COREOPSIS.*

LEPTOTAENIA: *LOMATIUM.* **Leptotaenia multifida**: *Lomatium dissectum* var. *multifidum.* **Leptotaenia purpurea**: *Lomatium columbianum.*

LEPTOTES Lindl. *Orchidaceae.* Six spp. of small epiphytes, native to Brazil; sts. short, thickened, 1-lvd.; lvs. fleshy, semicylindrical; infl. terminal, short, few-fld.; sepals and petals spreading, not united, lip not united with column, 3-lobed, column short, fleshy, obscurely 2-winged, pollinia 6. For structure of fl. see *Orchidaceae.*

For culture see *Orchids.*

bicolor Lindl. [*Tetramicra bicolor* (Lindl.) Benth.]. Lvs. to 4 in. long, recurved, channelled; scape short, 1–3-fld.; sepals and petals white, lateral lobes of lip white or green, midlobe purple with white apex. Spring, late autumn. Brazil.

LESPEDEZA Michx. BUSH CLOVER. *Leguminosae.* (subfamily *Faboideae*). About 120 spp. of per. herbs or low shrubs, native to temp. e. N. Amer., e. Asia, and Australia; lvs. alt., of 3 lfts.; fls. in dense or loose, axillary racemes, papilionaceous or petals 0, stamens 10, 9 united and 1 separate; fr. a flat, ovate-acuminate, very small legume, 1-seeded and indehiscent.

The ornamental species are hardy (Zone 5) and thrive in any upland soil. Propagated by seeds and division, or *L. Thunbergii* also by softwood cuttings. *Lespedeza cuneata, L. striata,* and *L. stipulacea* are grown as forage, hay, and green-manure crops, especially in the southeastern U.S.; seeds should be sown early in spring.

bicolor Turcz. Shrub, to 10 ft.; lfts. elliptic, to 1½ in. long, pale beneath; fls. purple, in erect racemes longer than lvs., calyx lobes blunt. Summer, autumn. Japan.

Buergeri Miq. Similar to *L. Thunbergii,* but with lfts. elliptic-ovate, more pubescent, and fls. purple to white in shorter, ascending racemes. Summer, autumn. Japan.

capitata Michx. Per., to 5½ ft., silvery-pubescent; lfts. oblong to narrowly elliptic, petioles to ³⁄₁₆ in. long; fls. yellowish-white, with purple spot on standard, in dense headlike racemes shorter than subtending lvs., calyx longer than fr. Ont. to Fla. and La. Many vars. have been recognized.

cuneata (Dum.-Cours.) G. Don [*L. sericea* (Thunb.) Miq.]. CHINESE L. Subshrub, to 3 ft.; lfts. linear-oblong to linear, to ¾ in. long, obtuse, pubescent beneath; fls. whitish, to ¼ in. long, 2–4 together in dense axillary clusters to 1 in. long; fr. rarely to ⅛ in. long. China, Japan; naturalized in se. U.S. Cult. as a forage plant, and for erosion control.

cyrtobotrya Miq. To 6 ft.; lfts. broadly elliptic-obovate, emarginate, pubescent beneath; racemes nearly headlike, to 1½ in. long, shorter than lvs.; fls. rose-purple. Japan, Korea.

formosa (Vogel) Koehne. Differs from *L. Thunbergii* in having lfts. varying from elliptic to obovate and often retuse. Se. China.

hirta (L.) Hornem. Differs from *L. capitata* in having lfts. obovate to elliptic, racemes cylindrical, longer than lvs., and calyx about as long as fr. E. N. Amer.

japonica L. H. Bailey. Similar to *L. Thunbergii,* but herbage nearly glabrous, lfts. broader, and fls. pure white. Japan.

sericea: *L. cuneata.*

Sieboldii: *L. Thunbergii.*

stipulacea Maxim. KOREAN L., KOREAN CLOVER. Differs from *L. striata* in having lvs. mostly with distinct petioles to ⁵⁄₁₆ in. long, lfts. broader, emarginate, conspicuously ciliate on margin and on midrib beneath when young, and calyces covering only ⅓–½ of pods. Ne. China to Korea; naturalized in e.-cent. U.S.

striata (Thunb. ex J. Murr.) Hook. & Arn. JAPANESE CLOVER, COMMON L. Ann., to 1½ ft., sometimes prostrate; lfts. many, small, obovate to narrowly elliptic, nearly sessile, stipules conspicuous, ovate-lanceolate, to ³⁄₁₆ in. long; fls. axillary, small, pink to lavender. China, Japan; widely naturalized in se. U.S.

Thunbergii (DC.) Nakai [*L. Sieboldii* Miq.; *Desmodium penduliflorum* Oudem.]. Per. herb or subshrub, to 10 ft.; lfts. elliptic, to 2 in. long; fls. rose-purple, in long drooping racemes, calyx lobes long-pointed. Autumn. Japan, China.

LESQUERELLA S. Wats. BLADDERPOD. *Cruciferae.* About 40 spp. of small, ann. or per., grayish herbs, with the look of *Alyssum,* mostly in N. Amer.; lvs. simple, entire to toothed, densely pubescent in per. spp., usually in rosettes as well as on the st.; fls. small but often showy because of their number, sepals 4, petals 4, commonly yellow, spatulate; fr. a short, more or less inflated silicle. Closely related to *Physaria,* which differs in having silicles often paired, much larger, more papery, and conspicuously retuse.

alpina (Nutt.) S. Wats. [*L. spatulata* Rydb.]. Cespitose per., with branched caudex, sts. erect, unbranched, to 5 in.; lvs. linear to oblanceolate-spatulate, to 1½ in. long; fls. yellow, on curved pedicels, infl. elongating in fr. Rocky Mts., w. N. Dak. to Utah, to Alta. and Sask.

montana (A. Gray) S. Wats. Grayish, stellate-pubescent per., caudex usually branched; sts. decumbent, to 8 in. high, basal lvs. usually narrowly oblanceolate, to 1½ in. long, entire or toothed, narrowed to slender petiole; fls. yellow, on curved pedicels. S. Dak., Wyo., Colo., New Mex.

spatulata: *L. alpina.*

LESSINGIA Cham. *Compositae* (Aster Tribe). Seven or more spp. of branching ann. herbs in Calif.; lvs. alt., sessile, woolly and usually glandular, entire to lobed; fl. heads discoid, small, few-fld.; fls. all tubular, yellow, white, or light purple, the marginal ones slightly enlarged; pappus of many tan bristles.

Propagated by seeds.

leptoclada A. Gray. Erect, 1–3 ft., with many slender branchlets; lvs. tomentose, later glabrate, the lowest spatulate, toothed, the upper bractlike, glandular-dotted; heads in a panicle; fls. purple to white. Open slopes, Sierras of cent. Calif.

LETTSOMIA: *ARGYREIA.*

LETTUCE. Lettuce, *Lactuca sativa,* is a leading salad vegetable, grown for its developed thin radical leaves and, in one odd race, for the thick edible stem. See *Lactuca sativa.*

Lettuce is a hardy annual of simple culture, but the best results are obtainable only with well-selected strains and on suitable, open, moisture-holding soil. The plant must grow rapidly and continuously to produce a good crop of tender leaves, but heading is usually better if the growth rate is not too rapid. In the more highly developed kinds, the leaves form a dense rosette or clump, known as head or cabbage lettuce, in contradistinction to leaf or loose lettuce, in which the basal leaves are hardly consolidated into a ball or head; sometimes leaf lettuces are crisped and curled. The cos lettuces or romaine are summer lettuces with leaves aggregated into an erect, oblong head or column, the leaves being mostly long-oblong rather than the usual broad type. Bibb lettuce is a semiheading type of excellent quality. Slow-bolting varieties are available. A kind that is little known in this country and that would hardly pass as a lettuce is the so-called asparagus lettuce, grown for its long, thick main stem before the plant goes to seed; the leaves are long and narrow and tapering to the point; it may be grown to some extent in this country by Chinese and perhaps by Europeans.

Large areas are now devoted to lettuce for the general market, under intensive methods both as to growing and handling. Muck lands are well adapted to the crop. This large-area growing requires special experience, and is not covered in the present entry.

Lettuce seed can be sown in a seed bed, either under glass or in the open ground. From this bed the little plants are transferred to their permanent positions 6–12 inches apart in rows far enough apart to permit hand tillage; or they may be set closer and thinned as they grow. Lettuce plants that are crowded do not produce the firm rosettes of good substance that the best markets or the best tastes demand.

As lettuce soon runs to seed, particularly in warm weather, only a small space should be grown at each sowing for home use, and the sowings may be made every week or two until summer approaches; some cultivars do well in warm weather. The cos lettuces are summer kinds but do not thrive in the hot suns and soils in most parts of North America. As a rule, 5–8 feet of row supplies sufficient lettuce to each person for each sowing. Head lettuces are more difficult to bring to perfection than the ordinary loose lettuces, unless one has soils and conditions specially adapted. Soils for lettuce should be fertile and well drained. The crop is better if cut in the morning before the plants have become soft, and care should be taken not to expose it to the sun. Lettuce is soon ruined by careless cutting and handling.

Lettuce is usually followed by a succession crop, as cabbages *(Brassica),* celery *(Apium),* late beets *(Beta),* green beans *(Phaseolus),* and sometimes it is grown as a companion crop along with early cabbages, cauliflowers, or other longer-season plants. Good lettuce should be had for the table in six to eight weeks from sowing, and the thinnings may be used still sooner.

LEUCAENA Benth. *Leguminosae* (subfamily *Mimosoideae*). About 50 spp. of unarmed trees or shrubs, mostly of trop. Amer., 1 sp. in Polynesia; lvs. alt., 2-pinnate; fl. heads axillary and clustered or terminally racemose; fls. 5-merous, stamens 10, separate; fr. a flat, oblong-linear, nearly membranous legume, with a stalk.

glauca (L.) Benth. WHITE POPINAC. Shrub or small tree, to 30 ft.; lvs. with 3–10 pairs of pinnae, lfts. in 10–20 pairs, acute, about ½ in. long, pale beneath; fls. in heads to more than 1 in. in diam., calyx about half as long as corolla; fr. puberulent, to 6 in. long, ⅝ in. wide, with stout stalk. Trop. Amer.; naturalized in s. Fla., Hawaii, and elsewhere. Grown for forage and as shade for coffee. Seeds are used in necklaces.

pulverulenta (Schlechtend.) Benth. Tree, to 60 ft.; herbage white-tomentose; lvs. with 15–18 pairs of pinnae, lfts. many, small, linear-curved, obtuse; fls. white, fragrant, in oblong heads, calyx 3–4 times shorter than corolla; fr. to 7 in. long. Tex., e. Mex.

retusa Benth. Glabrate shrub or tree, to 25 ft.; lvs. with 2–5 pairs of pinnae, lfts. in 4–8 pairs, oblong-elliptic or the uppermost obovate, to 1 in. long, obtuse or retuse, reticulate-veined; fr. 6–10 in. long, ⅜ in. wide. Tex., New Mex.

trichodes (Jacq.) Benth. Glabrate shrub; lvs. with 2–3 pairs of remote pinnae, lfts. in 2–5 pairs, ovate, about 1 in. long, usually apically rounded; fls. in heads to ⅜ in. in diam., calyx little shorter than corolla; fr. 6 in. long or more, ¾ in. wide, membranous, lustrous. Peru.

LEUCANTHEMUM: *CHRYSANTHEMUM.* **L. coronopifolium:** *C. atrata.*

LEUCHTENBERGIA Hook. *Cactaceae.* One sp., a small cactus, native to Mex.; sts. bearing 3–4-angled, elongate tubercles with apical areoles; spines weak, papery; fls. from young areoles, funnelform-campanulate, opening several days, scales on ovary few, naked in their axils; seeds dark brown, tubercled. Resembles *Mammillaria* with elongate tubercles, but the fls. from the spiniferous areoles.

For culture see *Cacti.*

principis Hook. AGAVE CACTUS, PRISM C. Sts. simple or branched, to 2 ft. high and 3 in. thick, tubercles bluish, 4–5 in. long, axils woolly; radial spines 8–14, to 2 in. long, central spines 1–2, to 4 in. long; fls. yellow, fragrant, 4 in. across.

LEUCOCARPUS D. Don. *Scrophulariaceae.* One sp., a tall per. herb, native from Mex. to Bolivia; sts. 4-angled, winged; lvs. opp., simple; fls. yellow, in axillary, several-branched cymes on conspicuous peduncles, calyx 5-lobed, corolla 2-lipped, upper lip 2-lobed, lower lip 3-lobed, central lobe with 2 hairy, prominent ridges extending to throat, stamens 4; fr. indehiscent, fleshy, white.

For cultivation see **Mimulus.**

perfoliatus (HBK) Benth. Rank herb, to 3 ft., shrubby at base; lvs. lanceolate, cordate-clasping, to 10 in. long, toothed; fls. to ¾ in. long.

LEUCOCORYNE Lindl. *Amaryllidaceae.* Four or 6 spp. of bulbous herbs, native to Chile; lvs. basal, sheathing the bulb; fls. in an umbel terminal on a scape and subtended by 2 spathe valves, perianth tube cylindrical, longer or shorter than lobes, stamens 3, inserted on tube, staminodes 3, inserted at throat, ovary superior; fr. a loculicidal caps.

Culture as for *Ixia.*

ixioides (Hook.) Lindl. [*L. odorata* Lindl.; *Brodiaea ixioides* Hook., not (Ait.f.) S. Wats.]. GLORY-OF-THE-SUN. To 1 ft.; lvs. 1 ft. long; umbel 4–6-fld.; fls. white or pale blue, fragrant, tube ½ in. long, lobes ¾ in. long. Var. **purpurea** (C. Gay) Bak. Taller; fls. larger, deep lilac.

odorata: *L. ixioides.*

uniflora: *Ipheion uniflorum.*

LEUCOCRINUM Nutt. SAND LILY, STAR L., MOUNTAIN L. *Liliaceae.* One sp., a stemless herb, native from Ore. and n. Calif. to S. Dak., Nebr., and New Mex.; rhizome deep-seated, roots fleshy; lvs. narrowly linear; fls. arising from the rhizome and borne in clusters near surface of ground, perianth salverform, 6-lobed, stamens 6, attached near top of perianth tube; fr. a loculicidal caps., seeds black, angled.

montanum Nutt. Lvs. several, to 5 in. long; fls. pure white, fragrant, perianth tube 1–5 in. long, anthers yellow. Spring.

LEUCODENDRON R. Br. *Proteaceae.* About 60 spp. of dioecious trees and shrubs, native to S. Afr.; lvs. entire, leathery; male fls. in terminal, sessile heads, female fls. in terminal conelike heads subtended by woody bracts; fr. a nut.

Grown outdoors in Calif. (Zone 10) and rarely under glass in the North. Propagated by seeds.

adscendens R. Br. Low-growing shrub, to 1 ft., brs. slightly angular, usually glabrous; lvs. narrowly lanceolate, to 1 in. long, those surrounding male infl. linear-oblanceolate, those surrounding female infl. lanceolate; infl. solitary, to 1 in. long.

argenteum R. Br. SILVER TREE. Tree, to 30 ft.; lvs. sessile, lanceolate, to 6 in. long, densely covered with silvery-silky pubescence; male infl. to 2½ in. across; fr. heads large and heavy. Sw. Cape Prov.

plumosum R. Br. Shrub, to 7 ft.; lvs. linear or linear-lanceolate, to 2½ in. long, pubescent; male infl. ½ in. long, female infl. to 1¾ in. long.

Stokoei E. P. Phillips. Lvs. oblong or oblong-lanceolate, to 3½ in. long, glabrous; male infl. 1 in. across, surrounded by brown bracts.

venosum R. Br. Shrub, to 4 ft.; lvs. oblanceolate, to 3¼ in. long, glabrous; male infl. 1 in. across, female infl. similar to male when young, becoming ovoid-globose, 1½ in. long, 2 in. in diam. in fr.

LEUCOGENES Beauverd. NEW ZEALAND EDELWEISS. *Compositae* (Inula Tribe). Two or 3 spp. of silvery-tomentose per. herbs of New Zeal.; resembling *Leontopodium*, but differing in the structure of the fl. heads; lvs. imbricate, the uppermost bractlike, larger, spreading, subtending the terminal glomerules of small discoid heads; involucral bracts imbricate, scarious; fls. all tubular and fertile, the inner ones many, narrowly campanulate, bisexual, the outer row filiform, female; achenes angled, hairy, pappus of 20–25 scabrous bristles.

grandiceps (Hook.f.) Beauverd. To 8 in., sts. decumbent, woody at base, branched; lvs. in rosettes, oblong-spatulate, to ⅜ in. long, obtuse, recurved at apex; heads ³⁄₁₆ in. across, several in a dense glomerule subtended by white-woolly, ovate bractlike lvs.

Leontopodium (Hook.f.) Beauverd [*Helichrysum Leontopodium* Hook.f.]. Differs from *L. grandiceps* in having lvs. linear-oblong, to ¾ in. long, erect at apex, and glomerule subtended by lanceolate bractlike lvs.

LEUCOJUM L. SNOWFLAKE. *Amaryllidaceae.* Nine spp. of small herbs with membranous-coated bulbs, native to Eur. and w. Medit.; lvs. basal; fls. nodding, solitary or in an umbel on a hollow scape and subtended by a spathe splitting along one side or into 2 papery valves, perianth segms. separate, white, tinged with yellow, red, or green, ovary inferior; fr. a berry.

Hardy; bulbs should remain undisturbed for a number of years. Plant 3 in. deep in well-drained soil.

aestivum L. GIANT S., SUMMER S. To 1 ft.; lvs. to 1½ ft. long and ½ in. wide; fls. 2–8, on long, nodding pedicels, white, tipped with green, ¾ in. long. Late spring. Cent. and s. Eur.

autumnale L. To 9 in.; lvs. threadlike, developing after fls.; spathe split on one side; fls. 1–3, usually 2, on nodding pedicels, white, tinged with red, ½ in. long. Autumn. Medit. region.

carpathicum: *L. vernum* var.

hiemale: see *L. nicaeense.*

nicaeense Ardoino [*L. hiemale* of auth., not DC.]. Lvs. 2–4, threadlike, to 1 ft. long, developing with fls.; fls. usually solitary, on short, nodding pedicels, white, tinged with green outside, to ½ in. long, with 6-lobed receptacular disc. Early spring. Medit. region.

vernum L. SPRING S. To 1 ft.; lvs. to 9 in. long, ½ in. wide; fls. solitary, on short, somewhat nodding pedicels, white, tipped with green, ¾ in. long. Early spring. Cent. Eur. Var. **carpathicum** Sweet [*L. carpathicum* (Sweet) Sweet]. Fls. often 2, perianth segms. and style tipped with yellow.

LEUCOPHAE: *SIDERITIS.*

LEUCOPHYLLUM Humb. & Bonpl. *Scrophulariaceae.* About 12 spp. of shrubs, native to New Mex., Tex., and Mex.; lvs. simple, entire, silvery-tomentose or glabrate; fls. rosylavender or purple, solitary in lf. axils, calyx 5-lobed, corolla funnelform or campanulate, 5-lobed, slightly 2-lipped, stamens 4; fr. a caps.

Grown as a low ornamental hedge plant in its native region and sometimes as a lawn plant.

compactum: *L. frutescens* cv.

frutescens (Berland.) I. M. Johnst. [*L. texanum* Benth.]. CENIZA, BAROMETER BUSH. Compact shrub, to 8 ft.; lvs. elliptic to obovate, to 1 in. long, felty on both sides with stellate hairs; fls. rosy-lavender, to 1 in. across. Tex. and Mex. Cvs. 'Floribundum' and 'Compactum' [*L. compactum* Hort.] are listed.

minus A. Gray. Shrub, to 3 ft., finely stellate-hairy throughout; lvs. spatulate-obovate, to ½ in. long; fls. purple, to 1 in. long. W. Tex., s. New Mex., n. Mex.

texanum: *L. frutescens.*

LEUCOPOGON R. Br. *Epacridaceae.* About 130 spp. of shrubs and small trees, native to Australia, New Zeal., and other Pacific Is.; lvs. alt., usually sessile; fls. solitary or in spikes or clusters, 5-merous, calyx usually white, corolla tubular, white to pink, lobes valvate and bearded inside, tube short and lacking scales or tufts of hair inside below middle, but glabrous or hairy above, stamens subsessile and inserted in throat, ovary 2–5-celled, each cell 1-ovuled; fr. a drupe, small, nearly dry, stone several-celled.

Cultivation as for *Erica.* Seeds soon lose their viability.

Fraseri A. Cunn. [*Cyathodes Fraseri* (A. Cunn.) Allan]. OTAGO HEATH. Low, spreading shrub, to 6 in.; lvs. obovate- to linear-oblong, to ⅜ in. long, closely imbricate, acute, glossy on upper surface; fls. solitary in lf. axils, pinkish, ¼–½ in. long, fragrant; fr. broadly oblong, to ⁵⁄₁₆ in. long, yellowish-orange, edible. Australia, New Zeal. Zones 9 and 10 on Pacific Coast.

LEUCOSPERMUM R. Br. PINCUSHION, PINCUSHION FLOWER. *Proteaceae.* About 40 spp. of erect or procumbent S. Afr. shrubs; lvs. crowded, entire, leathery, hairy; fls. yellow or reddish, in solitary or clustered, bracted heads, perianth tubular, 2–4-lobed, stamens 4, borne at base of lobes, ovary sessile, 1-ovuled; fr. a whitish nutlet.

incisum E. P. Phillips. Lvs. densely crowded and concealing st., oblong, to 2½ in. long, deeply 6–7-toothed toward apex; fl. heads sessile, 2½ in. long and nearly as wide.

nutans R. Br. NODDING P. Lvs. sessile, ovate, to 2½ in. long, cordate, entire or broadly and shortly 3-toothed at apex; fl. heads large, about 4 in. across; fls. spreading, but directed upward.

reflexum Buek ex Beissn. ROCKET P. Lvs. crowded but with st. partly exposed, oblong, to 1½ in. long, 3-toothed or entire; fl. heads on stout peduncle, large, 2½ in. long, about 4 in. across; fls. becoming directed downward in the later stages of flowering.

LEUCOSPORA Nutt. *Scrophulariaceae.* One sp., a pubescent, ann. herb, with cylindrical sts., native to cent. U.S.; lvs. opp., pinnatifid; fls. pale lavender or white, axillary, solitary, sepals 5, linear, corolla 2-lipped, upper lip 2-lobed, lower lip 3-lobed, stamens 4; fr. an ovoid caps.

multifida (Michx.) Nutt. [*Conobea multifida* (Michx.) Benth.]. Muchbranched herb, to 10 in.; lvs. to ¾ in. long; fls. to ⅛ in. long. Summer, autumn. S. Ont. to e. Iowa and n. Kans., s. to nw. Ga. and Tex.

LEUCOTHOE D. Don [*Eubotrys* Nutt.]. FETTERBUSH. *Ericaceae.* About 50 spp. of deciduous or evergreen shrubs, widely distributed in e. Asia, Madagascar, N. and S. Amer.; lvs. alt., simple; fls. white to pink, in axillary or terminal racemes, sometimes in panicles, calyx 5-parted, corolla urceolate to cylindrical, stamens 10, awned or awnless, ovary superior; fr. a 5-valved, many-seeded caps.

Leucothoes require protection in the North. They thrive in a moist soil of peat and sand. Propagated by seeds under glass in sphagnum and sand, the seedlings then set outdoors, and also by division, cuttings, and underground runners.

acuminata: *L. populifolia.*

axillaris (Lam.) D. Don [*L. Catesbaei* (Walt.) A. Gray; *L. platyphylla* Small; *Andromeda Catesbaei* Walt.]. Depressed, evergreen shrub, to 6 ft.; lvs. elliptic to oblong-lanceolate, abruptly pointed, remotely toothed; fls. in axillary racemes to 3 in. long, bracts ovate to orbicular. Va. to Fla. and Miss. Zone 7?

Catesbaei: *L. axillaris,* but material offered as *L. Catesbaei* is *L. Fontanesiana.*

Davisiae Torr. ex A. Gray. SIERRA LAUREL. Evergreen shrub, to 5 ft.; lvs. to 3 in. long, obscurely serrate to entire; fls. in panicles to 6 in. long, corolla urceolate, ⁵⁄₁₆ in. long. Summer. Mts., n.-cent. Calif. to s. Ore. Zone 6.

editorum: *L. Fontanesiana.*

elongata: *L. racemosa* var.

Fontanesiana (Steud.) Sleum. [*L. editorum* Fern. & Schub.]. DOGHOBBLE, SWITCH IVY, DROOPING L. Evergreen shrub, to 6 ft., brs. spreading, arching; lvs. oblong-lanceolate to ovate-lanceolate, to 6½ in. long, tapering to a long-acuminate tip, teeth ciliate-spinose; fls. in axillary racemes to 3 in. long, bracts lanceolate-acuminate. Spring. Va. to Ga. and Tenn. Zone 5. Commonly offered under the names *L. Catesbaei* or *Andromeda Catesbaei.*

Grayana Maxim. Deciduous shrub, to 4 ft.; lvs. sessile or nearly so, elliptic to obovate, to 4 in. long, abruptly acuminate, ciliate; fls. in terminal, 1-sided racemes to 4 in. long. Summer, early autumn. Japan. Zone 6.

Keiskei Miq. Half-evergreen to evergreen shrub, to 3½ ft.; lvs. oblong-lanceolate to ovate, to 3 in. long, long-acuminate, somewhat crenate-serrate; fls. in axillary and terminal racemes to 1½ in. long, corolla cylindrical, ½–¾ in. long. Japan. Zone 6.

platyphylla: *L. axillaris.*

populifolia (Lam.) Dipp. [*L. acuminata* (Ait.) G. Don]. Evergreen shrub, to 12 ft.; lvs. lanceolate to ovate-lanceolate, to 4 in. long, tapering to an acute or acuminate tip, entire to obscurely serrulate; fls. in axillary racemes, to ⁵⁄₁₆ in. long, on long pedicels. Spring. S.C. to Fla. Zone 7?

racemosa (L.) A. Gray [*Andromeda racemosa* L.; *Eubotrys racemosa* (L.) Nutt.]. SWEETBELLS. Upright, deciduous shrub, to 12 ft.; lvs. oblong to ovate or elliptic, to 3 in. long, acute, serrulate, pubescent beneath, at least on veins; fls. in 1-sided, terminal racemes, to ⁵⁄₁₆ in. long, anthers 4-awned; fr. not lobed. Late summer. Moist places and swamps, Mass. to Fla. and La. Zone 6. Var. **elongata** (Small) Fern. [*L. elongata* Small; *Eubotrys elongata* (Small) Small]. Branchlets pilose; sepals ciliate. Ga. and Fla. to La.

recurva (Buckl.) A. Gray [*Eubotrys recurva* (Buckl.) Britt.]. RED-TWIG L. Spreading, deciduous shrub, to 12 ft.; lvs. elliptic-lanceolate to obovate, to 4 in. long, tapering to an acute or acuminate tip, serrulate; fls. in 1-sided, curved, terminal racemes, corolla cylindrical, anthers 2-awned; fr. 5-lobed. Spring, late spring. Va. to Ga. and Ala. Zone 6.

LEUZEA DC. *Compositae* (Carduus Tribe). Four spp. of per. herbs, native to s. Eur. and N. Afr.; lvs. in a rosette or alt. on the sts., usually pinnately dissected or pinnatifid, rarely entire; fl. heads large, solitary, involucre ovoid or globose, involucral bracts imbricate in several rows, with a lanceolate to orbicular terminal appendage, receptacle flat, bristly, slightly chaffy-scaly; fls. all tubular, bisexual, anthers short-tailed; achenes glabrous, pappus plumose, in several rows, united in a ring at the base and falling as a unit.

Sometimes grown as an ornamental. Propagated by seeds or division.

conifera (L.) DC. [*Centaurea conifera* L.]. Erect per., to 1½ ft.; lvs. lanceolate or lyrate, to 6 in. long, white-tomentose beneath; heads solitary, to 2 in. across, involucre conelike, involucral bracts yellowish or purple-tipped, blunt, splitting; fls. purple. S. Eur., Algeria.

LEVISTICUM J. Hill. *Umbelliferae.* One sp., a per. herb grown for the aromatic frs. used in confectionary and cooking, and also for its striking ornamental appearance.

officinale W. D. J. Koch. LOVAGE. To 6 ft.; lvs. ternately compound, segms. coarsely toothed above the middle; fls. greenish-yellow, in compound umbels subtended by narrow, deflexed bracts. S. Eur.; naturalized from Penn. and N.J., to Va., w. to Mo. and New Mex. Prop. by seeds and division.

LEWISIA Pursh. *Portulacaceae.* About 15–20 spp. of fleshy per. herbs, with thick starchy roots or corms, native to w. N. Amer.; basal lvs. in rosettes, st. lvs. few; fls. white, rose, or red, solitary or in panicles, sepals 2–6, petals 4–18, stamens 5 to many, styles 3–8, united at base; fr. a caps. opening by top falling as a lid, seeds few to many, dark, glossy.

The thick starchy roots of some species are edible. Many are useful in the rock garden. They do well in a deep, loose, gritty soil made up of about 1 part earth, 2 parts peat moss, and 3 parts very coarse sand, in locations that are moist during the spring, when foliage and flowers are produced, and dry in the summer. Best effects are obtained when planted several in a group rather than singly. Propagated by seeds or division of roots in spring. Storage of seeds at low temperature for 3–4 weeks before sowing improves and hastens germination. Deciduous species thrive in the sun. Flowers and leaves appear in spring and early summer, the leaves mature, and then the roots lie dormant. Evergreen species have rosettes of fleshy, persistent leaves and perhaps are more hardy. They require good drainage; a collar of chipped stone to a depth of 1 in. about the crown is desirable. Plant in partial shade, except in damp regions where full sun is desirable.

bernardensis: error for *L. bernardina.*

bernardina: *L. nevadensis.*

brachycalyx Engelm. ex A. Gray. Deciduous; lvs. in rosettes, spatulate or oblanceolate, to 3 in. long, somewhat fleshy; fls. solitary, on scapes to 2 in. high, with usually 2 ovate bracts next to calyx, petals

white, to 2 in. across. Late spring. Mt. meadows, s. Calif., Ariz., Utah, New Mex.

Cantelowii J. T. Howell. Evergreen, to 16 in.; basal lvs. many, oblanceolate, to 2 in. long, sharply dentate, apex obtuse or subtruncate to retuse; fls. many, in panicles, on slender pedicels, petals light pink with dark veins, about ¼ in. long. Late spring. Wet cliffs, nw. Sierra Nevada of Calif.

columbiana (J. T. Howell) B. L. Robinson. Evergreen, root fleshy; basal lvs. linear-spatulate, to 2 in. long; fls. in panicles on scapes to 1 ft. high, sepals 2, petals 7–9, white or pink, veined with red, to ½ in. long, stamens 5–6. Spring, summer. Gravelly and rocky slopes, s. B.C., s. to Calif., e. to Idaho. Var. **rupicola** (English) C. L. Hitchc. [*L. rupicola* English]. Lvs. generally rounded at apex; fls. light to dark pink or rose. Mts., Wash. and Ore.

Cotyledon (S. Wats.) B. L. Robinson [*L. Finchiae* Purdy; *L. longifolia* Hort.; *L. Millardii* Hort.; *L. Purdyi* Gabr.; *L. Whiteae* Purdy.]. Evergreen, root fleshy; basal lvs. many, spatulate, to 3 in. long, margins flat, entire to undulate; fls. in panicles on scapes to 10 in. high, pedicels stout, petals 8–10, white with red tinge or stripe, to ½ in. long. Early spring to summer. Rocky places in mts., n. Calif. and s. Ore. Var. **Heckneri** (C. V. Mort.) Munz [*L. Heckneri* (C. V. Mort.) J. T. Howell]. Lvs. strongly toothed; petals to ¾ in. long. Var. **Howellii** (S. Wats.) Jeps. [*L. Howellii* (S. Wats.) B. L. Robinson]. Lf. margins crisped, sometimes fimbriate-toothed; petals to ⅝ in. long.

Edithae: a listed name of no botanical standing; may refer to a form of *L. columbiana.*

Finchiae: *L. Cotyledon.*

Heckneri: *L. Cotyledon* var.

Howellii: *L. Cotyledon* var.

Leana (T. C. Porter) B. L. Robinson. Evergreen, root thick and fleshy; basal lvs. many, narrow-linear, to 2½ in. long, glaucous; fls. in panicles on scapes to 9 in. high, petals 6–8, red or white, to ¼ in. long. Summer. Rocky places in mts., n. Calif., and s. Ore.

longifolia: *L. Cotyledon.*

Millardii: *L. Cotyledon.*

minima: *L. pygmaea.*

nevadensis (A. Gray) B. L. Robinson [*L. bernardina* A. Davidson]. Deciduous, resembles *L. pygmaea* in habit and foliage; to 4 in., with fleshy tuberlike root; lvs. linear, to 2½ in. long; fls. on scape shorter than lvs., with pair of bracts near middle, solitary, petals white, to ¾ in. long. Summer. Wet places in mts., Calif., n. to Wash., e. to Rocky Mts.

oppositifolia (S. Wats.) B. L. Robinson. Deciduous, root short, thick; sts. slender, to 6 in.; basal lvs. few, linear, to 3 in. long; fls. in 2–4-fld. umbels, on scapes to 8 in. high, petals white or pink, to ¾ in. long. Late winter to late spring. Moist rocky places, extreme n. Calif. and s. Ore.

Purdyi: *L. Cotyledon.*

pygmaea (A. Gray) B. L. Robinson [*L. minima* A. Nels.]. Deciduous, root fleshy, carrot-shaped, sts. several, to 3 in.; basal lvs. few to many, linear, to 2 in. long; fls. on scapes to 2 in. high, petals white, sometimes pink, to ⅜ in. long. Summer. Gravelly damp places in high mts., Sierra Nevada of Calif., n. to Wash., e. to Rocky Mts. Subsp. **glandulosa** (Rydb.) Ferris. Sepals with dark, stalked glands. Cent. Sierra Nevada of Calif.

rediviva Pursh. BITTER ROOT. Deciduous, root fleshy, thick; basal lvs. fleshy, linear, 2 in. long; fls. on scapes to 2 in. high, petals many, rose or white, to 1 in. long. Early spring to summer. Rocky or gravelly places on foothills and mts., n. Calif. to B.C., e. to Rocky Mts. The thick root shaped like a forked radish or short carrot was a much-used food plant by Indian tribes.

rosea: a listed name of no botanical standing.

rupicola: *L. columbiana* var.

Tweedyi (A. Gray) B. L. Robinson. Evergreen, root large, thick, reddish, sts. to 4 in.; basal lvs. fleshy, obovate, to 4 in. long; fls. 1–3, on scapes more or less longer than lvs., petals usually 8–9, salmon-pink, nearly 2 in. across, to 1½ in. long, stamens 12–25. Spring to summer. Rocky slopes of mts., cent. Wash. and s. B.C. The large fls. make it the most attractive of all lewisias for the garden.

Whiteae: *L. Cotyledon.*

LEYCESTERIA Wallich. *Caprifoliaceae.* Six spp. of deciduous shrubs, native to the Himalayas; lvs. opp., simple; fls. in leafy-bracted spikes, calyx 5-lobed, corolla 5-lobed, funnelform, stamens 5, ovary inferior, 5–8-celled; fr. a berry.

One species grown outdoors in Zone 7 and in protected places in the North. Propagated by seeds and cuttings.

formosa Wallich. HIMALAYA HONEYSUCKLE. To 6 ft.; lvs. cordate-ovate to ovate-lanceolate, to 7 in. long; spikes drooping, to 4 in. long; fls. purplish, bracts purple, corolla nearly regular, ¾ in. long. Autumn.

LHOTSKYA Schauer (also but incorrectly spelled *Lhotzkya*). *Myrtaceae.* Ten spp. of heathlike shrubs in Australia; lvs. alt., rarely opp., small, semicylindrical, or 3- or 4-angled, rigid, entire, glabrous or pubescent; fls. sessile or short-pedicelled, solitary in each axil or forming terminal, leafy heads, calyx tube elongated, surrounded by 2 bracteoles, calyx lobes 5, scarious, petals 5, stamens many; fr. formed by the ovary and lower fusiform part of the calyx tube, crowned by the persistent lobes. Similar to *Calytrix,* but calyx lobes lacking long hairlike awn.

alpestris (Lindl.) Druce [*L. genetylloides* F. J. Muell.]. Branchlets stiffly hairy; lvs. to ¼ in. long, hairy; bracteoles obtuse; calyx tube cylindrical, hairy, somewhat longer than bracteoles, petals pinkish, to $^3/_{16}$ in. long. S. Australia.

brevifolia Schauer. Branchlets sparsely short-hairy; lvs. to ½ in. long, glabrous; calyx tube glabrous, longer than bracteoles, narrowed above into short neck, petals to ¼ in. long. W. Australia.

ericoides Schauer. Branchlets sparsely hairy; lvs. to ½ in. long, glabrous; calyx tube cylindrical, shorter than bracteoles, glabrous or scabrid along the ribs, petals white, ¼ in. long. S. and W. Australia.

genetylloides: *L. alpestris.*

LIATRIS Gaertn. ex Schreb. BLAZING-STAR, BUTTON SNAKEROOT, GAY-FEATHER. *Compositae* (Eupatorium Tribe). About 40 spp. of per. herbs, usually from a corm, or less often from a rhizome or an elongated root crown, native to N. Amer.; lvs. alt., simple, mostly linear to linear-lanceolate, entire, usually resin-dotted; fl. heads discoid, in a spicate or racemose infl. or sometimes panicled, the uppermost head always flowering first, involucral bracts imbricate in several rows, lanceolate to orbicular, margins scarious, ciliate to deeply erose, receptacle flat, naked; fls. tubular, bisexual, purple or rose-purple; achenes cylindrical, about 10-ribbed, pappus of 15–40 plumose or minutely barbed, sessile bristles, in 1 or more rows. White-fld. forms occur in most spp.

Suitable for the wild garden or border, flowering in late summer and autumn. Propagated by seeds, division of the clumps, and some species by offsets.

aspera Michx. Stout, stiffly erect, to 6 ft., sts. 1 or sometimes several, short-hairy to glabrous, or sometimes rough; lowest lvs. rhombic-lanceolate, to 16 in. long including petiole, upper lvs. linear to linear-lanceolate, progressively reduced upward, the uppermost sessile; heads to 1 in. across, 25–40-fld., 20–150 in a spicate infl., involucre campanulate to nearly globose, involucral bracts wrinkled, glabrous, purple, with lacerate margins. S. Ont. and Ohio to S. Dak., s. to Tex. and S.C.

callilepis: a listed name; plants cult. under this name usually are *L. spicata.*

cylindracea Michx. Slender, to 2 ft., sts. 1 to several, mostly glabrous; lvs. linear, usually glossy, punctate, glabrous or rarely with short white hairs, lowest lvs. to 10 in. long, the upper progressively reduced, upward; heads to 1¼ in. long and ⅝ in. across, 30–60-fld., solitary or few in a racemose infl., involucre cylindrical to cylindric-campanulate, involucral bracts rounded but mucronate to abruptly acuminate. S. Ont. and w. N.Y. to Minn., s. to n. Ark.

elegans (Walt.) Michx. To 4 ft., sts. 1 or 2, finely pubescent; lvs. sessile, linear to linear-lanceolate, glabrous, punctate, lowest lvs. to 4 in. long, upper lvs. progressively reduced upward; heads to 1¼ in. long, mostly 5-fld., many in a spicate or racemose infl. to 2½ ft. long, involucral bracts pink, the inner with rounded, petal-like, serrulate apex. Tex., Okla., and Ark., e. to S.C.

glabrata: *L. squarrosa* var.

graminifolia Willd. To 4 ft., sts. 1 or few, nearly glabrous to hairy; lvs. linear or linear-lanceolate, ciliate or with hairs on margins of petioles, lowest lvs. to 1 ft. long, upper lvs. progressively reduced upward; heads to ⅝ in. long, 5–15-fld., in a spicate to paniculate infl., involucre turbinate to nearly cylindrical, involucral bracts thin, flat, scarious, minutely ciliate. Coastal, s. Penn. and N.J. to Ala. and Fla.

ligulistylis (A. Nels.) K. Schum. To 3 ft., sts. 1 or several, glabrous or pubescent; lvs. glabrous to densely pubescent, ciliate, basal lvs. lanceolate-oblong to oblanceolate, to 6 in. long, sometimes longer, usually petioled, upper lvs. lanceolate, abruptly reduced, the uppermost sessile; heads to 1¼ in. across, 40–70-fld., 2–30 in a racemose infl., involucre broadly campanulate or hemispherical, involucral bracts often purplish apically, with scarious, lacerate margins. Wisc. to Alta., s. to Colo. and n. New Mex.

montana: a listed name of no botanical standing; perhaps for *L. spicata* forma *montana.*

novae-angliae (Lunell) Shinn. To 3 ft., sts. 1 to several, pubescent or glabrous below inlf.; lvs. linear to narrowly lanceolate, usually glabrous, but sometimes hairy or even scabrous, somewhat succulent, lowest lvs. to 2¾ in. long including petiole, upper lvs. reduced, sessile; heads to ⅝ in. long, 30–80-fld., 6–50 in a racemose infl., involucre nearly hemispherical, involucral bracts reddish-purple toward apex. S. Me. to n. Mich., s. to W. Va., Mo., and Ark.

punctata Hook. Glabrous, to 1 ft., sts. many, stiff, arising from a crown; lvs. rigid, conspicuously punctate, basal lvs. linear, to 4 in. long, conspicuously ciliate, upper lvs. gradually reduced; heads ¾ in. long, 4–8-fld., in a dense spicate infl., involucre cylindrical, involucral bracts white-ciliate. Man. to Alta., s. to Iowa, Kans., Tex., and n. New Mex.

pycnostachya Michx. Coarse, strict, to 5 ft., sts. 1 to many, usually hairy; lvs. linear, punctate, glabrous or hairy, lowest lvs. to 16 in. long, upper lvs. progressively reduced upward; heads to ⅜ in. across, 5–12-fld., many in a dense, cylindrical, spicate infl. to about 1½ ft. long, involucre cylindrical to narrowly turbinate, involucral bracts with spreading tips. Ind. to S. Dak., s. to Fla., La. and Tex. Cv. **'Alba'.** Fls. white.

scariosa (L.) Willd. Pubescent, to 3 ft., sts. 1 to several; lvs. pubescent to scabrous, basal lvs. lanceolate to narrowly ovate or obovate, to 10 in. long including petiole, upper lvs. oblanceolate, reduced, to 2¾ in. long, sessile; heads to 1 in. across, 25–50-fld., 15–30 in a racemose or occasionally paniculate infl., involucre globose, involucral bracts recurved, the inner rounded and often purple at apex. Mts., s. Penn. to S.C. and n. Ga.

spicata (L.) Willd. To 5 ft., sts. mostly 1, stiff, erect, nearly glabrous; lvs. glabrous or slightly hairy, lower lvs. linear or linear-lanceolate, to 16 in. long, upper lvs. linear, reduced; heads about ⅜ in. across, 10–18-fld., many in a dense, spicate infl. to 2½ ft. long, involucre cylindrical to turbinate-campanulate, involucral bracts often purple, with narrow, scarious margins. Moist areas, Long Is. to Mich., s. to Fla. and La. Forma **montana** (A. Gray) Gaiser. Shorter and dwarfer; lvs. broader; infl. shorter. Mts., Va. to Ga.

squarrosa (L.) Michx. Stout, to 3 ft., sts. several to many, pubescent; lvs. linear, rigid, punctate, glabrous or hairy, lowest lvs. to 10 in. long, upper lvs. to 6 in. long; heads to 1¼ in. long, 20–45-fld., or the terminal head up to 60-fld., solitary to many in a racemose to paniculate infl., involucre cylindrical, involucral bracts with long, tapered, spreading tips. Del. to Ill., s. to Ala. and Mo. Var. **glabrata** (Rydb.) Gaiser [*L. glabrata* Rydb.]. Glabrous. S. Dak. to Tenn., Mo., and Tex.

LIBERTIA K. Spreng. *Iridaceae.* About 20 spp. of herbs with fibrous roots, native to Australia, New Zeal., and S. Amer.; lvs. mostly crowded at base of sts., linear; fls. clustered in axils of sheathing bracts, perianth tube none, segms. united only basally, inner segms. much longer and usually showier than the outer; fr. a caps.

Propagated by division and seeds.

caerulescens Kunth. To 2 ft.; lvs. to 1 ft., stiff; fls. in sessile clusters along a usually unbranched axis, blue, about ½ in. across, outer perianth segms. greenish-brown. Chile. Less hardy than most other cult. spp.

formosa R. C. Grah. Sts. 2–4½ ft.; lvs. to 1½ ft. long, stiff; infl. a terminal, bracted panicle of umbel-like clusters, the pedicels shorter than the bracts; fls. white, to ¾ in. long, outer perianth segms. greenish-brown. Mts., Chile.

grandiflora (R. Br.) Sweet. To 3 ft.; lvs. to 2½ ft. long, $^5/_{16}$–½ in. wide, stiff; infl. with pedicels longer than bracts; fls. white, inner perianth segms. about ⅝ in. long, outer segms. about ¼ in. long, greenish outside; caps. about ¼ in. long, yellow. New Zeal.

ixioides (J. R. Forst.) K. Spreng. To 2 ft.; lvs. to 1 ft. long or more, to $^5/_{16}$ in. wide, with pale midrib; infl. a bracted panicle of many corymbs, the pedicels longer than bracts; fls. white, inner perianth segms. about ⅜ in. long, outer much shorter, greenish outside; caps. about ½ in. long. New Zeal.

pulchella K. Spreng. To 10 in. or more; lvs. tufted, grasslike, 2–6 in. long; fl. clusters 3–8-fld., pedicels to 1 in. long; fls. small, perianth segms. white, to ¼ in. long. New Zeal., Tasmania, s. Australia, New Guinea.

LIBIDIBIA: *CAESALPINIA.*

LIBOCEDRUS Endl. INCENSE CEDAR. *Cupressaceae.* Five spp. of coniferous, evergreen, mostly monoecious trees, native to New Zeal. and New Caledonia; branchlets 2-ranked, compressed; lvs. scalelike, decurrent; male cones oblong, female cones ovoid, scales in 2 pairs, erect, woody, valvate, with prominent spine on the back, only larger upper scales fertile; seeds 1–2 to each scale, 2-winged, 1 wing broad, longer than the seed, the other minute. *L. Bidwillii* Hook.f. and *L. plumosa* (D. Don) Endl. [*L. Doniana* (Hook.) Endl.] from New Zeal. are rarely cult. in Eur. and may be in collections, but have not been offered in U.S.

chilensis: *Austrocedrus chilensis.*

decurrens: *Calocedrus decurrens.*

macrolepis: *Calocedrus macrolepis,* but material so offered may be *C. formosana.*

LIBONIA: *JUSTICIA.* **L. floribunda:** *J. Rizzinii;* **L.** ×**penrhoziensis:** see *J. Rizzinii.*

LICUALA Thunb. *Palmae.* More than 100 spp. of mostly small, clustered or solitary palms with bisexual fls., in wet trop. forests from Asia to Australia and the New Hebrides; lvs. palmate or shortly costapalmate, petiole usually armed with spinose teeth, blade sometimes undivided but usually deeply divided into several-ribbed segms. with blunt, shallowly toothed tips; infls. among the lvs., peduncle with rarely 1–2 but more often several sheathing bracts, usually terminating in a rachis bearing several brs., rarely in a spikelike axis, brs. subtended by a sheathing bract, spikelike or more often once- to twice-branched into slender rachillae; fls. solitary or in clusters of a few, calyx tubular or subcampanulate, 3-lobed, corolla tubular or urceolate below, 3-lobed above, stamens 6, inserted at the throat of the corolla tube, filaments separate or often variously united, carpels 3, separate except the united styles, usually only 1 maturing; fr. usually orange or red, with apical stigmatic residue, seed with homogeneous endosperm but seed coat intruded on 1 side, embryo lateral.

Small, very ornamental fan palms much grown in tropics and subtropics; hardy in warmer parts of Zone 9b in Fla. Species with clustering habit are useful pot or tub plants indoors. For culture see *Palms.*

amplifrons Miq. St. solitary (?); lvs. divided to the base into about 13 firm, glossy segms.; infl. elongate, reddish when young, brs. once-branched into about 7, slender, minutely reddish-hairy rachillae; fls. arranged singly. Sumatra. A poorly known sp. perhaps not distinct from *L. paludosa* Griff.

elegans: *L. pumila.*

gracilis: *L. pumila.*

grandis H. Wendl. St. solitary, to about 6 ft.; lvs. nearly orbicular or broader than long, to 3 ft. wide, normally undivided but continuously lobed along the margin; infl. elongate, brs. several, each divided once into slender rachillae; fls. arranged singly, ³⁄₁₆ in. long, staminal ring 3-lobed with 3 anthers borne on lobes, 3 between lobes; fr. orange, ½ in. in diam. New Hebrides Is.

Lauterbachii Dammer & K. Schum. [*L. Lauterbachii* var. *bougainvillensis* Becc.]. To 20 ft. or more, sts. to 2½ in. in diam.; lvs. stiff, dark glossy green above, green beneath, to about 2 ft. long, with many segms., sheath brown-fibrous; infl. erect, becoming arched in fr.; fls. solitary or in clusters of 2–3, straw-colored in bud, hairy outside when young, white when open, to ³⁄₁₆ in. long, petals twice as long as calyx, staminal ring 3-lobed, 3 anthers in notches of lobes, 3 in sinuses; fr. globose, orange-red, ½ in. in diam. New Guinea to Solomon Is.

peltata Roxb. ex Buch.-Ham. Sts. usually several, to 15 ft.; lvs. orbicular, 4–5 ft. wide, appearing peltate, divided into 12–30 wedge-shaped segms.; infl. longer than lvs., brs. several, elongate, brown-tomentose, undivided; fls. nearly ¾ in. long, velvety-hairy, filaments not united; fr. orange-red, ¾ in. long. India, Burma, Andaman Is.

pumila Blume [*L. elegans* Blume; *L. gracilis* Blume]. Sts. to 5 ft. or sometimes very short; lvs. variable, about 18 in. wide, divided into as few as 7–8 several-ribbed segms. or as many as 20–24, mostly 2-ribbed segms.; infls. shorter than lvs., brs. 2–3, spikelike, to 4 in. long, or the lower lvs. again divided into 2–3 spikelike rachillae; fls. singly and irregularly arranged, glabrous, to ³⁄₁₆ in. long, stamens united in a ring with 6 equal, broad-based, abruptly awl-shaped filaments; fr. globose to globose-oblong, red, orange, or purple, about ³⁄₈ in. long. Java, Sumatra.

Rumphii Blume. To 12 ft.; lvs. nearly orbicular in outline, segms. 12–15, the central ones to 20 in. long, several-ribbed; infl. elongate, brs. few, rachillae to 6 in. long; fls. solitary, somewhat pedicelled, ¼ in. long, calyx brown-dotted, staminal ring 3-lobed, 3 anthers in notches of lobes, 3 in sinuses. A poorly known sp. said to occur in the Molucca Is and Celebes.

spinosa Thunb. Sts. several, to 15 ft.; lvs. nearly orbicular or broader than long, to 4½ ft. across, divided into about 18–19 several-ribbed segms.; infl. to 6 ft. long, brs. several, each divided into 5–10 or fewer finely hairy rachillae with fls. in clusters of 3 basally or single above; fls. finely hairy, to ⅛ in. long, stamens united in a ring with 6 equal filaments; fr. slightly longer than broad, to ³⁄₈ in. long. Swampy places near the sea, Thailand to Malay Pen., Indonesia, Philippine Is.

LIGHTING: see *House Plants* and *Photoperiod.*

LIGULARIA Cass. [*Farfugium* Lindl.]. *Compositae* (Senecio Tribe). About 50–150 coarse, showy, per. herbs in Eur. and Asia; lvs. basal and alt. on sts., long-petioled, broad; fl. head radiate, short-peduncled, few to many, racemose, corymbose, or panicled, involucral bracts broad, in 1 row; disc fls. several, ray fls. 1 to many, yellow or orange; achenes glabrous (except in *L. tussilaginea*), pappus of rough hairs. Sometimes included in *Senecio*, but distinct in having the petiole bases sheathing the st., and every other bract of the involucre overlapping the 2 adjacent bracts.

Summer-flowering; of easy culture in moist, sunny places; propagated by seeds or division.

altaica DC. [*Senecio altaicus* (DC.) Schultz-Bip.]. To 2 ft. or more; lf. blades elliptic, to 7 in. long, cuneate-attenuate basally, entire; heads few to 25, racemose; disc fls. 10–20, ray fls. 4–5. Altai Mts. (Asia).

clivorum: *L. dentata.*

dentata (A. Gray) Hara [*L. clivorum* (Maxim.) Maxim.; *Senecio clivorum* Maxim.]. To 4 ft.; lf. blades orbicular-reniform, to 12 in. long, cordate, dentate; infl. corymbose, heads 2½–5 in. across, lacking the 2 small narrow bractlets present beneath the involucre in *L. Hodgsonii;* ray fls. 12–14, to 2 in. long, orange. China, Japan. Cvs. are: 'Desdemona', compact, sts., petioles, and lower lf. surfaces dark purple; 'Orange Queen', more luxuriant, green throughout, heads larger, deeper orange; 'Othello', similar to cv. 'Desdemona', but less deeply purple-flushed.

Fischeri: *L. sibirica* var. *speciosa.*

×**Hessei** (Hesse) Bergmans [*Senecio* ×*Hessei* Hesse]. Hybrid believed to involve *L. dentata* and *L. Wilsoniana*, and possibly *L. Veitchiana;* to 6 ft.; lf. blades cordate-reniform; infl. paniculate, heads 3 in. across; fls. orange-yellow.

Hodgsonii Hook. Similar to *L. dentata,* but of smaller proportions; heads 2½ in. across, with 2 narrow bractlets on peduncle beneath involucre; ray fls. to 1 in. long. Japan.

japonica DC. [*Senecio japonicus* Schultz-Bip., not Thunb.]. To 4 ft. or more; blades of basal lvs. cordate-ovate in outline, to 12 in. long, cut almost to base into 3 coarsely lobed and serrate divisions; infl. corymbose, heads 2–8 or more, about 4 in. across; fls. orange-yellow. Japan, Korea, China.

Kaempferi: *L. tussilaginea.*

macrophylla (Ledeb.) DC. [*Senecio Ledebourii* Schultz-Bip.]. To 6 ft.; blades of basal lvs. elliptic to ovate-oblong, to 2 ft. long, dentate, tapering to winged petiole; infl. densely paniculate, heads many, ½–¾ in. across; disc fls. 4–8, ray fls. mostly 3, canary-yellow. Altai Mts. (Asia).

×**palmatiloba:** a hort. name of no botanical standing for a hybrid between *L. dentata* and *L. japonica.* To 4 ft.; blades of basal lvs. rounded in outline, cordate, margined all around with serrate lobes; infl. corymbose, heads several; fls. yellow.

Przewalskii (Maxim.) Diels [*Senecio Przewalskii* Maxim.]. Sts. deep purple, to 6 ft.; blades of basal lvs. deeply palmately lobed, lobes again lobed or toothed; infl. long, narrow, racemose, heads many, small; fls. yellow, disc fls. 3, ray fls. 2. N. China.

sibirica (L.) Cass. [*Senecio sibiricus* C. B. Clarke, not L.f.]. To 3 ft.; blades of basal lvs. cordate, to 6 in. long, acute, denticulate; infl. racemose, heads about 30, 1–1½ in. across, each peduncle subtended by a linear to lanceolate bract; fls. yellow, disc fls. 20–30, ray fls. 7–11. A very variable sp. France to the Himalayas and Japan. Var. **speciosa** (Schrad. ex Link) DC. [*L. Fischeri* (Ledeb.) Turcz.; *L. speciosa* (Schrad. ex Link) Fisch. & C. A. Mey.]. Larger and showier; infl. usually with additional short basal brs., heads 1½–2 in. across, each peduncle subtended by an ovate bract. E. Siberia, Manchuria, Korea, Japan.

speciosa: *L. sibirica* var.

stenocephala (Maxim.) Matsum. & G. Koidz. [*Senecio stenocephalus* Maxim.]. Sts. dark purple, to 5 ft.; blades of basal lvs. hastate-cordate to triangular, to 14 in. long, acuminate, dentate, the basal lobes acute; infl. long, slender, racemose, heads many, 1¼ in. across; fls. yellow, disc fls. 5–12, ray fls. 1–3. China, Japan, Taiwan.

tangutica: *Senecio tanguticus.*

tussilaginea (Burm.f.) Mak. [*L. Kaempferi* Siebold & Zucc.; *Senecio Kaempferi* (Siebold & Zucc.) Benth.; *Farfugium grande* Lindl.]. Sts. to 2 ft., scapelike, with a few bracts but no lvs.; lvs. all basal, evergreen, blades leathery, reniform, to 6 in. long, 12 in. wide, somewhat angled and irregularly low-dentate, floccose-tomentose when young, glabrate and glossy later; infl. loose, corymbose, heads few, 1½–2½ in. across; fls. light yellow, disc fls. many, ray fls. 10–12. Differs from all other cult. spp. in its nonsheathing petiole bases, involute rather than revolute young lvs., and pubescent achenes. China, Korea, Japan, Taiwan. Less hardy than other spp.; the green-lvd. typical form is seldom cult., but the cvs. are grown outdoors in the South and the Pacific states, and as house plants elsewhere. Cvs. include: 'Argentea' [cvs. 'Albovariegata', 'Variegata'], lvs. irregularly mottled deep green, gray-green, and ivory-white; 'Aureo-maculata', LEOPARD PLANT, lvs. randomly spotted with round yellow blotches; 'Crispata' [cv. 'Cristata'], PARSLEY LIGULARIA, lvs. green, ruffled and crisped marginally.

Veitchiana (Hemsl.) Greenm. [*Senecio Veitchianus* Hemsl.]. To 8 ft.; blades of basal lvs. triangular-cordate, to 12 in. long and somewhat broader, dentate, petioles solid, channelled; infl. racemose, often 30 in. long, heads many, 2½ in. across, each peduncle subtended by an ovate bract; fls. bright yellow, disc fls. many, ray fls. 8–12, 1 in. long. China.

Wilsoniana (Hemsl.) Greenm. [*Senecio Wilsonianus* Hemsl.]. GIANT GROUNDSEL. To 6 ft.; blades of basal lvs. as in *L. Veitchiana*, but petioles hollow and cylindrical; infl. racemose above, paniculate toward base, heads many, crowded, 1 in. across, each peduncle subtended by a small filiform bract; disc fls. 10–12, ray fls. 6–8, to ½ in. long. China.

LIGUSTICUM L. *Umbelliferae.* From 40–50 spp. of circumboreal per. herbs; lvs. decompound; fls. white, in large compound umbels, involucre and involucels absent or inconspicuous; fr. ribbed, not flattened.

Sometimes planted as an ornamental in borders.

acutilobum: *Angelica acutiloba.*

lucidum Mill. [*L. pyrenaeum* Gouan]. To 4 ft., sts. erect; lvs. 4–5-pinnately decompound, segms. linear; umbel to 40-rayed, rays spreading in fl., becoming erect and pressed together in fr.; fr. slightly compressed. Eur.

pyrenaeum: *L. lucidum.*

LIGUSTRUM L. [*Parasyringa* W. W. Sm.]. PRIVET, HEDGE PLANT. *Oleaceae.* About 50 spp. of deciduous or evergreen shrubs or rarely trees, chiefly in e. Asia to Malay Arch. and nw. Australia, 1 in Eur. and N. Afr.; lvs. opp., entire, often thick, mostly oblong or ovate; fls. small, white, in terminal panicles, bisexual, corolla funnelform; fr. a black, berrylike drupe, seeds 1–4.

Privets are commonly planted for hedges and in shrubberies as ornamentals, and sometimes as single specimens for their handsome foliage and profusion of small white flowers. They are not particular as to soil. Propagated by cuttings of young or mature wood under glass, by division, by seeds, and varieties by grafting on *L. vulgare* or *L. ovalifolium.* Many of them are very hardy and durable, and well adapted to mass plantings.

acuminatum: *L. Tschonskii.*

acutissimum Koehne. Deciduous shrub, to 9 ft.; lvs. ovate to ovate-lanceolate, to 3½ in. long, lower surface light green, pubescent along midrib; fls. white, in narrow panicles to 2½ in. long, corolla ¼ in. long, stamens not exserted; fr. ovoid, to ⅜ in. long. China. Zone 6.

amurense Carrière. AMUR P. To 15 ft., deciduous or semievergreen; lvs. to 2½ in. long, pubescent on midrib beneath; fls. in panicles to 2 in. long, corolla ⅜ in. long, stamens not exserted; fr. ovoid, to ¼ in. long. Early summer. N. China. Zone 4.

atrovirens: a listed name of no botanical standing, used for *L. vulgare* cv.

buxifolium: a listed name of no botanical standing, used for *L. vulgare* cv.

californicum: a listed name of no botanical standing for *L. ovalifolium.*

ciliatum: see *L. Tschonskii.*

confusum Decne. Evergreen shrub or small tree, to as much as 40 ft.; lvs. lanceolate, to 4 in. long, glabrous; fls. in pubescent panicles to 4 in. long; fr. globose, to ⅜ in. across. Early summer. E. Himalayas.

cordiformis: a listed name of no botanical standing, probably used for a form of *L. lucidum.*

coriaceum: *L. japonicum* var. *rotundifolium.*

Delavayanum Hariot [*L. ionandrum* Diels; *L. Prattii* Koehne]. Evergreen shrub, to 10 ft.; lvs. elliptic to ovate, to 1¼ in. long, glabrous, glossy above; fls. in pubescent panicles to 2 in. long, corolla to ¼ in. long, tube twice as long as lobes, stamens not exserted; fr. globose, ¼ in. across. Late spring. W. China, Burma. Zone 8.

erectum: a listed name of no botanical standing.

excelsum superbum: a listed name of no botanical standing, used for *L. lucidum* cv.

Fraseri: a listed name of no botanical standing.

gracile Rehd. Deciduous, to 10 ft., brs. gracefully spreading; lvs. 1½ in. long, glabrous; fls. in panicles to 3 in. long and broad, corolla tube about as long as lobes. China.

Henryi Hemsl. Evergreen shrub, to 12 ft.: lvs. orbicular-ovate to ovate or ovate-lanceolate, to 2 in. long, glossy above, glabrous; fls. in pubescent, pyramidal panicles to 5 in. long, corolla ¼ in. long, tube twice as long as lobes, stamens nearly as long as corolla; fr. ovoid-oblong, to ⅜ in. long. Summer. Cent. China. Zone 8. Similar to *L. Delavayanum* but having larger lvs. and infl.

×**ibolium** E. F. Coe: *L. obtusifolium* × *L. ovalifolium.* Shrub, young brs., infl., and midrib on lower surface of lvs. pubescent; fls. in loose pyramidal panicles to 5 in. long, corolla to ¼ in. long, stamens as long as corolla; fr. subglobose, to ¼ in. across. Useful as hedge plant. Zone 5.

Ibota Siebold ex Siebold & Zucc. Not cult.; material grown under this name is *L. obtusifolium* or *L. Tschonskii.*

indicum (Lour.) Merrill [*L. nepalense* Wallich]. Semievergreen shrub or small tree; lvs. ovate-elliptic, to 3 in. long, pubescent beneath, especially along midrib; fls. in loose pyramidal panicles to 5 in. long, corolla 3/16 in. long, lobes spreading, longer than tube, stamens exserted; fr. subglobose, to 3/16 in. across. Himalayas and Indochina. Cv. 'Variegatum' is listed.

ionandrum: *L. Delavayanum.*

iwata: a listed name of no botanical standing, probably used for a form of *L. japonicum.*

japonicum Thunb. [*L. Kellermannii* Van Houtte]. WAX-LEAF P., JAPANESE P. Evergreen, to 10 ft. or more; lvs. to 3 or 4 in. long, short-pointed or nearly obtuse, glabrous, leathery; fls. in panicles to 6 in. long, corolla tube slightly longer than lobes. Summer to early autumn. Japan, Korea. Zone 7. Grown in s. states. Cv. 'Variegatum'. Lvs. variegated, edged with white. Var. **rotundifolium** Blume [*L. coriaceum* Carrière]. Lvs. nearly orbicular, to 2½ in. long, obtuse or emarginate at apex.

Kellermannii: *L. japonicum.*

koreanum: a listed name of no botanical standing.

laurifolium: a listed name of no botanical standing, used for *L. vulgare* cv.

lodense: *L. vulgare* cv.

lucidum Ait. GLOSSY P., CHINESE P., NEPAL P., WAX-LEAF P., WHITE WAX TREE. Evergreen, to 30 ft.; lvs. to 4 or 6 in. long, acuminate, glossy, glabrous; fls. in panicles to 10 in. long, corolla tube as long as lobes. Late summer. China, Korea. Zone 8. Much used as street tree. The following cvs. are listed in the trade under *L. lucidum,* but may be referable to *L. japonicum:* 'Aureo-marginatum', lvs. yellow-margined; 'Ciliatum', lvs. small; 'Compactum', dense, lvs. dark waxy green; 'Excelsum Superbum', lvs. variegated creamy-white; 'Gracile', fastigiate; 'Macrophyllum', lvs. large; 'Microphyllum', lvs. small; 'Nigrifolium', lvs. very dark green; 'Nobile', fastigiate; 'Pyramidale', habit narrowly conical; 'Recurvifolium', lf. margins recurved; 'Repandum', lvs. narrow, crisped; 'Tricolor', lvs. variegated with yellow, pink when young.

Massalongianum Vis. [*L. myrtifolium* Hort.]. Evergreen, to 10 ft.; lvs. linear-lanceolate, to 3 in. long, glabrous; fls. in panicles to 3½ in. long, corolla tube much longer than lobes; fr. subglobose, to ¼ in. across. Summer. Himalayas. Zone 9. Distinguished by its lanceolate lvs.

medium: *L. ovalifolium.*

myrtifolium: a listed name of no botanical standing for *L. Massalongianum.*

nanum compactum: a listed name of no botanical standing and of uncertain application.

nepalense: *L. indicum.*

nobile: a listed name of no botanical standing, used for *L. lucidum* cv.

obtusifolium Siebold & Zucc. Deciduous, to 10 ft.; lvs. to 2½ in. long, pubescent beneath; fls. in nodding panicles to 1½ in. long, corolla tube about 3 times as long as lobes. Early summer. Japan. Zone 4. This is commonly known as *L. Ibota* in hort. Var. **Regelianum** (Koehne)

Rehd. [*L. Regelianum* Koehne; *L. ovalifolium* var. *Regelianum* Hort.]. REGEL'S P. Low, brs. spreading horizontally, prominently pilose. Zone 5.

ovalifolium Hassk. [*L. californicum* Hort.; *L. medium* Franch. & Sav.]. CALIFORNIA P. Semievergreen shrub, to 15 ft.; lvs. elliptic-ovate to elliptic-oblong, to 2½ in. long, dark and glossy above, pale beneath; fls. nearly sessile, in panicles to 5 in. long, corolla ¼ in. long, tube 1 ½ times as long as spreading lobes. Early summer. Japan. Zone 6. Cvs. include: '**Albo-marginatum**', lvs. edged with white; '**Aureo-marginatum**', [cv. '**Aureum**'], lvs. edged with yellow; '**Compactum**', denser growth habit; '**Globosum**' and '**Nanum**', dwarf in habit; '**Variegatum**', lvs. marbled with pale yellow. Var. **Regelianum**: *L. obtusifolium* var.

pendulum: a listed name of no botanical standing: see cvs. in *L. Quihoui* and *L. sinense*.

Prattii: *L. Delavayanum*.

Quihoui Carrière. Deciduous shrub, to 6 ft.; lvs. oblanceolate, oblong, or lanceolate, to 2¼ in. long, glabrous; fls. sessile, paniculate, panicle narrow or broadly pyramidal, pubescent, 2 in. to as much as 12 in. long, with brs. spreading horizontally, corolla to ³⁄₁₆ in. long, tube flaring in upper half and about 1½ times as long as spreading lobes, stamens exserted; fr. obovoid or almost globose, to ¼ in. long. China. Zone 7. Cv. '**Pendulum**'. Brs. drooping.

Reevesii: a listed name of no botanical standing.

Regelianum: *L. obtusifolium* var.

repandum: a listed name of no botanical standing, used for *L. lucidum* cv.

sempervirens (Franch.) Lingelsh. [*Parasyringa sempervirens* (Franch.) W. W. Sm.]. Evergreen shrub, to 6 ft.; lvs. suborbicular to ovate, to 1¾ in. long, glabrous, thick and lustrous, paler with dark dots beneath; fls. sessile or nearly so, in dense panicles to 4 in. long, corolla to ¼ in. long, tube about twice as long as lobes, stamens barely exserted; fr. at first fleshy, later becoming a dry caps. W. China. Zone 7.

sinense Lour. Deciduous shrub, to 12 ft.; lvs. elliptic to elliptic-oblong, to 3 in. long, pubescent on midrib beneath; fls. on slender pedicels, in open, narrow, pubescent panicles to 4 in. long, corolla ³⁄₁₆ in. long, tube shorter than spreading lobes, stamens exserted. Spring to early summer. China. Zone 7. Cv. '**Pendulum**'. Brs. pendulous. Var. **Stauntonii** (A. DC.) Rehd. [*L. Stauntonii* A. DC.]. Lower; panicles broader.

Stauntonii: *L. sinense* var.

strongylophyllum Hemsl. Evergreen shrub or tree; lvs. rounded to nearly ovate, to 1 in. long, smooth; fls. in loose panicles to 4 in. long, corolla ¼ in. long, tube about 1½ times as long as spreading lobes, stamens exserted, anthers yellow; fr. obovoid, to ⁵⁄₁₆ in. long. Cent. China. Zone 8.

texanum: a listed name of no botanical standing, has been applied to *L. japonicum*.

Thompsonii: a listed name of no botanical standing, used for *L. vulgare* cv.

Tschonskii Decne. [*L. acuminatum* Koehne; *L. ciliatum* in the sense of Rehd., not Siebold or Blume]. Deciduous shrub; lvs. usually broadly lanceolate to ovate, to 2 in. long, occasionally 3 in., usually appressed-puberulent above and pilose beneath especially on the veins; fls. in narrowly pyramidal, densely puberulent panicles to 2½ in. long, corolla ¼ in. long, tube slender, 1½–2 times as long as lobes, stamens reaching tips of corolla lobes; fr. ovoid, to ⅜ in. long. Japan. Zone 5. Some material grown as *L. Ibota* may belong here.

vulgare L. COMMON P., PRIM. Deciduous shrub, to 15 ft.; lvs. oblong-ovate to lanceolate, to 2½ in. long; fls. pedicelled, in dense panicles to 1½ in. long, corolla tube about as long as spreading lobes, stamens scarcely longer than corolla tube. Early summer. Medit. region; naturalized in e. U.S. Zone 5. Cult. for centuries, much used as a hedge plant. Cvs. include: '**Albo-variegatum**': 'Glaucum'; '**Argenteo-variegatum**', lvs. variegated white; '**Atrovirens**', lvs. small; '**Aureum**', lvs. yellow; '**Aureo-variegatum**', lvs. variegated yellow; '**Buxifolium**', semievergreen, lvs. to 1 in. long; '**Chlorocarpum**', fr. greenish-yellow; '**Foliosum**', an improved, more vigorous form; '**Glaucum**' [cv.'Albo-variegatum'], **lvs. glaucous, edged with white**; '**Laurifolium**', lvs. broadly elliptic, laurel-like; '**Leucocarpum**', fr. white; '**Lodense**' [cv. 'Nanum'; *L. lodense* Glogau], low-growing, compact form; '**Nanum**': 'Lodense'; '**Pyramidale**', pyramidal in habit; '**Thompsonii**', a listed name; '**Xanthocarpum**', fr. yellow.

Walkeri Decne. Shrub or small tree, twigs conspicuously white-speckled; lvs. ovate to lanceolate, to 3 in. long, acute at apex and base, entire, glabrous; fls. in erect, terminal panicles 4–6 in. long with hairy brs.; fr. purple, about ¼ in. long. Ceylon. Zone 10.

LILIACEAE Juss. LILY FAMILY. Monocot.; about 240 genera and perhaps 3,000 spp., generally distributed over the earth, but most abundant in temp. and subtrop. areas; mostly per. herbs from bulbs, corms, rhizomes, or tubers; lvs. basal or cauline, usually alt., sometimes whorled, rarely opp.; fls. usually bisexual and regular, mostly showy, in various types of infls.; perianth generally of 6 distinct segms., stamens usually 6, sometimes 3, filaments commonly distinct, ovary superior or sometimes inferior, mostly 3-celled, with axile placentation; fr. a berry or caps., seeds few to many. Some plants called lilies belong to other families.

The Liliaceae include medicinal plants, plants with edible parts, and a wide range of ornamental plants. The cult. genera are: *Albuca, Aletris, Aloe, Amianthium, Anemarrhena, Anthericum, Aphyllanthes, Arthropodium, Asparagus, Asphodeline, Asphodelus, Aspidistra, Astelia, Astroloba, Bellevalia, Blandfordia, Bowiea, Brimeura, Bulbine, Bulbinella, Bulbocodium, Calochortus, Camassia, Cardiocrinum, Chamaelirium, Chionodoxa, Chionographis, Chlorogalum, Chlorophytum, Clintonia, Colchicum, Convallaria, Danae, Dianella, Disporum, Endymion, Eremurus, Erythronium, Eucomis, Eustrephus, Fritillaria, Galtonia, Gasteria, × Gastrolea, Gloriosa, Haworthia, Helonias, Heloniopsis, Hemerocallis, Hesperocallis, Hosta, Hyacinthella, Hyacinthus, Kniphofia, Lachenalia, Lapageria, Ledebouria, Leucocrinum, Lilium, Liriope, Littonia, Lloydia, Maianthemum, Medeola, Melanthium, Muscari, Narthecium, Nomocharis, Notholirion, Ophiopogon, Ornithogalum, Paradisea, Paris, Pasithea, Periboea, Philesia, Polygonatum, Puschkinia, Reineckia, Ripogonum, Rohdea, Ruscus, Sandersonia, Scilla, Semele, Smilacina, Smilax, Stenanthium, Streptopus, Tofieldia, Trichopetalum, Tricyrtis, Trillium, Tulipa, Urginea, Uvularia, Veltheimia, Veratrum, Xanthorrhoea, Xerophyllum*, and *Zigadenus*.

LILIUM L. LILY. *Liliaceae*. Between 80 and 90 spp. of per. herbs of the N. Temp. Zone; bulbous, the bulb scaly, not tunicate, sometimes stoloniferous or rhizomatous, sts. unbranched, leafy; lvs. alt. or whorled, usually many; fls. solitary and terminal or in terminal racemes, panicles, or umbels, white, yellow, orange, red, purple, or maroon, never blue, usually spotted inside, perianth funnelform, cup-shaped, or campanulate, segms. 6, spreading or reflexed, each with a basal nectar-bearing gland, stamens 6, anthers versatile; fr. a 3-valved, loculicidal caps., the margins of valves flat, seeds many, flat, in 2 rows in each cell.

Lilies are among the most stately of garden plants. They are usually of easy cultivation, particularly the many hybrid clones. They are hardy in the North, although sometimes needing winter protection, and always profiting by it. In well-prepared ground and a suitable location, the plants may be allowed to stand year after year. Remove the seed pods immediately after flowering, and allow the foliage to mature naturally. A light, fertile, sandy or loamy soil is suitable, with some leaf mold added. As a rule, lilies do better in partial shade or not fully exposed to heat and winds. A handful of sand or gravel may be placed under each bulb and the top of the bulb should be at least 4 in. below the surface in those kinds that produce roots above the bulb, or deeper with *L. auratum* and others with very large bulbs, but shallow planting is the rule with those that produce roots only from the bottom of the bulb. Propagation by division of the offsets as soon as the tops die or early in autumn; also by bulb scales, or in some species by aerial bulblets, which will produce flowering plants in 2 or 3 years. Seeds yield variations.

Lilies may be forced in the greenhouse. The bulbs should be potted and placed in a coldframe and covered with sphagnum, coal ashes, or other porous material, until they are well rooted in the pots. They may then be taken to the greenhouse and kept in a temperature of about 50° F. for 10 days, and when growth begins, the night temperature should be raised to 60° F. The plants should flower in about 13 weeks.

Lilies are subject to serious diseases, for the nature and treatment of which consult the most recent literature by specialists in the subject. Perhaps the most serious is lily mosaic, a virus disease transmitted form plant to plant by aphids. It infects all parts of the plant except the seed; thus, plants grown from seed are free from the disease until infected. Certain cultivated species are more resistent than others, as *L. Martagon* and its varieties, *L. Hansonii, L. paradalinum, L. Brownii,*

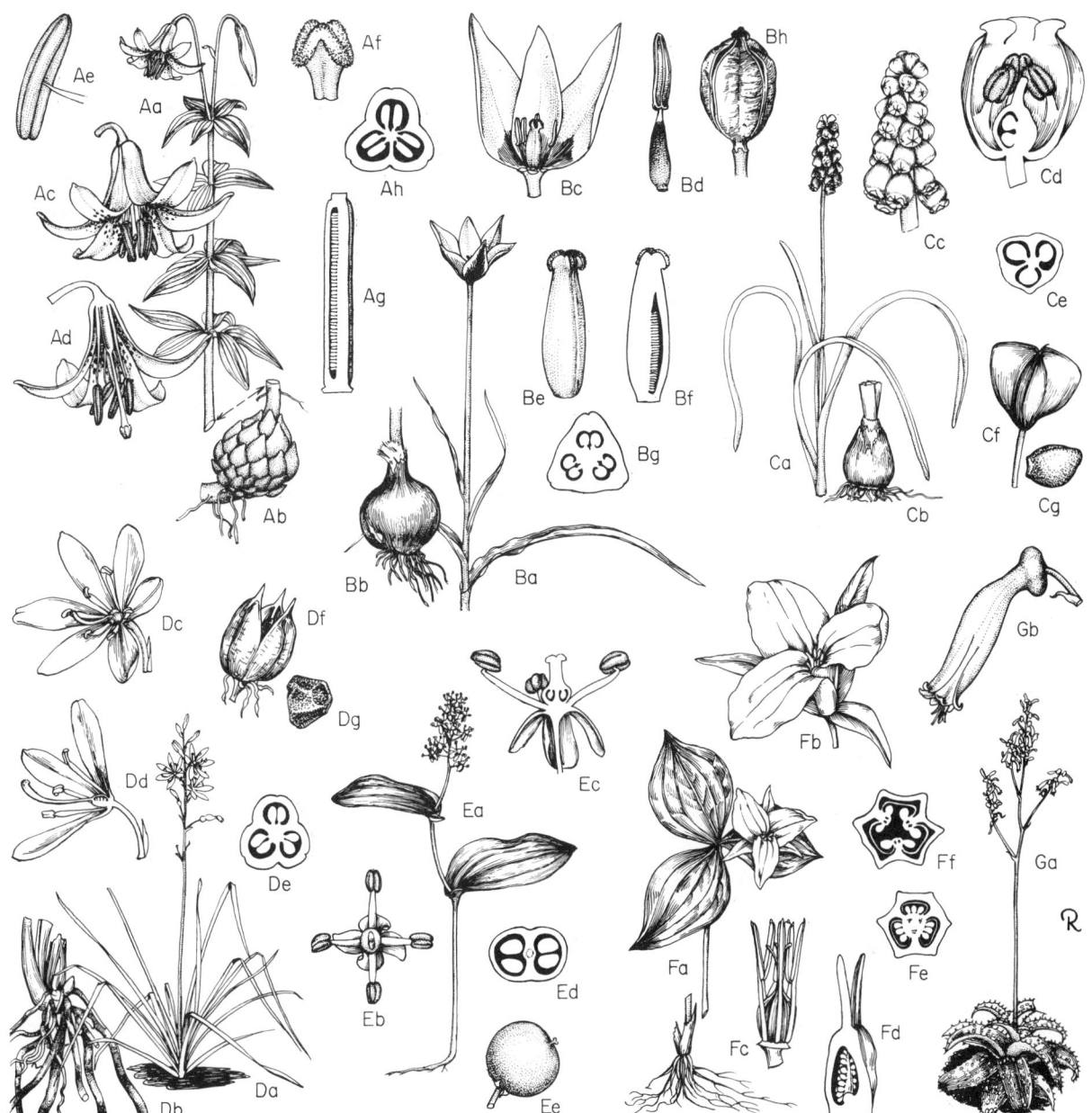

LILIACEAE. **A,** *Lilium canadense:* **Aa,** flowering stem, × ⅙; **Ab,** bulb, × ½; **Ac,** flower, × ⅓; **Ad,** flower, vertical section, × ⅓; **Ae,** anther, × 2; **Af,** stigma, × 2; **Ag,** ovary, vertical section, × 2; **Ah,** ovary, cross section, × 5. **B,** *Tulipa Clusiana:* **Ba,** flowering stem, × ¼; **Bb,** bulb, × ½; **Bc,** flower, vertical section, × ½; **Bd,** stamen, × 1½; **Be,** pistil, × 1½; **Bf,** pistil, vertical section, × 1½; **Bg,** ovary, cross section, × 3; **Bh,** capsule, × ¾. **C,** *Muscari botryoides:* **Ca,** flowering scape and basal leaves, × ¼; **Cb,** bulb, × ½; **Cc,** inflorescence, × 1; **Cd,** flower, vertical section, × 5; **Ce,** ovary, cross section, × 5; **Cf,** capsule, × 1½; **Cg,** seed, × 3. **D,** *Anthericum Liliago:* **Da,** flowering plant, × ⅙; **Db,** fleshy roots, × ⅜; **Dc,** flower, × 1; **Dd,** flower, vertical section, × 1; **De,** ovary, cross section, × 5; **Df,** capsule, × 1½; **Dg,** seed, × 3. **E,** *Maianthemum canadense:* **Ea,** flowering plant, × ½; **Eb,** flower, viewed from above, × 3; **Ec,** flower, vertical section, × 4; **Ed,** ovary, cross section, × 8; **Ee,** berry, × 2. **F,** *Trillium grandiflorum:* **Fa,** flowering stem and rhizome, × ¼; **Fb,** flower, × ½; **Fc,** stamens and pistil, × 1; **Fd,** ovary, vertical section, × 1½; **Fe,** ovary, cross section near base, × 2; **Ff,** ovary, median cross section, × 2. **G,** *Aloe barbertoniae:* **Ga,** flowering plant, × ¹⁄₁₄; **Gb,** flower, × ¾. (Aa-Ah from Lawrence, *Taxonomy of Vascular Plants.*)

L. Henryi, L. Davidii, L. regale, L. pumilum, L. amabile, L. monadelphum. The most susceptible species include *L. auratum, L. canadense, L. concolor, L. pensylvanicum, L. formosanum, L. superbum, L. × maculatum. Lilium lancifolium* [*L. tigrinum*] is easily infected, but not apparently injured, and so often becomes a reservoir of the disease for infection of other species.

Many lilies produce annual fibrous roots from the underground part of the stem above the bulb. Lilies developing these stem roots usually bloom well the first summer after planting, whereas those that are not stem-rooting rarely flower until the second summer. Stem-rooting species include: *L. amabile, L. auratum, L. Bakeranum, L. Brownii,*

L. bulbiferum, L. callosum, L. carniolicum, L. concolor, L. × dalhansonii, L. distichum, L. Duchartrei, L. formosanum, L. Hansonii, L. Henryi, L. lancifolium, L. leucanthum, L. × maculatum, L. medeoloides, L. Michauxii, L. myriophyllum, L. neilgherrense, L. nepalense, L. pensylvanicum, L. philippinense, L. primulinum, L. pumilum, L. regale, L. Sargentiae, L. speciosum, L. Wallichianum, and *L. Wardii.* Those producing few or no stem roots include: *L. Bolanderi, L. canadense, L. candidum, L. chalcedonicum, L. columbianum, L. Grayi, L. Humboldtii, L. Kelloggii, L. maritimum, L. Martagon, L. monadelphum, L. pardalinum, L. pomponium, L. pyrenaicum, L. superbum, L. × testaceum,* and *L. Washingtonianum.*

Further information on *Lilium* culture, hybridizing, and cultivars may be found in publications of The North American Lily Society.

album: *L. candidum,* but material offered as *L. album* may be a cv. of *L. auratum, L. Martagon,* or *L. speciosum.*

Alexandrae: *L. nobilissimum.*

amabile Palib. Sts. to 3 ft., with gray, hispid hairs, leafless in lower ⅓; lvs. alt., lanceolate, to 3½ in. long, finely hairy; fls. 1–6, in a raceme, nodding, unpleasantly scented, grenadine-red, spotted black, segms. 2 in. long, strongly reflexed, anthers chocolate-brown. Korea. Cv. **'Luteum'** [var. *luteum* Hort. ex Constable]. Fls. clear orange-yellow. Cv. **'Unicolor'.** Fls. orange, not spotted.

aurantiacum: see *L. bulbiferum* and *L.* × *maculatum.*

auratum Lindl. GOLD-BANDED L., GOLDEN-RAYED L., MOUNTAIN L. Sts. to 8 ft., purple-green, glabrous; lvs. alt., linear-lanceolate, to 9 in. long, mostly 5-nerved; fls. 1–35, in a raceme, to 1 ft. across, bowl-shaped, horizontal, fragrant, white, spotted with crimson, each segm. with central yellow stripe, pollen chocolate-red. Japan. Bulbs are used for food in Japan. Cv. **'Album'.** Fls. white, not spotted. Cv. **'Pictum'.** Fls. densely spotted with crimson, stripes on segms. crimson at tip. Cv. **'Praecox'.** Blooming earlier. Cv. **'Rubro-vittatum'.** Stripes on segms. changing from yellow to crimson, spots larger, anthers bright red. Cv. **'Rubrum'.** Stripes on segms. very broad, crimson. Cv. **'Tricolor'.** Of robust habit; lvs. suberect; fls. spotted, stripes yellow. Cv. **'Variegata'.** Fls. with gold stripes and yellow spots. Var. **macranthum:** var. *platyphyllum.* Var. **platyphyllum** Bak. [var. *macranthum* Hort.]. Lvs. broader, more numerous, mostly 7-nerved; fls. more than 1 ft. across, with fewer spots. Japan.

×**aurelianense** Debras: *L. Henryi* × *L. Sargentiae.* To 8 ft.; lvs. alt., lanceolate, to 4¾ in. long; fls. 1–25 in a raceme, horizontal or nearly so, fragrant, to 5 in. across, yellow-orange, segms. spreading, tending to recurve.

×**Backhousei:** a catalogue name for the group of hybrids known as Backhouse Hybrids, derived from *L. Hansonii* × *L. Martagon.* To 6 ft.; lvs. whorled; fls. 20–30 in a raceme, cream, yellow, pink, or maroon, with dark spots, segms. reflexed. The original plant from this cross was called 'Marhan'.

Bakeranum Collett & Hemsl. To 3 ft.; lvs. alt., linear to lanceolate, to 4 in. long, veins and margins scabrous; fls. 1–5, in a raceme, campanulate, nodding, fragrant, to 3 in. long, greenish-yellow, changing to creamy-white, spotted with red-brown inside, segms. reflexed at apex, filaments to 1½ in. long, anthers brown, pollen orange. W. China, n. Burma.

Barryi: *Lilium* cv. 'Barryi', one of the Aurelian Strain Hybrids, presumably developed from cv. 'T. A. Havemayer'. Fls. white and green to soft yellow and bright orange, segms. reflexed.

Batemanniae: *L.* × *maculatum* cv.

×**Beecheri:** a name applied to *L. auratum* × *L. speciosum* hybrids. Fls. deep pink, opening wide, segms. slightly reflexed.

Bloomeranum: *L. Humboldtii* var.

Bolanderi S. Wats. [*L. Howellii* I. M. Johnst.]. THIMBLE L. To 3½ ft.; lvs. whorled, oblanceolate to obovate, to 2¾ in. long, glaucous; fls. 2–9, in a raceme, funnelform, to 1¾ in. long, deep crimson, spotted with purple, anthers dull purple, pollen orange. N. Calif. and adjacent Ore.

Brownii Hort. ex Gheld. To 4 ft.; lvs. alt., lanceolate, to 1 ft. long, glossy; fls. 1–6, in an umbellate raceme, funnelform, horizontal, slightly fragrant, to 6 in. long, pure white inside, rose-purple outside, filaments papillose, anthers brown, pollen red-brown. Probably s. China. Var. **australe** (Stapf) Stearn. Lvs. linear to linear-lanceolate. China. Var. **colchesteri** (Hort. Wallace ex Van Houtte) E. H. Wils. [var. *viridulum* Bak.]. Lvs. of middle of st. oblanceolate; fls. large, white, stained with rose-purple outside, fragrant. Cent. China. Var. **viridulum:** var. *colchesteri.*

bulbiferum L. [*L. aurantiacum* Weston]. ORANGE L. Sts. to 4 ft., slightly woolly above, often with bulbils in upper lf. axils; lvs. alt., many, lanceolate, to 4 in. long; fls. 1–20, in an umbellate raceme, cup-shaped, erect, to 3⅜ in. long and 4 in. across, orange-red with a central orange patch, filaments pinkish-orange, anthers brown, pollen orange. E. cent. Eur. Var. **croceum** (Chaix) Pers. [*L. croceum* Chaix]. To 5 ft.; lvs. linear-lanceolate, to 6 in. long; fls. orange, to 3 in. long. Pyrenees, e. to Switzerland, s. Germany, cent. Italy.

×**Burbankii** Hort. van Tuberg.: *L. pardalinum* × *L. Parryi.* To 7 ft.; lvs. whorled; fls. many, in a raceme, campanulate, horizontal, fragrant, yellow, spotted chocolate, segms. strongly reflexed.

callosum Siebold & Zucc. To 3 ft.; lvs. alt., many, linear to linear-lanceolate, to 5 in. long; fls. 1–19, in a raceme, nodding, to 2 in. across, orange-red with faint black spots, segms. strongly reflexed. China, Korea, Japan, Taiwan. Cv. **'Flaviflorum'** [cv. 'Flavum']. Fls. yellow. Cv. **'Flavum':** cv. 'Flaviflorum'. Cv. **'Luteum'.** Fls. pale citron-yellow.

canadense L. [*L. canadense* var. *flavum* Pursh]. CANADA L., WILD YELLOW L., MEADOW L., YELLOW-BELL L., YELLOW L. Bulb renewed annually at end of a stolon, sts. to 5 ft.; lvs. whorled, lanceolate to oblanceolate, to 6 in. long, margins often scabrous; fls. 1–20, in 1–4 umbels from upper lf. axils, campanulate, nodding, to 3 in. long and 3 in. across, orange-yellow to red, spotted with purple-brown, segms. recurving outward but not reflexed. Nov. Sc. to Va., w. to Ohio and Ky. Cv. **'Coccinea'** [var. rubrum Hort. ex T. Moore]. Fls. brick-red, with a yellow, spotted throat. Var. **editorum** Fern. Lvs. elliptic to oblong; fls. red, with a short tube. Drier sites, Penn. and s. Ind, s. to Ala. Var. **flavum:** *L. canadense.* Var. **rubrum:** cv. 'Coccinea'. Var. **superbum:** *L. superbum.*

candidum L. [*L. album* Houtt.]. MADONNA L. To 6 ft.; basal lvs. oblanceolate, to 9 in. long, persisting through winter, st. lvs. alt., oblanceolate, the upper lvs. lanceolate or linear and shorter; fls. 5–20, in a raceme, campanulate, horizontal, fragrant, to 3 in. long, clear waxy white, segms. gently recurved, anthers yellow. Probably native in the Balkans, perhaps also in Israel and Lebanon, but spread early by cult. to s. Eur., N. Afr., and se. Asia. Fls. yield an essential oil used in perfumery. Var. **cernuum** Weston [var. *peregrinum* (Mill.) Pers.]. Plant more slender; outer perianth segms. scarcely overlapping the narrow inner segms. Var. **peregrinum:** var. *cernuum.* Var. **salonikae** Hort. Basal lvs. narrow, wavy; perianth segms. widely spreading, filaments short, pollen yellow. Macedonia.

carniolicum Bernh. ex W. D. J. Koch. To 3 ft.; lvs. alt., lanceolate, to 3 in. long, ascending, veins hairy beneath; fls. 1–6, in a raceme, nodding, fragrant, to 2 in. across, red or orange, segms. strongly reflexed, anthers red. Mts. of se. Eur. Var. **albanicum** (Griseb.) Bak. Shorter; lvs. glabrous; fls. amber-yellow or red, pollen brilliant red. Yugoslavia, Albania. Var. **Jankae** (A. Kern.) Wehrh. [*L. Jankae* A. Kern.]. Fls. bright yellow, usually spotted with black, anthers red. Yugoslavia, Bulgaria.

carolinianum: *L. Catesbaei,* but material offered as *L. carolinianum* is probably *L. Michauxii.*

Catesbaei Walt. [*L. carolinianum* Bosc ex Lam.]. LEOPARD L., PINE L., SOUTHERN RED L. To 2 ft.; basal lvs. linear, persisting through winter, st. lvs. alt., linear to linear-lanceolate, to 3¼ in. long; fls. solitary, cup-shaped, erect, to 5 in. long, red, yellow toward base, brown-spotted, segms. narrow-clawed, recurved toward tip. Bogs and wet pinelands, N.C. to Fla. and La. Also called TIGER L. where it is native. Var. **Longii** Fern. LONG'S RED L. Basal lvs. absent, st. lvs. broader; perianth segms. without long recurving tips. Se. Va. to Ga. and Ala.

cathayanum: *Cardiocrinum cathayanum.*

centifolium: *L. leucanthum* var.

cernuum Kom. To 3 ft.; lvs. alt., linear, to 7 in. long, glabrous; fls. 1–6, in a raceme, nodding, fragrant, to 1½ in. long, purplish-pink, with wine-purple spots, segms. strongly reflexed, pollen lilac. Korea, Manchuria, adjacent Siberia.

chalcedonicum L. SCARLET TURK'S-CAP L. Sts. to 4½ ft., thinly hairy; lvs. alt., many, crowded, lanceolate or oblanceolate, to 4½ in. long, becoming smaller upwards, erect and appressed to st., with silver margins; fls. 1–10, in a raceme, nodding, to 3 in. across, vermilion-scarlet, not spotted, segms. strongly reflexed. Greece. Cv. **'Maculatum'.** Fls. spotted with purple.

colchicum: *L. Szovitsianum.*

columbianum Hanson ex Bak. COLUMBIA L., OREGON L. To 5 ft., or more in the wild; lvs. whorled, lanceolate to oblanceolate, to 4 in. long; fls. few to many, in a raceme, nodding, to 2 in. long, yellow or golden to red, usually maroon-spotted, segms. strongly reflexed. N. Calif. to B.C. and Idaho. Cv. **'Ingramii'.** More robust; fls. large, more numerous, deep orange.

concolor Salisb. STAR L. Sts. to 3 ft., purplish, with stiff, white hairs; lvs. alt., linear to linear-lanceolate, to 4 in. long; fls. 1–10, often in an umbellate raceme, star-shaped, erect, to 2 in. long, vermilion, glossy, stamens scarlet, style slightly shorter than ovary. China. Cv. **'Racemosum'.** Vigorous, sts. taller; fls. 18–26, brilliant red. Var. **coridion:** var. *partheneion* cv. Var. **partheneion** (Siebold & De Vriese) Bak. [var. *coridion* (Siebold & De Vriese) Bak.]. Sts. nearly smooth, green; lvs. sessile, linear; fls. 1–5, usually spotted, segms. woolly outside. Korea, Manchuria, Japan. Cvs. of this var. include: **'Partheneion',** with fls. red, streaked with yellow and green, sparsely spotted with black, and **'Coridion',** with fls. citron-yellow, spotted with purplish-brown. Var. **pulchellum** (Fisch.) Regel. Sts. green; fls. spotted, vermilion to apricot-colored, anthers orange. Korea, Manchuria, adjacent Siberia.

cordatum: *Cardiocrinum cordatum.*

cordifolium: *Cardiocrinum cordatum.*

corbellatum: a listed name of no botanical standing, used for *L.* × *hollandicum* cv. 'Orange Triumph'.

croceum: *L. bulbiferum* var.

Croftii: a listed name of no botanical standing for *L. longiflorum* cv. 'Croft'.

dahuricum: *L. pensylvanicum.*

×**dalhansonii** C. B. Powell: *L. Hansonii* × *L. Martagon* var. *Cattaniae.* To 6 ft.; fls. many, in a raceme, segms. maroon toward the recurved tips, orange-spotted in the middle, style purplish.

dauricum: *L. pensylvanicum.* Var. **luteum:** *L. pensylvanicum* cv.

Davidii Duchartre ex Elwes. Sts. to 4 ft., usually rough; lvs. alt., many, linear, to 4 in. long, becoming shorter upwards, margins finely toothed and usually inrolled; fls. 1–20, in a raceme, nodding, to 3 in. long, orange-red or scarlet, spotted with black, segms. strongly reflexed. W. China. Var. **macranthum** Raffill. To 6 ft.; fls. 1–2 on a pedicel, bright orange. Var. **unicolor** (J. M. C. Hoog) Cotton [*L. Willmottiae* E. H. Wils. var. *unicolor* J. M. C. Hoog]. To 3 ft.; fls. 10–15, pale, with small purplish or reddish spots. N. China. Var. **Willmottiae** (E. H. Wils.) Raffill [*L. sutchuenense* Franch.; *L. Willmottiae* E. H. Wils.]. St. to 7 ft., purple-spotted; fls. up to 40, on drooping pedicels to 6 in. long, in a loose pyramidal infl., vivid orange, spotted with black. W. China.

×**davimottiae** a hort. name applied to hybrids between *L. Davidii* var. *Davidii* and *L. Davidii* var. *Willmottiae.*

davuricum: *L. pensylvanicum.*

distichum Nakai ex Kamib. Sts. to 3 ft., hollow, ribbed in lower part; lvs. in 1 whorl, with some lvs. scattered above, oblong-lanceolate to oblanceolate-ovate, to 6 in. long; fls. 3–8, in a raceme, pale orange-red and spotted, segms. to 1⅜ in. long, filaments pale yellow, anthers orange-red. Ne. Manchuria and Korea.

Duchartrei Franch. [*L. Duchartrei* var. *Farreri* (Turrill) Grove; *L. Farreri* Turrill]. Stoloniferous, sts. to 3 ft., rarely to 5 ft.; lvs. alt., many, lanceolate or oblanceolate, to 4 in. long, sometimes with a tuft of white hairs in the axils; fls. 1–12, in an umbel, nodding, fragrant, to 3 in. long, marble-white, spotted with purple, segms. strongly reflexed, papillose along the nectary, filaments green, anthers yellow. W. China.

elegans: *L.* × *maculatum.* Var. **alutaceum, atropurpureum, atrosanguineum, aureum, Batemanniae, bicolor, biligulatum, incomparabile, sanguineum:** *L.* × *maculatum* cvs.

Erabu: *L. longiflorum* var. *insulare* cv.

×**excelsum:** *L.* × *testaceum.*

Farreri: *L. Dutchartrei.*

×**formolongi:** a catalogue name for a hybrid between *L. longiflorum* var. *Takeshima* and *L. formosanum.*

formosanum A. Wallace [*L. philippinense* Bak. var. *formosanum* (Bak.) E. H. Wils.]. Sts. to 5 ft., rarely to 7 ft., purple-brown; lvs. alt., many, linear, to 8 in. long, dark green, with 2–4 prominent lateral veins on under surface; fls. solitary, paired, or 3–10 in an umbel, funnelform, fragrant, 5–8 in. long, white inside, suffused wine-purple outside, filaments papillose toward base, pollen yellow. Taiwan. Var. **Pricei** Hort. Dwarfer; fls. fewer, heavily suffused reddish-purple outside. Mt. Morrison in Taiwan. Var. **Wilsonii** Hort. is listed.

formosum: *L. pensylvanicum;* see also *L. leucanthum.*

giganteum: *Cardiocrinum giganteum.*

Glehnii: *Cardiocrinum cordatum.*

×**gloriosum** Hort.: *L. Humboldtii* × (*L. Humboldtii* var. *ocellatum* × *L. Parryi*). Fls. many, large, light orange, spotted crimson, segms. strongly reflexed. Material presently offered under this name may be something else.

Grayi S. Wats. ORANGE-BELL L., BELL L., ROAN L., GRAY'S L. Stoloniferous, sts. to 4 ft.; lvs. in 3–6 whorls or 4–8 lvs., lanceolate or elliptic to oblong-lanceolate, to 4¾ in. long, margins rough; fls. 1–8, campanulate, horizontal or slightly nodding, to 2 in. long, reddish-orange, spotted with purplish-brown. Va., N.C., Tenn.

Hansonii Leichtl. ex D. D. T. Moore. JAPANESE TURK'S-CAP L. To 5 ft.; lvs. in whorls, oblanceolate to elliptic, to 5 in. long; fls. in a loose raceme, nodding, fragrant, to 2½ in. across, orange-yellow, spotted purplish-brown, segms. strongly reflexed, thick and waxy, pollen yellow. Japan, Korea, adjacent Siberia.

Harrisii: *L. longiflorum* var. *eximium.*

Henryi Bak. Sts. to 8 ft., or sometimes more, flexible, usually arching, purple-spotted, glabrous; lvs. alt., many, crowded, lanceolate, to 6 in. long, those just below infl. ovate, shorter; fls. 4–20, in a loose raceme, to 3 in. long, orange, spotted with brown, papillose, segms. strongly reflexed, anthers dark orange. Cent. China. Cv. 'Citrinum'. Fls. pale yellow, sparsely spotted with chocolate. Cv. 'Erectum'. Sts. stiffer, more erect.

×**hollandicum** Bergmans ex Woodcock & Stearn [*L.* × *umbellatum* Hort., not Pursh]. CANDLESTICK L. A group of lilies derived from crossing *L. bulbiferum* or *L. bulbiferum* var. *croceum* with forms of *L.* × *maculatum.* To 2½ ft. or more; lvs. alt., many, mostly 3-nerved;

fls. in an umbel or short raceme, cup-shaped, erect, to 4 in. long, red, orange, or yellow. Cv. 'Orange Triumph' [*L.* × *crobellatum* Hort.]. To 3 ft.; fls. 10–12, vivid orange, with faint, fine, maroon spots.

Hollissii: a listed name of no botanical standing.

Howardii: a listed name of no botanical standing for *L. longiflorum* cv. 'Howard'.

Howellii: *L. Bolanderi.*

Humboldtii Roezl & Leichtl. ex Duchartre. HUMBOLDT L. Bulb scales not jointed, sts. to 6 ft., stout, often rough-hairy; lvs. in 4–8 whorls, oblanceolate, to 5 in. long, margins pubescent; fls. few to 15, in a pyramidal raceme, nodding, 3½ in. long, orange-yellow, spotted with purple or maroon, segms. strongly reflexed, anthers purple, pollen orange. Sierras of cent. Calif. Var. **Bloomeranum** (Kellogg) Jeps. [*L. Bloomeranum* Kellogg]. Bulb scales with several joints, sts. shorter; perianth segms. dark-spotted, red-margined. S. Calif. Var. **magnificum:** var. *ocellatum.* Var. **ocellatum** (Kellogg) Elwes [var. *magnificum* Purdy]. Perianth segms. with maroon spots encircled with red. S. Calif.

×**imperiale** E. H. Wils. [*L.* × *princeps* E. H. Wils.]: *L. regale* × *L. Sargentiae.* Sts. to 4 ft., wiry; lvs. alt., many, linear; fls. open-funnelform, white, purplish outside, with yellow throat, anthers orange-brown.

iridollae M. Henry. POT-OF-GOLD L. Stoloniferous, sts. to 5 ft.; lvs. usually whorled, mostly oblanceolate to obovate, to 3½ in. long, hairy on margins and veins beneath; fls. solitary or as many as 8, nodding, slightly fragrant, to 4 in. long, golden-yellow, spotted brown, segms. strongly reflexed, pollen brownish-red to brownish-yellow. Acid bogs, nw. Fla. and S. Ala.

Jankae: *L. carniolicum* var.

japonicum Thunb. ex Houtt. [*L. Krameri* Hook.f.; *L. Makinoi* G. Koidz.]. JAPANESE L. To 3 ft.; lvs. alt., lanceolate to oblong, to 6 in. long, firm, dark green, 3–5-nerved; fls. 1–5, broadly funnelform, fragrant, to 6 in. long, rose-pink, pollen orange-brown. Japan. Cv. 'Album' [var. *album* (Hort. Teutschel ex A. Wallace) E. H. Wils.]. Fls. white. Cv. 'Albomarginatum' [var. *albomarginatum* Mak.]. Lvs. white-margined. Var. **platyfolium:** a listed name.

Kelleyanum Lemm. [*L. nevadense* Eastw.; *L. nevadense* var. *shastense* Eastw.; *L. pardalinum* Kellogg var. *nevadense* (Eastw.) Stoker; *L. shastense* (Eastw.) Beane]. Rhizomatous, sts. 2–6 ft.; lvs. mostly whorled, oblong-lanceolate, to 6 in. long; fls. 1–25, in a loose raceme, nodding, fragrant, to 1½ in. long, yellow, often orange at tip, dotted with maroon, segms. strongly reflexed. Mts. of cent. to n. Calif.

Kelloggii Purdy. To 4 ft.; lvs. whorled, lanceolate or oblanceolate, to 4 in. long; fls. up to 20, in a loose raceme, or few and umbellately arranged, nodding, fragrant, to 2 in. long, cream to pink, aging dull purple, pollen orange. Nw. Calif.

Kesselringianum Misch. To 2 ft.; lvs. alt., many, lanceolate, to 5 in. long; fls. 1–3, creamy-white or straw-yellow, with faint brown dots, segms. to 3⅜ in. long, recurved at tip, stamens 2 in. long, filaments separate, anthers and stigma chestnut-purple. Caucasus.

Krameri: *L. japonicum.*

lancifolium Thunb. [*L. sinense* Nois. ex Steud.; *L. tigrinum* Ker-Gawl.]. TIGER L. Sts. to 6 ft., purplish, scabrous, cobwebby-hairy, with bulbils in lf. axils; lvs. alt., many, broadly linear to lanceolate, to 7½ in. long; fls. 1–25, in a raceme, nodding, to 5 in. across, orange- or salmon-red, spotted with purple-black, segms. strongly reflexed, pollen purplish-brown. China, Korea, Japan; escaped in e. U.S. Bulbs used for food in Japan. Cv. 'Flore-pleno' [cv. 'Floribundum'; *L. tigrinum* Ker-Gawl. var. *flore-pleno* Regel]. Fls. double. Cv. 'Floribundum': cv. 'Flore-pleno'. Cv. 'Giganteum'. Listed as an improved form. Cv. 'Splendens' [*L. tigrinum* Ker-Gawl. var. *splendens* Leichtl. ex Van Houtte]. Fls. larger, more abundant, rich red, with bolder spots. Cv. 'Superbum'. Fls. bright orange spotted with black. Var. **flaviflorum** Mak. [*L. tigrinum* Ker-Gawl. var. *flaviflorum* (Mak.) Stearn]. Fls. yellow with purple spots except toward tips of segms., anthers brick-red. Japan. Var. **Fortunei** Hort. Sts. densely woolly; fls. up to 30 or 50, salmon-orange. Late-flowering. Dagelet Is., Korea. Var. **simplex:** a listed name for the typical single-fld. form. Material offered or grown as *L. lancifolium* is likely to be *L. speciosum.*

lankongense Franch. Stoloniferous, sts. to 4 ft.; lvs. alt., many, oblong to oblong-lanceolate, to 4 in. long, dark green; fls. 1–15, in a raceme, nodding, fragrant, to 2½ in. long, white, tinged rose-purple, spotted with purple, segms. strongly reflexed, pollen rusty-brown. W. China.

Leichtlinii Hook.f. Stoloniferous, sts. to 4 ft.; lvs. alt., many, linear-lanceolate, to 6 in. long; fls. 1–5, nodding, 3 in. long, lemon-yellow, spotted purplish-brown, segms. strongly reflexed, anthers and pollen reddish. Japan. Var. **Maximowiczii:** var. *tigrinum.* Var. **tigrinum** (Regel) Nichols. [var. *Maximowiczii* (Regel) Bak.; *L. Maximowiczii* Regel].

To 8 ft., more slender; fls. 1–12, orange-red, copiously spotted with purplish-brown. Manchuria, Korea, Japan.

leucanthum (Bak.) Bak. [*L. formosum* Franch., not Lem.]. CHINESE WHITE L. To 4 ft.; lvs. alt., many, lanceolate, to 4 in. long, 3-nerved; fls. 3–5, funnelform, slightly drooping, fragrant, to 6 in. long, greenish-white outside, flushed pale yellow in lower half inside, filaments and style pubescent basally, pollen brown. Cent. China. Var. **centifolium** (Stapf) Stearn [*L. centifolium* Stapf]. To 10 ft.; lvs. to 10 in. long; fls. trumpet-shaped, fragrant, to 6½ in. long, white, flushed green and purple outside with rose-purple or brownish keel. Nw. China. Var. **chloraster** (Bak.) E. H. Wils. Sts. to 3 ft., glaucous; lvs. to 3 in. long; fls. open-funnelform, to 5 in. long, white, with a distinct green keel. Cent. China.

longiflorum Thunb. TRUMPET L., WHITE T. L. To 3 ft.; lvs. alt., many, sessile, lanceolate, to 7 in. long; fls. few to several, funnelform, horizontal, fragrant, to 7 in. long, white, filaments glabrous, pollen yellow. Japan. Cv. **'Croft'** [*L. Croftii* Hort.]. To 2 ft., rather pyramidal in habit; lvs. downward-curving; fls. slightly longer than broad. Var. **Croftii:** cv. 'Croft'. Var. **eximium** (Courtois) Bak. [var. *Harrisii* Hort.; *L. Harrisii* Carrière]. EASTER L., BERMUDA E. L., BERMUDA L. Taller; fls. larger, more narrowly cylindrical, with more revolute tips. Cv. **'Howard'** [*L. Howardii* Hort.]. A much earlier-flowering cv. of var. *eximium*, with fls. firmer, smaller. Var. **formosum:** var. *insulare.* Var. **giganteum:** var. *Takeshima.* Var. **Harrisii:** var. *eximium.* Var. **insulare** Hort. ex Mallett [var. *formosum* Hort.]. An improved strain; fls. horizontal, borne at right angles to their stalks. Cv. **'Erabu'** [*L. Erabu* Hort.]. A more floriferous cv. of var. *insulare.* Var. **praecox** is listed. Var. **Takeshima** (Siebold ex Duchartre) Duchartre [var. *giganteum* Hort.]. Vigorous, sts. purple-brown; fls. 6–10, pure white, pollen orange-yellow.

Mackliniae Sealy. To 5 ft.; lvs. alt. except for the whorl just below the infl., elliptic to linear-oblong, to 2 in. long or longer; fls. few to several, cup-shaped to widely campanulate, nodding, to 2¼ in. across, white or pale pink inside, flushed with pink to purple outside, with a basal crimson spot. Ne. India.

macrophyllum: *Notholirion macrophyllum.*

×**maculatum** Thunb. [*L. aurantiacum* Paxt., not Weston; *L. elegans* Thunb.; *L. Thunbergianum* Schult. & Schult.f.]. Sts. to 2 ft., sparsely hairy to glabrous; lvs. alt., many, lanceolate to elliptic, to 4 in. long, 5–7-nerved; fls. 1 to several, in an umbel, cup-shaped, open, erect, lemon-yellow to deep red, scarcely to densely spotted, segms. clawed. Japan. Much-cult., with many cvs. Cv. **'Alutaceum'** [*L. elegans* var. *alutaceum* (Bak. & Dyer) Bak.; *L. Thunbergianum* var. *alutaceum* Bak. & Dyer]. To 9 in.; fls. apricot-colored, spotted with purple. Cv. **'Atropurpureum'** [*L. elegans* var. *atropurpureum* Hort.; *L. Thunbergianum* var. *atropurpureum* Hort.]. Fls. crimson-red, spotted with black. Cv. **'Atrosanguineum'** [*L. elegans* var. *atrosanguineum* Bak. & Dyer) Bak.; *L. Thunbergianum* var. *atrosanguineum* Bak. & Dyer]. Fls. very dark red, spotted with black. Cv. **'Aureum'** [*L. elegans* var. *aureum* Hort.; *L. Thunbergianum* var. *aureum* Duchartre]. Fls. orange-yellow, strongly spotted with black. Cv. **'Batemanniae'** [*L. elegans* var. *Batemanniae* Hort. ex Bak.]. Sts. to 3½ ft.; fls. apricot-colored, not spotted. Cv. **'Bicolor'** [*L. elegans* var. *bicolor* Hort.; *L. Thunbergianum* var. *bicolor* Dombr.]. Segms. red, marked with central orange stripe. Cv. **'Biligulatum'** [*L. elegans* var. *biligulatum* Hort.; *L. Thunbergianum* var. *biligulatum* Hort.]. Early-flowering, fls. deep chestnut-red, spotted. Cv. **'Incomparabile'** [*L. elegans* var. *incomparabile* Voss]. Fls. bright crimson-scarlet. Cv. **'Sanguineum'** [*L. elegans* var. *sanguineum* (Hort. ex Lindl.) Bak.; *L. Thunbergianum* var. *sanguineum* (Hort. ex Lindl.) Bak. & Dyer]. Fls. blood-red, slightly tinged orange, spotted purple-black. Cv. **'Wallacei'** [*L. Wallacei* A. Wallace]. Fls. erect, apricot-colored, spotted with slightly raised spots at base inside.

magnificum: a listed name of no botanical standing; plants offered under this name are probably variants of *L. Humboldtii, L. speciosum,* or *L. longiflorum.*

Marhan: see under *L. Backhousei.*

Makinoi: *L. japonicum.*

maritimum Kellogg. COAST L. To 4 ft., sometimes taller; lvs. mostly alt., linear to oblanceolate, to 5 in. long; fls. 1–12, campanulate, horizontal, 1½ in. long, dark red, spotted with maroon, segms. slightly recurved. Coastal n. Calif.

Martagon L. MARTAGON L., TURK'S-CAP L., TURK'S-CAP, TURBAN L. Sts. to 6 ft., purplish, sometimes hairy; lvs. mostly whorled, mostly oblanceolate, to 6½ in. long, occasionally hairy; fls. 3–50, in a raceme, nodding, disagreeably scented, purple and spotted with black, or varying from white and pink to dull red or nearly black in the cvs. and vars., segms. strongly recurved, stamens long-exserted, pollen orange-yellow. Eur. and w. Asia, e. to Mongolia. Var. **album** Weston. Sts. green; fls. pure white, anthers yellow. Var. **Cattaniae** Vis. [var. *dalmaticum* Elwes]. Fls. dark burgundy-red, not spotted. Dalmatia. Var. **dalmaticum:** var. *Cattaniae.* Var. **hirsutum** Weston. Sts. and lower lf. surfaces hairy; fls. shorter, purplish-pink. Widespread. Var. **unicolor:** a listed name, for a plant described as growing to 5 or 6 ft., fls. nasturtium-red, not spotted.

Maximowiczii: *L. Leichtlinii* var. *tigrinum.*

medeoloides A. Gray. WHEEL L. To 2 or 2½ ft.; lvs. whorled, the upper ones alt., all lanceolate to oblanceolate, to 4¾ in. long; fls. 1–10, in an umbel, nodding, 2 in. long, apricot to scarlet, spotted with black, segms. strongly reflexed, anthers purplish, pollen red. China, s. Korea, Japan.

Michauxii Poir. [*L. carolinianum* Michx., not Bosc]. CAROLINA L, TURK'S-CAP L. To 4 ft.; lvs. whorled, the upper ones alt., all oblanceolate to obovate, to 4¾ in. long, glaucous, rather fleshy; fls. 1–5, nodding, slightly fragrant, to 4 in. long, orange-scarlet, spotted with purple-brown, yellowish-white in the throat, segms. strongly reflexed. S. Va. and W. Va., s. to Fla. and La.

michiganense Farw. MICHIGAN L. Stoloniferous, sts. to 5 ft.; lvs. whorled, lanceolate, to 4½ in. long, margins and lower lf. surface minutely spiculate; fls. 1–8, in an umbel, nodding, to 2¾ in. long, orange-red, spotted reddish-maroon and with a green basal spot inside, segms. strongly recurved, stigma purple. Ont. to s. Man., s. to Tenn., Ark., and Kans. The westward extension of the *L. canadense* type, and by some taxonomists included with *L. canadense* or treated as a variant of it.

monadelphum Bieb. CAUCASIAN L. To 5 ft.; lvs. alt., many, lanceolate or oblanceolate, to 5 in. long; fls. many, in a raceme, campanulate, nodding, fragrant, to 5 in. across, golden-yellow, sometimes tinged or spotted with purple, segms. reflexed, filaments separate or united into a tube, pollen yellow. N. Caucasus. Var. **Szovitsianum:** *L. Szovitsianum.*

montanum: *L. philadelphicum.*

myriophyllum: see *L. sulphureum* and *L. regale.* Var. **superbum:** *L. sulphureum.*

nanum Klotzsch [*Nomocharis nana* (Klotzsch) E. H. Wils.]. To 16 in.; lvs. alt., linear, to 6 in. long; fls. solitary, campanulate, nodding, to 1½ in. long, lilac or rose to purple, with minute reddish-purple dots. Himalayas, se. Tibet, w. China.

neilgherrense Wight. To 3 ft., sometimes taller; lvs. alt., lanceolate, to 5 in. long, glabrous; fls. usually 1 or 2, funnelform, horizontal, fragrant, to 10 in. long, white, flushed with yellow, pollen bright yellow. S. India.

nepalense D. Don. St. running horizontally underground for 1–2 ft., to 3 ft. high above ground; lvs. alt., lanceolate to oblong-lanceolate, to 5½ in. long, 5-nerved; fls. 2 or 3, funnelform, nodding, to 6 in. long, yellow or greenish-yellow, stained or blotched with purple inside, anthers purplish, pollen orange-brown. Himalayas. Cv. **'Robusta'.** Fls. larger, of better texture.

nevadense: *L. Kelleyanum.* Var. **shastense:** *L. Kelleyanum.*

nobilissimum (Mak.) Mak. [*L. Alexandrae* Hort. Wallace]. To 2 ft.; lvs. alt., lanceolate, to 6 in. long; fls. 1–3, in an umbel, broadly funnelform, fragrant, to 6 in. long, white, anthers dark brown, pollen yellow-brown. Ryukyu Is.

occidentale Purdy. WESTERN L., EUREKA L. Bulb rhizomatous, sts. to 6 ft.; lvs. whorled, but upper ones alt., narrowly oblanceolate, to 5 in. long; fls. 1–5, in a raceme, nodding, orange with maroon dots and green centers, segms. to 2½ in. long, the upper half recurved, anthers purple, pollen orange-red. In wet places, coastal n. Calif. and s. Ore.

ochraceum: *L. primulinum* var.

oxypetalum (Royle) Bak. [*Nomocharis oxypetala* (Royle) E. H. Wils.]. To 10 in.; lvs. alt., linear or lanceolate, to 3 in. long; fls. solitary, campanulate, nodding, greenish-yellow. Nw. Himalayas.

papilliferum Franch. Sts. to 2 ft., papillose; lvs. alt., many, linear, to 4 in. long; fls. 1–3, nodding, fragrant, deep crimson to deep purple-maroon, segms. strongly reflexed, to 1½ in. long, anthers brown, pollen orange. Nw. Yunnan.

×**pardaboldtii** Hort. ex Woodcock & Coutts: *L. Humboldtii* × *L. pardalinum.* To 5 ft.; lvs. whorled; fls. many, in a raceme, red-orange, spotted dark crimson, segms. strongly reflexed. The Bellingham Hybrids were developed from this cross.

pardalinum Kellogg [*L. pardalinum* var. *angustifolium* Kellogg; *L. Roezlii* Regel]. LEOPARD L., PANTHER L. Bulb rhizomatous, sts. to 8 ft.; lvs. whorled, but the upper ones alt., linear to lanceolate, to 7 in. long; fls. solitary or several in a raceme, nodding, to 4 in. across, orange-red with crimson tip, spotted with maroon, segms. strongly reflexed, anthers reddish, pollen orange. Sw. Ore. to s. Calif. Cv. **'Californicum'.** Lvs. smaller; fls. larger. Cv. **'Giganteum'.** SUNSET L. Probably actually a hybrid between *L. Humboldtii* and *L. pardalinum;* fls. yellow, tipped bright red, spotted with brown. Cv. **'Johnsonii'.** With a large proportion of bright red in fls. Var. **nevadense:** *L. Kelleyanum.*

Parryi S. Wats. LEMON L. Bulb rhizomatous, sts. to 6 ft.; lvs. mostly alt., the lower ones sometimes whorled, all lanceolate or linear-oblanceolate, to 6 in. long; fls. 1–25, in a raceme, funnelform, horizontal, fragrant, to 4 in. long, clear lemon-yellow, sometimes with maroon spots, anthers brown. S. Calif., s. Ariz. Var. **Kessleri** A. Davids. Lvs. ovate-lanceolate; fls. coarser, anthers smaller. S. Calif.

parvum Kellogg. ALPINE L., SMALL TIGER L., SIERRA L. Bulb rhizomatous, sts. to 5 ft.; lvs. whorled, sometimes alt., linear to lanceolate, to 5 in. long; fls. few to many, in a raceme, campanulate, ascending to erect, to 1¼ in. long, bright orange to dark red, spotted with purplish-brown. Along streams, and in wet meadows in the mts., cent. Calif. to s. Ore. Forma **crocatum** Stearn [var. *luteum* of auth., not Purdy]. Fls. clear orange-yellow, finely dotted with maroon. Mts., Calif.

pensylvanicum Ker-Gawl. [*L. dahuricum* of auth.; *L. dauricum* Ker-Gawl.; *L. davuricum* of auth.; *L. formosum* Lem.]. CANDLESTICK L. St. horizontal and stolonlike below ground, to 3 ft. high above ground, ribbed, somewhat cobwebby; lvs. alt., linear to oblong-lanceolate, to 6 in. long, sometimes hairy; fls. 1 to several, in an umbellate to racemose infl., erect, to 5 in. across, red to scarlet, yellow at base, spotted with purplish-black. Ne. Asia. Cv. **'Luteum'** [*L. dauricum* var. *luteum* R. W. Wallace]. Fls. yellow, spotted with black. Var. **Wilsonii:** *L. Wilsonii*. The misleading epithet, *pensylvanicum*, was given to this sp. from a mistaken belief that it was native to N. Amer.

philadelphicum L. WOOD L., ORANGE-CUP L., WILD ORANGE-RED L. To 3 ft.; lvs. in whorls of 4–8, linear-lanceolate, to 4 in. long; fls. 1–5, open-campanulate, erect, to 4 in. across, orange to vivid orange-red, spotted purple, segms. long-clawed. Me. to s. Ont., s. to Del., Ky. and N.C. Var. **andinum** (Nutt.) Ker-Gawl. [*L. montanum* A. Nels.; *L. umbellatum* Pursh, not Hort.]. WESTERN ORANGE-CUP L. Smaller; lvs. mostly alt.; perianth segms. with smaller claws. W. Que. to B.C., s. to Ky., Nebr., New Mex.

philippinense Bak. To 3 ft.; lvs. alt., many, linear, to 6 in. long, grasslike; fls. 1–2, funnelform, horizontal, fragrant, to 10 in. long, white, tinged with green, anthers yellow. Philippine Is. Var. **formosanum:** *L. formosanum*.

pitkinense Beane & Vollmer. Sometimes with short stolons, sts. to 6 ft.; lvs. whorled or alt., linear, to 5½ in. long, yellow-green; fls. in an umbel, scarlet-vermilion, with yellow zone basally, spotted black, segms. 2 in. long, strongly reflexed from middle, anthers brown-purple, pollen rusty-brown. Pitkin Marsh, Sonoma Co., Calif.

polyphyllum D. Don. To 4 ft., or taller in the wild; lvs. alt., the lower ones occasionally whorled, many, linear to lanceolate, to 5 in. long; fls. several, in a raceme, narrowly campanulate, nodding, fragrant, to 3 in. across, yellowish-green outside, creamy-white inside, with lilac streaks and spots, segms. forming a tube for half their length, then strongly reflexed, anthers yellow, pollen orange. W. Himalayas.

pomponium L. LESSER TURK'S-CAP L., LITTLE T.-C. L., MINOR T.-C. L., TURBAN L. To 3 ft.; lvs. alt., many, linear, to 5 in. long, margins silvery, ciliate; fls. 1–10, in a raceme, nodding, with disagreeable odor, brilliant scarlet, spotted with dark purple, segms. strongly reflexed. S. France, n. Italy.

primulinum Bak. To 8 ft.; lvs. alt., lanceolate, to 6 in. long; fls. 2–7, in a raceme, nodding, primrose-yellow, unblotched, segms. to 6 in. long, strongly reflexed, filaments green. Burma. Var. **ochraceum** (Franch.) Stearn [*L. ochraceum* Franch.]. St. to 4 ft., brown; fls. many, greenish-yellow, marked with purple in throat. W. China.

× **princeps:** *L.* × *imperiale.*

pumilum Delile [*L. tenuifolium* Fisch.]. CORAL L. Sts. to 1½ ft. or rarely more, wiry; lvs. alt., many, linear, to 4 in. long; fls. 1–20, in a raceme, nodding, fragrant, to 2 in. across, light scarlet, sometimes spotted with black, segms. strongly reflexed, pollen scarlet. Siberia, e. China. Cv. **'Golden Gleam'.** Fls. golden-yellow.

pyrenaicum Gouan. YELLOW TURK'S-CAP L. To 4 ft.; lvs. alt., many, dense, linear-lanceolate, to 5 in. long, finely ciliate; fls. 1–12, in a raceme, nodding, unpleasantly scented, to about 1½ in. across, sulphur-yellow, spotted with purplish-black, segms. strongly reflexed, anthers brownish, pollen orange. Pyrenees. Cv. **'Aureum'.** Fls. deeper yellow. Cv. **'Rubrum'.** Fls. orange-scarlet, with maroon spots.

regale E. H. Wils. [*L. myriophyllum* E. H. Wils., not Franch.]. REGAL L., ROYAL L. Sts. to 6 ft.; lvs. alt., many, to 5 in. long, 1-nerved, somewhat recurved, rough-margined; fls. in an umbel, funnelform, horizontal, fragrant, to 6 in. long, lilac or purple outside, white inside with yellow base, anthers yellow, pollen golden-yellow, style and stigma green. W. China. Cv. **'Album'.** Fls. pure white.

Roezlii: *L. pardalinum.*

rubellum Bak. To 2¾ ft.; lvs. alt., many, broadly lanceolate to narrowly oblong, to 4 in. long, distinctly petioled; fls. 1–9, in an umbel, funnelform, horizontal, fragrant, to 3 in. long, clear rose-pink. Japan.

rubescens S. Wats. CHAPARRAL L., REDWOOD L., CHAMISE L. To 6 ft.; lvs. whorled, oblanceolate, to 4 in. long, glaucous beneath; fls. 3 to many, in a raceme, funnelform, ascending to erect, fragrant, to 2 in. long, white or pale lilac with purple spots, turning to rose-purple, anthers golden. Coast Ranges, s. Ore. to cent. Calif.

rubrum: *L. pomponium,* but material offered as *L. rubrum* may be *L. canadense* cv. 'Coccineum', *L. auratum* cv. 'Rubrum', or *L. speciosum* cv. 'Rubrum'.

Sargentiae E. H. Wils. Sts. to 5 ft., purplish, with bulbils in lf. axils; lvs. alt., many, linear-oblong to lanceolate, to 8 in. long, 3–7-nerved; fls. 1–8, in an umbel, funnelform, horizontal, fragrant, to 6 in. long, rose-purple flushed with brown and green outside, white inside with yellow throat, anthers purplish, pollen brown. W. China.

× **Scottiae** F. Skinner: *L.* × *maculatum* cv. 'Mahogany' × *L. Davidii* var. *Willmottiae.* To 3 ft.; lvs. alt., linear, to 4½ in. long, glossy, dark green; fls. open, to 5¾ in. across, deep orange-red, shading to orange, sparsely spotted, the segms. recurved.

shastense: *L. Kelleyanum.*

sikkimense: a listed name of no botanical standing.

sinense: *L. lancifolium.*

speciosum Thunb. [*L. lancifolium* of auth., not Thunb.]. SHOWY L., JAPANESE L., SHOWY J. L. Sts. to 5 ft. or sometimes more, glabrous; lvs. alt., broadly lanceolate to oblong, to 7 in. long, leathery; fls. 1 to many, in leafy panicle, nodding, fragrant, to 4 in. long, white, suffused inside with rose and spotted with rose-red, segms. strongly reflexed, papillate, undulate. Late summer. S. Japan. Cv. **'Album'** [var. *album* M. T. Mast. ex Bak.]. Sts. purplish-brown; fls. white. Cv. **'Kraetzeri'** [var. *Kraetzeri* Grove]. Fls. white, segms. with a central green stripe, pollen orange-brown. Cv. **'Magnificum'.** Sts. red; fls. large, suffused with crimson and spotted with pink, pollen red. Cv. **'Melpomene'.** Fls. deep carmine, segms. margined with white. Cv. **'Punctatum'** [var. *punctatum* Hort. ex Marnock]. Fls. white, flushed with pink, spotted with red, pollen orange. Cv. **'Roseum'** [var. *roseum* M. T. Mast. ex Bak.]. Sts. green; fls. rose. Cv. **'Rubrum'** [var. *rubrum* M. T. Mast. ex Bak.]. Sts. purplish-brown; fls. carmine. Var. **gloriosoides** Bak. Lvs. narrower; perianth segms. very undulate, scarlet-spotted. Cent. China, Taiwan.

sulphureum Bak. ex Hook.f. [*L. myriophyllum* Franch.; *L. myriophyllum* var. *superbum* (Bak.) E. H. Wils.]. Sts. to 8 ft. or sometimes more, with bulbils in upper lf. axils; lvs. alt., many, linear-lanceolate, to 8 in. long, 3–7-nerved; fls. 1–15, in a racemose to subumbellate infl., funnelform, horizontal or nodding, fragrant, to 9 in. long, or sometimes longer, sulphur-yellow with claret-red flush outside, pollen orange-brown. Burma, w. China.

× **sulphurgale** Hort.: *L. regale* × *L. sulphureum.* Similar to *L. regale,* but blooming 2–3 weeks later.

superbum L. [*L. canadense* L. var. *superbum* Hort.]. TURK'S-CAP L., AMERICAN T.-C. L., LILY-ROYAL, SWAMP L., TURK'S-CAP. Bulbs stoloniferous, sts. to 8 ft.; lvs. whorled, or the upper ones alt., lanceolate, to 6 in. long; fls. few to many in a raceme or umbel, nodding, to 4 in. across, orange-scarlet, spotted with purplish-brown, green basally, segms. strongly reflexed, anthers orange-red, filaments strongly curved outward. Wet areas, se. New Hamp. to Ga. and Ala.

sutchuenense: *L. Davidii* var. *Willmottiae.*

Szovitsianum Fisch. ex Avé-Lall. [*L. colchicum* Steven ex Ledeb.; *L. monadelphum* var. *Szovitsianum* (Fisch. & Avé-Lall.) Bak.]. To 5 ft.; lvs. alt., many, oblong-lanceolate, to 5 in. long, pubescent on veins beneath; fls. 1–20, in a raceme, campanulate, nodding, yellow, sometimes dotted near edges, segms. to 4⅜ in. long, recurved, filaments free at base, anthers brown. Caucasus.

taliense Franch. Sts. running horizontally below ground for a short distance, to 4 ft. high, often scabrous, purple or green, blotched with purple; lvs. alt., many, linear-lanceolate, to 5 in. long; fls. 1–12, in a raceme, nodding, fragrant, to 2 in. across, white, with purple spots, anthers purple, pollen yellow. W. China.

tenuifolium: *L. pumilum.*

× **testaceum** Lindl. [*L. excelsum* Endl. & Hartinger]: *L. candidum* × *L. chalcedonicum.* NANKEEN L. Sts. to 6 ft., purplish, glaucous; lvs. alt., many, linear, to 4 in. long, gradually shorter upward along the st., twisted; fls. 1–12, in an umbellate raceme, nodding, fragrant, to 3 in. across, apricot or nankeen-yellow, often flushed with pink, occasionally with a few red spots, segms. to 3 in. long, recurved, pollen orange.

Thomsonianum: *Notholirion Thomsonianum.*

Thunbergianum: *L.* × *maculatum.* Vars. **alutaceum, atropurpureum, atrosanguineum, aureum, bicolor, biligulatum, sanguineum:** *L.* × *maculatum* cvs.

tigrinum: *L. lancifolium.* Vars. **flaviflorum, flore-pleno, giganteum, splendens, superbum:** *L. lancifolium* cvs. Var. **floribundum:** *L. lancifolium* cv. 'Flore Pleno'.

tsingtauense Gilg. To 3 ft.; lvs. whorled, the upper ones alt., oblanceolate to oblong-oblanceolate, to 4 in. long, glabrous; fls. 1–7, in a subumbellate infl., open, erect, to 2 in. across, orange, sparsely spotted, stamens and pollen orange. E. China, Korea.

umbellatum: *L. philadelphicum* var. *andinum;* however, in hort. the name *L. umbellatum* has been commonly applied to *L.* × *hollandicum.*

Vollmeri Eastw. Bulb rhizomatous, sts. to 3 ft.; lvs. mostly alt., or a few whorled, linear-lanceolate, to 6 in. long; fls. 1–3 or sometimes many, nodding, yellow to reddish-orange, spotted on lower part of inner surface, segms. strongly reflexed, to 3 in. long. Bogs, nw. Calif. and adjacent Ore.

Wallacei: *L.* × *maculatum* cv.

Wallichianum Schult. & Schult.f. Sts. often running horizontally underground before emerging, to 6 ft. high; lvs. alt., many, linear to lanceolate, to 10 in. long, 3–5-nerved; fls. usually solitary but sometimes several, funnelform, horizontal, fragrant, to 10 in. long, greenish-white outside, creamy-white inside, pollen bright yellow. E. Himalayas.

Wardii F. C. Stern. St. usually running horizontally underground before emerging, to 5 ft. high, purplish-brown, finely scabrous; lvs. alt., many, narrowly lanceolate to oblong-elliptic, to 3 in. long, margin finely scabrous; fls. few to 40, in a raceme, nodding, fragrant, to 2½ in. across, rose-pink, spotted with reddish-purple, segms. reflexed, smooth inside, anthers purple, pollen orange. Se. Tibet.

Washingtonianum Kellogg. WASHINGTON L. To 6 ft.; lvs. whorled, oblanceolate, to 6 in. long; fls. few to 20, in a raceme, funnelform, horizontal, fragrant, to 4 in. long, white, with reddish dots, anthers yellow. Mts., cent. to n. Calif. Var. **minus** Purdy. SHASTA L. Fls. fewer and smaller. Foot of Mt. Shasta (Calif.).

Wigginsii Beane & Vollmer. Rhizomatous, sts. to 3 ft.; lvs. alt. or in 2–4 whorls at middle of st., linear-lanceolate, to 9 in. long; fls. horizontal to nodding, clear yellow, spotted with purple or sometimes only dotted, segms. to 2¾ in. long, strongly reflexed from the middle, pollen yellow. N. Calif.

Willmottiae: *L. Davidii* var. Var. **unicolor:** *L. Davidii* var.

Wilsonii Leichtl. To 3 ft.; lvs. alt., lanceolate, to 4 in. long; fls. several, in an umbel, cup-shaped, erect, to 5 in. across, reddish-orange, segms. golden-yellow centrally and black spotted, clawed, recurved toward tip, filaments and style red-orange. Nativity uncertain, supposedly Japan.

LIMNANTHACEAE. *Limnanthes Douglasii:* **a,** plant, × ⅓; **b,** flower, × ¾; **c,** flower, vertical section, × 1; **d,** base of flower, vertical section, × 4; **e,** apex of style and stigmas, × 4; **f,** fruit, × 1; **g,** nutlet, × 2.

LIMNANTHACEAE R. Br. MEADOW FOAM FAMILY. Dicot.; 2 genera of ann. herbs, native to N. Amer.; lvs. alt., pinnately dissected; fls. solitary, bisexual, regular, sepals 3–5, valvate, petals 3–5, stamens twice as many as petals; pistil of 3–5 1-ovuled carpels, carpels nearly separate in the ovary but united in the stylar region, stigmas 3–5; fr. 3–5 nutlets. Only *Limnanthes* is cult.

LIMNANTHEMUM: *NYMPHOIDES.*

LIMNANTHES R. Br. MEADOW FOAM. *Limnanthaceae.* Seven spp. of small ann. herbs, native to w. coast of N. Amer.,

with characters of the family, but sepals, petals, and carpels 4 or 5.

Of easy culture in moist soil, but of short duration; propagated by seeds as a flower garden subject.

Douglasii R. Br. To 1 ft. or more; lvs. 2-pinnatifid, glabrous, yellowish-green; fls. 5-merous, fragrant, 1 in. across, petals yellow with white tips, or white, pinkish, or yellow in vars. Calif. and s. Ore., making sheets of color on low ground in early spring. Var. **sulphurea** C. T. Mason. Petals yellow. Point Reyes (Calif.).

LIMNOBIUM L. Rich. AMERICAN FROG'S-BIT. *Hydrocharitaceae.* Three spp. of stoloniferous, floating, aquatic herbs, native to the New World; lvs. basal, with a spongy layer of tissue on the under surface, long-petioled; fls. unisexual, in axillary, solitary spathes, sepals and petals 3, male spathes 1-valved, 3-fld., stamens 6–12, filaments united into a column, female spathes 2-valved, 1-fld., ovary 6–9-celled, stigmas as many as the cells; fr. a many-seeded, dry berry. Occasionally grown in aquaria or pools.

Spongia (Bosc) Steud. Lf. blades elliptic or ovate to suborbicular, to 3 in. long, cordate at base, upper surface spotted with red-brown, lower surface purplish, petioles to 4 in. long. E. U.S. to Del. and se. Ill.; trop. Amer.

stoloniferum (G. F. Mey.) Griseb. Lf. blades elliptic to ovate, to 1 in. long, undulate, pale green, glossy above, petioles to 1½ in. long. W. Indies; Mex. to s. Brazil.

LIMNOCHARIS Humb. & Bonpl. *Butomaceae.* Two spp. of erect, aquatic herbs with milky sap, native to trop. Amer.; lvs. tufted, petioles long, blades emersed; peduncles naked, with terminal umbels; fls. bisexual, sepals 3, persistent, petals 3, withering early, stamens many, pistils 15–20, with many ovules, stigmas sessile; fr. a caps., seeds many.

Grown in shallow-water pools or ponds, or in tubs. Propagated by seeds, offsets, and suckers.

flava (L.) Buchenau. To about 2 ft. or more, stout; lf. blades mostly lanceolate to broadly elliptic or ovate, to 10 in. long or more, velvety-green; umbels 3–15-fld.; fls. pedicelled, yellow, to about 1 in. across. W. Indies, Mex., trop. S. Amer. Tender.

Humboldtii: *Hydrocleys nymphoides.*

LIMNOPHILA R. Br. [*Ambulia* Lam.]. *Scrophulariaceae.* About 40 spp. of aromatic, marsh or aquatic herbs, native to warmer parts of Afr., and from Asia to Australia; lvs. whorled or opp., submersed ones often dissected or multifid, often with pellucid dots; fls. solitary in uppermost lf. axils or in racemes or spikes, sessile or pedicelled, calyx of 5 nearly equal lobes, corolla 2-lipped, stamens 4, included; fr. a caps.

Suitable for indoor aquaria, although seldom flowering except when growth extends well above water level.

gratioloides: *L. indica.*

heterophylla Benth. [*Ambulia heterophylla* Hort.]. Per., to 2 ft.; lower, submersed lvs. in whorls of 6–12, multifid into filiform segms., ½ in. long, upper lvs. 4–6 in a whorl, sometimes opp., pinnatifid, those above water level oblong, crenulate to entire; fls. sessile, solitary. Indonesia to Japan.

indica (L.) Druce [*L. gratioloides* R. Br.]. Much-branched glabrous or pubescent herb, to 8 in. or more, smelling of turpentine; lower, submersed lvs. 6 to many in a whorl, multifid, lvs. above water opp., linear to elliptic-oblong or pinnatifid; fls. pedicelled, solitary. Trop. Afr., India and China to Australia.

sessiliflora Blume. Slender herb, to 8 in.; lower, submersed lvs. pinnatisect, in whorls, upper lvs. pinnatifid to lanceolate, entire or toothed; fls. sessile or almost sessile, solitary. Indonesia to Japan.

LIMNORCHIS: *HABENARIA.*

LIMODORUM Boehmer. *Orchidaceae.* Not in general cult. **L. tuberosum:** *Calopogon tuberosus.*

LIMONIUM Mill. [*Statice* Willd., and of L. in part, not Mill.]. SEA LAVENDER, MARSH ROSEMARY, STATICE. *Plumbaginaceae.* About 150 spp. of mostly per. herbs, sometimes woody at base, widely distributed on all continents; lvs. in basal rosettes, or alt. in shrubby spp., entire or pinnatifid; fls. sessile or nearly so, in panicles or spikes, calyx tubular, often colored, 10-ribbed at base, petals united only at base, clawed, stamens 5, borne at base of petals, ovary 1-celled; caps. enclosed in calyx, dehiscent or indehiscent, 1-seeded.

Often grown in rock gardens, in greenhouses, or for cut flowers, some are useful in dry bouquets.

auriculifolium: see *L. binervosum.*

bellidifolium (Gouan) Dumort. [*L. caspium* (Willd.) Gams; *L. reticulatum* Mill.; *Statice bellidifolia* Gouan; *S. caspia* Willd.; *S. reticulata* Huds., not L.]. Glabrous per., to 10 in.; lvs. obovate to lanceolate, to 2 in. long, narrowed into long petiole; fl. scapes to 12 in., scabrous, decumbent, much-branched from near base, with many zigzag sterile brs. in lower part, spikelets 2–3-fld., 1-sided, at ends of branchlets; calyx white, teeth cuspidate, denticulate, tube hairy in lower ⅓, corolla pale blue or lilac, to ¼ in. long, longer than calyx. Eur., e. Asia.

binervosum (G. E. Sm.) Salmon [*L. auriculifolium* of auth., not (Vahl) Druce; *Statice auriculifolia* of auth., not Vahl; *S. binervosa* G. E. Sm.]. Per., with stout, woody rhizome and many lf. rosettes; lvs. obovate to spatulate, 1–5 in. long; fl. scapes to 18 in., infl. dichotomously branched, with few or no sterile brs.; spikelets in 2 rows on upper side of spike; calyx teeth blunt, entire, lower ⅓ of calyx tube hairy on nerves, corolla violet-blue, ⅜ in. long, longer than calyx. W. Eur.

Bonduellii (Lestib.) O. Kuntze [*Statice Bonduellii* Lestib.]. Ann. or bien., hairy at base; lvs. basal, lyrate-pinnatifid, to 6 in. long; fl. scapes to 2 ft., infl. dichotomously paniculate, brs. winged, spikelets 1–3-fld., in terminal corymbs; calyx yellow, tubular at first, later funnelform, corolla yellow, longer than calyx. Algeria. Sometimes considered conspecific with *L. sinuatum,* but differs in having fls. yellow.

brasiliense: *L. carolinianum.*

brassicifolium (Webb & Berth.) O. Kuntze [*Statice brassicifolia* Webb & Berth.]. Per., with stout, woody rhizome; lvs. basal, broadly obovate, to 12 in. long, shallowly pinnately lobed, tapering to winged petiole; fl. scapes prominently winged, infl. dichotomously paniculate; calyx tubular at first, becoming funnelform, purple, corolla white, longer than calyx. Canary Is.

caesium (Girard) O. Kuntze [*Statice caesia* Girard]. Per., branched from base; lvs. deciduous, obovate-spatulate, to 1¼ in. long; sterile and fertile sts. slightly zigzag, to 3 ft., infl. paniculate, showy, densely fld., spikelets 1-fld.; calyx goblet-shaped, ¼ in. long, upper half whitish-hyaline, with 5 short lobes, corolla deep pink, tubular, longer than calyx. Spain.

callicomum: *Goniolimon callicomum.*

carolinianum (Walt.) Britt. [*L. brasiliense* (A. Gray) Small; *Statice brasiliensis* A. Gray, not Boiss.; *S. caroliniana* Walt.]. Per.; lvs. basal, spatulate to elliptic or obovate-elliptic, to 7 in. long; fl. scapes to 24 in., erect, infl. paniculate; calyx to ¼ in. long, glabrous or nearly so, teeth between calyx lobes about half as long as lobes, corolla lavender. N.C. to Fla.

caspium: *L. bellidifolium.*

cosyrense (Guss.) O. Kuntze [*Statice cosyrensis* Guss.]. Low per., glabrous, woody at base; lvs. in basal tufts, linear-spatulate, to 1¼ in. long; fl. scapes to 6 in., slender, cylindrical, infl. dichotomously branched, spikelets mostly 1-fld. S. Eur.

delicatulum (Girard) O. Kuntze [*Statice delicatula* Girard]. Per.; lvs. basal, elliptic to elliptic-lanceolate, to 4 in. long, with 2 pairs of lateral veins; infl. dichotomously branched, open, spikelets 2–3-fld.; calyx tubular, to ½ in. long, lobes short. N. Afr.

Dregeanum (K. Presl) O. Kuntze [*L. tetragonum* Hort., not (Thunb.) Bullock; *Statice Dregeana* K. Presl; *S. tetragona* in the sense of Drège, not Thunb.]. Per., tufted, becoming woody, with bases of old scapes sometimes persisting; lvs. mostly linear-spatulate, to 1½ in. long, tapered to base, clasping; fl. scapes erect, to 10 in., somewhat scabrous with scattered minute raised pits, spikelets 3–8-fld; fls. opening successively, pedicelled, calyx tubular, ⅛ in. long, with few hairs, lobes short, corolla pink, longer than calyx. Arid parts of Cape region of S. Afr.

dumosum: a listed name of no botanical standing.

gangitanum: a listed name of no botanical standing.

globosum: a listed name of no botanical standing.

globulariifolium: *L. ramosissimum.*

Gmelinii (Willd.) O. Kuntze [Statice Gmelinii Willd.]. Per.; lvs. in basal rosettes, ovate to obovate, to 5 in. long, tapered to short petiole; fl. scapes to 2 ft., branched, spikelets mostly 2–3-fld.; calyx tubular, to ¼ in. long, pubescent, lobes short, corolla blue. E. Eur., Siberia.

Gougetianum (Girard) O. Kuntze [*Statice Gougetiana* Girard]. Per., mostly glabrous; lvs. in basal rosettes, obovate to spatulate, to 2 in. long, tapering to base, margins revolute; fl. scapes to 10 in., infl. panicled, spikelets 2–3-fld., continuous with and somewhat over-lapping

adjacent ones; calyx tubular, reddish beneath, white above, corolla lavender. Algeria.

incanum: *Goniolimon callicomum.*

insigne (Coss.) O. Kuntze. Per. herb; lvs. all basal, obovate, small, tapered to long petiole; infl. dichotomously panicled; corolla rich rose. Spain. Closely related to *L. caesium,* but of more robust habit, and with sts. and sterile brs. somewhat thicker, infl. smaller, narrower, spikelets fewer, larger, usually 2-fld., and corolla larger.

latifolium (Sm.) O. Kuntze [*Statice latifolia* Sm.]. Per., with woody base, stellate-hairy; lvs. all basal, few, oblong-elliptic, to 10 in. long, narrowed to petiole about as long as blade; fl. scapes to 2 ft., very much branched, infl. strongly spreading to almost spherical, spikelets 1–2-fld.; calyx ⅛ in. long, lobes about half as long as tube, white, corolla blue-violet. Rumania, Bulgaria, s. Russia. Distinguished by its stellate hairs.

macrophyllum (Brouss.) O. Kuntze [*Statice macrophylla* Brouss.]. Subshrub, to 3–4 ft.; lvs. basal, obovate, to 12 in. long, narrowed to short, winged petiole; fl. scapes glabrous, infl. paniculed, brs. broadly winged; calyx funnelform, limb corollalike, to ½ in. across, blue or purple, corolla white or yellow-white. Canary Is.

minimum: a listed name of no botanical standing.

minutum (L.) O. Kuntze [*Statice minuta* L.]. Per., with woody rhizome; lvs. closely tufted, basal, linear, to 1 in. long, margins recurved; fl. scapes to 6 in., dichotomously branched, sometimes zigzag, infl. with many sterile brs. in lower ⅓, spikelets 2–3-fld.; calyx tubular, white, corolla violet. Medit. region. Useful in the rock garden.

Mouretii (Pit.) Maire [*Statice Mouretii* Pit.]. Per., with woody base; lvs. basal, oblanceolate, to 8 in. long, irregularly lobed; fl. scapes to 2 ½ ft., brs. winged, infl. a 1-sided spike; calyx tube green, lobes purplish, corolla white. Morocco.

otolepis (Schrenk) O. Kuntze [*Statice otolepis* Schrenk]. Per.; basal lvs. few, obovate-spatulate, to 3 in. long, gradually tapering to short, flat petiole, mostly dying off by flowering time, st. lvs. sessile to clasping, suborbicular, ½–1¼ in. long, mostly on lower st. nodes; fl. scapes mostly many, infl. paniculate, with many sterile brs., spikelets 1–2-fld., densely clustered in short, terminal spikes; calyx narrowly funnelform, ⅛ in. long, white, petals blue. Iran, Soviet cent. Asia. Characterized by its many fertile and sterile brs. and small fls. Has been erroneously known in Calif. as *L. perfoliatum* (Karel.) O. Kuntze, a synonym of *L. reniforme* (Girard) Linchevskii.

Perezii (Stapf) F. T. Hubb. [*Statice Perezii* Stapf]. Subshrub, to 2 ft.; lvs. basal, broadly ovate to triangular, to 12 in. long, petiole about as long as blade; fl. scapes much-branched, infl. paniculate, spikelets 2-fld.; calyx funnelform, tube pubescent, limb corollalike, blue, corolla white. Canary Is.

perfoliatum: see *L. otolepis.*

peregrinum (Bergius) R. A. Dyer [*L. roseum* (Sm.) O. Kuntze; *Statice peregrina* Bergius; *S. rosea* Sm.; *S. rhytidophylla* Hook. may also be a synonym]. Shrub, to 3 ft., brs. leafy, covered below by persistent lf. bases; lvs. obovate, to 3 in. long, tapering to a clasping base, scabrous on 1 or both surfaces with pitted glands; fl. scapes scabrous, infl. dichotomously branched, spikelets 1-fld., few to many, close-set in spikes; calyx to ½ in. long, funnelform, limb 5-ribbed, pink, corolla pink, longer than calyx. S. Afr.

peticulum: a listed name of no botanical standing.

Preauxii (Webb) O. Kuntze [*Statice Preauxii* Webb]. Subshrub, to 2 ft.; lvs. orbicular-triangular, to 9 in. long, petiole longer than blade; fl. scapes much-branched, brs. flattened but not winged, spikes 1-sided; calyx funnelform, lavender, corolla white. Canary Is.

puberulum (Webb) O. Kuntze [*Statice puberula* Webb]. Subshrub, puberulous to white-pilose; lvs. basal, obovate, to 1 in. long, stellate-pubescent, tapered to narrowly winged petiole; fl. scapes to 10 in., infl. paniculate, brs. more or less angled; calyx narrow-funnelform, purple, corolla white, longer than calyx. Canary Is.

pulchellum: a listed name of no botanical standing.

ramosissimum (Poir.) Maire [*L. globulariifolium* (Desf.) O. Kuntze; *Statice globulariifolia* Desf.; *S. ramosissima* Poir.]. Glabrous per., woody at base; lvs. in rosettes, obovate to spatulate, to 3 in. long, glaucous, dotted, with limy deposits; fl. scapes to 20 in., infl. paniculate, spikelets 2-fld.; calyx to ¼ in. long, tubular, lobes short, corolla pale violet. Algeria.

reticulatum: *L. bellidifolium.*

roseum: *L. peregrinum.*

Sieberi (Boiss.) O. Kuntze [*Statice Sieberi* Boiss.]. Per.; basal lvs. obovate, to 2 in. long, narrowed to petiole as long or longer than blade; infl. dichotomously paniculate, lower brs. mostly sterile, spikelets 1–2-fld., erect, scattered on 1-sided branchlets; calyx tubular, to ¼ in. long, appressed-pilose beneath, corolla longer than calyx. S. Eur.

sinense (Girard) O. Kuntze [*Statice sinensis* Girard]. Glabrous per.; lvs. basal, obovate, to 2 in. long, gradually narrowed to cuneate base; fl. scapes to 10 in., infl. paniculate, brs. angled, spikelets 2-fld.; calyx narrow, funnelform, pinkish-white, lobes irregular, short, corolla yellow, longer than calyx. China.

sinuatum (L.) Mill. [*Statice sinuata* L.]. Bien. or per., rough-hairy throughout; lvs. all basal, lyrate-pinnatifid, mostly 4 in. long; infl. corymbose-paniculate, brs. prominently winged, spikelets 3–4-fld.; calyx funnelform, to ½ in. long, tube minutely hairy, lobes blue-violet, corolla white, longer than calyx. Medit. region to Asia Minor.

spathulatum (Desf.) O. Kuntze [*Statice spathulata* Desf.]. Per.; lvs. all basal, spatulate, to 1½ in. long, glaucous, narrowed to short petiole; fl. scapes to 10 in., infl. dichotomously paniculate; fls. in 2 rows on upper side of branchlets, calyx tubular, to 5/16 in. long, white, lobes obtuse, corolla purple, longer than calyx. Medit. region.

speciosum: *Goniolimon speciosum.*

spicatum: *Psylliostachys spicata.*

Suworowii: *Psylliostachys Suworowii.*

tataricum: *Goniolimon tataricum.*

tetragonum: see *L. Dregeanum.*

Thouinii (Viv.) O. Kuntze [*Statice Thouinii* Viv.]. Ann., glabrous, glaucous, to 18 in.; lvs. in basal rosette, oblong-oblanceolate, to 2 in. long, coarsely pinnatifid, tapering to short petiole; infl. dichotomously paniculate, brs. winged; calyx white, funnelform, 5-lobed, corolla yellow, shorter than calyx. Medit. region.

transwallianum (Pugsl.) Pugsl. Per.; lvs. oblanceolate or linear-oblong, to 2 in. long, gradually narrowed to petiole; fl. scapes mostly to 6 in., rarely 12 in., branched from base, spikelets close-set, overlapping with those adjacent; calyx teeth deeply triangular, corolla violet-blue. Brit. Isles.

virgatum (Willd.) O. Kuntze [*Statice virgata* Willd.]. Per.; lvs. in basal rosettes, oblanceolate to spatulate, to 1¼ in. long; fl. scapes to 12 in., infl. paniculate, sterile brs. many in lower ⅔ of infl., spikelets 2–3-fld.; calyx tubular, corolla violet. Medit. region. Related to *L. minutum*, but lvs. broader, larger, flat.

vulgare Mill. [*Statice Limonium* L.]. Per.; lvs. in basal rosettes, oblong-lanceolate, to 6 or rarely 10 in. long, strongly pinnately veined, narrowed to long, winged petiole; fl. scapes to 12 in., rarely 18 in., infl. corymbosely branched, usually lacking sterile brs., spikelets 1–3-fld., closely imbricate in 1-sided, spreading spikes; calyx pale purple, somewhat flared at apex, hairy at base, with 5 acute teeth, corolla blue-purple. W. Eur., N. Afr.

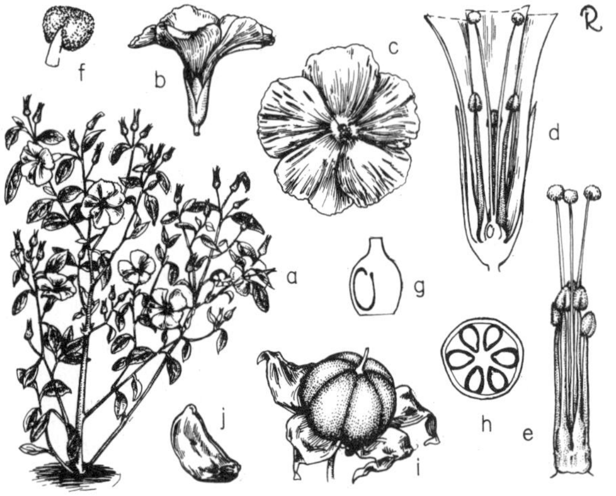

LINACEAE. *Reinwardtia indica:* **a,** flowering plant, × ⅛; **b,** flower, side view, × ½; **c,** flower, face view, × ½; **d,** flower, vertical section (apices of petals cut away), × 1½; **e,** stamens surrounding pistil, × 2; **f,** stigma, × 5; **g,** ovary, vertical section, × 5; **h,** ovary, cross section, × 8; **i,** capsule, × 1½; **j,** seed, × 2.

LINACEAE S. F. Gray. FLAX FAMILY. Dicot.; about 14 genera and 275 spp. of ann. or per. herbs., or sometimes shrubs, of cosmopolitan distribution, but chiefly of temp. regions; lvs. usually alt., rarely opp. or whorled, simple, entire; fls. mostly in cymes, sometimes corymbose, racemose, or panicled, bisexual, regular, sepals 4 or 5, petals 4 or 5, falling early, often clawed, stamens 5, united at the base, alternating with staminodes, pistil 1, ovary superior, usually 5-carpelled, often 10-celled, with axile placentation; fr. a septicidal caps., rarely a drupe. *Linum* and *Reinwardtia* are cult. as ornamentals in the open or under glass, and *L. usitatissimum* for its fiber and oil.

LINANTHUS Benth. *Polemoniaceae.* About 35 spp. of erect or spreading, mostly ann. or rarely per. herbs, native chiefly to w. N. Amer., also Chile; lvs. opp., palmately parted into 3–11 linear segms., rarely linear-filiform and simple; fls. blue, white, or yellow, in open cymes or congested in heads, calyx 5-parted, corolla campanulate to funnelform or salverform, 5-lobed, stamens 5, equally inserted; fr. a 3-celled caps. Differs from *Gilia* in having lvs. opp. and palmately parted.

Of easy cultivation; seeds are sown where plants are to grow, in sunny open places.

androsaceus (Benth.) Greene [*Gilia androsacea* (Benth.) Steud.]. Ann., to 1 ft., sts. simple or much-branched; lvs. 5–9-parted; fls. white, pink, rose, lilac, or yellow, in dense heads, corolla salverform, tube 1½–3 times as long as the calyx. Calif. Subsp. **luteus** (Benth.) H. L. Mason [*Gilia lutea* (Benth.) Steud.]. Corolla limb subfiliform, styles scarcely exserted. Subsp. **micranthus** (Steud. ex Benth.) H. L. Mason [*Gilia micrantha* Steud. ex Benth.]. Corolla limb subfiliform, style long-exserted.

aureus (Nutt.) Greene [*Gilia aurea* Nutt.]. Glabrous, hairy, or glandular ann., to 8 in.; lvs. 3-cleft; fls. yellow, in cymes, corolla often with purple spot in throat, filaments glabrous. S. Calif. and Baja Calif.

dianthiflorus (Benth.) Greene [*Gilia dianthoides* Endl.]. GROUND PINK. Tufted ann., to 6 in.; lvs. simple, filiform, entire; fls. lilac or pink, varying to white, to ¾ in. long, solitary or in few-fld. leafy cymes, corolla lobes toothed. S. Calif. and Baja Calif.

dichotomus Benth. [*Gilia dichotoma* (Benth.) Benth.]. EVENING-SNOW. Ann., to 1 ft., usually glabrous and somewhat glaucous; lvs. 3–5-parted or rarely simple; fls. in cymes, opening in evening, corolla white or with a brown or purple throat, to nearly 1¼ in. long. Calif., Nev., Ariz.

floribundus: *L. Nuttallii* subsp.

grandiflorus (Benth.) Greene [*Gilia densiflora* (Benth.) Benth.]. Erect ann., to 2 ft.; lvs. 5–11-cleft; fls. white to pale lilac, to 1 in. long, in dense heads, corolla funnelform, tube 1–2 times the calyx. Calif.

liniflorus (Benth.) Greene [*Gilia liniflora* Benth.]. Erect ann., to 1½ ft.; lvs. 3–9-cleft; fls. white, pale pink or blue, in cymose panicle, filaments hairy at base. Calif.

Nuttallii (A. Gray) Greene ex Milliken [*Gilia Nuttallii* A. Gray; *Leptodactylon Nuttallii* (A. Gray) Rydb.]. Erect per., from a woody base, to 1 ft.; lvs. 5–9-cleft; fls. white to cream-yellow, usually sessile or almost sessile, in headlike cymes. E. Wash. to Calif., e. to Rocky Mts. Subsp. **floribundus** (A. Gray) Munz [*L. floribundus* (A. Gray) Greene; *Gilia floribunda* A. Gray]. Lvs. 3-5-cleft; fls. short- to long-pedicelled. Calif. to Colo., s. to adjacent Mex.

LINARIA Mill. TOADFLAX, SPURRED SNAPDRAGON. *Scrophulariaceae.* Between 75 and 100 spp. of ann. and per. herbs of temp. Eur., Asia, N. Amer., but mainly of the Medit. region; lvs. opp., whorled, or the upper alt., entire, toothed, or lobed; fls. yellow, blue, purple, or violet, in terminal racemes, calyx 5-parted, corolla 2-lipped, corolla tube long-spurred at base, a palate often nearly closing the throat, stamens 4; fr. a caps.

The linarias are of easy culture. The annuals are propagated by seeds; the perennials usually by division, although seeds sown one year should produce flowering plants the following year.

aequitriloba: *Cymbalaria aequitriloba.*

aeruginea (Gouan) Cav. Glaucous per., glabrous except for glandular-pubescent infl., sts. decumbent or ascending; lvs. linear, to 1¼ in. long, lower lvs. in whorls, upper lvs. alt.; corolla to 1⅛ in. long, yellow with purple palate to nearly entirely purple, yellow, violet, or whitish-cream-colored, spur to ½ in. long; seeds winged. Spain, Portugal, Balearic Is. Var. **nevadensis** (Boiss.) Valdés [*L. nevadensis* (Boiss.) Boiss. & Reut.]. Small; infl. 2–30-fld., dense; corolla yellow, spur shorter than lower lip. Mts. of Spain and Portugal.

alpina (L.) Mill. Tufted, glaucous, glabrous per., to 6 in.; lvs. linear or lanceolate, sessile; corolla blue or violet, with orange palate, spur as long as corolla. Alps. Cv. **'Rosea'**. Fls. rose, with orange-yellow palate. Cv. **'Unicolor'** is listed.

amethystea (Lam.) Hoffmanns. & Link [*L. Broussonnetii* (Poir.) Chav.]. Glabrous to viscid-pubescent ann., to 14 in., sts. ascending; lvs.

linear to oblanceolate, to ¾ in. long, lower lvs. in whorls of 4, upper lvs. alt.; racemes mostly 2–5-fld., rarely to 10-fld.; corolla bluish-violet, yellow, white, or cream-colored, spotted with purple, to 1 in. long, spur to ⅝ in. long; seeds winged, wing papillose. Spain and Portugal.

angustifolia: *L. angustissima.*

angustissima (Loisel.) Borb. [*L. angustifolia* Rchb.; *L. italica* Trevir.]. Erect, glabrous per., to 2 ft.; lvs. linear-lanceolate; corolla yellow, with orange palate, spur slightly shorter than corolla; seeds winged. S. and e.- cent. Eur.

anticaria Boiss. & Reut. Much-branched per., to 1 ft., with ascending sts.; lvs. whorled, elliptic-lanceolate; corolla white, with blue throat, spur lilac, shorter than corolla. S. Spain. Var. **cuarjanensis** is listed.

azurea: a listed name.

bipartita (Venten.) Willd. CLOVEN-LIP T. Glabrous ann., to 1 ft.; lvs. linear, 1–2 in. long; fls. violet-purple, with orange palate, upper lip deeply 2-parted, spur curved, slightly shorter than corolla. Portugal and N. Afr.

Broussonnetii: *L. amethystea.*

caesia (Lag.) DC. ex Chav. Glabrous per., to 1 ft., sts. prostrate to ascending; lvs. linear, to ½ in. long; corolla 1 in. long, yellow, with orange-yellow, bearded palate, spur straight, about as long as corolla. Portugal.

canadensis (L.) Dum.-Cours. OLD-FIELD T. Ann. or bien., to 2½ ft., fl. sts. erect, basal offshoots trailing; lvs. linear to oblong; corolla ¼ in. long, blue or violet-blue, with white palate, spur filiform, curved, as long as corolla. N. Amer.

Cymbalaria: *Cymbalaria muralis.*

dalmatica: *L. genistifolia* subsp. *dalmatica.*

excelsior: *L. maroccana* cv.

faucicola Levier & Leresche. Glabrous ann., to 6 in. and more; lvs. lanceolate, lower lvs. in whorls of 4, upper lvs. opp. or alt.; corolla to ¾ in. long, violet with paler throat, and blue-violet, hairy palate. N. Spain.

genistifolia (L.) Mill. Glabrous per., to 3 ft., sts. erect, branched; lvs. linear to ovate, to 1⅜ in. long, more or less clasping at base; raceme to 8 in., bracts about as long as pedicels; corolla to 2 in. long, yellow, with orange-bearded palate, spur straight, to 1 in. long; seeds not winged. Italy to Russia. Subsp. **dalmatica** (L.) Maire & Petitm. [*L. dalmatica* (L.) Mill.; *L. Jattae* Palanza; *L. macedonica* Griseb.]. Lvs. mostly less than 4 times as long as wide; corolla ¾–2 in. long. Subsp. **genistifolia.** The typical subsp.; lvs. usually 4 times as long as wide; corolla to ⅞ in. long; probably not cult. in U.S.

glareosa: *Chaenorrhinum glareosum.*

hepaticifolia: *Cymbalaria hepaticifolia.*

italica: *L. angustissima.*

Jattae: *L. genistifolia* subsp. *dalmatica.*

macedonica: *L. genistifolia* subsp. *dalmatica.*

maroccana Hook.f. Erect ann., to 1½ ft., glabrous in lower part, viscid-pubescent above; lvs. narrowly linear; corolla bright violet-purple, with small yellow patch on palate, spur pointed, often 1½ times as long as corolla. Morocco; naturalized in ne. U.S. Cv. **'Excelsior'.** Perhaps of mixed origin; fls. varying from pink to dark blue.

minor: *Chaenorrhinum minus.*

monspessulana: *L. repens.*

nevadensis: *L. aeruginea* var.

origanifolia: *Chaenorrhinum origanifolium.*

pallida: *Cymbalaria pallida.*

pilosa: *Cymbalaria pilosa.*

purpurea (L.) Mill. Glabrous, glaucous per., to 3 ft.; lvs. linear or linear-lanceolate, lower lvs. whorled; corolla $^5/_{16}$ in. long, bright purple, with white-bearded palate, spur incurved, more than half as long as corolla. S. Eur.

repens (L.) Mill. [*L. monspessulana* (L.) Mill.]. STRIPED T. Glabrous, glaucous per., to 2 ft., erect or decumbent at base, with creeping rhizomes; lvs. linear, mostly in whorls of 4 at base, alt. above; fls. fragrant, corolla less than ½ in. long, white with purplish veins and orange palate. Eur.; naturalized in ne. U.S. and Canada. Cv. **'Alba'.** Fls. white.

reticulata (Sm.) Desf. PURPLE-NET T. Glaucous ann., to 4 ft.; lvs. linear, lower lvs. whorled, upper lvs. alt.; corolla purple, netted-veined, with orange or yellow palate, spur as long as corolla. Portugal and N. Afr. Cv. **'Aureo-purpurea'.** Deeper in color.

saxatilis (L.) Chaz. Viscid-pubescent per., to 10 in., sts. ascending; lvs. lanceolate to linear, lower lvs. whorled; corolla yellow, spur slightly incurved, shorter than corolla. Spain and Portugal.

supina (L.) Chaz. Pubescent per., to 9 in., sts. decumbent; lvs. whorled, linear; corolla nearly 1 in. long, pale yellow, spur about as long as corolla. Eur.; naturalized sparingly in e. U.S.

triornithophora (L.) Willd. THREE-BIRDS-FLYING. Erect, glabrous, glaucous per., to 4 ft.; lvs. whorled, ovate-lanceolate; corolla 1½ in. long, pale lavender, striped with dark lavender or lavender-purple, with yellow palate, spur longer than corolla. Spain and Portugal.

tristis (L.) Mill. DULL-COLORED LINARIA, SAD-COLORED L. Per., to 1 ft.; lvs. linear-oblong, lower lvs. whorled; corolla yellow, with brown palate, spur curved, shorter than corolla. Canary Is., N. Afr., s. Spain.

ventricosa Coss. & Bal. Glaucous, glabrous per., to 3½ ft.; lvs. alt., lanceolate-attenuate; corolla to ¾ in. long, pale yellow, with reddish veins, with hairy palate, tube broadly swollen, spur half as long as corolla. Sw. Morocco.

villosa: *Chaenorrhinum villosum.*

vulgaris Mill. COMMON T., BUTTER-AND-EGGS, WILD SNAPDRAGON. Erect per., to 3 ft.; lvs. linear or linear-lanceolate; corolla 1¼ in. long, yellow, with orange-bearded palate, spur about as long as corolla. Eur. and Asia; naturalized in N. Amer.

LINDELOFIA Lehm. *Boraginaceae.* About 14 spp. of herbaceous per. of N. Afr., w. and cent. Asia; plants hairy; lvs. simple, alt., basal and cauline; fls. yellow, blue, or purple, in racemose or paniculate scorpioid cymes, calyx deeply 5-lobed, corolla 5-lobed, with scales in the throat, stamens 5; fr. of 4 spiny nutlets.

anchusoides: *Adelocaryum anchusoides.*

longiflora (Benth.) Baill. [*L. spectabilis* Lehm.]. Per., to 2 ft., with leafy sts.; lvs. lanceolate to oblong-lanceolate, st. lvs. sessile; fls. deep blue, ⅝ in. long. Himalayas. Thrives in any soil, but requires a sheltered position and winter protection in the North. Prop. by division and seeds.

spectabilis: *L. longiflora.*

LINDENBERGIA Lehm. ex Link & Otto. *Scrophulariaceae.* About 20 spp. of ann. or per. herbs or subshrubs, native from trop. Afr. to the Himalayas and se. Asia, sts. decumbent to erect; lvs. simple, opp., or the upper alt.; fls. yellow, purple, or red, in spikes, or racemes, or axillary, calyx 5-lobed, corolla 2-lipped, upper lip notched or 2-lobed, lower lip 3-lobed, throat with 2 large swellings, stamens 4; fr. a loculicidal caps.

grandiflora Benth. Soft-hairy per., to 1½ ft. or more, sts. flexuous, nearly climbing; lvs. ovate, 2–8 in. long, toothed, petioled; fls. in loose, leafy racemes, corolla to 1 in. long, yellow, with a red-spotted palate. Himalayas.

LINDERA Thunb. [*Benzoin* Schaeff.]. *Lauraceae.* About 100 spp. of aromatic trees and shrubs, native primarily to temp. and trop. regions of s. and e. Asia, 2 in e. N. Amer.; lvs. deciduous or sometimes evergreen, alt.; infl. axillary, umbellate, with involucre at base; fls. small, yellow, unisexual, perianth segms. 6, deciduous or sometimes persistent, male fls. with 9 stamens, the inner 3 with 2 glands, staminodes absent, female fls. with many staminodes, ovary globose; fr. a 1-seeded berry seated in a usually very shallow cupule.

Propagated by seeds sown as soon as ripe, by layers, and by cuttings of green wood under glass.

aestivalis: *L. Benzoin.*

Benzoin (L.) Blume [*L. aestivalis* Blume; *Benzoin aestivale* Nees]. SPICEBUSH, BENJAMIN BUSH. Deciduous shrub, 6–15 ft., brs. and buds glabrous; lvs. oblong-obovate, to 5 in. long, tapering at base; fls. greenish-yellow, opening before the lvs.; fr. ellipsoid, scarlet (or yellow in one form), to ½ in. in diam., showy. Damp woods, e. N. Amer. from s. Me. and Ont. to Fla. and Tex.

melissifolia (Walt.) Blume [*Benzoin melissifolium* (Walt.) Nees]. JOVE'S FRUIT. Deciduous shrub, 1–6 ft., brs. and buds pubescent; lvs. ovate-elliptic or oblong, to 6 in. long, rounded to cordate at base, minutely pilose; fr. ellipsoid, red. Wet places, very local, N.C. and s. Mo., s. to Fla. and La.

obtusiloba Blume [*Benzoin obtusilobum* (Blume) O. Kuntze]. Deciduous shrub or tree, to 30 ft.; lvs. broad-ovate, to 5 in. long, usually 3-lobed, 3-nerved from base; fls. yellow, opening before the lvs.; fr. globose, red, about $^5/_{16}$ in. in diam. Mts., China, Korea, Japan.

praecox: *Parabenzoin praecox.*

triloba: *Parabenzoin trilobum.*

umbellata Thunb. Erect, deciduous shrub, to 16 ft.; lvs. narrowly oblong to ovate-oblong, to 4 in. long, acute, cuneate, pubescent on midrib and glaucous beneath, with 4–6 pairs of lateral veins; infl. pubescent; fls. appearing with lvs.; fr. subglobose, black, about ¼ in. in diam. Japan, China.

LINDHEIMERA A. Gray & Engelm. STAR DAISY. *Compositae* (Helianthus Tribe). Two ann. herbs of Mex. and Tex.; lower st. lvs. alt., petioled to sessile, upper lvs. opp., bractlike; fl. heads radiate, peduncled, corymbose, with 2 rows of unlike, herbaceous involucral bracts; disc fls. several, bisexual but sterile; ray fls. 4 or 5, female, fertile; ray achenes compressed, winged, each attached to an involucral bract and 2 receptacular scales, pappus of 2 awns.

texana A. Gray & Engelm. Erect, hispid ann., to 2 ft., branching above; lower lvs. oblanceolate, coarsely lobed, upper lvs. ovate-lanceolate, entire; heads to 1½ in. across; fls. yellow. W. Tex.

LINDLEYELLA: *BIFRENARIA.*

LINDMANIA Mez. *Bromeliaceae.* Not cult. L. **penduliflora:** *Fosterella penduliflora.*

LINNAEA L. TWINFLOWER. *Caprifoliaceae.* One circumboreal sp., a trailing evergreen subshrub; lvs. opp., simple, roundish; fls. nodding, campanulate, paired on slender terminal peduncles, calyx and corolla 5-lobed, stamens 4, ovary inferior, 3-celled, but only one fertile; fr. a 1-seeded achene.

Suitable for the wild garden, where it thrives in moist peaty or woodsy soil. Propagated by division and cuttings under glass.

americana: *L. borealis* var.

borealis L. Lvs. crenate, to 1 in. long; fls. rose or white, to ⁵⁄₁₆ in. long, fragrant; fr. yellow, ⅛ in. long. Circumboreal. Zone 2. Var. **americana** (J. Forbes) Rehd. [*L. americana* J. Forbes]. Differs in having fls. more tubular, to ½ in. long. N. Amer. Var. **longiflora** Torr. Differs in having lvs. slightly larger, corolla longer, the tube longer than the calyx. B.C., to n. Calif.

LINOSPADIX H. Wendl. [*Bacularia* F. J. Muell. ex Hook.f.]. *Palmae.* Perhaps 12 spp. of small, solitary or mostly clustered, unarmed, monoecious palms without a crownshaft, native in trop. e. Australia and New Guinea; lvs. pinnate or 2-cleft at apex only and pinnately ribbed, pinnae 2-toothed at apex; infl. solitary among lvs., spicate, bearing 2 thin bracts, the upper cylindrical, inserted at apex of elongate peduncle, the lower short; fls. in triads (2 male and 1 female) sunken in pits, male fls. with sepals imbricate, petals valvate, stamens 6–15, filaments erect, pistillode minute, female fls. with sepals and petals imbricate, ovary 1-celled; fr. small, red, globose to fusiform, with apical stigmatic residue, endocarp not operculate, seed with homogeneous endosperm and basal embryo.

Small ornamental palms sometimes grown in the tropics and subtropics and especially suitable as pot or tub plants for indoor planting. Warmer parts of Zone 10. For culture see *Palms.*

minor (W. Hill) F. J. Muell. ex Burret [*Bacularia minor* (W. Hill) F. J. Muell. ex F. M. Bailey]. Sts. clustered, to 5 ft.; lvs. to 3½ ft. long, pinnae 12–14; male fls. ⅛ in. long, stamens 12; fr. cylindrical, ⅝ in. long. Queensland.

monostachya (Mart.) H. Wendl. [*Bacularia monostachya* (Mart.) F. J. Muell. ex Hook.f.]. WALKING-STICK PALM. St. solitary, to 12 ft.; lvs. to 4 ft. long, irregularly pinnate; male fls. to ⁵⁄₁₆ in. long, stamens about 10; fr. ovoid or globose, ½ in. long. E. Australia.

LINUM L. [*Cathartolinum* Rchb.]. FLAX. *Linaceae.* About 200 spp. of ann. or per. herbs or subshrubs, native mostly to temp. or subtrop. regions of all continents, but chiefly to the N. Hemisphere; lvs. simple, usually alt., narrow, entire; fls. red, yellow, blue, or white, in terminal or axillary racemes, corymbs, cymes, or panicles, sepals 5, petals 5, falling early, stamens 5, united at the base, pistil 1, styles 5; fr. a 5- or 10-celled caps.

Linum usitatissimum furnishes fiber (flax) and linseed oil; the other species are grown for summer bloom. They have simple cultural requirements. The annuals may be grown from seeds sown where the plants are to stand; the perennials are propagated by seeds, division, or cutting.

africanum L. Shrubby per., to 3 ft.; lvs. opp., except the uppermost, sessile, narrowly lanceolate, to ⅝ in. long, acute; fls. yellow, in loose or dense, forking corymbs. S. Afr.

album Kotschy ex Boiss. Glabrous, glaucous, per. herbs, to 1 ft.; lvs. sessile, elliptic-oblanceolate, to ¾ in. long, becoming narrower in the infl.; fls. white, in few-fld., loose cymes. Iran.

alpinum: *L. perenne* subsp. Subsp. **julicum:** *L. perenne* subsp. *alpinum.*

altaicum Ledeb. ex Juz. Glabrous, cespitose per., to 2 ft.; lvs. oblong, to 1¼ in. long, crowded, upper lvs. linear-lanceolate or lanceolate; sepals ovate-lanceolate to ovate, ¼ in. long, scarious-margined, petals violet-blue, to ⅞ in. long. Cent. Asia.

angustifolium: *L. bienne.*

arboreum L. Compact shrub, usually to 1 ft., occasionally higher; lvs. obovate, to 1½ in. long, cuneate, obtuse to mucronate, 1-nerved, glaucous, persistent; fls. clear yellow, to 1½ in. across, in erect, few-fld. cymes, sepals narrow-acuminate. E. Medit. region. Not hardy.

austriacum L. Glabrous, erect per., to 2 ft.; lvs. linear, to ⅝ in. long, 1- or obscurely 3-nerved; fls. blue, to ¾ in. across, sepals elliptic, obtuse, rarely mucronate, to ⅓ as long as caps.; caps. to ³⁄₁₆ in. long. S. Eur. Cv. 'Loreyi'. Semidecumbent; fls. lilac, with darker lines. Subsp. **collinum** Nym. [var. *collinum* Boiss.; *L. collinum* Guss.]. Lower than typical subsp., lvs. shorter, caps. ³⁄₁₆–⁵⁄₁₆ in. long. S. Eur., Asia Minor.

bienne Mill. [*L. angustifolium* Huds.]. Glabrous ann. or per., to 2 ft., with several sts. from the base; lvs. linear, to 1 in. long, 1–3-nerved; fls. blue, to ½ in. across, in loose cymes, sepals ovate, more than half as long as caps., acuminate, or the inner apiculate and glandular-ciliate. Medit. region, w. Eur.

bulgaricum: *L. tauricum.*

caeruleum: *L. grandiflorum* cv.

campanulatum L. Glabrous per., to 15 in., woody at base; basal and st. lvs. spatulate to lanceolate, 1-nerved, with narrow transparent margins, minutely glandular on each side at the base; fls. yellow, with orange veins, to 1¼ in. across, in loose cymes, sepals lanceolate-acuminate, white-margined. S. Eur.

capitatum Kit. Per., to 18 in., with stout sts.; lvs. acute to obtuse, with marginal glands toward base, basal lvs. obovate-lanceolate, upper st. lvs. lanceolate; fls. golden-yellow, to 1 in. across, in a many-fld. head, sepals lanceolate-acuminate, glandular-fimbriate. S. Eur. Much of the material offered under this name is *L. flavum.*

collinum: *L. austriacum* subsp.

compactum A. Nels. Pubescent per. herb, to 4 in.; lvs. linear, to ⅜ in. long, 1-nerved; fls. yellow, sepals glandular-ciliate, half as long as petals, styles separate ⅓ their length. E. Wyo. Perhaps not distinct from *L. rigidum.*

dolomiticum Borb. Tufted per. herb, to 6 or 8 in.; basal lvs. linear-oblanceolate, to 1¾ in. long, st. lvs. oblong to lanceolate, to ½ in. long; petals yellow, ¾–1 in. long, twice as long as sepals. Hungary.

flavum L. GOLDEN F. Erect, somewhat woody per., to 2 ft., with stout sts.; lvs. 3–5-nerved, with glands on each side of lf. base, lower lvs. spatulate, obtuse, upper st. lvs. lanceolate, acute; fls. golden-yellow, to 1 in. across, usually 20–50 in a much-branched cyme, sepals lanceolate-acuminate, glandular-ciliate, keeled. Cent. and s. Eur. Cv. 'Compactum'. Listed as a dwarf form. Some material grown as *L. flavum* is *Reinwardtia indica.*

grandiflorum Desf. FLOWERING F. Erect glabrous ann., to 2 ft.; lvs. linear-lanceolate to ovate-lanceolate, to 1¼ in. long, acuminate, remotely ciliate; fls. in shades of red, to 1½ in. across, in a loose panicle, sepals lanceolate-acuminate, to ½ in. long, margins membranous and ciliate. N. Afr. Cvs. include: 'Caeruleum', fls. bluish-purple; 'Coccineum', fls. scarlet; 'Roseum', fls. rose-pink; 'Rubrum', fls. bright red.

hirsutum L. Per., to 2 ft., hirsute except for petals and caps.; lvs. broadly lanceolate, to ⅝ in. long, 3–5-nerved; fls. lavender-blue, with pale yellow or white eye, to ½ in. across, sepals broadly lanceolate, densely hirsute. Cent. Eur. and Medit. region.

hologynum Rchb. Glabrous per., to 2 ft.; lvs. linear or lanceolate, 1-nerved; fls. to 1 in. across, petals blue, 2 or 3 times as long as calyx, styles twisted or united about half their length. Mts., cent Eur.

julicum: *L. perenne* subsp. *alpinum.*

Lewisii: *L. perenne* subsp.

maritimum L. [*L. Muelleri* Moris]. Per., to 2 ft.; lvs. oblanceolate or elliptic to linear-lanceolate, revolute, lower lvs. 3-nerved, upper 1-nerved; fls. ¾ in. across, in loose panicles, sepals elliptic to ovate, glandular-ciliate, petals yellow, more than 4 times as long as calyx. Sardinia.

monogynum G. Forst. Glabrous per., to 2 ft.; lvs. subsessile, linear to lanceolate, to 1 in. long, acute to acuminate; fls. white, to 1 in. across, sepals ovate to lanceolate-ovate, white-margined, as long as caps. New Zeal.

Muelleri: *L. maritimum.*

narbonense L. Glabrous, glaucous per., to 2 ft.; lvs. linear-lanceolate, to ¾ in. long, usually 3-nerved, the uppermost lvs. or bracts with scarious margins; fls. azure-blue with white eye, to 1¾ in. across, in few-fld. cymes, sepals lanceolate-acuminate, white-margined, longer than caps. Medit. region. Distinguished from *L. perenne* in its stouter habit, scarious-margined bracts, and longer sepals and petals.

perenne L. [*L. sibiricum* DC.]. PERENNIAL F. Glabrous per., to 2 ft.; lvs. linear to lanceolate, to 1 in. long, lower part of st. usually leafless or nearly so, upper lvs. 1-nerved, uppermost lvs. and bracts without scarious margins; fls. to 1 in. across, usually in a much-branched panicle, sepals shorter than caps., the inner ones longer than the outer, petals chicory-blue. Eur. Cv. **'Alba'**. Fls. white. Cv. **'Caerulea'**. Fls. clear blue. Subsp. **alpinum** (Jacq.) Ockend. [*L. alpinum* Jacq.; *L. julicum* Hayek; *L. alpinum* subsp. *julicum* (Hayek) Hayek]. Sts. 2–12 in., rarely more; lvs. linear-subulate, to ¾ in. long, usually close together on lower ⅓ of st.; fls. to ¾ in. across, inner and outer sepals of equal length. Mts., Eur. Subsp. **Lewisii** (Pursh) Hult. [*L. Lewisii* Pursh]. PRAIRIE F. Slightly more robust than the typical subsp.; lvs. to 1¼ in. long, sepals and caps. somewhat larger. W. N. Amer. See also *L. narbonense*.

rigidum Pursh. Glabrous per., to 20 in.; brs. rigid, fastigiate, angled; lvs. few, erect, linear, with stipular glands; fls. yellow, to 1¼ in. across, sepals with marginal glands, inner ones shorter than outer. Man. to Alta., s. to Mo., Tex., New Mex.

rubrum: *L. grandiflorum* cv.

salsoloides: *L. suffruticosum* subsp.

sanctum Small. Deep green herb, to 1 ft., brs. angled; lvs. spatulate to oblong, 3-nerved; fls. yellow, about 1 in. long, inner sepals shorter than the outer. Tex.

sibiricum: *L. perenne.*

strictum L. Ann., to 18 in.; lvs. linear-lanceolate, to 1 in. long, strongly revolute; fls. yellow, to nearly ¼ in. across, in tight, compact, headlike clusters, sepals much longer than caps. Cent. Eur. and Medit. region, e. to Iran and Afghanistan.

suffruticosum L. Woody-based per., with many short, sterile shoots, fl. sts. procumbent, 10–20 in. high; lvs. linear, involute, without basal glands; fls. white, with purple veins, 1½–2 in. across, sepals ovate-acuminate, glandular-ciliate, longer than caps. Spain. The typical subsp. is apparently not in cult. Subsp. **salsoloides** (Lam.) Rouy [*L. salsoloides* Lam.]. Less woody at base, sts. 2–10 in.; lvs. narrower, filiform or subulate; fls. to 1½ in. across. Spain to n. Italy. Cv. **'Nanum'**. Of prostrate habit, forming clumps 18 in. across, to 3 in.; lvs. usually longer. None of the forms of this sp. withstand severe cold.

sulcatum Ridd. Erect ann., to 2½ ft., sts. angled; lvs. linear, to nearly 1 in. long, with minute glands on each side of lf. base; fls. yellow, to ½ in. across, sepals lanceolate, glandular-serrate, longer than caps. Man. and Ont., s. to Tex. and Ga.

tauricum Willd. [*L. bulgaricum* Podp.]. Rhizomatous per., to 16 in., with many sterile lf. rosettes; basal and lower st. lvs. narrow-spatulate, acute, 3-nerved, upper st. lvs. lanceolate, narrower, usually 1-nerved; fls. pale yellow, sepals linear-lanceolate, acuminate, ⅓ as long as petals, about twice as long as caps. Se. Eur.

tenuifolium L. Glabrous, shrubby per., to 18 in.; lvs. linear, to ¾ in. long, 1-nerved; fls. to 1 in. across, sepals ovate-lanceolate, acuminate, glandular-ciliate, petals pink-lilac or white, with purple veins or center, very short-acuminate. Cent. Eur. and Medit. region, e. to Iran.

trigynum L., not Roxb. Ann., to 1 ft.; lvs. linear-lanceolate, without basal glands; fls. yellow, sepals short-acuminate, glandular-ciliate, longer than caps. S. Eur. Probably not cult.; material grown under this name may be *Reinwardtia indica.*

usitatissimum L. FLAX. Ann., to 4 ft.; lvs. linear to lanceolate, 3-nerved; fls. blue, sometimes white, to ½ in. across, in terminal, leafy panicles, sepals ovate, half as long as petals, the inner scarious-margined and ciliate, nearly as long as caps. Probably Asia; escaped in much of N. Amer. An ancient cultigen widely grown in temp. regions as a fiber plant, and as a seed crop for linseed oil. See *Flax.*

viscosum L. Glandular-hairy per., to 2 ft.; lvs. oblong-lanceolate, to ⅝ in. long, 3–5-nerved, densely glandular-ciliate; fls. to 1¼ in. across, in corymbs, sepals lanceolate, glandular-ciliate, petals pink with violet lines. S. Eur.

LIPARIS L. Rich. TWAYBLADE. *Orchidaceae*. About 250 spp. of cosmopolitan, terrestrial herbs arising from a corm or pseudobulb; lvs. 1 or more, basal, fleshy or plicate; infl. a terminal, loosely few- to many-fld. raceme; fls. small, petals commonly much narrower than sepals, lip 3-lobed, midlobe entire to emarginate, column curved, dilated toward base. for structure of fl. see *Orchidaceae.*

Sometimes transplanted to the wild garden. For culture see *Orchids.*

elata: *L. nervosa.*

liliifolia (L.) L. Rich. ex Lindl. LARGE T., MAUVE SLEEKWORT, PURPLE SCUTCHEON. Erect, to 9 in., sts. often tinged with purplish-brown; lvs. 2, to 7 in. long; infl. to 7 in. long, few-fld.; fls. to ⅜ in. across, sepals pale greenish-white, petals filiform, madder-purple, lip entire, mauve-purple, tinged with green. Late spring–summer. E. U.S.

Loeselii (L.) L. Rich. BOG T., YELLOW T., LOESEL'S T., FEN ORCHID, OLIVE SCUTCHEON, RUSSET-WITCH. Erect, slender, to 10 in., glabrous; lvs. 2, oblong-elliptic, to 7 in. long; infl. few-fld., to 4 in. long; fls. to ½ in. across, whitish- or yellowish-green. Late spring–late summer. N. Amer., Eurasia.

longipes: *L. viridiflora.*

nervosa (Thunb.) Lindl. [*L. elata* Lindl.]. Erect, to 2 ft., pseudobulbs conical; lvs. 3–5, ovate to elliptic, to 10 in. long, plicate; scape naked, suffused with madder-purple; fls. small, to ¼ in. long, sepals and petals greenish, streaked with madder-purple, lip madder-purple, obcordate to oblong-fan-shaped, emarginate, disc with 2 fleshy tubercles. Pantrop.

viridiflora Lindl. [*L. longipes* Lindl.]. Pseudobulbs orbicular, compressed, to 6 in. long; lvs. 2, apical, to 6 in. long; infl. longer than lvs., pendent, many-fld.; fls. minute, green, lip orange, ovate, without lateral lobes. Late autumn. Sikkim Himalayas, s. India, Ceylon, Java.

LIPPIA L. *Verbenaceae*. Not cult. **L. canescens:** *Phyla nodiflora* var. **L. citriodora:** *Aloysia triphylla.* **L. lanceolata:** *Phyla lanceolata.* **L. nodiflora:** *P. nodiflora.* **L. repens:** *P. nodiflora* var. *rosea.*

LIQUIDAMBAR L. SWEET GUM. *Hamamelidaceae*. About 4 spp. of monoecious, deciduous trees, native to N. Amer. and Asia; lvs. palmately lobed, toothed, somewhat maplelike; fls. unisexual, without petals, male fls. with many stamens, in terminal racemes or panicles, female fls. in globose heads hanging by slender peduncles below male infl. or on separate brs.; fr. head with spiny, persistent styles, pendent.

Liquidambars produce valuable timber and an aromatic balsam, called storax or styrax, important in medicine and perfumery. They are hardy ornamental shade trees, with brilliant autumn coloring, used for street or home plantings. Propagated by seeds which may not germinate until the second year. Thrive best on fertile moist soils.

formosana Hance. FORMOSAN GUM. To 120 ft., shoots often downy when young; lvs. usually 3-lobed, to 6 in. wide, often downy beneath. S. China, Taiwan.

orientalis Mill. ORIENTAL S. G. To 25 ft., young shoots glabrous; lvs. usually 5-lobed, to 3 in. wide, lobes often ⅔ the length of blade, coarsely toothed. Asia Minor. Source of Levant styrax.

sinensis: a listed name of no botanical standing.

Styraciflua L. SWEET GUM, AMERICAN S. G., RED GUM, BILSTED. To 120 ft., brs. becoming corky-winged; lvs. 5- or 7-lobed, to 7 in. wide, lobes finely serrate. Conn. to Fla. and Cent. Amer. Source of Amer. styrax. Clones, such as cv. **'Palo Alto'**, have been selected for especially good autumn foliage color.

LIRIODENDRON L. TULIP TREE. *Magnoliaceae*. Two spp. of deciduous trees, native to China and N. Amer.; lvs. alt., long-petioled, lobed, with broad, truncate or retuse apex; fls. terminal, erect, cup-shaped, solitary; fr. of long narrow carpels congested into a "cone."

Tulip trees do not transplant readily, and should be moved only in spring. They thrive on rich, moist land. Propagated by seeds, stratified and sown in spring, or cultivars by layering and grafting.

chinense (Hemsl.) Sarg. CHINESE T. T. To 50 ft.; lvs. to 6 in. long, with 4 acuminate lobes, glaucescent and papillose beneath; peduncles somewhat curved, fls. to 1½ in. long, petals dull olive-green, with faint splash of yellow at base. Cent. China. Distinguished from *L. Tulipifera* by smaller fls. and different petal colors.

Tulipifera L. TULIP TREE, TULIP POPLAR, WHITEWOOD. To 200 ft., trunk eventually columnar and unbranched below; lvs. to 5 in. long and broad, lobed, pale beneath; fls. greenish-yellow with broad orange band at base, to 2 in. long; fr. brown, to 3 in. long. Mass. to Fla. and Miss. One of the noblest of Amer. trees; the wood known in the trade as poplar or yellow poplar. Cvs. are: **'Aureo-marginatum'**, lvs. margined with yellow; **'Fastigiatum'** [cv. **'Pyramidale'**], narrow pyramidal habit; **'Integrifolium'**, lvs. rounded at base and unlobed.

LIRIOPE Lour. LILYTURF. *Liliaceae*. About 5 spp. of stemless, evergreen, per. herbs, native to Japan, China, and Vietnam; plants tufted or rhizomatous; lvs. grasslike; fls. white or lilac-blue, in axillary fascicles arranged in terminal spikes or racemes, perianth segms. 6, separate, stamens 6, ovary superior; fr. berrylike, black, seeds 1 or 2, fleshy.

Liriopes make good ground cover in both shade and sun, and are hardy in parts of Zone 6. Propagated readily by division.

exiliflora (L. H. Bailey) H. Hume [*L. Muscari* var. *exiliflora* L. H. Bailey]. Rhizomatous, to 1½ ft. high; lvs. dark green, to 1½ ft. long; fls. violet, in an open raceme on a violet rachis and violet-brown scape. Japan, China.

graminifolia (L.) Bak. Rhizomatous, to 8 in. high; lvs. to 16 in. long, serrulate with translucent teeth; fls. pale violet, in an open raceme on a slender, violet-tinted, green scape. China, Vietnam. Probably not in cult.; material grown under this name is probably *L. spicata*. Var. **densiflora:** *L. Muscari.*

grandiflora: a listed name of no botanical standing for *L. Muscari* cv.

japonica: *Ophiopogon japonicus.*

majestica: a listed name of no botanical standing for *L. Muscari* cv.

Muscari (Decne.) L. H. Bailey [*L. Muscari* var. *densiflora* Hort.; *L. graminifolia* var. *densiflora* Bak.]. BIG BLUE L. Tufted, with thick tubers, to 1½ ft. high; lvs. to 2 ft. long and ¾ in. wide, firm; fls. dark violet, in a dense raceme. Japan, China. There are cockscombed and fasciated forms. Var. **exiliflora:** *L. exiliflora.* Cvs. are: 'Grandiflora' [*L. grandiflora* Hort.], fls. light lavender; 'Majestic' [*L. majestica* Hort.], lvs. narrow, infls. fasciated, fls. violet; 'Munroe White' [var. *Monroei* Hort.], shade plant, scape green, fls. pure white; 'Variegata' [*L. variegata* Hort.], young lvs. yellow-striped, becoming completely green with age, fls. dark violet.

spicata Lour. CREEPING L. Rhizomatous, to 10 in. high; lvs. grasslike, to 17 in. long and ¼ in. wide, serrulate with translucent teeth; fls. pale violet to nearly white, with distinct tube, on a violet rachis, scape erect, light violet-brown. China, Vietnam.

variegata: a listed name of no botanical standing for *L Muscari* cv.

LISIANTHUS L. *Gentianaceae.* Perhaps more than 15 spp. of ann. or per. usually branched herbs, in the W. Indies, Mex., Cent. Amer., and n. S. Amer.; lvs. mostly lanceolate or ovate; fls. purple-black or yellow-green, in cymes or corymbs, 5-merous; fr. a caps.

nigrescens Cham. & Schlechtend. To 6 ft., branched; lvs. sessile, oblong-lanceolate, almost united basally; fls. purple-black, 1½–2 in. long. Chiapas (s. Mex.) and Cent. Amer.

Russellianus: *Eustoma grandiflorum.*

LISSOCHILUS R. Br. *Orchidaceae.* About 50 spp. of terrestrial herbs with creeping rhizomes, native to S. Afr.; sts. short, leafy, pseudobulbous; lvs. long, usually narrow, plicate; scapes lateral, long, bearing loose racemes; fls. of medium size or large, lip saccate or spurred at base, column curved-cylindric, footless. Differs from the closely allied genus *Eulophia* in having petals much broader than sepals and of a different color. For structure of fl. see *Orchidaceae.*

For culture see *Orchids.*

Krebsii Rchb.f. Pseudobulbs to 3 in. long, with concentric scars; lvs. to 6, elliptic-lanceolate, to 2 ft. long; racemes to 5 ft. long, 20- to many-fld.; fls. to 1¼ in. across, sepals reddish-brown, mottled with green, petals butter-yellow, lip 3-lobed, saccate between lateral lobes, red-brown inside, yellow outside, midlobe nearly orbicular, folded in middle, yellow, with 2 purple blotches, spur short. Natal.

LISTERA R. Br. TWAYBLADE. *Orchidaceae.* About 30 spp. of terrestrial herbs of boreal and temp. regions of the N. Hemisphere; lvs. 2, opp., sessile; infl. a terminal raceme; fls. greenish or purplish, sepals and petals similar, lip 2-lobed, column slender, curved. For structure of fl. see *Orchidaceae.*

Sometimes planted in the wild garden. For culture see *Orchids.*

convallarioides (Swartz) Nutt. BROAD-LIPPED T., BROAD-LEAVED T. To 16 in.; lvs. ovate to elliptic, to 2½ in. long; racemes to 4½ in. long, loosely many-fld.; fls. small, yellowish-green, lip notched at apex. Early summer–early autumn. Nfld. nw. to Alaska, s. to S.C. and Calif.

cordata (L.) R. Br. [*Ophrys cordata* L.]. HEART-LEAF T. To 10 in.; lvs. ovate-cordate, to 1½ in. long; racemes to 4 in. long, loosely fld.; fls. small, greenish to dark purple, sepals to ⅛ in. long, lip with filiform segms. Spring–early autumn. Circumboreal.

LITCHI Sonn. *Sapindaceae.* Several spp. of polygamous trees, native from s. China and the Philippine Is. to India; lvs.

alt., pinnate; fls. greenish-white or yellowish, in terminal panicles, regular, calyx 4- or 5-lobed, petals 0, stamens usually 8; fr. a tubercled drupe, aril separate from the seed coat.

When well established, the litchi will stand a few degrees of frost. It requires abundant moisture and thrives in deep loamy soil. Trees should be set 30–40 ft. apart. Propagated by seeds, air-layering, and inarching.

chinensis Sonn. [*Nephelium Litchi* Camb.]. LITCHI, LEECHEE, LYCHEE, LICHI. To 40 ft.; lvs. to 9½ in. long, lfts. 2–8, elliptic-oblong to lanceolate, to 8 in. long, acuminate, leathery; infl. to 1 ft. long; fr. bright red, to 1½ in. across, seed single and large with white, fleshy, juicy, edible aril. S. China. Zone 10. Widely grown in the Orient and elsewhere in the tropics and subtropics for the edible fresh or dried fr.; particularly prized in China.

LITHOCARPUS Blume [*Pasania* Ørst.]. *Fagaceae.* About 275 spp. of evergreen, monoecious, oaklike shrubs or trees, native to Asia, 1 to w. N. Amer.; lvs. alt., leathery; fls. unisexual, male fls. in erect catkins, female fls. usually at base of male catkins; fr. a solitary nut, partly or wholly enclosed in a cuplike spineless involucre.

Sometimes grown in the South and in Calif. Propagated by cuttings, layers, or seeds.

chinensis (Abel) A. Camus [*Castanopsis sclerophylla* (Lindl.) Schottky]. To 50 ft., bark dark gray, almost smooth; lvs. elliptic-lanceolate, to 6 in. long, entire or serrate above middle, glabrous and bluish-green above, rusty-brown to yellowish-green and pubescent beneath; nuts conical, to ½ in. long, cup scaly, almost completely enclosing nut. China.

cleistocarpus (Seemen) Rehd. & E. H. Wils. To 40 ft., bark dark gray, shallowly fissured; lvs. elliptic to elliptic-ovate, to 4½ in. long, entire, glabrous, glossy above, glaucescent and reticulate beneath; fr. in compact clusters, cup scaly, almost entirely enclosing nut. China.

corneus (Lour.) Rehd. [*Quercus cornea* Lour.]. Bushy tree, to 25 ft.; lvs. oblong-elliptic, to 4 in. long, toothed above middle, glabrous, shining, and with impressed lateral veins above, pubescent on prominent lateral veins beneath; fr. in clusters, cup scaly, enclosing nut. W. China.

densiflorus (Hook. & Arn.) Rehd. [*Quercus densiflora* Hook. & Arn.]. TANBARK OAK. Tree, 60–80 ft., sometimes 150 ft.; lvs. elliptic to oblong, to 5 in. long, serrate, rusty-tomentose at first, becoming glabrous; frs. 1 or 2, cup shallow, partly enclosing nut. Ore., Calif. Zone 8. A tanbark sp.

echinoides: a listed name of no botanical standing for *L. densiflorus.*

edulis (Mak.) Nakai [*Quercus edulis* Mak.]. Shrub or tree, to 30 ft., twigs glabrous; lvs. narrowly elliptic to oblanceolate, to 6 in. long, entire, glabrous; cup shallow, partly enclosing nut. Japan. Zone 8. Sometimes confused with *L. glaber*, but differs in having twigs and lvs. always glabrous.

fissus (Champ.) A. Camus [*Quercus fissa* Champ.]. To 60 ft.; lvs. obovate or lanceolate, to 8 in. long, coarsely serrate, with 15–20 pairs of veins, glabrous above, silvery-pubescent beneath. Se. Asia.

glaber (Thunb.) Nakai [*L. thalassica* (Hance) Rehd.; *Quercus glabra* Thunb.]. Shrub or tree, to 30 ft., twigs at first pubescent; lvs. elliptic-oblong to lanceolate, to 5 in. long, entire or serrate above middle, gray-pubescent beneath when young. E. China, Japan. Zone 8.

glabrescens: a listed name of no botanical standing.

Hancei (Benth.) Rehd. [*Quercus Hancei* Benth.]. To 80 ft.; lvs. elliptic-ovate, to 4 in. long, glabrous, leathery, pale beneath; cup half enclosing the nut, densely silky-pubescent, the scales united into rings. E. China.

Harlandii (Hance) Rehd. [*Quercus Harlandii* Hance]. To 50 ft.; lvs. elliptic-ovate, to 3 in. long; entire or dentate in upper half, glabrous, leathery, pale beneath; cup enclosing about ¼–½ the nut, the scales thick and overlapping. E. China.

Henryi (Seemen) Rehd. & E. H. Wils. To 50 ft., glabrous except when young; lvs. narrowly oblong, to 10 in. long, entire, becoming glabrous beneath; fr. clustered along a stout spike, cup shallow, partly enclosing the nut. China. Zone 8.

ternaticupula (Hayata) Hayata [*Quercus ternaticupula* Hayata]. Medium-sized tree; lvs. oblong to elliptic, to 5 in. long, with conspicuous, reticulate veins on both surfaces, glabrous, leathery; cup enclosing ½ the nut, the scales united into rings. Taiwan.

LITHODORA Griseb. *Boraginaceae.* Seven spp. of low, hairy shrubs or subshrubs of w. and s. Eur., N. Afr., and Asia Minor; lvs. simple, alt., entire; fls. blue or purple, in small, few-fld. cymes, calyx and corolla 5-lobed, corolla throat without appendages, glabrous within or sometimes with hairs or glands, stamens 5; fr. of 4 nutlets, often only 1 nutlet maturing, nutlets circumscissile above the base, leaving a cup-shaped appendage.

diffusa (Lag.) I. M. Johnst. [*L. prostrata* (Loisel.) Griseb.; *Lithospermum diffusum* Lag.; *Lithospermum prostratum* Loisel.]. Dwarf or prostrate evergreen shrub; lvs. linear-lanceolate; corolla deep blue, striped with reddish-violet, ½ in. long, throat hairy or glandular within, hairy on the outside, filaments of unequal length and attached at different levels in the throat; nutlets striate. S. and w. Eur., Morocco.

oleifolia (Lapeyr.) Griseb. [*Lithospermum oleifolium* Lapeyr.]. Much-branched prostrate subshrub, to 1 ft.; lvs. oblong to elliptic-oblong, densely white-silky on lower surface; corolla blue, to ½ in. long, hairy outside, throat with a few glands inside, stamens all at the same level; nutlets smooth and shiny. Pyrenees.

prostrata: *L. diffusa.*

LITHOPHRAGMA (Nutt.) Torr. & A. Gray. WOODLAND-STAR. *Saxifragaceae.* About 9–10 spp. of simple-stemmed, rather small, delicate, per. herbs with tuberous rhizomes, native to w. N. Amer.; lvs. mostly basal, long-petioled, broadly ovate to orbicular, deeply or shallowly lobed or cleft; fls. small, white or pink, in terminal racemes, calyx tube cup-shaped, partly united to ovary, petals 5, clawed, stamens 10, ovary partly inferior, styles 3, forming short beaks in fr.; fr. a 3-valved caps.

Useful in wild gardens and rock gardens.

affine A. Gray [*Tellima affinis* (A. Gray) A. Gray]. Robust, to 24 in., variously pubescent; basal lvs. orbicular to reniform, 3-lobed, long-petioled; petals white, shallowly 3-lobed at apex. Calif. and s. Ore.

bulbiferum: *L. glabrum.*

glabrum Nutt. [*L. bulbiferum* Rydb.]. Plant slender, to 12 in., sparingly pubescent to nearly glabrous; basal lvs. orbicular, 3-parted, short-petioled, st. lvs. reduced, 3-parted, often with bulbils in the axils; fls. pink or occasionally white, 2–5 in a raceme. B.C. to Calif., e. to Rocky Mts. The fls. are sometimes replaced by bulbils.

parviflorum (Hook.) Torr. & A. Gray [*Tellima parviflora* Hook.]. Slender, to 20 in., densely pubescent to nearly glabrous; basal lvs. orbicular, 3–5-parted, segms. shallowly 3-cleft; petals 3–7-parted. B.C. to Calif., e. to Rocky Mts.

tenellum Nutt. Slender, to 12 in., foliage light green, sparingly pubescent, basal lvs. orbicular, simple, irregularly 3–5-lobed or palmately compound, sometimes appearing almost pinnatifid, st. lvs. 3-parted, appearing pinnatifid; petals pink, occasionally white, palmately 5-parted. B.C. to Calif., e. to Rocky Mts., s. to Ariz. and New Mex.

LITHOPS N. E. Br. LIVING-STONES, STONEFACE, FLOWERING STONES, MIMICRY PLANT. *Aizoaceae.* About 50 spp. of dwarf, per. succulents, native to S. Afr. and S.-W. Afr.; plants essentially stemless, forming clumps, in their native habitat normally buried in the sand with only tips of their lvs. exposed; lvs. resembling stones, opp., paired, united over half their length to form an obconical or top-shaped body (growth) with a transverse fissure between the 2 lvs., apex of each lf. semicircular to lunate, flat to convex or rounded, usually with transparent areas (windows) and with various markings; fls. solitary, arising in fissure, calyx 4–7-lobed, petals many, stamens many, in a column, ovary superior, 4–7-celled, stigmas 4–7, filiform; fr. a 4–7-lobed caps., cell lids absent, expanding keel central, with membranous wings.

These are summer-growing plants capable of withstanding temperature to about 120° F. Cultivate in pots sunk in gravel in full sun in a well-ventilated greenhouse, hot frame, or window ledge, keep moist in summer, but withhold water from early autumn to early spring; in winter should provide maximum illumination with a relatively cool temperature of about 60° F. Propagation by cuttings less easy than by seeds, which give flowering plants in 3–4 years. See also *Succulents.*

alpina: *L. pseudotruncatella.*

Aucampiae L. Bolus. Growths solitary or in clumps, to ½ in. high and 2 in. wide at apex, top-shaped, apex concave, sienna-brown with olive-green windows, fissure to ⅛ in. deep; fls. 1 in. across, petals in 3–4 series, golden-yellow. Bechuanaland, Transvaal. Var. **Koelemanii** (DeBoer) DeBoer & Boom [*L. Koelemanii* DeBoer]. Apex with dark brown lines, dark gray dots and many light gray, translucent dots. Cape Prov.

bella N. E. Br. Growths solitary or in small clumps, to 1 in. high and 1 in. wide at apex, apex slightly convex to flat, brownish-yellow-ocher with green islands; fls. to 1 in. across, fragrant, petals white. S.-W. Afr. Var. **Lericheana** (Dinter & Schwant.) DeBoer & Boom [*L. Lericheana* (Dinter & Schwant.) Dinter & Schwant. ex N. E. Br.]. Growths with darker bands and brownish-yellow islands. S.-W. Afr.

Bromfieldii L. Bolus. Growths forming clumps of 4–6, to ⅝ in. high, top-shaped, apex essentially flat, windows irregular, dark olive-green with many dark red lines and yellow-brown islands within the windows; fls. to 1⅝ in. across, petals golden-yellow. Cape Prov.

Comptonii L. Bolus. Growths solitary or forming a clump, to 1½ in. high and wide, top-shaped, olive-green, window dark green or purple-green, solitary or divided into confluent windows with islands having a rugose, white-dotted surface, outer margin irregularly toothed; fls. to 1 in. across, petals yellow. Cape Prov.

dendritica: *L. pseudotruncatella* var.

Dinteri Schwant. Growths solitary or in small clumps, 1¼ in. high and wide, obconical, sides whitish to pearl-gray, fissure to ¼ in. deep, apex rounded, window transparent brown-green, with a dark yellow border, with few islands and scattered blood-red dots; petals yellow. S.-W. Afr.

divergens L. Bolus. Growths solitary or in small clumps, apex oblique, often rounded, lvs. unequal, diverging in age, sides green, apex with large, transparent, gray-green windows, often appearing cobwebby; petals yellow. Cape Prov.

Dorotheae Nel. Growths in clumps of 5–7, obconical, apex convex to flat, windows large, transparent, with irregularly incised margins and irregularly shaped, buff-colored islands lined and dotted with red; petals yellow. Cape Prov.

Edithae: *L. pseudotruncatella* var.

Erniana Loesch & Tisch. Growths in clumps of 2 or more, to ¾ in., obconical, apex convex, rough, reddish-gray with maroon lines that pale with maturity, windows few, blue-green, opaque; fls. to 1¼ in. across, petals white. S.-W. Afr. Var. **witputzensis** DeBoer. Growths larger, apex flat, fissure glaucous or with paler lines. S.-W. Afr.

farinosa: *L. pseudotruncatella* var. *dendritica.*

floris-alba: a listed name of no botanical standing; growths described as reddish, suffused with brown, and with pencilled markings on apex.

fossulifera: a listed name of no botanical standing.

Framesii: *L. marmorata.*

Fulleri N. E. Br. Growths solitary or forming clumps of 2–6, ⅝–1¼ in. high, obconical, fissure ¼ in. deep, sides dove-gray with a violet cast, apex strongly convex, rough, windows dark green with rust-brown lines and row of dark brown spots around margin; fls. 1 in. across, petals white. Cape Prov.

fulviceps (N. E. Br.) N. E. Br. [*L. Lydiae* Hort.]. Growths solitary or in clumps of 2–4, to 1 in. high, obconical, sides purple, apex nearly flat to slightly convex, light brown to rust-brown, windows reduced to dark green, transparent dots; fls. to 1¼ in. across, petals yellow above, whitish beneath. S.-W. Afr.

gracilidelineata Dinter. Growths solitary or rarely in clumps of 2–3, to ⅝ in. high, top-shaped, sides yellow-gray, fissure to ¼ in. deep, apex truncate, buff to red, with dark brown, branching lines, the surface bumpy; fls. to 1¼ in. across, petals yellow. S.-W. Afr.

Gulielmi: *L. Schwantesii* var. *Triebneri.*

Helmutii L. Bolus. Growths solitary or in clumps of 10–21, top-shaped; lvs. unequal in size, apex obliquely convex, sometimes tapered to a point, windows bright green often spotted or mottled with gray, with irregularly lobed margins; fls. to 1¼ in. across, fragrant, petals golden-yellow. Cape Prov.

Herrei L. Bolus [*L. translucens* L. Bolus]. Growths in clumps of 10–15, to 1 in. high and ⅝ in. across, top-shaped, sides gray-white, apex convex, brownish-green, windows opaque with transparent lines making many islands and giving the surface a rugose appearance; fls. to ⅝ in. across, petals yellow, in 2 series, stamens white. Cape Prov.

Inae: *L. verruculosa* var.

inornata: a listed name of no botanical standing for *L. Marthae.*

insularis L. Bolus. Growths solitary or in small clumps, to 1 in. high, top-shaped, apex flat or convex, windows dark green, smooth or bumpy, with many blood-red, unevenly distributed dots or lines, the bumpy area with white spots, outer margin serrate; fls. about 1½ in. across, petals bright yellow, in 2–3 series, stamens white. Cape Prov.

Julii (Dinter & Schwant.) N. E. Br. [*L. lactea* Schick & Tisch.]. Growths forming clumps, to 1¼ in. high, obconical, apex flat to slightly convex, pale gray, the sides reddish, top rugose when young with depressed, dark red lines surrounding the irregularly shaped islands; fls. to 1¼ in. across, petals white. S.-W. Afr. Var. **reticulata** Tisch. ex

DeBoer & Boom. Apex of growths with dark brown reticulations. S.-W. Afr.

karasmontana (Dinter & Schwant.) N. E. Br. [*L. Ursulae* Hort.]. Growths solitary or in clumps, to ½ in. high, obconical, apex flat to convex, sides pearl-gray to mauve-gray, top rugose to sometimes bullate, light grayish-yellow to reddish-brown, windows usually opaque; fls. to 1⅜ in. across, petals white. S.-W. Afr. Var. **mickbergensis** (Dinter) DeBoer & Boom [*L. mickbergensis* Dinter]. Apex of growths yellowish-red with distinct, delicate reticulations and darker, often starlike branched lines. S.-W. Afr. Var. **opalina** (Dinter) DeBoer & Boom [*L. opalina* Dinter]. Apex of growths opaline to amethyst with vague markings. S.-W. Afr. Var. **summitata** (Dinter) DeBoer & Boom [*L. summitata* Dinter]. Apex of growths reddish-brown, unlined, and with less impressed reticulations. S.-W. Afr.

Koelemanii: *L. Aucampiae* var.

kuibisensis: *L. Schwantesii.*

kunjasensis: *L. Schwantesii* var.

lactea: *L. Julii.*

Lericheana: *L. bella* var.

Lesliei (N. E. Br.) N. E. Br. Growths solitary or in clumps of 3–4, to 1¾ in. high, obconical, apex flat or slightly convex, sides purplish-gray to green, windows olive-green with orange or irregular rust-colored spots; fls. to 1¼ in. across, petals golden-yellow, whitish or pinkish on the back. Transvaal, Orange Free State. Var. **Venteri** (Nel) DeBoer & Boom [*L. Venteri* Nel]. Apex with gray-green margin and islands. Cape Prov.

lineata: *L. Ruschiorum.*

localis (N. E. Br.) Schwant. Growths solitary or only a few per clump, to ½ in. high, top-shaped, apex truncate, ocher or pink to almost red; petals yellow. Cape Prov. Var. **localis.** The typical var.; windows usually absent, with many isolated violet-green dots. Var. **Peersii** (L. Bolus) DeBoer & Boom [*L. Peersii* L. Bolus]. Apex of growths with or without distinct windows, surface bluish-purple or violet, with many translucent dots. Cape Prov. Var. **terricolor** (N. E. Br.) DeBoer & Boom [*L. terricolor* N. E. Br.]. Apex of growths with greenish windows, surface grayish to yellow-green, with many dark green, translucent dots. Cape Prov.

Lydiae: a listed name of no botanical standing for *L. fulviceps.*

marmorata (N. E. Br.) N. E. Br. [*L. Framesii* L. Bolus; *L. umdausensis* L. Bolus]. Growths solitary or in small clumps, to 1⅜ in. high, top-shaped, apex slightly convex, fissure ⅜ in. deep, window large, gray-green and mottled with creamy-green or gray, with irregular islands in the windows; fls. to 1¼ in. across, petals white, filaments white, anthers yellow. Cape Prov.

Marthae Loesch & Tisch [*L. inornata* Hort.]. Growths 4–5 in a clump, to ¼ in. high, obconical, sides gray with a purplish tint, fissure to ⅛ in. deep with red lines radiating from it, apex slightly convex, mouse-gray to violet-green, window dull; fls. 1 in. across, petals yellow, stamens yellow. S.-W. Afr.

Mennellii L. Bolus. Growths up to 8 in a clump, to ¾ in. high, top-shaped, fissure ⅛ in. deep, apex slightly convex, without windows, grayish-buff, with dark brown dots and lines resembling Hebrew script; fls. to almost 1¼ in. across, petals golden-yellow. Cape Prov.

Meyeri L. Bolus. Growths solitary or 3–4 in a clump, to 1¼ in. high, obconical, fissure ¾ in. deep, lobes divergent, dark blue to green-gray, apex rounded and lighter bluish-green; fls. to 1⅜ in. across, petals yellow. Cape Prov.

mickbergensis: *L. karasmontana* var.

Mundtii: *L. pseudotruncatella* var.

olivacea L. Bolus. Growths to 9 in a clump, to ¾ in. high, top-shaped, fissure ¼ in. deep, apex flat or convex in age, window transparent, olive-green to brownish, sometimes with white islands; fls. to about 1¾ in. across, petals bright yellow, white toward base, filaments white, anthers yellow. Cape Prov.

opalina: *L. karasmontana* var.

optica (Marloth) N. E. Br. Growths in clumps of 4–15 or sometimes 20–30, to 1¼ in. high, obconical, lobes divergent, pale gray or brownish, apex convex, windows nearly transparent, with a few, small, greenish-white or pale grayish-white islands; fls. to ¾ in. across, petals yellow, filaments white, anthers yellow. S.-W. Afr.

Otzeniana Nel. Growths to 20 in a clump, to 1¼ in. high, top-shaped, sides mauve-gray, apex flat to convex, windows semitransparent, greenish, olive-green or even tinted violet, margin of window gray to yellow-gray, irregularly lobed; fls. to ¾ in. across, petals golden-yellow. Cape Prov.

Peersii: *L. localis* var.

pseudotruncatella (A. Berger) N. E. Br. [*L. alpina* Dinter]. Growths solitary to many in a clump, to 1¼ in. high, obconical, sides gray or tinted with purple, apex flat to slightly convex, brownish-gray, with branching lines forming more or less confluent, rust-colored grooves; fls. to 1⅜ in. across, petals golden-yellow. Widely distributed in S.-W. Afr. Var. **dendritica** (Nel) DeBoer & Boom [*L. dendritica* Nel; *L. farinosa* Dinter]. Apex mostly gray-brown with branching markings. S.-W. Afr. Var. **Edithae** (N. E. Br.) DeBoer & Boom [*L. Edithae* N. E. Br.]. Apex light bluish-gray with light chocolate-brown markings and rather distinct translucent dots. S.-W. Afr. Var. **Mundtii** (Tisch.) Tisch. [*L. Mundtii* Tisch.]. Growths rather flat, evenly yellowish-brown with distinct branching lines. S.-W. Afr. Var. **pulmonuncula** (Dinter ex Jacobsen) Dinter ex Higgins [*L. pulmonuncula* (Dinter ex Jacobsen) Dinter ex Jacobsen]. Apex uniformly brownish-gray, lines and translucent dots sometimes indistinct, windows bluish-green or indistinct. S.-W. Afr.

pulmonuncula: *L. pseudotruncatella* var.

Ruschiorum (Dinter & Schwant.) N. E. Br. [*L. lineata* Nel]. Growths solitary or in clumps to 5–6, to 1¾ in. high, top-shaped, fissure to ¾ in. deep, apex convex, gray-green to pearl-gray or sometimes tinged with yellow or reddish-ocher, without distinct markings; fls. to 1 in. across, petals yellow. S.-W. Afr.

salicola L. Bolus. Growths solitary or up to 20 in a clump, to 1 in. high, top-shaped, sides gray, apex flat to slightly convex, windows more or less transparent, olive-green to dark green, divided into small areas and islands, the surface appearing roughened; fls. to 1 in. across, petals white. Orange Free State.

Schwantesii Dinter [*L. kuibisensis* Dinter ex Jacobsen]. Growths usually in pairs, to 1⅝ in. high, obconical, old growths often persisting for up to 2 years, fissure to ¼ in. deep, sides mauve-gray, apex flat to strongly convex, reddish-brownish-gray, with rusty-yellow-bordered semitransparent windows irregularly marked with blood-red dots and lines; fls. 1¼ in. across, petals yellow. S.-W. Afr. Var. **kunjasensis** (Dinter) DeBoer & Boom [*L. kunjasensis* Dinter]. Apex more rugose, paler, with more red and less gray (discernible only in summer). S.-W. Afr. Var. **Triebneri** (L. Bolus) DeBoer & Boom [*L. Triebneri* L. Bolus; *L. Gulielmi* L. Bolus]. Apex gray to light leather-brown. S.-W. Afr.

summitata: *L. karasmontana* var.

terricolor: *L. localis* var.

translucens: *L. Herrei.*

Triebneri: *L. Schwantesii* var.

turbiniformis (Haw.) N. E. Br. [*L. aurantiaca* L. Bolus]. Growths 1–4 in a clump, to 1 in. high, top-shaped, sides gray, apex flat or slightly convex, unevenly tubercled, brownish with dark brown, branched lines between tubercles; fls. to 1¾ in. across, petals bright yellow, whitish on back, filaments yellow with white bases, anthers orange-yellow. Cape Prov.

umdausensis: *L. marmorata.*

Ursulae: a listed name of no botanical standing for *L. karasmontana.*

vallis-mariae (Dinter & Schwant.) N. E. Br. Growths in clumps of 2 or more, to ⅝ in. high, top-shaped, sides purplish, apex slightly convex, yellowish to bluish-milky-colored, with impressed lines and vermiform ridges; fls. to 1⅜ in. across, petals yellow. S.-W. Afr.

Vanzylii: *Dinteranthus Vanzylii.*

Venteri: *L. Lesliei* var.

verruculosa Nel. Growths up to 6 in a clump, to 1¼ in. high, top-shaped, apex flat or slightly convex, bluish-gray, windows reduced to grooves formed by confluent depressions bearing many tiny, more or less raised, dark red or gray warts; fls. orange-brown. Cape Prov. Var. **Inae** (Nel) DeBoer & Boom [*L. Inae* Nel]. Apex bearing broader windows. Cape Prov.

Villettii L. Bolus. Growths to 1⅞ in. high, oblong-obovate, lobes divergent, apex convex, window transparent or white, with 1 or 2 paler spots; fls. to 1¼ in. across, petals white. Cape Prov.

Weberi Nel. Growths 2–10 in a clump, obconical, apex flat to slightly rounded, windows large, transparent, light green to gray-green or even purple-green, islands absent or present, variously shaped, mauve or mauve-gray, slightly raised above surface of window; petals yellow. Cape Prov.

Werneri Schwant. & Jacobsen. Growths solitary or several in a clump, the size of a pea, in resting stage, but to ¾ in. high and 1¾ in. wide, when growing actively in cult., obconical, apex slightly convex, gray, yellowish-gray or brownish-gray, with 2–3 dark green, branched furrows transverse to fissure, and usually with small, rounded, isolated dots; petals yellow. S.-W. Afr.

LITHOSPERMUM L. [*Batschia* J. F. Gmel.]. GROMWELL, PUCCOON. *Boraginaceae.* About 44 spp. of hairy per. herbs, or rarely subshrubs, represented on all continents except Australia; roots commonly with a red- or purple-staining dye;

lvs. simple, alt., sessile, entire, cauline and sometimes some lvs. basal; fls. yellow, orange, or white, in simple or branched scorpioid cymes, calyx and corolla 5-lobed, corolla throat bearing glands, sometimes hairy, and sometimes with appendages, stamens 5, never exserted, some spp. heterostylic; fr. of 4 nutlets, usually polished, white, and porcelainlike.

Planted in rock gardens and borders. Propagated by seeds and cuttings.

angustifolium: *L. incisum.*

canescens (Michx.) Lehm. [*Batschia canescens* Michx.]. PUCCOON, INDIAN-PAINT. Per., to 1½ ft. with a hoary pubescence; lvs. oblong to linear; fls. orange-yellow, ½ in. long, corolla lobes entire, tube glabrous within. Ont. to Tex., e. to Ga. Roots contain a red dye.

diffusum: *Lithodora diffusa.*

distichum Ort. Erect, silky-hairy per., with a stout tap root; lvs. oblong-lanceolate to oblanceolate; fls. white or white with a yellow throat, to ½ in. long, the throat with appendages. Mex., Guatemala.

Doerfleri: *Moltkia Doerfleri.*

×**Froebelii:** *Moltkia* × *intermedia* cv.

graminifolium: *Moltkia suffruticosa.*

incisum Lehm. [*L. angustifolium* Michx.; *L. linearifolium* J. Goldie; *L. mandanense* K. Spreng.]. Per., to 2 ft.; lvs. linear; fls. of two kinds, the earlier ones bright yellow, showy, to 1 in. long, corolla lobes fimbriate, later fls. pale yellow, small. Ont., Ind. to B.C., s. to Ariz., Tex. and adjacent Mex.

×**intermedium:** *Moltkia* × *intermedia.*

linearifolium: *L. incisum.*

mandanense: *L. incisum.*

multiflorum Torr. Branching per., to 2 ft.; lvs. linear or linear-lanceolate; fls. heterostylic, yellow or orange, ½ in. long, many, corolla lobes rounded, corolla tube glabrous within. Wyo., s. to Ariz., w. Tex. and adjacent Mex.

officinale L. Per., to 3 ft. or more; lvs. lanceolate to ovate- or linear-lanceolate, to 4 in. long, rough; fls. yellowish- or greenish-white, to ¼ in. long. Eur. and Asia; naturalized in e. U.S.

oleifolium: *Lithodora oleifolia.*

petraeum: *Moltkia petraea.*

prostratum: *Lithodora diffusa.*

purpurascens: *Buglossoides purpureocaeruleum.*

purpureocaeruleum: *Buglossoides purpureocaeruleum.*

ruderale Dougl. ex Lehm. Erect or decumbent per., to about 2 ft.; lvs. linear-lanceolate to lanceolate, many, crowded toward the tip of st.; fls. greenish-yellow, in many small cymes from upper lf. axils, corolla tube not much longer than the calyx. Wash. to n. Calif., e. to Mont. and Colo., adjacent Canada.

LITHREA Miers ex Hook. & Arn. *Anacardiaceae.* Three spp. of evergreen trees and shrubs, native to S. Amer.; lvs. leathery, simple or pinnate; fls. small, in panicles, stamens 10; fr. a drupe.

Planted in Calif. as an ornamental.

caustica (Mol.) Hook. & Arn. Shrub or small tree, 10–20 ft.; lvs. simple, ovate or oblong-ovate, 1–2½ in. long, undulate; fls. creamy-yellow; fr. white, lustrous, to 5 mm. in diam. Chile. The sap is sometimes poisonous to the skin, causing extensive and painful swelling lasting for many days.

molleoides (Vell.) Engl. Shrub, to 12 ft.; lvs. pinnate, lfts. 3 or 5, very narrowly elliptic or lanceolate, 1–2 in. long; fls. greenish or whitish; fr. ¼ in. in diam., whitish and lustrous. Argentina, Bolivia, s. Brazil.

LITSEA Lam. *Lauraceae.* About 400 spp. of widespread, dioecious trees and shrubs, abundant in trop. Asia and Australia, a few in Afr. and Amer.; lvs. commonly alt., pinnately veined; infl. cymose-umbellate, subtended by 4–6 involucral bracts; fls. unisexual, perianth segms. 6, usually deciduous, male fls. with 9–12 stamens, female fls. with 9–12 staminodes; fr. a 1-seeded, usually black berry, seated in a more or less developed cupule or disc.

aciculata: *Neolitsea aciculata.*

aestivalis (L.) Fern. [*L. geniculata* (Walt.) Benth. & Hook.f.]. POND-SPICE. Spreading, deciduous shrub, to 9 ft., branchlets zigzag; lvs. leathery, narrowly oblong, to 2½ in. long, entire; fls. yellow, few, terminal, opening before the lvs.; fr. red, globose, ¼ in. across. Se. U.S.

geniculata: *L. aestivalis.*

glauca: *Neolitsea sericea.*

glutinosa (Lour.) C. B. Robinson. Evergreen shrub or small tree, to 20 ft.; lvs. elliptic, to 4 in. long; infl. axillary, cymose, few-fld.; fr. brown, globose, ⅛ in. across. Trop. Asia.

LITTONIA Hook. *Liliaceae.* Six or 7 spp. of tender, per. herbs, native to Afr. and Arabia; rhizome tuberous, sts. prostrate to erect, leafy; lvs. alt., opp., or whorled; fls. campanulate, solitary in lf. axils, perianth segms. 6, separate, each segm. with basal nectar-bearing scale, stamens 6, anthers versatile; fr. a loculicidal, 3-valved caps., seeds globose, brown.

For culture see *Gloriosa.*

modesta Hook. St. 2–6 ft., simple, more or less erect, often prostrate or runnerlike; lvs. linear to ovate, the upper ones alt. or opp., the middle ones whorled, all bright green, glossy, with tip produced into a tendril; fls. bright orange, to 1¼ in. long, on pedicels to 2 in. long. S. Afr. Cv. 'Keitii' [var. *Keitii* Leichtl.]. More robust; fls. more numerous, larger.

LITTORELLA O. Berg. *Plantaginaceae.* Two spp. of monoecious, aquatic, per. herbs, native to Eur. and temp. S. Amer.; lvs. in rosettes at nodes along stolons; fls. solitary on a scape, male fls. 4-merous, stamens 4, female fls. 3–4-merous, ovary 1-celled; fr. hard, indehiscent.

uniflora (L.) Asch. SHOREWEED, SHORE GRASS. Lvs. variable, semicylindrical to linear-subulate or even flat, to 4 in. long or sometimes longer; scapes shorter than lvs.; fls. not produced on submersed plants. Eur., Azores. Sometimes grown in aquaria.

LIVERWORTS: see *Mosses and Liverworts.*

LIVISTONA R. Br. FAN PALM. *Palmae.* Perhaps 30 spp. of solitary, mostly tall palms with bisexual fls., native to trop. and subtrop. Asia, Indonesia, Australia, New Guinea, Solomon and Philippine Is.; lvs. costapalmate, petioles usually armed with spinose marginal teeth, blades deeply divided, sometimes to the main axis, into 1-ribbed, shallowly or deeply 2-cleft segms.; infls. among the lvs., bracts tubular, sheathing on peduncle and subtending each of several brs., each br. bearing 1 or more bracts at the base, divided 1–3 times into slender rachillae; fls. solitary or in clusters, sepals united in a low, 3-lobed cupule, petals 3, separate and valvate above a briefly united base, stamens 6, filaments united basally, carpels 3, separate except united styles, usually only 1 maturing; fr. globose to ellipsoid, green, blue, black, or orange-red, seed with homogeneous endosperm but the seed coat intruded on 1 side, embryo lateral.

Livistonas are widely cultivated as ornamentals in the tropics and subtropics; certain of the hardier species thrive in Zone 9b. They are also used as pot plants in the home or greenhouse. For culture see *Palms.*

altissima: *L. rotundifolia.*

australis (R. Br.) Mart. [*Corypha australis* R. Br.]. GIPPSLAND PALM, CABBAGE P., AUSTRALIAN C.P., AUSTRALIAN F.P. To 60 ft. or more; lvs. orbicular in outline, to 8 ft. wide, divided to beyond the middle into about 70 soft, deeply 2-cleft segms. with pendulous apices resembling *L. chinensis*, drying with conspicuous cross-veinlets, lacking scales on surface beneath but veins with soft scales near base at least when young, petiole toothed to or nearly to apex, teeth stout basally, finer apically; infl. with hairy bracts, rachillae glabrous, yellow, bearing fls. in 2's or 3's on very short, pedicel-like, axillary branchlets; fls. glabrous, calyx with very short solid base and longer membranous spreading lobes; fr. purple-black, to ⅞ in. long, ¾ in. in diam. E. Australia. One of the hardier sp. of the genus.

chinensis (Jacq.) R. Br. ex Mart. CHINESE F.P., CHINESE FOUNTAIN P. To 30 ft. or more; lvs. many, petiole toothed basally, blade with a prominent undivided central area and many deeply 2-cleft segms., apices pendulous; infl. of several brs. along a single main rachis, each 2–3 times divided into rachillae; fls. in clusters of up to 6; fr. blue-green to green, ellipsoid, subglobose, or pear-shaped. Var. **chinensis** [*L. oliviformis* (Hassk.) Mart.]. The typical var.; fr. ellipsoid, to ⅞ in. long, ⁹⁄₁₆ in. broad. S. Japan, China (?). One of the hardier palms in the genus. Var. **subglobosa** (Hassk.) Becc. [*L. subglobosa* (Hassk.) Mart.]. Fr. subglobose, ⅝–¾ in. long. Ryukyu Is.

cochinchinensis: *L. Saribus.*

decipiens Becc. Smaller than *L. australis;* lvs. to 5 ft. long, very deeply divided into about 80 segms. to or within about 3 in. of the main axis, apices pendulous, very deeply 2-cleft, drying with conspicuous cross-veinlets, lacking scales on surface beneath but veins with soft scales near base, petioles often toothed only near the base; infl. with glabrous bracts or with hairs only on the margins of smaller bracts, rachillae glabrous, bearing fls. mostly in 2's or 3's on very short but separate pedicel-like axillary branchlets, sepals with solid base as long as erect narrow lobes; fr. blackish, ½ in. in diam or slightly more. Described from cult., supposedly Australian.

Hoogendorpii: *L. Saribus.*

humilis R. Br. Sts. low but sometimes to 20 ft.; lvs. divided more than halfway to the base into 30–35 rather stiff, more or less deeply 2-cleft segms. to about 1½ ft. long, petiole toothed to the apex, with scurfy deciduous scales leaving elongate shining brown bases; infls. longer than lvs., with hairy bracts and brs., these 2–3 times divided into finely hairy rachillae; fls. in sessile clusters of 2–4, very small, sepals rounded; fr. obovoid-ellipsoid, black, ⅝ in. long. N. Australia.

Jenkinsiana Griff. To 30 ft.; lvs. to 6 ft. across, pale beneath, with large, entire, central portion and many rather briefly 2-cleft segms., petioles toothed nearly to apex; infls. with hairy bracts and brs. divided 2–3 times into puberulous rachillae; fls. in sessile clusters of 2 or more; fr. globose, about 1 in. in diam., deep blue. Himalayan foothills, Sikkim to Assam.

Mariae F. J. Muell. To 80 or rarely 100 ft.; lvs. bronze-red on young plants, blue-green on mature plants, with a large, entire, central portion and many stiff, rather deeply 2-cleft segms.; fr. about ½ in. in diam., blackish. Cent. Australia.

mauritiana: a listed name of no botanical standing for *L. chinensis.*

Merrillii Becc. To 60 ft.; lvs. large, to 4½ ft. long, paler beneath than above, regularly divided into deeply 2-cleft segms. with pendulous apices, petioles slightly toothed near the base, tomentose when young; infl. of 3 essentially equal brs. from near the base, each br. with tubular bracts and about two further brs. divided into rachillae; fls. arranged singly, about ⅛ in. long; fr. globose, nearly 1 in. in diam. Philippine Is.

Muelleri F. M. Bailey. To 20 ft. or more; lvs. green, stiff, divided about ⅔ to the base into 50 or more very briefly 2-cleft segms., petiole toothed in lower half; infl. with several brs. along a single main axis, these branched into glabrous rachillae; fls. in sessile clusters of 2–3; fr. black, globose-obovoid, about ½ in. long. E. Australia.

okinawensis: a listed name of no botanical standing, probably for *L. chinensis* var. *subglobosa.*

oliviformis: L. *chinensis* var. *chinensis.*

Robinsoniana Becc. Similar to *L. rotundifolia* but bracts of infl. straw-colored when dry and fr. orange, ⅝ in. in diam. Philippine Is.

rotundifolia (Lam.) Mart. [*L. altissima* Zoll.]. To 80 ft. or more, trunk rather slender and prominently ringed; lvs. nearly orbicular, pale beneath, with large, entire, central portion, divided into many short, stiff, briefly 2-cleft segms., petiole sometimes nearly lacking teeth on older trees; infl. of 3 essentially equal brs. from near the base, each br. with tubular reddish-brown bracts and several branchlets divided into slender rachillae; fls. borne singly, very small, slightly more than $\frac{1}{16}$ in. long; fr. black at maturity, globose, to ¾ in. in diam. Indonesia, Philippine Is. Tender, excellent as an indoor pot palm.

Saribus (Lour.) Merrill ex A. Cheval. [*L. cochinchinensis* (Blume) Mart.; *L. Hoogendorpii* Teysm. & Binn. ex Miq.]. To 75 ft. or more; lvs. large, to 5 ft. long, unevenly divided into several-ribbed primary segms., these again less deeply divided into deeply 2-cleft segms., petiole stoutly toothed at base; infl. with 7–8 brs. along a single main axis, these divided into slender glabrous rachillae, with fls. arranged in clusters of 3–5; fr. globose, blue, ½ in. in diam. Se. Asia, Indonesia, Philippine Is.

subglobosa: *L. chinensis* var. *subglobosa.*

Woodfordii Ridl. To 40 ft.; lvs. powdery waxy beneath, about 3 ft. long, divided into deeply 2-cleft segm.; infl. of several nearly equal brs. from near the base, to 3 ft. long; fls. very small, in clusters of 4–6 on the rachillae; fr. about ½ in. in diam. Solomon Is.

LLAVEA Lag. *Polypodiaceae.* One sp., a fern of the New World tropics; rhizomes short, stout, scaly; lvs. 3-pinnate, sterile pinnules ovate, 1–2 in. long, fertile pinnules toward apex of blade linear, veins separate, repeatedly forked, petiole scales large, needle-shaped, lemon-colored when young; sporangia along the veins, spreading over entire surface when mature, slightly protected by reflexed lf. margins.

For culture see *Ferns.*

cordifolia Lag. [*Ceratodactylis osmundioides* John Sm.] To 2 ft.; lvs. yellow-green, petioles yellow; fertile pinnule contracted, borne at apex of blade. Cent. Mex., Guatemala. Tender.

LLOYDIA Salisb. ex Rchb. ALP LILY. *Liliaceae.* About 12 spp. of alpine, per. herbs, native to Eur., Asia, and w. N. Amer.; bulbs tunicate, from a creeping rhizome; lvs. basal and cauline, linear, grasslike; fls. white, solitary or in a terminal raceme, perianth segms. 6, separate, each segm. with a basal gland, stamens 6, anthers basifixed; fr. an apically loculicidal caps., seeds 3-angled, many, in 2 rows in each cell.

serotina (L.) Salisb. ex Rchb. Bulb fibrous-coated, sts. to 6 in.; lvs. several, to 4 in. long; fls. yellowish-white, veined with purple, $\frac{5}{16}$ in. long, usually solitary. Mts. of Eur., Asia, N. Amer. from Alaska to Ore., Mont., and New Mex. Suitable for the alpine garden.

LOASA Adans. *Loasaceae.* About 105 spp. of herbs or subshrubs, usually with stinging hairs, native from Mex. to S. Amer.; fls. yellow, white, or red, petals saclike or hooded (in the cult. spp.), with colored nectar scales; fr. a caps.

Propagated by seeds and cuttings.

acanthifolia Desr. ex Lam. Erect per., covered with stinging hispid hairs; lvs. opp., to 4 in. long, pinnately lobed to pinnate, lobes coarsely sinuate-toothed, dark green; fls. yellow, to ¾ in. across, petals recurved, nectar scales with 3 linear appendages arising from the middle. Chile.

aurantiaca: *Cajophora lateritia.*

hispida: *L. urens.*

lateritia: *Cajophora lateritia.*

triphylla Juss. Ann., to 1½ ft.; lvs. alt., mostly trifoliolate or the upper often simple, the lobes coarsely toothed or serrate; fls. few, white, ⅞ in. across, nectar scales forming deep yellow crown, barred with red and white, and having 2 inflated, horned sacs at base. N. S. Amer. Var. **papaverifolia** (HBK) Urb. & Gilg. Lower lvs. usually pinnately 2–4-lobed, lobes narrow, irregularly toothed; fls. 1 in. across. Var. **vulcanica** (André) Urb. & Gilg [*L. vulcanica* André]. Lvs. less coarsely toothed; fls. about 2 in. across.

urens Jacq. [*L. hispida* L.]. Ann., to 1½ ft., sts. densely brown-hispid; lvs. alt., deeply pinnatifid to 2-pinnate; fls. yellow, 2 in. across, nectar scales with 2 inflated, horned sacs near base. Peru.

vulcanica: *L. triphylla* var.

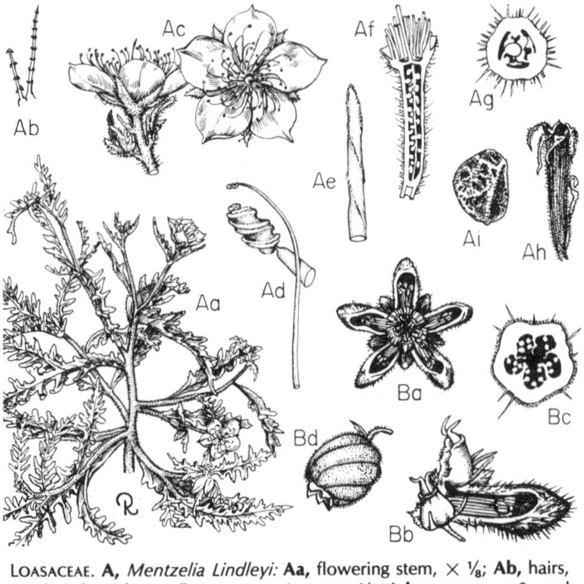

LOASACEAE. **A,** *Mentzelia Lindleyi:* **Aa,** flowering stem, × ⅛; **Ab,** hairs, much enlarged; **Ac,** flower, two views, × ½; **Ad,** stamen, × 2, and anther, × 8; **Ae,** stigma, × 5; **Af,** ovary and base of flower, × 1; **Ag,** ovary, cross section, × 4; **Ah,** fruit, × ¾; **Ai,** seed, × 5. **B,** *Blumenbachia insignis:* **Ba,** flower, × 1; **Bb,** petal with basal scales and stamen cluster, × 2; **Bc,** ovary, cross section, × 3; **Bd,** fruit, × ½.

LOASACEAE Dumort. LOASA FAMILY. Dicot.; 13 genera and about 250 spp., mostly native to temp. parts of N. and S. Amer., usually herbs, sometimes twining, usually with rough, bristly, and often stinging hairs; fls. regular, bisexual, sepals and petals 4–5, stamens many, ovary inferior, 1–3-celled; fr. a caps. *Blumenbachia, Cajophora, Eucnide, Loasa,* and *Mentzelia* are cult. as ornamentals.

LOBEIRA: *NOPALXOCHIA.*

LOBELIA L. *Lobeliaceae.* About 375 spp. of herbs, shrubs, or sometimes trees, native mostly to trop. and warm-temp. regions; lvs. alt., simple; fls. mostly in bracted racemes, inverted by the twisted pedicel, calyx 5-toothed, corolla blue, violet, red, yellow, or white, often spotted, irregular, mostly 2-lipped, the upper lip of 2 distinct lobes, the lower larger and 3-cleft, tube slit along the upper edge almost to base, stamens not united to petals, anther tube with lower 2 or all anthers with tufted hairs at apex, ovary 2-celled, stigma lobes rounded, spreading; fr. a caps., dehiscing below calyx teeth, seeds many.

Lobelias are grown in borders and the flower garden. The native perennial species that are cultivated thrive in moist locations. Seeds of the annual kinds sown in early winter will produce flowering plants by early spring. Propagated also by cuttings, and the perennials by division. One species, *L. inflata*, is a drug plant.

aberdarica R. E. Fries & T. C. E. Fries. Columnar, unbranched, to 9 ft.; lvs. congested below infl., linear to oblong-lanceolate, to 15 in. long; fls. in terminal, bracted racemes to 6 ft. long, corolla 1–1½ in. long, blue or white, anthers to ½ in. long, the lower 2 tufted. Wet places above 9,000 ft., Kenya and Uganda.

aquatica Cham. Aquatic, decumbent herb, sts. to 20 in. long, rooting at nodes or floating; lvs. mostly sessile, ovate to oblong, to 1 in. long; fls. solitary in axils, corolla about ¼ in. long, blue, with white markings, anthers all white-tufted. Mostly swamps and streams, W. Indies, S. Amer.

campanulata: *Monopsis campanulata.*

Cardinalis L. CARDINAL FLOWER, INDIAN PINK. Per., to 3 ft., sts. mostly glabrous, often purple-red; lvs. lanceolate to oblong, to 4 in. long, acute; fls. in bracted racemes, corolla to 1½ in. long, scarlet, rarely pink or white, anthers exserted, lower 2 tufted; caps. subglobose, about ⅜ in. across, seeds rough. Late summer. New Bruns. to Minn., s. to Fla. and e. Tex. Cv. **'Alba'**. Fls. white Cv. **'Rosea'**. Fls. pink.

comosa L. [*L. triquetra* L.]. Mostly glabrous, unbranched herb, to 2 ft.; lvs. linear to oblanceolate, to 2 in. long, ¼ in. wide; fls. in loose, corymbose racemes, corolla about ½ in. long, deep blue, throat yellowish, swollen, glabrous, lower 2 anthers tufted; caps. oblong-obovate, to ⅜ in. long, seeds smooth. S. Afr.

compacta: a listed name of no botanical standing, probably for *L. Erinus* cv. or *L. tenuior* cv.

coronopifolia L. Hirsute, branched, per. herb, to 2 ft.; lvs. crowded at base, to 1½ in. long, ¼ in. wide, pinnately dentate; fls. 1–3, on axillary and terminal peduncles, corolla 1–1 ½ in. long, blue, purplish, pink, or white, glabrous outside, anthers black, all tufted. S. Afr.

Davidii Franch. Erect subshrub, to 3 ft.; lvs. subsessile, oblong-elliptic to lanceolate, to 6 in. long, doubly serrate to denticulate; fls. in elongate racemes, bracts leafy, corolla to 1 in. long, purple or violet, lobes linear, anthers bright blue, lower 2 tufted. China, Burma.

Dortmanna L. WATER L. Aquatic, glabrous herb, sts. hollow, leafless except for a few small scales; lvs. clustered at base, linear, to ½ in. long; fls. few, nodding above water, corolla ½–¾ in. long, lilac, anthers more or less included, lower 2 penicillate-tufted, upper 3 bearded; seeds brown, rough. Summer. N. N. Amer., w. Eur.

dresdensis: a listed name of no botanical standing.

Erinus L. EDGING L. Ann. or per., mostly less than 8 in.; lower lvs. elliptic to obovate, upper lvs. linear, ½–1 in. long, all serrate; fls. in loose racemes, corolla ½–¾ in. long, blue or violet, throat yellowish or whitish, anthers slightly exserted, blue, lower 2 penicillate-tufted. S. Afr. Cvs. include: **'Alba'**, used for various white-fld. kinds; **'Compacta'**, for low, dense kinds; **'Erecta'**, erect, compact habit; **'Gracilis'**, sts. slender; **'Pendula'**, sts. pendulous; **'Pumila'**, of dwarf habit; **'Speciosa'**, loosely branched, fls. large, blue; **'Rosea'**, fls. pinkish-violet.

fenestralis Cav. Erect, mostly unbranched, ann. or bien., to 2 ft. or more; lvs. narrow-oblong, to 3 in. long, dentate-crisped, sometimes prickly on margins and lower surface; fls. in spikelike racemes, corolla to ½ in. long, blue, violet, or white, anthers included, all tufted; caps. generally with prickly calyx teeth, seeds smooth, lustrous. Tex. to New Mex. and Ariz., s. to Mex.

fulgens: *L. splendens.*

×**Gerardii** Chabanne & Goujon ex Sauv.: *L. Cardinalis* cv. 'Queen Victoria' × *L. siphilitica.* Robust per., to 5 ft.; lvs. clasping at the base, obovate to elliptic, the largest to 6 in. long or more; fls. in dense elongate racemes, corolla 1–1¾ in. long, pinkish-violet to purplish, lower lip with 2 triangular white spots. Late summer.

gracilis Andr. Glabrous ann., to 18 in.; lvs. linear-lanceolate to oblong, less than 1 in. long, dentate; fls. in loose, 1-sided racemes, corolla about ⅝ in. long, intense blue, throat yellow, median lobe of lower lip much longer than lateral lobes, anthers conspicuously exserted, all tufted. Summer. Australia Cv. **'Rosea'**. Fls. more reddish.

heterophylla: see *L. tenuior.*

hybrida: a listed name of no botanical standing, variously employed but generally referring to hybrids involving *L. Cardinalis, L splendens,* and *L. siphilitica.*

inflata L. INDIAN TOBACCO. Hirsute ann., usually branched, to 3 ft.; lvs. obovate to lanceolate, mostly less than 3 in. long, serrate; fls. in open racemes, pedicels bracted at base, corolla about ¼ in. long, bluish-violet or white, lower 2 anthers tufted, calyx tube inflated, to ½ in. long, enclosing caps., seeds rough. Early summer–autumn. Lab., s. to La. and Ga. The dried sts. and lvs. are the source of an alkaloid, lobeline, used medicinally.

Kalmii L. Matlike to erect, to 2 ft.; basal lvs. spatulate to obovate, upper lvs. linear; fls. in loose, often 1-sided racemes, pedicels bracted at middle, corolla about ½ in. long, blue, with a conspicuous white eye, or all white, anthers bluish-gray, lower 2 tufted. Summer. Nfld. to N.J., w. to S. Dak. and Colo.

laxiflora HBK. Shrubby or sometimes herbaceous, to 3 ft. or more; lvs. lanceolate-linear to elliptic, to about 3 in. long, serrate; fls. on pedicels to 4 in. long, subtended by bracts to 6 in. long, corolla 1–1½ in. long, red with yellowish lobes or all yellow, filaments reddish or yellowish, anthers nearly ½ in. long, gray, lower 2 tufted, upper 3 hirsute. Summer. Ariz., s. to Mex. and Colombia.

pendula: a listed name of no botanical standing for *L. Erinus* cv.

pinifolia L. Shrub, to 2 ft.; lvs. crowded, needlelike, to 1 in. long; fls. in narrow racemes, corolla ½–⅝ in. long, blue, violet, or sometimes pink or white, anthers more or less included, brownish, all tufted. S. Afr.

ramosa: *L. tenuior.*

siphilitica L. GREAT L., BLUE CARDINAL FLOWER. Simple-stemmed per., to 3 ft.; lvs. ovate to broadly lanceolate, mostly 2–4 in. long, acute, irregularly serrate; fls. in dense racemes, pedicels bracted at middle, calyx lobes auricled at base, corolla about 1 in. long, blue, sometimes white, lower 2 anthers tufted; seeds rough. Late summer. Me. to S. Dak., s. to N.C., Miss., Kans. Cv. **'Alba'**. Fls. white. Cv. **'Nana'**. Of dwarf habit.

×**speciosa** Sweet: *L. cordigera* Cav. × *L. siphilitica.* Hirsute per.; lvs. sessile, oblong, acuminate; calyx lobes short-auricled at base, corolla 1–1¼ in. long, purplish or purple-violet. More generally the name *L. speciosa* is used incorrectly to refer to *L. Erinus* cv. 'Speciosa'.

spicata Lam. PALE-SPIKE L. Simple or few-branched per. or bien., to 4 ft.; distinguished from *L. inflata* in having base of st. short-puberulent, calyx tube scarcely inflated, about ¼ in. long, and not enclosing the caps. Late spring–summer. New Bruns. to Minn., s. to Ga. and Ark.

splendens Willd. [*L. fulgens* Hemsl.]. Similar to *L. Cardinalis* but differing in having lvs. mostly lanceolate to linear, 2–7 in. long, infl. more or less 1-sided, and corolla and caps. slightly larger. Mex.

tenuior R. Br. [*L. heterophylla* Lindl., not Labill.; *L. ramosa* Benth.]. Diffuse ann., to 2 ft.; lvs. to 2½ in. long, linear, irregularly pinnately cut, lower lvs. often broader, trifid; fls. in open racemes or nearly panicled, pedicels to 2½ in. long, bracted at middle, corolla about 1 in. long, bright blue, throat yellow-spotted, tube yellowish, anthers all tufted. Late summer. W. Australia. Cv. **'Compacta'** is listed.

tomentosa L.f. Shrub, less than 2 ft.; differing from *L. coronopifolia* in having lvs. tomentose; corolla to ¾ in. long, purplish, hirsute. S. Afr.

triquetra: *L. comosa.*

vedraiensis: a listed name of no botanical standing.

LOBELIACEAE R. Br. LOBELIA FAMILY. Dicot.; about 25 genera, usually herbs, sometimes shrubs or trees, native mostly to trop. regions, sap often acrid, milky; lvs. alt., sometimes in rosettes, simple, entire, toothed, or pinnately parted; fls. solitary or in spicate, racemose, or paniculate infls., calyx limb 5-lobed or -parted, the divisions equal or unequal, corolla irregular, often 2-lipped, 5-lobed, the tube often split nearly to the base on one side, stamens 5, sometimes inserted on petals, anthers united into a tube around style, ovary inferior, rarely superior, 2–5-celled, stigma fringed at base; fr. a caps. or berry. The genera cult. as ornamentals are: *Centropogon, Downingia, Hippobroma, Hypsela, Laurentia, Lobelia, Monopsis,* and *Pratia.*

LOBIVIA Britt. & Rose [*Acantholobivia* Backeb.; *Soehrensia* Backeb.]. COB CACTUS. *Cactaceae.* Perhaps 70 spp. of low, ribbed cacti of Peru, Bolivia, and Argentina; sts. simple or cespitose, globose to short-cylindrical, ribs mostly 10–25, rarely 60, more or less tubercled; fls. lateral, diurnal, cam-

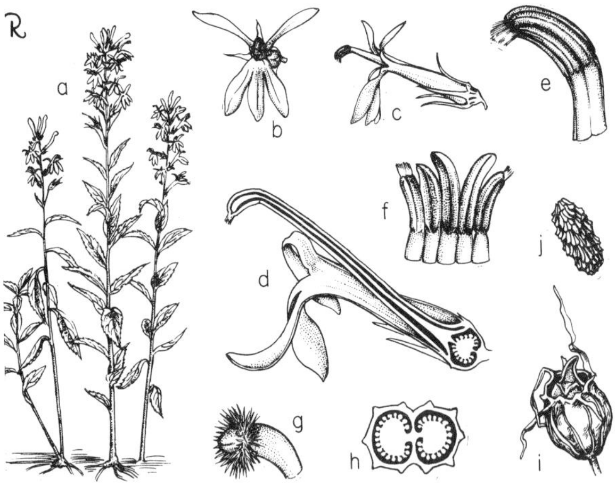

LOBELIACEAE. *Lobelia Cardinalis:* **a,** plant, × 1/16; **b,** flower, face view, × ½; **c,** flower, side view, × ½; **d,** flower, vertical section, × 1; **e,** anthers, × 3; **f,** anther tube, expanded, × 2; **g,** stigma, × 2; **h,** ovary, cross section, × 3; **i,** dehiscing capsule within calyx, × 1; **j,** seed, × 10.

panulate to short-funnelform, mostly red to yellow, perianth tube scarcely or not exceeding the limb, scales of tube and ovary mostly with long axillary hairs, upper stamens in a distinct circle at the mouth; fr. globose, small, hairy. Intermediate between *Echinopsis* and *Rebutia.* Generally differs from *Echinopsis* in shorter, colored, diurnal fls. and from *Rebutia* in ribbed, not strongly tubercled sts. and stamens in 2 series; but the three genera intergrade.

For culture see *Cacti.*

Allegraiana Backeb. Sts. mostly simple, globose, to 3 in. thick, ribs spiralled; spines to 12, yellowish, becoming brown, to 1¼ in. long; fls. red, 2 in. long; fr. green, ½ in. in diam. S. Peru.

andalgalensis (A. Web.) Britt. & Rose. Sts. to 1 ft. high and 2–4 in. thick, ribs about 14; spines fine-needle-shaped, white to brownish, to ⅜ in. long, radial spines 8–12, central spine 1, stouter; fls. red, 4 in. long. Argentina.

aurea: *Echinopsis aurea.*

Backebergii (Werderm.) Backeb. [*Echinopsis Backebergii* Werderm.]. Sts. cespitose, to 4 in. high and 2½ in. thick, ribs 14–15, weakly cross-furrowed; spines commonly 5–7, sometimes more, needle-shaped, radial, short, irregularly arranged, to 2 in. long; fls. red, 2 in. long. Bolivia.

Binghamiana Backeb. Sts. cespitose, subglobose, to 3½ in. thick, ribs about 22, slightly crenate; spines to 12, needle-shaped, yellow, central spines 3, longer, to ⅝ in. long; fls. purplish-red, 2 in. long; fr. green, ½ in. in diam. Se. Peru.

boliviensis Britt. & Rose. Roots fleshy, sts. cespitose, globose, to 4 in. thick, ribs about 20, of oblong tubercles; spines 6–8, needle-shaped, brown, to 3½ in. long; fls. red, 2½ in. long, open 1 night and day, perianth tube longer than segms., Bolivia.

breviflora Backeb. Sts. depressed-globose, ribs 22–25, obtuse, becoming acute, tubercled; spines to 25, nearly equal, to ½ in. long, radial spines comblike, curved, brown, becoming gray, central spines thickened at base; fls. cinnabar-red, 1¼ in. long. N. Argentina.

Bruchii Britt. & Rose [*Soehrensia Bruchii* (Britt. & Rose) Backeb.]. SOUTH AMERICAN GOLDEN-BARREL. Sts. simple, globose, to 1 ft. thick, ribs to 50 or more, somewhat tubercled, tubercles chinlike; spines about 15 or more, spreading, needle-shaped; fls. red. N. Argentina.

caespitosa (J. Purpus) Britt. & Rose. Sts. cespitose, to 6 in. high and 2 in. thick, ribs 10–12, nearly crenate; radial spines about 12, needle-shaped, the upper longer, dark, to ¾ in. long, central spine 1, dark, to 2 in. long: fls. orange, to 3 in. long. Bolivia.

chrysantha (Werderm.) Backeb. Sts. simple, to 2½ in. high and 3 in. thick, ribs 5–13, continuous, broad; spines mostly 5–7, radial, slender-awl-shaped, straight, appressed; fls. orange-yellow with purple center, 2 in. long, tube longer than segms. Argentina. Var. **Hossei** (Werderm.) Backeb. To 6 in., ribs about 16; central spines 1–3, to 1¼ in. long. Var. **Janseniana** (Backeb.) Backeb. [*L. Janseniana* Backeb.]. To 8 in., ribs 13–18; spines 7–12, radial, thinner.

chrysochete (Werderm.) Wessn. Sts. simple or clustered, globose, to 3 in. thick, ribs 15–20; spines 4–10, to 30 on old plants, spreading, slender, straight or some hooked, yellowish, unequal, to 3 in. long; fls. orange-red with white throat, to 1½ in. across. Argentina.

churinensis: a listed name of no botanical standing.

cinnabarina (Hook.) Britt. & Rose. Sts. simple, globose, to 7 in. thick, ribs about 20, irregular, divided into oblong tubercles; spines stout-needle-shaped, curved, radial spines 8–11, recurved, to ¾ in. long, central spines 1–3, stouter; fls. scarlet. Bolivia.

corbula: *L. Pentlandii.*

cylindrica Backeb. Sts. simple, to 5 in. high and 2½ in. thick, ribs about 11; radial spines about 7, awl-shaped, to 5/16 in. long, central spine 1, stouter, to 1¼ in. long; fls. golden, to 2¼ in. long; fr. green. N. Argentina.

densispina: *L. famatimensis* var.

Drijverana Backeb. Root thick, sts. simple, to 3 in. thick, ribs about 15, irregular, divided into oblong tubercles; radial spines 10–12, bristlelike, whitish, appressed, central spines late in appearing, 1–4, curved, yellow to black, short, or to 2½ in. long; fls. yellow, with green throat. N. Argentina. Var. **aurantiaca** Backeb. Fls. orange, style purple. Var. **nobilis** Backeb. Fls. dark red-orange, style pale purple.

Ducis-Paulii: a listed name of no botanical standing, perhaps referring to *L. longispina.*

famatimensis (Speg.) Britt. & Rose. Sts. to 6 in. high and 2 in. thick, often smaller, ribs about 20–24, shallowly cross-furrowed; spines needle-shaped, whitish, radial spines about 8–14, appressed, about ¼ in. long, central spines 1–3; fls. yellow to red or white, 1½–3 in. long. N. Argentina. Variable. Cv. **'Longispina'.** Spines to ¾ in. long. Cvs. **'Nigra'** and **'Nigricans'** are also listed. Var. **aurantiaca** (Backeb. ex Wessn.) Backeb. Sts. dark bronze-green; fls. orange-yellow to golden-yellow, with green throat. Var. **densispina** (Werderm.) Backeb. [*L. densispina* (Werderm.) Backeb.]. Sts. dark green; radial spines 20 or more, central spines 4–7, red-brown. Var. **haematantha** (Backeb. ex Wessn.) Backeb. Sts. light to dark green; fls. blood-red with green throat. Var. **setosa** Backeb. Central spines lacking, radial spines bristlelike, whitish; fls. yellow or red.

ferox: *Echinopsis ferox.*

formosa (Pfeiff.) Dodds [*Soehrensia formosa* (Pfeiff.) Backeb.]. Sts. solitary or cespitose, perhaps to 10 ft. high and 1½ ft. thick, but flowering when globose, ribs 15–60; spines needle-shaped, white to brown, radial spines 8–20, central spines 2–5, to 1½ in. long; fls. yellow, to 3 in. long, perianth segms. papery-tipped. N. Argentina. Cv. **'Rubra'** is listed.

grandis Britt. & Rose [*Soehrensia grandis* (Britt. & Rose) Backeb.]. Sts. subglobose to oblong, to 10 in. high, ribs 14–16, ¾ in. high; spines 10–15, needle-shaped, yellow, to 3 in. long; fls. dull honey-yellow, 2½ in. long. N. Argentina.

Haageana Backeb. Sts. simple, to 1 ft. high and 3 in. thick, ribs 22; spines stout-needle-shaped, brown, becoming gray, radial spines about 10, to ½ in. long, central spines 2–3, to 1½ in. long; fls. light yellow, with red throat, 3 in. long. N. Argentina.

Hermanniana Backeb. Sts. cespitose, to 8 in. long and 2 in. thick, ribs about 13; spines uniform, slender, brown, becoming gray, interlacing, the older to 2½ in. long; fls. greenish-rose, 3 in. long. Ne. Bolivia.

Hertrichiana Backeb. Sts. simple or branching, to 4 in. thick, ribs 11, cross-furrowed and -ridged above areoles; radial spines about 5–7, needle-shaped, yellow-brown, to ⅝ in. long, central spine 1, upcurved, to 1 in. long; fls. red, to 3 in. long. Se. Peru.

Higginsiana Backeb. Sts. subglobose, to 4 in. thick, ribs 15–17; spines needle-shaped, curved, red, radial spines to 10, ¼–1½ in. long, central spine 1, to 3 in. long; fls. rose, with yellowish center, 2½ in. long. Bolivia.

Huascha: *Trichocereus Huascha.*

incaica Backeb. Sts. branching, to 6 in. high and 3 in. thick, ribs about 15, deeply crenate; spines 14–20, awl-shaped, brown, to ¾ in. long, about 7 stouter than remainder, appearing central; fls. red, 1½ in. across. Se. Peru.

Jajoiana Backeb. Sts. usually simple, cylindrical, 2 in. thick, ribs 10–18, divided into sharp, oblong tubercles; spines needle-shaped, radial spines about 10, to ⅜ in. long, central spines 1–3, often curved or even hooked, black, ¾–2½ in. long; fls. dark red, 2½ in. long. N. Argentina. Var. **Fleischerana** Backeb. Central spines to 2 in. long; fls. tomato-red.

Janseniana: *L. chrysantha* var.

Johnsoniana Backeb. Sts. cespitose, to 1¼ in. high and twice as thick, ribs 16; areoles white-woolly, radial spines 1–7, appressed, to ⅜ in. long or an upper one to 1¼ in. long, central spine usually 0; fls. lilac-rose, to 2⅝ in. across. Bolivia.

lateritia (Gürke) Britt. & Rose. Sts. simple, oblong, to 2½ in. thick, ribs 16–18, slightly sinuous; spines curved, thickened at base, brown, radial spines 8–10, to ¾ in. long, central spines 1–2, upcurved, 1 in. long; fls. scarlet to brick-red, to 2 in. long, stamens in 3 series, the lower bowed inward. Bolivia.

longispina: *Echinopsis longispina.*

Marsoneri (Werderm.) Backeb. Sts. simple, globose, 3 in. thick, ribs about 20, divided below into thin, oblong tubercles; radial spines 8–12, needle-shaped, the lateral longest, to 1¼ in. long, central spines 2–5, mostly 3–4, awl-shaped, to 2 in. long, sometimes hooked; fls. yellow, 2 in. long, throat purple. N. Argentina.

mistiensis (Werderm. & Backeb.) Backeb. Sts. simple, to 8 in. high and 4 in. thick, ribs 25–30, thin, notched above the areoles; spines 7–9, radial, thin-awl-shaped, the longest upcurved, to 2 in. long; fls. orange, 3¼ in. long. S. Peru.

Nealeana Backeb. Sts. simple, to 3 in. high and 1 in. thick, ribs about 14, low; spines about 8, radial, needle-shaped, thickened at base, yellow, to ⁵⁄₃₂ in. long; fls. bright red, 2 in. long. N. Argentina.

neohaageana: *L. pygmaea.*

orurensis Backeb. Sts. cespitose, to ¾ in. thick, ribs about 9, tubercled above; spines about 10, comblike, yellowish, to about ¹⁄₁₆ in. long; fls. said to be red. Bolivia. Probably only a var. of *L. pectinata.*

pectinata Backeb. [*Mediolobivia pectinata* (Backeb.) Backeb.]. Similar to *M. pygmaea*, but having sts. more sharply tubercled, radial spines more nearly regularly arranged, looser, often bent or curved.

Pentlandii (Hook.) Britt. & Rose [*L. corbula* (Herrera) Britt. & Rose]. Sts. simple, about 2 in. thick, ribs about 12, divided into thin, oblong tubercles; spines 5–8, radial, needle-shaped, recurved, brownish, to 1¼ in. long; fls. rose, 1½ in. long; fr. subglobose, to ½ in. in diam. Bolivia.

polycephala Backeb. Root thick, sts. cespitose, subglobose, ribs about 16, divided into acute tubercles; radial spines about 10, less than ¹⁄₁₆ in. long, central spines 3–4, thickened at base, longer; fls. red, 2 in. long. N. Argentina.

pseudocachensis Backeb. Sts. cespitose, globose, 2 in. thick, ribs about 15, low; radial spines about 10, needle-shaped, recurved, yellowish, to ¼ in. long, central spine 1, similar, upcurved, dark; fls. dark red, 2½ in. long. N. Argentina.

pygmaea (R. E. Fries) Backeb. [*L. neohaageana* Backeb.; *Mediolobivia Haagei* (Frič & Schelle) Backeb.; *M. pygmaea* (R. E. Fries) Backeb.; *Rebutia Haagei* Frič & Schelle; *R. pygmaea* (R. E. Fries) Britt. & Rose]. Root thick, sts. simple, to 1½ in. high and ¾ in. thick, ribs divided into low tubercles in 8–12 spiral rows; spines 9–12, radial, needle-shaped, appressed, mostly directed sideways, swollen at base, to ⅛ in. long; fls. rose-purple, to 1¼ in. long; fr. ¼ in. in diam. Bolivia, n. Argentina.

raphidacantha Backeb. Sts. cespitose, depressed-globose, ribs acute; spines about 7, uniform, dark brown, becoming gray, curved, interlacing, central spine 1, to 3 in. long; fls. light red. Bolivia.

rebutioides Backeb. Roots thick, sts. cespitose, globose, to ¾ in. thick, ribs 10–12, low, somewhat tubercled; spines bristlelike, to ⅛ in. long, radial spines 5–9, white, central spine 1, darker; fls. red, 1½ in. long. S. Bolivia and n. Argentina.

rhaphidacantha: an erroneous spelling of *L. raphidacantha.*

rubescens (Backeb.) Backeb. Probably only a phase of *L. Haageana*, having sts. red-tinged, radial spines 12, central spines 4, to 1½ in. long. N. Argentina.

saltensis (Speg.) Britt. & Rose. Sts. cespitose, to 2½ in. high and 2 in. thick, ribs 17–18, low, crenate; spines needle-shaped, straight, yellowish, radial spines 12–14, to ¼ in. long, central spines 1–4, stouter, to ½ in. long; fls. red, 1½ in. long, perianth segms. short, scales with naked axils. N. Argentina.

sanguiniflora Backeb. Sts. mostly simple, globose, to 4 in. thick, ribs obtuse, crenate; spines dark, radial spines about 10, to ⅝ in. long, central spines several, 1 of them hooked, to 3 in. long; fls. red, to 2 in. across. N. Argentina.

Schreiteri Castell. Sts. cespitose from a thick root, to 1¼ in. thick, ribs 9–14, continuous; areoles few, radial spines 6–8, bristlelike, white, to ⅜ in. long, rarely 1 central; fls. purple, 1¼ in. long. N. Argentina.

Shaferi Britt. & Rose. Sts. cespitose, to 6 in. high and 1½ in. thick, ribs about 10, low; radial spines 10–15, needle-shaped, white or brown, to ⅜ in. long, central spines several, often 1 stout, to 1¼ in. long; fls. yellow, to 2½ in. long. N. Argentina.

Steinmannii (Solms-Laub.) Backeb. [*Rebutia Steinmannii* (Solms-Laub.) Britt. & Rose]. Sts. about ¾ in. high and ½ in. thick, ribs low, tubercled; spines about 8, needle-shaped. Bolivia. Probably not cult.; material offered under this name is *L. pectinata* or a var. of it.

Teglerana Backeb. [*Acantholobivia Teglerana* (Backeb.) Backeb.]. Sts. mostly simple, subglobose, 2 in. thick, ribs about 14, divided into thin, acute tubercles; radial spines 7–8, bristlelike, central spines 1–4, stouter, dark, to ¾ in. long; fls. pink to orange-red, 2 in. long; fr. spiny, splitting. Peru. Cv. 'Eckardtiana'. Spines very long.

Walterspielii Böd. Sts. simple, to 3 in. high and 4½ in. thick, ribs 20 or more, divided into acute tubercles ¾ in. long; radial spines about 8–10, thick-needle-shaped, to 1¼ in. long, central spines 0–2, similar, thickened at base; fls. carmine, 1½ in. long. Bolivia.

Wegheiana Backeb. Root thick, sts. solitary, subglobose, 2 in. thick, ribs about 20, divided into oblong, acute tubercles; radial spines 7–8, dark, becoming gray, to 1¼ in. long, central spine 1, 1½ in. long; fls. pale violet, 1½ in. long. Bolivia.

LOBULARIA Desv. *Cruciferae.* About 5 spp. of ann. or per. herbs in Medit. region with forked and simple, but not stellate, hairs; lvs. entire; fls. white, sepals 4, petals 4, entire; fr. a silicle, valves slightly inflated. Differs from *Alyssum* in lacking stellate hairs and having white fls.

maritima (L.) Desv. [*Alyssum maritimum* (L.) Lam.; *A. minimum* L., not Willd.]. SWEET ALYSSUM. Per., but usually grown as an ann., much-branched, widely spreading on the ground, rising to 12 in.; grayish-white-pubescent; lvs. linear to lanceolate, entire, tapering to base; fls. small, many, on slender pedicels; silicles small, nearly orbicular. Fls. vary in size and color and sometimes double, lasting over a long season. S. Eur. The dwarf, compact form is sometimes known as *Alyssum Benthamii* Hort. or *A. minimum.* Grown from seeds.

LOCHNERA: *CATHARANTHUS.*

LOCKHARTIA Hook. *Orchidaceae.* About 25 spp. of trop. epiphytes, native to Cent. and S. Amer.; sts. simple, leafy; lvs. many, 2-ranked, equitant, entirely concealing st.; infl. short, racemose or loosely paniculate; sepals and petals similar, lip deeply 3- or 4-lobed, not united to column. For structure of fl. see *Orchidaceae.*

For culture see *Orchids.*

acuta (Lindl.) Rchb.f. [*L. pallida* Rchb.f.]. Sts. to 20 in. long; lvs. obliquely triangular, to 1 in. long, sharply apiculate; panicles 1–3, from axils of upper lvs., spreading, to 3 in. long, few- to many-fld.; fls. small, less than ⅝ in. across, white, lip yellow, rectangular, 4-lobed, deeply cleft apically, disc with 2-lobed puberulent callus. Winter. Costa Rica to Colombia and Venezuela.

amoena Endres & Rchb.f. To 20 in., sts. erect; lvs. triangular, to 1½ in. long; racemes loosely few-fld.; fls. to ½ in. across, yellow, lip with brown or red markings, 3-lobed, to ¼ in. long, lateral lobes linear-strap-shaped, midlobe distinctly lobed, with undulate margins. Cent. Amer.

elegans Hook. Sts. to 8 in. long; lvs. to 1 in. long; infl. to 1 in. long, 1- to several-fld.; fls. less than ¼ in. across, pale yellow or yellowish-green, lip uppermost, 3-lobed, midlobe notched and curved upward, yellow, spotted with red. Late summer–winter. Guyana, Trinidad, Venezuela.

lunifera Rchb.f. Sts. to 15 in. long; lvs. broadly triangular, to 1 in. long; infl. to ¾ in. long, 1- to several-fld.; fls. erect or pendent, to ⅜ in. across, lemon-yellow, lip yellow with small purplish spots, midlobe 2-lobed. Winter–late summer. Brazil.

micrantha Rchb.f. Sts. erect or pendent, to 16 in. long; lvs. narrowly triangular, to ¾ in. long; infl. simple or paniculate, to ¾ in. long, 1–3-fld., from axils of upper lvs.; fls. small, yellow, sepals and petals to less than ¼ in. long, lip complexly 3-lobed, to ¼ in. long, lateral lobes filiform, midlobe squarish, cleft apically. Winter. Nicaragua to Surinam.

Oerstedii Rchb.f. Sts. to 16 in. long, flattened; lvs. narrowly triangular in profile, to 1¼ in. long; racemes very short, 1–3-fld., from axils of upper lvs.; fls. variable in size, to ½ in. across, yellow, spotted with red, lip 3-lobed, to ⅜ in. long, yellow with reddish markings at base. Late winter–summer. Mex. to Panama.

pallida: *L. acuta.*

Pittieri Schlechter. Sts. to 8 in. long; lvs. to 1½ in. long, narrowly triangular-lanceolate in outline, completely enclosing st.; scapes 1-fld., from axils of upper lvs.; fls. to ½ in. across, yellow, lip to ¼ in. long, entire, oblong-quadrate, with orange callus at base. Spring. Brit. Honduras, Costa Rica, Panama.

serra Rchb.f. Sts. to 8 in. long; lvs. triangular, to 1 in. long; infl. simple or paniculate, 1- to few-fld.; fls. to ½ in. across, yellow, marked with purple, lip 3-lobed, to ⅜ in. long, midlobe obscurely 4-lobed. Late spring. Ecuador.

LODOICEA Comm. ex Labill. DOUBLE COCONUT. *Palmae*. One sp., a solitary, tall, stout, dioecious palm of Praslin and Curieuse Is. (Seychelles Is.); lvs. costapalmate to apex, petioles elongate, margins not toothed; infls. among lvs., unlike, peduncles sheathed by several tubular bracts, the male with 1 or rarely 2 elongate, thick, spikelike flowering axes covered with imbricate bractlets, the female with a short axis bearing few sessile fls.; male fls. many, in clusters sunken in pits formed by bractlets, sepals and petals 3, much alike, separate, stamens many, female fls. much larger than male, with 2 large bractlets, sepals and petals 3, similar, thick, imbricate, pistil 3-celled, 3-ovuled; fr. very large, fibrous, with 1 or rarely 2–3 large seeds, each 2-lobed in a 2-lobed, thick, bony, endocarp, hollow in center, endosperm homogeneous.

Rarely cultivated; a tender, very slow-growing fan palm, noteworthy for its giant seeds, largest in the plant kingdom. The nuts, floating in the Indian Ocean, were once thought to have come from the Maldive Is., an error preserved in the name *L. maldivica*. Suitable for gardens in the tropics or indoors under glass. For culture see *Palms*.

maldivica (J. F. Gmel.) Pers. [*L. sechellarum* Labill.]. SEYCHELLES NUT, COCO-DE-MER, DOUBLE COCONUT. To 100 ft.; lf. blades to 20 ft. long, 12 ft. wide, glossy; male infl. to 6 ft. long, 3 in. in diam., female infl. shorter, with fls. to 4 in. in diam; fr. ovoid, to 20 in. long, flattened when 1-seeded.

sechellarum: *L. maldivica*.

LOGANBERRY: see *BOYSENBERRY*.

LOGANIA R. Br. *Loganiaceae*. About 20–30 spp. of herbs or shrubs, native mostly to Australia, but also to New Zeal. and New Caledonia; lvs. opp.; fls. small, white or pink, mostly in terminal cymes or panicles, 5(-4)-merous, ovary 2-celled; fr. a dehiscent caps.

longifolia: *L. vaginalis*.

vaginalis (Labill.) F. J. Muell. [*L. longifolia* R. Br.]. Shrub, to 6 ft. or more; lvs. elliptic or lanceolate, to 3 in. long; fls. small, white, in leafy panicles. W. and S. Australia. Cult. in Calif. in Zone 10.

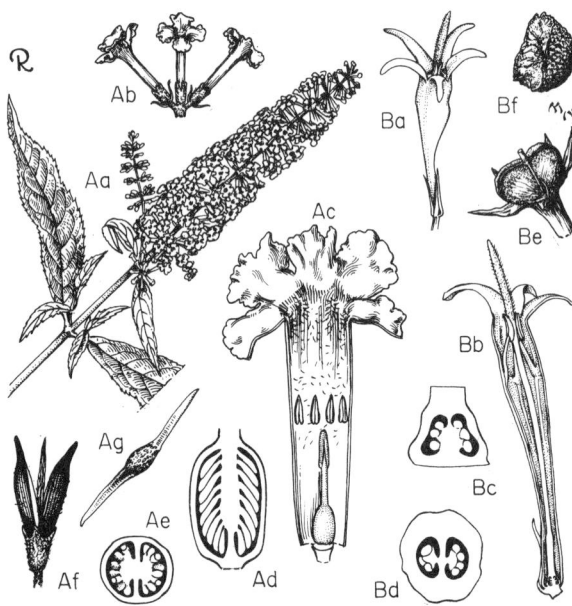

LOGANIACEAE. **A,** *Buddleia Davidii:* **Aa,** inflorescence, × ¼; **Ab,** flowers, × 1; **Ac,** pistil and expanded corolla, × 4; **Ad,** ovary, vertical section, × 10; **Ae,** ovary, cross section, × 10; **Af,** capsule, × 3; **Ag,** seed, × 6. **B,** *Spigelia marilandica;* **Ba,** flower, × ¾; **Bb,** flower, vertical section, × 1; **Bc,** ovary, vertical section, × 6; **Bd,** ovary, cross section, × 6; **Be,** capsule, × 1; **Bf,** seed, × 4.

LOGANIACEAE Mart. LOGANIA FAMILY. Dicot.; 32 genera and nearly 800 spp. of herbs, shrubs, or trees, native to warm temp. or trop. regions; lvs. commonly opp., simple; fls. bisexual, regular, in panicles, cymes, heads, or spikes, or sometimes solitary, calyx and corolla commonly 4–5-lobed, stamens 4–5, ovary superior, 2-celled; fr. a caps., berry, or drupe. Several genera yield drugs and poisonous substances; others are grown as ornamentals. *Anthocleista, Buddleia, Desfontainea, Fagraea, Gelsemium, Geniostoma, Logania, Nuxia, Spigelia,* and *Strychnos* are cult.

LOISELEURIA Desv. *Ericaceae*. One circumpolar sp., an evergreen, prostrate shrub; lvs. opp., crowded, simple, entire; fls. white or rose, in few-fld. terminal clusters, calyx 5-parted, corolla campanulate, stamens 5, anthers dehiscing longitudinally, ovary superior; fr. a 2–3-valved, many-seeded caps.

procumbens (L.) Desv. [*Azalea procumbens* L.; *Rhododendron procumbens* (L.) E. H. L. Krause]. ALPINE AZALEA. Glabrous, mat-forming per., 6–8 in. high; lvs. elliptic to oblong, to ⁵⁄₁₆ in. long, revolute. Useful in alpine and rock gardens in cold climates. Zone 2.

LOLIUM L. RYEGRASS, DARNEL. *Gramineae*. About 10 spp. of ann. or per. grasses in Eurasia; lf. blades flat; spikes slender, usually flat; spikelets several-fld., solitary, placed edgewise to the continuous rachis, one edge fitting the alt. concavities, the rachilla disarticulating above the glumes and between the florets, first glume usually lacking, the second strongly 3–5-nerved, equalling or exceeding the second floret, lemma rounded on the back, 5–7-nerved, obtuse, acute, or awned. For terminology see *Gramineae*.

italicum: *L. multiflorum*.

multiflorum Lam. [*L. italicum* A. Braun]. ITALIAN R., AUSTRALIAN R. Distinguished from *L. perenne* by more robust habit, sts. to over 3 ft., cylindrical, pale or yellowish at base; spikelets 10–20-fld., to 1 in. long, glume shorter than the spikelet, lemmas to ⁵⁄₁₆ in. long, at least the upper one awned. Eur. The hybrid, *L. multiflorum* × *L. perenne,* COMMON R., DOMESTIC R., OREGON R., WESTERN R., is closer to *L. multiflorum,* although usually shorter. Used in the nw. and se. states as a lawn or pasture grass.

perenne L. PERENNIAL R., ENGLISH R., LYME GRASS, TERRELL G., STRAND WHEAT. Short-lived per., sts. to 2 ft., erect or decumbent at the commonly reddish base; lf. blades glossy, to ⅛ in. wide; spike often subfalcate, mostly 6–10 in. long; spikelets mostly 6–10-fld., lemma ¼ in. long, awnless or nearly so. Eur.; introd. for lawns or pastures and widely naturalized in cool temp. N. Amer. Cv. 'Paceyi'. PACEY'S ENGLISH R. seeds smaller. Used in lawn mixtures. For the hybrid with *L. multiflorum,* see under *L. multiflorum*.

LOMATIA R. Br. *Proteaceae*. Twelve spp. of trees and shrubs, native to Australia and S. Amer.; lvs. alt., entire or pinnately divided; fls. bisexual, in pairs in simple or branched loose racemes; fr. a leathery follicle, differing from *Grevillea* in having several seeds.

They require cool greenhouse treatment or are grown outdoors in warm regions. Propagated by cuttings of well-ripened wood.

fraxinifolia F. J. Muell. Small tree; lvs. pinnately divided, segms. stalked, ovate or ovate-lanceolate, to 3 in. long, toothed, leathery, glossy; racemes to 8 in. long. Queensland.

hirsuta (Lam.) Diels [*L. obliqua* (Ruiz & Pav.) R. Br.]. Small tree, to 20 ft.; lvs. ovate, to 4 in. long, crenate, brown-tomentose at first, leathery; racemes axillary, to 3 in. long; fls. white, about ⁵⁄₁₆ in. long. Ecuador, Peru, Chile, Argentina. In Chile, wood used for making furniture.

ilicifolia R. Br. Shrub or small tree; lvs. ovate to lanceolate, to 3 in. long or more, prickly-toothed or -lobed, silky-pubescent beneath, rarely pinnately divided. Queensland, New S. Wales, Victoria.

obliqua: *L. hirsuta*.

silaifolia R. Br. Shrub, to 3 ft.; lvs. to 8 in. long, rarely pinnate, mostly 2–3-pinnately divided, segms. sessile, linear or lanceolate, toothed. Australia. Dyed sprays are used by florists and decorators, as "CRINKLEBUSH."

LOMATIUM Raf. [*Cogswellia* K. Spreng.; *Leptotaenia* Nutt.]. *Umbelliferae*. About 70 spp. of short-stemmed or stemless per. herbs, native mostly in w. N. Amer.; roots thickened; lvs. often dissected; fls. small, yellow, white, or purple, in compound umbels, involucre usually absent or inconspicuous, involucels usually present; fr. flattened dorsally corky- or membranous-winged.

Sometimes planted in wild gardens.

ambiguum (Nutt.) J. Coult. & Rose. To 1 ft.; lvs. 1–2-pinnately divided, lfts. linear; fls. yellow; fr. glabrous, wings very narrow. B.C. to Ore. and Utah.

angustatum: *L. Martindalei.*

columbianum Mathias & Const. [*Leptotaenia purpurea* J. Coult. & Rose]. To 20 in.; lvs. ternately compound, the divisions 2–4-pinnate, segms. linear to filiform, glabrous; fls. purple, in 6–10-rayed umbels to 6 in. across; fr. to 1 in. long and ½ in. wide. Columbia R. region of Ore. and Wash.

dissectum (Nutt.) Mathias & Const. To 4½ ft.; lvs. ternately compound, the divisions 2–4-pinnate, segms. linear, puberulent, or glabrate; fls. yellow or purple, pedicels to ¾ in. long; fr. oblong-ovoid, ½ in. long. Var. **dissectum** [*Leptotaenia dissecta* Nutt.]. The typical var.; leaf segms. more than ⅛ in. wide; pedicels shorter than sterile fls. Idaho, Wash. to n. Calif. Var. **multifidum** (Nutt.) Mathias & Const. [*Leptotaenia multifida* Nutt.]. Leaf segms. to ⅛ in. wide; pedicels longer than sterile fls. Alta. and B.C., s. to Colo., Ariz., and s. Calif.

Grayi (J. Coult. & Rose) J. Coult. & Rose. Stemless or short-stemmed, to 2 ft.; lvs. ternately to biternately compound, the divisions pinnately divided into narrow segms.; fls. yellow; fr. ovate-oblong to oblong, to ⅝ in. long. Wyo. and Colo., w. to Wash., Ore., and Nev.

Hallii (S. Wats.) J. Coult. & Rose. To 14 in., mostly glabrous; lvs. oblong in outline, ultimate segms. less than ¹⁄₁₆ in. wide; peduncles longer than lvs., rays of umbel 9–17, to 2 in. long, involucels of slender bractlets, pedicels to ¼ in. long; fls. yellow; fr. glabrous, oblong, ⅛ in. wide. W. Ore.

macrocarpum (Hook. & Arn.) J. Coult. & Rose. Short-stemmed, 4–20 in., tomentose to villous or glabrate; lvs. ternately compound, the divisions 2–3-pinnate into linear or oblong segms.; involucral bracts conspicuous, pedicels ⅝ in. long; fls. white, yellow, or purplish; fr. oblong, to ¾ in. long, glabrous to villous. Man. to N. Dak., w. to B.C., Calif., and Nev.

Martindalei J. Coult. & Rose [*L. angustatum* (J. Coult. & Rose) St. John]. To 8 in.; lvs. ternately compound, the divisions 2–3-pinnate, lfts. ovate, overlapping; involucels absent; fls. creamy-white to lemon-yellow; fr. narrow-oblong, wings very narrow. Mts. of w. B.C. to Cascade Mts., Ore.

multifidum: *L. dissectum* var.

nudicaule (Pursh) J. Coult. & Rose [*Cogswellia nudicaulis* (Pursh) M. E. Jones]. PESTLE PARSNIP. To 2 ft., glabrous; lvs. biternately compound, ovate to lanceolate, entire or toothed, to 2 in. long; peduncle inflated at apex; fr. elliptic, glabrous, to ½ in. long. Idaho to B.C. and Calif.

triternatum (Pursh) J. Coult. & Rose [*Cogswellia triternata* (Pursh) M. E. Jones]. BUCK PARSNIP. To 2½ ft., puberulent to glabrate; lvs. biternately to triternately compound, segms. linear to linear-lanceolate, to 4 in. long; fls. yellow; fr. narrowly oblong, to ½ in. long. Alta., s. to Wyo. and n. Calif. Material listed as *Cogswellia trinervata* may be this sp.

utriculatum (Nutt.) J. Coult. & Rose [*Cogswellia utriculata* (Nutt.) M. E. Jones]. SPRING-GOLD, BLADDER PARSNIP. Low to caulescent, to 1 ft.; lvs. pinnately decompound, segms. linear, to ⅜ in. long; bractlets of involucels obovate, often toothed; fls. yellow; fr. glabrous. B.C. to Calif., w. of Cascade Mts. and Sierra Nevada.

LONAS Adans. *Compositae* (Anthemis Tribe). One sp., an ann. herb, native to Medit. region; lvs. alt., pinnately divided, segms. linear; fl. heads in dense corymbs, discoid, involucral bracts imbricate in several rows, scarious-margined, receptacle chaffy; fls. all tubular, ray fls. absent; achenes 5-angled, pappus a toothed crown.

annua (L.) Vines & Druce [*L. inodora* (L.) Gaertn.]. AFRICAN DAISY, YELLOW AGERATUM. To 1 ft., branched; heads about ⅜ in. across, in corymbs 1–2 in. across; fls. yellow. Italy, nw. Afr.

inodora: *L. annua.*

LONCHOCARPUS HBK. LANCEPOD. *Leguminosae* (subfamily *Faboideae*). About 100 spp. or more of mostly trees, widespread in tropics; lvs. alt., odd-pinnate; fls. in racemes, white to violet, stamens 10, 1 of them separate at base but united above with the other 9; fr. a flat, few-seeded, indehiscent legume.

Roots of several shrubby S. Amer. species yield the fish poisons cubé, timbo, and barbasco, now utilized as commercial sources of the insecticide rotenone; others are grown in tropical and subtropical areas for their very showy flowers.

Griffonianus (Baill.) S. T. Dunn. To 50 ft.; lfts. in 3–4 pairs, elliptic, to 4 in. long, acuminate; racemes erect, to 12 in. long; fls. dark purple,

solitary or clustered; fr. linear-lanceolate, over 3 in. long. Tropics, W. Afr.

latifolius (Willd.) HBK. To 50 ft., branchlets brown, silky-hairy; lfts. in 2–4 pairs, ovate to oblong, to 4¾ in. long, gray-hairy beneath; racemes axillary, dense; fls. dark red- or greenish-purple, standard silky-hairy, more than ½ in. long; fr. to 2½ in. long and 1 in. wide. Caribbean area. Wood used for general construction.

punctatus HBK [*L. violaceus* of auth., not Benth.]. Differs from *L. violaceus* in having lfts. in 2–4 pairs, ovate-oblong, to 2 in. long, light green above, and petals densely dotted. Ne. Venezuela, Trinidad.

violaceus Benth. Small, glabrous tree; lfts. in 3–5 pairs, ovate, translucent-dotted, to 3½ in. long, dark green above; racemes axillary, to 10 in. long; calyx truncate, petals whitish outside, pale purple or pinkish inside; fr. lanceolate, to 2⁵⁄₁₆ in. long and half as broad, 1-seeded. W. Indies. Often cult. in Zone 10b. *L. violaceus* of most authors is *L. punctatus.*

LONICERA L. HONEYSUCKLE. *Caprifoliaceae.* More than 150 spp. of usually deciduous, sometimes more or less evergreen, erect or climbing shrubs, widespread in the N. Hemisphere; lvs. opp., simple; fls. small but showy or sometimes large, often in axillary pairs subtended by 2 bracts and 4 bractlets, or in sessile whorls at ends of brs.; calyx 4–5-toothed, corolla 4–5-lobed, stamens 5, ovary inferior, 2–3(–5)-celled; fr. berrylike, fls. of pairs sometimes united.

The name honeysuckle is sometimes also applied to some Amer. azaleas *(Rhododendron).* Honeysuckles are very popular ornamental plants, mostly hardy north (Zone 5), except for the Himalayan species, which require winter protection. They thrive in any good garden soil. Propagated by seeds in autumn or stratified, by cuttings of ripe wood, by layers, or by cuttings of green wood under glass.

Alberti: *L. spinosa* var.

albiflora Torr. & A. Gray. Somewhat climbing; lvs. elliptic or ovate, to 1½ in. long, upper pair united at base, fls. in clusters yellowish-white, 2-lipped, 1 in. long; fr. orange. Spring. Zone 6. Var. **albiflora.** The typical var.; lvs. glabrous. Okla., Tex. Var. **dumosa** A. Gray. Lvs. pubescent. Okla., Tex., w. to Ariz.

alpigena L. To 10 ft.; lvs. elliptic to oblong, to 4 in. long; fls. in pairs, yellowish, tinged red, 2-lipped, ½ in. long; fr. scarlet. Late spring. Eur. Cv. 'Nana'. Dwarf form, lower lf. surface and peduncles pubescent. Zone 6.

alesuosmoides Graebn. Twining, evergreen; lvs. lanceolate, to 2½ in. long and ⅝ in. wide, rounded at base; fls. in pairs, orange-red, to ⅝ in. long, corolla tube longer than limb; fr. reddish. Summer. W. China. Similar to *L. Henryi.*

×**amoena** Zab.: *L. Korolkowii* × *L. tatarica.* To 9 ft., lvs. ovate, to 2 in. long; fls. in pairs, pink or white, 2-lipped, ¾ in. long. Early summer. Cv. 'Arnoldiana'. Fls. almost white on opening. Cv. 'Rosea'. Fls. pink.

aureoreticulata: *L. japonica* cv.

belgica: a listed name of no botanical standing for *L. Periclymenum* var.

×**bella** Zab.: *L. Morrowii* × *L. tatarica.* Lvs. ovate, to 2 in. long; fls. in pairs, white or pink changing to yellow, 2-lipped, ½ in. long; fr. red. Early summer. Cvs. are: 'Albida', 'Candida', fls. white; 'Atrorosea', fls. red; 'Chrysantha', fls. yellow; 'Incarnata', 'Rosea', fls. red.

Billardii: a listed name of no botanical standing.

×**Brownii** (Regel) Carrière: *L. hirsuta* × *L. sempervirens.* Closely resembling *L. sempervirens,* but fls. somewhat 2-lipped. Cvs. include: 'Fuchsioides', fls. scarlet outside; 'Plantierensis', fls. coral-red with scarlet lobes; 'Punicea', fls. orange-red.

caerulea L. [*L. emphyllocalyx* Maxim.]. To 5 ft., much-branched; lvs. ovate to oblong, to 3 in. long, bright green; fls. in pairs, yellowish-white, ½ in. long; fr. dark blue, with a bloom, the 2 berries united at base and enveloped by the united bractlets. Spring. Eur., Asia; naturalized in N. Amer. Var. **dependens** (Dipp.) Rehd. [*L. caerulea* var. *graciliflora* Dipp.]. Lvs. elliptic to ovate, to 1¼ in. long, pubescent; corolla tube slender. Turkestan. Var. **edulis** Regel. Lvs. pubescent, oblong-lanceolate, stamens longer than limb. Tibet, e. Siberia. Var. **glabrescens** Rupr. [*L. caerulea* var. *praecox* Dipp.]. Lvs. usually oblong, to 2½ in. long, pubescent when young; corolla with short, thick tube, glabrous on outside. Eur. to ne. Asia. Var. **graciliflora:** var. *dependens.* Var. **praecox:** var. *glabrescens.*

canadensis Bartr. FLY H. To 5 ft.; lvs. ovate or elliptic, to 3 in. long, ciliate; fls. in pairs, yellowish or tinged red, to ¾ in. long; fr. red. Spring. Que. to Penn. and Minn. Zone 4.

Caprifolium L. [*L. verna* Hort. ex Lavall.]. ITALIAN WOODBINE. Twining, to 20 ft.; lvs. elliptic, to 4 in. long, bluish-green beneath, upper lvs. united at base; fls. in whorls, white or purplish, 2-lipped, 2 in. long, fragrant; fr. orange-red. Late spring. Eur., w. Asia; naturalized in e. U.S. Zone 6.

Chamissoi Bunge. To 3 ft., twigs glabrous; lvs. ovate to elliptic, to 2 in. long, usually obtuse, glabrous, nearly sessile; fls. in pairs, dark violet, to ½ in. long; fr. red. Ne. Asia. Zone 5.

chrysantha Turcz. To 12 ft.; lvs. ovate to ovate-lanceolate to 5 in. long; fls. in pairs, yellowish-white changing to yellow, 2-lipped, to ¾ in. long; fr. coral-red. Late spring. Asia. Zone 4. Var. **latifolia** Korsh. Lvs. elliptic, broad, sparingly pilose beneath, somewhat thickish.

ciliosa (Pursh) Poir. Usually twining, more or less evergreen; lvs. ovate to oblong-elliptic, to 4 in. long, ciliate, blue-green beneath, petiole to ½ in., upper lvs. united at base; fls. in terminal, 3-fld., sessile, headlike cymes, yellow, sometimes tinged purple, 2-lipped, swollen at base, to 1½ in. long, stamens longer than limb; fr. red. Mont. to Utah., w. to B.C. and Calif. Zone 6.

Claveyi: a listed name of no botanical standing for a compact, dwarf cv. perhaps of *L. tatarica* or *L. xylostoides* or *L. xylosteum.*

compacta: a lised name of no botanical standing for dwarf plants.

conjugialis Kellogg. To 5 ft., much-branched; lvs. elliptic to obovate, to 2 in. long, acute, ciliate; fls. in pairs, dark red, about 5/16 in. long; fr. red. Early summer. Nev. to Calif. and Wash. Zone 6.

demissa Rehd. To 12 ft., much-branched; lvs. obovate, to 1¼ in. long, pubescent; fls. in pairs, whitish, changing to yellow, 2-lipped, ½ in. long; fr. scarlet. Late spring. Japan. Zone 6.

dioica L. Often twining; lvs. elliptic or oblong, to 3 in. long, glaucous beneath, upper pair united at base; fls. in whorls, greenish or yellowish, 2-lipped, ½ in. long, style usually glabrous; fr. red. Late spring. Que. to N.C. and Iowa. Zone 2.

discolor Lindl. To 6 ft., glabrous; lvs. elliptic to elliptic-oblong, glaucous beneath, to 3 in. long; fls. in pairs, yellowish-white, often tinged red, to 1 in. long; fr. black. Late spring. Kashmir to Afghanistan. Zone 6.

emphyllocalyx: *L. caerulea.*

etrusca Santi. Climbing, evergreen or partly so; lvs. obovate to elliptic, to 3 in. long, glaucous and pubescent beneath, upper lvs. united at base; fls. in dense spikes, yellowish-white, 2-lipped, 2 in. long, fragrant; fr. red. Summer. Medit. region. Zone 7. Cv. **'Superba'.** A vigorous form; fl. heads forming large terminal panicles.

flava Sims. YELLOW H. Climbing; lvs. elliptic, to 3 in. long, bluish-green beneath, upper lvs. united at base; fls. in whorls, orange-yellow, 2-lipped, 1¼ in. long, fragrant; fr. red, ¼ in. in diam. Late spring. N.C. to Okla. Zone 6.

fragrantissima Lindl. & Paxt. To 8 ft., partly evergreen; lvs. ovate or elliptic, to 3 in. long, bluish-green beneath; fls. in pairs, creamy-white, 2-lipped, ½ in. long, very fragrant; fr. red. Spring. China. Zone 6. Fls. tending to precede lvs. where the shrub is deciduous.

fuchsioides: a listed name of no botanical standing for *L.* × *Brownii* cv.

Geraldii: a misspelling of *L. Giraldii.*

Giraldii Rehd. Climbing; lvs. oblong-lanceolate, to 3 in. long, pubescent; fls. in pairs, purplish-red, yellow-pubescent outside, ¾ in. long; fr. purple-black. Summer. China. Zone 6.

glaucescens (Rydb.) Rydb. Differs from *L. dioica* in having lvs. pubescent beneath; corolla about ¾ in. long, style usually pubescent. Que. to Alta., s. to Va. and Nebr. Zone 4.

gracilipes Miq. To 6 ft.; lvs. ovate, to 3 in. long, bluish-green beneath; fls. usually solitary and drooping, pink to carmine, ½ in. long; fr. scarlet. Spring. Japan. Zone 6. Var. **glabra** is listed.

grandiflora: a listed name of no botanical standing, perhaps *L. tatarica* cv.

Halliana: *L. japonica* cv.

Heckrottii Rehd. Origin unknown, may be a hybrid between *L. americana* and *L. sempervirens;* lvs. elliptic, to 2 in. long, glaucous beneath; fls. in spikes, purple outside, yellow inside, 2-lipped, to 2 in. long; fr. red. Summer. Zone 4.

Henryi Hemsl. Twining or prostrate, partly evergreen; lvs. oblong-lanceolate, to 3 in. long, ciliate; fls. in pairs, yellowish- or purple-red, to ¾ in. long; fr. black. Summer. China. Zone 6.

Hermanii: a listed name of no botanical standing.

Hildebrandiana Collett & Hemsl. GIANT BURMESE H., GIANT H. Climbing, evergreen; lvs. ovate, to 6 in. long; fls. in pairs, yellow changing to orange-red, to 7 in. long, tube very slender. Burma. Zone 10, thrives in Calif. Outstanding for its large lvs. and fls.

hirsuta Eat. HAIRY H. Climbing; lvs. elliptic, to 4 in. long, gray-pubescent beneath, upper lvs. united at base; fls. in short spikes, orange-yellow, 2-lipped, 1 in. long; fr. red. Summer. Que. to Penn. and Nebr. Zone 4.

hispidula Dougl. ex Torr. & A. Gray. Brs. sarmentose; lvs. ovate or ovate-oblong, to 2½ in. long, pubescent beneath, upper lvs. united at base; fls. in whorls, whitish or purplish, 2-lipped, ½ in. long; fr. red. Summer. B.C. to Calif. Var. **vacillans** A. Gray. More vigorous, lvs. and fls. larger.

iberica Bieb. To 6 ft., much-branched; lvs. orbicular-ovate, to 1½ in. long, hairy; fls. in pairs, yellowish-white, 2-lipped, ½ in. long; fr. bright red. Early summer. W. Asia. Zone 6.

interrupta Benth. CHAPARRAL H. Twining, evergreen; lvs. orbicular to elliptic, to 1½ in. long, glaucous beneath, uppermost pair usually united at base; fls. sessile, in interrupted spikes, yellowish, to ¾ in. long; fr. red. Early summer. Ariz. and s. Calif.

involucrata (Richardson) Banks ex K. Spreng. TWINBERRY. To 3 ft.; lvs. ovate to oblong-lanceolate, to 5 in. long, glabrous or slightly hairy beneath; fls. in pairs, yellow or tinged red, ½ in. long, corolla tubular; fr. purple-black, shining. Late spring. Que. to Alaska and Mex. Zone 4. Forma **humilis** Rehd. Dwarf shrub, to 1½ ft. Colo. Forma **serotina** Rehd. Corolla orange-yellow, flushed with scarlet, to ¾ in. long. Colo. Var. **flavescens** (Dipp.) Rehd. Lvs. glabrous or nearly so, corolla gibbous at base. B.C. to Ore., Utah, & Wyo.

japonica Thunb. JAPANESE H., GOLD-AND-SILVER FLOWER. Climbing, wholly or partly evergreen; lvs. ovate, to 3 in. long; fls. in pairs, white or purplish, 2-lipped, to 1½ in. long, the limb as long as tube, fragrant; fr. black. Summer. E. Asia; naturalized in N. Amer. and a serious woodland weed in the Middle Atlantic states. Zone 5. Cvs. include: **'Aureo-reticulata'** [*L. aureoreticulata* Hort. ex T. Moore], lvs. small, veined with yellow; **'Halliana'** [*L. Halliana* Hort. ex C. Koch], HALL'S JAPANESE H., fls. white, changing to yellow, upper lip divided nearly to middle; **'Purpurea'**, lvs. purple; **'Variegata'**, lvs. variegated yellow. Var. **chinensis** (S. Wats.) Bak. Lvs. usually ciliate, often slightly pubescent on veins beneath, often tinged red-purple when young; corolla carmine on outside, upper lip divided more than halfway. Var. **repens** (Siebold) Rehd. Lf. veins often purplish; corolla white or tinged pale purple, limb longer than tube, upper lip divided about ⅓.

Koehneana Rehd. To 12 ft.; lvs. ovate, to 4 in. long, densely pubescent beneath; fls. in pairs, yellowish-white, ¾ in. long, 2-lipped; fr. dark red. China.

Korolkowii Stapf. To 12 ft.; lvs. ovate or elliptic, to 1 in. long, bluish-green and pubescent beneath; fls. in pairs, rose or rarely white, 2-lipped, ½ in. long; fr. bright red. Late spring. Turkestan. Zone 5. Var. **Zabelii** (Rehd.) Rehd. Lvs. broadly ovate, subcordate, glabrous.

Ledebourii Eschsch. Sometimes united with *L. involucrata,* from which it differs in having lower lf. surface pubescent and stamens not longer than corolla tube. Coastal, Calif. Zone 6.

Maackii (Rupr.) Maxim. To 15 ft.; lvs. ovate to ovate-lanceolate, to 3 in. long; fls. in pairs, white changing to yellowish, 2-lipped, ¾ in. long; fr. dark red. Early summer. Asia. Zone 3. Forma **podocarpa** Franch. ex Rehd. Spreading; lvs. pubescent; corollas small, pubescent.

magnifica: a listed name of no botanical standing for *L. sempervirens* cv.

Maximowiczii (Rupr.) Maxim. To 10 ft.; lvs. ovate, to 2½ in. long, pubescent beneath; fls. in pairs, violet-red, 5/16 in. long, 2-lipped; fr. red. Late spring. Manchuria, Korea. Zone 5. Var. **sachalinensis** Friedr. Schmidt [*L. sachalinensis* (Friedr. Schmidt) Nakai]. Fls. dark purple.

microphylla Willd. To 3 ft., twigs glabrous to puberulous; lvs. obovate to oblong-elliptic, to 1 in. long, obtuse or acutish, usually puberulous; fls. in pairs, yellowish-white, nearly ½ in. long; fr. orange-red. Cent. Asia. Zone 6.

× **minutiflora** Zab.: *L. Morrowii* × *L.* × *xylosteoides.* Lvs. oblong, to 1½ in. long; fls. whitish, 2-lipped, ½ in. long; fr. red. Late spring.

modesta Rehd. To 7 ft., brs. brownish-gray, fibrous; lvs. rhombic-ovate to oblong, to 1¾ in. long, obtuse to mucronate, dull green and glabrous above, pale green and villous-pubescent beneath at least on veins; fls. in pairs on short peduncles in axils of upper lvs., white, becoming yellowish with reddish base, to ½ in. long. W. China. Zone 8.

Morrowii A. Gray. To 8 ft.; lvs. elliptic to oblong, to 2 in. long, pubescent beneath; fls. in pairs, white, changing to yellow, 2-lipped, ½ in. long; fr. red. Late spring. Japan. Zone 4. Cv. **'Xanthocarpa'.** Fr. yellow.

nitida E. H. Wils. [*L. pileata* forma *yunnanensis* (Franch.) Rehd.]. Evergreen, to 6 ft.; lvs. ovate, to ½ in. long, shining above; fls. creamy-white, ¼ in. long, scentless or nearly so; fr. amethyst, spherical, to ¼ in. across. China. Zone 7. The cvs. listed are: **'Elegant'**, spreading, to 3 ft., leading shoots arching with lvs. suborbicular to narrowly ovate, to ⅝ in. long, lateral shoots often erect, with lvs. slightly smaller, narrower, fls. and frs. freely produced; **'Ernest Wilson'**, leading shoots erect or arching, with lvs. 4-ranked, ovate or broadly triangular, to ⅜ in. long, lateral shoots mostly horizontal, with lvs. narrower, fls. and frs. few in number; **'Fertilis'**, habit stiff, leading shoots erect, with lvs. 4-ranked, broadly ovate or broadly elliptic, to ⅝ in. long, lateral shoots mostly long and arching, with lvs. smaller and sometimes slightly falcately curved, fls. and frs. freely produced; **'Graziosa'**, densely branched, low and matforming, leading shoots arching, with lvs. narrowly triangular-ovate, to ½ in. long, lateral shoots many, short, with lvs. smaller and narrower, fls. and frs. rare; **'Yunnan'**, leading shoots erect, with lvs. 4-ranked, broadly ovate or ovate-triangular, to ½ in. long, lateral shoots mostly erect, with lvs. smaller, narrower, fls. and frs. usually freely produced.

×**notha** Zab.: *L. Ruprechtiana* × *L. tatarica.* Lvs. ovate-oblong, to 2½ in. long; fls. in pairs, pinkish changing to yellowish, 2-lipped, ¾ in. long; fr. red.

oblongifolia (J. Goldie) Hook. SWAMP FLY H. To 5 ft.; lvs. oblong, to 3 in. long, gray-pubescent beneath; fls. in pairs, yellowish-white, 2-lipped, ½ in. long; fr. red. Late spring. New Bruns., to Penn. and Minn. Zone 2.

obovata Royle ex Hook.f. & T. Thoms. To 7 ft., twigs glabrous; lvs. obovate, 3/16–½ in. long, tapering toward base, whitish beneath; fls. in pairs, whitish, nearly ½ in. long; fr. blue-black. Cent. Asia. Zone 6.

orientalis Lam. To 10 ft.; lvs. ovate or ovate-lanceolate, to 4 in. long, pale and pubescent beneath; fls. in pairs, pink or violet, 2-lipped, ½ in. long; fr. black. Asia Minor. Var. **caucasica** (Pall.) Rehd. Lvs. elliptic, glabrous beneath. Zone 4. Var. **longifolia** (Dipp.) Rehd. Lvs. oblong or lanceolate; fls. smaller and reddish.

Periclymenum L. WOODBINE. Climbing; lvs. ovate or ovate-oblong, to 3 in. long, bluish-green beneath; fls. in whorls, yellowish-white, 2-lipped, to 2 in. long; fr. red. Summer. Eur., N. Afr., w. Asia. Zone 5. Cv. **'Aurea'**. Lvs. variegated. Var. **belgica** Ait. DUTCH WOODBINE. Shrubby, lvs. glabrous, somewhat thickish; fls. purple outside, usually fading to yellowish. Var. **serotina** Ait. Differs from preceding in having fls. dark purple outside, yellow inside.

×**permixta** Zab. A name applied to a Eur. garden hybrid, presumably between *L. micranthoides* Zab., a plant of probable hybrid origin, and *L. Xylosteum.*

pileata D. Oliver. Often prostrate, evergreen or partly so; lvs. ovate to oblong-lanceolate, to 1½ in. long, shining above; fls. in pairs, whitish, 5/16 in. long, fragrant; fr. purple, translucent. Spring. China. Zone 6. Closely related to *L. nitida,* but having prostrate habit, stiffer horizontal branching, and larger lvs. Forma **yunnanensis:** *L. nitida.*

prolifera (Kirchn.) Rehd. [*L. Sullivantii* A. Gray]. GRAPE H. Climbing; lvs. elliptic or oblong, to 4 in. long, very glaucous, upper lvs. united at base; fls. in whorls, pale yellow, marked with purple, 2-lipped, 1 in. long; fr. red. Summer. Ohio to Tenn. and Mo. Zone 5.

pulcherrima Ridl. Not cult. See *L. tatarica* cv. 'Latifolia'.

×**Purpusii** Rehd.: *L. fragrantissima* × *L. Standishii.* Lvs. to 3 in. long, 1½ in. wide, dark green above, light green beneath, midrib hairy; fls. mostly as in *L. fragrantissima.*

pyrenaica L. To 3 ft.; lvs. oblong to oblong-lanceolate, to 1½ in. long, pale beneath; fls. in pairs, white, to ¾ in. long; fr. red. Late spring. Pyrenees. Zone 6.

quinquelocularis Hardw. To 15 ft.; lvs. ovate or elliptic, to 3 in. long, grayish and pubescent beneath; fls. in pairs, yellowish, 2-lipped, ¾ in. long; fr. translucent, white. Early summer. W. Asia. Zone 6.

reticulata Champ. Similar to *L. confusa,* but having lvs. obtusish, strongly netted beneath, petioles ½–⅝ in. long; ovary glabrous. Se. China. Cv. **'Aurea'** is listed.

Ruprechtiana Regel. To 12 ft.; lvs. oblong to lanceolate, to 4 in. long, pale and pubescent beneath; fls. in pairs, white changing to yellow, 2-lipped, ½ in. long; fr. red. Late spring. Manchuria. Zone 2.

saccata Rehd. To 6 ft.; lvs. oblong, to 2 in. long; fls. in pairs, pinkish, ½ in. long; fr. scarlet. Late spring. China. Zone 6.

sachalinensis: *L. Maximowiczii* var.

×**salicifolia** Zab.: *L. Ruprechtiana* × *L.* ×*xylosteoides.* Lvs. narrow, pointed; fls. small.

sempervirens L. TRUMPET H., CORAL H. Evergreen in the South, climbing; lvs. ovate to oblong, to 3 in. long, glaucous beneath, upper lvs. united at base; fls. in spikes, orange-scarlet, yellow inside, 2 in. long; fr. red. Summer. Conn. to Fla. and Tex. Zone 4. Cvs. include: **'Magnifica'**, late flowering; **'Minor'**, partly evergreen; **'Sulphurea'**, fls. yellow; **'Superba'**, fls. bright scarlet.

spinosa Jacquem. ex Walp. To 4 ft., brs. somewhat spiny; lvs. linear-oblong, to 1 in. long; fls. in pairs, ¾ in. long; fr. whitish or purple, with a bloom. Himalayas. Var. **Alberti** (Regel) Rehd. [*L. Alberti* Regel]. Lvs. glaucous; fls. rose, ½ in. long, fragrant. Turkestan. Zone 4.

Standishii Jacques. To 8 ft., partly evergreen; lvs. ovate-oblong to lanceolate, to 4 in. long, hairy; fls. in pairs, white, 2-lipped, ½ in. long, fragrant; fr. red. Early spring. China. Zone 6.

strophiophora Franch. To 7 ft., twigs glandular-pilose; lvs. ovate to elliptic-ovate, to 3 in. long, acuminate, glabrous to hairy above, densely pilose beneath; fls. in pairs, white, to ¾ in. long; fr. red, pilose. Early spring. Japan. Zone 6.

subaequalis Rehd. Lvs. elliptic to obovate-oblong, to 4 in. long; fls. in sessile whorl, subtended by upper pair of lvs.; corolla funnelform, to 1 in. long, stamens about as long as limb. W. China. Zone 7.

subspicata Hook. & Arn. Clambering, evergreen, to 7–8 ft.; lvs. linear-oblong to oblong, to 1¼ in. long, pubescent, especially beneath; fls. several, in whorls, in short, compact, leafy spikes to 5 in. long, yellowish, to ½ in. long; fr. yellowish or red. S. Calif. Var. **Johnstonii** Keck. Lvs. oblong-ovate to suborbicular; fls. to slightly more than ½ in. S. and cent. Calif.

Sullivantii: *L. prolifera.*

syringantha Maxim. To 10 ft.; lvs. elliptic to oblong, to 1 in. long; fls. in pairs, pinkish or lilac, ½ in. long, fragrant; fr. red. Late spring. China. Zone 4. Cv. **'Grandiflora'** is listed. Var. **Wolfii** Rehd. Lvs. larger, narrower; fls. carmine.

tatarica L. TATARIAN H. To 10 ft.; lvs. ovate or ovate-lanceolate, to 2½ in. long, pale beneath; fls. in pairs, pink or white, 2-lipped, to 1 in. long; fr. red. Late spring. Russia to Turkestan. Zone 5. Cvs. include: **'Alba'**, fls. pure white; **'Angustifolia'**, lvs. narrow; **'Claveyi'**, listed name, may be *L. xylosteoides* cv. 'Clavey's Dwarf'; **'Grandiflora'**, fls. pure white, large; **'Latifolia'** [cv. 'Pulcherrima'], lvs. to 4 in. long, 2 in. wide; **'Lutea'**, fr. yellow; **'Nana'**, low compact shrub, lvs. oblong-ovate, to 2 in. long, fls. many, small, pink; **'Pulcherrima':** cv. 'Latifolia'; **'Rosea'**, fls. rose outside, pink inside; **'Rubra':** cv. 'Sibirica'; **'Sibirica'** [cv. 'Rubra'], fls. deep pink; **'Virginalis'**, fls. white. Var. **Zabelii:** probably *L. Korolkowii* var. *Zabelii.*

×**Tellmanniana** Hort. Späth: *L. sempervirens* × *L. tragophylla.* Fls. showy, deep yellow, to 1¼ in. long, in peduncled heads of usually 2 whorls.

tenuipes Nakai. To 7 ft., twigs glabrescent to pilose; lvs. elliptic to oblong or ovate, to 1 5/16 in. long, pilose above, densely so beneath, petioles glandular-hairy; fls. in pairs, red, to ¾ in. long, pilose outside; fr. red. Spring. Japan. Zone 6.

thibetica Bur. & Franch. To 5 ft.; lvs. oblong-lanceolate, to 1¼ in. long, shining above, white-tomentose beneath; fls. in pairs, pale purple, ½ in. long, pubescent outside; fr. red. China. Zone 5.

tragophylla Hemsl. Climbing; lvs. oblong, to 5 in. long, glaucous beneath, upper lvs. united at base; fls. in terminal heads, bright yellow, 2-lipped, to 3 in. long; fr. red. Early summer. China. Zone 6.

trichosantha Bur. & Franch. To 6 ft.; lvs. ovate or obovate, to 2 in. long, hairy on veins beneath; fls. in pairs, yellow, ½ in. long, 2-lipped; fr. bright red. Early summer. China, Tibet. Zone 6.

Tschonoskii Maxim. Upright shrub; lvs. elliptic-oblong, to 3½ in. long, glabrous; fls. in pairs, on slender peduncles to 1½ in. long, white, 2-lipped, glabrous outside; fr. red. Summer. Japan.

utahensis S. Wats. Low shrub; lvs. ovate to oblong, to 2 in. long; fls. in pairs, pale yellow, to ¾ in. long; fr. red. B.C. to Ore. and Utah. Zone 6.

verna: *L. Caprifolium.*

Wheeleri: a listed name of no botanical standing.

×**xylosteoides** Tausch: *L. tatarica* × *L. Xylosteum.* Lvs. rhombic-ovate, bluish-green; fls. pinkish, small. Cv. **'Clavey's Dwarf'**. Slow-growing, almost rounded shrub, densely branched to the ground, to 3 ft.; lvs. blue-green; fls. white.

Xylosteum L. FLY H., EUROPEAN F.H. To 10 ft.; lvs. ovate or obovate, to 2½ in. long, pale and pubescent beneath; fls. in pairs, yellowish-white, 2-lipped, ½ in. long, pubescent outside; fr. dark red. Late spring. Eur., Asia. Zone 5. Cv. **'Mollis'**. Lvs. pubescent on both sides.

yunnanensis Franch. Twining; lvs. oblong to obovate-lanceolate, to 3 in. long, acutish, glaucous, upper lvs. united at base; fls. in several peduncled whorls forming a head, yellow, to 1 in. long, hairy inside; fr. red. Sw. China. Zone 7.

LOPEZIA Cav. *Onagraceae.* About 18 spp. of herbaceous to somewhat woody plants, native to Mex. and Cent. Amer.; lvs. mostly lanceolate; fls. usually small, many, in racemes, sepals 4, petals 4, the 2 upper ascending, more or less clawed and geniculate, usually with 1 or 2 glands or tubercles at the junction of claw and blade, the 2 lower larger, not bent or tubercled, stamens 2, the upper fertile and enfolded by the expanded, lower, sterile one; fr. a caps.

Grown under glass, or in mild climates in the open. Propagated by seeds and by cuttings of firm wood.

albiflora Schlechtend. Of uncertain application; but cult. material under this name is probably *L. hirsuta*.

coccinea: a listed name of no botanical standing.

coronata Andr. CROWN-JEWELS. To 3 ft.; lvs. ovate to lanceolate, not much reduced up the st.; racemes leafy, to 1 ft. long; sepals ¼ in. long, red, petals lilac-pink, the 2 upper with single tubercles. S. Mex., El Salvador.

grandiflora Zucc. [*L. macrophylla* Benth.]. Woody, to 6 ft.; lvs. ovate, to 6 in. long; racemes bracted, in panicles; sepals and petals ⅝ in. long, deep rose. Chiapas (Mex.), Guatemala.

hirsuta Jacq. [*L. lineata* Zucc.]. MOSQUITO FLOWER. Ann. to suffrutescent per., sts. 1–3 ft. long, mostly cylindrical, slender, hairy; lvs. ovate, blades ½–1 in. long, the uppermost reduced to bracts; petals pink to rose, the 2 upper less than ³⁄₁₆ in. long, with single tubercles. Mex. to El Salvador.

lineata: *L. hirsuta*.

macrophylla: *L. grandiflora*.

miniata Lag. ex DC. Ann. to per., to 4 ft.; lvs. ovate, 1–4 in. long; racemes bracted, often paniculate; sepals ¼ in. long, dark red, petals paler, the 2 upper with paired tubercles. Mex.

rosea: a listed name of no botanical standing.

LOPHANTHERA A. Juss. *Malpighiaceae.* Three spp. of shrubs and trees, native to Brazil; lvs. opp., simple, 8–12 in. long; fls. yellow, in terminal panicles 10–20 in. long, calyx 5-parted, with 10 basal glands on exterior, petals clawed, glabrous, stamens 10, all fertile; fr. a caps.

lactescens Ducke. To 45 ft., the younger parts with latex; lvs. obovate, 8–12 in. long, entire, thin; panicles 300–500-fld., to 20 in. long, pendant. Brazil.

LOPHANTHUS: *AGASTACHE.* L. **anisatus**: *A. Foeniculum.*

LOPHIOLA Ker-Gawl. *Haemodoraceae.* Two spp. of per. herbs growing in wet pine barrens from Nov. Sc. to Fla.; fls. small, in densely white-woolly panicles, perianth segms. 6, stamens 6, ovary superior.

americana (Pursh) A. Wood [*L. aurea* Ker-Gawl.]. GOLDCREST. To 2 ft.; lvs. mostly basal, linear, much shorter than sts.; fls. yellowish.

aurea: *L. americana.*

LOPHOCEREUS (A. Berger) Britt. & Rose. *Cactaceae.* Perhaps 2 spp. of bushy to treelike cacti of nw. Mex. and s. Ariz.; sts. branching from the base or forming a short trunk, brs. simple, erect, 5–15-ribbed, at first short-spined; upper areoles fertile, with many long, bristlelike spines; fls. usually several at an areole, small, nocturnal, perianth tube short, limb rotate, scales of ovary few, small, with scant axillary wool; fr. with persistent perianth, globose, bursting, edible. Differs from *Myrtillocactus* in the elongate spines of the upper areoles and in the pink nocturnal fls.

For culture see *Cacti.*

australis: *L. Schottii* var.

Gatesii M. E. Jones. Sts. branching from the base, to 10 ft. high and 3½ in. thick, ribs 10–15, acute, ⅜ in. high; lower areoles ⅜ in. apart, radial spines 8–10, needle-shaped, central spines 3–5, awl-shaped, to ⅝ in. long, upper areoles with 15–20 bristlelike spines 1½–2½ in. long; fls. pink, 1¼ in. across, segms. acuminate. Local, s. Baja Calif.

Mieckleyanus: *L. Schottii* cv. 'Monstrosus'.

Sargentianus: *L. Schottii.*

Schottii (Engelm.) Britt. & Rose [*Lophocereus Sargentianus* (Orcutt) Britt. & Rose]. WHISKER CACTUS, SENITA. Sts. branching from the base, erect, to 15 ft. high and 8 in. thick, ribs 5–7, obtuse; spines conical, swollen at base, gray, to ⁵⁄₃₂ in. long, radial spines 4–10, central spine 1, upper areoles with 15–50 twisted, gray, bristlelike spines 1–4 in. long; fls. pink, to 1½ in. across; fr. 1 in. in diam. Spring, summer. S. Ariz. and w. Mex. Cv. '**Monstrosus**' [*L. Mieckleyanus* (Weing.) Backeb. & F. M. Knuth]. TOTEM-POLE CACTUS. Ribs irregularly interrupted and nearly spineless. Var. **australis** (K. Brandeg.) Borg [*L. australis* (K. Brandeg.) Britt. & Rose]. Distinct short trunk often formed, brs. taller and more slender, ribs to 10; appearing very different from the few-ribbed northern form, but these are merely the extremes of a series.

LOPHOMYRTUS Burret. *Myrtaceae.* Two spp. of evergreen shrubs or small trees, endemic to New Zeal.; lvs. opp., simple, leathery, gland-dotted; fls. white, axillary, solitary, 4-merous, calyx tube not extended beyond ovary, calyx lobes persistent, stamens many, ovary inferior, 2-celled, with many ovules attached to ribbonlike lobe of the placenta; fr. a many-seeded berry. Closely related to *Myrtus* but differing in its placenta.

bullata (Soland. ex A. Cunn.) Burret [*Myrtus bullata* Soland. ex A. Cunn.]. To 18 ft.; lvs. broad-ovate to suborbicular, to 2 in. long, somewhat leathery, puckered, often reddish-tinged; fls. about ½ in. across; berries dark red to black, to ⅜ in. across.

obcordata (Raoul) Burret [*Myrtus obcordata* (Raoul) Hook.f.]. To 15 ft.; lvs. obcordate, to ½ in. long, cuneate, emarginate at apex; fls. about ¼ in. across; berries red, to ¼ in. across.

×**Ralphii** (Hook.f.) Burret [*Myrtus Ralphii* Hook.f.]: *L. bullata* × *L. obcordata*. Intermediate between parents. Occurs in wild or in cult. where the two spp. grow together.

LOPHOPHORA J. Coult. PEYOTE, MESCAL-BUTTON. *Cactaceae.* Two variable spp. of small, spineless cacti, native to s. Tex. and n. Mex.; root turnip-shaped, st. dome-shaped, with low rounded tubercles more or less confluent into ribs, glaucous; areole with a tuft of wool; fls. subapical, funnelform-campanulate, ovary and fr. naked.

The buttonlike crowns of the plants yield the hallucinogenic alkaloid peyote, long used by Indians in the area where *Lophophora* is native.

For culture see *Cacti.*

diffusa (Croiz.) Bravo. Sts. yellow-green, ribs and furrows usually unequally spaced on prominent tubercles; fls. whitish to yellow-white. Cent. Mex.

echinata: *L. Williamsii.*

Lewinii: *L. Williamsii.*

Williamsii (Lem.) J. Coult. [*L. echinata* Croiz.; *L. echinata* var. *lutea* Rouhier; *L. Lewinii* (Hennings) Rusby; *L. Williamsii* vars. *pentagona* Croiz. and *pluricostata* Croiz.; *L. Ziegleri* Werderm.]. PEYOTE, DUMPLING CACTUS. Solitary, st. blue-green, to 3 in. thick, tubercles low and obscure, confluent into about 7–10 ribs separated by nearly straight vertical grooves, hairs in tufts equally spaced on ribs; fls. pink or rarely whitish, ½ in. across, perianth tube short. Tex. and n. Mex. Var. **decipiens** Croiz. Ribs about 11, breaking up into tubercles below; fls. longer. Var. **pentagona**: *L. Williamsii.* Var. **pluricostata**: *L. Williamsii.*

Ziegleri: *L. Williamsii.*

LOPHOSPERMUM: *ASARINA.* L. **scandens**: *A. Lophospermum.*

LOPHOTOCARPUS: *SAGITTARIA.*

LOQUAT. The loquat, an evergreen, broad-leaved tree, *Eriobotrya japonica*, of China and Japan, is sometimes seen as an ornamental pot subject under glass but is grown in Zone 9 in California, the lower Gulf regions, and Florida for its yellow, oblong-pyriform to spherical, acid fruits that are eaten raw or in jellies, jams, pies, and preserves. The fruits reach a length of 3 inches in large-fruited cultivars. The fragrant, white, panicled flowers appear in autumn, followed by ripe fruits in spring. The trees attain a height of 25 feet. In orchard formation they may be set 20–24 feet apart either way. The requirements are not peculiar. In northern Florida and similar regions, frost may limit fruitfulness in some seasons. For best results improved cultivars should be grown, being budded on seedling stocks; as commonly seen in yards, the trees are often unimproved seedlings with undersized fruits.

LORANTHACEAE Juss. MISTLETOE FAMILY. Dicot.; perhaps 20 genera of mostly erect or pendent shrubs of wide distribution, mainly trop., chiefly parasitic on trees, but possessing chlorophyll; sts. jointed; lvs. mostly opp., broad, entire, and leathery, or reduced to scales; fls. regular, bisexual or unisexual, very small or sometimes large and showy, calyx united to ovary, 2–5-lobed, petals green, yellow, or red, sometimes absent, separate or united into a tube, the tube often split down one side, stamens 2–6, ovary inferior, 1-celled; fr. a small berry with sticky pulp, distributed by birds.

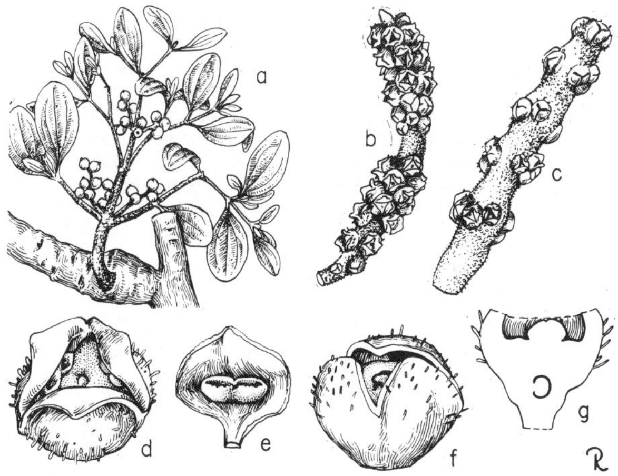

LORANTHACEAE. *Phoradendron serotinum:* **a,** fruiting plant on host, × 1/6; **b,** spike of male flowers, × 2; **c,** spike of female flowers, × 2; **d,** male flower, × 15; **e,** sepal and stamen, × 15; **f,** female flower, × 15; **g,** female flower, vertical section, perianth partially cut away, × 15. (From Lawrence, *Taxonomy of Vascular Plants.*)

Seeds of *Phoradendron* and *Arceuthobium* are sometimes offered, especially by botanical gardens, but mistletoes, although certain tropical genera are very showy, are not ordinarily horticultural subjects. Seeds of parasitic sorts germinate on the host and attach themselves to it by haustoria through which they absorb fluids from the host plant. The MISTLETOE of N. Amer. holiday markets is *Phoradendron serotinum,* parasitic on many species of deciduous trees of eastern N. Amer.; the MISTLETOE of literature is the Old World *Viscum album* L.; *Arceuthobium pusillum* Peck, the DWARF MISTLETOE, is a very small parasite on conifers in eastern N. Amer.; the very showy red-flowered mistletoes of tropical Amer. belong to the genus *Psittacanthus.*

LOROPETALUM R. Br. *Hamamelidaceae.* One sp., an evergreen, stellate-pubescent shrub or small tree, native to Japan, China, and the Himalayas; lvs. alt., entire; fls. white or yellow, in clusters at ends of short peduncles; sepals, petals, and stamens 4, petals long and strap-shaped, ovary inferior, 2-celled; fr. a woody caps., each cell 1-seeded.

Grown outdoors in mild climates (Zone 8) and in a cool greenhouse in the North, although it may be root hardy in colder climates. Propagated by seeds and by grafting on *Hamamelis.*

chinense (R. Br.) D. Oliver. Shrub, to 12 ft., but usually shorter; lvs. ovate, to 2 in. long, slightly asymmetrical at base; petals to 1 in. long. Early spring. China, Japan.

LOTONONIS (DC.) Eckl. & Zeyh. *Leguminosae* (subfamily *Faboideae*). About 100–110 spp. of shrubs and herbs, native to S. Afr., s. Eur., and cent. Asia; lvs. alt., of 3 lfts. or rarely of 1 or 5 lfts.; fls. commonly yellow, papilionaceous, stamens 10, united, alternately of 2 lengths; fr. a flat, elongate, many-seeded legume.

cytisoides Benth. Stout shrub, to 3 ft., sts. slender, little-branched; lfts. cuneate-obovate, varying from 3/32–5/8 in. long, stipules resembling lfts.; fls. axillary, solitary, short-peduncled, calyx lobes acute; fr. to 3/4 in. long, pubescent. S. Afr. Zone 10.

LOTUS L. *Leguminosae* (subfamily *Faboideae*). Perhaps 100 spp. of herbs and subshrubs of mostly temp. regions; lvs. alt., odd-pinnate; fls. in axillary umbels or sometimes solitary, papilionaceous, keel beaked, stamens 10, 9 united and 1 separate; fr. a narrow, dehiscent legume.

Grown as ornamentals, and some species for the edible pods and for forage. Propagated by seeds, or woody kinds also by cuttings, division, or layering.

Berthelotii Masf. PARROT'S-BEAK, PELICAN'S-BEAK, WINGED PEA, CORAL-GEM. Silvery shrub, with scrambling brs., to 2 ft.; lfts. 3–7, very narrow, 1/2 in. long; fls. scarlet, 1 in. long, standard narrow and recurved. Cape Verde, Canary Is.

corniculatus L. BIRD'S-FOOT TREFOIL. Per., to 2 ft. high, sts. often decumbent; lfts. 3, obovate to oblanceolate, stipules resembling lfts.; umbels long-peduncled, 3–6-fld.; petals yellow or tinged with red; fr. narrow, about 1 in. long. Eur., Asia. Sometimes grown for forage. Var. **arvensis** (Schkuhr) Ser. ex DC. BROADLEAF BIRD'S-FOOT TREFOIL. Lfts. cuneate-obovate. Var. **tenuifolium** L. NARROWLEAF BIRD'S-FOOT TREFOIL. Sts. weak, prostrate; lfts. linear-oblanceolate or linear.

crassifolius (Benth.) Greene. Per. herb, to 4 ft., differing from *L. pinnatus* in having 3–7 pairs of lfts., peduncle bearing a 1–5-pinnate bract and 8–15 fls., corolla greenish-yellow with keel marked purple-red, and fr. broader, to 3/16 in. wide. S. Calif. to Wash.

mascaensis Burchard. Low silvery shrub, main sts. decumbent; lfts. 3, very narrow, about 5/16 in. long, stipules resembling lfts.; fls. bright yellow, 1/2 in. long. Canary Is.

pedunculatus Cav. [*L. uliginosus* Schkuhr]. Differs from *L. corniculatus* in having a stoloniferous rootstock, hollow sts., and 6–12-fld. umbels. Eur.

pinnatus Hook. Per., to 16 in.; lfts. in 2–4 pairs, obovate, to 3/4 in. long, glabrous; fls. yellow with white wing petals, 3–7 on bractless peduncles longer than lvs.; fr. linear, cylindrical, to 2½ in. long. Cent. Calif., n. to Wash. and Idaho.

tetragonolobus L. WINGED PEA. Trailing ann., sts. to 16 in. long; lfts. 3, broadly elliptic to obovate, about 1 in. long; fls. purplish-red, 1 or 2 on peduncles shorter than to as long as lvs., 3/4 in. long; fr. 4-angled, to 3 in. long. S. Eur. Seeds and young fr. edible.

uliginosus: *L. pedunculatus.*

LOWIACEAE Ridl. ORCHIDANTHA FAMILY. Monocot; 1 genus, *Orchidantha,* of Asiatic herbs with prostrate sts.; lvs. in 2 ranks, petioles elongate, with sheathing base, blades with several pairs of longitudinal nerves connected by cross veins; infl. a reduced, bracted, 1–2-fld. cyme from the crown; fls. showy, bisexual, irregular, fl. parts united in a cylinder above the ovary, calyx lobes 3, corolla lobes 3, 2 small and 1 developed into a flat lip, stamens 5, ovary inferior, 3-celled, many-ovuled; fr. a woody caps., seeds with aril.

LOXANTHOCEREUS: *BORZICACTUS.* **L. eriotrichus:** *B. acanthurus.* **L. Faustianus:** *B. acanthurus.* Listed names of no botanical standing are: **L. acranthus, L. aureisetosus, L. decumbens, L. ferruginospinus, L. matucanensis** vars. **senilis** and **speciosus, L. paucispinus,** and **L. polygonus.**

LOXOGRAMME (Blume) K. Presl. *Polypodiaceae.* Not in cult. **L. immersa:** a listed name of uncertain application. **L. involuta:** *Polypodium scolopendria.*

LOXOSTIGMA C. B. Clarke. *Gesneriaceae.* Three spp. of herbs, native to the e. Himalayan region of India; lvs. opp., those of a pair unequal; fls. several on axillary peduncles, corolla tubular, slightly swollen below throat, somewhat 2-lipped, stamens 4, borne at base of corolla tube, anthers united in pairs, disc ringlike, ovary superior, linear, stigma obliquely 2-lobed; fr. an elongate, loculicidal caps., seeds many, small.

For cultivation see *Gesneriaceae.*

Griffithii (Wight) C. B. Clarke. Lvs. ovate, to 7 in. long, 3½ in. wide, green, short-hairy; peduncles to 3¼ in. long; calyx lobes lanceolate, 1/4 in. long, corolla to 1⅝ in. long, flecked with brown outside, lobes spreading.

LUCULIA Sweet. *Rubiaceae.* About 5 spp. of evergreen shrubs, native to the Himalayas and Yunnan; lvs. opp., leathery, stipules interpetiolar, deciduous; fls. white or pink, in terminal corymbs or panicles, 5-merous, corolla salverform; fr. a caps., seeds many, winged.

Grown outside in warm areas, or in colder regions in the greenhouse and planted out in summer. Propagated by cuttings of ripe wood.

fragrantissima: a listed name of no botanical standing.

grandifolia Ghose. Shrub or small tree, to 20 ft.; lvs. elliptic to broadly ovate, to 15 in. long, petioles and midveins reddish; fls. fragrant, corolla white, tube cylindrical, to 2½ in. long. Bhutan.

gratissima Sweet. Shrub or tree, to 16 ft.; lvs. ovate-oblong, to 8 in. long; fls. in corymbs to 8 in. across, corolla pink or rose, to 1½ in. across, tube slender, to 1 in. long, lobes 5, spreading. Himalayas. Distinguished by the hairs on the ovary and the lack of appendages in the throat of the corolla.

intermedia Hutch. To 12 ft.; lvs. oblong or oblong-lanceolate, to 6 in. long; fls. reddish, to 2 in. long. Yunnan. Distinguished by the appendages continuous between the lobes of the corolla.

limosella: a listed name of no botanical standing.

Pinceana Hook. To 6 ft.; lvs. elliptic-lanceolate, to 6 in. long, slender-pointed; fls. fragrant, corolla white, tinged with pink, tube to 2 in. long. Nepal and Assam. Distinguished by the pairs of appendages between the corolla lobes.

speciosa: a listed name of no botanical standing.

tsetensis: a listed name of no botanical standing.

LUCUMA Mol., not of auth. A genus no longer recognized. Cult. plants belonging to Sapotaceae and formerly assigned to it are referred as follows: **L. hypoglauca:** *Pouteria hypoglauca;* **L. mammosa:** see *Pouteria Sapota;* **L. nervosa:** *Pouteria campechiana;* **L. Roxburghii:** a listed name of no botanical standing; some material so named is *Mimusops Balata;* **L. salicifolia:** *Pouteria campechiana;* **L. serpentaria:** *Pouteria domingensis.*

LUDVIGIA: *LUDWIGIA.*

LUDWIGIA L. [*Isnardia* L.; *Jussiaea* L.; *Ludvigia* L.; *Ludwigiantha* (Torr. & A. Gray) Small]. FALSE LOOSESTRIFE. *Onagraceae.* About 75 spp. of aquatic or moist places in the Old and New World, especially in warmer regions; herbaceous and often floating or creeping, to woody and erect; lvs. mostly alt., sometimes opp., simple; fls. yellow or white, solitary and axillary or in terminal clusters, sepals 4–7, persistent, petals 0–7, deciduous, ovary inferior; fr. a cylindrical to obconical caps., many-seeded.

Aquatic forms may be used in aquaria, terrestrial forms in damp places; propagated by seeds or cuttings. Summer bloomer.

alternifolia L. RATTLEBOX, SEEDBOX. Erect per., to 3 ft.; lvs. lanceolate, 1½–4 in. long; fls. solitary in upper axils, 4-merous, sepals ovate, 5/16 in. long, petals yellow, quickly shed, 5/16 in. long; caps. cubical, slightly wing-angled, ¼ in. long. E. U.S.

arcuata Walt. [*Ludwigiantha arcuata* (Walt.) Small]. Per., sts. creeping, to 10 in. long; lvs. elliptic-linear to oblanceolate, to ¾ in. long, essentially sessile; fls. golden-yellow; caps. curved, to ⅜ in. long. S.C. to Fla.

californica: a listed name; probably *L. peploides.*

decurrens Walt. [*Jussiaea decurrens* (Walt.) DC.]. Erect ann., with decurrent wings from lf. bases; lvs. lanceolate, 2–4 in. long; fls. solitary in upper axils, petals 4, 5/16–½ in. long, yellow; caps. obpyramidal, elongate, angled. Se. U.S. and Mex. to S. Amer.

helminthorrhiza (Mart.) Hara [*Jussiaea helminthorrhiza* Mart.; *J. natans* Humb. & Bonpl.]. Floating herb, rooting at nodes and with spongy pneumatophores; lvs. roundish, blades ½–2 in. long; fls. solitary in axils, mostly 5-merous, petals 5/16–½ in. long, broad, white with basal yellow spot; caps. nearly cylindrical. S. Mex. to S. Amer. Aquarium plant.

longifolia (DC.) Hara [*Jussiaea longifolia* DC.]. Erect per., to 6 ft., sts. narrowly winged, glabrous; lvs. lanceolate, 4–8 in. long, much reduced up the sts.; fls. solitary in upper axils, sepals 4, lanceolate, ¼–½ in. long, petals ½–1 in. long, pale yellow; caps. elongate-pyramidal, 4-angled. Brazil to Argentina.

Mulertii: a listed name of no botanical standing used for *L. natans.*

natans Elliott. Aquatic herb, rooting at nodes; lvs. opp., petioled, elliptic to obovate, purplish beneath; fls. axillary, sepals 4, triangular, ⅛ in. long, petals yellow, quickly shed; caps. somewhat 4-sided, tapering at base, ⅛–⅜ in. long. U.S., W. Indies.

octovalvis (Jacq.) Raven [*J. suffruticosa* of New World auth., not L.]. Herb or shrub, to 8 ft., smooth to hairy; lvs. lanceolate to ovate, 1–4 in. long; fls. in upper axils, sepals 4, ovate, 5/16–½ in. long, petals ½–¾ in. long, deep yellow; caps. cylindrical. W. Indies and Mex. to S. Amer.; Old World tropics. Var. **linearifolia** (Hassl.) Munz [*Jussiaea salicifolia* HBK; *J. suffruticosa* var. *linearifolia* Hassl.]. Lvs. linear.

palustris (L.) Elliott [*Isnardia palustris* L.]. WATER PURSLANE. Much like *L. natans,* but lvs. lanceolate to elliptic-ovate; caps. with 4 longitudinal green bands. Wet places, U.S. and Canada to Costa Rica, W. Indies; Eurasia.

peploides (HBK) Raven [*Jussiaea californica* (S. Wats.) Jeps.; *J. peploides* HBK; *J. repens* var. *peploides* (HBK) Griseb.]. Per. herb, sts. creeping or floating; lf. blades oblong, ½–2 in. long, glossy, petioles to 1 in. long; fls. axillary, solitary, 5-merous, sepals ¼–½ in. long, petals ¼–1 in. long, yellow; caps. cylindrical, 1–1½ in. long; fr. pedicels to 1 in. long. Ore. to S. Amer., W. Indies. Subsp. **glabrescens** (O. Kuntze) Raven [*Jussiaea repens* var. *glabrescens* O. Kuntze]. Petioles 1–1½ in. long; lf. blades 1–3½ in. long; fr. pedicels 1–3 in. long. E. and s. U.S.

peruviana (L.) Hara [*Jussiaea peruviana* L.]. Suffrutescent to woody, to 9 ft., hairy; lvs. more or less ovate, 2–6 in. long; fls. solitary in upper axils, sepals lanceolate, ½–⅝ in. long, petals 4, ½–1 in. long, broad, yellow; caps. obconical, 4-angled. Fla. and Mex. to S. Amer.

pulvinaris Gilg. Plants creeping, rooting at nodes; lvs. oblong-obovate, to ½ in. long, glabrous, petioles to 3/16 in. long; fls. greenish-yellow; caps. to ¼ in. long. Trop. Afr.

uruguayensis (Camb.) Hara [*Jussiaea grandiflora* Michx., not Ruiz & Pav.; *J. uruguayensis* Camb.]. Per., with creeping rhizomes, sts. floating or emersed; lvs. of erect hairy brs. lanceolate, 1–3 in. long, pointed; fls. in upper axils, 5-merous, petals ½–¾ in. long, bright yellow; caps. nearly cylindrical. Wet places, se. U.S., Guatemala to S. Amer.

LUDWIGIANTHA: *LUDWIGIA.*

LUEHEA Willd. *Tiliaceae.* About 15 spp. of large shrubs or trees, native to trop. Amer.; lvs. alt., short-petioled, simple, mostly toothed only in the upper half, glabrous or glabrescent above, variously pubescent beneath; fls. mostly large, white or pink, solitary or in racemes or panicles, subtended by several long involucral bracts, sepals and petals 5, stamens many, outer ones sterile, style simple, stigma rounded or 5-lobed; fr. a caps., large, woody, 5-celled, 5-valved, loculicidally dehiscent only in upper half, many-seeded.

Suitable for cultivation in Zone 10.

candida (Sessé & Moç, ex DC.) Mart. Shrubs or small trees, seldom over 35 ft.; lvs. broadly ovate to elliptic, to 8 in. long, abruptly short-acuminate; fls. white, fading cream or brownish, 2–3½ in. across, solitary, on thick peduncles, involucral bracts 1–1½ in. long, slender, densely tomentose; caps. deeply 5-angled, to 3 in. long, acuminate. Mex. to n. S. Amer.

divaricata Mart. Shrub or small tree, to 30 ft.; lvs. oblong, 3–6 in. long, unequally rounded at base; fls. rose, about 1 in. across, in apical racemes or panicles, involucral bracts 6–8, half as long as sepals, narrow, pubescent, sepals about as long as petals, sometimes recurved at apex; caps. ovate, about 1 in. long, appressed-stellate, cells 3–4-seeded. Brazil. Wood used for general carpentry and interior construction.

grandiflora Mart. Tree, to 25 ft.; lvs. oblong-ovate, 3–5 in. long, short-acute; fls. white, large, in terminal racemes or few-branched panicles, pedicels bracted, involucral bracts about 8, shorter than sepals, lanceolate-ovate, grayish- or olive-tomentose; caps. ovate, cylindrical or obscurely 5-angled, 5-celled, cells many-seeded. Brazil.

Seemanii Triana & Planch. To 90 ft., often with buttresses; lvs. oblong-ovate, to 8 in. long, 5 in. wide; fls. white, many in terminal panicles, involucral bracts about ¼ in. long, petals about ½ in. long; caps. angular, furrowed, to 1 in. long. Late winter to early spring. Guatemala to Colombia.

speciosa Willd. Shrub, or tree to 75 ft., often with buttresses; lvs. deciduous, oblong-lanceolate to obovate, to 8 in. long; fls. white, 2–3 in. across, in naked, terminal racemes or panicles, involucral bracts nearly ¾ in. long; caps. subcylindrical to angular, to 1½ in. long. W. Indies and Mex., s. to n. S. Amer.

LUETKEA Bong. *Rosaceae.* One sp., a cespitose, somewhat woody, decumbent or creeping per. herb, native to w. N. Amer.; lvs. 2–3 times ternately dissected; fls. bisexual, small, racemose, sepals and petals 5, stamens about 20, pistils 5; frs. 5 small follicles.

Adapted to the rock garden and propagated by cuttings of green wood and by division.

pectinata (Pursh) O. Kuntze [*Saxifraga pectinata* Pursh, not Schott, Nym., & Kotschy]. Sts. 2–6 in.; lvs. 3/16–⅝ in. long; racemes to 2 in. long; fls. white, ¼ in. across. High mts., Calif. to Alaska. Zone 6.

LUFFA Mill. LOOFAH, DISHCLOTH GOURD, RAG G., VEGETABLE-SPONGE, STRAINER VINE. *Cucurbitaceae.* Six spp. of monoecious, tender, tendril-bearing vines of trop. regions; lvs. angled or lobed; fls. large, conspicuous, yellow or whitish, petals 5, male fls. racemose, stamens 3–5 on the campanulate or top-shaped fl. tube, anthers flexuous, female fls. solitary; fr. glabrous, becoming dry and more or less papery, dehiscent by an apical lid, seeds flat, black, narrowly winged.

The two commonly cultivated species are annuals from the Old World tropics. Grown in the U.S. mostly as ornamentals or for the "vegetable sponge" provided by the dried, reticulate, fibrous interior of the fruit. They grow easily from seeds.

acutangula (L.) Roxb. ANGLED L., SING-KWA. Lvs. angled, but little if at all lobed except on young shoots; stamens 3; fr. club-shaped, 1 ft. long or less, strongly 10-angled, seeds wrinkled, wingless. Young frs. used for food in the Orient.

aegyptiaca Mill. [*L. cylindrica* of auth., not M. J. Roem.; *L. gigantea* Hort.; *L. macrocarpa* Hort.; *L. marylandica* Hort.]. SPONGE GOURD, DISHCLOTH G., SMOOTH L., SZE-KWA. Lvs. mostly 3–7-lobed; stamens 5; fr. cylindrical, to 2 ft. long, sometimes curved, not angled, seeds smooth, girdled by a thin wing. The most commonly cult sp.

cylindrica: see *L. aegyptiaca.*

gigantea: a listed name of no botanical standing for *L. aegyptiaca.*

macrocarpa: a listed name of no botanical standing for *L. aegyptiaca.*

marylandica: a listed name of no botanical standing for *aegyptiaca.*

LUINA Benth. [*Cacaliopsis* A. Gray]. *Compositae* (Senecio Tribe). Four spp. of more or less tomentose per. herbs, in s. B.C. and nw. U.S.; lvs. simple, entire to lobed; fl. heads discoid, involucre of a single row of equal bracts; fls. all tubular, fertile, yellow or yellowish; pappus of many capillary bristles.

hypoleuca Benth. Sts. several, from a stout, woody root crown, to 16 in., tomentose, leafy; lvs. sessile, ovate to elliptic, entire, 1–2 in. long, white-tomentose beneath, green above; heads ½ in. long, corymbose; fls. creamy-white or pale yellow. Mts., s. B.C. to n. Calif. Sometimes grown in the rock garden, for its foliage.

Nardosmia (A. Gray) Cronq. [*Cacaliopsis Nardosmia* (A. Gray) A. Gray]. St. from a rhizome, 2–3 ft.; lvs. largely basal, long-petioled, blades 4–8 in. wide, broader than long, palmately veined and cleft, tomentose beneath, upper lvs. few, much-reduced; heads to 1 in. long, several, racemose or corymbose; fls. yellow. Cascade Mts., Wash. to n. Calif.

LUMA A. Gray [*Myrceugenella* Kausel]. *Myrtaceae.* Four spp. of evergreen shrubs in Chile and adjacent Argentina; lvs. opp., simple, pinnately veined; fls. in 3-fld. cymes or solitary in lf. axils, calyx lobes and petals 4, stamens many, exserted; fr. a berry.

apiculata (DC.) Burret [*Eugenia apiculata* DC.; *Myrceugenella apiculata* (DC.) Kausel; *Myrceugenia apiculata* (DC.) Niedenzu]. TEMU. Densely branched shrub or small tree, 5–15 ft., bark becoming golden-brown, flaking; lvs. crowded, ovate, to 1 in. long, sharply apiculate; fls. cream-white, suffused with pink, to ½ in. across; fr. black, globose, to ⅜ in. across, crowned with calyx lobes. Chile and adjacent Argentina.

Chequen (Mol.) A. Gray [*Myrceugenella Chequen* (Mol.) Kausel]. Similar to *L. apiculata,* but having lvs. conspicuously punctate, more regularly crowded, and paler green.

LUNARIA L. HONESTY, MONEY PLANT, MOONWORT, SATIN FLOWER. *Cruciferae.* Two or 3 spp. of erect, branching, bien. or per. herbs of Eur.; lvs. simple, broad, toothed; fls. white to purple, in terminal racemes, sepals 4, petals 4, long-clawed; fr. a flat, oblong-elliptic to nearly orbicular silicle with satiny, paper-white septum.

The fruiting stems are used in dry bouquets after the valves and seeds drop late in the season. Plants come readily from seeds; partial shade is desirable.

annua L. [*L. biennis* Moench]. HONESTY, BOLBONAC, SILVER-DOLLAR, PENNY FLOWER. Bien., to 3 ft.; lvs. ovate or narrower, coarsely toothed, upper lvs. sessile or subsessile; fls. white or purple; silicles to 2 in. long and nearly as broad, obtuse or rounded at both ends. S. Eur.; naturalized in Eur. and N. Amer. A form with variegated lvs. is offered.

biennis: *L. annua.*

redeviva *L.* PERENNIAL H. Per., to 4½ ft.; lvs. more closely and sharply toothed than in *L. annua,* upper lvs. distinctly petioled; silicles oblong-lanceolate, much longer than wide, tapering at both ends. Eur.

LUPINUS L. LUPINE. *Leguminosae* (subfamily *Faboideae*). Perhaps 200 spp. of ann. or per. herbs or subshrubs of wide distribution, especially numerous in w. N. Amer.; lvs. palmately compound, rarely reduced to solitary lfts., stipules united to petioles; fls. in terminal spikes or racemes, showy, papilionaceous, standards erect, with reflexed margins, stamens 10, united; fr. a flat legume, often constricted between seeds.

Lupines are grown in the U.S. mostly as ornamentals, although a few species have value as cover crops, forage, and human food. They grow on any well-drained soil, thriving even on poor sandy loams. Propagated by seeds sown where the plants are to grow, or the perennial kinds also by division.

Through hybridization and selection, many highly ornamental lupines have been developed. The most popular group are the Russell hybrids. Of uncertain parentage, they are about 3 ft. high with long racemes of closely set, uniformly colored or bicolored flowers in a wide range of colors.

albifrons Benth. Shrub, to 5 ft.; lfts. 7–10, spatulate to obovate, silvery-silky, to 1 in. long; fls. mostly whorled, about ½ in. long, petals blue or purplish with white or yellow center, standard somewhat pubescent on the back; fr. yellowish, to 2 in. long. Calif. Var. **albifrons.** The typical var.; fls. ⅜–½ in. long, pedicels with spreading hairs. Var. **Douglasii** (J. Agardh) C. P. Sm. Differs in having larger lvs., to $2\frac{5}{16}$ in. long, and fl. bracts much longer than fl. buds. Var. **eminens** (Greene) C. P. Sm. [*L. Brittonii* Abrams]. Fls. $\frac{9}{16}$–⅝ in. long, pedicels sometimes with appressed hairs.

albus L. WHITE L., FIELD L., WOLF BEAN. Hairy ann., to 4 ft.; fls. white or lightly tinted; fr. to 4 in. long, seeds white, large. S. Eur. Grown as forage and green-manure crop.

angustifolius L. Slender ann., to 20 in., sts. pilose; lfts. 5–9, linear, 1½ in. long, blunt, silky beneath; fls. bright blue; fr. 2½ in. long, ½ in. wide. Early summer. Medit. region.

arboreus Sims. TREE L. To 6–8 ft.; lfts. 5–12, oblanceolate, to $2\frac{5}{16}$ in. long, strigose on both sides or glabrous above; racemes loose; fls. sulphur-yellow, standard glabrous on the back; fr. to 3 in. long, seeds small. Summer. Calif.

arcticus S. Wats. To 15 in.; differs from *L. nootkatensis* in having basal lvs. with petioles twice to several times longer than width of lvs., and acute lfts. Alaska and Yukon, s. to n. Wash.

argenteus Pursh. Per., 6–24 in., silvery-pubescent; lvs. mostly on st., lfts. 6–9, narrow-lanceolate to oblanceolate, about 1 in. long; fls. white to rose, blue, or violet, standard glabrous, with a whitish spot; fr. very hairy, to 1 in. long. Ore. and Calif., Alta., s. to New Mex. and S. Dak. Var. **depressus** (Rydb.) C. L. Hitchc. [*L. depressus* Rydb.]. To 10 in.; fls. congested in racemes. Subalpine.

aridus: *L. lepidus* var.

Benthamii A. Heller. Villous ann., to 2 ft.; lfts. 7–10, linear, to 2 in. long; bracts linear, longer than buds, fls. ½ in. long, petals light to dark blue, standard with a yellow spot; fr. $2\frac{5}{16}$ in. long. Calif.

bicolor Lindl. Villous ann., to 16 in.; lfts. 5–7, oblanceolate to cuneate, to 1 in. long; racemes short; fls. in 1–3 whorls, standard reflexed, red-purple, central white spot purple-dotted, other petals blue; fr. pubescent, less than 1 in. long. Coastal, Calif. to B.C. Subsp. **bicolor.** The typical subsp.; fls. in indistinct whorls, standard ¼ to more than ⅝ in. long. Subsp. **tridentatus** (Eastw. ex C. P. Sm.) D. Dunn [var. *tridentatus* Eastw. ex C. P. Sm.]. Racemes longer, to $4\frac{5}{16}$ in.; fls. in separated whorls, standard ⅛ to nearly ⅝ in. long.

Brittonii: *L. albifrons* var. *eminens.*

Burkei: *L. polyphyllus* var.

Chamissonis Eschsch. Shrubby, to 6 ft., silky-tomentose; lfts. 6–9, oblanceolate; fls. blue or lavender, standard broad, yellow-spotted, pubescent on the back; fr. strigose. Coastal, Calif.

concinnus J. Agardh. Densely hairy ann., to 8 in.; lfts. 5–9, narrow, oblanceolate, to ¾ in. long; racemes mostly 1 in. long; petals usually lilac, margined red-purple, standard with yellow spot; fr. hairy, ½ in. long. Calif.

Cruckshanksii: *L. mutabilis* var.

cytisoides: *L. latifolius.*

densiflorus Benth. Hairy ann., to 16 in.; lfts. 7–9, obtuse to mucronate, to ¾ in. long, glabrous above; calyx subtended by narrow reflexed bracts, petals white, yellow, or rose to purple; fr. shaggy, ⅝ in. long. Calif. Var. **densiflorus.** The typical var.; fls. white, tinged or veined violet or rose. Var. **aureus** (Kellogg) Munz [*L. Menziesii* J. Agardh]. Fls. to ⅝ in. long, petals yellow or margined red-purple. Var. **glareosus** (Elmer) C. P. Sm. Fls. about ½ in. long, petals light blue, with white spot on standard. Var. **lacteus** (Kellogg) C. P. Sm. Pubescence of sts. and peduncles to $\frac{1}{16}$ in. long; fls. white, rose, or purple.

depressus: *L. argenteus* var.

excubitus M. E. Jones. Perhaps not specifically distinct from *L. albifrons,* from which it is separated by having fls. with the keel not narrowed toward the base. S. Calif. Var. **excubitus.** The typical var.; fls. ⅜–½ in. long. Deserts. Var. **Hallii** (Abrams) C. P. Sm. Fls. larger than in var. *excubitus,* to nearly ¾ in. long, lvs. greenish, less silky-hairy, and the whorls of fls. usually not more than 1 in. apart. Mts.

formosus Greene. Per., with decumbent or ascending sts., to 2½ ft.; lfts. 7–9, oblanceolate, silky on both surfaces, to 2½ in. long; fls. purple to blue, lilac, or white, ½ in. long; fr. silky, 1¼ in. long. Calif.

Hartwegii Lindl. Ann., to 3 ft., with shaggy pubescence; fls. blue, standard partly rose-colored; fr. about 1 in. long, seeds small. Summer, early autumn. Mex.

hirsutissimus Benth. Robust ann., to 2½ ft., densely clothed with yellowish, stinging hairs; lfts. 5–8, broadly cuneate-obovate, to 2 in. long; fls. reddish-purple, standard more or less yellow-blotched; fr. bristly, to 1½ in. long. Spring. Cent. Calif. to Baja Calif.

hirsutus L. BLUE L. Ann., to 2 ft. but usually lower, brown-hairy; flts. 5–7, to 1½ in. long; fls. blue, keel usually white-tipped; fr. very hairy, to 3 in. long and ¾ in. wide, seeds large. Summer. S. Eur.

latifolius J. Agardh [*L. cytisoides* J. Agardh]. Erect per., to 4 ft.; lfts. 5–9, mostly acute, to 4 in. long, glabrous above or nearly so, petioles 2–8 in. long; fls. blue to purple, rarely yellowish, to ½ in. long, in loose racemes to 18 in. long; fr. hairy, dark brown, to 1¼ in. long. Calif. to Wash. Var. **latifolius.** The typical var.; fls. ⅜ to nearly ⅝ in. long, keel partly exposed, wings curved inward on lower edges. Coast Ranges of Calif. Var. **columbianus** (A. Heller) C. P. Sm. To 6 ft.; wing petals broader than in var. *latifolius,* covering most of the keel. Sierra Nevada of Calif. Var. **subalpinus** (Piper & B. L. Robinson) C. P. Sm. [*L. subalpinus* Piper & B. L. Robinson; *L. volcanicus* Greene]. Plants dwarf, 4–10 in., mostly whitish- to rufous-villous. Mts., Alaska to Wash.

laxiflorus Dougl. ex Lindl. Per., to 2 ft.; lfts. 7–11, mostly to 2 in. long, pubescent on both surfaces or glabrous above; racemes short-peduncled; calyx 2-lipped, spurred, petals white, sometimes tinged with blue, pink, or violet, varying to rose or purple, standard basally pubescent on the back; fr. to 1¼ in. long. Wash. to Calif.

lepidus Dougl. ex Lindl. Tufted per., to about 1 ft., gray- to rusty-pubescent; lfts. 5–9, very hairy on both surfaces; racemes dense, to 6 in. long; fls. to ½ in. long, violet-blue, standard often paler or darker, glabrous; fr. hairy, to ¾ in. long. B.C. to Calif., Mont., Wyo., and Colo. Var. **lepidus.** The typical var.; racemes longer than lvs.; fls. about ½ in. long. B.C. to Ore. Var. **aridus** (Dougl. ex Lindl.) Jeps. [*L. aridus* Dougl. ex Lindl.]. Lfts. usually longer than ⅝ in.; racemes 2 in. long or more, partly concealed by the longer lvs.; fls. smaller than in var. *lepidus.*

littoralis Dougl. To 2½ ft., sts. decidedly spreading-villous near the nodes, roots bright yellow; lfts. 5–9, strigose on both surfaces, to 1³⁄₁₆ in. long; fls. blue to lilac, to ½ in. long; fr. to 1½ in. long. Coastal, Calif. to B.C.

longifolius (S. Wats.) Abrams. Shrubby, to 5 ft., grayish-pubescent throughout; lfts. 6–9, elliptic- or oblong-oblanceolate, obtuse, to 2¼ in. long; fls. deep blue to nearly white, standard with a whitish or rose-purple spot; fr. to 2¼ in. long. S. Calif., Baja Calif.

luteus L. YELLOW L. Ann., to 2 ft., densely pilose; lfts. 7–11, acute; fls. yellow, fragrant, verticillate on long, pubescent stalks. Early summer. Medit. region. Differs from *L. densiflorus* chiefly in having calyx not subtended by bracts, and much longer, and fr. to 2 in. long and with large seeds.

Lyallii A. Gray. Per., to 4 in., silky-pubescent throughout; lfts. 5–6, less than ½ in. long, acute; racemes nearly headlike; fls. dark blue or with a pale center, nearly ½ in. long; fr. ½ in. long. Wash. to Calif.

Menziesii: *L. densiflorus* var. *aureus.*

micranthus Dougl. Hairy ann., to 1½ ft.; lfts. 5–7, linear to oblanceolate, to 1½ in. long, glabrous or slightly hairy above; fls. deep blue, standard emarginate, about ¼ in. long, with a purple-dotted white spot; fr. about 1 in. long. B.C. to Calif.

Moerheimii: a listed name of no botanical standing for *L. polyphyllus* cv.

mutabilis Sweet. Ann., to 6 ft., glabrous; lfts. 7–11, to 3 in. long, obtuse; fls. white, standard retuse, with yellow spot and sometimes tinged violet, to ¾ in. long; fr. to 3 in. long, seeds large. Summer. Andean S. Amer. Var. **Cruckshanksii** (Hook.) L. H. Bailey [*L. Cruckshanksii* Hook.]. Fls. large, fragrant, with purplish standard and dark blue wing petals. Peru.

nanus Dougl. Pubescent ann., to 20 in.; lfts. 5–7, mostly acute; fls. fragrant, bright blue, standard with purple-dotted white or yellowish spot, reflexed; fr. strigose, to 1¼ in. long, seeds small. Spring, summer. Calif. Var. **apricus:** *L. vallicola* subsp.

nootkatensis J. Donn. Villous per., to 3 ft.; lfts. 5–9, to 2¾ in. long, obtuse; petioles about as long as width of lvs.; fls. blue variegated with light purple, to white or yellow, ¾ in. long; fr. to 1¼ in. long. Spring, summer. Coastal Wash. to Aleutian Is.; introd. Nfld. to n. New Eng.

perennis L. SUNDIAL L., WILD L. Pubescent per., to 2 ft.; lower lvs. with 7–11 lfts. to 2 in. long; racemes to 1 ft. long; fls. blue, varying to pink and white; fr. 1½ in. long. Late spring. Me. to Fla.

plattensis S. Wats. Hairy per., to 2 ft.; lfts. 7–9, thick, somewhat glaucous, to 1½ in. long; fls. pale blue, standard with dark spot; fr. to 1¼ in. long. Early summer. Wyo., Colo., Kans.

polyphyllus Lindl. Stout per., to 5 ft., scarcely pubescent except for the woolly fr.; lfts. 12–18 on lower lvs., acute, to 5 in. long; racemes dense, to 2 ft. long; fls. blue to reddish; fr. 1½ in. long, seeds small. Summer. Calif. to B.C. Var. **Burkei** (S. Wats.) C. L. Hitchc. [*L. Burkei* S. Wats.]. To 2 ft. or less, sts. only slightly hollow; sts., petioles, and lower surfaces of lfts. glabrous or with white spreading hairs. Cv. **'Moerheimii'.** Fls. rose and white. Other color forms include cvs.: **'Albiflorus'** [var. *albiflorus* Bergmans], **'Albus'** [var. *albus* Bergmans], **'Atroviolaceus'**, **'Caeruleus'**, **'Carmineus'**, and **'Roseus'** [var. *roseus* Bergmans].

pubescens Benth. Soft-pubescent ann., to 3 ft.; lfts. 7–9, stipules very small; fls. violet-blue with white center, whorled in long racemes; fr. very hairy, 1 in. long, seeds whitish, small. Mex., Guatemala. Important parent in production of a large group of hybrids.

rivularis Dougl. ex Lindl. Similar to *L. latifolius,* but more or less villous, lfts. to only 1½ in. long, petioles to 2 in. long, keel of fls. ciliate along upper margin, fr. to 2 in. long. Calif. to B.C.

sericatus Kellogg. Per., to 1 ft. or more, finely whitish-pubescent; lfts. 6–7, spatulate-obovate, to 1½ in. long, rounded or retuse; racemes dense; fls. purplish-blue; fr. pubescent, to 1 in. long. N. Calif.

sparsiflorus Benth. Differs from *L. Benthamii* in having shorter sts. mostly 8–16 in. high, shorter, linear to oblanceolate lfts. to 1³⁄₁₆ in. long, bracts of racemes scarcely longer than fl. buds, fls. light blue to lilac, and smaller fr. to ¾ in. long. S. Calif. to Baja Calif., Nev., Ariz.

Stiversii Kellogg. Ann., to 1½ ft.; lfts. 6–8, to 1½ in. long, strigose on both surfaces; racemes about 1 in. long; fls. ½ in. long with bright yellow standard, rose or purple wings, and whitish keel; fr. glabrous, to 1 in. long. Calif.

subalpinus: *L. latifolius* var.

subcarnosus Hook. TEXAS BLUEBONNET. Ann., to 1 ft., silky-hairy; lfts. mostly 5–6, obtuse or rounded; fls. blue with white or yellow spot on standard, wing petals inflated, light blue, pubescence of fl. buds and mature pods yellowish-gray or brown; fr. 1½ in. long, seeds small. Tex.

succulentus Dougl. ex C. Koch. Stout ann., to 2 ft. or more, usually succulent or hollow-stemmed; lfts. 7–9, to 2¾ in. long, glabrous above; fls. deep purple-blue or sometimes white, standard usually with yellow center; fr. dark, pubescent, to 2 in. long. Calif., Baja Calif.

sulfureus Dougl. ex Hook. Hairy per., to 3 ft. or more; lfts. 9–11, narrowly oblanceolate, less than 2 in. long, usually acutish, densely pubescent on both surfaces or glabrous above; fls. small, yellowish to bluish or purple, standard glabrous, slightly reflexed; fr. 1 in. long. B.C. to Calif.

texensis Hook. TEXAS BLUEBONNET. Differs from *L. subcarnosus* by its often acute lfts., fls. with dark blue wings not inflated, and whitish pubescence of fl. buds and mature fr. Tex.

Tidestromii Greene. Differs from *L. littoralis* in having sts. strigose, lfts. to ¾ in. long, and petioles to 1³⁄₁₆ in. long. Cent. Calif.

vallicola A. Heller. To 14 in.; lfts. mostly 6–8, linear, to 1 in. long; peduncles to 2¾ in. long, racemes to 4 in. long; fls. bright blue, small, keel ciliate toward apex; fr. to 1 in. long, almost silky. Subsp. **vallicola.** The typical subsp.; standard wider than long, with pale central spot; seeds flesh-colored, scarcely mottled. Calif. Subsp. **apricus** (Greene) D. Dunn [*L. nanus* var. *apricus* (Greene) C. P. Sm.]. Standard longer than wide; seeds gray, mottled with brown. Calif. to B.C.

villosus Willd. Per., to 3 ft.; lvs. long-petioled, of 1 lft., lfts. elliptic-lanceolate to oblanceolate, to 6 in. long; fls. lilac to purple with deep red-purple spot on standard, in elongate, dense racemes; fr. to 1¾ in. long. N.C. to Fla., w. to Miss.

volcanicus: *L. latifolius* var. *subalpinus.*

LURONIUM Raf. [*Elisma* Buchenau]. *Alismataceae.* One sp., a rootless, floating herb, native to Eur.; lvs. submersed or floating; fls. axillary, long-pedicelled, sepals and petals 3, stamens 6, ovaries 10–12, separate; fr. a head of achenes.

natans (L.) Raf. [*Elisma natans* (L.) Buchenau]. Sts. to 20 in.; submersed lvs. linear, to 4 in. long, floating lvs. ovate or elliptic, to 1 in. long, petioles to about 2 ft. long; fls. white, yellowish in center, floating; fr. oblong-ovate.

LUZULA DC. WOOD RUSH. *Juncaceae.* About 80 spp. of usually hairy, per. herbs, native to cold or temp. regions, especially Eurasia; lvs. flat, pliant; fls. in spikes, umbels, or heads, sepals and petals 3, scalelike, stamens 6, ovary 1-celled; fr. a caps., seeds 3.

Plants mostly of acid soils; for dry, shaded woods, adapted to naturalizing in colonies or for the border. Propagated by seeds and division.

campestris (L.) DC. COMMON W.R., FIELD W.R. Tufted, with short stolons; fl. sts. 5–24 in., usually solitary; basal lvs. to 5 in. long, ⅛–¼ in. wide, flat, very hairy; fls. in 2–6 subglobose spikes ⁵⁄₁₆ in. in diam., peduncles mostly recurved. Eurasia; naturalized in N. Amer. and N. Afr.

lutea (All.) DC. Similar to *L. campestris* and perhaps only a variant of it; differing in having lvs. glabrous and broader, and fls. yellow. Cent. Eur.

maxima: *L. sylvatica.*

multiflora (Retz.) Lej. Densely tufted, with few or no stolons, fl. sts. 8–20 in., wiry, erect; basal lvs. mostly ⅔ as long as fl. sts., to ³⁄₁₆ in. wide, flat, sparsely hairy; infl. umbellate; fls. chestnut-brown. Eurasia, N. Afr.

nivea (L.) Lam. & DC. Tufted, stoloniferous, fl. sts. 1–2 ft., slender, flexuous; basal lvs. nearly as long as fl. sts., margins pilose; infl. umbellate; fls. white, many, perianth segms. twice as long as caps. Mts., w. and cent. Eur.

pilosa (L.) Willd. Tufted per., rootstock short, upright, stolons slender; lvs. ⅛ in. wide, grasslike, sparsely hairy; infl. a loose cyme; seeds with a long hooked appendage. Eur., Asia, N. Amer.

sylvatica (Huds.) Gaud.-Beaup. [*L. maxima* (Reichard) DC.]. GREATER W.R. Robust stoloniferous per., forming bright green tussocks; fl. sts. to 3 ft., erect, with 4 cauline lvs. to 2 in. long, basal lvs. 4–12 in. long, to ⅝ in. wide, glossy, spreading; infl. a loose, terminal cyme; fls. chestnut-brown. Eur. and Asia Minor; naturalized in E. Indies and S. Amer.

LYCASTE Lindl. *Orchidaceae.* About 40 spp. of epiphytes, native to trop. Amer.; pseudobulbs 1–3-lvd. at apex; lvs. petioled, plicate; scapes basal, 1-fld.; fls. commonly showy, sepals forming a conical mentum with column foot, petals shorter and narrower than sepals, lip 3-lobed, midlobe entire or fringed, disc with 1 to several calluses. For structure of fl. see *Orchidaceae.*

Grown in the shaded intermediate greenhouse. For culture see *Orchids.*

acuminata: *Maxillaria acuminata.*

aromatica (R. C. Grah. ex Hook.) Lindl. Pseudobulbs to 4 in. long, several-lvd.; lvs. to 20 in. long; scapes to 5 in. long; fls. yellow, fragrant, sepals to 1½ in. long, lip to 1¼ in. long, yellow, dotted with orange inside, lateral lobes sickle-shaped, midlobe clawed, variously shaped, disc pubescent and thickened along center. Mex. to Honduras.

Barringtoniae (Sm.) Lindl. [*L. ciliata* Lindl.]. Pseudobulbs ellipsoid to 3½ in. long, 2–3-lvd.; lvs. to 20 in. long; scapes to 5 in. long; fls. drooping, to 2 in. across, sepals and petals spreading, oblong-ovate, yellowish to olive-green, lip to 1¾ in. long, light buff, lateral lobes curved-ovate, midlobe round, fringed. Spring–early summer. W. Indies.

brevispatha Klotzsch ex Lindl. [*L. candida* Lindl. ex Rchb.f.]. Pseudobulbs ovoid, compressed laterally, to 2½ in. long, 2–4-lvd.; lvs. to 8 in. long; scapes 1 to many, to 2¾ in. long; sepals to 1 in. long, pale green to olive-green, rarely rose, petals white, marked with rose, lip to 1 in. long, white with rose markings, disc with elongate, 2-keeled, tongue-shaped callus. Late winter–spring. Costa Rica, Panama.

candida: *L. brevispatha.*

ciliata: *L. Barringtoniae.*

costata: *L. fimbriata.*

cruenta Lindl. Pseudobulbs ovoid-oblong, to 4 in. long, several-lvd.; lvs. to 18 in. long; scapes several, to 6 in. long; fls. showy, sepals ovate, to 2 in. long, yellow-green, petals ovate, to 1½ in. long, bright yellow or orange-yellow, lip to 1 in. long, yellow, flecked with maroon, with crimson blotch at saccate base, lateral lobes ovate-triangular, midlobe ovate, with whitish hairs in saccate part. Flowering throughout year. Mex. to El Salvador.

Deppei (Lodd.) Lindl. Pseudobulbs ovoid, to 4 in. long, several-lvd.; lvs. to 20 in. long; scapes to 6 in. long, with inflated red-brown scarious sheaths to 2 in. long; sepals broadly ovate, to 2½ in. long, pale green flecked with red, petals white, flecked red, lip to 1½ in. long, bright yellow with red spots and red lateral striations, lateral lobes triangular, midlobe lanceolate. Early summer–early autumn. Mex., Guatemala.

Dowiana: *L. macrophylla.*

fimbriata (Poepp. & Endl.) Cogn. [*L. costata* Lindl.]. Pseudobulbs to 6 in. long, 2–3-lvd.; lvs. to 28 in. long; scapes to 10 in. long; fls. white to pale greenish, sepals and petals ovate, to 3 in. long, lip to 2 in. long, lateral lobes semiovate, midlobe orbicular, margin minutely toothed to fringed, disc with 5 keels extending into a broad, retuse callus in middle. Colombia to Peru.

gigantea Lindl. Large, showy, pseudobulbs oblong-ovoid, to 6 in. long, 2–3-lvd.; lvs. to 2½ ft. long; scapes to 2 ft. long; fls. yellowish or greenish, suffused with brown or pink, petals and sepals ovate-lanceolate, sepals to 4 in. long, petals shorter, lip red, brown, or purple, to 2 in. long, broadly rounded apically, midlobe minutely toothed or fringed. Venezuela to Peru.

Harrisoniae: *Bifrenaria Harrisoniae.*

lanipes Lindl. Pseudobulbs to 6 in. long, 2–3-lvd.; lvs. to 25 in. long; scapes to 4 in. long; fls. to 4 in. high, sepals greenish-white, petals and lip ivory-white, lip fringed apically, plate of disc dilated at apex and with 3–5 parallel raised lines, column hairy in front. Autumn. Ecuador.

locusta Rchb.f. Pseudobulbs oblong-ovoid, to 4 in. long, 1–3-lvd.; lvs. to 22 in. long; scapes to 12 in. long; fls. fleshy, green with white column and white margin on midlobe of lip, sepals, petals, and lip ovate, to 2 in. long, midlobe fringed apically, disc with pair of fleshy keels. Spring. Peru.

macrobulbon Lindl. Pseudobulbs ovate, to 3 in. long, 2-lvd., old pseudobulbs tipped with a pair of short spinelike lf. remnants; lvs. to 20 in. long; scape to 10 in. long; fls. to 3 in. across, fragrant, sepals ovate-oblong, greenish-yellow, petals similar but shorter, bright yellow, lip bright yellow with red spots, lateral lobes subovate, midlobe ovate, disc with a longitudinal callus. Colombia.

macrophylla (Poepp. & Endl.) Lindl. [*L. Dowiana* Endres & Rchb.f.; *L. plana* Lindl.]. Pseudobulbs ovoid, to 4 in. long, 2–3-lvd.; lvs. to about 2½ ft. long; scapes to 20 in. long; sepals to 2¾ in. long, ovate-oblong, to 2 in. long, brownish-green outside, brownish-purple inside, petals white or cream-colored, lip white, flushed with rose, disc with central linear concave callus spotted pink on margin and terminating between lateral lobes of lip. Cent. Amer. to Bolivia.

plana: *L. macrophylla.*

Powellii Schlechter. Pseudobulbs ovoid, laterally compressed, to 2½ in. long, 2–3-lvd.; lvs. to 14 in. long; scapes 1–4, to 5½ in. long; fls. fragrant, sepals ovate-ovate, to 1½ in. long, pale translucent-green, blotched with chestnut-brown, or wine-red with yellow margins, petals cream-yellow to nearly white, spotted rose-pink or wine-red, lip to 1 in. long, obscurely 3-lobed, disc with short, fleshy, concave callus. Summer–early autumn. Panama.

Schillerana Rchb.f. Pseudobulbs 2-lvd.; lvs. to 2 ft. long; scapes to 8 in. long; sepals lanceolate, to 4 in. long, brown, petals similar, to 1½ in. long, white, dotted with brown on back, lip as long as petals, white, speckled and tinged with rose, disc with tongue-shaped callus. Summer. Colombia. Cv. 'Magnifica'. Sepals longer, olive-tinted, petals and lip white.

Skinneri: *L. virginalis.*

tricolor (Klotzsch) Rchb.f. Pseudobulbs to 3 in. long, several-lvd.; lvs. to 14 in. long; scapes several, to 14 in. long; sepals to 1½ in. long, narrow, greenish, tinged with rose-pink, petals white or pink, often striped and spotted with rose, lip stained and marked with deep rose, to 1 in. long, midlobe toothed. Guatemala, Costa Rica, Panama.

virginalis (Scheidw.) L. Linden [*L. Skinneri* (Batem. ex Lindl.) Lindl.]. Pseudobulbs to 4 in. long, several-lvd.; lvs. to 2 ft. long or more; scapes to 6 in. long; fls. to 6 in. across, sepals ovate, to 3 in. long, white to violet-pink, lateral sepals joined at base and forming a blunt mentum, petals similar but shorter than sepals, reddish-violet, fading, especially toward apex, lip to 2 in. long, flecked or veined with reddish-violet, sometimes unmarked. Winter–late spring, late autumn. Mex. to Honduras. The wild flower-fld. form, called the NUN ORCHID, WHITE NUN, or WHITE NUN ORCHID, is the national fl. of Guatemala. Cvs. include: 'Alba', fls. white, lip with yellow crest; 'Armeniaca', sepals white, petals and lip suffused with apricot-yellow; 'Candida', fls. pure white; 'Delicatissima', fls. rose-white, lip white, blotched with rose; 'Denholmiana', fls. rich crimson, lip almost white; 'Grandiflora', fls. larger; 'Hellemense', fls. bright rose-purple; 'Nigro-rubra', sepals tinted with rose-carmine, petals purplish-crimson, lip maroon-crimson; 'Picturata', sepals and petals light rose, lip white, stained with crimson at base, midlobe spotted with crimson; 'Purpurata', sepals and petals rose-white, lip crimson-purple; 'Rosea', fls. deep rose, lip white, spotted with crimson; 'Superba', sepals white with flush of light rose, petals dark carmine, lip white with yellow crest.

LYCHNIS L. [*Coronaria* Schaeff.; *Viscaria* Röhling]. CAMPION, CATCHFLY. *Caryophyllaceae.* About 35 spp. of ann. or per. herbs, native to n. temp. and arctic regions; lvs. opp., stipules absent; infl. cymose; fls. bisexual or sometimes unisexual, white, scarlet, or pink to purple, calyx 5-toothed, 10-veined, sometimes inflated, not subtended by epicalyx, petals 5, with coronal scales at juncture of blade and claw, stamens 10, ovary 1-celled, or sometimes 5-celled at base, styles usually 5; fr. a 5-toothed caps., enclosed by calyx, usually borne on a stalk.

Useful in the border or rock garden. Easily grown from seeds and the perennials readily propagated by division.

alba: *Silene alba.*

alpina L. [*Viscaria alpina* (L.) G. Don]. Cespitose per., to 12 in., glabrous; lvs. of basal rosette linear-spatulate; infl. capitate to elongate,

6–20-fld.; calyx ³⁄₁₆ in. long, petals ⁵⁄₁₆ in. long, 2–lobed, rosy-purple, rarely white. Eur., ne. N. Amer. Cv. **'Alba'**. Fls. white. Cv. **'Rosea'**. Fls. rose-pink.

apetala: *Silene uralensis* subsp.

arida: a listed name of no botanical standing.

×**Arkwrightii** Heydt: *L. chalcedonica* × *L.* × *Haageana.* Infl. capitate, 5–10-fld.; fls. scarlet, about 1½ in. across. A garden hybrid.

atropurpurea: *L. Viscaria* subsp.

chalcedonica L. MALTESE-CROSS, JERUSALEM-C., SCARLET-LIGHT-NING, LONDON-PRIDE. Per., sts. 1–2 ft., erect, usually simple, stout, hispid; lvs. ovate, acute, sparsely hispid, st. lvs. clasping, lower lvs. 2–4 in. long; infl. capitate, 10–50-fld.; calyx to ¾ in. long, petals 2-lobed, vivid scarlet. N. U.S.S.R. Cvs. include: **'Alba'**, fls. white; **'Grandiflora'**, fls. very large, flaming scarlet; **'Rosea'**, fls. rose; **'Salmonea'**, fls. salmon-rose.

Coeli-rosa (L.) Desr. [*Agrostemma Coeli-rosa* L.]. ROSE-OF-HEAVEN. Glabrous ann., sts. 8–20 in.; lvs. linear-lanceolate, acute; calyx club-shaped, to 1 in. long, teeth linear-filiform, petals to 1 in. across, rose-pink. W. Medit. region. Cvs. are: **'Candida'**, fls. white; **'Kermesina'** [*Viscaria cardinalis* Hort. Vilm.-Andr.], fls. red; **'Nana'**, plant dwarf; **'Nobilis'**, a listed name; **'Oculata'**, fls. with purple eye.

cognata: *L. fulgens.*

Coronaria (L.) Desr. [*Agrostemma Coronaria* L.; *Coronaria coriacea* (Moench) Shishk. ex Gorshchk.]. MULLEIN PINK, ROSE CAMPION, DUSTY-MILLER. Densely white-woolly bien. or per., sts. to 3 ft., erect, often branched; lvs. ovate, 1–4 in. long, lower lvs. petioled, upper lvs. sessile; infl. few-fld., pedicels long; calyx to ¾ in. long, petals purplish, rarely white. Nw. Afr., se. Eur., to cent. Asia. Cvs. are: **'Alba'**, fls. white; **'Atrosanguinea'** [*Agrostemma atrosanguinea* Hort.], fls. dark red; **'Bicolor'**, a listed name.

coronata Thunb. GAMPI. Glabrous per., sts. 15–30 in., green, nodes thickened; lvs. sessile, ovate, to 3 in. long, margin scabrous; calyx ⅛ in. long, glabrous, teeth short, ciliate, petals yellowish-red, blades ⅛ in. long, deeply and irregularly toothed. E. China.

Dammeri: a listed name of no botanical standing.

dioica: *Silene dioica.*

Flos-cuculi L. CUCKOO FLOWER, RAGGED-ROBIN. Per., sts. to 3 ft., often branched, sparsely scabrous-puberulent; basal lvs. petioled, oblanceolate, slightly scabrous, st. lvs. clasping, linear-lanceolate; infl. panicled; calyx glabrous, to ⅜ in. long, petals deep rose-red or white. Eur.; naturalized from Que. to Penn.

Flos-Jovis (L.) Desr. [*Agrostemma Flos-Jovis* L.]. FLOWER-OF-JOVE. White-tomentose per., sts. to 3 ft., erect, little branched; lvs. of basal rosette lanceolate, st. lvs. clasping; infl. capitate, 4-10-fld.; calyx ½ in. long, petals 2-lobed, purplish, red, rarely white. Alps.

×**Forrestii:** a listed name of no botanical standing, used for a strain of garden hybrids; sts. to 2 ft.; fls. crimson, carmine, and pink to white.

fulgens Fisch. ex Sims [*L. cognata* Maxim.]. Per., rhizome thickened; sts. to 30 in., sparsely white-hairy; lvs. sessile, ovate-lanceolate, to 2 in. long, 1 in. wide; calyx to ¾ in. long, petals deeply 2-lobed, ¾ in. long, toothed, deep red. Siberia, Manchuria, Korea, Japan.

gracillima: *Silene gracillima.*

×**Haageana** Lem.: *L. coronata* × *L. fulgens.* Hairy per., to 1 ft.; fls. about 2 in. across, petals orange-red, scarlet, or crimson, toothed. Cvs. are: **'Grandiflora'**, fls. large, red; **'Hybrida'**, fls. red; **'Salmonea'**, fls. salmon-rose.

Lagascae: *Petrocoptis glaucifolia.*

Miqueliana Rohrb. ex Franch. & Sav. Per., sts. to 3 ft., pubescent to glabrous; lvs. sessile, ovate, to 5 in. long, glabrescent; pedicels to ¼ in. long, calyx ⅛ in. long, glabrous, petals red, rarely white. Mts., cent. and s. Japan.

montana: *Silene Hitchguirei.*

Sartorii: *L. Viscaria* subsp. *atropurpurea.*

sibirica L. Pubescent per., sts. 3–12 in., usually simple; lvs. of basal rosette linear-lanceolate, st. lvs. in 3–8 pairs; infl. loose, 1-8-fld.; calyx ¼ in. long, petals 2-lobed, pale yellow or white. Arctic regions, U.S.S.R. Subsp. **villosula** (Trautv.) Tolm. Plants more dwarf, 2–6 in., villous. Arctic Siberia.

silvestris: *Silene dioica.*

taimyrense: *Silene taimyrense.*

tomentosa: a listed name of no botanical standing.

utriculata: a listed name of no botanical standing.

Viscaria L. [*L. vulgaris* Hort.; *Viscaria viscosa* Asch.; *V. vulgaris* Bernh.]. GERMAN CATCHFLY. Per., to 3 ft., sts. glabrous to hairy above, viscid just below nodes; lvs. mostly basal, petioled, linear to lanceolate, glabrous, basally ciliate; infl. panicled, 3-6-fld.; calyx to ½ in. long,

petals often emarginate, dark purple, pinkish-purple, rarely white. Eur. and Turkey, e. to cent. Asia and Siberia. Cvs. are: **'Alba'**, fls. white; **'Nana'**, plants dwarf; **'Rosea'**, fls. pink; **'Splendens'**, fls. rose-pink. Subsp. **atropurpurea** (Griseb.) Chater [*L. atropurpurea* (Griseb.) Nym.; *L. Sartorii* (Boiss.) Hayek; *Viscaria atropurpurea* Griseb.]. Calyx campanulate, stalk of ovary short, about ¹⁄₁₆ in. long. Balkan Pen. and Romania.

vulgaris: a listed name of no botanical standing for *L. Viscaria.*

×**Walkeri** Hort. [*Agrostemma* × *Walkeri* Hort. Dicksons ex Düesb.]: *L. Coronaria* × *L. Flos-Jovis.* Silvery, hairy, sts. usually many-fld.; fls. carmine-red, pedicels shorter than in *L. Coronaria.*

Wilfordii (Regel) Maxim. Per., sts. 20–30 in., pubescent to glabrescent, simple; lvs. slightly clasping, ovate, to 3 in. long; pedicels to ⅜ in. long, yellowish-pubescent, calyx to ¾ in. long, glabrescent, petals deep red, blades ¾ in. long, finely laciniate. N. and cent. Japan, Korea, Manchuria. Related to *L. fulgens.*

yunnanensis Bak.f. Cespitose per., to 8 in., sts. hairy, slender; lvs. sessile, linear to lanceolate, acute, hairy; calyx usually 10-nerved, teeth ovate, glandular, margins reddish, petals longer than calyx, white, blades bifid. Yunnan (sw. China).

LYCIUM L. MATRIMONY VINE, BOX THORN. *Solanaceae.* About 100 spp. of deciduous or evergreen, erect or clambering woody shrubs, native in trop. or warm temp. parts of both hemispheres, often in dry regions; lvs. alt., often clustered, small, commonly narrow, entire, usually grayish-green, without stipules; fls. solitary or clustered in lf. axils, not large but often many on the long brs., calyx campanulate, 3-5-toothed, not enlarged in fr., corolla funnelform, greenish, whitish, or purplish, stamens mostly 5, often with a bearded ring near base of filament; fr. a berry, usually scarlet.

Lyciums grow in all usual soils; because they produce suckers, plants should not be set near flower beds. Propagated by hardwood cuttings, suckers, layers, and seeds.

barbarum L. Distinguished from *L. halimifolium* in having lvs. smaller, linear to linear-oblong, to 1 in. long, corolla pale rose, often fading to whitish, and stamens with glabrous filaments. N. Afr. to Iraq. Zone 8 in the Southwest.

carnosum: see *L. chinense.*

chinense Mill. [*L. carnosum* Hort., not Poir.]. CHINESE M.V. Shrub, with arching or prostrate brs., to 12 ft. long, generally unarmed; lvs. ovate or ovate-lanceolate, to 3 in. long; fls. usually 2–3(–6) at a node, ½ in. long, purplish, stamens pubescent at the base; berry scarlet or orange, to 1 in. long. Temp. e. Asia; naturalized in Eur. and e. U.S. Similar to *L. halimifolium* and perhaps not distinct.

europaeum L. BOX THORN. Differs from *L. halimifolium* in having lvs. smaller, narrower, corolla tube more slender, and 3 short and 2 long stamens with glabrous filaments. Asia Minor.

halimifolium Mill. COMMON M.V. Shrub, with arching or spreading brs., to 10 ft. long, generally spiny; lvs. to 2½ in. long, generally lanceolate, obtuse or acute; fls. 1–3 at a node, to ½ in. long or more, dull lilac-purple, stamens exserted, filaments pubescent at base. Se. Eur. and w. Asia; naturalized in e. N. Amer.

horridum Thunb. Spiny shrub, to 7 ft.; lvs. ovate or oblong-elliptic, to ¼ in. long, obtuse or acute; fls. solitary, ¼ in. long, whitish, stamens exserted, filaments pubescent at base. S. Afr.

LYCOPERSICON Mill. TOMATO. *Solanaceae.* About 7 spp. of unarmed herbs of Pacific S. Amer. and the Galapagos Is.; sts. weak, clambering, often glandular-pilose; lvs. pinnate or pinnatifid, segms. unequal, coarsely dentate; fls. in loose, peduncled cymes or racemes, calyx usually 5-parted, corolla yellow, rotate, usually deeply 5-lobed, stamens usually 5, anthers prolonged into sharp or narrow sterile tips, dehiscing from top to bottom; fr. a pulpy berry, red, sometimes yellow, cells 2 or few in the wild form, more numerous under cult. Sometimes included in *Solanum,* with which it intergrades and with which graft hybrids (called pomato or topato) can be formed.

A few species are cultivated for their fruit. For culture see *Tomato.*

esculentum: *L. Lycopersicum.*

Lycopersicum (L.) Karst. ex Farw. [*L. esculentum* Mill.]. TOMATO, LOVE APPLE, GOLD A. Tender per., grown as ann. in temp. regions, erect to decumbent, to 10 ft.; lvs. to 18 in. long, lfts. 5–9, to 3 in. long, coarsely toothed, margin often crisped or curled; infl. 3-20-fld., shorter than lvs.; calyx and corolla 5-lobed, lobes acuminate, calyx to ⅜ in. long, corolla yellow, to 1 in. across; fr. usually red, rarely golden-orange, mostly 2–4 in. in diam., 2- to many-celled, usually lobed near calyx, flattened at apex, the sides sometimes furrowed, seeds many. Andean S. Amer. Widely cult. as a vegetable crop for its fr. There are many cvs. Var. **cerasiforme** (Dunal) Alef. CHERRY T. Fls. more numerous, in longer clusters; fr. globose, unlobed, about ¾–1 in. in diam., 2-celled, red or yellow-orange. Locally naturalized in the sw. U.S. Var. **pyriforme** (Dunal) Alef. PEAR T. Fr. pear-shaped, about 1½–2 in. long, red or yellow-orange.

peruvianum (L.) Mill. Odoriferous herb, sts. tomentose; lvs. pinnately incised, tomentose; racemes often paired, lateral or terminal, leafy, villous; calyx 5-parted, corolla very large, yellow; fr. about ⁵⁄₁₆ in. across, villous. Andean Peru.

pimpinellifolium (Jusl.) Mill. CURRANT T. Herb without pronounced odor, sts. slender, weak, finely pubescent; lvs. pinnate, to 8 in. long, lfts. 5–7, long-stalked; infl. longer than lvs., 10–25-fld.; fls. yellow, 5-lobed; fr. red, currantlike, about ½ in. in diam., 2-celled. Andean Peru and Ecuador.

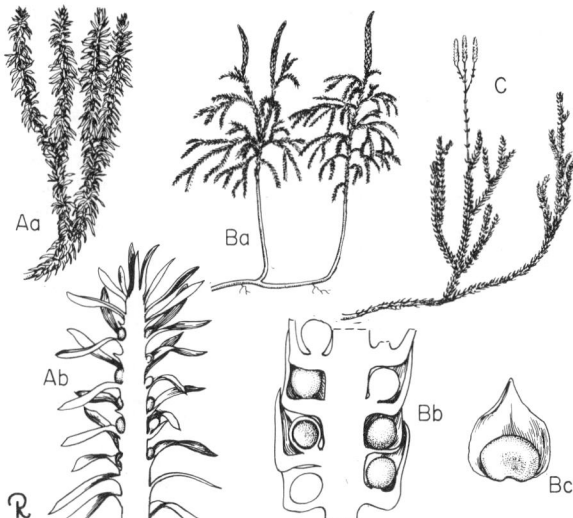

LYCOPODIACEAE. **A.** *Lycopodium lucidulum*: **Aa,** fertile branch, × ⅙; **Ab,** branch tip, vertical section, showing sporangia, × 1. **B,** *L. obscurum*: **Ba,** fertile branches, × ¼; **Bb,** part of strobilus, vertical section, × 5; **Bc,** sporophyll with sporangium, × 5. **C,** *L. clavatum*: fertile and sterile branch, × ¼. (From Lawrence, *Taxonomy of Vascular Plants.*)

LYCOPODIACEAE Beauvois ex Mirb. CLUB MOSS FAMILY. Fern allies; 2 genera and about 450 spp. of primitive, spore-bearing, vascular, evergreen herbs or epiphytes of wide distribution; sts. dichotomously branched; lvs. many, scalelike or needlelike; sporangia borne in a terminal spike-like cone (strobilus) or in the axils of the lvs., spores all alike. *Lycopodium* is sometimes cult.

LYCOPODIUM L. CLUB MOSS. *Lycopodiaceae.* About 450 spp. of evergreen per. herbs of wide distribution, with characters of the family.

The native species often used for Christmas greens. Sometimes grown in moist shady places. The spores of some temperate species are collected for industrial uses. The tropical epiphytic species with pendent branches make attractive greenhouse plants when grown in hanging baskets. Propagated by cuttings.

clavatum L. GROUND PINE, RUNNING P. Sts. creeping, to 9 ft., brs. very leafy, ascending; lvs. bristle-tipped; peduncles to 4 in. long, with 1–4 terminal strobili. N. Amer., Eur., Asia. Spores used medicinally and in industry.

complanatum L. GROUND PINE, GROUND CEDAR. Sts. trailing, leafy, brs. flat, glaucous, few-forked, erect or ascending; peduncles about 1½ in. long, with 1–3 strobili. Eur., Asia, n. N. Amer. Var. **flabelliforme** Fern. [*L. flabelliforme* (Fern.) W. Blanchard]. Brighter green, brs. many-forked, more horizontal; peduncles 2–3 in. long, mostly with 4 strobili. Ne. N. Amer.

dendroideum: *L. obscurum* var.

flabelliforme: *L. complanatum* var.

lucidulum Michx. SHINING C.M. Sts. to 10 in. high, decumbent at base; lvs. glossy green; sporangia in axils of lvs.; upper lvs. commonly with separable buds (gemmae). N. Amer.

obscurum L. GROUND PINE, PRINCESS P. Main st. creeping underground, brs. erect, to 10 in., branchlets horizontal or reflexed; strobili nearly sessile. N. Amer.; Asia. Var. **dendroideum** (Michx.) D. C. Eat. [*L. dendroideum* Michx.]. More compact, branchlets ascending or erect.

Selago L. Sts. forming tufts, stiff, erect, to 8 in.; sporophylls shorter than other lvs., not in strobili, upper lvs. commonly bearing separable buds (gemmae). Alaska to Ore. and mts. of N.C.; Eur., Asia. Useful in the alpine garden.

tristachyum Pursh. GROUND CEDAR. Sts. creeping underground, brs. narrow, glaucous; lvs. 4-ranked, imbricate; peduncles to 5 in. long. Me. to Ga. and Minn., Eur.

LYCOPUS L. BUGLEWEED, GYPSYWORT, WATER HOREHOUND. *Labiatae.* About 4 spp. of stoloniferous per. herbs of N. Temp. Zone and Australia, not aromatic; sts. mostly square in cross section; lvs. opp., serrate to pinnatifid; fls. small, in axillary verticillasters, bracts leaflike, bractlets small; calyx campanulate, 13-nerved, 5-toothed, corolla tube shorter than calyx, limb 4-lobed, stamens 2, divergent, exserted, anther cells parallel; fr. of 4 four-sided nutlets.

For use in wet places and in the wild flower garden.

americanus Muhlenb. ex W. Barton. Glabrescent, 1–3 ft.; lvs. lanceolate to linear, to 3 in. long, bluntly dentate to pectinate; verticillasters small, dense; corolla pink, scarcely longer than calyx. Summer. N. Amer.; widespread.

europaeus L. Sts. to 3 ft., sparsely to densely hairy, brs. ascending; lvs. ovate-lanceolate, to 4 in. long, pinnately lobed, lobes many, triangular, acute; calyx teeth spiny, corolla about ⅛ in. across, white, dotted purple on lower lip. Summer. Wet places, Eur. and Asia; naturalized in N. Amer.

LYCORIS Herb. *Amaryllidaceae.* Eleven or perhaps more spp. of bulbous herbs, native from China and Japan to Burma; lvs. narrow, basal, dying away before fls. develop; fls. in an umbel on a solid scape, perianth segms. separate or united into a short tube, red, pink, white, or yellow, ovary inferior; fr. a caps., seeds few, round, smooth, black.

Grown under glass, and some species hardy outdoors to Zone 7 with winter protection.

africana (Lam.) M. J. Roem. [*L. aurea* (L'Hér.) Herb.; *Amaryllis aurea* L'Hér.]. GOLDEN HURRICANE LILY, GOLDEN SPIDER L. Lvs. to ¾ in. wide; spathe valves lanceolate, to 3 in. long; fls. golden-yellow, 3 in. long, perianth tube ½–¾ in. long, wavy-margined, lobes about ⅜ in. wide, recurved, stamens exserted. Summer. China, Taiwan, to Burma. Once thought to have come from Afr., hence the name.

albiflora G. Koidz. Similar to *L. radiata*, but lvs. ⅜–½ in. wide, fls. white, smaller. Japan. Cv. 'Carnea' is listed.

aurea: *L. africana.*

Caldwellii Traub. To 21 in.; lvs. dark green, to 14 in. long, ½ in. wide; umbel 5-fld.; fls. pale yellow becoming creamy-white, perianth tube ¾ in. long, lobes to 2¾ in. long, margin slightly undulate, stamens shorter than lobes. Late summer. China.

cinnabarina: a listed name of no botanical standing.

Haywardii Traub. Similar to *L. Sprengeri*, but fls. appearing in late summer, reddish-violet or orchid-purple, hyacinth-blue at tips, lobes about 1¾ in. long. Japan.

incarnata Comes ex Sprenger. To 1¾ ft.; lvs. strap-shaped; umbel 6–12-fld.; fls. salmon to bright rose, fragrant, large, perianth tube absent or indistinct, lobes only slightly reflexed and undulate. Autumn. Cent. China.

japonica: a listed name of no botanical standing.

purpurea: a listed name of no botanical standing; plants so named may be *L. incarnata, L. Sprengeri,* or *L. squamigera* cv. 'Purpurea'.

radiata (L'Hér.) Herb. [*Amaryllis radiata* L'Hér.]. SPIDER LILY, RED S. L. Lvs. linear, ³⁄₁₆–⁵⁄₁₆ in. wide; fls. bright red, 1½ in. long, lobes irregular, reflexed, wavy-margined, stamens exserted. Autumn. China, Japan; Zone 8, extensively naturalized in the South. Long mistakenly distributed as *Nerine sarniensis.* Cv. 'Alba'. Fls. white.

sanguinea Maxim. Lvs. linear; fls. bright red, 2 in. long, perianth tube very short, lobes scarcely reflexed or wavy-margined, stamens included. Summer. Japan. Cv. '**Major**' is listed.

Sprengeri Comes ex Bak. Similar to *L. incarnata*, but fls. with rose throat and purple, carmine, and blue lobes. Cent. China.

squamigera Maxim. [*Amaryllis Hallii* Hovey ex Bak.]. MAGIC LILY, RESURRECTION L. Lvs. to 1 in. wide; fls. rose-lilac or pink, 3 in. long, fragrant, lobes not reflexed or wavy-margined. Late summer. Japan;

Zone 5. Cv. '**Purpurea**' is listed, but some material so named is *L. incarnata.*

Traubii Hayw. Similar to *L. africana*, but hardier, lvs. appearing later, spathe valves ovate, 1½ in. long, fls. saffron-yellow, perianth tube ¾ in. long, lobes to ⅝ in. wide. Taiwan. Zone 7.

LYGODIUM Swartz. CLIMBING FERN. *Schizaeaceae.* Forty spp. of climbing ferns, mainly of trop. and subtrop. regions; lvs. of indeterminate growth, main rachis stemlike, long and twining, pinnae alt., short-stalked, forking into 2 pinnules, the pinnules palmately lobed or pinnate; fertile pinnules contracted, with 2 rows of sporangia on marginal lobes, indusia hard, scalelike.

Temperate species may be grown outdoors, but the tropical species are usually seen as greenhouse plants. For culture see *Ferns.*

circinatum (Burm.f.) Swartz. MALAY C.F. Pinnules almost sessile, 1-forked and the divisions deeply 5–6-lobed, or sometimes 2-forked, sterile pinnules 4–12 in. long, ½–¾ in. wide. Malay Arch., where sts. are used in basketry.

japonicum Swartz. JAPANESE C.F. Pinnae triangular, 4–8 in. long and as wide, terminal pinnules pinnatifid, lateral pinnules 2–3 on each side, very unequal, lower ones stalked and pinnate, margins serrate. E. temp. Asia. Zone 8. The commonly cult. sp.

palmatum Swartz.HARTFORD FERN, CLIMBING F. Pinnules cordate-palmate, 1½–2 in. long, short-stalked, fertile pinnules 3–4-pinnatifid, ultimate lobes linear. Mass. to Fla. and Tenn. Locally in Zone 6. Requires light moist soil and partial shade.

scandens Swartz. Like *L. japonicum*, but pinnules less divided, the segms. simple and ovate, or lobed at base. Tropics, Afr., Asia, Australia.

volubile Swartz. Pinnae 6–12 in. long, 4–10 in. wide, 1-pinnate, pinnules 5–13, tongue-shaped, 2–6 in. long, ½–1¼ in. wide, truncate or somewhat cuneate and jointed at base, stalked. Trop. Amer., Cuba to Brazil.

LYONIA Nutt. [*Arsenococcus* Small; *Desmothamnus* Small; *Neopieris* Britt.; *Xolisma* Raf.]. *Ericaceae.* Between 40 and 50 spp. of evergreen or deciduous shrubs or rarely small trees, native to e. Asia and N. Amer., but most abundant in the W. Indies; lvs. alt., simple; fls. white to pink, in racemose, axillary clusters or panicles, from old wood, calyx usually 5-lobed, corolla urceolate to cylindrical, stamens usually 10, ovary superior; fr. a 5-angled caps., the valves with thickened margins.

Lyonias are adapted for colonizing and shrub collections. They are mostly plants of moist soil. Cultivation as for *Leucothoe.*

arborea: *Oxydendrum arboreum.*

ferruginea (Walt.) Nutt. [*Xolisma ferruginea* (Walt.) A. Heller]. Evergreen shrub or small tree, to 15 ft.; lvs. elliptic or ovate to obovate, to 2¾ in. long, strongly revolute, with lepidote scales beneath; fls. in dense axillary clusters. Coastal plain, S.C. to Fla.

foliosiflora: a listed name of no botanical standing for *L. ligustrina* var.

fruticosa (Michx.) G. Torr. ex B. L. Robinson [*Xolisma fruticosa* (Michx.) Nash]. Evergreen shrub, to 10 ft.; lvs. elliptic to oblanceolate or obovate, to 2 in. long, greatly reduced toward ends of brs., not revolute, with lepidote scales beneath; fls. in axillary clusters. Coastal plain, S.C. to Fla.

ligustrina (L.) DC. [*Arsenococcus ligustrinus* (L.) Small; *Xolisma ligustrina* (L.) Britt.]. MALE BERRY, HE HUCKLEBERRY, MALE BLUEBERRY. Deciduous shrub, to 12 ft., but often less; lvs. lanceolate, oblong, elliptic, or obovate, to 3 in. long, entire to finely toothed; fls. white, in panicles to 6 in. long. Late spring, early summer. Me. to Fla. and Tex. Zone 4. Var. **foliosiflora** (Michx.) Fern. [*Arsenococcus frondrosus* (Pursh) Small; *Xolisma foliosiflora* (Michx.) Small]. Glabrescent shrub, to 6 ft.; panicle with brs. leafy-bracted. Se. Va. to Fla.

lucida (Lam.) C. Koch [*Desmothamnus lucidus* (Lam.) Small; *Pieris lucida* (Lam.) Rehd.; *P. nitida* (Bartr.) Benth. & Hook.f.]. TETTERBUSH. Glabrous, evergreen shrub, to 6 ft., branchlets sharply 3-angled; lvs. lanceolate to oblong-ovate, to 3 in. long, entire, leathery, shining above; fls. white to pink, in axillary clusters. Spring. Low woods and barrens, Va. to Fla. and La. Zone 7.

mariana (L.) D. Don [*Andromeda mariana* L.; *Neopieris mariana* (L.) Britt.; *Pieris mariana* (L.) Benth. & Hook.f.]. STAGGERBUSH. Deciduous shrub, to 6 ft., branchlets cylindrical; lvs. elliptic, oblong, or obovate, to 2½ in. long, entire; fls. white or pink, in umbellate-racemose clusters on leafless old brs. Late summer. R.I. to Fla. and Ark. Zone 6.

ovalifolia (Wallich) Drude [*Pieris ovalifolia* (Wallich) D. Don]. Deciduous or half-evergreen shrub or small tree, to 40 ft.; lvs. elliptic, ovate to ovate-oblong, to 5 in. long; fls. in 1-sided axillary racemes. Late summer. W. China and Himalayas. Var. **elliptica** (Siebold & Zucc.) Hand.-Mazz. [*Pieris elliptica* (Siebold & Zucc.) Nakai]. Lvs. thinner, deciduous; racemes shorter. China, Japan. Zone 7?

LYONOTHAMNUS A. Gray. CATALINA IRONWOOD. *Rosaceae.* One sp., an evergreen tree of the islands off the coast of s. Calif.; bark exfoliating in narrow strips; lvs. opp., thickish, simple and entire to pinnate; fls. many, in large corymbose panicles, bisexual, white, sepals and petals 5, stamens about 15, pistils 2; frs. a pair of small woody follicles.

Planted in warm regions; propagated by basal sprouts, with difficulty by cuttings, or by seeds.

floribundus A. Gray. Slender, to 50 ft., with narrow crown; lvs. 4–6 in. long, entire to crenate-serrate; petals less than $^3/_{16}$ in. long. Santa Catalina Is. Intergrading with subsp. **asplenifolius** (Greene) Raven. Lvs. pinnate into 2–7 lfts., then pinnatifid into many lobes. San Clemente, Santa Rosa, and Santa Cruz Is.

LYSIAS: *HABENARIA.*

LYSICHITON Schott (sometimes but incorrectly spelled *Lysichitum*). *Araceae.* Two spp. of robust, stemless, hardy per. herbs of swamps in ne. Asia and nw. N. Amer.; lvs. arising from thick rhizomes, simple; infl. before the lvs., spathe showy, stalked, spadix subtended by spathe and longer-stalked, stout; fls. bisexual, perianth 4-parted. Ill-scented when bruised.

Of easy culture in wet ground; propagation by division or seeds.

americanum Hult. & St. John [*L. camtschatcense* (L.) Schott, in part]. SKUNK CABBAGE, YELLOW S.C., WESTERN S.C. Lvs. oblanceolate to elliptic, to 5 ft. long and 1 ft. wide, narrowed to a winged petiole, bright green; spathe bright yellow, the upper part inflated, to 7 in. long, the lower narrow, sheathing the stout, elongate peduncle, spadix greenish, stout, to 6 in. long in age and exceeding the spathe. Late spring. Calif. to Alaska, e. to Idaho and Mont.

camtschatcense (L.) Schott [*L. camtschatcense* var. *album* Hort. ex Besant]. Distinguished from *L. americanum* in having lvs. shorter, blunter, glaucous-green, especially when young, spathe broader, white, spadix generally smaller, and flowering several weeks later. Kamchatka, Sakhalin and Kurile Is., n. Japan.

LYSIDICE Hance. *Leguminosae* (subfamily *Caesalpinioideae*). One sp., a shrub or small tree of Asia; lvs. alt., even-pinnate; fls. racemose, calyx tubular, 4-parted, petals 3, fertile stamens 2, elongate; fr. a flat, dehiscent legume.

rhodostegia Hance. To 25 ft.; lfts. in 4 pairs, oblong-elliptic, acuminate, the larger terminal ones to 6 in. long; racemes in showy, terminal panicles to 1 ft. long, bracts rose; calyx lobes reflexed, petals violet, spoon-shaped; fr. oblanceolate-oblong, to 7 in. long, nearly woody. Se. China, Vietnam.

LYSILOMA Benth. *Leguminosae* (subfamily *Mimosoideae*). About 30–35 spp. of unarmed trees and shrubs of trop. Amer.; lvs. alt., 2-pinnate; fls. in heads or spikes, small, 5-merous, stamens many, 12–30, exserted, united basally; fr. flat, oblong-linear, thin.

bahamensis Benth. Tree, to 50 ft.; lvs. large, with 2–5 pairs of pinnae, with a large gland below the lowest, lfts. in 10–30 pairs, oblong, obtuse, $^5/_{16}$–⅝ in. long; fl. heads on long peduncles in racemes, whitish; fr. to 6 in. long, 1 in. wide, glabrous, tip pointed. S. Fla., Bahamas, Cuba, Yucatan (Mex.).

latisiliqua (L.) Benth. [*L. Sabicu* Benth.] SABICU. Large tree, differing from *L. bahamensis* in having only 3–7 pairs of ovate to obovate lfts., and fr. rounded at tip. Bahamas, Cuba, Hispaniola.

Sabicu: *L. latisiliqua.*

Thornberi Britt. & Rose. Shrub or small tree; lvs. with 6–8 pairs of pinnae, to 6 in. long, lfts. in 20–35 pairs, linear-oblong, about $^3/_{16}$ in. long, obtuse; fl. heads white; fr. oblong, 4–6 in. long, glaucous. Rincon Mts. (Ariz.).

LYSIMACHIA L. [*Naumbergia* Moench; *Steironema* Raf.]. LOOSESTRIFE. *Primulaceae.* About 165 spp. of ann. or per. herbs, rarely shrubby, widely distributed in temp. and subtrop. regions, sts. leafy; lvs. simple, alt., opp., or whorled, often dotted with glands; fls. yellow or white, rarely pink, bluish, or purplish, calyx 5–6-parted, corolla rotate or campanulate, 5–7-parted, stamens 5–7, inserted on corolla tube; fr. a 5-valved caps.

Grown as an ornamental in moist locations; propagated by division.

ciliata L. [*Steironema ciliatum* (L.) Baudo]. To 3½ ft.; lvs. opp., ovate to ovate-lanceolate, to 6 in. long, petioles conspicuously ciliate; fls. yellow, to 1 in. across, solitary in upper lf. axils. N. Amer.; naturalized in Eur.

clethroides Duby. GOOSENECK L. Pubescent per., to 3 ft.; lvs. alt., ovate-lanceolate, tapering at both ends, to 6 in. long; fls. white, in slender, curving racemes, corolla lobes oblong or linear. China, Japan.

decurrens G. Forst. Glabrous, to 1½ ft.; lvs. alt. or subopp., lanceolate to ovate, to 4 in. long; fls. white, fragrant, in terminal racemes. Old World tropics, India to Taiwan and New Caledonia.

Ephemerum L. Glabrous, glaucous per., to 3 ft.; lvs. opp., sessile, joined at the base, linear-lanceolate; fls. white, in terminal racemes. Sw. Eur.

Fortunei Maxim. Sts. to 1½ ft., with short glandular hairs in upper part; lvs. alt. or opp., lanceolate to elliptic, to 2 in. long or more; fls. white, in terminal, straight racemes, corolla lobes ovate. China, Japan.

lanceolata Walt. [*Steironema lanceolatum* (Walt.) A. Gray]. Per., to 2½ ft., sts. 4-angled in upper part; lvs. opp., lower lvs. elliptic to ovate, upper lvs. linear or lanceolate; fls. yellow, solitary in upper lf. axils or becoming panicled. E. U.S.

Leschenaultii Duby. Small, tufted, glabrous per., to 1 ft.; lvs. opp., whorled, or alt., lanceolate, to 3½ in. long; fls. pink, bluish, or purple, in dense terminal racemes. India.

lichiangensis Forr. Glabrous per., to 2 ft.; lvs. alt., lanceolate, to 2 in. long; fls. pinkish-white, in terminal racemes. China.

lobelioides Wallich. Glabrous, to 1 ft., sts. slender, erect or ascending; lvs. opp., lanceolate to widely ovate, to nearly 2 in. long; fls. white, broadly campanulate, stamens exserted. Nw. Himalayas.

mauritiana Lam. Glabrous per., to 1½ ft. or more; lvs. alt., spatulate, margin revolute; fls. white, in a dense leafy raceme, calyx white-margined. Mauritius, e. Asia to Hawaii and New Caledonia.

Nummularia L. MONEYWORT, CREEPING JENNIE, CREEPING CHARLIE. Glabrous, creeping per.; lvs. opp., nearly orbicular, to 1 in. long; fls. yellow, solitary, axillary. Eur.; naturalized in e. N. Amer. Cv. 'Aurea'. Foliage yellow.

punctata L. GARDEN L. Per., to 4 ft.; lvs. whorled, in 3's or 4's, sometimes opp., ovate-lanceolate; fls. yellow, in axillary whorls, petals margined with minute glandular hairs. Eur.; naturalized in U.S.

ramosa Wallich ex Duby. Glabrous, to 4 ft.; lvs. alt., linear-lanceolate to oblong, to 4¾ in. long; fls. yellow, axillary, on long pedicels. E. Himalayas, Ceylon, Java, Philippine Is.

thyrsiflora L. [*Naumbergia thyrsiflora* (L.) Rchb.]. TUFTED L. To 2½ ft.; sts. from creeping rhizomes; lvs. opp., lanceolate to elliptic, to 6 in. long, sessile; fls. pale yellow, in short, axillary, spicate racemes from lower lf. axils. Swamps, Eurasia, N. Amer.

vulgaris L. GARDEN L. Coarse, bushy per., 3–5 ft.; lvs. whorled or opp., lanceolate, elliptic, or lanceolate-ovate; fls. yellow, in leafy panicles, calyx lobes dark-margined. Eurasia; naturalized in N. Amer.

LYSIONOTUS D. Don. *Gesneriaceae.* About 20 spp. of glabrous, rhizomatous, epiphytic shrubs in Asia; lvs. opp. or in 3's, those of a pair nearly equal, short-petioled; fls. few or many in peduncled, axillary cymes, calyx 5-parted, segms. lanceolate, corolla tubular, inflated above base, white or purplish, with yellow lines in throat, limb more or less 2-lipped, lobes spreading, stamens 2, borne on corolla tube, anthers included, connivent and with a hooked connective, disc ring-like, ovary superior, linear, stigma shortly 2-lipped; fr. a linear, loculicidal caps., seeds many, small.

For cultivation see *Gesneriaceae.*

serratus D. Don. To 1½ ft.; lvs. elliptic, to 5 in. long, 2½ in. wide, serrate, green with pale margins; fls. several to many on peduncle to 4 in. long, calyx segms. ¼ in. long, corolla pale lavender, yellow in throat, tube 1¼ in. long, lower lobes to ½ in. long. N. India.

LYTHRACEAE. LOOSESTRIFE FAMILY. Dicot.; about 22 genera of widely distributed herbs, shrubs, or trees, many of them native to trop. Amer.; lvs. mostly opp. or whorled, rarely alt., entire; fls. bisexual, calyx tube tubular, calyx lobes 4–6, often alternating with 3–5 triangular appendages, petals (3–)4–6(–16), inserted toward top of calyx tube, or sometimes absent, stamens few to many, ovary superior, 2–6-celled, with

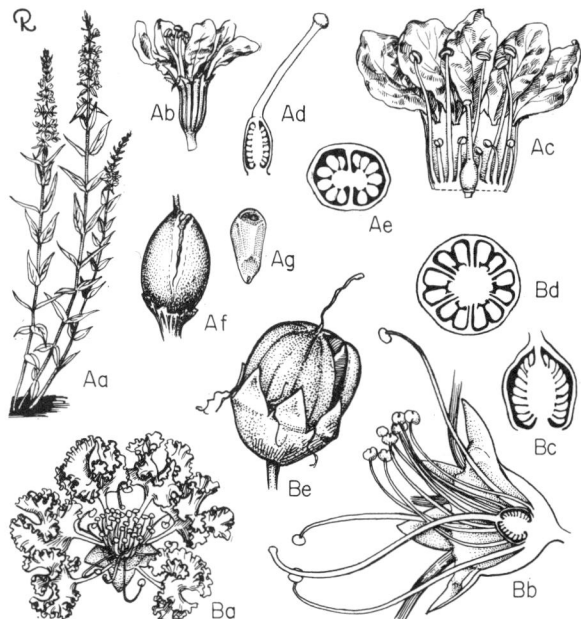

LYTHRACEAE. **A,** *Lythrum Salicaria:* **Aa,** flowering plant, × ¹⁄₂₀; **Ab,** flower, × 1; **Ac,** flower, expanded, × 1½; **Ad,** pistil, vertical section, × 3; **Ae,** ovary, cross section, × 4; **Af,** capsule, × 5; **Ag,** seed, × 12. **B,** *Lagerstroemia indica:* **Ba,** flower, × ¾; **Bb,** flower, vertical section, × 1½; **Bc,** ovary, vertical section, × 5; **Bd,** ovary, cross section, × 6; **Be,** capsule, × 1½.

axile placentas; fr. a caps. Several genera furnish medicinal and dye products, others timber. *Cuphea, Decodon, Ginoria, Heimia, Lafoensia, Lagerstroemia, Lawsonia, Lythrum, Peplis, Rotala,* and *Woodfordia* are cult. as ornamentals.

LYTHRUM L. LOOSESTRIFE. *Lythraceae.* About 30 spp. of ann. or per. herbs in N. Amer. and the Old World; sts. 4-angled or winged; lvs. mostly opp., or alt. in upper part of plant, entire; fls. purple to white, regular, solitary, paired in lf. axils, or in clusters in axils of terminal leafy infl.; calyx tube with calyx lobes alternating with appendages, petals 4–8, stamens 2–12, often very unequal; fr. a 2-valved caps.

Planted in borders and wild gardens. Easily cultivated in moist soil; propagated by division or seeds.

alatum Pursh. Erect per., to 4 ft.; lvs. oblong-ovate to linear-lanceolate, acute; fls. purple, solitary, axillary, calyx tube not much expanded upward from a thickish base, appendages longer than lobes, ovary with a fleshy, thickened ring at base. Ont. to B.C., s. to Ga., and Tex.; more or less naturalized in ne. U.S. This sp. has been hybridized with *L. virgatum.*

Dalcana: a listed name of no botanical standing; plants so named are *L. virgatum.*

flexuosum Lag. [*L. Graefferi* Ten.]. Per., to 2½ ft., sts. prostrate or ascending; lvs. oblong to linear, rounded to acute at apex; fls. purple, solitary, axillary, calyx tube funnelform, expanded upward from a very narrow base, appendages not longer than lobes or only slightly longer, ovary without thickened ring. Eur., Asia Minor, N. Afr.

Graefferi: *L. flexuosum.*

Salicaria L. PURPLE LOOSESTRIFE, SPIKED L. Erect, more or less downy per., to 6 ft.; lvs. lanceolate, to 4 in. long, cordate at base; fls. purple, often in whorled clusters in axils of leafy, interrupted, terminal spikes, appendages of calyx tube 2 or more times as long as calyx lobes. Old World; naturalized in N. Amer. Cv. 'Atropurpureum'. Fls. dark purple. Cv. 'Roseum Superbum'. Fls. larger, rose-colored. Var. **tomentosum** (Mill.) DC. Calyx and bracts white-tomentose.

virgatum L. Similar to *L. Salicaria,* but glabrous, with lvs. narrower, acute at base, fls. mostly paired or clustered in leafy, open racemes, appendages not longer than the lobes of calyx tube. Eur. and Asia; naturalized in Mass. and New Hamp. Cv. 'Dropmore Purple'. Fls. purple. Cv. 'Morden Pink'. A mutant; this cv. crossed with *L. alatum* has given hybrids, 'Morden Gleam', to 4½ ft., fls. deep rose-pink; and 'Morden Rose', more compact, fls. rose-red.

MAACKIA Rupr. & Maxim. *Leguminosae* (subfamily *Faboideae*). Six to 12 spp. of deciduous trees of e. Asia; lvs. alt., odd-pinnate, with opp. lfts.; fls. in erect, paniculate racemes, white, papilionaceous, stamens 10, united basally; fr. a flat, dehiscent legume.

amurensis Rupr. & Maxim. [*Cladrastis amurensis* (Rupr. & Maxim.) C. Koch]. To 40 ft.; lfts. in 3–5 pairs, ovate to elliptic, to 3 in. long, short-acuminate, glabrous; infl. to 8 in. long; fls. ⁵⁄₁₆ in. long; fr. to 2 in. long. Summer. Manchuria, Korea. Var. **Buergeri** (Maxim.) C. K. Schneid. Lfts. almost obtuse, pubescent beneath.

chinensis Takeda. To 70 ft.; differing from *M. amurensis* in having 5–6 pairs of obtuse lfts., pubescent beneath, and slightly larger fls., ⅜ in. long. Cent. China.

MABA J. R. Forst. & G. Forst. *Ebenaceae*. About 70 spp. of mostly dioecious trees and shrubs, native to warmer parts of world; lvs. alt., entire; fls. solitary or in cymes, unisexual, usually 3-merous; fr. a berry.

natalensis Harv. Much-branched, evergreen shrub, to 20 ft.; lvs. elliptic to ovate, to 1¼ in. long, obtuse or mucronate, revolute, glossy dark green above, petioles very short; fls. small, solitary, corolla silky, stamens or staminodes 6–9; berry subglobose, ⅜ in. long, glabrous, chestnut-brown, 1-seeded. S. Afr. Grown as an ornamental.

MACADAMIA F. J. Muell. *Proteaceae*. About 10 spp. of trees or shrubs, native from Madagascar to Australia; lvs. whorled; fls. small, bisexual, in pairs in simple racemes; fr. a hard, globose drupe.

One species grown commercially in Hawaii, and elsewhere for the edible nuts.

alternifolia: a listed name of no botanical standing; probably a misspelling for *M. ternifolia.*

integrifolia Maiden & Betche [*M. ternifolia* of auth., in part, not F. J. Muell.]. MACADAMIA NUT, QUEENSLAND NUT, AUSTRALIAN NUT. Tree to 60 ft. high, 50 ft. wide, branchlets dark-colored, new growth mostly pale green; lvs. in whorls of mostly 3, occasionally 4, petioled, the juvenile coarsely dentate-serrate, the adult oblanceolate to obovate, 4–12 in. long, rounded at apex, entire or with 1–12 teeth on each side; fls. white, in 100–300-fld. racemes 4–12 in. long; fr. nearly glabrous, often not dehiscing while on the tree, seeds ½–1¼ in. in diam., sweet, edible. Queensland (Australia). The principal sp. grown commercially; long confused with *M. ternifolia.*

minor: *M. ternifolia.*

ternifolia F. J. Muell. [*M. minor* F. M. Bailey]. SMALL-FRUITED QUEENSLAND NUT. Tree to 15 ft. high and wide, branchlets paler than in *M. integrifolia*, new growth pink to red; lvs. in whorls of mostly 3, occasionally 4, petioled, the juvenile coarsely dentate-serrate, the adult lanceolate, to 6 in. long, acute, serrate but less obviously so, teeth 8–10 on each side; fls. pink, in 50–100-fld. racemes 2–5 in. long; fr. pubescent, dehiscing while still on tree, seeds ¼ in. in diam., bitter, inedible. Queensland (Australia). Rarely cult.; trees cult. for their nuts, under this name, are *M. integrifolia* or *M. tetraphylla.*

tetraphylla L. A. S. Johnson [*M. ternifolia* of auth., in part, not F. J. Muell.]. MACADAMIA NUT, ROUGH-SHELL M. N., ROUGH-SHELL QUEENSLAND NUT, AUSTRALIAN NUT. Tree to 50 ft. high, 60 ft. wide, branchlets dark-colored, new growth usually pink to red, occasionally yellow-green; lvs. in whorls of mostly 4, occasionally 3 or 5, sessile, the juvenile finely serrate, the adult oblanceolate, 4–20 in. long, acute, finely serrate, with 15–40 teeth on each side; fls. pink, rarely white or cream, in 100–300-fld. racemes 6–18 in. long; fr. pubescent, dehiscing while still on tree, seeds ½–1½ in. in diam., sweet, edible. Queensland and New S. Wales (Australia). Often grown commercially along with *M. integrifolia* and not usually distinguished from it by growers; long confused with *M. ternifolia.*

MACARANGA Thouars. *Euphorbiaceae*. About 240 spp. of dioecious or rarely monoecious shrubs and trees, native to Afr., se. Asia, Philippine Is., Malay Arch., Melanesia, Australia; lvs. simple, alt., entire or lobed, palmately or pinnately veined, petioled, sometimes peltate; fls. without petals, in axillary panicles, ovary 2–6-celled; fr. a caps.

grandifolia (Blanco) Merrill. CORAL TREE. Tree, to 15 ft. or more; lvs. orbicular-ovate, to 2 ft. across, peltate, petioles to 2 ft. long; fls. small, ovary 2-celled. Philippine Is.

MACFADYENA A. DC. [*Doxantha* Miers]. *Bignoniaceae*. Three or 4 spp. of woody vines, native to trop. Amer.; lvs. with 2 lfts. and a terminal, 3-parted, clawlike tendril; fls. bright yellow, axillary, solitary or in clusters of 2 or 3, calyx truncate at apex and irregularly lobed, or spathelike and split, corolla campanulate-funnelform, stamens 4, ovary sharply 4-angled; fr. an elongate-linear, leathery-valved caps., seeds with reduced wings and opaque, shiny, or with 2 wings, the wings hyaline at least apically.

Grown outdoors in the South where it will stand a few degrees of frost, and also in the greenhouse. Propagated by cuttings under glass.

cynanchoides: *Dolichandra cynanchoides.*

Unguis-cati (L.) A. Gentry [*Bignonia Tweediana* Lindl.; *B. Unguis-cati* L.; *Doxantha Unguis-cati* (L.) Rehd.]. CAT'S-CLAW, CAT'S-CLAW-TRUMPET, FUNNEL CREEPER, CAT'S-CLAW CREEPER. Lfts. lanceolate-oblong to oblong-ovate, to 2 in. long; fls. to 3 in. long and 4 in. across; fr. 1 ft. long or more. Yucatan (Mex.), Guatemala, Argentina.

MACHAERANTHERA Nees. *Compositae* (Aster Tribe). Between 25 and 30 spp. of taprooted ann., bien., or per. herbs or shrubs, native to w. N. Amer.; lvs. alt., spinulose-dentate to pinnately parted or pinnatifid, rarely entire; fl. heads usually radiate, solitary or corymbose or paniculate, involucres hemispherical to turbinate, involucral bracts in several rows, receptacle flat to slightly convex, rough; disc fls. many, bisexual, fertile, yellowish, ray fls. female, fertile, blue, purple, or white, rarely absent; achenes turbinate to linear, more or less compressed, with several nerves, glabrous to hairy, pappus of somewhat unequal, minutely barbed, often brownish bristles.

Bigelovii (A. Gray) Greene [*Aster Bigelovii* A. Gray; *A. Pattersonii* A. Gray]. Ann. or bien., to 3 ft., sts. glandular-puberulent to glandular-hispid; lvs. oblong to lanceolate or oblanceolate, to 4 in. long, scabrous, toothed; heads to 2½ in. across, corymbose; ray fls. purple to violet. Colo., New Mex., Ariz.

tanacetifolia (HBK) Nees [*Aster tanacetifolius* Nees]. TAHOKA DAISY. Ann., to 2 ft., sts. densely leafy, nearly glabrous; lvs. mostly 2-pinnately parted, to 3 in. long; heads to 2⅜ in. across, on peduncles to 1¼ in. long; ray fls. violet-blue or whitish. Alta. to S. Dak., s. to n.-cent. Mex.

tortifolia (Torr. & A. Gray) Cronq. & Keck [*Aster tortifolius* Torr. & A. Gray]. MOJAVE ASTER. Suffruticose per., to 2½ ft., from a woody root crown, hairy, at least when young; lvs. sessile, linear to lanceolate or oblong, spiny-toothed; heads to 2½ in. across, solitary on ends of nearly naked peduncles; ray fls. blue-violet to lavender, or nearly white. Desert slopes, e. Calif. to sw. Utah and n. and w. Ariz.

MACHAEROCARPUS Small. *Alismataceae*. One sp., an aquatic per. herb, native to n. Calif. and se. Ore.; lvs. erect to floating, long-petioled; fls. bisexual, in a panicle, sepals and petals 3, stamens 6, carpels few, in a whorl, not united, 1-ovuled; fr. a head of beaked achenes.

californicus (Torr. ex Benth.) Small [*Alisma californica* (Torr. ex Benth.) P. Micheli; *Damasonium californicum* Torr. ex Benth.]. Lf. blades linear-oblong to ovate, to 3⅛ in. long; scapes 2 or more, to 16 in. high; fls. white or pink.

MACHAEROCEREUS: *LEMAIREOCEREUS.*

MACHILUS: *PERSEA*. **M. arisanensis**: *P. acuminatissima.*

MACKAYA Harv. *Acanthaceae*. One sp., a S. Afr. evergreen shrub; lvs. opp., short-petioled; fls. in terminal, loose racemes, calyx 5-parted nearly to base, segms. linear-lanceolate, corolla tube cylindrical in lower half, as long as calyx segms., campanulate above, lobes 5, nearly equal, stamens 2, anther sacs 2, staminodes 2, ovary 2-celled, each cell with 2 ovules; fr. an ellipsoid caps., on long woody stalk, seeds 2, somewhat ovate, rugose with prominent folds.

Grown in the open in southern U.S. and under glass. Propagated by cuttings in spring or summer.

bella Harv. [*Asystasia bella* Hort.]. Shrub, to 4–5 ft.; lvs. glabrous, glossy, dark green, 3–5 in. long, sinuate-dentate; calyx lobes ¼ in. long, corolla 2 in. long, pale lavender, with dark veining on each lobe.

MACLEANIA Hook. *Ericaceae.* About 32 spp. of evergreen, often epiphytic shrubs, native from s. Mex. to Peru; lvs. alt., simple, leathery; fls. in axillary or terminal racemes or fascicles, calyx mostly 5-lobed, corolla cylindrical to elongate-urceolate, stamens 10, separate or united, ovary inferior; fr. a berry.

insignis M. Martens & Galeotti. Glabrous shrub, to 12 ft.; lvs. ovate, to 3 in. long; fls. scarlet, to 1½ in. long, in axillary fascicles. S. Mex. to Guatemala.

MACLEAYA R. Br. *Papaveraceae.* Two spp. of large, per., more or less glaucous herbs, with yellow sap, native to temp. e. Asia; lvs. palmately nerved and lobed; fls. small, many, lacking petals, in showy panicles; fr. a caps. with membranous valves. Closely related to *Bocconia,* but differs in having lvs. palmately lobed, and fr. membranous, opening from the top downward.

Grown in borders and as specimen plants for their bold attractive habit. Propagated by suckers.

cordata (Willd.) R. Br. [*Bocconia cordata* Willd.; *B. japonica* André]. PLUME POPPY, TREE CELANDINE. To 8 ft.; lvs. to 8 in. across, white and rather densely short-pubescent beneath; panicles to 1 ft. long; stamens 24–30; caps. 4–6-seeded. China, Japan. Var. **Thunbergii** (Miq.) Miq. [*Bocconia cordata* var. *Thunbergii* Miq.]. Lvs. glabrous beneath.

microcarpa (Maxim.) Fedde [*Bocconia microcarpa* Maxim.]. Differs from *M. cordata* in having 8–12 stamens, and a 1-seeded caps. Cent. China.

MACLURA Nutt. *Moraceae.* One sp., a dioecious, spiny tree, native to Ark. and Tex.; lvs. alt., ovate to oblong-lanceolate, entire; male fls. in racemes; syncarp globose, bearing achenes embedded in pulp.

Propagated readily from seeds, cuttings of young wood, and root cuttings under glass. Long grown as a good spiny hedge plant, which succeeds on poor soil.

pomifera (Raf.) C. K. Schneid. OSAGE ORANGE, BOWWOOD. Tree, to 60 ft., brs. often spiny, but sometimes spineless; lvs. oblong-ovate, 3–6 in. long, 1–2 in. wide, acuminate, glabrous, entire, petioles to 1 in. long, rarely longer; syncarp heavy, rough-textured, to 5 in. in diam. Naturalized in e. U.S.

MACODES Lindl. *Orchidaceae.* Ten spp. of terrestrial herbs, native to Malay Arch. and Solomon Is.; lvs. variegated, petioled; fls. small, in long racemes, sepals and petals spreading, petals narrower than sepals, lateral sepals enclosing base of lip, lip 3-lobed, not resupinate, column twisted. For structure of fl. see *Orchidaceae.*

For culture see *Orchids.*

petola (Blume) Lindl. Lvs. few, near ground, dark green with golden veins; scape to 6 in. long, hairy, with sessile bracts, to 15-fld.; fls. red-brown with white lip, dorsal sepal less than ¼ in. long, lip shorter than sepals, midlobe with short, narrow claw. Malay Pen., Sumatra to Philippine Is.

MACRADENIA R. Br. [*Serrastylis* Rolfe]. *Orchidaceae.* Eight spp. of epiphytes, native to trop. Amer.; pseudobulbs slender, 1-lvd. at apex; infl. a short, lateral, nearly erect to arching, loosely fld. raceme; fls. small, sepals and petals separate, similar, spreading, lip 3-lobed, continuous with base of column, lateral lobes broad, erect and enclosing column, column without a foot. For structure of fl. see *Orchidaceae.*

Warm greenhouse. For culture see *Orchids.*

brassavolae Rchb.f. Small, in dense clumps, to 10 in., pseudobulbs to 1¾ in. long; lvs. somewhat leathery, to 6 in. long; racemes from base

of pseudobulb, pendent, to 10 in. long; fls. chestnut-brown, sepals and petals lanceolate, with translucent green margins, to 1 in. long, lip sessile at base of column, broadly cuneate at base, to ¾ in. long, lateral lobes semiorbicular, midlobe filiform. Guatemala to n. S. Amer.

modesta (Rolfe) Rolfe [*Serrastylis modesta* Rolfe]. Pseudobulbs cylindrical, to 2¼ in. long; lvs. leathery, to 7 in. long; sepals and petals ovate-lanceolate, light reddish-brown margined with pale yellow, lip to ¾ in. long, whitish-yellow, lateral lobes erect, midlobe long, narrow, acuminate. Colombia.

×**MACRANGRAECUM** Costantin: *Angraecum* × *Macroplectrum. Orchidaceae.* A group of bigeneric hybrids intermediate in character between the parents.

For culture see *Orchids.*

Veitchii (Hort. Veitch) Costantin [*Angraecum Veitchii* Hort. Veitch]: *Angraecum superbum* × *Macroplectrum sesquipedale.* Intermediate in all respects between its parents; fls. similar to those of *Macroplectrum sesquipedale* but half the size.

MACROCARPAEA (Griseb.) Gilg. *Gentianaceae.* About 30 spp. of usually tall, more or less woody per. herbs or shrubs, in Cent. and S. Amer., mostly in the Andes; lvs. large; fls. showy, yellowish or greenish, in terminal few- to many-fld. panicles or racemes, 5-merous; fr. a somewhat compressed caps.

glabra (L.f.) Gilg. Shrub, to 7 ft., with short internodes and leafy brs.; lvs. elliptic or lanceolate-ovate, to 5 in. long, nearly sessile, or the uppermost pairs united and clasping at the base; fls. in narrow panicles, corolla tube 2 in. long, lobes deltoid-ovate. Colombia.

MACROLOBIUM Schreb. *Leguminosae.* Not cult. **M. coeruleoides** and **M. coeruleum:** *Paramacrolobium coeruleum.*

MACROPIPER Miq. *Piperaceae.* About 6 spp. of shrubs or small trees, native in Polynesia, w. to New Guinea, and in New Zeal.; lvs. alt., entire, stipules united to petioles; fls. reduced, very small, unisexual, in axillary spikes, stamens 2–3, with distinct anther cells, stigmas 3; fr. of small drupes united to the bracts and fleshy axis.

Culture as for *Piper.*

excelsum (G. Forst.) Miq. To 20 ft., glabrous, aromatic, sts. dark, with swollen nodes; lf. blades nearly orbicular to broadly ovate, to 4(–8) in. long, rounded with short-acuminate tip, cordate to obtuse at base, undulate, mostly 7(–9)-nerved from base, petioles to 1½ in. long, with broad stipular wing in basal half, reddish; spikes solitary or paired, erect, slender, to 2(–6) in. long; frs. crowded, small, broadly obovoid, yellow to orange. New Zeal., where it is called KAWA-KAWA and PEPPER TREE.

MACROPLECTRUM Pfitz. Orchidaceae. Four spp. of robust epiphytes, native to Madagascar; lvs. completely enclosing st., fleshy, 2-ranked; infl. axillary, 1- to several-fld.; sepals and petals similar, spreading, lip united to base of column, prolonged into a long, slender spur, column short, fleshy. For structure of fl. see *Orchidaceae.*

Warm greenhouse. For culture see *Orchids.*

Leonis (Rchb.f.) Nash [*Angraecum Leonis* (Rchb.f.) Hort. Veitch]. Sts. short; lvs. to 8 in. long; infl. 3–5-fld.; sepals and petals yellowish, tongue-shaped, to 1½ in. long, lip roundish, shallowly concave, spur filiform, to 6 in. long. Winter–spring. Comoro Is.

sesquipedale (Thouars) Pfitz. [*Angraecum sesquipedale* Thouars]. Sts. to 3 ft. high; lvs. oblong-strap-shaped, to 1 ft. long, unequally 2-lobed; infl. 2–5-fld.; fls. white, star-shaped, to 7 in. across, sepals and petals triangular-lanceolate, acuminate, lip cordate, acuminate, irregularly serrate, spur to 1 ft. long. Early winter–late winter. Madagascar.

MACROSIPHONIA Müll. Arg. *Apocynaceae.* Ten. spp. of suffrutescent herbs and subshrubs, native to trop. Amer., differing from *Mandevilla* only in habit and in having fls. opening in the evening.

macrosiphon (Torr.) A. Heller. Erect per., to 1 ft.; sts. minutely tomentose when young, becoming glabrate; lvs. opp., ovate-elliptic to nearly orbicular, to 2 in. long, densely tomentose, petioles ⅜ in. long; fls. terminal, solitary; calyx lobes foliaceous, densely and minutely tomentose, corolla white, funnelform, about 4 in. long and mostly 2 in. across, puberulent-papillate outside; follicles slender, 4–6 in. long. Texas to n.-cent. Mex.

MACROZAMIA Miq. *Zamiaceae.* Fourteen spp. of dioecious palmlike plants, of Australia; sts. usually unbranched, mostly underground, clothed with persistent, densely silky- or woolly-tomentose petiole bases; lvs. few to many, in crowns, pinnate, rachis sometimes strongly twisted, pinnae more or less linear or deeply divided, not articulated with the rachis; cones axillary, solitary or clustered, stalked, cone scales not in vertical rows, ovules sessile; seeds red or yellow. Distinguished from *Dioon, Encephalartos,* and *Lepidozamia* in having ends of scales spine-tipped.

Grown as ornamentals under glass or outdoors in Zone 10. Viable seeds easily produced with artificial pollination. For culture see *Cycads.*

communis L. A. S. Johnson. Plant large, sts. to 6 ft. high but more commonly underground; lvs. to about 100, to 6 ft. long, pinnae 70–130, straight, entire, to 14 in. long, the lower few progressively reduced and spinelike, petiole 5–16 in. long; male and female cones cylindrical, to 18 in. long. New S. Wales. Material offered as *M. spiralis* is often this sp.

corallipes: *M. spiralis.*

Denisonii: *Lepidozamia Peroffskyana.*

diplomera (F. J. Muell.) L. A. S. Johnson. Plant large, sts. usually underground; lvs. up to 50, 2–4 ft. long, pinnae 70–120, spreading, mostly dichotomously divided at the apex, 6–8 in. long, rigid, several of the lowest spinelike; male and female cones cylindrical, to 10 in. long. Queensland.

Fawcettii C. Moore. Plant small, sts. usually underground; lvs. 2–12, to 4 ft. long, rachis spirally twisted, pinnae 50–112, more or less spreading, broadly linear, more or less curved, 7–12 in. long, 2–7-toothed at apex, often loose, drooping; male cones cylindrical, 6–10 in. long, female cones more ovoid, 4–7 in. long. New S. Wales.

flexuosa: *M. Pauli-Guilielmi* subsp.

Fraseri: *M. Riedlei.*

heteromera C. Moore. Plant small, sts. usually underground; lvs. 2–10, 1½–2½ ft. long, rachis not twisted or only slightly so at apex, pinnae 80–130, spreading but the 2 ranks not in the same plane, mostly once- to twice-divided to near the base, 4–8 in. long; male cones cylindrical, 5–8 in. long, female cones broader, to 11 in. long. New S. Wales.

lucida L. A. S. Johnson. Similar to *M. spiralis* with which it has often been confused and from which it differs in having pinnae 6–14 in. long with bases whitish. Queensland, New S. Wales.

Miquelii (F. J. Muell.) A. DC. Plant large, sts. usually underground, rarely to 3 ft. high; lvs. mostly 50–100, 2–6 ft. long, pinnae 70–160, spreading, linear, 6–12 in. long, loose, thin, flexible, petioles 4–16 in. long; male and female cones cylindrical, to 16 in. long. Queensland, New S. Wales. Material offered as *M. spiralis* is often this sp.

Moorei F. J. Muell. Plant large, sts. sometimes to 3 ft. high but more often underground; lvs. to 100, to 7 ft. long, pinnae 150–250, spreading and directed forward, 40 or more of the lower ones progressively reduced and spinelike, petiole 4 in. long or less; cones cylindrical, the female salmon-pink inside. Queensland, New S. Wales.

Pauli-Guilielmi W. Hill & F. J. Muell. Plant small, sts. mostly underground but sometimes to 6 in. high; lvs. 2–12, to 3½ ft. long, rachis spirally twisted, pinnae 50–200, more or less spreading, twisted at base, linear, straight or curved, 4–12 in. long, entire or 2-toothed at apex; male cones cylindrical or ellipsoid-cylindrical, 4–10 in. long, female about as long, somewhat wider. Subsp. **Pauli-Guilielmi.** The typical subsp.; petioles flattened, 2–6 in. long, pinnae 140–200, mostly about ¼ in. wide, 3–5-veined, pale at base. Queensland. Subsp. **flexuosa** (C. Moore) L. A. S. Johnson [*M. flexuosa* C. Moore]. Petioles rounded, 8–14 in. long, pinnae 80–150, mostly about ¼ in. wide, 5–6(–7)-veined, pale or red at base. New S. Wales. Subsp. **plurinervia** L. A. S. Johnson. Petioles flattened or rounded, 2–8(–10) in. long, pinnae 50–150, to ⅜ in. wide or more, 5–10-veined, usually orange or reddish at base. New S. Wales, s. Queensland.

Peroffskyana: *Lepidozamia Peroffskyana.*

plurinervia: a listed name of no botanical standing for *M. Pauli-Guilielmi* subsp.

Riedlei (Fisch. ex Gaud.-Beaup.) C. Gardn. [*M. Fraseri* Miq.]. Plant large, sts. to 15 ft., sometimes underground; lvs. 50–100 or more, to 7 ft. long, pinnae 100–150, directed forward, to 10 in. long, lower ones progressively reduced, petiole 5–12 in. long; male cones cylindrical, to 16 in. long or more, female cones ovoid-cylindrical, to 18 in. long, salmon-pink inside. W. Australia.

secunda C. Moore. Plant small, sts. mostly underground; lvs. 2–12, in a crown, 3 ft. long, pinnae 80–170, in 2 ranks at an acute angle to each other, straight or somewhat curved, directed forward; cones cylindrical to ellipsoid- or ovoid-cylindrical, 6–10 in. long. New S. Wales.

spiralis (Salisb.) Miq. [*M. corallipes* Hook.f.]. Plant small, sts. mostly underground; lvs. 2–12, 2–3 ft. long, pinnae 45–120, more or less spreading but the 2 ranks not in the same plane, 4–8 in. long, petioles 6–16 in. long; male cones cylindrical to ellipsoid-cylindrical, 6–8 in. long, the female about the same length but ovoid. New S. Wales. Material offered under this name may be *M. communis, M. lucida,* or *M. Miquelii.*

stenomera L. A. S. Johnson. Similar to *M. heteromera,* but differs in having rachis more strongly twisted and pinnae divided into more numerous, slender, loose segms. New S. Wales.

MADDENIA Hook.f. & T. Thoms. *Rosaceae.* A few spp. of dioecious trees or shrubs of Asia; lvs. alt., deciduous, glandular-toothed; fls. without petals, in racemes or corymbs, calyx tube turbinate, 10-lobed, stamens 20–30, pistil 1; fr. a drupe.

Infrequently planted; hardy north.

hypoleuca Koehne. MADDEN CHERRY. Shrub, to 20 ft.; lvs. oblong to ovate-oblong, whitish beneath, to 3 in. long, short-petioled, stipules narrow, to ½ in. long; racemes 1–2 in. long, on longer peduncles; sepals 10, unequal, to ⅛ in. long, greenish or purplish-brown; fr. 5/16 in. long. China. Zone 6.

hypoxantha Koehne. Like the preceding, but lvs. yellowish beneath, somewhat hairy on the veins. China.

MADIA Mol. TARWEED. *Compositae* (Helianthus Tribe). About 17 or 18 spp. of usually heavy-scented, glandular and hairy, ann., bien., or per. herbs, native to w. N. Amer. and Chile; lvs. linear to oblong, entire or toothed; fl. heads radiate, involucral bracts herbaceous, receptacle with a ring of chaffy scales between the disc and ray fls.; fls. yellow; ray achenes almost completely enclosed by the involucral bracts, pappus of awns or scales or lacking. The heads close at midday in most spp.

elegans D. Don ex Lindl. COMMON M., COMMON T. Ann., 1–4 ft., glandular in upper part; heads long-peduncled, corymbose; ray fls. conspicuous, ½–¾ in. long, yellow throughout or with brown-red spot at base. Wash. to Baja Calif.

sativa Mol. CHILE T., MADIA OIL PLANT. Ann., to 4 ft., glandular throughout; heads short-peduncled, racemose or glomerate; ray fls. inconspicuous, ¼ in. long, yellow. A coarse, weedy plant. Chile and w. coast of N. Amer. Seeds used in Chile for their oil.

MAESA Forssk. *Myrsinaceae.* About 100 spp. of evergreen, erect or straggling shrubs or small trees, native chiefly to Old World tropics; lvs. alt., simple, often pellucid-punctate; fls. small, white, in axillary racemes or panicles, calyx 5-lobed, corolla usually campanulate, stamens 5, ovary half-inferior; fr. a drupe.

Propagated by seeds and cuttings.

indica (Roxb.) Wallich. Shrub or small tree, to 30 ft.; lvs. elliptic to elliptic-oblong, to 7½ in. long, leathery, toothed; fls. white, fragrant; fr. creamy-white, edible. India.

japonica (Thunb.) Moritzi. Shrub or small tree, 3–15 ft., sometimes decumbent; lvs. elliptic-lanceolate to oblong-ovate or obovate, to 6 in. long, entire to serrate, glossy above, pale beneath; fls. in short axillary racemes or racemose panicles. E. Asia.

MAGNOLIA L. *Magnoliaceae.* About 85 or more spp. of deciduous and evergreen trees and shrubs, native in Asia from Himalayas to Japan and in Amer. from e. N. Amer. to Cent. Amer. and Venezuela; lvs. alt., entire, often leathery; fls. large, solitary, terminal, often very showy, sepals 3, petal-like, petals 6–23, white, pink, purple, or yellow; fr. of many separate carpels congested into a "cone," seeds often red or orange, suspended at maturity by a slender thread.

Magnolias are very ornamental as specimen trees and are sometimes used as street trees. The evergreen species are not hardy far north. Those from eastern Asia that flower in early spring before the leaves unfold are very striking in appearance. Fertile, well-drained, loamy soil that holds moisture is best. Magnolias usually transplant with difficulty and should be moved before new growth starts. Propagated by seeds sown in autumn or stratified; also by green cuttings under glass, by layers put down in spring and transplanted to pots the following summer, and named cultivars by grafting, particularly on *M. acuminata*.

acuminata (L.) L. CUCUMBER TREE. Deciduous tree, to 100 ft., twigs glabrescent to tomentose; lvs. elliptic to oblong-ovate, to 10 in. long, glabrous to tomentose beneath; fls. appearing with the lvs., greenish-yellow to yellow, to 3 in. long; fr. purplish-red, to 4 in. long. Var. **acuminata**. The typical var.; twigs glabrous except at terminal bud scar and adjacent node; lvs. tomentose beneath; petals greenish to greenish-yellow. S. Ont. to Ga., Ala., and La. Over a dozen cvs. are known. Forma **aurea** (Ashe) Hardin. Fls. yellow inside. Mts., N.C., Ga., Tenn. Var. **cordata** (Michx.) Sarg. [*M. cordata* Michx.]. YELLOW CUCUMBER TREE. Seldom over 35 ft., twigs short-tomentose or roughened with bases of hairs; lvs. tomentose beneath; petals greenish-yellow or yellow outside, golden-yellow inside. Rare, piedmont and coastal plain, N.C., S.C., Ga. Cv. 'Miss Honeybee'. Fls. larger, paler yellow.

alba superba: a listed name of no botanical standing for *M.* × *Soulangiana* cv.

Alexandrina: a listed name of no botanical standing for *M.* × *Soulangiana* cv.

Ashei Weatherby. ASHE M. Similar to *M. macrophylla*, but differing in its smaller habit; fls. 4–6 in. wide, petals less irregular; fr. cylindric-ovoid. W. Fla. and Tex.

auriculata: *M. Fraseri*.

×**brooklynensis** Kalmb.: *M. acuminata* × *M. quinquepeta*. Tree with fls. intermediate between the parents. Cvs. 'Evamaria' and 'Woodsman' are listed.

Campbellii Hook.f. & T. Thoms. Deciduous tree, to 80 ft.; lvs. elliptic-oblong to ovate, to 1 ft. long, glaucous beneath; fls. appearing before the lvs., erect, pink outside, pink and white inside, or entirely white, large, to 10 in. across; fr. greenish-brown, oblong, contorted, to 8 in. long. Himalayas. A variable sp., distinguished from other spp. in having the 4 innermost petals erect and more or less united, enclosing the stamens and carpels. Subsp. **Campbellii**. The typical subsp.; trunk usually single; fls. cup-shaped because of stiff and horizontally spreading position of the 8 outermost perianth parts. Cult. trees need about 20 years to reach flowering stage. Cvs. are: 'Darjeeling', fls. dark rose-purple; 'Late Pink', fls. pink, appearing late in flowering season; 'Stark White'. Subsp. **mollicomata** (W. W. Sm.) Johnstone [*M. mollicomata* W. W. Sm.]. Usually hardier with several basal trunks giving a more open, branching habit; fls. not cup-shaped, the outermost perianth parts flaccid and tending to hang downward. Cult. trees need only about 10–12 years to reach flowering stage. Here belong the cvs.: 'Lanarth', fls. cyclamen-purple, very large; 'Maharajah', fls. large, petals white, base purple; 'Maharanee', fls. white; 'Strybing White', fls. large. Interspecific hybrids include cvs.: 'Charles Raffill'; 'Kew's Surprise', fls. larger, rich pink; 'Sidbury'; 'Wakehurst'.

Candolleana: a listed name of no botanical standing for *M.* × *Soulangiana* cv.

compressa: *Michelia compressa*.

conspicua: *M. heptapeta*.

cordata: *M. acuminata* var.

cylindrica E. H. Wils. Deciduous shrub or tree, to 30 ft.; lvs. oblong-lanceolate, to 6 in. long; fls. appearing before lvs.; fr. cylindrical, to 3 in. long. Anhwei Prov. (China). Related to the Japanese *M. salicifolia* and *M. Kobus*, but differs from both in its cylindrical fr. Probably not in cult. here; plants prop. under this name appear to represent a different sp. or a hybrid related to *M. heptapeta*.

Dawsoniana Rehd. & E. H. Wils. Deciduous tree, to 40 ft.; lvs. obovate to elliptic, to 6 in. long, leathery, dark green and shining above, hairy along midrib and somewhat glaucous beneath, reticulate on both surfaces; fls. borne facing sideways, large, to 10 in. across, perianth parts 9–12, whitish to pale rose, suffused with rose-purple on outer lower portion. W. China. Closely related and similar to *M. Sargentiana*, but hardier, a densely twiggy shrub or thick small tree, having mature lvs. darker green, more leathery, and more noticeably reticulate, and fls. somewhat larger but with fewer perianth parts. Cv. 'Chyverton'. Fls. red, fading to carmine pink. Cv. 'Lanarth'. Fls. lilac-purple in bud, fading to white.

Delavayi Franch. Evergreen, spreading tree, to 35 ft.; lvs. ovate-oblong to ovate, about 10 in. long, glaucescent beneath; fls. white, 6–8 in. across; fr. about 5 in. long. Sw. China. Less hardy than *M. grandiflora*. Differs from other cult. magnolias in having large, gray-green, evergreen lvs.

denudata: *M. heptapeta*.

discolor: *M. quinquepeta*.

exoniensis: a listed name of no botanical standing for *M. grandiflora* cv. 'Exmouth'.

foetida: *M. grandiflora*.

Fraseri Walt. [*M. auriculata* Bartr.]. EAR-LEAVED UMBRELLA TREE. Deciduous tree, to 50 ft.; lvs. spatulate-obovate, to 1¼ ft. long, cordate-auriculate at base; fls. appearing with lvs., white or pale yellow, fragrant, to 10 in. across; fr. oblong, rose-red, to 5 in. long. Mts., Va. to Ga. and n. Ala.

fuscata: *Michelia Figo*.

glauca: *M. virginiana*.

globosa Hook.f. & T. Thoms. Tender, deciduous shrub or small tree, to 20 ft., branchlets reddish-pubescent when young; lvs. ovate to elliptic, to 8 in. long, short-pointed, dark, shining green above, downy beneath especially along midrib; fls. borne facing sideways or nodding, creamy-white, more or less globose, 3 in. across, stamens reddish-purple, carpels green; fr. oblong, pendent, to 3 in. long. E. Himalayas to nw. Yunnan (w. China).

gloriosa: a listed name of no botanical standing for *M. grandiflora* cv.

gracilis: *M. quinquepeta* cv.

grandiflora L. [*M. foetida* Sarg.]. BULL BAY, SOUTHERN M. Noble evergreen tree, to 100 ft.; lvs. obovate-oblong, to 8 in. long, very thick, shining above, mostly rusty-tomentose beneath, at least when young; fls. white, fragrant, to 8 in. across; fr. conelike, rusty-tomentose, to 4 in. long. N.C. to Fla. and Tex. Zone 7b-10. Variable in habit, in lf. shape and size, in amount of tomentum on lower surface of lf., and in size of fls. Of many cvs. grown the following are select: 'Cairo', lvs. very glossy, flexible, early and long-flowering; 'Charles Dickens' [cv. 'Rotundifolia'], lvs. very broad, nearly blunt, fls. large, fr. large, red; 'Edith Bogue', among hardiest of all cvs.; 'Exmouth' [cvs. 'Exoniensis', 'Lanceolata', 'Stricta'], of conical habit, lvs. narrow; 'Gallissonniere' [cv. 'Gallissoniensis'], very hardy; 'Gloriosa', fls. large, to 12 in. across; 'Goliath', fls. large, to 12 in. across, long-flowering; 'Lanceolata': 'Exmouth'; 'Praecox', early- and long-flowering; 'Praecox Fastigiata', similar, narrow tree; 'Rotundifolia': 'Charles Dickens'; 'Samuel Sommer', lower lf. surface covered with soft brown hairs, fls. large, to 14 in. across; 'St. Mary', lvs. to 10 in. long, lustrous above, rusty-red beneath, fls. cupped, to 5 in. across; 'Victoria', tree hardy, lvs. rusty-red beneath, fls. small.

Halleana: *M. stellata*.

heptapeta (Buc'hoz) Dandy [*M. conspicua* Salisb.; *M. denudata* Desr.; *M. Yulan* Desf.]. YULAN. Deciduous spreading tree, to 50 ft.; lvs. obovate, to 7 in. long, slightly pubescent beneath; fls. appearing before lvs., erect, white, fragrant, to 6 in. across; fr. brownish, oblong, to 5 in. long. China. Cv. 'Japanese Clone'. Fls. larger, hardier in bud. Cv. 'Lacey'. Fls. up to 8 in. across.

×**highdownensis** Dandy. A hybrid, presumably between *M. sinensis* and *M. Wilsonii*. Similar to *M. sinensis* in habit; lvs. pointed; fls. nodding, white, fragrant.

Hudsonii: a listed name of no botanical standing.

hypoleuca Siebold & Zucc. [*M. obovata* Thunb.]. Deciduous tree, to 100 ft.; lvs. obovate, 1 ft. long and more, glaucous and pubescent beneath, not tapering at base; fls. appearing with lvs., white, fragrant, to 7 in. across; fr. scarlet, to 8 in. long. Early summer. Kurile Is. to Japan. Fls. not as conspicuous as in the earlier-flowering spp.

×**kewensis** Pearce: *M. Kobus* × *M. salicifolia*. Commonly occurring among seedlings of *M. salicifolia;* tree; lvs. ovate-lanceolate, to 5 in. long; fls. profuse, pure white, about 4 in. across. Cv. 'Wada's Memory'. Early-blooming, larger fls.

Kobus DC. [*M. Thurberi* Parsons]. Deciduous shrub or tree, to 75 ft.; lvs. oblong-obovate or obovate, to 6 in. long; fls. appearing before lvs., creamy-white to pink, to 4 in. across, usually erect. Japan. A variable sp. Var. **Kobus**. The typical var.; tree, to 30 ft., shoots mostly glabrate; lvs. usually less than 4 in. long; fls. with 6–12 petals. Cent. Honshu (Japan) southward. Var. **borealis** Sarg. To 75 ft., differing from preceding var. in its more vigorous growth and larger lvs., to 6 in. long. N. Honshu and Hokkaido (Japan). Var. **stellata**: *M. stellata*.

Lennei: *M.* × *Soulangiana* cv.

liliiflora: *M. quinquepeta*.

×**Loebneri** Kache: *M. Kobus* × *M. stellata*. Similar to *M. stellata* in habit, but having lvs. larger, more obovate; fls. larger, with about 12 petals. Cvs. include: 'Ballerina', with more numerous petals; 'Leonard Messel'; 'Merrill', a taller tree; 'Spring Snow'; and 'Willowwood'.

macrophylla Michx. LARGE-LEAVED CUCUMBER TREE, GREAT-LEAVED M. Deciduous tree, to 50 ft.; lvs. oblong-obovate, to 3 ft. long, cordate-auriculate, glaucous and pubescent beneath; fls. appearing after lvs., creamy-white, fragrant, to 1 ft. across, petals 6, the 3 inner usually with purple blotch at base; fr. broadly ovoid, rose, to 3 in. long. Ky. to Fla. and La. Zone 7–9. Cv. 'Holy Grail' is listed.

major: *M. Thompsoniana.*

mollicomata: *M. Campbellii* subsp.

nigra: a listed name of no botanical standing for *M. quinquepeta* cv.

nigricans: a listed name of no botanical standing for *M. quinquepeta* cv. 'Nigra'.

obovata: *M. hypoleuca.*

Norbertiana: *M.* × *Soulangiana* cv. 'Norbertii'.

officinalis Rehd. & E. H. Wils. Deciduous tree, to 50 ft., young shoots silky-hairy; lvs. obovate, to 20 in. long, glabrous above, finely downy beneath; fls. white, fragrant, to 8 in. across, perianth parts 9–12; fr. ovate, to 5 in. long. W. China. Cv. **'Biloba'.** Lvs. notched. Comes true from seed.

parviflora: *M. Sieboldii.*

portoricensis Bello. Evergreen tree, to 70 ft.; lvs. broadly elliptic to obovate, to 10 in. long, leathery, glabrous; fls. white, 2–5 in. across, fragrant; fr. conelike, to 2 in. long. Puerto Rico. The foliage and bark have a spicy taste, and a spicy odor when crushed.

×**Proctoriana** Rehd.: *M. salicifolia* × *M. stellata.* Differs from *M. salicifolia* in having lf. buds pubescent, lvs. generally broader about or above the middle, and petals more numerous (6–13); and from *M. stellata* in having a treelike cylindrical habit, lvs. narrower, smaller, more pointed; fls. white, not as many as those of *M. stellata,* but more conspicuous than those of *M. salicifolia,* sepals 3, petals larger, broader, and more upright. Cv. **'Slavin's Snowy'** [*M. Slavinii* Harkn.]. Fls. white, with a pink flush near the base of petals.

purpurea: *M. quinquepeta.*

pyramidata Bartr. ex Pursh. Deciduous tree, to 30 ft., glabrous, brs. ascending; lvs. rhombic-obovate, to 9 in. long, short-pointed, auricled, grayish-pubescent beneath; fls. creamy-white, to 5 in. across; fr. oblong, to 3 in. long, rose-red. Coastal plain, S.C. to Ga., Ala. to se. Tex. Resembles *M. Fraseri,* but lvs. smaller, more rhombic, and bluntly pointed; fls. smaller; brs. ascending.

quinquepeta (Buc'hoz) Dandy [*M. discolor* Venten.; *M. liliiflora* Desr.; *M. purpurea* Curtis]. Deciduous shrub, to 12 ft.; lvs. obovate to elliptic, to 7 in. long, pale beneath; fls. appearing before lvs., bell-shaped, with 6 petals, purple outside, white inside, to 4 in. long; fr. brownish. China. Cv. **'Gracilis'** [*M. liliiflora* var. *gracilis* (Salisb.) Rehd.; *M. gracilis* Salisb.]. Lvs. narrow; fls. small, pale purple. Cv. **'Nigra'** [cv. 'Nigricans'; *M. liliiflora* (Nichols.) Rehd., not Desr.; *M. nigricans* Hort.]. Fls. large, dark purple outside, pale purple inside, with more petals.

rostrata W. W. Sm. Tender, deciduous tree, young shoots glabrous, purplish; lvs. obovate, to 20 in. long, purplish-red and covered with rusty hairs when young, later glabrous above and glaucous and reddish-hairy along veins beneath; fls. white; fr. to 6 in. long, bright red. Yunnan, Tibet, n. Burma.

rustica: *M.* × *Soulangiana* cv. 'Rustica Rubra'.

salicifolia (Siebold & Zucc.) Maxim. [*M. salicifolia* var. *fasciata* Millais]. Deciduous shrub or small tree, to 30 ft.; lvs. elliptic to oblong-lanceolate, to 5 in. long, glaucous beneath, with distinct anise scent when crushed; fls. appearing before lvs., white or sometimes purplish at base, fragrant, to 5 in. across; fr. rose, to 3 in. long. Japan. Related to *M. Kobus,* but having lvs. lanceolate, broadest at or below middle, and glaucous on lower surface. Cv. **'Else Frye'.** A vigorous, floriferous form.

Sargentiana Rehd. & E. H. Wils. Deciduous tree, to 60 ft.; lvs. obovate, to 8 in. long, generally rounded at apex or emarginate, smooth and dark green above, densely gray-pubescent beneath; fls. borne facing sideways or nodding, to 8 in. across; perianth parts generally 12–16, white on inside, flushed rose-purple outside, especially toward base; fr. slender, oblong, usually contorted, to 5 in. long. W. China. Var. **robusta** Rehd. & E. H. Wils. The var. generally cult.; of shrubby habit, branching from base; fls. appearing before lvs., large, showy, to 12 in. across, perianth parts 12–16, deep rose-purple, especially when first opening.

Schiedeana Schlechtend. Large, evergreen tree; lvs. ovate or elliptic, to 7 in. long, glabrous, with prominent reticulate venation; fls. creamy-white, petals 6, about 2 in. long. S. Mex.

Sieboldii C. Koch [*M. parviflora* Siebold & Zucc., not Blume]. Deciduous tree, to 30 ft. or more, frequently a wide-spreading shrub; lvs. elliptic to obovate, to 6 in. long, glaucous beneath; fls. appearing with lvs., nodding or facing sideways, white, fragrant, to 4 in. across, sepals pink, stamens red, carpels green; fr. crimson, to 1½ in. long. Japan, Korea. Cvs. **'Kwanso'** and **'Semiplena'** are double-fld.

sinensis (Rehd. & E. H. Wils.) Stapf. CHINESE M. Deciduous shrub or small tree, to 20 ft., brs. silky-pubescent when young, later becoming glabrous; lvs. obovate, to 7 in. long, bright green above, silvery-pubescent beneath; fls. appearing with lvs., fully pendent, white, saucer-shaped, fragrant, to 4 in. across, stamens red, carpels green; fr. pendulous, oblong, to 3 in. long, pale pink. Late spring. W. China. Resembles *M. Wilsonii* in its pendent white fls., but differs in having lvs. obovate, silvery-gray beneath.

Slavinii: *M. Proctoriana* cv. 'Slavin's Snowy'.

×**Soulangeana:** a common misspelling of *Soulangiana.*

×**Soulangiana** Soul.-Bod.: *M. heptapeta* × *M. quinquepeta.* CHINESE M., SAUCER M. Small tree; lvs. obovate; fls. appearing before and with lvs., purplish outside, white inside, to 6 in. across. Zone 5b-9. This hybrid is hardy north and common in cult. in many cvs. some of which are: **'Alba Superba'**, fls. large, almost white; **'Alexandrina'**, fls. large, petals white inside and purplish-pink outside; **'Amabilis'**, fls. lighter than the type; **'André Leroy'**, fls. cup-shaped, dark rose to purple outside, white inside; **'Brozzonii'**, fls. late, large, nearly white, shaded purple; **'Burgundy'**, fls. large, purple about halfway up on the outside of petals, earlier than in most cvs.; **'Candolleana'**, fls. white, tinged with purple at base; **'Grace McDade'**, fls. large, light pink with reddish color outside and at base of petals; **'Lennei'** [*M. Lennei* Van Houtte], fls. very large, saucer-shaped, petals deep purple on outside and white on inside; **'Lennei Alba'**, fls. pure white; **'Lombardy Rose'**, a seedling of 'Lennei', petals dark rose outside and white inside; **'Niemetzii'**, columnar tree, fls. purple; **'Norbertii'** [cv. 'Norbertiana', *M. Norbertiana* Hort. ex Dipp.], late-flowering, fls. large, purple; **'Picture'**, fls. very large, thick-textured, purple outside, white inside, early; **'Rosea'**, fls. white with center carmine-rose, fragrant; **'Rustica Rubra'** [cvs. 'Rubra', 'Rustica'; *M. rustica* Hort. ex DC.], fls. rounded, lighter purple than cv. 'Lennei'; **'Spectabilis'**, fls. white, smaller than cv. 'Brozzonii'; **'San Jose'**, fls. appearing early, white, slightly flushed with pink; **'Verbanica'**, fls. large, light purplish-pink, unopened buds long, slender, pointed, later than most cvs.

Sprengeri Pamp. Deciduous tree, to 60 ft.; lvs. obovate, to 7 in. long; fls. appearing before lvs., erect, rose-pink outside, paler with dark streaks inside, to 8 in. across; fr. red, to 8 in. long. Late winter, early spring. W. China. Related to *M. Campbellii,* but a hardier tree with all perianth parts spreading apart, so that the stamens and carpels are exposed. Cv. **'Diva'** [*M. Sprengeri* var. *diva* Stapf]. Fls. darker in color.

stellata (Siebold & Zucc.) Maxim. [*M. Halleana* Parsons; *M. Kobus* DC. var. *stellata* (Siebold & Zucc.) Blackb.]. STAR M. Shrub or small tree, to 25 ft., compact and rounded in habit; lvs. obovate-oblong, to 5 in. long, dull green above; fls. appearing before lvs., white, fragrant, to 3 in. across, perianth parts 12–18, narrow-oblong, spreading, becoming reflexed; fr. red, 2 in. long. Cent. Japan. Zone 5b-9. Its small size and many showy fls. make it useful in the small garden. Cvs. include: **'Centennial'**, **'Rosea'**, **'Royal Star'**, **'Rubra'**, **'Waterlily'**, perianth parts more numerous than in typical sp.

stricta: a listed name of no botanical standing for *M. grandiflora* cv. 'Exmouth'.

subrotunda: a listed name of no botanical standing.

×**Thompsoniana** (Loud.) Vos [*M. major* C. K. Schneid.]: *M. tripetala* × *M. virginiana.* Lvs. intermediate in size between parents, glaucescent; fls. fragrant, to 6 in. across, creamy-white, less globular than in *M. virginiana.* Original hybrid is less hardy than either parent. Cv. **'Urbana'.** Hardier.

Thurberi: *M. Kobus.*

tripetala L. UMBRELLA-TREE, UMBRELLA M. To 40 ft.; lvs. oblong-obovate, to 2 ft. long, pale and pubescent beneath, tapering at base; fls. appearing with lvs., white, of unpleasant odor, to 10 in. across; fr. rose, to 4 in. long. Penn. to Ala. and Miss. The large lvs. are crowded at the ends of the brs., giving an umbrellalike effect.

×**Veitchii** Bean: *M. Campbellii* × *M. heptapeta.* Lvs. larger than in *M. heptapeta;* fls. blush-pink, to 10 in. across. Flowering before lvs. Although the fls. are not so handsome as those of the tender *M. Campbellii,* grafted plants of this vigorous hybrid have the advantage of flowering at an earlier age and are hardy in the e. U.S. Cvs. **'Isca'** and **'Peter Veitch'** are listed.

verbanica: a listed name of no botanical standing for *M.* × *Soulangiana* cv.

Victoria: a listed name of no botanical standing for *M. grandiflora* cv.

virginiana L. [*M. glauca* L.]. SWEET BAY. Shrub, or tree to 60 ft., deciduous or evergreen in the South; lvs. oblong to elliptic, to 5 in. long, glaucous-gray beneath; fls. appearing with lvs., white, fragrant, to 3 in. across; fr. red, to 2 in. long. Often coastal, Mass. to Fla., Tenn. and Tex. Zone 5b-10a. Cv. **'Havener'.** Fls. large, petals many. Cv. **'Mayer'.** Shrubby. Var. **australis** Sarg. Larger, more pubescent, more nearly or fully evergreen. Occupies s. part of range of the sp. Cv. **'Henry Hicks'** is listed.

×**Watsonii** Hook.f. A hybrid, presumably *M. hypoleuca* × *M. Sieboldii.* Tree, to 25 ft.; lvs. obovate, to 7 in. long, glaucous and pubescent beneath; fls. appearing with lvs., to 6 in. across, fragrant, petals white, sepals pink; fr. crimson, about 2 in. long. In e. U.S. not hardy north of Zone 6.

Wilsonii (Finet & Gagnep.) Rehd. Deciduous tree, to 25 ft.; lvs. oblong, to 5 in. long, silky-tomentose beneath; fls. appearing with lvs., pendent, white, fragrant, to 5 in. across; fr. crimson, 2½ in. long. China. Related to *M. sinensis.* Doubtfully hardy in e. U.S. beyond Zone 8.

Yulan: *M. heptapeta.*

MAGNOLIACEAE Juss. MAGNOLIA FAMILY. Dicot.; about 12 genera and over 200 spp. of evergreen or deciduous trees or shrubs, native mostly to temp. regions of the N. Hemisphere, extending into the Amer. and Asiatic tropics; lvs. alt., simple, usually entire, pinnately veined, stipules often present and enclosing the young bud, but early-deciduous and leaving a scar on st.; fls. often large and showy, usually solitary, terminal or axillary, usually bisexual, regular, sepals often 3, petals 6 or more, or perianth undifferentiated, stamens and carpels many, spirally arranged; fr. a follicle or samara, often in conelike aggregations. Genera cult. as ornamentals are: *Alcimandra, Liriodendron, Magnolia, Michelia,* and *Talauma.*

MAHERNIA: *HERMANNIA.*

×**MAHOBERBERIS** C. K. Schneid.: *Berberis* × *Mahonia. Berberidaceae.* A hybrid genus including offspring of several crosses, mostly sterile; lvs. simple or compound on the same plant, spines mostly lacking.

aquisargentii Krüssm.: *Berberis Sargentiana?* × *Mahonia Aquifolium.* Shrub, to 3 ft., brs. upright; lvs. simple, or compound with usually 1 pair of lfts. and a terminal one to 3 in. long, with very spiny margins, becoming bronze in autumn. Resistant to st. rust.

Miethkeana Melander & Eade: *Berberis* 'Renton' (= *B. manipurana?*) × Mahonia Aquifolium. Evergreen, brs. erect; lvs. dimorphic, some deeply spinose-sinuate, others spinulose-serrate, simple or with 1–2 small lateral lfts.; fls. yellow to cream-colored, umbellate; fr. black. Resistant to st. rust.

Neubertii (Hort. ex Lem.) C. K. Schneid.: *Berberis vulgaris* × *Mahonia Aquifolium.* Shrub, to 6 ft., evergreen or nearly so, without spines; lvs. variable on the same plant, simple, to 3 in. long, toothed or spiny, or sometimes of 3–5 lfts.; not known to bloom. This has often been grown mistakenly under the name *Berberis ilicifolia.* Immune to st. rust; hardy North.

MAHONIA Nutt. OREGON GRAPE, HOLLY G. *Berberidaceae.* More than 100 spp. of evergreen, thornless shrubs, native to Asia, n. and Cent. Amer.; lvs. alt., odd-pinnate, lfts. mostly spiny-toothed; fls. yellow, in often fascicled racemes or in panicles, rarely umbellate, sepals in 3 series, petals in 2 series, stamens 6, ovary 1-celled; fr. a berry, commonly dark blue-black with a bloom. By some included in *Berberis.*

Some mahonias are hardy in the North in sheltered places. They should be protected from the wind and hot sun. Some are excellent for ground cover and similar uses wherever hardy, for the foliage is attractive and durable. Propagated by seeds, suckers, layers, and cuttings of half-ripe wood under glass.

As with barberries, some of the mahonias are susceptible to stem rust and should not be planted in grain-growing areas; susceptible species in cultivation are *M. Fremontii, M. Nevinii,* and *M. trifoliolata.*

Aquifolium (Pursh) Nutt. [*Berberis Aquifolium* Pursh]. OREGON GRAPE, MOUNTAIN G., HOLLY MAHONIA, HOLLY BARBERRY, BLUE B. To 3 ft. or more; lvs. with 5–9 pairs of lfts., lfts. ovate, to 3 in. long, with about 6–12 spiny teeth, lustrous above, green on both sides, not papillose beneath, petioles 1–2 in. long; racemes fascicled, to 3 in. long, basal bracts short, deciduous, pedicels seldom with bracts at middle; petals longer than inner sepals; fr. globose, black with blue bloom, style lacking. Nw. N. Amer. Cv. **'Compacta'.** Dwarfer, more compact. Cv. **'Gracilis'.** A listed name. Cv. **'Moseri'.** Lvs. light green, becoming brownish-rose. Cv. **'Vicarii'.** Of broad growth habit; lvs. at first reddish, then becoming green and remaining green in winter.

Bealei (Fort.) Carrière. To 7 ft.; lvs. to 18 in. long, with 5–8 pairs of lfts., lfts. ovate, spiny-margined, dull gray-green above, paler yellow-green beneath, the terminal one broad, to 8 in. wide; racemes erect, to 4 in. long, basal bracts long, persistent, pedicels to ¼ in.; fr. ovoid, black with gray bloom, style short or lacking. Confused in cult. with *M. japonica.*

californica (Jeps.) Ahrendt. To 6 or rarely 10 ft.; lvs. to 4 in. long, with 2–4 pairs of lfts., lfts. to 2 in. long, grayish and pale, with 8–12 coarse teeth; racemes dense, many-fld., basal bracts short, deciduous. Calif.

dictyota (Jeps.) Fedde [*Berberis dictyota* Jeps.]. To 6 ft.; lvs. with 2–3 pairs of lfts., lfts. overlapping, ovate, with 3–4 teeth, lustrous above, dull beneath; racemes fascicled, basal bracts short, deciduous; fr. ellipsoid, black with blue bloom, style lacking. Ariz. and Calif.

Forrestii: a listed name of no botanical standing.

Fortunei (Lindl.) Fedde. To 6 ft.; lvs. with 1–4 pairs of lfts., lfts. remote, oblong-lanceolate to elliptic-lanceolate, oblique, thin, with 6–10 teeth, dull deep green above, yellow-green beneath; racemes to 2 in., fascicled, basal bracts long, persistent. China.

Fremontii (Torr.) Fedde [*Berberis Fremontii* Torr.]. To 9 ft.; lvs. to 4 in. long, with usually 2–3 pairs, rarely 1 or 4 pairs of lfts., lfts. thick, oblong-lanceolate, to 2⅜ in. long, with 3–4 or 6 spiny teeth; infl. fascicled or racemose-subumbellate, 3–5-fld., to 2 in. long, basal bracts short, deciduous; fr. ovoid, black with blue bloom, seeds black. Colo. to Mex.

gracilis (Hartweg ex Benth.) Fedde [*Berberis gracilis* Hartweg ex Benth.]. To 5 ft.; lvs. with usually 3–5 pairs of lfts., lfts. overlapping, ovate, to 1⅝ in. long, with 10–12 spiny teeth, bright green above; racemes fascicled, to 3 in. long, basal bracts very short, deciduous; fr. ovoid, black with blue bloom. Mex. Cv. **'Compacta'** is listed. Not in

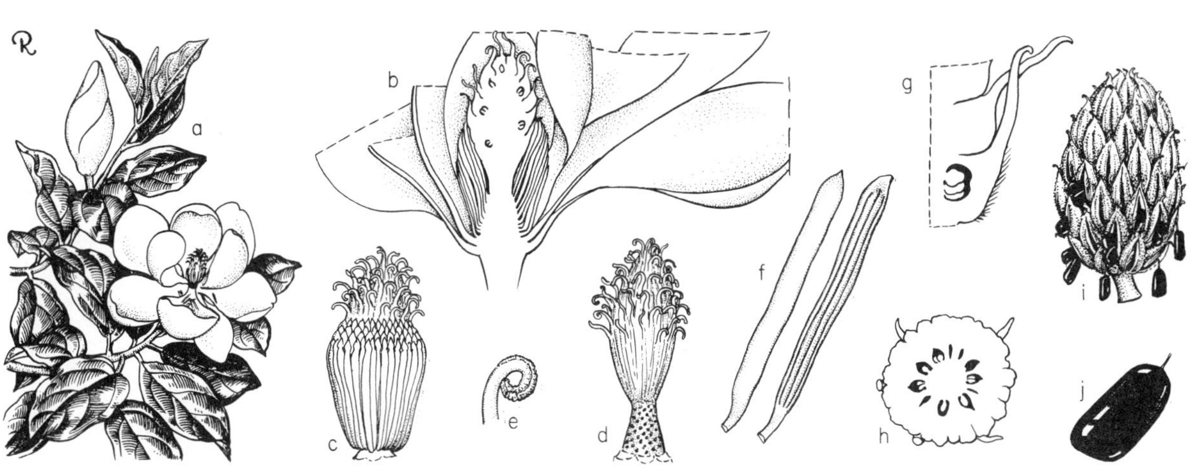

MAGNOLIACEAE. *Magnolia grandiflora:* **a,** flowering branches, × ⅛; **b,** flower, vertical section (apices of perianth parts cut off), × ½; **c,** stamens surrounding carpels, × ½; **d,** "cone" of carpels, × ½; **e,** stigma, × 2; **f,** stamens, back (abaxial) view at left, front (adaxial) view at right, × 1½; **g,** carpel, vertical section, × 1½; **h,** "cone" of carpels, cross section, × 1; **i,** fruiting "cone," × ¼; **j,** seed, × 1.

cult.; material offered under this name is probably a cv. of *M. Aquifolium.*

Higginsiae (Munz) Ahrendt [*Berberis Higginsiae* Munz]. Similar to *M. Fremontii,* but fr. yellowish-red, seeds red-brown. S. Calif. and Baja Calif.

japonica (Thunb.) DC. Similar to *M. Bealei* and confused with it, but distinguished by having terminal lft. narrow, to 1⅜ in. wide, racemes pendulous, to 10 in. long, pedicels to ⅜ in. long. China; cult. in Japan.

lomariifolia Takeda. To 12 ft.; lvs. with 12–20 pairs of lfts., lfts. rigid, narrow, oblong-ovate to oblong-lanceolate, to nearly 3 in. long at mid-leaf, with 3–7 spiny teeth; racemes to 6 in., fascicled, basal bracts long, persistent; fr. ovoid, black with blue bloom, style very short. China.

nervosa (Pursh) Nutt. [*Berberis nervosa* Pursh]. OREGON GRAPE. To 2 ft.; lvs. with 3–10 pairs of lfts., lfts. separated, thick, to nearly 3 in. long, with 8–15 spiny teeth; racemes to 8 in., fascicled, basal bracts long, persistent; fr. globose, black with blue bloom. B.C., s. to Calif. and Idaho.

Nevinii (A. Gray) Fedde [*Berberis Nevinii* A. Gray]. To 5 ft.; lvs. with 2 pairs of lfts., lfts. remote, thin, lanceolate, to 1⅜ in. long, with 10–18 spiny teeth; infl. racemose-subumbellate, 3–8-fld., basal bracts short, deciduous; fr. globose, red, without bloom. S. Calif.

pinnata (Lag.) Fedde [*Berberis pinnata* Lag.]. To 10 ft.; lvs. with 3–5 pairs of lfts., lfts. overlapping, mostly to 2 in. long, undulate, with 4–6 spiny teeth, petioles mostly less than 1 in. long; racemes fascicled, basal bracts short, deciduous; pedicels with 1–2 bracts near the middle; fr. subglobose, black with blue bloom. Calif.

Piperana Abrams [*Berberis Piperana* (Abrams) McMinn]. Similar to *M. Aquifolium,* but lfts. with 7–10 teeth on each side, lustrous bright green above, gray and papillose beneath; petals shorter than inner sepals. Ore.

pumila (Greene) Fedde. To 1 ft.; lvs. with 2–3 pairs of lfts., lfts. separated, finely serrate with 5–8 spiny teeth, at first red, becoming purple and deep gray-green; racemes fascicled, basal bracts short, deciduous; fr. globose-obovoid, blue-black. Ore. and Calif. Differs from *M. californica* in lacking minute bracts at middle of pedicel.

repens (Lindl.) G. Don [*Berberis repens* Lindl.]. Stoloniferous shrub, to 3 ft.; lvs. with 2–3 pairs of lfts., lfts. ovate, rounded at apex, undulate, with 5–9 spiny teeth, or not undulate and scarcely toothed, dull above, paler and densely papillose beneath; racemes fascicled, basal bracts short, deciduous; fr. globose, black with blue bloom. B.C., s. to Calif. and Colo. Var. **repens.** The typical var.; lfts. with margin undulate, spiny. Var. **rotundifolia** (May) Fedde. Lfts. with margin scarcely undulate, teeth few, inconspicuous. Of cult. origin.

trifoliolata (Moric.) Fedde [*Berberis trifoliata* Lem.]. To 7 ft.; lvs. with 3 lfts., lfts. thick, with 1–3 spiny teeth; infl. 3–6-fld.; fr. subglobose, black with blue bloom. Tex. to cent. Mex.

MAIANTHEMUM Wiggers. FALSE LILY-OF-THE-VALLEY. *Liliaceae.* Three spp. of low, per. herbs, with slender roots and creeping rhizomes, native to Eur., Asia, and N. Amer.; lvs. 2–3, simple; fls. white, in terminal racemes, perianth segms. 4, separate, spreading, stamens 4, ovary 2-celled; fr. a 1–2-seeded berry.

Of easy culture and useful for colonizing in shady places. Propagated by division.

bifolium (L.) F. W. Schmidt [*Smilacina bifolia* (L.) Schult. & Schult.f.]. To 9 in., st. white-hairy in upper part, glabrous below; st. lvs. triangular-ovate, cordate with deep and open sinus, petiole to 1 in. long; raceme about 1 in. long; fr. red. Eur., Asia. Var. **kamtschaticum:** *M. kamtschaticum.*

canadense Desf. TWO-LEAVED SOLOMON'S-SEAL, WILD L.-OF-T.-V. To 8 in.; lvs. 1–3, ovate to ovate-oblong, to 4 in. long, glabrous, subcordate, with a narrow, V-shaped sinus, almost sessile; fls. fragrant, in racemes to 2 in. long; fr. pale red. Nfld. to S. Dak., s. to Ga. and Tenn. Var. **interius** Fern. Lvs. larger, ciliate and hairy on lower surface and petiole. Mackenzie dist. of Northwest Territories and n. B.C. to Ont., s. to Ind. and w. N.Y.

dilatatum: *M. kamtschaticum.*

kamtschaticum (Cham.) Nakai [*M. bifolium* var. *kamtschaticum* (Cham.) Trautv. & C. A. Mey.; *M. dilatatum* (A. Wood) A. Nels. & Macbr.]. To 14 in., glabrous; lvs. ovate, to 8 in. long and 4 in. wide, cordate with deep sinus, petioles to 6 in. long; fls. in raceme to about 2 in. long on peduncle to 2 in. long; fr. red. Alaska to Idaho and cent. Calif.; e. Asia.

MAIHUENIA Phil. ex K. Schum. *Cactaceae.* About 5 spp. of low, cespitose cacti of Chile and Argentina; sts. jointed, the

joints globose to short-cylindrical; lvs. cylindrical; spines 3, the lateral ones short; fls. sessile, white, yellow, or red, rotate, perianth segms. separate, persistent. Resembling *Opuntia* subgenus *Tephrocactus,* but having thin, black seed coats and no glochids, and so perhaps more closely allied to *Pereskia.*

For culture see *Cacti.*

Poeppigii (Otto ex Pfeiff.) A. Web. ex K. Schum. Joints cylindrical, to 2½ in. long, ½ in. thick, spiny all over; lvs. persistent, to ¼ in. long; central spine to ¾ in. long; fls. yellow; fr. 2 in. long. Chile.

MAIRANIA: *ARCTOSTAPHYLOS.* M. japonica: *A. alpina* var.

MAJORANA: *ORIGANUM.* M. hortensis: *O. Majorana.*

MALACHODENDRON: *STEWARTIA.* M. pentagynum: *S. ovata.*

MALACHRA L. *Malvaceae.* Perhaps as many as 9 spp. of coarse, usually hispid, ann. or per. herbs in trop. and subtrop. Amer., of which 2 or 3 are now naturalized in the Old World; lvs. simple, unlobed to palmately lobed or parted; fls. in terminal and axillary, headlike, conspicuously bracted infl., involucral bracts present or absent, petals white, yellow, or reddish, stamens united in a tubular column, the column usually shorter than the bracts, style brs. 10, stigmas capitate, ovary 5-celled, each cell with 1 ovule; fr. a schizocarp, mericarps 5, essentially indehiscent, 3-angled.

Best treated as tender annuals; propagated by seeds.

radiata L. Erect, yellow-hispid herb, to 8 ft.; lvs. deeply 3-, or 5-lobed or -parted; fls. in terminal heads subtended by leafy, ovate bracts to 1 in. long or more, involucral bracts 9–12, filiform, petals pink, about ½ in. long; mericarps about ⅛ in. long. Cent. and S. Amer., W. Indies; trop. Afr.

MALACOCARPUS: *WIGGINSIA.* M. Kovaricii: a listed name of no botanical standing, perhaps for a form of *W. corynodes.* M. pauciareolatus: *W. sessiliflora.* M. pulcherrimus: *Frailea pulcherrima.* M. Sellowii: *W. tephracantha.*

MALACOTHAMNUS Greene. CHAPARRAL MALLOW. *Malvaceae.* About 20 spp. of suffruticose to nearly arborescent shrubs in Calif. and n. Baja Calif.; lvs. simple, mostly palmately lobed; fls. cymosely arranged in very open to dense clusters disposed in terminal heads, spikes, racemes, or panicles, rarely solitary, involucral bracts 3, filiform to ovate, sometimes united basally, petals whitish to deep mauve, stamens united in a tubular column, style brs. as many as the mericarps, stigma capitate; fr. a depressed-globose, apically pubescent schizocarp, mericarps 7–14, each 1-seeded, splitting completely into 2 separate valves at maturity.

Suitable for cultivation in Calif. and similar climates; not hardy in the North. Propagated by seeds or cuttings over heat.

Davidsonii (B. L. Robinson) Greene [*Malvastrum Davidsonii* B. L. Robinson]. Coarse subarborescent shrub, to 9 ft. or more, sts. stout; lvs. thick, 3-, 5-, or 7-lobed, to about 4 in. across; infl. racemose to thyrsoid-paniculate, with many fls. abortive; involucral bracts to ³⁄₁₆ in. long, calyx about ¼ in. long, corolla mostly pale mauve, about 1 in. across. Late spring–summer. San Fernando Valley in Calif.

fasciculatus (Nutt. ex Torr. & A. Gray) Greene [*Malvastrum fasciculatum* (Nutt. ex Torr. & A. Gray) Greene; *M. fasciculatum* var. *laxiflorum* (A. Gray) Munz & I. Johnst.; *M. Thurberi* A. Gray; *Sphaeralcea fasciculata* (Nutt. ex Torr. & A. Gray) Arth.]. Erect, slender-branched shrub, to 6 ft. or more, mostly closely stellate-pubescent; lvs. sometimes unlobed but mostly 3-, 5-, or occasionally 7-lobed, generally less than 2 in. long and wide, thin, but sometimes leathery, paler beneath than above; fls. many in interrupted spikes to open panicles, calyx less than ⅜ in. long, longer than involucral bracts, corolla pale to deep mauve, up to 1½ in. across. Coast ranges, Calif. and n. Baja Calif.

MALACOTHRIX DC. *Compositae* (Cichorium Tribe). About 15 spp. of herbs or woody-based plants with milky sap, in w. N. Amer.; lvs. mostly basal; fl. heads on scapelike sts.; fls. all ligulate, yellow, white, or pink; pappus of white bristles coherent basally.

californica DC. Ann., to 1 ft.; lvs. all basal, pinnately parted into narrow linear segms., woolly at least when young; heads $1\frac{3}{4}$ in. across, solitary; fls. pale yellow. Calif.

MALAXIS Soland. ex Swartz [*Microstylis* Eat.]. ADDER'S-MOUTH. *Orchidaceae.* About 300 spp. of mostly inconspicuous, cosmopolitan, terrestrial herbs; sts. with bulbous swelling at base, 1–5-lvd. or more; lvs. usually at middle or near base of st.; infl. a terminal, few- to many-fld. raceme or corymb; fls. small, sepals spreading, separate, or lateral sepals united basally, petals narrower than sepals, often filiform, lip sessile, entire or 3-lobed, sometimes 3-toothed at apex, column short, fleshy. For structure of fl. see *Orchidaceae.*

Sometimes planted in the wild garden. For culture see *Orchids.*

ophioglossoides: *M. unifolia.*

unifolia Michx. [*M. ophioglossoides* Muhlenb. ex Willd.; *Microstylis ophioglossoides* (Muhlenb. ex Willd.) Eat.; *M. unifolia* (Michx.) BSP]. GREEN A.-M., WIDE A.-M., TENDERWORT, ADDER'S-TONGUE T., GREEN M. Erect, to 20 in., lower part of st. concealed by tubular lf. sheath; lf. solitary, orbicular-ovate, sessile, clasping st., to $3\frac{1}{2}$ in. long; raceme umbellate to slender-elongate, densely fld., to 6 in. long; fls. minute, green, petals filiform, lip 3-lobed, variable in shape, 3-toothed at apex. E. N. Amer., W. Indies, Mex.

MALCOLMIA R. Br. MALCOLM STOCK. *Cruciferae.* About 25–30 spp. of ann. and per. herbs in the Medit. region; mostly grayish with branched hairs; lvs. entire or pinnatifid; fls. small but profuse, lilac, pink-purple, or rarely white, sepals 4, petals 4, long-clawed; fr. an elongated silique, valves 3-veined.

Propagated by seeds, either started indoors or sown where plants are to stand.

maritima (L.) R. Br. [*Cheiranthus maritimus* L.]. VIRGINIA STOCK. Diffuse ann., main st. often decumbent; lvs. with broad petioles, oblong or elliptic, obtuse, entire; petals lilac or reddish to white, about $\frac{1}{2}$ in. long; siliques erect or spreading, not fleshy.

MALEOPHORA N. E. Br. *Aizoaceae.* About 15 spp. of procumbent to erect, branched, succulent shrubs, native to S. Afr.; lvs. opp., semicylindrical to triangular-prismatic, slightly united basally, soft to the touch, often bluish; fls. axillary or terminal, subsessile, calyx 4–6-lobed, petals yellow or pink, many, stamens many, ovary inferior, 8–9-celled, styles 8–9; fr. a caps., cell lids horizontal, expanding keels with well-developed wings.

Planted out in summer, but in the cool greenhouse in winter. Propagated by seeds or cuttings; seedlings often flowering the first year. See also *Succulents.*

crocea (Jacq.) Schwant. Brs. gray-brown; lvs. erect at first, spreading in age, pale green with a powdery bloom, to $1\frac{3}{4}$ in. long, $\frac{1}{4}$ in. wide, slightly compressed laterally and 3-angled; fls. to $1\frac{5}{16}$ in. across, solitary, terminal, on pedicels to $1\frac{3}{4}$ in. long, petals golden-yellow inside, reddish outside. Cape Prov. Var. **purpureocrocea** (Haw.) Jacobsen & Schwant. Fls. bright red. Cape Prov.

Englerana (Dinter & A. Berger) Schwant. To 1 ft. high; lvs. arched upward, green with waxy coat, to $1\frac{5}{8}$ in. long, obtusely 3-angled; fls. to $\frac{3}{4}$ in. across, solitary, terminal, on pedicels to $\frac{3}{8}$ in. long, petals orange-yellow inside, orange-red outside. S.-W. Afr.

MALOPE L. *Malvaceae.* Three spp. of glabrous or pilose, ann. herbs from the Medit. region; lvs. simple, unlobed or palmately lobed; fls. axillary, solitary, on elongate pedicels, involucral bracts 3, separate, leafy, cordate-ovate, petals white, pink, or violet, stamens united in a tubular column, style brs. filiform, stigmatic along the inner edge, as many as the mericarps; fr. a schizocarp, mericarps many, 1-seeded, appearing to be arranged in superposed whorls.

Propagated by seeds.

grandiflora: *M. trifida.*

trifida Cav. [*M. grandiflora* F. Dietr.]. Glabrous, 2–3 ft.; lvs. rounded, dentate, unlobed or acutely 3-lobed; fls. white to rose or purple, with a darker center, 2–3 in. across. Spain, N. Afr. Cvs. are: **'Alba'**, fls. white; **'Grandiflora'**, fls. large, deep rose-red; **'Rosea'**, fls. rose-red.

MALORTIEA: *REINHARDTIA.*

MALPIGHIA L. *Malpighiaceae.* About 30 spp. of evergreen shrubs and trees, native to trop. Amer., but mostly to Mex., Cent. Amer., and W. Indies, plants glabrous or hairy, the hairs sometimes stinging; lvs. opp., simple, entire or spiny-toothed, short-petioled; fls. white, rose, or red, in axillary panicles, corymbs, or umbels, sepals 5, with 6–10 glands on exterior, petals 5, clawed, stamens 10, all fertile, styles 3; fr. a drupe with 3 stones and 3 seeds, red, orange, scarlet, or purple.

Grown as ornamentals, and the Barbados cherry (see *M. glabra*) for the edible fruit, which has a high content of vitamin C and is also made into jam or preserves. Propagated by seeds and cuttings.

clarensis: a listed name of no botanical standing.

coccigera L. MINIATURE HOLLY, SINGAPORE H., DWARF H. Glabrous shrub, to 3 ft.; lvs. elliptic to obovate, to $\frac{3}{4}$ in. long, entire or spiny-toothed, glossy above; fls. rose, to $\frac{1}{2}$ in. across; fr. red, nearly globose. W. Indies. Var. **prostrata** is listed.

glabra L. Shrub, to 10 ft.; lvs. ovate-lanceolate or elliptic-lanceolate, to 4 in. long, cuneate, entire, dark green above; fls. rose or red, about $\frac{5}{8}$ in. across, in peduncled, 3–5-fld. umbels, calyx with 8 glands, glabrous or sparsely hairy on exterior, stamens nearly equal, styles nearly equal; fr. red, about $\frac{3}{8}$ in. in diam. Tex., s. to n. S. Amer. and W. Indies. The plant known as BARBADOS CHERRY is usually referred to *M. glabra,* but is perhaps actually a hybrid between this sp. and *M. punicifolia.*

punicifolia L. Shrub, to 8 ft.; lvs. oblong-ovate or lanceolate-obovate, to 3 in. long, cuneate, entire; fls. rose or purple, about $\frac{1}{2}$ in. across, in umbels, calyx with 6 glands, setose-pubescent on exterior, stamens unequal, 2 styles longer than the third; fr. red, about $\frac{5}{8}$ in. in diam. W. Indies and Mex., s. to Venezuela and Peru.

suberosa Small. Lvs. oblong to oblong-ovate, to 4 in. long, crenulate, bright green; infl. sessile; fls. white or pink, calyx glabrous; fr. yellowish-red. Cuba.

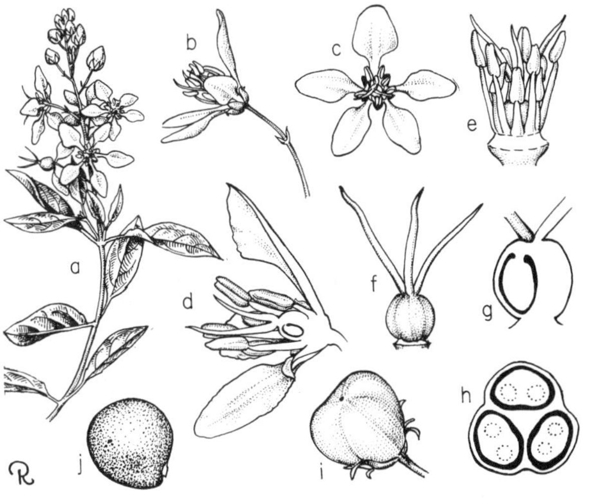

MALPIGHIACEAE. *Galphimia glauca:* **a,** flowering twig, × ½; **b,** flower, side view, × 1; **c,** flower, face view, × 1; **d,** flower, vertical section, × 2; **e,** stamens and pistil, × 2; **f,** pistil, × 3; **g,** ovary, vertical section, × 10; **h,** ovary, cross section, × 15; **i,** capsule, × 2; **j,** seed, × 4.

MALPIGHIACEAE Juss. MALPIGHIA FAMILY. Dicot.; about 60 genera and 850 spp. of trees or shrubs, often trailing or scandent, mostly native to trop. Amer. but also to Old World tropics; lvs. usually opp., simple; fls. in axillary or terminal racemes, panicles, umbels, or corymbs, calyx 5-merous, often with 8–10 glands on exterior, petals 5, prominently clawed, stamens 5 or 10, ovary superior, 3-lobed or -parted; fr. of samaras, drupes or caps. Several genera yield narcotics widely used by Amazonian aborigines. *Bunchosia, Byrsonima, Galphimia, Gaudichaudia, Hiptage, Lophanthera, Malpighia, Mascagnia, Sphedamnocarpus, Stigmaphyllon,* and *Tristellateia* are grown as ornamentals or for their edible fr.

MALUS Mill. APPLE. *Rosaceae.* About 25 spp. of small, much-branched, deciduous trees or shrubs of the N. Temp. Zone; sometimes treated as a subgenus of *Pyrus,* from which it is here distinguished by its soft, more or less pubescent lf. surfaces with acute rather than callous-tipped marginal teeth, broad, pubescent or tomentose winter-buds, fl. clusters prevailingly simple without a columnar central stalk, pome lacking stone cells or grit cells, calyx tube open in flowering and not closed about the styles, which are more or less united basally.

Apples are grown for fruit and as ornamentals. The most important fruit trees of cool temperate regions are the various descendants of *M. pumila,* the wild or original apple. The pomological crabs or crab apples may be *M. baccata* or derivatives, and a few hybrids have been produced by crossing *M. ioensis* with cultivated apples. The native crab apples are sometimes grown as ornamentals, chiefly for their pink-white flowers. The oriental crab apples of the *M. floribunda* group are among the choicest of small, hardy decorative trees with an abundance of showy flowers and fruit. They may be budded on closely related stock or the species grown directly from seeds.

Many of the binomials of cultivated apples are difficult to determine and probably represent hybrid forms; in some cases they may be clones perpetuated asexually, sometimes apomictically. For culture see *Apple.*

×**adstringens Zab.** [*Pyrus* ×*adstringens* Hort.]: *M. baccata* × *M. pumila.* A group of hybrids with lvs. soft-hairy underneath; fls. mostly pink, calyx pubescent; fr. about 2 in. in diam., red, yellow, or green.

×**aldenhamensis:** a listed name of no botanical standing for *M.* ×*purpurea* cv.

angustifolia (Ait.) Michx. [*Pyrus angustifolia* Ait.]. SOUTHERN WILD CRAB A., AMERICAN CRAB, WILD C. Trees to 25 ft., fl. branchlets and lvs. soon glabrous; lvs. oblong to narrow-elliptic, round-tipped to short-mucronate, firm, often evergreen, 1–3 in. long, pedicels glabrous; fls. 1 in. across, petals pink, fading to white; fr. to 1½ in. in diam., yellowish-green. Md. to Ky. and Mo., s. to Fla. and La.

×**arnoldiana** (Rehd.) Rehd. [*Pyrus* ×*arnoldiana* (Rehd.) Bean]: *M. baccata* × *M. floribunda.* Shrub, to about 6 ft., like *M. floribunda;* lvs. 2–3 in. long, more or less double-serrate; fls. 4–6, petals pink, becoming white, narrow-elliptic, to 1¼ in. long; fr. yellowish, to ⅝ in. in diam.

×**astracanica** Hort. ex Dum.-Cours.: *M. prunifolia* × *M. pumila.* Differing from *M. pumila* by the more coarsely and sharply serrate lvs., longer pedicels, and bright red fls. and frs.

×**atrosanguinea** (F. L. Späth) C. K. Schneid. [*Pyrus atrosanguinea* F. L. Späth]: *M. Halliana* × *M. Sieboldii.* Habit like *M. floribunda,* with arching branchlets; lvs. ovate, serrate, dark green, shiny; buds deep carmine, petals darker outside than inside.

baccata (L.) Borkh. [*Pyrus baccata* L.]. SIBERIAN CRAB. Tree or shrub, to 16 ft., young twigs glabrous, slender; lvs. ovate, 1–3 in. long, finely serrate, shining above, mostly glabrous, petioles 1–2 in. long; fls. white, 1–1½ in. across; fr. about ⅜ in. in diam., yellow with red cheek, calyx deciduous. E. Asia. Zone 2. Var. **Jackii** Rehd. Broad-crowned; lvs. broadly elliptic; fls. 1⅜ in. across, white; fr. ⅜ in. in diam., bright red. Korea. Var. **mandshurica** (Maxim.) C. K. Schneid. [*M. cerasifera* Spach; *M. mandshurica* (Maxim.) Kom.; *Pyrus baccata* var. *mandshurica* Maxim.]. Lvs. elliptic, remotely serrate, petioles pubescent; fls. white, 1⅝ in. across, sepals hairy; fr. to ½ in. in diam., broadly ellipsoid. Manchuria, China. Cv. **'Columnaris'.** Growth erect, willowlike; fr. yellow, with large red cheek.

brevipes (Rehd.) Rehd. [*Pyrus brevipes* (Rehd.) L. H. Bailey]. Resembling *M. floribunda,* but of denser growth, stiff-branched, usually a shrub; lvs. 2–3 in. long, finely and closely serrate; fls. many, white, 1³⁄₁₆ in. across; fr. ⅝ in. in diam., subglobose, sepals mostly deciduous. Origin unknown.

calocarpa: a listed name of no botanical standing for *M. Zumi* var.

cerasifera: *M. baccata* var. *mandshurica.*

communis: *M. pumila.*

coronaria (L.) Mill. [*Pyrus coronaria* L.]. AMERICAN CRAB A., WILD SWEET CRAB, WILD C., SWEET-SCENTED C., GARLAND C. Differing from *M. angustifolia* in having lvs. with more acute tips and rounded to cordate bases, lvs. of the flowering branchlets ovate, elliptic, or lanceolate-ovate. Ont. and Wisc., s. to N.C., Tenn., Mo. Var. **lancifolia** (Rehd.) Fern. [*Pyrus lancifolia* (Rehd.) L. H. Bailey]. Lvs. lanceolate, more pointed, 1½–4½ in. long. Penn. to Ill., s. to N.C., Tenn., Mo. Cvs. **'Charlottae'** [*Pyrus Charlottae* Hort.], and **'Nieuwlandiana'** [*Pyrus Nieuwlandiana* Hort.]. Fls. larger, partly double.

crataegifolia: *M. florentina.*

×**Dawsoniana** Rehd. [*Pyrus* ×*Dawsoniana* (Rehd.) L. H. Bailey]: *M. fusca* × *M. pumila.* Habit of *M. fusca;* lvs. mostly broader, more elliptic, 2½–3 in. long, pointed, sharper-serrate; fls. 1–1½ in. across, pale pink at first, later white; fr. to 1½ in. long, yellow.

Dolgo: *Malus* cv. 'Dolgo', a cv. close to *M. baccata* with white fls. 2 in. across; fr. deep red, ovoid, 1 in. in diam.

domestica: *M. pumila.*

×**Eleyi:** *M.* ×*purpurea* cv.

florentina (Zuccagni) C. K. Schneid. [*M. crataegifolia* (Savi) Koehne; *Pyrus florentina* (Zuccagni) O. Targ.-Tozz.]. Small tree with round crown and soft-hairy twigs; lvs. broadly ovate, 2–3 in. long, lobed, hawthornlike, gray-yellow underneath, hairy; fls. white, ¾ in. across; fr. red, ⅜ in. in diam., broadly ellipsoid. Italy.

floribunda Siebold ex Van Houtte [*M. pulcherrima* (Asch. & Graebn.) K. R. Boynt.; *Pyrus floribunda* Siebold ex Kirch., not Lindl.]. SHOWY CRAB A., PURPLE CHOKEBERRY. Shrub or tree, to 25 ft., crown thick, branchlets mostly arched, pubescent, becoming reddish when exposed to sun; lvs. ovate to oblong, 2–3 in. long, sharp-serrate; fls. many, deep carmine in bud, rose in early bloom, later paler, 1–1¼ in. across; fr. about ⁵⁄₁₆ in. in diam., yellow. Introd. from Japan; perhaps of hybrid origin. Zone 5.

formosana Kaw. & G. Koidz. Tree, to 50 ft.; lvs. oblong to elliptic-oblong, to 6 in. long, coarsely serrate, white-tomentose when young; fls. about 1 in. across, pedicels white-tomentose; fr. globose, yellowish-red, to 2 in. in diam., calyx persistent. Rather astringent, but edible when cooked.

fusca (Raf.) C. K. Schneid. [*Pyrus fusca* Raf.; *P. rivularis* Dougl.]. OREGON CRAB A. Large shrub or small tree, 15–30 ft., more or less thorny; lf. blades 1–3 in. long, ovate to lanceolate-ovate, serrate, sometimes 3-lobed, eventually rusty beneath, petioles to 1½ in. long; pedicels and calyx tube tomentose; fr. oblong, ½ in. long, purplish-black. Cent. Calif. to Alaska.

glabrata Rehd. Like *M. glaucescens,* but lvs. green beneath, glabrous, deeply lobed, cordate; fls. pink, 1³⁄₁₆ in. across, calyx glabrous, reddish. N.C. to Ala.

glaucescens Rehd. [*Pyrus glaucescens* (Rehd.) L. H. Bailey]. Large shrub or small tree, to 25 ft., sparingly sharply thorny; lvs. glabrate, triangular-ovate, deeply serrate, distinctly 3–5-lobed, 2–3 in. long, bluish-green beneath; fls. white to pink, 1½ in. across, petals gradually narrowed at base; fr. flat-globose, yellow, fragrant, 1¼–1¾ in. in diam. N.Y. to Ala.

Halliana Koehne [*Pyrus Halliana* (Koehne) Voss]. Shrub or small tree, 6–18 ft., twigs somewhat purplish, soon glabrous; lvs. ovate to elliptic or oblong-ovate, 1½–3 in. long, acuminate; fls. bright rose, 1–1½ in. across, on slender, nodding pedicels, sepals obtusish, ovate; fr. obovoid, purplish, ripening late, to ⁵⁄₁₆ in. in diam. From cult. in Japan, China. Zone 6. Cv. **'Parkmanii'** [*M. Parkmanii* Hort.]. Fls. double.

×**Hartwigii** Koehne [*Pyrus* ×*Hartwigii* Hort.]: *M. baccata* × *M. Halliana.* Habit willowlike; lvs. ovate, 2½–3 in. long; fls. double, 1½ in. across, at first dark red, fading white; fr. yellow-green, ½ in. in diam.

×**heterophylla** Spach: *M. coronaria* × *M. pumila.* Resembling *M.* ×*Soulardii,* but lvs. wider, less hairy; pedicels pubescent; fl. buds rose, opening white, fls. 1⁵⁄₁₆ in. across; fr. green, to 2¼ in. in diam.

Hillieri: a listed name of no botanical standing for *M.* ×*Scheideckeri* cv.

hupehensis (Pamp.) Rehd. [*M. theifera* Rehd.; *Pyrus hupehensis* Pamp.; *P. theifera* (Rehd.) L. H. Bailey]. Tree, to 25 ft., brs. stiff, spreading, pubescent on young growth only; lvs. ovate to ovate-oblong, 2–4 in. long, acuminate, sharply serrulate, petioles to 1 in. long; pedicels slender, to 1½ in. long; fls. white or pinkish, 1½ in. across, sepals purplish, glabrous; fr. globose, scarcely ½ in. in diam., greenish-yellow with red cheek. China, Assam. Zone 5.

ioensis (A. Wood) Britt. [*Pyrus ioensis* (A. Wood) L. H. Bailey]. WILD CRAB, PRAIRIE C.A. Tree, to 30 ft., tomentose on young parts and mostly on the underside of lvs.; lvs. oblong-ovate, short-acute, serrate, sometimes with lateral lobes, to 2–4 in. long; fls. 1–2 in. across, white or pinkish; fr. about 1 in. long, short-oblong, slender-pedicelled. Minn. and Wisc., s. to Mo. and Kans. Var. **Palmeri** Rehd. Lvs. smaller, obtusish, lvs. on fl. shoots crenate. Mo. Cv. **'Plena'.** BECHTEL'S CRAB. Fls. double.

Kaido: see *M.* ×*micromalus* and *M. Prattii.*

kansuensis (Batal.) C. K. Schneid. [*Pyrus kansuensis* Batal.]. Shrub or small tree, to 25 ft., finely pubescent on young growth; lvs. broadly ovate, 3–5-lobed, closely serrate, 2–3 in. long, dark green above, lighter and hairy beneath; pedicels to 1½ in. long, fls, white, ⅝ in. across, sepals hairy; fr. ellipsoid, ⅜ in. long, yellow to purple. Nw. China. Zone 5.

×**Lemoinei:** a listed name of no botanical standing for *M.* ×*purpurea* cv.

×**magdeburgensis** Hartwig [*Pyrus* ×*magdeburgensis* Hort.]: *M.*

pumila × *M. spectabilis*. Like *M. spectabilis*, but lvs. broader, narrowed at both ends, 2½–3 in. long, pubescent underneath; fls. bright pink, calyx pubescent; fr. yellow-green with red cheek, 1 in. in diam.

Malus: *M. sylvestris.*

mandschurica: *M. baccata* var.

×**micromalus** Mak. [*M.* × *Kaido* (Siebold ex Wenz.) Pardé; *Pyrus* ×*micromalus* (Mak.) L. H. Bailey]: *M. baccata* × *M. spectabilis*. Erect, to 15 ft.; brs. long, dark brown, pubescent when young; lvs. long-elliptic, 2–4 in. long, finely serrate, attenuate at base; fls. deep pink, to almost 2 in. across; fr. round, ⅝ in. in diam., yellow, somewhat angled. Zone 5.

Niedzwetzkyana: *M. pumila* cv.

Parkmanii: a listed name of no botanical standing for *M. Halliana* cv.

×**platycarpa** Rehd. [*Pyrus* × *platycarpa* (Rehd.) L. H. Bailey]: *M. coronaria* × *M. pumila*. Tree, to 20 ft., unarmed, soon glabrous; lvs. ovate to elliptic, rounded at ends, 2–3 in. long, sharply, mostly doubly serrate, often 3-lobed; fls. white, 1⁵⁄₁₆ in. across, calyx glabrous; fr. yellow-green, to 2 in. in diam. Cv. 'Hoopesii'. Lvs. slightly or not lobed; calyx pubescent.

Prattii (Hemsl.) C. K. Schneid. [*M. Kaido* Dipp., not (Siebold ex Wenz.) Pardé; *Pyrus Prattii* Hemsl.]. To 25 ft., young growth soon glabrous; lvs. ovate to elliptic-lanceolate, acuminate, rounded at base, 2–6 in. long, pubescent beneath on veins; fls. white, ¾ in. across; fr. about ½ in. long, red or yellow, spotted, calyx persistent. China. Hardy north.

prunifolia (Willd.) Borkh. [*Pyrus prunifolia* Willd.]. PLUM-LEAVED A., CHINESE A., CRAB A. Small tree, to 30 ft., soft-hairy on young growth; lvs. elliptic to ovate, 2–4 in. long, short-acuminate, serrate, pubescent underneath, subglabrate; fls. white, about 1½ in. across, sepals long, glabrous; fr. yellow or red, long-persistent on tree, about 1 in. long. Ne. Asia. Zone 4. Var. **Rinkii** (G. Koidz.) Rehd. [*M. Ringo* Carrière; *Pyrus Ringo* Wenz.]. Lvs. pubescent beneath; fls. pink, calyx somewhat hairy. China.

pulcherrima: *M. floribunda.*

pumila Mill. [*M. communis* Poir.; *M. domestica* Borkh; *Pyrus pumila* (Mill.) C. Koch, not J. Neumann ex Tausch]. COMMON A. Like *M. sylvestris*, but rarely thorny, twigs at first tomentose, later glabrous; lvs. obtuse to acuminate, rather persistently tomentose beneath; pedicels, calyx tube, and outside of calyx tomentose; fr. usually large, often sweet. Se. Eur., sw. Asia. Zone 4. Var. **paradisiaca** (Medic.) C. K. Schneid. PARADISE A. A self-perpetuating form of very small stature; petals bright pink; frs. small, ½ in. in diam. Asia to s. Russia. Cv. 'Apetala'. BLOOMLESS A. Fls. lacking fertile stamens and showy petals, styles 10–15, calyx end of fr. open. Cv. 'Niedzwetzkyana' [*M. Niedzwetzkyana* Dieck; *Pyrus Niedzwetzkyana* (Dieck) Hemsl.]. Shrub, to 12 ft., with reddish bark and wood; lvs. tinged red on veins; fls. deep red; fr. purple-red inside and out.

×**purpurea** (Hort. Barbier) Rehd. [*Pyrus purpurea* (Hort. Barbier) Woolley]: *M.* × *atrosanguinea* × *M. pumila* cv. 'Niedzwetzkyana'. Large shrub or small tree; lvs. ovate, acute, ¾ in. long, coarsely serrate, sometimes small-lobed; fls. 1–1½ in. across, purple-red, later paler; fr. purple-red, to 1 in. in diam. Cvs. are: 'Aldenhamensis' [*M.* × *aldenhamensis* Hort.; *Pyrus* × *aldenhamensis* Hort.], shorter, with thinner twigs, lvs. reddish to bronze; 'Eleyi' [*M.* × *Eleyi* (Bean) Hesse; *Pyrus* × *Eleyi* Bean], a large, erect bush, fls. dark, single; 'Lemoinei' [*M.* × *Lemoinei* Hort.; *Pyrus* × *Lemoinei* Hort.], erect bush, lvs. dark purple, often 1–2-lobed, fls. single to somewhat double.

Ringo: *M. prunifolia* var. *Rinkii.*

×**robusta** (Carrière) Rehd. [*Pyrus* × *robusta* Hort.]: *M. baccata* × *M. prunifolia*. Vigorous shrub or small tree with spreading, arching branchlets; lvs. elliptic, acute, 3–4 in. long, somewhat narrower than in *M. baccata;* fls. mostly white, 1–1½ in. across; fr. round to ellipsoid, to 1 in. in diam., yellow or red.

Sargentii Rehd. [*Pyrus Sargentii* (Rehd.) Bean]. Shrub, to 6 ft., more or less thorny; lvs. ovate, 2–3 in. long, acute to acuminate, sharply serrate, at first pubescent, later glabrate, those on young shoots 3-lobed; fls. white, 1 in. across; fr. round, ⅜ in. in diam., dark red, calyx deciduous. Japan. Hardy north.

×**Scheideckeri** F. L. Späth ex Zab. [*Pyrus Scheideckeri* (F. L. Späth ex Zab.) Wittm.]: *M. floribunda* × *M. prunifolia*. To about 10 ft., erect; lvs. ovate, sharply serrate, bright green above, pubescent beneath; fls. bright pink, to 2 in. across, petals 10; fr. yellow to orange, ¾ in. in diam. Cv. 'Hillieri' [*M.* × *Hillieri* Hort.; *Pyrus* × *Hillieri* Hort.]. Fls. half-double.

Sieboldii (Regel) Rehd. [*M. Toringo* Carrière; *Pyrus Sieboldii* Regel]. TORINGO CRAB A. Shrub, to 12 ft., with spreading, arching brs.; lvs. ovate-elliptic, acute, coarsely serrate, 3–5-lobed on young shoots;

fls. ¾ in. across, bright pink, fading whitish, petals obovate; fr. round, red to yellow-brown, ⁵⁄₁₆ in. in diam., long-persistent. Japan. Hardy north. Var. **arborescens** Rehd. To 30 ft.; lvs. larger, not so deeply lobed, less pubescent; fls. to 1³⁄₁₆ in. across; fr. ⅜ in. in diam. Korea, Japan.

sikkimensis (Wenz.) Koehne ex C. K. Schneid. [*Pyrus sikkimensis* (Wenz.) Hook.f.]. Like *M. baccata*, but lvs. ovate or ovate-lanceolate, to 5 in. long, serrulate, tomentose beneath, peduncle and calyx woolly. Himalayas. Zone 6.

×**Soulardii** (L. H. Bailey) Britt. [*Pyrus* × *Soulardii* L. H. Bailey]: *M. ioensis* × *M. pumila*. SOULARD CRAB. Tall shrubs resembling *M. ioensis;* lvs. broadly elliptic, 2–3 in. long, somewhat lobed, densely pubescent underneath; pedicels short, stiff; fls. pink, 1⁵⁄₁₆ in. across; fr. depressed-globose, yellow-green, to 2 in. in diam., with reddish cheek.

spectabilis (Ait.) Borkh. [*Pyrus spectabilis* Ait.]. CHINESE FLOWERING A. Tall shrub or small tree, to 25 ft., broadening in age, branchlets at first sparingly pubescent; lvs. elliptic to lanceolate, 2–3 in. long, acute, pubescent beneath; pedicels about 1 in. long, glabrous to somewhat pubescent; fls. bright pink, to 2 in. across; fr. globose, 1 in. in diam., yellow, sour. From cult. in China, but not known wild. Zone 5. Cv. 'Riversii'. Lvs. large; fls. large, double, pink. Cv. 'Van Eseltinei' [*Pyrus Van-Eseltinei* Hort.]. Fls. bright rose, 2 in. across, with about 15 petals.

×**sublobata** (Dipp.) Rehd. [*Pyrus* × *sublobata* Hort.]: *M. prunifolia* × *M. Sieboldii*. Conical tree; lvs. 2–3 in. long, with 1–2 short lobes if on young brs.; fls. pale pink, to 1½ in. across, calyx hairy, sometimes deciduous; fr. ½ in. in diam., yellow.

sylvestris Mill. [*M. Malus* (L.) Britt.; *Pyrus Malus* L.]. APPLE, CRAB A. Small tree with dense round crown or a shrub, 6–40 ft., glabrous or somewhat pubescent when young, usually thorny; lf. blades 1-1½ in. long, twice as long as petiole, ovate or elliptic, cuneate or rounded at base, crenate-serrate, acuminate or cuspidate; fls. 4–7, in umbel-like infl., pedicels and exterior of calyx tube glabrous, petals ⅜–¾ in. long, white, usually suffused with pink; fr. to 1 in. in diam., sour. Eur., sw. Asia.

theifera: *M. hupehensis.*

Toringo: *M. Sieboldii.*

toringoides (Rehd.) Hughes [*Pyrus toringoides* (Rehd.) Osborn]. Shrub or tree, to 25 ft., branchlets hairy only at first; lvs. ovate, 1–3 in. long, mostly with 2 serrate lobes, finally pubescent only on the veins beneath; fls. white, ¾ in. across, calyx hairy; fr. round or somewhat pear-shaped, yellow or with reddish tinge, ⅝ in. long. W. China. Hardy north.

transitoria (Batal.) C. K. Schneid. Like *M. toringoides*, but smaller, more slender; lvs. to 1 in. long, with deeper narrower lobes, more pubescent; fr. bright red. Nw. China.

trilobata (Labill.) C. K. Schneid. Erect; lvs. deeply 3-lobed, serrulate, becoming glabrous and glossy above; fls. white, 1⅜ in. across; fr. ellipsoid, red, to ¾ in. long, calyx persistent. W. China. Hardy north.

Tschonoskii (Maxim.) C. K. Schneid. [*Pyrus Tschonoskii* Maxim.]. Erect tree, to 30 or 40 ft., twigs white-pubescent; lvs. ovate to elliptic, broad at base, acuminate, coarsely sharp-serrate, remaining pubescent beneath; pedicels stout, pubescent; fls. white, about 1 in. across; fr. round, 1 in. in diam., yellow-green with reddish cheek, calyx persistent. Japan. Hardy north.

yunnanensis (Franch.) C. K. Schneid. Tree, to 30 ft.; lvs. broadly ovate, 2–5 in. long, round at base, sharply and doubly serrate, often 3–5-lobed on each side, thick-pubescent beneath; fls. many, white, ⅝ in. across; pedicel and calyx pubescent; fr. subglobose, ½ in. in diam., red-dotted. W. China. Var. **Veitchii** Rehd. Lvs. cordate, more or less lobed, becoming nearly glabrous beneath. Cent. China.

×**Zumi** (Matsum.) Rehd. [*Pyrus* × *Zumi* Matsum.]: *M. baccata* var. *mandshurica* × *M. Sieboldii*. Tree, to 20 ft., pyramidal; lvs. ovate, acute, 2–4 in. long, serrate, lobed if on young shoots, becoming glabrous beneath; fls. rose in bud, white on opening, 1³⁄₁₆ in. across; fr. ⅜ in. in diam., red, globose. Zone 6. Var. **calocarpa** (Rehd.) Rehd. [*M. calocarpa* Hort.]. Of more spreading habit; lvs. on young shoots more deeply lobed; fls. smaller.

MALVA L. MALLOW, MUSK M. *Malvaceae.* About 30 spp. of glabrate to densely pubescent, prostrate to erect ann., bien., or per. herbs in Eur., N. Afr., and temp. Asia; lvs. mostly palmately angled, lobed, or dissected; fls. axillary, solitary or in loose to dense clusters, involucral bracts 3, separate, petals white to pink or purple, stamens united in a tubular column, style brs. filiform, stigmatic along inner edge, as many as the mericarps; fr. a discoid schizocarp, mericarps beakless, each 1-seeded.

Mallows are easily cultivated. Sow seeds where the plants are to stand. The perennials may also be propagated by division.

Alcea L. Similar to *M. moschata*, but having sts. stellate-pubescent, involucral bracts ovate, and mericarps glabrous. Early summer. Eur.; naturalized in e. U.S. Var. **fastigiata** (Cav.) C. Koch. Brs. more numerous, congested.

crispa: *M. verticillata* var.

mauritiana: *M. sylvestris* var.

moschata L. MUSK M. Leafy-branched per., to 3 ft., sts. hirsute, with spreading, simple hairs; basal lvs. reniform, shallowly 3-lobed, st. lvs. divided into 3–5–7 segms., the divisions pinnatifid; involucral bracts usually linear-lanceolate, fls. slender-pedicelled, axillary, white or rose-mauve, 1–2 in. across; mericarps hispid-pubescent. Early summer. Eur., N. Afr.; naturalized in ne. U.S. Cv. 'Alba'. Fls. white. Cv. 'Rosea'. Fls. rose-mauve.

nicaeenis All. [*M. setosa* Moench]. Ann., sts. more or less ascending, hispid-pubescent, to 1½ ft.; lvs. rounded-reniform, 5- or 7-lobed, lobes of the upper lvs. rather acute; fls. 2–6 in axillary clusters, petals bluish-lilac, about ½ in. long; mericarps glabrous or puberulous, strongly reticulate. Early spring–early autumn. Eurasia; naturalized in U.S.

setosa: *M. nicaeensis.*

sylvestris L. HIGH M., CHEESES. Bien., usually grown as an ann., up to 3 ft., sts. hirsute, with sparse, spreading hairs; lvs. cordate-orbicular or reniform, basal lvs. with 5 or 7 shallow lobes, upper lvs. with deeper, triangular lobes; fls. 2–6 in axillary clusters, petals rose-purple with darker veins, up to 1 in. long; mericarps brownish-green, the outer edges sharply angled, the lateral walls reticulate. Early spring–late summer. Eur.; naturalized in U.S. Lvs. and fls. used medicinally. Var. **mauritiana** (L.) Boiss. [*M. mauritiana* L.]. Glabrous or nearly so; lf. lobes broad and rounded; fls. deeper colored.

verticillata L. Ann. or bien., sts. erect, to 6 ft.; lvs. rounded, 5- or 7-lobed; fls. in dense axillary clusters, petals white or purplish, about ½ in. long; mericarps glabrous, conspicuously transverse-ridged. Summer–early autumn. Eurasia; naturalized in U.S. Var. **crispa** L. [*M.*

crispa (L.) L.]. CURLED M. Lvs. strongly crisped. Eurasia; naturalized in U.S. Sometimes grown as a salad plant.

MALVACEAE Juss. MALLOW FAMILY. Dicot.; about 95 genera of herbs, shrubs, and trees in trop. and temp. regions; lvs. alt., generally stipuled, simple, usually palmately veined or lobed, or palmately compound; fls. mostly regular, bisexual; calyx 5-lobed, often subtended and in bud sometimes enclosed by an involucre of distinct or united bracts, lobes 5, shallow to deep, valvate, petals generally 5, obovate, united at base to staminal column, stamens united into a single tubular column enclosing the pistil, the column with free filaments over most of its length or only terminally, anthers 1-celled, ovary superior, carpels 5 to many, rarely 1–2, in a single whorl or sometimes seemingly superposed whorls, each carpel with 1 to many ovules, style brs. as many as the carpels or sometimes twice as many, stigmas capitate or decurrent or sometimes twice as many, stigmas capitate or decurrent along the style brs.; fr. a loculicidally dehiscent caps. or a schizocarp separating at maturity into individual carpels, termed mericarps. The cult. genera are: *Abelmoschus, Abutilon, Alcea, Althaea, Alyogyne, Anisodontea, Anoda, Callirhoe, Corynabutilon, Eremalche, Goethea, Gossypium, Hibiscus, Hoheria, Howittia, Iliamna, Kitaibelia, Kokia, Kosteletzkya, Lagunaria, Lavatera, Malachra, Malacothamnus, Malope, Malva, Malvaviscus, Montezuma, Napaea, Pavonia, Phymosia, Plagianthus, Robinsonella, Sida, Sidalcea, Sphlaeralcea, Thespesia, Triplochlamys,* and *Wercklea.*

The family furnishes many ornamental, fiber, and medicinal plants as well as some food plants; it is most important as the source of cotton.

MALVASTRUM A. Gray. *Malvaceae.* Not in cult. **M. capense:** *Anisodontea capensis;* **M. coccineum:** Sphaeralcea

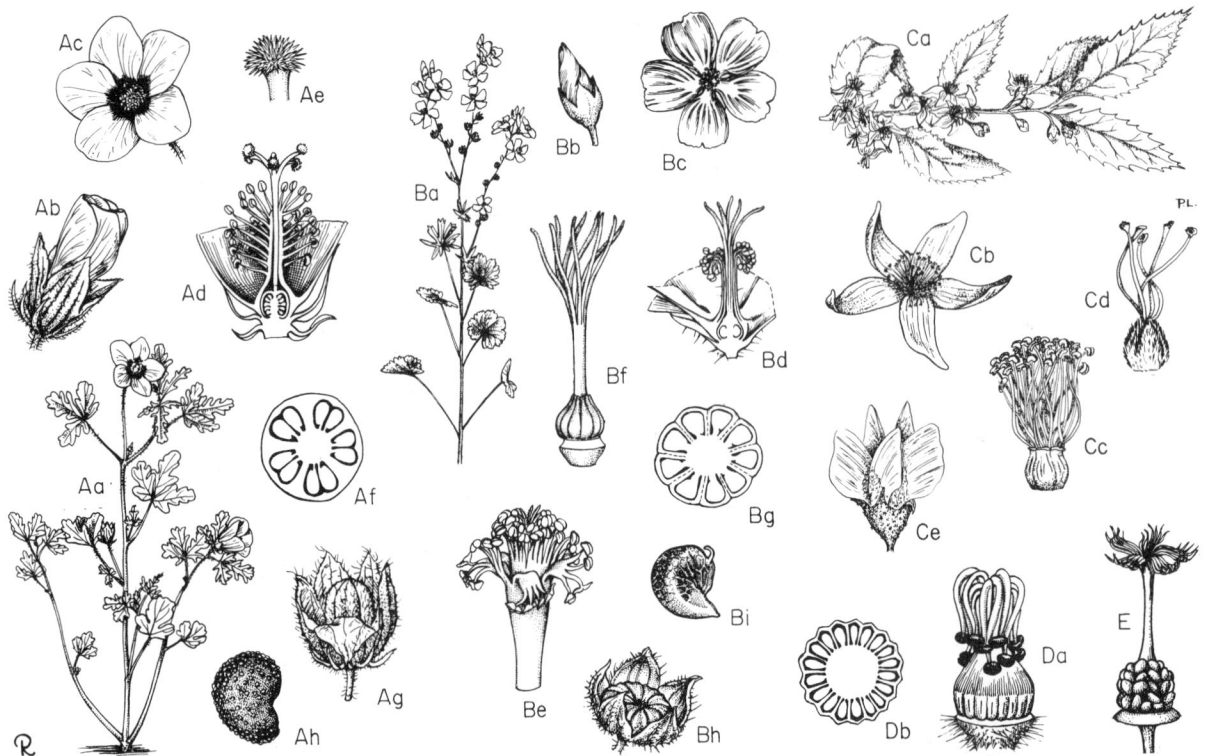

MALVACEAE. **A,** *Hibiscus Trionum:* **Aa,** flowering plant, × ⅛; **Ab,** flower bud, showing involucre and calyx, × ¾; **Ac,** flower, × ⅓; **Ad,** flower, vertical section (upper part of corolla cut off), × 1; **Ae,** stigma, × 5; **Af,** ovary, cross section, × 4; **Ag,** fruit (capsule), × ¾; **Ah,** seed, × 5. **B,** *Sidalcea neomexicana:* **Ba,** flowering stem, × ⅛; **Bb,** flower bud, × 1; **Bc,** flower, × ¾; **Bd,** flower, vertical section (part of perianth cut off), × 2; **Be,** upper part of double staminal column, × 4; **Bf,** pistil, × 3; **Bg,** ovary, cross section, × 7; **Bh,** fruit (schizocarp), × 2; **Bi,** single carpel (mericarp), × 4. **C,** *Hoheria populnea:* **Ca,** flowering branch, × ¼; **Cb,** flower, × 1; **Cc,** stamens surrounding pistil, × 2; **Cd,** pistil, × 2; **Ce,** fruit (schizocarp), × 1½. **D,** *Anoda cristata:* **Da,** pistil, × 3; **Db,** ovary, cross section, × 4. **E,** *Malope trifida:* pistil, × 4. (E from Bailey, *Manual of Cultivated Plants,* ed. 2.)

coccinea; **M. Davidsonii:** *Malacothamnus Davidsonii;* **M. fasciculatum:** *Malacothamnus fasciculatus;* **M. fasciculatum** var. **laxiflorum:** *Malacothamnus fasciculatus;* **M. prostratum:** *Sphaeralcea Philippiana;* **M. rotundifolium:** *Eremalche rotundifolia;* **M. scabrosum:** *Anisodontea scabrosa;* **M. Thurberi:** *Malacothamnus fasciculatus;* **M. virgatum:** *Anisodontea capensis.*

MALVAVISCUS Adans. SLEEPY MALLOW. *Malvaceae.* Three spp. of shrubs, sometimes vinelike or arborescent, in subtrop. and trop. Amer.; lvs. simple, unlobed or palmately angled or lobed; fls. usually solitary in upper axils, but sometimes in terminal, few-fld. racemes or cymes, involucral bracts 6-16, corolla funnelform, usually bright red, each petal with prominent auricle basally, stamens united in a column longer than the petals, style brs. 10, stigmas capitate, ovary 5-celled, each cell with 1 ovule; fr. a schizocarp, red-fleshy at first, the individual mericarps falling away as they dry.

Introduced as ornamentals and sometimes naturalized in subtropical and tropical regions of the Old World. Grown under glass or in the open in southern U.S. and Calif. Propagated by softwood cuttings.

arboreus Cav. [*M. mollis* (Ait.) DC.]. WAX MALLOW. A polymorphic sp., including many forms that have previously been recognized as distinct spp.; in the typical state usually densely velvety-pubescent; lvs. lobed or unlobed, ovate to suborbicular in outline, stellate-pubescent above; petals 1–2 in. long. Mex. to Peru and Brazil. Var. **Drummondii** (Torr. & A. Gray) Schery [*M. Drummondii* Torr. & A. Gray]. Lvs. about as broad as long, symmetrically lobed, with predominantly simple pubescence above; petals 1–1¼ in. long. Fla., w. to Tex. and Mex. Var. **mexicanus** Schlechtend. [*M. Conzattii* Greenm.; *M. grandiflorus* HBK; *M. penduliflorus* Sessé & Moç. ex DC.]. TURK'S-CAP. More or less glabrate; lvs. lanceolate to ovate, unlobed or scarcely lobed; petals mostly 1–2 in. long. Mex. to Colombia.

Conzattii: *M. arboreus* var. *mexicanus.*

Drummondii: *M. arboreus* var.

grandiflorus: *M. arboreus* var. *mexicanus.*

mollis: *M. arboreus.*

penduliflorus: *M. arboreus* var. *mexicanus.*

MAMILLOPSIS (E. Morr.) A. Web. ex Britt. & Rose. *Cactaceae.* Two spp. of low, tubercled cacti of Mex.; sts. cespitose, globose or short-cylindrical, with watery sap, tubercles conical, obtuse, not grooved, their axils with hairs and bristles; spines many, slender, central spines hooked; fls. nearly apical, axillary, red or orange, open several days and nights, stamens in 2 series, exserted, style exserted, stigma lobes erect, green. Resembling *Mammillaria,* but fls. salverform, the ovary and long perianth tube scaly.

For culture see *Cacti.*

senilis (Lodd. ex Salm-Dyck) Britt. & Rose. Sts. to 7 in. high and 5 in. thick, hidden by spines; radial spines 30–40, bristlelike, white, 1 in. long, central spines 5–6, thicker, the lower hooked, yellow at apex; fls. orange-yellow, 2–3 in. long, 2½ in. across, segms. serrate. Mts., w. Mex.

MAMMEA L. *Guttiferae.* About 50 spp. of trop., polygamous trees; lvs. opp., simple; fls. solitary or few in the axils, sepals 2, petals 4–6, stamens separate or united basally, ovary 2–4-celled, each cell 1–2-ovuled, style subulate, stigma 2–4-lobed; fr. drupaceous.

One species, *M. americana,* the mamey, widely cultivated in the Caribbean area for the edible fruit, and in the French Antilles for a liqueur distilled from the flowers. The mamey will not stand more than 2–3 degrees of frost. Propagated by seeds and probably also by inarching and budding. Seedlings bear in 6–8 years.

americana L. MAMEY, MAMMEE, MAMMEE APPLE, SOUTH AMERICAN APRICOT. Handsome tree, to 60 ft.; lvs. to 8 in. long, blunt, thick and glossy, with many lateral veins; fls. white, fragrant, 1 in. across; fr. to 6 in. in diam., with russet, roughened skin and bright yellow, firm, juicy flesh. The 1–4 large seeds are toxic to fish, chicks, and certain types of insects. W. Indies. Zone 10b in Fla. Cult. in the tropics in Mex., Cent. and S. Amer., and occasionally elsewhere. Fr. usually stewed or made into candies.

MAMMILLARIA Haw. [*Cactus* L., *Dolichothele* (K. Schum.) Britt. & Rose; *Krainzia* Backeb.; *Neomammillaria* Britt. & Rose; *Pseudomammillaria* Buxb.]. PINCUSHION, STRAWBERRY CACTUS. *Cactaceae.* Perhaps 150 spp. of low cacti, native to N. Amer., W. Indies, n. S. Amer., but mostly Mex.; sts. simple or cespitose, hemispherical to oblong, with milky or watery juice, covered with ungrooved tubercles, each with a terminal spine-bearing (spiniferous) areole and an axillary flower-bearing (floriferous) areole, tubercles succulent, cylindrical or angled, spirally arranged (the number of spiral rows to the left and to the right given in the descriptions below), axils (flower-bearing areoles) commonly with wool or hairs, sometimes with bristlelike spines; fls. mostly lateral, diurnal, small, perianth tube short, segms. petaloid, stamens rather few, included, ovary naked, stigma lobes spreading; fr. naked, mostly club-shaped, red, and exserted, sometimes the same plant also with fr. persistent, globose, green. The genus sometimes incorrectly spelled *Mamillaria.* Many spp. recognized here are probably subspp. or vars.

The genus has been divided into 6 subgenera and 6 sections, all of which, except for 2 sections, have sometimes been treated as genera. The species of a section possess the characteristics of that section and of the subgenus to which the section belongs. These characteristics are not repeated in the brief descriptions of the species; instead, the following symbols are used to indicate the subgenus and section to which each species belongs: B, *Bartschella;* Cc, *Crinitae;* Cph, *Phellosperma;* Cps, *Pseudomammillaria;* Cs, *Stelligerae;* Mc, *Conothele;* Mm, *Mammillaria;* Ml, *Mammilloydia;* P, *Porfiria;* S, *Solisia.*

The distinguishing characters of the subgenera and sections follow:

Subgenus **Bartschella** (Britt. & Rose) Moran [*Bartschella* Britt. & Rose] (B). Seeds black, pitted, hilum basal, micropyle next to the hilum, perisperm absent; sts. with watery juice, tubercles almost rhombic, truncate; central spines often hooked; fr. circumscissile.

Subgenus **Chilita** (Orcutt) Moran [*Chilita* Orcutt] (C). Seeds dark, pitted, hilum mostly basal or nearly basal; sts. with watery juice, tubercles mostly cylindrical, separated; spines often puberulent, at least in seedlings, central spines often hooked.

Section **Crinitae** Salm-Dyck (Cc). Central spines often hooked; seeds mostly black, micropyle next to the hilum, perisperm absent.

Section **Phellosperma** (Britt. & Rose) Moran [*Phellosperma* Britt. & Rose] (Cph). Central spines hooked; seeds black, with conspicuous aril, perisperm absent.

Section **Pseudomammillaria** (Buxb.) Moran [*Pseudomammillaria* Buxb.] (Cps). Tubercles elongate, soft; central spines straight or none; seeds brown, micropyle small or closed, distant from the nearly lateral hilum, perisperm absent.

Section **Stelligerae** Salm-Dyck (Cs). Central spines often hooked; seeds mostly black, micropyle next to the hilum, perisperm present.

Subgenus **Mammillaria** (M). Seeds light brown, smooth or rugose, testa soft, micropyle small or closed, distant from the mostly lateral hilum, perisperm present; sts. mostly gray-green, with milky juice; spines glabrous, rarely hooked.

Section **Conothele** Salm-Dyck (Mc). Tubercles with watery juice, milky juice confined to the central part of the st.

Section **Mammillaria** (Mm). Tubercles with milky juice.

Subgenus **Mammilloydia** (Buxb.) Moran [*Mammilloydia* Buxb.] (Ml). Seeds black, verrucose, hilum basal, perisperm absent; sts. with watery juice; spines straight.

Subgenus **Porfiria** (Böd.) Moran [*Porfiria* Böd.] (P). Seeds almost black, pitted, perisperm absent; body top-shaped, with a thick tap root and with milky juice; spines straight.

Subgenus **Solisia** (Britt. & Rose) Moran [*Solisia* Britt. & Rose] (S). Seeds black, pitted, hilum large, perisperm absent; sts. with milky juice; areoles elongate, spines comblike, all radial, straight.

For culture see *Cacti.*

acanthophlegma: *M. elegans.*

albescens Tiegel. Cps; sts. cespitose, to 3 in. high and 2 in. thick, tubercles in 5 and 8 spirals, ¾ in. long, ¼ in. in diam., axils with 2–4 yellowish bristles; radial spines 4–6, slender, yellowish, becoming white, to ⅝ in. long, central spine 0, rarely 1, similar to radial spines; fls. greenish-white, to ¾ in. long; fr. greenish, to 1 in. long. Cent. Mex. Cv. **'Senilis'** is listed. Perhaps a var. of *M. decipiens.*

albicans (Britt. & Rose) A. Berger. Cc; sts. simple or few-branched, to 8 in. high and 2½ in. thick, tubercles in 13 and 21 spirals, conical, to ¼ in. long and thick, axils with wool and bristles; spines densely interlacing, straight, sometimes brown-tipped, becoming white, radial spines 15–20, bristlelike, mostly lateral, central spines 3–8, needle-shaped, to ⅜ in. long; fls. pinkish, ¾ in. across; fr. to ¾ in. long. Islands of Gulf of Calif.

albicoma Böd. Cc?; sts. cespitose, to 2 in. high and 1¼ in. thick, tubercles in 8 and 13 spirals, ¼ in. long, ⅛ in. in diam., axils with wool and slender bristles; radial spines 30–40, capillary, soft, white, to ⅜ in. long, central spines 0–4, needle-shaped, white, brown-tipped, to ⅜ in. long; fls. whitish, to ⅝ in. long. Ne. Mex. Allied to *M. bocasana.*

albilanata Backeb. Mc?; sts. mostly simple, to 6 in. high and 3 in. thick, tubercles in 13 and 21 spirals, cylindric-conical, to ¼ in. long and 5/32 in. in diam., axils woolly; radial spines 15–20, stellate, needle-shaped, white, to 5/32 in. long, central spines mostly 2, thicker, brown-tipped, to ⅛ in. long; fls. red, to 5/16 in. long. S. Mex. Incompletely known; perhaps a var. of *M. Haageana.*

angularis: *M. compressa.*

applanata: *M. Heyderi* var. *Heyderi*

armillata K. Brandeg. [*M. capensis* (H. E. Gates) R. T. Craig]. Cc; sts. simple or few-branched, to 1 ft. high and 2 in. thick, tubercles in 5 and 8 spirals, conical to cylindrical, 3/16 in. long and nearly as thick, axils with wool and 1–3 bristles; radial spines 9–15, needle-shaped, yellow to white, brown-tipped, to ½ in. long, central spines 1–4, yellowish to brown, the lower hooked, to ¾ in. long; fls. white to pink, to ¾ in. long; fr. to 1¼ in. long, seeds constricted above the hilum.

aureilanata Backeb. [*M. cephalophora* Quehl, not Salm-Dyck]. Cc; roots tuberous, sts. simple, globose, to 3 in. thick, tubercles in 8 and 13 spirals, ⅜ in. long and 5/16 in. in diam., punctate, axils naked; radial spines 25–30, in 2 series, slender, yellowish-white, to ⅝ in. long, the tips thin and flexuous, making the crown woolly, central spines 0; fls. pink, to 1¼ in. long; fr. pinkish. Cent. Mex.

aurihamata Böd. Cc; cespitose, sts. to 2½ in. high and 1½ in. thick, tubercles in 8 and 13 spirals, conical, to ¼ in. long and ⅛ in. in diam., axils with about 8 thin white bristles; radial spines 15–20, bristlelike, yellowish, to 5/16 in. long, central spines 4, soon golden, the upper 3 nearly straight, to ⅜ in. long, the lower directed outward, hooked, to 1 in. long; fls. yellow, ⅝ in. long. Cent. Mex.

Bachmanii Böd. Mm; sts. simple, globose, to 7 in. thick, tubercles in 13 and 21 spirals, ovoid, to 5/16 in. long, slightly thicker, axils with abundant white wool; radial spines 6–10, capillary, brown, to 3/16 in. long, central spines 4, in form of a cross, needle-shaped, black, the lower longest, to ¾ in. long; fls. deep pink, ¾ in. long; fr. ¾ in. long. Spring. Presumably Mex.

Balleotii: a listed name of no botanical standing.

barbata Engelm. Cc; sts. cespitose, globose, to 2 in. thick, tubercles in 8 and 13 spirals, 5/16 in. long, ⅛ in. in diam., axils naked; radial spines to 5/16 in. long, the outer 30–40 capillary, white, the inner 10–15 thicker, brown, central spine 1, brown, hooked, to ⅝ in. long; fls. rose, ¾ in. long, outer segms. ciliate; fr. ½ in. long. Spring. N. Mex.

Baumii Böd. [*Dolichothele Baumii* (Böd.) Werderm. & Buxb.]. Sts. to 2½ in. wide, tubercles to ⅜ in. long and 3/16 in. thick; 5–6 radial spines needle-shaped, yellowish, to ¾ in. long, 30–35 of them capillary, sinuous, white, to ⅝ in. long, central spine 0; fls. to 1¼ in. long, with solid column from ovary to tube; fr. ovoid, green, to ⅝ in. long. Spring. Ne. Mex.

Baxterana (H. E. Gates) Böd. [*M. pacifica* (H. E. Gates) Böd.]. Mm; sts. simple or forked, to 6 in. high and thick, tubercles in 13 and 21 spirals, 4-angled, to ½ in. long and 5/16 in. thick, axils slightly woolly; radial spines 7–13, needle-shaped, white, to ⅜ in. long, central spine 1, directed outward, stouter, to ¾ in. long; fls. greenish-yellow, ⅝ in. long; fr. to 1 in. long. S. Baja Calif. Perhaps a var. of *M. Brandegeei,* which has 2–4 central spines and smaller fls.

Beneckii C. A. Ehrenb. Sts. cylindrical, to 2¾ in. high and thick, tubercles columnar, 4-angled at base, axils woolly at first; radial spines 12–15, horizontal, whitish or yellowish, brown-tipped, central spines 2–6, brown, black-tipped, 1–2 of them longer and hooked; fls. yellow. W. Mex.

Blossfeldiana Böd. Cc; root thick, sts. mostly simple, deep-seated, globose to oblong, to 2 in. thick, tubercles in 5 and 8 spirals, to 5/16 in. long and ¼ in. in diam., axils slightly woolly; radial spines 15–20, needle-shaped, grayish, dark-tipped, ¼ in. long, central spines 4, dark, the lower hooked, to ⅜ in. long; fls. pink, to 1½ in. long; fr. ¾ in. long. Baja Calif. Var. **Shurliana** (H. E. Gates) Wiggins [*M. Shurliana* H. E. Gates]. Main root thinner.

bocasana Poselg. SNOWBALL CACTUS, POWDER-PUFF C., FISH-HOOKS. Cc; sts simple or cespitose, globose to oblong, to 2 in. thick, tubercles in 8 and 13 spirals, cylindrical, flabby, to ⅜ in. long and 5/32 in. in diam., axils naked; radial spines 25–30, capillary, sinuous, white, to ¾ in. long, interlacing, central spines mostly 1, directed outward, yellowish, pubescent, hooked, to 5/16 in. long; fls. yellow, to ¾ in. long. Cent. Mex. Cv. **'Inermis'.** Central spine 0.

bogotensis: *M. columbiana.*

bombycina Quehl. Cc; sts. simple or cespitose, to 8 in. high and 2½ in. thick, tubercles in 11 and 18 spirals, to ⅝ in. long and ⅜ in. in diam., axillary wool covering tubercles at apex; radial spines 30–40, needle-shaped, white, pubescent, to ⅜ in. long, central spines 2–4, yellowish, with dark tips, the lower hooked, to ¾ in. long; fls. red, ⅝ in. long; fr. ⅝ in. long. N. Mex.

Brandegeei (J. Coult.) K. Brandeg. Mm; sts. simple or cespitose, globose to oblong, to 3½ in. thick, tubercles in 13 and 21 spirals, 4-angled, to ⅜ in. long, axils woolly; radial spines 9–16, needle-shaped, whitish, dark-tipped, to ⅜ in. long, central spines 2–4, stouter, dark, to ¾ in. long; fls. greenish-yellow, to 5/16 in. long, outer segms. ciliate; fr. to ⅝ in. long. Baja Calif. Var. **Gabbii** (J. Coult.) R. T. Craig. Central spines 1–2.

Brauneana Böd. Mm; sts. mostly simple, globose, to 3 in. thick, tubercles in 21 and 34 spirals, to 5/32 in. long and thick, axils with dense wool and slender bristles; radial spines 25–30, capillary, white, to 3/16 in. long, central spines 2–4, awl-shaped, ¼ in. long; fls. violet-red, to ½ in. across. Ne. Mex.

Bravoae R. T. Craig. Mm; sts. solitary or cespitose, globose, to 2½ in. thick, tubercles in 13 and 21 spirals, axils with wool covering apex and with slender bristles; radial spines 28–30, needle-shaped, white, to ¼ in. long, interlacing, central spines 2, stouter, black-tipped, to ⅛ in. long; fls. deep pink, to ⅜ in. long; fr. to ⅜ in. long. Cent. Mex.

bucareliensis R. T. Craig. Mm; sts. simple, to 3½ in. high and 2 in. thick, tubercles in 8 and 13 or in 13 and 21 spirals, 4-angled, to ⅜ in. long and ½ in. thick, axils woolly; radial spines mostly 3–5, needle-shaped, whitish, to 3/16 in. long, central spines 2–4, stouter, brown, the lower to 1½ in. long; fls. deep pink, to ⅝ in. long; fr. to ⅝ in. long. Spring. Cent. Mex.

Bullardiana: *M. Hutchisoniana.*

calacantha Tiegel. Mc; sts. simple, to 5 in. high and 2½ in. thick, tubercles in 13 and 21 spirals, conoid, to ½ in. long and 5/16 in. in diam., young axils short-woolly; radial spines 25–35, needle-shaped, pale yellow, becoming gray, ¼ in. long, central spines 2–4, stouter, reddish, to ⅝ in. long; fls. carmine, ½ in. long; fr. ¾ in. long. Cent. Mex.

camptotricha Dams. BIRD'S-NEST CACTUS, GOLDEN B.-N. C. Cps; sts. cespitose, globose, to 1¼ in. thick, tubercles in 8 and 13 spirals, cylindrical, to ¾ in. long and ¼ in. in diam., axils with little wool and 2–5 yellowish bristles; spines radial, 4–8, slender, flexuous, the upper longest, to 1¼ in. long; fls. white, ½ in. long; fr. ¾ in. long. Cent. Mex.

candida Schneidw. SNOWBALL P. Ml; sts. cespitose, oblong, to 3 in. thick, tubercles in 13 and 21 spirals, cylindrical, ⅜ in. long and 3/16 in. in diam., axils with 4–7 white bristles; radial spines 50 or more, needle-shaped, white, stellate to somewhat spreading, to 5/16 in. long, central spines 8–12, a little heavier and shorter, brown-tipped; fls. pink, ¾ in. long. Cent. Mex.

capensis: *M. armillata.*

caput-Medusae: *M. sempervivi.*

carnea Zucc. Mm; sts. mostly simple, to 4 in. high and 3½ in. thick, tubercles in 8 and 13 spirals, 4-angled, ½ in. long, ⅜ in. thick, axils with yellowish wool; radial spines 0 or 1–2 upper bristles, central spines 4, in form of a cross, awl-shaped, black-tipped, the longest ¾–2 in. long; fls. flesh-colored, to ¾ in. long; fr. to 1 in. long. Cent. Mex. Cv. **'Rosea'** is listed.

Carretii Rebut [*M. Saffordii* (Britt. & Rose) Bravo]. Cc; sts. mostly simple, to 3 in. high and 2 in. thick, tubercles in 8 and 13 spirals, cylindrical, flabby, 5/16 in. long and 3/16 in. in diam., axils slightly woolly; radial spines 14–15, needle-shaped, pubescent, brownish, curved, to ½ in. long, central spine 1, hooked, brown, to ¾ in. long; fls. rose, 1 in. long. N. Mex.

Celsiana Lem. Mc; sts. simple or cespitose, to 5 in. high and 3 in. thick, tubercles in 13 and 21 spirals, to ⅜ in. long and 5/16 in. in diam., axils white-woolly; radial spines 24–30, needle-shaped, white, to 5/16 in. long, central spines 4–6, awl-shaped, often curved, yellow, the lower to 1¼ in. long; fls. carmine, to ½ in. long. Cent. Mex.

centricirrha: *M. magnimamma.*

cephalophora: see *M. aureilanata.*

chionocephala J. Purpus. Mm; sts. mostly simple, globose, to 5 in. thick, tubercles in 13 and 21 spirals, 4-angled, dotted, to 5/16 in. long, axils white-woolly and with short hairs; radial spines 22–24, bristlelike, white, to 5/16 in. long, central spines 2–4, awl-shaped, white to brownish, to ¼ in. long; fls. rose, to ¾ in. long. N. Mex.

cirrhifera: *M. compressa.*

coahuilensis (Böd.) Moran [*Porfiria coahuilensis* Böd.; *P. Schwarzii* (Frič) Böd.]. P; sts. simple, to 1½ in. thick, tubercles in 8 and 13 spirals, 3-angled, to ½ in. long and ⅜ in. thick, axils woolly; spines scaly, grayish, to ¼ in. long, radial spines about 16, needle-shaped, to ¼ in. long, central spine 1, stouter; fls. rose, 1¼ in. wide. N. Mex.

collina J. Purpus. M?; sts. mostly simple, globose, to 5 in. thick, tubercles in 13 and 21 spirals, obscurely 4-angled, ⅜ in. long, axils woolly, radial spines 16–18, needle-shaped, white, to 3/16 in. long, central spines 1–2, stouter, gray-brown, to 5/16 in. long; fls. rose, to ¾ in. long; fr. to 1 in. long, seeds brown, pitted. S. Mex.

columbiana Salm-Dyck [*M. bogotensis* Werderm.]. Mc; sts. simple, to 10 in. high and 3½ in. thick, tubercles in 13 and 21 spirals, to ¼ in. long and thick, axils woolly; radial spines 20–30, needle-shaped, white, to ¼ in. long, central spines 3–6, yellow to brown, to 5/16 in. long; fls. deep pink, to ⅜ in. long. Colombia, Venezuela.

compressa DC. [*M. angularis* Link & Otto; *M. cirrhifera* Mart.]. Mm; cespitose, forming clumps to 3 ft. wide, sts. to 8 in. high and 3 in. thick, tubercles in 8 and 13 spirals, 4-angled, to ¼ in. long and ½ in. thick, axils with white wool and bristles; spines 4–6, spreading, needle-shaped, often flexuous, unequal, the lowest ¾–2¾ in. long; fls. purplish-red, to ⅝ in. long; fr. to 1 in. long. Spring. Cent. Mex. Cvs. **'Angularis'**, **'Longiseta'**, and **'Superba'** are listed.

confusa (Britt. & Rose) Orcutt. Mm; sts. cespitose, to 6 in. high and 4 in. thick, tubercles in 8 and 13 spirals, somewhat 4-sided, to ⅜ in. long and thick, axils with wool and with 10–12 exserted, flexuous, white bristles; radial spines 4–6, needle-shaped to awl-shaped, black, becoming chalky, to 1¼ in. long, central spines usually 0; fls. greenish, to ¾ in. long; fr. ¾ in. long. Spring, summer. S. Mex. Perhaps not distinct from *M. Karwinskiana.*

conspicua J. Purpus. Mc; sts. simple, to 6 in. high and 4 in. thick, tubercles conical or somewhat 4-angled, ¼ in. long, axils with wool and bristles; radial spines 16–25, needle-shaped, white, to ¼ in. long, central spines 2, stouter, brown-tipped, to ⅜ in. long; fls. rose. S. Mex.

Craigii G. Lindsay. Mm; sts. mostly simple, to 3 in. high and 6 in. thick, tubercles in 13 and 21 spirals, somewhat 4-angled, ⅝ in. long, ½ in. thick, axils slightly woolly; spines needle-shaped, golden-brown, radial spines 7–8, spreading, to 1 in. long, central spines 1–3, stouter, to 1¼ in. long; fls. purplish, to ¾ in. long; fr. ½ in. long. Spring. N. Mex.

crocidata Lem. [*M. Webbiana* Lem.]. Mm; sts. mostly simple, to 4 in. high and 3 in. thick, tubercles in 13 and 21 spirals, at first 4-angled, to ⅜ in. long and ½ in. thick, axils very woolly; spines 2–4, needle-shaped, white, dark-tipped, unequal, to ¾ in. long; fls. carmine, ⅝ in. long; fr. ¾ in. long. Cent. Mex.

crucigera Mart. Mm; sts. simple or forked, globose to oblong, to 6 in. high, tubercles in 8 and 13 spirals, to ¼ in. long and thick, the sap milky in growing season, axils densely woolly; radial spines 24 or more, needle-shaped, white, to 3/32 in. long, central spines mostly 4, in the form of a cross, awl-shaped, dark-tipped, to ⅛ in. long; fls. purplish-red. Spring. S. Mex.

dealbata: *M. Parkinsonii;* see also *M. elegans* var.

decipiens Scheidw. Cps; sts. cespitose, globose, to 4 in. thick, tubercles in 5 and 8 spirals, cylindrical, to ½ in. long and 3/16 in. in diam., axils slightly woolly, with to 4 bristles; spines needle-shaped, radial spines 7–8, yellowish, to ⅜ in. long, central spine 1, brown toward apex, to ¾ in. long; fls. pink, to ¾ in. long; fr. to ¾ in. long. N. Mex.

densispina (J. Coult.) Orcutt. Cs; sts. simple, globose to oblong, to 4 in. thick, tubercles in 8 and 13 spirals, to 3/16 in. long and thick, axils woolly; spines needle-shaped, interlacing, radial spines 20–25, white to yellow, to ½ in. long, central spines 5–6, yellow, dark-tipped, to ¾ in. long; fls. yellow, to ¾ in. long. Cent. Mex.

denudata: *M. lasiacantha.*

Dietrichiae: *M. Parkinsonii.*

dioica K. Brandeg. Cc; sts. simple or branched, to 1 ft. high and 4 in. thick, but mostly smaller, tubercles in 8 and 13 spirals, to ¼ in. long and 5/32 in. in diam., axils with wool and 5–15 bristles; radial spines 11–22, needle-shaped, white, ¼ in. long, central spines 1–4, stouter, brown, the lower hooked, to ⅝ in. long; fls. yellowish, to 1½ in. long, sometimes unisexual; fr. dimorphic. Spring. Sw. Calif. and Baja Calif.

discolor Haw. Mc; sts. simple, oblong, to 3 in. thick, tubercles in 8 and 13 spirals, about ¼ in. long and thick, axils with little wool; spines needle-shaped, to ⅜ in. long, radial spines 16–20, white, central spines 6–8, stouter, yellow, becoming gray; fls. pink, ¾ in. long; fr. 1 in. long. S. Mex.

dolichocentra: *M. tetracantha.*

dumetorum: *M. Schiedeana.*

durispina Böd. Mc; sts. simple, to 8 in. high and 4½ in. thick, tubercles in 21 and 34 spirals, to ½ in. long and 5/16 in. in diam., axils woolly; radial spines 6–8, awl-shaped, stellate, banded, the upper longest, ⅝ in. long, central spines 0 or rarely 1–2, similar; fls. purplish, ⅝ in. long; fr. ¾ in. long. Cent. Mex.

echinaria: *M. elongata* var. *echinata.*

Eichlamii Quehl. Mm; sts. cespitose, to 10 in. high and 2½ in. thick, tubercles in 8 and 13 spirals, scarcely angled, to 5/16 in. long, axils with yellowish wool and with 5–6 exserted, flexuous bristles; radial spines 6–8, needle-shaped, yellowish, dark-tipped, ¼ in. long, central spine 1, stouter, reddish, to ⅜ in. long; fls. red, ¾ in. long. Autumn. Guatemala.

elegans DC. [*M. acanthophlegma* Lehm.; *M. Kunthii* C. A. Ehrenb.]. Mc; sts. simple or cespitose, to 6 in. high and 2½ in. thick, tubercles in 13 and 21 spirals, cylindrical, 3/16 in. long and thick, axils woolly; radial spines 20–30, needle-shaped, white, to ¼ in. long, interlacing, central spines 1–4, stouter, dark-tipped, ¼ in. long; fls. red, to ⅝ in. long; fr. ¾ in. long. Cent. Mex. Cvs. **'Microthele'** and **'Potosina'** are listed. Var. **dealbata** Borg [*M. dealbata* Hort., not A. Dietr.]. Sts. more cylindrical, with central spine mostly 1 and erect. Var. **supertexta** (Mart.) Schelle [*M. supertexta* Mart.]. Central spines 0–2, to 3/32 in. long.

elongata DC. [*M. stella-aurata* Mart.]. LACE CACTUS, GOLDEN-STAR C., GOLD LACE C., GOLDEN-LACE, LADYFINGER. Cs; sts. cespitose, to 4 in. high and 1¼ in. thick, tubercles in 3 and 5 or 5 and 8 spirals, to nearly 3/16 in. long, axils naked or slightly woolly; radial spines 15–20, slightly spreading and recurved, needle-shaped, yellow, to ½ in. long, central spines 0 or rarely 1; fls. yellowish, to ⅝ in. long. Cent. Mex. Cvs. **'Longispina'**, **'Microthele'**, **'Minima'**, **'Rufocrocea'**, and **'Schmollii'** are listed. Var. **echinata** (DC.) K. Schum. [*M. echinaria* DC.]. Central spines 1–2, to ¾ in. long. Var. **tenuis** (DC.) K. Schum. Sts. to ⅜ in. thick, tubercles in 3 and 5 spirals; radial spines 20–25, bristlelike, central spines 0.

erectohamata Böd. Cc; sts. cespitose, globose, to 2½ in. thick, tubercles in 13 and 21 spirals, cylindrical, 5/16 in. long and 3/16 in. in diam., axils with slender bristles; radial spines about 25, needle-shaped, white, ¼ in. long, central spines 2, dark, the lower hooked, to ¾ in. long; fls. white, ¾ in. across; fr. ½ in. long. Cent. Mex.

eriacantha Link & Otto. Mc; sts. simple or cespitose, to 6 in. high and 2 in. thick, tubercles in 8 and 13 spirals, to 5/16 in. long and ¼ in. in diam., axils woolly; spines needle-shaped, pubescent, yellow, radial spines 20–25, to ¼ in. long, central spines 2, stouter, to ⅜ in. long; fls. yellow, ⅝ in. long; fr. ⅜ in. long. Cent. Mex.

erythrosperma Böd. Cc; sts. simple or cespitose, to 2 in. high and 1½ in. thick, tubercles in 8 and 13 spirals, dotted, ⅜ in. long, 3/16 in. in diam., axils with slender bristles; radial spines 15–20, needle-shaped, white, at first pubescent, to ⅜ in. long, central spines 1–4, yellow, brown-tipped, pubescent, the lower hooked, to ⅜ in. long; fls. carmine, ⅝ in. long; fr. ¾ in. long. Cent. Mex.

Essaussieri: a listed name of no botanical standing.

fasciculata Engelm.: *Echinocereus fasciculatus;* but material listed as *M. fasciculata* is *M. Thornberi.*

Fischeri: *M. Karwinskiana.*

flavovirens Salm-Dyck. Mm; sts. mostly simple, to 3 in. high, tubercles in 8 and 13 spirals, 4-sided, to ⅜ in. long, axils woolly; radial spines 4–5, slender-awl-shaped, to ¼ in. long, central spine 1, awl-shaped, deflexed, to ⅝ in. long; fls. white with pink, ¾ in. long; fr. ¾ in. long. Mex. Perhaps referable to *M. pentacantha,* which is incompletely known.

formosa Galeotti. Mm; sts. mostly simple, subglobose, to 3 in. thick, tubercles in 13 and 21 spirals, obscurely 4-angled, dotted, 5/16 in. long, less than 3/16 in. thick, axils woolly; radial spines 20–25, needle-shaped, white, to ¼ in. long, central spines 4–6, awl-shaped, black-tipped, to 5/16 in. long; fls. pink, to ⅝ in. long; fr. to ⅝ in. long. Cent. Mex.

fragilis Salm-Dyck. THIMBLE M., THIMBLE CACTUS. Cc?; sts. cespitose, oblong, to 1 in. thick, easily disarticulating, tubercles in 5 and 8 spirals, to 3/16 in. long and 5/16 in. in diam., axils woolly; radial spines 12–16, needle-shaped, white, to 3/16 in. long, central spine 0–1, directed outward, stouter, brown-tipped, to ⅜ in. long; fls. pale yellow, ½ in. long; fr. ½ in. long. Cent. Mex. Cvs. **'Cristata'**, **'Minima'**, and **'Prolifera'** are listed.

Fraileana (Britt. & Rose) Böd. Probably a var. or form of *M. armillata*, having longer central spines and slightly larger fls. Baja Calif.

fuliginosa Salm-Dyck. Mc; sts. simple, globose, to 3 in. thick, tubercles in 21 and 34 spirals, cylindrical, ¼ in. long, axils slightly woolly; radial spines 16, bristlelike, white, to 3/32 in. long, central spines 4, in the form of a cross, needle-shaped, black-tipped, to ⅜ in. long; fls. deep pink, ⅝ in. long; fr. ¾ in. long. Probably Venezuela.

fuscata Pfeiff. [*M. Pfeifferi* Hort. Booth]. Mc; sts. simple, globose, tubercles to ⅜ in. long and ¼ in. wide, axils naked or somewhat woolly; radial spines 25–28, needle-shaped, white to yellow, to 5/16 in. long, central spines 4–6, stouter, yellow to brown, straight or curved, to 1¼ in. long; fls. purplish, ⅝ in. wide; fr. ¾ in. long. Spring. Cent. Mex. Perhaps a var. of *M. rhodantha*.

Galeottii: *M. tetracantha* var.

geminispina Haw. Mm; sts. cespitose, to 7 in. high and 3 in. thick, tubercles in 13 and 21 spirals, cylindrical above, to 5/16 in. long and thick, axils with wool and with 10–20 sinuous bristles; radial spines 16–20, needle-shaped, white, ¼ in. long, central spines 2–4, stouter, brown-tipped, the upper longest, to 1½ in. long; fls. carmine, ¾ in. long; fr. to ½ in. long. Cent. Mex.

gigantea Hildm. Mm; sts. simple, to 4 in. high and 7 in. wide, tubercles in 13 and 21 spirals, 4-angled, to ⅜ in. long and ½ in. thick, axils woolly; radial spines 12, needle-shaped, whitish, to 3/16 in. long, central spines 4–6, awl-shaped, becoming yellowish, the lower longest, to ¾ in. long; fls. yellowish, ⅝ in. long; fr. 1¼ in. long. Spring. Cent. Mex.

globosa: *M. longimamma* cv.

glochidiata Mart. Cc; sts. cespitose, oblong, to 1½ in. thick, tubercles in 5 and 8 spirals, cylindrical, flabby, to ⅝ in. long and ¼ in. in diam., axils with 1–5 fine bristles; radial spines 12–15, bristlelike, white, to ½ in. long, central spines 3–4, pubescent, yellow to brown, the lower directed outward, hooked, to ½ in. long; fls. white with pink, ⅝ in. long; fr. ⅝ in. long. Cent. Mex.

Grahamii Engelm. Cc; sts. simple, ovoid to globose, to 4 in. high and 4½ in. thick; spines dense, radial spines 20–35, white, to 5/16 in. long, central spines 2–4, dark reddish-brown or red to nearly black, 1 hooked or straight, to 1 in. long; fls. white or pale pink, to ¼ in. across. Var. **Grahamii.** The typical var.; 1 or more central spines hooked. Tex. to Ariz. Var. **Oliviae** (Orcutt) L. Bens. [*M. Oliviae* Orcutt]. Central spines not hooked. Se. Ariz. and n. Mex.

Guelzowiana Werderm. [*Krainzia Guelzowiana* (Werderm.) Backeb.]. Cph; sts. cespitose, to 2½ in. high and 3 in. thick, tubercles in 8 and 13 spirals, cylindrical, flabby, ½ in. long and 3/16 in. in diam., axils naked; radial spines 60–80, capillary, white, flexuous, to ¾ in. long, central spines 1–2, directed outward, yellowish to brown, hooked, to ⅜ in. long; fls. purplish-red, to 2 in. long; fr. subglobose, to 5/16 in. in diam. Spring to autumn. Cent. Mex.

guerreronis (Bravo) Backeb. & F. M. Knuth. Cs?; sts. cespitose, to 28 in. high and 2½ in. thick, tubercles in 8 and 13 spirals, 5/16 in. long, 3/16 in. in diam., the sap semimilky, axils with wool and 15–20 slender bristles; radial spines 20–30, fine-needle-shaped, white, to ⅜ in. long, central spines 2–5, needle-shaped, orangish, becoming white, the lowest longest, deflexed, sometimes slightly hooked, to ⅝ in. long; fr. greenish, ¾ in. long. S. Mex.

guirocobensis R. T. Craig. Cc; sts. simple or cespitose, to 4½ in. high and 2 in. thick, tubercles in 8 and 13 spirals, somewhat angled, ¼ in. long and thick, axils mostly naked; radial spines 18–20, needle-shaped, yellowish to gray, to 5/16 in. long, central spines 1–3, brown, the lowest often hooked, to ⅜ in. long; fls. whitish, ¾ in. long; fr. ½ in. long. Nw. Mex.

gummifera: *M. Heyderi* var. Var. **applanata:** *M. Heyderi* var. *Heyderi*. Var. **hemisphaerica:** *M. Heyderi* var.

Haageana Pfeiff. Mc; sts. mostly simple, to 3 in. high and 2 in. thick, tubercles in 13 and 21 spirals, 4-sided, 3/16 in. long, ⅛ in. thick, axils woolly; radial spines 18–20, needle-shaped, white, ⅛ in. long, central spines 2, stouter, brown to black, ascending and deflexed, the lower longer, to 5/16 in. long; fls. purplish-pink, ½ in. long; fr. to ½ in. long. Cent. Mex.

Hahniana Werderm. OLD-WOMAN CACTUS, OLD-LADY C., OLD-LADY-OF-MEXICO. Mm; sts. cespitose, subglobose, to 4 in. thick, tubercles in 13 and 21 spirals, nearly triangular, to ¼ in. long and 5/32 in. thick, axils woolly, with 20 or more slender, white, unequal bristles to 1½ in. long; radial spines 20–30, capillary, white, soft, to ⅝ in. long, central spines 1 or more, soon shed, needle-shaped, reddish-tipped, to 5/16 in. long; fls. purplish-red, to ¾ in. long. Summer. Cent. Mex. Var. **Giseleana** Neale. Axillary bristles fewer, to ⅝ in. long; radial spines to 40.

Hamiltonhoytiae (Bravo) Werderm. Mm; sts. mostly simple, subglobose, to 7 in. thick, tubercles in 13 and 21 spirals, somewhat 4-sided, ½ in. long, ⅜ in. thick, axils woolly; radial spines 5–8, needle-shaped, white, dark-tipped, the lower to ¾ in. long, central spines 2–3, awl-shaped, the lower longest, to 1½ in. long; fls. pinkish, ¾ in. long; fr. ¾ in. long. Cent. Mex.

Haseltonii: a listed name of no botanical standing.

Heeseana: *M. Petterssonii*.

hemisphaerica: *M. Heyderi* var.

Herrerae Werderm. Ml?; sts. cespitose, subglobose, to 1½ in. thick, tubercles in 8 and 13 spirals, cylindrical, to ¼ in. long and 3/32 in. in diam., axils naked; spines about 100, radial, in several series, appressed, bristlelike, white or gray, to 3/16 in. long, interlacing; fls. rose, to 1 in. long; fr. subglobose, under the spines. Cent. Mex.

Heyderi Mühlenpf. [*M. gummifera* Engelm.]. CORAL CACTUS. Mm; sts. simple, hemispherical or top-shaped, to 5 in. wide, tubercles in 13 and 21 spirals, 4-angled at base, cylindrical above, to ½ in. long and ¼ in. thick, axils woolly; radial spines needle-shaped, white, brown-tipped, to ½ in. long, central spines 0–2, directed outward, stouter, to ⅜ in. long; fls. white with pink or red, to 1¼ in. long; fr. dimorphic. Spring. Ariz. to Tex., n. Mex. Var. **Heyderi** [*M. applanata* Engelm.; *M. gummifera* var. *applanata* (Engelm.) L. Bens.]. The typical var.; sts. somewhat flattened; radial spines 10–22. Tex. Var. **gummifera** (Engelm.) L. Bens. [*M. gummifera* Engelm.]. Sts. hemispherical or top-shaped; radial spines 20–22, central spine 1, directed outward, to 5/16 in. long; fls. white, with pink or red. N. Mex. Var. **hemisphaerica** (Engelm.) Engelm. [*M. gummifera* var. *hemisphaerica* (Engelm.) L. Bens.; *M. hemisphaerica* Engelm.; *M. Waltheri* Böd.]. Radial spines 9–13, outer segms. entire. Tex., n. Mex. Var. **Macdougalii** (Rose) L. Bens. [*M. Macdougalii* Rose]. Radial spines 9–15; fls. greenish-yellow, outer segms. erose to fimbriate. S. Ariz. Var. **meiacantha** (Engelm.) L. Bens. [*M. meiacantha* Engelm.]. Hemispherical, tubercles nearly pyramidal; radial spines 10–22, to ⅜ in. long, central spine 0–1, to ¼ in. long; fls. pink or pink and white, to 1¼ in. across, segms. mostly entire. Tex. to Ariz., Mex.

hidalgensis J. Purpus. Mm; sts. to 5 in. thick; tubercles with watery sap; spines to ⅜ in. long. Perhaps a var. of *M. polythele*.

Hoffmanniana (Tiegel) Bravo. Mc; sts. simple, to 1 ft. high and 5 in. thick, tubercles in 13 and 21 spirals, ⅜ in. long and thick, axils densely woolly; radial spines 18–20, bristlelike, white, to ⅛ in. long, sometimes deciduous, central spines 4–7, thin-awl-shaped, curved, whitish, brown-tipped, to 1 in. long; fls. magenta, ⅜ in. long; fr. ¾ in. long. Spring. Cent. Mex.

Humboldtii C. A. Ehrenb. Cc; sts. simple or cespitose, globose to cylindrical, tubercles in 13 and 21 spirals, cylindrical, ½ in. long, ⅛ in. in diam., axils with wool and 7–8 bristles; radial spines 80 or more, in several series, thin-needle-shaped, white, unequal, to 5/16 in. long, central spines 0; fls. red, ⅝ in. across. Cent. Mex.

Hutchisoniana (H. E. Gates) Böd. [*M. Bullardiana* (H. E. Gates) Böd.]. Cc; sts. cespitose; to 6 in. high and 2½ in. thick, tubercles in 8 and 13 spirals, 3/16 in. long and thick, axils naked; radial spines 15–20, thin-needle-shaped, becoming whitish, to 5/16 in. long, central spines 3, purple-tipped, the lowest hooked, to 5/16 in. long; fls. pinkish, ¾ in. long; fr. ¾ in. long. Baja Calif.

jaliscana (Britt. & Rose) Böd. Cc; sts. cespitose, globose, 2 in. thick, tubercles in 13 and 21 spirals, cylindrical, 3/16 in. long, ⅛ in. diam; radial spines 30 or more, needle-shaped, white, to 5/16 in. long, central spines 4–8, dark-tipped, the lower hooked, to ½ in. long; fls. purplish, ⅜ in. across; fr. 5/16 in. long. Sw. Mex.

Johnstonii (Britt. & Rose) Orcutt. Mm; sts. simple, globose, to 8 in. thick, tubercles in 13 and 21 spirals, 4-angled above, to ½ in. long and ⅜ in. thick, axils with scant wool; radial spines 10–18, needle-shaped, whitish, darker-tipped, 5/16 in. long, central spines 2–6, stouter, straight or curved, dark, ⅜–1 in. long; fls. pinkish, to ¾ in. long; fr. 1 in. long. Nw. Mex.

Karwinskiana Mart. [*M. Fischeri* Pfeiff.]. ROYAL-CROSS. Mm; sts. simple or cespitose, globose to oblong, tubercles in 13 and 21 spirals, angled below, to 5/16 in. long and thick, axils with wool and brown-tipped bristles; radial spines 4–6, needle-shaped to awl-shaped, whitish, dark-tipped, to 1¼ in. long, central spine 0–1, similar; fls. cream with red, ¾ in. long; fr. ¾ in. long. S. Mex.

Kellerana Schmoll. Mc; sts. simple, to 5 in. high and 3 in. thick, tubercles in 13 and 21 spirals, cylindrical, ⅜ in. long, 5/16 in. in diam., axils with scant wool; radial spines 6, spreading, stout-needle-shaped, purplish, to ¾ in. long, central spine 0–1, similar; fls. magenta, ⅜ in. long; fr. ¾ in. long. Summer. Cent. Mex.

kewensis Salm-Dyck. Mc; sts. simple or cespitose, to 5 in. high and 3½ in. thick, tubercles in 8 and 13 spirals, conical, to 5/16 in. long and ⅝ in. in diam., axils woolly; spines 6, radial, spreading, stout-needle-shaped, at first dark, the lower to 1¼ in. long; fls. purplish, to ¾ in. long; fr. to ¾ in. long. Summer. Cent. Mex. Var. **Craigiana** Schmoll.

Tubercles only 3/16 in. in diam.; spines shorter and more spreading. Cent. Mex.

Klissingiana Böd. Mm; sts. simple or cespitose, to 6 in. high and 3½ in. thick, tubercles in 13 and 21 spirals, nearly cylindrical above, 3/16 in. long, 3/32 in. thick, axils with dense wool and sinuous bristles; radial spines 30–35, slender, white, to ¼ in. long, interlacing, central spines 2–5, stouter, to ¼ in. long; fls. rose, ⅜ in. long; fr. ½ in. long. N. Mex.

Knebeliana Böd. Cc; sts. simple or cespitose, to 2½ in. high and 2 in. thick, tubercles in 13 and 21 spirals, cylindrical, ¼ in. long, 5/32 in. thick, axils with 5–8, sinuous bristles; radial spines 20–25, bristlelike, white, ¼ in. long, central spines 4–7, stouter, reddish-brown, the lowest hooked, to ⅝ in. long; fls. yellow, ⅝ in. wide. Cent. Mex.

Kunthii: *M. elegans.*

Kunzeana Böd. & Quehl. Cc; sts. simple or cespitose, to 3½ in. high and 2½ in. thick, tubercles in 8 and 13 spirals, cylindrical, to ⅝ in. long and 3/16 in. in diam., axils with many slender bristles; radial spines 20–25, bristlelike, white, at first pubescent, to ⅜ in. long, central spines stouter, black-tipped, the lowest hooked, to ¾ in. long; fls. white or with pink, to ¾ in. long; fr. ⅝ in. long. Cent. Mex.

lanata (Britt. & Rose) Orcutt. Mc; sts. simple or cespitose, oblong, to 2 in. thick, tubercles in 13 and 21 or 21 and 34 spirals, to 5/32 in. long and 3/32 in. in diam., axils woolly; radial spines 12–20, needle-shaped, to 3/32 in. long, central spines rudimentary; fls. pink, ⅜ in. long; fr. 3/16 in. long, with few seeds. S. Mex. Intergrades with *M. elegans.*

lasiacantha Englem. [*M. denudata* (Engelm.) A. Berger]. Cc; sts. simple or cespitose, globose, to 1 in. thick, tubercles in 8 and 13 spirals, cylindrical, 5/32 in. long, 3/32 in. in diam., axils naked; spines 40–60, radial, bristlelike, white, pubescent, to 5/32 in. long; fls. white with red, ½ in. long; fr. to ¾ in. long. Spring. W. Tex., New Mex.

lenta K. Brandeg. Cc?; sts. cespitose, globose, to 2½ in. thick, tubercles in 13 and 21 spirals, to ⅜ in. long and 3/32 in. in diam., axils woolly; spines 30–40, radial, bristlelike, white or yellowish, to 3/16 in. long; fls. whitish, ¾ in. long; fr. ⅜ in. long, seeds few, tubercled(?). N. Mex.

Lloydii (Britt. & Rose) Orcutt. Mm; sts. simple, to 4 in. high and 3 in. wide, tubercles in 8 and 13 spirals, 4-angled, to ¼ in. long and thick, axils woolly; spines 3–4, spreading, awl-shaped, to ¼ in. long; fls. white with pink, to ⅝ in. across; fr. 5/16 in. long. Cent. Mex.

longicoma (Britt. & Rose) A. Berger. Cc; sts. cespitose, subglobose, to 2 in. thick, tubercles in 13 and 21 spirals, 5/32 in. long and thick, axils with long white hairs; radial spines 25 or more, capillary, flexuous, white, pubescent, to 5/16 in. long, central spines 4, thicker, brown, pubescent, 2-hooked, to ½ in. long; fls. white or pinkish; fr. ⅝ in. long. Cent. Mex.

longiflora (Britt. & Rose) A. Berger [*Krainzia longiflora* (Britt. & Rose) Backeb.]. Cph; sts. simple or cespitose, globose, to 1¼ in. thick, tubercles in 5 and 8 spirals, cylindrical, to ⅜ in. long, axils naked or slightly woolly; spines pubescent, radial spines 25–30, bristlelike, yellowish, to ½ in. long, central spines 4, stouter, reddish-brown, to ½ in. long, the lower 1 hooked; fls. pink, 1½ in. long, the tube ¾ in. long; fr. depressed, long-persistent (and dimorphic?). N. Mex.

longimamma DC. [*Dolichothele longimamma* (DC.) Britt. & Rose]. Sts. to 6 in. wide, tubercles 1–2½ in. long, to ½ in. in diam.; spines puberulent, pale yellow, becoming brown, weak-tipped, to 1 in. long, radial spines 6–10, stellate, central spines mostly 1; fls. to 3 in. long and nearly as wide, with solid column from ovary to tube. Summer. Cent. Mex. Cv. **'Globosa'** [*M. globosa* Link]. Radial spines to 12, central spines 2–3. Var. **sphaerica** (A. Dietr.) K. Brandeg. [*Dolichothele sphaerica* (A. Dietr.) Britt. & Rose]. Tubercles to 1 in. long and ¼ in. in diam.; spines glabrous, pale yellow, to 5/16 in. long, radial spines 12–15, stellate. Tex., n. Mex. Var. **uberiformis** (Zucc.) K. Schum. [*Dolichothele uberiformis* (Zucc.) Britt. & Rose]. Tubercles to 1¼ in. long; radial spines 4–5, central spine 0; fls. smaller. Cent. Mex.

Macdougalii: *M. Heyderi* var.

macrantha DC. Sts. simple, to 2 in. high and 6 in. thick, tubercles ovoid or somewhat 4-sided, axils woolly; spines 1–2, white to brownish, angled, to 2 in. long; fls. and fr. unknown. Mex.

magnimamma Haw. [*M. centricirrha* Lem.]. Mm; sts. mostly cespitose, globose, or depressed, to 4 in. thick, tubercles in 8 and 13 spirals, 4-sided, about ½ in. long and thick, axils woolly; spines 3–5, awl-shaped, recurved, black-tipped, unequal, the lower longer, to 1 in. long; fls. cream, to 1 in. long and across; fr. ¾ in. long. Cent. Mex.

Mainiae K. Brandeg. Cc; sts. simple or cespitose, globose or depressed, to 3 in. thick, tubercles in 8 and 13 spirals, cylindrical, to ⅝ in. long and ⅜ in. in diam., axils naked; spines often pubescent, radial spines 10–15, needle-shaped, yellowish, becoming chalky, to ⅜ in. long, central spines 1–3, stouter, hooked, dark-tipped, to ¾ in. long; fls. white with pink, to ¾ in. long; fr. globose to obovoid, to 5/16 in. long. Summer. S. Ariz. and nw. Mex.

mammillaris (L.) Karst. [*M. microthele* (K. Spreng.) Mühlenpf.]. Mm; sts. simple or cespitose, globose to oblong, to 8 in. high, tubercles in 8 and 13 spirals, nearly cylindrical, to ½ in. long and 5/16 in. in diam., axils slightly woolly; radial spines 10–16, needle-shaped, reddish, becoming gray, to 5/16 in. long, central spines 3–5, similar; fls. cream, to ½ in. long; fr. to ¾ in. long. Summer. Venezuela and nearby islands.

Martinezii Backeb. Sts. simple, cylindrical, to nearly 6 in. high and 3 in. thick, tubercles small, many, thick, axils woolly; radial spines about 20, very thin, white with yellow base, central spines 2, similar; fls. carmine. S. Mex.

mazatlanensis K. Schum. Cc; sts cespitose, to 5 in. high and 1½ in. thick, tubercles in 5 and 8 spirals, cylindrical, to 5/16 in. long and ⅜ in. in diam., axils with 0–2 bristles; radial spines 13–15, needle-shaped, white, to ⅜ in. long, central spines 3–4, brown-tipped, to ⅝ in. long; fls. red, 1¼ in. long; fr. to ¾ in. long. Nw. Mex.

meiacantha: *M. Heyderi* var.

melanocentra Poselg. Mm; sts. simple, subglobose, to 6 in. high, tubercles in 8 and 13 spirals, 4-angled, to ¾ in. long and ⅝ in. thick, axils at first woolly; radial spines 7–9, needle-shaped, gray, black-tipped, the upper to ¼ in. long, the lower to 1 in. long, central spine 1, stouter, black, becoming brown, ¾–2 in. long; fls. rose-red, ¾ in. long; fr. to 1¼ in. long. Spring. Tex., New Mex., n. Mex. Var. **Runyonii** (Britt. & Rose) R. T. Craig [*M. Runyonii* (Britt. & Rose) Böd., not (Britt. & Rose) V. L. Cory]. Central spine about ½ in. long. N. Mex. Close to *M. Heyderi*

Mendeliana (Bravo) Werderm. Mm; sts. simple, subglobose, to 3½ in. thick, tubercles in 13 and 21 spirals, nearly cylindrical above, 5/16 in. long, ¼ in. in diam., axils with wool and many long white hairs; radial spines capillary, short, white, central spines 2–4, needle-shaped, black-tipped, brownish, becoming gray, the lowest to ¾ in. long; fls. pink, ⅜ in. long; fr. ¾ in. long. Spring. Cent. Mex.

microcarpa Engelm. [*M. Milleri* (Britt. & Rose) Böd.]. Cc; sts. simple or few-branched, to 6 in. high and 2½ in. thick, tubercles in 13 and 21 spirals, cylindrical, about ¼ in. long and thick, axils naked; radial spines 20–30, needle-shaped, white, to ½ in. long, central spines 1–3, stouter, tan to black, 1 hooked, to ¾ in. long; fls. pink, 1 in. long, inner segms. acuminate; fr. dimorphic. Spring, summer. Se. Calif. to w. Tex., n. Mex.

microhelia Werderm. Cs; sts. simple or few-branched, to 6 in. high and 2 in. thick, tubercles in 8 and 13 spirals, ¼ in. long and thick, axils at first slightly woolly; radial spines about 50, spreading and recurved, bristlelike, yellow with brownish base and white tips, to ¼ in. long, central spines 0–4, needle-shaped, red to brown, to ½ in. long; fls. white to yellowish, to ¾ in. long; fr. to ½ in. long. Cent. Mex. Cv. **'Rubrispina'** is listed.

microheliopsis Werderm. Cs; sts. simple, to 5 in. high and 2 in. thick, tubercles in 8 and 13 spirals, dotted, 5/16 in. long and thick, axils at first slightly woolly; radial spines 30–40, fine-needle-shaped, whitish or yellowish, to 5/16 in. long, central spines 6–8, needle-shaped, brownish, to ½ in. long; fls. pale violet, ⅝ in. long; fr. pale, to ¾ in. long. Cent. Mex.

micromeris: *Epithelantha micromeris.*

microthele: *M. mammillaris;* but plants cult. as *M. microthele* are probably some other sp.

Miehiana Tiegel. Probably a form of *M. densispina* having more slender sts.

Milleri: *M. microcarpa.*

missouriensis: *Coryphantha missouriensis.*

Moellerana Böd. Cc; sts. simple, globose, to 2½ in. thick, tubercles in 8 and 13 spirals, 5/16 in. long and thick, axils naked; radial spines 35–40, needle-shaped, white, 5/16 in. long, central spines 8–9, stouter, yellow, reddish-brown below, the 4 lower hooked, to ¾ in. long; fls. cream to yellow, ⅝ in. wide; fr. greenish, ⅝ in. long. N. Mex.

Muehlenpfordtii C. F. Först. [*M. neopotosina* R. T. Craig]. Mm; sts. simple, to 4 in. high and 3 in. thick, tubercles in 13 and 21 spirals, angled, dotted, to 5/16 in. long and ¼ in. thick, axils with wool and bristles; radial spines 40–50, bristlelike, white, to ¼ in. long, central spines 4, needle-shaped, yellow, brown-tipped, the upper to ½ in. long, the lower to 1½ in. long; fls. purplish-red, ⅝ in. long; fr. to ¾ in. long. Spring, summer. Cent. Mex. Material offered as *M. potosina* may be this sp.

multiceps Salm-Dyck. Cc; sts. cespitose, globose to oblong, to 1 in. thick, tubercles in 8 and 13 spirals, 5/32 in. long and thick, axils with long, sinuous bristles; radial spines 30–50, capillary, pubescent, white, to 3/16 in. long, central spines 6–8, needle-shaped, reddish above, to 5/16 in. long; fls. yellowish; fr. ½ in. long. Spring. Tex., n. Mex.

multiformis (Britt. & Rose) Böd. Cc; sts. cespitose, globose to oblong, tubercles cylindrical, to 5/16 in. long, axils with wool and long bristles; radial spines 30 or more, needle-shaped, yellow, to 5/16 in. long, central spines 4, stouter, reddish above, to ⅜ in. long, the lower hooked; fls. purplish-red, to ⅜ in. long; fr. subglobose. N. Mex.

Mundtii K. Schum. Mc; sts. solitary, globose, to 3 in. thick, tubercles in 8 and 13 spirals, about ¼ in. long and thick, axils naked; radial spines 10–12, needle-shaped, white, dark-tipped, to $^3/_{16}$ in. long, central spines 2, stouter, brown, becoming gray, to ⅜ in. long; fls. carmine, ½ in. long. Cent. Mex.

mystax Mart. Mm; sts. mostly simple, to 6 in. high and 4 in. thick, tubercles in 13 and 21 spirals, 4–6-angled, to ⅝ in. long and $^5/_{16}$ in. thick, axils with wool and bristles; radial spines 5–10, needle-shaped, white, brown-tipped, to $^5/_{16}$ in. long, central spines 3–4, needle-shaped, purplish, 3 about ¾ in. long, 1 to 3 in. long, sinuate; fls. rose-purple, 1 in. long; fr. to 1 in. long. Cent. Mex.

napina J. Purpus. Sts. simple, subglobose, to 2½ in. thick, tubercles in 8 and 13 spirals, to ⅜ in. long and $^5/_{16}$ in. thick, axils naked or slightly woolly; radial spines 10–12, needle-shaped, yellowish, $^5/_{16}$ in. long, comblike, central spine 0–1, directed outward; fls. rose, 1½ in. across. S. Mex.

neocoronaria F. M. Knuth. Cc?; sts. cespitose, to 6 in. high and 3 in. thick, tubercles in 8 and 13 spirals, $^5/_{16}$ in. long, axils naked; radial spines 16–18, white, to ⅜ in. long, central spines 4–6, red, becoming gray, to ⅝ in. long, the lower hooked; fls. carmine, ¾ in. long. Cent. Mex.

neopalmeri R. T. Craig. Cc; sts. cespitose, to 5 in. high and 3 in. thick, tubercles in 8 and 13 spirals, to ¼ in. high and thick, axils with wool and bristles; radial spines 20–30, needle-shaped, white, to ¼ in. long, central spines 3–5, brownish, mostly straight, to $^5/_{16}$ in. long; fls. cream, to ¾ in. long; fr. to 1 in. long. Spring. Islands of Baja Calif.

neopotosina: *M. Muehlenpfordtii.*

nigra C. A. Ehrenb. Sts. to 4 in. high and 3 in. thick, tubercles ovoid-conic, to ½ in. high, axils slightly woolly; radial spines 16–18, bristlelike, brownish, becoming white, dark-tipped, the upper to ⅛ in. long, the lower to ¼ in. long, central spines 4–7, needle-shaped, dark red, the lower ones hooked; fls. and fr. unknown. Mex.

nivosa Link. Mm; sts. cespitose, to 7 in. thick, tubercles in 8 and 13, 11 and 17, or 13 and 21 spirals, to ⅝ in. long and ⅜ in. thick, axils densely woolly; spines yellow, becoming brown, radial spines 6–8, needle-shaped, spreading, to 1¼ in. long, central spine 1, stouter, to ¾ in. long; fls. cream or yellowish, to ¾ in. long; fr. to ⅝ in. long. W. Indies.

Nunezii (Britt. & Rose) Orcutt. Cc?; sts. mostly simple, to 6 in. high and 3 in. thick, tubercles in 13 and 21 spirals, cylindrical, about ¼ in. long and thick, axils with 8–10 bristles; radial spines 25–30, needle-shaped, white, ¼ in. long, central spines 2–6, mostly 4, awl-shaped, yellowish, dark-tipped, to ⅝ in. long; fls. rose, ⅝ in. across; fr. greenish, to 1 in. long. S. Mex.

obscura Hildm. [*M. Wagnerana* Böd.]. Mm; sts. simple, to 3 in. high and 4½ in. thick, tubercles in 13 and 21 spirals, pyramidal, about $^5/_{16}$ in. long and thick, axils at first woolly; radial spines 6–8, needle-shaped, whitish, to ⅝ in. long, central spines 2–4, awl-shaped, rough, reddish, becoming gray, the lower 1–2 in. long, sometimes tortuous; fls. yellowish, ⅝ in. across. Cent. Mex.

occidentalis (Britt. & Rose) Böd. Cc; sts. cespitose, to 6 in. high and 1¼ in. thick, tubercles in 5 and 8 spirals, about ¼ in. long and thick, axils sometimes with bristles; radial spines 12–18, needle-shaped, white or yellowish, to $^5/_{16}$ in. long, central spines 4–5, stouter, reddish-brown, to ½ in. long, the lower 1 mostly hooked; fls. pink to purple, ⅜ in. long. W. Mex.

Ochoterenae (Bravo) Werderm. Mc; sts. simple, depressed-globose, to 3 in. thick, tubercles in 13 and 21 spirals, conical, keeled, about ¼ in. long and thick, axils naked; radial spines 17–18, needle-shaped, white or yellowish, to $^5/_{16}$ in. long, central spines 5–6, stouter, yellowish, becoming brown, to ¾ in. long; fls. white with rose, ⅜ in. long; fr. ¾ in. long. S. Mex.

ocotillensis R. T. Craig. Mm; sts. simple, globose, to 3 in. thick, tubercles in 13 and 21 spirals, ovoid, keeled, to $^5/_{16}$ in. long and ¼ in. in diam., axils naked; radial spines 2–4, needle-shaped, white, to ⅜ in. long, central spines 1–3, stouter, dark, the upper ⅛–⅝ in. long, the lower ½–1½ in. long; fls. cream; fr. ¾ in. long. Cent. Mex.

Oliviae: *M. Grahamii* var.

Orcuttii Böd. Mm; sts. simple, subglobose, to 3 in. thick, tubercles in 13 and 21 spirals, ovoid, keeled, about ¼ in. long and thick, axils woolly; radial spines 6–8, capillary, white, to $^3/_{32}$ in. long, soon deciduous, central spines 4, needle-shaped, black, becoming gray, the upper to ⅜ in. long, the lower to ¾ in. long; fls. carmine, ½ in. long; fr. ½ in. long. S. Mex.

Ortiz-Rubiona (Bravo) Werderm. Ml; sts. cespitose, subglobose, to 4 in. thick, tubercles in 8 and 13 spirals, cylindrical, to ¾ in. long and ⅜ in. in diam., axils with many exserted hairs; radial spines 25–30, bristlelike, white, to ⅝ in. long, interlacing, central spines 4–6, needle-shaped, white, to ⅝ in. long; fls. white to pink, 1½ in. long. Cent. Mex.

pacifica: *M. Baxterana.*

Painteri Rose. Cc; sts. simple, globose, to 1 in. thick, tubercles in 8 and 13 spirals, cylindrical, ¼ in. long, $^3/_{32}$ in. in diam.; spines pubescent, radial spines 20 or more, bristlelike, white, to $^3/_{16}$ in. long, central spines 4–5, stouter, dark brown, to ⅜ in. long, the lower hooked; fls. white, to ⅝ in. long; fr. ⅜ in. long. Spring. Cent. Mex.

Parkinsonii C. A. Ehrenb. [*M. dealbata* A. Dietr.; *M. Dietrichiae* Tiegel]. Mm; sts. cespitose, to 6 in. high and 3 in. thick, forking, tubercles in 8 and 13 spirals, pyramidal, dotted, to ⅜ in. long and ¼ in. thick, axils with dense wool and sinuous bristles; radial spines 30–35, needle-shaped, white, to ¼ in. long, central spines 2–4, awl-shaped, angled, dark-tipped, the upper to $^5/_{16}$ in. long, the lower to 1½ in. long; fls. white with pink, to ⅝ in. long; fr. ⅜ in. long. Cent. Mex. Var. **brevispina** R. T. Craig. Tubercles in 13 and 21 spirals; central spines to $^3/_{16}$ in. long.

pectinifera (Rümpler) A. Web. [*Solisia pectinata* (Stein) Britt. & Rose]. S; sts. cespitose, to 2½ in. high and 1½ in. thick, tubercles in 8 and 13 spirals, to $^5/_{32}$ in. long and thick, axils naked; spines 20–40, appressed, united at base, white, to $^3/_{32}$ in. long; fls. small, yellowish; fr. ¼ in. long. S. Mex.

peninsularis (Britt. & Rose) Orcutt. Mm; sts. simple or cespitose, depressed, 1½ in. wide, tubercles in 5 and 8 spirals, 4-angled, $^5/_{16}$ in. long, $^3/_{16}$ in. thick, axils at first woolly; spines 4–8, stout-needle-shaped, yellowish, ¼ in. long; fls. greenish-yellow, ⅝ in. long. S. Baja Calif.

pentacantha Pfeiff. An incompletely known sp., perhaps the same as *M. flavovirens.*

perbella Hildm. Mc; sts. simple or forking, to 3½ in. high and 2½ in. thick, tubercles in 13 and 21 spirals, about $^3/_{16}$ in. long and thick, axils woolly; radial spines 14–18, needle-shaped, white, to ⅛ in. long, central spines 2, awl-shaped, white, the upper longer, to ¼ in. long; fls. carmine, ⅜ in. long; fr. ⅝ in. long. Cent. Mex. Cv. **'Lanata'** is listed. Perhaps a var. of *M. Haageana.*

petrophila K. Brandeg. Mm; sts. cespitose, globose, to 6 in. thick, tubercles in 8 and 13 spirals, faintly angled, ⅜ in. long, ¼ in. in diam., axils with tan wool and 3–6 bristles; radial spines 8–10, needle-shaped, spreading, to ⅝ in. long, central spines 1–2, stouter, brown, to ¾ in. long; fls. greenish-yellow, ¾ in. long. S. Baja Calif.

Petterssonii Hildm. [*M. Heeseana* McDow.]. Mm; sts. simple or cespitose, to 8 in. high and 5 in. thick, tubercles in 13 and 21 spirals, ovoid, keeled, ⅜ in. long and thick, axils woolly; radial spines 10–12, needle-shaped, white, the upper ⅛ in. long, the lower to ⅝ in. long, central spines 1–4, stouter, tan, becoming pale, the upper to ¾ in. long, the lower to 2 in. long; fls. pink, 1 in. long. Cent. Mex.

Pfeifferi: *M. fuscata.*

phaeacantha Lem. Mc; sts. simple, globose, to 3 in. thick, tubercles in 8 and 13 spirals, to $^5/_{16}$ in. long and thick, axils with wool and long bristles; radial spines 16–20, bristlelike, white, $^3/_{16}$ in. long, central spines 4, in the form of a cross, awl-shaped, black, to ⅝ in. long; fls. pink; fr. ⅝ in. long. Mex.

phellosperma: *M. tetrancistra.*

phitauiana Baxter. Cc; sts. cespitose, to 7 in. high and 2½ in. thick, tubercles in 8 and 13 spirals, to $^5/_{16}$ in. long and thick, axils with to 20 exserted bristles; radial spines 18–24, needle-shaped, white or brown-tipped, to ½ in. long, central spines 4, stouter, reddish-brown or white at base, to ⅜ in. long, the lower hooked; fls. pink, to ⅝ in. long; fr. ⅜ in. long. S. Baja Calif.

phymatothele A. Berger. Mm; sts. mostly simple, to 3 in. high and 3½ in. thick, tubercles in 8 and 13 spirals, keeled, to ⅝ in. long and ¾ in. in diam., axils at first woolly; radial spines 3–7, spreading, needle-shaped, grayish, brown-tipped, the upper to ¼ in. long, the lower to 1½ in. long, central spine mostly 1, stouter, red, deflexed, to ¾ in. long; fls. carmine, to ⅝ in. long. Cent. Mex. Var. **Trohartii** (Hildm.) R. T. Craig [*M. Trohartii* Hildm.]. Sts. cespitose; central spines 1–2; fls. purplish-pink.

pilispina J. Purpus. Cc?; sts. cespitose, globose, to 1½ in. thick, tubercles cylindrical, papillose, to ⅜ in. long and ¼ in. in diam., axils with long curly hairs; spines puberulent, outer radial spines capillary, curly, white, inner 4–5, spreading, awl-shaped, brown-tipped, ¼ in. long, central spine 1, similar; fls. and fr. unknown. Cent. Mex.

plumosa A. Web. FEATHER CACTUS. Cc; sts. cespitose, globose, to 3 in. thick, hidden by spines, tubercles in 8 and 13 spirals, cylindrical, ½ in. long, to ⅛ in. in diam., axils woolly; spines to 40, radial, plumose, soft, white, to ¼ in. long; fls. greenish-white, ⅝ in. long. N. Mex.

polyedra Mart. [*M. villifera* Otto]. Mm; sts. simple or cespitose, globose to oblong, to 4 in. thick, tubercles in 13 and 21 spirals, angular, to ½ in. long and thick, axils woolly, later with bristles; spines 2–6, needle-shaped, dark, becoming gray, the upper to $^5/_{32}$ in. long, the lower to 1 in. long; fls. pink, to 1 in. long; fr. to ¾ in. long. Spring. S. Mex.

polythele Mart. Mm; sts. mostly simple, to 20 in. high and 4 in. thick, tubercles in 13 and 21 spirals, nearly cylindrical, to ½ in. long and ⅜ in. thick, axils at first woolly; spines 1–4, needle-shaped, brown, the lower longest, to 1 in. long; fls. rose to carmine, to ¾ in. long. Cent. Mex.

potosiana Jacobi: probably *Coryphantha clavata;* but plants listed as *M. potosiana* or *M. potosina* may be *M. Muehlenpfordtii.*

Pottsii Scheer. Cs?; sts. cespitose, to 6 in. high and 1½ in. thick, tubercles in 8 and 13 spirals, $^{3}/_{16}$ in. long and thick, axils slightly woolly; radial spines to 35, needle-shaped, white, to $^{3}/_{16}$ in. long, interlacing, central spines 7–9, stouter, yellowish to purple, the upper longest and often curved, to ⅜ in. long; fls. rose, to ⅜ in. long. W. Tex., n. Mex.

Pringlei (J. Coult.) K. Brandeg. LEMON-BALL. Mc; sts. simple, to 6½ in. high and 3 in. thick, tubercles in 13 and 21 spirals, to ⅜ in. long and ¼ in. in diam., axils woolly; spines needle-shaped, yellow, often curved, radial spines 15–20, to $^{5}/_{16}$ in. long, central spines mostly 6, stouter, to ¾ in. long; fls. red, to ⅜ in. long; fr. to ⅝ in. long. Cent. Mex. Var. **columnaris** Schmoll. More cylindrical; spines shorter, more slender.

prolifera (Mill.) Haw. LITTLE-CANDLES, SILVER CLUSTER CACTUS. Cc; sts. cespitose, to 2½ in. high and 1½ in. thick, tubercles in 5 and 8 spirals, to $^{5}/_{16}$ in. long and $^{3}/_{16}$ in. thick, axils with wool and exserted bristles; radial spines to 40, bristlelike, white, to ⅜ in. long, central spines 5–9, needle-shaped, pubescent, yellowish, to $^{5}/_{16}$ in. long; fls. yellowish, to ⅝ in. long; fr. few-seeded, to ⅜ in. long. Spring. W. Indies.

pseudocrucigera R. T. Craig. Mm; sts. simple, depressed, to 2 in. thick, tubercles in 8 and 13 spirals, 4-angled, ¼ in. long and thick, axils woolly; radial spines 12–13, needle-shaped, white, to $^{3}/_{32}$ in. long, central spines 4, awl-shaped, white, dark-tipped, to $^{5}/_{32}$ in. long; fls. white, ½ in. long; fr. ¾ in. long. Spring. Cent. Mex.

pseudoperbella Quehl. Mc; sts. simple or few-branched, globose to oblong, to 6 in. thick, tubercles in 13 and 21 spirals, ¼ in. long, ⅛ in. in diam., axils slightly woolly; radial spines 20–30, bristlelike, white, to ⅛ in. long, central spines 2, awl-shaped, brown, the upper longer, $^{3}/_{16}$ in. long; fls. carmine, ⅝ in. long. Cent. Mex.

pubispina Böd. Cc; sts. simple, globose, to 1½ in. long, tubercles in 13 and 21 spirals, cylindrical, $^{5}/_{16}$ in. long, $^{3}/_{32}$ in. in diam., axils with some wool and slender bristles; spines pubescent, radial spines 15, capillary, white, tortuous, to ½ in. long, central spines mostly 4, dark, to ⅜ in. long, the lower hooked; fls. white, ¾ in. long. Cent. Mex.

pygmaea (Britt. & Rose) A. Berger. Cc; sts. simple or cespitose, globose, to 1¼ in. thick, tubercles in 13 and 21 spirals, cylindrical, to ⅜ in. long and $^{5}/_{32}$ in. in diam., axils with sinuous, slender bristles; radial spines to 15, bristlelike, slightly puberulent, white, to ½ in. long, central spines 4, needle-shaped, yellow, to $^{5}/_{16}$ in. long, the lower hooked; fls. cream, ½ in. long. Cent. Mex.

pyrrhocephala Scheidw. Mm; sts. simple or cespitose, oblong, to 4 in. high, tubercles in 13 and 21 spirals, keeled, ⅜ in. long, ¼ in. in diam., axils with wool and bristles; spines 4–6, spreading, awl-shaped, dark, to $^{5}/_{32}$ in. long; fls. pink, ¾ in. long; fr. ¾ in. long. Cent. Mex.

Rekoi (Britt. & Rose) Vaup. Cc; sts. simple, to 5 in. high and 2½ in. thick, tubercles in 8 and 13 spirals, cylindrical, with watery to semi-milky sap, to ⅜ in. long, axils with wool and 1–8 bristles; radial spines 20, needle-shaped, white, to ¼ in. long, central spines 4, stouter, brown, to ⅝ in. long, the lower curved or hooked; fls. purple, ⅝ in. long; fr. ½ in. long. S. Mex. Var. **pseudorekoi** (Böd.) R. T. Craig. Central spines 4–7; fls. red.

rhodantha Link & Otto. Mc; sts. simple or cespitose, to 1 ft. high and 4 in. thick, tubercles in 13 and 21 spirals, cylindrical, to ½ in. long and $^{5}/_{16}$ in. in diam., axils with wool and bristles; radial spines 16–20, needle-shaped, white and yellow, to ⅜ in. long, central spines 4–7, stouter, white, yellow, red, or brown, straight or curved, to 1 in. long; fls. purplish-pink, to ¾ in. long; fr. 1 in. long. Cent. Mex. Cvs. **'Chrysacantha'**, **'Pfeifferi'**, **'Rubra'**, and **'Sulphurea'** are listed.

Ritterana Böd. Mm; sts. simple, globose, to 2½ in. thick, tubercles in 13 and 21 spirals, cylindrical above, dotted, ¼ in. long and ⅛ in. in diam., axils with wool and strong bristles; radial spines 18–20, bristlelike, white, mostly lateral, about ¼ in. long, central spines 1–2, awl-shaped, white to nearly black, to ⅜ in. long; fls. white with rose, ½ in. long; fr. ½ in. long. N. Mex.

roseoalba Böd. Mm; sts. simple, to 2½ in. high and 7 in. wide, tubercles in 8 and 13 spirals, strongly 4-angled, to ⅝ in. long and $^{5}/_{16}$ in. thick, axils at first slightly woolly; spines 4–6, needle-shaped, to ⅝ in. long, the upper 1–2 small, often deciduous; fls. white with pink, ⅝ in. long; fr. ⅝ in. long. Ne. Mex.

Ruestii Quehl. Mc; sts. simple or cespitose, to 3 in. high and 2 in. thick, tubercles in 13 and 21 spirals, about ¼ in. long and thick, axils with wool and bristles; radial spines 16–20, needle-shaped, white, to ¼ in. long, central spines mostly 4, stouter, red, to $^{5}/_{16}$ in. long; fls. carmine, ¾ in. long. Honduras and Guatemala.

Runyonii: see *M. melanocentra* var. and *Coryphantha macromeris* var.

Saffordii: *M. Carretii.*

Sartorii J. Purpus. Mm; sts. cespitose, globose to oblong, to 5 in. thick, tubercles in 8 and 13 spirals, strongly 4-angled, dotted, to ½ in. long, axils woolly; radial spines mostly 4, needle-shaped, brown, to $^{5}/_{16}$ in. long, central spines 0 or 1 to several, similar; fls. carmine, to ¾ in. long; fr. ⅝ in. long. Cent. Mex.

Scheidweilerana Otto. Cc; sts. cespitose, about 2 in. high and 1½ in. thick, tubercles in 8 and 13 spirals, cylindrical, ¼ in. long, axils woolly; spines pubescent, radial spines 25–30, bristlelike, white, to ½ in. long, central spines 1–4, needle-shaped, dark, the lower longest and hooked; fls. rose, to ⅝ in. across. Cent. Mex.

Schelhasii Pfeiff. Cc; sts. cespitose, about 2½ in. high and 1½ in. thick, tubercles in 8 and 13 spirals, cylindrical, ¾ in. long, $^{5}/_{16}$ in. thick, axils slightly woolly; radial spines 15–20, bristlelike, white, to ⅜ in. long, central spines 3, reddish-brown, the upper 2 bristlelike, shorter, the lower stouter, hooked, to ¾ in. long; fls. white with rose, to 1 in. long. Cent. Mex.

Schiedeana C. A. Ehrenb. [*M. dumetorum* J. Purpus]. Cc; sts. cespitose, to 4 in. high and 1½ in. thick, tubercles in 13 and 21 spirals, cylindrical, to ⅜ in. long and $^{5}/_{32}$ in. in diam., axillary wool exceeding tubercles; spines to about 75, radial, in several series, bristlelike, puberulent, white, yellow-tipped, to $^{3}/_{16}$ in. long; fls. white, to ¾ in. long; fr. to 1 in. long. Cent. Mex.

Schmollii (Bravo) Werderm. Sts. simple, depressed-globose, to 3 in. thick, tubercles in 8 and 13 spirals, with watery sap, axils naked; radial spines to 25, needle-shaped, white, to $^{3}/_{16}$ in. long, central spines 11–15, stouter, yellow, to ⅜ in. long; fls. yellow. S. Mex. Plants so listed are often *M. elegans.*

Schumannii Hildm. [*Bartschella Schumannii* (Hildm.) Britt. & Rose]. B; sts. cespitose, to 4 in. high and 2 in. thick, tubercles in 8 and 13 spirals, crowded, subrhombic, depressed at apex, to ¼ in. long and ½ in. thick, axils woolly; spines needle-shaped, white, brown-tipped, radial spines 7–15, to ½ in. long, central spines usually 1, mostly hooked, to ¾ in. long; fls. purple, to 1½ in. long. Summer. S. Baja Calif.

Seideliana Quehl. Cc; sts. cespitose, to 3 in. high and 2 in. thick, tubercles in 8 and 13 spirals, cylindrical, ⅜ in. long, $^{3}/_{16}$ in. in diam., axils naked; spines white, at first pubescent, radial spines 18–25, bristlelike, to $^{5}/_{16}$ in. long, central spines 3–4, needle-shaped, brown-tipped, the lower hooked, to ⅝ in. long; fls. yellow, to ¾ in. long; fr. 1¼ in. long. Summer. N. Mex.

sempervivi DC. [*M. caput-Medusae* Otto]. Mm; sts. simple or cespitose, subglobose, to 4 in. thick, tubercles in 13 and 21 spirals, pyramidal, ⅜ in. long and ¼ in. thick, axils woolly; radial spines 3–7, capillary, white, to ⅛ in. long, usually soon shed, central spines 2–4, awl-shaped, brownish, $^{5}/_{32}$ in. long; fls. white, ⅜ in. long; fr. $^{5}/_{16}$ in. long. Cent. Mex.

Sheldonii (Britt. & Rose) Böd. Cc; sts. cespitose, to 10 in. high and 2½ in. thick, tubercles in 8 and 13 spirals, $^{5}/_{16}$ in. long, ¼ in. thick, axils naked; radial spines 10–15, needle-shaped, dark-tipped, to $^{5}/_{16}$ in. long, central spines 1–3, stouter, reddish-brown, to ½ in. long, the lower hooked; fls. pink, ¾ in. long; fr. to 1¼ in. long. Spring, summer. Nw. Mex. Perhaps a var. of *M. microcarpa.*

Shurliana: *M. Blossfeldiana* var.

sinistrohamata Böd. Cc; sts. simple, globose, to 2 in. thick, tubercles in 13 and 21 spirals, cylindrical, $^{5}/_{16}$ in. long, $^{5}/_{32}$ in. thick, axils naked; radial spines 20 or more, needle-shaped, white or yellowish, to ⅜ in. long, central spines 4, stouter, yellow, the lowermost hooked, to ⅝ in. long; fls. creamy, ⅝ in. long. N. Mex.

Solisii (Britt. & Rose) Böd. Cc; sts. simple or cespitose, to 8 in. high and 4 in. thick, tubercles in 13 and 21 spirals, to ⅜ in. long and thick, axils with sinuous bristles; radial spines 20–25, needle-shaped, white, to ⅜ in. long, central spines 3–6, stouter, yellowish, dark-tipped, the lower one longest, hooked, to ¾ in. long; fls. rose, ⅝ in. long; fr. to ¾ in. long. Cent. Mex.

sonorensis R. T. Craig. Mm; sts. simple or cespitose, globose, to 4 in. thick, tubercles quadrangular-ovoid, to ⅝ in. long and ¾ in. thick, axils with wool and sometimes bristles; radial spines 8–15, needle-shaped, white, to ¾ in. long, central spines 1–4, needle-shaped to awl-shaped, reddish-brown, $^{3}/_{16}$–2 in. long; fls. pink, ¾ in. long; fr. ½ in. long. Spring. Nw. Mex. Var. **Hiltonii** R. T. Craig. Central spines 1–3, to ⅝ in. long.

sphacelata Mart. Cc; sts. cespitose, to 8 in. high and 1½ in. thick, tubercles in 5 and 8 spirals, cylindrical, ¼ in. long and thick, axils with wool and sometimes bristles; spines white, dark-tipped, radial spines

10–15, needle-shaped, to $\frac{5}{16}$ in. long, central spines 1–4, stouter, to $\frac{1}{4}$ in. long; fls. dark red, $\frac{5}{8}$ in. long. S. Mex.

sphaerica: *M. longimamma* var.

spinosissima Lem. Mc?; sts. simple, to 1 ft. high and 4 in. thick, tubercles in 13 and 21 spirals, to $\frac{1}{4}$ in. long and $\frac{5}{32}$ in. thick, axils with wool and bristles; radial spines 20–30, bristlelike, white, to $\frac{3}{8}$ in. long, interlacing, central spines 7–15, needle-shaped, white to red, to $\frac{3}{4}$ in. long, rarely 1 of them hooked; fls. pink to purplish, to $\frac{3}{4}$ in. long; fr. $\frac{3}{4}$ in. long. Cent. Mex. Named vars. are mostly spine-color forms. Cv. 'Sanguinea' is listed.

Standleyi (Britt. & Rose) Orcutt. Mm; sts. simple or cespitose, subglobose, to 6 in. thick, tubercles in 13 and 21 spirals, about $\frac{5}{16}$ in. long and thick, axils with wool and bristles; radial spines 16–19, needle-shaped, white, brown-tipped, to $\frac{5}{16}$ in. long, central spines 4, stouter, brown, to $\frac{5}{16}$ in. long; fls. purplish, $\frac{1}{2}$ in. wide; fr. $\frac{5}{8}$ in. long. Spring. Sonora (Mex.).

stella-aurata: *M. elongata.*

supertexta: *M. elegans* var.

surculosa Böd. Cc; sts. cespitose, globose, $1\frac{1}{2}$ in. thick, tubercles in 5 and 8 spirals, cylindrical, dotted, $\frac{5}{16}$ in. long, $\frac{5}{32}$ in. in diam., axils naked or slightly woolly; radial spines to 15, needle-shaped, white or yellowish, to $\frac{3}{8}$ in. long, central spine 1, reddish-brown, hooked, to $\frac{3}{4}$ in. long; fls. yellow, to $\frac{3}{4}$ in. across. N. Mex.

Swinglei (Britt. & Rose) Böd. Probably a var. or form of *M. Sheldonii,* having sometimes axillary bristles, and perianth segms. and fr. shorter.

tarajensis: a listed name of no botanical standing for *M. Hahniana* var. *Giseliana.*

tetracantha Salm-Dyck [*M. dolichocentra* Lam.]. RUBY-DUMPLING. Mc; sts. simple or cespitose, to 12 in. high and 5 in. thick, tubercles in 13 and 21 spirals, 4-sided, to $\frac{3}{8}$ in. long and $\frac{5}{32}$ in. thick, axils woolly; radial spines 0 or a few deciduous bristles, central spines mostly 4, needle-shaped, sometimes curved, reddish, becoming gray, the lower longest, to $1\frac{1}{4}$ in. long; fls. red, $\frac{3}{4}$ in. long; fr. to 1 in. long. Cent. Mex. Var. **Galeottii** (Scheidw.) Borg [*M. Galeottii* Scheidw.]. Axils naked; spines recurved, yellowish.

tetrancistra Engelm. [*M. phellosperma* Engelm.; *Phellosperma tetrancistra* (Engelm.) Britt. & Rose]. Cph; sts. simple or cespitose, to 10 in. high and 3 in. thick, tubercles in 8 and 13 spirals, cylindrical, to $\frac{5}{8}$ in. long, $\frac{1}{4}$ in. in diam., axils with wool and bristles; radial spines 30–60, in 2 series, bristlelike to needle-shaped, white or brown-tipped, to $\frac{3}{8}$ in. long, central spines 3–4, needle-shaped, dark, 1 or all of them hooked, to $\frac{1}{2}$ in. long; fls. rose, to $1\frac{1}{2}$ in. long; fr. to 1 in. long. Se. Calif., s. Nev., w. Ariz., n. Mex.

Thornberi Orcutt [*M. fasciculata* of auth., not Engelm.]. Cc; sts. solitary but individual plants in clumps, to 4 in or rarely $16\frac{1}{2}$ in. high and $1\frac{1}{2}$ in. thick, tubercles in 5 and 8 spirals, cylindrical, to $\frac{1}{4}$ in. long, axils naked; radial spines 13–20, needle-shaped, white, $\frac{1}{4}$ in. long, central spine 1, hooked, brown, to $\frac{3}{4}$ in. long; fls. reddish to purplish, to $1\frac{1}{4}$ in. long; fr. dimorphic. Spring. S. Ariz. and n. Sonora.

tolimensis R. T. Craig. Similar to *M. mystax* and perhaps a var. of it, but having central spines 5–7, variable in length. Said also to approach *M. compressa.*

trichacantha K. Schum. Cc; sts. simple, globose to oblong, to 2 in. thick, tubercles in 13 and 21 spirals, cylindrical, to $\frac{3}{8}$ in. long and $\frac{3}{16}$ in. in diam., axils with slender bristles; spines needle-shaped, pubescent, radial spines 15–18, yellow above, to $\frac{5}{16}$ in. long, interlacing, central spines mostly 2, stouter, brown, the lower hooked, to $\frac{1}{2}$ in. long; fls. yellowish, to $\frac{5}{8}$ in. long; fr. $\frac{3}{8}$ in. long. Cent. Mex.

Trohartii: *M. phymatothele* var.

uncinata Zucc. Mm; sts. simple, to 3 in. high and 4 in. thick, tubercles in 8 and 13 spirals, to $\frac{3}{8}$ in. long and thick, axils at first woolly; radial spines 4–7, thick-needle-shaped, white, black-tipped, to $\frac{1}{4}$ in. long, the upper shorter, central spine usually 1, awl-shaped, hooked, to $\frac{1}{2}$ in. long; fls. pink, to $\frac{3}{4}$ in. long. Cent. Mex.

Vaupeliana: a listed name of no botanical standing for *Coryphantha Vaupeliana;* but see also *M. Vaupelii.*

Vaupelii Tiegel. Mm; sts. simple, to $1\frac{1}{2}$ in. high and $2\frac{1}{2}$ in. thick, tubercles in 13 and 21 spirals, dotted, to $\frac{1}{4}$ in. long and thick, axils with wool and bristles; radial spines 16–21, needle-shaped, white, to $\frac{1}{4}$ in. long, central spines 2–4, awl-shaped, brown, the lower longest, to $\frac{5}{8}$ in. long; fls. pink, $\frac{3}{4}$ in. long; fr. $\frac{5}{8}$ in. long. S. Mex.

Viereckii Böd. Cc; sts. mostly simple, globose, to $1\frac{1}{2}$ in. thick, tubercles in 8 and 13 spirals, cylindrical, to $\frac{3}{8}$ in. long and $\frac{1}{8}$ in. in diam., axils with wool and 8–10 bristles; spines 15–18, radial, needle-shaped, the outer white, to $\frac{3}{16}$ in. long, the inner yellowish, to $\frac{1}{2}$ in. long; fls. cream, $\frac{1}{2}$ in. long. N. Mex.

villifera: *M. polyedra.*

viperina J. Purpus. Cs; sts. decumbent, branching laterally, to 1 ft. long or more and $\frac{3}{4}$ in. thick, tubercles in 3 and 5 spirals, cylindrical, to $\frac{3}{16}$ in. long and $\frac{1}{8}$ in. in diam., axils naked or perhaps sometimes with hairs; spines 15–30, radial, recurved, needle-shaped, white to yellow or dark; fls. carmine, $\frac{5}{8}$ in. long; fr. $\frac{5}{16}$ in. long. S. Mex.

viridiflora: *M. Wrightii.*

vivipara: *Coryphantha vivipara.* Var. **aggregata:** *Echinocereus triglochidiatus* var. *melanacanthus,* but material sold as var. *aggregata* is probably *Coryphantha vivipara* var. *bisbeeana.* Var. **chlorantha:** *Coryphantha vivipara* var. *deserti.*

Wagnerana: *M. obscura.*

Waltheri: *M. Heyderi* var. *hemisphaerica.*

Webbiana: *M. crocidiata.*

Wiesingeri Böd. Mc; sts. simple, to $1\frac{1}{2}$ in. high and 3 in. thick, tubercles in 16 and 26 spirals, weakly angled, to $\frac{3}{8}$ in. long and $\frac{5}{32}$ in. thick, axils naked or with 1–2 thin bristles; radial spines 18–20, needle-shaped, white, to $\frac{1}{4}$ in. long, central spines mostly 4, stouter, reddish-brown, to $\frac{1}{4}$ in. long; fls. rose, $\frac{1}{2}$ in. long; fr. $\frac{3}{8}$ in. long. Cent. Mex.

Wilcoxii: *M. Wrightii.*

Wildii A. Dietr. FISHHOOK PINCUSHION CACTUS. Cc; sts. cespitose, to 6 in. high and $2\frac{1}{2}$ in. thick, axils with 1 to several hairs; spines pubescent, radial spines 8–10, bristlelike, white, to $\frac{5}{16}$ in. long, central spines 3–4, needle-shaped, yellowish, becoming brown, to $\frac{3}{8}$ in. long, the lower hooked; fls. white, $\frac{1}{2}$ in. long. Cent. Mex.

Winterae Böd. Mm; sts. simple, hemispherical, to 12 in. thick; tubercles in 8 and 13 spirals, 4-angled, to $\frac{5}{8}$ in. long and 1 in. thick, axils woolly; spines 4, needle-shaped, yellowish, brown-tipped, to $1\frac{1}{4}$ in. long, lateral spines to $\frac{5}{8}$ in. long; fls. yellowish, to $1\frac{1}{4}$ in. long. N. Mex.

Winterana: a listed name of no botanical standing, perhaps for *M. Winterae.*

woburnensis Scheer. Mm; sts. cespitose, to 2 in. high and $1\frac{1}{4}$ in. thick, tubercles in 8 and 13 spirals, pyramidal, to $\frac{3}{8}$ in. long and $\frac{5}{16}$ in. thick, axils woolly; spines needle-shaped, whitish, with brown tips, radial spines 9, to $\frac{3}{16}$ in. long, central spines 1–3, $\frac{1}{4}$ in. long; fls. yellow with red, to $\frac{3}{4}$ in. long; fr. to 1 in. long. Guatemala.

Woodsii R. T. Craig. Mm; sts. simple, subglobose, to 3 in. thick, tubercles in 13 and 21 spirals, keeled, $\frac{1}{4}$ in. long and thick, axils woolly and with bristles to 1 in. long; radial spines 25–30, capillary, sinuous, white, to $\frac{5}{16}$ in. long, central spines 2 or 4, needle-shaped, white, black-tipped, the lower to $\frac{5}{8}$ in. long, the upper to $\frac{3}{16}$ in. long; fls. pink, $\frac{1}{2}$ in. long; fr. $\frac{5}{8}$ in. long. Spring. Cent. Mex.

Wrightii Engelm. [*M. viridiflora* (Britt. & Rose) Böd.; *M. Wilcoxii* Toumey]. Cc; sts. simple, subglobose, to 3 in. thick, tubercles in 8 and 13 spirals, cylindrical, to $\frac{5}{8}$ in. long and $\frac{5}{32}$ in. in diam., axils naked; spines needle-shaped, pubescent, radial spines 12–14, white, dark-tipped, to $\frac{1}{2}$ in. long, central spines 2 or 4, stouter, dark, to $\frac{1}{2}$ in. long, one hooked; fls. purplish, 1 in. long; fr. ovoid, to 1 in. long. Summer. W. Tex., New Mex., n. Mex.

Zahniana Böd. & F. Ritter. Mm; sts. simple, to $2\frac{1}{2}$ in. high and 4 in. thick, tubercles in 8 and 13 spirals, pyramidal, $\frac{3}{4}$ in. long and thick, axils slightly woolly; spines 4, awl-shaped, whitish, dark-tipped, the 3 upper to $\frac{5}{16}$ in. long, the lower to $\frac{5}{8}$ in. long; fls. yellow, $1\frac{1}{4}$ in. long. N. Mex.

Zeilmanniana Böd. ROSE-PINCUSHION. Cc; sts. mostly simple, to $2\frac{1}{2}$ in. high and 2 in. thick, tubercles in 13 and 21 spirals, cylindrical, $\frac{1}{4}$ in. long, $\frac{5}{32}$ in. in diam., axils naked; radial spines 15–18, bristlelike, pubescent, $\frac{3}{8}$ in. long, central spines 4, needle-shaped, reddish-brown, $\frac{5}{16}$ in. long, the lower hooked; fls. purple, $\frac{3}{4}$ in. across. Cent. Mex.

zephyranthoides Scheidw. Cc; sts. simple, to 3 in. high and 4 in. thick, tubercles in 5 and 8 spirals, to 1 in. long and $\frac{1}{2}$ in. in diam., axils naked; spines pubescent, radial spines 12–18, capillary, white, to $\frac{1}{2}$ in. long, central spine mostly 1, hooked, red-brown, $\frac{1}{2}$ in. long; fls. white to yellow, $1\frac{1}{2}$ in. across; fr. ovoid. S. Mex.

Zeyerana F. A. Haage, jr. Mm; sts. simple, subglobose, to 4 in. thick, tubercles in 13 and 21 spirals, ovoid, to $\frac{1}{2}$ in. long, axils naked; radial spines 10, needle-shaped, white, to $\frac{3}{8}$ in. long, central spines 4, stouter, red, becoming brown, to 1 in. long; fls. orange. N. Mex.

Zuccariniana Mart. Mm; sts. simple, globose to oblong, to 8 in. high, tubercles in 16 and 26 spirals, somewhat angled, to $\frac{5}{8}$ in. long and $\frac{3}{8}$ in. thick, axils at first woolly; radial spines 0–4, often deciduous, bristlelike, white, brown-tipped, to $\frac{1}{4}$ in. long, central spines 2 or 4, needle-shaped, straight or recurved, white, dark-tipped, the upper to $\frac{1}{2}$ in. long, the lower to 1 in. long; fls. magenta, 1 in. long; fr. $\frac{3}{8}$ in. long. Cent. Mex.

MAMMILLOYDIA: *MAMMILLARIA* subgenus *Mammilloydia.*

MANDEVILLA Lindl. [*Dipladenia* A. DC.]. *Apocynaceae.* About 100 spp. of often scandent shrubs and, infrequently, herbs, native to trop. Amer., sap milky; lvs. opp. or whorled, entire, usually glandular at base of, or along, midrib; infls. mostly lateral, racemose, few- to many-fld.; fls. diurnal, 5-merous, bisexual, corolla funnelform to tubular-salverform, stamens borne on corolla, anthers connivent, adhering to stigma; fr. a pair of cylindrical follicles, seeds many, with tuft of hairs.

Planted as ornamentals in tropical and subtropical areas, and in tubs under glass; usually bloom in profusion over long periods. Grown in soil consisting of equal parts of peat and loam, with sand; they should not be planted in pots. Easily propagated by cuttings under mist or over bottom heat.

×**amabilis** (Hort. Backh.) Dress [*Dipladenia* ×*amabilis* Hort. Backh.]. Reputedly *M. splendens* × *M. crassinoda* (G. Gard.) Woodson, but identity of the latter parent in error; woody twiner; lvs. ovate-oblong to elliptic-oblong, acuminate; fls. large, showy, very freely produced, corolla funnelform, opening pale blush-pink but changing to deep rose, lobes rounded, short-acuminate. The backcross hybrid, *M.* × *amabilis* × *M. splendens,* has been called *Dipladenia* ×*amoena,* but this is only a nomenclatural synonym of *M.* × *amabilis.* The cv. 'Alice du Pont' probably represents this backcross.

boliviensis (Hook.f.) Woodson [*Dipladenia boliviensis* Hook.f.]. Glabrous woody twiner; lvs. opp., leathery, elliptic to obovate-elliptic, to 4 in. long, caudate-acuminate, obtuse at base, petioles to ¾ in. long; infl. 3–7-fld., shorter than subtending lvs.; corolla funnelform, white, tube and throat to 1¾ in. long, lobes acuminate, to 1¾ in. long. Ecuador, Bolivia.

laxa (Ruiz & Pav.) Woodson [*M. suaveolens* Lindl.]. CHILEAN JASMINE. Woody twiner; lvs. ovate, to 6 in. long, cordate, thin, glabrous except for tufted hairs in axils of veins underneath, petioles about 1 in. long; infls. 5–15-fld., longer than subtending lvs.; fls. fragrant, corolla funnelform, white to cream-colored, tube and throat to 2¼ in. long, lobes obtuse, 1¼ in. long; follicles relatively stout, to 16 in. long, glabrous. Bolivia and n. Argentina.

Sanderi (Hemsl.) Woodson [*Dipladenia Sanderi* Hemsl.]. Glabrous woody twiner; lvs. opp., leathery, broadly oblong-elliptic, to 2½ in. long, short-acuminate, rounded at base, petiole to ⅜ in. long; infl. 3–5-fld., about as long as subtending lvs.; corolla funnelform, rose-pink, tube and throat to 1¾ in. long, lobes slightly acuminate, to 1⅜ in. long. Brazil.

splendens (Hook.f.) Woodson [*Dipladenia splendens* (Hook.f.) A. DC.]. Woody twiner, sts. finely hairy, becoming glabrate; lvs. opp., membranous, broadly elliptic, to 8 in. long, acuminate, subcordate, minutely hairy, sessile or subsessile; racemes 3–5-fld., as long as subtending lvs.; corolla funnelform, 3–4 in. across, rose-pink, tube and throat to 1⅜ in. long, lobes short-acuminate, wide-spreading, to 1½ in. long. Se. Brazil.

suaveolens: *M. laxa.*

MANDRAGORA L. MANDRAKE. *Solanaceae.* About 6 spp. of per. herbs, native to the Medit. region and the Himalayas, with thick or tuberous roots; lvs. all basal or nearly so, ovate to obovate, undulate; fls. rather large, solitary or clustered among the foliage, calyx 5-parted, somewhat enlarged in fr., corolla whitish, blue-violet, or purple, campanulate, 5-lobed, stamens 5, borne on the corolla tube below the middle, ovary 2-celled, with long style and expanded stigma; fr. a fleshy, many-seeded, globose berry.

Propagated by seeds and division.

officinarum L. To 1 ft., with spindle-shaped, often branching roots; lvs. ovate, to 1 ft. long, sinuate-toothed; fls. greenish-yellow, to 1 in. long. Spring. S. Eur. Mandrake root contains the alkaloid hyoscyamine; in earlier times magical properties were ascribed to it because of its sometimes humanlike form and medicinal properties. It is occasionally cult. in collections of drug or medicinal plants.

MANETTIA Mutis ex L. [*Lygistum* P. Br.]. *Rubiaceae.* Over 100 spp. of evergreen herbs or shrubs of twining habit, native to trop. Amer.; lvs. mostly opp., stipules interpetiolar, sometimes dentate or fimbriate; fls. solitary and axillary or in cymes or panicles, white, yellow, or red, 4-merous, corolla tubular or funnelform; fr. a caps., seeds small, winged.

Manettias are grown for their bright-colored flowers, as trellis and rafter vines in the greenhouse or planted out in the summer and in southern U.S. They need a night temperature of 55° F. and above. Propagated by cuttings of young growth over heat, and by seeds when available.

bicolor: see *M. inflata.*

cordifolia Mart. FIRECRACKER VINE. Herbaceous vine, st. pubescent; lvs. cordate-ovate to lanceolate-oblong, to 3 in. long, membranous, pubescent or glabrous beneath; fls. mostly axillary and solitary, corolla bright red, tubular, slender at base and broadened above, to 2 in. long, lobes short. S. Amer. Var. **glabra** (Cham. & Schlechtend.) Standl. [*M. glabra* Cham. & Schlechtend.]. Lvs. glabrous beneath.

discolor Standl. ex Steyerm. Scandent shrub, glabrous or nearly so; lvs. elliptic or elliptic-oblong, to 2 in. long; fls. 1–7, in axillary, nearly racemose clusters, corolla whitish, tube broadly cylindrical, to ¼ in. long, lobes 4, shorter than tube. Colombia.

glabra: *M. cordifolia* var. *glabra.*

inflata T. Sprague [*M. bicolor* Hook.f., not Paxt.]. BRAZILIAN-FIRE-CRACKER, TWINING FIRECRACKER, FIRECRACKER VINE. Much-branched, more or less pubescent climber; lvs. ovate to ovate-lanceolate, to 6 in. long; fls. axillary, solitary, on long stalks, calyx lobes leafy, reflexed, corolla reddish with yellow tips, tube cylindrical, slightly narrowed toward apex, hispid with red hairs, lobes 4, short, yellow. Paraguay, Uruguay.

MANFREDA Salisb. [*Runyonia* Rose]. *Agavaceae.* Fewer than 20 spp. of per. herbs in s. U.S. and Mex., with fleshy underground sts. and fusiform, succulent roots; lvs. unarmed, soft and fleshy, in one or more rosettes on the rhizome, lacking a terminal spine, margins entire or finely serrulate, often crisped or undulate; infl. erect, spicate or racemose; fls. mostly solitary at each node of infl., segms. 6, united basally in a narrow tube, reflexed or recurved at flowering, stamens 6, long-exserted or rarely nearly included, ovary inferior, 3-celled; fr. a caps., seeds many, flat, black.

Culture as for *Agave,* but with somewhat more moisture required.

gigantea: a listed name of no botanical standing, perhaps referable to *M. variegata.*

longiflora (Rose) Verhoek-Williams [*Runyonia longiflora* Rose]. Lvs. to 10½ in. long, ¾ in. wide, green with darker green or brown spots, margins toothed; infl. to 3 ft. high; fls. pink to brick-red, to 2 in. long, lobes shorter than tube, stamens included. S. Tex. and n. Mex.

maculosa (Hook.) Rose. Lvs. to 1 ft. long, ¾ in. wide, mottled; infl. to 3 ft.; fls. fragrant, whitish or greenish, turning pink with age, 2 in. long, lobes nearly as long as tube, stamens scarcely longer than perianth. S. Tex., n. Mex.

undulata (Klotzsch) Rose. A name of uncertain application.

variegata (Jacobi) Rose [*Agave variegata* Jacobi]. Lvs. to 1½ ft. long, 1½ in. wide, mottled, margin somewhat toothed; infl. to 4 ft.; fls. brownish-green, to 1½ in. long, lobes equalling tube, stamens long-exserted. S. Tex. and e. Mex. Cv. 'Gigantea' is listed.

virginica (L.) Salisb. [*Agave virginica* L.]. Lvs. to 2 ft. long, 2 in. wide, dark green, sometimes reddish-striped or -mottled; infl. to nearly 6 ft.; fls. fragrant, greenish-yellow, about 2 in. long, lobes shorter than tube, stamens long-exserted. Ohio, W. Va., and e. Va., s. to Tex. and Fla.

MANGIFERA L. *Anacardiaceae.* About 40 spp. of polygamous trees of Asia; lvs. leathery, simple; fls. small, in terminal panicles, stamens 1–5, often only 1 fertile; fr. pendent, large, fleshy, drupaceous, the seed flat and fibrous.

The genus is known mostly for the mango, planted in southern Fla., the warmest parts of Calif., and widely grown in the tropics as an excellent dessert fruit. There are now many select cultivars. Propagated by seeds, but budding, grafting, and inarching must be used for named cultivars.

indica L. MANGO. Handsome, symmetrical, evergreen tree, to 90 ft., sometimes with a spread of 125 ft.; lvs. stiffish, lanceolate, to 16 in. long; fls. pinkish-white; mature fr. fragrant, variable in size, shape, and color, mostly ovoid-pointed or heart-shaped, commonly 3–5 in. long, but sometimes shorter or longer, the tough, thin, smooth skin mostly green, yellow, reddish, or yellow and reddish when ripe, the large fibrous seed adhering to the juicy pulp. Winter, early spring. N. India, Burma, Malay Pen. Zone 10. One of the most important trop. frs., used as food or dessert, and in the preparation of chutneys and preserves. Among selected cvs. found in the U.S. are: 'Borsha', fr. oblong, bright green with yellow spots when ripe, excellent flavor; 'Haden', very productive, frs. large, of good quality, brilliant reddish color, with low fiber content; 'Irwin'; 'Kent'; 'Mulgoba', frs. fairly large, blotched yellow and green, fiber-free, of sweet flavor; 'Paheri' or 'Pairi', frs. of medium size, skin rich crimson, pulp deep yellow, excellent quality, fiber-free; 'Sundersha' frs. large, clear yellow, with distinct beak, juicy, fiber-free; 'Zill'. See also *Mango.*

MANGO. The mango, *Mangifera indica,* is a handsome evergreen tree widely grown in the drier tropics for its superb and often very colorful fruit (the "peach of the tropics") and in the continental United States locally in Zone 10b (subtropical Florida). Centuries of selection and subsequent maintenance of the best types in tropical Asia, especially its native India, have yielded many cultivars free of the annoying fibers surrounding the seed and the turpentiny flavor often found in seedling mangos. The latter are, however, invariably more productive than grafted kinds and are the usual kinds seen in tropical America. There are two major groups of mangos, the Indian race (monoembryonic) and the Philippine or Manila race (polyembryonic). Seedlings of the latter race arise from nucellar embryos and are essentially of vegetative origin, hence are remarkably uniform, reproducing characteristics of the parent. Most mangos grown in this country, and primarily in subtropical Florida, are derived from Indian clones, such as 'Borsha', 'Mulgoba', 'Paheri', and 'Sundersha', introduced early in the century. Although generally superior as fruits on all counts, they have failed to meet commercial needs of productivity in Florida, at least, and have been largely replaced in large orchards by second or third generation seedling selections from these or other introductions. 'Haden', a 'Mulgoba' seedling, was for years a prominent Florida commercial mango but, although still a fine home garden mango, it has now been replaced by more recent seedling selections such as 'Irwin', 'Keitt', 'Kent', 'Palmer', and 'Zill'.

Mangos do best on rich, well-drained soils in hot, rather dry lowland climates. Although trees thrive and make handsome ornamental specimens under continually rainy tropical conditions, no fruiting occurs. Propagation may be by seeds but chip budding, side-veneer grafting, or inarching are normally used to reproduce named cultivars. In Florida, budding or grafting is done during the warmest months of summer on seedlings four to six weeks from germination. Mango trees are rarely pruned, and young grafted trees of most cultivars bear in three to five years. Bees are helpful in pollinating the large flower clusters to assure a good fruit set. At full maturity on the tree, the fruit softens and will fall, so the crop requires selective picking.

MANIHOT Mill. *Euphorbiaceae.* About 160 spp. of monoecious herbs, shrubs, or trees, with milky juice, native to N. and S. Amer.; lvs. alt., usually palmately veined and parted, sometimes peltate; fls. without petals, borne in axillary racemes or panicles; fr. a caps.

Manihot Glaziovii Müll. Arg. is the source of Ceara rubber. *M. esculenta* is one of the most important tropical root crops and is extensively cultivated in many forms in most lowland tropical regions for the staple starchy roots, which yield tapioca, cassava, starch, and other food products. It thrives on rich sandy land. Propagated by 4–6-in. cuttings and planted 4 ft. apart each way. In the U.S., the canes should be buried until spring and then cut into lengths. Some early-maturing kinds may be grown from seeds. Roots should not be dug until ready for use, as they decay readily.

dulcis (J. F. Gmel.) Pax. SWEET CASSAVA. Distinguished from *M. esculenta* in lvs. sometimes to 13-lobed, frequently fiddle-shaped; fr. cylindrical, not winged. S. Amer. The tuberous edible roots are largely free of bitter, poisonous prussic acid.

esculenta Crantz [*M. utilissima* Pohl; *M. Manihot* (L.) Cockerell; *Jatropha Manihot* L.]. YUCA, BITTER CASSAVA, CASSAVA, MANIOC, TAPIOCA, TAPIOCA PLANT, SWEET-POTATO TREE. Shrub, to 9 ft., with long tuberous edible roots; lvs. deeply parted into 3–7 lobes; fr. ½ in. in diam., 6-angled, narrowly winged. Brazil. Includes the bitter cassava, having much poisonous prussic acid in the roots, which is destroyed by cooking.

Manihot: *M. esculenta.*

utilissima: *M. esculenta.*

MANILKARA Adans. [*Achras* L.; *Sapota* Mill.]. *Sapotaceae.* About 85 spp. of trop. evergreen trees, with milky latex, native to both hemispheres; lvs. alt., thick; fls. small, whitish, solitary or in clusters, sepals 6, in 2 series, corolla 6-lobed, each lobe with 2 petal-like appendages or these obsolete, stamens as many as corolla lobes and opp., usually alternating

with another row of stamens or staminodes, ovary superior; fr. an ovoid or globose, large-seeded berry, seeds with narrow ventral scar.

The genus includes species important for their commercial latexes as well as for their edible fruit.

bidentata (A. DC.) A. Cheval. BALATA. To 100 ft. or more wood hard, purplish; lvs. oblong-obovate, to 12 in. long; fls. 10 or more in a cluster, outer corolla lobes lobed; fr. globose or ellipsoid-globose, about 1 in. long. W. Indies, Panama, n. S. Amer. This sp. has generally but erroneously been called *Mimusops Balata.* The principal source of a nonelastic rubber, balata, obtained from trees in the wild. The durable wood, called bulletwood or bullywood, has many uses.

Kauki (L.) Dubard [*Mimusops Kauki* L.]. Large tree; lvs. obovate-elliptic, long-petioled, to 4 in. long, 2 in. wide, silky-white beneath; fls. in clusters, on pedicels 1 in. long, corolla ⅜ in. long, staminodes 6–8; fr. to 1 in. across. Asia.

Roxburghiana (Wight) Dubard [*Mimusops Roxburghiana* Wight]. Large tree; lvs. to 3 in. long, 1¾ in. wide, glabrous; fls. 2–4 in a cluster, on pedicels 1 in. long. Asia.

Zapota (L.) Van Royen [*M. Zapotilla* (Jacq.) Gilly; *Achras Zapota* L.; *Sapota Achras* Mill.]. SAPODILLA, NISPERO, CHICOZAPOTE, NASEBERRY. To 100 ft. or more; lvs. clustered toward ends of twigs, elliptic or nearly so, to 6 in. long, 2½ in. wide; fls. solitary, corolla lobes entire or 3-toothed at apex; fr. variable in shape, to 4 in. across, the thin skin rusty-brown, roughened, the edible flesh yellow-brown, translucent, sweet, seeds black, glossy. Mex., Cent. Amer. Now widely cult. in tropics for its fr. Zone 10b, in Fla. Wild trees, when tapped, yield a milky latex, chicle, original base for chewing gum. The sapodilla is an attractive ornamental and grows well in any usual soil, though doing best in fertile sandy loam. Prop. is usually by seeds, but shield budding or grafting on seedling stocks is preferred.

Zapotilla: *M. Zapota.*

MARAH Kellogg. BIGROOT, MANROOT. *Cucurbitaceae.* Seven spp. of per., tendril-bearing, monoecious vines with large tubers, native to w. N. Amer.; lvs. more or less deeply 5–7-lobed; male fls. in axillary racemes or panicles, calyx lobes small, corolla rotate or campanulate, mostly 5-lobed, sometimes 4–8-lobed, filaments and 3–4 anthers fused, female fls. mostly solitary, in same axil as male infl., often larger than male fls., ovary usually 4-, sometimes 2–8-celled; fr. an inflated, spiny caps., irregularly dehiscent near apex.

fabaceus (Naud.) Greene [*Echinocystis fabacea* Naud.]. Sts. to 20 ft. or more; lvs. suborbicular, more or less deeply lobed, to 4 in. long; male fls. 8–25 in racemes or panicles to 10 in. long, corolla rotate, yellowish-white; fr. globose, to 2 in. in diam. Calif.

macrocarpus (Greene) Greene [*Echinocystis macrocarpa* Greene]. CHILICOTHE. Sts. to 12 ft. or more; lvs. orbicular, to 6 in. wide, rather deeply lobed; male fls. 5–12 in racemes to nearly 10 in. long, corolla slightly cup-shaped, white, to about ½ in. wide; fr. cylindrical, to 5 in. long, 3⅝ in. in diam. S. Calif. and Baja Calif.

oreganus (Torr. & A. Gray) T. J. Howell [*Echinocystis oregana* (Torr. & A. Gray) Cogn.]. Sts. to 20 ft. or more; lvs. suborbicular, shallowly lobed, to 8 in. wide or more; male fls. 5–20 in racemes to 1 ft. long, corolla campanulate, white, to ¼ in. wide; fr. oblong-ovoid, to about 3 in. long. Coast ranges and hills, cent. Calif. to Ore.

MARANTA L. *Marantaceae.* Perhaps 20 spp. of per. herbs with branching sts. forming clumps, native to trop. Amer.; lvs. thin, petioles sheathing; racemes loose, often paniculate, with few deciduous bracts; fls. irregular, sepals 3, petals 3, fertile stamen 1, staminodes 4, the outer 2 usually large and petal-like, ovary inferior, with 1 fertile cell; caps. 1-seeded.

One species the source of West Indian arrowroot. Culture as for *Calathea.*

amabilis: *Stromanthe amabilis.*

arundinacea L. ARROWROOT, OBEDIENCE PLANT. To 6 ft., rhizomes thick, starchy, sts. slender; lf. blades lanceolate, to 1 ft. long and 4 in. wide, attenuate-acuminate; infl. often branched; fls. white. Trop. Amer. Rhizomes yield arrowroot starch, produced mainly on the island of St. Vincent, W. Indies. Cv. 'Aurea' is listed. Cv. **'Variegata'** [*Phrynium variegatum* N. E. Br.]. Lvs. variegated with dark green, light green, and greenish-yellow.

bicolor Ker-Gawl. To 15 in., bearing tubers at base; lf. blades oblong-elliptic to ovate, to 6 in. long and 4 in. wide, undulate, glaucous-green and with brown spots and a light central strip above, light purple beneath; infl. slender, with 4 bracts; fls. white, marked with violet lines. Brazil and Guiana.

Closonii L. H. Bailey. Lvs. dark green, variegated with pale yellow. Brazil.

insignis: *Calathea lancifolia.*

Kelgeljanii: *Calathea bella.*

Kerchoviana: a listed name of no botanical standing for *M. leuconeura* var.

leuconeura E. Morr. PRAYER PLANT, TEN-COMMANDMENTS. Sts. usually spreading to pendent in age, without tubers; lf. blades more or less elliptic, mostly to 5 in. long and 3½ in. wide, upper surface variegated, light and dark green or brown, with satiny luster, sometimes with gray or red main lateral veins, lower surface glaucous or marked with red-purple, petioles shorter than lf. blades; infl. slender, with 2 bracts; fls. white, with purple spots. Brazil. Var. **leuconeura** [var. *Massangeana* E. Morr.; *M. Massangeana* Hort.]. The typical var.; lvs. broadly elliptic, upper surface black-green with silvery-gray, median, feathered zone and silver-gray veins, lower surface red-purple. Var. **erythroneura** Bunting. Lvs. oblong-elliptic to obovate, main lateral veins rose-red, otherwise colored like var. *Kerchoviana*, or with the darker blotches above coalescing into a zone reaching nearly to margins, lower surface marked with red-purple. Var. **Kerchoviana** E. Morr. [*M. Kerchoviana* Hort., often misspelled *Kerchoveana*]. RABBIT'S-FOOT, RABBIT'S-TRACKS. Lvs. oblong-elliptic, upper surface light green, with a row of dark brown or dark green blotches in a line on each side of midrib, lower surface glaucous-gray, or blotched red when young.

Lietzei: *Calathea Lietzei.*

Massangeana: a listed name of no botanical standing for *M. leuconeura* var. *leuconeura.*

Oppenheimiana: *Ctenanthe Oppenheimiana.*

orbifolia: *Calathea rotundifolia.*

Porteana: *Stromanthe Porteana.*

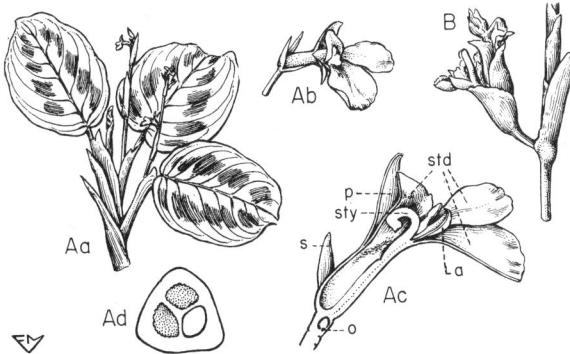

MARANTACEAE. **A,** *Maranta bicolor:* **Aa,** flowering stem, × ⅙; **Ab,** flower, × 1; **Ac,** flower, vertical section, × 2; **Ad,** ovary, cross section, × 15. **B,** *Calathea Lietzei:* inflorescence, × ½. (a anther, o ovary, p petal, s sepal, std staminode, sty style.) (From Bailey, *Manual of Cultivated Plants*, ed. 2.)

MARANTACEAE Petersen. MARANTA or ARROWROOT FAMILY. Monocot.; about 25 genera and 400 spp. of mostly trop., per. herbs with rhizomes or tubers, forming clumps or colonies; lvs. simple, entire, pinnately veined, petioles sheathing, with a characteristic pulvinus and joint at juncture with blade; fl. clusters subtended by prominent bracts and arranged in heads, spikes, racemes, or panicles; fls. bisexual, very irregular, sepals 3, separate, subequal, petals 3, unequal, united into tube at base, fertile stamen 1 with petal-like filament, staminodes 1–5, petal-like, ovary inferior, 1–3-celled; fr. a caps. or berry, 1–3-seeded. *Calathea, Ctenanthe, Hybophrynium, Maranta, Pleiostachya, Stromanthe,* and *Thalia* are cult.

Mostly grown for the very ornamental foliage. West Indian arrowroot is obtained from the rhizomes of one species of *Maranta*, a vegetable wax from the leaves of *Calathea lutea*, and the stems of some species are used in basketry.

MARATTIA Swartz. *Marattiaceae.* About 60 spp. of large ferns of the tropics and of temp. areas in the S. Hemisphere; sts. short, thick, more or less globose; lvs. ovate, large, to 15 ft. long, 2–3-pinnate; sori near margins of pinnules, sporangia fused to form synangia.

Sometimes cultivated as an ornamental in tropical or temperate gardens and occasionally in greenhouse collections, but not known to be offered in the trade. Propagated by spores. For culture see *Ferns.*

attenuata Labill. Lvs. to 4 ft. long, 3-pinnate, pinnae to 2 ft. long, pinnules to 6 in. long, petioles to 4 ft. long. New Caledonia.

Douglasii (K. Presl.) Bak. PALA. Lvs. to 8 ft. long, 3-pinnate, dark green, glossy, pinnules ovate or oblong, to 1 in. long, toothed, petioles to 5 ft. long. Hawaii, where occasionally cult. as a garden ornamental.

fraxinea Sm. [*M. salicina* Sm.]. KING FERN, PARA F. Basal st. thickened, turniplike; lvs. to 15 ft. long, dark green, glossy, 2-pinnate, the thick, fine-toothed pinnules to 6 in. long, petioles to 2 ft. long. New Zeal. and S. Afr. The thick st. was formerly much eaten by the Maoris.

salicina: *M. fraxinea.*

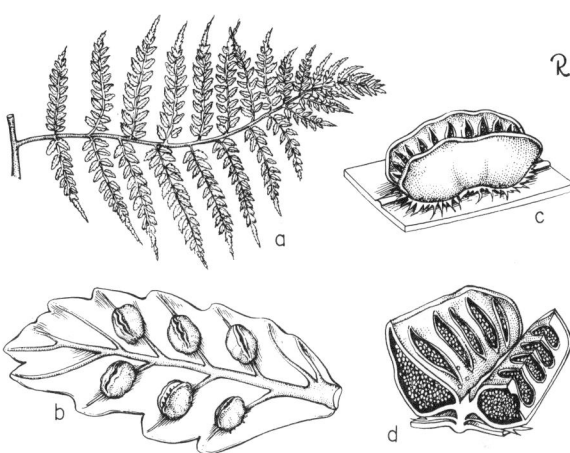

MARATTIACEAE. *Marattia alata* Swartz: **a,** a pinna, × ¼; **b,** pinnule, underside with sori, × 3; **c,** sorus, × 7; **d,** sorus, cross section, × 12. (Species representative, but not in general cultivation; from Lawrence, *Taxonomy of Vascular Plants.*)

MARATTIACEAE Bercht. & J. Presl. MARATTIA FAMILY. Ferns; about 7 genera and 145 spp. of herbaceous to woody, sometimes arborescent ferns of mostly trop. regions; lvs. articulated on st. or rhizome, stipuled, pinnate; sori on lower surface of lvs., sporangia opening by slits, sometimes closely united, those of each sorus maturing together. *Angiopteris* and *Marattia* are occasionally grown in greenhouse collections.

MARCETELLA Svent. *Rosaceae.* Two spp. of shrubs, native to Canary Is., like *Dendriopoterium*, but differing in having winged, samaralike, not angled fr., and in being dioecious.

Moquiniana (Webb & Berth.) Svent. Shrub, to 6 ft.; lvs. 5–6 in. long, pinnate into several oblong-ovate lfts.; fls. racemose, sepals 5, concave, ¹⁄₁₆ in. long, purplish-tomentose; fr. samaralike, cuneate at base, unequally winged. Tenerife.

MARCGRAVIA L. SHINGLE PLANT. *Marcgraviaceae.* About 45 spp. of trop. Amer. scandent shrubs, mostly epiphytic, with 2 kinds of brs. and lvs.; juvenile, vegetative shoots creeping, attached to support by aerial roots, with lvs. small, rounded, sessile, oriented in 1 plane, fl. shoots with lvs. alt., entire, petioled; infl. terminal, racemose or more or less umbellate; outer fls. fertile, sepals 4, petals 4–5, united into a deciduous cap, stamens 10 to many, central fls. abortive, the bracts modified into saccate nectaries; fr. a 4–12-celled, globose, many-seeded caps.

rectiflora Triana & Planch. Epiphytic, to 40 ft. long; lvs. of juvenile shoots elliptic to oblong, to 1 in. long, lvs. of fl. brs. oblong to oblong-lanceolate, acuminate, to 4½ in. long, petioles ⅛ in. long; infl. few-fld., pedicels stout, about 2 in. long; corolla ⅝ in. long, nectaries cylindric-clavate, ¾ in. long; fr. to ⅝ in. in diam. W. Indies.

MARCGRAVIACEAE Choisy. MARCGRAVIA FAMILY. Dicot.; 5 genera of scandent, often epiphytic shrubs of trop. Amer.; lvs. of juvenile shoots thin, oriented in 1 plane, lvs. of adult shoots alt., entire, leathery; infl. terminal, racemose, spicate, or more or less umbellate, with colored bracts variously modified into nectaries; fls. bisexual, 4–5-merous, stamens 3 to many; fr. a caps. *Marcgravia* is occasionally cult.

MARCOT: see *Propagation.*

MARGINATOCEREUS: *LEMAIREOCEREUS.*

MARGYRICARPUS Ruiz & Pav. *Rosaceae.* About 10 spp. of evergreen shrubs, native to the Andes; lvs. alt., pinnate, the rachis spiny; fls. inconspicuous, without petals; fr. a berry or drupe.

Suitable for the rock garden, but not hardy in the North.

setosus Ruiz & Pav. PEARL FRUIT, PEAR FRUIT, PEARLBERRY. Brs. prostrate, to 1 ft. high, densely leafy; lvs 1 in. long or less, lfts. linear and revolute at margins; fls. green, anthers dark red; fr. a white berry about ⁵⁄₁₆ in. in diam. Ecuador to Patagonia. Zone 8.

MARIANTHUS Hüg. *Pittosporaceae.* About 15 spp. of procumbent or twining, slender-stemmed shrubs, native to Australia; lvs. alt., mostly entire or the lower sometimes lobed; fls. in terminal or axillary clusters, sepals, petals, and stamens 5, petals blue, white, or red, coming together and appearing united; fr. a membranous, compressed caps., seeds many, not winged. Related to *Billardiera*, in which, however, fr. is a berry.

erubescens Putterl. Vine with brilliant red fls. W. Australia.

ringens (J. Drumm. & Harv.) F. J. Muell. Vine, to 10 ft.; fls. orange-yellow. W. Australia.

MARICA: see *NEOMARICA.*

MARISCUS: *Cyperus.* M. umbilensis: *C. Owanii.*

MARITIMOCEREUS: *BORZICACTUS.* M. gracilis: *B. Sextonianus.*

MARKHAMIA Seem. ex K. Schum. *Bignoniaceae.* About 12 spp. of evergreen shrubs or trees, native to trop. Afr. and se. Asia; lvs. opp., pinnate; fls. in large terminal or axillary racemes or in panicles; calyx spathelike, corolla usually yellow, with red or purple stripes or spots inside, funnelform or campanulate-funnelform, often strongly 2-lipped, stamens 4; fr. a linear caps.

acuminata K. Schum. Shrub or small tree, to 10–20 ft.; lvs. to 9 in. long, lfts. 5–7, elliptic, to 4 in. long, entire or serrulate, scaly; fls. to 2 in. long, corolla brownish-purple to maroon, tube yellow; fr. to 1¼ ft. long. Trop. Afr.

Hildebrandtii (Bak.) T. Sprague. Shrub or tree, to 30 ft.; lvs. to 17 in. long, lfts. 7–9, ovate to ovate-oblong, to 4 in. long, entire; fls. in panicles, yellow, to 2¼ in. long. E. Trop. Afr.

lutea (Benth.) K. Schum. Shrub or tree, to 30 ft.; lvs. to 20 in. long, lfts. 7–11, ovate to ovate-oblong or lanceolate, to 7½ in. long; fls. in panicles, to 2¼ in. long; fr. curved, to 22 in. long. W. Trop. Afr. Planted in s. Fla.

obtusifolia (Bak.) T. Sprague. Shrub or tree, to 30 ft.; lvs. to 17 in. long, lfts. 5–11, ovate-oblong, elliptic, or obovate, to 6¾ in. long; fls. to 2⅝ in. long, corolla yellow, striped with chocolate-brown, lobes glandular; fr. nearly straight to curved, to 2 ft. long, velvety-tomentose. Trop. Afr.

platycalyx (Bak.) T. Sprague. To 40 ft. or more; lvs. to 1½ ft. long, lfts. 7–11, elliptic to oblong-lanceolate, to 8 in. long; fls. to 2 in. long, corolla yellow, striped and spotted red; fr. to 4 ft. long, prominently ribbed. Trop. Afr.

speciosa: a listed name of no botanical standing.

MARRUBIUM L. HOREHOUND. *Labiatae.* About 30 spp. of whitish-woolly, bitter-aromatic, per. herbs of Medit. region, Eur., and Asia; sts. mostly square in cross section, branched at base; lvs. opp., crenate or dissected, rugose; fls. small, crowded, in many-fld., axillary verticillasters, calyx 5–10-nerved, spreading in fr., teeth spiny, corolla 2-lipped, upper lip erect, often notched, lower lip spreading, 3-lobed, stamens 4, in 2 pairs; fr. of 4 ovoid, glabrous nutlets.

Propagated by seeds or division.

candidissimum: see *M. incanum.*

incanum Desr. [*M. candidissimum* of auth., not L.]. White-woolly, 15–24 in.; lvs. ovate, to 2 in. long, finely crenate to dentate; bractlets

subulate, a little shorter than the calyx tube; calyx 5-toothed, corolla whitish. Late summer. Italy, w. Balkan Pen.

leonuroides Desr. Per., short-tomentose-hirsute, pale green, sts. fleshy; lvs. ovate, coarsely incised, gray-pubescent beneath, petioled; bractlets subulate, villous, spiny; calyx white-lanate, 5-toothed, teeth subulate, corolla twice as long as calyx, rose-pink, tube exserted. Caucasus.

vulgare L. COMMON H., WHITE H. To 18 in., white-pubescent; lvs. broadly round-ovate, to nearly 2 in. long, crenate, petioled; verticillasters globose; calyx with 10 recurved teeth, the alt. ones shorter, corolla small, white. Waste places, cent. and w. Asia, s. Eur., n. Afr., Canary Is., Azores; naturalized in N. Amer. An old-time herb, used in confections and medicines.

MARSDENIA R. Br *Asclepiadaceae.* Over 100 spp. of generally twining shrubs or subshrubs, chiefly native to trop. and subtrop. regions; lvs. opp.; fls. in axillary or terminal, panicled or umbellate cymes, 5-merous, corolla campanulate to urceolate, corona 5-lobed; fr. a follicle, usually thick, often fleshy.

Roylei Wight. Young parts mostly finely pubescent; lvs. cordate-ovate, 3–6 in. long, acuminate, often velvety beneath; cymes corymbose, about 1½ in. across, corolla campanulate, to ⁵⁄₁₆ in. across, lobes pubescent, corona lobes subulate; follicle beaked, to 3 in. long, turgid, transversely rugose. Indian Himalayas.

MARSHALLIA Schreb. *Compositae* (Helianthus Tribe). Ten spp. of per., tufted herbs of N. Amer.; lvs. basal or alt., entire; fl. heads discoid, solitary, long-peduncled, receptacle convex, scaly; fls. all tubular, pink, purple, or white; achenes turbinate, 5-angled, pappus of 5 scales.

grandiflora Beadle & Boynt. To 2–3 ft., sts. leafy chiefly at the base; lvs. elliptic-spatulate, 4–8 in. long, acute, upper lvs. linear-elliptic; heads to 1¼ in. across, involucral bracts obovate, acute; fls. ¾ in. long. Penn. to N.C. and Tenn.

MARSHALLOCEREUS: *LEMAIREOCEREUS.*

MARSILEA L. PEPPERWORT, WATER CLOVER. *Marsileaceae.* About 65 spp. of widely distributed aquatic or marshy ferns of trop. and temp. regions; lvs. 4-parted resembling a "4-leaf" clover *(Trifolium)*, long-petioled, floating in deep water, or erect on land or in shallow water; sporocarps containing sporangia that produce megaspores and microspores.

Grown in pools, aquaria, or as pot plants in greenhouses. Propagated by division or by pieces of the rhizome. See also *Ferns.*

crenata K. Presl. Floating lvs. with lfts. obovate, to 1 in. long, petioles to 8 in. long, lvs. raised out of the water, smaller, shorter-petioled; sporocarps usually 1 or 2, oblong, to ⅛ in. long, hairy when young. Tropics, India, Indonesia, Philippine Is.

Drummondii A. Braun. Lfts. obovate-cuneate, variable in size, crenate to entire, silky-hairy, may become glabrous in age; sporocarps to ⅜ in. long, hairy, on stalks 2–8 times their length. Australia. Zone 9.

hirsuta R. Br. Young rhizomes densely rusty-hairy; lfts. narrowly oblong or obovate-oblong, hairy when young, becoming glabrous in age; sporocarps nearly globose, hairy, subsessile. E. and w. Australia. Zone 9.

pubescens: *M. strigosa.*

quadrifolia L. EUROPEAN W. C. Lfts. obdeltoid, to ¾ in. long, glabrous, petioles to 8 in. long; sporocarps ellipsoid, to ³⁄₁₆ in. long, dark brown, on stalks to ¾ in. long, attached to base of petioles. Eur. and Asia; naturalized in e. N. Amer. Zone 5.

strigosa Willd. [*M. pubescens* Ten.]. Usually cespitose; lfts. cuneate to obdeltoid, to ⅝ in. long, glabrous to sparsely hairy, rounded at apex, entire to crenulate, petioles to 1 ft. long; sporocarps obovoid, essentially sessile. S. Eur.

MARSILEACEAE Mirb. MARSILEA OR PEPPERWORT FAMILY. Ferns; 3 genera and about 70 spp. of trop. and temp., aquatic or amphibious, rhizomatous, herbaceous ferns; lvs. 2- or 4-parted and long-petioled, or threadlike; sporocarps 1–20, stalked, borne on petioles of the lvs., bean-shaped, hard, containing sporangia that produce large spores (megaspores) and small spores (microspores). *Marsilea* and *Pilularia* are sometimes planted as ornamentals.

MARTINEZIA: see *AIPHANES.*

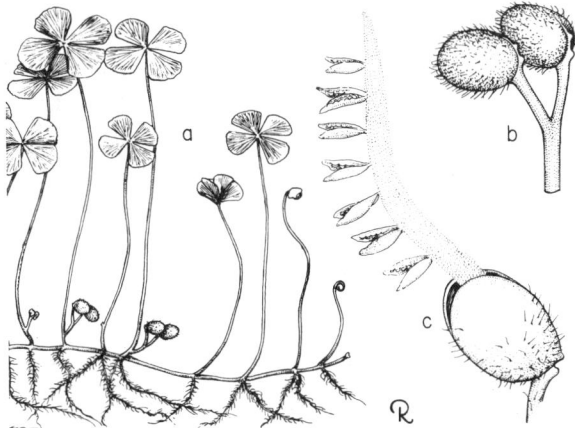

MARSILEACEAE. *Marsilea quadrifolia:* **a,** fertile plant, × ½; **b,** sporocarps, × 2; **c,** dehiscent sporocarp, releasing sori pendant on gelatinous tissue, × 3. (c from Lawrence, *Taxonomy of Vascular Plants*.)

MARTYNIA L. *Martyniaceae.* One sp., differing from *Proboscidea* in having calyx of 5 separate sepals, only 2 fertile stamens, and fr. with beak shorter than body.

Fruit sometimes used in pickles; see *Proboscidea* for culture.

annua L. Ann. herb, to 6(-10) ft., viscid-hairy, especially when young; lvs. opp., broadly ovate to triangular, 5–7-lobed, blades to 15 in. long, palmately veined, coarsely dentate; racemes of 10–20 fls.; corolla campanulate, creamy-white to reddish-purple, usually dotted with yellow or red in throat, blotched with purple on lobes, to 2 in. long; caps. ovoid, to 1½ in. long, 8-ribbed, beak shorter than body. Trop. Amer.; naturalized from India to Malay Arch.

fragrans: *Proboscidea fragrans.*

Proboscidea: *Proboscidea louisianica.*

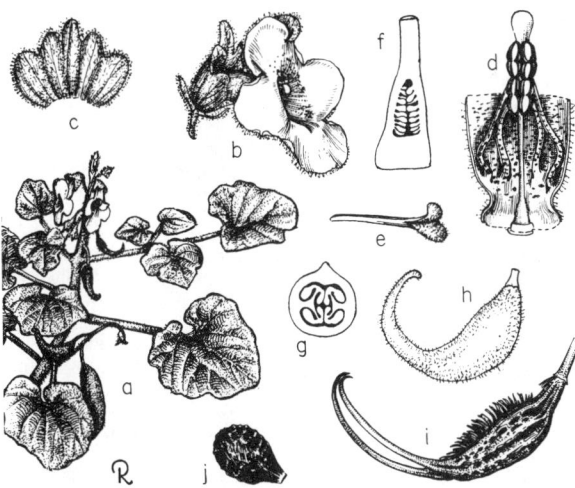

MARTYNIACEAE. *Proboscidea fragrans:* **a,** flowering plant, × ⅛; **b,** flower, × ½; **c,** calyx, expanded, × ½; ×**d,** tube of corolla, expanded (upper part cut away), showing stamens and pistil, × 1; **e,** stigma, × 2; **f,** ovary, vertical section, × 2; **g,** ovary, cross section, × 5; **h,** fruit, × ⅙; **i,** woody interior of fruit, × ⅓; **j,** seed, × 1.

MARTYNIACEAE Stapf. MARTYNIA FAMILY. Dicot.; 5 genera of sticky-hairy herbs, native to trop. and subtrop. Amer.; lvs. opp. or alt., palmately-veined; fls. irregular, corolla 5-lobed, stamens 4 or 2, ovary superior, 1-celled; fr. a curved, long-beaked caps. *Ibicella, Martynia,* and *Proboscidea* are grown in N. Amer. as ornamentals and for their curious fr., which is sometimes used in pickles.

MASCAGNIA Bertero ex Colla. *Malpighiaceae.* Between 40 and 50 spp. of shrubs or woody climbers, native to trop. Amer.; foliage glabrous or pubescent, lvs. opp., simple; fls. usually yellow, in simple or panicled racemes or sometimes

umbellate, sepals 5, with 8 (rarely 10) glands on exterior, petals 5, clawed, stamens 10, all fertile, styles 3, separate; fr. of 3 samaras.

macroptera (Sessé & Moç. ex DC.) Niedenzu. Shrub, brs. slender, vinelike; lvs. oblong, oblong-lanceolate to ovate, to 2 in. long, short-petioled; fls. yellow, glands on sepals half as long as sepals; samaras with 2 large lateral wings and a smaller dorsal wing. Mex.

MASCARENA: *HYOPHORBE.*

MASDEVALLIA Ruiz & Pav. *Orchidaceae.* About 300 spp. of epiphytes, native to highlands of continental trop. Amer.; pseudobulbs absent, sts. short, 1-lvd.; lvs. commonly leathery, generally long and narrow toward base; infl. terminal, racemose, 1- to many-fld.; sepals more or less united at base into a cup or tube, often terminating in an elongate tail, petals much smaller, narrow, lip small, similar to petals, variously shaped, jointed to column foot, pollinia 2. For structure of fl. see *Orchidaceae.*

Cool greenhouse with frequent watering. For culture see *Orchids.*

abbreviata Rchb.f. Densely tuft-forming, st. very short; lvs. spatulate, minutely 3-toothed at apex, long-petioled, to 6 in. long; racemes to 7 in. long, loosely several- to 7-fld.; fls. small, sepals white, spotted, with crimson, united below into an urceolate tube, upper sepal toothed on margins, terminating abruptly in yellow tail to ½ in. long, petals smaller, lip larger than petals, pale yellow, 3-lobed in front. Ecuador, Peru.

amabilis Rchb.f. & Warsz. Tuft-forming, medium-sized, with large, glossy fls.; lvs. to 7 in. long, oblanceolate; scapes 1-fld., to 9 in. long; sepals united at base into narrow tube, upper sepal orange, shaded with crimson, tapering into slender tail to nearly 1½ in. long, lateral sepals red, shaded with crimson, with tails about ¾ in. long, petals small, lip as long as petals. Peru.

attenuata Rchb.f. Densely tuft-forming; lvs. petioled, to 6 in. long, toothed at apex, grooved in front; scapes 1-fld., shorter than lvs.; fls. white, pale green along sepal tube, with bright yellow tails nearly twice as long as tube, petals short-clawed, lip yellow, clawed, with 2 keels on disc. Winter. Costa Rica, Panama.

Backhousiana: *M. chimaera* cv.

Barleana Rchb.f. Small; lvs. petioled, elliptic-lanceolate, to 4 in. long; scapes twice as long as lvs., 1-fld.; sepal tube prominently keeled, coral-red above, pinkish beneath, in free part of upper sepal ovate-triangular, orange-yellow with red lines, contracted to a filiform tail 1½ in. long, lateral sepals round-triangular, with slender tails, more deeply united with each other than with upper sepal, bright carmine with 3 sunken crimson lines, petals and lip minute, white, lip with purple spot at apex. Peru.

bella Rchb.f. Lvs. oblong-lanceolate, to 7 in. long, scapes pendent, dull purple, with appressed bract at each joint; fls. solitary, sepals triangular in shape, pale yellow, spotted with brownish-crimson, upper sepal contracted into long, slender, reddish-brown tail 3–4 in. long, lateral sepals somewhat rhomboidal, contracted to long slender tails similar to upper one, petals small, obcordate, yellow, spotted with red, lip large, with short, fleshy claw and concave, shell-like blade, in hollow of which are many raised lines radiating from claw, ovary blackish-purple. Late spring–summer, late autumn. Colombia.

caloptera Rchb.f. Lvs. oblong-oblanceolate to spatulate, to 3½ in. long, petioles grooved; racemes to 6 in. long, loosely 2–6-fld.; sepals united below into a small cup, white with crimson streaks, upper sepal round-triangular, minutely toothed, with yellow tail ⅜ in. long, lateral sepals ovate-oblong, with tails similar to that of upper sepal, petals minute, oblong-spatulate, minutely toothed above, with prominent longitudinal keel, lip larger than petals, oblong-fiddle-shaped, with erect lateral lobes. Colombia, Peru.

Carderi Rchb.f. Lvs. spatulate-lanceolate, to 5 in. long; scapes pendent, with 2–3 appressed membranous bracts, 1-fld.; fls. campanulate, white, blotched externally at base of united sepals with brown-purple, inner surface covered with short hairs and spotted with brown-purple at base, tails of sepals equidistant, 2 in. long, pale yellow, sometimes spotted with purple-brown, petals linear-oblong, white with purplish-brown midline, lip somewhat fiddle-shaped, basal half with longitudinal cleft, apical half shell-like, glabrous inside. Autumn. Colombia.

caudata Lindl. [*M. Shuttleworthii* Rchb.f.]. Lvs. obovate-oblong, to 4 in. long; scapes to 4 in. long, 1-fld.; fls. to 6 in. across from tip to tip of sepals, sepals united ⅓, upper sepal ovate, hooded, golden-yellow with many minute crimson spots and 5 deep crimson veins, lateral sepals slightly pouched toward base, ovate-triangular for 1 in., rose, covered with small transverse crimson spots, all sepals terminating in slender, orange-yellow to greenish tails to 3 in. long, petals to ¼ in.

long, white, lip ¼ in. long, oblong-fiddle-shaped, with many rose spots. Late winter–late spring. Venezuela, Colombia. Cv. **'Xanthocorys'** [var. *xanthocorys* Rchb.f.]. Fls. smaller, upper sepal golden-yellow with thin brownish-red-dotted veins, lateral sepals pale yellow, tinted and spotted with rose.

Chestertonii Rchb.f. Lvs. narrowly oblanceolate, to 7 in. long; scapes to 7 in. long, pendent, 1-fld.; sepals ovate-oblong, keeled on back, with slender tails to 1 in. long, blades greenish-yellow, spotted with blackish-purple, petals minute, oblong, yellowish-red with apical black tumor, lip large, with grooved claw, kidney-shaped, concave, pale orange-yellow with many radiating, raised, reddish lines. Colombia.

chimaera Rchb.f. Lvs. narrowly oblanceolate, to 9 in. long; scapes slender, to 15 in. long, pendent, 3–5-fld.; fls. produced singly by successive prolongations of scape, sepal tube campanulate, short, sepals broadly ovate, with tails to 8 in. long, lateral sepals united for about half their length, with a deep boat-shaped depression at suture and covered with warty spots, petals spatulate, expanded at tip into lobes bearing a blackish-purple spot, lip saccate, with fleshy claw, blade concave with 3 parallel or divergent raised lines and many smaller ribs radiating from outside, margins toothed. Winter–early autumn. Colombia. Cvs. include: **'Backhousiana'** [var. *Backhousiana* (Rchb.f.) Hort. Veitch; *M. Backhousiana* Rchb.f.], fls. large, tails reddish-brown, shorter, with hispid pubescence, sepals light yellow with crimson-red warty spots, lip white; **'Roezlii'** [var. *Roezlii* (Rchb.f.) Hort. Veitch; *M. Roezlii* Rchb.f.], sepal spots blackish and densely placed, leaving only small traces of ground color, lip broader and shorter, white or faintly tinted rose, the raised lines within the sac bright rose; **'Wallisii'** [var. *Wallisii* (Rchb.f.) Hort. Veitch; *M. Wallisii* Rchb.f.], sepals with hispid pubescence, whitish or pale yellow, more or less covered with brown-purple warty spots, tails red-purple, lip white, sometimes yellowish within sac; **'Winniana'** [var. *Winniana* (Rchb.f.) Hort. Veitch; *M. Winniana* Rchb.f.], fls. large, sepals elongated and more acuminate than in var. *Roezlii*, tails more slender, pubescence close, spots dense and blackish, dorsal sepal with basal yellow transverse band dotted with purple.

civilis Rchb.f. & Warsz. Lvs. linear-oblong, to 6 in. long; scapes short, mottled blackish-purple, 1-fld.; fls. leathery, with fetid odor, sepal tube cylindrical, swollen at base, greenish-yellow externally, deep purple at base internally, spotted in upper part, free part of sepals triangular, with short, recurved tails, greenish-yellow, petals somewhat spatulate, white with deep purple sunken midline on inner side, lip oblong, channelled, mottled and dotted with purple. Venezuela to Peru.

coccinea Linden ex Lindl. Lvs. obovate-lanceolate, to 9 in. long, long-petioled; scapes to 12 in. or more, 1-fld.; fls. variable in size and color, magenta-purple to scarlet, sepal tube compressed, bent, slightly swollen below, upper sepal linear, with recurved tail to 2 in. long, lateral sepals united about ⅓ their length, semiovate, tapering to short, blunt tails, petals small, 2-lobed at apex, with longitudinal keel close to anterior margin, lip similar to petals in size, ⅜ in. long, oblong, fiddle-shaped above middle, rounded at apex, 2-keeled. Spring–early summer. Colombia, Peru. Cvs. include: **'Armeniaca'**, fls. apricot-yellow, veined with red, throat of tube yellow; **'Atrosanguinea'**, fls. large, deep crimson-purple; **'Coerulescens'**, lateral sepals broadly semiovate, apiculate, crimson-magenta, spotted with bluish-purple; **'Conchiflora'**, fls. larger, lateral sepals broader, more rotund, shell-like; **'Denisonii'**, fls. deep blood-red-purple; **'Grandiflora'**, fls. large, rose-purple; **'Gravesiae'**, fls. white; **'Harryana'** [var. *Harryana* (Rchb.f.) Hort. Veitch; *M. Harryana* Rchb.f.], fls. variable in size and color, lateral sepals dilated into broad, curved-elliptic blades, terminating in acuminate tips turned towards each other.

coriacea Lindl. Lvs. linear-lanceolate, very leathery, fleshy, to 7 in. long; scapes as long as lvs., pale green dotted with purple, 1-fld.; fls. greenish-white, sepal tube broadly cylindrical, dotted with purple along veins, free part of upper sepal triangular, with short broad tail, lateral sepals oblong, yellowish, curved, acuminate, petals oblong, white with purple midline, lip tongue-shaped, reflexed, hairy, greenish-yellow with purple midline of margined dots. Early winter, summer. Colombia.

corniculata Rchb.f. Lvs. oblong-lanceolate, to 6 in. long; scapes to 3 in. long, 1-fld.; fls. brownish-red, mottled pale yellow, sepal tube broadly cylindrical, bent, swollen below, free part of upper sepal triangular, with tail 2 in. long, lateral sepals oblong, reflexed, with short tails pointing downward, petals strap-shaped, white with yellow tips, lip fiddle-shaped, yellowish, spotted with purple. Colombia. Cv. **'Inflata'**. Fls. larger, perianth tube more inflated, bright orange-yellow, mottled with brown, paler beneath, tails bright yellow.

Davisii Rchb.f. Lvs. to 8 in. long, narrowly oblanceolate, leathery; scapes more than 8 in. long, 1-fld.; fls. to 2 in. across the lateral sepals, yellow with orange markings at base externally, sepal tube subcylindrical, with prominent keel and swollen at base, free part of upper sepal ovate-triangular, with tail 1 in. long, lateral sepals oblong, united

for more than half their length, contracted at apex into slender cusps, petals and lip very small, concealed, white, lip clawed, linear-oblong, brownish. Peru.

elephanticeps Rchb.f. Lvs. spatulate-cuneate, to 10 in. long, very leathery; scapes stoutish, shorter than lvs., dotted with dull purple, 1-fld.; fls. large, horizontal or deflexed, sepal tube broadly cylindrical, yellowish above, dull purple beneath, upper sepal triangular, with long, leathery, yellowish tail to 3 in. long, lateral sepals reddish-purple on inner side, dull purple outside, oblong, united nearly to middle, with yellowish tails, petals oblong, lip strap-shaped or oblong, papillose above. Colombia.

ephippium Rchb.f. Lvs. elliptic-lanceolate, to 7 in. long; scapes 3-angled, to 12 in. long, racemose, bearing several fls. in succession; sepal tube cylindrical, short, upper sepal nearly orbicular, keeled, yellow, stained with brown outside, tawny-yellow within, with yellow reflexed tail, to 2 in. long in total length, lateral sepals nearly orbicular, forming hemispherical cup, ribbed, chestnut-brown, with long, flexuous, yellow tails to 5 in. long, petals white, linear, sometimes 2–3-toothed at apex, lip small, oblong, clawed, toothed at apex, reddish-brown. Colombia, Ecuador.

Estradae Rchb.f. Dwarf, densely tufted; lvs. elliptic-spatulate, leathery, to 3 in. long, often bifid at apex; scapes longer than lvs., 1-fld.; sepal tube short, campanulate, free part of upper sepal concave, almost helmet-shaped, lateral sepals oblong, nearly flat, with recurved margins, with tails to 2 in. long, basal half and tails yellow, apical half mauve-purple, petals and lip linear-oblong, white. Autumn. Colombia.

Harryana: *M. coccinea* cv.

infracta Lindl. Lvs. glossy, lanceolate, leathery, to 6 in. long; scapes 3-angled, twisted, longer than lvs., producing fls. in succession; sepal tube broadly campanulate, bent, with prominent rib above, swollen below at base, yellowish-white, free part of upper sepal triangular-rotund, concave, yellowish-white, with tail to 1½ in. long, lateral sepals oblong-rotund, united to below middle, keeled at suture, outer half yellowish-white, inner half pale violet-purple, tails yellow, to 2 in. long, petals white, small, linear-oblong, toothed at apex, lip oblong, reflexed at the red-brown apex. Brazil, Peru.

ionocharis Rchb.f. Dwarf, tuft-forming; lvs. elliptic-lanceolate, to 4 in. long; scapes many, as long as lvs., each bearing a solitary fl. ½ in. across; sepal tube campanulate, yellowish, sepals keeled at back, free parts short, white, blotched with violet-purple, tails slender, as long as tube, yellow, petals and lip minute, lip clawed, tongue-shaped, purplish. Peru.

leontoglossa Rchb.f. Lvs. linear-lanceolate, to 7 in. long, leathery, sometimes tinged with deep, dull purple; scapes short, to 2 in. long; sepal tube broadly cylindrical, swollen below, pale yellow-green with 3 purple-spotted ribs above, spotted dull purple beneath, free part of upper sepal triangular, with broad tail 1 in. long, yellow-green, with 3 purple lines on inner side, lateral sepals oblong, united for half of their length, free parts triangular with short tails, yellow-green, spotted with blackish-purple warts arranged in rows with lines of same color between, petals oblong, white with purple median line, lip tongue-shaped, hairy, densely spotted with wine-purple papillae. Venezuela.

macrura Rchb.f. Robust, sts. to 6 in. long; lvs. elliptic-oblong, to 12 in. long, very leathery; scapes as long as lvs., 1-fld.; fls. large, sepal tube short, cylindrical, ribbed, dull tawny-yellow shaded with brown externally as are free parts, studded inside with many blackish-purple warts, tails pale, without warts, free portion of upper sepal lanceolate, with tail to 5 in. long, lateral sepals united to 1 in. beyond tube, with tails to 5 in. long, petals and lip oblong, tawny-yellow, lip papillose, reflexed at tip, spotted with purple below. Colombia, Ecuador.

maculata Klotzsch & Karst. Lvs. linear-lanceolate, to 5 in. long; scapes 3-angled, to 5 in. long, few-fld.; sepal tube short, with prominent rib above, orange-yellow, free part of upper sepal triangular, with tail to 3 in. long, lateral sepals united to below middle, inner half brown-purple, outer half yellow, tails pale yellow, petals and lip oblong, petals white, lip dull purple, papillose, recurved at apex. Late summer–early winter. Venezuela, Colombia.

pachyura Rchb.f. Lvs. elliptic-oblong, to 5 in. long; scapes to 8 in. long, loosely 5–7-fld.; fls. straw-colored, spotted red, sepal tube short, campanulate, upper sepal hooded, with short yellow tail, lateral sepals narrowly ovate, with short, recurved, yellow tails, petals oblong, 3-toothed at apex, lip oblong, 3-keeled. Early spring. Ecuador.

Peristeria Rchb.f. Lvs. oblanceolate-oblong, to 6 in. long; scapes shorter than lvs., 1-fld.; fls. to 5 in. across from tip to tip of sepals, sepal tube broadly cylindrical, swollen at base, 6-ribbed, dull yellowish-green externally, free parts of sepals triangular, yellow, spotted with purple, with stout tawny-yellow tail to 1½ in. long, petals pale greenish-yellow, linear-oblong, lip with claw and oblong, subacute limb dilated in middle and contracted beyond it, upper surface studded with amethystine papillae, recurved at apex. Spring. Colombia.

platyglossa Rchb.f. Lvs. oblong-lanceolate, to 6 in. long, rigid, erect; scapes decumbent, shorter than lvs., 1-fld.; fls. small, 1 in. long, pale yellow, of semitransparent texture, light green, sepal tube cylindrical, swollen below, free parts of sepals triangular, contracted to sharp points, each with 3 prominent veins, petals strap-shaped, with triangular lacinia above middle, lip large, elliptic-oblong, reflexed, with many papillae at apex. Colombia.

polysticta Rchb.f. Lvs. more or less spatulate, emarginate, to 6 in. long; scapes longer than lvs., pale green, spotted with dull purple, 5–7-fld.; fls. short-pedicelled, white, spotted with purple, 2½ in. across from tip to tip of sepals, sepal tube short, free part of upper sepal ovate, concave, with tail 1 in. long, lateral sepals narrowly oblong, convex, with yellow midline and ciliate margins, keeled on back, with white tails spotted dull purple, apical half bright ochraceous-yellow, petals and lip minute, petals spatulate, lip oblong. Ecuador, Peru.

racemosa Lindl. Sts. erect, to 3 in.; lvs. elliptic-oblong, to 4 in. long; scapes to 15 in. long, 8–15-fld.; fls. brilliant orange-red, shaded with crimson, sometimes paler and approaching yellow, sepal tube cylindrical, ribbed, ¾ in. long, free part of upper sepal triangular, reflexed, shortly apiculate, lateral sepals united into a broadly obcordate, tailless blade 1½ in. across, petals and lip minute, whitish, oblong. Colombia.

radiosa Rchb.f. Lvs. oblanceolate, to 8 in. long; scapes decumbent, shorter than lvs., 3- or more-fld., producing fls. successively; sepal tube broadly campanulate, free parts of sepals similar, very short, broadly elliptic, keeled on back, concave, tawny-yellow, pubescent, densely spotted with blackish-purple, with warty papillae in front, and with deep depression at suture of lateral pair, tails to 3 in. long, dull blackish-purple, paler toward tips, petals oblong, keeled, dilated and with blackish wart at apex, lip with fleshy claw and saccate shell-like blade, white with many rose-colored radiating keels within sac. Colombia.

Reichenbachiana Endres. Lvs. oblanceolate, to 6 in. long; scapes erect, longer than lvs., 2–4-fld., producing fls. in succession from pedicels springing from joint below ovary; sepal tube funnel-shaped, bent, reddish-crimson above, pale yellow beneath, free part of upper sepal triangular, yellowish-white, with slender tail to 1½ in. long, lateral sepals deflexed, united for half their length, suddenly contracted into slender awns that cross each other at extremities, yellowish-white, petals, lip, and column minute and concealed within tube. Costa Rica.

Roezlii: *M. chimaera* cv.

rosea Lindl. Lvs. elliptic-lanceolate, to 5 in. long; scapes longer than lvs., 1-fld.; sepal tube to 1½ in. long, angled, compressed, reddish above, orange-yellow at base, free part of upper sepal filiform, to 2 in. long, red above, yellow on inner side, lateral sepals dilated into ovate-lanceolate, concave, rosy-carmine lobes, united to ⅓ their length from base, terminating in short, red tails, petals and lip reduced, minute, strap-shaped, lip with tuft of blackish hairs at apex. Colombia, Ecuador.

Schlimii Linden ex Lindl. Lvs. elliptic-obovate, to 12 in. long or more; scapes longer than lvs., 5–8-fld.; fls. 1¼ in. across vertically, exclusive of tails, sepal tube short, open, light orange-yellow above, upper sepal triangular, concave, light yellow, lateral sepals united to middle, broadly ovate, free parts divergent, yellow, densely mottled with brownish-purple papillae, tails to 2 in. long, golden-yellow, petals linear-oblong, white, lip linear-oblong, reflexed at apex. Late winter–late spring. Venezuela, Colombia.

Shuttleworthii: *M. caudata.*

tovarensis Rchb.f. Lvs. elliptic-spatulate, to 6 in. long; scapes as long as lvs., 3-angled, 2–5-fld.; fls. 1 in. across, pure white, sepal tube cylindrical, slightly swollen below, upper sepal filiform, to 1½ in. long, with dilated triangular base, lateral sepals elliptic-oblong, united for ⅔ their length, abruptly contracted at apex into short awns, petals and lip oblong, petals unequally 2-lobed, lip pointed and reflexed at apex. Early winter. Venezuela, Colombia.

triaristella Rchb.f. Dwarf, densely tufted; lvs. erect, to 1½ in. long, slender, narrowed at both ends, channelled; scapes 1–2-fld.; fls. nearly 1 in. long, reddish-brown with yellow tails, upper sepal small, ovate, contracted into a flexuous, ascending tail ½ in. long, lateral sepals united into a linear-oblong, boat-shaped blade notched at tip, each margin with a filiform tail about as long as that of upper sepal, petals yellow, linear-oblong, erect, 3-toothed at apex, lip tongue-shaped, recurved, 2-lobed at base. Costa Rica, Colombia.

Veitchiana Rchb.f. Lvs. linear-oblong, to 8 in. long; scapes to 18 in. long, 1- to rarely 2-fld.; fls. brilliant orange-red, among largest and most showy in the genus, 2–3 in. across vertically, exclusive of tails, sepal tube campanulate, free parts of sepals broadly ovate, with slender tails (the upper narrowest and longest) of brilliant orange-red with minute crimson-purple papillae, inner surface of sepals studded with minute papillae of brilliant cadmium-yellow, lateral sepals united beyond middle, petals and lip minute, white. Early spring. Peru.

Wagenerana Lindl. Dwarf; lvs. spatulate, leathery, to 2 in. long; scapes as long as lvs., 1-fld.; fls. light buff-yellow with many red dots over sepals and some crimson-red lines at base, sepals broadly elliptic-oblong, with yellow tails to 2 in. long and sharply bent backwards, lateral sepals united to beyond middle, petals hatchet-shaped, 2-toothed at apex, lip rhomboidal, with reflexed, toothed margin, whitish, spotted with red-brown. Flowering throughout year. Venezuela.

Wallisii: *M. chimaera* cv.

Winniana: *M. chimaera* cv.

MASTICHODENDRON Cronq. *Sapotaceae.* Seven spp. of trees, mainly trop., native to Fla., W. Indies, Mex., Cent. Amer.; lvs. alt. to nearly opp., entire; fls. many, in clusters, axillary or at defoliated nodes, sepals 5, imbricate, corolla 5-lobed, without lateral appendages, stamens 5, staminodes 5, ovary superior, usually 5-celled; fr. usually 1-seeded, seed with scar less than half its length.

foetidissimum (Jacq.) Cronq. [*Sideroxylon foetidissimum* Jacq.; *S. Mastichodendron* Jacq.]. To 75 ft.; lvs. broadly elliptic, to 4 in. long, glabrous; fls. yellow or yellowish, to $^3/_{16}$ in. long; fr. yellow or perhaps becoming black, to $1^3/_{16}$ in. long. Fla. and W. Indies, to Mex. and Brit. Honduras.

MATELEA Aubl. *Asclepiadaceae.* About 130 spp. of twining herbs or subshrubs, native to the Americas; similar to *Gonolobus,* but having the anthers relatively simple, without dorsal appendages.

carolinensis (Jacq.) Woodson [*Gonolobus carolinensis* (Jacq.) Schult.; *Vincetoxicum carolinense* (Jacq.) Britt.]. Per. herbs, sts. twining, spreading-pubescent; lvs. suborbicular to oblong, to 8 in. long, acuminate to mucronate, deeply cordate; cymes umbellate, axillary, shorter than lvs.; corolla brownish-purple, to 1 in. across, lobes oblong to narrow-elliptic; follicles to about 4 in. long, with fleshy spines. Se. U.S., n. to Md. and Mo.

MATRICARIA L. MATRICARY. *Compositae* (Anthemis Tribe). About 35 spp. of ann., bien., or per. herbs, often aromatic, native in Eur., Asia, S. Afr., and w. N. Amer.; lvs. alt., pinnatifid or finely pinnately dissected; fl. heads solitary and terminal on brs., or sometimes in corymbs, radiate or discoid, involucre saucer-shaped, involucral bracts imbricate in 2–3 rows, scarious-margined, receptacle hemispherical to conical, often hollow, naked; fls. white or yellow, disc fls. tubular, 4–5-lobed, ray fls. present or absent; achenes 3–5-ribbed or -nerved on inner surface, smooth on outer surface, oil glands lacking on outer surface, scar of point of attachment to receptacle on one side near base, pappus an entire or toothed rim or absent.

Matricarias require only the usual treatment for annuals and perennials, as described for *Chrysanthemum.*

africana Bergius [*M. capensis* L.]. Erect or spreading ann., to 1 ft., sometimes taller; lvs. 1- or 2-pinnately lobed, 1–2 in. long, glabrous or sparsely hairy; receptacle hemispherical or conical; disc fls. yellow, 4-lobed, ray fls. white; achenes 4-angled. S. Afr. Material offered under this name may be *Chrysanthemum Parthenium.*

aurea Schultz-Bip. Much-branched, erect ann., to about 1 ft.; lvs. finely pinnately dissected; heads about ¼ in. across, receptacle hemispherical; disc fls. yellow, ray fls. absent; achenes with 3–5 ribs on inner face. Spain, N. Afr., Caucasus.

capensis: *M. africana,* but material offered as *M. capensis* is usually *Chrysanthemum Parthenium.*

Chamomilla: see *M. recutita* and *Tripleurospermum maritimum* subsp. *inodorum.*

eximia: *Chrysanthemum Parthenium.*

globifera (Thunb.) Fenzl ex Harv. Much-branched ann., to 1½ ft., sts. glabrous or sparsely hairy; lvs. to 1½ in. long, 2–3-pinnately dissected; heads variable in size, involucral bracts glabrous, receptacle globose; disc fls. 4-lobed, ray fls. absent. S. Afr.

grandiflora Fenzl ex Harv. Erect, much-branched ann., to 1½ ft., sts. pubescent, corymbosely branched; lvs. to 2⅜ in. long, 2–3-pinnately lobed; heads to $^5/_{16}$ in. across, involucral bracts tomentose, receptacle flat; disc fls. 4-lobed, ray fls. absent. S. Afr. Material offered under this name may be *Tripleurospermum maritimum* subsp. *inodorum.*

inodora: *Tripleurospermum maritimum* subsp.

maritima: *Tripleurospermum maritimum.*

matricarioides (Less.) C. L. Porter. PINEAPPLE WEED. Erect, glabrous, strongly aromatic ann., to 1 ft.; lvs. to 2 in. long, 1–3-pinnatifid, segms. linear or filiform; heads to 5/16 in. across, involucral bracts with broad, scarious margins, receptacle conical; disc fls. dull greenish-yellow, 4-lobed, ray fls. absent. Common weed of waste places, ne. Asia, Alaska to Baja Calif.; naturalized in e. N. Amer. and other parts of the world.

oreades: *Tripleurospermum oreades.*

parthenoides: *Chrysanthemum Parthenium.*

recutita L. [*M. Chamomilla* of auth., not L.]. SWEET FALSE CHAMOMILE. Sweet-scented, much-branched, glabrous ann., to 2½ ft.; lvs. to 2⅜ in. long, 2-pinnatifid into linear segms.; heads 1 in. across, receptacle conical; disc fls. yellow, 5-lobed, ray fls. 10–20, white, reflexed; achenes 5-ribbed. Eur., w. Asia; naturalized in N. Amer.

suffruticosa (L.) Druce. Erect, strongly aromatic, semiwoody, corymbosely branched ann., sometimes to 1½ ft.; lvs. to 1½ in. long, 2-pinnately lobed; heads densely corymbose, to ¼ in. across; disc fls. bright yellow, 4-lobed, ray fls. absent. S. Afr.

Tchihatchewii: *Tripleurospermum Tchihatchewii.*

MATTEUCCIA Tod. [*Pteretis* Raf.; *Struthiopteris* Willd., not Weiss]. OSTRICH FERN. *Polypodiaceae.* Three spp. of large ferns of temp. N. Amer., Eur., and Asia; lvs. dimorphic, sterile lvs. leafy, longer than fertile lvs., forming a vaselike crown surrounding the fertile lvs., deeply 2-pinnatifid, with separate veins, fertile lvs. with pinnule margins contracted around the sori.

Often transplanted from the wild and easily cultivated outdoors in the North as bold subjects, thriving in half or full shade, in moderately moist to not too dry situations, preferably in rich loamy soil. See also *Ferns.*

nodulosa: *P. pensylvanica.*

pensylvanica (Willd.) Raym. [*M. nodulosa* (Michx.) Fern.; *Onoclea nodulosa* Michx.; *O. Struthiopteris* of Amer. auth., not Hoffm., *O. Struthiopteris* var. *pensylvanica* (Willd.) C. V. Mort.; *Pteretis nodulosa* (Michx.) Nieuwl.; *P. pensylvanica* (Willd.) Fern.; *Struthiopteris germanica* of Amer. auth., not Willd.]. Lvs. 6–9 ft. high, pinnules often revolute, petioles to 14 in. long, 4-angled, green, rachis grooved on upper sides. Cool temp. N. Amer.

Struthiopteris (L.) Tod. [*Pteretis Struthiopteris* (L.) Nieuwl.; *Onoclea Struthiopteris* (L.) Hoffm.]. Differs from *M. pensylvanica* in less erect habit, lvs. shorter, 3–5 ft. long, and petioles to 5 in. long. Cool temp. Eur. and Asia. Var. **pensylvanica:** *M. pensylvanica.*

MATTHIOLA R. Br. STOCK. *Cruciferae.* About 50 spp. of ann. and per. herbs, or subshrubs, mostly in s. Eur., n. Afr., and sw. Asia, gray-pubescent with branched hairs; lvs. long, entire or sinuate or pinnatifid; fls. lilac, purple, to white, in terminal racemes, sepals 4, petals 4, long-clawed; fr. a long, narrow silique with a deeply 2-lobed stigma, the lobes usually with swellings or horns on the outer side.

bicornis: *M. longipetala* subsp.

incana (L.) R. Br. STOCK, GILLYFLOWER, BRAMPTON S., IMPERIAL S. Felty bien. or per., stiffly erect, to 2½ ft.; lvs. oblong to oblanceolate, to 4 in. long; fls. in terminal racemes, about 1 in. long, purple or reddish, varying to white, bluish, and yellowish, fragrant, often fully double; siliques flattened, lacking conspicuous horns. S. Eur.; naturalized in Calif. There are dwarf compact races and races intermediate between bien. and the following. Cv. **'Annua'**. TEN-WEEKS S. Grown as an ann., flowering early from seed.

Stock is grown for summer and autumn bloom in the open, and also under glass. It is a standard garden flower for beds, borders, bouquets, and floral decorations.

The annual or ten-weeks stock is treated as a half-hardy subject, grown for summer and autumn flowers from seeds started in late winter or very early spring, or sometimes later for autumn use. Plants are transplanted as needed to maintain continuous growth and to produce stocky plants. They make good pot plants for the house, from seeds sown in summer.

The intermediate stock requires a longer season; sown at the same time as ten-weeks stock, it succeeds that kind in bloom and, since it is hardier, may be expected to bloom up to cold weather. For spring bloom, the hardy biennial strains are used, the seeds being sown the spring or summer before and the plants carried over winter in a cool house or frame; or they may be lifted in autumn and potted for winter bloom.

longipetala (Venten.) DC. EVENING S., PERFUME PLANT. Straggly-branched ann., low or as much as 1½ ft.; lvs. lanceolate or narrower, to 3½ in. long, entire or few-toothed, lower lvs. sinuate-dentate to pinnatifid; fls. scattered, yellow, pink, or purple; siliques somewhat cylindrical, terminated by stigmatic horns. Se. Eur. Subsp. **bicornis** (Sibth. & Sm.) P. W. Ball [*M. bicornis* Sibth. & Sm]. Fls. pink or purple, very fragrant, opening in evening, siliques with conspicuous, upturned horns. Frequently cult.; escaped in Ariz. and Calif.

MATTIASTRUM (Boiss.) Brand. *Boraginaceae.* About 30 spp. of mostly per. or bien. herbs, native in w. Asia, 1 in India; lvs. simple, alt., narrow; fls. in scorpioid cymes, calyx 5-parted, corolla funnelform, or cylindrical to campanulate, corolla throat with 5 scales, stamens included; fr. of 4 nutlets, each nutlet with a flat, shiny margin.

Propagated by seeds.

racemosum (Schreb.) Brand [*Paracaryum racemosum* Schreb.]. Subcespitose per., to 1 ft., with appressed hairs; lvs. linear to linear-lanceolate, to 3 in. long, often cobwebby; fls. bright blue, funnelform, ⅝ in. long, in scorpioid cymes aggregated into a corymbose panicle. Asia Minor.

MATUCANA: *BORZICACTUS.* **M. Blancii, M. breviflora, M. cereoides, M comacephala, M. elongata, M. Herzogiana, M. hystrix, M. multicolor, M. yanganucensis:** *B. Haynei.*

MAURANDYA [MAURANDIA]: *ASARINA.* **M. purpurea:** *A. Purpusii.* **M. scandens:** *A. scandens* or *A. Lophospermum*, but material cult. as *M. scandens* is usually *A. erubescens.*

MAURITIA L.f. MORICHE PALM. *Palmae.* About 16 spp. of solitary or cespitose, dioecious palms of trop. Amer.; sts. slender to stout, sometimes armed with short, stout spines; lvs. costapalmate, sheaths splitting opp. petiole, petioles elongate, blades divided partly to the base into 1-ribbed segms.; infls. among lvs., elongate, peduncle and bases of primary brs. sheathed with tubular bracts, brs. again divided into short to long rachillae sheathed with tubular bractlets; fls. similar, the male with calyx cupular, petals 3, stamens 6, the female with pistil 3-celled; fr. covered with imbricate scales, seed with ruminate endosperm.

Tender fan palms best suited for tropical planting; require standing water or high water table for best development. For culture see *Palms.*

flexuosa L.f. [*M. setigera* Griseb. & H. Wendl.]. ITA PALM, TREE-OF-LIFE. Sts. columnar, to 100 ft.; lvs. 12–20, petioles to 13 ft. long, cylindrical, blades to 6 ft. long, deeply divided; infls. to 4 ft. long, the male with rachillae elongate, zigzag, slender, the female with rachillae shorter and stouter; fr. to 2 in. in diam., 1¾ in. long. Flooded savannahs or marshlands; Trinidad, n. S. Amer., where used for food, fiber, and building.

setigera: *M. flexuosa.*

MAXILLARIA Ruiz & Pav. [*Camaridium* Lindl.; *Ornithidium* Salisb.]. *Orchidaceae.* About 400 spp. of small to large epiphytes, native to trop. Amer.; sts. pseudobulbous or stemlike, pseudobulbs when present 1- to rarely 4-lvd. at apex; lvs. narrow; scapes lateral, basal, or axillary, 1 to many, 1-fld.; fls. small to large, sepals all separate, lateral sepals united to column foot, forming a mentum, petals similar to sepals, lip erect, concave, deeply 3-lobed, with lateral lobes erect-incurved, column fleshy, arching, with a basal foot, pollinia 2. For structure of fl. see *Orchidaceae.*

Culture as for *Lycaste.* See also *Orchids.*

acuminata Lindl. [*Lycaste acuminata* (Lindl.) Rchb.f.]. Small, with creeping rhizome, pseudobulbs ellipsoid, to 1 in. long, 2-lvd.; lvs. oblong, to 4 in. long; scapes 2–5, lateral, shorter to longer than lvs.; fls. yellow, sepals linear-lanceolate, to 1 in. long, petals elliptic-linear, shorter than sepals and half as wide, lip erect, parallel to column, simple, fleshy, elliptic-oblong, to ⅜ in. long, disc with prominent ovate, sulcate or 2-lobed callus. Colombia to Peru.

camaridii Rchb.f. Rhizomes ascending, branched, clothed with 2-ranked, overlapping lf. sheaths from which lower lvs. have fallen, pseudobulbs ellipsoid, to 2½ in. long, 1–2-lvd. at apex; lvs. sessile, to 15 in. long; fls. many, solitary in axils of lvs., yellowish-white to white with yellow lip, sometimes barred with lilac, sepals elliptic-lanceolate, to 1¼ in. long, petals oblanceolate-oblong, smaller than sepals, lip nearly orbicular, 3-lobed, to ¾ in. long, disc with a central band and dense tubercled papillae, terminating in a transverse many-lobed callus. Flowering throughout year. Trop. Amer.

Colleyi: *Xylobium Colleyi.*

crassifolia (Lindl.) Rchb.f. Pseudobulbs inconspicuous, to 1 in. long, 1-lvd.; lvs. leathery, linear, to 18 in. long; scapes short, to 1 in. long; fls. yellow to orange, marked with purple, campanulate, sepals lanceolate, concave at base, to ¾ in. long, petals linear-oblanceolate, to ½ in. long, lip yellow or orange, tinged with lavender, obscurely 3-lobed, with tomentose callus. Fla., W. Indies, Mex. to n. S. Amer.

cucullata Lindl. Rhizomes with scattered pseudobulbs, pseudobulbs ellipsoid-oblong, to 2½ in. long, 1-lvd.; lvs. linear, to 12 in. long; scapes to 8 in. long; fls. fleshy, deep red, sepals deep red inside, yellow outside, margined with orange, oblong-lanceolate, petals of same color as sepals, linear-oblong, to ¾ in. long, with tips meeting to form hood over column, lip hinged to column foot, deep yellow, spotted and striped with red-brown, to ¾ in. long, disc papillose-puberulent, with thick, broad, papillose callus. Mex., Guatemala, Costa Rica.

curtipes Hook. [*M. Houtteana* Rchb.f.]. Rhizomes elongated, with scattered pseudobulbs, pseudobulbs ellipsoid-oblong, to 2½ in. long, 1-lvd.; lvs. leathery, to 16 in. long; fls. deep red, sepals yellowish on outer surface, deep red within, margined with orange, lateral sepals arching, deep yellow, spotted and striped with red-brown, disc papillose-puberulent, with thick, broad, tumid, papillose callus. Early winter–late spring. Mex., Guatemala, Costa Rica.

densa Lindl. [*Ornithidium densum* (Lindl.) Rchb.f.]. Rhizomes elongated, with many congested leafless pseudobulbs and few terminal leafy pseudobulbs, pseudobulbs elliptic-oblong, to 2¾ in. long, 1-lvd.; lvs. linear-oblong, to 16 in. long, olive-green, leathery; scapes densely clustered; fls. greenish-white and yellowish-white with purplish tinge, to deep maroon or reddish-brown, sepals linear-elliptic, to ⅜ in. long, petals elliptic-lanceolate, lip 3-lobed, fleshy, disc with concave, platelike, obtuse callus between lateral lobes. Mex., Brit. Honduras, Guatemala, Honduras.

elatior Rchb.f. Large, erect, leafy, rhizomes with few scattered pseudobulbs, to 18 in. long, pseudobulbs often solitary, ovoid, to 1¾ in. long, 1–2-lvd.; lvs. linear, leathery, to 16 in. long; scapes to 3 in. long; fls. fleshy, reddish-yellow to brick-red, often mottled, spotted, or striped, sepals oblong-elliptic, to 1 in. long, petals similar to sepals, recurved at apex, to 1 in. long, lip entire, ovate-oblong, arching, to ¾ in. long, disc with blackish smooth callus. Mex., Guatemala, Honduras, Costa Rica.

elegantula Rolfe. Pseudobulbs flattened-ellipsoid, to 2¼ in. long, 1-lvd.; lvs. oblong-elliptic, to 12 in. long; scapes erect, to 10 in. long; fls. large, showy, white, suffused with brownish-purple or dark blue, segms. spreading, upper sepal elliptic-oblong, to 1½ in. long, lateral sepals oblong-lanceolate, petals lanceolate, shorter than upper sepal, lip elliptic in outline, to ½ in. long, disc thickened below. Ecuador, Peru.

Endresii Rchb.f. Pseudobulbs elliptic or rotund, 1-lvd.; lvs. elliptic-oblong, long-petioled, to 16 in. long; scapes several, erect, to 8 in. long; fls. showy, to 4 in. across, sepals and petals linear-lanceolate, cream to light ochre-colored, lip 3-lobed, lateral lobes triangular, erect, parallel with column, dark red, midlobe triangular-ovate, yellow with white margin, disc with a fleshy, apically hairy basal callus. Costa Rica.

exaltata (Kränzl.) C. Schweinf. Sts. erect, to 2½ ft., without pseudobulbs; lvs. leathery, linear-lanceolate, to 10 in. long; scapes several, to 2¼ in. long; fls. of medium size, sepals spreading, separate, pale pinkish-tan, upper sepal linear-lanceolate, to 1 in. long, lateral sepals strapshaped, to 1 in. long, petals linear-lanceolate, pale pinkish-tan, ¾ in. long, lip 3-lobed, reddish-brown, ¾ in. long, conspicuously thickened and minutely papillose, with prominent tubercle on underside of apex, disc with strap-shaped, concave, obtuse callus. Peru.

Friedrichsthalii Rchb.f. Rhizomes creeping, with clustered or distant pseudobulbs, pseudobulbs ellipsoid, 2–4-lvd.; lvs. elliptic, to 10 in. long; scapes to ¾ in. long; fls. arching, fleshy, not showy, sepals and petals olive-green to light yellow, marked with deep yellow or light purple, sepals lanceolate, to 1½ in. long, petals elliptic-lanceolate, to 1 in. long, lip greenish-yellow, spotted with purple on margins or tinted with lavender, elliptic-lanceolate, to 1 in. long. Cent. Amer.

galeata: *Gongora galeata.*

grandiflora (HBK) Lindl. [*M. Lehmannii* Rchb.f.]. Pseudobulbs oblong-ovoid, flattened, to 2¼ in. long, 1-lvd.; lvs. to 10 in. long, leathery, stout-petioled; scapes 1 or 2, to 10 in. long; fls. fleshy, milk-white, upper sepal ovate-oblong, to 1¾ in. long, lateral sepals triangularovate, longer than dorsal sepal, petals elliptic-lanceolate, shorter and narrower than upper sepal, lip buff-yellow, erect, 1 in. long, entire and slightly undulate-crenulate on margins, obscurely 3-lobed, disc densely scurfy, with 3 central calluses, lateral lobes streaked with wine-purple. N. Andean S. Amer.

Houtteana: *M. curtipes.*

Lehmannii: *M. grandiflora.*

lepidota Lindl. Pseudobulbs oblong, to 1½ in. long, 1-lvd.; lvs. linearlanceolate, to 6 in. long; scapes to 6 in. long; sepals all about equal, pale yellow, long-attenuate, twisted, brown-red, to 1½ in. long, petals shorter, pale yellow, to 1¼ in. long, lip 3-lobed, to ¾ in. long, boatshaped, pale yellow, edged with red at apex, densely furry inside from the blunt, oblong callus forward. Venezuela to Ecuador.

Lindeniae Cogn. Pseudobulbs 1-lvd.; lvs. large, to 12 in. long; infl. to 10 in. long; fls. showy, to 5 in. across, sepals milk-white, somewhat fleshy, upper sepal to 2¾ in. long, lateral sepals ovate-triangular, petals triangular, shorter than sepals, milk-white with pale rose-colored stripes, lip much shorter, to 1 in. long, obovate, strongly concave, plicate, crisped near the rounded apex, yellow, with 5 or 6 reddish stripes on lateral lobes, and lemon-yellow through center, disc with central tomentose band in lower half. Peru.

luteoalba Lindl. Erect, pseudobulbs oblong-ovoid, to 2 in. long, 1-lvd.; lvs. leathery, linear-lanceolate, to 20 in. long; scapes to 3, erect, to 5½ in. long; fls. conspicuous, sepals spreading, strap-shaped, white on outer surface, pale yellow within, to 2 in. long, petals strap-shaped, to 1¾ in. long, white outside, pale yellow within, lip 3-lobed, deep yellow, margined with white, to 1 in. long, disc with a tongue-shaped, laterally 2-keeled, acute callus. Costa Rica to Ecuador.

maleolens Schlechter. Erect, to 1½ ft., pseudobulbs close together or solitary, oblong, to 3 in. long, 1-lvd.; lvs. leathery, strap-shaped, to 18 in. long; scapes solitary, to 3 in. long; fls. of medium size, fragrant, sepals elliptic-lanceolate, spreading, yellow, to 1 in. long, petals yellow, strap-shaped, to ¾ in. long, lip obscurely 3-lobed, reddish-brown to rich purple, sometimes with yellow lateral lobes, to 1 in. long, disc with narrow, thickened central vein. Honduras, Costa Rica, Panama.

neglecta (Schlechter) L. O. Williams. Rhizomes branched, pseudobulbs close together to widely separated, suborbicular, to 1¾ in. long, 1-lvd.; lvs. strap-shaped, to 7 in. long; scapes short; fls. small, sepals separate, concave, yellow or white, to ¼ in. long, upper sepal ellipticovate, lateral sepals rhombic, petals oblong-strap-shaped, shorter than sepals, of same color as sepals, lip yellow, ¼ in. long, 3-lobed, with narrow transverse callus on disc. Nicaragua to Panama.

nigrescens Lindl. Pseudobulbs ovoid, to 3½ in. long, 1-lvd.; lvs. narrow, to 14 in. long; scapes to 5½ in. long, clothed in 4–5 brown-flecked sheaths; sepals and petals oblong-strap-shaped, maroon-red to yellow at base, to maroon-orange at apex, petals generally darker, sepals 1¾ in. long, petals 1½ in. long, lip to ¾ in. long, dark maroon-puce, glossy except for fleshy apex, column ovate-elliptic, acute, dark maroon-red. Venezuela, Colombia.

picta Hook. Pseudobulbs ovate, to 2 in. long, 1–2-lvd.; lvs. oblonglanceolate, to 10 in. long; scapes to 6 in. high; sepals white, spotted with purple outside, orange-yellow and spotted with purple inside, incurved, oblong-linear, petals similar, lip pale dirty-white or creamcolored, spotted with purple, 3-lobed, disc with an oblong downy swelling, column almost purple-black. Colombia, Brazil.

porphyrostele Rchb.f. Pseudobulbs orbicular-ovoid, to 1¼ in. long, 2-lvd; lvs. erect, to 8 in. long; scapes to 2¾ in. long; fls. showy, segms. greenish-yellow outside, orange-yellow inside, to 1¼ in. long, sepals fleshy, spreading, oblong-strap-shaped, petals linear-strap-shaped, somewhat shorter than sepals, lip distinctly 3-lobed in middle, lateral lobes arching, midlobe oblong-orbicular, with a central callus. Brazil.

Reichenheimiana Endres & Rchb.f. Pseudobulbs less than ½ in. long, 1-lvd.; lvs. broadly ovate, thick, stiff, dull green with maroon tinge on margins and white spots on upper surface, to 5 in. long; scapes longer than lvs.; sepals linear-lanceolate, orange, to 1½ in. long, petals triangular-lanceolate, yellow-orange, to 1 in. long, lip ½ in. long, 3-lobed, lateral lobes semiovate, maroon, the small orbicular midlobe and callus yellow, underside dark maroon except for midlobe, which bears scattered white glandular hairs, column pale brown, flushed with red-maroon. Costa Rica to Venezuela.

rufescens Lindl. Extremely variable, pseudobulbs ovoid, 4-angled, to 2¼ in. long, 1-lvd.; lvs. sessile or short-petioled, elliptic-oblong, to 12 in. long; scapes 1 to several; fls. commonly yellow to orange with red or purple spots on lip, rarely white, reddish-green, or salmon-pink, sepals to ⅜ in. long, elliptic-oblong, petals oblong-lanceolate, as long as sepals, lip erect, 3-lobed, to ¾ in. long, lateral lobes acute, midlobe squarish, disc with median linear-oblong callus below middle. Cent. Amer., n. S. Amer.

Sanderana Rchb.f. Pseudobulbs clustered, ovoid, to 2 in. long, 1-lvd.; lvs. petioled, elliptic-oblong, to 16 in. long, leathery; scapes 1 to several, to 6 in. long; fls. fleshy, to 4 in. across, sepals and petals white with blotches of deep purple at base, upper sepal oblong, concave, to 3 in. long, lateral sepals triangular-ovate, a little longer than dorsal sepal, petals lanceolate-triangular, a little shorter than upper sepal, lip erect, parallel to column, recurved, half as long as sepals, elliptic, crisped-undulate on margin, bright yellow inside, streaked with purple. Ecuador, Peru.

sanguinea Rolfe. Rhizomes with pseudobulbs at short intervals, pseudobulbs ellipsoid, flattened, to 1¼ in. long, 1-lvd.; lvs. grasslike, to 16 in. long; scapes to 1¼ in. long; fls. fleshy, deep red or bronze with yellowish blotches, sepals oblong-elliptic, to 1 in. long, petals elliptic-oblanceolate, to ¾ in. long, lip obscurely 3-lobed, oblong-elliptic with whitish tip, to ½ in. long. Costa Rica, Panama.

setigera Lindl. Pseudobulbs round, somewhat compressed, 1–2-lvd.; lvs. to 5 in. long; sepals and petals linear-oblong, green-yellow in apical half, blending to white at base, with minute spicules at apices, petals with roughly recurved margins, to 2 in. long, lip to 1 in. long, 3-lobed, thickened axially, rigid, callus and disc of midlobe yellow, covered with fine hairs, margin and acute lateral lobes white with purple stripes. Guyana to Colombia.

striata Rolfe. Pseudobulbs clustered, ovoid, to 3 in. long, 1-lvd.; lvs. elliptic-oblong, leathery, to 9 in. long; scapes several, arching, to 12 in. long; fls. showy, sepals greenish-yellow, closely striped with red-purple, upper sepal to 2½ in. long, oblong-lanceolate, lateral sepals triangular-lanceolate, petals lanceolate, lip erect, 3-lobed near apex, disc with apically rounded callus. Ecuador, Peru.

tenuifolia Lindl. Rhizomes straggly, pendent or ascending, with pseudobulbs at short intervals, pseudobulbs ovoid, to 2¼ in. long, 1-lvd.; lvs. linear, to 20 in. long; scapes to ¾ in. long; fls. showy, dark red, variously marked with yellow or red, sepals elliptic-lanceoate, to 1 in. long, petals linear-lanceolate, to 1 in. long, lip dark red and yellow or whitish, marked with purple dots, ovate-oblong, to ¾ in. long, disc papillose, with narrow, dark maroon, puberulent callus on lower ⅓. Cent. Amer.

uncata Lindl. Dense, varying from leafy clumps to straggly pendent rhizomes, pseudobulbs small, cylindric-spindle-shaped, to ½ in. long, 1-lvd.; lvs. linear, to 2¾ in. long; scapes to ½ in. long; fls. white, pink, or greenish, tinged or veined with reddish-brown and purple, upper sepal lanceolate, to ½ in. long, lateral sepals triangular-lanceolate, to ⅝ in. long, petals linear, to ⅜ in. long, disc with flat, round, yellowish callus. Brit. Honduras to Peru and Brazil.

Valenzuelana (A. Rich.) Nash. Lvs. in fan-shaped spray, to 7 in. long, fleshy; scapes to 2 in. long; sepals ovate, light green, fleshy, to ⅜ in. long, petals oblong, pale green, thin, to ⅜ in. long, lip fleshy, to ⅜ in. long, rhomboid, pale brown with dark puce spots, callus divided into apical median and basal sections of clotted masses of water-white glandular hairs. Trop. Amer.

variabilis Batem. ex Lindl. Rhizomes erect or pendent, to 12 in. long, pseudobulbs elliptic, to 2¼ in. long, 1-lvd.; lvs. linear, to 10 in. long; scapes several, to 1 in. long; fls. inconspicuous, white to dark red, often orange or greenish-yellow marked with red, sepals ovate, wine-red, marked with orange-yellow on upper margins, to ¾ in. long, petals oblong, about as long as sepals, lip jointed to column foot, erect and then arching, fleshy, wine-red except for yellowish blotch on apex, somewhat mottled on inner surface at base, 3-lobed, to ½ in. long. Cent. Amer.

venusta Linden & Rchb.f. Pseudobulbs close together, ovoid, to 1½ in. long, 1-lvd.; lvs. oblong-strap-shaped, to 12 in. long; scapes to 6 in. long; sepals and petals triangular-lanceolate, white, with recurved margins, sepals to 2½ in. long, petals to 1¾ in. long, lip to ¾ in. long, fleshy, rhombic, yellow with a touch of maroon flush on margins, callus inconspicuous, covered in basal half with mealy material, column white. Venezuela, Colombia.

Wercklei (Schlechter) L. O. Williams. Rhizomes erect or pendent, pseudobulbs distantly spaced, linear, to 1 in. long, 1-lvd.; lvs. leathery, elliptic, to 1¼ in. long; scapes slender, to ½ in. long; fls. variable in size, usually tan striped with red or brown, to dark reddish-purple, sepals lanceolate, spreading, to ½ in. long, petals oblong-lanceolate, to ½ in. long, lip 3-lobed, to ⅜ in. long, callus fleshy. Costa Rica to Colombia.

MAXIMILIANA Mart. *Palmae*. A few spp. of solitary, monoecious palms of humid trop. Amer.; lvs. large, pinnate, pinnae many, 1-ribbed, acute; infls. long-peduncled, among lvs., often pendulous at least in fr., bracts 2, the upper very thick, woody, grooved outside, often beaked, enclosing the infl. in bud, rachillae simple, bearing fls. of one sex only or with fls. of both sexes; male fls. with sepals very small, petals small, shorter than the 6 stamens, anthers straight, female fls. with pistil 1–3-celled; fr. usually beaked, 1–3-seeded, mesocarp fleshy-fibrous, endocarp bony, with 3 pores near base, seed with homogeneous endosperm.

Tender; for culture see *Palms*.

caribaea: *M. Maripa.*

Maripa (Corréa) Drude [*M. caribaea* Griseb. & H. Wendl.; *M. Martiana* Karst.; *M. regia* Mart.]. CUCURITE PALM, INAJA P. To 60 ft., trunk to 1 ft. in diam., with obscure lf. scars; lvs. 10–15 or more, erect-arching, to 20 ft. long or more, pinnae 170–260 on each side of rachis, borne in groups of 4–9 and in several planes; infls. to 3 ft. long or more, upper bract to 3 ft. long, rachillae 200–350, male fls. with petals to about ¼ in. long; fr. ovoid to ovoid-ellipsoid, to 2¾ in. long. Trinidad, ne. S. Amer., where used locally for thatching.

Martiana: *M. Maripa.*

regia: *M. Maripa.*

MAXIMILIANEA: *COCHLOSPERMUM.*

MAYTENUS Mol. [*Gymnosporia* (Wight & Arn.) Hook.f.]. *Celastraceae*. About 200 spp. of polygamous trees and shrubs, native to tropics and subtropics of New and Old World, sts. spiny or unarmed; lvs. alt. or sometimes clustered, simple, leathery; fls. small, white, greenish, yellowish, or red, in cymes or clusters, or rarely in panicles, bisexual or unisexual, sepals, petals, and stamens 4–6; fr. a 2–3-valved caps.

A few species may be planted in warm regions. Propagated by seeds, cuttings, or suckers.

Boaria Mol. MAYTEN. Graceful, evergreen tree, to 25 ft. and more; lvs. lanceolate to ovate-lanceolate, to 2 in. long, finely serrate; fls. greenish, in axillary clusters; caps. 2-valved, seeds with scarlet aril. Chile.

serratus (Hochst. ex A. Rich.) R. Wilcz. [*Gymnosporia serrata* (Hochst. ex A. Rich) Loes.]. Evergreen shrub, to 6 ft. or more; lvs. elliptic or ovate to oblanceolate, to 3 in. long, finely toothed; fls. whitish; caps. 3-valved. Ethiopia.

MAZUS Lour. *Scrophulariaceae*. About 30 spp. of low, mat-forming herbs, native to Asia, Australia, and the Malay Arch.; lvs. toothed or cut, lower lvs. opp. or in a rosette, upper lvs. mostly alt.; fls. blue or white, in terminal, more or less one-sided racemes, calyx 5-lobed, corolla 2-lipped, upper lip 2-lobed, lower lip 3-lobed, with 2 prominent ridges in the throat, stamens 4; fr. a caps.

Grown as ground cover or in rock gardens; of simple requirements and increased by division or seeds.

japonicus (Thunb.) O. Kuntze [*M. rugosus* Lour.]. Trailing per., fl. sts. to 1 ft.; lvs. obovate, 2½ in. long, coarsely toothed; fls. to ¾ in. long, blue, the ridges of the lower lip brown-spotted and bearded with club-shaped hairs. E. Asia; naturalized locally in U.S. in waste ground and lawns.

pumilio R. Br. Tufted per., with creeping underground sts.; lvs. obovate, to 3 in. long, entire or coarsely toothed; fls. white or bluish, with yellow center, to 5/16 in. long. New Zeal. and Australia.

radicans (Hook.f.) Cheesem. Creeping per., to 3 in., sts. stout, rooting at nodes; lvs. obovate, often narrowly so, to 2 in. long, obtuse, mostly entire, usually pilose; fls. 1–3 on terminal peduncles, corolla to ¾ in. long, white, with yellow center. New Zeal.

reptans N. E. Br. Tufted per., to 2 in., sts. rooting at nodes; lvs. lanceolate to elliptic, to 1 in. long, coarsely toothed; corolla to ¾ in. long, purplish-blue, lower lip spotted white, yellow, and purple. Probably Himalayas. Material offered in the trade as *M. rugosus* probably belongs to this sp.

rugosus: *M. japonicus*, but material grown as *M. rugosus* is probably *M. reptans.*

MECONELLA Nutt. *Papaveraceae*. Three or 4 spp. of ann. herbs, native to w. N. Amer.; sts. slender; lvs. opp.; fls. solitary, petals falling early. Closely related to *Platystemon*, but differing in having only 6–12 stamens and mostly 3 carpels.

linearis (Benth.) A. Nels. & Macbr. To 10 in.; lvs. basal, linear, to 2½ in. long; fls. scapose, cream-colored, to ¾ in. long. Ore. and Calif.

MECONOPSIS Vig. ASIATIC POPPY. *Papaveraceae*. About 45 spp. of ann., bien., or per. herbs with yellow sap, native mostly to the Himalayas and w. China, one in w. Eur.; lvs. entire, lobed, or dissected; fls. yellow, reddish, or blue, solitary or in racemes or panicles, sepals 2, soon falling, petals 4–9, stamens many; fr. an oblong, ovoid or obovoid, or cylindrical caps. opening at the top.

Grown in the flower and rock garden under cool temperate conditions. Some species are monocarpic; others remain in the garden for many years. Hardy or semihardy, but most species require special treatment, in general a soil sufficiently well drained to be dry during winter, but moist during the growing season. A mixture of equal parts of leafmold, granulated peat, and sharp coarse sand to a depth of one ft. or more is sometimes recommended. They should be planted in a somewhat shaded situation where they are protected from excessive summer heat and strong winds. The plants are deep-rooted and long-lived and are best not disturbed after becoming established. They are best grown from seeds.

aculeata Royle. Monocarpic, st. to 2 ft., leafy, spiny; lvs. irregularly pinnatifid, basal and lower st. lvs. petioled, to 11 in. long, sparsely spinose, upper st. lvs. sessile; fls. blue, purplish, or red, to 3 in. across, solitary, on axillary pedicels 1–9 in. long. W. Himalayas.

×**Aliceae** G. Tayl.: *M. napaulensis* × *M. paniculata* Prain. Monocarpic, st. to 6 ft., reddish-bristly; basal lvs. in rosette, lower lvs. to 12 in. long, pinnatifid, upper lvs. sessile, pinnately lobed; fls. yellow, flushed with red, solitary or in pairs, in upper lf. axils.

alpina: a listed name of no botanical standing, perhaps for *M. cambrica*.

Baileyi: *M. betonicifolia*.

×**Beamishii** Prain: *M. grandis* × *M. integrifolia*. Per., to 4 ft.; basal lvs. petioled, to 10 in. long, upper st. lvs. in a false whorl; fls. yellow, sometimes with purple marking at base of petals.

bella Prain. Stemless per.; lvs. basal, crowded, to 4 in. long, pinnately cut; fls. pale blue, to 2 in. across, solitary, on scapes to 3 in. high. Himalayas.

betonicifolia Franch. [*M. Baileyi* Prain; *M. Baileyi* var. *pratensis* F. K. Ward]. BLUE POPPY. Monocarpic or persistent per., to 6 ft.; lvs. ovate to oblong, to 6 in. long, cut-toothed or nearly lobed, glaucous beneath; fls. blue-violet or purple, about 2 in. across, in cymes. China.

cambrica (L.) Vig. WELSH POPPY. Per., st. erect, branched, leafy, to 2 ft.; basal lvs. from a tufted rootstock, long-petioled, to 8 in. long, pinnately divided, upper st. lvs. similar, but petiole shorter; fls. yellow, to 3 in. across, solitary. W. Eur. Cv. 'Aurantiaca' [var. *aurantiaca* Hort.ex Wehrh.]. Fls. orange. Cv. 'Flore Pleno' [var. *flore-pleno* Nichols.]. Fls. double, orange or yellow.

Cathcartii: a listed name of no botanical standing.

chelidonifolia Bur. & Franch. Per., st. branched, to 3 ft.; basal lvs. petioled, deeply pinnately lobed, st. lvs. sessile; fls. yellow, to 1 in. across, on slender pedicels in upper lf. axils. W. China.

Delavayi (Franch.) Franch. ex Prain. Per., st. short, branched; lvs. basal, broadly ovate to narrowly oblanceolate, to 6 in. long, 1½ in. wide, entire, glaucous beneath; fls. somewhat pendulous, on a scape to 11 in. long, petals 4–8, deep purple or rarely rose, to 1¼ in. long. W. China.

Dhwojii G. Tayl. ex T. Hay. Monocarpic, st. branched in upper part, to 2 ft.; basal and lower lvs. long-petioled, to 13 in. long, pinnatifid, bristly, upper lvs. similar, but smaller; fls. yellow, to 3 in. across, many, on axillary brs. Nepal. A woodland plant requiring well-drained soil, especially at crown, and shade.

gracilipes G. Tayl. Monocarpic, st. branched, to 2 ft.; basal lvs. in a rosette, petioled, to 10 in. long, deeply lobed, sparsely bristly; fls. yellow, to 2¼ in. across, on 1–3-fld. brs. Nepal.

grandis Prain. Per., st. erect, rigid, bristly, to 4 ft.; basal and lower lvs. petioled, oblanceolate, to 7 in. long, entire or coarsely toothed; fls. purple or deep blue, to 5 in. across, solitary, on scapes or in upper lf. axils. Himalayas.

heterophylla: *Stylomecon heterophylla*.

horridula Hook.f. & T. Thoms. [*M. Prattii* (Prain) Prain; *M. rudis* (Prain) Prain]. Monocarpic, to 3½ ft.; basal and lower lvs. elliptic to linear-oblong, to 10 in. long, entire or irregularly lobed, covered with yellow or purple spines; fls. light blue or claret-colored, rarely white, many, solitary, in upper lf. axils or on scapes. High elevations, Himalayas and w. China.

integrifolia (Maxim.) Franch. YELLOW CHINESE POPPY. Monocarpic, covered with soft spreading hairs, st. to 3½ ft.; basal lvs. in dense rosette, lvs. linear-lanceolate, to 8 in. long, entire; fls. yellow, to 6 in. across, usually in upper lf. axils. E. Himalayas and w. China.

latifolia (Prain) Prain. Monocarpic, st. to 3½ ft., more or less covered with spreading spines; basal and lower st. lvs. oblong to broadly lanceolate, to 8 in. long, serrate to crenulate, covered with spines; fls. pale blue to white, to nearly 3 in. across, many, solitary in upper lf. axils. Kashmir. Best in gritty soil and partial shade.

napaulensis DC. [*M. Wallichii* Hook.f.]. SATIN POPPY. Monocarpic, st. branched, to 8 ft.; basal lvs. in rosette, petioled, to 20 in. long, pinnately cut or lobed, upper st. lvs. sessile, entire or lobed; fls. blue, red, or purple, rarely white, to 3 in. across, many, nodding, solitary in upper lf. axils. E. Himalayas to w. China.

paniculata (D. Don) Prain. Monocarpic, st. to 6 ft., branched; basal lvs. in a rosette, long-petioled, variable, pinnately toothed or divided, to 31 in. long, 8 in. wide, st. lvs. similar but petiole shorter; fls. pendulous, solitary in upper lf. axils, petals yellow, to 2 in. long. Himalayas.

Prattii: *M. horridula*.

quintuplinervia Regel. HAREBELL POPPY. Per., to 1 ft.; lvs. in basal rosettes, obovate to lanceolate, to 10 in. long, usually with 3–5 longitudinal nerves, bristly; fls. lavender-blue to purplish, to 3½ in. across. Ne. Tibet. Best on stony ledges of rock gardens in stony scree.

regia G. Tayl. Monocarpic, covered with soft hairs, to 2 ft.; lvs. petioled, elliptic, to 16 in. long, basal lvs. in a dense rosette, upper lvs. sessile; fls. yellow, to 3 in. across, solitary on upper brs., in 4's on lower brs. High elevations, Nepal.

rudis: *M. horridula*.

×**Sarsonsii** Sars.: *M. betonicifolia* × *M. integrifolia*. Monocarpic or per., to 3 ft.; fls. yellow, solitary in upper lf. axils. Resembles *M. betonicifolia* in habit, *M. integrifolia* in fl. color.

×**Sheldonii** G. Tayl. *M. betonicifolia* × *M. grandis*. Per., to 4 ft.; basal and lower st. lvs. oblong-lanceolate, to 8 in. long, serrate, bristly, upper lvs. sessile; fls. blue, on pedicels in upper lf. axils.

simplicifolia (D. Don) Walp. Monocarpic or per., to 2 ft.; lvs. all basal, lanceolate, to 6½ in. long, usually entire, weakly spinose-hairy; fls. purple to sky-blue, to 3 in. across, solitary, nodding. Nepal and Tibet.

superba King ex Prain. Monocarpic, to 3½ ft.; lvs. oblanceolate to ovate, to 16 in. long, basal lvs. persistent, in a rosette, with petiole to 2 in. long, upper st. lvs. sessile; fls. white, to 5½ in. across, solitary in upper lf. axils, on pedicels to nearly 5 in. long. Tibet. Suited to woodland planting with good drainage, especially at crown.

villosa (Hook.f.) G. Tayl. Per., st. unbranched, to 2 ft., reddish-bristly; basal lvs. long-petioled, cordate-ovate, 3–5-lobed, the lobes cut; fls. yellow, 2 in. across, in cymes. Himalayas.

Wallichii: *M. napaulensis*.

MEDEMIA Württemb. *Palmae*. Not cult. **M. nobilis**: *Bismarckia nobilis*.

MEDEOLA L. INDIAN CUCUMBER ROOT. *Liliaceae*. One sp., a per. herb native to e. N. Amer.; rhizome thickened, tuberlike; lvs. in 2 whorls; fls. in a sessile, few-fld., terminal umbel, perianth segms. 6, separate, recurved, stamens 6, anthers versatile; fr. a globose berry, seeds few.

asparagoides: *Asparagus asparagoides*.

virginica L. To 2½ ft.; lvs. of lower whorl to 5 in. long and 2 in. wide, lvs. of upper whorl to 2 in. long; fls. 2–9, greenish-yellow, to ½ in. long; fr. dark purple. Nov. Sc. to Minn., s. to Fla., Ala., La. The rhizomes are crisp and edible, with a cucumberlike flavor.

MEDICAGO L. MEDIC, MEDICK. *Leguminosae*. (subfamily *Faboideae*). About 50 spp. of ann. and per. herbs, rarely shrubby, native to the Old World; lvs. of 3 small lfts., stipules united to petioles; fls. in short, axillary racemes or heads, small, papilionaceous, stamens 10, 9 united and 1 separate; fr. a curved or spirally twisted legume.

Several species are important for fodder and green manure . Alfalfa (*M. sativa*), the most important of our forage crops, should be grown on deep, well-drained, nonacid soil. Propagated by seeds sown in drills or broadcasted. The annual species grown as ornamentals require no special treatment.

arborea L. Shrubby, to 12 ft., new brs. white-tomentose; lfts. obovate-cuneate, entire or minutely toothed at apex; fls. golden, ⁵⁄₁₆ in. long; fr. a flat, spiral legume, not spiny. S. Eur.

denticulata: *M. hispida*.

hispida Gaertn. [*M. denticulata* Willd.]. BUR CLOVER, TOOTHED B.C. Glabrous ann.; lfts. emarginate, minutely toothed at apex, stipules deeply incised; fls. yellow, in loose heads of 3–8; fr. coiled, spiny. Eur., Asia; naturalized in N. Amer.

lupulina L. BLACK MEDIC, HOP CLOVER, YELLOW TREFOIL, NONE-SUCH. Ann., sts. procumbent or ascending; lfts. minutely toothed at apex; fls. yellow; fr. curved, nearly glabrous. Eurasia; naturalized in N. Amer. A fodder plant.

orbicularis (L.) Bartal. Glabrous ann.; racemes 1–5-fld.; petals yellow; fr. spiral, smooth. S. Eur., w. Asia.

sativa L. ALFALFA, LUCERNE. Per.; lfts. oblong-cuneate; fls. in heads of 8–25, purplish, ⁵⁄₁₆ in. long; fr. loosely spiral, pubescent, not spiny. Sw. Asia; naturalized in N. Amer. Widely cult. since ancient times.

MEDINILLA Gaud.-Beaup. [*Hypenanthe* (Blume) Blume]. *Melastomataceae*. About 150 spp. of shrubs or epiphytes, native to trop. Afr., se. Asia, and Pacific Is.; lvs. simple, entire; fls. in panicles or cymes, white or pink, stamens 8–10, equal or nearly so, appendaged; fr. a berry, crowned by persistent calyx lobes.

Grown in greenhouses or in the open in tropics where used for hedges and in foundation plantings. The plants should be given plenty of light, but shaded from direct sunlight. Propagated by cuttings from growing points of young shoots potted singly in a mixture of finely sifted sand and peat, and kept fairly moist and in a humid atmosphere.

magnifica Lindl. Evergreen shrub, to 8 ft., sts. 4-angled to 4-winged; lvs. sessile, ovate to ovate-oblong, to 1 ft. long; panicles pendulous, to 18 in. long, bracts pinkish, showy, 1–4 in. long; fls. 1 in. across, pink to coral-red. Rain forest epiphyte, Philippine Is.

Scortechinii King. Epiphyte, to 4 ft., sts. wiry, warty; lvs. leathery, oblong-ovate, 4–7 in. long, 1½–3 in. wide, short-acuminate; panicles cymose, pendent, many-fld., to 4 in. long, peduncle cherry-red; fls. to ½ in. long, bright red; fr. globular, to ¼ in. long. Mts., Malay Pen.

Teysmannii Miq. Sts. 4-winged; lvs. subsessile, ovate to elliptic-oblong, 8–20 in. long, reddish beneath; panicles erect, pyramidal, 10–20 in long, bractless; fls. ¾ in. across, rose-pink. Celebes, New Guinea, Philippine Is.

venosa (Blume) Blume [*Hypenanthe venosum* (Blume) Blume; *Melastoma venosum* Blume]. Sts. cylindrical, densely reddish-brown-tomentose; lvs. oblong-elliptic, 3–6 in. long, mostly 7-nerved, nearly glabrous above, stellate-pubescent beneath, especially along the veins; fls. about 1 in. across, pink, pedicels reddish-brown-tomentose. Philippine Is., Molucca Is.

MEDIOCACTUS: *SELENICEREUS.* **M. coccineus:** *S. setaceus.*

MEDIOLOBIVIA: *REBUTIA.* **M. elegans:** *R. aureiflora.* **M. Haagei:** *Lobivia pygmaea.* **M. pygmaea:** *Lobivia pygmaea.*

MEEHANIA Britt. MEEHAN'S MINT. *Labiatae.* A few spp. of low, usually stoloniferous, per. herbs of temp. e. Asia and e. N. Amer.; sts. mostly square in cross section; lvs. opp., toothed, petioled; fls. in few-fld. verticillasters arranged in short, erect spikes, calyx tubular, 15-nerved, 5-toothed, limb 2-lipped, upper lip 3-lobed, lower lip 2-lobed, shorter, corolla showy, purplish to lavender, tubular, expanded at throat, 2-lipped, upper lip concave, 2-lobed, lower lip 3-lobed, broad, stamens 4, in 2 pairs, not exserted, anther cells parallel; fr. of 4 glabrous nutlets.

Hardy; plants of rich mountain woods; of easy culture.

cordata (Nutt.) Britt. [*Cedronella cordata* (Nutt.) Benth.]. CREEPING MINT, MEEHAN'S M. Low, with slender stolons, hairy; lvs. opp., broadly cordate, 1–2 in. long, crenate, petioled; spikes terminal on short, ascending st.; calyx ⅜ in. long, puberulent, corolla bright lavender or lilac, hairy inside, to 1¼ in. long. Early summer. Rich woods, sw. Penn. to N.C. and Tenn. Good ground cover for shady spots.

MEGACLINIUM: *BULBOPHYLLUM.*

MEGASEA: *BERGENIA.*

MEGASKEPASMA Lindau. *Acanthaceae.* One sp., a shrub of Venezuela; lvs. opp., large, ovate, short-petioled; fls. in a terminal spike, bracts large, conspicuous, brightly colored, calyx 5-parted, segms. equal, corolla narrowly tubular, abruptly 2-lipped, stamens 2; fr. an oblong caps., with 4 seeds in slightly enlarged upper half.

erythrochlamys Lindau. BRAZILIAN RED-CLOAK. To 6 ft., sts. somewhat quadrangular; lvs. to 12 in. long or more; spikes to 12 in. long, bracts red, ovate to ovate-lanceolate, to 1½ in. long, 3-nerved from base; corolla white, to 3 in. long. Cult. in warm regions, as Fla. Has been cult. erroneously under the name *Adhatoda cydoniifolia,* which is a synonym of *Justicia cydoniifolia.*

MELALEUCA L. HONEY MYRTLE, BOTTLEBRUSH. *Myrtaceae.* More than 100 spp. of shrubs or small trees, nearly all Australian, several n. to New Guinea and the Malay Arch.; lvs. usually alt., sometimes opp. or whorled, usually subsessile, entire, flat, concave, or semicylindrical; fls. sessile, in heads or cylindrical spikes, the axis usually growing beyond into a leafy shoot; calyx tube 5-lobed, petals 5, stamens many, much longer than petals, in 5 bundles opp. petals, the united basal part (claw) of each bundle flattened; fr. a caps., enclosed by the enlarged, woody calyx tube. The long-exserted stamens make infl. resemble a bottlebrush. Similar to *Callistemon,* (also called bottlebrush), but having stamens united in bundles opp. petals.

For culture see *Callistemon.*

acuminata F. J. Muell. Glabrous shrub, to 15 ft., bark rough, brs. rather slender, wandlike; lvs. mostly opp., lanceolate-acuminate, to ½ in. long, often pungent, nerveless; fls. in few-fld. rounded clusters in lf. axils or lateral on the previous year's branchlets, petals minute, pink or white, filaments white. New S. Wales, w. to W. Australia.

alba: a listed name of no botanical standing; used for *M. armillaris.*

armillaris (Soland. ex Gaertn.) Sm. BRACELET H.M. Shrub or small tree, to 30 ft., bark firm, gray, furrowed, peeling in strips; lvs. narrow-linear, to ¾ in. long, acute, often recurved at tip; spikes dense, 2 in. long or more, on old wood, bracts subtending unopened fl. buds; fls. pure white. Se. Australia. Thrives in poor, well-drained soil.

cordata Benth. Shrub, to 10 ft.; lvs. alt., ovate-cordate, to ½ in. long, somewhat clasping, several-nerved from base; heads terminal, dense, globose; fls. red-purple, calyces densely tomentose-villous. W. Australia.

crassifolia: *M. laxiflora.*

decora (Salisb.) Britten [*M. genistifolia* Sm.]. Shrub or tree, to 40 ft., bark whitish, many-layered, papery; lvs. alt., scattered, linear-lanceolate, to ⅝ in. long, acute, narrowed to very short petiole, with prominent midrib, sometimes 3-nerved; spikes to 2¼ in. long; fls. white. Queensland and n. New S. Wales. Perhaps not cult. in Calif.; has been mistaken for *M. styphelioides.*

decussata R. Br. ex Ait.f. Shrub or small tree, to 20 ft., bark firm, but shredding, brs. pendent; lvs. 2-ranked, oblong-lanceolate, to ½ in. long, acute, narrowed to very short petiole, nerveless or faintly 1–3-nerved; spikes cylindrical or almost globose, to 1 in. long, fls. lavender, 2-ranked. S. Australia and Victoria.

densa R. Br. Shrub, to 5 ft.; lvs. opp., overlapping, ovate, to 3/16 in. long; spikes short. W. Australia.

elliptica Labill. Shrub, to 10 ft., bark thinly furrowed, peeling in thin strips; lvs. opp., ovate, to ½ in. long, leathery, glaucous-gray, inconspicuously veined; spikes lateral, to 3 in. long; fls. red, claws of staminal bundles long, narrow. W. Australia.

ericifolia Sm. SWAMP PAPERBARK. Shrub or small tree, to 30 ft., bark thick, soft, papery; lvs. alt., narrow-linear or semicylindrical, to ½ in. long, often recurved; infl. terminal, heads or short cylindrical spikes to 1 in. long; fls. yellowish-white. New S. Wales, Victoria, Tasmania. Numerous basal sprouts eventually produce a clump. Lvs. of sprouts lanceolate, to 1 in. long.

erubescens (Benth.) Otto. Shrub, to 6 ft.; lvs. erect or recurved at apex, linear, more or less cylindrical, not prominently veined; spikes dense, to 2 in. long; fls. purplish. New S. Wales.

fulgens R. Br. Shrub, to 6 ft. or more, bark peeling in strips; lvs. opp., linear or linear-lanceolate, to 1 in. long, conspicuously glandular-dotted, midrib obscure; spikes showy, lateral, few-fld.; fls. scarlet, staminal bundles about 1 in. long, claws conspicuous. W. Australia.

genistifolia: *M. decora,* but plants grown in Fla. as *M. genistifolia* are *Callistemon speciosus.*

Huegelii Endl. HONEY MYRTLE. Nearly glabrous shrub, to 10 ft., bark firm, pale; lvs. alt., spirally arranged, overlapping, ovate-acuminate, to ¼ in. long, striate with 3–7 nerves; spikes dense, narrow, to 5 in. long; fls. white, pink in bud, staminal bundles to ½ in. long. W. Australia. Distinguished by whipcord brs. with small, overlapping, appressed lvs., and axis continuing to grow before flowering is over.

hypericifolia Sm. Glabrous shrub, to 6 ft. or more; lvs. opp., oblong-elliptic, obtuse or mucronulate, to 1½ in. long, conspicuously glandular-dotted; spikes lateral, dense, about 2 in. long, on short shoots from old wood; fls. crimson-red, staminal bundles to 1 in. long, claws conspicuous, about ½ in. long. New S. Wales. May be mistaken for a *Hypericum* when not in flower.

imbricata Link. A name of uncertain application.

incana R. Br. Shrub, to 10 ft., pubescent; lvs. alt. or subopp., spreading, linear or linear-lanceolate, to ½ in. long, narrowed to very short petiole, obscurely 1-nerved; spikes terminal, dense, ovoid or oblong, the axis rarely growing out until after flowering; fls. whitish, staminal bundles less than ½ in. long. W. Australia.

lanceolata Otto [*M. pubescens* Schauer]. MOONAH. Shrub or small tree, to 30 ft., bark dark, rough, fissured, young shoots and lvs. pubescent; lvs. scattered, linear or linear-lanceolate, to ¾ in. long, acute, mostly recurved at margin, narrowed to short petiole, not glandular-dotted, indistinctly 3-nerved; spikes to 2 in. long, the axis often growing out before fls. open; fls. whitish, staminal bundles ¼ in. long, claws very short. S. and e. Australia.

lateritia Otto. ROBIN-REDBREAST BUSH. Shrub, to 10 ft., nearly glabrous, bark soft-corky, becoming fibrous; lvs. alt., scattered, linear, to ¾ in. long, 1/16 in. wide; spikes showy, to 2½ in. long; fls. scarlet-red, staminal bundles ¾ in. long, very shortly united at base. W. Australia.

laxiflora Turcz. [*M. crassifolia* Benth.; *M. parviflora* Lindl., not Rchb.; *M. Preissiana* var. *leiostachya* Benth.]. Shrub, to 5 ft., bark smooth, gray, papery; lvs. lanceolate, sometimes sickle-shaped, flat, to ½ in. long, mucronate, narrowed to base, obscurely 1–3-nerved; spikes loose; fls. reddish-purple. W. Australia.

Leucadendron (L.) L., not of auth. RIVER TEA TREE, WEEPING T.T. Tree, bark papery; lvs. lanceolate, to 7 in. long, widest below middle, thinly leathery. N. Territory of Australia, n. to New Guinea and the Moluccas. Not cult. in this country; material so named is *M. quinquenervia.* The name *M. Leucadendron* (L.) L. has been used in a broad sense for a group of related spp. but correctly refers to only one of them.

lilacinas: a listed name of no botanical standing.

linariifolia Sm. Shrub or tree, to 20 ft. or more, bark soft, spongy, exfoliating, young parts somewhat pubescent; lvs. mostly opp., rigid, linear or linear-lanceolate, to 1½ in. long, midrib prominent beneath; spikes rather loose, to 2 in. long, fls. white, distinctly paired, staminal bundles to ¾ in. long, claws long, with short filaments along entire length. Queensland, New S. Wales, ne. S. Australia. Lvs. yield an essential oil.

longicoma: *M. macronycha.*

macronycha Turcz. [*M. longicoma* Benth.]. Shrub, to 8 ft.; lvs. alt., lanceolate to oblanceolate, to 1½ in. long, glandular-dotted, narrowed to short petiole, midrib inconspicuous beneath; spikes showy, to 2½ in. long, on old wood; fls. red, staminal bundles to 1 in. long, claw to ½ in. long. W. Australia.

micromeria Schauer. Tall shrub, brs. many, short, slender, white-tomentose; lvs. mostly in whorls of 3, closely appressed, ovate, scale-like, to $^1/_{16}$ in. long; heads rounded, small, about ¼ in. across. W. Australia. The minute, scalelike lvs. are distinctive.

microphylla Sm. Shrub; lvs. alt., scattered, spreading or recurved, linear, to ⅜ in. long; spikes short; fls. whitish. W. Australia.

nesophylla F. J. Muell. WESTERN TEA MYRTLE. Shrub or small tree, to 20 ft. or more, bark thick, spongy, peeling in broad strips; lvs. alt., obovate-oblong to oblong-cuneate, to 1 in. long, obscurely 1–3-nerved; heads terminal, dense, to 1 in. across; fls. lavender or rose-pink, staminal clusters to ½ in. long, claws short. W. Australia. Lvs. resembling *Leptospermum laevigatum,* but distinguished by their venation.

nodosa Sm. Tall, nearly glabrous shrub; lvs. alt., linear, to 1 in. long, straight, rigidly sharp-pointed; heads dense, rounded, the axis not growing out until after flowering; fls. pale yellow, staminal clusters to ⅜ in. long, claws short. New S. Wales.

paludosa: *Callistemon salignus* var. *australis.*

parviflora: see *M. laxiflora.*

Preissiana Schauer. Shrub, resembling *M. lanceolata* in habit but having bark whitish, papery; lvs. with nearly parallel sides, and blunt, more or less callose tip. Sw. Australia. Var. **leiostachya:** *M. laxiflora.*

pubescens: *M. lanceolata.*

quinquenervia (Cav.) S. T. Blake. PAPERBARK TREE, PUNK T., TEA T., SWAMP T.T. Tree, to 25 ft. or more, bark spongy, white, peeling in thin layers, brs. often pendulous; lvs. alt., lanceolate to oblanceolate, to 3½ in. long, narrowed to short petiole, usually 5-nerved; spikes dense, to 3 in. long; fls. white, staminal bundles ¾ in. long, claws about ⅛ in. long. E. Australia, along coast; se. New Guinea, New Caledonia. Cult. plants known as *M. Leucadendron* belong here.

radula Lindl. Shrub, to 8 ft.; lvs. opp., linear, to 2 in. long, somewhat cylindrical, glandular-dotted; fls. lilac-purple, in spaced pairs forming loose "bottlebrushes." W. Australia.

rhaphiophylla Schauer. SWAMP PAPERBARK. Tree, to 20 ft. or more; lvs. linear, to 1¼ in. long, cylindrical, pungent; spikes with axis growing out before flowering is over; fls. cream-white. W. Australia.

spathulata Schauer. Shrub, to 3 ft.; lvs. alt., obovate, to ¼ in. long, narrowed to base; fls. pink or reddish, clusters terminal, globose; staminal bundles ¼ in. long, claws less than half as long. W. Australia.

squamea Labill. Shrub, to 6 ft.; lvs. alt., crowded, lanceolate, to ⅜ in. long, incurved toward apex, 3-nerved; heads terminal; fls. reddish, purple, or whitish, staminal bundles $^3/_{16}$ in. long, basally united. New S. Wales to S. Australia, Tasmania.

squarrosa Sm. Shrub or tree, to 20 ft. or more, bark papery; lvs. opp., 2-ranked, spreading, rigid, ovate, to $^5/_{16}$ in. long, acute, very short-petioled, 5–7-nerved; spikes crowded, to 1½ in. long; fls. whitish, staminal bundles ¼ in. long, shortly united at base. New S. Wales to S. Australia, Tasmania.

Steedmanii C. Gardn. Shrub, to 3 ft.; lvs. opp., lanceolate to elliptic, to ¾ in. long, flat, inconspicuously veined; spikes lateral, short, loose, the axis continuing to grow during flowering; fls. crimson, staminal bundles ¾ in. long or more, claws long. W. Australia.

styphelioides Sm. Tree, to 25 ft. or more, bark spongy; lvs. alt., more or less twisted, ovate, to ½ in. long, tapering to a sharp rigid point, sessile, striate with 11 or more fine veins; spikes dense, to 2 in. long, axis continuing to grow after flowering; fls. whitish, staminal bundles to ¼ in. long, claws long. New S. Wales. See *M. decora.*

tenella Benth. Shrub, to 15 ft.; lvs. alt., linear, to ¼ in. long; spikes terminal, globose or short-cylindrical; fls. white. W. Australia.

teretifolia Endl. Tall shrub; lvs. alt., linear-subulate, cylindrical, to 2 in. long; heads sessile, axillary or lateral; fls. white. W. Australia.

thymifolia Sm. Shrub, to 3 ft.; lvs. mostly opp., lanceolate, concave above, to ½ in. long, glandular-dotted; spikes lateral, few-fld., ovoid, the axis continuing to grow during flowering; fls. red-purple, staminal bundles ½ in. long. New S. Wales.

thymoides Labill. Shrub, to 3 ft., branchlets often spine-tipped; lvs. alt., stiff, lanceolate, to ½ in. long; heads terminal, dense, globular; fls. yellow. W. Australia.

viminalis pendula: a listed name of no botanical standing, may refer to *Callistemon viminalis.*

Wilsonii F. J. Muell. Shrub, to 6 ft.; lvs. crowded, rigid, 2-ranked, linear-lanceolate, to ½ in. long; clusters few-fld., axillary, or rarely in terminal heads or spikes; fls. rose or red, staminal bundles to ½ in. long, claws long, narrow. Victoria and S. Australia. Yields an essential oil.

MELAMPODIUM L. *Compositae* (Helianthus Tribe). Twelve spp. of taprooted, per. herbs, native to sw. U.S., Cent. and S. Amer., and W. Indies; lvs. opp., entire to pinnatifid; fl. heads radiate, peduncled, in leafy cymes, involucral bracts imbricate, the inner ones enclosing the ray achenes and falling with them, receptacle scaly; disc fls. bisexual, sterile, ray fls. female, fertile, white or yellow; achenes obovate-oblong, pappus lacking.

Sometimes grown in the rock garden.

cinereum DC. To 1 ft., gray- or silvery-pubescent; lvs. linear to lanceolate, entire or undulate, sometimes pinnatifid; disc fls. yellow, ray fls. white, to ½ in. long. Tex., Colo., New Mex.

leucanthum Torr. & A. Gray. Differs from *M. cinereum* in its more entire lvs., larger heads, and longer ray fls. veined with purple beneath; often regarded as not specifically distinct. Kans. and Colo. to Ariz., Tex., and n. Mex.

MELANDRIUM: *SILENE.* **M. diurnum:** *S. dioica.* **M. rubrum:** *S. dioica.*

MELANTHIUM L. *Liliaceae.* About 4 spp. of rhizomatous, per. herbs, native to e. N. Amer.; sts. leafy; lvs. linear to ovate or oblanceolate; fls. greenish or white, both bisexual and unisexual fls. in a large terminal panicle, perianth segms. 6, separate, spreading, clawed, persistent, stamens 6, anthers 1-celled; fr. a septicidal, 3-celled caps., seeds several, elliptic, winged.

Sometimes transplanted to the wild or bog garden.

hybridum Walt. [*M. latifolium* Desr.]. To 3¼ ft.; lvs. oblanceolate, to 2¼ in. wide; fls. green, segms. suborbicular, ¼ in. long, undulate-crisped. Conn. to Ga.

latifolium: *M. hybridum.*

virginicum L. BUNCHFLOWER. Plant stout, to 5 ft.; lvs. linear, to 1 ft. long and 1⅛ in. wide; fls. greenish-yellow, turning dark in age, segms. oblong to ovate, $^5/_{16}$ in. long, flat. N.Y. to Ind., s. to n. Fla. and Tex.

MELASPHAERULA Ker-Gawl. *Iridaceae.* One sp., a cormous herb, native to the sw. tip of S. Afr.; lvs. grasslike; fls. irregular, style brs. 3; distinguished from *Sparaxis* in having acuminate perianth segms. separate almost to the base, and ovary acutely 3-angled.

Cultivation as for *Ixia.*

graminea: *M. ramosa.*

ramosa (L.) N. E. Br. [*M. graminea* (L.f.) Ker-Gawl.]. FAIRY-BELLS. Corms scarcely ½ in. in diam., tunic of dark leathery fibers; sts. 18–30 in., slender, much-branched, weak, the brs. often drooping and twisted; lvs. 6–7, basal, 2-ranked, 2–10 in. long, ½ in. wide, basally sheathing, midrib whitish; infl. a 3–7-fld., very short, headlike spike, borne on a wiry peduncle ¾–1¼ in. long, the bracts lanceolate-acuminate, with scarious margins; fls. sessile, white on opening, becoming greenish-yellow the third day, sometimes veined purple, starlike, to ¾ in. across, perianth segms. lanceolate-acuminate.

MELASTOMA L. *Melastomataceae.* About 70 spp. of shrubs or small trees, native to se. Asia; lvs. opp., entire; infl. cymose, terminal, few- to many-fld.; fls. white, pink, or purple, stamens 10 or rarely to 14, dimorphic; fr. a berry. Distinguished from *Medinilla* in having calyx lobes alt. with bristle-tipped appendages.

Grown in greenhouse or outdoors in warm climates. Propagated by cuttings in spring over bottom heat.

Banksii: *M. malabathricum.*

candidum D. Don [*M. septemnervium* Lour., not Jacq.; *Tibouchina alba* Hort., not Cogn.]. Shrub, to 10 ft., brs. nearly cylindrical, densely covered with appressed, brown scales; lvs. oblong-ovate, to 5 in. long, 7-nerved, strigillose, petioles to ¾ in. long, villous; fls. in 4–7-fld. cymes, 1–3 in. across, fragrant, petals white or reddish; fr. globose, to ½ in. in diam., with hairy calyx. Taiwan and Ryukyu Is., s. to se. Asia and Philippine Is. Fls. very showy.

decemfidum: *M. sanguineum.*

malabathricum L. [*M. Banksii* A. Cunn. ex Triana]. INDIAN RHODO-DENDRON. Spreading shrub, to 8 ft., brs. nearly 4-angled, densely covered with appressed scales; lvs. ovate to broadly lanceolate, 3–4 in. long, 3–5-nerved, hairy, bracts to ⅝ in. long; petals to ½ in. long, purple; fr. ⁵⁄₁₆ in. across, reddish pulp edible. India, se. Asia, Malay Arch., New Guinea, Philippine Is. Used medicinally by native peoples.

sanguineum Sims [*M. decemfidum* Roxb.]. Shrub, to 20 ft., brs. reddish-hairy, with hairs to ¼ in. long; lvs. lanceolate, to 8 in. long, 5-nerved, usually glabrous; fls. 2–3 in. across, calyx densely coarse-hairy, petals purple; berry to ½ in. across. Malay Pen. to Java.

sempervirens: a listed name of no botanical standing.

septemnervium: see *M. candidum.*

venosum: *Medinilla venosa.*

MELASTOMATACEAE Juss. (incorrectly spelled Melastomaceae). MELASTOMA FAMILY. Dicot.; about 240 genera and 3,000 spp. of mostly trop. herbs, shrubs, and trees in both hemispheres; lvs. simple, opp. or whorled, usually with 3–9 longitudinal, parallel nerves; fls. usually bisexual, regular, calyx 3–5(–10)-lobed, petals 3–5(–10), stamens 3–10(–90), either all similar or dimorphic, often with appendages, anthers usually dehiscing by apical pores, ovary superior or inferior, 2- to many-celled; fr. a berry or caps. Genera grown as ornamentals in greenhouses or outdoors in warm climates are: *Amphiblemma, Arthrostema, Bertolonia, Calvoa, Centradenia, Conostegia, Dissotis, Heterocentron, Medinilla, Melastoma, Memecylon, Miconia, Monochaetum, Oxyspora, Rhexia, Sonerila, Tetrazygia, Tibouchina,* and *Triolena.*

MELIA L. BEAD TREE. *Meliaceae.* About 10 spp. of trees or large shrubs, native to Asia and Australia; lvs. alt., pinnate or 2-pinnate, lfts. entire or toothed; fls. white or purple, in axillary panicles, calyx 5–6-lobed, petals 5 or 6, spreading, stamens 10–12, filaments united in a cylindrical tube, ovary 3–6-celled; fr. a berry, usually mistakenly called a drupe.

One species, widely cultivated in warm regions and withstanding several degrees of frost. Propagated by seeds sown as soon as ripe, and by cuttings under glass.

australis: *M. Azedarach.*

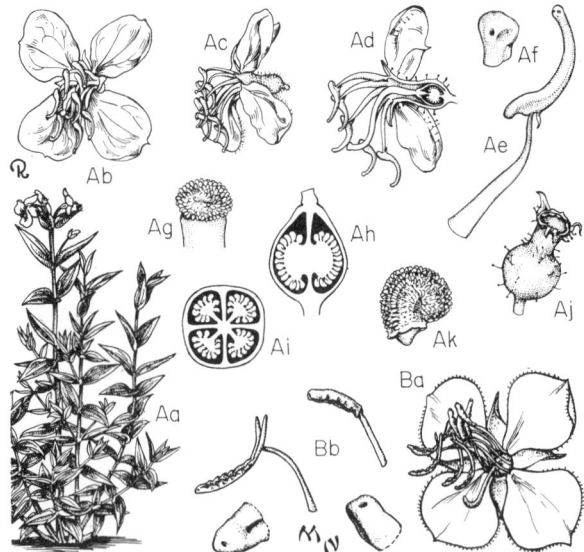

MELASTOMATACEAE. **A,** *Rhexia virginica:* **Aa,** plant, × ⅛; **Ab,** flower, face view, × ¾; **Ac,** flower, side view, × ¾; **Ad,** flower, vertical section, × 1; **Ae,** stamen, × 3; **Af,** tip of anther with apical pore, × 10; **Ag,** stigma, × 8; **Ah,** ovary, vertical section, × 3; **Ai,** ovary, cross section, × 3; **Aj,** fruit, × 1; **Ak,** seed, × 15. **B,** *Heterocentron subtriplinervium:* **Ba,** flower, × 1½; **Bb,** the two kinds of stamens, × 2, with detail (below) of anther tips showing apical pore, × 10.

Azedarach L. [*M. australis* Sweet; *M. japonica* G. Don; *M. sempervirens* Swartz]. CHINABERRY, CHINA TREE, PRIDE-OF-INDIA, PRIDE-OF-CHINA, PERSIAN LILAC, INDIAN L., PARADISE TREE, BEAD TREE, SYRIAN B.T., JAPANESE B.T. Spreading deciduous tree, to 40 ft. or more; lvs. 2-pinnate, 1–3 ft. long, petioled, lfts. many, toothed or lobed; fls. purplish, fragrant, stamen tube purple; fr. yellow, to ¾ in. across, persisting after lvs. fall. Asia; naturalized in trop. Amer. and planted in warm-temp. and trop. regions around the world; sometimes escapes. Zone 7b. Wood used in cabinet making; frs. medicinal, seeds used for rosaries. Cv. 'Floribunda' [*M. floribunda* Carrière]. Bushy, very floriferous. Cv. 'Umbraculifera': 'Umbraculiformis'. Cv. 'Umbraculiformis' [cv. 'Umbraculifera']. TEXAS UMBRELLA TREE. Foliage drooping and brs. radiating giving an umbrellalike effect.

floribunda: *M. Azedarach* cv.

japonica: *M. Azedarach.*

sempervirens: *M. Azedarach.*

umbraculiformis: a listed name of no botanical standing for *M. Azedarach* cv.

MELIACEAE Juss. MAHOGANY FAMILY. Dicot.; 50 genera and about 1,400 spp. of trop. trees and shrubs, native to Old

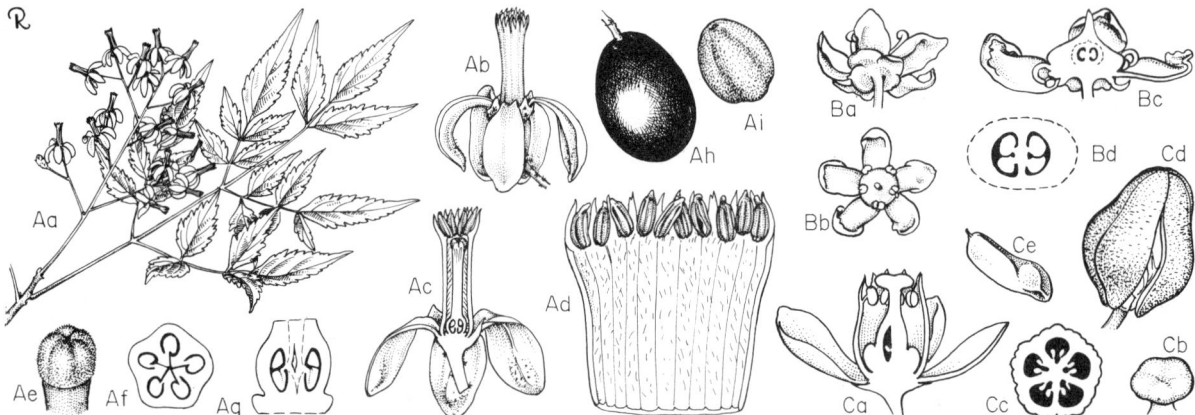

MELIACEAE. **A,** *Melia Azedarach:* **Aa,** flowering twig, × ³⁄₁₀; **Ab,** flower, × 1½; **Ac,** flower, vertical section, × 2; **Ad,** staminal tube, expanded, × 4; **Ae,** stigma, × 8; **Af,** ovary, cross section, × 8; **Ag,** ovary, vertical section, × 8; **Ah,** fruit, × 1; **Ai,** seed, × 1. **B,** *Cedrela odorata:* **Ba,** flower, back view, × 1½; **Bb,** flower, face view, × 1½; **Bc,** flower, vertical section, × 3; **Bd,** ovary, cross section, × 10. **C,** *Swietenia Mahagoni:* **Ca,** flower, vertical section, × 5; **Cb,** stigma, × 8; **Cc,** ovary, cross section, × 12; **Cd,** fruit, × ¼; **Ce,** seed, × ¼.

and New World; lvs. alt., usually pinnate or 2-pinnate (rarely simple), without stipules; fls. mostly bisexual (unisexual in *Aphanamixis*), in axillary or terminal panicles, spikes, cymes, or clusters, sometimes borne singly in lf. axils, sepals 4 or 5, petals 4 or 5 (rarely 3–8), stamens mostly 8–10, filaments united in a tube (except in *Cedrela*), disc usually present between the stamens and ovary, ovary superior, usually 2–5-celled, stigmas capitate or discoid; fr. a caps. or berry (frequently mistakenly referred to in the literature as a drupe), seeds often winged. Cult. genera are: *Aphanamixis, Cedrela, Ekebergia, Entandrophragma, Khaya, Melia, Nymania, Soymida, Swietenia, Trichilia,* and *Turraea.*

Cedrela, Khaya, and *Swietenia* are important sources of commercial timber in the tropics; however, with the exception of *Melia* and *Swietenia,* members of the family are infrequently cultivated in the U.S.

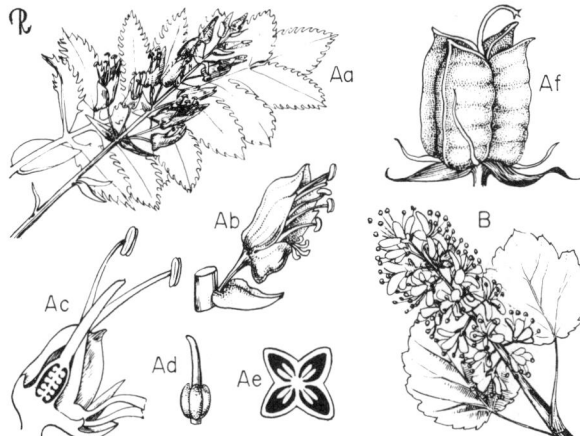

MELIANTHACEAE. **A,** *Melianthus major:* **Aa,** inflorescence, × ¼, and leaf, × ⅛; **Ab,** flower, × ¾; **Ac,** flower, vertical section, × 2; **Ad,** pistil, × 1; **Ae,** ovary, cross section, × 3; **Af,** fruit, × 1. **B,** *Greyia Sutherlandii:* flowering branch, × ¼. (From Bailey, *Manual of Cultivated Plants,* ed. 2.)

MELIANTHACEAE Link. MELIANTHUS FAMILY. Dicot.; 3 genera of trees, shrubs, and per. herbs, native to Afr. and India; lvs. alt., simple or compound, often large; infl. racemose; fls. mostly showy, sometimes irregular, bisexual, sepals and petals 4–5, stamens 4, 5, or 10, ovary superior, 4–5-celled, stamens and styles prominently exserted; fr. a lobed caps. *Greyia* and *Melianthus* are grown as ornamentals.

MELIANTHUS L. HONEYBUSH. *Melianthaceae.* Six spp. of shrubby, tender per. herbs, native to S. Afr. and India; foliage with unpleasant odor when bruised; lvs. alt., odd-pinnate, lfts. toothed, stipules prominent; fls. in racemes, showy, nectar-bearing, irregular, sepals and petals 5, stamens 4, exserted; fr. a 4-celled inflated caps.

Ornamental plants that grow well in Zone 10 in southern Calif.; propagated by seeds and cuttings. The plants are very strong-scented and are valued for medicine in Afr.

major L. HONEY FLOWER. To 10 ft., sts. hollow; lvs. 1 ft. long or more, clasping the st., stipules united into a single lanceolate blade to 5 in. long, lfts. 6–9, to 6 in. long, elliptic-oblong, glabrous, glaucous, rachis winged; racemes terminal, erect, 1 ft. long or more; fls. brown-red, about 1 in. long, calyx gibbous at base; caps. 4-lobed, to 1¼ in. long. S. Afr. and India.

minor L. To 5 ft.; similar to *M. major,* but lvs. smaller, to 7 in. long, lfts. to 2 in. long, downy beneath, stipules in distinct pairs, fls. dull red, calyx and pedicel downy. S. Afr.

MELICA L. MELIC, MELIC GRASS. *Gramineae.* About 60 spp. of rather tall, per. grasses in temp. regions; st. base often swollen into a corm; lvs. with closed sheaths, blades usually flat; panicles narrow or sometimes open, usually simple; spikelets relatively large, 2- to several-fld. (rarely with 1 bisexual floret), rachilla usually disarticulating above the glumes and between the fertile upper florets, upper florets sterile,

often rudimentary and enclosed by broad upper lemmas, glumes papery, 3–5-nerved, lemma convex, with several strong nerves, membranous or rather firm, scarious-margined, awnless or awned. For terminology see *Gramineae.*

altissima L. SIBERIAN M. Sts. to 3 ft. or more; lf. blades to 8 in. long and ⅜ in. wide; panicle narrow, dense, tawny to purple; spikelets about ½ in. long, glumes and lemma broad, papery. Eurasia; introd. and sometimes cult. for ornament.

ciliata L. SILKY-SPIKE M. Sts. to 2 ft.; lf. blades flat, folded, or involute, with a long, usually torn ligule; panicle spikelike, pale, silky; spikelets 1–2-fld., glumes nearly equal, lemma ovate-lanceolate, acute, with long, silky, whitish hairs in the lowest floret. Eurasia, N. Afr.

transsilvanica Schur. Similar to *M. ciliata,* but sts. to 3 ft., panicle shorter, glumes strongly unequal, the lower ⅛ in. long, the upper ¼ in. long. Eurasia.

MELICOCCA: *MELICOCCUS.* Melicocca bijuga: *Melicoccus bijugatus.*

MELICOCCUS P. Br. [*Melicocca* L.]. *Sapindaceae.* Two spp. of polygamous or dioecious trees, native to trop. Amer.; lvs. alt., pinnate; fls. small, in racemes or panicles, regular, calyx 4–5-lobed, petals 4 or 5, stamens 8; fr. a drupe with fleshy pulp, seed single, surrounded by a large fleshy aril.

When well established, melicoccas will stand several degrees of frost; propagated by seeds.

bijugatus Jacq. [*Melicocca bijuga* L.]. SPANISH LIME, GENIP, GENIPE, MAMONCILLO, HONEYBERRY. Slow-growing tree, to 60 ft.; lvs. 6 in. long, lfts. 4–6, elliptic-lanceolate, to 4 in. long, glabrous; fls. fragrant; fr. round, 1 in. in diam., the rind green and leathery, the juicy pulp yellowish, translucent, edible. Circum-Caribbean, trop. Amer. Zone 10. Grown in s. Fla. Locally popular as a fresh fr. in trop. Amer., where much planted as a dooryard tree in dry areas.

MELICOPE J. R. Forst. & G. Forst. *Rutaceae.* About 20 spp. of trees or shrubs, native from trop. Asia to Australia and New Zeal.; lvs. opp. or alt., with 1–3 lfts., glandular-dotted; fls. in few- to many-fld. cymes or panicles, bisexual or unisexual, sepals and petals 4, stamens 8; fr. separating into 4 1-seeded sections. The name has 4 syllables.

Propagated by seeds or cuttings.

ternata J. R. Forst. & G. Forst. Tree, to 20 ft.; lfts. 3, obovate-cuneate to ovate-oblong, to 4 in. long, entire; fls. greenish, 5⁄16 in. across, in axillary cymes; seeds black, glossy. New Zeal.

MELICYTUS J. R. Forst. & G. Forst. *Violaceae.* About 4 spp. of dioecious trees and shrubs, native to New Zeal. and Pacific Is.; lvs. alt.; fls. small, in clusters, regular, unisexual, 5-merous; fr. a few-seeded berry.

ramiflorus J. R. Forst. & G. Forst. MAHOE (of New Zeal.). Tree, to 30 ft., bark white; lvs. oblong-lanceolate, to 5 in. long, toothed; fls. greenish, ⅛ in. across; berries blue, 3⁄16 in. across. New Zeal. to Norfolk, Tonga, and Fiji Is. Sometimes planted in Calif.

MELILOTUS Mill. SWEET CLOVER, MELILOT. *Leguminosae* (subfamily *Faboideae*). Perhaps 20 spp. of ann. or bien., fragrant herbs of the Old World; lvs. of 3 lfts., lfts. minutely toothed; fls. in slender racemes, small, papilionaceous, stamens 10, 9 united and 1 separate; fr. a short, straight, mostly ovoid legume, tardily or not dehiscent.

Grown as green-manure or forage crops, or as bee plants; widely naturalized. Propagated by seeds.

alba Desr. WHITE S.C., WHITE M., BUKHARA CLOVER. Bien., to 10 ft.; lfts. oblong, to 1½ in. long, obtuse or emarginate, fragrant when dry; fls. white, less than ¼ in. long, fragrant; fr. to 3⁄16 in. long. Eurasia; naturalized in N. Amer. Var. **annua** H. S. Coe. HUBAM CLOVER. Maturing in one growing season.

indica (L.) All. To 3 ft., glabrous; lfts. obovate-cuneate, to 1¼ in. long, truncate or retuse apically, denticulate above middle; fls. yellow, smaller than in *M. alba,* in loose racemes to 2 in. long; fr. nearly globose, conspicuously reticulate. Eurasia; naturalized in N. Amer. Cover crop on Pacific Coast.

officinalis (L.) Pall. YELLOW S.C., MELILOT, YELLOW M., MELIST. To 4 ft. or more; lfts. obovate or oblanceolate, to 1 in. long, blunt, minutely toothed nearly all around; fls. yellow, in dense racemes to 4 in. long; fr. slightly reticulate. Eurasia; naturalized in N. Amer.

MELINIS Beauvois. *Gramineae.* About 20 spp. of per. grasses in Afr., 1 in trop. Amer., sts. slender, branching, decumbent; panicles narrow, many-fld., with capillary branchlets and pedicels; spikelets small, compressed on the back, 1-fld., with an awned sterile lemma below the fertile floret, rachilla disarticulating below the strongly unequal glumes, first glume minute, second glume and sterile lemma similar, membranous, strongly nerved, slightly exceeding the fertile floret. For terminology see *Gramineae.*

minutiflora Beauvois. MOLASSES GRASS. Sts. to about 3 ft., ascending from a much-branched base; lvs. viscid-pubescent, blades flat, to 6 in. long and ⅜ in. wide; panicle to 8 in. long, purplish; spikelets less than ⅛ in. long, awn of 2-lobed sterile lemma from between the lobes, to ⅜ in. long. Afr. Cult. for forage in tropics and s. Fla.

MELIOSMA Blume. *Sabiaceae.* About 45 spp. of trees and shrubs, native to trop. and warm temp. Asia and Amer.; lvs. alt., petioled, simple or odd-pinnate; fls. small, in panicles, usually bisexual, sepals (3–)5, petals 5, the inner 2 much reduced, stamens 3–5, opp. the petals, only 2 fertile; fr. drupaceous.

Sometimes grown as ornamentals; propagated by seeds, layering, and cuttings of young wood.

myriantha Siebold & Zucc. Tree, to 30 ft.; lvs. simple, obovate-elliptic to oblong-obovate, to 8 in. long, serrate, acute; panicles erect, to 8 in. long; fls. greenish-yellow; fr. red, about ¼ in. in diam. Japan.

pendens Rehd. & E. H. Wils. Shrub, to 15 ft.; lvs. simple, elliptic-obovate, to 6 in. long, serrate, hairy on midrib above and on veins beneath; panicles pendulous, to 8 in. long; fls. white, fragrant. Cent. China.

MELISSA L. BALM. *Labiatae.* About 3 spp. of per. herbs of Eur. to cent. Asia and Iran; sts. mostly square in cross section; lvs. opp., toothed, petioled; fls. in few- to many-fld. verticillasters, usually whitish, calyx campanulate, 13-nerved, 2-lipped, upper lip 3-toothed, lower lip 2-lobed, corolla tube longer than calyx, glabrous inside, limb 2-lipped, upper lip erect, emarginate, lower lip spreading, 3-lobed, stamens 4, in 2 pairs, anther cells coherent.

Propagated by seeds, division, or cuttings.

officinalis L. COMMON B., BEE B., LEMON B., SWEET B. Upright per., to 2 ft., pubescent; lvs. broadly ovate, often cordate, 1–3 in. long, crenate-serrate, petioled, lemon-scented; verticillasters 4–12-fld.; calyx to ¼ in. long, teeth mucronate, lower teeth longer, corolla about ½ in. long, white. Summer. S. Eur.; naturalized elsewhere in Eur. and in e. U.S. A sweet herb for the kitchen garden, cult. for the lemon-scented lvs. used in seasoning and in medicine. A variegated cv. is sometimes used in borders.

MELOCACTUS Link & Otto. *Cactaceae.* About 36 spp. of ribbed, ovoid cacti of trop. Amer. and W. Indies; sts. hemispherical to oblong, strongly ribbed, spiny; flowering structure (cephalium) terminal, permanently differentiated from the sterile lower part, smaller in diam., not evidently ribbed, hidden by a mass of white wool and brown bristlelike spines; fls. nearly apical, diurnal, small, red or pinkish, perianth segms. few, petaloid, spreading; fr. club-shaped, naked, red, seeds black.

For culture see *Cacti.*

amoenus (Hoffmanns.) Pfeiff. [*Cactus amoenus* Hoffmanns.]. Sts. to 8 in. high, ribs 10–15, ¾ in. high; spines white, radial spines 9, curved, to ¾ in. long, central spine 1, to 1 in. long; cephalium 1 in. high and 3 in. thick; fls. red, ⁵⁄₁₆ in. across. N. Colombia.

Antonii: *M. intortus* var.

bahiensis (Britt. & Rose) Lützelb. [*Cactus bahiensis* Britt. & Rose]. Sts. to 4 in. high and 6 in. thick, ribs 10–12, 1 in. high, each with 6–7 areoles; spines straight, brown, radial spines 10, to 1 in. long, central spines 4, to 1½ in. long; cephalium low; fls. pinkish. Brazil.

Broadwayi (Britt. & Rose) A. Berger [*Cactus Broadwayi* Britt. & Rose]. Sts. to 8 in. high and nearly as thick, ribs 14–18, ½ in. high; spines curved, horn-colored or brown, slender-awl-shaped, radial spines 8–10, nearly stellate, about ½ in. long, central spine usually 1, stouter; cephalium about 1 in. high and 3 in. thick; fls. purplish; fr. 1 in. long. W. Indies.

caesius H. L. Wendl. [*Cactus caesius* (H. L. Wendl.) Britt. & Rose]. Sts. to 8 in. high and 6 in. thick, ribs 10–15, ¾ in. high, each with about 6 areoles; spines straight, awl-shaped, horn-colored, radial spines about 8, central spine 1, to ¾ in. long; cephalium about 1½ in. high and 3 in. thick; fr. 1¼ in. long. Colombia, Venezuela, Trinidad.

communis (Ait.) Link & Otto [*Cactus Melocactus* L.]. MELON CACTUS, TURK'S-CAP C., TURK'S-HEAD C. Sts. to 3 ft. high and 1 ft. thick, ribs 10–14, to 1¼ in. high; spines 10–12, stout, cylindrical, yellowish to brown, to 2 in. long; cephalium to 2 in. high and 4 in. thick; fls. to 1½ in. long; fr. to 2 in. long. Jamaica.

Ernesti Vaup. Sts. conical, ribs 10, high, sharp, with about 12 areoles; spines about 10, lower radial spines wider than others. Brazil. Incompletely known.

intortus (Mill.) Urb. [*Cactus intortus* Mill.]. TURK'S-CAP CACTUS. Sts. to 3 ft. high and 16 in. thick, ribs 14–22, to 1½ in. high; spines 7–13, awl-shaped, straight, yellow to brown or reddish, to 1½ in. long; cephalium to 1½ ft. high and 4 in. thick; fls. pinkish, to ¾ in. long; fr. to 1 in. long, seeds tubercled. W. Indies. Var. **Antonii** (Britt.) Backeb. [*M. Antonii* (Britt.) F. M. Knuth; *Cactus Antonii* Britt.]. Sts. more ovoid, ribs broad; spines thinner.

Jansenianus Backeb. [*Cactus Jansenianus* (Backeb.) Borg]. Sts. globose, 5 in. thick, ribs about 10, obtuse, each with about 6 areoles; spines black, awl-shaped, radial spines about 8, recurved, the lower longer, to 1 in. long, central spine 1, slightly upcurved, to 1¼ in. long; cephalium to 6 in. high and 2½ in. thick; fls. red. Peru.

macracanthus (Salm-Dyck) Link & Otto [*Cactus macracanthus* Salm-Dyck]. Sts. globose, to 1 ft. thick, ribs 11–15, rounded; spines brown to yellow, radial spines 11–15, needle-shaped, to 1½ in. long, central spines 4 or more, awl-shaped, unequal, to 3 in. long; cephalium to 8 in. high and 4 in. thick; fls. and fr. ¾ in. long. Curaçao and nearby islands.

matanzanus Leon [*Cactus matanzanus* (Leon) Borg]. Sts. to 3½ in. high and 4 in. thick, ribs 8–9, each with about 5 areoles; spines awl-shaped, curved, reddish, becoming yellowish, to ¾ in. long, radial spines 7–8, central spine 1; cephalium to 1½ in. high and 2½ in. thick; fls. rose, to ¾ in. long. Cuba.

Maxonii (Rose) Gürke [*Cactus Maxonii* Rose]. Sts. globose, to 1 ft. high, ribs 11–15, each with about 5 areoles; spines awl-shaped, red or yellow, becoming gray, radial spines 7–11, stellate or recurved, to ⅝ in. long, central spine 1, directed outward or ascending, to 1 in. long; cephalium about 3 in. thick; fls. rose, 1½ in. long; fr. to 1¼ in. long. Guatemala.

melocactoides (Hoffmanns.) DC. [*M. violaceus* Pfeiff.; *Cactus melocactoides* Hoffmanns.]. Sts. to 4 in. high and 5 in. thick, ribs 9–12, each with 5–6 areoles; spines 5–8, radial, awl-shaped, brown, becoming gray, to ¾ in. long; cephalium to 2 in. high and 3 in. thick; fls. pinkish, to ¾ in. long; fr. white or pink, to 1 in. long, seeds tubercled, crested. Brazil.

Neryi K. Schum. [*Cactus Neryi* (K. Schum.) Britt. & Rose]. Sts. to 5 in. high and 6 in. thick, ribs 10, each with 3–4 areoles; spines 7–9, spreading, awl-shaped, gray, to 1 in. long; cephalium to 2 in. high and 3 in. thick; fls. rose, nearly 1 in. long; fr. red, ¾ in. long. Brazil. Originally but incorrectly spelled "Negryi."

oaxacensis (Britt. & Rose) Backeb. [*Cactus oaxacensis* Britt. & Rose]. Sts. ovoid, to 6 in. thick, ribs 11–15, each with about 7 areoles; spines awl-shaped, reddish, becoming gray, radial spines 8–12, recurved, to ¾ in. long, central spines 1–2, erect or directed outward; cephalium about 1 in. high and 1½ in. thick; fls. dark rose, ¾ in. long; fr. scarlet, to nearly 2 in. long. S. Mex.

violaceus: *M. melocactoides.*

MELON, MUSKMELON. Treated here are the common melons that belong to the species *Cucumis Melo;* for the watermelon, which is of a different genus, see *Watermelon.*

The dessert melons familiar in this country are of two types or groups: the netted melons (*C. Melo,* Reticulatus Group); and the winter melons (*C. Melo,* Inodorus Group), including honeydew and casaba. The culture of the two is similar except that the latter group requires a longer season and is not grown to any extent in the northern and central melon regions. The true cantaloupes (*C. Melo,* Cantalupensis Group) are seldom grown in North America, although the name is commonly but inaccurately applied to cultivars of the netted melon group. They are, however, the melons most commonly grown in Europe; while the exterior is distinctive in its lack of netting, the flesh is much like that of netted melons.

All melons are alike in requiring well-drained, fertile soil and a sunny location, continuous rapid growth, and freedom from frost. They are grown to some extent in the home garden in nearly all regions of the United States, except where the growing season is too short. The commercial supply is produced in regions such as the Imperial Valley of California and other warm and relatively dry areas. Most of the commercial crop is started directly in the field, but in northern regions seeds are started in small pots, plant bands, or blocks in the greenhouse two or three weeks before it is safe to set them in the open. The use of plastic film as a mulch has become almost indispensable in commercial melon-growing in the northern United States because it promotes earlier and higher yields and, if the plastic is black, it greatly simplifies weed control. Home gardeners will usually find it helpful, in growing melons, to start with greenhouse-grown plants and use black plastic mulch.

Control of insects and diseases is very important in melon growing, and local recommendations should be followed. Some disease problems can be minimized by choosing resistant cultivars. In cooler areas, fusarium wilt may be a problem; a number of good resistant cultivars are available. Powdery mildew is a threat in almost any area, and adapted cultivars with resistance to the disease are available for much of the United States. In the more humid parts of the southern United States, cultivars with resistance to both downy mildew and powdery mildew should be chosen.

Except for the winter melons, which do not "slip," melons should be picked at full slip, that is, when the fruit separates easily from the vine. If melons are to be held longer than two or three days, they should be stored at 50–55° F rather than at lower temperatures, which may cause chilling injury.

MELOTHRIA L. *Cucurbitaceae.* About 85 spp. of diffuse, slender, climbing or prostrate, monoecious or dioecious, herbaceous vines, native to warm parts of both hemispheres, a few to the U.S.; lvs. entire or lobed; fls. small, inconspicuous, male fls. racemose or corymbose, stamens 3, filaments separate, anthers straight, female fls. solitary or clustered, disc present at base of style; fr. small, berrylike, smooth or warty.

lupulina: a listed name of no botanical standing.

punctata (Thunb.) Cogn. Dioecious per., from thick root; lvs. cordate-ovate, angled or lightly 3–5-lobed, scabrous beneath; male fls. corymbose; fr. short-peduncled, about ¼ in. in diam., slightly pitted, brown. Afr. Raised from seeds. In autumn the tops may be cut back, and the roots brought in for the winter, and grown in window gardens; or they may be stored till spring; or plants may be carried over by means of green cuttings.

scabra Naud. Monoecious, ann. or grown as such; lvs. triangular-ovate, lobed; male fls. racemose; fr. long-peduncled, to 1 in. long, glabrous, more or less spotted with green. Mex.

MEMECYLACEAE: *MELASTOMATACEAE.*

MEMECYLON L. *Melastomataceae.* About 150 spp. of shrubs or trees of trop. Afr., Asia, and Malay Arch.; lvs. opp.; infl. of axillary or terminal and panicled cymes, few- to many-fld.; fls. 4-merous, white or blue, stamens 8, all similar, ovary inferior, 1-celled; fr. a berry. Sometimes placed in the segregate family Memecylaceae.

caeruleum: *M. floribundum.*

floribundum Blume [*M. caeruleum* Jack]. Shrub, to 10 ft.; lvs. leathery, ovate-elliptic, to 7 in. long and 1–3 in. wide, obtuse, petiole to ¼ in. long; fls. with petals to ¼ in. long, bluish-purple inside, reddish outside; fr. ovoid, to ⅝ in. long. Java.

umbellatum Burm.f. Small tree, to 25 ft., sts. and brs. densely covered with lenticels; lvs. leathery, oblong-ovate, 3–6 in. long, acuminate; cymes axillary, 1–2 in. long, on old wood; fls. many, petals deep blue to purple; fr. globose, ¼–½ in. across, purple to black. India, se. Asia, Philippine Is., Malay Arch., n. Australia.

MENDONCELLA Hawkes [*Galeottia* A. Rich.]. *Orchidaceae.* Four spp. of epiphytes, native to trop. Cent. and S. Amer.; pseudobulbs 2-lvd.; lvs. plicate; infl. lateral, short, distantly few-fld.; fls. large, sepals and petals spreading, lip fleshy, hypochil with ridged crest, epichil fringed, disc with longitudinal crests, column with foot. For structure of fl. see *Orchidaceae.*

For culture see *Orchids.*

grandiflora (A. Rich.) Hawkes [*Galeottia grandiflora* A. Rich.; *Zygopetalum grandiflorum* (A. Rich.) Benth. & Hook.f.]. Pseudobulbs ovoid, to 2¼ in. long; lvs. elliptic-lanceolate, to 20 in. long; infl. basal, to 7 in. long; fls. 1–5, sepals unequal, green, striped with reddish-brown, upper sepal lanceolate-acuminate, to 1¾ in. long, petals nearly as long as sepals, obliquely curved, to 1½ in. long, united to sides of column foot, green, striped with reddish-brown, lip 3-lobed, contracted at base to short claw, jointed to column foot, white with dull red or purple longitudinal markings, midlobe obovate, concave, fimbriate, disc with a lunate, ridged, many-toothed callus. Cent. Amer.

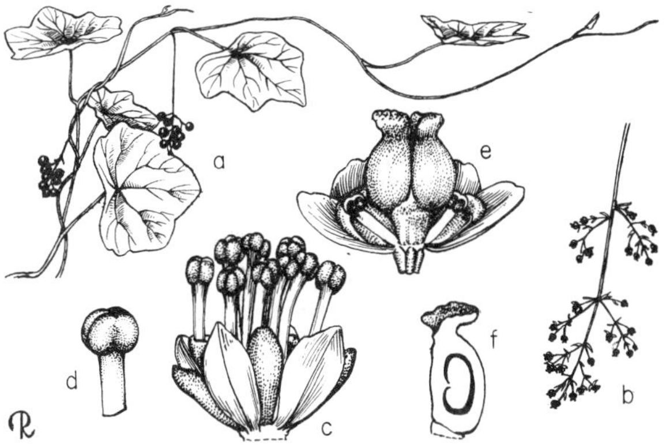

MENISPERMACEAE. *Menispermum canadense:* **a,** fruiting stem, × ⅙; **b,** female inflorescence, × ½; **c,** male flower, × 6; **d,** anther, × 12; **e,** female flower, part of perianth removed, × 6; **f,** pistil, vertical section, × 6. (From Bailey, *Manual of Cultivated Plants,* ed. 2.)

MENISPERMACEAE Juss. MOONSEED FAMILY. Dicot.; about 65 genera of dioecious, largely twining shrubs and herbs, mostly trop.; lvs. alt., simple, sometimes lobed; fls. inconspicuous, small, regular, sepals usually 6, petals 6 or 0, stamens 6 or more, ovaries usually 3, separate; fr. a drupe. *Cocculus* and *Menispermum* are cult.

Grown as ornamentals over arbors or walls, mostly for the foliage, although the fruits may be attractive. The family includes a number of species with alkaloids, some of which are used in arrow poisons, including *Chondrodendron tomentosum* Ruiz & Pav. of tropical Amer., one of the chief ingredients of curare, now used medicinally.

MENISPERMUM L. MOONSEED. *Menispermaceae.* Two spp. of dioecious, woody, twining vines, native to e. N. Amer. and e. Asia; lvs. peltate; infl. racemose or paniculate; fls. white or yellowish, sepals 4–10, petals 6–9, male fls. with 12–24 stamens, female fls. with 6–12 staminodes and 2–4 separate ovaries; fr. a subglobose drupe, about 5/16 in. across.

Cultivated outdoors in the North for its foliage. Propagated by seeds, and cuttings of mature wood.

canadense L. YELLOW PARILLA. To 12 ft.; lvs. circular-ovate, to 8 in. long, entire or shallowly lobed, pubescent beneath when young; fr. black, glaucous. Temp. e. N. Amer. Zone 4. Dried rhizome used medicinally.

MENODORA Humb. & Bonpl. *Oleaceae.* Perhaps 20 spp. of subshrubs, 16–18 in N. and S. Amer., and 2 spp. and a var. of a third in S. Afr.; lvs. alt., simple or pinnately lobed; fls. white or yellow, in terminal paniculate or cymose infl., or solitary, calyx tube 5–15-parted, corolla nearly rotate to campanulate or salverform; fr. a 2-celled caps. usually dehiscing circumscissilely.

integrifolia (Cham. & Schlechtend.) Steud. To 2 ft.; lvs. lanceolate or linear-lanceolate, to 1 in. long, margins entire, recurved; fls. ½ in. long, in terminal cymes, corolla campanulate. Bolivia s. to Uruguay.

MENTHA L. [*Menthella* Pérard]. MINT. *Labiatae.* About 25 spp. of erect or decumbent, aromatic, per. herbs of temp. regions of Old World; sts. mostly square in cross section; lvs. opp., rarely alt., sessile or petioled; fls. in dense, many-fld. verticillasters arranged in terminal spikes or heads, calyx tubular or campanulate, 10–13-nerved, 5-toothed, corolla lavender or white, tube shorter than calyx, limb 4-lobed, upper lobe emarginate, larger, stamens 4, in 2 pairs, usually exserted; fr. of 4 smooth, reticulate, or tubercled nutlets.

Although over 600 species have been named, the conservative view is that these are mainly variants or hybrids of about 25 well-defined species, most of which readily hybridize among themselves in nature. Most hybrids, usually sterile, can be recognized as such by their parental resemblance. Some hybrids, however, are distinct and are here treated under the names usually associated with them.

Several kinds are cultivated commercially for their valuable essential oils; others are ornamental garden plants or sweet herbs. Mints are propagated easily by cuttings, division, stolons, or runners; they tend to be weedy.

anisata: a listed name of no botanical standing.

aquatica L. WATER M. To 3 ft., strong-scented, nearly glabrous to tomentose; lvs. petioled, ovate to ovate-lanceolate, usually truncate at base, serrate; infl. short, headlike, ½–1 in. in diam., sometimes interrupted below; fls. purple, pedicels hairy. A variable fertile sp. Summer. Eur., n. Afr., Asia. Var. **citrata:** *M.* × *piperita* var. Var. **crispa** (L.) Benth. [*M. crispa* L.]. Glabrous or slightly pubescent; lvs. usually ovate to orbicular, lacerate, crisped.

arvensis L. [*M. austriaca* Jacq.]. FIELD M. To 2 ft., hairy; lvs. petioled, ovate to elliptic, broadest below the middle, serrate; bracts leafy, not much smaller than lvs.; fls. lilac, white, or rarely pink. Summer. Eur., Asia. Var. **villosa** (Benth.) S. R. Stewart [*M. canadensis* L.; *M. lanata* Rydb.]. Lvs. lanceolate to lanceolate-oblong, broadest at or above the middle; sts. more heavily pubescent at angles than on the sides. Forma **lanigera** S. R. Stewart. St. angles and sides about equally pubescent. U.S. Var. **piperescens** Malinv. JAPANESE M. To 3 ft. Important source of menthol in Japan.

austriaca: *M. arvensis.*

canadensis: *M. arvensis* var. *villosa.*

cardiaca: *M.* × *gentilis.*

citrata: *M.* × *piperita* var.

crispa: *M. aquatica* var.

Gattefossei Maire. Per., 8–12 in., glabrous to glabrescent; lvs. linear-oblong to linear-lanceolate, to 1 in. long; infl. elongate, bracts subtending lower verticillasters longer than fls.; fls. lilac. Summer. Morocco.

×**gentilis** L. [*M. cardiaca* (S. F. Gray) Bak.]: *M. arvensis* × *M. spicata.* RED M., SCOTCH M. Per., usually glabrous, often red-tinged, sweet-scented like *M. spicata;* similar to *M. arvensis,* but bracts leafy, distinctly smaller than lvs. Cult. somewhat for the production of spearmint oil under the name *M. cardiaca.*

lanata: *M. arvensis* var. *villosa.*

longifolia (L.) Huds. [*M. sylvestris* L.; *M. tomentosa* D'Urv.]. HORSEMINT. Per., 1–4 ft., usually white- or gray-hairy; lvs. sessile or nearly so, oblong-elliptic, 2–3⅝ in. long, serrate, pubescent above and generally gray- or white-villous beneath; infl. usually branched, spicate, verticillasters many, usually congested; calyx narrow-campanulate, hairy, corolla lilac or white. Summer. Eur. Extremely variable and parent of many hybrids. Has been confused with *M. spicata.*

×**niliaca:** *M.* × *rotundifolia;* but material generally known by this name is *M. spicata.*

×**piperita** L.: *M. aquatica* × *M. spicata.* PEPPERMINT. To 3 ft., usually glabrescent, often purple-tinged, pungent; lvs. petioled, lanceolate, to 2½ in. long, acute, serrate; spikes oblong, verticillasters congested; fls. sterile, calyx tubular, glabrous, teeth ciliate, corolla lilac-pink. Summer. Eur. Var. **citrata** (J. F. Ehrh.) Briq. [*M. aquatica* var. *citrata* (J. F. Ehrh.) Benth.; *M. citrata* J. F. Ehrh.]. BERGAMOT M., LEMON M. Herbage with a characteristic lemon odor when crushed. Var. **vulgaris** Sole. Sts. dark red, lvs. dark green; distinguished from *M. spicata* in having petioles up to ⅜ in. long. The nomenclature of commercial variants of this hybrid is complex; they can best be treated as cvs.

Pulegium L. PENNYROYAL. More or less decumbent, to 1 ft. or more, glabrescent to tomentose; lvs. ovate to nearly orbicular, to 1 in. long, acute or obtuse, entire to serrate; infl. elongate, verticillasters many, densely fld., distant; fls. lilac. Summer. Eur., W. Asia. Var. **gibraltarica** (Willd.) Batt. & Trab. White-tomentose.

Requienii Benth. [*Menthella Requienii* (Benth.) Pérard]. MENTHELLA, CORSICAN M., CREME-DE-MENTHE PLANT. Creeping herb, sts. filiform, glabrescent; lvs. petioled, nearly orbicular, to ⅜ in. long; verticillasters few-fld.; fls. lavender. Summer. Corsica, Sardinia; naturalized locally in w. Eur.

×**rotundifolia** (L.) Huds. [*M.* × *niliaca* Juss. ex Jacq.]: *M. longifolia* × *M. suaveolens.* Rarely cult.; most material grown under this name is *M. suaveolens.*

suaveolens J. F. Ehrh. [*M. rotundifolia* of auth., not (L.) Huds.]. APPLE M. To 3 ft., pubescent to tomentose, sweet-scented; lvs. sessile, oblong to nearly ovate, acute or obtuse, with or without an apical cusp, serrate, rugose, somewhat pubescent above and often heavily so beneath; infl. usually branched, spicate, verticillasters many, usually congested; calyx campanulate, hairy, corolla whitish or pink. Summer. S. and w. Eur. A much-cult. sweet herb. Cv. **'Variegata'**. Variegated, sometimes listed as PINEAPPLE M.

spicata L. [*M. longifolia* of auth., not (L.) Huds.; *M. niliaca* of auth., not Juss. ex Jacq.; *M. viridis* L.]. SPEARMINT. To 30 in., glabrous, usually with strong, sweet scent; lvs. sessile, lanceolate, to 2 in. long, acute, serrate, petioles about 1/16 in. long; infl. variable; calyx campanulate, glabrous or hairy, teeth nearly equal, corolla lilac, pink, or white. Summer. Origin not known; naturalized widely in Eur. Widely cult. as sweet herb and for essential oils. Cvs. **'Crispii'** and **'Crispata'**. Crisp-lvd.

sylvestris: *M. longifolia.*

tomentosa: *M. longifolia.*

viridis: *M. spicata.*

MENTHELLA: *MENTHA*.

MENTOCALYX: *GIBBAEUM*.

MENTZELIA L. [*Bartonia* Sims; *Nuttallia* Raf.]. *Loasaceae.*

About 60 spp. of Amer. herbs or shrubs with barbed hairs, often with shredding bark; lvs. mostly alt.; fls. white, yellow, or orange, often very showy, petals not united, stamens not clustered, ovary with 3 placentas; fr a caps.

Propagated by seeds sown where the plants are to grow.

albescens (Gillies) Griseb. Ann. or bien., to 2 ft., sts. white-hairy; lvs. ovate-lanceolate to linear-lanceolate, pinnately lobed; fls. in corymbose cymes, pale yellow, to ¾ in. across, petals 5, stamens 20–40. Dry habitats; Okla. to Mex., Chile, Argentina.

aurea: see *M. Lindleyi.*

decapetala (Pursh) Urb. & Gilg [*M. ornata* (Pursh) Torr. & A. Gray; *Nuttallia decapetala* (Pursh) Greene]. Bien. or per., to 4 ft.; lvs. lanceolate to oblong-lanceolate, pinnately lobed; fls. white or yellowish, to 5 in. across, opening in evening, fragrant, petals 10, stamens about 200. Plains and foothills, w. Iowa to Alta., s. to Tex. and n. Mex.

gronoviifolia: *Eucnide bartonioides.*

involucrata S. Wats. Ann. or bien., to 1½ ft., sts. very white; lvs. coarsely toothed; fls. cream-colored, to 2½ in. long, subtended by large white bracts with deeply toothed green margins. Desert areas, Ariz., Calif.

laevicaulis (Dougl.) Torr. BLAZING-STAR. Bien., to 3½ ft., sts. shining white; lvs. wavy-toothed; fls. light yellow, to 4 in. across. Canyons, valleys, and dry foothills, Mont. to Wash., s. to Nev. and Calif.

Lindleyi Torr. & A. Gray [*M. aurea* Hort., not Nutt.; *Bartonia aurea* Lindl.]. Ann., to 2 ft.; lvs. pinnately cut or toothed; fls. golden-yellow, vermilion at base, to 2½ in. across, opening in evening, fragrant, petals 5. Desert areas, cent. Calif.

multiflora (Nutt.) A. Gray. Per., to 2½ ft.; lvs. pinnately lobed, narrowly lanceolate; fls. usually 3–4 in corymbose cluster, yellow, to 1 in. across, petals 10. Sandy open places, Wyo. to Calif., s. to Tex. and New Mex.

nuda (Pursh) Torr. & A. Gray. Bien. or per., to 2 ft.; lvs. toothed or pinnatifid; fls. creamy-white, to 2½ in. across, usually without bracts, opening toward evening, petals 10. Gravelly and open places, Nebr. and Colo., s. to Tex.

ornata: *M. decapetala.*

Stella-Polaris: a listed name of no botanical standing, applied to plants said to be taller and larger-fld. than *M. Lindleyi.*

stricta (Osterh.) O. Stevens ex Jeffs & Little [*Nuttallia stricta* (Osterh.) Greene]. Per., to 3½ ft., st. not much-branched at base; lvs. linear-lanceolate, to 4 in. long, sinuate; fls. yellow, subtended by toothed bracts, petals 10. Nebr. to Wyo., s. to Tex. and Colo.

MENYANTHACEAE: see *GENTIANACEAE.*

MENYANTHES L. BUCKBEAN, BOGBEAN. *Gentianaceae*

(sometimes placed in separate family *Menyanthaceae*). One sp., a per. herb, in wet places, of circumboreal distribution; lvs. alt., of 3 lfts., long-petioled; fls. racemose, regular, bisexual, 5-merous, corolla funnelform, bearded on whole upper surface, stamens borne on corolla tube, ovary 1-celled, with many ovules; fr. a caps., bursting irregularly.

Sometimes planted in bog gardens.

trifoliata L. MARSH TREFOIL. With creeping rhizome; lfts. elliptic to obovate, to 4 in. long, entire to crenate, petioles to 10 in. long, broadly sheathing in basal half; fls. in 10–20-fld. racemes, at ends of axillary scapes to 1 ft. long, corolla white to purplish, with white beard, to 1 in. across. Early spring to early summer.

MENZIESIA Sm. MOCK AZALEA. *Ericaceae.*

About 6 or 7 spp. of deciduous shrubs of e. Asia and N. Amer.; lvs. alt., simple; fls. in terminal clusters, calyx 4–5-lobed, corolla campanulate or urceolate, 4–5-lobed, stamens 5–10, ovary superior; fr. a woody caps.

Suitable for rock gardens; for cultivation see *Andromeda*.

alba: a listed name of no botanical standing; probably a form of *Daboecia cantabrica*.

azorica: a listed name of no botanical standing, used for *Daboecia azorica*.

ciliicalyx (Miq.) Maxim. To 2½ ft.; lvs. elliptic to obovate, to 2 in. long, entire; clusters 3–8-fld.; fls. yellowish-green, tipped with purple, ½ in. long, stamens pubescent. Japan. Var. **multiflora** (Maxim.) Mak. [*M. lasiophylla* Nakai; *M. multiflora* Maxim.]. Clusters 6–10-fld.

ferruginea Sm. RUSTYLEAF. Erect or straggling shrub, to 12 or 15 ft.; lvs. elliptic-oblong to obovate, to 2½ in. long, finely serrate, glandular-ciliate, with rusty hairs above; fls. yellowish-red, ½ in. long, stamens glabrous. N. Calif. to Alaska.

lasiophylla: *M. ciliicalyx* var. *multiflora*.

multiflora: *M. ciliicalyx* var.

pentandra Maxim. To 6 ft.; lvs. elliptic to obovate, to 1¾ in. long, ciliate; fls. whitish, ¼ in. long, stamens glabrous. Japan.

pilosa (Michx.) Juss. MINNIEBUSH. To 6 ft.; lvs. elliptic to obovate-oblong, to 2 in. long, ciliate, hairy; fls. yellowish-white to pinkish, ¼ in. long, stamens glabrous. Late spring. Penn. to Ga. and Ala. Zone 6.

poliifolia: *Daboecia cantabrica*.

purpurea Maxim. To 6 ft.; lvs. elliptic to obovate, to 1½ in. long, pubescent beneath on midrib; fls. bright red, ½ in. long, corolla campanulate. Japan. Zone 6?

MERIANA: *WATSONIA*.

MERREMIA Dennst. ex H. G. Hallier. *Convolvulaceae.* About 80 spp. of circumtrop. herbaceous or woody twiners; lvs. entire, dentate, or palmately lobed or divided; fls. axillary, solitary or few, corolla campanulate or funnelform, white or yellowish to orange, stigma 2-lobed, lobes rounded; fr. a 4-valved caps. or more or less irregularly dehiscent. Differs from *Ipomoea* in having white or yellowish fls., characteristic globular stigma lobes, and often irregularly dehiscent fr.

dissecta (Jacq.) H. G. Hallier [*Ipomoea dissecta* (Jacq.) Pursh; *Operculina dissecta* (Jacq.) House]. Per. twiner, often rampant, coarsely hirsute at first, becoming nearly glabrous; lvs. deeply palmately 5–7-parted, segms. lanceolate, to 4 in. long, coarsely sinuately dentate, middle segm. larger than lateral ones; corolla white, with purple or dull reddish throat, to 1½ in. long; caps. globose, surrounded by enlarged sepals. Fla. to Ga. and Tex., s. to Argentina; occasionally escapes from cult. in trop. regions.

tuberosa (L.) Rendle [*Ipomoea tuberosa* L.; *Operculina tuberosa* (L.) Meissn.]. WOOD ROSE, HAWAIIAN W.R., YELLOW MORNING-GLORY, CEYLON M., SPANISH WOODBINE. Per., glabrous twiner; lvs. deeply palmately 7-parted, segms. oblong-lanceolate, to 6 in. long, entire, middle segm. larger than lateral ones; corolla yellow, to 2 in. long; fr. globose, to 1½ in. across, surrounded by enlarged sepals, loosening circumscissilely at base, in addition to dehiscing irregularly. Circumtrop., although perhaps of trop. Amer. origin.

MERTENSIA Roth. BLUEBELLS, LUNGWORT. *Boraginaceae.* About 40 to 45 spp. of glabrous or hairy, per. herbs, largely of woods and thickets, native to Asia, Eur. and N. Amer.; roots mostly thickened; lvs. simple, alt., entire, often with pellucid dots, basal lvs. petioled, cauline lvs. often sessile; fls. blue, purplish, or white, in loose or congested bractless scorpioid, racemose, or panicled cymes, calyx 5-lobed, corolla 5-lobed, with or seldom without crests in the throat, stamens 5, exserted or included, ovary 2-lobed; fr. of 4 erect, rough or seldom smooth nutlets.

A few species are planted in wild or rock gardens. Propagated by seeds sown as soon as ripe and with difficulty by division.

alpina (Torr.) G. Don [*M. Tweedyi* Rydb.]. Glabrous per., to 8 in.; lvs. spatulate to lanceolate, hairy above, glabrous beneath; corolla dark blue, ¼ in. long, with prominent crests. Rocky Mts.

Bakeri Greene. Soft-hairy per. to 16 in.; lvs. linear-lanceolate to ovate-elliptic, grayish-pubescent on both surfaces; corolla blue, ½ in. long, with prominent crests. Mts., Colo., Utah, New Mex.

ciliata (James) G. Don [*M. platensis* (Rydb.) Rydb.]. Per., to 4 ft., with many erect or ascending sts.; basal lvs. ovate to lanceolate, glabrous beneath, ciliate on the margin; corolla bright blue, to ¾ in. long, with crests. Mont. to Ore., New Mex.

coriacea: *M. viridis* var. *dilatata*.

echioides Benth. Soft-hairy per. to 15 in.; lvs. oblong or spatulate, pubescent beneath; corolla deep blue, to ⅜ in. long, without crests; nutlets white and shining. Himalayas.

lanceolata (Pursh) A. DC. Glabrous per., to 1½ ft., with erect or ascending sts.; lvs. broadly lanceolate to oblong, glabrous beneath; corolla blue, ¼–½ in. long, with crests; nutlets black at maturity. N. Dak., Sask., s. to New Mex.

longiflora Greene [*M. pulchella* Piper]. Per., to 12 in., from a tuberous root; lvs. oblong-lanceolate to ovate, glabrous beneath; corolla bright blue, to ¾ in. long, with conspicuous crests, tube twice as long as the limb. Mont. to B.C., s. to n. Calif.

maritima (L.) S. F. Gray. Glabrous, glaucous per., to 2 ft.; lvs. spatulate, obovate, or lanceolate, to 2⅜ in. long; fls. pink, becoming blue and pink, ¼ in. across, with crests. Coastal, n. Eur.

oblongifolia (Nutt.) G. Don. Per., to 1 ft., with an elongated rhizome; lvs. oblong or spatulate to oblong-ovate, glabrous beneath, hairy above; corolla blue, to ¾ in. long, with conspicuous crests. Mont. to Wash., and n. Calif. Var. **nevadensis** (A. Nels.) L. O. Williams. More robust; lvs. glabrous above.

paniculata (Ait.) G. Don. Erect per., to 3 ft.; lvs. ovate to lanceolate, rough-hairy on both surfaces; corolla blue, pinkish when young, sometimes white, to ½ in. long, with crests. Que. to Alaska, s. to Mich. and Wash. Var. **borealis** (Macbr.) L. O. Williams. Lvs. glabrous on both surfaces, or pubescent beneath. Var. **subcordata:** *M. platyphylla* var. *subcordata*.

platensis: *M. ciliata*.

platyphylla A. Heller. Erect per., to 2½ ft.; lvs. ovate, cordate, acuminate, hairy on both surfaces; corolla blue, to ⅝ in. long, with crests, calyx lobes to ¼ in. long increasing to ½ in. in fr., acute. W. Wash. Var. **subcordata** (Greene) L. O. Williams [*M. paniculata* var. *subcordata* (Greene) Macbr.]. Calyx lobes to ⅛ in. long, obtuse, basal lvs. subcordate and sometimes entirely glabrous.

primuloides C. B. Clarke. Rough-hairy, dwarf per., to 6 in.; lvs. elliptic, narrowed at both ends, hairy on both surfaces; corolla deep blue, varying to white and yellow, about ¼ in. long, with crests; nutlets shining. Himalayas.

pulchella: *M. longiflora*.

Tweedyi: *M. alpina*.

umbratilis Greenm. Per., to 2 ft.; lvs. glabrous beneath, basal lvs. ovate to oblong-ovate, st. lvs. oblong-lanceolate; corolla blue, to ¾ in. long, with crests. Wash., Ore.

virginica (L.) Pers. BLUEBELLS, VIRGINIA B., COWSLIP, VIRGINIA C., ROANOKE-BELLS. Erect, glabrous per., to 2 ft.; lvs. elliptic to ovate, glabrous; fls. in nodding clusters, corolla 1 in. long with inconspicuous crests, tube purple, limb blue. N.Y. to Tenn. and Ala., w. to Kans. Cv. 'Rubra'. Fls. pink. Cv. 'Alba'. Fls. white.

viridis A. Nels. Per., to 14 in.; lvs. lanceolate to ovate, hairy above, glabrous beneath; corolla blue, to ¾ in. long, with crests. Mts., Mont., Colo., Utah. Var. **dilatata** (A. Nels.) L. O. Williams [*M. coriacea* A. Nels.]. Lvs. glabrous on both surfaces.

MERYTA J. R. Forst. & G. Forst. *Araliaceae.* About 16 spp. of small, dioecious trees, native to New Zeal., Australia, New Caledonia, and Pacific Is.; lvs. alt. or crowded at ends of brs., large, simple, leathery; fls. in dense umbels arranged in panicles; male fls. commonly 5-merous, female fls. with petals 4–5, ovary 3- to many-celled; fr. an ovoid or globose drupe.

Sinclairii (Hook.f.) Seem. PUKA. Evergreen tree, to 25 ft.; lvs. oblong-obovate, to 10–20 in. long, obtuse, entire, glossy, petioles 4–15 in. long; fls. greenish-white, in erect, terminal panicles to 1½ ft. long, petals and stamens 4 in male fls.; fr. to ½ in. long, fleshy, glossy black. Islands n. of New Zeal. Zone 10, in s. Calif.

MESEMBRYANTHEMACEAE: *AIZOACEAE*.

MESEMBRYANTHEMUM L. emended by L. Bolus [*Cryophytum* N. E. Br.]. ICICLE PLANT, ICE PLANT, FIG MARIGOLD, PEBBLE PLANT. *Aizoaceae.* About 74 spp. of ann. or bien. succulents, native to s. Eur., sw. Asia, N. Afr., Canary Is., Madeira, and S. Afr., 1 sp. in w. N. Amer. and Chile; sts. often thick and fleshy, erect or prostrate, much-branched, often with glistening papillae; lvs. alt. or opp., sometimes in a basal rosette, flat or nearly cylindrical, sometimes with glistening papillae; fls. solitary or in cymes, calyx 4–5-lobed, with a distinct tube, petals white, pink, red, or rarely yellow, many, joined basally into a short, distinct tube, stamens many, erect, ovary at least half-superior, 4–5-celled, stigmas

4–5; fr. a 4–5-valved caps., expanding keels winged, placental tubercles absent.

Propagated by seeds sown in spring. The seedlings should be placed in pots and kept dry during summer. See also *Succulents*.

aequilaterum: *Carpobrotus aequilaterus;* see also *Carpobrotus chilensis*.

agninum: *Stomatium agninum.*

anemoniflorum: *Cephalophyllum anemoniflorum.*

aureum: *Lampranthus aureus.*

barbatum: *Trichodiadema barbatum.*

bellidiforme: *Dorotheanthus bellidiformis.*

Brownii: *Lampranthus Brownii.*

chilense: *Carpobrotus chilensis.*

cordifolium: *Aptenia cordifolia.*

crassum: *Ruschia crassa.*

criniflorum: *Dorotheanthus bellidiformis.*

crystallinum L. [*Cryophytum crystallinum* (L.) N. E. Br.]. ICE PLANT. Ann., sts. much-branched, prostrate, to 2 ft. long, glistening; lvs. ovate or spatulate, to 4 in. long, with glistening papillae; fls. to 1¼ in. across, in 3–5-fld. cymes, white to reddish. S.-W. Afr., Cape Prov; naturalized in Calif., Medit. region, and the Canary Is. Lvs. sometimes eaten like spinach.

deltoides: *Oscularia deltoides.*

Derenbergianum: *Ruschia Derenbergiana.*

edentulum: *Ruschia edentula.*

exacutum: *Ruschia acuminata.*

karrooicum: *Ruschia karrooica.*

multiradiatum: *Lampranthus roseus.*

pomeridianum: *Carpanthea pomeridiana.*

roseum: *Lampranthus multiradiatus.*

rostellum: *Ruschia rostella.*

Steingroeveri: *Ruschia Steingroeveri.*

tricolor: *Dorotheanthus tricolor.*

MESPILUS L. MEDLAR. *Rosaceae.* One sp., a small deciduous tree from Eur. and Asia Minor; fls. solitary, calyx lobes leafy, persistent, stamens 30–40, ovary inferior, the carpels becoming bony at maturity; fr. a pome, open at apex, with 1–5 nutlets.

Grown for the fruit, which is edible after frost. Propagated by seeds which are slow in germinating, and by grafting or budding on pear, quince, or hawthorn.

germanica L. To 20 ft., sometimes thorny; lvs. oblong, to 5 in. long, finely toothed; fls, white, to 2 in. across; fr. apple-shaped, brown, 1–2 in. in diam. Edible when fully ripe, or made into preserves. Zone 6.

MESUA L. *Guttiferae.* About 3 spp. of trop. trees, native to Asia; lvs. opp., leathery; fls. solitary, large, showy, sepals and petals 4, stamens many, ovary 2-celled, each cell 2-ovuled; fr. with thin, woody wall.

ferrea L. Medium-sized tree; lvs. linear-lanceolate to oblong-lanceolate, to 6 in. long, glaucous beneath; fls. white, 3 in. across, fragrant; fr. subglobose or ovoid-conical, to 2 in. long. India, Thailand, Malay Pen.

METASEQUOIA Miki. *Taxodiaceae.* One sp., endemic to Szechwan, China, allied to *Sequoia*, but differing in having brs. ascending; lvs. linear, decussate or appearing 2-ranked, on deciduous, lateral branchlets; male cones sessile, in long drooping spikes, female cones subglobose, pendulous on naked peduncles, scales 20–30; seeds 5–8 to each scale, 2-winged. The genus was first described in 1941 from fossil material, and the first living plants were brought to the attention of botanists in 1948.

Propagated easily by seeds or cuttings, like *Taxodium distichum*, thriving along water courses. For culture see *Conifers*.

glyptostroboides H. H. Hu & Cheng. DAWN REDWOOD. Monoecious tree, to 100 ft. or more, trunks to 9 ft. in diam., bark gray, fissured; lvs. on young trees to 1½ in. long, on mature trees to ½ in. long, blue-green above; female cone globose-ellipsoid, to 1 in. long, dark brown. Zone 5b.

METROSIDEROS Banks ex Gaertn. BOTTLEBRUSH, IRON TREE. *Myrtaceae.* About 60 spp. of evergreen shrubs, trees, or woody climbers, in S. Afr., New Zeal., Australia, n. to Polynesia and to Malay Pen.; lvs. opp., simple, pinnately veined; fls. in various shades of red, white, rarely yellow, usually showy, in dense terminal cymes or racemes, calyx lobes and petals 5, inconspicuous, stamens many, long-exserted, conspicuous; fr. a leathery caps., seeds linear, small.

Five species are known to be cultivated in Calif. as ornamentals; others described here may not be in cultivation but are confused with those that are. Propagated by cuttings.

carmineus W. Oliver [*M. diffusus* Hook.f., not (G. Forst.) Sm.]. Climber, with slender sts.; lvs. broadly ovate to round, usually ¼ in. long, but to 1¼ in.; fls. bright carmine-red, usually in terminal compound cymes, stamens to ½ in. long. New Zeal. Fls. only rarely produced in cult.

Colensoi Hook.f. [*M. pendens* Colenso]. Climbing shrub; lvs. ovate-lanceolate, to ¾ in. long, densely pubescent when young; fls. white or pink, in few-fld. cymes, stamens about ⅜ in. long. New Zeal. May not be cult.

collinus (J. R. Forst.) A. Gray [*M. diffusus* (G. Forst.) Sm., not Hook.f.]. Tree or shrub; lvs. elliptic-oblong or obovate to orbicular, to 3 in. long, leathery, variously pubescent; fls. crimson. Hawaii. May not be cult.

diffusus: see *M. collinus* and *M. carmineus*.

excelsus Soland. ex Gaertn. [*M. tomentosus* A. Rich.]. CHRISTMAS TREE, NEW ZEALAND C.T. Much-branched tree, brs. erect; lvs. elliptic to oblong, 2–4 in. long, usually twice as long as wide, gray-hairy beneath; fls. red, in dense cymose clusters, stamens 1 in. long or more. Summer. New Zeal.

floridus: see *M. robustus* and *M. fulgens*.

fulgens Soland. ex Gaertn. [*M. floridus* Sm., not Hook.f.; *M. scandens* (J. R. Forst. & G. Forst.) Druce, not Soland. ex Gaertn.; *M. speciosus* Colenso, not Sims]. Climber; lvs. elliptic-oblong, to 3 in. long, leathery; fls. orange-red, in terminal cymes, stamens to 1 in. long. New Zeal. Cv. 'Aurata'. Fls. yellow. May not be cult.

kermadecensis W. Oliver [*M. polymorphus* Hook.f., not Gaud.-Beaup.; *M. villosus* T. Kirk, not Sm.]. Tree, lvs. broadly ovate, to 1 in. long, usually less than twice as long as wide; fls. red, stamens less than 1 in. long. Summer, but flowering sporadically during year. New Zeal. Confused in cult. with *M. excelsus*, but differing in shape of lvs.

lucidus: *M. umbellatus*, but see also *M. robustus*.

Parkinsonii J. Buchan. Usually a straggling shrub or tree, to 20 ft., glabrous; lvs. ovate-lanceolate, to 2 in. long, rarely longer, leathery; fls. bright crimson, stamens to 1 in. long. New Zeal. May not be cult.

pendens: *M. Colensoi.*

perforatus (J. R. Forst. & G. Forst.) A. Rich. [*M. scandens* Soland. ex Gaertn., not (J. R. Forst. & G. Forst.) Druce]. Slender climber; lvs. crowded, ovate to suborbicular, to ½ in. long, leathery, subsessile; fls. white or pink, in axillary, few-fld. cymes, stamens to ⅜ in. long. New Zeal. May not be cult.

polymorphus: see *M. kermadecensis.*

robustus A. Cunn. [*M. floridus* Hook.f., not Sm.]. NEW ZEALAND CHRISTMAS TREE. Tree; lvs. elliptic-lanceolate, to 2 in. long, glabrous; fls. dull red, in many-fld. terminal cymes, stamens to ¾ in. long. Summer. New Zeal. Confused in cult. with *M. umbellatus* (M. lucidus), but having fls. dull red, and stamens shorter.

scandens: see *M. perforatus* and *M. fulgens.*

speciosus: see *M. fulgens* and *Callistemon speciosus.*

tomentosus: *M. excelsus.*

tremuloides (A. Heller) P. Knuth. Small tree; lvs. narrow-lanceolate, to 2 in. long, leathery, glossy above, pale beneath; fls. bright red, in few-fld. terminal panicles, stamens to ¾ in. long. Hawaii. May not be cult.

umbellatus Cav. [*M. lucidus* (G. Forst.) A. Rich.]. Tree; lvs. lanceolate, to 2½ in. long, leathery, glabrous; fls. coral-red, in terminal cymes, stamens to 1 in. long. Summer. New Zeal. Distinguished from *M. robustus* in having fls. bright coral-red, and stamens longer.

villosus: *M. kermadecensis.*

MEUM Jacq. *Umbelliferae.* One sp., a per., tufted, aromatic herb to 2 ft., native in the mts. of Eur. and planted as an ornamental.

athamanticum Jacq. Lvs. mostly basal, pinnately divided into fine segms.; fls. white to pink, in compound terminal umbels, bractlets of involucels long, narrow; fr. ribbed. Prop. by seeds and division.

MEYENIA Nees. *Acanthaceae.* Not cult. **M. erecta:** *Thunbergia erecta.*

MIBORA Adans. *Gramineae.* One sp. of small, ann. grasses in the w. Medit. region; racemes lax; spikelets minute, compressed laterally, 1-fld., glumes nearly equal, obtuse, rounded on the back, lemma and palea shorter, palea narrower than the lemma. For terminology see *Gramineae.*

minima (L.) Desv. [*M. verna* Beauvois]. Sts. to 4 in.; lf. blades narrow and short; racemes slender; spikelets 6–8, appressed, purple, less than ⅛ in. long, lemma and palea pubescent.

verna: *M. minima.*

MICHAUXIA: *MINDIUM.*

MICHELIA L. *Magnoliaceae.* About 50 spp. of evergreen trees or shrubs native to temp. and trop. Asia, resembling *Magnolia,* but with fls. axillary, and the cluster of carpels borne on a long stipe.

Planted as an ornamental in southern U.S. and Calif. Propagated by seeds and cuttings of ripe wood under glass.

Cathcartii: *Alcimandra Cathcartii.*

Champaca L. CHAMPACA, FRAGRANT C. Tall evergreen tree; lvs. lanceolate-ovate, to 10 in. long; fls. yellow or orange, very fragrant, to 2½ in. across. Himalayas. Champaca oil, used in perfumery in the Orient, is distilled from the fls.

compressa (Maxim.) Sarg. [*Magnolia compressa* Maxim.]. Tender tree, to 50 ft., semiglobular in form; lvs. oblong, to 4 in. long; fls. yellow, fragrant, 1 in. across, appearing in early spring. Cent. Japan to Ryukyu Is.

Doltsopa Buch.-Ham. ex DC. [*M. excelsa* (Wallich) Blume ex Wallich]. To 90 ft., but shorter in cult.; lvs. elliptic to oblong, to 6 in. long or more, thinly leathery, glabrous or nearly so; fls. whitish, fragrant, perianth parts 12–16, to 3 in. long. E. Himalayas, Tibet, w. China. The large white fls. are magnolialike. A valuable timber tree in the Himalayas.

excelsa: *M. Doltsopa.*

Figo (Lour.) K. Spreng. [*M. fuscata* (Andr.) Blume; *Magnolia fuscata* Andr.]. BANANA SHRUB. Evergreen shrub, to 15 ft., branchlets brown-tomentose; lvs. elliptic to oblong, to 3 in. long; fls. cream-yellow, edged with purple, with banana fragrance, to 1½ in. across. China. Seeds seldom viable here. Prop. by cuttings.

formosana (Kaneh.) Masam. To 60 ft.; lvs. leathery, lanceolate to oblong-elliptic, to 4 in. long. Taiwan, where important as a timber tree.

fuscata: *M. Figo.*

lanuginosa: *M. velutina.*

nilagirica Zenk. Shrub or tall tree; lvs. oblong or elliptic, to 4 in. long, glabrous or puberulous only on veins beneath; fls. white, 3–4 in. across, with 9–12 obovate perianth parts. S. India and Ceylon.

repens: a listed name of no botanical standing.

sinensis Hemsl. & E. H. Wils. To 45 ft.; lvs. obovate-oblong or oblanceolate, to 6 in. long, strongly reticulate, glaucous beneath; fls. ivory-white. W. China. A handsome tree with conspicuous fls.

velutina DC. [*M. lanuginosa* Wallich]. Small tree, branchlets white-silky-pubescent; lvs. elliptic-lanceolate, to 8 in. long, pale beneath; fls. creamy-white, to 4 in. across, fragrant, with about 18 narrow-oblong petals. Himalayas.

MICONIA Ruiz & Pav. *Melastomataceae.* About 1,000 spp. of shrubs and trees mostly of trop. Amer.; lvs. opp., entire or dentate; infl. terminal, racemose or panicled, many-fld.; fls. white, rose, purple, or yellow, sessile or short-pedicelled, calyx tube shorter than ovary, stamens usually appendaged; fr. an edible berry.

Miconias should be grown in fibrous soil, given abundant moisture, and screened from direct sunlight. Propagated by cuttings of firm wood over bottom heat.

calvescens DC. [*M. magnifica* Triana]. Shrub, to 15 ft.; lvs. broadly ovate, to 2 ft. long, wavy-margined, with white or light green veins, reddish-bronze beneath. Continental tropics of the New World.

magnifica: *M. calvescens.*

MICRANTHEMUM Michx. *Scrophulariaceae.* Three spp. of aquatic, ann. herbs, native to N. and S. Amer., and Cuba; lvs. opp., sessile; fls. white to purplish, solitary, axillary, calyx 4-parted, corolla 1- or 2-lipped, stamens 2, borne at throat of corolla, styles bifid; fr. a caps. enclosed in the calyx, dehiscing irregularly.

Sometimes grown in aquaria.

micranthemoides (Nutt.) Wettst. Creeping, sts. ascending, to 8 in. long; lvs. elliptic, to ³⁄₁₆ in. long, entire; fls. white, corolla 1-lipped, lip 3-lobed. N.Y. to Va.

umbrosum (J. F. Gmel.) S. F. Blake. Creeping, sts. to 1 ft. long; lvs. broadly elliptic to orbicular, to ⅜ in. long; fls. white, corolla 2-lipped. Trop. Amer.; in U.S. from se. Va. to Fla. and Tex.

MICRANTHES: *SAXIFRAGA.*

MICROCACHRYS Hook.f. *Podocarpaceae.* One sp., a low, straggling, evergreen, monoecious shrub, native to Tasmania, with slender, 4-angled branchlets; lvs. scalelike, in 4 rows, persistent; male and female cones terminal on separate shoots, the female ovoid to globose, fleshy; seeds enclosed in a scarlet aril.

Suitable for frost-free areas on the Pacific Coast. Zone 10. For culture see *Conifers.*

tetragona Hook.f. Lvs. to ³⁄₁₆ in. long; female cones ovoid to globose, to nearly ⅜ in. long, bright red at maturity.

MICROCITRUS Swingle. AUSTRALIAN WILD LIME. *Rutaceae.* Five or 6 spp. of spiny, evergreen shrubs or trees, native to e. Australia, and 1 in New Guinea; lvs. alt., of 1 lft., glandular-dotted, petioles not winged, lfts. of juvenile plants often very small; fls. solitary or paired in axils of lvs., sepals and petals 4 or 5, stamens 10–25, separate; fr. a thick-skinned, 4–8-celled berry, cylindrical to round-ovoid, with juicy pulp, the juice acid.

Introduced as a possible parent in hybridization or a stock for citrus.

australasica (F. J. Muell.) Swingle. AUSTRALIAN FINGER LIME. Tree, 30–40 ft.; mature lfts. obovate or rhombic, to 1½ in. long; fls. usually solitary, stamens 20–25; fr. elongate, to 4 in. long and 1 in. in diam., greenish-yellow, 5–7-celled. E. Australia.

australis (Planch.) Swingle [*Citrus australis* Planch.]. AUSTRALIAN ROUND LIME. Tree, 30–60 ft.; mature lfts. obovate or rhombic, to 1½ in. long, entire; fls. solitary, stamens 16–20; fr. green, globose to subglobose, to 2 in. in diam., 6-celled. Ne. Australia.

MICROCOELUM Burret & Potzt. *Palmae.* Two spp. of slender, unarmed, monoecious palms of Brazil; lvs. pinnate, petiole not toothed along the margin, pinnae slender, obliquely 2-cleft-acuminate or emarginate-acuminate; infl. among the lvs., simply branched, long-peduncled, bracts 2, the upper woody, deeply sulcate, rachillae with fls. borne in triads (2 male and 1 female) in lower part and above these with paired or solitary male fls.; male fls. asymmetrical, sepals 3, small, petals 3, valvate, much broader than thick, stamens 6, pistillode minute, female fls. with sepals 3, broadly imbricate, petals 3, broadly imbricate except briefly valvate apices, staminodes united in a low ring, pistil 3-celled, 3-ovuled; fr. ovoid, 1-seeded, exocarp and fibrous mesocarp splitting at length into 3 valves exposing the smooth papery endocarp with basal pores, seed with homogeneous, hollow endosperm and embryo basal at one side.

One species widely planted in the tropics and hardy in warmer parts of Zone 9b in Fla. For culture see *Palms.*

Weddellianum (H. Wendl.) H. E. Moore [*Coccos Weddelliana* H. Wendl.; *Syagrus Weddelliana* (H. Wendl.) Becc.]. WEDDEL PALM. To 10 ft.; lvs. to 4 ft. long, with red-black scales along margin of petiole and rachis, pinnae 50–60 on each side, regularly arranged, narrowly linear, grayish beneath; infl. to 3 ft. long; male fls. to ⅛ in. long, smaller than female fls.; fr. to 1 in. long.

MICROCYCAS (Miq.) A. DC. *Zamiaceae.* One sp., a rare palmlike, dioecious tree, with rather slender, cylindrical trunk, native to w. Cuba; lvs. 20–40, pinnate, in a crown; cones with sporophylls (cone scales) in vertical rows, scales of male cones flat and obtuse, scales of female cones thickened at the base and truncate.

Rarely cultivated as an ornamental. For culture see *Cycads.*

calocoma (Miq.) A. DC. PALMA CORCHO. To 30 ft., trunk roughened by persistent lf. bases; lvs. about 3 ft. long, pubescent, pinnae in about 80 pairs, each linear-acuminate, revolute, parallel-veined and lacking a distinct midvein; male cones cylindrical, 12–20 in. long, female cones narrowly conical, 20–30 in. long. Zone 10b. On verge of extinction in wild so needs to be maintained in cult. wherever possible.

MICROGRAMMA: *POLYPODIUM.*

MICROLEPIA K. Presl. *Polypodiaceae.* About 45 spp. of terrestrial, trop. and subtrop. ferns, similar to *Dennstaedtia,* but having indusia nearly marginal, shaped like shallow hoods, slightly broader than long.

Graceful plants requiring the usual greenhouse treatment although the hardier species thrive outdoors in shade in mild climates. Zone 9. For culture see *Ferns.*

firma Mett. Lvs. evergreen, to 3 ft. long, triangular, dull green, mostly 3-pinnate to 3-pinnate-pinnatifid at the base, the lower pinnae broad, 3 in. wide or more, the rachises and midribs densely hairy above, with hairs extending to the lf. surfaces. India. Zone 10. More delicate than *M. substrigosa,* the lvs. more arching.

hirta K. Presl. A confused name; much of the material so listed is *M. pyramidata.*

platyphylla (D. Don) John Sm. Lvs. to 4 ft. long, glabrous and glossy when old, 3-pinnatifid, pinnules broad, toothed, petioles to 3 ft. long. India, e. Asia.

pyramidata (Wallich) Lacaita [*M. hirta* of auth., not K. Presl]. Robust fern; lvs. leathery, triangular, to 6 ft. long, often 4-pinnatifid, pubescent on veins beneath and on rachis, petioles 1–2 ft. long. China, trop. Asia. Most Asiatic material passing in cult. as *M. hirta* is this sp.

speluncae (L.) T. Moore. Not known in cult.; lvs. 3–4-pinnate. Material offered under this name is *M. strigosa.*

strigosa (Thunb.) K. Presl. Lvs. evergreen, erect, to 3 ft. long, to 1 ft. wide, 2–3-pinnate at base, pinnules light green, the rachises and midribs essentially without hairs. E. and se. Asia, Polynesia. Zone 9. Material offered as *M. speluncae* is this sp. Forma **Macfaddeniae** C. V. Mort. Smaller; lvs. to 1 ft., very narrow, pinnae so condensed as to have imbricate fan-shaped pinnules, the lower pinnae often less condensed and much longer than those above. Zone 9. The name is sometimes misapplied to *Nephrolepis Duffii.*

substrigosa Tagawa. Lvs. evergreen, much like *M. strigosa,* but more arching, to 3 ft. long, broader, to 2 ft. wide, usually widest at the base, pinnae acuminate, usually drooping at the apex, the lower pinnae usually with basal pinnule pair much longer than the other pinnules. Taiwan, s. Japan. Zone 9. More sun tolerant than most spp. of this genus.

MICROMELES: *SORBUS.*

MICROMERIA Benth. SAVORY. *Labiatae.* About 70 spp. of per. herbs or shrubs of the Canary Is., Medit. region, Caucasus to Himalayas, and sw. China; sts. mostly square in cross section; lvs. opp., often entire and revolute, mostly sessile or short-petioled; fls. in verticillasters, calyx tubular to campanulate, 13-nerved, nearly equally 5-toothed, corolla tube as long as calyx or longer, naked inside, limb 2-lipped, upper lip erect, lower lip 3-lobed, stamens 4, in 2 pairs, anthers 2-celled; fr. of 4 nutlets.

Adapted to the rock garden; propagated by seeds, cuttings, or division. Many are tender in the North.

Chamissonis: *Satureja Douglasii.*

corsica: a listed name of no botanical standing; plants offered under this name may be *Acinos corsica.*

croatica (Pers.) Schott. Cespitose shrub, to 8 in., pubescent; lvs. broadly ovate, to 3/8 in. long, acute, entire; verticillasters 2–12-fld.; calyx to 3/16 in. long, corolla about twice as long as calyx, violet. Yugoslavia.

dalmatica Benth. Per., sts. to 18 in., pubescent; lvs. ovate, obtuse, obscurely dentate; verticillasters 10–60-fld.; calyx 3/32 in. long, corolla to 5/32 in. long, white to pale lilac. Balkan Pen.

Douglasii: *Satureja Douglasii.*

ericifolia (Roth) Bornm. [*Thymus ericifolius* Roth]. Procumbent per., sts. woody at base; lvs. ovate to lanceolate, obtuse, revolute; verticillasters 2–10-fld.; fls. small, nearly sessile, corolla scarcely longer than calyx, purple. Canary Is.

graeca (L.) Benth. [*Satureja graeca* L.]. Dwarf shrub, sts. many, to 15 in., simple, erect; lvs. to 5/16 in. long, lowermost ovate, uppermost lanceolate to linear, sessile; verticillasters 6–18-fld., loose; calyx densely villous in throat, corolla purple. Medit. region, cent. and s. Portugal.

Juliana (L.) Benth. [*Satureja Juliana* L.]. SAVORY. Dwarf shrub, to 12 in., pubescent; lvs. ovate to linear-lanceolate, to 1/2 in. long. 1/8 in. wide, entire, revolute, sessile; verticillasters 4–20-fld.; fls. sessile, calyx to 3/16 in. long, corolla only slightly longer than calyx, purplish. Medit. region to se. France, also cent. Portugal.

Piperella (Bertol.) Benth. Per., to 6 in., woody at base, pubescent; lvs. ovate to nearly orbicular, to 5/16 in. long, sessile; fls. in an interrupted spike, verticillasters 2–12-fld. S. Eur.

rupestris: *M. thymifolia.*

thymifolia (Scop.) Fritsch [*M. rupestris* (Wulfen ex Jacq.) Benth.; *Satureja rupestris* Wulfen ex Jacq.; *S. thymifolia* Scop.]. Per., sts. ascending, to 1 1/2 ft., woody at base, pubescent; lvs. ovate or oblong, to 1/2 in. long, obtuse, petioled; verticillasters densely 10–30-fld.; calyx to 1/2 in. long, corolla to 3 times longer than calyx, white. S. Eur.

MICROSERIS D. Don. *Compositae.* Not cult. **M. cuspidata:** *Nothocalais cuspidata.*

MICROSORIUM: *POLYPODIUM.*

MICROSTYLIS: *MALAXIS.*

MIKANIA Willd. *Compositae* (Eupatorium Tribe). About 150 spp., of climbing per. herbs, shrubs, or rarely erect herbs, native to N. and S. Amer.; lvs. opp., rarely whorled, usually petioled; fl. heads panicled, discoid, involucral bracts 4, of equal size, with an occasional small one, receptacle naked; fls. tubular, bisexual, pink-purple, white, or occasionally greenish-yellow; achenes 5-angled, pappus of capillary bristles.

hemisphaerica Schultz-Bip. ex Bak. Glabrous, herbaceous vine; lvs. opp., blade simple, cordate-ovate, 3–4 in. long, acuminate, serrate-dentate, petiole to 2 in. long; heads in corymbose panicles; fls. pinkish; pappus reddish. Brazil.

scandens (L.) Willd. CLIMBING HEMPWEED, CLIMBING HEMP-VINE. Glabrous, herbaceous vine, to 15 ft.; lvs. simple, triangular-cordate or hastate, to 4 in. long, acuminate, entire or with few teeth; heads corymbose; fls. lilac or purplish. Me. to Fla. and Tex.; pantrop. Adaptable for colonizing in wild places.

ternata (Vell.) B. L. Robinson. Half-woody vine, sts. purple-hairy; lvs. palmately compound, lfts. 5–7, oblong-rhomboideal to oblanceolate-rhomboideal, entire to pinnatifid or 3-lobed, dark green above, purple beneath; heads loosely corymbose; fls. yellowish. S. Brazil. Grown as a hanging-basket plant.

MILA Britt. & Rose. *Cactaceae.* Perhaps 11 spp. of small, cespitose, low-ribbed cacti of Peru; sts. oblong; fls. nearly apical, small, perianth tube short, scales of ovary and tube few, small, with a few long axillary hairs or none; fr. nearly naked.

For culture see *Cacti.*

caespitosa Britt. & Rose. Sts. to 6 in. high and 1 1/4 in. thick, ribs about 10; areoles close-set, brown, spines needle-shaped, yellowish, becoming brown, radial spines 20 or more, 3/8 in. long, central spines to 1 1/4 in. long; fls. yellow, 5/8 in. long; fr. globose, green, at first juicy, to 3/8 in. in diam.

Nealeana Backeb. Differs from *M. caespitosa* in having sts. to 1 3/4 in. thick; radial spines about 12, bristlelike, glassy, central spines 3–4, deflexed, to 3/4 in. long; fls. 1 in. long.

MILIUM L. MILLET GRASS. *Gramineae.* About 6 spp. of ann. and per. grasses in N. Amer. and Eurasia; lf. blades flat; panicles open; spikelets 1-fld., disarticulating above the glumes, glumes nearly equal, obtuse, 3-nerved, lemma a little shorter, elliptic, obscurely nerved, rounded on the back, compressed on the back, leathery, palea leathery. For terminology see *Gramineae.*

effusum L. Per., sts. to 5 ft., smooth, slender, erect, bent at base; lf. blades to 8 in. long; brs. of panicle isolated, in drooping pairs or fascicles, naked at base; spikelets pale, 1/8 in. long. Que. and Nov. Sc. to Minn., s. to Md. and Ill.; Eurasia. Sometimes cult. as an ann.

MILLA Cav. *Amaryllidaceae.* Six or 7 spp. of herbs with membranous-coated corm, native to sw. U.S., Mex., and Guatemala; lvs. 2–7, linear or cylindrical; fls. in an umbel or rarely solitary, on a naked scape, subtended by 4 spathe valves, perianth salverform, white with green stripes, pink, or blue, lobes 6, shorter than tube, stamens 6, inserted at throat of tube, ovary superior, 3-celled, borne on a long stalk united to the tube on 3 angles; fr. a loculicidal caps., seeds flat, black.

Bulbs may be planted in pots and grown in the greenhouse for late winter and early spring bloom; or in cold regions the bulbs may be planted outdoors in spring, and lifted and stored over winter.

biflora Cav. MEXICAN-STAR. To 1 ft.; lvs. 2–7, grasslike; fls. 1–6, sessile, to 8 in. long, waxy-white with green nerves. Sw. U.S. to Guatemala. Sometimes cult. erroneously as *Bessera elegans.*

magnifica H. E. Moore. To 2 ft.; lvs. dark green, cylindrical, hollow, to 3 ft. long; fls. 15–30, pedicelled, to 4 in. long, waxy-white with green nerves. Cent. Mex.

uniflora: *Ipheion uniflorum.*

MILLETTIA Wight & Arn. *Leguminosae* (subfamily *Faboideae*). Perhaps 150 spp. of trop. trees, shrubs, and lianas of the Old World; lvs. alt., odd-pinnate; fls. in axillary racemes, often forming terminal panicles, papilionaceous, calyx 4-lobed, petals 5, long-clawed, purple or reddish; fr. a flat, thick, nearly woody, tardily dehiscent legume. Differs from *Lonchocarpus* in the dehiscent fr.

albata: a listed name of no botanical standing.

atropurpurea: *Whitfordiodendron atropurpureum.*

caffra Meissn. Tree, to 30 ft.; lfts. lanceolate-oblong, acute, in 5–6 pairs, to 2½ in. long, thinly silky-hairy beneath; panicles to 8 in. long; standard silky-hairy on the back; fr. brown-velvety, lanceolate, obtuse, 2-seeded. S. Afr.

dura S. T. Dunn. To 40 ft.; lvs. rusty-pubescent when young, becoming glabrate, lfts. in 8–11 pairs, oblanceolate-oblong, acuminate, terminal ones larger, to 3 in. long; panicles pendent, 4–8 in. long; fls. rose-violet, fragrant, petals 1 in. long; fr. glabrous, blunt, linear-oblong, to 8 in. long. Tropics, Afr.

Laurentii de Wild. Tree, to 100 ft.; lfts. in 6–7 pairs, oblong, to 6 in. long, 1½ in. wide, with prominent raised veins, glabrous; panicles narrow, to 16 in. long; petals mauve to violet or blue-purple, standard glabrous on the back; fr. linear to oblanceolate, acuminate, to 10 in. long and 2 in. wide, glabrous, 2–4-seeded. Rio Muni and Gabon to Congo.

nitida Benth. Liana, branchlets and young petioles rusty-tomentose; lfts. about 5, ovate or elliptic-oblong, to 3 in. long, short-acuminate; fls. large, purple, in dense, rusty-pubescent panicles, standard silky-hairy, 1 in. long; fr. rusty-villous, to 4 in. long. China, Hong Kong.

oblata S. T. Dunn. Tree, to 100 ft.; lfts. in 8–10 pairs, lanceolate-oblong, somewhat hairy beneath; fls. lilac; fr. linear, to 4¾ in. long, woody, glabrous, 3–4-seeded. Tanganyika, Nyasaland.

ovalifolia Kurz. Glabrous tree of medium size; lvs. to 18 in. long, lfts. in 3 pairs, ovate-elliptic, acuminate, glaucescent beneath; racemes slender, to 3 in. long, solitary or several together; calyx purplish, nearly truncate, petals blue, standard ¼ in. long, glabrous on the back; fr. glabrous, to 2 in. long, somewhat woody. Burma.

pendula Benth. Tree, with silky-hairy branchlets; lvs. to 6 in. long, lfts. in 3 pairs, obovate-oblong, cuspidate, thin, densely gray-silky-hairy beneath; racemes short and dense; petals shorter than calyx, standard glabrous; fr. woody, oblong, glabrous, 3–5 in. long, tubercled. Burma.

reticulata Benth. Twining, woody vine; lvs. persistent, lfts. elliptic-lanceolate to lanceolate, to 3 in. long, acute, glabrous, almost leathery; racemes dense, stout, to 8 in. long, sometimes paniculate; fls. pinkish-blue, to ½ in. long; fr. to 6 in. long. China. Zone 8.

Stuhlmannii Taub. Tree; lfts. in 3–4 pairs, elliptic-obcordate, slightly pubescent beneath; fls. purple-blue; fr. woody, to 10½ in. long, glabrescent. Tanganyika, Mozambique.

MILLINGTONIA L. f. *Bignoniaceae*. One sp., a tall tree, native to Burma and the Malay Arch., also escaped and running wild in cent. India; lvs. opp., 2–3-pinnate; fls. white, in corymbose panicles, calyx truncate to shortly 5-toothed, corolla salverform, slightly 2-lipped, stamens 4; fr. a linear, 2-valved caps.

hortensis L. f. Fast-growing, evergreen, to 80 ft., bark corky, branchlets drooping; lvs. to 1½ ft. long, lfts. ovate to lanceolate, 2–3 in. long, sinuate or crenate; fls. 2–3 in. long, fragrant; fr. to 1 ft. long.

MILTONIA Lindl. PANSY ORCHID. *Orchidaceae*. About 25 spp. of epiphytes, native to highlands of trop. Cent. and S. Amer.; pseudobulbs 1–2-lvd., with sheathing lf. bases; infl. axillary, basal, loosely racemose, 1- to several-fld.; sepals and petals nearly equal, lip showy and large, spreading, entire, often bifid at apex, sessile at base, united to base of column at a right angle, column short, without a foot. For structure of fl. see *Orchidaceae.*

For culture see Orchids.

×**Bleuana** Hort. ex L. Linden & Rodig.: *M. Roezlii* × *M. vexillaria.* The first *Miltonia* hybrid; infls. loosely racemose, 2–7-fld.; fls. usually white or light pink, similar to those of *M. vexillaria,* to 3 in. across lip. Cv. 'Reine Elisabeth' is one of the parents of the modern red hybirds.

×**Bluntii** Rchb.f.: natural hybrid, *M. Clowesii* × *M. spectabilis.* Fls. whitish-yellow, blotched with purple-cinnamon, sepals and petals lanceolate, similar to those of *M. Clowesii,* lip similar in shape to that of *M. spectabilis,* white with purple at base. Autumn. Brazil.

candida Lindl. Pseudobulbs ovoid, 2-lvd.; lvs. fleshy, linear-oblanceolate, to 12 in. long; infls. lateral, erect, racemose, few-fld.; fls. showy, to 3 in. across, sepals and petals similar, spreading, ovate to ovate-oblong, yellow with large chestnut-brown blotches and spots, wavy, lip nearly orbicular, clasping column basally, strongly frilled along margin, front of disc with a yellow callus with light purple central blotch. Autumn. Brazil. Cv. 'Grandiflora' [var. *grandiflora* Lindl.]. Differs from typical form in having fls. twice as large, sepals and petals almost completely deep brown, only tips yellow, lip pure, brilliant white.

Clowesii Lindl. Pseudobulbs ovate-oblong, flattened, to 4 in. long, 2-lvd.; lvs. linear-strap-shaped, to 18 in. long; infls. racemose, several-fld., to 18 in. long; fls. 2–3 in. across, sepals and petals similar, lanceolate, chestnut-brown barred and tipped with yellow, lip somewhat fiddle-shaped, apex sharply pointed, basal half violet-purple, apical half white, crest with 5–7 raised lines, the lines sometimes yellow or white. Autumn. Brazil.

cuneata Lindl. Pseudobulbs ovate-oblong, flattened, to 4 in. long, 2-lvd.; lvs. narrowly lanceolate, to 15 in. long; infls. erect, 5–8-fld., to 1 ft. long; fls. to 3 in. across, sepals and petals similar, oblong-lanceolate, recurved at tips, undulate on margins, chestnut-brown tipped with yellow, occasionally with few yellow streaks at base, lip white, with long narrow claw and squarish, undulate blade, disc with 2 divergent raised keels spotted with rose. Winter–early spring. Brazil.

Endresii Nichols. Pseudobulbs ellipsoid, 1-lvd.; lvs. linear-lanceolate, to 12 in. long; infls. erect or arching, racemose, few-fld., to 12 in. long; fls. flat, large, to 2½ in. across, sepals broadly ovate, white with a bright red-purple blotch at base, or pure white, petals elliptic-obovate, similar in color to sepals, lip entire, broadly fiddle-shaped, emarginate at apex, white with 2 purple blotches at base or with a yellow disc. Late winter. Costa Rica, Panama.

flavescens Lindl. Pseudobulbs elliptic-oblong, to 5 in. long, flattened, 2-lvd.; lvs. linear-strap-shaped, to 1 ft. long; infls. longer than lvs., racemose, 7–10-fld.; sepals and petals linear-oblong, to 2 in. long, straw-yellow, lip shorter, ovate-oblong, undulate on margin, contracted below middle, white, streaked and marked with red-purple on basal half, pubescent, traversed by 4–6 radiating lines. Autumn. Brazil, Paraguay. Cv. 'Grandiflora' [var. *grandiflora* Regel]. Differs from typical form in having fls. larger, sepals and petals pale yellow, bracts yellow. Cv. 'Stellata' [var. *stellata* (Lindl.) Rchb.f.]. Fls. to 3½ in. across, sepals and petals white, lip white, bracts rose-colored.

laevis: *Odontoglossum laeve.*

Moreliana: *M. spectabilis* cv.

Phalaenopsis (Linden & Rchb.f.) Nichols. Pseudobulbs ovoid, flattened, to 1½ in. long, 2-lvd.; lvs. linear, to 9 in. long; infls. shorter than lvs., 3–5-fld.; fls. flat, 2½ in. across, sepals and petals white, sepals elliptic-oblong, petals broader, lip 4-lobed, white with some purple streaks or blotches, crest with 3 small blunt teeth with yellow spot on each side. Spring–late summer. Colombia. Cv. 'Alba'. Fls. white except for yellow markings at base of lip.

Regnellii Rchb.f. Pseudobulbs ovate-oblong, to 3 in. long, pale yellow-green, 2-lvd.; lvs. linear-strap-shaped, to 1 ft. long; infls. longer than lvs., 3–5-fld.; fls. flat, to 2½ in. across vertically, sepals and petals white or faintly suffused with rose at base, sepals oblong-lanceolate, petals elliptic-oblong, lip broadly obcordate, obscurely 3-lobed, light rose, streaked with rose-purple and with white margin, crest of 7–9 radiating yellow lines. Early autumn. Brazil. Cv. 'Purpurea' [var. *purpurea* Hort. ex Pynaert]. Sepals and petals light rose-purple, margined with white, lip rich magenta-purple with darker veining, lines of crest white except for bright yellow middle one.

Reichenheimii: *Odontoglossum Reichenheimii.*

Roezlii (Rchb.f.) Nichols. Pseudobulbs ovate-oblong, to 2½ in. long, 1-lvd.; lvs. linear, to 12 in. long; infls. shorter than lvs. or as long, 2–5-fld.; fls. flat, to 4 in. across, white with purple blotch at base of each petal and orange-yellow disc at base of lip, sepals ovate-oblong, petals similar but broader, lip broadly obcordate, with small hornlike auricle on each side of base and 3 raised lines on disc with 2 small teeth in front. Winter–spring. Colombia. Cv. 'Alba'. Fls. lacking purple blotch on petals.

Russelliana Lindl. Pseudobulbs ovate-oblong, flattened, to 3 in. long, 2-lvd.; lvs. narrowly lanceolate, to 9 in. long; infls. to 2 ft. long, green, mottled with dull purple, 5–9-fld.; fls. to 2 in. across when flattened, sepals and petals similar, oblong-lanceolate, reddish-brown, tipped with pale yellow, lip cuneate-oblong, lateral margins somewhat sinuate, basal ⅔ rose-lilac, apical ⅓ white or light yellow, disc with 3 raised lines. Early winter. Brazil.

spectabilis Lindl. Pseudobulbs on rhizomes at short intervals, ovate-oblong, flattened, to 4 in. long, 2-lvd.; lvs. linear-strap-shaped, to 6 in. long, brownish-yellow-green; infls. as long as lvs., completely enclosed by overlapping, flattened sheaths; fls. nearly flat, to 3 in. across, sepals and petals lanceolate-oblong, white or suffused with rose at base, lip large, obovate-orbicular, wine-purple with 6–8 longitudinal veins of deeper shade, margins white or pale rose, crest 3-keeled, usually yellow. Late winter. Brazil. Cv. 'Lineata' [var. *lineata* Linden & Rodig.]. Sepals and petals white, lip white in front part, purple-rose at base, with 7–8 carmine-rose veins running to front margins. Cv. 'Moreliana'. Fls. deep plum-purple with deeper veining on lip.

vexillaria (Rchb.f.) Nichols. Pseudobulbs elliptic-oblong, to 2½ in. long; lvs. as many as 8, linear-lanceolate, 2-ranked, light pea-green; infls. usually 2 from each pseudobulb, arching, to 20 in. long, 4–7-fld.; fls. variable in size and color, to 4 in. across vertically, white or white flushed with rose to pink, lavender, or rose-carmine, sepals and petals similar, obovate-oblong, lip flat, nearly orbicular, 2-lobed, with small, ascending auricle at base on each side, crest yellow, 2-lobed at base, and with 3 short teeth in front. Spring–early summer. Colombia. Cv. 'Alba'. Fls. pure white, sometimes with light pink suffusion at base of sepals and petals. Cv. 'Rubella'. Fls. smaller than in typical form, rose-pink, sepals and petals bordered with white, lip with large white area in front of yellow disc. Cv. 'Rubra'. Fls. deep rose, lip with darker veins and with 3 divergent blood-red streaks in front of yellow disc.

Warscewiczii Rchb.f. [*Oncidium fuscatum* Rchb.f.]. Pseudobulbs oblong, flattened, to 5 in. long, 1-lvd.; lvs. linear-oblong, to 7 in. long; infls. simple or paniculate, many-fld., to 14 in. long; fls. to 2 in. across, sepals and petals bluntly cuneate-strap-shaped and undulate, red-brown with yellow or white tips, lip 2-lobed, broadly oblong, rose-purple with brown blotch above middle, white margins, and base with 2 small yellow teeth. Late winter–early spring. Colombia, Peru.

✕**MILTONIDIUM** Hort.: *Miltonia* ✕ *Oncidium*. Orchidaceae. Bigeneric hybrids generally intermediate in character between the parents.

For culture see *Orchids*.

MIMOSA L. *Leguminosae* (subfamily *Mimosoideae*). About 400–500 spp. of herbs, shrubs, trees, or woody vines of warm regions; lvs. alt., mostly 2-pinnate; fls. in globose heads or spikes, mostly 4–5-merous, regular, stamens separate, long-exserted, as many as or twice as many as the petals; fr. a legume, mostly flat, oblong-linear, dehiscent.

Culture as for *Acacia*.

Bracaatinga Hoehne. Tall shrub, or slender tree, to 50 ft., unarmed, branchlets densely lepidote; lvs. small, with 5–7 pairs of pinnae, lfts. in 25–35 pairs, oblong-linear, obtuse; fl. heads solitary or clustered, white, ¼ in. in diam.; fls. 4-merous; fr. oblong-linear, warty-pubescent, to 1 in. long. S. Brazil.

illinoensis: *Desmanthus illinoensis.*

Nemu: *Albizia Julibrissin.*

nigra: a listed name of no botanical standing.

polycarpa Kunth. Much-branched shrub or subshrub, to 10 ft., differing from *M. pudica* in having the sensitive lvs. with 1 pair of pinnae, with lfts. to ⅝ in. long, and fr. usually hairy on the face as well as marginally bristly. S. Amer. Var. **Spegazzinii** (Pirotta) Burkart [*M. Spegazzinii* Pirotta]. Lfts. generally smaller, to ½ in. long, finely pubescent on the upper surface.

pudica L. SENSITIVE PLANT, TOUCH-ME-NOT, ACTION PLANT, HUMBLE PLANT, SHAME PLANT, LIVE-AND-DIE. Shrubby, with spiny sts. to 3 ft. long; lvs. small, exceedingly sensitive, long-petioled, with mostly 2 pairs of pinnae, lfts. oblong, in 15–25 pairs, glabrate above; fl. heads mauve; fls. 4-merous; fr. about ½ in. long, constricted between seeds, margins long-setose. Trop. Amer.; widespread weed in tropics; naturalized in Zone 9. Often grown in the greenhouse as a curiosity, the lvs. being sensitive and closing when touched.

rubicaulis Lam. Small, spiny tree; lfts. in 6–12 pairs, to ½ in. long; fl. heads axillary, to ½ in. in diam., reddish, becoming white; fr. curved, 3–4 in. long. India to Afghanistan.

Spegazzinii: *M. polycarpa* var.

viva L. Differs from *M. pudica* in having no spines, and the sensitive lvs. with only 1 pair of pinnae to ¾ in. long; lfts. in 4 pairs, to ³⁄₁₆ in. long; fr. bristly on face, with 1 segm. Jamaica.

MIMULUS L. [*Diplacus* Nutt.]. MONKEY FLOWER. *Scrophulariaceae*. About 150 spp. of spring- and summer-blooming ann. and per. herbs, or shrubs, native to S. Afr.,

Asia, Australia, N. and S. Amer., particularly abundant in w. N. Amer.; plants decumbent to erect, glabrous or hairy, often viscid or glandular-pubescent; lvs. opp., simple, entire or toothed; fls. yellow, orange, red, blue, violet, or purple, solitary, axillary or terminal, sometimes in spikelike racemes, calyx 5-angled, 5-toothed, corolla 2-lipped to nearly regular, upper lip 2-lobed, lower lip 3-lobed, throat open, or closed by a palate, stamens 4; fr. a caps.

Monkey flowers are grown in the greenhouse and in the border, and some of the large kinds in the general garden in Calif. In the open, greenhouse kinds of mimulus do well in a shady or semishady location with plenty of water, but some of the semishrubby kinds of the Pacific Coast may not require such protection. The greenhouse and florist's kinds are propagated by seeds sown from Jan. to Apr., in a mixture of equal parts of loam, leafmold, and sand, and kept at a temperature of 60° F. until germination; cuttings and division are also used.

alsinoides Dougl. ex Benth. Ann., to 10 in., sts. much-branched, decumbent or ascending; lvs. ovate, to 1½ in. long, toothed; corolla to ½ in. long, yellow, with dark purple spot on lower lip. Vancouver Is. to n. Calif.

aridus (Abrams) A. L. Grant [*Diplacus aridus* Abrams]. Much-branched sticky shrub, to 1½ ft.; lvs. crowded, oblanceolate to oblong, to 1¾ in. long; fls. on stout pedicels to ¼ in. long, corolla to 2 in. long, pale buff to yellow. S. Calif.

aurantiacus Curtis [*M. glutinosus* J. C. Wendl.; *Diplacus aurantiacus* (Curtis) Jeps.; *D. glutinosus* (J. C. Wendl.) Nutt.]. BUSH M.F. Sticky, finely glandular-pubescent shrub, to 4 ft.; lvs. oblong, to 2 in. long, glabrous above, densely pubescent beneath; corolla to 1½ in. long, orange or deep yellow, lobes spreading, toothed, or notched. Ore. and Calif.

✕**Bartonianus** Rivoire: *M. cardinalis* ✕ *M. Lewisii*. Corolla rose-red, throat yellow, spotted brownish-red.

bifidus Penn. [*M. longiflorus* var. *grandiflorus* Hort.; *Diplacus glutinosus* var. *grandiflorus* Lindl. & Paxt.; *D. grandiflorus* (Lindl. & Paxt.) Groenl., not *M. grandiflorus* T. J. Howell]. Sticky shrub, to 2½ ft. or rarely to 4 ft.; lvs. elliptic-oblong, to 2½ in. long, serrate, glabrous on both sides; corolla to 2½ in. long, pale yellow, lobes bifid ¼–½ their length. Calif.

brevipes Benth. Sticky-pubescent ann., to 2 ft.; basal lvs. broadly oblong or obovate, st. lvs. lanceolate or linear, to 3 in. long; corolla to 2 in. long, yellow, funnelform, 2-lipped. S. Calif. to n. Baja Calif.

cardinalis Dougl. ex Benth. SCARLET M.F. Sticky-pubescent, freely branching per., to 4 ft., sts. weak or erect; lvs. obovate to oblong, to 4½ in. long, sessile; corolla to 2 in. long, scarlet to pale reddish-yellow, seldom yellow, strongly 2-lipped, stamens exserted. S. Ore. to n. Mex., e. to Nev., Utah, Ariz.

cupreus Dombr. Compact ann., to 8 in.; lvs. ovate, to 1¼ in. long, 3–5-nerved from the base; corolla to 1½ in. long, yellow, becoming a brilliant copper color, lobes spreading. S. Chile. Cv. 'Whitecroft Scarlet'. Fls. red.

Flemingii Munz [*M. parviflorus* (Greene) A. L. Grant, not Lindl.; *Diplacus parviflorus* Greene]. Sticky shrub, to 2 ft.; lvs. ovate-oblong to obovate, to 2¾ in. long, entire or toothed; corolla to 1¾ in. long, red. Channel Is. (s. Calif.).

Fremontii (Benth.) A. Gray. Sticky-pubescent ann., to 8 in.; lvs. oblong-lanceolate or oblanceolate, to 1 in. long; corolla 1 in. long, rose-red or purple, broadly funnelform. Calif. and n. Baja Calif.

glutinosus: *M. aurantiacus.* Var. **puniceus:** *M. puniceus.*

grandiflorus: *M. guttatus,* but see also *M. bifidus.*

guttatus Fisch. ex DC. [*M. grandiflorus* T. J. Howell; *M. Langsdorfii* J. Donn ex Greene]. COMMON M.F. Ann. or per. herb, to 2 ft., sts. erect or decumbent, sometimes stoloniferous; lvs. ovate to oblong-lanceolate, to 6 in. long; fls. several in a raceme, corolla to 2½ in. long, yellow, usually with red-spotted throat, 2-lipped, with palate; fr. with calyx much-inflated. Alaska to Mex.

✕**hybridus** Hort. ex Siebert & Voss [*M. tigrinus* Hort.]: *M. luteus* ✕ *M. guttatus*. Fls. large, variously colored. Cv. 'Grandiflorus' is listed.

Langsdorfii: *M. guttatus.*

Lewisii Pursh. Erect, sticky-pubescent, per. herb, to 2½ ft.; lvs. oblong-elliptic, to 3 in. long; corolla to 2 in. long, rose-red to pink, rarely white. Se. Alaska to cent. Calif., e. to Mont. and Colo.

linearis: *M. longiflorus* var.

longiflorus (Nutt.) A. L. Grant [*Diplacus longiflorus* Nutt.]. Much-branched sticky shrub, to 3 ft.; lvs. lanceolate, to 3 in. long, pubescent beneath; corolla to 3 in. long, cream-colored to salmon-yellow, lobes cut or wavy. S. Calif. to n. Baja Calif. Subsp. **longiflorus.** The typical subsp.; lvs. linear-lanceolate to oblong; calyx tube gradually expanded to a slightly wider throat, corolla orange-yellow to deep orange, buff, dark red, or almost white. Var. **grandiflorus:** *M. bifidus.* Var. **linearis** (Benth.) A. L. Grant [*M. linearis* Benth.]. Lvs. linear-lanceolate, fls. pale yellow. Var. **rutilus** A. L. Grant [*Diplacus rutilus* (A. L. Grant) McMinn]. Fls. dark red. Subsp. **calycinus** (Eastw.) Munz [*Diplacus calycinus* Eastw.]. Lvs. elliptic-oblong; calyx tube abruptly expanded to a more inflated throat, corolla light lemon-yellow.

luteus L. Glabrous, per. herb, sts. prostrate or decumbent, to 1 ft. long, rooting at the nodes; lvs. broadly ovate, 1 in. long, toothed, 5–7-nerved from base; corolla 1½ in. long, yellow, spotted with red or purple. Chile.

moschatus Dougl. ex. Lindl. MUSK PLANT, MUSK FLOWER. Sticky-hairy, per. herb, to 1 ft., from spreading and creeping rhizomes, often with a musky odor; lvs. ovate or oblong-ovate, to 2 in. long; corolla to 1 in. long, pale yellow, lightly dotted with brown. B.C. and Mont. to s. Calif., also ne. N. Amer.

multiflorus Penn. Much-branched, sticky-hairy ann., to 8 in.; lvs. lanceolate-ovate, to ¾ in. long; corolla to ½ in. long, yellow, with fine brown spots in throat. Cent. Calif.

nasutus Greene. Hairy to nearly glabrous ann., to 3¼ ft.; lvs. orbicular-ovate or oblong, to 4 in. long, toothed or lobed; corolla to 1 in. long, yellow, spotted brown, usually with a reddish-brown blotch on lower lip, with a prominent palate. B.C. to n. Baja Calif., e. to Rocky Mts.

nepalensis Benth. Nearly glabrous per. herb, sts. weak, rooting at nodes; lvs. ovate or ovate-oblong, to 1½ in. long, toothed; corolla to ¾ in. long, yellow, the throat often dotted red, densely bearded along lower side. Japan, China, India.

parviflorus: *M. Flemingii.*

puniceus (Nutt.) Steud. [*M. glutinosus* J. C. Wendl. var. *puniceus* (Nutt.) A. Gray; *Diplacus puniceus* Nutt.]. Much-branched, sticky shrub, to 5 ft.; lvs. linear-lanceolate to elliptic, to 3 in. long; corolla to 1¾ in. long, red. S. Calif. to n. Baja Calif.

ringens L. ALLEGHENY M.F. Glabrous, per. herb, to 4 ft., sts. 4-angled; lvs. oblong, elliptic, or oblanceolate, to 4 in. long, toothed; corolla to 1½ in. long, blue to blue-violet, varying to pink or white, 2-lipped, throat very narrow. Nov. Sc. to Man. and N. Dak., s. to Va., Tex., Colo.

tigrinus: a listed name of no botanical standing for *M. hybridus.*

Tilingii Regel. Mat-forming, per. herb, to 8 in., with slender rhizomes, sts. decumbent; lvs. ovate, 3–5-nerved from the base, toothed; fls. terminal, 1–3 or rarely 5, corolla to 1½ in. long, yellow, spotted red, throat with prominent palate. Mont. to B.C., s. to Calif.

MIMUSOPS L. *Sapotaceae.* About 20 spp. of evergreen trees or shrubs, native to Old World tropics; lvs. mostly obovate to elliptic, closely nerved, thick; fls. white or whitish, not showy, in axillary clusters, sepals 6–8, in 2 series, corolla 6–8-lobed, each lobe with 2 petal-like appendages, ovary superior; fr. an ovoid to globose, large-seeded berry, seeds with small, circular, basal scar.

acuminata: *Payena acuminata.*

Balata (Aubl.) Gaertn. Large tree; lvs. obovate or obovate-oblong, to 6 in. long, obtuse or emarginate; fls. 3–4 in an axil, on elongate pedicels; fr. subglobose, 1½ in. in diam. Madagascar. Some material cult. as *Lucuma Roxburghii* belongs here. The balata of trop. Amer. has long been identified incorrectly with this name, but is now known as *Manilkara bidentata.*

caffra E. H. Mey. ex A. DC. Large shrub or small tree; lvs. obovate, to 1½ in. long, 1 in. wide, retuse, twigs and lower lf. surface appressed-hairy; fls. 2–3 in a cluster, on pedicels longer than petiole, sepals 8; fr. ovoid. S. Afr.

Elengi L. SPANISH CHERRY, MEDLAR. Tree, to 30 ft. or more; lvs. elliptic or ovate, to 4 in. long, obtuse or bluntly acute; fls. white, about ½ in. across, perianth parts acute; fr. ovoid, yellow, nearly 1 in. long, edible. India, Malay Pen. and Arch.

Kauki: *Manilkara Kauki.*

Nechodomii: a listed name of no botanical standing.

Roxburghiana: *Manilkara Roxburghiana.*

Zeyheri Sond. Shrub or tree, differing from *M. caffra* in having twigs reddish-tomentose, lvs. long-petioled, oblong-lanceolate, glabrous. S. Afr.

MINA Cerv. *Convolvulaceae.* One sp., an herbaceous twiner of Mex., Cent. and S. Amer.; lvs. palmately lobed, or nearly entire; infl. axillary, peduncled, several-fld., often 1-sided; corolla slightly irregular, abruptly widening above a short basal tube, forming a curved tube, with 5 small, scarcely spreading lobes, stamens much exserted; fr. a 4-valved caps.

lobata Cerv. Climber, 15–20 ft.; lvs. to 3 in. across, the lobes acuminate, middle one narrowed basally; fls. crimson, fading to yellow, to ¾ in. long.

MINDIUM Adans. [*Michauxia* L'Hér.]. *Campanulaceae.* About 7 spp. of erect herbs, native to sw. Asia; lvs. alt., simple, mostly oblong-ovate, irregularly toothed or lobed; fls. in spikes, racemes, or panicles, (6–)8–10-merous, calyx with acutely flaring lobes, appendaged at base of sinus, corolla white to pale lavender, lobes narrow, reflexed, stamens separate, exserted with the style; fr. a caps., dehiscing by 8 basal valves.

Thrives in well-drained, sunny locations; propagated by seeds.

campanuloides (L'Hér.) Rech.f. & Schiman-Czeika. [*Michauxia campanuloides* L'Hér.]. Stout-stemmed, bristly bien., to 4 or 5 ft.; lvs. lyrate to lanceolate, to about 8 in. long, lobed, toothed; fls. in naked racemes or panicles, drooping, petals white, tinged purple outside, first spreading, then reflexed, 1–1½ in. long, style strongly exserted, pubescent, ¾–1½ in. long. E. Medit. region.

MINUARTIA: *ARENARIA.* **M. caucasica:** *A. circassica.* **M. condensata:** *A. recurva.* **M. flaccida:** *A. Villarsii.* **M. juniperifolia:** probably a misspelling of *M. juniperina.* **M. juniperina:** *A. juniperina.* **M. Kitaibelii:** *A. laricifolia* subsp. **M. poliifolia robusta:** a listed name of no botanical standing. **M. pulvinaris:** a listed name of no botanical standing.

MIRABILIS L. [*Oxybaphus* L'Hér. ex Willd.]. UMBRELLAWORT. *Nyctaginaceae.* Sixty or more spp. of per. or ann. herbs in warmer parts of Amer., 1 Himalayan; roots often tuberous, sts. usually branched; lvs. opp.; fls. 1 to several within calyxlike, more or less deeply 5-lobed involucres, in axillary, corymbose or panicled infls., calyx corollalike, funnelform to tubular, campanulate, or rotate, stamens 3–5, filaments glabrous; fr. an ellipsoid to globose or ovoid achene, with persistent calyx, smooth or tubercled, often angled or ribbed. Spp. with involucres enlarged and papery in fr. and the fr. 5-ribbed are sometimes separated as *Oxybaphus.*

Grown as tender annuals from seeds sown where plants are to stand; roots may be taken up and stored over winter.

Froebelii (Behr) Greene. Per., with tuberous roots, sts. decumbent, to 2 ft. long, much-branched, sticky-pubescent; lvs. ovate, to 3 in. long; fls. usually 3–10 in an involucre, purplish-red, to nearly 2 in. long. Dry stony regions, Colo., Nev., s. Calif.

Jalapa L. [*M. uniflora* Schrank]. FOUR-O'CLOCK, MARVEL-OF-PERU, BEAUTY-OF-THE-NIGHT. To 3 ft., glabrous or nearly so; fls. in shades of red, pink, yellow, or white, often striped and mottled, opening in late afternoon, calyx tube 1–2 in. long. Trop. Amer. Commonly grown as an ann., but the roots are deep and tuberous, and weigh more than 40 lbs. when grown as a per. in warmer regions.

linearis (Pursh) Heimerl [*Allionia linearis* Pursh]. To 2 ft. or more, sts. glabrous or puberulent in lower part, sticky above; lvs. sessile or nearly so, linear to linear-lanceolate, to 4 in. long; fls. usually 3 in an involucre, pale pink to purplish-red. S. Dak. to Mont., s. to Mex.

longiflora L. To 3 ft., glandular-pubescent; lvs. short-petioled to nearly sessile, cordate-ovate to ovate-lanceolate; fls. white or marked or tinged with rose or violet, calyx tube 4–6 in. long. W. Tex., Ariz., Mex. Var. **Wrightiana:** *M. Wrightiana.*

multiflora (Torr.) A. Gray Much-branched, to 3 ft. high, 3 ft. in diam., glaucous or glaucescent; lvs. broadly ovate-triangular to ovate-oblong, to 3 in. long; fls. 6–8 in an involucre to 1⅜ in. long, calyx purplish-red, 1½–2⅛ in. long. S. Utah, Colo. to Tex., n. Ariz.

nyctaginea (Michx.) MacMill. [*Allionia nyctaginea* Michx.; *Oxybaphus nyctagineus* (Michx.) Sweet]. To 3 ft. or more, sts. nearly glabrous; lvs. petioled, triangular to ovate-oblong, to 4 in. long; fls. usually 3 in an involucre, white or pale pink; involucre enlarged in fr.; fr. obovoid, 5-angled. Mont. to Wisc., s. to Mex.

uniflora: *M. Jalapa.*

viscosa Cav. To 3 ft., sticky-pubescent, sts. to 2 in. thick; lvs. ovate, to 4 in. long, usually cordate at base, fleshy, petioled; fls. usually solitary, purple, red, pink, or white, to ¾ in. long or less. Mex., Colombia, Ecuador.

Wrightiana A. Gray [*M. longiflora* var. *Wrightiana* (A. Gray) Kearn. & Peebles]. To 4 ft., minutely puberulent, scarcely viscid; lvs. conspicuously petioled, cordate-ovate to ovate-triangular; fls. white, tinged with pink or purple, 4–5½ in. long. Tex., New Mex., Ariz.

MISCANTHUS Anderss. *Gramineae.* About 20 spp. of robust per. grasses in Asia; lf. blades long, flat; panicles terminal, of spreading, slender racemes; spikelets paired, alike, bisexual, surrounded by hairs, usually awned, unequally pedicelled along a slender continuous rachis, glumes equal, sterile lemma a little shorter than the glumes, fertile lemma smaller, usually with flexuous awn. For terminology see *Gramineae*.

Grown for the ornamental terminal silky panicles. Propagated by division or seeds.

floridulus (Labill.) Warb. [*M. japonicus* Anderss.]. Sts. to more than 6 ft.; lf. blades elongate, pale glaucous-green, to 1¼ in. wide; infl. paniculate, pyramidal, white, to 20 in. long, with axis longer than racemes; spikelets with awned lemmas. Japan, Pacific Is.

japonicus: *M. floridulus*, but some material cult. under the name *M. japonicus* may be *M. sinensis*.

nepalensis (Trin.) Hack. HIMALAYA FAIRY GRASS, NEPAL SILVER G. To 6 ft.; lvs. to 18 in. long; panicles yellowish-brown; spikelets less than ⅛ in. long, hairs of the callus about ⅜ in. long. Nepal, India. Occasionally cult. for ornament.

sacchariflorus (Maxim.) Hack. AMUR SILVER GRASS. Sts. to 7 ft., rhizomes thick, horizontal, elongate; lf. blades to ¾ in. wide; panicles very silky; spikelets dull gray-brown, usually awnless, surrounded by silky hairs about twice as long as spikelet. Asia. Cult. for ornament; escaped in Iowa.

sinensis Anderss. EULALIA. Sts. to 10 ft., robust, in large clumps, rhizomes short, thick; lf. blades mostly basal, flat, to 3½ ft. long and ⅜ in. wide, tapered to a slender tip, sharply serrate; infl. a corymbose panicle, of racemes to 8 in. long, axis shorter than or about as long as racemes; spikelets with a tuft of silky hairs at base about as long as glumes. E. Asia. Cult. for ornament and naturalized in some e. states. Cv. 'Gracillimus' [var. *gracillimus* A. S. Hitchc.]. Lf. blades usually ¼ in. or less wide and strongly channelled. Cv. 'Variegatus' [var. *variegatus* Beal]. Lf. blades striped with white or yellowish. Cv. 'Zebrinus' [var. *zebrinus* Beal; *M. zebrinus* (Beal) Nakai ex Matsum.]. ZEBRA GRASS. Lf. blades banded or zoned with white or yellow.

zebrinus: *M. sinensis* cv.

MITCHELLA L. PARTRIDGEBERRY. *Rubiaceae*. Two spp. of evergreen, per. herbs, native to e. N. Amer. and e. Asia, barely woody, with trailing, rooting sts. to 1 ft. long; lvs. opp., stipules minute, interpetiolar; fls. in axillary or terminal pairs, white, mostly 4-merous, corolla funnelform, tube elongate, lobes short, the ovaries united; fr. a twin berry, red, rarely white, 8-seeded.

Sometimes cultivated, used in rock gardens or as ground cover beneath trees.

repens L. PARTRIDGEBERRY, TWO-EYED BERRY, RUNNING BOX, TWINBERRY, SQUAWBERRY, SQUAW VINE. Lvs. orbicular-ovate, to ¾ in. long, dark green and glossy above and often with white lines; fls. to ½ in. long, bearded inside; fr. to ⅜ in. across, insipid, but edible. Nov. Sc. to Ont. and Minn., s. to Fla., e. Tex. and e. Mex. Forma **leucocarpa** Bissell. Fr. white.

MITELLA L. BISHOP'S-CAP, MITERWORT. *Saxifragaceae*. About 12 spp. of delicate, per., rhizomatous, glandular-puberulent herbs of N. Amer. and ne. Asia; lvs. mostly basal, cordate, long-petioled; fls. small, in simple racemes, calyx tube saucer-shaped, calyx lobes 5, petals 5, pinnately cut, stamens 5 or 10, ovary partly or nearly entirely inferior, with 2 short styles; fr. an apically dehiscent caps.

Useful for the rock garden and the wild garden.

Breweri A. Gray. Scapes slender, to 8 in.; fls. greenish-yellow, on short spreading pedicels, usually 4–20 in a raceme, petals pinnately dissected into 5–9 lateral segms., stamens 5. Late spring and summer. Mts., B.C. to Calif., e. to Alta., Mont., Idaho.

caulescens Nutt. Scapes to 1 ft., with 1–3 lvs.; fls. yellowish-green, in loose racemes, opening from top downward, otherwise resembling those of *M. Breweri*. Late spring and early summer. Damp woods and wet ground, B.C. to Calif., e. to Idaho and Mont.

diphylla L. COOLWORT. Scapes to 1½ ft., with 1 pair of opp., sessile or nearly sessile lvs.; fls. white, about ¼ in. across, in racemes to 8 in. long, petals white, deeply fimbriate-pinnatifid. Spring. Que. and Ont. to Minn., s. to Va., Ala., Mo. Forma **oppositifolia** (Rydb.) Rosend. [*M. oppositifolia* Rydb.]. St. lvs. definitely petioled.

nuda L. Scapes to 8 in., usually leafless; fls. yellowish-green, about ⅜ in. across, in few-fld. racemes, petals fimbriate-pinnatifid into usually 8 opp. lateral segms., stamens 10. Spring. N. N. Amer., e. Asia.

oppositifolia: *M. diphylla* forma.

ovalis Greene. Scapes to 1 ft., leafless; fls. greenish-yellow, to ⅜ in.

across, in dense racemes, petals fimbriate-pinnatifid into 2–7 lateral segms. Spring. B.C., s. to cent. Calif.

pentandra Hook. Scapes to 1 ft., leafless; fls. greenish, about ¼ in. across, in loose racemes, petals fimbriate-pinnatifid into usually 8 lateral segms. Summer. Alaska to ne. Calif., e. to Alta. and Colo.

stauropetala Piper. Scapes to 20 in., glandular-puberulent or hirsute; lvs. reniform-orbicular, obtusely 5–9-lobed, somewhat hirsute on both sides; fls. white, in elongate, 1-sided racemes, petals 3-parted to the middle into linear segms. Late spring. Mont. to Colo., w. to Wash. and Ore.

trifida R. C. Grah. Scapes to 1 ft., leafless; fls. white to purplish-tinged, in elongate, partly 1-sided racemes, petals 3-parted at apex into short, blunt lobes. Late spring and early summer. B.C. to n. Calif., e. to Rocky Mts.

MITRAGYNA Korth. [*Stephegyne* Korth.]. *Rubiaceae*. About 12. spp. of trees and shrubs, native to trop. Afr. and Asia; lvs. opp., stipules large, interpetiolar, deciduous; fls. in globose, solitary or panicled heads, 5-merous, corolla funnelform, tube sometimes with ring of hairs in throat; fr. a caps., seeds many, small.

parvifolia (Korth.) Korth. [*Stephegyne parvifolia* Korth.]. Deciduous tree, to 50 ft.; lvs. variable in size and shape, more or less oblong-ovate, to 6 in. long, membranous; fl. heads 1 in. across; corolla about ⁵⁄₁₆ in. long, sparsely hairy in throat. India, Ceylon, Malay Pen.

MITRARIA Cav. *Gesneriaceae*. One sp., a vine of s. Chile; sts. woody, obscurely 4-angled; lvs. opp., ovate, acute, toothed; fls. solitary on drooping axillary peduncles with a 2-lobed bract at apex, calyx lobes lanceolate, ⅜ in. long, partially enfolded by subtending bract, corolla tubular, slightly inflated, limb 5-lobed, lobes spreading, nearly equal, stamens 4, exserted, anthers united in pairs, disc ringlike, ovary superior; fr. a fleshy caps.

For cultivation see *Gesneriaceae*.

coccinea Cav. Lvs. to ¾ in. long, green, nearly glabrous above; calyx lobes ⅜ in. long, corolla to 1¼ in. long, scarlet or orange-red, lobes to ¼ in. long; caps. rosy-green, ½ in. in diam.

MITRIOSTIGMA Hochst. *Rubiaceae*. Two spp. of shrubs, native to Afr.; related to *Gardenia*, but having stipules interpetiolar, lanceolate, scarcely sheathing; fls. 3 or more together in lateral cymes, corolla funnelform, calyx tube usually short; fr. a berry.

axillare Hochst. [*Gardenia citriodora* Hook.]. Shrub of medium size; lvs. elliptic-lanceolate, to 4 in. long; fls. white, corolla tube about ½ in. long; fr. subglobose, about ½ in. across. S. Afr.

MOEHRINGIA: *ARENARIA*.

MOHAVEA A. Gray. *Scrophulariaceae*. Two spp. of viscid-pubescent, ann. herbs of sw. U. S.; lvs. alt., simple, entire; fls. yellow, in dense leafy spikes, calyx 5-parted, corolla with 2 fan-shaped lips, the throat almost closed with a hairy palate, stamens 2; fr. a caps.

confertiflora (Benth.) A. Heller. Sticky, glandular-pubescent ann., to 1 ft.; lvs. lanceolate-linear to ovate-lanceolate, to 2½ in. long; corolla about 1 in. long, pale yellow, palate with purple dots arranged in lines. Mohave and Colo. deserts to s. Nev. and w. Ariz., s. to Baja Calif.

MOHRODENDRON: *Halesia*.

MOLINIA Schrank. *Gramineae*. About 5 spp. of per. grasses in Eurasia, sts. slender, clustered; lf. blades flat; panicles narrow, rather open; spikelets 2–4-fld., rachilla disarticulating above the glumes, florets distant, glumes somewhat unequal, acute, 1-nerved, lemma, membranous, narrowed to an obtuse point, 3-nerved. For terminology see *Gramineae*.

caerulea (L.) Moench. MOOR GRASS. Sts. to 3 ft., erect; lf. blades to ¼ in. wide, erect, tapering to a fine point; panicle to 8 in. long, purplish; spikelets short-pedicelled, to ¼ in. long, lemma about ⅛ in. long. Eurasia; introd. from Me. to Penn. Cv. 'Variegata'. Lvs. striped green and cream.

MOLTKIA Lehm. *Boraginaceae*. Six spp. of hairy subshrubs and per. herbs, native to s. Eur. and Near East; lvs. simple, alt., entire; fls. blue, purple, or yellow, in cymes, calyx and corolla 5-lobed, lobes erect, glabrous outside, throat without appendages and glands, stamens 5, all at the same level, style exserted from the corolla; fr. of 4 nutlets, the nutlets distinctly bent. Differs from *Lithospermum* in having throat of corolla not crested and its nutlets distinctly bent.

Sometimes cultivated in the rock garden.

Doerfleri Wettst. [*Lithospermum Doerfleri* Hort.]. Sts. herbaceous, leafy, erect, 12–15 in., from a per. rhizome; lvs. lanceolate, cauline; fls. purple, about 1 in. long, anthers yellow, longer than their filaments, included within the corolla tube. Ne. Albania.

×**Froebelii**: a listed name of no botanical standing for *M.* ×*intermedia* cv.

graminifolia: *M. suffruticosa*.

×**intermedia** (Froeb.) J. Ingram [*Lithospermum* ×*intermedium* Froeb.]: *M. petraea* × *M. suffruticosa*. Intermediate in characters and having bright blue fls. Cv. **'Froebelii'** [*Lithospermum* ×*Froebelii* Sünderm.]. Fls. azure.

petraea (Tratt.) Griseb. [*Lithospermum petraeum* (Tratt.) DC.]. Hoary, much-branched bush, to 1 ft. and more; lvs. oblanceolate to linear-oblong; fls. blue to deep violet-blue, to ½ in. long, anthers blue, exserted beyond the corolla lobes. Albania to Dalmatia.

suffruticosa (L.) Brand [*M. graminifolia* (Viv.) Nym.; *Lithospermum graminifolium* Viv.]. Subshrub, to 1½ ft.; lvs. linear, white-tomentose on their lower surfaces; fls. blue to purple-blue, ½ in. long, anthers yellow, not or scarcely exserted beyond the corolla lobes. N. Italy.

MOLUCCELLA L. *Labiatae.* About 4 spp. of glabrous, ann. herbs of Medit. region to nw. India; sts. mostly square in cross section; lvs. opp., crenately incised, petioled; fls. in axillary, many-fld. verticillasters, bractlets subulate, spiny, calyx conspicuous, campanulate, 5–10-nerved, 5–10-toothed, teeth mucronate to spiny, corolla inconspicuous, shorter than calyx, 2-lipped, upper lip erect, concave, lower lip 3-lobed, stamens 4, in 2 pairs, anthers 2-celled; fr. of 4 three-angled, glabrous nutlets. Characterized by the inflated calyx.

Propagated by seeds.

laevis L. BELLS-OF-IRELAND, MOLUCCA BALM, SHELLFLOWER. Glabrous, to 3 ft.; lvs. ovate-triangular, to 2 in. long, usually deeply crenate; calyx inflated, to ¾ in. long, light green, corolla white. Late summer. Asia Minor. Grown for the curious green, shell-like calyces.

MOMORDICA L. *Cucurbitaceae.* About 42 spp. of monoecious or rarely dioecious, tendril-bearing vines of Old World tropics; lvs. in the cult. spp. compound or deeply lobed; fls. yellow or white, corolla rotate or campanulate, deeply lobed, to 1 in. across or more, rather showy, solitary (in the cult. spp.), peduncle of male fls. bearing a broad bract, stamens 3, filaments separate, borne at throat of tube, anthers flexuous; fr. berrylike, nearly spherical to oblong, often splitting at maturity.

Grows quickly from seeds. Fruits bitter, but cooked and eaten in the Orient.

Balsamina L. BALSAM APPLE. Lvs. thin, 1–4 in. across, with very sharp lobes and teeth, the lobes half as long as the width or less; bract on upper part of peduncle, serrate; fr. ovoid or ellipsoid, orange, to 3 in. long, narrowed at both ends, with many protuberances or nearly smooth, bursting at maturity. Afr., Asia, Australia; naturalized in Amer. tropics.

Charantia L. BALSAM PEAR, LA-KWA, BITTER GOURD, BITTER CUCUMBER. Lvs. deeply lobed, mostly less pointed than in *M. Balsamina;* bract at middle of peduncle or lower, entire; fr. oblong or ovoid, orange-yellow, 1–8 in. long, warty, bursting at maturity and showing red arils. Widespread in tropics; naturalized in se. U.S. The more commonly cult. sp. Juice from fr. and lvs. has been used medicinally.

Elaterium: *Ecballium Elaterium.*

MONADENIUM Pax. *Euphorbiaceae.* About 46 spp. of monoecious dwarf per. herbs, with succulent sts. or tuberous rhizomes and milky juice, native to E. Afr.; lvs. simple, alt., more or less succulent; fls. in cyathia (see *Euphorbiaceae*), arranged in solitary, axillary cymes, involucre bracteate, cuplike, open on one side to below the middle, truncate at the summit, and bearing a continuous gland around its top margin, as long as the inner series of 5 membranous, fringe-toothed lobes, or longer, ovary 3-celled; fr. a caps.

For culture see *Succulents.*

Lugardiae N. E. Br. Sts. simple or branched at base, 4–24 in., cylindrical, glabrous, with rhomboidal or hexagonal tessellations; lvs. in small terminal tuft or spaced along upper part of st., spatulate to obovate, to about 4 in. long, attenuate, subsessile, deciduous and leaving prominent lf. scars; cyathia of 3 nodding involucres; ovary triangular, with 2 rows of serrated wings on each ridge, becoming long-exserted on a recurved stalk. Se. Afr.

MONANTHES Haw. *Crassulaceae.* About 15 spp. of small, succulent, mostly per. herbs or subshrubs of the Salvage and Canary Is.; lvs. mostly alt. and very thick, often papillose; infl. cymose or racemose; fls. long-pedicelled, mostly 6–7-merous, petals greenish, yellowish, or purplish, stamens twice as many as petals, nectar glands very large, 2-lobed.

For culture see *Succulents.*

anagensis Praeg. Subshrub, to 6 in.; lvs. scattered, alt., linear-elliptic, ½–1 in. long, somewhat obtuse, nearly round in cross section, channelled above, smooth; infl. terminal. Late spring. Canary Is.

atlantica: *Sedum atlanticum.*

brachycaulon (Webb & Berth.) Lowe [*Sempervivum Lowei* Paiva]. Sts. short, erect, thick, unbranched; lvs. about 20, in a loose rosette, oblanceolate-spatulate, ½–¾ in. long, $^3/_{16}$ in. wide, papillose; infl. lateral. Spring. Canary Is.

laxiflora (DC.) C. Bolle. Sts. erect or sprawling; lvs. opp., ovoid but somewhat flattened, to ¾ in. long, ¼ in. wide, glabrous; infl. terminal. Spring. Canary Is.

muralis (Webb) Christ. Shrublike, to 3 in., st. single, erect, much-branched; lvs. obovate to oblanceolate-spatulate, ¼ in. long, ⅛ in. wide, thick, papillose; infl. terminal. Late spring. Canary Is.

polyphylla Haw. Sts. creeping, much-branched, forming a mat of ovoid rosettes each about ½ in. wide; lvs. many, closely imbricate, cuneate-spatulate, ¼ in. long, fleshy, mammillate on face and edges; infl. terminal. Early summer. Canary Is.

MONARDA L. WILD BERGAMOT, HORSEMINT. *Labiatae.* About 12 spp. of ann. or per., aromatic herbs of N. Amer. to Mex.; sts. mostly square in cross section; lvs. opp., entire or toothed; verticillasters densely fld., subtended by many, often leafy bracts; calyx tubular, 15-nerved, 5-toothed, tube often hairy inside, corolla tube longer than calyx, limb 2-lipped, upper lip erect, often emarginate, lower lip spreading, 3-lobed, middle lobe largest, emarginate, fertile stamens 2, usually exserted, anthers 2-celled; fr. of 4 glabrous nutlets.

Horsemints are rather coarse plants but striking in masses in the border or wild garden. Of easy cultivation; propagated by division of plants in spring.

Bradburiana: *M. Russeliana.*

citriodora Cerv. ex Lag. [*M. dispersa* Small]. LEMON MINT. Ann. or bien., to 2 ft., pubescent; lvs. narrowly lanceolate to oblong, to 2 in. long, awn-tipped, remotely serrate or nearly entire, glabrescent; fls. in 2 or more superposed headlike verticillasters to 1½ in. across, calyx to ½ in. long, teeth to ¼ in. long, long-awned, hirsute in throat, corolla white to pink, spotted purple, tube to ¾ in. long, lips equal, shorter than tube. Spring to summer. On limestone, S.C. and Fla., w. to Mo., w. Tex., Mex.

clinopodia L. Per., to 4 ft., glabrous to glabrescent; lvs. ovate, to 5 in. long, acute to acuminate, serrate; fls. in a solitary, terminal, headlike verticillaster, bracts leafy, white or white-tinged, calyx tubular, to ⅜ in. long, bearded in throat, teeth bristly, corolla to 1 in. long, white to flesh-pink, spotted purple. N.Y. to Ill., s. to Md. and in mts. to Ala. and Ky.

coccinea: *M. didyma.*

didyma L. [*M. coccinea* Michx.]. BEE BALM, OSWEGO TEA. Per., to 4 ft., usually glabrescent; lvs. ovate-acuminate, to 4 in. long, serrate-dentate, sparsely pubescent, petioles over ¼ in. long; fls. usually in a solitary, terminal, headlike verticillaster, bracts tinged scarlet, leafy, calyx to ½ in. long, glabrous or pubescent in throat, teeth bristly, corolla to 1¼ in. long, vivid scarlet-red. Summer. Rich woods, New Eng., s. to Ga. and Tenn. Cvs. include: **'Adam'**, fls. rose-red; **'Alba'**, fls white; **'Cambridge Scarlet'**, fls. bright crimson; **'Coccinea'**, fls. scarlet; **'Croftway Pink'**, fls. pink; **'Granite Pink'**, plant dwarf, to 10 in., fls. pink; **'Mahogany'**, fls. deep red-brown; **'Rosea'**, fls. rose-pink; **'Salmon Queen'**, fls. salmon-pink; **'Salmonea'**, fls. salmon; **'Snow Queen'**, fls. large, white; **'Splendens'**, a listed name; **'Sunset'**, fls. dark red; **'Superba'**, a listed name; **'Violacea'** and **'Violet Queen'**, fls. violet.

dispersa: *M. citriodora.*

fistulosa L. [*M. hybrida* Wender.; *M. mollis* L.; *M. Ramaleyi* A. Nels.; *M. stricta* Woot.]. Per., to 4 ft., sometimes pubescent above; lvs. ovate-lanceolate to broadly ovate, to 4 in. long, acute to acuminate, weakly serrate to nearly entire, generally pubescent, petioles over ¼ in. long; fls. usually in a solitary, terminal, headlike verticil-laster, calyx to ⅜ in. long, hirsute in throat, teeth bristly, corolla to 1¼ in. long, bright lavender, pubescent outside. Summer. E. N. Amer. Forma **albescens** Farw. Fls. white. Var. **menthifolia** (R. C. Grah.) Fern. [*M. menthifolia* R. C. Grah.]. Petioles short, less than ¼ in. long. W. N. Amer.

hybrida: *M. fistulosa,* but some material may be garden hybrids.

lasiodonta: *M. punctata* var.

menthifolia: *M. fistulosa* var.

mollis: *M. fistulosa.*

pectinata Nutt. Ann., to 1 ft., generally branched, pubescent; lvs. oblong-lanceolate to oblong, to 2 in. long, serrate or nearly entire, glabrous or glabrescent; fls. in 2 or more superposed, headlike verticil-lasters, calyx to ¼ in. long, hirsute in throat, teeth bristly, corolla to ¾ in. long, pink or whitish. Summer. Dry soil, Nebr. and Colo., s. to Ariz. and Tex.

punctata L. DOTTED MINT, HORSEMINT. Ann., bien., or per., usually less than 3 ft., more or less branched, pubescent; lvs. lanceolate to oblong, to 3½ in. long, serrate to nearly entire; fls. in 2 or more super-posed, headlike verticillasters, calyx to ⅜ in. long, teeth narrowly triangular, corolla to ¾ in. long, yellowish, spotted purple. Sandy soil of coastal plain, Long Is., s. to Fla. and La. Var. **lasiodonta** A. Gray [*M. lasiodonta* (A. Gray) Small]. Lvs. 1–2 in. long, calyx teeth triangu-lar, silky-villous. Sw. Ill. and Kans., s. to sw. U.S. and Mex.

Ramaleyi: *M. fistulosa.*

Russeliana Nutt. ex Sims [*M. Bradburiana* L. Beck.]. Per., to 2 ft., simple or sparingly branched, usually glabrous; lvs. ovate to lanceo-late, to 2¼ in. long, remotely serrate to nearly entire, glabrescent to sparsely pubescent, sessile; fls. in a solitary, terminal, headlike verticil-laster, calyx to ½ in. long, teeth subulate, corolla to 1½ in. long, pinkish or whitish, with purple spots. Early summer. Dry sites, Ill. and La., s. to n. Ala., Ark., ne. Tex.

stricta: *M. fistulosa.*

MONARDELLA Benth. *Labiatae.* About 20 spp. of aro-matic, ann. or per. herbs of w. N. Amer.; sts. mostly square in cross section; lvs. opp., small, entire or serrate; fls. in dense, terminal, bracted, globose, headlike verticillasters, calyx tubular, 10–13-nerved, 5-toothed, corolla usually rose-purple, 2-lipped, stamens 4, scarcely exserted; fr. of 4 nutlets.

Sometimes grown in the rock garden; propagated by seeds or divi-sion.

lanceolata A. Gray. Ann., 12–15 in., puberulent; lvs. lanceolate, to 1½ in. long, obtuse, entire; fl. heads dense, to 1 in. in diam., bracts ovate-lanceolate, calyx shorter than bracts, to ⅜ in. long, corolla ½–⅝ in. long, rose-purple. Summer. Calif., Nev., Ariz.

linoides A. Gray. Per., to 12–15 in., sts. decumbent, woody, silvery-pubescent; lvs. narrowly oblong to lanceolate, to 1½ in. long, acute or obtuse, silvery-pubescent beneath; fl. heads to 1 in. in diam., bracts ovate to lanceolate, acuminate; calyx as long as bracts or shorter, to ⅜ in. long, corolla to ⅝ in. long, rose-purple or paler. Summer. Calif., Nev., Ariz.

macrantha A. Gray. Rhizomatous per., brs. erect, to 12 in., pubes-cent; lvs. somewhat leathery, ovate to lanceolate, to 1½ in. long, ob-tuse, entire or obscurely crenate, glabrous to pubescent; fl. heads more or less open, to 1½ in. in diam., bracts oblong-elliptic; calyx as long as bracts, ¾–1 in. long, corolla about 1½ in. long, scarlet to yellowish. Early summer. Calif.

menthifolia: a listed name of no botanical standing; possibly *Monarda menthifolia.*

nana A. Gray. YELLOW M. Similar to *M. macrantha,* but calyx ½–⅝ in. long, corolla 1–1¼ in. long, pale yellow. Calif.

nervosa: *M. odoratissima.*

odoratissima Benth. [*M. nervosa* Greene; *M. purpurea* T. J. Howell]. MOUNTAIN M. Per., to 18 in., sts. decumbent, woody at base, brs. erect, pubescent; lvs. oblong, lanceolate, or ovate, to 1 in. long, obtuse to acute, entire or weakly serrate, pubescent; fl. heads to 2 in. in diam., bracts ovate to orbicular, obtuse or acute; calyx as long as bracts, to ⅜ in. long, corolla about twice as long as calyx, rose-purple. Summer. Wash. to New. Mex.

purpurea: *M. odoratissima.*

villosa Benth. COYOTE MINT. Per., to 2 ft., sts. decumbent, woody at base; lvs. orbicular to lanceolate, to 1¼ in. long, obtuse, entire to serrate; fl. heads to 1½ in. in diam., bracts leafy; calyx about as long as bracts, to ⅜ in. long, corolla about twice as long as calyx, rose-purple. Summer. Calif. and Ore.

MONDO: *OPHIOPOGON.*

MONESES Salisb. *Pyrolaceae.* One sp., a glabrous per. herb, with slender rhizome, native to cool woods of Eurasia and n. N. Amer.; lvs. simple, in basal clusters; fls. white or pink, nodding, solitary on scapes, sepals and petals 5, stamens 10, filaments expanded at base; fr. a 5-angled, 4-5-valved caps.

Sometimes planted in the wild garden.

uniflora (L.) A. Gray [*Pyrola uniflora* L.]. ONE-FLOWERED SHIN-LEAF, ONE-FLOWERED PYROLA. Lvs. orbicular or ovate, to 1 in. long, wavy-toothed; fls. white or pink, fragrant, to ¾ in. across; caps. ¼ in. across. Summer.

MONILARIA Schwant. *Aizoaceae.* About 11 spp. of low, clump-forming, succulent shrubs, native to S. Afr., sts. con-stricted, forming buttonlike or beadlike joints; lvs. opp., of 2 types, but only 1 type produced each year, first pair short, sheathlike with circular tips, protecting second young pair during the dry season, second pair long, nearly cylindrical, united basally, upper side flattened, surface papillose; fls. soli-tary, terminal, pedicelled, calyx 5-lobed, petals white, yellow-ish, or red, many, in 3–4 series, stamens many, filaments not bearded basally, ovary inferior, 5–7-celled; fr. a caps., expand-ing keels narrowly winged, placental tubercles lacking.

The growth period is autumn and winter; cultivate in fairly sandy soil. Propagated by seeds; the seedlings grow quickly, but produce only the long, cylindrical leaves the first year. See also *Succulents.*

Peersii L. Bolus. To 5 in. high, brs. short, to ¾ in. long and ⅜ in. thick, pale brown when young, gray in age, surface papery after 2–3 years; lvs. glaucous, minutely papillate, short or not visible in resting stage and ¼ in. long, ⅛ in. across, variable in shape when expanded, then to 2½ in. long with sheath to ⅛ in. long, or to 1½ in. long and 1⅛ in. thick, upper side flat, lower side rounded, obscurely keeled below the blunt to rounded apex; fls. ¾ in. across, on pedicels ¼ in. long, petals white. Cape Prov.

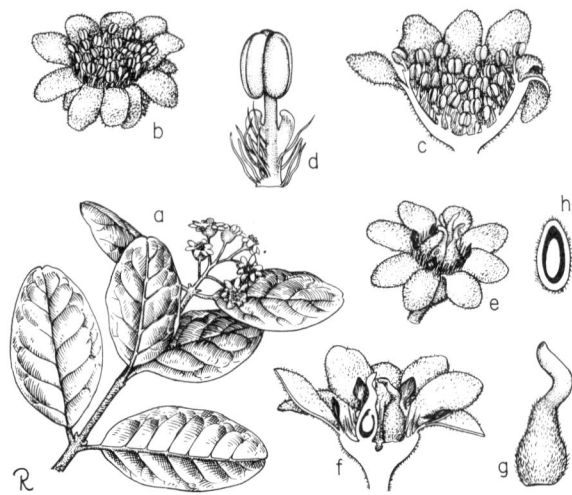

MONIMIACEAE. *Peumus Boldus:* **a,** flowering branch, × ½; **b,** male flower, × 2; **c,** male flower, vertical section, × 3; **d,** stamen, × 10; **e,** female flower, × 2; **f,** female flower, vertical section, × 3; **g,** pistil, × 6; **h,** ovary, cross section, × 10. (From Lawrence, *Taxonomy of Vas-cular Plants.*)

MONIMIACEAE Juss. MONIMIA FAMILY. Dicot.; about 30 genera of widely distributed trop. and subtrop. trees and shrubs; lvs. usually opp., simple, aromatic, gland-dotted; fls. in cymes or racemes, bisexual or unisexual, inconspicuous, perianth united in lower half into cuplike tube, bearing sev-eral to many stamens, carpels several, 1-celled; fr. an achene or drupe. *Hedycarya, Laurelia,* and *Peumus* may be cult. in warm climates.

MONNINA Ruiz & Pav. *Polygalaceae.* About 150 spp. of herbs, shrubs, or trees, native from New Mex. and Ariz. and through Mex. and Cent. Amer. to Brazil and Chile, but princi-pally in Andes in nw. S. Amer.; lvs. alt., simple, entire; fls. in axillary or terminal racemes or panicles, sepals 5, the inner

2 petal-like (wings), petals 3, the lower petal (keel) boat-shaped, not crested, stamens 8 or 6, filaments united into sheath, split on the upper side; fr. a drupe, or rarely samara-like, narrowly and nearly equally winged.

xalapensis HBK. Much-branched shrub, to 10 ft.; lvs. oblanceolate or obovate-elliptic to elliptic, to 3¼ in. long, acute to acuminate at base and apex, sparsely hairy; fls. purple, small, in racemes; fr. a black drupe. Mex., s. to Costa Rica.

MONOCHAETUM (DC.) Naud. *Melastomataceae.* About 50 spp. of trop. Amer. herbs or shrubs, usually branching freely; lvs. many, 3- to many-nerved, usually pubescent, frequently glandular; fls. in cymules arranged in panicles, calyx lobes 4, petals 4, stamens 8, dimorphic, ovary hairy; fr. a caps.

vulcanicum Cogn. Shrub, to 3 ft., sts. strigose, densely branched and densely leafy; lvs. elliptic to ovate-lanceolate, small, to ¾ in. long, ciliate, 3- to many-nerved, strigillose, dark green above, pale beneath; fls. in cymes or solitary, purple-pink, to 1½ in. across, short-pedicelled. Volcanic soil, Costa Rica.

MONOCOTYLEDON (Monocotyledones, one of the two primary divisions of the angiosperms). A monocotyledon is a plant bearing only one cotyledon or seed leaf, in contrast to those (dicotyledons) that have two or more seed leaves in the embryo; the cotyledons may become apparent in germination. The monocotyledons (sometimes shortened to monocots) usually lack cambium tissue and hence the woody tissues typical of many dicotyledons. Often these plants have parallel-veined leaves, and the floral parts are mostly in threes or multiples of three. Lack of a woody cylinder means that few of them are tall trees, many of the palms being exceptions. Monocotyledonous, pertaining to monocotyledons, is the adjectival form. Monocotyledonous plants include, among others, all the grasses (Gramineae), sedges (Cyperaceae), bananas (Musaceae), lilies (Liliaceae), aroids (Araceae), bromeliads (Bromeliaceae), irids (Iridaceae), cannas (Cannaceae), orchids (Orchidaceae), and palms (Palmae).

MONODORA Dunal. *Annonaceae.* About 15 spp. of shrubs and trees, native to trop. Afr.; lvs. alt., entire; fls. large, pendulous, solitary or in pairs, bisexual, 3-merous, petals 6, in 2 series, usually undulate-crisped marginally, inner ones connivent apically, stamens and pistils many; fr. a globose or ellipsoid fleshy syncarp formed by fusion of the pistils.

Myristica (Gaertn.) Dunal. AFRICAN NUTMEG, JAMAICA N. To 100 ft.; lvs. obovate-oblong to elliptic, drooping, to 20 in. long, 6–8 in. wide; fls. on pedicels to 10 in. long, pendulous, fragrant, petals white to yellowish, spotted with red, the outer ones to 4 in. long, 1 in. wide, the inner ones to 2 in. long; fr. subglobose, to 6 in. in diam., seeds aromatic, sometimes used like nutmeg. Sierra Leone, w. to Cameroons and Uganda, s. to Angola.

MONOLOPIA DC. *Compositae* (Helenium Tribe). Four spp. of white-woolly ann. herbs in Calif.; lvs. sessile, the lower ones opp., the upper ones alt.; fl. heads radiate, solitary; disc and ray fls. golden-yellow; pappus absent.

major DC. To 1½ ft., usually branched; lvs. oblong-lanceolate, to 4 in. long, entire or slightly toothed; heads 1–2 in. across, involucral bracts united half their length.

MONOPSIS Salisb. [*Dobrowskya* K. Presl]. *Lobeliaceae.* Sixteen spp. of ann. or per. herbs, native to S. Afr., 1 apparently naturalized in Australia; lvs. alt., opp., or whorled; fls. nearly regular or 2-lipped. Similar to *Lobelia* but having stigma lobes filiform and revolute.

campanulata (Lam.) Sond. [*Lobelia campanulata* Lam.]. Branching, procumbent ann., to 10 in.; lvs. alt., lowermost lvs. oblong-lanceolate, entire or few-toothed, to 1 in. long, upper lvs. linear, to ½ in. long; fls. solitary, on erect pedicels 1–1¾ in. long, corolla nearly regular, blue, to ½ in. long, lobes 5, spreading, subulate, about ¼ in. long, anthers yellow, calyx tube nearly globose, about ³⁄₁₆ in. in diam. S. Afr. Often confused with *M. simplex.*

debilis: *M. simplex.*

simplex (L.) F. E. Wimm. [*M. debilis* (L.f.) K. Presl]. Similar to *M. campanulata*, but having pedicels spreading and calyx tube obconical. S. Afr. and Australia, where it is probably naturalized.

unidentata (Ait.f.) F. E. Wimm. [*Dobrowskya tenella* (Thunb.) Sond.]. Mostly scabrous, procumbent per.; lvs. opp., alt., or whorled, mostly less than ¾ in. long, the lower oblong-elliptic to suborbicular, the upper linear, 1–2 toothed, with revolute margins; fls. solitary on pedicels 1–3 in. long, corolla 2-lipped, violet or blue, to ⅝ in. long. S. Afr.

MONOTROPA L. *Pyrolaceae.* About 6 spp. of per., saprophytic, fleshy herbs without chlorophyll, native to the temp. parts of N. Hemisphere; sts. white, red, or tawny, drying black; lvs. alt., bractlike; fls. white, yellowish-white, red or pink, nodding, solitary or in scaly racemes, sepals 2–5, scaly, deciduous, petals 4–6, saccate at base, stamens 8–12; fr. an erect caps., 8–10-grooved.

Sometimes transferred from the wild for curiosity, to suitable woodland conditions.

Brittonii Small. To 16 in.; lvs. ovate to oblanceolate; fls. yellowish-white or salmon-colored, solitary, petals densely ciliate and hairy inside. Winter. N.C. to s. Fla.

uniflora L. INDIAN-PIPE, CORPSE PLANT, CONVULSION ROOT, PINE-SAP, FITSROOT. To 1 ft., sts. several, white; lvs. lanceolate or elliptic-lanceolate; fls. white, to 1 in. long, solitary; caps. ½ in. long. Summer–early autumn. N. Amer., Japan, Himalayas.

MONOTROPACEAE: *PYROLACEAE.*

MONSONIA L. *Geraniaceae.* About 30 spp. of herbs or subshrubs, native to Afr. and Asia; lvs. opp. or alt., crenate-dentate or dissected; peduncles axillary, 2- to many-fld.; fls. regular, 5-parted, stamens 15, filaments united in threes at the base, pistil 5-celled, beaked; fr. 5-valved, the valves coiling and twisting toward the beak.

Grown in cool greenhouse; propagated by root cuttings and seeds.

speciosa L.f. To 1 ft.; lvs. palmately 5-parted, segms. 2-pinnate; peduncles 1-fld.; petals cream to pink with dark base, to 1½ in. long; beak of fr. to 4 in. long. S. Afr.

MONSTERA Adans. WINDOWLEAF. *Araceae.* About 25 spp. of often large, epiphytic climbers, native to trop. Amer.; lvs. mostly inequilateral, entire or pinnatifid, sometimes perforated, leathery, petioles geniculate, long-sheathing; fls. unisexual, spathe boat-shaped, fugacious, spadix densely fld., surrounded by spathe, carpels mostly apically truncate, ovary 2-celled, each cell with 2 ovules. Identification of young plants is often difficult, since their small, entire lvs. rarely resemble those of the adult stage; juvenile shoots of some spp. form "shingle plants."

Strictly tropical; for culture see *Philodendron.*

acuminata C. Koch. SHINGLE PLANT. Lf. blades ovate, very inequilateral, to 11 in. long and 5 in. wide, basally cordate, entire, sometimes pinnatifid with 1 or 2 segms. 1–2 in. wide, petioles 5½ in. long, sheath wide, persistent; peduncle less than 2 in. long, spadix 2 in. long, pistils apically subconical. Cent. Amer.

Adansonii Schott [*M. pertusa* (L.) De Vriese, not Schott; *M. pertusa* var. *Jacquinii* (Schott) Engl.]. A variable sp.; lf. blades ovate to oblong-ovate or -elliptic, to 2 or 3 ft. long and 10 in. wide, very inequilateral, with the larger half basally rotund-truncate, the other subcuneate, irregularly perforate with a few large, elliptic-oblong holes in a single series on one or both sides of midrib, these rarely reaching and cutting through margin, petioles shorter than blades, sheathing to geniculum, sheath green, persistent; spathe white, to 8 in. long, spadix to 4 in. long, relatively slender. Trop. Amer.

deliciosa Liebm. [*Philodendron pertusum* Kunth & Bouché]. CERIMAN, SWISS-CHEESE PLANT, BREADFRUIT VINE, HURRICANE PLANT, MEXICAN BREADFRUIT, FRUIT-SALAD PLANT, WINDOW PLANT, SPLIT-LEAF PHILODENDRON, CUT-LEAF P. To 30 ft. or more; lf. blades orbicular-ovate, to 3 ft. wide, basally cordate, regularly pinnatifid half-way to midrib into many oblong-curved, 1-nerved segms., perforate with elliptic to oblong holes in 1–4 series on each side of midrib, petioles as long as blades, sheath early drying and evanescent, geniculum flattened and winged; peduncle elongate, spathe creamy, to 1 ft. long, expanding at flowering and drying in place, spadix to 10 in. long, maturing into edible fr. of good aroma and acceptable flavor. Mex. and Cent. Amer. Var. **Borsigiana** (C. Koch ex Engl.) Engl. & Kurt Krause. Differs in having lvs. smaller, less perforated, and geniculum narrowly winged.

dubia (HBK) Engl. & Kurt Krause. Lf. blades oblong in outline, to 4 ft. long and 2 ft. wide, basally truncate, regularly pinnatisect, segms. 12–20, linear, petioles about 18 in. long, sheath evanescent; spathe white inside, splitting away irregularly, spadix to 17 in. long, white, pistils apically truncate. Nicaragua, Costa Rica.

egregia Schott. Lf. blades broadly lanceolate-oblong, to 28 in. long and 13 in. wide, basally oblique-obtuse, entire, perforate, with holes in 2 series on each side, polished, petioles to 21 in. long, winged, the wings wide-spreading, continuous to the lf. blade, persistent, green; spathe creamy, to 14 in. long, spadix to 7 in. long. S. Mex. Not known to be in cult.; material offered under this name is *M. Karwinskyi*, with which this sp. has long been confused.

epipremnoides Engl. [*M. Leichtlinii* Hort.]. Huge climber; lf. blades of adult shoots ovate- to oblong-elliptic, to 3 ft. long and 22 in. wide, basally truncate or emarginate, pinnatifid, the segms. ½–1½ in. wide, perforate, with 2 or 3 series of holes on each side, inner ones elliptic to oblong-elliptic, ¼ or 1–2 in. long, outermost ones linear-oblong, very large and extending nearly to the margin, or cutting it, petioles sheathing nearly to geniculum, sheath broad, persistent, apically auriculate, lvs. of juvenile shoots smaller but similar in form, or more broadly ovate; spathe white, to 16 in. long, spadix to 7 in. long, pistils apically nearly conical and white. Costa Rica.

falcifolia: *M. obliqua.*

Friedrichsthalii Schott [*Philodendron Friedrichsthalii* Hort.]. Allied to *M. Adansonii* but having lf. blades entire, thin, perforations oblong to elliptic, in 2 or 3 series on each side, lateral veins very prominent, uniting and forming an antemarginal connecting vein. Cent. Amer.

guttifera: a listed name of no botanical standing for *M. Standleyana.*

Karwinskyi Schott. To 15 ft. or more; lf. blades ovate to oblong-elliptic, 22–33 in. long and 13–22 in. wide, entire, basally truncate, leathery, perforate, with narrowly oblong holes in a single series on each side, 1 between each primary lateral vein, petioles as long as width of blade, sheath continuous to geniculum, very early drying and shredding off; spathe green outside, white inside, splitting open irregularly, spadix shorter than spathe, 5½ in. long, stout, cream-colored. S. Mex.

latiloba Kurt Krause. Lf. blades ovate-oblong, to 18 in. long and 12 in. wide, basally truncate, pinnatifid nearly to midrib, the segms. 3–4, wide-spreading, broad, separated by wide sinuses, each with 1–3 primary lateral veins, petioles little shorter than blades; spadix orange. Peru.

Leichtlinii: a listed name of no botanical standing for *M. epipremnoides.*

maxima Engl. & Kurt Krause. Distinguished from *M. latiloba* in having lf. blades to 28 in. long and 16 in. wide, irregularly pinnatifid, basally cordate, with small holes along midrib; spadix white. Ecuador.

Nechodomii: a listed name of no botanical standing for *Epipremnum pinnatum.*

obliqua (Miq.) Walp. [*M. falcifolia* Engl.]. Lf. blades elliptic to oblong-lanceolate, to 8 in. long and about ⅓ as wide, basally oblique, entire, petioles to 5 in. long; peduncle 3 in. long, slender, spadix to 1½ in. long, slender, few-fld. N. S. Amer. Doubtfully in the trade; material listed under this name is described as a fancy-lvd. variant with large lvs.

perforoides: a listed name of no botanical standing.

pertusa: see *M. Adansonii.*

Pittieri Engl. Differs from *M. obliqua* in having lf. blades to 6 in. long and half as wide, peduncle less than 1 in. long, and spadix stout, densely-fld. Costa Rica.

punctulata Schott. Differs from *M. deliciosa* in having lf. blades ovate- to oblong-elliptic, to 4 ft. long and half as wide, petioles heavily dotted with white, geniculum nearly cylindrical, fibrous remains of scalelike lvs. persistent on st., juvenile growth forming a shingle plant with lf. blades ovate, oblique, and spathe pinkish-buff outside, white inside, to 5½ in. long, splitting irregularly at flowering. S. Mex.

Schleichtlinii: misspelling for *Leichtlinii.*

Standleyana Bunt. [*M. guttifera* Hort.; *Philodendron guttiferum* Hort., not Kunth]. Lf. blades entire, very dark green, not perforate, petioles very broadly winged nearly or quite to blade; in adult shoots, sts. stout, lf. blades oblong-ovate, to 2 ft. long, 13 in. wide, basally obtuse, with many lateral veins very prominent beneath, petioles to 21 in. long; peduncle solitary, 1 ft. long, spathe creamy, 11 in. long, expanded at flowering, spadix about 6 in. long, creamy; commonly seen in juvenile phase with sts. slender, lf. blades narrowly oblong-lanceolate, 6–8 in. long and 2 in. wide, with 3 pairs of primary lateral veins ascending at a very sharp angle from midrib, and petioles 4–5 in. long and ½ in. wide or more at midpoint. Costa Rica.

subpinnata (Schott) Engl. [*Raphidophora laciniosa* Hort.]. Lf. blades orbicular-ovate, to 13 in. long, with 3–4 pairs of narrowly oblanceolate segms. distant from one another, each segm. about 6 in. long and to 1 in. wide with a single primary lateral vein and several smaller, parallel ones, petioles to 10 in. long, sheath evanescent; spathe dirty yellow, to 6 in. long, spadix shorter; pistils apically subconical and yellowish. Peru.

Uleana Engl. Distinguished from *M. dubia* in having lf. blades ovate in outline, smaller, to 12 in. long and 10 in. wide, irregularly pinnatifid, segms. 6–7; spadix 3 in. long; pistils apically conical. Peru.

MONTANOA Cerv. *Compositae* (Helianthus Tribe). Between 30 and 50 spp. of pithy-stemmed shrubs or small trees, native from n. Mex. to Colombia and Venezuela; lvs. opp., serrate to lobed or even coarsely pinnatifid; fl. heads radiate or discoid, in corymbs or panicles, involucre nearly cylindrical to hemispherical, involucral bracts in 1–2 rows, receptacle conical, with persistent, sometimes spinescent-tipped scales; disc fls. bisexual, fertile or the outer row sometimes sterile, ray fls. neutral, white to rose or purplish, sometimes lacking; achenes obovate, laterally compressed, pappus lacking.

Propagated by seeds under glass and by cuttings; grown under glass, and outside in warm climates, for the large leaves and bold habit, as well as for the showy heads.

bipinnatifida (Kunth) C. Koch. Shrubby per., to 10 ft., sts. 4-angled; lvs. pinnatifid to 2-pinnatifid, upper lvs. not divided, the blade to 3 ft. long, hairy; heads to 3 in. across. Mex.

hibiscifolia (Benth.) C. Koch. Shrub, to 20 ft.; lvs. orbicular to reniform in outline, to 1 ft. across, palmately lobed to about the middle, cordate, pubescent beneath, petioles usually with 1 or 2 pairs of auricles near the apex just below the blade; heads to 1½ in. across. S. Mex. and Guatemala to Costa Rica.

MONTBRETIA: *TRITONIA.* **M.** ×**crocosmiiflora:** *Crocosmia* × *crocosmiiflora.* **M. miniata:** *Tritonia crocata* var. **M. Pottsii:** *Crocosmia Pottsii.*

MONTEZUMA Sessé & Moç. ex DC. *Malvaceae.* One sp., a tree in Puerto Rico, once thought to be native to Mex.; closely related to *Thespesia,* but having upper part of the calyx dehiscing transversely after flowering.

speciosissima Sessé & Moç. ex DC. [*Thespesia grandiflora* DC.]. To 50 ft.; lvs. 2–8 in. long, ovate to orbicular, acuminate or acute, cordate, entire, leathery; fls. solitary, on long axillary pedicels, calyx about 1 in. long, truncate, petals 2½–4½ in. long, rose shading to crimson inside, tan or orange and densely pubescent outside; fr. about 1 in. long, ovoid, indehiscent, rather fleshy when young but becoming woody and dry. Spring. Planted as an ornamental and as a street tree in s. Fla. The wood is used for making furniture.

MONTIA L. MINER'S LETTUCE. *Portulacaceae.* About 50 spp. of small, soft, ann. or per. herbs, native mostly to N. Amer., a few to Eur., Asia, Australia; basal lvs. petioled, rather fleshy, st. lvs. often several and alt., or only 2 and then opp., usually sessile; fls. small, whitish or pinkish, usually several in simple to compound, axillary or terminal racemes, sepals 2; fr. a 3-valved caps., seeds 1–3, usually black and glossy.

One species sometimes grown as a salad and potherb and others for interest in moist places. Seeds may be sown where plants are to stand, any time in spring or summer.

Chamissoi (Ledeb. ex K. Spreng.) T. Durand & B. D. Jacks. Floating aquatic or creeping per., rooting at nodes; st. lvs. of several opp. pairs, spatulate to oblanceolate, to nearly 2 in. long; fls. pale rose, to ⁵⁄₁₆ in. long, 1–9 in a raceme. Wet places and springs, Alaska, s. to Calif. and New Mex. Adapted to bog garden or shallow pools or ponds.

flagellaris: *Claytonia parvifolia* var.

parviflora: *M. perfoliata* forma.

parvifolia: *Claytonia parvifolia.* Subsp. **flagellaris:** *C. parvifolia* var.

perfoliata (J. Donn) J. T. Howell [*Claytonia parviflora* Dougl. ex Hook.; *C. perfoliata* J. Donn]. MINER'S LETTUCE, WINTER PURSLANE, CUBAN SPINACH. Ann., glabrous, bright green, 4–12 in. or more; lvs. basal, rhombic-ovate to lanceolate, long-petioled; fls. white, in racemes subtended by 2 lvs. united into a round disc and on scapes to 1 ft. high. B.C. to Mex. Forma **parviflora** (Dougl.) J. T. Howell [*Montia parviflora* (Dougl.) J. T. Howell]. Basal lvs. linear to oblanceolate; infl. elongate; fls. with sepals only about ¹⁄₁₆ in. long.

sibirica (L.) J. T. Howell [*Claytonia sibirica* L.]. SIBERIAN PURSLANE. Ann., or of longer duration, to 15 in.; basal lvs. usually many, rhombic-ovate to lanceolate, petioles 2–3 times as long as blades, some becoming fleshy at base or having bulbils in the axils, st. lvs. 2, opp., sessile to short-petioled; fls. white to pink, in many-fld. terminal racemes to 12 in. long. Moist places at lower and middle elevations, Alaska, s. to Calif., e. to Mont. and Utah.

MONVILLEA Britt. & Rose. *Cactaceae.* About 16 spp. of slender, ribbed cacti, native to S. Amer.; sts. nearly erect to creeping, ribs mostly 3–7, low; fls. nocturnal, white, funnel-form, perianth persistent in fr., scales of tube and ovary few, small, with naked axils; fr. mostly juicy, with white flesh. Some spp., including the type of the genus perhaps referable to *Cereus*, but others apparently close to *Pilocereus*.

For culture see *Cacti*.

Anisitsii: *M. Spegazzinii.*

Cavendishii (Monv.) Britt. & Rose. Sts. branching at base, nearly erect or decumbent, to 10 ft. long and 1¼ in. thick, ribs 9–10, low; areoles ⅜ in. apart, spines 8–10, needle-shaped, brown; fls. white, to 5 in. long; fr. globose, red, to 2 in. in diam. S. Brazil, Paraguay, n. Argentina.

diffusa Britt. & Rose [*Cereus diffusus* (Britt. & Rose) Werderm.]. Sts. erect or arching, to 2 in. thick, ribs 8, high and thin; areoles 1 in. apart, radial spines 6–10, needle-shaped, to ½ in. long, central spines 1–3, unequal, awl-shaped, to 1¼ in. long; fls. 3 in. long, scales long-decurrent, perianth deciduous? S. Ecuador and n. Peru.

insularis: *Cereus insularis.*

maritima Britt. & Rose. Sts. erect or clambering, to 18 ft. high and 3 in. thick, ribs 4–6, undulating; areoles 1 in. apart, in the depressions, spines about 8, gray, black-tipped, central spines 1–2, 1 of them stouter, to 2½ in. long; fls. 2½ in. long. Ecuador. Position doubtful; perhaps allied to *M. diffusa.*

marmorata: a listed name of no botanical standing, probably for *M. Spegazzinii.*

mocupensis: a listed name of no botanical standing.

phatnosperma (K. Schum.) Britt. & Rose. Sts. creeping, to 7 ft. long and 1 in. thick, ribs 4–5, sinuous, to ⁵⁄₁₆ in. high, concave on the sides; spines awl-shaped, brown, radial spines 5–6, to ½ in. long, central spines 0–1, to 1 in. long; fls. white, 5 in. long; fr. ellipsoid, to 3 in. long. Paraguay. Cv. 'Grossei' is listed.

pucuraensis: a listed name of no botanical standing.

Spegazzinii (A. Web.) Britt. & Rose [*M. Anisitsii* (K. Schum.) Backeb. & F. M. Knuth]. Sts. clambering, few-branched, to 7 ft. long and ¾ in. thick, bluish, spotted, ribs 3–4, strongly undulate to serrate; areoles to 1 in. apart, spines at first 3, conical, black, to ⁵⁄₃₂ in. long, later 5 radial and 1 central to ⅝ in. long; fls. white, 5–7½ in. long. Paraguay. Material offered as *M. marmorata* is probably this sp.

Vargasiana: a listed name of no botanical standing.

MORACEAE Link. MULBERRY FAMILY. Dicot.; about 53–75 genera and 1,400–1,850 spp. of trees, shrubs, climbers, or herbs, widely distributed, often with milky latex; lvs. mostly alt., simple; fls. small, unisexual, usually in spikes or heads (in *Ficus*, on the inside of a hollow receptacle, constituting a fig), perianth usually 4–merous, stamens 4, ovary superior, 1-celled; fr. an achene or drupe. The cult. genera are: *Antiaris, Artocarpus, Brosimum, Broussonetia, Castilla, Cecropia, Chlorophora, Cudrania, Dorstenia, Ficus, Maclura, Morus,* and *Treculia.* For *Cannabis* and *Humulus,* see Cannabaceae.

In addition to ornamentals, the family furnishes many economic products such as timber, edible fruits, rubber, dyes, medicines, and leaves as food for silkworms.

MORAEA Mill. BUTTERFLY IRIS, NATAL LILY. *Iridaceae.* About 100 spp. of per. herbs with tunicate corms, native to trop. and S. Afr.; sts. simple or branched; lvs. usually few, linear; fls. fugacious, in clusters on cylindrical st., perianth tube none, perianth segms. 6, clawed, outer 3 reflexed or spreading, inner 3 usually smaller, sometimes reduced and 3-toothed, stamens 3, filaments often more or less united into a tube, style brs. 3, petal-like, stigmas bifid or rarely feathery; fr. a 3-valved caps.

Tender in the North; they thrive in Fla. and Calif. Cultivation as for *Iris,* which these plants much resemble. Some species are poisonous to cattle.

angustata (Thunb.) Ker-Gawl. Sts. simple, to 1 ft.; lvs. 2 or 3, cylindrical, to 16 in. long; perianth dull yellow or pale brown, veined with purple, outer segms. with a bright yellow basal spot. S. Afr.

bicolor: *Dietes bicolor.*

catenulata: *Dietes vegeta.*

collina var. **ochroleuca:** *Homeria ochroleuca.*

edulis (L.f.) Ker-Gawl. Sts. to 2½ ft., slender, cylindrical; lvs. 3–7, linear or cylindrical, to 4½ ft. long; infl. branched; fls. about 2 in. across, fragrant, perianth mauve or white, outer segms. with yellow basal spot, claws pubescent. S. Afr.

glaucopis: *M. tricuspidata.*

gracilis Bak. Sts. simple, to 15 in.; lvs. 2, basal, cylindrical, shorter than sts.; perianth less than 1 in. long, yellow. Angola.

grandiflora: *Homeria Breyniana.*

Huttonii (Bak.) Oberm. Similar to *M. spathulata,* with which it has been confused, but sheaths of old lvs. absent or inconspicuous, fls. smaller, buttercup-yellow, basal spot of segms. dark yellow edged with short dark brown lines, caps. smaller and rounder. S. Afr.

iridoides: *Dietes vegeta.*

juncea L. [*M. tristis* Ker-Gawl.]. Sts. to 1 ft.; lvs. 3 or 4, mostly basal, linear, grasslike, to 1½ ft. long; perianth to 1 in. long, yellow-brown, marked with blue, outer segms. with a bright yellow basal spot. S. Afr.

neopavonia R. Foster [*M. Pavonia* (L.f.) Ker-Gawl.; *Iris Pavonia* L.f.]. PEACOCK IRIS. Sts. 1–2 ft.; lf. solitary, linear, pilose; perianth about 1¼ in. long, orange-red, outer segms. with blue-black or green-black basal spot. S. Afr. Var. **villosa:** *M. villosa.*

Pavonia: *M. neopavonia.* Var. **villosa:** *M. villosa.*

polystachya (Thunb.) Ker-Gawl. Sts. to 3½ ft.; lvs. 4, linear, to 2 ft. long, prominently ribbed; infl. corymbose; perianth to 1½ in. long, lilac, outer segms. with large, yellow basal spot. S. Afr.

ramosa: *M. ramosissima.*

ramosissima (L.f.) Druce [*M. ramosa* (Thunb.) Ker-Gawl.]. Sts. to 3 ft., stout, much-branched; basal lvs. 3, linear, to 2½ ft. long, with cormlets in axils; infl. corymbose; fls. fragrant, perianth bright yellow, outer segms. with brown or gray basal spot. S. Afr.

Robinsoniana: *Dietes Robinsoniana.*

spathacea: *M. spathulata.*

spathulata (L.f.) Klatt [*M. spathacea* (Thunb.) Ker-Gawl.]. Sts. to 4 ft.; lf. solitary, sword-shaped, to 2 ft. long, with long, fibrous, often reticulate old sheaths persisting; fls. fragrant, perianth to 2 in. long, bright yellow. S. Afr.

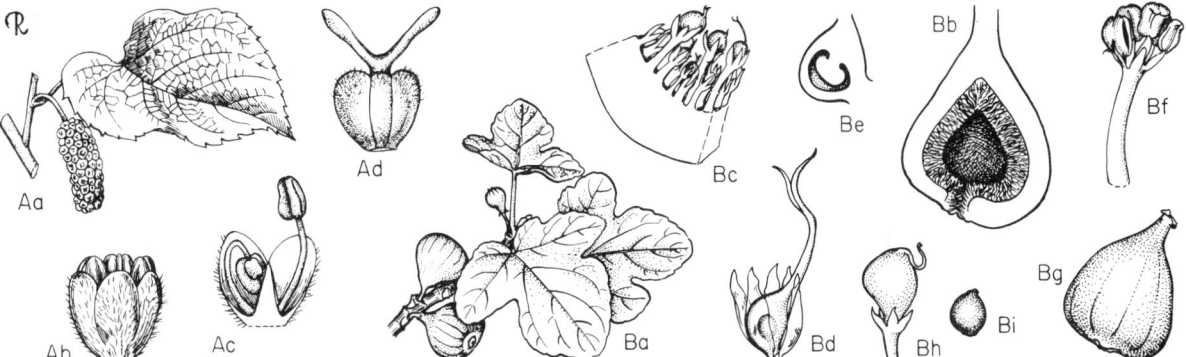

MORACEAE. **A,** *Morus alba:* **Aa,** fruiting spike and leaf, × ½; **Ab,** male flower, × 6; **Ac,** male flower, vertical section, × 6; **Ad,** female flower, × 6. **B,** *Ficus Carica:* **Ba,** fruiting branch, × ⅙; **Bb,** receptacle in flower, vertical section, × 1; **Bc,** segment of receptacle bearing flowers on inner surface, × 1½; **Bd,** female flower, × 5; **Be,** ovary, vertical section, × 6; **Bf,** male flower, × 3; **Bg,** fruiting receptacle ("fruit"), × ½; **Bh,** achene, × ⅓; **Bi,** seed, × ⅓. (Aa-Ad from Bailey, *Manual of Cultivated Plants,* ed. 2.)

tricuspidata (L.f.) G. J. Lewis [*M. glaucopis* (DC.) Drap.]. Sts. to 2 ft.; lvs. 3 or 4, linear, to 2½ ft. long; perianth 1¼ in. long, white, outer segms. with a circular, blue-black basal spot. S. Afr.

tripetala (L.f.) Ker-Gawl. Sts. to 1½ ft.; lvs. 3 or 4, linear, to 20 in. long; fls. faintly fragrant, perianth to 1¼ in. long, lilac or pale blue, outer segms. with a triangular, yellow basal spot. S. Afr.

tristis: *M. juncea.*

undulata Ker-Gawl. Sts. to 6 in. long; lf. solitary, linear, to 1 ft. long, margin somewhat wavy; fls. few, perianth to 1 in. long, lilac. S. Afr.

vegeta: *Dietes vegeta.*

villosa (Ker-Gawl.) Ker-Gawl. [*M. Pavonia* var. *villosa* (Ker-Gawl.) Bak.]. Sts. to 1 ft.; lf. solitary, linear, to 2 ft. long, hairy; perianth to 1¼ in. long, segms. bright purple, with a narrow area of bluish-black and a basal yellow spot streaked with purple-brown, outer segms. bearded. S. Afr.

zambesiaca Bak. Sts. to 1 ft.; lf. solitary, linear, to 1½ ft. long; perianth to 2 in. long, lilac-purple. Trop. Afr.

MORANGAYA Rowley. *Cactaceae.* One sp., a sprawling cactus of Baja Calif.; sts. elongate, low-ribbed, with aerial roots; areoles indeterminate; fls. diurnal, funnelform, regular; fr. bristly-spiny. Allied to *Aporocactus* but larger, with smooth epidermis and minutely pitted seeds.

For culture see *Cacti.*

pensilis (K. Brandeg.) Rowley [*Echinocereus pensilis* (K. Brandeg.) J. Purpus]. Sts. to 12 ft. long, 1–2 in. thick, ribs 8–11, rounded, cross-grooved between areoles; spines 6–11, later to 70, needle-shaped, yellowish, ¼–1 in. long; fls. red, 2–2½ in. long, stigma lobes 6–9, erect; fr. 1–2 in. long. Spring, summer.

MORAWETZIA: *BORZICACTUS.*

MORELLA: *MYRICA.* **Morella caroliniensis:** *Myrica pensylvanica.*

MORICANDIA DC. *Cruciferae.* Not cult. **M. hesperidiflora:** *Diplotaxis acris.*

MORINA L. *Dipsacaceae.* About 10 spp. of thistlelike per. herbs, native from se. Eur. to cent. Asia; lvs. basal and opp. or whorled on sts., simple, usually spiny-toothed; fls. yellow, white, pink, red, or purple, in congested axillary whorls, subtended by leaflike, spiny-toothed bracts, calyx 2-lipped, enveloped by an involucel with several bristly teeth, corolla 5-lobed, somewhat 2-lipped, with a long tube, fertile stamens 2 or 4; fr. an achene.

Sometimes planted as an ornamental; propagated by division or seeds.

betonicoides Benth. Sts. to 1½ ft.; st. lvs. opp., linear-lanceolate, to 8 in. long, margins prickly; corollas bright rose-red, about 1 in. long, lobes 3 or 4, with a basal crimson blotch, fertile stamens 4, anthers of unequal length, included. Sikkim.

kokanica Regel. Sts. to 3 ft., cylindrical; basal lvs. lanceolate, to 14 in. long, st. lvs. whorled, entire; bracts yellow-tipped; corollas lilac, about ½ in. long, fertile stamens 2, exserted. Turkestan.

longifolia Wallich ex DC. WHORLFLOWER. Sts. to 4 ft., ridged; lvs. linear to oblong, to 1 ft. long, pinnatifid, margins undulate, spiny-toothed, st. lvs. whorled; corollas white, changing to crimson, to 1½ in. long, fertile stamens 2, exserted. Himalayas.

MORINDA L. *Rubiaceae.* About 80 spp. of trees and shrubs or sometimes vines, native to the tropics; lvs. opp. or whorled, stipules interpetiolar; fls. in dense, terminal or axillary, capitate clusters, white or red, corolla funnelform or salverform, tube short, lobes 4–7; fr. a head of coherent or nearly separate drupes enclosed in succulent, enlarged calyces.

citrifolia L. [*M. Royoc* Blanco, not L. or Lour.]. INDIAN MULBERRY, AWL TREE. Small, glabrous tree; lvs. narrow-oblong to broad-elliptic, to 10 in. long, entire, with prominent curving lateral veins, stipules large, soon falling; fls. white, corolla ½ in. long; aggregate fr. yellow, subglobose or ovoid, to 2 in. long, fleshy. Se. Asia, Australia. The fls. contain a red dye and the roots a yellow dye. The fr. has been reported to be poisonous.

Royoc L. ROYOC. Vinelike shrub or sometimes erect, to 4 ft.; lvs. narrow-oblong, to 3 in. long or more, acute; fls. mostly white or reddish, corolla ¼ in. long; aggregate fr. yellow, subglobose, to 1 in. across. Fla., W. Indies. See also *M. citrifolia.*

MORINGA Adans. *Moringaceae.* Three or more spp. of deciduous trees with characters of the family.

One species is grown as an ornamental in the tropics, and for the edible roots, young leaves, and fruits, and for the seeds, from which oil is often extracted. Propagated by seeds and cuttings.

oleifera: *M. pterygosperma.*

pterygosperma C. F. Gaertn. [*M. oleifera* Lam.]. HORSERADISH TREE. To 30 ft.; lvs. to 2 ft. long, 2- or 3-pinnate, lfts. less than 1 in. long; fls. white, to 1 in. across, fragrant; fr. pendulous, linear, 3-angled, to 18 in. long. India; widely cult. and naturalized in the tropics.

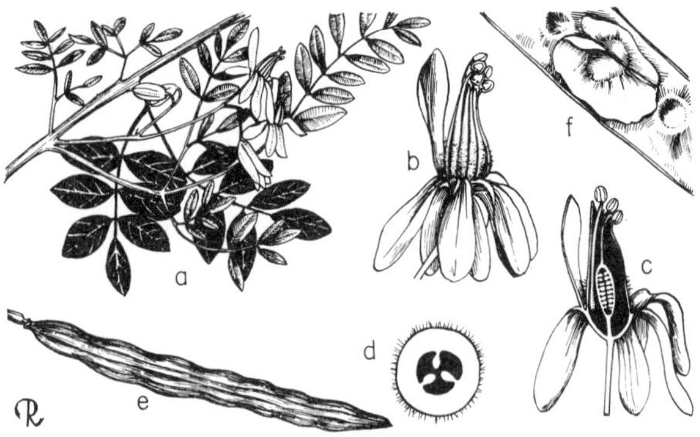

MORINGACEAE. *Moringa pterygosperma:* **a,** flowering branch, reduced; **b,** flower, × 1; **c,** flower, vertical section, × 1; **d,** ovary, cross section, × 5; **e,** capsule, × ⅙; **f,** seed on portion of capsule valve, × ½. (From Bailey, *Manual of Cultivated Plants,* ed. 2.)

MORINGACEAE Dumort. MORINGA FAMILY. Dicot.; 1 genus of trees, *Moringa,* native to Old World tropics and subtropics; lvs. alt., 2- or 3-pinnate; fls. in axillary panicles, bisexual, irregular, 5-merous, with 5 fertile and 5 sterile stamens, ovary superior, stipitate, 1-celled; fr. an elongate, podlike caps., seeds many, winged.

MORISIA J. Gay. *Cruciferae.* One sp., a small, stemless, per. herb of sandy places in Corsica and Sardinia; lvs. in a basal rosette; fls. solitary, yellow, sepals and petals 4; fr. a short, 2-jointed silique.

hypogea: *M. monanthos.*

monanthos (Viv.) Asch. [*M. hypogea* J. Gay]. Lvs. lanceolate, to 3 in. long, pinnately cut; pedicels elongating to 2½ in., curling downward and burying the fr. Spring or early summer. Adapted to the alpine or rock garden.

MORMODES Lindl. *Orchidaceae.* About 30 spp. of epiphytes, native to trop. Amer.; pseudobulbs jointed, many-lvd.; lvs. deciduous, plicate; infl. lateral, from lower joints of pseudobulbs, racemose, few- to many-fld.; fls. fleshy, bisexual or unisexual, sepals and petals similar, spreading, lip clawed, fleshy, with revolute margins, column cylindrical, twisted to 1 side of claw of lip, pollinia 2. For structure of fl. see *Orchidaceae.*

For culture see *Orchids.*

buccinator Lindl. Pseudobulbs spindle-shaped, to 6 in. long, leafless during flowering; infl. to 12 in. long; fls. variable in color, green suffused with pink and with creamy-white lip, or bright yellow-green with clear yellow lip, or maroon with paler maroon lip, or entirely white, sepals and petals ovate-lanceolate, to 1 in. long, lip kidney-shaped, with sides recurved. Uncommon but widespread in trop. Amer. Cv. **'Aurantiaca'** [var. *aurantiaca* Rolfe]. Fls. deep orange-yellow. Cv. **'Rolfei'.** Sepals and petals bronzy-green, lip rosy-crimson.

colossus Rchb.f. Pseudobulbs to 12 in. long; lvs. elliptic-ovate; infl. to 2½ ft. long; fls. to 6 in. across, sepals and petals narrowly lanceolate, with recurved margins, light rose basally, yellow apically, lip short-clawed, ovate-cordate, with revolute margins, bright yellow with some red dots towards base of tip. Costa Rica, Panama.

histrio Linden & Rchb.f. Pseudobulbs elongate, to 6 in. long; lvs. linear-lanceolate, to 9 in. long; infls. several, to 20 in. long, several-fld.; fls. polymorphic, variable in size and coloration, sepals and petals 1¼ in. long, fleshy to leathery, maroon, green, or yellowish, marked with brownish-purple or brick-red stripes and dots, sepals oblong-lanceolate, recurved at thickened apex, reflexed at margins, petals elliptic-lanceolate, recurved at apex, lip 3-lobed, to 1¼ in. long, brown-purple, greenish-white, or yellow, marked with a few purple or reddish dots. Mex., Guatemala, Honduras.

Hookeri Lem. Pseudobulbs to 4 in. long; infl. short, erect, densely fld.; fls. dark reddish-brown or red, sepals and petals lanceolate, to ¾ in. long, reflexed, lip obovate, to ⅝ in. long, truncate, abruptly apiculate, lateral margins reflexed, pubescent. Costa Rica, Panama.

igneum Lindl. & Paxt. Pseudobulbs stout, cylindrical, to 12 in. long, 5–15-lvd.; lvs. 2-ranked, lanceolate; infls. 1 to several, erect, arching; fls. few to many, variable in size, color, and texture, sepals reflexed, membranous, to 1 in. long, yellow, olive-green, tan-brown, or red, with minute spots, petals similar, lip fleshy, nearly orbicular, short-apiculate, white, yellow, olive-green, tan-brown, or reddish-brown, often with brown spots, lateral margin reflexed. Costa Rica, Panama, n. S. Amer.

lineatum Batem. ex Lindl. Similar to *M. histrio;* infl. to about 9 in. long; fls. dull olive-green, striped and spotted with dull brown, sepals linear-oblong, to 1 in. long, on reflexed margins, petals elliptic-lanceolate, to 1 in. long, undulate-crisped and somewhat reflexed on margins, lip linear, slightly dilated at apex, with small, subulate, incurved tooth on each side near base. Guatemala.

luxatum Lindl. Pseudobulbs ovoid, completely enclosed by base of overlapping sheaths; lvs. lanceolate, much longer than infl.; infl. erect, densely many-fld.; fls. fleshy, to 3 in. across, yellow with white margin, sepals and petals ovate to ovate-elliptic, with scarious margins, upper sepal, right petal, and lateral sepal arching over lip to form a hood, lip concave, obscurely 3-lobed, with revolute margin, deep yellow, suffused with bronze inside. Mex. Cv. 'Eburneum' [var. *eburneum* Rchb.f.]. Fls. larger, ivory-white, sweet-scented.

maculatum (Klotzsch) L. O. Williams [*M. pardinum* Batem.]. Pseudobulbs to 6 in. long, several-lvd.; lvs. lanceolate, membranous, infl. to 1 ft. long or more, racemose, densely fld.; sepals and petals ovate-lanceolate, directed upward at apex, lip 3-lobed, lobes lanceolate, bright yellow spotted with rich brownish-crimson. Mex. Var. **unicolor** (Hook.) L. O. Williams [*M. pardinum* var. *unicolor* Hook.]. Fls. clear lemon-yellow, without spots.

pardinum: *M. maculatum.* Var. **unicolor:** *M. maculatum* var.

MORMOLYCA Fenzl. *Orchidaceae.* Five spp. of epiphytes, native to Cent. and S. Amer.; pseudobulbs fleshy, 1–3-lvd.; lvs. leathery, strap-shaped; scapes slender, from axils of bracts subtending pseudobulbs, 1-fld.; sepals separate, petals similar, smaller than sepals, lip shorter than sepals and petals, disc with a callus, column arching, wingless, footless, pollinia 2. For structure of fl. see *Orchidaceae.*

For culture see *Orchids.*

ringens (Lindl.) Schlechter. Pseudobulbs congested along a wiry rhizome, ellipsoid, flattened, to 1½ in. long, 1-lvd.; lvs. to 14 in. long; scapes several, to 13 in. long; fls. fleshy, yellowish-green to light lavender, veined with lavender or maroon, lip lavender or dark maroon, sepals oblong-elliptic, longer than petals, to ¾ in. long, lip jointed to base of column and parallel with it, 3-lobed, ovate-elliptic, to ⅜ in. long, disc with fleshy thickening in center below middle which terminates in triangular 3-toothed callus. Cent. Amer.

MORPHIXIA: *IXIA.*

MORUS L. MULBERRY. *Moraceae.* About 10 spp. of deciduous, monoecious trees, native from N. to S. Amer., Afr., Asia; lvs. alt., simple, often lobed, usually crenate to dentate-serrate, glabrous to scabrous; fls. unisexual, in drooping catkins; fr. a juicy syncarp, resembling a blackberry.

Grown for the edible fruits, attractive to birds, and some for the foliage used as food for silkworms. For culture see *Mulberry.*

alba L. WHITE M. Tree, to 80 ft.; lvs. ovate, to 4 in. long or more, coarsely toothed, often lobed, glossy green above; fr. white, pinkish, or blackish-purple, 1–2 in. long, sweet. Late spring. Cent. and E. China.; naturalized in Eur. and N. Amer. Cv. 'Macrophylla'. Lvs. undivided, large, to 9 in. long. Var. **multicaulis** (Perrotet) Loud. [*M. multicaulis* Perrotet]. SILKWORM M. Lvs. large, coarse, dull green, rough above, long used for silk worm cult.; fr. black, sweet. Cvs. are: 'Pendula', brs. weeping; 'Striblingii', male fls. falling early, fr. not formed; 'Tatarica' [*M. tatarica* Pall., not L.], RUSSIAN M., trees small, very hardy, but fr. of poor quality.

australis Poir. [*M. indica* Roxb., not L.]. AINO M. Small tree; lvs. ovate, caudate-acuminate, sharply serrate, often deeply lobed, scabrous. Warm temp. e. Asia.

indica: see *M. australis.*

laevigata: *M. macroura.*

macrophylla: a listed name of no botanical standing for *M. alba* cv.

macroura Miq. [*M. laevigata* Wallich ex Brandis]. Small tree, shoots hairy; lvs. 3–7 in. long, sparsely pubescent, base round to cordate, petiole 1 in. long, pubescent; fr. insipid. Himalaya, Burma, s. China.

multicaulis: *M. alba* var.

nigra L. BLACK M. Tree, to 30 ft.; lvs. broadly ovate, to 8 in. long, cordate, coarsely toothed, unlobed or deeply lobed, dull green and scabrous above, pubescent to glabrescent beneath; fr. purple to black, to 1 in. long. Late spring. W. Asia. Zone 5. Has the largest and juiciest frs.

pendula: a listed name of no botanical standing for *M. alba* cv.

platanifolia: a listed name of no botanical standing, used for plants described as sterile, lvs. glossy, large, lobed. Possibly a cv. of *M. alba.* Reported introd. from France.

rubra L. RED M., AMERICAN M. Tree, to 60 ft.; lvs. ovate, to 5 in. long or more, sharply toothed, sometimes lobed, pubescent to glabrescent beneath, rough above; fr. red to dark purple, to 1 in. long, edible. Late spring. Rich bottomland soils, e. N. Amer. More useful for ornament than fr.

Striblingii: a listed name of no botanical standing for *M. alba* cv.

tatarica: see *M. alba* cv.

tropicana: a listed name of no botanical standing.

MOSCHARIA Ruiz & Pav. *Compositae* (Mutisia Tribe). One sp., a musk-scented ann. herb, native to Chile; fl. heads in small terminal clusters, involucral bracts 5–6, receptacle scaly; fls. all 2-lipped, the outer (lower) lip raylike, the other shorter and coiled, inner fls. sterile, the outer fertile, the scales of receptacle inflated, each clasping one fertile and one sterile fl.; pappus of achenes of fertile fls. with 1 row of short, fringed scales.

pinnatifida Ruiz & Pav. To 2 ft., diffusely branched; lvs. clasping, pinnatifid, the upper ones lobed only at base; fls. white or light rose.

MOSIERA: *Psidium.* **M. bahamensis:** *P. longipes.*

MOSSES AND LIVERWORTS. These are a well-defined group *(Bryophyta)* of nonflowering, nonvascular, rootless plants that, although diminutive, often form conspicuous parts of the world's vegetation, especially in areas of high humidity and shade. Mosses have simple stems and leaves, whereas most liverworts lack these organs and grow flat upon the ground or substrate.

Mosses are perhaps best known to most home gardeners in the form of dried peat or sphagnum, important components of standard soil mixes for plantings; both materials are largely if not entirely derived from the so-called bog or peat mosses of the genus *Sphagnum,* live material of which is often used as a medium in which to grow certain bog species such as carnivorous plants. In this country, miscellaneous species of living terrestrial mosses collected from the wild are often combined with other plants in terraria or to make the necessary attractive soil covering for pots holding bonsai specimens. The aquatic floating species of the liverwort genera *Riccia* and *Ricciocarpus* are sometimes grown for ornament or as protection for fish fry in aquaria; species of submerged aquatic moss genera such as *Fontinalis* may also be planted occasionally in cool water aquaria or clear pools. In Japan, many native terrestrial mosses have been used for centuries as attractive garden subjects and indeed some Japanese gardens are devoted primarily to plantings of mosses. Moss gardening of this type is feasible elsewhere, especially wherever a mild, humid climate prevails, as in the coastal Pacific Northwest. Many native mosses are easily transplanted from the wild for naturalistic evergreen plantings in similar sites under trees. Recommended species include the pincushion moss, *Leucobryum glaucum* (J. Hedw.) Ångstr., broom mosses (*Dicranum* J. Hedw.), and for moist sites the attractive mat-forming genera *Hypnum* J. Hedw. and *Thuidium* BSG; the familiar haircap moss (*Polytrichum* J. Hedw.) is unusual in its drought resistance and ability to withstand considerable direct sunlight.

The classification of mosses requires special knowledge, and, with the exception of *Fontinalis* and the Fontinalaceae, the genera and families of mosses, as with other kinds of nonvascular plants, are not treated separately in *Hortus*

Third. The interested grower can find appropriate literature on mosses and their identification in botanical libraries. The so-called club mosses are not true mosses but vascular plants treated under *Lycopodium* and *Selaginella;* Spanish moss is a flowering plant, *Tillandsia usneoides.*

MUCUNA Adans. [*Stizolobium* P. Br.]. *Leguminosae* (subfamily *Faboideae*). More than 100 spp. of trop., scandent herbs and shrubs of both hemispheres; lvs. alt., of 3 lfts.; fls. in axillary clusters with peduncles often very long and pendent, showy, papilionaceous, stamens 10, 9 united and 1 separate, anthers of 2 sorts; fr. a thick, leathery legume, often clothed with stinging hairs.

Some species are useful for forage and some have spectacular flowers. One species extensively grown for forage in the South and as an ornamental; another as an ornamental vine in tropical gardens or warm greenhouses. Plants are frost-tender; they need support and are often planted with maize. Propagated by seeds.

Bennettii F. J. Muell. NEW GUINEA CREEPER. Woody climber; lfts. oblong, pointed, glabrous; fls. orange or red to scarlet, to 3 in. long, in very showy, pendent clusters. New Guinea. Occasionally grown in gardens in the tropics. Prop. by air-layering or seeds (obtained by artificial pollination).

Deeringiana (Bort) Merrill [*Stizolobium Deeringianum* Bort]. VELVET BEAN, FLORIDA V.B., BENGAL B. Climbing to 60 ft.; lfts. rhomboid-ovate, lateral lfts. very oblique, to 6 in. long, pubescent, especially beneath; racemes pendent, 6–12 in. long, many-fld.; fls. to 1½ in. long, standard green-purplish, about half as long as the red-violet wings; fr. about 2½ in. long, densely covered with irritating, dark, velvety pubescence, seeds nearly globose, to ½ in. long, whitish, marked with brown or black. Probably trop. Asia.

MUEHLENBECKIA Meissn. WIRE PLANT. *Polygonaceae.* About 20 spp. of prostrate, vining or climbing, woody plants, with wirelike sts., native to New Zeal., Australia, and S. Amer.; lvs. alt.; fls. small, unisexual, in axillary clusters, or clusters in axillary or terminal spikes, racemes, or panicles, sepals 5, united basally, enlarging in fr., stamens or staminodes 8, stigmas 3; fr. an achene, 3-angled, partly fused with fleshy calyx.

Several are grown in greenhouses and hanging baskets and outdoors in warm climates. Propagated by cuttings, when seeds are not available.

australis (G. Forst.) Meissn. Stout dioecious vine, up to 25 ft., brs. interlacing, tangled, slender branchlets essentially glabrous; lvs. variable in shape, mostly broadly oblong, 1–3 in. long; panicles to 3½ in. long, densely fld.; fls. small, greenish; fr. glossy black. New Zeal.

axillaris (Hook.f.) Walp. [*M. nana* Thurst.]. Much-branched, prostrate or sprawling, small shrub, forming matted clumps 1 ft. across or less, or at other times straggling; lvs. oblong to nearly orbicular, ⅜ in. long or less, rounded at base; fls. solitary or in 2's. New Zeal.

chilensis: *M. hastulata.*

complexa (A. Cunn.) Meissn. MAIDENHAIR VINE, WIRE VINE, MATTRESS VINE, NECKLACE VINE. Similar to *M. australis,* but small branchlets mostly pubescent; lvs. elliptic to fiddleform, ½–¾ in. long; infl. a simple or small dense panicle ½ in. long or more. New Zeal. Cult. in Calif.; in colder climates adapted to basket cult. Var. **trilobata** (Colenso) Cheesem. Lvs. fiddleform, deeply lobed.

hastulata (Sm.) I. M. Johnst. [*M. chilensis* Meissn.]. Twining; lvs. ovate to oblong, about ½ in. long, triangular at base; fls. in axillary and terminal racemes. Chile, Peru.

nana: *M. axillaris.*

platyclada: *Homalocladium platycladum.*

varians Meissn. Smooth-stemmed, twining plant, of garden origin; much like *M. complexa,* and probably the same as *M. complexa* var. *trilobata.*

MUILLA S. Wats. *Amaryllidaceae.* Three spp. of herbs with fibrous-coated corms, native to sw. U.S. and to Mex.; lvs. very narrow; umbel on a scape and subtended by several papery spathe valves; fls. small, greenish-white, perianth tube scarcely evident, filaments separate, unappendaged, ovary superior; fr. a loculicidal caps.

maritima (Torr.) S. Wats. [*Allium maritimum* (Torr.) Benth.]. To 1 ft.; lvs. nearly cylindrical, margins very sparsely scabrous; fls. on long, unjointed pedicels, in loose umbels, anthers blue, green, or purple. Calif., Baja Calif.

MULBERRY. Mulberries are trees of the genus *Morus.* In North America, the mulberry is planted both for ornament and for fruit, the latter being highly attractive to birds. In silk-producing countries, especially in the Orient, mulberries are grown as forage for silkworms. The tree is naturally open-centered and round-headed, and is an interesting subject; some of the cultivars have finely cut leaves. A weeping mulberry (*Morus alba* cv. 'Pendula') is frequently planted as an ornamental oddity, being grafted 4 or 5 feet high on a straight form.

In orchard plantations, mulberries may be placed 25–30 feet apart. About the borders of a place they may go closer. The Russian cultivars are often planted for windbreaks, for they are very hardy and thrive under the greatest neglect, and for this purpose they may be planted 8–20 feet apart; they make excellent screens and stand clipping well. 'New American', 'Trowbridge', and 'Thornburn' are leading kinds of fruit-bearing mulberries for the North. The true 'Downing' is not hardy in the northern states, but 'New American' has been sold under this name. Cultivars true to name are rare in the trade. 'Wellington' (which may be 'New American' renamed) and 'Illinois Everbearing' are currently available. The pomological mulberries for planting in the North are forms of *Morus alba.* The more tender black mulberry (*M. nigra*) is grown in the Middle South and beyond. Certain named fruit cultivars of the native *M. rubra* are also known.

Mulberries thrive in any good soil, and need no special treatment. They should not be planted near patios, sidewalks, or any place where staining from the fruits is undesirable. Mulberries grow readily from seeds and, in fact, they frequently become weed trees. Named kinds may be scion-budded on seedlings or on stocks grown from ripe hardwood cuttings.

MULCHES. Included under this term are various substances spread upon the ground and used in horticulture primarily to protect plant roots against heat, cold, and drought; they may also serve to discourage weeds or to keep certain berry fruits clean and free from rot. Mulches help conserve moisture, and those of organic origin, if renewed annually like the leaf fall in our deciduous forests, release important nutrients from decay of the material next to the soil. For some plants, mulching is almost mandatory—as in strawberry beds to keep the fruit clean and free from rot, or under certain members of the heath family (*Rhododendron, Vaccinum,* etc.), whose shallow roots usually benefit greatly from annual applications of organic mulch.

Generally speaking, mulching is a good practice, especially when cheap and appropriate mulching materials are available, such as old hay, straw, sawdust, pine needles, wood chips, shredded bark, and many kinds of leaves. Commercial mulches are no better and usually more expensive, but black plastic is convenient and of easy use, especially in the home vegetable garden, where it also helps in conserving hand labor during the producing season. Mulches have drawbacks as well as advantages. Some may be fire hazards or may harbor mice that destroy or injure woody plants by girdling under the protection of the mulch. Plastic mulches may hinder application of fertilizers or the practice of tillage. Also, under some conditions in the spring, frost damage is greater over a mulch than over bare ground.

MULGEDIUM: *LACTUCA.*

MUNTINGIA L. *Elaeocarpaceae.* One sp., a tree to 30 ft., native to and widespread in trop. Amer., somewhat naturalized in the Asiatic tropics; lvs. alt., asymmetrical; fls. solitary or clustered in axils, pedicelled, sepals and petals 5, imbricate in bud, stamens many, disc bowl-shaped, bearing long bristles; fr. a 5-celled berry, seeds small, many.

Calabura L. CALABUR. Lvs. oblong-lanceolate, to 5 in. long, toothed, tomentose beneath; fls. white, 1 in. across; fr. white, globose, about ½ in. in diam.

MURRAYA J. König ex L. [*Chalcas* L.]. MOCK ORANGE. *Rutaceae.* About 4 spp. of spineless trees or shrubs, native to se. Asia; lvs. alt., odd-pinnate, glandular-dotted; fls. large, solitary or in axillary or terminal cymes, calyx 5-cleft, petals 4 or 5, stamens 8 or 10; fr. a few- to several-seeded berry.

Grown as ornamentals in southern Fla., southern Calif., and the tropics, as a pot plant, and as a stock for citrus. Propagated by seeds.

exotica: *M. paniculata.*

Koenigii (L.) K. Spreng. CURRY-LEAF TREE, CURRY-LEAF. Small tree; lfts. 11–21, lanceolate to ovate, 1–2 in. long, strong-smelling; fls. white, to 5⁄16 in. long, in many-fld. terminal cymes; fr. black, 5⁄16 in. diam. India and Ceylon, cult. occasionally in tropics. Zone 10. Pungent aromatic lvs. a standard ingredient of curries where native.

paniculata (L.) Jack [*M. exotica* L.; *Chalcas exotica* (L.) Millsp.; *C. paniculata* L.]. ORANGE JASMINE, ORANGE JESSAMINE, SATINWOOD, COSMETIC-BARK TREE, CHINESE BOX. Shrub or small tree, 10–12 ft.; lfts. 3–9, ovate, rhombic-ovate, to obovate, to 2¾ in. long, glossy; fls. white, fragrant; fr. red, ovoid, ½ in. in diam. or less. Se. Asia and Malay Pen. Cult. widely in tropics as an ornamental. Zone 10. Blooms several times a year.

MUSA L. BANANA. *Musaceae.* About 25 spp. of giant, cespitose, rhizomatous, treelike herbs in Asia; lf. sheaths forming a uniform pseudostem which produces blooms and frs. once and then dies, being supplanted by younger pseudostems; lvs. spirally arranged, blades elongate, fraying in the wind; fls. in axils of bracts, on long, drooping or erect stalks, lower fls. female or bisexual, upper fls. male, perianth of 5 united segms. and 1 separate segm.; fr. elongate, fleshy, seeds with straight embryo.

Some species are widely grown in the tropics for the staple edible fruits, some for ornament, and one for fiber. Bananas are suited only to warm climates, although they often withstand a few degrees of frost. They are gross feeders and thrive best on rich alluvial soil. As ornamentals they are grown in mild climates and are often used for subtropical effects. When so planted, a sheltered site is desirable to protect the attractive large leaves from wind damage. The edible hybrid kinds are propagated by rhizome cuttings or offsets planted in warm beds and transplanted as soon as 1 or 2 leaves have matured. The ornamental species normally produce seeds and these are sown in beds with bottom heat. Bananas may be grown for decoration in greenhouses with a night temperature of about 65° F. See also *Banana.*

acuminata Colla [*M. Cavendishii* Lamb. ex Paxt.; *M. chinensis* Sweet; *M. nana* of auth., not Lour.; *M. zebrina* Van Houtte ex Planch.]. EDIBLE B., PLANTAIN. Pseudostems to 20 ft. or more, few to many in a clump, usually blotched with brown or black; lvs. erect or ascending, to about 9 ft. long, to 2 ft. wide, green or dark-flecked above, green or purple beneath; infl. nearly horizontal or turned downward (becoming pendulous when fr. matures), peduncle usually brown-hairy; female fls. in 2 rows, about 16 in each of as many as 10 lower bracts, male bud acute, bracts acute, grooved, more or less glaucous, bright red to dark purple or sometimes yellow outside, paler red or purple to yellowish inside, only 1 bract lifted at a time, male fls. in 2 rows, about 20 in each bract; fr. to 5 in. long or more, 1¼ in. in diam., bright yellow, usually parthenocarpic in cult. forms, pulp whitish to yellow, seeds angular-depressed, about ¼ in. wide. Five subspp. range from Burma to Malay Pen. and Arch., New Guinea, Australia, Samoa, with other forms probably in E. Afr., s. India, Philippine Is. One of the parents of many edible bananas and largely diploid in the wild forms. Some diploids and especially the polypoid forms are edible and usually seedless. Among the diploid cvs. are: 'Bande', 'Mjengo Maua', 'Paka', 'Palembang', 'Pisang Lilan', 'Sikazani', 'Sucrier', 'Tongat'. Triploids include: 'Dwarf Cavendish' (DWARF B., LADYFINGER B., CHINESE B., CHINESE DWARF B., GOVERNOR B., CANARY ISLAND B.), 'Giant Cavendish', 'Gitigi', 'Grand Nain', 'Green Red', 'Gros Michel', 'Lacatan' or 'Musak Hijau', 'Kitarasa', 'Lujugira', 'Lwekilo', 'Maruthuva', 'Mutika', 'Nambi', 'Ntobe', 'Oratava', 'Palimbang', 'Rajah', 'Rio', 'Robusta', 'Valery'.

Arnoldiana: *Ensete ventricosum.*

Balbisiana Colla. Pseudostems several in a cluster, to more than 20 ft. high, 1 ft. in diam., green or yellowish-green; lvs. to more than 9 ft. long, more or less glaucous beneath; infl. pendulous, peduncle glabrous; female fls. in 10–15 clusters, male bud obtuse, bracts obtuse, grooved, more or less glaucous, purple outside, crimson inside, several bracts lifted at a time, male fls. in 2 rows, about 20 in each bract; fr. about 4 in. long, 1⅝ in. in diam., pale yellow with whitish pulp, seeds irregularly globose, about ¼ in. wide. India from Ceylon to Assam, Sikkim, n. Burma, s. China, Phillippine Is., e. New Guinea and New Britain. Cult. and naturalized in Thailand, Malay Pen., and Indonesia to Philippine Is., and New Guinea. A diploid, seeded sp. which is much used in banana breeding because of its disease resistance; one of the

parents of many edible bananas, but probably not cult. outside special collections.

Basjoo Siebold & Zucc. ex Iinuma. Pseudostems to about 8 ft. high, green or yellowish-green; lvs. about 4½ ft. long, not glaucous; infl. horizontal, but bud turning down above female fls., peduncle puberulent; female fls. in 2 rows, 10–16 in each of as many as 6 clusters, male bud with bracts grooved, yellowish-green or brownish-tinged on outside, pale yellow inside and there transversely corrugate between ridges, often 2 or more bracts lifted at a time, male fls. in 2 rows, about 20 in each bract; fr. to 2¾ in. long, ¾–1⅛ in. wide, greenish-yellow with white pulp. Ryukyu Is. Cult. for fiber and in s. Japan as a prized ornamental. A variegated cv. is grown. Perhaps the hardiest of the spp. Zone 9, and perhaps in sheltered sites in Zone 8.

Cavendishii: *M. acuminata.*

chinensis: *M. acuminata.*

coccinea Andr. Pseudostems to 4½ ft. high, 2 in. in diam., clustered, green; lvs. to 3½ ft. long, dark green above, paler beneath; infl. erect, short-peduncled, bracts scarlet, with green or yellow apex; female fls. 1–3 in each of 1–4 clusters, male bud not closely overlapped, bracts not grooved but firm, glossy, persisting unwithered for many days, fls. 2 in each bract; fr. oblong, to 2 in. long, 1 in. in diam., orange-yellow with white pulp, seeds nearly cylindrical, black, ¼ in. long. Indochina. This ornamental sp. may be found, on further study, to be identical with the earlier *M. uranoscopos* Lour.

Ensete: *Ensete ventricosum.*

Fehi: the names *Musa Fehi* Bertero ex Vieill. and *M. troglodytarum* L. have been used for the FEHI or FE'I BANANA widely cult. in many forms throughout the Pacific Is. (Polynesia and Melanesia) and perhaps originally from New Guinea. Until studies comparable to those on the *M. acuminata-M. Balbisiana* complex have been completed, the correct name must remain in doubt, and the use of generic cv. names may be continued, as *Musa* 'Aiuri', *M.* 'Borabora', *M.* 'Rureva', *M.* 'Soaga', and others, Distinguishing marks of these taxa are the generally violet-purple sap of cut petioles and the erect infls. These are both seeded and seedless cvs. Pseudostems to 20 ft. or more, green or becoming dark purple or black below on exposure; lvs. green, to 12 ft. long, 2 ft. wide; infl. erect; female fls. 2–12 in each of several clusters, male fls. cream-white, pink-tinged, 2–4 in axils of smooth, green, blunt or pointed bracts; fr. to 6½ in. long, coppery-orange with astringent raw pulp, edible when roasted or cooked.

gigantea O. Kuntze. Pseudostems solitary, to nearly 30 ft.; infl. to nearly 10 ft. long, bracts green; fls. white, 20–40 in each bract; fr. short, angled, seeds to ⅛ in. wide. An incompletely known sp. described from plants cult. in Java and Sumatra and perhaps referable to *Ensete*.

Koae: a listed name of no botanical standing for *M.* × *paradisiaca* cv. 'Aeae', a striped mutant of *M.* × *paradisiaca* cv. 'Maiamaoli'.

Mannii H. Wendl. Pseudostems to 2 ft. high, 1 in. in diam., tinged black; lvs. to 2½ ft. long, green; infl. erect, 6 in. long; female fls. in a single row, 3 in each of 3 clusters, male bracts somewhat grooved, pale crimson. Assam.

Martinii Van Geert: a confused name not clearly applicable to any sp.; plants so named have proved in some instances to be *M. Balbisiana*.

Maurelii: a listed name of no botanical standing for an ornamental red-lvd. plant, probably belonging to *Ensete*.

nana Lour. DWARF B. A dwarf sp. of Indochina not certainly identified; cult. material under this name is referable to *M. acuminata* cv. 'Dwarf Cavendish'.

nepalensis Wallich. A doubtful sp.; perhaps, if it actually exists, to be referred to *Ensete*.

oranocensis: a listed name of no botanical standing.

ornata Roxb. [*M. rosacea* of auth., not Jacq.]. FLOWERING B. Pseudostems to about 9 ft. high, 4 in. in diam., pale green and waxy, developing black blotches; lvs. to 6 ft. long, 14 in. wide, medium green and slightly glaucous, often red-flushed on midrib beneath; infl. erect, glabrous; female fls. in a single row, 3–5 in each of as many as 7 clusters, male bud top-shaped, acute, bracts more or less grooved, somewhat glaucous, pale pink, tipped with yellow, similar to darker within, usually only 1 lifted at a time, male fls. in a single row, 3–6 in each bract; fr. to 3⅛ long, ¾ in. in diam., pale greenish-yellow with white pulp, seeds warty, black, angular-depressed, about ¼ in. wide, ⅛ in. thick. Widely cult. as an ornamental, probably native in e. Pakistan to Burma. Most material cult. as *M. rosea* probably belongs here.

×paradisiaca L. [*M.* × *sapientum* L.]: *M. acuminata* × *M. Balbisiana*. EDIBLE B. PLANTAIN. The proper name to be applied to those cult., edible, seedless bananas of hybrid rather than autopolyploid origin, including both dessert and cooking bananas. These, however, are generally known by cv. names, as the origin of most clones is not readily ascertained except by experts. *Musa* 'French Plantain' is probably the type of *M.* × *paradisiaca; Musa* 'Silk' is probably the type of *M.* × *sapientum.* Var. *seminifera* of both *M.* × *paradisiaca* and *M.* × *sapientum* has been variously applied to seeded bananas, either to a wild form of *M. acuminata* or to *M. Balbisiana.* There are many named clones, among them cv. 'Aeae' from the Hawaiian Is., which has striped lvs. This is also known as 'Koae' or KOAE B. and has been listed as *M. Koae.* A cv. 'Variegata' is also listed. Named edible clones known to belong here are: 'Ney Poovan' (diploid), 'Awk Legor', 'Bluggoe', 'Celat', 'French Plantain', 'Grindy', 'Horn Plantain', 'King', 'Mysore', 'N. Podaththi', 'Nadan', 'Ney Mannan', 'P. B. Bathees', 'Peyan', 'Pome', 'Septsemaines', 'Silk' (triploid), and 'Tiparot' (tetraploid).

religiosa: *Ensete Gilletii.*

rosacea Jacq. A poorly known, seedless sp. probably closely related to *M. Balbisiana;* the name has generally been misapplied to *M. ornata.*

rosea Hort. ex Bak. Similar to *M. coccinea* but having lvs. 1 ft. long, 6 in. wide, green; infl. short, erect, peduncle hairy, bracts pale red, the male part 2 in. long, obtuse, fls. 2–3 in a cluster. A poorly known ornamental sp.; most material cult. as *M. rosea* is probably *M. ornata.*

×**sapientum:** *M.* × *paradisiaca.*

sumatrana Becc. An incompletely described sp. based on a juvenile plant; confused in the literature, and probably referable to *M. acuminata.*

superba: *Ensete superbum.*

textilis Née. ABACA, MANILA HEMP. Pseudostems in large clumps, to 15 ft. high or more, green to purplish or black near base; lvs. to 6½ ft. long, green; infl. nearly horizontal; female fls. in 2 rows, about 10 in each of as many as 6 clusters, male bud blunt, bracts not grooved, firm, glossy, greenish-brown or purplish-brown outside, rounded, sometimes green at tip, glossy and paler inside, male fls. in 2 rows, 10–12 in each bract; fr. to 2¾ in. in diam., yellow with scant pale buff pulp, inedible, seeds many, irregular, about ⅛ in wide. Philippine Is., where cult. for the strong durable fiber obtained from the sheathing petioles and much used in making marine cordage.

troglodytarum: see *M. Fehi.*

velutina H. Wendl. & Drude. Pseudostems to 4½ ft. high, yellowish-green; lvs. to 3¼ ft. long, dark green above, paler beneath, midrib red beneath; infl. erect, peduncle white-hairy; bisexual fls. in a single row, 3–5 in each of 2–4 clusters, male bud acute or acuminate, with bracts not conspicuously grooved, pale pink outside, darker inside, one raised at a time; fr. to 2¾ in. long, outer coat hairy, splitting, revealing white pulp and angular-depressed, black seeds to ¼ in. long. Assam. Grown as an ornamental.

zebrina: *M. acuminata.*

MUSACEAE Juss. BANANA FAMILY. Monocot.; 2 genera and about 42 spp. of large, trop., rhizomatous or cormous per. herbs of Afr., Asia, and Australia; plants to 20 ft. high, pseudostems often of very large size; lf. blades large, rolled in bud, pinnately veined; infl. terminal, erect or pendulous; fls. in clusters in axils of large bracts, mostly unisexual, female or

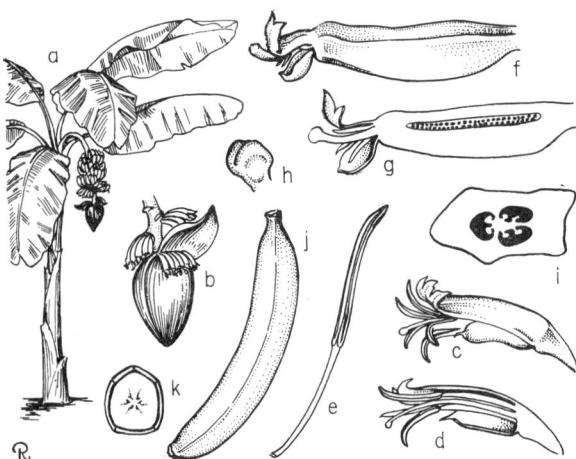

MUSACEAE. *Musa acuminata:* **a,** plant, much reduced; **b,** apex of inflorescence, × ⅛; **c,** male flower, × ½; **d,** male flower, vertical section, × ½; **e,** stamen, × 1; **f,** female flower, × ⅓; **g,** female flower, vertical section, × ⅓; **h,** stigma, × 1; **i,** ovary, cross section, × 1; **j,** fruit, × ⅙; **k,** fruit, cross section, × ¼.

bisexual fls. in lowermost clusters, male fls. above, sepals 3, petals 3, or perianth of 5 united and 1 separate segm., stamens 5–6, rarely to 8, ovary inferior, 3-celled; fr. a many-seeded berry, seeds absent in edible forms, with straight or T-shaped embryo. Cult. genera are *Ensete* and *Musa.*

Both genera are cultivated as ornamentals, but *Musa* also supplies an important edible fruit and fiber.

MUSCARI Mill. GRAPE HYACINTH. *Liliaceae.* About 40 spp. of bulbous, scapose, spring-flowering per. herbs, native to Medit. region and sw. Asia; bulb tunicate; lvs. usually more than 2, all basal; fls. urceolate to subglobose, usually constricted at apex, blue, white, olive, or rarely yellow, nodding or pendulous, in terminal, bracted racemes, perianth with 6 tiny reflexed, toothlike lobes, stamens 6, filaments arising from middle of perianth tube, anthers versatile; fr. a loculicidal, obtusely 3-angled caps. with rounded valves, seeds black, wrinkled to reticulate.

Of easy culture, and useful for colonizing. Propagated by offsets or seeds.

album: plants offered under this name are cvs. of *M. botryoides* or *M. conicum.*

alpinum J. Gay ex Bak. To about 4 in.; lvs. 4–5, linear, to 3 in. long; fls. tubular-urceolate, greenish, to ³⁄₁₆ in. long, in 12–20-fld. racemes. Asia Minor.

ambrosiacum: *M. racemosum.*

amethystinum: a listed name of no botanical standing; material offered under this name may be *Brimeura amethystina.*

Argaei album: a listed name of no botanical standing, for *Muscari* cv. 'Argaei Album', a late-flowering, white-fld. form of uncertain affinity.

armeniacum Leichtl. ex Bak. To 9 in.; lvs. 6–8, linear, to 1 ft. long and ¼ in. wide, appearing in autumn; fls. oblong, deep violet with white teeth, to ⁵⁄₁₆ in. long. Ne. Asia Minor. Cvs. 'Blue Spike', 'Fairway Seedling', and 'Ramosum', perhaps scarcely distinguishable from one another, have infls. branched, with fls. tightly clustered at ends of brs.

atlanticum Boiss. & Ruet. [*M. racemosum* of auth., not Mill.]. To 10 in.; lvs. 3–5, linear, to 1 ft. long, semicylindrical; fls. ovoid, fragrant, dark blue, with white or pale teeth, to ¼ in. long, in a dense, 10–30-fld. raceme. Eur., Asia.

Aucheri (Boiss.) Bak. To 4 in.; lvs. 2, linear-tongue-shaped, to 3 in. long, rather thick; fls. subglobose, blue, to about ⅛ in. long, in a 6–10-fld. raceme. Asia Minor.

azureum Fenzl [*Hyacinthella azurea* (Fenzl) Chouard; *Hyacinthus azureus* (Fenzl) Bak.]. To 8 in.; lvs. 2–5, linear, to 6 in. long; fls. tubular, not constricted, bright blue, to about ³⁄₁₆ in. long, in a dense 20–40-fld. raceme. Very early spring. Asia Minor. Cv. 'Album'. Fls. white. Cv. 'Amphibolis'. Fls. light blue.

botryoides (L.) Mill. COMMON G.H. To 1 ft.; lvs. 2–4, linear, to 1 ft. long; fls. globose, blue, with white teeth, about ⅛ in. long, in a dense, short, 12–20-fld. raceme. Cent. and s. Eur. to Caucasus. Cvs. are: 'Album', fls. white; 'Caeruleum', fls. bright blue; 'Carneum', fls. flesh-colored.

comosum (L.) Mill. TASSEL HYACINTH. Scape to 1½ ft., spotted brown; lvs. 3–4, linear-strap-shaped, to 1½ ft. long, rather thick; lower fls. fertile, brownish-olive, to ⁵⁄₁₆ in. long, horizontal or nodding, in a loose, 40–100-fld. raceme terminating in 20–30 sterile, smaller, upright, purple-blue fls. W. Eur., N. Afr. The bulbs are eaten in some Medit. countries and are sometimes sold in the U.S. as CIPOLLINO. Cv. 'Monstrosum'. FEATHER HYACINTH. Fls. all sterile, violet-blue, and cut into fine shreds. Cv. 'Plumosum' [*M. plumosum* Hort.; *Hyacinthus plumosus* Hort.]. FEATHER HYACINTH. Fls. reddish-purple, cut into long, fine shreds.

conicum (Jord. & Fourr.) Bak. To 6 in.; lvs. 6, linear, to 1 ft. long; fls. violet-blue, ³⁄₁₆ in. long, with white teeth, in a dense raceme, sterile fls. few, light blue. S. Eur.?

elegans Misch. ex Grossh. Lvs. linear, to 1¼ in. long; fls. bright violet-blue, ovoid-spherical, with longitudinal pleats, scape red in lower part. Caucasus.

latifolium Armitage, J. Kirk, & Playne ex J. Kirk. To 1 ft.; lvs. 1, rarely 2, oblanceolate, to 1 ft. long; fls. in a dense, many-fld. raceme, lower fls. fertile, oblong-urceolate, dark blackish-violet, about ¼ in. long, upper fls. sterile, violet-blue. Asia Minor.

macrocarpum Sweet [*M. moschatum* Willd. var. *flavum* Lam.]. To 8 or 10 in.; lvs. 5–7, linear-lanceolate to strap-shaped, to 15 in. long; fls. oblong-ellipsoid, yellow with brownish-purple lobes, ⅜ in. long, in an open, 20–30-fld. raceme. Aegean Is.

massayanum: a listed name of no botanical standing for a plant with rose-colored fls.

moschatum: *M. racemosum.* Var. **flavum:** *M. macrocarpum.*

neglectum Guss. To 9 in.; lvs. many, strap-shaped, to 1 ft. long, channelled; fls. fragrant, dark blue, in a 20–40-fld. raceme. Medit. region.

paradoxum (Fisch. & C. A. Mey.) C. Koch. To 9 in.; lvs. 3 or 4, to 1½ ft. long and ¾ in. wide; fls. oblong-campanulate, blackish-blue, green inside and at tips, to ⁵⁄₁₆ in. long, in a dense, many-fld. raceme on a stout scape. Caucasus. Cv. 'Album'. Fls. white.

Pinardii (Boiss.) Boiss. To 2½ ft.; lvs. narrowly linear, to 6 in. long, channelled; fertile fls. tubular-clavate, yellowish with brownish tips, in an open raceme, sterile fls. pale violet. Sw. Asia Minor.

plumosum: *M. comosum* cv.

polyanthum Boiss. To 1 ft.; lvs. linear, to ¼ in. wide, channelled; fertile fls. oblong-tubular, deep blue, in a dense, many-fld. raceme. E. cent. Asia Minor. Cv. 'Album'. Fls. white.

racemosum Mill., not of auth. [*M. ambrosiacum* Moench; *M. moschatum* Willd.]. MUSK HYACINTH, NUTMEG H. To 10 in.; lvs. 5–6, to 1 ft. long and ¾ in. wide; fls. musk-scented, purplish, aging to yellowish or brownish, in a dense, 20–50-fld. raceme. Asia Minor. This name has long been misapplied to *M. atlanticum.* Cvs. 'Majus' (incorrectly, 'Major'), and 'Minus' (incorrectly, 'Minor') are offered.

Szovitsianum Bak. To 7 in.; lvs. many, linear, to 9 in. long, channelled; fls. obovoid-oblong, bright to purplish-blue, with white teeth, to ³⁄₁₆ in. long, in a dense, conical, many-fld. raceme. Caucasus, Iran.

Tubergenianum T. Hoog ex Turrill. To 1 ft.; lvs. 2–3, linear to strap-shaped, to about 10 in. long; fls. ellipsoid, blue, to ³⁄₁₆ in. long, in a dense, many-fld. raceme. Nw. Iran.

MUSHROOMS. Mushrooms are higher fungi, of which *Agaricus bisporus,* the common mushroom, is the only species usually cultivated in the United States. Four distinct cultivars (white, golden-white, light cream, and brown) are grown. The life cycle of mushrooms begins with the germination of a spore, which gives rise to a mass of threadlike growths called the mycelium. The mycelium develops an extensive underground system by which it concentrates food in a central point. Here the threads enlarge, eventually forming a group of buttons or small mushrooms. See *Fungi.*

Mushrooms are produced horticulturally from an especially prepared material, called spawn, filled with living mushroom mycelium, with which the prepared beds are inoculated. The spawn originally had a manure base, but since 1930 there has been a gradual change to a base of whole kernels of wheat *(Triticum),* rye *(Secale),* milo *(Sorghum),* or millet *(Panicum miliaceum).* This new type is economical to produce and will inoculate approximately three times as much bed area as an equal volume of the manure spawn.

Mushrooms are grown where the temperature can be kept between 55° and 65° F, provided the relative humidity is high and the ventilation controlled. Sunlight is not harmful to mushrooms, but they are usually grown in the dark because it is easier and cheaper to control the temperature and humidity in structures without windows. Cellars, caves, old barns, and specially constructed mushroom houses are employed.

Horse manure with straw bedding has been used almost exclusively in the past as the raw material for mushroom compost. However, experiments at the Pennsylvania State University have shown that a compost of hay, straw, crushed corncobs, and certain organic and inorganic nitrogen supplements produced as many mushrooms to a ton as did horse manure. It is usually composted as soon as a pile is assembled sufficient to fill the mushroom house or a definite unit of bed space; less than one ton of manure is difficult to compost. Aeration, moisture, and temperature are the most important factors affecting the composting process. These are largely dependent on the size, shape, and compactness of the pile, the quantity of water added, and the number of days between turnings. Manure containing a moderate amount of straw is usually piled 4–6 feet high when first assembled. The piles are allowed to stand undisturbed for ten days before the first turning. Three or four turnings are made at intervals of two to three days. The compost should be kept moist at all times, neither wet nor dry. The practical test is to squeeze

a ball of it tightly in the hand. If the hand is not moistened, the compost is too dry; if water oozes out freely between the fingers, it is too wet.

Compost should be placed in the beds at about the rate of 1 bushel to 2 square feet of bed space. As soon as the beds are filled, the house, or that section of the structure containing the beds, is sealed tightly for a few days to allow the compost to go through a final period of fermentation. High temperatures are generated in the beds and in the air surrounding them. Both compost and air temperatures should reach 140° F for several hours, after which a compost temperature of approximately 130° F should be maintained until all odor of ammonia has been dissipated. This eradicates most of the harmful insects and fungi and seems to bring about a condition which later encourages a healthier and more rapid run of spawn. A still more complete control of insects and diseases may be obtained by the use of approved pesticides.

After heating, the temperature is gradually lowered to 75° F for spawning. Mycelium develops most rapidly from the spawn inoculations if this temperature is maintained for a week or ten days after spawning. The beds are then allowed to cool slowly until a cropping temperature of 55°–65° F is reached. Spawn pieces about half as large as hen's eggs should be spaced 8 inches to 1 foot apart in the beds and about 1–1½ inches deep. An imperial quart bottle of manure spawn will inoculate 30–40 square feet of bed area. The grain spawn will inoculate about twice this area.

Casing is the term applied to spreading soil about 1 inch thick over the entire bed. This is performed two to four weeks after spawning. Silt loams to light clay loams, containing a fair amount of organic matter and with a reaction approximately neutral, are best. Acid soils should be avoided or limed. Watering the beds usually begins as soon as they have been cased. Light watering may be necessary before this if the compost becomes too dry. Care should be taken to avoid excess watering. After casing, mushrooms should appear in two or three weeks, and the crop should continue, under proper conditions, for two or three months.

MUSINEON Raf. [*Daucophyllum* Rydb.]. *Umbelliferae.* Four spp. of caulescent, cespitose, per. herbs of w. N. Amer.; lvs. pinnate to 3-pinnate; fls. cream-colored to yellow, in dense umbels, involucre usually lacking, involucels usually present; fr. ovate to oblong, flattened laterally.

tenuifolium Nutt. [*Daucophyllum tenuifolium* (Nutt.) Rydb.]. Cespitose, to 10 in.; lvs. 2–3-pinnate, segms. filiform; peduncle hirtellous below umbel, bractlets of involucels green, longer than fls.; fr. creamy-white. S. Dak., Nebr., Wyo., Colo.

MUSKMELON: see *Melon.*

MUSSAENDA L. *Rubiaceae.* About 200 spp. of erect or twining shrubs, rarely herbs, native to trop. Afr., Asia, and Pacific Is.; lvs. opp. or in 3's, stipules interpetiolar, persistent or deciduous; fls. in open, terminal, few- or many-fld. corymbs, yellowish, red, or white, 5-merous, one sepal usually enlarged, leaflike and brightly colored, corolla funnelform; fr. a berry, rarely a caps.

erythrophylla Schumach. & Thonn. Erect or climbing shrub, to 30 ft.; lvs. roundish-ovate to elliptic, to 6 in. long, more or less hairy beneath; fls. sulphur-yellow, leaflike sepal scarlet, round-ovate, to 3½ in. long, nearly as broad, corolla tube ¾ in. long. Trop. W. Afr.

glabra Vahl. Climbing shrub, brs. mostly glabrous; lvs. elliptic, oblong or elliptic-lanceolate, to 6 in. long, glabrous; fls. many, yellow or orange, leaflike sepal white, oblong or elliptic, to 5 in. long, corolla tube to 1 in. long. Himalayas at lower elevations and se. Asia.

incana Wallich. Erect shrub, to 3 ft.; lvs. ovate-oblong, to 4½ in. long, hairy above, white-villous beneath; fls. few, leaflike sepal white, ovate or broadly oblong, to 2½ in. long, corolla tube to 1 in. long. Himalayas at lower elevations.

Roxburghii Hook.f. Erect shrub, to 30 ft., brs. almost glabrous to densely hirsute; lvs. oblong-lanceolate, ovate or elliptic, to 12 in. long, minutely hairy above, sparsely to densely hairy beneath; fls. many, leaflike sepal white, oblong-lanceolate, to 4½ in. long, corolla tube green, to 1 in. long, lobes orange or yellow. Himalayas at lower elevations.

MUSTARD. Several species of *Brassica* are known as mustard; they are mostly annuals, grown for the cluster of basal leaves used as greens, and also for the oil seeds employed in the manufacture of table mustard and in other countries for rape (or colza) oil. They are half-hardy, coming quickly from seeds. For greens the plants are usually planted in rows far enough apart to permit hand cultivation; in the row they may stand 5 or 6 inches apart and be thinned as used. They may be sown at intervals, in early spring for early summer use and up to August or even later for autumn use; in warm countries they are sown in autumn for an early spring crop. They are usually little attacked by pests. If allowed to seed, they may become weedy.

The commonest vegetable-garden species is *Brassica juncea,* particularly var. *crispifolia* in the cultivars known as 'Ostrich Plume' and 'Southern Curled'.

MUTISIA L.f. *Compositae* (Mutisia Tribe). About 60 spp. of erect or climbing shrubs, native to S. Amer.; lvs. alt., simple or compound, frequently terminating in a tendril; fl. heads solitary, terminal, involucral bracts imbricate in several rows, often with an apical, leafy appendage, receptacle naked; disc fls. 2-lipped, bisexual, usually yellow, anthers tailed at base, ray fls. 2-lipped or ligulelike, female, purple, rose, yellow, scarlet, orange, or rarely white; achenes cylindric-fusiform, glabrous, pappus of 1 row of tawny or white, plumose hairs.

Mutisias may be grown outdoors in Calif., or in a cool greenhouse. Propagated by seeds or cuttings.

Clematis L.f. Vine, to 10 ft.; lvs. pinnate, lfts. in 3–5 pairs, elliptic, to 2¾ in. long, tomentose beneath, ending in a 3-parted tendril; heads pendulous, to 2 in. across; ray fls. ligulelike, scarlet. Colombia.

decurrens Cav. Much-branched, glabrous vine; lvs. simple, oblong-lanceolate, ending in a 2-parted tendril, decurrent, basally entire or toothed; heads 4–5 in. across; disc fls. yellow, ray fls. 2-lipped, brilliant orange. Cent. Chile and adjacent Argentina.

ilicifolia Cav. Climbing shrub, to 15 ft.; lvs. simple, ovate to elliptic-ovate, to 2⅜ in. long, notched at apex and ending in a simple tendril, cordate or semiclasping basally, spiny-dentate; heads 2–3 in. across; disc fls. yellow, ray fls. 2-lipped, rose. Cent. Chile.

oligodon Poepp. & Endl. Vine, to 1½ ft.; lvs. simple, oblong to elliptic, to 1½ in. long, acute to obtuse at apex and ending in a simple tendril, clasping basally, glossy above, woolly beneath, entire or with 3–6 teeth; heads to 2½ in. across; disc fls. yellow, ray fls. ligulelike, pink. Cent. Chile and adjacent Argentina.

retusa: *M. spinosa.* Var. **glaberrima:** *M. spinosa.*

spinosa Ruiz & Pav. [*M. retusa* Rémy; *M. retusa* var. *glaberrima* Phil.]. Subshrubby vine, to 20 ft.; lvs. simple, elliptic to elliptic-ovate, to 2¼ in. long, notched at apex and ending in a simple tendril, cordate to semiclasping basally, essentially glabrous, usually with only a few spiny marginal teeth; heads to 2½ in. across; disc fls. yellow, ray fls. ligulelike, pale rose. Chile and adjacent Argentina.

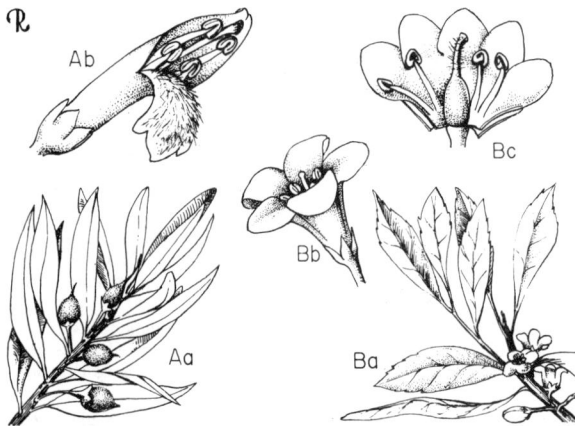

MYOPORACEAE. **A,** *Bontia daphnoides:* **Aa,** fruiting branch, × ¼; **Ab,** flower, × 1½. **B,** *Myoporum laetum:* **Ba,** flowering branch, × ¼; **Bb,** flower, × 3; **Bc,** flower, expanded, × 3. (From Bailey, *Manual of Cultivated Plants,* ed. 2.)

MYOPORACEAE R. Br. MYOPORUM FAMILY. Dicot.; 5 genera and perhaps 180 spp. of shrubs or trees, often with stellate or glandular hairs or glandular-dotted, native mostly to the Old World tropics and subtropics, chiefly Australia; lvs. mostly alt., simple, entire; fls. bisexual, regular or irregular, calyx 5-parted, corolla 5–6-lobed, stamens 4, staminode 1, ovary superior, usually 2-celled; fr. a drupe. *Bontia, Eremophila,* and *Myoporum* are occasionally grown as ornamentals in warm regions and in greenhouses.

MYOPORUM Banks & Soland. ex G. Forst. *Myoporaceae.* About 30 spp. of evergreen shrubs and trees, native mostly to Australia, and a few to New Zeal., Hawaiian Is., China, and Japan; lvs. alt., glandular-dotted, entire or toothed; fls. solitary or in axillary clusters among the foliage, small, white, usually regular, bell-shaped, calyx and corolla usually 5-lobed, stamens usually 4; fr. a small, more or less succulent drupe.

The several species in cultivation are useful for hedges and windbreaks. They are difficult to distinguish from one another. Grown in the open in warm regions and under glass in the North. Propagated by cuttings.

acuminatum R. Br. Erect glabrous shrub; lvs. usually elliptic-oblong, lanceolate, or linear, 1½–3 in. long, more or less acuminate, narrowed to base, entire or rarely toothed; corolla almost campanulate, about ¼ in. long, bearded inside, lobes usually shorter than tube, stamens 4; fr. rounded, to ¼ in. across. Extremely variable in stature, size and shape of lvs., and size of fls. Australia.

debile R. Br. Low shrub, to 3 ft. high and 4 ft. across, brs. trailing, shoots glandular-tubercled; lvs. lanceolate to narrow-oblong, to 4 in. long, sparsely toothed, short-petioled; fls. 1 or 2 in lf. axils, pink, calyx lobes broadly ovate, corolla about ⁵⁄₁₆ in. across, bearded inside; fr. ovoid, flattened, ½ in. wide, rose-colored, edible. Australia. Useful for rock gardens and banks.

insulare R. Br. BOOBYALLA. Tall shrub or tree, to 30 ft.; lvs. lanceolate to obovate, to 3 in. long, remotely serrate to entire, thick and usually glabrous; fls. usually 2–4 in axils, corolla white, purple-bearded, to ¼ in. across; fr. purplish-blue, globular, to ¼ in. across. Australia.

laetum G. Forst. Shrub or tree, to 15 ft.; lvs. lanceolate, to 4 in. long, shining; fls. white, purple-spotted, ⅝ in. across; fr. reddish-purple, to ¼ in. across. New Zeal. Differs from other cult. spp. in having young lvs. clammy and brownish-green. Cv. 'Carsonii'. Vigorous, fast-growing; lvs. large, broad. Prop. by cuttings. Grown in Calif. Zone 10.

montanum R. Br. Shrub, to 9 ft.; lvs. lanceolate, to 2 in. long, entire; fls. white, corolla purple-spotted in throat, bearded inside, lobes as long as tube; fr. rounded, becoming purple, to ¼ in. across. Australia.

procumbens: a listed name of no botanical standing.

sandwicense (A.DC.) A. Gray. BASTARD SANDALWOOD, NAIO. To 60 ft., wood hard, dark yellow-green with odor of sandalwood; lvs. ovate-lanceolate, to 6 in. long; fls. white or pink, ⁵⁄₁₆ in. across, corolla lobes 5–6, rarely 7, stamens as many as lobes of corolla; fr. white. Hawaiian Is. Zone 10. Wood once used as a substitute for sandalwood.

serratum R. Br. Shrub or tree, to 30 ft., usually glabrous; lvs. elliptic-oblong to lanceolate, more or less serrate; fls. white, ¼ in. long, corolla bearded inside, lobes usually as long as tube; fr. rounded, to ⅜ in. across. Australia. Variable in shape and size of lf., and size of fl.

tomentosum: a listed name of no botanical standing.

MYOSOTIDIUM Hook. *Boraginaceae.* One sp., a pubescent, per. herb, of the Chatham Is., New Zeal.; lvs. simple, alt., basal and cauline; fls. blue, in dense, bractless, corymbose cymes, calyx deeply 5-lobed, corolla 5-lobed, with 5 yellow scales in the throat, stamens included; fr. of 4 smooth, winged nutlets.

Propagated by seeds.

Hortensia (Decne.) Baill. [*M. nobile* (Hook.f.) Hook.]. Sts. 1–2 ft.; basal lvs. ovate, cordate, glossy, to 1 ft. long, glabrous, fleshy, st. lvs. smaller, sessile; fls. dark blue, paler toward outside, ½ in. across, in dense cymes to 6 in. across.

nobile: *M. Hortensia.*

MYOSOTIS L. FORGET-ME-NOT, SCORPION GRASS. *Boraginaceae.* About 50 spp. of hairy, ann., bien., or per. herbs, native to temp. zones of all continents; lvs. simple, entire, basal lvs. petioled, st. lvs. sessile; fls. pink, blue, or white, solitary or in bractless terminal infls. or branched scorpioid cymes, calyx 5-lobed, corolla salverform, 5-lobed, with scales in the throat, stamens 5, included or exserted; fr. of 4 smooth, shining nutlets.

Forget-me-nots are cultivated mostly outdoors and thrive in partly shady positions in moist soil. Winter protection is desirable. Propagated by seeds which will give bloom in autumn or the second year, also by division of the clumps.

alpestris F. W. Schmidt [*M. rupicola* Sm.]. Densely tufted per.; lf. bases forming a loose papery sheath at base of st.; similar to *M. sylvatica* from which it differs in shorter habit, shorter-stalked fls., and larger nutlets. Eur. Not known in cult.; plants grown under this name are referable to *M. sylvatica*.

alpina Lapeyr. Mat forming per., to nearly 6 in.; basal lvs. not petioled, tongue-shaped, glabrous beneath; fls. blue, pedicels and calyx with hooked bristles, corolla to ⁵⁄₁₆ in. across. Pyrenees.

arvensis (L.) J. Hill. Ann. or bien., to 1½ ft.; lvs. oblong to oblong-lanceolate; fls. blue or white, to ³⁄₁₆ in. across, calyx with hooked hairs. Eur., Asia; naturalized in N. Amer.

australis R. Br. Erect, hispid per., to 1½ ft.; sts. branched from base; lvs. oblong- to linear-spatulate, to 2 in. long, hispid on both surfaces; fls. yellow or white, to ¼ in. long. New Zeal.

azorica H. Wats. Coarse per., to 1½ ft., with decumbent base, lower part of st. with white, retrorse hairs; basal lvs. broadly oblanceolate, to 4 in. long; fls. blue with white eye, ¼ in. across. Azores, Canary Is., Algeria.

cespitosa K. F. Schultz. Similar to *M. laxa,* but more pubescent, and fls. longer-pedicelled. Eur.

dissitiflora Bak. Similar to *M. sylvatica,* but differing in being of lower habit and having nutlets stalked. Switzerland. Plants cult. under this name are *M. sylvatica.*

explanata Cheesem. Per., to 1 ft., sts. white-hairy, ascending; basal lvs. linear to spatulate, to 4 in. long, st. lvs. narrowly oblong-lanceolate; fls. white, to ⅝ in. across. New Zeal.

hybrida: a listed name of no botanical standing.

laxa Lehm. Per., to 1½ ft., with slender, decumbent, cylindrical sts.; lvs. oblong to spatulate; fls. blue with yellow eye, ³⁄₁₆ in. across, calyx without hooked hairs. Nfld. to Ont., s. to La.; B.C. to n. Calif.; Chile, Eur., Asia.

oblongata: *M. sylvatica.*

palustris: *M. scorpioides.*

robusta D. Don. Not cult.; *M. robusta grandiflora* is *M. sylvatica* cv.

rosea: a listed name of no botanical standing for *M. sylvatica* cv.

rupicola: *M. alpestris.*

scorpioides L. [*M. palustris* Lam.]. FORGET-ME-NOT. Per., to 1½ ft., sts. angled, decumbent, from stolonlike rhizome; lvs. oblong-lanceolate or oblanceolate; fls. bright blue with yellow, pink, or white eye, ¼ in. across, calyx without hooked hairs. Eur., Asia; naturalized in N. Amer. Var. **semperflorens** Bergmans [*M. semperflorens* Hort.]. Dwarf, to 8 in.; fls. in summer.

semperflorens: *M. scorpioides* var.

stricta Link. Ann. or bien., to 8 in., branching from the base; lvs. lanceolate or oblong, with straight and hooked hairs; fls. blue, tiny, pedicel shorter than calyx, calyx with hooked hairs. Eur.; naturalized in N. Amer. The plant listed under this name is probably a cv. of *M. sylvatica.*

sylvatica Hoffm. [*M. oblongata* Link]. GARDEN FORGET-ME-NOT. Erect, hairy ann. or bien., to 2 ft.; lvs. oblong-linear to oblong-lanceolate; fls. blue with yellow eye, varying to pink or white, to ⁵⁄₁₆ in. across, pedicel nearly twice as long as calyx, calyx with hooked hairs; nutlets sessile. Eur. and Asia; sparingly naturalized in N. Amer. A variable plant in cult. and hort. variants are often confused and listed under *M. alpestris* and *M. dissitiflora.* Some of these cvs. are: 'Alba', fls. white; 'Compacta', a dense form, lower than the type; 'Fischeri', dwarf, with bluish-pink fls.; 'Oblongata Perfecta', early blooming with large blue fls.; 'Robusta Grandiflora', vigorous, fls. large; 'Rosea', fls. rose; 'Stricta', brs. erect and strict.

Welwitschii Boiss. & Reut. Tufted ann. or bien., to 4 in.; lvs. ovate-lanceolate; fls. bright blue with yellowish-white eye. Spain.

MYRCEUGENELLA: *LUMA.*

MYRCEUGENIA O. Berg. *Myrtaceae.* Not cult. **M. apiculata:** *Luma apiculata.*

MYRCIA DC. ex Guillem. *Myrtaceae.* About 200–300 spp. of shrubs or trees in trop. Amer.; lvs. opp.; fls. white, mostly small, 4–5-merous, usually many in terminal or axillary panicles, stamens many; fr. a berry, 1–3-seeded, crowned with persistent calyx lobes.

tomentosa (Aubl.) DC. [*Eugenia tomentosa* Aubl.]. Shrub or tree, branchlets densely villous; lvs. obovate, to 2½ in. long or longer, short-petioled; fr. orange, subglobose, to ⁵⁄₁₆ in. across. Panama to Brazil.

MYRCIANTHES O. Berg [*Anamomis* Griseb.]. *Myrtaceae.* About 50 spp. of evergreen trees or shrubs, native from Fla. and W. Indies to S. Amer.; lvs. opp., simple; fls. white, 1–7 in usually solitary, axillary cymes, the terminal or central fls. usually sessile, fl. tube not extending beyond the ovary, calyx lobes 4, persistent, petals 4, spreading, stamens many, ovary inferior, 2-celled, ovules many in each cell; fr. a berry, 1-(rarely 2–4-)seeded, crowned by the persistent calyx lobes.

Mato (Griseb.) McVaugh [*Eugenia Mato* Griseb.]. Tree, to 25 ft.; lvs. ovate-oblong, punctate, margins yellowish; fls. solitary. Argentina.

Simpsonii (Small) K. A. Wils. [*Anamomis Simpsonii* Small; *Eugenia Simpsonii* (Small) Sarg.]. Tree, to 60 ft.; lvs. narrowly obovate or nearly elliptic; fls. several in a cyme. S. Fla. Lvs. contain a volatile oil resembling nutmeg in flavor.

MYRCIARIA O. Berg. *Myrtaceae.* About 40 spp. of evergreen trees or shrubs in trop. Amer.; lvs. opp., simple; fls. subsessile, clustered in lf. axils or on trunk and brs., calyx tubular, 4-lobed, tube prolonged above the ovary, circumscissile at base after flowering, petals 4, small, stamens many; fr. a globose berry. Has in the past been placed in the larger genus *Eugenia,* but differs in having calyx tube prolonged above the ovary.

cauliflora (DC.) O. Berg [*Eugenia cauliflora* DC.]. JABOTICABA. Tree, to 40 ft.; lvs. lanceolate or somewhat broader, to 4 in. long, acuminate; fls. white, in clusters along trunk and brs.; fr. globose, ¾–1½ in. across, white to purple, edible. S. Brazil, where much cult. for the fr. Occasionally grown elsewhere in the tropics and subtropics, where it requires a deep rich soil, and a moist rather cool climate without frost.

edulis (Vell.) Skeels [*Eugenia edulis* Vell.]. Tree, to 20 ft., brs. pendent; lvs. willowlike, 2–3 in. long, rusty-pubescent when young; fls. ½ in. across, in axillary or terminal clusters; fr. pear-shaped, about 2 in. long, orange-yellow, downy, ill-smelling. Late winter. Brazil. Material cult. under this name may be *Eugenia aggregata.*

floribunda (West ex Willd.) O. Berg [*Eugenia floribunda* West ex Willd.]. Tree, to 30 ft.; lvs. lanceolate to ovate-lanceolate, to about 3 in. long, acuminate; fls. white, sessile, 2–5 in lateral clusters; fr. globose, to ½ in. across, red or yellow, edible. W. Indies, s. Mex. to Cent. Amer., Guyana, Brazil.

myriophylla (Casar.) O. Berg [*Eugenia myriophylla* Casar.]. Much-branched shrub; lvs. very narrow and crowded (at least on juvenile plants), to 1½ in. long or more, midrib obscure above, but prominent underneath; fls. white, solitary on axillary peduncles. S.-cent. Brazil.

MYRICA L. [*Cerothamnus* Tidestr.; *Morella* Lour.]. *Myricaceae.* About 50 spp. of deciduous or evergreen shrubs or small trees of wide distribution; lvs. alt., simple, mostly oblanceolate, short-petioled; fls. small, unisexual, in short spikes or catkins, perianth absent, stamens 2–8, ovary 1-celled; fr. drupaceous, grayish or purple, the surface covered with granules of resin or wax.

Cultivated as ornamentals, or *M. rubra* for the edible fruit. Propagated by seeds, layering, and suckers.

asplenifolia: *Comptonia peregrina* var.

californica Cham. & Schlechtend. CALIFORNIA WAX MYRTLE, CALIFORNIA BAYBERRY. To 35 ft.; lvs. evergreen, to 4 in. long; fr. purple, to ¼ in. long. Wash. to Calif. Zone 8. Will grow on sterile sandy soils.

caroliniensis: see *M. cerifera* and *M. pensylvanica.*

cerifera L. [*M. caroliniensis* Mill.; *Cerothamnus ceriferus* (L.) Small; *Morella cerifera* (L.) Small]. WAX MYRTLE, WAXBERRY, CANDLEBERRY. To 35 ft.; lvs. evergreen, to 3 in. long, acute, entire to sharply serrate above middle; fr. grayish-white, less than ⅛ in. in diam. N.J. to Fla. and Tex. Zone 7. Yields wax used in making candles. Grows best in moist peaty soil.

Faya Ait. CANDLEBERRY MYRTLE. To 25 ft.; lvs. glabrous, to 4¼ in. long; male catkins branched, to ¾ in. long, female catkins essentially simple, ovaries united, forming an irregularly lobed syncarp ¼ in. in diam. without waxy coating. Canary and Madeira Is., s. Portugal. Zone 10.

Gale L. SWEET GALE, BOG MYRTLE, MEADOW FERN. To 5 ft.; lvs. deciduous, to 2½ in. long; fr. yellowish, enclosed by 2 winglike bracts, in dense catkins ¼ in. long or more. N. N. Amer., Eurasia. Zone 4. Lvs. used medicinally. Grows best on moist peaty soil. Specific epithet pronounced in two syllables.

pensylvanica Loisel. [*M. caroliniensis* of many auth. and Hort., not Mill.; *Cerothamnus caroliniensis* Tidestr.; *Morella caroliniensis* Small]. BAYBERRY, CANDLEBERRY, SWAMP C. To 9 ft.; lvs. deciduous or sometimes evergreen, broadly oblanceolate, to 4 in. long, acutish or obtuse; fr. grayish-white, scarcely more than ⅛ in. in diam. Nov. Sc. to Fla. and Ala. Zone 5. Grows well on poor soil. Yields wax used in making bayberry candles. The name *M. caroliniensis* was originally used by Miller for the plant correctly known as *M. cerifera* and is not available for the bayberry.

rubra Siebold & Zucc. Small tree, or rarely to 60 ft.; lvs. oblong-lanceolate to obovate, to 5 in. long, entire or serrate above middle; fr. deep red-purple, succulent, to 1 in. in diam. Japan, s. China, Korea, Philippine Is. Zone 8. The fr. is edible and is also used for making a drink.

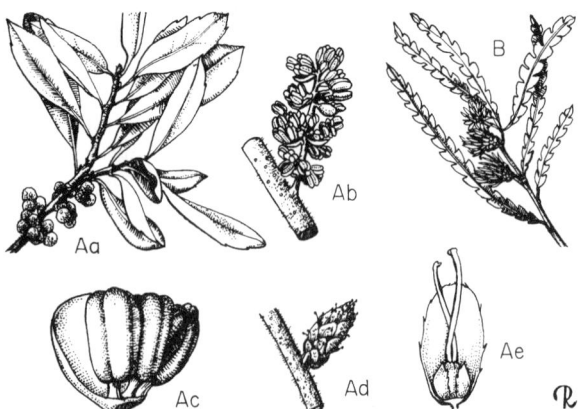

MYRICACEAE. **A,** *Myrica pensylvanica:* **Aa,** fruiting branch, × ⅜; **Ab,** male inflorescence, × 2; **Ac,** male flower, × 8; **Ad,** female inflorescence, × 2; **Ae,** female flower, × 8. **B,** *Comptonia peregrina* var. *asplenifolia:* branch with young fruit, × ⅜. (From Bailey, *Manual of Cultivated Plants,* ed. 2.)

MYRICACEAE Blume. BAYBERRY or WAX MYRTLE FAMILY. Dicot.; 2 genera of small monoecious or dioecious trees and shrubs of wide distribution; lvs. alt., simple or pinnatifid; fls. small, unisexual, in axillary spikes or catkins, perianth lacking, stamens 2–16, ovary superior, 1-celled; fr. a small drupe or nutlet. Both *Comptonia* and *Myrica* are cult.

MYRICARIA Desv. FALSE TAMARISK. *Tamaricaceae.* About 10 spp. of deciduous shrubs, native to s. Eur. and Asia; lvs. alt., closely placed, scalelike; fls. small, white or pink, in dense racemes, sepals and petals 5, stamens 10, filaments united; fr. a caps., seeds with terminal tuft of hairs. Closely related to *Tamarix.*

germanica (L.) Desv. [*Tamarix germanica* L.]. To 6 ft., brs. many, close-ascending; fls. in terminal, bracted racemes to 2 in. long. Summer. S. Eur., w. Asia. Zone 5.

MYRIOPHYLLUM L. MILFOIL, WATER M. *Haloragaceae.* About 45 spp. of mostly aquatic or wet-ground herbs, of world-wide distribution; lvs. alt., opp., or whorled, often of 2 kinds, the submersed ones pinnatifid into capillary segms., the emersed ones entire or toothed; fls. small, axillary or in spikes, bisexual or unisexual, calyx lobes and petals usually 4, stamens 4 or 8; fr. a 4-lobed nutlet.

Several aquatic species are grown in aquaria and pools for their long, flexuous stems with feathery foliage; propagated by cuttings.

alterniflorum DC. Sts. slender, to 3 ft.; lvs. in whorls of 3–5, of 2 kinds, usually shorter than internodes and less than ⅜ in. long; female fls. in whorls of 3, male fls. alt. E. N. Amer., Eur.

aquaticum (Vell.) Verdc. [*M. brasiliense* Camb.; *M. proserpinacoides* Gillies ex Hook. & Arn.]. PARROT'S-FEATHER, WATER-FEATHER. Tips of sts. rising out of water for several in.; lvs. all alike, in whorls of 4–6, pinnatifid, with short segms., to 1 in. long or more, bright yellow-green; fls. axillary. Brazil, Argentina, Chile; naturalized in se. U.S.

brasiliense: *M. aquaticum.*

elatinoides Gaud.-Beaup. Sts. to 3 ft.; lvs. in whorls of 3–5, submersed lvs. pinnatifid, to ¾ in. long, emersed lvs. oblong-ovate, be-

coming successively more entire, not over ⅜ in. long. Mex., S. Amer., Falkland Is., New Zeal., Australia.

exalbescens: *M. spicatum* subsp.

heterophyllum Michx. Sts. rather stout; lvs. in whorls of 4–6, submersed lvs. pinnate, to 2 in. long, emersed lvs. lanceolate to elliptic, to 1¼ in. long, entire to serrate; fr. conspicuously beaked. Temp. e. N. Amer.

hippuroides Nutt. ex Torr. & A. Gray. WESTERN MILFOIL, RED WATER M. Sts. to 2 ft.; lvs. in whorls of 4–6, submersed lvs. pinnately dissected, to 1½ in. long, emersed lvs. linear to lanceolate, to ⅝ in. long, pectinate to entire; fls. axillary. Cent. Calif. to s. Wash.

oguraense Miki. Lvs. in whorls of 4, pinnately cleft, submersed lvs. to 2 in. long, emersed lvs. to ⅜ in. long, whitish with fine white papillae above. Japan.

pinnatum (Walt.) BSP. [*M. scabratum* Michx.]. Lvs. in whorls of 3–5, or frequently scattered to nearly whorled, submersed lvs. pinnate, with linear capillary segms., to 1¼ in. long, emersed lvs. linear or lanceolate, pectinate; fls. in a spike. S. New Eng. to Kans., s. to Fla. and Tex.

proserpinacoides: *M. aquaticum.*

scabratum: *M. pinnatum.*

spicatum L. Sts. to 8 ft.; lvs. usually in whorls of 4, submersed lvs. to 1¼ in. long, pinnate, mostly with 12–17 pairs of segms., emersed lvs. pectinate to entire, shorter than fls. and fr.; fls. in an interrupted spike. N. Amer., Eur., Asia, N. Afr. Subsp. **exalbescens** (Fern.) Hult. [*M. exalbescens* Fern.]. Lvs. with 6–12 pairs of segms. N. Amer.

ussuriense (Regel) Maxim. Plants dioecious; lvs. in whorls of 3 or 4, submersed lvs. pinnately parted, to ⅜ in. long, emersed lvs. usually linear, entire; fls. in a spike. Temp. e. Asia.

verticillatum L. MYRIAD LEAF. Lvs. in whorls of 4–5, submersed lvs. finely pinnatifid, ½–1½ in. long, emersed lvs. smaller, pinnately dissected, as long as fls. and fr. or longer; fls. in a spike. N. N. Amer., Eur., Asia.

MYRISTICA Gronov. *Myristicaceae.* About 80 spp. of dioecious trees, native to se. Asia, n. Australia, and the Pacific Is., with characters of the family; lvs. often whitish or glaucous beneath, veins slightly sunken in upper surface; fls. in axillary cymose or subumbellate panicles, calyx 3–5-toothed, filaments united, anthers elongate, united; fr. fleshy, dehiscent, seeds partly covered by aril.

One species, *M. fragrans,* grown commercially, chiefly in Indonesia and the W. Indian island of Grenada, provides nutmeg and mace. It is sometimes cultivated for interest, thriving in a hot moist climate, in well-drained rich soil. Propagated by seeds and grafting.

fragrans Houtt. NUTMEG. Glabrous tree, to 70 ft.; lvs. alt., oblong-lanceolate, to 5 in. long; fls. pale yellow, small, corolla lacking; fr. yellow, to 2 in. long, splitting into 2 halves, the brown seed (nutmeg) surrounded by a thin, scarlet, netlike aril (mace). Moluccas. Widely cult. in tropics and sometimes escaped.

MYRISTICACEAE R. Br. NUTMEG FAMILY. Dicot.; 15 genera of trop., evergreen, dioecious trees; lvs. alt., entire; fls. small, regular, unisexual, in axillary clusters, calyx mostly

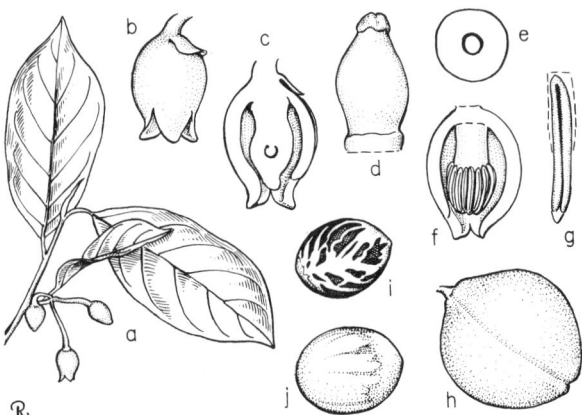

MYRISTICACEAE. *Myristica fragrans:* **a,** flowering twig, × ½; **b,** female flower, × 1½; **c,** female flower, vertical section, × 2; **d,** pistil, × 3; **e,** ovary, cross section, × 3; **f,** male flower, part of calyx cut away, × 2; **g,** anther, × 6; **h,** fruit, × ⅓; **i,** seed surrounded by aril, × ⅜; **j,** seed, × ⅜.

3-lobed, corolla lacking, stamens 2–30, filaments united, ovary superior, 1-celled; fr. fleshy, dehiscent, 1-seeded, seeds surrounded by aril. *Myristica* furnishes nutmeg and mace.

MYROXYLON J. R. Forst. & G. Forst., not L.f.: *XYLOSMA*.

MYROXYLON L.f. *Leguminosae* (subfamily *Faboideae*). Two spp. of trees of trop. Amer.; lvs. odd-pinnate, lfts. alt., translucent-lined and -dotted; fls. in racemes, whitish, papilionaceous, standard large, clawed, stamens 10, separate; fr. a flat, 2-winged legume, with solitary seed toward the tip.

Species of this genus provide two true balsams, important in medicine and perfumery, as well as a valuable mahoganylike wood. Cultivated in the tropics.

Balsamum (L.) Harms. Tall tree; lfts. 5–13, ovate-oblong, to 3½ in. long, reticulate, glossy; racemes pubescent, pedicels more than ½ in. long; fls. fragrant, standard less than ½ in. long; fr. about 3 in. long, 1 in. across. Venezuela to Peru. Source of balsam of Tolu. Var. **Pereirae** (Royle) Harms [*M. Pereirae* (Royle) Klotzsch]. Fr. thicker, often curved. Cent. Amer. Source of balsam of Peru.

Pereirae: *M. Balsamum* var.

MYRRHINIUM Schott. *Myrtaceae*. One or a few spp. of shrubs or small trees in S. Amer.; lvs. opp., simple; fls. in ternately-dichotomous cymes lateral on old wood, with a sessile fl. in each fork of the cyme, calyx lobes 4, petals 4, small, reddish-purple to grayish-purple, rounded, short-clawed, stamens 4–8, red, twice folded in bud, long-exserted; fr. few-seeded, berrylike, crowned with persistent calyx lobes.

atropurpureum Schott [*M. lanceolatum* Burret; *M. loranthoides* (Hook. & Arn.) Burret; *M. rubriflorum* (Camb.) O. Berg; *M. salicinum* Gand.]. To 15 ft. or more; lvs. elliptic, to 4 in. long, leathery, nearly sessile; petals to ⅜ in. long, stamens ¾ in. long, conspicuous. Ecuador to n. Argentina and s. Brazil.

lanceolatum: *M. atropurpureum.*

loranthoides: *M. atropurpureum.*

rubriflorum: *M. atropurpureum.*

salicinum: probably *M. atropurpureum.*

MYRRHIS Mill. *Umbelliferae*. One sp., a Eur. per. herb, sometimes grown for the sweet-scented herbage.

odorata (L.) Scop. MYRRH, SWEET CICELY, ANISE, SWEET CHERVIL. To 3 ft.; lvs. 2–3-pinnate, segms. lanceolate, toothed or cut; fls. small, whitish, in compound umbels; fr. shining, nearly 1 in. long, strongly ribbed. Prop. by seeds sown as soon as ripe, or by division.

MYRSINACEAE R. Br. MYRSINE FAMILY. Dicot.; about 32 genera and 1,000 spp. of evergreen shrubs and trees (only

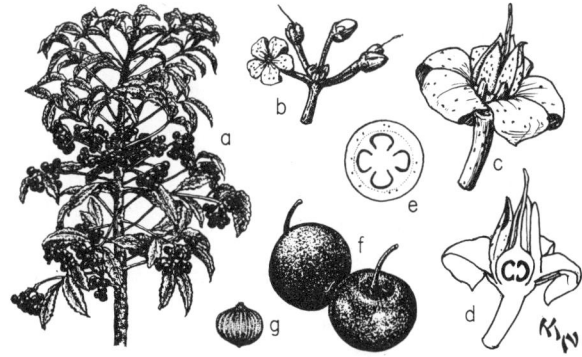

MYRSINACEAE. *Ardisia crenata:* **a,** fruiting stem, × ¹⁄₁₂; **b,** branch of inflorescence, × 1; **c,** flower, × 3; **d,** flower, vertical section, × 3; **e,** ovary, cross section, × 5; **f,** fruits, × 1; **g,** seed, × 1.

Ardisia primulifolia is herbaceous), native to tropics and subtropics; lvs. simple, mostly alt., often leathery; fls. small, white to pinkish-red, mostly bisexual, rarely unisexual, regular, in panicles or cymose clusters, calyx 4–6-lobed, sometimes of separate sepals, corolla usually rotate to salverform, stamens as many as corolla lobes and opp. them, pistil 1, with 4–6 carpels, ovary superior (half-inferior in *Maesa*); fr. a drupe. *Ardisia, Maesa, Myrsine,* and *Suttonia* are grown as ornamentals.

MYRSINE L. *Myrsinaceae*. About 5 spp. of dwarf shrubs to small trees, native to Asia and Afr.; lvs. alt., simple; fls. small, unisexual, in few-fld., axillary, umbellate clusters, calyx 4–5-lobed, corolla 4–5-lobed or -parted, stamens 4 or 5; fr. a 1-seeded drupe.

Grown outdoors in warm climates.

africana L. CAPE MYRTLE, AFRICAN BOXWOOD. Shrub or small tree, to 6 ft.; lvs. lanceolate to orbicular or obovate, mostly elliptic-ovate, to 1¼ in. long, finely toothed above the middle, glabrous; fls. 4-merous, minute, in 3–8-fld. clusters; fr. red. The Azores to China and Taiwan.

MYRSIPHYLLUM: *ASPARAGUS.*

MYRTACEAE Juss. MYRTLE FAMILY. Dicot.; about 80 genera and 3,000 spp. of trees or shrubs, largely trop., particularly in Asia and Amer., and in Australia where those with capsular frs. occur; lvs. usually opp., simple, glandular-dotted; fls. regular, bisexual, in cymes, umbels, racemes, or panicles,

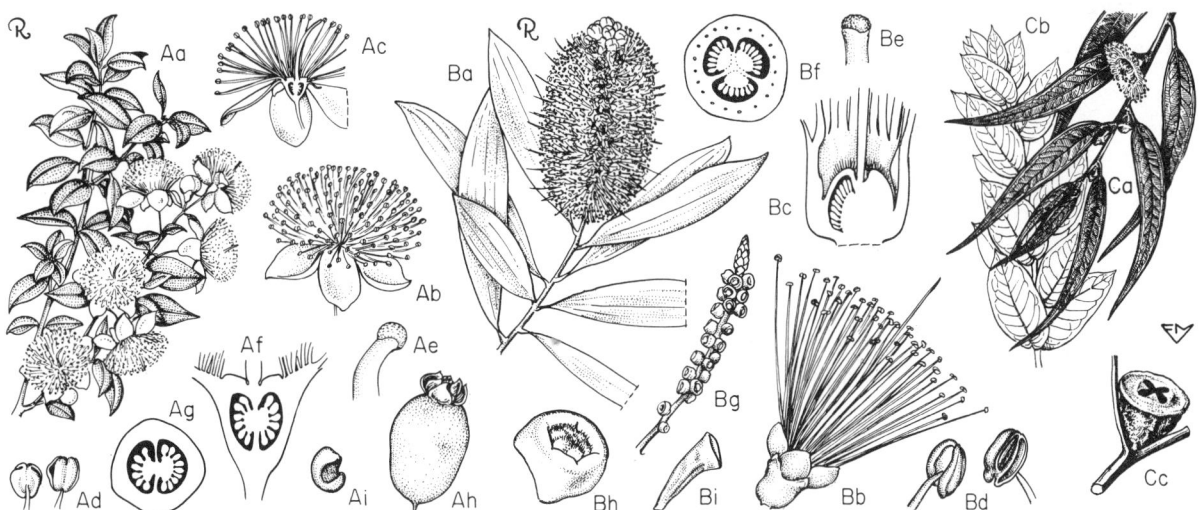

MYRTACEAE. **A,** *Myrtus communis:* **Aa,** flowering branch, × ½; **Ab,** flower, × 1; **Ac,** flower, vertical section, × 1; **Ad,** anthers, two views, × 6; **Ae,** stigma, × 15; **Af,** ovary, vertical section, × 4; **Ag,** ovary, cross section, × 5; **Ah,** fruit, × 1; **Ai,** seed, × 2. **B,** *Melaleuca Leucadendron:* **Ba,** flowering branch, × ½; **Bb,** flower, × 2; **Bc,** base of flower, vertical section, × 5; **Bd,** anthers, two views, × 10; **Be,** stigma, × 10; **Bf,** ovary, cross section, × 8; **Bg,** fruiting branch, × ½; **Bh,** fruit, × 2; **Bi,** seed, × 2. **C,** *Eucalyptus globulus:* **Ca,** flowering branch, × ⅙; **Cb,** branch with juvenile foliage, × ⅙; **Cc,** fruit, × ½. (Ca-Cc from Bailey, *Manual of Cultivated Plants*, ed. 2.)

rarely solitary, calyx lobes usually 4–5, separate or united at base, petals 4–5, stamens usually many, sometimes in bundles, occasionally fewer than 20, ovary usually inferior, sometimes nearly half-inferior, with 1–3 or more cells; fr. a berry or caps., rarely a drupe or nutlike, seeds few to many. Genera cult. are: *Acmena, Agonis, Amomyrtus, Angophora, Backhousia, Baeckea, Callistemon, Calothamnus, Calytrix, Chamelaucium, Cleistocalyx, Darwinia, Eucalyptus, Eugenia, Feijoa, Kunzea, Leptospermum, Lhotskya, Lophomyrtus, Luma, Melaleuca, Metrosideros, Myrcia, Myrcianthes, Myrciaria, Myrrhinium, Myrtus, Neomyrtus, Phymatocarpus, Pimenta, Psidium, Rhodomyrtus, Syncarpia, Syzygium, Thryptomene, Tristania, Ugni,* and *Verticordia.*

The family is important economically for several edible fruits: guava *(Psidium),* rose-apple *(Syzygium Jambos),* jaboticaba *(Myrciaria cauliflora),* Surinam cherry *(Eugenia uniflora);* a few spices, allspice (unripe fruit of *Pimenta dioica*), clove (dried flower buds of *Syzygium aromaticum*), oil of bay *(Pimenta racemosa);* timber *(Eucalyptus);* and many ornamentals.

MYRTILLOCACTUS Console. MYRTLE CACTUS. *Cactaceae.* One or more spp. of treelike cacti, native to Mex.; trunk short, brs. many, erect, with 5–8 ribs; areoles all similar, spines angled, awl-shaped; fls. several at an areole, diurnal, small, white, tube short, limb rotate, scales of ovary few, small, woolly in the axils; fr. small, subglobose, edible.

For culture see *Cacti.*

Cochal: *M. geometrizans.*

geometrizans (Mart. ex Pfeiff.) Console [*M. Cochal* (Orcutt) Britt. & Rose; *Cereus geometrizans* Mart. ex Pfeiff.]. BLUE-CANDLE, BLUE-FLAME. To 20 ft. high, crown to 25 ft. wide, joints 1–3 ft. long, 3–4 in. thick, often bluish, ribs 5–8, about 1 in. high; areoles to 1 in. apart, radial spines 5–9, to ½ or rarely 1¼ in. long, central spine 1, laterally flattened, ½–3 in. long; fls. 4–9 per areole, 1–1½ in. across; fr. purplish, to ¾ in. in diam. Mex.

Schenckii (J. Purpus) Britt. & Rose. Areoles close-set, spines short; perhaps a var. of *M. geometrizans.*

MYRTUS L. MYRTLE. *Myrtaceae.* Evergreen shrubs or small trees; lvs. opp., entire, pinnately-veined; fls. white to pink, in few-fld. cymes, or solitary in axils, calyx 4–5-lobed, lobes separate, persistent, petals 4, white, spreading, stamens many, in several series, separate, longer than petals, ovary 2–3-celled, each cell with many ovules; fr. a berry, crowned by persistent calyx lobes. Many spp. traditionally placed in *Myrtus* are now regarded as belonging in other genera. Recent workers interpret *Myrtus* as consisting of about 16 spp., 1 in Eur., 1 in Afr., and about 14 in Fla. and the W. Indies.

Myrtle is grown outside in the South, in greenhouses or in pots for lawn specimens in the North. Propagated by cuttings of partially ripened wood under glass; also by seeds.

acris: *Pimenta racemosa.*

bahamensis: *Psidium longipes.*

boetica: *M. communis.*

bullata: *Lophomyrtus bullata.*

buxifolia: *M. communis* cv.

communis L. [*M. boetica* Mill.; *M. italica* Mill.; *M. latifolia* Raf.; *M. romana* Hoffmanns.]. The classic MYRTLE, GREEK M., SWEDISH M. Shrub, to 15 ft., with dense foliage; lvs. ovate to lanceolate, to 2 in. long, strongly scented when crushed; fls. white or pinkish, to ¾ in. across, calyx lobes often 5; fr. blue-black, to ½ in. long. Spring–autumn. Medit. region and sw. Eur. Zone 9. Cult. for centuries; its native range is therefore uncertain. Subsp. **communis**. The typical subsp.; to 15 ft.; lvs. to 2 in. long, not crowded. Cvs. include: 'Albocarpa', fr. white; 'Buxifolia' [*M. buxifolia* Raf.], lvs. elliptic; 'Compacta', dwarf and dense; 'Flore Pleno', fls. white, double; 'Microphylla' DWARF M., GERMAN M., POLISH M., lvs. overlapping, linear-lanceolate, less than 1 in. long; 'Minima' [*M. minima* Mill.] and 'Nana', of dwarf habit, lvs. small; 'Variegata', lvs. white-margined. Subsp. **tarentina** (L.) Arcang. Not more than 6 ft.; lvs. less than 1 in. long, crowded.

italica: *M. communis.*

latifia: *M. communis.*

Lechlerana: *Amomyrtus Luma.*

Luma: *Amomyrtus Luma.*

minima: *M. communis* cv.

obcordata: *Lophomyrtus obcordata.*

pedunculata: *Neomyrtus pedunculata.*

Ralphii: *Lophomyrtus Ralphii.*

romana: *M. communis.*

tarentina: *M. communis* subsp.

Ugni: *Ugni Molinae.*

verrucosa: *Psidium longipes.*

MYSTACIDIUM Lindl. *Orchidaceae.* Twelve spp. of epiphytes, native to E. and S. Afr.; sts. leafy, short or elongated; lvs. 2-ranked, leathery or fleshy, jointed to a persistent sheath; infl. lateral, simple; fls. small to medium-sized, racemose or solitary, sepals and petals nearly equal, separate to somewhat connivent, lip joined to base of column, extended at base into a short or somewhat elongate spur, lateral lobes small or obsolete, column short, broad, concave in front, without wings or foot. For structure of fl. see *Orchidaceae.*

For culture see *Orchids.*

distichum (Lindl.) Pfitz. [*Angraecum distichum* Lindl.]. Sts. tufted, to 9 in. long; lvs. overlapping, 2-ranked, broadly elliptic-oblong, falcately recurved, to 9 in. long; fls. solitary, axillary, white, on short peduncles, sepals ovate-oblong, about ¹⁄₁₆ in. long, petals oblong, slightly smaller than sepals, lip hooded, broadly ovate, 3-lobed, shorter than petals, midlobe triangular. Trop. Afr.

NAEGELIA: *SMITHIANTHA.*

NAGELIELLA L. O. Williams [*Hartwegia* Lindl.]. *Orchidaceae.* Two spp. of rhizomatous epiphytes, native to Cent. Amer. and Venezuela; pseudobulbs 1-lvd.; lvs. fleshy, nearly sessile; infl. a terminal, dense, few- to many-fld. raceme; sepals and petals similar, lip swollen or saccate at base, united to middle of the winged column. For structure of fl. see *Orchidaceae.*

For culture see *Orchids.*

purpurea (Lindl.) L. O. Williams [*Hartwegia purpurea* Lindl.]. To 1½ ft., slender, erect, pseudobulbs to 3 in. long; lvs. leathery, ovate-lanceolate, usually spotted with bronze-purple, to 6 in. long; racemes to 19 in. long, subumbellate-paniculate or racemose; fls. purplish-red, upper sepal elliptic, to ¼ in. long, petals elliptic-lanceolate, shorter than sepals, lip to ⅜ in. long, united to base of column, extended below into a short, nearly globose, saclike spur. Spring–autumn. Mex. to Honduras.

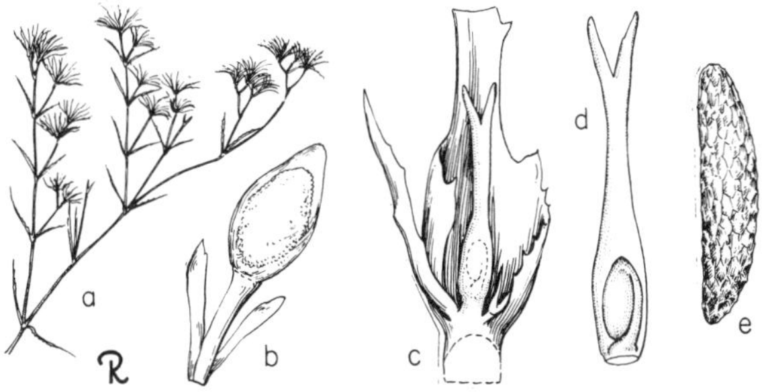

NAJADACEAE. *Najas gracillima* (Alex. Br.) Magnus: **a,** vegetative branch, × ⅙; **b,** male flower, × 15; **c,** leaf base with female flower in axil, × 10; **d,** female flower (with position of ovule indicated), × 15; **e,** seed, × 10. (Species representative, but not in general cultivation; from Lawrence, *Taxonomy of Vascular Plants.*)

NAJADACEAE Juss. NAIAD FAMILY. Monocot.; 1 cosmopolitan genus, *Najas,* of slender, dioecious or monoecious, aquatic ann. herbs; lvs. narrow, opp., with conspicuous basal sheaths; fls. unisexual, solitary in axils of lf. sheaths, male fl. with a single anther usually in a membranous involucre, female fl. with a single naked, 1-celled, 1-ovuled pistil; fr. an achene. Includes some aquarium plants.

NAJAS L. NAIAD, WATER-NYMPH. *Najadaceae.* About 35 spp. of aquatic herbs, with characters of the family.

Sometimes grown in aquaria.

falciculata: *N. indica.*

flexilis (Willd.) Rostk. & W. L. Schmidt. Monoecious; lvs. linear to narrowly lanceolate, margins often slightly inrolled, with 20–40 minute spinules, sheath not auriculate. Shallow, brackish or fresh water, Eur., n. U.S.

graminea Delile. Monoecious, sts. slender, much-branched, to 1½ ft. long; lvs. linear, mostly flat, to 1⅜ in. long, margins with many conspicuous teeth, sheath auriculate; male and female fls. not enclosed in an involucre. Eurasia, Afr., Australia; naturalized in rice fields in Calif.

guadalupensis (K. Spreng.) Magnus [*N. microdon* A. Braun]. COMMON W.-N. Monoecious, sts. threadlike, to 2 ft.; lvs. linear, flat, to 1 in. long, entire or only remotely finely spiny, sheath not auriculate; male fls. enclosed in an involucre, female fls. without an involucre. U.S. to S. Amer.

indica (Willd.) Cham. [*N. falciculata* A. Braun; *N. Kingii* Rendle]. Monoecious, sts. to 16 in.; lvs. linear, to 1¾ in. long, margins conspicuously spiny-toothed, sheath often auriculate; male fls. enclosed in an involucre, female fls. usually without an involucre. Japan, Philippine Is., Malay Arch.

Kingii: *N. indica.*

microdon: *N. guadalupensis.*

minor All. Monoecious, sts. much-branched, to 10 in. long; lvs. linear, flat, to ¾ in. long, margins coarsely dentate, with conspicuous, spiny teeth, sheath auriculate, spiny; male fls. with or without an involucre. Asia, N. and trop. Afr.

NAMA L. *Hydrophyllaceae.* Not cult. **N. Parryi:** *Turricula Parryi.*

NANANTHUS N. E. Br. *Aizoaceae.* About 9 spp. of dwarf, cespitose, succulent herbs, native to S. Afr., rhizomes fleshy, divided apically into short brs.; lvs. in rosettes, opp., united basally, essentially flat, ascending or spreading, dotted; fls. solitary, nearly sessile, calyx 5-lobed, petals yellow, many, in 2–3 series, stamens many, in a cone, ovary inferior, 7–10-celled, stigmas 7–10; fr. a caps., cell lids reduced or absent, expanding keels broadly winged, placental tubercles lacking.

The plants grow chiefly in summer in a light, dry location, requiring very tall or tubular pots with a sandy, stony, loamy soil, and in winter a relatively cool temperature of about 60° F. See also *Succulents.*

albinotus: *Rabiea albinota.*

aloides (Haw.) Schwant. Lvs. 6–8, crowded, dark green, covered with many prominent, white-tubercled dots, younger lvs. erect, older ones spreading, 2 in. long, the edges slightly roughened toward apex, upper side flat or flatly grooved, obliquely lanceolate or narrowly rhombic in outline, 3-angled toward apex, lower side keeled; fls. 1 in. across, nearly sessile, petals yellow. Cape Prov.

crassipes: *Aloinopsis spathulata.*

Jamesii: a name used in 2 different senses, see *Aloinopsis Jamesii* and *Rabiea Jamesii.*

Malherbei: *Aloinopsis Malherbei.*

Orpenii: *Aloinopsis Orpenii.*

Peersii: *Aloinopsis Peersii.*

Pole-Evansii N. E. Br. Lvs. 4–6, smooth, reddish, glaucous, powdery white, dark-dotted, ascending, 1⅛ in. long, ⅜ in. across, upper side flat, oblong, upper ⅓ long-triangular in outline, mucronate, lower side boat-shaped and obliquely keeled, edges and keel reddish; fls. 1 in. across, petals golden-yellow with a red midrib. Cape Prov.

rubrolineatus: *Aloinopsis rubrolineata.*

Schooneesii: *Aloinopsis Schooneesii.*

Triebneri: a listed name of no botanical standing.

Villetii: *Aloinopsis Villetii.*

vittatus (N. E. Br.) Schwant. Lvs. 6–8, dull green, rough from many prominent tubercled dots, spreading, of various lengths in each pair, to 1¼ in. long and ⅜ in. wide, obliquely lanceolate in outline above, acute, shortly mucronate, semicylindrical, with an expanded oblique keel toward apex; fls. to 1 in. across, on pedicels to 1¼ in. long, opening in the afternoon, petals light yellow with a fine red central line. Orange Free State.

NANDINA Thunb. *Berberidaceae.* One sp., an evergreen shrub native from India to e. Asia; lvs. 2–3-pinnate; fls. small, in panicles to 1 ft. long, perianth in several series, mostly 3-merous, sepals merging with the petals; fr. a berry.

Thrives in shady or sunny locations, but should be well watered; attains full growth only in Zone 7, but is root-hardy in Zone 6 in protected places. Propagated by seeds.

domestica Thunb. HEAVENLY BAMBOO, SACRED B. To 8 ft.; lvs. turning red in fall, lfts. narrow, to 2 in. long; fls. white; berries bright red, ¼ in. across. Cv. **'Alba'.** Berries white.

NANNORRHOPS H. Wendl. *Palmae.* Four spp. of small, bushy, cespitose or stoloniferous, branching, unarmed palms with bisexual fls., native from n. India to s. Arabia; lvs. shortly costapalmate, arched, petiole smooth, lacking well-defined hastula, segms. 2-cleft; infls. compound, terminating the st. on main or lateral brs. or arising from a rhizome, composed of several to many lateral infls. in axils of reduced lvs. or bracts; fls. in groups of 2–7, each group and fl. subtended by a short tubular bractlet or bracteole, calyx 3-lobed, petals 3, stamens 6, carpels 3, united by their inner surfaces; fr. usually 1-seeded, globose or oblong-ellipsoid, with basal stigmatic residue, seed globose or ovoid, endosperm homogeneous.

Infrequently cultivated but includes one of the hardiest of exotic palms. For culture see *Palms.*

Ritchiana (Griff.) Aitch. [*Chamaerops Ritchiana* Griff.]. MAZARI PALM. Sts. clustered, to 10 ft. or more, often branched; lvs. glaucous, becoming green in age, petiole 3 ft. long or more, segms. 8–20 or more, to 3 ft. long or more, deeply 2-cleft to middle or lower and becoming pendulous; infl. terminating st.; fls. white with dark purple anthers and pink carpels; fr. orange when ripe, ¾ in. in diam. In arid and cold regions, Afghanistan, nw. India, Iran. Slow-growing, cult. outside in s. Calif. and Fla., and probably adapted for more northerly plantings. Zone 8b.

NAPAEA L. GLADE MALLOW. *Malvaceae.* One sp., a dioecious, coarse, per. herb in the e.-cent. U.S.; lvs. large, palmately parted; fls. in cymose panicles, involucral bracts 0, petals white, stamens united in a tubular column, male fls. with 15–20 anthers at the apex of the staminal column, female fls. with style brs. enclosed and subtended by ring of sterile anthers, style brs. stigmatic on inner edge, as many as the mericarps; fr. a schizocarp, mericarps 10, scarcely dehiscent, apiculate, 1-seeded.

Propagated by seeds.

dioica L. [*Sida dioica* (L.) Cav.]. Erect, 4–8 ft.; lvs. 5-, 7-, 9-, or 11-lobed or -parted, segms. serrate to lacerate or pinnatifid, lower lvs. often 1–2 ft. long and wide; calyx about ¼ in. long, petals of male fls. about ½ in. long, those of female fls. slightly smaller. Early summer. Ohio, w. to Ill. and Minn.

NAPOLEONA Beauvois. *Barringtoniaceae.* About 15 spp. of evergreen trees and shrubs in W. Trop. Afr.; lvs. simple, usually entire; fls. borne in lf. axils or sometimes on trunk or brs.; calyx lobes 5, petals 0, stamens many, inserted in 4 whorls on a glandular disc, those of the outer 3 whorls sterile and more or less united to form a showy pseudocorolla and corona, those of the innermost whorl fertile or sterile; fr. a berry. Of uncertain family affiliation, sometimes placed in the Lecythidaceae, or in a separate family, the Napoleonaceae Beauvois.

Occasionally grown in tropical gardens and in Zone 10b in Fla.

cereifera: a listed name of no botanical standing.

imperialis Beauvois. Shrub or small tree, to 10 ft.; lvs. elliptic-oblong, abruptly acuminate, to 7 in. long; fls. sessile in the lf. axils, pseudocorolla blue, 1½ in. across, corona rose, fertile stamens 5. Nigeria.

NARCISSUS L. DAFFODIL. *Amaryllidaceae.* About 26 spp. of spring- or autumn-flowering herbs with tunicate bulbs, native to Eur. and N. Afr.; lvs. basal; fls. 1 or several on a scape, subtended by a 1-valved spathe, perianth yellow or white, generally salverform, with a long and tubular or short and ringlike corona (crown) separate from the filaments, ovary inferior, ovules many; fr. a caps., seeds subglobose, black.

Narcissus may be divided into three subgenera:

Subgenus **Ajax** Spach. Spathes 1-fld.; fls. regular, stamens straight, equal, anthers essentially basifixed, surrounding the style, corona nearly as long as perianth; includes *N. Pseudonarcissus* and its close allies, *N. minor, N. asturiensis,* and *N. cyclamineus.*

Subgenus **Corbularia** (Salisb.) Pax. Spathe 1-fld.; fls. irregular, stamens declinate, corona as long as perianth tube; includes *N. Bulbocodium, N. cantabricus, N. Romieuxii,* and their subspp. and vars.

Subgenus **Narcissus.** Spathe 1- to several-fld.; fls. regular, stamens straight, unequal, in 2 ranks, anthers dorsifixed, corona varying from well developed to rudimentary; includes the remaining spp. This subgenus comprises 6 sections:

Section **Jonquilleae** DC. Includes *N. rupicola, N. Watieri, N. scaberulus, N. juncifolius, N. Jonquilla, N. viridiflorus.*

Section **Ganymedes** (Salisb.) Schult. Includes *N. triandrus* and its vars.

Section **Serotini** Parl. Includes only *N. serotinus.*

Section **Hermione** (Salisb.) K. Spreng. Includes *N. Tazetta* and *N. Broussonetii.*

Section **Narcissus** [Section Helena (Haw.) Asch. & Graebn.]. Includes *N. poeticus* and its vars.

Section ×**Queltia** (Salisb.) K. Spreng. Includes *N.* × *incomparabilis* [*N. poeticus* × *N. Pseudonarcissus*].

The narcissi hybridize in nature and have long been the subject of horticultural hybridization and selection. Named cultivars run to many hundreds; only the most common or well-marked crosses are listed here. Persons interested in named cultivars are referred to *The Classified List of Daffodil Names* published by the Royal Horticultural Society of London, and supplementary lists in *The Daffodil and Tulip Year Book.*

Effective Jan. 1, 1950, a revised system for the horticultural classification of daffodils was adopted by the Royal Horticultural Society (*Daffodil and Tulip Year Book* 1948, pp. 101–103) in which the LEEDSII, BARRII, and INCOMPARABILIS groups were abandoned and incorporated into categories based on flower proportions, with further subdivision based on color combinations. Eleven divisions are now recognized as follows, all except no. 10 of garden origin:

1. TRUMPET NARCISSI. Fl. 1, corona as long as segms. or longer.
2. LARGE-CUPPED NARCISSI. Fl. 1, corona ⅓ to nearly as long as segms.; of *N.* × *incomparabilis* origin.
3. SMALL-CUPPED NARCISSI. Fl. 1, corona less than ⅓ as long as segms.; of *N.* × *incomparabilis* origin.
4. DOUBLE NARCISSI.
5. TRIANDRUS NARCISSI. Characteristics of *N. triandrus* clearly evident.
6. CYCLAMINEUS NARCISSI. Characteristics of *N. cyclamineus* clearly evident.
7. JONQUILLA NARCISSI. Characteristics of any of the *N. Jonquilla* group (Section *Jonquilleae*) clearly evident.
8. TAZETTA NARCISSI. Characteristics of any of the *N. Tazetta* group (Section *Hermione*) clearly evident.
9. POETICUS NARCISSI. Characteristics of the *N. poeticus* group (Section *Narcissus*) clearly evident.
10. SPECIES AND WILD FORMS AND [WILD] HYBRIDS.
11. MISCELLANEOUS NARCISSI not referable to other groups.

Narcissi are hardy outdoors and are frequently naturalized. They are also forced in the greenhouse for winter and spring bloom. Bulbs should be planted in Sept. or Oct. in good loamy soil and will bloom the following spring if of flowering size. They do better if lifted every few years, separated, and the poor bulbs discarded. A few kinds, as *N. Tazetta,* may be grown in the house without soil, merely putting the bulbs in a bowl of water and propping them up with stones.

asturiensis (Jord.) Pugsl. To 5 in.; lvs. 2–3, erect-spreading, to 4 in. long, glaucous; scape nearly cylindrical, spathe greenish; fls. solitary, to 1 in. long, nearly uniform soft yellow, corona longer than perianth tube, longer than perianth segms., constricted in center, expanded apically, filaments inserted near base of tube. Spain, cent. Portugal. Most garden material labelled *N. minumus* belong here.

×**Barrii** Hort. ex Burb. [*N.* × *Burbidgei* Hort. ex Bak.]: *N.* × *incomparabilis* × *N. poeticus.* A hybrid group intermediate between the parents and very variable. Fls. solitary, yellow or bicolored, corona crenulate, about ⅓ as long as perianth segms. or less. Cv. 'Conspicuus' is said to have a short, broad corona, edged with red. The name BARRII was formerly applied to a hort. division including all plants with yellow, or white-and-yellow fls., the corona sometimes red or red-stained and less than ⅓ as long as perianth segms. These forms are now referred to hort. division no. 3, the small-cupped narcissi. The name *N.* × *Barrii* has generally been used for forms more nearly resembling *N.* × *incomparabilis,* and *N.* × *Burbidgei* for those nearer *N. poeticus.*

bicolor L. Similar to *N. pseudonarcissus;* fls. large, nearly erect, usually bicolored, perianth segms. broad, corona somewhat expanded and obscurely lobed. Pyrenees?

×**biflorus:** *N.* × *medioluteus.*

borealis: a listed name of no botanical standing.

Broussonetii Lag. To 1 ft.; lvs. linear, as long as scape; fls. white, to 1¾ in. across, corona very short or seemingly absent, segms. oblong-lanceolate, acutish. Morocco. Perhaps not hardy north.

Bulbocodium L. HOOP-PETTICOAT D., PETTICOAT D. Outer bulb scales whitish to maroon; lvs. to 15 in. long, very slender, nearly cylindrical, longer than scapes; fls. bright yellow, nearly odorless, solitary, somewhat irregular, pedicels more or less prominent, perianth segms. very narrow, corona to 1 in. long, longer than segms., stamens more than half as long as corona, declinate. Portugal, Spain, s. France. Var. **citrinus** Bak. Fls. lemon-yellow, to 2 in. long. Var. **conspicuus** (Haw.)

Burb. Fls. larger, style exserted. Cv. 'Tenuifolius' [*N. tenuifolius* Salisb.]. Early-flowering; lvs. slender, erect; corona 6-lobed. Var. **foliosus:** *N. cantabricus* var. *foliosus.* Var. **Graellsii** (Webb) Bak. Fls. whitish or primrose-yellow. Var. **monophyllus:** *N. cantabricus* subsp. *monophyllus.* Subsp. **Romieuxii:** *N. Romieuxii.*

×**Burbidgei:** *N.* × *Barrii.*

calathinus: *N.* × *odorus,* but material named *N. calathinus* may be *N. triandrus* var. *Loiseleurii.*

Campernellii: *N.* × *odorus.*

canaliculatus: *N. Tazetta.*

cantabricus DC. Differs from *N. Bulbocodium* in outer bulb scales deep maroon to nearly black, and fls. subsessile, white, very fragrant, corona clearly flaring apically. S. Spain, nw. Afr. Subsp. **cantabricus.** The typical subsp.; includes vars. *cantabricus* and *foliosus.* Var. **cantabricus** [*N. Clusii* Dunal]. Lvs. spreading. Var. **foliosus** (Maire) A. Fernand. [*N. Bulbocodium* var. *foliosus* (Maire) Maire]. Lvs. 3–8, erect, incurved; fls. to 2³⁄₁₆ in. long. Subsp. **monophyllus** (Durieu) A. Fernand. [*N. Bulbocodium* var. *monophyllus* (Durieu) Bak.]. Usually with only 1 lf. per bulb.

cernuus: *N. triandrus* var., but much garden material known as *N. cernuus* is *N. moschatus.*

Clusii: *N. cantabricus* subsp. *cantabricus.*

concolor: *N. triandrus* var.

cyclamineus DC. ex Redouté. To 12 in.; lvs. bright green, narrowly linear, keeled, to ³⁄₁₆ in. wide; fls. solitary, to 1¾ in. long, deep yellow, drooping or declining, perianth tube very short, segms. reflexed, corona wavy-edged, as long as segms., stamens half as long as corona, in 1 series, anthers basifixed, surrounding style. Spain, Portugal. Cv. 'Major' is listed.

festinus: a listed name of no botanical standing; see *N. Pseudonarcissus* var.

Gayi (Hénon) Pugsl. Similar to *N. Pseudonarcissus* and perhaps only a subsp. of it, with fls. larger, yellow, pedicels neither deflexed nor very short, perianth tube short, segms. narrow, corona large, caps. 3-angled. Origin unknown.

giganteus: a listed name of no botanical standing, applied to large-fld. kinds of *N.* × *incomparabilis.*

×**gracilis** Sab.: *N. Jonquilla* × *N. poeticus.* To 1 ft.; lvs. grasslike, ³⁄₁₆ in. wide or less; fls. light lemon-yellow, corona usually deeper colored, perianth segms. oblong, acute, imbricate. Parentage believed by some to be *N. Jonquilla* × *N. Tazetta.* S. France.

hispanicus Gouan. To 2 ft.; lvs. erect, flat and more or less spirally twisted, to ½ in. wide, glaucous; pedicel erect but curved above, 1 in. long or more; fls. to 2 in. long or more, deep golden-yellow, perianth tube ¾ in. long, segms. spirally twisted, corona as long as segms., abruptly dilated at the widely spreading, ruffled margin, filaments inserted ⅛ in. above base of tube. Spain. Much hort. material grown as *N. maximus* belongs here.

×**incomparabilis** Mill. [*N.* × *Leedsii* Hort.; *N.* × *Nelsonii* Hort. ex Bak.]: *N. poeticus* × *N. Pseudonarcissus.* Lvs. 1 ft. long, ¼–½ in. wide, somewhat glaucous; fls. solitary, yellow, perianth tube ¾ in. long, corona wavy-edged, about half as long as segms. Spain to Tyrol. Var. **albus** (Haw.) Bak. Segms. white. There are also double-fld. cvs. of this hybrid. *N.* × *Leedsii* and *N.* × *Nelsonii* are variants of this parentage; the name LEEDSII was once applied to a hort. division which included plants with white perianth and the corona white, cream, or pale citron, sometimes tinged with pink or apricot, and less than ⅓ to nearly as long as the perianth segms. These forms are now placed in hort. divisions 2 and 3.

×**Johnstonii** (Bak.) Pugsl.: *N. Pseudonarcissus* × *N. triandrus* var. *cernuus.* To 10 in.; lvs. erect, obscurely keeled, to ½ in. wide, slightly glaucous; fls. solitary or rarely in pairs, to 2 in. long, horizontal or nodding, pale lemon-yellow, perianth tube narrow, to ¾ in. long, segms. spreading-reflexed, corona straight, about as long as segms., stamens in 1 series, anthers basifixed, surrounding style. Portugal.

Jonquilla L. JONQUIL. Lvs. to 1½ ft. long, narrow, rushlike; fls. 2–6, yellow, fragrant, perianth tube 1 in. long, corona wavy-edged, much less than half as long as segms. S. Eur., Algeria. Var. **minor** (Haw.) Bak. Dwarf, lvs. slender, fls. ½ in. in diam. S. Spain, Algeria. Cvs. 'Citrinus', 'Simplex', and 'Varicolor' are listed.

juncifolius Lag. Lvs. to 6 in. long, narrow, cylindrical, rushlike; fls. 1–4, bright yellow, perianth tube ½ in. long, segms. imbricate, to ½ in. long, corona darker yellow, wavy-edged, about half as long as segms. S. France, Spain. Subsp. **rupicola:** *N. rupicola.*

Leedsii: *N.* × *incomparabilis.*

lobularis: *N. obvallaris,* but some material grown as *N. lobularis* is *N. nanus.*

maximus: *N. obvallaris* var., but much material grown as *N. maximus* is *N. hispanicus.*

×**medioluteus** Mill. [*N.* × *biflorus* Curtis; *N.* × *poetaz* Hort. ex L. H. Bailey]: *N. poeticus* × *N. Tazatta.* PRIMROSE PEERLESS N., POETAZ N. Lvs. to 2 ft. long and ½ in. wide; fls. usually 2, white, perianth tube 1 in. long, corona pale yellow, wavy-edged, several times shorter than segms. in the naturally occurring hybrid and in old garden plants as cv. 'Primrose Peerless', but 2–6, fragrant, white to yellow with yellow to orange cup in the Poetaz Group of cvs.

minimus: *N. minor* var., but most garden material labelled *N. minimus* is *N. asturiensis.*

minor L. To 6 in.; lvs. suberect-spreading, to 5 in. long, ¼ in. wide, glaucous; fl. solitary, small, horizontal or nodding, to 1⅜ in. long, soft yellow, perianth tube ½ in. long, segms. ovate-lanceolate, spreading, corona lobed, deep-yellow, nearly as long as segms.; caps. nearly circular in cross section. Eur. Var. **minimus** (Haw.) Pugsl. [*N. minimus* Haw.]. More dwarf; lvs. spreading, slender; scape nodding, fls. very small, to 1³⁄₁₆ in. long; probably no longer cult.

monophyllus: *N. cantabricus* subsp.

monspieliensis: a listed name of no botanical standing, perhaps for a dwarf form of *N. Tazetta.*

moschatus L. Similar to *N. Pseudonarcissus,* fls. nodding, of moderate size, sulphur-white, with slightly dilated and lobed corona. Pyrenees? Most garden material known as *N. cernuus* is this sp.

nanus Spach. Differs from *N. minor* in stiffer, more erect growth, broader, more obtuse lvs., and paler fls. with broader perianth segms. and corona. Some material grown as *N. lobularis* belongs here.

×**Nelsonii:** *N.* × *incomparabilis.*

obvallaris Salisb. [*N. lobularis* (Haw.) Schult.f.]. Similar to *N. Pseudonarcissus,* but the pedicels not deflexed or short, fls. moderate-sized, perianth tube broad, generally short, segms. broad, imbricate, corona broad, variously lobed, spreading apically. England? Var. **maximus** (Haw.) Pugsl. [*N. maximus* (Haw.) D. Don]. Fls. larger, to 2 in. long.

×**odorus** L. [*N. calathinus* L.; *N. Campernellii* Hort. ex Haw.]: *N. Jonquilla* × *N. Pseudonarcissus.* CAMPERNELLE JONQUIL. Lvs. about 1 ft. long, very narrow; fls. 2–4, bright yellow, fragrant, perianth tube ¾ in. long, segms. ¾–1¼ in. long, imbricate only at base, corona crenately lobed, about half as long as segms. France, Spain, and eastward. Cv. 'Rugulosus' [*N. rugulosus* (Haw.) Link]. Segms. shorter, imbricate.

orientalis: *N. Tazetta* var.

ornatus: *N. poeticus,* but most material grown as *N. ornatus* is *N. poeticus* var. *ornatus.*

pallidiflorus Pugsl. [*N. pallidus* var. *praecox* Hort.]. Similar to *N. Pseudonarcissus;* fls. moderate-sized, straw-yellow, perianth tube long, corona generally expanded and distinctly lobed. Pyrenees.

pallidus var. **praecox:** *N. pallidiflorus.*

×**poetaz:** *N.* × *medioluteus.*

poeticus L. [*N. ornatus* Haw.]. POET'S N., PHEASANT'S-EYE. LVS. TO 1½ ft. long and ¼ in. wide; fls. mostly solitary, white, very fragrant, perianth tube 1 in. long, corona very short, with wavy red edge, much shorter than segms. France to Greece. Fls. used in making perfume. Var. **ornatus** Hort. Barr. Early-flowering, corona yellow, edged with red. Var. **radiiflorus** (Salisb.) Bak. ex Burb. [*N. radiiflorus* Salisb.]. Lvs. and segms. narrower, corona less flaring. Var. **recurvus** (Haw.) Bak. ex Burb. [*N. recurvus* Haw.]. Lvs. and segms. recurved.

polyanthos: *N. Tazetta* var.

Pseudonarcissus L. DAFFODIL, TRUMPET N. Lvs. to 15 in. long and ¾ in. wide; fls. solitary, horizontal or deflexed, sulphur-yellow with greenish perianth tube to ⅞ in. long, corona frilled, deep yellow, about length of segms. or to 2 in. long, sometimes double. Eur. Var. **festinus** (Jord.) Pugsl. Dwarf, lvs. narrow, glaucous; fls. horizontal, pedicels longer, corona deep yellow, abruptly dilated, spreading and scalloped apically. France. The following spp. have been considered by one authority to be no more than subspp. of *N. Pseudonarcissus: N. bicolor, N. Gayi, N. moschatus, N. obvallaris, N. pallidiflorus.*

pulchellus: *N. triandrus* var.

pumilus Salisb. Similar to *N. minor* and probably opnly a var. of it, larger in all parts, segms. very narrow, corona frilled. Portugal.

radiiflorus: *N. poeticus* var.

recurvus: *N. poeticus* var.

Romieuxii Br.-Bl. & Maire [*N. Bulbocodium* subsp. *Romieuxii* (Br.-Bl. & Maire) Emberger & Maire]. A tetraploid sp., probably derived from *N. Bulbocodium* and *N. cantabricus* and resembling them; spathe whitish; fls. sulphur-yellow, perianth segms. linear, corona nearly as long as segms. N. Afr.

rugulosus: *N. odorus* cv.

rupicola Dufour. [*N. juncifolius* subsp. *rupicola* (Dufour.) Bak.]. Similar to *N. juncifolius*, but pedicels greatly reduced or absent, and perianth tube about ¾ in. long. Spain, Portugal.

scaberulus Henriq. To 4 in.; lvs. 2, linear, arching to prostrate, channelled; fls. deep orange-yellow, perianth tube narrowly cylindrical, to 1 in. long, segms. obovate, acute, somewhat reflexed. Portugal. Requires much moisture at blossoming time, but little or none for remainder of season.

serotinus L. To 10 in.; lvs. narrowly linear, developing after fls.; fls. 1–2, perianth tube greenish-white, to ½ in. long, segms. small, white, corona less than half as long as segms. Autumn. Spain to Palestine. Perhaps not hardy north.

Tazetta L. [*N. canaliculatus* Guss.]. POLYANTHUS N. Lvs. to 1½ ft. long and ¾ in. wide; fls. usually 4–8, white, fragrant, perianth tube to 1 in. long, segms. obovate, corona light yellow, much shorter than segms. Medit. Cv. **'Paper-white'**. PAPER-WHITE N. Fls. pure white. Can be brought into flower before Christmas. Var. **orientalis** (L.) Hort. [*N. orientalis* L.]. CHINESE SACRED LILY. Perianth segms. sulphur-yellow, corona dark yellow, about ⅓ as long as segms.; probably a hybrid of *N.* ×*incompararabilis* × *N. Tazetta*. Var. **polyanthos** (Loisel.) Bak. ex Burb. [*N. polyanthos* Loisel.]. Fls. in umbels of 12–20, perianth segms. ovate, shorter than tube. S. France. The various kinds of *N. Tazetta* are commonly grown for winter bloom, often in water and gravel.

tenuifolius: *N. Bulbocodium* cv.

×**tenuior** Curt. Perhaps of same parentage as *N.* ×*gracilis;* differs from that hybrid in more slender habit and paler fls.

triandrus L. ANGEL'S-TEARS. Lvs. about 1 ft. long, narrow, rushlike; fls. 1–6, pure white to pale yellow, perianth tube to ¾ in. long, corona entire, cuplike, white or yellow, half as long as segms. or more. Spain, Portugal. Var. **triandrus** [var. *albus* (Haw.) Bak.]. The typical var.; fls. pure white. Var. **albus:** var. *triandrus*. Var. **cernuus** (Salisb.) Bak. ex Burb. [*N. cernuus* Salisb.]. Fls. larger, segms. pale yellow, corona golden-yellow. Var. **concolor** (Haw.) Bak. [*N. concolor* (Haw.) Link]. Fls. pale yellow. Var. **Loiseleurii** Rouy [*N. calathinus* of some auth.]. Fls. pale yellow, corona nearly as long as segms. Var. **pulchellus** (Salisb.) Bak. [*N. pulchellus* Salisb.]. Fls. yellow, corona white.

viridiflorus Schousb. To 1½ ft.; lvs. slender, cylindrical, to 1 ft. long; fls. on slender, erect scape, usually 2–4, green, nodding, to 1 in. long, perianth segms. linear-lanceolate, reflexed. Morocco.

Watieri Maire. To 6 in.; lvs. narrowly linear, about ⅛ in. wide, obtuse; fl. solitary, perianth tube to ½ in. long, greenish-white, segms. pure white or occasionally flushed pink, to 1 in. across. Morocco. Does best in sun in not too dry a soil.

NARDOSTACHYS DC. *Valerianaceae.* Three spp. of erect, per. herbs, with woody rhizomes and fragrant roots, native to the Himalayas and China; lvs. opp., simple, mostly basal; fls. red to purplish, in headlike cymes, calyx 5-lobed, enlarging in fr., corolla 5-lobed, stamens 4, ovary inferior, 3-celled; fr. with 2 sterile and 1 fertile cell, 1-seeded, crowned by persistent calyx.

Jatamansi (D. Don) DC. Plant cespitose, covered with black, shredded remains of old petioles at base, sts. to 10 in.; lvs. elliptic-lanceolate to spatulate, 2–4 in. long; fls. rose-purple, ¼ in. across. Himalayas. Yields an essential oil.

NARTHECIUM Huds. BOG ASPHODEL. *Liliaceae.* About 6 spp. of rhizomatous, per. herbs, native to Eur., Asia, and N. Amer.; lvs. mostly basal, grasslike, equitant; fls. greenish-yellow, in simple terminal racemes, perianth segms. 6, separate, persistent, stamens 6, filaments white-woolly; fr. a loculicidal, many-seeded caps., seeds with a bristlelike appendage at each end.

americanum Ker-Gawl. YELLOW ASPHODEL. To 1½ ft.; lvs. linear, to 8 in. long and ⅛ in. wide; fls. ¼ in. long, on pedicels ¼ in. long, in dense racemes to 2 in. long, perianth segms. linear, anthers yellow. Swamps, N.J. and Del. to S.C.

asiaticum Maxim. To 2 ft.; lvs. linear, to 10 in. long and ⅜ in. wide; fls. ⅜ in. long, on pedicels to ⅝ in. long, in racemes to 4¾ in. long, perianth segms. linear, anthers pale yellow. Wet places, Japan.

californicum Bak. To 20 in.; lvs. linear, to 1 ft. long and ¼ in. wide; fls. ⅜ in. long, on pedicels to ⅝ in. long, in racemes to 6 in. long, perianth segms. linear-lanceolate, anthers red. Marshes, sw. Ore to cent. Calif.

NASTURTIUM R. Br. WATERCRESS. *Cruciferae.* Six spp. of succulent, essentially glabrous per. herbs of running water or wet soils, of temp. regions; lvs. pinnate to pinnatisect; petals white, about twice as long as calyx; fr. a plump, linear-cylindrical silique, the valves convex, without nerves, seeds in 1 or 2 rows in each cell. Nasturtium as a common name is applied to *Tropaeolum.*

One species almost worldwide from cultivation for its pungent herbage used in salads.

Armoracia: *Armoracia rusticana.*

microphyllum Boenn. ex Rchb. [*Rorippa microphylla* (Boenn. ex Rchb.) Hyl.]. Resembles *N. officinale*, but fls. slightly larger, siliques ½–1 in. long, each cell usually with 1 row of seeds, seed coat with as many as 150 reticulations. W. Eur.; introd. as a salad plant and naturalized over most of n. U.S.

officinale R. Br. [*Rorippa Nasturtium-aquaticum* (L.) Hayek]. WATERCRESS. Aquatic per., sts. floating or ascending, rooting freely at nodes; juvenile lvs. often ovate or cordate and entire, adult lvs. pinnate, lfts. 3–11, round or broadly elliptic, essentially entire, somewhat fleshy; fls. white; siliques less than ½ in. long, each cell with 2 rows of seeds, seed coat with about 35 reticulations on each side. Eur.; introd. as a salad plant and naturalized over most of the U.S. Hybridizes with *N. microphyllum*, the hybrid also used as a salad plant, and reproducing vegetatively.

NAUCLEA L. [*Sarcocephalus* Afzel. ex Sab.]. *Rubiaceae.* About 25–35 spp. of scandent shrubs or trees, native to trop. Afr., Asia, Malay Pen., to Australia, and Polynesia; lvs. opp., somewhat leathery, stipules interpetiolar, deciduous; fls. crowded on common globose receptacles forming compact heads, calyx tubes cohering, corolla narrowly funnelform; fr. a fleshy, globose syncarp.

latifolia Sm. [*N. esculenta* (Afzel. ex Sab.) Merrill; *Sarcocephalus esculenta* Afzel. ex Sab.]. Straggling shrub or small tree, to 25 ft.; lvs. elliptic, to 8 in. long; fl. heads about 2 in. across; fls. white, ½ in. long, fragrant; fr. reddish, to 3½ in. across. Trop. Afr. The fr. is edible, and has an applelike flavor.

esculenta: *N. latifolia.*

NAUMBERGIA: *LYSIMACHIA.*

NAUTILOCALYX Linden ex Hanst. *Gesneriaceae.* More than 12 spp. of erect or decumbent, per. herbs in trop. Amer.; lvs. opp., usually elongate, sometimes wedge-shaped and winged at base; fls. solitary, clustered, or several on short peduncles in lf. axils, often subtended by 2 or more leafy bracts, calyx irregular, lobes unequal, thin, corolla more or less tubular, oblique in the calyx, short-spurred, somewhat flattened top and bottom, lobes nearly regular, large, stamens 4, filaments united to one another and to the narrowed base of the corolla tube, anthers united in pairs by their tips, disc of 1 gland at back of ovary or of 2 opp. glands, ovary superior; fr. a 2-valved caps.

For cultivation see *Gesneriaceae.*

bullatus (Lem.) T. Sprague [*N. tessellatus* Hort.; *Episcia tessellata* Hort. Linden ex Lem.]. To 2 ft.; lvs. elliptic, to 9 in. long, 3½ in. wide, tapering to winged base, dark green to olive-green and embossed above, rosy and with 10–12 pairs of prominent lateral veins beneath; fls. 8–10 on very short pedicels in an axillary cluster subtended by 2 green bracts, calyx pale green, lobes 1 in. long, toothed, corolla 1⅜ in. long, pale yellow, densely hairy outside, lobes about ½ in. long. Peru.

Forgetii (T. Sprague) T. Sprague. Similar to *N. Lynchii*, but petioles to 2 in. long, hairy, not winged, lf. blades bright green, with red pattern about veins, calyx lobes brownish or reddish. Peru.

Lynchii (Hook.f.) T. Sprague [*Alloplectus Lynchii* Hook.f.]. To 2 ft.; lvs. elliptic-lanceolate, toothed, narrowed to short, thick petiole ½ in. long or less, surface glabrous except for 6–8 pairs of sunken hairy veins, glossy and dark green or red-purple above, red or red-purple beneath; fls. 2–3 in axils, bracts lanceolate, calyx lobes erect, ovate, to 1 in. long, ½ in. wide, reddish, corolla 1½ in. long, pale yellow, reddish-hairy outside, with minute purple dots inside, lobes ⅜ in. long, red-hairy outside. Colombia?

melittifolius (L.) Wiehl. [*Episcia melittifolia* (L.) Mart.]. Sts. decumbent, rooting at nodes, succulent; lvs. ovate, to 10 in. long, 4 in. wide, coarsely crenate, green, sparsely appressed-hairy above, puberulent beneath; fls. many, on long pedicels, from short peduncles in axils, calyx lobes narrowly ovate, ⁵⁄₁₆ in. long, puberulent, corolla to ¾ in. long, cerise, hairy, lobes ¼ in. long. Lesser Antilles.

picturatus Skog. Compact, sts. to 8 in.; lvs. elliptic, to 5¼ in. long, 2 in. wide, finely toothed, rugose, dark green with pale green veins and softly hairy above, red-flushed and with pale veins and softly hairy beneath; fls. clustered in axils, short-pedicelled, bracts obovate, small, calyx lobes to ⅝ in. long, green, softly hairy, corolla 1¼ in. long, white, with purple lines in tube, hairy outside, lobes ⅜ in. long. Peru.

tessellatus: a listed name of no botanical standing for *N. bullatus.*

villosus (Kunth & Bouché) T. Sprague. To 2 ft., densely villous; lvs. long-petioled, elliptic or ovate, to 7 in. long, 4½ in. wide, crenate, green; fls. 1 to several in axils, on villous pedicels, calyx lobes ovate-lanceolate to ovate, to ¾ in. long, green or red-veined, villous, corolla white, hairy, tube 1½ in. long, purple-veined inside, lobes to ⅜ in. long. Venezuela, Guyana.

NAVARRETIA Ruiz & Pav. *Polemoniaceae.* Thirty spp. of ann. herbs, native to w. N. Amer., 1 sp. to Argentina and Chile; sts. rigid, variously hairy, but never cobwebby-woolly; lvs. alt., entire to toothed, lobed or parted, spine-tipped; fls. pink, violet, blue, yellow, or white, in spiny, bracted heads, calyx 4–5-parted, lobes unequal, corolla funnelform or salver-form, stamens 4 or 5, equally or unequally inserted; fr. a caps.

Seeds are sown where plants are to grow, in sunny open places.

mellita Greene. Glandular, erect ann., to 8 in.; lvs. pinnately dissected; fls. blue, throat of corolla with purple veins. Spring to summer. Calif.

NEANTHE: a generic name of no botanical standing. **N. bella:** a listed name of no botanical standing for *Chamaedorea elegans.*

NECTARINE. The nectarine is a smooth-skinned peach, the fruit of a botanical variety (var. *nucipersica*) of *Prunus Persica.* Usually nectarines are smaller than peaches, of a sweeter, richer quality, and have a distinct aroma, but there are no essential differences. The trees are the same. One may originate from the other, reciprocally, by seed and by bud variation. Cultural requirements and propagation are the same. Where space is limited, top-worked dwarf trees are sometimes offered in which a nectarine, peach, and almond are available on a single plant. Nectarines are more susceptible than peaches to plum curculio and brown rot, and therefore need a thorough spray program. Nectarines are most frequently grown in the Pacific Coast states, California in particular, and are only infrequently planted in the eastern United States. There are clingstone and freestone, white- and yellow-fleshed cultivars. In the West, cultivars are available which ripen from the first week of June through the first of September. Among them are 'Early Flame', 'Fantasia', 'Flavorop', 'Grandeur', 'Independence', 'John Rivers', 'Late Le Grand', 'Le Grand', 'Red Grand', 'Stanwick', 'Star Grand', 'Sun Grand', and 'Sunrise'. 'Arm King', 'Panamount', 'Pioneer', and 'Silver Lode' do best where winter climates are mild. Good cultivars for the East are 'Cherokee', 'Lexington', 'Morton', 'Nectarcrest', and 'Pocahontas'.

NECTAROSCORDUM Lindl. *Amaryllidaceae.* Two or 3 spp. of bulbous herbs, native to s. Eur., Caucasus, and Asia Minor; bulbs solitary, membranous-coated, without a rhizome; lvs. linear, sheathing the scape for some distance; scape solitary, with a many-fld. umbel subtended by a 1-valved, early-deciduous spathe, pedicels enlarged apically into a disc; perianth segms. separate, 3–7-nerved, stamens 6, separate, united to perianth for short distance at base, ovary half-inferior, somewhat sunken in the pedicel disc, cells with 5 or more ovules; fr. a caps. When bruised, plants emit an unpleasant leeklike odor.

bulgaricum Janka [*Allium bulgaricum* (Janka) Hayek]. Similar to *N. siculum,* but more slender in all parts; scape enclosed at base by a short, tubular, bladeless sheath. Bulgaria. Apparently not cult.; material offered under the name *Allium bulgaricum* has been found to be *A. sphaerocephalum* or other spp. of *Allium.*

siculum (Ucria) Lindl. [*Allium siculum* Ucria]. Lvs. linear-lanceolate, ⅜–2 in. wide; scape to 4 ft., pedicels unequal, pendulous in fl., becoming erect in fr.; perianth segms. dull green, purplish, pink, and buff. Sicily, Italy, Sardinia, Corsica, France.

NEGUNDO: *ACER.* **N. californicum:** *A. Negundo* subsp. **N. fraxinifolium:** *A. negundo.*

NEILLIA D. Don. *Rosaceae.* About 10 spp. of deciduous, spiraealike shrubs, native to China and the Himalayas; lvs. alt., simple, toothed, sometimes lobed, with caducous stipules; fls. pink or white, in terminal racemes or panicles, calyx prominent, sepals 5, almost equalling the petals, stamens 10–30, staminal disc absent, pistils usually 2; frs. dehiscent, not inflated follicles.

Grown as ornamentals, hardy in Zone 4. Propagated by greenwood cuttings under glass and by seeds.

affinis Hemsl. Close to *N. longiracemosa,* to 6 ft., young shoots glabrous; lvs. 2–4 in. long, ovate to lanceolate, cordate; fls. pink, campanulate, in racemes 1–3 in. long. W. China. Zone 6?

longiracemosa Hemsl. To 10 ft., young shoots pubescent, angular; lvs. ovate to elliptic, round to cuneate at base, 2–4 in. long; fls. pink, tubular, in dense racemes 4–6 in. long, calyx pubescent. China. Zone 7?

sinensis D. Oliver. Three to 6 ft., young shoots glabrous, cylindrical; lvs. lanceolate, 2–3 in. long; fls. whitish-pink, in nodding racemes 1–2 in. long, calyx glabrous. China.

thibetica Franch. To 6 ft., young shoots finely pubescent, cylindrical; lvs. ovate, 2–3 in. long, almost cordate; infl. a short, dense raceme, to 3 in. long; calyx finely pubescent. China. Zone 6?

thyrsiflora D. Don. Upright, to 4 ft., young shoots glabrous, angular; lvs. ovate to lanceolate-ovate, 2–4 in. long, 3-lobed, glabrous beneath or pubescent on veins; racemes 1–3 in. long; fls. white, calyx pubescent. Himalayas.

NELUMBIUM: *NELUMBO.* **N. Nelumbo:** *N. nucifera.*

NELUMBO Adans. [*Nelumbium* Juss.]. LOTUS, WATER L., SACRED BEAN. *Nymphaeaceae.* Two spp. of large, aquatic herbs, with wide-spreading, horizontal, thickened rhizomes rooted in mud, native in Asia and N. Amer.; lvs. nearly orbicular, concave, peltate, usually above the water on long petioles; fls. solitary, large, showy, mostly overtopping lvs., sepals 4–5, petals and stamens many, attached at base of an obconical, flat-topped receptacle in which the many 1-ovuled carpels are embedded.

The seeds and thickened rhizomes (lotus root) of nelumbos are edible. Lotuses are hardy north if the rootstocks are not allowed to freeze. Propagation by division of rhizomes, by seeds sown in shallow pans in the garden, or rolled in a ball of clay and dropped into pond; seed coats are hard and seeds may germinate better if scarified.

alba grandiflora: a listed name of no botanical standing for *N. nucifera* cv.

alba striata: a listed name of no botanical standing for *N. nucifera* cv.

flavens: a listed name of no botanical standing for *N. lutea* cv. 'Flavescens'.

flavescens: *N. lutea* cv.

lutea (Willd.) Pers. [*N. pentapetala* (Walt.) Fern.; *Nelumbium luteum* Willd.]. AMERICAN L., WATER CHINQUAPIN, YANQUAPIN, WONKAPIN, YELLOW N., POND NUTS. To 3–7 ft.; lvs. circular, mostly aerial, 1–2 ft. across, entire, bluish-green; fls. pale yellow, to 10 in. in diam. S. Ont. to Fla., Minn. and Tex. Formerly an important Indian food plant. Cv. 'Flavescens' [*N. flavescens* Hort. ex L. H. Bailey]. More floriferous, but fls. smaller, lvs. with red spot in center.

Nelumbo: *N. nucifera.*

nucifera Gaertn. [*N. Nelumbo* (L.) Karst.; *N. speciosa* Willd.; *Nelumbium Nelumbo* (L.) Druce]. SACRED L., EAST INDIAN L. Differs from *N. lutea* in being usually larger, and having lvs. glaucous, 1–3 ft. across, with often sinuate margins, petioles and peduncles rough, and fls. very fragrant, pink, rose, or sometimes white. S. Asia to Australia; sometimes naturalized. Fls. are sacred to Buddhists; much grown in the Orient for the edible rhizomes and seeds. Cvs. are: 'Alba Grandiflora', lvs. deep green, fls. white; 'Alba Striata', sepals white, edged with rose-carmine; 'Pekinensis Rubra', fls. rosy-carmine; 'Pekinensis Rubra Plena', fls. large, very double, rose-carmine; 'Rosea Plena', fls. double, rose-pink, to 12 in. across. The Egyptian lotus is *Nymphaea caerulea,* or sometimes *Nymphaea Lotus.*

pekinensis rubra: a listed name of no botanical standing for *N. nucifera* cv.

pentapetala: *N. lutea.*

rosea plena: a listed name of no botanical standing for *N. nucifera* cv.

speciosa: *N. nucifera.*

NEMASTYLIS Nutt. CELESTIAL LILY. *Iridaceae.* About 25 spp. of bulbous herbs, native to N. and S. Amer.; allied to *Eustylis;* bulb globose to depressed-globose; fls. 2–3 in a spathe, perianth segms. similar, filaments separate or united only at the base, style brs. twice as long as style or more, radiating at right angles to it; caps. obovoid or top-shaped.

Propagated by seeds or offsets. Tender in the North.

acuta (Bartr.) Herb. [*N. geminiflora* Nutt.]. PRAIRIE IRIS. Sts. 6–18 in., simple or forked; lvs. to 1 ft. long; fls. 2–3 in a spathe, to 2½ in. across, blue, opening in the early morning. Spring, late spring. Prairies, La. to Tex.

coelestina: *Sphenostigma coelestina.*

floridana Small. Sts. ½–4½ ft., simple or forked; lvs. very narrow, to 1½ ft. long; fls. to 2 in. across, violet, with a small white eye, open 4–6 o'clock in afternoon in native habitat, earlier in more n. latitudes. Early autumn. Swamps, marshes, ne. Fla.

geminiflora: *N. acuta.*

purpurea: *Eustylis purpurea.*

NEMATANTHUS Schrad. [*Hypocyrta* Mart.]. *Gesneriaceae.* More than 30 spp. of epiphytic shrubs in S. Amer.; lvs. opp., those of a pair equal or unequal; fls. solitary or few in lf. axils, often resupinate, pedicels long or short, calyx deeply 5-parted, corolla oblique or erect in the calyx and usually short-spurred, narrowed above the base, then gradually expanded to a broad, laterally compressed throat, or abruptly expanded upward and then abruptly narrowed to a rounded throat, limb lobed, the lobes nearly equal, small, rounded, stamens 4, borne on the corolla tube, filaments prominently united to one another and to the base of corolla tube, anthers united in a square, disc a gland at back of ovary, ovary superior; fr. a fleshy caps., the valves tardily recurved or spreading to expose the placental mass and seeds.

For cultivation see *Gesneriaceae.*

fissus (Vell.) Skog [*N. Selloanus* (Klotzsch & Hanst. ex Hanst.) H. E. Moore; *Hypocyrta Selloana* Klotzsch & Hanst.]. Sts. stiff; lf. blades oblanceolate, to 3½ in. long, 1 in. wide, densely pale-hairy, dull green; fls. solitary or several in an axil, on pedicels shorter than the lvs., resupinate, calyx lobes very narrowly triangular, green, hairy, corolla scarlet, densely white-hairy, tube cylindrical at base, gradually expanded to a pouch ¼ in. deep, then abruptly narrowed to a throat ⅛ in. wide. Brazil.

fluminensis (Vell.) Fritsch. Similar to *N. longipes,* but fls. yellow, lvs. of a pair unequal, red-flushed beneath. Probably not cult., but *N. Fritschii* has been erroneously grown under this name.

Fritschii Hoehne. Sts. brown-hairy; lvs. of a pair unequal, the larger ovate, to 3 in. long, 1½ in. wide, dark green above, with red splotch beneath, glabrous above, finely hairy beneath; pedicels to 4 in. long, calyx lobes unequal, narrowly elliptic, glandular-toothed or -spotted, pale-hairy, corolla oblique in the calyx, resupinate, to 2 in. long, lavender-pink, tube with rose spots inside, narrow for more than half its length, then rather abruptly expanded into a pouch ½ in. deep, then again narrowed slightly to a broad, oblique throat, lobes ¹⁄₁₆ in. long. Brazil. This sp. was at first misidentified as *N. fluminensis* and has been grown under that name.

gregarius D. L. Denh. [*N. radicans* (Klotzsch & Hanst. ex Hanst.) H. E. Moore, not K. Presl; *Hypocyrta radicans* Klotzsch & Hanst. ex Hanst.]. Glabrous; lvs. opp. or in 3's, equal, elliptic, to 1¼ in. long, ½ in. wide, fleshy; fls. solitary on pedicels shorter than lvs., not resupinate, calyx angular, green flushed with red, lobes oblong-elliptic, to ½ in. long, corolla orange, ¾ in. long, abruptly expanded to pouch ⁵⁄₁₆ in. deep, then narrowed to a throat ⅛ in. wide, lobes small, yellow and red. Brazil.

longipes DC. [*Columnea splendens* Paxt.]. Sts. sparsely hairy; lvs. elliptic to obovate, to 3 in. long, 1 in. wide, not spotted beneath; pedicels to 4 in. long, calyx lobes to 1 in. long, glandular-toothed, long-hairy, corolla to 2¼ in. long, laterally compressed, scarlet, 1 in. deep at the orange-mottled throat. Brazil.

nervosus (Fritsch) H. E. Moore [*Hypocyrta nervosa* Fritsch]. Sts. minutely hairy when young; lvs. of a pair nearly equal, elliptic, to 1¾ in. long, ¾ in. wide, thick, finely hairy; fls. solitary in lf. axils, short-pedicelled, not resupinate, calyx lobes elliptic, to ½ in. long, 3–5-nerved, more or less reddish on nerves and margins, corolla ⅞ in. long, orange-red, minutely hairy, abruptly expanded to a pouch ⁵⁄₁₆ in. wide, then abruptly narrowed to a throat ⅛ in. wide, lobes erect, very short. Brazil.

perianthomegus (Vell.) H. E. Moore [*Hypocyrta perianthomega* (Vell.) Ten.]. Sts. stiff, in cult.; lvs. of a pair unequal, the larger with petiole to 1½ in. long, blade obovate, to 4 in. long, 1¾ in. wide, glossy green and very sparsely hairy above; fls. 2–3 in lf. axils, on pedicels shorter than lvs., resupinate, calyx dark orange, lobes ovate-elliptic, to ¾ in. long, prominently veined, corolla yellow with maroon stripes, hairy, curved and rather abruptly swollen into a pouch ⅜ in. deep, then narrowed to a throat ³⁄₁₆ in. wide. Brazil.

radicans: see *N. gregarius.*

Selloanus: *N. fissus.*

speciosus: a listed name of no botanical standing.

strigillosus (Mart.) H. E. Moore [*Hypocyrta strigillosa* Mart.]. Lvs. of a pair equal, blades elliptic, to 1¾ in. long, ¾ in. wide, minutely and densely hairy, soft; fls. solitary in axils, on pedicels shorter than the lvs., not resupinate, calyx lobes ovate-elliptic, ⁵⁄₁₆ in. long, green, hairy, corolla bright orange, finely hairy, tube abruptly expanded to a pouch ⅜ in. deep, then narrowed to a throat ⅛ in. wide. Brazil.

Wettsteinii (Fritsch) H. E. Moore [*Hypocyrta Wettsteinii* Fritsch]. Lvs. short-petioled, elliptic, to ¾ in. long, ⁵⁄₁₆ in. wide, fleshy, smooth; fls. solitary, on pedicels shorter than the lvs., not resupinate, calyx lobes subulate, ¼ in. long, green, corolla red with yellow limb, tube rather abruptly expanded to a pouch ⅜ in. deep, then narrowed to a throat ³⁄₁₆ in. wide. Brazil.

NEMESIA Venten. *Scrophulariaceae.* About 50 spp. of tender ann. or per. herbs and subshrubs, native mostly to S. Afr., a few to trop. Afr., lvs. opp.; fls. of various colors, in terminal racemes, rarely solitary in lf. axils, calyx 5-lobed, corolla 2-lipped, tube short, with a sac or spur, throat with a palate, stamens 4; fr. a caps.

Nemesias are easily grown as annuals. Seeds are commonly started indoors; plants, blooming from June to Sept., should stand about 6 in. apart in the garden.

compacta: a listed name of no botanical standing for *N. versicolor* cv.

foetens Venten. Somewhat shrubby per., to 2 ft.; lvs. linear or lanceolate, to 1½ in. long, entire or toothed; fls. in racemes, corolla to ⅝ in. long, blue, lavender, pink, or white, crest, spur, and throat yellow. S. Afr.

grandiflora Diels. Erect ann., to 1½ ft. or more; lvs. oblong or linear, to 2 in. long, with a few teeth; fls. in racemes, corolla to 1 in. long, lower lip large, palate hairy, spur conical, short. S. Afr. Plants grown under this name may be *N. strumosa* cv. 'Grandiflora'.

nana-compacta: a listed name of no botanical standing for *N. strumosa* cv.

strumosa Benth. Erect ann., to 2 ft.; st. lvs. lanceolate to linear, toothed, sessile; fls. in racemes to 4 in. long, corolla to 1 in. across, white or in shades of yellow and purple, often marked purple outside, throat bearded, spotted on a yellow ground, with pouch at base. S. Afr. Cvs. include: **'Grandiflora'**, fls. larger; **'Nana Compacta'** [*N. nana-compacta* Hort.], a dwarf form; **'Suttonii'**, fls. white, yellow, rose-pink, orange, crimson, and scarlet.

versicolor E. H. Mey. ex Benth. Erect ann., to 1 ft. or more; lvs. ovate, lanceolate, or linear, to 2 in. long, entire or toothed; fls. in racemes to 3 in. long, corolla to ½ in. long, in various colors, spur nearly straight or incurved. S. Afr. Cv. **'Compacta'** [*N. compacta* Hort.]. Compact, very free-flowering.

NEMOPANTHUS Raf. MOUNTAIN HOLLY. *Aquifoliaceae.* A single sp. of polygamodioecious, deciduous shrubs of e. N. Amer.; lvs. alt., simple, oblong-ovate, mucronate, entire or slightly toothed, smooth, glabrous; fls. axillary, solitary or few in clusters, calyx of male fls. of 4–5, minute, deciduous teeth, of female fls. absent or rudimentary, petals 4–5, yellowish, separate, stamens 4–5, ovary 3–5-celled, with 1 ovule in each cell; fr. drupaceous. Distinguished from *Ilex* by the separate petals and the absence of or early loss of the calyx.

mucronatus (L.) Trel. CATBERRY. Stoloniferous shrub, to 10 ft., brs. purplish when young, turning ashy-gray with age; lvs. to 1½ in. long, thin, dull bluish-green, turning yellow in autumn; fls. on pedicels to 1 in. long; fr. dark red, subglobose, to ⅝ in. in diam. In moist woods, thickets, and swamps, Nfld. to Minn., s. to Ind. and Va. Grown for its attractive fr. and colorful autumn foliage. Zone 5.

NEMOPHILA Nutt. ex W. Barton. *Hydrophyllaceae.* Eleven spp. of delicate, ann. herbs, native chiefly to w. N. Amer., 2 spp. to se. U.S.; plants glabrous, pubescent, or prickly-hairy, sts. soft, slightly succulent and brittle; lvs. opp. or alt., usually pinnatifid; fls. blue or white, usually solitary, rarely in racemelike cymes, calyx 5-parted, with 5 spreading or reflexed appendages in each sinus, or these rarely obsolete, corolla campanulate to rotate, 5-lobed, stamens 5, included; style 2-cleft; fr. a 1-celled caps.

Grown in the garden for continuous spring and summer bloom. Seeds may be sown where the plants are to grow, in early spring for summer bloom; the flowers are small, but usually profuse and bright.

atomaria: *N. Menziesii* var.

aurita: *Pholistoma auritum.*

discoidalis: *N. Menziesii* var.

insignis: *N. Menziesii.*

maculata Benth. ex Lindl. FIVE-SPOT. Sts. ascending or decumbent, to 1 ft. long, glabrate or thinly hispid; corolla white, with deep purple spot at tip of each lobe, to 1¾ in. across. Cent. Calif.

Menziesii Hook. & Arn. [*N. insignis* Dougl. ex Benth.]. BABY-BLUE-EYES. Sts. procumbent, to 1 ft. long, obscurely winged or angled; lvs. to 2 in. long, pinnatifid, segms. usually 9–11, lobed; corolla bright blue with white center, to 1½ in. across. Calif. Cvs. are: **'Alba'**, fls. white; **'Crambeoides'**, fls. light blue, veined purple, not spotted; **'Marginata'**, fls. blue, margined white. Var. **atomaria** (Fisch. & C. A. Mey.) Chandl. [*N. atomaria* Fisch. & C. A. Mey.]. Fls. white, dotted with black-purple. Var. **discoidalis** (Lem.) Voss [*N. discoidalis* Lem.]. Fls. brownish-purple, margined white.

NEOBENTHAMIA Rolfe. *Orchidaceae.* One sp., a tall and straggly herb, native to E. Afr.; sts. leafy, hardened; lvs. 2-ranked, drooping; infl. a terminal, many-fld., almost capitate raceme; sepals and petals nearly equal, spreading, lateral sepals united at base and slightly united to base of lip, petals similar, lip spreading, entire, fleshy, united to base of column, disc slightly hairy, without keels or crest, column short and stout. For structure of fl. see *Orchidaceae.*

For culture see *Orchids.*

gracilis Rolfe. Sts. branching, to 4 ft.; lvs. many, 2-ranked, linear, to 6 in. long; infl. densely fld., at end of long, naked peduncle; fls. less than ½ in. across, sepals and petals similar, spreading, white, lip with yellow midline bordered with a row of rosy spots, entire, somewhat narrowed and fleshy in lower half. Winter–spring, early autumn. Zanzibar (Tanzania).

NEOBESSEYA: *CORYPHANTHA* subgenus *NEOBESSEYA.* **N. Wissmannii:** *C. missouriensis* var. *robustior.*

NEOBUXBAUMIA: *CEPHALOCEREUS.*

NEOCHILENIA: *NEOPORTERIA.*

NEOCLEOME: *CLEOME.*

NEOCOGNIAUXIA Schlechter. *Orchidaceae.* Two spp. of cespitose epiphytes, native to W. Indies; pseudobulbs slender, stemlike, 1- or 2-lvd.; lvs. fleshy, occasionally with serrate edge; infl. terminal, 1- or 2-fld.; sepals and petals spreading, lip small, enveloping the column, column short, without a foot, pollinia 8. For structure of fl. see *Orchidaceae.*

For culture see *Orchids.*

monophylla (Griseb.) Schlechter [*Laelia monophylla* (Griseb.) N. E. Br.; *Trigonidium monophyllum* Griseb.]. To 1 ft., pseudobulb to 3½ in. long, covered with speckled sheaths, 1-lvd.; lvs. linear-oblong, to 4 in. long; infl. to 9 in. long; fls. vivid orange-scarlet except for purple anther cap, 1½ in. across, sepals and petals elliptic, to less than 1 in. long, lip ovoid, ⅜ in. long, 3-lobed, midlobe semicircular, somewhat apiculate, disc papillose with saclike outgrowth along median line. Jamaica.

NEODAWSONIA: *CEPHALOCEREUS.*

NEODONNELLIA: *TRIPOGANDRA.*

NEODYPSIS Baill. *Palmae.* About 14 spp. of Madagascar, differing from *Chrysalidocarpus* chiefly in having seeds with ruminate endosperm and probably ultimately to be joined with that genus.

For culture see *Palms.*

Decaryi Jumelle. St. solitary, to 30 ft. or more, 20 in. in diam., surface rough, brown; lvs. in 3 ranks, arched upward and curved at the apex, to 15 ft. long, sheaths overlapping, rusty-tomentose, petiole prominent, rusty-tomentose, pinnae more than 80 on each side, regularly arranged, linear, ascending from the rachis and curved at the apex; infl. among the lvs., lower brs. rusty-tomentose, twice-branched; fls. chartreuse; fr. obovoid, olive-green, glaucous, ⅞ in. long, 9/16 in. in diam. Zone 9b. The 3-ranked ascending lvs. give the plant an unusual aspect.

Lastelliana Baill. To 40 ft. or more, sts. to 9 in. in diam., brown; lvs. about 10, ascending, sheaths red-furfuraceous, more or less tubular and forming a crownshaft, petiole short, blade to 11 ft. long or more, pinnae about 95 on each side, regularly arranged; infl. among the lvs. or persisting below them, to 3 ft. long or more, 2–3 times branched; fr. obovoid, about ¾ in. long, ½ in. in diam.

NEOFINETIA H. H. Hu. *Orchidaceae.* One sp., an epiphyte, native to China and Japan; sts. short, completely enclosed by overlapping lf. bases; lvs. fleshy, arching; infl. a lateral, rather short, several-fld. raceme; fls. long, pedicelled, delicate in texture, sepals and petals similar, spreading, lip ovate-triangular, with a long spur, column short, fleshy, with short, 2-lobed rostellum. For structure of fl. see *Orchidaceae.*

For culture see *Orchids.*

falcata (Thunb.) H. H. Hu [*Angraecum falcatum* (Thunb.) Lindl.]. Lvs. thick, sickle-shaped, to 4 in. long; infl. 3–8-fld.; fls. fragrant, to 3¼ in. across, opening pure white, becoming light yellowish-orange, sepals and petals linear-oblong, lip 3-lobed, spur long, slender, to 1¾ in. long, yellow at tip. Summer.

NEOGLAZIOVIA Mez. *Bromeliaceae.* Two spp. of terrestrial herbs, native to arid Brazil; lvs. basal, few, spiny, linear to nearly cylindrical; fls. pedicelled, violet, in a simple raceme, sepals without spines, separate, petals with appendages, ovary inferior, each cell with up to 5 thickly tailed ovules; fr. a berry.

Grown in full sun in warm climates. For culture see *Bromeliaceae.*

variegata (Arr. Cam.) Mez. CAROÁ. Lvs. to 4½ ft. long, ⅝ in. wide, stiff, nearly cylindrical, banded and remotely spiny; fls. to ¾ in. long. Ne. Brazil. The lvs. of this sp. provide a strong fiber much used commercially in Brazil as a substitute for jute.

NEOGOMESIA: *ARIOCARPUS.*

NEOHENRICIA L. Bolus. *Aizoaceae.* One sp. of mat-forming, dwarf succulents, native to S. Afr.; lvs. opp., 4 on each br., erect, covered with white tubercles; fls. solitary, calyx 4–6-lobed, petals many, stamens many, ovary inferior, 5-celled, stigmas 5–6; fr. a caps., expanding keels winged, placental tubercles absent.

Cultivate in very sandy soil containing lime. See also *Succulents.*

Sibbettii (L. Bolus) L. Bolus. Lvs. more or less erect, to ⅜ in. long and to 1/16 in. wide at base, ¼ in. wide at apex, flat above, rounded on lower side, apex truncate to rounded with warts in groups or lines; fls. ½ in. across, on pedicels ⅝ in. long, nocturnal, petals white. Orange Free State.

NEOLITSEA Merrill. *Lauraceae.* About 80 spp. of evergreen, dioecious trees, native to e. and se. Asia; lvs. alt., entire, usually 3-nerved, leathery; infl. umbellate; fls. unisexual, male fls. with 6 fertile stamens, female fls. with 6 staminodes; fr. a berry.

aciculata (Blume) G. Koidz. [*Litsea aciculata* Blume]. Tree, to 12 ft.; lvs. oblong to obovate-oblong, 2–4¾ in. long, obtuse, whitish beneath, petioles to ⅝ in. long; fls. reddish; fr. black, ellipsoid. Spring. Cent. and s. Japan, Korea.

sericea (Blume) G. Koidz. [*Litsea glauca* Siebold]. Tree, to 20 ft., branchlets greenish; lvs. oblong or ovate-oblong, 3–7 in. long, obtuse, white beneath, densely yellow-hairy when young, petioles to 1¼ in. long; fls. yellow; fr. red, ellipsoid, to 5/16 in. long. Autumn. Temp. e. Asia.

NEOLLOYDIA Britt. & Rose [*Echinomastus* Britt. & Rose; *Gymnocactus* Backeb.]. *Cactaceae.* Perhaps 20 or more spp. of small, ovoid or cylindrical, mostly cespitose cacti, native to Tex. and Mex.; sts. globose to oblong, tubercles somewhat united into spiral ribs, grooved shortly or to the axils on the upper side; spines often curved but not hooked, radial spines 3–32, central spines 1–8; fls. subapical, from the groove and separated from spines, said to be diurnal, funnelform to campanulate, ovary with few or no scales; fr. subglobose, thin-walled, becoming papery, seeds black, tubercled, hilum large, nearly basal, with a narrow collar. Differs from *Thelocactus* in seeds and juvenile spines. Some spp. may not be correctly assigned here.

For culture see *Cacti.*

Beguinii (A. Web.) Britt. & Rose. Sts. simple, to 6 in. high and 3 in. thick, densely spiny, ribs 13, tubercles low, short-grooved; radial spines 12–20, stellate or somewhat spreading, white with dark tips, ⅛–¾ in. long, central spine 1, erect, to 1¼ in. long; fls. pink to violet, to 1½ in. long, ovary naked. N. Mex. Var. **senilis** Backeb. & F. M. Knuth. Spines larger, whiter, central spines 2–3, one of them directed outward.

ceratites (Quehl) Britt. & Rose. Sts. simple or in small clusters, to 4 in. high and 2 in. thick, ribs about 8, tubercles rhombic, grooved to base; radial spines 15–20, more or less spreading, white, to ⅝ in. long, central spines 5–6, stouter, dark-tipped, to 1 in. long; fls. purple, 1½ in. long. Mex.

conoidea (DC.) Britt. & Rose [*N. texensis* Britt. & Rose]. Sts. cespitose, to 4 in. high and 3 in. thick, ribs 4–8, tubercles rather loosely placed, ovoid, grooved to base; radial spines about 16, stellate, needle-shaped, white, ⁵⁄₁₆ in. long, central spines 1–5, black, spreading, to 1¼ in. long; fls. red-violet, 2½ in. across, perianth segms. narrow-lanceolate, acute. Tex. and ne. Mex.

durangensis (Runge) L. Bens. [*Echinomastus durangensis* (Runge) Britt. & Rose]. Sts. about 10 in. high and 4 in. thick, ribs 18–21; spine cluster circular, radial spines 15–30, awl-shaped, gray-black, the upper longer, to 1¼ in. long, central spines 4, the upper 3 like the radial spines, the lower shorter. N. Mex.

erectocentra (J. Coult.) L. Bens. [*Echinomastus erectocentrus* (J. Coult.) Britt. & Rose]. Sts. to 8 in. high and 4 in. thick, ribs 15–21, radial spines 13–15, somewhat comblike, needle-shaped, straight, white or red above, ½ in. long, central spines 1–2, one erect, reddish, to 1 in. long; fls. pink, to 2 in. long. Spring. Se. Ariz.

grandiflora (Otto) F. M. Knuth. Similar to and probably a var. of *N. conoidea,* but tubercles close-set; radial spines to 25, flattened laterally, central spines 0–2; perianth segms. wider, more obtuse. Ne. Mex.

horripila (Lem.) Britt. & Rose. Sts. cespitose, ovoid, to 5 in. high, ribs about 8, tubercles rounded, ⁵⁄₁₆ in. long, short-grooved; spines white, becoming gray, radial spines 8–10, needle-shaped, to ⅝ in. long, central spine 1, larger, directed outward; fls. purple, 1¼ in. long, ovary naked. Cent. Mex.

intertexta (Engelm.) L. Bens. [*Echinomastus intertextus* (Engelm.) Britt. & Rose]. Sts. ovoid to cylindrical, to 6 in. high and 4 in. thick, ribs 12–14; spines stiff, reddish, radial spines 13–20, central spines 4, the upper 3 ascending, the lower short, directed outward; fls. pink or lavender, 1 in. long; fr. green, oblong, ½ in. long, splitting lengthwise. Spring. Tex. to Ariz., n. Mex. Var. **intertexta.** The typical var.; radial and upper central spines appressed against st., to ⅝ in. long, lower central spines directed outward, to ⅛ in. long. Tex. to Ariz., n. Mex. Var. **dasyacantha** (Engelm.) L. Bens. [*Echinomastus dasyacanthus* (Engelm.) Britt. & Rose]. Radial and upper central spines not appressed against st., to ⅞ in. or 1⅝ in. long, lower central spine to ⅞ in. long. Tex., s. New Mex.

Johnsonii (Parry) L. Bens. [*Echinomastus Johnsonii* (Parry) Baxter; *Ferocactus Johnsonii* (Parry) Britt. & Rose]. Sts. to 10 in. high and 5 in. thick, ribs 17–21; spines red to gray, radial spines 10–14, to 1¼ in. long, central spines 4–8, stouter, alike, to 1½ in. long; fls. magenta or yellow, to 2½ in. long; fr. green, oblong, ¾ in. long, splitting lengthwise. Spring. S. Utah, s. Nev., nw. Ariz., se. Calif.

Mcdowellii (Rebut ex Quehl) H. E. Moore [*Echinomastus Mcdowellii* (Rebut ex Quehl) Britt. & Rose]. Sts. to 3 in. high or more and 5 in. thick, ribs 20–25, spine clusters elliptic, radial spines 15–20, awl-shaped, transparent-white, to ¾ in. long, central spines 3–4, yellow, the lower longest, flattened, to 2 in. long; fls. rose, to 1½ in. long. N. Mex.

subterranea (Backeb.) H. E. Moore [*Gymnocactus subterraneus* (Backeb.) Backeb. ex F. Schwarz]. Neck to 2 in. long, st. body to 2 in. long and 1 in. thick; areoles with long, white, woolly hairs, radial spines about 16, stellate, needle-shaped, white, the upper, longer, brown-tipped, central spines 2, the upper appressed. N. Mex.

texensis: *N.conoidea.*

unguispina (Engelm.) L. Bens. [*Echinomastus unguispinus* (Engelm.) Britt. & Rose]. Sts. to 5 in. high and 4 in. thick, ribs about 21; spine clusters circular, radial spines 4–8, blue-gray, mostly ascending, to 1½ in. long, but 1 deflexed, stouter, to 1 in. long; fls. reddish, 1 in. long. N. Mex.

NEOMAMMILLARIA: *MAMMILLARIA.*

NEOMARICA T. Sprague [*Marica* Ker-Gawl., not Schreb.]. FAN IRIS, HOUSE I., WALKING I., TWELVE-APOSTLES, TOAD-CUP LILY, FALSE FLAG. *Iridaceae.* About 15 spp. of rhizomatous per. herbs, native to trop. Amer. and w. Afr.; lvs. sword-shaped, many-veined; fls. blue, white, or yellow, fuga-

cious, in clusters near the ends of flat, winged, leaflike scapes, perianth tube none, perianth segms. 6, in 2 unlike series, stamens 3, filaments not united, style brs. 3, bifid or trifid at apex; fr. a 3-valved caps.

Hardy in mild regions with winter protection, they thrive in Fla. and similar climates; also an excellent house plant. Propagated by division.

caerulea (Ker-Gawl.) T. Sprague [*Marica caerulea* Ker-Gawl.]. To about 2 ft.; lvs. 3–6 ft. long, 1½ in. wide; fls. to 4 in. across, light blue or lilac, outer perianth segms. with transverse bars of brown, yellow, or white. Brazil.

gracilis (Herb. ex Hook.) T. Sprague [*Marica gracilis* Herb.]. To 2 ft., erect or reclining; lvs. to 2½ ft. long and 1 in. wide, veins conspicuous; fls. to 2 in. across, outer perianth segms. white, with yellow and brown markings, inner segms. blue, smaller. S. Mex. to Brazil.

longifolia (Link & Otto) T. Sprague [*Marica longifolia* Link & Otto]. To 3 ft.; lvs. 1 ft. long or more, 1 in. wide; fls. 2 in. across, perianth segms. yellow, barred with brown. Brazil.

Northiana (Schneev.) T. Sprague [*Marica Northiana* Schneev.]. APOSTLE PLANT. To 3 ft.; lvs. to 2 ft. long and 2 in. wide; fls. 4 in. across, very fragrant, outer perianth segms. white, inner segms. violet, both variegated at base. Brazil.

×**NEOMEA** M. B. Foster: *Aechmea* × *Neoregelia. Bromeliaceae.*

Marnieri M. B. Foster: *Aechmea Chantinii* × *Neoregelia Carolinae.* Lvs. lacking the banded appearance of *A. Chantinii;* infl. branched from a very short scape, with 2–4 compact, conelike heads low in the center of the rosette; sepals light orange, petals violet.

NEOMOOREA Rolfe. *Orchidaceae.* One sp., an epiphyte, native from Panama to Ecuador; pseudobulbs 2-lvd.; lvs. plicate; infl. a lateral, many-fld. raceme, shorter than lvs.; sepals and petals similar, spreading, lip 3-lobed, jointed to column foot, sessile, column fleshy, arching, dilated basally into a short, broad foot, pollinia 4, unequal, on long stalk. For structure of fl. see *Orchidaceae.*

For culture see *Orchids.*

irrorata: *N. Wallisii.*

Wallisii (Rchb.f.) Schlechter [*N. irrorata* (Rolfe) Rolfe]. Pseudobulbs ovoid, to 1½ in. long; lvs. to 3 ft. long, elliptic-lanceolate, plicate; raceme shorter than lvs., from base of pseudobulb, loosely many-fld., to 10 in. long; fls. 2 in. across, sepals and petals to 1 in. long, elliptic-ovate, orange-brown, pale at base, lip smaller, cream-colored, sessile, broader than long, lateral lobes ear-shaped, yellow, banded and spotted with purple, midlobe drawn out to a point, disc with horseshoe-shaped erect appendage with 2 linear-oblong, obtuse, red-spotted, yellow arms embracing 3 oblong calluses. Panama to Venezuela and Ecuador.

NEOMYRTUS Burret. *Myrtaceae.* One sp., an evergreen shrub or small tree, endemic to New Zeal.; lvs. opp., simple, gland-dotted; fls. axillary, solitary, 5-merous, white, stamens many, ovary inferior, 1-celled, ovules few; fr. a few-seeded berry. Related to *Lophomyrtus,* but 5-merous, and ovary 1-celled, with few ovules.

pedunculata (Hook.f.) Allan [*Myrtus pedunculata* Hook.f.]. To 18 ft.; lvs. obovate, to ¾ in. long, obtuse, cuneate at base; fls. to ¼ in. across; berry reddish or yellow, to ⅜ in. across, seeds 2–4.

NEOPANAX Allan. *Araliaceae.* Five spp. of evergreen, monoecious or dioecious, unarmed trees and shrubs, native to New Zeal; lvs. simple or palmately compound, mostly glabrous; infl. of compound, rarely simple umbels; fls. 5-merous, calyx minute, ovary 2-celled, styles 2, united at base; fr. a compressed drupe, pyrenes 2.

arboreus (J. Murr.) Allan [*Nothopanax arboreus* (G. Forst.) Seem.]. FIVE-FINGERS. Dioecious tree, much-branched, to 25 ft.; lvs. palmately compound, lfts. 5–7, to 7 in. long, coarsely serrate, thin-leathery; infl. a compound umbel; fr. black-purple. Zone 10.

laetus (T. Kirk) Allan [*Nothopanax laetus* (T. Kirk) Cheesem.]. Dioecious shrub or small tree, to 20 ft.; lvs. palmately compound, lfts. 5–7, from 6–12 in. long, lower ⅓ entire, upper ⅔ dentate, thick-leathery, petioles, petiolules, and midvein purplish-red; infl. a terminal, compound umbel; fr. dark purple. Zone 10.

×**NEOPHYTUM** M. B. Foster: *Neoregelia* × *Orthophytum. Bromeliaceae.*

Lymanii M. B. Foster: *Neoregelia bahiana* × *Orthophytum navioides* (L. B. Sm.) L. B. Sm. Resembling a giant form of *O. navioides* at flowering; lvs. thick, glossy, not red at base; fls. borne low in the lf. tube, on pedicels 1 in. long, blue, 3 in. long.

NEOPIERIS: *LYONIA.*

NEOPORTERIA Britt. & Rose [*Chilenia* Backeb.; *Horridocactus* Backeb.; *Islaya* Backeb.; *Neochilenia* Backeb.; *Pyrrhocactus* A. Berger]. *Cactaceae.* About 66 spp. of globose to short-cylindrical, ribbed cacti, native to Peru, Chile, and w. Argentina; sts. simple or rarely cespitose, crowns naked or woolly, ribs mostly with separate tubercles often swollen on one side; areoles central on tubercles, sunken and with feltlike hairs; fls. apical, campanulate or funnelform, tube prominent; fr. dry, hollow, and with a basal opening when mature, sometimes fleshy at first.

The genus has been divided into 2 subgenera. The species of a subgenus possess the characteristics of that subgenus which are not repeated in the brief descriptions of the species; instead, the following symbols are used to indicate the subgenus to which each species belongs: N, *Neoporteria;* P, *Pyrrhocactus.*

The distinguishing characters of the subgenera follow:

Subgenus **Neoporteria** (N). Crown not woolly; fls. campanulate, perianth segms. lanceolate, the innermost incurved, rose-carmine, tube narrow, scales with only traces of wool or bristles in axils; fr. often fleshy at first, becoming dry and hollow at maturity.

Subgenus **Pyrrhocactus** (A. Berger) Donald & Rowley (P). Crown naked or woolly; fls. funnelform, perianth segms. spatulate or lanceolate, mostly pale yellow, rarely orange or pale rose, tube conical, scales pilose to nearly naked in axils; fr. hollow from beginning.

For culture see *Cacti.*

acutissima: *N. subgibbosa.*

atrispina: *N. villosa* var.

bicolor (Akers & Buin.) Donald & Rowley [*Islaya bicolor* Akers & Buin.]. P; sts. simple, globose or short-cylindrical, to 8 in. high and 4 in. thick, ribs 20, low; radial spines 12–14, gray, needle-shaped, to ⅜ in. long; fls. to ¾ in. across, petaloid segms. yellow, red at apex; fr. obovoid, ¾ in. in diam. S. Peru.

castaneoides: *N. subgibbosa* var. *subgibbosa* forma.

cephalophora: *N. villosa* var.

chilensis (Hildm.) Britt. & Rose [*Neochilenia chilensis* (Hildm.) Backeb.]. P; sts. simple or branching at base, to 10 in. high and 4 in. thick, ribs 20–21, ½ in. high; radial spines more than 20, white or yellowish, glassy, to ½ in. long, central spines 6–8, stouter, to ¾ in. long; fls. pink, 2 in. across. Chile.

curvispina (Bertero) Donald & Rowley [*Horridocactus curvispinus* (Bertero) Backeb.; *Pyrrhocactus curvispinus* (Bertero) Backeb.]. P; sts. simple or cespitose, to 6 in. high, ribs 16, obtuse, divided into large tubercles; spines 15, straight or curved, flexuous; fls. yellow or reddish, to 2½ in. long, stigma green. Chile.

fusca (Mühlenpf.) Britt. & Rose [*Neochilenia fusca* (Mühlenpf.) Backeb.]. P; sts. globose to oblong, to 4 in. thick, ribs 12–13, of 6-sided tubercles swollen on one side; spines black, becoming gray, radial spines 5–7, central spines 4, the upper strongest, upcurved, to 1½ in. long; fls. yellow, 1¼ in. long, 1½ in. across; fr. reddish, ¾ in. long. Chile.

heteracantha: *N. subgibbosa* var. *subgibbosa* forma.

islayensis (C. F. Först.) Donald & Rowley [*Islaya islayensis* (C. F. Först.) Backeb.]. P; sts. simple, to 10 in. high and 4 in. thick, crown more or less woolly, ribs 19–25, low, obtuse; areoles close-set, spines grayish, radial spines 8–22, to ⅜ in. long, central spines 4–7, stouter, to ⅝ in. long; fls. yellow, ¾ in. long, stigmas yellow. S. Peru. Forma **minor** (Backeb.) Donald & Rowley [*Islaya minor* Backeb.]. Ribs to 17; central spines 4, in the form of a cross, to ¾ in. long.

mammillarioides: *N. subgibbosa* var.

napina (Phil.) Backeb. [*Neochilenia napina* (Phil.) Backeb.]. P; root large, tuberous, sts. globose, 1 in. thick or more, tubercles in 8 and 13 spirals; spines about 9, appressed, black, to ⅛ in. long; fls. yellow, 1 in. long. Chile.

nidus (Söhrens ex K. Schum.) Britt. & Rose [*Chilenia nidus* (Söhrens ex K. Schum.) Backeb.]. N; sts. to 3 in. high and 2½ in. thick, densely covered with ascending, connivent spines, ribs 16–18; areoles large, spines about 30, needle-shaped, weak, curved, white, unequal, the largest to 1¼ in. long; fls. pink, 1½ in. long. Chile. Forma **senilis** (Phil.)

Donald & Rowley [*Neoporteria senilis* (Phil.) Backeb.]. Spines softer; fls. twice as large.

nigricans: *N. tuberisulcata* var.

occulta (Phil.) Britt. & Rose [*Neochilenia occulta* (Phil.) Backeb.]. P; sts. globose, to 1 in. thick, sometimes proliferous, ribs 8–10; radial spines 6, the lower longest, to ⁵⁄₁₆ in. long or more, central spine 1, to ⅝ in. long or more; fls. pale yellow, 1 in. long. Chile.

Reichei (K. Schum.) Backeb. [*Neochilenia Reichei* (K. Schum.) Backeb.]. P; sts. globose, to 3 in. thick, tubercles rhombic, in 25 and 39 spirals; spines 7–9, appressed, weak, whitish, to ⅛ in. long; fls. yellow, to 1½ in. long. Chile.

senilis: *N. nidus* forma.

Strausiana (K. Schum.) Donald & Rowley [*Pyrrhocactus Strausianus* (K. Schum.) A. Berger]. P; sts. to 6 in. high and 3½ in. thick, ribs 13, obtuse; spines 9–20, awl-shaped, reddish, to 1½ in. long; fls. salmon, to ¾ in. long, stigma cream. W. Argentina.

subgibbosa (Haw.) Britt. & Rose [*Neoporteria acutissima* (Otto & A. Dietr.) Borg; *Chilenia acutissima* (Otto & A. Dietr.) Backeb.; *C. subgibbosa* (Haw.) Backeb.]. N; sts. erect or prostrate, to 3 ft. long, ribs many; areoles large, close-set, spines many, needle-shaped, brownish, to 1¼ in. long; fls. pink or red, 1½ in. long; fr. reddish, to ¾ in. long. Chile. Var. **subgibbosa.** The typical var.; tubercles not prominent; spines variable, light or dark amber. Forma **castaneoides** (J. F. Cels) Donald & Rowley [*Neoporteria castaneoides* (J. F. Cels) Werderm.]. Spines yellow to yellow-brown, radial spines to 20, central spines to 6. Forma **heteracantha** (Backeb.) Donald & Rowley [*Neoporteria heteracantha* (Backeb.) Backeb.; *Chilenia heteracantha* Backeb.]. Spines stiffly bristlelike to needle-shaped, thick, dirty-white to brown-gray. Var. **mammillarioides** (Hook.) Donald & Rowley [*Neoporteria mammillarioides* (Hook.) Backeb.; *Pyrrhocactus mammillarioides* (Hook.) Backeb.]. Tubercles pronounced; spines whitish to reddish.

tuberisulcata (Jacobi) Donald & Rowley [*Horridocactus horridus* (Colla) Backeb.; *Pyrrhocactus horridus* (Colla) Backeb.; *P. tuberisulcatus* (Jacobi) Borg]. P; sts. globose, to 8 in. thick, ribs 14–20, strongly tubercled; radial spines finally 10–12, brown, becoming gray, central spines 4–5, larger, to 1 in. long; fls. yellowish. Chile. Var. **tuberisulcata.** The typical var.; sts. dark green; spines yellowish; fls. about 1¾ in. long. Var. **Froelichiana** (K. Schum.) Donald & Rowley [*Pyrrhocactus Froelichianus* (K. Schum.) Backeb.]. Sts. light green; spines yellowish; fls. to 2⅝ in. long. Var. **nigricans** (A. Dietr.) Donald & Rowley [*Neoporteria nigricans* (A. Dietr.) Britt. & Rose; *Horridocactus nigricans* (A. Dietr.) Backeb. & Dölz]. Sts. dark green, becoming gray; spines black.

umadeave (Frič ex Werderm.) Donald & Rowley [*Pyrrhocactus umadeave* (Frič ex Werderm.) Backeb.]. P; sts. to 16 in. high and 12 in. thick, ribs 18–27, weakly tubercled; spines 30–35, awl-shaped, whitish to brownish, mostly ascending, to 1¼ in. long; fls. 1½ in. long. N. Argentina.

villosa (Monv.) A. Berger. N; sts. cylindrical, gray-green, becoming violet to blackish, to 6 in. high or more and 3 in. thick, ribs 13–15; areoles white-hairy to white-woolly, spines many, not strongly differentiated, central spines somewhat darker, about 4 of them stouter, to 1½ in. long; fls. white, about ¾ in. long. Chile. Var. **villosa.** The typical var.; spines hairlike or finally bristlelike, yellow to whitish or central spines blackish. Var. **atrispinosa** (Backeb.) Donald & Rowley [*Neoporteria atrispinosa* (Backeb.) Backeb.]. Spines bristlelike, dark, ascending, to 1½ in. long. Var. **cephalophora** (Backeb.) Donald & Rowley [*Neoporteria cephalophora* (Backeb.) Backeb.]. Dwarf; spines short, hairlike, light yellow to whitish.

NEORAIMONDIA Britt. & Rose. *Cactaceae.* One sp., a large, columnar cactus of Peru; sts. branching from base, strongly ribbed; areoles large with strong spines, short shoots from upper areoles, with close-set areoles and 1–2 fls.; fls. diurnal, campanulate, limb rotate, tube and ovary scaly, with axillary wool; fr. globose, with deciduous wool and short spines. Unique in having fls. on cylindrical short shoots.

For culture see *Cacti.*

arequipensis: see *N. macrostibas.*

macrostibas (K. Schum.) Britt. & Rose. To 15 ft., ribs 5–8; areoles brown, to 1 in. wide, spines 12 or more, unequal, black, to 10 in. long, eventually deciduous, short shoots to 4 in. long; fls. 1–1½ in. long, white; fr. purple, to 3 in. in diam. S. Peru. Also called *N. arequipensis* (Meyen) Backeb., but the identity of Meyen's plant is uncertain. Var. **roseiflora** (Werderm. & Backeb.) Backeb. About 6 ft. high; fls. rosy. Cent. Peru. Var. **gigantea** (Werderm. & Backeb.) Backeb. To 25 ft. high or more; fls. red. N. Peru.

NEOREGELIA L. B. Sm. [*Aregelia* Mez, not O. Kuntze]. *Bromeliaceae.* About 52 spp. of epiphytic herbs, mostly native to Brazil (1 sp. in Colombia and Peru); lvs. in a basal rosette, usually spiny, the inner often brightly colored; infl. central, usually simple, dense, appearing sessile; fls. pedicelled, violet, blue, or white, lasting 1 night, petals without scales, united into a tube, pollen sculptured, ovary inferior; fr. a berry, seeds without appendages.

For culture see *Bromeliaceae.*

ampullacea (E. Morr.) L. B. Sm. Lvs. few, to 5 in. long, 5/8 in. wide, forming a flasklike tube, rounded at apex, brown-banded beneath, the inner not red-margined; fls. blue, to 1 in. long. Cv. **'Tigrina'** is listed.

bahiana (Ule) L. B. Sm. Lvs. to 10 in. long, 1 in. wide, forming a cylindrical tube, minutely spiny, green, the inner bordered with red and sometimes purplish; infl. bracts entire, pedicels 3/8–3/4 in. long; fls. blue, about 2½ in. long.

Burchellii: a listed name of no botanical standing, used in error for *Nidularium Burchellii.*

carcharodon (Bak.) L. B. Sm. Plant very large; lvs. to 18 in. long, 3½ in. wide, fiercely spiny, green and unspotted; infl. bracts pale green or violet, acute; fls. violet, to 1½ in. long.

Carolinae (Beer) L. B. Sm. [*N. Marechalii* Hort.; *Aregelia Marechalii* Mez]. BLUSHING BROMELIAD. Lvs. many, to 16 in. long, 1⅜ in. wide, glabrous, green above, darker beneath, the inner purplish to red; fls. violet or lavender, to 1⅝ in. long. Cv. **'Meyendorffii'** probably the typical form. Cv. **'Tricolor'.** Lvs. variegated.

chlorosticta (Bak.) L. B. Sm. [*N. sarmentosa* var. *chlorosticta* (Bak.) L. B. Sm.]. Lvs. few, to 1 ft. long, 3/4 in. wide, sheath conspicuously pale-spotted, blade nearly glabrous, inner lvs. not red; sepals obtuse, to ½ in. long, petals white, to 7/8 in. long. Rio de Janeiro (Brazil).

concentrica (Vell.) L. B. Sm. Lvs. many, to 1 ft. long, 4 in. wide, light green with dark spines, pale scurfy beneath, the inner often violet or yellow-green and sparsely brown-spotted; infl. bracts obtuse; fls. lavender, to 2¾ in. long.

cruenta (R. Grah.) L. B. Sm. Lvs. green or cross-banded, distinctly toothed with red spines; infl. unbranched, fl. bracts hooded; fls. many, sepals acute, straight, petals violet.

eleutheropetala (Ule) L. B. Sm. Lvs. leathery, to 30 in a rosette, with dark spines, neither banded nor spotted, sheaths brown; infl. with short brs., many-fld., to 3 3/16 in. across; sepals not united at base.

farinosa (Ule) L. B. Sm. CRIMSON-CUP. Lvs. to 2 ft. long, 1½ in. wide, mucronate, bronzy-green above, densely mealy beneath, the inner crimson; fl. bracts about half as long as sepals; fls. violet, to 2 in. long.

Fosterana L. B. Sm. Lvs. not leathery; infl. with short, rusty-scurfy brs., fl. bracts about as long as sepals; sepals 5/8 in. long, petals united at base.

Johannis (Carrière) L. B. Sm. Lvs. few, to 3 in. wide, recurved, with very short, distant spines, green, red-spotted at tip; infl. unbranched; petals white.

laevis (Mez) L. B. Sm. Lvs. about 20, in a loose rosette, to 1 ft. long, 1⅜ in. wide, without spines, all light green; fls., white, 1⅜ in. long or more.

macahensis (Ule) L. B. Sm. Lvs. up to 15, sheaths maroon, spotted with green, constricted at apex, blades broad, rounded at apex, remotely spiny, those next to infl. not red; fls. white, about 1 in. long.

marmorata (Bak.) L. B. Sm. [*Aregelia marmorata* (Bak.) Mez]. MARBLE PLANT. Lvs. many, not stiff, to 16 in. long, 2⅜ in. wide, light green, sheath and base dark-mottled or -spotted, inner lvs. sometimes paler than the outer; fls. blue or lavender, 1⅜ in. long or more. Much material grown under this name, but with lvs. mottled and red-tipped, is probably of hybrid origin, involving this sp. and *N. spectabilis.* Cv. **'Rubra'** is listed.

Marechalii: a listed name of no botanical standing, used for *N. Carolinae.*

princeps (Bak.) L. B. Sm. Lvs. to 1 ft. long, 2 in. wide, mucronate, densely gray-scurfy beneath and often above, the inner purple-margined; fl. bracts shorter than pedicels; fls. violet, to 2 in. long.

sarmentosa (Regel) L. B. Sm. Lvs. few, to 10 in. long, 1 in. wide, nearly glabrous and green, the inner brownish-green; fls. white, to 1 in. long, sepals shortly acute, not mucronate. Var. **chlorosticta:** *N. chlorosticta.*

spectabilis (T. Moore) L. B. Sm. [*Aregelia spectabilis* (T. Moore) Mez]. PAINTED-FINGERNAIL, FINGERNAIL PLANT. Lvs. to 16 in. long, 1½ in. wide, gray-striped beneath, green above with red tips, the inner margined with purple; fls. blue, to 1⅝ in. long.

tricolor: a listed name of no botanical standing, probably referable to *N. Carolinae* cv.

tristis (Beer) L. B. Sm. [*Aregelia tristis* (Beer) Mez]. Lvs. 10–12, to 8 in. long, 3/4 in. wide, green with red spots and bars, the inner scarcely red; fls. lilac, to 1¼ in. long.

zonata L. B. Sm. Stoloniferous; lvs. few, to 14 in. long, spiny, pale scurfy and purple-banded; infl. 15-fld., fl. bracts toothed; fls. white with blue tip, to 1½ in. long.

NEOWASHINGTONIA: *WASHINGTONIA.*

NEOWERDERMANNIA Frič. *Cactaceae.* Two spp. of small, tubercled cacti, native to S. Amer.; with sts. deep-seated, obconical, the above-ground surface with broad conical tubercles; areoles axillary only; fls. nearly lateral, campanulate, small, scales of the perianth tube naked in the axils, stamens in 1 series, ovary naked; fr. globose, few-seeded, the perianth persistent. Probably not distinct from *Gymnocalycium.*

For culture see *Cacti.*

Vorwerkii Frič. Sts. simple or branched, about 3 in. thick, tubercles in 5 and 8 spirals; areoles woolly, spines about 10, mostly curved, glassy, to 5/8 in. long, the lower one hooked, black, to 1½ in. long; fls. white or rosy, 1 in. long; fr. red, dry, 3/16 in. in diam. Bolivia and n. Argentina.

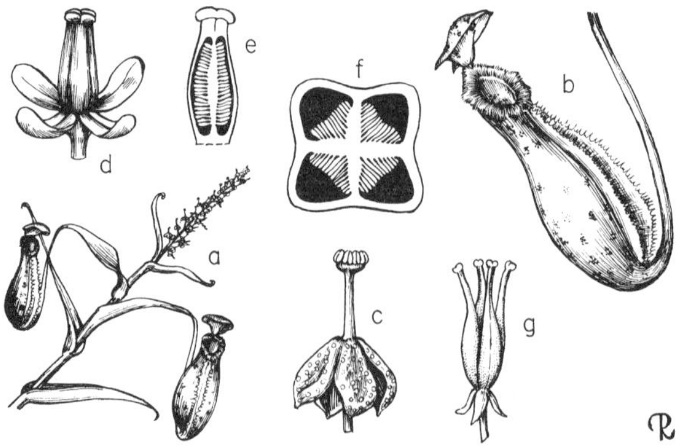

NEPENTHACEAE. *Nepenthes* ×*Balfouriana:* **a,** flowering stem, × 1/8; **b,** leaf-tip pitcher, × 1/6; **c,** male flower, × 2; **d,** female flower, × 3; **e,** pistil, vertical section, × 4; **f,** ovary, cross section, × 10; **g,** capsule, × 3. (From Bailey, *Manual of Cultivated Plants,* ed. 2.)

NEPENTHACEAE Dumort. NEPENTHES FAMILY. Dicot.; 2 genera of dioecious, mostly herbaceous, sometimes semi-woody, more or less climbing, epiphytic, or occasionally terrestrial, carnivorous plants, native from the Philippine Is. to n. Australia, Malay Pen., and the Seychelles; lvs. alt., simple, sessile or petioled, leathery, with midrib prolonged into a tendril, bearing at its end a hollow, cylindrical or unequally swollen, liquid-containing pitcher with 2 wings on 1 side, and a thickened rim and a lid at the apex; fls. small, greenish, unisexual, in panicles or racemes, sepals 3–4, petals 0, stamens 4–24, united, ovary superior, 3–4-celled; fr. a many-seeded caps. *Nepenthes* is cult. for its bizarre pitchers.

NEPENTHES L. PITCHER PLANT. *Nepenthaceae.* About 70 spp., with characters of the family, native from the Philippine Is. to n. Australia, Malay Pen. and Ceylon.

Nepenthes are grown under glass as curiosities. In addition to Latin-named hybrids, several fancy-named cultivars are in the American trade. Pitcher plants of this genus, as opposed to *Sarracenia* and *Darlingtonia,* are suitable for pots or baskets suspended from the roof of the greenhouse. They require high humidity and temperature not less than 70° F., and shade from bright sunshine. The best potting material is fibrous orchid peat, sphagnum moss, and sand. Propagated by cuttings of ripened shoots and by seeds in a closed propagating frame.

ampullaria Jack. Robust, scandent or prostrate; lvs. to 12 in. long, pitchers clustered, short-tubular, 1½–2 in. long, to 1½ in. wide, green, wings fringed. Malay Arch.

×**atrosanguinea** M. T. Mast.: probably *N. distillatoria* L. × *N.* ×*Sedenii* M. T. Mast. Pitchers cylindrical, unequally swollen, reddish-purple mottled with yellowish-green, wings fringed.

×**Balfouriana** Hort. ex M. T. Mast.: *N.* ×*Mastersiana* × *N.* ×*mixta.* Pitchers cylindrical, unequally swollen, green blotched with purple, wings fringed.

×**Boissiense:** a listed name of no botanical standing for a reputed hybrid, *N. gracilis* × *N.* ×*superba*, with lvs. green, succulent, dense, to 1 ft. long, pitchers funnelform, to 6 in. long, yellow-green, striped magenta, rim darker green and red, wings fringed.

×**Chelsoni** Hort. Veitch ex M. T. Mast.: *N.* ×*Dominii* × *N. Hookerana.* Pitchers broadly ovate, yellowish-green spotted with purple, wings fringed. Var. **excellens:** *N.* ×*edinensis.* Var. **excelsa** is listed, perhaps meant for *excellens.*

Curtisii: *N. maxima.*

×**Courtii** Hort. Veitch: *N.* ×*Dominii* × *N.* ? Pitchers cylindrical, unequally swollen, green mottled with purple, wings fringed.

×**Dicksoniana** R. Lindsay ex M. T. Mast.: *N. Rafflesiana* × *N. Veitchii* Hook.f Lvs. 8–20 in. long, 2–4 in. wide, pitchers 4–10 in long, 2–4 in. wide, cylindric-ventricose, villous, yellowish-green, purple-spotted, pale green and red-striped at the rim, wings long-fringed.

×**Dominiana:** *N.* ×*Dominii.*

×**Dominii** J. G. Veitch [*N.* ×*Dominiana* Nichols.]: *N. gracilis?* × *N. Rafflesiana.* Pitchers cylindrical, unequally swollen, green, blotched with purple, wings broad, fringed.

×**edinensis** W. E. Dixon [*N.* ×*Chelsoni* var. *excellens* Hort. Veitch]: *N.* ×*Chelsoni* × *N. Rafflesiana.* Pitchers ovate, yellowish-green, spotted with brownish-red, wings broad, fringed.

goettingensis: a listed name of no botanical standing, for a plant described as having mug-shaped pitchers, dull maroon, mottled with green.

gracilis Korth. Lvs. 4–8 in. long, pitchers 3–5 in. long, ½–1¼ in. wide, swollen below, cylindrical above, pale or yellowish-green, spotted purple, wings broad, fringed. Malay Pen., Indonesia.

Hookerana Lindl. Pitchers of 2 shapes, the lower ovate, to 4½ in. long, pale green, mottled with purple, wings broad, fringed, the upper funnelform, to 5 in. long, 1½ in. wide, wings reduced to ribs. Malay Pen., Sumatra, Borneo. Possibly a natural hybrid between *N. ampullaria* and *N. Rafflesiana.*

×**intermedia** Hort. Veitch: *N. Rafflesiana* × a Bornean sp. Pitchers cylindrical, unequally swollen, green, mottled and dotted with purple, wings long-fringed.

khasiana Hook.f. Pitchers green or reddish-green, of 2 shapes, the lower unequally swollen, wings short-fringed, the upper tubular, to 8 in. long, wings riblike. Assam.

×**Lawrenceana** M. T. Mast.: Probably *N. Hookerana* × *N. mirabilis.* Pitchers cylindrical, unequally swollen, pale green, heavily spotted with purple, wings fringed. *N.* ×*Morganiana* Hort. Veitch ex M. T. Mast. [*N.* ×*Morganiae* M. T. Mast.] closely resembles this and is believed to have the same parentage.

×**Mastersiana** Hort. Veitch ex M. T. Mast. [*N. khasiana* × *N. sanguinea*]. Pitchers tending to be of 2 shapes, the lower cylindrical, unequally swollen, wings fringed, the upper tubular with reduced wings, reddish-green, obscurely mottled with red, or purplish.

maxima Reinw. ex Nees [*N. Curtisii* M. T. Mast.]. Pitchers variable in shape, the lower to 8 in. long, 2½ in. wide, cylindrical, unequally swollen, with fringed wings, the upper to 12 in. long, 3 in. wide, funnelform, with wings reduced to ribs, pale green with many purple spots. Borneo, Celebes, New Guinea.

mirabilis (Lour.) Druce [*N. Phyllamphora* Willd.]. Pitchers nearly cylindrical, to 6 in. long, 1 in. wide, pale to reddish-green, wings narrow and fringed or reduced to ribs. S. China, Malay Pen. and Arch., Philippine Is.

×**mixta** M. T. Mast.: *N. Northiana* Hook.f. × *N. maxima.* Pitchers 4–14 in. long, 1½–3 in. wide, yellowish-green, sparsely purple-spotted toward the base, more densely so at the rim, wings ciliate.

×**Morganiana,** ×**Morganiae:** see *N.* ×*Lawrenceana.*

Phyllamphora: *N. mirabilis.*

Rafflesiana Jack. Pitchers pale green, mottled with purple, to 10 in. long, 4 in. wide, of 2 shapes, the lower unequally swollen, with broad, fringed wings, the upper funnelform, the narrow wings not or slightly fringed. Malay Pen., Sumatra, Borneo.

sanguinea Lindl. Lvs. 4–16 in. long, pitchers cylindrical, unequally swollen, 4–12 in. long, deep red to green and red, becoming paler toward the apex, purple-spotted, wings fringed. Malay Pen.

×**superba** B. S. Williams: parentage unknown, perhaps *N. Hookerana* × *N.* ×*Sedenii* M. T. Mast. Pitchers 6–8 in. long, green, blotched purple, wings ciliate.

ventricosa Blanco. Terrestrial or epiphytic; lvs. to 10 in. long, pitchers 4–7 in. long, swollen at the base, constricted in the middle, pale or whitish-green, tinged red, rim red or green and red. Philippine Is.

×**Williamsii** M. T. Mast.: parentage unknown, perhaps *N. Hookerana* × *N.* ×*Sedenii* M. T. Mast. Pitchers yellow-red or pale red with many bright red blotches.

NEPETA L. CATMINT. *Labiatae.* About 250 spp. of per. and sometimes ann. herbs of dry habitats of temp. Eur., Asia, n. Afr., and mts. of trop. Afr.; sts. mostly square in cross section; lvs. opp., usually petioled; fls. bisexual or unisexual, in verticillasters, calyx tubular, 5-toothed, corolla tube dilated, limb 2-lipped, upper lip erect, 2-lobed, lower lip 3-lobed, stamens 4, in 2 pairs, anther cells divergent, opening by a common slit; fr. of 4 glabrous, obovoid nutlets.

Grown as ground covers, as edging plants for borders, in rock gardens, and for medicinal purposes. Propagated by seeds or division; easily grown.

amethystina: *N. Nepetella* subsp.

camphorata Boiss. & Heldr. To 1½ ft., viscid-hairy; lvs. ovate, to ¾ in. long, cordate, crenate, viscid-hairy, with a camphor odor when crushed; infl. racemose, verticillasters spaced apart, bractlets linear, half as long as calyx; calyx gray, teeth much shorter than the tube, corolla to ½ in. long, white with purple spots. S. Greece.

Cataria L. CATNIP, CATMINT. To 3 ft., gray-pubescent; lvs. ovate, to 3 in. long, acute, cordate at base, crenate or serrate, gray-tomentose beneath; infl. spikelike, lower verticillasters spaced apart; calyx ovoid, about ³⁄₁₆ in. long, corolla to ⅜ in. long, white with pale purple spots. Summer. Eurasia; widely naturalized elsewhere. Attractive to cats and frequently grown for their enjoyment; a sweet herb sometimes used as a tea. Cv. '**Citriodora**'. Lemon-scented.

×**Faassenii** Bergmans ex Stearn [*N. pseudomussinii* Floto]: *N. Mussinii* × *N. Nepetella.* To 2 ft., short-pubescent; lvs. lanceolate to oblong-ovate, to 1¼ in. long, truncate at base, coarsely crenate-dentate; infl. an elongate or interrupted raceme, with axillary, peduncled cymes, bracts linear-lanceolate, very short; calyx about ⅔ as long as corolla tube, white-pubescent, slightly oblique, teeth short, acute, corolla to ½ in. long, violet-blue. Spring and summer. A sterile hybrid of hort. origin; sometimes confused with *N. Mussinii.*

Glechoma: *Glechoma hederacea.*

grandiflora Bieb. Sts. 1½–3 ft., glabrous or puberulent; lvs. ovate, to 2 in. long, cordate, crenulate; fls. in an elongate, interrupted raceme, bractlets subulate, short, calyx to about ½ in. long, often blue, corolla to ¾ in. long, lavender-blue. Summer. Caucasus; naturalized locally in e. Eur.

hederacea: *Glechoma hederacea.*

macrantha: *N. sibirica.*

melissifolia Lam. Sts. 8–16 in., ascending, pubescent to villous; lvs. ovate, to 1⅜ in. long, cordate at base, coarsely crenate, pubescent; infl. elongate, racemose; calyx to ⅜ in. long, corolla about ½ in. long, blue, with small red spots. Summer. Crete, Greece.

Mussinii K. Spreng. ex Henckel. Decumbent, sts. to 1 ft., short-pubescent; lvs. ovate-cordate, to 1 in. long, crenate, gray-green; infl. a loose terminal raceme; calyx about half as long as corolla, oblique, frequently blue, white-pubescent, corolla ⁵⁄₁₆ in. long, blue. Caucasus, Iran.

Nepetella L. Sts. to 4 ft., puberulent; lvs. lanceolate, to 1 in. long, truncate at base, crenate to deeply dentate, gray-green to green, pubescent, usually branched; infl. usually glandular; lower bracts leaflike, bractlets linear-lanceolate, about ⅛ in. long; calyx about half as long as corolla, slightly oblique, pubescent to villous, teeth triangular, often tinged pink or blue, corolla ½ in. long, white, pink, or blue. Sw. Eur. to s. Italy. A very polymorphic sp., especially in Spain. Subsp. **amethystina** (Poir.) Briq. [*N. amethystina* Poir.]. Corolla bluish-violet. Iberian Pen. and N. Afr.

nervosa Royle ex Benth. To 2 ft., glabrescent; lvs. narrowly lanceolate, to 4 in. long, entire or slightly dentate; infl. a dense raceme 5 in. long and ½ in. in diam.; calyx half as long as corolla, teeth subulate, as long as tube, ciliate, corolla to ½ in. long, blue or yellowish. Summer. Kashmir.

nuda L. [*N. pannonica* L.]. To 4 ft., glabrescent; lvs. ovate to ovate-oblong, to 2 in. long, somewhat cordate, acute or obtuse, crenate; infl. usually branched; calyx about half as long as corolla, teeth subulate, shorter than the tube, corolla ¼ in. long, pale violet or white. Summer. S. Eur. and Asia.

pannonica: *N. nuda.*

×**pseudomussinii:** *N.* ×*Faassenii.*

raphanorhiza Benth. To 18 in., glabrescent; lvs. ovate to ovate-cordate, to ½ in. long, crenate; infl. a dense, ovoid raceme, about 1 in. long; calyx half as long as corolla, teeth lanceolate, short, corolla to ⁵⁄₁₆ in. long, purplish-blue. W. Himalayas.

reticulata: *N. tuberosa* subsp.

sibirica L. [*N. macrantha* Fisch. ex Benth.]. To 3 ft., glabrous to glabrescent; lvs. lanceolate to ovate-lanceolate, to 3½ in. long, cordate or cuneate, serrate; infl. a raceme, with axillary, peduncled cymes;

calyx ⅓ as long as corolla, violet-tinged, mouth oblique, teeth short, acute, corolla to 1½ in. long, violet-blue, tube not curved. Summer. Siberia.

Stewartiana Diels. Differs from *N. sibirica* in having fls. smaller and corolla tube curved. Pakistan.

tuberosa L. Rhizome tuberous, sts. to 2½ ft., pubescent to woolly; lvs. ovate-lanceolate to oblong, to 3¼ in. long; infl. a simple spike, bracts broadly ovate to lanceolate, membranous, greenish-white, pink, or red-purple; calyx nearly as long as corolla, corolla to ½ in. long, purple or violet. Portugal, Spain, Sicily. Subsp. **tuberosa.** The typical subsp.; bracts nearly erect, overlapping, lanceolate, reddish-purple.

ucranica L. To 2 ft., erect, much-branched, glabrescent; lvs. oblong-lanceolate, to 1¾ in. long, obtuse or somewhat acute, crenate-serrate, glabrous; infl. cymose, loose, cymes many, few-fld.; calyx about ¼ in. long, often bluish, teeth linear or linear-lanceolate, longer than tube; corolla about ¼ in. long, blue-violet. Bulgaria, Romania, Asia.

NEPHELEA Tryon. TREE FERN. *Cyatheaceae.* About 30 spp. of evergreen tree ferns of the New World; trunks to 30 ft. or more, spiny; lvs. dark green, usually 2–3-pinnate, petioles with very sharp black spines and scales with a delicately differentiated margin and a black terminal bristle; sori on lower surface of pinnules near the midrib, indusia absent, or saucer-shaped to globose.

For culture see *Ferns.*

incana (Karst.) Gastony [*Cyathea incana* Karst.]. Trunk to 8 ft. or more; petioles straw-colored, with soft, scurfy scales, lvs. 2-pinnate-pinnatifid, with minute, fimbriate scales beneath; indusia shaggy with soft hairs. Colombia to nw. Argentina.

mexicana (Schlechtend. & Cham.) Tryon [*Cyathea mexicana* Schlechtend. & Cham.]. Petioles with very sharp blackish spines, lvs. 3-pinnate, pinnules jointed at point of attachment, rachis pubescent and with some whitish scales bearing darker marginal spinules. Mex. to Ecuador. Zone 10. Needs winter protection in s. Calif.

NEPHELIUM L. *Sapindaceae.* Not in cult. **N. Litchi:** *Litchi chinensis.* **N. Longan:** *Euphoria Longan.* **N. malaiense:** *E. malaiensis.*

NEPHROLEPIS Schott. SWORD FERN. *Polypodiaceae.* About 30 spp. of trop. and subtrop. terrestrial ferns of both hemispheres, usually stoloniferous with short, erect rhizomes; lvs. tufted, scaly, usually long and narrow, pinnate to decompound, pinnae jointed on the rachis, veins separate; sori terminal on the veins, indusia round to lunate, fixed by a point or along the base.

Sword ferns are favorite house or greenhouse plants. They are commonly propagated by rooting runners or by crown divisions, as good spores may not be produced by all of the many cultivars. The plants thrive under common or even poor conditions and produce dense, attractive crowns of long, often drooping lvs. See also *Ferns.*

acuminata (Houtt.) Kuhn [*N. davallioides* Kunze]. Lvs. drooping, 1-pinnate, to 3 ft. long and 1 ft. wide, pinnae linear-lanceolate, coarsely toothed, the fertile ones much contracted; sori solitary on small marginal lobes. Malay Pen.

biserrata (Swartz) Schott [*N. ensifolia* K. Presl]. SWORD FERN. Lvs. drooping or arching, 1-pinnate, to 4½ ft. long and 1 ft. wide, pinnae distant, to 6 in. long, toothed; indusia facing the margin but somewhat distant from it. Tropics. Cv. 'Furcans'. FISHTAIL FERN. Pinnules forked.

bostoniensis: *N. exaltata* cv.

cordata: *N. cordifolia.*

cordifolia (L.) K. Presl [*N. cordata* Hort.; *N. tuberosa* K. Presl]. ERECT S.F., LADDER F., SWORD F. Rhizomes usually bearing tubers; lvs. erect or nearly so, 1-pinnate, to 2 ft. long and 2½ in. wide, bright green, pinnae close together, to 1¼ in. long, sharp-toothed; indusia facing the apex of pinna, reniform to lunate. Tropics and subtropics. Cvs. include: 'Compacta', 'Gigantea', Plumosa', 'Tessellata', 'Variegata'.

coreacea: a listed name of uncertain application.

davallioides: *N. acuminata.*

Duffii T. Moore [*N. cordifolia* cv. 'Duffii']. DUFF'S S. F. Tufted, graceful; lvs. 1-pinnate, to 2 ft. long and ½ in. wide, usually forked or crested at tips, pinnae nearly orbicular, ¼ in. across, wavy-toothed. New Zeal. or Pacific Is. Probably a mutant of *N. cordifolia.*

ensifolia: *N. biserrata.*

exaltata (L.) Schott. Stiff, erect; lvs. 1-pinnate, to 4–5-pinnate in some cvs., to 5 ft. long and 6 in. wide, pinnae close together, to 3 in.

long, entire or slightly toothed; sori submarginal, indusia orbicular-reniform. Tropics. Cv. 'Bostoniensis'. BOSTON FERN. More graceful and drooping, a popular house fern; from cv. 'Bostoniensis' or its derivatives many additional cvs. have been selected, often with much-divided or even crested lvs. These include: 'Amerschlii', 'Anna Foster', 'Barrowsii', 'Childsii', 'Dreyeri', 'Edmontoniensis', 'Elegantissima' and its variant cvs. 'Compacta' (DWARF BOSTON FERN) and 'Compacta Cristata', 'Elmsfordii', 'Falcata', 'Fluffy Ruffles', 'Forsterana', 'Galvestonii', 'Giatrasii', 'Goodii', 'Gretnai', 'Harrisii', 'Hillsii', 'Lycopodioides', 'Maasil', 'Macawii', 'Magnifica', 'Milleri', 'M. P. Mills', 'Milsii', 'Muscosa', 'Neubertii', 'New York', 'Norwoodii', 'Ostrich Plume', 'Philippinensis', 'Piersonii', 'Randolphii', 'Robusta', 'Rooseveltii', 'Scholzelii', 'Schubertii', 'Scottii', 'Smithii', (LACE FERN), 'Sparrowii', 'Splendida', 'Superba', 'Superbissima', 'Tripartita', 'Todeoides', 'Verona', 'Victorii', 'Viridissima', 'Wanamakeri', 'Whitmanii' (LACE FERN, FEATHER FERN), 'Wicheri', 'Wilsonii', 'Wittboldii', 'Wredei'.

furcans: a listed name of no botanical standing for *N. biserrata* cv. 'Furcans'.

hirsutula (G. Forst.) K. Presl. Lvs. drooping, 1-pinnate, 2–4 ft. long and to 6 in. wide, with many brown scales on the rachis and lower surface, pinnae elongate, acuminate, sharply auricled at base on upper margin, auricles to 5/16 in. long. Tropics.

pectinata (Willd.) Schott. BASKET FERN, TOOTHED S. F. Small, compact; lvs. 1-pinnate, to 1½ ft. long and 1 in. wide, grayish-green, pinnae close together, ½ in. long, inequilateral at base, toothed. Trop. Amer.

tuberosa: *N. cordifolia.*

NEPHROPHYLLIDIUM: *FAURIA.*

NEPHROSPERMA Balf.f. *Palmae.* One sp., a solitary, monoecious palm in the Seychelles; lvs. pinnate, sheath whitish with black spines, not forming a crownshaft, petiole short, unarmed, pinnae 1-ribbed and paired or 2–3-ribbed, regularly arranged, midrib prominent; infl. interfoliar, long-peduncled, lower bract 2-edged, open at apex, often black-spiny, upper bract longer, prickly, beaked, deciduous, rachillae many, simple, with fls. in triads (2 male and 1 female); male fls. symmetrical, with sepals imbricate, petals valvate, stamens 40–50, filaments erect, pistillode small, female fls. with sepals and petals imbricate, staminodes 6, pistil 1-celled, 1-ovuled; fr. globose, with stigmatic residue in upper ⅓, endocarp operculate, seed slightly reniform, endosperm ruminate, embryo basal.

A tender palm suitable for gardens in the tropics. For culture see *Palms.*

Vanhoutteanum (H. Wendl. ex van Houtte) Balf.f. To 30 ft. or more, sts. to 6 in. in diam.; lvs. to 6 ft. long, pinnae 25–40 on each side; infl. with peduncle to 9 ft. long or more, rachis 30 in. long, upper bract 20 in. long; male fls. 3/16 in. long; fr. cherry-red at maturity, ⅜–½ in. in diam.

NEPHTHYTIS Schott. *Araceae.* Four spp. of herbs, native to Afr.; lvs. few, arising from short, horizontal rhizomes, sagittate or hastate with large basal lobes, petioles long, cylindrical; peduncle nearly as long as petiole, spathe expanded, erect or reflexed, green, persistent; fls. unisexual, perianth absent; fr. a berry, orange. Doubtfully in the trade and of little ornamental value except in fr. Material so listed is probably *Syngonium.*

Strictly tropical; for culture see *Callopsis.*

Afzelii Schott [*N. liberica* N. E. Br., not Hort.]. Lf. blades to 14 in. long and 10 in. wide; spathe oblong, to 2¾ in. long and 1⅜ in. wide, spadix nearly sessile; female fls. with broad, discoid, coronate stigmas; berries obovoid, less than ⅜ in. long. Sierra Leone and Liberia. Material of *Syngonium podophyllum* has been offered under this name.

Gravenreuthii Engl. Differs from *N. Poissonii* in having spathe ovate, about ¾ in. wide, and spadix on free stalk above spathe to ⅛ in. long. Cameroon. Probably not specifically distinct from *N. Poissonii.*

Hoffmannii: *Syngonium Hoffmannii.*

liberica: see *N. Afzelii* and *Syngonium podophyllum.* Var. **variegata:** see *Syngonium angustatum* cv. 'Albolineatum'.

picturata: *Rhektophyllum mirabile.*

Poissonii (Engl.) N. E. Br. Differs from *N. Afzelii* in having spathe oblong-ovate, about 2 in. wide, spadix on free stalk above spathe to ⅜ in. long, pistils with distinct, short styles, and berries ellipsoidal, to 1¼ in. long. Cameroon, Gabon.

triphylla: see *Syngonium podophyllum.*

Wendlandii: *Syngonium Wendlandii.*

NEPTUNIA Lour. *Leguminosae* (subfamily *Mimosoideae*). About 10 spp. of diffusely branched or prostrate per. herbs of worldwide distribution; lvs. alt., 2-pinnate, lfts. small, stipules obliquely cordate; fls. in solitary, axillary heads, regular, 5-merous, stamens 10(-5), separate, exserted, basal fls. with long, petal-like staminodes; fr. a flat legume, ⅓–½ as broad as long.

Grown as ornamentals; propagated by seeds.

lutea (Leavenw.) Benth. Prostrate or spreading, pubescent per. herb; lfts. in 9-17 pairs, oblong, to ⅛ in. long, with a short point; fls. yellow, in dense heads to ¾ in. long. Okla. and Tex.

NERINE Herb. *Amaryllidaceae*. Twenty or more spp. of autumn-flowering herbs with tunicate bulbs, native to S. Afr.; lvs. strap-shaped, basal, usually absent at flowering time; umbel terminal on a solid scape, subtended by 2 separate spathe valves; fls. funnelform, in shades of red to white, perianth tube very short or lacking, segms. equal, stamens nearly erect or declinate, ovary inferior, cells with few ovules; fr. a caps., seeds globose.

Nerines are tender and are grown mostly in pots in the greenhouse, or outdoors in Zone 9. They should be given plenty of water until after flowering, and the bulbs should then be rested for a few months. Propagated by offsets.

Bowdenii W. Wats. To 15 in.; lvs. strap-shaped, obtuse; umbel 8–12-fld.; fls. bright rose-pink, segms. to 3 in. long, spreading, margin wavy and crisped, reflexed at tip, stamens and style longer than segms., declinate.

coruscans: a hort. name, perhaps for *N. sarniensis* var.

curvifolia (Jacq.) Herb. To 1½ ft.; lvs. 1 ft. long, curved, glaucous, developing after fls.; umbel 8–12–fld.; fls. to 1½ in. long, scarlet, stamens and style nearly straight, about as long as segms. Var. **Fothergillii** (Andr.) Bak. [*N. Fothergillii* (Andr.) M. J. Roem.]. More vigorous; fls. many.

×**erubescens** Hort. ex Bak.: *N. flexuosa* × *N. undulata*.

falcata W. F. Barker. To nearly 2 ft.; lvs. sickle-shaped, erect or spreading and somewhat twisted, developing with the fls.; umbel 20–25-fld.; perianth segms. spreading, then recurved, white with rose-pink, tips slightly undulate, stamens declinate.

filifolia Bak. Lvs. nearly erect, grasslike, to 8 in. long; umbel 8–10-fld.; fls. bright red, to 1 in. long, segms. narrow, oblanceolate, stamens and style declinate, shorter than segms.

flexuosa (Jacq.) Herb. To 3 ft.; lvs. linear, strap-shaped, to ¾ in. wide; umbel 10–20-fld.; fls. pale pink, to 1½ in. long, segms. with crisped margins, stamens and style shorter than segms., declinate. Cv. **'Alba'**. Fls. white.

Fothergillii: *N. curvifolia* var.

laticoma: *N. lucida*.

lucida Burchell ex Herb. [*N. laticoma* (Ker-Gawl.) T. Durand & Schinz]. To 8 in.; lvs. 6–8, linear, developing with the fls.; umbel 20–40-fld.; fls. on pedicels to 4 in. long, pale or bright red, segms. ¼ in. wide, scarcely crisped, stamens and style declinate.

magnifica: a listed name of no botanical standing, for a plant said to be similar to *N. Bowdenii*, but with fls. larger, deeper pink.

×**Mansellii** Hort. ex Bak.. *N. curvifolia* var. *Fothergillii* × *N. flexuosa*.

Masonorum L. Bolus. To 9 in.; lvs. 4–5, suberect, filiform; umbel 4–12-fld.; fls. rose-pink with darker stripe, segms. undulate, recurved, to ½ in. long, stamens shorter than segms., declinate, with small appendages at base.

rosea: *N. sarniensis* var.

sarniensis (L.) Herb. GUERNSEY LILY. To 1½ ft.; lvs. green, to 1 ft. long and ¾ in. wide, developing after fls.; fls. crimson, 1½ in. long, segms. slightly crisped, stamens bright red, nearly straight, exserted. Cv. **'Maxima'** [cv. 'Major']. Fls. crimson-red. Var. **corusca** (Ker-Gawl.) Bak. Lvs. broader, with crossbars between veins; fls. salmon-red, large. Var. **rosea** (Herb.) Bak. [*N. rosea* Herb.]. Lvs. darker; fls. rose-red. *Lycoris radiata* has long been distributed as this sp.

undulata (L.) Herb. To 1½ ft.; lvs. 4–6, linear, to 1½ ft. long, ½ in. wide; umbel 8–12-fld.; fls. pale pink, to ¾ in. long, nodding, stamens declinate, about as long as segms.

NERIUM L. OLEANDER. *Apocynaceae*. Two spp. of evergreen, erect shrubs, native from Medit. region to Japan; sap not milky; lvs. mostly in whorls of 3, lanceolate, entire; fls. showy, in terminal branching cymes, 5-merous, bisexual, corolla funnelform, with a corona of 5 laciniate-dentate scales in the throat, lobes obovate, stamens borne at middle of corolla tube, anthers connivent, adhering to stigma, with slender basal lobes and apical awns; fr. a pair of slender, elongate follicles, seeds with tuft of hairs.

Oleanders are grown outdoors in mild climates. They require little attention, and are very drought resistant. In cold regions they are favorite pot or tub plants, and should be cut back and rested after flowering, then potted in loam and rotted manure. Propagated easily by cuttings of mature firm wood, sometimes in water. All parts are very poisonous if eaten.

indicum: *N. Oleander*.

odorum: *N. Oleander*.

Oleander L. [*N. indicum* Mill.; *N. odorum* Ait.]. COMMON O., ROSE-BAY. Shrub to 20 ft.; lvs. linear- to oblong-lanceolate, to 10 in. long, dark dull green; fls. yellowish to rose-pink, red-purple, or white, sometimes scented, 1-2 in. across; follicles 4-7 in. long. Medit. region to Japan. Cvs. include: **'Album'**, **'Atropurpureum'**, **'Roseum'**, **'Splendens'**, and **'Variegata'**. Sweet-scented oleanders, of which a double-fld. red is common, are often listed as *N. indicum* or *N. odorum*.

NERTERA Banks & Soland. ex Gaertn. *Rubiaceae*. About 12 spp. of creeping, slender, per. herbs, rooting at nodes, from s. China to Java, Australia, New Zeal., Society Is., Hawaii, S. Amer.; lvs. opp., small, stipules interpetiolar; fls. solitary, axillary or terminal, inconspicuous, 4–5-merous, corolla tube funnelform, anthers exserted; fr. a fleshy, 2–seeded drupe.

One species is cultivated as a ground cover in Calif. and under glass in the North. It should be grown in a shady place in sandy or light soil. Propagated by seeds and division.

depressa: *N. granadensis*.

granadensis (Mutis) Druce [*N. depressa* Banks & Soland. ex Gaertn.]. BEAD PLANT, CORAL MOSS, ENGLISH BABYTEARS, CORAL-BEAD PLANT. Sts. glabrous, to 10 in. long, matted; lvs. broad-ovate, to ³⁄₁₆ in. long; fls. greenish, minute; fr. orange, about ¼ in. across. S. Amer., New Zeal., Tasmania.

NESAEA Comm. ex Juss. *Lythraceae*. Not cult. **N. verticillata:** *Decodon verticillatus*.

NESTEGIS Raf. *Oleaceae*. Four spp. of dioecious or monoecious trees or shrubs of New Zeal.; lvs. opp., entire, those on adult plants differing from those on the juvenile; fls. in racemes, unisexual or bisexual, petals 0; fr. a drupe, usually red. Often placed in the genus *Olea* but having no petals.

Cunninghamii (Hook.f.) L. A. S. Johnson. To 60 ft.; lvs. of adult plants narrowly lanceolate to elliptic, to nearly 6 in. long, to 1³⁄₁₆ in. wide, glabrous, midrib and primary veins more or less impressed in upper surface, pubescent when young; infl. to 1⅝ in. long, 9–19-fld., densely pubescent; calyx tube short, less than ⅛ in. long; fr. ovoid or oblong-ovoid, to ⅝ in. long, red.

lanceolata (Hook.f.) L. A. S. Johnson [*Olea lanceolata* Hook.f.]. Tree, to 45 ft.; lvs. on adult plants lanceolate, to 5 in. long, entire, thickish and leathery, primary veins usually more or less visible; infl. to 1¼ in. long, 11–17-fld., puberulous; calyx divided almost to base; fr. elliptic, red or orange, to ½ in. long.

montana (Hook.f.) L. A. S. Johnson [*Olea montana* Hook.f.]. Differs from *N. lanceolata* chiefly in having lvs. of adult plants narrower, linear or very narrowly lanceolate, with venation usually obscure.

NEVIUSIA A. Gray. SNOW-WREATH. *Rosaceae*. One sp., a deciduous shrub, native to Ala.; lvs. simple, doubly serrate; fls. many, borne in short open cymes, calyx tube flattish, sepals 5, whitish, toothed, petals none, stamens many, filaments white, conspicuous, pistils 2–4; frs. 2–4 achenes.

Grown outdoors as an ornamental and sometimes forced under glass. Propagated by seeds and by cuttings of young wood in the greenhouse. Hardy in New Eng. and central N.Y. in protected places.

alabamensis A. Gray. To 6 ft.; lvs. to 3 in. long, sharp-pointed; sepals to ½ in.long, incised-serrate above the middle, stamens giving a feathery appearance to infl. Ala. Zone 6.

NEWBOULDIA Seem. *Bignoniaceae*. One sp., an evergreen tree or shrub, native to W. Trop. Afr.; lvs. opp. or in 3's, rarely alt., pinnate; fls. pink, purple, or purple and white, in terminal panicles, calyx spathelike, corolla campanulate-funnelform, slightly 2-lipped, stamens 4; fr. a linear caps.

laevis Seem. Shrub or tree, 10–40 ft.; lvs. 1–2 ft. long, lfts. 7–13, ovate-oblong, obovate, or lanceolate, 3–8 in. long; fls. to 2¼ in. long; fr. to 1 ft. long.

NEW ZEALAND SPINACH: see *Spinach.*

NEYRAUDIA Hook.f. *Gramineae.* About 6 spp. of tall, reedlike per. grasses in the Old World; panicles large, open, many-fld.; spikelets 4–8-fld., pedicelled, rachilla jointed about halfway between the florets, the part below the joint glabrous, the part above bearded, forming a stalk below the mature floret, glumes unequal, 1-nerved, shorter than first floret, lemma narrow, awned, conspicuously long-pilose on the margins. For terminology see *Gramineae.*

Reynaudiana (Kunth) Keng ex A. S. Hitchc. BURMA REED. Sts. to 10 ft.; lf. sheaths woolly at the throat and on the collar, blades flat, to ¾ in. wide; panicle nodding, 1–2 ft. long; spikelets to ⁵⁄₁₆ in. long, rather short-pedicelled, lemma somewhat curved, slender, awn flat, recurved. Introd. from s. Asia. Occasionally planted and escaped in the South.

NICANDRA Adans. *Solanaceae.* One sp., an erect, glabrous, ann. herb, native to Peru; lvs. alt., coarsely sinuate-dentate to slightly lobed; fls. solitary, large, calyx 5-parted, corolla blue, or violet and white, broadly campanulate, obscurely 5-lobed, stamens 5, borne on the corolla, ovary 3–5-celled; fr. a globose berry, not fleshy, enclosed by the enlarged calyx.

Planted in the open in southern U.S. or under glass in the North. Easily propagated by seeds.

Physalodes (L.) Gaertn. APPLE-OF-PERU, SHOO-FLY PLANT. Ann., 3–8 ft.; lvs. ovate, to 1 ft. long, acute, sinuately toothed; fls. axillary, long-pedicelled, corolla 1 in. across or more, blue. Escaped in U.S. and Amer. tropics, often weedy. Cv. **'Violacea'.** Corolla violet-blue on upper half, white on the lower.

NICODEMIA: *BUDDLEIA.*

NICOLAIA Horan. [*Phaeomeria* Lindl. ex K. Schum.]. *Zingiberaceae.* About 16 spp. of per., aromatic herbs from Ceylon to New Guinea; differing from *Amomum* in that the persistent lower bracts of infl. are brightly colored and reflexed and form an involucre.

For culture see *Zingiberaceae.*

elatior (Jack) Horan. [*Phaeomeria magnifica* (Roscoe) K. Schum.; *P. speciosa* (Blume) Koord.]. TORCH GINGER, PHILIPPINE WAXFLOWER. Leafy sts. to 15 ft.; lvs. linear- to oblong-lanceolate, to 2 ft. long or more, 6 in. wide, glabrous; fl. st. to 4 ft., spike pyramidal, to 5 in. long, outer bracts waxy, red margined with pink, to 5 in. long, inner bracts about 2 in. long; corolla red. Celebes and Java. Much cult. in Hawaii and the tropics generally.

NICOTIANA L. *Solanaceae.* About 70 spp. of ann. or per. herbs, rarely shrubs, native to trop. and warm temp. Amer. and Australasia, and Polynesia, usually sticky-hairy; lvs. alt., simple, entire, rarely sinuate; fls. in a terminal panicle, or in elongate, 1-sided racemose cymes, or the lower solitary in the axils, usually opening at night and then most fragrant, calyx tubular-campanulate, 5-lobed, persistent, corolla white, yellow, greenish, purple, or red, salverform, tube long, limb 5-lobed, often oblique, stamens 5, included or exserted; fr. a 2- or rarely 4-valved caps., seeds many, minute.

The genus yields tobacco and includes a number of ornamental species. Nicotianas are easily grown but are sensitive to frost. Some of them make good pot plants and border subjects. Propagated by seeds, the ornamental cultivars also by cuttings, and *N. alata* cv. 'Grandiflora' by root cuttings.

acuminata (R. C. Grah.) Hook. Viscid ann., to 6 ft.; lvs. ovate to triangular-lanceolate, mostly 4–10 in. long; infl. paniculate, large, but rather few-fld.; corolla greenish-white, with dark green veins, tube cylindrical, 2–3½ in. long, limb ¾ in. across, with shallow, entire or slightly notched lobes, stamens included. Chile, Argentina. Herbage has unpleasant acrid odor. Var. **multiflora** (Phil.) Reiche. Corolla less than 1¾ in. long. Chile.

affinis: *N. alata.*

alata Link & Otto [*N. affinia* T. Moore]. JASMINE TOBACCO, FLOWERING T. Coarse, viscid per., 3–4½ ft., sometimes with basal brs.; lvs. ovate to elliptic, 4–10 in. long, decurrent; infl. a short, few-fld. raceme; corolla chalky-white inside, greenish outside, tube 2–4 in. long, ex-

panding into a larger throat ⁵⁄₁₆ in. in diam., limb about 1 in. across, irregular, deeply cut into broadly ovate lobes, anthers purple, extending to mouth of throat. Warm temp. S. Amer. Cv. **'Grandiflora'.** Fls. 2 in. across, corolla with larger, more widely dilated throat. Cv. **Nana'.** Plants dwarf. Cv. **'Rubella'.** Fls. rose-red.

attenuata Torr. ex S. Wats. Erect, simple or branched, mostly viscid-pubescent ann., to 4½ ft.; lower lvs. elliptic, to 6 in. long, upper lvs. smaller, narrower; infl. racemose or paniculate; calyx to ⅜ in. long, corolla white, blushed pink outside, tube nearly cylindrical, to 1 in. long, limb to ½ in. across, with upper lobes slightly reflexed, stamens not exserted. B.C. to Baja Calif. Used by the Indians of w. N. Amer. for tobacco.

Bigelovii (Torr.) S. Wats. Glandular, ill-smelling ann., to 4 ft., brs. ascending; lvs. oblong-ovate to lanceolate, 2–8 in. long; fls. in racemes, calyx to ¾ in. long, corolla white, tinged with green, tube to 2½ in. long, limb to 2 in. across. S. Ore. to s. Calif. Used by the Indians of w. N. Amer. for tobacco.

glauca R. C. Grah. TREE TOBACCO, MUSTARD TREE. Mostly glabrous, glaucous, branched shrub or small tree, 10–30 ft.; lvs. thickish and rubbery, ovate to lanceolate, 2–10 in. long, petioles half as long; infl. a short, loose or dense panicle; corolla yellow, tube 1¼–1¾ in. long, dilated above, somewhat contracted at mouth, limb narrow, shallowly and acutely lobed, stamens included. S. Bolivia, n. Argentina; naturalized in the U.S. in Zones 9 and 10. Lvs. toxic to livestock.

longiflora Cav. LONG-FLOWERED TOBACCO. Glabrescent ann. or per., 1½–3½ ft.; st. lvs. ovate to lanceolate, undulate, sessile; infl. racemose; corolla white to lavender inside, purplish-gray outside, tube 1½–4½ in. long, dilated abruptly just below the mouth, limb about 1¾ in. across, deeply acuminately lobed. Warm-temp. S. Amer.; occasionally adventive in e. U.S.

rustica L. TOBACCO, WILD T. Coarse ann., 1½–3½ ft., sts. viscid-pubescent; lvs. ovate-cordate to elliptic, 4–8 in. long, fleshy; infl. a panicle; corolla greenish-yellow, tube broadly cylindrical, ½–¾ in. long, limb scarcely ½ in. across, with very short obtuse lobes. Andes, Ecuador to Bolivia; sporadically naturalized in e. U.S. Cult. in Eur. and Asia for the insecticidal nicotine, and as a fumitory. This is the original tobacco, smaller and hardier then *N. Tabacum* and cult. in pre-Columbian times by Indians of Mex. and e. N. Amer. and later by the colonists of Va.; the first tobacco introd. to the Old World. See also *N. Tabacum.*

×**Sanderae** Hort. Sander ex W. Wats.: *N. alata* × *N. Forgetiana* Hort. Sander ex Hemsl. Bushy, viscid-pubescent ann., 2–3 ft.; basal lvs. spatulate, 6–12 in. long, undulate; fls. in loose panicles, corolla tube greenish-yellow, tinted rose, 2–3½ in. long, limb usually red, but varying from white to rose or deep violet, to 2 in. across. Cv. **'Sutton's Scarlet'.** Fls. large, corolla deep red.

suaveolens Lehm. Glabrate ann., to 3½ ft.; lvs. oblanceolate to lanceolate, 4–10 in. long, petiole winged; infl. a panicle; corolla white inside, cream-colored with green to purple veins outside, tube to 1 in. long, throat dilated, limb 1–1½ in. across, with shallow, obtuse, entire to notched lobes. Se. Australia.

sylvestris Speg. & Comes. Similar to *N. alata*, but lvs. 8–20 in. long, not commonly decurrent, and corolla tube spindle-shaped, broadest at or slightly above the middle. Argentina.

Tabacum L. TOBACCO. Stout, viscid ann. or per., 3–10 ft.; lvs. ovate to lanceolate, cuneate; infl. a panicle; corolla varying from greenish-cream to pink or red, tube ½–⅝ in. long, dilated throat 1–1½ in. long, limb about 1 in. across, with acuminate lobes, anthers often slightly exserted. Trop. Amer., now widely cult. as principal source of commercial tobacco. A long-time cultigen, originating in pre-Columbian times.

NIDULARIUM Lem. *Bromeliaceae.* About 23 spp. of epiphytic herbs, native to Brazil; lvs. in dense basal rosettes, prickly-margined; fls. red, purplish, or white, in a sessile, compound, central infl. subtended by usually colored, modified lvs. or bracts, petals without appendages, united at the base, hooded, erect, pollen sculptured, ovary inferior; fr. a berry, seeds without appendages.

Grown outdoors in warm climates or under glass. Requires filtered light. For culture see *Bromeliaceae.*

amazonicum: *Wittrockia amazonica*, but most material cult. as *N. amazonicum* is *N. Innocentii* var. *Innocentii.*

billbergioides (Schult.f.) L. B. Sm. [*N. citrinum* (Burchell ex Bak.) Mez]. Stoloniferous; lvs. about 8, to 1 ft. long, minutely spiny, pale green with paler center and brown-dotted; infl. scapose, ¾ as long as lvs., bracts yellowish to pale rose; fls. white, 1 in. long.

Burchellii Mez. Lvs. few, narrowly sword-shaped above the tubular sheaths, to 16 in. long, 1¾ in. wide, minutely spiny, often red or purplish, at least beneath; infl. bracts sometimes orangish, fl. bracts and axis rusty-scurfy; fls. 1 in. long, white.

Chloro-Marechallii: a listed name of no botanical standing.

citrinum: *N. billbergioides.*

fulgens Lem. [*N. pictum* Hort.]. BLUSHING BROMELIAD. Lvs. to 1 ft. long, 2 in. wide, spotted with dark green, with spines to 3/16 in. long; infl. sessile, bracts bright scarlet; fls. in dense clusters, white, with violet limb.

Innocentii Lem. Lvs. to 1 ft. long, strap-shaped, with very short spines; infl. a dense, sessile head; fls. white, to 2 5/16 in. long or more. Var. **Innocentii.** The typical var.; lvs. dark red beneath or on both sides; primary infl. bracts red, sometimes tipped with green. Var. **lineatum** (Mez) L. B. Sm. [*N. lineatum* Mez]. Lvs. with many longitudinal white lines; primary infl. bracts green with red tips. Var. **striatum** Wittm. [*N. striatum* Hort. ex Mez]. Lvs. white-striped; primary infl. bracts mostly red-purple. Var. **Wittmackianum** (Harms) L. B. Sm. Lvs. green; primary infl. bracts mostly red-purple.

Lindenii: *Canistrum Lindenii.*

lineatum: *N. Innocentii* var.

Perringeanum: a listed name, apparently referable to *N. fulgens.*

pictum: *N. fulgens.*

procerum Lindm. Lvs. to 40 in. long, 2 in. wide, narrowed toward the spiny, acuminate tip; infl. scapose, longer than lf. sheaths, many-fld., star-shaped; fls. blue. Var. **Kermesianum** (Fritz Müll. ex Mez) Reitz. Lvs. only 16 in. long, not more than 1 3/16 in. wide.

regelioides Ule. Lvs. green, tubular, in a rosette, to 16 in. long, 2 3/8 in. wide, nearly smooth or minutely spiny; infl. sessile, bracts purple, fl. bracts toothed; fls. red, to 2 1/8 in. long.

rutilans E. Morr. Lvs. to 1 ft. long, 3 in. wide, sparsely short-spinose, green; infl. sessile; fls. red, to 1 5/8 in. long.

Scheremetiewii Regel. Lvs. narrowed above the sheath, with short spines, green; infl. short-stalked, bracts red, spiny, fl. bracts entire; fls. blue, to 2 1/8 in. long.

striatum: *N. Innocentii* var.

NIEREMBERGIA Ruiz & Pav. CUPFLOWER. *Solanaceae.* About 30 spp. of decumbent to erect, diffusely branched, mostly glabrous, per. herbs and subshrubs, native from Mex. to Chile and Argentina; lvs. alt., simple, entire; fls. axillary, solitary or in cymes, calyx tubular to campanulate, deeply 5-lobed, corolla pale violet to blue or white, salverform to cup-shaped, limb 5-lobed, stamens borne on the corolla, fertile stamens 4, in pairs, staminode 1; fr. a 2-valved caps., seeds many.

Grown for the showy flowers in the open border, rock garden, or as pot plants. Propagated by seeds or in autumn by cuttings of firm shoots, *N. repens* most easily by division of creeping rooted stems. The species listed are hardy in Zone 7.

caerulea: see *N. hippomanica* var. *violacea.*

frutescens: *N. scoparia.*

gracilis Hook. Brs. ascending, to 18 in., very slender, downy-pubescent; lvs. linear to spatulate, generally 1/2 in. long, but sometimes 1 1/8 in. long; fls. axillary, on pedicels to 5/16 in. long, corolla white, tinged blue or violet toward center, with yellow throat, tube to 5/8 in. long, limb to 1 in. across. Paraguay, Argentina.

hippomanica Miers. Per., to 6–12 in. or more, pubescent; lvs. linear-spatulate, to 5/8 in. long; fls. with pedicels to 1/8 in. long, corolla bluish, tube to 3/8 in. long, limb to 3/4 in. across. Argentina. Var. **violacea** Millán [*N. caerulea* Sealy, not Miers]. The commonly cult. var.; to 15 in.; lvs. linear or linear-lanceolate, 3/4–1 in. long; pedicels to 5/16 in. long, corolla violet, tube to 5/8 in. long, limb to 1 1/2 in. across. Argentina; naturalized locally in U.S., in Zone 9.

repens Ruiz & Pav. [*N. rivularis* Miers]. WHITECUP. Creeping per., sts. rooting at nodes; lvs. oblong or spatulate, to 1 1/4 in. long, petioled; corolla whitish or pale lilac, with golden-yellow throat, tube to 2 in. long, limb broadly campanulate, to 2 in. across. Andean and warm-temp. S. Amer.

rivularis: *N. repens.*

scoparia Sendtn. [*N. frutescens* Durieu]. TALL C. To 3 ft., shrubby, much-branched, nearly glabrous; lvs. spatulate, to 3/4 in. long, obtuse; fls. with pedicels to 1/8 in. long, corolla violet, tube to 5/8 in. long, limb to 1 1/2 in. across. Uruguay, Argentina. Blooms almost continuously as a pot plant. Var. **glaberrima** Millán. Pedicels 1/8–1/4 in. long, fls. smaller. Uruguay.

NIGELLA L. FENNEL FLOWER, WILD FENNEL. *Ranunculaceae.* About 20 spp. of ann. herbs, native to the Medit. region and w. Asia; lvs. rarely entire or palmately parted, usually 2–3-pinnate into linear or filiform segms.; fls. mostly solitary, often showy, white, blue, or yellow, sepals mostly 5, petal-like, petals 5, 2-lipped, with a hollow nectariferous claw; fr. of 2–14 more or less united follicles.

Nigellas are planted in the flower garden and are of easy culture. Propagated by seeds, which may be sown where the plants are to stand in open sunny location.

aristata Sibth. & Sm. Resembling *N. arvensis,* but glaucescent, with slender brs.; lf. lobes narrower, uppermost lvs. forming an involucre around fl.; follicles united about half their length. Greece, Macedonia.

arvensis L. WILD FENNEL. To 1 1/2 ft.; lf. segms. filiform, lvs. not forming involucre around fl.; fls. bluish-white, 1 in. across or more; follicles 3–5, strongly ribbed, united about 2/3 their length, styles long, beaklike. N. Afr., Eur., Asia.

damascena L. LOVE-IN-A-MIST, WILD FENNEL. To 1 1/2 ft. or more, much-branched; lf. segms. filiform; fls. with large, finely divided involucre, white to light blue, to 1 1/2 in. across; fr. globular, inflated, follicles united to base of long, erect styles. N. Afr., s. Eur.

diversifolia: *N. integrifolia.*

hispanica L. To 1 1/2 ft., branching; lf. segms. linear, but not filiform; fls. solitary or in 2's, without involucre, blue, to 2 1/2 in. across, stamens red; follicles ribbed, united nearly to the top, styles spreading. Spain, N. Afr. Cv. **'Alba'.** Fls. white. Cv. **'Atropurpurea'.** Fls. purple.

integrifolia Regel [*N. diversifolia* Franch.]. Lower lvs. oblong-linear, entire, st. lvs. sessile, palmately parted into linear segms.; fls. pale bluish, in cymes; follicles 3, united to about middle, with short beaks. Turkestan.

sativa L. BLACK CUMIN, NUTMEG FLOWER, ROMAN CORIANDER. To 1 1/2 ft., branching, rather hairy; lf. segms. linear, but not filiform; fls. solitary, without involucre, blue, to 1 1/2 in. across; fr. inflated, follicles 3–7, united to base of spreading styles. Medit. region. Seeds are used for seasoning.

NIOBE: *HOSTA.*

NIPHAEA Lindl. *Gesneriaceae.* A few spp. of per., hairy herbs with scaly rhizomes, native to trop. Amer.; lvs. mostly congested basally; fls. solitary or more or less corymbose in lf. axils, calyx 5-parted, corolla rotate, 5-lobed, the 2 upper lobes slightly smaller than the lower, stamens 4, borne at base of corolla, filaments shorter than or as long as the anthers, anthers separate, the 2 cells confluent at apex and dehiscing in an arc, disc lacking, ovary half-inferior, stigma capitate, mouth-shaped.

Propagated by the scaly rhizomes. For cultivation see *Gesneriaceae.*

oblonga Lindl. To 6 in.; lvs. petioled, blades ovate, to 5 in. long, 2 3/4 in. wide, serrate or doubly serrate, softly hairy, glossy green, sometimes with purple veins; fls. several in an axil, long-pedicelled, calyx lobes linear-lanceolate, corolla white with yellow center, 1 in. across, tube 3/16 in. long, lobes to 3/8 in. long. S. Mex., Guatemala.

NIPHOBOLUS: *PYRROSIA.*

NITELLA Agardh. STONEWORT. *Characeae.* About 100 or more spp. of fragile aquatic plants of cosmopolitan distribution; plant a thallus with the slender axis erect, anchored to substrate by rhizoids, with limp and flexible, regular and symmetrically whorled, filiform brs. of unlimited growth, branchlets leaflike; corona of oogonia 10-celled. Frequently cult. in aquaria.

flexilis (L.) Agardh. Brs. in whorls of 6–8, straight or slightly incurved, 1 1/2–2 times longer than internodes of the axis, the primary branchlets about twice as long as secondary branchlets. N. Amer., Eurasia.

gracilis (Sm.) Agardh. Brs. in whorls of mostly 5–8, straight, sometimes condensed into heads, mostly shorter than internodes. Cosmopolitan.

NOLANA L. *Nolanaceae.* About 60 spp. of herbs and subshrubs, native to semidesert coastal regions of Chile and Peru; lvs. generally fleshy; fls. solitary, axillary, pedicelled; fr. deeply lobed, breaking up into several 1–8-seeded nutlets or follicles.

Nolanas grow in sand and gravel in full sun; perennials, but treated as annuals.

acuminata (Miers) Miers [*N. lanceolata* (Miers) Miers]. Prostrate or decumbent per., to 4 in. high; lvs. opp., linear-lanceolate, to 3 1/2 in.

long and ½ in. wide, obtuse to acute, pubescent, fleshy, the lower ones petioled, the upper ones sessile; calyx to ½ in. long, lobes acuminate, ¼ in. long, corolla deep blue, with a white or yellowish center, to 1¼ in. long, 1½ in. across. Chile.

atriplicifolia: *N. paradoxa.*

grandiflora: *N. paradoxa.*

humifusa (Gouan) I. M. Johnst. [*N. prostrata* L.f.]. Similar in habit to *N. paradoxa;* lvs. alt., rhomboidal to ovate, to 1 in. long, ⅜ in. wide, petioled; calyx to ¼ in. long, teeth acuminate, to ⅛ in. long, corolla blue, to ½ in. long. Peru.

lanceolata: *N. acuminata.*

paradoxa Lindl. [*N. atriplicifolia* Hort. ex D. Don; *N. grandiflora* Lehm.]. Decumbent per., to 6–8 in. high, pubescent, fleshy; lvs. ovate, obtuse, 2¼ in. long, ¾ in. wide, petioled; calyx to ¾ in. long, lobes acuminate, to ⅜ in. long, corolla bright dark blue, with whitish or pale yellow throat, to 1½ in. long, 2 in. wide. Chile.

prostrata: *N. humifusa.*

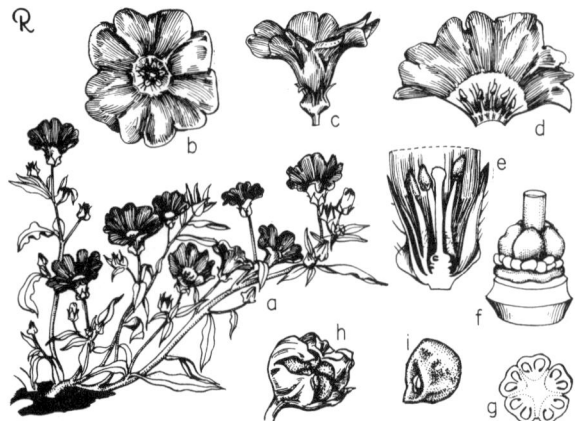

NOLANACEAE. *Nolana paradoxa:* **a,** flowering stems, × ¼; **b,** flower, face view, × ½; **c,** flower, side view, × ½; **d,** corolla expanded, × ½; **e,** flower, vertical section (upper part of corolla cut off), × 1½; **f,** base of pistil, × 4; **g,** ovary, cross section, × 4; **h,** fruit, × 1; **i,** nutlet, × 2.

NOLANACEAE Dumort. NOLANA FAMILY. Dicot.; 2 genera and 85 spp. of generally fleshy herbs or subshrubs, native to arid coastal regions of Peru and Chile; lvs. alt. or opp.; fls. solitary, bisexual, calyx 5-parted, corolla 5-lobed, stamens 5, ovary superior; fr. of 3 to many nutlets or follicles. Only *Nolana* is cult. Related to the Solanaceae.

NOLINA Michx. BEAR GRASS. *Agavaceae.* About 25 spp. of dioecious, acaulescent or caulescent per. plants of U.S. and Mex.; lvs. linear, stiff, often rough along the margin; infl. paniculate; fls. small, whitish, unisexual, segms. 6, stamens 6, ovary superior, 3-celled, each cell 2–3-ovuled; fr. deeply 3-lobed, often inflated, wingless, each cell 1-seeded.

Cultivated in warmer and drier parts of U.S. Cultivation as for *Yucca.*

Bigelovii (Torr.) S. Wats. To 6 ft.; lvs. in a dense crown, to 1 in. wide, shredding into brown fibers along margin, apex not brushlike; infl. with stout brs.; pedicel scarcely half as long as fr. Ariz. to Baja Calif.

erumpens (Torr.) S. Wats. Lvs. ¼–⅜ in. wide, brushlike at apex, thick, margin rough or rarely smooth; bracts as long as lower brs.; fr. on stout pedicels, not inflated, the seeds protruding. W. Tex., n. Mex.

glaucophylla: a listed name, probably referable to *Dasylirion glaucophyllum.*

gracilis: *Beaucarnea gracilis.*

Lindheimeri: a listed name, probably referable to *N. Lindheimerana.*

Lindheimerana (Scheele) S. Wats. Stemless; lvs. to ³⁄₁₆ in. wide, flat, grasslike but wiry, apex not becoming fibrous. Cent. Tex.

longifolia (Schult. & Schult.f.) Hemsl. [*Dasylirion longifolium* (Schult. & Schult.f.) Zucc.]. To 10 ft., swollen at base and with few brs. toward top; lvs. recurved over trunk, 3 ft. long or more, to 1¼ in. wide, with rough margins, apex somewhat brushlike; infl. nearly sessile, pedicels about as long as fr. Mex.

microcarpa S. Wats. SACAHUISTA. Stemless; lvs. coarse, linear, to ½ in. wide, concave, keeled, thickish, scabrous on margins; infl. with brs. to 18 in. long; fls. pale yellow to whitish; fr. somewhat inflated, seeds not protruding. Sw. New Mex. to Ariz. and southward.

Parryi S. Wats. To 6 ft., unbranched; lvs. in a dense crown, to 3 ft. long, ¾ in. wide, serrulate; infl. to 2 ft., with stout brs.; pedicels scarcely half as long as fr., style persistent on fr. S. Calif.

texana S. Wats. Stemless; lvs. to ³⁄₁₆ in. wide, concave, keeled; infl. often much shorter than lvs., bracts longer than lower brs. Tex.

tuberculata: *Beaucarnea recurvata.*

NOLTEA Rchb.f. *Rhamnaceae.* Two spp. of glabrous shrubs in S. Afr.; lvs. alt., simple; fls. small, in terminal and axillary panicles, calyx tube cup-shaped, petals inserted in sinuses between the calyx lobes; fr. a caps.

africana (L.) Rchb.f. To 12 ft.; lvs. oblong-lanceolate, to 2½ in. long, toothed, pale beneath; panicles about 1 in. long; fls. white, small; caps. ⁵⁄₁₆ in. diam. Cv. 'Aurea' is listed. Sometimes cult. in Calif. Prop. by seeds and cuttings of green or mature wood.

NOMAPHILA: *HYGROPHILA.*

NOMOCHARIS Franch. *Liliaceae.* About 10 spp. of bulbous, per. herbs, native to e. Himalayas, Tibet, and w. China; bulbs scaly, not tunicate; lvs. alt., opp., or whorled; fls. almost flat to saucer-shaped, white, pale yellow, pink, rose, or rose-purple, often spotted, 1 or more in upper lf. axils, perianth segms. 6, separate, outer segms. without nectaries, inner segms. ridged, with basal nectaries and a basal blotch on inside, and margins entire to fringed, stamens 6, filaments usually cylindrical and inflated, ending in a fine, threadlike appendage supporting the anther, style flaring, stigma 3-lobed; fr. a loculicidal, many-seeded caps. Allied to *Fritillaria* and *Lilium.*

aptera (Franch.) E. H. Wils. To 3 ft.; lvs. alt., elliptic to elliptic-lanceolate, to 4 in. long, with basal tufts of hairs; fls. rose, to 4 in. across, with maroon eye and a greenish to cream-colored area above eye, and crimson spots and blotches, segms. entire. Nw. Yunnan and sw. Szechwan.

Farreri (W. E. Evans) R. Harrow. To 3 ft. or more; lvs. whorled, narrowly lanceolate, to 3¾ in. long, narrowed to acuminate apex; fls. pink with maroon eye, often crimson-spotted, to 3 in. across, inner segms. nearly entire to serrate. Ne. Burma.

Mairei Lév. To 2½ ft.; lvs. whorled, lanceolate to ovate-lanceolate, to 4 in. long; fls. white, sometimes spotted red-purple, nodding, flat, to 4 in. across, margins of inner segms. fimbriate, anthers purple. N. Yunnan and sw. Szechwan.

nana: *Lilium nanum.*

oxypetala: *Lilium oxypetalum.*

pardanthina Franch. To 3 ft.; lvs. whorled, lanceolate to ovate-lanceolate, to 2 in. long; fls. pink, to 3 in. across, nodding, almost flat, inner segms. heavily purple-spotted on lower ⅓, margins toothed or fringed. W. Yunnan.

saluenensis Balf.f. To 3 ft.; lvs. opp. or in whorls of 3, lanceolate, to 3 in. long; fls. white, pale rose, or pale yellow, purple-spotted, saucer-shaped, to 3½ in. across, filaments slender. N. Burma, w. Szechwan, nw. Yunnan, se. Tibet.

NOPALEA Salm-Dyck. *Cactaceae.* About 10 spp. of shrubs and small trees, native to Mex. and Cent. Amer.; joints flattened, the lower ones forming a cylindrical trunk with age; lvs. small, early deciduous; glochids present; perianth segms. separate, erect, red or pinkish, stamens many, erect, long-exserted, not sensitive, style long-exserted, swollen just above the base; fr. deeply umbilicate, red, juicy, seeds flat, bony. Resembling *Opuntia* subgenus *Opuntia,* but having perianth erect, stamens and style long-exserted.

For culture see *Cacti.*

Auberi (Pfeiff.) Salm-Dyck [*Opuntia Auberi* Pfeiff.]. To 35 ft., not very spiny, joints narrow, bluish or glaucous, to 1 ft. long; areoles bearing wool and glochids, spines 0 or 1–2, to 1 in. long; fls. rose-pink, about 3½ in. long. Cent. and s. Mex.

cochenillifera (L.) Salm-Dyck [*Opuntia cochenillifera* (L.) Mill.]. COCHINEAL PLANT. To 15 ft., trunk sometimes 8 in. thick, joints obovate, to 20 in. long; spines mostly 0, glochids many, falling early; fls. on top of joints, 2 in. long or more, pink or rose. Long cult., but nativity unknown. Cochineal of commerce is the dried bodies of insects (mealy bugs) that feed on this plant; cochineal was formerly collected in bulk and extensively used as the source of the scarlet dye, carmine. This is one of several cacti on which the insect subsists.

dejecta (Salm-Dyck) Salm-Dyck [*Opuntia dejecta* Salm-Dyck]. To 6 ft., with definite trunk, very spiny, joints linear-oblong, 4–6 in. long, often drooping; spines usually 2 in each areole, to 1½ in. long; fls. 2 in. long, dark red. Probably Panama. Cult. in trop. Amer. Var. **variegata** is listed.

NOPALXOCHIA Britt. & Rose [*Lobeira* Alexand.]. *Cactaceae*. Four spp. of epiphytic cacti, native to s. Mex.; brs. flat, sometimes several-angled at the base, obliquely crenate; areoles marginal, spineless or short-spined; fls. lasting several days, funnelform, perianth segms. many, the outer somewhat recurved, stamens many, ovary scaly or nearly naked. Allied to *Epiphyllum*, but perianth segms. pink to red, longer than or about as long as the tube.

For culture see *Cacti*.

Ackermannii (Haw.) F. M. Knuth [*Epiphyllum Ackermannii* Haw.]. RED ORCHID CACTUS. Brs. 10–16 in. long, 1½–2 in. wide; fls. red, 5 in. long, 5–7 in. across, perianth segms. spreading, about twice as long as tube, series of stamens close together. Not widely grown; the common plant often so-called is apparently a hybrid of this sp. with *Heliocereus*.

Conzattiana MacDoug. Brs. 1 ft. long or more, about 1 in. wide; fls. bright red, 3 in. long, 2 in. across, perianth segms. ascending, longer than the tube; fr. ovoid, somewhat angled, green, 1½ in. long, the few scales with axillary bristles.

Macdougallii (Alexand.) W. T. Marsh. [*Lobeira Macdougallii* Alexand.]. Brs. 6–18 in. long or more, ¾–2 in. wide; fls. purplish-rose, 3 in. long, 2½ in. across, perianth segms. ascending, about as long as tube, series of stamens close together; fr. truncate-obpyriform, somewhat angled, with few woolly areoles, green, 1 in. long.

phyllanthoides (DC.) Britt. & Rose [*Epiphyllum phyllanthoides* (DC.) Sweet]. POND-LILY CACTUS, EMPRESS-OF-GERMANY. Brs. about ½–2 ft. long, 1½–2 in. wide; fls. rose-pink, 3–4 in. long, 2 in. across, perianth segms. ascending, about as long as the cylindrical tube, upper series of stamens separated from the others.

NORMANBYA F. J. Muell. ex Becc. *Palmae*. One sp., a solitary, unarmed, monoecious palm of rain forests in ne. Australia; lvs. pinnate, sheaths tubular, forming a conspicuous crownshaft, pinnae obliquely toothed at apex, broadly wedge-shaped and borne in 1 plane on young plants, longitudinally dissected into narrow segms. in several planes on mature plants; infl. below lvs., bracts 2, deciduous, peduncle short, rachis elongate, brs. many, the lower ones once-branched, rachillae with fls. in triads (2 male and 1 female) in lower part and above these with paired or solitary male fls.; male fls. symmetrical, sepals 3, imbricate, petals 3, valvate, stamens many, filaments erect in bud, anthers attached by back, pistillode ovoid-attenuate, as long as stamens, female fls. with sepals and petals 3, imbricate, staminodes 3, toothlike, pistil 1-celled, 1-ovuled; fr. ovoid, purple-brown at maturity, endocarp fibrous, with basal operculum, more or less adherent to seed, seed with ruminate endosperm and basal embryo.

For culture see *Palms*.

Normanbyi (W. Hill) L. H. Bailey. BLACK PALM. To 60 ft.; trunk with outer layer of hard black fibers; lvs. to 12 ft. long, sheaths silvery-brown, to 4 ft. long, pinnae about 35–36 on each side, each divided into as many as 9 segms. to 1½ ft. long, 1 in. wide, whitish below; male fls. ⁵⁄₁₆ in. long; fr. 1½ in. long. Warmer parts of Zone 10a in Fla.

NORONHIA Stadtm. ex Thouars. *Oleaceae*. About 40 spp. of evergreen, large shrubs or trees, of Madagascar and the Comoro Is.; fls. small, white, in panicles or racemes, corolla urceolate, 4-parted, thick and fleshy, with a basal nectary resembling a small second corolla inside; fr. a drupe, usually 1-seeded, pulp sweet, edible.

emarginata (Lam.) Thouars ex Hook. Shrub; lvs. broadly elliptic, to 4 in. long, entire, leathery; corolla to ¼ in. long; fr. globular, about 1 in. across. Madagascar. Zone 10?

NOTHOCALAIS (A. Gray) Greene. *Compositae* (Cichorium Tribe). Four spp. of scapose, per. herbs with milky sap, native to w. N. Amer.; taproot ropelike; lvs. in a basal rosette, erect, rather stiff; fl. heads solitary, always erect, involucral bracts nearly equal, often with purple lines or dots;

fls. all ligulate, yellow; achenes not beaked, pappus persistent, of 10 to many glossy bristles.

cuspidata (Pursh) Greene [*Agoseris cuspidata* (Pursh) D. Dietr.; *Microseris cuspidata* (Pursh) Schultz-Bip.]. Sts. to 14 in.; lvs. linear-lanceolate, to 1 ft. long, margin entire, villous-ciliolate, often wavy; pappus of many capillary bristles and scales. Great plains, Wisc. and Ill. to Mont., Colo., Okla.

NOTHOFAGUS Blume. *Fagaceae*. About 40 spp. of deciduous or evergreen beechlike trees or shrubs, native to temp. S. Amer., New Zeal., Tasmania, se. Australia, New Caledonia, and New Guinea; lvs. small, alt., 2-ranked; fls. unisexual, solitary or in 3's; fr. of usually 3 3-angled nuts enclosed in a 2–4-lobed scaly involucre.

The S. Hemisphere representatives of *Fagus*, and important timber trees there, second in importance to *Eucalyptus*. Hardy only in equable regions, such as the coastal areas of the Pacific states. Propagated by seeds and layers.

antarctica (G. Forst.) Ørst. Deciduous, to 100 ft.; lvs. to 1 in. long, toothed or slightly lobed, glabrous except on midrib. Chile, Argentina. Zone 8.

cliffortioides (Hook.f.) Ørst. Evergreen, to 40 ft.; lvs. to ⅝ in. long, acute, entire, grayish-pubescent beneath. New Zeal. Zone 8? Closely related to *N. Solandri*, but having lvs. ovate, acute.

Cunninghamii (Hook.f.) Ørst. [*Fagus Cunninghamii* Hook.f.]. Evergreen, to 200 ft.; lvs. to ½ in. long, glabrous. Se. Australia and Tasmania. Zone 8?

fusca (Hook.f.) Ørst. Evergreen, to 100 ft.; lvs. to 1½ in. long, coarsely toothed, glabrous except on margin. New Zeal. Zone 8.

Menziesii (Hook.f.) Ørst. Evergreen. to 80 or 100 ft.; lvs. ovate-rhomboid, to ½ in. long, double-toothed, glabrous except for petiole. New Zeal. Zone 8?

obliqua (Mirb.) Ørst. Deciduous, to 100 ft.; lvs. to 3 in. long, toothed. Chile, Argentina. Zone 8.

procera orst. Deciduous tree; lvs. to 4 in. long, finely toothed, pubescent beneath. Chile, Argentina. Zone 8.

Solandri (Hook.f.) Ørst. Evergreen, to 80 ft.; lvs. to ¾ in. long, blunt or obtuse, entire, grayish-pubescent beneath. New Zeal. Zone 8?

NOTHOLAENA R. Br. (sometimes, but not originally, spelled *Nothochlaena*). CLOAK FERN. *Polypodiaceae*. About 60 spp. of small, mostly xerophytic, rock-loving ferns, native to warm-temp. and trop. Amer., also 1 sp. in Eur.; lvs. 1–4-pinnate, mealy, densely chaffy, or hairy; sori usually nearly marginal, borne at or near the ends of unmodified veins, margins of pinnules unmodified, flattish, or less typically revolute and partly covering the sporangia. The genus intergrades with *Cheilanthes* and *Pellaea*.

Mostly plants for rock gardens. For culture see *Ferns*.

aurea (Poir.) Desv. GOLDEN C. F. Lvs. ovate to linear, gradually reduced at base, 1-pinnate, pinnae uniformly pinnatifid, oblong or triangular-oblong, covered with hairs beneath, not powdery. Sw. U.S. to n. Chile and Argentina.

californica D. C. Eat. CALIFORNIA C. F. Rhizomes with dense, denticulate scales; lvs. 3–8 in. long, triangular-pentagonal, about as wide as long, basally 3-pinnate, glabrous and mealy beneath, pinnule margins revolute, petioles brown; sori in a continuous marginal line. S. Calif., Ariz.

candida (M. Martens & Galeotti) Hook. Differs from *N. californica* in lvs. basally 1–2-pinnate and the petioles black, white-mealy beneath. Sw. Tex., New Mex., Mex.

cochisensis: *N. sinuata* var.

Fendleri Kunze. FENDLER'S C. F. Rhizomes with entire scales; lvs. to 9 in. long, broadly triangular-ovate, basally 4–5-pinnate, whitish-mealy beneath, with rachises and their brs. flexuous and zigzag. Colo. to Ariz. and Tex.

Newberryi D. C. Eat. COTTON FERN. Rhizomes with entire, blackish-brown scales; lvs. 5–14 in. long, ovate to linear, 1-pinnate, densely tomentose beneath, never mealy, pinnae 10–14 pairs, sessile, minutely tomentose above, petioles densely tomentose, becoming less so with age. S. Calif., Baja Calif.

Parryi D. C. Eat. PARRY'S C. F. Differs from *N. Newberryi* in scales of rhizomes cinnamon-brown, with darker midsection, pinnae 5–9 pairs, short-stalked, densely tomentose above, and petioles sparsely hirsute. S. Calif., Utah, Ariz.

sinuata (Swartz) Kaulf. WAVY C. F. Lvs. linear, pinnate-pinnatifid, scaly and not powdery beneath, pinnae 12 pairs or more, short-petioled, broadly oblong to triangular-ovate, less than 1 in. long and ½ in. wide, entire or cut into 4–6 oblong lobes. U.S. to Argentina. Var. **cochisensis** (L. Goodd.) Weatherby [*N. cochisensis* L. Goodd.]. Pinnae ⅜ in. long or less, very obtuse, somewhat square, with 1–2 pairs of broadly ovate lobes or entire. Tex., Calif. to cent. Mex.

NOTHOLIRION Boiss. *Liliaceae.* Four spp. of bulbous, per. herbs, native to Asia; bulb tunicate, producing small basal bulbils; basal lvs. very long, st. lvs. successively shorter upward; fls. red, rose, pink, or lavender, in racemes, perianth segms. 6, separate, more or less recurved at tip, stamens 6, anthers versatile, stigma deeply 3-cleft; fr. a loculicidal caps., seeds small, wingless.

bulbiferum (Lingelsh.) Stearn [*N. hyacinthinum* (E. H. Wils.) Stapf]. To 3 ft., stout; basal lvs. to 1½ ft. long and 1 in. wide; fls. broadly funnelform, pale rose to pale lavender, to 1 in. long. Se. Tibet and w. China, s. to n. Assam, Bhutan, Sikkim, Nepal.

hyacinthinum: *N. bulbiferum.*

macrophyllum (D. Don) Boiss. [*Lilium macrophyllum* D. Don]. Sts. flexuous, to 3 ft.; basal lvs. strap-shaped, to 1½ ft. long and 1 in. wide; fls. usually 4–6, funnelform, rose, to 1½ in. long. Himalayas.

Thomsonianum (Royle) Stapf [*Fritillaria Thomsoniana* Royle; *Lilium Thomsonianum* (Royle) Lindl.]. To 3 ft., stout; basal lvs. to 1 ft. long and ¾ in. wide; fls. funnelform, pink to rose, fragrant, perianth segms. 2 in. long and ½ in. wide. Afghanistan to nw. Himalayas.

NOTHOPANAX: *POLYSCIAS.* **N. arboreus:** *Neopanax arboreus.* **N. laetus:** *Neopanax laetus.*

NOTHOSCORDUM Kunth. FALSE GARLIC, GRACE G. *Amaryllidaceae.* About 20 spp. of *Allium*-like but not odorous herbs with tunicate bulbs, native mostly to N. and S. Amer.; lvs. linear, basal; fls. in an umbel subtended by 2 papery, basally united spathe valves, perianth yellow or white, segms. shortly united at the base, stamens 6, ovary superior; fr. a loculicidal caps.

Rarely cultivated; the following species are tender in the North.

bivalve (L.) Britt. [*Allium striatum* Jacq.]. Lvs. to 16 in. long and ³⁄₁₆ in. wide; scapes to 16 in.; fls. yellowish or white with green midrib, ½ in. long, ovary scarcely longer than thick; caps. nearly globose. Va. to Fla. and Mex.

fragrans: *N. inodorum.*

inodorum (Ait.) Nichols. [*N. fragrans* (Venten.) Kunth]. Lvs. to 1 ft. long and ¾ in. wide; scapes to 2 ft.; fls. white, with pink lines, fragrant, to ½ in. long, ovary much longer than broad; caps. obovoid. Nativity doubtful; naturalized in Bermuda and s. U.S.

NOTOCACTUS (K. Schum.) A. Berger [*Eriocactus* Backeb.]. BALL CACTUS. *Cactaceae.* About 25 spp. of cacti, native to s. S. Amer.; probably referable to *Wigginsia,* though fr. dry, sts. not woolly at apex.

For culture see *Cacti.*

apricus (Arech.) A. Berger. Sts. cespitose, subglobose, to 2 in. thick, ribs 15–20, almost tubercled; radial spines 18–20, needle-shaped, yellowish, central spines 4, reddish, the lowest curved; fls. yellow, 3 in. long, tube stout; fr. red, ¾ in. long. Uruguay.

caespitosus: *Frailea caespitosa.*

concinnus (Monv.) A. Berger. Sts. simple, to 3 in. thick, ribs 16–20; spines 10–12, bristlelike, radial spines ¼ in. long, central spines 1–4, 1 longer, spreading or deflexed; fls. yellow with red tips, to 3 in. long, tube slender. S. Brazil and Uruguay.

floricomus (Arech.) A. Berger. Sts. simple, to 7 in. high and 5 in. thick, ribs 20; radial spines 15–20, needle-shaped, reddish at base, central spines 4–5, awl-shaped, to 1 in. long; fls. yellow, to 2½ in. long; fr. ovoid. Uruguay and Argentina.

Graessneri (K. Schum.) A. Berger. Sts. simple, to 4 in. high and mostly thicker, ribs to 60 or more, low, tubercled; radial spines many, needle-shaped, glassy-yellow, to ¾ in. long, interlacing, central spines 5–6, thicker, darker; fls. yellowish-green, ¾ in. long. S. Brazil.

Grossei (K. Schum.) A. Berger. Sts. cylindrical, to 6 ft., ribs 16 or more, cross-furrowed; spines 3–7, needle-shaped, curved, yellowish, becoming gray, to 1½ in. long; fls. yellow, 1½ in. long. Paraguay. By some authors referred to *N. Schumannianus.*

Haselbergii (F. A. Haage, jr.) A. Berger. SCARLET B. C. Sts. globose, 5 in. thick, ribs 30 or more, tubercled; radial spines about 20, needle-shaped, yellowish, to ⅜ in. long, central spines 3–5, similar; fls. orange to red, ⅝ in. long, stigma yellow. S. Brazil.

Leninghausii (F. A. Haage, jr.) A. Berger [*Eriocactus Leninghausii* (F. A. Haage, jr.) Backeb.]. GOLDEN B. C. Sts. simple, to 3 ft. high and 4 in. thick, ribs 30 or more, ⅛ in. high; radial spines to 15, bristlelike, white or yellowish, to ¼ in. long, central spines 3–4, yellow, to 1½ in. long; fls. yellow, 2 in. long. Brazil.

Linkii: a listed name of no botanical standing.

mammulosus (Lem.) A. Berger. Sts. simple, subglobose, to 3 in. thick, ribs 18–25, strongly tubercled; radial spines 20–30, to 2 in. long, central spines 2–4, ¾ in. long; fls. yellow, to 1½ in. long. Brazil, Uruguay, Argentina.

Mueller-Melchersii Frič ex Backeb. & F. M. Knuth. Small; spines yellow, more or less appressed, central spine usually 1, spreading, to ³⁄₁₆ in. long. Uruguay.

muricatus (Otto) A. Berger. Sts. to 8 in. high and 4 in. thick, ribs 16–20; spines nearly bristlelike, yellow, radial spines 12–20, to ⁵⁄₁₆ in. long, central spines 3–4; fls. yellow, 1¼ in. long. S. Brazil.

Ottonis (Lehm.) A. Berger. Sts. simple or cespitose, subglobose, to 5 in. thick, ribs 10–13, broad, rounded; radial spines 10–13, needle-shaped, yellow or brown, central spines 3–4, darker, rarely 0; fls. yellow, to 2½ in. long. S. Brazil, Uruguay, n. Argentina. Cvs. **'Longispinus'**, **'Tenuispinus'**, and **'Uruguayensis'** are listed.

pampeanus: *N. submammulosus* var.

rutilans Däniker & Krainz. Sts. globose to cylindrical, blue-green, to 2 in. high and 2 in. thick or more, ribs 18–24, spiralled, with small, chin-shaped tubercles; radial spines 14–16, white, tipped with brown-red, becoming yellowish or gray, to ³⁄₁₆ in. long, central spines 2, the lower strongest, to ¼ in. long; fls. carmine-rose, white-woolly, to 2½ in. across. Uruguay.

Schumannianus (Hort. Nicolai) A. Berger [*Eriocactus Schumannianus* (Hort. Nicolai) Backeb.]. Sts. globose, in age cylindrical, to 5 in. thick, ribs to 30, acute, ¼ in. high; spines 4–7, bristlelike, red, becoming gray to black, the lower to 2 in. long; fls. yellow, to 2 in. long, stigma yellow; fr. yellow or reddish. Paraguay and n. Argentina.

Scopa (K. Spreng.) A. Berger. SILVER B. C. Sts. to 18 in. high, ribs 30–40, low, obtuse; radial spines 40 or more, bristlelike, white, central spines about 4, stouter, brown or purple; fls. yellow, 2½ in. wide. S. Brazil and Uruguay.

submammulosus (Lem.) Backeb. LEMON-BALL. Differs from *N. mammulosus* in having about 13 ribs. N. Argentina. Var. **submammulosus.** The typical var.; sts. clear green; radial spines 6, central spines 2, one directed up, the other down. Var. **pampeanus** (Speg.) Backeb. [*N. pampeanus* (Speg.) Backeb.]. DEVIL'S-PAW. Sts. darker, glossy green; radial spines 5–10, central spines 2–3.

tabularis (J. F. Cels) A. Berger. Sts. simple, globose or short-cylindrical, ribs 16–18, obtuse; radial spines 16–18, needle-shaped, central spines 4; fls. yellow, 2½ in. long. Brazil or Uruguay.

Velenovskyi Y. Ito. Sts. depressed-globose to oblong, dull green, ribs 16–20, spiralled, tubercles acutely angled; spines dark rose, becoming dark brown, radial spines 18–20, to ⅝ in. long, central spines 3–5, to 1 in. long; fls. yellow, to 2½ in. across. Uruguay.

NOTONIA: *SENECIO.* **N. petraea:** *S. Jacobsenii.*

NOTOSPARTIUM Hook.f. PINK BROOM, SOUTHERN B. *Leguminosae* (subfamily *Faboideae*). Three spp. of mostly leafless shrubs and trees with flattened, slender, pendent branchlets, native to s. New Zeal.; fls. in lateral racemes, small, papilionaceous, stamens 10, 9 united and 1 separate; fr. a linear, flat, indehiscent legume, with 1-seeded segms.

Grows best in sandy loam in sunny locations. Propagated by seeds and cuttings. Zone 8.

Carmichaeliae Hook.f. Shrub, to 16 ft.; lvs. small, obcordate or orbicular, present only on young plants; racemes many, crowded, to 2 in. long; fr. to 1 in. long.

NOTYLIA Lindl. *Orchidaceae.* About 60 spp. of small epiphytes, native to trop. Amer.; pseudobulbs, when present, small; lvs. 2-ranked, overlapping or sheathing one another in a fan, leathery or fleshy, erect, spreading; infl. basal or axillary, racemose or rarely paniculate, few- to many-fld.; sepals all alike, separate or with lateral sepals more or less united, petals similar to sepals but smaller, lip simple or variously lobed, attached to base of column with slender claw, column slender, erect, wingless, footless. For structure of fl. see *Orchidaceae.*

For culture see *Orchids.*

Barkeri Lindl. Clump-forming, erect, to 1 ft., pseudobulbs ellipsoid, flattened, 1-lvd., to 1½ in. long; lvs. oblong-strap-shaped, leathery, to

8 in. long; infl. elongate, pendent, racemose, to 12 in. long, loosely many-fld.; fls. small, variable, fragrant, sepals greenish, oblong-strap-shaped, with revolute apex, to ¼ in. long, petals white, often dotted or mottled with yellow, elliptic-oblong, lip white, variable, with short convex-conduplicate claw, blade ovate-rhombic, without a callus. Mex. to Panama.

NUPHAR Sm. [*Nymphaea* Small, not L.]. COW LILY, SPAT-TERDOCK, YELLOW POND LILY, WATER COLLARD, MARSH C. *Nymphaeaceae*. About 25 spp. of per., aquatic herbs, of wide distribution in the N. Hemisphere, with stout rhizomes creeping in mud; lvs. large, entire, with basal sinus, sub-mersed, floating, or standing erect above water; fls. solitary, yellow or purplish, usually standing above water surface, se-pals 5–12, conspicuous, yellow, at least inside, petals and sta-mens many, small, inserted below the compound ovary, style short, stigma disclike; fr. ovoid, many-seeded, maturing above water.

Spatterdocks grow near the margins of slow-running, mud-bottom streams, rivers, and lakes, or in stagnant pools. Cultivation and propa-gation as for hardy nymphaeas and nelumbos. For culture see *Water Lily.*

advena (Ait.) Ait.f. COMMON S. Lvs. thick, erect, usually above water surface, green, glabrous; fls. nearly globose, 1½ in. wide, sepals 6, broad, the inner 3 yellow, tipped with green, petals and stamens yellowish or tinged reddish, stigmatic disc 9–23-rayed. E. and cent. U.S.

japonicum DC. Blades of submersed lvs. narrow, thin, undulate, blades of lvs. above the water oblong to narrowly ovate, to 1 ft. long and 4¾ in. wide, almost leathery, saggittate at base, glabrous above, hairy beneath when young; fls. yellow, to 2 in. wide, stigmatic disc about 11-rayed, dentate. Japan.

luteum (L.) Sm. YELLOW WATER LILY. Blades of submersed lvs. broadly ovate to orbicular, thin, blades of floating lvs. ovate-oblong, to 16 in. long and 1 ft. wide, leathery; fls. to 2⅜ in. across, raised above the water, sepals bright yellow inside, broadly obovate, petals broadly spatulate; stigmatic disc 15–20-rayed, margin entire. E. N. Amer., W. Indies, Eurasia, N. Afr.

pumilum (Timm) DC. Blades of submersed lvs. thin and translu-cent, blades of floating lvs. broadly ovate to ovate-orbicular, to 5½ in. across; sepals yellow, stigmatic disc 8–10-rayed, wavy. Temp. Eurasia.

sagittifolium (Walt.) Pursh. Blades of submersed lvs. filmy, oblong to oblong-lanceolate, to 16 in. long and 4 in. wide, margins wavy, blades of floating lvs. like the submersed, but firm; fls. yellow and green, to 1⅜ in. across, stigmatic disc 14–18-rayed. Va. to S.C.

NURSERY. A nursery, in horticulture, is a place or estab-lishment in which plants are propagated and then grown until such time as they are placed in permanent quarters or sold to the customer. It is naturally concerned mostly with perennial plants.

The nursery establishment may be wholly or partly under glass, or wholly in the open. It may be devoted to the rearing of orchids, begonias, roses, dahlias, lilies, lilacs, hedge plants, forest trees, fruit trees, or any other kind of plant. Nursery growing practically constitutes a business or enterprise quite by itself, requiring special equipment, experience, and mar-ket, and it has its own literature, traditions, and professional associations.

NUTTALLIA: *MENTZELIA.*

NUXIA Lam. *Loganiaceae.* About 14 spp. of trees or shrubs with fibrous, stringy bark, native to Afr.; lvs. usually in whorls of 3, petioled; fls. small, in terminal panicles or umbels; fr. a caps.

floribunda Benth. Glabrous tree, to 25 ft. or more, sometimes shrubby, lf. scars prominent; lvs. oblong-elliptic, to 6 in. long, entire or obscurely dentate, petioles to 1½ in. long; fls. many, dull white, stamens exserted. S. and trop. Afr. Cult. in Calif. in Zone 10.

NYCTAGINIA Choisy. *Nyctaginaceae.* One sp., a viscid, branched per. herb of Tex., se. New Mex., and n. Mex.; roots tuberous; lvs. opp., sessile; fls. bisexual, in long-peduncled heads subtended by involucre of distinct bracts, calyx corolla-like, funnelform, with abruptly expanded 5-lobed limb, sta-mens 5–8; fr. an achene with persistent calyx, top-shaped, finely ribbed.

capitata Choisy. SCARLET MUSK FLOWER. Erect or decumbent, to 16 in.; lvs. petioled, broadly ovate to triangular, to 3½ in. long, 2⅛ in. wide; peduncles to 5½ in. long, fls. deep red, to 1½ in. long; fr. ³⁄₁₆ in. long.

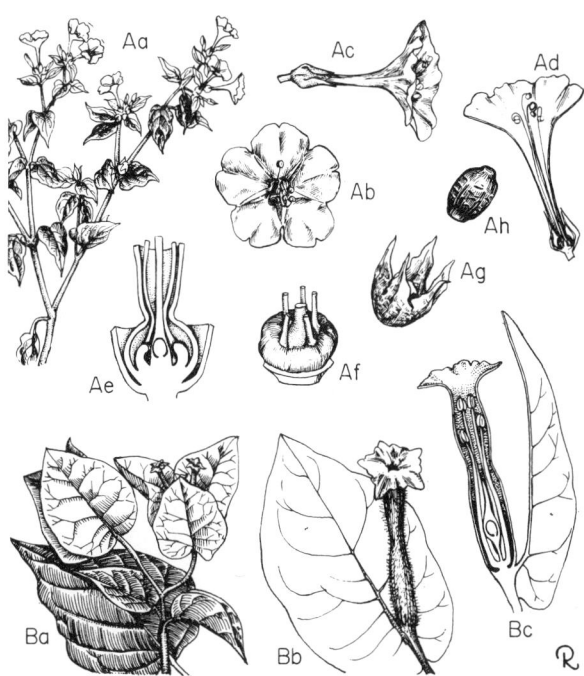

NYCTAGINACEAE. **A,** *Mirabilis Jalapa:* **Aa,** flowering branch, × ⅛; **Ab,** flower, face view, × ½; **Ac,** flower, side view, × ½; **Ad,** flower, vertical section, × ½; **Ae,** base of flower, vertical section, × 3; **Af,** ovary sur-rounded by gland and stamen bases, × 3; **Ag,** fruiting calyx, × ¾; **Ah,** achene, × 1. **B,** *Bougainvillea spectabilis:* **Ba,** flowering twig, × ⅓; **Bb,** flower and subtending bract, × 1; **Bc,** flower and bract, vertical section, × 1. (Ba-Bc from Bailey, *Manual of Cultivated Plants,* ed. 2.)

NYCTAGINACEAE Juss. FOUR-O'CLOCK FAMILY. Dicot; about 32 genera and 300 spp. of herbs, shrubs, and trees, widely distributed in warm and trop. countries; fls. often sub-tended by an involucre, which is sometimes petal-like and showy, calyx often or usually corollalike, petals 0, ovary su-perior, 1-celled, 1-seeded; fr. an achene on which the calyx is persistent (an anthocarp). Known to hort. as ornamentals, chiefly in *Abronia, Bougainvillea, Mirabilis, Nyctaginia,* and *Pisonia.*

NYCTANTHES L. *Verbenaceae.* One or two spp. of shrubs or small trees, native to se. Asia; lvs. opp.; fls. white, in termi-nal, few-fld. cymes subtended by involucrelike bracts, sta-mens 2; fr. a caps. This genus has traditionally been placed in the Oleaceae, but there is ample evidence for placing it in the Verbenaceae.

Sometimes cultivated under glass or out of doors in warm regions for its fragrant flowers, which open at night.

arbor-tristis L. NIGHT JASMINE, TREE-OF-SADNESS. Lvs. ovate-cor-date, to 4½ in. long; corolla tube orange, to ½ in. long, lobes 5–8, white, shorter than tube; fr. an orbicular caps., ¾ in. long. Fls. yield an orange dye and a perfume.

NYCTERINIA: *ZALUZIANSKYA.*

NYCTOCEREUS (A. Berger) Britt. & Rose. *Cactaceae.* Six spp. of slender, ribbed cacti of Mex. and Cent. Amer.; sts. erect to prostrate, lacking aerial roots, ribs 5–13; spines nee-dle-shaped or weak; fls. nocturnal, funnelform, white, inner segms. narrow, stamens in 1 series, tube and ovary with bris-tles or weak spines; fr. fleshy, seeds large.

For culture see *Cacti.*

chontalensis Alexand. Sts. prostrate, 2–3½ in. thick, joints 4–16 in. long, ribs 5–6, narrow, to ¾ in. high; areoles to ⅝ in. apart, spines weak, light, becoming dark, to ⅜ in. long, radial spines 5–7, central spines

1–4; fls. white, fragrant, to 3 in. long, style to 1 in. long; fr. globose, reddish, to ¾ in. in diam., seeds ⅛ in. long. S. Mex.

oaxacensis Britt. & Rose. Sts. branching, to 1¼ in. thick, ribs 7–10, low; areoles ⅜ in. apart, radial spines 8–12, to ⅝ in. long, central spines 3–5; fls. whitish, to 4 in. long. S. Mex.

serpentinus (Lag. & Rodr.) Britt. & Rose. SERPENT CACTUS, SNAKE C., NIGHT-BLOOMING CEREUS, QUEEN-OF-THE-NIGHT. Sts. clambering or creeping, to 10 ft. long and 1–2 in. thick, ribs 10–12, low-rounded; areoles to ¾ in. apart, radial spine 10–12, needle-shaped to bristlelike, brownish, to ½ in. long, central spine 0–1, stouter, red, becoming whitish; fls. white, to 10 in. long; fr. red, edible, seeds to ¼ in. long. Mex.

NYMANIA S. Lindb. *Meliaceae.* One sp., a much-branched shrub, native to S. Afr.; lvs. alt. or fascicled, simple, evergreen; fls. in lf. axils, calyx 4-lobed, petals 4, longer than calyx, stamens 8, united at base, exserted, ovary 4-celled; fr. a caps.

capensis (Thunb.) S. Lindb. Much-branched, densely leafy, rigid shrub, 5–10 ft.; lvs. linear, linear-oblong, or spatulate, 1–1½ in. long, tapering to a short petiole; fls. purplish, ovary pubescent; fr. inflated and membranous, 1½ in. in diam., pink or purple. S. Afr. Zone 10.

NYMPHAEA L. [*Castalia* Salisb.]. WATER LILY, WATER-NYMPH. *Nymphaeaceae.* About 35 spp. of cosmopolitan aquatic herbs; rhizomes horizontal or erect, often stout, sometimes tuberous; lvs. simple, commonly nearly orbicular, sinus reaching nearly or quite to petiole, usually long-petioled and floating, often colored on the undersurface; fls. mostly showy, floating on or standing above the water surface, opening during the day or some trop. ones at night, sepals 4, petals many, united to ovary, stamens many, carpels many; fr. subglobose, many-seeded, depressed and saucerlike at apex, maturing under water. The name *Nymphaea* has also been applied to *Nuphar*.

The cultivated water lilies occur in many colors and are largely of hybrid origin; some kinds cannot be definitely assigned botanically. Propagated by seeds either placed in a ball of clay and dropped into a pond, or sown in pots which are then submersed in shallow water, indoors or out; usually increased by division of rootstock, or viviparous kinds by new plantlets produced on the leaves at the junction of blade and petiole. For culture see *Water Lily.*

alba L. [*N. venusta* Hentze]. EUROPEAN WHITE W. L., PLATTER DOCK. Hardy, robust; lvs. to 1 ft. across, red when young, entire, crowded on rhizome; fls. white, 4–5 in. across, with yellow stigmas, open nearly all day. Eurasia, N. Afr. Cv. **'Candidissima'.** Possibly a hybrid between *N. alba* and *N. candida;* very robust, fls. larger, sterile, petals broad. Earliest flowering cv., continuing till frost. [Var.] **Gladstoniana:** see *N. Gladstoniana.* Var. **rubra** Lönnr. Fls. rose. Lake Faver (Sweden).

×**amabilis:** *Nymphaea* cv. 'Amabilis' [*N.* × *amabilis* Marliac]. Hybrid; hardy, robust; fls. tulip-shaped, to 11 in. across, standing above water surface, opening salmon-white, changing to rose and red.

ampla (Salisb.) DC. Robust; lvs. to 16 in. in diam., with small black spots on both sides, red-purple beneath; fls. white, 5 in. across, petals obtuse. Trop. and subtrop. Amer. Doubtfully in cult. Var. **speciosa** (Mart. & Zucc.) Casp. [*N. gracilis* Zucc., not Hort.]. Of medium size, tuber subglobose; lvs. repand-sinuate or dentate, with obtuse teeth.

caerulea Savigny. EGYPTIAN LOTUS, BLUE LOTUS. Tender, day-blooming, not showy; lvs. green, 12–16 in. in diam., with small purple blotches beneath, entire or basally wavy; fls. 3–6 in. across, light blue, standing above water surface. N. and cent. Afr. White- and red-fld. forms occur. This sp., and sometimes *N. Lotus,* are the "lotus" of ancient Egyptian art.

candida J. Presl. & K. Presl. Differs from *N. alba* in being smaller and in having the lowest pair of veins of basal lobes curved toward one another, and the line of attachment of sepals to the receptacle sharply angular, not rounded. N. Eurasia.

capensis Thunb. CAPE BLUE W. L. Tender, day-blooming; lvs. to 16 in. across, margins strongly sinuate-dentate; fls. 6-8 in. across, sky blue, pale in center. S. Afr. Var. **zanzibariensis** (Casp.) Conard [*N. zanzibariensis* Casp.]. Lvs. often smaller, purplish beneath; fls. larger, to 12 in. across, deep blue. Seedlings may produce fls. of light blue or reddish colors, and several cvs. have been named, including 'Azurea' and 'Rosea'. Zanzibar.

×**castaliiflora:** *Nymphaea* cv. 'Castaliiflora' [*N.* × *castaliiflora* Pring]. Developed from *N. capensis* var. *zanzibariensis* cv. 'Rosea'. Tender, day-blooming; lvs. to 15 in. across, marginally undulate to sinuate-dentate, marked with reddish-brown above, reddish beneath; fls. light pink, 8–10 in. across.

×**chromatella:** *Nymphaea* cv. 'Chromatella' [*N. Marliacea chromatella* Marliac]. Sterile hybrid, possibly either *N. alba* or *N. tuberosa* × *N. mexicana.* Hardy; lvs. bronzy-green, marked with brown-green, to 8 in. across, fls. large, canary-yellow, with deep yellow stamens.

×**chrysantha:** *Nymphaea* cv. 'Chrysantha' [*N.* × *chrysantha* Marliac]. Possibly, *N. alba* var. *rubra* × *N. mexicana.* Hardy; lvs. marbled with brown on upper surface; fls. medium-sized, changing from yellow to yellow-vermilion, with bright orange stamens.

colorata Peter. Tender, day-blooming, rhizome short, erect; lvs. 5 in. in diam., dark green with lighter veins, brownish-green beneath, irregularly coarsely sinuate-toothed, but entire in upper ⅓; fls. light blue, 4 in. across, sepals obtuse, with small dark dots. Tanzania.

×**Daubeniana:** *Nymphaea* cv. 'Daubeniana' [*N.* × *Daubeniana* Hort. ex O. Thomas]. Possibly, *N. caerulea* × *N. micrantha.* Tender, day-blooming, viviparous; fls. freely produced, to 8 in. across, creamy-white suffused violet, stamens orange, tipped violet. Material offered under this name, however, has small, pale blue, sterile fls. borne well above water surface. Also listed as cv. **'Daubenyana'** and **'Dauben'.**

dentata: *N. Lotus* var.

×**devoniensis:** *Nymphaea* cv. 'Devoniensis' [*N.* × *devoniensis* Hook.; *N.* cv. 'Devonshire']: *N. rubra* × ? Tender, night-blooming, large; lvs. red, changing to bronzy-green, greenish-brown beneath, to 18 in. in diam.; fls. many, bright rosy-red, 10–12 in. across, on peduncles well above the water surface.

flava: *N. mexicana.*

flavovirens Lehm. [*N. gracilis* Hort., not Zucc.]. Tender, day-blooming, tuberous, very vigorous; lvs. to 17 in. across, pale green beneath, irregularly sinuate to entire; fls. star-shaped, 6–8 in. across, standing above water surface, sepals pure green, petals white, acuminate, stamens yellow. Mex.

×**formosa:** *Nymphaea* cv. 'Formosa' [*N.* × *formosa* Marliac]. Hybrid; hardy; fls. large, lilac-pink, darker toward center, sepals white, stamens yellow.

×**fulva:** *Nymphaea* cv. 'Fulva' [*N.* × *fulva* Marliac]. Possibly, *N. alba* var. *rubra* × *N. mexicana.* Hardy; lvs. heavily mottled with red-brown; fls. with outer petals yellowish, shading, to deep red toward center, stamens orange-red.

gigantea Hook. AUSTRALIAN W. L. Tender, day-blooming, tuber-bearing; lvs. green above, purple beneath; fls. fragrant, standing above water surface, soft purplish-blue, shading to white toward base, stamens many, yellow, incurved. Australia. A white-fld. form is offered.

Gladstoniana: *Nymphaea* cv. 'Gladstoniana' [*N. Gladstoniana* (Richardson) Tricker; *N. alba Gladstoniana* Richardson]. Hardy, vigorous; fls. pure white, 6–8 in. across, fertile. Closely related to *N. alba;* possibly of hybrid origin.

×**gloriosa:** *Nymphaea* cv. 'Gloriosa' [*N.* × *gloriosa* Marliac]. Hybrid; hardy; lvs. floating, blotched with brown; fls. fragrant, with many currant-red petals and red stamens.

gracilis: *N. ampla* var. *speciosa,* but material offered under this name is probably *N. flavovirens.* [Var.] **rubra:** *Nymphaea* cv. 'Gracilis Rubra': *N. capensis* var. *zanzibariensis* cv. 'Rosea' × *N. flavovirens.* Tender, day-blooming; fls. deep pink.

×**helvola:** *Nymphaea* cv. 'Pygmaea Helvola'; see under *N. pygmaea* var. *helvola.*

Heudelotii Planch. Lf. blades floating, ovate to orbicular, to 3½ in. long, entire, reddish speckled with black beneath; fls. bluish-white, to 2 in. across, sepals black-spotted on exterior. Angola.

×**lactea:** *Nymphaea* cv. 'Lactea' [*N.* × *lactea* Marliac]. Hybrid; hardy; fls. fragrant, milk-white, with yellow stamens.

×**Laydekeri:** *Nymphaea* cv. 'Laydekeri' [*N.* × *Laydekeri* Marliac]. Possibly, *N. alba* var. *rubra* × *N. tetragona.* Hardy, vigorous, but not so robust as *N.* cv. 'Marliacea'; lvs. mottled with brown; fls. 2½–3 in. across. Var. **lilacea:** *Nymphaea* cv. 'Laydekeri Lilacea'. Fls. very fragrant, rosy-lilac, with orange-red stamens. Var. **fulgens:** *N.* cv. 'Laydekeri Fulgens'. Possibly, *N. alba* var. *rubra* × *N. mexicana.* Hardy; lvs. mottled with brown; fls. crimson-magenta, to 3½ in. across, with red stamens. Var. **purpurata:** *N.* cv. 'Laydekeri Purpurata' [*N.* cv. 'Purpurata']. Hardy; lvs. green above; fls. sterile, crimson, petals acute, stamens orange-red.

×**lilacea:** *Nymphaea* cv. 'Laydekeri Lilacea'.

Lotus L. EGYPTIAN W. L., LOTUS, EGYPTIAN L., WHITE L. (of Egypt). Tender, night-blooming, robust; lvs. 12–20 in. across, dark green above, greenish or brownish and usually puberulent beneath, margins serrate; fls. 5–10 in. across, white with outer petals pinkish, remaining open till noon. Egypt. This sp. and, more commonly, *N. caerulea* are the "lotus" of ancient Egyptian art. Var. **dentata** (Schumach. & Thonn.) Nichols. [*N. dentata* Schumach. & Thonn.]. Lvs. glabrous; fls. white, petals narrower, inner filaments with a purple spot near apex. Sierra Leone. Material cult. under this varietal name has lvs. densely pubescent beneath and fls. 12–14 in. across; it may not actually represent the var., and is perhaps better treated as *Nymphaea* cv. 'Dentata Superba'.

×**luciana:** *Nymphaea* cv. 'Luciana'. Possibly, *N. odorata* var. *rosea* × *N. tuberosa*. Hardy, vigorous; lvs. green above, reddish beneath; fls. rosy-pink, 3–5 in. across, petals evenly colored.

×**lucida:** *Nymphaea* cv. 'Lucida' [*N.* × *lucida* Marliac]. Possibly, *N. alba* var. *rubra* × *N. mexicana*. Hardy; lvs. mottled with red-brown; fls. large, rose-vermilion, with orange stamens.

×**Marliacea** Marliac: possibly, *N. alba* × *N. odorata* var. *rosea*. A group of hardy, vigorous, and robust hybrids with large fls. standing above water surface. [Var.] **albida:** *N.* cv. 'Marliacea Albida'. Fls. fragrant, white, sepals flushed pinkish, stamens yellow. [var.] **carnea:** *N.* cv. 'Marliacea Carnea'. Fls. sterile, fragrant, flesh-pink, becoming deep rose toward base of petals, with rose-pink sepals. [Var.] **chromatella:** *N.* cv. 'Chromatella', see *N.* × *chromatella*. [Var.] **rosea:** *N.* cv. 'Marliacea Rosea'. Similar to cv. 'Marliacea Carnea', but young lvs. purplish-red changing to deep green.

marmorata: *Nymphaea* cv. 'Marmorata'. Tender, day-blooming, viviparous; lvs. green, blotched with brown; fls. to 12 in. across, opening blue, becoming paler.

mexicana Zucc. [*N. flava* Leitn.; *Castalia flava* (Leitn.) Greene]. YELLOW W. L. Rhizome erect and tuberlike, spreading by runners; lvs. floating, 4–8 in. across, green blotched with brown above, crimson-brown with blackish dots beneath; fls. bright yellow, 4 in. across, standing above water surface. Fla., Mex. Hardy in Zone 8 when protected under cult.

micrantha Guillem. & Perrottet. Tender, viviparous; lvs. nearly orbicular, cordate, 3–10 in. across, reddish with dark dots beneath; fls. blue to white, 3–5 in. across, petals narrow, acute, filaments whitish. W. Afr.

×**Moorei:** *Nymphaea* cv. 'Moorei'. Possibly, *N. alba* × *N. mexicana*. Hardy; lvs. pale green, heavily spotted purple; fls. large, canary-yellow.

odorata Ait. [*Castalia odorata* (Ait.) Woodv. & W. Wood.] FRAGRANT W. L., WHITE W. L., POND LILY. Hardy; lvs. 3–10 in. across, rather thick, entire, dull green above, usually purplish beneath; fls. fragrant, white, 3–5 in. across, opening in the forenoon for 3 days. E. U.S. Cvs. 'Alba' and 'Major' are listed. Var. **gigantea** Tricker. Larger and more vigorous; lvs. bright red beneath; fls. larger, not as fragrant, sepals mostly green. Del. to Fla. and trop. Amer. Var. **minor** Sims [*Castalia minor* (Sims) DC.]. Plants ¼–½ as large as typical; fls. 2–3 in. across, sepals purple. Var. **rosea** Pursh. CAPE COD PINK W. L. Fls. very fragrant, deep pink, 4 in. across. Cape Cod, Mass. [Var.] **sulfurea:** *N.* cv. 'Sulfurea'; see under *N. sulfurea*.

×**Omarana:** *Nymphaea* cv. 'Omarana' [*N.* × *Omarana* Bisset]. *N. dentata* × *N.* cv. 'Sturtevantii'. Tender, night-blooming; lvs. large, dark bronzy-red, dentate; fls. magenta, 8–12 in. across, borne above water surface and opening very wide, stamens deep orange-red. Sometimes listed as *N.* cv. 'O'Marana'.

pubescens Willd. Lf. blades floating, ovate or broadly oblong, to 20 in. long and 18 in. wide, dark green above, dark purple and densely short-hairy beneath, margins wavy-dentate; fls. white or varying to pink or red, to 10 in. across, opening in the evening. India, Philippine Is., and Java, s. to Australia.

purpurata Peter. Tender; lvs. dark green, to 10 in. across, irregularly toothed, green beneath, becoming brownish toward margins; fls. to 7 in. across, petals light blue, becoming golden at base, stamens golden, purple-blue apically. Tanzania. Probably not commonly in cult.; *N.* cv. 'Laydekeri Purpurata' is sometimes offered under this name.

pygmaea: *N. tetragona*. [Var.] **alba** Marliac: *Nymphaea* cv. 'Pygmaea Alba'. Possibly, *N. alba* × *N. tetragona*. Hardy; differs from *N. tetragona* in having broader, more circular lvs. and sterile fls. [Var.] ×**helvola** Marliac: *Nymphaea* cv. 'Pygmaea Helvola' [*N.* × *helvola* Hort.]. *N. mexicana* × *N. tetragona*. Hardy, a little more dwarf than *N. tetragona;* lvs. blotched with brown; fls. canary-yellow, opening during afternoon.

×**Robinsonii:** *Nymphaea* cv. 'Robinsonii' [*N.* × *Robinsonii* Marliac]. Possibly, *N. alba* var. *rubra* × *N. mexicana*. Hardy; lvs. dark green, spotted red-brown above, deep red beneath, with a distinctive irregular notch at middle of the sides of the sinus; fls. 4 in. across, outer petals yellow, shading to rose and deep red toward center of fl., stamens orange-red.

Richardsonii: *N. tuberosa* cv.

rubra Roxb. INDIA RED W. L. Tender, night-blooming; lvs. 12–18 in. across, bronzy reddish-brown, becoming greenish in age, hairy beneath; fls. deep purplish-red, 6–10 in. across, remaining open till nearly noon. India. A parent of many hybrids. Cv. 'Rosea'. Fls. larger,

rosy-carmine, with longer, more pointed buds; lvs. not so dark, slightly spotted brown, dentate.

×**Seignouretii:** *Nymphaea* cv. 'Seignouretii' [*N.* × *Seignouretii* Marliac]. Possibly *N. alba* var. *rubra* × *N. mexicana*. Hardy; lvs. spotted with red-brown; fls. 5–6 in . across, borne above water surface, light yellow, shaded with soft rose and carmine, stamens orange-yellow.

×**somptuosa:** *Nymphaea* cv. 'Somptuosa' (sometimes misspelled *sumptuosa)* [*N.* × *somptuosa* Marliac]. Possibly, *N. alba* × *N. odorata* var. *rosea*. Hardy; fls. very large, fragrant, outer petals rose-pink, inner petals darker, spotted with carmine, stamens deep orange.

×**splendida:** *Nymphaea* cv. 'Splendida' [*N.* × *splendida* Marliac]. Hybrid; hardy; fls. large, petals deep red, shaded with white and carmine, stamens orange.

stellata Willd., not Casp. BLUE LOTUS (of India). Differs from *N. caerulea* in having lvs. irregularly sinuate-dentate, and pink or blue-violet beneath. S. and e. Asia. White- and pink-fld. forms occur in India.

×**Sturtevantii:** *Nymphaea* cv. 'Sturtevantii' [*N.* × *Sturtevantii* Hort. ex Tricker]. *N.* cv. 'Devoniensis' × *N. Lotus.* Tender, night-blooming; lvs. with brownish metallic cast, sinuate-dentate; fls. 8–12 in. across, petals broad, bright rosy-pink, stamens orange-brown.

sulfurea Gilg. Tender, day-blooming, rhizome erect, stout; lvs. ovate to nearly orbicular, entire, reddish above, deep red beneath; fls. fragrant, to 2¾ in. across, deep sulphur-yellow, sepals purplish on both sides or yellowish inside. Angola. Doubtfully in cult.; material offered under this name is probably *Nymphaea* cv. 'Sulfurea' [*N. odorata sulfurea* Marliac]: *N. mexicana* × *N. odorata*. Hybrid; hardy; lvs. mottled brownish-red above, red beneath; fls. sterile, large, fragrant, yellow, standing above water surface. Cv. 'Sulfurea Grandiflora'. Similar, but has larger, double fls.

tetragona Georgi [*N. pygmaea* Ait.]. PYGMY W. L. Hardy; lvs. ovate, entire, brown-blotched when young, reddish beneath, 3–4 in. across; fls. white, 1½–2½ in. across, open from noon to about 5 P.M. Siberia to Japan, also n. Idaho and Ont. Smallest sp. cult.; much used in hybridization, contributing to *N.* cv. 'Laydekeri' and other hybrids.

tuberosa Paine. MAGNOLIA W. L., TUBEROUS W. L. Hardy, robust, rhizome horizontal, bearing detachable, short, tuberlike brs.; lvs. to 15 in. across, entire, green beneath; fls. pure white, 4–9 in. across, with little or no fragrance, open until shortly after noon. N. Amer. Cv. 'Richardsonii' [*N. Richardsonii* Hort.]. Petals more numerous.

turicensis: *Nymphaea* cv. 'Turicensis'. Hardy; fls. light rose-colored, fragrant.

venusta: *N. alba;* the hardy plant with large, fragrant, pink fls. offered under this name is *Nymphaea* cv. 'Venusta'.

×**virginalis:** *Nymphaea* cv. 'Virginalis' [*N.* × *virginalis* Marliac]. Hybrid; hardy; fls. pure white with yellow stamens, to 11 in. across.

zanzibariensis: *N. capensis* var.

NYMPHAEACEAE Salisb. WATER LILY FAMILY. Dicot.; 8 genera of widely distributed per., aquatic herbs; lvs. usually large with long petioles, sometimes floating, commonly arising from submersed rootstocks; fls. solitary, axillary, often showy, regular, bisexual, sepals 4 or more, petals, stamens, and carpels few to many, carpels separate, united, or embedded in the receptacle; fr. various. Planted in ponds or aquaria. *Nelumbo* is cult. in e. Asia for its edible seeds and tuberous rhizomes. The cult. genera are: *Brasenia, Cabomba, Euryale, Nelumbo, Nuphar, Nymphaea,* and *Victoria. Brasenia* and *Cabomba* are sometimes separated as a distinct family, the Cabombaceae A. Rich.

NYMPHOIDES J. Hill [*Limnanthemum* S. G. Gmel.]. FLOATING-HEART. *Gentianaceae* (sometimes placed in separate family *Menyanthaceae*). Twenty spp. of polygamous, aquatic, per. herbs of wide distribution; lvs. floating, simple, at ends of elongate sts., deeply cordate at base, short-petioled; fls. in dense, axillary umbels, pedicelled, flowering nodes often with a cluster of short, spurlike roots; fls. 5-merous, corolla deeply parted, stamens borne on corolla tube, stigma 2-lobed, sessile, ovary 1-celled; fr. a caps., bursting irregularly.

Often grown in ponds and tubs, and *N. aquatica* also in fresh water aquaria. Outdoors they should be planted in loam covered with sand, in shallow water. Propagated by pieces having a flowering node and leaf.

aquatica (Walt.) O. Kuntze [*N. lacunosa* (Venten.) O. Kuntze; *Limnanthemum aquaticum* (Walt.) Britt.]. BANANA PLANT (of aquarists),

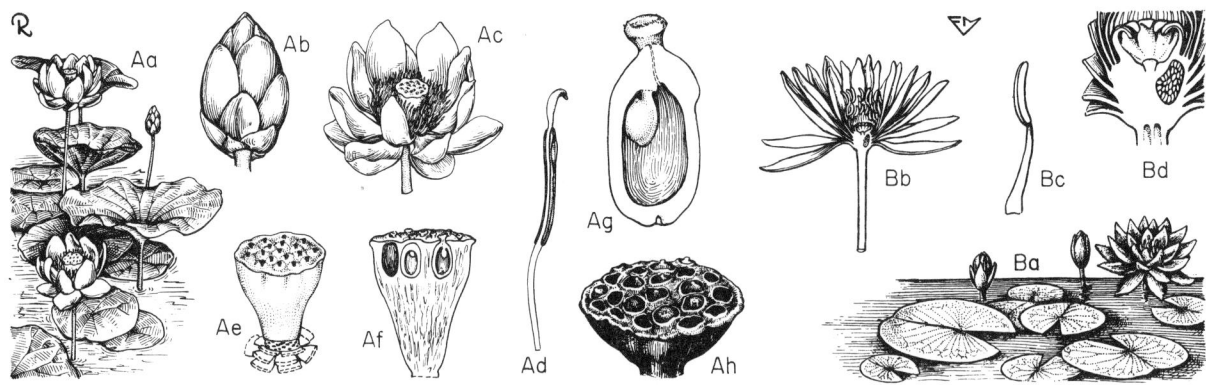

NYMPHAEACEAE. **A,** *Nelumbo lutea:* **Aa,** flowering plants, × ¹⁄₁₅; **Ab,** flower bud, × ¼; **Ac,** flower, × ⅙; **Ad,** stamen, × 1; **Ae,** receptacle (perianth and stamens removed), × ⅜; **Af,** receptacle, vertical section, × ½; **Ag,** carpel, vertical section, × 1½; **Ah,** receptacle in fruiting stage, × ⅕. **B,** *Nymphaea odorata:* **Ba,** flowering plant, × ⅛; **Bb,** flower, vertical section, × ¼; **Bc,** stamen, × 1; **Bd,** base of flower (perianth cut away), vertical section, × 1. (Ba-Bd from Bailey, *Manual of Cultivated Plants,* ed. 2.)

AQUATIC B. P., FAIRY WATER LILY. Lvs. nearly orbicular to reniform, to 6 in. across, lower surface and petioles usually purple-glandular; flowering nodes with clusters of short, blunt, tuberous roots, corolla white, to ¾ in. across; caps. to ⅜ in. long. Summer. N.J., s. to Fla. and Tex.

cordata (Elliott) Fern. [*N. lacunosa* Fern., not (Venten.) O. Kuntze]. Floating lvs. broadly ovate, deeply cordate, to 2½ in. long, purplish beneath; flowering nodes with cluster of slender, elongate tubers, corolla white or cream. E. N. Amer.

Humboldtiana (HBK) O. Kuntze. Per., with runners developing from petioles; lvs. orbicular, to 6 in. across, glandular-hairy beneath; corolla white, with yellow centers, lobes elliptic, ¾ in. long, fringed; caps. less than ⅜ in. long. Trop. Amer.

indica (Thwaites) O. Kuntze [*Limnanthemum indicum* Thwaites]. WATER SNOWFLAKE. Lvs. orbicular, to 8 in. across; corolla white, yellow toward center, lobes ⅜ long, fimbriate and papillose; caps. ⅜ in. long. Tropics.

lacunosa: see *N. aquatica* and *N. cordata.*

nymphaeoides: *N. peltata.*

peltata (S. G. Gmel.) O. Kuntze [*N. nymphaeoides* Britt.; *Limnanthemum Nymphoides* (L.) Hoffmans. & Link; *L. peltatum* S. G. Gmel.]. YELLOW F.-H., WATER-FRINGE. Spreading rapidly by runners; lvs. ovate-orbicular, to 4 in. across, wavy-margined, often mottled, upper lvs. mostly opp.; flowering nodes lacking clusters of roots, pedicels to 4 in. long, corolla bright yellow, 1 in. across or more, lobes fringed; caps. to 1 in. long. Late spring, early summer. Eur., Asia; naturalized in U.S.

NYPA Steck. *Palmae.* One sp., a gregarious, unarmed, monoecious palm with underground, forking sts. and no erect trunk, of estuaries and brackish swamps in India, Malay Arch. to Solomon Is., and Ryukyu Is.; lvs. pinnate, erect, petiole elongate, cylindrical, pinnae regularly arranged, acuminate, with prominent brown scales on midrib beneath; infl. among lvs., erect, branched, the axes subtended by brown tubular bracts; male fls. on short catkinlike lateral brs., perianth segms. 6, similar, separate, stamens 3, united, female fls. in dense terminal head, perianth segms. 6, similar, separate, carpels separate, usually 3; fr. obovoid, angled, fibrous, aggregated.

Grown in suitable locations with brackish water in southern Fla., Zone 10b. An ornamental plant when properly placed. For culture see *Palms.*

fruticans Wurmb. NIPA, NYPA PALM, MANGROVE P. Lvs. from the base, 10–30 ft. long, gracefully arching, pinnae many, rigid, 2–3 ft. long, somewhat glaucous below; fruiting head 10–12 in. in diam.; frs. angular, hard, 4–5 in. long.

NYSSA L. TUPELO. *Nyssaceae.* About 6 or 7 spp. of deciduous trees, native to N. Amer. and se. Asia; lvs. alt., simple; fls. minute, greenish-white, in axillary peduncled clusters, unisexual, petals 5, stamens 5–12, exserted; fr. a drupe.

The wood of the tupelos is valued in commerce. Sometimes grown as ornamentals in moist locations; prized also for the crooked, brushy branching of some of the species, and for the brilliant color of their foliage in autumn. Propagated by seeds sown at once or stratified, and by layers. Trees do not transplant well from the wild.

aquatica L. [*N. uniflora* Wangenh.]. COTTON GUM, TUPELO G., WILD OLIVE, LARGE T. To 100 ft.; lvs. oblong or ovate, to 10 in. long, entire or angular-toothed; fr. dark purple, 1 in. long, solitary. Swamps, Va. to Fla. and Tex. Bee plant.

biflora: *N. sylvatica* var.

multiflora: *N. sylvatica.*

orientalis: a listed name of no botanical standing.

sinensis D. Oliver. To 60 ft.; lvs. elliptic, to 6 in. long; fr. bluish, ⅝ in. long, 2–3 together on short peduncles. Cent. China.

sylvatica Marsh. [*N. multiflora* Wangenh.]. PEPPERIDGE, SOUR GUM, BLACK G., UPLAND T. To 100 ft.; lvs. elliptic or obovate, to 5 in. long, short-acuminate, entire; fr. dark blue, to ½ in. long. Me. to Fla. and Tex. Var. **biflora** (Walt.) Sarg. [*N. biflora* Walt.]. Lvs. mostly obtuse, fr. with much-flattened, ribbed stones. Del. and Md., s. to Fla. and La. Var **pendula.** A listed name of no botanical standing, used for a weeping form.

uniflora: *N. aquatica.*

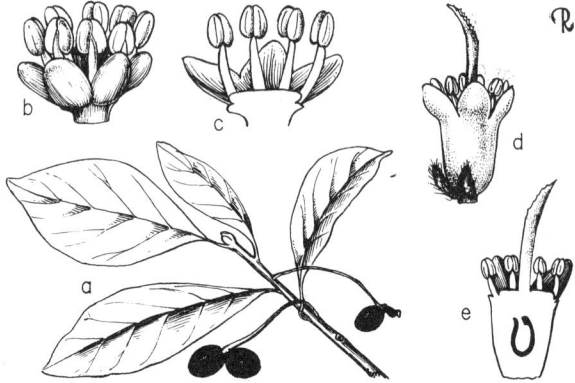

NYSSACEAE. *Nyssa sylvatica:* **a,** fruiting branch, × ½; **b,** male flower, × 6; **c,** male flower, vertical section, × 6; **d,** bisexual flower, × 4; **e,** bisexual flower, vertical section, × 4. (From Bailey, *Manual of Cultivated Plants,* ed. 2.)

NYSSACEAE Juss. NYSSA, TUPELO, or SOUR-GUM FAMILY. Dicot.; 3 genera of deciduous trees and shrubs, native to N. Amer. and Asia; lvs. alt., simple; fls. minute, unisexual or less commonly besexual, in axillary or terminal heads, calyx 5-toothed or obsolete, petals 5 or more, or lacking, stamens 5–10, exserted, pistil 1, ovary inferior, 1-celled or 6–10-celled; fr. a drupe. Species of *Nyssa* produce commercially important timber, and *Camptotheca, Davidia,* and *Nyssa* are cult. as ornamentals.

OAKESIA: *UVULARIA.*

OAKESIELLA: *UVULARIA.*

OBREGONIA Frič. *Cactaceae.* One sp., a small, globose, tubercled cactus, native to Mex.; plant turnip-shaped, crowned by a dense, globose rosette of leaflike tubercles, these triangular-ovate, truncate at apex, centrally convex, dorsally keeled, with acute margins; areoles terminal, deciduous, spines weak; fls. subapical, from spiniferous areoles, tube and ovary naked; seeds black, tubercled. Allied to *Leuchtenbergia,* in which it should perhaps be included, but the tubercles short and broad.

For culture see *Cacti.*

Denegrii Frič. Sts. mostly solitary, to 8 in. thick, tubercles to ⅝ in. long and 1 in. thick; spines 2–4, about ½ in. long; fls. white, to 1¼ in. long; fr. white, hidden in the woolly crown. Ne. Mex.

OCHAGAVIA Phil. [*Rhodostachys* Phil.]. *Bromeliaceae.* Five spp. of stiff, stemless or short-stemmed, suffruticose plants, native to Chile; lvs. many, narrow, spiny; infl. sessile or very short-stalked; fls. many, bisexual, sepals separate, petals separate, without appendages, shorter than stamens, ovary inferior, angled; fr. a berry, seeds large, globose.

Grown in full sun. For culture see *Bromeliaceae.*

Lindleyana (Lem.) Mez [*Rhodostachys andina* Phil.]. Lvs. in a rosette, to 1½ ft. long, 1 in. wide at base, broadly linear, silvery, fiercely spiny; infl. headlike; fls. many, rose, to 1⅝ in. long.

OCHNA L. [*Diporidium* Bartl. & H. L. Wendl.]. BIRD'S-EYE BUSH. *Ochnaceae.* About 90 spp. of trop., Old World trees and shrubs; lvs. alt., simple, mostly serrate, leathery; fls. large, yellow, in panicles, racemes, or umbels, sepals 5–6, colored, persistent, petals 5–12, disc thick, lobed, stamens many, opening mostly by terminal pores, ovary deeply 3–12-lobed, developing into 3–12 1-seeded drupes on the expanded receptacle.

Grown in gardens in the tropics; one species is cultivated under glass or outdoors in Zone 10 in southern Calif. The best soil in greenhouse culture is well-drained fibrous loam. Propagated by cuttings of half-ripened wood in summer or autumn, and by seeds.

atropurpurea DC. Shrub, to 4 ft.; lvs. ovate, sharply serrate; fls. solitary, sepals ovate, enlarged and deep purple in fr. S. Afr. Material cult. under this name is usually *O. serrulata.*

Jabotapita L. [*O. Moonii* Thwaites; *O. squarrosa* L.; *O. Wightiana* Wallich var. *Moonii* (Thwaites) Trimen]. Shrub or small tree; lvs. lanceolate, narrowed toward each end, 3–7 in. long, 2 in. wide, denticulate; fls. 6–12, terminal on short lateral brs., pedicels elongate; fls. about ¾ in. across, petals 5, oblong, as long as sepals, carpels 5–7. Ceylon.

japonica: *O. serrulata.*

Kirkii D. Oliver. To 15 ft.; lvs. oblong-elliptic to narrowly obovate, to 4 in. long, apically obtuse or rounded, mucronate, cuneate to cordate at base, margin entire or undulate, usually with many cilia; fls. in short panicles on short lateral branchlets, petals 1 in. long, calyx red, flat, spreading in fr., carpels to 12; drupes flattened-cylindrical. Tanzania, n. Mozambique, Kenya.

Moonii: *O. Jabotapita.*

mossambicensis Klotzsch. Bushy, to 10 ft.; lvs. obovate to oblanceolate, stiff, to 9 in. long and 3 in. wide, rounded and apiculate at apex, densely serrulate; fls. in many-fld. open panicles on short lateral brs., petals to ⅝ in. long, sepals red in fr., spreading, carpels 8–10, forming as many drupes. Mozambique.

multiflora DC. To 30 ft.; lvs. elliptic to oblong or obovate, to 6 in. long and 2½ in. wide, remotely spinulose-serrulate; fls. in simple, terminal, 12–20-fld. racemes, petals ⅜ in. long, sepals pink to red in fr., slightly reflexed, carpels 5; fr. reniform. Trop. Afr. Doubtfully in cult.; material offered under this name is usually *O. serrulata.*

obtusata DC. [*O. squarrosa* of auth., not L.]. Small, glabrous tree; lvs. very variable, oblanceolate to elliptic or narrowly obovate, to 5 in. long, crenate-serrulate, the teeth spiny, petioles ¼ in. long; fls. 1½ in. across or more, in short umbellate panicles terminal on lateral brs., pedicels elongate, petals 7–12; fr. ovoid, black, receptacle and sepals red. Ceylon and India.

pumila Buch.-Ham. ex D. Don. Subshrub, from woody root; lvs. oblanceolate to obovate, to 6 in. long, spiny-serrulate, tapering to a short petiole, stipules toothed; fls. fragrant, 2 in. across, subumbellate on long peduncles, sepals ½ in. long, petals obovate, much longer than sepals; drupes greenish, to ½ in. long. Assam and Nepal.

serratifolia Bak. [*Diporidium vaccinioides* (Bak.) van Tiegh. var. *serratifolium* (Bak.) van Tiegh. ex Humbert]. Glabrous shrub; lvs. oblong, obtuse, 1–2 in. long, finely serrulate, teeth bristle-tipped; cymes axillary, few, nearly sessile; fls. few, calyx nearly 1 in. across in fr., oblong, rigid, sepals brown and spreading. Madagascar. Doubtfully in cult.; material so listed may be *O. serrulata.*

serrulata (Hochst.) Walp. [*O. japonica* Hort.; *O. multiflora* Hort., not DC.; *O. serratifolia* Hort., not Bak.]. MICKEY-MOUSE PLANT, BIRD'S-EYE BUSH. Shrub, to 5 ft., brs. roughened by many lenticels; lvs. narrowly elliptic, to 2⅜ in. long, sharply serrulate; fls. 1 to several, on short spurs, sepals broadly elliptic, yellow-green, becoming enlarged and oblong in age, strongly reflexed and bright red in fr., petals obovate; drupes ellipsoid, becoming black when mature, on enlarged red receptacle. S. Afr. Perhaps not specifically distinct from *O. atropurpurea.*

squarrosa: *O. Jabotapita;* but the large-fld. sp. commonly cult. as *O. squarrosa* is *O. obtusata.*

Thomasiana Engl. & Gilg ex Gilg. Differs from *O. Kirkii* in having lvs. usually smaller and auriculate at base, with long basal cilia, and infl. with fewer, usually smaller fls. Coast, e. Afr.

Wightiana var. **Moonii:** *O. Jabotapita.*

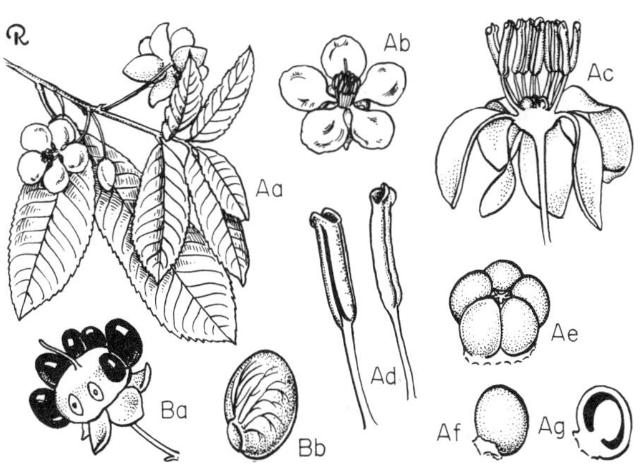

OCHNACEAE. **A,** *Ochna serrulata:* **Aa,** flowering branch, × ⅓; **Ab,** flower, × 1; **Ac,** flower, vertical section, × 2; **Ad,** stamens, two views, × 5; **Ae,** ovary, × 8; **Af,** single carpel, × 10; **Ag,** carpel, vertical section, × 10. **B,** *O. mossambicensis:* **Ba,** fruit, × ½; **Bb,** single drupe, × 1½.

OCHNACEAE DC. OCHNA FAMILY. Dicot.; about 20 genera of trop. trees, shrubs, and herbs; lvs. alt., simple or rarely pinnate; fls. bisexual, sepals 5, petals mostly 5, stamens 5 to many, inserted on a disc, filaments persistent, ovary superior, entire to deeply 3–12-lobed; fr. a berry, caps., or cluster of drupes. *Ochna* and *Ouratea* are sometimes planted as ornamentals.

OCHROMA Swartz. *Bombacaceae.* Probably one variable sp., a tree native to trop. Amer.; lvs. alt., simple, large, palmately-veined, mostly palmately-lobed, or -angled; fls. very large, solitary on stout, axillary peduncles, calyx campanulate, unequally 5-lobed, petals 5, stamens united in a tube bearing a spiral of anthers from the middle to the apex; fr. a 5-valved, linear caps., seeds many, embedded in dense, brownish wool.

Propagated by seeds.

Lagopus: *O. pyramidale.*

pyramidale (Cav.) Urb. [*O. Lagopus* Swartz]. BALSA, CORKWOOD. To 90 ft., trunk smooth, often with buttresses, to 3 ft. in diam.; lvs. broadly ovate to nearly circular, to 1 ft. across or more, sparsely to densely soft-pubescent beneath; petals off-white, 4–6 in. long, shorter than staminal column; caps. to 1 ft. long. Fast growing, pioneer tree of lowland trop. Amer. Zone 10. Furnishes the very light, commercially important balsa wood.

OCHROSIA Juss. *Apocynaceae.* About 36 spp. of trees and shrubs native to Australia and the Pacific and Mascarene Is.; sap milky; lvs. opp. or whorled, entire; cymes terminal or in upper axils; fls. 5-merous, regular, bisexual, corolla salverform, lobes contorted in bud, stamens included, borne on the corolla, anthers lanceolate, separate, pistil with 2 ovaries; fr. of 1 or 2 fleshy or fibrous, somewhat flattened, mostly 1-seeded drupelets, seeds broad and flat.

Propagated by cuttings or seeds.

elliptica Labill. To 20 ft.; lvs. in whorls of 3–4, obovate-oblong to elliptical, mostly 3–6 in. long, obtuse or abruptly acute; infls. small, dense; fls. sessile, corolla cream-white, tube ⅜ in. long, lobes linear and ¼ in. long; fr. ellipsoid, to 2 in. across, scarlet at maturity, pulp with odor of violets, seeds circular, with narrow wings. Coastal, New Caledonia to Australia.

OCIMUM L. [*Becium* Lindl.]. BASIL. *Labiatae.* About 150 spp. of herbs or shrubs, of warm-temp. or trop. regions, chiefly Afr.; sts. mostly square in cross section; lvs. opp., often toothed; fls. mostly small, in 6–10-fld. verticillasters arranged in terminal racemes or panicles, calyx campanulate, 2-lipped, lower lip usually with 4 mucronate teeth, corolla 2-lipped, upper lip 4-lobed, lower lip concave, stamens 4, in 2 pairs, exserted; fr. of 4 nutlets.

Sometimes grown for the fragrant foliage and as sweet herbs. Basils are tender and should be started indoors or in a hotbed, otherwise they are easily grown. The herbage is cut while the plant is growing and dried; a second crop is often obtained.

Basilicum L. [*O. bullatum* Lam.]. COMMON B., SWEET B. Glabrous or glabrescent ann., to 2 ft.; lvs. ovate to ovate-elliptic, 3–5 in. long, generally cuneate; infl. racemose; corolla about 5/16 in. long, white or purplish. Summer. Trop. Old World. Used in seasoning and grown for its pleasant fragrance. Cvs. are: 'Citriodorum', lemon-scented; 'Minimum' [*O. minimum* L.], lvs. much smaller, rarely to 2½ in. long, acute to acuminate, entire or weakly serrate, glabrous, green or purplish; 'Purpurascens', lvs. purplish.

bullatum: *O. Basilicum.*

canum Sims. HOARY B. Herb, to 2 ft., much-branched, pungent; lvs. elliptic-lanceolate, to nearly 3 in. long, acute at both ends, entire to shallowly serrate, essentially glabrous, gland-dotted; verticillasters close, 6-fld., arranged in spikelike racemes 3–8 in. long, bracts elliptic-lanceolate, stalked, pedicels shorter than calyx; calyx pubescent, teeth of lower lip lanceolate-subulate, longer than upper lip, corolla less than 3/16 in. long, white. Trop. and subtrop. Asia, trop. Afr.

crispum: *Perilla frutescens* cv.

frutescens: *Perilla frutescens.*

gratissimum L. Shrubby, to 6 ft., glabrescent or pubescent; lvs. ovate, to 4 in. long, cuneate, acute, serrate, glabrous; infl. racemose; corolla nearly ½ in. long, pale yellow. Se. Asia.

minimum: *O. Basilicum* cv.

obovatum E. H. Mey. ex Benth. [*Becium obovatum* (E. H. Mey. ex Benth.) N. E. Br.]. Per., 5–10 in., glabrescent, sts. woody at base; lvs. lanceolate to nearly orbicular, to 2¼ in. long, obtuse or acute, entire or slightly serrate, glabrous or glabrescent; infl. headlike to short-spicate; calyx to ¼ in. long, corolla white or pink. Trop. and s. Afr.

OCTOMERIA R. Br. *Orchidaceae.* About 120 spp. of epiphytes, native to trop. Amer.; tufted or with distinct creeping rhizomes, sts. elongate, 1-lvd. at apex, concealed by 1 or more tubular sheaths; lvs. erect, sessile; infls. fleshy, 1 to many, clustered, 1-fld.; fls. small, campanulate, sepals and petals nearly equal, separate, lip shorter, commonly with a pair of small lateral lobes and with a pair of calluses on disc, column fleshy, arching, with a distinct foot, pollinia 8. For structure of fl. see *Orchidaceae.*

For culture see *Orchids.*

erosilabia C. Schweinf. Sts. to 6½ in. high, 3–5-jointed; lvs. erect, short-petioled, leathery, oblong-linear, revolute on margins, to 6 in. long; infls. 1-fld., many, clustered; fls. small, creamy-white to yellow, sepals lanceolate, to ¼ in. long, petals similar but smaller, lip half as long as sepals, 3-lobed, oblong-ovate, ⅛ in. long, lateral lobes very small, midlobe toothed, disc with a pair of short, fleshy keels. Guyana and Venezuela to Peru.

graminifolia (L.) R. Br. Rhizome long, repent, sts. widely spaced, ascending, to 3 in. long; lvs. fleshy, narrowly lanceolate, to 4 in. long; fls. clustered, few, pale yellow to greenish-yellow, sepals and petals ovate, similar, to ¼ in. long, lip smaller, 3-lobed, yellow, lateral lobes squarish, midlobe ovate, disc with a pair of madder-purple keels. Early winter. W. Indies to Colombia and Brazil.

surinamensis Focke. Tuft-forming, sts. to 4 in. long; lvs. to 4 in. long, leathery, pale green on upper side, green to maroon-red on back; fls. pale yellow, to 5 in a cluster, sepals and petals ovate, similar, to ¼ in. long, lip shorter than sepals, 3-lobed, yellow, lateral lobes sickle-shaped, midlobe squarish, emarginate, disc with a pair of dark maroon keels, column pale brown with pink-maroon suffusion. Trop. lowlands, S. Amer.

×**ODONTIODA** Hort.: *Cochlioda* × *Odontoglossum.* Orchidaceae. Bigeneric hybrids intermediate in character between the parents.

For culture see *Orchids.*

×**ODONTOBRASSIA** Hort.: *Brassia* × *Odontoglossum.* Orchidaceae. Bigeneric hybrids intermediate in character between the parents.

For culture see *Orchids.*

×**ODONTOCIDIUM** Kupper: *Odontoglossum* × *Oncidium.* Orchidaceae. Bigeneric hybrids intermediate in character between the parents.

For culture see *Orchids.*

ODONTOGLOSSUM HBK. *Orchidaceae.* About 250 spp. of epiphytic or rock-dwelling herbs, native to cool highlands of trop. Amer.; pseudobulbs ovoid, 1–2-lvd.; lvs. folded lengthwise; infl. lateral, racemose or paniculate, few- to many-fld.; fls. small to large, often showy, long-lasting, sepals and petals similar, spreading, lip often with a distinct claw parallel to the column, blade of lip bent, disc with calluses, column footless, often united basally to lip. For structure of fl. see *Orchidaceae.*

Odontoglossums require a cool greenhouse. For culture see *Orchids.*

×**Adrianae** L. Linden: *O. crispum* × *O. Hunnewellianum.* Fls. to 2½ in. across, sepals and petals similar, ovate-lanceolate, light yellow with brown blotches, lip white with cinnamon spots and denticulate margins, column cylindrical, with denticulate wings at apex.

×**amabile** Hort.: *O. crispum* × *O. spectabile* Hort. Fls. large, to 5 in. across, firm in texture, sepals and petals similar, cream-white with violet-brown markings, lip lanceolate, white with many light cinnamon blotches.

Andersonianum: *O. crispum* cv.

apterum Llave & Lex. [*O. nebulosum* Lindl.]. Epiphytic, pseudobulbs to 4 in. long, 2-lvd.; lvs. fleshy, to 6 in. long; infl. a lateral, erect, loosely 3–7-fld. raceme; fls. large, to 3 in. across, white with red-brown spots on the basal half of sepals and petals, sepals keeled dorsally, lip with a keeled, folded claw and a nearly circular toothed or entire blade, disc with a pair of calluses in center. Mex.

×**ardentissimum:** *O.* ×*armainvillierense.*

×**armainvillierense** Hort. [*O.* ×*ardentissimum* Hort.]: *O. crispum* × *O. nobile.* Similar to *O. crispum,* but fls. more rounded, to 4 in. across, sepals and petals broad, blunt, white with a few red-brown blotches, lip somewhat fiddle-shaped, white, with yellow crest behind a large red-brown blotch.

×**aspersum** Rchb.f.: *O. maculatum* × *O. Rossii.* Pseudobulbs flattened, 2-lvd.; infl. racemose, few-fld.; fls. rather thin in texture, to 3 in. across, sepals and petals similar, spreading, cream or light yellow with many sepia blotches on sepals and a few at base of petals, lip white, ovate-cordate, crenulate, with a yellow callus, tip of column violet. Mex.

bictoniense Lindl. Pseudobulbs ovoid, 2–3-lvd.; lvs. lanceolate, to 1 ft. long; infl. erect, racemose, occasionally paniculate, many-fld., to

2½ ft. long; fls. fleshy, to 2 in. across, sepals and petals similar, linear, yellowish-green with reddish-brown cross bars, lip large, triangular-cordate, undulate, white with mauve or rose veins. Mex., Guatemala, El Salvador. Cv. **'Album'** [var. *album* André]. Similar to typical form in shape and size of fls., sepals and petals reddish-brown, lip pure white.

brevifolium Lindl. [*O. chiriquense* Rchb.f.; *O. coronarium* Lindl.]. Robust, to 2 ft., from a creeping rhizome, pseudobulbs flattened, 1-lvd.; lvs. fleshy, ovate to elliptic, to 1 ft. long; infl. lateral, erect, many-fld.; fls. showy, to 2½ in. across, sepals and petals similar, round-ovate, undulate-crisped, bright reddish-coppery-brown with yellow margin, lip fiddle-shaped, yellow with whitish crest. Highlands, Costa Rica to Venezuela and Peru.

cariniferum Rchb.f. Pseudobulbs flattened, 2-lvd.; lvs. strap-shaped, to 15 in. long; infl. lateral, paniculate, many-fld.; fls. fleshy, to 2 in. across, sepals and petals lanceolate, keeled, dark brownish-maroon with greenish-yellow margins, lip anchor-shaped, white with pale rose calluses at base. Autumn. Costa Rica, Panama.

Cervantesii Llave & Lex. Pseudobulbs small, 1-lvd.; lvs. oblong, to 6 in. long; infl. racemose, to 10 in. long, densely several-fld.; fls. showy, to 2 in. across, sepals and petals spreading, similar, petals somewhat broader, white or faintly pink with yellowish tips and transverse red-brown bars near base, lip white, ovate-cordate, with erose margins and 2-lobed callus at base. Mex., Guatemala. Cv. **'Decorum'** [var. *decorum* Rchb.f.]. Similar to typical form in shape and size of fls., sepals, petals, and lip covered with red spots.

chiriquense: *O. brevifolium.*

cirrhosum Lindl. Pseudobulbs flattened, 1–2-lvd.; lvs. sword-shaped, to 1 ft. long; infl. racemose or rarely branched, arching-pendent, densely many-fld.; fls. showy, to 4 in. across, sepals and petals similar, lanceolate, long-acuminate, white or milk-white, spotted with maroon-crimson, lip shorter than sepals, long-acuminate from an ovate base, base yellow with maroon lines, apical part white with maroon-crimson spots. Spring. Colombia, Ecuador.

citrosmum: *O. pendulum.*

constrictum Lindl. Pseudobulbs ovoid, 2-lvd.; lvs. linear-lanceolate, to 15 in. long; infl. racemose or with a few brs., slender, arching or pendent, many-fld.; fls. fleshy, to 1½ in. across, sepals and petals similar, yellow with red-brown blotches, lip squarish-fiddleform, white with a pair of rose-colored spots in front of the calluses. Winter. Venezuela. Cvs. are : **'Castaneum'** [var. *castaneum* Rchb.f.], similar to typical form in size and shape of fls., sepals and petals cinnamon-colored with a few greenish longitudinal stripes at base, lip pale peach with a cinnamon spot in center; **'Majus'** [var. *majus* Lindl.], fls. larger than in typical form, lip long, hastate; **'Pallens'** [var. *pallens* Rchb.f.], sepals, petals, and lip pale yellow, without spots; **'Sanderanum'** [var. *Sanderanum* (Rchb.f.) Hort. Veitch; *O. Sanderanum* Rchb.f.], differs from typical form in its larger and brighter fls., sepals lanceolate, yellow with sepia or red-brown markings, petals yellow with longitudinal stripes, lip white with a large rose-purple spot in front of callus.

convallarioides (Schlechter) Ames & Correll. Pseudobulbs small, ovoid, 2-lvd.; lvs. narrow, to 1 ft. long; infl. racemose, to 10 in. long, few-fld.; fls. gaping, to ¾ in. across, sepals and petals similar, all separate, ovate-elliptic, white, lip ovate, constricted in middle, orbicular in front, white with yellow callus at base. Autumn. Costa Rica.

cordatum Lindl. Rhizomatous, pseudobulbs flattened, 1-lvd.; lvs. oblong-elliptic, to 8 in. long; infl. racemose, erect, to 2 ft. long, loosely many-fld., scape 2-edged; fls. starlike, to 3 in. across, sepals and petals similar, spreading, long-acuminate, yellow or ochraceous with chestnut-brown or sepia markings, lip cordate, white with sepia markings. Mex., Guatemala.

coronarium: *O. brevifolium.*

crispum Lindl. Pseudobulbs flattened, to 3 in. long, 2-lvd.; lvs. linear, to 1 ft. long; infl. racemose, rarely branched, arching or pendent, densely many-fld.; fls. very variable, to 3½ in. across, sepals and petals similar, commonly white with violet-rose suffusion, petals with erose or dentate margins, lip strap-shaped, toothed, white, with a 2-lobed callus at base. Late winter–spring. Colombia. Cvs. include: **'Andersonianum'** [var. *Andersonianum* (Rchb.f.) Hort. Veitch; *O. Andersonianum* Rchb.f.], differs from typical form in its narrower and more pointed sepals and petals, yellowish or cream-white with chestnut-brown spots; **'Apiatum'** [var. *apiatum* Ballant.], differs from typical form in having fls. with large chocolate-brown blotches on white ground, sepals occasionally stained with violet-purple; **'Ashworthianum'** [var. *Ashworthianum* O'Brien], sepals and petals bright rosy-purple, shading to a white margin, lip yellow at base and with a dark reddish-purple blotch in front of callus; **'Fowleranum'** [var. *Fowleranum* O'Brien], sepals and petals white with bright, deep ruby-crimson blotches, lip white with a yellow crest and purple marking, reverse side of whole fl. heavily blotched with claret; **'Grairianum'**,

sepals and petals yellowish-rose with white margins and with a yellow crest on lip; **'Guttatum'** [var. *guttatum* Hook.], sepals and petals white with 4–6 central reddish-brown spots, lip white with many small reddish-brown spots in a semicircle in front of callus; **'Lehmannii'** [var. *Lehmannii* Rchb.f.], plant smaller than in typical form, with large panicle, up to 50 fls., sepals, petals, and lip white, tinted with purple and brown; **'Lucianii'** [var. *Lucianii* Warb.], sepals and petals white with deep plum-purple blotches, lip blotched also in front of callus; **'Mundyanum'**, sepals and petals white, tinged with rose-purple and heavily blotched with chestnut- or red-brown, central area of lip bright yellow; **'Pittianum'** [var. *Pittianum* O'Brien], sepals and petals white, slightly tinged with rose and heavily blotched with red-brown, lip with a yellow crest marked with reddish lines; **'Purpurescens'**, similar to var. *Pittianum,* but sepals and petals heavily tinged with rose, which on the lateral sepals obscures the fine reddish-purple spotting; **'Veitchianum'** [var. *Veitchianum* Rchb.f.], sepals and petals very broad, white, with mauve suffusion and with a few brown blotches, petals coarsely toothed along margins.

cristatum Lindl. [*Oncidium cristatum* (Lindl.) Beer]. Pseudobulbs ovoid, 2-lvd.; lvs. strap-shaped, to 10 in. long; infl. erect, densely many-fld.; fls. fleshy, to 2½ in. across, sepals and petals similar, spreading, starlike, yellow with chestnut-brown blotches and markings, lip similar, with crenulate margins, yellow with a large chestnut-brown blotch in front, disc with a basal rose callus with many fingerlike lobes. Spring. Colombia, Ecuador. Cv. **'Dayanum'** [var. *Dayanum* Rchb.f.]. Differs from typical form in having a rhomboid lip with toothed margin, and a basal callus in which the fingerlike lobes diagonally cross one another.

Dawsonianum: *O. Ehrenbergii.*

Egertonii Lindl. Pseudobulbs elongate, to 4 in. long, 2-lvd.; lvs. thin, linear, to 10 in. long; infl. racemose, erect, few-fld.; fls. fragrant, white, to 1 in. across, upper sepal and petals similar, ovate, lateral sepals united to middle, lip ovate, shell-like, with a yellow W-shaped callus at base. Late spring. Mex. to Panama.

Ehrenbergii Link, Klotzsch, & Otto [*O. Dawsonianum* Rchb.f.]. Plant small, pseudobulbs 1-lvd.; lvs. ovate, 2–3 in. long; infl. racemose, erect, 1–3-fld.; fls. rather delicate, showy, to 1½ in. across, sepals lanceolate, white with chestnut-brown transverse bars, petals white or pink, ovate, with a brown spot at base, lip ovate-cordate, white or pink with crenulate margin and a hollow callus at base. Mex., Guatemala.

gloriosum Linden & Rchb.f. Epiphyte, to 3 ft., pseudobulbs ovoid, 2-lvd.; lvs. long-strap-shaped; infl. paniculate, many-fld.; fls. fleshy, starlike, to 2½ in. across, sepals and petals lanceolate, pale to greenish-yellow, with cinnamon spots and blotches, lip hastate, pale yellow, with a large cinnamon blotch in front and a 2-lobed callus. Spring. Colombia, Ecuador.

grande Lindl. TIGER ORCHID. Pseudobulbs ovoid, 2–3-lvd.; lvs. oblong-ovate, to 6 in. long; infl. racemose, erect, few-fld.; fls. large, to 6 in. across, sepals oblong-strap-shaped, bright yellow, barred with cinnamon-brown, petals broader, basal half cinnamon-brown with yellow, apical half bright yellow, lip nearly orbicular, white or pale yellow with a few pale red blotches. Late autumn–early spring. Mex., Guatemala.

Hallii Lindl. Pseudobulbs ovoid, 2-lvd.; lvs. linear-lanceolate, to 15 in. long; infl. racemose, up to 5 ft. long, arching, many-fld.; fls. fleshy, showy, to 4 in. across, sepals and petals similar, ovate-lanceolate, light yellow with brown or red-brown markings, lip of same color, undulate, with fringed margins and a basal crest with many fingerlike lobes. Early spring. Ecuador.

Harryanum Rchb.f. Pseudobulbs ovoid, 2-lvd.; lvs. leathery, to 10 in. long; infl. racemose, erect, few-fld.; fls. fleshy, showy, to 3½ in. across, sepals oblong-elliptic, deep chestnut-brown with golden-yellow transverse bars and margin, petals ovate, dark chestnut-brown with greenish-yellow apex and margin, basally marked with close-set mauve-purple longitudinal lines, lip ovate-cordate, acuminate, white, yellow at base around the crest, central portion heavily checkered with mauve-purple. Late summer. Colombia to Peru.

Hunnewellianum Rolfe. Pseudobulbs ovoid, 2-lvd.; lvs. to 8 in. long; infl. racemose, slender, loosely few-fld.; fls. fleshy, to 2 in. across, orbicular, sepals and petals similar, broadly ovate, lemon-yellow with many dark brown spots, occasionally almost completely dark brown, lip ovate-elliptic, cream-white with light cinnamon spots and crenulate, undulate margins. Late autumn. Colombia.

hystrix: *O. luteopurpureum.*

Insleayi Lindl. Vegetatively similar to *O. grande;* fls. showy, to 3 in. across, sepals and petals similar, ovate, undulate, pale greenish-yellow, barred with reddish-brown, lip orbicular-reniform, with a cuneate base, yellow with red spots around margin, column with subulate horns. Late summer. Mex. Cv. **'Leopardinum'** [var. *leopardinum* Regel]. Sepals and petals broader than in typical form, chestnut-brown, barred and margined with yellow, lip yellow with red blotches around margin. Cv. **'Splendens'** [var. *splendens* Rchb.f.]. Fls. larger, sepals and petals unicolored, chestnut-brown, lip yellow with many purplish spots and orange callus.

Krameri Rchb.f. Pseudobulbs globose, 1-lvd.; lvs. oblong-lanceolate, to 9 in. long; infl. arching to ascending, slender, few-fld.; fls. delicate, showy, to 1½ in. across, sepals and petals similar, elliptic-oblong, white with a pale violet suffusion toward base, lip kidney-shaped, with a cuneate base, pale rose with white and reddish-brown bands in front of basal yellow callus. Mex. to Costa Rica.

laeve Lindl. [*Miltonia laevis* (Lindl.) Rolfe]. Robust, pseudobulbs flattened, 2-lvd.; lvs. oblong-lanceolate, to 12 in. long; infl. paniculate, to 3 ft. long, many-fld.; fls. fleshy, starlike, to 2¼ in. across, sepals and petals similar, oblong-ovate, cinnamon-brown barred with yellow-green, lip bent, somewhat fiddle-shaped, rosy-lilac and white with 3–5 thickened ridges at base, column with earlike wings. Mex., Guatemala. Cv. **'Auratum'** [var. *auratum* Rchb.f.]. Differs from typical form in having the lip not bent, and the fls. paniculate rather than racemose.

Lindleyanum Rchb.f. & Warsz. Pseudobulbs ovoid, 2-lvd.; lvs. oblong-linear, to 10 in. long; infl. racemose, rarely branched, several- to many-fld.; fls. rather firm in texture, to 3 in. across, sepals and petals similar, lanceolate, yellow with heavy brown markings and spots, lip narrow-clawed, hastate, acuminate, claw white, front lobe yellow with large brown spot in front and with a hornlike callus, column with 2 narrow wings. Late summer. Colombia.

Londesboroughianum Rchb.f. Rhizomes large, pseudobulbs widely spaced, ovoid, 2-lvd.; lvs. strap-shaped, to 15 in. long, deciduous; infl. racemose, to 3 ft. long, densely many-fld.; fls. showy, to 2 in. across, sepals and petals ovate-oblong, undulate, yellow with many, thin, transverse, brown or red-brown lines in the form of concentric rings, lip 3-lobed, bright yellow, lateral lobes strap-shaped, midlobe kidney-shaped, with a few brown markings at base and on basal callus. Mex. Cv. **'Pardinum'** [var. *pardinum* Burb.]. Differs from typical form in coloration of fls., sepals and petals pale yellow, completely covered with brownish-crimson spots, lateral lobes of lip white with crimson spots, midlobe deep yellow, densely dotted with crimson.

luteopurpureum Lindl. [*O. hystrix* Batem.]. Robust, to 3 ft., pseudobulbs ovoid, 2-lvd.; lvs. linear-oblong, to 2 ft. long; infl. racemose, suberect, arching, loosely many-fld.; fls. large, showy, to 4 in. across, sepals and petals similar, ovate-lanceolate, undulate, petals with scal-lopped-toothed margin, chestnut-brown with yellow tips and markings, lip somewhat fiddle-shaped, with dentate or fimbriate margin, yellow with a large chestnut-brown spot in front of fringed callus. Early spring. Colombia. Cv. **'Crispatum'** [var. *crispatum* Rchb.f.]. Differs from typical form in having nearly the whole front half of the lip convoluted into deep folds. Cv. **'Radiatum'** [var. *radiatum* (Rchb.f.) Rchb.f.]. Differs from typical form in having very dark sepia-brown sepals and petals and a finely toothed, fan-shaped lip. Cv. **'Sceptrum'** [var. *sceptrum* (Rchb.f.) Rchb.f.; *O. sceptrum* Rchb.f.]. Fls. smaller than in typical form, sepals chestnut-brown with a few yellow bars, petals yellow with 1 large and several small brown spots, lip yellow with several brown spots.

maculatum Llave & Lex. [*O. madrense* Rchb.f.]. Pseudobulbs ovoid, 1-lvd.; lvs. ovate, fleshy; infl. arching-pendent, many-fld.; fls. to 2½ in. across, sepals lanceolate, keeled, chocolate-brown inside, yellowish-green outside, petals ovate, slightly undulate, yellow with red-brown spots on basal half, lip clawed, cordate, yellow with red-brown spots on disc, claw provided with a folded callus, column hairy. Early spring. Mex., Guatemala. Cv. **'Thompsonianum'**. Differs from typical form in having more richly colored fls. to 3 in. across.

madrense: *O. maculatum.*

mirandum Rchb.f. Very similar to *O. Lindleyanum;* infl. racemose, several-fld.; fls. starlike, fleshy, to 2¼ in. across, sepals and petals similar, narrowly oblong-elliptic, reddish-brown with bright yellow tips and margins, lip shorter than in *O. Lindleyanum,* broadly triangular-hastate, chestnut-brown with yellow apex and margin in front of 2 prominent hornlike calluses. Colombia.

naevium Lindl. & Paxt. Pseudobulbs 2-lvd.; lvs. oblong-lanceolate, to 15 in. long; infl. racemose, arching, many-fld.; fls. showy, to 3 in. across, sepals and petals similar, linear-lanceolate, long-acuminate, wavy, white, spotted with deep reddish-purple, lip shorter than sepals, linear-lanceolate, white with a yellow base around callus, disc covered with reddish-purple spots. Spring. Venezuela, Colombia.

nebulosum: *O. apterum.*

nevadense Rchb.f. Pseudobulbs flattened, 2-lvd.; lvs. sword-shaped, to 1 ft. long; infl. racemose, arching, to 15-fld.; fls. showy, to 3½ in. across, sepals and petals similar, ovate-lanceolate, cinnamon-brown with yellow margin and occasionally with a few longitudinal yellow bars at base, lip 3-lobed, lateral lobes parallel with column, white with chestnut-brown stripes or spots, midlobe hastate, white or pale yellow, with toothed margin. Colombia.

nobile Rchb.f. [*O. Pescatorei* Lindl.]. Pseudobulbs flattened, 2-lvd.; lvs. strap-shaped, to 1 ft. long; infl. racemose, rarely branched, arching, to 2 ft. long, densely many-fld.; fls. orbicular, to 3 in. across, sepals and petals similar, ovate to ovate-elliptic, with undulate margins, white, sepals occasionally with rose hue in center, lip fiddle-shaped, white with yellow calluses at base, undulate-wavy. Spring. Colombia. Cv. **'Veitchianum'** [var. *Veitchianum* Rchb.f.]. Infl. paniculate, many-fld.; fls. larger than in typical form, sepals and petals white with large, irregular, transverse, magenta-purple bars, lip white with yellow calluses.

odoratum Lindl. Pseudobulbs ovoid, 2-lvd.; lvs. lanceolate, to 1 ft. long; infl. paniculate, much surpassing lvs., many-fld.; fls. starlike, to 2 in. across, sepals and petals similar, ovate-lanceolate, acuminate, straw-yellow with several reddish-brown spots, lip lanceolate, of same color as sepals, with a forked callus at base, column with lanceolate-sickle-shaped, long-acuminate wings. Venezuela, Colombia. Cv. **'Latemaculatum'** [var. *latemaculatum* André]. Fls. larger, with more intense purple-brown spots.

Oerstedii Rchb.f. To 6 in., pseudobulbs ovoid, 1-lvd.; lvs. fleshy, to 4 in. long; infl. slender, longer than lvs., 1–3-fld.; fls. delicate, to 1½ in. across, sepals ovate, spreading, white, petals oblong-elliptic, white, undulate, lip nearly orbicular, with cuneate base, deeply cleft in front, with a rhomboid, 2-lobed callus at base, column short, puberulent. Costa Rica.

pendulum (Llave & Lex.) Batem. [*O. citrosmum* Lindl.]. Pseudobulbs ovoid to globose, 2-lvd.; lvs. oblong-strap-shaped, fleshy, to 1 ft. long; infl. racemose, pendent, densely many-fld.; fls. showy, to 3 in. across, sepals and petals similar, ovate, obtuse, white or occasionally with rose suffusion in center, lip sagittate-reinform, with a long claw, 2-lobed, lobes orbicular, pale to intense rose, claw with a fleshy, 2-keeled yellow callus marked with reddish dots. Mex., Guatemala. Cvs. include: **'Album'**, fls. pure white except for yellow claw of lip; **'Punctatum'**, sepals and petals pale rose, dotted with purple; **'Rosellum'** [var. *rosellum* Lem.], fls. rose except for yellow claw of lip; **'Roseum'**, fls. similar to those of typical form except for deeper rose lip.

Pescatorei: *O. nobile.*

pulchellum Batem. ex Lindl. LILY-OF-THE-VALLEY ORCHID. Pseudobulbs ovoid, 2-lvd; lvs. linear, to 15 in. long; infl. racemose, as long as the lvs., many-fld., scape 2-edged; fls. showy, to 1 in. across, sepals and petals separate, similar, ovate to elliptic-ovate, white, lip fiddle-shaped, basal portion concave, enclosing the fleshy, W-shaped, yellow, red-dotted callus, apical portion nearly orbicular, column short, fleshy. Late winter–spring. Guatemala. Cv. **'Majus'**. Fls. larger.

ramosissimum Lindl. Pseudobulbs 2-lvd.; lvs. linear-lanceolate, to 4 ft. long; infl. paniculate, to 5 ft. long, many-branched, many-fld.; fls. showy, to 2 in. across, sepals and petals similar, ovate-lanceolate, undulate, white or pale pink or rose with darker rose spots or dots, lip ovate-hastate or triangular, elongate, reflexed, white or pale rose with a pale yellow basal crest with many fingerlike lobes. Early spring. Venezuela, Colombia.

Reichenheimii Linden & Rchb.f. [*Miltonia Reichenheimii* (Linden & Rchb.f.) Rolfe]. Pseudobulbs flattened, 2-lvd.; lvs. oblong-lanceolate, to 1 ft. long; infl. paniculate, to 2 ft. long, many-fld.; fls. showy, to 2 in. across, sepals and petals similar, ovate to ovate-elliptic, bright yellow with heavy, dark chocolate-brown bars, lip ovate, somewhat fiddle-shaped, pale lemon-yellow with a large semicrescent pink or rose spot, base of lip with a 5-parted, keeled callus, column wings aborted. Mex.

Rossii Lindl. Pseudobulbs ovoid, 1-lvd.; lvs. oblong-ovate, fleshy, to 4 in. long; infl. erect, to 8 in. long, 1- to few-fld.; fls. showy, to 2 in. across, sepals ovate-lanceolate, yellowish-green with red-brown spots, petals ovate, recurved, white with red-brown spots at base, lip ovate-cordate, white, ruffled, with a yellow callus on claw, anther purple. Late winter–spring. Mex., Guatemala. Cv. **'Rubescens'** [var. *rubescens* Rchb.f.]. Fls. larger, petals clear rose with dark purple spots at base.

Sanderanum: *O. constrictum* cv.

sceptrum: *O. luteopurpureum* cv.

Schlieperanum Rchb.f. Pseudobulbs ovoid, 2-lvd., similar to those of *O. grande;* infl. erect, surpassing lvs., several-fld.; fls. showy, to 4 in. across, sepals ovate-lanceolate, canary-yellow with red-brown bars and spots, petals ovate-elliptic, similar in color and markings, lip fiddle-shaped, pale yellow with a few red-brown bars in front of an orange-yellow callus, on both sides of which is a crimson blotch, column wings crimson. Costa Rica, Panama. Cv. **'Citrinum'** [var. *citrinum* O'Brien]. Differs from typical form in having pale yellow fls. with darker yellow bars and blotches.

tripudians Rchb.f. & Warsz. Vegetatively similar to *O. nobile;* infl. racemose, arching, several-fld.; fls. showy, fleshy, to 2½ in. across, sepals and petals similar, ovate to elliptic-ovate, almost dark sepia with yellow tips and a few markings on petals, lip large, fiddle-shaped, white with toothed margin, disc with several purple blotches in front and around the many-lobed callus. Early winter. Colombia, Peru. Cv. 'Harryanum' [var. *Harryanum* Rchb.f.]. Differs from typical form in having almost uniformly black-sepia sepals and petals tipped with rich mauve.

triumphans Rchb.f. Pseudobulbs ovoid, 2-lvd.; lvs. fleshy, sword-shaped, to 15 in. long; infl. racemose, occasionally branched, erect or arching, to 3 ft. long, many-fld.; fls. large, to 4 in. across, sepals oblong-strap-shaped, spreading, yellow, almost covered with large red-brown blotches and bars, petals ovate-elliptic, yellow with fewer and smaller red-brown spots, lip white, elliptic, with toothed margin, disc with large red-brown blotch in front of 2-lobed callus. Spring. Colombia.

Uroskinneri Lindl. Pseudobulbs 2-lvd.; lvs. ovate-lanceolate, to 10 in. long; infl. racemose, occasionally branched, erect, to 3 ft., many-fld.; fls. fleshy, to 2 in. across, sepals and petals similar, broadly ovate to ovate-elliptic, green with many chestnut-brown small spots, lip round-cordate, white with many rose spots, column wings rose. Summer. Guatemala.

Wallisii Linden & Rchb.f. Small, pseudobulbs ovoid, 2-lvd.; lvs. linear, grasslike, to 10 in. long; infl. racemose, arching, slender, to 15 in. long, few-fld.; fls. 2 in. across, sepals and petals similar, lanceolate, cinnamon-brown with yellow margins, petals with fewer markings, lip fiddle-shaped, apiculate, with a long claw, white with a few purple lines on claw and a large blotch in front of a comblike crest. Colombia.

Williamsianum Rchb.f. Vegetatively similar to *O. grande;* infl. few-fld.; fls. large, to 4½ in. across, sepals ovate-lanceolate, yellowish-green with large and coarse transverse chestnut-brown bars, petals elliptic-oblong, with a short claw, bright yellow, with basal half covered by a large chestnut-brown blotch, lip 3-lobed, lateral lobes small, earlike, midlobe nearly orbicular, pale yellow with concentric pale rust-colored lines at base. Costa Rica.

ODONTONEMA Nees [*Thyrsacanthus* Nees]. *Acanthaceae.* Perhaps more than 40 spp. of herbs and shrubs, in trop. regions of Amer.; lvs. opp., entire; fls. red, yellow, or white, in terminal spikelike racemes, corolla tubular, 5-lobed or 2-lipped, stamens 2, anther sacs 2, parallel, staminodes 2; fr. a clavate caps.

Three species are grown in southern U.S. and sometimes under glass. Propagated by cuttings.

callistachyum (Schlechtend. & Cham.) O. Kuntze. Shrub, to 15 ft.; lvs. oblong to elliptic-ovate, to 1 ft. long; fls. in racemelike panicles, corolla red or pink, to 1¼ in. long. Mex. and Cent. Amer.

Schomburgkianum (Nees) O. Kuntze [*Thyrscanthus rutilans* Planch.]. Shrub, to 6 ft.; lvs. oblong-lanceolate; fls. in drooping racemes to 3 ft. long, corolla red, 1½ in. long. British Guiana.

strictum (Nees) O. Kuntze. Shrub, to 6 ft.; lvs. oblong, to 6 in. long, often wavy-margined; fls. in erect, close, long infl., corolla crimson, to 1 in. long, with short lobes. Cent. Amer. Sometimes grown erroneously under the name *Justicia coccinea.*

×**ODONTONIA** Hort.: *Miltonia* × *Odontoglossum. Orchidaceae.* Bigeneric hybrids intermediate in character between the parents.

For culture see *Orchids.*

ODONTOPHORUS N. E. Br. *Aizoaceae.* About 6 spp. of dwarf, clump-forming, succulent shrubs with fleshy roots, native to S. Afr., sts. ascending or prostrate; lvs. 1–2 pairs, 4-ranked, very thick, triangular in section, tuberculate, velvety to the touch, margins and keel toothed; fls. solitary, sessile or pedicelled, calyx 5-lobed, petals many, yellow or white, stamens many, ovary inferior, 9–10-celled, stigmas 9–10; fr. a caps., expanding keels winged and toothed, apex ending in fine tip.

Growth occurs from winter to early summer. In summer, plants need full sun and moderate moisture; in winter, at a relatively cool temperature of about 60° F., with the soil kept almost dry. Cultivate in very porous soil containing much sand and rubble. See also *Succulents.*

albus L. Bolus. Low, brs. congested; lvs. 2 each year, nearly erect, dirty olive-green, dotted, softly pilose, to 1⅝ in. long, nearly ⅝ in. wide at middle and a little wider at tip, apex rounded in top view, middle narrowed, obscurely keeled beneath and nearly truncate in side view, compressed apically, margins entire or 1–2-toothed, keel 1-toothed; fls. on pedicels to 1⅜ in. long, petals white, to ⁹⁄₁₆ in. long. Cape Prov.

Marlothii N. E. Br. Shorter shoots with 2–3 pairs of 4-ranked lvs., longer shoots from lf. axils, erect becoming prostrate; lvs. gray to dark green, covered with roundish, prominent, finely whitish-hairy tuber-

cles, to 1⅜ in. long and ⅜ in. across, slightly vesicularly swollen at base, upper side only slightly convex, slightly expanded, long-triangular in outline toward apex, often obliquely acuminate, lower side roundish, keeled toward apex, laterally compressed, margins with 6–7 teeth above, teeth bearing a brown awnlike, downward-curved tip; fls. 1¼ in. across, on pedicels ½ in. long, petals yellow. Cape Prov.

nanus L. Bolus. Like *O. primulinus,* but smaller, shoots very short; lvs. crowded, ⅝ in. long, ⅜ in. wide, ⅜ in. thick, upper side nearly ovate in outline, gibbous-expanded, margins dentate, teeth stiff; fls. on pedicels ¼ in. long, petals white. Cape Prov.

primulinus L. Bolus. Low, compact, to 2¾ in. high in fl., brs. with persistent lf. sheaths; lvs. erect, becoming spreading, dirty green, velvety from finely hairy tubercles, to 1½ in. long, ¾ in. wide, ⅝ in. thick, nearly truncate in side view, upper side flat, lower side more or less rounded, obtusely keeled, edges with 4–5 short thick teeth toward the apex; fls. 1¾ in. across, on pedicels 1¼ in. long, petals straw-yellow. Cape Prov.

ODONTOSPERMUM: *ASTERISCUS.*

OEMLERIA Rchb. [*Osmaronia* Greene]. *Rosaceae.* One sp., a deciduous, dioecious shrub, native from B.C. to Calif.; lvs. entire, simple, oblong to oblanceolate; infl. racemose; fls. greenish-white, 5-merous, stamens 15, pistils 5; frs. thin-fleshed drupes.

Planted as an ornamental; hardy in Zone 4. Propagated by seeds and suckers.

cerasiformis (Torr. & A. Gray ex Hook. & Arn.) Landon [*Osmaronia cerasiformis* (Torr. & A. Gray ex Hook. & Arn.) Greene]. INDIAN PLUM, OSOBERRY. To 15 ft., slender-stemmed; lvs. 2–4 in. long, short-petioled; fls. white, fragrant, ⁵⁄₁₆ in. across; fr. blue-black, to ½ in. long.

OENANTHE L. *Umbelliferae.* About 30 spp. of glabrous, per. herbs, native to the Old World and N. Amer., with fascicled tuberous and fibrous roots, often rooting at the lower nodes; lvs. pinnate to pinnately decompound with serrate to pinnatifid segms., or reduced to hollow petioles; fls. white, in compound umbels, involucre small or absent, involucels of many small bractlets, calyx persistent; fr. oblong, nearly cylindrical, with corky ribs.

sarmentosa K. Presl. Sts. decumbent and ascending, to 5 ft.; lvs. pinnate to 2-pinnate, segms. ovate, coarsely toothed; involucral bracts few, linear, bractlets of involucels many, acute; fr. often purplish. Coastal marshes, B.C. to cent. Calif.

OENOTHERA L. [*Anogra* Spach; *Lavauxia* Spach; *Onagra* Spach]. EVENING PRIMROSE, SUNDROPS. *Onagraceae.* About 80 spp. of ann. to per. herbs of wide distribution in the W. Hemisphere, including the evening primroses, which are generally evening-flowering, and the sundrops or suncups, which are day-flowering; plants stemless to decumbent or erect and tall; lvs. mostly alt., simple, entire to pinnatifid; fls. solitary and axillary to racemose or paniculate, 4-merous, usually with a well-developed calyx tube, stamens usually 8, anthers versatile, ovary inferior, 4-celled, cylindrical or clavate, elongate to short, sometimes winged, stigma 4-lobed to discoid or nearly globose; fr. a caps.

Oenotheras are mostly sun-loving terrestrial plants of simple culture, commonly grown from seeds or division of clumps. Some are rather weedy, others low and attractive. The flowers are often large and showy.

acaulis Cav. [*O. taraxacifolia* Sweet]. Evening-flowering, stemless or short-stemmed per.; lvs. oblanceolate, 1–8 in. long, runcinate-pinnatifid, hairy; calyx tube 1–4 in. long, petals ½–1½ in. long, white; caps. obovoid, ½ in. long, 4-winged, woody. Chile. Cv. 'Aurea' is listed.

albicaulis Pursh [*Anogra albicaulis* (Pursh) Britt.]. Evening-flowering ann., more or less pubescent; rosette lvs. spatulate to obovate, 1–2 in. long, st. lvs. lanceolate, pinnatifid; fls. solitary in axils, buds nodding, calyx tube to 1 in. long, petals ½–1½ in. long, white, aging pink; caps. cylindrical, 1–1½ in. long. Rocky Mts. and adjacent plains.

argillicola Mackenz. Evening-flowering bien. to per., more or less fleshy, glabrous, sts. 2–4 ft. long; rosette lvs. oblanceolate-linear, 6–8 in. long, st. lvs. lanceolate-linear; infl. terminal; calyx tube 1½–2 in. long, petals 1–1½ in. long, yellow, aging orange-red; caps. attenuate, spreading, woody at base. Appalachian Mts.

Berlandieri (Spach) Walp. [*O. speciosa* var. *Childsii* (L. H. Bailey) Munz; *O. tetraptera* var. *Childsii* L. H. Bailey]. MEXICAN E.P. Near *O. speciosa,* but sts. very slender, to 6 in. long; petals to 1 in. long, rose. Tex., Mex.

biennis L. [*O. muricata* L.]. EVENING PRIMROSE, GERMAN RAMPION. Evening-flowering, variable, weedy sp., 1–6 ft.; lvs. of basal rosette 4–12 in. long, st. lvs. flat, usually lanceolate, 3–6 in. long, shallowly toothed; infl. elongate, spicate, or branched, bracted; calyx tube 1–2 in. long, petals ½–1 in. long, yellow, aging old gold, stigma lobes linear; caps. gradually attenuate upward, ½–1½ in. long. E. N. Amer. Roots may be eaten as a vegetable, and the shoots in salads.

bistorta Nutt. SUNCUP. Day-flowering ann., 1–2 ft., decumbent at base, hairy; lower lvs. petioled, spatulate to lanceolate, upper lvs. sessile, ovate to lanceolate; petals about ½ in. long, yellow, usually with a maroon-brown basal spot, drying green; caps. contorted, ½ in. long, scarcely beaked. Coastal, s. Calif. Var. **Veitchiana** Hook. More slender; caps. 1–1½ in. long, beaked. Away from the coast, s. Calif.

brachycarpa A. Gray. Evening-flowering, nearly stemless per., almost glabrous to hoary; lvs. tufted, narrow, 1–6 in. long, entire to wavy-toothed; calyx tube 2–6 in. long, petals broad, 1–2 in. long, yellow, drying reddish; caps. ovoid to nearly cylindrical, 1 in. long, winged above or throughout. Rocky Mts. to n. Mex.

caespitosa Nutt. Evening-flowering, stemless per.; lvs. 1–4 in. long, nearly entire to sinuate-toothed, glabrous; fls. fragrant, calyx tube 2–3 in. long, petals 1–2 in. long, white; caps. lanceolate-ovoid, ½–¾ in. long, leathery, tubercled on the angles. N. Rocky Mts. and adjacent plains. Subsp. **marginata** (Nutt. ex Hook. & Arn.) Munz [*O. marginata* Nutt. ex Hook. & Arn.]. Villous-hirsute throughout; lvs. pinnatifid; caps. 1–1½ in. long, pedicelled, tubercled. Wash. and Calif., e. to w. Colo. and New Mex. Subsp. **montana** (Nutt.) Munz. Stemless, hairy on veins and margins of lvs.; caps. without tubercles. Rocky Mts.

californica S. Wats. Resembling *O. deltoides* in having large white fls. and strigose or hairy foliage, but per., with running rhizomes. Calif.

cheiranthifolia Hornem. ex K. Spreng. BEACH E.P. Day-flowering, prostrate or decumbent per., with wiry sts.; lvs. ½–3 in. long, mostly grayish-pubescent; fls. axillary, petals ¼–⁵⁄₁₆ in. long, yellow, drying red or green; caps. coiled, 4-angled. Beaches, Ore., Calif. Subsp. **suffruticosa** (S. Wats.) Munz & Raven [*O. cheiranthifolia* var. *suffruticosa* S. Wats.]. Plants woodier; fls. larger, petals ½–1 in. long. Coast, s. Calif.

Childsii: a listed name of no botanical standing, probably for *O. Berlandieri.*

deltoides Torr. & Frém. DESERT E.P. Evening-flowering, coarse spring or winter ann., 2–10 in., sts. usually several, with peeling epidermis; lower lvs. crowded, rhombic-lanceolate to -oblanceolate, 1–3 in. long, entire to pinnatifid; fls. solitary, in axils, petals broad, ½–1½ in. long, white, turning pink; caps. elongate, 1–3 in. long, spreading, woody. Interior, Calif., sw. deserts of U.S. Confused with the per. *O. pallida* subsp. *trichocalyx.*

densiflora: *Boisduvalia densiflora.*

Drummondii Hook. Evening-flowering, prostrate, strigose per.; basal lvs. oblanceolate to obovate, ½–3 in. long, st. lvs. oblong, ½–1½ in. long; calyx tube 1–1½ in. long, sepals 1 in. long, petals 1 in. long, yellow; caps. nearly cylindrical. Tex. to ne. Mex.

erythrosepala Borb. [*O. Lamarckiana* de Vries, not Ser.]. Much like *O. Hookeri,* but lvs. broader, ⅓ as wide as long. Arose in cult. and now established in cooler n. areas.

flava (A. Nels.) Garrett. Per., stemless, cespitose; lvs. oblong-linear to oblanceolate, to 8 in. long, runcinate-pinnatifid; calyx tube to nearly 5 in. long, petals pale yellow, to ¾ in. long; caps. 4-winged. Wash., s. to Calif., Ariz., Mex.

Fraseri: *O. tetragona* var.

Fremontii S. Wats. Evening-flowering, nearly stemless per., strigose; lvs. lanceolate-linear, 1–2 in. long; fls. few, calyx tube 1–2 in. long, sepals and petals almost 1 in. long, petals yellow; caps. ½–1 in. long, wings ⅛ in. wide. Kans., Nebr.

fruticosa L. SUNDROPS. Day-flowering per., sts. 1–2 ft., slender, strigose; lower lvs. oblanceolate, 1–3 in. long, st. lvs. lanceolate; petals ½–1 in. long, yellow; caps. enlarged upward, the body ¼–½ in. long, basal part sterile, slender. E. U.S. Cv. **'Major'** is listed. Var. **Youngii:** *O. tetragona.* Many references to *O. fruticosa* in the hort. literature apply to *O. tetragona,* with which *O. fruticosa* has been confused.

Fyrverkeri: a listed name of no botanical standing; material grown under this name is usually *O. tetragona.*

glauca: *O. tetragona* var. *Fraseri.*

heterantha Nutt. [*O. subacaulis* (Pursh) Jeps.]. SUNCUP. Day-flowering, stemless per., largely glabrous; lvs. many, lanceolate, 1–6 in. long, entire to pinnatifid; petals ⁵⁄₁₆ in. long, yellow, ovary with the terminal sterile part 1–4 in. long. W. U.S.

Hookeri Torr. & A. Gray. Evening-flowering, erect, bien. to per., 2–8 ft., with a basal rosette, variable in pubescence; lvs. largely lanceolate, 2–5 in. long; fls. many, in terminal spikes, calyx tube 1–2 in. long, petals 1–1¾ in. long, yellow, aging orange or red; caps. gradually narrowed upward, 1–1¾ in. long. W. U.S.

Jamesii Torr. & A. Gray. Much like *O. Hookeri,* but st. lvs. 1–1½ in. wide, calyx tube 3–4 in. long. Okla. to n. Mex.

Kunthiana (Spach) Munz. Evening-flowering per., sts. slender, to 2 ft.; basal lvs. oblanceolate, 1–4 in. long, sinuate-pinnatifid, st. lvs. reduced; fls. few, petals ⁵⁄₁₆–⅝ in. long, whitish to pink; caps. obovoid, about ½ in. long, 4-winged above. Tex. to Guatemala.

laciniata J. Hill [*O. mexicana* Spach]. Evening-flowering ann. to per., green, sts. ½–2 ft., with some long hairs; lvs. mostly oblanceolate, 1–3 in. long, frequently toothed or pinnatifid; fls. in upper axils, petals ¼–¾ in. long, yellow, aging red; caps. cylindrical, ½–1½ in. long, thin-walled. Me. and S. Dak. to Tex.

Lamarckiana: see *O. erythrosepala.*

lavandulifolia Torr. & A. Gray. Evening-flowering, cespitose per., to 6 or 8 in., from a woody root crown, grayish-strigose; lvs. linear to obovate; calyx tube 1–2 in. long, petals rhombic, ½–1 in. long, yellow, aging reddish, stigma discoid. Sw. U.S.

longiflora L. Evening-flowering, bien. or per., erect or ascending, 1–3 ft.; basal lvs. oblanceolate, 4–6 in. long, soft-pubescent, st. lvs. sessile, oblong, smaller; fls. in upper axils, 2–3 in. across, petals yellow, aging red; caps. cylindrical, thin-walled. S. Amer.

macrocarpa: *O. missourensis.*

marginata: *O. caespitosa* subsp.

mexicana: *O. laciniata.*

missourensis Sims [*O. macrocarpa* Pursh]. Evening-flowering per., sts. decumbent to erect, to 15 in. long, strigose; lvs. petioled, lanceolate, blades 1–4 in. long, entire; fls. few, very showy, petals 1–2 in. long, yellow, often reddish in age; caps. 2–3 in. long, broadly 4-winged, leathery or almost woody. Mo. and Kans. to Tex. Var. **oklahomensis** (Norton) Munz [*O. oklahomensis* (Norton) A. S. Hitchc.]. Plants glabrous. Kans., Okla.

muricata: *O. biennis.*

odorata Jacq. Evening-flowering, ascending or erect per., 6–15 in., more or less strigose or pubescent; lvs. sessile, lanceolate, 1–6 in. long, crisped, glaucous; fls. not crowded, calyx tube ½–1 in. long, petals ½–1½ in. long, yellow, aging red; caps. 1 in. long, slightly enlarged upward. S. Amer.

oklahomensis: *O. missourensis* var.

pallida Lindl. [*Anogra pallida* (Lindl.) Britt.]. Evening-flowering per., 8–20 in., with running rhizomes, essentially glabrous; lvs. 1–2 in. long, lanceolate, nearly entire or remotely toothed; fls. fragrant, calyx tube 1–1½ in. long, sepals with free tips in bud, petals ½–1 in. long, white, aging pink; caps. cylindrical, sometimes contorted. W. U.S. Subsp. **trichocalyx** (Nutt. ex Torr. & A. Gray) Munz & W. Klein [*O. trichocalyx* Nutt. ex Torr. & A. Gray]. Lvs. grayish-green, usually sinuate-dentate; sepals with tips not free in bud. W. Wyo., Colo., e. Utah.

parviflora L. Evening-flowering bien. or per., 1–4 ft., strigose and hairy; rosette lvs. long-petioled, narrow, st. lvs. narrowly lanceolate, 2–4 in. long, rather fleshy; fls. in terminal spikes, petals ⁵⁄₁₆–⅝ in. long, yellow, aging orange; caps. cylindric-fusiform, tapering toward apex. E. N. Amer.

perennis L. [*O. pumila* L.; *O. pusilla* Michx.]. SUNDROPS. Day-flowering per., sts. 4–20 in.; lower lvs. oblanceolate to spatulate, 1–2 in. long; infl. nodding in bud; petals ¼–⁵⁄₁₆ in. long, yellow; caps. ellipsoid-clavate to -oblong. E. N. Amer. Var. **rectipilis** S. F. Blake [*O. Pilgrimii* Hort.]. Plant with short spreading hairs. E. N. Amer.

Pilgrimii: a listed name of no botanical standing for *O. perennis* var. *rectipilis.*

pilosella Raf. [*O. pratensis* (Small) B. L. Robinson]. SUNDROPS. Day-flowering erect per., 6–20 in., spreading-hairy; lower lvs. obovate to oblanceolate, st. lvs. lanceolate, 1–4 in. long; petals ½–1 in. long, conspicuously veined, yellow; caps. linear-clavate, sessile. Cent. U.S.

pratensis: *O. pilosella.*

primiveris A. Gray. Evening-flowering, stemless, winter ann., hairy; lvs. oblanceolate, 1–4 in. long, deeply pinnatifid, lobes toothed or lobed; petals ½–1½ in. long, yellow, aging orange; caps. gradually tapered upward, to 1 in. long, leathery to almost woody, hairy. Sw. deserts.

pumila: *O. perennis.*

pusilla: *O. perennis.*

rhombipetala Nutt. ex Torr. & A. Gray. Evening-flowering bien., with rosette of basal lvs., st. 1–2½ ft., appressed-pubescent; lvs. oblanceolate, entire to pinnatifid, blades 1–3 in. long; fls. many, in a long terminal spike, petals rhombic-obovate, yellow; caps. curved-cylindrical, tapering toward apex. Cent. U.S.

riparia: *O. tetragona* var.

rosea Ait. Per., brs. slender, 6–20 in. long; lvs. scattered, oblong-ovate, ½–1 in. long, sinuate-toothed; petals to 5/16 in. long, rose to purplish-red; caps. obovoid, 4-angled, 5/16 in. long. S. U.S. to S. Amer.

rubricalyx: a listed name of no botanical standing, used for a derivative of *O. erythrosepala.*

serrulata Nutt. Evening-flowering per., ½–1 ft., mostly several-stemmed, gray-pubescent in upper parts; lvs. largely lanceolate to oblanceolate, 1–2 in. long, entire to toothed; petals to ½ in. long, yellow, stigma discoid; caps. cylindrical. Great Plains. Subsp. **Drummondii** (Torr. & A. Gray) Munz [*O. spinulosa* Nutt. ex Torr. & A. Gray]. Taller; lvs. sharply toothed; petals ½–1 in. long, stigma and calyx tube often almost black. Tex.

speciosa Nutt. WHITE E.P. Day-flowering ann. to per., with running rhizomes, sts. fairly coarse, 1–2 ft.; lower lvs. oblanceolate to obovate, 1–3 in. long, sinuate-pinnatifid; fls. in upper axils, petals 1–1½ in. long, white, aging pink, sometimes pink when young; caps. enlarged upward, less than 3/16 in. thick above, base sterile, cylindrical. Kans. to Tex. Var. **Childsii:** *O. Berlandieri.*

spinulosa: *O. serrulata* subsp. *Drummondii.*

subacaulis: *O. heterantha.*

taraxacifolia: *O. acaulis.*

tetragona Roth [*O. fruticosa* var. *Youngii* L. H. Bailey; *O. Youngii* Hort.]. Confused with *O. fruticosa,* but caps. usually with some gland-tipped hairs and more oblong or oblong-ellipsoid, less clavate; sts. with spreading pubescence; petals less than ¾ in. long. E. U.S. Var. **tetragona.** The typical var.; sts. with spreading hairs; ovary and caps. with gland-tipped hairs only. Var. **Fraseri** (Pursh) Munz [*O. Fraseri* Pursh; *O. glauca Michx*.]. Plant glabrous; lvs. broad, glaucous underneath; petals 1 in. long or more. S. Appalachian Mts. Var. **riparia** (Nutt.) Munz [*O. riparia* Nutt.]. Petals ⅝–1 in. long; ovary and caps. with some nonglandular hairs among the gland-tipped ones. N.C. and S.C.

tetraptera Cav. Evening-flowering, branched ann., to 16 in., hairy; lvs. lanceolate to oblanceolate or narrowly elliptic, to 3⅝ in. long, 1 in. wide, sinuate to sinuate-pinnatifid; buds erect, calyx tube to 1 3/16 in. long, petals white, fading pink, to 1⅜ in. long. Tex., s. to S. Amer. Var. **Childsii:** *O. Berlandieri.*

trichocalyx: *O. pallida* subsp.

triloba Nutt. [*Lavauxia triloba* (Nutt.) Spach]. Evening-flowering, winter ann. or bien., mostly stemless, scarcely hairy; lvs. tufted, oblanceolate, 1–8 in. long, runcinate-pinnatifid; petals ⅜–¾ in. long, roundish, with apical sinus and sometimes a toothlike middle lobe, yellow; caps. ovoid, about ½ in. long, 4-winged, hard. Kans. and Ky., s. to Tex.

Youngii: a listed name of no botanical standing for *O. tetragona.*

OKRA. Okra is the large, green, erect pod of *Abelmoschus esculentus,* and is also known as gumbo. From these pods is made the well-known gumbo soup of the South, where the plant is more extensively grown than in the North. The pods are also employed in their green state for stews, and are dried and used in winter, when they form an important and nutritious part of the diet in certain sections of the country. 'Clemson Spineless' and 'Emerald' are important cultivars. They grow 3½–5 feet high. The seeds are sensitive to cold and moisture, and should not be sown until the ground has become warm. The seed should be sown in a drill 1 inch deep, the plants thinned to 12 inches in the row; the rows are usually far enough apart to permit cultivation. One ounce of seed supplies 50–100 feet of drill, depending on the thickness of sowing. The culture given corn or cotton is suitable.

OLDENLANDIA L. *Rubiaceae.* About 300 spp. of shrubs or herbs, native to the tropics, most of them in Afr.; lvs. opp., lanceolate or linear, stipules acute, sometimes setose; fls. usually in loose or dense terminal or axillary cymes or panicles, corolla tube cylindric-funnelform, lobes 4, spreading, stamens 4, often borne in upper part of corolla tube, style sometimes exserted; fr. a small caps., seeds few to many.

natalensis (Hochst.) O. Kuntze. Compact shrub, about 1 ft.; lvs. lanceolate or ovate-lanceolate, to 2½ in. long, stipules setose; fls. in a terminal, few-fld. umbel, corolla lavender, tube to ½ in. long. Natal and n. Transvaal.

OLEA L. OLIVE. *Oleaceae.* About 20 spp. of evergreen trees and shrubs, native to the E. Hemisphere; lvs. opp., commonly entire, silvery-scurfy beneath, but sometimes sparsely so; fls. small, white or whitish, in panicles, unisexual or bisexual, corolla tube short, lobes 4, valvate; fr. a drupe, usually 1-seeded.

One species is grown widely for the fruit, source of olive oil and edible olives, and others as ornamentals in Calif. and other mild climates.

The olive is propagated by softwood cuttings, 4 or 5 in. long, only the leaves on the tip being retained and those usually cut back somewhat. Cuttings are started in sand under artificial heat and then moved to the nursery. Suckers about the base of a tree, taken with a heel from the trunk are also employed. Seeds are also used in propagation, but the seedlings must be grafted to the desired variety. Cutting off the end of the stone or pit will hasten germination. When one year in the nursery, the seedlings may be whip-grafted or side-grafted. Olives attain great age, but require a deep fertile and well-drained soil. See also *Olive.*

africana Mill. [*O. chrysophylla* Lam.]. Tree, to 25 ft. or more; lvs. linear-lanceolate to narrowly oblong-elliptic, to 3½ in. long, dark green above, paler and usually densely covered with silvery, golden, or pale green scales beneath; fr. thinly fleshy, nearly globose, to ⅜ in. across, black when ripe. S. Afr. and sw. China. Closely related to *O. europaea,* but having frs. smaller and thinly fleshy. Some authorities suggest that the cult. olive was derived from this sp.

Aquifolium: *Osmanthus heterophyllus.*

chrysophylla: *O. africana.*

communis: see *O. europaea* var. *europaea.*

europaea L. COMMON O. To 25 ft. or more; lvs. elliptic to lanceolate, to 3 in. long, silvery-scaly beneath; fls. fragrant; fr. oblong, to 1½ in. long, glossy black when ripe. Medit. region, where widely cult. as an economic plant. Zone 9. Grown for its oil-rich fr. and as an ornamental in Calif. and to a lesser extent in Ariz., and as an ornamental elsewhere. Wood used for turning. Var. **europaea** [var. *communis* Ait.]. The typical var., the cult. olive, fr. large, fleshy, edible. Cvs. listed are: **'Ascolano'**, **'Barouni'**, **'Manzanillo'**, **'Mission'**, and **'Sevillano'**. Var. **Oleaster:** var. *sylvestris.* Var. **sylvestris** Brot. [var. *Oleaster* DC.]. The wild form, brs. thorny, fr. small, thinly fleshy.

fragrans: *Osmanthus fragrans.*

ilicifolia: *Osmanthus heterophyllus.*

lanceolata: *Nestegis lanceolata.*

manzanillo: a listed name of no botanical standing, used for *O. europaea* cv.

montana: *Nestegis montana.*

OLEACEAE Hoffmanns. & Link. OLIVE FAMILY. Dicot.; about 29 genera and 600 spp. of trees or shrubs, in temp. or trop. regions of both hemispheres; lvs. prevailingly opp., simple or pinnate; fls. regular, bisexual or unisexual, the plants then dioecious, calyx commonly 4-lobed, corolla 4-lobed, petals sometimes 0 in *Fraxinus,* stamens 2, ovary superior, 2-celled; fr. a berry, drupe, caps., or samara. Grown mostly as ornamentals and for shade, and the olive for its edible fr. Genera treated here are: *Abeliophyllum, Chionanthus, Fontanesia, Forestiera, Forsythia, Fraxinus, Jasminum, Ligustrum, Menodora, Nestegis, Noronhia, Olea, Osmanthus,* × *Osmarea, Phillyrea, Schrebera,* and *Syringa.*

OLEARIA Moench. TREE ASTER, DAISYBUSH. *Compositae* (Aster Tribe). About 130 spp. of evergreen shrubs or trees, native chiefly to New Zeal., Australia, and Tasmania, a few in New Guinea and Lord Howe Is.; lvs. alt. or opp., sometimes clustered, usually leathery; fl. heads radiate or discoid, solitary, corymbose or paniculate, involucre cylindrical or campanulate, involucral bracts in several rows, with dry or scarious margins, receptacle flat or convex, pitted; disc fls. bisexual, fertile, white, yellow, purple, or dark red to dark brown, ray fls. female, white, blue, or purple, sometimes absent; achenes cylindrical or slightly compressed, ribbed or striate, usually hairy, pappus of 1 or 2 rows of bristles.

Several species are grown outdoors in Calif. as ornamentals. Propagated by cuttings of half-ripened shoots, as well as by seeds.

albida (Hook.f.) Hook.f. Shrub or small tree, to 20 ft.; lvs. alt., oblong to ovate-oblong, to 4 in. long, glabrous above when mature, with white appressed hairs beneath, margins entire, often undulate, petioles to ¾ in. long; heads in panicles; disc and ray fls. white. New Zeal.

Allomii T. Kirk. Shrub, to 3 ft.; lvs. alt., obliquely elliptic-ovate to elliptic-oblong, to 2 in. long, glabrous above when mature, silvery-tomentose beneath; heads to ⅝ in. across, in branched corymbs. New Zeal.

arborescens (G. Forst.) Cockayne & Laing. Much-branched shrub or small tree, to 12 ft.; lvs. alt., broadly ovate to elliptic-ovate, to 3½

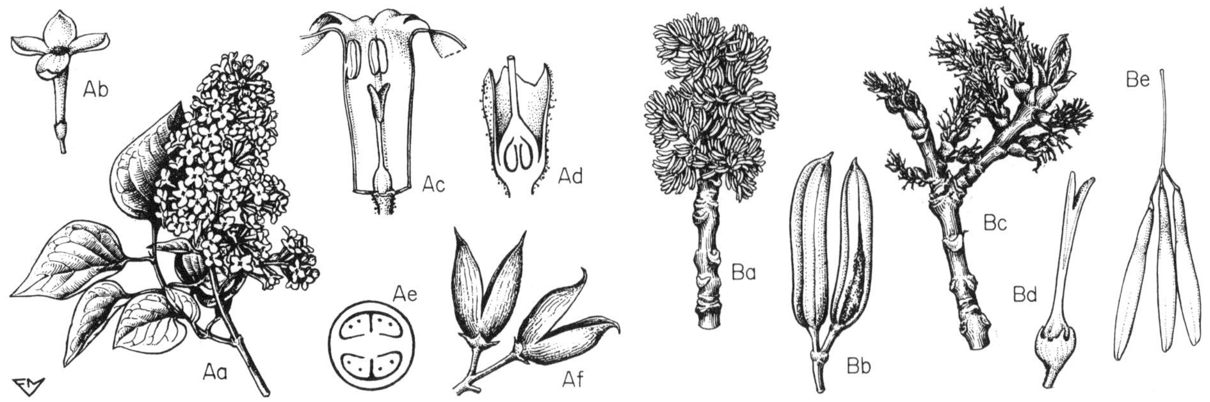

OLEACEAE. **A,** *Syringa vulgaris:* **Aa,** flowering branch, × ¼; **Ab,** flower, × 1; **Ac,** flower, perianth expanded, × 2; **Ad,** calyx and ovary, vertical section, × 5; **Ae,** ovary, cross section, × 10; **Af,** capsules, × 1. **B,** *Fraxinus americana:* **Ba,** twig with male inflorescence, × ½; **Bb,** male flower, × 4; **Bc,** twig with female inflorescence, × ½; **Bd,** female flower, × 4; **Be,** samaras, × ½. (From Bailey, *Manual of Cultivated Plants,* ed. 2.)

in. long, glabrous above when mature, with satiny-white hairs beneath, sinuate-dentate or rarely entire; heads in corymbs; ray fls. white. New Zeal. Var. **angustifolia:** *O. Cheesemanii.*

chathamica T. Kirk. Shrub, to 6 ft.; lvs. alt., lanceolate to elliptic or oblong-ovate, to 5 in. long including the short petiole, glabrous above, densely white-woolly and prominently 3-veined beneath, serrate; heads to 2¼ in. across, solitary on peduncles to 6 in. long; disc fls. violet-purple, ray fls. pale violet-purple to white. Chatham Is. (New Zeal.).

Cheesemanii Cockayne & Allan [*O. arborescens* var. *angustifolia* (Cheesem.) Cheesem.]. Much-branched, erect shrub or small tree, bark often flaking; lvs. alt., linear-lanceolate to lanceolate, sometimes oblong-lanceolate, to 3½ in. long, with appressed buff hairs beneath, serrate, petioles to ¾ in. long; heads in loose, much-branched corymbs to 6 in. across; disc fls. yellowish, ray fls. white. New Zeal.

cymbifolia: a listed name of no botanical standing, for *O. nummulariifolia* var.

furfuracea (A. Rich.) Hook.f. Shrub or tree, to 15 ft.; lvs. alt., obliquely ovate to elliptic-oblong, to 4 in. long, glabrous above when mature, with thin, appressed, glossy, brown hairs beneath, crenate-dentate to entire, petioles to 1 in. long; heads in large, loose, much-branched corymbs; disc fls. yellow, ray fls. white. New Zeal.

×**Haastii** Hook.f.: *O. avicenniifolia* (Raoul) Hook.f. × *O. moschata* Hook.f. Much-branched shrub, to 10 ft.; lvs. alt., crowded, oblong to elliptic-oblong or oblong-ovate, to 1¼ in. long, glabrous and glossy above, white-tomentose beneath; heads $^5/_{16}$ in. across, in long-peduncled corymbs to 3 in. across; disc fls. yellow, ray fls. white. New Zeal.

ilicifolia (Hook.f.) Hook.f. Shrub or small tree, to 15 ft., with musky scent; lvs. alt., linear-oblong to lanceolate, to 4 in. long, acute to acuminate, truncate at base, yellowish-tomentose beneath, coarsely and sharply toothed, petioles to ¾ in. long; heads in corymbs to 4 in. across; fls. fragrant, ray fls. white. New Zeal.

nummulariifolia (Hook.f.) Hook.f. Densely much-branched shrub, to 10 ft.; lvs. alt., crowded, broadly ovate to nearly orbicular, to ⅜ in. long including petiole, very thick and leathery, glabrous above when mature, white-, buff-, or yellow-tomentose beneath, margins more or less revolute; heads solitary, axillary; ray fls. yellowish. New Zeal. Var. **cymbifolia** Hook.f. Lvs. to ⅝ in. long, revolute almost to midrib, very viscid. New Zeal.

×**oleifolia** T. Kirk. Apparently a hybrid between *O. avicenniifolia* (Raoul) Hook.f. and *O. odorata* Petrie. Much-branched shrub, to 10 ft., brs. crowded, erect; lvs. alt., lanceolate to oblong-lanceolate, to 3 in. long including the short petiole, very leathery, glabrous above, appressed-white-tomentose beneath; heads in broad, loose corymbs; ray fls. white. New Zeal.

paniculata (J. R. Forst. & G. Forst.) Druce. Much-branched shrub or small tree, to 20 ft.; lvs. alt., elliptic to ovate-oblong, to 4 in. long including petiole, glabrous above, white- to buff-tomentose beneath, undulate to almost flat; heads in clusters arranged in corymbs; disc fls. solitary, whitish, ray fls. absent. New Zeal.

phlogopappa: *O. stellulata.*

stellulata (Labill.) DC. [*O. phlogopappa* (Labill.) DC.]. Erect shrub, to 5 ft.; lvs. alt., oblong to lanceolate, to 3 in. long, glabrous, scabrous, or stellate-hairy above, white or rusty with dense stellate hairs beneath, sinuate-toothed; heads in leafy panicles. Se. Australia, Tasmania.

OLIVE. The olive, *Olea europaea,* is a broad-leaved evergreen tree whose drupaceous fruits, when immature or nearly mature, are pickled and used as a food or relish, or, when fully mature, are crushed for their oil. Because of its attractive silver-gray foliage, the olive tree is also ornamental, and is often seen planted as a street tree.

The olive is grown commercially in all the countries surrounding the Mediterranean Sea, as well as in Argentina, Chile, and Peru in South America, and in the hot interior valleys of California, to which it is especially adapted. It is also grown to some extent in the southern part of Australia and in South Africa.

Olive trees have rather exact climatic requirements for flowering and fruit production. A certain amount of winter chilling is necessary for flower initiation in most cultivars; 12–15 weeks of a diurnally fluctuating temperature pattern, such as from 35° to 60° F, is satisfactory. Trees will be killed by temperatures below about 12° F. A long, hot growing season is conducive to good fruit development. The trees bloom in midspring, with table-olive harvest in autumn and oil harvest in winter. Trees respond to summer irrigation and annual fertilization with nitrogen by strong vegetative growth and increased fruit production. In some soils olives also respond to potassium, boron, and phosphorus fertilizers. Olive trees are very drought- and heat-resistant but will not tolerate poorly drained soils. Yields range from about 1–5 tons per acre, but year to year fluctuations can be pronounced.

Propagation is by rooting leafy cuttings in mist propagation beds. Treatments with root-promoting hormones, as indolebutyric acid, increase root initiation. Grafting or budding cultivars on seedlings or rooted cuttings is also practiced. The olive is quite susceptible to *Verticillium,* so where this fungus is present a resistant rootstock should be used.

The only serious insect pest in this country is *Saissetia oleae* (Bern.), black scale. A bacterium, *Pseudomonas Savastanoi* (Erw. Sm.) F. Stevens, causes galls to develop on twigs and limbs, particularly following cold winters that cause cracks in the bark. *Cycloconium oleaginum* Castagne is a fungus which attacks the leaves, sometimes defoliating the trees.

The fruits are quite bitter when harvested because of the presence of a certain glucoside. This is neutralized to some extent by prolonged washing or soaking the fruits in water, or better, in salt water. The bitterness is more completely removed by use of a lye solution, which is then thoroughly removed by rinsing. The fruits can then be stored in a brine solution for several months. Sealed canning of these nonacid fruits should be done only in commercial canneries so that they can be thoroughly autoclaved for at least 60 minutes at 240° F to prevent the buildup of toxic organisms.

OLIVERANTHUS: *ECHEVERIA.* **O. elegans:** *E. Harmsii.*

OLMEDIELLA Baill. *Flacourtiaceae.* One sp., an evergreen, dioecious tree, native to Guatemala; lvs. alt., leathery, usually with coarse, spine-tipped teeth, bearing 2 glands on the upper side at the base of blade; fls. small, petals 0, stamens many; fr. a berry.

Suitable for tropical plantings.

Betschlerana (Göpp.) Loes. COSTA RICAN HOLLY, PUERTO RICAN H., MANZANOTE. Glabrous tree, to 45 ft.; lvs. elliptic-oblong, to 6 in. long, nearly entire on flowering brs., otherwise spiny-toothed and hollylike.

OLNEYA A. Gray. *Leguminosae* (subfamily *Faboideae*). One sp., an armed tree, native to sw. deserts of N. Amer.; lvs. alt., even- or odd-pinnate, spines in pairs below lvs.; fls. in few-fld. axillary racemes, papilionaceous, the upper 2 calyx lobes united, stamens 10, 9 united and 1 separate; fr. a thick legume, slightly constricted between seeds.

The seeds formerly used as food by the Amer. Indians.

Tesota A. Gray. DESERT IRONWOOD. To 25 ft., with broad crown; lfts. in 4–12 pairs, oblong-cuneate, to ¾ in. long, gray-pubescent; racemes to 2 in. long; petals pale rose-purple, ⅜ in. long, standard emarginate; fr. to 2¼ in. long, hairy, seeds black. Calif., Ariz., nw. Mex.

OLSYNIUM: *SISYRINCHIUM.*

OMPHALODES Mill. NAVELWORT, NAVELSEED. *Boraginaceae.* About 24 spp. of glabrous or minutely hairy, ann. or per. herbs of Eur., Asia, and Mex.; lvs. simple, alt., basal ones long-petioled, st. lvs. few; fls. white or blue, in loose racemes, calyx 5-cleft, corolla 5-lobed, tube short, with scales in throat, stamens 5, included; fr. of 4 horizontal nutlets, the edge of the nutlet smooth or toothed.

A few species are grown in the flower garden. They succeed in moist, partly shady or sunny situations. Propagated by seeds sown in the spring or by division.

cappadocica (Willd.) DC. Per., to 10 in., from a creeping rhizome; basal lvs. ovate, to 4 in. long, cordate, lateral veins prominent; fls. blue with white centers, ⁵⁄₁₆ in. across; nutlets with entire, hairy margin. Spring. Asia Minor.

linifolia (L.) Moench [*Cynoglossum linifolium* L.]. Erect, glabrous ann., to 1 ft.; lvs. linear-lanceolate to spatulate; fls. white, to ½ in. across; nutlets with infolded, toothed margins. Summer, autumn. Spain, Portugal.

Luciliae Boiss. Tufted, glabrous per., 4–8 in.; lvs. ovate, elliptic to oblong; fls. rose turning to blue, ½ in. across; nutlets with entire margin. Summer. Greece, Asia Minor.

lusitanica: *O. nitida.*

nitida Hoffmanns. & Link. [*O. lusitanica* (L.) Pourr. ex J. Lange]. Per., to 2 ft.; lvs. oblong-lanceolate, upper surface shining, lower surface hairy; fls. blue with white centers, ⁵⁄₁₆ in. across; nutlets hairy, margin toothed. Spring. Portugal.

verna Moench. CREEPING FORGET-ME-NOT. Stoloniferous per., to 8 in., with ascending sts.; lvs. ovate to ovate-lanceolate; fls. blue, ½ in. across; nutlets hairy, with entire margin. Spring. Eur. Cv. 'Alba'. Fls. white.

OMPHALOGRAMMA (Franch.) Franch. *Primulaceae.* About 13 spp. of per. herbs, native to Asia; lvs. basal, simple, with sessile amber-colored glands beneath; fls. solitary on bractless scapes; calyx 5–8-lobed, corolla funnelform or rarely campanulate; fr. a caps. dehiscing by valves, seeds flat, with broad aril wing. Closely allied to *Primula* but differing in fls. without bracts and winged seeds.

Elwesianum (King ex G. Watt) Franch. [*Primula Elwesiana* King ex G. Watt]. To 5 in., with well-developed rhizome; lvs. oblanceolate, to 4 in. long or more in fr., tapering to a winged petiole, glabrous; fls. purple, with tube yellow inside, to 1 in. across, corolla lobes incised-dentate. Himalayas.

vinciflorum (Franch.) Franch. To 8 in., with little or no woody rhizome; lvs. oblong to ovate or oblong-ovate, to 8 in. long, longer in fr., usually tapering to a winged petiole, hairy; fls. purple-violet or blue, to 2 in. across. China.

ONAGRA: *OENOTHERA.* **Onagra pallida**: a listed name of no botanical standing for *Oenothera pallida.*

ONAGRACEAE Juss. EVENING PRIMROSE FAMILY. Dicot.; 21 genera and perhaps 600–700 spp. largely of the New

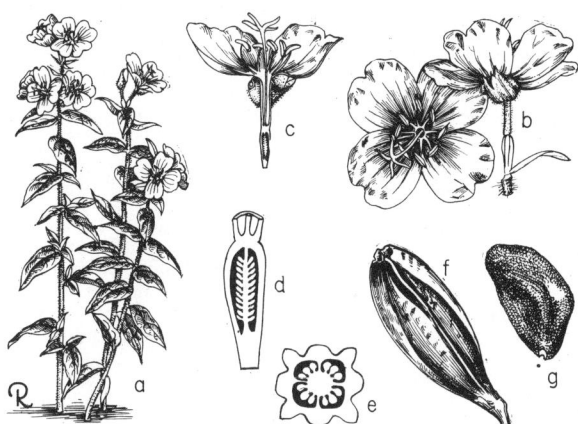

ONAGRACEAE. *Oenothera pilosella:* **a,** plant, × ⅙; **b,** flowers, × ½; **c,** flower, vertical section, × ½; **d,** ovary, vertical section, × 1½; **e,** ovary, cross section, × 3; **f,** capsule, × 3; **g,** seed, × 15.

World, but with some genera more widespread; ann. to per. herbs, shrubs, or trees, of various habit, terrestial or aquatic; fls. often showy, mostly 4-merous, sepals 4, petals 4, stamens often 8, ovary inferior, elongate; fr. a thin-walled or woody caps. or a berry. The cult. genera are: *Boisduvalia, Circaea, Clarkia, Epilobium, Fuchsia, Gaura, Hauya, Lopezia, Ludwigia, Oenothera, Semeiandra,* and *Zauschneria.*

×**ONCIDASIA** Hort.: *Aspasia* × *Oncidium. Orchidaceae.* Bigeneric hybrids intermediate in character between the parents.

For culture see *Orchids.*

×**ONCIDIODA** Rolfe: *Cochlioda* × *Oncidium. Orchidaceae.* Bigeneric hybrids intermediate in character between the parents.

For culture see *Orchids.*

ONCIDIUM Swartz. DANCING-LADY ORCHID. *Orchidaceae.* About 400 spp. of epiphytes, native to trop. Amer.; pseudobulbs well developed, occasionally reduced or rarely absent, 1- to several-lvd.; lvs. fleshy, flat or overlapping in 2 ranks, rarely cylindrical; infl. lateral, racemose or paniculate, few- to many-fld.; fls. small to showy, sepals separate, or the lateral ones rarely united, sepals occasionally clawed, petals spreading, lip simple to 3-lobed, with variously formed calluses at base, column without a foot, pollinia 2, on distinct stalks. For structure of fl. see *Orchidaceae.*

Oncidium species occur both in cool mountains and in lowlands in the tropics, hence they have varying cultural requirements, from coolhouse to warmhouse, depending on the species; they usually require considerable sun and air. For culture see *Orchids.*

altissimum (Jacq.) Swartz. Pseudobulbs flattened, ovoid, 2-lvd.; lvs. strap-shaped, to 1 ft. long; infl. pendent, to 3–4 ft. long, densely many-fld.; fls. to 1½ in. across, sepals and petals similar, ovate-lanceolate, yellow with pale chestnut-brown bars, lip 3-lobed, yellow, lateral lobes earlike, midlobe kidney-shaped, emarginate, disc with a basal crest with many fingerlike lobes. Early spring–summer. W. Indies.

ampliatum Lindl. Pseudobulbs close together, discoid, 2-lvd.; lvs. oblong-oblanceolate, to 1 ft. long; infl. paniculate, many-fld.; fls. to 1½ in. across, showy, sepals small, concealed, spatulate, pale yellow with red-brown blotches, petals larger, ovate-spatulate, canary-yellow with a few spots on base, almost white on the back, lip 3-lobed, canary-yellow, whitish on the underside, lateral lobes small, earlike, midlobe broadly kidney-shaped, 2-lobed, with a large basal callus. Spring. Mex. to Venezuela and Peru. Cv. 'Majus' [var. *majus* Van Houtte]. More robust; fls. larger, underside of lip pure white.

anthocrene Rchb.f. [*O. Powellii* Schlechter]. Pseudobulbs flattened, 2-edged, 2-lvd.; lvs. oblong-strap-shaped, to 1 ft. long; infl. racemose, rarely branching, arching, to 4 ft. long, many-fld.; fls. to 2½ in. across, sepals and petals similar, elliptic-oblong, undulate, chestnut-brown with yellow markings, lip 3-lobed, fiddle-shaped, yellow with a broad red-brown band in front of callus, lateral lobes small, midlobe ovate, cuspidate. Panama, Colombia.

asparagoides: *O. heteranthum.*

aurosum: *O. excavatum.*

barbatum Lindl. Pseudobulbs ovoid, 1-lvd.; lvs. oblong-ovate, to 4 in. long; infl. racemose or paniculate, many-fld.; fls. to 1 in. across, sepals ovate-lanceolate, clawed, yellow blotched with red-brown, petals broader, of same color, lip yellow, 3-lobed, lateral lobes ovate, midlobe toothed, with a short, squarish, 2-lobed apex, column without wings. Winter–late spring. Brazil.

Batemannianum Parm. ex Knowles & Westc. Pseudobulbs 2–3-lvd.; lvs. linear-lanceolate, to 10 in. long; infl. racemose or paniculate, to 4 ft. long, many-fld.; fls. to 1½ in. across, sepals and petals similar, ovate, undulate, light yellow with heavy chestnut-brown barring, petals broader, lip 3-lobed, yellow, lateral lobes small, orbicular, midlobe obovate-kidney-shaped, 2-lobed, disc with a sharp many-tubercled crest. Winter–spring. Peru, Bolivia, Brazil.

Baueri Lindl. Pseudobulbs 2-lvd.; lvs. sword-shaped, to 15 in. long; infl. branched, to 7 ft. long, many-fld.; fls. to 1¼ in. across, sepals and petals similar, linear-lanceolate, yellowish-green with red-brown spots, lip 3-lobed, lateral lobes triangular, blunt, midlobe transverse-oblong, above a narrowed base, yellow with a large red-brown blotch in front of callus, column with hatchet-shaped wings. Spring. W. Indies, Guyana, Venezuela to Bolivia.

bicallosum Lindl. Pseudobulbs inconspicuous, 1-lvd.; lvs. oblong-lanceolate, fleshy, to 1 ft. long; infl. erect, racemose, occasionally paniculate, many-fld.; fls. showy, to 2 in. across, sepals and petals similar, spatulate, undulate, yellow with greenish or bronze suffusion, lip 3-lobed, bright yellow, lateral lobes small, somewhat spatulate, midlobe kidney-shaped, with a shallow sinus in middle, crest white with red dots, column with a pair of hooked, sickle-shaped wings. Mex., Guatemala, El Salvador.

bryolophotum: *O. heteranthum.*

Cabagrae Schlechter. Pseudobulbs flattened, 2-lvd.; lvs. linear-strap-shaped, to 1 ft. long; infl. paniculate, tortuose, to 3 ft. long, loosely many-fld.; fls. to 1 in. across, sepals lanceolate-elliptic, clawed, petals elliptic, undulate, both sepals and petals chestnut-brown with yellow apex and margin, lip 3-lobed, yellow, lateral lobes small, semiorbicular, tapering into a broad, squarish, chestnut-brown neck, midlobe kidney-shaped, emarginate, column wings 2-lobed, hatchet-shaped. Late winter. Costa Rica.

carthagenense (Jacq.) Swartz. Pseudobulbs inconspicuous, 1-lvd.; lvs. fleshy, densely covered with green dots, to 1 ft. long; infl. paniculate, to 5 ft. long, loosely many-fld.; fls. small, about 1 in. across, sepals and petals similar, spatulate, undulate-crisped, white with purplish-rose spots, lip fiddle-shaped, of same color as sepals and petals, disc with a large crest at base, column wings triangular, rose-colored. Spring. Trop. Amer. Cv. 'Roseum' [var. *roseum* (Lem.) Hort. Sander]. Differs from typical form in having red-dotted lvs., sepals and petals pale rose-colored, spots on lip lighter.

Cavendishianum Batem. Pseudobulbs inconspicuous, 1-lvd.; lvs. leathery, elliptic-oblong, to 14 in. long; infl. paniculate, to 3 ft. long, many-fld.; fls. fragrant, to 1½ in. across, sepals and petals similar, ovate-elliptic, undulate, yellow or yellow-green, spotted with red, lip 3-lobed, bright yellow, lateral lobes large, ovate, midlobe oblong-kidney-shaped, emarginate, disc with a cross-shaped crest with many fingerlike lobes, column wings curved, yellow with red dots. Spring. Mex., Guatemala.

Cebolleta: See *O. longifolium.*

cheirophorum Rchb.f. COLOMBIA BUTTERCUP. Pseudobulbs globose, 1-lvd.; lvs. linear, to 6 in. long; infl. paniculate, longer than lvs., densely many-fld.; fls. to ½ in. across, bright yellow with a pale yellow or white crest, sepals and petals similar, orbicular-ovate, lip 3-lobed, lateral lobes oblong-ovate, midlobe entire, ovate, disc with a 4-parted crest, column wings hatchet-shaped. Costa Rica, Panama.

concolor Hook. Pseudobulbs ovoid, 2-lvd.; lvs. oblong-strap-shaped, to 6 in. long; infl. racemose, longer than lvs., several-fld.; fls. bright canary-yellow with orange crest, to 1½ in. across, upper sepal and petals similar, ovate, undulate, lateral sepals ovate-lanceolate, united at base, lip prominently clawed, cuneate-orbicular, 2-lobed in front, disc with a pair of parallel keels, column wings spreading, linear, toothlike. Spring. Brazil. Cv. 'Rhodoptera'. Column wings red.

confusum: *O. ensatum.*

crispum Lodd. Pseudobulbs flattened, 2-lvd.; lvs. lanceolate-oblong, to 8 in. long; infl. paniculate, erect, loosely many-fld.; fls. variable, to 3 in. across, bright chestnut-brown, barred and often margined with yellow, with a bright yellow spot in front of crest on lip, upper sepal and petals similar, crisped-undulate, spatulate, lateral sepals ovate-elliptic, undulate, united at base, lip 3-lobed, lateral lobes small, midlobe nearly orbicular, large, ruffled, crest with many fingerlike lobes. Late autumn. Brazil. Cv. 'Grandiflorum' [var. *grandiflorum* Dombr.]. Fls. to 3 in. across, sepals and petals deep rich brown with yellow margin, lip similarly colored, with yellow center.

crista-galli Rchb.f. Small, to 10 in., pseudobulbs ovoid, with 1 abortive lf., its base enclosed by 2-ranked, overlapping, lf. bearing sheaths; infl. short, 1–2-fld., scape filiform; fls. large for plant, to ¾ in. across, sepals greenish-yellow, spreading, petals oblong, bright yellow with reddish-brown transverse bars, lip bright yellow, 3-lobed, lateral lobes nearly orbicular, midlobe 4-lobed, with a deep sinus in front, crest many-keeled. Mex. to Panama, Colombia to Peru.

cristatum: *Odontoglossum cristatum.*

cucullatum Lindl. Pseudobulbs ovoid, 2-lvd.; lvs. linear-strap-shaped, to 8 in. long; infl. racemose, erect, several-fld.; fls. showy, to 1 in. across, sepals and petals similar, ovate, deep chestnut-brown, greenish, or olive-green, lateral sepals united, 2-lobed, lip 3-lobed, white or pale rose, densely spotted with crimson, lateral lobes nearly orbicular, midlobe kidney-shaped, emarginate, disc with 3-keeled crest, yellow, column hooded. Summer. Colombia, Ecuador. Var. **nubigenum** Lindl. Smaller throughout; lip white with a violet spot in front of crest.

dasystyle Rchb.f. Pseudobulbs small, 1-lvd.; lvs. linear-lanceolate, to 6 in. long; infl. racemose, slender, to 15 in. long, remotely few-fld.; fls. to 1½ in. across, sepals and petals similar, ovate-lanceolate, pale yellow, blotched with red-brown, lateral sepals united, 2-lobed, lip clawed basally, then broadly kidney-shaped above, yellow, crest occupying whole claw, blackish-crimson, column wings squarish. Autumn–late winter. Brazil.

divaricatum Lindl. Pseudobulbs nearly globose, small, 1-lvd.; lvs. fleshy, elliptic, to 1 ft. long; infl. paniculate, to 6 in. long, many-fld.; fls. 1 in. across, sepals and petals similar, spatulate, greenish-yellow with purple-brown markings at base, lip 3-lobed, bright yellow with red spots, crisped lateral lobes orbicular, midlobe smaller, emarginate, disc with 4 close-set, globose, puberulent calluses. Early winter. Brazil.

ensatum Lindl. [*O. confusum* Rchb.f.]. Pseudobulbs flattened, 1–3-lvd.; lvs. linear-lanceolate, to 3 ft. long; infl. paniculate, erect, often longer than lvs., many-fld.; fl. to 1¼ in. across, sepals and petals similar, separate, lanceolate-elliptic, undulate, greenish- or brownish-olive, lip 3-lobed, bright yellow, lateral lobes somewhat ear-shaped, midlobe dilated, nearly orbicular, emarginate, disc with a 7-parted crest behind a greenish-yellow spot. Autumn. Brit. Honduras, Costa Rica, Panama.

excavatum Lindl. [*O. aurosum* Rchb.f. & Warsz.]. Pseudobulbs flattened, 1-lvd.; lvs. strap-shaped, to 20 in. long; infl. paniculate, to 3 ft. long, many-fld.; fls. to 1½ in. across, upper sepal and petals obovate, lateral sepals ovate-lanceolate, all yellow with 2–3 red-brown bars on basal half, petals larger, lip 3-lobed, lateral lobes small, red-brown, midlobe between fan- and kidney-shaped, emarginate, bright canary-yellow, crest cushionlike, tubercled. Early winter. Ecuador, Peru.

flexuosum Sims. DANCING-DOLL ORCHID. Rhizome ascending, pseudobulbs widely spaced, ovoid, 2-lvd.; lvs. linear-lanceolate, to 7 in. long; infl. paniculate, erect, loosely many-fld.; fls. ½ in. across or more, sepals and petals similar, ovate-lanceolate, yellow with red-brown bars on basal half, lateral sepals united, lip 3-lobed, yellow with red-brown markings in front of crest, lateral lobes triangular, midlobe kidney-shaped, emarginate, crest many-keeled. Autumn–early spring. Brazil.

Forbesii Hook. Pseudobulbs flattened, 2-lvd.; lvs. oblong-strap-shaped, to 1 ft. long; infl. paniculate, to 3 ft. long, densely many-fld.; fls. showy, to 2½ in. across, dark chestnut-brown with yellow border, upper sepal ovate, wavy, lateral sepals similar, united for ⅓, petals obovate to nearly orbicular, crisped, lip 3-lobed, lateral lobes small, earlike, midlobe suborbicular-kidney-shaped, with a cuneate base, 2-lobed in front, crisped, disc with a 4-parted callus. Early spring. Brazil.

fuscatum: *Miltonia Warscewiczii.*

Harrisonianum Lindl. Pseudobulbs lens-shaped, 1-lvd.; lvs. fleshy, ovate-oblong, to 6 in. long; infl. paniculate, erect, to 1 ft. long, densely many-fld.; fls. ¾ in. across, sepals and petals similar, obovate-oblong, yellow blotched with red, lip fiddle-shaped, basal part semiorbicular, yellow with red spots, apical part cuneate-ovate, emarginate, pure yellow, disc with 4-parted, keeled callus. Spring. Brazil.

hastatum (Batem.) Lindl. Pseudobulbs flattened, 2-edged, 2-lvd.; lvs. oblong-lanceolate, to 10 in. long; infl. racemose or paniculate, to 5 ft. long, loosely many-fld.; fls. starlike, to 1½ in. across, sepals and petals lanceolate, chocolate-brown, bordered and barred with yellow-green, lip 3-lobed, lateral lobes squarish, pale yellow, midlobe obovate, pointed, claret-red, crest 4-keeled. Spring–early summer. Mex., Guatemala.

heteranthum Poepp. & Endl. [*O. asparagoides* Kränzl.; *O. bryolophotum* Rchb.f.]. Pseudobulbs 2–3-lvd.; lvs. oblong-lanceolate, to 5 in. long; infl. paniculate, many-branched, to 4 ft. long, many-fld.; fls. of 2 kinds, those along zigzag brs. abortive, small, with 5 lanceolate segms. but without a lip, those terminating the brs. well developed, to ¾ in. across, with lips, sepals oblanceolate, petals obovate, both pale cream-yellow with a few brown bars, lip 3-lobed, yellow with red-brown markings on basal half, lateral lobes broadly triangular, mid-lobe kidney-shaped, emarginate, crest tubercled. Early winter–spring. Trop. Amer.

hyphaematicum Rchb.f. Pseudobulbs flattened, 1-lvd.; lvs. lanceolate-strap-shaped, to 1 ft. long; infl. paniculate, to 5 ft. long, many-fld.; fls. to 1½ in. across, sepals and petals similar, ovate-lanceolate to oblong-lanceolate, undulate, red-brown with yellow tips, lip 3-lobed, canary-yellow on upper surface, pale yellow with crimson spots underneath, lateral lobes ear-shaped, midlobe kidney-shaped, emarginate at apex, crest a 3-parted keel. Ecuador.

incurvum G. Barker ex Lindl. Pseudobulbs flattened, 2–3-lvd.; lvs. linear-strap-shaped, to 15 in. long; infl. paniculate, to 5 ft. long, many-fld.; fls. to 1 in. across, sepals and petals similar, lanceolate, undulate, rose-pink with white spotting, lip fiddle-shaped, with rose-pink-blotched white disc in front of a yellow callus. Autumn. Mex.

iridifolium: *O. pusillum.*

Krameranum Rchb.f. BUTTERFLY ORCHID. Pseudobulbs orbicular, flattened, 1-lvd.; lvs. elliptic-oblong, mottled with blackish-green, to 10 in. long; infl. erect, with swollen nodes, to 2½ ft. long, 1-fld.; fls. showy, produced in succession, upper sepal and petals similar, erect, linear, with undulate margins, reddish-brown, lateral sepals oblong-sickle-shaped, undulate, orange-red with yellow markings, lip large, 3-lobed, lateral lobes nearly orbicular, yellow with red-brown spots, midlobe nearly orbicular, undulate, canary-yellow with a red border. Late summer–autumn. Costa Rica to Ecuador.

leucochilum Batem. Pseudobulbs 2-lvd.; lvs. strap-shaped, to 1 ft. long; infl. paniculate, many-fld.; fls. to 1½ in. across, sepals and petals similar, ovate-elliptic, yellow-green with brown markings, lip 3-lobed, white, lateral lobes ear-shaped, midlobe kidney-shaped, emarginate, disc with 5-parted crest, the center one upwardly curved. Mex., Guatemala.

longifolium Lindl. [*O. Cebolleta* of auth.]. Pseudobulbs inconspicuous, 1-lvd.; lvs. fleshy, cylindrical, to 15 in. long; infl. paniculate, longer than lvs., many-fld.; fls. very variable in size, to 1½ in. across, sepals and petals similar, ovate-spatulate, undulate, yellow with reddish-brown spots and dots, lip 3-lobed, canary-yellow, lateral lobes large, ovate, midlobe kidney-shaped, emarginate, disc with an elevated platelike crest, column wings small. Late autumn–summer. Trop. Amer. *O. Cebolleta* (Jacq.) Swartz is a name of doubtful application.

longipes Lindl. & Paxt. Pseudobulbs ovoid, 2-lvd.; lvs. linear, to 6 in. long; infl. racemose, short, few-fld.; fls. to 1½ in. across, sepals and petals spatulate, yellow with red-brown bars, lateral sepals longer than upper sepal, lip 3-lobed, canary-yellow, lateral lobes ovate, midlobe from a denticulate isthmus, kidney-shaped, 2-lobed, with a toothed, narrow base, crest many-tubercled. Autumn. Brazil.

luridum Lindl. Pseudobulbs inconspicuous, 1-lvd.; lvs. large, fleshy, to 20 in. long; infl. paniculate, to 6 ft. long, many-fld.; fls. to 1½ in. across, sepals and petals similar, spatulate, undulate, yellow with brown markings, lip 3-lobed, lateral lobes small, white, midlobe large, yellow with red spots, 2-lobed in front, column wings hooked. Late winter–late summer. Trop. Amer. Cv. 'Guttatum' [var. *guttatum* (L.) Lindl.]. Sepals and petals yellow with reddish-brown spots.

macranthum Lindl. Pseudobulbs 2-lvd.; lvs. lanceolate, to 20 in. long; infl. paniculate, flexuous, to 10 ft. long, many-fld.; fls. showy, to 4 in. across, sepals orbicular, clawed, undulate, yellowish-brown, petals similar, more undulate, sulphur-yellow, lip hastate, yellow, lateral lobes violet-purple, midlobe orangish with violet border, crest white. Ecuador.

maculatum Lindl. Pseudobulbs 2-lvd.; lvs. strap-shaped, to 10 in. long; infl. paniculate, many-fld.; fls. to 2 in. across, sepals and petals similar, ovate-elliptic, yellow-green with chocolate-brown markings, lip indistinctly 3-lobed, with a cuneate base, white with a few chocolate-brown lines along the keeled crest at base. Mex., Guatemala.

Marshallianum Rchb.f. Pseudobulbs 2-lvd.; lvs. oblong-lanceolate, to 15 in. long; infl. paniculate, many-fld.; fls. showy, to 3 in. across, upper sepal obovate, lateral sepals ⅓ united, oblong, all yellowish-green with pale reddish-brown bars, petals obovate, emarginate, undulate, canary-yellow with red-brown spots in center, lip 3-lobed, bright yellow, lateral lobes earlike, midlobe between fan- and kidney-shaped, emarginate, crest with many fingerlike lobes. Late spring. Brazil.

microchilum Batem. ex Lindl. Pseudobulbs nearly globose, 1-lvd.; lvs. oblong-elliptic, to 1 ft. long; infl. paniculate, to 4 ft. long, many-fld.; fls. to 1¼ in. across, sepals elliptic, clawed, pale brown with yellow borders and markings, petals ovate, chestnut-brown with yellow margins, lip 3-lobed, white with purple spots, lateral lobes semiorbicular, midlobe triangular, column wings triangular. Mex., Guatemala.

oblongatum Lindl. Pseudobulbs 2-lvd.; lvs. strap-shaped, to 1 ft. long; infl. paniculate, many-fld.; fls. to 1¼ in. across, sepals and petals similar, lanceolate, sulphur-yellow with light crimson spots at base, lateral lobes triangular, midlobe kidney-shaped, emarginate, crest with 3 parallel keels, the middle one shortest. Autumn–early winter. Mex.

obryzatum Rchb.f. Pseudobulbs 1-lvd.; lvs. linear-oblong, to 9 in. long; infl. paniculate, to 6 ft. long, many-fld.; fls. to 1 in. across, sepals and petals similar, oblong-spatulate, yellow with red-brown bars, petals broader, lip 3-lobed, lighter yellow with red-brown bar in front of crest, lateral lobes triangular, rounded, midlobe kidney-shaped, with tapering narrow base, emarginate, crest with many fingerlike lobes, column wings sickle-shaped, toothed. Trop. Amer.

ornithorhynchum HBK. Pseudobulbs 2-lvd.; lvs. linear-lanceolate, to 10 in. long; infl. paniculate, arching or pendent, much longer than lvs., many-fld.; fls. to ¾ in. across, rose-lilac except for yellow callus on lip, sepals and petals similar, oblanceolate, reflexed, lip fiddle-shaped, wider toward base, crest many-tubercled, column with a long rostellum. Mex. to Venezuela and Peru. Cv. 'Albiflorum' [var. *albiflorum* Rchb.f.]. Whole fl. white except for yellow callus on lip.

panamense Schlechter. Pseudobulbs 2-lvd.; lvs. linear-lanceolate, to 2½ ft. long; infl. paniculate, to 10 ft. long, many-fld.; fls. to 1 in. across, sepals and petals similar, ovate-lanceolate, undulate, yellow with olive-brown blotches and bars, lip fiddle-shaped, yellow with a large reddish-brown bar in front of crest, lateral lobes rounded, midlobe kidney-shaped, crest white, many-keeled, column wings toothed. Flowering throughout year. Panama.

papilio Lindl. BUTTERFLY ORCHID. Pseudobulbs globose, flattened, 1-lvd.; lvs. oblong-elliptic, green mottled with purplish-crimson, to 9 in. long; infl. to 4 ft. long, upper part of scape 2-edged; fls. large, showy, produced in succession, upper sepal and petals linear-filiform, reddish-crimson, lateral sepals oblong-elliptic, sickle-shaped, undulate, yellow with chestnut-red bars, lip 3-lobed, yellow, lateral lobes nearly orbicular, speckled with red, midlobe orbicular, 2-lobed in front, with a broad band of red around margin. Autumn–winter. Venezuela to Peru and Brazil. Cv. 'Eckhardtii' [var. *Eckhardtii* Linden & Rodig.]. Fls. larger, petals and lip marked with orange-red. Cv. 'Majus' [var. *majus* Rchb.f.]. Sepals and petals to 4 in. long, lip to 2 in. across.

Phalaenopsis Linden & Rchb.f. Pseudobulbs 2-lvd.; lvs. lanceolate, to 8 in. long; infl. racemose, to 10 in. long, few-fld.; fls. to 1 in. across, upper sepal elliptic, lateral sepals united, bifid, white with red-crimson bars and spots, lip 3-lobed, white with red-crimson spots around crest, lateral lobes nearly orbicular, midlobe kidney-shaped, emarginate. Colombia, Ecuador.

phymatochilum Lindl. Pseudobulbs flattened, 1-lvd.; lvs. elliptic-oblong, to 15 in. long; infl. paniculate, to 5 ft. long, many-fld.; fls. to 2 in. across, sepals and petals linear-lanceolate, reflexed, pale yellow with brown markings, petals shorter, lip 3-lobed, white with orange markings, lateral lobes nearly orbicular, undulate, midlobe ovate-lanceolate with cuneate base, undulate, crest with fingerlike lobes. Spring. Brazil.

Powellii: *O. anthocrene.*

pubes Lindl. Pseudobulbs narrow, 2-lvd.; lvs. oblong-lanceolate, to 6 in. long; infl. paniculate, erect, to 2 ft. long, many-fld.; fls. variable, to 1 in. across, sepals and petals similar, yellow with orange-brown bars, obovate, undulate, lateral sepals united, lip 3-lobed, yellow with red-orange markings, lateral lobes linear, midlobe obovate, crest tubercled, column wings somewhat sickle-shaped. Early winter–early spring. Brazil.

pulchellum Hook. Pseudobulbs lacking; lvs. flattened laterally or 3-angled, and overlapping in form of a fan; infl. racemose, to 15 in. long, several-fld.; fls. to 1 in. across, white with pink or rose suffusion on all segms., sepals and petals similar, obovate, lateral sepals united, bifid, lip with 4 equal lobes, crest yellow, column wings sickle-shaped. Late spring. Jamaica, Guyana.

pulvinatum Lindl. Pseudobulbs small, round, 1-lvd.; lvs. fleshy, narrowly oblong, to 1 ft. long; infl. paniculate, many-fld.; fls. to 1 in. across, sepals and petals similar, ovate-spatulate, undulate, yellow with crimson-brown base, lip 3-lobed, yellow with crimson-brown dots on lobes, lateral lobes nearly orbicular, frilled, midlobe kidney-shaped, emarginate, frilled, disc with a large cushionlike, papillose callus. Brazil. Cv. 'Grandiflorum' [var. *grandiflorum* Regel]. Fls. to 1½ in. across, lateral lobes of lip laciniate-toothed.

pumilum Lindl. Pseudobulbs small, inconspicuous, 1-lvd.; lvs. fleshy, ovate, to 4 in. long; infl. paniculate, longer than lvs., many-fld.; fls. small, less than ½ in. across, sepals and petals similar, spatulate, yellow, spotted with red-brown, lip 3-lobed, kidney-shaped, brown-yellow, lateral lobes semiorbicular, midlobe triangular-ovate, crest of 2 2-keeled calluses. Early summer. Brazil.

pusillum (L.) Rchb.f. [*O. iridifolium* HBK]. Dwarf, without pseudobulbs; lvs. 2-ranked, flattened laterally and overlapping in the form of a fan, to 2½ in. long; infl. racemose, as long as lvs., 1-fld.; fls. to ¾ in. across, produced in succession, sepals and petals spreading, yellow, irregularly barred with reddish-brown, lip 3-lobed, bright yellow, lateral lobes nearly orbicular, midlobe transverse-elliptic, 2-lobed on front, undulate, disc with a flat callus at base. Flowering throughout year. Trop. Cent. and S. Amer.

reflexum Lindl. Pseudobulbs flattened, 2-lvd.; lvs. linear-lanceolate, to 10 in. long; infl. paniculate, to 2½ ft. long, loosely many-fld.; fls. to 1 in. across, sepals and petals similar, linear-lanceolate, reflexed, yellow-green with red-brown bars, lip 3-lobed, yellow with red spots around the crest, lateral lobes roundish, midlobe kidney-shaped, emarginate, crest tubercled, column wings toothed. Mex.

robustissimum Rchb.f. Pseudobulbs robust, broadly elliptic, 1-lvd.; lvs. ovate-elliptic, to 16 in. long; infl. paniculate, to 6 ft. long, many-fld.; fls. to 1 in. across, sepals and petals similar, cuneate-obovate, golden-yellow with a large reddish-brown blotch on lower half, lip with 4 equal lobes, lobes nearly orbicular, golden-yellow with many red-brown spots, crest squarish. Brazil.

Rogersii: *O. varicosum* cv.

sarcodes Lindl. Pseudobulbs 2–3-lvd.; lvs. obovate-oblong, to 10 in. long; infl. paniculate, slender, arching, many-fld.; fls. to 2 in. across, sepals and petals similar, obovate, chestnut-brown with yellow margin, lip 3-lobed, yellow with a few red-brown spots around crest, lateral lobes nearly orbicular, midlobe transverse-elliptic, emarginate, crest a lobed plate, column wings triangular. Spring. Brazil.

serratum Lindl. Pseudobulbs 2-lvd.; lvs. lanceolate, to 15 in. long; infl. paniculate, many-fld.; fls. to 3 in. across, upper sepal nearly orbicular, clawed, undulate-crisped, chestnut-brown with yellow margin, lateral sepals ovate-lanceolate, clawed, of the same color, petals similar to lateral sepals, more undulate, incurved, basal half chestnut-brown, apical half bright yellow, lip hastate, purplish-brown with a white platelike crest. Peru.

sphacelatum Lindl. Pseudobulbs ovate-cylindric, 2-lvd.; lvs. oblong-linear, to 2 ft. long; infl. paniculate, to 5 ft. long, many-fld.; fls. to 1 in. across, sepals and petals similar, oblong-elliptic, yellow with dark brown bars, lip 3-lobed, bright yellow with dark maroonish-brown spot in front of crest, lateral lobes earlike, small, tapering into a squarish base, midlobe kidney-shaped, emarginate, disc with a platelike crest. Spring–early summer. Mex.

splendidum A. Rich. ex. Duchartre. Pseudobulbs close together, round, flattened, 1-lvd.; lvs. large, fleshy, ovate; infl. racemose, much longer than lvs., few-fld.; fls. to 2 in. across, variable, sepals and petals similar, ovate-lanceolate, yellow with rich red-brown bars and spots, lip 3-lobed, canary-yellow, lateral lobes poorly developed, round, midlobe nearly orbicular or elliptic, slightly emarginate, crest of 3 parallel keel-like calluses, the middle one longest. Guatemala.

stenotis Rchb.f. Pseudobulbs 2-lvd.; lvs. cuneate-oblong, to 10 in. long; infl. paniculate, to 4 ft. long, many-fld.; fls. to 1¼ in. across, sepals and petals similar, lanceolate-oblong, undulate, yellow with reddish-brown bars and spots, lip 3-lobed, yellow, lateral lobes elliptic, midlobe kidney-shaped, emarginate, disc with a many-toothed crest, column wings hatchet-shaped. Costa Rica, Ecuador.

stipitatum Lindl. Pseudobulbs inconspicuous, 1-lvd.; lvs. cylindrical, often pendent, to about 2½ ft. long; infl. paniculate, pendent, to 2½ ft. long, many-fld.; fls. to ¾ in. across, sepals and petals similar, rich yellow with reddish-brown markings, lip 3-lobed, canary-yellow, lateral lobes linear-sickle-shaped, midlobe transversely elliptic, with narrow base, 2-lobed at apex, crest an elevated callus. Panama.

stramineum Lindl. Pseudobulbs inconspicuous, 1-lvd.; lvs. ovate-oblanceolate, to 8 in. long; infl. paniculate, arching, longer than lvs., densely many-fld.; fls. to ¾ in. across, white or straw-colored, lip speckled with red, sepals and petals spreading, nearly orbicular, concave, lip 3-lobed, lateral lobes sickle-shaped, dotted with red, midlobe transversely elliptic, emarginate, crest a confluent set of platelike keels. Mex.

superbiens Rchb.f. Pseudobulbs 1-lvd.; lvs. linear-oblong, to 20 in. long; infl. paniculate, flexuous, to 5 ft. long, many-fld.; fls. showy, to 3 in. across, sepals and petals clawed, upper sepal orbicular, undulate, reddish-brown tipped with yellow, lateral sepals ovate, of same color, petals ovate, undulate, light yellow or white, barred with brown on basal half, lip obscurely 3-lobed, plum-purple, lateral lobes semiorbicular, midlobe ovate, disc with a many-keeled crest. Winter–spring. Venezuela, Colombia.

tetrapetalum (Jacq.) Willd. Pseudobulbs lacking; lvs. in tufts or in the shape of a fan, 3-angled, flattened laterally and overlapping, sickle-shaped; infl. racemose, occasionally branched, to 2 ft. long, many-fld.; fls. ¾ in. across, sepals ovate-spatulate, lateral sepals united at base, petals spatulate-fiddle-shaped, pale yellow or white with bright chestnut-red markings, lip 3-lobed, white or pink, lateral lobes linear, sickle-shaped, midlobe kidney-shaped, column wings sickle-shaped. W. Indies.

tigrinum Llave & Lex. [*O. unguiculatum* Lindl.]. Pseudobulbs 2–3-lvd.; lvs. linear-oblong, to 1 ft. long; infl. paniculate, to 3 ft. long, many-fld.; fls. to 3 in. across, sepals and petals similar, lanceolate, reflexed, yellow with brown blotches, lip 3-lobed, yellow, lateral lobes earlike, midlobe kidney-shaped, with a distinct narrow base, emarginate, crest many-keeled, column wings ear-shaped. Mex.

unguiculatum: *O. tigrinum.*

urophyllum Lodd. Pseudobulbs lacking; lvs. flattened laterally, overlapping, sword-shaped, to 6 in. long; infl. paniculate, drooping, to 2 ft. long, loosely many-fld.; fls. ¾ in. across, sepals and petals yellow with reddish-brown markings, sepals lanceolate, lateral sepals united, petals obovate, apiculate, lip 3-lobed, bright yellow above, pale cream-colored but fading to white underneath, lateral lobes sickle-shaped, midlobe kidney-shaped, emarginate, crest 3-parted, column wings hatchet-shaped. Lesser Antilles.

varicosum Lindl. Pseudobulbs flattened, 2–3-lvd.; lvs. lanceolate-strap-shaped, to 10 in. long; infl. paniculate, pendent, to 5 ft. long, many-fld.; fls. to 1½ in. across, sepals and petals similar, ovate, yellow with pale red-brown bars, lip large, 3-lobed, lateral lobes semiorbicular, midlobe nearly orbicular, cleft in front, bright yellow, crest many-tubercled. Brazil. Cv. 'Rogersii' [var. *Rogersii* Rchb.f.]. Panicle larger and more spreading; fls. larger, lip to 2 in. across.

variegatum Swartz. Pseudobulbs lacking; lvs. laterally flattened, overlapping in a fan-shaped cluster; infl. racemose, rarely branched, to 1½ ft. long, many-fld.; fls. to 1½ in. across, rose-purple with yellow crest, sepals and petals similar, obovate, lateral sepals united to bifid tip, lip 3-lobed, lateral lobes oblong, midlobe kidney-shaped, emarginate, crest 3-parted, column wings hatchet-shaped. W. Indies.

Wentworthianum Batem. ex Lindl. Pseudobulbs flattened, 2-lvd.; lvs. strap-shaped, to 15 in. long; infl. branched, flexuous, to 4 ft. long, many-fld.; fls. to 1 in. across, sepals and petals similar, linear-spatulate, undulate, yellow with red-brown blotches, lip 3-lobed, yellow, lateral lobes nearly orbicular, midlobe kidney-shaped, with a long basal neck, toothed, 2-lobed, crest of many fingerlike lobes, column wings narrow. Guatemala.

ONCOBA Forssk. [*Xylotheca* Hochst.]. *Flacourtiaceae.* About 39 spp. of often spiny trees or shrubs, native mostly to trop. and s. Afr., a few in Brazil; lvs. alt., simple, short-petioled; fls. white, reddish, or yellow, in clusters or solitary, sepals 3–4, petals 5–20, stamens many; fr. a globose, indehiscent, leathery berry, seeds many.

Kraussiana (Hochst.) Planch. [*Xylotheca Kraussiana* Hochst.]. Evergreen shrub or small tree, to 15 ft., without spines; lvs. elliptic-oblong, to 2 in. long, entire; fls. white, 2 in. across, solitary; berry orange-colored, smooth, about 1½–2 in. in diam. S. Afr. Zone 10b.

Routledgei T. Sprague. Shrub or small tree, to 20 ft., with spines; lvs. ovate-acuminate, crenate; fls. white, solitary, 2 in. across, fragrant. Trop. Afr. Zone 10. Closely related to *O. spinosa* and perhaps not distinct from it.

spinosa Forssk. Shrub or small tree, to 20 ft., spines straight, to 2 in. long; lvs. elliptic-acuminate, serrate, to 4 in. long; fls. white, camellialike, fragrant, solitary, 3 in. across; fr. smooth, glossy, reddish-brown, 2½ in. in diam. Trop. Afr. Zone 10b. The roots and lvs. are used for medicinal purposes; the frs. are hollowed and made into snuff boxes; the sour, edible fr. pulp tastes like pomegranate.

ONCOSPERMA Blume. *Palmae.* A few spp. of solitary or cespitose, spiny, monoecious palms of wet tropics from Ceylon to the Philippine Is.; lvs. pinnate, sheaths spiny, forming a crownshaft, petioles short, spiny, pinnae acute, spreading or pendulous; infl. infrafoliar, peduncle short, often spiny, bearing an often spiny lower bract enclosing a thinner upper bract, both splitting and deciduous at flowering, rachillae many, simple or forked, with fls. in triads (2 male and 1 female); male fls. asymmetrical, sepals 3, acute, imbricate basally, petals 3, valvate, acute to acuminate, stamens 6–12, filaments short, erect, anthers narrow, arrow-shaped basally, pistillode short, deeply 3-cleft, female fls. smaller, sepals and petals imbricate, staminodes 6, pistil 1-celled, 1-ovuled; fr. globose with lateral stigmatic residue, seed with deeply ruminate endosperm and basal embryo.

Tender, ornamental palms, mostly planted in Old World tropics. For culture see *Palms.*

fasciculatum Thwaites. To 50 ft., sts. usually clustered, densely spiny; lvs. to 8 ft. long, pinnae in groups along each side, ascending, with drooping apices, in several planes, the blade appearing ragged; infl. with bracts unarmed, to 2 ft. long; male fls. ¼ in. long, stamens 9; fr. black or purple, ½ in. in diam. Ceylon.

filamentosum: *O. tigillarium.*

tigillarium (Jack) Ridl. [*O. filamentosum* Blume]. NIBUNG PALM. Sts. usually clustered, to 60 ft., spiny; lvs. to 20 ft. long, pinnae slender, pendulous, regularly arranged; infl. with spiny bracts, to 2 ft. long; male fls. yellow, ¼ in. long, fragrant, stamens 6; fr. black or glaucous, ½ in. in diam. Se. Asia, Malay Pen., Borneo, Sumatra, and Philippine Is.

ONIONS. The onions are species of *Allium.* The best-known ones are the hardy cool-season biennials and perennials cultivated in the vegetable garden for their edible bulbs and sometimes for their leaves, which are used in seasoning. Others of the genus are grown for their ornamental flowers (see *Allium*).

The common onion is *Allium Cepa,* native to western Asia, ordinarily biennial, with hollow, cylindrical leaves and a prominent bulb. The Japanese bunching or Welsh onion is *A. fistulosum,* also Asian, a more leafy plant, with a soft bulb a little thicker than the neck. The shallot is *A. Cepa,* Aggregatum Group, probably Asian but not known as a wild plant; it differs from the common onion in its small stature, in being propagated vegetatively rather than by seed, and in producing from each planted bulb a group of bulbs cohering by the base. Most shallots are used as green onions since the mature bulbs are small, and, in fact, in some areas any green bunching onion is called a shallot, regardless of species.

Another hollow-leaved species is the perennial, tufted chive, *A. Schoenoprasum,* native to Europe and Asia. It does not produce distinct bulbs. The leaves are used for seasoning, being cut as needed. It is a hardy plant, which requires little care and makes an attractive border; the rose-purple flower-heads are ornamental when allowed to develop. The chive (or cive) is readily raised from seeds and also propagated easily by division. It is well to divide and reset the clumps when they become weak from overcutting or crowding.

Flat-leaved alliums grown for eating are the leek, *A. Ampeloprasum,* and garlic, *A. sativum;* see the separate articles on these plants. The leek has a simple bulb not much thicker than the crown. Garlic is a much smaller plant, with a thin-skinned bulb that breaks into several integral parts or cloves. Rocambole, *Allium Scorodoprasum,* is a larger plant than garlic, grown the same way but little seen in North America. Chinese chive, *Allium tuberosum,* is grown only a little in North America but extensively in China. This species has a growth habit much like *A. Schoenoprasum* but has flat leaves and a flavor somewhat like garlic.

The common field onion is propagated directly from seeds. Other races of the same species are propagated asexually, as by (a) sets, (b) multipliers, (c) top sets or bulbils; these races are grown for small green early bunch onions. (a) Sets are small onions, ideally ½–¾ inch in diameter, that were arrested in their development by being grown very thickly (from seed) and ripened off early in the season; when planted the next spring they resume their growth and produce mature bulbs earlier than direct-seeded onions of the same kind. (b) Multipliers or potato onions are a form in which the bulb divides into separable parts; each part is planted the following spring (or autumn far South) as are the sets. (c) Top set onions are little bulbils that appear in the flower cluster in the place of flowers; they are handled in the same way as sets.

Being hardy, onions are started as early in the spring as the ground can be prepared. The land should be in good tilth, fine and mellow. In the far South, they may be sown in autumn. Seed is sown in rows 12–18 inches apart at a rate to give plants 2–4 inches apart, and are covered ½–1 inch deep. Most commercial onions are grown on soils high in organic matter, which do not bake or dry out quickly. Many home gardeners have soils in which it is difficult to get good emergence of direct-seeded onions and therefore find it better to use either sets or transplants. Transplants may be from local greenhouses or from southern outdoor plant beds. Good crops can be grown from transplants or sets in the ordinary garden if the earth is deeply prepared, fertile, well supplied with humus, and in superior tilth.

When the onion tops have fallen over and the leaves are partially dry, the plants may be pulled or lifted and the tops allowed to dry completely, preferably under cover if outdoor conditions are not suitable for rapid drying. After curing, the tops are cut off, about a half inch above the bulb. For home use, onions are stored in the cellar, much as are potatoes.

There are many cultivars, differing in season, size, shape, color, flavor, and storage life. Time of bulbing is determined by day length and to some extent by temperature, and each cultivar has its own characteristic response. Short-day cultivars used in the southern United States from bulbs prematurely at an extremely small size in the North, while long-day cultivars fail to form bulbs under short days. Consequently, it is vital to choose a cultivar that is adapted to the day lengths prevailing when and where it is grown. Male sterility has made it possible to produce F_1 hybrid seed that gives a more uniform and higher-yielding crop than the standard open-pollinated cultivars, but because of this uniformity it is even more important that a hybrid be adapted to the region where it is used.

The onion is subject to serious diseases and pests, some of which are avoided in the home garden by using sets or transplants. The most recent advice should be available from the nearest state experiment station.

ONOBRYCHIS Mill. *Leguminosae* (subfamily *Faboideae*). More than 100 spp. of pubescent, per. herbs or spiny shrubs of the Old World; lvs. alt., odd-pinnate; fls. in axillary racemes or spikes, papilionaceous, stamens 10, 9 united and 1 separate; fr. an indehiscent, flat, nearly orbicular legume, often spiny or crested, with 1–2 seeds.

Onobrychis viciifolia is grown for forage, other species as ornamentals. Seeds should be sown in spring or autumn where plants are to grow.

arenaria (Kit. ex Schult.) DC. Differs from *O. viciifolia* in having fls. to ⅜ in. long in very slender racemes, and fr. to 3/16 in. long, with fewer (4–5) teeth, very short-puberulent. Temp. Eurasia.

viciifolia Scop. SAINFOIN, HOLY CLOVER, ESPARCET. Per., to 2 ft.; lfts. in 6–12 pairs, oblong or linear, 1 in. long; peduncles longer than lvs., racemes many-fld.; fls. pink, rarely white, to ½ in. long or more; fr. pubescent, toothed on 1 side, to ⅜ in. long. Temp. Eurasia. Adapted to dry soil.

ONOCLEA L. *Polypodiaceae.* One sp., a coarse terrestrial fern, native to n. temp. regions in both hemispheres; rhizomes creeping and forking, without scales; lvs. dimorphic.

Sometimes transferred to grounds, but can be weedy. For culture see *Ferns.*

nodulosa: *Matteuccia pensylvanicum.*

sensibilis L. SENSITIVE FERN. Sterile lvs. solitary and scattered, to 4½ ft. long, deeply pinnatifid, pinnae wavy-toothed, fertile lvs. to 2½ ft. long, dark brown or black at maturity, 2-pinnate, the pinnules rolled up into beadlike segms. which open to discharge the spores. In moist pastures and similar places. Common name refers to sensitivity to early frost.

Struthiopteris: see *Matteuccia pensylvanica* and *M. Struthiopteris.*

ONONIS L. REST-HARROW. *Leguminosae* (subfamily *Faboideae*). Over 70 spp. of herbs and shrubs of the Old World; lvs. of 3 (or 1) toothed lfts.; fls. axillary, papilionaceous, keel beaked, stamens 10, united; fr. an oblong, dehiscent legume.

Of easy culture; propagated by seeds or division.

arvensis: *O. spinosa.*

cenisia L. [*O. cristata* Mill.]. Per., to 10 in., slightly woody at base; lfts. obovate, small, minutely toothed; fls. rose, solitary on naked, jointed peduncles much longer than lvs.; fr. somewhat inflated, ½ in. long. Summer. S. Eur.

cristata: *O. cenisia.*

hircina Jacq. Shrubby, to 2 ft.; lfts. oblong-ovate; fls. usually paired, rose and white, to ¾ in. long; fr. ovate, glandular. Summer. S. Eur., N. Afr.

rotundifolia L. Shrubby, to 1½ ft., glandular-pubescent; lvs. long-petioled, lfts. round to ovate, crenate; fls. 2–3 together on long peduncles, bright rose, ¾ in. long; fr. inflated, pendent, about 1 in. long. S. Eur.

spinosa L. [*O. arvensis* L.]. Per., to 2 ft., sometimes spiny; lvs. of 3 lfts., or the upper with 1 lft., lfts. oblong or ovate; fls. 1–2 together, pink, to 1 in. long; fr. ovate, mostly 1-seeded. Eur.

ONOPORDUM L. *Compositae* (Carduus Tribe). About 25 spp. of coarse bien., occasionally triennial, woolly, thistlelike herbs, native to Eur., N. Afr., w. Asia; lvs. alt., large, prickly-toothed or lobed, with spiny decurrent wings along the st.; fl. heads solitary or clustered, large, involucral bracts usually spine-tipped, receptacle deeply pitted but without bristles; fls. all tubular, purple, violet, or white; pappus of plumose or only minutely barbed bristles.

Propagated by seeds.

Acanthium L. COTTON THISTLE, SCOTCH T., SILVER T., OAT T., ARGENTINE T. To 9 ft., white-tomentose throughout; lvs. oblong, lobed and toothed, spiny, lower lvs. to 2 ft. long, 1 ft. wide; heads to 2 in. across, involucral bracts narrowly lanceolate, attenuate, cobwebby, the outer ones recurving, the inner erect, much shorter than fls.; fls. reddish-purple, sometimes white, glabrous; pappus bristles only minutely barbed. Eur. to cent. Asia; naturalized in parts of N. and S. Amer.

acaulon L. Stemless, or st. to 3 in.; lvs. in a rosette, oblanceolate to narrowly elliptic, 6–15 in. long, gray-tomentose; heads 1 to several, sessile or short-peduncled, involucral bracts oblong-lanceolate, glabrous; fls. white. S. France, Spain, w. N. Afr.

arabicum: *O. nervosum.*

bracteatum Boiss. & Heldr. Tall, white-tomentose; lvs. oblong-lanceolate, shallowly lobed, spiny; heads large, subtended by many short bractlike lvs., involucral bracts broadly lanceolate, with short spines, glabrous, the outer ones reflexing, the inner longer, erect, about as long as fls.; fls. purple, glabrous; pappus minutely barbed. Sw. Asia Minor.

illyricum L. Tall, gray- to white-tomentose, occasionally greenish, sts. and peduncles narrowly winged; lvs. oblong-lanceolate, divided into spiny lobes; heads 2 in. across, involucral bracts glabrous or slightly cobwebby basally, the outer ones ovate-lanceolate, reflexing, short-pointed, the inner longer, erect, shorter than the fls.; fls. purple, glandular; pappus minutely barbed. Medit. region.

macracanthum Schousb. To 5 ft., gray-tomentose; sts. and peduncles broadly winged, the wings coarsely toothed and spinose; heads usually solitary, broader than long, involucral bracts lanceolate-acuminate, the outer ones spreading, the innermost erect, appressed; fls. purple. W. Medit. region.

nervosum Boiss. [*O. arabicum* Hort.]. To 6–9 ft.; lvs. oblong-lanceolate, lobed and toothed, white-tomentose, prominently veined on underside, spiny; heads 2 in. across, involucral bracts lanceolate, all erect, appressed, the outer ones cobwebby, short-pointed, much shorter than the inner, the inner ones acuminate, glabrate, slightly glandular, shorter than the fls.; fls. rose-purple, glandular; pappus bristles short-plumose. Spain, Portugal.

tauricum Willd. [*O. virens* A. DC.]. Tall, green, glandular-puberulent but otherwise nearly glabrous; lvs. oblong-lanceolate, with large spiny lobes; heads large, involucral bracts narrowly lanceolate, green, glandular-viscid, the outer ones recurving, not much shorter than the inner, the inner ones shorter than the fls.; fls. purple, glabrous; pappus minutely barbed. Medit. region.

virens: *O. tauricum.*

ONOSMA L. *Boraginaceae.* About 125–130 spp. of hispid, ann. or per. herbs or subshrubs, native from Medit. region to the Himalayas; lvs. simple, alt., entire, basal and cauline; fls. yellow, blue, red, or white, in bracted, scorpioid cymes, calyx 5-lobed, enlarging in fr., corolla tubular or ventricose, shortly 5-lobed, without scales in the throat, stamens 5, usually included; fr. of 4 erect or incurved, smooth or rough nutlets.

Sometimes grown in borders and rock gardens. Propagated by seeds and in summer by cuttings.

alboroseum Fisch. & C. A. Mey. Per., to 8 in.; lvs. spatulate-oblong, apex rounded; fls. white, changing to red and then bluish, to about 1 in. long, velvety. Asia Minor.

cassium Boiss. Herbaceous per. to 1½ ft.; lvs. oblong, obtuse, with few small bristles; fls. yellow, about ¾ in. long, glabrous, stamens slightly exserted. Syria.

helveticum (A. DC.) Boiss. Per., sts. several, to 20 in.; lvs. oblong-spatulate, to nearly 3 in. long, puberulent, stellate-bristly; fls. pale yellow, to 1 in. long. Alps.

heterophyllum Griseb. [*O. tubiflorum* Velen.]. Cespitose per., to 16 in.; lvs. oblong or linear-oblong, to 6 in. long, stellate-bristly; fls. pale yellow, to 1³⁄₁₆ in. long. Balkan Pen.

nanum DC. Per., to 5 in., with yellowish hairs; lvs. linear-lanceolate, hispid; fls. yellow, changing to blue, glabrous, to about ¾ in. long. Asia Minor.

pyramidale Hook.f. Stout, pyramidally branched per., to 2 ft.; lvs. linear, with white hairs from rough tubercles; fls. scarlet, becoming lilac, to ½ in. long, hairy. W. Himalayas.

rupestre Bieb. Per., to 9 in.; lvs. linear-lanceolate, to 1¾ in. long, soft-hairy, acute or obtuse, sessile; fls. pale yellow in bud, becoming ivory-white, narrowly urn-shaped, to ¾ in. long, velvety, on short red pedicels. Caucasus.

stellulatum Waldst. & Kit. Woody-based per., to 10 in., sts. several; lvs. oblong-spatulate, to nearly 6 in. long, stellate-bristly; fls. pale yellow, tubular, to ¾ in. long, glabrous, bracts shorter than the calyx. W. Yugoslavia.

tauricum Pall. GOLDEN-DROP. Very similar to *O. stellulatum;* lvs. linear-lanceolate; fls. sessile, to 1 in. long, lower bracts longer than calyx. S. Eur.

tubiflorum: *O. heterophyllum.*

ONYCHIUM Kaulf. CLAW FERN. *Polypodiaceae.* Six spp. of small, graceful, terrestrial ferns, native to trop. and subtrop. Asia and Afr.; lvs. 3–4-pinnate, finely dissected, fertile lvs. slightly contracted; sori along each margin of segms., linear, indusia flaplike, those of the 2 margins of pinnules meeting at center of the pinnule.

Grown usually as pot and pan plants in the greenhouse. See also *Ferns.*

auratum: *O. siliculosum.*

japonicum (Thunb.) Kunze. Lvs. thin, to 1½ ft. long, light green, 2–4-pinnate into very small, narrow pinnules, fertile lvs. scarcely different from sterile lvs. E. and se. Asia. Zone 9.

siliculosum (Desv.) C. Chr. [*O. auratum* Kaulf.]. Like *O. japonicum,* but lvs. distinctly dimorphic, fertile pinnules larger, to ½ in. long, ⅛ in. wide, noticeably enlarged; sori and indusia often yellow. Trop. Asia.

OOPHYTUM N. E. Br. *Aizoaceae.* Three spp. of tiny, tufted, per. succulents, native to S. Afr.; lvs. opp., united most of their length to form an ovoid body (growth) with a small apical fissure, texture pulpy, the old body drying to a papery shell and covering the new growth during the resting season; fls. solitary, bracted, calyx 6–7-lobed, petals many, in 2–3 series, stamens many, erect, ovary half-superior, 6-celled, stigmas 5 or 6; fr. a caps., expanding keels winged, cell lids lacking.

Growth occurs in spring. Cultivate in a warm place with maximum light and moderate moisture, but keep dry during the resting period. See also *Succulents.*

nanum (Schlechter) L. Bolus. Growths green, with fine, almost invisible papillae, to ¾ in. high, ¼ in. across; fls. ⅜ in. across, petals white inside, with reddish margins. Cape Prov.

oviforme (N. E. Br.) N. E. Br. Growths olive-green, sometimes red, minutely roughened with glossy papillae, to ¾ in. high, ½ in. wide; fls. to ⅞ in. across, petals white with purple-pink tips. Cape Prov.

OPERCULINA Manso. *Convolvulaceae.* Not cult. O. dissecta: *Merremia dissecta.* O. tuberosa: *Merremia tuberosa.*

OPHIOGLOSSACEAE (R. Br.) Agardh. ADDER'S-TONGUE FAMILY. Ferns; 3 genera and about 60 spp. of more or less fleshy ferns, native to trop. and temp. regions of both hemispheres; lvs. lacking circinate vernation, divided into fertile and a sterile blade, fertile blade spikelike to paniclelike; sporangia 2-valved, not in sori, spores many. *Botrychium* and *Ophioglossum* are cult.

Species of this family are planted sparingly in wild gardens. Tropical epiphytic species are grown under glass.

OPHIOGLOSSUM L. ADDER'S-TONGUE FERN, ADDER'S-TONGUE. *Ophioglossaceae.* About 30–50 spp. of small, mostly terrestrial ferns of wide distribution, several of the trop. spp. epiphytic; lvs. solitary or few, succulent, consisting of a sterile, usually entire blade and a contracted, long-stalked, fertile spike bearing 2 rows of fleshy spore clusters.

For culture see *Ferns.*

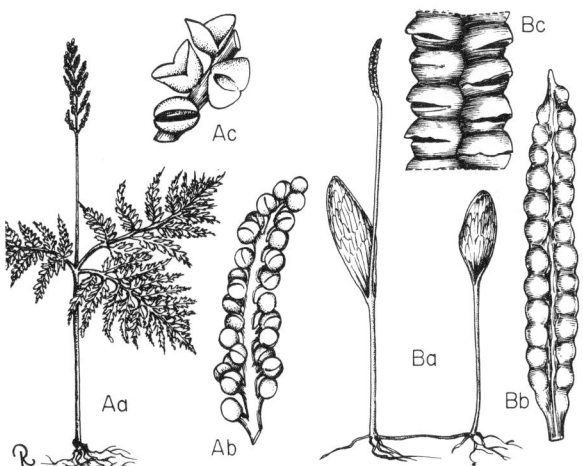

OPHIOGLOSSACEAE. **A,** *Botrychium virginianum:* **Aa,** plant, × ¼; **Ab,** division of fertile blade, × 2; **Ac,** sporangia, × 5. **B,** *Ophioglossum vulgatum:* **Ba,** plant, × ½; **Bb,** fertile blade, × 2; **Bc,** sporangia, × 4.

californicum Prantl. Terrestrial; differing from *O. vulgatum* in lvs. 2, rarely to 4 in. high, and the sterile blade sharply acute and narrower. S. Calif., Baja Calif.

Engelmanii Prantl. ENGELMANN'S A.-T. Terrestrial; lvs. usually 2–5, to 9 in. long, the sterile blade to 3½ in. long and 2 in. wide, apiculate; fertile spikes to 1 in. long, on stalks to 4 in. long. Va. to Ariz. and Mex.

pendulum L. Epiphytic; lvs. pendent, loose, membranous, strap-shaped, to 5¼ ft. long, to 2½ in. wide; fertile blade pendulous, inserted on and usually exceeded by sterile blade. Old World tropics from Madagascar to Hawaii. Cult. in trop. gardens and elsewhere occasionally under glass for the attractive foliage.

vulgatum L. Terrestrial; lvs. usually solitary, to 16 in. long, sterile blade to 5 in. long and 2 in. wide, obtuse or bluntly acute, fertile blade about 2 in. long, on stalks to 10 in. long. Mostly in moist meadows and woods, Nov. Sc. to Fla.; Eurasia.

OPHIOPOGON Ker-Gawl. [*Mondo* Adans.]. LILYTURF, MONDO GRASS. *Liliaceae.* Perhaps 10 spp. of evergreen, stemless, sod-forming per. herbs, native from India to Korea and Japan; lvs. grasslike; fls. white to pale purple, usually nodding, in simple racemes or in fascicles arranged in terminal racemes, perianth segms. 6, separate, stamens 6, anthers pointed, filaments very short, ovary inferior; fr. berrylike, blue.

Ophiopogons are valuable as ground covers in mild climates and as pot plants, sometimes seen in the conservatory. Culture is simple, in sun or shade.

arabicus: *O. planiscapus* cv.

Clarkei Hook. f. Plants tufted, rhizome creeping, roots not tuberous; lvs. linear, to 1 ft. long, and ⅛ in. wide; fls. 3–5, to ⅝ in. across. Sikkim.

intermedius D. Don. Plants tufted; lvs. linear, to 2 ft. long and ½ in. wide, margins serrulate toward base; fls. many, white, ½ in. across, in a loose raceme. India and Ceylon.

Jaburan (Siebold) Lodd. [*Mondo Jaburan* (Siebold) L. H. Bailey]. JABURAN L., WHITE L., SNAKEBEARD. Plants tufted, roots stout, cordlike, not tuberous; lvs. linear, to 2 ft. long or more, about ½ in. wide; fls. white, ½ in. long or more, in axillary fascicles in short racemes; fr. oblong, violet-blue. Japan. Often confused with *Liriope Muscari.* Cvs. 'Argenteo-vittatus', 'Aureo-variegatus', 'Javanensis', 'Variegatus', and 'Vittatus' have lvs. striped with white or yellow, and may not all be distinguishable from one another. Cv. 'Caeruleus' is listed as having violet fls.

japonicus (Thunb.) Ker-Gawl. [*Mondo japonicum* (Thunb.) Farw.; *Liriope japonica* Hort.]. DWARF L., MONDO GRASS. Plants with long underground stolons, roots tuberous; lvs. many, rather rigid, to 15 in. long, about ⅛ in. wide, dark green, commonly curved; fls. light lilac to white, in a short, loose, few-fld. raceme; fr. blue, size of a pea. Japan and Korea. An excellent sod-forming plant.

planiscapus Nakai. Plants often stoloniferous and with thickened roots; lvs. linear, to 20 in. long and ⅛–¼ in. wide, green, with several veins; fls. white or pale purple, ¼ in. long, in racemes; fr. dull blue. Japan. Cv. 'Arabicus' [*O. arabicus* Hort.]. Mature lvs. turning purple-black; scapes purple-black; fls. pinkish; fr. blue-green.

OPHRYS L. *Orchidaceae.* About 35 spp. of terrestrial herbs with ovoid tubers, native to Medit. region and Eurasia; sts. leafy or often with basal lvs.; infl. erect, racemose or spicate, few-fld.; fls. highly colored, sepals similar, spreading, petals smaller, lip velvety, usually dark-colored and with various markings, column short, fleshy, united with anther, pollinia 2. For structure of fl. see *Orchidaceae.* The lip in some spp. mimics the female of certain insects; in a misdirected attempt to copulate with the lip, male insects transfer pollen from one fl. to another and thus effect cross-pollination.

Sometimes planted in the wild garden. For culture see *Orchids.*

apifera Huds. BEE ORCHID. To 16 in.; lvs. oblong-lanceolate, keeled, paler and slightly glossy underneath; spike loosely 2–8-fld.; fls. sessile, sepals petal-like, reflexed, oblong, obtuse, pale rose to violet-rose, rarely white, more or less hooded apically, petals half as long as sepals, green or purple-brown, covered apically with whitish hairs, margins revolute, lip 5-lobed, recurved, red-brown or dark purple, with broad, glabrous, brownish or purplish collarette encircling the red-brown elliptic lip base, often with 2 or 3 yellowish spots near lip apex. Early summer. Cent. Eur. to N. Afr.

aranifera Huds. EARLY SPIDER ORCHID. To 2 ft., leafy; spikes loosely 1–7-fld.; sepals yellow-green, oblong, margins revolute, petals shorter than sepals, strap-shaped, wavy-margined, green or brownish, lip as long as sepals, rounded, elliptic-oblong, with or without 2 obtuse, conical humps near base, notched at apex, outside surface and sides with dense, long, brown-purple hairs, forming a kind of fur collar around central area, margin of lip often paler or yellowish-green. Spring–early summer. England, cent. and s. Eur., Asia Minor.

cordata: *Listera cordata.*

fuciflora Haller. LATE SPIDER ORCHID. Sts. to 16 in. high, leafy; spikes loosely 2–6-fld.; sepals petal-like, elliptic-oblong, pale rose, rarely white, margins revolute, petals short, dagger-shaped, rose, rarely white, densely velvety with short hairs, lip sessile, broad, entire, red-brown to purple-brown, conspicuously marked, with a small, shining, eyelike knob on each side of base of column. Late spring. Cent. and s. Eur.

fusca Link. Sts. erect, to 16 in.; lvs. in a basal rosette, herbaceous, to 4 in. long; racemes loosely few-fld.; fls. showy, to ¾ in. across, sepals ovate, greenish, petals smaller, strap-shaped, lip 4-lobed, hairy, dark puce with yellow margin, disc with a pair of large, glabrous, metallic-blue spots. Medit. region.

insectifera L. FLY ORCHID. Sts. to 16 in. high, leafy; spikes long, loosely 2–10-fld.; sepals lanceolate, yellow-green, margins reflexed, petals shorter than sepals, purplish- or brownish-red, margins revolute, lip longer than petals, 3-lobed, purplish- or reddish-brown, with a quadrangular, iridescent, bluish shield in middle and 2 dark, glossy, eyelike knobs at base, margins reflexed, midlobe deeply notched. Late spring–summer. Eur.

lutea Cav. Sts. erect; lvs. basal, linear-oblong, to 2 in. long; racemes to 7 in. long, many-fld.; fls. to 1 in. across, sepals oblong, green, incurved, petals smaller, linear-oblong, yellow or yellow-green, lip squarish, 3-lobed, golden-yellow with maroon-purple disc, polished in center. Medit. region.

speculum Link. MIRROR ORCHID, MIRROR-OF-VENUS. Sts. erect, to 1 ft.; lvs. basal, linear-oblong, to 2½ in. long; racemes 3–6-fld.; fls. to 1 in. across, sepals linear-oblong, green, with broad purple bands, petals small, triangular-lanceolate, dark purple or maroon-brown, lip squarish, 3-lobed, margins recurved, disc steel-blue, shining, with golden-yellow edge, margins of lip broadly maroon-purple, velvety and fringed. Medit. region.

tenthredinifera Willd. SAWFLY ORCHID. Sts. erect, to 5 in.; lvs. elliptic-oblong, to 3½ in. long; raceme few-fld.; sepals nearly orbicular, white with pink veins, petals white with pink suffusion, lip hairy, white to bright rose, disc carmine-rose, with blue markings, apex greenish. Spring. Medit. region.

OPHTHALMOPHYLLUM Dinter & Schwant. EYE-LEAVES. *Aizoaceae.* About 19 spp. of dwarf, stemless succulents, native to S. Afr.; lvs. opp., united for most of their length, forming cylindrical or obconical bodies (growths), the old growth drying to a papery shell and the new growth developing within it, in their native habitat normally buried in the sand with only apex exposed, apex usually with transparent areas (windows); fls. more or less pedicelled, calyx 6-lobed, petals white, pink, or violet-red, many, in several series, fused at base, stamens many, ovary inferior, 6-celled, stigmas 6; fr. a caps., expanding keels winged, cell lids rudimentary.

Cultivate in a sandy-loamy soil with maximum light in greenhouse or window with minimum temperature of 60° F. Overwatering will cause growths to burst and rot. Propagation easy by seeds, but seedlings require a resting period, which for mature plants is normally of 10 months duration. See also *Succulents.*

Friedrichiae (Dinter) Dinter & Schwant. Growths mostly solitary, smooth, green with a reddish tinge, coppery-red in the resting period, to 1¼ in. long, ⅝ in. wide, ½ in. thick, cylindrical, fissure ¼ in. deep, lobes roundish, distinctly and roundly keeled, ends of lobes with translucent windows passing into a few large light dots toward lower margin; fls. to ¾ in. across, petals white. S.-W. Afr.

griseum: a listed name of no botanical standing.

Herrei Lavis. Growths 1 or more, olive-green, soft-velvety, to 1¾ in. long, ⅜ in. wide at base, ⅞ in. wide at apex, fissure about ⅜ in. deep, to ⁵⁄₁₆ in. across, lobes saddle-shaped above; fls. to 1⅛ in. across, diurnal, slightly fragrant, petals white to pale pink. Cape Prov.

Larisae: a listed name of no botanical standing.

Maughanii (N. E. Br.) Schwant. Growths 1 or several, smooth, uniformly transparent or almost translucent, dull, to 1⅝ in. long and 1 in. wide, compressed-cylindrical, oblong or squarely oblong in profile, notched at apex or with 2 short lobes, fissure slightly open, to ⁵⁄₁₆ in. deep, lobes rounded or slightly conical at top, very blunt, often slightly keeled, windows light yellow-green, lower edge with transparent large dots; fls. ⅝ in. across, petals white. Cape Prov.

multipunctatum: a listed name of no botanical standing.

Schlechteri Schwant. ex Jacobsen. Growths 1–2, smooth, dull green to light flesh-colored or reddish, pale-dotted, to 1⅝ in. long and ⅝ in. wide at center, slightly less thick at base and at end, oblong-ovoid, fissure ¼ in. wide, lobes conically tapering, tops of lobes with light windows; fls. 1 in. across, petals white. Cape Prov.

Triebneri Schwant. ex Jacobsen. Growth solitary, smooth, lower part dark lilac to brown-red, darker ocher-colored above, to ¾ in. high, ⅞ in. wide, ⅝ in. thick, obconical, slightly laterally compressed, truncate above, fissure ¼ in. deep, lobes 2, thick, slightly flattened, faintly roundly keeled on lower side, upper part of the sides and lobes covered with large, transparent dots which coalesce to form a window; fls. 1 in. across, slightly fragrant, petals very broad, shining white. S.-W. Afr.

verrucosum Lavis. Growth solitary, red-brown, over 1 in. long, ⅝ in. wide, ⅞ in. across, cylindrical, truncate above, fissure ⅛–¼ in. deep, tops of lobes distinctly tubercled, finely papillose, ¼–⅜ in. across, dots many, large, transparent; fls. on pedicels ½ in. long, petals white. Cape Prov.

OPITHANDRA B. L. Burtt. *Gesneriaceae.* About 6 spp. of per., hairy herbs in Asia; lvs. in a basal rosette; fls. 1 to many in a scapose cyme, sepals 5, lanceolate, corolla tubular, limb 5-lobed, more or less 2-lipped, lobes spreading or erect, stamens 2, anthers free or coherent at tips, disc cuplike, short, ovary superior, cylindrical, stigma 2-lobed; fr. a caps.

For cultivation see *Gesneriaceae.*

primuloides (Miq.) B. L. Burtt [*Oreocharis primuloides* (Miq.) Benth. & Hook.f. ex C. B. Clarke]. Lvs. elliptic to orbicular or nearly cordate, to 2½ in. long, 1½ in. wide, coarsely toothed, pale-hairy; scapes 3–4 in. long, cymes 2–12-fld., congested; sepals linear, ¼ in. long, corolla to ¾ in. long, lilac with white tube, upper lobes erect or bent backward, lower lobes ¼ in. long. Japan.

OPLISMENUS Beauvois. *Gramineae.* About 20 spp. of ann. or per. grasses in the tropics and subtropics of both hemispheres, sts. freely branching, with erect flowering shoots; lf. blades flat, thin, lanceolate or ovate; racemes several, 1-sided, thickish, short, distant; spikelets solitary or in pairs on a hairy rachis, glumes about equal, awned from the apex or from between the lobes, sterile lemma exceeding the glumes and fr., fertile lemma convex or boat-shaped. For terminology see *Gramineae.*

An occasional greenhouse subject, propagated by rooting the stems.

hirtellus (L.) Beauvois. BASKET GRASS. Per., sts. widely creeping and branching, the fertile sts. to 1 ft., erect from an ascending base; lf. sheaths glabrous to papillose-hispid, blades to 4 in. long, ¾ in. wide, green; panicle 2–4 in. long, with 3–7 rather distant racemes; spikelets green with erect, purple awns to ⅜ in. long, Tex., Mex., and W. Indies to Argentina. Cv. 'Variegatus'. Lf. blades striped with white. Cult. in hanging baskets under the name *Panicum variegatum* Hort.

OPLOPANAX (Torr. & A. Gray) Miq. [*Echinopanax* Decne. & Planch. ex Harms]. *Araliaceae.* Two spp. of prickly, deciduous shrubs of N. Temp. Zone; lvs. alt., orbicular, pal-

mately lobed, deeply toothed; fls. greenish-white, in globose umbels arranged in dense, terminal racemes or panicles, petals 5, valvate, stamens 5, ovary 2-celled, styles 2, separate; fr. a drupe, pyrenes 2.

Propagated by seeds, suckers, and root cuttings.

horridus (Sm.) Miq. [*Echinopanax horridus* Hort.]. DEVIL'S CLUB. Shrub, 3–10 ft., sts., petioles, and rachises densely set with spines to ½ in. long; lvs. bright green, more or less orbicular, to 10 in. wide, 5–7-lobed, serrate, deeply cordate, prickly on both sides, lobes acuminate to cuspidate; infl. racemose, woolly-pubescent; fr. scarlet, ⁵⁄₁₆ in. in diam. Mich. to Ore. and se. Alaska. Zone 4.

japonicus (Nakai) Nakai [*Echinopanax japonicus* Nakai]. Differs from *O. horridus* in having the lvs. sometimes peltate, the lobes more deeply cut and long-acuminate. Japan. Zone 6.

OPSIANDRA O. F. Cook. *Palmae.* One sp., a solitary, unarmed palm, native from Mex. to Guatemala; lvs. pinnate, sheaths not forming a crownshaft, petiole short, pinnae 1-ribbed, acute; infl. below lvs., long-peduncled, long-persistent, with 4–5 tubular sheathing bracts on peduncle, brs. simple, stout, or the lower ones forked, rachillae with fls. in clusters of 2–3, the lower female, the upper 1–2 male; male fls. with sepals imbricate, petals valvate, stamens 6, female fls. with sepals imbricate, petals valvate, pistil 3-celled, 3-ovuled; fr. red, usually 1-seeded, subglobose to somewhat kidney-shaped, broader than long, seed with homogeneous endosperm, embryo lateral.

For culture see *Palms.*

Maya O. F. Cook. Trunk to 60 ft. or more, 6 in. in diam., brown, prominently ringed; lvs. arched, to 9 ft. long, sheath split nearly to base, pinnae about 90 on each side, regularly arranged, borne in 2 planes, light green; infls. many, often with fls. and fr. at same time; fr. maturing bright red, acrid to taste, ⅜–⁹⁄₁₆ in. in diam. Zone 10b in s. Fla.

OPULASTER: *PHYSOCARPUS.*

OPUNTIA Mill. PRICKLY PEAR, TUNA, CHOLLA, CHOLLA CACTUS. *Cactaceae.* Perhaps 300 spp. of prostrate to treelike, mostly jointed cacti, native from Mass. and B.C. to Straits of Magellan; sts. mostly divided, at least distally, into determinate joints, the primary st. sometimes indeterminate and unjointed, joints either flattened and commonly obovate, or cylindrical to globose; lvs. cylindrical to conical, either large and persistent or, mostly, small and early deciduous; larger spines naked or sheathed, sometimes 0, very minute spines (glochids) usually many in the upper part of the areole; fls. lateral, sessile, perianth tube not or scarcely extending beyond the ovary, segms. separate, mostly spreading, commonly yellow, but sometimes orange to purple or white, stamens shorter than segms., sensitive; fr. a dry or juicy berry, umbilicate after perianth falls, seeds flattened, whitish, with a thick bony covering in addition to the integuments. *Maihuenia, Nopalea, Pereskiopsis, Pterocactus,* and *Quiabentia,* formerly included in *Opuntia,* are here treated separately.

The genus has been divided into 4 subgenera and one of these into 5 sections, all of which have sometimes been treated as genera, the first 2 perhaps with most reason. The species of a section possess the characteristics of that section and of the subgenus to which the section belongs. These characteristics are not repeated in the brief descriptions of the species; instead, the following symbols are used to indicate the subgenus and section to which each species belongs: B, *Brasiliopuntia;* Con, *Consolea;* C, *Cylindropuntia;* Ca, *Austrocylindropuntia;* Cb, *Cylindraceae;* Cc, *Corynopuntia;* Cg, *Grusonia;* Ct, *Tephrocactus;* P, *Opuntia.*

The distinguishing characters of the subgenera and sections follow:

Subgenus **Brasiliopuntia** K. Schum. [*Brasiliopuntia* (K. Schum.) A. Berger] (B). Treelike, primary sts. unjointed, cylindrical, bearing cylindrical joints near the st. and flattened joints away from the st.; spines not sheathed; staminodes present between petals and stamens, ovary flattened; seeds solitary or few, woolly. S. Brazil to n. Argentina. Perhaps better treated as a genus.

Subgenus **Consolea** (Lem.) A. Berger [*Consolea* Lem.]

(Con). Mostly treelike, primary sts. cylindrical or at first flattened, bearing flattened joints; spines not sheathed; style with a glandular flange near the base, ovary flattened; seeds hairy on the sides. W. Indies and Fla. Perhaps better treated as a genus.

Subgenus **Cylindropuntia** Engelm. [*Cylindropuntia* (Engelm.) F. M. Knuth] (C). Prostrate to treelike, sts. globose to cylindrical, jointed or (especially the primary sts.) unjointed, smooth or commonly tubercled; spines sheathed or sheathless; ovary cylindrical; seeds glabrous. N. and S. Amer. There are 5 more or less intergrading sections.

Section **Austrocylindropuntia** (Backeb.) Moran [*Austrocylindropuntia* Backeb.] (Ca). Mostly erect, sts. unjointed or of mostly cylindrical joints, smooth or mostly tubercled, the tubercles commonly low; lvs. sometimes large and persistent; spines not sheathed. S. Amer.

Section **Corynopuntia** (F. M. Knuth) L. Bens. [*Corynopuntia* F. M. Knuth] (Cc). More or less prostrate and spreading, sts. of club-shaped or short-cylindric joints, tubercled; lvs. small, early deciduous; spines with rudimentary sheaths or mostly without. Mex., sw. U.S.

Section **Cylindraceae** DC. (Cb). CHOLLA. Mostly erect, primary st. unjointed, bearing cylindrical joints; lvs. small and early deciduous; spines sheathed. Mostly N. Amer.

Section **Grusonia** (F. Rchb. ex K. Schum.) Baxter [*Grusonia* F. Rchb. ex K. Schum.] (Cg). Erect, sts. more or less divided into cylindrical joints, tubercles confluent into ribs; lvs. small, early deciduous; spines with or without rudimentary sheaths. N. Mex.

Section **Tephrocactus** (Lem.) Moran [*Tephrocactus* Lem.] (Ct). Mostly cespitose and forming broad clumps, sts. of globose to short-cylindric joints, more or less tubercled; lvs. small, early deciduous; spines not sheathed, glochids often deep-set; seeds few. Andes of Peru to Chile and Argentina.

Subgenus **Opuntia** (P). PRICKLY PEAR, TUNA. Prostrate to treelike, sts. of flattened joints, commonly several in a series, the lower of which may in age form a cylindrical trunk, joints commonly obovate, but orbicular to linear or rarely subglobose to nearly cylindrical; lvs. small and early deciduous; spines not sheathed; ovary cylindrical; seeds mostly glabrous. N. and S. Amer.

Opuntias are mostly coarse and awkward plants not lending themselves well to pot or tub culture, and their spines and glochids do not encourage their use. Hence relatively few are well known to horticulture. However, their odd forms, showy flowers, and ability to withstand unfavorable growing conditions make them useful as ornamental subjects for exposed and rocky banks, rock gardens, and neglected corners. Several are hardy practically throughout the country. They may be propagated from the joints and also grown readily from seeds. *Opuntia Ficus-indica*, the Indian fig or tuna, and others are widely grown in tropical and subtropical countries for the abundant edible fruit. The stems of some spineless forms are used for forage and the joints for human food; in time of need, forage is made by burning the spines off some wild forms. Some kinds have run wild and become serious pests in Australia, S. Afr., India, and elsewhere.

Too many spp. of *Opuntia* are recognized in this treatment, particularly in subgenus *Opuntia*. Lack of field studies in other areas prevents a conservative treatment like that adopted for Ariz. spp.

For culture see *Cacti*.

acanthocarpa Engelm. & Bigel. Cb; densely spiny shrub, 4–15 ft., joints to 1 ft. long and 1 in. thick or more, with laterally compressed tubercles ¾–1¼ in. long and ¼ in. wide; spines 10–12, straw-colored, to 1½ in. long; fls. red to yellow, 1–1½ in. across; fr. dry, shriveled, deciduous, spines 8–12. Spring. Nev., Ariz., Calif., Mex. Differs from *O. Parryi* in having young joints hidden by spines, fr. more spiny.

aciculata: *O. Lindheimeri*.

albispina: a listed name of no botanical standing.

arborescens: *O. imbricata*.

arbuscula Engelm. [*O. vivipara* Rose]. Cb; dense shrub, usually 2–4 ft., joints to 3 in. long and ⅜ in. thick, scarcely tubercled; spines usually 1, to ½ in. long, with straw-colored sheath; fls. bronze-yellow, to 1 in. across; fr. club-shaped, 1–1½ in. long, often proliferous. Spring. Ariz., nw. Mex.

arenaria Engelm. P; prostrate, joints turgid, becoming thinner, to 3 in. long, half as wide; areoles brown-woolly; spines 5–8, unequal, to

1½ in. long; fls. red, 3 in. across; fr. dry, 1¼ in. long. W. Tex., s. New Mex.

articulata Pfeiff. ex Otto. Ct; cespitose, joints ellipsoid, brown- to gray-green, tubercles low; spines 0 or in some vars. or cvs. 1–4 and papery, glochids many, deep-set, reddish-brown; fls. rose to yellow, to ½ in. across; fr. dry, to 2 in. long, seeds round, with starlike, corky rim. W. Argentina. A variable sp.; the cvs. here listed have been treated as spp. or as vars. of *Tephrocactus articulatus*. Cv. 'Diademata' [*O. diademata* Lem.; *Tephrocactus diadematus* (Lem.) Lem.]. Spines 1–4, papery, brownish, 1–4 in. long, to 5/16 in. wide. Cv. 'Inermis' [*O. strobiliformis* A. Berger; *Tephrocactus strobiliformis* (A. Berger) Backeb.]. SPRUCE-CONES. Joints gray-green; spines 0 or rarely 1–2, brown, to 5/16 in. long. Cv. 'Papyracantha' [*O. papyracantha* Phil.]. Spines white. Cv. 'Syringacantha' [*O. Turpinii* Lem.; *Tephrocactus Turpinii* (Lem.) Lem.]. PAPER CACTUS, PAPER-SPINED PEAR, PAPER-SPINED O. Spines with brownish tinge.

atrispina Griffiths. P; low and spreading, joints nearly orbicular, 4–6 in. long; spines from upper areoles only, 2–4, flattened, dark at base, glochids yellow, becoming brown; fls. yellow, becoming orange; fr. purplish. W. Tex.

Auberi: *Nopalea Auberi*.

aurea: *O. basilaris* var.

basilaris Engelm. & Bigel. BEAVER-TAIL, ROSE TUNA. P; low, branching mostly from the base, joints obovate to spatulate, usually puberulent, gray or purplish, often transversely wrinkled, 2–13 in. long, 1–6 in. wide, ½ in. thick; areoles close-set, circular or elongate, sunken, spines 0 or 1–3 (in var. *Treleasei*); fls. cerise to rose, yellow, or rarely white, 2–3 in. across; fr. dry, spineless. Spring. Sw. U.S., n. Mex. Var. **basilaris** [var. *ramosa* S. Parish]. The typical var.; joints obovate to orbicular, to 13 in. long and 6 in. wide; areoles circular; fls. reddish. S. Utah, Ariz., s. Calif., n. Mex. Var. **aurea** (Baxter) W. T. Marsh. [*O. aurea* Baxter]. Joints elliptic to obovate, to 4 in. long and 2½ in. wide; areoles circular; fls. yellow. S. Utah, n. Ariz. Var. **brachyclada** (Griffiths) Munz. Joints small, nearly cylindrical to flat or nearly club-shaped, to 2½ in. long; fls. reddish. S. Calif. Var. **ramosa**: var. *basilaris*. Var. **Treleasei** (J. Coult.) Toumey [*O. Treleasei* J. Coult.]. Joints narrowly to broadly obovate, to 6 in. long; areoles circular, spines 1–3 in most areoles, to ¾ in. long; fls. reddish. Nw. Ariz., Calif.

Bergerana A. Web. P; clambering or erect and treelike, to 12 ft., joints narrowly oblong, to 10 in. long; areoles distant, gray-woolly, spines mostly 2–3, unequal, the longest to 1½ in. long, flattened; fls. many, red or orange, 2 in. across; fr. red, to 1¼ in. long. Nativity unknown; described from cult.

Bigelovii Engelm. TEDDY-BEAR CACTUS. Cb; trunk erect, 3–8 ft., joints 2–10 in. long, and to 2 in. thick, tubercled, hidden by the dense covering of spines, terminal joints easily detached; spines 7–10 or more, to 1½ in. long, sheathed, pale yellow, becoming black; fls. greenish-yellow, to 1½ in. across; fr. deciduous, fleshy, the upper tubercles larger than the lower. Spring. S. Nev., Ariz., s. Calif., n. Mex.

brasiliensis (Willd.) Haw. B; trunk cylindrical, to 18 ft., with a small rounded crown, ultimate joints obovate, 3 in. long; spines 1–3, or more on old trunks, to 2½ in. long; fls. yellow, to 2 in. across; fr. subglobose, yellow, to 1½ in. long. Brasil.

Bravoana Baxter. P; shrubby, to 6 ft., joints obovate, 12–15 in. long, glabrous; spines 1–5 or sometimes 0, especially on lower areoles, flattened, yellow, becoming gray, to 2½ in. long; fls. yellow, fading reddish, to 3 in. across, ovary pubescent, 1½ in. long. S. Baja Calif.

bulbispina Engelm. Cc; joints ovoid, 1 in. long, ½ in. thick, with prominent tubercles; radial spines 8–12, central spines 4, stouter, cylindrical with bulbous base, ½ in. long. Mex.

Burbankii: a listed name of no botanical standing.

Burrageana Britt. & Rose. Cb; bushy, to 3 ft., joints to 6 in. long and ¾ in. thick, with low tubercles about as wide as long; areoles brown-woolly, spines about 8–15, similar, sheathed, yellow, to ¾ in. long; fls. red, to 1½ in. across. S. Baja Calif.

camanchica: *O. phaeacantha* var.

caribaea Britt. & Rose. Cb; similar to *O. leptocaulis* but having fls. small, pale yellow; fr. large, sterile. W. Indies, Venezuela.

chlorotica Engelm. & Bigel. FLAPJACK CACTUS. P; shrubby, to 6 ft., with a distinct trunk, joints orbicular to obovate, 6–8 in. long; spines 1–6, deflexed, slender, flattened, yellow, to 1½ in. long; fls. yellow, to 3 in. across; fr. globose, purple, 1½ in. in diam. Spring. S. Calif. to New Mex., n. Mex.

Cholla A. Web. Cb; trunk to 10 ft. high and 6 in. thick, joints to 10 in. long and 2 in. thick, tubercles to 1 in. long; spines several, sheathed, brownish, ½ in. long; fls. pink, 1¼ in. across; fr. to 2 in. long, proliferous. Baja Calif.

clavarioides Pfeiff. CRESTED O., SEA-CORAL, FAIRY-CASTLES, GNOME'S-THRONE, BLACK-FINGERS. Ca; low, much-branched, often fasciate and handlike, joints cylindrical or club-shaped, not tubercled, ½ in. thick; areoles close-set, woolly, spines 4–10, hairlike, appressed; fls. rare, greenish-brown, 2 in. across; fr. ½ in. long, seeds solitary, woolly. Supposedly Chile. Usually grafted on another *Opuntia* or a *Cereus*. Requires half shade.

clavata Engelm. [*Corynopuntia clavata* (Engelm.) F. M. Knuth]. Cc; joints club-shaped, 1–2½ in. long; spines white, rough, radial spines 6–12, slender, central spines 4–7, longer, flattened, the longest dagger-like; fls. yellow; fr. to 2 in. long, with white bristles. Ariz.

cochenillifera: *Nopalea cochenillifera.*

compressa: *O. humifusa.* var. **austrina**: *O. humifusa* var. *austrina.*

Covillei: *O. littoralis* var. *Vaseyi.*

cylindrica (Lam.) DC. CANE CACTUS, EMERALD-IDOL. Ca; little-branched, to 13 ft., sts. scarcely jointed, to 2 in. thick, with low, rhomboid tubercles; areoles white-woolly, with some long hairs, spines at first 2–3, white, to ½ in. long, sometimes 0; fls. scarlet, 1 in. across. Ecuador, Peru. Cv. 'Cristata'. Crested.

decumbens Salm-Dyck. P; low, often creeping, to 1½ ft. high, joints elliptic to oblong, pubescent, to 8 in. long; areoles woolly, often surrounded by purple blotch, spines mostly solitary, yellow, to 1½ in. long, sometimes many or 0, glochids yellow; fls. yellow to reddish, 2 in. across; fr. purple, 1 in. long. Mex., Guatemala.

dejecta: *Nopalea dejecta.*

diademata: *O. articulata* cv.

echinocarpa Engelm. & Bigel. Cb; much-branched, to 5 ft., trunk usually well developed, joints 4–6 in. long, ¾ in. thick, tubercles ¼–⅜ in. long, ¼ in. wide; spines 3–10, to 1¼ in. long, yellow or silvery, with persistent, conspicuous sheaths; fls. greenish-yellow, to 1½ in. across; fr. dry, spiny, deciduous. Spring. S. Utah, s. Nev., w. Ariz., se. Calif., Baja Calif.

elata Link & Otto. ORANGE T. P; erect, to 3 ft., joints oblong, thick, dark green, to 10 in. long; areoles remote, white-woolly, spines commonly 0, sometimes 1–3 or on old brs. more, thick, whitish, to 1¼ in. long, glochids slow to appear, long-persistent; fls. orange-yellow, 2 in. across; fr. oblong, spineless, to 2½ in. long. Brazil, Paraguay. Cv. 'Oblongata'. Decumbent. Cv. 'Obovata'. Joints obovate.

elongata (Willd.) Haw. P; similar to *O. Ficus-indica* and perhaps only a var. of it, having joints narrower, 4–5 in. wide; glochids few, whitish.

Engelmannii: *O. Ficus-indica;* but plants cult. as *O. Engelmannii* may be *O. phaeacantha* var. *discata.*

erectoclada Backeb. DOMINOES. P; cushion-forming, older brs. prostrate, young shoots erect, joints to 2 in. long and slightly narrower, often nearly cylindrical and narrowed below; areoles small, spines at first 2, small, later several, among which 2–3 are deflexed; fls. unknown. N. Argentina.

erinacea Engelm. & Bigel. P; low and spreading, joints ovate to oblong, 2–8 in. long; areoles about ⅜ in. apart, spines 4–9, somewhat flattened, moderately rigid, white or pale gray, the longest ones about 2 in. long; fls. white to yellow or red, to 2½ in. across; fr. dry, spiny, 1¼ in. long. Spring. Se. Calif. to Utah and n. Ariz. Var. **hystricina** (Engelm. & Bigel.) L. Bens. [*O. hystricina* Engelm. & Bigel.]. PORCUPINE CACTUS. Joints obovate to orbicular, 3–4 in. long; longer spines 1½–4 in., mostly rigid, deflexed. N. Ariz., New Mex. Var. **ursina** (A. Web.) S. Parish [*O. ursina* A. Web.]. GRIZZLY-BEAR CACTUS, GRIZZLY-BEAR. Joints 4–6 in. long; spines 6–15, threadlike, flexible, 3–8 in. long, not deflexed, concealing the joints; fls. mostly yellow. Se. Calif., s. Nev., nw. Ariz. Var. **utahensis** (Engelm.) L. Bens. [*O. rhodantha* K. Schum.]. Joints obovate, 2–4 in. long; spines 1–8, the longer ones 1–1½ in. long, deflexed, mostly absent from the lower areoles. Se. Calif. to New Mex. and w. Nebr.

exaltata A. Berger. C; similar to *O. subulata,* of which it may be a var., but sts. grayish, lvs. ½–3 in. long, spines brownish. Andes, Ecuador to Bolivia.

falcata Ekm. & Werderm. [*Consolea falcata* (Ekm. & Werderm.) F. M. Knuth]. Con; trunk to 5 ft., joints obliquely lanceolate to curved, to 14 in. long and 4 in. wide; areoles distant, tomentose, spines 2–8, gray, rough, unequal, to 1½ in. long; fls. red, ⅜ in. long, ovary to 1½ in. long. Hispaniola.

Ficus-indica (L.) Mill. [*O. Engelmannii* Salm-Dyck; *O. megacantha* Salm-Dyck; *O. occidentalis* Engelm. &. Bigel.]. INDIAN FIG, SPINELESS CACTUS. P; bushy or treelike, to 18 ft., joints oblong to spatulate, 12–20 in. long; spines mostly 0, or 1–5, pale yellow or white, to 1 in. long, glochids many, yellow, soon deciduous; fls. yellow, 3–4 in. across; fr. edible, mostly red but also purple, white, or yellow, 2–3½ in. long. Origin unknown; now widely grown for fr. and forage in trop. and subtrop. regions and often naturalized. BURBANK'S SPINELESS CACTUS, a form completely without spines, belongs to this sp.

floccosa Salm-Dyck. CUSHION CACTUS, WOOLLY-SHEEP. Ct; joints oblong, 2–4 in. long, 1½ in. thick, tubercled; lvs. small, persistent; areoles with long white hairs that often conceal the plant, spines 1–3, yellow, to 1¼ in. long; fls. yellow, 1 in. across; fr. globose, 1¼ in. in diam. Andes, Peru and Bolivia.

fragilis (Nutt.) Haw. P; prostrate or decumbent, roots tuberous, joints ovoid to subglobose or flattened, 1–2 in. long, 1 in. wide, easily detached, especially the terminal ones; areoles white-woolly, spines 5–9, slender, white or pale gray, to 1¼ in. long; fls. yellow or greenish or purplish, 2 in. across; fr. dry, spiny. Spring, summer. E. Man. and B.C., s. to Tex. and Ariz.

fulgida Engelm. JUMPING CACTUS. Cb; treelike, 3–12 ft., trunk 3–8 in. thick, joints 4–8 in. long, 1¼–2 in. thick, easily detached, tubercles ½ in. long and ¼ in. wide; spines 2–12, straw-colored, ¾–1½ in. long, sheaths papery, persistent; fls. pink, ¾ in. across; fr. obovoid, smooth, to 1⅜ in. long, proliferous, persistent in chains. Summer. S. Ariz., n. Mex. The sts. yield a gum. Var. **mamillata** (Schott) J. Coult. [*O. mamillata* Schott]. CLUB CACTUS, BOXING-GLOVE. To 4 ft. high, brs. drooping, more succulent, tubercles more prominent; spines 2–6, ½ in. long, inconspicuous. S. Ariz. Cv. 'Cristata'. Crested.

fuscoatra: *O. humifusa.*

glomerata Haw. The correct application of this name is uncertain; plants so listed may be *O. articulata* cv. 'Diademata' or cv. 'Syringacantha'.

Gosseliniana: *O. violacea* var.

Grahamii: *O. Schottii* var.

grandiflora: *O. macrorhiza.*

Hamiltonii: a listed name of no botanical standing; see *O. rosarica.*

humifusa (Raf.) Raf. [*O. compressa* (Salisb.) Macbr.; *O. fuscoatra* Engelm.; *O. Opuntia* (L.) Karst.; *O. Rafinesquei* Engelm.; *O. vulgaris* of auth., not Mill.]. P; prostrate or spreading, roots fibrous, joints nearly orbicular to obovate, 2–6 in. long; areoles remote, spineless, or those of the edge spiny, spines 1–2, brown to whitish, slender, to ¾ in. long; fls. yellow, 3–4 in. across; fr. obovoid, green to purple, to 2 in. long. Early summer. Mass to Mont., s. to Fla. and e. Tex. Var. **austrina** (Small) Dress [*O. compressa* var. *austrina* (Small) L. Bens.; *O. Pollardii* Britt. & Rose; *O. polycarpa* Small]. Roots tuberous, sts. erect, to 3 ft.; upper areoles usually spiny, spines 1–2, white, becoming gray, twisted. Del. to Fla. and Miss.

humilis: *O. Tuna.*

hystricina: *O. erinacea* var.

imbricata (Haw.) DC. [*O. arborescens* Engelm.]. CHAIN-LINK CACTUS. Cb; treelike, to 10 ft. or more, trunk woody, to 3 in. thick, joints 3–8 in. long, about 1 in. thick, tubercles about 1 in. long and ¼ in. wide; spines 8–30, brown to whitish, about 1 in. long, with papery sheaths; fls. pink to purple, about 3 in. across; fr. yellow, becoming naked, 1½ in. long. Colo. to Mex.

invicta Brandeg. [*Corynopuntia invicta* (Brandeg.) F. M. Knuth]. Cc; to 1½ ft.; joints obovoid to club-shaped, 3–4 in. long, tubercles 1–1½ in. long, flattened laterally; areoles large, white-woolly, spines 15–20, flattened, gray in age, to 1½ in. long, glochids few; fls. yellow, 2 in. across, ovary very spiny. Baja Calif.

Kleiniae DC. Cb; shrub, to 7 ft. or more, joints about ½ in. thick, tubercles ½ in. long, ⅛ in. high and wide; spines 1–4, to 1 in. long, the sheaths deciduous; fls. to 1 in. across; fr. red, strongly tubercled, spineless, ¾ in. long, ½ in. in diam. Var. **Kleiniae**. The typical var.; petaloid segms. reddish to purple. Tex., New Mex. Var. **tetracantha** (Toumey) W. T. Marsh. [*O. tetracantha* Toumey]. Petaloid segms. green, edged with red or brown. Ariz., n. Mex.

Kunzei: *O. Stanlyi* var.

laevis: *O. phaeacantha* var.

leptocaulis DC. Cb; low-shrubby or sometimes to 6 ft., joints 1–12 in. long, ³⁄₁₆ in. thick; spines 1 or later 2–3, slender, 1–2 in. long, with a membranous sheath; fls. green to yellow, ½–¾ in. across; fr. obovoid, red, ½ in. long, persistent through winter, sometimes proliferous. Spring. Ariz. to Tex., n. Mex.

leucotricha DC. P; treelike, to 15 ft., joints oblong to orbicular, 4–10 in. long, pubescent; areoles close-set, with spines at first 1–3, short, but later several, to 3 in. long, white, bristlelike, glochids many, yellow; fls. yellow, 3 in. across; fr. white to red, about 2 in. long, aromatic, edible. Mex.

Lindheimeri Engelm. [*O. aciculata* Griffiths; *O. tardispina* Griffiths]. P; commonly erect, to 12 ft., joints orbicular to obovate, to 10 in. long; areoles remote, spines 1–6, pale yellow to white or brownish, the longest to 1½ in. long; fls. yellow to red; fr. purple, 1½–2¾ in. long. La., New Mex., n. Mex. Var. **Lindheimeri**. The typical var.; joints not continuing to grow at apex, to 1 ft. long. La. to New Mex., n. Mex. Var. **linguiformis** (Griffiths) L. Bens. [*O. linguiformis* Griffiths]. Joints continuing to grow at the apex, becoming 3–4 ft. long and oblong or lanceolate. Tex.

linguiformis: *O. Lindheimeri* var.

littoralis (Engelm.) Cockerell. P; prostrate to ascending, to about 5 ft., joints elliptic to obovate or orbicular, green or glaucous, to 1 ft. long and 6 in. wide; spines 1–11 in each areole, variously disposed on the joint, white, gray, yellow, brown, or red; fls. yellow; fr. obpyriform. S. Calif. to s. Utah, n. Ariz., n. Baja Calif. Var. **littoralis.** The typical var.; green, joints narrowly elliptic or obovate, to 7½ in. long; spines 5–11 in each areole, borne over entire joint, gray, yellow, white, or with red intermixed, to 1⅞ in. long. S. Calif., n. Baja Calif. Var. **Vaseyi** (J. Coult.) L. Bens. & Walkington [*O. Covillei* Britt. & Rose; *O. Vaseyi* (J. Coult.) Britt. & Rose]. Moderately glaucous, joints obovate, to 10 in. long; spines 1–6 in each areole, borne over most of the joint, brown or dark gray, to 2³⁄₁₆ in. long. s. Calif.

Mackensenii: *O. macrorhiza.*

macrocentra: *O. violacea* var.

macrorhiza Engelm. [*O. grandiflora* Engelm.; *O. Mackensenii* Rose; *O. tortispina* Engelm.]. Clump-forming, roots tuberous, joints orbicular to obovate, glaucous, to 4 in. long and 1½ in. wide; spines 1–6, white or gray, to 2¼ in. long; fls. yellow or tinged red at base, to 2½ in. across; fr. obovoid, reddish-purple, to 1½ in. long. Var. **macrorhiza.** The typical var.; joints moderately glaucous, to 4 in. long; fls. yellow or reddish in center. Calif., e. to s. Mich. and La. Var. **Pottsii** (Salm-Dyck) L. Bens. [*O. Pottsii* Salm-Dyck; *O. tenuispina* Engelm.]. Joints glaucous, to 2½ in. long; fls. reddish. Tex. to Ariz.

mamillata: *O. fulgida* var.

margaritana: *O. pycnantha* var.

maxima Mill. Similar to *O. Ficus-indica* and perhaps only a var. of it, having narrower joints, to 4 in. wide, and fls. orange-red. Nativity unknown.

megacantha: *O. Ficus-indica.*

microdasys (Lehm.) Pfeiff. RABBIT-EARS, BUNNY-EARS, YELLOW B.-E., GOLDPLUSH. P; shrubby, to 3 ft., joints orbicular to oblong, yellowish-green, velvety-pubescent, 3–6 in long; areoles close-set, with many yellow glochids in a conspicuous tuft, rarely with a short yellow spine; fls. yellow, 1½–2 in. across; fr. red, subglobose. N. Mex. Cvs. **'Alba'** and **'Albispina'**, POLKA-DOT CACTUS, HONEY-BUNNY, are listed. Var. **rufida** (Engelm.) K. Schum. [*O. rufida* Engelm.]. CINNAMON CACTUS, BLIND PEAR, RED BUNNY-EARS. Joints more elongated, grayish-green; glochids reddish. Tex., n. Mex.

mistiensis (Backeb.) Rowley. Ct; clump-forming, joints ovate or elongate, green, becoming olive-gray, tubercles large, elliptic; spines mostly 0, sometimes 1, white, ⁵⁄₃₂ in. long; fls. and fr. not known. S. Peru.

Moelleri A. Berger. Cc; joints club-shaped, 2–3 in. long and 1½ in. thick, tubercles 1 in. long, ½ in. wide; radial spines several, slender, brown to whitish, to ½ in. long, central spines about 6, thickened at base, the longest to ¾ in. long, deflexed, whitish, angular or flattened; fls. yellow-green, 2 in. across. Spring. Mex.

mojavensis: *O. phaeacantha* var. *major.*

monacantha: *O. vulgaris.*

moniliformis (L.) Haw. Con; trunk flattened above, to 15 ft., densely covered with spreading spines, joints oblong to obovate, oblique, 4–12 in. long, to 5 in. wide; areoles close-set, gray-woolly, spines yellowish or gray, at first 1–3, to 1 in. long, later 5–8, to 5 in. long; fls. yellow or orange, 1 in. across; fr. 2½ in. long. W. Indies. Fr. and small joints, rooting, form masses of subglobose or turgid joints very different from the tree form.

nigrispina K. Schum. [*Tephrocactus nigrispinus* (K. Schum.) Backeb.]. Ct; joints ellipsoid, to 1½ in. long and ¾ in. thick, tubercled; areoles woolly, spines 2–5 from the upper areoles, the largest purple-black, to 1 in. long, glochids brown; fls. purple, 1 in. long. Andes, Bolivia, Argentina.

occidentalis: *O. Ficus-indica.*

Opuntia: *O. humifusa.*

ovata Pfeiff. Ct; joints ellipsoid or nearly cylindrical, yellowish-green to purplish, 1½–3 in. long, 1 in. thick, tubercled; spines 5–9, awl-shaped, brown, becoming white, to ½ in. long; fls. brownish to reddish-yellow, to 2 in. long; fr. ovoid, yellow, spiny, ½ in. in diam. Andes, Argentina.

pallida Rose. Cb; shrub, to 3 ft., sts. 2 in. thick; spines 20 or more in old areoles, to 1½ in. long, with white, papery sheaths; fls. pale rose. Mex.

papyracantha: *O. articulata* cv.; but material cult. as *O. papyracantha* is probably *O. articulata* cv. 'Syringacantha'.

Parishii: *O. Stanlyi* var.

Parryi Engelm. Cb; prostrate to shrubby, to 4 ft., joints 3–12 in. long and ¾ in. thick; spines 1–20, brown, unequal, to 1¼ in. long, sheaths loose; fls. yellow, tinged with red; fr. dry, deciduous, spines solitary or few. Spring. Var. **Parryi.** The typical var.; shrubby, tubercles prominent, narrow, to 1 in. long; spines 1–5, to 1¼ in. long. S. Calif. Var. **serpentina** (Engelm.) L. Bens. [*O. serpentina* Engelm.]. Prostrate to ascending, tubercles flattened, to ½ in. long; spines 7–20, to ¾ in. long. S. Calif., n. Baja Calif.

Pentlandii Salm-Dyck [*Tephrocactus Pentlandii* (Salm-Dyck) Backeb.]. Ct; joints obovoid to oblong-cylindrical, 1–2 in. long or more and to 1½ in. thick; spines 0 or 2–10 in the upper areoles, yellow or brownish, cylindrical, to 2½ in. long; fls. yellow to red, to 2 in. across; fr. dry, spineless, 1 in. long. Andes, Peru to Argentina.

phaeacantha Engelm. P; prostrate or sprawling, joints orbicular to obovate, 4–16 in. long, to 9 in. wide and ¾ in. thick; spines 1–10, white, gray, or brown, 1–2½ in. long, glochids ¼–½ in. long; fls. yellow, the bases sometimes red, 2½–3¼ in. across; fr. red, spineless, 1¼ in. long. Spring. Tex. to Calif., n. Mex. Intergrades with *O. humifusa.* Var. **phaeacantha.** The typical var.; joints obovate, to 6 in. long and 4 in. wide, upper ¾ or more spiny; spines 1–9, dark or light brown, to 2½ in. long. Tex. to Ariz. Var. **camanchica** (Engelm. & Bigel.) L. Bens. [*O. camanchica* Engelm. & Bigel.]. Joints orbicular to ovate, to 7 in. long and 5½ in. wide, spiny nearly throughout; spines 5–8, red- or black-brown, flattened, to 2¼ in. long. W. Okla., Tex., New Mex. Var. **discata** (Griffiths) L. Bens. & Walkington. Joints orbicular to elliptic, to 16 in. long and 9 in. wide, spiny nearly throughout; spines 1–4 or sometimes to 10, white or ash-gray, to 3 in. long. Calif. to Tex., n. Mex. Material cult. as *O. Engelmannii* probably belongs here. Var. **laevis** (J. Coult.) L. Bens. [*O. laevis* J. Coult.]. Joints narrowly obovate, to 10 in. long and 6 in. wide; spines 0. Ariz. Var. **major** Engelm. [*O. mojavensis* Engelm. & Bigel.]. Joints obovate or nearly orbicular, to 12 in. long and 8 in. wide, spiny over the upper half or less; spines 1–3, angled, twisted, red-brown, to 2¾ in. long. Calif., e. to Kans. and Tex., n. Mex. Var. **rufispina** (Engelm.) L. Bens. [*O. rutila* Nutt.]. Spines in lower areoles stiff, to 1³⁄₁₆ in. long, spines in upper areoles sometimes reddish-brown, to 2 in. long. Calif. to Tex.

pilifera A. Web. P; treelike, to 18 ft., joints oblong to orbicular, 4–12 in. long, pale; areoles remote, with deciduous white hairs 1 in. long, spines 2–9, white, slender, ½ in. long; fls. red, 2½ in. across; fr. red, to 2 in. long. Mex.

Pollardii: *O. humifusa* var. *austrina.*

polyacantha Haw. P; low and spreading, joints orbicular, 2–4 in. wide; areoles close-set, spines 7–10, cylindrical, mostly deflexed, to ¾ in. long, those at the margin of the joint 1–2 in. long; fls. mostly yellow, 2 in. across; fr. obovoid, dry, spiny, ¾–1 in. long. Summer. Var. **polyacantha** [var. *borealis* J. Coult.]. The typical var.; joints to 4 in. long. N. Dak. to Alta., Wash., Ariz., and Tex. Var. **borealis:** var. *polyacantha.* Var. **Schweriniana** (K. Schum.) Backeb. [*O. Schweriniana* K. Schum.]. Joints 1–2 in. long. Colo.

polycarpa: *O. humifusa* var. *austrina.*

Pottsii: *O. macrorhiza* var.

prolifera Engelm. JUMPING CHOLLA. Cb; erect, 3–8 ft., joints 2–6 in. long, 1–2 in. thick, easily detached, with tubercles ½ in. long and somewhat narrower; spines 5–12, reddish-brown, ½–1 in. long, with yellowish or brown sheaths; fls. rose to purple, 1½ in. across; fr. globose, 1–1½ in. long, proliferous. Spring, summer. Coastal, s. Calif., n. Baja Calif.

pycnantha Engelm. P; creeping or to 4 ft. high, joints oblong to orbicular, 8–10 in. long, puberulent or papillose; areoles large, close-set, spines 8–12, ¼–1 in. long, bright yellow, glochids many, large, yellow; fls. bright yellow; fr. spiny, 1½ in. long. S. Baja Calif. Var. **margaritana** J. Coult. [*O. margaritana* (J. Coult.) Baxter]. Spines and glochids red-brown; fls. cream-yellow, fading maroon. S. Baja Calif. With the sp. and the var. there are said to be forms having 1–2 mostly deflexed spines to 2 in. long besides the shorter ones.

Quimilo K. Schum. P; shrub, to 15 ft., joints elliptic to obovate, 1–20 in. long; areoles remote, spines at first solitary, white, twisted, 3–6 in. long, later sometimes 2–3; fls. red, 3 in. across; fr. pear-shaped to globose, greenish-yellow, 2–3 in. long. N. Argentina.

Rafinesquei: *O. humifusa.*

ramosissima Engelm. PENCIL CACTUS. Cb; woody shrub, joints ¼ in. thick, not succulent after the first year, tubercles low, rhombic or obovate; areole in an apical notch, spines solitary, spreading, 1–2½ in. long, with loose papery sheaths; fls. yellowish-green, ½ in. across; fr. dry, to 1 in. long, densely covered with sheathless spines. Spring, summer. Se. Calif., s. Nev., w. Ariz., n. Mex. Difficult to grow.

repens Bello. P; prostrate or erect, to 2 ft., joints oblong to linear, 2–6 in. long and to 1½ in. wide, glabrous or pubescent, easily detached; areoles with brown wool, white hairs, yellow glochids, spines many, needle-shaped, pinkish, becoming brown, to 1½ in. long; fls. yellow, fading salmon, 1½ in. across; fr. red, 1 in. long. W. Indies.

retrorsa: *O. stenarthra.*

rhodantha: *O. erinacea* var. *utahensis.*

robusta H. L. Wendl. P; erect, to 18 ft., joints orbicular or nearly so, blue-glaucous, to 1 ft. long; areoles remote, spines 8–12, stout, white with brown or yellowish base, to 2 in. long; fls. yellow, 2 in. across, often unisexual; fr. red, 3–3½ in. long. Mex. Cult. forms have fewer and shorter spines.

rosarica G. Lindsay. Cb; spreading, to 3 ft. high, joints 4–8 in. long and 1–2 in. thick, tubercles prominent, ½–1¼ in. long, 5/16 in. wide, more or less confluent into ribs; spines 4–7, the longest reddish-brown, sheathed, to 1½ in. long, glochids many, yellow; fls. yellow with red, 1½ in. across; fr. dry or apparently sometimes proliferous. Baja Calif. Formerly listed as *Grusonia rosarica.* The plant listed as *Opuntia* or *Grusonia Hamiltonii,* from the same vicinity, is perhaps a var., but has lower tubercles and very short spines.

rubescens Salm-Dyck [*Consolea rubescens* (Salm-Dyck) Lem.]. Con; trunk flattened above, to 20 ft., joints oblong or oblong-obovate, to 10 in. long; areoles close-set, spines 0 or several, whitish, to 3 in. long; fls. yellow to red, ¾ in. across; fr. reddish, obovoid to globose, 3 in. in diam., often proliferous. W. Indies. The cult. form practically spineless.

rufida: *O. microdasys* var.

rutila: *O. polyacantha* var *rufispina;* but material cult. as *O. rutila* may not be this sp.

Salmiana Parm. Ca; bushy, to 6 ft., brs. often weak, joints to 10 in. long and about ½ in. thick, not tubercled; spines usually several, white, to ½ in. long; fls. pale yellow to white or pinkish, to 1½ in. across; fr. red, sterile. S. Brazil to n. Argentina. Resembles *O. leptocaulis,* but spines sheathless, fls. larger.

santa-rita: *O. violacea* var.

Scheeri A. Web. P; to 3 ft., joints oblong to orbicular, bluish, 6–12 in. long; areoles with long, white or yellow hairs, spines 10–12, yellow, slender, less than ½ in. long; fls. pale yellow, fading salmon, 4 in. across; fr. globose, red. Mex.

Schickendantzii A. Web. MULE'S-EARS, LION'S-TONGUE. P; shrub, to 6 ft., joints cylindrical or somewhat flattened, to 8 in. long and 1 in. thick, almost tubercled; spines 1–5, to ¾ in. long; fls. yellow, 1½ in. across; fr. green, sterile. N. Argentina.

Schottii Engelm. DEVIL CACTUS. Cc; joints club-shaped, to 3 in. long and ¾ in. thick, easily detached; spines 6–15, slender, brownish or gray, tinged pink or red, sheathed when young, to 2 in. long, glochids white, becoming brown; fls. yellow, 1½ in. across; fr. yellow, 1½ in. long. Var. **Schottii.** The typical var.; spines 6–12, flattened, brownish or yellowish, becoming gray. W. Tex., n. Mex. Var. **Grahamii** (Engelm.) L. Bens. [*O. Grahamii* Engelm.]. Spines 8–15, only slightly flattened, tan or gray, tinged pink or red. W. Tex., New Mex.

Schweriniana: *O. polyacantha* var.

serpentina: *O. Parryi* var.

Soehrensii Britt. & Rose. FAIRY-NEEDLES. P; prostrate, joints orbicular, thin, tubercled, 1½–2½ in. wide; spines several, slender, brown or yellow, to 2 in. long; fls. light yellow, 1 in. long; fr. naked. Highlands, s. Peru to n. Argentina.

sphaerica C. F. Först. THIMBLE T. Ct; often erect, but low, joints globose to obovate, easily detached, ½–2 in. thick, with broad, low tubercles; areoles brown-woolly, spines 10–15, brown, becoming gray, to 3 in. long; fls. orange, 1½ in. long; fr. globose, spiny. Andes, Peru to Chile. Cv. **'Violaciflora'.** Said to have violet fls.

spinosior (Engelm.) Toumey. Cb; shrubby or treelike, to 12 ft., joints 4–12 in. long and 1–1¼ in. thick, with close-set tubercles ⅜–¾ in. long; spines 10–20, gray, to ⅜ in. long, sheaths deciduous the first year; fls. white or red to yellow, 2 in. across; fr. obovoid, tubercled, yellow, 1–1½ in. long. Spring. Ariz., New Mex., n. Mex.

Stanlyi Engelm. Cc; joints 2½–6 in. long and 1½–2 in. thick, tubercles 1–1¾ in. long, ¼–½ in. wide; spines 10–18, brown or reddish, the larger ones rough, flattened, to 2 in. long, sometimes with rudimentary sheaths; fls. yellow, 1–1¼ in. across; fr. yellow, spiny, 2 in. long. Spring. Var. **Stanlyi.** The typical var.; joints 3–6 in. long or more, club-shaped, to 1½ in. thick, tubercles to 1¼ in. long. Ariz., New Mex. Var. **Kunzei** (Rose) L. Bens. [*O. Kunzei* Rose; *O. Wrightiana* (Baxter) Peebles]. Joints 1–1½ in. thick, tubercles ½–1 in. long, confluent into ribs. W. Ariz., se. Calif., n. Mex. Var. **Parishii** (Orcutt) L. Bens. [*O. Parishii* Orcutt]. Joints 2–3 in. long and ¾–1¼ in. thick, woody skeleton poorly developed. S. Nev., nw. Ariz., se. Calif. Var. **Peeblesiana** L. Bens. Joints club-shaped, ⅝–1 in. thick, tubercles ⅝–1 in. long. Ariz., n. Mex.

stenarthra K. Schum. [*O. retrorsa* Speg.]. P; prostrate, joints linear-lanceolate, 3–10 in. long and about 1 in. wide, often purplish below the areoles; spines 0 or 1–3, awl-shaped, whitish, to 1 in. long, glochids red; fls. yellow, 1–2 in. across; fr. ¾ in. long, seeds villous. Paraguay, n. Argentina.

stenopetala Engelm. P; bushy, joints obovate to orbicular, gray-green or purplish, 4–8 in. long; areoles remote, spines 2–4, reddish-brown to black or becoming pale, flattened, to 2 in. long; fls. unisexual, petals awl-shaped, erect, red, ½ in. long; fr. globose, 1¼ in. in diam. Mex.

streptacantha Lem. P; treelike, to 16 ft., joints obovate to orbicular, 10–12 in. long; spines several, white, to 1 in. long, 2 or more bristly and reflexed, glochids reddish-brown, short; fls. yellow to orange, 3–3½ in. across; fr. globose, red or yellow, 2 in. in diam. Mex.

Strigil Engelm. P; bushy, to 1½ ft., joints orbicular to obovate, 4–5 in. long; areoles close-set, spines 5–8, spreading or deflexed, red or reddish-brown, to 1 in. long; fr. subglobose, red, ½ in. in diam. W. Tex.

strobiliformis: *O. articulata* cv. 'Inermis'.

subulata (Mühlenpf.) Engelm. EVE'S-PIN CACTUS. Ca; coarse, branching shrub, to 12 ft., joints to 2 ft. long and 1½–2½ in. thick, tubercles large, depressed, rhomboid, retuse; lvs. persistent, nearly cylindrical, acute, 2–5 in. long; spines 0 or at first mostly 1–2, yellowish, to 3 in. long, glochids few, yellowish; fls. red or reddish, ovary branchlike; fr. leafy, 2–4 in. long, persistent and sometimes proliferous. Probably Argentina. Often grown; recognized by the large persistent lvs.

sulphurea G. Don. P; spreading, to 1 ft. high, joints oblong to obovate, strongly tubercled, green or purplish, 5–10 in. long, easily detached; spines 2–8, stout, straight or twisted, brownish, becoming pale, 1–4 in. long; fls. yellow, 1½ in. across; fr. small. W. Argentina, Chile, possibly Bolivia.

tardispina: *O. Lindheimeri.*

tenuispina: *O. macrorhiza* var. *Pottsii.*

teres J. F. Cels. Ca; to 1 ft., joints ovoid to cylindrical; lvs. more or less persistent, cylindrical, to 1 in. long; areoles with white hairs and glochids, central spines 1–2, gray or brownish, to ¾ in. long; fls. reddish-purple; fr. reddish, proliferous. Andes, Bolivia. *O. vestita* apparently differs in having longer hairs, shorter lvs., and more spines, *O. Verschaffeltii* in having no hairs.

Tesajo Engelm. Cb; to 1½ ft., sts. jointed throughout, the joints 2–3 in. long; spines 0 or 1–2 in upper areoles, 1–2 in. long, with yellowish sheaths; fls. yellow, 1 in. across. Baja Calif.

tetracantha: *O. Kleiniae* var.

tomentosa Salm-Dyck. P; treelike, to 20 ft., trunk smooth, to 1 ft. thick, joints oblong or narrowly obovate, velvety-pubescent, 4–8 in. long; spines 0 or sometimes 1–2, short, white, glochids yellow; fls. orange, 2 in. across; fr. ovoid, red. Mex.

tortispina: *O. macrorhiza.*

Treleasii: *O. basilaris* var.

Tuna (L.) Mill. [*O. humilis* Haw.]. P; to 3 ft., joints obovate to oblong, to 6 in. long but mostly smaller, brownish above the areoles; spines 3–6, light yellow; fls. yellow, tinged red, 2 in. across; fr. red, 1¼ in. long. Jamaica. Since "tuna" is the common Mex. name for the edible fr. of flat-jointed opuntias, the name *O. Tuna* has sometimes been misapplied to various Mex. spp.; its correct application is not entirely certain.

tunicata (Lehm.) Link & Otto. Cb; cespitose or to 2 ft., joints subglobose to oblong, to 10 in. long, 1¼ in. thick, tubercles about ¾ in. long and ½ in. wide; spines 6–10, reddish, to 2 in. long, with white papery sheaths; fls. yellow, 1 3/16 in. across; fr. tubercled, 1¼ in. long. Var. **tunicata.** The typical var.; joints easily detached, not woody, to 10 in. long; spines to 2 in. long. Tex., Mex., Ecuador to n. Chile. Var. **Davisii** (Engelm. & Bigel.) L. Bens [*O. Davisii* Engelm. & Bigel.]. Joints not easily detached, woody, to 6 in. long; spines about 1½ in. long. W. Okla., w. Tex., e. New Mex.

Turpinii: *O. articulata* cv. 'Syringacantha'.

ursina: *O. erinacea* var.

Vaseyi: *O. littoralis* var.

velutina A. Web. VELVET O. P; erect, to 14 ft., joints oblong to obovate, 6–8 in. long, pubescent; spines 2–6, yellow, becoming white, unequal, to 1½ in. long, bristles many, yellow, becoming brownish; fls. yellow, 2 in. across, petals retuse; fr. red, pubescent, with close-set areoles. S. Mex.

Verschaffeltii J. F. Cels. Ca; low-growing, joints in the wild globose, 1½ in. long, in cult. cylindrical, to 8 in. long and ½ in. thick, somewhat tubercled; lvs. persistent, cylindrical, to 1¼ in. long; spines 1–3, slender, whitish, to 2½ in. long, in cult. often absent, glochids small, yellow; fls. red, 1½ in. across. N. Bolivia.

versicolor Engelm. Cb.; treelike, 3–12 ft., joints 4–12 in. long and ⅝–1 in. thick, tubercles ¾ in. long and ¼ in. wide; spines 5–10, gray or purplish, ¼–⅝ in. long, sheaths white or yellowish, shed the first year; fls. yellow, green, red, or brown, but commonly orange, 1½ in. across; fr. fleshy, 1–1½ in. long, somewhat proliferous. Spring. S. Ariz., nw. Mex.

vestita Salm-Dyck [*Austrocylindropuntia vestita* (Salm-Dyck) Backeb.]. OLD-MAN O., COTTON-POLE CACTUS. Ca; cespitose, joints in the wild globose, in cult. elongate, to 8 in. long or more and 1 in. thick; lvs. awl-shaped, to ⅝ in. long, persistent; areoles with long, white hairs almost covering the sts., spines 4–8, to ¾ in. long; fls. red, 1½ in. across; fr. red, woolly. Bolivia.

vilis Rose. LITTLE TREE O., MEXICAN DWARF TREE CACTUS. Cc; ultimate joints club-shaped, to 2 in. long, tubercles low; radial spines 12 or more, central spines 3–4, white or reddish, cylindrical or somewhat flattened, to 1½ in. long; fls. purple, 1½ in. across; fr. pale green, to 1 in. in diam., with few white bristles. Mex.

violacea Engelm. P; shrubby or treelike, to 7 ft., joints obovate to orbicular, green, tinged with reddish-purple, to 8 in. long and wide; spines 0 or 1–3 in each areole and on upper part or margin of joint, to 7 in long; fls. yellow, red at base inside, to 3½ in. across; fr. red or purplish-red, smooth, to 1½ in. long, ¾ in. in diam. Var. **violacea.** The typical var.; joints obovate, to 6 in. long, spiny near upper margin; spines 1–3, dark reddish-brown, to 2½ in. long. Sw. New Mex., se. Ariz. Var. **Gosseliniana** (A. Web.) L. Bens. [*O. Gosseliniana* A. Web.]. Joints orbicular or broadly obovate, to 7 in. long, spiny on upper margin and flat sides; spines 1–2, light reddish-brown to pink or partly yellow, to 2½ in. long. Se. Ariz., n. Mex. Var. **macrocentra** (Engelm.) L. Bens. [*O. macrocentra* Engelm.]. Joints obovate, to 7 in. long, spiny on upper margin and below; spines 1–2, nearly black, to 7 in. long. W. Tex. to Ariz., n. Mex. Var. **santa-rita** (Griffiths & Hare) L. Bens. [*O. santa-rita* Griffiths & Hare]. BLUE-BLADE, DOLLAR CACTUS. Joints orbicular, to 8 in. long, spineless or with 2–4 spines on upper margin; spine 1, reddish-brown to pink, to 2½ in. long. Tex. to Ariz.

vivipara: *O. arbuscula.*

vulgaris Mill. [*O. monacantha* (Willd.) Haw.]. PRICKLY PEAR, BARBARY FIG, IRISH-MITTENS. P; shrub or treelike, to 20 ft., trunk to 6 in. thick, joints obovate to oblong, to 1 ft. long, glossy green, rather thin; spines at first 1–2, later more, yellowish-brown to reddish, to 1½ in. long; fls. yellow or reddish, 3 in. across; fr. pear-shaped, red, spineless, 2–3 in. long, sometimes proliferous. Brazil to n. Argentina. Frequently grown. Once widely planted as a host for cochineal insects, and now naturalized in many trop. and subtrop. lands. The name is often misapplied to *O. humifusa.* Cv. **'Variegata'.** JOSEPH'S-COAT CACTUS. Some joints green, some yellow or white, some mottled.

Whipplei Engelm. & Bigel. Cb; low or shrubby, joints 2–12 in. long, ½–¾ in. thick, tubercles ⅜ in. long; spines 4–12, to ¾ in. long, sheaths persistent, straw-colored or silvery; fls. pale yellow, to 1 in. across; fr. subglobose, fleshy, yellow, to 1¼ in. long. Summer. S. Utah, w. Colo., New Mex., Ariz.

Wrightiana: *O. Stanlyi* var. *Kunzei.*

ORBIGNYA Mart. ex Endl. *Palmae.* About 25 spp. of unarmed, monoecious palms native to Cent. and S. Amer.; sts. not emergent or often very tall and stout; lvs. large, ascending-erect on young plants, pinnate, pinnae many, acute, midrib prominent; infls. among lvs., often pendulous in fr., of 2 kinds on same tree, male only or female with usually a few male fls. on each rachilla, peduncles long, bracts 2, the upper fusiform in bud, woody, often beaked, deeply sulcate externally, rachillae simple; male fls. spirally arranged or in 2 rows along rachillae, sepals small, petals much wider than thick, stamens 12–24, anthers spirally coiled, female fls. with sepals and petals imbricate, pistil 3–7-celled, stigmas 3–7; fr. usually beaked, 1- to several-seeded, mesocarp fleshy-fibrous, endocarp very thick, with 3–7 pores near base, seed with homogeneous endosperm. The spp. are poorly understood.

Slow-growing, often very large palms requiring many years to produce an emergent trunk. They yield useful palm kernel oil making them commercially important where native. Cultivated for ornament or interest in the tropics and subtropics. Most species hardy in the warmer parts of Zone 9b in Fla. For culture see *Palms.*

Barbosiana Burret [*O. speciosa* (Mart.) Barb.-Rodr., not *O. speciosa* Barb.-Rodr.]. BABASSÚ. To 60 ft. or more; lvs. many, pinnae many, regularly arranged; infl. elongate; male fls. in 2 rows on rachillae, stamens 24; fr. to 4½ in. long, 1–3-seeded. Brazil. A source of babassu oil.

Cohune (Mart.) Dahlgr. ex Standl. [*Attalea Cohune* Mart.; *O. speciosa* Barb.-Rodr.]. COHUNE PALM. To 45 ft., trunk to 1 ft. in diam. or more; lvs. many, plumelike, to 30 ft. long or more, with many regularly arranged pinnae; infl. to 4½ ft. long or more; male fls. spirally arranged on rachillae, cream-colored, petals oblanceolate, ⅝ in. long, to nearly ⅜ in. wide; fr. to about 3 in. long, 2 in. in diam., 1–3-seeded. Cent. Amer. Source of cohune oil.

Guacuyule (Liebm.) Hernández Xoloc. Similar to *O. Cohune,* but having male fls. with petals spatulate, ½ in. long, $^3/_{16}$ in. wide, and fr. to 2¾ in. long, 1⅝ in. in diam. W. Mex.

speciosa: a name used in two senses, the earlier (1891) being synonymous with *O. Cohune,* the later (1903) with *O. Barbosiana.*

spectabilis (Mart.) Burret. Trunk short or none; lvs. erect, petiole short, pinnae linear-acuminate, regularly arranged; fr. ellipsoid or obovoid, 2 in. long, 1¼ in. in diam., 2–3-seeded. Brazil.

ORCHIDACEAE Juss. ORCHID FAMILY. Monocot.; variously estimated at 600–800 genera and 17,000–30,000 spp. of per. herbs of nearly worldwide distribution, especially abundant in the tropics but absent from desert regions; terrestrial or epiphytic, sometimes vines, occasionally saprophytic and without chlorophyll, often rhizomatous, roots of terrestrial spp. fibrous or cordlike to tuberous, those of epiphytic spp. usually cordlike and with a spongy water-absorbing exterior layer (velamen), sts. leafy or scapose, elongating indefinitely from terminal bud (i.e., growth monopodial) or of definite, limited terminal growth but with growth continued by axillary shoots (i.e., growth sympodial), often more or less swollen or thickened and forming a pseudobulb of 1 to many internodes; lvs. usually alt., rarely opp. or whorled, simple, often 2-ranked (distichous) and then sometimes closely overlapping (imbricate), occasionally reduced to bracts, of various shapes, linear, strap-shaped, elliptic, to orbicular, membranous and pleated (plicate) to leathery or fleshy and then usually folded or channelled lengthwise (conduplicate), the base sheathing the st.; infl. apical or axillary and then lateral or basal, spicate, racemose, or paniculate, or fl. sometimes solitary; fls. very small and inconspicuous to large and showy, bisexual or unisexual (the plants then monoecious or dioecious), irregular, pedicelled or sessile (ovary often slender and pedicel-like), pedicel or ovary usually twisted 180° so that the originally upper side of fl. is lowermost, the fls. then resupinate, sepals 3, usually narrow, often colored and petal-like, all alike or the middle one (i.e., the upper or dorsal one in resupinate fls.) larger and differently colored, separate or all 3 or only the lateral 2 more or less united, petals 3, lateral ones alike, variously shaped, the middle one (the lip or labellum —i.e., the lowermost one in resupinate fls.) usually different and much-modified in size, shape, and color, usually 3-lobed, sometimes extended at base into a spur or sac, stamens, style, and stigmas united in various degrees into a single structure (column, gynandrium, or gynostegium), in most genera only 1 anther fertile and terminal on column above stigmas, in a few genera the fertile anthers 2 (rarely 3) and lateral on column just below stigmas, pollen sometimes of separate grains or merely joined in groups of 4 (tetrads), but most frequently more or less united into 2–8 soft to waxy or bony masses (pollinia) in an anther, stigmas 2 or 3, on front of column, ovary inferior, 3-carpelled, 3-celled and with axile placentation in a few genera, but mostly 1-celled and with parietal placentation, ovules numerous; fr. a caps., opening by 3–6 lateral valves remaining united at base and apex, seeds numerous, minute, without endosperm.

Generally conceded to be the largest family of flowering plants in terms of number of spp. There is great diversity in habitat, habit, and details of morphology, with many exceptions to the general characterization of the family given above. All spp. of the arctic and most spp. of temp. regions are terrestrial, but the majority of those of the tropics are epiphytic or lithophytic (growing on rocks); a few completely subterranean spp. are known. At least one sp., *Zeuxine strateumatica* (L.) Schlechter, is known to be an ann. Members of the subfamily *Apostasioideae* (see below), rarely found in cult., are believed to be the most primitive orchids and depart in important details from the generalized description of the floral morphology of the family already given.

Except for a few self-pollinating spp., orchids are

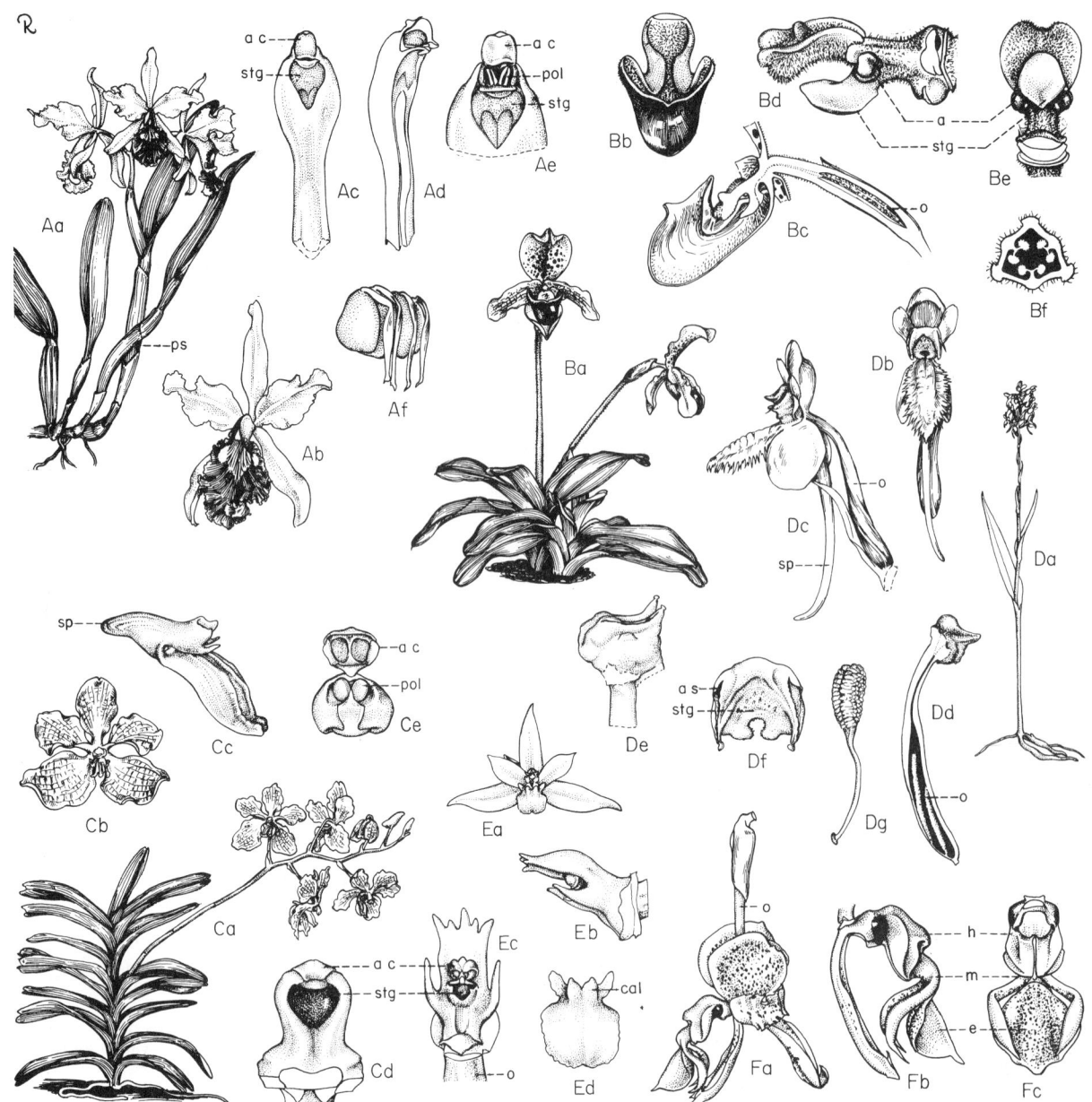

ORCHIDACEAE. **A,** *Cattleya Warscewiczii:* **Aa,** plant, × ¹/₁₂; **Ab,** flower, × ¹/₆; **Ac,** column, face view, × ½; **Ad,** column, vertical section, × ½; **Ae,** apex of column with anther cap lifted, × 1½; **Af,** pollinia, greatly enlarged. **B,** *Paphiopedilum insigne:* **Ba,** plant, × ¹/₆; **Bb,** lip, × ½; **Bc,** flower, longitudinal section (perianth cut off, excepting lip), × ½; **Bd,** column, side view, × 1½; **Be,** column, face view, × 1; **Bf,** ovary, cross section, × 1½. **C,** *Vanda coerulea:* **Ca,** plant, × ¹/₈; **Cb,** flower, × ¼; **Cc,** lip, × 1; **Cd,** column, face view, × 2; **Ce,** anther with anther cap lifted, × 2. **D,** *Habenaria blephariglottis:* **Da,** plant, × ¹/₆; **Db,** flower, face view, × 1½; **Dc,** flower, side view, × 1½; **Dd,** column and ovary, vertical section, × 2; **De,** column and apex of ovary, side view, × 4; **Df,** column, face view, × 4; **Dg,** pollen mass, × 8. **E,** *Dendrochilum glumaceum:* **Ea,** flower, × 2; **Eb,** column, side view, × 10; **Ec,** column and apex of ovary, face view, × 10; **Ed,** lip, × 6. **F,** *Stanhopea Wardii:* **Fa,** pendent flower, × ¹/₃; **Fb,** column (left) and lip, side view, × ½; **Fc,** lip, face view, × ½. (a anther, a c anther cap, a s anther sac, cal callus, e epichil, h hypochil, m mesochil, o ovary, pol pollinia, ps pseudobulb, sp spur, stg stigma.)

obligatorily insect- or humming-bird-pollinated. The lip and column are sometimes complex and variously elaborated as an adaptation ensuring cross-pollination, often by a particular sp. of insect. The attractant may be nectar or the succulent tissue of the lip or column or, as in *Ophrys,* the lip may even mimic the female of certain insect spp. and thus lure the males to it. In some genera the lip is longitudinally differentiated into 2 or 3 distinct and usually more or less modified segms., a basal (hypochil), an apical (epichil), and sometimes a middle (mesochil) segm. The upper surface of the midlobe of the lip (the disc) frequently bears fleshy calluses, papillae,

keels, or ridges, various in number, size, form, and color, and the margins may be entire, lobed, toothed, fringed, or diversely appendaged. The base of the lip may end in a sac or spur, from very short to a ft. long. The column may be short and stout or relatively long and slender, the sides sometimes winged, lobed, or toothed. In some genera, it has a basal forward extension (column foot) that is sometimes united with the bases of the lip and lateral sepals to form a chinlike projection (mentum). In many 1-anthered orchids there is a flaplike or beaklike tissue (rostellum) of diagnostic importance that separates the stigmas from the anther; part of this may form a sticky organ (viscidium) to which the pollinia may be attached and with which they adhere to the bodies of visiting pollinators. The seeds are dustlike, very small, and exceedingly numerous, as many as 4 million in a caps. in some instances. There is no endosperm and the embryo is undifferentiated. Development after germination depends, in nature, on infection of the roots by a mycorrhizal fungus and the subsequent symbiotic relationship.

The orchid family is divided taxonomically into subfamilies, tribes, and subtribes. The five subfamilies generally accepted today are listed below, with their characterization.

Apostasioideae Wettst. Perianth nearly regular, lip shallow, fertile anthers 2 or 3, elongate, filaments incompletely to almost entirely united with style but stigmas and terminal part of style separate from filaments, pollen dry, of separate grains, stigmas 3, rostellum absent, ovary 3-celled, with axile placentation. The most primitive of the orchids. Two genera: *Apostasia* Blume, *Neuwiedia* Blume; not in general cult.

Cypripedioideae Garay [*Diandrae* Kunth]. Perianth irregular, lip deeply saccate (slipper-shaped), fertile anthers 2, nearly globose, at either side of and slightly below the stigmas, staminode large, flattened, terminal, filaments and style completely united, pollen grains sticky, in tetrads, but not united into pollinia, stigmas 3, terminal on column, rostellum absent, ovary either 3-celled and with axile placentation or 1-celled and with parietal placentation. Four genera: *Cypripedium, Paphiopedilum, Phragmipedium, Selenipedium* Rchb.f.; the last not in general cult.

Neottioideae Garay [*Monandrae* Kunth, in part]. Perianth irregular, lip variously but well differentiated, fertile anther 1, filaments, style, and stigmas united into a short column, stigmas 2 or 3, separate or confluent, rostellum absent, pollen grains coherent into soft, powdery pollinia, ovary usually 1-celled and with parietal placentation, but in a few genera 3-celled and with axile placentation. Many genera.

Orchidoideae [*Ophrydoideae* Garay; *Monandrae* Kunth, in part]. Perianth irregular, lip variously but well differentiated, filaments, style, and stigmas united into a cylindrical column, fertile anthers 1, rarely 2, pollen grains united in small masses further coherent into soft pollinia, stigmas 2 or 3, confluent, rostellum absent, ovary 1-celled, with parietal placentation. Many genera.

Epidendroideae Dressl. [*Kerosphaeroideae* Garay; *Monandrae* Kunth, in part]. Perianth irregular, lip variously but well differentiated, fertile anther 1, filaments, style, and stigmas united into a column, pollen grains united into hard, compact, waxy or bony pollinia, stigmas 2, confluent, rostellum always present, ovary 1-celled, with parietal placentation. Many genera.

The cult. genera and hybrid genera include: *Acineta, Ada, Aerides,* × *Aeridovanda, Amblostoma, Angraecum, Anguloa, Anoectochilus, Anota, Ansellia, Anthogonium, Aplectrum, Arachnis, Arethusa, Arpophyllum, Arundina, Ascocentrum, Ascotainia, Aspasia, Batemannia, Bifrenaria, Bletia, Bletilla, Bollea, Bothriochilus, Brassavola, Brassia,* × *Brassocattleya,* × *Brassolaelia,* × *Brassolaeliocattleya, Broughtonia, Bulbophyllum, Calanthe, Calopogon, Calypso, Catasetum, Cattleya, Caularthron,* × *Caulocattleya, Cephalanthera, Chloraea, Chysis, Cleistes, Cochleanthes, Cochlioda, Coelia, Coelogyne, Comparettia, Corallorhiza, Coryanthes, Cychnoches, Cymbidium, Cypripedium, Cyrtopodium, Dendrobium, Dendrochilum, Dendrophylax, Disa,* × *Doritaenopsis, Doritis,* × *Epicattleya, Epidendrum, Epigenium, Epipactis,* × *Epiphronitis, Eria, Eriopsis, Erythrodes, Eulophia, Eulophidium, Galeandra, Galeola, Gomesia, Gongora, Goodyera, Grammatophyllum, Graphorkis, Habenaria, Haemaria, Hexisea, Houlletia, Huntleya, Ionopsis, Isochilus, Isotria, Jacquiniella, Laelia,* × *Laeliocattleya, Laeliopsis, Leptotes, Liparis, Lissochilus, Listera, Lockhartia, Lycaste, Macodes, Macradenia,* × *Macrangraecum, Macroplectrum, Malaxis, Masdevallia, Maxillaria, Mendoncella, Miltonia,* × *Miltonidium, Mormodes, Mormolyca,*

Mystacidium, Nageliella, Neobenthamia, Neocogniauxia, Neofinetia, Neomoorea, Notylia, Octomeria, × *Odontioda,* × *Odontobrassia,* × *Odontocidium, Odontoglossum,* × *Odontonia,* × *Oncidasia,* × *Oncidioda, Oncidium, Ophrys, Orchis, Ornithochilus, Paphinia, Paphiopedilum, Paraphalaenopsis, Pecteilis, Peristeria, Pescatorea, Phaius, Phalaenopsis, Pholidota, Physosiphon, Phragmipedium, Pleione, Pleurothallis, Pogonia, Polyradicion, Polystachya,* × *Potinara, Promenaea, Renanthera, Restrepia, Restrepiella, Rhynchostylis, Rodriguezia, Saccolabium, Sarcanthus, Sarchochilus, Scaphyglottis, Schomburgkia, Scuticaria, Sigmatostalix, Sobralia,* × *Sophrocattleya,* × *Sophrolaeliocattleya, Sophronitis, Spathoglottis, Spiranthes, Stanhopea, Stelis, Stenoglottis, Tainiopsis, Tetramicra, Thrixspermum, Thunia, Tipularia, Trichocentrum, Trichoglottis, Trichopilia, Trigonidium, Trizeuxis, Vanda, Vandopsis, Vanilla, Warrea, Xylobium,* × *Zygopabstia, Zygopetalum,* and *Zygosepalum.*

The hardy, terrestrial, temperate-region orchids are grown outdoors in the woodland, bog, wild garden, or shaded rock garden. The many species, varieties, and hybrids of terrestrial and epiphytic orchids of the tropics and subtropics are, in colder regions, grown in glasshouses or sometimes as houseplants, but in frost-free regions are grown in lath-houses or planted out in the ground or on trees. (For culture see *Orchids.*) They are largely collector's or specialist's plants, and many kinds with small, inconspicuous flowers are cultivated for the interesting structure of their flowers or just because they are orchids. The family is remarkable for the number of fertile interspecific and intergeneric hybrids that have been created by growers, some involving as many as four or more genera generally accepted as distinct. A number of genera with large, showy flowers, especially *Cattleya, Cymbidium, Paphiopedilum, Phalaenopsis,* and *Odontoglossum,* furnish cut flowers to the florist trade; the commercial production of orchid plants for the hobbyist and for their cut flowers is a specialized division of the horticultural industry. Species of *Vanilla* are grown commercially in the tropics for their immature capsules, which are the source of the flavoring vanilla.

There are many societies and journals around the world devoted to orchids and their culture; the American Orchid Society publishes its Bulletin for members, and this is one source of further information on the family.

ORCHIDANTHA N. E. Br. *Lowiaceae.* Four to 5 spp. of low Asiatic per. herbs; lvs. in 2 ranks; fls. solitary or paired in a bracted infl. from the crown, calyx irregular, tubular, 3-lobed, corolla 3-lobed, 2 lobes small and 1 (the lip) large, stamens 5, grouped on 1 side.

maxillarioides (Ridl.) K. Schum. To 16 in.; lvs. long-petioled, oblong, to 9 in. long, $3\frac{9}{16}$ in. wide; infl. a panicle with 2–3 brs.; calyx lobes to $1\frac{3}{8}$ in. long, violet-purple, tipped with green, lip to $\frac{3}{4}$ in. long, green, variegated with purple. Malacca.

ORCHIDS. Orchids are members of the very large family Orchidaceae (see *Orchidaceae*). Many genera are grown by fanciers and producers of commercial plants, a number by florists for cut flowers, and some others as garden plants or in the home; many artificial hybrids have been produced, often between genera. Any number of genera and hybrid genera are to be found in the special collections of fanciers, but those most generally cultivated or known within the scope of this book may be found listed under *Orchidaceae*.

The native terrestrial orchids of the continental United States and Canada are many. They usually inhabit cool bogs, though they are also represented on sandy plains and in moist grasslands, but invariably the soils and habitats are specialized. Many of them are not showy, such as most members of the genera *Aplectrum, Epipactis, Goodyera, Liparis, Listera, Malaxis, Spiranthes,* and *Tipularia;* others have showy or very prominent flowers, as in *Arethusa, Calopogon, Calypso, Cypripedium, Habenaria,* and *Orchis,* and *Pogonia.* These orchids are sometimes transferred to grounds and some of them are offered by dealers in native plants. In nature the native orchids live symbiotically with specific fungi under highly specialized soil conditions, and this combination of factors makes it almost impossible for most gardeners to grow these plants from seed and difficult also to maintain them as mature transplanted specimens. Unfortunately, many species are now becoming rare because of the destruction of their natural habitats. In most cases it is better to leave these plants to live where they are native and protected than to move them to gardens under conditions where they may not thrive or increase. If they are to be grown, one must learn the exact conditions required for success in culture and then reproduce those conditions before moving in any plants.

The commercial orchids of house culture are of tropical origin, although many come from high elevations. Most of them are epiphytes of the tree tops, but a few are terrestrial. These orchids are principally of the genera *Brassavola, Calanthe, Cattleya, Coelogyne, Cymbidium, Dendrobium, Epidendrum, Laelia, Lycaste, Miltonia, Odontoglossum, Oncidium, Paphiopedilum, Phalaenopsis,* and *Vanda.* One undertaking the culture of these and other exotic orchids should become familiar with the rather exacting conditions of moisture, temperature, shade, and sunlight that the various species and hybrids require for successful culture.

Most orchids are not difficult to grow, even in the house, but their culture requires close observation and adaptability on the part of the grower. The niceties of orchid culture are the result of much devotion to the subject. A difference of two or three degrees in temperature, a change in humidity, or a slight variation in watering or shading may make the difference between success and failure. The resting period of the different kinds must be carefully understood and adjusted. In the greenhouse, nearness to the glass or remoteness from it are important. If one is growing the usual run of commonly cultivated orchids, a whole greenhouse may be devoted to them, but if a wide assortment of fancier's species is to be grown, the home greenhouse will need three separate compartments, each with different temperature and moisture conditions. For the warmest species, the winter temperature should not go below 65–70° F at night and the day temperature should be near 80°; in such conditions a starter collection might include species such as *Angraecum distichum, Cattleya luteola, C. violacea, Epidendrum atropurpureum, E. phoeniceum,* most species and hybrids of *Phalaenopsis,* and *Paphiopedilum × Harrisianum, P. × Maudiae,* and *P. venustum;* later one might add representative kinds of *Aerides, Calanthe, Dendrobium,* and *Vanda.* For an intermediate greenhouse where the night temperature is about 60° F, rising to 70–75° F in daytime, recommended orchids include *Catasetum saccatum, Cattleya Forbesii, C. Mossiae, Calanthe vestita* and its hybrids, *Epidendrum cochleatum, E. tampense, Laelia pumila, Leptotes bicolor, Maxillaria tenuifolia, M. sanguinea, Nageliella purpurea, Oncidium* 'Java'. For the cool greenhouse compartment, where temperatures at night range 50–55° F and in the day 65–70° F, one can try *Dendrobium nobile, D. Kingianum,* species of *Epidendrum,* cultivars of *Odontoglossum, O. pulchellum, Paphiopedilum insigne,* and *P. × nitens.* The orchid greenhouse should be moist but well ventilated, and in hot weather the roof may be sprayed outside with cold water; shading in summer is also necessary, both to protect the plants and to reduce the temperature.

Some orchids may be grown successfully in the house, either under artificial light or in normal daylight in a bright window, where, for most, an abundance of morning and late afternoon sun will produce good growth, though the tropical Old World lady's-slipper orchids *(Paphiopedilum)* prefer the light of a north window. Orchids require less routine maintenance than many common house plants, but watering is the most important concern. The commonest cause of failure with orchids is over-watering. Among orchid taxa that have proved amenable to home culture are *Brassavola nodosa, Cattleya Gaskelliana, C. labiata, C. Mossiae, C. Percivaliana, C. Trianaei, Cycnoches ventricosum* var. *chlorochilon, Dendrobium nobile,* species of *Epidendrum, Laelia anceps, L. autumnalis, L. rubescens, Odontoglossum grande, Oncidium cheirophorum, O. ornithorhynchum, O. papilio,* and *O. splendidum;* the genera *Catasetum, Lockhartia, Maxillaria, Miltonia,* and *Phalaenopsis* also yield species amenable to culture in the home.

The two cultural groups of tropical orchids are the terrestrials and the epiphytes, although these divisions are not absolute; some growers make one cultural group the deciduous kinds and another the evergreen. As classes, the terrestrials and epiphytes do not differ in temperature and moisture requirements, but the terrestrials are grown in pots of soil and the epiphytes in pots with special mixes, though often also on cork or other bark, blocks made of tree-fern trunk, or in baskets.

In general, terrestrial orchids thrive in a rich soil composed of about one-half fibrous loam to which is added approximately equal parts of leaf mold and sharp sand. Some growers make a mixture of one-third good chopped sod with part of the fine silty soil removed, one-third live chopped sphagnum, and one-third leaf mold; ground bone may be added for vigorous plants. The purpose is to provide a medium containing sufficient plant food and, though thoroughly well drained and aerated, yet retaining the necessary constant moisture that these plants prefer.

The epiphytic orchids require a well-ventilated mix of fibrous or peaty material in which to grow. Long-lasting osmunda fiber, obtained from the rhizomes of wild ferns, particularly species of the genus *Osmunda,* has long been a favorite potting medium for orchids, for it holds moisture well and is at the same time well aerated. Other materials used are shredded fir bark, peat moss, or leaf mold. Mixes of several substances are often used and some of the newer ones combine fir bark with redwood fiber, peat, and perlite. Potting media eventually deteriorate, and for this reason orchids are often repotted every two years, usually in spring or early summer so as to give plants a good chance to become reestablished while humidity is high.

Orchids are propagated by seeds (usually in aseptic flasks by the Knudson method), or vegetatively by separation of offsets (as in *Dendrobium*), by division, by cuttings, or by the production of mericlones by the new technique of apical meristem culture (meristemming). Seeds and meristem culture require very special techniques demanding aseptic conditions similar to those used in the laboratory culture of bacteria. Such culture is suited primarily for commercial orchid production. Details of seed and meristem culture should be sought in the numerous special publications on orchid culture. Established seedlings are often offered by commercial orchidists to orchid hobbyists to grow on, first in a community pot or flat. Again, cultural techniques are best sought out in special orchid publications. The home grower of orchids, who seldom needs more than a few propagations, will probably find the time-tried process of simple vegetative division best suited to his needs, especially since it assures the reproduction of genetically identical plants.

Vegetative propagation by division differs slightly depending upon which type of growth habit is exhibited by the plant to be divided. Well-established plants of terrestrial orchids, such as species of *Paphiopedilum,* may be divided just before active growth begins. Epiphytic orchids usually show either so-called sympodial or monopodial growth. In the former type, the axis of the plant is horizontal, with new growth coming from the development of lateral buds produced from the bases of the pseudobulbs of the parent plant; in the latter type, the axis of the plant is vertical, the main growing tip extending upward and producing leaves in a two-ranked (distichous) arrangement. Sympodial orchids are mostly species of the New World and dominate the family, the familiar *Cattleya, Coelogyne,* and *Odontoglossum* being examples. The rhizomes of such pseudobulbous genera, when well grown, regularly develop one or more new pseudobulbs each season. Eventually the plant overgrows its pot and requires dividing and repotting. The rhizome bearing the older pseudobulbs (backbulbs) may then be partially severed and allowed to remain until new growth begins on it, or the rhizome may be completely severed and potted at once. In the case of *Cattleya* and similar orchids, each new plant should have at least three pseudobulbs, though with other orchids, for example *Cymbidium,* a single back bulb separated off and potted up is usually adequate.

Growth of monopodial, nonpseudobulbous orchids is typified by the genus *Vanda.* As such orchids grow upward, they develop side shoots, which are also upward-growing. Both main and lateral shoots are supported by whitish adventitious prop roots. Once lateral shoots with roots have developed, they may be cut off with a sharp knife as stem cuttings and potted up. Other shoots are likely to arise near such cuts and these can also be used as propagations.

The American Orchid Society, with its many local affiliated societies, is the major promoter of information on orchids and their culture in this country.

ORCHIS L. [*Galeorchis* Rydb.]. *Orchidaceae.* About 50 spp. of terrestrial herbs with tuberous roots or rhizomes, native to N. Amer. and Eurasia; sts. leafy; lvs. 1 or more; fls. few to many in a congested or loose raceme, sepals separate, spreading, nearly equal, petals similar but smaller, meeting with upper sepal to form a hood over the column, lip simple or more or less 3-lobed, united with lower part of column, extended at base into a prominent spur, column short. For structure of fl. see *Orchidaceae.*

Sometimes planted in moist situations in the wild garden. For culture see *Orchids.*

militaris L. SOLDIER ORCHID. Sts. to 16 in. high, light green, tinged with violet; lvs. basal, oblong-lanceolate, without spots; racemes densely or loosely many-fld.; fls. large, rose or pale red-violet, fragrant, sepals elliptic-lanceolate, pale ashen-gray with rose or violet suffusion, petals linear, lip longer than sepals, rose, nearly white in center, with scattered tufts of red-violet hairs, 3-lobed, lobes filiform, bright rose or red-violet, spur saclike, half as long as ovary. Late spring. Eur.

morio L. SALEP ORCHID, GANDERGOOSE, GREEN-WINGED ORCHID. Sts. to 1 ft. high; lvs. basal, lanceolate, bluish-green, upper lvs. often purplish; racemes loosely 6–12-fld., bracts conspicuous, green or purple; fls. red-purple or blue-purple to mauve, rarely white, sepals veined with green, center of lip paler and spotted, sepals forming a globular helmet, petals linear-oblong, forming an interior hood beneath helmet, lip 3-lobed, midlobe toothed or crenate on margins, densely covered with minute papillae, spur shorter than ovary, densely covered inside with minute papillae, column purplish. Late spring. Gr. Brit. and Eur., Asia Minor, Siberia.

pallens L. Sts. to 10 in. high; lvs. basal; racemes loosely 12–20-fld.; fls. to ½ in. across, pure yellow, lip 3-lobed, midlobe lobed, spur saclike, longer than lip. Eur.

rotundifolia Banks ex Pursh. SMALL ROUND-LEAVED O., SPOTTED KIRTLE PINK. Stoloniferous, sts. to about 1 ft.; racemes naked, to 8 in. long, with a basal elliptic lf. to 4 in. long, loosely 1–16-fld.; fls. showy, sepals white to mauve-pink, squarish-elliptic, to ⅜ in. long, lateral sepals longer than the upper, petals ovate-oblong, pale white to mauve, lip white, spotted with magenta or purple, 3-lobed, ovate in outline, to ⅜ in. long, spur to ¼ in. long. Spring–summer. Canada to s. U.S.

spectabilis L. [*Galeorchis spectabilis* (L.) Rydb.]. SHOWY ORCHID, WOODLAND O., PURPLE-HOODED O., KIRTLE PINK. Sts. to 10 in. high, naked, 4–5-angled; lvs. basal, oblong-ovate, to 6 in. long; racemes to 4 in. long, loosely 2–15-fld.; fls. showy, gaping, sepals and petals pink to mauve, rarely white, sepals elliptic, ¾ in. long, petals linear-oblong, to ½ in. long, lip white, entire, orbicular-ovate, to ¾ in. long, crenate on margin, spur conspicuous, slender. N. Amer.

OREOCALLIS R. Br. *Proteaceae.* Five spp. of evergreen trees or shrubs, native to S. Amer., Australia, and Malay Arch.; lvs. alt., simple or pinnate; fls. bisexual, pedicelled, paired in solitary or clustered racemes, perianth tube cylindrical, limb 4-lobed, anthers sessile, ovary stalked; fr. a 1-celled follicle, seeds many, winged.

pinnata (Maiden & Betche) Sleum. [*Embothrium Wickhamii* W. Hill & F. J. Muell. var. *pinnata* Maiden & Betche]. Lvs. 9–18 in. long, pinnate, lfts. 7–9; fls. red, in terminal corymbs. Queensland and New S. Wales.

OREOCEREUS: *BORZICACTUS.* **O. neocelsianus:** *B. Celsianus.*

OREOCHARIS Benth. *Gesneriaceae.* Not cult. **Oreocharis primuloides:** *Opithandra primuloides.*

OREODOXA: see *ROYSTONEA.*

OREOPANAX Decne. & Planch. *Araliaceae.* About 80 spp. of polygamodioecious, glabrous or hairy shrubs or trees, widespread in trop. Amer.; lvs. simple, unlobed to palmately lobed or compound, entire or toothed; fls. in small heads arranged in panicles or racemes, petals (4–)5(–7), valvate, stamens as many as the petals, ovary 3–5-celled, rarely more, styles separate or united; fr. a drupe, pyrenes 3 or more.

Hardier species grown outdoors in Zone 10 and indoors in their juvenile form, which frequently may be scandent and epiphytic. Propagated by cuttings and seeds.

capitatus (Jacq.) Decne. & Planch. Tall tree, but may be grown as a shrub or juvenile epiphyte; lvs. simple, entire, ovate to elliptic, variable in length but mostly about 5 in. long, long-petioled; infl. large, paniculate, puberulent. Trop. Amer.

peltatus Linden ex Regel. [*O. Salvinii* Hemsl.]. Slender tree, to 40 ft.; lvs. mostly 7-lobed, suborbicular, to 20 in. wide, truncate to deeply cordate or sometimes peltate, at maturity glabrous above, densely tomentose beneath, thin-leathery; fls. greenish-white, in a terminal panicle. Mex.

Salvinii: *O. peltatus.*

Thibautii: *O. xalapensis.*

xalapensis (HBK) Decne. & Planch. [*O. Thibautii* (Versch.) Hook.f.]. Shrub or tree, to 30 ft.; lvs. palmately compound, lfts. 5–9, to 12 in. long, juvenile lvs. shorter, entire or variously serrate; fls. in heads ½ in. across in a long raceme; fr. black. Mex., Cent. Amer.

OREOXIS Raf. *Umbelliferae.* Three spp. of dwarf, stemless, alpine, per. herbs of w. N. Amer.; lvs. pinnate or 2-pinnate; umbels small, involucre usually absent, involucels of small bracts; fls. yellow; fr. globose-oblong and slightly compressed laterally.

Propagated by division or seeds; adapted to the rock garden.

alpina (A. Gray) J. Coult. & Rose. To 7 in.; lvs. 1–2-pinnate, lfts. 1–7, linear, to $^3/_{16}$ in. long, pale green; fls. yellow to whitish, in umbels to nearly ¾ in. across; fr. smooth, slightly flattened laterally, to $^3/_{16}$ in. long. High elevations, Wyo. to New Mex., w. to Utah and ne. Ariz.

ORGANIC GARDENING. Organic gardening relies on the use of organic rather than inorganic materials to provide the necessary chemical elements for plant growth and for control of insects and disease. The necessary nutrient elements are identical whether obtained indirectly from decomposing organic matter or more directly from inorganic compounds (chemical fertilizers), but an appreciation of the value of organic matter in maintaining the structure and fertility of soils is as old as agriculture and is the basis for one of the standard agronomic practices of growing important cover crops for incorporation into the soil. The gardener with an abundance of natural organic materials available for recycling as compost may utilize them to improve the tilth through granulation of soil particles, to increase water-holding capacity, to slow erosion, and to release nitrogen and other nutrients to growing plants through decay. In most major agricultural areas, however, manpower and adequate organic material are insufficient for major production of crops by strictly organic means, and chemical fertilizers and sprays are required.

ORIGANUM L. [*Amaracus* Benth.; *Majorana* Mill.]. MARJORAM. *Labiatae.* About 15–20 spp. of dwarf shrubs, or ann., bien., or per. herbs of Eur., the Medit. region, to cent. Asia; sts. mostly square in cross section; lvs. opp., simple; fls. in few- to many-fld. verticillasters arranged in spikelets, these arranged in racemes, panicles, cymes, or corymbs, bracts imbricate, sometimes colored; calyx campanulate to tubular, bearded at the mouth, nearly equally 5-toothed, or obliquely truncate at apex, with entire upper lip and slightly toothed lower lip, or with entire margin but deeply slit on one side, corolla 2-lipped, upper lip entire or emarginate, lower lip 3-lobed, stamens 4, in 2 pairs, exserted or included; fr. of 4 nutlets.

Species of dry, often rocky places. Several are grown as potherbs and one, *O. Majorana,* yields an essential oil. Most species are easily grown in warm garden soils; propagated by seeds or the perennials by division in spring or early autumn. *O. Majorana* is grown from seeds as an annual, since it winter-kills easily unless carefully protected; it is harvested just before blooming.

Dictamnus L. [*Amaracus Dictamnus* (L.) Benth.]. CRETE DITTANY, HOP M. White-woolly, dwarf shrubs, to 12 in.; lvs. ovate to orbicular, to 1 in. across, short-petioled; fls. in compact, hoplike spikelets arranged in loose panicles, bracts to ⅜ in. long, conspicuous, purple; calyx shorter than bracts, to ⅛ in. long, 2-lipped, lower lip shorter, teeth indistinct, corolla tubular, twice as long as calyx tube, to ½ in. long, pink. Late summer and autumn. Mts., Greece and Crete. Not reliably hardy north. Prop. by summer cuttings. An attractive plant for pots, window boxes, and hanging baskets.

heracleoticum L. [*O. hirtum* Link]. POT M., WINTER SWEET M. Closely related and similar to *O. vulgare*, but having bracts shorter, to ⅛ in. long, green, densely glandular on the outer surface. Se. Eur.

hirtum: *O. heracleoticum*.

×**hybridum** Mill. [*Amaracus ×hybridus* (Mill.) A. K. Jacks.]: *O. Dictamnus ×* *O. sipyleum*. Decumbent subshrub, to 18 in.; often confused with *O. sipyleum*, but st. lvs. larger, to 1 in. long, pubescent, and bracts larger. Late summer to autumn. Of garden origin.

Majorana L. [*Majorana hortensis* Moench]. SWEET M., ANNUAL M. Per., sts. to 2 ft., glabrous to tomentose, not papillose; lvs. ovate, ¼–1 in. long, entire; spikelets ½–¾ in. long, in racemes or panicles, bracts closely imbricate, ovate, to ⅛ in. long, obtuse; calyx 1-lipped, with a deep slit on one side, ciliate, corolla about ⁵⁄₃₂ in. long, white, purplish, or pink. N. Afr., sw. Asia; naturalized in s. Eur. Widely used as a culinary herb. Tender, usually cult. as an ann.

Onites L. [*Majorana Onites* (L.) Benth.]. POT M. Per., sts. erect, papillose, hirsute; lvs. ovate, cordate at base, sparingly serrate, villous to tomentose, sessile; fls. in dense, terminal corymbs, spikelets about ¾ in. long, bracts imbricate, about ⅛ in. long, acute; corolla larger than in *O. Majorana*, about ¼ in. long or more, purplish or whitish. Se. Eur., Turkey, Syria. Tender, not widely cult.

pulchellum (Boiss.) O. Kuntze [*Amaracus pulchellus* (Boiss.) Briq.]. Similar to *O. Dictamnus*, but lvs. smaller, to ¾ in. long, less pubescent, calyx markedly toothed, the corolla rose, tube to 1½ in. long, not gibbous. Perhaps Asia Minor; named from cult. plants from the Orient.

sipyleum L. [*Amaracus sipyleus* (L.) Raf.]. Per., to about 2 ft., pilose at base, otherwise glabrous, sts. wandlike, flexuous; lvs. small, ovate, entire, glaucous; panicles leafy, spikes peduncled, ovate-oblong, bracts ovate, glabrous; calyx with upper lip 3-toothed, lower lip deeply 2-lobed, corolla twice as long as calyx. Turkey. *O.* × *hybridum* has sometimes been confused with this sp.

virens Hoffmanns. & Link. Similar to *O. vulgare*, but bracts twice as long as calyx, obovate to orbicular, short-pointed, glandular-punctate, glabrous, membranous, pale green, calyx glabrous, corolla white. Sw. Eur.

vulgare L. MARJORAM, POT M., WILD M., ORIGANO, ORGANY. Per., to 2½ ft., usually branched above, pubescent, rarely glabrous or hirsute; lvs. ovate to lanceolate-ovate, to 1½ in. long, entire to somewhat toothed, glabrous or hairy, petioled; infl. corymbose or paniculate, spikelets to 1⅛ in., ovoid, oblong, or angular, bracts usually purple, without glands or sparsely glandular on outer surface; calyx about ⅔ as long as bracts, yellow-glandular-punctate, hairy or glabrous, corolla longer than calyx, white or purplish. Late summer. Eur. to cent. Asia; naturalized in e. U.S. An extremely variable sp. Cv. 'Aureum'. Lvs. yellow or golden. Cv. 'Viride'. Bracts green, fls. white. Var. **prismaticum** Gaudin. Spikelets longer, angular, bracts strongly imbricate.

ORIXA Thunb. *Rutaceae.* One sp., a dioecious, deciduous shrub, endemic to Japan; lvs. alt., simple, glandular-dotted; male fls. in racemes, female fls. solitary, calyx 4-parted, petals 4, stamens 4; fr. of 4 2-valved sections.

Propagated by greenwood cuttings, root cuttings, layers, and seeds.

japonica Thunb. To 10 ft.; lvs. oblong to obovate, to 5 in. long; fls. greenish; seeds black.

ORMOCARPUM Beauvois. *Leguminosae* (subfamily *Faboideae*). About 19–20 spp. of trop. shrubs or small trees of the Old World, often glandular-hairy; lvs. alt. or somewhat clustered, odd-pinnate or rarely even-pinnate or with 1 lft.; fls. axillary, solitary, or in racemes or clusters, papilionaceous, stamens united basally; fr. a flat, straight or curved legume, constricted into 2 or more indehiscent, oblong or ellipsoid segms. with prominent veins, often papillate, long-hairy, or minutely warty.

setosum: *O. trichocarpum*.

trichocarpum (Taub.) Engl. [*O. setosum* Davy]. Shrub or small tree, to 15 ft., with very rough bark; lfts. narrowly oblong, ⅛ in. wide, petioles and peduncles with soft, brown bristles; fls. cream or bluish, veined with deep purple, standard to ⅝ in. long. Uganda and Kenya to S. Afr.

ORMOSIA G. Jacks. NECKLACE TREE. *Leguminosae* (subfamily *Faboideae*). More than 50 spp. of trop. trees in Amer., Asia, and Madagascar; lvs. alt., leathery, odd-pinnate; fls. usually in terminal panicles, papilionaceous, purple, stamens 10, separate, unequal; fr. a flat, mostly thick, leathery, dehiscent legume, with circular, mostly red, or red and black seeds.

The ornamental seeds of several species are made into necklaces. Propagated by seeds.

calavensis Azaola ex Blanco. Lvs. glabrous, glossy, the nerves obscure, lfts. in 2–3 pairs, elliptic-oblong, to 5½ in. long, 1⁵⁄₁₆ in. wide; fls. purplish, ⅜ in. long; fr. mostly rhomboid-elliptic and 1-seeded, or elongate and 2-seeded. Philippine Is.

coarctata G. Jacks. Similar to *O. monosperma*, but the oblong-elliptic lfts. to 6 in. long, the lower surfaces and rachises of lvs. as well as infls. and frs. rusty-pubescent. Guyana, Trinidad.

coccinea (Aubl.) G. Jacks. Lfts. in 3–5 pairs, ovate to oblong, glossy above, to 4½ in. long, main veins very prominent beneath; panicles and calyces tawny-pubescent; standard reflexed, less than ½ in. across; fr. glabrous, to 1¾ in. long, 1 in. wide, 1-seeded. Amazon Basin.

emarginata Benth. Glabrous throughout; lfts. 3 or 5, obovate-oblong, to 3 in. long, blunt or emarginate; panicles small; fls. less than ½ in. long; fr. 1–2 in. long, seeds scarlet. Hong Kong.

Krugii Urb. Tree, to 75 ft., differing from *O. monosperma* in having lfts. obtuse or abruptly acuminate, larger, to 8 in. long and 5½ in. wide on petiolules to more than ½ in. long; fls. dark violet, petals about ½ in. long; fr. 2–4 in. long, pointed at either end, constricted between the red or black-spotted seeds. Puerto Rico.

monosperma Urb. Large timber tree; lfts. in 3–4 pairs, oblong to obovate-oblong, to 4½ in. long, gradually acuminate, at most puberulous beneath except pubescent on midrib, petiolules to ⅛ in. long; panicles, calyces, and frs. rusty-woolly; fls. blue, standard to ¾ in. long; fr. nearly circular, rostrate, about 1½ in. long, seed 1, large, scarlet with black spot. Lesser Antilles.

panamensis Benth. To 50 ft.; lvs. 1 ft. long, lfts. 5–7, elliptic-oblong, obtusely acuminate, pubescent on both surfaces, terminal lfts. larger, 4 in. long; racemes simple; fls. lilac. Panama, where called PERONIL.

ORNITHIDIUM: *MAXILLARIA.*

ORNITHOCHILUS Wallich ex Lindl. *Orchidaceae.* One sp., an epiphyte, native to India and China; sts. short, not pseudobulbous; lvs. few, crowded, oblong, flat, leathery; infls. borne above the lf. axils, racemose or paniculate; sepals nearly equal, spreading, lateral sepals obliquely obovate, petals smaller, cuneate-oblong, lip longer than sepals, united to column foot by a long, broad claw, spurred, midlobe entire, mouth of spur closed by 2 calluses projecting from its back and front walls, the latter hairy, column short, stigma circular, surrounded by hairy rim. For structure of fl. see *Orchidaceae*.

For culture see *Orchids*.

fuscus Wallich ex Lindl. Lvs. oblong, to 6 in. long, narrowed to sessile sheathing base; infl. 2–3 times as long as lvs., branched; fls. to ¼ in. across, sepals and petals greenish-yellow, sepals with 4 and petals with 2 broad brown vertical bands, lip 3-lobed, brown, shading to purple basally, margins of midlobe lacerate, lateral lobes comblike, spur longer than lip, saccate. India, Burma, China.

ORNITHOGALUM L. *Liliaceae.* About 100 spp. of scapose, bulbous, per. herbs, native to Afr., Eur., and w. Asia; bulb tunicate; lvs. basal; fls. white, greenish-white, or yellow to orange-red, in racemes or corymbs, sometimes even more or less umbellate, perianth segms. 6, separate, stamens 6, filaments often flattened and dilated, anthers versatile; fr. a loculicidal, 3-angled caps., seeds ovoid or globose.

Mostly winter- and spring-flowering. The hardy kinds may be planted outdoors and left undisturbed. The tender species, from Afr. and the Medit. region, may be grown in pots in the greenhouse or in frames, sometimes in window gardens. Propagated by offsets.

arabicum L. [*O. corymbosum* Ruiz & Pav.]. STAR-OF-BETHLEHEM. To 2 ft.; lvs. linear, to 2 ft. long and 1 in. wide, glaucous-green; fls. white, to 1 in. long, showy, fragrant, on pedicels to 3 in. long, in corymbose racemes, pistil black. Medit. region. Useful in conservatory.

aureum: *O. miniatum*.

Balansae Boiss. To 2 in.; lvs. linear-tongue-shaped, 3–4 in. long, ⅜ in. wide; fls. to ⅝ in. long, on short pedicels, in a corymbose raceme, perianth segms. pale, with broad green stripes; caps. 6-winged. Asia Minor.

caudatum Ait. SEA ONION, FALSE S. O., GERMAN ONION. To 3 ft.; lvs. strap-shaped, to 2 ft. long and 1½ in. wide, fleshy; fls. white, 1 in. across, in stout, 50–100-fld. racemes, perianth segms. with wide green midvein, pistil green. S. Afr.

corymbosum: *O. arabicum.*

lacteum Jacq. To 2 ft.; lvs. lanceolate, to 1½ ft. long, 1 in. wide, ciliate; fls. milk-white, to ¾ in. long, in many-fld. dense racemes on stout, erect scapes, perianth segms. not keeled, pistil green. S. Afr.

longibracteatum Jacq. To 2 ft.; lvs. strap-shaped-lanceolate, to 2 ft. long and 1 in. wide; fls. greenish-white, to ⁵⁄₁₆ in. long, in dense, many-fld. racemes, perianth segms. keeled, with broad, green midvein. S. Afr.

miniatum Jacq. [*O. aureum* Curtis; *O. thyrsoides* var. *aureum* (Curtis) Bak.]. To 1 ft.; lvs. lanceolate to ovate-lanceolate, to 4 in. long and ¾ in. wide, ciliate; fls. white, yellow, orange, or red-orange, 1¼ in. across, in few- to many-fld., dense, corymbose racemes. S. Afr.

narbonense L. To 1½ ft.; lvs. linear, to 1½ ft. long and ½ in. wide; fls. milk-white, to 2 in. across, in many-fld., loose racemes, pedicels of older fls. to 1¼ in. long, perianth segms. keeled, with green midvein. S. Eur.

niveum Ait. To 4 in.; lvs. filiform, to 6 in. long; fls. ⁵⁄₁₆ in. long, in slender, few-fld., loose racemes, perianth segms. white, keeled with green. S. Afr.

nutans L. To 2 ft.; lvs. linear, to 2 ft. long and ⅜ in. wide; fls. to 2 in. across, nodding, in few-fld., 1-sided racemes, perianth segms. white inside, green with white margins outside. Eur., sw. Asia; naturalized in e. U.S.

oligophyllum E. D. Clarke. To 6 in.; lvs. linear-lanceolate, to 6 in. long, glaucescent; fls. pale, to 1 in. across, in few-fld. racemes, perianth segms. creamy-white, with narrow pure-white margins. Greece to Asia Minor.

pyramidale L. To 2 ft.; lvs. linear, to 1½ ft. long and ½ in. wide; fls. white, 1 in. across, in long, narrow, 20–50-fld. racemes, perianth segms. keeled with green. S. Eur.

pyrenaicum L. PRUSSIAN ASPARAGUS, STAR-OF-BETHLEHEM. To 3 ft.; lvs. linear, 1–2 ft. long and ½ in. wide, glaucous, withering before flowering ends; fls. greenish-white, ⅜ in. long, on pedicels to ¾ in. long, in 30–50-fld. racemes, perianth segms. keeled with green. S. Eur., Asia Minor, Morocco.

Saundersiae Bak. GIANT CHINCHERINCHEE. To 3 ft. or more; lvs. many, limp and strap-shaped, to 1 ft. long and 2 in. wide; fls. white, to 1 in. across, on long pedicels, in many-fld., corymbose racemes, pistil prominent, shining, greenish-black. S. Afr.

Schelkovnikovii Grossh. To 2 ft.; lvs. linear-oblong, withering before flowering ends; fls. white, ½ in. long, in many-fld., dense racemes, perianth segms. keeled with green. Armenian S.S.R.

speciosum Bak. To 1 ft., rarely to 1½ ft.; lvs. usually 4, linear, short, thick; fls. 3–5, in a raceme with flexuous rachis, white, perianth segms. with distinct purplish-black spot at tip, to 1 in. long, not keeled, style short and thick. S. Afr.

spirale Schinz. To 5 in.; lvs. linear-lanceolate, to 8 in. long and ³⁄₁₆ in. wide, channelled, coiled at apex; fls. yellow, to ¾ in. long, in loose, 20-fld. racemes, perianth segms. keeled, 3–4-nerved. S. Afr.

thyrsoides Jacq. WONDER FLOWER, AFRICAN W. F., CHINCHERIN-CHEE. To 1½ ft., rarely to 2 ft.; lvs. linear to lanceolate, to 1 ft. long and 2 in. wide, ciliate, withering before flowering ends; fls. cream-colored or white, brownish-green basally, ¾ in. long, in few- to many-fld., dense, corymbose racemes. S. Afr. Frequently used by florists as an early-winter cut fl. because of its long-lasting quality. Var. **aureum:** *O. miniatum.*

umbellatum L. STAR-OF-BETHLEHEM, NAP-AT-NOON, SUMMER SNOWFLAKE, DOVE'S-DUNG. To 1 ft.; lvs. linear, to 1 ft. long and ⁵⁄₁₆ in. wide, with a broad, white midvein; fls. white, 1 in. across, in 5–20-fld., corymbose racemes, lower pedicels to 4 in. long, perianth segms. green and margined with white outside. Eur., N. Afr.; a weedy sp., naturalized in e. U.S.

OROBUS: *LATHYRUS.*

ORONTIUM L. *Araceae.* One sp., a hardy per., aquatic herb, native to se. U.S.; lvs. many, tufted, arising from a thick rhizome rooted in the mud; spathe tubular, spadix slender; perianth 6(–4)-parted; fr. a berry.

Rhizomes should be planted in about 1 ft. of water, in sunny locations; propagated by division or by seeds.

aquaticum L. GOLDEN-CLUB. Lf. blades floating or aerial, oblong-elliptic, to 1 ft. long and 4 in. wide, blue-green, petioles to 1½ ft. long; spathe basal, inconspicuous, spadix aerial, yellow, to about 4 in. long, on a white stalk to 3 ft. long; berries blue-green. Mid-spring to summer. La. to Fla., n. to Mass.

OROSTACHYS Fisch. *Crassulaceae.* About 10 spp. of glabrous, succulent herbs of n. Asia; rosettes flowering and dying, but often with offsets, withering in autumn, leaving compact winter bud of mostly callose lvs. that grow basally in spring to form callus-tipped foliage lvs.; infl. a terminal, crowded raceme, spike, or thyrse; fls. 5-merous, sepals nearly equal, petals spreading, nearly separate, stamens 10. Closely related to *Sedum,* but lvs. in dense rosettes, mostly callus-tipped, of 2 different lengths at some seasons.

For culture see *Succulents.*

Chanetii (Lév.) A. Berger [*Sedum Chanetii* Lév.]. Lvs. linear, to 1 in. long, ³⁄₁₆ in. wide, glaucous, callus entire, with terminal spine; infl. a pyramidal thyrse 6–12 in. high, 2–3 in. wide; fls. pedicelled, white or pink, ½ in. wide. Late summer, autumn. China.

fimbriata (Turcz.) A. Berger [*Sedum fimbriatum* (Turcz.) Franch.]. Lvs. oblong, to 1¼ in. long, callus spiny-toothed and with terminal spine; infl. a narrow thyrse 4–6 in. high; fls. pedicelled, reddish. Late summer. Se. Siberia.

spinosa (L.) Sweet [*Cotyledon spinosa* L.; *Sedum spinosum* (L.) Willd.; *Sempervivum cuspidatum* Haw.; *Umbilicus spinosus* (L.) DC.]. Lvs. oblong, 1 in. long, to ¼ in. wide, callus entire, with terminal spine to ³⁄₁₆ in. long; infl. a dense spike 4–12 in. high; fls. nearly sessile, greenish-yellow, to ½ in. wide. Summer. E. Russia, n. and cent. Asia.

OROXYLUM Venten. *Bignoniaceae.* One sp., a night-blooming, small tree, native from India to the Malay Arch. and the Philippine Is.; lvs. 2–3 pinnate; fls. white or purplish, in terminal racemes, calyx truncate or irregularly 5-toothed, leathery, corolla campanulate-ventricose, 5-lobed, stamens 5; fr. a linear, 2-valved caps.

Grown in the open in southern U.S. It thrives in rich soil; propagated by seeds and cuttings over heat.

flavum: *Radermachia pentandra.*

indicum (L.) Venten. Glabrous tree, to 40 ft.; lvs. to 5 ft. long, lfts. ovate, to 5 in. long, entire; racemes 3–6 ft. long; fls. to 2½ in. long and 3½ in. across, with a disagreeable odor; fr. to 3 ft. long, flat, pendulous.

OROYA Britt. & Rose. *Cactaceae.* Perhaps 6 spp. of globose, tubercled-ribbed cacti, native to Peru; fls. subapical, campanulate, perianth tube thick-walled, scales of tube and ovary with axillary hairs, stamens included, in a distinct close series at the mouth; fr. short-club-shaped, glabrous. Perhaps not distinct from *Lobivia.*

For culture see *Cacti.*

neoperuviana Backeb. Said to be thicker than *O. peruviana,* with more ribs and more radial spines.

peruviana (K. Schum.) Britt. & Rose. Sts. deep-seated, to 8 in. thick, ribs about 20–25; radial spines about 15–20, spreading, needle-shaped, brown, to ¾ in. long, central spines 0–4, stouter, red; fls. rose, with yellow center, to 1¼ in. long.

ORPHANIDESIA Boiss. & Bal. *Ericaceae.* One sp., a prostrate, evergreen shrub, native to ne. Asia Minor; lvs. alt., simple, leathery; fls. pink, in 1–3-fld. spikes, sepals 5, corolla broadly campanulate, stamens 10, anthers opening by longitudinal slits, ovary superior; fr. a 5-valved caps.

Culture as for *Epigaea.*

gaultherioides Boiss. & Bal. Young branchlets densely pubescent with red, glandular hairs; lvs. elliptic, elliptic-oblong, to oblanceolate-elliptic, to 5 in. long at maturity, entire but wavy, with red bristles; fls. to 1¾ in. across. Zone 7.

ORPHIUM E. H. Mey. *Gentianaceae.* One sp., an erect, somewhat pubescent shrub of S. Afr.; lvs. opp., sessile; fls. pink, 1 to several, terminal or in the axils of the upper lvs., calyx and corolla 5-lobed, stamens 5, anthers slightly twisted; fr. a caps.

frutescens (L.) E. H. Mey. To 2 ft.; lvs. linear to oblong, to 2 in. long; calyx tube ½ in. long, about as long as corolla tube and loosely enveloping it, corolla lobes broadly rounded, mucronate.

ORTHIOPTERIS: *SACCOLOMA.*

ORTHOCARPUS Nutt. OWL'S CLOVER. *Scrophulariaceae.* About 25 spp. of ann. herbs of w. N. and S. Amer., chiefly of w. U.S.; allied to *Castilleja;* lvs. alt., entire or cut; fls. yellow, cream-colored, white, crimson, or purple, in bracted spikes, bracts often colored, calyx 4-cleft, corolla tubular, 2-lipped, stamens 4, anthers 1- or 2-celled; fr. a caps.

Sometimes grown in the flower garden.

imbricatus Torr. Erect hairy ann., to 1 ft.; lvs. linear or linear-lanceolate, to 1½ in. long; fl. bracts purple-tipped, closely imbricate; corolla to ½ in. long, purple, with partly white lower lip. Wash. to n. Calif.

purpurascens Benth. ESCOBITA. Ann., frequently much-branched, to 15 in., sts. hairy, often purplish; lvs. deeply pinnatifid into linear or filiform segms.; fl. bracts rose-purple-tipped; corolla to 1¼ in. long, crimson or purple, lower lip tipped white, or with yellow or purple markings. Calif., Ariz., adjacent Mex.

tenuifolius (Pursh) Benth. Hairy ann., to 1 ft.; lvs. narrow, upper lvs. with 3–5 filiform segms.; fl. bracts purple-tipped; corolla to ¾ in. long, yellow, sometimes purplish-tipped. B.C. to e. Ore., e. to Mont.

ORTHOPHYTUM Beer. *Bromeliaceae.* Seventeen spp. of epiphytic herbs, native to Brazil; sts. short to long, leafy at base; lvs. spiny; infl. of heads or panicles of sessile fls. in axils of modified or leaflike bracts; sepals separate, petals separate, ovary inferior; fr. berrylike, seeds without appendages.

Grown in bright light in warm climates or under glass. For culture see *Bromeliaceae.*

foliosum L. B. Sm. To 16 in.; lvs. to 2½ ft. long or more, closely spiny, narrowly triangular, pale beneath; scape bracts similar to lvs. but more loosely arranged; fls. white, petals to ¾ in. long.

saxicaule: a listed name, probably for *O. saxicola.*

saxicola (Ule) L. B. Sm. Stoloniferous; lvs. 15–20, to 2 ft. long, ⅝ in. wide, spiny; infl. scapose, compact, headlike; fls. clustered, white.

speciosum: a listed name of no botanical standing.

vagans M. B. Foster. Similar to *O. saxicola,* but trailing, with elongate branched st.

ORTHROSANTHUS Sweet. MORNING FLAG, MORNING FLOWER. *Iridaceae.* About 8 or 9 spp. of per. herbs with short rhizomes, native to Australia and trop. Amer.; closely allied to *Sisyrinchium,* but having filaments separate or nearly so, and young caps. partly enclosed by the spathe valves.

chimboracensis (HBK) Bak. Sts. 1½–3 ft.; lvs. basal, 2-ranked, grass-like, 12–15 in. long, mostly ¼–½ in. wide, margins scabrid-pubescent; infl. racemose, overtopping lvs., with 2–3 fls. in clusters, each cluster subtended by a spathelike bract or reduced lf., spathes surrounding each fl. 2, ovate-lanceolate, margins broadly scarious; fls. light violet-blue, rotate, about 1½ in. across, perianth segms. nearly equal, anthers yellow, style brs. purple, horizontal to reflexed; caps. to ⅝ in. long. Temp. highlands, Mex. to Bolivia and Peru.

ORYZA L. RICE. *Gramineae.* About 15–20 spp. of ann. or sometimes per., trop. swamp grasses in Asia and Afr.; lf. blades flat; panicles open; spikelets 1-fld., flattened laterally, disarticulating below the glumes, glumes 2, much shorter than the lemma, narrow, lemma rigid, keeled, 5-nerved, sometimes awned, palea similar to the lemma but narrower. For terminology see *Gramineae.*

sativa L. RICE. Sts. to 6 ft., erect; lf. blades elongate; panicle dense, drooping, to 16 in. long; spikelets ¼–⅜ in. long, ⅛ in. wide, lemma mucronate to long-awned, both lemma and palea papillose-roughened with scattered appressed hairs. Se. Asia. Cult. in Calif. and the South, sometimes introd. from Va. to Fla. and Tex. One of the most important economic plants of the world; widely cult. in trop. and warm-temp. regions for the grain, usually requiring flooded conditions for part of its development.

ORYZOPSIS Michx. RICEGRASS, MOUNTAIN RICE. *Gramineae.* About 20 spp. of mostly per. grasses in N. Amer. and Eurasia; lf. blades flat or involute; panicles terminal, narrow or open; spikelets 1-fld., pedicelled, disarticulating above the glumes, glumes about equal, obtuse to acuminate, lemma usually about as long, with a short deciduous awn; fr. hard, cylindrical. For terminology see *Gramineae.*

hymenoides (Roem. & Schult.) Ricker. INDIAN R., SILK GRASS, INDIAN MILLET. Per., sts. to 2 ft., densely clustered; lf. blades slender, involute, nearly as long as sts.; panicle to 6 in. long, the slender brs. and capillary pedicels divaricately spreading; spikelets with glumes

about ¼ in. long, lemma about ⅛ in. long, nearly black at maturity, densely long-pilose with white hairs ⅛ in. long, awn about ⅛ in. long, straight. Man. to B.C., s. to Tex., Calif., and n. Mex.

miliacea (L.) Benth. & Hook.f. ex Asch. & G. Schweinf. SMILO GRASS. Per., sts. to 5 ft., stout, branching, erect but base sometimes decumbent; lf. blades flat, to ⅜ in. wide; panicle to 1 ft. long, loose; spikelets many, short-pedicelled, glumes ⅛ in. long, lemma smooth, less than ⅛ in. long, awn about ⅛ in. long, straight. Medit. region; introd. in Calif., N.J., and Penn. Used for forage, as a sand binder, and for seeding burned areas.

OSCULARIA Schwant. *Aizoaceae.* Three spp. of small, succulent subshrubs, native to S. Afr., sts. erect or spreading; lvs. opp., 3-angled, gray-green, shortly united at base, apex short-pointed, margins toothed, keel entire or toothed; fls. in 3's, subsessile, calyx 5-lobed, petals many, pink to red, stamens many, in a cone, staminodes present, ovary inferior, 5-celled, stigmas 5; fr. a caps. with expanding keels with narrow wings, cell lids present, placental tubercles lacking.

Growth occurs from spring to summer. Easily grown outdoors in a sunny place with minimum water, as excessive moisture causes straggly growth. Keep in a light place in window or greenhouse at a relatively cool temperature of about 50° F in winter. Propagation easy by seeds, but cuttings are quicker, especially for mass plantings, for which this genus is especially suited. See also *Succulents.*

caulescens (Mill.) Schwant. Brs. spreading, reddish, branchlets many; lvs. erect, incurved, light gray, powdery-pruinose, to ¾ in. long and ⅜ in. wide, slightly tapering apically, mucronate, margins reddish, entire or armed toward tip with 2–3 small, reddish teeth, keel toothed or often entire; fls. ½ in. across, fragrant, petals pink. Cape Prov.

deltoides (L.) Schwant. [*Mesembryanthemum deltoides* L.]. Small, sts. reddish, brs. compressed, branchlets many; lvs. bent inward, blue-gray, powdery-pruinose, to ⅜ in. long and ⅜ in. wide, narrowed toward base, not much united, edges and keel with 2–4, reddish, acute teeth; fls. ½ in. across, on pedicels to 1⅝ in. long, petals pale pink. Cape Prov.

glauca: a listed name of no botanical standing.

paardebergensis: a listed name of no botanical standing.

OSMANTHUS Lour. [*Siphonosmanthus* Stapf]. DEVILWEED. *Oleaceae.* About 30–40 spp. of evergreen shrubs and trees mostly in e. Asia, a few in N. Amer., Hawaii, and New Caledonia; lvs. opp., entire or toothed, green and glabrous beneath; fls. small, usually white or cream-colored, rarely yellow or orange, in clusters or racemes, usually fragrant, bisexual or unisexual, corolla 4-lobed, imbricate; fr. a 1-seeded drupe.

Grown under glass, or in the open in mild or warm regions. Propagated in late summer by cuttings of half-ripe wood under glass: seeds do not germinate until the second year, and are not often obtainable.

americanus (L.) A. Gray. DEVILWOOD, AMERICAN OLIVE, WILD O. To 45 ft.; lvs. elliptic to lanceolate, to 7½ in. long, entire, glossy above; fls. creamy or yellowish-white, in short, axillary panicles, fragrant, corolla tube about as long as lobes. N.C. to Fla. and Miss., Mex. Zone 7.

Aquifolium: *O. heterophyllus.*

armatus Diels. Shrub or tree, to 30 ft.; lvs. oblong-lanceolate, to 5½ in. long, spiny-toothed, with 6–14 teeth on each side, mostly less than ¼ in. long, rarely to ½ in. long, reticulate, leathery; fls. white, in clusters, fragrant. Autumn. China. Zone 7.

auriantiacus: *O. fragrans* forma *aurantiacus.*

Delavayi Franch. [*Siphonosmanthus Delavayi* (Franch.) Stapf]. Shrub, usually to 6 ft., occasionally to 15 ft.; lvs. ovate to lanceolate, to 1 in. long, toothed, thick, leathery, usually punctate with very small black dots, venation obscure but with 4 pairs of primary veins visible beneath; fls. white, in axillary or terminal clusters, fragrant, corolla tubular, to ⅜ in. long, lobes shorter than tube. W. China.

×**Forrestii:** *O. yunnanensis.*

×**Fortunei** Carrière. Presumably a hybrid between *O. fragrans* and *O. heterophyllus;* shrub; lvs. broadly elliptic, usually to 2½ in. long, sharply toothed, with 10–12 teeth on each side to 3⁄16 in. long, thick, leathery; fls. white, on pedicels ⅜ in. long, in axillary clusters, fragrant, corolla to ¼ in. long, lobes longer than tube. Known only in cult., first originated in Japan, where it has been grown for a long time. Zone 8. Cv. 'Aurea' is listed. Cv. 'San Jose' belongs here.

fragrans (Thunb.) Lour. [*Olea fragrans* Thunb.]. FRAGRANT OLIVE, SWEET O., TEA O. To 30 ft.; lvs. elliptic to oblong-lanceolate, to 4 in. long, entire or finely toothed; fls. white, fragrant, corolla to ¼ in. long, divided nearly to base. Early spring. E. Asia, but cult. for so long that it is difficult to define the area of its natural distribution. Fls. used in China to add a scent to tea. Zone 8. Forma **aurantiacus** (Mak.) P. S. Green [*O. aurantiacus* (Mak.) Nakai]. Fls. orange. Probably occurs in the wild in e. Asia.

heterophyllus (G. Don) P. S. Green [*O. Aquifolium* Siebold & Zucc.; *O. ilicifolius* (Hassk.) Hort. ex Carrière; *Olea Aquifolium* Siebold & Zucc.; *Olea ilicifolia* Hassk.]. HOLLY OLIVE, CHINESE HOLLY, FALSE H. To 20 ft.; lvs. elliptic to oblong, to 2½ in. long, with few, large, spiny teeth, glossy; fls. white, fragrant, corolla divided nearly to base. Early to late autumn. Japan, Taiwan. Zone 7. Cvs. include: **'Argenteo-marginatus'**: 'Variegatus'; **'Aureus'** [cv. 'Aureo-marginatus'], lvs. margined with yellow; **'Myrtifolius'**, lvs. entire, unarmed except for spine-tipped apex, elliptic to elliptic-oblong, to 1¾ in. long; **'Purpureus'** [cv. 'Purpurascens'], young lvs. purplish-black, mature lvs. green with purple tinge; **'Rotundifolius'**, dwarf, lvs. obovate, to 1½ in. long, entire; **'Variegatus'** [cv. 'Argenteo-marginatus'], lvs. margined with white.

ilicifolius: *O. heterophyllus.*

latifolius: a listed name of no botanical standing; material offered under this name is probably *Phillyrea latifolia.*

purpureus: a listed name of no botanical standing, used for *O. heterophyllus* cv.

serrulatus Rehd. Shrub or small tree; lvs. usually oblanceolate or narrowly obovate, to 5 in. long, mostly entire or with 29–35 small teeth on each side, leathery, primary veins usually 10–12 pairs, raised above; fls. white, fragrant, corolla to ¼ in. long, cut nearly to base. W. China. Zone 7.

suavis King ex C. B. Clarke [*Siphonosmanthus suavis* (King ex C. B. Clarke) Stapf]. Shrub or small tree, to 25 ft.; lvs. lanceolate to rarely ovate, usually more than 1¼ in. long, usually punctate with small black dots, somewhat crenate, rarely with sharp teeth, thick, nearly leathery, venation obscure, but usually 5–9 pairs of primary veins visible beneath; fls. white or cream, fragrant, corolla tube to ⅜ in. long, lobes shorter. Himalayas of w. China. Closely related to *O. Delavayi*, but having larger lvs.

yunnanensis (Franch.) P. S. Green [*O. Forrestii* Rehd.]. Shrub or small tree, to 45 ft.; lvs. usually lanceolate, to 7 in. long, entire or spinose-dentate, with 20–38 teeth on each side ¹⁄₁₆–⅛ in. long, thick to nearly leathery, venation reticulate, 10–12 pairs of primary veins; fls. white or cream, corolla to ¼ in. long, lobes cut nearly to base. W. China. Zone 7. Probably most closely related to *O. serrulatus* but having lvs. broadest at the middle, more prominently reticulate, and teeth, when present, as much as ⅛ in. long.

×**OSMAREA** Hort. Burkw. & Skipw.: *Osmanthus* × *Phillyrea. Oleaceae.* Hardy evergreen shrub, more or less intermediate between the parents; fls. small, white, in axillary clusters, fragrant.

Burkwoodii Hort. Burkw. & Skipw.: *Osmanthus Delavayi* × *Phillyrea decora.* To 8–10 ft.; lvs. elliptic to elliptic-ovate, to 2 in. long, entire or sparsely serrate; fls. on slender pedicels to ½ in. long, corolla to ⅜ in. long, 4-lobed to middle. Zone 7.

OSMARONIA: *OEMLERIA.*

OSMIA: *EUPATORIUM.*

OSMORHIZA Raf. SWEET CICELY. *Umbelliferae.* Eleven spp. of per. herbs, native to N. and S. Amer. and e. Asia, with fleshy roots; lvs. ternately compound; fls. very small, white or yellow, in few-rayed umbels with or without involucre and involucels; fr. cylindrical.

brevistylis: *O. Claytonii.*

Claytonii (Michx.) C. B. Clarke [*O. brevistylis* DC.]. WOOLLY S. C., HAIRY S. C., SWEET JAVRIL, SWEET JARVIL. To 3 ft., hairy; lvs. to 1 ft. across, segms. ovate, deeply toothed; fr. oblong, about 1 in. long, the slender base nearly as long as the body, styles very short. Nov. Sc. to N.C. and Ala., w. to Man., Mo., Nebr.

longistylis (Torr.) DC. SMOOTH S. C., ANISEROOT. Differs from *O. Claytonii* in having lvs. less coarsely and irregularly toothed, styles to ⅛ in. long, fr. slightly smaller, and the slender base about half as long as the body. Glabrous and pubescent forms occur. Que. to Ga., w. to Alta., Colo., and Tex.

OSMUNDA L. FLOWERING FERN. *Osmundaceae.* About 10 spp. of rather coarse but attractive deep-rooted ferns, native to temp. and trop. areas in e. Asia, and N. and S. Amer.; lvs. in large crowns, 2-pinnate or -pinnatifid; fertile pinnules

much contracted, segregated on wholly fertile lvs. or at the end or the middle of otherwise sterile lvs.

The young croziers of some osmundas, prepared like garden asparagus, are occasionally eaten in rural areas where the plants are native. The fibrous roots are used as a medium for growing orchids and other epiphytes. Osmundas are hardy ferns in the shaded, moist, wild garden and are easily transplanted from the wild. For culture see *Ferns.*

cinnamomea L. CINNAMON FERN, FIDDLEHEADS, BUCKHORN. Sterile lvs. to 5 ft. long, rusty-tomentose when young, pinnate-pinnatifid, margins usually entire, petioles 1 ft. long, fertile lvs. in the center, 2-pinnate, becoming cinnamon-brown as spores mature. N. Amer., W. Indies, S. Amer., e. Asia. Zone 4. Young croziers edible.

Claytoniana L. INTERRUPTED FERN. Lvs. to 4 ft. long, pinnate-pinnatifid, margins usually entire, petioles to 2 ft. long; sporangia confined to a few of the central pinnae. N. Amer., Asia. Zone 4. Young croziers edible.

regalis L. ROYAL FERN, FLOWERING F. Lvs. to 6 ft. long, 2-pinnate, margins finely toothed, the fertile pinnae toward apex of lf. forming a terminal panicle, rachis with many black hairs. Eur., Afr. Var. **spectabilis** (Willd.) A. Gray. Rachis of fertile panicle glabrous or nearly so. Nfld. to Sask., s. to Fla. and La.; S. Amer. Zone 3.

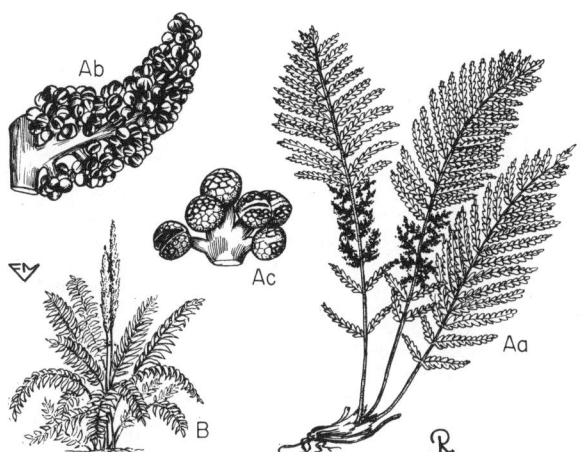

OSMUNDACEAE. **A,** *Osmunda Claytoniana:* **Aa,** plant with one sterile and two fertile leaves, × ¹⁄₁₂; **Ab,** pinnule from central pinna of fertile leaf, × 3; **Ac,** sporangia, × 9. **B,** *O. cinnamomea:* plant with two central fertile leaves, × ¹⁄₃₀. (B from Bailey, *Manual of Cultivated Plants,* ed. 2.)

OSMUNDACEAE Bercht. & J. Presl. FLOWERING FERN or OSMUNDA FAMILY. Ferns; 3 genera and about 17 spp. of per. ferns, native to both the Old and the New World, rhizomes erect, sts. enveloped in persistent lf. bases and coarse roots; lvs. 1–3-pinnate or -pinnatifid; sori on the lower surface of lvs. or on modified lvs., indusium absent, sporangia stalked, opening by 2 valves, annulus lateral, poorly developed, spores many, maturing at one time. *Leptopteris, Osmunda,* and *Todea* are cult. as ornamentals.

OSTEOMELES Lindl. *Rosaceae.* A few spp. of evergreen or deciduous shrubs from China to Hawaii and New Zeal.; lvs. alt., pinnate, lfts. entire, bristle-tipped; fls. hawthornlike, white, in terminal corymbs; fr. a small pome.

Grown as ornamentals, mostly in mild regions, where they prefer well-drained soil and a sunny location. Propagated by seeds, which germinate slowly, by cuttings under glass, or by grafting on cotoneaster.

anthyllidifolia Lindl. Evergreen, to 6 ft., young shoots silvery-villous; lfts. 13–19, oblong-obovate, to ½ in. long, remaining silvery-pubescent beneath; fls. ½ in. across; fr. pubescent, red, more or less bell-shaped. Hawaii, Polynesia. Zone 7.

microphylla: a listed name of no botanical standing for *O. Schweriniae* var.

Schweriniae C. K. Schneid. Deciduous to semievergreen, to 10 ft., branchlets pendulous, gray-pubescent; lfts. 15–31, elliptic to oblong-obovate, ³⁄₁₆–½ in. long, gray-pubescent beneath; fls. ½ in. across; fr. glabrous, blue-black, ⁵⁄₁₆ in. in diam., round-ovoid. W. China. Zone 7?

Var. **microphylla** Rehd. & E. H. Wils. Lfts. ⅛–³⁄₁₆ in. long, becoming glabrous; infl. smaller, denser. W. China.

  subrotunda C. Koch. Smaller, growing more slowly and stiffly; lfts. 9–17, rounded to obovate, to ⁵⁄₁₆ in. long, thinly strigose beneath; racemes about 1 in. long. E. China. Zone 7?

OSTEOSPERMUM L. [*Tripteris* Less.]. *Compositae* (Calendula Tribe). About 70 spp. of ann. or per. herbs, sub-shrubs, or shrubs, native chiefly to S. Afr., but extending to Arabia; sts. glabrous or variously hairy; lvs. alt., rarely opp., entire, toothed, pinnatifid, or pinnately parted; fl. heads solitary on terminal peduncles or in loose umbellate or corymbose panicles, radiate, involucral bracts in 1–3 rows, receptacle flat or convex, naked; disc fls. tubular, male, anthers sagittate, ray fls. ligulate, female; achenes all alike or dimorphic or rarely even polymorphic, straight or incurved, cylindrical or often 3-angled or 3–9-keeled, rough or tubercled, winged or unwinged, with or without an apical cavity, beaked or, mostly, not beaked, pappus absent.

  amplectans (Harv.) Norl. Ann., to about 3 ft.; lvs. alt., lower ones elliptic to ovate or rhombic, to 3 in. long or more, often auricled, petioled, more or less sinuate-dentate, upper lvs. lanceolate or linear-lanceolate, dentate, sessile, often clasping; heads in corymbose panicles; disc fls. yellow, tipped with purple, ray fls. yellow to orange; achenes triangular-pear-shaped, 3-winged, with an apical cavity. S. Afr.

  Barberae (Harv.) Norl. [*Dimorphotheca Barberae* Harv.]. Straggling, somewhat shrubby per., minutely glandular-pubescent; lvs. linear-oblong to spatulate, lower ones to 3 in. long, short-petioled, upper ones to 2 in. long, entire to remotely denticulate, sessile; heads to about 2½ in. across, on peduncles to 8 in. long; disc fls. deep purple, the outer ones with 5 spreading, bearded lobes, the inner not opening, ray fls. deep purple above, duller underneath. S. Afr.

  Ecklonis (DC.) Norl. [*Dimorphotheca Ecklonis* DC.]. Subshrubs or shrubs, to 3 ft.; lvs. alt., oblong or elliptic to oblanceolate, to 4 in. long, remotely denticulate to coarsely serrate-dentate, glandular-pubescent; heads 2–3 in. across, solitary or in loose corymbs; disc fls. azure-blue, ray fls. white above, blue to violet underneath, often with white margins; achenes narrowly triangular-ovoid, acutely 3-angled in cross section, faintly reticulate. S. Afr.

  fruticosum (L.) Norl. Herbaceous or somewhat shrubby per., sts. decumbent to prostrate, to 2 ft. long; lvs. alt., obovate to spatulate, glandular-hairy, becoming glabrescent, sessile or almost clasping; heads to 1¾ in. across, on peduncles to 4 in. long; disc fls. dull violet-purple, ray fls. white above, violet, lilac, or rosy-lilac underneath; achenes narrowly triangular-obovoid, 3-angled in cross section, essentially smooth. S. Afr.

  hyoseroides (DC.) Norl. [*Tripteris hyoseroides* DC.]. Aromatic ann. herb, to about 2 ft., sts. erect, glandular-pubescent; lvs. alt., glandular-hairy to nearly glabrous, lower lvs. oblong or oblanceolate, to about 4 in. long, sinuate-dentate, nearly clasping, upper lvs. oblong-linear to oblanceolate, sessile; heads in loose corymbs; disc fls. yellow, tipped with dark violet, ray fls. orange-yellow. S. Afr.

  jucundum (E. P. Phillips) Norl. [*Dimorphotheca jucunda* E. P. Phillips]. Glandular-pubescent per. herb, sts. decumbent to ascending, to about 1½ ft.; lvs. alt., linear-oblong, elliptic, or oblanceolate, sparingly and irregularly dentate; heads about 2 in. across, solitary, disc fls. dark purple, outer ones 5-lobed, lobes not bearded, ray fls. cerise, paler underneath; achenes triangular-ovoid to ellipsoid, 3-angled in cross section. S. Afr.

OSTROWSKIA Regel. *Campanulaceae.* One sp., a per. herb, native to Turkestan, distinguished from *Campanula* by its whorled lvs., 5–9-merous fls., and caps. dehiscing by twice as many slits as the calyx lobes.

  A showy and commanding plant, flowering from seed in 3–4 years, or more commonly grown from tubers that may flower the year after planting; best grown in sandy soil in full sun with protection from strong winds. Mature plants are not easily transplanted; propagated by cuttings of young growth or roots, by division of tubers, or by seeds.

  magnifica Regel. GIANT BELLFLOWER. Clump-forming, glabrous per., with milky sap, 5–8 ft.; lvs. 4–5 in remote whorls, ovate, to 6 in. long, serrate; fls. few to many in long-pedicelled, terminal racemes, calyx lobes long-acute, half as long as the corolla or more, without appendages in the sinuses; corolla pale lilac, 4–6 in. across, lobes broad and short; fr. obconical, about 1 in. across.

OSTRYA Scop. HOP HORNBEAM. *Betulaceae.* About 10 spp. of deciduous, monoecious, small trees, native to the N. Hemi-

sphere; lvs. alt., toothed; male fls. in slender, drooping catkins, female fls. in erect catkins; fr. a nutlet enclosed in a bladderlike, green involucre. Distinguished by the hopslike fr. clusters.

  Propagated by seeds sown in autumn or stratified.

  carpinifolia Scop. [*O. vulgaris* Willd.]. EUROPEAN H. H. To 60 ft., bark gray; lvs. ovate to elliptic, usually rounded at base, veins 11–15 pairs, petioles ⅜ in. long, glabrous; fruiting clusters to 2 in. long, nutlets ovoid, to ³⁄₁₆ in. long, with a tuft of hairs at apex. S. Eur. and Asia Minor.

  virginiana (Mill.) C. Koch. AMERICAN H. H., LEVERWOOD. To 60 ft., similar to *O. carpinifolia* but differing in having bark dark brown, lvs. usually subcordate, petioles shorter, often with stalked glands, and nutlets slightly larger, fusiform, glabrous at apex. E. N. Amer. Wood has many uses.

  vulgaris: *O. carpinifolia.*

OSTRYODERRIS S. T. Dunn: *AGANOPE* Miq. *Leguminosae.* Not cult. **O. Stuhlmannii**: *Xeroderris Stuhlmannii.*

OTANTHUS Hoffmanns. & Link [*Diotis* Desf., not Schreb.]. *Compositae* (Anthemis Tribe). One sp., a maritime per. herb, native to w. Eur. and Medit. region to Near East; lvs. alt.; fl. heads in dense corymbs, discoid, involucre campanulate-hemispherical, involucral bracts many, imbricate in several rows, receptacle conical, scaly; fls. all tubular, bisexual, base of tube extending downward in 2 spurs nearly enclosing ovary; achenes compressed, ribbed, pappus absent.

  Propagated by seeds or cuttings.

  maritimus (L.) Hoffmanns. & Link [*Diotis maritima* (L.) Desf. ex Cass.]. COTTONWEED. Sts. stout, ascending, to 1 ft., branching only above; lvs. oblong to oblong-lanceolate, to ½ in. long, covered with dense, white, cottony felt; fls. yellow.

OTHAKE: *PALAFOXIA.*

OTHONNA L. *Compositae* (Senecio Tribe). About 150 spp. of shrubs and herbs, chiefly in S. Afr.; often tuberous-rooted; lvs. basal or st. lvs. alt. or clustered at ends of brs.; fl. heads radiate, solitary or corymbose, involucral bracts in 1 row, united in lower half; fls. yellow, disc fls. sterile, ray fls. fertile; achenes 5–10-ribbed, pappus of many bristles.

  Othonnas thrive in any soil with good drainage. Propagated by cuttings of the stems, which often root naturally where they rest on the soil.

  capensis L. H. Bailey [*O. crassifolia* Harv., not L.]. LITTLE-PICKLES. Sts. trailing, slender, branching; lvs. scattered or clustered along sts., fleshy, cylindric-obovoid to cylindrical, 1 in. long, acute, pale green; heads 1 or 2 on slender terminal peduncles, ½ in. across, opening only in sun. Grown in hanging baskets under glass, or as ground cover in Calif.; more or less everblooming.

  carnosa Less. Shrubby, to 9 in., sts. fleshy, branching; lvs. crowded at ends of brs., fleshy, linear-cylindrical, to 2½ in. long; heads ¾ in. across, in long-peduncled corymbs.

  crassifolia: see *O. capensis.*

OTTELIA Pers. *Hydrocharitaceae.* Perhaps 40 spp. of trop. and subtrop., submersed aquatic herbs, native mostly to the Old World, with 1 sp. in Brazil; lvs. basal, long-petioled; fls. unisexual or bisexual, solitary in a 2-lobed spathe, sepals and petals 3, stamens 6–15, not united, ovary incompletely 6-celled, beaked, styles 6, bifid; fr. enclosed within spathe.

  A beautiful though fairly uncommon aquarium plant.

  alismoides (L.) Pers. Juvenile lvs. linear to lanceolate, older lvs. with blades broadly ovate to suborbicular, to about 8 in. long, thin, transparent, pale green, margins wavy, petioles to 20 in. long, 3-angled; fls. bisexual, white or yellow, sessile in the spathe, peduncle to 1 ft. long, sometimes spirally contracted in fr. China and Japan to Australia and ne. Afr.

OUGEINIA Benth. *Leguminosae* (subfamily *Faboideae*). One sp., a tree, native to India; lvs. alt., of 3 lfts.; fls. clustered in axillary, short racemes, papilionaceous, stamens 10, 9 united and 1 separate; fr. a flat, linear legume, divided into 2–5 large segms.

  dalbergioides Benth. To 40 ft., brs. gray, slender; lfts. rigid, leathery, nearly orbicular or obovate, obtuse, entire or slightly crenate; fls. abundant, whitish or pale rose, on pedicels to ¾ in. long; fr. to 3 in.

long, segms. to 3 times longer than broad. India. Wood useful for general carpentry.

OURATEA Aubl. *Ochnaceae.* About 200 spp. of trop. shrubs and trees; lvs. alt., simple, stipules small, deciduous; fls. yellow, mostly in panicles or racemes, sepals and petals 5, imbricate, stamens 10, opening by terminal pores, ovary 5–10-lobed, developing into 5 or fewer drupes on an expanded, fleshy receptacle.

littoralis Urb. Shrub or small tree, to 20 ft.; lvs. elliptic to ovate, to 4½ in. long, indistinctly denticulate or entire, short-petioled; panicles to 4 in. long; fls. fragrant, petals fan-shaped, 5⁄16 in. long; drupes obovoid, 5⁄16 in. long. Puerto Rico, and St. Thomas (Virgin Is.).

OURISIA Comm. ex Juss. *Scrophulariaceae.* About 25 spp. of per. herbs, native in the Andean region of S. Amer., in New Zeal., and Tasmania; sts. prostrate, decumbent, or erect; lvs. mostly basal, opp., entire or crenate; fls. mostly white, sometimes purple or with yellow centers, in some spp. scarlet, in scapose racemes, corymbs, or superposed whorls, or sometimes solitary and axillary, calyx 5-lobed or -parted, corolla 2-lipped to almost regular, stamens 4; fr. a caps.

Sometimes grown in rock gardens and shady places.

elegans Phil. To 1½ ft.; lvs. elliptic to orbicular, cordate, dentate-lobed, long-petioled; fls. scarlet, nodding, in scapose racemes. Chile. More or less hardy north.

macrocarpa Hook.f. Sts. stout, to 2 ft., but usually shorter, from a creeping rhizome; lvs. persistent, oblong to orbicular, to 8 in. long, crenate and ciliate, leathery; fls. in 4–8 superposed whorls, corolla to 1 in. across, white, with more or less yellow centers. New Zeal. Hardy north in cool woods or rock gardens.

macrophylla Hook. Differs from *O. macrocarpa* in more slender habit, in being pubescent rather than glabrous, and in having less leathery lvs. and smaller fls. New Zeal.

OUVIRANDRA: *APONOGETON.* **O. fenestralis:** *A. madagascariensis.*

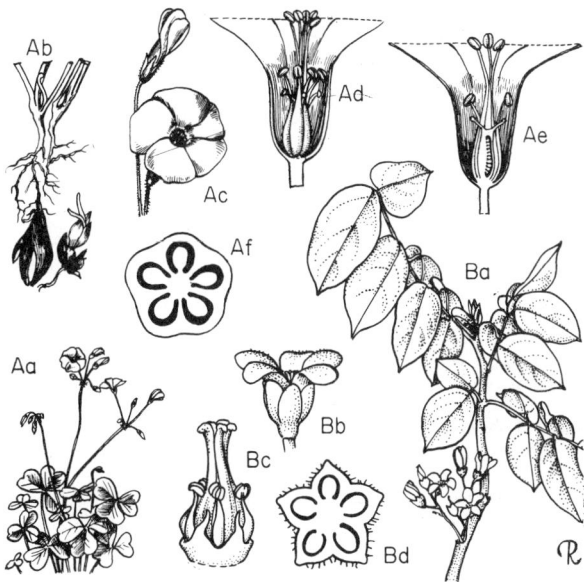

OXALIDACEAE. **A,** *Oxalis Bowiei:* **Aa,** flowering plant, × ⅛; **Ab,** stems with subterranean bulbs, × ¼; **Ac,** flower and bud, × ½; **Ad,** flower, part of perianth removed, × 2; **Ae,** flower, vertical section, × 2; **Af,** ovary, cross section, × 10. **B,** *Averrhoa Carambola:* **Ba,** flowering branch, × ½; **Bb,** flower, × 2; **Bc,** stamens and pistil, × 5; **Bd,** ovary, cross section. (Aa–Af from Bailey, *Manual of Cultivated Plants,* ed. 2.)

OXALIDACEAE R. Br. OXALIS or WOOD-SORREL FAMILY. Dicot.; 7 genera and about 1,000 spp. of herbs, shrubs, or rarely trees, native mostly to tropics, but also in temp. regions; lvs. pinnately or palmately compound, alt., often crowded, lfts. 1 to many; fls. solitary, racemose, cymose, or umbellate, bisexual, regular, sepals 5, petals 5, stamens 5 or 10, pistil 1, ovary superior, 5-celled, styles and stigmas 5; fr. a caps., rarely a berry. *Averrhoa* is grown primarily for its edible fr., *Biophytum* and *Oxalis* as ornamentals.

OXALIS L. [*Bolboxalis* Small; *Hesperoxalis* Small; *Ionoxalis* Small; *Xanthoxalis* Small]. WOOD SORREL, LADY'S SORREL. *Oxalidaceae.* About 850 spp. of herbs and suffrutescent plants of all continents, with the greatest number in S. Afr. and S. Amer.; small, stemmed or stemless ann. or per. herbs, often bulbous, tuberous, or rhizomatous, rarely subshrubs or shrubs; lvs. alt., cauline or basal, cloverlike, palmate and 3- to many-foliolate, or pinnately 3-foliolate, or sometimes reduced to 1 or 2 lfts., often closing at night; fls. in most colors except blue, in 1- to several-fld., scapose, umbellate cymes, sepals 5, petals 5, cohering basally, stamens 10, in 2 series, the outer shorter than the inner, all fertile, united or separate at base; fr. a caps.

Grown as ornamentals and one, *O. tuberosa* Mol., the OCA of the high Andes, for its edible tubers (ocas). Propagated by bulbs or division of the roots and by seeds; for bloom in late winter or early spring in window garden and conservatory, bulbs should be divided in early autumn. After blooming, the bulbous kind should be placed in a cool cellar for a resting period. Some species are weedy.

Acetosella L. EUROPEAN W. S., IRISH SHAMROCK. Low, scapose per., with scaly rhizomes, early blooming; petioles to 3 in. long, lfts. 3, obcordate; fls. white with purple or rose-purple veins, solitary on peduncles longer than petioles, petals ovate, obtuse, not emarginate. Eur., n. and cent. Asia to Japan.

adenophylla Gillies. Scapose, bulbous per., to 6 in.; petioles 2–5 in. long, lfts. 9–22, obcordate, ½ in. long, glaucous; fls. pink, purple at base, ½–1½ in. across, in 1–3-fld. umbels, peduncles 10–12 in. long, as long as petioles. Chile and Argentina.

amplifolia (Trel.) R. Knuth [*Ionoxalis amplifolia* (Trel.) Rose]. Bulbous per., to 14 in.; lfts. 3, V-shaped to obreniform, to 1½ in. wide, glabrous; fls. violet, to ⅝ in. long, in 7–12-fld. cymes, peduncles longer than petioles. Sw. Tex. to Ariz.

asinina: *O. fabifolia.*

Bowieana: *O. Bowiei.*

Bowiei Herb. [*O. Bowieana* Lodd.]. Pubescent, scapose per., with thickened roots and scaly bulbs; petioles stout, lfts. 3, suborbicular to obovate, to 2 in. long, emarginate; fls. pink to rose-purple, 1–1½ in. across, in 3–12-fld. umbels, peduncles 10–12 in. long, longer than petioles. Summer. S. Afr.

braziliensis Lodd. ex Westc. & Knowles. Scapose, bulbous per., 6–10 in.; lfts. 3, obcordate, 1 in. long, purplish and hairy beneath, margins hairy; fls. rosy-purple with darker veins, paler beneath, 1–1¼ in. across, on 1–3-fld. peduncles. Brazil.

caprina L. Nearly stemless or very short-stemmed per., 6–8 in., with rhizomes and scaly bulbs; lvs. all basal or crowded toward tip of st., lfts. 3, triangular, to ⅜ in. long, tapering toward base, 2-lobed to about the middle, lobes obovate; fls. pale violet, rarely white, in 2–4-fld. umbels, peduncles frequently twice as long as petioles. S. Afr.

carnosa: *O. megalorrhiza.*

cernua: *O. Pes-caprae.*

corniculata L. [*Xanthoxalis corniculata* (L.) Small]. CREEPING O., CREEPING L. S. Much-branched, creeping per., from a slender root, without rhizomes or bulbs but rooting at nodes; lfts. 3, cuneate-obcordate; fls. light yellow, in 1–5-fld. umbels; caps. on reflexed pedicels. Eur.; cosmopolitan weed. Frequent on the floor of greenhouses. Var. atropurpurea Planch. [var. *purpurea* Parl.; *O. tropaeoloides* Schlachter ex Planch.]. Lvs. purple.

corymbosa DC. [*O. Martiana* Zucc.; *Ionoxalis Martiana* (Zucc.) Small]. Scapose per., to 1 ft., with loosely scaly, compound bulbs; lfts. 3, obcordate or orbicular-obcordate; fls. violet to rose-purple, to ¾ in. long, in many-fld. cymes, peduncles longer than petioles. Trop. Amer.; introduced into Old World tropics.

crassipes Urb. Nearly stemless or very short-stemmed per., sts. densely or loosely clustered on rhizome, to 1 in. thick, the older parts with persistent old lf. bases; lvs. all at ends of sts., lfts. 3, obcordate, cut ½–⅓ their length, dotted with rust-colored spots on lower surface; fls. white or rose-pink, in umbellate cymes, peduncles 6–18 in. long. Nativity unknown, perhaps S. Amer.

Deppei Lodd. ex Sweet [*Ionoxalis Deppei* (Lodd. ex Sweet) Small]. GOOD-LUCK LEAF, GOOD-LUCK PLANT, LUCKY CLOVER. Scapose per., to 1¼ ft., with simple, scaly bulbs; lfts. 4, obovate to orbicular, to 1½ in. long; fls. red, in 5–12-fld. umbels. Mex. A white-fld. form is also grown.

depressa Eckl. & Zeyh. [*O. inops* Eckl. &. Zeyh.]. Nearly stemless, bulbous, rhizomatous per., to 4 in.; lfts. 3, rotund or subtriangular, ¼ in. long, cuneate or attenuate at base, glabrous or sparingly ciliate; fls. white, rosy, or violet, with yellow tube, to 1¼ in. long, solitary on peduncles longer than lvs. S. Afr.

Drummondii A. Gray [*O. vespertilionis* Torr. & A. Gray, not Zucc.; *Ionoxalis Drummondii* (A. Gray) Rose; *I. vespertilionis* (Torr. & A. Gray) Small, not Rose]. Scapose, bulbous per., to 1 ft.; lfts. 3, deeply 2-lobed, lobes lanceolate, oblong to ovate; fls. violet, to ¾ in. long, in 4–8-fld. umbels, peduncles longer than petioles. Tex.

enneaphylla Cav. SCURVY GRASS. Scapose per. with tuberous roots; petioles 4–6 in. long, lfts. 9–20, in 2 whorls, obcordate, glaucous, somewhat fleshy; fls. solitary, white with lavender veins. Falkland Is. A form with rose-pink fls. is also grown.

fabifolia Jacq. [*O. asinina* Jacq.]. Glabrous, bulbous, rhizomatous per.; petioles winged, to 4 in. long, lfts. 2, occasionally up to 5, suborbicular to elliptic, oblanceolate, or obovate, to 3 in. long; fls. yellow, white, or mauve, to 1¼ in. long, solitary on peduncles to 3½ in. long. S. Afr.

flava L. Scapose, bulbous, rhizomatous per., to 10 in.; petioles to 2½ in. long, lfts. mostly 5–12, linear, oblong to cuneate-obovate; fls. yellow, rarely white or violet, solitary. S. Afr.

floribunda: *O. rosea.*

gigantea Barnéoud. Erect shrub, to 6 ft.; lfts. 3, obcordate, to about ³⁄₁₆ in. long; fls. yellow, to ¾ in. long, solitary or in 3–6-fld. umbels. Chile.

hedysaroides HBK. Subshrub, to about 3 ft.; petioles to 2¼ in. long, lfts. 3, ovate or orbicular-ovate, to 1 in. long, stalked; fls. yellow, in axillary cymes, peduncles about as long as petioles. Venezuela, Colombia, Ecuador. Cv. 'Rubra'. FIRE FERN, RED-FLAME. Lvs. maroon.

Herrerae R. Knuth. Branching shrublet, to 4 in.; petioles ¾ in. long, dilated, lfts. 3, broadly obcordate, ¼ in. long, glabrous; fls. reddish, ½ in. long, in 5–7-fld. cymes. Peru.

hirta L. Erect or decumbent, bulbous per., to 1 ft.; sts. branched and leafy; lvs. nearly sessile, lfts. 3, linear to oblong or obovate; fls. violet, purple, white, or rarely yellow, solitary on axillary peduncles longer than petioles, petals hairy on exterior. S. Afr.

incarnata L. Bulbous per., to 8 in., sts. branched; lvs. opp., becoming crowded, lfts. 3, obcordate, ⅝ in. long, glabrous; fls. pale lilac with darker veins, solitary on peduncles as long as petioles. S. Afr.

inops: *O. depressa.*

lasiandra Zucc. [*Ionoxalis lasiandra* (Zucc.) Rose]. Scapose per., to 1 ft., with simple, scaly bulbs; petioles reddish, lfts. 5–10, lingulate-cuneate, to 3 in. long, entire; fls. crimson, in many-fld. umbels. Mex.

latifolia HBK [*Ionoxalis latifolia* (HBK) Rose]. Scapose per., to 8 in., with scaly bulbs; petioles to 6 in. long, lfts. 3, very broadly wedge-shaped, ¾ in. long, to 1¼ in. wide at apex, truncate-emarginate, glaucous, sometimes ciliate; fls. pink to violet, to ¼ in. across, in 6–13-fld. umbels. Mex. to S. Amer., W. Indies.

lobata Sims. Scapose, bulbous per., to 4 in., with tuberous roots; lfts. 3, obovate, to ¼ in. long, deeply emarginate to retuse, occasionally almost 2-lobed; fls. yellow, streaked and dotted with red, solitary on peduncles longer than petioles. Chile.

magellanica J. R. Forst. Stoloniferous per., to 2½ in.; lfts. 3, obcordate, ³⁄₁₆ in. long; fls. white, ⁵⁄₁₆ in. long, solitary on peduncles to 1½ in. long. S. S. Amer., S. Australia, New Zeal.

Martiana: *O. corymbosa.*

megalorrhiza Jacq. [*O. carnosa* Mol.]. Per., to 4 in., with fleshy rhizomes, at first nearly stemless, but with age producing sts., scaly with old lf. bases; lvs. borne at ends of sts., petioles to 3 in. long, lfts. 3, obcordate, to ½ in. long, somewhat fleshy; fls. yellow, in 2–5-fld. umbellate clusters, peduncles as long as petioles. Chile, Bolivia, Peru, Galapagos Is.

melanosticta Sond. Short, nearly stemless, rhizomatous per., from bulbs with blackish-brown scales; lfts. 3, cuneate-obovate, ciliate, usually pubescent on both sides, dotted with tiny orange spots that become black on drying; fls. yellow, solitary, peduncles to 1 in. long, half as long as petioles. S. Afr.

Nelsonii (Small) R. Knuth [*Ionoxalis Nelsonii* Small]. Scapose per., 10–18 in., with scaly bulbs; lfts. 4 or 5, obcordate, to 1½ in. long; fls. deep purple, in 5–11-fld. cymes. Mex.

oregana Nutt. REDWOOD SORREL. Nearly stemless per., to 10 in., with creeping rhizomes, more or less rusty-pubescent; petioles to 6 in. long, lfts. 3, broadly obcordate, to 1½ in. wide; fls. pink, white, or rose, solitary on peduncles as long as petioles. Wash. to n. Calif.

Ortgiesii Regel. TREE O. Leafy-stemmed per., to 1½ ft., sts. hairy, purplish; lfts. 3, to 2 in. long, the middle one deeply lobed to ⅓ its length, the lateral ones with one lobe smaller than the other; fls.

yellow with darker veins, to ½ in. long, in axillary cymes, peduncles somewhat longer than petioles. Andes of Peru.

peduncularis HBK. Erect, leafy-stemmed per., to 2 ft., sts. fleshy, glabrous; petioles 3½–4½ in. long, lfts. 3, obovate, to ½ in. long; fls. yellow with red veins, in 9–16-fld. axillary cymes, peduncles to 1 ft. long. Ecuador, Peru.

Pes-caprae L. [*O. cernua* Thunb.; *Bolboxalis cernua* (Thunb.) Small]. BERMUDA BUTTERCUP. Scapose per., with thickened roots and deep scaly bulbs; petioles to 5 in. long, lfts. 3, deeply obcordate, often dotted; fls. bright yellow, showy, to 1½ in. across, nodding, in 3–20-fld. umbellate cymes, peduncles to 1 ft. long. S. Afr.; naturalized widely in tropics and subtropics. A double-fld. form is also known.

purpurea L. [*O. variabilis* Jacq.]. Robust, scapose, bulbous per., to 6 in.; petioles to 3 in. long, lfts. 3, orbicular-obovate, to ¾ in. long, ciliate, with pellucid dots that become black on drying; fls. showy, rose, violet, or white, with yellow throat, to 2 in. across, solitary on peduncles shorter or longer than petioles. Cape of Good Hope.

Regnellii Miq. Scapose per., to 10 in., with scaly rhizomes; lfts. 3, broadly obtriangular, to 1 in. long, almost entire to incised, purple beneath; fls. white, in 3–7-fld. umbels, peduncles 4–6 in. long. Peru, Brazil, Bolivia, Paraguay, Argentina.

rosea Jacq. [*O. floribunda* Lehm. ex Lindl.]. Erect, much-branched, leafy-stemmed ann., to 18 in.; petioles to 1 in. long, lfts. 3, obcordate, to ½ in. long; fls. rose with darker veins and white throat, in loose, several-fld. cymes, peduncles 3–8 in. long. Chile. Probably much of the material cult. under this name is *O. rubra*. Cv. 'Delicata'. A listed name.

rubra St.-Hil. Scapose per., with a thick woody root crown and tuber; petioles to 1 ft., lfts. 3, obcordate, about ¾ in. long; fls. pink or rose with darker veins, varying to lilac, ½–¾ in. long, several to many in umbellate cymes, peduncles longer than petioles. Brazil. Frequently grown as a window plant, and in the open in mild regions; probably sometimes grown as *O. rosea*. Cv. 'Alba'. Fls. white.

Suksdorfii Trel. [*Xanthoxalis Suksdorfii* (Trel.) Small]. Per., with slender rhizomes, sts. trailing or decumbent, to 1 ft.; lfts. 3, cuneate-obcordate, to ¾ in. long, ciliate; fls. yellow, in 1–3-fld. cymes, peduncles about as long as petioles. S. Wash. to n. Calif.

tetraphylla Cav. [*Ionoxalis tetraphylla* (Cav.) Rose]. Scapose per., to 1 ft., with brown scaly bulbs; lvs. 3–6, lfts. usually 4, broadly obcordate, 1–2 in. long; fls. lilac or rose, in 4–9-fld. umbels, peduncles about as long as petioles. Mex.

trilliifolia Hook. [*Hesperoxalis trilliifolia* (Hook.) Small]. Scapose per., 5–12 in., with stout rhizome; petioles 5–10 in. long, lfts. 3, obcordate, 1–1½ in. long; fls. white or pink, in 2–8-fld. umbellate cymes, peduncles about as long as petioles or longer. N. Calif. to Wash.

tropaeoloides: *O. corniculata* var. *atropurpurea.*

valdiviensis Barnéoud. Grown as an ann., but perhaps per., sts. 2–8 in. long; lvs. many, petioles to 5 in. long, lfts. 3, broadly obcordate, to ¾ in. long; fls. bright yellow, striped with brown inside, in close, 4–6-fld., umbellate cymes, peduncles axillary, longer than petioles. Chile.

variabilis: *O. purpurea.*

vespertilionis Zucc. [*Ionoxalis vespertilionis* (Zucc.) Rose]. Scapose per., 4–12 in., with scaly bulbs; petioles to 5 in. long, lfts. 3, V-shaped, lobes linear to linear-lanceolate; fls. purple, in 3–10-fld. umbels, peduncles as long as petioles. Mex. Not known to be in cult.; material offered under this name is *O. Drummondii.*

violacea L. [*Ionoxalis violacea* (L.) Small]. VIOLET W. S. Scapose per., to 10 in., with brown scaly bulbs; lfts. 3, obreniform, to 1 in. wide; fls. violet to rose-purple or seldom white, in 3–10-fld. umbels, peduncles to 10 in. long, longer than petioles. Me. to Fla., w. to Rocky Mts. Rarely cult. but useful in borders and rock gardens.

OXERA Labill. ROYAL CLIMBER. *Verbenaceae.* About 20 spp. of often climbing shrubs, native to New Caledonia; lvs. opp., simple, leathery; fls. white or yellowish, in axillary cymes, calyx 4–5-parted, corolla 4-lobed, stamens 2; fr. a drupe.

Grown in greenhouses or out of doors in southern Calif. and Fla. Requires a rich loamy soil and a winter temperature of 55–60° F. Propagated by cuttings and seeds.

pulchella Labill. Glabrous, woody climber; lvs. oblong-lanceolate, to 5 in. long, entire or shallow-toothed; fls. pendulous, calyx conspicuous, corolla white, trumpet-shaped, 2 in. long or more, stamens long-exserted.

OXYBAPHUS: *MIRABILIS.*

OXYCOCCUS: *VACCINIUM.*

OXYDENDRUM DC. *Ericaceae.* One sp., a deciduous tree of e. U.S.; lvs. alt., simple, turning scarlet in autumn; fls. in drooping, terminal panicles, calyx deeply 5-lobed, corolla urceolate, stamens 10, ovary superior; fr. a 5-valved caps.

Planted as an ornamental and hardy north, but of slow growth. Propagated by seeds.

arboreum (L.) DC. [*Andromeda arborea* L.; *Lyonia arborea* (L.) D. Don]. SOURWOOD, SORREL TREE, TITI. To 80 ft.; lvs. oblong-lanceolate, to 8 in. long, pointed, serrulate; panicles to 10 in. long; fls. white, 5/16 in. long. Summer. Penn. to s. Ill., s. to Fla. and La. Zone 5. A honey plant.

OXYPETALUM R. Br. *Asclepiadaceae.* About 125 spp. of per. herbs and subshrubs, native from Cent. Amer. to trop. S. Amer.; lvs. opp.; fls. in axillary, open cymes, corolla deeply 5-parted, lobes ligulate to lanceolate, corona of 5 scales, united at the base to the corolla and staminal column; fr. a follicle.

caeruleum (D. Don) Decne. [*Tweedia caerulea* D. Don]. Suffrutescent, weakly twining per., to 3 ft. or more, densely but minutely white-pubescent throughout; lvs. oblong-lanceolate, to about 4 in. long, cordate-hastate; fls. 1 to few, axillary, corolla rotate, to 1 in. across, fleshy, pale blue but becoming darker with age, corona scales erect, dark blue, to 1/8 in. long; follicle spindle-shaped, smooth, to 6 in. long. Brazil, Uruguay. Not hardy north, but may be treated as an ann. if seeds are sown early.

OXYRIA J. Hill. MOUNTAIN SORREL. *Polygonaceae.* Two spp. of low per. herbs, native to alpine and arctic regions of N. Amer. and n. Eurasia; lvs. basal, palmately veined; fls. small, greenish, in terminal panicles, sepals 4, stamens 6, stigmas 2; fr. an achene, lenticular, broadly winged.

For damp rockeries; propagated by division or seeds.

digyna (L.) J. Hill. To 2 ft.; lvs. reniform to orbicular, to 1½ in. wide, petioles long; fls. many; fr. red. Arctic, N. Amer., Eurasia.

OXYSPORA DC. *Melastomataceae.* About 20 spp. of shrubs with drooping brs., native to China and Malay Arch.; lvs. opp., long-petioled, 5–7-nerved; infl. terminal, panicled; fls. rose-purple, 4-merous, stamens 8, dimorphic, anthers 4, purple, lacking appendage in front but often with a spur on the back; fr. a caps.

Grown in greenhouses.

paniculata (D. Don) DC. Shrub, to 5 ft., brs. stellate-pubescent; lvs. ovate, mostly 4–5 in. long, rarely to 15 in., acuminate, bristly toward apex, stellate-pubescent on nerves beneath, petiole 1–2 in. long; panicles loose, with stellate hairs; fls. rose-purple; fr. a caps., to 3/8 in. long. Himalayas, s. China, se. Asia.

OXYTROPIS DC. LOCOWEED, CRAZYWEED. *Leguminosae* (subfamily *Faboideae*). Perhaps 300 spp. of low, per. herbs of N. Temp. Zone; lvs. odd-pinnate, lfts. oblique basally; fls. in racemes or spikes, papilionaceous, keel beaked, stamens 10, 9 united and 1 separate; fr. a legume, often inflated. Some of the spp. are extremely variable and difficult to delimit.

Sometimes grown as ornamentals; propagated by seeds sown where they are to grow, and by division.

albiflora: see *O. sericea.*

Besseyi (Rydb.) Blankinsh. Differs from *O. Lambertii* in having hispid-villous calyces, thin-walled, villous frs., and simple pubescence. Mont., Idaho, Wyo., Colo., Utah.

campestris (L.) DC. Very variable; lvs. to 6 in. long, lfts. linear-oblong to oblong-lanceolate, to 1 in. long; scapes to 1 ft., racemes to 30-fld., to 4¼ in. long in fr.; fls. white to yellow to bright purple, standard to ¾ in. long; fr. thin-walled, not rigid, to 5/8 in. long. N. Asia, Amer. Var. **gracilis** (A. Nels.) Barneby [*O. olympica* St. John]. Lfts. 17–33; petals uniformly white or yellowish. Wash. and B.C. to Colo., S. Dak., and Man.

Halleri Bunge [*O. sericea* (Lam.) Simonk., not Nutt.]. To about 6 in., from stout rhizome, densely hairy; lfts. in about 10 pairs, elliptic, acutish, ¼ in. long; racemes 6–10-fld., 1 in. long, longer than lvs.; fls. pale purple with tip of keel dark purple, ¾ in. long; fr. pubescent, 1 in. long. Scotland, Pyrenees, Alps. Often considered a part of *O. uralensis.*

Lambertii Pursh. PURPLE LOCO, LOCOWEED. Cespitose, herbage sometimes silky-gray-pubescent, hairs 2-armed; lvs. to 8 in. long, lfts. 7–15, linear to ovate, acute; scapes longer than lvs., racemes 10–25-fld., to 6 in. long in fr.; fls. mostly purple, but varying to pink-purple to white, standard to 1 in. long; fr. leathery, ovoid to lanceolate in outline, pubescent. Sask., Mont. to Mo., Tex., and Ariz.

megalantha Boissieu. Herbage reddish-villous; lfts. in 8–20 pairs, lanceolate, acute, pubescent on both sides; scapes 8 in. long, much longer than lvs., spikes ovate, congested, 2¼ in. long; fls. large, purple, to more than 1 in. long; fr. oblong, turgid, leathery. Japan.

ochroleuca Bunge. Sts. short, glaucous; lvs. to 4 in. long, lfts. oblong-lanceolate; scapes elongate, racemes short; fls. small, yellowish-white, drooping. Cent. Asia.

olympica: *O. campestris* var. *gracilis.*

podocarpa A. Gray. Herbage pilose-hispidulous, sometimes gray-pubescent, especially when young; lvs. to 2 in. long, lfts. 9–13, linear-lanceolate or linear, crowded on short rachises; scapes to 1½ in. long, racemes 1–3-fld., almost headlike; fls. with purple petals, standard to 5/8 in. long; fr. papery, bladderlike, about 1 in. long, hairy. Colo. to Alta., coastal Lab. to Baffin Is.

sericea Nutt. ex Torr. & A. Gray [*O. albiflora* (A. Nels.) K. Schum., not Bunge]. Silky-pubescent with simple hairs; lvs. to 1 ft. long, lfts. ovate to lanceolate, to 1½ in. long; racemes as long as or longer than lvs., to 27-fld., to 7 in. long in fr.; fls. commonly white, or yellowish, sometimes with keel dotted, rarely entirely lilac to purple, standard deeply emarginate; fr. oblong, leathery, erect, to 1 in. long. Mont. to New Mex., Okla., and Nev. *O. sericea* (Lam.) Simonk. is *O. Halleri.*

shokanbetsuensis Miyabe & Tatew. Petioles and scapes white-hairy, lfts. in 7–9 pairs, oblong or ovate, about 5/16 in. long, glabrous above; scapes longer than lvs., infl. 2–5-fld.; petals purple, standard ¾ in. long; fr. ovoid, to ¾ in. long, hirsute. Japan.

splendens Dougl. To 18 in., densely silky-pubescent throughout; lvs. to 10 in. long, lfts. elliptic to lanceolate or oblong, acute, unequal, to ¾ in. long, in 7–15 groups of 2–4 along rachis; scapes longer than lvs., racemes to 6 in. long in fr.; corolla rose or carmine, drying violet; fr. thin-papery, 5/8 in. long. Alaska and Yukon, s. to New Mex., Minn., and Ont.

uralensis (L.) DC. Differs from *O. Halleri* in having more vigorous growth, lfts. in 12–16 pairs, and rather glandular floral bracts. Ural Mts. Material cult. under this name may be *O. Halleri.*

PACHIRA Aubl. [*Carolinea* L.f.]. SHAVING-BRUSH TREE. *Bombacaceae.* Two spp. of trees, native to trop. Amer.; lvs. alt., palmately compound; fls. very large, solitary or in 2's or 3's near ends of brs., calyx persistent, truncate or undulate, petals 5, linear, stamens 200–700, separate above, united into a long tube, nearly as long as petals; fr. a large, heavy, woody, 5-celled caps., seeds embedded in a fleshy pulp, sometimes eaten.

Cultivated as ornamentals in the tropics and in southern Fla. Propagated by seeds and cuttings.

aquatica Aubl. [*P. macrocarpa* (Schlechtend. & Cham.) Walp.; *Carolinea princeps* L.f.]. GUIANA CHESTNUT, WATER C., PROVISION TREE, WILD COCOA. Tree, 15-60 ft.; lfts. 5–9, more or less elliptic, to 12 in. long; fls. soon falling, calyx campanulate to tubular, about ¾ in. long, with 5 basal glands, petals greenish- or yellowish-white, sometimes pinkish, to 14 in. long, 1 in. wide, stamens 200–250, conspicuous, filaments white, purplish above, tube to 5 in. long, anthers red; caps. subglobose to elliptic, brown, to 12 in. long, 5 in. in diam. An estuarine sp., Mex. to n. S. Amer. Zone 10.

fastuosa: *Pseudobombax ellipticum.*

insignis (Swartz) Sav. WILD CHESTNUT. To 90 ft.; differing from *P. aquatica* in having calyx mostly open-campanulate, often without glands, petals brownish-red to scarlet, stamens more numerous, 400–700, wide-spreading, shorter than petals, purplish below, whitish above or purplish above and below and whitish centrally, anthers yellow; lfts. and caps. sometimes larger. Dry sites, Brazil. Trees cult. under this name may be *Pseudobombax ellipticum.*

macrocarpa: *P. aquatica;* but material offered as *P. macrocarpa* may be *Pseudobombax ellipticum.*

PACHISTIMA: see *Paxistima.*

PACHYCEREUS (A. Berger) Britt. & Rose. *Cactaceae.* About 5 spp. of treelike cacti, native to Mex.; ribs about 10–25; fls. campanulate, opening at night but often remaining open next morning, stamens many, included; fr. densely covered with felt and spines. Differs from *Carnegiea* in the more felty and bristly areoles of ovary and tube and in the dry fr. Perhaps to be united with *Carnegiea* or *Cereus,* but the boundaries with other genera such as *Cephalocereus* are also uncertain.

For culture see *Cacti.*

chrysomallus: see *Cephalocereus militaris* and *C. fulviceps.*

grandis Rose. To 35 ft., simple or branched, trunk to 3 ft. thick, sts. pale green, at first glaucous, ribs 9–13, high; lower areoles circular, about 1 in. apart, spines awl-shaped, radial spines 9–10, central spines 3, the lower flattened, to 2½ in. long, fertile upper areoles elliptic, with needle-shaped to bristlelike spines; fls. 1½ in. long, scales small, acuminate; fr. with yellow bristles and felt. Cent. Mex.

marginatus: *Lemaireocereus marginatus.*

pecten-aboriginum (Engelm.) Britt. & Rose. HAIRBRUSH CACTUS, COMB C., INDIAN-COMB. To 35 ft., trunk to 1 ft. thick, brs. many, erect, to 6 in. thick, ribs 10–11; areoles connected, spines to 1¼ in. long, mostly shorter, radial spines 8–12, central spines 1–3, flowering areoles with many short, weak spines; fls. white, to 3½ in. long; fr. to 3 in. in diam., with yellow wool and many long, yellow bristles. W. Mex.

Pringlei (S. Wats.) Britt. & Rose. GIANT MEXICAN CEREUS, MEXICAN-GIANT. To 70 ft., trunk to 5 ft. thick, brs. glaucous, to 1½ ft. thick, ribs 11–17, to 2 in. high; areoles large, all but the lowermost confluent or connected by a groove, spines at first 10–20, later to 50 or more, needle-shaped to awl-shaped, white to black, ½–5 in. long, absent from upper areoles; fls. white, ill-smelling, to 3½ in. long, areoles of tube and ovary densely brown-hairy, stamens in 1 series. Spring. W. Mex.

Tetetzo: *Cephalocereus Tetetzo.*

PACHYPHYTUM Link, Klotzsch, & Otto. *Crassulaceae.* Twelve spp. of glabrous, succulent, per. herbs or subshrubs of Mex., sts. elongating; lvs. alt., in rosettes to scattered, turgid, with broadly rounded margins; fl. st. axillary, cincinnus solitary, often with overlapping bracts when young; fls. 5-merous, sepals erect, petals erect or with tips outcurved, nearly separate, overlapping above but separated near base, where margins infolded to form the appendages. Close to *Echeveria,* but each petal with 2 scalelike appendages inside at middle. Hybrids with *Echeveria* are described under × *Pachyveria.*

The genus has been divided into 3 sections. The species of a section possess the characteristics of that section. These characteristics are not repeated in the brief descriptions of the species; instead, the following symbols are used to indicate the section to which each species belongs: D, *Diotostemon:* I, *Ixiocaulon;* P, *Pachyphytum.*

The distinguishing characters of the sections follow:

Diotostemon (Salm-Dyck) A. Berger (D). Lvs. fusiform to nearly cylindrical; bracts not overlapping, pedicels ¼–1¼ in. long; sepals nearly equal, shorter than corolla, petals unicolored or with darker tips.

Ixiocaulon Moran (I). Lvs. flattened; bracts overlapping, pedicels about 1/16–5/16 in. long; sepals unequal, shorter than corolla at least in later fls., petals unicolored.

Pachyphytum (P). Lvs. half-cylindrical or mostly broader; bracts overlapping, pedicels less than ¼ in. long; sepals markedly unequal, longer than corolla, petals white, each with full-width red spot below apex.

Sometimes grown in greenhouses and perhaps in the open in the warm regions. For culture see *Succulents.*

aduncum: *P. Hookeri.*

amethystinum: *Graptopetalum amethystinum.*

bracteosum Klotzsch. P; st. ½–1 in. in diam.; lvs. 15–30, obovate to spatulate, 3–4½ in. long, 1–2 in. wide, to ½ in. thick, obtuse to rounded, glaucous; fl. st. ½–2 ft.; fls. 10–28, calyx ½–1 in. long, petals ⅜ in. long. Late autumn, winter.

brevifolium Rose. Not in cult.; plants cult. under this name are probably *P. glutinicaule.*

compactum Rose. THICK PLANT. D; st. to ½ in. in diam.; lvs. 30–60, crowded, lanceolate, ¾–1¼ in. long, ½ in. wide, nearly round in cross section, low-angled, nearly acute, broadly minutely pointed, glaucous, often purplish; fl. st. 12–16 in.; fls. 3–10, pedicels to 1¼ in. long, calyx 5/16 in. long, pink with bluish tips, petals ⅜ in. long, orange-red with blue-glaucous tips. Spring.

Fittkaui Moran. I; st. ½–1½ in. in diam.; lvs. 10–40, elliptic-oblanceolate, 1¼–4 in. long, ¾–1½ in. wide, ½ in. thick, obtuse, slightly glaucous; fl. st. 8–15 in.; fls. 12–25, pedicels to ¼ in. long, calyx ½–1 in. long, petals pink, ½–¾ in. long. Winter, spring.

glutinicaule Moran. I; st. glutinous, to ⅝ in. in diam.; lvs. 20–35, obovate, 1–2½ in. long, ¾–1¼ in. wide, to ⅝ in. thick, obtuse to rounded, minutely pointed, glaucous; fl. st. 6–10 in.; fls. 6–23, pedicels to ⅝ in. long, calyx 5/16–⅝ in. long, petals red, ½–¾ in. long, outcurved in age. Fls. all year, especially winter, early spring. Formerly often misidentified as *P. brevifolium. P. glutinicaule* is believed to be one parent of the hybrid cv. **'Cornelius Hybrid',** with lvs. bluish-gray, turgid, obovate, often tinged pink and tipped red, and with red fls.

glutinosum: a listed name of no botanical standing; perhaps referring to *P. glutinicaule.*

Haagei: a listed name of no botanical standing; probably for × *Pachyveria Haagei.*

heterosepalum: *Echeveria heterosepala.*

Hookeri (Salm-Dyck) A. Berger [*P. aduncum* (Bak.) Rose; *P. uniflorum* Rose]. D; st. ⅜–¾ in. in diam.; lvs. 25–40, separated, club-shaped to fusiform, 1–2 in. long, ¼–⅝ in. wide, obtuse, minutely pointed, green or glaucous; fl. st. 4–10 in.; fls. 3–15, pedicels to 1¼ in. long, calyx 3/16–5/16 in. long, petals deep pink, ¼–½ in. long. Fls. all year in one form but mostly spring.

longifolium Rose. P; st. ½–1 in. in diam.; lvs. 20–60, separated, oblanceolate, 2½–4¼ in. long, ⅝–1 in. wide, to ⅜ in. thick, acute to obtuse, channelled on back, glaucous, often purplish; fl. st. 8–16 in.; fls. 10–50, calyx ½–⅝ in. long, petals ⅜ in. long. Summer to winter.

Orpettii: a listed name of no botanical standing; perhaps referring to ×*Pachyveria* cv. 'E. O. Orpet'.

oviferum J. Purpus. MOONSTONES. P; st. to ½ in. in diam.; lvs. 12–25, crowded, obovate, 1¼–2 in. long, ¾–1¼ in. wide, to ¾ in. thick, rounded at apex, glaucous, often lavender; fl. st. 2–5 in.; fls. 7–15, calyx ½–1 in. long, petals ⅜ in. long. Winter, spring.

uniflorum: *P. Hookeri.*

virens: a listed name of no botanical standing; perhaps a misspelling of *P. viride.*

viride Walth. P; st. ¾–1¼ in. in diam.; lvs. 12–40, separated, elliptic-oblong, 2½–5½ in. long, ¾–1¼ in. wide, to ⅝ in. thick, obtuse, green or purplish-red; fl. st. 8–15 in.; fls. 10–22, calyx ½–1 in. long, petals ½ in. long. Late autumn to spring.

Werdermannii Poelln. P; st. ½ in. in diam.; lvs. 10–35, separated, elliptic, 1½–4 in. long, ¾–1¼ in. wide, to ½ in. thick, obtuse, glaucous; fl. st. 6–10 in.; fls. 10–22, calyx to ½ in. long, petals ⅜ in. long. Winter, early spring.

PACHYRHIZUS L. Rich. ex DC. *Leguminosae* (subfamily *Faboideae*). Six spp. of erect or vining herbs with tuberous roots, native to trop. Amer.; lvs. alt., of 3 lfts., strigose; infl. an axillary raceme; fls. papilionaceous, calyx 4-lobed, standard eared at base, wings curved, stamens 10, 9 united and 1 separate; fr. a flat, strigose legume constricted between seeds.

Some species are cultivated for their edible tuber; the seeds are poisonous.

erosus (L.) Urb. YAM BEAN. Herbaceous vine, to 15 ft. or more; lateral lfts. ovate or rhomboidal, to 6 in. long, entire, toothed, or lobed, terminal lft. rhomboidal, to ovate-reniform, to 7½ in. long, toothed or 5-lobed; racemes to 28 in. long; fls. clustered at nodes, to 1 in. long, deep violet to white; fr. to 5⅝ in. long, seeds square or rounded, flattened, yellow, brown, or red. Mex., Cent. Amer.; naturalized in s. Fla.

tuberosus (Lam.) A. Spreng. YAM BEAN, POTATO B. Herbaceous vine, to 20 ft. or more; lfts. rhomboid-ovate, entire, terminal lft. to about 10 in. long and nearly as wide; racemes to 8 in. long; fls. clustered at nodes, to ⅞ in. long, violet or white, standard with green spot at base; fr. to 1 ft. long, seeds reniform, plump, red, black, or black and white. Amazon Basin.

PACHYSANDRA Michx. SPURGE. *Buxaceae.* Five spp. of monoecious, per. herbs or subshrubs, one in N. Amer., the others in e. Asia; lvs. simple, often crowded at ends of brs.; fls. in erect spikes, the male borne above the female, petals 0, male fls. with stamens 4, long-exserted, opp. the sepals, female fls. with 4 or 6 sepals; fr. a 3-beaked caps., or sometimes drupaceous.

Useful ground cover for shady areas. Propagated by division or by cuttings in summer.

procumbens Michx. ALLEGHANY P., ALLEGHANY S. To about 1 ft. high; lvs. broadly ovate to suborbicular, up to 3 in. long, toothed apically and narrowed to a long petiole; fls. greenish or purplish, in spikes from near the base of st. Spring. Rich woods, e. Ky. to Fla. and La.

terminalis Siebold & Zucc. JAPANESE P., JAPANESE S. To about 1 ft. high; lvs. obovate, 2–4 in. long, toothed above the middle, cuneate; fls. whitish, in terminal spikes. Spring. Japan. Zone 5. Widely grown evergreen ground cover. Cv. **'Variegata'.** Lvs. bordered and variegated white.

PACHYSTACHYS Nees. *Acanthaceae.* About 6 spp. of shrubs or herbs of trop. Amer.; lvs. opp., usually large; fls. in a large, terminal spike with large, green bracts, calyx segms. equal, or the uppermost one narrower, corolla large, showy, yellow, purple, or red, 2-lipped, stamens 2, short staminodes sometimes present; fr. a caps., seeds 4.

Related to *Justicia,* but differing in technical characters of pollen and of stamens, which are borne near base of corolla tube. Culture as for *Justicia.*

coccinea (Aubl.) Nees [*Jacobinia coccinea* (Aubl.) Hiern; *Justicia coccinea* Aubl.]. CARDINAL'S-GUARD. Shrub, to 5 ft. or more; lvs. ovate, to 8 in. long, entire, short-petioled; spike to 6 in. long, lower bracts 4-ranked, ovate, to 1 in. long, apiculate; corolla scarlet, about 2 in. long. W. Indies and n. S. Amer.

lutea Nees. Shrub, glabrous, to 3 ft. or more; lvs. narrowly ovate, to 5 in. long, entire, narrowed to base; spike to 4 in. long, bracts cordate, to 1 in. long, golden-yellow; corolla white, about 2 in. long Peru.

PACHYSTEGIA Cheesem. *Compositae* (Aster Tribe). One sp., a robust, spreading shrub, endemic to New Zeal.; lvs. crowded in rosettes at ends of brs., entire; fl. heads radiate, solitary on long peduncles, involucre nearly globose, involucral bracts very numerous, densely imbricate in many rows, receptacle slightly convex, pitted; disc fls. bisexual, yellow, ray fls. in 2–3 series, female, white; achenes linear, grooved, silky-hairy, pappus of 1 row of rough capillary bristles.

insignis (Hook.f.) Cheesem. Shrub, occasionally to 6 ft.; lvs. thick, leathery, blades oblong to obovate-oblong or ovate-oblong, to 6⅜ in. long, glabrous above when mature, with dense, soft, white to yellowish hairs beneath, petioles stout, to 2 in. long; heads to 3 in. across, peduncles to 1 ft. long. Var. **minor** Cheesem. Smaller and more slender in all parts; lvs. to 4 in. long including petiole; heads to 1⅜ in. across, peduncles to 4 in. long.

PACHYSTIMA: see *PAXISTIMA.*

×PACHYVERIA Hort. Haage & Schmidt ex A. Berger: *Echeveria* × *Pachyphytum. Crassulaceae.* The petal appendages characteristic of *Pachyphytum* are present in some hybrids, lacking in others.

Fancy-named hybrids are: ×*Pachyveria* cvs. **'E. O. Orpet'** [*Echeveria* sp.? × *Pachyphytum bracteosum*], lvs. obovate-spatulate, to 7 in., purplish, infl. 2–3-branched; **'La Rochette No. 1'** [*Echeveria gibbiflora* cv. 'Flammea'? × *Pachyphytum bracteosum*], lvs. few, to 4 in., red-tinged; **'Mrs. Scannavino'** [*Echeveria* sp.? × *Pachyphytum bracteosum*], lvs. obovate, glaucous. For culture see *Succulents.*

brevifolia: a listed name of no botanical standing; perhaps referring to *Pachyphytum brevifolium.*

clavata Walth.: *Echeveria* sp.? × *Pachyphytum bracteosum.* Lvs. gray, broadest near middle; cincinni mostly 2; fls. short-pedicelled, crowded, sepals broad, as long as corolla, appressed, petals with appendages. Has been misidentified with ×*Pachyveria clavifolia* (A. Berger) Walth., which apparently is not cult. in Amer. Cv. **'Cristata'** is crested.

clavifolia: see ×*Pachyveria clavata.*

Clevelandii Walth.: *Echeveria secunda?* × *Pachyphytum bracteosum.* Lvs. about 70, cuneate-spatulate, 3–4 in. long, 1 in. wide, acute and mucronate, purple-tinged; sepals ascending, half as long as corolla, petals without appendages, ⅜ in. long. Also known as *Echeveria nobilis.*

Corneliusii: a listed name of no botanical standing; probably for *Pachyphytum* cv. 'Cornelius Hybrid'.

Curtisii: a listed name of no botanical standing; plants said to form rosettes of about 25 turgid, narrowly obovate, minutely pointed lvs., bluish-green tipped with red.

glauca Hort. Haage & Schmidt ex A. Berger. Lvs. about 40, crowded, angled and nearly angular-cylindrical, to 2 in. long, slightly flattened, acute, glaucous; fl. st. 1 ft. or more, slender, cincinnus 1, about 8-fld., pedicels to ⅜ in. long, bracts small, not overlapping; sepals equal, appressed, ¼ in. long, petals appendaged, ½ in. long, the tips spreading. Parentage given as *Echeveria* sp. × *Pachyphytum Hookeri,* but *Pachyphytum compactum* seems more likely.

Haagei: a listed name of no botanical standing, to be treated as ×*Pachyveria* cv. 'Haagei', for the hybrid ?*Pachyphytum compactum* × ?. JEWEL PLANT. Said to have compact rosettes of 30–45 oblong, minutely pointed, turgid but flattened lvs., these bluish-green, with purplish-red towards apex; fls. yellow and orange.

mirabilis (Deleuil) Walth.: *Echeveria* sp.? × *Pachyphytum bracteosum.* Lvs. about 60, oblanceolate, 2½ in. long, ¾ in. wide, acute, glaucous, concave above; fl. st. 8 in., cincinnus 1, pedicels ¼ in. long; sepals appressed, as long as corolla, acute, petals with appendages.

Orpetii: a listed name of no botanical standing; perhaps referring to ×*Pachyveria* cv. 'E. O. Orpet'.

pachyphytoides (De Smet) Walth.: *Echeveria gibbiflora* cv. 'Metallica' × *Pachyphytum bracteosum.* Like *Pachyphytum bracteosum* but larger; lvs. tinged purple; fl. st. with larger acute lvs., cincinni 2–3; petals pink, appendaged.

Scheideckeri (De Smet) Walth. [*Echeveria Scheideckeri* De Smet]: *Echeveria secunda* × *Pachyphytum bracteosum.* Cespitose; lvs. about 50, cuneate-spatulate, about 2 in. long, acute, turgid, blue-glaucous; fl. st. about 5 in., cincinnus 1, about 10-fld., bracts overlapping; sepals appressed, broad, nearly as long as corolla, petals ½ in. long, without appendages. Cv. **'Albocarinata'**. Lvs. white-striped. Cv. **'Cristata'**. JEWELLED-CROWN. Lvs. crested.

Schickendantzii: a listed name of no botanical standing.

sobrina (A. Berger) Walth.: *Echeveria* sp.? × *Pachyphytum Hookeri.* Lvs. about 20, oblanceolate, 2 in. long, ⅜ in. wide, $^{3}/_{16}$ in. thick, acute, nearly cylindrical, glaucous; fl. st. to 10 in., cincinni 1–2, 6–15-fld.; sepals nearly equal, triangular-lanceolate, to ½ in. long, petals with appendages, to ½ in. long.

sodalis (A. Berger) Walth.: *Echeveria* sp.? × *Pachyphytum bracteosum.* Sts. short; lvs. 15–25, spatulate to cuneate, to 3½ in. long and 1½ in. wide, glaucous, apex broadly acute to nearly truncate, minutely pointed; fl. st. 16–20 in., infl. trailing, of 2–3 cincinni, pedicels ¼ in. long, bracts overlapping; sepals unequal, lanceolate, about as long as corolla, petals with appendages.

PAEDEROTA L. *Scrophulariaceae.* Two spp. of per. herbs, native to s. Eur.; lvs. opp., simple; fls. blue or yellow, in terminal, bracted, spikelike racemes, calyx 5-lobed, corolla 2-lipped, upper lip usually entire, lower lip 3-lobed, stamens 2, exserted from tube; fr. a caps.

Bonarota (L.) L. [*Veronica Bonarota* L.]. To 8 in.; lvs. to 1¼ in. long, orbicular to lanceolate, with 3–6 or to 9 teeth on each side; corolla ⅜–½ in. long, violet-blue or rarely pink. E. Alps.

PAEONIA L. PEONY. *Paeoniaceae.* About 33 spp. of n. temp. Eurasia and w. N. Amer.; stout to coarse per. herbs or diffuse shrubs, the herbaceous kinds rhizomatous and with thickened and tuberous roots; lvs. alt., large, compound; fls. 1 or few at ends of sts., petals 5–10, purple, red, pink, yellow, or white, stamens many, pistils 2–8; fr. a cluster of horizontally spreading follicles.

Peonies are among the most popular flower garden plants and are very hardy, blooming in spring and early summer. They thrive in any soil, but fertile loam is best. Being gross feeders they should in late autumn be given a top dressing, which is worked into the soil in spring. Propagated by division of clumps in late summer or autumn, by layers, and by cuttings; also by seeds, which will not produce blooming-size plants for about 3 years and, in the case of cultivars, cannot be expected to reproduce the parent exactly. Cultivars may be propagated by grafting on a piece of tuber with eyes removed, in late summer or early autumn, which is then stored over winter and planted out in spring. Peonies may also be forced in the greenhouse.

The common herbaceous peonies are mostly derivatives of *P. lactiflora,* and the tree peonies of *P. suffruticosa,* although other species are now used in the development of newer cultivars. In the past many cultivars were given Latin names. Most of these have since been discarded, but among those currently in the trade are such as **'Atrosanguinea'**, **'Aurea'**, **'Candidissima'**, **'Carnea Elegans'**, **'Delicatissima'**, **'Edulis Superba'**, **'Festiva Maxima'**, **'Gigantea'**, **'Grandiflora'**, **'Humei'**, **'Ligulata'**, **'Nigricans'**, **'Odorata'**, **'Umbellata Rosea'**, **'Violacea'**, and **'Whittleyi Major'**. Descriptions and classification of cultivars are to be found in publications of the American Peony Society.

albiflora: *P. lactiflora.*

anomala L. [*P. laciniata* Pall.]. Sts. to 2 ft., 1-fld.; lvs. 2-ternate, lfts. pinnately dissected, narrowly oblong, acuminate, with minute bristles along veins above; fls. 3–4 in. across, bright crimson, filaments yellow, pistils 3–5, glabrous, stigmas yellow or crimson. Ural Mts. to Siberia and cent. Asia. Very hardy. Var. **intermedia** (C. A. Mey.) O. Fedtsch. & B. Fedtsch. Pistils villous. More commonly cult. than the typical var. Some material offered as this sp. or its var. may be *P.* ×*Smouthii.*

arborea: *P. suffruticosa.*

arietina: *P. mascula* subsp.

banatica: *P. officinalis* subsp., but the name has often been misapplied to *P. mascula.*

Banksii: a listed name of no botanical standing for *P. suffruticosa* cv.

Beresowskii: *P. Veitchii* var.

Broteri Boiss. & Reut. Sts. 1–1½ ft., glabrous, 2–3-fld.; lower lvs. 2-ternate, terminal and often lateral lfts. deeply divided into 2–3 segms., acute, glabrous, glossy green above, glaucous beneath; fls. 3–4 in. across, rose, filaments yellow, pistils 2–4, tomentose. Spain, Portugal.

Brownii Dougl. ex Hook. Sts. 1–1 ½ ft., with 5–8 lvs.; lvs. 2-ternate, dark green above, glaucous beneath, primary divisions short-stalked, divided into three 3–4-lobed segms.; fls. about 1 in. across, globose, petals to ½ in. long, deep maroon or bronze, shorter than inner sepals, pistils 5, glabrous. Early summer. B.C. to n. Calif., e. to Wyo. and Nev. Difficult in cult.

californica Nutt. ex Torr. & A. Gray [*P. Brownii* subsp. *californica* (Nutt. ex Torr. & A. Gray) Abrams]. Sts. 1½–2½ ft., with 7–12 lvs.; lvs. 2-ternate, dark green above, paler green beneath, primary divisions nearly sessile, divided into three 2–3-lobed segms.; fls. about 1¼ in. across, globose, petals to 1 in. long, blackish-red, longer than inner sepals, pistils 3. Spring. Coastal mts., s. Calif.

Cambessedesii Willk. MAJORCAN P. Sts. 1–1½ ft.; lvs. deep purple beneath, leathery, glabrous, lower lvs. 2-ternate, upper lvs. ternate; fls. 2½–4 in. across, deep rose, pistils 5–8, glabrous, dark purple; follicles 2¼ in. long. Spring. Balearic Is. Tender, needing protection from heavy freezes.

caucasica: *P. mascula* subsp. *mascula.*

chinensis: *P. lactiflora.*

corallina: *P. mascula* subsp. *mascula.*

coriacea Boiss. Sts. about 20 in., glabrous; lvs. leathery, the lower ones 2-ternate, lfts. ovate to elliptic, some lfts. divided, the lf. then with 14–16 segms.; fls. 3–6 in. across, rose, pistils 2, glabrous. Late spring. S. Spain to Morocco.

daurica Andr. [*P. triternata* Pall.]. Sts. 1¼-2 ft., glabrous; lower lvs. 2-ternate, lfts. broadly ovate to orbicular, with undulate margins; fls. 3–3¾ in. across, rose-red, pistils 2–3, densely hairy. Nw. Yugoslavia to Asia Minor.

decora: *P. peregrina.*

Delavayi Franch. Shrub (a "tree peony"), 4–6 ft.; lvs. 2-ternate, lfts. oblong-elliptic, the 3 terminal lfts. set ahead of the laterals; fls. about 3 in. across, dark maroon-red, with 8–12 bracts forming an involucre immediately below the calyx, sepals 5, pistils 4–5, glabrous, the lobes of the fleshy basal disc conspicuous. W. China. Zone 5. Var. **angustiloba:** *P. Potaninii.* Var. **lutea:** *P. lutea.*

edulis: *P. lactiflora.*

emodi Wallich ex Royle. Sts. 1–3 ft., glabrous; lower lvs. 2-ternate, upper lvs. ternate, lfts. elliptic, often decurrent, minutely puberulous along veins above; fls. 3–5 in. across, white, pistils usually 1, yellow-hairy. Himalayas of Kashmir. Differs from *P. lactiflora* in having margins of lfts. not scabrid, fls. always white, and pistil solitary, with yellow hairs. Requires winter protection.

festiva maxima: a listed name of no botanical standing for *P. lactiflora* cv.

fragrans: *P. lactiflora.*

fulgida Sab. ex Salm-Dyck. A name of unknown application and of no botanical standing. Cult. material of this name may be *P. lactiflora* cv. 'Fulgida', a century-old cv. with double magenta fls.

Henryi: a listed name of no botanical standing.

humilis: *P. officinalis* subsp. Var. **villosa:** *P. officinalis* subsp.

japonica (Mak.) Miyabe & Takeda [*P. obovata* var. *japonica* Mak.]. Related to *P. obovata,* but lfts. villous beneath, fls. to 2 in. across, nearly globose, white, stigmas slightly recurved. Mt. woodlands, Japan. Difficult to cult. Plants offered as *P. japonica* may sometimes be cvs. of the "Japanese" class of *P. suffruticosa.*

laciniata: *P. anomala;* see also *P. tenuifolia* cv.

lactea: *P. lactiflora.*

lactiflora Pall. [*P. albiflora* Pall.; *P. chinensis* Hort. Vilm.-Andr.; *P. edulis* Salisb.; *P. fragrans* (Sab.) Redouté; *P. lactea* Pall.; *P. Reevesiana* (Paxt.) Loud.; *P. sinensis* Hort.]. CHINESE P., COMMON GARDEN P. Sts. 1½–3 ft., glabrous, each 2- or more-fld.; lower lvs. 2-ternate, lfts. elliptic to lanceolate, entire or occasionally lobed, margins rough-scabrous; fls. 2¾–4 in. across, fragrant, typically white, but often in shades of pink and red, pistils 4–5, glabrous, or hairy in some garden plants. Tibet to China and Siberia. Hundreds of named cvs. have been derived from this sp.; **'Festiva Maxima'**, with double white fls. flecked with crimson, may be mentioned as an old and still highly rated favorite (introd. in 1851).

lobata: a confused name, which has been applied to several spp., including *P. latiflora, P. Broteri, P. peregrina,* and *P. officinalis* subsp. *villosa.*

lutea Delav. ex Franch. [*P. Delavayi* var. *lutea* (Franch.) Finet & Gagnep.]. Shrub (a "tree peony"), to 5 ft., glabrous, differing from *P. Delavayi* in absence of involucre immediately beneath calyx, the bracts and sepals together not more than 8 in number, and in having fls. yellow, 2–3 in. across, pistils 3–4. W. China. Zone 6. Cvs. include: **'Speciosa'**, **'Splendens'**, **'Superba'**. Var. **Ludlowii** F. C. Stern & G. Tayl. TIBETAN P. To 8 or 9 ft.; fls. 3–5 in. across, pistils 1–2. Earlier-flowering than the typical var. Tibet.

Ludlowii: a listed name for *P. lutea* var.

macrophylla (Albov) Lomak. [*P. Wittmanniana* var. *macrophylla* (Albov) N. Busch ex Grossh.]. Sts. to 3 ft. or more; lvs. very large, lfts. elliptic-lanceolate, ovate- or obovate-rounded to nearly orbicular, 6–10 in. long, 4–6 in. wide, glaucous beneath, with sparse long hairs along main veins; fls. large, 3 in. across or more, white with tinge of yellow, pistils glabrous. W. Caucasus. Considered by some to be conspecific with *P. Wittmanniana*, but apparently a much larger plant, with white rather than yellow fls.

mascula (L.) Mill. Sts. 2–3 ft.; lvs. mostly 2-ternate, lfts. narrowly to broadly elliptic, cuneate, acute; fls. 3–5½ in. across, rose-red, pistils 3–5, usually pubescent. Subsp. **mascula** [*P. caucasica* (Shipch.) Shipch.; *P. corallina* Retz.]. The typical subsp.; lvs. glabrous beneath. Widespread in s. Eur. Subsp. **arietina** (G. Anderson) Cullen & Heyw. [*P. arietina* G. Anderson]. Lvs. pubescent beneath, upper lvs. with 12–15 narrow-elliptic lfts. E. Eur., Asia Minor. A white-fld. cv. is known. Subsp. **Russi** (Biv.) Cullen & Heyw. [*P. Russi* Biv.]. Lvs. pubescent beneath, lower lvs. with 9–10 broad-elliptic to ovate lfts. Corsica, Sardinia. Several variants occur. This subsp. is rare in cult.

microcarpa: *P. officinalis* subsp. *villosa.*

Mlokosewitschii Lomak. Sts. to 3½ ft., glabrous; lvs. 2-ternate, lfts. broadly oblong to ovate or obovate, mostly 2½–4 in. long, obtuse, sparsely short-hairy beneath; fls. 3–4¾ in. across, yellow, pistils 2–4, densely white-hairy. Early-flowering. Cent. Caucasus. By some considered conspecific with *P. daurica*, with which it produces fertile hybrids.

mollis G. Anderson [*P. pubens* Sims]. Sts. 1–1½ ft., rigidly upright, glabrous to villous; lvs. mostly 2-ternate, lfts. sessile, 2–3-lobed, the lf. with 20 or more segms., green and glabrous above, glaucous and densely white-hairy beneath; fls. about 3 in. across, cup-shaped, red or white, short-pedicelled, pistils 2–3, densely hairy. Probably of garden origin.

Moutan: *P. suffruticosa.*

multifida: *P. peregrina.*

obovata Maxim. Sts. 1½–2 ft., glabrous; lvs. 2-ternate, terminal lft. usually obovate, other lfts. ovate to oblong, all glabrous to sparsely hairy beneath; fls. 3 in. across, opening widely, rose to white, filaments white to pink, pistils 2–3, glabrous, stigmas coiled. China and Manchuria to Japan and Sakhalin. Only the white-fld. form is known to be in cult. Var. **japonica:** *P. japonica.* Var. **Willmottiae:** *P. Willmottiae.*

officinalis L. Sts. 1¼–2 ft.; lvs. mostly 2-ternate, lfts. more or less deeply cut into narrowly elliptic segms. 3–4 in. long, to 1 in. wide, glabrous above, pubescent beneath; fls. 3½–5 in. across, opening wide, red, filaments red, pistils 2–3. Subsp. **officinalis** [*P. fulgida* Sab. ex Salm-Dyck]. PINEY. The typical subsp.; most or all lfts. cut into segms. nearly to base; pistils tomentose. France to Hungary and Albania. There are several cvs. of this subsp., with single or double, white, pink, to red fls. Subsp. **banatica** (Rochel) Soó [*P. banatica* Rochel]. Only central lft. cut into segms. nearly to base; pistils tomentose. Hungary, Yugoslavia, Romania. Subsp. **humilis** (Retz.) Cullen & Heyw. [*P. humilis* Retz.; *P. paradoxa* G. Anderson]. Lfts. cut into segms. to about ⅓ their length; sts. and petioles pubescent; follicles glabrous. Sw. Eur. Subsp. **villosa** (Huth) Cullen & Heyw. [*P. humilis* var. *villosa* (Huth) F. C. Stern; *P. microcarpa* Salm-Dyck]. Lfts. as in subsp. *humilis*; sts. and petioles floccose; follicles tomentose. S. France, Italy.

paradoxa: *P. officinalis* var. *humilis.*

peregrina Mill. [*P. decora* G. Anderson; *P. multifida* Salm-Dyck]. Sts. 1½–3 ft., glabrous; lvs. mostly 2-ternate, some lfts. divided, the lf. with about 15–17 segms.; fls. 3–4½ in. across, red, cup-shaped, filaments red, pistils 2–3, tomentose. Italy, Balkan Pen.

Potaninii Kom. [*P. Delavayi* var. *angustiloba* Rehd. & E. H. Wils.]. Shrub (a "tree peony"), allied to *P. Delavayi*, but stoloniferous, lacking an involucre immediately below calyx, and having fls. 2–2½ in. across, deep red to white. Szechwan (w. China). Var. **trollioides** (Stapf ex F. C. Stern) F. C. Stern [*P. trollioides* Stapf ex F. C. Stern]. Plant more erect; lf. segms. more acuminate; fls. yellow, cup-shaped. Tibet.

pubens: *P. mollis.*

Reevesiana: *P. lactiflora.*

Russi: *P. mascula* subsp.

sinensis: *P. lactiflora.*

×**Smouthii** Van Houtte: *P. lactiflora* × *P. tenuifolia.* Sts. usually 2–4-fld.; lvs. finely dissected; fls. single, crimson-red, fragrant. A very early-flowering sterile hybrid, often sold as *P. anomala* or its var. *intermedia.*

suffruticosa Andr. [*P. arborea* J. Donn; *P. Moutan* Sims]. TREE P. Coarsely branched shrub, to 7 ft.; lvs. 2-pinnate, lfts. mostly deeply and incisedly divided, acute, with a few hairs along midrib; fls. 6–8 in. across, rose-pink to white, with magenta blotch at base of petals, pistils 5, green, at first enveloped by a thin, white lobe of the disc that splits as the follicles develop. Bhutan to Tibet and China. Zone 5. Many named cvs. are cult., with fls. varying from single to double and from white to pink, red, purple, and even light yellow. Cv. **Banksii.** Fls. double, flesh-pink. Var. **spontanea** Rehd. Lfts. smaller, more or less bluntly 3-lobed. Shensi (China).

tenuifolia L. Sts. 1½–2 ft., densely leafy, 1-fld.; lvs. fernlike, mostly 2-ternate, lfts. dissected into narrowly linear segms., glabrous; fls. 2¼–3½ in. across, deep crimson, appearing to rest on the lvs., filaments yellow, pistils 2–3, tomentose. Early-flowering. Se. Eur. to Caucasus. Cv. **'Laciniata'** [*P. laciniata* DC., not Pall.]. Taller; lft. segms. broader. Perhaps not different from material passing as cv. 'Latifolia'. Cv. **'Plena'.** Fls. double. Cv. **'Rosea'.** Fls. rose-red.

triternata: *P. daurica.*

trollioides: *P. Potaninii* var.

Veitchii Lynch. Sts. glabrous, 2–4-fld.; lvs. 2-ternate, glabrous except for minute, scattered bristles on veins above and sometimes beneath, lfts. deeply cut into 2–4 mostly lobed, long-attenuate segms.; pistils 2–4, densely tomentose. W. China. Var. **Veitchii.** The typical var.; sts. to 1¾ ft.; fls. 2–4 in. across, various shades of rose-purple, innermost sepal rounded or notched apically but with a definite mucro ³⁄₃₂–¼ in. long. Var. **Beresowskii** (Kom.) Shipch. [*P. Beresowskii* Kom.]. Sts. to 1¾ ft.; fls. 2–4 in. across, innermost sepal attenuate to a definite mucro, petals notched at apex, cream to light pink, stigmas cream. W. China. Var. **Woodwardii** (Stapf ex Cox) F. C. Stern [*P. Woodwardii* Stapf ex Cox]. Sts. to 1 ft.; fls. to about 2½ in. across, innermost sepal as in var. *Beresowskii*, petals entire at apex, deep rose-pink, stigmas pink. Flowering earlier than var. *Beresowskii*. Mts., nw. China. This sp. and its vars. have by some been considered merely ecological variants of *P. anomala.*

Willmottiae: *P. obovata* var.

Wittmanniana Hartwiss ex Lindl. Sts. 3–3½ ft., glabrous; lvs. mostly 2-ternate, lfts. broadly ovate to elliptic, villous beneath, densely so on veins; fls. 4–5 in. across, pale yellow, pistils 2–4, tomentose, stigmas red. Nw. Caucasus. Var. **macrophylla:** *P. macrophylla.* Var. **nudicarpa** Shipch. Pistils glabrous. Common in cult. and passes as typical *P. Wittmanniana.*

Woodwardii: *P. Veitchii* var.

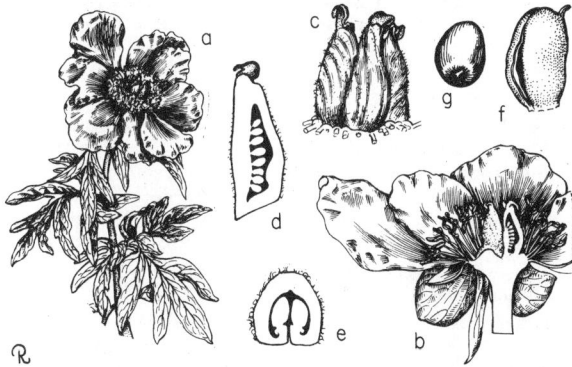

PAEONIACEAE. *Paeonia lactiflora:* **a,** upper part of flowering stem, × ¼; **b,** flower, vertical section, × ½; **c,** pistils, × 1; **d,** pistil, vertical section, × 1; **e,** ovary, cross section, × 1; **f,** follicle, × ½; **g,** seed, × 1.

PAEONIACEAE F. Rudolphi. PEONY FAMILY. Dicot.; 1 genus, *Paeonia*, of coarse, per., rhizomatous herbs or diffuse shrubs of temp. Eurasia, except for 2 spp. in w. N. Amer.; lvs. alt., pinnate or 2-ternate, without stipules; fls. showy, bisexual, sepals 5, persistent, petals many, stamens many, spirally arranged, the inner ones maturing before the outer (centrifugal), pistils 2–8, 1-celled, borne on a fleshy disc; fr. 2–8 follicles, leathery or woody at maturity, seeds subtended or basally enveloped by an aril. Related to the Ranunculaceae, but differing in having sepals persistent, stamens maturing centrifugally, pistils borne on a disc, and seeds with aril.

PAHUDIA: *AFZELIA.*

PALAFOXIA Lag. [*Othake* Raf.; *Polypteris* Nutt.]. *Compositae* (Helenium Tribe). About 10 spp. of ann. herbs, sometimes overwintering, native from Fla. to Colo., s. Calif., and n. Mex.; lvs. alt., simple, entire; fl. heads discoid or radiate, corymbose, involucre turbinate to hemispherical or cylindrical, involucral bracts in 2–3 rows, receptacle flat, naked; disc fls. bisexual, fertile, ray fls. absent or, if present, female and fertile; achenes obpyramidal, 4-angled, pappus of 7–10 scales.

Hookerana Torr. & A. Gray [*Othake Hookerana* (Torr. & A. Gray) Bush; *Polypteris Hookerana* (Torr. & A. Gray) A. Gray]. To 4 ft., sts. robust, branched at or below middle, usually glandular; lvs. lanceolate, to 4 in. long, rough on both sides; heads to 1 in. across or more, involucre broadly turbinate to campanulate; ray fls. rose-purple, ligules deeply 3-lobed. Se. Tex.

sphacelata (Torr.) V. L. Cory [*Othake sphacelata* (Torr.) Rydb.]. To 2 ft., sts. branching at or below middle; lvs. lanceolate to ovate-lanceolate, to 2¾ in. long; heads to 1 in. across or more, involucre narrowly turbinate to cylindrical; ray fls. reddish-pink, ligules 3-lobed. Ne. Colo. and sw. Kans. to n. Mex.

PALANDRA O. F. Cook. IVORY PALM, TAGUA. *Palmae.* One sp. of Ecuador and probably w. Colombia, related to *Phytelephas* but having a well-developed trunk and male fls. borne in small heads on short lateral brs. from a thick central axis.

May be found in tropical gardens. For culture see *Palms.*

aequatorialis (Spruce) O. F. Cook. To 12 ft. or more; lvs. to nearly 20 ft., petiole rounded below, slightly convex above, pinnae more than 100 on each side, nearly regular in arrangement or in groups of 2–5 at midleaf; male infl. more than 1 ft. long; fruiting heads about 1 ft. across.

PALICOUREA Aubl. *Rubiaceae.* About 200 spp. of shrubs or small trees, native to trop. Amer.; lvs. opp. or whorled, stipules interpetiolar; fls. in terminal panicles or racemes, usually 5-merous, corolla tube more or less elongate, straight or curved, often swollen at base, hairy inside, stamens exserted or included; fr. a berry, usually globular, seeds 2–4.

barbinervia DC. Shrub or tree, to 25 ft.; lvs. elliptic, to 10 in. long, glossy above; corolla white, tomentose, to ⅜ in. long, stamens included; berry ¼ in. long. W. Indies and Trinidad.

crocea (Swartz) Roem. & Schult. Shrub or sometimes a small tree, to 20 ft.; lvs. ovate or elliptic, to 8 in. long; fls. red, corolla glabrous, to ⅜ in. long, stamens included; berry purple-black, to ¼ in. long. Trop. Amer.

PALISOTA Rchb. ex Endl. *Commelinaceae.* About 25 spp. of per. herbs, native to trop. Afr.; lvs. often edged with reddish or brownish hairs; fls. white, rose, or bluish, in thyrses sometimes nearly hidden at base of foliage, stamens 5–6, the 3 opp. the petals fertile, the other 2–3 sterile and with a tuft of hairs at apex, ovary with 1–8 ovules in each cell; fr. a purple or red berry.

Occasionally grown in greenhouse collections. Propagated by cuttings over heat or by seeds.

Barteri Hook.f. Lvs. to 2 ft. long, 4½ in. wide, mostly basal; infl. short, dense, to 2 in. or rarely 4½ in. long; fls. white or tinged with purple, fertile stamens all alike, ovary hairy; fr. red.

bracteosa C. B. Clarke. Similar in habit to *P. Barteri;* lvs. elliptic-lanceolate to somewhat obovate, to 18 in. long, 4½ in. wide, nearly glabrous except for hairy margin; infl. to 3½ in. long, with bracts prominently exserted; fls. white, ovary glabrous; fr. red.

Elizabethae: *P. Pynaertii* cv.

hirsuta (Thunb.) K. Schum. [*P. thyrsiflora* Benth.]. Sts. to 15 ft.; upper lvs. opp. or whorled, lanceolate-obovate or oblong-elliptic, to 15 in. long, 4 in. wide; thyrse open, to 10 in. long, 2 in. wide, of cincinni on peduncles to 1 in. long; fls. white, ovary glabrous; fr. blue.

Mannii C. B. Clarke. Similar to *P. bracteosa,* but differing in having infl. bracts concealed by the fls.

Pynaertii De Wild. Sts. short; lvs. to 1½ ft. long, 6 in. wide, glabrous above, gray-pubescent beneath; infl. dense, to 3 in. long, pedicels to ⅜ in. long, bracts ovate-lanceolate, not longer than fls.; fls. white, ¼ in. long, some with fertile stamens all short, some with the front stamen twice as long as others. Cv. 'Elizabethae' [*P. Elizabethae* Gentil]. Lvs. with midvein greenish-yellow.

thyrsiflora: *P. hirsuta.*

PALIURUS Mill. *Rhamnaceae.* About 6–8 spp. of spiny trees or shrubs from s. Eur. to e. Asia; lvs. alt., simple; fls. in cymes, small, bisexual, 5-merous; fr. small, spherical, with a broad wing or rim surrounding it.

Sometimes grown as ornamentals but not hardy north of Washington, D.C. The species commonly grown, *P. Spina-Christi,* needs a sunny location and well-drained soil. Propagated by seeds sown in autumn or stratified, by layers and root cuttings.

aculeatus: *P. Spina-Christi.*

orientalis Hemsl. [*P. sinicus* C. K. Schneid.]. Tree, to 15 ft., spiny; lvs. ovate, to ½ in. long, petiole ⅛ in. long; fr. to ¾ in. diam. W. China.

sinicus: *P. orientalis.*

Spina-Christi Mill. [*P. aculeatus* Lam.]. CHRIST THORN, JERUSALEM T. Tree, to 20 ft., with straight and hooked spines; lvs. ovate, to 1½ in. long, mostly finely toothed, 3-ribbed; fls. greenish-yellow; fr. brownish-yellow, to 1 in. in diam. S. Eur. to n. China. Zone 7.

PALMAE Juss. or, alternatively, **ARECACEAE** Schultz-Bip. PALM FAMILY. Monocot.; about 210 genera and 2,780 spp. of evergreen, shrublike or treelike plants or vines in trop., subtrop., and occasionally warm-temp. regions of both hemispheres; sts. woody, solitary or clustered, or colonial from elongate rhizomes, rarely branched aerially, erect, prostrate, creeping, or climbing, slender to very thick, smooth, prickly, or covered with persistent lf. sheaths; lvs. alt., sheaths tubular in bud, at maturity tubular and sometimes forming a prominent cylinder (crownshaft) below the lvs., or split, petiole usually present, sometimes toothed at the margin or prickly, blades palmate, costapalmate, pinnate (2-pinnate in *Caryota*), or undivided and palmately or pinnately veined, always with a prominent midrib (costa or rachis), segms. or pinnae 1- to several-ribbed, acute to 2-cleft, truncate, or oblique and toothed at the apex; infl. among, below, or above the lvs., paniculate to spicate, peduncle always bearing a basal, 2-edged bract (prophyll) and usually 1 or more persistent or deciduous upper bracts, infl. brs. usually subtended by a small to prominent bract; fls. bisexual or unisexual (the plants then monoecious or dioecious), sessile, pedicelled, or sometimes sunken in pits, borne singly or in clusters of several (cincinni), or in 3's (triads), of 2 male and 1 female, or in lines (acervuli) of several male and a female, or in pairs of a bisexual and neuter, or bisexual and male, or male fls. often paired towards ends of fl. brs. (rachillae), sepals and petals usually 3 in each whorl, but sometimes 2 or more than 3, separate and imbricate, or valvate, or united, or the perianth of one series and lobed, stamens often 6, sometimes 3 or to more than 250, carpels usually 3, sometimes 2, 1, or more than 3, separate or united, superior, ovule 1 in each cell; fr. fleshy or dry, sometimes covered with scales, hairs, or prickles, sometimes with a bony endocarp, seeds 1–3 or more, endosperm copious, homogeneous or ruminate. The cult. genera are: *Acanthophoenix, Acoelorrhaphe, Acrocomia, Actinorhytis, Aiphanes, Allagoptera, Archontophoenix, Areca, Arecastrum, Arenga, Arikuryroba, Asterogyne, Astrocaryum, Attalea, Bactris, Balaka, Basselinia, Bismarckia, Borassus, Brahea, Brassiophoenix, Butia, Calamus, Calyptrocalyx, Calyptrogyne, Calyptronoma, Carpentaria, Caryota, Ceroxylon, Chamaedorea, Chamaerops, Chambeyronia, Chrysalidocarpus, Clinostigma, Coccothrinax, Cocos, Colpothrinax, Copernicia, Corypha, Cryosophila, Cyrtostachys, Daemonorops, Deckenia, Desmoncus, Dictyosperma, Drymophloeus, Elaeis, Eleiodoxa, Euterpe, Gastrococos, Gaussia, Geonoma, Gronophyllum, Hedyscepe, Heterospathe, Howea, Hydriastele, Hyophorbe, Hyphaene, Johannesteijsmannia, Juania, Jubaea, Jubaeopsis, Kentiopsis, Laccospadix, Latania, Lepidorrhachis, Licuala, Linospadix, Livistona, Lodoicea, Mauritia, Maximiliana, Microcoelum, Nannorrhops, Neodypsis, Nephrosperma, Normanbya, Nypa, Oncosperma, Opsiandra, Orbignya, Palandra, Parajubaea, Phoenicophorium, Phoenix, Phytelephas, Pinanga, Polyandrococos, Pritchardia, Pseudophoenix, Ptychococcus, Ptychosperma, Raphia, Reinhardtia, Rhapidophyllum, Rhapis, Rhopaloblaste, Rhopalostylis, Rhyticocos, Roystonea, Sabal, Salacca, Satakentia, Scheelea, Schippia, Serenoa, Siphokentia, Syagrus, Synechanthus, Thrinax, Trachycarpus, Trithrinax, Veitchia, Verschaffeltia, Vonitra, Wallichia, Washingtonia,* and *Zombia.*

Besides furnishing many ornamental species for horticulture, the family is of major economic importance, including two of the world's most important cultivated trees, the coconut palm and African oil palm, which are primary sources of industrial vegetable fats. In addition, various species provide a wide range of other necessities of life, especially in the tropics, such as: edible fruits and seeds, masticatories, sugar and starch, fresh, fermented, and distilled beverages, vegetable wax, fibers for brushes and ropes, stems for construction and furniture,

PALMAE. **A,** *Cocos nucifera:* **Aa,** tree in fruit, much reduced; **Ab,** inflorescence and bracts, × ¹⁄₁₂; **Ac,** segment of rachilla with unopened female (below) and open male flowers, × ½; **Ad,** segment of rachilla with male flower, × 1; **Ae,** female flower, × ½; **Af,** female flower, vertical section, × ½; **Ag,** fruit, × ⅛; **Ah,** fruit, longitudinal section, × ⅛; **Ai,** "nut," × ⅙. **B,** *Chrysalidocarpus lutescens:* trunk apex, showing inflorescence, crownshaft, and petioles, much reduced. **C,** *Washingtonia filifera:* **Ca,** tree, much reduced; **Cb,** fruit, × 1. **D,** *W. robusta:* **Da,** flower, × ½; **Db,** flower, vertical section, × ½. (Aa-Ac, Ag-Ai, B, Ca, Cb from Bailey, *Manual of Cultivated Plants,* ed. 2.)

and leaf material for thatching, basketry, and similar crafts. See also *Palms.*

PALMS. Palms are highly ornamental and decorative, evergreen, mainly tropical, woody plants of the family Palmae, much prized in the juvenile state under glass or in the home, and extensively planted in tropical and warm-temperate regions around the globe, many of them yielding economic products of great importance. See *Coconut* and *Date.*

Palms are mostly treelike, but some are extensive climbers and others are shrubby, at times even diminutive. The trunk is various in character, and in some kinds is wholly subterranean. In most cases the trunk is unbranched, but in *Hyphaene* and a few others it may be naturally forked, sometimes extensively; multiple heads now and then occur in various palms following injury. The flowers of palms are mostly small but commonly numerous, bisexual or unisexual, borne on a simple or usually branching, often very large inflorescence that is mostly contained in or subtended by one to many sheathing bracts. Plants are most often monoecious but in some genera are dioecious, in others hermaphroditic.

The inflorescence is borne among the leaves in some genera, below them in others, and sometimes above the crown; the fruit may be small or large, one-seeded or three- to several-seeded, dry or fleshy, and sometimes brilliantly colored.

To the general observer and the horticulturist, the palms fall into two groups, (1) the fan-leaved or palmate kinds, and (2) the feather-leaved or plumose kinds, in which the veining or the division is pinnate on either side of a continuing rachis; these distinctions, however, do not hold strictly, for there are intermediate types. For positive identification, the inflorescence, flowers, and fruits must be known. The palms seen under glass are mostly in the juvenile state and their exact identification may be difficult or impossible.

The species planted represent most palm regions of the world. (For listed genera, see *Palmae.*) In the United States, ten genera are native, with about 44 species, most of the latter representing species of *Pritchardia* in Hawaii. Of the balance, the largest number (11, in the genera *Acoelorrhaphe, Coccothrinax, Pseudophoenix, Rhapidophyllum, Roystonea, Sabal, Serenoa,* and *Thrinax*) occur in Florida. California and Arizona share one species of *Washingtonia,* and Texas has one species of *Sabal. Rhapidophyllum, Sabal,* and *Serenoa* are represented also in the middle Gulf Coast area; and the cabbage palmetto, *Sabal Palmetto,* extends north along the Atlantic Coast to Cape Fear, North Carolina. All these native species have ornamental value and are especially suited to the geographical areas where they occur naturally.

Formerly many kinds of palms were grown in greenhouses and for decoration in residences, but the number has been reduced to those that can be grown most easily commercially in quantity production. However, in tropical areas like Hawaii, as well as in Zone 10, there are many ornamental palms available for outdoor plantings and as tub subjects for use in patio or lath house. A very large number of these same species are adaptable to indoor use as pot palms by home gardeners and others throughout the United States. The dwarf or semidwarf species especially suitable as ornamentals for indoor container culture include: *Balaka Seemannii,* species of *Chamaedorea* (especially *C. cataractarum, C. costaricana, C. elegans, C. erumpens, C. Klotzschiana,* and *C. Seifrizii*), *Chamaerops humilis, Coccothrinax argentata, Licuala grandis, L. spinosa, Microcoelum Weddellianum, Phoenix Roebelenii, Pinanga Kuhlii, Reinhardtia gracilis, Rhapis excelsa,* and *R. humilis.* Juvenile specimens of the following, among others, are also satisfactory as pot plants in the home: *Acoelorrhaphe Wrightii, Aiphanes caryotifolia, Archontophoenix Alexandrae, A. Cunninghamiana, Areca triandra, Arecastrum Romanzoffianum, Butia capitata, Caryota mitis, C. urens, Chrysalidocarpus lutescens, Cocos nucifera, Dictyosperma album, Drymophloeus Beguinii, Hedyscepe Canterburyana, Heterospathe elata, Howea Belmoreana, H. Forsterana, Livistona rotundifolia, Phoenix canariensis, P. reclinata, P. rupicola, Ptychosperma elegans, P. Macarthurii, Thrinax radiata, Trachycarpus Fortunei, Veitchia Merrillii,* and *Washingtonia robusta.*

Where they thrive outdoors, palms are outstanding as ornamentals. They are mostly durable plants, long-lived, relatively free of pests and diseases, and usually require a minimum of maintenance. Since most palms are tropical, frost is the major limiting factor in their use outdoors. In this volume, the plant hardiness zone numbers, when known, provide an indication of palm hardiness, but one should be aware that zone numbers are relative and not entirely satisfactory for all these plants. Some palms that grow quite well in Florida, because of higher average temperatures, cannot be grown satisfactorily in the same zone in California. Similarly, palms from areas with a Mediterranean climate like that in Zone 10 of southern California may thrive there but may not do so in the same zone in Florida. Palm species lacking a hardiness zone number are essentially tropical in their requirements (Zone 10b).

Within the United States, most of the palms listed will probably thrive outdoors in Hawaii, where many others, not yet introduced to cultivation, might also be grown. In the continental United States, the number of species capable of culture outdoors decreases rapidly in passing from the subtropical parts of Zone 10 to the normal limits of cultivation of a few of the hardiest species in Zone 8. *Trachycarpus Fortunei* appears to be the hardiest arborescent palm and has been cultivated on the coasts in Zone 8 as far north as Norfolk, Virginia, and Vancouver, British Columbia. Even hardier (to Zone 8) are our native nonarborescent species, *Rhapidophyllum hystrix* and *Sabal minor,* certain cultivated specimens of which have withstood temperatures of −12° F.

Most palms grow readily from good seed in mild heat under glass. Ideally, seed for planting should be fully ripe, planted within several days of harvest (most palm seed is short-lived), and under conditions that will induce rapid germination. A well-drained mix of peat and perlite, or peat and sand, or a comparable mixture kept warm (about 80° F) and moist is suitable. Most seeds need to be covered by the mix to a depth of ¼–½ inch. However, the large seeds of the coconut (planted with husks) are only half buried when planted. Some kinds of palms germinate quickly, others may take as long as two years. Germinated seedlings are trans-

planted when the first leaf is fully developed or as the second leaf begins to emerge. Seedlings should be grown in 50–70 percent shade, must be transplanted with much care to avoid injury to the delicate roots, and should be kept at temperatures of about 60° F at night and 70° to 80° during the day. Very few species can be propagated from offshoots (suckers) or by division, but this is the only way to multiply date cultivars for orchard plantings; however, for use in the home as potted ornamentals, young date palms are readily raised from seed of commercial fruits. Some small palms that produce adventitious roots, such as species of *Chamaedorea,* may become leggy with age, but can be reduced in height by marcotting (or air layering) the stem and replanting the rooted top once the air layer has developed a new root system.

Palms are relatively easy to manage as container subjects, but when they become too large it is better to discard them, replacing them with younger plants. In the home, palms thrive mostly in partial shade. Potting media may vary but should provide a fair amount of organic matter. Sand, perlite, peat moss, ordinary topsoil, wood shavings, rotted leaves, pulverized manure, or other substances may be used in various combinations as preferred to make up an adequate medium which should be light, sweet, and open. For a recommended mix see Foliage Plant Mix under *Soils.*

Good drainage is essential, and in the bottom of a large container 1 inch of gravel plus 2 inches of coarse sand is needed. Great care must be given not to overwater, for although actively growing young palms require constant moisture, they will not tolerate soggy soil. Transplanting to other pots should be undertaken in spring or summer when the roots are active, but one should not overpot, for growth may be checked. In summer, potted palms may be plunged in soil outdoors in partial shade in locations well protected from wind.

Palms should be moved only when their roots are active and may reestablish themselves. Palms require good soil and, in the growing season, abundant water to produce their best foliage. When young palms are planted outdoors, they should be placed where they are to stay. The hole to receive them should be much larger than the root ball and should be dug out and backfilled with topsoil mixed liberally with manure or the very best organic matter obtainable. If the soil is extremely sandy it should be replaced with soil high in organic matter. Before large palms are transplanted, they should be root-pruned so as to allow the initiation of new roots; after replanting, which should be done during a period of active growth, half to three-fourths of the leaf area should be removed.

The palms have great potential in landscape planting in climates adapted to them, but they are commonly very poorly placed for the best effect; the subject needs careful study by landscape architects. A palm, like any other plant, is not pleasing unless thrifty and exhibiting the characteristics of its kind. Often the plants are neglected or carelessly grown, and if placed where they must be constantly trimmed of their leaves they soon lose character and become valueless.

The intending grower may learn much about the needs of these plants through a knowledge of the climate and soils of the areas where his particular subjects are native. Desirable palm species for home gardens in subtropical Florida, southern California, or Hawaii may be seen in the living collections maintained by gardens and arboreta, especially in Miami, greater Los Angeles, and Honolulu. Botanical and horticultural interest in palms is actively sponsored internationally by The Palm Society, mainly through its journal *Principes.*

PAMIANTHE Stapf. *Amaryllidaceae.* Two or 3 spp. of bulbous herbs, native to n. S. Amer.; bulbs tunicate, with a long false neck; lvs. linear; fls. 1–4 in an umbel terminal on a scape and subtended by separate, linear spathe valves; perianth white or green-flushed, tube long, cylindrical, lobes nearly equal, thickened basally, stamens 6, filaments short and incurved, united at the base into a campanulate, 6-lobed corona, anthers versatile, exserted from the corona, style basally joined to perianth tube by 3 wings, ovary inferior, 3-celled, ovules many, one above another; fr. a caps., seeds pale brown, flat, winged apically.

peruviana Stapf. Lvs. 5–7, to 20 in. long, ¾–1½ in. wide; scape longer than lvs., umbel 2–4-fld.; fls. fragrant, white or flushed with cream, tube green, to 5 in. long, lobes to 5 in. long, the inner to 1¼ in. wide, corona 3 in. long, the lobes bifid or mucronate, free portions of filaments about ½ in. long. Peru.

PANAX L. GINSENG. *Araliaceae*. About 6 spp. of glabrous herbs, with thick roots and simple sts., native to N. Amer. and e. Asia; lvs. borne in whorls, palmately compound, lfts. toothed or lobed; fls. small, polygamous, in mostly single, terminal umbels, petals 5, imbricate, sometimes united, stamens 5, ovary 2–3-celled, styles 2–3, separate or in male fls. united; fr. a drupe, pyrenes 2–3.

The roots and rhizomes of several species are used medicinally in the Orient. Propagated by seeds, which should be stratified before sowing.

Ginseng: *P. pseudoginseng*.

pseudoginseng Wallich [*P. Ginseng* C. A. Mey.; *P. Schinseng* Nees]. GINSENG. To 2½ ft., root fusiform; lfts. 3–7, long-petioluled, obovate, 3–9 in. long, abruptly acuminate to caudate, serrate; umbels solitary or 2–4; fls. yellowish-green, styles 2–4; fr. red, globose, about ¼ in. long. Korea, Manchuria.

quinquefolius L. GINSENG, AMERICAN G. Mostly 1–2 ft., sometimes more, roots fusiform; lfts. 3–5, long-petioluled, somewhat obovate, to 6 in. long, abruptly acuminate, coarsely toothed, thin; fls. mostly bisexual, greenish-white, styles 2; fr. bright red, nearly ½ in. in diam. Que. to Minn., s. to Ga. and Okla. Cult. sporadically for export of roots and rhizomes.

trifolius L. DWARF G., GROUNDNUT. To 8 in., root globose; lfts. 3–5, to 1½ in. long, sessile or nearly so, acute, finely toothed; fls. often unisexual, white tinged with pink, styles 3; fr. yellowish. Nov. Sc. to Wisc. and Ga.

Schinseng: *P. pseudoginseng*.

PANCRATIUM L. *Amaryllidaceae*. Mostly summer-flowering bulbs, native to the Old World; lvs. basal; fls. in an umbel terminal on a solid scape and subtended by 1 or more separate spathe valves; perianth white, tube long, lobes narrow, stamens united at base into a cup or corona, ovary inferior, 3-celled, ovules many in each cell, one above another; fr. a caps., seeds black, angular. Plants grown under this name are likely to be *Hymenocallis*, which differs in number and arrangement of ovules, and type of seed.

Pancratiums should be kept at a night temperature of 60–70° F and well watered. Bulbs should be rested and kept dry through the winter. In late winter, they may be repotted or given a top dressing. Propagated by offsets or seeds.

canariense Ker-Gawl. To 2 ft.; lvs. sword-shaped, glaucous, to 2 ft. long; umbel 6–10-fld., outer spathe valves 2, pedicels very long; fls. white, to 2½ in. long, perianth tube about 1½ in. long, corona with bifid teeth. Canary Is.

caribaeum: *Hymenocallis caribaea*.

illyricum L. Lvs. strap-shaped, to 2 in. wide; scapes 1 ft. long or more, outer spathe valves solitary, pedicels short; perianth tube green, 1 in. long, lobes 1½ in. long, corona with bifid teeth, ¼ in. long, filaments to ¾ in. long. Medit. region.

maritimum L. SEA DAFFODIL. Lvs. to 2½ ft. long, linear, evergreen; outer spathe valves 2, pedicels short; fls. very fragrant, perianth tube to 3 in. long, lobes linear, 1½ in. long, corona with short triangular teeth, 1 in. long, filaments short. Medit. region.

zeylanicum L. Lvs. lanceolate, less than 1 ft. long, developing with the fls.; scape shorter than lvs., spathe valve 1, fl. solitary; perianth tube 2 in. long, lobes as long as tube, corona ¼ in. long, with large bifid teeth, filaments to 1¼ in. long. Trop. Asia.

PANDANACEAE R. Br. SCREW-PINE FAMILY. Monocot.; 3 or 4 genera of dioecious trees and shrubs, some scandent, native to warm regions of Old World, especially oceanic islands; lvs. crowded toward ends of brs., stiff, leathery, swordlike, keeled, usually spiny-margined, sheathing at base; fls. in panicles or crowded into spadixlike infls. subtended by often showy bracts, unisexual, perianth mostly 0, male fls. with many stamens, anthers basifixed, female fls. rarely with stami-

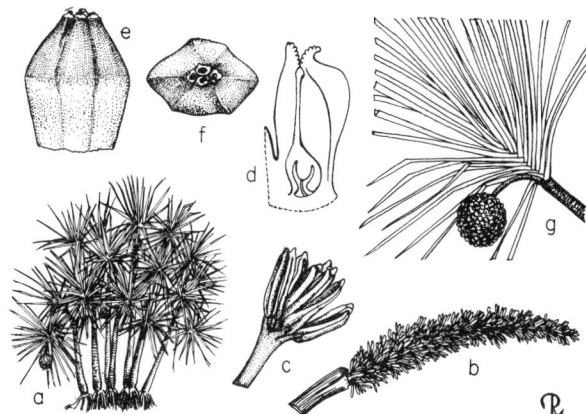

PANDANACEAE. *Pandanus utilis:* **a,** tree in fruit, much reduced; **b,** branch of male inflorescence, × ½; **c,** male flower, × 3; **d,** female flower, vertical section, enlarged; **e, f,** drupe, side and top views, × ½; **g,** fruiting branch, much reduced. (From Bailey, *Manual of Cultivated Plants,* ed. 2.)

nodes, ovary superior, 1-celled, ovaries of adjacent fls. often united into groups, becoming woody, drupelike, or berrylike, and forming an oblong or globose multiple fr. (syncarp). *Freycinetia* and *Pandanus* are cult. as ornamentals.

PANDANUS L. SCREW PINE. *Pandanaceae*. More than 650 spp. of dioecious shrubs and trees, native to Old World tropics; sts. with aerial prop roots and many brs. bearing crowns of spirally arranged lvs.; lvs. stiff, long-linear, keeled, usually spiny-margined, sometimes white-striped, or young lvs. essentially all white; infls. terminal, pendent; fls. without perianth, male fls. in branched spadices subtended by often showy, fragrant bracts, stamens many, female fls. mostly without staminodes, crowded in solitary dense heads or spikes, the ovaries becoming woody or drupaceous, and sometimes united, forming a multiple fr. (syncarp). A difficult genus taxonomically. Several so-called spp. are known only from sterile plants in cult., and have not yet been correlated with wild spp.

Screw pines may be planted outdoors in tropical or semitropical regions. Where they are native, their leaves are much used for thatch, and for making baskets, mats, etc. In the North plants in the juvenile stage are grown in greenhouses and window gardens, usually having a tuft of gracefully arching leaves and little or no apparent stem. They require constant moisture and heat, thriving in conditions suitable for palms. Propagation is by suckers that arise around the base, removed and planted in pots over bottom heat, or by seeds when available. Seeds should be soaked for 24 hours before planting.

Baptistii Hort. Veitch ex Misonne. Lvs. 1 in. wide, without spines, dark green or with 1 wide or 1–4 narrow, white, median stripes; fls. and fr. unknown. New Britain Is. Cv. 'Aureus'. Lvs. yellow-striped.

dubius K. Spreng. Straight-trunked tree, to 60 ft.; lvs. bright green, to 12 ft. long or more and 7 in. wide, broadly keeled, spiny on margins and underneath on keel, abruptly narrowed to a caudate tip to 3 in. long or more; syncarps large, globose, drupes 4 or 5 in. long, with 2–4 stigmas. New Guinea, Moluccas, Marianna Is. Prop roots yield a fiber for cordage. Juvenile plants of this sp., with lvs. bright green, to 20 in. long and 4–5 in. wide, have been called *P. pacificus*.

furcatus Roxb. [*P. urophyllus* Hance]. Tree, to 30 ft.; lvs. to 9 ft. long or more and 2¾ in. wide, spiny-margined, glaucous beneath; syncarp ellipsoid, to 9 in. long, ovaries separate, becoming 1-celled drupes to 1½ in. long, styles bifurcate, spinelike. Bengal and Burma. Lvs. made into mats.

Nelsonii: *P. Veitchii* cv. 'Compacta'.

odoratissimus L.f. BREADFRUIT, PANDANG. To 20 ft., much-branched; lvs. 3–5 ft. long, acuminate-caudate and becoming pendent at apex, with very long sharp spines on keel and margins, male spadices 3–4 in. long, bracts white, lanceolate, 4–12 in. long, fragrant, anthers caudate-acuminate, female infl. globose, 2 in. in diam., enclosed in yellow bracts, pistils united in groups of 6–10, stigmas short and reniform; syncarp oblong or globose, 6–10 in. in diam., orange-red, ovaries angular, apically smooth and convex. Ceylon, extending perhaps to Malay Arch. and Philippine Is. An overused name, incorrectly applied to diverse elements, its correct application still imperfectly understood. Male fls. yield an essential oil; lvs. are made into mats, baskets, floor covering, and used for thatching.

pacificus H. J. Veitch ex M. T. Mast. Apparently only the juvenile stage of *P. dubius.*

pygmaeus Thouars. Spreading, to 2 ft.; lvs. to 16 in. long, ⅜ in. wide, long-pointed at apex, spiny on margins and underneath on keel, glaucous beneath; syncarps elliptic, drupes 1-celled, united at base, stigmas broad and 2-lobed. Madagascar.

Rumphii: a confused name of variable application.

Sanderi Hort. Sander ex M. T. Mast. Lvs. to 2½ ft. long, 2 in. wide or more, with narrow, golden-yellow, central stripes, minutely spiny on margins; fr. unknown. Reputedly from Timor. Cv. **'Roehrsianus'**. Young lvs. golden-orange.

tectorius Parkins. PANDANUS PALM, THATCH S.P. Similar to, but different from *P. odoratissimus,* with much shorter spines on lf. margins. Tahiti. Further study is necessary to determine the correct application of the name.

urophyllus: *P. furcatus.*

utilis Bory. COMMON S.P. Tree, to 60 ft., much-branched, trunk smooth; lvs. to 6 ft. long and 4 in. wide, stiff, erect, markedly glaucescent, especially on lower surface, with small, reddish marginal spines; syncarp of 100–200 drupes, each 4–8-celled and about 1¼ in. long, the separate upper half green, the base with a purple or red band. Madagascar; now widespread. Much used for making baskets and mats.

Veitchii Hort. Veitch ex M. T. Mast. & T. Moore. VEITCH S.P. Lvs. 2–3 ft. long, 3 in. wide, light green, with broad, longitudinal, white stripes on or near margins, margins finely spinose; fls. and fr. unknown. Polynesia. The most popular house and florist's pandanus. Cv. **'Compacta'** [*P. Nelsonii* Hort.]. More compact; lvs. more rigid.

PANDOREA (Endl.) Spach. *Bignoniaceae.* Seven or 8 spp. of evergreen, woody vines, climbing without tendrils, native from the Malay Arch. to Australia; lvs. opp., odd-pinnate; fls. white or pink, in terminal panicles, calyx truncate or shortly 5-toothed, corolla funnelform-campanulate, slightly 2-lipped, stamens 4, ovary ovoid; fr. an oblong, woody-valved caps.

Pandoreas are grown outdoors in southern U.S., but may withstand a little frost. They require rich soil and sunny exposure. Propagated by seeds, and by cuttings of green wood under glass.

Brycei: *Podranea Brycei.*

jasminoides (Lindl.) K. Schum. [*Bignonia jasminoides* Hort., not Thunb.; *Tecoma jasminoides* Lindl.]. BOWER PLANT. Lfts. 5–9, ovate to lanceolate, to 2 in. long, entire, glabrous; fls. in few-fld. panicles, corolla white with pink throat, to 2 in. long. Australia. Cv. **'Alba'**. Fls. pure white. Cv. **'Rosea'**. Fls. pink.

pandorana (Andr.) Steenis [*Bignonia australis* (R. Br.) Ait.f.; *B. pandorana* Andr.; *Tecoma australis* R. Br.]. WONGA-WONGA VINE. Lfts. 3–9 or more, ovate to ovate-lanceolate, 1–3 in. long, entire or coarsely crenate, glabrous; fls. in many-fld. panicles, corolla yellowish-white, streaked with purple and often spotted, ¾ in. long. Malay Arch., Australia. Cv. **'Rosea'**. Fls. pale rose.

Ricasoliana: *Podranea Ricasoliana.*

PANICUM L. PANIC GRASS. *Gramineae.* About 600 spp. of ann. or per. grasses throughout the world, habits various; infl. an open or compact panicle, rarely racemose; spikelets more or less compressed dorsiventrally, with a bisexual terminal floret above a sterile floret and 2 glumes, glumes membranous, usually very unequal, the first often minute, the second typically equalling and resembling the sterile lemma, fertile lemma and palea hard-papery, the margins inrolled over an enclosed palea. For terminology see *Gramineae.*

A few species are grown for grain and forage and others for ornament.

antidotale Retz. GIANT P., BLUE P. Robust, rhizomatous per., sts. to 10 ft., glabrous, branching, leafy; lf. blades elongate, flat, to ½ in. wide; panicle to 1 ft. long, brs. many-fld., ascending; spikelets to ⅛ in. long, strongly nerved, pointed, the first glume ⅓–½ as long as the spikelet. India; introd. into the sw. states, escaped in Ariz. and Calif.

bulbosum HBK. BULB P. Per., sts. to 7 ft., clustered, lowest internode thickened, cormlike, budding at base; lf. sheaths glabrous or pilose toward the summit, blades to 2 ft. long and ½ in. wide, scabrous above, glabrous beneath; panicle to 20 in. long, open; spikelets ⅛ in. long. W. Tex. to Ariz., s. to Mex.

capillare L. WITCHGRASS, OLD-WITCH GRASS. Ann., sts. to 3 ft., erect or somewhat spreading at base, papillose-hispid to nearly glabrous; lvs. hispid, blades to 10 in. long and to ⅝ in. wide; panicles with divaricately spreading brs., often half the height of plant; spikelets less than ⅛ in. long. Me. to Mont., s. to Fla. and Tex., occasionally w. of this area. Sometimes used in dry bouquets; a weed in cult. ground.

crus-galli: *Echinochloa crus-galli.*

germanicum: *Setaria italica.*

maximum Jacq. GUINEA GRASS. Per., sts. in large clumps from short, stout rhizomes; lvs. glabrous to hairy, blades to 2½ ft. long and 1⅝ in. wide; panicles to 20 in. long, brs. naked at the base, the lower in whorls with short branchlets; spikelets short-pedicelled, ⅛ in. long, first glume about ⅓ the length of the spikelet. Afr.; naturalized and cult. in s. Fla., s. Tex., and Calif. Now the most important cult. forage grass of lowland trop. Amer.

miliaceum L. BROOMCORN, MILLET, HOG M., PROSO. Ann., sts. to 40 in., stout, erect or decumbent at base; lf. blades more or less pilose or glabrate, to 1 ft. long and ¾ in. wide; panicles usually more or less included at base, to 12 in. long, usually nodding, rather compact, brs. many, ascending, bearing spikelets toward the ends; spikelets to ¼ in. long; fr. to ⅛ in. long. Asia; escaped from cult. in the ne. states and occasional elsewhere. Used for forage, or the seed for hog feed.

obtusum HBK. VINE MESQUITE. Per., sts. clustered, compressed, to 32 in. high, stolons sometimes 7 ft. long or more, with long internodes, the nodes geniculate, swollen, conspicuously villous; lf. blades elongate, to ¼ in. wide, glabrous or nearly so; panicles to 4¾ in. long, about ⅜ in. wide; spikelets ⅛ in. long, obovoid, brownish, obtuse, first glume nearly as long as the spikelet. W. Mo. to Colo., s. to Tex., Ariz., and Mex.

palmatum: a name of no botanical standing for *Setaria palmifolia* or perhaps *S. Poiretiana.*

palmifolium: *Setaria palmifolia.*

purpurascens Raddi. PARA GRASS. Per., sts. to 18 ft., decumbent, rooting at base, nodes densely villous; lf. sheaths villous or the upper glabrous, densely pubescent on the collar, blades to 12 in. long and ⅝ in. wide, flat, glabrous; panicle to 8 in. long, brs. separated, ascending or spreading; spikelets subsessile, ⅛ in. long, second glume and sterile lemma 5-nerved. Afr.; naturalized in Fla., Ala., Tex., and Ore. Cult. as an important forage grass in tropics and warm-temp. regions.

ramosum L. BROWNTOP MILLET. Ann., sts. to 3 ft., erect or spreading from a decumbent base, sometimes branched near base; lf. sheaths glabrous to papillose-hispid, blades to 2 in. long and ½ in. wide, glabrous; panicle to 4 in. long; spikelets to ⅛ in. long, tawny or dull brown, glabrous to finely pubescent. Trop. Asia; introd. in N.C. to Fla., Ark., and La. Cult. for bird food.

variegatum: see *Oplismenus hirtellus* cv. 'Variegatus'.

virgatum L. SWITCH-GRASS. Per., sts. to 7 or rarely 10 ft., usually in large clumps, rhizomatous; lf. sheaths glabrous, blades to 2 ft. long and ⅝ in. wide, flat, glabrous or sometimes pilose; panicle to 20 in. long, open; spikelets to ¼ in. long, first glume shorter than the spikelet. Nov. Sc. to Wyo., s. to Fla., Ariz., Mex., and Cent. Amer. Sometimes grown as an ornamental.

PAPAVER L. POPPY. *Papaveraceae.* About 50 spp. or more of ann. or per. herbs or rarely subshrubs, with milky sap, native mostly to the Old World, but a few to w. N. Amer.; lvs. lobed or dissected; fls. showy, nodding in bud, solitary on long stalks, sepals 2, falling early, petals 4, crumpled in bud, red, white, violet, or yellow, stamens many; fr. a subcylindrical to nearly globose caps., opening by terminal pores.

In some countries, the drug opium, edible seeds, and an edible oil are important commercial products of *P. somniferum,* the opium poppy, whose culture in the U.S. is strictly controlled. Poppies are popular in borders and rock gardens. Seeds should be sown where plants are to grow, since they do not transplant well.

alpinum L. A name of doubtful application; some material grown under this name may be *P. Burseri.*

amurense: *P. nudicaule* cv.

Argemone L. Hispid ann., to 1½ ft.; lvs. pinnately dissected, segms. linear- to oblong-lanceolate; petals red, sometimes with a dark spot at base, to 1 in. long; caps. oblong-cylindrical, to ¾ in. long. N. Afr. and s. Eur.

atlanticum (J. Ball) Coss. Hairy per., to 2 ft.; lvs. toothed or pinnately lobed; petals orange-red or scarlet, to 1½ in. long; caps. narrowly club-shaped, to 1½ in. long, glabrous except on ridges at apex. Morocco.

bracteatum: *P. orientale.*

Burseri Crantz. Nearly stemless per., to 10 in.; lvs. 2–3-pinnate, segms. 3–4 on each side, lanceolate to linear, ¼–⅝ in. wide; petals usually white, to ¾ in. long; caps. oblong, to ½ in. long. Mts., cent. Eur. May be offered under the name *P. alpinum.*

californicum A. Gray. WESTERN P. Slender, glabrous ann., to 2 ft.; lvs. pinnately dissected; petals red, spotted with green at base, to 2 in. across; caps. top-shaped. Calif.

caucasicum: *P. fugax.*

commutatum Fisch. & C. A. Mey. [*P. Rhoeas* L. var. *commutatum* (Fisch. & C. A. Mey.) Elkan]. Spreading- and appressed-hairy ann., to 20 in.; lvs. pinnatifid, to 6 in. long, segms. 3–5 on each side, ovate to oblong in outline, to 1¼ in. long, entire or sparsely toothed; pedicels up to 1 ft., fls. nodding in bud, then erect, petals bright red with large dark blotch at base, rotund-obovate, to 1½ in. long, ovary constricted at base, stalked. Caucasus and Asia Minor. Closely related to *P. Rhoeas,* but having appressed hairs on pedicels, petals conspicuously blotched, and ovary and caps. stalked.

croceum: *P. nudicaule* cv.

dubium L. [*P. Mairei* Batt.]. Hispid ann., to 2 ft.; lvs. somewhat glaucous, basal lvs. pinnately dissected or pinnatifid, st. lvs. often bipinnatifid; petals red, sometimes with dark spot at base, suborbicular, to 1 in. long; caps. obovoid, to ¾ in. long. A variable sp. Eur., w. Asia; naturalized in N. Amer.

Fauriei Fedde. Hairy per.; lvs. basal, long-petioled, mostly ovate, pinnately lobed; scapes to 8 in. high; petals yellow, to ¾ in. long; caps. broadly ellipsoidal, to ⅜ in. long, hairy. N. Japan.

fugax Poir. [*P. caucasicum* Bieb.]. Sparsely hairy to glabrous bien., to 2 ft.; lvs. pinnately dissected, segms. triangular, ¼ in. wide or more; buds erect, petals orange. Caucasus.

glaucum Boiss. & Hausskn. TULIP P. Ann., similar to *P. somniferum,* but having lvs. pinnately lobed, the segms. triangular-oblong to linear-oblong; fls. to 4 in. across, petals red, with black blotch at base. Syria, Iraq, Iran.

Heldreichii: *P. spicatum.*

heterophyllum: *Stylomecon heterophylla.*

Kerneri Hayek. Scapose per., related to *P. Burseri;* lvs. 2- to 3-pinnate; petals yellow, ⅝ in. long or more; caps. broadly top-shaped, to ⅜ in. long. Mts., cent Eur.

lateritium C. Koch. Many-stemmed, hairy per., to 2 ft.; lvs. lanceolate, pinnatifid at base, upper half irregularly serrate, to 10 in. long; petals brick-red or bright orange. Turkey.

Macounii: *P. nudicaule.*

Mairei: *P. dubium.*

Miyabeanum: *P. nudicaule.*

monstrosum: a listed name of no botanical standing; has been applied to a form of *P. somniferum.*

Mursellii: a listed name of no botanical standing; has been applied to a form of *P. somniferum.*

Nordenhagenianum Á. Löve. Hairy per., with yellow sap; lvs. variable, usually long-petioled, 3-lobed or pinnately dissected; scapes many, to 12 in. high; petals yellow, deciduous or persistent; caps. ellipsoid or subglobose, to ¾ in. long. Iceland, Faeroe Is., Scandinavia. Subsp. *islandicum* Á. Löve. Petals persistent.

nudicaule L. [*P. Macounii* Greene; *P. Miyabeanum* Tatew.]. ICELAND P., ARCTIC P. Nearly stemless, hairy per., to 1 ft.; lvs. mostly basal, petioled, pinnately lobed or cleft; fls. fragrant, 1–3 in. across, sometimes double, petals white with yellow at base, orange, or reddish; caps. oblong or subglobose, about ⅝ in. long, usually hispid. Arctic regions, N. Amer., s. to Colo.; Eurasia. Color forms are grown under such names as cvs. 'Amurense' [*P. amurense* Hort. ex Karrer], 'Croceum' [*P. croceum* Ledeb.]., 'Delicatum', and 'Rubro-aurantiacum'.

oreophilum Rupr. Hispid, densely tufted per., sts. somewhat branched; lvs. pinnatifid or coarsely toothed, upper lvs. sessile; fls. brick-red, 3–4 in. across. Summer. Caucasus. Closely related to *P. lateritium.*

orientale L. [*P. bracteatum* Lindl.]. ORIENTAL P. Robust hispid per., to 4 ft.; lvs. pinnately dissected, segms. lanceolate or oblong; petals 4–6, red, usually with a dark basal spot, sometimes orange or pale pink, obovate, to 3 in. long, fls. sometimes double. Sw. Asia. Widely cult. and sometimes naturalized. Color forms include cvs. 'Album' and 'Atrosanguineum'. Oriental poppies are easily prop. by division or root cuttings made after flowering. They are among the longest-lived poppies and do best when left undisturbed.

pseudocanescens M. Popov. Cespitose per., to 6 in.; lvs. pinnately lobed; fl. buds globose, nearly ½ in. long, densely black-hairy, fls. about 2 in. across, petals yellow, rarely white. Alpine zone, Siberia, Mongolia. Closely related to *P. radicatum,* but having lf. segms. wider, and stamens many, much longer than ovary.

pyrenaicum (L.) A. Kern. A name of doubtful application; material cult. under this name may be *P. rhaeticum.*

radicatum Rottb. Cespitose per., with yellow or whitish sap; lf. bases persistent, lvs. pinnately lobed or cut; petals usually yellow, sometimes whitish, or rarely pink. Nw. Eur. Extremely variable. Closely related to *P. nudicaule.*

rhaeticum Leresche. Tufted, nearly stemless per., to 4 in.; lvs. pinnately parted; petals yellow or orange, to 1 in. long; caps. oblong. Pyrenees.

Rhoeas L. CORN P., FIELD P., FLANDERS P. Ann., to 3 ft., erect, branched, with spreading, bristly hairs; lvs. irregularly pinnate or rarely entire, to 6 in. long; fls. to 2 in. across, on long, hairy peduncles, petals cinnabar-red, deep purple, scarlet, or sometimes white. Eur., Asia; naturalized in N. Amer. The common field poppy of Eur. SHIRLEY POPPIES are a strain of this sp. Fls. used medicinally, and pigment used to color medicines and wine. Cv. 'Coccineum Aureum'. A color form. Var. **commutatum:** *P. commutatum.*

rupifragum Boiss. & Reut. Nearly stemless per., to 18 in.; lvs. pinnately cut, segms. irregular, oblong or lanceolate, bristle-tipped; fls. to 3 in. across, petals brick-red Spain.

Schinzianum Fedde. Gray-hairy per., to 1½ ft.; lvs. obovate-lanceolate, irregularly pinnately lobed; fls. 1¼ in. long, petals brick-red; obovoid. Nativity unknown.

setigerum: *P. somniferum* subsp.

somniferum L. OPIUM P. Erect, glaucous ann., to 4 ft.; lvs. coarsely toothed or lobed, lower lvs. short-petioled, upper lvs. clasping; fls. often double, to 4 in. across, white, pink, red, or purple, petals sometimes fringed or with dark spot at base, suborbicular. Se. Eur. and w. Asia. Crude opium is the hardened milky sap of the unripe fr. Subsp. **setigerum** (DC.) Corb. [*P. setigerum* DC.]. Hairy; lvs. deeply cut and acutely lobed.

spicatum Boiss. & Bal. [*P. Heldreichii* Boiss.]. Densely white-hairy per., to 2½ ft.; lvs. oblong, basal lvs. long-petioled, densely pilose, crenate-serrate; fls. arranged in spikelike racemes on short peduncles, petals orange-red. Asia Minor.

stylosum: a listed name of no botanical standing.

triniifolium Boiss. Glaucous bien., to about 1 ft.; basal lvs. to 3 in. long, 2–3-pinnately cut, segms. narrow-linear, terminated by a yellow bristle; fls. 1 in. across, petals pale red, falling soon. Summer. Asia Minor.

PAPAVERACEAE Juss. POPPY FAMILY. Dicot.; about 25 genera and 200 spp. of herbs, rarely shrubs or trees, of worldwide distribution; sap usually milky or colored; lvs. mostly alt., rarely opp. or whorled, entire to pinnately or palmately cleft; fls. mostly solitary, showy, bisexual, regular, sepals 2–3, falling early, petals 4–8 or 8–12, deciduous, stamens many, ovary superior, 1-celled, rarely many-celled; fr. a caps., usually opening by valves or pores, rarely of separate carpels. Genera grown as ornamentals are: *Arctomecon, Argemone, Bocconia, Chelidonium, Dendromecon, Dicranostigma, Eomecon, Eschscholzia, Glaucium, Hunnemannia, Macleaya, Meconella, Meconopsis, Papaver, Platystemon, Roemeria, Romneya, Sanguinaria, Stylomecon,* and *Stylophorum.*

The family is economically important for opium, the dried exudate obtained by cutting unripe capsules of *Papaver somniferum,* for poppy seeds, and for poppy oil, an edible drying oil much used in commerce.

PAPAYA. The papaya, *Carica Papaya,* is a frost-tender, tropical, fruit-producing species, originally native to Middle America but now widely cultivated for its large melonlike fruits in warm climates and to a limited extent in the warmest parts of Zone 10. The plant, which may grow to a height of 25 feet, is a giant herb rather than a tree, for it lacks woody tissue. It is fast-growing, producing flowers in about five months from seed. Fruit production continues to be profitable for three or four years. Commonly and typically the papaya is dioecious, but there are many variations from this habit and cultivars are available with perfect flowers. The latter are more desirable for garden culture, as plants derived from typical dioecious forms will produce male and female plants in about equal numbers, with the sex indeterminate until the first flowers appear.

Papayas thrive on many different soils but require good

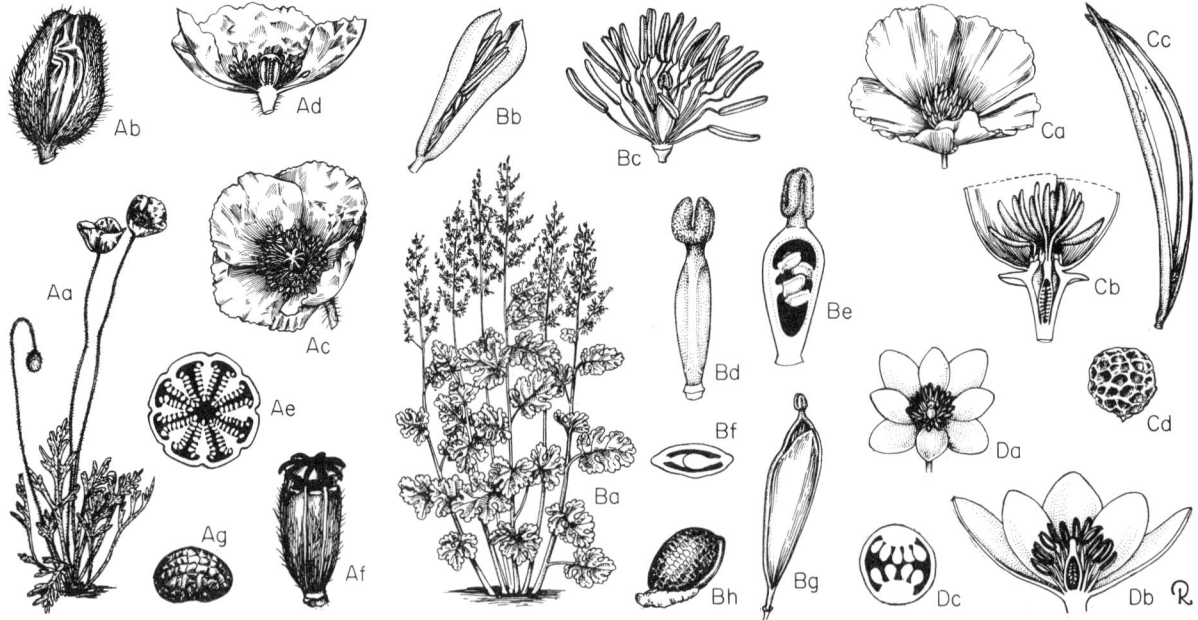

PAPAVERACEAE. **A,** *Papaver nudicaule:* **Aa,** plant, × ⅛; **Ab,** flower bud, × 1; **Ac,** flower, × ½; **Ad,** flower, vertical section, × ½; **Ae,** ovary, cross section, × 3; **Af,** capsule, × 1; **Ag,** seed, × 5. **B,** *Macleaya cordata:* **Ba,** plant, × ⅟₃₀; **Bb,** flower bud, × 2; **Bc,** flower, × 2; **Bd,** pistil, × 6; **Be,** pistil, vertical section, × 6; **Bf,** ovary, cross section, × 8; **Bg,** capsule, × 2; **Bh,** seed, × 6. **C,** *Eschscholzia californica:* **Ca,** flower, × ½; **Cb,** flower, vertical section, × 1; **Cc,** capsule, × ½; **Cd,** seed, × 6. **D,** *Sanguinaria canadensis:* **Da,** flower, × ½; **Db,** flower, vertical section, × 1; **Dc,** ovary, cross section, × 4.

drainage. The best quality fruit is produced in a warm low-land tropical climate where rainfall is not excessive.

PAPHINIA Lindl. *Orchidaceae.* Five spp. of epiphytes, native to trop. Amer.; pseudobulbs 2–3-lvd.; lvs. plicate; infl. pendent, 1–3-fld.; fls. showy, sepals and petals similar, lip 3-lobed, the disc with a prominent callus, column slender, with a large foot, pollinia 2, on a slender stalk. For structure of fl. see *Orchidaceae.*

For culture see *Orchids.*

cristata (Lindl.) Lindl. Pseudobulbs ovoid, to 2 in. long; lvs. elliptic-lanceolate, to 10 in. long; infl. short, 1–3-fld.; sepals and petals lanceolate, to 2 in. long, white with heavy red stripes, lateral sepals shortly united at base, lip purple, lateral lobes sickle-shaped, midlobe triangular, with long, white cilia along margin, disc with a fleshy laciniate crest. Late winter–early autumn. Colombia to Trinidad, Guyana, and Brazil.

PAPHIOPEDILUM Pfitz. [*Cordula* Raf.]. CYPRIPEDIUM, LADY-SLIPPER, LADY'S-SLIPPER. *Orchidaceae.* About 60 spp. of terrestrial herbs or epiphytes without pseudobulbs, native to trop. Asia; lvs. basal, 2-ranked, folded lengthwise, leathery, sometimes mottled with dark and pale green; scape terminal; fls. solitary or in a raceme, dorsal sepal usually larger, lateral sepals always united to form a synsepal, petals spreading horizontally or pendent, lip slipper-shaped, the pouch usually half the total length, with lateral lobes incurved toward the base, column with a flattened staminode between and in front of the 2 anthers. For structure of fl. see *Orchidaceae.*

Grown in the warm greenhouse, or some of them at intermediate temperatures; they require a good moisture supply. For culture see *Orchids.*

Albertianum: *P.* × *Leeanum* cv.

Appletonianum (Gower) Rolfe. Fls. 1 or 2 on long scape, 4 in. across, dorsal sepal yellow-green, striped with brown or brownish-purple, revolute at base, synsepal small, green, petals horizontal, longer than upper sepal, green, with apical ⅓ pink-magenta, dotted with small spots on the green area, lip longer than synsepal, green with brown overlay, staminode green, to ¼ in. across. Thailand. Cv. **'Poyntzianum'** [var. *Poyntzianum* (O'Brien) Pfitz.]. Petals pale green with lilac apices, lip white, marked inside with purple.

barbatum (Lindl.) Pfitz. Lvs. mottled; scape long, dark purple, pubescent; fls. to 4 in. across, sepals white, pale green at base, veined with brown-purple, petals greenish at base and purple toward apex,

with black warts along upper margin, lip brown-purple, staminode green. Winter–late summer. Java, Straits of Malacca, Malay Pen. Cv. **'Warneri'** [var. *Warneri* Pfitz.]. Dorsal sepal very large, white with dark green lines and stained with red-magenta, with wide white margin, petals glossy dark green above, lip deep maroon.

×**Beeckmannii** L. Linden: *P. bellatulum* × *P. villosum* var. *Boxallii.* Scape long, 1-fld.; fls. to 4½ in. across, dorsal sepal emerald-green with narrow white margin, spotted with blackish dots, revolute at base, petals very large, maroon, margined with yellow and with some purple spots, lip maroon, margined with yellow.

bellatulum (Rchb.f.) Pfitz. Lvs. dark green above with pale green mottling, dull purple underneath; scape shorter than lvs.; fls. to 3 in. across, white or very pale yellow or cream, spotted with brown-purple throughout, more heavily so at base of segms., dorsal sepal orbicular, synsepal small, elliptic, petals elliptic, lip shorter than petals, staminode rhomboid-orbicular, keeled. E. Burma and Thailand.

Boxallii: *P. villosum* cv.

Bullenianum (Rchb.f.) Pfitz. Lvs. mottled; scape longer than lvs., 1-fld., hirsute; fls. 3½ in. across, dorsal sepal ovate, with reflexed basal margins, olive-green suffused with brown, petals deflexed, dilated from a narrow, oblong base, ciliate, with hairless brown warts along upper margin, olive-green in lower half, rose-violet in upper half, lip green, marked with greenish-brown, longer than sepals, shorter than petals, the inflexed lobes with warts. Early spring. Borneo.

callosum (Rchb.f.) Pfitz. Lvs. green, mottled with blackish-green; scape long, 1- or sometimes 2-fld.; fls. to 4 in. across, sepals white with radiating purple and green veins, petals greenish, pale rose at apex, with several black warts on upper margin, lip helmet-shaped, brown-purple outside, the infolded lobes purple-spotted. Late winter. Thailand. Cv. **'Sanderae'** [var. *Sanderae* Pfitz.]. Fls. white, dorsal sepal with green venation.

Charlesworthii (Rolfe) Pfitz. Lvs. mottled; scape about as long as lvs., 1-fld., purple-spotted; fls. 3 in. across, dorsal sepal broadly ovate, nearly flat, white, suffused and veined with brilliant purple-rose, petals horizontal, spreading, hairy at base on inner surface, sparsely ciliate, yellowish-green, lip greenish. India.

concolor (Batem.) Pfitz. Lvs. green, mottled with grayish-green on upper surface, spotted with deep crimson on lower surface; scape shorter than lvs., 1–2-fld.; fls. 2 in. across, pale yellow, dotted with purple, sepals and petals ciliolate, dorsal sepal orbicular, petals oblong-elliptic, deflexed, lip small, nearly cylindrical, somewhat laterally flattened. Burma, Vietnam.

Curtisii (Rchb.f.) Pfitz. Lvs. mottled above; scape longer than lvs., 1-fld., pubescent; fls. to 4 in. across, segms. ciliolate, dorsal sepal ovate, grass-green, white-margined, with many green veins, purple toward base, petals strap-shaped, deflexed, recurved at apex, pale purple, white along midvein, spotted with purple and veined with green, with black hairs and warts on margin, lip helmet-shaped, brownish-purple, the infolded narrow purple lobes with dark warts. Late spring. Sumatra.

×**Dauthieri:** *P.* × *Harrisianum.*

Delenatii Guillaum. [*Cypripedium Delenatii* Hort.]. Lvs. mottled light green above, marked with purple underneath; scape 8 in. long, purple, 1–2-fld.; fls. soft rose with purplish shading, dorsal sepal ovate-elliptic, petals broadly ovate, lip inflated, ovoid, staminode ovate, cordate, tomentose along margin, rose-colored with yellow center. Vietnam.

Fairieanum (Lindl.) Pfitz. Lvs. bright green; scape 6 in. long, 1-fld.; fls. to 3 in. high, dorsal sepal cordate-oblong, ciliate, undulate on margin, reflexed at apex, with hairy keel behind, white with pale yellow-green stain at base and with purple longitudinal and anastomosing veins, synsepal smaller, ovate, ciliate, green, streaked with purple, petals oblong-strap-shaped, deflexed and recurved like a buffalo's horn, undulate and with minute blackish hairs on margins, yellow-white with longitudinal streaks and marginal bands of purple, lip brownish-green with net of purplish veining, the infolded lobes white, spotted with purple, staminode orbicular-lunate, with a proboscis between horns of crescent, ivory-white mottled with green. Assam.

glaucophyllum J. J. Sm. Lvs. glaucous, to 9 in. long; scape erect, to 1½ ft., with dull brownish-green hairs, gradually elongating and producing up to 21 fls. in succession; dorsal sepal yellowish-green with primrose-yellow margin, suborbicular, undulate, 1¼ in. across, synsepal narrower than dorsal sepal, hirsute, petals spreading, 1¾ in. long, horizontal, linear-oblong, spirally twisted and undulate, ciliate, white with many bright red-purple blotches, lip 1½ in. long, inflated, light rose-purple with darker dots and light green margin, staminode ovate, convex, pilose, purple with green base. Java, New Guinea.

Godefroyae (Godefr.) Pfitz. Lvs. dark green, mottled with greenish-white; scape short, 1–2-fld.; fls. to 2½ in. high, pure white to cream to pale yellow, spotted with red-purple to magenta-purple, sparingly pubescent, dorsal sepal nearly orbicular, keeled behind, synsepal smaller, petals elliptic-oblong, deflexed, lip subcylindrical, minutely spotted, staminode oblong, minutely spotted like lip and with yellow stain in center. Thailand, S. Vietnam. Cv. 'Leucochilum' [var. *leucochilum* (Rolfe) Pfitz.]. Sepals and petals white, spotted with purple, lip white.

×**Goeranum** Hort.: *P. Curtisii* × *P. Lawrenceanum.* Lvs. mottled; scape long, 1–2-fld.; fls. 4½ in. across, sepals pale magenta with radiating magenta veins, petals greenish at base shading to bright rose-magenta at apex, with many dark black-purple spots, margins ciliate, lip helmet-shaped, brownish-purple, the infolded lobes magenta, spotted.

×**Harrisianum** (Rchb.f.) Stein [*P.* × *Dauthieri* (Desb.) Hort.]: *P. barbatum* × *P. villosum.* The first *Paphiopedilum* hybrid. Lvs. mottled with dark and light green; scape long, 1-fld.; fls. 5 in. across, dorsal sepal deep blackish-purple, passing into green at apex, with white margin and blackish veins, synsepal pale green with deep green veins, petals horizontal, with blackish-purple midvein, brown-purple with purple veins in upper half, buff-yellow with green veins in lower half, lip pale purple with deeper colored veins, pale yellow-green in front, with green veins underneath, staminode dull brown, tinged with green.

Haynaldianum (Rchb.f.) Pfitz. Lvs. to 16 in. long; scape much longer than lvs., bearing a 2–6-fld. raceme; fls. 7 in. across, dorsal sepal green and with large brown spots at revolute base, cream to rosy above, petals spatulate-linear, to 4 in. long, twisted and recurved apically, ciliate, yellowish-green with large brown spots in lower half, dull purple in upper half, lip pale green tinged with dull purple, staminode oblong, 2-lobed in front. Winter–late spring. Philippine Is.

hirsutissimum (Lindl.) Pfitz. Lvs. uniformly green, to 1 ft. long; scape to 1 ft. long, with dark purple hairs; fls. 4 in. across, all segms. ciliate, dorsal sepal cordate, keeled behind, central and basal area densely spotted with blackish-purple, broad marginal area deeper or paler green, synsepal small, pale green with purplish markings along veins, petals horizontal, spatulate, slightly twisted, with crisp margins, undulate in basal half, blotched with green and spotted with deep purple and studded with blackish hairs in basal half, bright violet-purple in apical half, lip prominent, helmet-shaped, dull green stained purplish-brown and dotted with black warts, staminode squarish, green with 2 white spots near basal edge. Himalayas.

insigne (Wallich) Pfitz. Lvs. green, to 1 ft. long; scape usually shorter than lvs., 1–2-fld., purple-pubescent; fls. 4–5 in. across, dorsal sepal revolute on margins, yellow-green spotted with brownish-purple along veins, white at apex, petals linear-oblong, spreading, undulate, yellow-green with brown venation, lip yellow-green with brown suffusion, staminode squarish, pubescent, with orange-yellow tubercle. Au-

tumn–early spring. Himalayas. Cvs. include: 'Albomarginatum' [var. *albomarginatum* Pfitz.], dorsal sepal olive-green, dotted with brown, with white margin, petals undulate on margins, yellowish, reticulated with rose-salmon, lip large, brilliant maroon, bordered with yellow; 'Aureum' [var. *aureum* Pfitz.], dorsal sepal yellow, petals and lip clear yellow-brown; 'Chantinii' [var. *Chantinii* (Rafarin) Pfitz.], dorsal sepal large, bordered with white, basal part olive-green, dotted with purple, synsepal clear green with small brown dots, petals clear mahogany, lip large, glossy, mahogany; 'Harefield Hall', a fine cv. with large fls., dorsal sepal large, round, with broad white margin and large bright brown spots; 'Illustre' [var. *illustre* Pfitz.], fls. yellowish, sepals, petals, and lip suffused with clear red-brown; 'Macfarlanei' [var. *Macfarlanei* (Rolfe) Pfitz.], fls. clear yellow, dorsal sepal with large white border, without warty spots; 'Mandevillianum' [var. *Mandevilliana* Pfitz.], fls. similar to those of 'Albomarginatum', dorsal sepal with white border at apex, petals with many spots in lines; 'Maulei' [var. *Maulei* (T. Moore) Pfitz.], upper part of dorsal sepal pure white with spotting of purple; 'Maximum' [var. *maximum* Pfitz.], dorsal sepal very large, margin undulate, deep green with brown-black dots, and with violet dots in the white apex; 'Sanderae' [var. *Sanderae* (Rchb.f.) Pfitz.], dorsal sepal primrose-yellow with a few minute reddish-brown spots, upper part white, petals yellow, lip waxy-yellow; 'Sanderanum', resembling 'Sanderae', but fls. smaller, dorsal sepal greenish-yellow, without spots; 'Sylhetense' [var. *sylhetense* Pfitz.], dorsal sepal with large dark spots somewhat confluent in lines along center.

Lawrenceanum (Rchb.f.) Pfitz. Lvs. mottled; scape longer than lvs., 1–2-fld., brownish-purple, pubescent; fls. to 5 in. across, dorsal sepal orbicular, white, with alternating longer and shorter purple veins, central veins green at base, petals spreading, ciliate, green, purple at apex, with 5–10 black warts on each margin, lip dull purple, tinged with brown above, green beneath. Early spring–summer. Borneo. Cv. 'Hyeanum' [var. *Hyeanum* (Rchb.f.) Pfitz.]. Dorsal sepal white with green venation, petals horizontal, long, white, dotted with green, lip olive.

×**Leeanum** (Rchb.f.) Stein: *P. insigne* × *P. Spiceranum.* Fls. 4 in. across, dorsal sepal nearly orbicular, white, green at base, with broken lines of magenta radiating toward apex, synsepal green, petals green with longitudinal magenta lines and spots, lip green with longitudinal reddish stripes. Himalayas. Cv. 'Albertianum' [var. *Albertianum* Cogn.; *P. Albertianum* (Cogn.) Hort.]. Differs from typical *P.* × *Leeanum* in having more pronounced magenta spotting on dorsal sepal, petals suffused with magenta and horizontally striped with broken magenta lines, lip of uniform color.

×**Leoniae** (L. Linden) Kerch.: *P. callosum* × *P. insigne.* Fls. intermediate between parent spp. in color, shape of lip and petals similar to that of *P. callosum.*

Lowii (Lindl.) Pfitz. Lvs. strap-shaped, to 15 in. long; scape to 3 ft. long, arching, 3–6-fld.; fls. to 6 in. across, segms. fringed with black hairs, dorsal sepal ovate, somewhat hooded at apex, revolute and stained with brownish-purple at base, pale green in upper part, synsepal pale green, petals spatulate, 3 in. long, greenish-yellow basally and marked with large blackish-purple spots, clear bright magenta apically, lip purplish-green on upper surface, greenish underneath, staminode inversely cordate, with tooth at base. Sabah (Malay Arch.).

×**Maudiae** Hort.: *P. callosum* cv. 'Sanderae' × *P. Lawrenceanum* cv. 'Hyeanum'. Lvs. mottled; scape long, 1-fld.; dorsal sepal semiorbicular, white or pale greenish-white, marked with green veins, petals green at base, white at apex, lip yellow-green.

×**nitens** (Rchb.f.) Pfitz. [*P. Sallieri* (Godefr.) Hort.]: *P. insigne* cv. 'Maulei' × *P. villosum.* Lvs. green; scape longer than lvs.; dorsal sepal apple-green at base, white at apex, blotched with purple, veined with green, synsepal light green with small spots, petals orchre-yellow with reddish-brown venation, lip greenish-yellow, suffused with brown, staminode yellow with a yellow tubercle.

niveum (Rchb.f.) Pfitz. Lvs. to 6 in. long, dull dark green mottled with gray-green, purple underneath; scape longer than lvs., 1–2-fld.; fls. white, 3 in. across, dorsal sepal orbicular, concave, reddish-purple on back, with purple dots on front toward base, petals nearly orbicular, deflexed, lip short, ovoid, snow-white. Se. Asia. Cv. 'Album' [var. *album* Pfitz.]. Fls. pure white. Cv. 'Punctatum' [var. *punctatum* Pfitz.]. Base of petals densely dotted with violet. Cv. 'Reticulatum' [var. *reticulatum* Pfitz.]. Apex of petals reticulate with brilliant purple veins, spotted with purple.

Parishii (Rchb.f.) Pfitz. Lvs. green, to 16 in. long; scape 4–8-fld., downy; fls. 3 in. across, dorsal sepal oblong-elliptic, pale yellow, with green venation, petals linear, twisted, to 6 in. long, pendent, green basally with blackish dots, blackish-purple apically with lighter margin, lip dark green, stained with brown-purple, staminode pale yellow, mottled green. Autumn. Burma.

philippinense (Rchb.f.) Pfitz. Lvs. to 1 ft. long, waxy; scape to 1½ ft. long, 3–5-fld.; fls. 3 in. high, dorsal sepal ovate, whitish, striped with purple-brown, synsepal whitish with green venation, petals linear, twisted, to 6 in. long, ciliate, with hairy basal warts, yellowish-green at base blending to dull purple, lip buff-yellow with brown lines. Spring. Philippine Is.

praestans (Rchb.f.) Pfitz. Lvs. to 1 ft. long; scape as long as lvs., black-purple, several-fld.; dorsal sepal oblong, 2 in. long, whitish, with 15 purplish veins, yellowish on back, petals 5 in. long, yellowish-green, margins undulate, with dark red hair-bearing warts, lip as long as sepals, yellow with suffusion of red, laterally flattened. Late summer. New Guinea. Cv. **'Kimballianum'**. Purplish veins on sepals wider, petals broader at base, with dense red lines at base, warts larger, lip white suffused with rose.

purpuratum (Lindl.) Pfitz. Lvs. to 5 in. long, mottled; scape longer than lvs., 1-fld., purple, hirsute; fls. 3½ in. across, dorsal sepal orbicular, folded at middle, revolute at base, white with green in center and purple venation, petals spreading, undulate, elliptic, somewhat sickle-shaped, ciliate, purplish-crimson with purple-green veins and with many small warts at base, lip brownish-purple, with darker venation and reticulation, the unfolded lobes purple, with many warts. Early autumn–winter. China.

×**Rossettii** Hort.: *P. insigne* cv. 'Sanderae' × *P.* ×*Maudiae.* Scape longer than lvs., 1-fld.; fls. similar to those of *P. insigne* in shape, but without color.

Rothschildianum (Rchb.f.) Pfitz. Lvs. to 2 ft. long, glossy green; scape erect, longer than lvs., violet, pubescent, bract yellow-green, ciliate, with black-purple lines; fls. 5 in. high, dorsal sepal ovate, ciliate, yellow, veined with black-purple, petals 5 in. long, linear, undulate, pale green, spotted with purple, 7-veined, lip as long as sepals, flattened laterally, dull purple, apex yellow. Borneo, Sumatra.

×**Sallieri**: *P.* ×*nitens.*

×**selligerum** (Rchb.f.) Stein: *P. barbatum* × *P. philippinense.* Dorsal sepal with green stain at base and with alternately longer and shorter purple veins, synsepal white with paler purple veining, petals 4 in. long, greenish at base, with black warts along upper margin, remainder rose-purple, lip brownish-purple with darker venation, staminode green, with purple hairs.

Spiceranum (Rchb.f.) Pfitz. Lvs. to 9 in. long, dark green, spotted with purple underneath; scape as long as lvs., 1-fld.; fls. 3 in. high, dorsal sepal transversely elliptic, 1½ in. long, deeply channelled, with retroflexed margins, white with crimson-purple band down center and with green blotch speckled with dull red at base, synsepal greenish-white, petals strap-shaped, deflexed, curved toward front, undulate on margins, yellow-green, spotted with dull red and with crimson midline, lip longer than sepals, violet with pale green margin, staminode purplish-crimson, margined with white. Autumn–early winter. Assam.

Stonei (Hook.f.) Pfitz. Lvs. to 1 ft. long, grass-green; scape to 2 ft. long, greenish-purple, 3–5-fld.; fls. 4 in. high, dorsal sepal cordate, white with 2 to several blackish-crimson longitudinal streaks, synsepal similar, petals linear, to 6 in. long, pendent, twisted, with a few black ciliate hairs on each margin, pale tawny-yellow for ⅔ their length, spotted with brownish-crimson, lip dull rose, veined and reticulated with crimson, whitish underneath, the unfolded lobes narrow, whitish, staminode elliptic-oblong, whitish, fringed with close-set hairs except in front. Borneo.

tonsum (Rchb.f.) Pfitz. Lvs. narrow, to 8 in. long, mottled, purple underneath; scape reddish-brown, hirsute, longer than lvs., 1-fld.; fls. 5 in. across, dorsal sepal elliptic, whitish, green-veined, petals oblong-strap-shaped, green, washed with sepia and with a few black spots, lip greenish, tinged with crimson and brown, the infolded lobes broadly warty. Autumn. Sumatra.

venustum (Wallich) Pfitz. Lvs. to 6 in. long, mottled with pale grayish-green, strongly violet-mottled underneath; scape as long as lvs., 1-fld., purple; fls. 3 in. across, dorsal sepal ovate, white with green venation, petals spatulate, spreading, ciliate, longer than sepals, green with blackish warts basally, dull brownish-purple apically, lip pale yellowish-green, tinged with rose and reticulated with green, the unfolded lobes yellow, staminode semiblunate. Winter–early spring. Himalayas. Cv. **'Pardinum'** [var. *pardinum* (Rchb.f.) Pfitz.]. Petals yellow, suffused with copper and with warts over their entire upper surface, lip of brighter color, with more prominent reticulation.

villosum (Lindl.) Pfitz. Lvs. green, paler underneath and spotted with purple toward base, to 1½ ft. long; scape hairy, almost as long as lvs., 1-fld.; fls. to 6 in. high, glossy, dorsal sepal ciliate, broadly elliptic, hooded at apex, with revolute margin basally, brown-purple at base and center, otherwise green, with narrow white margin, synsepal smaller, pale yellow-green, petals spatulate, ciliate, undulate, with purple hairs at base and broad purple midvein, yellow-brown in upper half, paler in lower half, lip brownish-yellow, with yellow margin at opening, the infolded lobes tawny-yellow, staminode yellow, oblong-cordiform, with small glandular boss in center. Winter. Borneo. Cv. **'Aureum'** [var. *aureum* Pfitz.]. Dorsal sepal bright yellow-green, margined with white, petals and lip suffused with bright golden-yellow. Cv. **'Boxallii'** [var. *Boxallii* (Rchb.f.) Pfitz.]. Dorsal sepal narrower at base and with margins more reflexed, central area covered with many blackish spots which become confluent in middle and at base, white margin broader, petals more mottled.

virens (Rchb.f.) Pfitz. Lvs. to 6 in long, obscurely mottled above; scape longer than lvs., brown, 1-fld.; fls. 4 in. across, dorsal sepal ovate, ciliate, with reflexed margin at base, pale green, striated with darker green, petals spreading, green and with small black warts at base, pale purple at apex, lip as long as sepals, green, suffused with rose, the inflexed lobes with many contiguous warts. Java, n. Borneo.

Volonteanum (Hort. Sander) Pfitz. Lvs. to 8 in. long, somewhat mottled above, paler underneath; infl. longer than lvs., 1-fld., pale brown with white hairs; fls. 4 in. across, dorsal sepal ovate, ciliate, with reflexed margin at base, yellowish-green, petals nearly twice as long as sepal, undulate, spatulate, sickle-shaped, minutely toothed, long-ciliate and barbed at base, green, rose at apex and with black spots on upper margin, lip pale green with rose suffusion, staminode orbicular. Borneo.

PARABENZOIN Nakai. *Lauraceae.* Two spp. of dioecious, deciduous shrubs or small trees, native to China and Japan; lvs. alt., entire or 3-cleft; infl. umbellate; fls. unisexual; fr. globose, dry, splitting irregularly into 5–6 parts, exposing the single yellow-brown seed. Some botanists combine this genus with *Lindera,* with fls. similar but fr. an indehiscent berry.

Culture like that of *Lindera.*

praecox (Siebold & Zucc.) Nakai [*Benzoin praecox* Siebold & Zucc.; *Lindera praecox* (Siebold & Zucc.) Blume]. Shrub to small tree; lvs. ovate-elliptic, to 3 in. long, entire, not 3-nerved from the base; fls. lemon-yellow, opening before the lvs. Early spring. Mts., Japan. Hardy.

trilobum (Siebold & Zucc.) Nakai [*Benzoin trilobum* Siebold & Zucc.; *Lindera triloba* (Siebold & Zucc.) Blume]. Shrub; lvs. triangular-obovate, to 5 in. long, usually 3-cleft, 3-nerved from base. Mts., cent. and s. Japan, China.

PARACARYUM Boiss. *Boraginaceae.* Not cult. **P. racemosum:** *Mattiastrum racemosum.*

PARADISEA Mazz. *Liliaceae.* Two spp. of rhizomatous, per. herbs, native to Eur.; roots fleshy and clustered; lvs. basal; fls. funnelform, showy, in loose racemes on slender bracted scapes, perianth segms. 6, separate, 3-nerved, anthers versatile; fr. a 3-valved, loculicidal caps., seeds many, angled.

Of easy culture in the hardy border. Propagated by division and seeds.

Liliastrum (L.) Bertol. [*Anthericum Liliastrum* L.]. ST. BRUNO'S LILY, PARADISE L. To 2 ft.; lvs. linear, to 2 ft. long and 5/16 in. wide; fls. white, to 2 in. long, in 1-sided racemes, pedicels not articulated, perianth segms. with apical green spot. Mts., s. Eur. Cv. **'Major'**. Taller; fls. larger. Var. **lusitanica:** *P. lusitanica.*

lusitanica (Coutinho) Samp. [*P. Liliastrum* var. *lusitanica* Coutinho]. To 5 ft., more robust; lvs. to ¾ in. wide; fls. white, to ¾ in. long, in symmetrical racemes, pedicels articulated. Portugal.

PARADRYMONIA Hanst. *Gesneriaceae.* A few spp. of terrestrial or epiphytic herbs in Cent. and n. S. Amer.; sts. creeping or ascending, with many adventitious roots; lvs. opp., those of a pair equal or unequal, usually large, blades mostly cuneate basally; fls. many in lf. axils, sepals linear, acuminate, corolla funnelform or trumpet-shaped, with spreading prominent limb, stamens 4, borne at base of corolla tube, anthers coherent in pairs or in a square, often bearded, disc of 1 or 2 glands, ovary superior.

For cultivation see *Gesneriaceae.*

decurrens (C. V. Mort.) Wiehl. [*Episcia decurrens* (C. V. Mort.) Leeuw.]. Epiphytic, creeping; lvs. elongate, to 11 in. long including the petiole, to 1½ in. wide, blades elliptic, green, shallowly toothed, softly hairy, cuneate basally and decurrent along the petiole; fls. creamy-white, red-brown-hairy outside, yellowish in throat, sepals to ½ in. long, corolla to 1½ in. long, trumpet-shaped, oblique and prominently spurred in the calyx, lobes 3/16 in. long, anthers bearded at apex, ovary red-hairy. Nicaragua, Costa Rica.

PARAHEBE W. Oliver. *Scrophulariaceae.* About 12 spp. of herbs or subshrubs, native to New Zeal.; sts. prostrate, decumbent, or suberect; lvs. opp., simple, usually toothed; fls. white, pink, or blue, solitary or in axillary racemes, calyx mostly 4-lobed, corolla 4- or 5-lobed, stamens 2; fr. an emarginate, laterally flattened caps., with the septum across narrower diam. Differs from *Hebe* mainly in its habit, infl., and compression of caps.

For culture see *Hebe*.

×**Bidwillii** (Hook.) W. Oliver [*Hebe Bidwillii* (Hook.) Allan; *Veronica Bidwillii* Hook., not Hook.f.]: *P. decora* Ashw. × *P. Lyallii* (Hook.f.) W. Oliver. Sts. procumbent; lvs. rounded, usually with 3–5 crenate lobes, leathery; fls. in about 12-fld. racemes; caps. longer than calyx.

canescens W. Oliver [*Hebe canescens* Hort.; *Veronica canescens* T. Kirk, not Schrad.]. Per., sts. creeping, matted, much-branched, to 4 in.; lvs. broadly ovate, to ⅛ in. long, with loose, grayish-white hairs; fls. solitary, pale blue, ⁵⁄₁₆ in. across.

cataractae (G. Forst.) W. Oliver [*Hebe cataractae* (G. Forst.) Allan; *Veronica cataractae* G. Forst.; *V. irrigans* T. Kirk]. Sts. decumbent to ascending, to 2 ft.; lvs. linear-lanceolate to ovate or elliptic, to 3½ in. long, serrate, dark green above; fls. in many-fld. racemes, corolla white with pink to purple veins, to ⅜ in. across.

decora Ashw. [*Veronica Bidwillii* Hook.f., not Hook.]. Prostrate, forming mats, sts. to 2 in.; lvs. ovate to suborbicular, to ³⁄₁₆ in. long, entire or lobed at base; fls. in 6–10-fld. racemes, corolla white or pink, to ⅜ in. across; caps. much longer than calyx.

linifolia (Hook.f.) W. Oliver [*Hebe linifolia* (Hook.f.) Allan; *Veronica linifolia* Hook.f.]. Much-branched, glabrous subshrub, sts. more or less erect, to 10 in.; lvs. linear to linear-lanceolate, to 1 in. long, obtuse, entire; fls. in mostly 2–4-fld. racemes, corolla white to pale rose, to ½ in. across; caps. as long as or shorter than calyx.

Lyallii (Hook.f.) W. Oliver [*Hebe Lyallii* (Hook.f.) Allan; *Veronica Lyallii* Hook.f.]. Diffusely branched per., sts. prostrate, rooting, to 1½ ft. long; lvs. ovate, linear-obovate, or suborbicular, to ½ in. long, coarsely toothed; fls. in many-fld. racemes, corolla white to pink, ⅜ in. across.

PARAJUBAEA Burret. *Palmae*. Two spp. of solitary, unarmed, monoecious palms in Andean S. Amer.; lvs. pinnate, sheaths not forming a crownshaft, pinnae acuminate; infl. among lvs., pendulous, long-peduncled, rachillae many, simple, with fls. in triads (2 male and 1 female) near the base and above these with predominantly paired male fls.; male fls. asymmetrical, sepals 3, small, acute, basally imbricate, petals 3, flat, much wider than thick, valvate, stamens many, pistillode short, 3-cleft, female fls. with sepals 3, imbricate, about as long as the 3 imbricate petals, staminodes united in a low, 3-lobed cupule, pistil 3-celled, 3-ovuled; fr. with apical stigmatic residue, mesocarp fibrous, endocarp blackish, irregularly pitted, apically 3-crested, pores basal, sunken, seeds 1 or more, endosperm homogeneous.

Grown as ornamentals in cool tropical or subtropical locations; suitable for Zone 9b in Calif. and perhaps other Pacific states. For culture see *Palms*.

cocoides Burret. To more than 20 ft.; lvs. long-petioled, pinnae many, regularly arranged; male fls. ½ in. long, stamens about 15; fr. ovoid, 1¾ in. long, 1⅜ in. in diam. Ecuador.

PARAMACROLOBIUM J. Léonard. *Leguminosae* (subfamily *Caesalpinioideae*). One sp., a tree of trop. Afr.; lvs. alt., even-pinnate, with 1 to several pairs of lfts.; infl. compact, corymblike, fl. buds completely enveloped by sepal-like bracts; sepals 4(–5), petals 5, unequal, 1 large, 2 intermediate, 2 small, stamens 9, unequally united at base, 3 fertile, 6 smaller, sterile; fr. a flat, leathery, dehiscent, few-seeded legume.

coeruleum (Taub.) J. Léonard [*P. coeruleoides* De Wild; *P. coeruleum* (Taub.) Harms]. Tree, to 100 ft. or more, branchlets blackish; lfts. in 3–5 pairs, elliptic to oblong, to 6 in. long, acuminate, golden-silky-hairy beneath; infl. to 3 in. long; petals 2-lobed at apex, the largest spatulate and nearly 2 in. long, blue-violet with basal green-blue spot; fr. to 8 in. long and 2⁵⁄₁₆ in. wide, glabrous, slightly winged on 1 side, seeds rectangular. Sierra Leone to Congo region, Kenya, and Tanzania.

PARAMIGNYA Wight. *Rutaceae*. Twelve spp. of evergreen shrubs, climbing by sharp, recurved spines, native from India, s. China, and Philippine Is. s. to ne. Australia; lvs.

alt., of 1 lft., glandular-dotted; fls. white, solitary or in axillary clusters, fragrant, calyx 4- or 5-lobed, petals 4 or 5, stamens 8 or 10; fr. berrylike, elliptic or globose, gummy inside.

Grown experimentally as a possible stock for citrus.

monophylla Wight. Lvs. mostly oblong or elliptic, to 5 in. long; fls. 1 in. across; fr. yellow, about 1 in. in diam. India.

PARAMONGAIA Velarde. *Amaryllidaceae*. One sp., native to Peru; related to *Pamianthe*, from which it differs in having bulbs without a false neck, perianth lobes yellow, not thickened basally, filaments inserted well below the margin of the prominent staminal corona and anthers not exserted from it, style not united to the perianth tube or winged; fr. a caps.

Propagated by seeds or offsets.

Weberbaueri Velarde. Lvs. 6–8, 2-ranked, glaucous, to 30 in. long, 2 in. wide; scape erect, 1–2-fld.; fls. bright yellow, fragrant, tube 4 in. long, lobes to 3¾ in. long, 1½ in. wide, spreading, corona 3⅜ in. long, ¾ in. across; caps. 1½ in. long, seeds many.

PARAPHALAENOPSIS Hawkes. *Orchidaceae*. Three spp., native to w. Borneo; lvs. cylindrical; sepals and petals about equal, lip 3-lobed, lateral lobes narrow, with 2-lobed callus between, midlobe narrow, not keeled, widened at apex. For structure of fl. see *Orchidaceae*.

For culture see *Orchids*.

Denevei (J. J. Sm.) Hawkes [*Phalaenopsis Denevei* J. J. Sm.]. Sts. short; lvs. to 2½ in. long, dark bluish-green; infl. lateral, to 6 in. long, 3–15-fld.; fls. 2 in. across, fragrant, long-lasting, sepals and petals 1 in. long, undulate, light greenish-yellow to dark yellow-brown, with paler margins, lateral lobes of lip triangular, strongly curved, subulate-acuminate at apex, midlobe clawed, fleshy, spatulate, white, but violet or crimson apically, yellow at margins, callus square, yellow. Early spring–summer. Borneo.

serpentilingua (J. J. Sm.) Hawkes. Sts. short; infl. many-fld.; fls. white, sepals and petals to ¾ in. long, transversely banded with yellow and purple, deeply 2-lobed at apex, with acute, diverging lobes like a snake's tongue, callus strongly toothed. W. Borneo.

PARAQUILEGIA J. R. Drumm. & Hutch. *Ranunculaceae*. Four spp. of small, tufted, per. herbs, native to mts. of cent. Asia; lvs. 2–3-ternately divided; sepals 5, petal-like, petals almost round, more or less emarginate, follicles usually 3–7, seeds narrowly winged. Like *Isopyrum*, but having several follicles; like *Semiaquilegia*, but lacking staminodes.

grandiflora (Fisch. ex. DC.) J. R. Drumm. & Hutch. Lvs. glaucous, delicately cut; fls. lavender-blue, gracefully pendulous, 1¼ in. across. Cent. Asia.

PARASYRINGA: *LIGUSTRUM*.

PARDANTHUS: *BELAMCANDA*.

PARIS L. *Liliaceae*. Perhaps 20 spp. of rhizomatous, per. herbs, native to temp. Asia and Eur.; lvs. 4–9, in a whorl near apex of the unbranched st.; fls. solitary, terminal, 4-merous, filaments flat, anthers basifixed; fr. a rather fleshy, loculicidal caps. Differing from *Trillium* mainly in its 4-merous fls.

Sometimes planted in the hardy border or wild garden.

polyphylla Sm. To 3 ft.; lvs. 4–9, linear to oblong-lanceolate, to 6 in. long, acuminate, petiole to ½ in. long; fls. to 4 in. across or more, inner perianth segms. 4–6, yellow, filiform, outer perianth segms. 4–6, green, ovate-lanceolate; fr. to 2½ in. in diam., seeds scarlet. Himalayas. Size of parts very variable.

PARITIUM: *HIBISCUS*.

PARKERIACEAE Hook. WATER-FERN FAMILY. Ferns; 1 genus, *Ceratopteris*, of 4 spp. of pantrop., floating ferns; lvs. dimorphic, sterile lvs. broad and laminate, producing new plants asexually in axils; fertile lvs. with narrower pinnules; sporangia in 1–4 rows, sessile, globose, enclosed in revolute margins of lf., annulus incomplete, vertical.

PARKIA R. Br. *Leguminosae* (subfamily *Mimosoideae*). About 40 spp. of unarmed trees in tropics of both hemispheres; lvs. alt., large, evenly 2-pinnate, with many small lfts.; fls. in long-peduncled, mostly pendent, globose or pear-shaped heads, sessile, bisexual or female or sterile, petals lin-

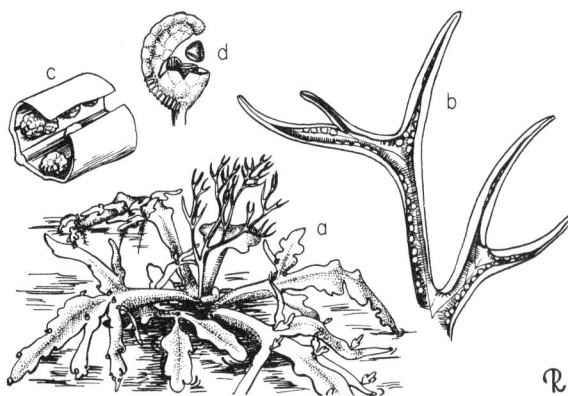

PARKERIACEAE. *Ceratopteris pteridoides:* **a,** floating plant with sterile and fertile leaves, × ⅙; **b,** segment of fertile leaf, × 1; **c,** section of fertile leaf, showing sporangia, × 4; **d,** sporangium shedding spores, × 12. (From Bailey, *Manual of Cultivated Plants,* ed. 2.)

ear, separate or united at base, stamens 10, exserted; fr. a legume.

africana: *P. biglobosa.*

biglandulosa: *P. pedunculata.*

biglobosa (Jacq.) Benth. [*P. africana* R. Br.]. AFRICAN LOCUST. To 50 ft., with wide-spreading crown; pinnae in 15–30 pairs, each with 50–70 pairs of lfts., these somewhat curved, ¼–½ in. long, basally eared on 1 side, 1-nerved; peduncles 6–8 in. long, fl. heads pear-shaped, orange or red, 1½ in. in diam.; fr. stalked, flat, 8–12 in. long, 1 in. wide. Trop. Afr.; introd. in W. Indies. Seeds edible.

filicoidea Welw. ex D. Oliver. AFRICAN LOCUST BEAN. To 90 ft.; pinnae in mostly 4–9 pairs, lfts. in 12–28 pairs, oblong, basally eared on 1 side, ½–1½ in. long, more or less distinctly 3-nerved; peduncles to 14 in. long; fl. heads pear-shaped, to 2¾ in. long, rose to red; fr. long-stalked, slender, nearly cylindrical, to 18 in. long, somewhat fleshy. Tropics, Afr.

javanica (Lam.) Merrill. To 150 ft.; differing from *P. biglobosa* in having lfts. acute, peduncles 10–16 in. long, corolla yellowish-white, and fr. 15–20 in. long and 1½ in. wide. Java.

pedunculata (Roxb.) Macbr. [*P. biglandulosa* Wight & Arn.]. Differs from *P. biglobosa* in having pinnae with 75–100 pairs of lfts., fertile fls. tawny, basal fls. whitish, and fr. downy when immature. Malay Pen.

speciosa Hort. ex Hassk. Differs from *P. filicoidea* in having lfts. ¼ in. long, minutely mucronate, and fls. white. Malay Arch. Seeds used for food.

PARKINSONIA L. *Leguminosae* (subfamily *Caesalpinioideae*). Two spp. of spiny shrubs or small trees with green brs., 1 in Amer. and 1 in Afr.; lvs. alt., 2-pinnate, with 1–2 pairs of long pinnae from a very short, spine-tipped rachis, lfts. many, alt.; fls. in racemes, large, yellow, almost regular, 5-merous, stamens 10; fr. a slender, leathery legume.

Planted in warm regions. Propagated by seeds.

aculeata L. JERUSALEM THORN, MEXICAN PALO VERDE. To 20 ft. or more, with stout spines to 1 in. long; pinnae to 16 in. long, flat, lfts. small, distant, in 10–25 pairs, linear to obovate, deciduous; racemes axillary, loose, shorter than pinnae; petals to ⅝ in. long; fr. to 6 in. long, greatly constricted between seeds. Trop. Amer. Widely cult.

microphyllum: *Cercidium microphyllum.*

Torreyana: *Cercidium floridum.*

PARMENTIERA DC. *Bignoniaceae.* Three or 4 spp. of trees, native to Mex. and Cent. Amer., with branchlets often spiny at the nodes; lvs. opp. to alt., sometimes in clusters, simple or with 3 lfts.; fls. white, greenish, or greenish-yellow, solitary or in fascicles on the older brs., calyx spathelike, corolla campanulate, somewhat curved, slightly 2-lipped, stamens 4; fr. long-cylindrical, indehiscent.

Occasionally planted in tropical and subtropical gardens.

alata (HBK) Miers [*Crescentia alata* HBK]. Spineless, to 30 ft.; lfts. oblanceolate to spatulate, entire, terminal one often 3 in. long, petiole broadly winged and long; fls. greenish and purplish-brown or reddish; fr. 2–4¾ in. in diam. Baja Calif. and Sonora (Mex.), s. to Guatemala and El Salvador.

cereifera Seem. CANDLE TREE. Small, spineless; lfts. obovate, to 2 in. long, entire or toothed; fls. white, to 3 in. long, calyx large, brownish; fr. pendent from the older brs., to 4 ft. long, yellowish, resembling candles. Panama. Planted in the tropics and subtropics as an oddity. Zone 10b in Fla.

edulis DC. GUAJILOTE, CUACHILOTE. Spiny, to 30 ft., with broad head; lfts. ovate, entire, petiole very narrowly winged; fls. greenish-yellow, about 2½ in. long; fr. 4–6 in. long, about 1 in. in diam., yellowish-green, edible. Mex., Guatemala. Fr. eaten but of poor quality.

PARNASSIA L. GRASS-OF-PARNASSUS, BOG-STARS. *Saxifragaceae.* About 15 spp. of small, per. herbs in temp. and arctic N. Amer. and Eurasia; basal lvs. long-petioled, entire; fl. st. with 1 sessile lf. and a solitary terminal white fl.; calyx tube short, calyx lobes 5, petals 5, stamens 5, staminodes always present, opp. the petals, usually as fingerlike or filiform projections from a broad scalelike base, ovary superior, stigmas 4, sessile; fr. a 4-valved caps.

Useful for planting in damp locations, blooming in summer. Propagated by seeds or division.

asarifolia Venten. To 20 in.; lvs. reniform, wider than long, to 3 in. across, st. lf. orbicular and clasping, at about the middle of fl. st.; fls. 1 in. across, petals clawed, entire, staminodial scales 3-lobed to below the middle, slightly shorter than stamens. Va. to Ga., and Ark.

californica: *P. palustris* var.

caroliniana: see *P. glauca.*

fimbriata K. König. To 1 ft.; lvs. reniform or broad-cordate, to 1½ in. long, st. lf. clasping; petals fringed on sides, staminodial scales fleshy, with several stout lobes or fingerlike projections. Alaska, s. to Colo. and Calif. Var. **intermedia** (Rydb.) C. L. Hitchc. [*P. intermedia* Rydb.]. Staminodial scales much flared and divided into 7–9 filaments or more, some with apical knobs.

foliosa Hook.f. & T. Thoms. To 12 in.; sts. acutely 4-angled, winged; st. lf. sessile, orbicular-cordate, about 1 in. across, lobed, 5–7-nerved; fls. to 1 in. across, petals fringed at base, staminodial scales 3-lobed, with a globose gland terminating each lobe. Himalayas, w. China, Japan.

glauca Raf. [*P. caroliniana* of auth., not Michx.]. To 1½–2 ft.; lvs. ovate to orbicular-ovate, to 2 in. long, st. lf. at or below middle of st., sometimes absent, smaller than basal lvs., sessile; fls. 1–1½ in. across, petals entire, staminodial scales 3-lobed to below middle, slightly shorter than stamens. Nfld. to Sask., s. to Va., Ind., S. Dak.

grandifolia DC. To 2 ft.; lvs. ovate to orbicular, st. lf. clasping, at or below middle of st., ovate; fls. to 2 in. across, petals entire, staminodial scales divided nearly to base into 3–5 slender filaments, much longer than stamens. Va. to Mo., s. to Fla. and La.

intermedia: *P. fimbriata* var.

montanensis: *P. palustris* var.

nubicola Wallich. To 12 in.; lvs. elliptic, 2–4 in. long, 5–7-nerved from base, basal lvs. petioled, st. lf. sessile; fls. to 1½ in. across, staminodial scales 3-lobed. Himalayas.

palustris L. To 1 ft.; lvs. ovate, to 1½ in. long, cordate, st. lf. clasping at or below middle of st., ovate; fls. to 1 in. across, petals entire, 7–13-veined, staminodial scales dilated, divided into 5–11 or more slender filaments, each terminating in a knob. N. Amer., Eur., Asia. Var. **californica** A. Gray [*P. californica* (A. Gray) Greene]. St. lf. above middle of st., very small, not clasping; staminodial scales with mostly 17–27 filaments. Sierra Nevada of Calif. Var. **montanensis** (Fern. & Rydb.) C. L. Hitchc. [*P. montanensis* Fern. & Rydb.]. St. lf. rarely at all clasping, staminodial scales with 5–9 filaments. Rocky Mts., Alta. to Colo., Utah, and s. Sierra Nevada of Calif.

parviflora DC. To 1 ft.; lvs. elliptic, to 1 in. long, narrowed at base, st. lf. clasping, at about middle of st., elliptic; fls. about ½ in. across, petals usually 5-veined, staminodial scales divided into mostly 5–7 filaments tipped with knobs, shorter than stamens. B.C. to Que., s. to Idaho, Mont., and Minn.

PAROCHETUS Buch.-Ham. ex D. Don. *Leguminosae* (subfamily *Faboideae*). One sp., an herb of the Old World; lvs. alt., of 3 lfts.; fls. axillary, papilionaceous, stamens 10, 9 united and 1 separate; fr. a linear, dehiscent legume.

Propagated by seeds or cuttings.

communis Buch.-Ham. ex D. Don. SHAMROCK PEA, BLUE OXALIS. Per., sts. long, slender, trailing; lfts. obcordate, to ¾ in. long, marked with brown crescent at base, petioles 3–4 in. long; peduncles solitary or 2–3 together, longer than petioles; petals cobalt-blue, with pink wings; fr. 1 in. long. Himalayas, Mozambique. Zone 9. Useful for rock gardens or hanging baskets.

PARODIA Speg. *Cactaceae.* About 20 spp. of small, ribbed or tubercled, globose cacti of S. Amer.; sts. mostly solitary; central spines straight or hooked; fls. subapical, nearly campanulate, yellow to red, scales on ovary small, with axillary wool and bristles, stamens many, in 1 series, included; fr. oblong, thin-walled, dehiscent, many-seeded, seeds minute, brown, glossy, with prominent corky hilum. Closely related to *Notocactus.*

For culture see *Cacti.*

aureicentra Backeb. Sts. cespitose, subglobose, to 6 in. thick, ribs about 15, continuous; radial spines about 40, bristlelike, interlacing, central spines stouter, reddish or yellowish-brown, thick at base, 1 or more hooked; fls. light red, 1½ in. long. N. Argentina.

aureispina Backeb. TOM-THUMB, GOLDEN T.-T. Sts. globose, to 2½ in. thick, ribs divided into tubercles; radial spines about 40, bristlelike, white, ¼ in. long, central spines about 6, needle-shaped, thick at base, golden, 1 of them hooked, to ¾ in. long; fls. yellow, 1 in. long; seeds minute. N. Argentina.

catamarcensis Backeb. Sts. cylindrical, ribs divided into low, flattened tubercles; radial spines about 9, slender, white, central spines 4, curved, dark purple, the lowest deflexed, robust, hooked; fls. pale yellow. N. Argentina.

chrysacanthion (K. Schum.) Backeb. Sts. to 2½ in. high and 2 in. thick, ribs divided into tubercles to ¼ in. high; spines 30–40, bristlelike, ½ in. long, central spines longer, thicker, yellow; fls. yellow, ¾ in. long, ovary nearly naked; seeds small. N. Argentina.

erythrantha (Speg.) Backeb. Sts. small, globose, ribs spiral, tubercled; radial spines about 20, bristlelike, white, central spines 4, thin, 1 hooked; fls. red, to 1¼ in. long. N. Argentina.

Faustiana Backeb. Sts. subglobose, to 2½ in. thick, ribs divided into tubercles; radial spines about 20, glassy, to ⅜ in. long, central spines 4, the lower robust, curved, brown, to 1½ in. long; fls. yellow. N. Argentina.

Maassii (Heese) Backeb. & F. M. Knuth. Sts. mostly simple, ovoid, to 6 in. thick, ribs 13–21, strong, somewhat spiral; radial spines 8–15, needle-shaped, yellowish, to ⅝ in. long, central spines 4, stouter, thickened at base, the longest deflexed, often curved or hooked, to 1½ in. long; fls. red. Bolivia, n. Argentina.

microsperma (A. Web.) Speg. Sts. subglobose, to 4 in. thick, tubercles in about 20 spirals, scarcely joined; radial spines 11–25, needle-shaped, white, to ¼ in. long, central spines 3–4, awl-shaped, reddish, to ⅜ in. long, the lowest hooked; fls. yellow or orange, 1½ in. across; seeds minute. N. Argentina.

mutabilis Backeb. Sts. globose, to 3 in. thick, tubercled; radial spines about 50, bristlelike, white, ⅜ in. long, central spines 4, needle-shaped, red to orange, the lower hooked, ½ in. long; fls. yellow or with red throat; seeds small. N. Argentina.

nivosa Backeb. Sts. to 6 in. high and 3 in. thick, tubercled; radial spines about 18, needle-shaped, glassy, to ½ in. long, central spines 4, stouter, straight, white, to ¾ in. long; fls. red, 1¼ in. long; seeds minute. N. Argentina. Perhaps a var. of *P. microsperma.*

sanguiniflora Backeb. Related to *P. microsperma* and perhaps only a var. of it with red fls.

Schwebsiana (Werderm.) Backeb. Sts. to 2½ in. high and thick, ribs 13–20, low, scarcely tubercled; radial spines about 10, needle-shaped, brownish, to ½ in. long, central spine 1, awl-shaped, decurved, thickened at base, to ¾ in. long; fls. red, to 1¼ in. long; seeds small. Bolivia.

scopaoides Backeb. Sts. ovoid, ribs divided into close-set tubercles; radial spines many, bristlelike, glassy-white, central spines 4, stouter, the lower hooked, red; fls. orange-yellow with red throat, 1¼ in. across. N. Argentina. Perhaps a form of *P. microsperma.*

setifera Backeb. Sts. globose, about 2 in. thick, ribs 17–18, nearly tubercled; radial spines about 20, bristlelike, white, to ⁵⁄₁₆ in. long, central spines 3–4, pink to black, the lower hooked, to ¾ in. long; fls. yellowish-white, 1½ in. across; seeds rather small. N. Argentina.

Stuemeri (Werderm.) Backeb. Sts. globose, to 4 in. thick, ribs about 20, tubercled; radial spines about 25, needle-shaped, white, to ¾ in. long, central spines 4, thicker, brown, the lowest sometimes hooked, to 1¼ in. long; fls. orange-yellow, 1½ in. long; seeds small. N. Argentina.

tilcarensis (Werderm. & Backeb.) Backeb. Perhaps a var. of *P. Stuemeri* with 9–12 radial spines and smaller orange fls. N. Argentina.

PARONYCHIA Mill. WHITLOWWORT, NAILWORT, CHICK-WEED. *Caryophyllaceae* (sometimes placed in a separate family, *Illecebraceae).* About 45 spp. of small, tufted, ann. and per. herbs of wide distribution; lvs. opp. or whorled; fls. minute, greenish, usually clustered, often hidden among silvery stipules or bracts, sepals 5, petals minute or 0, stamens 2–5, styles bifid; fr. dry, enclosed in the calyx, 1–seeded.

Useful in rock gardens. Easily cultivated; propagated by seeds, and the perennials also by division.

argentea Lam. Procumbent per., sts. to 1 ft., matted; lvs. ovate to lanceolate, mostly to ⁵⁄₁₆ in. long; fls. in dense clusters among lvs., concealed by silvery bracts, calyx apically hooded and awned on the back. Medit. region.

argyrocoma (Michx.) Nutt. SILVER W., SILVERLING. Tufted per., to 1 ft., freely branching, silky-hairy; lvs. linear to linear-lanceolate, to 1¼ in. long; fls. in dense clusters, sepals to ¼ in. long, appressed-hairy, with a hairy awn at apex. Mts., Va. and W. Va. to Ga.

bonariensis: *P. brasiliana.*

brasiliana DC. [*P. bonariensis* DC.]. Per., 4–10 in., pubescent to glabrous; lvs. lanceolate, to ⅜ in. long, mucronate, pilose, stipules lanceolate, acuminate; fls. in axillary clusters, sepals largely mucronate, stamens 5, staminodes 5. Sandy soil, in the pampas, Argentina, Uruguay, probably s. Brazil.

canadensis (L.) A. Wood. FORKED C. Glabrous ann., much-branched, bushy, to 16 in., internodes elongated; lvs. elliptic, thin, to ⅝ in. long, stipules and bracts short; infl. diffuse; fls. in lf. axils, minute. New Hamp. to Ga., Minn. to Ark.

capitata (L.) Lam. [*P. nivea* DC.]. Cespitose per., to 6 in.; lvs. narrowly oblong-lanceolate, acute, ciliate, pubescent, gray-green; fls. concealed by bracts longer than lvs. and fls., calyx lobes very unequal. Medit. region. See also *P. Kapela.*

dichotoma: *P. virginica.*

Kapela (Hacq.) A. Kern. [*P. capitata* of auth., not (L.) Lam.]. Per., 2–6 in.; lvs. crowded, ciliate; fl. clusters conspicuous, to ½ in. across or more, bracts silvery; calyx lobes nearly equal in length, usually obtuse. Medit. region, n. to Austria. Subsp. **Kapela.** The typical subsp.; sts. prostrate or ascending, lvs. crowded, ovate-lanceolate, to ³⁄₁₆ in. long, glabrous; calyx half as long as lvs. Subsp. **serpyllifolia** (Chaix) Graebn. [*P. serpyllifolia* (Chaix) Poir.]. Procumbent, mat-forming; lvs. densely crowded, usually 2-ranked, elliptic to ovate, strongly ciliate; calyx about ¹⁄₁₆ in. long. Spain, Pyrenees, Alps, Apennines.

nivea: *P. capitata.*

serpyllifolia: *P. Kapela* subsp.

sessiliflora Nutt. Cespitose per., forming mats to 8 in. across, yellowish-green; fl. sts. mostly 1(–5) in.; lvs. very crowded, linear-subulate, to ³⁄₁₆ in. long; fls. terminal, solitary or clustered, calyx brownish-yellow, awned. Sask. to Alta., s. to New Mex. and Tex.

virginica K. Spreng. [*P. dichotoma* Nutt., not DC.]. Tufted per., to 16 in., glabrous; lvs. subulate, to 1¼ in. long; fls. in terminal, branched cymes, longer than the short silvery bracts. W. Md. to Tenn., w. to Okla. and Tex.

PAROSELA: *DALEA.*

PARROTIA C. A. Mey. *Hamamelidaceae.* One sp., a deciduous tree, native to Iran, with stellate pubescence; lvs. like those of *Hamamelis,* short-petioled; fls. without petals, clustered in dense heads, surrounded by large bracts, sepals and stamens 5–7, filaments slender, pendulous, ovary superior, 2-celled; fr. a caps., each cell 1-seeded. Related to *Parrotiopsis,* but differs in having lvs. of different form, brownish bracts, and fewer stamens.

Propagated by seeds, layers, and cuttings.

persica C. A. Mey. To 15 ft.; lvs. ovate to obovate, to 4 in. long, coarsely toothed above middle; fls. before lvs., in dense heads to ½ in. across surrounded by brown-tomentose bracts. Lvs. scarlet, orange, and yellow in autumn. Zone 8.

Jacquemontiana: *Parrotiopsis Jacquemontia.*

PARROTIOPSIS (Niedenzu) C. K. Schneid. *Hamamelidaceae.* One sp., a deciduous, stellate-pubescent tree, native to the Himalayas; lvs. alt., simple, toothed, alderlike; fls. many, in heads surrounded by large white bracts; sepals 5–7, petals none, stamens about 15, filaments erect, ovary superior, 2-celled; fr. an ovoid, 2-beaked caps. Related to *Parrotia.*

Rather tender in the North. Propagated by seeds, layers, and greenwood cuttings under glass.

Jacquemontiana (Decne.) Rehd. [*Parrotia Jacquemontia* Decne.]. To 20 ft.; lvs. broadly ovate to nearly orbicular, to 3 in. long, stellate-pubescent on both surfaces; fls. in spring, with the lvs., about 20 in bracted heads to 2 in. across, bracts creamy-white, conspicuous. Lvs. yellow in autumn. Zone 8.

PARRYA R. Br. *Cruciferae.* Not cult. **P. Menziesii:** *Phoenicaulis cheiranthoides.*

PARSNIP. The parsnip, *Pastinaca sativa*, is a root vegetable, native of Eurasia, which can be grown widely in the cool-temperate United States, although the seeds are difficult to germinate during hot weather and roots maturing during summer are of poor quality. In the southern states, the species can be grown so that the edible roots mature in spring or early summer. Like similar root crops, parsnips require deep fertile soils that are well drained, light and friable, and with good tilth. Parsnips are not sensitive to high soil acidity. Soil should be enriched with 3 to 5 pounds of complete fertilizer thoroughly mixed into each 100 feet of row.

Recommended cultivars include 'All American', 'Hollow Crown', and 'Model'. Freshly purchased seed should always be used, for viability falls rapidly after a year. Seeds are planted at a depth of ½ inch in rows 20 to 24 inches apart and later thinned so plants stand 3 inches apart in the rows. Parsnips are much sweeter if allowed to remain in the ground over winter or if placed for some weeks in cold storage. There is no basis for the belief that parsnips overwintered in the garden are poisonous.

PARSONIA: *CUPHEA.*

PARTHENIUM L. *Compositae* (Helianthus Tribe). Sixteen spp. of aromatic shrubs and per. or ann. herbs in N. Amer. and the W. Indies; lvs. alt., entire to pinnately divided; fl. heads solitary or corymbose, small, radiate, white or yellowish, involucral bracts in 2 rows, receptacle scaly; disc fls. many, sterile, ray fls. 5, short, inconspicuous, fertile, their achenes basally attached to and falling with an involucral bract and 2 adjacent disc fls.; pappus of 2–3 awns or scales, or lacking.

Propagated by seeds.

argentatum A. Gray. GUAYULE. Shrub, to 3 ft., much-branched; lvs. oblanceolate, to 2 in. long, entire or few-toothed, closely silvery-pubescent; heads ¼ in. across, many in a close corymb on a peduncle 4–8 in. long. Tex., n. Mex. Select cvs. were grown during wartime in the sw. U.S. as a potential emergency source of natural rubber, obtained from the sts.

integrifolium L. Pubescent per. herb, to 3–4 ft., from a swollen root; lvs. ovate to lanceolate, coarsely dentate, basal lvs. to 15 in. long, long-petioled, the upper st. lvs. shorter, sessile; heads ¼ in. across, many in broad flat-topped corymbs; fls. whitish. Mass., s. to Ga., w. to Minn. and Ark.

PARTHENOCISSUS Planch. WOODBINE. *Vitaceae.* About 15 spp. of deciduous, woody vines, climbing by tendrils often with disclike tips, native to temp. Asia and N. Amer.; lvs. alt., unlobed or palmately lobed to compound; fls. small, greenish, in compound cymes, usually 5-merous, petals expanding and falling separately, disc absent, ovary 2-celled; fr. a black or blue-black berry.

These vines are grown as covering for walls, fences, and arbors, and are allowed to grow on trees. They thrive in any good soil. Propagated by seeds, cuttings of hard and green wood, and by layers.

Engelmannii: *P. quinquefolia* cv.

Henryana (Hemsl.) Graebn. ex Diels & Gilg [*Ampelopsis Henryana* (Hemsl.) Rehd.; *Cissus Henryana* Hort.; *Vitis Henryana* Hemsl.]. Young brs. 4-angled, tendrils 5–7-branched; lfts. 5, ovate to obovate, to 2½ in. long, toothed above middle, marked with white above, purplish beneath; infl. narrow, to 6 in. long; fr. dark blue. Cent. China. Zone 7?

Henryi: a listed name of no botanical standing for *P. Henryana.*

heterophylla (Blume) Merrill. Lvs. of 2 kinds, those of sterile brs. simple, small, those of fl. brs. palmately compound, lfts. 3–5, with the lateral lfts. subcordate. Taiwan to Indonesia. Zone 10.

inserta (A. Kern.) Fritsch [*P. quinquefolia* var. *vitacea* (Knerr) L. H. Bailey; *P. vitacea* (Knerr) A. S. Hitchc.]. Similar to *P. quinquefolia*, but differs in having tendrils tapering to tip and not disc-tipped, hence does not cling to walls; cymes usually solitary; lvs. glossy above; fr. smaller, about ¼ in. long. Que. to Ariz. Zone 3.

quinquefolia (L.) Planch. [*Ampelopsis quinquefolia* (L.) Michx.; *Vitis quinquefolia* (L.) Lam.]. VIRGINIA CREEPER, WOODBINE, AMERICAN IVY, FIVE-LEAVED I. High-climbing, brs. with adhesive, disc-tipped tendrils; lfts. 5, elliptic-ovate, to 6 in. long, coarsely toothed, dull green above, paler beneath; cymes paniculate; fr. about ⅜ in. long. Ne. U.S. to Fla., Tex., and Mex. Zone 4. Bark used medicinally. Cvs. include: 'Engelmannii' [*P. Engelmannii* Koehne & Graebn.], lfts. smaller; 'Hirsuta', lvs. pubescent beneath; 'Murorum', tendrils short, many; 'Saint-Paulii', brs. often with aerial rootlets, lfts. hairy beneath. Var. **vitacea:** *P. inserta.*

tricuspidata (Siebold & Zucc.) Planch. [*Ampelopsis tricuspidata* Siebold & Zucc.]. BOSTON IVY, JAPANESE I. Glabrous, high-climbing, tendrils disc-tipped; lvs. simple, ovate to orbicular, to 8 in. across, 3-lobed or -parted, glossy above; cymes usually on short, 2-lvd. brs.; fr. blue-black, about ¼ in. long. Cent. China to Japan. Zone 5. Cvs. include: 'Lowii', lvs. to 1½ in. long, purplish when young; 'Minutifolia', lvs. mostly 1–2 in. across; 'Purpurea', lvs. dark purple; 'Veitchii' [*P. Veitchii* Koehne & Graebn.], young lvs. 1–2 in. across, purplish; 'Veitchii Robusta', more vigorous.

Veitchii: *P. tricuspidata* cv., but sometimes applied to the sp.

vitacea: *P. inserta.*

PASANIA: *LITHOCARPUS.*

PASITHEA D. Don. *Liliaceae.* One sp., a rhizomatous, per. herb, native to Chile; lvs. basal; fls. blue, in loose panicles on slender scapes, perianth segms. 6, united basally into a short tube, stamens 6, 3 with short filaments alternating with 3 on longer filaments, anthers versatile; fr. a 3-valved, loculicidal caps.

caerulea (Ruiz & Pav.) D. Don. To 2 ft.; lvs. linear, grasslike, to 10 in. long, keeled; fls. blue, to 1 in. across, spreading.

PASPALUM L. *Gramineae.* About 400 spp. of ann. or mostly per. grasses throughout the world; racemes 1 to many, spikelike; spikelets compressed but slightly convex on the sides, usually obtuse, nearly sessile, solitary or paired, in 2 rows on one side of the rachis, fertile lemma with back toward rachis, first glume usually absent, second glume and sterile lemma usually about equal or the former rarely lacking, fertile lemma usually obtuse, hard-papery, with inrolled margins. For terminology see *Gramineae.*

dilatatum Poir. DALLIS GRASS. Per., sts. to 5 ft., clustered, ascending or erect from a decumbent base; lf. blades to 10 in. long and ½ in. wide; racemes usually 3–5, spreading, to 3¼ in. long; spikelets ⅛ in. long, fringed with long, white, silky hairs and sparsely silky on the surface. S. Amer.; introd. and naturalized from N.J. to Tenn. and Fla., w. to Okla. and Tex.

malacophyllum Trin. RIBBED P. Per., sts. to 7 ft., rather coarse; lf. blades flat, to ⅜ in. wide, the lower narrowed to a slender base; panicles nodding, racemes usually many; spikelets less than ⅛ in. long, glabrous, second glume absent, fertile lemma strongly ridged. Mex. to Bolivia and Argentina; introd. into the s. states for hay or in soil conservation work.

Nicorae Parodi. Per., rhizomatous, sts. slender, erect or ascending; lf. sheaths and blades, at least the lower, sparsely pilose, the blades sometimes minutely pubescent on the upper surface; racemes 3–4, appressed or ascending; spikelets about ⅛ in. long, brown at maturity, glabrous or the glume appressed-pubescent, sterile lemma with short, transverse wrinkles just inside the slightly raised margin. S. Amer.; introd. in Ga. and Fla.

notatum Flügge. BAHIA GRASS. Per., sts. to 20 in., from a rhizome; lf. blades flat or folded; racemes mostly paired, recurved-ascending, to 2¾ in. long; spikelets ovate to obovate, ⅛ in. long, smooth and glossy. Mex., W. Indies, S. Amer.; introd. in N.J., N.C., Fla., La., and Tex. Var. **Saurae** Parodi. PENSACOLA B.G., PARAGUAY B.G., WILMINGTON B.G. Sts. taller; lf. blades to over 1 ft. long; racemes 2–3, rarely to 5, suberect; spikelets shorter. Paraguay, Argentina; introd. in the s. states as a lawn grass.

racemosum Lam. PERUVIAN P. Ann., sts. branching; lf. blades to 4¾ in. long and to ¾ in. wide; racemes many in a tawny or purple panicle; spikelets nearly ⅛ in. long, pointed, sterile lemma transversely fluted on each side of the midnerve. Peru. Sometimes cult. for ornament.

Urvillei Steud. VASEY GRASS. Per., sts. to 7 ft., in large clumps; lower lf. sheaths coarsely hirsute or occasionally glabrous, blades mostly elongate, to ⅝ in. wide, pilose at base; panicle erect, to 16 in. long, racemes 12–20, to 5½ in. long; spikelets to ⅛ in. long, fringed with long, white, silky hairs, the glume appressed-silky. S. Amer.; naturalized from Va. to Fla., w. to Tex. and in s. Calif.

PASSIFLORA L. [*Tacsonia* Juss.]. PASSIONFLOWER. *Passifloraceae.* About 400 spp. of vines climbing by tendrils, native to New and Old World but principally to trop. Amer.; lvs. alt., entire or lobed, often with glands on the petiole, stipuled; fls. solitary or racemose, each usually subtended by 3–5 green bracts, bisexual, regular but complex in structure, the 5 sepals and 5 petals united basally to form a tubular calyx tube usually bearing a fringelike crown or corona composed of 1 to several rings of filamentous, tubercular, or tubelike structures, and inside the corona a circular membrane (the operculum), stamens 5–10, filaments separate above but basally united and adherent to the elongated stalk bearing the ovary, styles 3; fr. a firm-walled, many-seeded berry.

Many species are grown as ornamentals, but several are important economically in the tropics for their edible fruits: purple granadilla (*P. edulis*), yellow granadilla (*P. laurifolia*), sweet granadilla (*P. ligularis*), sweet calabash (*P. maliformis*), curubá (*P. mollissima*), giant granadilla (*P. quadrangularis*). The fruit is also known as passion fruit or water lemon. The arillate pulp covering the seeds is the part eaten or used for flavoring beverages and ices. One hybrid, *P.* ×*alatocaerulea*, has been used in perfumery.

Passifloras are hardy only in the southernmost U.S., but are sometimes grown under glass or in the home for the striking flowers. Propagated by seeds and cuttings. Many of the species are highly susceptible to nematodes, which are often responsible for failure in culture.

alata Dryand. Sts. 4-angled and -winged; lvs. simple, ovate-oblong, 3–6 in. long; fls. 4–5 in. across, fragrant, sepals green outside, carmine-crimson inside, petals white outside, carmine-crimson inside, corona variegated red, purple, and white, the outer 2 rows filamentous; fr. 3–5 in. long, yellow, edible. E. Brazil, ne. Peru. Closely related to *P. quadrangularis*, but petioles with only 2–4 glands.

×**alatocaerulea** Lindl. [*P. Pfordtii* M. T. Mast.]: *P. alata* × *P. caerulea*. Sts. angled or narrow-winged; lvs. 3-lobed; fls. 4 in. across, fragrant, sepals white inside, petals white outside, pink to purple inside, corona variegated. Of garden origin. Fls. used in the manufacture of perfumes.

alba: *P. subpeltata;* but see also *P. Eichlerana.*

×**Allardii** Lynch: *P. caerulea* cv. 'Constance Elliott" × *P. quadrangularis.* A free-flowering hybrid; lvs. usually 3-lobed; petals white, suffused pink, corona deep cobalt-blue.

antioquiensis Karst. [*P. Van-Volxemii* (Lem.) Triana & Planch.; *Tacsonia Van-Volxemii* Lem.]. BANANA PASSION FRUIT. Sts. cylindrical, red-hairy; lvs. lanceolate or with 3 elliptic-lanceolate lobes, sharp-serrulate; fls. 4–5 in. across, bright rose-red, calyx tube 1–2 in. long, glabrous; fr. ellipsoidal, edible. Colombia.

×**atropurpurea** Nichols.: probably *P. racemosa* × *P. kermesina* Link & Otto. Fls. 3 in. across, sepals purple inside, petals dark blood-red, corona violet, spotted with white.

Banksii Benth. Sts. obtusely angled, glabrous; lvs. 2–3 in. long, shallowly 3-lobed, lobes ovate, bluntly acute; bracts setaceous; fls. 2½–4 in. across, sepals linear-oblong, pale pink, petals half as long as sepals, orange- to brick-red but paler on opening, outer part of corona of deep red filaments, inner part tubular; fr. ovoid, 1½ in. long. Queensland (Australia). A white-fld. form is known in cult.

biflora Lam. Sts. 5-angled; lvs. variable, but mostly twice as wide as long or wider, often sausage-shaped in outline; fls. 1–1½ in. across, white, petals shorter than sepals; fr. globose, nearly ¾ in. across. Mex. to Venezuela, and Bahama Is.

bryonioides HBK. Sts. obtusely angled, hispidulous; lvs. deeply 3-lobed, lateral lobes often 2-lobed, about 3 in. long; fls. ¾–1¼ in. across, sepals greenish-yellow, petals linear, white, less than ¼ in. long, corona purplish basally; fr. oblong, 1½ in. long. Ariz. to s. Mex.

caerulea L. BLUE PASSIONFLOWER. Sts. somewhat angled and grooved; lvs. deeply 5–9-lobed, stipules ovate, leaflike; fls. 2–4 in. across, sepals and petals white or pinkish inside, of equal length, corona filamentous, in 4 rings, all purple at base, white at middle, blue at apex; fr. ovoid, 2½ in. long, yellow to orange. Brazil to Argentina; naturalized in various parts of the tropics. One of the more hardy spp., capable of withstanding some frost; can be flowered in a 4-in. pot. Garden hybrids between this and *P. alata, P. kermesina* Link & Otto, *P. racemosa*, and other spp. have been produced. Cv. **'Grandiflora'**. Fls. 5–6 in. across. Cv. **'Constance Elliott'**. Sepals, petals, and corona white.

cinnabarina Lindl. Sts. slender, glabrous; lvs. mostly 3-lobed, 2–4 in. long and wide, petioles lacking glands; bracts setaceous; fls. 2½ in. across, sepals 1 in. long, oblong, scarlet, petals about half as long as sepals, scarlet, corona yellow. Australia. Early-flowering.

coccinea Aubl. RED PASSIONFLOWER, RED GRANADILLA. Sts. nearly cylindrical, obtusely angled, finely red-hairy; lvs. oblong to nearly orbicular, 2½–5 in. long, not lobed, doubly serrate, petioles with glands; fls. 3–5 in. across, sepals and petals acute, scarlet to deep orange, sepals with keel terminating in an awn to ½ in. long, petals as long as sepals or shorter, corona in 3 rings with the outer 2 filamentous, pale pink to white at base and deep purple towards apex; fr. ovoid, about 2 in. across, orange or yellow, mottled green, hard and brittle at maturity. Venezuela to Bolivia.

×**Colvillii** Sweet: *P. caerulea* × *P. incarnata.* Lvs. deeply 3–5-lobed, toothed; fls. 3½ in. across, white, spotted with red-brown, corona banded with purple, white, and blue.

coriacea Juss. BAT-LEAF PASSIONFLOWER. Sts. angled, densely puberulent when young; lvs. not lobed, peltate, broader than long, leathery; fls. in a terminal raceme or in lf. axils, not showy, 1–1½ in. across, sepals obtuse, yellowish-green inside, petals 0; fr. globose, to ¾ in. across. Mex. to Bolivia.

edulis Sims. PURPLE GRANADILLA, PASSION FRUIT. Sts. obtusely angled, glabrous; lvs. 2–4 in. long, 3-lobed, deeply toothed, glabrous, glossy above; bracts ½ in. long or more; fls. 2–3 in. across, white, corona filaments purple at base, white at apex; fr. ovoid, 2 in. across, greenish-yellow to purple, edible. Brazil; naturalized in n. S. Amer. and W. Indies. Cult. for its fr. in Australia, Hawaii, Mex., and s. Calif.

Eichlerana M. T. Mast. Sometimes confused with *P. subpeltata* [*P. alba*], from which it differs in having lobes of lvs. entire, petioles with 6–8 stalked glands, and, within the corona, an operculum membranous at the base and filamentous above. E. Brazil to Paraguay. Usually passes in the trade under the name *P. alba.*

×**exoniensis** Hort. ex L. H. Bailey: *P. antioquiensis* × *P. mollissima.* Lvs. deeply 3-lobed; fls. 4–5 in. across, petals brick-red outside, rose-pink inside.

foetida L. RUNNING POP, LOVE-IN-A-MIST, WILD WATER LEMON. Sts. glabrous to hispid; foliage fetid, lvs. 3–5-lobed, membranous, petioles without glands; fls. 1–2 in. across, white, pink, lilac, to purplish, petals slightly shorter than sepals, corona filaments white, banded with purple; fr. globose, bright red to yellow, edible. A polymorphic sp. of Amer. tropics; naturalized in Old World tropics.

gracilis Jacq. ex Link. Sts. 4-angled, very slender; lvs. not peltate, 3-lobed, entire, thin-membranous; fls. nearly 1 in. across, sepals pale green, white inside, petals 0; fr. ellipsoidal, about 1 in. long, scarlet, the walls parchmentlike. Venezuela; widely naturalized or escaped from cult. in Amer. tropics and subtropics.

grandiflora: *P. caerulea* cv.

incarnata L. WILD PASSIONFLOWER, MAYPOP, APRICOT VINE. Sts. cylindrical, or angular when young; lvs. deeply 3-lobed, mostly 4–6 in. long, toothed, dull above, petioles with 2 glands; fls. 2–3 in. across, white or pale lavender, outer 2 rings of corona filamentous, mostly pink to purple; fr. ovoid, to 2 in. long, yellow, edible. Va. to Fla., w. to Mo. and Tex. Differs from *P. edulis* in having herbage usually minutely pilose, lvs. dull above, and bracts ⅜ in. long or less.

Jamesonii (M. T. Mast.) L. H. Bailey [*Tacsonia Jamesonii* M. T. Mast.]. Sts. angled; lvs. 1½–3 in. long, deeply 3-lobed, spiny-toothed, somewhat leathery, glossy above; stipules and bracts deeply cleft; fls. 3–4 in. across, rose to coral-red, calyx tube 3–4 in. long, corona of minute tubercles, purplish. Andes, Ecuador.

laurifolia L. YELLOW GRANADILLA, WATER LEMON, JAMAICA HONEYSUCKLE, BELLE APPLE, VINEGAR PEAR, POMME-DE-LIANE. Sts. cylindrical; lvs. ovate to oblong, 2½–4½ in. long, entire, petioles with 2 glands near apex, stipules setaceous, falling early; bracts not united basally, glandular-serrate apically; fls. 2–3 in. across, purple-red, corona banded with blue, purple, and rose; fr. ovoid, 2–3½ in. long, lemon-yellow to orange, edible. W. Indies to e. Brazil and Peru. Widely cult. in tropics as an ornamental and for the fr.

ligularis Juss. SWEET GRANADILLA. Glabrous, sts. cylindrical; lvs. broadly ovate, 3–6 in. long, cordate, abruptly acuminate, entire, petioles with 2 glands at apex and middle; bracts united at base, lobes entire; fls. 2½–4 in. across, sepals greenish-white inside, petals white or tinged pink, corona banded basally with white and red-purple, blue at tips; fr. ovoid, 2½–3 in. long, yellow to purplish with white pulp, edible. Mex. to w. Bolivia. Cult. in tropics for its sweet fr., considered superior to that of *P. laurifolia.*

lutea L. Lvs. mostly 3-lobed, usually wider than long, 1½–2½ in. long, rounded or rarely nearly acute at apex; bracts 0; fls. ½–¾ in. across, sepals pale greenish-yellow, petals minute, white, corona pink at base, white apically; fr. globose-ovoid, ⅝ in. long. Penn. to Fla., w. to Okla. and Tex.

macrocarpa: *P. quadrangularis.*

maculifolia: *P. organensis.*

maliformis L. SWEET CALABASH, SWEETCUP, CONCH APPLE. Sts. cylindrical; lvs. ovate-lanceolate to orbicular-ovate, 1½–4, in. long, undulate to serrulate; bracts united at base; fls. 3 in. across, sepals green, petals green, densely mottled with reddish-purple, rings of outer corona white, banded with purple basally and with violet apically; fr. globose, 1½ in. in diam., rind hard, yellowish-green, with fleshy pulp inside. W. Indies to n. S. Amer. Cult. in W. Indies for its grape-flavored pulp, used in beverages.

manicata (Juss.) Pers. [*Tacsonia manicata* Juss.]. RED PASSION-FLOWER. Sts. angled; lvs. 3-lobed, 1½–3½ in. long, serrate, tomentose beneath; fls. on peduncles to 3 in. long, perianth to 3 in. across, calyx tube to ¾ in. long, sepals pale green to pink-tinged outside, scarlet inside, petals scarlet, corona blue and white; fr. ovoid, to 2 in. long, dark glossy green. Venezuela to Peru.

mixta L. f. [*Tacsonia mixta* (L.f.) Juss.]. Sts. angled; lvs. 3-lobed, lobes ovate-oblong, serrate; bracts united at base, forming a tube ¾–2 in. long, petioles with 4–8 stalked glands; fls. 3–4 in. across, calyx tube 3–4 in. long, sepals and petals pink to orange-red, white at base, corona deep lavender to purple; fr. ovoid, 2–2½ in. long. Venezuela to Bolivia.

mollissima (HBK) L. H. Bailey [*Tacsonia mollissima* HBK]. CURUBÁ, BANANA PASSION FRUIT. Sts. cylindrical, densely and softly red- to yellow-villous; lvs. 3-lobed, 2–4 in. long, sharply serrate-dentate, reddish-tomentose beneath, lobes and sinuses acute; bracts united; fls. 2½–3 in. across, with calyx tube 2½–3½ in. long, glabrous, sepals white inside, petals pale pink inside, corona reduced to a purple, tubercled band; fr. oblong-ovoid, 2½ in. long, yellowish, pubescent, edible. Venezuela to Bolivia; naturalized in Mex. Material grown as *P. tomentosa* probably belongs here.

morifolia M. T. Mast. Similar to *P. Warmingii* and often confused with it, but lvs. 3–5-lobed, the central lobe extending well below middle of blade, somewhat narrowed at base; fls. 1–1¾ in. across, sepals either whitish, mottled purple, or greenish without mottling, petals inconspicuous. Mex. to Argentina.

Oerstedii M. T. Mast. Sts. glabrous, cylindrical; lvs. ovate-lanceolate, unlobed or rarely 2–3-lobed, entire or with a few teeth at base; bracts deciduous; fls. 1½–2½ in. across, sepals white, petals white, tinged pink, corona purple; fr. ovoid, to 2½ in. long. Mex. to Colombia and Venezuela.

organensis G. Gardn. [*P. maculifolia* M. T. Mast.]. Sts. somewhat angled; lvs. 2-lobed, rarely 3-lobed, the lobes broadly ovate to lanceolate, mucronulate, upper surface zoned silver between veins; fls. 1¼ in. across, cream-colored to dull purple, corona of 1 ring, dark violet to purple; fr. globose, ⅝ in. in diam. Brazil.

Pfordtii: *P. alatocaerulea.*

princeps: *P. racemosa.*

quadrangularis L. [*P. macrocarpa* M. T. Mast.]. GRANADILLA, GIANT G. Glabrous, sts. 4-winged; lvs. broadly ovate to ovate-oblong, 4–8 in. long, abruptly acuminate, entire, petioles with 6 glands; fls. 3 in. across, fragrant, white, pink, or violet inside, corona banded with reddish-purple and white at base, blue at middle, pinkish-blue at apex; fr. oblong-ovoid, often 3-grooved, 8–12 in. long, edible, the rind thick. Nativity unknown. Widely cult. in trop. Amer. for its fr. Cv. 'Variegata'. Foliage blotched yellow.

racemosa Brot. [*P. princeps* Lodd.]. Glabrous, sts. somewhat 4-angled; lvs. ovate, unlobed to mostly 3-lobed, entire; fls. in racemes, to 4 in. across, deep red, corona purple, banded with white; fr. narrowly ovoid, 2–3 in. long, with leathery skin. Se. Brazil.

subpeltata Ort. [*P. alba* Link & Otto]. GRANADINA. Sts. cylindrical; lvs. 3-lobed, 1½–3½ in. long, somewhat cordate, lobes glandular-serrulate in sinuses; bracts not united, ovate-oblong, cordate; fls. 2 in. across, pure white, corona white, operculum membranous with margin finely toothed or shallowly fringed; fr. ovoid to subglobose, about 1½ in. in diam., greenish. Cent. Mex. to Colombia and Venezuela; naturalized in W. Indies. Material cult. as *P. alba* may be *P. Eichlerana.*

tetrandra: *Tetrapathaea tetrandra.*

tomentosa: see *P. mollissima.*

trifasciata Lem. Glabrous, sts. angled; lvs. always 3-lobed, 2–4 in. long, dark green above, mottled white or yellowish-green along veins, reddish to violet beneath; bracts setaceous; fls. fragrant, 1–1½ in. across, sepals and petals pale green inside, corona green, operculum white with pinkish edge; fr. globose, to 1 in. in diam., glaucous. Peru.

Van-Volxemii: *P. antioquiensis.*

violacea Vell. Glabrous, sts. cylindrical to somewhat angled; lvs. 3-lobed, to 4¾ in. long, entire or the lobes glandular-serrate in sinuses; bracts elliptic-oblong; fls. to 4 in. across, sepals purple, awned, petals purplish-blue, obtuse, corona white basally and violet apically, oper-

culum deeply filamentous, ovary villous-tomentose. E. Brazil to Paraguay and Bolivia.

viridiflora Cav. [*Tacsonia viridiflora* (Cav.) Juss.]. Glabrous, sts. angled and flattened; lvs. peltate, deeply 3-lobed, 1½–3 in. long, leathery, dark glossy green above, lobes mostly obtuse, the middle one narrowed at base; bracts 0; fls. 1½ in. across, sepals green, petals 0, corona of 1 ring, green; fr. nearly globose, to ¾ in. in diam. S. Mex.

vitifolia HBK. Sts. cylindrical, sts., petioles, and peduncles densely reddish-tomentose; lvs. 3-lobed, 3–6 in. long, usually glossy above, lobes acuminate, the central one narrowed at base, all irregularly toothed; bracts oblong-lanceolate; fls. 5–7 in. across, sepals and petals obtuse, bright scarlet to vermilion, corona red to bright yellow; fr. ovoid, 2 in. long, puberulent, very fragrant. Nicaragua, s. to Venezuela and Peru.

Warmingii M. T. Mast. Sts. angled and grooved; lvs. 3-lobed, 1½–2½ in. long, mucronate, repand-dentate, lobes cut about to middle, the central lobes not narrowed at base; bracts setaceous; fls. 1 in. across, sepals greenish-white, petals white, corona purple-violet at base, becoming white at apex; fr. ovoid, pilose. Brazil to Paraguay and Colombia. Often confused with *P. morifolia*, which has lvs. deeply lobed, the central lobe narrowed at base, and usually larger fls.

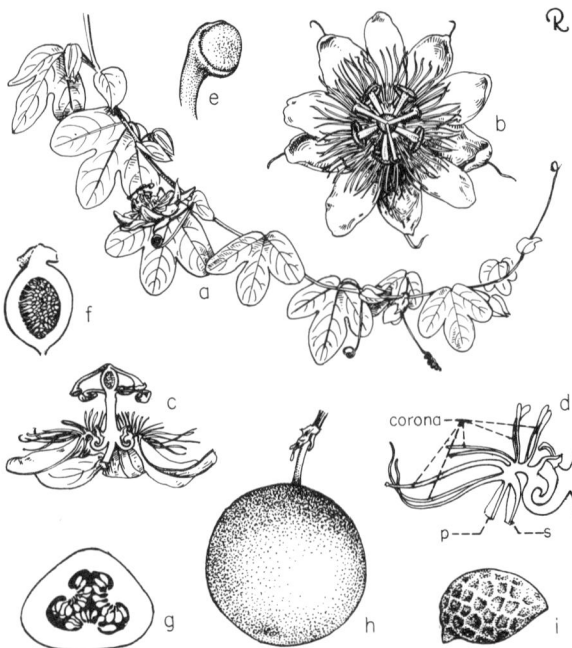

PASSIFLORACEAE. *Passiflora subpeltata:* **a,** flowering branch, × ⅙; **b,** flower, × ½; **c,** flower, vertical section, × ½; **d,** diagram of one side of perianth, vertical section (part of sepal and petal cut off), × 1½; **e,** stigma, × 8; **f,** ovary, vertical section, × 2; **g,** ovary, cross section, × 3; **h,** fruit, × ½; **i,** seed, × 3. (p petal, s sepal.)

PASSIFLORACEAE Juss. PASSIONFLOWER FAMILY. Dicot.; about 12 genera of herbaceous or woody, tendril-bearing vines, or sometimes erect shrubs, of trop. and warm temp. regions of both hemispheres; lvs. alt., simple or lobed; fls. regular, mostly bisexual, usually with a conspicuous, often showy, fringed crown (corona) in the center, sepals 3–5, petals present or 0, stamens 3–5(–10), ovary 1-celled, styles 1–5; fr. a berry or caps., seeds many. The cult. genera are *Passiflora* and *Tetrapathaea.*

PASTEURIZATION: see *Propagation* and *Soils.*

PASTINACA L. PARSNIP. *Umbelliferae.* About 14 spp. of mostly bien., thick-rooted Eurasian herbs; lvs. pinnate; fls. yellow or red, in compound umbels; fr. dorsally flattened.

Parsnips should be grown in deep, loamy soil so that the roots may develop straight and unbranched. Seeds may be sown in spring; the entire season is needed for full development. Parsnips may be dug in autumn and stored in a cellar, or left in the ground till spring. See *Parsnip.*

sativa L. PARSNIP. To 3 ft., st. grooved, hollow, roots to 20 in. long; lvs. with 7–9 ovate, toothed or lobed lfts.; fls. greenish-yellow. Eurasia; naturalized in N. Amer. Cult. for the edible root.

PATERSONIA R. Br. *Iridaceae.* About 18 spp. of summer-flowering, rhizomatous, per. herbs, native to Australia; lvs. basal, 2-ranked, stiff, linear; fl. sts. slender, erect; fls. blue, fugacious, in 2 clusters of 1 to many fls. enclosed by 2 stiff, brown, boat-shaped spathes, perianth tube present, segms. in 2 series, the inner erect, much smaller than the outer, filaments united, style brs. 3, obovate, petal-like; fr. a linear caps.

Propagated by seeds or division, thriving in moist, peaty soil, in full or partial sun; not hardy at ground-freezing temperatures.

glauca R. Br. Lvs. narrowly linear, to 18 in. long, acute, pale green; fls. blue, 2–4 in a cluster, spathes lanceolate, 1–1½ in. long, glabrous, outer perianth segms. ovate, about ½ in. long, filaments united half-way. New S. Wales to Tasmania.

umbrosa Endl. Lvs. linear, to 24 in. long, more rigid than in *P. glauca;* spathes keeled, glabrous, 2–3 in. long; outer perianth segms. obovate, to 1½ in. long, filaments united to apex. W. Australia.

PATRINIA Juss. *Valerianaceae.* About 15 spp. of hardy, rhizomatous or stoloniferous, per. herbs, native to e. and cent. Asia; lvs. opp. or basal, simple to pinnatifid or pinnate; fls. yellow or white, in corymbose-paniculate cymes, calyx 5-toothed, corolla 5-lobed, sometimes spurred, stamens mostly 4, ovary inferior, 3-celled; fr. an achene, with 1 fertile and 2 sterile cells.

Patrinias flower in early summer and are adapted to the rock garden or border. Propagated by seeds or by division.

gibbosa Maxim. Sts. stout, erect, to 2¼ ft.; lvs. elliptic-ovate to broadly ovate, to 6 in. long, pinnately cut and coarsely toothed; cymes to 4 in. across; fls. yellow, ³⁄₁₆ in. across, with a basal spur, stamens exserted; achenes broadly winged. Japan.

intermedia (Hornem.) Roem. & Schult. Sts. to 1½ ft.; lvs. pinnatifid, to 5 in. long, segms. linear; fls. yellow; achenes winged. Siberia.

palmata: *P. triloba* var.

rupestris (Pall.) Dufr. Sts. to 2 ft., or occasionally taller; lvs. pinnatifid, 3–4 in. long, segms. linear to linear-lanceolate, entire to lobed; fls. bright yellow; achenes winged. Siberia.

scabiosifolia Fisch. ex Link. Sts. to 3 ft. or occasionally taller; st. lvs. pinnatifid, to 6 in. long, coarsely toothed, somewhat hairy to nearly glabrous, terminal segm. lanceolate, longer than the others, basal lvs. ovate-oblong, lyrate; fls. yellow; achenes wingless. Temp. e. Asia.

sibirica (L.) Juss. Sts. usually less than 1 ft.; leafless or with 1–2 pairs of lvs., basal lvs. elliptic to obovate, usually pinnately cut, to 1½ in. long, with petioles to 2 in. long; fls. yellow, fragrant; achenes winged. Japan, e. Siberia.

triloba Miq. Sts. to 2 ft.; lvs. palmately 3–5-lobed or -cut, to 3 in. long, coarsely serrate to dentate, petioles 1–3½ in. long; fls. golden-yellow, in clusters to 4 in. across; achenes winged. Var. **palmata** (Maxim.) Hara [*P. palmata* Maxim.]. Fls. with spurs to ⅛ in. long. Japan.

villosa (Thunb.) Juss. Coarse per., to 3 ft.; lvs. ovate, simple to pinnatifid, 1¼–6 in. long, more or less white-hairy; fls. white; achenes winged. Temp. e. Asia.

PAULOWNIA Siebold & Zucc. *Bignoniaceae.* Six spp. of deciduous trees, native to China; lvs. opp., simple, entire, or 3-lobed; fls. in axillary cymes, blue-violet to almost white, calyx 5-cleft, corolla funnelform, with 5 spreading lobes, slightly 2-lipped, stamens 4; fr. a 2-valved caps., seeds winged. Sometimes placed in the *Scrophulariaceae.*

Paulownias are tender in the far North, but on the margin of their natural climatic zone they are root-hardy and in the spring send up strong new shoots with very large leaves. They thrive in a light deep loam, and, in the North, in a sheltered position. Propagated by seeds sown in spring or by root cuttings, and from greenwood cuttings in the greenhouse; also by leaves, taken when unfolding and about 1 in. long.

Fortunei (Seem.) Hance. To 20 ft.; lvs. ovate-oblong, to 10 in. long, densely tomentose beneath; fls. before lvs., to 4 in. long, corolla white, spotted inside with purple; fr. oblong-ellipsoid, to 3⅛ in. long. China. Grown in Calif.

imperialis: *P. tomentosa.*

Kawakamii T. Ito. To 36 ft.; lvs. cordate-ovate, to 1 ft. long, 3- or 5-lobed, glandular-hispid above, glandular-villous or lanate beneath;

fls. to 1¾ in. long, corolla pale purplish-white with purple lines in throat, or white; fr. ovoid, to 1 in. long. Taiwan, e. and s. China.

tomentosa (Thunb.) Steud. [*P. imperialis* Siebold & Zucc.; *P. tomentosa* var. *lanata* (Dode) C. K. Schneid.]. PRINCESS TREE, KARRI TREE. Pubescent tree, to 40 or 60 ft., much like *Catalpa* in habit; lvs. broad-ovate, to 1 ft. long or more, entire to 3-lobed, tomentose beneath; infl. a pyramidal panicle, to 1 ft. long; fls. 2 in. long or more, fragrant, corolla pale violet, darker spotted inside; fr. ovoid, to 1¼ in. long. China. Cult. widely in temp. countries, naturalized in U.S. Zone 7. Yields an excellent cabinet wood, much used in Orient.

PAUROTIS: *ACOELORRHAPHE.*

PAVETTA L. *Rubiaceae.* Perhaps 400 spp. of shrubs or trees, native to tropics of Old World; lvs. opp., sometimes colored, stipules joined at base; fls. usually in terminal corymbs, white or greenish, corolla usually funnelform, tube slender, lobes 4–5, stamens 4–5, inserted at throat of corolla, style much exserted; fr. a somewhat fleshy berry.

indica L. Shrub or small tree; lvs. variable in shape and size, elliptic to obovate or oblanceolate or orbicular, to 9 in. long; fls. fragrant, corolla white, tube to ¾ in. long; fr. 2-seeded, about the size of a pea. India, s. China, Malay Arch., n. Australia.

PAVONIA Cav. *Malvaceae.* Over 150 spp. of herbs and shrubs in temp. and trop. regions of the world; lvs. simple, unlobed to palmately parted; fls. axillary and solitary or in corymbose to paniculate infl. with reduced lvs., involucral bracts 5 to many, petals white to yellow, pink, or deep purple, often spotted basally, stamens united into a tubular column, the column mostly closely anther-bearing beneath 5-toothed apex, style brs. 10, twice as many as the mericarps, stigmas capitate; fr. a schizocarp, mericarps 5, smooth, wrinkled or awned, each 1-seeded, more or less dehiscent.

Propagated by seeds or softwood cuttings.

hastata Cav. Branching shrub, to 6 ft.; lvs. lanceolate to ovate, to about 2 in. long, hastate, dentate; involucral bracts 5–6, lanceolate to obovate, less than ¼ in. long, shorter than calyx, petals to 1 in. long, pale red to nearly white, red-spotted at base; mericarps brown, ribbed and reticulate, but not armed. S. Amer.; naturalized in s. U.S.

multiflora: *Triplochlamys multiflora.*

sepium St.-Hil. Similar to and sometimes grown as *P. spinifex,* but smaller and having lvs. narrower, cuneate; calyx and involucral bracts mostly less than ¼ in. long, petals ½–¾ in. long; mericarp awns erect or ascending, less than ¼ in. long. S. Amer.

spinifex (L.) Cav. Shrub, 5–15 ft.; lvs. ovate to oblong-ovate, mostly 3–4 in. long, obtuse or subcordate, serrate; fls. solitary, sometimes congested apically, involucral bracts longer than calyx, about ½ in. long, longer in fr.; petals yellow, 1–1½ in. long; mericarps brown, reticulate, with a median and 2 generally divergent lateral awns up to ½ in. long. Trop. Amer.; naturalized in s. U.S.

PAXISTIMA Raf. (sometimes misspelled *Pachistima* or *Pachystima*). *Celastraceae.* Two spp. of small, glabrous, evergreen shrubs, native to N. Amer.; lvs. opp., simple, leathery; fls. small, reddish-brown, solitary or in axillary cymes, bisexual, sepals, petals, and stamens 4; fr. a 2-valved caps., seeds with a white, many-lobed aril.

Paxistimas may be grown in the border, wild garden, or rock garden, where they thrive in any well-drained soil. Propagated by seeds, layers, cuttings under glass, and *P. Canbyi* also by division; they are hardy in southern New Eng.

Canbyi A. Gray. CLIFF-GREEN, MOUNTAIN-LOVER. Sts. decumbent to ascending, to 16 in.; lvs. linear-oblong, to 1 in. long, obtuse at apex, revolute, minutely serrulate toward apex. Mts., Va. and W. Va.

Myrsinites (Pursh) Raf. OREGON BOXWOOD. Almost prostrate to spreading, to 40 in.; lvs. ovate, oblong, or oblanceolate, to 1¼ in. long, acute to obtuse, finely serrate, dark glossy green above. B.C. to Calif., e. to Mont., Colo., New Mex.

PAYENA A. DC. *Sapotaceae.* About 16 spp. of medium to large trees, native from Burma to Philippine Is., s. to Java and Borneo; lvs. alt., mostly acuminate, stipules early deciduous; fls. 1 to many, in axillary or pseudoterminal clusters, long-pedicelled, sepals 4, in 2 series, corolla with 8 lobes in 2 series from a short tube, stamens 16, in 1–2 series, ovary superior, 6–8-celled; fr. a dryish berry, seeds 1–2.

A gutta percha is obtained from certain species.

acuminata (Blume) Pierre [*Mimusops acuminata* Blume]. To more than 100 ft.; lvs. broadly elliptic to lanceolate, acuminate, to 9½ in. long, 3½ in. wide; fls. 2–13 in axillary clusters, sepals ³⁄₁₆ in. long; fr. ovoid to obovate, to 1½ in. long, about ¾ in. thick. Thailand, Malay Pen. and Arch.

PEA. The garden and field pea, *Pisum sativum*, is a cool-season, hardy, annual, tendril-climbing plant. It occupies the land only part of the season. Peas are grown for the fresh edible green seeds, and one race for the whole, edible pods with the seeds intact, eaten in the same way as the green bean. They are also grown for the dry, mature seeds, even in tropical areas, but there at high elevations where temperatures are cool. Commercial production in the United States is largely limited to the northern tier of states, particularly in the Great Lakes area, the Pacific Northwest, and, to a lesser extent, in New York, Pennsylvania, Delaware, and Maryland. Seed production is centered mainly in Washington and Idaho, which are also the centers for production of dry edible peas used in soup and for export.

In the home garden, peas should be planted in a fertile, well-drained soil and in an unshaded location. In the North, seeds may be planted as early in spring as possible, provided the soil is suitable for working. This provides maximum exposure to the cool part of the growing season, which favors the growth and development of this vegetable. In the South and in parts of the Southwest and southern California, peas are grown in winter and early spring. Width between rows may vary from 1 to 3 feet or more depending on availability of space and on convenience. A planting depth of 1–2 inches and spacing of 2 inches apart in the row are right for most conditions. A succession of harvests is best achieved by planting cultivars of different maturation times at the same time rather than planting a single kind at different times. For the sake of neatness and economy of space, and for convenience in cultivating and picking, it may be considered desirable to use trellises, especially for tall, late peas.

Pods should be picked and shelled just after they are fully swollen but before they become crinkled or discolored. Prime maturity occurs about 18–20 days after the first open flowers appear on the plants. Edible-podded (sugar pea) cultivars are picked when the pods are still flat and when the seeds inside are still small. Garden peas produce either smooth or wrinkled seeds; the smooth kinds are inferior to the wrinkled in quality. Both tall-growing and dwarf cultivars are available.

Many of the cultivars available in seed packets (e.g., 'Little Marvel', 'Telephone', 'Thomas Laxton') were introduced early in the century and most of them are susceptible to commonly occurring diseases. Some of the cultivars of more recent origin, such as 'Frosty' and 'Sparkle', were developed for the processing trade but have been found useful in the home and market garden. Cultivars differ in the relative size of the edible green seed, those with large pods and seeds being easier to pick and shell. There is a relationship between seed size and maturity on the one hand and tenderness and sweetness on the other, but since each cultivar has its own characteristic seed size, the relationship applies only within a given cultivar. Thus large seeds harvested from one cultivar may be succulent and sweet, but the same size from another cultivar may be hard and lacking in flavor.

Although peas may be attacked by any one or more of 20 known diseases, those most commonly encountered in the garden are the root rots, powdery mildew, and one or another of several virus diseases. Control for the root rots is confined to avoidance of infested sites and rotation, and for the other diseases the use of resistant cultivars is recommended. Little injury is to be expected from insects except when an occasional severe infestation of the pea aphid may occur. Malathion is effective against the aphid.

PEACH. The peach, *Prunus Persica*, is considered the queen of temperate-zone fruits and, next to the apple, *Malus pumila*, is the world's most widely grown tree fruit. It is also highly ornamental in bloom, and suitable for the home gar-

den since trees do not become very large. Its range is somewhat south of the apple, for it is less hardy. Peaches thrive in clear, hot weather and thus reach perfection in middle temperate latitudes. In some of its forms the peach can be grown in nearly all parts of the United States and southern Ontario where winter temperatures do not fall below −12° to −15° F and where late spring frosts are not common. Although dormant flower buds may withstand a temperature of −20° under the most favorable conditions, ordinarily −10° is critical and lower temperatures may cause damage. Temperatures of −15° to −25° F may seriously injure the sapwood or kill the tree outright. Cultivars do not differ enough in hardiness to make possible the extension of peach growing by the choice of hardy cultivars as can be done with the apple. Commercial peach growing is, therefore, confined to the southern and middle states and those parts of the northern states that have the protection of bodies of water, such as the fruit districts along the Great Lakes and some of the larger inland lakes. Outside these regions, peach growing is too uncertain to be commercially profitable, but may be undertaken in home plantings where occasional crop failure is not of great importance. In the warmer parts of the United States peaches often fail because of insufficient cold weather to break the rest period. The 'Honey' and 'Peen-to' races are adapted to southern conditions. Large quantities of clingstone peaches are raised in California for canning.

Peach trees begin to bear when young, often producing a partial crop the third year and peaking at eight to 12 years. The average life of peach trees is only about eight years. Valsa canker, which invades the tree through areas of winter injury and pruning wounds, is the chief cause of the short life of trees. Commercial growers have successive orchards coming on, but in the home garden young trees may be set every four or five years to replace older ones, thus having trees at a bearing age at all times on a small place. Peach trees are set when one year old, that is, one season's growth from the grafted bud. Trees should be set 18–20 feet apart each way in spring or autumn, the former being the better time in the North. In regions where the trees attain large size, they should be planted as much as 24 feet apart either way.

Although peaches may be grown with fair success on practically any good agricultural soil that is well drained and reasonably warm, the fruit attains its best development in color and quality on good sands, sandy loams, or the lighter clay loams. In some regions, good commercial crops are grown in almost pure sand with abundant fertilizers. Heavy or very fertile lands, which prolong the growing season, should be avoided in the North as late growth does not become sufficiently hardened to withstand the winter.

Peach cultivars are budded on seedling stocks. The pits are planted in the nursery row in late summer, or they may be stratified and sown in spring; in either case germination does not take place until the spring following the ripening of the seed. The first-year seedlings are budded to the desired cultivar in June in the southern states and in late August or September in the North. The buds inserted in late summer or autumn remain dormant until the following spring, when the stock (or young tree) is cut off just above the bud; this bud is forced into growth, and all other sprouts from the stock are pulled off. The age of the tree is reckoned from the bud, but the root, of course, is one year older. In June-budded trees in the South, the bud grows the same year in which it is inserted and the resulting tree is ready for planting that autumn. The best rootstocks for peaches in the North are 'Siberian C' seedlings. In the South, 'Nemaguard' (nematode resistant) seedlings are preferred. Seedlings raised from cannery seeds are not widely used. Dwarf peach trees are sometimes produced by budding named cultivars on sand cherry *(Prunus Besseyi)*, Nanking cherry *(P. tomentosa)*, or on *Prunus* 'St. Julien A.', a plum.

Commercial peach orchards are usually cultivated until midsummer, when a cover crop is sown. In the home garden, mulching or herbicides to control weeds is easier. Suitable mulches are black plastic, tree leaves, rain-spoiled hay, or straw. Herbicides currently in use for fruit trees are simazine (Princep), diuron (Karmex), and dichlobenil (Casoron G-4). Newly set trees should be mulched or clean-cultivated, but herbicides may be used on trees after two or three years.

Peach trees on good soils are most likely to respond to nitrogen, but occasionally potash may be needed on infertile, sandy, or gravelly soils. Mature trees should make about 12–15 inches of annual growth. Trees that are too vigorous may be susceptible to winter injury. Newly set trees should ordinarily not be fertilized, but thereafter a few ounces of ammonium nitrate per year may be applied, increasing the amount until trees five to ten years old are receiving from four to eight ounces per tree or the equivalent amount of nitrogen in other materials. The amounts should vary according to tree vigor as determined by growth and foliage color.

Severe pruning at the time of setting is the common practice. The trees are headed to the desired height, usually 20–30 inches, all but the three or four branches wanted for the head are removed, and these are cut back to stubs 2–3 inches long. As the young shoots appear in the spring, the trees should be disbudded by removing all young shoots except those desired for permanent scaffold branches. From this time until the first crops are borne, the tree as grown in the northern states should be pruned little except to keep it in shape and the head somewhat open. In the South and West, where the trees grow more rapidly, the scaffold branches must be headed back to prevent them from becoming leggy. Mature trees must be heavily pruned to maintain vigor of growth of the fruiting wood, to keep the tree low so that the fruit can be harvested from the ground or a six-foot step-ladder, and to open up the center of the tree. All this is accomplished by heading back the most vigorous growth to side branches and thinning out where necessary. The best time for pruning peach trees is in the late winter or early spring, before the buds start. Peaches may set fruit too heavily, and so the young fruits must be thinned so that the remaining ones will be of good size and quality. Thinning is done when the fruits are about 1¼ inches in largest diameter; one peach should be left every 6–10 inches along the branch.

Peaches are harvested when full-sized and well colored but still firm. The time of picking is very important and requires experience to determine with nicety. Care must be taken not to tear the flesh about the stem. In its fourth or fifth year a well-grown tree may yield ½–1 bushel of fruit and when in full bearing 3–4 bushels are not exceptional.

Cultivars of peaches are many, with regional adaptations. There are clingstones and freestones, and yellow- and white-fleshed kinds. Most home gardeners prefer yellow-fleshed freestones. Many new peaches are being introduced yearly. The commercial grower should choose cultivars suited to the particular market. The following cultivars, listed in order of ripening, give a succession for either home or commercial use. All listed are self-fruitful except 'J. H. Hale', which is pollen-sterile and requires a second cultivar planted nearby for fruit set.

Cultivars with hardy fruit buds that are suitable for culture at the northern limits of peach growing are: 'Reliance', 'Polly', 'Prairie Dawn', and 'Veteran'. In Florida and southern California only cultivars with low chilling requirements should be planted. Cultivars for fruit sections of New England, New York, and Michigan where temperatures do not drop below −15° F in midwinter, when peach fruit buds are at their maximum hardiness, include: 'Candor', 'Garnet Beauty', 'Jerseyland', 'Redhaven', 'Triogem', 'Canadian Harmony', 'Cresthaven', 'Redskin', and 'Jefferson'. Cultivars for the Southeast are: 'Springgold', 'Candor', 'Early Coronet', 'Cardinal', 'Dixired', 'Coronet', 'Ranger', 'Redglobe', 'Blake', and 'Redskin'; for central and northern Florida: 'Maygold' and 'June Gold'; for southern Florida and other subtropical regions: 'Jewell', 'Suber', 'Waldo', 'Angel', 'Florida Gem', 'Honey', 'Imperial', and 'Luttichau'; for the Midwest: 'Harbinger', 'Garnet Beauty', 'Redhaven', 'Glohaven', 'Loring', 'Cresthaven', 'Redskin', 'Canadian Harmony', and 'Rio Oso Gem'.

Cultivars for California include: 'Springcrest', 'Early Coronet', 'Cardinal', 'Regina', 'Redtop', 'Suncrest', 'Redglobe', 'Fay Elberta', 'Rio Oso Gem', and 'Summerset'. 'Altair' and 'Saturn' (of standard size) and 'Bonanza' (a very dwarf cultivar) are dual-purpose peaches, bearing ornamental flowers and good fruit but adapted to the warm winters of southern California. Cultivars for the Pacific Northwest include: 'Cardinal', 'Dixired', 'Early Redhaven', 'Redhaven', 'Redglobe', Earlihale', 'Delp Early Hale', 'J. H. Hale', 'Gold Medal', 'Redskin', and, 'Rio Oso Gem'.

The spraying of the commercial orchard should be carefully planned to meet local conditions. In most cases a satisfactory program for home planting consists of two sprays. The first spray should be applied in autumn after the leaves are off or early in the spring before the buds start, using lime-sulfur 1–15 or an oil spray for the control of scale, leaf curl, and brown rot; the second spray is applied when the "shucks" or calyx rings are falling from the fruit, using wettable sulfur at manufacturer's directions, lead arsenate 2 pounds, hydrated lime 16 pounds, water 100 gallons. This is to control curculio, scab, and brown rot. The Oriental peach moth, now widely distributed, cannot be controlled by spraying, but is kept in check by liberating larval parasites.

The peach borer, one of the worst pests in many regions, can be controlled with ethylene dichloride emulsion or by digging larvae out with a knife. Ethylene dichloride emulsion has the advantage of being applied as a liquid in October after the rush of orchard work is past. In using paradichlorobenzene, all gum is removed from the base of the tree and the ground made level for a space of about 1 foot. The dry white powder is spread on the ground in a narrow ring about 2 inches from the base of the tree. The base of the tree is then mounded up with finely pulverized earth to a height of about 2 inches above the highest visible borer injury and the surface of the mound paced with a shovel. This mound should be left undisturbed for three weeks and then torn down. One ounce of powder for a tree six years old, ½ ounce for a three- to five-year tree, ¼–⅜ ounce for a one- to two-year tree is sufficient. An excess may cause serious injury. Application should be made in the autumn, about September 1 in a region like New Jersey, when the soil temperature is about 55–70° F.

PEAR. In North America, pomological pears are of three botanical groups: (1) the European pear, *Pyrus communis*, including all of the old standard cultivars; (2) the Asian, Oriental, or sand pear, *P. pyrifolia (P. serotina)*, native to eastern Asia and characterized by sharply serrate, long-pointed leaves and a mostly apple-shaped fruit of long-keeping quality, without a calyx and with speckled, russet-colored skin and often very gritty, hard (but in the best cultivars very juicy) flesh (the species is not much grown in America); and (3) the Eurasian race, *P. ×Lecontei*, a hybrid between the two, represented principally by cultivars 'Kieffer' and 'Leconte'.

Pear trees in a favorable climate are usually long-lived and experience less trouble from insects and diseases than other temperate tree fruits. No home fruit plantation is complete without trees of various kinds of pears, ripening from early August till winter. The late cultivars are generally good keepers, and extend the season into February, thus supplying fruit for six or seven months. The pear is also a good commercial fruit, although perhaps not maintaining its former importance in many of the fruit regions. Compared with the apple, *Malus pumila*, the pear is much more restricted in its geography. It cannot endure the low temperatures of many parts of the northern states nor the humid heat of the South, thriving only in those favored regions that have a fairly equable climate. Commercially, therefore, plantings of the European type of pear are largely confined to the fruit districts of New England, the Great Lakes region, and the Pacific Coast. In home plantings, by the selection of cold-resistant cultivars, the range can be extended somewhat farther north and, by blight-resistant cultivars, particularly those derived from the Oriental or Asian pear, into the southern states.

Soils for the pear should be of the strong or heavy types. It thrives on the heavier sandy loams or clay loams, which have good humus content and moisture-holding capacity. Good drainage and a porous subsoil are essential for its best development. On the average, the European pear is adapted to heavier soils than the apple. 'Kieffer' and Oriental pears, however, thrive better on rather light soils.

Pears are propagated by budding on seedlings of the European pear, *P. communis,* which are produced on the Pacific Coast, mostly in Oregon. Seedlings of the Oriental pear have been used much in the past, but the trees are short-lived and are not recommended now. Pears for espaliering, growing in tubs, or for dwarfing are budded on quince *(Cydonia oblonga)* 'Angers' and 'Provence' roots, but the trees are not as long-lived and do not perform as well as trees on *P. communis* roots. Some cultivars are incompatible with quince roots, so the trees are produced with an interstem of the inedible cultivar 'Old Home'.

Pruning is similar to that described for the apple except that more scaffold limbs can be left on the young pear tree. As the trees mature their tops should be thinned out by removing crossing or crowded limbs and, in case the head becomes spurry, by cutting out many of the smaller branches. Severe pruning is to be avoided, as the resulting succulent growth is susceptible to fire blight. 'Kieffer' and Oriental pears are cut back much more severely than cultivars of the European pear. Pruning may be undertaken at any time when the trees are dormant, ordinarily in late winter or early spring.

The fruit is always picked by hand when mature (full-sized) but still green and firm. The fruit is raised and the pedicel ("stem") separates from the twig; it should not be pulled off. Pears should not be tree-ripened, even for home use. In home storage, the fruit should be kept as cool as possible without freezing.

The question of cultivars is very important inasmuch as there is great variation in regional adaptation and resistance to disease. In the following lists, cultivars are given in order of ripening.

Cultivars of more than average hardiness, adapted to growing in the colder parts of the pear regions, are: 'Tyson', 'Clapp', 'Seckel', 'Flemish Beauty', and 'Anjou'. Cultivars adapted to milder fruit sections, such as the fruit districts of New England, New York, Ohio, and Michigan, are: 'Tyson', 'Clapp', 'Aurora', 'Bartlett', 'Gorham', 'Seckel', 'Sheldon', 'Bosc', 'Anjou', 'Dana Hovey', and 'Winter Nellis'. Cultivars for the Pacific Coast are: 'Bartlett', 'Seckel', 'Comice', 'Easter Buerre', 'Hardy', 'Bosc', 'Anjou', and 'Winter Nellis'. Cultivars resistant to fire blight are: 'Magness', 'Moonglow', 'Maxine', and 'Kieffer'.

All pears normally require cross pollination, which should be provided by planting two or more compatible cultivars. 'Bartlett' and 'Seckel' do not pollinate each other but 'Bartlett', 'Comice', and 'Hardy' are usually self-fruitful in California, though not elsewhere. 'Seckel' is one of the best pears for the home garden.

Insects and diseases play an important part in pear culture. Of those common to both apple and pear, the codling moth and borers are important and may be controlled as described under the former. Fire blight is the most serious disease, becoming the factor limiting pear growing in the southern part of the pear regions. It is caused by bacteria that gain entrance through flowers and insect punctures and cause the young growth and fruit to blacken and die. Frequently trees of susceptible cultivars are killed outright. It can sometimes be kept in check by cutting out the diseased branches as soon as they are observed, making the cuts a foot or more below the point where the tissue is killed. The cut stub should be disinfected with clorox. Dormant cankers on the trunk and limbs should have the bark removed from the diseased area and at least ½ inch beyond, and the wound should be disinfected. After disinfection, the wounds should be protected with some good wound dressing. Blossom blight can be controlled in part by spraying the trees in early full bloom with

bordeaux mixture 2–6–100. The trees should be maintained in moderate vigor to prevent soft growth, which is susceptible to fire blight. In some regions pear psylla is a very troublesome pest, as are also the pear midge and the pear thrip. The control of these insects is complicated and difficult, and in the commercial orchard requires expert advice. For the home orchard, about the only spray that is practicable is the calyx application for codling moth control as for apple.

PECAN. One of the hickory nuts, the pecan, *Carya illinoinensis,* is of special value and attractiveness. In the United States, the species is indigenous throughout most of the valley of the Mississippi River and its principal tributaries as far north as Iowa, especially on the lowlands along the rivers and creek bottoms. Farther west, it is found along most of the major streams in Texas and Oklahoma. In Mexico, the pecan is native over areas in the northern and central parts. The cultural range of the pecan, as is usual with most fruits and nuts, is much larger than its natural range. Pecans have been planted successfully from the Atlantic Coast to the western part of Iowa, Oklahoma, and Texas, from the forty-third Parallel in the North to the Gulf of Mexico in the South. In addition, successful plantings have been made in New Mexico and Arizona. However, most of the commercial production comes from Georgia, Texas, Alabama, Louisiana, Oklahoma, and Mississippi. Trial plantings have been made in the Pacific states, especially California.

The first pecan cultivar was propagated in 1846 by a slave gardener. This cultivar was named 'Centennial' and is still in existence. For about 50 years following, however, most plantings were of seedlings. During this interval some grafted seedlings were sold, but their expense prohibited widespread planting. With the perfection of ring budding in the 1890's, the supply of improved named cultivars increased and they became less expensive. About 500 cultivars of pecans have been named and propagated. These cultivars show great variation in precocity, productivity, alternate-bearing tendency, nut size, shell thickness, kernel quality, cracking percentage, type of tree growth, disease resistance, and length of time required to mature their crop satisfactorily. Thin-shelled nuts are often advertised and sold as "paper shell" pecans. This is not a pecan cultivar but a characteristic of many cultivars. Pecan cultivars adapted to the southern range require a growing season of 270 to 290 days. Cultivars adapted to the northern range, particularly southern Indiana and parts of Iowa, require 170 to 190 days. Some northern cultivars are 'Colby', 'Fritz', 'Giles', 'Major', and 'Witte'; 'Major' is the standard northern cultivar, while 'Fritz' and 'Witte' are cultivars for the most northern range of the pecan. In the South, 'Stuart' and 'Mahan' are the cultivars most widely planted by the homeowner. However, 'Mahan', a big nut, does not fill well, especially when the tree matures, and often this cultivar is a disappointment. 'Candy' and 'Caddo' are also suitable cultivars for the southern homeowner since they have some resistance to scab, a major disease. In the arid parts of the United States, diseases are not an important factor in cultivar selection. However, in almost all areas insects can be serious pests. The yellow and black aphids, in particular, can turn a beautiful shade tree into an unattractive one. Commercially, in the South, 'Stuart' and 'Schley' are important cultivars in old established groves, but in new plantings 'Wichita' and 'Desirable' are popular. In the West, the standard cultivar is 'Western Schley', but 'Wichita' is being widely planted. As new and better cultivars are being released, the cultivar situation is apt to change drastically. Since 1953 the United States Pecan Field Station (USDA), Brownwood, Texas has released 14 cultivars. Their names are those of Indian tribes. In the pecan belt as a whole, these cultivars are the ones that are being most widely planted.

Pecans are usually propagated by budding or grafting named cultivars on seedling stocks. In the Southeast, 'Curtis' nuts are often used as the stock; in the West, 'Riverside' nuts; and in the North, 'Giles'. The seeds are stratified naturally by planting in the nursery in late autumn, or the seeds are artificially stratified for ten weeks at 45° F and planted in early spring. In the West, seeds are often planted in early spring but are soaked in water for three days before planting. Soaking, however, is of dubious value. Budding, usually ring or patch, is done during July and August, and grafting, usually whip grafting, is done in the dormant season, December to February. Nursery trees are usually sold with a two- or three-year-old root and a one-year-old scion. Nursery trees are harder to transplant successfully than other fruit trees. This is due to the long taproot, which often has few laterals, particularly so after digging, and to improper nursery practices that often lead to general damage and especially desiccation.

Pecans will grow on a variety of soils; however, the tree growth and the yield increase in proportion to soil depth and drainage. Pecans are tolerant of excessive soil water during the dormant season, but they must have a well-drained soil during the growing season. A soil with a pH of 5.8 to 7.0 is desirable. Pecans have a high nutrient requirement. Nitrogen, especially, must be applied in liberal amounts if high yields are to be attained. At one time pecan rosette was a serious threat to the industry, until the disorder was found to be zinc deficiency. Homeowners in the southwestern United States often find zinc deficiency a problem unless new leaves and shoots are periodically sprayed with a 2 percent solution of zinc sulfate. Throughout most of the commerical pecan belt, trees are fertilized according to leaflet and soil analysis. This service is available to and should be used by the homeowner.

Trees were formerly planted at distances of 50–70 feet, but at present plantings of 30–40 feet are usual. Closer spacings have been tried commercially but high yields cannot be maintained once the trees begin to crowd. The pecan is very sensitive to inadequate sunlight, and as trees grow, mutual shading increases and yields decrease. Mutual shading from excessive crowding is one of the major factors limiting production in old groves. Consequently, trees must be thinned periodically. With very large trees, the final spacing may allow only four trees per acre.

Pecans are wind-pollinated. The trees are monoecious, the sexes separated but on the same tree. Often within a cultivar the period of receptivity of the female flower does not coincide with pollen-shedding of the male flower. Hence, within a planting, cultivars must be included that allow for adequate cross pollination. Provision for cross pollination becomes especially important when pecans are planted in areas where other pecan plantings or native pecan trees are not nearby.

Historically pecans are noted for their alternate bearing habit. Normally, young trees do not bear alternately. As the tree matures and the leaf area per fruit becomes less, the tendency to bear alternately increases. Alternate bearing is more severe in pecan trees than in most other fruit trees. This is because of the high oil content of the kernel, which requires a large amount of carbohydrates, and because the nut matures late in the season. Late maturity does not allow much time before frost for accumulation of carbohydrates that are utilized in next season's growth and fruiting. Hence alternate bearing is greatly accentuated if leaves are lost prematurely. Premature leaf drop is usually due to lack of insect and disease control, although lack of soil water is another fairly common cause.

Scab, which infests leaves and fruits, is the most serious disease. Pecan aphids, both yellow and black, shuckworm, nut casebearer, and weevil are serious insects. If these pests are controlled by appropriate sprays, many other diseases and insects are also controlled at the same time.

PECTEILIS Raf. *Orchidaceae.* Four spp., native to trop. Asia; tuberous, sts. more or less elongate, leafy; infl. erect, scape 1- to few-fld.; fls. showy, upper sepal and the petals forming a hood, lateral sepals spreading, lip 3-lobed, the lateral lobes denticulate or lacerate, spur prominent, column short, united with anther, basally extended into distinct canals, stigma cushionlike. For structure of fl. see *Orchidaceae.*

For culture see *Orchids.*

radiata (K. Spreng.) Raf. [*Habenaria radiata* K. Spreng.]. To 16 in.; lvs. 3–5 at base, linear, upper lvs. scalelike; fls. 1–3, about 1¼ in. across, sepals green, petals white, lip white, 3-lobed, about 1 in. long, lateral lobes deeply fringed on outer margin, spur to 1½ in. long, cylindrical. Summer. Japan.

PECTINARIA Haw. *Asclepiadaceae.* About 7 spp. of leafless, dwarf, succulent per. herbs, native to S. Afr.; distinguished from *Stapelia* and the other succulent asclepiads in having the apices of the corolla lobes remaining united at flowering; fr. a follicle.

For culture see *Succulents.*

arcuata N. E. Br. Sts. to 4 in. or more long, arching, with the tips buried in the ground; fls. in 1–3-fld. fascicles, corolla ovoid-acuminate, to ½ in. long, glabrous, the outside pale yellow with lobes purple-tinted, the inside dark purple basally with lobes whitish, purple-spotted, corona yellow, apparently in a single whorl.

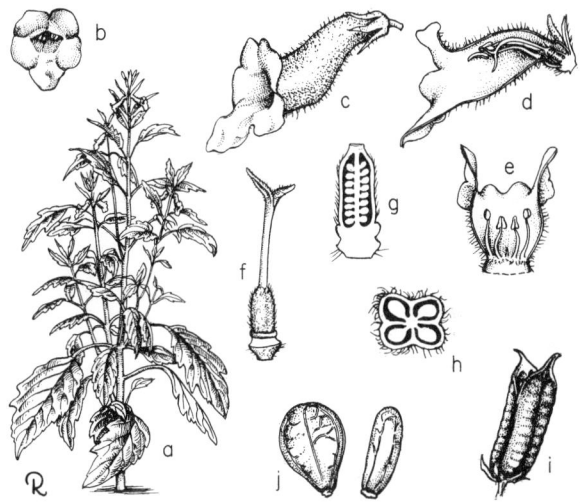

PEDALIACEAE. *Sesamum indicum:* **a,** flowering plant, × ¹⁄₁₂ ; **b,** flower, face view, × ½; **c,** flower, side view, × 1; **d,** flower, vertical section, × ¾; **e,** corolla, split longitudinally along upper side and expanded, × ½; **f,** pistil, × 1½; **g,** ovary, vertical section, × 3; **h,** ovary, cross section, × 5; **i,** capsule, × ¾; **j,** seeds, two views, × 4.

PEDALIACEAE R. Br. PEDALIUM FAMILY. Dicot.; about 16 genera and 50 spp. of mostly ann. or per. herbs, native to tropics and subtropics of the Old World, a few naturalized in the New World; lvs. opp., the upper ones sometimes alt., simple to deeply lobed, covered with slime-secreting hairs or glands; fls. bisexual, irregular, usually solitary, axillary, calyx 5-parted, corolla broadly tubular, 5-lobed, stamens usually 4, in 2 pairs, borne on the corolla tube, pistil 1, ovary usually superior, carpels 2, style 1, with 2 stigmas; fr. a nut or caps., often hooked or horned. *Ceratotheca* is cult. as an ornamental, and *Sesamum* as a source of an important seed oil.

PEDICELLARIA: *CLEOME.*

PEDICULARIS L. WOOD BETONY, LOUSEWORT. *Scrophulariaceae.* Over 350 spp. of ann., bien., or per. herbs, native in the N. Hemisphere, one sp. in Andean Colombia and Ecuador; lvs. basal and cauline, alt., opp., or rarely whorled, toothed or lobed to pinnatifid; fls. purple, red, rose-colored, white, or yellow, axillary or in showy terminal bracted racemes or spikes, calyx tubular, 2–5-toothed, corolla tubular, 2-lipped, upper lip helmetlike, often beaked, lower lip 3-lobed, tube cylindrical, stamens 4; fr. a caps.

Sometimes planted in the border or the rock garden. Propagated by seeds and division. Some species are probably partly parasitic on roots and under cultivation may not find the proper hosts.

bracteosa Benth. ex Hook. Per., to 3 ft., glabrous below infl.; lvs. to 6 in. long, divided to the midrib into lanceolate, laciniately toothed divisions, st. lvs. alt.; corolla pale yellow, ¾ in. long, upper lip not beaked. Early summer. Alta., s. to e. Wash. and Mont.

canadensis L. COMMON L., WOOD BETONY. Pubescent per., to 1½ ft., sts. simple, clustered; lvs. to 5 in. long, pinnately parted, st. lvs. alt.; corolla yellow or reddish, rarely white, to ¾ in. long; caps. 3 times as long as calyx. Spring. Que. to Fla., w. to Tex. and n. Mex.

contorta Benth. ex Hook. [*P. ctenophora* Rydb.]. Glabrous per., to 2 ft.; lvs. to 6 in. long, pinnately parted into linear divisions, st. lvs. alt.; corolla white or light yellow, spotted purple, to ⅝ in. long. Summer. B.C. to n. Calif., e. to Alta. and Mont.

ctenophora: *P. contorta.*

densiflora Benth. ex Hook. INDIAN-WARRIOR. Pubescent or nearly glabrous per., to 1 ft. or more, sts. simple, clustered; st. lvs. alt., to 4 in. long or more, pinnately parted into oblong, toothed or cut divisions, basal lvs. sometimes as long as st.; corolla crimson, to 1 in. long. Winter to late spring. S. Ore. to s. Calif.

groenlandica Retz. ELEPHANT-HEADS. Glabrous per., to 2 ft.; lvs. to 6 in., pinnatifid, st. lvs. alt.; corolla red or purple, upper lip compressed into decurved beak to ¾ in. long. Summer. Labrador to B.C., s. to New Mex. and Calif. Var. **surrecta** (Benth. ex Hook.) A. Gray [*P. surrecta* Benth. ex Hook.]. Beak longer, lower lip pale.

lanceolata Michx. Nearly glabrous per., to 3 ft.; lvs. opp. or subopp., oblong-lanceolate, to 5 in. long, pinnately lobed, sessile; corolla yellow, to ¾ in. long; caps. about as long as calyx. Summer, autumn. Mass. to Man., s. to N.C., Mo., Nebr.

nepalensis Prain. Glabrous, cespitose per., to 3 in.; lvs. basal, to 2½ in. long; pinnately lobed; fls. axillary, on pedicels 1½ in. long, corolla deep purple, to 1½ in. long. Nepal.

ornithorhyncha Benth. ex Hook. Per., to 1 ft., glabrous below infl.; lvs. mostly basal, to 4 in. long, pinnately parted into oblong-lanceolate, toothed divisions; corolla purple, to ¾ in. long. Summer. Se. Alaska to w. Wash.

Parryi A. Gray. Glabrous per., to 1½ ft.; lvs. to 4¾ in. long, pinnately parted into toothed or cut divisions, st. lvs. alt.; corolla pale yellow, to ¾ in. long. Summer, early autumn. Mont. to New Mex. and Ariz.

racemosa Dougl. ex Hook. Cespitose per., to 20 in., sts. glabrous below infl.; lvs. all cauline, lanceolate to linear, to 3½ in. long, crenate; corolla white or purple-tinged, to ⅝ in. long. Summer. B.C. to Alta., s. to n. Calif., e. Ariz., New Mex.

siifolia Rydb. Per., to 2¼ ft., glabrous or nearly so; st. lvs. alt., to 6 in. long, pinnately parted into linear-lanceolate, toothed divisions, almost sessile; corolla greenish-yellow, to ¾ in. long, upper lip short-beaked. Spring, summer. Sw. Wash. to w. Mont. By some authors not considered specifically different from *P. Canbyi* A. Gray.

siphonantha D. Don. Glabrous or pubescent per., to 1 ft.; sts. decumbent to ascending; basal lvs. to 6 in. long, pinnately divided, st. lvs. alt.; corolla pink, rose-pink, or purple, variable in size, to 2 in. long, tube very slender, 2–5 times as long as calyx. Himalayas.

surrecta: *P. groenlandica* var.

PEDILANTHUS Poit. SLIPPER S. *Euphorbiaceae.* About 30 spp. of odd, monoecious, succulent shrubs with milky juice, native to drier sites in trop. N. and S. Amer., s. Fla., Bahamas, and the W. Indies; lvs. alt., simple, with thickened midrib; fls. in showy cyathia (see *Euphorbiaceae*), arranged in cymes, involucre slipper-shaped, oblique, strongly 2-lipped, and spurred, ovary 3-celled; fr. a caps.

Grown as ornamentals in warm climates. For culture see *Succulents.*

aphyllus: *P. cymbiferus.*

bracteatus (Jacq.) Boiss. Shrubby, to 3 ft., leafless before flowering; lvs. oblong, to 4 in. long, subsessile; infl. terminal, repeatedly forked, subtending bracts longer than the involucre. Mex.

cymbiferus Schlecdend. [*P. aphyllus* Boiss. ex Klotzch & Garcke]. Brs. straight and slender, whitish, to 3 ft., leafless; involucre red, ¾ in. long, pubescent, subtending bracts deciduous. Mex.

macrocarpus Benth. To 3 ft. or more, sts. whitish, forking; lvs. minute, early deciduous; infl. of few cyathia, bracts red, elliptic-obovate to oblanceolate, involucre to 1¼ in. long, red, lobe of involucre above spur 2-parted. Mex.

Smallii: *P. tithymaloides* subsp.

tithymaloides (L.) Poit. [*Euphorbia tithymaloides* L.]. JAPANESE POINSETTIA, REDBIRD FLOWER, REDBIRD CACTUS, RIBBON C., SLIPPER FLOWER, SLIPPER PLANT, JEWBUSH, DEVIL'S-BACKBONE. To 6 ft.; lvs. ovate to obovate, to 4 in. long, subsessile, acute and often recurved, midrib winged below; cyathia in dense terminal cymes, involucre red to purple, to ¾ in. long, pointed. Fla., W. Indies, Mex. to n. S. Amer. Subsp. **tithymaloides.** The typical subsp.; sts. straight; lvs. more than half as long as wide, acute, cuneate. [Subsp. or var.] **cucullatus:** a listed name of no botanical standing; material offered under this name is

subsp. *Smallii.* Cv. 'Nana Compacta'. Lvs. closely set on upright brs., dark green. Subsp. **Smallii** Millsp.) Dressl. [*P. Smallii* Millsp.]. JACOB'S-LADDER. Sts. zig-zag. Fla., Cuba. Cv. 'Variegatus'. Lvs. green, variegated white and red.

PEDIOCACTUS Britt. & Rose [*Toumeya* Britt. & Rose; *Utahia* Britt. & Rose]. *Cactaceae.* Seven spp. of small, globose to ovoid or cylindrical, tubercled cacti, native to w. U. S. ; sts. solitary or cespitose, tubercles not grooved; fls. subapical from spine-bearing areoles, diurnal, campanulate, scales of ovary few, with naked axils; fr. dry, opening by an apical cap and a slit on the back, seeds black or gray, roughened.

For culture see *Cacti.*

Bradyi L. Bens. Sts. subglobose to obovoid, to 2½ in. high and 2 in. thick, tubercles elongate-ovoid to cylindric-ovoid; spines dense, radial spines 14–15, spreading, white or yellowish-tan, to ¼ in. long, central spines 0; fls. yellow, to 1¼ in. across; fr. ⁵⁄₁₆ in. in diam., seeds black, minutely beaded. N. Ariz.

Knowltonii L. Bens. Sts. solitary or cespitose, to 1½ in. high and ¾ in. thick, tubercles conical or pyramidal; spines dense, white to reddish-tan or pink, finely white-hairy, radial spines 18–23, less than ¹⁄₁₆ in. long, central spines 0; fls. pink, about ¾ in. across. Colo.

Paradinei B. W. Bens. Sts. depressed, to 2 in. high and 3¼ in. thick, tubercles blunt-conical; spines flexible, hairlike, white to pale gray, becoming straw- or cream-colored, radial spines about 20, central spines 4-6, not clearly different from radial spines, to 1⁵⁄₁₆ in. long; fls. white, to 1 in. across, petaloid segms. with pink midribs; fr. ¼ in. in diam., seeds nearly black, tubercled. Ariz.

papyracanthus (Engelm.) L. Bens. [*Toumeya papyracantha* (Engelm.) Britt. & Rose]. Sts. simple, elongate, to 3 in. long and ¾ in. thick, tubercles in 8 oblique rows, cylindrical or domelike; spines flattened, awl-shaped, dense, minutely hairy, radial spines 6–8, spreading, ash-white or pale gray, central spines 1 or sometimes 2–4, white to pale brown, becoming gray, to 1¼ in. long; fls. white, to 1 in. across, petaloid segms. with brownish midribs; fr. subglobose, to ³⁄₁₆ in. in diam., seeds black. Ariz., New Mex.

Sileri (Engelm. ex J. Coult.) L. Bens. [*Utahia Sileri* (Engelm.) Britt. & Rose]. Sts. simple, depressed-ovoid to ovoid, to 5 in. high and 4 in. thick, tubercles in 8–16 spirals, blunt-conical, ⅜ in. long; spines dense, needle-shaped, radial spines 11–13, white, to ¾ in. long, central spines 3–7, stouter, somewhat directed outward, brownish-black, becoming pale gray or nearly white, to 1⅛ in. long; fls. yellowish, about ³⁄₁₆ in. across, sepaloid segms. fringed, petaloid segms. minutely toothed, with maroon veins; fr. to ⅜ in. in diam., seeds gray, tubercled. N. Ariz.

Simpsonii (Engelm.) Britt. & Rose. SNOWBALL CACTUS. Sts. simple or cespitose, globose or depressed-ovoid, to 6 in. high and 5 in. thick, tubercles in 8 and 13 spirals; spines densely interlacing, needle-shaped, radial spines 15–25, white, to ½ in. long, central spines 5–11, spreading to erect, reddish-brown to yellow or cream-colored, to 1¹⁄₁₆ in. long; fls. pink or yellowish, to 2 in. across. Var. **Simpsonii.** The typical var.; sts. to 6 in. high and 5 in. thick; central spines to ¾ in. long. W. Kans., w. to New Mex., Mont., Idaho. Var. **minor** (Engelm.) Cockerell. Sts. to 3 in. high and 2 in. thick; central spines to about ½ in. long. Mts., Colo.

PELARGONIUM L'Hér. ex Ait. GERANIUM of florists, STORKSBILL. *Geraniaceae.* About 280 spp. of ann. or per. herbs or shrubs, native mostly to S. Afr.; lvs. entire, lobed, or dissected, stipules usually prominent; infl. a 1- to many-fld. umbel, terminal, axillary, or opp. the lvs.; fls. irregular, calyx with a spur united to the pedicel, sepals 5, petals 5, rarely 4 or 2, the upper pair usually larger, stamens 10, only 5–7 with fertile anthers, the rest present only as filaments; fr. 5-valved, the valves coiling upward as they dehisce.

Geraniums are commonly grown as house and bedding plants. When propagated by cuttings, bloom can be obtained in four or five months. Plants over a year old are not satisfactory for common house or conservatory kinds and should be discarded after cuttings are taken, although plants of the *P. domesticum* group may be kept longer. Plants of the common or FISH GERANIUM, *P.* × *hortorum,* grown outdoors may be lifted in autumn and kept until cuttings can be taken from them for next year's plants. If wanted for winter bloom in the window, cuttings should be taken in summer. The SHOW GERANIUMS, *P.* × *domesticum,* may be kept several years; cuttings taken late in spring will produce blooming plants the following winter or summer.

The important cultivated pelargoniums fall into 4 major groups, *P.* × *domesticum, P* × *hortorum, P. peltatum* and its derived forms, and the species or their derivatives having pungent or fragrant leaves. Most important in this last group are: *P. abrotanifolium, P.*

acerifolium, P. capitatum, P. crispum, P. cucullatum, P. denticulatum, P. graveolens, P. grossularioides, P. odoratissimum, P. quercifolium P. radens, P. scabrum, and *P. tomentosum.* A number of named clones in this fragrant-leaved group are hybrids; some of these are listed below with the species to which they are most closely related: 'Attar of Roses', *P. capitatum;* 'Beauty Oak', *P. quercifolium;* 'California Brilliant', *P.* × *domesticum;* 'Camphor Rose', *P. graveolens;* 'Capri', *P.* × *domesticum;* 'Carlton Corsage', *P. capitatum;* 'Carlton Oak', *P. denticulatum;* 'Clorinda', *P.* × *domesticum;* 'Cody's Fragrans', *P.* × *fragrans;* 'Countess of Scarborough', *P.* × *Scarboroviae;* 'Dr. Livingston', *P. radens;* 'Elkhorn', *P. capitatum;* 'Fair Ellen', *P. quercifolium;* 'French Lace', *P. crispum;* 'Fringed Oak', *P. capitatum;* 'Granelous', *P. graveolens;* 'Grey Lady Plymouth', *P. graveolens;* 'Godfrey's Pride', 'Haviland', 'Joy Lucille', all *P. quercifolium;* 'Lady Mary', *P.* × *limoneum;* 'Lady Plymouth', *P. graveolens;* 'Little Gem', *P. graveolens;* 'Logeei', *P. odoratissimum;* 'Logee's Snowflake', *P. capitatum;* 'Mrs. Kingsley', of unknown origin (lvs. slightly pungent, hairy, curled like parsley, fls. rich cerise; 'Mrs. Taylor', *P. graveolens;* 'Pheasant's Foot', *P.* × *jatrophifolium;* 'Pretty Polly', *P. quercifolium;* 'Prince of Orange', *P. crispum* or *P.* × *citrosum;* 'Prince Rupert', *P. crispum;* 'Red-flowered Rose' and 'Rober's Lemon Rose', *P. graveolens;* 'Rollison's Unique', of unknown parentage (large grower, lvs. fragrant, capitatumlike, fls. deep red); 'Round-Leaf Rose', *P. capitatum;* 'Scarlet Unique', *P.* × *ignescens;* 'Shrubland Pet', *P. capitatum, P. fulgidum;* 'Skelton's Unique', *P. capitatum;* 'Staghorn', *P. quercifolium;* 'Toronto', *P. nervosum;* 'Village Hill Oak', *P. quercifolium.* More complete listings of cultivars in all complexes may be found in current books on pelargoniums or "geraniums".

abrotanifolium (L.f.) Jacq. SOUTHERNWOOD G. Aromatic shrub; lvs. clustered at tips of sts., velvety-canescent, fan-shaped in general outline, 3-parted, lobes divided into linear teeth resembling those of *Artemisia Abrotanum,* stipules minute; umbels axillary, 1–3-fld.; fls. nearly sessile, calyx spur 1–3 times as long as sepals, petals ⅜ in. long, white veined with red at base, or rose, the upper shorter and broader than the lower.

acerifolium L'Hér. ex Ait. [*P. citriodorum* (Cav.) Mart.]. MAPLE-LEAVED G. Similar to *P. angulosum* and by some considered a variety of it, but differing in having lvs. lobed to middle, petals to ¾ in. long.

acetosum (L.) L'Hér. ex Ait. Shrubby, sts. and brs. fleshy; lvs. rounded, shallowly lobed and toothed at apex, cuneate at base, bluish-green, glabrous, stipules about ³⁄₁₆ in. long, umbels axillary, 2–6-fld.; calyx spur more than twice as long as sepals, petals to 1³⁄₁₆ in. long, white or pale rose, narrow, long-clawed, nearly equal in length.

adcifolium: a listed name of no botanical standing; material so labeled may be *P. capitatum* or a derivative.

alchemilloides (L.) L'Hér. ex Ait. [*P. malvifolium* Jacq.f.]. Sts. to 1½ ft., slender, erect or ascending; lvs. pubescent, zoned with red, to 3 in. across, deeply 5–7-lobed, lobes sharply toothed; umbels 3–6-fld.; calyx spur twice as long as sepals or more, petals to 1 in. long, white, veined with rose.

alternans J. C. Wendl. Shrubby, to 1 ft., branched, sts. short and knobby; lvs. small, pilose, pinnately lobed, lobes cuneate, trifid or 3–4-parted and toothed, stipules very small; umbels 3–4-fld.; calyx spur about as long as sepals, petals nearly equal, white, the upper streaked with red.

angulosum (Mill.) L'Hér. ex Ait. Shrubby, to 3 ft.; lvs. to 2½ in. across, cuneate at base, 5-angled and toothed but scarcely lobed, usually soft-hairy; umbels 3–7-fld., calyx spur shorter than to as long as sepals, petals carmine-purple, darker veined, the upper larger, to 1 in. long or more.

apiifolium Jacq.f. Roots thick, sts. short; lvs. glabrous, glaucous, pinnately parted, lobes wedge-shaped, pinnate; umbels simple, 20–30-fld.; calyx spur 3–4 times as long as sepals, petals deep purple, pale-margined, nearly equal. A poorly known sp., perhaps of hybrid origin. Plants so labeled in the U.S. are probably incorrectly identified.

× **ardens** Lodd.: *P. fulgidum* × *P. lobatum* (L.) L'Hér. ex Ait. Tuberous-rooted, sts. short; lvs. similar to *P. fulgidum* but not as deeply divided; umbels many-fld.; calyx spur 3–4 times as long as sepals, petals scarlet, shaded with dark red.

× **asperum** J. F. Ehrh. ex Willd.: *P. graveolens* × *P. radens.* Intermediate between the parents, usually resembling *P. graveolens* but lvs. with narrower, more deeply cut lobes and with the harsh pubescence of *P. radens.*

australe Willd. Sts. slender, herbaceous; lvs. cordate, slightly lobed and toothed, to 1½ in. across, softly hairy above, densely so beneath; umbels nearly capitate, 6–25-fld.; calyx spur very short, to about ¹⁄₁₆ in. long, much shorter than sepals, petals to ⅜ in. long, white to rose, red-spotted. Australia. Cult. plants so named are likely to be misidentified and are apparently derivatives of *P. capitatum.*

balkanum: a listed name of no botanical standing.

bicolor (Jacq.) L'Hér. ex Ait. Tuberous-rooted, to 18 in., sts. short, thick, brs. erect, herbaceous; lvs. hairy, rounded to cordate in outline, 3-lobed, lower lobes trifid, upper lobes 5-toothed; umbels many-fld.; calyx spur 2 or more times as long as sepals, petals nearly equal, deep purple, paler at base and on margins.

× **Blandfordianum** (Andr.) Sweet: *P. echinatum* × *P. graveolens.* Habit of *P. graveolens;* lvs. palmately 5–7-lobed, lobes with rounded teeth; umbels many-fld.; fls. distinctly pedicelled, calyx spur ⅜ in. long, slightly longer than to 1½ times as long as sepals, petals white or very pale pink, the 2 upper ⅜ in. long, broader, with 2 red central spots and purplish basal veins.

capitatum (L.) L'Hér. ex Ait. ROSE-SCENTED G. Sts. to 1 ft. or more, weak and trailing, woody at base; lvs. to 2 in. across, cordate, 3–5-lobed above the middle, softly long-hairy, long-petioled; umbels capitate, 9–20-fld.; fls. sessile, calyx spur about as long as sepals, petals rose, the upper veined with red-purple, to ¾ in. long, the lower smaller, not veined. Cv. **'Major'** ['Large-Leaf Rose'] is listed. Hybridized with *P. odoratissimum* to produce *P.* cv. **'Carlton Diana',** with *P. quercifolium* to produce *P.* cv. **'Elkhorn',** *P.* cv. **'Fringed Oak',** *P.* cv. **'Logee's Snowflake',** *P.* cv. **'Round-Leaf Rose',** *P.* cv. **'Skelton's Unique';** and with *P. radens* to produce *P.* cv. **'Carlton Corsage'.** *P.* cv. **'Shrubland Pet'** is a complex derivative of *P. capitatum,* with characters also from *P. quercifolium* and fl. color from *P. fulgidum.* Other derived cvs. are *P.* cv. **'Attar of Roses'** and *P.* cv. **'Shotesham Pet'.**

carnosum (L.) L. Hér. ex Ait. Sts. to 6 in., fleshy, branched, swollen at nodes; lvs. to 4 in. long, nearly glabrous, pinnately lobed, lobes ovate, pinnatifid; umbels 6–8-fld., peduncle 2–4 times as long as pedicels; sepals uniformly colored, calyx spur shorter than sepals, petals white or rarely rose or flame-colored, the upper abruptly narrowed on outer margin to a short claw.

citriodorum: *P. acerifolium;* but material grown as *P. citriodorum* is *P.* × *citrosum* or a derivative.

× **citrosum** Voigt ex T. Sprague [*P.* × *citriodorum* Schrank, not (Cav.) Mart.]. ORANGE G. A hybrid related to *P. crispum* and *P.* × *limoneum,* having the narrow lower petals of the former and fl. color of the latter. *Pelargonium* cv. **'Prince of Orange',** commonly listed, may belong here.

× **concolor** Sweet: *P. capitatum* × *P.* × *ignescens.* Like *P. capitatum* in habit, but lvs. deeply 3–5-lobed and toothed, fls. usually distinctly pedicelled, somewhat larger, petals bright red, veined with violet-black.

conduplicatum Willd. Shrubby; lvs. nearly round to ovate, truncate or cordate at base, densely white-hairy beneath; umbels few-fld.; petals pink, the upper spotted, much broader than the lower. A poorly known sp. or perhaps a hybrid of garden origin, probably related to *P. cordifolium.* Plants cult. as *P. conduplicatum* in U.S. may actually belong to the *P.* × *hortorum* complex.

cordifolium (Cav.) Curtis. Shrubby, to 2 ft. or more; lvs. cordate; peduncles 4–7-fld.; petals pale or intense rose, the upper to 1 in. long.

coriandrifolium: *P. myrrhifolium* var.

crassicaule L'Hér. ex Ait. [*P. mirabile* Dinter]. Sts. short, thick, fleshy; similar to *P. echinatum,* but lf. blades less lobed and attenuate at base; petals white, all or only the upper spotted purple.

crassipes Harv. Sts. short, fleshy, with persistent thickened petioles; lvs. once or twice pinnately parted, pubescent; umbels many-fld., peduncles elongate, branched; fls. nearly sessile, calyx spur 4–6 times as long as sepals, petals small, deep purple.

crispum (L.) L'Hér. ex Ait. LEMON G. Woody, to 3 ft., lemon-scented; lvs. many, small, 3-lobed, 1 in. long or less, margin crisped; umbel 1–3-fld.; calyx spur ⁵⁄₁₆–⅜ in. long, about as long as sepals, petals rose or rosy-white, the upper broader and deeply veined. A number of cvs. are associated with the sp. or its hybrids, among them: *P.* cv. **'French Lace',** *P.* cv. **'Latifolium',** *P.* cv. **'Minor',** *P.* cv. **'Prince Rupert',** and *P.* cv. **'Variegatum'.** See also *P.* × *citrosum, P.* × *limoneum, P.* × *melissinum, P.* × *Scarboroviae. P.* cv. **'Prince of Orange',** belongs either here or with *P.* × *citrosum.*

crithmifolium Sm. Sts. fleshy, branched, swollen at nodes; lvs. nearly glabrous, bluish-green, nearly twice pinnately parted, lobes oblong-linear, toothed; umbels in a panicle, 4–6-fld., peduncles twice as long as pedicels or less; petals white, the upper splotched with red at base, abruptly narrowed on outer margin to a short claw.

cucullatum (L.) L'Hér. ex Ait. Shrubby, to 6 ft.; lvs. to 3 in. across, reniform, crenate, long-hairy, blades more or less cupped; umbels 5–10-fld.; calyx spur to ½ in. long, slightly shorter than sepals, petals to 1 in. long or more, red, with deep red veins.

dasycaule Haw. Similar to *P. crithmifolium* and perhaps not distinct, differing essentially in having lvs. less divided, lobes oblong or ovate, pinnately toothed.

×**decipiens** Tratt. A complex hybrid with large white fls. splotched and veined with red, best considered a form of *P.* × *domesticum.* Some material offered as *P. decipiens* is referable to *P. vitifolium* or a derivative.

×**Dennisianum** Sweet. A hybrid derived from *P. cucullatum,* having petals dark red marked with blackish streaks and red lines; best considered a form of *P.* × *domesticum.* Some material offered as *P. Dennisianum* is referable to *P. vitifolium* or a derivative.

denticulatum Jacq. PINE G. To 3 ft.; lvs. glabrous and viscid above, pinnately lobed, lobes long, linear, deeply and sharply toothed; umbels 1–3-fld.; calyx spur to ⁵⁄₁₆ in. long, about as long as sepals, petals lilac or pink, the upper larger, notched, spotted and veined purple. Cv. 'Filicifolium' [*P. filicifolium* Hort.]. FERN-LEAF G. Lvs. finely divided, lacy. Cv. 'Majus' is listed. Hybridized with *P. quercifolium* to produce *P.* cv. 'Carlton Oak'.

deserti: a listed name of no botanical standing.

×**divaricatum** F. Dietr. A hybrid derived from *P. fulgidum,* but not known to be in cult.; plants offered as *P. divaricatum* have not been identified with certainty.

×**domesticum** L. H. Bailey. SHOW G., FANCY G., LADY WASHINGTON G., MARTHA WASHINGTON G., PANSY-FLOWERED G., SUMMER AZALEA, REGAL G. A cultigen of complex hybrid origin but largely derived from *P. cucullatum, P. angulosum* and *P. grandiflorum,* with an admixture of other spp. and now familiar in hort. primarily as a florist's cultural group with many fancy-named cvs. Sts. usually long, to 1½ ft. or more, soft-hairy throughout; lvs. 2–4 in. across, mostly obscurely lobed and toothed like those of the principal parents but sometimes more deeply divided; fls. few to many, large, petals white, pink, red, or purple, the 2 upper with dark blotches and veins. Hybridized with *P. quercifolium* to produce *P.* cv. 'Clorinda'. *P.* cv. 'California Brilliant' and *P.* cv. 'Capri' may be derived from this complex, with fl. color from *P. fulgidum.*

echinatum Curtis. CACTUS G., SWEETHEART G. Sts. short and fleshy, with persistent, spinelike stipules; lvs. cordate-ovate, with 3–7 shallow, wavy-toothed lobes, white-tomentose beneath; umbels 3–6-fld.; calyx spur as long as sepals, petals white to red-purple, the upper deeply spotted.

Endlicheranum Fenzl. Per. herb., to 18 in.; sts. little-branched or simple, downy; lvs. few, basal, cordate, obscurely 5-lobed, upper lvs. often more deeply divided; umbels 5–15-fld., peduncles long; fls. short-pedicelled, calyx spur to 1 in., twice as long as sepals or more, petals deep rose, the 2 upper 1 in. long or more, long-clawed, purple-veined basally, the 3 lower shorter than sepals, stamens united in a tube at base and declinate. Asia Minor. May be hardy north.

ferulaceum (Burm.f.) Willd. [*P. parviflorum* J. C. Wendl.]. To 2 ft., sts. fleshy, swollen at nodes; lvs. oblong, pinnatifid to pinnatisect, hairy on both sides, flat, segms. incised; umbels 2–5-fld., peduncles 3–4 times as long as pedicels; sepals white-margined, calyx spur about as long as sepals, petals to ⅜ in. long, white, narrow, the upper abruptly narrowed on the other margin to a short claw, rose-spotted. Probably not cult.

filicifolium: a listed name of no botanical standing for *P. denticulatum* cv.

filtrum: a listed name of no botanical standing; material so labeled is usually *P.* cv. 'Mrs. Taylor'.

formosa: a listed name of no botanical standing.

×**fragrans** Willd.: *P. exstipulatum* (Cav.) L'Hér. ex Ait. × *P. odoratissimum.* NUTMEG G. Similar to *P. odoratissimum* and not always easily distinguished, but brs. generally more woody, lvs. 3-lobed above the middle, fls. slightly larger, calyx spur about twice as long as sepals, petals more prominently spotted and veined with red. Nutmeg-scented. Cv. 'Cody's Fragrans'. A more compact form. Cv. 'Logee': see *P. Logeei.* Cv. 'Variegatum' is also listed.

frutetorum R. A. Dyer. Similar to *P. inquinans* and *P. zonale;* lvs. softly hairy, zoned; fls. salmon-colored.

fulgidum (L.) L'Hér. ex Ait. Shrubby; lvs. softly hairy, pinnately divided, to 3 in. long, lobes broad, again lobed, stipules ¼ in. long, united to petiole half their length; umbels axillary, 5–12-fld., peduncles long, villous; fls. nearly sessile, calyx spur ¾–1 in. long, swollen toward top, sepals ¼ in. long, petals scarlet, the upper larger, to 1 in. long, veined but not blotched with deep red. Hybrids and cvs. cult. today showing influence of *P. fulgidum* are *P.* × *ignescens, P.* cv. 'Mrs. Taylor', *P.* cv. 'Scarlet Unique', and *P.* cv. 'Shrubland Pet'.

gibbosum (L.) L'Hér. ex Ait. KNOTTED G., KNOTTED S. Shrubby, sts. swollen at nodes; lvs. pinnately divided, to 3 in. long, glaucous, glabrous, stipules ³⁄₁₆ in. long, free from petiole; umbels 5–10-fld., axillary, peduncles to 4 in. long; fls. nearly sessile, calyx spur ¾–1 in. long or more, somewhat swollen at top, sepals ⁵⁄₁₆ in. long, petals to ¾ in. long, yellow-green, the upper 2 larger.

×**glaucifolium** Sweet: *P. gibbosum* × *P. lobatum* (L.) L'Hér. ex Ait. BLACK-FLOWERED G., LITTLE-LEAF ROSE G. Similar to *P. gibbosum;* lvs. large, ternately to pinnately lobed, glaucous, umbels long-peduncled, petals nearly equal, purplish-black, margined with pale yellowgreen.

glutinosum (Jacq.) L'Hér. ex Ait. [*P. viscosum* (Cav.) Harv. & Sond.]. PHEASANT'S-FOOT G. Shrubby, to 3 ft.; lvs. glabrous above, 5-lobed nearly to the base, lobes broad, sharply toothed; umbels 2–7-fld.; fls. nearly sessile, calyx spur to ⅜ in. long, about as long as sepals, petals rose, the upper broader, red-spotted.

gratum Willd. An obscure sp. or hybrid, perhaps related to *P. crispum* but not certainly known; plants cult. under this name are probably incorrectly named.

graveolens L'Hér. ex Ait. [*P. terebinthinaceum* (Cav.) Small, not Harv.]. ROSE G., SWEET-SCENTED G. Woody, to 3 ft.; lvs. softly hairy, fragrant, deeply 5–7-lobed, the lobes again lobed and crenately toothed; umbels 5–10-fld.; fls. nearly sessile, calyx spur ¼–⁵⁄₁₆ in. long, about as long as sepals, petals rose, the upper larger, red-spotted and -veined. Hybridizes with other spp., especially *P. radens* and much material cult. as *P. graveolens* is probably of this hybrid origin, including the plants used as the source of commercial geranium oil. See *P.* × *asperum.* Also hybridized with *P. tomentosum,* producing *P.* cv. 'Joy Lucille' and *P.* cv. 'Rober's Lemon Rose'. Other cvs. derived from *P. graveolens* are *P.* cv. 'Camphor Rose', *P.* cv. 'Fragrantissimum', *P.* cv. 'Giganteum', *P.* cv. 'Granelous', *P.* cv. 'Grey Lady Plymouth', *P.* cv. 'Lady Plymouth', *P.* cv. 'Little Gem', *P.* cv. 'Marginata', *P.* cv. 'Minor', *P.* cv. 'Mrs. Taylor', *P.* cv. 'Red-flowered Rose', and *P.* cv. 'Variegatum', the mint-scented ROSE G.

grossularioides (L.) L'Hér. ex Ait. GOOSEBERRY G., COCONUT G. Sts. herbaceous, slender, branched, spreading, nearly glabrous; lvs. to 1½ in. across, reniform-cordate, slightly lobed and crenate-dentate, turpentine-scented; umbels 3–10-fld., often many on axillary brs., peduncles slender, to 4 in. long; sepals ⅛–³⁄₁₆ in. long, calyx spur about as long as sepals, petals deep rose-purple, not much longer than the sepals. Naturalized in Calif. Some material so named is *P. crispum* cv. 'Variegatum'. The sp. has been erroneously offered as *P. parviflorum.*

hirsutum (Burm.f.) L'Hér. ex Ait. Tuberous, stemless; lvs. to 3 in. long, hirsute with long white hairs, lanceolate or ovate in outline, entire to pinnatifid, segms. toothed; umbels compound, 5–10-fld.; fls. nearly sessile, calyx spur to ⁹⁄₁₆ in. long, petals spatulate, longer than sepals, dark purple to red, rose, or white.

×**hortorum** L. H. Bailey. FISH G., ZONAL G., HOUSE G., HORSESHOE G., BEDDING G. A cultigen of complex hybrid origin, largely derived from *P. inquinans* and *P. zonale;* familiar in hort. as a garden culture group used as pot plants or for bedding. Sts. 1–2 ft. or more, succulent, smooth or slightly hairy; lvs. rounded to reniform, 3–5 in. across, cordate, scalloped and crenate-toothed, often zoned or variegated; umbels densely many-fld.; calyx spur elongate, petals nearly equal, red, pink, salmon, or white, usually uniform in color but sometimes varicolored. Double-fld., cactus-fld., miniature, and spotted forms are known. Offered in many fancy-named cvs.

×**ignescens** Lodd. An old hybrid of *P. fulgidum* and very similar to it; perhaps represented in cult. today by *P.* cv. 'Scarlet Unique'.

inquinans (L.) L'Hér. ex Ait. Shrubby, sts. fleshy; lvs. cordate-orbicular, crenate; softly hairy; umbels many-fld.; calyx spur several times as long as sepals, densely glandular and long-hairy, petals ¾ in. long, uniformly pale rose to, usually, deep red. One of the principal parents of *P.* × *hortorum;* the sp. itself probably not cult.

×**jatrophifolium** DC: *P. denticulatum* × *P. quercifolium.* PHEASANT'S-FOOT G. Similar to *P. denticulatum* but lobes of lvs. broader, more sinuate, upper petals not notched. Generally known today as *P.* cv. 'Pheasant's Foot'.

lateripes L'Hér. ex Ait. Similar to *P. peltatum,* differing chiefly in having lvs. cordate, not peltate.

×**latifolium** Sweet. A hybrid of undetermined parentage, best referred to *P.* × *domesticum;* fls. bright red, upper petals white at base, splotched and streaked with red. Material cult. under the name *P. latifolium* perhaps belongs to *P.* cv. 'Latifolium' (see *P. crispum*).

×**limoneum** Sweet. ENGLISH FINGER-BOWL G. A hybrid derived from *P. crispum,* with lvs. 3–5-lobed, more strongly toothed, less crisped, upper petals bright lilac tinged with purple, dark-veined and spotted with violet in the center, the lower pale lilac, unspotted. Lemon-scented. Generally known in the trade as *P.* cv. 'Lady Mary'.

Logeei: *P.* cv. 'Logeei', a hybrid of *P. fragrans* and *P. odoratissimum.*

malvifolium: *P. alchemilloides.*

×**mellissinum** Sweet: *P. crispum* × *P. graveolens.* Similar to *P. crispum* but the lvs. larger, more deeply divided, scarcely crisped, umbels few-fld., fls. pedicelled, upper petals white, with strong red flush and nearly black spotting, much broader than the narrow, white, lower petals; scented like *Melissa officinalis*. Most hort. material is erroneously named and appears to be of *P. graveolens* origin but with another parent involved, perhaps *P. quercifolium*.

mirabile: *P. crassicaule*.

×**monstrum** L'Hér. ex Ait. An early hybrid of *P. zonale*, best referred to *P. × hortorum*.

multibracteatum Hochst. Herbaceous, to 30 in.; lvs. hairy on both sides, cordate and 5-angled in outline, to 2½ in. wide, palmately deeply 5–7-lobed, lobes coarsely toothed; umbels 3–12-fld., peduncles 2–6 times as long as lvs.; calyx spur shorter than sepals, petals obovate, to twice as long as sepals, white. E. Afr.

myrrhifolium (L.) L'Hér. ex Ait. Sts. several, to 2 ft., ascending or decumbent at base; lvs. pilose or hirsute, elongate-cordate, pinnately lobed, lobes incised or divided; calyx spur to 1 in. long, petals white, striped with red at base, the upper longer than the lower. Var. **coriandrifolium** (L.) Harv. [*P. coriandrifolium* (L.) Jacq.]. Lvs. 2-pinnately divided.

×**nervosum** Sweet. LIME G. A hybrid of undetermined parentage, softly hairy, sts. shrubby, branching; lvs. reniform to ovate, about 1 in. long, deeply and sharply toothed but not lobed, densely hairy, lime-scented; umbels few-fld.; calyx spur as long as sepals, petals rose-purple, the upper broader, more deeply colored than the lower, veined and splotched with dark crimson. *P.* cv. '**Torento**', is similar, but has lvs. more sharply toothed, densely hairy beneath.

odoratissimum (L.) L'Hér. ex. Ait. APPLE G. Plant sprawling, brs. to 1½ ft. long; lvs. 1 in. across, obtusely cordate, crenate, fragrant; umbels 5–10-fld.; calyx spur to 5⁄16 in. long, not much longer than sepals, swollen at top, petals to 3⁄8 in. long, white, sometimes veined with red. A source of geranium oil. Often confused with *P. × fragrans* and hybridized with it to produce *P.* cv. '**Logeei**'. Also hybridized with *P. capitatum*.

odoratum Hoffmanns. An old, obscure sp. or hybrid, not definitely known in cult.; the name has been used erroneously in hort. for *P. × limoneum* [*P.* cv. 'Lady Mary'].

palmatum: a listed name of no botanical standing.

papilionaceum (L.) L'Hér. ex Ait. Shrubby, to 3 ft.; lvs. cordate, to 4 in. across, dentate and sometimes shallowly lobed, softly hairy; umbel 5–10-fld.; calyx spur to ¼ in. long, shorter than sepals, petals strongly unequal, the upper 5⁄8 in. long, rose, marked with red, the lower white, shorter than to as long as sepals. Material cult. under this name is probably erroneously named and of hybrid derivation, perhaps from *P. capitatum* or *P. vitifolium*.

paradoxum Dinter. Sts. to 2 ft., thick, gnarled; lvs. spatulate, fleshy, to 4 in. long, 1 in. wide or more, undulate-crisped and crenate-lobed, rough-hairy; umbels clustered, 4–10-fld.; calyx spur short, petals white, nearly equal.

parviflorum: *P. ferulaceum*, but most hort. material called *P. parviflorum* is *P. grossularioides*.

patulum Jacq. Similar to *P. alchemilloides*, but lvs. glabrous above, petals to 5⁄8 in. long, rosy, veined and spotted red.

peltatum (L.) L'Hér. ex Ait. IVY G., HANGING G. Trailing or climbing, brs. to 3 ft. long or more; lvs. 2–3 in. across, peltate, broadly ovate, somewhat obtuse, shallowly 5-angled or -lobed, sometimes zoned with red; umbels axillary, 5–7-fld.; fls. short-pedicelled, calyx spur more than twice as long as sepals, petals rose-carmine varying to white, the upper dark-veined, ¾ in. long, longer than the lower. The IVY GERANIUMS thrive outdoors in Calif. A number of named cvs. and hybrid derivatives are cult.

pinnatum (L.) L'Hér. ex Ait. Stemless; lvs. basal, long-petioled, hirsute, pinnate, lfts. few to many, ovate to nearly round; umbels several on an erect fl. st. from rootcrown, calyx spur several times as long as sepals, petals white or pinkish, the upper spotted. Plants cult. as *P. squarrosum* belong here.

quercifolium (L.f.) L'Hér. ex Ait. [*P. terebinthinaceum* (Murr.) Harv. & Sond., not Small]. OAK-LEAVED G., ALMOND G., VILLAGE-OAK G. Shrubby, to 4 ft.; lvs. deeply and sinuately pinnately lobed, often dark-marked in center, lobes rounded, denticulate, 2–3 on each side; umbels 3–7-fld.; fls. subsessile, calyx spur about as long as sepals, petals rose, the upper larger, entire, with large red spot and red veins. Cvs. are: '**Giganteum**', approaching *P. glutinosum* but with rounded lobes; '**Pinnatifidum**', lvs. deeply divided, '**Prostratum**', a low form. Hybridizes with other spp. such as *P. capitatum* and *P. denticulatum;* also with *P. tomentosum* to produce *P.* cv. '**Beauty Oak**'. Other cvs. derived from this sp., some perhaps hybrids, are: *P.* cv. '**Fair Ellen**', *P.* cv. '**Godfrey's Pride**', *P.* cv. '**Haviland**', *P.* cv. '**Pretty Polly**', *P.* cv. '**Staghorn**', *P.* cv. '**Village Hill Oak**'.

radens H. E. Moore [*P. Radula* (Cav.) L'Hér. ex Ait.]. CROWFOOT G. Shrubby, to 3 ft.; lvs. rough-bristly-hairy, deeply lobed, lobes much divided into very slender revolute divisions; umbels about 5-fld.; fls. short-pedicelled, calyx spur not longer than sepals, petals rose, the upper larger, to ¾ in. long, spotted with red. Frequently confused with *P. denticulatum;* hybridizes with *P. capitatum* and *P. graveolens*. Cv. '**Dr. Livingston**' ['Skeleton Rose']. A large form.

Radula: *P. radens*.

rapaceum (L.) L'Hér. ex Ait. Stemless, with tuberous-thickened root; lvs. 2-pinnately divided, to 3 in. long, glaucous, more or less densely hairy, stipules to 1 in. long or more, united to petiole ¾ their length; umbels 3–12-fld., simple or compound, peduncle to 8 in.; fls. nearly sessile, calyx spur long, sepals to 3⁄8 in. long, petals slender, to 1 in. long or more, rose-white to flesh or yellow, the upper recurved and spotted with red, the lower straight and connivent. Most material offered under this name has been *P.* cv. '**Mrs. Kingsley**'.

reniforme Curtis. Sts. to 1½ ft., thick and woody at base; lvs. cordate to bluntly triangular, densely white-tomentose beneath, stipules not spiny; umbels 5–20-fld.; calyx spur several times as long as sepals, petals red-purple, narrow.

×**rutaceum** Sweet: *P. gibbosum* × *P. multiradiatum* J. C. Wendl. Similar to *P. gibbosum*, lvs. much-divided, like those of rue; umbels many-fld.; petals chocolate, margined pale yellow, the upper yellow-spotted at base, with scent of rue in the evening.

×**saepeflorens** Sweet: *P. echinatum* × *P. reniforme*. Habit of *P. echinatum*, but stipules less pronounced, lvs. not lobed or only slightly so, white-tomentose beneath, petals rose, with red spot in center, upper broader, with red splotches at base.

salmoneum R. A. Dyer. Similar to *P. frutetorum*, with salmon-pink fls., lvs. rounded in outline but minutely glandular and thinly hairy, not zoned but often more or less glaucous.

scabroviride: a listed name of no botanical standing, perhaps in error for *P. × Scarboroviae*.

scabrum (L.) L'Hér. ex Ait. APRICOT G., STRAWBERRY G. Shrubby, to 6 ft.; lvs. to 1 in. long, deeply 3-lobed, cuneate at base, glabrous above, scabrous beneath; umbels 2–6-fld.; calyx spur not longer than sepals, petals to ¾ in. long, rose to white, the upper larger, spotted and veined with red.

scandens J. F. Ehrh. Similar to *P. zonale*, but plants less compact, lvs. retuse or broadly cuneate at base, glabrous, glaucous-green, petals narrowly linear, pale rosy-white, with intensely colored veins.

×**Scarboroviae** Sweet. A hybrid of obscure origin, probably derived from *P. crispum*, but lvs. more deeply divided, coarsely toothed, not crisped, the upper petals spotted and veined with red or pink-violet; the lower petals narrower, pale lilac. Generally known in the trade as *P.* cv. '**Countess of Scarborough**'.

squarrosum Dinter. Shrubby, to 3 ft.; lvs. fan-shaped, 3⁄8 in. long, 5–7-toothed, shortly rough-hairy; umbels few-fld.; petals yellow, the lower streaked with purple. Plants cult. under this name are *P. pinnatum*.

×**Stapletonii** Sweet: *P. echinatum* × *P. × saepeflorens*. Similar to *P. × saepeflorens*, but lvs. more deeply divided, upper petals white at base and center.

×**strictum** F. Dietr. An obscure hybrid of undetermined parentage and affinity; plants cult. under this name are probably erroneously named.

terebinthinaceum: see *P. quercifolium* or *P. graveolens;* most hort. material so named is referable to *P.* cv. '**Little Gem**' (see *P. graveolens*).

tetragonum (L.f.) L'Hér. ex Ait. SQUARE-STALK CRANESBILL. Sts. fleshy, obtusely 3–4-angled; lvs. few, to 1½ in. wide, cordate, deeply 5-lobed, bluish-green; umbels axillary, 1–3-fld., peduncles short; fls. sessile, calyx spur to 1 in. or more, several times as long as sepals, petals usually 4, the 2 upper 1 in. or more long, obovate on a long claw, rose with purple lines at base, the 2 lower half as long or less, spatulate, white.

tomentosum Jacq. HERB-SCENTED G., PEPPERMINT G. Shrubby, to 3 ft.; lvs. cordate-ovate, angled, more or less 3-lobed, softly hairy above, densely white-tomentose beneath; umbels 4–20-fld.; calyx spur shorter than sepals, petals to 5⁄16 in. long, white, the upper splotched with red. Peppermint-scented. Hybridizes with *P. graveolens* and *P. quercifolium*.

tricolor Curtis [*P. violareum* Jacq.]. Plant short-hairy, sts. to 8 in. or more, branched, ascending; lvs. lanceolate in outline, coarsely and irregularly toothed or divided, pale-tomentose; peduncles 2–3-fld.; upper petals red, shading to very deep red at base, lower petals white, or veined with red.

triste (L.) L'Hér. ex Ait. To 2 ft., st. short, thick; lvs. 3-pinnately divided into oblong or lanceolate, acute teeth, to 10 in. long, densely hirsute; peduncles to 20 in.; fls. nearly sessile, calyx spur to 1⅝ in. long, petals dark purple.

violareum: *P. tricolor.*

viscosum: *P. glutinosum.*

vitifolium (L.) L'Hér. ex Ait. GRAPE-LEAVED G. Similar to *P. capitatum* and perhaps not distinct, differing in its more erect habit, and in having lvs. less deeply lobed, more harshly pubescent. May be offered as *P.* × *decipiens* or *P* × *Dennisianum.*

xerophyton Schlechter. Sts. low, densely branched, woody, often armed with persistent petioles; lvs. many, cuneate-obovate, to ⅜ in. long and broad, dentate, stipules minute; umbels 1–2-fld.; calyx spur 2 or more times as long as sepals, petals subequal, narrow, white, the upper purple-red-spotted.

zonale (L.) L'Hér. ex Ait. Shrubby, sts. fleshy; lvs. reniforme-orbicular, crenate, smooth or lightly hairy, often zoned; umbels many-fld.; calyx spur 1 in. long or more, nearly glabrous, several times as long as sepals, petals to ¾ in. long, narrow, uniformly pale pink or less frequently in shades of red. One of the principal parents of *P.* × *hortorum;* unmodified material of the sp. is probably not cult.

PELECYPHORA C. A. Ehrenb. [*Encephalocarpus* A. Berger]. HATCHET CACTUS. *Cactaceae.* Two spp. of small, tubercled cacti, native to Mex.; sts. solitary or cespitose, globose to club-shaped, with watery sap, tubercles rhombic at base, laterally flattened above, the truncate end vertically elliptic; areoles elongate, spines radial, comblike-appressed; fls. subapical, next to spine cluster or from an adaxial groove, diurnal, rosy to violet, tube short, ovary naked; seeds reniform, black, smooth. Differs from *Mammillaria* in form of tubercles and areoles and position of fls.

For culture see *Cacti.*

asseliformis C. A. Ehrenb. Sts. simple or cespitose, to 4 in. high and 2 in. thick, tubercles not overlapping, elliptic in outline, $^{3}/_{16}$ in. long, with a faint adaxial furrow; spines 8–60, blunt, united, to $^{5}/_{32}$ in. long; fls. axillary, rose, ¾ in. long, 1 in. across. Cent. Mex.

pseudopectinata: *Thelocactus pseudopectinatus.*

Valdeziana: *Thelocactus Valdezianus.*

strobiliformis (Werderm.) Frič & Schelle [*Ariocarpus strobiliformis* Werderm.; *Encephalocarpus strobiliformis* (Werderm.) A. Berger]. Sts. to 1⅝ in. high and 2⅜ in. thick, tubercles overlapping, triangular in outline, to ½ in. long; spines comblike at tips of tubercles; spines 7–14, not persistent; fls. light to dark magenta, to $1^{3}/_{16}$ in. across. N. Mex.

PELLAEA Link. CLIFF BRAKE. *Polypodiaceae.* About 80 spp. of small, rock-loving ferns, of wide distribution, but mostly in temp. and cool trop. regions of the New World; lvs. often leathery, 1–4-pinnate; sori rounded or oblong, often in a marginal band, covered by reflexed margins of the pinnules.

Some of them are grown in rock gardens and a few in cool greenhouses; some species prefer limestone sites. See also *Ferns.*

adiantoides: *P. viridis.*

andromedifolia (Kaulf.) Fée. COFFEE FERN. Lvs. to 2½ ft. long, 2–4-pinnate, pinnules oblong to elliptic, ½ in. long, veins visible beneath, petioles 1½ ft. long, flesh-colored. Calif., n. Baja Calif.

atropurpurea (L.) Link. PURPLE C.B. Lvs. tufted, leathery, to 1 ft. long and 6 in. wide, 1–2-pinnate, pinnae to 2 in. long, petioles to 8 in. long, dark purple. N. Amer. Zone 5.

brachyptera (T. Moore) Bak. SIERRA C.B. Lvs. to 1½ ft. long, 2-pinnate, pinnules 3–5 pairs, narrow-linear, to ¾ in. long, rachis of primary pinnae mostly shorter than the pinnules, petioles 1½ ft. long, purplish-brown. Sw. Ore., n. Calif.

Breweri D. C. Eat. BREWER'S C.B. Lvs. to 10 in. long, 1-pinnate, pinnae mostly 2-parted, petioles to 4 in. long, slender, brown. Much like *P. glabella* but basal pinnae with persistent stalks. Wash. to Calif. and Utah.

Bridgesii Hook. BRIDGES' C.B. Lvs. tufted, leathery, to 1 ft. long, blue-green, 1-pinnate, pinnae nearly equal, elliptic or oblong, petioles to 8 in. long, glossy, brownish. Sierra Nevada (Calif.), ne. Ore., cent. Idaho.

compacta: *P. mucronata* var. *californica.*

cordata: *P. sagittata* var. Var. **flexuosa:** *P. ovata.*

densa: *Cheilanthes siliquosa.*

falcata (R. Br.) Fée. AUSTRALIAN C.B. Lvs. leathery, to 1½ ft. long and 3 in. wide, 1-pinnate, pinnae lanceolate or oblong, to 2 in. long. India to New Zeal.

flexuosa: *P. ovata.*

glabella Mett. ex Kuhn. SMOOTH C.B. Plants 6–12 in., allied to *P. atropurpurea* but having lower pinnae 3-lobed or with 3–5 sessile pinnules. Vt. to B.C., s. to Ariz. Var. **occidentalis** [*P. occidentalis* (A. Nels.) Rydb.; *P. pumila* Rydb.]. Smaller, 1–6 in.; lvs. not commonly 2-pinnate basally, pinnules more broadly ovate. S. Dak. to Wyo. and Colo.

gracilis: *Cryptogramma Stelleri.*

hastata (Thunb.) Prantl. Pinnae with very strongly hastate bases. Transvaal (S. Afr.). Not known to be cult.; material cult. under this name is *P. viridis.*

intermedia Mett. ex Kuhn. Rhizomes cordlike, scales with dark center; lvs. leathery, mostly 2-pinnate, pinnules 10–30, ovate, veins obscure, petioles and rachis straw-colored or darker. Sw. Tex. to Ariz. and n. Mex.

mucronata D. C. Eat. [*P. ornithopus* Hook.]. BIRD'S-FOOT C.B. Lvs. to 1½ ft. long, bluish-green to lead-colored, 2–3-pinnate, pinnules elliptic or linear-oblong, to ¼ in. long, lower pinnules sessile in groups of 3, petioles to 10 in. long, purplish. Calif. to Tex. and Colo. Var. **californica** (Lem.) Munz and I. M. Johnst. [*P. compacta* (Davenp.) Maxon]. Pinnae linear, imbricate. Calif.

occidentalis: *P. glabella* var.

ornithopus: *P. mucronata.*

ovata (Desv.) Weatherby [*P. cordata* var. *flexuosa* (Kaulf. ex Schlechtend. & Cham.) Hook. & Bak.; *P. flexuosa* Kaulf. ex Schlechtend. & Cham.]. Lvs. clambering, to 4 ft. or more, 4-pinnate, pinnules 3–20 on each pinna, stalked, mostly ½ in. long, ovate, obtuse at apex, nearly cordate at base, petioles and rachises pale tan-colored, rachises and rachillae zigzag; sori along each margin, contiguous. Tex., s. to n. Argentina, Hispaniola. Plants grown on trellises or in hanging baskets under glass in the North.

pumila: *P. glabella* var. *occidentalis.*

rotundifolia (G. Forst.) Hook. BUTTON FERN, NEW ZEALAND C.B. Lvs. to 1 ft. long and 1½ in. wide, 1-pinnate, pinnae many, oblong to orbicular, to ¾ in. long, petioles bristly or scaly, dark brown-black. New Zeal. Sometimes seen in greenhouses, grown outdoors in Calif. Zone 10.

sagittata (Cav.) Link. Lvs. to 2 ft. long, light green, pinnae with 3–18 sagittate pinnules of firm texture, petioles straw-colored to ruddy-tan. N. Mex. to Bolivia. Var. **cordata** (Cav.) A. Tryon [*P. cordata* (Cav.) John Sm.]. Pinnules cordate-orbicular. Tex. to s. Mex.

viridis (Forssk.) Prantl [*P. adiantoides* John Sm.; *P. hastata* Hort., not (Thunb.) Prantl; *Pteris adiantoides* Bory]. GREEN C.B. lvs. to 2 ft. long, 2–3-pinnate, pinnules broad-ovate to lanceolate, lobed or auricled at truncate base, terminal pinnule longest, petioles purple-brown. Afr.

virgata: a listed name of no botanical standing.

PELLIONIA Gaud.-Beaup. *Urticaceae.* About 50 spp. of monoecious or dioecious herbs or sometimes shrubs, native to trop. and e. Asia and Pacific Is.; lvs. alt., 2-ranked, asymmetrical at base; fls. minute, mostly in dense cymes, calyx segms. 4–5; fr. an achene enclosed by the calyx.

Grown for the attractively colored stems and leaves; make good basket plants, but require warmth and moisture. Propagated by cuttings and division.

argentea: a listed name of no botanical standing for *P. Daveauana* var. *viridis.*

Daveauana (Godefr.) N. E. Br. TRAILING WATERMELON BEGONIA. Creeping herb, sts. succulent, glabrous, pinkish, to about 2 ft. long; lvs. subsessile, oblong to oblong-orbicular, or lanceolate in upper part of plant, 1–2½ in. long, obtuse and crenate apically or acuminate, upper side dark bronzy-olive-green with purplish margins and a broad central stripe of pale green, lower side pinkish. Vietnam, Malay Arch. Var. **viridis** N. E. Br. [*P. argentea* Hort.]. Lvs. green, sometimes with whitish veins.

pulchra N. E. Br. SATIN P., RAINBOW VINE. Glabrate, creeping herb, sts. purple-tinged; lvs. oblong to broadly elliptic, obtuse at apex, upper side dull blackish along midrib and veins and green between, lower side pale purplish. Vietnam.

PELTANDRA Raf. ARROW ARUM. *Araceae.* Two or 3 spp. of stemless, hardy per. herbs, of swamps and margins of slow streams and ponds in N. Amer.; lvs. arising from stout rhizomes, entire, sagittate-hastate, petioles long; fls. unisexual, perianth absent.

Sometimes planted in wet locations for their attractive foliage. Of easy culture; propagated by seeds or division.

virginica (L.) Schott & Endl. VIRGINIAN WAKE-ROBIN, ARROW ARUM, TUCKAHOE. To 3 ft.; lf. blades glossy, to 15 in. long, petioles stout; spathe green, hidden among lvs., to 8 in. long, convolute with wavy margins, constricted basally; fr. cluster about 2 in. long, berries green. Midspring to summer. Me. to Fla., w. to Tex. and Mo.

PELTARIA Jacq. SHIELDWORT. *Cruciferae.* Four or more spp. of per., glabrous herbs in Medit. region; lvs. simple, entire; fls. small, white or rose, sepals 4, petals 4, short-clawed; fr. a pendent, strongly compressed, nearly orbicular silicle.

alliacea Jacq. GARLIC CRESS. Erect, to 24 in., branched, with onion-like odor; lvs. ovate or lanceolate, to 3 in. long, clasping st.; fls. white, on slender pedicels, many in short terminal racemes; silicles shield-shaped, to ⅜ in. across. Spring or early summer. Se. Eur. An ornamental, grown readily from seeds, blooming the following year; also prop. by division.

PELTIPHYLLUM Engl. *Saxifragaceae.* One sp., a rhizomatous, per. herb, in streams of sw. Ore. and mts. of n. Calif.; lvs. large, peltate, arising from the rhizome; fl. sts. tall, leafless, arising from the rhizome and developing before lvs.; fls. in showy, terminal, branched infl., calyx tube united to base of ovary, calyx lobes 5, longer than the tube, petals 5, stamens 10, carpels 2, united only at the base; fr. of 2 follicles.

peltatum (Torr. ex Benth.) Engl. [*Saxifraga peltata* Torr. ex Benth.]. UMBRELLA PLANT. Fl. sts. stout, up to 5–6 ft., hirsute-glandular; lf. blades nearly orbicular, peltate, to 10 in. across, nearly glabrous, 10–15-lobed, lobes coarsely serrate, petioles roughly hirsute, to 3 ft. long; calyx lobes ⅛ in. long, reflexed, petals obovate, to ¼ in. long, entire, pink, stamens erect; follicles purplish, to ⅜ in. long. Easily grown in wet places.

PELTOBOYKINIA (Engl.) Hara. *Saxifragaceae.* Two spp. of rather large per. herbs with short, thick, creeping rhizomes, native to Japan; basal lvs. long-petioled, large, peltate, palmately lobed, st. lvs. few; fls. in terminal cymes, yellow; calyx tube campanulate, united to ovary in lower half, calyx lobes 5, petals 5, toothed, deciduous, stamens 10, ovary half-inferior, 2-celled, styles 2; fr. a caps., enclosed in the somewhat inflated calyx tube. Distinguished from *Boykinia* by the 10 stamens, and large peltate lvs.

tellimoides (Maxim.) Hara [*Boykinia tellimoides* (Maxim.) Engl.; *Saxifraga tellimoides* Maxim.]. To 2 ft., st. sparingly leafy; basal lvs. 1–3, almost orbicular in outline, to 6 in. across, 7–9-lobed; petals greenish-yellow, twice as long as calyx lobes or longer. Japan.

PELTOPHORUM (Vogel) Walp. *Leguminosae* (subfamily *Caesalpinioideae*). Perhaps 15 spp. of pantrop., unarmed, tall, more or less evergreen trees; lvs. alt., 2-pinnate; fls. in terminal panicles of racemes, showy, yellow, 5-merous, stamens 10, separate; fr. a thin, flat, oblong legume with a broad wing on each side.

Fast-growing, commonly cultivated in the tropics and subtropics for shade and the showy flowers; propagated by seeds that have been scarified, or immersed in dilute acid or boiling water for 2 minutes before planting. Young trees flower in 4–5 years.

brasiliense (L.) Urb. [*P. Linnaei* Benth.]. To 40 ft. or more; lfts. in 6–8 pairs, elliptic, to 1½(–2) in. long; racemes solitary or clustered; 1 calyx lobe 1½ times as large as the others, with a glandular, comblike margin; fr. to 4 in. long, 1 in. wide. Jamaica.

dasyrachis Kurz ex Bak. Similar to *P. pterocarpum,* but with axillary racemes 8–14 in. long, conspicuous antlerlike stipules to ¾ in. long, longer pedicels, to 1⁵⁄₁₆ in. long, and fr. larger and flatter, sharp-pointed, greenish-yellow, becoming pale brownish. Thailand, Malay Pen., Sumatra.

dubium (K. Spreng.) Taub. Differs from *P. pterocarpum* in having smaller mucronate lfts., to ⅜ in. long, and fr. to 3 in. long. Brazil. Zone 10b.

ferrugineum: *P. pterocarpum.*

inerme: *P. pterocarpum.*

Linnaei: *P. brasiliense.*

pterocarpum (DC.) Bak. ex K. Heyne [*P. ferrugineum* (Decne.) Benth.; *P. inerme* (Roxb.) Naves ex Fern.-Vill.]. YELLOW POINCIANA, YELLOW-FLAME. To 50 ft., rusty-tomentose; lvs. with 4–12 pairs of pinnae, lfts. in 10–15 pairs, oblong, to ¾ in. long, blunt, oblique, panicles 12–18 in. long, pedicels ⁵⁄₁₆ in. long; fls. fragrant, 1½ in. across, petals yellow, crinkled, with reddish median mark; fr. purple-brown, to 3½ in. long. Seashores, Ceylon, Malay Arch., n. Australia. Zone 10b.

PENIOCEREUS (A. Berger) Britt. & Rose. *Cactaceae.* About 6 spp. of night-flowering cacti of Mex. and sw. U.S.; roots tuberous, sts. slender, strongly 3–6-ribbed, or upper shoots sometimes nearly cylindrical; spines mostly small, thickened at base; fls. large, funnelform, white, tube exceeding the limb, ovary spiny, stamens in 1 series; fr. ovoid, spiny, fleshy.

For culture see *Cacti.*

Diguetii: *Wilcoxia striata.*

Greggii (Engelm.) Britt. & Rose [*Cereus Greggii* Engelm.]. NIGHT-BLOOMING CEREUS, REINA-DE-LA-NOCHE. Tuber to 2 ft. thick, sts. 3–8 ft. long and ½–1 in. thick, at first pubescent, ribs 4–5, acute; spines bulbous-based, acuminate, dark, to ⅛ in. long, radial spines 6–9, central spines 1–2; fls. white, fragrant, to 8 in. long; fr. ovoid, beaked, scarlet, spiny, to 5 in. long, edible. Spring. Sw. Tex. to s. Ariz., n. Mex.

Johnstonii Britt. & Rose. Tuber to 8 in. thick or more, sts. clambering, to 10 ft. long and ½ in. thick, glabrous, ribs 3–5; areoles ½–1 in. apart, radial spines 5–12, reddish, becoming dark, to ¼ in. long, the upper swollen at base, the lower bristlelike, central spines 1–3, to ⁵⁄₁₆ in. long; fls. 6 in. long, perianth tube with bristles to 1 in. long, ovary with black spines; fr. 2½ in. long. S. Baja Calif.

PENNISETUM L. Rich. *Gramineae.* About 80 spp. of ann. or per. grasses in trop. regions, sts. often branched; lf. blades usually flat; infl. dense, spikelike; spikelets alike, with 1 bisexual floret above a sterile floret, solitary or in groups of 2–3, surrounded by an involucre of bristles, these not united except at the very base, often plumose, falling attached to the spikelets, glumes and sterile lemma membranous, first glume shorter than the spikelet or absent, second glume shorter than or equaling the sterile lemma, fertile lemma papery, smooth, the margin thin, enclosing the palea. For terminology see *Gramineae.*

alopecuroides (L.) K. Spreng. [*P. japonicum* Trin.]. CHINESE P. Per., sts. to 3½ ft., compressed; lf. blades elongate, scabrous; infl. bristly, to 6¼ in. long; bristles of spikelets to ¾ in. long. Asia. Sparingly cult. for ornament; escaped in Penn.

americanum (L.) K. Schum. [*P. glaucum* of auth., not (L.) R. Br.; *P. spicatum* (L.) Willd. ex Roem. & Schult.; *P. typhoides* (Burm.) Stapf & C. E. Hubb.]. PEARL MILLET, INDIAN M., AFRICAN M. Ann., sts. to 7 ft., robust, densely villous below the panicle; lf. blades flat, cordate, to 3¼ ft. long and 2 in. wide; infl. cylindrical, stiff, to 20 in. long and 1 in. thick, pale, bluish-tinged or sometimes tawny; spikelets short-pedicelled, about ⅛ in. long, the grain at maturity protruding. Old World cultigen, origin unknown. A food crop of trop. Asia and Afr.; cult. for forage in the s. states.

atrosanguineum: a listed name of no botanical standing for *P. setaceum* cv.

caudatum: a listed name of no botanical standing.

ciliare (L.) Link. BUFFEL GRASS. Per., sts to 20 in., geniculate from the crown; infl. to 4 in. long; bristles united at the very base, flexuous, purple, to ⅜ in. long, the inner plumose. S. Afr.; introd. in N.Y. Occasionally cult. for forage in the South as far n. as Okla.

cupreum: *P. setaceum* cv.

glaucum: see *P. americanum.*

japonicum: *P. alopecuroides.*

latifolium K. Spreng. URUGUAY P. Per., sts. to 5 ft., nodes appressed-pubescent; lf. blades to 1¼ in. wide, tapering to a long point; infl. terminal and axillary, nodding, to 3¼ in. long; bristles of spikelets prominent. S. Amer. Occasionally cult. for ornament.

longistylum: see *P. villosum.*

macrostachyum (Brongn.) Trin. Distinguished from *P. setaceum* in having lf. blades to 1 in. wide, infl. denser, brownish-purple; bristles not plumose. E. Indies. Sparingly cult. for ornament.

purpureum Schumach. NAPIER GRASS, ELEPHANT G., ELEPHANT'S G. Robust, leafy per., sts. to 14 ft.; lf. blades elongate, to 1¼ in. wide; infl. dense, elongate, stiff, tawny or purplish; bristles sparsely plumose, about ⅜ in. long. Afr.; introd. as a forage plant in Fla.

Ruppelianum: *P. setaceum.*

Ruppelii: *P. setaceum.*

setaceum (Forssk.) Chiov. [*P. Ruppelii* Steud.; *P. Ruppelianum* Hort.]. FOUNTAIN GRASS. Per., sts. simple, about 3½ ft. high, clustered; lf. blades narrow, elongate, scabrous; infl. to 14 in. long, nodding, loose, pink or purple; bristles plumose toward base, unequal, the longer to 1⅝ in. long. Afr. Cult. for ornament. Cv. 'Atrosanguineum'. Foliage and spikes purple. Cv. 'Cupreum' [*P. cupreum* A. S. Hitchc. ex L. H. Bailey]. Foliage reddish; spikes copper-colored. Cv. 'Rubrum' [*P. Ruppelii.* cv. 'Rubrum']. Foliage and spikes rose.

spicatum: *P. americanum.*

typhoides: *P. americanum.*

villosum R. Br. ex Fresen. [*P. longistylum* Vilm., not Hochst.]. FEATHERTOP. Per., sts. to 2 ft., clustered; lf. blades to ¼ in. wide; infl. tawny, to 4 in. long and 2 in. wide, including bristles, dense, feathery; bristles many, spreading, the inner very plumose, the longer to 2 in. long. Afr. Cult. for ornament, sparingly escaped in Mich., Tex., and Calif. Called *P. longistylum* by florists in error.

PENSTEMON Mitch. [*Pentastemon* Batsch; *Pentstemon* Mitch.]. BEARD-TONGUE. *Scrophulariaceae.* About 250 spp. of per. herbs or shrubs, 1 sp. native to ne. Asia, the rest to N. Amer., chiefly w. U.S.; lvs. opp., rarely in whorls of 3, or the upper alt., sessile in upper part of plant, petioled in lower part; fls. scarlet, purple, blue, white, or yellow, solitary or in terminal racemes or panicles, calyx 5-parted, corolla tubular, more or less 2-lipped, fertile stamens 4, staminode 1, naked or bearded; fr. a caps., seeds many.

Nearly all penstemons succeed in full sun, but may not persist in a hot dry location. Many species are not hardy north, but many others are, especially if given winter protection. Some variants of *P. gloxinioides* are treated successfully as annuals. Propagated by seeds, somewhat by division, rarely by cuttings in summer.

abietinus Penn. Much-branched, heathlike, matted per., sts. prostrate and ascending; lvs. linear, to ½ in. long, mucronate, entire; corolla ⅝ in. long, blue, with red-purple tube, without lines, staminode golden-yellow-bearded. Utah.

acaulis L. O. Williams. Tufted per., to 2 in., with underground sts.; lvs. linear, about ¾ in. long, acute; fls. solitary, corolla to ⅝ in. long, azure blue, throat golden-hairy, staminode golden-brown-bearded. Wyo. and Utah.

acuminatus Dougl. ex Lindl. Erect, stout, glaucous, glabrous per., to 2 ft.; lvs. entire, leathery, basal lvs. lanceolate, elliptic, or spatulate, st. lvs. ovate to cordate and clasping, to 3 in. long, acuminate; corolla pale blue, funnelform, staminode dilated, gold-bearded at apex. Wash. to Tex.

aggregatus: *P. Rydbergii* subsp.

alamosensis Penn. & Nisbet. Sts. solitary or few, glabrous; lvs. mostly basal, elliptic to broadly lanceolate, st. lvs. reduced; corolla to 1 in. long, bright red, staminode glabrous. New Mex.

albertinus Greene. Glabrous or rarely glandular per., to 16 in., sts. clustered; lvs. entire to serrate-denticulate, thin, basal lvs. lanceolate to elliptic, st. lvs. lanceolate-oblong; corolla blue to blue-violet, ¾ in. long, staminode gold-bearded. B.C. to Alta., s. to Idaho and Mont.

albidus Nutt. Per., to 16 in., sts. puberulent in lower part, glandular-pubescent above; basal lvs. spatulate or oblong, entire, st. lvs. lanceolate or oblong, to 2½ in. long, denticulate; corolla white, ¾ in. long, glandular-puberulent inside, staminode slightly bearded. Alta. and Man. to Tex.

alpinus Torr. [*P. glaber* var. *alpinus* (Torr.) A. Gray]. Glabrous to puberulent per., to 2½ ft.; lvs. entire, often glaucous and thick, basal lvs. oblanceolate, st. lvs. lanceolate to cordate and clasping, to 5 in. long; corolla 1 in. long, blue to bluish-purple, staminode glabrous or bearded at apex. Rocky Mts., Wyo., Colo., New Mex.

amabilis: *P. pruinosus.*

ambiguus Torr. Much-branched, woody-based per., to 2 ft.; lvs. linear-filiform, 1¼ in. long; corolla salverform, white inside, with deep rose throat, usually purplish outside, with a definite sheen, staminode glabrous. Colo. to Mex. and Ariz.

anguineus Eastw. [*P. Rattanii* var. *minor* A. Gray]. Per., to 2½ ft.; lvs. almost entire to denticulate, glabrous, basal lvs. elliptic to ovate, st. lvs. oblong, triangular-ovate to cordate and clasping; corolla ¾ in. long, deep lavender to blue-violet, tube purple, staminode exserted, glabrous or sparingly bearded. S. Ore. to n. Calif.

angustifolius Nutt. ex Pursh [*P. caeruleus* Nutt.]. Glabrous, glaucous per., to 1 ft.; lvs. to 3 in. long, entire, basal lvs. linear-lanceolate to broader, st. lvs. linear to linear-lanceolate; corolla ¾ in. long, blue, lilac, or white, staminode bearded. Plains, S. Dak. to Mont., s. to New Mex. Subsp. **caudatus** (A. Heller) Keck [*P. caudatus* A. Heller]. Bracts ovate, caudate-tipped.

antirrhinoides Benth. Much-branched shrub, to 6 ft.; lvs. linear-elliptic to elliptic-ovate, to ½ in. long, entire; corolla ¾ in. long, very broad, yellow, staminode yellow-bearded. S. Calif., Baja Calif. Subsp.

microphyllus (A. Gray) Keck [*P. microphyllus* A. Gray]. Twigs gray, herbage canescent throughout.

aridus Rydb. Slightly pubescent, cespitosely clumped per., 4–20 in., from a compact root crown; basal lvs. many, linear-oblanceolate, to 2¼ in. long, often involute, obscurely scabrid-denticulate; corolla ½ in. long, blue or blue-purple, staminode yellow-bearded. W. Mont., Wyo., Idaho.

aristatus: a listed name of no botanical standing.

arizonicus: *P. Whippleanus.*

arkansanus Penn. Per., to 2 ft., sts. clumped, grayish-puberulent; lvs. lanceolate, to 2¾ in. long, crenate-serrate, essentially glabrous; corolla to ¾ in. long, white, with violet lines, staminode yellow-bearded. Mo., Ark. to e. Tex.

attenuatus Dougl. ex Lindl. [*P. Nelsoniae* Keck & J. W. Thomps.]. Per., to 2 ft., from a basal rosette, glabrous except infl.; lvs. entire to finely denticulate, basal lvs. linear-lanceolate to elliptic, st. lvs. reduced, clasping; corolla pale yellow to shades of blue-purple, staminode densely golden-bearded. Idaho, Wash., Ore. Subsp. **pseudoprocerus** (Rydb.) Keck [*P. pseudoprocerus* Rydb.]. Shorter, fls. smaller, blue-purple.

auriberbis Penn. Per., to 8 in., sts. pubescent; lvs. linear to linear-lanceolate, to 3 in. long, entire or subentire, usually puberulent; corolla lilac to purplish-blue, staminode yellow-bearded its entire length. Colo.

australis Small. Pubescent per., to 2½ ft. or more; basal lvs. oblanceolate to obovate, st. lvs. mostly narrowly lanceolate, acuminate, entire to toothed; corolla cream, with reddish-purple lower lip, paler inside, staminode densely bearded. Se. Va. to cent. Fla., w. to Miss.

azureus Benth. [*P. Jaffrayanus* Hook.]. Blue-glaucous, glabrous subshrub, to 2½ ft.; basal lvs. oblanceolate to obovate, st. lvs. oblong or lanceolate to ovate, clasping, entire; corolla to 1½ in. long, deep blue-purple, staminode glabrous. Sw. Ore. to n. Calif. Subsp. **angustissimus** (A. Gray) Keck. Herbage paler yellow-green, lvs. very narrow. Cent. Calif.

barbatus (Cav.) Roth [*Chelone barbata* Cav.]. Glabrous per., to 6 ft.; sts. glaucous; basal lvs. oblong to ovate, st. lvs. linear or lanceolate, entire; corolla to 1 in. long, strongly 2-lipped, red, lower lip yellow-bearded, staminode glabrous. Utah to Mex. Cvs. include: 'Coccineus', fls. scarlet; 'Praecox', listed as early flowering; 'Roseus', fls. rose-pink. Subsp. **Torreyi** (Benth.) Keck [*P. Torreyi* Benth.]. Lower lip essentially glabrous.

Barrettiae A. Gray. Much-branched per., to 1 ft., forming dense clumps; lvs. ovate or elliptic-ovate, to 3 in. long, serrate, blue-glaucous, glabrous, leathery; corolla 1½ in. long, lilac to rose-purple, anthers of fertile stamens woolly, staminode glabrous. Ore.

Berryi: *P. Newberryi* subsp.

bicolor (Brandeg.) Clokey & Keck. Coarse, glaucous per., to 3 ft. or more, glabrous below infl.; lvs. ovate, to 3½ in. long, toothed, glaucous, glabrous, thick, leathery, upper lvs. connate-perfoliate; infl. glandular-pubescent, not leafy; corolla to about 1 in. long, yellow, staminode exserted, yellow-bearded. S. Nev. Subsp. **roseus** Clokey & Keck. Fls. pink.

Bradburii: *P. grandiflorus.*

Brandegei T. C. Porter ex Rydb. Puberulent, robust per., to 2½ ft., sts. ascending; st. lvs. lanceolate-ovate, to 4 in. long, entire, clasping; corolla to 1½ in. long, blue to reddish-purple, staminode exserted, sparingly bearded. S.-cent. Colo. to n. New Mex.

breviflorus Lindl. Glabrous, glaucous shrub, to 7 ft.; lvs. lanceolate, to 2¾ in. long, serrulate to entire; fl. bud yellowish, glandular-pubescent outside, corolla to ¾ in. long, white with rose or purplish veins, staminode glabrous. Calif.

brevifolius (A. Gray) A. Nels. Much-branched, cespitose per., to 1 ft., finely puberulent, glandular-pubescent in infl.; lvs. ovate to elliptic-ovate, to 1 in. long, entire, thin; corolla to ½ in. long, blue, staminode bearded. Utah.

Bridgesii A. Gray. Subshrub, to 2 ft. or more, glandular-pubescent in infl.; lvs. to 3 in. long, entire, basal lvs. linear-oblanceolate to spatulate, st. lvs. linear to elliptic; corolla to 1¼ in. long, red to scarlet, strongly 2-lipped, staminode glabrous. Calif., adjacent Baja Calif., Ariz., e. to Colo. and New Mex.

Buckleyi Penn. Glabrous, glaucous per., to 1 ft. or more; lvs. entire, basal lvs. elliptic-oblong, st. lvs. lanceolate to ovate or cordate, clasping; corolla pale lavender, staminode moderately bearded. Kans., Okla., Tex.

caelestinus Penn. Per., to 1½ ft., from a woody rhizome; lvs. entire to dentate, mostly glabrous, st. lvs. oblong-lanceolate, to 1¾ in. long, rounded-clasping; corolla to ¾ in. long, violet-blue, staminode yellow-bearded at apex. Mont.

caeruleus: *P. angustifolius.*

caesius A. Gray. Loosely cespitose, glaucous per., to 1½ ft., sts. glabrous in lower part, glandular-pubescent in infl.; lvs. entire, leathery, basal lvs. orbicular, st. lvs. oblanceolate; corolla to 1 in. long, purplish-blue, staminode glabrous. Mts., cent. and s. Calif.

caespitosus Nutt. ex A. Gray. Mat-forming per., to 2 in., sts. prostrate, creeping; lvs. linear to oblanceolate, entire, usually puberulent; corolla to ¾ in. long, light blue with purplish throat, mostly tubular, anther sacs as broad as long, staminode densely bearded. Wyo., s. to Colo. and Utah. Subsp. **desertipictus** (A. Nels.) Keck. Corolla inflated, with blue throat, anther sacs not much more than half as broad as long. Subsp. **perbrevis** Penn. Forms mats to 20 in. across; lvs. elliptic or ovate; fls. pale lilac. Subsp. **suffruticosus** (A. Gray) Keck. To 4 in.; sepals glandular.

californicus (Munz & I. M. Johnst.) Keck. Woody-based, tufted per., to 9 in., herbage with closely appressed white hairs; lvs. linear-oblanceolate, to ½ in. long, mucronate, entire, thick; corolla to ¾ in. long, purplish-blue, staminode yellow-bearded. Calif. to n. Baja Calif.

calycosus Small. Nearly glabrous per., to 4 ft.; lvs. spatulate to lanceolate or ovate, to 6 in. long, sharply serrate to nearly entire; corolla 1 in. long, purple, anthers glabrous, staminode bearded at apex. Me. to n. Ala. and Ga., w. to Mich.

campanulatus (Cav.) Willd. [*P. pulchellus* Lindl.]. Per., to 2 ft., glabrous in lower part, glandular-pubescent in infl.; lvs. linear to lanceolate, to 4 in. long, long-acuminate, sharply serrate; corolla 1 in. long, rose-purple or violet, sometimes white, staminode bearded at apex. Mex. and Guatemala.

canescens (Britt.) Britt. Densely puberulent to glabrous per., to 3 ft.; lvs. oblong, lanceolate to ovate, irregularly serrate; corolla 1 in. long, pale purple, white inside lined with purple, staminode densely bearded. Penn., s. to N.C. and Ala.

cardinalis Woot. & Standl. Erect, glabrous per., to 2½ ft., forming clumps; lvs. entire, basal lvs. elliptic-spatulate, st. lvs. oblong, lanceolate to ovate, to 5 in. long, thin; corolla to 1 in. long, red, throat and staminode yellow-bearded. New Mex.

Cardwellii T. J. Howell. Loosely tufted per., to 10 in., glabrous in lower part, sparsely glandular-puberulent in infl.; lvs. oblong-elliptic to elliptic, to 1½ in. long, serrate; corolla 1½ in. long, bright purple, anthers densely hairy, staminode yellow-bearded. Wash. and Ore. Cv. 'Roseus'. Fls. rose.

caudatus: *P. angustifolius* subsp.

centranthifolius Benth. SCARLET-BUGLER. Glabrous, glaucous per., to 4 ft.; lvs. entire, thick, basal lvs. spatulate, st. lvs. linear-lanceolate to ovate-lanceolate, upper pairs clasping; corolla 1 in. long, scarlet, tubular, staminode glabrous. Coastal Calif. to n. Baja Calif.

cinereus Piper. Tufted, gray-pubescent per., to 20 in., from a well-developed rosette; lvs. mostly entire, somewhat leathery, basal lvs. lanceolate to ovate, st. lvs. lanceolate to nearly linear, to ¾ in. long, clasping; corolla to ½ in. long, dark blue, staminode golden-bearded. Ore., n. Calif., Nev.

Clevelandii A. Gray. Glabrous per., to 2½ ft.; lvs. entire to serrate, glaucous or green, basal lvs. ovate, st. lvs. deltoid-lanceolate to cordate, to 2 in long; fls. in infl. to 1 ft. long, corolla 1 in. long, crimson to purplish-red, tubular-funnelform, anthers glabrous, staminode weakly bearded or glabrous. S. Calif. to n. Baja Calif. Subsp. **connatus** (Munz & I. M. Johnst.) Keck. Lvs. blue-glaucous, upper lvs. connate-perfoliate; anthers ciliolate.

Clutei A. Nels. Glabrous per., to 3¼ ft.; lvs. lanceolate-ovate to ovate, upper lvs. connate-perfoliate, to 2 in. long, sharply serrate-dentate, somewhat leathery, glaucous; infl. leafy basally; corolla to 1 in. long, pink to rose, ventricose, staminode yellow-bearded or glabrous. Ariz. Cv. 'Albiflorus' is listed.

Cobaea Nutt. Stout, pubescent per., to 2½ ft., glandular-pubescent in infl.; lvs. oblong to ovate, to 2½ in. long, dentate, upper lvs. clasping; corolla 2 in. long, white or pale violet-purple, scarcely 2-lipped, abruptly inflated, staminode bearded. Se. Nebr. to s. Tex. Subsp. **purpureus** Penn. Fls. deep purple.

coloradoensis: *P. linarioides* subsp.

comarrhenus A. Gray. Mostly puberulent per., to 3 ft.; lvs. entire, somewhat glaucous, basal lvs. oblong-oblanceolate, st. lvs. linear-oblanceolate to linear-lanceolate, to 4 in. long; corolla to 1½ in. long, pale blue to purplish-blue, anthers woolly, staminode glabrous or bearded at apex. Sw. Colo., Utah, ne. Ariz.

concinnus Keck. More or less puberulent, erect, woody-based per., to 6 in.; lvs. entire to toothed, thick, glabrous to hairy, basal lvs. linear-oblanceolate or spatulate, st. lvs. linear to linear-oblong; corolla to ⅜ in. long, pale blue-purple, staminode hooked, bearded. Utah.

confertus Dougl. ex Lindl. Glabrous per., to 2 ft.; lvs. lanceolate to oblanceolate, to 2 in. long or more, entire; corolla ½ in. long, pale sulphur-yellow, tubular, staminode brownish-bearded at apex. Alta. and Mont. B.C., s. to Ore. Cv. 'Violaceus' is listed.

confusus M. E. Jones. Glabrous per., to 1 ft.; lvs. glabrous, glaucous, leathery, basal lvs. lanceolate, st. lvs. lanceolate-oblong, to 3 in. long, clasping; corolla ¾ in. long, rose-lavender or purplish, staminode hooked, papillose-bearded at apex or glabrous. Utah and Nev.

congestus: *P. pachyphyllus* subsp.

connatifolius: *P. pseudospectabilis* subsp.

cordifolius Benth. Somewhat pubescent, scandent shrub, to 10 ft., glandular in infl.; lvs. lanceolate-ovate to cordate, to 2 in. long, glossy, toothed; corolla to 1½ in. long, scarlet, tubular, staminode densely yellow-bearded at apex. S. Calif.

corymbosus Benth. Shrub, to 2 ft., with glabrous to hairy herbage and glandular-pubescent in infl.; lvs. elliptic, to 1½ in. long, entire to remotely serrate, leathery; corolla 1¼ in. long, brick-red, tubular, staminode densely yellow-bearded throughout. Calif.

Crandallii A. Nels. [*P. xylus* A. Nels.]. Slightly pubescent, tufted per., to 8 in., sts. erect or ascending; lvs. linear-oblanceolate, to ¾ in. long, entire, pubescent or glabrous apically; corolla dark blue-purple, with lines in throat, deeply 2-lipped, staminode golden-bearded. Colo. Subsp. **glabrescens** (Penn.) Keck. Lvs. linear, glabrous above the petiole. Var. **taosensis** (Keck) Nisbet & R. C. Jacks. [*P. linarioides* subsp. *taosensis* Keck]. Lvs. puberulous. Subsp. **procumbens** (Greene) Keck [*P. procumbens* Greene]. Sts. decumbent; lvs. elliptic to obovate.

crassifolius: *P. fruticosus.*

cristatus: *P. eriantherus.*

Cusickii A. Gray. Tufted, pubescent, woody-based per., to 1½ ft.; lvs. linear to oblanceolate, to 2½ in. long, entire, gray-green; corolla to 1 in. long, purple to blue, anthers black-purple, staminode glabrous. Ore. and w. Idaho.

cyananthus Hook. [*P. glaber* var. *cyananthus* (Hook.) A. Gray]. Glabrous per., to 3 ft.; lvs. entire, thick, glaucous, basal lvs. lanceolate to spatulate, st. lvs. ovate to subcordate; corolla 1 in. long, blue to blue-purple, anthers and staminode bearded. Idaho, Utah, Wyo.

cyaneus Penn. Glabrous, tufted per., to 2½ ft.; lvs. lanceolate, entire, st. lvs. to 4½ in. long, clasping; corolla sky blue with purplish tube, anthers bearded, staminode yellow-bearded at apex. Cent. Idaho to nw. Wyo.

dasyphyllus A. Gray. Per. herb, to 2½ ft., with herbage gray-pubescent throughout and infl. glandular-pubescent; lvs. linear, to 3½ in. long, entire; corolla to 1½ in. long, purple or violet, staminode glabrous. W. Tex. to se. Ariz. and adjacent Mex.

Davidsonii Greene. [*P. Menziesii* Hook. subsp. *Davidsonii* (Greene) Piper]. Creeping, mat-forming, woody-based, puberulent per., to 6 in., glandular-pubescent in infl.; lvs. elliptic to orbicular, to ½ in. long, entire, thick; corolla to almost 1½ in. long, purple-violet, anthers woolly, staminode bearded. B.C. to Ore. Cv. 'Albus' is listed. Subsp. **Menziesii** Keck [*P. Menziesii* of auth., not Hook.]. Lvs. toothed. Subsp. **Thompsonii** Penn. & Keck [*P. Thompsonii* Hort.]. Plants, lvs., and fls. larger.

deustus Dougl. ex Lindl. Glabrous or glandular-pubescent, much-branched, clump-forming per., to 2 ft.; lvs. linear-lanceolate to elliptic-ovate, coarsely toothed; corolla ½ in. long, yellowish-white with purple lines, nearly tubular, staminode usually glabrous. Wash. to n. Calif., e. to Wyo.

diffusus: *P. serrulatus.*

Digitalis Nutt. [*P. laevigatus* var. *Digitalis* (Nutt.) A. Gray]. Per., to 5 ft., with sts. glabrous except for slender decussate lines of hairs from lf. bases, and infl. glandular-pubescent; lvs. entire to toothed, basal lvs. oblanceolate to elliptic, st. lvs. lanceolate, oblanceolate to oblong-ovate, to 7 in. long; corolla 1 in. long, white or pinkish, anthers bearded, staminode bearded. Me., s. to S. Dak. and Tex.

diphyllus: *P. triphyllus* subsp.

dissectus Elliott. Puberulent per., to 16 in.; st. lvs. bipinnatifid, segms. linear; corolla to 1 in. long, purple, staminode exserted, yellow-bearded at apex. Ga.

dolius M. E. Jones ex Penn. Gray-hairy per., to 6 in.; lvs. entire, gray-hairy, basal lvs. lanceolate to elliptic, st. lvs. linear-lanceolate; corolla ¾ in. long, blue-purple, staminode yellow-bearded. Nev. and Utah.

dracophyllum: a listed name of no botanical standing.

Eatonii A. Gray. Glabrous, erect per., to 3¼ ft.; lvs. entire, thick, glabrous, basal lvs. oblanceolate, long-petioled, st. lvs. lanceolate-oblong, to 4 in., clasping; corolla 1¼ in. long, scarlet, scarcely 2-lipped, staminode glabrous to sparsely bearded. S. Calif., e. to Ariz.,

Nev., Utah. Subsp. **exsertus** (A. Nels.) Keck. Sts. puberulent, stamens long-exserted. Subsp. **lancifolius:** a listed name of no botanical standing. Subsp. **undosus** (M. E. Jones) Keck. Sts. puberulent, stamens included or barely exserted.

×**Edithae** English: *P. Barrettiae* × *P. rupicola.* Glabrous, mat-forming per., to 10 in.; lvs. elliptic to suborbicular, to 1¾ in. long, toothed or entire, glaucous, glabrous; corolla to 1½ in. long, pink, anthers woolly, staminode slightly bearded at apex.

ellipticus J. Coult. & E. Fisher. Procumbent per., forming loose mats to 6 in. high; lvs. elliptic to obovate, to ¾ in. long, glabrous; corolla to 1½ in. long, light violet, anthers woolly, staminode yellow-bearded. B.C. and Alta., s. to Mont. and n. Idaho.

eriantherus Pursh [*P. eriantherus* subsp. *saliens* (Rydb.) Penn.; *P. cristatus* Nutt.; *P. saliens* Rydb.]. Pubescent per., to 16 in., glandular-pubescent in infl.; lvs. entire to toothed, basal lvs. lanceolate to ovate, st. lvs. lanceolate to oblong; corolla 1 in. long, purplish, staminode exserted, strongly yellow-bearded. N. Dak. and Nebr., w. to B.C. and Wash.

euglaucus English. Glabrous, somewhat glaucous per., to 20 in., from a well-developed rosette; lvs. entire, basal lvs. elliptic, st. lvs. linear-oblong to lanceolate-ovate; calyx lobes with caudate tip, corolla ½ in. long, blue, staminode yellow-bearded at apex. Ore., Wash.

exilifolius: *P. laricifolius* subsp.

Fendleri Torr. & A. Gray. Erect per., to 1½ ft., with glabrous, glaucous herbage; lvs. entire, leathery, basal lvs. ovate or obovate, st. lvs. ovate or oblong, to 2 in. long; corolla to ¾ in. long, blue with violet-purple lines, staminode bearded at apex. Sw. Kans., s. to se. Ariz. and adjacent Mex.

flavescens Penn. Per., to 16 in., from a well-developed rosette; lvs. entire, glabrous, leathery, basal lvs. lanceolate to elliptic, to 4¾ in. long, st. lvs. lanceolate-oblong; corolla to ½ in. long, pale yellow, staminode yellow-bearded at apex. Idaho and Mont.

floridus Brandeg. Erect per., to 4 ft., with blue-glaucous, glabrous herbage, and glandular-pubescent infl.; lvs. toothed, basal lvs. oblong-ovate, st. lvs. lanceolate-ovate, to 4 in. long; corolla to 1¼ in. long, rose-pink, abruptly inflated, staminode glabrous. Calif. and Nev.

fruticiformis Cov. Much-branched, shrubby-based per., to 2 ft., herbage glaucous, glabrous; lvs. linear-lanceolate, entire, rarely toothed; corolla to 1 in. long, white or flesh-colored, with pale lavender limb, abruptly inflated, staminode exserted, densely yellow-bearded. Death Valley (Calif.).

fruticosus (Pursh) Greene [*P. crassifolius* Lindl.]. Woody-based per., to 16 in., forming dense clumps; lvs. lanceolate, oblanceolate to elliptic, to 2 in., entire or toothed, leathery; corolla to 1½ in. long, lavender-blue, stamens woolly, staminode yellow-bearded. Cvs. 'Alba' and 'Major' are listed. Var. **azureus:** a listed name of no botanical standing, perhaps for *P. azureus.* Subsp. **Scouleri** (Lindl.) Penn. & Keck [*P. Scouleri* Lindl.]. Lvs. linear-lanceolate, to ³⁄₁₆ in. wide; fls. to 2 in. long. Subsp. **serratus** Keck. More shrubby and shorter than the typical subsp.; lvs. prominently serrate-dentate.

Gairdneri Hook. Tufted, gray-pubescent per., to 1 ft.; lvs. alt., usually recurved, linear, to 1½ in. long, entire, revolute; corolla ¾ in. long, lavender-purple with blue limb, staminode yellow-bearded. E. Ore. Subsp. **oreganus** (A. Gray) Keck [*P. oreganus* (A. Gray)]. Lvs. appearing opp.; corolla pale blue or lavender to almost white.

Garrettii Penn. Nearly glabrous per., to 1½ ft., sparingly glandular-pubescent in infl.; basal lvs. lanceolate, to 4 in. long, somewhat glaucous, st. lvs. clasping; corolla ¾ in. long, blue, staminode yellow-bearded. Utah.

gentianoides (HBK) Poir., not Lindl. Robust, short-lived per., to 4 or 5 ft.; lvs. lanceolate, to 4½ in. long, acuminate, entire to toothed, upper lvs. often in whorls of 3; infl. leafy; corolla 1¼ in. long, bluish-purple, staminode slightly bearded. Mex. and Guatemala. Material cult. under this name is usually *P. Hartwegii.*

glaber Pursh [*P. Gordonii* Hook.]. Glabrous per., to 2 ft.; st. lvs. lanceolate, elliptic to oblanceolate, to 6 in. long, entire; corolla to 1¼ in. long, blue or purple, stamens and staminode slightly hairy. N. Dak., s. to Nebr. and Wyo. Var. **alpinus:** *P. alpinus.* Var. **cyananthus:** *P. cyananthus.* Var. **speciosus:** *P. speciosus.*

glandulosus Dougl. ex Lindl. Glandular-pubescent, stout-stemmed per., to 3 ft.; lvs. serrate, thin, basal lvs. lanceolate to elliptic, st. lvs. lanceolate-ovate to cordate; corolla 1¾ in. long, lilac to violet, staminode glabrous. W. Idaho, w. to Wash. and Ore.

glaucus: *P. gracilis.* Var. **stenosepalus:** *P. Whippleanus.*

globosus (Piper) Penn. & Keck. Glabrous per., to 16 in. and more, from a well-developed rosette; lvs. entire, thin, basal lvs. lanceolate, st. lvs. lanceolate, oblong to ovate, clasping; corolla to ¾ in. long, blue or blue-purple, staminode densely golden-bearded. Ore. and Idaho.

gloxinioides: a listed name of no botanical standing for variants of *P. Hartwegii,* or hybrids between *P. Hartwegii* and *P. Cobaea,* in many colors.

Gordonii: *P. glaber.*

Gormanii Greene. Glabrous per., to 1 ft., glandular-pubescent in infl.; lvs. mostly entire, basal lvs. narrowly lanceolate to spatulate, st. lvs. lanceolate; corolla to ¾ in. long, blue-purple, staminode yellow-bearded. Alaska and Yukon.

gracilentus A. Gray. Glabrous per., to 2 ft., from a compact crown, glandular-pubescent in infl.; lvs. mostly basal, entire, glabrous, basal lvs. oblanceolate, st. lvs. linear-lanceolate; corolla to ½ in. long, violet-blue, anthers black-purple, staminode yellow-bearded. Ore., s. to n. Calif., Nev.

gracilis Nutt. [*P. glaucus* R. C. Grah.]. Slender per., to 2 ft., glandular-pubescent in infl.; lvs. finely toothed to subentire, thin, glabrous, basal lvs. oblanceolate to elliptic, st. lvs. linear-lanceolate; corolla ¾ in. long, lilac to whitish, strongly 2-lipped, staminode densely yellow-bearded. B.C. to Ont., s. to New Mex. and Wisc.

grandiflorus Nutt. [*P. Bradburii* Pursh]. Glabrous, glaucous per., to 4 ft.; lvs. entire, thick, fleshy, basal lvs. obovate, st. lvs. obovate to round-ovate or orbicular, clasping; corolla to 2 in. long, lilac or blue-lavender, staminode hooked, minutely bearded at apex. Ill. to N. Dak. and Wyo., s. to Tex. Cv. 'Albus' is listed.

Grinnellii Eastw. [*P. hians* I. M. Johnst.]. Similar to *P. Palmeri,* but having upper lvs. separate, bright green, infl. loose, and ovary glabrous. Calif.

Hallii A. Gray. Erect, glabrous, tufted per., to 8 in., sparingly glandular-pubescent in infl.; lvs. oblanceolate or linear-lanceolate, to 2 in. long, entire; corolla ¾ in. long, violet, abruptly inflated from a very short tube, staminode short-bearded. Colo.

Harbourii A. Gray. Per., to 6 in., from creeping rhizomes, glandular-pubescent in infl.; lvs. spatulate, oblanceolate or lanceolate-ovate, to ¾ in. long, entire, hairy; corolla ¾ in. long, lilac-purple, staminode densely bearded. Colo.

Hartwegii Benth. [*P. gentianoides* Lindl., not (HBK) Poir]. Glabrous per., to 4 ft., glandular-pubescent in infl.; lvs. lanceolate to ovate-lanceolate, to 4 in. long, acuminate, entire; corolla 2 in. long, scarlet, staminode slightly bearded at apex. Mex.

Harvardii A. Gray. Glabrous per., to 2 ft.; lvs. elliptic to oblong, entire, leathery; corolla 1 in. long, blue or violet, staminode glabrous. Tex.

Haydenii S. Wats. Glabrous per., to 2 ft., sts. decumbent; st. lvs. linear-lanceolate to linear, to 5 in. long, clasping, entire; corolla 1 in. long, blue, staminode bearded at apex. Nebr.

heterophyllus Lindl. Glabrous shrub, to 2 ft.; lvs. linear to lanceolate, to 2 in. long, entire; corolla to 1½ in. long, purple, staminode glabrous. Calif. Cv. 'Erectus' is listed. Subsp. **australis** (Munz & I. M. Johnst.) Keck. Densely puberulent; lvs. clustered. Subsp. **Purdyi** Keck. Decumbent, mat-forming; corolla blue to light purple; sometimes listed as *Penstemon* cv. **'California Blue Bedder'.**

hians: *P. Grinnellii.*

hirsutus (L.) Willd. [*P. pubescens* Soland.]. Per., to 3 ft., with fine, often glandular hairs, glandular-pubescent in infl.; st. lvs. lanceolate to oblong, to 4½ in. long, toothed, at first hairy then glabrate; corolla 1 in. long, purplish or violet, throat nearly closed, staminode bearded. Me. to Va. and Wisc. Cvs. 'Caeruleus', 'Purpureus', 'Pygmaeus', 'Roseus', and 'Rosinus' are listed.

humilis Nutt. ex A. Gray. Gray-puberulent, cespitose per., to 1 ft. or more, glandular-pubescent in infl.; st. lvs. oblanceolate to oblong in lower part, linear-lanceolate above, entire; corolla to ½ in. long, deep blue to blue-lavender, staminode golden-bearded. Calif. to Idaho, Wyo. and w. Colo.

hybridus: a listed name of no botanical standing.

imberbis (HBK) Trautv. Per., to 20 in.; lvs. linear, to 3 in. long, entire, glabrous; corolla to ¾ in. long, pinkish-red, staminode glabrous. Mex.

incertus Brandeg. Glaucous, shrubby per., to 3 ft., forming clumps, glabrous except moderately glandular-pubescent in infl.; lvs. linear-lanceolate, entire; corolla 1 in. long, violet or purple, limb deep blue, staminode included, densely bearded. Calif.

Jaffrayanus: *P. azureus.*

Jamesii Benth. Glabrate to pubescent per., to 1½ ft., glandular-pubescent in infl.; lvs. linear to oblanceolate, to 4 in. long, entire to serrate; corolla to 1¼ in. long, blue-lavender, staminode exserted, yellow-bearded. E. New Mex. to sw. Tex. Subsp. **ophianthus** (Penn.) Keck [*P. ophianthus* Penn.]. Fls. smaller, less than 1 in. long.

Keckii Clokey. Usually glaucescent per., to 6 in., glandular-pubescent in infl.; lvs. oblanceolate or lanceolate, entire; corolla to 1 in. long, deep blue, staminode densely yellow-bearded. S. Nev.

Kirkwoodii: a listed name of no botanical standing.

labrosus (A. Gray) Hook.f. Glabrous, somewhat glaucescent per., to 2½ ft.; lvs. entire, leathery, basal lvs. linear-oblanceolate, to 4½ in. long, st. lvs. linear; corolla 1½ in. long, scarlet, tubular, staminode glabrous. S. Calif. to n. Baja Calif.

laetus A. Gray. Hairy subshrub, to 2½ ft., glandular-pubescent in infl.; lvs. linear to lanceolate, to 4 in. long, entire; corolla to 1 in. long, blue-lavender to blue-violet, staminode glabrous. Calif. Subsp. **Roezlii** (Regel) Keck [*P. Roezlii* Regel]. Fls. ¾ in. long.

laevigatus (L.) Ait. [*Chelone Pentstemon* L.]. Nearly glabrous per., to 3 ft., glandular-pubescent in infl.; lvs. oblong to lanceolate, to 6 in. long, toothed; corolla to 1 in. long, purplish, staminode bearded. Penn., s. to n. Fla. and Miss. Var. **Digitalis:** *P. Digitalis.*

laricifolius Hook. & Arn. Glabrous or finely puberulent, cushion-forming per., to 10 in., from a much-branched subterranean root crown; lvs. in a dense rosette, filiform, to 1¼ in. long; corolla to ¾ in. long, purple, staminode yellow-bearded. Wyo. Subsp. **exilifolius** (A. Nels.) Keck [*P. exilifolius* A. Nels.]. Fls. smaller, corolla white, tinged greenish-yellow.

lemhiensis (Keck) Keck & Cronq. [*P. speciosus* subsp. *lemhiensis* Keck]. Glabrous or minutely pubescent per., to 2½ ft.; lvs. entire, basal lvs. lanceolate to oblanceolate; calyx to ½ in. long, segms. long-acuminate or subcaudate, corolla blue-purple. Lemhi Co. (Idaho).

leiophyllus Penn. Slightly glaucous per., to 2 ft., glabrous except glandular-pubescent in infl.; st. lvs. lanceolate, entire, clasping; corolla 1 in. long, blue, staminode slightly bearded to glabrous. S. Utah.

lentus Penn. Glaucous, glabrous per., to 1 ft.; lvs. thick, entire, basal lvs. elliptic, st. lvs. lanceolate to ovate, to 2¾ in. long, clasping; corolla ¾ in. long, purple-blue, staminode yellow-bearded. Colo. and Ariz. Subsp. **albiflorus** Keck. Fls. white.

linarioides A. Gray. Per., to 1½ ft., from a suffruticose root crown, herbage gray-pubescent with scalelike hairs, or glabrous; lvs. linear, to 1 in. long, entire; corolla ½ in. long, lilac to purple, staminode yellow-bearded. W. New Mex., se. Ariz. Subsp. **coloradoensis** (A. Nels.) Keck [*P. coloradoensis* A. Nels.]. Staminode bearded only at apex. Subsp. **taosensis:** *P. Crandallii* subsp. *glabrescens* var.

linearifolius: *P. Lyallii.*

Lyallii (A. Gray) A. Gray [*P. linearifolius* J. Coult. & E. Fisher]. Woody-based per., to 2½ ft., glabrous to finely pubescent, glandular-pubescent in infl.; lvs. linear to lanceolate, to 4¾ in. long, entire to serrate; corolla 1½ in. long, lavender, staminode glabrous. N. Idaho and w. Mont.

Manscanteri: a listed name of no botanical standing.

Menziesii: see *P. Davidsonii* subsp. Subsp. **Davidsonii:** *P. Davidsonii.*

micranthus: *P. procerus.*

microphyllus: *P. antirrhinoides* subsp.

miser A. Gray. Woody-based per., to 10 in., gray-pubescent, glandular-pubescent in infl.; lvs. mostly entire, basal lvs. linear-lanceolate to elliptic, st. lvs. linear to oblong; corolla to 1 in. long, dull purple, staminode stiffly orange-bearded. Ore. and adjacent Idaho, s. to cent. Nev. and n. Calif.

missouliensis: a listed name of no botanical standing.

montanus Greene. Glandular-pubescent per., to 8 in., forming loose clumps; lvs. elliptic to ovate, to 1½ in. long, serrate; corolla to 1½ in. long, lilac-purple, anthers woolly, staminode glabrous. Wyo., w. to Idaho and Mont.

Murrayanus Hook. Glabrous, glaucous per., to 3 ft.; lvs. ovate to oblong, to 4 in. long, entire, upper lvs. connate-perfoliate; corolla to 1 in. long, scarlet, tubular, staminode glabrous. E. Tex and adjacent Okla. and Miss.

Nelsoniae: *P. attenuatus.*

nemorosus (Dougl. ex Lindl.) Trautv. Puberulent, erect per., to 2½ ft., herbaceous to the base; lvs. lanceolate to ovate, to 4 in. long, serrate, thin; corolla to 1¼ in. long, rose-purple, anthers woolly, staminode densely short-bearded. Vancouver Is. to n. Calif.

neomexicanus Woot. & Standl. Glabrous, erect per., to 2½ ft.; basal lvs. linear-oblanceolate, st. lvs. linear to oblong, to 4 in. long, thick; corolla to 1 in. long, bright blue, throat hairy, staminode glabrous. New Mex.

Newberryi A. Gray. MOUNTAIN-PRIDE. Woody-based, decumbent or creeping, mat-forming per., to 1 ft. or more, mostly glabrous, glandular-pubescent in infl.; lvs. elliptic to ovate, to 1½ in. long, serrate, leathery; corolla to about 1¼ in. long, rose-red, anthers exserted,

woolly, staminode yellow-bearded. N. Calif. and adjacent Nev. Subsp. **Berryi** (Eastw.) Keck [*P. Berryi* Eastw.]. Fls. slightly larger, anthers included.

nitidus Dougl. ex Benth. Glaucous, glabrous per., to 1 ft.; lvs. entire, leathery, st. lvs. oblong to ovate; corolla to ¾ in. long, blue, staminode bearded its entire length. Man. and Sask., s. to w. N. Dak., ne. Wyo., Mont. Subsp. **polyphyllus** Penn. Plant larger; lvs. lanceolate to oblanceolate.

Olgae: a listed name of no botanical standing.

oliganthus Woot. & Standl. Slender per., to 1 ft., from a well-developed rosette, glabrous or puberulent, glandular-pubescent in infl.; lvs. entire, basal lvs. lanceolate to elliptic, to 5 in. long, st. lvs. lanceolate to linear-attenuate; corolla to 1 in. long, purplish-blue, staminode yellow-bearded. Colo., New Mex., e. Ariz.

ophianthus: *P. Jamesii* subsp.

oreganus: *P. Gairdneri* subsp.

Osterhoutii Penn. Glabrous, slightly glaucous per., to 3½ ft.; lvs. ovate to lanceolate-ovate, to 3½ in. long, fleshy-thickened, upper lvs. clasping; corolla to ¾ in. long, light purple to violet-purple, staminode densely golden-yellow-bearded. Nw. Colo. and adjacent Utah.

ovatus Dougl. ex Hook. Per., to 3 ft., glabrous or finely hairy, glandular-pubescent in infl.; lvs. toothed, basal lvs. lanceolate to ovate, to 6 in. long, st. lvs. triangular-ovate; corolla ¾ in. long, deep blue-purple, staminode bearded or rarely glabrous. S. B.C. to Ore.

pachyphyllus A. Gray ex Rydb. Glabrous, glaucous per., to 1 ft.; lvs. entire, thick, basal lvs. elliptic, st. lvs. lanceolate to ovate, to 2 in. long, clasping; corolla to ¾ in. long, blue-purple, throat hairy, staminode yellow-bearded. Utah. Subsp. **congestus** (M. E. Jones) Keck [*P. congestus* (M. E. Jones) Penn.]. Corolla throat nearly glabrous, staminode pale yellow-bearded.

pallidus Small. Per., to 2½ ft., soft hairy, glandular-pubescent in infl.; st. lvs. lanceolate to lanceolate-oblong, to 3½ in. long, remotely toothed or entire, leathery; corolla to 1 in. long, white with violet-purple lines, staminode densely yellow-bearded. Me., s. to Ga. and Kans.

Palmeri A. Gray. Robust, gray-glaucous, glabrous per., to 5 ft., glandular-pubescent in infl.; lvs. mostly toothed, basal lvs. oblong-ovate, st. lvs. lanceolate-ovate, to 6 in. long, clasping, upper pairs connate-perfoliate; corolla to 1¼ in. long, white, tinged pink or lilac, abruptly inflated, staminode exserted, shaggy-yellow-bearded. Calif., e. to Utah and Ariz. Subsp. **eglandulosus** Keck. Infl. glabrous.

Parryi (A. Gray) A. Gray. Erect, glabrous, glaucous per., to 4 ft.; lvs. entire, leathery, st. lvs. lanceolate to lanceolate-oblong, to 5 in. long, clasping; corolla to ¾ in. long, rose-magenta, abruptly inflated, staminode included, yellow-bearded. Ariz. to s. Sonora (Mex.).

payettensis A. Nels. & Macbr. Glabrous, clump-forming per., to 2 ft.; lvs. entire, thickish, basal lvs. oblanceolate, to 7 in. long, st. lvs. lanceolate-oblong to ovate; corolla to 1 in. long, purplish-blue, staminode glabrous. Ore. to cent. Idaho.

Peckii Penn. Clump-forming per., to 2 ft., puberulent to glabrous, glandular-pubescent in infl.; lvs. entire, basal lvs. lanceolate, to 2 in. long, st. lvs. linear-lanceolate; corolla ⅜ in. long, purplish-blue to white, staminode yellow-bearded at apex. Ore.

perpulcher A. Nels. Related to *P. speciosus*, but having corolla smaller, to 1 in. long, pollen sacs straight, and staminode bearded. Idaho.

pinetorum: *P. Wilcoxii.*

pinifolius Greene. Glabrous or finely puberulent, shrubby, much-branched per., to 2 ft.; lvs. crowded, filiform, ¾ in. long; corolla 1½ in. long, scarlet, tubular, staminode yellow-bearded. Sw. New Mex., se. Ariz., and adjacent Mex.

platyphyllus Rydb. Per., to 2 ft., with slightly glaucous herbage, somewhat hairy on younger shoots; lvs. to 2 in. long, upper lvs. lanceolate-elliptic to lanceolate-ovate; corolla to 1 in. long, lavender or violet, staminode glabrous. Utah and Nev.

polyphyllus: a listed name of no botanical standing, probably *P. nitidus* subsp.

pratensis Greene. Glabrous per., to 1½ ft., from a well-developed rosette; lvs. entire, thin, basal lvs. linear-oblanceolate to elliptic, to 3 in. long, st. lvs. oblong; corolla ½ in. long, white, staminode densely golden-bearded at apex. Ore. to sw. Idaho and ne. Nev.

procerus Dougl. ex R. C. Grah. [*P. micranthus* Nutt.]. Essentially glabrous per., to 1½ ft. or more; lvs. entire, thin, basal lvs. lanceolate to oblanceolate, st. lvs. oblong to lanceolate, to 3 in. long; corolla to ½ in. long, blue-purple, staminode short-yellow-bearded at apex. S. Alaska and Yukon to s. Colo. Subsp. **Tolmiei** (Hook.) Keck [*P. Tolmiei* Hook.]. More compact; lvs. basally tufted.

procumbens: *P. Crandallii* subsp.

pruinosus Dougl. ex Lindl. [*P. amabilis* G. N. Jones]. Viscid-puberulent, clump-forming per., 1–2 ft.; lvs. toothed, basal lvs. lanceolate to ovate, to 4 in. long, st. lvs. oblong to lanceolate-ovate; corolla ½ in. long, deep blue-purple, staminode sparingly yellow-bearded at apex. S. B.C. to cent. Wash.

pseudoprocerus: *P. attenuatus* subsp.

pseudospectabilis M. E. Jones. Robust per., to 40 in., glabrous, glandular-pubescent in infl.; lvs. prominently toothed, glaucous, basal lvs. lanceolate-ovate to ovate, st. lvs. connate-perfoliate; corolla 1 in. long, rose-purple, staminode glabrous. Deserts, Calif., Ariz. Subsp. **connatifolius** (A. Nels.) Keck [*P. connatifolius* A. Nels.]. Lvs. finer-toothed; infl. glabrous.

pubescens: *P. hirsutus.*

pulchellus: *P. campanulatus.*

pumilus Nutt. Gray-pubescent, tufted per., to 5 in.; lvs. linear to linear-oblanceolate or spatulate, to 1 in. long; corolla ¾ in. long, blue-violet, staminode yellow-bearded. Idaho.

Purdyi: a listed name of no botanical standing.

pygmaeus: a listed name of no botanical standing, probably for *P. hirsutus* cv.

Rattanii A. Gray. Often stout per., to 4 ft., glabrous, glandular-pubescent in infl.; lvs. undulate-serrate, basal lvs. lanceolate to elliptic, st. lvs. oblong, to 2¼ in. long; corolla to 1 in. long, lavender to red-purple or violet-purple, staminode exserted, bearded. Ore. to n. Calif. Var. **minor:** *P. anguineus.*

rex: *P. speciosus.*

Richardsonii Dougl. ex Lindl. Subshrub, to 2½ ft., glabrous to hairy, glandular-pubescent in infl.; lvs. lanceolate to narrowly ovate, to 3 in. long, toothed to pinnatifid; corolla to 1¼ in. long, pink, rose-lilac, or bluish, staminode exserted, usually bearded. S. B.C. to cent. Ore.

Roezlii: *P. laetus* subsp.

rubicundus Keck. Erect per., to 4 ft., glaucous, glabrous, sparingly glandular-pubescent in infl.; lvs. toothed, basal lvs. oblong-ovate, st. lvs. ovate-lanceolate, to 4 in. long, clasping; corolla to 1½ in. long, rose, staminode exserted, hooked, yellow-bearded. Nev.

rupicola (Piper) T. J. Howell. Woody-based, mat-forming per., to 4 in., with herbage usually glaucous, glabrous to pubescent and infl. glandular-pubescent; lvs. elliptic to orbicular, to ¾ in. long, toothed; corolla to 1¼ in. long, deep rose, anthers woolly, staminode bearded at apex. Wash. to n. Calif. Cvs. **'Albus'** and **'Roseus'** are listed.

Rydbergii A. Nels. Usually glabrous per., to 1½ ft. or more, from a well-developed rosette; lvs. elliptic to oblanceolate to oblong, to 6 in. long, entire; corolla to ¾ in. long, deep indigo-blue, staminode golden-bearded at apex. S. Wyo., s. to n. Ariz. and New Mex. Subsp. **aggregatus** (Penn.) Keck [*P. aggregatus* Penn.]. Corolla lighter blue to purple.

saliens: *P. eriantherus.*

Scouleri: *P. fruticosus* subsp.

secundiflorus Benth. Glabrous, usually glaucous per., to 2 ft.; lvs. entire, basal lvs. oblanceolate, to 3 in. long, st. lvs. lanceolate to ovate-lanceolate, clasping; corolla ¾ in. long, lilac, staminode golden-bearded. Wyo. to cent. New Mex. Subsp. **lavendulus** Penn. Fls. smaller, corolla lavender-pink to lavender-blue.

sepalulus A. Nels. Glabrous, blue-glaucous subshrub, to 2½ ft.; lvs. linear to elliptic, to 3 in. long, entire; corolla to 1 in. long, pale lavender to pale violet, staminode glabrous. Utah.

serpyllifolius: a listed name.

serrulatus Menz. ex Sm. [*P. diffusus* Dougl. ex Lindl.] Subshrub, to 2 ft., herbage often glabrous, but puberulent in upper part and in infl.; lvs. elliptic, lanceolate to ovate, to 3½ in. long, subentire to deeply toothed; corolla to 1 in. long, blue to purple, staminode yellow-bearded. S. Alaska to nw. Ore. Cv. **'Albus'** is listed.

Smallii A. Heller. Per., to 2½ ft. or more, finely puberulent, glandular-pubescent in infl.; lvs. serrate, basal lvs. elliptic or ovate, st. lvs. lanceolate to triangular-ovate, to 5 in. long; corolla 1 in. long, pink-purple striped with white inside, staminode yellow-bearded. N.C. and Tenn.

speciosus Dougl. ex Lindl. [*P. glaber* var. *speciosus* (Dougl. ex Lindl.) Rydb.; *P. rex* A. Nels. & Macbr.]. Clump-forming, glabrous or hairy per., to 2½ ft.; lvs. entire, basal lvs. lanceolate to oblanceolate, to 6 in. long, st. lvs. linear-lanceolate; corolla 1–1½ in. long, blue-purple, pollen sacs twisted, staminode glabrous. Cent. Wash. to s. Calif., e. to sw. Idaho and Utah. Subsp. **lemhiensis:** *P. lemhiensis.*

spectabilis Thurb. ex A. Gray. Erect, glabrous, glaucous per., to 4 ft.; lvs. oblanceolate to ovate, to 4 in. long, upper lvs. connate-perfoliate, serrate; corolla to 1¼ in. long, lavender-blue, staminode glabrous. S. Calif. to n. Baja Calif.

stenosepalus: *P. Whippleanus.*

strictus Benth. Mostly glabrous, often somewhat glaucous per., to 2½ ft. or more; lvs. entire, basal lvs. oblanceolate, to 6 in. long, st. lvs. linear-lanceolate to ovate-lanceolate or oblanceolate; corolla to 1 in. long, deep blue, anthers hairy, staminode glabrous to sparingly bearded. S. Wyo., Utah to n. New Mex. and ne. Ariz.

subglaber Rydb. Glabrous per., to 1½ ft.; lvs. entire, basal lvs. oblanceolate or linear, to 4 in. long, st. lvs. linear to lanceolate; corolla 1 in. long, blue or violet, anthers hairy, staminode yellow-bearded at apex. Utah and Wyo.

subulatus M. E. Jones. Erect, glabrous per., to 2 ft.; lvs. entire, green or glaucescent, basal lvs. oblanceolate to elliptic, st. lvs. linear-lanceolate to linear-subulate, to 3 in. long, clasping; corolla to 1 in. long, scarlet, tubular, staminode usually glabrous. Ariz.

ternatus Torr. ex A. Gray. Glabrous, glaucous, straggly or sometimes scandent shrub, to 5 ft.; lvs. in whorls of 3, linear-lanceolate, to 2 in. long, toothed; corolla to 1¼ in. long, scarlet, tubular, staminode densely yellow-bearded. S. Calif. Subsp. **septentrionalis** (Munz & I. M. Johnst.) Keck. Calyx and pedicels glandular-pubescent.

teucrioides Greene. Ascending to erect, gray-pubescent per., to 4 in., from a stout woody root crown; lvs. linear, to ½ in. long, mucronate, involute; corolla to ¾ in. long, pale blue to blue-purple, staminode golden-bearded. Colo.

Thompsoniae (A. Gray) Rydb. Gray-puberulent, prostrate or ascending per., forming mats or tufts to 2 in. high and to 1 ft. across; lvs. spatulate-oblong to obovate, to ¾ in. long, entire, thick; corolla to ¾ in. long, blue-violet, nearly tubular, staminode golden-bearded. S. Nev. and adjacent Calif., s. Utah, n. Ariz. Subsp. **Jaegeri** Keck. Corolla tubular-campanulate, ½ in. long.

Thompsonii: a listed name of no botanical standing for *P. Davidsonii* subsp.

Thurberi Torr. Glabrous, intricately branched bush, to 2 ft.; lvs. linear, to 1¼ in. long, involute; corolla to ½ in. long, lavender-rose, staminode glabrous. S. Calif. to n. Baja Calif., e. to Ariz. and New Mex.

Tidestromii Penn. Puberulent per., to 1½ ft.; lvs. oblanceolate, to 4¾ in. long, entire, somewhat glaucous, upper lvs. clasping; corolla to ¾ in. long, blue, staminode yellow-bearded. Utah.

Tolmiei: *P. procerus* subsp.

Torreyi: *P. barbatus* subsp.

triflorus A. Heller. Erect per., to 3 ft., glabrous, except glandular-puberulent in infl.; lvs. toothed, basal lvs. spatulate, st. lvs. oblong to ovate-lanceolate, to 4 in. long; corolla to almost 1½ in. long, rose-purple, staminode glabrous. Cent. Tex. Subsp. **integrifolius** Penn. Lvs. linear to lanceolate, mostly entire.

triphyllus Dougl. ex Lindl. Subshrub, to 2½ ft., with herbage more or less puberulent, and infl. glandular-pubescent; lvs. usually in whorls of 3, linear to linear-lanceolate, to 2 in. long, nearly entire to cleft; corolla to ¾ in. long, pale lavender to lilac-blue, staminode densely yellow-bearded. W. Idaho to e. Wash. and Ore. Subsp. **diphyllus** (Rydb.) Keck [*P. diphyllus* Rydb.]. Lvs. opp., wider, staminode lightly bearded.

tubiflorus Nutt. Per., to 3 ft., glabrous, except glandular-pubescent in infl.; lvs. elliptic-lanceolate to ovate, to 4 in. long, entire to finely serrate; corolla to 1 in. long, white, staminode bearded. Wisc., sw. to Nebr., s. to La. and e. Tex.; also Me. to Penn.

unilateralis Rydb. Glabrous per., to 2 ft. or more; lvs. entire, sometimes glaucous, basal lvs., oblanceolate, st. lvs. linear-lanceolate to ovate-lanceolate, to 4 in. long, clasping; fls. in one-sided infl., corolla to 1 in. long, blue, staminode usually glabrous. Se. Wyo. to n. New Mex.

utahensis Eastw. Glabrous per., to 2 ft.; lvs. entire, leathery, glaucous, basal lvs. lanceolate, st. lvs. lanceolate-oblong, to 3 in. long, clasping; corolla to 1 in. long, carmine, tubular, staminode hooked, glabrous. E. Calif. to Utah.

variabilis Suksd. Woody-based, much-branched per., to 2 ft., glabrous, except glandular-pubescent in infl.; lvs. linear to lanceolate-oblong, to 2 in. long, 2–4 at a node, toothed; corolla ½ in. long, yellowish-white striped with red, staminode sparingly bearded at apex. Wash. and Ore.

venustus Dougl. ex Lindl. Nearly glabrous, often glaucescent subshrub, to 2½ ft.; lvs. elliptic or oblong to lanceolate, to 4¾ in. long, toothed; corolla 1 in. long, light violet to violet-purple, stamen filaments and staminode white-bearded toward apex. Wash., Ore. to n. cent. Idaho.

virens Penn. Slender per., to 1 ft. or more, forming dense clumps; lvs. mostly entire or toothed, glabrous, basal lvs. lanceolate to elliptic, to 3 in. long, st. lvs. lanceolate, often clasping; corolla to ½ in. long, bright blue, staminode golden-bearded. Se. Wyo. to Colo.

virgatus A. Gray. Per., to 2 ft. or more; lvs. entire, basal lvs. linear-spatulate, st. lvs. linear to linear-lanceolate, to 4 in. long; corolla to

¾ in. long, blue, lilac, or white, staminode dilated at apex, glabrous. Ariz. and New Mex.

Watsonii A. Gray. Erect, clump-forming per., to 2 ft., from a woody root crown; lvs. lanceolate, to 3 in. long, puberulent or glabrous; corolla ¾ in. long, light blue to blue-purple, staminode densely golden-bearded. S. Idaho to n. Ariz. and sw. Colo.

Wherryi Penn. Per., to 2 ft., grayish-puberulent, glandular-pubescent in infl.; lvs. entire to serrate, thin, basal lvs. elliptic, to 2 in. long, st. lvs. lanceolate, clasping; corolla ¾ in. long, pale lilac, staminode yellow-bearded. E. Okla. and w. Ark.

Whippleanus A. Gray [*P. arizonicus* A. Heller; *P. glaucus* var. *stenosepalus* A. Gray; *P. stenosepalus* (A. Gray) T. J. Howell]. Often stout, clump-forming per., to 2 ft. or more, usually glabrous, glandular-pubescent in infl.; lvs. entire or toothed, thin, basal lvs. elliptic-oblong to ovate, to 4 in. long, st. lvs. lanceolate to oblong; corolla 1 in. long, purple or lavender, staminode exserted, yellow-bearded at apex. Sw. Mont. to Ariz. and New Mex.

Whitedii Piper. Per., to 1 ft., with herbage glabrous to gray-puberulent, and infl. glandular-pubescent; lvs. linear, lanceolate or oblanceolate, upper lvs. cordate, clasping, entire to toothed; corolla to 1 in. long, red-purple, staminode densely golden-yellow-bearded. Cent. Wash.

Wilcoxii Rydb. [*P. pinetorum* Piper]. Per., to 3 ft. or more, usually glabrous, lightly glandular-pubescent in infl.; lvs. lanceolate to ovate, nearly entire to toothed, st. lvs. to 3 in. long; corolla to 1 in. long, bright blue to bluish-purple, staminode yellow-bearded. E. Wash. and Ore. to w. Mont.

Wrightii Hook. Rather stout, glabrous, slightly glaucous per., to 2 ft.; lvs. obovate or oblong, entire, upper lvs. clasping; corolla ¾ in. long, bright rose-red, staminode bearded. W. Tex. and New Mex.

xylus: *P. Crandallii.*

PENTACHONDRA R. Br. *Epacridaceae.* About 3 spp. of small shrubs, native to se. Australia and New Zeal.; lvs. crowded; fls. axillary at ends of brs., with several small bracts, 5-merous; corolla tubular, lobes recurved or revolute, bearded inside, tube short, stamens inserted at rim of tube and shortly exserted; fr. drupelike, stones usually 5, each 1-seeded.

Cultivation as for *Erica;* prefers cool summers. Zone 9.

pumila (J. R. Forst. & G. Forst.) R. Br. Procumbent, much-branched, to 6 in. high and about 16 in. across; lvs. many, ovate to oblong, to ³⁄₁₆ in. long, 3–5-veined, subsessile; fls. white to reddish, solitary, subsessile, sepals and bracts fringed with hairs, corolla lobes recurved; fr. ellipsoid or globose, ¼ in. in diam., red to orange, pulpy, with 3–10, mostly 5, stones. Se. Australia, New Zeal.

PENTAGLOTTIS Tausch. *Boraginaceae.* One sp., a hairy per. herb, native to Eur.; lvs. ovate, with conspicuous netted venation; fls. blue, in bracted, racemose, scorpioid cymes, calyx 5-lobed, corolla 5-lobed, with scales in the throat, stamens 5, included; fr. of 4 stalked nutlets.

sempervirens (L.) Tausch [*Anchusa sempervirens* L.]. Per., 1–3 ft.; basal lvs. broadly ovate, petioled, st. lvs. sessile; fls. rich blue, to ¼ in. long, nearly sessile, in long-peduncled, axillary infl. Spring, summer. Eur.

PENTAPTERYGIUM: *AGAPETES.*

PENTAS Benth. *Rubiaceae.* About 34 spp. of herbs or shrubs, native to Afr. and Madagascar; lvs. opp., sometimes whorled, usually ovate to lanceolate, stipules divided; fls. in terminal corymbs, often dimorphic or trimorphic, usually 5-merous, corolla tube long; fr. a caps., seeds many, minute.

Grown in warm greenhouses or bedded out in southern U.S. Propagated by cuttings of half-ripe wood over heat.

Bussei Kurt Krause [*P. coccinea* Stapf]. Shrub, to 4 ft. or more, erect or somewhat scrambling, pubescent; lvs. usually ovate, to 6 in. long, white-hairy beneath; fls. dimorphic, calyx lobes unequal, 1–3 of them enlarged, lanceolate, to ½ in. long, the remainder linear, to ¼ in. long, corolla bright scarlet, tube to ¾ in. long. E. Trop. Afr.

carnea: *P. lanceolata.*

coccinea: *P. Bussei.*

lanceolata (Forssk.) Deflers [*P. carnea* Benth.]. STAR-CLUSTER, EGYPTIAN S. Herb or subshrub, to 4½ ft.; lvs. ovate to lanceolate, to 3½ in. long, hairy; fls. variously colored, magenta, pink, lilac, or white, dimorphic, calyx lobes unequal, ⅛–½ in. long, corolla tube variable in length, ¾–1½ in. long. E. Trop. Afr. to s. Arabia.

mussaendoides Bak. Shrub, to 15 ft., erect, sts. brown-pubescent; lvs. elliptic to elliptic-oblong, to 4 in. long; fls. probably dimorphic, calyx lobes unequal, one lobe enlarged, leaflike, corolla tube to 1 in. long. Madagascar.

PEPEROMIA Ruiz & Pav. [*Rhynchophorum* (Miq.) Small]. RADIATOR PLANT. *Piperaceae.* Perhaps 1,000 spp. of mostly small, succulent herbs of wide distribution in trop. and subtrop. areas; sts. commonly stout; lvs. alt., opp., or whorled, simple, entire, usually fleshy and petioled, often ciliate even when otherwise glabrous, commonly with several to many main veins palmately disposed or arising near base of blade; spikes terminal or lateral, mostly cylindrical; fls. very small, sessile, unisexual, perianth none, but each fl. subtended by a bract, stamens 2, pistil 1, stigma 1, sometimes 2-cleft; frs. small, drupelike, 1-seeded, occasionally stalked.

Peperomias require warm temperatures, but little light. Many of the species are epiphytes, preferring high atmospheric humidity but little soil moisture. Potting in mixtures of low water-holding capacity with excellent drainage prevents overwatering. Propagated by stem cuttings, or some species by division of crowns, or by leaves in sand over bottom heat.

acuminata Ruiz & Pav. To 2 ft. or more, little-branched, glabrous; lvs. alt., elliptic, lanceolate, or oblanceolate, to 5 in. long and 1½ in. wide, sharply acuminate, cuneate, pinnately veined, short-petioled; spikes solitary, terminal, to 5 in. long, peduncles 1–2 in. long. N. S. Amer. Material offered under this name may be *P. elongata* var. *guianensis.*

angulata: *P. quadrangularis.*

argyreia E. Morr. [*P. peltifolia* Hort., not C. DC.; *P. Sandersii* C. DC.]. WATERMELON BEGONIA, WATERMELON P. To 6–12 in., glabrous, sts. very short; lvs. more or less tufted, alt., orbicular-ovate, to 5½ in. long and 4 in. wide, acute-acuminate, nearly centrally peltate, dark green and with gray zones between the 9–11 radiating veins above, pale green beneath, petioles 3–10 in. long, reddish; spikes commonly 3–5 in an open panicle, to 4 in. long, peduncles about as long as petioles. Tropics, S. Amer.

arifolia Miq. Very similar to *P. argyreia,* but lvs. not silver-striped, spikes simple, to 8 in. long, on peduncles to twice as long as spikes. Brazil, Argentina. Var. **litoralis:** a listed name of no botanical standing; see *P. Verschaffeltii.*

Berlandieri Miq. Creeping, brs. ascending, to 4 in. long, sts. and petioles finely puberulent; lvs. in whorls of 4, broadly to narrowly obovate, to ⁵⁄₁₆, rarely ⅜ in. long, obtuse or emarginate, 1-nerved, short-petioled; spikes equal, peduncles terminal, solitary, to ¾ in. long; fls. sunken in pits having ciliate-hirtellous margins. Mex. to Costa Rica.

bicolor Sodiro. To 10 in., branched, stoloniferous, somewhat pubescent; lvs. alt., elliptic to obovate, to 2 in. long and half as wide, progressively smaller upward, acute at each end, purplish beneath, petioles short, channelled; spikes to 2⁵⁄₁₆ in. long. Ecuador. May not be distinct from *P. velutina.*

blanda (Jacq.) HBK. To 2 ft. or more, decumbent at base, villous, sts. and petioles reddish; lvs. mostly opp., sometimes in 3's, elliptic to oblanceolate or obovate, often nearly rhombic, to 4 in. long, acute, palmately 3(–5)-nerved, red beneath, short-petioled; spikes many, slender, to 5 in. long. W. Indies, n. S. Amer., Mex. Var. **blanda.** The typical var.; to 1 ft. or more; lvs. to 2 in. long and 1 in. wide. Var. **Langsdorfii** (Miq.) Henschen [*P. Langsdorfii* Miq.]. To 20 in. or more; lvs. to 4 in. long and 1½ in. wide. W. Indies, n. S. Amer.

brevipes: *P. rotundifolia* var. *pilosior.*

camptotricha Miq. Similar to *P. Liebmannii,* but lower lvs. (3–)4 in a whorl, nearly orbicular, about ½ in. in diam., upper lvs. opp., obovate-rhombic, 1 in. long and ⅝ in. wide. S. Mex.

caperata Yunck. EMERALD-RIPPLE P., GREEN-RIPPLE P., LITTLE-FANTASY P. Compact, tufted plant, to 6 in. or more, sts. very short; lvs. alt., ovate or suborbicular-ovate, to 2 in. long, acute, cordate, slightly peltate, palmately 5–7-veined, glossy dark green above, strongly plicate-bullate, petioles to 4 in. long, reddish; spikes many, to 4 in. long, whitish, peduncles to 6 in. long, reddish. Brazil? Cv. **'Variegata'.** Lvs. with small, irregular, central zone of green, and broad white margin.

clusiifolia (Jacq.) Hook. RED-EDGE P. To 10 in. or more, sts. red; lvs. alt., oblanceolate-oblong to obovate, to 3½(–6) in. long, obtuse to emarginate, nearly cuneately narrowed and abruptly truncate or somewhat auriculate basally, green or suffused purplish with red-purple margins, petioles to ¾ in. long; spikes terminal, solitary or paired, about 4 in. long. W. Indies, Venezuela. Cv. **'Variegata'.** Lvs. with broad, irregular, creamy-yellow border edged with red.

crassifolia Bak. LEATHER P. Sts. about 1 ft. long, decumbent, glabrous; lvs. alt., orbicular, ½ in. across, obtuse at apex, slightly pubescent beneath, short-petioled; spikes 2–3 in. long, peduncles short. Uganda. Doubtfully in cult.; material offered under this name has rhombic to obovate lvs. 3 in. long, and may represent *P. magnoliifolia.*

cubensis C. DC. Creeping or scandent, glabrous, internodes 2–4 in. long; lvs. alt., ovate, acuminate, cordate, to 3 in. long, margins minutely ciliate, 5–7-veined from the base, petioles to 2 in. long; spikes paired and lateral, or 3–4 in a terminal cluster, to ¾ in. long. Cuba. Cv. **'Variegata'.** Lvs. white-margined.

Dahlstedtii C. DC. [*P. Fosteri* Hort.]. VINING P. Trailing, nearly glabrous, sts. rooting at nodes, rather stiff, angular, reddish-purple, internodes 1–2 in. long; lvs. mostly 3(2–4) at a node, elliptic to obovate-elliptic, to 2 in. long or more, obtuse to shortly acuminate, dark green with 3–5 paler and sunken veins from base, short-petioled; spikes lateral, in groups of 3, to 5 in. long, subtended by small bracts on a common stalk to 1½ in. long. S. Brazil.

dolabriformis HBK. PRAYER P. Similar to *P. nivalis,* but larger throughout, with lvs. subsessile, to 1³⁄₁₆ in. long. Peru.

elongata HBK. Stoloniferous, essentially glabrous, sts. ascending, internodes to 2 in. long or more; lvs. alt., blades lanceolate-elliptic, to 3 in. long, 1 in. wide, acuminate, mostly obtuse to truncate at base, ciliate, obscurely 3-nerved from near base on each side, petioles to ¾ in. long, channelled, strongly ciliate; spikes 1 or more on a short stalk arising opp. lvs., to 5 in. long, peduncles subtended by a lanceolate bract to 1 in. long. Trop. S. Amer. Var. **guianensis** Yunck. More robust, sts. more pendulous, to about 2 ft. long; lvs. larger, to 4½ in. long and 2 in. wide. Guyana and Venezuela. Some material offered as *P. acuminata* may belong here.

emarginella (Swartz ex Wikstr.) C. DC. [*P. minima* C. DC.]. Prostrate, sts. filiform, long, glabrous; lvs. alt., orbicular-obovate to obcordate, to ³⁄₁₆ in. in diam., commonly emarginate apically, slightly peltate, palmately 3-veined, short-petioled; spikes to ¾ in. long but usually ⅜ in. long, glabrous. Tropics, N. and S. Amer.

Fenzlei Regel. Distinguished from *P. Liebmannii* in lvs. mostly in whorls of 4, rarely 3–6, with sts. and lvs. minutely puberulent. Nativity unknown.

floridana Small [*Rhynchophorum floridanum* (Small) Small]. Similar to *P. obtusifolium,* but lf. blades typically nearly orbicular or elliptic, to 3½ in. long. S. Fla.

Fosteri: a listed name of no botanical standing for *P. Dahlstedtii.*

Fraseri C. DC. [*P. resediflora* Linden & André]. FLOWERING P. To 2 ft., branched, tuberous, internodes 4–6 in. long; sts., petioles, and peduncles red; lvs. orbicular-ovate, to 1¾ in. long, acute to acuminate, palmately 5–9-veined, basal lvs. in a rosette, very succulent, sometimes nearly obovate, petioles to 4 in. long, st. lvs. in whorls of 3–5 in lower part, or opp. to alt. above, scarcely succulent, with petioles to 1½ in. long or uppermost lvs. subsessile; spikes in long-stalked, terminal panicles to 2 in. long, filiform, ⅜ in. long, white. Ecuador.

galioides HBK. Sts. nearly erect, to 3 ft. long, hirtellous; lvs. 4–5(3–9) at a node, elliptic-oblong to oblanceolate, to 1 in. long and ³⁄₁₆ in. wide, obtuse at apex, acute at base, petioles very short, hirtellous; spikes solitary or in whorls of 3–6, to 2¾(–6) in. long. Tropics, N. and S. Amer.

glabella (Swartz) A. Dietr. To 6 in. or more, stoloniferous; lvs. alt. or uppermost rarely opp., ovate to elliptic-lanceolate, to 3 in. long and 1 in. wide, acute to acuminate at both ends, palmately 3–5-veined, petioles short, sometimes ciliate; spikes slender, 3–6 in. long. Tropics, N. and S. Amer. Var. **glabella.** The typical var.; lvs. to 1⁵⁄₁₆ in. long and ½ in. wide, with 2 lines of hairs decurrent on the internodes from the margins of the petioles. Var. **nervulosa** (C. DC.) Yunck. Lvs. lanceolate, to 3 in. long and 1 in. wide. Material offered as *P. glabella* has broadly elliptic lvs. and doubtless represents a different but as yet undetermined sp.; a white-margined cv. of this is offered as *P. glabella* cv. **'Variegata'.**

griseoargentea Yunck. [*P. hederifolia* Hort.]. IVY-LEAF P., IVY P., PLATINUM P., SILVER-LEAF P. Compact, tufted plant, to 6 in. or more, sts. very short; lvs. alt., orbicular-ovate, to 2¾ in. long and 2⁵⁄₁₆ in. wide, rounded or blunt-acute at apex, cordate, peltate, glossy and gray to silvery-green above, darker along the 7–9 depressed, palmately disposed veins, moderately to strongly bullate, petioles to 4 in. long, red-marked; spikes 4–5 in. long, peduncles nearly equal, reddish. Brazil. Cv. **'Nigra'.** Lvs. black-green along veins.

hederifolia: a listed name of no botanical standing for *P. griseoargentea.*

Hoffmannii C. DC. Differentiated from *P. Berlandieri* in lvs. 3–5 in a whorl, spikes shorter, and peduncles swollen toward apex. Costa Rica to Colombia.

incana (Haw.) Hook. To 15 in., white-tomentose throughout; lvs. alt., close together, thick-fleshy, ovate-suborbicular, 2 in. long, obtuse or acuminate and blunt, cordate and often nearly peltate, 9-nerved, petioles 1⅜ in. long; spikes terminal, solitary or paired, 4–6 in. long. Brazil.

lanceolata C. DC. Sts. ascending, to 3 ft. long, densely villous at nodes, internodes 2–4 in. long; lvs. in whorls of 3–6, elliptic-lanceolate to nearly oblanceolate or rhombic, to 1½ in. long, acuminate at each end, with 3–5 pubescent veins above, petioles short; spikes terminal and axillary, to 3 in. long. Ecuador. Doubtfully in cult.; material offered under this name is described as having "lvs. very rich green with chartreuse veins along midrib."

Langsdorfii: *P. blanda* var.

leptostachya Hook. & Arn. To 8 in. high, hirtellous throughout, sts. decumbent; lvs. opp. or sometimes in 3's, thick, elliptic-obovate to elliptic or ovate, mostly to 1 in. long, acute or rounded apically, acute basally, sometimes red beneath, petioles to ⁵⁄₁₆ in. long; spikes many, axillary and terminal, to 4 in. long, peduncles short. Hawaii and other Pacific Is.

Liebmannii C. DC. To 18 in., rhizomatous, sts. densely hirsute, branched above; lvs. obovate to rhombic-obovate, to 1¼ in. long, acute apically, cuneate basally, 3-nerved, densely pubescent on both surfaces, short-petioled, lower lvs. in whorls of 5(4–6), thick-succulent, reddish beneath, lvs. of brs. 2–4 at a node, thinner, undulate, green; spikes many, axillary and terminal, very slender, to 3½ in. long, peduncles short, hairy. S. Mex.

maculosa (L.) Hook. [*P. variegata* Ruiz & Pav.]. To 1 ft., robust, sts. red-spotted, hairy; lvs. alt., elliptic-ovate to ovate or nearly orbicular, to 7 in. long, abruptly short-acuminate apically, peltate near base, faintly 7–11-veined or more from below middle, very dark green above, petioles 3–6 in. long, red-spotted, pubescent; spikes terminal, solitary or paired, to 12 in. long, maroon, peduncles 2–6 in. long. W. Indies, Panama, n. S. Amer.

magnoliifolia (Jacq.) A. Dietr. [*P. tithymaloides* Vahl?]. To 10 in. or more; lvs. alt., orbicular to obovate-elliptic or nearly spatulate, to 6 in. long, rounded to emarginate or acutish apically, cuneate or abruptly narrowed basally, 7–9- to many-veined from near base, petioles to 1 in. long; spikes 1–3, to 7 in. long, peduncles shorter than spikes, generally glabrous; frs. with sharp, curved beaks. W. Indies, Panama, n. S. Amer. Very closely related to *P. obtusifolia.* Cv. **'Variegata'.** Sts. spotted red; lvs. green, variegated yellow-green.

marmorata Hook.f. To 6 in. or more, glabrous throughout; lvs. opp., ovate, to 5 in. long and 3 in. wide, acute, not peltate but with basal lobes rounded and overlapping, dull green and with gray zones between the 5–7 radiating veins above, pale with reddish veins beneath, petioles shorter than blades; spikes to 6 in. long. S. Brazil.

metallica L. Linden & Rodig. Small, much-branched, glabrous, internodes short, reddish; lvs. alt., lanceolate to lanceolate-ovate, about 1 in. long, acute at apex, obtuse basally, pinnately-veined, bronzy with gray midrib above, pale with red veins beneath, short-petioled; spikes terminal, to 1½ in. long. Peru.

microphylla HBK. Spreading, brs. erect, to 6 in.; lvs. 4–5 at a node, oblong-elliptic to spatulate or occasionally orbicular-elliptic, to ⅜ in. long, obtuse apically, acute basally, faintly 1-nerved, nearly sessile; spikes terminal, to 1³⁄₁₆ in. long. Nw. S. Amer.

miniata: a listed name of no botanical standing, applied to a plant of very reduced size with red sts.

minima: *P. emarginella,* but the name *P. minima* has been variously applied to *P. rubella, P. galioides,* and to a cv. of *P. obtusifolia.*

Moninii C. DC. Erect, about 8 in., pubescent; lvs. opp., elliptic, 1⅜ in. long, narrowed toward each end, 3-veined, veins pubescent beneath, petioles about ⅜ in. long; spikes axillary, densely fld., peduncles 1 in. long, pubescent. Réunion Is. Material offered under this name may be misidentified, having sts. mostly pendent, to 1 ft. long, reddish-brown; lvs. opp., 1½ in. long, from elliptic to elliptic-subrhomboid, lower surfaces evenly pubescent and red especially in lower lvs.; spikes terminal, to 3½ in. long, subtended by a whorl of 4–5 lvs.

nigra: a listed name of no botanical standing for *P. griseoargentea* cv.

nivalis Miq. About 6 in. high in vegetative state, glabrous or powdery-glaucous, with pungent odor, sts. decumbent, finally elongating, ascending, bearing infl.; lvs. alt., very fleshy, hatchet-shaped, to ¾ in. long, laterally compressed and ¼ in. wide, to ⁵⁄₁₆ in. across in side view, mucronate, petioles to ⅜ in. long; spikes 10–12, slender, 2–3 in. long, in a terminal, bracted, loose panicle 8–10 in. long. Peru. Perhaps not specifically distinct from *P. dolabriformis.*

nummulariifolia: *P. rotundifolia.*

obtusifolia (L.) A. Dietr. [*Rhynchophorum obtusifolium* (L.) Small]. BABY RUBBER PLANT, AMERICAN R.P., PEPPER-FACE. To 6 in. or more; lvs. alt., spatulate-obovate, to 5(–8) in. long and 2(–3) in. wide, rounded to emarginate at apex, cuneate, petioles to 1½ in. long; spikes solitary or paired, to 6 in. long, peduncles 2–4 in. long; frs. with slender, strongly hooked beaks, usually minutely hirtellous. Trop. Amer. and s. Fla. Cv. **'Alba'**. Young growth entirely white-yellow, marked with bright red. Cvs. are: **'Albo-marginata'**, SILVER-EDGE P., lvs. gray-green centrally, with silvery border; **'Albo-marginata Minima'**, dwarf form of the preceding; **'Minima'**, compact plant, lvs. only 1½–2 in. long; **'Variegata'**, lvs. with broad irregular creamy-white margin, and central green area blotched with gray-green.

orba Bunt. [*Peperomia* cv. 'Astrid'; *P.* cv. 'Pixie'; *P.* cv. 'Princess Astrid', *P.* cv. 'Teardrop']. Much-branched, downy-pubescent, sts. ascending-decumbent, to 7 in. long or more, dotted purplish-red; lvs. alt., blades narrowly ovate to elliptic, to 2 5/16 in. long, half as broad, acute apically, truncate to obtuse basally, glossy on both sides, upper surface mottled with gray especially along midrib and lateral veins scarcely discernible, petioles to about 1 in. long, channelled; spikes terminal, solitary, to 6 in. long. Nativity unknown.

ornata Yunck. To 6 in. or more, glabrous throughout, internodes short; lvs. alt., mostly elliptic, to 5 in. long, obtuse at both ends, palmately 5(–7)-veined, dark green above, paler with red veins beneath, petioles to nearly 5 in. long, red; spikes in large, open panicles well above lvs., about 3 in. long, peduncles red. S. Venezuela.

peltifolia C. DC. Sts. villous; lvs. alt., ovate, to 11 in. long and 7 in. wide, acute apically, rounded or notched basally, peltate, hairy, radiately 9–11-veined, midrib with pinnate brs., petioles to 4¾ in. long, villous; spikes 6 in. long or more, with villous rachis and peduncle. W. Bolivia. Doubtfully in cult. Material offered under this name is probably *P. argyreia.*

pereskiifolia (Jacq.) HBK. Sts. to 10 in. long or more, weak, essentially glabrous, internodes 2–5 in.; lvs. in whorls of 3–6, often of unequal size in the same whorl, elliptic to elliptic-obovate, to 2 5/16 in. long, acute apically, palmately 3–5-veined, nearly acute at base and narrowed to a short petiole; spikes terminal, to 7 in. long, peduncles 2–3 in. long. Venezuela and Colombia.

pericata, pericatii: listed names of no botanical standing, probably synonyms of *P. polybotrya* or *P. tristachya.*

polybotrya HBK [*P. pericatii* Hort.?]. COIN-LEAF P. To 10 in. or more, glabrous; lvs. alt., orbicular-ovate, to 4 in. long, abruptly acute to acuminate, peltate, truncate to cordate basally, with 9–12 faint, radiating veins, glossy, petioles to 4½ in. long; spikes many, 1–2½ in. long, in large, terminal panicles to 1 ft. long and 6 in. wide. Colombia and Peru. Sometimes confused with *P. tristachya.*

prostrata: *P. rotundifolia* var. *pilosior.*

pseudovariegata C. DC. Sts. short, erect or procumbent; lvs. alt., oblong-lanceolate, to 5½ in. long, acute, pinnately veined, glabrous above, petioles to 3 in. long; spikes solitary or paired, to 7 in. long, peduncles to 2¾ in. long. Var. **pseudovariegata.** The typical var.; lvs. pubescent beneath. W. Colombia. Var. **sarcophylla** (Sodiro) Trel. & Yunck. [*P. sarcophylla* Sodiro]. Lvs. glabrous beneath. Ecuador and sw. Colombia.

pulchella: *P. verticillata.*

puteolata Trel. Sts. pendent, to 18 in. long or more, angular, purplish, leafless in basal 6 in. or more; lvs. 2–3 at a node, to 4½ in. long and 1¼ in. wide, long-acuminate, with 5 pale veins from the base, very dark green above, pale green beneath, petioles short; spikes lateral, paired, on short, common stalks bearing a pair of lanceolate bracts to ½ in. long, to 7 in. long or more. Peru.

quadrangularis (J. V. Thomps.) A. Dietr. [*P. angulata* HBK]. Sts. prostrate, slender, 4-angled; lvs. mostly opp., obovate, elliptic-rhombic to orbicular, to 1 3/16 in. long, obtuse, palmately 3-veined, bronzy when young with green veins, petioles short, hirtellous; spikes solitary or paired on equal, lateral peduncles, 1–2 in. long. W. Indies, Panama, n. S. Amer.

resediflora: *P. Fraseri.*

rotundifolia (L.) HBK [*P. nummulariifolia* HBK]. YERBA LINDA. Sts. creeping, filiform; lvs. alt., orbicular or orbicular-elliptic or -ovate, to nearly ½ in. long and ⅛ in. thick, obtuse at apex, faintly 3-veined, petioles to 3/16(–⅜) in. long; spikes terminal, to 1 5/16 in. long. Tropics, N. and S. Amer. Var. **rotundifolia.** The typical var.; commonly glabrescent; lvs. all green. Var. **pilosior** (Miq.) C. DC. [*P. brevipes* (Benth.) C. DC.; *P. prostrata* B. S. Williams ex M. T. Mast. & T. Moore]. Young sts. hairy; lvs. mostly orbicular-ovate, red-margined, ciliate, densely hairy above when young, green to red-brown with pale green reticulate pattern above.

rubella (Haw.) Hook. To about 6 in., hairy, sts. erect, much-branched, sts. and petioles crimson; lvs. in whorls of 4(3–6), obovate to elliptic, to ½ in. long, acute at apex, 3-nerved, dark green and sometimes with paler reticulate pattern above, crimson beneath, petioles very short; spikes axillary or terminal, slender, to 1 in. long. Jamaica. May not be specifically distinct from *P. verticillata.*

Sandersii: *P. argyreia.*

sarcophylla: *P. pseudovariegata* var.

scandens: *P. serpens,* but material offered as *P. scandens* differs in being larger, hairy, having sts. stout, with swollen nodes, lvs. ovate to nearly orbicular, to 3 in. long and 2 5/16 in. wide, long-acuminate, truncate to nearly cordate basally, 7-veined from below middle, and with petioles to 1¼ in. long. A white-margined cv. of this cult. material is offered as *P. scandens* cv. **'Variegata'.**

serpens (Swartz) Loud. [*P. scandens* Ruiz & Pav., not Hort.]. Sts. prostrate or scandent, slender, internodes to 1½ in. long; lvs. alt., orbicular-triangular, mostly to ¾ in. across, acute or obtuse apically, truncate-subcordate basally, palmately 3–5-veined, petioles to 1 3/16 in. long; spikes to 1 3/16 in. long, peduncles nearly equal. W. Indies; Panama to Peru and Brazil.

tithymaloides: apparently a variant of *P. magnoliifolia.*

trinervis Ruiz & Pav. To 10 in. high or more, stoloniferous, pubescent, sts. decumbent, red; lvs. alt., elliptic-ovate to elliptic-obovate, or lower ones nearly orbicular, to 1 5/16 in. long, acute to acuminate apically, acute or rounded at base, palmately 3–5-veined, villous on both sides at least along veins, petioles 5/16 in. long; spikes to 4 in. long, peduncles short. W. S. Amer.

tristachya HBK [*P. pericatii* Hort.?]. Erect, to 18 in.; differing from *P. polybotrya* in spikes only 3–4, white. Andes, Colombia.

urocarpa Fisch. & C. A. Mey. Sts. decumbent, to 6 in. long or more, appressed-pubescent; lvs. alt., orbicular-ovate, about 1–2 in. wide, abruptly short-acuminate, mostly truncate basally, palmately about 7-veined, petioles to 1½ in. long; spikes lateral toward tips of brs., to 1½ in. long, peduncles nearly equal. W. Indies, n. S. Amer.

variegata: *P. maculosa.*

velutina Linden & André. To about 1 ft., sts. zigzag, reddish, soft-hairy; lvs. alt., ovate-elliptic, to 3 in. long, acute-acuminate, 7-veined from near base, dark green and with silvery band along midrib and with silvery veins above, purplish-salmon with green veins beneath, petioles ⅜ in. long, hirtellous; spikes 2½ in. long. Ecuador.

Verschaffeltii Lem. To 6 in., sts. short; lvs. more or less tufted, alt., ovate-elliptic, obtuse, cordate at base, bluish-green with silvery bands between veins above, palmately 5–7-veined, petioles elongate, red; spikes solitary, stout, white. Peru? Material offered as *P. arifolia* var. *litoralis* Hort. with lvs. somewhat shorter and less regular stripes may belong here.

verticillata (L.) A. Dietr. [*P. pulchella* A. Dietr.]. To 1 ft. or more, sts. stout in lower part, slender above, hirsute; lvs. in whorls of 3–5, acute, pubescent on both sides, petioles very short, hairy, lower lvs. nearly orbicular to obovate, about ½ in. long, upper lvs. elliptic, seldom more than 1 in. long, blunt; spikes axillary and terminal, very slender, to 3 in. long. W. Indies.

viridis: a listed name of no botanical standing, applied to a plant with sts. decumbent, stout, elongate, with swollen nodes, lvs. lanceolate-ovate, of moderate size, acuminate, truncate at base, glossy green, and petioled.

PEPLIS L. [*Didiplis* Raf.]. WATER PURSLANE. *Lythraceae.* Eight spp. of ann. herbs, growing near or in water, native to Eur. and e. U.S.; lvs. opp. or alt., linear or oblanceolate; fls. regular, calyx tube broadly campanulate to globose, calyx lobes 4–6, appendages lacking or long-subulate, petals 6 and deciduous, or 0, stamens (2-?)4–6; fr. a caps., dehiscing irregularly.

diandra Nutt. ex DC. [*Didiplis diandra* (Nutt. ex DC.) A. Wood]. Submersed or rooting in mud, sts. to 16 in. long; lvs. many, submersed lvs. linear, to 1 in. long, emersed lvs. oblanceolate; calyx lobes 4, petals and appendages lacking, stamens 4. N.C. to Fla., w. to Minn. and e. Tex. Sometimes grown in aquaria.

PEPPER. The black or white condiment pepper of world commerce and spice markets is the small fruit or berry of a tropical Old World vine, *Piper nigrum.*

The green and red peppers of our vegetable gardens and markets, including hot chili peppers, are the fruits of several species of a very different New World genus, *Capsicum, Capsicum* plants are tender while young, although they endure some frost in autumn. Their culture is that recommended for eggplant, being grown as annuals although they are actually perennials. A small seedsman's packet of seed is sufficient for a large number of plants, say 200. The large bell peppers of the *C. annuum* Grossum Group are the mildest and are used for making stuffed peppers and other dishes. Paprika is made from the long, pointed type of fruit. The small, hot chili peppers are used for seasoning and sauces. It is better to start seeds indoors for the northern states, although early cultivars bear well from seed sown in the open ground as soon as it is thoroughly warm. The little seedlings may be transplanted from the original pan or flat to other flats or to pots before putting them in the garden. Rows should be as far apart as will admit of good tillage, usually 2–3 ft., and the plants may stand 10–18 inches apart in the row depending on the cultivar.

PERAMIUM: *GOODYERA.*

PERENNIAL. Derived from the Latin *perennis*, meaning enduring, perpetual, the word *perennial* is both noun and adjective denoting, in horticulture, a plant that persists more than two years, a one-year plant being an annual and a two-year plant a biennial. All shrubs and trees are perennial, but the word ordinarily connotes an enduring herbaceous plant, one that remains year after year. The perennial border is made up of such plants, among which are the larkspurs *(Delphinium)*, peonies *(Paeonia)*, columbines *(Aquilegia)*, and sedums *(Sedum)*. A perennial may not endure indefinitely, however; many of them are at their best in about the third year and then gradually decline; but some, like tansy *(Tanacetum vulgare)* and bouncing Bet *(Saponaria officinalis)*, may remain long after the house they were planted around falls down. It is enjoyable work to grow perennials from seed. Sown one spring, or sometimes in midsummer, the seeds should in most cases give blooming plants the following season.

PERESKIA Mill. LEAF CACTUS, BLADE APPLE. *Cactaceae.* Perhaps 20 spp. of leafy trees, shrubs, and vines of Mex., W. Indies, and Cent. and S. Amer., a few long cult. in warm countries; sts. woody, not jointed; lvs. alt., broad, deciduous; areoles spiny, without glochids; fls. stalked, solitary or corymbose or panicled, rotate, white or yellow to red, ovary superior to half-inferior. Sometimes incorrectly spelled *Peireskia* or *Peirescia.*

Although the pereskias are leaf-bearing plants, their culture does not differ particularly from that of other cacti. They are used as stocks on which to graft other kinds, but otherwise they are not much known in greenhouses. They are propagated from cuttings. For culture see *Cacti.*

aculeata Mill. [*P. Pereskia* (L.) Karst.]. BARBADOS GOOSEBERRY, LEMON VINE, LEAFY CACTUS. Erect at first, but becoming a vine to 30 ft. long; lvs. thick, lanceolate to ovate, acute, short-petioled, to 3 in. long; spines 1–3, recurved; infl. paniculate or corymbose; fls. white, yellow or pinkish, 1–1¾ in. across, ovary superior; fr. yellow, spiny, ¾ in. in diam. Widely grown for its fr. Trop. Amer. Cv. **'Godseffiana'** [*P. Godseffiana* Hort. Sander]. Often bushy; lvs. purplish beneath, blotched with crimson and yellow above. Cv. **'Rubescens'**. Lvs. red-variegated.

Bleo (HBK) DC. WAX ROSE. Tree, to 20 ft., trunk to 4 in. thick, becoming naked; lvs. oblong to oblanceolate, thin, to 8 in. long, petioles 1 in. long; fls. terminal, rose-colored, petals entire, ovary top-shaped-truncate, naked; fr. yellow, 2 in. long. Panama, Colombia. Plants cult. under this name are likely to be *P. grandifolia.*

Conzattii: *P. Pititache.*

Godseffiana: *P. aculeata* cv.

grandiflora: *P. grandifolia.*

grandifolia Haw. [*P. grandiflora* Hort. ex Pfeiff.]. ROSE CACTUS. Shrub or tree, to 15 ft., trunk very spiny; lvs. oblong, to 6 in. long, short-petioled; spines at first 1–2, to 2 in. long; fls. in mostly few-fld. terminal clusters, rose-colored or white, 1½ in. across, sepals green, style and stigma lobes white; fr. pear-shaped, with cuneate lvs. Brazil. Usually cult. under the name *P. Bleo.*

Pereskia: *P. aculeata.*

Pititache Karw. [*P. Conzattii* Britt. & Rose]. Tree, to 40 ft., trunk spiny, bark smooth; lvs. orbicular to obovate, acute, to 1 in. long; spines 2–6 on small sts. and 10–20 on large brs., to 1 in. long, yellowish to dark brown; ovary superior; fr. pear-shaped, naked, to 2 in. long. Mex.

sacharosa Griseb. Shrub or small tree, to 25 ft.; lvs. lanceolate to oblanceolate, acute, to 5 in. long, short-petioled; spines 1–3 on young and 3–6 on old brs., to 2 in. long, unequal; fls. in terminal clusters, white to rose-pink, to 3½ in. across, petals entire, ovary superior; fr.

1–1½ in. in diam., leafy, with wool and sometimes a spine in the axils. Paraguay and Ecuador.

PERESKIOPSIS Britt. & Rose. *Cactaceae.* About 10 spp. of trees and shrubs of Mex. and Cent. Amer.; lvs. broad and flat but thick; areoles with glochids; fls. lateral, mostly sessile, rotate, yellow to red, ovary leafy; fr. umbilicate by abscission of the perianth, seeds few, bony, covered with matted hairs. Allied to *Opuntia* but more similar to *Pereskia* in habit and foliage.

For culture see *Cacti.*

Chapistle (A. Web.) Britt. & Rose. Glabrous, branching shrub, to 16 ft.; lvs. obovate to nearly orbicular, acute, to 1½ in. long; areoles white, with few glochids, spines solitary, stout, to 2½ in. long; fls. yellow; fr. red. Mex.

Porteri (Brandeg.) Britt. & Rose. Glabrous, branching, to 4 ft.; lvs. obovate, acute, 1 in. long; areoles with many brown glochids, spines 1–8, sometimes more on trunk, to 2 in. long; fls. yellow, 1½ in. across; fr. orange, 2 in. long. Mex.

PEREZIA Lag. *Compositae* (Mutisia Tribe). About 70–80 spp. of ann. or per. herbs, rarely shrubby, native from sw. U.S. to Argentina; lvs. alt. or basal, mostly sessile, frequently clasping, margins often spinulose; fl. heads mostly in panicles or corymbose or thyrsoid cymes, involucral bracts imbricate in 2 to many rows, receptacle flat, naked or pilose; fls. all 2-lipped, bisexual, rose, purple, blue, or white, anthers sagittate at base; achenes nearly cylindrical to fusiform, pappus of many scabrous bristles.

multiflora (Humb. & Bonpl.) Less. Erect ann., to 1½ ft.; lvs. dentate-spinose, st. lvs. alt., sessile, ovate-lanceolate, 1½–3 in. long, basal lvs. oblong-lanceolate, much longer; heads to about 1 in. across, in a corymbose panicle; fls. bluish; pappus reddish. Peru to Argentina.

PERIBOEA Kunth. *Liliaceae.* About 2 spp. of scapose, bulbose, per. herbs, native to S. Afr.; bulb tunicate; lvs. basal; fls. rose to lilac, in few-fld. racemes, perianth 6-lobed, deciduous, stamens 6, mostly in 2 series, filaments arising from perianth tube, anthers versatile; fr. a 3-valved, loculicidal caps., seeds globose, black, 1–2 in each cell.

corymbosa (L.) Kunth [*Hyacinthus corymbosus* L.]. To 3 in.; lvs. 3–6, linear, to 5 in. long, channelled, rather fleshy; fls. lilac-rose, to ⅝ in. long, in a 4–8-fld. corymbose raceme, perianth tube ½ or ⅓ as long as segms., stamens exserted from tube.

PERIDERIDIA Rchb. YAMPAH. *Umbelliferae.* About 9 spp. of tuberous, per., branched herbs, often of damp places, native to cent. and w. U.S.; lvs. pinnate or ternately compound, ultimate divisions ovate to linear; umbels compound, usually with more or less scarious involucre and involucels; fls. small, white or pink; fr. compressed.

The tubers were eaten by Indians and early settlers.

Gairdneri (Hook. & Arn.) Mathias [*Carum Gairdneri* (Hook. & Arn.) A. Gray]. SQUAWROOT, EDIBLE-ROOTED CARAWAY, FALSE C., INDIAN C. To 4 ft.; lvs. pinnate, lfts. linear, upper lvs. usually simple; involucels of linear or setaceous bractlets; fls. white; fr. nearly orbicular. Mts., S. Dak. to B.C., s. to New Mex. and Calif.

PERILEPTA: *STROBILANTHES.*

PERILLA L. *Labiatae.* About 6 spp. of ann. herbs of se. Asia, naturalized elsewhere; sts. mostly square in cross section; lvs. opp., often colored or variegated; verticillasters 2-fld., in dense or loose terminal racemes, bracts short; fls. small, pedicelled, calyx campanulate, 10-nerved, 5-toothed, 2-lipped, corolla tube shorter than calyx, limb shortly 5-lobed, stamens 4, in 2 pairs, anthers 2-celled; fr. of 4 reticulate nutlets.

Propagated by seeds. Used for summer bedding, requiring a sunny or half-sunny location, and the same treatment as other half-hardy annuals. One species, *P. frutescens,* is widely cultivated in eastern Asia and Japan for its oil seeds.

atropurpurea: a listed name of no botanical standing for *P. frutescens* cv.

crispa: *P. frutescens* cv.

frutescens (L.) Britt. [*P. ocimoides* L.; *Ocimum frutescens* L.]. Erect, to 3 ft., sts. branched, densely pubescent; lvs. broadly ovate, to 5 in.

long, more or less acuminate, toothed, long-pubescent especially on nerves, greenish or purplish, long-petioled; calyx to ⅛ in. long, corolla white. Early autumn. Himalayas to e. Asia, where much cult. Cv. 'Atropurpurea'. Lvs. dark purple. Cv. 'Crispa' [*P. crispa* (Thunb.) Tanaka; *P. frutescens* var. *nankinensis* (Lour.) Britt.; *P. laciniata* Hort. ex W. Mill. & L. H. Bailey; *P. nankinensis* (Lour.) Decne.; *Ocimum crispum* Thunb.; *O. frutescens* var. *crispum* (Benth.) Decne.]. Lvs. laciniate-dentate, with wrinkled margins, often brightly colored purple or bronze. Naturalized in e. U.S., weedy.

laciniata: *P. frutescens* cv. *crispa.*

nankinensis: *P. frutescens* cv. *crispa.*

ocimoides: *P. frutescens.*

PERIPLOCA L. SILK VINE. *Asclepiadaceae.* About 12 spp. of woody twiners, native to s. Eur., Asia, and Afr.; lvs. opp., entire; fls. in terminal or axillary cymes, corolla rotate, corona of 5 or 10 lobes, united at the base to the corolla, stamens with very short, free filaments, anthers united at apex, villous on the back; fr. a cylindrical, glabrous follicle.

Silk vines grow in well-drained soil in sunny locations and may need winter protection in the North. Best propagated by division, but may be increased by layering or by cuttings under glass in summer, or may be grown from seeds.

graeca L. Deciduous, glabrous twiner, to 40 ft.; lvs. ovate to oblong-lanceolate, 2–5 in. long; fls. in long-peduncled terminal cymes, corolla purplish inside, greenish outside, 1 in. across, lobes oblong, spreading, villous-margined, corona of 5 slender threadlike appendages; follicles paired, slender, to 5 in. long. Se. Eur. and w. Asia.

sepium Bunge. Similar to *P. graeca*, but smaller and more delicate, having lvs. lanceolate, to 3 in. long, ¾ in. broad; fls. about ¾ in. across, with recurved corolla lobes; follicles slender, twisted. China.

PERISTERIA Hook. *Orchidaceae.* Nine spp. of epiphytes, native to trop. Amer.; pseudobulbs 1–5-lvd.; lvs. plicate, often seasonally deciduous; infl. basal, racemose; fls. fleshy, conspicuous, globose, upper sepal separate, concave, lateral sepals somewhat united at base, petals smaller, lip very fleshy, 2-parted, the basal part (hypochil) jointed to column foot, lobed, the apical part (epichil) entire. For structure of fl. see *Orchidaceae.*

For culture see *Orchids.*

Barkeri: *Acineta Barkeri.*

cerina Lindl. Pseudobulbs ovoid, to 3 in. long, 3–4-lvd.; lvs. oblong-lanceolate, to 1 ft. long; racemes pendent, short, densely 6–10-fld.; fls. 1 in. across, with the fragrance of juniper, pale lemon-yellow, waxy, sepals and petals broadly ovate, concave, hypochil of lip 3-lobed, the lateral lobes ovate, epichil emarginate, crisped. Costa Rica.

elata Hook. HOLY GHOST FLOWER, DOVE F., DOVE ORCHID. Pseudobulbs ovoid, to 5 in. long, 3–5-lvd.; lvs. lanceolate, plicate at apex, to about 3 ft. long; racemes solitary, erect, simple, to 4 ft. long, bearing 10–15 fls. or more; fls. waxy, white, fragrant, opening in succession from the lowermost upward, sepals ovate, concave, 1¼ in. long, petals elliptic-ovate, 1 in. long, hypochil of lip broad, white, spotted with rose-red, epichil white, column and beaked anther white. Summer. Costa Rica to Colombia and Venezuela. The national fl. of Panama. Requires a liberal supply of moisture during growth, and the general treatment given *Calanthe.*

Humboldtii: *Acineta superba.*

PERISTROPHE Nees. *Acanthaceae.* About 15 spp. of herbs or subshrubs in tropics of the Old World; lvs. opp., entire; fls. solitary or in clusters in the axils, calyx deeply 5-lobed, mostly shorter than the bracts, corolla with 2 equal lips, rose or purple, tube slender, stamens 2, borne in throat of corolla; fr. an ellipsoid caps., seeds 4.

Grown in the greenhouse where they need abundant air and rich loamy soil. Propagated by cuttings.

angustifolia: *P. hyssopifolia.*

aurea-maculata: a listed name of no botanical standing; may refer to *P. hyssopifolia* cv. 'Aureo-variegata'.

hyssopifolia (Burm.f.) Bremek. [*P. angustifolia* Nees; *P. salicifolia* (Blume) Hassk.]. Per.; lvs. lanceolate, to 3 in. long; fls. rose, in terminal clusters. Perhaps Java. Cv. 'Aureo-variegata'. MARBLELEAF. Lvs. variegated centrally with yellow.

salicifolia: *P. hyssopifolia.*

speciosa (Roxb.) Nees. Woody per., to 3 ft.; lvs. ovate, to 5 in. long; fls. violet-purple, 2 in. across, 2–3 together on slender brs. or peduncles in upper lf. axils. India.

PERNETTYA Gaud.-Beaup. *Ericaceae.* About 25 spp. of low, evergreen shrubs, native to New Zeal. and Tasmania and from Mex. to s. S. Amer.; lvs. alt., simple, leathery; fls. white, usually solitary and axillary, calyx 5-parted, corolla urceolate or campanulate, stamens 10, anthers usually awned, ovary superior; fr. a white or bright-colored berry, persisting throughout the winter.

Pernettyas thrive in sunny locations in rather moist, peaty soil. Fairly hardy north. Propagated by seeds, cuttings of half-ripe wood, layers, and suckers.

angustifolia: *P. mucronata* var.

leucocarpa: *P. pumila* var.

macrostigma Colenso [*Gaultheria macrostigma* Hort.; *G. perplexa* T. Kirk ex Cheesem.]. Trailing shrub, to 3 ft., brs. wiry; lvs. linear to oblong, to ½ in. long, bristly-serrate; corolla campanulate; fr. rosy-pink. New Zeal.

mucronata (L.f.) Gaud.-Beaup. ex K. Spreng. [*P. rupicola* Phil.]. Rigid, much-branched shrub, to 3 ft.; lvs. ovate-lanceolate to ovate, to ¾ in. long, sharp-pointed; fls. white to pinkish, corolla urceolate, ¼ in. long. Late spring. Straits of Magellan region to Chile. Zone 7. Var. **angustifolia** (Lindl.) Reiche [*P. angustifolia* Lindl.]. Lvs. narrower, smaller; fls. smaller.—Cvs. are: 'Alba', fr. white; 'Coccinea', fr. scarlet; 'Rosea', fr. rosy-pink; 'Rubra', fr. dark red.

nana Colenso. Low, creeping, mat-forming shrub, to 3 in. high; lvs. oblong-lanceolate, to ³⁄₁₆ in. long, entire or remotely toothed; calyx lobes acute, corolla campanulate, less than ³⁄₁₆ in. long, filaments smooth, longer than the styles, anthers with 4 rigid awns; fr. reddish. New Zeal. Some material offered under this name may be *P. tasmanica.*

Pentlandii: *P. prostrata* subsp.

prostrata (Cav.) Sleum. Rigid, prostrate shrub, to 1 ft.; lvs. ovate to ovate-lanceolate, to ⅝ in. long, glabrous, shining; corolla globose-urceolate, ⁵⁄₁₆ in. long; fr. blue-black. Costa Rica to n. Chile. Zone 7. Subsp. **Pentlandii** (DC.) B. L. Burtt [*P. Pentlandii* DC.]. Lvs. narrowly elliptic to oblong-lanceolate, to 1⅛ in. long; fls. urceolate; fr. purplish-black.

pumila (L.f.) Hook. Straggling, cespitose shrub; lvs. oblong-elliptic, to ⅛ in. long, glabrous; corolla campanulate, ⅛ in. long; fr. pink or white. S. S. Amer. Var. **leucocarpa** (DC.) Kausel [*P. leucocarpa* DC.]. Taller; lvs. to ⅝ in. long. S. Chile. Zone 7.

rupicola: *P. mucronata.*

tasmanica Hook.f. Creeping, glabrous per., to 3 in. long; lvs. oblong, to ⁵⁄₁₆ in. long, obscurely crenate; corolla campanulate, to ¼ in. long, filaments papillose, swollen at base, anthers not awned; fr. bright red. Tasmania. Zone 7. Material so listed in cult. may be *P. nana.*

PEROVSKIA Kar. *Labiatae.* About 7 spp. of per. herbs, native from e. Iran to nw. India; sts. mostly square in cross section, woody at base; lvs. opp., incised or dissected; fls. small, in 2- to many-fld. verticillasters arranged in terminal racemes or panicles, calyx tubular, 2-lipped, hirsute or pilose, corolla tube slightly longer than calyx, limb 5-lobed, stamens 2, anthers 2-celled, staminodes 2; fr. of 4 glabrous nutlets.

Easily grown in full sun in average soil. Hardy; propagated by seeds or cuttings of young wood kept under glass or mist.

abrotanoides Kar. To 3 ft.; upper st. lvs. ovate, 2-pinnately cut, to 2 in. long; infl. narrowly paniculate; fls. blue. Turkestan to ne. Iran.

artemesioides Boiss. To 3 ft.; upper lvs. ovate-oblong, pinnately parted, to 1¼ in. long, ¾ in. wide, petioled; infl. narrowly paniculate; fls. blue-purple. Se. Iran, e. to w. Pakistan.

atriplicifolia Benth. To 3 ft., or more; upper lvs. ovate-oblong, to 1½ in. long, obtuse or acute, entire or weakly dentate; infl. spreading-paniculate; fls. lavender-blue. W. Pakistan.

PERSEA Mill. [*Machilus* Nees]. *Lauraceae.* About 150 spp. of trop. evergreen trees; lvs. alt., entire, pinnately veined; fls. in axillary panicles, small, greenish, not showy, bisexual, perianth segms. 6, fertile stamens 9, anthers 4-celled, introrse in first 2 whorls, extrorse in whorl 3; fr. a berry or drupe, usually globose, seated on the persistent calyx tube.

Persea americana is grown for fruit, while others are planted for their ornamental laurel-like foliage. Most of them have greenish, reddish, or glaucous young shoots. The ornamental kinds require no special treatment. Propagated by seeds and cuttings.

acuminatissima (Hayata) Kosterm. [*Machilus arisanensis* (Hayata) Hayata]. Tree; lvs. lanceolate, to 4 in. long, acute, petioles about ½ in. long; panicle terminal, to 2½ in. long; fr. ovoid, about ⅜ in. long. Taiwan.

americana [*P. gratissima* C. F. Gaertn.]. AGUACATE, ALLIGATOR PEAR, AVOCADO, PALTA. Much-branched tree, to 60 ft. or more; lvs. elliptic or ovate, 4–8 in. long, acuminate, acute or short-pointed; panicles terminal, tawny-pubescent; fls. small, greenish, the parts gray-pubescent; fr. pear-shaped to oblong or globose, medium to large, skin to ¼ in. thick, sometimes woody, varying from yellow-green or green to maroon, brown, or deep purple, flesh greenish-yellow, usually becoming bright yellow when ripe and of a buttery consistency, seed single, large. Trop. Amer., probably originally Cent. Amer. Cult. widely, including warmest parts of U.S., for the highly nutritious fr., used as a vegetable or in salads. Horticulturists recognize 3 groups or races of avocados: Mexican, Guatemalan, and West Indian, the geographical names reflecting areas where each race was originally most abundant in cult. Besides botanical distinctions noted below, there are others of horticultural importance (See *Avocado*). Var. americana [*P. leiogyna* S. F. Blake]. The typical var.; lvs. not anise-scented when crushed. The so-called "Guatemalan" and "West Indian" races of avocado belong here. Var. drymifolia (Schlechtend. & Cham.) S. F. Blake. Lvs. mostly elliptic, acute at each end, anise-scented when crushed; perianth more or less persistent; fr. small, skin very thin and soft. The "Mexican" race of avocados.

Borbonia (L.) K. Spreng. RED BAY, SWAMP R. B., SWEET B., LAUREL TREE, TISSWOOD, FLORIDA MAHOGANY. Tree, 30–40 ft.; lvs. lanceolate to lanceolate-oblong, to 6 in., tapering to base, glabrous and somewhat glaucous; panicles few- or several-fld., short-peduncled; fr. about ½ in. in diam., dark blue or blackish, peduncle red. Swamps, Del. to Fla. Sometimes planted as an ornamental.

breviflora (Benth.) Pax [*Machilus breviflora* (Benth.) Hemsl.]. Tree; lvs. lanceolate, to 2 in. long, short-petioled; panicles short, almost contracted to umbels. Hong Kong.

gratissima: *P. americana*.

indica (L.) K. Spreng. Small tree, young shoots finely pubescent or nearly glabrous; lvs. oblong to lanceolate-oblong, to 6 in., mostly acute, pubescent beneath, leathery; panicles few-fld., peduncled clusters in upper axils; fls. small; fr. oblong, scarcely fleshy, ¾ in. long. Canary Is., Madeira, Azores. Planted as ornamental in s. Calif. and Fla.

japonica (Siebold & Zucc.) Kosterm. [*Machilus japonica* Siebold & Zucc.]. To 40 ft.; lvs. obovate-oblong to lanceolate or oblanceolate, to 8 in. long, leathery, usually tapered; panicles axillary, about as long as lvs.; fr. globose, ⅜ in. across, greenish-black. S. Japan, Korea.

Kusanoi (Hayata) H. L. Li [*Machilus Kusanoi* Hayata]. Large tree; lvs. thinly leathery, oblong to oblanceolate, 4½–8 in. long, acuminate, petioles 1–2 in. long; panicles terminal, to 5 in. long; fr. globose, about ½ in. across. Taiwan.

leiogyna: *P. americana* var.

Thunbergii (Siebold & Zucc.) Kosterm. [*Machilus Thunbergii* Siebold & Zucc.]. Tree, to 45 ft., the young buds bright red; lvs. obovate to oblong, 2½–4 in. long, abruptly obtuse, leathery; fls. greenish-yellow; fr. globose, dark purple, about ⅜ in. in diam. Korea, Japan, China, Taiwan. An ornamental shade tree for parks, borders, or windbreaks; resists salt spray.

zuihoensis (Hayata) H. L. Li [*Machilus zuihoensis* Hayata]. Large tree; lvs. lanceolate to oblanceolate, 4–5½ in. long, acuminate, thick, leathery petioles ⅜ in. long; fr. globose, about ¼ in. in diam. Taiwan.

PERSIMMON. Certain species of the genus *Diospyros* are known as persimmon. Although noteworthy selections of the American persimmon, *Diospyros virginiana*, native to the eastern United States, have been introduced, no important orchard industry is based on it and they are primarily home garden plants. The small size of the fruit and its pulpy character when mature have been drawbacks not offset by its high quality and delicious flavor. Hence, persimmon culture has been undertaken with cultivars of *Diospyros Kaki*, introduced from Japan and China, commonly known as Oriental or Japanese persimmons and as kaki, the Japanese name.

Roughly, the Oriental persimmon is best adapted climatically to Zone 8, the cotton belt. Cultivars are grown as garden fruits over wide areas, including parts of Zone 5, but commercially only in California, Texas, Florida, southern Georgia, and the southern parts of those states bordering on the Gulf of Mexico. In the latter area Oriental persimmons are rather short-lived.

The persimmon is not particular in its soil requirements.

It may be grown on any good farming land, provided water is available for irrigation in dry sections and drainage is satisfactory where rainfall is heavy. Soils of good quality produce more abundant crops of finer fruits than do lighter soils.

Stocks of *D. virginiana* are employed for propagation in the South and East entirely, while in California seedling *D. Kaki* and *D. Lotus* stocks are also used. *Diospyros virginiana* roots are adapted to moist soils, *D. Lotus* to dry soils, while *D. Kaki* is intermediate in its moisture requirements; *D. Lotus* has a fine, fibrous root system, while *D. Kaki* and *D. virginiana* have well-developed taproots, naturally very deficient in lateral and fibrous roots. Their root systems can be greatly improved by transplanting and by root pruning, but persimmons are generally difficult to transplant. Propagation is by whip-grafting in winter just below the surface of the ground on one- or two-year seedling stocks or by shield-budding with long heavy buds just before the stocks become dormant in summer.

While many kinds of Oriental persimmons may be found in gardens, the most frequent cultivars are 'Tanenashi' and 'Fuyu' in the Southeast and 'Hachiya' and 'Fuyu' in the West. 'Fuyu' may be eaten firm-ripe, like an apple, because its flesh is nonastringent at all stages, whereas both 'Tanenashi' and 'Hachiya' are astringent until they are extremely soft, when they have a rich flavor. Pollination is required for 'Fuyu' in the East, and a good pollinator such as 'Gailey' is required.

Persimmons are relatively free of pests and hence one of the best species for home planting, where little care need be given, yet delicious fruit is assured. Additionally, the size and shape of the Oriental persimmon and the beauty of the foliage and decorative fruits, which persist for a long time on the tree, make it an outstanding ornamental for landscaping and in the home garden.

PERSOONIA Sm. *Proteaceae*. About 60 spp. of small trees or shrubs, native to Australia and New Zeal.; lvs. mostly alt., entire; fls. small, yellowish or white; fr. a drupe.

Toru A. Cunn. To 40 ft.; lvs. linear-lanceolate, to 8 in. long, thick, leathery; fls. yellowish-brown, to ⁵⁄₁₆ in. long, in rusty-pubescent, axillary racemes; fr. reddish, to ⅝ in. long. New Zeal.

PERUVOCEREUS: *HAAGEOCEREUS*. P. rubrispinus: *H. chosicensis* var.

PESCATOREA Rchb. f. *Orchidaceae*. About 17 spp. of tufted epiphytes without pseudobulbs, native to Cent. and S. Amer.; lvs. plicate, 2-ranked, arranged fanwise; infl. short, arching, 1-fld.; fls. large, conspicuous, sepals fleshy, upper sepal erect, separate, lateral sepals united at base, obliquely inserted on column foot, petals similar, lip 3-lobed, contracted into a strap-shaped claw basally, lateral lobes forming a deep concavity below column surrounded by a semicircular, many-grooved callus, midlobe convex with recurved margins. For structure of fl. see *Orchidaceae*.

For culture see *Orchids*.

cerina (Lindl.) Rchb.f. [*Zygopetalum cerinum* (Lindl.) Rchb.f.]. Lvs. linear-lanceolate, to 2 ft. long; scape to 4 in. long; sepals concave, spreading, upper sepal separate, elliptic, 1¼ in. long, white, lateral sepals white with greenish-yellow blotch near base, petals similar to upper sepal, white, inserted on base of column, lip 1¼ in. long, rich yellow, basal callus reddish-brown, column white, anther lavender. Costa Rica, Panama.

PESTS. See *Diseases and Pests*.

PETALOSTEMON Michx. PRAIRIE CLOVER. *Leguminosae* (subfamily *Faboideae*). About 36–50 spp. of glandular-dotted herbs of N. Amer.; lvs. alt., crowded, odd-pinnate; fls. in dense heads or spikes, with 4 petals united basally to stamen tube and the standard separate; fr. a short, indehiscent legume, included in calyx.

May be planted in the rock garden, perennial border, or wild garden.

candidum (Willd.) Michx. [*P. oligophyllum* (Torr.) Rydb.]. WHITE P.C. Per., to 2½ ft.; lfts. 7–9, linear or oblong; fls. white, in oblong spikes to 3 in. long. Sask. to Miss., w. to Ariz. and Colo.

mollis: *P. purpureum.*

oligophyllum: *P. candidum.*

purpureum (Venten.) Rydb. [*P. mollis* Rydb.]. Per., to 3 ft.; lfts. 3–5, linear, to ¾ in. long; fls. violet to crimson, in dense spikes 2 in. long. Ind. to Sask., s. to Tex. and New Mex.

villosum Nutt. SILKY P.C. Per., to 2 ft., ascending or decumbent, densely soft-hairy; lfts. elliptic to oblong or oblanceolate, 13–19, to ½ in. long; fls. rose-purple or rarely white, in cylindrical spikes to 4 in. long. Mich. to Sask. and Tex.

PETASITES Mill. BUTTERBUR, SWEET COLTSFOOT. *Compositae* (Senecio Tribe). About 15 spp. of more or less dioecious, stoloniferous per. herbs, in Eur., n. Asia, and N. Amer.; lvs. basal, large, long-petioled, appearing with or after fls.; fl. heads usually radiate, in scapose racemes or panicles, white or purplish, the fertile heads with many mostly female and fertile fls. with or without ligules, the sterile heads with many bisexual but sterile disc fls. and with or without a few female but sterile ray fls.; achenes cylindrical, ribbed, pappus of white hairs.

Of easy cultivation. Usually propagated by division; also by seeds.

albus (L.) Gaertn. WHITE B. Lf. blades somewhat orbicular, to 16 in. wide, cordate, sinuately lobed and denticulate, glabrous above, white-woolly beneath at maturity; scape to 12 in. in fl., elongating in fr., with scattered bracts, heads in panicles; fls. whitish. Eur., w. Asia.

japonicus (Siebold & Zucc.) Maxim. FUKI. Lvs. reniform-orbicular, to 16 in. wide, shallowly dentate, pubescent above, tomentose beneath when young; scape to about 6 in. in fl., elongating in fr., bracts crowded, to 2½ in. long, green, the upper ones more or less forming an involucre under the infl.; fls. white. Korea, China, Japan. Grown in Japan for the edible petioles used as a vegetable.

PETREA L. PURPLE-WREATH, QUEEN'S-WREATH, BLUE-BIRD VINE, SANDPAPER V. *Verbenaceae.* About 30 spp. of deciduous shrubs, trees, or woody vines, native from Mex. and W. Indies to Brazil; lvs. opp. or whorled, simple; fls. blue, violet, purple, or white, in axillary or terminal racemes, calyx 5-lobed, the lobes blue, violet, purple, or white, becoming green and rigid in fr., corolla 5-lobed, stamens 4; fr. a drupe.

Grown out of doors in the South and under glass. Propagated by cuttings of shoots over heat and by seeds.

arborea HBK. Shrub or low tree, sometimes vinelike, to 25 ft.; lvs. sessile or with petiole less than ⅛ in. long, elliptic, to 6 in. long, cordate, obtuse to emarginate, entire to undulate; racemes axillary, 2–6 in. long; fls. blue. Trinidad, Venezuela, Guyana. Much of the cult. material grown under this name is *P. volubilis.* Cv. '**Broadwayi**'. Fls. white.

Kohautiana K. Presl. Woody vine, or tortuous, nearly self-supporting shrub, to 30 ft. or more; lvs. with petioles to ⅜ in. long, elliptic to elliptic-ovate, to 6 in. long, cordate, usually obtuse to emarginate, glabrous; racemes terminal, 6–20 in. long; fls. lilac-blue to dark purple. W. Indies, particularly the Fr. Antilles. Sometimes cult. as *P. volubilis.* Var. **anomala** Moldenke. Lvs. narrowed at ends; fls. white.

volubilis L.. QUEEN'S-WREATH. Woody vine or subshrub, to 35 ft.; lvs. with petioles to ½ in. long, elliptic, 2–8 in. long, acute or obtusely cuneate at base, mostly acute to short-acuminate at apex, rough-scabrous; racemes axillary, 3–12 in. long; fls. pale lilac to purple. W. Indies, Mex., Cent. Amer. Cv. '**Albiflora**'. Fls. white.

PETROCALLIS R. Br. *Cruciferae.* Two spp. of per. herbs in mts. of cent. and s. Eur. and Iran; closely related to *Draba,* but lvs. palmately lobed, hairs unbranched, seeds 1 or 2 in each cell.

pyrenaica (L.) R.Br. [*Draba pyrenaica* L.] Matlike, 3–4 in. tall; lvs. in compact rosettes, stiff, wedge-shaped, to ¼ in. long, 3–5-lobed, grayish; fls. about ⅛ in. long, white changing to pink, in few-fld. corymbs; silicles short, little longer than broad. Lime-loving alpine, cent. and s. Eur. Grown in rock gardens.

PETROCOPTIS A. Braun ex Endl. *Caryophyllaceae.* Seven spp. of suffrutescent per. herbs of the mts. of Spain; lvs. usually in basal rosettes; infl. cymose, 1–10-fld.; calyx conic-campanulate, 10-veined, petals 5, imbricate, with long claws, coronal scales present at junction of claw and blade, stamens 10, ovary 1-celled, styles 5; fr. a caps., 5-toothed, seeds reniform, black, hairy on scar.

Propagated by seeds or division.

glaucifolia (Lag.) Boiss. [*P. Lagascae* (Willk.) Willk.; *Lychnis Lagascae* (Willk.) Hook.f.]. Per., fl. sts. without basal rosettes, sts. diffusely branched basally; st. lvs. ovate-lanceolate, to ¾ in. long, thick, glaucous, petioles to ¾ in. long, uppermost lvs. ovate; bracts ¹⁄₁₆ in. long, scarious; calyx ⁵⁄₁₆ in. long, glabrous, whitish to purplish, the teeth obtuse, petals purplish, to ¾ in. long, emarginate. Cantabrian Mts. and Pyrenees, n. Spain.

hispanica (Willk.) Pau. Cespitose per.; basal lvs. in rosettes, obovate, to 2⅜ in. long including petiole, thick, leathery, glaucous, st. lvs. elliptic to ovate, upper ones nearly orbicular, to 1¼ in. long; bracts less than ⅛ in. long; calyx to ⁵⁄₁₆ in. long, teeth ovate, obtuse, petals white, to ⅝ in. long, emarginate. W.-cent. Pyrenees.

Lagascae: *P. glaucifolia.*

pyrenaica (Bergeret) A. Braun. Cespitose per., fl. sts. with rosettes at base, to 6 in., glabrous; lvs. to ¾ in. long, green to slightly glaucous, the basal lvs. ovate-lanceolate, with petioles to 1 in. long, ciliate, the lower st. lvs. lanceolate, the upper ovate; bracts ⅛ in. long, margins scarious; calyx to ⁵⁄₁₆ in. long, whitish, glabrous, petals white or pale purplish, to ⅝ in. long, emarginate. W. Pyrenees.

PETROCOSMEA D. Oliver. *Gesneriaceae.* About 29 spp. of per., hairy, rhizomatous herbs, in mts. of Asia; lvs. in a rosette; fls. 1 to several on a scape, calyx 5-parted or 2-lipped, corolla tubular to campanulate, limb 2-lipped, lobed, the lobes about equal or the upper shorter than the lower, stamens 2, anthers dehiscent by slits at tips or lengthwise, disc lacking, ovary superior; fr. a caps.

For cultivation see *Gesneriaceae.*

Kerrii Craib. Lvs. ovate-lanceolate to oblong, to 4 in. long, 2⅜ in. wide, irregularly toothed, with 4–6 pairs of nerves; scapes to 2 in.; fls. 1–3, calyx 2-lipped, corolla white, blotched with yellow at base of the 2 upper lobes, tube ⅛ in. long, limb 2-lipped, upper lip shallowly 2-lobed, ¼ in. long, lower lip longer, with lobes ³⁄₁₆ in. long, anthers dehiscent by short slits at tips. Thailand.

Parryorum C. E. Fisch. Lvs. nearly round to oblong, to 4½ in. long; fls. 1–12, corolla campanulate, violet, tube ⅜ in. long, lobes ⅛ in. long, nearly equal. India.

PETRONYMPHE H. E. Moore. *Amaryllidaceae.* One sp., native to Mex.; corm membranous-coated; lvs. linear, 5–7-keeled; fls. nodding, in an umbel on a naked scape, subtended by 3–4 spreading, separate spathe valves; perianth tubular, lobes 6, short, spreading, anthers 6, inserted at throat of tube, ovary superior, 3-celled, on a short stalk united to the perianth tube on 3 angles.

decora H. E. Moore. To 2 ft.; lvs. to 2 ft. long; scape arched toward apex, about 14-fld., pedicels slender, to 3 in. long; perianth 2 in. long, pale yellow with green lines, lobes spreading, ¼ in. long, filaments pale yellow, anthers blue-violet.

PETROPHILA R. Br. *Proteaceae.* About 40 spp. of shrubs, native to Australia; lvs. stiff; fls. bisexual, white or yellow, solitary in the axils of scales or bracts, these adhering to st. and forming dense spikes or cones; fr. indehiscent, small, dry.

biloba R. Br. Lvs. flat, ternately divided, segms. obliquely ovate or oblong, to ½ in. long, sharp-pointed; fls. hairy, about ¾ in. long; cones ¼ in. across.

media R. Br. Lvs. cylindrical, 2–3 in. long, occasionally to 10 in.; fls. hairy, about ½ in. long; cones ½ in. across.

Shuttleworthiana Meissn. Lvs. flat, divided, segms. 1 in. long, sharp-pointed; fls. glabrous, ⁵⁄₁₆ in. long; cones 1 in. long.

PETROPHYTUM Rydb. ROCK SPIRAEA. *Rosaceae.* A few spp. of matted, woody plants with prostrate brs., growing on rocks, native to w. N. Amer.; lvs. persistent, crowded, entire, oblanceolate to spatulate; fls. white, bisexual, racemose, sepals and petals 5, stamens about 20, pistils 3–5; frs. 3–5 follicles dehiscent along both sutures.

Does best in sunny places in limy soil; propagated by seeds and division. Suitable for the rock garden.

caespitosum (Nutt.) Rydb. [*Spiraea caespitosa* Nutt.]. Mats 1–3 ft. across, densely silky-pubescent; lvs. ¼–½ in. long, 1-nerved; peduncles 1–4 in. high, bearing a spike 1–1½ in. long; fls. less than ³⁄₁₆ in. across. Mont. and S. Dak., s. to New Mex. and Calif. Zone 6.

cinerascens (Piper) Rydb. Lvs. to 1 in. long, 3-nerved, rather sparsely gray-pubescent; peduncles 2–6 in. long, racemes often branched below; sepals acute. Wash. Zone 7.

Hendersonii (W. Canby) Rydb. [*Spiraea Hendersonii* (W. Canby) Piper]. Lvs. to ¾ in. long, more or less 3-nerved beneath, sparingly if at all pubescent; peduncles 2–3 in. high; sepals obtuse. Wash.

PETRORHAGIA (Ser.) Link [*Tunica* Mert. & W. D. J. Koch, not Ludw.]. *Caryophyllaceae*. About 25 spp. of ann. or per. herbs of sandy or dry, limy soils, native from the Canary Is. through Medit. region to Kashmir; lvs. opp., subulate to oblong; infl. a dichasial cyme; fls. in clusters, heads, or solitary, bracts present or absent; calyx 5-toothed, petals 5, usually not clawed, without coronal scales at junction of claw and blade, entire to bifid, or irregularly toothed, or 4-lobed, stamens 10, ovary 1-celled, styles 2; fr. a caps., dehiscent by 4 teeth, seeds many, compressed.

Propagated by seeds, the perennials by division. Some species may be tender in the North; probably better suited to the Southwest and Calif.

illyrica (L.) P. W. Ball & Heyw. Per., to 16 in., sts. glandular-pubescent; lvs. linear-subulate, to 1 in. long; infl. loose, sometimes 1-fld.; calyx to ³⁄₁₆ in. long, densely glandular-pubescent, petals showy, oblanceolate to ⁵⁄₁₆ in. long, white or pale yellow, spotted purple at base, sometimes veined pink. Greece, Crete. Subsp. **Haynaldiana** (Janka) P. W. Ball & Heyw. [*Tunica rhodopea* Velen.]. Sts. glabrous in lower part to entirely glabrous; calyx to ¼ in. long, glabrous, petals to ⅜ in. long. Balkan Pen., s. Italy.

prolifera (L.) P. W. Ball & Heyw. [*Dianthus prolifer* L.; *Tunica prolifera* (L.) Scop.]. CHILDING PINK. Ann., to 20 in., glabrous, or scabrous-pubescent; lvs. 3-veined, lf. sheaths as long as broad; infl. capitate, bracts mucronate; petals ½ in. long, pink or purplish, blade obcordate. Nw. Afr., Eur., Turkey, s. Russia.

Saxifraga (L.) Link [*Tunica Saxifraga* (L.) Scop.]. COAT FLOWER, TUNIC FLOWER. Per., sts. many, woody at base, glabrous to scabrous; lvs. linear-lanceolate, setose-serrate; infl. lax, sometimes a cluster; fls. with 4 bracts, calyx to ¼ in. long, pubescent to glandular, petals to ⁵⁄₁₆ in. long, white or pink. Cent. and s. Eur., to cent. Asia. Cv. 'Alba'. Fls. white. Cv. 'Rosea'. Fls. rose-pink.

velutina (Guss.) P. W. Ball & Heyw. [*Tunica velutina* Fisch. & C. A. Mey.]. Ann., about 12 in., sts. densely glandular-tomentose; lf. sheaths twice as long as broad, upper lvs. smooth-margined; outer bracts acute or mucronate; blade of petals pink or purplish, to ⅛ in. wide; seeds papillate. Medit. region; introd. in S. Afr., Australia, Hawaii.

PETROSELINUM J. Hill. *Umbelliferae*. Three spp. of Old World herbs; lvs. pinnate; fls. greenish-yellow or reddish, in compound umbels, involucels present; fr. ovate, compressed.

One species is cultivated as a garnish and for salads. It is grown from seeds, but since germination is very slow, it is well to soak them in warm water before sowing. For winter use, roots may be transplanted to boxes or pots and kept in a sunny window.

crispum (Mill.) Nyman ex A. W. Hill [*P. hortense* Hoffm.; *P. sativum* Hoffm.; *Carum Petroselinum* (L.) Benth. & Hook.f.]. PARSLEY. Bien., to 3 ft.; lvs. ternately decompound. Eur., w. Asia. Var. **crispum**. The typical var.; roots fibrous; lf. segms. curled and crisped. Var. **neapolitanum** Danert [*P. crispum* var. *latifolium* of auth., not (Mill.) Airy-Shaw]. ITALIAN P. Roots fibrous; lf. segms. flat, not crisped. Var. **tuberosum** (Bernh.) Crov. [*P. hortense* var. *radicosum* (Alef.) L. H. Bailey]. TURNIP-ROOTED P. Roots thick, parsniplike, edible; lf. segms. flattened, not crisped.

hortense: *P. crispum.* Var. **radicosum:** *P. crispum.* var. *tuberosum.*

latifolium: a listed name of no botanical standing; see *P. crispum* var. *neapolitanum.*

neapolitanum: a listed name of no botanical standing, for *P. crispum* var.

sativum: *P. crispum.*

PETTERIA K. Presl. *Leguminosae* (subfamily *Faboideae*). One sp., a deciduous shrub, native to Balkan Pen.; lvs. of 3 lfts.; fls. in terminal racemes, papilionaceous, keel united to stamen tube; fr. linear, wide.

Cultivated as for *Laburnum*.

ramentacea (Sieber) K. Presl. To 6 ft.; lfts. obovate, to 2 in. long; racemes erect, to 3 in. long; fls. fragrant, yellow, to ¾ in. long; fr. glabrous, to 1½ in. long. Late spring. Yugoslavia, Albania.

PETUNIA Juss. *Solanaceae*. About 30 spp. of mostly viscid-pubescent, branching ann. or per. herbs, native to trop. and warm temp. S. Amer.; lvs. alt., entire, often small; fls. axillary, solitary, calyx 5-parted, corolla violet to white, or pale yellow,

bluish, pink, and red in cvs., funnelform or salverform, stamens borne on the corolla, 4 fertile, 1 smaller or rudimentary; fr. a 2-celled caps., seeds many.

Grown for their showy, fragrant flowers; petunias bloom all summer and often well into autumn. They are treated as annuals in gardens and are excellent for bedding, to fill spaces in the border, and in windows and porch boxes; also grown in the greenhouse. Petunias require a sunny exposure and are propagated by seeds, usually started indoors; the large frilled and double cultivars are sometimes propagated from cuttings.

axillaris (Lam.) BSP. LARGE WHITE P. Sts. erect or decumbent, viscid-pubescent, the upright ones to 2 ft.; lvs. ovate to ovate-lanceolate, to 4½ in. long, decurrent; fls. fragrant at night, corolla dull white, salverform, tube to 2½ in. long, limb to 2 in. across. S. Brazil, Uruguay, Argentina. Occasionally persists as an escape in Zone 7.

fimbriata: see under *P.* × *hybrida.*

grandiflora: see under *P.* × *hybrida.*

×**hybrida** Hort. Vilm.-Andr. COMMON GARDEN P. Cultigen; apparently a complex of hybrids involving *P. axillaris, P. inflata,* and *P. violacea*; fls. 2–3½ in. long, corolla tube funnelform, limb mostly very broad; corolla tube broader than in *P. axillaris,* longer with broader limb than in *P. violacea,* differing from both in its much larger and variously formed fls. in many colors, and its more stocky growth. Various cvs. have fls. varying in size, form, and color, sometimes measuring 4–5 in. across, often deeply fringed or full-double, ranging from white to deep red-purple, variously striped and barred or with starlike markings radiating from the throat; these often are designated in catalogues by such hort. names as *P. fimbriata, P. grandiflora, P. multiflora, P. nana,* and *P. superbissima.* This hybrid complex comprises all the highly developed garden petunias. Certain cvs. may be maintained only through closely controlled breeding and are best prop. by cuttings, others come reasonably true from seed.

inflata R. E. Fries. Perhaps not specifically distinct from *P. axillaris,* differing in having lvs. narrower, and corolla tube swollen or inflated. Argentina.

multiflora: see under *P.* × *hybrida.*

nana: see under *P.* × *hybrida.*

parviflora Juss. WILD P., SEASIDE P. Diffuse, much-branched ann., slightly viscid-pubescent; lvs. fleshy, linear-oblong to spatulate, to ⅜ in. long; corolla purple, tube yellow, to ⅜ in. long, limb to ⅜ in. across. Trop. Amer.; naturalized from Va. to s. Calif. in low wet places in Zone 8.

superbissima: see under *P.* × *hybrida.*

violacea Lindl. VIOLET-FLOWERED P. Viscid-pubescent, decumbent ann., upright sts. to 10 in. high; lvs. elliptic-ovate or elliptic-lanceolate, to 3½ in. long; corolla rose-red or violet, tube to 1 in. long, limb irregular, to 1½ in. across. Brazil, Uruguay, Argentina; naturalized locally in U.S. in Zone 7. Considered by some botanists not to be distinct from *P. axillaris.* Some material offered as *P. violacea* may be only color forms of *P.* × *hybrida.*

PEUCEDANUM L. *Umbelliferae*. Not cult. **P. graveolens:** *Anethum graveolens.*

PEUMUS Mol. [*Boldea* Juss.; *Boldoa* Endl., not Cav.]. *Monimiaceae*. One sp., a dioecious tree, native to Chile; lvs. opp., entire; fls. in terminal, cymose panicles, unisexual, perianth tube campanulate, segms. 10–12, spreading, stamens many, carpels 3–5; fr. 2–5 drupes, each 1-seeded.

Propagated by cuttings of young wood, and by seeds.

Boldus Mol. [*Boldoa fragrans* Lindl.]. BOLDO. To 25 ft., aromatic, evergreen; lvs. broadly ovate or ovate-elliptic, to 2 in. long, young lvs. pilose on both surfaces, mature lvs. glabrous, punctate above; fls. whitish, ¼ in. across. Chile. Grown in Calif. Zone 10. Bark used for tanning and dyeing; lvs. have medicinal properties; drupes edible.

PFEIFFERA Salm-Dyck. *Cactaceae*. One sp., an epiphytic or terrestrial cactus of N. Argentina; sts. erect or pendent, 3–4-ribbed, without aerial roots; fls. small, diurnal, stamens in 2 series. Often considered closely allied to *Rhipsalis* because of the nearly separate petals, but with spiny sts. and ovary.

For culture see *Cacti*.

ianothele (Monv.) A. Web. Sts. 1–2 ft. long and ¾ in. thick, ribs undulate; areoles ½ in. apart, spines 6–7, needle-shaped, yellowish, ¼ in. long; fls. campanulate, about ¾ in. long, white inside, pinkish outside; fr. red, globose, ½ in. in diam.

PHACELIA Juss. SCORPION WEED. *Hydrophyllaceae.* Between 150 and 200 spp. of per., bien., or ann. herbs, native chiefly to w. U.S. and Mex., a few spp. to e. U.S. and S. Amer.; plants variously hairy, often glandular; lvs. mostly alt., simple to compound; fls. violet, blue, or white, sessile to long-pedicelled, in simple or branched, loose or dense scorpioid cymes often arranged in panicles, calyx 5-parted, corolla tubular to rotate, 5-lobed, stamens 5, exserted or included, style 2-cleft, sometimes nearly to base; fr. a 1- or 2-celled caps.

Grown for spring and summer bloom in the flower garden. The individual flowers are commonly not showy, but produce a bold effect in mass. Seeds of the annual species may be sown in spring where the plants are to stand. The perennials are propagated by division as well as by seeds.

bipinnatifida Michx. Hairy bien., to 2 ft.; lvs. pinnately 3–5 times divided, the divisions cut or pinnatifid; fls. violet or blue, in glandular-pubescent infl., filaments hairy. W. Va. to s. Ill., s. to Ark., Ala., Ga.

campanularia A. Gray. CALIFORNIA BLUEBELL. Glandular-hispid ann., to 20 in.; lvs. elliptic to broadly ovate, angular or coarsely toothed, petiole longer than blade; fls. long-pedicelled, in loose cymes, corolla campanulate-funnelform, bright blue, rarely white. Colo. and Mojave deserts of s. Calif.

cicutaria Greene. Hispid and somewhat glandular ann., to 2 ft.; lvs. oblong-ovate to ovate in outline, pinnately parted, segms. 5–9, oblong to ovate-lanceolate, cut or toothed; fls. many, yellowish-white, short-pedicelled, in dense cymes, calyx elongating in fr. Cent. Calif. Var. **hispida** (A. Gray) J. T. Howell [*P. hispida* A. Gray]. Fls. lavender. Cent. Calif., s. to Baja Calif. and Mex.

ciliata Benth. Rough-pubescent ann., to 1 ft.; lvs. oblong or ovate in outline, pinnately parted, segms. oblong, toothed or cut; fls. almost sessile, calyx enlarging and becoming scarious in fr., corolla bright blue with paler center. Cent. Calif., s. to Baja Calif. and Mex.

ciliosa: *P. sericea* subsp.

congesta Hook. BLUE-CURLS. Hairy ann. to 2½ ft.; lvs. pinnatifid, often finely dissected, upper lvs. petioled; fls. blue. Tex., New Mex.

crenulata Torr. ex S. Wats. Glandular-pubescent ann. or bien., to 5 ft.; lvs. oblong or elliptic in outline, to 4½ in. long, pinnate or pinnately lobed, the lobes crenate or lobed; fls. many, violet or bluish-purple, in corymbs or panicles of short-peduncled cymes. Se. Calif., s. to Baja Calif. and Mex., e. to Utah and Ariz.

divaricata (Benth.) A. Gray [*P. divaricata* var. *Wrangeliana* (Fisch. & C. A. Mey.) Jeps.]. Straggling pubescent ann., to 1 ft.; lvs. oblong to ovate, to 6 in. long, entire or with few teeth at base; fls. many, purplish-blue, subsessile, in compact cymes. N. Calif.

gloxinioides: a listed name of no botanical standing for *P. minor* cv.

grandiflora (Benth.) A. Gray [*Eutoca grandiflora* Benth.]. Coarse, erect, glandular-hispid ann., to 3 ft.; lvs. elliptic, ovate, to ovate-orbicular, to 8 in. long or more, truncate or cordate, dentate or serrate; fls. many, in dense cymes, pale purplish-blue, sometimes white at the center. Coastal s. Calif. to n. Baja Calif. and Mex. Some material grown under this name may be *P. minor.*

hastata Dougl. ex Lehm. [*P. leucophylla* Torr. ex Frém.]. Densely silky-pubescent or somewhat hispid per., sts. several, decumbent, to 20 in. high; lvs. linear-lanceolate to ovate-lanceolate, mostly entire, prominently veined, silvery; fls. white to lavender. B.C. to ne. Calif., e. to Mont., Colo., and Nebr. Sometimes confused with *P. heterophylla*, which has foliage grayish-green and some lvs. divided.

heterophylla Pursh. Bien., to 4 ft., sts. usually solitary, erect, simple, densely short-hairy; foliage grayish-green, basal lvs. simple to pinnate, to 3½ in., prominently veined, terminal lft. much larger than lateral lfts., uppermost st. lvs. entire; fls. yellow or greenish-white, in dense panicled cymes. Wash. to Calif., e. to Mont., Wyo., and Utah.

hirsuta Nutt. Ann. with stiff, spreading hairs, to 1½ ft.; basal lvs. oblong in outline, to 2½ in. long, pinnate or pinnatifid, petioled, st. lvs. oblong to orbicular, short-petioled or sessile; corolla bluish-lavender with whitish center and 2 purple spots on each lobe. Sw. Mo. and Ark., s. to Okla. and Tex.

hispida: *P. cicutaria* var.

leucophylla: *P. hastata.*

linearis (Pursh) Holzing. Nonglandular, hairy ann., to 20 in.; lvs. essentially sessile, linear to lanceolate, to 3 in. long, entire or pinnately lobed; fls. many, violet to white. B.C. to Alta., s. to n. Calif. and Wyo.

Lyallii (A. Gray) Rydb. Tufted, pubescent per., to 8 in.; lvs. oblanceolate, to 5 in. long, divided half-way to midrib; fls. dark blue or purple, to 5⁄16 in. long, in short, dense infl., calyx lobes hairy. Mont.

minor (Harv.) Thell. ex F. Zimm. [*P. Whitlavia* A. Gray; *Whitlavia grandiflora* Harv.; *W. minor* Harv.]. WHITLAVIA. Glandular-hispid

ann., to 2 ft.; lvs. oblong-ovate to broadly ovate, to 4 in. long, coarsely serrate; corolla violet, rarely white, tubular-campanulate, tube 3 times as long as lobes, filaments glabrous. S. Calif. Cv. **'Gloxinioides'.** Fls. white, with blue center.

Parryi Torr. Glandular-hispid ann., to 2 ft.; lvs. oblong-ovate to broadly ovate, to 4 in. long, toothed or lobed; corolla violet with white- or yellow-marked center, nearly rotate, lobes as long as or longer than tube, filaments hairy. Calif., n. Baja Calif., Mex.

platycarpa (Cav.) K. Spreng. Pubescent, prostrate to ascending per., to 1½ ft., branching from the base; basal lvs. in a rosette, linear to oblanceolate or oblong, to 6 in. long, pinnate, lfts. 4–8 pairs, entire or pinnatifid, st. lvs. pinnate to merely toothed; fls. pinkish-lavender to pale blue or white. Mts. of Mex.

Purshii Buckl. MIAMI-MIST. Hairy, erect or ascending ann., to 2½ ft.; lvs. oblong to elliptic in outline, to 2 in. long, pinnate or pinnatifid, the lobes lanceolate or elliptic, st. lvs. sessile, clasping; corolla pale blue with white center, lobes short-fringed. Penn. to Mo., s. to Ga. and Ala.

ramosissima Dougl. ex Lehm. Sprawling, finely gray-pubescent, usually glandular, hispid per., to 4 ft.; lvs. oblong to broadly ovate in outline, to 4 in. long, pinnately divided, segms. elliptic or oblong, toothed, cut or pinnatifid; fls. many, bluish or sordid white, in short, dense, scattered cymes. Cent. Wash. to cent. Calif.

sericea (R. C. Grah.) A. Gray. Bien. or woody-based, silvery-silky per., to 1½ ft.; lvs. oblong or oblong-elliptic in outline, to 4 in. long, pinnatifid, segms. linear or oblong, entire or sometimes cleft; fls. many, lavender, purple, or dark blue, in short cymes arranged in narrow panicles, stamens prominently exserted. Subsp. **sericea.** The typical subsp.; lvs. narrow-lobed, silky-hairy; stamens 2–3 times as long as the campanulate corolla. B.C. to Alta., s. to Wash. and Colo. Subsp. **ciliosa** (Rydb.) G. W. Gillett [*P. ciliosa* Rydb.]. Lvs. with broad lobes, lightly silky-hairy; stamens to twice as long as the urceolate-campanulate corolla. Ore., s. to ne. Calif., Ariz., w. to Wyo.

tanacetifolia Benth. FIDDLENECK. Erect, sparsely bristly ann., to 4 ft.; lvs. oblong-elliptic to ovate in outline, to 9 in. long, pinnately divided, segms. oblong to lanceolate; fls. many, blue or lavender, in dense corymbosely branched cymes. Cent. Calif. to Ariz., s. to n. Baja Calif. and Mex. Cult. in some countries as a honey plant.

viscida (Benth. ex Lindl.) Torr. [*Eutoca viscida* Benth. ex Lindl.]. Erect, glandular-hirsute ann., to 2½ ft.; lvs. ovate to ovate-orbicular, to 3 in. long, toothed; fls. blue with white or purplish center, or entirely white, in loose cymes; filaments hairy. Coastal, cent. and s. Calif. and adjacent is.

Whitlavia: *P. minor.*

Wrangeliana: *P. divaricata.*

PHAEDRANASSA Herb. *Amaryllidaceae.* A few spp. of bulbous herbs, native to Cent. and S. Amer., allied to *Urceolina*, but differs in having the corolla nearly cylindrical, the lobes spreading at the tip, and a corona of small hyaline teeth present between the 6 filaments.

Carmiolii Bak. to 2 ft., bulb to 3 in. in diam.; lvs. 1–3, appearing at flowering time, oblanceolate, to 15 in. long and 2 in. wide, obtuse, petiole to 8 in. long; umbel 6–10-fld., scape cylindrical, pedicels 1 in. long; fls. to 2 in. long, scarlet with green lobes, margined yellow; fr. a caps. Cult. in and described from Costa Rica, but perhaps actually native to Peru.

PHAEDRANTHUS: *DISTICTIS.*

PHAEOMERIA: *NICOLAIA.* **P. magnifica:** *N. elatior.* **P. speciosa:** *N. elatior.*

PHAIUS Lour. *Orchidaceae.* About 50 spp. of terrestrial herbs, native from Malay Arch. n. into China; sts. various, from short and pseudobulbous to slender and leafy; infls. 1 or more, lateral on pseudobulb or st.; fls. rather large, sepals and petals separate, spreading, lip united to base of column, 3-lobed, saccate or spurred at base, with longitudinal ridges on upper surface, lateral lobes enclosing column, column slender, pollinia 8, in 2 groups of 4. For structure of fl. see *Orchidaceae.*

For culture see *Orchids.*

bicolor: *P. Tankervilliae.*

Blumei: *P. Tankervilliae.*

flavus (Blume) Lindl. [*P. maculatus* Lindl.]. Pseudobulbs conical, 5–8-lvd.; lf. blades to 1½ ft. long, sheaths overlapping to form a false st. to 2 ft. high; infl. basal, racemose, to 3 ft. long, many-fld.; fls. light yellow with brown markings on lip, sepals 1½ in. long, petals smaller, lip as long as sepals, hairy, 3-keeled within, spur ¼ in. long, column ¾ in. long, hairy. Ne. India, Sumatra to Philippine Is.

grandifolius: *P. Tankervilliae.*

Gravesii: *P. Tankervilliae.*

Humblotii Rchb.f. Pseudobulbs globose; lvs. broadly lanceolate, to 20 in. long; infl. longer than lvs., racemose, with 7–10 fls. or more; fls. 2 in. across, sepals and petals obovate, light rose-purple, suffused with white, lip fiddle-shaped, with crisped, undulate margins, rose-purple with white center with 2 large bright yellow teeth pointing inward, column slender. Madagascar.

maculatus: *P. flavus.*

mishmensis Rchb.f. Sts. to 3 ft. high, from a tuberous, lobed base, leafless below, leafy above; lvs. elliptic-lanceolate, to 10 in. long; infl. axillary, racemose, to 2 ft. long, with up to 10 fls.; fls. to 2 in. across, pale or dark rose with paler, speckled lip, sepals and petals linear-oblong, petals narrower, lip as long as sepals, lateral lobes orbicular, midlobe squarish, spur to ⅝ in. long. Sikkim, Assam.

Tankervilliae (Ait.) Blume [*P. bicolor* Lindl.; *P. Blumei* Lindl.; *P. grandifolius* Lindl.; *P. Gravesii* O'Brien; *P. Wallichii* Hook.f.]. NUN'S ORCHID, NUN'S-HOOD O. Pseudobulbs to 6 in. long, 2–3-lvd.; lvs. elliptic-oblong, to 2½ ft. long; infl. racemose, to 4 ft. long, to 20-fld.; fls. showy, sepals and petals linear-lanceolate, 2½ in. long, tawny-brown margined with yellow, whitish on reverse, lip elliptic, with lateral lobes wrapped around column, basal half orange-yellow with pale purple spot on each side, apical half white with yellow disc with 4–5 red lines, spur yellow. Himalayas.

tuberculosus Blume. Pseudobulbs spindle-shaped, 3 in. long; lvs. oblong-lanceolate, to 15 in. long; infl. racemose, to 1½ ft. long, 5–7-fld.; fls. 2½ in. across, sepals and petals white, elliptic-oblong, lateral lobes of lip forming a funnel, orange-yellow, spotted with red-purple and studded with white hispid hairs, midlobe squarish, with crisped margins, white, blotched with rose and with deep yellow callus on disc. Madagascar.

Wallichii: *P. Tankervilliae.*

PHALAENOPSIS Blume. MOTH ORCHID. *Orchidaceae.* About 55 spp. of epiphytes or rock-dwelling herbs, native to trop. Asia, Malay Arch., and Oceania; sts. short, without pseudobulbs; lvs. 2-ranked, occasionally bractlike and deciduous, fleshy, erect or arching, rarely petioled; infl. lateral, a 1- to many-fld. raceme or panicle, bracts small, scarious; fls. small to large, variously colored, fleshy to delicate, lip small, often more brightly colored than other fl. segms., deeply 3-lobed, with various callosities between lateral lobes and at base of midlobe, column dilated toward base into a foot. For structure of fl. see *Orchidaceae.*

Cultivated in greenhouse with minimum temperature not less than 65° F. in osmunda fiber or sphagnum; requiring humid atmosphere and unfailing moisture at the roots. See also *Orchids.*

amabilis (L.) Blume [*P. Elisabethae* Hort.; *P. gloriosa* Rchb.f.; *P. grandiflora* Lindl.; *P. Rimestadiana* (Linden) Rolfe]. St. leafy; lvs. green, few, lanceolate, to 10 in. long; infl. a many-fld. raceme, longer than lvs.; fls. white, to 2½ in. across, sepals elliptic-ovate, petals transverse-elliptic, distinctly rounded above, contracted below into a cuneate, almost petioled base, lip 3-lobed, continuous with column foot, lateral lobes erect, obovate-oblanceolate, midlobe cruciform to linear-oblong, hastate at base, with pair of filiform appendages at apex. Palawan Is., Java, Borneo, Moluccas, Celebes, ne. Queensland. Var. **Aphrodite:** *P. Aphrodite.* Var. **aurea** Rolfe. Fls. larger, with front half of lateral lobes and opposing margins of midlobe, including appendages, bright yellow. Var. **formosa:** *P. Aphrodite.* Var. **moluccana** Schlechter. Midlobe of lip linear-oblong, lateral lobes either absent or merely suggested. Moluccas. Var. **papuana** Schlechter [var. *Rosenstromii* (F. M. Bailey) Nicholls; *P. Rosenstromii* F. M. Bailey]. Midlobe of lip narrowly triangular. New Guinea and ne. Queensland. Var. **Rosenstromii:** var. *papuana.*

amboinensis J. J. Sm. Lvs. elliptic, to 10 in. long; infl. a few-fld. raceme, to 1½ ft. long, fls. produced in succession; sepals and petals elliptic to ovate, spreading, ½ in. long, white with rather broad cinnamon-red bars, bars on inner half of lateral sepals much narrower, lip 3-lobed, ⅞ in. long, lateral lobes oblong-strap-shaped, midlobe ovate, with keel with double-serrated edge, calluses present on disc between lateral lobes and at junction of midlobe. Molucca Is.

Aphrodite Rchb.f. [*P. amabilis* var. *Aphrodite* (Rchb.f.) Ames; *P. amabilis* var. *formosa* Shimadzu]. Similar to *P. amabilis;* scape and rachis purplish; fls. white, lateral sepals occasionally spotted with minute carmine dots, base of lateral lobes of lip dotted or striped with carmine, midlobe of lip sagittate-hastate, with broadly triangular,

acute lateral lobes and with 2 tendril-like appendages at apex. Philippine Is., Taiwan.

cochlearis Holttum. Lvs. thin, oblong-ovate, to 8 in. long; infl. branched, to 20 in. long, few-fld.; fls. delicate, segms. spreading, pale yellow to white with 2 faint brown bars at base of segms., sepals and petals elliptic to ovate, to ⅝ in. long, lip 3-lobed, fleshy, lateral lobes oblong-linear, notched at apex, white with broken crimson-yellow marking at base, midlobe nearly orbicular, strongly concave, rounded at apex, disc with five parallel shallow ridges, calluses present between lateral lobes and at junction of midlobe. Sarawak.

cornu-cervi Blume & Rchb.f. Lvs. oblong-strap-shaped, to 8 in. long; infls. 1 to several, to 15 in. long, simple or branched, commonly several-fld.; fls. fleshy, waxy, with spreading segms., several open simultaneously, yellow or yellowish-green, upper sepal ¾ in. long, covered with reddish-brown or cinnamon blotches or spots, obovate-elliptic, margins recurved, lateral sepals elliptic, similarly colored but blotches and spots present only on apical half, petals lanceolate, similar to upper sepal in color, lip 3-lobed, whitish, with parallel reddish-brown or cinnamon stripes on lateral lobes and at base of column, lateral lobes squarish, midlobe anchor-shaped, base swollen, with elevated keel. Java.

Denevei: *Paraphalaenopsis Denevei.*

denticulata: *P. pallens* cv.

Elisabethae: a listed name of no botanical standing for a hybrid between vars. of *P. amabilis.*

equestris (Schauer) Rchb.f. [*P. rosea* Lindl.]. Lvs. fleshy, oblong-elliptic, to 8 in. long; infl. simple or branched, many-fld., rachis purple; fls. variable in size and color, pale rose to white with rose suffusion, lip darker rose, sepals oblong-elliptic, ¾ in. long, petals elliptic, constricted at base, slightly shorter than sepals, lip ½ in. long, 3-lobed, lateral lobes oblong-ovate, midlobe ovate, acute and fleshy at apex, squarish, with peltate callus at junction of lateral and midlobes. Philippine Is.

Esmeralda: *Doritis pulcherrima.*

fasciata Rchb.f. Lvs. elliptic, to 8 in. long; infl. longer than lvs., racemose; fls. fleshy, yellow to yellow-green, with many transverse cinnamon bars, sepals elliptic, to 1 in. long, petals ovate, 1 in. long, lip 1 in. long, 3-lobed, lateral lobes strap-shaped, with sicklelike tip, midlobe oblong-ovate, convex, with median keel terminating in an elevated, ovate callus with a few hairs on the ridge, disc between lateral lobes with elongated, retrorse papillae and a forked, needlelike callus at apex. Philippine Is.

fimbriata J. J. Sm. Lvs. oblong-elliptic, to 9 in. long; infl. loosely many-fld., to 10 in. long; fls. fleshy, white with a few fine transverse striations of magenta-purple, sepals elliptic, to ¾ in. long, petals oblong-elliptic, somewhat shorter than sepals, lip 3-lobed, white, ⅝ in. long, lateral lobes oblique, quadrangular-oblong, somewhat sicklelike at apex, midlobe ovate-rhomboid, with upcurved dentate-fimbriate margins at apex and cushionlike callus densely covered with stiff hairs, a central serrate keel, and forked calluses on disc between lateral lobes and at junction with midlobe. Java.

fuscata Rchb.f. Lvs. obovate-oblong, to 1 ft. long; infl. few-fld., sometimes branched, as long as lvs.; fls. yellow with brown markings, upper sepal ovate, with revolute margins, ⅝ in. long, lateral sepals elliptic, with revolute margins, as long as dorsal sepal, petals obovate-oblong, shorter than sepals, lip ½ in. long, 3-lobed, lateral lobes squarish, midlobe ovate, flat, with fleshy median keel, various calluses present on disc between lateral lobes and junction of midlobe, column cylindrical. Philippine Is.

gigantea J. J. Sm. Lvs. large, pendent, oblong-ovate, to 20 in. long; infl. a pendent, densely many-fld. raceme, to 16 in. long; fls. all open simultaneously, aromatic, 2 in. across, fleshy, greenish-yellow, fading to white at base, densely covered with many red-brown or maroon blotches, sepals elliptic, petals shorter than sepals, lip white with crimson lines and blotches, 3-lobed, lateral lobes triangular-sickle-shaped, midlobe ovate, with a few teeth on margins and an ovoid callus at apex, calluses present on disc between lateral lobes and at junction of midlobe. Borneo.

gloriosa: *P. amabilis.*

grandiflora: *P. amabilis.*

hieroglyphica (Rchb.f.) Sweet [*P. Lueddemanniana* var. *hieroglyphica* Rchb.f.]. Lvs. oblong-strap-shaped, to 1 ft. long; infl. to 1 ft. long, often branched, many-fld.; fls. fleshy, waxy, sepals and petals ovate-elliptic, 1½ in. long, white to greenish, covered with small cinnamon-colored circles, ovals, and dots, lip white, 1 in. long, 3-lobed, lateral lobes oblong-linear, with truncate, emarginate apex, midlobe cuneate-fan-shaped, obscurely erose at apex, with keel from base to middle merging into an ovoid callus covered with prominent hairs, various papillae and calluses present on disc between lateral lobes and junction of midlobe. Philippine Is.

×**intermedia** Lindl.: *P. amabilis* × *P. equestris.* Lvs. elliptic, to 8 in. long, brownish-purple; infl. a many-fld. raceme; fls. 2 in. across, intermediate in size between those of the parent spp., sepals white suffused with rose, oblong, petals much larger, transverse-elliptic, with rose dots at base, lip 3-lobed, lateral lobes ovate, violet with a few crimson dots and spots, midlobe ovate, deeper colored, with 2 short, filiform appendages at apex and a peltate, deep yellow, crimson-spotted callus present at junction of midlobe and lateral lobes. Philippine Is.

Kunstleri Hook.f. Lvs. pendent, obovate, to 9 in. long; infl. often branched, to 16 in. long, with several fls. open simultaneously; fls. fleshy, segms. spreading, sepals obovate, with revolute margins, yellow with large brown or cinnamon blotches, ¾ in. long, petals elliptic, shorter than sepals, lip 3-lobed, yellow with 1 or 2 cinnamon-colored stripes on either side of a median keel, lateral lobes squarish, midlobe orbicular, rounded in front, flat or slightly concave, with fleshy median keel, calluses present on disc between lateral lobes and at junction of midlobe, column short, constricted in middle. Malay Arch.

Lindenii Loher. Lvs. green, mottled silvery-white, oblong-lanceolate, to 10 in. long; infl. occasionally branched, many-fld., rachis green; fls. whitish, suffused with rose and with rose dots at base of sepals and petals, sepals oblong-elliptic, ⅝ in. long, petals elliptic-rhombic, slightly shorter than sepals, lip ½ in. long, 3-lobed, lateral lobes oblong-ovate, white with minute orange dots at base and 3 purple lines above, midlobe orbicular, apiculate and amethyst-rose at apex, with 5–7 radiating darker rose lines shading to brownish at base and with a 6–8-sided peltate callus at junction of midlobe and lateral lobes, column purple. Philippine Is.

Lueddemanniana Rchb.f. Lvs. oblong-elliptic, to 1 ft. long; infl. a suberect to pendent, often branched, several-fld. raceme, longer than lvs.; fls. fleshy, to 2¼ in. across, white with magenta-purple transverse bars, sepals oblong-elliptic, to 1½ in. long, petals slightly smaller, lip bright carmine with yellow at base and on calluses on lateral lobes, 3-lobed, lateral lobes quadrangular-oblong, truncate at apex, midlobe variable, linear-oblong, with median longitudinal keel terminating in a swollen cushionlike apex covered with coarse hairs, various papillae and calluses present on disc between lateral lobes and at junction of midlobe. Philippine Is. Cv. 'Delicata' [var. *delicata* Rchb.f.]. Sepals and petals white, marked on apical half with transverse bars of cinnamon or ochre, barred transversely on basal half with amethyst. Cv. 'Ochracea' [var. *ochracea* Rchb.f.]. Sepals and petals yellowish, barred or striped transversely with ochre, suffused basally with pale amethyst-purple. Var. **hieroglyphica:** *P. hieroglyphica.* Var. **pulchra:** *P. pulchra.*

maculata Rchb.f. Lvs. oblong-strap-shaped, to 8 in. long; infl. a few-fld. raceme, as long as lvs.; fls. small, sepals and petals cream-white to greenish-white with a few dark purple-brown blotches, oblong-lanceolate, sepals ½ in. long, petals smaller, lip 3-lobed, purple, with yellow calluses on lateral lobes, lateral lobes squarish, midlobe oblong-elliptic, with indistinct longitudinal grooves, calluses present on disc between lateral lobes and at junction of midlobe. Sarawak, Malay Pen.

Mannii Rchb.f. Lvs. oblong-lanceolate, to 14 in. long; infls. several, pendent, rarely branched, as long as lvs., many-fld.; fls. opening in succession, waxy, yellow with many cinnamon dots and blotches, upper sepal obovate-lanceolate, with revolute margins, 1 in. long, petals lanceolate-sickle-shaped, with revolute margins, shorter than sepals, lip white and purplish, 3-lobed, lateral lobes squarish, midlobe anchor-shaped, covered with papillae, margins toothed, column yellow. India.

Mariae Burb. Lvs. oblong-strap-shaped, to 1 ft. long; infl. a pendent, occasionally branched, few- to many-fld. raceme, shorter than lvs.; fls. white or cream-colored with large maroon to chestnut-brown blotches and wide transverse bars on sepals and petals, sepals and petals spreading, oblong-elliptic, ¾ in. long, lip pale mauve with yellow calluses on lateral lobes, 3-lobed, lateral lobes oblong-strap-shaped, midlobe ovate, with margins erose-dentate at apex, with keel at base and callus at apex covered with short, soft hairs, calluses present on disc between lateral lobes and at junction of midlobe. Philippine Is.

pallens (Lindl.) Rchb.f. Lvs. fleshy, elliptic, to 5 in. long; infl. a slender, 1- to few-fld. raceme, rarely longer than lvs.; fls. 2 in. across, delicate, sepals and petals spreading, oblong-elliptic, yellowish, barred with slender short bars and dots, lip 3-lobed, white, lateral lobes oblong-strap-shaped, truncate, with semilunate callus in middle, midlobe ½ in. long, ovate, with cuneate base, dentate laterally at apex, with keel from base to middle and a hairy callus at apex, calluses present between lateral lobes and at junction with midlobe. Philippine Is. Cv. 'Denticulata' [var. *denticulata* (Rchb.f.) Sweet; *P. denticulata* Rchb.f.]. Midlobe of lip with 2 or 3 parallel magenta lines on either side of central keel.

Parishii Rchb.f. St. very short; lvs. ovate, at times asymmetrical, to 4½ in. long; infl. few- to several-fld., to 6 in. long, rachis zigzag; fls. all open simultaneously, small, sepals and petals milk-white, upper sepal elliptic, ¼ in. long, lateral sepals and the petals obovate, lip 3-lobed, purple-violet or magenta, with distinct short claw fused to column foot, lateral lobes directed forward, triangular, with distinct longitudinal fleshy keel, midlobe movable, triangular-kidney-shaped, with basal semicircular fleshy callus with long marginal fringe. Burma. Cv. 'Lobbii' [var. *Lobbii* Rchb.f.]. Midlobe of lip with a pair of large vertical chestnut-brown or rusty-brown bands on each side, callus either entire-margined or obscurely toothed.

pulchra (Rchb.f.) Sweet [*P. Lueddemanniana* var. *pulchra* Rchb.f.]. Similar to *P. Lueddemanniana;* raceme few-fld.; fls. deep magenta-purple, fleshy, sepals and petals elliptic, to 1 in. long, lip 3-lobed, midlobe fan-shaped, lateral lobes oblong-linear, with truncate apex, midlobe erose-dentate at apex, with median keel on basal half and a calluslike thickening at apex with few scattered hairs, various papillae-like protuberances and calluses present on disc between lateral lobes and at junction with midlobe. Philippine Is.

Rimestadiana: *P. amabilis.*

rosea: *P. equestris.*

Rosenstromii: *P. amabilis* var. *papuana.*

×**Rothschildiana:** *P. amabilis* × *P. Schillerana.* Lvs. mottled with gray as in *P. Schillerana;* fls. 3 in. across, with shape of *P. amabilis,* upper sepal and petals white, lateral sepals white, the basal half light yellow, spotted with purple toward base, lateral lobes of lip as in *P. amabilis,* midlobe stained with yellow and spotted with red in basal half, white in apical half, with pair of long, filiform appendages at apex.

Sanderana Rchb.f. Lvs. green, elliptic, to 14 in. long; infl. similar to that of *P. amabilis;* fls. deep pink, 3 in. across, sepals elliptic-ovate, petals transverse-elliptic, with upper margin more curved than lower one, lip 3-lobed, lateral lobes ovate, midlobe triangular-hastate, with pair of diverging filiform appendages at apex, base of lip with orange-red suffusion spotted with crimson, a peltate callus present at junction of midlobe and lateral lobes. Philippine Is.

Schillerana Rchb.f. Lvs. oblong, to 10 in. long, dark green mottled with silver or gray above, purple underneath; infl. a panicle to 3 ft. long, with 200 fls. or more; fls. to 3 in. across, rich rose-lilac, sepals obovate, petals rhomboid, lip 3-lobed, spotted with reddish-brown, with a yellow callus, lateral lobes oblong, midlobe elliptic, with 2 divergent, hornlike appendages at apex. Winter–early spring, late summer. Philippine Is.

serpentilingua: *Paraphalaenopsis serpentilingua.*

Stuartiana Rchb.f. Lvs. elliptic-oblong, 1 ft. long, blotched with gray above when young, purplish-red underneath; infl. a pendent, many-fld. panicle; fls. 2 in. across, white or greenish-white, lateral sepals speckled with red, petals quadrangular, with purple dots at base, lip 3-lobed, golden-yellow or orange, spotted with crimson, white at tip, lateral lobes obovate, with a peltate callus, midlobe orbicular, with 2 white diverging hornlike appendages at apex. Winter. Philippine Is. Cv. 'Punctatissima' [var. *punctatissima* Rchb.f.]. Upper sepal, petals, and upper and inner side of lateral sepals with many small mauve spots.

sumatrana Korth. & Rchb.f. Lvs. oblong-elliptic, to 1 ft. long; infl. a several- to many-fld. raceme, to 1 ft. long; fls. to 2 in. across, fleshy, sepals and petals oblong-lanceolate, off-white to pale lemon-yellow, transversely barred with cinnamon to brownish-red, lip 3-lobed, white to cream, with 2 magenta stripes on either side of median keel on midlobe, midlobe convex, oblong-elliptic, heavily thickened toward densely hirsute apex, lateral lobes linear-oblong, various calluses present on disc between lateral lobes and at junction of midlobe, column fleshy. Malay Pen., Sumatra, Java, Borneo.

violacea Witte. Lvs. fleshy, elliptic, to 10 in. long; infl. remotely few-fld.; fls. fleshy, waxy, rose-magenta, sepals ovate-lanceolate, 1⅜ in. long, petals elliptic, 1¼ in. long, lip 1 in. long, deep magenta-purple, lateral lobes linear-oblong, midlobe ovate, with median keel tapering into an ovoid callus at apex, various calluses and papillae present between lateral lobes and midlobe. Malay Pen., Sumatra, Borneo.

PHALARIS L. CANARY GRASS. *Gramineae.* About 15 spp. of ann. or per. grasses in N. Amer., Eur., and N. Afr.; lf. blades many, flat; panicles narrow or spikelike; spikelets laterally compressed, with 1 terminal bisexual floret and 2 neuter florets reduced to scalelike lemmas below, rachilla disarticulating above the glumes, glumes equal, boat-shaped, fertile lemma leathery, shorter than the glumes. For terminology see *Gramineae.*

arundinacea L. REED C.G. Per., rhizomatous, sts. to 5 ft., glaucous; panicles to 7 in. long, narrow, brs. spreading during flowering; glumes ¼ in. long, fertile lemma lanceolate, ⅛ in. long, with a few appressed hairs, sterile lemmas villous, ¹⁄₁₆ in. long. N. Amer., from New Bruns. to Alaska, s. to N.C., Okla., Ariz.; Eurasia. Var. **erecta:** a listed name of no botanical standing. Var. **picta** L. [var. *variegata* Parn.]. RIBBON GRASS, GARDENER'S-GARTERS. Lf. blades striped with white. Cult. for ornament. Var. **variegata:** var. *picta.*

canariensis L. CANARY GRASS, BIRDSEED G. Ann., sts. to 2 ft., erect; panicles ovate to oblong-ovate, dense, to ⅝ in. long; spikelets broad, imbricate, pale with green stripes, glumes to ⁵⁄₁₆ in. long, broadly winged, fertile lemma ¼ in. long, acute, densely appressed-pubescent, sterile lemmas at least half as long as fertile one. W. Medit.; introd. and adventive from Nov. Sc. to Alaska, s. to Va., Ariz. and Calif. Furnishes the canary seed of commerce.

stenoptera: *P. tuberosa* var.

tuberosa L. Per., sts. to 4 ft., spreading to erect, lower internodes swollen; lf. blades to ³⁄₁₆ in. wide; panicles to 6 in. long, ⅝ in. wide; spikelets with lanceolate glumes, awnless, narrowly winged on the upper ⅔, fertile lemma ⅛ in. long, appressed-pubescent, sterile lemmas usually solitary, ⅓ as long as fertile lemma. Medit. region. Not in cult. Var. **stenoptera** (Hack.) A. S. Hitchc. [*P. stenoptera* Hack.]. HARDING GRASS. Rhizome short, vertical or ascending, sometimes branching, not swollen. Origin unknown; cult. for forage.

PHANEROPHLEBIA: see *CYRTOMIUM.*

PHARIUM: *BESSERA.*

PHASEOLUS L. BEAN. *Leguminosae* (subfamily *Faboideae*). Twenty spp. or more of mostly twining herbs, native from warm temp. to trop. regions of the New World; lvs. of 3 lfts., stipules not produced beyond their point of attachment; fls. clustered to racemose, papilionaceous, standard orbicular, spreading or somewhat contorted, keel beaked, together with thickened part of style twisted more than 360°, uppermost stamen separate; fr. a flat, dehiscent legume. Many spp. previously included in *Phaseolus* are now placed in the genus *Vigna,* which differs from *Phaseolus* in having stipules often basally appendaged and the thickened part of the style less strongly twisted, and in a number of technical characters related to pollen and biochemistry.

Extensively grown for the edible seeds and pods. Many species have a scandent "pole" form as well as an erect "bush" form. For cultivation of annual garden beans see *Beans.*

aconitifolius: *Vigna aconitifolia.*

acutifolius A. Gray. Ann., sts. short, twining; lfts. thin, almost linear to ovate, to 2½ in. long, attenuate-acuminate; fls. white to pale purple, few on very slender peduncles shorter than lvs.; fr. 2–3 in. long, seeds roundish, ¼ in. long or more, variable in color. Tex. to Ariz., s. to Mex. Var. **latifolius** G. Freem. TEPARY B. Broad-lvd. cult. form.

angularis: *Vigna angularis.*

aureus: *Vigna radiata.*

calcaratus: *Vigna umbellata.*

Caracalla: *Vigna Caracalla.*

coccineus L. [*P. multiflorus* Lam.]. SCARLET RUNNER B., DUTCH CASE-KNIFE B. Tall, twining per., with thickened roots, grown as an ann.; lfts. broadly ovate, to 5 in. long; fls. bright scarlet, to 1 in. long; fr. flat, 4–12 in. long, seeds broad, to 1 in. long, blackish, mottled red. Trop. Amer. Fls. ornamental. Cv. 'Albus' [var. *albus* L. H. Bailey]. WHITE DUTCH RUNNER B. Fls. and seeds white. Grown mostly for the edible seeds. Dwarf, erect strains of the sp. are also offered.

giganteus: a listed name of no botanical standing applied to a plant apparently not different from *Vigna Caracalla.*

limensis Macfady. LIMA B. Often included in *P. lunatus,* from which it may be distinguished by its more robust growth, lfts. to 5 in. long, weakly veined linear calyx bracts, thick-edged large pods with blunt or short tips and larger seeds, and later flowering. Trop. S. Amer. Important edible bean. Var. **limenanus** L. H. Bailey. BUSH LIMA B. DWARF L.B. Plants having "bush" form.

lunatus L. SIEVA B., BUTTER B., CIVET B., SEWEE B., CAROLINA B. Also often called LIMA B. Twining or erect, grown as an ann.; lfts. broadly ovate, to 3½ in. long, long-pointed; fls. in long, open racemes, white or yellowish, to ⅜ in. long, calyx bracts ovate, strongly veined; fr. to 3½ in. long and ¾ in. wide, sharply beaked, seeds flat, thin, ½ in. long. Trop. S. Amer. An important edible bean. Var. **lunonanus** L. H. Bailey. DWARF SIEVA B. Plants having "bush" form.

multiflorus: *P. coccineus.*

Mungo: *Vigna Mungo.*

radiatus: *Vigna radiata.*

sublobatus: *Vigna radiata.*

vulgaris L. KIDNEY B., GREEN B., SNAP B., HARICOT, COMMON B., FRENCH B., FRIJOL, RUNNER B., STRING B., SALAD B., WAX B. Erect or scandent ann.; lfts. thin, ovate to rhombic-ovate, acuminate; peduncles shorter than petioles and bearing few whitish or purplish fls. at tip; fr. narrow, to 8 in. long, flat or nearly cylindrical, seeds elongate or globose, about ½ in. long, red, brown, black, white, or mottled. Trop. Amer. Cv. 'Kentucky Wonder', one of the commonly offered "pole" green beans. Cvs. with yellow edible pods are called WAX BEANS. The ROMANO or ITALIAN GREEN BEAN is scandent with very broad, edible pods. One of the most important of legumes, supplying edible young pods (snap or string beans), unripe seeds (shell beans), or dried, mature seeds (dry beans), as well as valuable forage (the whole plant). Mature seeds of other variants furnish PEA BEANS, PINTO BEANS, and others. Var. **humilis** Alef. The widely grown "bush" bean.

PHEGOPTERIS: *THELYPTERIS.*

PHELLODENDRON Rupr. CORK TREE. *Rutaceae.* About 10 spp. of dioecious, deciduous trees, native to e. Asia; lvs. opp., odd-pinnate, glandular-dotted; fls. greenish, in terminal panicles or corymbs, unisexual, sepals, petals, and stamens 5–6; fr. black, berrylike, 5-seeded.

Cork trees are hardy in the North (Zone 4) and adapted to most soils. Propagated by seeds, cuttings over heat, and root cuttings stored over winter in moist sand or sphagnum.

amurense Rupr. To 50 ft., with corky bark, branchlets orange-yellow; lfts. 5–13, ovate to ovate-lanceolate, to 4 in. long, long-acuminate, ciliate, dark green and glossy above, glabrous and glaucous beneath; infl. pubescent. China, Japan.

chinense C. K. Schneid. To 30 ft., branchlets red-brown; lfts. 7–13, oblong-ovate to oblong-lanceolate, to 5½ in. long, rounded at base, with almost parallel margins, dark yellow-green above, pubescent beneath; infl. compact, higher than wide. Cent. China. Var. **glabriusculum** C. K. Schneid. Lfts. pubescent only on veins beneath. Cent. and w. China.

japonicum Maxim. To 30 ft., branchlets red-brown; lfts. 9–13, ovate-oblong, to 4 in. long, oblique at base, dull green above, pubescent beneath; infl. loose, as wide as high. Japan. Sometimes treated as a var. of *P. amurense.*

Lavallei Dode. To 30 ft. or more, branchlets purplish-brown; lfts. 5–13, elliptic-ovate to oblong-lanceolate, to 4 in. long, dull yellow-green above, pubescent beneath when young; infl. loose. Japan. Sometimes treated as a var. of *P. amurense.*

sachalinense (Friedr. Schmidt) Sarg. Tree, to 45 ft., bark not corky, branchlets red-brown; lfts. 7–11, ovate to oblong-ovate, to 4¾ in. long, usually not ciliate, dull green above, glabrous beneath; infl. essentially glabrous. China, Korea, n. Japan, Sakhalin. Sometimes treated as a var. of *P. amurense.*

Wilsonii Hayata & Kaneh. Tree; lfts. 9–11, ovate-oblong, to 3½ in. long; infl. to about 3 in. long and wide. Taiwan.

PHELLOSPERMA: *MAMMILLARIA* section *Phellosperma.*

PHILADELPHUS L. MOCK ORANGE. *Saxifragaceae.* About 65 spp. of shrubs, mostly erect but with curving or drooping brs., native to N. Amer., e. Asia, and Eur.; lvs. opp., simple, commonly deciduous; fls. white, often fragrant and showy, solitary or in small clusters or racemes, calyx tube united to ovary, sepals and petals usually 4, stamens many, ovary inferior or half-inferior, styles usually 4; fr. a caps., seeds many.

Many species are popular in cultivation; some have given rise to attractive, often double-flowered cultivars. Garden plants have been known popularly as SYRINGA, but that is the scientific name of the lilac.

Mock oranges commonly bloom in late spring. They are well adapted to shrubberies. If pruning is needed, it should be done after flowering, since the blossoms appear from wood of the previous year. Propagated by seeds, layers, suckers, and cuttings, the last usually of mature wood. Well-marked varieties are grown from cuttings of soft wood taken in summer and placed in frames.

argenteus Rydb. Low, spreading shrub, older brs. with exfoliating bark; lvs. almost sessile, elliptic to ovate, to ⅝ in. long, entire, leathery, white-silky beneath, strigose above; fls. in leafy panicles, sepals white-silky outside, tomentose inside, petals obtuse to retuse. Calif., Nev., Ariz., Colo.

aureus: a listed name of no botanical standing for *P. coronarius* cv.

×**Billardii:** *P.* ×*insignis.*

blandus: a listed name of no botanical standing.

brachybotrys Koehne. Shrub, to 9 ft., bark of the second year's growth brownish-gray, not exfoliating; lvs. ovate, to 2¼ in. long, sparsely strigose above and along veins beneath; fls. to 1¼ in. across, petals suborbicular. Closely related to *P. pekinensis* and perhaps not distinct from it.

burfordiensis: a listed name of no botanical standing for *P. virginalis* cv.

californicus: *P. Lewisii* subsp.

columbianus: *P. Lewisii.*

cordifolius J. Lange. A name used for a cult. plant of Amer. origin; may be synonymous with *P. Lewisii* subsp. *californicus.*

coronarius L. To 10 ft.; lvs. ovate to ovate-oblong, to 3 in. long, hairy only on veins beneath; fls. to 1½ in. across, very fragrant, in 5–7-fld. racemes, calyx usually glabrous, petals creamy. Eur., sw. Asia. Zone 5. A heterogeneous sp., widely cult. and with many cvs., including: 'Aureus' [cv. 'Foliis Aureis'], lvs. yellow; 'Deutziiflorus' [cv. 'Multi-florus Plenus'], dwarf, fls. double, petals narrow, pointed; 'Dianthi-florus', dwarf, fls. double, differing from 'Deutziiflorus' in petals rounded at apex; 'Duplex' [cv. 'Nanus'; cv. 'Pumilus'], dwarf, fls. double, differing from the 2 preceding cvs. in having hairy pedicels and in not flowering until shrubs are several years old; 'Multiflorus Plenus': 'Deutziiflorus'; 'Nanus': 'Duplex'; 'Primuliflorus' [cv. 'Rosi-florus Plenus'], closely related to 'Dianthiflorus', but taller, with hairy pedicels; 'Pumilus': 'Duplex'; 'Rosiflorus Plenus': 'Primuliflorus'; 'Salicifolius', lvs. lanceolate; 'Speciosissimus', low-growing, lvs. small; 'Variegatus', lvs. bordered with white; 'Zeyheri' [*P. Zeyheri* Schrad. ex DC.], erect, to 6 ft., fls. single, about 1 in. across.

Coulteri S. Wats. To 10 ft.; lvs. ovate to ovate-oblong, to 2 in. long, white-tomentose beneath; fls. about 1 in. across, solitary, calyx white-tomentose, petals with red spot at base. Mex. Not hardy north.

×**cymosus** Rehd. [*P.* ×*floribundus* Schrad. ex DC., not Roem. & Usteri]. A hybrid of uncertain parentage; shrub, to 7 ft.; lvs. ovate, to 4½ in. long; fls. 1–5, sometimes double, calyx tube glabrous. Zone 6. Cvs. include: 'Banniere', 'Conquête', 'Mer de Glace', 'Perle Blanche', and 'Rosace'.

Delavayi L. Henry. To 15 ft.; lvs. ovate-oblong, to 4 in. long, grayish-tomentose beneath; fls. 1½ in. across, very fragrant, in 5–13-fld. racemes, calyx glabrous, purple W. China. Zone 5.

dianthiflorus: a listed name of no botanical standing for *P. coronarius* cv.

×**Falconeri** Sarg. A hybrid of uncertain parentage; lvs. ovate, to 2½ in. long; fls. single, 3–5 to 22 in compound cymes, petals elliptic, acute, stamens sterile. Zone 5.

×**floribundus:** *P.* ×*cymosus.*

floridus Beadle. Closely related to *P. inodorus* var. *grandiflorus*, but lvs. pubescent beneath, and calyx and pedicels densely hairy. A rare sp., known in the wild only from Floyd Co. (Ga.) Zone 6.

gloriosus: *P. inodorus* var. *grandiflorus.*

Gordonianus: *P. Lewisii.* Var. **columbianus:** *P. Lewisii.*

grandiflorus: *P. inodorus* var.

hirsutus Nutt. Low, spreading shrub, brs. slender, slightly twisted, arching; lvs. ovate, to 3 in. long, densely grayish-pubescent beneath; fls. 1 in. across, usually in 3's, calyx pubescent, petals creamy. N.C. to Ga., w. to Ark. Zone 6.

incanus Koehne. To 10 ft. or more; lvs. ovate to oblong-ovate, to 3 in. long, densely gray-pubescent beneath; fls. 1 in. across, in 5–7-fld. racemes, calyx densely tomentose. W. China. Zone 6.

inodorus L. To 10 ft.; lvs. ovate, to 4 in. long, usually entire, glabrous beneath except on veins; fls. 2 in. across, 1–3 together, calyx glabrous. Penn. to Ala. Zone 6. Var. **grandiflorus** (Willd.) A. Gray [*P. gloriosus* Beadle; *P. grandiflorus* Willd; *P. speciosus* Schrad. ex DC.]. Moundlike shrub, brs. slender, arching; lvs. ovate, to 4 in. long, denticulate, sparsely pubescent on both surfaces, bearded at the principal nerve axils beneath; corolla campanulate at first, later nearly flat, petals suborbicular, becoming oblong. Va. to Ala. Zone 5. Var. **laxus** (Schrad.) S. Y. Hu [*P. laxus* Schrad.]. Differs in lvs. lanceolate, to 2½ in. long, sparsely pubescent beneath. Known in the wild only from Swain Co. (N.C.) Zone 5.

×**insignis** Carrière [*P.* ×*Billardii* Koehne]. A name used for a plant of cult. origin; presumably a hybrid, with *P. Lewisii* subsp. *californicus* and *P. pubescens* possibly the parents. Zone 6.

Karwinskyanus Koehne. Evergreen, somewhat scandent shrub, to 12 ft.; lvs. ovate, to 3 in. long, 5-nerved, sparsely hairy; fls. about 1 in. across, in 5–30-fld. panicles, calyx hairy. Mex. See *P. mexicanus.*

Keteleeri Carrière. A name given to a plant of cult. origin, said to have been a seedling of *P. coronarius;* fls. double, petals fringed. Perhaps now extinct.

latifolius: *P. pubescens.*

laxus: *P. inodorus* var.

×**Lemoinei** Hort. Lemoine: *P. coronarius* × *P. microphyllus.* Lvs. ovate to ovate-lanceolate, to 2 in. long, slightly hairy beneath; fls. 1½ in. across, very fragrant, in 3–7-fld. racemes. Zone 5. Cvs. include: 'Avalanche', 'Candelabra', 'Coupe d'Argent', 'Erectus', 'Manteau d'Hermine'. Var. **purpureomaculatus:** *P.* ×*purpureomaculatus.*

Lewisii Pursh [*P. Lewisii* var. *Gordonianus* (Lindl.) Jeps.; *P. colum-bianus* Koehne; *P. Gordonianus* Lindl.; *P. Gordonianus* var. *colum-bianus* (Koehne) Rehd.]. Shrub to 10 ft.; lvs. mostly ovate to 2¾ in. long, entire to remotely denticulate on older brs., strigose or strigose-villous on both surfaces to glabrous above and sometimes glabrous beneath except along the veins; fls. to 2 in. across, fragrant, 3–11 in terminal racemes on lateral brs. W. N. Amer. Zone 5. Variable in both floral and vegetative characters. Subsp. **californicus** (Benth.) Munz [*P. californicus* Benth.]. Lvs. more or less glabrous above, strigose on veins beneath. Mts., n. and cent. Calif. Zone 7.

Magdalenae Koehne. To 12 ft.; lvs. ovate, to 3 in. long, rough-pubescent beneath; fls. 1 in. across, in 7–11-fld. racemes, calyx-pubes-cent. China. Zone 6.

×**maximus** Rehd.: *P. pubescens* × *P. tomentosus.* Lvs. tomentose beneath; calyx tomentose.

mexicanus Schlechtend. To 15 ft. or more, brs. long, climbing; lvs. ovate to lanceolate, to 3 in. long, slightly hairy beneath; fls. to 1½ in. across, fragrant, 1–3 together, calyx hairy, petals creamy. Mex., Guatemala. Rare in cult.; not hardy north. Plants cult. under this name are commonly the related *P. Karwinskyanus*, with fls. somewhat smaller and more numerous in loose panicles.

microphyllus A. Gray. Much-branched shrub, to 6 ft.; lvs. ovate to lanceolate-elliptic, to 1¼ in. long, 3-nerved; fls. to 1 in. across, fragrant, usually solitary, calyx usually nearly glabrous, less often with silvery, feltlike pubescence. A variable sp. Se. U.S., s. to cent. Mex. Zone 6.

nepalensis: *P. tomentosus.*

×**nivalis** Jacques: *P. coronarius* × *P. pubescens.* Lvs. ovate, slightly pubescent beneath; fls. 1½ in. across, in 5–8-fld. racemes, calyx hairy.

pekinensis Rupr. To 6 ft.; lvs. oblong-ovate, to 3 in. long, glabrous except in axils of veins beneath, petioles purplish; fls. about 1 in. across, slightly fragrant, in 5–9-fld. racemes, calyx glabrous, petals creamy. N. China to Korea. Zone 6.

×**polyanthus** Rehd.: *P. Lemoinei* × (probably) *P. insignis.* Lvs. ovate, 1 in. long, usually entire, hairy beneath; fls. 1½ in. across, in cymes or racemes, calyx pubescent. Cvs. include: 'Favorite', 'Gerbe de Neige', 'Pavillon Blanc'.

pubescens Loisel. [*P. latifolius* Schrad. ex DC.]. To 10 ft.; lvs. ovate, to 4 in. long, gray-pubescent beneath; fls. 1½ in. across, in 5–9-fld. racemes, calyx pubescent. Tenn. to Ala., w. to Ark. Zone 5. Var. **ver-rucosus** (Schrad.) S. Y. Hu [*P. verrucosus* Schrad. ex DC.]. Lvs. elliptic or elliptic-ovate, acute or obtuse at base. Zone 5.

purpurascens (Koehne) Rehd. To 12 ft.; lvs. elliptic- to lanceolate-ovate, to 2 in. long, pubescent beneath; fls. 1 in. across, very fragrant, in 5–9-fld. racemes, calyx purple, glabrous, petals pure white. China. Zone 6.

×**purpureomaculatus** Hort. Lemoine: *P. Coulteri* × *P. Lemoinei.* Lvs. ovate, to 2 in. long, hairy beneath; fls. about 1 in. across, 1–3 together, calyx slightly pubescent, petals with purple spot at base. Zone 7? Cvs. include: 'Fantasie', 'Nuage Rose', 'Ophelia', 'Romeo', 'Surprise', 'Sybille'.

pyramidalis: a listed name of no botanical standing.

satsumanus Siebold ex Miq. To 8 ft.; lvs. ovate to ovate-lanceolate, to 3 in. long, hairy only in axils of veins beneath; fls. 1 in. across, somewhat fragrant, in 5–9-fld. racemes, calyx nearly glabrous. Japan. Zone 6.

Schrenkii Rupr. To 6 ft. and more; lvs. ovate to oblong-lanceolate, to 5 in. long, hairy only on veins beneath; fls. 1½ in. across, in 5–7-fld. racemes, calyx hairy on nerves. Manchuria to Korea. Zone 5.

sempervirens: a listed name of no botanical standing; has been ap-plied to cult. plants of *P. mexicanus.*

sericanthus Koehne. To 12 ft.; lvs. ovate to 4 in. long, hairy on veins beneath, petioles often reddish; fls. 1 in. across, in 5–9-fld. racemes, calyx pubescent. China. Zone 6.

speciosissimus: *P. coronarius* cv.

speciosus: *P. inodorus* var. *grandiflorus.*

×**splendens** Rehd.: *P. grandiflorus* × (probably) *P. Lewisii.* Lvs. nearly glabrous; fls. 2 in. across, in 5-fld. racemes, calyx glabrous.

subcanus Koehne. To 10 ft.; lvs. oblong-ovate, to 5 in. long, pubescent on veins beneath; fls. 1 in. across, in 5–9-fld. racemes, calyx densely pubescent. China. Zone 6. Var. **Wilsonii** (Koehne) Rehd. [*P. Wilsonii* Koehne]. Larger in all parts.

tomentosus Wallich [*P. nepalensis* Wallich ex Loud.]. To 10 ft.; lvs. ovate, to 3 in. long, grayish-pubescent beneath; fls. 1 in. across, fragrant, in 5–7-fld. racemes, calyx nearly glabrous. Himalayas. Zone 6.

verrucosus: *P. pubescens* var.

×**virginalis** Rehd. A hybrid of doubtful parentage; lvs. ovate, to 3 in. long, pubescent beneath; fls. double or partly so, in 3–7-fld. racemes, calyx pubescent. Zone 5. Cv. 'Burfordiensis'. Fls. large, single, stamens conspicuous. Other cvs. include: 'Argentine', 'Fleur de Neige', 'Glacier', 'Virginal'.

Wilsonii: *P. subcanus* var.

Zeyheri: *P. coronarius* cv.

PHILESIA Comm. ex Juss. *Liliaceae.* One sp., an evergreen shrub native to s. Chile; lvs. alt.; fls. red, borne toward ends of brs., perianth segms. 6, the outer ½–⅓ as long as the inner ones, stamens 6, filaments fused below middle into a tube, anthers basifixed; fr. a berry with rough surface.

Philesia thrives in cool temperatures and partly shaded locations, and requires peaty soil; sometimes grown under glass. Propagated by cuttings of ripened wood, which are slow in rooting.

buxifolia: *P. magellanica.*

magellanica J. F. Gmel. [*P. buxifolia* Lam. ex Poir.]. From ¼–4 ft.; lvs. linear-oblong, 1–1½ in. long, leathery, glaucous beneath, mucronate; fls. tubular, to 2 in. long, nodding, bracted at base.

PHILLYREA L. *Oleaceae.* Four spp. of evergreen, small, spring-flowering trees or shrubs in the Medit. region; lvs. opp., simple, entire or toothed; fls. small, white or greenish-white, unisexual, in racemes, corolla 4-lobed; fr. a black, one-seeded drupe.

Grown in mild and warm climates as ornamentals. Propagated by seeds, cuttings of half-ripe wood under glass, by layers, and by grafting on privet.

angustifolia L. To 15 ft.; lvs. oblong or linear-lanceolate, to 2 in. long, commonly entire; fr. ¼ in. long. S. Eur., N. Afr., Asia Minor.

decora Boiss. & Bal. [*P. Vilmoriniana* Boiss. & Bal.]. To 10 ft.; lvs. oblong to oblong-lanceolate, to 5 in. long, commonly entire, glossy above; fr. ½ in. long. W. Asia. Zone 6. The large, deep-green, leathery lvs. give this sp. a superficial resemblance to the Portugal laurel, *Prunus lusitanica.*

latifolia L. To 30 ft.; lvs. ovate, to 2½ in. long, toothed, glossy above; fr. ¼ in. long. S. Eur., Asia Minor. Zone 7. The lvs. are variable in shape. Cv. 'Spinosa'. Lvs. spiny-toothed. Var. **media** (L.) C. K. Schneid. [*P. media* L.]. To 6 ft., lvs. entire or wavy-toothed, to 2 in. long,

media: *P. latifolia* var.

Vilmoriniana: *P. decora.*

PHILODENDRON Schott. *Araceae.* Perhaps 200 spp. of mostly epiphytic herbs of trop. Amer., sts. mostly stout, climbing with aerial roots or rarely erect; lvs. often large, entire to variously lobed or pinnatifid, with parallel venation, petioles often stout, rarely geniculate; peduncle commonly very short, spathe fleshy, green or variously colored red to white, surrounding spadix, persistent until fr. ripens; fls. unisexual, perianth absent, spadix stout, with zones of female and male fls. contiguous, female fls. without staminodes; fr. a berry, white to orange.

Identification is complicated by differences in form and size of leaves between juvenile and adult phases, as well as by the great number of hybrids that have been produced. Small plants of many species have similar leaves, and often are nearly impossible to identify. Typical leaf forms of adult phase, noted in descriptions below, afford more positive identification. The adult phase is attained only under ideal growth conditions, and in many species, only when stems are also climbing on vertical supports.

Philodendrons are popular foliage plants for interior decoration and for landscaping in warm climates. They are of easy culture in any rich loam soil having good drainage and a constant supply of moisture. Though mostly native in humid forests, many species thrive under conditions of low humidity. Propagation by stem cuttings, and seeds when available.

There are white-variegated forms in cultivation, but they are generally unstable and have not been noted. Many hybrids have received names of Latin form, which have not been validated by publication of Latin descriptions of the plants and which are here treated as cultivars, as *Philodendron* cv. 'Fosteranum' and *Philodendron* cv. 'Mandaianum'. The parentage given for hybrids is that stated in the published records, and is not verifiable.

Species may be grouped according to their habit, indicated for each species, by the following symbols: Sh, "self-heading", with very abbreviated stems; Sc, scandent; or Ea, erect-arborescent, stems very stout, elongate, with very short internodes and a crown of lvs., but appearing to be "self-heading" in the juvenile phase.

alatum Poepp. Sc; similar to *P. lingulatum,* but having lvs. prominently inequilateral, and petioles more broadly winged, to 1 in. across or more. Peru. Doubtfully in cult.; some material offered under this name is *P. latilobum.*

Andersonii: a listed name of no botanical standing.

Andreanum: *P. melanochrysum.*

angustisectum Engl. [*P. elegans* Kurt Krause]. Sc; internodes 2 in. long (much longer in juvenile phase); lf. blade reflexed, broadly ovate in outline, to 2 ft. long, 18 in. wide, glossy dark green above, pinnately parted, segms. to 16 on each side, linear, acute, to about 1 in. wide, basal sinus open, petioles as long as blades, cylindrical; spathe about 6 in. long, tube light green with rose margin outside, blade yellowish, rose inside. Colombia.

argyreum: a listed name of no botanical standing.

auriculatum Standl. & L. O. Williams. Sc; sts. stout, internodes very short; lf. blades erect, narrowly elliptic-oblong, to 3 ft. long and 12–15 in. wide, basally auriculate, midrib and the many primary lateral veins pale, petioles somewhat shorter than blades, nearly cylindrical; peduncle 5 in. long, spathe to 11 in. long, greenish-white. Costa Rica.

auritum: *Syngonium auritum.*

bahiense Engl. Sc; differs from *P. Ruizii* in having lf. blades smaller, to 14 in. long and 5 in. wide, primary lateral veins 5–6 pairs, and petioles 6 in. long, sheathing in lower half. Bahia (Brazil).

Barrosoanum Bunt. [*P. deflexum* Hort., not Poepp. ex Schott]. Sc; lf. blades reflexed, hastate, 3-lobed, middle lobe ovate, 16 in. long and 10 in. wide, lateral lobes elliptic-ovate, 12 in. long and 7 in. wide, midrib and basal ribs broad, petioles 30 in. long, cylindrical; spathe 8 in. long, green, suffused with red, base reddish inside. S. Amer.

Barryi: a listed name of no botanical standing; to be treated as *Philodendron* cv. 'Barryi', applied to hybrids between *P. Selloum* and *P. bipinnatifidum;* lf. blades deeply cut, segms. narrow, irregularly toothed and lobed, undulate.

biauriculatum: a listed name of no botanical standing.

bipennifolium Schott [*P. panduriforme* Hort., not (HBK) Kunth]. HORSEHEAD P., FIDDLE-LEAF P., PANDA PLANT. Sc; internodes elongate; lf. blades reflexed, glossy, dark green, 5-lobed, to 18 in. long, 6–10 in. wide across lateral lobes, the terminal lobes oblanceolate, 3–4 in. wide and half as long as blade, lateral lobes angular, blunt, basal lobes oblong-triangular, flaring and separated by an open sinus, petioles shorter than blades, cylindrical; spathe 4½ in. long, greenish. Se. Brazil.

bipinnatifidum Schott ex Endl. Ea; lf. blades reflexed, ovate in outline, to 3 ft. long, sagittate, deeply pinnatifid, segms. many, overlapping, blunt, each with 1–4 secondary lobes of various sizes on each side, petioles scarcely longer than blades, flat on upper surface; spathe to 7 in. long, purple outside, white inside. S. Brazil.

Brenesii Standl. Sc; lvs. lanceolate- to ovate-oblong, to 20 in. long and half as wide, deeply cordate, thick-leathery, midrib broad, convex, primary lateral veins 8 or more pairs, petioles nearly as long as blades; spathe 6 in. long, green outside, tube inflated, dark red inside. Costa Rica.

calophyllum: *P. insigne.*

cannifolium: see *P. Martianum.*

chartaceum: a listed name of no botanical standing.

coerulescens: *P. inaequilaterum.*

colombianum R. E. Schult. Sts. short, decumbent, covered with remains of fibrous, scalelike lvs.; lf. blades erect, triangular-ovate, to 15 in. long, 9 in. wide, cordate, thin, with many very prominent, parallel veinlets between the 4–5 pairs of primary lateral veins, petioles to 20 in. long; peduncle 3–4 in. long, spathe to 2½ in. long, greenish. Colombia. Material cult. under this name or as *Philodendron* cv. 'Colombia' differs in having sts. scandent, with elongate internodes, without fibrous covering, and lf. blades ovate, of firm texture, without conspicuous veinlets; infl. unknown.

cordatum (Vell.) Kunth. HEART-LEAF P. Sc; internodes short; lf. blades reflexed, ovate, to 18 in. long and 10 in. wide, or larger, sagittate, undulate, basal lobes nearly oblong, rounded-angular and separated by a narrow sinus 5–6 in. long or slightly overlapping, primary lateral veins about 5 pairs, petioles shorter or longer than blades; spathe about 6 in. long, greenish. Rio de Janeiro (Brazil). Material of *P. scandens* subsp. *oxycardium* is often offered under this name.

×**Corsinianum** Hort. Makoy: *P. lucidum* Hort.? × *P. verrucosum.* Sc; internodes short, with fibrous remains of scalelike lvs. persistent at nodes; lf. blades somewhat reflexed, ovate, to 30 in. long and 24 in. wide, cordate, somewhat irregularly sinuate-lobed, new lvs. red-purple beneath with green veins, becoming green in age, petioles nearly as long as blades; spathe 7 in. long, tube purple outside, blade greenish-white, dotted with red. Has been misidentified as *P. Lindenii.*

corrugosum: a listed name of no botanical standing; applied to a vining plant with lf. blades reflexed, ovate, cordate, primary lateral veins many, impressed, petioles winged.

crassinervium Lindl. Sc; internodes 2–4 in. long; lf. blades narrowly elliptic-oblong, to 2 ft. long and 4 in. wide, attenuate-acuminate, cuneate, leathery, midrib convex, to ½ in. wide, lateral veinlets many, nearly equal, petioles 4–7 in. long, nearly cylindrical; peduncle mostly longer than petiole, spathe to 6 in. long, green below, whitish above, base cherry-red inside. Se. Brazil.

crassum: *P. Martianum.*

crenulatum: a listed name of no botanical standing; applied to a plant similar to *P. Selloum,* but having lf. segms. not lobed, narrow, strongly undulate-crisped. Origin uncertain.

crestifolium: a listed name of no botanical standing; applied to a plant similar to *P. lacerum.*

cruentum Poepp. REDLEAF. Sc; differs from *P. Ruizii* in having lf. blades narrower, to 16 in. long and 4 in. wide, basally acute, petioles 7 in. long; spathe longer, 6 in. long, white outside, red inside. Peru. Material offered under this name differs in having lf. blades cordate-sagittate, thin in texture, primary lateral veins 5–6 pairs, prominent, and lvs. of juvenile phase purple-red beneath.

cymbispathum Engl. Ea; differs from *P. Tweedianum* in having lf. blades ovate-triangular, acute, cordate-sagittate, undulate-sinuous, and spathe purplish. Minas Gerais (Brazil). Material offered under this name may be *P. saxicola.*

deflexum Poepp. ex Schott. Sc; lf. blades linear-oblong, 15 in. long, sagittate-hastate, terminal lobe 2 in. wide, midrib broad, lateral veinlets many, nearly equal, basal lobes oblong, narrow, spreading. Peru. Doubtfully in cult.; material of *P. Barrosoanum* has been offered under this name.

distantilobum Kurt Krause. Sc; lf. blades erect, ovate-oblong in outline, to 16 in. long and almost as wide, pinnatifid nearly to midrib, segms. 5–6 on each side, widely separated by wide, angular sinuses, oblanceolate to linear, to 2 in. wide, acuminate, entire, basal lobes bifid, petioles nearly as long as blades; peduncles several together, 5 in. long, spathe about 3½ in. long, greenish-white. Amazon region (Brazil).

domesticum Bunt. [*P. hastatum* Hort., not C. Koch & H. Sello]. SPADE-LEAF P. Sc; lf. blades reflexed, elongate-triangular, to 2 ft. long and 1 ft. wide, or larger, sagittate, undulate, bright green above, midribs paler, basal lobes oblong-rounded to triangular, petioles as long as blades, the upper side flattened toward apex and with a central longitudinal ridge; peduncle to 6 in. long, spathe 7 in. long, green outside, blade cherry-red with greenish border inside, tube darker red. Origin unknown.

dubium Chodat & Vischer. Not cult. Material grown under this name is *P. radiatum.*

Duisbergii: *P. Fendleri.*

Dursii: a listed name of no botanical standing.

Eichleri Engl. Ea; to 15 ft.; differs from *P. undulatum* in having lf. blades elongate-triangular, larger, to 3 ft. long or more, lobed, the lobes separated by prominent sinuses, obtuse, 3 in. long and 2 in. wide, or larger. Minas Gerais (Brazil).

elegans: *P. angustisectum.*

erubescens C. Koch & Augustin. RED-LEAF P., BLUSHING P. Sc; internodes elongate, new sts. red-purple; lf. blades reflexed, ovate-triangular, to 10 in. long and 7 in. wide, or larger, sagittate-cordate, shiny dark green above, coppery beneath, petioles as long as blades, red-purple at base; spathe boat-shaped, about 6 in. long, dark purple outside, crimson inside, fragrant, spadix white. Colombia.

Evansii: a listed name of no botanical standing; applied to hybrids between *P. Selloum* and *P. speciosum,* lf. blades large, lobed less than halfway to midrib.

Fendleri Schott [*P. Duisbergii* Epple ex Bunt.]. Sc; foliage suggestive of *P. pinnatifidum,* but scalelike lvs. drying and deciduous, sts. thus exposed and nearly bare, lf. blades reflexed, midrib convex, peti-

oles cylindrical; peduncle and spathe each 4¾ in. long, spathe maroon outside, tube inflated, 2 in. long. Colombia, Venezuela, Trinidad.

Fenzlii Engl. Sc; separated from *P. tripartitum,* in having lf. segms. broader, to 5 in. wide, the middle segm. narrowly obovate, lateral segms. not more than ¾ as long. Mex.

fibrillosum Poepp. Sc; internodes 2 in. long, fibrous remains of scalelike lvs. persistent at nodes; lf. blades erect, oblong-elliptic, 16 in. long and 7 in. wide, equally narrowed toward each end, membranous, primary lateral veins many, prominent, petioles to 7 in. long, geniculate at apex; spathe to 3 in. long, purplish at base. Peru. *Philodendron* cv. 'Jet Streak' may belong here. Material of *P. Grazielae* has been offered under this name.

ficutissimum: a listed name of no botanical standing; applied to climber, having lvs. oblong, cordate, with prominent veins.

flavens: a listed name of no botanical standing.

Fosteranum: a listed name of no botanical standing; to be treated as *Philodendron* cv. 'Fosteranum', applied to hybrids between *P. bipinnatifidum* and an unidentified sp.

fragrantissimum (Hook.) Kunth. Sh; differs from *P. Melinonii* in being much smaller, having a climbing habit in the juvenile phase, lf. blades triangular-ovate, petioles more or less V-shaped in cross section, lvs. of juvenile phase ovate, small, petioles winged; spathe with tube bright red outside, cherry-red inside, ovary with many ovules in each cell. N. S. Amer.

Friedrichsthalii: *Monstera Friedrichsthalii.*

giganteum Schott. GIANT P. Sc; huge, sts. to 4 in. in diam., internodes short, covered with remains of scalelike lvs.; lf. blades reflexed, ovate, to 3 ft. long and 2 ft. wide, or larger, cordate-sagittate, basal lobes often overlapping, petioles as long as blades, stout; spathe about 9 in. long, tube inflated-globose, cherry-red, blade white. W. Indies and Trinidad.

gloriosum André. Sts. prostrate, internodes short, fibrous remains of scalelike lvs. persistent; lf. blades reflexed, orbicular-ovate, to 16 in. long and 13 in. wide, sagittate-cordate with semicircular basal lobes, upper surface deep green with silky sheen, midrib and primary lateral veins ivory, petioles to 30 in. long, flattened dorsiventrally toward apex, dashed with white; peduncle as long as spathe, with white lines, spathe 6½ in. long, tube pale green flushed rosy outside, blade cherry-rose. Colombia.

Grazielae Bunt. [*P. fibrillosum* Hort., not Poepp.]. Sc; lf. blades leathery, nearly reniform, to 3½ in. long and 4¼ in. wide, nearly caudate at apex, cordate, primary lateral veins many, nearly equal, petioles 3 in. long, those of juvenile phase broad-sheathing in basal half; spathe 1 in. long, slender, greenish-white. Peru.

guatemalense: *P. inaequilaterum.*

guttiferum Kunth [*P. talamancae* Engl.]. LEATHERLEAF P. Sc; sts. slender; lf. blades ovate- to obovate-oblong, to 7 in. long and 3 in. wide, acuminate, basally obtuse, thin, petioles to 3½ in. long, winged nearly to apex; spathe 3½ in. long. Peru. Doubtfully in the trade; material of *Monstera Standleyana* has been offered under this name.

hastifolium Regel. Sc; differs from *P. mexicanum* in having basal lobes nearly oblong, less spreading, and petioles shorter than blades. Bahia (Brazil). Doubtfully in cult.

hastatum C. Koch & H. Sello, not Hort. Sc; lf. blades reflexed, oblong-hastate, to 18 in. long, terminal lobe oblong, 3 in. wide, basal lobes oblong, curved, 3 in. long, petioles as long as blades, lvs. of juvenile phase oblong, smaller, shallowly cordate; spathe green, 4 in. long. Brazil. The popular spade-leaf philodendron, long offered as *P. hastatum,* has been named *P. domesticum.*

Houlletianum Engl. Sc; apparently conspecific with *P. radiatum.* French Guiana.

Ilsemannii Hort. Sander. Sc; lf. blades reflexed, arrow-shaped, cordate-sagittate, mostly ivory, blotched with pale and dark green. Brazil. Possibly merely a variegated cv. of the juvenile phase of a well-known sp.

Imbe Schott ex Endl. [*P. Sellowianum* Kunth]. Sc; lf. blades reflexed, ovate-oblong, to 13 in. long and 7 in. wide, cordate to sagittate, rather thin, but firm-textured, basal lobes rounded, separated by narrow sinus about 3 in. long, primary lateral veins wide-spreading, petioles nearly as long as blades, cylindrical; spathe 6 in. long, white, becoming red toward base, spadix slender. Se. Brazil. Rope made from aerial roots.

imperiale: *P. ornatum;* but material offered as *P. imperiale* is very similar to *P. speciosum.*

inaequilaterum Liebm. [*P. coerulescens* Engl.; *P. guatemalense* Engl.]. Sc; sts. slender, woody; lf. blades papery, not reflexed, ovate to elliptic-oblong, to 10–12 in. long and about 6 in. wide, acuminate, obtuse to truncate basally, primary lateral veins many, wide-spreading, petioles 7–8 in. long, winged up to geniculum; spathe about 6 in. long, greenish-white. Mex., s. to Colombia.

inconcinnum Schott. Sc; internodes 2 in. long; lf. blades oblong to elliptic-narrow-obovate, to 8 in. long and 3½ in. wide, or larger, acuminate, usually emarginate basally, with broad midrib and 5–7 pairs of primary lateral veins, petioles to 7½ in. long or more, flattened on upper surface, wide-winged in basal half in lvs. subtending infl.; spathe to 5½ in. long, greenish-yellow outside, cream inside, marked with cherry-red at base. Venezuela.

insigne Schott [*P. calophyllum* Brongn. ex Linden & André]. Sh; sts. short, erect; lf. blade erect, oblanceolate-spatulate, to 40 in. long and 8½ in. wide, long-cuneate, rounded or acute at base, acuminate, leathery, midrib to 1 in. wide at base, primary lateral veins spreading, about 1 in. apart, petioles to 5 in. long, stout, sheathing in basal half; peduncle 10–15 in. long, spathe 7 in. long, greenish outside, becoming yellow or suffused with rose-purple in age, cherry inside. Guianas, s. to e. Colombia.

Johnsii: a listed name of no botanical standing for a juvenile phase of *P. Selloum.*

Karstenianum Schott, not Hort. Sc; sts. slender; lf. blades elliptic-ovate to -oblong, 8–13 in. long and 4–5 in. wide, basally obtuse to truncate, papery, petioles about ⅔ as long as blades, wide-winged except in apical ⅛–½ in.; spathe to 6 in. long, greenish-white. Panama, s. to Venezuela and Trinidad. Doubtfully in cult.; material offered under this name may be *P. inconcinnum.*

Krebsii Schott. Sc; internodes 1–4 in. long; lf. blades scarcely reflexed, ovate to oblong-elliptic or elongate-triangular, to 14 in. long and 8 in. wide or larger, cordate, nearly leathery, glossy, dark green, midrib broad, primary lateral veins many, nearly equal, petioles about 5 in. long, cylindrical; peduncle about as long as petiole, spathe to 4 in. long, green. W. Indies.

lacerum (Jacq.) Schott. Sc; internodes elongate; lf. blades reflexed, ovate in outline, to 30 in. long and nearly as broad, cordate, pinnately lobed, the lobes obtuse, midrib and primary lateral veins very prominent, petioles to 3 ft. long, cylindrical; peduncle to 8 in. long or more, spathe to 5 in. long, tube inflated, dull red-purple outside, purplish inside, blade green-yellow. Cuba, Jamaica, Hispaniola.

laciniatum: *P. pedatum.*

laciniosum: *P. pedatum.*

lanceanum: a listed name of no botanical standing.

latilobum Schott. Sc; young lvs. entire or nearly so, adult lvs. leathery, ovate-triangular, to 1 ft. long and nearly as wide, rounded-subtruncate basally, 3-lobed past the middle, middle lobe broadly ovate, about 6 in. wide, acute, lateral lobes broadly rounded from the base to a shorter and slightly curved upper margin, obtuse, with about 6 primary nerves alternating with weaker nerves. Peru. Some material offered as *P. amoenum* is apparently this sp.

ligulatum Schott. Sc; lf. blades oblong or lanceolate-oblong, 10 in. long and 4¾ in. wide, basally obtuse, petioles 4 in. long, stout, winged to apex; peduncle to 6 in. long, spathe slightly shorter. Costa Rica to Colombia. Material offered under this name may be *P. inconcinnum.*

Lindenii Schott. Not cult. Material offered under this name is *P.* × *Corsinianum.*

lingulatum (L.) C. Koch. Sc; sts. relatively slender; lf. blades oblong-elliptic to ovate, to 16 in. long, abruptly acuminate, basally truncate to subcordate, papery, glossy dark green above, petioles slightly longer than blades, to about ½ in. across, prominently winged except in apical ½–2½ in.; spathe about 6 in. long, creamy-white, becoming green. W. Indies.

Linnaei Kunth [*P. nobile* Bull]. Sc; differs from *P. insigne* in being smaller in all parts, lf. blades with primary lateral veins many, nearly equal, less than ⅛ in. apart, petioles sheathing to apex, and spathe at flowering with tube red-purple and blade white outside. Guianas to e. Colombia.

longilaminatum Schott. Sc; similar to *P. crassinervium,* but generally larger, lf. blades to 4 ft. long, petioles to 18 in. long, and spathe to 11 in. long. Bahia (Brazil).

longistilum Kurt Krause. Sc; internodes 2–4 in. long; lf. blades oblong-elliptic to oblanceolate, to 7 in. long and 3 in. wide, abruptly acuminate, acute-obtuse at base, midrib convex and prominent, primary lateral veins nearly equal, petioles about 2 in. long, broadly sheathing in basal ⅜ in. or less; spathe greenish-white, to 2 in. long. Ne. Peru, nw. Brazil. Doubtfully in cult.; material of *P. Linnaei* has been offered under this name.

Lundii Warm. Ea; doubtfully distinct from *P. bipinnatifidum,* having lf. blades more ample, 2–3-pinnatifid, and spathe green. S. Brazil. *Philodendron* cv. **'Seaside'** is probably referable here.

Lynette: a listed name of no botanical standing; to be treated as *Philodendron* cv. **'Lynette',** a reported hybrid between *P. elaphoglossoides* Schott and *P. Wendlandii,* differing from *P. Wendlandii* in being smaller, and having lf. blades thinner, primary lateral veins very many, wide-spreading, petioles more slender, nearly cylindrical, and spathe to only 2½ in. long, reddish toward base.

Macneilianum: a listed name of no botanical standing; to be treated as *Philodendron* cv. **'Macneilianum',** applied to hybrids between *P. Selloum* and an unidentified sp., having lvs. nearly triangular in outline, large, deeply 2-pinnatifid, with wavy margins.

magnificum: a listed name of no botanical standing; to be treated as *Philodendron* cv. **'Magnificum',** applied to hybrids between *P. Eichleri* and *P. Selloum.*

Mamei André. Similar to *P. gloriosum,* but having lf. blades somewhat narrower, irregularly marked with pale green blotches, and lacking silky sheen, with basal lobes somewhat rhombic, undulate, midrib green, primary lateral veins green, prominently impressed, petioles shorter and slightly winged toward apex, peduncle only 2 in. long, red-purple, and spathe red-maroon outside. Ecuador.

Mandaianum: a listed name of no botanical standing; to be treated as *Philodendron* cv. **'Mandaianum',** a supposed hybrid between *P. domesticum* and *P. erubescens,* but differing little from the latter except in its more intense red coloration.

Martianum Engl. [*P. cannifolium* Mart. ex Kunth, not (Dryand.) G. Don or (Rudge) Engl.; *P. crassum* Rendle]. Sc; internodes very short; lvs. leathery, lf. blades erect, lanceolate to ovate, to 18 in. long or more, 6–8 in. wide, acute-acuminate, basally cuneate to truncate, midrib very broad, primary lateral veins many, nearly equal, petioles 12–16 in. long, very swollen and spongy, deeply V-channelled on upper surface; spathe 5–6 in. long, green below and cream above outside, base cherry-red inside. Se Brazil.

maximum Kurt Krause [*Philodendron* cv. 'Baleza do Acre']. Sc; st. 2 in. in diam. or more, internodes short, remains of scalelike lvs. persistent; lf. blades reflexed, elongate-ovate, to 4½ ft. long and 29 in. wide, sagittate, undulate-sinuate, dark green above, midrib and primary lateral veins pale, basal ribs naked for some distance in sinus, petioles 3½ ft. long, flat on upper surface; peduncle to 1 ft. long, spathe 8 in. long, greenish. Acre (Brazil).

melanochrysum Linden & André [*P. Andreanum* Devans.]. BLACK-GOLD P. Internodes elongate; lf. blades of adult phase reflexed-pendent, oblong-lanceolate, to 32 in. long and 1 ft. wide, acuminate, sagittate, with basal lobes separated by narrow sinus or overlapping, upper surface black-green with a velvet sheen, midrib and primary lateral veins pale green, petioles to 20 in. long, rough, new lvs. coppery-salmon, lvs. of juvenile phase much smaller, ovate, cordate, with basal lobes often shortly united, and petioles sheathing in basal half or more; spathe 8 in. long, apically nearly caudate, tube greenish, blade white. Colombia.

Melinonii Brongn. ex Regel. Sh; fibrous remains of scalelike lvs. persistent, obscuring st.; lf. blades erect, elongate-ovate-triangular, to 3 ft. long, 16 in. wide, shallowly cordate, midrib broad, concave, pale, primary lateral veins 8–9 pairs, lvs. of juvenile phase oblong, basally truncate, rose-purple beneath, petioles stout, D-shaped in cross section and narrowly winged on angles, marked with purple spots; spathe 6½ in. long, tube inflated, pale olive, flushed with red outside, rose-purplish inside, blade cream, ovary with few ovules, stalks attached near base of each cell. N. S. Amer.

Mello-Barretoanum Burle Marx ex G. Barroso. Ea; differs from *P. bipinnatifidum* in having lf. blades triangular in outline, basal lobes larger, nearly as long as terminal lobe, with more slender, acute-tipped secondary lobes; and spathe green. Goias (Brazil).

mexicanum Engl. Sc; internodes elongate; lf. blades reflexed, elongate-triangular, subhastate to hastate, terminal lobe to 15 in. long and 7 in. wide, basal lobes unequal, lanceolate to oblong, somewhat curved, to 9 in. long and 3½ in. wide, petioles about 2 ft. long; spathe 5 in. long or more, green outside, ruby inside. Mex.

micans: *P. scandens* subsp. *scandens* forma.

microstictum Standl. & L. O. Williams. Sc; lf. blades wide-triangular to subreniform, to 9 in. long and almost as wide, long-acuminate, shallowly cordate or in lvs. of juvenile phase truncate, leathery, primary lateral veins many, nearly equal, petioles as long as blades, broadly sheathing in basal 2 in.; peduncle longer than petiole, spathe 6 in. long, green outside, tube burgundy-red at base inside. Costa Rica. Material of this sp. has been offered erroneously as *P. Pittieri.*

nobile: *P. Linnaei.*

ochrostemon Schott. Sc; sts. slender; lf. blades not reflexed, oblong-elliptic to oblong, to 11 in. long and 3–4½ in. wide, basally truncate, midrib slender, primary lateral veins about 10–12 on each side, petioles shorter than blades, narrow-winged nearly to blade, wings auriculate at apex; spathe about 6 in. long, tube greenish outside, yellow-green inside, blade yellow. Se Brazil. Doubtfully in cult.; some material offered under this name is an undetermined sp. of *Monstera*.

ornatum Schott [*P. imperiale* Schott; *P. Sodiroi* Hort. ex Bellair & St.-Léger]. Sc; internodes less than 1 in. long, to 4 in. in juvenile phase, covered with fibrous remains of scalelike lvs.; lf. blades reflexed, broadly ovate, to 2 ft. long (much smaller in juvenile phase), deeply cordate, dark green, sometimes splotched with gray, veins red beneath; petioles as long as blades, flat on upper surface, especially toward apex, reddish at apex; peduncle red, with white streaks, spathe 7 in. long, long-subulate apically, cream-colored inside, tube green outside, blade white suffused with red outside. Se Brazil.

oxycardium: *P. scandens* subsp.

panduriforme (HBK) Kunth. Imperfectly known sp.; doubtfully in cult.; material offered under this name is *P. bipennifolium*.

pedatum (Hook.) Kunth [*P. laciniatum* (Vell.) Engl.; *P. laciniosum* Schott]. Sc; internodes elongate; lf. blades reflexed, ovate in outline, irregularly pinnatifid or lobed, terminal lobe to 1½ ft. long and 1 ft. wide, with 1–3 triangular-oblong or -linear segms. on each side and an elliptic to rhombic terminal segm., basal lobes variously lobed, each to 11 in. long and 7 in. wide, petioles longer than blades, rarely warty toward apex; spathe 5 in. long, greenish outside, whitish toward apex, creamy inside, except red-purple toward base. Guianas and adjacent Venezuela and Brazil. Var. **palmatisectum** (Engl.) A. Jonker & F. Jonker. Differs in having lf. blades deeply pinnatifid into several very narrow segms. Brazil. Material of this var. has been offered as *P. quercifolium*. The sp. and its var. have served as parents of hybrids listed as cvs. following *P. squamiferum*.

Pennockii: a listed name of no botanical standing.

pertusum: *Monstera deliciosa.*

Pittieri: *P. scandens;* but material of *P. microstictum* has been offered erroneously as *P. Pittieri.*

pinnatifidum (Jacq.) Schott [*Philodendron* cv. 'British Guiana']. Sh; sts. covered by fibrous remains of scalelike lvs. and base of petioles; lf. blades triangular-ovate in outline, to 2 ft. long, acuminate, pinnatifid, terminal lobes with slightly channelled midrib and 5–6 pairs of oblong, blunt-tipped secondary lobes 6–8 in. long and 1–2 in. wide, basal lobes 2–4-cleft, separated by usually very open sinus, petioles as long as blade or longer, prominently channelled on upper surface, spotted, purple-brown; spathe 5–6 in. long, tube fusiform, green to purplish, blade white. Venezuela, Trinidad.

pinnatilobum Engl. [*Philodendron* cv. 'Fernleaf'] Sc; sts. angular, internodes to 1½ in. long (to 4 in. in juvenile phase); lf. blades erect, ovate-orbicular in outline, to 20 in. across, pinnately parted, lobes up to 13 on each side, narrow, about ½ in. wide, acuminate, basal lobes bifid (in juvenile phase, lobes fewer and often to 1 in. wide, with basal lobes very reduced), petioles as long as blades, channelled on upper surface; peduncles several together, 8½ in. long, spathe about 4 in. long, green, base marked rose inside. Amazon region (Brazil).

quercifolium Engl. Sc; a juvenile phase, possibly of *P. pedatum*, with lobes of lf. blades less deeply cut than in typical *P. pedatum.* Plants of *P. pedatum* var. *palmatisectum*, as well as of *P. Fendleri,* have been offered under this name.

radiatum Schott [*P. dubium* Hort., not Chodat & Vischer.]. DUBIA P. Sc; lf. blades reflexed, of firm texture, ovate in outline, to 3 ft. long and 28 in. wide, or larger, cordate-sagittate, deeply lobed, terminal segm. with about 8 pairs of linear-oblong to 3-lobed segms. separated by narrow sinuses, basal segms. 5-parted, with primary lateral veins fused and naked in sinus for 2–3 in., petioles longer than blades, cylindrical; peduncles several together, spathe 8–10 in. long, tube inflated, dull red-purple outside, cherry-red inside, blade greenish outside, cream-colored inside. Mex. and Cent. Amer.

rubens Schott. Sc; internodes elongate; lf. blades reflexed, elongate-ovate, to 20 in. long and 11 in. wide, sagittate-cordate, with rounded basal lobes, basal ribs shortly naked in sinus, petioles to 2 ft. long, nearly cylindrical, slightly rough toward apex; peduncle red, streaked with white, spathe 6 in. long, greenish, dotted and streaked with white outside, red-purple inside. Venezuela.

rubrum: a listed name of no botanical standing; applied to plants similar to *Philodendron* cv. 'Mandaianum'.

Ruizii Schott. Sc; lf. blades narrowly elliptic- or oblanceolate-oblong, to 2 ft. long or more and 9 in. wide, obtuse to truncate or auriculate at base, thick-leathery, primary lateral veins about 10 pairs, poorly defined with many prominent, striate veinlets between, petioles to 10 in. long; peduncles several together, spathe light green, to 4 in. long. Peru. Doubtfully in cult.

sagittatum: a listed name of no botanical standing for *P. sagittifolium.*

sagittifolium Liebm. [*P. sagittatum* Hort.]. Sc; internodes short; lf. blades elongate-triangular-oblong, to 2 ft. long and 8–12 in. wide, or larger, sagittate, firm, glossy, bright green, midrib broad, primary lateral veins 6–7 pairs, widely spreading, basal lobes nearly triangular, obtuse, about 3–5 in. long, petioles nearly as long as blades, flattened-convex on upper surface; spathe 5–7 in. long, green, base purple inside. Se. Mex. Baskets made from aerial roots by native peoples.

sanguineum Regel. Very similar to *P. sagittifolium,* but new lvs. mottled red beneath. E. Mex.

saxicola Kurt Krause. Ea; differs from *P. undulatum* in having lf. blades more broadly ovate, cut about half way to midrib, the segms. overlapping, oblong, obtuse, and peduncle and spathe shorter. Bahia (Brazil).

scandens C. Koch & H. Sello. HEART-LEAF P. Sc; sts. slender, internodes elongate; lf. blades reflexed, ovate, to 12 in. long and 9 in. wide, or larger, acuminate, cordate, primary lateral veins 2–3 pairs, petioles shorter than blades, rather slender, nearly cylindrical, channelled; spathe greenish, about 6 in. long, sometimes red-purple inside toward base. Subsp. **scandens** [*P. Pittieri* Engl.]. The typical subsp.; lvs. of juvenile phase green, with a silky sheen above, green to red-purple beneath. Trop. Amer. Forma **micans** (C. Koch) Bunt. [*P. micans* C. Koch]. VELVET-LEAF P. Lvs. of juvenile phase dark green above and red-purple beneath. Panama. Subsp. **oxycardium** (Schott) Bunt. [*P. cordatum* Hort., not (Vell.) Kunth; *P. oxycardium* Schott]. PARLOR IVY, COMMON P. Lvs. glossy and green on both surfaces in both juvenile and adult phase. E. Mex.

Schottii C. Koch. Sc; sts. slender; lf. blades lanceolate or oblong-lanceolate, to 7 in. long and 1½ in. wide, acuminate, obtuse to nearly cordate, petioles to 2 in. long, winged to apex; spathe 3 in. long, greenish-white. Jamaica. Doubtfully in cult.

Schottianum H. Wendl. ex Schott. Sc; internodes short; lf. blades broadly ovate, to 24 in. long and 16 in. wide, or larger, cordate, primary lateral veins 5–6 pairs, petioles longer than blades, nearly cylindrical; peduncle reddish, spathe 5 in. long, green outside, red-purple inside. Costa Rica.

Selloum C. Koch [*P. Johnsii* Hort.]. Ea; perhaps not specifically distinct from *P. bipinnatifidum,* from which it has been separated in having primary lf. segms. merely somewhat dentate to pinnatifid, and spathe green outside. S. Brazil. Frs. are eaten. Cvs. offered include: 'German Selloum', 'Miniature Selloum', 'Seaside', and 'Uruguay'. Has been widely used as one parent in production of many hybrids. *Philodendron* cv. 'Golden Selloum': *P. Warscewiczii* cv. 'Flavum'.

Sellowianum: *P. Imbe;* but material similar to *P. Selloum* has been offered under this name.

Simsii (Hook.) Kunth. Sh; very similar to *P. fragrantissimum,* from which it has been differentiated in having lf. blades with veins purple beneath, and petioles cylindrical. Venezuela.

Sodiroi: *P. ornatum.*

speciosum Schott ex Endl. Ea; differs from *P. Williamsii* in having lf. blades broader, 24 in. long and 16 in. wide, or larger, basal lobes nearly rhombic, peduncle shorter, 2 in. long, and spathe to 9 in. long, crimson inside. S. Brazil.

squamiferum Poepp. Sc; differs from *P. pedatum* in having lf. blades smaller, divided into only 5, mostly entire lobes separated by broader sinuses, with basal lobes smaller, central lobes somewhat curved, petioles reddish, clothed in fleshy bristles or scales ³⁄₁₆ in. long; peduncle warty, spathe smaller, flushed reddish below. Surinam, French Guiana, adjacent Brazil. One parent of the following hybrids: *Philodendron* cv. 'Florida': *P. pedatum* × *P. squamiferum;* similar to the latter but lobes of lf. blade sometimes apically lobed, and petioles merely minutely warty. *Philodendron* cv. 'Florida Compacta'. *P. pedatum* var. *palmatisectum* (mistakenly reported to be *P. quercifolium*) × *P. squamiferum;* very similar to *Philodendron* cv. 'Florida'.

stenophyllum Kurt Krause. Sc; probably not specifically distinct from *P. Ruizii,* from which it has been separated by its narrower lf. blades not more than 5 in. wide. Peru.

talamancae: *P. guttiferum.* Material similar to *Philodendron* cv. 'Wend-imbe' has been offered as *P. talamancae;* see *P. × Wend-imbe.*

trifoliatum: *Synogonium auritum.*

tripartitum (Jacq.) Schott. Sc; internodes elongate; lf. blades sometimes reflexed, 3-parted, divided nearly or quite to base, segms. elongate-oblong-elliptic, middle segm. sometimes oblanceolate, to 10 in. long and 3 in. wide, or larger, lateral ones nearly as large, but very inequilateral and rounded on outer side, petioles little longer than blades; spathe about 6 in. long, tube greenish, the base purple inside, blade whitish. Trop. Amer.

trisectum Standl. Sc; differs from *P. tripartitum* in being smaller; and having lf. segms. nearly equal, to 7½ in. long and 1½ in. wide, shortly united at base, the lateral segms. somewhat curved and nearly equilateral, petioles to 13 in. long; peduncle 4½ in. long, spathe greenish-white, 4 in. long. Costa Rica.

triumphans: a listed name of no botanical standing for *P. verrucosum.*

Tweedianum Schott. Ea; lf. blades reflexed, broadly ovate-triangular, 1 ft. long and 10 in. wide, apically obtuse and apiculate, sagittate, basal lobes obtuse, separated by oblong sinus to 4 in. long, petioles as long as blades; peduncle 8–12 in. long, spathe greenish, 4 in. long, thickened toward base. S. Brazil, Uruguay.

undulatum Engl. Ea; lf. blades reflexed, ovate, to 2 ft. long and 16 in. wide, or larger, sagittate, sinuately lobed, petiole 30 in. long; spathe nearly as long as peduncle, to 8 in. long, green outside, purplish inside W. Mato Grosso (Brazil), Paraguay.

variifolium Schott. Sc; lf. blade oblong, 8–11 in. long and 3–5 in. wide, long-acuminate, cordate, primary lateral veins many, nearly equal, or varying to wider and hastate with basal lobes obtuse, curved, separated by a very open sinus, petioles nearly as long as blades; infl. unknown. Peru. Doubtfully in cult.; material offered under this name resembles a juvenile phase of *P. ornatum.*

verrucosum Mathieu ex Schott [*P. triumphans* Hort.]. Sc; internodes 3–6 in. long, petioles, peduncles, and outside of scalelike lvs. and spathes covered with greenish, fleshy bristles; lf. blades reflexed, ovate, to 2 ft. long and 16 in. wide, sagittate-cordate, weakly sinuate, upper surface shimmering dark green, with pale zones along midribs and primary lateral veins, lower surface red-purple between veins, petioles to 20 in. long, reddish; peduncle 4–8 in. long, spathe about 3 in. long, yellowish outside, the base sometimes purplish in age, tube cherry-burgundy inside. Costa Rica to Ecuador.

Wallisii Regel ex Engl. St. erect, abbreviated; lf. blades broadly ovate, 17 in. long and 1 ft. wide, cordate, firm, petioles 16 in. long, broadly and shallowly channelled toward apex; spathe 5 in. long, greenish-brown. Colombia.

Warscewiczii C. Koch. Sc; semideciduous, sts. huge; lvs. few, in a crown, lf. blades reflexed, membranous, triangular in outline, 2-pinnatifid, primary segms. rather few, each deeply lobed, the ultimate lobes sometimes toothed, basal sinus very open, with basal ribs naked for some distance; spathe green outside, creamy inside. W. Mex. and Cent. Amer. Cv. **'Flavum'.** Lvs. yellow; sometimes called *Philodendron* cv. 'Golden Selloum'.

×**Wend-imbe:** a listed name of no botanical standing; to be treated as *Philodendron* cv. 'Wend-imbe', applied to hybrids reportedly between *P. Imbe* and *P. Wendlandii,* having internodes abbreviated, lf. blades erect, nearly oblong, subcordate, undulate, petioles elongate, flattened on upper surface, and spathe large, salmon-rose. A similar sort with variegated lvs. is offered as *Philodendron* cv. **'Tricolor'.**

Wendlandii Schott. Sh; lf. blades erect, narrowly oblanceolate, to 30 in. long and 8 in. wide, nearly truncate to somewhat auriculate basally, firm, midrib convex, to 1 in. wide at base, primary lateral veins lightly impressed, petioles to 1 ft. long and 1½ in. wide, thick, spongy, flat on upper surface; spathe to 7 in. long, tube pale olive, flushed purplish outside, the base purplish inside, blade creamy. Nicaragua to Panama. *Philodendron* cv. **'Orlando'.** A hybrid between *P. Wendlandii* and an undetermined sp.; similar to *Philodendron* cv. 'Wend-imbe', with lvs. erect, elongate, sagittate, and spathe red-brown.

Williamsii Hook.f. Ea; st. 2–3 in. in diam.; lf. blades reflexed, firm, oblong-triangular, to 30 in. long, sagittate, terminal lobe to 14 in. wide, weakly sinuate, basal lobes oblong-ovate, to about 8½ in. long, obtuse, with basal ribs naked for some distance in nearly rhombic sinus, midrib and primary lateral veins dull purple beneath, petioles as long as blades; spathe as long as peduncle, 12 in. long, greenish outside, cream-colored inside. Bahia (Brazil). Material offered under this name differs in having lf. blades nearly hastate, to 3 ft. long with terminal lobes narrower, only 8–11 in. wide.

Wilsonii: a listed name of no botanical standing; to be treated as *Philodendron* cv. 'Wilsonii', applied to hybrids between *P. giganteum* and *P. radiatum;* similar to *P. lacerum.*

PHILOTRIA: *ELODEA.*

PHINAEA Benth. *Gesneriaceae.* A few spp. of low, per., hairy herbs with scaly rhizomes, native to trop. Amer.; lvs. opp., often more or less congested; fls. solitary or clustered or on short brs. in lf. axils, calyx 5-lobed, corolla rotate or more or less cup-shaped, tube short, lobes spreading to nearly erect, nearly equal, stamens 4, borne at base of corolla tube, filaments slender, anthers shorter than filaments, united, cells not confluent at apex, disc lacking, ovary half-inferior, stigma mouth-shaped; fr. a caps.

Propagated by the scaly rhizomes. For cultivation see *Gesneriaceae.*

multiflora C. V. Mort. To 3 in.; lvs. petioled, blades ovate to rhombic, crenate, green with pale veins and soft, erect hairs above, green or red with hairs on nerves beneath; fls. 1 to many, pedicels and calyx tube villous, calyx lobes oblong, ⅛ in. long, pilose on both sides, corolla white, about ¼ in. long, the lobes about as long as tube and nearly erect, densely glandular at margins and outside, ovary pilose. Mex.

PHLEBODIUM: *POLYPODIUM.*

PHLEUM L. TIMOTHY. *Gramineae.* About 10 spp. of mostly per. grasses in the temp. zone of both hemispheres, sts. erect; lf. blades flat; infl. dense, cylindrical; spikelets 1-fld., laterally compressed, disarticulating above the glumes, glumes equal, membranous, compressed, ciliate on the keel, acute to awned, lemma shorter, 3–5-nerved, palea nearly as long as the lemma. For terminology see *Gramineae.*

alpinum L. ALPINE T. Sts. to 20 in., clustered from a decumbent, somewhat creeping base; lf. blades to 4 in. long and ¼ in. wide; panicle not more than twice as long as wide; bristly; glumes about ¼ in. long, awned, the awns less than ⅛ in. long. Greenland to Alaska, s. to Me. and Calif.; Mex. to S. Amer.; Eurasia.

pratense L. COMMON T., MOUNTAIN T., HERD'S GRASS. Sts. 2–3 ft., from a bulblike base, forming large clumps; lf. blades elongate, mostly ¼–⁵⁄₁₆ in. wide; panicle more than twice as long as wide; spikelets crowded, spreading, glumes ⅛ in. long, truncate, with a stout minute awn. Eurasia. Common meadow grass, cult. as forage and commonly escaped throughout the U.S.

PHLOGACANTHUS Nees. *Acanthaceae.* About 15 spp. of shrubs or herbs in India; lvs. often large; fls. in often long, dense, terminal panicles, corolla 2-lipped, tube broad, curved, stamens 2, anther sacs 2, parallel; fr. a 4-sided caps., seeds many.

thyrsiflorus Nees. To 7 ft., lvs. elliptic-lanceolate, to 7 in. long; fls. in showy terminal clusters to 12 in. long, corolla orange.

PHLOMIS L. *Labiatae.* About 100 spp. of per. herbs or shrubby plants from Medit. region to cent. Asia and China; sts. mostly square in cross section, woody at base, usually densely pubescent or woolly; lvs. opp., simple; fls. sessile, tomentose to villous, in axillary, few- to many-fld. verticillasters, bractlets often many, calyx tubular, 5–10-nerved, 5-toothed, corolla yellow to purple or white, tube shorter than calyx or longer, often hairy-ringed inside, limb 2-lipped, upper lip concave, lower lip 3-lobed, stamens 4, in 2 pairs, anthers 2-celled; fr. of 4 glabrous or pubescent nutlets.

Coarse plants suited to the wild garden or perennial border. Propagated by seeds, cuttings, division, and *P. tuberosa* by tubers.

alpina Pall. Herb, to 18 in., pubescent; lvs. ovate-lanceolate to cordate, 8 in. long; fls. in 20–30-fld. verticillasters, bractlets subulate, hirsute, calyx teeth short, bristly, corolla purplish, upper lip pilose. Altai Mts., Mongolia. Material cult. under this name may be *P. tuberosa.*

cashmeriana Royle ex Benth. Per., to 3 ft., white-tomentose; lvs. ovate-lanceolate, to 7 in. long, acute; fls. in 2–3 verticillasters, bractlets linear-subulate, ciliate, as long as calyx or longer, calyx to ¾ in. long, teeth subulate, to ¼ in. long, corolla to 1⅛ in. long, lavender, upper lip pilose. Summer. Kashmir.

fruticosa L. JERUSALEM SAGE. Per., to 4 ft., much-branched, densely white-tomentose; lvs. elliptic to lanceolate-ovate, 2–4 in. long, entire or crenate, tomentose; fls. in usually 14–36-fld. verticillasters, bractlets obovate to elliptic, to ¾ in. long, often ciliate, tomentose, calyx to ¾ in. long, teeth very short, subulate, corolla slightly longer than calyx, intense yellow. Spring, summer. Medit. region, w. to Sardinia.

herba-venti L. Herb, to 18 in., pubescent, roots without tubers; lvs. lanceolate, to 6 in. long, crenate-dentate; fls. in 2–14-fld. verticillasters, bractlets subulate, longer than the calyx, strongly pubescent, calyx to ⅜ in. long, teeth subulate, to ³⁄₁₆ in. long, corolla about twice as long as calyx, purple or pink. Summer. S. and e. Eur.

laciniata: *Eremostachys laciniata.*

Leonurus: *Leonotis Leonurus.*

Russeliana (Sims) Benth. [*P. viscosa* Hort., not Poir.]. Shrubby, pubescent; lvs. ovate, truncate to subcordate basally, obtuse, crenate; bractlets longer than verticillaster, lanceolate-linear, ciliate; calyx ½ in. long, viscid, slightly 2-lipped, the 2 lower teeth longer, corolla yellow. Asia Minor.

samia L. Per., to 3 ft., sts. glandular, roots without tubers; lvs. ovate-cordate, tomentose, long-petioled; verticillasters 12–20-fld., bractlets subulate, glandular-tomentose; calyx teeth subulate, corolla purple. Greece.

tuberosa L. Per., to 6 ft., glabrescent, pubescent at the nodes and on the petioles, roots with small tubers; lvs. ovate-cordate, to 10 in. long, crenate, sparsely to densely pubescent, petioled; infl. to 1 ft. long or more, verticillasters 40–40-fld., bractlets about as long as calyx, subulate, pubescent; calyx to ½ in. long, teeth very short, corolla longer than calyx, purple or pink, upper lip pilose. Summer. Cent. and se. Eur. to cent. Asia.

villosa: a listed name of no botanical standing.

viscosa: see *P. Russeliana.*

PHLOX L. *Polemoniaceae.* About 60 spp. of erect, diffuse, or cespitose ann. or per. herbs or subshrubs, native to N. Amer.; 1 sp. to Siberia; lvs. opp., or the upper lvs. sometimes alt., simple; fls. blue, purple, crimson, pink, and white, solitary, or in terminal cymes or panicles, calyx 5-cleft, corolla salverform, 5-lobed, stamens 5, unequal in length, or unequally inserted on corolla tube; fr. a 3-valved caps., rupturing the calyx at maturity.

Popular flower garden subjects with many forms. The annual phloxes are of easy culture in any garden soil, but will bloom longer if given abundant moisture and plant food. Seeds should be sown in early spring or started in boxes and transplanted. The perennial summer phloxes require fertile soil and plenty of water and should be set 2–3 ft. apart. Clumps will bloom for three or four years and should then be divided. Seeds do not reproduce the type, and named or special forms are multiplied from the strong young shoots that arise from the rootcrown or root as the plant spreads, or clumps may be divided. Most of the phloxes are hardy north.

adsurgens Torr. ex A. Gray. Per., with decumbent or creeping shoots, fl. sts. to 1 ft.; lvs. elliptic to ovate upward, to 1¼ in. long, thin, glossy, evergreen; fls. purple, lilac, or pink, with white eye, to 1 in. across. Ore. and n. Calif.

abdita: *P. alyssifolia* subsp.

advena: a listed name of no botanical standing.

albomarginata M. E. Jones. Cespitose per., to 3 in. high; lvs. elliptic-lanceolate or oblong, to ¼ in. long, pointed at apex, margin white, thickened; fls. pink to white, 1–3 in glandular-pubescent infl. Mts., e. Idaho and w. Mont.

alyssifolia Greene. Tufted per., to 4 in. high; lvs. linear to oblong, to 1 in. long, margins ciliate and thickened; infl. glandular-pubescent; fls. purple to pink, with a pale center, rarely white, to ⅝ in. across, calyx shorter than corolla tube. Sask. to Mont., s. to Wyo. and nw. Nebr. Subsp. **abdita** (A. Nels.) Wherry [*P. abdita* A. Nels.]. Somewhat larger in all its parts. W. S. Dak. and adjacent Wyo. Subsp. **collina** (Rydb.) Wherry [*P. collina* Rydb.]. Infl. hairy, but not glandular. Sw. Mont.

amoena Sims. Pilose per., to 1 ft., decumbent at base; lvs. oblong-lanceolate, to 2 in. long; fls. purple or pink, rarely lavender or white, to ¾ in. across, in terminal compact infl. subtended by leafy involucre. S. Ky. to n. Fla. Rarely cult.; plants offered under this name are *P.* × *procumbens.*

andicola Nutt. ex A. Gray. Erect per., to 5 in., spreading by rhizomes; lvs. linear-subulate, to ¾ in. long; fls. white, rarely yellowish or purplish, to ¾ in. across, on short pedicels. N. Dak., w. to Nebr. and ne. Colo.

× Arendsii: a listed name of no botanical standing for the hybrid *P. divaricata* × (probably) *P. paniculata.* Per., to 2 ft.; lvs. lanceolate-ovate to linear-lanceolate, to 4 in. long; fls. lavender or mauve, 1 in. across, in loose clusters to 6 in. across.

austromontana Cov. [*P. Douglasii* var. *austromontana* (Cov.) Jeps. & H. L. Mason]. Cespitose per., to 4 in., herbage gray-hairy but not glandular; lvs. linear-subulate, to 1 in. long, firm, sharp-pointed; fls. pink, lavender, or white, usually solitary. Ore. and s. Calif., w. to Idaho and n. Ariz.

bifida L. Beck. SAND P. One of the subulate-lvd. phloxes, cespitose per., to 8 in., with well-separated nodes; lower lvs. mostly 1–2 in. long, linear to lanceolate; infl. glandular-pubescent; fls. lavender or rarely lilac, corolla lobes conspicuously notched to about ⅛ in. Sw. Mich. to Tenn., w. to Kans. and Ark. Cv. 'Alba'. Fls. white. Subsp. **Stellaria** (A. Gray) Wherry [*P. Stellaria* A. Gray]. Glabrous or with nonglandular hairs, corolla lobes less deeply notched.

borealis Wherry. Cespitose per., to 3½ in.; lvs. linear, to 6 in. long, ciliate; fls. lilac, lavender, or white, 1–3 in infl. with glandless and glandular hairs intermixed. Alaska.

Brittonii: *P. subulata* subsp.

bryoides Nutt. Cushion-shaped per., to 2 in.; lvs. densely imbricate, oblong, to 3⁄16 in. long, cuspidate, cobwebby; fls. white or lilac, solitary, sessile. Cent. Ore. and w. Mont., s. to Nev. and w. Nebr.

Buckleyi Wherry. SWORD-LEAF P. Rhizomatous per., to 1½ ft.; lvs. linear-ensiform, to 5 in. long, long-acuminate, evergreen; infl. glandular-pubescent; fls. bright purple to pink. W. Va.. and Va.

caespitosa Nutt. Densely cespitose per., to 5 in.; lvs. linear-subulate, to ½ in. long, 3-ribbed; fls. white to lilac, mostly solitary. Ore. and Mont., s. to New Mex. Subsp. **caespitosa.** The typical subsp.; forming mound 6–10 in. high. Subsp. **condensata** (A. Gray) Wherry [*P. condensata* (A. Gray) E. E. Nels.]. Forming mound to 1½ in. high; lvs. appressed. Colo. Subsp. **pulvinata** Wherry. Forming mound to 1½ in. high; lvs. spreading. Cent. Colo. to n. New Mex.

camlaensis: a listed name of no botanical standing for *P. nivalis* cv. 'Camla'.

canadensis: *P. divaricata.*

carolina L. THICK-LEAF P. Per., to 4 ft.; lvs. lanceolate to ovate-oblong, to 5 in. long, thick and scarcely veiny; fls. purple to pink, rarely white, about ¾ in. across, in panicles, calyx lobes broad-linear, prominently nerved. N.C. to nw. Fla., w. to Mo. and Miss. Some material cult. as *P. maculata* belongs here; early-blooming phases are widely cult. as *P. suffruticosa* Hort., not Venten. in several hort. cvs. Cv. 'Gloriosa'. Fls. salmon-pink. Cv. 'Miss Lingard'. Fls. white. Var. **triflora:** *P. glaberrima* subsp.

collina: *P. alyssifolia* subsp.

condensata: *P. caespitosa* subsp.

cuspidata Scheele. Delicate ann., to 10 in.; lower lvs. opp., oblanceolate, to 1⅜ in. long, upper lvs. alt., linear; fls. purple to lilac, often with pale centers, in compound cymes. E. Tex. Material offered under this name is often *P. Drummondii* cv. 'Twinkle'.

decussata: *P. paniculata,* but the name *P. decussata* is sometimes misapplied to *P. maculata* or *P. carolina.*

diffusa Benth. Freely branching, prostrate or spreading per., forming clumps to 6 in. high and wide; lvs. linear or linear-subulate, to about ½ in. long; fls. pink, lilac, or white, ½ in. across, usually solitary on leafy brs. S. Ore., s. to n. Nev. and s. Calif. Subsp. **scleranthifolia** (Rydb.) Wherry [*P. scleranthifolia* Rydb.]. Lvs. rigid, sharp-pointed. Wash. and Mont., s. to e. Ore., Utah, S. Dak.

divaricata L. [*P. canadensis* Sweet]. WILD SWEET WILLIAM, BLUE P. Spreading per., to 1½ ft., with many sterile, decumbent, creeping shoots rooting at nodes; lvs. elliptic, ovate, to oblong, to 2 in. long; fls. pale violet-blue to lavender, to 1½ in. across, corolla lobes mostly notched or erose. Que. to Mich., s. to Ga. and n. Ala. Cv. 'Alba'. Fls. white. Cv. 'Grandiflora'. Fls. larger. Cv. 'Rosea'. A listed name. Subsp. **Laphamii** (A. Wood) Wherry. Fls. large, rich blue-violet, corolla lobes entire.

Douglasii Hook. Loosely cespitose per., to 8 in., herbage glandular-pubescent throughout; lvs. subulate to linear-subulate, to ½ in. long, sharp-pointed, firm; fls. lavender, pink, or white, 1–3 in infl. Wash. and ne. Ore., e. to nw. Mont. Var. **austromontana:** *P. austromontana.* Var. **macrantha:** a listed name of no botanical standing. Subsp. **rigida** (Benth.) Wherry [*P. rigida* Benth.]. Lower, more compact; lvs. rigid, more pungent.

Drummondii Hook. ANNUAL P., DRUMMOND P. Ann., to 20 in.; lvs. ovate to lanceolate, to 3 in. long, upper lvs. alt.; fls. rose-red varying to white, buff, pink, red, and purple, to 1 in. across, in dense cymose clusters. S.-cent. Tex. Color forms are represented by such cvs. as: 'Alba Oculata', 'Atropurpurea', 'Caerulea-striata', 'Carnea', 'Coccinea', 'Isabellina', 'Rosea', 'Violacea'. Cv. Gigantea'. Large-fld. strain with a wide range of colors. Cv. 'Grandiflora' [var. *grandiflora* Regel]. Fls. purple, white beneath. Cv. 'Rotundata' [var. *rotundata* Voss]. Corolla lobes broad. Cv. 'Twinkle' [var. *stellaris* Voss; *P. cuspidata* Hort.]. STAR P. A group with narrow, cuspidate corolla lobes, which are often cut and fringed; also known as cv. 'Sternenzauber'. Other cvs. listed are: 'Leopoldii' and 'Nana Compacta'.

floridana Benth. Erect or ascending per., to 20 in. or more, glabrous in lower part; lvs. linear to oblong or lanceolate, to 3½ in. long; fls. purple to pink, with pale eye, in compact, glandular-pubescent infl. Ga., Fla., Ala. Subsp. **bella** Wherry. Shorter; lvs. glossy; fls. pastel-pink.

frondosa: Hort. Vilm.-Andr. Inferred to be a hybrid between *P. subulata* and *P. nivalis;* to 6 in., with rose fls.

glaberrima L. SMOOTH P. Per., to 5 ft.; lvs. linear to linear-lanceolate, to 4 in. long or more, mostly glabrous; fls. purple to pink, rarely white, to ¾ in. across, in panicled cymes. Se. Va. to S.C. Subsp. **triflora** (Michx.) Wherry [*P. carolina* var. *triflora* (Michx.) Wherry]. Sts. shorter, with fewer (7–9) nodes, calyx larger. Md. to Ga., w. to Ind. and Ala.

glabrata: *P. Hoodii* subsp.

×**Henryae** Wherry: *P. bifida* × *P. nivalis.* To 6 in.; lvs. narrow, to ⅝ in. long; fls. lilac-purple, to 1 in. across, corolla with deeply notched lobes. Cv. 'Blanda'. Listed as being smaller, foliage blue-gray.

Hoodii Richardson. Tufted per., to 2 in.; lvs. subulate, to ⅜ in. long, woolly; fls. mostly white, to 5/16 in. across, solitary. Nw. N. Amer. Material offered under this name is likely to be *P. diffusa* or some similar sp. Subsp. **glabrata** (E. E. Nels.) Wherry [*P. glabrata* (E. E. Nels.) Brand]. Lvs. ciliate, but otherwise glabrous. Subsp. **muscoides** (Nutt.) Wherry. Lvs. smaller, more compact. Subsp. **viscidula** Wherry. Infl. with both glandless and gland-tipped hairs.

idahonis Wherry. Finely pubescent per., to 3 ft., from a shallow rhizome; lvs. oblong to ovate, to 3 in. long, cordate; fls. lilac to lavender, rarely white, in glandular-hairy, compound cymes. Idaho.

Kelseyi Britt. Dwarf shrub, to 6 in., sts. very leafy; lvs. linear-lanceolate, to 1 in. long; fls. lilac to lavender, about ¾ in. across, 1–5 in infl. E. Mont., s. to Wyo.

laplantica: a listed name of no botanical standing; material so listed is probably *P. ovata.*

longiflora: *P. maculata* subsp. *pyramidalis.*

longifolia Nutt. Woody-based per. or low shrub, to 1 ft. or more; lvs. linear to lanceolate, to 3 in. long, long-acuminate; fls. usually lilac to pink, or white, to ¾ in. across, in corymbs. Nw. U.S. Subsp. **humilis** (Dougl. ex Hook.) Wherry. Lvs. narrower, crowded, to 1½ in. long.

maculata L. WILD SWEET WILLIAM. Per., to 5 ft., with slender rhizomes, sts. often purple-spotted; lvs. linear to lanceolate or ovate, to 5 in. long; fls. purple to pink, or white, ½ in. across, in elongated, cylindrical, paniceled cymes. Conn. to N.C., w. to Iowa. Rarely cult.; material offered under this name is usually a form of *P. carolina.* Subsp. **pyramidalis** (Sm.) Wherry [*P. longiflora* Sweet]. Later blooming and usually taller.

mesoleuca Greene. Sparsely glandular-pubescent per., to 1 ft. or more; lvs. linear, to 3¼ in. long; fls. purple with pale centers, pink, yellow or white. New Mex. and n. Mex. Material offered under this name is probably a white-eyed form of *P. pilosa.*

missoulensis Wherry. Tufted per., to 4 in.; lvs. linear to linear-lanceolate, to 1 in. long, glandular-pubescent; fls. lavender to pink, solitary, sepals united less than half their length. Mont. to Nev. and Colo.

multiflora A. Nels. Mat-forming per., to 6 in.; lvs. linear, to 1 in. long, ciliate or glabrous; fls. lilac to pink, or white, ¾ in. across, solitary on numerous branchlets. Mont. to Colo. Subsp. **patula** (A. Nels.) Wherry [*P. patula* A. Nels.]. Lvs. and pedicels longer.

nana Nutt. Tufted per., to 1 ft.; lvs. narrowly elliptic to lanceolate, to 1¾ in. long, glandular-pubescent; fls. purple to lilac, pink or white, or light yellow, to 1 in. across, in few-fld. corymbs. New Mex., to w. Tex., se. Ariz., n. Mex. Material cult. under this name may be cv. of *P. Drummondii.*

nana compacta: a listed name of no botanical standing for *P. Drummondii* cv.

nivalis Lodd. ex Sweet. TRAILING P. Glandular-pubescent, trailing-decumbent per., to 6 in.; lvs. subulate to linear-subulate, to ½ in. long; fls. purple to pink or white, nearly 1 in. across, corolla lobes entire to erose or shallowly notched, styles much shorter than calyx. Va. to Fla. and Ala. Has been confused with *P. subulata,* from which it differs by its short styles. Cv. 'Azurea'. Fls. pale blue. Cv. 'Camla' [*P. camlaensis* Hort.]. Fls. salmon-pink. Cv. 'Sylvestris'. Fls. rose-pink, to ½ in. across.

ovata L. MOUNTAIN P. Mostly glabrous per., to 20 in.; sts. arising from leafy, decumbent brs.; lvs. variable in shape and size, elliptic to ovate, to 6 in. long, lower lvs. long-petioled, upper lvs. sessile; fls. purple, pink, or rarely white, 1 in. across. Penn. and ne. Ind., s. to Ala. Var. **latifolia** (Michx.) Wherry. Lvs. wider. Var. **pulchra:** *P. pulchra.*

paniculata [*P. decussata* Lyon ex Pursh]. PERENNIAL P., SUMMER P. P., FALL P. Clump-forming per., to 6 ft.; lvs. elliptic to elliptic-lanceolate or ovate, to 6 in. long, thin, veiny; fls. pink-purple, but varying into many colors as white, salmon, scarlet, lilac, purple, 1 in. across, in large panicles. Summer. N.Y. to Ga., w. to Ill., s. to Ark. The common per. garden phlox.

patula: *P. multiflora* subsp.

perennis: a listed name of no botanical standing.

pilosa L. Hairy per., to 1½ ft.; lvs. linear to lanceolate, to 3 in. long; fls. purple to pink, or white, to ¾ in. across, in small clusters. Se. Conn. to s. Fla., w. to Wisc., and Tex. Some material cult. as *P. mesoleuca* may belong here. Subsp. **fulgida** (Wherry) Wherry. Infl. with white, glandless hairs. Minn., and N. Dak., s. to Ill. and Kans. Subsp. **ozarkana** (Wherry) Wherry. Often glandular pubescent; upper lvs. often ovate-cordate, Mo. to e. Okla., s. to n. La.

×**procumbens** Lehm.: *P. stolonifera* × *P. subulata.* Per., to 1 ft., decumbent at base; lvs. elliptic or oblanceolate, to 1 in. long; fls. bright

purple, to ¾ in. across. Cv. 'Folio-variegata'. Foliage variegated. Cv. 'Rosea'. Fls. rose-pink. Often grown mistakenly as *P. amoena.*

pulchra (Wherry) Wherry [*P. ovata* var. *pulchra* Wherry]. Differs from *P. ovata* in having the lower lvs. short-petioled and fls. pastel-pink. Ala.

reptans: *P. stolonifera.*

rigida: *P. Douglasii* subsp.

scleranthifolia: *P. diffusa* subsp.

setacea: *P. subulata;* but material offered as *P. setacea* is probably *P. nivalis.*

sibirica L. Woody-based per., forming mats to 4 in.; lvs. linear, to 2¼ in. long, long-acuminate; fls. with corolla lobes entire to erose. Siberia.

speciosa Pursh. Shrub, with herbaceous flowering shoots, to 2 (rarely 4) ft.; lvs. linear to lanceolate, to 3 in. long; fls. purple to pink, or white, to 1 in. across, in corymbs. Wash. and Ore., e. to Mont.

Stellaria: *P. bifida* subsp., but most material in cult. as *P. Stellaria* is a hybrid between *P. bifida* and *P. subulata.*

stolonifera Sims [*P. reptans* Michx.]. CREEPING P. Hairy per., to 1 ft., with long, creeping, sterile shoots; lvs. spatulate-obovate, or oblong to ovate, to 3¾ in. long; fls. purple or violet, to 1 in. across, in glandular-pubescent cymes. Penn. to Ga. Cvs. are: 'Blue Ridge', lvs. shiny, fls. blue; 'Grandiflora' a listed name; 'Rosea', fls. rose; 'Violacea', fls. violet.

subulata L. [*P. setacea* L.]. MOSS PINK, MOSS PHLOX, MOUNTAIN P. Mat-forming per., to 6 in.; lvs. linear to subulate, to 1 in. long, crowded, evergreen; fls. red-purple to violet-purple, pink, or white, ¾ in. across, corolla lobes shallowly notched. N.Y. to Md., w. to Mich. Cvs. include: 'Camla': *P. nivalis* cv.; 'Garyi', fls. large, rose-pink; 'Moerheimii' [var. *Moerheimii* Ruys], fls. deep pink; 'Nelsonii', of compact habit, fls. white, with rose centers. Many other cvs. are listed: 'Alba', 'Atrolilacina', 'Atropurpurea', 'Atroviolacea', 'Caerulea', 'Coccinea', 'Frondosa', 'Lilacina', 'Major', 'Rosea', 'Rubra', 'Violacea', 'Wilsonii'. Some cvs. offered as this sp. belong to *P. nivalis.* Subsp. **Brittonii** (Small) Wherry [*P. Brittonii* Small]. Fls. lavender-white, corolla lobes deeply notched. Appalachians and Potomac Valley.

suffruticosa: see *P. carolina.*

sylvestris: a listed name of no botanical standing for *P. nivalis* cv.

PHOENICAULIS Nutt. *Cruciferae.* One sp., a tufted per. herb of w. N. Amer., with simple or branched, pubescent caudex; lvs. basal, in thick rosettes; fls. racemose, showy, sepals 4, petals 4, pinkish or purple, sometimes white, long-clawed; fr. a flattened, oblong-lanceolate to linear, dehiscent silique.

cheiranthoides Nutt. [*Parrya Menziesii* Greene]. Caudex covered with remains of old lvs., sts. to 8 in.; lvs. spatulate to oblanceolate, to 4 in. long, entire; fls. many; siliques spreading horizontally, to 1½ in. long. Cent. Wash., s. to mts. of Calif., e. to Idaho and Nev. A useful rock garden plant.

PHOENICOPHORIUM H. Wendl. [*Stevensonia* J. Duncan ex Balf.f.]. *Palmae.* One sp., a solitary, monoecious palm of the Seychelles Is.; trunk erect, spiny when young, becoming spineless in age; lvs. pinnately ribbed, large, shallowly to deeply dissected marginally into short or long, toothed lobes, ribs prominent, sheath usually spiny near the base, not forming a regular crownshaft, petiole spiny at least on juvenile plants; infls. interfoliar, becoming infrafoliar, long-peduncled, lower bract 2-edged, open, upper bract cylindrical, enclosing infl. in bud, splitting and deciduous in flowering, rachis with many brs., these simple or the lower branched, rachillae slender, with fls. in triads (2 male and 1 female); male fls. asymmetrical, sepals low, imbricate, petals much longer, acute, valvate, stamens 15–18, filaments short, erect, female fls. with sepals and petals imbricate, staminodes 6, pistil 1-celled, 1-ovuled; fr. narrowly ovoid, endocarp operculate, seed with ruminate endosperm and basal ovule.

For culture see *Palms.*

Borsigianum (C. Koch) Stuntz [*Stevensonia grandifolia* J. Duncan ex Balf.f.]. To 45 ft. or more, trunk to 4 in. in diam. at top; lf. blades to 6 ft. long or more, orange beneath on young plants; infl. to 3 ft. long or more, rachillae to 30 in. long or more; male fls. about ¼ in. long; fr. black, to ⅜ in. long. Zone 10b in Fla.

PHOENIX L. DATE PALM. *Palmae.* Perhaps 17 spp. of dioecious palms of trop. and subtrop. Afr. and Asia, unarmed, except for the stiff basal spines or modified pinnae on the lvs.; sts. solitary or clustered, sometimes very short, covered with bases of old petioles, at least toward the top; lvs. pinnate, pinnae trough-shaped in cross section, narrow, acute to acuminate, without midrib but with a vein on each side of a sharp central fold or ridge, regularly arranged or often paired or otherwise clustered along rachis; infl. among lvs., subtended by a single deciduous bract, peduncle compressed, often elongate, rachillae often fascicled on rachis; fls. small, yellowish, borne singly, male fls. with sepals united in a lobed cupule, petals obtuse or rarely acute to acuminate, valvate, stamens usually 6, female fls. with sepals 3, united in a cupule, petals 3, imbricate, carpels 3, separate, only one usually maturing; fr. an oblong or nearly globose drupe with a single grooved seed, endosperm homogeneous except for intrusion of seed coat below the groove, embryo lateral or rarely basal.

It is often difficult to identify trees of *Phoenix* in cultivation. Some of the surest characters for separation are in the male flowers and the fruits; but since these palms are dioecious, trees of both sexes may not be available together. Also, there is much natural variation in some of the species and hybridization occurs in cultivation so that many horticultural forms are probably of hybrid origin. Species of the genus are important as a source of fruit and palm sugar, and are also used as ornamentals, thriving mostly in warm dry climates. For culture see *Date* and *Palms*.

abyssinica Drude. Similar to *P. reclinata* but said to differ in having the calyx of female fls. urn-shaped, more than half as long as the corolla, and the endocarp hard. Ethiopia. A poorly known sp.

acaulis Roxb. Apparently stemless, the trunk represented by an ovoid, bulbiform structure 1 ft. in diam. or less; lvs. to 3 ft. long, somewhat glaucous, pinnae not many, to 18 in. long, ⅜ in. wide with strong marginal veins, arranged in groups of 2–4 at intervals along rachis; infl. less than 1 ft. long, peduncle very short or not evident; male fls. with petals obtuse, female fls. with calyx about half as long as corolla; fr. ovoid, to ¾ in. long, ⅜ in. in diam., red to blue-black, edible. Assam to Burma.

Andersonii: a listed name of no botanical standing, probably referable to *P. rupicola.*

canariensis Hort. ex Chabaud. CANARY ISLAND DATE, CANARY D.P. Solitary, stout palm, to 50 ft. or more, trunk nearly 3 ft. in diam., in age with petiolar scars broader than high; lvs. many, to 20 ft. long, in a dense crown, not appearing ragged, apices or nearly the whole lf. sometimes twisted at an angle from the horizontal, pinnae green, many, more or less regularly arranged or paired along rachis but essentially in 1 plane; infl elongate; male fls. about ⅜ in. long, petals not acuminate, female fls. with calyx nearly as long as the petals; fr. oblong-ellipsoid, yellow to reddish, ¾ in. long, ½ in. in diam. Canary Is., but widely cult. One of the hardiest and most massive (when grown on fertile moist soil) palms, thriving in cent. Calif., cent. and n. Fla. and along the Gulf Coast. Warmer parts of Zone 9a.

cycadifolia Hort. ex Regel. A sp. described without reference to reproductive characters, possibly an older name for *P. canariensis* but impossible to determine precisely.

dactylifera L. DATE, DATE PALM. Tree, to 100 ft. and more, trunk slender, suckering unless pruned, petiolar scars as high as or higher than wide, upper part of crown with erect-ascending foliage, lower part with down-curving foliage; lvs. grayish-glaucous, sometimes bluish, pinnae 18 in. long or less, narrow, stiff, borne in pairs, clusters, or regular arrangement at a somewhat acute angle from the rachis; infl. elongate; male fls. not acuminate, female fls. with calyx half as long as petals; fr. cylindrical or oblong-ellipsoid, 1–3 in. long, with thick, sweet, edible flesh and slender, often pointed seed. One of the oldest crops, a cultigen probably originating in w. Asia and n. Afr. over 5000 years ago; cult. commercially in Iraq, N. Afr., and in the U.S. in Calif. and Ariz.; widely planted for ornament. Warmer parts of Zone 9a. See also *Date.*

formosana: a listed name of no botanical standing, perhaps for a form of *P. Loureirii.*

Hanceana: *P. Loureirii.*

humilis: a listed name of no botanical standing, but long used for plants now referred to *P. Loureirii.*

hybrida a listed name of no botanical standing, variously applied in hort.

leonensis: a listed name of no botanical standing, but plants so named in hort. may be *P. canariensis* or a hybrid.

Loureirii Kunth [*P. Hanceana* Naud.; *P. humilis* of auth.]. Variable, nearly stemless to 6 ft. or more, rarely 15 ft., sts. often clustered; lvs. more or less glaucous, pinnae in groups along the rachis, not prominently scaly beneath but with deciduous pale scales and persistent linear brown scales on midribs beneath; peduncle of fruiting infl. to 3 ft. long; male fls. ³⁄₁₆ in. long, petals rather blunt, female fls. with calyx

half as long as corolla, lobes very brief, petals with very short central lobe; fr. red, ½–¾ in. long, ⁵⁄₁₆–½ in. in diam. India to China; a poorly understood sp., sometimes confused with *P. Roebelenii.*

paludosa Roxb. Sts. clustered, slender, to 30 ft. or more, 3½ in. in diam.; lvs. graceful, spreading, petiole elongate, pinnae many, variously paired, clustered and 2-ranked basally or nearly regularly arranged and in 1 plane near apex, green above, densely white-waxy or -floury below, secondary veins 4–8 on each side of central ridge, prominent, separated, with persistent linear brown scales, ridged with deciduous, membranous scales attached by base and persistent, linear, brown bases; infl. elongate, orange; male fls. slender, to ⁵⁄₁₆ in. long, petals acutish, female fls. with calyx half as long as corolla; fr. orange ripening black, ½ in. long, ¼–⁵⁄₁₆ in. in diam. Estuarine shores, Bengal to Malay Pen., Andaman Is. Zone 9b. Distinctive in whitish under surface of pinnae. Most material cult. under this name is *P. reclinata.*

pumila: *P. reclinata.*

pusilla Gaertn. Shrubby, stoloniferous, with very short, little evident trunk entirely covered with sheaths; lvs. pale green, appearing ragged, pinnae many, rigid, more or less regularly arranged in 4 planes; fr. ½ in. long, dull purple-black. Near the sea, s. India and Ceylon.

reclinata Jacq. [*P. pumila* Regel]. SENEGAL D.P. Sts. clustered, to 20 ft. or more, slender; lvs. to 9 ft. long or more, graceful, arcuately spreading or the lower more or less pendulous, apices often twisted nearly to a vertical plane, petiole elongate, orangish, with spines to 6 in. long, pinnae to 80 or more on each side of rachis, with grayish scales along central ridges beneath when young, to 15 in. long, 1 in. wide, acuminate, finely and closely veined; infl. to 5 ft. long; male fls. ¼ in. long, petals acute to acuminate, female fls. with calyx ringlike, 3-lobed, about half as long as petals; fr. oblong-ellipsoid, ½–¾ in. long, ¼–⁵⁄₁₆ in. in diam., orange-red to black. A variable sp. widespread in trop. Afr. Sometimes grown under the name of *P. paludosa.* Zone 9b. Useful for large hedges and screens because of attractive clustering habit.

Roebelenii O'Brien. MINIATURE D.P., PYGMY D.P., ROEBELIN P. Sts. solitary or sometimes clustered, to 6 ft. or more, slender, 2–6 in. in diam., roughened by old petiole bases; lvs. to 4 ft. long, pinnae about 50 on each side, soft, green, more or less regularly arranged throughout and borne in a single plane, to 10 in. long, ¼–⅜ in. wide, with prominent yellowish or grayish scales on veins beneath; infl. to 18 in. long; male fls. about ⁵⁄₁₆ in. long, petals acuminate, female fls. to ³⁄₁₆ in. long, calyx less than half as long as petals, lobes 3, prominent, petals with prominent, acute center; fr. blackish, ½ in. long, ³⁄₁₆ in. in diam. Laos. Widely cult. as an elegant pot plant or outdoors in warm regions. Warmer parts of Zone 9b.

rupicola T. Anderson. CLIFF DATE, WILD D.P., INDIA D.P., EAST INDIAN WINE P. Slender, solitary, to 20 ft.; lvs. to 10 ft. long, bright green, with 80 or more soft pinnae on each side regularly arranged in one plane but apex or entire blade often twisted nearly to the vertical, lower lvs. more or less pendulous, pinnae with a line of grayish, peltate scales on central ridges beneath; infl. to 4 ft. long; male fls. about ⁵⁄₁₆ in. long, petals not acuminate, female fls. with calyx half as long as corolla or less; fr. oblong-ellipsoid, ¾ in. long, glossy yellow. Himalayan India, Sikkim, Assam. One of the most graceful sp. for cult.

sylvestris (L.) Roxb. WILD DATE, INDIA D. Trunk stout, solitary, to 50 ft., to 1 ft. in diam., at length with petiolar scars higher than wide; lvs. many, appearing ragged, to 15 ft. long, grayish-green, petiole short, pinnae many, arranged in clusters and borne in 2–4 planes, to 18 in. long, 1 in. wide; infl. to 3 ft. long; male fls. to ⁵⁄₁₆ in. long, petals obtuse, female fls. with calyx half as long as petals; fr. to 1¼ in. long, oblong-ellipsoid, orange-yellow, embryo lateral. Widespread in India, where used as source of palm sugar. Zone 9a.

tenuis: a listed name of no botanical standing, used in literature for *P. canariensis* but in hort. apparently applied to other spp. as well.

tomentosa: a listed name of no botanical standing.

zeylanica Trimen. CEYLON DATE. Trunk solitary, to 20 ft.; lvs. with many stiff short pinnae to 10 in. long, ¾ in. wide, borne in 4 ranks; infl. to 1 ft. long or more; male fls. about ¼ in. long, petals obtuse, female fls. with calyx about half as high as petals; fr. red, becoming violet-blue, ½ in. long, ¼ in. in diam. Ceylon.

PHOLIDOTA Lindl. *Orchidaceae.* About 55 spp. of epiphytes, native to trop. Asia, Malay Arch., and Oceania; pseudobulbs 1- or 2-lvd.; infl. slender, several- to many-fld., rachis often zigzag, fls. 2-ranked; sepals concave, lateral sepals often keeled on back, petals similar, narrower, lip rarely 3-lobed, saccate at base, column short, with wide wing around anther. For structure of fl. see *Orchidaceae.*

Warm greenhouse. For culture see *Orchids.*

articulata Lindl. Pseudobulbs 2-lvd., 4 in. long; lvs. elliptic, to 4 in. long; infl. pendent, to 6 in. long; fls. ½ in. across, purplish to dull brownish, sepals and petals spreading, lip with 5 longitudinal yellow ridges at base, blade slightly twisted, 2-lobed, orange at base. Late spring–autumn. Burma to Java.

chinensis Lindl. Pseudobulbs oblong, to 2 in. long; lvs. oblong, to 8 in. long; infl. loosely several-fld.; fls. pale reddish-brown, sepals oblong, ½ in. long, petals linear, lip oblong, base concave, apical part reflexed, lateral lobes broadly oblong. China.

conchoidea: *P. imbricata.*

imbricata Lindl. [*P. conchoidea* Lindl.]. RATTLESNAKE ORCHID. Pseudobulbs ovate, to 3 in. long, 1-lvd.; lvs. oblong-lanceolate, to 1 ft. long; infl. pendent, to 10 in. long, many-fld.; fls. to ¼ in. across, light brown, upper sepal orbicular, lateral sepals ovate, lip nearly globose, hooded, lateral lobes orbicular, midlobe oblong. Late spring–late summer. Himalayas, Malay Pen., Philippine Is.

PHOLISTOMA Lilja ex Lindbl. *Hydrophyllaceae.* Three or 4 spp. of prostrate or reclining ann. herbs, native to sw. U.S. and adjacent Mex.; sts. brittle, succulent, with retrorse prickles on angles; lvs. pinnately divided, lower lvs. opp., upper lvs. alt.; fls. white, blue, or violet, cymose or less commonly solitary, calyx 5-parted, corolla 5-lobed, stamens 5, style 2-cleft less than half its length; fr. a 1-celled, prickly or bristly caps.

auritum (Lindl.) Lilja ex Lindbl. [*Nemophila aurita* Lindl.]. FIESTA FLOWER. Scrambling herb, to 4 ft.; lvs. to 6 in. long, petiole broadly winged, clasping; fls. lavender to blue or violet, with darker markings, to 1¼ in. across. Spring. Calif. For cult. see *Nemophila.*

PHORADENDRON Nutt. MISTLETOE, FALSE M. *Loranthaceae.* Perhaps 200 spp. of dioecious or monoecious shrubs, native mostly to trop. Amer., parasitic on other woody plants but possessing chlorophyll; lvs. opp., simple, entire, or sometimes reduced to scales; fls. small, usually embedded in rachis of spike, male fls. with calyx 3-lobed and 3 very short stamens, female fls. with calyx fused to the inferior, 1-celled, 1-ovuled ovary; fr. a small berry with viscid pulp.

Seeds of mistletoes are sometimes offered, but no attempts to cultivate members of this group are known to have succeeded.

flavescens: *P. serotinum.*

serotinum (Raf.) M. C. Johnst. [*P. flavescens* (Pursh) Nutt.]. AMERICAN M. Sts. to 1 ft. or more, forming masses in tops of various deciduous host trees, glabrous; fl. spikes ⅜–¾ in. long; lvs. obovate or oblanceolate, short-petioled, to 2 in. long; berries whitish, translucent. N.J. to Fla., w. to s. Ill. and Tex. This is the common mistletoe familiar to Americans; the mistletoe of Eur. and Eur. literature is *Viscum album.*

PHORMIUM J. R. Forst. & G. Forst. FLAX LILY. *Agavaceae.* Probably 2 spp. of large per. herbs, native to New Zeal.; lvs. basal, sword-shaped, equitant; infl. a panicle on a leafless scape; fls. tubular at base, segms. 6, spreading, stamens 6, ovary superior, 3-celled; fr. a caps.

One species is important for its leaf fibers. Propagated by seeds sown in Feb. out of doors (where hardy) or in pots of rich compost; also by division.

Colensoi Hook.f. [*P. Cookianum* Le Jolis]. MOUNTAIN FLAX. To 7 ft.; lvs. to 5 ft. long, 2½ in. wide, less rigid than in *P. tenax;* fls. yellow, to 1½ in. long; caps. 4–7 in. long, pendulous, twisted, cylindrical.

Cookianum: *P. Colensoi.*

tenax J. R. Forst. & G. Forst. NEW ZEALAND FLAX, NEW ZEALAND HEMP. To 15 ft.; lvs. to 9 ft. long, 5 in. broad, stiff, tough and leathery, splitting at apex, margined with red or orange line; fls. dull red, to 2 in. long; caps. short, 2–4 in. long, erect, 3-angled. Cvs. include: **'Atropurpureum'**, lvs. reddish-purple; **'Aureum'**, lvs. with broad yellow stripes; **'Powerscourtii'** and **'Purpureum'**, listed names; **'Rubrum'**, lvs. red; **'Tricolor'**, a listed name; **'Variegatum'**, lvs. striped with creamy-yellow and white; **'Veitchianum'**, lvs. with broad, creamy-white stripes.

PHOTINIA Lindl. *Rosaceae.* About 40 spp. of trees and shrubs of s. and e. Asia; lvs. alt., toothed or entire, simple, short-petioled; fls. mostly white, in terminal corymbs or short panicles, sepals 5, persistent, petals 5, round, stamens about 20; fr. a round, red, berrylike pome.

The deciduous species are mostly hardy north and succeed in sunny places. Propagated by seeds, by cuttings of young wood under glass, by layers, and by grafting on hawthorn or quince.

arbutifolia: *Heteromeles arbutifolia.*

Beauverdiana C. K. Schneid. Deciduous shrub or small tree, to 20 ft., entirely glabrous; lvs. narrow-ovate to lanceolate, pointed, 2–5 in. long, finely serrate; infl. to 1 in. long, 2 in. wide; fls. 5/16 in. across; fr. ovoid, ¼ in. long, purplish. China. Zone 8.

Davidsoniae Rehd. & E. H. Wils. Evergreen, to 30 ft., young branchlets reddish, pubescent; lvs. oblanceolate, tapering at both ends, 3–6 in. long, glossy above, pubescent beneath on veins; infl. pubescent, 3–4 in. wide; fls. ⅜ in. across; fr. globose, orange-red, 5/16 in. in diam. Cent. China. Zone 8.

deflexa: *Eriobotrya deflexa.*

dentata: a listed name of no botanical standing.

×Fraseri Dress: *P. glabra* × *P. serrulata.* Lvs. elliptic-obovate to elliptic, 3–3½ in. long, broadly cuneate at base; petals bearded inside at very base. Zone 8.

glabra (Thunb.) Maxim. JAPANESE P. Evergreen, to 20 ft., glabrous; lvs. elliptic to narrowly obovate, 2–3 in. long, red when young; infl. 2–4 in. wide; petals bearded inside at base; fr. globose, 3/16 in. in diam., at first red, then black. Late spring. Japan. Zone 8. An important hedge plant.

integrifolia Lindl. Small tree, quite glabrous; lvs. oblanceolate, 3–5 in. long, acuminate, entire; corymb large, spreading; fls. less than 3/16 in. across; fr. globose, ¼ in. in diam., blue, glaucous. Himalayas. Zone 8.

parvifolia (E. Pritz.) C. K. Schneid. [*P. subumbellata* Rehd. & E. H. Wils.]. Deciduous, to 10 ft., young shoots glabrous, dark red; lvs. ovate, 1–2 in. long, acute, broadly cuneate at base, sharply serrate; infl. about 1 in. wide, 5–6-fld.; fr. ellipsoid, ⅜ in. long, bright red. China. Zone 7.

serrulata Lindl. Evergreen, to 40 ft., almost or quite glabrous; lvs. oblong, to 8 in. long, serrate, somewhat leathery, dark green above, yellowish-green beneath; infl 4–6 in. wide; petals glabrous. China. Zone 7. Cv. **'Aculeata'** [cv. 'Lineata']. Young sts. reddish; lvs. with longer teeth.

subumbellata: *P. parvifolia.*

villosa (Thunb.) DC. Deciduous shrub to small tree, to 15 ft., pubescent on young growth, later glabrous; lvs. obovate to lanceolate-ovate, short-acute, 1–3 in. long, leathery; infl. 2 in. wide; fr. ellipsoid, 5/16 in. in diam., red. Japan, Korea, China. Zone 5. Var. **laevis** (Thunb.) Dipp. Lvs. smaller, narrower, more glabrous. Japan.

PHOTOPERIOD. The length of the period of light relative to that of the period of darkness experienced by a plant in a 24-hour period is known as the photoperiod. Like most higher organisms, many flowering plants throughout the world respond to seasonal changes in day length, the response being known as photoperiodism. The response best known to the gardener is the plant's transformation from vegetative growth to the flowering state. However, other phenomena are associated with photoperiodism, including tillering of grasses, formation of tubers or storage roots, autumn coloration, leaf fall, and the beginning of winter dormancy. Plants fall generally into three groups with respect to photoperiodism. One group, like the China aster *(Callistephus chinensis),* requires long days to start flowers; another group, typified by the chrysanthemum *(Chrysanthemum × morifolium),* Christmas cactus *(Schlumbergera Bridgesii),* and poinsettia *(Euphorbia pulcherrima),* needs shorter days to initiate bloom; a third group is insensitive to varying photoperiods or length of day, and examples like the African violet *(Saintpaulia ionantha)* consequently flower the year around. The terms photoperiodism, long-day-plant, short-day-plant, etc., though widely used, are now known to be misnomers, for scientists have found that plants respond primarily to length of night, not of day. Further research has shown that a special plant pigment, phytochrome, a protein, is involved in the photoperiodic response. Whatever the names, the knowledge that plants do respond to varying periods of light and darkness has made it possible to control flowering artificially in many plants important to the florist industry, which, for example, is now able to produce flowering chrysanthemums the year around. The average gardener, with a little ingenuity in controlling amounts of light and darkness, can also put the knowledge now widely available to good use in manipulating the flowering of certain ornamentals, especially in the home and greenhouse.

PHRAGMIPEDILUM: *PHRAGMIPEDIUM.*

PHRAGMIPEDIUM (Pfitz.) Rolfe [*Phragmipedilum* Rolfe]. LADY-SLIPPER, LADY'S-SLIPPER. *Orchidaceae.* Twelve spp. of terrestrial herbs, native to trop. Cent. and S. Amer.; lvs. strap-shaped, folded lengthwise, leathery; infl. a terminal raceme or panicle, commonly several-fld.; sepals spreading, petals similar to sepals or long-caudate, lip sessile, inflated, slipper-shaped, the margins inrolled near base, fertile anthers 2, the third stamen represented by a petal-like staminode. For structure of fl. see *Orchidaceae.*

Warm greenhouse. For culture see *Orchids.*

Boisseranum (Rchb.f.) Rolfe. To 20 in.; lvs. 6–8 on lower part of st., strap-shaped, to 20 in. long; raceme as long as lvs., loosely 3–10-fld.; fls. large, yellow-green, reticulated with dark green, petals bordered with white or brown, upper sepal oblong-lanceolate, to 2 in. long, undulate, lateral sepals united into an oblong-ovate blade more than twice as broad as upper sepal, petals much longer than sepals, 2¾ in. long, lanceolate-linear, twisted, with undulate margins, lip pendent, obovate-saccate, clawed, with pair of conical horns between claw and sac, staminode transversely elliptic-kidney-shaped. Peru.

caricinum (Lindl. & Paxt.) Rolfe. To 1 ft.; lvs. 3–6 at base of st., linear, to 20 in. long; raceme as long as lvs., 3–7-fld.; sepals and petals pale green or whitish with green veins and spotted with madder on lip, upper sepal lanceolate-ovate, 1½ in. long, lateral sepals united into an oblong-ovate blade, petals pendent, lanceolate-linear, to 5 in. long, twisted, with undulate margins, lip obovoid, as long as blades of lateral sepals. Early spring–autumn. Peru, Bolivia, Brazil.

caudatum (Lindl. & Paxt.) Rolfe. Tuft-forming; lvs. about 6 at base of st., strap-shaped, to 2 ft. long; raceme longer than lvs., loosely 1–4-fld.; fls. the largest of genus, sepals whitish to greenish-yellow, upper sepal lanceolate, to 7 in. long, lateral sepals united into an ovate-lanceolate blade, petals pendent, elongate-linear, to 30 in. long, twisted, purplish-brown, lip slipper-shaped, 2½ in. long, green at base to purplish-brown apically, with purple spots on the white infolded margins. Spring-early summer. Mex. to Venezuela and Peru. Cv. 'Giganteum' [var. *giganteum* (Carrière) Pfitz.]. Sepals yellow with purple striations, petals very long, lip brown, with green apex. Cv. 'Lindenii' [var. *Lindenii* (Benth.) Pfitz.]. Lip not saccate, but ribbonlike and pendent.

Hartwegii (Rchb.f.) Pfitz. Lvs. oblong-linear; raceme many-fld.; fls. greenish-yellow, 6 in. across, sepals ovate, petals linear-strap-shaped, with obscurely crisped margin, lip ovoid, narrowly oblong, with infolded margin, staminode triangular-cordate, velvety-hairy. Peru.

Klotzschianum (Rchb.f.) Rolfe. Lvs. 6–8 on each st., linear, to 15 in. long; raceme to 2 ft. long, pubescent; fls. 2 in. high, upper sepal lanceolate, lateral sepals united into an ovate blade, petals pendent, linear, 3 in. long, lip cylindrical. Guyana.

Schlimii (Rchb.f.) Rolfe. Lvs. strap-shaped, to 1 ft. long; infl. longer than lvs., sometimes branched, pale greenish-purple, few-fld.; fls. 2 in. across, segms. covered with soft, velvety down, upper sepal elliptic-oblong, greenish-white, stained with pale rose-pink, lateral sepals concave, whitish with pale green veins, petals elliptic-oblong, white, spotted and stained with rose-purple, lip inflated, ovoid, rose-carmine, whitish underneath, the infolded margin streaked with white and rose-carmine, staminode rhomboid, with central keel, bright yellow. Colombia.

×**Sedenii** (Rchb.f.) Pfitz.: *P. longifolium* (Rchb.f.) Rolfe × *P. Schlimii.* Sepals ivory-white with faint flush of pale rose, rose-pink on exterior, petals twisted, white, tinted with pale rose at margins and apex, lip rose-pink, the infolded lobes ivory-white, spotted with rose, staminode white with a few pink spots and fringe of purple hairs on each side.

PHRAGMITES Trin. REED. *Gramineae.* Four spp. of per. reeds, on all continents; lf. blades broad, flat, linear; panicles large, terminal, plumelike; spikelets several-fld., pedicelled, the rachilla clothed with long, silky hairs, disarticulating above the glumes and between the florets, lowest floret male or neuter, glumes 3-nerved, or the upper 5-nerved, the first about half as long as the upper, the second shorter than the florets, lemmas glabrous, 3-nerved, the florets successively smaller, the summit of all about equal. For terminology see *Gramineae.*

australis (Cav.) Trin. ex Steud. [*P. communis* Trin.]. COMMON R., CARRIZO. Sts. erect, to 19 ft., rhizomatous and often also stoloniferous; lf. blades to 2 in. wide; infl. tawny or purplish; spikelets to ¾ in. long, hairs of the rachilla longer than florets. Cosmopolitan, in marshes and wet places. Used in latticework. Subsp. **australis.** [*P. communis* var.

Berlandieri (Fourn.) Fern.]. The typical subsp.; to 12 ft.; panicle erect, to 12 in. long; spikelets smaller, glumes entire, acute. Eurasia, Australia, Afr., S. Amer.; N. Amer., from Nov. Sc. to B.C., s. to Fla. and Calif. Not in cult. Subsp. **altissimus** (Benth.) W. D. Clayt. [*P. maximus* of auth., probably not (Forssk.) Chiov.]. To 19 ft.; panicle nodding, to 16 in. long; spikelets large, glumes 3-toothed. Medit.

communis: *P. australis.* Var. **Berlandieri:** *P. australis* subsp. *australis.*

maximus (Forssk.) Chiov. A name of uncertain application used for *P. australis* subsp. *altissimus.*

PHRYNIUM Loefl. ex O. Kuntze. *Marantaceae.* Not cult. **P. variegatum:** *Maranta arundinacea* cv.

PHYCELLA Lindl. *Amaryllidaceae.* About 7 spp. of bulbous herbs, native to S. Amer.; lvs. narrowly linear; fls. in 2–12-fld. umbels, perianth red, purple, red and yellow, or yellowish-green, narrowly funnelform, declinate, tube usually short, lobes 6, stamens 6, in 2 series at mouth of tube, usually with subulate marginal teeth at base, ovary inferior, stigma obscurely trifid or headlike; fr. a caps., seeds many, flat, black.

phycelloides (Herb.) Traub [*Amaryllis phycelloides* (Herb.) Steud.; *Habranthus phycelloides* Herb.; *Hippeastrum phycelloides* (Herb.) Bak.]. To 1 ft.; lvs. linear, glaucous, developing with the fls.; umbel 3–6-fld.; fls. bright red, yellowish inside, lobes connivent except at tip, stigma minutely trifid. Chile.

PHYGELIUS E. H. Mey. ex Benth. *Scrophulariaceae.* Two spp. of subshrubs, native to S. Afr.; woody at the base, with more or less herbaceous sts., glabrous or nearly so; lvs. opp., simple, crenate, petioled; fls. scarlet or salmon, drooping, in terminal panicles, calyx 5-parted, corolla tubular, lobes 5, nearly equal, rounded, tube curved or nearly straight, stamens 4, exserted; fr. a caps.

Grown as pot plants under glass or in the open in sheltered locations as far north as Philadelphia. Propagated by seeds or cuttings taken from the shoots of outdoor plants in late autumn.

aequalis Harv. ex Hiern. Differs from *P. capensis* in having infl. denser, fls. on short pedicels, calyx segms. lanceolate, and corolla salmon, tube nearly straight. By some not considered a different sp. from *P. capensis.*

capensis E. H. Mey. ex Benth. CAPE FUCHSIA. To 3 ft., sts. 4-angled or narrowly winged; lvs. ovate or ovate-lanceolate, to 5 in. long, toothed; fls. in panicles to 1½ ft. long, corolla to 2 in. long, somewhat curved, scarlet. Cv. 'Coccineus' is listed.

PHYLA Lour. FROGFRUIT. *Verbenaceae.* About 15 spp. of procumbent or creeping per. herbs, native to warm and trop. regions; plants glabrous or with 2-armed hairs; lvs. opp., toothed or lobed; fls. small, violet, blue, pink, or white, in dense spikes on axillary peduncles, calyx 2-lobed, enlarging and enclosing the fr., corolla 2-lipped, stamens 4; fr. dry, of 2 nutlets.

canescens: *P. nodiflora* var.

lanceolata (Michx.) Greene [*Lippia lanceolata* Michx.; *L. lanceolata* var. *recognita* Fern. & Grisc.]. NORTHERN F. Sts. procumbent or ascending, to 2 ft. long; lvs. oblong to oblong-lanceolate or ovate, to 3 in. long, acute, cuneate, toothed below middle, bright green; peduncles usually longer than lvs., spikes to 1½ in. long; corolla pale blue, purplish, or white. Wet areas, cent. and s. U.S., n. Mex.

nodiflora (L.) Greene [*Lippia nodiflora* L.]. FROGFRUIT, MATGRASS, CAPEWEED, TURKEY-TANGLE. Creeping and spreading, rooting at the nodes; lvs. spatulate to cuneate-obovate, to 1¾ in. long, toothed toward apex, green or gray-hairy; fls. white or lilac, peduncles much longer than subtending lvs. A variable sp. of wide trop. and subtrop. distribution. Var. **canescens** (HBK) Moldenke [*Lippia canescens* HBK]. CARPET GRASS. Corolla lilac, with yellow throat. Var. **rosea** (D. Don) Moldenke [*Lippia repens* Hort.]. Fls. rose-colored. Grown as a groundcover in warm climates. Best increased by planting small sods a few ft. apart.

PHYLLANTHUS L. [*Cicca* L.; *Xylophylla* L.]. *Euphorbiaceae.* About 650 spp. of monoecious or rarely dioecious herbs, shrubs, and trees, native to trop. and subtrop. regions of both hemispheres, often with flattened leaflike brs. (cladophylls); lvs. simple, alt., sometimes 2-ranked on lateral brs. giving the appearance of pinnately compound lvs., entire, usually glabrous, petioles always shorter than the blades; fls.

without petals, pedicelled or sessile, disc usually evident, ovary usually 3-celled; fr. usually a caps., sometimes a berry or drupe, each cell 2-seeded.

Two arborescent species are grown in warm climates for the edible fruits, which are made into preserves, and a few others are grown under glass. Propagated by seeds, green wood cuttings, and *P. Emblica* by layers.

acidus (L.) Skeels [*P. distichus* (L.) Müll. Arg.; *Cicca disticha* L.]. OTAHEITE GOOSEBERRY, GOOSEBERRY TREE. Tree, to 30 ft.; lvs. ovate-lanceolate to broadly ovate, 2½–3 in. long, 2-ranked; cymes many-fld., small; fls. tiny, reddish; fr. angled, to ¾ in. in diam. S. Asia; naturalized in s. Fla. and W. Indies.

angustifolius (Swartz) Swartz [*Xylophylla angustifolia* Swartz]. FOLIAGE FLOWER. Shrub, to 10 ft.; cladophylls to 4 in. long and ⅜ in. wide, primary axis ending abruptly or with a very short tip; fls. reddish or cream-colored or yellowish-green. Jamaica, Swan Is., Cayman Is.; naturalized in s. Fla.

arbuscula (Swartz) J. F. Gmel. [*P. speciosus* Jacq.; *Xylophylla arbuscula* Swartz; *X. speciosa* (Jacq.) Sweet]. FOLIAGE FLOWER. Shrub or small tree, to 20 ft.; cladophylls to 3 in. long and ¾ in. wide, primary axis ending abruptly or with a very short tip; fls. cream-colored, greenish, or scarlet. Jamaica.

atropurpureus: a listed name of no botanical standing for *Breynia disticha* cv.

distichus: *P. acidus.*

×elongatus (Jacq.) Steud.: *P. arbuscula* × *P. epiphyllanthus* L. Shrub, cladophylls 2-ranked, lanceolate, 2–3 in. long, ⅜ in. wide, primary axis ending in a floriferous cladophyll, 4–5 in. long.

Emblica L. EMBLIC, MYROBALAN. Deciduous tree, to 50 ft., bark flaking; lvs. 2-ranked, linear-oblong, ½–¾ in. long; fls. small, yellow, clustered in axils of lvs.; fr. somewhat lobed, to 1 in. in diam. Trop. Asia.

myrtifolius Moon. Small shrub; lvs. narrowly oblanceolate, ½–¾ in. long, petioles very short; fls. minute, pink, on long pedicels; caps. about size of a pea. Ceylon.

Niruri L. Ann., to 15 in.; lvs. 2-ranked on branchlets, ¼–⅜ in. long, oblong to oblanceolate; fls. minute, white. W. Indies.

nivosus: *Breynia disticha.*

roseopictus: a listed name of no botanical standing for *Breynia disticha* cv.

speciosus: *P. arbuscula.*

PHYLLAUREA: *CODIAEUM.*

PHYLLITIS J. Hill. *Polypodiaceae.* Eight spp. of mostly small ferns of temp., subtrop., and trop. regions; lvs. simple, strap-shaped; sori long, at right angles to midrib. Sometimes united with *Asplenium*, but differing in its lvs. simple, commonly auricled at base, and sori often in pairs on opp. sides of veins.

One hardy species, of simple cultural requirements, is sometimes grown in the open. See also *Ferns.*

Scolopendrium (L.) Newm. [*Scolopendrium vulgare* Sm.]. HART'S-TONGUE, HART'S-TONGUE FERN, DEER-TONGUE F. Lvs. straight or curved, to 1½ ft. long and 3 in. wide, entire or sometimes wavy-margined, vein tips reaching the margin, some midrib scales lanceolate. Eur.; naturalized locally in U.S. Var. **americana** Fern. Vein tips not reaching the margin, scales of midrib narrowly linear or thread-like. Very local on limestone, ne. Amer. Zone 5. There are a number of crested, divided, crisped, and dwarf cvs. known to fanciers including: **'Crispifolia'**, **'Cristata'**, **'Lacerata'**, **'Marginata'**, **'Undulata'**.

PHYLLOCACTUS: *EPIPHYLLUM.*

PHYLLOCARPUS Riedel ex Endl. *Leguminosae* (subfamily *Caesalpinioideae*). Two spp. of unarmed trees of trop. Amer.; lvs. alt., even-pinnate; fls. in short racemes clustered at leafless nodes, scarlet, petals 3, obovate, stamens 10, separate above, united in a split tube at base; fr. an oblong, flat, thin legume, winged on 1 side, indehiscent.

Propagated by seeds.

septentrionalis J. D. Sm. To 60 ft. or more, with spreading crown; lvs. deciduous, lfts. in 4–6 pairs, obovate or oblong, to 3 in. long; racemes few-fld.; fr. 6 in. long or more, 1–2-seeded. Guatemala, Honduras. Zone 10b. Very showy in fl. where native, but rarely flowering in s. Fla.

PHYLLOCLADUS L. Rich. *Podocarpaceae.* Perhaps 7 spp. of monoecious or dioecious, coniferous, evergreen trees and shrubs, native to the S. Hemisphere; lvs. reduced to scales, branchlets flattened into leathery, leaflike cladophylls, which are often toothed or lobed; male cones in terminal clusters, female cones usually of several clustered, 1-ovuled scales or reduced to a single scale, borne on or at base of cladophylls; seeds 1 to several, each in a cup-shaped, fleshy aril.

Grown in cooler parts of Zone 10 in Calif. For culture see *Conifers.*

trichomanoides D. Don. CELERY PINE. To 70 ft.; cladophylls alt. and 2-ranked on whorled brs., resembling pinnate lvs., ½–1 in. long, reddish-brown. New Zeal. Yields tanbark and a valuable timber.

PHYLLODOCE Salisb. MOUNTAIN HEATHER. *Ericaceae.* About 8 circumboreal spp. of low, evergreen, heathlike shrublets; brs. prostrate or ascending; lvs. crowded, alt., simple, linear, needlelike, revolute; fls. greenish, yellow, white, pink, or purple, in terminal, umbellate clusters, pedicels usually glandular-hairy, calyx 5-parted, corolla campanulate to urceolate, stamens 7–10, ovary superior; fr. a 5-celled caps.

Phyllodoces are suitable for the rock garden, where they thrive if in moist, peaty soil. Propagated by seeds, cuttings, or layers.

aleutica (K. Spreng.) A. Heller. To 10 in. or more; lvs. to ½ in. long, scabrous; corolla whitish to yellowish-green, urceolate, glabrous, filaments glabrous, anthers pale violet. E. Asia, Aleutian Is., Alaska.

Breweri (A. Gray) A. Heller. RED HEATHER. To 1 ft.; lvs. to ⅝ in. long; corolla rose-purple, open-campanulate, divided to the middle, stamens long-exserted, anthers dark purple. Summer. Mts., Calif. Zone 7?

caerulea (L.) Bab. To 6 in., brs. ascending; lvs. to ⅜ in. long; corolla purple, urceolate, ⅜ in. long, glandular, anthers dark violet. Circumpolar, s. to Me., New Hamp. and Alta. Zone 1.

empetriformis (Sm.) D. Don. Matted shrub, to 20 in.; lvs. to ⅝ in. long; corolla rose-purple, campanulate, ⅝ in. long, stamens included, anthers purple-brown. Summer. N. Calif. to Alaska and Rocky Mts. Zone 6.

glanduliflora (Hook.) Cov. Matted rigid shrub, to 1½ ft.; lvs. to ½ in. long; corolla sulphur-yellow, urceolate, 5/16 in. long, pubescent on the tube outside, filaments pubescent, anthers purple. Summer. Alaska to s. Ore., e. to Rocky Mts.

nipponica Mak. Compact shrub, to 6 in.; lvs. to ½ in. long; pedicels glandular-hairy throughout; sepals green, corolla white, campanulate, stamens not exserted, filaments glabrous, anthers brown. N. Japan. Zone 6. Var. **amabilis** (Stapf) Stoker. Sepals red, corolla pinkish, anthers crimson.

tsugifolia Nakai. To 6 in.; lvs. to ½ in. long; pedicels glandular-hairy only on their upper ⅓ or ½; corolla white, urceolate. N. Japan.

PHYLLOSTACHYS Siebold & Zucc. BAMBOO. *Gramineae.* About 30 spp. of usually tall, evergreen, rhizomatous grasses in temp. e. Asia and Himalayas, rhizomes slender, wide-ranging, sts. woody, with rather short, hollow internodes, flattened or grooved on 1 or both sides, nodes prominent, st. brs. usually 2 at each node, quite unequal, with a much smaller third br. sometimes developing between the 2; st. sheaths promptly deciduous; lf. blades petioled, tessellate, small or moderately large, articulated, with a patch of antrorse hairs each side of midrib at base; infl. a terminal, leafy panicle, appearing usually only after an interval of many years; spikelets 2–3, 1–4-fld., subtended by imbricate bracts, glumes usually unequal, many-nerved, glabrous, lemma ovate-lanceolate, acuminate, palea 2-keeled, often with 2 short points. For terminology see *Gramineae.*

Because of the habit of rarely flowering, garden bamboos are best identified on the basis of vegetative characters, the most useful being those of the stem sheaths (culm sheaths) that temporarily clothe the young shoots in the spring.

The species of this genus include the largest and most frequently grown of the hardy temperate bamboos. The plants are vigorous growers, sometimes weedy, with wide-ranging rhizomes producing thicketlike groves. All species are attractive as ornamentals. Young shoots are edible and the stems of some, when fully mature (3 years old) and adequately cured, have a wide range of uses. Most thrive in Zones 8 and 9 but are killed by a temperature of 0° F; they do not thrive in warm tropical and subtropical areas.

Propagation is by division or by 12-in. cuttings of young rhizomes made in late winter or early spring during dormancy, well before the new shoots begin growth. The new plants require 6 or more years to attain mature size. See *Bamboos.*

argentea: a listed name of no botanical standing; see *Arundinaria viridistriata.*

argenteostriata: a listed name of no botanical standing; see *Arundinaria viridistriata.*

aurea Carrière ex A. Rivière & C. Rivière [*Bambusa aurea* Hort.]. FISHPOLE B., GOLDEN B. Sts. erect, to 20 ft. high and 1⅝ in. thick, yellow or yellowish, nodes usually crowded at the base and obliquely inclined, upper internodes to 6 in. long, with a swollen band below each node; st. sheaths brown-spotted, with very short, smoothly convex, ciliate ligule, auricles lacking; lf. sheaths with 2 tufts of bristles at apex, blades linear, to 4 in. long and ¾ in. wide, 8–10-nerved, long-pointed, cuneate at base, denticulate on one side, dark green above, glaucous underneath, glabrous. China, Cult. in Japan and elsewhere; in the U.S., widely cult. in Zone 8. Shoots appearing in midspring are edible, well-matured sts. are tough and have many uses.

aureosulcata McClure. YELLOW-GROOVE B., STAKE B., FORAGE B. Sts. to 30 ft. high and 1⅜ in. thick, the internodes to 1⅜ in. long, more or less farinose, retrorsely scabrous to touch at first, dull green with a panel striped green and yellow above the insertion of buds and brs., especially in the first year, nodes glabrous, rather prominent, farinose zone usually extending both above and below the sheath scar; st. sheaths never spotted, striped with white, yellow, wine, and green, ligule well-developed, broadly convex, margin irregularly toothed, auricles variable in the same st., sparsely fringed with crinkly bristles, sheath blade erect or strongly reflexed on the lower sheaths, triangular, not crinkled, scabrous, brs. with 3–5 lvs.; lf. sheaths glabrous or rarely setose, blades to 6 in. long and ¾ in. wide, densely pilose at base; infl. unknown. China. Widely cult. in the U.S. in Zone 8; perhaps the hardiest sp. in the genus. Shoots appearing in midspring are edible; sts. are useful but wood is of inferior quality. Originally distributed as *Phyllostachys Nevinii* Hance, a sp. not known in cult. in the U.S.

bambusoides Siebold & Zucc. TIMBER B., HARDY T.B., GIANT T.B., JAPANESE T.B., MADAKE. Sts. erect, to 72 ft. high and 5¾ in. thick, glossy dark green without any white powder, the brs. long; st. sheaths greenish to reddish-buff densely spotted with dark brown, auricles often 2, fringed with bristles, ligule moderately developed with margin ciliolate or with coarse bristles, sheath blades short, lanceolate, reflexed, to strap-shaped and recurved, green or colored in pastel shades; lf. sheaths with auricles and tufts of bristles at apex, blades to 7½ in. long and 1¼ in. wide. China. Long cult. in Japan; widely planted in Zones 8 and 9. The most important timber bamboo in the Orient and the most versatile sp. in the genus. Edible shoots appear in the late spring. Cv. **'Allgold'** [*P. sulphurea* A. Rivière & C. Rivière]. ALLGOLD B. Internodes yellow, the groove not green. China. Cult. in Japan. Var. **Castillonii:** Cv. 'Castillon'. Cv. **'Castillon'** [var. *Castillonii* Marliac ex Houz. de Leh.; *Bambusa Castillonii* Marliac ex Carrière]. CASTILLON B. Internodes yellow, with a broad green panel; a few lf. blades with cream stripes. China. Long cult. in Japan.

dulcis McClure. SWEETSHOOT B. Sts. to 40 ft. high and 2½ in. thick, more or less strongly curved at the base, glabrous, the internodes copiously farinose, more or less ribbed, often visibly striped with narrow cream or pale yellow lines, lower nodes usually thickened asymmetrically; st. sheaths glabrous, dark-spotted, auricles thick, green when fresh, pale straw-colored when dry, blades narrowly triangular or linear, very strongly crisped, brs. short, nearly equal, usually with 2–3 lvs.; lf. blades to 5¼ in. long and ⅞ in. wide, usually densely pilose at least toward base; infl. unknown. Cent. China. Zone 8. The shoots appear in early spring; this is the most important edible-shoot bamboo of cent. China. St. strength is inferior to other spp.

edulis: *P. pubescens.*

fastuosa: *Semiarundinaria fastuosa.*

flexuosa A. Rivière & C. Rivière. Sts. to 31 ft. high and 2¾ in. in diam., green, glaucous, especially below nodes, straight or more often zigzag; st. sheaths greenish-beige with purplish veins and brown spots, auricles absent, ligule dark maroon, blades narrow, bent back or arched, brs. rather long, flexuous; lf. sheaths on brs. without bristles, ligules not maroon, blades to 6 in. long and ¾ in. wide, 8–12-nerved, slender-pointed, abruptly narrowed at base, serrulate on one margin, dark green above, glaucous beneath. China. Zone 8. Shoots are edible, appearing in midspring.

Henonis: *P. nigra* cv. 'Henon'.

Meyeri McClure. MEYER B. Sts. to 33 ft. high and 1⅞ in. in diam., straight or rarely somewhat flexuous near base, green, glaucous, glabrous, not ribbed; st. sheaths greenish-buff, glaucous, brown-spotted, auricles absent, ligule of medium length, exserted, sheath blade lanceolate to strap-shaped; lf. sheaths on brs. with weak auricles or none, ligules prominently exserted, blades to 6 in. long or more and 1½ in. wide, pilose at base. Cent. China. Zone 8. Resembles *P. aurea* but lacks crowding of lower nodes of sts. and ligules of st. sheaths lack a fringe of hairs. The edible shoots appear in midspring. The mature sts. are rated among the strongest in the genus. Sometimes used for hedges.

Nevinii: see *P. aureosulcata.*

nigra (Lodd. ex Lindl.) Munro [*Bambusa nigra* Lodd. ex Lindl.]. BLACK B. Sts. to 26 ft. high and 1¼ in. in diam., green at first, then becoming speckled and changing at maturity to brownish- or purple-black, nodes conspicuously edged with white below, the brs. usually spotted, st. sheaths greenish- to reddish-buff, not spotted, sparsely hairy, auricles and bristles at mouth weak or absent, sheath blades boat-shaped; lf. blades many, to 3⅝ or rarely 5 in. long and ½ or rarely ¾ in. wide, 6–12-nerved, very thin, denticulate, usually glabrous, glaucous and rarely pilose beneath. China. Long cult. in Japan; also cult. in Eur. and elsewhere. Zone 8, but less hardy than cv. 'Henon'. A favorite ornamental bamboo. The edible shoots appear in midspring. Var. *Henonis:* cv. 'Henon'. Cv. **'Henon'** [var. *Henonis* (Mitf.) Stapf ex Rendle; *P. Henonis* Mitf.]. HENON B. Larger than usual for the typical var., sts. to 50 ft. high, to 3 in. in diam. or more, rough to touch when young, green or reddish, finally yellowish, not spotted; st. sheaths tawny or reddish-brown, not spotted. S. China. Long cult. in Japan. Zone 8, but hardier than most of the larger spp. of *Phyllostachys.*

nuda McClure. Sts. to 34 ft. high and to 1½ in. in diam., internodes green, glabrous; st. sheaths grayish-wine, white-powdery, with prominent, exserted, truncate ligules, without auricles and bristles, sheath blades relatively short, narrowly triangular to lanceolate; lf. blades without auricles and bristles. China. Zone 8; one of the hardiest of the medium-sized spp. The edible shoots appear in early spring; mature sts. of inferior quality.

pubescens Mazel ex Houz. de Leh. [*P. edulis* Houz. de Leh.]. MOSO B. To 70 ft. high and 5 in. in diam. or more, sts. strongly tapered, pale green, densely velvety at first, gradually glabrescent, lower internodes short; st. sheaths greenish-smoky-buff, with dark brown spots and erect brown hairs, auricles fringed with very long, coarse, wavy bristles, ligules long, exserted, narrowly convex at apex, fringed with long, coarse, dark bristles, sheath blades lanceolate to nearly strap-shaped, green; lvs. of brs. unusually small with sheaths usually lacking auricles, ligules short, blades to 5 in. long and ⅝ in. wide or less. China. Long cult. in Japan. Zone 8. The largest and handsomest of the running bamboos. The sts. have many uses in the Orient and in Japan this sp. is the major source of edible bamboo shoots, which appear in midspring. The sp. is difficult to propagate and establish.

sulphurea: *P. bambusoides* cv. 'Allgold'. Var. **viridis:** *P. viridis.*

viridiglaucescens (Carrière) A. Rivière & C. Rivière [*Bambusa viridiglaucescens* Carrière]. Sts. very straight, erect, to 34 ft. high or more and 2 in. in diam., farinose, not ribbed, the outer arching; st. sheaths glabrous, pale green, spotted with brown, auricles usually 2, sometimes 1 or 0, dark wine-red, with prominent bristles at the mouth, ligules long and narrow, finely to coarsely ciliate, blades narrow; lf. blades to 4 in. long and ¾ in. wide, indistinctly 8–14-nerved, long-pointed, abruptly narrowed at base, denticulate on one margin, bright green above, glaucous beneath and pubescent near base. China. Cult. in Eur.; hardy in Zone 8. Shoots edible, appearing in early spring.

viridis (R. A. Young) McClure [*P. sulphurea* var. *viridis* R. A. Young]. Sts. to nearly 48 ft. high and 3¼ in. in diam., usually somewhat curved, not zigzag, pale green, glabrous, glaucous, surface of internode with a visible pigskinlike pattern; st. sheaths glabrous, often glaucous, rosy-buff with green veins and brown spots, ligule truncate to convex, auricles absent, blades narrowly triangular to ribbon-shaped; lf. sheaths on brs., with exserted ligules, blades to 5 in. long, rarely to 1 in. wide. China. Cult. in Eur.; Zone 8. St. wood of good technical quality; shoots edible, appearing in midspring.

vivax McClure. Sts. erect, to 46 ft. high and 3¾ in. in diam.; internodes green, glaucous, glabrous, strongly ribbed-striate; st. sheaths creamy-buff, spotted brown, auricles absent, bristles absent at the mouth, ligule strongly decurrent, relatively short, with convex apex, margin with bristles; lvs. pendulous, blades to 8 in. long, ¾ in. wide. China. Zone 8. Shoots edible, appearing in midspring. The most vigorous in growth of the hardy timber bamboos.

PHYMATOCARPUS F. J. Muell. *Myrtaceae.* Two spp. of shrubs in W. Australia; lvs. small, opp., mostly 3-nerved or more; fls. purple to white, in dense globose heads, calyx tube united to ovary at base, calyx lobes 5, persistent, petals 5, spreading, stamens many, in bundles opp. each petal, anthers opening by transverse slits, ovary inferior, 3-celled; fr. a 3-valved caps., dehiscing loculicidally.

porphyrocephalus F. J. Muell. To 3 ft., usually glabrous except the infl.; lvs. orbicular or broadly ovate, to ¼ in. long, thick; stamens in bundles of 10–15; fr. crowned by the thick calyx lobes. W. Australia.

PHYMATODES: *POLYPODIUM*.

PHYMOSIA Desv. *Malvaceae*. About 9 spp. of stellate-pubescent shrubs or small trees, 1 in the W. Indies the others in Cent. Amer.; lvs. simple, palmately lobed; fls. in loose, naked, nearly umbellate cymes in the upper lf. axils, involucral bracts 3, separate or united basally, sometimes early deciduous, petals 5, rose-red to mauve, stamens united in a tubular glabrous column, style brs. as many as the mericarps, stigmas terminal or sometimes slightly decurrent; fr. a schizocarp, mericarps to 60, large, thin-walled, oblong-reniform, stellate-pubescent on back, 2–3-seeded, eventually splitting into 2 separate valves, seeds glabrous or glabrate.

Not hardy in the North; propagated by softwood cuttings or seeds.

rosea (DC.) Kearn. [*Sphaeralcea rosea* (DC.) Standl.; *S. vitifolia* (Zucc.) Hemsl.]. Shrub or small tree, to 15 ft.; lvs. to 10 in. long, deeply 3-, 5-, or 7-lobed, lobes acute or acuminate, irregularly crenate-dentate; involucral bracts thin, laterally united and enclosing the bud, splitting irregularly at flowering, calyx ¾–1½ in. long, only slightly longer than the bracts, corolla more or less bell-shaped, rose to dark red, to 2½ in. long; mericarps about ¾ in. long. Mex. and Guatemala.

umbellata (Cav.) Kearn. [*Sphaeralcea umbellata* (Cav.) G. Don]. Shrub or small tree, to 20 ft.; lvs. to 9 in. long, rather shallowly lobed into 3, 5, or 7 lobes, sinuate-dentate; involucral bracts separate, spatulate, narrowed abruptly into a claw, calyx up to 1 in. long, corolla bell-shaped, rose-red, to 1½ in. long; mericarps about ⅝ in. long. Mex.

PHYSALIS L. [*Quincula* Raf.]. GROUND CHERRY, HUSK TOMATO. *Solanaceae*. About 80 spp. of erect or decumbent, sometimes rhizomatous, cosmopolitan ann. or per. herbs, chiefly of the New World; sts. glabrous or pubescent; lvs. alt., simple, petioled, mostly variously toothed, commonly soft in texture; fls. mostly solitary in lf. axils, small, pedicelled, calyx 5-toothed, becoming bladderlike in fr., prominently 10-veined, corolla usually yellowish, sometimes blue or white, usually dark-spotted and hairy toward center, rotate or short-campanulate, mostly 5-lobed, stamens 5; fr. a yellow or greenish globose berry, enclosed in the inflated calyx, seeds many.

A few species are grown for the edible fruit, used fresh or in preserves and pickles, and some also for the ornamental fruiting calyx. Most cultivated species need a warm sunny exposure. Since they are long-season plants and the high colors of the calyx in the ornamental species do not develop until the fruit is ripe, the seeds should be sown early in the spring indoors or in a hotbed. The perennial kinds may be propagated by division or by soft cuttings.

Alkekengi L. [*P. Bunyardii* Mak.; *P. Franchetii* M. T. Mast.]. ALKEKENGI, WINTER CHERRY, CHINESE-LANTERN PLANT, CHINESE-LANTERN, JAPANESE-LANTERN, STRAWBERRY TOMATO. Per., but sometimes grown as an ann., to 2 ft., with long rhizomes, glabrous or glabrescent; lvs. ovate to ovate-rhombic, to 3½ in. long, entire or undulate; fls. nodding, corolla whitish; fr. red, edible, mature calyx nearly globose, vermillion-red, to 2 in. long. Se. Eur. to Japan. Grown as an ornamental. Cvs. are: 'Gigantea' and 'Monstrosa', frs. large; 'Pygmaea', of dwarf habit.

Bunyardii: *P. Alkekengi.*

edulis: *P. peruviana,* but plants listed as *P. edulis* may be *P. ixocarpa.*

Franchetii: *P. Alkekengi.*

heterophylla Nees. CLAMMY G. C. Rhizomatous per., to 3 ft., densely glandular-pubescent; lvs. ovate, to 3 in. long, cordate, sinuate-dentate; corolla yellowish, with darker center; fr. small, yellow, edible, mature calyx conical, greenish, to 1 in. across. E. N. Amer. A highly variable sp.

ixocarpa Brot. MEXICAN H. T., TOMATILLO, JAMBERRY. Ann., to 4 ft., glabrous or glabrescent; lvs. ovate to rhombic, to 3 in. long, acuminate, base cuneate, margins dentate to entire; corolla to 1 in. across, bright yellow, with 5 dark spots at base; fr. viscid, yellow to purple, to 2¼ in. in diam., mature calyx globose, buff with purple streaks, to 1 in. long or more, frequently split by the enlarging fr. Mex.; naturalized in e. N. Amer. Cult. for food in Mex. Cv. 'Golden Nugget'. Fr. yellow; sometimes offered incorrectly as *P. peruviana* cv.

lobata Torr. [*Quincula lobata* (Torr.) Raf.]. PURPLE G. C. Branching, scurfy per. herb; lvs. ovate-lanceolate to linear-lanceolate, narrowed to winged petiole, to 4 in. long, to 1¼ in. wide, usually pinnatifid; corolla blue or violet, rarely white, rotate, to ¾ in. across; fr. to ⁵⁄₁₆ in. in diam. Sw. U.S. and adjacent Mex.

peruviana L. [*P. edulis* Sims]. CAPE GOOSEBERRY, BARBADOS G., POHA, GROUND CHERRY, WINTER C., CHERRY TOMATO, STRAWBERRY

T., GOOSEBERRY T. Per., to 3 ft., partly erect, much-branched, densely glandular-villous; lvs. ovate to triangular, to 4 in. long, cordate at base, entire to coarsely toothed; corolla yellow, with purple markings, to 2½ in. long; fr. small, yellow, edible. Trop. S. Amer. Cv. 'Golden Nugget': *P. ixocarpa* cv.

pruinosa L. STRAWBERRY TOMATO, DWARF CAPE GOOSEBERRY. Ann., to 20 in., diffusely branching, viscid-pubescent; lvs. ovate, to 3¼ in. long, coarsely and unevenly dentate to base; corolla buff-yellow, to ½ in. long; fr. yellowish, edible. E. N. Amer. The common edible husk tomato of gardens, eaten raw or cooked.

pubescens L. GROUND CHERRY, DOWNY G.C., STRAWBERRY TOMATO. Differs from *P. pruinosa* in being less pubescent, more slender, and having lvs. entire or with 1–7 teeth on each side. E. N. Amer., s. Calif., trop. Amer. Fr. edible.

subglabrata Mackenz. & Bush. Per., from a stout rhizome, to 4 ft., glabrous or glabrescent; lvs. ovate to broadly lanceolate, to 4 in. long, entire or weakly dentate; corolla yellowish, with purple throat, to 1 in. across; fr. reddish or purplish. E. N. Amer.

PHYSARIA (Nutt.) A. Gray. *Cruciferae*. About 14 spp. of tufted per. herbs in w. N. Amer., mainly in drier parts of mts.; lvs. in basal rosettes, simple, entire to toothed, stellate-pubescent; fls. yellow, rather showy, in bractless racemes, sepals 4, petals 4, somewhat spatulate; fr. a somewhat inflated silicle, strongly 2-lobed at apex, with style emerging from sinus. Closely related to *Lesquerella,* which differs in fr. smaller, less papery, not 2-lobed.

Propagated by seeds, cuttings, or division and adapted to rock gardens in well-drained soil.

didymocarpa (Hook.) A. Gray. Sts. erect to decumbent, to 6 in. long, short-pubescent; lvs. broadly obovate, to 3 in. long, entire or sinuately toothed; fls. ½ in. long; silicles deeply cordate at base, strongly inflated. Utah to Colo., n. to Sask. and Alta. Var. **lanata** A. Nels. Long- and loose-pubescent throughout; lf. bases lanate.

Geyeri (Hook.) A. Gray. Sts. ascending or decumbent, to 6 in. long; basal lvs. obovate to orbicular, to 2 in. long, petiole winged; fls. to ½ in. long; silicles not much inflated, the upper sinus shallow. Wyo., Mont. to Wash.

PHYSOCARPUS (Camb.) Maxim. [*Opulaster* Medic. ex Rydb.]. NINEBARK. *Rosaceae*. About 10 spp. of deciduous, spiraealike shrubs with exfoliating bark, native to N. Amer. and Asia; lvs. alt., petioled, simple, toothed or palmately lobed; fls. white or pinkish, in umbel-like corymbs, sepals and petals 5, stamens 20–40, inserted on a disc; fr. an inflated follicle.

Hardy in the North and of easy culture. Propagated by seeds and cuttings of young or old wood.

amurensis (Maxim.) Maxim. Similar to *P. opulifolius,* but lvs. 2–4 in. long, 3–5-lobed, sharply serrate; fls. ⅝ in. across. Manchuria, Korea. Zone 5.

bracteatus (Rydb.) Rehd. [*Opulaster bracteatus* Rydb.]. Like *P. monogynus,* but young shoots glabrous, yellowish; lvs. 1–3 in. long, mostly 3-lobed; infl. surrounded by leaflike bracts; fls. more numerous. Colo. Zone 6.

capitatus (Pursh) O. Kuntze. Erect or spreading, 3–8 ft., pubescent on young growth; lvs. 1–2½ in. long, round-ovate, 3–5-lobed, lobes serrate to incised; fls. many, sepals stellate-pubescent; follicles more or less stellate-pubescent to glabrous, ¼ in. long. B.C. and Mont., s. to Calif. and Utah.

intermedius: *P. opulifolius* var.

malvaceus (Greene) A. Nels. [*P. pauciflorus* Piper; *Opulaster malvaceus* (Greene) O. Kuntze ex Rydb.]. Erect, 3–7 ft.; lvs. round or nearly so, to 2½ in. wide, 3–5-lobed, doubly crenate-serrate; umbels few-fld.; fls. white, to ½ in. across; follicles usually 2, flattened and keeled, stellate-pubescent, styles erect. B.C. to Mont., s. to Ore., Utah, Wyo. Zone 6.

missouriensis: *P. opulifolius* var. *intermedius.*

monogynus (Torr.) Coult. To 3½ ft., young shoots glabrous to stellate-pubescent; lvs. broadly ovate to reniform, to 1½ in. long, 3–5-lobed, incised-serrate, glabrous; fls. few in a cluster, pinkish to white, to ½ in. across; follicles 1 or 2, stellate-pubescent, turgid, styles divergent. S. Dak. to Tex., Ariz., Nev. Zone 6.

opulifolius (L.) Maxim. [*Opulaster opulifolius* (L.) O. Kuntze ex Rydb.; *Spiraea opulifolia* L.]. To 10 ft., old bark separating in many thin layers; lvs. rounded, to 3 in. long, somewhat 3-lobed, cordate; pedicels and calyx glabrous to tomentulose, fls. many, to ¼ in. across; follicles usually 3, glabrous, conspicuous. Que. to Va., and Tenn. Zone 2. Var. **intermedius** (Rydb.) B. L. Robinson [*P. intermedius* (Rydb.)

C. K. Schneid.; *P. missouriensis* Daniels]. Follicles permanently pubescent. W. N.Y. to Minn. and Colo., s. to Ill., Ind., Ark. Zone 5. Cv. 'Luteus'. Lvs. yellow when young, later yellow-green or bronze-yellow. Cv. 'Nanus'. Dwarf, with smaller, less lobed lvs.

parviflorus: a listed name of no botanical standing; perhaps in error for *P. pauciflorus*.

pauciflorus: *P. malvaceus.*

PHYSOSIPHON Lindl. *Orchidaceae.* Ten spp. of epiphytes, native to highlands of Cent. and trop. S. Amer.; sts. slender, 1-lvd. at apex; lvs. oblong; infls. 1 or 2, axillary, racemose, many-fld.; fls. small, sepals partly united, forming a campanulate or urceolate tube, their apices spreading, petals concealed in tube, cuneate, lip larger than petals, commonly 3-lobed, column with a foot, pollinia 2. For structure of fl. see *Orchidaceae.*

Cool greenhouse. For culture see *Orchids.*

Loddigesii: *P. tubatus.*

tubatus (Lodd.) Rchb.f. [*P. Loddigesii* Lindl.]. BOTTLE ORCHID. Erect, to 16 in.; lvs. elliptic, to 6 in. long; raceme to 10 in. long, with fls. closely spaced; fls. varying from greenish-yellow to brick-red, sepals to 1 in. long, lip small, 3-lobed, lateral lobes semicircular, midlobe ovate, crenulate. Mex., Guatemala.

PHYSOSTEGIA Benth. FALSE DRAGONHEAD, LION'S-HEART, OBEDIENCE, OBEDIENT PLANT. *Labiatae.* About 15 spp. of glabrous to puberulous per. herbs of N. Amer.; sts. mostly square in cross section; lvs. opp., often toothed; fls. showy, solitary in axils, in solitary or panicled leafless spikes, bracts small, calyx tubular or campanulate, 10-nerved, slightly inflated in fr., corolla whitish to red and pink, tube much longer than calyx, limb 2-lipped, upper lip erect, nearly entire, lower lip 3-lobed, stamens 4, in 2 pairs, anthers 2-celled; fr. of 4 glabrous nutlets.

Useful ornamentals for borders and wild gardens; easily cultivated. Usually propagated by division of clumps, also by seeds.

denticulata (Ait.) Britt. Stoloniferous, sts. slender, 1½–3 ft.; lvs. membranous, oblong-lanceolate, blunt to acute, undulate to dentate, lowermost petioled; spikes slender, 4–16 in. long; corolla to 1 in. long, 5/16 in. wide at throat, bright magenta. Swamps and bottomlands, Va. to Fla.

Digitalis Small. Tall, stout ann., to 5 ft.; middle and lower st. lvs. oblong-ovate or obovate, to 3 in. wide; corolla to 1 in. long, pale lavender to whitish, often with red-purple dots. Sandy or gravelly soils, e. Tex. to La. and Ark.

grandiflora: a listed name of no botanical standing for *P. virginiana* cv.

parviflora Nutt. ex Benth. [*Dracocephalum Nuttallii* Britt.]. Similar to *P. virginiana,* but upper lvs. not much reduced, and fls. smaller, with corolla to ½ in. long. Miss., w. to Colo., Ore., B.C.

speciosa: *P. virginiana* var.

virginiana (L.) Benth. OBEDIENCE. Stoloniferous, glabrous per., to 4 ft. or more; lvs. lanceolate, to 5 in. long, acute, often sharp-serrate, uppermost lvs. much reduced; spikes closely fld., usually panicled, with calyces overlapping in fr.; calyx tubular-campanulate, viscid-glandular, teeth sharp, triangular, corolla showy, to 1¼ in. long, rose-purple, inflated at the mouth. N. Bruns. to Minn., s. to S.C. and Mo. Cvs. include: 'Alba', fls. white; 'Gigantea', to 7 ft.; 'Grandiflora', fls. bright pink; 'Nana', of dwarf habit; 'Rosea', fls. rose-pink; 'Rubra', fls. red; 'Splendens' and 'Superba', listed names; 'Vivid', fls. claret-colored. Var. **speciosa** (Sweet) A. Gray [*P. speciosa* Sweet]. Coarser habit; upper lvs. more gradually or not much reduced; calyx essentially without glands.

PHYTELEPHAS Ruiz & Pav. *Palmae.* Several spp. of stemless or short-trunked, unarmed, dioecious palms of wet lowland forests in nw. S. Amer. and Panama; lvs. regularly pinnate, pinnae acute; infl. among lvs., subtended by 2 fibrous bracts; male fls. in a long, thick, catkinlike spike, perianth shallowly lobed, ringlike, stamens many, long, female fls. in a dense head, very large, sepals and petals many, long, slender, pistil 7–10-celled, 7–10-ovuled; frs. aggregated, large, coarsely tubercled, seeds with very hard, homogeneous endosperm and subbasal embryo.

For culture see *Palms.*

macrocarpa Ruiz & Pav. IVORY-NUT PALM, IVORY P., TAGUA. Trunk sometimes to 5 ft. high, but mostly prostrate or not evident; lvs. very long, erect-curving, to 20 ft. or more, pinnae about 80 pairs, to 3 ft. long, 2 in. wide, strongly veined, stiffish. Brazil, Peru. Fruiting heads sometimes weigh 25 lbs.; the hard durable endosperm of the seeds is a source of "vegetable ivory," used as substitute for true ivory.

PHYTEUMA L. HORNED RAMPION. *Campanulaceae.* Perhaps 40 spp. of per. herbs, native to Eur. and temp. Asia; sts. mostly simple, from a loose, basal rosette; fls. mostly many, small, in dense spikes or terminal heads, sometimes somewhat umbellate, 5-merous, corolla blue, purplish, or white, divided to near the base but with the linear petals coherent at first in a curved tube, later often spreading, style long-exserted, stigma 2–3-lobed; fr. a caps., opening by lateral slits.

Phyteumas are plants for the rock garden and border, where they succeed in any good soil. Propagated by seeds or division in the spring.

austriacum: *P. orbiculare* var.

Balbisii A. DC. Sts. erect, 4–6 in., glabrous, rosette lvs. broadly cordate-ovate, acute, petioled, st. lvs. few, ovate-acuminate, entire to remotely dentate, sessile; fls. in cylindric-oblong spikes about 1 in. long, corolla white, stigma 3-lobed. Italy.

betonicifolium Vill. Glabrous or puberulent, sts. to 18 in.; lvs. lanceolate-ovate to linear, to about 2 in. long, cordate to obtuse, entire or toothed, the lower long-petioled; fls. in ovoid spikes, with obscure bracts, corolla blue or violet, sometimes white, stigmas 3. S. Eur. Var. **sessilifolium** A. DC. [*P. scaposum* R. Schulz]. Lower lvs. linear-lanceolate, not cordate, sessile.

campanuloides: *Asyneuma campanuloides.*

canescens: *Asyneuma canescens.*

Charmelii Vill. Glabrous, sts. suberect to erect, 6–12 in.; lower lvs. cordate-ovate, deeply serrate, long-petioled, st. lvs. lanceolate; fls. in globose heads, bracts linear to lanceolate, mostly longer than fls., corolla dark blue, stigmas 2. Alps.

comosum L. Glabrous, decumbent herb, sts. to 6 in. long; lvs. ovate to lanceolate, to 2 in. long, cuneate to obtuse, coarsely serrate, the lower long-petioled; fls. in sessile, umbellate clusters, corolla dark purple apically, lilac and inflated below, to 1 in. long, stigmas 2. Alps.

Halleri: *P. ovatum.*

hemisphaericum L. Tufted, sts. erect, nearly leafless, 3–8 in.; lvs. erect, linear, 2–4 in. long, entire; fls. in dense, globose heads about 1 in. across, bracts ovate to lanceolate, not as long as head, corolla blue or sometimes whitish. Alps.

humile Schleich. Tufted, 2–5 in.; lvs. linear, lower ones nearly reaching fl. heads; fls. in dense, globose heads about ¾ in. across, bracts long, linear, corolla dark violet. Alps.

Laibachianum: a listed name of no botanical standing.

limonifolium: *Asyneuma limonifolia.*

lobelioides: *Asyneuma lobelioides.*

Michelii All. [*P. scorzonerifolium* Vill.]. Erect, sts. simple, 1–2 ft.; lvs. ovate to lanceolate, serrate, subcordate to cuneate, the lower long-petioled; fls. in dense, oblong-spicate heads 2–3 in. long, bracts reflexed, corolla longer than bracts, pale blue to violet or nearly white, stigmas 2–3. S. Eur.

nigrum F. W. Schmidt. Erect, 8–12 in.; basal lvs. ovate, obtuse, weakly toothed, long-petioled, st. lvs. linear or oblong-ovate; fls. in ovate heads, corolla dark blue, strongly recurved after flowering. Cent. Eur.

orbiculare L. Variable, 6–24 in., glabrous; lower lvs. broadly ovate to elliptic, obscurely serrate, st. lvs. linear, 2–4 in. long including petiole; fls. in dense, globose heads to about 1 in. across, bracts serrate, spreading or reflexed, corolla dark blue. Alps. Var. **austriacum** (G. Beck) G. Beck [*P. austriacum* G. Beck]. St. lvs. ovate-lanceolate, bracts erect.

ovatum Honck. [*P. Halleri* All.]. Erect, to 2 ft., glabrous; lower lvs. cordate-ovate, acute, serrate, long-petioled, upper lvs. more lanceolate; fls. in oblong-ovate heads 1–2 in. long, bracts 2, spreading or reflexed, corolla dark violet, sometimes white. Alps.

pauciflorum L. Tufted, to 3 in.; lvs. obovate to lanceolate, to about 1½ in. long, obtuse, entire or toothed near apex; fls. few, in globose heads to ¾ in. across, bracts closely subtending fls., broadly ovate, acute, usually denticulate and minutely ciliate, corolla blue. Alps.

scaposum: *P. betonicifolium* var.

Scheuchzeri All. Loose, to 18 in.; lower lvs. ovate-lanceolate, bluntly toothed, long-petioled, grading above to linear, 2–5 in. long, nearly entire, sessile; fls. in globose heads to about 1 in. across, bracts leaflike, corolla deep blue, stigmas 3. S. Eur.

scorzonerifolium: *P. Michelii.*

Sieberi K. Spreng. To 6 in.; lower lvs. ovate to lanceolate, crenate, petioled, upper lvs. lanceolate, clasping; fls. in globose heads to 1 in.

across, subtending bracts usually longer than fls., corolla deep blue. S. Eur.

spicatum L. SPIKED RAMPION. One to 3 ft.; lower lvs. cordate-ovate, 2–3 in. long, coarsely serrate, petioles longer than blades, upper lvs. lanceolate to linear, sessile; fls. in dense, bracted, oblong spikes mostly 2–3 in. long, corolla white with greenish tips or sometimes bluish, about ½ in. long. Eur.

Vagneri A. Kern. Erect, to 1 ft. or more; lower lvs. cordate-ovate, serrate, long-petioled, upper lvs. remote, linear-lanceolate, 2–4 in. long, sessile; fls. in globose heads to 1 in. across, eventually becoming elongate, corolla dark blue. Hungary.

Zahlbruckneri Vest. Probably not distinct from *P. Michelii;* erect, glabrous, sts. 1–3 ft.; lower lvs. oblong-lanceolate, crenate, not cordate, long-petioled, upper lvs. linear-lanceolate, nearly entire; fls. in bracted, oblong spikes 1–2 in. long, corolla blue. Eur.

PHYTOLACCA L. POKEWEED, POKEBERRY. *Phytolaccaceae.* About 25 spp. of coarse, sometimes dioecious herbs, shrubs, or treelike plants, native to trop. and warm regions; lvs. often large, alt., simple; fls. small, in racemes or panicles, sometimes unisexual, sepals 5, petals 0, stamens 6–33, carpels 5–16, separate or somewhat united; fr. a depressed-globose berry, each carpel 1-seeded.

Grown as ornamentals, and *P. esculenta* as a potherb in some countries. Of easy culture; propagated by seeds.

acinosa Roxb. INDIAN POKE. Herb, with succulent sts., to 5 ft.; lvs. elliptic-ovate or lanceolate, to 10 in. long; racemes to 6 in. long; fls. 5/16 in. across, sepals white-margined, stamens 8. China, Japan; naturalized in India.

americana L. [*P. decandra* L.]. POKE, VIRGINIAN P., SCOKE, POCAN, GARGET, PIGEON BERRY. Herb, to 12 ft., with unpleasant odor and large poisonous root; lvs. oblong- to ovate-lanceolate, to 6(–14) in. long; racemes to 6 in. long or more; fls. bisexual, white or purplish, stamens and styles 10; fr. a black-purple berry with red juice. Me. to Fla., w. to Mex. Young shoots when about 6 in. high often used as a potherb, but cooking water must be discarded, since the plant is more or less poisonous in all parts.

decandra: *P. americana.*

dioica L. Evergreen, dioecious, soft-wooded tree, with thick trunk, to 60 ft. or more; lvs. elliptic or ovate, to 7 in. long, glabrous; racemes to 4 in. long; fls. white, stamens 20–30. Paraguay, s. Brazil, Uruguay, n. Argentina.

esculenta Van Houtte. Herb, to 3 ft. or more, slightly woody at base; lvs. broad-elliptic, to 10 in. long, short-petioled, edible; racemes to 4 in. long; fls. bisexual, white, stamens 8. China, Japan.

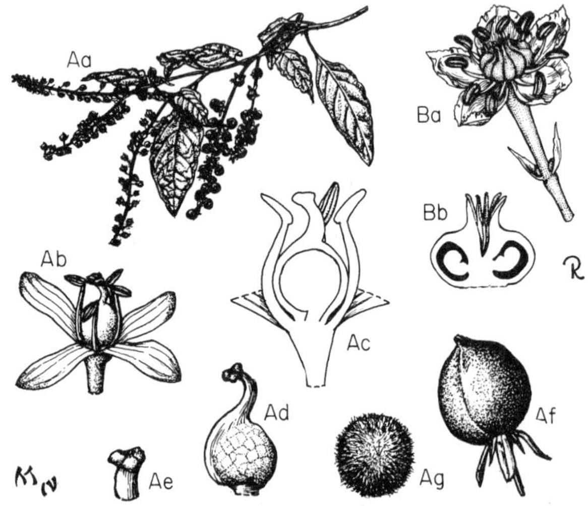

PHYTOLACCACEAE. **A,** *Rivina humilis:* **Aa,** flowering and fruiting branch, × 1/4; **Ab,** flower, × 5; **Ac,** flower, vertical section (perianth lobes cut off), × 10; **Ad,** pistil, × 10; **Ae,** stigma, × 15; **Af,** fruit, × 2; **Ag,** seed, × 4. **B,** *Phytolacca americana:* **Ba,** flower, × 3; **Bb,** pistil, vertical section, × 6. (Ba, Bb from Lawrence, *Taxonomy of Vascular Plants.*)

PHYTOLACCACEAE R. Br. POKEWEED FAMILY. Dicot.; about 20 genera of herbs, shrubs, and trees, sometimes climbing, native to Amer. and Afr.; foliage sometimes ill-scented; lvs. alt., entire; fls. bisexual or unisexual, mostly in racemes, calyx 4–5-parted, petals usually 0, stamens 3 to many, pistils united or separated, ovary superior or partly inferior; fr. dry, fleshy, or drupelike. *Agdestis, Phytolacca, Rivina,* and *Trichostigma* are sometimes cult.

PIARANTHUS R. Br. *Asclepiadaceae.* About 15 spp. of dwarf, succulent, leafless per. herbs, native to S. and S.-W. Afr.; distinguished from *Stapelia* and other succulent asclepiads in having one rather than two whorls of corona lobes.

For culture see *Succulents.*

disparilis N. E. Br. Sts. very stout, moderately tubercled-angled; fls. solitary, erect, near apex of st., corolla rotate, less than 1 in. across, pale pinkish-purple, marked with transverse yellow lines, velvety-puberulous. S. Afr.

elegans: a listed name of no botanical standing.

foetidus N. E. Br. Sts. tufted, to 2½ in. long, ovoid to globose or indistinctly 4–5-angled; fls. 1–6, usually paired at apex of st., corolla rotate, ¾ in. across, yellow, marked with purplish-crimson lines or spots, evenly pubescent, corona orange-yellow, marked with purple-brown. S. Afr. Var. **diversus** N. E. Br. Corolla lobes dark purple-crimson, with creamy-yellow lines and spots on the lower ⅔. Var. **purpureus** N. E. Br. Corolla lobes brighter purple-crimson, with dull yellow markings at base.

globosus A. C. White & Sloane. Sts. ovoid to globose, less than 1 in. long; fls. solitary or in pairs near apex of st., corolla about ½ in. across, light greenish-yellow, dotted red or lavender, velvety-puberulous, corona yellow, with a red-spotted crest. Known only in cult.

Nebrownii: *P. pulcher* var.

pallidus Lückh. Sts. globose to oblong, obtusely 4-angled; fls. in clusters of 2–4 near apex of st., corolla rotate, without distinct tube, to 1 in. across, pale yellow, without spots, velvety-puberulous, corona lobes yellow. S. Afr.

parvulus N. E. Br. Sts. to 2 in. long, ovoid to oblong-ovoid, obtusely 4-angled; fls. in clusters of up to 12 at middle or apex of st., corolla rotate, ½ in. across, straw-yellow, without spots, corona lobes yellow, conspicuously tubercled at apex. S. Afr.

Pillansii N. E. Br. Sts. to 1½ in. long, subcylindrical to obtusely 4–5-angled, obscurely tubercle-toothed; fls. mostly in apical pairs, corolla up to 1½ in. across, dull greenish-yellow or pale yellow, without spots, velvety-puberulous, corona lobes yellow. S. Afr.

pulcher N. E. Br. Sts. to 1 in. or more long, obscurely 4-angled, with small teeth; fls. single or paired at middle or apex of st., corolla with ascending lobes, to ¾ in. across, greenish-yellow, marked with purple-brown spots, velvety-pubescent with white and purple hairs. S. Afr. Var. **Nebrownii** (Dinter) A. C. White & Sloane [*P. Nebrownii* Dinter]. Said to differ in characters of the corona and purple-margined corolla lobes.

Ruschii Nel. Apparently differs from *P. foetidus* only in having short but conspicuous white hairs on corolla lobes and a pleasant odor. S.-W. Afr.

PICEA A. Dietr. SPRUCE. *Pinaceae.* Perhaps 45 spp. of monoecious, coniferous, evergreen trees of conical habit, with undivided main axis, native to cooler parts of N. Hemisphere; lvs. linear, 4-angled or compressed, the bases persistent and raised on brs.; male cones catkinlike, female cones woody, pendulous, scales persistent, each bearing 2 small, 1-winged seeds. Differs from *Abies* in the persistent, raised lf. bases and pendulous cones with persistent scales; from *Tsuga* in having lvs. sessile with lateral resin ducts; and from *Pseudotsuga* in having bracts shorter than the cone scales.

The spruces produce strong light wood having many uses, the most important being a source of paper pulp. As ornamentals they are hardy at least through Zone 6. For culture see *Conifers.*

Abies (L.) Karst. [*P. excelsa* (Lam.) Link]. NORWAY S. To 150 ft., branchlets usually drooping; lvs. 4-angled, to ¾ in. long, dark green and shiny; cones to 7 in. long. Eur. Zone 3. One of the most commonly planted conifers in N. Amer. Important timber tree in Eur. Some of the cvs. are: **'Argentea'**, lvs. variegated with white; **'Argenteospica'**, tips of young branchlets white; **'Attenuata'**, brs. slender, lvs. sparse; **'Aurea'**, lvs. golden-yellow; **'Aurescens'**, lvs. golden-yellow when young, becoming yellowish-green; **'Barryi'**, conical, brs. thick; **'Borealis'**, a listed name; **'Brevifolia'**, lvs. about ¼ in. long; **'Capitata'**, shoots close together at ends of brs., forming heads; **'Chlorocarpa'**, cones green when young; **'Cincinnata'**, lvs. long, spirally twisted; **'Clanbrasiliana'**, compact bush, to 7 ft., branchlets whitish; **'Columnaris'**, columnar, brs. very short; **'Compacta'**, dense, nearly globose;

'**Conica**', conical; '**Costickii**', dwarf, upright; '**Cranstonii**', brs. long, irregular, lateral brs. few; '**Cupressina**', broadly columnar; '**Diffusa**', dense, wide-spreading, lvs. light yellowish-green; '**Dumosa**', prostrate; '**Echiniformis**', dwarf, slow-growing, lvs. long and prickly, resembling a hedgehog; '**Elegans**', narrow-conical; '**Ellwangerana**', broadly conical, with crowded branchlets; '**Erimata**', conical habit, brs. fastigiate; '**Erythrocarpa**', cones violet-purple; '**Finedonensis**', lvs. pale yellow, becoming bronzy, then green; '**Gregoryana**', dwarf, to 2 ft., with crowded pale branchlets; '**Highlandia**', low, domelike, lvs. glossy dark green; '**Humilis**', very dwarf, lvs. small, dark green; '**Inversa**' [cv. 'Inverta'], brs. drooping, densely branched; '**Maxwellii**', dwarf, to 2 ft., with very short, thick branchlets; '**Merkii**', low, lvs. thin, grass green; '**Microsperma**', dense, bushy; '**Monstrosa**', with only an unbranched single st. clothed with stiff lvs.; '**Mucronata**', shrub, with crowded, red-yellow branchlets; '**Mutabilis**', slow-growing, cushionlike; '**Nana**', branchlets short, orange-yellow; '**Nidiformis**', low, with very dense head and a nestlike mass of branchlets; '**Nigra**', conical, densely branched; '**Ohlendorffii**', compact, globose, lvs. pale yellowish-green; '**Parsonii**', straggling dwarf, with drooping branchlets; '**Parviformis**', broadly conical; '**Pendula**', brs. drooping; '**Phylicoides**', st. erect, with few lateral brs., lvs. sparse, thickened; '**Procumbens**', prostrate, branchlets horizontal, bright yellow; '**Prostrata**', a listed name; '**Pseudomaxwellii**', cushionlike, brs. in horizontal layers; '**Pumila**', dense, dwarf, lvs. bluish-green; '**Pungens Semiglauca**', a listed name; '**Pygmaea**', dense, dwarf; '**Pyramidalis Gracilis**', dwarf, nearly globose, lvs. bright green; '**Pyramidata**', narrow-conical; '**Reflexa**', mat-forming; '**Remontii**', dense, conical, branchlets crowded, yellow; '**Repens**', low, brs. procumbent or arching, lvs. crowded; '**Robusta**', '**Sherwoodii**', '**Smithii**', listed names; '**Tabuliformis**', prostrate, brs. horizontal; '**Tenuifolia**', a listed name; '**Variegata**', some lvs. variegated with yellow; '**Veitchii**', dwarf, conical; '**Viminalis**', brs. nearly horizontal, with long slender branchlets.

alba: *P. glauca.*

albertiana: *P. glauca* var.

Alcockiana: a variant spelling for *Alcoquiana.*

Alcoquiana (J. G. Veitch ex Lindl.) Carrière [*P. bicolor* (Maxim.) Mayr]. ALCOCK S. To 75 ft. or more, branchlets yellow or reddish-brown, glabrous or gray-pubescent; lvs. rhombic in section, to ¾ in. long, with white bands on all 4 angles; cones to 4¾ in. long. Japan. Zone 5. Much material originally cult. as *P. Alcockiana* in England and Eur. is *P. jezoensis.*

asperata M. T. Mast. To about 75 ft., branchlets yellow, mostly pubescent; lvs. 4-angled, to ¾ in. long, dark green; cones gray, to 4 in. long. W. China. Zone 6. Used by the Chinese for many building purposes. Var. **notabilis** Rehd. & E. H. Wils. Lvs. and cones longer. Var. **ponderosa** Rehd. & E. H. Wils. Bark thicker, cones larger.

Balfouriana: *P. likiangensis* var.

bicolor: *P. Alcoquiana.*

borealis: a listed name of no botanical standing; perhaps for *P. Omorika* cv., but may also have been used for material referable to *P. Abies* or *P. obovata* var. *fennica.*

Brewerana S. Wats. To 100 ft. or more, branchlets drooping and whiplike; lvs. more or less flattened, to 1 in. long, with white bands above; cones light orange-brown, to 5 in. long. S. Ore. and n. Calif. Zone 6.

canadensis: *P. glauca.*

Engelmannii Parry ex Engelm. To 150 ft.; lvs. 4-angled or slightly flattened, to 1 in. long, bluish-green; cones to 3 in. long. B.C. to New Mex. Zone 3. Yields tanbark and timber. Cvs. are: '**Argentea**', lvs. silvery-gray; '**Fendleri**', lvs. longer, branchlets drooping; '**Glauca**', lvs. steel-blue; '**Microphylla**', lvs. shorter.

excelsa: *P. Abies.*

glauca (Moench) Voss [*P. alba* (Ait.) Link; *P. canadensis* (Mill.) BSP, not Link]. WHITE S., CAT S. Mostly less than 100 ft., branchlets commonly drooping; lvs. 4-angled, to ¾ in. long, bluish-green; cones to 2 in. long. Across Canada and n. U.S. Zone 3. Wood used for timber and pulp. Cvs. listed are: '**Aurea**', lvs. golden-yellow; '**Caerulea**', lvs. glaucous; '**Conica**', dwarf, narrowly conical; '**Densata**', BLACK HILLS S., a very hardy form from the Black Hills of S. Dak., slow-growing and of compact, dense, symmetrical habit, sometimes erroneously grown as var. *albertiana;* '**Echiniformis**', dwarf, cushionlike, lvs. very glaucous-blue; '**Gloriosa**', a listed name; '**Nana**', dwarf, dense; '**Parva**' [var. *tabuliformis* (Slav.) L. H. Bailey], dwarf, flat-topped, brs. horizontal, layered. Var. **albertiana** (S. Br.) Sarg. [*P. albertiana* S. Br.]. ALBERTA S. Lvs. more crowded, cones to 1½ in. long and nearly as broad; B.C. to Mont. Plants grown under this name may be cv. 'Densata'. Var. **tabuliformis:** 'Parva'.

Glehnii (Friedr. Schmidt) M. T. Mast. SAKHALIN S. To 100 ft. or more, branchlets densely villous; lvs. 4-angled, to ½ in. long, deep green; cones to 3 in. long. Japan, Sakhalin Is. Zone 4.

hondoensis: *P. jezoensis* var.

Hunnewelliana: a listed name of no botanical standing for *P. pungens* cv.

jezoensis (Siebold & Zucc.) Carrière. YEDDO S. To 150 ft.; lvs. flattened, to ¾ in. long, silvery-white above, glossy dark green beneath; cones to 3½ in. long. N. Asia, Japan. Zone 5. Important timber tree in Japan. Var. **hondoensis** (Mayr) Rehd. [*P. hondoensis* Mayr]. HONDO S. Lvs. shorter, dull green beneath.

koraiensis: *P. Koyamai.*

Kosterana: a listed name of no botanical standing for *P. pungens* cv. 'Koster'.

Koyamai Shiras. [*P. koraiensis* Nakai]. To 60 ft.; lvs. 4-angled, to ½ in. long, with 2 white bands above; cones to 4 in. long. Japan. Zone 5.

likiangensis (Franch.) E. Pritz. To about 90 ft., branchlets pale yellow; lvs. 4-angled, with white bands above; cones to 3½ in. long, green when young. W. China. Zone 6. Var. **Balfouriana** (Rehd. & E. H. Wils.) Cheng ex Rehd. [*P. Balfouriana* Rehd. & E. H. Wils.]. Branchlets densely villous; cones violet-purple when young.

mariana (Mill.) BSP [*P. nigra* (Ait.) Link]. BLACK S., DOUBLE S., BOG S. Mostly less than 60 ft.; lvs. 4-angled, to ¾ in. long, dull or bluish-green; cones to 1½ in. long. Alaska and n. states to mts. of Va. Zone 2. Yields spruce gum. Some of the cvs. are: '**Beissneri**', conical, lvs. light bluish-green; '**Doumetii**', dense, conical; '**Ericoides**', slow-growing, conical, lvs. very thin; '**Fastigiata**', columnar; '**Globosa**', dense, rounded; '**Nana**', dwarf; '**Procumbens**', low, spreading.

Maximowiczii Carrière. JAPANESE BUSH S. To about 75 ft. but mostly much shorter; lvs. 4-angled, spreading, radially arranged, to ½ in. long, dark green, stiff; cones to 2½ in. long. Japan. Zone 5.

Moerheimii: a listed name of no botanical standing for *P. pungens* cv.

montigena M. T. Mast. To about 90 ft., lvs. 4-angled, to ½ in. long, bluish-green, with 2 white bands above; cones to 4 in. long. W. China. Zone 6. Allied to *P. likiangensis,* but having shorter lvs.

Morinda: *P. Smithiana.*

morrisonicola Hayata. Branchlets glabrous; lvs. 4-angled, to ¾ in. long, dark green; cones to 2½ in. long. Mt. Morrison (Taiwan).

nigra: *P. mariana.*

obovata Ledeb. [*Abies obovata* (Ledeb.) D. Don]. SIBERIAN S. To 100 ft. or more, branchlets slightly drooping; lvs. 4-angled, to ¾ in. long, dull or bluish-green; cones to 2½ in. long. N. Eurasia. Zone 3. Var. **alpestris** (Brügg.) A. Henry. Slow-growing, with larger cones. Var. **fennica** (Regel) A. Henry. FINNISH S. Lvs. dark green.

Omorika (Panč.) Purk. SERBIAN S. To 100 ft.; lvs. flattened, to ½ in. long, with 2 white bands above, glossy dark green beneath; cones to 2½ in. long. S. Eur. Zone 4, but requires shelter from winter winds. Cvs. include: '**Borealis**', similar to *P. Abies* but with lvs. longer and narrower; '**Nana**', dwarf, to 5 ft. high; '**Pendula**', brs. pendulous.

orientalis (L.) Link. To 120 ft. or more, branchlets slightly drooping, pale brown, pubescent; lvs. 4-angled, to ½ in. long, crowded, glossy dark green; cones to 3¼ in. long. Caucasus and Asia Minor. Zone 5, but does best in sheltered positions. Cv. '**Aurea**'. Lvs. bronzy-golden. Cv. '**Gracilis**'. Dense, rounded, dwarf.

polita: see *P. Torano.*

pungens Engelm. COLORADO S., COLORADO BLUE S. To 100 ft. or more, branchlets yellowish-brown, glabrous; lvs. 4-angled, to 1¼ in. long, spreading radially, stiff and spiny-pointed, usually bluish-green; cones to 4 in. long. Wyo., Utah, Colo., New Mex. Zone 3. Cvs. are: '**Argentea**', lvs. silvery-white; '**Aurea**', lvs. golden-yellow; '**Bakeri**', lvs. longer, deeper blue than 'Argentea'; '**Caerulea**', lvs. bluish-white; '**Compacta**', dense, dwarf; '**Glauca**', BLUE S., lvs. bluish; '**Hoopsii**', lvs. very silvery; '**Hunnewelliana**', dense, dwarf; '**Koster**' [cv. 'Kosterana'], branchlets drooping, lvs. bluish; '**Moerheimii**', compact, lvs. blue; '**Nana**', dwarf; '**Prostrata**', low, spreading; '**Royall**', a listed name; '**Semiglauca**', a listed name; '**Spekii**', lvs. bluish-white; '**Thompsonii**', a listed name; '**Viridis**', lvs. dull green.

retroflexa M. T. Mast. To 120 ft., branchlets bright yellow, glabrous; lvs. 4-angled, to 1 in. long; cones to 5 in. long. W. China. Zone 6.

rubens Sarg. [*P. rubra* (Du Roi) Link, not A. Dietr.]. RED S., HE BALSAM. To about 90 ft., branchlets brown, pubescent; lvs. 4-angled, ½ in. long, dark or bright green; cones to 2 in. long. Nov. Sc. to mts. of N.C. Zone 2. Important timber tree and main source of spruce gum. Cv. '**Monstrosa**' is listed. Cv. '**Virgata**'. SNAKE S. Brs. long, slender, without branchlets.

rubra: *P. rubens.*

Schrenkiana Fisch. & C. A. Mey. To 100 ft. or more, branchlets drooping; lvs. 4-angled, to 1½ in. long, spreading radially, dull green; cones to 4 in. long. Cent. Asia. Zone 6. Cv. '**Glauca**' is listed.

sitchensis (Bong.) Carrière. SITKA S. To 120 ft. or more, branchlets light brown, glabrous; lvs. flattened, to 1 in. long, spiny-pointed, silvery-white above, glossy green beneath; cones to 4 in. long. Alaska to Calif. Zone 6b, does best under cool, humid conditions. Wood has many uses. Cv. 'Speciosa'. More compact, slower growing.

Smithiana (Wallich) Boiss. [*P. Morinda* Link]. HIMALAYAN S. To 150 ft., branchlets drooping, glossy, gray; lvs. 4-angled, to 1½ in. long, spreading radially, bright or dark green; cones to 7 in. long. Himalayas. Zone 7, in sheltered positions.

Torana Koehne [*P. polita* of auth., not (Siebold & Zucc.) Carrière]. TIGER-TAIL S. To 90 ft. or more, branchlets yellowish, glabrous; lvs. 4-angled, to 1 in. long, spreading radially, stiff, dark glossy green; cones to 5 in. long. Japan. Zone 6.

Watsoniana: *P. Wilsonii.*

Wilsonii M. T. Mast. [*P. Watsoniana* M. T. Mast.]. To about 75 ft., densely branched, branchlets light gray, glabrous; lvs. 4-angled, ½ in. long, sharp-pointed, dark green; cones to 2½ in. long. Cent. China. Zone 6.

PICKERINGIA Nutt. ex Torr. & A. Gray. CHAPARRAL PEA. *Leguminosae* (subfamily *Faboideae*). One sp., a spiny, evergreen shrub of N. Amer.; lvs. alt., of 1 or 3 palmately arranged lfts., without stipules; fls. axillary, solitary, papilionaceous, stamens 10, separate; fr. a flat, linear legume.

montana Nutt. ex Torr. & A. Gray. To 7 ft., much-branched, branchlets spine-tipped; lvs. nearly sessile, lfts. obovate to oblanceolate, to 1 in. long; fls. large, purple, to ¾ in. long; fr. to 2 in. long. Calif.

PICRIDIUM: *REICHARDIA.*

PICRIS L. BITTERWEED, OX-TONGUE. *Compositae* (Cichorium Tribe). About 50 spp. of leafy-stemmed, ann., bien., or per. herbs with milky sap, native to Eur., Asia, and N. Afr.; lvs. alt., entire to pinnatifid; fl. heads solitary or in corymbs, involucral bracts imbricate in 2 to many rows, receptacle flat, pitted, naked; fls. all ligulate, bisexual, yellow; achenes curved, often 5–10-ribbed, pappus of 2 rows of deciduous hairs, the inner plumose, the outer plumose or simple.

hieracioides L. Stout bien. or per. herb, to 3 ft., bristly especially below; lower lvs. oblanceolate, to 8 in. long, upper lvs. lanceolate, all undulate, bristly on veins beneath, margins bristly-ciliate; heads to 1⅜ in. across, in a corymbose infl.; fls. bright yellow; achenes reddish-brown, to ¼ in. long, only shortly if at all beaked, pappus cream-colored. Eur. and Asia; naturalized in N. Amer., Australia, and New Zeal. Subsp. **kamtschatica** (Ledeb.) Hult. [*P. kamtschatica* Ledeb.]. Achenes slightly longer, beaked, pappus dirty-white. Kamchatka.

kamtschatica: *P. hieracioides* subsp.

PIERIS D. Don [*Ampelothamnus* Small; *Arcterica* Cov.]. *Ericaceae*. About 8 spp. of evergreen shrubs or small trees, native to e. Asia, the Himalayas, and N. Amer.; lvs. alt., or rarely opp. or whorled, simple, leathery; fls. white, in axillary racemes or terminal panicles, calyx deeply 5-lobed, corolla urceolate, stamens 10, filaments sometimes S-shaped, anthers spurred, ovary superior; fr. a 5-valved caps.

Pierises require moist, peaty, or sandy soil and partial shade. They are sometimes forced under glass. Propagated by seeds, by layers, and by cuttings of ripe wood under glass, which root slowly.

elliptica: *Lyonia ovalifolia* var.

floribunda (Pursh ex Sims) Benth. & Hook. [*Andromeda floribunda* Pursh ex Sims]. FETTERBUSH. Dense shrub, to 6 ft., brs. with appressed, brown hairs; lvs. ovate to oblong-lanceolate, to 3 in. long, ciliate, petioles hairy; panicles erect, to 5 in. long; fls. ¼ in. long. Spring. Va. to Ga. Zone 5.

formosa (Wallich) D. Don. Small shrubby tree, to 20 ft.; lvs. elliptic-oblong to lanceolate, to 6 in. long, acuminate, margins finely toothed, glabrous; panicles more or less erect, to 6 in. long; sepals green, corolla white, often tinged pink. E. Himalayas. Zone 7? Var. **Forrestii**: *P. Forrestii.*

Forrestii R. Harrow ex W. W. Sm. [*P. formosa* var. *Forrestii* (R. Harrow ex W. W. Sm.) Airy-Shaw; *Andromeda Forrestii* Hort.]. To 10 ft., young shoots and lvs. scarlet; lvs. elliptic, lanceolate, or oblanceolate, to 4½ in. long; sepals white, corolla white, ⅜ in. long. Himalayas.

japonica (Thunb.) D. Don ex G. Don [*Andromeda japonica* Thunb.]. LILY-OF-THE-VALLEY BUSH. Shrub or small tree, to 10 or sometimes 30 ft.; lvs. oblanceolate to obovate-oblong, to 3 in. long, serrulate, glabrous; panicles drooping, to 6 in. long; fls. ¼–⅜ in. long. Spring. Japan. Zone 6. Cvs. are: **'Bonsai'**, a very dwarf form; **'Compacta'**, a dwarf compact form; **'Crispa'**, lvs. with undulate-crisped margins;

'Pygmaea', a minute, bushy shrub, lvs. smaller; **'Variegata'**, lvs. with whitish margins.

lucida: *Lyonia lucida.*

mariana: *Lyonia mariana.*

nana (Maxim.) Mak. [*Arcterica nana* (Maxim.) Mak.]. Prostrate shrub, brs. puberulous; lvs. usually in whorls of 3, elliptic to elliptic-oblong, to ½ in. long, entire, mucronulate; racemes terminal, short, 3- or 4-fld.; fls. less than 3/16 in. long. Ne. Asia. Zone 1.

nitida: *Lyonia lucida.*

ovalifolia: *Lyonia ovalifolia.*

phillyreifolia (Hook.) DC. [*Ampelothamnus phillyreifolius* (Hook.) Small]. Shrub or woody vine, brs. hairy; lvs. oblong to elliptic or obovate, to 2¾ in. long, toothed toward apex; racemes axillary; fls. to ⅜ in. long. Coastal plain, n. Fla. to Ga. and Ala.

taiwanensis Hayata. Erect, compact shrub, to 4–10 ft., brs. glabrous; lvs. elliptic, oblanceolate to obovate, to 5 in. long, toothed in the upper half; panicles dense, more or less erect; fls. nodding, ¼ in. long. Taiwan. Zone 7.

PILEA Lindl. [*Adicea* Raf.]. *Urticaceae*. More than 200 spp. of monoecious or dioecious, ann. or per. herbs, rarely suffrutescent, without stinging hairs, widespread in most trop. and warm-temp. regions; lvs. opp., petioled, stipuled, those of a pair often of unequal size, mostly toothed or entire, usually with 3 principal nerves from the base and containing many linear to stellate cystoliths (calcium carbonate concretions); fls. minute, unisexual, in axillary cymes or panicles composed of clusters of one or both sexes, calyx of male fls. 4-parted, that of female fls. 3-parted with the middle segm. the largest; fr. an achene.

Grown as pot plants or for edging in greenhouses or outside in the South. The trailing species are particularly suited for hanging baskets. Of easy culture, but require shade and abundant moisture. Propagated by cuttings.

Cadierei Gagnep. & Guillaum. ALUMINUM PLANT, WATERMELON PILEA. Succulent herb, to 1 ft., sts. smooth, brownish, somewhat 4-angled; lvs. ovate, to about 3 in. long, acuminate, rounded or obtuse at base, crenate-dentate, green, with broad, interrupted bands of silver centrally and along margins; female fls. in loose, peduncled heads. Vietnam. Cv. **'Minima'**. A dwarf form.

callitrichoides: *P. microphylla.*

colioides: a listed name of no botanical standing, applied to a plant with pubescent, light green lvs. and trailing sts.

depressa (Swartz) Blume. Succulent, glabrous or glabrate, creeping herb, differing from *P. nummulariifolia* in having lvs. obovate to subspatulate, crenate at apex. W. Indies.

fontana (Lunell) Rydb. RICHWEED, CLEARWEED, COOLWORT. Similar to and perhaps not specifically distinct from *P. pumila*, but of smaller stature and having lvs. smaller and achenes roughened, blackish or black, with white margins. N.Y. to Fla., w. to N. Dak. and Nebr.

involucrata (Sims) Urb. PANAMIGA, FRIENDSHIP PLANT. Herb, trailing to erect, hirsute or pilose; lvs. clustered near ends of sts., ovate to broadly obovate, up to 1½ in. long, rounded apically, crenate-dentate, rugose, bronzy-green above, purplish beneath; male fls. few at the base of branched, many-fld. female cymes. W. Indies and Panama, s. to n. S. Amer.

microphylla (L.) Liebm. [*P. callitrichoides* (HBK) Kunth; *P. muscosa* Lindl.]. ARTILLERY PLANT. Glabrous, succulent ann. or short-lived per., to about 1 ft.; lvs. crowded, mostly subsessile, mostly obovate, up to ⅜ in. long, entire, 1-veined, transversely striate above with linear cystoliths; cymes small, sessile or nearly so, with fls. of both sexes or only one; mature anthers ejecting pollen forcefully, thus the common name. Widespread in Amer. tropics. Cv. **'Variegata'** [cv. **'Confetti'**]. Lvs. blotched white and pink.

muscosa: *P. microphylla.*

nummulariifolia (Swartz) Wedd. CREEPING CHARLIE. Per. herb, creeping, branched, rooting at the nodes, mostly villous, leafy, usually dioecious; lvs. orbicular, mostly ¼–¾ in. across, rounded at apex, crenate, 3-nerved; female fls. generally clustered in dense axillary cymes scarcely longer than the subtending petiole. W. Indies and Panama, s. to n. S. Amer.

prostrata: a listed name of no botanical standing; applied to a trailing plant with small, dark green, wrinkled lvs.

pubescens Liebm. Decumbent, strigulose-stemmed herbs, differing from *P. involucrata* in having lvs. thin, broadly ovate to elliptic, up to 3 in. long, deeply crenate, mostly smooth, and the female fls. in loose, paniculate cymes often longer than subtending lf. W. Indies and

Mex., s. to n. S. Amer. Cv. 'Liebmannii'. SILVER-LEAF PANAMIGA. Lvs. silvery.

pumila (L.) A. Gray. RICHWEED, CLEARWEED, COOLWORT. Simple or branched herb, to 2 ft., erect or decumbent at base; lvs. thin, translucent, ovate, 1–6 in. long, acuminate, cuneate, with few, large, crenate-dentate teeth; cymes branching, usually not longer than subtending petiole; achenes smooth, yellowish to green, sometimes spotted purple, without pale margins. Prince Edward Is. to Fla., w. to S. Dak. and Tex.

repens (Swartz) Wedd. BLACK-LEAF PANAMIGA. Sts. repent, brs. erect, pilose; lvs. thin, ovate to obovate, 1¼ in. long, obtuse, crenate to serrate; female cymes long-peduncled, in loose heads often longer than subtending lf. W. Indies.

serpyllacea (HBK) Liebm. Very succulent, reddish-tinged herb, similar to *P. microphylla*, but having lvs. nearly orbicular, to about ¼ in. across, entire or crenulate; and female cymes peduncled. Trop. n. S. Amer.

serpyllifolia (Poir.) Wedd. Apparently distinguishable from *P. microphylla* and *P. serpyllacea* by its ciliate lvs.; not known to be cult., however, and material listed as *P. serpyllifolia* may be one of the other 2 spp.

Spruceana Wedd. Sparsely villous herb, similar to *P. involucrata*, but having lvs. oblong to oblong-ovate, 1–3 in. long, acute. Peru and Bolivia. Material offered under this name seems generally to be *P. involucrata*.

PILEOSTEGIA Hook.f. & T. Thoms. *Saxifragaceae*. Three spp. of evergreen, climbing shrubs in e. Asia; lvs. opp., simple, mostly entire; fls. small, white, all fertile, in terminal pyramidal clusters, sepals 4–5, petals 4–5, coherent and falling as a cap, stamens 8–10, with long filaments, ovary inferior, style short, stigma lobed; fr. a caps., top-shaped, ribbed, dehiscing between ribs. Related to *Decumaria*, but evergreen, and with fewer sepals, petals, and stamens.

viburnoides Hook.f. & T. Thoms. Climbing to 25 ft. or more; lvs. elliptic, to 5 in. long, glabrous, dark green and glossy above. Himalayas. Zone 7.

PILIOSTIGMA: *BAUHINIA.*

PILOCEREUS: *CEPHALOCEREUS.*

PILOSOCEREUS: *CEPHALOCEREUS.*

PILULARIA L. PILLWORT. *Marsileaceae*. About 6 spp. of herbaceous, rhizomatous, aquatic ferns, native to Eur., N. Amer., Australia, and New Zeal.; lvs. filiform or subulate, entire; sporocarps globose, blackish, 2–4-chambered, each chamber bearing a sorus with sporangia producing megaspores and microspores.

Culture as for *Marsilea*. See also *Ferns.*

globulifera L. Lvs. to 2 in. long and ³⁄₁₆ in. wide; sporocarps essentially sessile, 4-chambered, about ⅛ in. in diam. Eur. Sometimes grown in pools or aquaria.

PIMELEA Banks & Soland. ex Gaertn. RICEFLOWER. *Thymelaeaceae*. About 80 spp. of evergreen shrubs or subshrubs, native to New Zeal. and Australia, with a few in Timor and Lord Howe Is.; lvs. opp. or alt., simple, entire, usually small; fls. white, pink, or reddish, unisexual or sometimes bisexual, mostly in terminal heads usually surrounded by involucre of leaflike, often colored bracts; fr. a drupe.

Pimeleas are grown outdoors in warm climates and in the greenhouse. Propagated in early spring by cuttings of half-ripened shoots under glass at a temperature of 55–60° F.

coarctica: a listed name of no botanical standing, applied to *P. prostrata.*

decussata: *P. ferruginea.*

ferruginea Labill. [*P. decussata* R. Br.]. To 3 ft.; lvs. opp. and crowded, ovate or oblong, to ½ in. long, revolute; fls. rose, in round heads subtended by pink or red bracts. W. Australia.

graciliflora (Endl.) Hook. To 2½ ft.; lvs. opp., lanceolate, to ¾ in. long, dotted on upper surface; fls. white, in globular heads. W. Australia.

humilis R. Br. Dwarf shrub, to 8 in., sometimes procumbent; lvs. opp., overlapping, oblong or ovate-oblong, to ½ in. long; fls. white, in heads subtended by greenish bracts. Se. Australia, Tasmania.

ligustrina Labill. Erect shrub, to 6 ft., glabrous except for infl.; lvs. opp., ovate or oblong, to 2 in. long; fls. white, many in globular heads subtended by reddish bracts. Se. Australia, Tasmania.

prostrata (J. R. Forst. & G. Forst.) Willd. [*P. coarctica* Hort.]. Low, prostrate, much-branched shrub; lvs. 4-ranked, oblong, to ¼ in. long, leathery; fls. white, somewhat fragrant, on short side brs. gathered into terminal heads. New Zeal.

spectabilis (Fisch. & C. A. Mey.) Lindl. To 4 ft.; lvs. opp., crowded, linear-oblong to lanceolate, to 1½ in. long; fls. white or pinkish, in large, globular heads subtended by bracts tinged pinkish on margins. W. Australia.

tomentosa (J. R. Forst. & G. Forst.) Druce [*P. virgata* Vahl.]. Erect shrub, to 20 in., sts. with appressed grayish to white hairs; lvs. linear to lanceolate to oblong-lanceolate, to ¾ in. long, sessile or nearly so, smooth above, hairy beneath; fls. 6–12 in each head. New Zeal.

virgata: *P. tomentosa.*

PIMENTA Lindl. *Myrtaceae*. About 5 spp., or perhaps only 2, of aromatic trees in trop. Amer.; lvs. opp., simple, leathery; fls. small, in many-fld. cymes in the upper lf. axils; fr. a drupe. Allied to *Myrtus*, but having ovary 2-celled, with 1–6 ovules pendulous from the apex of each cell, and to *Eugenia* from which it differs in its spiral embryo.

Two species are of economic importance. Adapted to tropical and subtropical climates. Zone 10b.

dioica (L.) Merrill [*P. officinalis* Lindl.]. ALLSPICE, PIMENTO. Tree, to 40 ft.; lvs. oblong-lanceolate, to 6 in. long, veins prominent beneath; fls. white, about ¼ in. across, calyx 4-lobed; fr. globose, about ¼ in. across, dark brown. Late spring. W. Indies, Cent. Amer. Allspice is the dried, unripe fr.

officinalis: *P. dioica.*

racemosa (Mill.) J. W. Moore [*Myrtus acris* Swartz]. BAY, BAY-RUM TREE. Similar to *P. dioica*, but having lvs. elliptic to obovate, with fine reticulate venation, and calyx 5-lobed. W. Indies, Venezuela, Guiana. Oil of bay, distilled from lvs. and twigs, is used in perfumery and to prepare bay rum.

PIMPINELLA L. *Umbelliferae*. About 140 spp. of herbs, native to Eurasia and Afr.; lvs. pinnate; fls. small, white or yellow, in compound umbels, involucre usually absent, involucels present or absent; fr. ovoid.

Anisum L. COMMON ANISE. Ann., to 2 ft.; basal lvs. simple, pinnate, or ternately compound, st. lvs. 1–2-pinnate or ternately compound, entire or toothed; fls. white. Greece to Egypt. Cult. for its use in medicine and cookery; prop. by seeds sown where plants are to stand.

magna: *P. major.*

major (L.) Huds. [*P. magna* L.]. To 3½ ft., stout; lvs. pinnate, segms. 7–13, usually undivided, ovate to lanceolate, to 1½ in. long, teeth or lobes very pointed; fls. white. Var. **rubra** (Hoppe) Fiori & Béguinot. Fls. pink, in large terminal umbels of 10–15 rays. Eur.

PINACEAE Lindl. PINE FAMILY. Gymnosperms; 9 genera and about 210 spp. of coniferous, resinous, mostly evergreen, monoecious trees or rarely shrubs, of wide distribution but especially in temp. regions of the N. Hemisphere; brs. opp. or whorled, rarely alt., elongate or sometimes spurred and bearing seemingly whorled or fascicled lvs.; lvs. linear, often needle-shaped; male cones small, herbaceous, female cones woody, mostly with many spirally arranged scales, each usually with 2 ovules borne basally on the upper surface and subtended by a small or large, more or less united bract; seeds usually 2 on each scale, winged. The family includes many spp. grown as sources of timber, wood pulp, turpentine, rosin, other economic products, and ornamentals. The cult. genera are: *Abies, Cedrus, Keteleeria, Larix, Picea, Pinus, Pseudolarix, Pseudotsuga,* and *Tsuga.*

PINANGA Blume. *Palmae*. More than 100 spp. of dwarf to moderate, solitary or cespitose, unarmed, monoecious palms native to wet tropics from India to the Philippine Is. and New Guinea; lvs. pinnate or 2-cleft at apex only and pinnately ribbed, sheaths often tubular, forming a slender crownshaft, pinnae slender and acuminate or frequently several-ribbed and at least the terminal pair with coarsely toothed apices; infls. below or rarely among lvs., with a single bract, simply branched or spicate, rachillae with fls. in triads (2 male and 1 female) spirally arranged or more often in 2–6

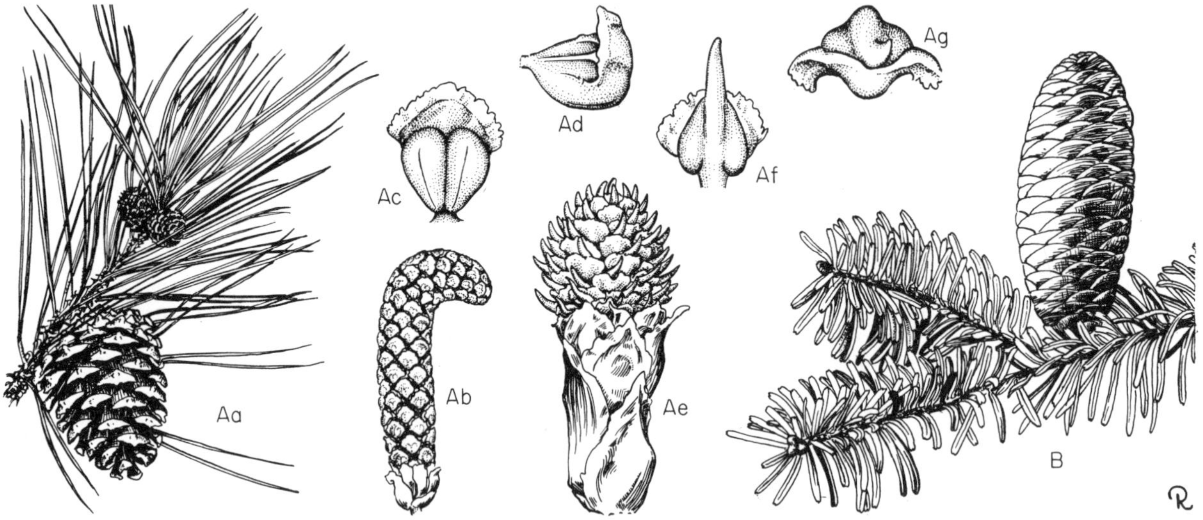

PINACEAE. **A,** *Pinus Taeda:* **Aa,** branch with one- and two-year-old cones, × ¼; **Ab,** male cone, × 2; **Ac,** lower (abaxial) surface of scale from male cone, showing the two microsporangia, ×15; **Ad,** three-quarter view of upper (adaxial) surface of scale from male cone, × 15; **Ae,** very young female cone, × 4; **Af,** upper (adaxial) surface of scale from young female cone, showing the two ovules, × 6; **Ag,** end view of scale from young female cone, × 8. **B,** *Abies homolepis:* branch with cone, × ½. (Aa-Ag from Lawrence, *An Introduction to Plant Taxonomy;* B from Bailey, *Manual of Cultivated Plants,* ed. 2.)

vertical rows; male fls. asymmetrical, sepals 3, separate, scarcely imbricate, petals 3, acute, valvate, stamens 9 to many, filaments erect, pistillode usually lacking, female fls. with sepals 3, imbricate or united, petals 3, imbricate, with briefly valvate apices, staminodes lacking, pistil 1-celled, 1-ovuled; fr. ellipsoid to ovoid, sometimes curved, with apical stigmatic residue, mesocarp fibrous, endocarp thin, seed with ruminate endosperm and basal or subbasal embryo, often asymmetrical at the base.

Attractive ornamental palms grown mostly in the tropics. For culture see *Palms.*

furfuracea Blume. Sts. to 4 ft., slender; lvs. to about 18 in. long, petiole short, less than 4 in. long, rachis densely scurfy, pinnae about 6 on each side, linear-lanceolate, to about 1¼ in. wide, acuminate except the broader terminal pair; infl. recurved, rachillae about 3, to 5¼ in. long; fr. ellipsoid, about ⅝ in. long. Celebes.

Kuhlii Blume. Sts. cespitose, to 10 ft. high, 1⅝ in. in diam.; pinnae many, curved-lanceolate, acuminate, several-ribbed; infl. recurved, rachillae 7–15, elongate; fr. black, ½ in. long, 5/16 in. in diam. Java, Sumatra. Zone 10a in Fla.

malaiana (Mart.) Scheff. Sts. cespitose, to 10 ft. high, 1⅝ in. in diam.; lvs. to 6 ft. long or more, petiole to 16 in. long, pinnae 18–20, several-ribbed, to 28 in. long, acuminate; infl. reflexed, rachillae 3–5; fr. ovoid, red-purple on red rachillae at maturity, to 1 in. long, ½ in. in diam. Malay Pen., Sumatra, Borneo.

patula Blume. Sts. cespitose, to nearly 8 ft. high, 1 in. in diam.; pinnae few, 2- to several-ribbed, double curved, acuminate; infl. recurved, rachillae 2–5; fr. ovoid-ellipsoid, to about ⅝ in. long, ¼ in. in diam. Sumatra, Borneo.

pectinata Becc. Sts. cespitose, to 15 ft. high, 3½ in. in diam.; lvs. to 4 ft. long, pinnae 1–5-ribbed, glaucous below, to 16 in. long, 1¾ in. wide; infl. with 3–9 short rachillae to 5 in. long; fr. elongate-ovoid, about ⅝ in. long, 3/16 in. in diam. Malay Pen.

Scortechinii Becc. St. solitary, to 10 ft.; lvs. with elongate petiole, pinnae many, narrowly lanceolate, doubly curved, 2–5-ribbed, acuminate; infl. erect in fr., rachillae 5–6, ascending, triads in 4 vertical rows; fr. oblong-ovoid, to about ⅝ in. long, ⅜ in. in diam. Malay Pen.

Tashiroi Hayata. Sts. ashy-white, to 15 ft. high, 7 in. in diam.; lvs. 7–8 ft. long, including elongate petiole, pinnae to 2 in. wide, several-ribbed, acuminate; infl. pendulous, to 16 in. long, rachillae about 30, to 9 in. long; fr. ovoid, red, about ⅝ in. long, ½ in. in diam. Taiwan.

PINCKNEYA Michx. *Rubiaceae.* One sp., a shrub or tree, native to se. U.S., lvs. opp., deciduous, membranous, stipules interpetiolar, deciduous; fls. in terminal and axillary corymbs, showy, 5-merous, calyx lobes unequal, in some fls. 1 or 2 expanded, leaflike, showy, rose, corolla tube elongate, stamens exserted; fr. a caps., seeds many, winged.

pubens Michx. FEVER TREE. Small tree, to 30 ft.; lvs. ovate or elliptic, sometimes broadly so, to 8 in. long, hairy, paler beneath; leaflike calyx lobe to 2½ in. long, corolla yellowish, to 1½ in. long; caps. to ¾ in. long. S.C. to Fla.; rare. Bark, called Georgia bark or fever bark, contains cinchonin and has been used in treatment of intermittent fevers.

PINEAPPLE. The pineapple is a terrestrial bromeliad, originally native to tropical South America, with a large compound fruit also called pineapple (see *Ananas*).

Although it was once extensively grown in Florida, commercial pineapple culture, widespread in the tropics, is now centered in Mexico, Puerto Rico, Hawaii, Taiwan, and the Philippine Islands. Elsewhere in the tropics, pineapples are often planted in the home garden, and cultivars with ornamental leaves are sometimes grown for decorative purposes outdoors where feasible or under glass in temperate regions.

Cultivars of the pineapple in commercial plantings have never been great in number, compared with other fruits. Only two, 'Smooth Cayenne' and 'Red Spanish', are of major importance, and of these the former, because it cans well, now produces 95 percent of the world crop of commercial pineapples. Until recently 'Red Spanish', hardy and with medium-sized fruits that ship well, was the main commercial cultivar in the Caribbean area, but it is being replaced by the much larger-fruited 'Smooth Cayenne'. Sometimes grown are 'Porto Rico', with large fruits, and 'Abbaka', with small fruits of very high quality. Although it may be grown from seed, the pineapple is usually propagated by suckers developed along the stem of mature plants, by slips produced on the peduncle just below the fruit, or by the crown or leafy part on top of the fruit. When propagated from the crown, the plant is slow in coming into fruit. Plants also develop from old stems if these are cut up and partly buried in the earth.

Pineapples can be grown in a wide range of soils, but they thrive best in those that are loose and light. Excellent drainage is important, for although the pineapple requires abundant water for its development, it fails where drainage is poor and water stagnates. In some localities excess lime and manganese have caused trouble. Manganese affects the availability of iron and its presence may be compensated for by using iron sulfate spray.

Pineapples are usually planted in beds of three or more rows. Slips are set 8–14 inches apart and just deep enough to keep them in an upright position. Tillage must be shallow (an inch or so) inasmuch as pineapple roots are near the surface. The favorite tool is the scuffle hoe, with which shallow cultivation and weed destruction are readily accomplished, or rows may be mulched with polyethylene. Fertilizer should be used as needed.

Pineapples for shipment are commonly picked a week or so before reaching full maturity, but those intended for home consumption or for nearby canning should be allowed to become much riper, thereby developing their full flavor. There is perhaps no more delicious fruit than a well-grown, field-ripened pineapple.

Insect and disease control presents a serious problem. Wilt is caused by a virus spread by mealy bugs, and another virus is spread by thrips. Spraying with approved contact insecticides controls these insects and thus checks the spread of the diseases. Nematodes are often troublesome. They are best handled by rotating the crop and planting *Crotalaria* or Natal grass, *Rhynchelytrum repens*, to starve them out. Other problems should be referred to the local experiment station.

PINGUICULA L. BUTTERWORT. *Lentibulariaceae*. About 45 spp. of small carnivorous herbs of wide distribution in moist locations; lvs. in basal rosettes, entire, usually viscid above, trapping small insects; fls. solitary, on naked scapes, calyx 4–5-lobed, corolla 5-lobed, 2-lipped, spurred at base, stamens 2; fr. a caps.

Butterworts are grown mostly on moist rocks or rock gardens, or under glass as curiosities. Propagated by seeds, by offsets when produced, and by single leaves laid on sand under a glass.

caudata Schlechtend. Lvs. glabrous, obovate to nearly orbicular, to 4 in. long (only 1 in. long in dry season), blunt, with margins rolled inward; peduncles to 7 in. long; corolla deeply 5-parted, violet-purple to rosy, lobes obtuse, spreading, spur very long and slender. Mex. Showiest of the cult. spp.

montana: a listed name of no botanical standing.

vulgaris L. To 6 in.; lvs. somewhat fleshy, ovate to elliptic, very obtuse, to 2 in. long; fls. violet or purple, to ¾ in. long, spur slender, ⅜ in. long. N. N. Amer., Eurasia.

PINUS L. PINE. *Pinaceae*. About 90 spp. of often tall, coniferous, evergreen, monoecious trees, native to the N. Hemisphere; lvs. of two kinds, the scalelike ones soon deciduous, the needle-shaped ones long and usually borne in clusters (fascicles) of 2–5, or rarely 1; male cones catkinlike, clustered, female cones cylindrical to nearly globose, cone scales woody, persistent, thickened at the end, usually with a terminal or subterminal projection or scar (umbo); seeds 2 to each scale, with or without wing, maturing in 2–3 years.

Pines are sources of valuable timber, turpentine, and rosin, edible pine nuts, as well as many ornamentals. Most of the ornamentals are best suited to large areas and extended grounds, but a few are dwarf and compact. For culture see *Conifers*.

albicaulis Engelm. WHITE-BARK P. Prostrate shrub or tree to 30 ft.; lvs. in fascicles of 5, to 2½ in. long, stiff, dark green; cones purple-brown, ovoid, to 3 in. long. Mts., B.C. to Calif. Zone 4.

aristata Engelm. BRISTLE-CONE P., HICKORY P. Mostly 10–40 ft., sometimes shrubby, prostrate, branchlets light orange, glabrous or pubescent; lvs. in fascicles of 5, to 1½ in. long, dark green with whitish exudations of resin; cones cylindric-ovoid, to 3½ in. long. Mts., Calif. to Colo. Zone 6, grows very slowly.

arizonica: *P. ponderosa* var.

Armandii Franch. To 60 ft., brs. spreading, branchlets glabrous; lvs. in fascicles of 5, to 6 in. long, bright green, thin; cones conic-oblong, 6 in. long and more. Temp. e. Asia. Zone 6.

attenuata Lemm. [*P. tuberculata* Gord., not D. Don]. KNOB-CONE P. Shrub or tree, 6–40 ft.; lvs. in fascicles of 3 or rarely 2, to 5 in. long or more, pale yellowish or bluish-green; cones conic-oblong, to 6 in. long. Ore. to Calif. Zone 7.

×**attenuradiata** Stockw. & Righter: *P. attenuata* × *P. radiata*. Similar to *P. radiata* in habit, but with more brs. and hardier (Zone 7a), otherwise more or less intermediate between the parents.

australis: *P. palustris*.

austriaca: *P. nigra* subsp. *nigra*.

Ayacahuite C. A. Ehrenb. MEXICAN WHITE P. To 100 ft. or more; lvs. in fascicles of 5, to 6 in. long, bluish-green; cones cylindric-conical, to 15 in. long, scales reflexed; wing of seed 5–8 times as long as seed. Mts., Mex., Guatemala. Zone 8.

Balfouriana Grev. & Balf. FOXTAIL P. Small tree, 20–50 ft., branchlets hairy; lvs. in fascicles of 5, to 1½ in. long, stiff, dark green; cones cylindrical, to 5 in. long, drooping. Calif. Zone 6. Resembles *P. aristata*, but lvs. shorter and cones smaller.

Banksiana Lamb. JACK P., GRAY P., SCRUB P. To 75 ft., but usually smaller and sometimes shrubby; lvs. in fascicles of 2, to 1½ in. long, stiff and twisted, bright or dark green; cones conic-oblong, to 2 in. long. Nov. Sc. to N.Y. and Minn. Zone 2. Produces pulp. Thrives on poor soils.

brevispica: *P. taiwanensis*.

Bungeana Zucc. ex Endl. LACE-BARK P. To 75 ft. or more, bark flaky, becoming chalky-white, branchlets gray-green, glabrous; lvs. in fascicles of 3, to 4 in. long, stiff, light green; cones conic-ovoid, to 3 in. long. Nw. China. Zone 5, but may remain bushy.

canariensis Sweet ex K. Spreng. CANARY ISLAND P. To 100 ft., branchlets drooping, yellow, glabrous; lvs. in fascicles of 3, to 12 in. long, glossy light green, drooping; cones cylindric-ovoid, to 8 in. long. Canary Is. Zone 8. Resembles *P. Roxburghii*, but differs in having tips of cone scales with low-pyramidal umbo.

caribaea Morelet. CUBAN P. To 100 ft.; lvs. in fascicles of 3 or sometimes 4 or 5, to 12 in. long, glossy dark green; cones conic-oblong, to 6½ in. long. W. Indies and Cent. Amer. Zone 9? A useful pine for lowland trop. areas. Material offered under this name may be *P. Elliottii*.

Cembra L. SWISS STONE P., RUSSIAN CEDAR. Mostly to 75 ft., branchlets densely brown-tomentose; lvs. in fascicles of 5, to 5 in. long, dark green; cones ovoid, to 3½ in. long. Eur., n. Asia. Zone 3, but very slow growing.

cembroides Zucc. MEXICAN STONE P. Shrub or small tree, to 25 ft. or more, branchlets dark orange, pubescent; lvs. in fascicles of 3 or sometimes 2, 4, or 5, to 2¾ in. long, dark green, stiff and generally curved; cones subglobose, to 2½ in. in diam., seeds wingless. Ariz., Mex. Zone 7. Var. **edulis:** *P. edulis*. Var. **monophylla:** *P. monophylla*. Var. **Parryana:** *P. quadrifolia*.

chiapensis (Martinez) Andresen [*P. Strobus* var. *chiapensis* Martinez]. Similar to *P. Strobus*, but having the lvs. longer, tips of cone scales truncate, with thin and wavy margins, and basal cone scales not reflexed against the peduncle. S. Mex., Guatemala. Zone 8.

contorta Dougl. ex Loud. SHORE P., BEACH P. Shrub, or small tree to 30 ft.; lvs. in fascicles of 2, to 2 in. long, stiff and twisted, dark green; cones conic-ovoid, to 2 in. long. Alaska to Calif. Zone 7b. Var. **latifolia** Engelm. ex S. Wats. [*P. Murrayana* Grev. & Balf.]. LODGEPOLE P. Tree, 70–150 ft.; lvs. longer and broader, lighter green. Alaska to Calif. and Colo. Zone 4.

Coulteri G. Don. BIG-CONE P. To about 75 ft.; lvs. in fascicles of 3, to 12 in. long, dark bluish-green; cones cylindric-ovoid, to 14 in. long, drooping. Calif. Can be grown in sheltered sites in Zone 7.

densiflora Siebold & Zucc. JAPANESE RED P. To 100 ft. or more; lvs. in fascicles of 2, to 5 in. long, bright bluish-green; cones conic-ovoid to oblong, 2 in. long. Japan. Zone 5, but sometimes damaged in severe winters. Cvs. are: 'Alboterminata', tips of lvs. yellowish-white; 'Oculus-draconis', lvs. with 2 yellow bands; 'Pendula', brs. drooping or prostrate; 'Prostrata', low, spreading; 'Umbraculifera', TANYOSHO, JAPANESE UMBRELLA P., dwarf, with umbrellalike head. Material sometimes offered as *P. Tanyosho*.

echinata Mill. SHORTLEAF P., YELLOW P., LONG-TAG P. To 100 ft. or more; lvs. usually in fascicles of 2, to 5 in. long, dark bluish-green; cones conic-oblong, to 2 in. long. N.Y. to Fla. and Tex. Zone 6.

edulis Engelm. [*P. cembroides* var. *edulis* (Engelm.) Voss]. PINYON, PINYON P., NUT P., TWO-LEAVED N. P. Similar to *P. cembroides* from which it differs in having generally stouter lvs. mostly in fascicles of 2. Wyo. to Tex., Calif., and n. Mex. Zone 5. A source of edible piñon nuts.

Elliottii Engelm. SLASH P. To 100 ft.; lvs. in fascicles of 2 or 3, deep green, more than 5 in. long; cones broadly ovoid when open, to 6 in. long. Se. U.S. Zone 8. Yields timber, turpentine, rosin, and pulp.

Engelmannii Carrière. APACHE P. To 75 ft. or more; lvs. in fascicles of 3 or 4, clear green, thick, to 16 in. long; cones ovoid to conic-oblong, to 7 in. long, heavy. S. New Mex., Ariz., Mex. Zone 7. Differs from *P. ponderosa* in its longer lvs.

excelsa: see *P. Wallichiana*.

flexilis James. LIMBER P. To 60 ft., branchlets stout, greenish-orange, pubescent; lvs. in fascicles of 5, to 3 in. long, stiff, yellowish-green; cones ovoid, to 3–10 in. long, glossy, yellowish, seeds wingless. Alta. s. to Calif. and Tex. Zone 4.

formosana: *P. morrisonicola*.

Gerardiana Wallich ex D. Don. CHILGHOZA P., GERALD'S P., NEPAL NUT P. To 80 ft., bark flaky; lvs. in fascicles of 3, to 4 in. long, bluish-green; cones to 9 in. long. Himalayas. Zone 7? Nuts edible.

glabra Walt. CEDAR P., SPRUCE P. To 80 ft. or more; lvs. in fascicles of 2, to 3 in. long, soft; cones ovoid, to 2½ in. long. S.C. to Fla. and La. Zone 8.

Griffithii: see *P. Wallichiana.*

halepensis Mill. ALEPPO P., JERUSALEM P. To about 50 ft., branchlets glabrous, glaucous; lvs. in fascicles of 2 or rarely 3, to 4 in. long, soft, light green; cones conic-ovoid, to 3½ in. long. Medit. region. Zone 8. Yields turpentine. Var. **brutia** (Ten.) A. Henry. CALABRIAN P. Lvs. 4–6 in. long, rigid, darker green.

Heldreichii var. **leucodermis**: *P. leucodermis.*

insignis: *P. radiata.*

insularis Endl. [*P. khasyana* Griffith]. BENGUET P. To 100 ft. or more but mostly smaller; lvs. in fascicles of 3 or rarely 2, to 10 in. long, pliable, bright green; cones conic-ovoid, to 4 in. long. Philippine Is. to Burma and s. China. Zone 10. Suitable for trop. plantings.

Jeffreyi Grev. & Balf. Branchlets glaucous; lvs. in fascicles of 3, 5–10 in. long, pale bluish-green; cones conic-ovoid, 5–12 in. long. S. Ore., to Baja Calif. Zone 6.

khasyana: *P. insularis.*

koraiensis Siebold & Zucc. KOREAN P. To 100 ft. or more, branchlets yellow-brown-tomentose; lvs. in fascicles of 5, to 4 in. long, dark green; cones conic-oblong, to 6 in. long. Japan, Korea. Zone 4, but grows slowly north and needs sheltered sites. Cv. 'Glauca'. Lvs. bluish-green.

Lambertiana Dougl. SUGAR P., GIANT P. To 200 ft. or more; lvs. in fascicles of 5, to 4 in. long, sharp-pointed, with white lines on back; cones cylindrical, 12–20 in. long. Ore. to Baja Calif. Zone 6, but needs protection from winter winds.

Laricio: *P. nigra* subsp.

leucodermis Ant. [*P. Heldreichii* Christ var. *leucodermis* (Ant.) Markgr. ex Fitschen]. To nearly 90 ft., bark flaky, branchlets glabrous, glaucous; lvs. in fascicles of 2, rigid, to 3½ in. long; cone slightly glossy, 2–3 in. long. Italy, Balkan Pen. Zone 6.

longifolia: see *P. Roxburghii.*

luchuensis Mayr. To 100 ft., bark of young trees smooth, flaky when old; lvs. in fascicles of 2, to 6 in. long; cones conic-ovate, 2 in. long. Ryukyu Is. Zone 10.

maritima Mill. A name that cannot be applied with certainty; *P. maritima* has also been used by other authors for *P. nigra* and *P. Pinaster.*

Massoniana Lamb. To 80 ft., branchlets glabrous; lvs. in fascicles of 2, to 8 in. long, thin, light green; cones ovoid, to 3 in. long. China. Zone 8. Important timber tree in China. The material usually cult. under this name is *P. densiflora* or *P. Thunbergiana.*

Maximinoi H. E. Moore [*P. tenuifolia* Benth., not Salisb.]. To nearly 100 ft.; lvs. thin, flexible, pendulous, in fascicles of 5, to 11 in. long; cones oblong or elongate-ovoid, scales thin, with rounded apices. W. Mex. Zone 8.

Kerkusii Jungh. & de Vriese. TENASSERIM P. Differs from *P. insularis* in having lvs. in fascicles of 2 and cones narrow-cylindrical, to 3 in. long. Philippine Is. to Cambodia and Sumatra. Zone 10. Useful for trop. plantings.

monophylla Torr. & Frém. [*P. cembroides* var. *monophylla* (Torr. & Frém.) Voss]. SINGLE-LEAF PINYON P., NUT P., STONE P. Similar to *P. cembroides* from which it differs in having lvs. mostly single, cylindrical. Idaho to Calif. and n. Mex. Zone 6. A source of edible piñon nuts.

montana: *P. Mugo.*

Montezumae Lamb. ROUGH-BARKED MEXICAN P. To 70 ft. or more; lvs. spreading or drooping, usually in fascicles of 5, to 12 in. long, stiff, bluish-green; cones cylindrical, 5–8 in. long. B.C. to Calif. Zone 6. Source of valuable timber.

monticola Dougl. ex D. Don. WESTERN WHITE P. To 200 ft.; lvs. in fascicles of 5, to 4 in. long, stiff, bluish-green; cones cylindrical, 5–8 in. long. B.C. to Calif. Zone 6. Source of valuable timber.

morrisonicola Hayata [*P. formosana* Hayata; *P. parviflora* var. *morrisonicola* (Hayata) C. Wu; *P. uyematsui* Hayata]. To 75 ft.; lvs. in fascicles of 5, to 3¼ in. long; cones ovoid to oblong-ovoid, to 4 in. long, seeds winged. Mts., Taiwan. Perhaps not distinct from *P. parviflora,* or only a var. of it.

Mugo Turra [*P. montana* Mill.]. MOUNTAIN P., SWISS M. P. Shrub or small tree, to 30 ft.; lvs. in fascicles of 2, to 2 in. long, crowded, bright green; cones ovoid, to 2 in. long, cone scales flat or concave-convex at apex. Eur. Zone 3. Var. **Mugo**. The typical var.; commonly a prostrate shrub with short cones. Cv. 'Compacta'. Dense, globose. Cv. 'Slavinii'. Low, compact and spreading, with erect branchlets, foliage bluish-green. Var. **pumilo** (Haenke) Zenari. Usually shrubby,

brs. erect. Var. **rostrata**: *P. uncinata*. Var. **rotundata**: *P. uncinata* var. *rotundata.*

muricata D. Don [*P. remorata* H. L. Mason]. BISHOP P. Usually 40–50 ft., sometimes more; lvs. in fascicles of 2, 3–6 in. long, stiff, usually twisted, dark green; cones oblong-ovoid, to 3½ in. long. Calif. Zone 8.

Murrayana: *P. contorta* var. *latifolia.*

nepalensis: see *P. Wallichiana.*

nigra Arnold. AUSTRIAN P. To 100 ft. or more; lvs. in fascicles of 2, to 6½ in. long, stiff, dark green; cones ovoid, to 3½ in. long. Eur. and Asia Minor. Zone 4. Variable, with several subsp. recognized in Eur. Subsp. **nigra** [*P. austriaca* Hoess; *P. nigra* var. *austriaca* (Hoess) Badoux]. The typical subsp.; lvs. rigid, thick, dark green. E. Eur. Subsp. **Laricio** Maire [*P. Laricio* Poir., not Savi; *P. Poiretiana* (Ant.) Hort. ex Gord.]. Lvs. thinner, flexible, bluish-green or gray-green. W. Eur.

oocarpa Schiede. Tree, to 50 ft.; lvs. in fascicles of 3–5, to 12 in. long, bright green; cones ovoid, to 3½ in. long, persistent, hanging from usually curved, elongated peduncle. Mts., Mex., Cent. Amer. Zone 9?

palustris Mill. [*P. australis* Michx.f.]. LONGLEAF P., SOUTHERN YELLOW P., GEORGIA P. To 100 ft.; lvs. in fascicles of 3, forming tufts at ends of branchlets, to 18 in. long on young trees, 9 in. long on mature trees, dark green; cones cylindrical, to 10 in. long. Va. to Fla. and Miss. Source of timber, pulp, and turpentine. Zone 7.

Parryana: *P. quadrifolia.*

parviflora Siebold & Zucc. [*P. parviflora* var. *pentaphylla* (Mayr) A. Henry; *P. pentaphylla* Mayr]. JAPANESE WHITE P. To 50 ft. or more, branchlets greenish-brown, mostly glabrous; lvs. in fascicles of 5, forming tufts at ends of branchlets, to 1½ in. long, bluish-green; cones ovoid, to 3 in. long. Japan. Zone 6. Cv. 'Glauca'. Lvs. glaucous. Cv. 'Nana'. Less vigorous; lvs. shorter. Var. **morrisonicola**: *P. morrisonicola.*

patula Schlechtend. & Cham. MEXICAN YELLOW P. To about 50 ft., often with 2 or more main sts.; lvs. usually in fascicles of 3, 6–12 in. long, drooping, grass-green; cones conic-ovoid, to 4½ in. long. Mex. Zone 8.

pentaphylla: *P. parviflora.*

Peuce Griseb. MACEDONIAN P. To 60 ft. or more; lvs. in fascicles of 5, to 4 in. long, bluish-green; cones cylindrical, to 6 in. long. Balkans. Zone 5.

Pinaster Ait. CLUSTER P. To 100 ft. or more; lvs. in fascicles of 2, 7–10 in. long, stiff, glossy green; cones conic-ovoid, to 5–10 in. long. Medit. region. Zone 7. Var. **Hamiltonii** (Ten.) Gord. Lvs. shorter, cones large.

pinea L. ITALIAN STONE P., UMBRELLA P., STONE P. To 80 ft., with a flat-topped crown; lvs. in fascicles of 2, to 6 in. long, stiff, bright green; cones ovoid, to 5½ in. long. N. Medit. region. Zone 8. Seeds edible, the pignolia nut of s. Eur.

Poiretiana: *P. nigra* subsp. *Laricio.*

ponderosa Dougl. ex P. Laws. & C. Laws. WESTERN YELLOW P. To 200 ft. or more but mostly smaller; lvs. usually in fascicles of 3, 5–11 in. long, dark green; cones ovoid-oblong, 3–8 in. long. B.C. to Tex. and Mex. Zone 6. Very valuable timber tree. Cv. 'Pendula'. Brs. drooping. Var. **arizonica** (Engelm.) Shaw [*P. arizonica* Engelm.]. Lvs. 4–7 in. long, commonly in fascicles of 5; cones 2–3 in. long. Ariz., New Mex. Var. **scopulorum** Engelm. [*P. scopulorum* (Engelm.) Shaw]. ROCKY MOUNTAIN YELLOW P. Brs. usually drooping; lvs. 3–6 in. long, commonly in fascicles of 3; cones to 3 in. long.

pseudostrobus Lindl. To 75 ft. or more, branchlets very glaucous; lvs. in fascicles of 5, to 8 in. long, thin and flexible; cones ovoid, to 4 in. long, cone scales usually with only a small apical cusp. Mex. Zone 8. Var. **oaxacana** (Mirov) S. G. Harrison. Cone scales with prolonged cusp.

pumila (Pall.) Regel. DWARF STONE P., DWARF SIBERIAN P. Shrub, more or less prostrate but sometimes to 9 ft. high; lvs. in fascicles of 5, to 3 in. long; cones ovoid, to 1¾ in. long. Alpine areas, e. Siberia and Japan. Zone 4.

pungens Lamb. TABLE MOUNTAIN P., PRICKLY P. To about 50 ft.; lvs. in fascicles of 2 or 3, to 2½ in. long, stiff and twisted, dark green; cones conic-ovoid, to 3½ in. long. N.J. to Ga. Zone 6.

quadrifolia Parl. ex Sudw. [*P. cembroides* var. *Parryana* Voss; *P. Parryana* Engelm., not Gord.]. PARRY PINYON P. Similar to *P. cembroides* from which it differs in having lvs. more or less glaucous, in fascicles of 4. S. Calif., n. Baja Calif. Zone 9. A source of edible piñon nuts.

radiata D. Don [*P. insignis* Dougl. ex Loud.]. MONTEREY P. To 75 ft. or more; lvs. in fascicles of 3, 4–6 in. long, bright green; cones conic-ovoid, to 7 in. long. Calif. to Baja Calif. Zone 7. Much planted worldwide in Medit. climates for timber. Var. **binata** (S. Wats.) Lemm.

Lvs. in fascicles of 2, stouter. Santa Rosa Is. (Calif.), Guadalupe Is. (Mex.).

remorata: *P. muricata*.

resinosa Ait. RED P., NORWAY P. To 90 ft.; lvs. in fascicles of 2, 5–6 in. long, flexible, glossy; cones conic-ovoid, to 2½ in. long. Nfld. to Penn. and Minn. Zone 3. Cv. 'Globosa'. Dwarf, rounded.

rigida Mill. PITCH P. To 60 ft. or more; lvs. in fascicles of 3, mostly 3–4 in. long, stiff, spreading, dark green; cones ovoid, 1½–4 in. long. New Bruns. to Ky. and Ga. Zone 5. Thrives on poor soils.

Roxburghii Sarg. [*P. longifolia* Roxb., not Salisb.]. CHIR P., EMODI P. To 150 ft. or more; lvs. in fascicles of 3, to 1 ft. long, drooping, light green; cones conic-ovoid, to 7 in. long, scales arching or reflexed at tip. Himalayas. Zone 9?

rudis Endl. To 75 ft. or more; lvs. in fascicles of 5, rarely 4 or 6, rigid, to 6¾ in. long; cones ovoid, to 5 in. long. N. and cent. Mex. Related to and perhaps only a var. of *P. Montezumae*.

Sabiniana Dougl. ex D. Don. DIGGER P. To 40–80 ft.; lvs. in fascicles of 3, 9–12 in. long, pale bluish-green; cones ovoid, 6–10 in. long. Calif. Zone 8. Seeds edible.

scopulorum: *P. ponderosa* var.

sinensis: see *P. tabuliformis*.

Strobus L. WHITE P., EASTERN W. P. To 120 ft. or more; lvs. in fascicles of 5, to 5 in. long, soft, bluish-green; cones cylindrical, 4–6 in. long, basal cone scales reflexed against the peduncle. E. N. Amer. Zone 3. Valuable timber tree. Cvs. are: 'Brevifolia', a listed name; 'Compacta', dense, slow growth; 'Contorta', brs. twisted, bearing tufts of lvs.; 'Dawsoniana', dwarf, spreading; 'Densa': 'Nana'; 'Fastigiata', narrow-conical head; 'Globosa', a listed name; 'Inversa', a listed name; 'Nana' [cv. 'Densa'], dwarf, bushy; 'Pendula', brs. drooping; 'Prostrata', dwarf, with trailing brs.; 'Pumila', seemingly not distinct from 'Nana'; 'Pyramidalis', markedly conical; 'Umbraculifera', dwarf, umbrella-shaped. Var. **chiapensis**: *P. chiapensis*.

sylvestris L. SCOTS P., SCOTCH P., SCOTCH FIR. To 100 ft. or more; lvs. in fascicles of 2, to 3 in. long, stiff and twisted, glaucous, bluish-green; cones conic-oblong, to 2½ in. long. Eurasia. Zone 3, one of the hardiest pines. Important timber tree in Eur. Cvs. include: 'Argentea', lvs. silvery; 'Aurea', lvs. golden-yellow when young; 'Beauvronensis', very dwarf; 'Compressa', dwarf, conical; 'Fastigiata', with narrow-conical head; 'Nana', low dense bush; 'Pendula', brs. drooping; 'Watereri', columnar, lvs. steel-blue. Var. **rigensis** Loud. Usually tall, crown conical, bark red. Baltic region.

tabuliformis Carrière [*P. sinensis* Mayr, not Lamb; *P. Wilsonii* Shaw]. CHINESE P. To 80 ft. or more; lvs. in fascicles of 2 or 3, 4–6 in. long, stiff; cones ovoid, to 2 in. long. China. Zone 6. Var. **yunnanensis** (Franch.) Shaw [*P. yunnanensis* Franch.]. Lvs. in fascicles of 3, to 10 in. long; cones to 3½ in. long.

Taeda L. LOBLOLLY P., OLD-FIELD P., FRANKINCENSE P. To 100 ft.; lvs. in fascicles of 3, 6–9 in. long, bright green; cones conic-oblong, 3–5 in. long. N.J. to Tex. Zone 7. Yields timber and pulpwood.

taiwanensis Hayata [*P. brevispica* Hayata]. FORMOSA P. To 80 ft. or more; lvs. in fascicles of 2, to 4½ in. long, clustered near ends of brs.; cones conic-oblong, 2 in. long. Taiwan. Zone 10. Perhaps not distinct from *P. luchuensis*.

Tanyosho: a listed name of no botanical standing, used as a common name for *P. densiflora* cv. 'Umbraculifera'.

tenuifolia: see *P. Maximinoi*.

Teocote Schlechtend. & Cham. TWISTED-LEAF P. From 30–90 ft.; lvs. in fascicles of 3, 4–7 in. long, stiff; cones cylindric-ovoid, to 2½ in. long. Mex. Zone 8.

Thunbergiana Franco [*P. Thunbergii* Parl., not Lamb.]. JAPANESE BLACK P. To 130 ft.; lvs. in fascicles of 2, 3–4½ in. long, sharp-pointed, bright green; cones conic-ovoid, to 2½ in. long. Japan. Zone 5. Cv. 'Oculus-draconis'. Lvs. with 2 yellow bands. Cv. 'Variegata'. Some lvs. variegated with yellow.

Thunbergii: see *P. Thunbergiana*.

Torreyana Parry ex Carrière. TORREY P., SOLEDAD P. From 30–40 ft.; lvs. in fascicles of 5, 7–10 in. long, stiff, dark green; cones ovoid, to 6 in. long. S. Calif. Zone 7. Seeds edible.

tuberculata: *P. attenuata*.

uncinata Mill. ex Mirb. [*P. Mugo* var. *rostrata* (Ant.) Hoopes]. Similar to *P. Mugo* but a tree, to 75 ft.; lvs. in fascicles of 2; cones to 2¾ in. long, cone scales with tip prominent, recurved-hooked. Eur. Zone 4. Var. **rotunda** (Link) Ant. [*P. Mugo* var. *rotundata* (Link) Hoopes]. Shrubby, cone scales with rounded or hooded tips.

uyematsui: *P. morrisonicola*.

virginiana Mill. JERSEY P., SPRUCE P., POVERTY P., SCRUB P. To 30–50 ft.; lvs. in fascicles of 2, to 3 in. long, stiff, twisted; cones conic-

ovoid, to 2½ in. long. N.Y. to Ga. and Ala. Zone 5. Thrives on barren soil.

Wallichiana A. B. Jacks. [*P. excelsa* Wallich ex D. Don, not Lam.; *P. Griffithii* of auth., not Parl.; *P. nepalensis* Chambr., not J. Forbes]. HIMALAYAN WHITE P., BHUTAN P., BLUE P. To 150 ft., branchlets glabrous, glaucous; lvs. in fascicles of 5, to 8 in. long, drooping, gray-green; cones cylindrical, to 6–12 in. long. Himalayas. Zone 6. Cv. 'Zebrina'. Lvs. with yellow areas.

Watereri: a listed name of no botanical standing for *P. sylvestris* cv.

Wilsonii: *P. tabuliformis*.

yunnanensis: *P. tabuliformis* var.

PIPER L. PEPPER. *Piperaceae*. About 1,000 spp. or more of pantrop., shrubby or treelike plants, some scandent, with pungent odor and nodes often swollen; lvs. alt., simple, mostly entire, often oblique basally, petioles commonly sheathing at base; fls. in cylindrical spikes opp. lvs., very small, reduced, sessile, bisexual or unisexual, perianth none, but each fl. subtended by a bract, stamens 2–5, pistil 1, stigmas usually 3; fr. a 1-seeded drupe with a thin fleshy layer.

Several species are sources of important economic products. Of easy culture in warm temperatures and with constant soil moisture. Propagated by cuttings under glass, or by seeds when available.

Betle L. BETEL, BETLE P. Shrubby vine, glabrous, dioecious; lvs. leathery, oblong-ovate to orbicular-ovate, to 6 in. long and 4 in. wide, acute to sharp-acuminate, obtuse to shallowly cordate at base, 5–7-veined from near base, petioles to 1½ in. long; spikes solitary, the female to 3 in. long, the male 3–6 in. long; frs. embedded in rachis and coalescing into a fleshy red mass to 5 in. long. Malay Pen. to India. Widely cult. especially in se. Asia for the fresh lvs. called "pan," which are chewed with slaked lime and betel nut (the fr. of *Areca Catechu*).

bicolor: *P. magnificum*.

celtidifolium: *P. unguiculatum*.

Cubeba L.f. CUBEB, CUBEB P. Scandent shrub; lvs. elliptic-ovate or narrower, short-acuminate, obliquely cordate, glabrous; fr. pedicelled, nearly globose, with remains of stigma at top, to ¼ in. in diam., brownish. Se. Asia. Cult. in tropics in Orient and W. Indies for the fr. The dried unripe frs. are the medicinally important cubebs of commerce. Sometimes grown in collections of economic plants.

Futokadsura: *P. Kadsura*.

Kadsura (Choisy) Ohwi [*P. Futokadsura* Siebold & Zucc.]. Climbing shrub, dioecious; lvs. stiff, ovate to lanceolate, long-acuminate, evenly rounded to nearly cordate at base, to 4 in. long and 1½ in. wide, 5–7-nerved, dark green above, petioles to 1 in. long; spikes nodding or pendulous, the male as long as the lvs., the female shorter, rachis hairy; frs. globose, ⅛ in. in diam., red. S. Korea, cent. to s. Japan, Ryukyu Is.

magnificum Trel. [*P. bicolor* Yunck.]. Shrub, to 2 ft. or more, sts. stout, with 6–8 longitudinal, frilled wings; lf. blades oblong-elliptic to obovate, to 9 in. long, oblique and subcordate-auriculate at base, glossy dark green above with very pale midrib, purple-red and pubescent beneath, petioles sheathing st., about 1½ in. long; spikes solitary, axillary, to 1⅝ in. long, green, peduncles short, pendent, winged, red-purple. Peru.

methysticum G. Forst. KAVA, KAVA-KAVA. Erect shrub, to 8–20 ft., dioecious; sts. fleshy, from a stout rhizome; lvs. suborbicular-ovate, to 10 in. long, 8 in. wide, acuminate, unevenly deeply cordate at base, with 9–13 radiating veins, puberulent beneath; mature spikes solitary, to 2⁵⁄₁₆ in. long. Pacific Is., especially Fiji, where much cult. for preparation of kava drink.

nigrum L. BLACK P., WHITE P., PEPPER PLANT. Monecious or dioecious vine, glabrous, sts. stout; lf. blades elliptic to ovate-elliptic, to 5–7 in. long and 2–5 in. wide, sharp-acuminate, acute to cordate and oblique at base, palmately 5–7-veined, petioles to about 1 in. long, with sheath to middle; spikes pendulous, as long as lvs.; frs. globose, red, peppery. S. India and Ceylon. Widely cult. in Old World tropics for its frs., the source of pepper of commerce. Black pepper is obtained from the dried unripe fr.; when the pericarp is removed the product obtained is white pepper.

ornatum N. E. Br. CELEBES P. Differs from *P. porphyrophyllum* in being more slender, and having lvs. smaller, distinctly peltate, to 5 in. long and 4 in. wide, pale green beneath, and more heavily spotted with pinkish-white over a greater area above. Celebes Is.

porphyrophyllum (Lindl.) N. E. Br. Tall-climbing, sts. slender, red, with lines of white cilia; lf. blades broadly ovate, to 6 in. long and 5 in. wide, acuminate, cordate at base, 5–7-veined, bullate, olive-green marked with pinkish spots above, especially along veins, petioles reddish; infl. unknown. Malay Pen.

sylvaticum Roxb. MOUNTAIN LONG P. Creeping shrub, to several ft. long, brs. ascending, short; lower lvs. broadly ovate, 3–4 in. long, acuminate, evenly cordate at base, 5–7-veined, glabrous, petioles to 4 in. long, upper lvs. narrower, elliptic to oblong-lanceolate, shorter-petioled; male spikes threadlike, 2–3 in. long, female ones erect, short cylindrical, to 1½ in. long in fr.; frs. ³⁄₁₆ in. in diam. Ne. India, Burma.

unguiculatum Ruiz & Pav. [*P. celtidifolium* Desf.]. Bushy shrub, to 8 ft. or more; lf. blades lanceolate, to 3 in. long, long-attenuate, truncate to acute basally, 5-veined, or lower lvs. broader, subcordate, 7-veined, all with petioles ½ in. long; spikes pendent, to 1¾ in. long, yellowish; fls. fragrant, stamens generally 5. Peru.

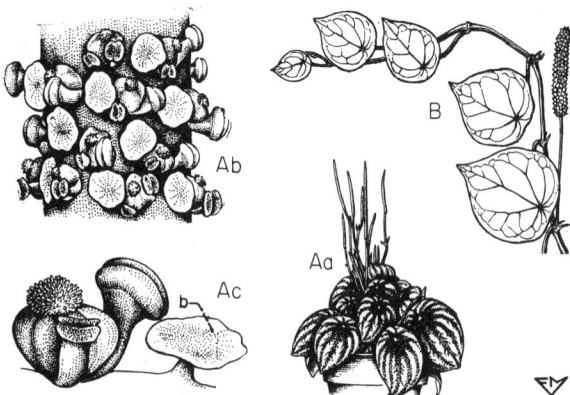

PIPERACEAE. **A,** *Peperomia argyreia:* **Aa,** flowering plant, × ⅙; **Ab,** segment of inflorescence, × 10; **Ac,** flower and bract (b), × 25. **B,** *Piper Betle:* flowering branch, × ⅙. (From Bailey, *Manual of Cultivated Plants,* ed. 2.)

PIPERACEAE Agardh. PEPPER FAMILY. Dicot.; about 9 genera of succulent herbs or woody plants of wide distribution in tropics and subtropics; lvs. simple, mostly entire, sometimes stipuled; fls. very small and reduced, borne in usually dense spikes, bisexual or unisexual, each fl. subtended by a bract, without a perianth, stamens 2–6, ovary superior, 1-celled, with 1 ovule, stigmas 1 to several; fr. drupelike. *Macropiper, Peperomia,* and *Piper* are grown for their decorative foliage, and *Piper* also for economic products.

PIPTADENIA Benth. *Leguminosae.* Not cult. **P. macrocarpa:** *Anadenanthera colubrina* var. *Cebil.*

PIPTANTHOCEREUS: *CEREUS.* **P. coerulescens:** a listed name of no botanical standing for *C. aethiops.*

PIPTANTHUS Sweet. *Leguminosae*(subfamily *Faboideae*). Eight to 9 spp. of shrubs, native to Asia; lvs. alt., of 3 lfts., stipules united; fls. racemose, yellow, papilionaceous, keel petals united, stamens separated; fr. a linear, flat, dehiscent legume.

Adapted to southern U.S.

laburnifolius: *P. nepalensis.*

leiocarpus Stapf. Differs from *P. nepalensis* in having the mature fr. glabrous. W. Himalayas.

nepalensis (Hook.) Sweet [*P. laburnifolius* (D. Don) Stapf]. To 10 ft.; lfts. lanceolate, to 5½ in. long, glaucous beneath; fls. more than 1 in. long, in rather dense racemes; fr. to 5 in. long, pubescent. Nepal to Sikkim and Bhutan. Material offered under this name may be *P. leiocarpus.*

PIQUERIA Cav. *Compositae* (Eupatorium Tribe). About 20 spp. of ann. or per. herbs and shrubs, from n. Mex. to n. Chile, 1 sp. in Haiti; lvs. opp. or alt., entire or toothed; heads discoid, 3- to many-fld., in dense cymose panicles, involucral bracts in 2 rows; fls. tubular, bisexual, white or bluish, apex of anthers blunt, neither thickened nor appendaged; pappus absent or rudimentary.

Florists grow *Piqueria trinervia* (as "stevia") for its profuse winter bloom, and also as a bedding plant. Propagated by seeds, cuttings, or division.

trinervia Cav. [*Stevia serrata* Hort., not Cav.]. STEVIA. Erect per. herb, to 3 ft.; lvs. opp., lanceolate to narrowly ovate, to 3 in. long, cuneate, serrate-dentate; heads usually 4-fld.; fls. white, fragrant. Mex., Cent. Amer., Haiti.

PIQUETIA: *KENSITIA.*

PISCARIA: *EREMOCARPUS.*

PISCIDIA L. [*Ichthyomethia* P. Br.]. *Leguminosae* (subfamily *Faboideae*). About 8–10 spp. of trees of Caribbean area; lvs. alt., odd-pinnate; fls. in lateral panicles, papilionaceous, stamens 10, all united, but the uppermost separate at base; fr. a linear, indehiscent legume, with 4 broad, longitudinal wings.

One species grown as an ornamental. Propagated by seeds or cuttings.

piscipula (L.) Sarg. [*Ichthyomethia piscipula* (L.) A. S. Hitchc. ex Sarg.]. JAMAICAN DOGWOOD, WEST INDIAN D. To 50 ft.; lfts. in 3–4 pairs, ovate to obovate, to 4 in. long, undulate or weakly toothed; petals white, striped red, ⅝ in. long; fr. to 4 in. long, wings with irregular margins. S. Fla., W. Indies. Source of a fish poison.

PISONIA L. [*Heimerliodendron* Skottsb.]. *Nyctaginaceae.* About 50 spp. of trees and shrubs of trop. and subtrop. regions; lvs. opp. or whorled, simple; fls. small, unisexual or bisexual, subtended by involucre of 2–4 small bracts, or lacking involucre and borne in panicles or cymes, or sometimes on the sts. or brs., calyx corollalike, lobed, stamens 3–40; fr. an achene topped with persistent calyx, smooth or often with glandular tubercles.

Brunoniana: *P. umbellifera.*

umbellifera (J. R. Forst. & G. Forst.) Seem. [*P. Brunoniana* Endl.; *Heimerliodendron Brunonianum* (Endl.) Skottsb.]. BIRD-CATCHER TREE, PARA-PARA. Small tree, to 20 ft. or more, glabrous; lvs. oblong, to 15 in. long; fls. pinkish or yellowish, to ⁵⁄₁₆ in. long, calyx 5-lobed, stamens 6–14; fr. an achene with persistent calyx, to 1⅜ in. long, with 5 viscid ribs. Mauritius to Australia, New Zeal., Bonin Is.

Zapallo Griseb. Tree; lvs. broadly elliptic, to 5 in. long, 3 in. wide; fls. in small clusters in peduncled cymes, stamens 5; fr. ¾ in. long. Argentina.

PISTACHIO. The pistachio tree, *Pistacia vera,* of western Asia, produces the edible pistachio nut of commerce, actually the seed (containing two large green cotyledons) of a drupaceous fruit. Pistachio trees grow slowly to a height and spread of 20–25 feet, and are both deciduous and dioecious. In the home garden they may be kept small by pruning. The trees thrive under long, hot summers with low humidity, but need moderately cold winters to satisfy their chilling requirements. They are about as cold resistant as the almond and thrive in the Sacramento and San Joaquin Valleys of California, where pistachio-growing is centered in the United States.

Since the pistachio cannot be propagated from cuttings, seedling rootstocks are T-budded with the desired cultivar. *Pistacia atlantica* and *P. Terebinthus* are the rootstocks used in California, primarily because they are more resistant to nematodes and soil-borne fungi than is *P. vera.* The ornamental *P. chinensis,* with its brightly colored autumn foliage, is not a satisfactory stock for *P. vera.* There is often considerable loss when bare-rooted trees are transplanted. Consequently, the trees are grown in the nursery in individual containers and then are transplanted into the field. Budding can be done from early April to the middle of October, but buds set in the autumn are most successful.

As the pistachio is wind-pollinated, male trees are spaced throughout the orchard to take advantage of the prevailing winds. One male tree is usually adequate for ten to 12 female trees. Topworking a male limb into each female tree is feasible, but it is not recommended because the male portion outgrows the female unless held in bounds by pruning. 'Kerman', 'Red Aleppo', and 'Trabonella' are the common female cultivars, while 'Peters' is a good male cultivar.

Four to five years are required for the trees to begin bearing fruit. The female inflorescences, composed of 100–200 flowers that bloom in April, are produced from lateral buds on growth made the previous year. Fruits on some clones may mature as early as mid-August, whereas others may not mature until early October. The hull (exocarp and mesocarp) of the semidry, drupaceous fruit is removed either in the fresh state immediately after harvest, or after drying. In the latter case the shells become stained and unattractive, and artificial coloring is necessarily applied for commercial nuts. The bony shell (endocarp) of *P. vera,* unlike that of other *Pistacia* species, splits partly along the ventral suture, enabling easy removal of the kernel with the fingers. Pistachio kernels contain less than 10 percent sugar, but their protein and oil content of about 20 and 40 percent respectively make them high in food value. To process home-grown fruits, remove the husk or covering, dip the hulled nuts in water, spread in the sun to dry and to split the shell, or boil the nuts in a salt solution for a few minutes and then redry.

Most mature trees produce at least 50 pounds of dry nuts in a good crop year. However, the pistachio is an alternate-bearing species, producing a heavy crop one year but little or no crop the next. In contrast to other alternate-bearing fruit and nut trees, in which there is limited flower bud production in the year of a heavy crop, the number of inflorescence buds formed in the pistachio is actually greater in the bearing than in the nonbearing year. Most of them absciss, however, and only a few remain, to produce little or no crop the following year.

The production of blank (empty) nuts is another important problem wherever pistachios are grown. 'Kerman', the predominant cultivar in California, produces about 25 percent blank nuts. This is primarily the result of seed abortion, as well as parthenocarpy. In other fruits and nuts seed abortion generally results in fruit abscission, but aborted pistachios do not absciss because of the strong parthenocarpic tendency.

Pistachio trees are relatively free of above-ground diseases. However, oak root fungus (*Armillaria mellea* (Vahl) Sacc.) and verticillium wilt (*Verticillium* spp.), both soil-borne diseases, seriously affect pistachio trees. Limited experience with the trees in California has revealed no serious insect pests.

PISTACIA L. PISTACHIO. *Anacardiaceae.* About 10 spp. of deciduous or evergreen, dioecious trees or shrubs, native to sw. U.S., Mex., Canary Is., Medit. region, and the Caucasus to Asia; lvs. pinnately compound; fls. small, petals 0, stamens 5, ovary 1-celled; fr. dry, drupaceous.

One species (*P. vera*) is grown for the edible seed; other species yield resins and oils. Pistachios may be grown in climates suited to the olive; although *P. chinensis* is hardy to Zone 6b. Propagated by budding and grafting, also by seeds. The species listed are deciduous, except for *P. Lentiscus.*

atlantica Desf. [*P. mutica* Fisch. & C. A. Mey.]. MT. ATLAS MASTIC TREE. To 60 ft.; lvs. odd-pinnate, lfts. 7–11, oblong or lanceolate, to 2 in. long, petiole somewhat winged; fr. dark blue, to ⁵⁄₁₆ in. in diam. Canary Is., Medit. region, Caucasus to Pakistan. Wood has many uses.

chinensis Bunge. Tree, to 60 ft.; lvs. nearly sessile, pinnate, lfts. in 6–10 pairs, 1½–2½ in. long, to ¾ in. wide, acuminate, entire, oblique; infl. axillary, male fls. in compound racemes, female fls. in panicles; fr. a globose drupe, reddish-brown, to 1½ in. in diam. China, Taiwan, Philippine Is.

integerrima J. L. Stewart ex Brandis. Tree, to 40 ft.; lfts. in 4–6 pairs, nearly opp. and sessile, lanceolate, acuminate, to 10 in. long; fls. reddish; fr. gray, ¼ in. in diam. W. Himalayas.

Lentiscus L. MASTIC TREE, CHIOS M.T. Shrub, to 15 ft.; lfts. in 3–5 pairs, oblong-elliptic, to 1 in. long, mucronulate, revolute, petiole winged; fr. reddish, turning black. Medit. region, cult. principally on the Greek is. of Chios for mastic, one of the oldest known of high grade resins. Zone 9, in w. U.S.

mexicana HBK. Related to *P. texana,* but having lfts. thinner, usually falcate, ovate-lanceolate, to 1 in. long, obtuse or acuminate, oblique, and more densely pubescent; fr. to ⁵⁄₁₆ in. in diam. Mex. and Guatemala.

mutica: *P. atlantica.*

Simaruba: *Bursera Simaruba.*

Terebinthus L. CYPRUS-TURPENTINE. Large shrub, to 15 ft.; lfts. 9–13, ovate or oblong-lanceolate, to 2 in. long, petiole somewhat winged; fr. dark purple, wrinkled. Medit. region. Source of a tanning material and formerly of turpentine.

texana Swingle. AMERICAN P., LENTISCO. Tree, to 30 ft.; lfts. 7–21, obovate, obtuse, mucronate; fr. ovoid, reddish-brown, to ¼ in. in diam. Spring. Tex.

vera L. PISTACHIO, GREEN ALMOND, PISTACIA NUT. Spreading, deciduous tree, to 30 ft.; lfts. in 1–5 pairs; fr. reddish, containing a green or yellow edible seed. Iran to cent. Asia. Several cvs. are known. Much cult. where native, also in the Medit., and in the w. U.S. (Zone 9) for the edible seeds, the pistachio nuts of commerce. Often budded or grafted onto other spp. of the genus. See also *Pistachio.*

PISTIA L. *Araceae.* One sp., a pantrop., free-floating per. of quiet ponds nearly throughout tropics and subtropics; lvs. in rosettes; infl. inconspicuous; fls. few, unisexual, enclosed in a leaflike spathe.

Tender; often grown in ponds and aquaria; sometimes a serious pest in the tropics.

stratiotes L. WATER LETTUCE, SHELLFLOWER. Stoloniferous, forming colonies, rosettes to 6 in. across, with long, feathery, hanging roots; lvs. obovate to spatulate-oblong, truncate to emarginate at the apex, long-cuneate at base, with many prominent longitudinal veins, light green, velvety-hairy; infl. to ½ in. long.

PISUM L. PEA. *Leguminosae* (subfamily *Faboideae*). Perhaps 6 spp. of glabrous, more or less scandent herbs, native to Old World; lvs. alt., pinnate, terminal lfts. represented by a bristle or branched tendril, stipules leafy; fls. large, papilionaceous, axillary, solitary or in few-fld. racemes; fr. a flat legume.

Widely grown since ancient times for the edible seeds and pods, and some forms for forage. For cultivation see *Pea.*

arvense: *P. sativum* var.

sativum L. GARDEN P., ENGLISH P., GREEN P., COMMON P. Glaucous ann., climbing to 6 ft.; lfts. in (1–)2–3 pairs, ovate to oblong; fls. 1–3 together; fr. to 4 in. long, dehiscent. Eurasia. Var. **sativum.** The typical var.; fls. white; seeds globose, green, yellow, or white, smooth or wrinkled, sweeter than in other vars., eaten fresh, or dried, canned, or frozen. Var. **arvense** (L.) Poir. [*P. arvense* L.]. FIELD P. Standard pinkish, wings purple, keel greenish; seeds angular, colored. Seeds used for meal; plants grown for forage and silage. Var. **macrocarpon** Ser. EDIBLE-PODDED P., SUGAR P., SNOW P. Pods thicker, soft, lacking the fibrous inner lining present in the typical var., to 6 in. long, not dehiscent. Young pods eaten.

PITCAIRNIA L'Hér. *Bromeliaceae.* About 260 spp. of generally stemless, terrestrial herbs, native to trop. Amer., 1 sp. in trop. Afr.; lvs. in rosettes, narrow, usually spiny; infl. a sessile or mostly scapose raceme, panicle, or spike; fls. usually pedicelled, mostly red or yellow, slightly irregular, petals separate, with or without appendages, ovary partly inferior; fr. a usually dehiscent caps., seeds with annular wings or with tail at each end.

Grown in warm climates or under glass. Requires filtered light. For culture see *Bromeliaceae.*

Andreana Linden. Lvs. persistent, petioled, lanceolate, to 1 ft. long, 1¼ in. wide; infl. short, unbranched, few-fld., bracts about as long as pedicels; fls. orange-yellow, to 2½ in. long. Colombia.

angustifolia Ait. To 6 ft.; lvs. all alike, to 3 ft. long or more, ¾ in. wide, spiny, glabrous above, white- or brown-scurfy beneath; infl. unbranched or branched; fls. red, pedicels to ½ in. long, petals appendaged, to 2 in. long. Lesser Antilles. Some material cult. under this name is *P. bromeliifolia.*

bromeliifolia L'Hér. Lvs. mostly alike, linear, densely spiny at base, glabrous above, white-scurfy beneath; infl. unbranched or branched; fls. red, pedicels to 1 in. long, petals appendaged, acute, to 2 in. long. Jamaica.

bulbosa L. B. Sm. Lvs. all alike, sheaths compacted into a pseudobulb, blades spiny-toothed, to 20 in. long, 1 in. wide; infl. 2-branched, bracts as long as sterile base of brs.; fls. spreading, sepals acute, 1⅜ in. long, petals greenish-white. Colombia.

Carolinae: a listed name of no botanical standing.

chiapensis Miranda. To 15 in.; outer lvs. reduced, inner lvs. long-petioled, blade elliptic-oblanceolate, to 16 in. long, 2¾ in. wide; infl. an unbranched raceme, shorter than lvs., loosely fld., more or less 1-sided; petals yellow. Mex.

coerulea: *Puya coerulea.*

consimilis: *Puya ferruginea.*

corallina Linden & André. Lvs. of 2 types, some small, ovate, and acute, some elongate, more elliptic, spiny on the petiole only, to 3 ft. long, 4 in. wide; infl. prostrate, trailing, unbranched; fls. erect, coral-red, petals appendaged, to 2¾ in. long. Colombia and Peru.

ferruginea: *Puya ferruginea.*

flammea Lindl. Lvs. petioled, narrowly sword-shaped, to 3 ft. long, 1¼ in. wide, not toothed; infl. slender, unbranched, bracts longer than pedicels; fls. red, to 2⅝ in. long. Brazil.

heterophylla (Lindl.) Beer. Low plants; outer lvs. reduced to spiny-serrate spines, inner lvs. linear, spiny near base, green; infl. sessile; fls. red or white, to 2 in. long or more, petals with appendages. Mex., Cent. Amer., S. Amer.

imbricata (Brongn.) Regel. Lvs. with long, spiny petiole, blade narrow, to 20 in. long, 1¾ in. wide, nearly spineless; infl. stout, bracts imbricate; fls. dense, to 2¾ in. long, petals white. Mex.

latifolia Ait. Lvs. linear, to 3 ft. long, 1½ in. wide, often spiny at base and tip; scape erect, scape bracts long, infl. unbranched or sometimes branched; fls. suberect, pedicels slender, to ½ in. long, sepals acuminate, petals red, about 2 in. long. W. Indies.

maidifolia (C. Morr.) Decne. Lvs. of 2 types, the outer reduced and nearly black, the inner petioled, green and glabrous; infl. scapose, unbranched, subcylindrical, fl. bracts green, yellow, or reddish, as long as sepals; fls. white or greenish-white, nearly sessile, to 2 in. long or more, petals without appendages. Cent. and S. Amer.

platyphylla Schrad. Lvs. all alike, in basal rosette, to 32 in. long, ⅝ in. wide, blades linear-lanceolate, closely serrate; scape erect, red, scape bracts narrowly triangular, infl. unbranched or few-branched, fl. bracts shorter than pedicels; fls. spreading, pedicels to $1\frac{3}{16}$ in. long, petals red, to 2 in. long. Jamaica.

Schultzei Harms. Lvs. of 3 types, the outermost reduced to sheaths with short, spine-toothed blades, the middle ones longer, lanceolate, spiny at base, the innermost ones to 20 in. long, entire; scape slender, infl. unbranched or few-branched; fls. suberect to spreading, pedicels to ⅜ in. long, petals red, to ⅝ in. long. Colombia.

Tuerckheimii J. D. Sm. Lvs. not alike, the outer spinelike, toothed, dark brown, the inner to 10 in. long, ⅜ in. wide, green; infl. to 10 in., racemose; fls. red, pedicels ⅜ in. long, petals without appendages, 3⅛ in. long. Guatemala.

Whitei: a listed name of no botanical standing.

xanthocalyx Mart. Lvs. all alike, to 3 ft. long or more, 1 in. wide or more, green above, whitish beneath; infl. unbranched; fls. pedicelled, yellow, to 2 in. long or more, petals with appendages. Mex. Has apparently been used as a parent of some hybrids.

PITHECELLOBIUM Mart. [*Ebenopsis* Britt. & Rose; *Pithecolobium* Mart.]. *Leguminosae* (subfamily *Mimosoideae*). About 100–200 spp. of trees and shrubs of trop. or warm-temp. regions; lvs. alt., 2-pinnate; fls. small, in heads or spikes, commonly white, 5–6-merous, stamens more than twice as many as corolla lobes, united into a tube; fr. a flat, often curved and contorted dehiscent legume, with thickened valves, seeds sometimes with an aril.

Grown as an ornamental in tropical and semitropical regions. Some species yield tannin and wood useful for many purposes.

arboreum (L.) Urb. Tree, to 60 ft., trunk to 3 ft. in diam., bark thick and very rough; lvs. to 16 in. long, with many pinnae and lfts., lfts. linear, to ⅝ in. long; fr. red, nearly cylindrical, constricted between seeds, twisted after dehiscence, blood-red inside, seeds black. Mex., Cent. Amer., W. Indies.

dolichoides: a listed name of no botanical standing.

dulce (Roxb.) Benth. [*Inga dulcis* (Roxb.) Willd.]. HUAMUCHIL, OPIUMA, MANILA TAMARIND. Very spiny tree, to 60 ft.; lvs. with 1 pair of pinnae, lfts. in 1 pair, elliptic, to 2 in. long or more, obtuse; fls. in dense, sessile heads; fr. red, to 5 in. long, spiralled. Mex., Cent. Amer.; introd. in Philippine Is. and other trop. regions.

flexicaule (Benth.) J. Coult. [*Ebenopsis flexicaulis* (Benth.) Britt. & Rose]. TEXAS EBONY. Tree, to 50 ft., trunk to 4 ft. in diam., or shrub, twigs with stipular spines ½ in. long; lfts. in 3–5 pairs, oblong to obovate, to ½ in. long, obtuse; fls. fragrant, yellow, in dense, slender spikes 1½ in. long; fr. woody, to 6 in. long, tardily dehiscent. S. Tex., ne. Mex.

guadalupense (Pers.) Chapm. [Inga guadalupensis (Pers.) Desv.]. BLACKBEAD. Differs from *P. Unguis-cati* in having no spines, petioles shorter than petiolules, fls. pink, and ovary pubescent. S. Fla.; W. Indies, n. S. Amer.

Junghuhnianum Benth. Similar to *P. pruinosa,* but peduncles longer and fls. orange-yellow. Java.

pruinosa Benth. Tree, young growth rusty-pubescent or glabrous; lvs. 8 in. long or more, with 2–4 pinnae, terminal pinna mostly with 3–4 pairs of lfts. to 3 in. long, mostly oblong or rhomboidal, but number, size, and shape variable; fls. white, pedicelled, heads peduncled, 2–3 together in axils or shortly racemose; fr. flat, very curved and twisted, several in. long, red inside. Ne. Australia.

Saman: *Samanea Saman.*

Unguis-cati (L.) Benth. CAT'S-CLAW, BLACKBEAD. Shrub or tree, to 25 ft., very spiny; lvs. with 1 pair of pinnae, lfts. in 1 pair, obovate or elliptic, petioles longer than petiolules; fls. in peduncled heads, greenish-yellow, stamens long, purplish, ovary glabrous; fr. red-brown, spiralled, 4–5 in. long. S. Fla., W. Indies, Mex., to n. S. Amer.

PITHECOCTENIUM Mart. ex Meissn. MONKEYCOMB. *Bignoniaceae.* About 20 spp. of evergreen woody vines, native from Mex. to Argentina, branchlets angular with fibrous ribs which eventually become detached; lvs. opp., with 2 lfts. and sometimes a terminal, 3-parted, threadlike tendril, or with 3 lfts.; fls. white, in terminal racemes or panicles, calyx truncate or with small teeth, corolla funnelform to funnelform-campanulate, curved, stamens 4; fr. a woody, prickly caps.

Hardy only in warm climates; propagated by cuttings.

clematideum: *P. cynanchoides.*

cynanchoides DC. [*P. clematideum* Griseb.]. Lfts. ovate, to 2 in. long; fls. to 2 in. long, corolla white with yellow throat; fr. 2½ in. long, covered with yellowish spines. Argentina, Uruguay.

echinatum (Jacq.) K. Schum. [*P. muricatum* Moç. ex DC.; *Bignonia muricata* Hort.]. Lfts. ovate, to 4 in. long; fls. white turning yellow, to 2 in. long; fr. to 8 in. long, covered with sharp tubercles. Cuba, Jamaica, Mex., s. to Brazil and Paraguay.

muricatum: *P. echinatum.*

PITHECOLOBIUM: *PITHECELLOBIUM.*

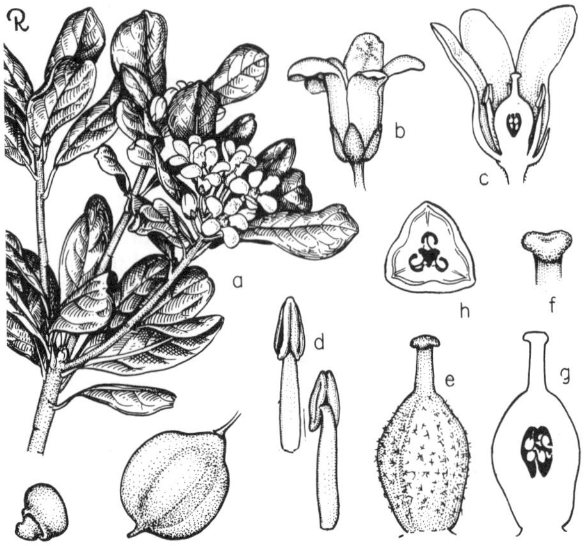

PITTOSPORACEAE. *Pittosporum Tobira:* **a,** flowering branch, × ½; **b,** flower, × 1½; **c,** flower, vertical section, × 2; **d,** stamens, two views, × 4; **e,** pistil, × 4; **f,** stigma, × 6; **g,** pistil, vertical section, × 4; **h,** ovary, cross section, × 4; **i,** fruit, × 1½; **j,** seed, × 15.

PITTOSPORACEAE R. Br. PITTOSPORUM FAMILY. Dicot.; 9 genera and about 200 spp. of trees, shrubs, or sometimes woody climbers, native to the warmer parts of the Old World; lvs. simple, alt.; fls. mostly bisexual, regular, solitary or in cymes or panicles, sepals, petals, and stamens 5, ovary superior; fr. a dehiscent caps. or a berry. *Billardiera, Bursaria, Hymenosporum, Marianthus, Pittosporum,* and *Sollya* are grown as ornamentals in the warmer parts of the country and sometimes under glass.

PITTOSPORUM Banks ex Gaertn. *Pittosporaceae.* About 100 spp. of evergreen trees or shrubs, native to warm-temp., subtrop., and trop. regions of the Old World; lvs. alt. or sometimes whorled, simple; fls. solitary or in few- to many-fld.

clusters or panicles; fr. a 2- or 3-(4-) valved woody or leathery caps., seeds many, not winged, often sticky.

Pittosporums are useful ornamentals and are cultivated in the Pacific Coast states and southern states because of their good habit, attractive foliage, flowers, and fruits. A number make good hedge plants. *Pittosporum Tobira* is sometimes seen under glass. Propagated by seeds sown in a cool greenhouse, by cuttings of half-ripened wood, or by grafting, principally on *P. undulatum*.

bicolor Hook. Shrub or tree, to 30 ft., bark smooth, gray; lvs. oblong, to 2½ in. long, leathery, tomentose beneath, margins usually recurved; fls. yellow, with reddish-purple markings, to ½ in. long, solitary or in few-fld. clusters; fr. globose, 2-valved, about 5/16 in. long, seeds yellowish-red. Se. Australia.

Buchananii Hook.f. A name of doubtful application.

Colensoi: *P. tenuifolium* subsp.

crassifolium Banks & Soland. ex A. Cunn. KARO. Shrub or small tree, to 35 ft., bark smooth, dark gray; lvs. obovate or oblanceolate, to 3 in. long, leathery, whitish-tomentose beneath, with about 5 pairs of secondary veins, margins thickened and revolute; fls. dark red to purple, to ½ in. long, in 10-fld., terminal clusters; caps. globose to elliptic, usually 3-valved, to 1½ in. long, gray-tomentose, seeds black. New Zeal.

daphniphylloides Hayata. Shrub or small tree, to 10 ft.; lvs. oblong-lanceolate, to 6 in. long, acute at both ends, leathery, petiole to 1 in. long; fls. yellow, fragrant, to ¼ in. long, in terminal panicles; caps. leathery, 2-valved, globose, 5/16 in. in diam., brown, glabrous, seeds reddish-brown. Taiwan.

eriocarpum Royle. Small tree, to 10 ft. or more; young brs., lvs., and infls. conspicuously covered with brownish tomentum; lvs. broadly obovate-oblong, obovate, or oblanceolate-oblong, to 6 in. long, leathery; fls. yellow, fragrant, to ⅜ in. long, in terminal panicles; caps. 2-valved, globose, to ½ in. in diam., laterally compressed, more or less hairy. W. Himalayas.

erioloma C. Moore & F. J. Muell. Shrub, to 15 ft.; lvs. more or less whorled, oblanceolate to obovate, to 2 in. long, glabrous, leathery, margins revolute; fls. creamy-white, with reddish markings, in 2–7-fld. terminal clusters; caps. 3-valved, to ¾ in. in diam., glabrous. Lord Howe Is.

eugenioides A. Cunn. TARATA. To 40 ft., trunk pale gray, smooth; lvs. elliptic, to 4 in. long, margins usually undulate; fls. yellow, fragrant, to ¼ in. long, in many-fld. terminal panicles; caps. 2-valved, to ¼ in. in diam., glabrous. New Zeal.

Fairchildii Cheesem. Shrub, to 15 ft.; lvs. obovate to elliptic-oblong, to 3 in. long, obtuse or acute, leathery; fls. purple, solitary or in 2–4-fld. terminal clusters; fr. globose, 3-valved, to 1 in. in diam. New Zeal.

ferrugineum Ait. Shrub or tree, to 60 ft.; lvs. ovate to lanceolate, to 4 in. long, rusty-tomentose when young, long-petioled; fls. yellowish, in many-fld. terminal clusters; caps. globose, 2-valved, to 5/16 in. in diam., glabrous. Australia to Malay Arch.

floribundum Wight & Arn. Small tree, trunk pale gray; lvs. lanceolate, to 8 in. long, glabrous, margins somewhat undulate; fls. small, greenish-yellow, to ¼ in. long, in many-fld. terminal panicles; caps. globose, 2-valved, to ¼ in. in diam., seeds few. Himalayas.

glabratum Lindl. Shrub, to 8 ft.; lvs. narrowly obovate, to 5 in. long, usually acuminate, cuneate, glossy green, glabrous; fls. pale yellow, fragrant, to ½ in. long, in 6–10-fld. terminal clusters; caps. 3-valved, to 1 in. long or more. China.

grandiflorum: a listed name of no botanical standing.

hawaiiense Hillebr. Small tree, to 18 ft., trunk smooth, white; lvs. obovate-oblong, to 8 in. long, papery in texture, glabrous, veins deeply impressed on upper surface; fls. creamy-white, in few-fld. clusters in lf. axils or on st. below lvs.; caps. globose, to 1 in. in diam. or more, valves woody, deeply wrinkled. Is. of Hawaii.

heterophyllum Franch. Shrub, to 12 ft.; lvs. of various shapes, small, glabrous; fls. pale yellow, fragrant, few, terminal, on slender pedicels to ½ in. long; caps. globose, 2-valved, to ⅜ in. in diam. W. China.

Hosmeri Rock. Tree, to 30 ft.; lvs. oblong, to 24 in. long, nearly leathery, brown-tomentose beneath, margins revolute; fls. creamy-white, to ½ in. long, in about 10-fld. racemose clusters in lf. axils or on st. below lvs.; caps. globose, to 2 in. in diam., 2-, 3-, or 4-valved, becoming orange. Is. of Hawaii.

Kirkii Hook.f. ex T. Kirk. Shrub, to 15 ft.; lvs. linear-obovate, to 5 in. long, glabrous, leathery, margins thickened and slightly revolute; fls. yellow, in few-fld. terminal umbels; caps. ellipsoid, 2- or rarely 3-valved, to 1½ in. long. New Zeal.

Mayii: *P. tenuifolium*.

nigricans: *P. tenuifolium*.

odoratissimum: a listed name of no botanical standing.

pentandrum (Blanco) Merrill. Shrub or small tree, branchlets brownish-pubescent; lvs. ovate to oblong, to 3½ in. long; fls. white, small, in many-fld., terminal, brown-pubescent panicles; caps. globose, 2-valved, to 3/16 in. in diam. Philippine Is., Taiwan.

phillyraeoides DC. NARROW-LEAVED P., WILLOW P. Shrub or small tree, to 30 ft., brs. pendulous; lvs. linear-lanceolate, to 4 in. long; fls. yellow, 5/16 in. long, solitary or in few-fld. axillary clusters; caps. 2- or rarely 3-valved, globose, to ¾ in. in diam., deep yellow. Australia.

Ralphii T. Kirk. Not always readily distinguished from *P. crassifolium*, but having lvs. somewhat larger, to 4½ in. long, with 9–12 pairs of secondary veins, and margins flat or revolute, not thickened. New Zeal.

revolutum Ait. Shrub, to 9 ft., young branchlets rusty-tomentose; lvs. elliptic, to 4 in. long or more, rusty-tomentose beneath, margins thickened and revolute; fls. yellow, to ½ in. long, in 1–11-fld. terminal, cymose clusters; caps. 2–4-valved, globose to ellipsoid, to 1 in. long. Australia.

rhombifolium A. Cunn. ex Hook. QUEENSLAND P. Tree, to 80 ft.; lvs. rhombic-ovate, to 4 in. long, coarsely toothed, rarely entire; fls. white, to ¼ in. long, in many-fld. compound corymbs; caps. 2-valved, subglobose, to ⅜ in. long. E. Australia.

tenuifolium Banks & Soland. ex Gaertn. [*P. Mayii* Hort.; *P. nigricans* Hort.]. TAWHIWHI, KOHUHU. Tree, to 30 ft., bark dark gray, almost black; lvs. oblong, obovate, or elliptic, to 4½ in. long, margins flat, revolute, or undulate; fls. to ½ in. long, dark purple, solitary or 2–3, axillary or terminal; caps. 2–4-valved, subglobose, to ½ in. in diam. New Zeal. Subsp. **tenuifolium.** The typical subsp.; lvs. more or less membranous, to 2½ in. long, margins undulate. Subsp. **Colensoi** (Hook.f.) T. Kirk [*P. Colensoi* Hook.f.]. Lvs. larger, to 4½ in. long, leathery, margins usually flat.

Tobira (Thunb.) Ait. JAPANESE P., AUSTRALIAN LAUREL, MOCK ORANGE, HOUSE-BLOOMING M.O. Shrub or small tree, to 18 ft.; lvs. obovate, to 4 in. long, thick and leathery, margins revolute; fls. white to lemon-yellow, fragrant, to ½ in. long, in many-fld. umbellate clusters; caps. 3-valved, globose, to ½ in. in diam., tomentose. Early summer. China, Japan. Now widely cult. Zone 8. Especially useful for seaside plantings. Cv. **'Variegata'.** Lvs. variegated with white.

umbellatum Banks & Soland. ex Gaertn. Tree, to 30 ft.; lvs. elliptic to oblong-lanceolate, to 4 in. long, leathery, margins revolute; fls. reddish, to ½ in. long, up to 20 in terminal umbels; caps. 2-valved, 4-sided or -lobed, to ½ in. in diam. New Zeal.

undulatum Venten. VICTORIAN BOX, MOCK ORANGE. Tree, to 40 ft.; lvs. oblong to lanceolate, to 6 in. long, membranous, margins undulate or flat; fls. yellowish, fragrant, to ½ in. long, in 4–15-fld., terminal, umbellate clusters; caps. 2-valved, subglobose, to ½ in. in diam., yellow to brown. Australia.

viridiflorum Sims. CAPE P. Shrub or small tree, to 25 ft.; lvs. obovate, to 3 in. long, leathery, margins sometimes revolute; fls. yellowish-green, to ¼ in. long, in many-fld., terminal panicles; caps. 2-valved, subglobose, to ¼ in. in diam. S. Afr.

PITYOPSIS Nutt. *Compositae* (Aster Tribe). Eight spp. of mostly autumn-flowering per. herbs of e. and se. U.S. and Cent. Amer.; usually stoloniferous, sts. solitary or clustered, slender, erect, leafy; lvs. alt., linear-filiform to linear-oblanceolate, often grasslike, entire, parallel-nerved, mostly pubescent with appressed silky hairs; fl. heads small, in corymbose infl.; involucre turbinate, involucral bracts imbricate in several rows, linear-lanceolate, scarious or partly herbaceous, receptacle naked, disc and ray fls. yellow; achenes linear or fusiform, pappus double, the inner of long capillary bristles, the outer of shorter bristles.

Occasionally cultivated in the rock garden or wild garden; an acid, sandy soil and full sun are required. Propagated by division or by seeds.

falcata (Pursh) Nutt. [*Chrysopsis falcata* (Pursh) Elliott; *Heterotheca falcata* (Pursh) V. L. Harms]. Stoloniferous, sts. often in clumps, 4–16 in. high, white-cottony; lvs. broadly linear, to 3½ in. long, silky-villous, spreading or ascending, those of infl. curved; heads about ¾ in. across, involucral bracts silky-villous to glabrate. Cape Cod to s. N.J.

graminifolia (Michx.) Nutt. [*P. microcephala* (Small) Small; *Chrysopsis graminifolia* (Michx.) Elliott; *C. microcephala* Small; *Heterotheca graminifolia* (Michx.) Shinn.; *H. microcephala* (Small) Shinn.]. SILK GRASS. Stoloniferous, sts. solitary or loosely clumped, 12–40 in. high, with appressed silky pubescence; lvs. silvery with appressed silky pubescence; the basal lvs. numerous, spreading or recurving, forming a rosette, long-linear, 4–8 or even 20 in. long, lower st. lvs. similar but progressively shorter upward, middle and upper st. lvs. abruptly shorter and of nearly uniform length, appressed to st.; heads to ½ in.

across, involucral bracts spreading, the outer cobwebby, the inner with stalked glands but otherwise nearly glabrous. N.C. to n. Fla., w. to La. The names *P. graminifolia* and *Chrysopsis graminifolia* have long but incorrectly been applied to *P. nervosa*, which is most obviously distinguished by having the involucre rather uniformly silky-hairy, rather than cobwebby in the lower half and glandular but otherwise glabrous in the upper half.

microcephala: *P. graminifolia.*

nervosa (Willd.) Dress [*Chrysopsis nervosa* (Willd.) Fern.; *Heterotheca nervosa* (Willd.) Shinn.]. SILK GRASS. Very variable, stoloniferous or not, sts. often forming clumps, to 2 ft. high, with appressed silky pubescence; lvs. various, linear-filiform to oblanceolate, usually grasslike, with appressed silvery-silky pubescence, basal lvs. few to many, ascending to spreading, gradually reduced upward along st.; heads 1 in. across or smaller, involucral bracts silky-hairy, the inner only rarely also somewhat glandular. S. Ohio and se. Va., s. to Tex. and Fla., also s. Mex., Guatemala, Brit. Honduras, Bahama Is. See *P. graminifolia*, with which this sp. has long been confused.

pinifolia (Elliott) Nutt. [*Chrysopsis pinifolia* Elliott; *Heterotheca pinifolia* (Elliott) Ahles]. Nearly glabrous except for rosette lvs., stoloniferous, sts. often forming clumps, 8–16 in. high, densely leafy, basal lvs. in a rosette, short, ½–1½ in. long, silky-villous, st. lvs. spreading-erect, linear-filiform, 2–3 in. long, 3-nerved, green, glabrate; heads ¾ in. across, involucre glabrous. W.-cent. Ga. and e.-cent. N.C.

PITYROGRAMMA Link [*Ceropteris* Link; *Gymnogramma* Desv.]. GOLD FERN, SILVER F. *Polypodiaceae*. About 15 spp. of terrestrial ferns, mainly of trop. Amer. and Afr., naturalized in Asia; lvs. tufted, 2–3-pinnate, veins separate, with white or bright yellow, waxy powder on lower surface, petioles scaly at base, dark glossy above; sori linear, along veins on under surface of pinnules, indusia absent.

Grown in the conservatory and in the open in warm countries. They are plants of simple requirements, readily grown in an intermediate temperature in pots and pans. See also *Ferns*.

calomelanos (L.) Link [*Gymnogramma calomelanos* Kaulf.]. SILVER FERN. Lvs. 2–3-pinnate, to 3 ft. long and 10 in. wide, pinnae equilateral, powdery-white to pale yellow beneath, pinnules toothed or cut, petioles as long as blades. Trop. Amer. and Afr. Var. **aureoflava** (Hook.) Weatherby ex L. H. Bailey. GOLD FERN. With bright gold-colored powder. Trop. Amer.

chrysophylla (Swartz) Link. GOLD FERN. Scales at tip of rhizome and base of petiole with a short portion 1 cell wide below the terminal cell, otherwise much like *P. calomelanos*, which has a long portion 1 cell wide below the terminal cell. Puerto Rico, Lesser Antilles.

×**hybrida** Domin. *P. calomelanos* × *P. chrysophylla*. Much like *P. calomelanos* var. *aureoflava*, but blade longer and wider, pinnules fuller, margins mostly doubly serrate-dentate and hardly revolute.

sulphurea (Swartz) Maxon [*Gymnogramma sulphurea* (Swartz) Desv.]. JAMAICA G.F. Lvs. to 1 ft. long and 5 in. wide, sulphur-yellow-powdery beneath, pinnules toothed to deeply laciniate, petioles much shorter than blades. W. Indies.

tartarea (Cav.) Maxon [*Gymnogramma tartarea* (Cav.) Desv.]. Lvs. to 2½ ft. long and 1 ft. wide, pinnae inequilateral, white-powdery beneath, pinnules entire or cut, petioles as long as blades. Trop. Amer.

triangularis (Kaulf.) Maxon [*Gymnogramma triangulare* Kaulf.]. CALIFORNIA G.F., GOLDEN-BACK F., GOLDBACK. Lvs. triangular, to 7 in. long and 6 in. wide, deep golden-yellow beneath, sometimes white, petioles to 1 ft. long, dark brown. B.C. to Baja Calif. Var. **viscosa** (D. C. Eat.) Weatherby. SILVER-BACK FERN. Lvs. viscid with stalked resinous glands above, white-powdery beneath, petioles reddish-brown. S. Calif. Var. **pallida** Weatherby. Lvs. glandular (but not viscid) and mealy above, petioles black, glandular, with whitish meal. S. Calif.

PLAGIANTHUS J. R. Forst. & G. Forst. *Malvaceae*. Two spp. of shrubs or trees in New Zeal.; lvs. alt., simple, stipules falling early; fls. small, in terminal or axillary panicles or solitary, unisexual or bisexual, involucral bracts 0, petals yellowish or white, stamens united in a tubular column with 8–20 anthers, ovary 1–2-celled, each cell with 1 or rarely 2 ovules, style brs. 2 (rarely 3) and stigmas decurrent or brs. sometimes joined to near the apex and the stigma forked; fr. somewhat asymmetrical, splitting irregularly at maturity.

betulinus: *P. regius.*

divaricatus J. R. Forst. & G. Forst. Erect shrub, to about 8 ft., densely branched, brs. divaricate; lvs. linear-spatulate to narrow-obovate, to 1 in. long; fls. solitary or in few-fld. cymes on short lateral brs., bisexual, corolla yellowish, about ¼ in. across, ovary 1–2-celled, stigmas club-shaped; fr. globose or 2-lobed, about ¼ in. across. Early spring in Calif.

Lyallii: *Hoheria Lyallii.*

regius (Poit.) Hochr. [*P. betulinus* A. Cunn.]. RIBBONWOOD. Polygamodioecious tree, to 45 ft.; lvs. ovate to lanceolate-ovate, to 3 in. long, acuminate, cuneate to narrow-truncate basally, coarsely serrate; fls. mostly unisexual, in paniculate cymes to about 10 in. long, corolla white, less than ¼ in. across; fr. ovoid, to ¼ in. long, acute at apex, 1-seeded. Early spring in Calif.

PLAGIOBOTHRYS Fisch. & C. A. Mey. POPCORN FLOWER. *Boraginaceae*. About 50 spp. of mostly hairy, ann. and per. herbs, mainly of w. N. Amer. and S. Amer.; lvs. simple, alt. above, opp. below, or in a basal rosette; fls. white, in scorpioid, racemose cymes, calyx deeply 5-lobed, corolla 5-lobed, salverform, with crests in the throat, stamens 5, included; fr. of 1–4 erect or incurved, rough, or rarely nearly smooth nutlets.

nothofulvus A. Gray. Slender, softly hairy ann., to 1½ ft., from a purple-stained root; lvs. with purple-stained midribs, basal lvs. in a rosette, oblanceolate, to 4 in. long, st. lvs. linear-lanceolate, smaller; fls. white, to ¼ in. across, in mostly bractless, twice-forked infl. Wash. to Calif.

PLANCHONELLA Pierre. *Sapotaceae*. About 60 spp. of trees or shrubs, native from e. Asia to w. Polynesia; lvs. alt., leathery; fls. small, whitish, in axillary clusters, sepals 4–5, small, corolla 4–5-lobed, ovary superior; fr. a berry, seeds with long, narrow ventral scar.

costata (Endl.) Pierre ex H. J. Lam [*Sideroxylon novozeylandicum* (F. J. Muell.) Hemsl.]. To 45 ft.; lvs. obovate, to 4 in. long, shining; fr. 1 in. long, New Zeal. May be cult. in Calif. Zone 10.

PLANERA J. F. Gmel. PLANER TREE, WATER ELM. *Ulmaceae*. One sp., a deciduous, elmlike tree, native to N. Amer.; lvs. serrate, pinnately veined; fls. unisexual and bisexual; fr. a small, muricate, symmetrical drupe with crested ribs.

Propagated by seeds sown in spring, by layers, and by grafting on *Ulmus.*

aquatica (Walt.) J. F. Gmel. WATER ELM. To 35 ft.; lvs. ovate, to 2½ in. long; fls. appearing with lvs.; fr. to ¼ in. across. Ky. to Fla., w. to Ill. and Tex. Zone 7.

PLANTAGINACEAE Juss. PLANTAIN FAMILY. Dicot.; 3 genera of herbs and subshrubs of wide distribution; lvs. often all basal, sometimes cauline and alt. or opp.; fls. mostly bisexual, small, not showy, in heads or spikes, calyx 4-parted, corolla 4-lobed, scarious, stamens 4, exserted, ovary superior; fr. a caps. or nutlet, enclosed by calyx. *Plantago* and *Littorella* are occasionally cult., the former for its useful seeds.

PLANTAGO L. PLANTAIN, RIBWORT. *Plantaginaceae*. About 200 or more spp. of herbs or rarely subshrubs, mostly native to temp. regions, with fl. characters of the family; fr. a dehiscent caps., 1- to many-seeded.

Several species are cultivated abroad for psyllium, the seed, which becomes mucilaginous when moist and is used as a mild laxative. A few species rarely planted in gardens, but mostly weedy plants. Propagated by seeds.

arborescens Poir. To 1 ft., shrubby, much-branched, very leafy, pilose; lvs. opp., linear, to 2 in. long; scapes axillary, to 3 in. long, spikes subcapitate, ³⁄₁₆–½ in. long. Canary Is.

lanceolata L. NARROW-LEAVED P., RIBGRASS, ENGLISH P., RIPPLE-GRASS, BUCKHORN. Per.; lvs. all basal, lanceolate to lanceolate-oblong, tapering to petiole, to 9 in. long and 1½ in. wide, strongly ribbed, veins impressed on upper surface; scapes 8–32 in. long, spikes dense, to 2–3 in. long. Eur.; widely naturalized, a common weed of lawns.

major L. COMMON P., WHITE-MAN'S-FOOT, CART-TRACK PLANT. Stout per.; lvs. all basal, lanceolate or elliptic to ovate, blades 4–6 in. or sometimes to 1 ft. long, abruptly tapering to winged petiole 4–6 in. long or sometimes longer, margin entire or irregularly toothed; spikes dense, to about 8 in. long, on scapes to about 1½ ft. long. Eur., n. and cent. Asia; naturalized in N. Amer. and most parts of the world. Cvs. are: 'Atropurpurea', lvs. bronzy-purple above, bronzy-green beneath; 'Nana', lvs. prostrate, green, scapes decumbent; 'Rosularis', scapes terminating in rosettes of lvs.

Psyllium L. FLEAWORT, SPANISH PSYLLIUM. Branched ann., to 2 ft.; lvs. opp., linear, to 3 in. long, sticky-hairy, entire; fls. in dense spikes to ½ in. long, fl. bracts scarious-margined, rounded at apex. E. Medit. region; naturalized in e. U.S. An important source of psyllium.

PLANT HORMONES. These are complex chemical substances occurring naturally in higher plants and upon which most of their developmental processes depend. Among the more familiar classes of plant hormones are auxins (promoting stem elongation and bending, fall of leaves and fruits, etc.), gibberellins (controlling flowering and germination processes), and kinins (concerned with the activities of cell-producing tissues). Hormone production in plants is sometimes regulated by day length (see *Photoperiod*). Certain plant alkaloids, for example colchicine, which is obtained from the corms of *Colchicum* and is much used in genetics and plant breeding, may be used as plant hormones. Scientific studies of plant hormones fall in the domain of plant physiology, but a number of important modern techniques in horticulture are now based on the use of commercially produced plant hormones. Among them are the speedy rooting of cuttings, weed killing and defoliation control, improvement of fruit set, and the prevention of premature fruit drop in orchard fruits.

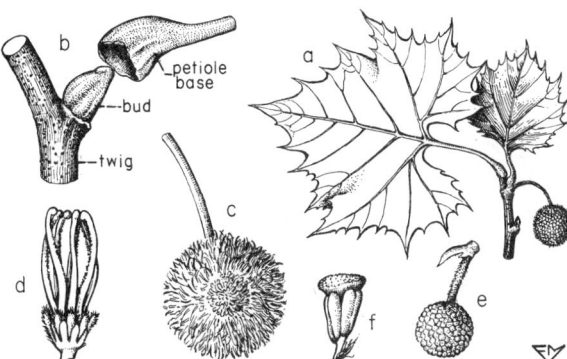

PLATANACEAE. *Platanus occidentalis:* **a,** fruiting twig, × ⅙; **b,** bud (uncovered) and sheathing petiole base, × 2; **c,** female inflorescence, × 2; **d,** female flower, × 4; **e,** male inflorescence, × 1; **f,** male flower, × 4. (From Bailey, *Manual of Cultivated Plants,* ed. 2.)

PLATANACEAE Dumort. PLANE TREE or SYCAMORE FAMILY. Dicot.; 1 genus, *Platanus,* of deciduous, monoecious trees, native to n. temp. regions; bark shedding in thin plates, herbage stellate-pubescent; lvs. alt., large, palmately lobed and veined, conspicuously stipuled, petioles long, the bases enlarged and covering the axillary buds; fls. unisexual, in dense, globular heads on nodding peduncles, sepals, petals (when present), and stamens or pistils 3–8, stamens with short filaments and peltate apical appendages, ovary superior, oblong, with 1–2 pendulous ovules; fr. heads hard, of many 1-seeded nutlets surrounded by long hairs.

PLATANTHERA: *Habenaria.* **P. fimbriata:** *H. psycodes* var. *grandiflora.*

PLATANUS L. SYCAMORE, BUTTONWOOD, PLANE, PLANE TREE. *Platanaceae.* Six or 7 spp. of large trees of wide distribution; with characters of the family; fls. inconspicuous, in spring.

Sycamores are useful as street trees and for large properties; they will stand heavy pruning. They thrive in rich, moist soil, and withstand transplanting well. Propagated by seeds, cuttings, layering, and the cultivars sometimes by grafting.

× **acerifolia** (Ait.) Willd.: *P. occidentalis × P. orientalis.* LONDON P. To 120 ft.; lvs. 3–5-lobed, lobes about ⅓ as long as blade; fr. heads mostly in pairs, bristly. Origin unknown; a common street tree in N. Amer. Zone 5. Cv. 'Pyramidalis' [forma *pyramidalis* (Janko) C. K. Schneid.]. Of upright habit, lower brs. not drooping as in typical cv.; lvs. mostly 3-lobed, lobes only slightly toothed.

americana: a listed name of no botanical standing.

mexicana Moric. To 60 ft.; lvs. to 8 in. wide, mostly 5-lobed, lobes entire, acuminate, lower surface whitish-tomentose; fr. heads 1 or 2 on a peduncle, rough, tawny-hairy, 1½ in. in diam. Ne. Mex. Zone 7.

occidentalis L. EASTERN S., BUTTONWOOD, BUTTONBALL, AMERICAN P. To 150 ft., with broad open head; lvs. to 10 in. wide, shallowly 3–5-lobed, lobes broader than long and sharply sinuate-dentate, surface becoming glabrous except on veins beneath; fr. heads usually solitary, smooth, about 1 in. in diam. Me. to Minn., s. to Fla. and Tex. Zone 4. Wood used for furniture, crates, and fuel. Var. **glabrata** (Fern.) Sarg. Lvs. usually smaller, mostly truncate at base, usually more deeply lobed, with sinus about ⅓ as long as blade, often entire or coarsely and sparsely dentate. Iowa to Tex. and n. Mex.

orientalis L. ORIENTAL P. To 100 ft.; lvs. with 5–7 narrow, coarsely toothed lobes about half as long as blade, surface becoming glabrous; fr. heads bristly, 2–6 on a peduncle. Se. Eur. and w. Asia. Zone 6. Wood used for pulp. Name often incorrectly applied to *P. × acerifolia.* Var. **insularis** Kotschy ex A. DC. Lvs. smaller, deeply cut into narrow, lanceolate lobes, basally wide-cordate but cuneate near petiole. Crete, Cyprus.

racemosa Nutt. To 90 ft.; lvs. thick, tomentose beneath, with 3–5 deep, entire or remotely dentate lobes; fr. heads bristly, 2–7 on a peduncle, sessile. S. Calif and Baja Calif. Zone 10. Var. **Wrightii:** *P. Wrightii.*

Wrightii P. Wats. [*P. racemosa* var. *Wrightii* (P. Wats.) L. Bens.]. Perhaps not specifically distinct from *P. racemosa,* from which it differs in having fr. heads mostly smooth and usually stalked, and lvs. with longer lobes. Ariz., New Mex., n. Mex. Zone 7.

PLATYCARYA Siebold & Zucc. *Juglandaceae.* A single sp., a deciduous, monoecious tree, with solid pith, native to China; lvs. alt., odd-pinnate, lfts. 7–15, opp.; male catkins in clusters, female catkins solitary, terminal, ovate; fr. a small, winged nutlet in the axils of stiff, lanceolate bracts, forming a small conelike catkin.

Propagated by seeds and layers.

strobilacea Siebold & Zucc. To 40 ft.; lfts. oblong-lanceolate, to 4 in. long, doubly serrate; male catkins to 3 in. long, female catkins to 1½ in. long. Cent. and e. China. Zone 6. Bark yields black dye commonly used in the Orient.

PLATYCERIUM Desv. STAGHORN FERN, ELK'S-HORN F., ANTELOPE-EARS. *Polypodiaceae.* About 17 spp. of large, spreading or drooping, epiphytic ferns of the tropics and subtropics, mainly in the Old World; lvs. dimorphic, sterile lvs. rounded to oblong, shieldlike, entire or lobed above, turning brown-papery, clasping the support on which they grow, fertile lvs. entire or typically dichotomously forked into antlerlike lobes, covered with stellate hairs; sporangia dense, in zones or clusters on lower surface of lf., not forming sori, indusia absent.

Staghorn ferns are striking plants when old and well grown. *Platycerium bifurcatum* does well in a cool temperature, but the others are tropical. They thrive on pieces of tree-fern trunks or on boards if provided with a thick piece of peat moss for a foothold, with perhaps some charcoal; small amounts of dried blood or bonemeal may be added now and then if needed. Their growth may be slowed in winter. Propagated by spores or suckers. See also *Ferns.*

aethiopicum: *P. Stemaria.*

alcicorne: *P. Vassei,* but material cult. as *P. alcicorne* is usually *P. bifureatum* cv. 'Ziesenhenne'.

angolense Welw. ex Bak. ELEPHANT'S-EAR FERN. Sterile lvs. round to oblong, to 2 ft. long, fertile lvs. cuneate, to 1½ ft. long, undivided, entire, hairs stellate, tawny to rusty-brown; sporangia apical or almost covering the under surface of lf. Trop. Afr.

biforme: *P. coronarium.*

bifurcatum (Cav.) C. Chr. [*P. alcicorne* Hort., not (Willem.) Tardieu]. COMMON S.F. Rhizome scales with multicellular, gland-tipped hairs; lvs. typically grayish-green, tomentose, sterile lvs. roundish-reniform, to 1 ft. across, undulate or shallowly lobed, fertile lvs. semierect to drooping, to 3 ft. long, the blade divided into narrow segms., petioles to 3 in. long or more; sporangia on upper part of ultimate lobes or covering them completely, extending to, or within 1 in. from, the apex. Australia, Polynesia. There are many variants, some of which intergrade into *P. Hillii, P. Veitchii,* and *P. Willinckii.* Some of the named cvs. are: **'Majus',** lvs. greener than in typical form, erect, branching apically, segms. short; **'Netherlands'** [*P. alcicorne* Hort. cv. 'Regina Wilhelmina'], fertile lvs. fuller, shorter than in the typical form, spreading in all directions, gray-green; **'Regina',** a listed name; **'Regina Wilhelmina':** 'Netherlands' (not to be confused with *P. Wilhelminae-Reginae*); **'Roberts',** lvs. gray-green, thicker than those of the typical form, suberect, stiffish; **'San Diego'** [*P. Bloomei* Hort.], lvs. dark green, glabrate, ultimate segms. long, attenuate; **'Ziesenhenne',**

like the typical form, but smaller and very slow-growing. Var. **lanciferum** Domin. Fertile lvs. deeply forked, segms. elongate, oblong-linear, to ¾ in. wide. Queensland (Australia).

Bloomei: a listed name of no botanical standing for *P. bifurcatum.* cv. 'San Diego'.

coronarium (J. König ex O. F. Müll.) Desv. [*P. biforme* Blume]. Sterile lvs. lobed above, fertile lvs. drooping, much-forked into narrow lobes; sporangia borne on reniform lobes. Se. Asia.

diversifolium Bonap. Not in cult.; material cult. under this name is a form of *P. Hillii.*

Ellisii Bak. Fertile lvs. cuneate-obovate, to 1 ft. long, 2-lobed apically, lobes separated by a broad sinus; sporangia borne below sinus and part way up the lobes. Madagascar. Material listed in the trade under this name is a variant of *P. Hillii* cv. 'Drummond'.

grande (Fée) John Sm. ex K. Presl. Nearly glabrous; sterile lvs. ascending, divided into broad, blunt lobes apically, fertile lvs. drooping, to 6 ft. long; sporangia borne in semicircular patch at the sinus of the first fork on a broadened area. Australia.

Hillii T. Moore. ELK'S-HORN. Deep green; fertile lvs. erect, 3 ft. long, lobed in upper ⅓ of the lf., the ultimate lobes broad, to 3 in. wide, with sporangia usually covering the underside. Australia. Cv. 'Drummond'. Fertile lvs. very broadly fan-shaped, to 1 ft. long; plants of this cv. often pass under the names *P. Ellisii, P. pumila* Hort., or *P.* "Cass Hybrid."

Lemoinei: *P. Willinckii* cv. 'Lemoinei'.

madagascariense Bak. Sterile lvs. roundish, deeply pitted into a waffle-like pattern, fertile lvs. broadly fan-shaped, laciniate or deeply cleft apically; sporangia borne on upper half of lf. except at tips of lobes. Madagascar.

pumilum: a listed name of no botanical standing for *P. Hillii* cv. 'Drummond'.

Stemaria (Beauvois) Desv. [*P. aethiopicum* Hook.]. TRIANGULAR S.F. Fertile lvs. to 3 ft. long, twice forked, from base to first fork typically broadly wedge-shaped; sporangial area V- or crescent-shaped, around the sinus of the fork. Trop. Afr.

sumbawense: *P. Willinckii,* but material cult. as *P. sumbawense* is *P. Willinckii* cv. 'Payton'.

Vassei Poiss. [*P. alcicorne* (Willem.) Tardieu]. Distinguished from *P. bifurcatum* by erect habit, the fertile area near base or on the last forking of the lf., but never reaching the apex, and by the unicellular, conical white hairs on rhizome scales. Some forms approach *P. Stemaria.* Cv. 'Regina Wilhelmina': *P. bifurcatum* cv. 'Netherlands'. Afr. Most material cult. as *P. alcicorne* is *P. bifurcatum* cv. 'Ziesenhenne'.

Veitchii (Underw.) C. Chr. Sterile lvs. deeply to shallowly lobed or laciniate, fertile lvs. rigid, erect, to 2 ft. long, narrow at base, becoming 4 in. wide, then 6–8-lobed, whitish above, very white-hairy beneath; sporangia as in *P. bifurcatum.* Australia.

Wallichii Hook. Similar to *P. grande,* but smaller, densely yellowish- or gray-green-tomentose, fertile lvs. about as long as sterile lvs., sporangia in 2 semicircular patches, each in the sinus of the second fork. Malay Pen.

Wilhelminae-Reginae Alderw. Sterile lvs. as in *P. grande,* but laciniate on inner lateral margin just above the base, fertile lvs. drooping, to 6 ft. long, divided into 2 unequal wedge-shaped segms., one short, with 2 triangular-lanceolate, widely divergent terminal lobes, the other longer, the 2 lobes broader, much-divided; sporangia borne at the apex of each of the 2 main wedge-shaped lobes, between the 2 terminal lobes. Papua, New Guinea.

Willinckii T. Moore [*P. sumbawense* Christ]. JAVA S. F. Sterile lvs. ascending, deeply lobed apically, fertile lvs. drooping, to 2½ ft. long, pale gray-green, petioles less than ½ in. long below a wedge-shaped base, segms. many, long, strap-shaped, densely stellate-hairy beneath; sporangia like *P. bifurcatum* but rarely extending around the sinus onto ultimate lobe. Java, Australia. Cv. 'Lemoinei' [*P. Lemoinei* Hort. Lemoine]. Lvs. white-tomentose when young, lobes of sterile lvs. stiff, rigid, narrower, fertile lvs. more rigid. Cv. 'Payton'. Fertile lvs. with about 8 segms. to 15 in. long; passing in trade as *P. sumbawense.* Cv. 'Pygmaeum'. Dwarf form, fertile lvs. as long as broad, semierect. Cv. 'Scofield'. Sterile lvs. erect, not as deeply lobed as in the typical form, fertile lvs. with very wide base and lobes, the lobes to 1½ in. wide.

PLATYCLADUS Spach [*Biota* (D. Don) Endl.]. *Cupressaceae.* One sp., a coniferous, evergreen, monoecious shrub or tree, native to China and Korea; differing from *Thuja* in having branchlets 2-ranked, in a vertical plane, female cones larger, erect, the 3–9 pairs of scales fleshy when young, becoming woody, strongly hooked at apex, the innermost pair united, the rest each bearing 1–2 large, thick, wingless seeds.

For culture see *Conifers.*

orientalis (L.) Franco [*Biota orientalis* (L.) Endl.; *Thuja orientalis* L.]. ORIENTAL ARBORVITAE. Densely branched, to 40 ft. or more; lvs. bright green, scalelike, less than ⅛ in. long, glandular, grooved; female cones to 1 in. long, seeds wingless. China, Korea. Zone 5b. Less hardy than the American arborvitae. Some of the cvs. are: 'Argenteus' [cv. 'Variegatus Argenteus'], tips of young shoots cream-white; 'Aureus', lvs. golden-yellow in spring; 'Azureus', lvs. glaucous-blue-green; 'Bakeri', lvs. pale green, adapted to hot, dry locations; 'Berckmannii', a listed name; 'Beverleyensis', pyramidal, lvs. golden-yellow; 'Bonita', cone-shaped, lvs. tipped golden-yellow; 'Burtonii', a listed name; 'Caesius', lvs. blue-gray; 'Chinensis', variable, dwarf, globose to pyramidal, lvs. variable; 'Columnaris', narrow-columnar, lvs. green; 'Compactus': 'Sieboldii'; 'Conspicuus' [cv. 'Aureus Conspicuus'], compact, lvs. golden-yellow, suffused with green; 'Decussatus', dwarf, juvenile form, lvs. acute, bluish-green; 'Elegantissimus', compact, lvs. bright yellow in spring; 'Excelsus', dwarf, compact, pyramidal, lvs. bright green; 'Filiformis': 'Flagelliformis'; 'Flagelliformis' [cvs. 'Pendulus', 'Filiformis'], brs. drooping, threadlike; 'Fruitlandii', listed as dwarf, globose, lvs. dark green; 'Funiculatus', branchlets drooping, lvs. of 2 kinds; 'Glaucus', pyramidal, lvs. blue-green; 'Globosus', dwarf, globose; 'Gracilis', slender, pyramidal; 'Gracillimus', narrow-globose, lvs. compact, dark green; 'Hohmanii', a listed name; 'Howardii', pyramidal, to 10 ft.; 'Hudginsii', a listed name; 'Intermedius', branchlets drooping, lvs. of 2 kinds; 'Maurieanus', very slender-columnar, lvs. green; 'Mayhewiana', compact, pyramidal, branchlets tipped yellow; 'Meldensis', narrow-pyramidal, bluish-green, needlelike; 'Nanus': 'Sieboldii'; 'Nanus Compactus', dwarf, columnar or conical; 'Pendulus': 'Flagelliformis'; 'Pygmaeus', dwarf; 'Pyramidalis': 'Strictus'; 'Ramsayi', a listed name; 'Semper-aurescens', dwarf, lvs. golden-yellow; 'Sieboldii' [cvs. 'Nanus', 'Compactus'], low, globose; 'Sikesii' and 'Stans', listed names; 'Strictus' [cv. 'Pyramidalis'], dense, pyramidal; 'Tataricus', branchlets yellow-tipped; 'Texanus Glaucus', pyramidal, lvs. blue-green; 'Weaveri', a listed name.

PLATYCLINIS: *DENDROCHILUM.*

PLATYCODON A. DC. BALLOON FLOWER. *Campanulaceae.* One sp., a showy per. herb, native to e. Asia; distinguished from *Campanula* chiefly by the apically dehiscent, 5-valved caps.; fl. buds inflated, balloonlike before opening, corolla broadly bell-shaped to nearly rotate, filaments dilated at the base, anthers separate, stigmas 5.

Plants thrive in loamy soils in full sun, hardy in the North; propagated by seeds or division in the spring; bloom the second year.

glaucus: *P. grandiflorus.*

grandiflorus (Jacq.) A. DC. [*P. glaucus* (Thunb.) Nakai; *Campanula grandiflora* Jacq.]. Glabrous, erect, sts. 1½–2½ ft., branched above; lvs. ovate to ovate-lanceolate, to 3 in. long, sharply dentate, glaucous-blue beneath; fls. erect, solitary and terminal on brs., corolla deep to pale blue, lilac, or white, 2–3 in. across. Summer. Cvs. include: 'Albus', fls. white; 'Alpinus' and 'Apoyama', dwarf; 'Autumnalis', late-flowering; 'Azureus' and 'Caeruleus', fls. blue; 'Japonicus', corolla 10-lobed, starlike; 'Micranthus', fls. small; 'Nanus', dwarf; 'Praecox' [cv. 'Praecox Giganteus'], early-blooming; 'Pumilus', dwarf; 'Semiduplex' and 'Semiplenus', partly double-fld. Var. Mariesii (Hort.) Nichols. [*P. Mariesii* Hort.]. DWARF B.F. To about 1½ ft.; corolla greatly expanded. Japan. Cvs. of this var. are 'Albus', fls. white, and 'Roseus', fls. rose-lilac.

Mariesii: *P. grandiflorus* var.

PLATYLOBIUM Sm. *Leguminosae* (subfamily *Faboideae*). Three to 6 spp. of slender shrubs of e. Australia; lvs. opp., simple; fls. solitary, yellow, papilionaceous, standard much longer than other petals, stamens united; fr. a very flat, dehiscent legume, winged on 1 side.

formosum Sm. To 5 ft.; lvs. broadly ovate or ovate-lanceolate, to 2 in. long, acute, with small rigid point, strongly reticulate; pedicels hairy, ½ in. long, calyx hairy, standard to ¾ in. long; fr. to 1½ in. long. Queensland to Tasmania.

PLATYMISCIUM Vogel. *Leguminosae* (subfamily *Faboideae*). About 15 spp. of trees and shrubs of trop. Amer.; lvs. opp., odd-pinnate; fls. in often clustered axillary racemes, yellow, papilionaceous, keel petals united near apex, stamens 10, all united or 1 separate; fr. an oblong, flat, membranous, indehiscent legume, with 1 seed.

pinnatum (Jacq.) Dug. Erect shrub, to 12 ft., with weak brs.; lvs. to 6 in. long, lfts. 7, ovate, to 3 in. long, acuminate, with petiolules; racemes loose, solitary, 4 in. long; fls. with odor of fresh-cut hay, standard reflexed, stamens 10, united. Colombia.

trinitatis Benth. Tree, to 100 ft.; lfts. 3–5(–7), ovate, to 4 in. long, glabrous, with petiolules; racemes yellow-pubescent; petals ⅝ in. long, stamens 10, united; fr. to 4 in. long and 1½ in. wide. Trinidad, Guyana.

PLATYSTEMON Benth. CREAMCUPS. *Papaveraceae.* One sp., a low, hairy ann., native to w. N. Amer.; lvs. mainly opp., entire; fls. solitary, cream-colored or yellow, sepals 3, petals 6, stamens many, carpels 6–25, united in fl. but separating in fr. into 1-seeded segms.

Suitable for cultivation in the flower garden; propagated by seeds.

californicus Benth. To 12 in., branched from near base; lvs. subsessile, lanceolate-linear, to 3 in. long; fls. to 1 in. across. In Calif. it covers great areas of open country in spring. Very variable, and many spp. have been proposed on the basis of trivial and inconstant characters. Var. **crinitus** Greene. More hairy; fls. yellow, often tipped with pink or green. Dry regions and desert slopes, cent. Calif., s. to n. Baja Calif.

PLECTRANTHUS L'Hér. SWEDISH BEGONIA, SWEDISH IVY, PROSTRATE COLEUS, SPUR FLOWER. *Labiatae.* About 250 spp. of herbs and shrubs of Old World tropics; sts. mostly square in cross section; lvs. opp., often toothed; fls. small, in 6- to many-fld. verticillasters, these arranged in cymes, racemes, or panicles, bracts deciduous, calyx campanulate, 5-toothed, corolla tube longer than calyx, swollen at base, limb 2-lipped, upper lip 3–4-lobed, lower lip concave, stamens 4, in 2 pairs; fr. of 4 smooth or granular nutlets. Allied to *Coleus,* but having filaments separate.

Cultivated in homes or greenhouses in the North; propagated by seeds or cuttings.

australis R. Br. Erect, pubescent per., 2–3 ft.; lvs. fleshy, broadly ovate, to 1½ in. long, obtusely incised-crenate, rugose; verticillasters about ½ in. apart, in racemes to 8 in. long; upper calyx teeth ovate-acuminate, lower teeth bristly-acuminate, corolla to 3 times as long as calyx, pale purple. Se. Australia.

ciliatus E. H. Mey. Subshrub, sts. and brs. densely pubescent; lvs. ovate, to 3 in. long, acute, crenate-serrate, sparsely pubescent; fls. in a raceme or a sparsely branched panicle, calyx 2-lipped, to ⁵⁄₁₆ in. long, corolla to ½ in. long or more, tubular, straight or slightly deflexed at base, with a pouch above base. Trop. Afr.

coleoides Benth. Succulent herb., to 3 ft., sts. purple; infl. to 12 in. long, 8 in. in diam., bracts large, rounded, falling early; corolla lilac; nutlets black, glossy. Wet places, sw. India.

fruticosus L'Hér. Erect shrub, to 3 ft. or more, sparsely hairy; lvs. broadly ovate, to 4 in. long, acute, cordate or rounded basally, coarsely serrate-dentate; fls. in terminal panicles, pedicels ¼ in. long, corolla blue, tube to ⅜ in. long, cylindrical, spurred at base. S. Afr.

glaucocalyx Maxim. Erect per., to 3 ft.; lvs. ovate-acuminate, to 2½ in. long, coarsely serrate, pubescent beneath; fls. many, in cymose panicles, corolla bluish. E. China.

myrianthus Briq. Erect herb; lvs. broadly ovate, to 3 in. long, obtuse to subacute, incised-serrate, somewhat pubescent; fls. in racemose infl. to 6 in. long, 2 in. in diam., calyx tubular, less than ³⁄₁₆ in. long, nearly equally 5-toothed, corolla blue, to ⁵⁄₁₆ in. long, tubular, deflexed and inflated. Trop. Afr.

nummularius Briq. Decumbent per., to 12 in. or more, often rooting at lower nodes, pubescent with slender hairs interspersed with orange-colored glands; lvs. somewhat fleshy, nearly orbicular, to 2½ in. long, coarsely dentate; fls. in a long, loose raceme, to 12 in. long, corolla pale lavender, tube to ⅜ in. long, cylindrical, slightly swollen at base. S. Afr. Differs from *P. Oertendahlii* in having lvs. entirely green, and corolla tube only slightly swollen at base. Used in hanging baskets.

Oertendahlii T. C. E. Fries. BRAZILIAN COLEUS, PROSTRATE C., CANDLE PLANT. Decumbent, pubescent per., 15–18 in.; lvs. orbicular, to 2½ in. long, obtuse or acute, truncate at base, crenate to crenate-dentate, pubescent, veins somewhat fleshy, whitish above and purplish beneath; fls. in a long, loose raceme to 12 in. long, calyx campanulate, 2-lipped, tube to ¹⁄₁₆ in. long, enlarging to ⅛ in. in fr., teeth as long as tube to twice as long, corolla pale lavender, to ¾ in. long, tubular-compressed, with pouch toward the base. Probably Afr.; described from cult. Used in hanging baskets.

purpuratus: a listed name of no botanical standing.

purpureus: a listed name of no botanical standing; some material offered under this name is *P. Oertendahlii.*

saccatus Benth. Not in cult.; the name is sometimes erroneously used for *P. Oertendahlii* and *P. nummularius.*

tomentosus Benth. ex E. H. Mey. Densely pubescent, sts. woody at base; lvs. broadly ovate, to 3½ in. long, obtuse, crenate, pubescent; fls. in a raceme or panicle, calyx to ⁵⁄₁₆ in. long, corolla purple, ½ in. long or more, deflexed about the middle, enlarged above. S. Afr.

PLECTRITIS DC. *Valerianaceae.* Four spp. of ann. herbs, native to the Pacific Coast of N. Amer., and 1 sp. in Chile; lvs. simple, opp., mostly entire; fls. white, pink, or rose, in headlike or dense, interrupted spikes; calyx obsolete, corolla 2-lipped or 5-lobed, usually with a basal spur, stamens 3, ovary inferior, 1-celled; fr. a winged or wingless achene.

congesta (Lindl.) DC. St. rather stout, to 1½ ft., usually simple but sometimes branched; lvs. obovate to oblong-ovate, to 2 in. long; fls. pink to rose, to ⁵⁄₁₆ in. long, in headlike clusters, corolla 2-lipped, spurred; achenes winged. B.C. to n. Calif.

PLEIOBLASTUS: *ARUNDINARIA.* **P. aureus:** a name of no botanical standing, perhaps referable to *Phyllostachys aurea.* **P. Fortunei:** *Arundinaria variegata.* **P. niger:** a name of no botanical standing, perhaps referable to *Phyllostachys nigra.*

PLEIOGYNIUM Engl. *Anacardiaceae.* Two spp. of trop., deciduous, dioecious trees from the Philippine Is., Lesser Sunda Is., New Guinea, and ne. Australia; lvs. odd-pinnate, lfts. 7–9, ovate, to 4 in. long, obtuse; fls. sessile, crowded in short, axillary spikes or panicles, calyx deeply lobed, petals 5, obtuse, less than ³⁄₁₆ in. long, stamens 10, inserted on a disc, ovary with 3 or 4 conical styles; fr. drupaceous.

cerasiferum (F. J. Muell.) R. Parker [*P. Solandri* (Benth.) Engl.; *Spondias Solandri* Benth.]. QUEENSLAND HOG PLUM, BURDEKIN PLUM. Evergreen tree, to 60 ft.; lfts. 7–9, ovate to oblong, to 4 in. long, entire; fls. greenish, densely clustered; fr. 1½ in. in diam. Early summer. Queensland. Cult. in Calif., Fla., and Hawaii; used for jellies and jams.

Solandri: *P. cerasiferum.*

PLEIONE D. Don. *Orchidaceae.* Ten spp. of terrestrial herbs, native to India, China, Thailand, Taiwan; pseudobulbs cormlike, ovate, 1- or 2-lvd.; lvs. plicate; scape 1-fld.; fls. showy, sepals and petals similar, lip much broader, 3-lobed, with fringed keels, lateral lobes enveloping the column, disc of lip crested. For structure of fl. see *Orchidaceae.*

Cool greenhouse. For culture see *Orchids.*

Hookerana (Lindl.) T. Moore. Pseudobulbs 1-lvd., ½ in. long; lvs. elliptic-lanceolate, to 3½ in. long; scapes to 3 in. long; fls. nodding, amethyst-colored, sepals ovate, 1 in. long, petals oblong, lip white with yellow spots, broadly truncate, obscurely 3-lobed, lateral lobes orbicular, midlobe erose-denticulate. Himalayas.

humilis (Sm.) D. Don. Pseudobulbs conical, ovate, 1-lvd., 1½ in. long; lvs. oblong-obovate, to 8 in. long; scapes erect; fls. showy, white, sepals and petals lanceolate, to 2 in. long, lip elliptic, to 1¼ in. long, margins lacerate, disc yellow, spotted with brown, crest brown, apex of lip spotted with amethyst. Himalayas.

maculata Lindl. & Paxt. Pseudobulbs small, 2-lvd.; lvs. elliptic-oblong, to 8 in. long; fls. 2 in. across, white, sepals and petals lanceolate, lip white, elliptic, lateral lobes narrow, with oblique purple lines, midlobe broader than long, spotted with purple, emarginate, with 5–7 lines between side lobes, column winged at apex. Autumn. Himalayas.

praecox (Sm.) D. Don [*P. Wallichiana* (Lindl.) Lindl. & Paxt.]. Pseudobulbs variable, mottled brown to purple, 2-lvd.; lvs. elliptic, to 8 in. long; scapes basal, as long as pseudobulbs, 1- or 2-fld.; fls. large, to 4 in. across, rose-colored, sepals and petals lanceolate, lip ovate-orbicular, without lateral lobes, slightly bifid at apex, disc with 5 laciniate crests, column expanded into a wide, undulate, lobed hood at apex. Late autumn. Himalayas.

Reichenbachiana T. Moore. Pseudobulbs 2½ in. long, pitcher-shaped, green, reticulated with dark brown, 1- or 2-lvd.; lvs. to 2½ in. long; scapes to 2 in. long; sepals narrow-oblong, 2 in. long, pale rose with white margins, petals narrower, paler, lip white, lateral lobes convolute, midlobe bifid, white with pale red-purple spots, with toothed margin, disc streaked purple, with 3 crests. Burma.

Wallichiana: *P. praecox.*

PLEIOSPILOS N. E. Br. [*Punctillaria* N. E. Br.]. LIVING-ROCK, STONE MIMICRY PLANT. *Aizoaceae.* About 35 spp. of occasionally clump-forming, stemless, per. succulents, native to S. Afr.; lvs. opp., usually 2–4 but sometimes 6–8 on a shoot, thick, firm, often as broad as long, united at base, usually conspicuously covered with more or less translucent dots, upper side flat, lower side convex, keeled; fls. solitary to several in a group, bracted, sessile or nearly so, often with the scent of coconut, calyx 5–6-lobed, petals many, yellow, sometimes the faces white, stamens many, erect, staminodes lacking, ovary inferior, 9–15-celled, styles 9–15; fr. a caps., expanding keels with narrow wings, cell lids stiff, placental tubercles glossy, seeds large, brown, reniformly D-shaped, minutely papillose.

Growth occurs from late spring to summer, flowering at the end of the growth period. Cultivate in deep pots using very sandy loam, watering only during the growth period. Propagation easy by seeds. Species hybridize readily. See also *Succulents.*

beaufortensis L. Bolus. Lvs. 2–4, rosy-brown with many, prominent, dark green dots, to 2⅞ in. long with a sheath to ¾ in. long, about 2 in. wide and 1¾ in. thick at middle, ⅜ in. wide near tip, nearly flat and obliquely almost ovate in top view, gradually expanded on lower side, rounded, and then truncate in side view, sides compressed in upper ⅓ and obtusely keeled above middle; fls. included, petals to 1⅜ in. long, golden above, pale rose beneath. Cape Prov.

Bolusii (Hook.f.) N. E. Br. MIMICRY PLANT, AFRICAN L., LIVING-ROCK CACTUS. Lvs. slightly spreading, gray-green or brownish with many conspicuous dark green dots, to 2 in. long and to 2 in. thick at tip, upper side flat, broadly ovate in outline, upper part of lf. more or less half-ovoid in section; fls. 2 in. across or more, 1–3, sessile, opening in the afternoon, petals bright yellow fading to white at base, paler outside. Cape Prov.

borealis L. Bolus. Lvs. 4, somewhat unequal, nearly glaucous or at length yellow-green with inconspicuous dots, to 2¾ in. long with sheath ⅜ in. long, to ⅞ in. wide, ¾ in. thick, larger lf. nearly curved in outline, keel central or eccentric; fls. to 2 in. across, solitary, sessile, opening in the afternoon, petals gold above, reddish and basally white outside. Orange Free State.

compactus: *P. nobilis.*

Dekenahii (N. E. Br.) Schwant. Lvs. 4, spreading, gray-green, roughened by prominent dark green dots, becoming pruinose, to 2½ in. long, ⅝ in. wide at base, 1 in. wide at center, apex acuminate, upper side slightly concave, lower side rounded at base, sharply keeled toward apex, margins and keel more or less reddish; fls. to 1⅜ in. across, petals light yellow. Cape Prov.

dimidiatus L. Bolus. Lvs. 4–6, gray-green, uniformly covered with many large dark green dots, to 3¼ in. long, ¾ in. wide at base, a little widened at center and tapered above, upper side flat, tip often recurved, lower side rounded near base, sharply keeled toward apex, margins and keel reddish; fls. to 2¾ in. across, sessile, petals yellow. Cape Prov.

Hilmarii L. Bolus. Lvs. 2, glaucous-green suffused with rose, covered with more or less dark green dots, these coalescing at tip to form a more or less distinct window, to 1 in. long, ⅝ in. wide at base and semicylindrical, little narrowed toward apex, upper side slightly rounded, lower side rounded, apex very obtuse and rounded, edges much-rounded; fls. to 1$^{5}/_{16}$ in. across, sessile, opening in afternoon, petals golden-yellow, white at base. Cape Prov.

Kingiae L. Bolus. Lvs. 2, bluish, prominently dotted, 2 in. long with sheath ¼ in. long, to ⅝ in. wide at middle, ½ in. thick, symmetrical or asymmetrial on upper side, nearly rhombic in outline above middle in top view, acute to acuminate, very broad above middle in side view, tip rounded to narrowed, lower side keeled, compressed toward apex; fls. to 1½ in. across, on peduncles to ¼ in. long, petals yellow, to 1 in. long. Cape Prov.

latipetalus L. Bolus. Lvs. 6, green, covered with prominent large dots, to 3½ in. long, to 1⅜ in. wide and 1 in. thick at center, obtuse or nearly acute in side view, upper side flat or concave at center, expanded and broadly acuminate in top view, lower side rounded near base, keeled toward apex, keel central or eccentric, compressed; fls. to 3¼ in. across, 1–3, nearly sessile, opening in the afternoon, petals yellow, paler beneath, white at center. Cape Prov.

magnipunctatus (Haw.) Schwant. Lvs. 2–4 on a br., green, gray-green, or brownish, covered with rather prominent dots, to 2¾ in. long and ½ in. wide at center, upper side flat or convex or concave, tip slightly recurved, edges blunt, lower side rounded at base, bluntly keeled toward apex, 3-angled in section, sides convex, slightly 3-angled, concave toward apex, tip blunt; fls. to 2 in. across, solitary, sessile, petals light yellow. Cape Prov. Var. **inaequalis** L. Bolus. Lvs. unequal, variously shaped, laterally keeled, concave above.

minor L. Bolus. Lvs. 4–6, gray-green, uniformly and loosely covered with dark green dots, to 1¼ in. long, ⅜ in. wide at base, in outline forming a roundish triangle ¾ in. long in upper ⅓ above, rounded beneath, keeled, margins rounded, tip recurved; fls. to 2¼ in. across, sessile, petals yellow, whitish basally. Cape Prov.

multipunctatus: a listed name of no botanical standing.

Nelii Schwant. SPLITROCK, CLEFTSTONE, MIMICRY PLANT. Similar to *P. Bolusii*, but lvs. dark gray-green or often reddish with many little dots, thicker at tip, this rounded and semiglobose in cross section; fls. 2¾ in. across, petals salmon-pink-yellow. Cape Prov.

nobilis (Haw.) Schwant. [*P. compactus* (Ait.) Schwant.]. Lvs. 4–6, dull gray-green with many prominent dots, to 2⅜ in. long, ¾ in. wide toward apex, broadly linear and curved in outline, upper side flat basally, somewhat concave above, lower side rounded at base, keeled toward the bluntish apex where 3-angled in cross section, keel more or less sinuate; fls. to 2⅜ in. across, solitary, nearly sessile, petals yellow. Cape Prov.

optatus (N. E. Br.) Schwant. Lvs. 2–4, spreading, brownish or reddish-green, tinged with purple to nearly bluish, with dense, indistinct dark green dots, to 1¾ in. long, ¼ in. wide and slightly thicker, upper side flat or slightly concave, lower side rounded, bluntly keeled toward the blunt or slightly acute apex; fls. to 1$^{3}/_{16}$ in. across, petals light yellow. Cape Prov.

simulans (Marloth) N. E. Br. Lvs. spreading, reddish to yellowish, brown or green, with upper side much-dotted, to 3¼ in. long, 2¾ in. wide, ⅝ in. thick, ovate-triangular in outline in top view, upper side flat or somewhat concave, troughlike and then recurved, lower side keeled; fls. fragrant, petals light yellow to yellow or orange. Cape Prov.

sororius (N. E. Br.) Schwant. Lvs. 4–6, ascending to spreading, green, covered with slightly prominent dots, to 2 in. long, ⅜ in. wide, ⅜ in. thick, often curved to one side in upper portion, expanded at center, narrowed toward tip, lower side rounded basally, keeled toward apex; fls. to 2 in. across, on pedicels ⅜ in. long, petals bright yellow. Cape Prov.

willowmorensis L. Bolus. Lvs. 2–4, green-purple, prominently dotted, to 2¾ in. long, ⅞ in. wide, ⅝ in. thick, upper lvs. shorter, curved to nearly falcate, upper side flat to concave, lower side widened laterally and keeled below apex; fls. to 2¾ in. across, solitary, petals yellow, white at base. Cape Prov.

PLEIOSTACHYA K. Schum. *Marantaceae.* Two spp. of rhizomatous per. herbs, native to trop. Amer.; basal lvs. long-petioled; panicles of a few flattened spikes; fls. paired, sepals 3, corolla 3-lobed, the tube almost as long as the sepals, fertile stamen 1, outer staminode 1, ovary inferior, 1-celled.

Culture as for *Calathea.*

pruinosa (Regel) K. Schum. To 6 ft. or more; lvs. oblong-lanceolate, to 20 in. long and 6 in. wide, shimmering deep green and with many lateral veins deeply impressed above, purple beneath, petioles pubescent, longer than lf. blades; spikes to 4 in. long, bracts glabrous, pruinose; fls. white and violet. Honduras to Panama.

PLEOMELE: *DRACAENA.* **P. gracilis:** *D. cincta.*

PLEROMA: *TIBOUCHINA.* **P. splendens:** *T. Urvilleana.*

PLEUROTHALLIS R. Br. *Orchidaceae.* About 1,000 spp. of epiphytes of trop. Amer.; sts. in tufts or creeping, 1-lvd.; infl. racemose or reduced to 1 fl., peduncled or sessile; fls. small, sepals and petals separate, lateral sepals sometimes united, lip jointed to column foot, pollinia 2. For structure of fl. see *Orchidaceae.*

Greenhouse culture similar to that given *Cattleya;* cultivated in shallow pans near the glass. For culture see *Orchids.*

Broadwayi: *P. foliata.*

calyptrostele Schlechter. Creeping, to 1 in. high, sts. much reduced; lvs. fleshy, oblanceolate, to ½ in. long; scape to 1 in. long, filiform, few-fld.; fls. ⅛ in. long, sepals ovate-lanceolate, united basally, petals much smaller, obovate, lip fleshy, narrowly oblong, column with broad wings. Costa Rica, Panama.

foliata Griseb. [*P. Broadwayi* Ames]. To 2 in., sts. in tufts, covered with funnel-shaped sheaths; lvs. ovate, to ½ in. long; scape surpassing lvs., filiform, several-fld.; fls., ⅛ in. long, pale yellow, sepals separate, lanceolate, petals filiform, lip lanceolate-strap-shaped, obtuse, disc of lip with a pair of keels, column with a prominent foot. Trop. Amer.

fulgens Rchb.f. Tufted, sts. short, concealed by red-brown sheaths; lvs. long-petioled, fleshy, oblong-elliptic, to 5 in. long; scape shorter than lvs., erect, usually 1-fld.; fls. appearing in succession, ⅜ in. long, red-orange, sepals ovate, petals obliquely ovate-lanceolate, lip strap-shaped, obtuse, 2-keeled in middle, column slender, ciliate. Winter. Costa Rica.

gelida Lindl. Tufted, to 20 in., sts. erect, completely enclosed by loose, overlapping sheaths; lvs. short-petioled, fleshy, elliptic, to 8 in. long; scapes 1 to many, as long as lvs. or longer, slender, loosely many-fld.; fls. ¼ in. long, yellow, partially pubescent, sepals oblong-lanceolate, lateral sepals united to their middle, petals shorter than sepals, oblong-obovate, lip cuneate-oblong, S-curved, disc with a pair of calluses, column lacerate. Trop. Amer.

Ghiesbreghtiana: *P. quadrifida.*

Grobyi Batem. ex Lindl. [*P. picta* Lindl.]. Tufted, to 6 in., sts. short, covered with overlapping sheaths; lvs. petioled, oblong-elliptic, commonly 1 in. long, rarely to 7 in. long; scape slender, loosely fld.; fls. few, to ⅜ in. long, commonly shorter, yellow, streaked with red, upper sepal elliptic, lateral sepals united up to apex, elliptic, petals obliquely obovate, lip linear-oblong. Trop. Amer.

macrophylla HBK [*P. Roezlii* Rchb.f.]. WIDOW ORCHID. Robust, to 20 in., sts. erect, with a single sheath at middle; lvs. fleshy, elliptic or oblong-elliptic, to 10 in. long, 4 in. wide; scapes 1 to 2, to 10 in. long, loosely many-fld.; fls. relatively large, to 1 in. long, dark purple, sepals ovate-elliptic, lateral sepals united up to apex, petals oblanceolate, lip strap-shaped, with a rough disc and margin. Late spring. Colombia.

ophiocephala: *Restrepiella ophiocephala.*

Ospinae: *Restrepia antennifera.*

ornata: *P. Schiedei.*

picta: *P. Grobyi.*

quadrifida (Llave & Lex.) Lindl. [*P. Ghiesbreghtiana* A. Rich. & Galeotti]. Tufted, to 2 ft., sts. enclosed by overlapping sheaths; lvs. fleshy, oblong, obtuse, to 7 in. long; scapes 1 to few, commonly much longer than lvs., many-fld.; fls. yellow, to ⅜ in. long, upper sepal ovate, lateral sepals united to apex, elliptic, petals lanceolate, lip fiddle-shaped. Cent. Amer., W. Indies, Venezuela, Colombia.

Roezlii: *P. macrophylla.*

saurocephala Lodd. To 20 in., sts. robust, basal half enclosed by 3 loose-fitting sheaths; lvs. fleshy, elliptic or elliptic-oblong, to 6 in. long; scapes 1 or 2, longer than lvs., many-fld.; fls. to ⅜ in. long, fleshy, green or greenish-brown, hairy, upper sepal elliptic-spatulate, lateral sepals united in lower ⅔, elliptic, petals obliquely rhombic, lip fleshy, 3-lobed, lateral lobes rounded, midlobe squarish, disc with 2 prominent keel-like calluses obliquely inserted. Late autumn. Brazil.

sertularioides (Swartz) K. Spreng. Small, rhizome slender, long, creeping, sts. short; lvs. fleshy, linear-spatulate, to 1 in. long; scape to 1 in. long, filiform, 1-fld.; fls. to ⅛ in. long, white with yellow tips, sepals separate, lanceolate, petals linear-triangular, acuminate, lip oblong, 3-lobed, lateral lobes triangular, midlobe lanceolate, column minutely serrate. Winter–spring. Trinidad.

Schiedei Rchb.f. [*P. ornata* Rchb.f.]. Tufted, to 3 in., sts. short, completely enclosed by overlapping sheaths; lvs. fleshy, oblanceolate, dotted with green-purple; scape few-fld.; fls. black-brown with white fringes, sepals ovate, lateral sepals united to middle, their margins with movable long white cilia, petals spatulate, lip long-clawed, squarish, disc with a pair of keel-like calluses. Spring. Mex.

PLOIDY. Chromosomes, through which heredity is transmitted by way of genes, occur within the nucleus of each living cell of the plant body in sets which are known technically as genomes. Ploidy, as used in *Hortus Third*, refers to the degree of duplication of genomes or of individual chromosomes making up the genome, although there are other and more complex uses of the term. While both kinds of duplication in chromosome number are important features of plant evolution, only reference to those changes involving whole genomes are commonly encountered in horticultural literature. Normally each vegetative cell of the plant body contains two genomes and the plant is known as a diploid. If the cells have only a single set of chromosomes, a situation rare among the higher plants, the plant is termed a monoploid. Continued duplication of genomes leads to the formation of polyploid plants with three (triploid), four (tetraploid), five (pentaploid), six (hexaploid), or more sets of chromosomes. If the genomes included in the polyploid are duplicates of each other, that is, derived from the same individual or the same species, the plant is termed an autopolyploid. If the genomes are dissimilar, derived from parents belonging to different species, the plant is an allopolyploid. The degree of duplication in an autopolyploid or an allopolyploid may be designated with the appropriate prefix, as autotetraploid or allohexaploid. Allotetraploids are often referred to as amphidiploids or amphiploids.

While it is relatively easy to create terms to categorize polyploids, it is often difficult to apply these terms in a strict sense. In the extremes, the differences between auto- and allopolyploid are clear, but all degrees of intermediacy exist between the extremes as various combinations of similar and dissimilar genomes are brought together. Many species of plants are known or thought to be of polyploid origin, but the details of their origin are lost in antiquity, and for all practical purposes they are considered to be normal diploids. While the plant breeder needs acquaintance with the complexities and subtleties of polyploidy, especially as these relate to sterility and the expression of desired traits, most horticulturists need only recognize that polyploidy, and in particular allopolyploidy, is a widespread phenomenon in the plant kingdom and that many of our most important plants are of polyploid origin, for example, the bread wheats *(Triticum aestivum)*, oats *(Avena sativa)*, white potatoes *(Solanum tuberosum)*, sweet potatoes *(Ipomaea Batatas)*, and sugar cane *(Saccharum officinarum)*. In the horticultural trade, polyploidy tends to be publicized only in those instances where it confers desirable characteristics such as gigantism of floral parts, increased vigor, or adaptability to a wide range of soils and climates.

PLUM, PRUNE. True plums and prunes are several species of the genus *Prunus,* which also includes the almonds, apricots, peaches, and cherries. Plum fruits (drupes), unlike cherries, usually have a bloom, and they lack the pubescence and prominently furrowed stone of apricots. Furthermore, species of plums produce solitary axillary buds rather than the three buds characteristic of almonds and peaches. The cultivated plums are of widely different nativities and also involve hybrids between some of the diploid types. An understanding of these sources is essential to a clear analysis of plum culture.

(A) The domesticas are cultivars of *Prunus domestica,* the so-called common or European plum, probably originating in southwestern Asia. Here are included the familiar blue plums and prunes long grown in Europe and the eastern states and on the Pacific Coast. Such cultivars as 'Bradshaw', 'Grand Duke', 'Green Gage', 'Italian Prune', 'Lombard', 'Stanley', and 'Washington' belong here. The tart damson plums *(P. insititia),* used for jams and jellies, cross freely with the domestica cultivars as both are hexaploid types of diverse background.

(B) The usually red-colored Japanese or Oriental plums derive from the Asiatic *P. salicina,* and are represented by 'Abundance', 'Formosa', 'Santa Rosa', 'Shiro', and other cultivars. The Japanese types thrive over a wide range of territory but lack the winter hardiness of the domestica types, and because of their earlier flowering habit are more susceptible to spring frosts. The Japanese plums are diploids and can be crossed with other diploid species, but are incompatible with the hexaploid domestica types. The ornamental *Prunus Mume,* called "plum" in its native Japan, is actually an apricot.

(C) The native American plums are of several species, which, with some of their cultivars, include: the wild plum, *P. americana* ('De Soto', 'Forest Garden', 'Hawkeye', 'Wolf'); chickasaw or sand plum, *P. angustifolia* ('Caddo Chief', 'Strawberry', 'Yellow Transparent'); hortulan plum, *P. hortulana* ('Golden Beauty', 'Miner', 'Wayland'); beach plum, *P. maritima* ('Autumn', 'Raritan', 'Stearns'); wild-goose plum, *P. Munsoniana* ('Newman', 'Robinson', 'Wild Goose'); Canada plum, *P. nigra* ('Cheney', 'Hasca', 'Oxford'); and the Pacific plum, *P. subcordata* ('Sisson'). Although these native species thrive over a wide area in the interior of the country, their fruits are of relatively poor quality and are used primarily for jams and jellies. Some, like the beach plum, are also planted as ornamentals or as sand binders.

(D) Hybrids of the Japanese and American species combine the qualities of both to give types that will survive in the north-central area where the domestica and Japanese cultivars are not sufficiently hardy. Extensive breeding work in the Midwest, especially Minnesota, has produced a number of hybrid cultivars such as 'Ember', 'Kahinta', 'La Crescent', and 'Superior' that approach the quality of the Japanese types while retaining the hardiness of the native species. Recent hybrids have also contributed some disease resistance necessary for southern plum growing.

These more than half a dozen species, by their diverse climatic requirements, contribute to the growing of plums over much of the United States and north into Canada. The European plum is of the greatest importance, being largely grown as a source of prunes in the Great Lakes and Pacific Coast areas. The Japanese plum is grown over much of the same region and somewhat further south along the Atlantic Coast and Mississippi Valley. The native American species are valuable in extending plum culture north and south because of their resistance to disease, heat, and cold. The main value of these native species will probably continue to be in their ability to pass on their resistant characteristics to higher-quality hybrids.

Soil requirements are variable although any well-drained agricultural land is suitable for some type of plum. In general, the European cultivars grow best on the heavier loams and can tolerate some poor drainage, while the Japanese and American types prefer lighter, better-drained soils.

Propagation is by budding, rarely grafting, on many different seedling stocks, the method being similar to that described for the apple. Myrobalan stock *(P. cerasifera)* is the most widely used in both the East and West. Japanese cultivars are sometimes worked on peach stocks, especially for growth on light soils and in the South. American species may be used as stocks when unusual hardiness is desired.

Planting distance for plums has normally been 20 X 20 feet, but the smaller-growing kinds may be planted 20 X 10 feet and later thinned, if necessary. One-year-old nursery trees are preferred, set usually early in the spring.

Tillage and fertilizer, together with cover-cropping, can be done as with the peach. Maintenance of a sod cover in the row in conjunction with chemical control of weeds under the tree gives satisfactory growth and cropping under eastern conditions. A light application of nitrogen fertilizer (1–2 pounds per tree of ammonium sulphate) is usually all the fertilizer necessary for deep-rooted plum trees. In some soils, potash deficiency may develop so that a potash source must be applied every few years to maintain healthy growth.

Pruning at planting time is essentially similar to that for the apple. After the scaffold limbs are started, little pruning is advisable until the trees come into bearing, except to thin out unwanted growth and shape the tree to a modified leader system. The mature trees may be thinned out by removing crowding or crossing limbs, and if the trees are not making vigorous growth or are becoming taller than is desirable, the limbs may be headed back. Some Japanese cultivars have more vigorous growth and require some renewal pruning as done for the peach. Pruning is done when the trees are dormant, preferably in late winter or early spring in the East.

Harvesting and marketing of plums is similar to that of other perishable fruits. The best-quality fruits for home use or nearby markets are tree-ripened or nearly so, mature but still firm. Yields vary greatly with cultivars, species, and care. In the eastern states, 1 to 3 or 4 bushels may be expected from a mature tree under good conditions. Larger yields are frequent on the West Coast. Plums may be stored a few days or weeks at 32° F in firm condition, but the flavor is soon lost and long storage is not advisable. Fresh prunes keep longer than other plums because of their firmer flesh and higher sugar content, the latter characteristic permitting them to be sun-dried as prunes without fermenting at the pit. They may be eaten fresh but are very sweet. 'French', small and yellow-fleshed, is a commercial cultivar in California; 'Imperial' is very large; 'Sugar', often sold fresh, may also be canned. Prunes for drying are allowed to fall from the tree, then carefully gathered. They are dipped in lye to prevent fermentation and to hasten the drying, often being rinsed thereafter. They may then be dried in kilns or, in warm sunny regions like California, on trays in the open air. In this country prunes are raised and prepared commercially on the Pacific Coast.

Cultivars of plums are many and one should know what class or group they belong to before planting. Some of the European plums such as 'Iroquois' and 'Stanley' are self-fruitful, that is, will produce fruit from their own pollen. The Japanese and hybrid types, on the other hand, and many European types, require another cultivar of the same type to supply the pollen to produce fruit. For example, two or more Japanese plums must be planted together to produce fruit, and some cultivars such as 'Formosa' produce poor pollen so that a minimum of three cultivars would be necessary to insure pollination when 'Formosa' is one of those involved. The hybrids are especially difficult to pollinate and it is sometimes necessary to provide a special pollination cultivar, such as 'North Dakota' (a *P. americana* cultivar), to insure a crop. The hexaploid plums (European) will not pollinate the diploid types (Japanese-American), so that one must be sure the type of plum involved will insure proper pollination.

It is recommended that the local experiment station or extension service be consulted to insure that trees suitable for a particular area and compatible for pollination purposes are planted.

European cultivars suitable for the fruit regions of the East Coast and Great Lakes area include, in order of ripening: 'Laxton Gage', 'De Montfort', 'Oullins', 'Mohawk', 'Seneca', 'Green Gage', 'Richards Early Italian', 'Iroquois', 'Stanley', 'Italian Prune', 'French Damson', 'Valor', and 'Oneida'. 'Stanley' and 'Italian Prune' are the main commercial cultivars in this area. Japanese plums for the same eastern area include 'Early Golden', 'Shiro', 'Formosa', 'Santa Rosa', 'Ozark Premier', 'Burbank', and 'Redheart'.

Important Japanese cultivars for the West Coast region include: 'Beauty', 'Burmosa', 'Formosa', 'Santa Rosa', 'Burbank', 'Duarte', 'Laroda', and 'Late Duarte'. European cultivars for the West Coast include: 'Tragedy', 'Early Italian', 'Standard', 'Grand Duke', and 'President', with 'Italian Prune', and 'Agen' in the cooler areas.

Recent introductions for the southern region include 'Crimson' and 'Purple' plums (hybrids of a parent of uncertain origin crossed with Japanese cultivars), which are disease resistant and may help extend plum culture to warmer areas where other types fail or are very difficult to grow successfully.

Pests and diseases can be a serious problem with the plum, especially plum curculio and brown rot. These can be controlled with methoxychlor for the curculio and Zineb or other fungicide for the brown rot fungus. Black knot is a fungus disease that causes black warty excrescences on the twigs and limbs and may cause serious damage. Control is to cut out and remove the affected parts as the disease appears, and to clean out any nearby sources of infection such as wild or abandoned trees or orchards. Spraying with Zineb in preblossom and blossom sprays and cover sprays helps control further spread. Detailed spraying instructions and timing should be obtained from a local agricultural extension service or experiment station.

PLUMBAGINACEAE Juss. PLUMBAGO or LEADWORT FAMILY. Dicot.; about 10 genera and 300 or more spp. of cosmopolitan shrubs or per. herbs, often of sea coasts or alpine, saline, or limestone locations; plants stemless and with a basal rosette of lvs., or with branched sts. and alt. lvs.; fls. in heads, spikes, or panicles, bisexual, regular, 5-merous, calyx tubular or funnelform, pleated, often scarious or colored, corolla tubular or sometimes with petals united only at base, stamens borne on corolla tube or opp. petals, ovary superior, 1-celled and with 1 ovule, styles 5, separate or united; fr. usually enclosed in calyx, dehiscent or indehiscent. The cult. genera are: *Acantholimon, Armeria, Ceratostigma, Goniolimon, Limonium, Plumbago,* and *Psylliostachys.*

PLUMBAGO L. LEADWORT. *Plumbaginaceae.* About 20 spp. of mostly trop. per. herbs or subshrubs, sometimes climbing; lvs. alt., simple, entire, sometimes auricled or clasping at base; fls. in terminal, spikelike racemes, calyx tubular,

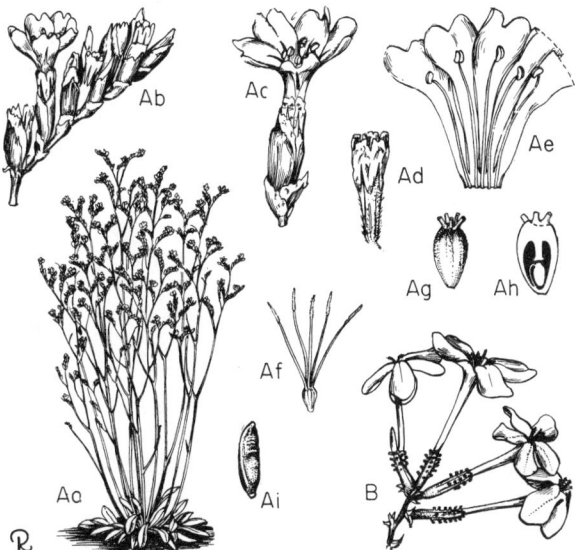

PLUMBAGINACEAE. **A,** *Limonium binervosum:* **Aa,** plant, × ⅙; **Ab,** spike (branch of inflorescence), × 2; **Ac,** spikelet, × 3; **Ad,** calyx, × 3; **Ae,** corolla, expanded, × 3; **Af,** pistil, × 3; **Ag,** ovary, × 8; **Ah,** ovary, vertical section, × 10; **Ai,** seed, × 5. **B,** *Plumbago auriculata:* flowers, × ½. (B from Bailey, *Manual of Cultivated Plants,* ed. 2.)

glandular, 5-ribbed, corolla tube slender, twice as long as calyx, lobes 5, spreading, stamens 5, free from corolla tube, ovary 1-celled; fr. a caps., splitting into 5 parts, 1-seeded.

Propagated by cuttings of nearly mature wood, by division, and by seeds.

auriculata Lam. [*P. capensis* Thunb.]. CAPE L. Evergreen shrub, sts. long, arching, semiscandent; lvs. oblong or oblong-spatulate, to 2 in. long, tapering to a short petiole; fls. blue or white, in short spikes, corolla to 1½ in. long. S. Afr. Cv. 'Alba'. Fls. white.

capensis: *P. auriculata.*

coccinea: *P. indica.*

Griffithii: a listed name, probably for *Ceratostigma Griffithii.*

indica L. [*P. coccinea* Salisb.; *P. rosea* L.]. Semiscandent, evergreen shrub; lvs. ovate-elliptic, to 4 in. long; fls. in long racemes, corolla red, tube about 1 in. long. Se. Asia.

Larpentiae: *Ceratostigma plumbaginoides.*

rosea: *P. indica.*

rubra: a listed name, probably referring to *P. indica.*

scandens L. Decumbent or scandent shrub; lvs. oblong to oblong-lanceolate, to 4 in. long, narrowed at base to a short petiole; fls. in spikes paniculately arranged, calyx glabrous except for conspicuous, stalked, glandular hairs, corolla to ¾ in. long, white or blue. Se. U.S. to Ariz., s. to W. Indies and n. S. Amer.

Willmottiae: a listed name, probably for *Ceratostigma Willmottiae.*

zeylanica L. Scandent, much-branched shrub, sts. angled; lvs. ovate to oblong, narrowed to short petiole; fls. white, in dense spikes. Se. Asia.

PLUMERIA L. FRANGIPANI, TEMPLE TREE. *Apocynaceae.* About eight spp. of deciduous trees and shrubs, with stout, weak brs. and abundant milky sap, native to trop. Amer.; lvs. alt., simple, entire; fls. large, showy, 5-merous, bisexual, in terminal thyrsiform clusters, usually when plants are leafless, calyx deeply cleft, lobes gland-tipped, corolla funnelform, lobes convolute in bud, stamens borne on the corolla, pistil with 2 half-inferior ovaries and a single spindle-shaped style; fr. a pair of leathery follicles, seeds with an eccentric, basal wing.

Widely grown in warm regions and in greenhouses as an ornamental and for the fragrance of the flowers. Propagated by cuttings in early spring.

acuminata: *P. rubra* forma *acutifolia.*

acutifolia: *P. rubra* forma.

alba L. Tree, to 40 ft.; lvs. oblong-lanceolate, to 1 ft. long, usually long-acuminate at apex, obtuse to rounded at base, without a well-

developed marginal connecting vein, usually densely pubescent beneath; corolla salverform, to 3 in. across, white with yellow center, tube to ⅞ in. long; follicles to 6 in. long. Puerto Rico and Lesser Antilles.

emarginata: *P. obtusa.*

obtusa L. [*P. emarginata* Griseb.]. Shrub or small tree, to 24 ft.; lvs. obovate to oblong-obovate, to 7 in. long, rounded or emarginate to short-acuminate, essentially glabrous, with well-developed marginal connecting vein, petioles ⅜–1½ in. long; corolla salverform, to 3 in. across, white with yellow center, tube to ¾ in. long; follicles to 9 in. long. Var. **obtusa.** The typical variety; glabrous throughout. Bahamas and Greater Antilles. Var. **sericifolia** (C. H. Wright) Woodson. Lower lf. surfaces, and often petioles and infl., rather conspicuously pubescent. Hispaniola, Cuba, Yucatan Pen.

pudica Jacq. Shrub or small tree, to 10 ft.; lvs. obovate-oblong, somewhat spoon-shaped or fiddle-shaped, to 1 ft. long, obtuse to short-acuminate at apex, cuneate, subsessile; corolla almost funnelform, to about 3 in. across, yellowish-white, tube 1 in. long, twice as wide at the throat as at the base; follicles 6–7 in. long. Colombia, Venezuela, Curaçao.

rubra L. NOSEGAY, FRANGIPANI. Tree, to 25 ft.; lvs. broadly elliptic to obovate or oblong-oblanceolate, to 20 in. long, obtuse to acuminate, with prominent marginal connecting vein, glabrous to densely pubescent beneath, petioles to 4¼ in. long; infls. rather open; corolla salverform, to 4½ in. across, white with yellow center to various shades of rose and yellow, tube to 1 in. long; follicles to 1 ft. long. Mex. to Panama. Much cult. Forma **rubra.** The typical form; corolla predominantly rose of varying intensity, usually with yellow center. Forma **acutifolia** (Poir.) Woodson [Var. *acutifolia* (Poir.) L. H. Bailey; *P. acutifolia* Poir.; *P. acuminata* Ait.]. PAGODA TREE. Corolla white, usually with yellow center, sometimes flushed rose. Forma **lutea** (Ruiz & Pav.) Woodson. Corolla predominantly yellow, sometimes flushed rose-pink on outside. Forma **tricolor** (Ruiz & Pav.) Woodson [*P. tricolor* Ruiz & Pav.]. Corolla usually white, generally with yellow center, margin of lobes rose.

tricolor: *P. rubra* forma.

POA L. BLUEGRASS, MEADOW GRASS, SPEAR G. *Gramineae.* About 250 spp. of slender ann. or usually per. grasses in temp. and cool regions of the world; lf. blades relatively narrow, flat, folded or involute, ending in a boat-shaped tip; infl. an open or contracted panicle; spikelets 2- to several-fld., small, rachilla disarticulating above the glumes and between the florets, the uppermost floret reduced or rudimentary, glumes acute, keeled, the first usually 1-nerved, the second usually 3-nerved, lemma awnless, usually keeled on the back, membranous, 5-nerved. For terminology see *Gramineae.*

Bluegrasses are palatable and nutritious forage plants, hence important in pastures and ranges; some are also cultivated for lawns.

ampla Merrill. BIG B. Per., sts. to 4 ft., green or glaucous; lf. sheaths smooth, rarely minutely scabrous, ligule short, rounded, lf. blades flat, to ⅛ in. wide; panicle narrow, to 6 in. long, usually rather dense; spikelets 4–7-fld., little compressed, longer than wide, to ⅜ in. long, lemma glabrous, to ¼ in. long. N. Dak. to Yukon, s. to Nebr. and Calif.

annua L. ANNUAL B., LOW S. G., SIX-WEEKS G., DWARF M. G. Ann., sts. clustered, flattened, bright green, erect to spreading, usually 2–10 in. high, forming mats; lf. blades soft, lax, mostly ¹⁄₁₆–⅛ in. wide; panicle pyramidal, open, to 2¾ in. long; spikelets 3–6-fld., crowded, compressed, ⅛ in. long, first glume to ⅛ in. long, the second slightly longer, lemma distinctly 5-nerved, with long hairs on the lower part of the keel. Eur.; introd. and naturalized from Nfld. to Alaska, s. to Fla. and Calif., trop. Amer. at high altitudes. Sometimes a troublesome weed.

arachnifera Torr. TEXAS B. Per., dioecious, rhizomatous, sts. cylindrical, clustered, to 2½ ft. high; lf. blades to ⅛ in. wide, scabrous above; panicle oblong, to 4¾ in. long; spikelets mostly 5–10-fld., compressed, female conspicuously webbed, male essentially glabrous, lemma ¼ in. long. S. Kans. to Tex. and Ark.; introd. eastward to N.C. and Fla., also Idaho. Sometimes cult. for winter pasture and as a lawn grass.

bulbosa L. BULBOUS B. Per., sts. to 2 ft., densely clustered, more or less bulbous at base; lf. blades flat or loosely involute, less than ⅛ in. wide; panicle ovoid, to 3¼ in. long, somewhat contracted, brs. ascending or appressed; spikelets mostly proliferous, some florets converted to bulblets with a dark purple base, unaltered spikelets about 5-fld., compressed, lemma less than ⅛ in. long, webbed at base; seed usually not produced. Eurasia, N. Afr.; introd. and naturalized, N.Y. to N.C., N. Dak. to B.C. and Calif., Colo. and Okla.

compressa L. CANADA B., WIRE GRASS. Per., rhizomatous, sts. to 2½ ft., strongly flattened, solitary or few together, often gregarious, bluish-green; lf. blades mostly rather short, ¹⁄₁₆–⅛ in. wide; panicle narrow, to 4 in. long, brs. usually short, in pairs, spikelet-bearing to the base; spikelets 3–6-fld., crowded, compressed, to ¼ in. long, glumes, keeled, to ⅛ in. long, lemma firm, same size as the glumes, keeled, the web at base scant or absent. Eurasia, N. Afr.; introd. and naturalized from Nfld. to Alaska, s. to Ga., Okla., New Mex., and Calif. Cult. for pasture in the ne. states and Canada.

nemoralis L. [*Agrostis alba* L.]. WOOD B. Per., sts. clustered, to 2½ ft.; lf. blades rather lax, less than ⅛ in. wide, ligules very short; panicle to 4 in. long, brs. spreading; spikelets 2–5-fld., compressed, to ¼ in. long, glumes narrow, sharply acuminate, about as long as the first floret, lemma to ⅛ in. long, sparsely webbed at base. Eurasia, N. Afr.; introd. and naturalized from Me. to Va. and Mich. to Wash.

pratensis L. KENTUCKY B., JUNE GRASS, SPEAR G. Per., rhizomatous, sts. to 3½ ft., clustered, erect, slightly compressed, glabrous; lf. sheaths glabrous, ligule ³⁄₃₂ in. long, blades soft, flat or folded, mostly ⅛ in. wide or less; panicle pyramidal or open-pyramidal, lower brs. in whorls of usually 5; spikelets 3–5-fld., crowded, compressed, to ¼ in. long, lemmas webbed at base, with keel and marginal nerves, pubescent in lower part. Eurasia, N. Afr.; introd. and naturalized in all the states. Commonly cult. for lawns and pasture in the humid n. regions where soils are limy.

rostrata: a listed name of no botanical standing.

secunda J. Presl. & K. Presl. Not cult., but the name sometimes used for *P. Sandbergii.*

Sandbergii Vasey. SANDBERG B. Per., sts. to 2 ft., erect from a dense, often extensive clump of short basal foliage; lf. blades short, soft, flat, folded or involute, ligule acute, rather prominent; panicle narrow, 3–4 in. long, brs. short; spikelets 3–5-fld., to ¼ in. long, lemma convex and obscurely keeled, crisp-puberulent toward base. Yukon to N. Dak., s. to Calif., New Mex., and Nebr. Has been misidentified as *P. secunda* of Chile.

trivialis L. ROUGH B., ROUGH-STALK B., ROUGH-STALKED M. G. Per., sts. to 3½ ft., erect from a decumbent base, scabrous below the panicle; lf. sheaths retrorsely scabrous, at least toward the summit, blades scabrous, to ⅛ in. wide; panicle oblong, 2¼ in. long; spikelets usually 2–3-fld., compressed, ⅛ in. long, lemma with a conspicuous web at base, nerves prominent. Eurasia, N. Afr.; introd. and naturalized from Nfld. to s. Alaska, s. to n. Calif. and N.C. Cult. in mixtures for meadows and pastures.

violacea Bellardi. Per., sts. to 16 in.; lf. blades involute, stiffly erect; panicle usually tinged with purple, oblong, brs. with 1–5 spikelets; spikelets 3–5-fld., lemma acute, 5-nerved, membranous at the apex and terminated by a point, callus webbed. Eurasia.

POACEAE: see *Gramineae.*

PODACHAENIUM Benth. *Compositae* (Helianthus Tribe). Two spp. of shrubs, native from s. Mex. to n. S. Amer.; lvs. opp., simple; fl. heads radiate, in terminal corymbs, involucral bracts in 2–3 rows, receptacle convex to conical, scaly; disc fls. bisexual, yellow, ray fls. female, fertile, white; achenes obovoid, stalked, 3-angled, pappus of scales.

Grown outdoors in southern Calif., but not hardy outside Zone 10.

eminens (Lag.) Schultz-Bip. Shrub, to 25 ft., sts. gray-tomentose; lf. blades ovate to nearly orbicular, to 9 in. long, rather membranous, finely scabrous above, gray-hairy beneath, margins nearly entire, toothed, or with 5–7 shallow lobes, petioles to 5 in. long; heads to 1 in. across. S. Mex., Cent. Amer.

PODALYRIA Lam. ex Willd. *Leguminosae* (subfamily *Faboideae)*. About 20 spp. or more of shrubs, native to S. Afr.; lvs. alt., simple; infl. few-fld., on axillary peduncles; fls. purple to rose or whitish, papilionaceous, stamens separate or scarcely united basally; fr. a leathery, swollen, pubescent legume.

calyptrata Willd. Vigorous shrub, to 9 ft.; lvs. obovate-elliptic, to 2 in. long, obtuse, green, finely pubescent; fl. bracts very wide, united into a cap over the buds, early deciduous; petals pink, standard to ¾ in. long; fr. a woolly legume, to 1½ in. long, ⅝ in. wide.

sericea R. Br. Silvery shrub, usually about 2 ft., silky-hairy throughout, sts. sometimes procumbent; lvs. oblong, cuneate, longer than 1 in.; fls. solitary, pink, standard about ⅜ in. long, with purple blotch toward center; fr. cylindrical, about 1 in. long.

PODOCARPACEAE Endl. PODOCARPUS FAMILY. Gymnosperms; 7 genera and about 100 spp. of evergreen, coniferous, dioecious, rarely monoecious, resinous trees, native principally to the S. Hemisphere; lvs. usually alt., scalelike to linear or broadly oblong; male cones catkinlike, with many

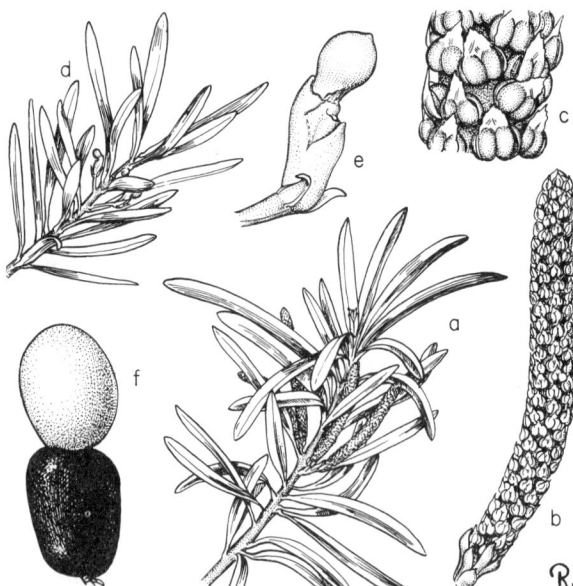

PODOCARPACEAE. *Podocarpus macrophyllus:* **a**, branch of male plant, with cones, × ½; **b**, male cone, × 1½; **c**, segment of male cone, showing sporangia, × 5; **d**, branch of female plant, with cones, × ½; **e**, female cone, × 3; **f**, seed (above) and aril (below), × 1½.

bracts, each bract bearing 2 sporangia, female cones with few bracts, usually only 1 seed maturing; seeds drupelike, surrounded or subtended by a fleshy aril or stalk. Once united with the Taxaceae. *Dacrydium, Microcachrys, Phyllocladus, Podocarpus,* and *Saxegothaea* are cult.

Includes a number of important timber species of the S. Hemisphere. Grown as ornamentals in southern and western U.S., or rarely in the greenhouse.

PODOCARPUS L'Hér. ex Pers. *Podocarpaceae.* About 75 spp. of mostly dioecious, coniferous trees and shrubs, native to the temp. S. Hemisphere and to mts. and highlands of the tropics, n. to the W. Indies and Japan; lvs. flat, mostly spirally arranged, usually narrow but sometimes broad, persistent; male cones yellow, catkinlike, female cones mostly of 2–4 scales, usually only 1 or 2 ovules and a seed; seeds drupelike, often on fleshy red or purple receptacle.

Some species of *Podocarpus* produce valuable timber and many are ornamentals. Most species may be grown outdoors in Zone 9 or under glass as tub plants. For culture see *Conifers.*

acutifolius T. Kirk. Much-branched shrub, to 10 ft. or more; lvs. linear, to 1 in. long, thin, almost spinescently acute; fr. to nearly ⅜ in. long, on fleshy red receptacle. New Zeal. Zone 9.

alpinus R. Br. ex Hook.f. Densely branched shrub, to 12 ft.; lvs. crowded, linear-spatulate, to ½ in. long, pale beneath, obtuse; fr. bright red. Tasmania, Australia. Zone 8.

andinus Poepp. ex Endl. PLUM FIR. To 45 ft., but often shrubby in cult.; lvs. more or less 2-ranked, linear, to 1 in. long, bright green above, with 2 glaucous bands beneath, mostly abruptly mucronulate or obtuse; fr. yellowish-white. Chile. Zone 8. Some of the material offered under this name may be *P. salignus.*

chilinus: *P. salignus.*

chinensis: *P. macrophyllus* var. *Maki.*

coriaceus L. Rich. To 60 ft. or more; lvs. crowded, linear-lanceolate, straight or curved, 3–7 in. long, ¾ in. wide, long-acuminate, leathery. Puerto Rico to Trinidad. Zone 10b.

Cowgillii: a listed name of no botanical standing.

dacrydioides A. Rich. KAHIKA, WHITE PINE, RED P. To 100 ft. or more; lvs. overlapping and spreading, awl-shaped, apiculate, on young trees to ⅜ in. long, often reddish, with green tinge, on mature trees scalelike. New Zeal. Zone 9b. Valuable timber tree.

elatus R. Br. ex Endl. To 90 ft., brs. solitary or in whorls; lvs. leathery, linear-lanceolate, straight or curved, 2–4½ in. long, often mucronate, light green and glossy above; fr. globose, about ½ in. in diam.

Australia. Zone 10. Produces a durable wood. Has been cult. under the names *P. macrophyllus, P. neriifolius,* and others.

elongatus (Ait.) L'Hér. ex Pers. AFRICAN YELLOWWOOD, FERN P., WEEPING P. To 70 ft., twigs brown; lvs. linear-lanceolate, mostly 3 in. long and more, ⅛ in. wide, thin, pointed. S. and trop. Afr. Zone 9. Useful for railroad ties, furniture, and for planks. Most, perhaps all, of the material cult. under this name is *P. gracilior.*

falcatus (Thunb.) R. Br. ex Mirb. To 100 ft.; lvs. spirally arranged or subopp., linear, 2 in. long; fr. glaucous-green, globose, to ½ in. in diam. S. Afr. Zone 10. Yields valuable timber.

ferrugineus D. Don. MIRO. To 80 ft.; lvs. 2-ranked, crowded, linear, to ¾ in. long, long-acute; fr. to ¾ in. long, reddish-purple, glaucous. New Zeal. Zone 9. Yields a medicinal gum and a valuable timber.

gracilior Pilg. AFRICAN FERN PINE. To 75 ft., twigs green, bark thin and flaky; lvs. linear-lanceolate, to 4 in. long, ¼ in. wide, often with apiculate black tip; fr. ⅝ in. long, glaucous-blue. E. Afr. Zone 10. A valuable timber tree. This sp. is commonly, but erroneously, grown as *P. elongatus* in Calif.

Hallii T. Kirk [*P. Totara* var. *Hallii* (T. Kirk) Pilg.]. To 60 ft.; lvs. linear-lanceolate, to 1¼ in. long, leathery, glaucous beneath, with spinescent tip; fr. red, to ⅛ in. long. New Zeal. Zone 9.

Henkelii Stapf ex Dallim. & A. B. Jacks. Tree with pendent brs.; lvs. on mature trees 2–7 in. long, drooping, attenuate and often curved; fr. globose, ⅜ in. in diam., glaucous, green. S. Afr. Zone 10.

latifolius (Thunb.) R. Br. ex Mirb. To 100 ft., bark shreading in long strips, brs. stiff, erect; lvs. rigid, oblong to lanceolate, 1–2 in. long; fr. globose, to ⅜ in. in diam., glaucous, green. S. Afr. Zone 10.

longifolius: *P. macrophyllus.*

macrophyllus (Thunb.) D. Don [*P. longifolius* Salisb.]. SOUTHERN YEW, JAPANESE Y., BUDDHIST PINE. To 45 ft.; lvs. linear-lanceolate, 2–4½ in. long, to ⅜ in. wide, glossy dark green above, paler beneath. Cent. and sw. Japan. Zone 8. Var. **macrophyllus.** The typical var.; brs. horizontal, twigs crowded, leafy; lvs. 3–4 in. long, about ⅜ in. wide. Var. **angustifolius** Blume. Narrow tree, new shoots light green or yellow-green; lvs. abundant, 2–4½ in. long, sometimes curved, cuneate at base, long-tapering at apex; fr. bluish, about ⅜ in. long, on peduncles to ⅝ in. long. Var. **appressus** (Maxim.) Matsum. Low shrub, with short lvs. Var. **Maki** Endl. [*P. chinensis* Wallich ex Endl.; *P. sinensis* Hort.]. Brs. more erect than in var. *angustifolius,* twigs densely leafy; lvs. 1½–3 in. long, to ¼ in. wide, straight, obtuse or abruptly narrowed at tip. China; much cult. in Japan and elsewhere.

Nagi (Thunb.) Zoll. & Moritzi ex Mak. BROADLEAF P. To 90 ft.; lvs. elliptic to ovate, 2–3 in. long and mostly ⅝–1 in. wide, like those of *Agathis,* pale beneath; fr. globose, to ½ in. in diam., glaucous. Cent. and sw. Japan, Ryukyu Is. Zone 9.

neriifolius D. Don. To 70 ft. or more; lvs. lanceolate, to 6 in. long, leathery, slightly glaucous beneath, midrib raised on both surfaces; fr. ellipsoid, to ½ in. long. China to New Guinea. Zone 10.

nivalis Hook. Much-branched shrub, to 6 ft.; lvs. to ¾ in. long, leathery, with thickened margins, obtuse; receptacle fleshy, red. New Zeal. Zone 9.

Reasoneri: a listed name of no botanical standing.

salignus D. Don [*P. chilinus* L. Rich.]. To 60 ft., brs. slender, drooping; lvs. linear-lanceolate, often curved, 2½–5 in. long, about ¼ in. wide, blue-green above and pale beneath; fr. to ⅜ in. long. Chile. Zone 10 in Calif.

sinensis: *P. macrophyllus* var. *Maki.*

Totara D. Don. TOTARA PINE, MAHOGANY P. To 100 ft., bark silvery-gray; lvs. linear, oblong, to 1 in. long, apiculately acute, dull green, leathery; fr. red, about ½ in. long. New Zeal. Zone 9. A valuable timber tree. Sometimes, but not originally, spelled "Totarra." Var. **Hallii:** *P. Hallii.*

tropicana: a listed name of no botanical standing.

PODOLEPIS Labill. *Compositae* (Inula Tribe). About 15 spp. of ann. or per. herbs, native to Australia and Tasmania; lvs. alt., often clasping; fl. heads radiate, usually solitary and peduncled, rarely clustered, involucre usually hemispherical, rarely ovoid, involucral bracts in several rows, scarious, not radiating, receptacle flat, naked; disc fls. tubular, bisexual, anthers tailed, ray fls. female, yellow, pink, or purple; achenes usually cylindrical, pappus of capillary bristles often united at base.

Grown as everlastings, thriving in sunlight in porous soil. Propagated by seeds sown under glass in Apr. or outdoors when the soil is in proper condition.

acuminata: *P. jaceoides.*

jaceoides (Sims) Voss [*P. acuminata* Ait.f.]. Erect per., to 2½ ft., sts. scapelike; basal lvs. linear to oblanceolate, to 8 in. long, upper lvs. lanceolate or linear, sessile, clasping, decurrent; heads to 1¼ in. across, solitary or 2–8 in a cluster; fls. yellow. E. Australia, Tasmania.

robusta (Maiden & Betche) Willis. Robust per., to 2 ft., sts. unbranched, scapelike, white-woolly; basal lvs. spatulate, to 8 in. long, glabrous, margins often crinkled, st. lvs. broadly linear, to 5¾ in. long, clasping and decurrent; heads to 1 in. across, 6–11 in a dense cluster; fls. yellow. Mts., e. Australia.

PODOPHYLLUM L. *Berberidaceae.* Two or perhaps more spp. of rhizomatous per. herbs, native to N. Amer. and Asia; radical lvs. large, peltate, solitary, lobed, those on fl. sts. paired, palmately lobed; fl. solitary in fork between lvs., waxy, sepals 6, petals 6 or 9, stamens as many as or twice as many as petals; fr. a fleshy, ellipsoid berry.

Useful for shady places in the wild garden. The drug podophyllum is obtained from the rhizomes of both species. Propagated by division and seeds.

emodi: *P. hexandrum.*

hexandrum Royle [*P. emodi* Wallich ex Hook.f. & T. Thoms.]. HIMALAYAN MAYAPPLE. To 1½ ft.; lvs. to 10 in. across, deeply 3–5-lobed, often purplish-brown-spotted; fls. to 2 in. across, white or pinkish, stamens usually 6; fr. red, to 2 in. across, pulp edible. Himalayas. Cv. 'Majus'. Fls. pink.

peltatum L. MAYAPPLE, MANDRAKE, WILD LEMON, RACCOON BERRY, WILD JALAP. To 1½ ft.; lvs. to 1 ft. across, 5–9-lobed; fls. 2 in. across and more, white, stamens 12–18; fr. yellowish or rarely red, 2 in. long, pulp edible. Que. to Fla. and Tex.

PODRANEA T. Sprague. *Bignoniaceae.* Two spp. of climbing shrubs, native to trop. and s. Afr.; similar to *Pandorea;* lvs. opp., odd-pinnate; fls. pink or lilac, in terminal panicles, calyx 5-lobed, inflated, corolla funnelform or campanulate above, narrowed below, slightly 2-lipped, stamens 4, ovary oblong; fr. a linear, leathery caps., to 1 ft. long or more.

See *Pandorea* for cultivation.

Brycei (N. E. Br.) T. Sprague [*Pandorea Brycei* (N. E. Br.) Rehd.; *Tecoma Brycei* N. E. Br.; *T. Reginae-Sabae* Franceschi]. QUEEN-OF-SHEBA VINE. Lfts. 9–11, lanceolate to ovate, to 2 in. long; fls. in many-fld. panicles, corolla 1½ in. long and 2 in. across, abruptly campanulate in the upper part, pale pink marked with red, throat yellow. Rhodesia.

Ricasoliana (Tanfani) T. Sprague [*Pandorea Ricasoliana* (Tanfani) Baill.; *Tecoma Mackenii* W. Wats.; *T. Ricasoliana* Tanfani]. PINK TRUMPET VINE. Lfts. 7–9, ovate, to 2 in. long; fls. in loose panicles, corolla pale pink, striped with red, funnelform, 2 in. long. S. Afr.

POGONIA Juss. *Orchidaceae.* Ten spp. of erect, terrestrial herbs, native to temp. Asia and N. Amer.; sts. with 1 lf. at about middle, 1–3-fld. at apex; perianth parts separate, lip bearded, column separate, coarsely toothed at apex. For structure of fl. see *Orchidaceae.*

Planted in the wild garden in shady or moist situations. For culture see *Orchids.*

divaricata: *Cleistes divaricata.*

ophioglossoides (L.) Ker.-Gawl. ROSE P., ADDER'S-TONGUE-LEAVED P., BEARDFLOWER, SNAKE-MOUTH, ADDER'S-MOUTH, ETTERCAP, CRESTED E., ROSE CREST-LIP. Sts. to about 2½ ft. high, green or brownish-green; lf. ovate, to 5 in. long; fls. rose to white, fragrant, sepals and petals oblong-elliptic, to 1 in. long, lip oblong-spatulate, 1 in. long, lacerate-toothed apically, prominently bearded with short, fleshy, yellow-white bristles along the 3 central veins of disc. Early spring–late summer. Canada and U.S.

verticillata: *Isotria verticillata.*

POGONOPUS Klotzsch. *Rubiaceae.* About 3 spp. of trees or shrubs, native to Cent. and S. Amer.; lvs. opp., membranous, large, stipules interpetiolar, deciduous; fls. in terminal panicles, showy, 5-merous, calyx lobes unequal, one often expanded, leaflike, large, brightly colored, corolla tubular, anthers exserted; fr. a caps., seeds many.

speciosus (Jacq.) K. Schum. Shrub or tree, to 30 ft.; lvs. obovate to elliptic-obovate, to 8 in. long, more or less pubescent beneath; enlarged calyx lobe purple-red, rounded-ovate, to 2 in. long; caps. to ¼ in. long. Cent. Amer. Showy in fl. because of the brightly colored, enlarged calyx lobe.

POINCIANA: *CAESALPINIA.* **P. elata:** *Delonix elata.* **P. regia:** *D. regia.*

POINSETTIA: *EUPHORBIA.*

POISONOUS PLANTS. Ornamental plants are cultivated for beauty, not to be eaten. Yet everyone who grows ornamentals, wherever he lives, should be aware that many species, often very familiar ones planted as horticultural subjects, contain poisonous compounds that may be deadly if parts of the plants are eaten. One or two castor bean *(Ricinus)* seeds or a single seed of the attractive precatory bean *(Abrus)*, if chewed and swallowed, can kill a child. Although poisons are to be found throughout the whole range of cultivated and wild plants, they are especially prevalent in members of certain plant families such as the Euphorbiaceae, Ranunculaceae, and Solanaceae. Poisons may be distributed throughout all plant parts or they may be concentrated in one organ, as in the rootstock *(Iris)*, foliage *(Nerium Oleander)*, or fruit *(Daphne)*.

Such a specific distribution in the plant makes it possible for us to eat the innocuous petioles of rhubarb *(Rheum)* but not the poisonous leaf blades. Some plant parts that are edible when cooked may be poisonous when raw, like the roots of certain kinds of cassava *(Manihot)*, a staple food in the tropics, in which the poison is dispelled by cooking.

More familiar species like poison ivy *(Rhus)* and nettles *(Urtica)* are sometimes occasional weeds in horticultural plantings. They may induce allergenic reactions when brought in contact with human skin. Some cultivated plants produce similar reactions. They are exemplified by the spurges *(Euphorbia* species) and some of the aroids, like dumbcane *(Dieffenbachia)*, with acrid, often milky juice, one of the primroses *(Primula obconica)* with soft irritating hairs, and tropical relatives of poison ivy like the mango *(Mangifera)* and cashew *(Anacardium)*, whose fresh fruits sometimes produce similar skin rashes on persons especially sensitive to such poisoning.

Much more serious are the poisons in many other common garden plants. Horticultural plant materials of poisonous nature are the bulbs (in *Colchicum, Galanthus, Hyacinthus, Narcissus, Ornithogalum*) or rhizomes (in *Convallaria*) of many ornamentals, seeds of popular fruits (in *Malus, Prunus)*, and foliage or other parts of plants in such genera as *Abrus, Aconitum, Aleurites, Atropa, Buxus, Celastrus, Daphne, Datura, Delphinium, Dicentra, Digitalis, Hypericum, Hyoscyamus, Iris, Kalmia, Leucothoe, Ligustrum, Lupinus, Nerium, Pieris, Rhododendron, Ricinus, Solanum, Taxus,* and *Wisteria.*

Most poisons in these plants can act only if ingested, and the seriousness depends upon the amount eaten—an adult must eat proportionately much more than a child to be similarly affected. Prevention of poisoning is the best approach to the problem of poisonous plants. Since children are the usual victims, the rule to observe and enforce in all families is: "Don't put into your mouth any plant or plant part that is not good, wholesome food." If poisoning is suspected, a physician should be called immediately. The best defense is knowledge. Get to know the horticultural plants that have poisonous properties—by scientific names, if possible, to avoid the confusion inherent in common names—and keep younger children away from them, at the same time educating all others to the hazards of tasting or eating these or any unidentified plants.

POLANISIA Raf. *Capparaceae.* Six spp. of coarse, weedy, ann. herbs of temp. N. Amer., related to the Old World spp. of *Cleome* but having a relatively massive, truncate gland at base of ovary, petals notched to laciniate, and caps. erect and nearly sessile. The 2 spp. below sometimes grown under the names *Cleome gigantea* and *C. grandis.*

trachysperma Torr. & A. Gray [*Cleome trachysperma* (Torr. & A. Gray) Pax & K. Hoffm.]. To 2 ft., clammy-viscid, with strong odor; lfts. 3, about 1 in. long; fls. in bracted racemes, petals white, to ½ in. long, narrow, notched at apex, stamens 10–16, purplish, unequal, to ½ in. long, gland orange, style deciduous, slender; caps. narrow, dehiscing at the top. Intergrading with the next sp. Cent. U.S., s. to Tex.

and New Mex. Grown from seeds sown where plants are to stand; reseeds and is hardy.

uniglandulosa (Cav.) DC. [*Cleome uniglandulosa* Cav.]. Very similar to *P. trachysperma*, but fls. and fr. larger, petals to 1½ in. long, stamens as many as 22, to 1¾ in. long. Tex. and Ariz., s. to cent. Mex.

POLASKIA: *LEMAIREOCEREUS.*

POLEMONIACEAE. **A,** *Phlox Drummondii:* **Aa,** flowering branch, × ¼; **Ab,** flower, side and face views, × ½; **Ac,** pistil and expanded corolla, × 1; **Ad,** pistil, × 4; **Ae,** ovary, vertical section, × 10; **Af,** ovary, cross section, × 10; **Ag,** fruit, × 1. **B,** *Cobaea scandens:* **Ba,** plant, × ¹⁄₁₂; **Bb,** flower, × ⅓; **Bc,** flower, vertical section, × ⅓; **Bd,** ovary, cross section, × 2; **Be,** fruit, × ¼.

POLEMONIACEAE Juss. PHLOX FAMILY. Dicot.; 18 genera and about 316 spp. of mostly ann. or per. herbs, rarely shrubs, vines, or trees, native chiefly to N. Amer. but extending into Eur., Asia, and S. Amer.; lvs. alt. or opp., simple or compound; fls. bisexual, mostly regular, terminal or axillary, solitary or in cymose clusters, panicled cymes, or dense heads, calyx and corolla 5-lobed, stamens 5, equally or unequally inserted, pistil 1, ovary superior, usually 3-celled, style 1, stigma 3-lobed; fr. a caps. The family includes many ornamentals, as: *Cantua, Cobaea, Collomia, Eriastrum, Gilia, Ipomopsis, Langloisia, Leptodactylon, Linanthus, Navarretia, Phlox,* and *Polemonium.*

POLEMONIUM L. JACOB'S-LADDER, GREEK VALERIAN. *Polemoniaceae.* Between 20 and 25 spp. of decumbent, ann. or rhizomatous per. herbs, native to Eur., Asia, S. Amer., and N. Amer., but chiefly to w. N. Amer.; lvs. alt., pinnate; fls. blue, purple, yellow, or white, solitary to capitate, in terminal or axillary cymes, calyx 5-lobed, enlarging with the fr. but not rupturing, corolla campanulate to funnelform, stamens equal, regularly inserted; fr. a 3-celled caps.

Grown in the flower garden or border. Of easy cultivation in rich loam. Propagated by division or seeds sown in autumn.

acutiflorum: *P. caeruleum* subsp. *villosum.*

album: material offered under this name may be cvs. of *P. boreale, P. carneum,* or *P. reptans.*

boreale Adams [*P. humile* Willd. ex Roem. & Schult., not Salisb.; *P. lanatum* Pall.; *P. Richardsonii* R. C. Grah.]. Per., to 9 in., sts. villoushairy; lvs. mostly basal, lfts. 13–23, elliptic to nearly orbicular; fls. blue to purplish, ½ in. across, on pedicels shorter than calyx. Summer. Circumboreal. Cv. '**Album**'. Fls. white.

caeruleum L. [*P. sibiricum* D. Don]. JACOB'S-LADDER, GREEK VALERIAN, CHARITY. Per., to 3 ft.; lfts. 19–27, lanceolate to elliptic, terminal lft. distinct; fls. blue, to 1 in. across, stamens longer than corolla; seeds not mucilaginous when moistened. Late spring, summer. Eur., Asia. Material grown as *P. cashmirianum* belongs here. Var. **album** Hort.: var. *lacteum*. Var. **gracile** is listed. Var. **grandiflorum:** var. *himalayanum*. Var. **himalayanum** Bak. [var. *grandiflorum* Manning; *P. himalayanum* Hort.]. Fls. lilac-blue, to 1½ in. across. Var. **lacteum** (Lehm.) Benth. [var. *album* Hort.]. Fls. white. Var. **tanguticum:** probably not distinct from var. *lacteum*. Subsp. **amygdalinum** (Wherry) Munz [*P. caeruleum* subsp. *occidentale* (Greene) J. F. Davids.; *P. occidentale* Greene]. Infl. erect; stamens shorter than corolla, style long-exserted. Alaska, s. to Colo. and Calif. Subsp. **Van-Bruntiae** (Britt.) J. F. Davids. [*P. Van-Bruntiae* Britt.]. Stamens and styles long-exserted. Vt. to Md. Subsp. **villosum** (J. H. Rudolph ex Georgi) Brand [*P. acutiflorum* Willd. ex Roem. & Schult.; *P. villosum* J. H. Rudolph ex Georgi]. St. lvs. smaller; corolla lobes ciliate. B.C. and Alaska, through Siberia to Finland.

californicum Eastw. Glandular-pubescent per., to 1 ft., sts. solitary or clustered; lvs. mostly basal, lfts. 11–23, ovate, lanceolate, or oblong; fls. blue, white, or yellow, to ⅝ in. across. Late spring–summer. Wash. to Calif., e. to Mont.

carneum A. Gray. Per., to 2½ ft.; lvs. mostly cauline, lfts. 13–21, ovate to oblong-lanceolate, to 1½ in. long; fls. salmon, fading purplish, to 1½ in. across. Spring–autumn. Ore. and Calif. Cv. '**Album**'. Fls. white.

cashmirianum: a listed name of no botanical standing; material offered under this name is probably *P. caeruleum*.

confertum: *P. viscosum*.

elegans Greene. Dwarf, cespitose per., to 6 in.; lvs. mostly basal; lfts. many, crowded, obovate to orbicular, very small, glandular-pubescent; fls. in a subcapitate cyme, corolla blue with yellow throat, about ½ in. long. Summer. Mts., Wash. and Ore.

filicinum: *P. foliosissimum*.

flavum Greene. Per., to 3 ft.; lfts. ovate- to oblong-lanceolate; fls. tawny-red outside, yellow inside, about 1 in. across, corolla lobes acuminate. Summer. Ariz. and sw. New Mex.

foliosissimum A. Gray [*P. filicinum* Greene]. Per., to 2½ ft.; lvs. mostly cauline, lfts. 11–25, elliptic to narrowly lanceolate, 5 apical lfts. commonly confluent; fls. white, cream, violet, or blue, ⅝ in. across; seeds mucilaginous when moistened. Summer. Idaho and Wyo., s. to Ariz. and New Mex.

Haydenii: *P. pulcherrimum*.

himalayanum: see *P. caeruleum* var.

humile: see *P. boreale* and *P. reptans*.

lanatum: *P. boreale*.

Lindleyi: *P. pulcherrimum*.

mexicanum Cerv. ex Lag. Erect per., to 2 ft.; lvs. mostly cauline, lfts. ovate to elliptic; corolla blue, to ½ in. across, slightly longer than calyx. Summer. Mex.

occidentale: *P. caeruleum* subsp. *amygdalinum*.

pauciflorum S. Wats. Glandular-pubescent per., to 2 ft., sometimes ann. in cult.; lvs. mostly cauline, lfts. 11–25, lanceolate, to 1 in. long; corolla funnelform, almost tubular, yellow, tinged red, to 1½ in. long. Summer. Tex., Ariz., Mex.

pulcherrimum Hook. [*P. Haydenii* A. Nels.; *P. Lindleyi* Wherry]. Per., to 1 ft., becoming cespitose; lvs. mostly basal, lfts. 11–23, ovate to orbicular or elliptic, to ¾ in. long; corolla blue, with yellowish tube, 5/16 in. long. Summer. Mts., Alaska to Calif., Nev., Wyo.

reptans L. [*P. humile* Salisb.]. Tufted per., to 2 ft.; lfts. 7–19, ovate to lanceolate, to 2 in. long; fls. blue, to ¾ in. long; fr. stipitate. Spring–summer. New Hamp. to Ga., w. to Minn., Okla., Ala. Cv. '**Album**'. Fls. white.

Richardsonii: *P. boreale*.

sibiricum: *P. caeruleum*.

Van-Bruntiae: *P. caeruleum* subsp.

vera nana: a listed name of no botanical standing.

villosum: *P. caeruleum* subsp.

viscosum Nutt. [*P. confertum* A. Gray]. Ill-scented, glandular-pubescent per., to 1 ft.; lvs. mostly basal, lfts. 3–5-parted, seeming verticillate, to ⅜ in. long; fls. blue, sometimes white, to ¾ in. long, corolla lobes shorter than tube. Summer. Mts., B.C. to Mont., s. to n. Ariz. and New Mex.

POLIANTHES L. [*Bravoa* Llave & Lex.]. *Agavaceae.* About 12 spp. of per. herbs of Mex., with usually elongate, bulblike bases, often from a short, thick rhizome with thickened roots; lvs. grasslike, mostly basal; infl. a terminal raceme or spike; fls. red or white, mostly in pairs, the tube bent near base or middle, lobes 6, stamens 6, ovary inferior, 3-celled; fr. a caps.

One species widely grown commercially as a cut flower and in southern France as a source of perfume. Rhizomes should be set out early in June and covered with about 1 in. or more of fine light soil. They should be dug before frost and stored over winter in a dry warm place. Tuberoses are summer and autumn bloomers; they may be forced for bloom in Apr. to June by starting them in Jan. and keeping them at a temperature of 75°–80° F. The bulbs may also be retarded in a cool dry place and forced for Nov. bloom.

geminiflora (Llave & Lex.) Rose [*Bravoa geminiflora* Llave & Lex.]. To 2 ft. or more; lvs. to ½ in. wide, 20 in. long, st. lvs. shorter; fls. red or orange, to ¾ in. long, strongly bent downward near base. Mex.

tuberosa L. TUBEROSE. To 3½ ft.; lvs. to 1½ ft. long, ½ in. wide, st. lvs. clasping and successively smaller; fls. waxy-white, very fragrant, 2½ in. long. Unknown in the wild. A double-fld. form is most frequently grown.

POLIOTHYRSIS D. Oliver. *Flacourtiaceae.* One sp., a monoecious, deciduous tree, native to cent. China; fls. in terminal panicles, sepals 5, petals none, stamens many; fr. a caps., seeds many, winged.

Propagated by seeds, greenwood cuttings, or by roots.

sinensis D. Oliver. To 40 ft.; lvs. ovate, acuminate, to 7 in. long, toothed, 3–5-nerved at base; caps. oblong-ovoid, ¾ in. long.

POLYALTHIA Blume. *Annonaceae.* Over 100 spp. of trees and shrubs, native to Old World tropics; lvs. alt., simple; fls. axillary, bisexual, 3-merous, petals 6, often large and showy, valvate in 2 series, stamens and pistils many; frs. several on a receptacle, each with 1–2, rarely to 5, seeds.

cerasoides Benth. & Hook.f. ex Hook.f. Tree, young branchlets tomentose; lvs. membranous, lanceolate or oblong-lanceolate, acuminate, softly pubescent beneath, to 8 in. long, 1–2 in. wide; peduncles 1–3-fld., on axillary tubercles; petals ovate-oblong, ½ in. long, thick-leathery, greenish; fr. small, dark red, on 1-in. stalks. India.

suberosa (Roxb.) Thwaites. Shrub, to 6 ft., bark with corky ridges; lvs. thin, oblong or oblong-lanceolate, to 5 in. long, obtuse at both ends; fls. mostly solitary, opp. the lvs., on pedicels to 1 in. long, fragrant, petals reddish-brown, to ½ in. long, silky outside; fr. stalked, globose, glabrous, to ⅜ in. long. India and Ceylon to Malay Pen.

POLYANDROCOCOS Barb.-Rodr. *Palmae.* One sp., a solitary, unarmed, monoecious palm in Brazil; lvs. pinnate, sheath fibrous, open, petiole not toothed along the margin, pinnae acute or briefly 2-dentate, midrib prominent; infl. among lvs., spicate, pendulous, long-peduncled, bracts 2, the upper not deeply sulcate externally, spike with bright yellow fls. mostly in triads (2 male and 1 female) but apical portion with paired male fls. only; male fls. asymmetrical, sepals 3, elongate, basally united, attenuate apically, petals 3, valvate, acute, not much longer than sepals, stamens 55–60, pistillode lacking, female fls. ovoid, sepals 3, imbricate, petals 3, imbricate except the briefly valvate apices, longer than sepals, staminodes united in a low cupule, pistil 3-celled, 3-ovuled; fr. angled by mutual pressure, yellow to deep orange, fleshy, endocarp bony, thick, with pores near the base, seed with ruminate endosperm.

For culture see *Palms*.

caudescens (Mart.) Barb.-Rodr. [*Diplothemium caudescens* Mart.]. To 20 ft. or more; lvs. stiff, elongate, pinnae to 32 in. long or more, 1½ in. wide; spike to 30 in. long or more; male fls. to ¾ in. long; fr. to 2 in. long, edible. Warmer parts of Zone 9b in Fla.

POLYCODIUM: *VACCINIUM*.

POLYGALA L. MILKWORT. *Polygalaceae.* Between 500 and 600 spp. of trees, shrubs, and herbs, widely distributed around the world; lvs. alt., opp., or whorled, simple, entire; fls. in terminal or axillary racemes, irregular, sepals 5, the inner 2 petal-like (wings), petals 3–5, often united, the lower petal (keel) often crested, stamens 8, rarely 6, filaments united into a sheath split on upper side; fr. a caps., seeds usually pubescent or with an aril.

Some species may be transplanted from the wild; these should mostly be placed in shady locations in light soil. Planted outdoors in warm climates or grown in the greenhouse; propagated by seeds.

alba Nutt. Sts. many, to 1 ft., from a per. root; lvs. alt., mostly linear, to 1 in. long; fls. white, with green centers, crest often purple, wings elliptic; caps. elliptic. Minn. to Mex.

apopetala Brandeg. Shrub or small tree, to 15 ft.; lvs. alt., lanceolate to ovate, to 3 in. long, obtuse; fls. pinkish-purple, wings nearly orbicular; caps. elliptic. Baja Calif. Planted on the Pacific Coast.

arillata Buch.-Ham. ex D. Don. Shrub, 4–8 ft.; lvs. lanceolate, ovate-lanceolate, or elliptic-oblong, 4–6 in. long; fls. in drooping, usually panicled racemes, the wings ovate, red-purple, keel yellow, amply crested; caps. broadly reniform. India, Ceylon, se. Asia.

calcarea F. W. Schultz. Sts. several, to 8 in. long, prostrate, from a per. root; lvs. in rosettes at base of sts. but more widely spaced above, spatulate, obovate, or linear-lanceolate, variable in size; fls. blue, seldom white or rose, wings obovate; caps. obovate, retuse. Eur.

Chamaebuxus L. Evergreen shrub, to 1 ft., sts. creeping; lvs. alt., lanceolate to obovate, to 1 in. long, leathery; fls. 1 or 2 together, white to yellow, wings obovate; caps. obovate, retuse. Eur. Var. **grandiflora** Gaudin [cv. 'Atropurpurea'; *P. Chamaebuxus* var. *purpurea* Neilr.]. Wings purple, petals yellow. Eur.

Cowellii (Britt.) S. F. Blake. VIOLETA, VIOLET TREE, TORTUGUERO. Small to medium-sized, deciduous tree, 15–40 ft.; lvs. alt., elliptic, 2–5 in. long, 1–2½ in. wide, slightly thickened and leathery, yellow-green, lateral veins many, nearly parallel, slightly raised, thin; fls. in short lateral racemes, violet, showy, about ¾ in. across, sepals 5, wings elliptic, petals ⁹⁄₁₆ in. long; caps. flattened, 1¼–1½ in. long, unequally 2-winged. Hillside tree, Puerto Rico. Cult. in subtrop. Fla.

×**Dalmaisiana** Hort.: *P. oppositifolia* L. var. *cordata* Harv. × *P. myrtifolia* var. *grandiflora*. Shrub, 3–8 ft.; lvs. alt. or opp. on same plant, elliptic, lanceolate, or ovate, to 1 in. long; fls. purplish or rosy-red. Flowering almost continuously. Grown in greenhouse, planted out in the southernmost states and Calif.

diversifolia: *Securidaca diversifolia*.

lutea L. YELLOW M., CANDYWEED, YELLOW BACHELOR'S-BUTTON. Bien., sts. to 1 ft.; lvs. in a rosette, lanceolate, oblanceolate, obovate, or spatulate, 1–2 in. long; fls. in dense, spikelike racemes to 1½ in. long, orange-yellow, wings obliquely elliptic; caps. cuneate-obovate. Long Is., s. to Fla. and La.

myrtifolia L. Erect, much-branched shrub, to 8 ft.; lvs. alt., elliptic-oblong or obovate, to 1 in. long; fls. in short, terminal racemes, greenish-white veined with purple, wings obliquely obovate, keel crested; caps. obovate. S. Afr. Grown in the greenhouse or in the open in warm regions. Var. **grandiflora** Hook. Fls. large, rich purple.

paucifolia Willd. FRINGED P., FLOWERING WINTERGREEN, BIRD-ON-THE-WING. Per., to 6 or 7 in., rhizomatous, stoloniferous; upper lvs. clustered, ovate to oblong, to 1½ in. long, lower lvs. distant and scale-like; fls. 1–4 together, rose-purple or rarely white, wings obovate, keel fringed, stamens 6; caps. nearly orbicular. New Bruns. and Que. to Sask. and Minn., s. in mts. to Ga.

Senega L. SENECA SNAKEROOT. Sts. several, to 1½ ft., from a thick per. root; lvs. alt., linear-lanceolate, to 2 in. long; fls. in terminal racemes, white or greenish, very small, wings nearly orbicular; caps. nearly globose. New Bruns. and Que. to Alta., s. to Ga. and Ark. Dried root used medicinally.

Vayredae Costa. Per., to 8 in.; lvs. alt., linear-lanceolate to linear; fls. axillary, solitary or paired, wings and upper petals pinkish-purple, keel yellowish, with 5–9-lobed, fimbriate crests; caps. obcordate-orbicular. E. Pyrenees.

virgata Thunb. Shrub or small tree, to 15 ft., brs. straight and erect; lvs. alt., linear to lanceolate, to 3 in. long; fls. in terminal racemes, purple or pink, wings nearly orbicular, keel crested; caps. obcordate. S. Afr. Sometimes planted in warm regions.

POLYGALACEAE. MILKWORT FAMILY. Dicot.; 10 genera and about 1,000 spp. of herbs, shrubs, or small trees, often scandent or climbing, of worldwide distribution except in New Zeal. and Arctic regions; lvs. alt., infrequently opp. or whorled, simple; fls. solitary, spicate, racemose or panicled, sometimes cleistogamous, irregular, bisexual, sepals 4–7 but mostly 5, the inner 2 usually winglike or petal-like, petals 3–5, the upper 2 united with each other or to the stamens, lower petal (keel) often crested or fringed, stamens 6–8, in 2 whorls, united into a sheath split on the upper side, pistil 1, ovary

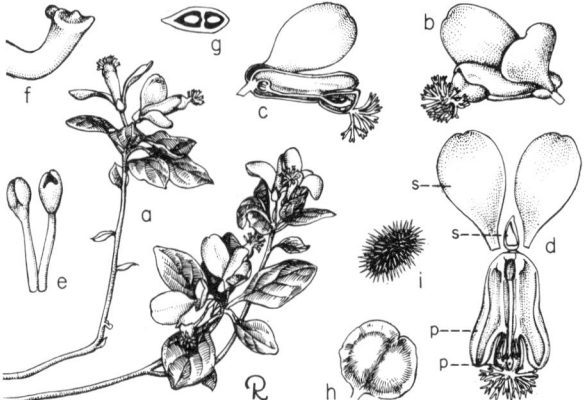

POLYGALACEAE. *Polygala paucifolia:* **a,** flowering stems, × ½; **b,** flower, × 1; **c,** flower, vertical section, × 1; **d,** flower, expanded, × 1; **e,** stamens, × 5; **f,** stigma and apex of style, × 5; **g,** ovary, cross section, × 5; **h,** fruit, × 2; **i,** seed, × 4. (p petal, s sepal.)

superior, usually 2-celled, each cell with 1 ovule, style 1, stigma 2-lobed; fr. a caps., nut, samara, or drupe, seeds often hairy, and often with an aril. The fl. resembles a papilionaceous fl. of the Leguminosae, but the similar parts are not strictly comparable. The genera grown as ornamentals are: *Monnina, Polygala,* and *Securidaca.*

POLYGONACEAE Juss. BUCKWHEAT FAMILY. Dicot.; 40 genera and 800 spp. of herbs, shrubs, vines, or trees, with jointed sts., cosmopolitan, but chiefly N. Temp.; lvs. simple, stipules usually united into a more or less tubular sheath (ocrea); fls. small, sepals or calyx lobes 2–6, petal-like, often with wings, spines, or hooks, petals none, ovary superior, 1-celled; fr. an achene. Of the cult. genera, the more tender are: *Antigonon, Coccoloba, Ruprechtia,* and *Triplaris;* those grown in cool-temp. regions are: *Atraphaxis, Chorizanthe, Eriogonum, Fagopyrum, Homalocladium, Muehlenbeckia, Oxyria, Polygonella, Polygonum, Rheum,* and *Rumex.*

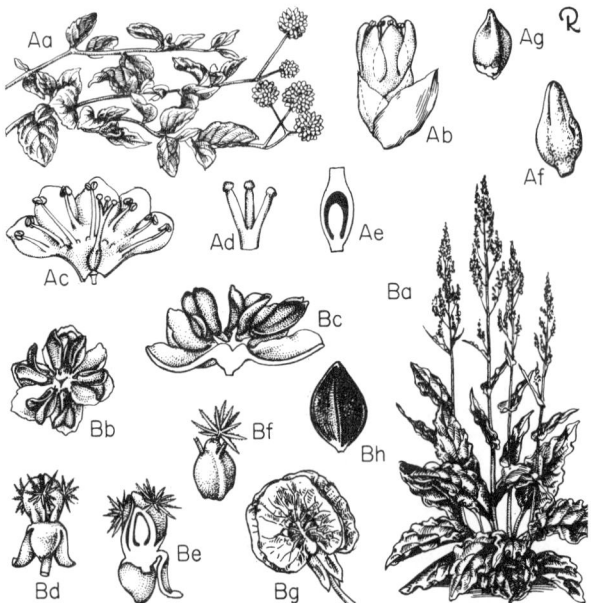

POLYGONACEAE. **A,** *Polygonum capitatum:* **Aa,** flowering stems, × ½; **Ab,** flower with bracts, × 5; **Ac,** pistil and expanded perianth, × 5; **Ad,** stigmas, × 10; **Ae,** ovary, vertical section, × 10; **Af,** perianth in fruiting state, × 5; **Ag,** achene, × 5. **B,** *Rumex Acetosa:* **Ba,** plant, × ¹⁄₁₆; **Bb,** male flower, × 3; **Bc,** male flower, vertical section, × 5; **Bd,** female flower, × 6; **Be,** female flower, vertical section, × 8; **Bf,** pistil (two stigmas removed), × 10; **Bg,** perianth in fruiting state, × 3; **Bh,** achene, × 5.

POLYGONATUM Mill. SOLOMON'S-SEAL, KING-SOLOMON'S-SEAL. *Liliaceae*. About 30 spp. of rhizomatous, per. herbs, native to temp. N. Amer., Eur., and Asia; rhizome horizontal, much-jointed, with many scars; sts. arching to erect; lvs. alt., opp., or whorled; fls. greenish to yellow, axillary, solitary or in clusters, perianth cylindrical, 6-lobed, stamens 6, on perianth tube; fr. a blue-black or red berry with several seeds.

Solomon's-seals thrive in shady locations in deep, rich soil; suitable for the wild garden. Propagated by division.

biflorum (Walt.) Elliott [*P. canaliculatum* (Muhlenb.) Pursh]. SMALL S-S. Sts. to 3 ft. or more, erect or arching; lvs. alt., sessile, elliptic-lanceolate, to 4¼ in. long, glabrous and glaucous beneath; fls. greenish-white, on mostly 1–3-fld. peduncles. Conn. to Ont. and Nebr., s. to Fla. and Tex. Forma **racemosum** (McGivney) Fern. [*P. commutatum* forma *racemosum* McGivney and var. *racemosum* Hort.]. Fls. borne on axillary brs. instead of peduncles. N. Ind. and s. Mich.

canaliculatum: *P. biflorum;* but material offered as *P. canaliculatum* is *P. commutatum*.

commutatum (Schult.f.) A. Dietr. [*P. giganteum* A. Dietr.]. GREAT S.-S. Sts. to 6 ft., stout, arching, naked below; lvs. alt., ovate-lanceolate to ovate, to 7 in. long, glabrous; fls. yellowish-green to greenish-white, to ¾ in. long, on mostly 2–10-fld. peduncles. New Hamp. to Man., s. to Ga. and Nuevo León (Mex.). Var. **racemosum**: *P. biflorum* forma.

giganteum: *P. commutatum.*

japonicum: *P. odoratum* var. *Thunbergii.*

latifolium (Jacq.) Desf. Sts. to 4 ft., erect, angled; lvs. alt., oblong, to 6 in. long, pubescent beneath; fls. white with green lobes, pubescent, to ¾ in. long, on 1–5-fld. peduncles. Eur.; naturalized locally in e. Mass.

macrophyllum: *P. verticillatum.*

multiflorum (L.) All. Sts. to 3 ft., cylindrical, arching; lvs. alt., elliptic-oblong to ovate, 2–6 in. long, glabrous; fls. white, to ⅝ in. long, constricted in middle, on 2–5-fld. peduncles, filaments hairy. Eur., Asia. Var. **major** is listed.

odoratum (Mill.) Druce [*P. officinale* All.]. Sts. to 1½ ft. or more, angled, arching; lvs. alt., elliptic-oblong to ovate, to 4 in. long; fls. greenish-white, to ⅞ in. long, fragrant, on 2-fld. peduncles, filaments glabrous. Eur., Asia. Var. **Thunbergii** (C. Morr. & Decne.) Hara [*P. japonicum* C. Morr. & Decne.; *P. Thunbergii* C. Morr. & Decne.]. Plant stout, sts. to 3⅜ ft. tall; lvs. to 6 in. long; fls. to 1 in. long. Japan.

officinale: *P. odoratum.*

pubescens (Willd.) Pursh. Sts. slender, to 3 ft.; lvs. alt., elliptic to ovate, to about 5 in. long, veins on lower surface hairy; fls. yellowish-green, to ½ in. long, mostly on 1–2-fld. peduncles. Nov. Sc. to Man., s. to N.C., n. Ga., and Ind.

sibiricum Redouté. Sts. 2–4 ft., flexuous; lvs. whorled, linear, to 6 in. long, coiled at apex; fls. greenish-white or purplish, to ½ in. long, on 2–4-fld. peduncles, filaments ciliate. Himalayas to n. Asia.

Thunbergii: *P. odoratum* var.

verticillatum (L.) All. [*P. macrophyllum* Sweet]. Sts. to 4 ft., angled, erect; lvs. whorled, linear-lanceolate, to 4¾ in. long, not coiled at apex; fls. greenish-white, ⁵⁄₁₆ in. long, constricted in middle, on 1–4-fld. peduncles, filaments papillose; fr. red. Eur. to Asia Minor and Afghanistan.

POLYGONELLA Michx. JOINTWEED. *Polygonaceae*. Nine spp. of ann. or per. herbs with jointed sts., native to e. U.S. and se. Canada; lvs. alt.; fls. small, white, pinkish or greenish, in panicled racemes, bisexual or unisexual, sepals 5, stamens 8, styles 3; fr. an achene, usually 3-angled. Closely related to *Polygonum.*

The species are similar in appearance and of little horticultural value.

americana (Fisch. & C. A. Mey.) Small. Suffrutescent per., st. at first depressed, later erect, to 3 ft. or more, flexuous; lvs. club-shaped, about ½ in. long; racemes to about 3 in.; fls. small, many, white or pinkish, from jointed rachis; achenes glossy brown. S.C., Ga., w. to New Mex.

articulata (L.) Meissn. Ann. herb, sts. to 1 ft. or more, habit as in *P. americana;* lvs. small, linear-club-shaped, fls. pink, often drying brown; achenes glossy brown. Sandy places, Que., s. to N.C., w. to Great Lakes.

Croomii: *P. polygama.*

polygama (Venten.) Engelm. & A. Gray [*P. Croomii* Chapm.]. OCTOBER FLOWER. Similar to *P. americana* in habit; lvs. narrowly to

widely spatulate, ⅛ in. to more than ½ in. long; achenes yellow to dark brown. A variable sp. N.C. to Fla., w. along Gulf Coast to e. Tex.

POLYGONUM L. [*Bilderdykia* Dumort.; *Reynoutria* Houtt.]. KNOTWEED, SMARTWEED, FLEECE FLOWER. *Polygonaceae*. About 150 spp. of mostly ann. or per. herbs of wide distribution, a few more or less woody, sometimes twining or aquatic, sts. usually appearing to be jointed; lvs. alt., simple, entire, variously shaped, stipular sheaths usually well developed; fls. small but sometimes showy, in racemes, spikes, or heads, sepals 5, stamens 8, stigmas 2 or 3; fr. a small achene, lenticular or 3-angled, partly or wholly enclosed by sepals.

A few are of ornamental value for their profusion of small, white, greenish, or red flowers and sometimes for the abundant foliage. Of easy cultivation; propagated by seeds and division.

affine D. Don. Tufted, evergreen per., to 1½ ft.; lvs. to 4 in. long, tapering to the base, finely serrate, dark green; fls. small, bright rose, in dense, erect spikes 2–3 in. long. Autumn. Himalayas.

amplexicaule D. Don. MOUNTAIN-FLEECE. Per., to 3 ft.; lvs. ovate to lanceolate, to 6 in. long, the upper clasping; fls. rose-red or white, in spikes to 6 in. long. Midsummer. Himalayas. Cv. 'Rubrum'. Fls. red.

Aubertii L. Henry [*Bilderdykia Aubertii* (L. Henry) Moldenke]. CHINA FLEECE VINE, SILVER LACE VINE. Twining, per. vine, to 20 ft.; lvs. ovate-lanceolate, to 2½ in. long; fls. white, fragrant, in long, erect, panicled racemes. Late summer. W. China and Tibet.

baldschuanicum Regel. BUKHARA F.F. Closely resembling *P. Aubertii*, but fls. larger, rose-colored, in denser, drooping panicles. Bukhara.

Bistorta L. SNAKEWEED, BISTORT. Per., to 2 ft.; like *P. bistortoides* in habit, differing in having both basal and st. lvs. oblong-ovate, and tending toward winged petioles. N. Eur. and Asia. Dried rhizome has been used medicinally. Cv. 'Superbum'. More than 2 ft.; fls. in dense spikes.

bistortoides Pursh. Per., to 2½ ft.; lvs. mostly basal, oblong or lanceolate, to 10 in. long; fls. white, in dense racemes to 2 in. long. In marshes and meadows, mts. of B.C. to Calif. and Rocky Mts. Differs from *P. Bistorta* in having lvs. longer, narrower, commonly tapering to unwinged petioles. Lf. characteristics are variable. Var. **linearifolium** (S. Wats.) Small. Lvs. linear.

campanulatum Hook.f. Variable, slender-stemmed herb, stoloniferous at base, sts. to 3 ft.; lvs. petioled, ovate to elliptic, to 5 in. long, sparsely hairy, mostly deciduous; fls. pink or white, campanulate, ⅛ in. long, in nodding panicles. Himalayas.

capitatum Buch.-Ham. ex D. Don. Per., brs. trailing, to 10 in. long; lvs. elliptic, to 1½ in. long; fls. pink, in dense heads to ¾ in. across. Himalayas.

compactum: *P. cuspidatum* var.

coccineum Muhlenb. [*P. Muhlenbergii* (Meissn.) S. Wats.]. WATER S. Aquatic or semiaquatic per., sts. to 20 ft., rooting at nodes; lvs. 4 in. long, thickish; infl. a dense spike 1 in. long, borne above floating lvs.; fls. small, rose-colored. Throughout N. Amer.

cuspidatum Siebold & Zucc. [*Reynoutria japonica* Houtt.]. JAPANESE K., MEXICAN BAMBOO. Per. from vigorous rhizome, to 8 ft.; lvs. elliptic to nearly orbicular, to 5 in. long, abruptly pointed; fls. small, greenish-white, in axillary, panicled racemes. Late summer and autumn. Japan; often becomes weedy. Var. **compactum** (Hook.f.) L. H. Bailey [*P. compactum* Hook.f.; *P. Reynoutria* Hort., not Mak.]. A condensed form, stamens aborted, sepals enlarging over the ovary and turning red. Cv. 'Spectabilis'. Lvs. red, becoming yellow-marbled.

emodi Meissn. Shrub, sts. creeping, rooting at nodes; much like *P. affine*, but having lf. margins entire; fls. crimson, in loose, narrower spikes on slender sts. Himalayas.

hayachinensis Mak. A Japanese form of *P. macrophyllum.*

hydropiperoides Michx. MILD WATER PEPPER. Per. herb, more or less hairy, sts. to 3 ft., rooting at nodes; fls. small, greenish-white to pinkish, in loose spikelike racemes. U.S. For damp or boggy places; of little or no hort. value.

macrophyllum D. Don. Stout, leafy-stemmed plant, erect, from thickened rootcrown; basal lvs. long-petioled, blades oblong to lanceolate, to 9 in. long; fls. small, pink, in a single, dense, terminal spike about 4 in. long. Himalayas and China.

molle D. Don. Bushy per., to 5 ft. high, brs. strong, compact; lvs. narrow, hairy beneath; fls. white, in large, terminal, tomentose panicles. Himalayas northward.

Muhlenbergii: *P. coccineum.*

multiflorum Thunb. Climber, with tuberous root; lvs. cordate-ovate, 2–5 in. long, evergreen in mild climates; fls. greenish, in slender panicles. Autumn. Japan.

POLYPODIACEAE (All details show lower surface of a fertile leaf). **A,** *Hemionitis arifolia:* **Aa,** plant, × ⅕; **Ab,** fertile leaf blade, × ⅜; **Ac,** segment of leaf with massed sporangia, × 20. **B,** *Polypodium virginianum:* **Ba,** plant, × ¼; **Bb,** pinna, × 2; **Bc,** segment of pinna with sorus, × 8. **C,** *Asplenium Trichomanes:* **Ca,** plant, × ½; **Cb,** pinna, × 4; **Cc,** segment of pinna with sorus, × 10; **Cd,** sorus, vertical section, × 20; **Ce,** sporangium, × 40; **Cf,** sporangium dehisced, × 40. **D,** *Dryopteris austriaca* var. *spinulosa:* **Da,** plant, × 1/12; **Db,** segment of pinna, × 2; **Dc,** segment of pinnule with sorus, × 10; **Dd,** sorus, vertical section, × 12. **E,** *Dennstaedtia punctilobula:* **Ea,** segment of pinna, × 2; **Eb,** segment of pinnule with sorus, × 18; **Ec,** sorus, vertical section, × 24. **F,** *Davallia trichomanoides:* **Fa,** segment of pinna, × 2; **Fb,** segment of pinnule with sorus, × 10. **G,** *Phyllitis Scolopendrium:* **Ga,** plant, × ⅙; **Gb,** segment of leaf, × 2; **Gc,** detail with two facing sori, × 3; **Gd,** two sori, vertical section, × 18. **H,** *Adiantum pedatum:* **Ha,** plant, × ⅛; **Hb,** pinnule, × 2; **Hc,** pinnule lobe with reflexed margin, × 12; **Hd,** pinnule margin with sorus, vertical section, × 24. **I,** *Pteris multifida:* **Ia,** plant, × ⅙; **Ib,** segment of pinnule, × 4; **Ic,** segment of pinnule with sorus, vertical section, × 24. **J,** *Onoclea sensibilis:* **Ja,** plant, × ⅛; **Jb,** fertile pinna, × 1½; **Jc,** pinnule enclosing sori, × 4. (Fa, Fb from Bailey, *Manual of Cultivated Plants,* ed. 2.)

orientale L. [*P. Spaethii* Dammer]. PRINCE'S-FEATHER, PRINCESS-FEATHER, KISS-ME-OVER-THE-GARDEN-GATE. Hairy ann., to 6 ft.; lvs. broadly ovate, to 10 in. long; fls. bright pink or rose, in dense spikes to 3½ in. long. Autumn. Asia, Australia; naturalized in N. Amer.

polystachyum Wallich. Shrub, to 6 ft., resembling *P. cuspidatum;* lvs. more narrowly elliptic; panicle large, spreading, essentially glabrous. N. India to Siberia.

Reynoutria: see *P. cuspidatum* var. *compactum.*

sachalinense Friedr. Schmidt ex Maxim. GIANT K., SACALINE. Coarse per., to 12 ft.; lvs. elliptic-oblong, 1 ft. long or more, slightly cordate; fls. greenish, in short axillary clusters. Autumn. Sakhalin. Sometimes grown for rough forage or as a coarse cover or screen.

Spaethii: *P. orientale.*

vacciniifolium Wallich. Per., to 1 ft., brs. trailing; lvs. orbicular, to ⅝ in. long, slightly glaucous beneath; fls. rose, $^5/_{16}$ in. across, in racemes to 3 in. long. Himalayas.

viviparum L. SERPENT GRASS, ALPINE BISTORT. Per., to 1 ft.; lvs. oblong to linear, to 8 in. long; fls. pale rose or white, in narrow, terminal racemes. N. Amer., Asia, Eur.

Weyrichii Friedr. Schmidt ex Maxim. Per., to 3 ft.; lvs. ovate, to 7 in. long, white-tomentose beneath; fls. white or greenish, in racemes forming a large terminal panicle. Sakhalin.

POLYPLOID: see *Ploidy.*

POLYPODIACEAE Bercht. & J. Presl. POLYPODY FAMILY. Ferns; about 180 genera and perhaps 7,000 spp., representing the largest family of ferns and comprising most of the common, low ferns without treelike trunks; delimited by the technical characters of sporangia; rhizomes erect or creeping; lvs. simple to pinnate, less commonly palmate, petioled, in compound lvs. the lfts. (pinnae) disposed on a rachis, sometimes divided or compounded into sessile or short-stalked segms. (pinnules); clusters (sori) of sporangia usually produced on the lower surface of lvs., scattered, along midvein, or sometimes marginal, usually with a covering (indusium) that shrivels after spores mature. By some authors the genera are treated as constituting several families rather than the single one here recognized. The cult. genera are: *Acrostichum, Adiantum, Aglaomorpha, Anopteris, Arachniodes, Arthropteris, Asplenium, Athyrium, Blechnum, Bommeria, Camptosorus, Cheilanthes, Coniogramme, Cryptogramma, Ctenitis, Cyrtomium, Cystopteris, Davallia, Dennstaedtia, Diplazium, Doodia, Doryopteris, Drynaria, Dryopteris, Elaphoglossum, Gymnocarpium, Hemionitis, Histiopteris, Humata, Hypolepis, Llavea, Matteuccia, Microlepia, Nephrolepis, Notholaena, Onoclea, Onychium, Pellaea, Phyllitis, Pityrogramma, Platycerium, Polypodium, Polystichum, Pteridium, Pteris, Pyrrosia, Rumohra, Saccoloma, Sadleria, Sphenomeris, Stenochlaena, Tectaria, Thelypteris, Vittaria, Woodsia,* and *Woodwardia.*

Planted in the open or under glass. Most species of the following are hardy and can be grown in the open in most northern states: *Athyrium, Camptosorus, Cheilanthes, Coniogramme, Cystopteris, Dennstaedtia, Dryopteris, Matteuccia, Notholaena, Onoclea, Onychium, Pellaea, Phyllitis, Polypodium, Polystichum, Pteridium, Pyrrosia, Sphenomeris, Woodsia,* and *Woodwardia.* For details of relationships and culture and of other fern families, see *Ferns.*

POLYPODIUM L. [*Campyloneurum* K. Presl; *Microgramma* K. Presl; *Microsorium* Link; *Phlebodium* John Sm.; *Phymatodes* K. Presl]. POLYPODY. *Polypodiaceae.* A large genus of cosmopolitan ferns, largely trop., usually epiphytic, with creeping, branching rhizomes; lvs. attached to the rhizome with a distinct joint, simple or compound; sori round, in 1 or more rows on each side of the midvein, indusia absent. Recent monographers subdivide the genus into 20 or more separate genera, and it is to be anticipated that many of these genera will be accepted more widely in the future. *Aglaomorpha* and *Drynaria* are accepted here as segregates from *Polypodium.*

The hardier native species are useful for growing on rocks or trees in the woodland garden, but most, being from the humid tropics, are plants for the warm greenhouse, where they should be treated as epiphytes. Propagation is by spores, or by divisions of clumps or rhizomes. See also *Ferns.*

angustifolium Swartz. NARROW-LEAVED STRAP FERN. Epiphyte; lvs. leathery, long, narrow, strap-shaped, to 2 ft. long, to ⅝ in. wide, tapered at both ends, entire, veins inconspicuous; sori in 1–4 irregular rows. Trop. Amer.

aristatum variegatum: a listed name of uncertain application; perhaps a variegated form of *Arachniodes aristata.*

aureum L. [*Phlebodium aureum* (L.) John Sm.]. RABBIT'S-FOOT FERN, HARE'S-FOOT F., GOLDEN P. Rhizomes surface-creeping, thick, brown-scaly; lvs. pinnatifid, to 4 ft. long, 2 ft. wide, the lobes to 1 ft. long, 2 in. wide; sori in 2 irregular rows, often bright yellow. Fla. to Argentina. Cvs. include: **'Mandaianum'** [*P. Mandaianum* Hort.], BLUE FERN, margins deeply laciniate, lobes undulate; **'Mayi'** [cv. 'Undulatum'], lobes strongly undulate; **'Cristatum'** [cv. 'Crested'], end of lvs. and lobes crested. Var. **areolatum** (Willd.) De la Sota. Lvs. erect, leathery, somewhat smaller, glaucous; sori in 1 row. Includes many glaucous forms listed under the incorrect trade names *P. glaucopruinatum, P. glaucophyllum, P. glaucophyllum crispum,* and *P. glaucum.*

Brownii Wikstr. Epiphyte; lvs. leathery, 6–18 in. long, ¼–½ in. wide, obtuse at apex, narrowed gradually at base, entire or slightly wavy; sori in single row between margin and midrib, large, oblong, slightly sunken. Australia, New Caledonia, Fiji Is.

californicum Kaulf. CALIFORNIA P. Lvs. deciduous, herbaceous, 10–20 in. long, 2½–5 in. wide, ovate to broadly triangular, pinnatifid to nearly pinnate, pinnae oblong to linear-oblong, acute or obtuse, mostly decurrent at base, unevenly serrate to crenulate, veins often more or less netted; sori closer to midrib than margin. N. Calif., to Baja Calif. Some plants resemble *P. vulgare* of Eur.

coronans: *Aglaomorpha coronans.*

crassifolium L. Epiphyte, rhizomes about ½ in. thick, with light brown scales; lvs. simple, narrow-ovate, to 3 ft. long, 5 in. wide, tapered at base, main veins oblique to midrib and parallel; sori in even rows between main veins, ⅛ in. in diam. Trop. N. and S. Amer.

decumanum Willd. [*Phlebodium decumanum* (Willd.) John Sm.]. Like *P. aureum,* but lvs. to 6 ft. long, lateral veins of lobes prominent, nearly straight and parallel, and sori in 4–7 rows on each side of midrib. Trop. N. and S. Amer.

diversifolium Willd. [*Microsorium diversifolium* (Willd.) E. Copel.]. Lvs. leathery, entire and about 9 in. long and 2 in. wide, to irregularly lobed or deeply pinnatifid and 1½ ft. long and 9 in. wide, pinnae to 5 in. long, main veins visible; sori in single row, slightly sunken. New Zeal., Australia, Tasmania. Closely allied to *P. nigrescens* except for diversity of lvs.

Dryopteris: *Gymnocarpium Dryopteris.*

fraxinifolium Jacq. ASH-LEAF P. Lvs. to 4 ft. long, 1½ ft. wide, 1-pinnate, pinnae entire, to 9 in. long, petioles to 2 ft. long. Trop. S. Amer.

glaucopruinatum C. Chr. [*P. glaucum* Kunze, not Thunb.]. Lvs. to 1½ ft. long, 8 in. wide, simple or deeply pinnatifid, with needlelike, blackish scales, pinnae ½ in. wide or more, entire, margins cartilaginous and minutely notched. Philippine Is. Most material cult. under this name is a glaucous form of *P. aureum.*

glaucophyllum and **glaucophyllum crispum:** listed names used for glaucous forms of *P. aureum.*

glaucum. Material listed under this name is *P. aureum* or *P. glaucopruinatum. Polypodium glaucum* Thunb. is a sp. of *Dicranopteris* Bernh. (Gleicheniaceae), not known to be cult.

glycyrrhiza D. C. Eat. [*P. vulgare* var. *occidentale* Hook.]. LICORICE FERN. Lvs. herbaceous, oblong-triangular to narrow-ovate, to 18 in. long and 7 in. wide, pinnatifid, sometimes almost to midrib, pinnae mostly linear-attenuate, dilated at base, serrate, veins free; sori nearer midrib than margin. Mostly coastal, Alaska to cent. Calif. Differs from *P. vulgare* in longer, attenuate segms.

heracleum: *Aglaomorpha heraclea.*

hesperium Maxon [*P. vulgare* var. *columbianum* Gilb.]. WESTERN P. Lvs. firm, herbaceous, to 10 in. long, 2 in. wide, pinnatifid, sometimes almost to midrib, pinnae oblong to elliptic, rounded at apex, entire or crenate; sori few, midway between midrib and margin. Pine forests, Alaska to Calif., e. to S. Dak. Differs from *P. vulgare* in shorter, rounder segms.

hexagonopterum: *Thelypteris hexagonoptera.*

incanum: *P. polypodioides.*

integrifolium: *P. punctatum.*

irioides: *P. punctatum.*

Knightiae: *P. subauriculatum* cv.

latipes Langsd. & Fisch. Rhizomes branching, creeping; lvs. widely spaced on rhizome, to 30 in. long, pinnatifid, petioles ½–⅓ as long as blade, pinnae many, oblong to linear or oblong-lanceolate, attenuate, areoles in 2–3 series; sori in 1 or 2 rows, borne on single enclosed veinlet. Argentina, Brazil, Bolivia, Paraguay.

lepidopteris (Langsd. & Fisch.) Kunze. Lvs. pinnatifid, 6–18 in. long, 1½–3 in. wide, blade gradually long-attenuate in the basal half, with many pairs of lower pinnae minute or even vestigial, all surfaces clothed with hairs and fringed, peltate scales; sori superficial. Trop. Amer.

lepidotrichum (Fée) Maxon. Lvs. to 2½ ft. long, 9 in. wide, ovate, covered with fringed, peltate scales, deeply pinnatifid but 1-pinnate at base, pinnae to 5 in. long and ⅜ in. wide; sori sunken, visible as impressions on the upper surface. Mex.

Lingua: *Pyrrosia Lingua.*

Mandaianum: *P. aureum* cv.

Meyenianum: *Aglaomorpha Meyenianum.*

musifolium Blume [*Microsorium musifolium* (Blume) Ching]. Epiphyte, rhizomes stout, covered with brownish scales; lvs. simple, sessile, mostly 2–3 ft. long, 3–4 in. wide, acute; sori very minute, covering almost the entire lower surface. E. Indies.

nigrescens Blume [*Phymatodes nigrescens* (Blume) John Sm.]. Like *P. scolopendria,* but lvs. darker green, margins wavy, veins visible; sori in 1 series. Ceylon, s. India, Malay Arch. Grown outdoors in s. Calif. Zone 10.

normale D. Don. Epiphyte, like *P. crassifolium,* but rhizome black-scaly, blade to 2 in. wide, veins not prominent; sori large, next to midrib. India, Malay Pen., s. China.

Palmeri Maxon. Epiphyte, rhizomes very thick, white-scaly; lvs. to 8 in. long, 3 in. wide, entire, fertile lvs. smaller, oblong to linear. Mex. to Panama.

pennigerum: *Thelypteris pennigera.*

percussum Cav. Rhizomes wiry; lvs. very leathery, to 1 ft. long, 1½ in. wide, narrowed toward both ends, entire, covered with fine scales beneath; sori in rows between midrib and margin, distinctly sunken. Trop. S. Amer.

Phegopteris: *Thelypteris Phegopteris.*

phyllitidis L. [*Campyloneurum phyllitidis* (L.) K. Presl]. STRAP FERN., RIBBON F. Epiphyte; lvs. simple, leathery, to 3 ft. long, 4 in. wide, sometimes wavy-margined, glossy; sori in 2 rows between parallel major veins. Trop. Amer. Zone 10.

phymatodes: *P. scolopendria.*

piloselloides L. [*Microgramma piloselloides* (L.) E. Copel.]. Scandent epiphyte with wide-creeping rhizomes; lvs. closely spaced on rhizome, simple, leathery, ovate to obovate, to 2 in. long, entire, glossy, veins not visible. Tropics, N. and S. Amer. Best grown in a hanging basket or on a bark standard.

polycarpon: *P. punctatum.*

polypodioides (L.) D. Watt [*P. incanum* Swartz]. RESURRECTION FERN. Creeping epiphyte; lvs. evergreen, leathery, to 7 in. long, 2 in. wide, pinnatifid, pinnae oblong, entire, gray-scaly beneath. Trop. and warm-temp. N. and S. Amer. Var. **Michauxianum** Weatherby. Scales of lower lf. surface entire, orbicular to triangular, those of rhizome fimbriate-serrulate, lvs. glabrous above. Del. to s. Ill., s. to Fla., Tex., and trop. Amer.

pteropus Blume [*Microsorium pteropus* (Blume) Ching]. Rhizomes fleshy, younger parts of rhizomes, petioles, and midribs with dense, dull brown, latticed scales; lvs. simple to deeply 3-lobed, 8–10 in. long, petioles ¾–8 in. long. On stream beds and banks and often submersed in rainy season; India, s. China, Malay Arch. Sometimes grown in aquariums.

punctatum (L.) Swartz [*P. integrifolium* Lowe; *P. irioides* Lam.; *P. polycarpon* Cav.; *Asplenium squamulatum* Hort., not Blume]. CLIMBING BIRD'S-NEST FERN. Epiphyte; lvs. thick, leathery, to 3 ft. long, 3 in. wide, entire, light green; sori small, irregularly scattered. Afr., Asia, Polynesia. There are hort. forms crested or forked at apex.

pustulatum G. Forst. [*Microsorium pustulatum* (G. Forst.) E. Copel.]. FRAGRANT FERN. Epiphyte; lvs. thin, variable, tapering gradually at base, acuminate at apex, the entire ones to 9 in. long and ⅝ in. wide, the deeply pinnatifid ones to 1½ ft. long and 6 in. wide, segms. linear-lanceolate, 3–6 in. long. New Zeal., Australia.

pyrrholepis (Fée) Maxon. Epiphyte; like *P. lepidotrichum,* but lvs. narrowly linear-oblong, long-attenuate at apex, and sori not sunken or visible as impressions on upper surface. Mex.

quercifolium: *Drynaria quercifolia.*

recurvatum Kaulf. Epiphyte; lvs. 1–3 ft. long, 10 in. wide, pinnatifid, pinnae slender, to 5 in. long, ⅛–¼ in. wide, dilated at base, entire, midrib finely pubescent; sori in single median row between midrib and margin. Brazil.

rhodopleuron Kunze. Epiphyte; lvs. narrowly ovate to linear-ovate, to about 18 in. long, 5 in. wide, deeply pinnatifid, pinnae oblong, round to acute, often with reddish color, midrib of lf. and all major veins of segms. reddish, the enclosed veinlet next to midrib with enlarged whitish tip, conspicuous. Trop. Amer.

rigidula: *Drynaria rigidula.*

scolopendria Burm.f. [*P. phymatodes* L.; *Loxogramme involuta* K. Presl.; *Phymatodes scolopendria* (Burm.f.) Ching]. WART FERN. Epiphyte, rhizomes creeping, fleshy, ⅜ in. in diam., sea-green, bearing scattered dark scales, which are denser near apex; lvs. thick-leathery, to 3 ft. long, deeply pinnatifid, pinnae to 8 in. long, about 1–2 in. wide, light green, glossy above, margin entire, flat, veins sunken but not visible; sori in 1–2 irregular rows on each side of segms., midrib deeply sunken. Tropics, Old World. Tender, needs greenhouse during winter in s. Calif. Zone 10.

Scouleri Hook. & Grev. LEATHERY P. Lvs. leathery, to 1½ ft. long, 6 in. wide, pinnatifid, pinnae to ¾ in. wide, rounded at apex, slightly wavy; sori next to midrib, ⅛ in. in diam. Coastal, B.C. to Calif.

sempervivoides: a listed name of no botanical standing; plants offered under this name are *P. virginianum.*

subauriculatum Blume. JOINTED PINE. Epiphyte; lvs. to 3 ft. long or more, to 1 ft. wide, 1-pinnate, pinnae to 5 in. long, ½ in. wide, truncate at base, entire or toothed. Trop. Asia to Australia. Cv. **'Knightiae'** [*P. Knightiae* Hort. Sander]. Margins fringed. Less tender, can be grown outdoors the year around in s. Calif. Zone 10.

subpetiolatum Hook. Epiphyte; lvs. to 2 ft. long, 1 ft. wide, 1-pinnate, pinnae tapered at base, sessile. Cuba, Mex., Guatemala.

vacciniifolium Langsd. & Fisch. Epiphyte, rhizomes creeping; lvs. widely spaced on rhizome, firm, ovate, less than 2 in. long, entire, veins visible. Trop. Amer.

venosum: a name of varied application; some plants offered under this name are *P. diversifolium.*

virginianum L. ROCK P., AMERICAN WALL FERN. Like *P. vulgare,* but rhizomes not sweet to the taste; lvs. smaller, to 10 in. long, narrower, to 3 in. wide, usually deeply pinnatifid, pinnae mostly attenuate, midrib straight at base; sori nearly marginal, mixed with glandular hairs. Cliffs and rocks, cool-temp. e. N. Amer.

vulgare L. EUROPEAN P., WALL P., WALL FERN, ADDER'S F. Forming mats, rhizomes sweet to the taste; lvs. evergreen, ovate-oblong, to 3 ft. long, 5 in. wide, green on both sides, deeply pinnatifid, pinnae to 2½ in. long, acute to rounded at apex, midribs curved at base; sori midway between margin and midrib, without glandular hairs. Rocks, banks, and trees, Eur., Asia. There are many Latin- and fancy-named crested, dissected, and plumed cvs. Var. **cambricum** (L.) Lightf. [*P. cambricum* L.]. Lvs. 2-pinnatifid. Brit. Isles. Var. **columbianum:** *P. hesperium.* Var. **occidentale:** *P. glycyrrhiza.*

POLYPOGON Desf. BEARD GRASS. *Gramineae.* About 10 spp. of usually decumbent ann. or per. grasses in temp. regions; lf. blades flat, scabrous; panicles dense, bristly, spike-like; spikelets 1-fld., pedicelled, articulated below the glumes, falling entire, glumes equal, long-awned, lemma much shorter than the glumes, bearing a shorter awn than glumes. For terminology see *Gramineae.*

monspeliensis (L.) Desf. RABBIT-FOOT GRASS, RABBIT'S-FOOT, ANNUAL B.G. Ann., sts. to 20 in.; lf. blades usually about ¼ in. wide; panicle to 6 in. long and ¾ in. wide, tawny-yellow; spikelets with hispidulous glumes less than ⅛ in. long, the awns mostly ¼–$^{5}/_{16}$ in. long, lemma smooth and glossy, half as long as the glumes. Eur.; introd. and weedy in the U.S., s. to Argentina.

POLYPTERIS: *PALAFOXIA.*

POLYRADICION Garay. *Orchidaceae.* Two spp. of leafless epiphytes, native to Fla. and W. Indies; sts. short, with densely entwined chlorophyllous roots; scape short, 1-fld.; sepals and petals separate, spreading, lip sessile at base of column, with a long spur, column short, 2-winged, pollinia 2, with separate stalks and glands. For structure of fl. see *Orchidaceae.*

For culture see *Orchids.*

Lindenii (Lindl.) Garay [*Polyrrhiza Lindenii* (Lindl.) Cogn.]. PALM-POLLY, WHITE BUTTERFLY ORCHID. Roots flexuous, glaucous-green, closely appressed to bark of trees; peduncle glabrous, brownish-black, to 8 in. long; fls. large, showy, fragrant, sepals and petals white, suffused with green, sepals lanceolate, to ¾ in. long, petals linear-lanceolate, sickle-shaped, recurved, 1 in. long, lip white, 1¼ in. long, 3-lobed, lateral lobes semicuneate, 1 in. wide, midlobe dilated from base into pair of retrorse, elongate-linear, acuminate lobes 2¾ in. long. Late winter–summer. S. Fla., W. Indies.

POLYRRHIZA Pfitz.: *DENDROPHYLAX.* **P. funalis:** *D. funalis:* **P. Lindenii:** *Polyradicion Lindenii.*

POLYSCIAS J. R. Forst. & G. Forst. [*Nothopanax* Miq.]. *Araliaceae.* About 80 spp. of mostly unarmed, glabrous shrubs and trees with aromatic foliage, native to Polynesia and trop. Asia; lvs. mostly 2–3-pinnate; fls. very small, in heads or umbels, usually arranged in panicles, pedicels jointed, (4–)5(–8)-merous, ovary 5–8-celled, styles 5–8, separate; fr. a drupe.

Widely grown in the North as greenhouse foliage plants and outdoors in the tropics and subtropics (Zone 10b) for hedges and other landscape use. Rarely flowering in cultivation. Propagated mainly by cuttings of mature wood.

Balfouriana (Hort. Sander) L. H. Bailey [*Aralia Balfouriana* Hort. Sander]. BALFOUR ARALIA. Small tree, to 25 ft., but compact shrub in cult., sts. green, speckled gray; lvs. commonly trifoliolate, lfts. broadly ovate to orbicular, mostly 2–4 in. wide, cordate, margins crenate to dentate or somewhat lacerate, often white. New Caledonia. Cv. 'Marginata'. Lfts. white-margined. Cv. 'Pennockii'. Lfts. large.

filicifolia (C. Moore ex E. Fourn.) L. H. Bailey [*Aralia filicifolia* C. Moore ex E. Fourn.]. FERN-LEAF ARALIA. Shrub, to 8 ft., brs. usually purple; lvs. pinnate, lfts. varying, sometimes on the same plant, from oblong and entire to 7 in. long, to very narrow, pinnatifid, sharply toothed, and to 1 ft. long. Pacific Is. Cvs. 'Marginata' and 'Variegata', lfts. white-margined. Common hedge plant in Key West, Fla.

fruticosa (L.) Harms. [*Aralia fruticosa* Hort., probably not Moç. & Sessé]. MING ARALIA. Shrub, 6–8 ft.; lvs. at least 3-pinnate, appearing much-divided into fine segms., lfts. varying from narrowly ovate to lanceolate, to 4 in. long, toothed or deeply cut. India to Polynesia. Cv. 'Deleauana', dwarf, lvs. much divided, lfts. variably shaped, irregularly lobed and toothed, bright green, white-margined; 'Elegans', compact with dense, leathery lvs.; 'Plumata' [*Panax excelsus* Hort.], lfts. small, narrow, very fine.

Guilfoylei (Bull) L. H. Bailey [*Aralia Guilfoylei* Bull]. GERANIUM-LEAF ARALIA, WILD COFFEE, COFFEE TREE. Shrub, 15–20 ft., usually few-branched; lvs. pinnate, to 16 in. long, lfts. ovate to orbicular, remotely toothed, to 5 in. long, usually with white margins or splashes. Polynesia. Cv. 'Laciniata'. Lfts. of various shapes, white-margined, cut into unequal, sharp teeth. Cv. 'Victoriae'. Compact; lfts. small, much-divided and cut, white-margined.

POLYSTACHYA Hook. *Orchidaceae.* About 200 spp. of pantrop. epiphytes; sts. thickened or pseudobulbous, leafy, 1- to several-lvd.; lvs. 2-ranked; infl. a simple or paniculate raceme; fls. small, nonresupinate, upper sepal separate, lateral sepals attached to foot of column, forming a mentum, petals linear, lip 3-lobed, disc with conspicuous callus covered with mealy hairs, column short, with prominent foot. For structure of fl. see *Orchidaceae.*

For culture see *Orchids.*

flavescens (Blume) J. J. Sm. [*P. luteola* (Swartz) Hook.; *P. minuta* (Aubl.) Frapp. ex Cordem.]. Erect, to 2 ft., pseudobulbs 3 in. long, set closely together, 1- to several-lvd.; lvs. oblong-elliptic, to 1 ft. long; infl. a many-fld., short-branched panicle, to 6 in. long; fls. very small, bright yellow-green, mentum well developed, sepals triangular-ovate, ⅛ in. long, petals linear-spatulate, as long as sepals, paler, lip 3-lobed, less than ¼ in. long, cream, midlobe fleshy, squarish-oblong, with undulate-crenulate margins, disc covered with inconspicuous glandular hairs. Pantrop.

foliosa (Lindl.) Rchb.f. [*P. stenophylla* Schlechter]. To 2 ft., sts. close together, to 5 in. long, 2- to several-lvd.; lvs. more or less clustered at base of st., oblong-linear, to 1 ft. long; infl. as long as lvs., either a densely fld. raceme or a panicle; fls. minute, fleshy, greenish to pale yellow or yellowish-white, sometimes tinged with purple, mentum short, sepals nearly orbicular, ¼ in. long, petals linear, shorter than sepals, lip erect, parallel to column, tubular-concave, 3-lobed, to less than ¼ in. long, midlobe squarish-oblong, disc covered with papillae or mealy hairs. W. Indies, Cent. Amer. to Venezuela and Peru.

luteola: *P. flavescens.*

minuta: *P. flavescens.*

stenophylla: *P. foliosa.*

POLYSTICHUM Roth. SHIELD FERN. *Polypodiaceae.* About 120 spp. of cosmopolitan, woodland, terrestrial ferns, with erect rhizomes; lvs. elongate, usually pinnatifid to 2-pinnate, with sharp-toothed margins; sori round, indusia peltate. Differs from *Dryopteris,* in which indusia are cordate or reniform and attached at the sinus (not strictly peltate), and lvs. rarely with sharp-toothed margins.

Our native species are sometimes transferred to the wild garden; others are cool or warm greenhouse plants of easy culture. See also *Ferns.*

acrostichoides (Michx.) Schott [*Asplenium acrostichoides* (Michx.) Swartz; *Dryopteris acrostichoides* (Michx.) O. Kuntze]. CHRISTMAS FERN, DAGGER F., CANKER BRAKE. Lvs. evergreen, to 2 ft. long and 5 in. wide, 1-pinnate, pinnae linear-lanceolate, those bearing spores contracted, with apices bluntly acute to obtuse. There are many variants and forms. E. N. Amer. Zone 4.

aculeatum (L.) Roth [*P. lobatum* (Huds.) Chevall.]. PRICKLY S.F., HEDGE F. Lvs. to 2 ft. long and 6 in. wide, rigid, dark green, glossy, pinnate-pinnatifid to 2-pinnate, lower pinnae shorter, each pinna with 10–15 pairs of pinnules, the pinnules acute at base. Widely distributed in Old World and S. Amer. Very variable; most material listed under this name is *P. setiferum.* Cv. 'Proliferum': *P. setiferum* cv.

adiantiforme: *Rumohra adiantiformis.*

alaskense: see *P. Braunii.*

Andersonii L. S. Hopk. ANDERSON'S HOLLY FERN. Lvs. to 3 ft. long and 8 in. wide, 2-pinnate, or nearly so, pinnules slightly scaly beneath, teeth long-awned, rachis proliferous below tip; indusia erose-dentate; otherwise much like *P. Dudleyi.* Alaska to Wash. and Mont. Some plants in the trade under this name are *P. californicum.*

angulare: *P. setiferum.*

aristatum: *Arachnioides aristata.*

×**Bicknellii** (Christ) Hahne: *P. aculeatum* × *P. setiferum.* Lvs. somewhat arching, leathery, 30 in. long, 8 in. wide, long-triangular, not narrowed at base, fully 2-pinnate, glossy, dark green, pinnules 15–20, auricled on upper surface. Material grown as *P. setosum* may be this hybrid.

Braunii (Spenn.) Fée. SHIELD FERN, BRAUN'S HOLLY F. Lvs. to 2 ft. long, 2-pinnate, pinnules broadly oblong, rounded, spine-tipped at apex, sharp-toothed, the rachis bearing 1 or 2 proliferating buds, covered with hairlike scales. Eur. Hardy. Var. **Purshii** Fern. PURSH'S HOLLY FERN. Lvs. thicker, veins more obscure, rachis with scales more broad than threadlike. N. N. Amer. to n. China. Some material of Alaskan origin passing as *P. Braunii* is *P. alaskense* Maxon, which lacks proliferating buds on the rachis.

californicum (D. C. Eat.) Underw. CALIFORNIA HOLLY FERN. Lvs. to 2½ ft. long and 8 in. wide, 1-pinnate, pinnae large, linear, pinnatifid into elliptic segms., the basal segms. largest and almost separate. Wash. to Calif.

capense: *Rumohra adiantiformis.*

coriaceum: *Rumohra adiantiformis.*

Dudleyi Maxon. DUDLEY'S HOLLY FERN, DUDLEY'S S.F. Lvs. to 3 ft. long, to 10 in. wide, 2-pinnate, oblong-lanceolate to narrow-ovate, long-acuminate to attenuate, not proliferous, copiously scaly beneath, dull dark green above, with curved, short-awned teeth; sori many, indusia delicate, long-ciliate. Calif.

falcatum: *Cyrtomium falcatum.*

Lemmonii Underw. Lvs. to 1 ft. long and 2 in. wide, 1-pinnate to pinnatifid toward apex, pinnae pinnately lobed or divided into many small crenulate-dentate segms.; sori few. Alaska to n. Calif.

lobatum: *P. aculeatum.*

Lonchitis (L.) Roth. HOLLY FERN, MOUNTAIN H.F., NORTHERN H.F. Lvs. leathery, evergreen, to 2 ft. long, 1-pinnate, pinnae lanceolate, to 1½ in. long, spiny-toothed and strongly auricled at base, the lowest pinnae reduced to small triangular lobes. Mts., N. Amer., Eur., Asia. Hardy.

montanum: *Thelypteris Oreopteris.*

munitum (Kaulf.) K. Presl [*Aspidium munitum* Kaulf.]. GIANT HOLLY FERN, WESTERN SWORD F. Lvs. leathery, evergreen, to 3½ ft. long and 10 in. wide, 1-pinnate, pinnae linear, sharp-toothed or cut, acuminate, petioles to 2 ft. long. Alaska to Mont. and Calif. Hardy. Var. **imbricans** (D. C. Eat.) Maxon. IMBRICATE SWORD FERN. Lvs. smaller, pinnae crowded, obliquely imbricate.

plumosum compactum and **plumosum densum:** listed names, probably for variations of *P. munitum.*

proliferum: *P. setiferum* cv.

Richardii (Hook.) John Sm. Lvs. oblong-ovate, about 15 in. long, 3 in. wide, 2-pinnate, pinnae narrow-triangular, 2–3 in. long, often woolly or scaly beneath, basal pinnules stalked, sharp-toothed; indusia white, with small black dot in center. New Zeal., Fiji Is.

scopulinum (D. C. Eat.) Maxon. WESTERN HOLLY FERN, EATON'S S.F. Lvs. to 1 ft. long and 2½ in. wide, 1-pinnate, pinnae pinnately lobed or divided into few, large, sharp-toothed segms., 2–3 lowermost segms. nearly distinct and separate, alt.; sori many. Que., Wash. to Idaho, Utah, and s. Calif.

setiferum (Forssk.) Woyn. [*P. angulare* (Kit.) K. Presl]. HEDGE FERN, ENGLISH H.F. Similar to *P. aculeatum*, but larger, more vigorous; lvs. arching, duller, fully 2-pinnate and more finely divided, less tapered at base, with brown scales at least beneath, pinnae lanceolate to curved, with 12–20 pairs of pinnules, pinnule base truncate and parallel to the axis of the pinna. Eur. Most material grown as *P. aculeatum* belongs here. The many cvs. include: 'Densum', lvs. dense; 'Multifidum', reported to have much-dissected segms.; 'Proliferum' [*P. proliferum* K. Presl], PLUME FERN, a proliferous form.

setosum: most material cult. under this name may be the hybrid *P.* × *Bicknellii*, or a variant of *P. aculeatum*.

Standishii: *Arachniodes Standishii*.

tsus-simense (Hook.) John Sm. [*Aspidium tsus-simense* (John Sm.) Hook.]. Lvs. narrow-triangular, 2-pinnate at base, to 2 ft. long or usually less, pinnae pinnatifid, the upper basal pinnule stalked, or nearly so, longer than others and auricled. Asia. Small and suitable for fern baskets; also much used in dish gardens.

varium: *Dryopteris varia*.

viviparum Fée. Lvs. to 1½ ft. long, 6 in. wide, 2-pinnate basally, pinnae many, lanceolate, deeply lobed, central pinnae 2 in. long, ½–⅝ in. wide, the upper side auricled, petiole scales large, lanceolate, lower ones nearly black at center; sori in 2 or 4 rows. W. Indies.

POMADERRIS Labill. *Rhamnaceae*. About 40 spp. of shrubs and trees of Australia and New Zeal.; lvs. alt., simple, mostly tomentose and stellate-hairy; fls. small, greenish, in cymes, corymbs, or panicles; fr. a small caps.

Grown as ornamentals in the South and Calif. Propagated by cuttings of half-ripened shoots under glass.

apetala Labill. To 20 ft.; lvs. oblong, to 4 in. long, white-tomentose beneath, rusty on veins; fls. in panicles to 7 in. long, greenish-white, petals 0. Australia, New Zeal. Planted as a yard and street tree in Calif.

elliptica Labill. To 8 ft.; lvs. oblong, to 3 in. long, white-tomentose beneath; fls. in much-branched panicles, ¼ in. across, petals bright yellow. Tasmania.

Kumeraho A. Cunn. Shrub, to nearly 10 ft., brs. slender; lvs. elliptic, to 2½ in. long, 1¼ in. wide, blue-green and stellate-hairy beneath; fls. in corymbs, calyx tube villous with simple and stellate hairs, petals yellow. New Zeal.

phylicifolia Lodd. ex Link. To 4 ft.; lvs. linear or linear-oblong, to ⁵⁄₁₆ in. long, revolute to midrib, rough-hairy above; fls. in small cymes, petals 0. New Zeal.

rugosa Cheesem. To 8 ft.; lvs. oblong-lanceolate, to 1½ in. long, pubescent beneath, rusty on veins; fls. in cymes, petals 0. New Zeal.

POMEGRANATE. A shrub native to southwestern Asia, the pomegranate, *Punica Granatum*, has been cultivated for centuries in hot, arid lands for its refreshing fruit and as an ornamental. In the United States it thrives best in the hot desert valleys of California and the Southwest (Zone 9), but a dwarf kind (cv. 'Nana') is also often grown as a greenhouse ornamental. Although pomegranates can be grown throughout the tropics and subtropics, like the date palm they only produce good crops under semiarid conditions where heat accompanies the ripening season and abundant water is available at the roots. Propagation is by seeds, cuttings, and layers, but select cultivars are normally reproduced by hardwood cuttings. The species does best on deep, rather heavy loams, and under such conditions fruits at three or four years of age. Fruit is borne terminally on short spurs produced on slow-growing, mature wood. Since fruit is liable to splitting if left on the plant, it is normally picked by clipping before full maturity and will keep well for months if stored in a cool, dry place. Cultivars include 'Paper-Shell', 'Spanish Ruby', and 'Wonderful'.

POMOLOGY: see *Horticulture*.

PONCIRUS Raf. *Rutaceae*. One sp., a spiny, deciduous tree of cent. and n. China; lvs. alt., of 3 lfts., glandular-dotted; fls. solitary or in pairs, sepals and petals 5, stamens 20–60, unequal, separate; fr. like a small orange, yellow, densely pubescent, 6–8-celled.

Planted as an ornamental and for hedges in many countries; in the U.S. hardy in Zone 8 but in protected places on the coasts as far north as Seattle and Boston; also much used as a stock for citrus to make them more hardy, and as parent in hybridization. Propagated by seeds. See *Citrus Fruits*.

trifoliata (L.) Raf. [*Aegle sepiaria* DC.; *Citrus trifoliata* L.]. TRIFOLIATE ORANGE, HARDY O. Brs. stiff, angled; lfts. elliptic to obovate, 1½ in. long, petiole winged; fls. white, to 2 in. across, in axils of thorns, appearing before the lvs.; fr. to 2 in. in diam., very fragrant, pulp scant, acid.

PONGAMIA Venten. *Leguminosae* (subfamily *Faboideae*). One sp., a tree of trop. Asia and Australia; lvs. alt., odd-pinnate; fls. in loose, axillary racemes, purplish, pink, or white, papilionaceous, standard basally eared, keel petals coherent at tips; fr. a thick, flat, woody, indehiscent legume, with 1 seed.

Grown as an ornamental in southern U.S.; the seeds furnish an oil. Propagated by seeds.

pinnata (L.) Pierre. KARUM TREE, POONGA-OIL TREE. To 40 ft.; lfts. 5 or 7, ovate, to 4 in. long, with strong odor; racemes to 5 in. long; standard about ½ in. across; fr. oblong, to 2 in. long and 1 in. wide.

PONTEDERIA L. *Pontederiaceae*. A few spp. of aquatic, per. herbs, native to N. and S. Amer.; lvs. thick, parallel-veined, long-petioled; fls. blue, in spikes, ovary with 1 fertile cell; fr. 1-seeded, achenelike.

Grown in ponds and bog gardens; the water should be about 1 ft. deep or less. Propagated by division.

cordata L. PICKEREL WEED. To 4 ft.; lvs. to 10 in. long and 6 in. wide, narrowly ovate, cordate at base; upper lobe of perianth with 2 yellow spots. Nov. Sc. to Fla. and Tex. Forma **angustifolia** (Pursh) Solms-Laub. [*P. montevidensis* Hort.]. Lvs. lanceolate to linear-lanceolate, truncate or tapering at base.

montevidensis: *P. cordata* forma *angustifolia*.

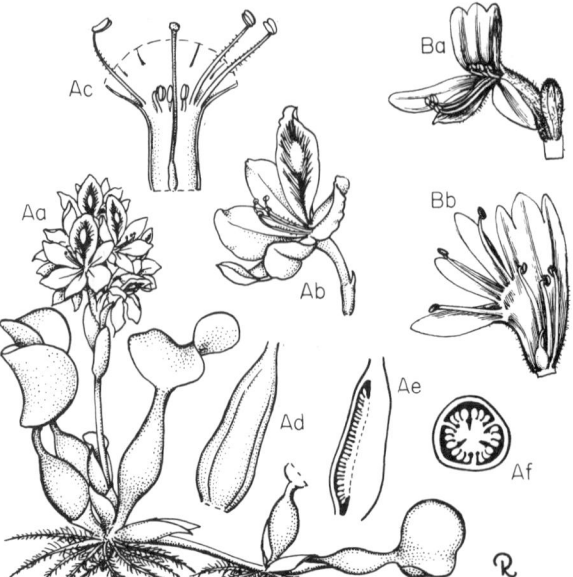

PONTEDERIACEAE. **A,** *Eichhornia crassipes:* **Aa,** flowering plant, ¼; **Ab,** flower, × ½; **Ac,** flower, perianth expanded (lobes cut off), × ¾; **Ad,** ovary, × 3; **Ae,** ovary, vertical section, × 3; **Af,** ovary, cross section, × 6. **B,** *Pontederia cordata:* **Ba,** flower and bud, × 1½; **Bb,** flower, perianth expanded, × 1½.

PONTEDERIACEAE Kunth. PICKEREL WEED FAMILY. Monocot.; 6 genera of trop. and temp. herbs, native to swamps or ponds, and floating or rooted in mud; lvs. various; fls. bisexual, somewhat irregular, perianth 6-parted, corolla-like, usually showy; stamens 3 or 6, ovary superior; fr. a caps. or achene. *Eichhornia*, *Heteranthera*, and *Pontederia* are grown in ponds and pools.

POPULUS L. POPLAR, ASPEN, COTTONWOOD. *Salicaceae*. About 30–40 spp. of dioecious, large or small trees with soft white wood, widely distributed in the N. Hemisphere; lvs. alt., mostly broad, petioles long, often flattened sidewise; fls. in drooping catkins appearing before the lvs.; fr. a small caps., seeds surrounded by copious hairs. The name cottonwood is applied mostly to *P. deltoides* and other spp., such as *P. Sargentii, P. Fremontii, P. Wislizenii,* in which the female tree becomes objectionable because of the copious "cotton" discharged from the caps.

Much planted for pulpwood, windbreaks, avenues, and as ornamentals. Poplars are of easy cultivation in almost any soil and grow promptly and rapidly. The roots are likely to stop drains or cause heaving of sidewalks, so poplars should be planted with caution. Propagated by hardwood cuttings, suckers, or sometimes by seeds, and the weeping sorts by grafting on upright forms.

×**acuminata** Rydb.: *P. angustifolia* × *P. Sargentii.* To 45 ft.; lvs. rhombic-lanceolate, to 4 in. long, broadly cuneate, glossy dark green above, light green beneath. Alta. and Sask., s. to New Mex. Zone 3.

adenopoda Maxim. CHINESE A. To 75 ft. or more; lvs. ovate, to 4 in. long or more, truncate or cordate at base, pale green beneath, with grayish pubescence at least when young. China. Zone 6.

alba L. WHITE P., SILVER-LEAVED P., ABELE. To 90 ft. or more; lvs. ovate, to 5 in. long, palmately 3–5-lobed or -toothed, rounded or slightly cordate, white- or gray-tomentose beneath. Eur., Asia; naturalized in N. Amer. Zone 4. Wood used for turning, matches, and excelsior. Cvs. are: 'Bolleana'; 'Pyramidalis'; 'Globosa' [var. *globosa* Hort. Späth], small, with dense oval crown; 'Nivea' [vars. *argentea* Hort. and *nivea* Ait.], lvs. lobed, densely white-tomentose beneath; 'Pendula' [var. *pendula* Loud.], brs. drooping; 'Pyramidalis' [vars. *Bolleana* (Lauche) Otto and *pyramidalis* Bunge; *P. Bolleana* Lauche], columnar in habit; 'Richardii', lvs. yellow above. Var. **argentea:** cv. 'Nivea'. Var. **Bolleana:** cv. 'Pyramidalis'. Var. **globosa:** cv. 'Globosa'. Var. **nivea:** cv. 'Nivea'. Var. **pendula:** cv. 'Pendula'. Var. **pyramidalis:** cv. 'Pyramidalis'.

angustifolia James. To 60 ft.; lvs. lanceolate or ovate-lanceolate, to 4 in. long, rounded or cuneate, light green beneath. Alta. and Sask., s. to New Mex., Tex., Chihuahua (n. Mex.). Zone 3.

balsamifera L. [*P. candicans* Ait.; *P. Tacamahacca* Mill.]. BALSAM P., HACKMATACK, TACAMAHAC. To 75 or 100 ft. at maturity, branchlets and winter buds viscid, appearing varnished; lvs. ovate to ovate-lanceolate, to 4½ in. long, rather thick and firm, glabrous, whitish beneath. N. N. Amer. Zone 2. Wood used for excelsior, plywood, boxes, and paper pulp. Var. **subcordata** Hyl. Lvs. subcordate or rounded at base, sometimes slightly pubescent on veins beneath. Ne. N. Amer.

×**berolinensis** Dipp.: *P. laurifolia* × *P. nigra* cv. 'Italica'. Columnar in habit; lvs. ovate, to 4 in. long, long-pointed, margin narrow, translucent. Zone 2.

Bolleana: *P. alba* cv. 'Pyramidalis'.

×**canadensis** Moench: *P. deltoides* × *P. nigra.* CAROLINA P. Vigorous upright tree; lvs. triangular-ovate, to 4 in. long, truncate at base, somewhat ciliate. Zone 4. Cvs. are: 'Aurea', lvs. yellow; 'Erecta', pyramidal in form; 'Eugenei' [*P. Eugenei* Hort. Simon-Louis ex C. Koch], EUGENE P., narrow-pyramidal in habit; 'Gelrica' [*P. gelrica* (Houtz.) Houtz.], male, a vigorous grower with narrow crown and reddish shoots, lvs. 3-angled, broader than long, coarsely toothed, bright green, glabrous; 'Marilandica' [*P. marilandica* Bosc ex Poir.], brs. wide-spreading; 'Serotina' [var. *serotina* (T. Hartig) Rehd.; *P. serotina* T. Hartig], brs. wide-spreading, ascending.

candicans: *P. balsamifera.*

canescens (Ait.) Sm. GRAY P. Tall tree, resembling *P. alba,* but having lvs. smaller, only obscurely lobed, and gray beneath. Zone 4. Cv. 'Macrophylla'. A vigorous grower; lvs. on long shoots, to 6 in. long.

carolinensis, caroliniana: listed names of no botanical standing; in the trade they may be applied to more than one sp., but probably refer to *P.* × *canadensis.*

cathayana Rehd. [*P. suaveolens* of auth., not Fisch.]. To 90 ft.; lvs. ovate to ovate-lanceolate, to 4 in. long and 2¼ in. wide, rounded or cuneate at base, glossy above, whitish beneath. Asia. Zone 6. Likely to be confused with *P. Maximowiczii.*

deltoides Bartr. ex Marsh. [*P. deltoides* var. *missouriensis* (A. Henry) A. Henry]. COTTONWOOD, NECKLACE P. To 90 ft., with broad crown; lvs. ovate, to 7 in. long, truncate or somewhat cordate at base, glossy above. Que. to Fla., w. to Tex. Zone 2.

Eugenei: *P* × *canadensis* cv.

fastigiata: *P. nigra* cv. 'Italica'.

Fremontii S. Wats. FREMONT C. To 90 ft.; lvs. triangular, to 2½ in. long and 3 in. wide, truncate or slightly cordate at base, glossy above. Calif., Ariz. Zone 7. Var. **Wislizenii** S. Wats. RIO GRANDE C., WISLIZENUS C. To 90 ft.; lvs. triangular-ovate, to 4 in. long and as broad, truncate at base, yellowish-green. S. Colo. and s. Utah, s. to New Mex., w. Tex., n. Mex.

gelrica: *P.* × *canadensis* cv.

×**generosa** A. Henry: *P. deltoides* × *P. trichocarpa.* Vigorous grower; lvs. coarsely serrate, pale beneath, margin narrow, translucent, petiole nearly cylindrical.

×**gileadensis** Rouleau. BALM-OF-GILEAD. Presumed to be a hybrid between *P. balsamifera* and *P. deltoides.* Known only as female plants, to 60 ft. with broad crown, twigs stout, angled, brown-hairy; lvs. triangular-ovate, to 6 in. long, usually cordate, densely pubescent on veins beneath. Spreads by suckering, persists, and sometimes escapes from cult. The status and origin of the balm-of-Gilead poplar is uncertain; by some it is considered to be a clone of *P. balsamifera* var. *subcordata.*

grandidentata Michx. LARGE-TOOTHED A. To 60 ft.; lvs. ovate, to 4 in. long, truncate or cuneate at base, coarsely toothed, grayish-tomentose beneath but becoming glabrous. Que. to Ont., e. U.S. Zone 4.

heterophylla L. SWAMP C., BLACK C., DOWNY P. To 90 ft., or shrubby in cult.; lvs. broad-ovate, to 7 in. long, cordate or rounded, pale green and often slightly pubescent beneath. Conn., s. to Ga. and La. Zone 6.

koreana Rehd. To 75 ft.; lvs. to 6 in. long and 3¼ in. across, rounded at base, dark green and wrinkled above, whitish beneath, with red midrib. Korea. Zone 6.

lasiocarpa D. Oliver. To 60 ft.; lvs. ovate, to 1 ft. long, cordate, light green and pubescent beneath, with red midrib. China.

laurifolia Ledeb. To 45 ft., branchlets pubescent toward apex, sharply angled; lvs. elliptic-ovate to lanceolate, to 5 in. long, rounded at base, whitish and slightly pubescent beneath. Siberia. Zone 5.

Lombardi: a listed name of no botanical standing; probably refers to *P. nigra* cv. 'Italica'.

marilandica: *P.* × *canadensis* cv.

Maximowiczii A. Henry. To 90 ft.; lvs. leathery, elliptic to nearly orbicular, to 5 in. long, slightly cordate, whitish beneath and pubescent on veins. Ne. Asia. Wood used for matches, boxes, and wood pulp.

Meyeri: a listed name of no botanical standing.

nigra L. BLACK P. To 90 ft.; lvs. triangular, to 4 in. long and 3 in. wide, cuneate or rounded at base, light green beneath. Eur., Asia. Zone 2. Cv. 'Italica' [var. *italica* Muenchh.; *P. fastigiata* Desf.; *P. pyramidalis* Salisb.; *P. pyramidata* Moench]. LOMBARDY P. Narrow-columnar in habit; lvs. mostly narrowly cuneate. Usually only male trees; the few known female trees have brs. less strictly erect and a broader crown. Its formal columnar habit makes it a striking tree. Much planted in U.S. and s. Canada; persists and escapes locally. Var. **betulifolia** (Pursh) Torr. Lvs. pubescent when young. Var. **elegans** L. H. Bailey [var. *plantierensis* (Hort. Simon-Louis ex C. K. Schneid.) C. K. Schneid.]. Columnar in form, with brs. and petioles pubescent. Var. **italica:** cv. 'Italica'. Var. **plantierensis:** var. *elegans.* Var. **thevestina** (Dode) Bean. Trunk whitish, bark of older brs. grayish, otherwise like cv. 'Italica'.

×**Petrowskiana** (Regel) C. K. Schneid.: *P. deltoides* × ?*P. laurifolia.* Lvs. ovate, to 6 in. long, pale beneath.

Purdomii Rehd. Lvs. ovate or oblong-ovate, to 10 in. long, rounded or slightly cordate. China. A handsome, large-lvd. poplar.

pyramidalis: *P. nigra* cv. 'Italica'.

pyramidata: *P. nigra* cv. 'Italica'.

Richardii: a listed name of no botanical standing, probably for *P. alba* cv.

×**robusta** C. K. Schneid.: *P. deltoides* × *P. nigra* var. *elegans.* A vigorous tree, brs. ascending; lvs. cuneate to subcordate at base.

Sargentii Dode. GREAT PLAINS C. Resembling *P. deltoides,* but having branchlets light yellow, buds pubescent, and lvs. mostly smaller. Sask., s. to New Mex. and Tex. Zone 2.

serotina: *P.* × *canadensis* cv.

Sieboldii Miq. JAPANESE A. To 60 ft.; lvs. ovate, to 3 in. long, rounded or cuneate, pubescent when young. Japan. Zone 6.

Simonii Carrière. To 35 ft.; lvs. rhombic-ovate, to 4 in. long and 3 in. wide, rounded at base, whitish or pale green beneath. China. Zone 2. Attractive slender-branched tree with rather small, bright green lvs. Cv. 'Fastigiata'. Narrow-pyramidal in habit. Cv. 'Pendula'. Brs. drooping.

suaveolens: see *P. cathayana.*

Tacamahacca: *P. balsamifera.*

tremula L. EUROPEAN A. To 90 ft., with open crown; lvs. orbicular to elliptic, to 3 in. long, truncate at base, with large teeth, becoming glabrous beneath, petioles flattened. Eur., N. Afr., Asia. Zone 2. Cv. 'Pendula'. Brs. drooping.

tremuloides Michx. QUAKING A., TREMBLING A., QUIVERLEAF. To 90 ft.; lvs. ovate to orbicular, to 3 in. long, truncate at base, finely toothed, petioles flattened. N. Amer. Zone 1. Cv. 'Pendula'. Brs. drooping.

trichocarpa Torr. & A. Gray. WESTERN BALSAM P., BLACK C. To 180 ft.; lvs. broad-ovate, to 5 in. or sometimes 10 in. long, truncate or rounded at base, whitish or rusty beneath. Alaska and Yukon, s. to Calif. and Baja Calif. Zone 5.

tristis Fisch. Small tree; lvs. narrow-ovate, 4 in. long and 2 in. wide, rounded at base, whitish and pubescent beneath. Cent. Asia. Zone 6.

Vanderi: a listed name of no botanical standing.

PORANA Burm.f. *Convolvulaceae*. About 25 spp. of twining herbs of Afr., se. Asia, Malay Arch., and Australia; lvs. alt., cordate-ovate, entire; fls. small, white, blue, or purple, in cymes or panicles, some or all of sepals becoming enlarged, scarious, prominently veined and falling with the fr.

paniculata Roxb. BRIDAL-BOUQUET, CHRIST VINE, SNOW CREEPER, SNOW-IN-THE-JUNGLE, WHITE CORALLITA. To 30 ft.; lvs. to 6 in. long, white-pubescent beneath; fls. white, to 5/16 in. across, in many-fld. panicles. N. India to Upper Burma. Grown in s. U.S. for its dense masses of white fls.

PORFIRIA: *MAMMILLARIA* subgenus *Porfiria.* **P.** Schwarzii: *M. coahuilensis.*

PORTEA C. Koch. *Bromeliaceae*. Seven spp. of herbs, native to Brazil; lvs. in basal rosettes, spiny; infl. scapose, bracted, paniculate; fls. violet or blue, pedicelled, sepals united, mucronate, petals separate, pollen sculptured, ovary inferior; fr. a berry, seeds without appendages.

Grown outdoors in warm climates or under glass. Requires bright light. For culture see *Bromeliaceae.*

petropolitana (Wawra) Mez. To 2 ft. or more; lvs. green, with many dark spines; scape many-fld., pedicels to 5/8 in. long; fls. blue, to 1 3/16 in. long. Var. **extensa** L. B. Sm. Brs. and pedicels more elongate, pedicels 1½ in. long or more.

PORTLANDIA P. Br. *Rubiaceae*. Twenty-five spp. of shrubs or small trees, native to Mex., Cent. Amer., W. Indies; lvs. opp., large, leathery, stipules interpetiolar, united with the petioles to form a sheath; fls. white or purple, large, 5–6-merous, corolla campanulate or funnelform; fr. a leathery caps., seeds many.

Propagated by cuttings.

grandiflora L. Shrub, to 10 ft.; lvs. oblong to ovate, to 1½ in. long, glossy above, venation prominent on both surfaces; fls. axillary, solitary, on stout pedicels 3/8 in. long, corolla white, to 8 in. long. W. Indies. A handsome evergreen shrub, the large white fls. shaped much like an Easter lily.

platantha Hook. A doubtful sp.; said to be similar to *P. grandiflora,* but corolla smaller.

PORTULACA L. PURSLANE, MOSS ROSE. *Portulacaceae.* Over 100 spp. of fleshy or trailing, mostly ann. herbs, widely distributed in warm regions; lvs. alt., sometimes cylindrical, the upper forming a leafy involucre subtending the often showy and variously colored fls.; calyx 2-cleft, petals 4–6, usually 5, stamens 8 to many; fr. a caps., opening by the top falling as a lid.

A few species grown as annuals in the flower garden, one sometimes grown or collected as a potherb.

grandiflora Hook. ROSE MOSS, SUN PLANT, ELEVEN-O'CLOCK. Prostrate, or to 1 ft. high; lvs. cylindrical, to 1 in. long; fls. rose, red, yellow, white, often striped, 1 in. across, or more. Brazil, Argentina, Uruguay. A favorite garden ann. for warm, sunny places.

oleracea L. PURSLANE, PUSLEY. Sts. thick and soft, prostrate, forming mats; lvs. spatulate to obovate, to 1¼ in. long; fls. bright yellow, to 3/8 in. across. Cosmopolitan and weedy, but probably originally from India. The wild, weedy form may be eaten as greens or salad, but is not cult. Cv. 'Giganthes' [var. *giganthes* L. H. Bailey]. Prostrate; fls. double, 1 in. across. Grown as an ornamental. Var. **sativa** DC. KITCHEN-GARDEN P. Sts. to 1½ ft., erect, thicker, very succulent; lvs. obovate; fls. ½ in. across. Grown as a pot or salad herb.

pilosa L. Sts. with tufts of white shaggy hairs; lvs. cylindrical, ½ in. long; fls. red, ½ in. across or less. N.C. to Fla. and Mex. Cv. 'Hortualis' [var. *hortualis* L. H. Bailey]. SHAGGY GARDEN P. Grown as an ornamental; fls. red-purple, larger, to ¾ in. across.

PORTULACACEAE Juss. PURSLANE FAMILY. Dicot.; about 16 genera and 500 spp. of ann. or per., cosmopolitan

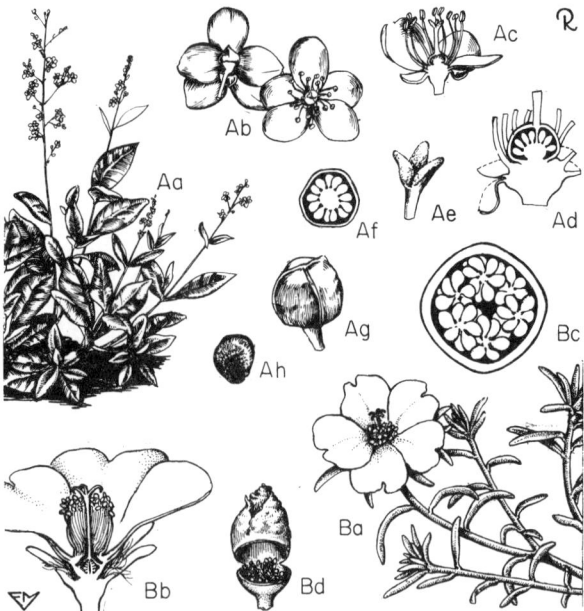

PORTULACACEAE. **A,** *Talinum paniculatum:* **Aa,** plant, × ⅛; **Ab,** flower, back and face views, × 1½; **Ac,** flower, vertical section, × 2; **Ad,** base of flower and ovary, vertical section, × 5; **Ae,** stigma, × 8; **Af,** ovary, cross section, × 6; **Ag,** fruit, × 2; **Ah,** seed, × 5; **B,** *Portulaca grandiflora:* **Ba,** flowering stem, × ½; **Bb,** flower, vertical section, × 1; **Bc,** ovary, cross section, × 4; **Bd,** fruit, dehiscing, × 1. (Ba-Bd from Bailey, *Manual of Cultivated Plants,* ed. 2.)

herbs or subshrubs; lvs. alt. or opp., simple, entire, often fleshy; fls. in cymes or racemes or solitary, often showy, regular, bisexual, sepals usually 2, sometimes more, petals 4–5, rarely fewer or to 18, falling early, stamens few or many, ovary superior or rarely half-inferior, 1-celled, but often 3–7-celled basally; fr. a caps. Some grown as ornamentals and a few as potherbs: *Anacampseros, Calandrinia, Calyptridium, Claytonia, Lewisia, Montia, Portulaca, Portulacaria,* and *Talinum.*

PORTULACARIA Jacq. *Portulacaceae*. One sp., a succulent shrub or small tree, nearly horizontally branched, native to arid parts of S. Afr.; lvs. opp., sessile, obovate, deciduous; fls. small, pale pink.

Grown under glass or in the open in coastal Calif. Zone 10.

afra (L.) Jacq. ELEPHANT BUSH. To 12 ft., with soft wood; lvs. to ¾ in. long; fls. about 1/16 in. long, in clusters. Used where native as a fodder for livestock. Cvs. 'Tricolor' and 'Variegata' are listed.

POSOQUERIA Aubl. *Rubiaceae*. About 12 spp. of trees or shrubs, native to trop. Amer.; lvs. opp., usually leathery, stipules large, interpetiolar, deciduous; fls. in terminal corymbs, large, fragrant, 5-merous, white to red, corolla funnelform, tube elongate, slender, lobes unequal, stamens unequal, anthers exserted; fr. a large, fleshy berry, seeds many.

Propagated by cuttings.

latifolia (Rudge) Roem. & Schult. [*P. trinitatis* DC.]. NEEDLE-FLOWER TREE. Tree, to 20 ft.; lvs. elliptic to oblong, to 8 in. long; fls. white, salverform, to 6 in. long; fr. yellow, globose, 2 in. across, fragrant. Mex. to S. Amer. Fr. sometimes eaten, but not considered flavorful.

longiflora Aubl. Small tree; lvs. oblong or narrowly oblong, to 8 in. long; corolla to 10 in. long. S. Amer.

multiflora Lem. To 4 ft.; lvs. broad, elliptic-oblong, to 12 in. long, soft-hairy beneath; fls. white, corolla tube slender, to 4 in. long, lobes spreading, to 2½ in. across. Brazil.

trinitatis: *P. latifolia.*

POTAMOGETON L. PONDWEED. *Potamogetonaceae*. Between 80 and 100 spp. of aquatic plants; lvs. often of 2 kinds, submersed or floating; fls. inconspicuous, in small spikes, mostly aerial.

Sometimes grown in ponds or aquaria.

acutifolius Link. Sts. to 3 ft., flattened, branched; lvs. all submersed, sessile, linear, to 2¾ in. long, with 3 main longitudinal veins, sharp-pointed at apex; fls. 4–8, in densely fld. spikes. Eur., Asia, Australia.

americanus: *P. nodosus.*

coloratus Hornem. Sts. to 3 ft., cylindrical; submersed lvs. linear-lanceolate to narrowly elliptic, to 4 in. long, sometimes longer, blade 2–3 times longer than petiole, often reddish, thin, distinctly reticulate-veined, floating lvs. elliptic-ovate; spikes densely fld. Eur., N. Afr.

crispus L. Lvs. linear-oblong, to 4 in. long, obtuse, sharply serrulate and crisped; spikes ½ in. long, on peduncles to 2 in. long. Eur.; naturalized in e. U.S. and Calif.

densus L. FROG'S LETTUCE. Lvs. ovate-lanceolate, entire, sessile, opp., densely arranged; spikes few-fld., on short peduncles. Eur., s. Asia.

filiformis Pers. Sts. filiform, to 16 in.; lvs. all submersed, blade narrowly linear, to 8 in. long, thin, 1-nerved, stipular sheath tubular; spikes interrupted, with 2–5-fld. whorls. N. Amer., Eur., Asia, Egypt, Australia.

Gayii A. Benn. Sts. filiform, much-branched; lvs. all submersed, sessile, linear, to 4¼ in. long, pale green to reddish-brown, thin; spikes few-fld. S. Amer.

gramineus L. Sts. to 3 ft. or longer; submersed lvs. sessile, linear or linear-lanceolate to oblanceolate, thin, margins finely serrate, floating lvs. petioled, elliptic, to 2¾ in. long; spikes densely fld., cylindrical. Circumboreal.

lucens L. Sts. stout, to 6 ft., or even to nearly 20 ft. long; lvs. all submersed, short-petioled, oblong-lanceolate, to 8 in. long, glossy, thin, margins finely toothed; spikes densely fld. Eur., w. Asia.

malaianus Miq. Sts. simple to sparsely branched; lvs. all submersed, linear-oblong to lanceolate, to 4¾ in. long, margins undulate, obscurely toothed, petioles to 1⅛ in. long; spikes densely fld. Japan, and China to India and Malay Arch.

nodosus Poir. [*P. americanus* Cham. & Schlechtend.]. Lvs. petioled, submersed lvs. linear to elliptic-lanceolate, floating lvs. lanceolate-oblong to elliptic; spikes many-fld., on thick peduncles to 6 in. long. N. Amer.

pectinatus L. Sts. and lvs. threadlike; spikes interrupted, flexuous, on flexuous peduncles. Saline, brackish, or limy waters, n. and e. U.S. to S. Amer.; Afr., Eurasia.

POTAMOGETONACEAE. *Potamogeton Richardsonii* (A. Benn.) Rydb.: **a,** flowering plant in water, × ¼; **b,** inflorescence, × 2; **c,** flower, × 8; **d,** pistil, vertical section, × 10; **d,** achene, × 8. (Species representative, but not in general cultivation; from Lawrence, *Taxonomy of Vascular Plants.*)

POTAMOGETONACEAE Dumort. PONDWEED FAMILY. Monocot.; 1 cosmopolitan genus, *Potamogeton*, of aquatic herbs, mostly of fresh waters; lvs. threadlike to broad, often of 2 kinds, submersed or floating; fls. in spikes, stamens 4, appendaged, pistils 4, 1-celled; fr. an achene.

POTATO. The potato, *Solanum tuberosum*, is the leading vegetable in the United States in terms of annual value. It ranks with the major cereals as one of the leading food crops in the world. Because the potato is a starchy vegetable there is a widely held misconception that potatoes are fattening. Actually, a five-ounce potato supplies only about 90 calories. It also contains 30 percent of the daily adult requirement for vitamin C and a significant amount of protein.

Although the potato is of Andean origin, 90 percent of the world production is now in Europe and the Soviet Union. The United States ranks fourth in world production, behind the Soviet Union, Poland, and West Germany. Potatoes are grown commercially in every one of the 50 states and are harvested somewhere in the United States each month of the year. About four-fifths of the crop is harvested in the autumn in such states as Idaho, Maine, Washington, North Dakota, Oregon, Minnesota, and New York. The cool summer temperatures of these northern areas are ideal for potato production. It is also essential to have ample soil moisture for optimum yields. Unless natural rainfall is abundant, supplemental irrigation will usually improve yields. Tuber formation in potatoes is favored by short days. In fact, clones of potatoes from Peru and Bolivia typically fail to form any tubers at all when grown under the long summer days of northern latitudes. Over the centuries there has been a selection by potato breeders in Europe and North America for insensitivity to day length. The result is that standard cultivars can be grown even as far north as Alaska.

Wild potatoes in South America are propagated both from true seeds and from the underground storage organs or tubers. When temperatures are cool, some North American cultivars will blossom and form fruits that resemble small green tomatoes. These fruits are inedible, due to the presence of toxins. Some fruits lack seeds, but others may contain several hundred. The potato does not breed true, and seeds may differ genetically in the same fruit and from the parent plant. Therefore, the seeds are of value only to the plant breeder who wishes to develop new genetic types. Ordinary propagation is through the planting of tubers or pieces of tubers.

Tubers represent the greatly enlarged tips of underground, horizontal stems called rhizomes and hence the tuber is actually a modified stem rather than a root. Each eye of a potato tuber is made up of a rudimentary scale leaf (the "eyebrow") and a multiple bud cluster. At least one eye must be present on each piece of tuber planted. Seed tubers should be cut into block-shaped pieces that average about 2 ounces in weight. Tubers weighing less than 3 ounces may be planted whole. There are many serious diseases that may be carried in seed potatoes. The only protection against such diseases is to use certified seed potatoes. Potatoes sold as "one year from certification" are not a satisfactory substitute, since there is no assurance that diseases have not multiplied significantly during the intervening year.

Seed pieces should be planted 3–4 inches deep, with 9–12 inches between pieces in a row and 36 inches between rows. High rates of nitrogen, phosphorus, and potash are required for best yields in most locations, and magnesium is frequently needed in acid soils.

Potatoes may be planted before the usual date of the last killing frost, since one to two weeks ordinarily elapse between planting and emergence even in warm soils. Although the foliage is only moderately tolerant of frosts, new shoots will emerge if the seed pieces are still sound at the time of any frost damage. Many soils are suitable for potatoes, but it is essential that the soil be well drained. Acid soils are preferable for control of scab, a disease which causes corky lesions on the skin of the potato. The potato grows well at a soil pH as low as 4.8, whereas the scab organism is usually not a problem if the pH is below 5.4. If acid soils are not available, then it is important to select a variety with scab resistance. 'Norchip', 'Superior', and 'Wauseon' are examples of white-skinned cultivars with resistance. 'Chieftain' and 'Norland' are two red-skinned cultivars with scab resistance. Cultivars lacking scab resistance but otherwise acceptable for the home garden include 'Katahdin', 'Kennebec', and 'Sebago'. 'Norland' and 'Superior' mature earliest of the cultivars named above. The potato most widely grown in the United

States on a commercial scale is 'Russet Burbank', also known as 'Netted Gem'. Although it has good scab resistance and excellent culinary quality, its tendency to produce misshapen tubers makes it very unsatisfactory for the amateur.

A number of insects attack the developing plant. Perhaps the most serious of these is the wireworm, which tunnels through the tubers. The best control against wireworms is to avoid planting potatoes in soils which were previously planted to sod, grassy weeds, or cereal grains. Another control measure is to apply a recommended insecticide to the soil before planting. Insects attacking potato foliage include flea beetles, leaf hoppers, Colorado potato beetles, and aphids. These may be controlled by regular application of appropriate insecticides. Regular application of fungicide is also necessary in most areas to control such diseases as late blight and early blight. Local agricultural authorities should be consulted for current recommendations of insecticides and fungicides.

Before plants are 10 inches tall, it is best to ridge up the soil in each row of potatoes. The purpose is to prevent exposure of the developing tubers to light. Tubers exposed to the light turn green and develop a bitter flavor, which renders them unfit for consumption. For the same reason, potatoes should be stored in a dark place after harvest. Harvesting may be started at any time after the tubers have reached a desirable size. For optimum yields and best storage quality, it is preferable to wait until the foliage has become senescent or killed by frost. However, it is important to harvest the crop before the surface layer of soil has been exposed to hard freezing conditions. Frozen tubers quickly decompose and cause decay of other tubers in storage. The ideal storage temperature for potatoes is 40° F. Temperatures close to freezing will cause tubers to develop excessive amounts of sugar and, under some circumstances, internal discoloration. Warm temperatures will hasten the development of sprouts, although cultivars differ greatly as to the natural length of the dormant period. Commercial growers frequently use sprout inhibitors to control sprouting. The actual sprout should never be eaten; like the fruit, it contains toxic substances.

A prime factor in culinary quality of potatoes is percentage of dry matter. Potatoes of high dry-matter content will be mealy rather than moist or soggy. Most people prefer mealy potatoes for baking, but tubers excessively high in dry matter tend to slough apart when boiled. High dry-matter content is associated with certain cultivars and with a cool growing season, but is affected by many cultural practices and even by position of the tuber on the plant. Tubers may be separated into dry-matter categories by dissolving exactly 1 pound of table salt in 1 gallon of water. Tubers that float in such a brine are best suited for frying or boiling; tubers that sink in it will be mealy when baked.

POTENTILLA L. [*Drymocallis* Fourr.]. CINQUEFOIL, FIVE-FINGER. *Rosaceae.* Perhaps 500 spp. of ann. and per. herbs and a few shrubs, native in the n. temp. boreal, and arctic regions and somewhat in the S. Hemisphere; lvs. compound, palmate or pinnate; fls. yellow, white, or red, mostly bisexual, solitary to cymose, sepals 5, with alternating bractlets, petals 5, usually broad, stamens many, pistils many; frs. achenes.

Potentillas are grown mostly in the border or rock garden, but some are useful in the flower garden; most of them are hardy north. Propagated by seeds and division.

alba L. Low, vigorous, spreading per.; lvs. palmate, lfts. 5, lanceolate, glabrous above, white-silky beneath, toothed at apex, 1–2½ in. long; fls. 3, white, on erect peduncles, to 1 in. across. Cent. Eur. to Caucasus.

alchemilloides Lapeyr. To 1 ft., whitish-silky; lower lvs. digitate, lfts. 5–7, oblong to lanceolate, glabrous above, white-silky beneath, slightly toothed at apex; fls. white, to 1½ in. across, corymbose, bractlets linear, sepals wider. Pyrenees.

alpestris: see *P. Crantzii.*

alpina Dalla Torre. A name of doubtful application.

ambigua Camb. Tufted per. with creeping or ascending sts., silky to glabrous; lfts. 3, obovate- or orbicular-cuneate, ¼–½ in. long, obtusely 3-toothed at the broad tip; fls. solitary on short-peduncles, yellow, to 1 in. across. Himalayas. Sometimes cult. under the name *P. cuneata* or *Sibbaldia maxima.*

andicola Benth. Cespitose per., silky-villous, sts. with many-fld. brs., ascending, few-lvd.; lower lvs. pinnate, lfts. 3–5, ovate, toothed; fls. yellow, petals obcordate, twice as long as sepals. Colombia.

Anserina L. SILVERWEED, GOOSE GRASS, GOOSE TANSY. Low, stoloniferous per.; lvs. in rosettes, pinnate, 4–8 in. long, lfts. 9–31, ½–2 in. long, with smaller ones interspersed, oblong to lanceolate-oblong, obtuse, deeply serrate, silvery-silky beneath, green above; peduncles axillary, solitary; fls. yellow, to 1 in. across, bractlets mostly exceeding sepals; achenes many, corky, thick, deeply grooved dorsally. Alaska and Nfld., s. to Calif., New Mex., N.Y.; Eur., Asia. Var. **sericea** Hayne. White-silky on both lf. surfaces.

arbuscula: *P. davurica.*

argentea L. HOARY C., SILVERY C. Per., to 1½ ft., more or less tomentose; basal lvs. palmate, lfts. 5, ½–1 in. long, obovate-cuneiform, pinnately lobed, with 2–5 lobes on each side, green to grayish above, white-tomentose beneath; fls. several, cymose, ½ in. across, sulphur-yellow. Eur., Asia; naturalized in e. N. Amer. Var. **calabra:** *P. calabra.*

arguta Pursh. TALL C. Per., to 3 ft., sts. erect, purplish, brownish glandular-villous; basal lvs. pinnate, lfts. 7–11, elliptic to ovate, cut-serrate, downy beneath; cyme narrow, capitate; fls. whitish or creamy, ½ in. across. New Bruns. to B.C., s. to Md., Ohio, Okla., Colo. Subsp. **Convallaria** (Rydb.) Keck [*P. Convallaria* Rydb.]. Sts. only slightly purplish or villous; lvs. sparingly hairy; cyme less crowded. B.C. to Alta., s. to Ore., Ariz.

argyrophylla Wallich ex Lehm. Hairy per., 2–3 ft.; lvs. palmate, lfts. 3, elliptic-ovate to obovate, sharply toothed, white-tomentose beneath; fls. yellow, ¾–1¼ in. across, in panicled cymes. Himalayas. Cv. **'Atrosanguinea'**: probably *P. atrosanguinea.* Cvs. **'Insignis'**, **'Leucochroa'** are listed.

atrosanguinea Lodd. ex D. Don. Like *P. argyrophylla,* but fls. dark purplish-red. Himalayas.

aurea L. To 1 ft.; lvs. digitate, lfts. 5, oblong, with 3–5 sharp teeth at apex, smooth or pubescent above, silvery-hairy on veins beneath; fls. few, in loose clusters, golden-yellow, with darker base, ½–¾ in. across. Eur.

Beesiana: *P. davurica* cv. 'Beesii'.

×**bicolor** Lindl.: ?*P. argyrophylla* × *P. atrosanguinea.* Fls. yellow with red and orange.

Blaschkeana: *P. gracilis* subsp. *Nuttallii.*

×**Brennia** Huter ex A. Kern.: *P. Crantzii* × *P. nivea.* Basal lvs. 4–5-parted.

Breweri S. Wats. Like *P. Drummondii,* but lf. blades narrower, white with a dense tomentum at least when young, lfts. 4–6 pairs, to 1 in. long, broadly flabelliform. Ore., Calif.

Buccoana Clementi. To 2 ft., ascending; basal lvs. parted into 3 coarsely toothed lfts. 2 in. long; fls. many, cymose, yellow, ½ in. across; petals obcordate. W. Asia.

calabra Ten. [*P. argentea* var. *calabra* (Ten.) Fiori & Paol.]. Like *P. argentea,* but lvs. smaller, silvery above and beneath, with narrower segms. Sicily.

canadensis L. Small creeping per., silky-pilose, sts. soon prostrate, not tuber-bearing at tips; cauline lvs. not fully expanded at flowering time, lfts. mostly 5, cuneate-obovate, coarsely 5–15-toothed in upper half; first fl. usually from the node above the first well-developed internode, about ½ in. across, yellow. Nov. Sc. to Ont., s. to S.C. and Ohio. Plants offered under this name may be *P. simplex.*

caulescens L. Per., 4–12 in., soft-silky, woody at base; basal lvs. digitate, lfts. 5–7, oblong-obovate to elliptic, silvery-silky beneath, 3–7-toothed at apex; fls. corymbose, white or rarely pink, to ¾ in. across, petals obovate, emarginate, longer than calyx. Cent. to s. Eur.

chrysantha Trevir. Per. from branched rootstock, sts. slender, ascending, to 1½ ft.; lower lvs. digitate, long-petioled, lfts. 5–9, elliptic to obovate, 1–2½ in. long, hairy, with 6–12 teeth on a side; fls. cymose, golden-yellow, to 1 in. across; petals longer than the sepals. Cent. and s. Eur.

cinerea Chaix ex Vill. [*P. Tommasiniana* F. W. Schultz]. Tufted, to 4 in., abundantly spreading-hairy; lvs. palmate, lfts. 5, oblong to obovate, conspicuously toothed, about 1 in. long; fls. mostly 3–5, pale yellow, ⅜–¾ in. across, bractlets broad, blunt. Alps.

Climanii: a listed name of no botanical standing.

Clusiana Jacq. Sts. slender, hairy, 4–6 in.; lower lvs. palmate, petioled, lfts. 5, obovate, 3-toothed on the rounded apex, smooth above, silky-downy beneath; fls. few, cream-white, about 1 in. across, sepals lanceolate, bractlets linear. E. Alps.

coccinea: *P. nepalensis.*

Convallaria: *P. arguta* subsp.

Crantzii (Crantz) G. Beck ex Fritsch [*P. alpestris* Haller f.; *P. verna* L., in part]. Per., to 1 ft.; sts. from a rosette of lvs., arching and ascending, pubescent, not glandular; basal lvs. palmate, lfts. 5, obovate-cuneiform, ⅜–¾ in. long, with 2–5 teeth on each side, green, more or less hairy especially on veins beneath; fls. 1 to few, in a loose cyme, yellow, often with basal orange spot, to 1 in. across, bractlets narrower than sepals. Eur., w. Asia.

crinita A. Gray. Per., to 1 ft., silky-pilose; basal lvs. many, pinnate, lfts. 11–17, crowded, ⅜–¾ in. long, oblong, toothed near apex, silky-villous beneath; fls. many, yellow, ½ in. across. Colo., Utah, Ariz., New Mex.

cuneata Wallich ex Lehm. Sts. erect, leafless; lvs. all basal, petioles pilose, nearly as long as sts., lfts. 3, obovate, coarsely toothed, hairy; fls. crowded at top of sts., short-pedicelled. Himalayas. Probably not cult.; material grown under this name is likely to be *P. ambigua*.

dahurica: in error for *P. davurica.*

davurica Nestl. [*P. arbuscula* D. Don]. Close to *P. fruticosa*, but with obovate to oblong-obovate lfts.; bractlets usually broader than sepals; petals white. China, e. Siberia. Cvs. are: **'Albicans'** ['cv. Farreri'], lvs. densely glandular beneath, fls. bisexual; **'Beesii'** [cv. 'Beesiana'; *P. Beesiana* Siegfr.], sts. less than 1½ ft., fls. yellow; **'Farreri'**: 'Albicans'; **'Mandshurica'**, sts. less than 1½ ft., lvs. more or less silky-hairy; **'Veitchii'** [*P. Veitchii* E. H. Wils.], sts. to 5 ft., lvs. more or less silky-hairy; **'Vilmoriana'**, sts. to 3 ft., fls. cream-white.

delphinensis Gren. & Godr. To 1½ ft., leafy, strigose; lvs. digitate, the lower long-petioled, lfts. 5, obovate, green, toothed in apical ⅔; fls. yellow, 1 in. across, in open infl., petals emarginate, longer than sepals. Alps.

diversifolia Lehm. Sts. to 1 ft., from woody rootstocks; lvs. mostly digitate, lfts. 5 or 7, oblanceolate, ½–2 in. long, 3–7-toothed or -incised above the middle, glabrous to silky-strigose especially beneath; fls. few to several, yellow, ½ in. across, petals obcordate. B.C. to Alta., s. to Calif. and New Mex.

divisa: *P. quinquefolia.*

Dombeyi Nestl. Cespitose, greenish-brown, sparsely long-pilose, to 6 in.; lvs. roundish, to ½ in. long, ⅝ in. wide, with 3 lfts. or deeply 3-lobed, lobes dentate halfway to midrib with mostly 6 teeth; fls. few, petals yellow, ¼ in. long. Peru.

Drummondii Lehm. Per., to 1½ ft., slightly hairy, few-fld.; lower lvs. ovate-oblong in outline, pinnate, lfts. 2–5 pairs, 1–2½ in. long, cuneate-obovate, sharply and deeply serrate; fls. bright yellow, ¾ in. across. Mts., B.C. to Alta. and Calif.

Egedii Wormsk. var **grandis** (Rydb.) J. T. Howell [*P. pacifica* T. J. Howell]. Habit of *P. Anserina*, but with stolons, petioles, peduncles nearly glabrous; lvs. 8–20 in. long, lfts. 7–31, oblong to obovate, 1–2 in. long, green above, white-tomentose to glabrate beneath, pubescence opaque, dull; fls. yellow, 1¼–1½ in. across; achenes not corky or grooved. Coastal, Calif. to Alaska; e. Asia.

×**engadinensis** Brügg.: *P. chrysantha* × *P. Crantzii.*

erecta (L.) Räuschel [*P. Tormentilla* J. Stokes]. TORMENTIL. Per., with slender, leafy, ascending sts. to 1½ ft.; lfts. 3, to ½ in. long; fls. many, to ½ in. across. Eur., Asia. Dried rhizome has been used medicinally.

eriocarpa Wallich ex Lehm. Per. with ascending rhizomes to 10 in. long, densely clothed with stipular sheaths; sts. slender, 2–18 in. high; lvs. few, long-petioled, lfts. 3, cuneate, incised and toothed above the middle, ¼–1½ in. long; fls. 1–2, yellow, 1–1½ in. across. Himalayas.

Farreri: a listed name of no botanical standing; see *P. parvifolia* cv. 'Gold Drop'.

fissa Nutt. [*Drymocallis fissa* (Nutt.) Rydb.]. To 1 ft., glandular-hirsute; lvs. pinnate, lfts. 9–13, orbicular, deeply incised; fls. many, in a narrow cyme, cream-white, to ¾ in. across, petals much longer than sepals. S. Dak. and Wyo. to New Mex.

flabellifolia Hook. ex Torr. & A. Gray. Sts. slender, to 1 ft.; lvs. few, mostly basal, lfts. 3, nearly sessile, cuneate-flabelliform, ½–1½ in. long, incised-serrate; fls. few, cymose, ¾ in. across, bright yellow. B.C. to Calif.

formosa: *P. nepalensis.*

fragiformis Willd. ex Schlechtend. Sts. to 10 in., from thick rhizome, with stipules brown, persistent, villous; lfts. 3, elliptic to obovate, with 3–5 teeth on each margin; infl. corymblike; fls. golden-yellow, to 1³⁄₁₆ in. across. Ne. Asia.

×**Friedrichsenii** F. L. Späth.: *P. davurica* × *P. fruticosa*. Lvs. ovate to oblong; fls. pale yellow to white.

frutescens: a listed name of no botanical standing; possibly *P. fruticosa.*

fruticosa L. SHRUBBY C., GOLDEN HARDHACK, WIDDY. Deciduous, densely leafy, dioecious shrub, about 2–4 ft., more or less pilose, much-branched; lvs. many, pinnate, lfts. mostly 5, ovate to oblong-lanceolate, acute, entire, with revolute margins, ⅜–¾ in. long, petioles to ½ in. long; fls. 1 to few in a terminal cyme, 5-merous, bright yellow, to 1¼ in. across, sepals triangular-ovate, alternating bractlets narrow; petals rounded. N. Temp. Zone, circumpolar. Zone 2. Many cvs. include: **'Arbuscula'**: probably *P. davurica;* **'Beesii'** ['cv. Beesiana']: *P. davurica* cv.; **'Compacta'**, compact; **'Davurica'**: *P. davurica;* **'Farreri'**: probably *P. parvifolia* cv. 'Gold Drop'; **'Friedrichsenii'**: *P.* × *Friedrichsenii;* **'Jackmannii'**, a listed name; **'Mandshurica'**, spreading, less than 18 in. high, fls. single; **'Minima'**, **'Montana'**, and **'Nana'**, listed names; **'Parvifolia'**: *P. parvifolia;* **'Pumila'**, a listed name; **'Veitchii'**: *P. davurica* cv.; **'Waltoniensis'** and **'Wilsonii'**, listed names.

fulgens Wallich ex D. Don. To 2 ft., with many spreading hairs, underside of lvs. and infl. shining-silvery-pubescent; lvs. 2–6 in. long, lfts. in many pairs, unequal, ½–1½ in. long, with many acute teeth; fls. panicled or corymbose, yellow, about ½ in. across. Himalayas.

Gibsonii: a listed name of no botanical standing; fls. brilliant scarlet.

glandulosa Lindl. Per. from a woody caudex, sts. erect, 1–2½ ft., leafy, glandular- or viscid-villous, branching above; lower lvs. pinnate, lfts. 5–9, obovate, ½–1½ in. long, serrate; cyme open, many-fld.; fls. pale yellow to cream-white, ½ in. across. B.C. to Baja Calif.

Gordonii: *Ivesia Gordonii.*

gracilis Dougl. ex Hook. Per. with short caudex, sts. slender, 1½–2 ft., more or less silky-villous; basal lvs. digitate, lfts. 5–7, oblanceolate, 1–2½ in. long, green and silky above, white-tomentose beneath, with deep, coarse, lanceolate teeth; fls. many, to ½ in. across, petals yellow, obcordate; achenes smooth. Calif. to Alaska. Subsp. **Nuttallii** (Lehm.) Keck [*P. Blaschkeana* Turcz.; *P. Nuttallii* Lehm.]. Lvs. showing less pronounced contrast between upper and lower surface. Alaska, Alta., s. to S. Dak. and Calif.

grandiflora L. Per., pubescent, 4–18 in.; lfts. 3, obovate, coarsely toothed in upper half, ½–1¼ in. long; fls. few, golden-yellow, about 1 in. across, petals obcordate, sepals half as long as petals, lanceolate. Cent. Eur.

heptaphylla L. [*P. opaca* L.]. Close to *P. Crantzii*, but with red glands, bractlets like the sepals. E. Eur.

Matsumurae T. Wolf. Sts. ascending, to 6 in.; lfts. 3, obovate to orbicular, toothed, to ½ in. long, slightly hairy; fls. yellow, long-pedicelled, ½ in. across. Japan.

megalantha Takeda. Somewhat cespitose, to about 6 in.; basal lvs. to 3 in. wide, lfts. 3, broad, deeply crenate, green and sparsely hairy above, grayish long-hairy beneath; fls. solitary, bright yellow, 1½ in. across. Japan.

multifida L. Per., to 4 in., softly white-tomentose; lvs. pinnate or nearly digitate, with 3–5 lfts., glabrous above, tomentose beneath, lfts. linear-oblong to obovate, pinnatifid nearly to base into narrow segms.; fls. corymbose, yellow, ½–⅝ in. across. Eur., Asia.

nepalensis Hook. [*P. coccinea* Hoffmeist.; *P. formosa* D. Don]. Per., to 1½ ft., spreading-hairy; lvs. palmate, with 5 lfts., lfts. 1–2½ in. long, obovate-oblong to oblanceolate, coarsely dentate; fls. rose-red, 1 in. across, in forking panicles. Himalayas. Cv. **'Willmottiae'**. Dwarf, with many magenta-rose fls.

nevadensis Boiss. Cespitose, pilose-silky, sts. slender, almost prostrate, 6–12 in. long; lfts. 5, obovate, coarsely toothed, silky-pubescent beneath, to about ½ in. long; fls. 3–4, about ½ in. across, petals obcordate. Spain.

nitida L. Forming mats 1 in. high or more, and several in. across, silky-hairy; lfts. 3, about ½ in. long, oblanceolate to narrowly obovate, entire or 3–7-toothed at apex; fls. solitary, short-peduncled, rose, rarely white, to 1 in. across, sepals often purplish on inner face, petals broadly obovate, about twice as long as sepals. Alps. Cvs. **'Alba'**, **'Compacta'**, and **'Rubra'** are listed.

nivalis Lapeyr. Soft-hairy, woody at base, 4–12 in. high; lfts. 5–7, obovate, entire to toothed at apex, silky-hairy on both sides, to about 1 in. long; fls. few, clustered, white, to ¾ in. across, sepals and bractlets narrow, longer than petals. S. Eur.

nivea L. Per., 4–8 in., densely white-tomentose on sts. and lower surface of lvs.; lfts. 3, sometimes 5, obovate, coarsely toothed, ¼–1 in. long; fls. 1–3, yellow, ½ in. across, calyx woolly, petals obcordate. Arctic and alpine regions, N. Amer., Eurasia.

norvegica L. Ann. to short-lived per., erect or ascending, to 1½ ft.; lvs. all ternately compound, lfts. 1½–3 in. long, obovate to oblong, coarsely serrate, green on both sides; fls. cymose, yellow, sepals and bractlets subequal, enlarging in fr.; petals ⁵⁄₁₆ in. long, carpels rugulose. Eur., Asia; n. N. Amer., s. to S.C. and Calif.

Nuttallii: *P. gracilis* subsp.

opaca: *P. heptaphylla.*

pacifica: *P. Egedii* var. *grandis.*

palustris (L.) Scop. MARSH C., MARSH F.-F. Decumbent per., sts. to 1½ ft., ascending; lower lvs. with 5–7 lfts., these 1–2½ in. long, oblong, sharply and coarsely serrate, somewhat galucous and more or less hairy underneath; infl. a loose cyme, pedicels glandular-pubescent; fls. red to purple, to 1¼ in. across, petals ovate-lanceolate, acuminate, sepals longer than petals. N. N. Amer., s. to N.J., Iowa, Calif.; Eurasia.

parvifolia Lehm. Differing from *P. fruticosa* in more uniformly fine foliage, lvs. to ½ in. long, densely clothing sts., lfts. ¼ in. long; peduncles shorter, style filiform instead of club-shaped. China. Cvs. are: 'Farreri': 'Gold Drop'; 'Gold Drop' [cv. 'Farreri'], supposed to have lfts. ¼–⅜ in. long; 'Pumila', depressed, very dwarf, lfts. very silky, ⅛–¼ in. long; 'Tenuiloba', lfts. nearly linear, more pubescent.

peduncularis D. Don. Rootstock long, stout, ascending, sts. erect or ascending, 4–8 in.; lvs. as long as sts., lfts. many, oblong, deeply serrate, silvery-silky beneath, silky or glabrous above, ½–1½ in. long; fls. few, corymbose, ¾ in. across, yellow. Himalayas.

Purdotaii: *P. × Rehderana.*

pyrenaica Ramond ex DC. Somewhat cespitose, stout, to 1 ft., pilose or somewhat gray-pubescent; lfts. 5, to ¾ in. long, cuneate-obovate to somewhat cuneate-oblong, dentate toward apex, almost silky beneath; infl. a few-fld. raceme; fls. golden-yellow, 1 in. across, petals obovate, emarginate, much longer than sepals. Pyrenees.

quinquefolia Rydb. [*P. divisa* Rydb.]. Per., to 8 in. high, spreading or ascending, more or less pubescent; basal lvs. many, digitate, lfts. 3 or 5, obovate to oblanceolate, to 1 in. long, deeply cleft into oblong or lanceolate lobes, silky-villous to greenish above, white-tomentose beneath; fls. few to several, less than ½ in. across, yellow. B.C. to Sask., s. to Utah and Colo.

recta L. Per., sts. erect, 1–2 ft., with both short stiff and long flexuous hairs; basal and lower lvs. palmate, lfts. 5 or 7, 1–4 in. long, oblong to oblanceolate, serrate-dentate, green and strigose on both sides; fls. many, cymose, to 1 in. across, calyx glandular, villous, petals yellow, carpels rugose. Cent. and S. Eur., N. Afr.; naturalized in e. N. Amer. Cvs. 'Macrantha' and 'Warrenii' [cv. 'Warrensii'; *P. Warrenii* Hort.], fls. large, bright yellow.

× Rehderana Hand.-Mazz. [*P. fruticosa* var. *Purdomii* Rehd.; *P. Purdomii* N. E. Br.]: *P. davurica* × *P. parvifolia.* Sepals reddish on back, fls. sulphur-yellow.

repens: a listed name of no botanical standing.

reptans L. Pubescent per. with creeping sts. to 3 ft. long; basal lvs. long-petioled, palmate, lfts. 5–7, obovate, to 1 in. long, with 6–10 teeth on each side, sparingly pilose; fls. solitary, ⅝–1 in. across, yellow, petals obovate, emarginate. Eur., Asia; introd. into e. N. Amer. and S. Amer.

rupestris L. ROCK C., PRAIRIE TEA. Pubescent per., 8–18 in.; basal lvs. 3–6 in. long, pinnate, with 2–4 pairs of main lfts., lfts. 1–2½ in. long, more or less ovate, obtuse, doubly toothed, green and pubescent on both sides; fls. several in a loose forking cyme, white, to 1 in. across. Nw. N. Amer., s to Calif. and Nev.; Eurasia. Var. **pygmaea** Duby. Sts. 1–4 in.; fls. 1 to few, smaller. Corsica, Sardinia. cvs. 'Alba' and 'Nana' are listed.

simplex Michx. OLD-FIELD C. Like *P. canadensis*, but stolon tips bear tuberous enlargements late in season, fl. st. arching; cauline lvs. well developed at flowering time; first fl. usually from the node above the second well-developed internode. Nov. Sc. to Minn., s. to N.C., Mo., Okla.

speciosa Willd. Sts. 2–10 in., few-lvd.; basal lvs. long-petioled, ternately compound, lfts. obovate, crenate-dentate above the base, less than 1 in. long, white-tomentose, especially beneath; fls. 3–8, short-pedicelled, ½–¾ in. across, petals white, scarcely longer than the sepals. S. Eur.

Tabernaemontani Asch. [*P. verna* L., in part]. Per., sts. to 20 in. long, with prostrate, usually rooting brs. forming mats; basal lvs. palmate, lfts. 5, obovate-cuneiform, with 2–9 teeth on each side, ³⁄₁₆–¾ in. long, green and more or less strigose; fls. few, in loose cymes, yellow, ⅜–⅝ in. across, achenes rugose. Eur.

Thurberi A. Gray. Rather coarse, to 2½ ft., pubescent, also with some long and some gland-tipped hairs; lvs. palmate, lfts. 5–7, broadly oblanceolate, green, coarsely toothed, 1–2 in. long, rounded at apex; fls. in loose clusters, red-purple, ½–¾ in. across. Ariz., New Mex., and adjacent Mex.

Tommasiniana: *P. cinerea*, but plants offered as *P. Tommasiniana* may be incorrectly identified.

× Tonguei: a listed name of no botanical standing for the hybrid *P. anglica* Laicharding × *P. nepalensis.* Prostrate, pubescent per., sts. to 1 ft. long; lvs. with 3–5 lfts., lfts. obovate, coarsely dentate; fls. ½ in. across, petals obovate, yellow with red base. This hybrid is often listed under the unacceptable name *P. Tormentilla-formosa.*

Tormentilla: *P. erecta.*

Tormentilla-formosa: see *P. × Tonguei.*

transcaspia T. Wolf. Robust per., to 2 ft., green, with scattered, long, soft hairs; lfts. 5–7, narrow-oblanceolate, 1–3 in. long, ½–¼ in. wide, coarsely serrate with few spreading teeth; cyme large, many-fld., grayish-strigose with long hairs; fls. yellow, ½ in. across. Asia.

tridentata Ait. THREE-TOOTHED C. Per., woody at base, sts. to 1 ft.; lvs. palmate, lfts. 3, leathery, evergreen, cuneate-oblong, 3–5-toothed at tip, nearly glabrous; fls. white, few to many in stiff cymes, ¼ in. across. Greenland and Wisc., s. to Ga., and Iowa.

valderia L. Whitish-tomentose, 5–16 in.; basal lvs. palmately compound, lfts. 5–7, silvery-silky beneath, toothed, to 1½ in. long; fls. white, corymbose, ½ in. across, sepals and bractlets lanceolate, acuminate, longer than the petals. S. Eur.

Veitchii: *P. davurica* cv.

verna: a Linnean name now considered ambiguous; plants so named are usually *P. Crantzii* or *P. Tabernaemontani.*

villosa Pall. ex Pursh. Villous with white or yellowish hairs, sts. ascending, to 1 ft.; basal lvs. ternately compound, silky above, white-tomentose beneath; lfts. obovate, coarsely toothed, 1–1½ in. long; fls. few, 1 in. across, yellow, petals emarginate. Wash. to Alaska, Asia.

Warrenii, Warrensii: listed names of no botanical standing for *P. recta* cv.

Willmottiae: a listed name of no botanical standing for *P. nepalensis* cv.

POTERIUM L. *Rosaceae.* About 25 spp. of herbs or subshrubs, native to Eur., w. Asia, and N. Afr., distinguished from *Sanguisorba* by being monoecious or polygamous; sepals green, stamens of male fls. many, exserted, pistils 2, rarely 3, stigmas feathery.

obtusatum: a listed name of no botanical standing for *Sanguisorba obtusa.*

obtusum: *Sanguisorba obtusa.*

Sanguisorba L. [*Sanguisorba minor* Scop.]. BURNET, GARDEN B. Somewhat glaucous per., 6–18 in., glabrous except for some long hairs toward base of plant; basal lvs. pinnate, lfts. 4–12 pairs, ³⁄₁₆–¾ in. long, rounded to elliptic, serrate, cauline lvs. few, reduced; head globose, to ½ in. in diam., green or purplish-tinged; lower fls. male, middle fls. bisexual, upper fls. female; calyx tube, in fr., with 4 entire ridges, the surface between them with fine raised reticulations. Eur., w. Asia; naturalized in N. Amer.

spinosum L. Subshrub, 2–3 ft., brs. rather hairy, often ending in a thorn; lvs. unequally pinnate, lfts. 9–15, petiolulate, ovate, scarcely ¼ in. long, sharply toothed, densely hairy beneath; spike 1–1¼ in. long, cylindrical to ovoid, greenish. E. Medit. region, Asia Minor. Zone 7?

POTHOS L. *Araceae.* About 70 spp. of mostly scandent vines, with tough slender sts., native to Old World tropics; lvs. 2-ranked, entire, petioles bladelike, often wide-winged; infl. lateral, spathe small, spadix stalked, mostly globose to ovoid, rarely cylindrical; fls. bisexual, perianth 6-parted.

For culture see *Philodendron.*

argyraeus: *Scindapsus pictus* cv.

aureus: *Epipremnum aureum.*

hermaphroditus (Blanco) Merrill. Large, branched climber; lf. blades lanceolate to linear-lanceolate, to 4½ in. long and 1 in. wide, petioles winged, 3½ in. long, ½ in. wide at apex, long-cuneate basally, auriculate-rounded apically; peduncle about ⅜ in. long, spadix long-stalked, obovoid, ¼ in. long, slightly shorter than spathe. Philippine Is., Indonesia.

jambea: a listed name of no botanical standing; material so listed may be *P. Seemannii.*

Seemannii Schott. Differs from *P. hermaphroditus* in having lf. blades elliptic or oblanceolate, shorter, to 4 in. long, petioles much shorter, rarely to 1 in. long; peduncle longer than petiole, spathe ½ in. long, spadix on stalk to ¾ in. long, ellipsoidal, shorter than spathe, yellow. China, Taiwan.

tricolor: *Epipremnum aureum* cv.

Wilcoxii: *Epipremnum aureum* cv.

× POTINARA Hort. Charlesworth: *Brassavola × Cattleya × Laelia × Sophronitis.* Orchidaceae. A group of quadrigeneric hybrids, usually involving the spp. *Brassavola Digbyana* and *Sophronitis coccinea*, and then showing the influence of the large, fringed lip of the former and the intense color of the latter. There are many named cvs.

For culture see *Orchids.*

POUTERIA Aubl. [*Calocarpum* Pierre; *Lucuma* of auth., not Mol.]. *Sapotaceae.* About 50 spp. of shrubs and trees, native to tropics of both hemispheres; lvs. alt., short-petioled, leathery, mostly oblong-lanceolate, entire; fls. usually several in axillary clusters, sometimes solitary, sepals 4–12, imbricate, paired (when 4) or in a spiral, corolla nearly rotate to cylindrical, 4–7-lobed, white to yellow or green, stamens inserted on corolla, alternating with staminodes, ovary superior; fr. often fleshy, seeds 1 to several, with a long scar.

The edible pouterias are grown in the tropics and will not endure frost. They thrive best in clay or clay-loam soils. Usually propagated by seeds from which the fruit pulp should be removed before planting. The seeds should be only slightly covered and seedlings transferred into pots when 6 or 8 in. high. Superior fruit types should be propagated vegetatively. Several other pouterias, besides the species listed, are cultivated in the Amer. tropics for their edible fruits, but probably not in the U.S.

campechiana (HBK) Baehni [*Lucuma nervosa* A. DC.; *L. salicifolia* HBK]. CANISTEL, TI-ES, EGGFRUIT, SAPOTE BORRACHO, SAPOTE AMARILLO. To 50 ft., mostly smaller; lvs. elliptic to narrowly obovate, to 14 in. long, 4 in. wide, rounded to acuminate at apex, with 12–20 pairs of lateral veins, glabrous; fls. greenish-white, in clusters, sepals 4–6, mostly 5, minutely hairy outside, corolla lobes 4–7, mostly 5; fr. subglobose or pear-shaped, to 4 in. long, green or brownish to yellow, the skin membranous, with very sweet, orange or yellow, mealy, edible pulp and a musky flavor. Cuba and Mex. to Panama. The canistel is grown as a garden tree in Cuba, Mex., and other Caribbean countries, and also in s. Fla. (Zone 10b) for the fresh fr. It withstands poor soil.

domingensis (C. F. Gaertn.) Baehni [*Lucuma serpentaria* HBK]. Tree, to 30 ft.; lvs. oblanceolate to obovate, to 5 in. long, 2¾ in. wide or sometimes more, reticulate-veiny on both sides; fls. pedicelled, solitary or several in axils, sepals 4, to ⅜ in. long, the outer finely hairy, corolla yellow or white, 6-lobed, to ⅝ in. long; fr. yellow, edible, to 2¼ in. in diam. W. Indies.

hypoglauca (Standl.) Baehni [*Lucuma hypoglauca* Standl.]. To 60 ft.; lvs. oblanceolate to elliptic, to 10 in. long, 3$^{3}/_{16}$ in. wide; fls. small, nearly sessile, ⅛ in. long or less; fr. edible, to 4 in. in diam. Mex.

Sapota (Jacq.) H. E. Moore & Stearn [*Calocarpum mammosum* of auth., not (L.) Pierre; *C. Sapota* (Jacq.) Merrill; *Lucuma mammosa* of auth., not (L.) C. F. Gaertn.]. SAPOTE, MAMMEE S., MAMEY S., SAPOTA, MAMEY COLORADO, MARMALADE PLUM, MARMALADE FRUIT. To 90 ft.; lvs. obovate to oblanceolate, to 2 ft. long, 6 in. wide, with 20–50 pairs of lateral veins; fls. ½ in. across, sepals 8–12 in a spiral, appressed-hairy on outside; fr. ellipsoid or ovoid, to 8 in. long, russet-brown, roughened, flesh reddish, edible, very sweet, seed 1, large, ellipsoid, brown, glossy. Humid lowlands, Mex. and Cent. Amer. Widely cult. in trop. Amer., also in the Philippine Is. Tender, does not do well on limy soils. An important fr. in the lowland Caribbean area, eaten fresh or made into thick preserves, often in combination with guava fr.

PRATIA Gaud.-Beaup. *Lobeliaceae.* About 25 spp. of mostly prostrate herbs, native mostly to Australia, New Zeal., and trop. Asia, but also to trop. Afr. and the Americas; lvs. mostly sessile, alt., toothed; fls. usually solitary in lf. axils, often unisexual, corolla 2-lipped, tube split nearly to base on upper side, stamens separate from corolla or nearly so, anther tube with lower 2 anthers 2-awned at apex; fr. a berry. Allied to *Lobelia* but having berrylike fr.

Rock garden plants requiring moist but well-drained soil and a sheltered location; probably none hardy north, except on the Pacific Coast.

angulata (G. Forst.) Hook.f. Mat-forming, glabrous or glabrate per., sts. rooting at nodes; lvs. about ½ in. long and wide, dentate, fleshy; fls. on bractless pedicels to 2 in. long, corolla ⅜–¾ in long, white with purple veins; fr. about ½ in. in diam., reddish to crimson. New Zeal.

begoniifolia: *P. nummularia.*

lacticolor: a listed name of no botanical standing.

macrodon Hook.f. Creeping, glabrous, somewhat succulent per.; lvs. ovate to suborbicular, less than ½ in. long, broadly cuneate, coarsely toothed; fls. nearly sessile, corolla to ½ in. long, white or pale yellow; fr. purplish, to ⅜ in. in diam. New Zeal.

nummularia (Lam.) A. Braun & Asch. [*P. begoniifolia* (Wallich ex Roxb.) Lindl.]. Prostrate, slender-stemmed, somewhat pilose per.; lvs. orbicular, to ¾ in. wide, nearly cordate, serrate-dentate; fls. scarcely longer than lvs., corolla about ½ in. long, lilac, rose, or yellowish-green, throat yellow, lower lip marked purple; fr. purplish to purple-black, nearly ½ in. long. Trop. and subtrop. Asia.

Treadwellii: a listed name of no botanical standing for *P. angulata.*

PRENANTHES L. RATTLESNAKE ROOT. *Compositae* (Cichorium Tribe). About 30 spp. of per. herbs with milky sap, native to Eur., Asia, and N. Amer.; sts. erect, leafy, from tuberous roots; fl. heads in racemes or panicles, nodding, involucre cylindrical, receptacle naked; fls. all ligulate, white to purple; achenes all alike, cylindrical, truncate at apex, only weakly ribbed, pappus of capillary bristles.

purpurea L. Sts. to 6 ft. or more; lvs. thin, the lower narrow-obovate, pinnately cut, petioled, the upper oblanceolate, sinuate-toothed or entire, clasping; heads many, few-fld.; fls. violet to red-purple, rarely white. Cent. and s. Eur.

PRESTONIA R. Br. *Apocynaceae.* About 60 spp. of woody or suffrutescent twining vines, with milky sap, native to trop. Amer.; lvs. opp., entire, with stipules; fls. in lateral racemes, 5-merous, bisexual, corolla generally salverform, with 5 scale-like appendages in throat; stamens borne on the corolla, anthers connivent, adhering to stigma, connective enlarged; fr. a pair of follicles, seeds many, with tufts of hairs.

quinquangularis (Jacq.) K. Spreng. [*Echites rubrovenosa* Linden]. Lvs. oblong- to ovate-ellipitc, to 6 in. long, pointed, obtuse to rounded at base, thin, conspicuously veined with red or purple when young, or with white in age, nearly or quite glabrous, petioles to ¾ in. long; infls. 6–20-fld.; calyx lobes small, sharply reflexed, corolla greenish-yellow, nearly ⅝ in. long and ¾ in. across, lobes obovate, sharply reflexed, stamens borne slightly above middle of tube; follicles united at apex, rather stout, to 14 in. long, seeds with tufts of tawny hairs. Lesser Antilles, w. to Guianas and Venezuela.

PRIMULA L. PRIMROSE. *Primulaceae.* About 400 spp. of usually scapose per. herbs, sometimes short-lived, native mostly to temp. zone of the N. Hemisphere, a few spp. in the S. Hemisphere; lvs. basal, simple; fls. of many colors, in heads, umbels, or sometimes in superimposed whorls, calyx 5-toothed, corolla funnelform or salverform, the tube longer than the calyx, the lobes entire to 2-lobed, stamens 5; fr. a 5- or 10-valved caps.

Primulas have received much attention in recent years and are becoming fanciers' plants. The hardy species thrive in any good garden soil. Seeds should be sown in spring or early summer in flats or pans and the seedlings transplanted. Large plants may be propagated by division. Seeds of the greenhouse species (mostly *P. sinensis* and *P. malacoides*) should be sown in Jan. for Christmas bloom, in soil composed of equal parts loam, leaf mold, and sand. Frequent transplantings should be made until Sept., when the plants should be set in the pots in which they are to bloom. Shade and moisture should be provided during the summer. A good temperature for these primroses is 55–60° F. The hardy outdoor kinds bloom largely in spring and early summer.

acaulis: *P. vulgaris.*

albo-cincta: a listed name of no botanical standing.

algida Adams. To 8 in.; lvs. oblong to oblanceolate, to 2 in. long; fls. violet, $^{5}/_{16}$ in. across, in 3–12-fld., subcapitate umbels. Late spring. W. Asia.

Allionii Loisel. Dwarf; lvs. obovate to spatulate, to 1¾ in. long, gray-green, glandular-hairy; fls. rose-purple to pink with white eye, to ¾ in. across, in 1–7-fld. umbels. Spring. Maritime Alps.

alpicola Stapf [*P. alpicola* var. *luna* (Stapf) W. W. Sm. & H. R. Fletch.]. To 20 in.; lvs. elliptic to oblong-elliptic, to 6 in. long, abruptly narrowed or obscurely cordate, crenate, glabrous, upper side rugose; fls. yellow, in 1–2 superimposed umbels, corolla tube nearly ½ in. long, limb to ¾ in. across, spreading. Tibet. Var. **violacea** (Stapf) W. W. Sm. Fls. violet or purple.

alpina: *P. Auricula.*

amoena Bieb. To 8 in.; lvs. spatulate-oblong, elliptic, or oblong, to 3 in. long, remotely toothed, wrinkled and minutely pubescent; fls. violet-blue or lavender-blue, rarely white, with yellow eye, to 1 in. across, in 6–10-fld. umbels. Caucasus, ne. Turkey. Reputedly confused in cult. with the scapeless *P. vulgaris* subsp. *Sibthorpii.*

angustifolia Torr. [*P. angustifolia* var. *Helenae* Pollard & Cockerell; *P. Helenae* of auth.]. To 2 in.; lvs. linear-lanceolate to lanceolate-spatulate, to 2 in. long; fls. purple or occasionally white, ½ in. across, usually solitary. Summer. Colo., New Mex.

anisodora Balf.f. & Forr. To 2 ft., herbage aromatic; lvs. obovate, to 8 in. long, denticulate; fls. dark purple, almost black, in superimposed umbels. China.

aurantiaca W. W. Sm. & Forr. To 10 in.; lvs. oblanceolate to obovate, to 8 in. long, denticulate, tapering to winged petiole; fls. deep ruddy-orange, ½ in. long, in 6–12-fld. superimposed umbels. China.

Auricula L. [*P. alpina* Salisb.; *P. lutea* Vill.]. AURICULA. To 8 in.; lvs. thick, persisting, obovate to oblong-lanceolate, to 4 in. long, often mealy; fls. in many colors, about 1 in. across, in many-fld. umbels. Spring. Alps. Vars. **alpina** and **gigantea** are listed. Subsp. **Balbisii** (Lehm.) Widm. [*P. Balbisii* Lehm.]. Lvs. densely long-ciliate, not mealy; fls. scentless.

The auricula is a favorite spring, cool-season per., both a garden plant and, especially in Eur., a fanciers' plant. Some of the races may be of hybrid origin. Cvs. grown as exhibition plants by fanciers are usually maintained in cold frames or cold greenhouses over winter.

Balbisii: *P. Auricula* subsp.

Beesiana Forr. To 2 ft.; lvs. obovate, to 9 in. long or more in fr., tapering to winged petiole, denticulate; fls. rose-lilac, with yellow eye and orange tube, ¾ in. across, in 2–8 superimposed umbels. Early summer. China.

bellidifolia King ex Hook.f. To 14 in.; lvs. oblanceolate to spatulate, to 16 in. long, tapering to winged petiole, toothed; fls. mauve to pale blue-violet, ⅝ in. across, in heads, corolla lobes notched. Tibet, Bhutan, Sikkim.

×**berninae** A. Kern.: *P. rubra* × *P. viscosa*. Fertile hybrid, fls. violet, in 1-sided umbels. Alps.

bhutanica H. R. Fletch. To 3 in. high in fl., to 7 in. high in fr.; lvs. spatulate to oblong-spatulate, to 4 in. long, longer in fr., tapering to a membranously winged petiole, irregularly dentate; fls. blue with white eye, 1 in. across, in umbels, corolla lobes deeply 3-toothed. Himalayas.

×**biflora** Huter: *P. glutinosa* Wulfen × *P. minima*. To 2 in.; lvs. wedge-shaped, glossy, notched at apex; fls. rosy-purple, 2 on a 2–3-in. scape. Alps.

Bilekii: *P. Steinii.*

Briscoei: a listed name of no botanical standing.

×**Bullesiana** Hort.: *P. Beesiana* × *P. Bulleyana*. A strain of hybrids in shades of cream to orange, pink to crimson, or purple or lilac.

Bulleyana Forr. To 2½ ft.; lvs. ovate to ovate-lanceolate, 5–14 in. long, tapering to winged petiole, midrib red; fls. orange-yellow, to 1 in. across, in 5–7 superimposed umbels, calyx lobes awl-shaped. Summer. China.

burmanica Balf.f. & F. K. Ward. To 2 ft.; lvs. oblanceolate, to 1 ft. long, tapering to winged petiole, toothed; fls. reddish-purple with yellow eye, ½ in. across, in 10–18-fld. superimposed umbels. Burma, China.

cachemiriana: *P. denticulata.*

Calderana Balf.f. & R. Cooper. To 12 in., herbage with disagreeable odor; lvs. oblong, oblanceolate, or spatulate, to 1 ft. long, tapering to a winged petiole, regularly toothed; fls. maroon or royal-purple, with yellow eye, 1 in. across, in umbels. Himalayas.

calycina: *P. glaucescens* subsp.

canescens: a listed name of no botanical standing for *P. veris* subsp.

capitata Hook. To 1½ ft.; lvs. oblong, oblong-lanceolate, to oblong-spatulate, to 5 in. long, tapering to winged petiole, toothed, silvery beneath; fls. purplish-blue, ½ in. across, imbricate in dense heads. Himalayas. Subsp. **crispata** (Balf.f. & W. W. Sm.) W. W. Sm. [*P. crispata* Balf.f. & W. W. Sm.]. Lvs. green on both surfaces; fls. open, in a flattened head. Subsp. **Mooreana** (Balf.f. & W. W. Sm.) W. W. Sm. & Forr. [*P. Mooreana* Balf.f. & W. W. Sm.]. Lvs. rounded at apex, green above, snow-white beneath. Sikkim. Subsp. **sphaerocephala** (Balf.f. & Forr.) W. W. Sm. & Forr. Lvs. green on both surfaces; fls. funnelform, in globose heads. China.

carniolica Jacq. To 10 in., from stout rhizome; lvs. obovate to oblong, to 1¾ in. long, glossy; fls. rose to lilac with white eye, 1 in. across, in umbels. Alps.

carpathica: *P. elatior* subsp.

cashmeriana: *P. denticulata.*

Cawdoriana F. K. Ward. To 8 in.; lvs. obovate, oblanceolate, or spatulate, to 2 in. long, tapering to broad petiole, coarsely and irregularly toothed; fls. mauve with white eye, ¾ in. across, pendent, in umbels, corolla lobes 2–3-cleft. Se. Tibet.

chinensis: in error for *P. sinensis.*

chionantha Balf.f. & Forr. To 2½ ft.; lvs. oblanceolate or oblong-ovate, to 10 in. long or longer in fr., tapering to a membranously winged petiole, yellow-mealy beneath; fls. white, fragrant, 1 in. across, in 1–4 superimposed umbels on stout scapes. China.

chrysopa: *P. gemmifera* var. *zambalensis.*

chungensis Balf.f. & F. K. Ward. To 2 ft. or more; lvs. elliptic to oblong or oblong-obovate, to 1 ft. long, irregularly toothed, glabrous; fls. pale orange, ¾ in. across, tube red, fragrant, in 2–5 superimposed umbels. China, Bhutan, Assam.

Clarkei G. Watt. To 2 in.; lvs. scattered, not in rosettes, orbicular-reniform or broadly ovate, ¾ in. long including petiole, toothed; fls. rose-pink with yellow eye, ¾ in. across, solitary or in 2–6-fld. umbels, corolla lobes deeply notched. Kashmir.

Clusiana Tausch. To 7 in.; lvs. ovate to elliptic or oblong, to 3½ in. long, glossy, margin narrow, cartilaginous, with glandular hairs; fls. rose or lilac, with white eye, 1 in. across or more, in 1–6-fld. umbels, corolla lobes bifid. Alps.

Cockburniana Hemsl. To 16 in.; lvs. oblong to oblong-obovate, to 6 in. long, evenly denticulate; fls. dark orange tinged with red, ⅝ in. across, in 1–3 superimposed umbels. China.

Columnae: *P. veris* subsp.

commutata: *P. villosa* subsp.

concholoba Stapf & Sealy. To 8 in.; lvs. oblanceolate-oblong to oblong, to 3 in. long, tapering to winged petiole, pubescent on both sides; fls. bright violet, powdered with white meal outside, ½ in. long, in 10–20-fld. globose, compact heads, corolla lobes concave and connivent. Himalayas.

conspersa Balf.f. & Purdom. To 20 in.; lvs. oblong-lanceolate to narrowly elliptic, to 4 in. long, toothed; fls. lilac, with orange eye and yellow tube, to ¾ in. across, in 1–3 superimposed umbels, corolla lobes notched. China.

cortusoides L. To 1½ ft.; lvs. ovate to oblong, to 3½ in. long, cordate, lobed; fls. rose, to ¾ in. across, on pedicels less than ⅜ in. long, in a many-fld. umbel, corolla lobes notched. Late spring. W. Siberia.

cottia: *P. villosa* forma.

crispa: *P. glomerata.*

crispata: *P. capitata* subsp.

cuneifolia Ledeb. To 1 ft.; lvs. obovate-cuneate, to 3 in. long, coarsely toothed, often only so toward apex; fls. rose-red or crimson, with yellow eye, in 1–9-fld. umbels. E. Siberia and Hokkaido, Japan. Subsp. **hakusanensis** (Franch.) W. W. Sm. & Forr. Corolla twice as long as calyx. Cent. Honshu, Japan. Subsp. **heterodonta** (Franch.) W. W. Sm. & Forr. Larger in all respects. N. Honshu, Japan.

Cusickiana (A. Gray) A. Gray. To 6 in.; lvs. lanceolate to oblong-lanceolate, to 2 in. long; fls. violet-purple, ½ in. across, fragrant, in 1–4-fld. umbels. E. Ore., w. Idaho.

daonensis (Leyb.) Leyb. [*P. oenensis* E. Thomas ex Gremli]. Glandular-hairy, dwarf per., to 3 in.; lvs. oblanceolate to spatulate, to 3 in. long, toothed; fls. lilac or rose, to ¾ in. across, in 1–7-fld. umbels, corolla lobes notched. Spring. Rhaetian Alps.

darialica Rupr. To 4 in.; lvs. narrowly obovate to oblong or spatulate, to 3 in. long, tapering to short petiole, regularly and sharply denticulate; fls. rose or carmine-red, ½ in. across, in 2–5-fld. umbels, corolla lobes notched. Ne. Caucasus.

denticulata Sm. [var. *cashmeriana* Hort.; *P. cachemiriana* Munro; *P. cashmeriana* Carrière]. To 1 ft.; lvs. oblong to oblanceolate, to 6 in. long in fl., to 8 in. or more in fr., tapering to winged petiole; fls. in shades of purple or pinkish-purple, with yellow eye, occasionally white, ½ in. across, in dense heads. Early spring. Himalayas. Cv. 'Gigantea'. A vigorous hort. form. Cvs. 'Alba', 'Rosea', and 'Rubra' are listed color variations.

×**Deschmannii:** *P.* ×*vochinensis.*

Edgeworthii (Hook.f.) Pax [*P. Winteri* W. Wats.]. To 3 in.; lvs. to 6¾ in. long, spring lvs. spatulate to obovate-spatulate, tapering to short, winged petiole, summer lvs. ovate, truncate or cordate at base and long-petioled; fls. pale mauve with white eye, ¾ in. across, on pedicels to 2 in. long, in short, many-fld. umbels. W. Himalayas. Cv. 'Alba'. Fls. white.

elatior (L.) J. Hill. OXLIP. To 1 ft.; lvs. ovate to elliptic or oblong, to 8 in. long, tapering abruptly to winged petiole, pubescent beneath; fls. sulphur-yellow, to 1 in. across, in a 1-sided, many-fld. umbel. Eur. to Iran Cv. 'Atrocaerulea'. Fls. dark blue. Cvs. 'Aurantiaca' and 'Gigantea' are listed. Subsp. **carpathica** (Griseb. & Schenk) W. W. Sm. & Forr. [*P. carpathica* (Griseb. & Schenk) Fuss]. Lvs. rounder, ovate; calyx inflated. Carpathians. Subsp. **leucophylla** (Pax) Hesl.-Harr. [*P. leucophylla* Pax]. Lvs. gray-pubescent beneath; scape pubescent. E. Carpathians. Subsp. **Pallasii** (Lehm.) W. W. Sm. & Forr. [*P. Pallasii* Lehm.]. Lvs. scarcely wrinkled and glabrous; calyx tube narrow, with reflexed lobes. Ural Mts., Caucasus to n. Iran.

elongata G. Watt. To 1 ft.; lvs. obovate or oblanceolate to 9½ in. long, tapering to a membranously winged petiole, crenulate, sometimes mealy beneath; fls. sulphur-yellow, ⅝ in. across, in umbels, rarely in 2 superimposed umbels. Sikkim Himalayas.

Elwesiana: *Omphalogramma Elwesiana.*

Erikssonii: a listed name of no botanical standing for *P. malacoides* cv.

farinosa L. BIRD'S-EYE P. To 1 ft.; lvs. oblanceolate or oblong-obovate, to elliptic or almost ovate, to 4 in. long, tapering to winged petiole, silvery or mealy beneath; fls. lilac, purple, or rarely white, yellow in throat, ½ in. across or more, in many-fld. umbels. Early summer. Boreal or alpine regions of Old World. Plants of N. Amer. formerly assigned to this sp. have been separated into *P. laurentiana* and *P. intercedens.* Subsp. **modesta:** *P. modesta.*

Faurieae Franch. To 4 in.; lvs. ovate, rhomboid, or suborbicular, to 2¼ in. long, crenulate to nearly entire, yellow-mealy beneath; fls. rose or purplish, ½ in. across, in 2–9-fld. umbels. Japan.

floribunda Wallich. BUTTERCUP P. To 11 in.; lvs. ovate or elliptic to spatulate or obovate, to 8 in. long; fls. gold to sulphur-yellow, ½ in. across, in 2–6 superimposed, many-fld. umbels. Winter and spring in greenhouse. Himalayas.

Florindae F. K. Ward. To 4 ft.; lvs. broadly ovate-cordate, to 20 in. long including petiole, toothed, glossy above, petiole reddish; fls. bright sulphur-yellow, ¾ in. across, drooping, in 30–40-fld., mealy umbels. Summer. Se. Tibet.

Forbesii Franch. BABY P. To 14 in.; lvs. elliptic to ovate-elliptic, cordate, to 4 in. long including petiole; fls. rose or lilac, with yellow eye, to ½ in. across, in 1–4 superimposed, 4–8-fld. umbels, calyx pilose. Winter and spring in the greenhouse. China, Burma.

Forrestii Balf.f. Glandular-hairy, to 3 ft., rhizomes several ft. long; lvs. ovate-elliptic or elliptic-oblong to oblong, to 8 in. long including petiole, wrinkled above, mealy beneath; fls. yellow with orange eye, fragrant, ¾ in. across, in 10–25-fld. umbels. China.

frondosa Janka. To 5 in.; lvs. spatulate, oblong, or obovate, to 1–3½ in. long, tapering to winged petiole, silvery beneath; fls. rose-lilac or reddish-purple, with yellow eye, ½ in. across, in 10–30-fld. umbels. Spring. Balkans.

gemmifera Batal. To 1 ft.; lvs. oblong or spatulate, 3 in. long, tapering to winged petiole; fls. pink to purple, to 1 in. across, in 3–10-fld. umbels, corolla lobes notched. China. Var. **zambalensis** (Petitm.) W. W. Sm. & H. R. Fletch. [*P. chrysopa* Balf.f. & Forr.]. Of stouter habit; lvs. fleshier; fls. usually larger.

glaucescens Moretti. To 5 in., glabrous; lvs. oblong to oblanceolate or lanceolate, to 4 in. long, with broad cartilaginous margins, glossy and glaucous; fls. rose-lilac to purple, 1 in. across, in 2–6-fld. umbels, corolla lobes notched. Late spring. Italian Alps. Cvs. **'Albocaerulea'** and **'Parviflora'** are listed. Subsp. **calycina** (Duby) Pax [*P. calycina* Duby]. Lvs. and calyces larger.

glomerata Pax [*P. crispa* Balf.f. & W. W. Sm.]. To 1 ft.; lvs. oblong, oblanceolate, or obovate-spatulate, to 6 in. long, tapering to winged petiole, margins erose-denticulate; fls. blue, ⅜ in. across, erect, in globular heads, corolla lobes notched. Himalayas.

Halleri J. F. Gmel. [*P. longiflora* All.]. To 7 in.; lvs. lanceolate-elliptic or oblanceolate, to 3 in. long, yellow-mealy beneath; fls. violet, ¾ in. across, in 2–12-fld. umbels, corolla lobes deeply notched, tube 1 in. long or more. Alps.

✕**Heerii** Brügg.: *P. integrifolia* ✕ *P. rubra.* Lvs. almost glaucous-green, entire; fls. rosy-red, in few-fld. umbels. Pyrenees, Alps.

Helenae: see *P. angustifolia.*

helodoxa Balf.f. To 3 ft.; lvs. oblanceolate, oblong-obovate, or lanceolate, to 14 in. long, tapering to winged petiole, denticulate, glabrous; fls. bright golden-yellow, 1 in. across, fragrant, in 4–6 superimposed umbels. Summer. China. Requires protection in the North.

heucherifolia Franch. To 1 ft., from a slender creeping rhizome; lvs. orbicular, to 6 in. long, cordate, palmately 7–11-lobed, somewhat pilose, petioles red-villous; fls. mauve-pink to deep purple, 1 in. across, nodding, in 3–10-fld. umbels, corolla lobes notched. Tibet, China.

hirsuta: *P. rubra.*

Hopeana: *P. sikkimensis* var.

hyacinthina W. W. Sm. To 1½ ft.; lvs. oblanceolate to oblong, to 7 in. long, tapering to winged petiole, irregularly denticulate, pubescent; fls. violet, ½ in. across, fragrant, pendent, in many-fld. heads. Se. Tibet.

hybrida: *P. vulgaris;* but the name *P. hybrida* is generally used in hort. for hybrids of the *P. japonica* type with very large purple fls.

Inayatii Duthie. To 5 in. high in fl., to 10 in. high in fr.; lvs. narrowly oblanceolate, to 4 in. long in fl., to 14 in. long in autumn, tapering to membranously winged, reddish-brown petiole, yellow-mealy beneath; fls. bluish-purple with yellow eye, ¾ in. across, in 3–15-fld. umbels. Nw. Himalayas.

incana M. E. Jones. To 1½ ft.; lvs. elliptic to obovate or spatulate, to 3 in. long, tapering to winged petiole, white-mealy beneath; fls.

lilac, with yellow throat, ⅜ in. across, in 2–14-fld. umbels, calyx markedly mealy. Sask. to Colo. and Utah.

integrifolia L. To 2 in.; lvs. elliptic or oblong to spatulate, 1½–2¼ in. long, entire, glandular; fls. rose-lilac to rose-magenta, rarely white, to 1 in. across, in 1–3-fld. umbels, corolla lobes notched. Alps, Pyrenees.

intercedens Fern. Similar to *P. laurentiana* but more slender, scape less than ³⁄₃₂ in. in diam.; lvs. cuneate, to 2¾ in. long, yellow-mealy beneath; fls. lilac, calyx to ¼ in. long. Ont. to Minn.

✕**intermedia** Portenschl. [*P.* ✕ *Wettsteinii* Wiem.]: *P. Clusiana* ✕ *P. minima.* Dwarf; lvs. ovate-cuneate to oblong-lanceolate, to 1 in. long, dentate, glossy; fls. to 1½ in. across, in 1–3-fld. umbels. Alps.

involucrata Wallich. To 1 ft.; lvs. ovate or oblong, to 6 in. long including the petiole, glabrous; fls. white with yellow eye, ¾ in. across, in 2–6-fld. umbels, corolla lobes notched. Himalayas.

ioessa W. W. Sm. To 1 ft.; lvs. narrowly oblong or oblanceolate to spatulate, to 8 in. long, irregularly and sharply toothed; fls. pinkish-mauve to violet, to 1 in. across, inflated, in 2–8-fld. umbels, calyx almost black. Se. Tibet. Var. **subpinnatifida** (W. W. Sm.) W. W. Sm. & H. R. Fletch. Fls. white or creamy-white, sometimes tinged with violet or purple.

japonica A. Gray. To 2½ ft.; lvs. obovate-oblong to spatulate, to 10 in. long, tapering to winged petiole; fls. purplish-red, to 1 in. across or more, in 1–6 superimposed, many-fld. umbels. Many cvs. with fls. white, red, or purple are in cult., as **'Alba'**, **'Atrosanguinea'**, **'Rosea'**, **'Rubra'**, and **'Splendens'**.

jesoana Miq. To 2 ft.; lvs. erect, orbicular-cordate, palmately 7–8-lobed, to 4 in. across, and 14 in. long including petiole, purplish; fls. rose or rose-purple, rarely white, with yellow eye, ¾ in. across, in 2–6-fld. umbels. Japan.

Juliae Kuzen. To 3 in.; lvs. reniform-orbicular to ovate-orbicular, to 4 in. long including petiole, cordate, petiole winged; fls. rose or red, to 1 in. across, on pedicels to 2 in. long. Caucasus. Cv. **'Alba'.** Fls. white.

✕**juribella** Sünderm.: *P. minima* ✕ *P. tyrolensis.* Mat-forming per.; lvs. elliptic, finely and irregularly toothed; fls. rosy-purple to magenta, 1 or 2 on 1-in. scapes. Giurbella Alps, Tyrol.

✕**kewensis** W. Wats.: *P. floribunda* ✕ *P. verticillata.* To 1½ ft.; lvs. obovate, to 8 in. long, tapering to winged petiole; fls. bright yellow, ¾ in. across, in 2–5 superimposed umbels. Winter and spring in greenhouse.

Kingii G. Watt. To 8 in.; lvs. elliptic-lanceolate to lanceolate, to 2½ in. long, with short, broadly winged petiole; fls. dark claret, ¾ in. across, in 2–10-fld. umbels. Himalayas.

kisoana Miq. To 8 in.; lvs. orbicular-cordate, to 6 in. long including petiole, pubescent on both sides; fls. deep rose or rose-mauve, in 2–6-fld. umbels, corolla lobes deeply notched. Japan.

Kleynii: a listed name of no botanical standing for *P. veris* cv.

laurentiana Fern. BIRD'S-EYE P. To 1½ ft.; lvs. spatulate, oblanceolate, or narrowly rhombic, to 5 in. long, dentate, mealy beneath; fls. lilac, ½ in. across, with calyx to ½ in. long, on erect to ascending pedicels, to 2 in. long, in 1–17-fld umbels. Summer. Lab., e. Que. to ne. Me.

leucophylla: *P. elatior* subsp.

lichiangensis: *P. polyneura.*

Littoniana: *P. Vialii.*

longiflora: *P. Halleri.*

lutea: *P. Auricula.*

luteola Rupr. To 1 ft.; lvs. lanceolate-elliptic or oblanceolate, to 1 ft. long, tapering to winged petiole, sharply toothed, glabrous; fls. yellow, ½ in. across, in 10–25-fld. umbels. Summer. E. Caucasus.

macrocalyx: *P. veris* subsp.

macrocarpa Maxim. Glabrous per., to 3 in.; lvs. ovate or spatulate, to 1 in. long, irregularly toothed; fls. white, with yellow eye, ⅜ in. across, in 1–4-fld. umbels, corolla lobes notched. Japan.

malacoides Franch. FAIRY P., BABY P. Hairy ann., 4–18 in.; lvs. ovate to elliptic or oblong-elliptic, to 10 in. long including petiole, cordate, with toothed lobes; scapes 1–12; fls. rose to lavender to almost white, to ½ in. across, in 1–6 superimposed, many-fld. umbels. Winter and spring in greenhouse. China. Many color forms with simple and double fls. up to 1½ in. across are cult. Cvs. include: **'Alba'**, fls. white; **'Ericksonii'** and **'Superba'**, improved strains; and **'Rosea'**, fls. bright rose.

marginata Curtis. To 5 in., mealy; lvs. obovate to oblong, to 4 in. long, margins white-mealy, irregularly toothed; fls. violet-rose, to 1 in. across, in 2–20-fld. umbels, corolla lobes deeply notched. Spring. Alps.

melanops W. W. Sm. & F. K. Ward. To 14 in.; lvs. lanceolate to linear-lanceolate, to 10 in. long, tapering to winged petiole, irregularly toothed, mealy beneath; fls. purple with black eye, fragrant, ¾ in. across, in 1 or 2 umbels, these 5–12-fld. China.

microdonta: *P. sikkimensis.*

minima L. Dwarf; lvs. cuneate, to 1 in. long, in compact rosettes, toothed on truncate apex, smooth, glossy; fls. rose with white eye, or white, 1 in. across, 1 or 2 on very short scapes, corolla lobes bifid. Mts., Eur.

mistassinica Michx. BIRD'S-EYE P. To 8 in.; lvs. oblanceolate to cuneate-obovate, to 2¾ in. long, toothed; fls. pink to pale blue, with yellow eye, ½ in. across, in 2–8-fld. umbels. N. N. Amer. Forma **leucantha** Fern. [var. *alba* Hort.]. Fls. white.

modesta Bisset & S. Moore [*P. farinosa* subsp. *modesta* (Bisset & S. Moore) Pax]. To 6 in.; lvs. oblong-elliptic or spatulate, to 3 in. long including petiole, toothed, mealy; fls. lilac to purple, ⅝ in. across, in 2–10-fld. umbels, corolla lobes notched. Japan.

×**Moerheimii** Hort.: hybrids, in general resembling *P. japonica;* fls. large, red, pink, or orange.

mollis Nutt. ex Hook. To 2 ft.; lvs. reniform-cordate, to 1 ft. long including petiole, lobed, hairy on both surfaces; fls. rose to crimson, with yellow eye, ¾ in. across, in 2–10 superimposed, 4–9-fld. umbels, corolla lobes notched. Himalayas.

Mooreana: *P. capitata* subsp.

muscarioides Hemsl. To 16 in.; lvs. obovate-spatulate or elliptic to oblong, to 7 in. long, tapering to winged petiole, crenate-dentate; fls. deep purplish-blue, fragrant, pendent, in many-fld. compact heads or short spikes. China.

nipponica Yatabe. To 6 in.; lvs. obovate to spatulate, to 1½ in. long, toothed in upper widest part; fls. white, with golden-yellow eye, ⅝ in. across, in 1–8-fld. umbels, corolla lobes notched. Japan.

nutans Delav. ex Franch. To 20 in.; lvs. narrowly elliptic to broadly oblanceolate, to 8 in. long, tapering to winged petiole; fls. lavender-blue to violet, 1 in. across, nodding, in dense heads or compact spikes. China.

obconica Hance. GERMAN P., POISON P. To 1 ft.; lvs. ovate or elliptic to oblong-elliptic, to 10 in. long including petiole, with irritating hairs; fls. lilac to pink, to 1 in. across, in 2–13-fld. umbels. Winter in greenhouse. China. Cv. **'Gigantea'.** A large form. Cv. **'Grandiflora'.** Fls. to 1½ in. across. Var. **werringtonensis** (Forr.) W. W. Sm. & H. R. Fletch. [*P. werringtonensis* Forr.]. Corolla tube exserted from calyx. China.

obliqua W. W. Sm. To 1½ ft. or more; lvs. lanceolate or narrowly obovate, to 8 in. long, tapering to a membranously winged petiole, regularly toothed, yellow-mealy beneath; fls. pale yellow to white, to 1 in. across, in few-fld.umbels, upper corolla lobes reflexed. Himalayas.

obtusifolia Royle. To 1½ ft.; lvs. elliptic to obovate-oblong, to 8 in. long, tapering to winged petiole, rounded at apex, thin, white-mealy beneath; fls. bluish-purple, with white or yellow eye, to 1 in. across, in a 2–6-fld. umbel, or in 2 or 3 superimposed, 10–12-fld. umbels. Nw. Himalayas.

oenensis: *P. daonensis.*

officinalis: *P. veris.*

Pallasii: *P. elatior* subsp.

Parryi A. Gray. To 20 in.; lvs. oblanceolate to obovate-oblong, to 1 ft. long including winged petiole, glabrous; fls. reddish-purple, with yellow eye, to 1 in. across, in many-fld. umbels. Summer. Rocky Mts.

Poissonii Franch. To 1½ ft.; lvs. oblong-obovate, to 7 in. long, tapering to petiole, denticulate, glaucous; fls. purplish-crimson, with yellow eye, ¼ in. across, in 2–6 superimposed umbels. Summer. China.

×**polyantha** Hort. POLYANTHUS. A hybrid group probably having the parentage *P. veris, P. elatior,* and *P. vulgaris.* To 1 ft.; lvs. obovate, tapering to winged petiole; fls. of many colors, in many-fld. umbels or sometimes solitary. Spring. Cvs. include: **'Colossea', 'Caerulea',** and **'Rubra'.** An old garden plant.

polyneura Franch. [*P. lichiangensis* Forr.; *P. Veitchii* Duthie]. To 1½ ft.; lvs. triangular, ovate, or orbicular, to 1 ft. long including petiole, cordate to subcordate, lobed, glabrous to conspicuously hairy beneath; fls. pale rose to rich rose-red to crimson or purple, with yellow eye, 1 in. across, in 1 umbel or in 2–3 superimposed umbels. China.

prolifera Wallich. Per., to 2 ft., not mealy; lvs. oblong to nearly spatulate, to 1 ft. long, tapering to petiole, minutely toothed; fls. yellow, ¾ in. across, in 1 umbel or in 2–3 superimposed umbels. Assam.

×**pubescens** Jacq.: *P. Auricula* × *P. rubra.* To 6 in.; lvs. oblong to rounded-oblong; fls. rosy-crimson with white eye, in many-fld. umbels. Cvs. with violet, yellow, or white fls. are known. Cv. **'Decora'** is listed.

pudibunda: *P. sikkimensis* var.

pulverulenta Duthie. To 3 ft.; lvs. oblanceolate to obovate, to 1 ft. long, tapering to winged petiole, toothed; fls. red, with darker red or

purple eye, 1¼ in. across, in several superimposed, many-fld. umbels, corolla lobes notched. Summer. China.

Reinii Franch. & Sav. To 4 in.; lvs. round to reniform, to 10 in. long including petiole, cordate, lobed; fls. rose to purple, with yellow eye, to 1½ in. across, in 1–6-fld. umbels, corolla lobes bifid. Cent. Japan.

reticulata Wallich. To 1½ ft.; lvs. oblong to oblong-ovate, to 4 in. long, on petioles to 1 ft. long, cordate, toothed; fls. yellow or white, to ¾ in. across, in few- to many-fld. umbels. Himalayas.

rosea Royle. To 5 in. high in fl., to 20 in. high in fr.; lvs. oblong or obovate, to 8 in. long, tapering to winged petiole; fls. rose, with yellow eye, ¾ in. across, in 4–12-fld. umbels. Spring. Himalayas. Cvs. **'Grandiflora'** and **'Splendens'** are listed.

rotundifolia Wallich. To 1 ft. or more; lvs. cordate-orbicular to cordate-reniform, to 8 in. long including petiole, toothed, crenate or erose, mealy beneath; fls. purplish-pink, with golden-yellow eye, ¾ in. across, in 1 umbel or in 2 superimposed umbels. Himalayas.

rubra J. F. Gmel. [*P. hirsuta* All.]. Glandular-hairy per., to 4 in., from a stout rhizome; lvs. rhombic to obovate or spatulate, to 5 in. long, toothed, often mostly toward apex; fls. rose, lilac, or white, to 1 in. across, in many-fld. umbels. Mts., Eur.

×**salisburgensis** Floerke: *P. glutinosa* Wulfen × *P. minima.* Dwarf; lvs. cuneate, deeply notched, glossy; fls. red Alps.

sapphirina Hook.f. & T. Thoms. To 2 in.; lvs. oblanceolate to obovate, to ⅜ in. long; fls. violet-purple to blue, ¼ in. across, semipendent, in 1–4-fld. umbels. Himalayas.

saxatilis Kom. To 1 ft.; lvs. oblong to ovate-oblong, to 8 in. long including petiole, cordate, lobed and crisped; fls. rose-lilac, to ¾ in. across, on pedicels ½–2 in. long, in a 3–15-fld. umbel, occasionally in 2 superimposed umbels. Ne. Asia.

scapigera Craib. To 6 in.; lvs. oblong-spatulate to elliptic or obovate, to 6 in. long, coarsely and irregularly toothed; fls. pink, with yellow eye surrounded by white, 1¼ in. across. W. Himalayas.

scotia Hook. To 4 in.; lvs. elliptic, oblong, or spatulate, to 2 in. long, tapering to broadly winged petiole, mealy beneath; fls. dark purple, with yellow throat, rarely white, ¼ in. across, in 1–6-fld. umbels, corolla lobes notched. N. Scotland.

secundiflora Franch. [*P. vittata* Bur. & Franch.]. To 3 ft.; lvs. oblong to obovate, to 1 ft. long including petiole, finely toothed, often yellow-mealy beneath when young; fls. reddish-purple or deep rose-red, to 1 in. across, nodding, in a 5–20-fld. umbel, sometimes in 2 superimposed umbels. Himalayas.

serratifolia Franch. To 1½ ft.; lvs. oblong, obovate-oblong to obovate, to 8 in. long, tapering to winged petiole, irregularly toothed; fls. yellow, striped with orange, 1 in. across, in 1 umbel, occasionally in 2 superimposed umbels. Himalayas.

sibirica Jacq. To 1 ft., glabrous; lvs. oblong, ovate, or elliptic-orbicular, to 4¾ in. long, tapering to winged petiole; fls. lilac or pinkish-purple, with yellow eye, to ¾ in. across, in 1–10-fld. umbels. Arctic Eur., cent. Asia, Alaska.

Sibthorpii: *P. vulgaris* subsp.

Sieboldii E. Morr. To 1 ft.; lvs. ovate to oblong-ovate, to 8 in. long including petiole, cordate, lobed and toothed; fls. white, rose, or purple, with white eye, to 1½ in. across, in 6–10-fld. umbels, calyx lobes spreading and enlarged in fr. Japan, ne. Asia. Many cvs. cult., with fls. larger, fringed, and variously colored. Cv. **'Alba'.** Fls. white.

sikkimensis Hook. [*P. microdonta* Franch. ex Petitm.]. To 3 ft.; lvs. elliptic or oblong to oblanceolate, to 16 in. long including petiole, sharp-toothed, wrinkled; fls. yellow or creamy-white, 1¼ in. across, nodding, in many-fld. umbels. Late spring. Himalayas. Var. **Hopeana** (Balf.f. & R. Cooper) W. W. Sm. & H. R. Fletch. [*P. Hopeana* Balf.f. & R. Cooper]. Plant smaller. Var. **pudibunda** (W. W. Sm.) W. W. Sm. & H. R. Fletch. [*P. pudibunda* W. W. Sm.]. Slender alpine plant; fls. much smaller.

sinensis Sab. ex Lindl. [*P. chinensis* Hort.]. CHINESE P. To 1 ft.; lvs. broadly ovate-cordate to orbicular-cordate, to 5 in. across, on petioles to 7 in. long, toothed, lobed, pubescent on both sides; fls. in many colors, to 1½ in. across, in many-fld. umbels. Winter, in the greenhouse. China. Cvs. include: **'Filicifolia',** lvs. crisped; **'Fimbriata',** fls. fringed or crested; **'Stellata',** STAR P., fls. in superimposed umbels.

sinoplantaginea Balf.f. To 8 in. or more in fr., rhizome with reddish scales and remains of old lvs.; lvs. narrowly lanceolate, to ⅜ in. wide, to 3½ in. long or longer in fr., tapering to winged petiole, yellow-mealy beneath; fls. deep purple or bluish-purple, with gray eye, ¾ in. across, fragrant, in 5–12-fld. umbels, calyx lobes blackish-purple. China.

sinopurpurea W. Irving. Similar to *P. sinoplantaginea,* but more robust and lvs. ⅝–2 in. wide, brighter yellow-mealy, fls. to 1¼ in. across. China.

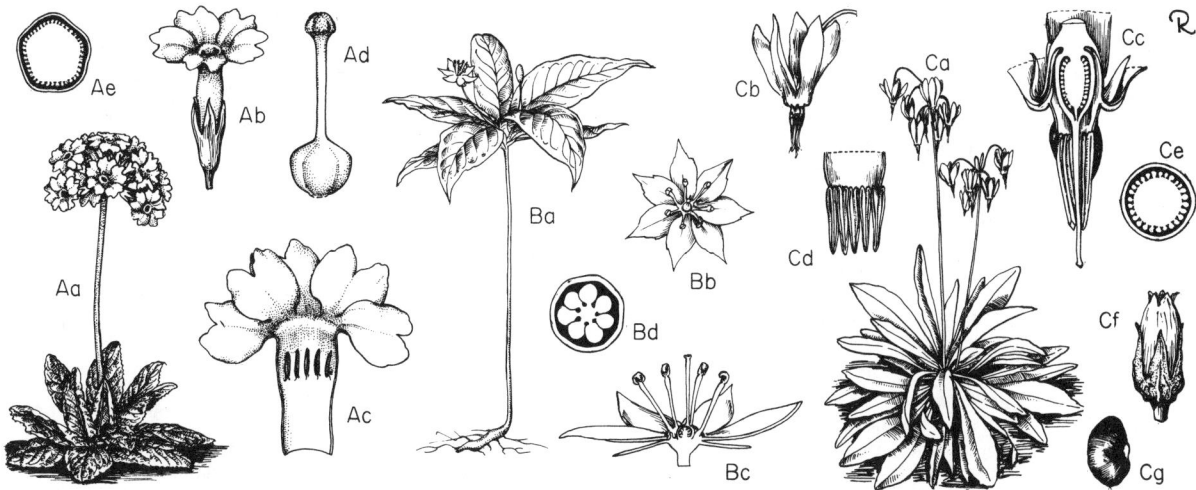

PRIMULACEAE. **A,** *Primula denticulata:* **Aa,** plant, × ¼; **Ab,** flower, × 1; **Ac,** corolla, expanded, × 1½; **Ad,** pistil, × 3; **Ae,** ovary, cross section, × 5. **B,** *Trientalis borealis:* **Ba,** plant, × ⅜; **Bd,** flower, × 1; **Bc,** flower, vertical section, × 2; **Bd,** ovary, cross section, × 10. **C,** *Dodecatheon Meadia:* **Ca,** plant, × ⅛; **Cb,** flower, × ½; **Cc,** flower, vertical section, × 1½; **Cd,** inner surface of staminal tube, expanded, × 1; **Ce,** ovary, cross section, × 4; **Cf,** fruit, × 1; **Cg,** seed, × 8. (Aa-Ae from Bailey, *Manual of Cultivated Plants,* ed. 2.)

Smithiana Craib. To 2 ft.; lvs. oblong-lanceolate to oblanceolate, to 8 in. long, obtuse, thin, usually glabrous, serrate; fls. pale yellow, to ¾ in. across, in 1–4 superimposed umbels. Himalayas.

sonchifolia Franch. To 1 ft. in fr.; lvs. oblong to obovate-oblong, to 8 in. long or more, tapering to winged petiole, irregularly lobed and coarsely toothed; fls. in various shades of blue, with yellow, white-margined eye, to 1 in. across, in 3–20-fld. umbels. Himalayas.

spectabilis Tratt. To 5 in.; lvs. ovate-lanceolate, to 4 in. long, stiff, with cartilaginous margins, glossy, glabrous; fls. rose-red, 1 in. across, in 1–7-fld. umbels. Summer. Alps.

specuicola Rydb. To 6 in.; lvs. spatulate, to 5 in. long, tapering to petiole, sinuate-dentate; fls. violet, with yellow eye, to ⅜ in. across, in 6–12-fld. umbels. Se. Utah.

stellata: a listed name of no botanical standing for *P. sinensis* cv.

×**Steinii** Obrist ex Stein [*P.* × *Bilekii* Sünderm.]: *P. minima* × *P. rubra.* Dwarf; lvs. spatulate, with 3–10 horny teeth toward apex; fls. deep red, in 2–5-fld. umbels on short scapes. Alps.

suaveolens: *P. veris* subsp. *Columnae.*

suffrutescens A. Gray. To 5 in.; lvs. cuneate-spatulate, to 1¼ in. long, glabrous, sharply toothed toward apex; fls. red-purple, ½ in. across, in 2–10-fld. umbels. Mts., Calif.

tyrolensis Schott. Dwarf per., from a stout rhizome; lvs. obovate or round, to 1 in. long, glandular-hairy; fls. rose to rose-violet, with white eye, to 1 in. across, in 1–2-fld. scapes, to ¾ in. long, corolla lobes notched. Tyrol.

uralensis: *P. veris* subsp. *macrocalyx.*

vaginata G. Watt. To 5 in., from a slender creeping rhizome; lvs. orbicular-cordate, to 2 in. across, on petioles to 4–8 in. long, palmately 7-lobed, lobes deeply dentate; fls. lilac to rosy-purple, ⅜ in. across, in 2–9-fld. heads, corolla lobes bifid. Himalayas.

Veitchii: *P. polyneura.*

veris L. [*P. officinalis* (L.) J. Hill]. COWSLIP. To 1 ft.; lvs. ovate to ovate-oblong, to 8 in. long including the abruptly narrowed and winged petiole, pubescent beneath, irregularly toothed; fls. bright yellow, ½ in. across, concave or almost flat, fragrant, in many-fld., often 1-sided umbels, calyx markedly 5-angled, somewhat inflated. Eur. Cvs. are: 'Alba', fls. white; 'Aurea' and 'Caerulea', listed names; 'Coccinea', fls. crimson; 'Colossea' and 'Gigantea', listed names; 'Kleynii', listed as having yellow fls. shading to apricot; 'Lilacina', a listed name; 'Lutea', fls. pale yellow. Grandiflora is a group name used for vigorous very large-fld. kinds. Subsp. **canescens** (Opiz) Hayek ex Lüdi [*P. canescens* Hort.]. Calyx as long as corolla tube. Cent. Eur. Subsp. **Columnae** (Ten.) Lüdi [*P. Columnae* Ten.; *P. suaveolens* Bertol.]. Lvs. densely white-hairy beneath; fls. slightly fragrant. S. Eur. Subsp. **macrocalyx** (Bunge) Lüdi [*P. macrocalyx* Bunge; *P. uralensis* Fisch. ex Rchb.]. Fls. orange-yellow, calyx ¾ in. long. Asia.

verticillata Forssk. Glabrous per., to 2 ft.; lvs. oblanceolate to obovate-spatulate, to 1 ft. long including petiole, tapering to winged petiole, toothed, mealy beneath; fls. yellow, to 1 in. across, fragrant, mostly in superimposed umbels. Winter, in greenhouse. S. Arabia.

Vialii Delav. ex Franch. [*P. Littoniana* Forr.]. To 2 ft.; lvs. lanceolate to oblong, to 1 ft. long, tapering to winged petiole, toothed, hairy on both surfaces; fls. bluish-violet, 3–8 in. long, fragrant, tubular, ½ in. across, in dense spikes, unopened calyx bright scarlet. China.

villosa Jacq. To 6 in.; lvs. in a compact rosette, oblong to spatulate or obovate, to ⅝ in. long including petiole, glandular-hairy; fls. rose to lilac, with white eye, 1 in. across, in 1–12-fld. umbels. Alps. Forma **cottia** (Widm.) Lüdi [*P. cottia* Widm.]. Lvs. broader, shorter-petioled, more densely hairy and smaller-toothed. Cottian Alps. Subsp. **commutata** (Schott) Widm. [*P. commutata* Schott]. Lvs. looser, larger, with definite petioles. Castle Herberstein, near Gleisdorf in se. Austria.

viscosa All. Glandular-hairy per., to 8 in., from a stout branching rhizome; lvs. oblanceolate, obovate, or elliptic, to 7 in. long, tapering to membranously winged, sheathing petiole, dentate above the middle, rank-smelling; fls. rose-lilac, ½ in. across, fragrant, in 1–25-fld. umbels. Alps, Pyrenees.

vittata: *P. secundiflora.*

×**vochinensis** Gusmus [*P.* × *Deschamannii* Gusmus]: *P. minima* × *P. Wulfeniana.* Dwarf; lvs. oblong, to oblong-lanceolate or oblong-cuneate, usually toothed; fls. deep red. Carinthia in Austria.

vulgaris Huds. [*P. acaulis* (L.) J. Hill; *P. hybrida* Schrank]. ENGLISH P. To 6 in.; lvs. oblanceolate to obovate, to 10 in. long, tapering to petiole, wrinkled, irregularly toothed; fls. yellow, purple, or blue, ½ in. across, solitary, on pedicels to 6 in. long, scape lacking. Spring. Eur. Cvs. listed are: 'Alba', 'Atropurpurea', 'Azurea', 'Caerulea', 'Grandiflora', 'Lilacina', 'Lutea', 'Rosea', and 'Rubra'. Var. hortensis is a term applied to cult. variations of many kinds. Subsp. **Sibthorpii** (Hoffmanns.) W. W. Sm. & Forr. [*P. Sibthorpii* Hoffmanns.]. Fls. purple, rose, lilac, red, crimson, or white. Se. Eur., Caucasus, n. Iran.

Waltonii G. Watt ex Balf.f. To 2½ ft.; lvs. elliptic-oblong to oblanceolate, to 1 ft. long including petiole, sharply toothed; fls. pink to deep wine-purple, to 1¼ in. across, powdered white or yellow inside, in few-to many-fld. umbels. China.

Wardii: *P. yargongensis.*

Wattii King ex G. Watt. To 7 in.; lvs. oblong to oblanceolate, to 4 in. long, coarsely dentate, pubescent beneath; fls. violet with white eye, ½ in. across, nodding, in compact 5–10-fld. umbels on glabrous scapes. E. Himalayas.

werringtonensis: *P. obconica* var.

Wettsteinii: *P.* × *intermedia.*

Wilsonii S. T. Dunn. To 3 ft.; lvs. oblanceolate, to 8 in. long, finely denticulate; fls. purple, ⅝ in. across, in 3–6 superimposed umbels. China.

Winteri: *P. Edgeworthii.*

Wulfeniana Schott. Tufted, glabrous per., to 3 in.; lvs. elliptic to oblanceolate, to 2 in. long, glossy, with cartilaginous margins; fls. rose with white eye and throat, to 1¼ in. across, in 1–3-fld. umbels. Alps.

yargongensis Petitm. [*P. Wardii* Balf.f.]. To 1 ft.; lvs. ovate, elliptic, or lanceolate-oblong, to 4¾ in. long, including sheathing, winged petiole; fls. mauve, pink, or purple, with white eye, sometimes entirely white, in 3–8-fld. umbels, corolla lobes notched. Himalayas.

PRIMULACEAE Venten. PRIMROSE FAMILY. Dicot.; about 20–28 genera and 800–1,000 spp. of mostly ann. or per. herbs, common in the N. Hemisphere but native to all continents; lvs. usually simple, mostly opp. or whorled, or occasionally all basal or alt.; fls. bisexual, regular, solitary or in various types of infl., calyx usually 5-lobed, corolla typically 5-lobed, stamens usually 5, opp. corolla lobes, pistil 1, compound, ovary superior, 1-celled, with free-central placentation; fr. a caps. The family furnishes many flower garden, rock garden, and greenhouse plants. The cult. genera are: *Anagallis, Androsace, Ardisiandra, Cortusa, Cyclamen, Dodecatheon, Douglasia, Hottonia, Lysimachia, Omphalogramma, Primula, Samolus, Soldanella,* and *Trientalis.*

PRINSEPIA Royle. *Rosaceae.* Three or 4 spp. of thorny, deciduous Asian shrubs; lvs. simple, mostly fascicled; fls. yellow or white, in axillary fascicles or racemes, sepals and petals 5; fr. a cherrylike drupe. Differing from *Prunus* in having sts. with chambered pith.

Grown as an ornamental; hardy north. Propagated by seeds sown as soon as ripe or stratified, also by cuttings of young wood under glass, and by layers.

sinensis (D. Oliver) D. Oliver ex Bean. To 6 ft. or more, spreading; lvs. oblong- to ovate-lanceolate, 1½–3½ in. long, sparsely toothed, ciliate; fls. yellow, usually 2–3 in a lf. axil, ½ in. across; fr. purple or red, ovoid, juicy, ½ in. long. Manchuria. Zone 5.

uniflora Batal. To 6 ft., glabrous; lvs. linear, 1–2 in. long, sparsely toothed; fls. 1–3, on short, leafy shoots, white, ⅝ in. across; fr. black with purple bloom, globose, $^5/_{16}$ in. in diam. N. China. Zone 6.

PRITCHARDIA Seem. & H. Wendl. [*Eupritchardia* O. Kuntze]. *Palmae.* About 36 spp. of tall or medium palms with bisexual fls., native to the Pacific Is.; trunks straight, not clothed with fibers at top; lvs. costapalmate, heavy and large but pliant, petiole with unarmed margins; infl. among the lvs., short- or long-peduncled, with swordlike or flaring bracts on the peduncle and on the 1 or few, long-stalked brs. when these present, rachis short, with simple or branched rachillae; fls. green, solitary, elongate in bud, calyx 3-lobed, petals deciduous, stamens 6, filaments united in a tube exceeding calyx, carpels 3, separate except united styles; fr. globose or ellipsoid, 1-seeded with abortive carpels at the apex and persistent pedicel-like calyx at base, seed with homogeneous endosperm.

The pritchardias are striking palms of regular form. Some thrive in protected places in southern Fla. and a few in central Calif.

Beccariana Rock. To nearly 60 ft., sts. to 1 ft. in diam.; lvs. large, nearly orbicular, with minute, fringed scales on lower surface; infl. with 3–5 nearly equal brs. from near the base, about 4½ ft. long; fls. about ½ in. long; fr. to 1⅜ in. long. Hawaiian Is. Zone 10a.

filifera: *Washingtonia filifera.*

Gaudichaudii H. Wendl. To 20 ft., trunk to 1 ft. in diam.; lvs. 3–4 ft. long, with prominent brown scales on lower surface when young but becoming nearly glabrous in age, segms. about 60, 1 ft. long, petiole 2–3 ft. long; infl. with 1 or rarely 2 axes, to 3 ft. long; fls. about $^5/_{16}$ in. long; fr. globose, to 1¾ in. in diam. Hawaiian Is. Zone 10a.

Martii H. Wendl. To 16 ft., trunk stout; lvs. with appressed, ciliate, confluent scales beneath; infl. with 3–4 nearly equal axes, about 3 ft. long; fls. to ⅜ in. long; fr. ovoid-ellipsoid to somewhat obovoid, to 1¾ in. in diam. Hawaiian Is. Zone 10a.

pacifica Seem. & H. Wendl. FIJI FAN PALM. Trunk to 30 ft., 1 ft. in diam.; lvs. to 4 ft. long and more, green on both surfaces, segms. about 90, petiole to 3 ft. long or more; infl. with a single axis, shorter than lvs.; fls. $^5/_{16}$ in. long; fr. globose, about ½ in. in diam. Fiji Is. Zone 10b.

robusta: *Washingtonia robusta.*

Thurstonii F. J. Muell. & Drude [*Eupritchardia Thurstonii* (F. J. Muell. & Drude) O. Kuntze]. Slender, to 15 ft.; lvs. glaucescent and bearing impressed elliptic scales beneath, segms. about 70; infl. with a single axis exceeding the lvs.; fls. about ¼ in. long; fr. about ¼ in. in diam. Fiji Is. Zone 10b.

PROBOSCIDEA J. C. Keller. UNICORN FLOWER, UNICORN PLANT. *Martyniaceae.* Nine spp. of broad-topped, sticky-pubescent Amer. herbs with stout sts.; lvs. large, long-petioled; infl. a loose axillary raceme of large, purple fls.; calyx 5-lobed, spathelike, corolla 5-lobed, stamens 4, all fertile; fr. a 2-valved caps., with fleshy, deciduous exterior, and woody interior, terminating in a long curved beak, which splits and is as long as or longer than the body.

Grown as an ornamental or for the young fruit, which is pickled like cucumbers or used in mixed pickles. In the South, seeds may be sown where the plants are to stand; in the North, they should be sown early in hotbeds and transplanted after danger of frost is past.

fragrans (Lindl.) Decne. [*Martynia fragrans* Lindl.]. Ann., to 2 ft.; lvs. opp. or subopp., broadly ovate or triangular, mostly broader than long, to 6 in. wide, usually 5-lobed in mature plants; fls. deep purple, often blotched, to 2 in. long, fragrant; fr. to 12 in. long, the body 4 in. long, the beak twice as long. Mex. Commonly grown under the name *P. Jussieui.*

Jussieui: *P. louisianica,* but material grown as *P. Jussieui* is *P. fragrans.*

louisianica (Mill.) Thell. [*P. Jussieui* J. C. Keller; *Martynia Proboscidea* Glox.]. COMMON U.F., PROBOSCIS FLOWER, RAM'S-HORN. Ann., clammy, low and spreading, to 3 ft. across, brs. in pairs; lvs. nearly orbicular to ovate-cordate, to 1 ft. across, wavy-margined but not lobed; fls. creamy-white to violet or light red, blotched with purple, to 2 in. long; fr. pendent, to 6 in. long, body and beak of nearly equal length. Del. to Ind., s. to New Mex.

lutea: *Ibicella lutea.*

petiolaris: a listed name of no botanical standing.

PROMENAEA Lindl. *Orchidaceae.* Six spp. of epiphytes, native to Brazil; pseudobulbs compressed, 1–3-lvd.; lvs. small, plicate; infl. shorter than lvs., 1-fld.; sepals and petals spreading, separate, similar, lip 3-lobed, jointed to column foot, disc with a transverse callus, column wingless, with a short foot. For structure of fl. see *Orchidaceae.*

Warm greenhouse. For culture see *Orchids.*

×**Crawshayana** Hort.: *P. stapelioides* × *P. xanthinum* Lindl. Pseudobulbs nearly globose, several-lvd.; lvs. oblong-lanceolate; fls. to 2¼ in. across, cream-yellow, sepals spotted red-brown, petals and lip more thickly spotted, lip 3-lobed, lateral lobes lanceolate, midlobe ovate-apiculate, disc with tubercled crest.

stapelioides (Link & Otto) Lindl. Pseudobulbs small, ovoid, 1–2-lvd.; lvs. lanceolate, to 2½ in. long; infl. longer than lvs., pendent, 2-fld.; fls. 1½ in. across, pale green, marked with purple, sepals and petals orbicular-ovate, lateral lobes of lip lanceolate, midlobe ovate, apiculate, disc with transverse ridge. Brazil.

PROPAGATION. In horticulture, propagation is the reproduction of plants by means of seeds or spores (sexual reproduction), or by vegetative parts (asexual reproduction) through division, bulblets and other specialized structures, layering, cuttings, tissue culture, and grafting (which is treated separately—see *Grafting*). Some forms of propagation require little equipment while others may require greenhouse facilities, hotbeds, coldframes, or lathhouses. A limited number of propagation techniques may be practiced in the home under artificial lighting (see *House Plants*).

In addition to facilities, diverse growing media and containers are used. For young plants, pots of clay, plastic, metal, or pressed peat are commonly used. Paraffined-paper or plastic cups punched for drainage, manufactured plant bands, or containers made of asphalt-treated building paper are also useful. Shallow trays or flats of plastic, metal, or wood and perforated for drainage are often used for germinating seeds or rooting cuttings. Seedlings and rooted cuttings are then transplanted to individual containers and ultimately may be moved to larger pots; in nursery or commercial operations, metal containers of one- to five-gallon size or polyethelene bags with drainage holes punched in them are often used. Containers, tools, and work area should be sterilized with steam or boiling water, two percent formaldehyde solution, Clorox, or other disinfectant.

The growing medium, whatever its nature, should be pasteurized by bringing the soil temperature to 140°–180° F with steam or other moist heat, or, if necessary, sterilized at 212° F for 30 minutes to kill undesirable insects, weed seeds, and disease organisms. Small quantities of moist medium can be pasteurized in the home oven if temperature is controlled by a thermostat or carefully monitored with a thermometer in the soil. Media may also be fumigated with chemicals such

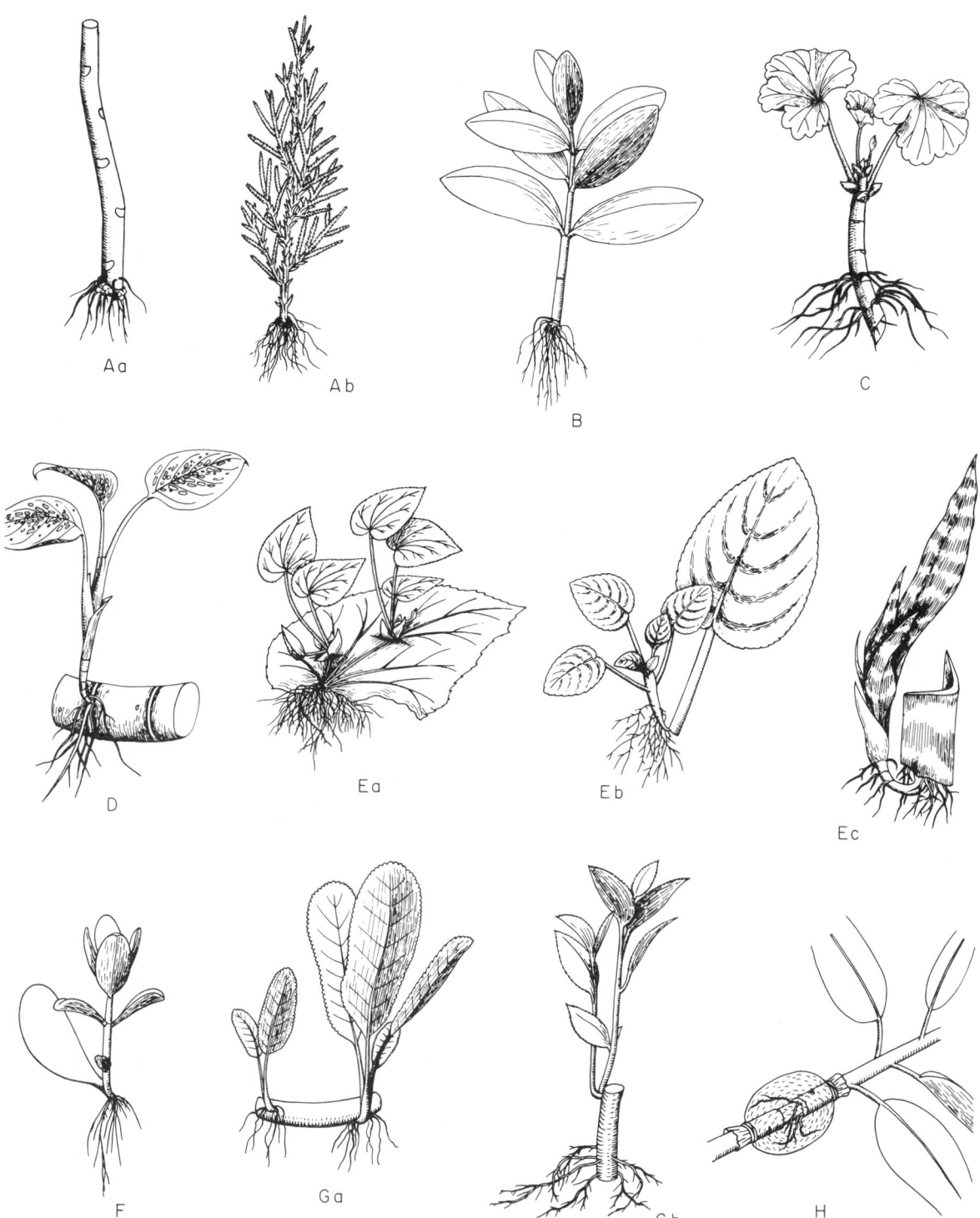

PROPAGATION. **A,** Hardwood cuttings: **Aa,** cutting of a deciduous hardwood; **Ab,** cutting of a narrow-leaved evergreen, *Juniperus.* **B,** Softwood cutting of *Hebe.* **C,** Herbaceous cutting of *Pelargonium.* **D,** Stem cutting of a monocot, *Dieffenbachia.* **E,** Leaf cuttings: **Ea,** blade of *Begonia* laid flat on rooting medium; **Eb,** leaf blade and petiole of *Saintpaulia* set vertically; **Ec,** portion of blade of *Sansevieria* with basal end cut on a slant. **F,** Leaf-and-bud cutting of *Crassula.* **G,** Root cuttings: **Ga,** root section of *Armoracia* set horizontally; **Gb,** root section of *Malus* set vertically. **H,** Air layering of *Ficus,* a diagrammatic sectional view showing girdling and formation of roots.

as chlorpicrin (tear gas), methyl bromide, formaldehyde, or other soil fumigants, but these require much care in handling and are more appropriate to commercial operations. It is well to seek advice from local county agents or experiment stations before using such chemicals. Formaldehyde may also be used for small amounts of a medium; for each bushel of medium, 2½ tablespoons of commercial formalin diluted with five to six parts of water, mixed well, and allowed to stand for 24 hours, is applied.

Containers are filled with a medium appropriate to the propagation technique. The medium may consist solely of soil, sand, organic material such as leaf mold, peat moss, sphagnum, shredded bark, sawdust, or wood shavings, or minerals such as vermiculite, perlite, and pumice, but usually is a mixture of several of the above. Sand and organic matter are usually added to loam for better consistency and water-holding capacity in ratios of approximately one part loam, one or two parts fine quartz building sand, and one part organic matter (peat moss, leaf mold, shredded bark) for potting rooted cuttings and young seedlings, or the same but with two parts loam and one part sand for use in containers. Soilless mixes using peat moss and perlite or vermiculite may also be used, especially for germinating seeds, but in such mixtures fertilizer must be added. Special mixtures such as those developed at the University of California at Los Angeles, the John Innes Horticultural Institute in England, and Cornell University were developed for commercial operations, and similar mixtures may be prepared for use in the home or small greenhouse (see *Soils*).

Sexual Propagation

Seeds and spores for sexual propagation may be purchased or they may be harvested from plants in the garden or in the wild state. For propagation by spores, see *Ferns and Fern Allies*. Seeds of some plants, such as spring-fruiting trees, germinate almost immediately and soon lose their viability if stored. Seeds of others, especially seeds with very hard coats, may remain viable for months to years if stored properly. Most kinds of seeds retain viability longest if stored in a sealed container with low moisture content at a low temperature, although seed of most common ornamental and crop plants may be stored without controls from one season to the next, preferably under cool, dry conditions. Some seeds, however, such as those of most Palmae and probably many tropical species, will not stand drying and should be stored under moist conditions or planted immediately. Cool, moist storage is required for seeds of *Acer, Citrus,* and many nut trees, as *Aesculus, Carya, Corylus, Fagus, Juglans,* and *Quercus.*

Seeds of annuals and herbaceous perennials may be germinated indoors or sown outdoors in spring or early summer. Most tree and shrub seeds are planted in outdoor seedbeds in autumn or early spring. If seeds are fresh, germination usually follows quickly as water is absorbed. Seeds of some plants, however, do not germinate quickly because an impermeable coat prevents the absorption of water, because the embryo requires a period of dormancy, because the seed contains a chemical inhibitor, or because of a combination of these factors. Such seeds require special treatment. Seeds with impervious coats, often found in the Cannaceae, Chenopodiaceae, Convolvulaceae, Geraniaceae, Leguminosae, Malvaceae, certain Palmae, and Solanaceae, may be scarified by mechanical means (breaking, scratching, rubbing, or cracking) or by treatment with concentrated sulfuric acid in the proportion of about two parts acid to one part seeds. Great care should be exercised, as the acid is very corrosive and splatters if water is added. Seeds should be soaked, with occasional stirring, until the coat is paper thin, at which time the acid is poured off outside on soil where it can be leached and the seeds are washed in running water for about ten minutes. Some impermeable seeds and those with chemical inhibitors may be prepared for germination by soaking in four to five times their volume of nearly boiling

water, which is allowed to cool for 12 to 24 hours or until seeds are swollen.

Seeds that require chilling to break dormancy may be stratified by soaking 12 to 24 hours and storing in moist vermiculite, sand, peat moss, sphagnum, or weathered sawdust in a refrigerator at 35–45° F or outdoors over winter. Some seeds require more than one exposure to cold, or they may require drying or exposure to light or combinations of treatments, and for these advice should be sought from local extension agents or experiment stations.

Seeds readied for planting may be sown on a soil mix or on clean pasteurized vermiculite in a flat or pot indoors for later transplanting, or directly in the seedbed or garden outdoors when temperatures permit, covering the seeds one to two times their diameter, except for very fine seed, which may be sown, sometimes mixed with sand or other inert material for more uniform distribution, without covering. The germination medium should be presoaked or moistened after sowing and kept moist; a glass or plastic covering may be used if necessary, or the containers may be put under mist if this is available. Most seeds germinate well at 68° F but some do better at a lower temperature, others require temperatures up to 86° F. It is helpful to treat seeds planted indoors with a disinfectant such as Clorox to lessen loss from disease after germination. The extremely small seeds of orchids usually require special techniques for germination (see *Orchids*).

Once germinated, uncovered seedlings should be kept moist but not wet, and light may be gradually increased and temperature lowered somewhat at night to produce vigorous, stocky young plants with good root development and to reduce loss from damping-off disease. When seedlings in a pot or flat have developed two to four true leaves, they should be transplanted with care, preferably into pots, bands, or other flats at a distance of one to two inches apart. When further developed, they may again be transplanted to their permanent location. If plants are to be grown in the open, it is well to transplant on a cloudy day or in the evening and just before a rain, if possible. Some shading may also be necessary for a day or two. Seedlings from the seedbed will need to be similarly transplanted; those from seeds sown directly in the garden will need to be thinned.

Asexual Propagation

Many plants can be propagated vegetatively by means of division, specialized organs such as bulbs and corms, layering, cuttings, and tissue culture to reproduce the individual without genetic change, although the appearance of the individual may be modified somewhat by age or by different environments. A plant and its offspring so propagated form a clone, which often has special characterisitics or combinations of characteristics that are not inherited through its seed.

The simplest form of asexual propagation is division of one parent plant with a branched crown, or with rhizomes, runners, suckers, offsets, tubers, tuberous roots, corms, bulbs, or plantlets, into two or more individuals. Early-flowering plants are usually divided in autumn, while those flowering in late summer may be divided before growth starts in the spring. Thus *Canna ✕ generalis, Rheum Rhabarbarum,* or *Rhapis excelsa* may be multiplied by dividing the crown into pieces, each piece having a portion of stem and root with bud attached; strawberries *(Fragaria ✕ Ananassa)* are propagated from new plants formed on runners; cultivars of the date, *Phoenix dactylifera,* are propagated by offsets; *Dahlia* cultivars are reproduced from tuberous roots with a portion of stem and bud; potatoes, *Solanum tuberosum,* are grown from pieces of tuber, each with a bud or eye; *Gladiolus* and *Tulipa* cultivars and species are multiplied by cormlets and bulblets; and some plants, such as *Chlorophytum comosum* and *Kalanchoe pinnata,* are propagated by plantlets formed on inflorescence or leaf.

Layering is the rooting of shoots while they are still attached to the parent plant. Some plants form natural layers, while in others the production of roots must be induced. The operation entails the covering of a part of shoot, stem, or branch with soil or other medium into which rooting is likely to take place, and is useful for plants that may be layered but which do not root well as cuttings. The initiation of roots may be encouraged by wounding the portion of the shoot so covered. Girdling, twisting, notching, and ringing are methods frequently practiced. When sufficient roots have been produced, the shoot is severed from the parent plant and potted or planted out.

In simple layering, a side shoot of a perennial such as a species of *Dianthus* or a branch of the previous season's growth of a shrub such as *Magnolia* or *Rhododendron* is notched or slit, preferably just below a node, bent down to the soil, held in place by a peg, bent wire, or stone, with the tip of the shoot exposed and bent up, and the region of the cut covered with soil. Layering may be done in spring, summer, or autumn and the branch may usually be severed from the parent at the end of a year. Quick-rooting layers may be transplanted immediately, but slower types, such as *Rhododendron*, should be left a second year for the formation of more roots.

In tip layering, the tip of the current season's growth may be bent to the ground, pegged, and lightly covered with soil, usually in late summer. By late autumn or spring the rooted tips can be separated from the parent plant and transplanted to a new location.

Serpentine layering is particularly adapted to vines such as *Clematis* or *Vitis*. In early spring, long, vigorous stems are taken down and undulated or arched so that occasional nodes, nicked by a knife, are pegged and buried beneath the soil; the intervening ones, with at least one bud, and the tip are left exposed. At the end of a year, the stem is cut from the parent plant and individual sections severed to leave an upper growing bud ahead of each root system. Transplanting can be done during the second year.

Mound layering is little used commercially now but is useful to the amateur gardener for propagating woody materials with stiff stems, such as *Hydrangea* and *Philadelphus*, that do not lend themselves to other types of layering. The parent shrub is cut off just above the ground in spring before new growth starts. Sandy loam is then mounded over the base of the plant until the tops of the stubs are buried half an inch deep. As new shoots develop, their bases are successively covered with additional soil into which they root. These young shoots may then be removed as rooted plants in autumn. Trench layering is a modification of this method, in which a plant, usually a small tree, or a branch of a plant is laid in a trench about two inches deep and covered by successive layers of soil or other medium until shoots have emerged and rooted.

Air layering or marcotting (Fig. H) is used mostly to propagate tropical and subtropical materials, including some small palms and tropical greenhouse plants. Layers are made after several new leaves have formed in greenhouse materials or, for hardy deciduous woody materials, in spring on wood formed in the previous season, or sometimes in late summer on partly hardened wood of the current season. The stem of dicotyledonous plants is girdled 6–12 inches from the tip or is cut halfway through with a slanting cut and the cut packed with sphagnum or a wood chip. A root-inducing growth regulator ("rooting hormone") is usually applied to the exposed upper edge of the girdle or cut and about two handfuls of only slightly moistened sphagnum moss are packed around the cut. The moss is wrapped in a piece of polyethylene about 8–10 inches square, the ends of which are tied or twisted and covered with waterproof tape or other material to prevent evaporation of the moisture and to prevent entry of additional water. When roots are visible through the plastic in greenhouse plants, the top may be severed and potted, but layers on hardy deciduous woody materials are usually left on the parent plant until shoots become dormant or even for two seasons in plants such as *Ilex, Magnolia, Rhododendron* (azalea types), and *Syringa*. Newly severed shoots may require pruning or they may be placed under mist propagation

(see below) or in a cool moist place for further development of roots and hardening. Air layering is particularly useful for reducing the height of foliage plants when they become too tall or become unsightly because of defoliation of the lower parts.

Propagation by cuttings is one of the most common methods, especially for ornamental deciduous and evergreen shrubs, greenhouse materials, some fruit trees, and such florist's crops as carnations *(Dianthus Caryophyllus)* and geraniums *(Pelargonium)*. The practice differs from layering in that portions of stem, leaf, or root are removed from the parent before roots are formed and are placed in a rooting medium such as sand, vermiculite, peat moss, perlite, or a mixture of these in a flat or container, or sometimes simply in water. A rooting hormone is often used to hasten the formation of roots. Cuttings of all sorts are often rooted in a chamber or on a greenhouse bench or outdoors under intermittent spray from a mist nozzle on a control system. Fine mist covers the leaves with a film of water and also cuts down transpiration and reduces temperature. Polyethylene sheeting or glass may be used to cover flats to maintain a high level of humidity. Light is required but direct sunlight on cuttings should be avoided.

Stem cuttings are most frequently used and are classified as hardwood, semihardwood, softwood, and herbaceous. Of these, hardwood cuttings (Figs. Aa, Ab) are the easiest, as they require no special equipment. For deciduous plants, portions of mature wood, commonly 6–8 inches long and with two or more nodes, are cut in late autumn, winter, or even early spring, with the basal cut just below a node, the upper cut ½–1 inch above a node. The cuttings may be stored in a moist, cool situation to callus until spring or they may be buried horizontally or upside down in a well-drained situation for rooting in spring, or cuttings in autumn may be planted immediately and protected by a mulch during the winter. Cuttings are usually planted at an angle or erect with only one bud above the soil. Some conifers may also be propagated by hardwood cuttings taken from late autumn to late winter, but they are often slow to root. These cuttings are treated with a rooting hormone and placed in a rooting medium such as sand or peat moss and perlite with bottom heat, high light intensity, and high humidity, preferably in a greenhouse. Whether terminal shoots of the previous year, small tip cuttings, or cuttings of older wood are used often depends on the species.

Semihardwood cuttings of partly matured wood of broadleaved evergreens and some deciduous plants are taken after a flush of growth has appeared on new shoots. Leaves are removed from the lower end of cuttings 3–6 inches long, and the upper leaves, if large, are trimmed to reduce loss of water. Cuttings are rooted most successfully under mist and over bottom heat after dipping in a rooting hormone.

Softwood cuttings (Fig. B), with leaves attached and made from new spring growth of deciduous or evergreen plants, generally root more quickly than other types but they require special attention. Such cuttings are usually 3–5 inches long, with two or more nodes, and should be taken from stems which are flexible but reasonably mature. They should be maintained at a temperature of 75–80° F where water loss will not be excessive, preferably under mist, under polyethylene sheeting, or in a glass-covered frame. Roots will usually form in 2–5 weeks.

Herbaceous cuttings (Fig. C) are those made from house plants, florist's crops, and many hardy herbaceous perennials in essentially the same way as softwood cuttings. In the home, they may be rooted in a flat of rooting medium with a simple frame and glass or polyethylene above it, and cuttings of some species, such as *Hedera Helix* or species of *Commelinaceae*, will root in water. Sections of stem of some *Araceae* may also be laid flat on the medium to produce new roots and shoots at the nodes. (Fig. D)

Leaf cuttings (Fig. Ea, Eb, Ec) are a common way of propagating plants such as cultivars of *Begonia* or *Saintpaulia*. The leaf blade and petiole, or the leaf blade with larger veins cut beneath, or even pieces of the leaf with a large vein, may be inserted in or laid flat on the rooting medium and kept moist as for herbaceous cuttings. When roots but not shoots originate from a leaf cuttings, a new plant may usually be obtained by including in the cutting a small portion of stem and an axillary bud (Fig. F).

Root cuttings (Fig. Ga, Gb) of some species may also be used, preferably taken in late winter or early spring before growth starts. Sections of fine roots 1–2 inches long are laid horizontally on the rooting medium and covered by about ½ inch of medium, or sections of larger roots 2–3 inches long may be set vertically in it. The medium is then watered and the flat or container covered with glass or polyethylene. Still larger roots may be propagated outdoors by cuttings 3–6 inches long packed in a moist material and kept cool for about three weeks, then planted. Care should be taken to have the top of the roots uppermost when planted vertically. Once rooted and with a new plant formed, cuttings are treated as are others.

Apart from the above, there are other and specialized techniques of propagation that involve the culturing of embryos, embryoids, shoot tips, callus tissues, and even single cells to produce new plants. These, like orchid seeds, are grown on a nutrient agar in glass flasks under aseptic conditions and generally require facilities not available to the usual gardener or grower. Details may be sought from books on propagation or from local county agents and experiment stations.

PROSERPINACA L. MERMAIDWEED. *Haloragaceae.* About 4 spp. of per. aquatic herbs, native from e. N. Amer. to Cent. Amer. and the W. Indies; lvs. alt., often of 2 kinds, submersed lvs. pinnately dissected, emersed lvs. pinnately dissected to serrate; fls. axillary, bisexual, sepals 3, petals 3 or 0, stamens 3; fr. a bony, 3-angled, 3-seeded nutlet.

Sometimes grown in pools or aquaria.

palustris L. Sts. leafy; submersed lvs. finely pinnately dissected, to 2⅜ in. long, emersed lvs. linear-lanceolate to linear-oblong, to 3¼ in. long, serrate. E. N. Amer., Mex., Cent. Amer., W. Indies.

PROSOPIS L. *Leguminosae* (subfamily *Mimosoideae*). Perhaps 25 spp. or more of mostly spiny trees or shrubs of warm regions; lvs. alt., 2-pinnate, with few pinnae and small lfts.; fls. in axillary heads, spikes, or racemes, yellowish, 5-merous, stamens 10, separate, exserted; fr. an elongate, indehiscent legume. Important as bee plants, and as range food plants, the seeds and young shoots are eaten by cattle; the seeds were also made into flour by Amer. Indians and early settlers.

chilensis (Mol.) Stuntz. Large tree, with few spines; lvs. with 1–2 pairs of pinnae, lfts. 13–20 pairs per pinna, ⅝–1½ in. long, 10 or more times as long as wide; fr. falcate. Argentina and Chile, where called ALGARROBO. Doubtfully in cult.; material so named being probably *P. glandulosa.* Var. **glandulosa:** *P. glandulosa.*

glandulosa Torr. [*P. chilensis* of auth., not (Mol.) Stuntz; *P. chilensis* var. *glandulosa* (Torr.) Standl.; *P. juliflora* of auth., not (Swartz) DC.; *P. juliflora* var. *glandulosa* (Torr.) Cockerell]. MESQUITE. Large shrub or small tree, to 30 ft., with large, deep root, brs. crooked, spines to 1 in. long or more; lvs. with usually 1, or more rarely 2, pairs of pinnae, lfts. 6–15 (–20) pairs per pinna, spaced ¼–¾ in. apart, bright green, usually glabrous; fr. nearly straight, 3–9 in. long, beaked, glabrous. Long confused with *P. chilensis* and *P. juliflora.* Var. **glandulosa.** HONEY MESQUITE. The typical var.; lfts. mostly 6–13 pairs per pinna, spaced ⁵⁄₁₆–¾ in. apart, linear to linear-lanceolate, 1–2¼ in. long, 8–15 times as long as wide; seeds narrowly elliptic. Kans. s. to Tex., New Mex., and ne. Mex. Var. **Torreyana** (L. Bens.) M. C. Johnst. [*P. juliflora* var. *Torreyana* L. Bens.; *P. odorata* Torr.]. WESTERN HONEY MESQUITE. Lfts. mostly 10–15 pairs per pinna, spaced about ¼ in. apart, linear, ⅜–1¼ in. long, 5–8 times as long as wide; seeds obovate. Tex., se. Ariz., s. Calif., n. Mex.

juliflora (Swartz) DC. MESQUITE, ALGARROBO. Lvs. with 1–2 pairs of pinnae, lfts. 11–19 pairs per pinna, spaced ¼–³⁄₁₆ in. apart, oblong or linear-oblong, ⅜–¾ in. long, less than 5 times as long as wide, glabrous or slightly ciliate; fr. nearly straight, beaked, glabrous. Coastal, from Mex. s. to Colombia and Venezuela, and islands of Caribbean. Not native and probably not cult. in U.S., plants so named being probably *P. glandulosa.* (The name *Acacia laevigata,* once associated with this sp., is a synonym of *P. laevigata.*)

laevigata (Humb. & Bonpl. ex Willd.) M. C. Johnst. [*Acacia laevigata* Humb. & Bonpl. ex Willd.]. MESQUITE. Small tree; lvs. with 1–3, but usually 2, pairs of pinnae, lfts. 20–30 pairs or more per pinna, closely spaced, mostly ⅜–½ in. long, 2–7 times as long as wide, densely hispidulous; fr. nearly straight, beaked. S. Tex., Mex.

odorata: *P. glandulosa* var. *Torreyana,* but the name *P. odorata* has long been confused in application, because it was based on mixed specimens.

pubescens Benth. SCREW BEAN, TORNILLO. Large shrub or small tree, 6–32 ft. high; lvs. with 1, sometimes 2, pairs of pinnae, lfts. 4–8 pairs per pinna, oblong to elliptic-oblong, ⅝–⅞ in. long, 2½–3 times as long as wide, finely appressed-gray-pubescent; fr. tightly coiled into a cylinder, not beaked, pubescent. S. Calif. and nw. Mex., e. to s. Utah and Tex.

PROSTANTHERA Labill. MINTBUSH. *Labiatae.* About 50 spp. of strongly aromatic shrubs or subshrubs of Australia; sts. mostly square in cross section; lvs. opp., simple; fls. usually solitary in the axils, bractlets 2, narrow, calyx campanulate, 10-nerved, 2-lipped, lips entire to notched, corolla tube short, limb 2-lipped, upper lip erect, hooded, 2-lobed, lower lip spreading, 3-lobed, stamens 4, in 2 pairs, anthers 2-celled, usually appendaged; fr. of 4 reticulate-rugose nutlets.

Floriferous shrubs for Mediterranean type climates; grown outdoors in southern Calif. Propagated by seeds or softwood cuttings.

lasianthos Labill. VICTORIAN CHRISTMAS BUSH. Shrub or small tree, to 20 ft.; lvs. petioled, lanceolate, to 3½ in. long, remotely serrate; infl. paniculate; calyx to ³⁄₁₆ in. long, upper lip somewhat larger than the lower, corolla to ½ in. long, pubescent, white, tinged or spotted with pink or pale blue. Se. Australia and Tasmania.

nivea A. Cunn. ex Benth. SNOWY M. Shrub, 3–6 ft.; lvs. sessile, linear or linear-lanceolate, to 1½ in. long; infl. racemose, with fls. in axils of uppermost lvs.; calyx to ³⁄₁₆ in. long, upper lip obscurely 3-lobed, lower lip smaller, entire, corolla twice as long as the calyx, pubescent, white, sometimes blue-tinged. Se. Australia and Tasmania. Var. **induta** Benth. Lvs. silvery; fls. lilac.

rotundifolia R. Br. ROUND-LEAF M. Shrub, to 12 ft.; lvs. petioled, obovate to orbicular, to ⅜ in. long and wide; fls. in short, loose or compact racemes on lateral branchlets, subtending lvs. reduced, calyx to ⅛ in. long at flowering, 2-lipped, the lips about equal, entire, corolla to ½ in. long, lilac. S. and se. Australia, including Tasmania.

Sieberi Benth. Shrub, to 6 ft.; lvs. ovate-lanceolate to oblong, to 1 in. long, bluntly toothed; infl. as in *P. rotundifolia;* corolla rose-violet. New S. Wales.

PROTEA L. *Proteaceae.* About 100 spp. of trees and shrubs, sometimes stemless, mostly from the Cape region of S. Afr., but also extending n. into trop. Afr.; lvs. alt., entire, leathery; fls. bisexual, irregular, many, in heads, these usually sessile, solitary, enclosed in an involucre of variously colored, imbricated bracts; fr. a densely bearded nut.

abyssinica: *P. Gaguedi.*

angolensis Welw. Shrub or rarely small tree, to 10 ft.; lvs. elliptic or ovate, to 5 in. long, glabrous, leathery; fl. heads terminal, to 5 in. in diam., outermost bracts rigid, innermost bracts short, to 2½ in. long, white to reddish, shortly white-ciliate, variably pubescent, slightly longer than the fls. Trop. Afr.

compacta R. Br. Shrub, to 10 ft.; lvs. strongly imbricate, ovate, to 4½ in. long, leathery; fl. heads terminal, to 4 in. long, bracts villous-pubescent, innermost bracts pink to carmine. S. Afr.

cynaroides L. GIANT P., KING P. Shrub, usually stemless, sometimes to 6 ft.; lvs. suborbicular to elliptic, to 5 in. long, petiole to 4 in. long; fl. heads terminal, 8 in. across, bracts light to dark pink, or nearly red, silky-hairy on outside, innermost ones spreading away from fls. S. Afr. The large fl. heads and petioled lvs. readily distinguish this attractive shrub.

Gaguedi J. F. Gmel. [*P. abyssinica* Willd.]. Shrub or small tree, to 10 ft. or more; lvs. sessile, lanceolate or oblong-lanceolate, to 6 in. long, glabrous; fl. heads terminal, top-shaped, to 4 in. long, bracts mostly in 6 series, pale green, densely silvery-pubescent, innermost ones shorter than fls. and spreading away from them. Trop. Afr.

grandiceps Tratt. PEACH P. Shrub, to 5 ft.; lvs. sessile, elliptic, to 5 in. long, obtuse, broad and somewhat cordate at base, usually with reddish margins, glaucous, leathery and strongly veined; fl. heads terminal, to 4½ in. long and 6 in. across, innermost bracts red to purplish, rounded at apex, with white, orange, purple, or black apical beard.

longiflora Lam. Shrub, to 10 ft.; lvs. sessile, elliptic, to 4 in. long, rounded or subcordate at base; fl. heads sessile, to 4 in. long, greenish-white or pink, bracts greenish-white, innermost ones ciliate, eventually spreading away from fls. S. Afr.

mellifera Thunb. SUGARBUSH, HONEY FLOWER, HONEY P. Shrub, to 8 ft.; lvs. narrowly oblong, to 4 in., glabrous; fl. heads terminal, to 5 in. long, innermost bracts sticky, white to nearly red, remaining erect. S. Afr. Excellent bee plant.

neriifolia R. Br. OLEANDER-LEAVED P. Shrub, to 5 ft., brs. tomentose; lvs. narrowly oblong, to 6 in. long, glabrous or woolly at base; fl. heads sessile, terminal, to 5 in. long, outermost bracts recurved in drying, innermost ones remaining erect, with black apical beard. S. Afr.

obtusifolia Buek. Shrub, to 10 ft.; lvs. oblong-elliptic, to 5 in. long, emarginate or obtuse, narrowed to base; fl. heads sessile, to 4 in. long, bracts ciliate, innermost ones slightly longer than fls., remaining erect. S. Afr.

petiolaris (Engl. ex Hiern) Bak. Tree, to 20 ft.; lvs. falcate, narrowly elliptic or oblanceolate, to 5½ in. long, narrowed at base, appearing petioled; fl. heads globose, to 3 in. across, bracts green to red, ciliate, glabrous or silky, outermost ones with a whitish bloom. Trop. Afr.

pulchella Andr. Shrub, to 5 ft.; lvs. linear to linear-lanceolate, to 6½ in. long, acute, narrowed at base, midrib prominent; fl. heads sessile, to 4 in. long, partly surrounded by upper foliage lvs., outermost bracts tomentose or pubescent, middle bracts acute, green with reddish tips, innermost bracts reddish, with rose or carmine-purple or black beard, longer than fls. S. Afr.

scolymocephala Reichard. Shrub, to 3 ft., stiffly branched; lvs. narrowly linear-lanceolate, to 2½ in. long, acute, long-attenuated at base; fl. heads sessile, to 1 in. long, about 1 in. across at base, bracts glabrous, pale green, innermost ones spreading away from fls. S. Afr.

Susannae E. P. Phillips. Shrub; lvs. lanceolate or oblong-lanceolate, to 5 in. long, obtuse, narrowed at base, midrib distinct; fl. heads subsessile, to 4 in. long, surrounded by upper foliage lvs., bracts brownish-pink, as long as fls. and spreading only slightly away from them. S. Afr.

PROTEACEAE. *Grevillea robusta:* **a,** flowering branch, × ⅙; **b,** flower just opening, × 1½; **c,** flower, × 1½; **d,** anther-bearing apex of perianth segment, × 8; **e,** perianth segments, two views, × 2; **f,** stigma, × 3; **g,** ovary, vertical section, × 3; **h,** ovary, cross section, × 5; **i,** fruit, × 1; **j,** seed, × 1.

PROTEACEAE Juss. PROTEA FAMILY. Dicot.; about 55 genera and 1,200 spp. of trees or shrubs, sometimes herbs, mostly native to the drier regions of the S. Hemisphere, especially S. Afr. and Australia; lvs. usually alt.; fls. in racemes, clusters, or sometimes in showy bracted heads, bisexual or unisexual, perianth 4-parted, stamens 4, ovary superior, 1-celled; fr. a nut, drupe, or caps. The cult. genera are: *Aulax, Banksia, Buckinghamia, Dryandra, Embothrium, Gevuina, Grevillea, Hakea, Hicksbeachia, Isopogon, Knightia, Lambertia, Leucodendron, Leucospermum, Lomatia, Macadamia, Oreocallis, Persoonia, Petrophila, Protea, Roupala, Serruria, Stenocarpus,* and *Telopea.*

A few genera yield edible nuts *(Gevuina, Macadamia),* dyes, and timber *(Grevillea),* and some are grown as ornamentals in warmer dry parts of the country, particularly in southern Calif.

PRUNE. See *Plum, Prune.*

PRUNELLA L. SELF-HEAL. *Labiatae.* About 7 spp. of per. herbs, chiefly of Asia, Eur., nw. Afr., N. Amer.; sts. mostly square in cross section; lvs. opp., simple; fls. in 6-fld. verticillasters arranged in dense, terminal, cylindrical spikes, bracts different from lvs., bractlets small or absent, calyx tubular-campanulate, 2-lipped, upper lip 3-toothed, lower lip 2-toothed, corolla tube longer than calyx, obconical, limb 2-lipped, upper lip hooded, stamens 4, in 2 pairs, anther cells diverging, filaments appendaged; fr. of 4 oblong, glabrous nutlets.

Useful in rock gardens or slightly shady borders; tend to be weedy. Propagated by seeds or division.

grandiflora (L.) Scholl. To 2 ft., sparsely pubescent; spikes often not subtended by lvs.; corolla usually 1 in. long or more, tube whitish, lips deep violet. Subsp. **grandiflora.** The typical subsp.; lvs. cuneate; infl. to 2 in. long. Limestone soils, Eur. except Portugal and sw. Spain. Cvs. include: 'Alba', 'Carminea', 'Pinnatifida', 'Rosea', and 'Rubra'. Subsp. **pyrenaica** (Gren. & Godr.) A. Bolós & O. Bolós. [*P. hastifolia* Brot.; *P. pyrenaica* (Gren. & Godr.) Philippe]. Lvs. hastate; infl. longer, to 3⅛ in. long. Summer. Not on limey soils, Eur.

hastifolia: *P. grandiflora* subsp. *pyrenaica.*

incisa: *P. vulgaris.*

laciniata L. Densely pubescent, sts. to 1 ft.; upper lvs. deeply pinnatifid or lobed; spikes subtended by lvs.; calyx with teeth of lower lip linear-lanceolate, corolla yellowish-white, rarely pink or purplish. Summer. Eur.

pyrenaica: *P. grandiflora* subsp.

vulgaris L. [*P. incisa* Link]. SELF-HEAL, HEAL-ALL. Decumbent or creeping, more or less pubescent, sts. to 20 in.; lvs. ovate to rhombic-ovate, cuneate, entire or crenulate; spikes usually subtended by lvs.; calyx with teeth of lower lip lanceolate, corolla deep violet-blue, rarely white. Summer. Eurasia; widely naturalized.

Webbiana Hort. ex J. B. Keller & W. Mill. Like *P. grandiflora;* lvs. shorter, blunt; corolla bright purple. May be *P. grandiflora* subsp. *grandiflora* × *P. grandiflora* subsp. *pyrenaica.* Cv. 'Rosea'. Fls. pink.

PRUNING. Pruning is the removal of unwanted branches, buds, or flowers from a plant to make it more vigorous and productive. The tools are a pruning knife or secateurs (clippers) of one or more types for cutting small twigs and branches, and saws of several types for removing larger branches of an inch or more in diameter. Methods are better demonstrated than described, hence an illustrated book on pruning is a useful adjunct to a gardener's pruning equipment. The pruning of fruit trees and vines is often a special process; for this see appropriate articles, as *Apple, Citrus Fruits, Grape,* etc. Pruning should not be confused with trimming or shearing plants in formal shapes, as in hedges and topiary work. For this, see *Hedge* and *Topiary.*

Timing is as important as technique in pruning ornamental shrubs and trees. Some of these, such as *Forsythia, Syringa,* and *Viburnum,* bear their flowers from buds on wood of the preceding year and the proper time to prune them is just after the flowers have passed. Flower buds then form later in the season for production of flowers the following spring. Other plants, such as *Clematis* and *Rosa,* flower in summer and autumn on wood of the current season. These should be pruned in winter and early spring.

Cuts should be made close to a branch or bud and back to living tissue, where healing may take place. Care should be taken to remove all dead or diseased tissue when pruning, and to relate cuts to the shape of the tree or shrub. Cuts should be made parallel to the parent stem when removing branches unless such a cut is likely to have a weakening effect; then a less acute angle should be chosen. A branch of any appreciable size should be removed with a saw by undercutting it from below to a depth at least ⅛ its diameter and then cutting it through from above at a distance from the main trunk, to remove weight and prevent tearing when a third, final cut is made closer to the trunk. Large limbs may need to be removed in several sections. Cuts for smaller branches and twigs may be made with a clean shear by knife or secateurs at an angle or straight across as the position and size of the portion to be removed dictate. Pruning of deciduous trees should be avoided in late winter or early spring lest rising sap cause the wound to "bleed."

The cut surface, if made in living tissue, will usually heal by itself, but cuts over an inch in diameter, and preferably smaller ones as well, should be covered with a waterproof sealant, usually a bituminous product to prevent entry of pests and infection or decay. If cracks appear in the wound, they should be filled and the surface covered again with additional sealant. If shoots proliferate from a cut, they should be removed.

PRUNUS L. [*Laurocerasus* M. J. Roem.]. *Rosaceae*. More than 400 spp. of trees and shrubs prevailingly of temp. climates and mostly of the N. Hemisphere; lvs. alt., simple, deciduous or persistent, mostly serrate, and sometimes with glands along the petiole or at the base of the blade, stipules small, falling early; fls. bisexual, white or pink, sepals and petals 5, stamens many, inserted with the petals on the calyx tube, pistil normally 1, with 2 ovules; fr. a drupe, with a fleshy outer layer surrounding a hard stone or pit containing the seed.

Prunus includes many desirable ornamentals as well as the stone fruits—plums, apricots, almonds, peaches, nectarines, cherries, and cherry laurels. The cherries fall into several groups, of which three may be mentioned: the *umbellate cherries*, in which the flowers are in small umbel-like clusters, as in the orchard kinds, although in some cases they may be only 1, 2, or 3; the *racemose cherries*, with flowers in distinctly elongated clusters or racemes, as the chokecherry; and the *cherry laurels*, with flowers racemose and leaves persistent (evergreen).

Widely cultivated for their fruits or nuts, or as ornamentals; most species of *Prunus* are hardy quite far north and are not particular as to soil, but are intolerant of polluted air. They may be propagated directly from seeds sown in autumn or stratified until spring. Named varieties are started from firm-wood cuttings under glass or are budded on closely related stock. The usual stocks are the common plum (*P. domestica*), myrobalan plum (*P. cerasifera*), peach (*P. Persica*), and cherry (*P. avium* or *P. Cerasus*). See *Cherry* and *Plum*.

acuminata: *P. maritima.*

alleghaniensis T. C. Porter. ALLEGHANY PLUM, SLOE. To 15 ft.; lvs. lanceolate to narrowly obovate, acuminate, 2–3 ⁵⁄₁₆ in. long, sharply serrate, becoming glabrous; fls. white, turning pink, ½ in. across, calyx pubescent outside; fr. dark purple, ⅜ in. in diam., glaucous. Conn. to W. Va. Zone 6.

americana Marsh. WILD PLUM, AUGUST P., AMERICAN P., GOOSE P., HOG P., SLOE. Coarse shrub or tree, to 25 ft., with shaggy bark, branchlets often thorny; lvs. obovate to lanceolate-ovate, acuminate, sharply serrate, 2–4½ in. long; fls. 1 in. across, white, sepals not glandular; fr. ¾ in. in diam., or larger, yellow or red, with a flattened stone. New Eng. to Man., s. to Fla. and New Mex. Zone 4. Includes cvs. 'Blackhawk', 'Hawkeye', 'De Soto', and other plums. Var. **lanata** Sudw. [*P. lanata* (Sudw.) Mackenz. & Bush]. Branchlets and petioles pubescent; lvs. soft-pubescent underneath. Ind. and Iowa, s. to Tenn. and Mex. Zone 6.

×**Amygdalo-persica:** an unacceptable name for the hybrid *P. dulcis* × *P. Persica*. Tree or bush; lvs. lanceolate, sharply toothed; fls. to 2 in. across, bright pink, with darker center; fr. peachlike but dry. Cv. 'Pollardii'. The form now in cult.

Amygdalus: *P. dulcis.*

Andersonii A. Gray. DESERT PEACH. Diffuse, deciduous, spreading, 3–6 ft., with short, stiff, spinescent brs.; lvs. fascicled, oblanceolate, about ½ in. long, obscurely serrulate, glabrous; fl. usually solitary, petals rose-colored, ¼ in. long; fr. roundish, ½ in. in diam., tomentulose, with thin dryish pulp. E. Calif., w. Nev.

angustifolia Marsh. CHICKASAW PLUM, SAND P. To 16 ft., with redbrown, glabrous, thorny branchlets; lvs. mostly longitudinally folded, 1–3 in. long, lanceolate to lanceolate-oblong, appressed teeth glandtipped; fls. with the lvs., ⁵⁄₁₆ in. across, white; fr. about ½ in. in diam., red or yellow, the stone plump. N.J. to Mo., s. to Fla. and Tex. Zone 6. Var. **Watsonii** (Sarg.) Waugh. SAND PLUM. Lvs. smaller, less conspicuously serrate; fls. smaller; fr. with thicker skin. Kans. to Tex., New Mex.

Ansu: *P. Armeniaca* cv.

apetala (Siebold & Zucc.) Franch. & Sav. Shrub or small tree, to 16 ft., pubescent on young growth; lvs. broadly obovate, 1–2 in. long, acuminate, doubly serrate, pubescent on both sides; fls. small, white, ½ in. across, calyx purple, petals falling early; fr. almost black, globose. Japan. Zone 6?

Armeniaca L. APRICOT. Small round-crowned tree, with reddish bark and glabrous twigs; lvs. ovate, sometimes subcordate, 2–3 in. long, abruptly short-pointed, closely simply serrate, pubescent beneath on veins; fls. before the lvs., more or less pinkish, 1 in. across; fr. smooth at maturity, pubescent when young, somewhat flattened, yellow, sometimes flushed with red, the stone flattened, ridged along suture. China, where cult. since about 2000 B.C. Zone 6. Cv. 'Ansu' [*P. Ansu* (Maxim.) Kom.]. Lvs. elliptic to broadly ovate; fls. mostly 2, pink; fr. globose, red. From cult. in Japan and Korea. Var. **mandshurica** Maxim. [*P. mandshurica* (Maxim.) Koehne]. Lvs. doubly serrate; fls. pedicelled. Manchuria, Korea. Zone 6. Var. **sibirica** (L.) C. Koch [*P. sibirica* L.]. Lvs. simply serrate, acuminate; fr. small, scarcely edible. E. Asia. Zone 5. For cult. see *Apricot*.

×**arnoldiana** Rehd.: *P. cerasifera* × *P. triloba.* Like *P. triloba*, but lvs. more elliptic; fls. white, sepals hairy inside.

autumnalis: *P. domestica;* but material cult. as *P. autumnalis* is probably *P. subhirtella* cv.

avium (L.) L. SWEET CHERRY, BIRD C., MAZZARD, GEAN. Large, deciduous tree with red-brown, birchlike bark; lvs. 2–6 in. long, obovate-elliptic, acuminate, crenate-serrate, glabrous above, persistently strigose beneath, petiole to 2 in. long, with 2 large glands; fls. 2–6, cup-shaped, white, about 1 in. across; fr. globular or oblong, long-pedicelled, 1 in. in diam., bright or dark red, sweet. Eurasia; naturalized in N. Amer. Zone 4. There are cvs. with double fls., cut lvs., pendent branchlets, etc., but they are little known in Amer. Var. **actiana** (L.) C. K. Schneid. [*P. avium* var. *sylvestris* G. Martens & Kemmler]. Fr. very small, sweet, dark. Var. **regalis:** *P.* ×*effusus.* Var. **sylvestris:** var. *actiana.*

Besseyi L. H. Bailey. SAND CHERRY, WESTERN S. C. Like *P. susquehanae*, but lvs. smaller, less than 2 in. long, leathery, acutely toothed; fr. ⅝ in. in diam., purple-black, fleshy, sweet, stone rounded at both ends. Man. to Wyo., s. to Minn. and Colo. Zone 3, very hardy. Used for pies, jams, and jelly. Selected cvs. are available in the Great Plains states.

×**blireiana** André.: *P. cerasifera* cv. 'Atropurpurea' × *P. Mume.* Broad shrub with arching brs.; lvs. red-brown, ovate, 1–2 in. long; fl. solitary, semidouble, pink, 1¼ in. across, sepals glandular. Cv. 'Moseri'. Stronger; lvs. intensely red; fls. smaller, sepals without glands.

Buergerana Miq. To 25–30 ft.; lvs. elliptic to oblong, acuminate, 3–4 in. long, finely serrate, glabrous except beneath in axils of veins; fls. ⁵⁄₁₆ in. across, white, in racemes, sepals toothed, persistent; fr. roundish, black, small. Japan, Korea. Zone 6.

campanulata Maxim. TAIWAN CHERRY. To 25 ft., glabrous on young growth; lvs. oblong-ovate, sharply serrate, about 3½ in. long, acuminate, nearly glabrous beneath; flowering with or before the lvs., fls. in umbels, long-pedicelled, deep rose-red, ¾ in. across; fr. ovoid, ½ in. long, red. Ryukyu Is. and Taiwan. Cult. in cent. and s. Japan. Zone 8. An early-flowering sp.

canescens Bois. Shrubby, to 6 ft., pubescent on young branchlets and lvs.; lvs. ovate, short-acuminate, serrate, 1–2 in. long; fls. 2–5, pink, ½ in. across; fr. red, ½ in. in diam. China. Hardy north.

caroliniana (Mill.) Ait. [*Laurocerasus caroliniana* (Mill.) M. J. Roem.]. CHERRY LAUREL, WILD ORANGE, MOCK O. Evergreen tree, 18–40 ft.; lvs. lanceolate-oblong, acuminate, 2–4 in. long, entire, glossy, slightly revolute; racemes dense, 1 in. long; fls. less than ³⁄₁₆ in. across; fr. short-ovoid, pointed, black, shining, dryish, ⁵⁄₁₆ in. long. N.C. to Tex. Zone 7.

cerasifera J. F. Ehrh. [*P. myrobalana* (L.) Loisel.]. CHERRY PLUM, MYROBALAN P. Deciduous shrub or small tree, to 25 ft., twigs glabrous; lvs. 1–3 in. long, ovate to obovate, acute, crenate-serrate, glabrous above, usually somewhat pubescent on midrib beneath; flowering before the lvs., fls. mostly solitary, white, to 1 in. across; fr. to 1 in. in diam., globose, sweet, yellow or reddish, stone little flattened. Cent. Asia to the Balkans; naturalized from cult. in Eur., N. Amer. Zone 4. Cv. 'Atropurpurea' [*P. Pissardii* Carrière]. Lvs. purple; fls. pale rose; fr. purple-red. Var. **divaricata** (Ledeb.) L. H. Bailey [*P. divaricata* Ledeb.]. Bushlike; lvs. rounder at base; flowering with the lvs., fls. smaller. Caucasus, Iran. Cv. 'Newportii' [*P. Newportii* Hort.]. Lvs. red; fls. white.

cerasoides D. Don [*P. Puddum* Ser.]. Close to *P. campanulata;* lvs. more leathery, ovate- or oblong-lanceolate, very sharply toothed; fr. pointed. Himalayas, W. China.

Cerasus L. SOUR CHERRY, PIE C. Shrub or small tree, suckering from the roots; lvs. 2–3 in. long, doubly serrate, ovate to obovate, dark green above, soon glabrous beneath, firm, petiole to 1 in. long; fls. clustered, white to pink, 1 in. across, flat; fr. ¾ in. in diam., sour, bright red. Origin uncertain. Widely cult. and naturalized. There are many cvs. with double fls. Var. **austera** L. MORELLO CHERRY. With colored juice, the fr. darker. Var. **Caproniana** L. AMARELLE. Fr. red, juice not colored.

×**cistena** N. E. Hansen: *P. cerasifera* cv. 'Atropurpurea' × *P. pumila.* PURPLE-LEAF SAND CHERRY. Weakly growing shrub; lvs. lanceolate-obovate, 1–2 in. long, reddish; pedicels and calyx reddish; fr. black-purple. Zone 3.

communis: *P. Amygdalus.*

commutata: a listed name of no botanical standing; possibly *P. Padus* var. *commutata.*

Davidiana (Carrière) Franch. Peachlike tree, glabrous, 10–30 ft.; lvs. narrow-lanceolate, 2–5 in. long; flowering before the lvs., fls. 1 in. across or more, white; fr. globose, 1 in. in diam., pubescent, dryish. China. Zone 4. Hardy north. Cv. **'Alba'.** Twigs and lvs. brighter green.

demissa: *P. virginiana* var.

depressa Pursh [*P. pumila* var. *depressa* (Pursh) Bean]. SAND CHERRY. Close to *P. pumila;* brs. trailing, forming mats 6 ft. across; lvs. spatulate-oblanceolate to -obovate, whitened beneath; fr. dark, ⅜ in. in diam., acid but pleasant, stone pointed at both ends. Que. to Ont., s. to Mass., Penn., Wisc.

divaricata: *P. cerasifera* var.

domestica L. [*P. autumnalis* Liegel]. PLUM, COMMON P., EUROPEAN P. Small, unarmed tree, young twigs more or less pubescent; lvs. ovate to obovate, dull green, pubescent beneath, to 4 in. long, crenate-serrate; fls. mostly before the lvs., 1 to few, whitish, to 1 in. across; fr. oblong-ovoid, 1½–3 in. long, variously colored, stone much flattened, usually free from the flesh. An ancient cultigen, known only in cult. or as an escape from cult. in Eurasia, N. Amer., mostly near houses. Zone 5. Many cvs. are known, especially in Eur. Cv. **'Plantierensis'.** Fls. white, semidouble; fr. violet.

dulcis (Mill.) D. A. Webb [*P. Amygdalus* Batsch; *P. communis* (L.) Arcang., not Huds.]. Broad-crowned tree, to 30 ft., twigs glabrous; lvs. lanceolate, 3–5 in. long, serrulate, glabrous; fls. before the lvs., 1–2, white to pinkish, 1–1½ in. across; fr. oblong, flattened, 1–2½ in. long, green and dry when ripe, inedible, finally splitting, stone smooth, pitted. W. Asia. Zone 7. Cvs. with double fls. in various tints, with variegated lvs., and with pendulous brs. are grown as ornamentals. Var. **dulcis.** ALMOND, SWEET A. The typical var.; lvs. widest toward the base; kernel sweet. Source of the important nut; many cvs. grown commercially in the Medit. region, Australia, S. Afr., and Calif. Var. **amara** (DC.) H. E. Moore [*P. Amygdalus* var. *amara* L. ex Focke]. BITTER ALMOND. Lvs. widest about the middle; kernel bitter, inedible. Kernels are source of oil of bitter almond, produced in s. Eur. Often used as understock for sweet almond. For cult. see *Almond.*

×**Dunbarii** Rehd.: *P. americana* × *P. maritima.* Like *P. maritima,* the twigs finally glabrous; lvs. larger, more sharply serrate, less pubescent beneath; fr. larger, purplish.

×**effusus** (Host) C. K. Schneid. [*P. avium* var. *regalis* (Poit. & Turpin) L. H. Bailey]: *P. avium* × *P. Cerasus.* DUKE CHERRY. Resembling *P. avium* in habit, but with fr. sour.

emarginata (Dougl. ex Hook.) Walp. BITTER CHERRY, OREGON C. Erect, 3–20 ft., twigs glabrous, red; lvs. oblong-obovate to elliptic, acutish to obtuse, finely serrulate, 1–2 in. long; corymbs 3–10-fld.; petals ¼ in. long; fr. red, bitter, 5/16 in. in diam., stone ellipsoid. B.C., Idaho to Calif. Zone 7.

eriogyna: *P. Fremontii.*

fasciculata (Torr.) A. Gray. DESERT ALMOND, WILD A., WILD PEACH. Divaricately and densely branched, deciduous, 3–8 ft., twigs short, stiff, minutely pubescent when young; lvs. fascicled, oblong-spatulate, mostly entire, ¼–½ in. long; fls. 1 to few, petals ⅛ in. long; fr. ovoid, dry, 5/16–½ in. long, pubescent, with a smooth stone. Deserts, Calif. to Utah and Ariz. Zone 7.

Fremontii S. Wats. [*P. eriogyna* S. C. Mason]. DESERT APRICOT. Rigidly branched, deciduous, 5–12 ft., twigs often spine-tipped, glabrous; lvs. roundish to broadly ovate, ⅜–¾ in. long, serrate; fls. 1 to few, petals white, ¼ in. long; fr. elliptic-ovoid, yellowish, to ½ in. long, dry. Deserts, s. Calif.

×**fruticans** Weihe: *P. insititia* × *P. spinosa.* Usually thornless; lvs. often acutish, about 2 in. long; fls. larger; fr. ½–¾ in. in diam. Occasional in Eur.

fruticosa Pall. EUROPEAN DWARF CHERRY, EUROPEAN GROUND C. Bush, 3–4 ft., glabrous or becoming so; lvs. elliptic-obovate to obovate-oblong, 1–2 in. long, short-pointed, closely serrate; fls. with the lvs., 2–4, in sessile umbels, white, ¾ in. across; fr. red-purple, globose, 5/16 in. in diam. Eur., Siberia. Zone 4.

glandulosa Thunb. [*P. glandulosa* var. *glabra* Koehne]. FLOWERING ALMOND. To 3–5 ft.; lvs. more or less oblong, 1½–4 in. long, pointed, serrulate, glabrous on both sides or somewhat pubescent on veins beneath; fls. white to pink, ½ in. across; fr. dark red, subglobose, ⅜ in. in diam. Japan, China. Zone 4. Cvs. are: **'Alboplena',** fls. double, white; **'Rosea',** fls. pink; **'Sinensis'** [*P. sinensis* Pers.], foliage dark, fls. double, pink.

gracilis Engelm. & A. Gray. OKLAHOMA PLUM, PRAIRIE CHERRY. Bush, to 15 ft.; lvs. elliptic to ovate-elliptic, slightly pubescent above, densely so beneath; fls. before the lvs., white, 5/16 in. across; fr. reddish with light bloom, ½ in. in diam. Ark. to Tex. Zone 6.

Gravesii Small. Like *P. maritima,* but smaller; lvs. roundish, subtruncate; fls. larger; fr. blacker. N. Long Is. (N. Y.).

Grayana Maxim. Tree, to 30 ft., like *P. Padus,* but lvs. with setaceous teeth and long point, petiole not glandular; fls. racemose, white, 5/16 in. across; fr. black, ¼ in. in diam. Japan. Zone 6.

hortulana L. H. Bailey. WILD-GOOSE PLUM, HORTULAN P. To 30 ft., branchlets glabrous; lvs. 3–4 in. long, ovate to lanceolate-oblong, long-acuminate, glabrate or pubescent beneath on the veins; fls. before lvs., ½ in. across, white; fr. 1 in. or less in diam., red to yellow, stone reticulate, pointed at both ends. S. Ind. to Iowa, Okla., Ark., Ala. Zone 6. Cvs. **'Cumberland', 'Golden Beauty', 'Wayland'** belong here. Cv. **'Mineri'.** Lvs. thicker, coarsely toothed; fr. later, firmer.

humilis Bunge. Shrub, to about 5 ft., pubescent on young growth; lvs. 1–2 in. long, obovate to elliptic, acute, serrulate, glabrous; fls. with the lvs., 1–2, pinkish-white, ½ in. across; fr. red, ½ in. in diam., globose. China. Zone 6.

ilicifolia (Nutt.) Walp. HOLLY-LEAVED CHERRY, EVERGREEN C., WILD C., MOUNTAIN HOLLY, ISLAY. Dense evergreen shrub or small tree, 3–25 ft., glabrous; lvs. shining, leathery, ovate to roundish, 1–2 in. long, coarsely spinose-toothed, crisped; fls. few to many, racemose, white, 5/16 in. across; frs. red, rarely yellow, ovoid-ellipsoid, ½ in. long, pulp thin, sweetish, stone smooth, large. Calif., n. Baja Calif.

incana (Pall.) Batsch. Erect shrub, 4–6 ft., twigs thin, somewhat hairy; lvs. ovate to obovate, 1–2 in. long, acute, sharply serrate, dark and shining above, gray-pubescent beneath; fls. 1–2, sessile, ⅜ in. across, bright pink; fr. ¼ in. in diam., round, red. Se. Eur., Asia Minor. Zone 6.

incisa Thunb. CHERRY. Small tree or large shrub, young twigs glabrous; lvs. reddish at first, ovate to obovate, acuminate, doubly serrate, pubescent on both sides; fls. with the lvs., nodding, red and pink, short-pedicelled, less than ½ in. across; fr. purple black, 5/16 in. in diam. Japan. Zone 6.

insititia L. BULLACE, DAMSON, DAMSON PLUM. To 20 ft., sometimes thorny, young growth tomentose; lvs. usually more or less hairy above, at first also beneath, elliptic to ovate, 1½–3 in. long, coarsely serrate; fls. 2, white, to 1 in. across; fr. pendulous, round to ovoid, blue-black, sweet. Eur., N. Afr. Zone 5. Var. **italica** (Borkh.) Neuman. GREENGAGE. Not thorny; lvs. obtuse; fr. usually greenish. Var. **syriaca** (Borkh.) Koehne. MIRABELLE. Fr. round, yellow, sweet.

integrifolia: see *P. Lyonii.*

Jacquemontii Hook.f. FLOWERING ALMOND. Shrubby, 4–8 ft., glabrous; lvs. dimorphic, elliptic to narrow-obovate, to 2½ in. long on new brs., mostly oblanceolate and about 1 in. long on brs. of the preceding year, sharply but shallowly serrate, pubescent only when young; fls. with the lvs., mostly 2, pink, ¾ in. across; fr. subglobose, red, ⅝ in. in diam., juicy. Himalayas. Zone 7.

japonica Thunb. JAPANESE BUSH CHERRY, JAPANESE PLUM, FLOWERING ALMOND. Small shrub, to 4½ ft., twigs fine, glabrous; lvs. ovate to broadly ovate, sharply serrate, 1–3 in. long, long-pointed, glabrous or pubescent beneath on the veins; fls. with the lvs., 2–3, white to pink, to ¾ in. across; fr. subglobose, wine-red, ⅜ in. in diam., stone pointed at the ends. China to Korea. Zone 4. Much cult. in Japan as an ornamental and for the edible frs. Cvs. **'Alba', 'Kuliensis', 'Koziensis', 'Kinkiensis', 'Rosea',** and **'Rubra'** are listed.

lanata: *P. americana* var.

Lannesiana: *P. serrulata* var.

Laurocerasus L. [*Laurocerasus officinalis* M. J. Roem.]. CHERRY LAUREL, ENGLISH L. Evergreen, glabrous shrub or small tree; lvs. oblong, remotely small-toothed, shining, leathery, acuminate, 2–7 in. long, petioles green, to ⅜ in. long; fls. many, in ascending racemes, white, 5/16 in. across; fr. dark purple, ½ in. long, ovoid. Se. Eur., sw. Asia. Zone 7. Many cvs. of different lf. shapes and growth habits: **'Angustifolia', 'Bertinii', 'Caucasica', 'Japonica', 'Latifolia', 'Magnoliifolia', 'Nana', 'Parvifolia', 'Reynvaanii', 'Rotundifolia'** [*Laurocerasus rotundifolia* (B. Verl.) Clemenc.], **'Schipkaensis'** [*Laurocerasus schipkaensis* (F. L. Späth) Morel], **'Serbica', 'Versaillensis', 'Zabeliana'** [*Laurocerasus Zabeliana* Hort.].

lusitanica L. [*Laurocerasus lusitanica* (L.) M. J. Roem.]. PORTUGAL LAUREL. Much like *P. Laurocerasus,* but a larger tree with crenate-dentate lvs., petioles longer, red, ⅝–1 in. long. Portugal, Spain, to Canary Is. Zone 7. Cvs. **'Angustifolia'**, **'Myrtifolia'**, and **'Variegata'** are listed.

Lyonii (Eastw.) Sarg. [*P. integrifolia* Sarg., not Walp.]. CATALINA CHERRY. Like *P. ilicifolia,* but more arboreous; lvs. darker green, more narrowly ovate, mostly entire, flat, 2–4 in. long; racemes many-fld.; fr. almost black, ½–1 in. long. Is. off s. Calif. Zone 8.

Maackii Rupr. To 50 ft., with rounded crown, pubescent on young growth; lvs. oblong to elliptic-ovate, acuminate, sharply glandular-serrate, to 3 in. long; fls. 6–10, in racemes, white, about 5⁄16 in. across; fr. black, globose, ¼ in. in diam. E. Asia. Zone 2.

Mahaleb L. MAHALEB, ST. LUCIE CHERRY, PERFUMED C. Green-twigged tree, to 30 ft., tomentulose on young growth; lvs. round-ovate, obtusish, crenate-dentate, glandular between the teeth, 1–2½ in. long; fls. 4–10, white, about ⅜ in. across; fr. subglobose or ovoid, nearly black, 5⁄16 in. long. Eur., w. Asia; introd. into N. Amer. Zone 6. Cult. as an ornamental. Cv. **'Pendula'**. Branchlets pendulous.

mandshurica: *P. Armeniaca* var.

maritima Marsh. [*P. acuminata* Michx.]. BEACH PLUM, SHORE P. Straggling, to 10 ft.; lvs. ovate to obovate, acute to obtuse, sharply crenate-serrate, pubescent beneath, 1–2½ in. long; fls. before lvs., white, ¾ in. across; fr. purple to yellow, ½–1 in. in diam., edible, with tart acid flesh. Coastal sand, Me. to Del. Frs. used for jams and jellies. Useful also as an ornamental and coastal soil binder. Prop. by seeds or better by root cuttings of selected forms taken in autumn.

Maximowiczii Rupr. Tree, to 35 ft., pubescent on young growth; lvs. mostly obovate, 1½–3 in. long, abruptly pointed, coarsely double-serrate, bright green and glabrous above, pubescent beneath on veins; fls. 5–10, in racemes, cream-white, ¾ in. across; fr. red to black, ¼ in. in diam. E. Asia. Zone 5.

melanocarpa: *P. virginiana* var.

Moseri: a listed name of no botanical standing for *P. × blireiana* cv.

Mume Siebold & Zucc. JAPANESE APRICOT, JAPANESE FLOWERING A. Round-crowned tree, to 30 ft., twigs thin, green; lvs. ovate to elliptic, long-pointed, 1½–4 in. long, sharply serrulate, pubescent beneath, at least on veins; fls. 1–2, white to dark red, to 1¼ in. across; fr. round, 1 in. in diam., yellow to greenish, slightly pubescent, sour and bitter, stone furrowed. China, sw. Japan. Zone 7. The winter-flowering "plum" of the Orient, a popular garden ornamental with many cvs. Much used in Japan for bonsai; frs. much pickled and source of a sweet liqueur.

Munsoniana F. W. Wight & Hedr. WILD-GOOSE PLUM. Differing from *P. hortulana* in having the lvs. longitudinally folded at maturity; fls. chiefly on short lateral spurs; stone obliquely truncate at base. Ohio to Kans., s. to Okla. and Tex. Zone 6.

myrobalana: *P. cerasifera.*

nana: *P. tenella.*

Newportii: a listed name of no botanical standing for *P. cerasifera* cv.

nigra Ait. CANADA PLUM. Close to *P. americana,* but teeth of lvs. gland-tipped, petiole with 2 glands; fls. larger, ¾–1 3⁄16 in. across, white, changing to pink, sepals glandular-serrate. Que. to Man., s. to Ga. and La. Zone 2.

nipponica Matsum. To about 15 ft., glabrous; lvs. mostly ovate, 1½–3 in. long, acuminate, doubly serrate, glabrous at maturity; fls. 2–4, in umbels, white, about 1 in. across; fr. round, 5⁄16 in. in diam., purple-black. High mts., n. Japan. Zone 6. Var. **kurilensis** (Miyabe) E. H. Wils. Petioles and pedicels pubescent; fls. larger. Kurile Is.

Padus L. BIRD CHERRY, EUROPEAN B. C., HAGBERRY. To 40 ft., with peeling bark; lvs. 2–4 in. long, elliptic to obovate, acuminate, sharply serrate, often subcordate, glabrous except sometimes with tufts of hairs beneath; fls. 10–40, in racemes, ½ in. across, white, fragrant, sepals obtuse, gland-fringed, pubescent inside, petals irregularly toothed, longer than stamens; fr. 5⁄16 in. in diam., ovoid, black, astringent, with rugose stone. Eur. to Japan. Zone 4. Wood used for furniture, boat building, and for interior work. There are cvs. with pendulous brs., and with red, double, and spotted fls. Var. **commutata** Dipp. Flowering earlier than the sp., lvs. coarsely toothed. E. Asia.

pedunculata (Pall.) Maxim. Shrub, to 6 ft., twigs tomentulose; lvs. elliptic to oblong, 1–1½ in. long, irregularly toothed, shining, pubescent beneath when young; fls. pink, solitary; fr. ovoid, ½ in. long, grooved, pubescent, with smooth stone. Siberia. Zone 6.

pendula: a listed name of no botanical standing.

pensylvanica L.f. WILD RED CHERRY, PIN C., BIRD C., FIRE C. To 35 ft.; lvs. oblong-lanceolate to narrow-ovate, membranous, gradually acute to acuminate, finely and sharply serrate, green and glabrous beneath; fls. with the lvs., umbellate or corymbose, ½ in. across, white; fr. globose, light red, ¼ in. in diam., with thin acid flesh. Lab. to B.C., s. to N.C., Iowa, Colo. Zone 2.

Persica (L.) Batsch. PEACH. Small, glabrous tree; lvs. long-lanceolate, serrulate, 3–6 in. long, acuminate; fls. before the lvs., 1–2, pink to red, 1–1½ in. across, sepals pubescent on exterior; fr. more or less spherical, 2–3 in. in diam., juicy, reddish on side exposed to the sun, not splitting, tomentulose, stone deeply sculptured. China, or a hort. derivative from the Chinese *P. Davidiana.* Zone 5. One of the most important frs. Widely cult. in many forms in temp. countries for the fr. and fls. Cvs. **'Alba'**, **'Alboplena'**, **'Atropurpurea'**, **'Pendula'**, **'Purpurea'**, **'Rosea'**, **'Rubra'**, **'Rubroplena'**, etc. are listed. Var. **Nectarina:** var. *nucipersica.* Var. **nucipersica** (Suckow) C. K. Schneid. [var. *Nectarina* (Ait.f.) Maxim.]. NECTARINE. Fr. smooth, not pubescent, smaller. For cult. see *Nectarine* and *Peach.*

pilosiuscula (C. K. Schneid.) Koehne. Shrub or tree, to 40 ft.; lvs. oblong to obovate, acuminate, serrate, 1½–3½ in. long, pubescent on veins beneath; fls. in umbels, with or just before the lvs., ¾ in. across, pink; fr. ellipsoid, red, 5⁄16 in. long. China. Zone 6.

Pissardii: *P. cerasifera* cv. 'Atropurpurea'.

Pollardii: a listed name of no botanical standing for *P. Amygdalo-persica* cv.

prostrata Labill. Dwarf, to 3 ft.; lvs. broadly ovate, 1 in. long, sharply serrate, white-tomentose to subglabrous beneath; fls. 1–2, pink, mostly sessile, ½ in. across; fr. ½ in. in diam., blackish-red. Medit. region. Zone 6.

Pseudocerasus Lindl. To 25 ft., sparingly pubescent on young growth; lvs. to about 4 in. long, broadly obovate to ovate, firm, sharply serrate, somewhat hairy on veins beneath; fls. before full foliage, to 1 in. across, white, fragrant; fr. early, red, edible, to ¾ in. in diam. China. Zone 6?

Puddum: *P. cerasoides.*

pumila L. SAND CHERRY, DWARF C. Decumbent shrub to 8 ft.; lvs. narrowly oblanceolate, attenuate at both ends, glabrous, 2–3 in. long, closely serrate toward apex; fls. white, 2–3 together, ½ in. across or more; fr. purple-black, ⅜ in. in diam., astringent, stone subglobose, apiculate at apex. Sandy shores, Great Lakes. Zone 4. A useful hardy ornamental. Var. **depressa:** *P. depressa.*

Reverchonii Sarg. HOG PLUM. Shrub, to 6 ft., forming thickets, glabrous on young growth; lvs. lanceolate, acuminate, glandular-serrate, somewhat pubescent beneath; fls. with the lvs., 2–4, white, 5⁄16 in. across; fr. round, ⅜–¾ in. in diam., mostly yellow with red, stone elliptic, reticulate. Okla., Tex. Zone 6.

rufa Hook.f. Close to *P. campanulata,* but young parts densely reddish-tomentose; lvs. narrower, glandular-serrate; fls. white to pale pink. Himalayas. Zone 7.

Salasii Standl. Tree with glabrous twigs; lvs. lanceolate-oblong, 3–6 in. long, long-acuminate, sharply serrate; racemes 6–7 in. long; petals white, roundish, less than 3⁄16 in. long; fr. globose, ½ in. in diam. Guatemala.

salicina Lindl. JAPANESE PLUM. Small tree, to 25 ft., glabrous; lvs. oblong-ovate to oblong-obovate, pointed, usually shining above, 3–4 in. long, closely serrate; fls. mostly 2–3, white, ½–¾ in. across, on slender pedicels to ½ in. long; fr. yellow or light red, often pointed. China. Zone 8. Cult. in Japan for its fr. Not to be confused with the better known "plum" of the Orient, *P. Mume.*

Sargentii Rehd. SARGENT CHERRY, NORTH JAPANESE HILL C. To 50 ft., glabrous; lvs. 2–5 in. long, elliptic to narrow-obovate, long-pointed, sharply serrate; fls. 2–4, before the lvs., deep red, 1½ in. across; fr. ovoid, ⅜ in. long, dark purple. N. Japan, Korea, Sakhalin. Zone 5. Very intolerant of smog. Cv. **'Columnaris'** is listed.

serotina J. F. Ehrh. BLACK CHERRY, WILD B. C., RUM C. To 80 ft. or more, with dark outer bark, aromatic inner bark; lvs. lanceolate-oblong to oblong-ovate, acuminate to acute, crenate-serrate, 1½–6 in. long, shining above, glabrous or nearly so beneath; racemes 2–6 in. long; fls. to 5⁄16 in. across, fragrant, calyx persistent in fr.; fr. globose, red to purple-black, sweetish or bitter. Nov. Sc. to N. Dak., s. to Fla. and Tex. Zone 4. Bark has been used medicinally and the wood used for cabinet making and interior work.

serrulata Lindl. JAPANESE FLOWERING CHERRY, ORIENTAL C. To 60 ft.; lvs. smooth, shining, ovate or narrower, long-acuminate, 2½–5 in. long, serrate, somewhat glaucous beneath; fls. with or before the lvs., 3–5, white, 1½ in. across, not fragrant; fr. black, pea-sized. E. Asia. Var. **serrulata.** The typical var.; fls. double. Var. **hupehensis** (C. Ingram) C. Ingram. Fls. small, white, single. China. Var. **Lannesiana** (Carrière) Mak. [*P. Lannesiana* Carrière]. Lvs. with long-aristate teeth; fls. pink, fragrant. Var. **pubescens** (Mak.) E. H. Wils. [*P. Veitchii*

Koehne]. Like var. *spontanea*, but more hairy, reddish on young growth. Korea, n. Japan. Var. **spontanea** (Maxim.) E. H. Wils. A wild Japanese var. with fls. single, pink or white, with cut petals. This or the preceding var. is probably the original wild form from which the typical var. was derived. Cvs. unassigned to var. are: 'Hisakura', sometimes spelled 'Hosakura', fls. single to half-double, pink; 'Kwanzan', fls. large, double, rose-pink; 'Pendula': *P. yedoensis*; 'Shirotae' [cv. 'Sirotae'; *P. Shirotae* Hort.], brs. spreading, hanging downward, lvs. with long teeth, fls. often single, 2 in. across, white; 'Takasago' [*P. Sieboldii* (Carrière) Wittm.], NADEN CHERRY, lvs. densely pubescent above and beneath, fls. semidouble, almost 2 in. across, bright pink. Zone 6. Other cvs. listed are 'Alborosea', 'Rosea', 'Spectabilis'.

Shirotae: *P. serrulata* cv.

sibirica: *P. Armeniaca* var.

Sieboldii: *P. serrulata* cv. 'Takasago'.

Simonii Carrière. APRICOT PLUM, SIMON P. Narrow-topped tree, glabrous; lvs. narrow-obovate, dull, rather thick, very veiny, 3–4 in. long, obtusely serrate; fls. before the lvs., 1–3, white, ¾ in. across; fr. 1–2 in. in diam., flattened at the poles, dull red, with yellow flesh clinging to the rounded stone. China, but not known wild. Zone 6.

sinensis: *P. glandulosa* cv.

×**Skinneri** Rehd.: *P. japonica* × *P. tenella*. To about 3 ft.; lvs. 1½–2 in. long, pubescent on midrib; fls. many, small, bright pink.

spinosa L. BLACKTHORN, SLOE. Rigid, deciduous, much-branched, suckering shrub or tree, 3–12 ft., twigs pubescent when young, later dark; lvs. 1–1½ in., oblong-obovate to oblanceolate, cuneate at base, acute or obtuse, crenate-serrate, more or less pubescent; fls. before the lvs., 1–2, white, to ¾ in. across; fr. globose, ½ in. in diam., blue-black, pruinose, astringent. Eur., w. Asia. Zone 5. Wood used for turnery, and frs. for flavoring liqueurs. Cvs. 'Atropurpurea' and 'Purpurea' are listed.

Ssiori Friedr. Schmidt. To 75 ft.; lvs. oblong to obovate, 3–6 in. long, obtuse, serrate, pubescent to glabrous beneath; fls. 10–23, in narrow racemes, white, ⅝ in. across; fr. ellipsoid, red or yellow, 1 in. long. Ne. Asia. Zone 5. Wood used in Japan for making furniture and utensils.

subcordata Benth. SIERRA PLUM, PACIFIC P. Tree, to 20 ft., with stiff crooked brs. and short thornlike branchlets; lvs. ovate to roundish, obtuse at both ends or subcordate at base, 1–2 in. long, serrulate, pubescent or glabrate beneath; fls. 2–4, white or pink in age, ⅝ in. across; fr. broadly ellipsoid, ⅝–¾ in. long, red-purple, edible, stone more or less flattened. Ore., Calif. Zone 7. Var. **Kelloggii** Lemm. SISSON PLUM. Fr. sweet, yellow. N. Calif.

subhirtella Miq. HIGAN CHERRY, ROSEBUD C. To 25 ft., twigs slender, pubescent; lvs. ovate to lanceolate, short-pointed, doubly serrate, hairy on veins beneath, 1–3 in. long; free-blooming, fls. 2–5, before the lvs., pink to nearly white, ¾ in. across, petals notched; fr. black, ovoid, ⁵⁄₁₆ in. long. Japan. Zone 6. An early-flowering, ornamental cherry. Intolerant of smog. Cvs. include: 'Autumnalis' [*P. autumnalis* Koehne ex Sarg., not Liegel], to 15 ft., fls. partly double; 'Pendula', twigs pendulous, crooked; 'Rosea', erect, the common garden form. Var. **ascendens** (Mak.) E. H. Wils. Tall tree, not weeping; lvs. lanceolate; fls. white. Japan.

×**sultana** Voss: *P. salicina* × *P. Simonii*. WICKSON PLUM. Hybrid represented by the cv. 'Wickson'; narrow upright tree; lvs. long-lanceolate; fr. very large, purplish-red with yellowish flesh.

tenella Batsch [*P. nana* (L.) J. Stokes]. DWARF RUSSIAN ALMOND. Hardy ornamental shrub, to 5 ft., glabrous; lvs. narrow, 1–3 in. long, stiffish, obtusish, serrate; fls. 1–3, rose, ¾ in. across; fr. ¾ in. long, pubescent. Eurasia. Zone 2.

tomentosa Thunb. NANKING CHERRY, HANSEN'S BUSH C., CHINESE BUSH FRUIT. Compact shrub, to 5 ft.; lvs. obovate, abruptly narrowed, tomentose beneath, serrate, 1½–2½ in. long; fls. appearing with the lvs., usually solitary, 1 in. across, white; fr. scarlet, ⅜ in. in diam., glabrous or pubescent, edible. Temp. e. Asia. Zone 3. Very winter hardy, fr. used for pies, jams, and jellies; attractive ornamental, one of the earliest flowering shrubs. Prop. by budding or suckers. Var. **endotricha** Koehne. Lvs. elliptic; a very profuse bloomer. China.

triloba Lindl. FLOWERING ALMOND. Bush to treelike, 10 ft. or more; lvs. broad-ovate to obovate, sometimes 3-lobed on new shoots, doubly serrate, 1½–3 in. long, pubescent beneath; fls. 1–2, double, pink or white, 1½ in. or less across; fr. red, ⁵⁄₁₆ in. in diam., pubescent. China, but not known wild except as forma **simplex** (Bunge) Rehd., with single fls. Cv. 'Multiplex'. Fls. double, pink. Zone 3.

Veitchii: *P. serrulata* var. *pubescens*.

virginiana L. CHOKECHERRY. Shrub or small tree; lvs. elliptic to obovate, short-acuminate, sharply serrulate, glabrous or nearly so beneath, 2–4½ in. long; fls. with the lvs., about ⁵⁄₁₆ in. across, white, in racemes; fr. red, becoming almost purple, acid, astringent, ¼–⁵⁄₁₆ in. in diam. Nfld. to Sask., s. to N.C., Mo., Kans. Zone 2. Cv. 'Xan-

thocarpa'. Fr. yellow. Var. **demissa** (Nutt.) Sarg. [*P. demissa* (Nutt.) Walp.]. Lvs. pubescent beneath; fr. dark red. Wash., Idaho, to Calif. Var. **melanocarpa** (A. Nels.) Sarg. [*P. melanocarpa* (A. Nels.) Rydb.]. Twigs and lvs. glabrous; fr. black. Calif. to Rocky Mts.

yedoensis Matsum. [*P. serrulata* cv. 'Pendula']. JAPANESE FLOWER-ING CHERRY, POTOMAC C., YOSHINO C. Like *P. serrulata*, but less hairy; fls. single, pink, becoming white with age; pistils, pedicels, and calyx pubescent. From cult. in Japan, where the most widely cult. ornamental cherry, but not known in the wild; believed to be a hybrid between vars. of *P. serrulata* and *P. subhirtella*. Zone 6. Fast-growing, profusely blooming, relatively short-lived tree. The single-fld. cherries of the Tidal Basin in Washington, D.C.

PSAMMOPHORA Dinter & Schwant. *Aizoaceae.* Four spp. of low, tufted, half-woody succulents, native to S. Afr., sts. densely leafy, often buried except for lvs.; lvs. 4-ranked, thick, nearly triangular to semicylindrical in section, dull blu-ish-gray-green, sticky, causing dust and sand to adhere, and so preventing excessive transpiration in the native habitat; fls. solitary, terminal, pedicelled, calyx 4-lobed, petals violet-pink or white, many, stamens many, white, staminodes absent, ovary inferior, 5–7-celled, stigmas 5; fr. a caps., cell lids and placental tubercles absent.

Growth occurs from spring to autumn. Cultivated in full sun under glass with moderate moisture, but should be kept completely dry and at a relatively cool temperature of about 60° F in winter. Propagated by seeds or cuttings. See also *Succulents.*

longifolia L. Bolus. Lvs. 4–6 on each br., very rough, light gray-green to brownish, olive-green when young, reddish basally, to 1¾ in. long, ½ in. wide and not as thick, semicylindrical, upper side long-rectangular in outline, short-acuminate at apex, flat, lower side rounded, keeled toward apex and there slightly oblique, margins rounded; fls. with white petals. S.-W. Afr.

modesta (Dinter & A. Berger) Dinter & Schwant. Lvs. gray-green tinged with red, rough, ½ in. long, ¼ in. wide, more or less 3-angled in section with rounded angles, acute at apex; petals violet. S.-W. Afr.

PSEUDANANAS Hassl. ex Harms. *Bromeliaceae.* One sp., a terrestrial herb, native to Brazil; similar to *Ananas,* but differing in producing stolons, in having the infl. terminating in a minute crown of reduced bracts that never produces offsets at its base, and in the petals' having lateral folds, not funnelform scales.

Grown in full sun in warm climates. For culture see *Bromeliaceae.*

macrodontes: *P. sagenarius.*

sagenarius (Arr. Cam.) F. Camargo [*P. macrodontes* (E. Morr.) Harms]. Lvs. 3 ft. long or more, to 3 in. wide, with spines 1 in. long or more; infl. to 7 in. long, 3½ in. thick; fls. rose, to 2 in. long.

PSEUDERANTHEMUM Radlk. *Acanthaceae.* About 60 spp. of glabrous herbs or shrubs in the tropics; lvs. entire or coarsely toothed; fls. 1–3 in axils of bracts, arranged in spikes, cymes, or racemes, calyx 5-parted, segms. narrow, corolla mostly whitish, flecked or flushed with lilac or mauve, tube long, narrow, lobes 5, spreading, nearly equal, stamens 2, borne in upper part of corolla tube, anther sacs 2, staminodes 2; fr. a caps., seeds 4 or fewer, flat, rough on both surfaces.

Grown in the greenhouse, and in the open in warm countries. Propagated by cuttings.

alatum (Nees) Radlk. [*Chamaeranthemum alatum* Hort.]. CHOCO-LATE PLANT. Low-growing herbs; lvs. broadly ovate, cordate at base, silver-blotched along midrib above, gray beneath, more or less pal-mately veined, the lowermost 3 pairs of veins arising nearly at same point, petioles winged; fls. purple, in racemes. Mex. and Cent. Amer.

atropurpureum L. H. Bailey [*Eranthemum atropurpureum* Hort. Bull, not Hook.f.]. PURPLE FALSE ERANTHEMUM. Shrub, to 4 ft.; lvs. ovate or elliptic, obtuse or nearly so, to 6 in. long, purple or sometimes green, variously marked with yellow along veins; fls. on short pedicels, in loose spikes, bracts inconspicuous, corolla to 1 in. across, white with purple markings, tube ½ in. long, lobes nearly equal, almost as long as tube. Probably Polynesia; escaped in trop. Amer.

bicolor (Schrank) Radlk. [*Eranthemum bicolor* Schrank]. Shrub, to 3 ft., differing from *P. atropurpureum* in having fls. sessile, corolla tube longer, more slender, up to 1–1½ in. long. Probably Polynesia.

kewense L. H. Bailey [*Eranthemum atropurpureum* Hook.f., not Hort. Bull.]. Shrub; lvs. purple and glossy above, green beneath; fls. pedicelled, in spikelike racemes, corolla tube slender, 1 in. long, lobes narrow, ciliate. Probably Solomon Is. May not be cult. in U.S.

reticulatum (Hook.f.) Radlk. [*Eranthemum reticulatum* Hook.f.]. To 3 ft.; lvs. ovate-lanceolate, to 10 in. long, wavy-margined, dark green, veined throughout with yellow; corolla 1½ in. across, tube ½ in. long, lobes nearly equal. Probably Polynesia.

seticalyx: *Ruspolia seticalyx.*

sinuatum: a listed name of no botanical standing.

tricolor: see *Eranthemum tricolor.*

tuberculatum (Hook.f.) Radlk. [*Eranthemum tuberculatum* Hook.f.]. Small shrub, brs. tubercled; lvs. elliptic, less than 1 in. long; fls. solitary in the axils, corolla to 1 in. across, pure white, tube long, slender, lobes slightly unequal. Polynesia and New Caledonia.

PSEUDOBOMBAX Dug. *Bombacaceae.* Twenty spp. of small or medium trees without spines, native to trop. Amer.; lvs. simple or palmately compound; fls. large, white, red, or purple; closely related to *Bombax* but lfts. not articulate at base, and calyx usually truncate, glandular, and persistent.

ellipticum (HBK) Dug. [*Bombax ellipticum* HBK; *Pachira fastuosa* (Moç. & Sessé ex DC.) Decne.]. SHAVING-BRUSH TREE. To 30 ft., bark smooth, greenish or gray; lfts. 3–6, more or less elliptic, to 12 in. long; fls. opening before lvs. appear; calyx to ⅝ in. long, usually with 10 basal glands, petals white to pink, oblong-linear, to 6 in. long, stamens very many, about ¾ as long as petals, separate nearly to base; caps. fusiform, to 6 in. long. Mex. to Guatemala. In s. Fla. this sp. is often cult. under the names *Pachira insignis* and *Pachira macrocarpa.*

grandiflorum (Cav.) A. Robyns [*Bombax cyathophorum* (Casar.) K. Schum.]. To 25 ft. or more; lfts. 5–9, obovate to nearly elliptic, to 12 in. long; fls. almost terminal, calyx sometimes 2–3-lobed, to ¾ in. long, sometimes glandular at base, petals deep purple-red outside, lighter inside, linear, to 6 in. long, stamens very many, separate almost to base; caps. oblong, pointed, 6–12 in. long. Brazil.

PSEUDOCYMOPTERUS J. Coult. & Rose. *Umbelliferae.* Not cult. **P. anisatus:** *Aletes anisatus.*

PSEUDOESPOSTOA: *ESPOSTOA.*

PSEUDOLARIX Gord. [*Chrysolarix* H. E. Moore]. GOLDEN LARCH. *Pinaceae.* One sp., a coniferous, deciduous, monoecious tree, native to e. China, distinguished from *Larix* in having acuminate rather than obtuse bud scales, male cones clustered rather than solitary, and scales of female cones deciduous, acuminate, spreading.

For culture see *Conifers.*

amabilis: *P. Kaempferi.*

Kaempferi Gord. [*P. amabilis* (J. Nels.) Rehd.; *Chrysolarix amabilis* (J. Nels.) H. E. Moore]. To 130 ft.; lvs. bright green, turning yellow in autumn, in dense clusters on short shoots, linear, to 3 in. long; cones pendent on peduncles, ovoid, to 3 in. long. Zone 6. Intolerant of limestone soils. Cv. **'Nana'**. Dwarf.

PSEUDOLOBIVIA: *ECHINOPSIS.*

PSEUDOMAMMILLARIA: *MAMMILLARIA* section *Pseudomammillaria.*

PSEUDOPANAX C. Koch. *Araliaceae.* About 10 spp. of dioecious shrubs or small trees of New Zeal. and Chile; lvs. in some spp. varying with age, from simple to compound; fls. unisexual, in simple or compound umbels, petals 4–5, valvate, stamens as many as the petals, ovary 4–5-celled, styles 4–5, separate; fr. a drupe, pyrenes mostly 4–5.

Grown under glass in the North or outdoors in mild cool climates. Zone 10 in Calif.

chathamicus T. Kirk. Small tree, to 20 ft.; lvs. simple, 2–8 in. long, juvenile lvs. lanceolate and toothed, adult lvs. linear-obovate, obscurely dentate or coarsely toothed at apex only; umbels terminal; fr. globose, ⁵⁄₁₆ in. in diam. New Zeal.

crassifolius (Soland. ex A. Cunn.) C. Koch. LANCEWOOD. Round-headed tree, 20–50 ft.; lvs. variable, those of seedlings simple, ovate-lanceolate, to 20 in. long, coarsely toothed or lobed, membranous, those of young plants narrow-linear, to 3 ft. long, rigid, leathery, remotely toothed, those of mature plants simple or trifoliolate, lfts. about 12 in. long, leathery, coarsely toothed or sinuate; fls. in terminal, compound umbels; fr. globose, about ⅛ in. in diam. New Zeal.

discolor (T. Kirk) Harms. Much-branched shrub, to 15 ft.; lfts. 3–5 and palmately arranged or solitary, obovate, to 3 in. long, sharply toothed, yellowish-green or bronzy, leathery; umbels terminal; fr. oblong, about ¼ in. long. New Zeal.

ferox (T. Kirk) T. Kirk. Small tree, to 20 ft.; lvs. always simple, but varying from narrow, linear-lanceolate in juvenile plants to thick, leathery, usually linear, 6–18 in. long, with margins bearing hooked lobes in immature plants, to linear-obovate, 2–6 in. long, nearly entire in mature plants; fr. oblong, ⁵⁄₁₆ in. in diam. New Zeal.

Lessonii (DC.) C. Koch. Shrub or small tree, to 20 ft., much-branched; lvs. palmately compound, lfts. 3–5, obovate, to 4 in. long, entire or wavy-toothed, glossy, leathery, similar in juvenile stage except larger and coarsely toothed; fr. oblong, about ¼ in. long. New Zeal.

PSEUDOPHOENIX H. Wendl. ex Sarg. CHERRY PALM. *Palmae.* Four spp. of medium-sized, stout, unarmed, polygamous palms of the Caribbean region; lvs. pinnate, crownshaft lacking, pinnae acute, arranged in several planes and in groups of 2–6 at the middle; infls. among lvs., long-peduncled, paniculate, erect to pendulous, bearing 2 large, flattened bracts; fls. not clustered, the bisexual with long pedicel-like base, sepals united in a short cup, petals valvate above a brief tubular base, stamens 6, filaments erect, pistil 3-celled, the male at ends of rachillae, similar but with reduced pistil; fr. red, fleshy, 1–3-seeded with stigmatic residue near base, seed with homogeneous endosperm and subbasal embryo.

Ornamental subtrop. or trop. palms with interesting trunks and showy frs. Zone 10b. For culture see *Palms.*

insignis: *P. vinifera.*

saonae: *P. Sargentii* var.

Sargentii H. Wendl. ex Sarg. Slow-growing, to 25 ft., trunk tapered; lvs. to nearly 10 ft. long, pinnae 87–127 on each side; infl. erect to spreading or pendulous in fr., to about 5 ft. long, stiffly and divaricately branched; fr. about ⅝ in. in diam. Var. **Sargentii.** The typical var.; infl. small, erect in fr., only ¼ as long as lvs. Fla., Mex., Brit. Honduras. Var. **saonae** (O. F. Cook) Read [*P. saonae* O. F. Cook]. Infl. half as long as lvs., arching and hanging in fr. Hispaniola, Cuba, Bahamas.

vinifera (Mart.) Becc. [*P. insignis* O. F. Cook]. To 75 ft., trunk swollen; lvs. to 10 ft. long, pinnae more than 150 on each side; infl. pendulous, to more than 9 ft. long; fr. about 1 in. in diam. Hispaniola.

PSEUDORHIPSALIS: *DISOCACTUS.*

PSEUDOSASA Mak. ex Nakai. BAMBOO. *Gramineae.* Three spp. of tall, evergreen, rhizomatous grasses in temp. e. Asia, sts. to 15 ft., cylindrical, fistulose, with 1 br. at each node; st. sheaths persistent, hispid outside; lf. sheaths with or without flexuous smooth bristles; spikelets 2–8-fld., lemma nearly awned, curving, palea bifid at apex, stamens 3, rarely 4, style short, with 3 stigmas. Sometimes combined with *Sasa,* which has lf. sheaths with scabrous rigid bristles and fls. with 6 stamens. For terminology see *Gramineae.*

Easily propagated by division. See *Bamboos.*

japonica (Siebold & Zucc. ex Steud.) Mak. [*Arundinaria japonica* Siebold & Zucc. ex Steud.; *A. Metake* Nichols.; *Bambusa Metake* Siebold ex Miq.; *Sasa japonica* (Siebold & Zucc. ex Steud.) Mak.]. ARROW B., HARDY B., METAKE. Rhizomes wide-creeping, sts. to 15 ft. or more, ¾ in. in diam., brs. semierect, borne singly at upper nodes; st. sheaths, except at lower nodes, equalling or longer than internodes, covered at first with compressed bristles, later smooth and turning pale brown, very persistent, terminated by a persistent awl-shaped tongue to 2¾ in. long; lf. blades to 13 in. long and 1⅝ in. wide, 12–20-nerved, tessellate, long-pointed, narrowed at base, serrulate on one margin, glossy dark green above, glaucescent beneath, except a green strip on one margin. Japan. Cult. in Eur. and elsewhere in Zone 8 and locally in milder parts of Zone 7. Spreads less rapidly than most other running bamboos, hence valued in decorative plantings, for screening and hedges; also suitable as a tub plant. Withstands shade.

PSEUDOTSUGA Carrière. *Pinaceae.* About 5 spp. of tall, evergreen, coniferous trees, native to w. N. Amer. and e. Asia; lvs. flat, linear, having 2 white bands beneath; female cones drooping, scales persistent, bracts conspicuous, exserted, sharply 3-lobed; seeds 2 to each scale, with large wing, maturing in 1 year.

For culture see *Conifers.*

Douglasii: *P. Menziesii.*

glauca: *P. Menziesii* var.

japonica (Shiras.) Beissn. To 70 ft. or more, branchlets glabrous, pale yellowish-gray; lvs. to 1 in. long, notched at apex, glossy; cones to 2 in. long, dark violet when young, bracts reflexed, scales glabrous. Japan. Zone 8.

macrocarpa (Vasey) Mayr. BIG-CONE SPRUCE. To 70 ft. or more, brs. usually drooping, branchlets usually pubescent; lvs. 1–1¼ in. long, acute, bluish-green; cones 4–7 in. long, bracts erect. S. Calif. to Baja Calif. Zone 9.

Menziesii (Mirb.) Franco [*P. Douglasii* (Sab. ex D. Don) Carrière; *P. mucronata* (Raf.) Sudw.; *P. taxifolia* (Lamb.) Britt.; *Abies Douglasii* (Sab. ex D. Don) Lindl.]. DOUGLAS FIR. To 300 ft., but usually smaller, branchlets rarely glabrous; lvs. 1–1¼ in. long, obtuse, dark or bluish-green; cones to 4½ in. long, bracts reflexed. B.C. to Mex. and Tex. Zone 6. A major timber tree in the regions of its best development. Some of the cvs. are: **'Argentea'**, lvs. silvery-white; **'Brevibracteata'**, smaller tree, bracts of cone shorter; **'Caesia'**, lvs. bluish-green; **'Compacta'**, dense, lvs. shorter; **'Densa'**, dwarf, flat-topped; **'Fastigiata'**, conical; **'Fretsii'**, lvs. shorter, broader; **'Glauca Pendula'**, branchlets drooping, lvs. bluish; **'Globosa'**, dwarf, rounded; **'Pendula'**, brs. drooping, lvs. dark green; **'Pyramidata'**, conical, partly dwarf; **'Viridis'**, lvs. green, cones larger. Var. **glauca** (Beissn.) Franco [*P. glauca* (Mayr) Mayr]. Lvs. and cones smaller; the Rocky Mt. form, hardy and adaptable as an ornamental in Zone 4.

mucronata: *P. Menziesii.*

sinensis Dode. Branchlets pubescent, reddish-brown; lvs. to 1½ in. long, notched at apex; cones to 2½ in. long, scales puberulous. W. China.

taxifolia: *P. Menziesii.*

PSEUDOWINTERA Dandy. *Winteraceae.* Two or 3 spp. of aromatic, evergreen shrubs or small trees, native to New Zeal.; lvs. alt., usually leathery; fls. small, axillary, usually clustered, calyx persistent, cup-shaped, petals 5–6, stamens 5–15, carpels 1–5, separate; fr. of 1 or more indehiscent berries.

axillaris (J. R. Forst. & G. Forst.) Dandy [*Drimys axillaris* J. R. Forst. & G. Forst.]. Shrub or small tree, to 30 ft., bark black; lvs. narrow-ovate to oblong, to 5 in. long, dark green and glossy above, glaucous beneath; fls. small, greenish-yellow, few in a cluster. Introd. in Calif., but not common.

PSIDIUM L. GUAVA. *Myrtaceae.* About 100 spp. of evergreen trees or shrubs in Amer. tropics; lvs. opp., simple, pinnately veined; fls. usually large, white, calyx tube prolonged above the ovary, splitting irregularly at flowering time, petals 5, stamens many; fr. a globose or pear-shaped berry, sometimes large and edible.

Several are cultivated in tropical regions for their edible fruits. The guava is grown throughout the tropics and subtropics and is used in many ways as fresh fruit, or the juice may be used for punch or ices. The greatest commercial use of guava fruit is for jelly.

Guavas require tropical temperatures, although they withstand a few degrees of frost. The guava grows wherever the orange thrives, and the cultural requirements are simple. Propagated by seeds sown in flats or pans of light sandy loam; seedlings should be kept in pots until transplanted permanently. Clones are propagated by shield and patch budding or less commonly by cuttings. See *Guava.*

araca: *P. guineense.*

Cattleianum: *P. littorale* var. *longipes.*

chinense: a listed name of no botanical standing.

Friedrichsthalianum (O. Berg) Niedenzu. COSTA RICAN G. Shrub or small tree, to 25 ft., branchlets 4-angled; lvs. to 3 in. long, glossy above, pubescent beneath; fls. 1 in. across, solitary; fr. sulphur-yellow, to 2½ in. long, with white flesh. Cent. Amer. Frequently cult.; fr. smaller than the COMMON G., with tart agreeable flavor, sometimes used for jellies.

Guajava L. COMMON G., YELLOW G., APPLE G. Shrub or small tree, to 30 ft., bark scaly, greenish-brown, branchlets 4-angled; lvs. ovate to oblong-elliptic, to 6 in. long, pubescent beneath, veins prominent; fls. white, solitary or few together on slender peduncles; fr. ovoid to pear-shaped, 1–4 in. long, with yellow or dark pink flesh. Spring. Trop. Amer. Cult. throughout tropics and subtropics and frequently naturalized. Zone 10b. Fr. varies in size, shape, color, and flavor, and has a musky, penetrating odor. Somewhat insipid when raw, it may be canned, preserved, spiced, and made into jam, relish, and chutney. The juice is used for punch. Its greatest commercial use is for jelly.

guineense Swartz [*P. araca* Raddi; *P. molle* Bertol.]. GUAVA. Shrub or small tree, to 20 ft., branchlets nearly cylindrical; lvs. ovate to oblong-elliptic, to 5 in. long or more, rusty-pubescent beneath; fls. white, solitary or few together on slender peduncles, fragrant; fr. ovoid, brownish-green, turning to a pale yellow when ripe, slightly acid. Early summer. Trop. Amer. Fr. smaller than the common guava; too bitter or resinous to be palatable.

littorale Raddi. Shrub or small tree, to 25 ft., bark smooth, gray-brown; lvs. elliptic to obovate, to 3 in. long, glabrous; fls. white, solitary, to 1 in. across; fr. to 1½ in. long, with white flesh. Early summer. Brazil. Planted in tropics and subtropics. Zone 10. Var. **littorale** [var. *lucidum* (Degener) Fosb.; *P. lucidum* Hort.]. YELLOW STRAWBERRY G., YELLOW CATTLEY G., WAIAWI. The typical var.; a rather loosely branched, small tree; fr. sulphur-yellow, somewhat translucent, acid when ripe. Useful in reforestation. Var. **longipes** (O. Berg) Fosb. [*P. Cattleianum* Sab.]. PURPLE G., PURPLE STRAWBERRY G., CATTLEY G. Small dense tree; fr. globose, purplish-red, sweet when ripe. Recommended for its edible fr. Var. **lucidum:** var. *littorale.*

longipes (O. Berg) McVaugh [*Eugenia longipes* O. Berg; *Mosiera bahamensis* (Kiaersk.) Small; *M. longipes* (O. Berg) Small; *Myrtus bahamensis* (Kiaersk.) Urb.; *M. verrucosa* O. Berg]. Erect shrub or small tree, to 3 ft. or more; lvs. elliptic to ovate or orbicular, to 1¾ in. long, ¾ in. wide, or rarely to 1⅜ in., obtuse to acute; fls. to ¾ in. across; fr. globose or obovoid-globose, to ⅜ in. across, black. Fla., Fla. Keys, Bahama Is., n. Lesser Antilles.

lucidum: *P. littorale* var. *littorale.*

molle: *P. guineense.*

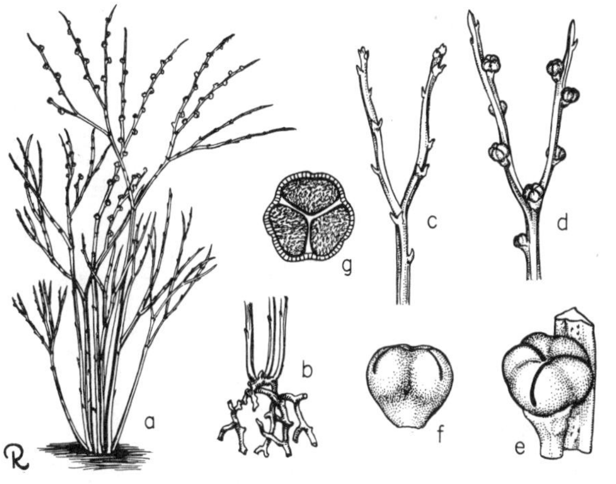

PSILOTACEAE. *Psilotum nudum:* **a,** plant, × ⅛; **b,** base of stems, with rhizomes, × ½; **c,** vegetative branch with bracts, × 1; **d,** fertile branch with sporangia, × 1; **e,** section of stem with sporangium, × 5; **f,** sporangium, × 5; **g,** sporangium, cross section, × 5.

PSILOTACEAE Kanitz. PSILOTUM FAMILY. Fern allies; 2 genera and about 9 spp. of primitive, spore-producing, vascular plants of wide distribution, with rootless, leafless, noncircinate, dichotomously branched sts. and large, solitary sporangia borne on bractlike or leaflike lateral appendages. *Psilotum* is sometimes cult. as a curiosity.

PSILOTHONNA: *GAMOLEPIS.*

PSILOTUM Swartz. *Psilotaceae.* Two spp. of epiphytic, clump-forming, rootless, leafless plants, widely distributed in tropics and subtropics; sts. dichotomously branched, angular, erect or pendent, green; spores produced in large, solitary sporangia borne on bractlike lateral appendages.

Humus-loving plants of easy culture, one hardy as far north as Okla. and N.C. and grown as a curiosity under glass in the North. Propagated by division or by spores. See also *Ferns.*

nudum (L.) Griseb. WHISK FERN. To 2½ ft.; sts. in brushlike clumps, rigid and withy, rarely more than 3/16 in. in diam.; sporangia nearly globose, to ⅛ in. across, mostly 3-chambered and -lobed, yellow at maturity. Hammocks and swamplands to dry rocky cliffs, S.C. to Fla. and south, pantrop. A number of distinct cvs. are occasionally grown by hort. hobbyists in Japan.

PSOPHOCARPUS Neck. ex DC. *Leguminosae* (subfamily *Faboideae*). Ten spp. of mostly climbing or prostrate herbs or subshrubs, native to trop. Old World; lvs. of 1 or 3 lfts.; fls. solitary, clustered, or in a raceme, papilionaceous, upper lobes of calyx forming a lip, standard broad, eared, stamens

10, united or the uppermost separate; fr. an oblong, 4-winged, dehiscent legume.

tetragonolobus (L.) DC. ASPARAGUS PEA, PRINCESS P., GOA BEAN, MANILA B., FOUR-ANGLED B., WINGED B. Twining herb, with tuberous roots; lfts. 3, ovate, to 6 in. long and wide, acute, entire; fls. reddish-brown, to 1$^3/_{16}$ in. long, in loose racemes; fr. to 9 in. long, 1 in. wide, with wings to $^1/_4$ in. wide. Asia, where cult. for the edible young frs.

PSORALEA L. SCURFY PEA. *Leguminosae* (subfamily *Faboideae*). Perhaps 130 spp. of scented herbs or shrubs, native mostly to N. Amer. and S. Afr.; lvs. alt., odd-pinnate, rarely with 1 lft., with translucent dots; fls. in heads, racemes, spikes, or sometimes clustered or solitary, papilionaceous, stamens 10, united or 1 separate; fr. a short, 1-seeded, indehiscent legume.

One species, *P. esculenta*, has an edible root; others are grown as ornamentals. Propagated by division.

bituminosa L. Per. herb, to 3 ft.; lfts. 3, lower ones ovate, upper ones lanceolate or linear; fls. light purple, in dense heads on very long axillary peduncles. Spring and early summer. Medit. region and Arabia.

candicans Eckl. & Zeyh. Slender, shrubby, with gray-pubescent brs.; lfts. 3, linear-oblong or cuneate-obovate, to $^3/_4$ in. long, black-dotted; racemes axillary, very short; fls. small. S. Afr.

esculenta Pursh. INDIAN TURNIP, BREADROOT, INDIAN B., PRAIRIE POTATO, POMME BLANCHE. Hirsute per., to 1$^1/_2$ ft., with edible, tuberous roots; lfts. 5, oblong to oblanceolate, to 2$^5/_{16}$ in. long, glabrous above; spikes dense, to 4 in. long; fls. yellowish to bluish. Late spring. Sask., s. to Mont. and Okla.

macrostachya DC. LEATHERROOT. Per., to 10 ft.; lvs. ovate, to 3 in. long; spikes to 4$^1/_2$ in. long, broad, villous; fls. small, purplish; fr. pubescent. Calif.

Onobrychis Nutt. Per., to 4$^1/_2$ ft.; lfts. 3, lanceolate, to 4 in. long, glabrous above, pubescent beneath; racemes narrow, spikelike, to 6 in. long; fls. pale purple; fr. rugose, $^1/_2$ in. long. Ohio to Iowa, s. to Tenn. and Mo.

pinnata L. Dense shrub, to 12 ft.; lfts. 7–11, linear or linear-lanceolate, about 1 in. long, acute; fls. solitary or clustered, blue and white. S. Afr.

PSYCHOTRIA L. WILD COFFEE. *Rubiaceae*. About 700 spp. of trop. shrubs or small trees; lvs. opp., rarely whorled, stipules persistent or deciduous; fls. in terminal or axillary corymbs or panicles, small, white, yellow or rose, 4–6-merous, corolla funnelform or subcampanulate, tube usually short, 2–3 times as long as lobes; fr. a drupe or few-seeded berry.

Sometimes grown in the warm greenhouse.

bacteriophila Val. Shrub, to 10 ft.; lvs. elliptic or ovate-oblong, to 3 in. long, glossy above, fleshy; fls. greenish-white, about $^1/_8$ in. long, stamens exserted; fr. $^1/_4$ in. across, reddish. Comoro Is. Lvs. warty with bacteria-inhabited nodules.

capensis Vatke. Compact shrub; lvs. obovate or oblong, to 5 in. long, glossy above, leathery; fls. yellow, $^1/_4$ in. long, fragrant; fr. globose, $^3/_{16}$ in. across, black, 2-seeded. S. Afr.

emetica L.f. FALSE IPECAC. Suffrutescent or shrubby, to 12 in. or more; lvs. elliptic-oblong, glabrous above, puberulent beneath, stipules persistent; fls. in axillary racemes, corolla white, $^1/_4$ in. long; fr. $^1/_4$ in. long, blue. Cent. and n. S. Amer. Roots have a strong and more or less nauseous odor, and are a source of ipecac, inferior to that obtained from *Cephaelis Ipecacuanha* A. Rich.

jasminiflora (Linden & André) M. T. Mast. Shrub, with white bark; lvs. oblong-ovate, to 3 in. long, pale beneath; corolla white, funnelform, to 1$^1/_4$ in. long, hairy outside, stamens exserted. Brazil.

nervosa Swartz [*P. undata* Jacq.] WILD COFFEE. Shrub, to 8 ft.; lvs. elliptic or elliptic-lanceolate, to 6 in. long, undulate, glabrous; fls. in a short terminal panicle, corolla white, tube $^1/_8$ in. long, lobes shorter than tube; drupe ellipsoid, to $^1/_4$ in. long, red or yellow. S. Fla. and W. Indies.

Sulzneri Small. WILD COFFEE. Similar to *P. nervosa*, but pubescent and having corolla lobes as long as the tube. S. Fla. and W. Indies.

undata: *P. nervosa*.

venosa (Hiern) Petit. Shrub, to 15 ft.; lvs. oblong-elliptic, to 7 in. long, glossy above; fls. many in spreading, paniculate cymes, white, small, about $^3/_{16}$ in. long. W. Trop. Afr.

PSYLLIOSTACHYS (Jaub. & Spach) Nevskiĭ. *Plumbaginaceae*. About 7 or 8 spp. of ann. herbs, in Soviet cent. Asia, the Caucasus, Afghanistan, Iran, w. to Syria and Israel; lvs. usually all basal, simple or pinnatifid; fl. scapes simple, infl. paniculate, composed of 2–4-fld. spikelets aggregated in long, narrow, terminal, or terminal and lateral, spikes; fls. white or pink. Related to *Limonium* but differing in its ann. habit and type of infl., and in having petals united in a funnelform corolla with a fairly long tube, and stamens united to corolla tube.

spicata (Willd.) Nevskiĭ [*Limonium spicatum* (Willd.) O. Kuntze; *Statice spicata* Willd.]. Lvs. oblanceolate, to 6 in. long, pinnatisect, hairy; infl. scapose, paniculate, to 16 in. high; calyx funnelform, to $^1/_4$ in. long, tube hairy, the expanded limb 5-lobed, lobes triangular-acuminate, corolla rose-pink, longer than calyx. Crimea, Soviet cent. Asia, Iran.

Suworowii (Regel) Roshk. [*Limonium Suworowii* (Regel) O. Kuntze; *Statice Suworowii* Regel]. Related to *P. spicata* but lvs. glabrous, and fls. slightly larger. Caucasus, Soviet cent. Asia, Iran.

PTELEA L. HOP TREE, SHRUBBY TREFOIL. *Rutaceae*. Three spp. of polygamous trees or shrubs, native to N. Amer.; lvs. alt., usually with 3 lfts., glandular-dotted, strongly aromatic; fls. greenish-white, in cymose panicles, unisexual and bisexual, sepals, petals, and stamens 4 or 5; fr. an orbicular, oblong, or cordate samara, with a reticulate wing.

Ornamental, treelike shrubs thriving in somewhat shady locations in porous soil and hardy north (Zone 5). Propagated by seeds sown in autumn, budding in summer, or layering or grafting in spring under glass.

crenulata Greene. Shrub or small tree, to 20 ft., bark red-brown; lfts. ovate to lanceolate or obovate, to 2$^3/_4$ in. long, yellow-green; filaments and ovary pubescent; samara orbicular, to 1 in. across. Cent. and n. Calif.

isophylla: *P. trifoliata*.

lutescens: *P. trifoliata* subsp. *pallida* var.

serrata: *P. trifoliata*.

trifoliata L. [*P. isophylla* Greene; *P. serrata* Small]. STINKING ASH, WATER A. Shrub or tree, to 25 ft., bark chestnut-brown; lfts. ovate, elliptic-ovate, to obovate, to 4 in. long or longer, dark green above; filaments hirsute, ovary usually glabrous; samara orbicular, to 1 in. across. N.Y., s. Ont., and Mich., s. to Fla. and Tex. Cv. **'Aurea'**. Lvs. bright yellow. Subsp. **pallida** (Greene) V. Bailey var. **lutescens** (Greene) V. Bailey [*P. lutescens* Greene]. Bark white; lfts. linear-lanceolate to oblong-lanceolate, 1$^1/_2$–3 in. long, pale green, glabrous. Nw. Ariz. and s. Utah. An extremely variable sp., comprising 5 subspp. and 10 vars.

PTELEOPSIS Engl. *Combretaceae*. About 5 spp. of polygamous trees and shrubs, native to E. Trop. Afr.; lvs. alt., petioled, leathery; racemes short, axillary; fls. small, 4-merous, stamens exserted; fr. elongate, 2(–4)-winged.

myrtifolia (M. Laws.) Engl. & Diels. To 50 ft., brs. drooping; lvs. oblong-elliptic, to 2$^1/_2$ in. long, glabrous; racemes to 1$^1/_2$ in. long; fls. white with yellow centers; fr. $^1/_2$ in. long, 2–4-winged. Kenya, Tanzania, ne. S. Afr.

PTERETIS: *MATTEUCCIA*.

PTERIDIUM Gled. BRACKEN, BRAKE. *Polypodiaceae*. One worldwide sp., a coarse terrestrial fern with 12 geographical vars.; lvs. triangular, 3–4-pinnate; sori borne in a marginal line, indusia double.

Foliage poisons livestock. Young croziers and rhizomes have been much eaten, but are now known to be carcinogenic. Easily transplanted and sometimes used as background in the rock garden or wherever large masses of ferns are desired; hardy, durable, but weedy. For culture see *Ferns*.

aquilinum (L.) Kuhn [*Pteris aquilina* L.]. BRAKE, PASTURE B., HOG-PASTURE B., BRACKEN. Lvs. to 4 ft. long and 3 ft. wide, densely pubescent beneath, 3-pinnate, pinnules oblong or lanceolate, petioles to 3 ft. long; indusia ciliate. Cosmopolitan. Var. **latiusculum** (Desv.) Underw. ex A. Heller [*P. latiusculum* (Desv.) Hieron. ex Fries]. The common form in e. N. Amer.; pinnules thinly pubescent along veins beneath; indusia not ciliate. Var. **pubescens** Underw. [*P. aquilinum* var. *lanuginosum* (Bong.) Fern.]. Lvs. strongly pubescent beneath and sometimes hairy above, pinnules linear-oblong. W. N. Amer., Mich., Ont., e. Que.

latiusculum: *P. aquilinum* var.

PTERIS L. BRAKE, DISH FERN, TABLE F. *Polypodiaceae.* About 280 spp. of mostly trop., terrestrial ferns; lvs. 1–4-pinnate; sori in a marginal line, covered by the revolute edge of lf.

For culture see *Ferns.*

adiantoides: *Pellaea viridis.*

Alexandrae: *P. cretica* cv.

aquilina: *Pteridium aquilinum.*

argyraea: *P. quadriaurita* cv.

Childsii: *P. cretica* cv.

comans G. Forst. Lvs. to about 3 ft. long, 1½ ft. wide, 1-pinnate-pinnatifid, the basal pinnae 2-pinnatifid, terminal pinnae pinnatifid into lobes, to 4 in. long, 1 in. wide, lateral pinnae coarsely lobed into blunt segms. New Zeal.

cordifolia: *Doryopteris cordifolia.*

crenata: *P. ensiformis.*

cretica L. CRETAN B. Lvs. to 1½ ft. long, 1-pinnate except for lower branched pinnae, pinnae over ¼ in. wide, rachis winged between upper first and second pairs of pinnae, petioles slender, straw-colored. Tropics and subtropics. Cv. 'Albo-lineata'. Lvs. white along center. Other cvs., among them crested, divided, or larger forms, are: 'Alexandrae' [*P. Alexandrae* Hort.], 'Childsii' [*P. childsii* Hort.], 'Cristata', 'Drinkwateri', 'Dutrei', 'Gautheri' [*P. Gautheri* Hort. ex Bernstiel], 'Magnifica', 'Major', 'Mayii', 'Nobilis', 'Ouvardii', 'Parkeri', 'Rivertoniana', 'Wilsonii', 'Wimsettii'.

crispa: *P. straminea.*

dentata Forssk. [*P. flabellata* Thunb.]. TOOTHED B. Lvs. herbaceous, erect, to 3 ft. long, glabrous, basally 3-pinnate, the pinnules folded. Afr.

ensiformis Burm.f. [*P. crenata* Swartz]. SWORD B. Fertile lvs. erect, to 20 in. long, 1-pinnate, pinnae to ¼ in. across, simple or coarsely lobed, sterile lvs. shorter, pinnae broader, to ¾ in. long and to ½ in. wide, simple or irregularly, coarsely lobed. E. Asia, Malay Pen., Australia. Cv. 'Victoriae' [*P. Victoriae* Bull]. VICTORIA B., SILVER-LEAF FERN. Pinnae banded with white.

flabellata: *P. dentata.*

Gautheri: *P. cretica* cv.

grandis: *P. Kunzeana,* but material listed as *P. grandis* may be a variant of *P. cretica* or *P. serrulata.*

heterophylla: *Anopteris hexagona.*

Kunzeana J. Agardh [*P. grandis* Hook.]. Plant large; lvs. 3 ft. long or more, 2-pinnate-pinnatifid at base, pinnate-pinnatifid above, pinnules linear-falcate, united basally, serrate, acuminate, glabrous. Tropics, New World.

longifolia L., not of auth. Similar to *P. vittata,* but differs in having articulate, deciduous pinnae. Tropics, New World. *P. longifolia* of most authors is *P. vittata.*

marginata: *P. tripartita.*

Mayii: a listed name of no botanical standing for *P. cretica* cv.

multiceps: a listed name of no botanical standing for a form with striking variegation.

multifida Poir. [*P. serrulata* of auth., not L.f.]. SPIDER B., CHINESE B. Lvs. to 1½ ft. long and 10 in. wide, 1-pinnate, pinnae very long, narrow, less than ¼ in. wide, lower pinnae 2–3-forked, rachis winged between upper 3 or more pairs of pinnae. E. Asia. There are many crested and other cvs., as 'Angustata', 'Charlesworthii', 'Corymbifera', 'Cristata', 'Nana', 'Variegata', 'Voluta'.

nodulosa: *Matteuccia pensylvanica.*

Ouvardii: a listed name of no botanical standing for *P. cretica* cv.

Parkeri: a listed name of no botanical standing for *P. cretica* cv.

quadriaurita Retz. Lvs. to 3 ft. long and 1½ ft. wide, 2-pinnate, 3-pinnate in lower part, lower pinnae forked, making 4 distinct divisions at base of lf. Tropics. Usually grown as the cv. 'Argyraea' [*P. argyraea* T. Moore], SILVER FERN, SILVER-LACE F., STRIPED B., pinnules with white stripes Cv. 'Tricolor'. Pinnules with whitish and reddish stripes.

Rivertoniana: a listed name of no botanical standing for *P. cretica* cv.

Roweii: a listed name of uncertain application.

semipinnata L. Lvs. to 18 in. long, 9 in. wide, triangular, pinnate-pinnatifid, the lowest pinnae to 2-pinnatifid on lower side, upper ones pinnatifid on lower side into oblong-linear pinnules. Asia.

serrulata: *P. multifida.*

straminea Mett. [*P. crispa* Hort.]. Lvs. to 18 in. long, narrowly triangular, pinnate-pinnatifid, pinnae ascending, lanceolate, 1½–2 in. wide, basal pinnae triangular, 2-pinnatifid, pinnules lanceolate, acute, dentate. Chile.

tremula R. Br. AUSTRALIAN B., AUSTRALIAN BRACKEN, POOR-MAN'S CIBOTIUM. Lvs. to 6 ft. long and 3 ft. wide, triangular, 2–4-pinnate, bright green. Australia, New Zeal.

tripartita Swartz [*P. marginata* Bory]. GIANT BRACKEN. Lvs. 3-parted, each division 1-pinnate, pinnae oblong, to 1 in. long, rachis winged. Tropics, Old World.

umbrosa R. Br. Lvs. to 3 ft. long, 2-pinnate at base, pinnae linear-lanceolate, to 12 in. long, toothed at apex, lower pinnae stalked, much-branched, giving lf. 3-parted appearance. Australia.

Victoriae: *P. ensiformis* cv.

vittata L. [*P. longifolia* of auth., not L.]. LADDER B. Lvs. to 4 ft. long and 1 ft. wide, 1-pinnate throughout, pinnae to 6 in. long and ⅜ in. wide, the fertile ones narrower. Tropics and subtropics, Old World. Cv. 'Mariesii'. Lvs. shorter.

Wilsonii: a listed name of no botanical standing for *P. cretica* cv.

Wimsettii: a listed name of no botanical standing for *P. cretica* cv.

PTEROCACTUS K. Schum. *Cactaceae.* Six spp. of low, more or less branched cacti, native to Argentina; roots tuberous, sts. cylindrical, joints mostly tubercled; lvs. minute, falling early; areoles with spines and glochids; fls. apical, perianth segms. separate, erect, ovary spiny; fr. dry, seeds winged, white.

For culture see *Cacti.*

Fischeri Britt. & Rose. Sts. to 4 in. high and ⅝ in. thick, tubercles spiralled; radial spines 12 or more, white, bristlelike, to ¼ in. long, central spines 4, brownish, to ⅝ in. long, glochids yellowish; ovary tubercled and spiny.

tuberosus (Pfeiff.) Britt. & Rose. Sts. branched from tuberous root, to 16 in. high and ⅜ in. thick, tubercles not prominent; spines many, white, appressed; fls. 1¼ in. long, ovary with long bristles; seeds to ½ in. across.

PTEROCARPUS Jacq. *Leguminosae* (subfamily *Faboideae*). Perhaps 100 spp. of trees, native to tropics of both hemispheres; lvs. alt., odd-pinnate, with alt. lfts.; fls. in racemes or panicles, showy, papilionaceous, frequently appearing before the lvs., petals yellow to orange, or whitish tinged violet, the standard and wings crisped, stamens united or the uppermost separate; fr. a flat, indehiscent legume, often with broad, membranous wings all around, 1–3-seeded.

Source of kino, dyes, and fine cabinet wood. Propagated by seeds or cuttings.

angolensis DC. To 40 ft., branchlets brown-villous; lfts. 12–20, ovate-oblong or sometimes nearly cordate, to 8 in. long, hairy when young, soon glabrate above, petiolules 5/16 in. long; infl. axillary, to 4½ in. long; fls. golden-yellow, standard obovate, to ⅝ in. wide; fr. orbicular, to 6 in. across. S.-W. Afr., S. Afr. to Angola and Tanzania.

echinatus Pers. Differs from *P. indicus* in having frs. with long spreading spines over the seeds. Philippine Is., Indonesia.

erinaceus Poir. SENEGAL ROSEWOOD, WEST AFRICAN KINO, BARWOOD. To 50 ft., buttressed in age, branchlets pubescent; lfts. to 12, oblong-elliptic, to 4 in. long, pubescent beneath; fls. bright yellow, produced when tree is nearly leafless; fr. orbicular, papery, to 3 in. across, prickly over the seeds, persistent. Senegal to Chad and Gabon. Wood useful in cabinetry and the source of a commercial red dye.

indicus Willd. PADAUK, PADOUK, BURMESE ROSEWOOD. To 80 ft. or more; lfts. ovate, to 4 in. long, blunt-acuminate, glabrous, with petiolules; panicles abundant; fls. yellow, more than ½ in. long, calyx brown-pubescent, petals longer than calyx; fr. orbicular, 2 in. across, silky-pubescent, veiny over the seeds. India to China, Malay Arch., Philippine Is. Planted in tropics. The durable wood, red with black stripes, is much in demand for furniture and cabinetwork.

macrocarpus Kurz. Branchlets, rachises, and infls. yellowish-pubescent; lfts. 7–11, leathery, ovate-oblong, to 2½ in. long, acute; racemes simple; calyx velvety, petals slightly longer than calyx; fr. nearly orbicular, to 2 in. across, gray-pubescent. Burma.

santalinus L.f. RED SANDERSWOOD, RED SANDALWOOD. Lfts. 3–5, ovate, to 4 in. long, obtuse, slightly emarginate, gray-pubescent beneath; standard not longer than calyx; fr. orbicular, 2 in. across, the center very turgid, wings less than ½ in. wide. Indonesia. A blood-red dye is obtained from the hard, fragrant wood.

violaceus Vogel. To 60 ft.; lfts. 5–9, ovate, to 3 in. long, glabrous; racemes axillary, to 3 in. long, infl. and calyx pubescent; fls. about ½ in. long, petals golden, standard orbicular, emarginate, violet-spotted; fr. flat, obovate to elliptic, to 2½ in. long, the wing leathery, wide, often undulate-irregular. Trop. e. Brazil.

PTEROCARYA Kunth. WINGNUT. *Juglandaceae.* About 10 spp. of deciduous, monoecious trees, with lamellate pith, mostly in China, 1 in Japan, and 1 in w. Asia; lvs. alt., odd-pinnate; male and female fls. in drooping catkins; fr. a winged nutlet.

Several species are grown as ornamental trees for the attractive foliage and pendent catkins. Of rapid growth, but some species require protection in the North when young. Propagated by seeds, layers, or suckers.

caucasica: *P. fraxinifolia.*

fraxinifolia (Lam.) Spach [*P. caucasica* C. A. Mey.]. CAUCASIAN W. To 100 ft.; lfts. 11–20, ovate-oblong or oblong-lanceolate, to 5 in. long; fr. with nearly orbicular wings, in racemes to 1½ ft. long. Caucasus to Iran. Zone 6.

japonica: *P. stenoptera.*

×**Rehderana** C. K. Schneid.: *P. fraxinifolia* × *P. stenoptera.* Lf. rachis more or less winged, lfts. somewhat smaller and narrower than those of parents; wings of fr. elliptic or ovate-oblong, longer than broad. Spreads by suckers, apparently more hardy than either of parents.

rhoifolia Siebold & Zucc. To 100 ft.; lfts. 11–21, ovate-oblong, to 5 in. long; fr. with wing broader than long, in racemes to 1 ft. long. Japan, where the wood is used for utilitarian articles. Zone 6.

sinensis: *P. stenoptera.*

stenoptera C. DC. [*P. japonica* Miq.; *P. sinensis* Hort. ex Rehd.]. CHINESE W. To 100 ft.; lvs. with a winged rachis, lfts. 11–23, oblong, to 4 in. long or more; fr. with oblong wings, in racemes to 1 ft. long. China. Zone 7.

PTEROCEPHALUS Adans. *Dipsacaceae.* About 20 spp. of ann. or per. herbs or subshrubs, native from Medit. region and trop. Afr. to the Himalayas and w. China; lvs. opp., entire to pinnatifid, often sessile; fls. pink to purple, in long-peduncled, involucrate heads, calyx with 10 or more pappuslike awns, enveloped by an involucel, corolla 5-lobed, marginal fls. 2-lipped, stamens 4; fr. an achene.

Hookeri (C. B. Clarke) Airy-Shaw & M. L. Green. Per. herb, to 1 ft.; lvs. basal, somewhat tufted, oblanceolate, to 8 in. long, entire to pinnatifid; heads to 2½ in. across; fls. pale violet, anthers dark purple. Bhutan, China.

parnassi K. Spreng. [*Scabiosa pterocephala* L.]. Spreading, deep-rooted per., sts. tufted, making broad cushions, 3 or 4 in. high; lvs. simple, ovate to lyrate-pinnatifid, to 1½ in. long, crenate, densely pubescent; heads about 1 in. across; fls. purplish-pink, anthers purplish-pink. Mts., Greece.

pyrenaicus: a listed name of no botanical standing; used for *Scabiosa pyrenaica.*

PTEROGYNE Tulasne. *Leguminosae* (subfamily *Caesalpinioideae*). One sp., an unarmed tree, native to s. S. Amer.; lvs. alt., odd-pinnate; fls. in short axillary racemes, small, regular, 5-merous, calyx tube short, stamens 10, separate; fr. a samaralike, 1-seeded legume.

nitens Tulasne. To 50 ft.; lvs. about 1 ft. long, lfts. mostly alt., 10–18, oblong or elliptic-obtuse, to 2¼ in. long, glossy above; racemes 3–5 together, to about 1½ in. long; fls. fragrant, whitish; fr. about 1½ in. long. Brazil, Bolivia, Paraguay, n. Argentina. Produces a useful hard wood.

PTEROLOBIUM R. Br. ex Wight & Arn. *Leguminosae* (subfamily *Caesalpinioideae*). About 10 spp. of trop. lianas, shrubs, or trees of the Old World; lvs. alt., 2-pinnate, with recurved spines in pairs at insertion of lvs. and pinnae; fls. in panicles or racemes, almost regular, 5-merous, with 1 sepal larger than others, petals oblong or obovate, nearly as long as sepals, stamens 10, separate; fr. an indehiscent, winged, samaralike legume, with flat seeds.

exosum (J. F. Gmel.) Bak.f. Liana, to 16 ft.; lvs. to 8 in. long, pinnae in 8–12 pairs, lfts. in 9–16 pairs, oblong, to ⅜ in. long, blunt, asymmetrical at base; racemes loose, spicate; fls. white or yellowish, about ⅛ in. long; fr. obliquely oblong-oblanceolate, to 2 in. long. Ethiopia to Rhodesia.

PTEROSPERMUM Schreb. *Byttneriaceae.* About 25 spp. of shrubs or tree, native to trop. Asia; lvs. alt., 2-ranked, simple, leathery; fls. mostly axillary, solitary or in few-fld. cymes, 5-merous, sepals linear, nearly separate, deciduous with the petals; androgynophore short, stamens 15, with long filaments but shorter than the 5 linear-subulate staminodes; fr. a woody or leathery, loculicidally dehiscent, 5-celled caps., seeds many, flattened, winged apically.

One species is cultivated in Zone 10 in Fla.; propagated by cuttings of the side shoots.

acerifolium (L.) Willd. Tree, to 100 ft.; lvs. ovate to orbicular in outline, to 14 in. across, mostly palmately lobed and nerved, peltate or cordate at base, truncate-mucronate at apex; sepals rusty-tomentose, to 6 in. long, slightly longer than the white petals; caps. to 6 in. long, seeds ¾–2½ in. long, including the wing. India to Java. Has a durable teaklike wood.

PTEROSPORA Nutt. PINEDROPS. *Pyrolaceae.* One sp., a stout, purple-brown, root-parasitic herb with clammy pubescence, native to N. Amer.; lvs. scalelike; fls. white to red, in a long, terminal raceme, calyx 5-parted, corolla urceolate, 5-lobed, stamens 10; fr. a 5-celled caps.

andromedea Nutt. GIANT BIRD'S-NEST. To 3 ft.; lvs. crowded in lower part, lanceolate, to 1⅜ in. long; caps. ½ in. across. Summer.

PTEROSTYRAX Siebold & Zucc. EPAULETTE TREE. *Styracaceae.* Four spp. of deciduous trees or shrubs, native to e. Asia; lvs. alt., petioled, serrate; fls. white, in large panicles, calyx 5-toothed, petals 5, separate or basally coherent, stamens 10, exserted, ovary partly inferior, 3(–5)-celled; fr. dry, oblong, ribbed or winged.

These ornamental plants thrive in rather moist sandy loam. Propagated by seeds, layering, and cuttings of young wood. Zone 7.

corymbosus Siebold & Zucc. Shrub or tree; lvs. elliptic to ovate, to 5 in. long; panicles corymbose, to 5 in. long; fr. obovoid, 5-winged, stellate-hairy. Japan, China.

hispidus Siebold & Zucc. To 50 ft.; lvs. oblong, to 7 in. long; panicles drooping, to 10 in. long; fls. fragrant; fr. spindle-shaped, prominently 10-ribbed but not winged, densely bristly. Japan, China.

PTERYGOTA Schott & Endl. *Sterculiaceae.* About 15 spp. of monoecious or polygamous trees, native to the New and Old World tropics, differing from *Sterculia* and *Brachychiton* chiefly in having winged seeds. One sp. introd. into s. Fla.

alata (Roxb.) R. Br. [*Sterculia alata* Roxb.]. Large tree with straight, ash-colored trunk buttressed at the base; lvs. clustered at ends of brs., cordate-ovate, sometimes lobed apically, to 12 in. long; fls. in axillary panicles, calyx about 1 in. long, rusty-tomentose; fr. of up to 5 woody, pubescent follicles, each to 5 in. across, seeds many, with large wing to 2½ in. long. Trop. Asia.

PTERYXIA Nutt. *Umbelliferae.* Not. cult. **P. anisata:** *Aletes anisatus.*

PTYCHANDRA: *HETEROSPATHE.*

PTYCHOCOCCUS Becc. *Palmae.* About 8 spp. of solitary, unarmed, monoecious palms from New Guinea to the Solomon Is.; lvs. pinnate, sheath tubular, forming a prominent crownshaft, pinnae broadest at middle, obliquely toothed at apex, midrib and marginal veins prominent; infls. below lvs., peduncle short, bracts 2, deciduous, the lower enclosing the upper, lower brs. 1–2 times branched, rachillae with fls. in triads (2 male and 1 female) nearly throughout, or near the apex with only paired or solitary male fls.; male fls. symmetrical, sepals 3, imbricate, petals 3, valvate, stamens many, anthers attached by back, pistillode ovoid-attenuate, as long as stamens, female fls. symmetrical, sepals 3, imbricate, petals 3, imbricate, staminodes toothed, pistil 1-celled, 1-ovuled; fr. red, ovoid, with apical stigmatic residue, endocarp thick, bony, black, acute, ribbed, seed acute, 5-ribbed, endosperm homogeneous or ruminate, embryo basal.

For culture see *Palms.*

paradoxus (Scheff.) Becc. To 25 ft. or more, sts. to 9 in. in diam.; lvs. 8 ft. long, petiole very short; pinnae to 32 in. long, 2 in. wide; male fls. ½ in. long; fr. 2 in. long, 1½ in. in diam., seed with ruminate endosperm. New Guinea.

PTYCHORAPHIS: *RHOPALOBLASTE.*

PTYCHOSPERMA Labill. [*Actinophloeus* (Becc.) Becc.; *Seaforthia* R. Br.; *Strongylocaryum* Burret]. *Palmae.* About 30 spp. of solitary or cespitose, unarmed, monoecious palms of Australia and New Guinea to the Solomon Is. and Micronesia; lvs. pinnate, sheath tubular, forming a prominent crownshaft, pinnae cuneate to linear, obliquely toothed at the apex, midrib and marginal veins prominent; infl. below lvs., usually short-peduncled, bracts 2, deciduous, the lower usually enclosing the upper, rachis elongate, lower brs. simple or forked to twice-branched, rachillae with fls. in triads (2 male and 1 female) nearly throughout, or near the apex with only paired or solitary male fls.; male fls. symmetrical, sepals 3, imbricate, petals 3, valvate, stamens many, filaments erect, anthers attached by back, pistillode usually ovoid-attenuate and as long as the stamens but sometimes conic-ovoid and short, female fls. with sepals 3, imbricate, petals 3, imbricate, staminodes 1–6, toothlike, pistil 1-celled, 1-ovuled; fr. ovoid to ellipsoid, with apical stigmatic residue, red, orange, or black, endocarp thin, seed longitudinally 3–5-sulcate, sometimes weakly so, endosperm homogeneous or ruminate, embryo basal.

Some species are attractive ornamentals for tropical or subtropical plantings. Zone 10a in Fla. For culture see *Palms.*

Alexandrae: *Archontophoenix Alexandrae.*

angustifolium Blume. An obscure sp. not identified with certainty, even to genus. For material cult. under this name see *P. Schefferi.*

Cunninghamianum: *Archontophoenix Cunninghamiana.*

elegans (R. Br.) Blume [*Seaforthia elegans* R. Br.]. ALEXANDER PALM, SOLITAIRE P. St. solitary, slender, to 25 ft. or more; lvs. to 8 ft. long, pinnae regularly arranged, about 28 on each side, to 2 ft. long, 3 in. wide, with many elongate, twisted scales beneath; infl. green, with lower brs. twice-branched; male fls. fragrant, green with white stamens; fr. red, ovoid, ¾ in. long, seed with ruminate endosperm. Ne. Australia; naturalized in s. Fla. Sometimes grown under the name *Hydriastele Wendlandiana.* Small size and delicate trunks make this a useful palm where garden space is limited.

hospitum: *P. Macarthurii.*

Kerstenianum (Hort. Sander) Burret. Described from a juvenile plant which cannot be identified with certainty. The name has become much confused in hort.

Macarthurii (H. Wendl.) Nichols. [*Actinophloeus Macarthurii* (H. Wendl.) Becc.; *Kentia Macarthurii* H. Wendl.; *P. hospitum* (Burret) Burret]. MACARTHUR PALM, MACARTHUR FEATHER P., HURRICANE P. Sts. slender, cespitose, to 20 ft. or more; lvs. several ft. long, pinnae regularly arranged, mostly 40–50 on each side, to about 1 ft. long, 2 in. wide, upper margin longest; fr. red, ovoid, ½–¾ in. long, seed with homogeneous endosperm. New Guinea. Suited to small garden or tub culture.

Nicolai (Hort. Sander ex André) Burret. Described from juvenile plants; the name cannot be applied clearly to any sp.

propinquum (Becc.) Becc. Sts. low, to about 6 ft. high, ¾ in. in diam.; lvs. to nearly 5 ft. long, pinnae 12–13 on each side, irregularly arranged, to 14 in. long, both margins longer than middle but upper margin longest; infl. densely brown-black-scaly, brs. all simple except the lower 2 forked; male fls. to ⁵⁄₁₆ in. long, stamens about 50; fr. not known. Aru Is. Plants cult. under this name are probably misidentified.

salomonense Burret [*Strongylocaryum latius* Burret]. To 20 ft. or more, sts. to 3 in. in diam.; lvs. about 4 ft. long, with 19–25 pinnae on each side; infl. brownish, lower brs. twice-branched; male fls. brownish, ¼ in. long, stamens 20–25; fr. orange-red, about ½ in. long, seed very shallowly grooved or nearly round in cross section, endosperm ruminate. Solomon Is.

Sanderanum Ridl. [*Actinophloeus Sanderanus* (Ridl.) Burret]. Cespitose, to 15 ft., sts. to 1 in. in diam.; lvs. to 4 ft. long, pinnae 40–50 or more on each side, regularly arranged, slender, to 18 in. long, ½ in. wide, notched at apex; infl. with few, densely brown-black-scaly, simple rachillae; male fls. ³⁄₁₆ in. long, stamens 15 or more; fr. red, crowded, ⅝ in. long, ⅜ in. in diam., endosperm homogeneous. New Guinea.

Schefferi Becc. [*P. angustifolium* Scheff., not Blume]. Sts. cespitose, to 20 ft.; lvs. to 6 ft. long, pinnae about 27 on each side, regularly arranged, to 18 in. long, 2 in. wide; infl. dull reddish in fr.; fr. black with pink perianth below, ⅝ in. long, seed with marginally ruminate endosperm. Sometimes grown under the name *Coleospadix oninensis.*

singaporense: *Rhopaloblaste singaporensis.*

Waitianum Essig. St. solitary, to 15 ft., about ¾ in. in diam.; lvs. to 2½ ft. long, pinnae 8–9 on each side, regularly arranged, cuneate, to 4½ in. long, apex concave, very coarsely toothed, lower surface bearing many narrow, dark, twisted scales; infl. to about 10 in. long and broad, few-branched, reddish and densely brown-black-scaly; fls. dark-scaly, male buds about ¼ in. long, stamens about 20; fr. black, ⅝ in. long, seed with homogeneous endosperm. New Guinea.

PUERARIA DC. *Leguminosae* (subfamily *Faboideae*). About 15 spp. of herbaceous or woody twiners, native to se. Asia; lvs. of 3 lfts.; fls. clustered in axillary racemes, blue or purple, papilionaceous, standard usually eared at base; fr. a linear, flat, dehiscent legume.

One species, *P. lobata,* is widely grown in southeastern U.S. as a fodder plant, to control erosion, and sometimes as an ornamental; in some areas it has become a rampant weed. Some species yield economic and medicinal products used in their native regions. Propagated by division, seeds, and cuttings.

hirsuta: *P. lobata.*

lobata (Willd.) Ohwi [*P. hirsuta* (Thunb.) C. K. Schneid.; *P. Thunbergiana* (Siebold & Zucc.) Benth.]. KUDZU VINE, KUDSU. Somewhat woody, hairy vine, to 60 ft.; lfts. wide-ovate or rhomboidal, to 6 in. long, entire or with shallow lobes; racemes to 1 ft. long; fls. fragrant, reddish-purple; fr. hairy, to 4 in. long. Late summer. China, Japan. Hardy in Zone 5, although sts. may be killed back to ground and not reach flowering stage.

phaseoloides (Roxb.) Benth. TROPICAL KUDZU. Sts. twining, 20 ft. or more, brown-hairy; lfts. roundish to rhomboid-ovate, to 6 in. long, entire to deeply 3-lobed, gray with densely matted hairs beneath; petals lavender and white; fr. glabrescent, to 4 in. long. Himalayas to China and Malay Arch.

Thunbergiana: *P. lobata.*

PULMONARIA L. LUNGWORT. *Boraginaceae.* About 12 spp. of hairy, spring-flowering, per. herbs of Eur. and Asia; rhizomes creeping; lvs. simple, green or white-spotted, basal lvs. long-petioled, st. lvs. few, alt.; fls. blue, purplish, pink, or white, in mostly bracted, terminal, forked cymes, calyx 5-lobed, corolla 5-lobed, without scales in the throat but with 5 tufts of hairs, stamens 5, included; fr. of 4 smooth nutlets, base of nutlets with a tubular annular rim.

Suitable for the flower garden and border. Of easy cultivation; propagated by division.

angustifolia L. [*P. azurea* Bess.]. Setose-hairy per., to 1 ft.; lvs. green, basal lvs. linear-lanceolate to oblong-lanceolate, st. lvs. linear-lanceolate to linear-elliptic; fls. blue. Eur. Color variations of rose and white have been given cv. names.

azurea: *P. angustifolia.*

lutea: a listed name of no botanical standing.

maculata: *P. officinalis.*

mollis: *P. montana.*

montana Lej. [*P. mollis* C. F. Wolff ex Heller; *P. rubra* Schott]. Soft-hairy per., to 1½ ft.; lvs. green, broadly elliptic-lanceolate to ovate, soft-hairy, acuminate; fls. violet, to ¾ in. long. Cent. Eur.

officinalis L. [*P. maculata* F. Dietr.]. BLUE L., JERUSALEM SAGE, JERUSALEM COWSLIP. Rough-hairy per., to 1 ft.; lvs. white-spotted, basal lvs. ovate, cordate, petioled, st. lvs. ovate, auriculate-cordate, sessile; fls. rose-violet to blue, seldom reddish, to ¾ in. long. Eur. Var. **immaculata** Opiz. Lvs. entirely green. Dried lvs. formerly used in medicine.

rubra: *P. montana.*

saccharata Mill. BETHLEHEM SAGE. Setose-hairy per., to 1½ ft.; lvs. white-spotted, basal lvs. elliptic, narrowed to petiole, acuminate, st. lvs. ovate-oblong, petioled or sessile; fls. whitish or reddish-violet, ¾–1 in. long. Eur.

PULSATILLA: *ANEMONE.* P. hirsutissima: *A. Nuttalliana.* P. vulgaris: *A. Pulsatilla.*

PULTENAEA Sm. *Leguminosae* (subfamily *Faboideae*). More than 90 spp. of shrubs, native to Australia; lvs. simple, alt. or rarely opp.; fls. solitary or in terminal heads, orange-yellow or variegated purple, papilionaceous, stamens separate; fr. a small, ovate legume.

Adapted to Calif. Propagated by seeds, or cuttings of the tips of shoots.

daphnoides H. L. Wendl. To 6 ft.; lvs. oblong-cuneate, to 1½ in. long, obtuse to truncate, mucronate; fls. in dense, sessile heads surrounded by an involucre of lvs., bright yellow with scarlet keels. Temp. Australia.

PUMPKIN, SQUASH. The various cultivars (as well as the fruits) of *Cucurbita Pepo, C. mixta, C. moschata,* and *C. maxima* are known as pumpkins and squashes, with usage varying according to time and location (see *Cucurbita*). There is confusion about the common names, since cultivars known as winter squashes and others known as pumpkins are found in all four species.

The clearest usage is of the term summer squash, which refers to fruits eaten when immature, from as early as the day of flowering to the stage when the rind is starting to harden. Essentially all summer squash is *C. Pepo,* but not all *C. Pepo* is summer squash; this species also includes winter squash, pumpkins, and certain ornamental gourds. Summer squash includes fruits with a range of shapes and colors, from the white scallops or pattypans to the cylindrical solid green zucchinis or striped cocozelles and the yellow straightneck and crookneck types. Cultivars with new combinations of colors and shapes appear from time to time.

Winter squash refers to fruits eaten when mature or stored for winter use. In contrast to summer squash, which is usually cooked by boiling, winter squash is most commonly baked. Examples of winter squash are cultivars 'Banana', 'Boston Marrow', 'Buttercup' (all *C. maxima*), 'Butternut' *(C. moschata),* 'Delicious' *(C. maxima),* 'Green-Striped Cushaw' *(C. mixta),* and 'Hubbard' *(C. maxima).* The winter squashes generally have flesh which is darker orange in color, less fibrous, and higher in sugar and dry matter than either pumpkins or mature summer squash.

No clear and consistent distinction can be made between winter squashes and pumpkins, both being used when mature and both having representatives in all four species of *Cucurbita.* However, in this country the cultivars used for pies, stock feed, or decorative jack-o-lanterns are commonly called pumpkins. Many of them tend toward spherical or at least symmetrical shape and orange exterior color, while internally the flesh is usually paler, more fibrous, and less sweet than in winter squashes. Among cultivars called pumpkins are 'Connecticut Field' and 'Small Sugar', which are *C. Pepo,* 'Japanese Pie' *(C. mixta),* 'Dickinson' *(C. moschata),* and 'Big Max' *(C. maxima).* 'Queensland Blue' *(C. maxima)* is called a pumpkin in Australia, where it is widely used, but in the United States it would be considered a typical winter squash, somewhat like 'Blue Hubbard'.

All squashes and pumpkins are similar in culture, being frost-tender annuals. They are usually direct-seeded but may be transplanted from pots, bands, or blocks, which minimize root disturbance. Transplanting should be done within seven to 14 days from seeding, since growth is very rapid. Most summer squashes are bush plants which can be grown 3 feet apart in rows 4–6 feet apart. Two to six plants will produce enough summer squash for the average family if picked frequently. Some bush forms of winter squash and pumpkin are available in *C. Pepo* and *C. maxima* and they can be spaced the same as summer squash. Many of these bush forms lack the quality of the viny ones, but some good ones are available. The traditional viny types will easily cover the ground if planted in rows 9–12 feet apart with plants 3–4 feet apart in the rows. In the North, winter squashes should be planted as early as weather permits and allowed to mature well on the vine in order to get the best quality. They should be harvested when fully mature or just after the first light frost.

Striped cucumber beetles are the main pest early in the season, with aphids, squash bugs, and vine borers occasionally causing trouble later. Control can be effected with a general purpose garden insecticide. Diseases are usually not a serious problem in the home garden, but if virus diseases or vine borers are present consistently, a cultivar of *C. moschata,* such as 'Butternut', should be chosen as a winter squash.

Choice of a summer squash cultivar depends largely on preference for color and shape, since none has a pronounced flavor. Winter squashes, however, vary considerably in depth of flesh, color intensity, texture, and flavor. 'Butternut' is one of the most dependably good ones, while 'Delicious' and 'Buttercup' *(C. maxima)* have somewhat different flavor and are preferred by some. 'Table Queen' *(C. Pepo)* is a very popular type, with the advantage of convenient fruit size and earlier maturity, but it is more susceptible to most diseases, and cultivars in the group vary considerably in quality.

Winter squash is best stored at 50–60° F. Storage below 50° causes chilling injury and reduces storage life. An initial curing period at 70–80° F for two to three weeks after harvest has been recommended for winter squash, but this is detrimental to quality in 'Table Queen'. It may improve the quality of the other types by hastening the conversion of starch to sugar. 'Table Queen' cannot be stored much longer than two to three months, but the other types can sometimes be kept for five to six months if they are free of disease and injury when put in storage. However, the quality of all types deteriorates gradually after the first two to three months. When quality of a lot of home-stored squash is at its best, it can be preserved by cooking the squash and freezing the edible flesh, frozen squash being essentially indistinguishable on the table from that which is freshly cooked.

PUNCTILLARIA: *PLEIOSPILOS.*

PUNICA L. *Punicaceae.* Two spp. of deciduous shrubs or small trees of se. Eur. and s. Asia, with characters of the family.

One species, the pomegranate, is widely cultivated in tropical and subtropical climates for its edible fruit and as an ornamental. It is also a popular greenhouse plant. It does best in deep, rather heavy loam. Propagated by hardwood cuttings in spring, softwood cuttings in summer, or by seeds or layering. See also *Pomegranate.*

Granatum L. POMEGRANATE. To 20 ft. or more, sometimes spiny; lvs. oblong to lanceolate, to 3 in. long, entire, glabrous, glossy; fls. to 1½ in. across, solitary or clustered at ends of branchlets, calyx purplish, petals crinkled, orange-red; fr. subglobose, 2½–5 in. in diam., brownish-yellow to purplish-red, with thick skin and persistent calyx, seeds many, each enclosed in a juicy, edible, red-purple pulp. Summer–autumn. Zone 9. Cult. for its fr. since ancient times. Cvs. include: **'Alba Plena'** [cv. 'Multiplex'], fls. double, creamy-white; **'Chico',** to 8 ft. or more, lvs. to 1½ in. long, fls. 1–2 in. across, double, orange-red, produced all summer, apparently not fruiting; **'Flore Pleno'** [cvs. Pleniflora', 'Rubra Plena'], fls. double, red; **'Legrellei'** [cvs. 'Mme. Legrelle', 'Variegata'], fls. double, orange-red, margined and streaked with yellowish-white; **'Mme. Legrelle':** 'Legrellei'; **'Multiplex':** 'Alba Plena'; **'Nana'** [var. *nana* (L.) Pers.] DWARF POMEGRANATE, dwarf, compact shrub, to 6 ft., often grown as a low hedge in the South and also as a pot plant, flowering when still very small, lvs. ¾–1½ in. long, fls. single, red-orange, 1 in. across, fr. 2 in. across; **'Pleniflora':** 'Flore Pleno'; **'Rubra Plena':** 'Flore Pleno'; **'Variegata':** 'Legrellei'; **'Wonderful',** commercial and also ornamental cv., fls. orange-red, double, to 3 in. across, frs. very large, pale green-yellow suffused with red.

Legrellei: a hort. name for *P. Granatum* cv.

sempervirens: a listed name of no botanical standing, doubtless to be referred to *P. Granatum.*

PUNICACEAE Horan. POMEGRANATE FAMILY. Dicot.; 1 genus, *Punica,* of shrubs or trees, native to se. Eur. and s. Asia; lvs. mostly opp.; fls. bisexual, tube campanulate to tubular, calyx lobes 5–8, persistent, the 5–8 petals and many stamens inserted on fl. tube, ovary inferior, cells 3–7 in 2 series, style and stigma 1; fr. a leathery-skinned berry, seeds many, surrounded by juicy, edible pulp.

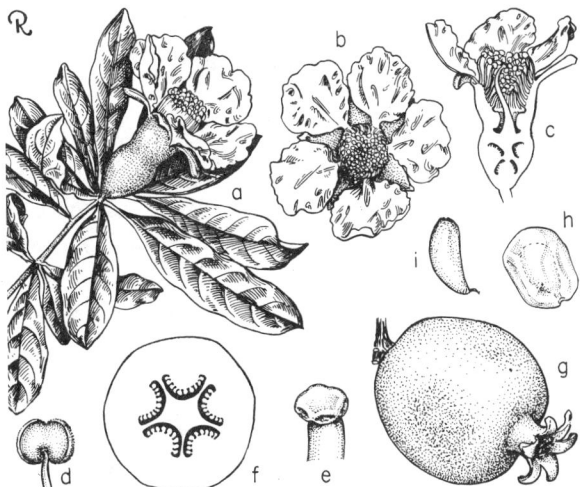

PUNICACEAE. *Punica Granatum:* **a,** flowering twig, × ½; **b,** flower, × ½; **c,** flower, vertical section, × ½; **d,** anther, × 5; **e,** stigma, × 4; **f,** ovary, cross section, × 1½; **g,** fruit, × ¼; **h,** seed enclosed by pulp, × 1; **i,** seed, × 1½.

PURSHIA DC. ex Poir. ANTELOPE BUSH. *Rosaceae.* Two spp. of unarmed shrubs in w. N. Amer.; lvs. crowded, apparently fascicled, deeply 3-cleft with revolute margins; fls. solitary, at ends of short brs., calyx tube more or less funnelform, persistent, sepals 5, petals 5, cream to yellow, stamens about 25; fr. an achene, style persistent, rather short.

glandulosa Curran. Greenish shrub, to 12 ft., twigs glabrous, glandular; lvs. to ½ in. long, slightly tomentose beneath, glabrous above, punctate-glandular; petals ⁵⁄₁₆ in. long. S. Calif., Nev., Ariz., n. Baja Calif.

tridentata (Pursh) DC. To 10 ft., twigs more or less glandular and tomentose; lvs. cuneate, to 1 in. long, white-tomentose beneath; petals ⁵⁄₁₆ in. long. Cent. Calif. to B.C., e. to Mont., New Mex. Zone 6.

PUSCHKINIA Adams. *Liliaceae.* Two spp. of spring-blooming, bulbous per. herbs, native to Asia Minor and the Caucasus; lvs. basal; fls. white or blue, in a raceme on a scape, perianth segms. 6, united into a short tube, stamens 6, filaments united into a cuplike crown, anthers versatile; fr. a 3-valved, loculicidal caps.

Sometimes grown in rock gardens or borders. For culture see *Scilla.*

libanotica: *P. scilloides* var.

scilloides Adams. To 6 in.; lvs. linear-strap-shaped, to 6 in. long and ½ in. wide; fls. bluish, ½ in. long. Asia Minor and Caucasus. Var. *libanotica* (Zucc.) Boiss. [*P. libanotica* Zucc.] Fls. smaller, crown sharply toothed. Lebanon. Cv. 'Alba'. Fls. white.

PUTORIA Pers. *Rubiaceae.* About 3 spp. of low, much-branched, unpleasant-smelling shrubs, native to Medit. region; lvs. opp., stipules interpetiolar, short, blunt; fls. in terminal clusters; fr. a small, linear-oblong drupe.

Propagated by seeds or division; does well in full sun in sandy soil; perhaps not hardy north.

calabrica (L.f.) Pers. To 8 in. or less, brs. velvety-hairy; lvs. short-petioled, linear-oblong, to ½ in. long or more, somewhat fleshy, margins scabrous; fls. red to reddish-purple, in terminal few-fld. corymbs, calyx tubular, 4-toothed, corolla tubular, to 1 in. long, 4-lobed.

PUTRANJIVA Wallich. *Euphorbiaceae.* Four spp. of dioecious or monoecious hardwood trees, native to India, Ceylon, and Borneo; lvs. alt., pinnately veined, serrate, short-petioled; fls. small, male fls. in axillary clusters, female fls. few, solitary in lf. axils, on long peduncles, ovary 2–3-celled; fr. a drupe.

Roxburghii Wallich. Fairly large, dioecious tree, brs. slender, drooping; lvs. 2-ranked, elliptic, 2½–5 in. long, glossy-green; fr. about ½ in. long. India.

PUTTERLICKIA Endl. *Celastraceae.* Two spp. of evergreen, glabrous, spiny shrubs, native to S. Afr.; lvs. alt. or in clusters, simple, leathery; fls. white, in loose, several-fld. cymes, sepals, petals, and stamens 5; fr. a 3-valved caps., seeds 6 in each cell, with an aril.

pyracantha (L.) Endl. Rigid shrub, 2–10 ft.; lvs. oblong to obovate, to 2 in. long, cuneate; caps. red, seeds black, partly enclosed in orange aril.

PUYA Mol. *Bromeliaceae.* About 168 spp. of terrestrial, stiff, often giant herbs, native to dry parts, mostly Andean, of S. Amer.; lvs. in dense rosettes, spiny-margined; fls. blue, purple, or yellow, in solitary or panicled spikes or racemes, petals separate, ovary superior; fr. a caps., seeds winged.

Grown occasionally outdoors in full sun in mild climates or in the greenhouse. Most puyas thrive without special treatment outdoors in Zone 10 in Calif. For culture see *Bromeliaceae.*

alpestris (Poepp.) C. Gay. Not cult., material cult. under this name is *P. Berteroniana.*

Berteroniana Mez. Lvs. to 3 ft. long, ½ in. wide, tapering to slender apex, light green above, pale beneath; infl. paniculate; fls. metallic greenish-blue. Chile. Sometimes grown as *P. alpestris.*

chilensis Mol. Sts. simple or branched, to 15 ft. high, 8 in. thick; lvs. to 3 ft. long, 2 in. wide, glaucous; infl. paniculate, brs. sterile above the middle; fls. yellow, to 3 in. long. Chile. Lvs. furnish a fiber used for making fish nets.

coerulea Lindl. [*Pitcairnia coerulea* (Lindl.) Benth. ex Bak.]. To 6 ft.; lvs. 2 ft. long, narrow; infl. branched, sterile bracts few or none; fls. deep blue, to 2 in. long, petals auricled inside. Chile.

ferruginea (Ruiz & Pav.) L. B. Sm. [*Pitcairnia consimilis* Bak.; *P. ferruginea* Ruiz & Pav.]. Woody-stemmed; lvs. many, all alike, to 6 ft. long, 2 in. wide, spiny; infl. paniculate, 3 ft. long or more, reddish-tomentose; fls. greenish-white, to 5½ in. long, petals without appendages. N. S. Amer.

floccosa (Linden) E. Morr. ex Mez. To 3 ft. or more; lvs. very many, to 3 ft. long or more, 1¼ in. wide, with stout spines, scurfy beneath; infl. paniculate, brs. fertile throughout, more than twice as long as subtending bracts; fls. to 1¾ in. long, erect, pedicels ³⁄₁₆ in. long, sepals densely hairy, petals blue. Mts., Guyana, Venezuela, Colombia.

hortensis L. B. Sm. Stemless, to 3 ft. or more; lvs. to 2½ ft. long, 2⅝ in. wide; infl. loosely 2-pinnate, pale tomentose, the naked base of brs. shorter than subtending primary bract, fl. bracts reaching to middle of sepals; fls. red-purple, petals without appendages, over 2⅝ in. long. Origin uncertain.

Raimondii Harms. Monocarpic, st. simple, to 10 ft. or more; lvs. to 4 ft. long; infl. to 25 ft. or more, dense, brs. to 1 ft. long, sterile above the middle, fl. bracts longer than sepals; fls. white, 2⅛ in. long. S. Peru, Bolivia.

spathacea (Griseb.) Mez. Stemless, to 3 ft.; lvs. to 16 in. long, ¾ in. wide; infl. 2-pinnate, sterile bracts few or 0; fls. pale blue, to 1⅜ in. long, petals without appendages. Argentina.

violacea (Brongn.) Mez. To 3 ft.; lvs. to 18 in. long, ¼ in. wide, spines short, ⅜–¾ in. apart; infl. usually paniculate, brs. suberect, more than twice as long as their subtending bracts, fertile throughout; fls. deep violet, pedicels suberect, soon glabrous, sepals rounded-mucronate, to ⅞ in. long. Chile.

PYCNANTHEMUM Michx. MOUNTAIN MINT. *Labiatae.* About 20 spp. of erect, per. herbs of N. Amer., with a pungent, mintlike odor when crushed; sts. mostly square in cross section; lvs. opp., entire or toothed; fls. in terminal or axillary heads or cymose clusters, calyx tubular, 10–13-nerved, 5-toothed, corolla whitish or pinkish, often dotted purple, 2-lipped, upper lip entire or emarginate, lower lip 3-lobed, stamens 4, in 2 pairs, anther sacs parallel; fr. of 4 smooth, pubescent or rugose nutlets.

Blooming in summer or autumn. Easily propagated by seeds or division.

flexuosum (Walt.) BSP. Sts. gray-green, to 3 ft. or more, puberulent; lvs. linear-oblong, to oblong-lanceolate, mostly 1–2 in. long, bluntly acute; heads solitary at br. tips or in upper axils; calyx teeth about ⅛ in. long, stiffly awned and yellowish, corolla white to pink, tube about ¼ in. long. On dry soils, Va. to Fla., w. to Tenn. and Ala. Much of the material offered under this name is *P. tenuifolium.*

muticum (Michx.) Pers. Sts. to 3 ft., hairy; lvs. of main st. short-petioled, ovate to broadly ovate-lanceolate, to 2½ in. long, acuminate, obtuse to subcordate, serrate, glabrous or nearly so; heads terminal and axillary, outer bracts leafy, pubescent; calyx teeth narrowly triangular, awnless, corolla pinkish. E. U.S.

pilosum Nutt. Similar to *P. muticum,* but having lvs. of main st. lanceolate, cuneate, entire or only shallowly dentate, densely hairy beneath; heads rarely axillary. E. U.S.

tenuifolium Schrad. Similar to *P. flexuosum,* but having sts. glabrous; lvs. sessile, linear; calyx teeth awnless, with firm sharp tips. E. U.S.

verticillatum (Michx.) Pers. Similar to *P. pilosum,* but having lvs. glabrate beneath or pilose only on primary veins; infl. corymbose, the heads solitary in axils and peduncled, or 2–3 in upper axils. Ne. U.S.

virginianum (L.) Pers. Similar to *P. muticum,* but sts. much-branched, to 3 ft., pubescent on the angles; lvs. sessile, lanceolate; outer bracts leafy, entire, glabrous. E. U.S.

PYCNOSTACHYS Hook. *Labiatae.* About 35 spp. of erect per. herbs of trop. and S. Afr. and Madagascar; sts. mostly square in cross section; lvs. opp., often toothed; fls. in dense verticillasters arranged in terminal spikes, bracts short, calyx campanulate, 5-toothed, teeth spiny, corolla blue, longer than calyx, limb 2-lipped, upper lip 4-toothed, lower lip concave, stamens 4, in 2 pairs, anthers 1-celled; fr. of 4 glabrous nutlets.

Tender; grown under glass and in the open far south; propagated by seeds or cuttings.

Dawei N. E. Br. Sts. stout, 4–6 ft., puberulous; lvs. linear-lanceolate to lanceolate, 5–12 in. long, cuneate, narrowly acuminate, serrate, hairy, rusty-glandular beneath; spikes to 5 in. long, to 1¾ in. in diam., bracts reddish-brown, with white cilia; fls. cobalt blue, to 1 in. long. Trop. cent. Afr.

Stuhlmannii Gürke. Sts. to 4 ft., pubescent; lvs. linear-lanceolate, 4–7 in. long, cuneate, acuminate, serrulate, mostly glabrous above and pubescent beneath, with skunklike odor when crushed; spikes to 1¼ in. long and scarcely ½ in. in diam., on naked axillary peduncles 2–6 in. long; fls. blue, about ⅜ in. long or less. Rhodesia.

urticifolia Hook. Sts. 5–7 ft., much-branched; lvs. ovate, to 4 in. long, acute, deeply incised-dentate, densely pubescent; spikes 2-3 in. long; corolla bright blue, about 1¼ in. long. Trop. and s. Afr. Some cult. material has lvs. crenate-serrate and only short-puberulent.

PYRACANTHA M. J. Roem. FIRE THORN. *Rosaceae.* About 6 spp. of evergreen, usually thorny shrubs from se. Eur. and Asia; closely allied to *Cotoneaster* and *Crataegus,* distinguished from the former by thorns, crenate or serrate lvs., and corymbose fls., and from the latter by having 2 fertile ovules instead of 1, leafy thorns, and unlobed persistent lvs.; fls. white; fr. a small red or orange pome.

Fire thorns are planted as ornamentals and hedges and are often espaliered. The fruit is showy and persistent in the winter. *P. coccinea* is fairly hardy in the central states, the other species only in a mild climate. Propagated by seeds, by cuttings of ripe wood under glass, by layers, and rare kinds by grafting on related species and genera. Care is needed in transplanting for they do not transplant easily.

angustifolia (Franch.) C. K. Schneid. Stiff upright shrub, to 12 ft., sometimes prostrate, twigs brownish-yellow, tomentose; lvs. linear to oblanceolate, ½–2 in. long, entire or somewhat toothed apically, glabrate above, permanently gray-tomentose beneath; fls. in dense tomentose corymbs, 1–1½ in. across; fr. orange-red, ⁵⁄₁₆ in. in diam. Sw. China. Zone 7. Cv. **'Variegata'.** Lvs. variegated.

atalantioides (Hance) Stapf [*P. Gibbsii* A. B. Jacks.]. To 15 ft.; lvs. elliptic to lanceolate, 1–3 in. long, acutish, mostly entire, glabrous and glaucescent at maturity; infl. 1–1½ in. wide; fr. ⁵⁄₁₆ in. in diam., scarlet or bright crimson. China. Zone 7. Cv. **'Aurea'** is listed. Cv. **'Bakeri'.** Fr. red.

Bakeri: a listed name of no botanical standing for *P. atalantioides* cv.

Bellii: a listed name of no botanical standing for *P. Koidzumii* cv.

Chadwickii: a listed name of no botanical standing for *Pyracantha* cv. 'Chadwickii'; fr. orange, abundant; extremely hardy.

coccinea M. J. Roem. To 6(–15) ft., grayish-pubescent on young growth; lvs. lanceolate to oblong-ovate, 1–1½ in. long, serrulate, glabrate, shining, dark green; infl. finely pubescent, 1–1½ in. wide; fls. ⁵⁄₁₆ in. across; fr. scarlet, ¼ in. in diam. Zone 7. Cvs. are many, including: **'Andenken an Heinrich Bruns', 'Bad Zivischenahn', 'Bosley', 'Boundsii', 'Bunch Bush', 'Cole Erect', 'Dauerbrand', 'Ebben', 'Fructo Luteo', 'Government Red', 'Heinrich Bruns', 'Improved', 'Kasan', 'Keessenii', 'Lalandei',** vigorous with orange-red fr., **'Lalandei Monrovia', 'Lalandei Thornless', 'Lindleyana', 'Lowboy', 'Minute Man', 'Orange King', 'Pauciflora'** [*P. pauciflora* André], **'Praecox', 'Red',**

'Royalii', 'Runyanii', 'Scarlet', 'Sensation', 'Sneed's Thornless', 'Telstar', 'Wayside Compact', 'Wyattii'.

Coolidgei: a listed name of no botanical standing for *P. Koidzumii* cv.

crenatoserrata: *P. Fortuneana.*

crenulata (D. Don) M. J. Roem. Shrub to small tree, to 20 ft., with rusty pubescence; lvs. oblong to oblanceolate, 1–2 in. long, usually acute to obtuse, crenate-serrulate, with bristle tips, glabrous, shining above; corymbs glabrous, 1 in. wide; fls. ⁵⁄₁₆ in. across; fr. subglobose, to ⁵⁄₁₆ in. in diam., orange-red. Himalayas. Zone 7? Cvs. listed are: **'Crimson Tide', 'Lowndes Early Red', 'Rubra', 'Superba'.** Var. **kansuensis** Rehd. [*P. kansuensis* Hort.]. Lvs. narrow, to 1 in. long; fr. smaller. Nw. China. Var. **Rogersiana:** *P. Rogersiana.*

Duvalii: a listed name of no botanical standing for *Pyracantha* cv. 'Duvalii', a cv. of *P. Fortuneana* × *P. Koidzumii.*

formosana: a listed name of no botanical standing for *P. Koidzumii.*

Fortuneana (Maxim.) H. L. Li [*P. crenatoserrata* (Hance) Rehd.; *P. yunnanensis* (M. L. Vilm. ex Mottet) Chitt.]. Differing from *P. atalantioides* in having lvs. crenate-serrate, obtuse, green beneath, broadest above the middle. China. Zone 7. Cvs. **'Graberi', 'Macrocarpa',** and **'Prostrata'** are listed.

Gibbsii: *P. atalantioides.*

Graberi: a listed name of no botanical standing for *P. Fortuneana* cv.

intermedia: a listed name of no botanical standing.

kansuensis: a listed name of no botanical standing for *P. crenulata* var.

Koidzumii (Hayata) Rehd. [*P. formosana* Hort.]. Ten to 12 ft., much-branched, densely leafy, young twigs reddish, pubescent, later purplish and glabrous; lvs. oblanceolate, 1–2 in. long, entire, rounded at apex; infl. pubescent; fr. flattened, ¼ in. in diam., orange-scarlet. Taiwan. Cvs. **'Arcadia'** and **'Bellii'.** Fr. red. Cvs. **'Coolidgei', 'Ellis', 'Government Orange', 'Lewisii', 'Low-Dense', 'Miller', 'Striblingii', 'Victory', 'Walderi Prostrata', 'Wilma'** are listed.

Lewisii: a listed name of no botanical standing for *P. Koidzumii* cv.

pauciflora: *P. coccinea* cv.

Rogersiana (A. B. Jacks.) Bean [*P. crenulata* var. *Rogersiana* A. B. Jacks.]. Like *P. crenulata* but shorter, lvs. unequally serrulate; fr. orange-red. Sw. China. Cvs. are: **'Aurantiaca',** fr. orange; **'Flava',** fr. yellow; **'Knaphill Buttercup',** a listed name.

Striblingii: a listed name of no botanical standing for *P. Koidzumii* cv.

Walderi: a listed name of no botanical standing; perhaps for *P. Koidzumii* cv. 'Walderi Prostrata'.

Watereri: a listed name of no botanical standing for *Pyracantha* cv. 'Watereri', a cv. of *P. coccinea* cv. 'Lalandei' × *P. crenulata.*

Winslowii: a listed name of no botanical standing.

Wyattii: a listed name of no botanical standing for *P. coccinea* cv.

yunnanensis: *P. Fortuneana.*

PYRETHRUM: *CHRYSANTHEMUM.* **P. atrosanguineum:** *C. coccineum.* **P. carneum:** *C. coccineum.* **P. hybridum:** *C. coccineum.* **P. ptarmiciflorum:** *C. ptarmiciflorum.* **P. ptarmicifolium:** *Achillea ptarmicifolia.* **P. roseum:** *C. coccineum.* **P. Tchihatchewii:** *Tripleurospermum Tchihatchewii.* **P. uliginosum:** *C. serotinum.*

PYROLA L. SHINLEAF, WINTERGREEN. *Pyrolaceae.* About 12 spp. of evergreen, per. herbs, with underground scaly rootstocks, native to temp. parts of N. Hemisphere; lvs. in basal clusters, simple; fls. white, greenish, pink, or purplish, in terminal scapose racemes, calyx 5-parted, petals 5, stamens 10; fr. a 5-valved caps.

Sometimes transplanted to the wild garden or colonized in woods, but they do not thrive in the usual garden soil.

americana: *P. rotundifolia* var.

asarifolia Michx. PINK P., PINK W. To 1 ft.; lf. blades reniform, to 2 in. long, about as long as petiole, leathery, shiny; fls. spiralled, corolla crimson to pale pink. Summer. New Bruns. to B.C., s. to New Mex. Var. **bracteata** (Hook.) Jeps. [*P. bracteata* Hook.]. Lf. blades elliptic-ovate, margins distinctly toothed; corolla rosy-purple or dull red. Early summer. B.C. and Mont., s. to n. Calif. Var. **purpurea** (Bunge) Fern. [*P. uliginosa* Torr. & A. Gray ex Torr.]. Lf. blades obovate to suborbicular, margins crenate; corolla pink to reddish-purple. Summer–early autumn. Asia, N. Amer.

bracteata: *P. asarifolia* var.

chlorantha: *P. virens.*

elliptica Nutt. SHINLEAF, WILD LILY-OF-THE-VALLEY. To 1 ft.; lf. blades elliptic, oblong, or obovate, to 3½ in. long, longer than petiole, thin, dull; fls. spiralled, calyx lobes ovate-triangular, corolla white or creamy. Summer. Japan, N. Amer.

grandiflora Radius. ARCTIC P., ARCTIC W. To 8 in.; lf. blades orbicular to ovate, leathery, glossy; fls. spirally arranged, corolla creamy-white, often tinged pink, conspicuously veined. Summer–early autumn. Arctic and boreal Eurasia and N. Amer.

minor L. To 10 in.; lvs. oblong to orbicular, to 1⅝ in. long, dull; fls. spirally arranged, corolla pink to white, nearly globose, style straight. Greenland to Alaska, s. to New Eng., New Mex.; Eurasia.

picta Sm. WHITE-VEINED S. To 8 in.; lvs. to 5½ in. long, including petiole, blades lanceolate-ovate to elliptic, mottled or white along veins, leathery, toothed; fls. spirally arranged, corolla greenish to cream, about ¼ in. long. Summer. W. N. Amer. Cv. 'Dentata' is listed.

rotundifolia L. WILD LILY-OF-THE-VALLEY. To 1 ft.; lf. blades nearly round, to 2 in. long, thick and leathery, glossy; fls. white, fragrant, spiralled, calyx lobes oblong, petals thick. Summer. Eurasia, Greenland to Nfld., e. Que., Nov. Sc. Var. **americana** (Sweet) Fern. [*P. americana* Sweet]. Differs only in being slightly larger. Summer. E. N. Amer.

secunda L. ONE-SIDED P., ONE-SIDED W. To 8 in.; lf. blades elliptic to ovate or orbicular, to 2 in. long, on somewhat shorter petioles, crenate-serrate, glossy; fls. in a 1-sided raceme, petals not spreading, style straight. Summer–early autumn. Eurasia, N. Amer. Var. **secunda.** The typical var.; lvs. nearly leathery, elliptic to ovate; racemes 6–20-fld.; corolla greenish-yellow. Eurasia, N. Amer. Var. **obtusata** Turcz. Lf. blades thinner, ovate to orbicular; racemes 2–10-fld.; corolla creamy-white. Summer. Asia, N. Amer.

uliginosa: *P. asarifolia* var. *purpurea.*

uniflora: *Moneses uniflora.*

virens Schweigg. [*P. chlorantha* Swartz]. To 1 ft.; lf. blade orbicular, reniform, or ovate, 1⅜ in. wide, shorter than petioles, thick, glossy; fls. spirally arranged, calyx lobes ovate-triangular, petals greenish-white. Summer. Eurasia, N. Amer.

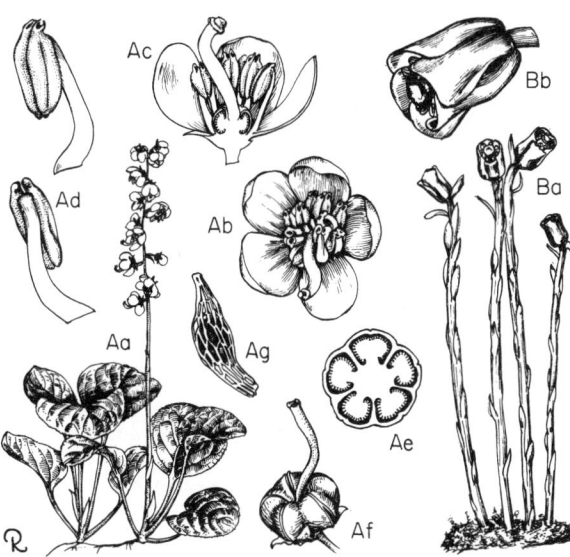

PYROLACEAE. **A,** *Pyrola rotundifolia* var. *americana*: **Aa,** plant, × ½; **Ab,** flower, × 1½; **Ac,** flower, vertical section, × 1½; **Ad,** stamens, two views, × 4; **Ae,** ovary, cross section, × 4; **Af,** capsule, × 2; **Ag,** seed, × 30. **B,** *Monotropa uniflora*: **Ba,** plant, × ¾; **Bb,** flower, × 1.

PYROLACEAE Lindl. [*Monotropaceae* Nutt.]. WINTER-GREEN FAMILY. Dicot.; About 10 or 12 genera and 40 spp. of low, per. herbs, native to cooler parts of N. Hemisphere; mostly evergreen plants with scaly, creeping rootstocks, or sometimes saprophytes or root parasites without chlorophyll varying from waxy-white to red or yellowish; lvs. alt., opp., basal, or in false whorls, simple, sometimes scalelike; fls. solitary or in scapose umbels or racemes, bisexual, regular or nearly so, sepals 4–5, separate or somewhat united, petals

4–5, separate or sometimes united, stamens 8–10, filaments often expanded at base, anthers often opening by a pore, pistil 1, ovary superior, 5-celled, style and stigma 1; fr. a caps., seeds minute, many. Sometimes included in the Ericaceae, or the saprophytes and root parasites sometimes segregated as Monotropaceae. Cult. genera are *Chimaphila, Moneses, Monotropa, Pterospora,* and *Pyrola.*

PYROLIRION: *ZEPHYRANTHES.* **P. aureum:** *Z. tubiflora.*

PYROSTEGIA K. Presl. *Bignoniaceae.* About 5 spp. of evergreen climbing shrubs, native to S. Amer., branchlets 6–8-ribbed; lvs. with 2 or 3 lfts., often with terminal, 3-parted tendril; fls. reddish-orange, in terminal or axillary panicled cymes, calyx truncate, corolla tubular, stamens 4, exserted; fr. a linear caps.

A common ornamental in the tropics and commonly planted as an arbor and roof vine in Zone 10 in Fla., southern U.S., and southern Calif., making a brilliant display when in bloom; sometimes grown in conservatories. Propagated by cuttings.

ignea: *P. venusta.*

venusta (Ker-Gawl.) Miers [*P. ignea* (Vell.) K. Presl; *Bignonia ignea* Vell.; *B. venusta* Ker-Gawl.]. FLAME VINE, FLAME FLOWER, FLAMING-TRUMPET, GOLDEN-SHOWER. Lfts. ovate, to 3 in. long, acuminate; fls. to 3 in. long, corolla lobes reflexed, margined with white hairs; fr. to 1 ft. long. Brazil, Paraguay.

PYRRHEIMA: *SIDERASIS.*

PYRRHOCACTUS: *NEOPORTERIA* subgenus *Pyrrhocactus.* **P. Froelichianus:** *N. tuberisulcata* var. **P. horridus:** *N. tuberisulcata.* **P. mammillarioides:** *N. subgibbosa* var.

PYRROSIA Mirb. [*Cyclophorus* Desv.; *Niphobolus* Kaulf.]. FELT FERN. *Polypodiaceae.* About 100 spp. of scandent epiphytic ferns of Asia and Malay Arch., rhizomes covered with stalked scales; lvs. leathery, usually simple, mostly lanceolate and entire, tomentose beneath, petioles usually conspicuous; sori covering lower surface of lvs., indusia lacking. Much like *Polypodium.*

Usually grown as basket ferns or on standards. May be propagated by division of rhizomes or by spores. See also *Ferns.*

lingua (Thunb.) Farw. [*Cyclophorus lingua* (Thunb.) Desv.; *Niphobolus lingua* (Thunb.) K. Spreng.; *Polypodium lingua* (Thunb.) Swartz]. TONGUE FERN, JAPANESE F. F. Rhizomes wide-creeping; lvs. including petiole to 15 in. long, entire, lanceolate or ovate-lanceolate, covered with stellate hairs beneath. China, Japan and south. Evergreen, drought-resistant basket fern. Cv. 'Corymbifera'. CRESTED F.F. Lvs. forked at the apex. Cv. 'Variegata'. Lvs. variegated.

stigmosa (Swartz) Ching [*Cyclophorus stigmosus* Desv.]. Much like *P. lingua* except rhizomes short, lf. thin-leathery, fertile lvs. not contracted, and sori small, not touching each other.

PYRUS L. PEAR. *Rosaceae.* About 20 spp. of deciduous or semievergreen small trees of Eurasia and N. Afr.; fls. showy, bisexual, in corymbs, before the lvs. or with them, white or nearly so, sepals and petals 5, stamens many, styles 3–5, separate to the base; fr. a pome, the flesh containing stone or grit cells.

Grown for its fruits or as an ornamental. The species and their varieties are hardy plants of simple culture in ordinary soils. They propagate readily from seeds sown or preferably stratified in autumn, and kinds not yet producing fruit may be grafted or budded on closely related stocks. For culture see *Pear.*

Adamsii: a listed name of no botanical standing.

×**adstringens:** a listed name of no botanical standing for *Malus* × *adstringens.*

×**aldenhamensis:** a listed name of no botanical standing for *Malus* × *purpurea* cv.

americana: *Sorbus americana.*

angustifolia: *Malus angustifolia.*

arbutifolia: *Aronia arbutifolia.*

×**arnoldiana:** *Malus* × *arnoldiana.*

×**atrosanguinea:** *Malus* × *atrosanguinea.*

Aucuparia: *Sorbus Aucuparia.*

baccata: *Malus baccata.*

betulifolia Bunge. Tree, to 20 ft. or more, branchlets tomentose; lvs. mostly ovate-acuminate, 2–3 in. long, sharply serrate, shining above and tomentose or glabrate beneath; fls. white, ⅝ in. across; fr. brown and dotted, about ½ in. in diam., sepals falling. N. China. Zone 5.

brevipes: *Malus brevipes.*

Calleryana Decne. Glabrous tree; lvs. ovate or broader, 1½–3 in. long, short-pointed, crenate, turning red in autumn; fls. white, 1 in. across or less, styles 2–3; fr. to ½ in. in diam., globose, dotted brown. China. Zone 6. Handsome ornamental, resistant to fire blight, a good street tree.

Charlottae: a listed name of no botanical standing for *Malus coronaria* cv.

communis L. PEAR, COMMON P. Long-lived tree; lvs. 1–2½ in. long, elliptic to oblong-ovate, somewhat leathery, short-pointed, crenate-serrulate to subentire, glabrous or becoming so; fls. with first lvs., 1 in. across or more, white or tinged pale pink; fr. mostly pear-shaped, variable. Eur. and w. Asia. Zone 5. Cult. as an orchard fr., with many cvs. Wood used for cutlery and turnery.

coronaria: *Malus coronaria.*

× **Dawsoniana:** *Malus × Dawsoniana.*

Dolgo: see *Malus Dolgo.*

elaeagrifolia Pall. Small, commonly thorny tree, tomentose on twigs and both sides or only on underside of lvs.; lvs 1½–3 in. long, lanceolate to very narrowly obovate, entire; fls. white, about 1 in. across, on tomentose pedicels; fr. about 1 in. in diam., green, short-pedicelled. Asia Minor. Zone 5.

× **Eleyi:** *Malus × purpurea* cv.

Ellwangerana: a listed name of no botanical standing.

florentina: *Malus florentina.*

floribunda: *Malus floribunda.*

fusca: *Malus fusca.*

glaucescens: *Malus glaucescens.*

Halliana: *Malus Halliana.*

Hartwigii: *Malus × Hartwigii.*

Hillieri: a listed name of no botanical standing for *Malus × Scheideckeri* cv.

Hoppii: a listed name of no botanical standing.

hupehensis: *Malus hupehensis.*

ioensis: *Malus ioensis.*

kansuensis: *Malus kansuensis.*

Kawakamii Hayata. EVERGREEN P. Shrub or small tree, to 30 ft., often thorny; lvs. 3–4 at ends of small branchlets, glabrous, leathery, ovate to obovate, 2–4 in. long, on petioles 1 in. long; fls. few, in a corymb, white; fr. globose, ½ in. in diam., glabrous. Taiwan.

lancifolia: *Malus coronaria* var.

× **Lecontei** Rehd.: *P. communis × P. pyrifolia.* Lvs. serrulate or crenate-serrulate; fr. yellow. Cv. 'Kieffer'. Vigorous; fr. ovoid, to 2¾ in. long, flesh yellowish-white, granular, undesirable raw but useful in canning. Cv. 'LeConte'. Fr. large, to 3 in. long, inferior to that of 'Kieffer' but can be grown further south.

× **Lemoinei:** a listed name of no botanical standing for *Malus × purpurea* cv.

× **magdeburgensis:** a listed name of no botanical standing for *Malus × magdeburgensis.*

Malus: *Malus sylvestris.*

melanocarpa: *Aronia melanocarpa.*

× **micromalus:** *Malus × micromalus.*

Niedzwetzkyana: *Malus pumila* cv.

Nieuwlandiana: a listed name of no botanical standing for *Malus coronaria* cv.

× **platycarpa:** *Malus × platycarpa.*

Prattii: *Malus Prattii.*

prunifolia: *Malus prunifolia.*

pumila: *Malus pumila.*

× **purpurea:** *Malus × purpurea.*

pyrifolia (Burm.f.) Nakai [*P. serotina* Rehd.]. SAND P., CHINESE P., JAPANESE P., ASIAN P., ORIENTAL P. Tree, to 50 ft., glabrous or becoming so; lvs. ovate or somewhat longer, long-acuminate, setose-serrate, 3–5 in. long; fls. with the lvs. or just before them, white, 1½ in. across, styles 5; fr. mostly apple-shaped, very hard, brown, the calyx deciduous. China, naturalized in Japan. Zone 6. Var. **culta** (Mak.) Nakai. NASHI. Cult. for its larger, edible, very juicy fr.

Ringo: *Malus prunifolia* var. *Rinkii.*

rivularis: *Malus fusca.*

× **robusta:** a listed name of no botanical standing for *Malus × robusta.*

salicifolia Pall. WILLOW-LEAVED P. Tree, often thorny, to 30 ft.; lvs. willowlike, ¾ in. wide or less, tapering at both ends, entire, tomentose when young, but glabrous later; fls. white, ¾ in. across; fr. pear-shaped, yellowish, about 1 in. long, the calyx persistent. Se. Eur., Caucasus, Armenia. Zone 5.

Sargentii: *Malus Sargentii.*

× **Scheideckeri:** *Malus × Scheideckeri.*

serotina: *P. pyrifolia.*

serrulata Rehd. Small tree differing from *P. pyrifolia* in having lvs. shorter, 2–4 in. long, the teeth acute but not setose; fls. smaller with 3–4 styles; fr. subglobose, ¾ in. in diam., the calyx often persistent. China. Zone 6.

Sieboldii: *Malus Sieboldii.*

sikkimensis: *Malus sikkimensis.*

× **Soulardii:** *Malus × Soulardii.*

spectabilis: *Malus spectabilis.*

× **sublobata:** a listed name of no botanical standing for *Malus × sublobata.*

theifera: *Malus hupehensis.*

toringoides: *Malus toringoides.*

Tschonoskii: *Malus Tschonoskii.*

ussuriensis Maxim. CHINESE P., SAND P. Tree; lvs. nearly orbicular to ovate, broad or subcordate at base, 2–4 in. long, acuminate, strongly setose-serrate, nearly or quite glabrous; fls. white, 1 in. across or more, short-pedicelled; fr. subglobose, to 1½ in. in diam., greenish-yellow, the calyx persistent. Ne. Asia. Zone 5. Var. **ovoidea** (Rehd.) Rehd. Lvs. ovate to oblong-ovate; fr. ovoid, long-stemmed. Ne. Asia.

Van-Eseltinei: a listed name of no botanical standing for *Malus spectabilis* cv.

× **Zumi:** *Malus × Zumi.*

PYXIDANTHERA Michx. *Diapensiaceae.* Two spp. of creeping, evergreen shrublets, forming cushionlike masses, native to pine barrens from N.J. to S.C.; lvs. simple, narrowly oblanceolate, subulate; fls. solitary, small, white or rose, sepals 5, corolla campanulate, 5-lobed, stamens 5; fr. a 3-celled caps.

Sometimes transplanted to the rock garden or wild garden, but difficult to cultivate; requires sandy, acid humus in sun.

barbulata Michx. PYXIE, FLOWERING MOSS, PINE-BARREN-BEAUTY. Brs. to 1 ft. long, closely set with bright green lvs. to about ¼ in. long; fls. sessile, many, toward ends of brs., about ⅛ in. across; calyx lobes obscurely ciliolate, corolla lobes suborbicular. Spring. N.J. to S.C.

brevifolia Wells. Differs from *P. barbulata* in having lvs. smaller, hoary, calyx lobes ciliate, and corolla lobes cuneate. N.C.

QUAMASIA: *CAMASSIA.* **Q.** hyacinthina: *C. scilloides;* **Q.** azurea: *C. Quamash* subsp. *azurea.*

QUAMOCLIT: *IPOMOEA.* **Q.** pennata: *I. Quamoclit.* **Q.** Sloteri: *I.* × *multifida.*

QUASSIA L. *Simaroubaceae.* One sp., a trop. Amer. shrub or small tree; lvs. alt., odd-pinnate, rachis conspicuously winged; infl. a raceme, pedicels jointed below fls.; fls. bisexual, sepals and petals 5, stamens 10, ovary of 5 weakly cohering carpels, style 1; fr. of several separate drupes.

Planted in the tropics for its showy flowers and sometimes planted in the warmest parts of the U. S.

amara L. BITTERWOOD, SURINAM Q. To 25 ft.; lvs. to 10 in. long, lfts. 3–7, elliptic, to 6 in. long, abruptly acuminate, usually cuneate; fls. crimson, to 2 in. long, stamens basally pilose. W. Indies, Mex., n. S. Amer. The yellowish-white wood is a source of a bitter drug, quassia.

QUERCUS L. OAK. *Fagaceae.* About 450 spp. of monoecious, deciduous or evergreen trees, rarely shrubs, native to N. Temp. Zone and in the tropics at high elevations, s. to Colombia and to Malay Arch.; lvs. alt., pinnately nerved, dentate, serrate, or pinnately lobed, rarely entire; male fls. many, in slender drooping catkins, female fls. in 1- to many-fld. spikes; fr. an acorn—a nut enclosed or surrounded at base by a cuplike involucre. Deciduous spp. commonly with striking color in autumn.

Grown as an ornamental and for timber. Because of the hard, tough, and durable wood, the species of the genus that are used for wood are among the most important commercially of temperate timber trees. The acorns are used as hogfeed, and the bark of some species yields dye, tannins, and cork. Propagated by seeds sown in autumn or stratified and the evergreen species also by cuttings and layers; protect the acorns from vermin. Varieties may be grafted on seedling stocks under glass in early spring or sometimes in Aug. Oaks usually thrive in rich, rather moist soil; although the scrub oaks grow on dry barren land. Most of the deciduous species are hardy north, but the evergreen kinds are adapted only to the southern and warmer parts of the country.

acuminata: see *Q. Muehlenbergii.*

acuta Thunb. JAPANESE EVERGREEN O., JAPANESE RED O. Small, evergreen tree; lvs. oblong, to 5 in. long, entire, wavy-margined; cup enclosing ¼ of nut, the scales united in several rings. Japan, Korea, China.

acutissima Carruth. [*Q. serrata* Siebold & Zucc., not Thunb.]. Deciduous, to 50 ft.; lvs. oblong, to 7 in. long, with bristlelike teeth, shining above; cup enclosing ⅔ of nut, the scales spreading, spinelike. Korea, Japan, China. Zone 7.

Aegilops: see *Q. macrolepis.*

agrifolia Née [*Q. oxyadenia* Torr.]. CALIFORNIA LIVE O., CALIFORNIA FIELD O. Evergreen, to 100 ft.; lvs. elliptic, to 3 in. long, spiny-toothed, convex above, somewhat stellate-pubescent, especially in axils of veins beneath; fr. maturing the first season, cup enclosing ¼–⅓ of nut, pubescent. Calif. Zone 9.

alba L. WHITE O. Deciduous, to 100 ft.; lvs. obovate, to 9 in. long, with 5–9 entire, obtuse lobes, glaucescent beneath; cup enclosing about ¼ of nut. Me. to Fla. and Tex. Zone 4. Furnishes one of the most important commercial woods.

aliena Blume. ORIENTAL WHITE O. Deciduous, to 70 ft.; lvs. oblong-obovate, to 8 in. long, coarsely toothed, gray-tomentose beneath; cup enclosing about ⅓ of nut, gray-tomentose. Japan, Korea, China. Zone 6.

Andrewsii: *Q. Havardii.*

aquatica: *Q. nigra.*

bambusifolia: *Q. myrsinifolia.*

bicolor Willd. SWAMP WHITE O. Deciduous, to 70 ft.; lvs. obovate, to 6 in. long, coarsely toothed or lobed, dark green above, whitish-tomentose beneath; cup enclosing about ⅓ of nut. Que. to Ga. and Ark. Zone 4. Furnishes a general-purpose wood.

borealis: *Q. rubra.*

Breweri: *Q. Garryana* var.

canariensis Willd. [*Q. Mirbeckii* Durieu ex Bory]. Semievergreen, to 100 ft.; lvs. ovate-oblong, to 5 in. long, coarsely toothed, with lateral veins parallel, shining above, glaucous beneath; cup enclosing about half of nut. Portugal, Spain, N. Afr. Zone 8?

carnea: a listed name of no botanical standing.

castanea: see *Q. Muehlenbergii.*

Catesbaei: *Q. laevis.*

cerris L. TURKEY O. Deciduous, to 100 ft.; lvs. oblong, to 5 in. long, with 3–8 pairs of entire or toothed lobes, grayish-pubescent beneath when young; fr. maturing second year, cup enclosing about half of nut, mossy. S. Eur., w. Asia. Zone 7. Cv. 'Laciniata'. Lvs. pinnatifid. Cv. 'Pendula'. Brs. drooping; lvs. pinnatifid. Var. **austriaca** (Willd.) Loud. AUSTRIAN T. O. Lobes of lvs. shallow, broad, triangular, obtuse and mucronate.

chinensis: *Q. variabilis.*

chrysolepis Liebm. CANYON O., MAUL O. Evergreen, to 90 ft.; lvs. elliptic, to 4 in. long, spiny-toothed, or with entire revolute margins, glaucous and tomentose beneath; cup enclosing about ¼ of nut, tomentose, scales almost hidden by feltlike tomentum. Ore. to Baja Calif. Zone 8.

coccinea Muenchh. SCARLET O. Deciduous, to 80 ft.; lvs. oblong or elliptic, to 6 in. long, with 7–9 very deep lobes, bright green, becoming brilliant red in autumn; cup enclosing ⅓–½ of nut. Me. to Fla. and Mo. Zone 4. Cv. 'Superba' is listed.

conferta: *Q. Frainetto.*

cornea: *Lithocarpus corneus.*

crispa: *Q. Ilex.*

crispula: *Q. mongolica* var. *grosseserrata.*

cuspidata: *Castanopsis cuspidata.*

Darlingtonia: a listed name of no botanical standing; has been used for a form of *Q. laurifolia* called the DARLINGTON OAK.

densiflora: *Lithocarpus densiflorus.*

dentata Thunb. DAIMYO O. Deciduous, to 80 ft.; lvs. ovate, to 1 ft. long, with 4–9 pairs of rounded lobes or teeth, pubescent beneath; cup enclosing half or more of nut, with spreading scales. Korea, China, Japan. Zone 6. Produces a tanbark. Remarkable for its large lvs. Cv. 'Pinnatifida'. Lvs. divided almost to midrib.

digitata: *Q. falcata.*

Douglasii Hook. & Arn. BLUE O. Deciduous, to 60 ft.; lvs. usually oblong, to 4 in. long, few-lobed, entire to somewhat undulate, blue-green above, paler and stellate-pubescent beneath; nuts ovoid, cup enclosing ¼ of nut. Calif.

dumosa Nutt. CALIFORNIA SCRUB O. Evergreen shrub, to 8 ft.; lvs. oblong to elliptic, to 1 in. long, spiny-toothed or entire, glossy dark green and nearly glabrous above, pale and pubescent beneath; cup enclosing about half of nut. Calif.

durata Jeps. LEATHER O. Spreading evergreen shrub, to 5 ft.; branchlets densely tomentose; lvs. elliptic, to 1 in. long, with sharp dentate teeth, dark green above, leathery; cup to ¾ in. across and nearly ½ in. deep, enclosing ⅓–½ of nut. Calif. Closely related to *Q. dumosa* but having lvs. stellate-pubescent and dull green above.

edulis: *Lithocarpus edulis.*

ellipsoidalis E. J. Hill. NORTHERN PIN O., JACK O. Deciduous, to 80 ft. or more; lvs. elliptic, to 4 or 5 in. long, with deep narrow lobes with pointed teeth, becoming glabrous beneath except in axils of veins; cup enclosing ⅓–½ of nut. Man. to Mich. and Iowa. Zone 3.

Emoryi Torr. EMORY O. Small or large tree, to 60 ft., evergreen or nearly so; lvs. ovate to oblong, to 2½ in. long, rarely 4 in. long, entire or with few awn-tipped teeth, leathery; nuts oblong, to ½ in. long, cup enclosing half of nut or less. Tex. to Ariz. and adjacent Mex. Acorns used for food by Indians.

Engelmannii Greene. ENGELMANN O. Evergreen, to 60 ft.; lvs. oblong, about 2 in. long, entire or sometimes toothed, pale beneath; cup enclosing half of nut. S. Calif., Baja Calif.

falcata Michx. [*Q. digitata* (Marsh.) Sudw.]. SPANISH RED O., SPAN-ISH O. Deciduous, to 80 ft. or more; lvs. obovate, to 8 in. long, with 1–3 pairs of deep, acute lobes, 1 pair falcate, pubescent beneath; cup enclosing ¼–⅓ of nut. N.J. to Fla. and Tex. Zone 7. Var. **pagodifolia** Elliott [*Q. pagodifolia* (Elliott) Ashe]. Lvs. pinnatifid, with 3–5 pairs of nearly equal, divergent lobes. N.J. to Ill., s. to n. Fla. and La. Zone 7.

fissa: *Lithocarpus fissus.*

Frainetto Ten. [*Q. conferta* Kit.]. ITALIAN O. Deciduous, to 120 ft.; lvs. obovate, to 7 in. long, with usually 7 very deep lobes, dark green above, pale and pubescent beneath; cup enclosing ⅓–½ of nut. S. Eur. Zone 6.

Gambelii Nutt. [*Q. utahensis* (A. DC.) Rydb.]. GAMBEL O. Decid-uous shrub, to 15 ft.; lvs. broad-obovate, divided about halfway into rounded lobes, glossy above, slightly pubescent beneath; cup enclos-ing about half of nut. Colo. to New Mex. Zone 6.

×**Ganderi** C. Wolf: *Q. agrifolia* × *Q. Kelloggii.* GANDER O. Inter-mediate between the two parents, but usually with tufts of hairs in axils of veins beneath.

Garryana Dougl. OREGON O., WESTERN O. Deciduous, to 100 ft.; lvs. oblong-obovate, to 6 in. long, divided about halfway into 3–5 pairs of entire or toothed lobes; cup pubescent, enclosing about ⅓ of nut. B.C. to Calif. Zone 7. Var. **Breweri** (Engelm.) Jeps. [*Q. Breweri* Engelm.]. Shrub, to 15 ft.; lvs. to 2 in. long. Mts., Calif.

gilva Blume. Evergreen tree; lvs. oblanceolate, to nearly 5 in. long, leathery, yellow-brown-tomentose beneath; cup scales united in rings, short-villous. China, Taiwan, Japan.

glabra: *Lithocarpus glaber.*

glandulifera Blume [*Q. serrata* Thunb., not Siebold & Zucc.]. KONARA O. Deciduous, to 50 ft.; lvs. oblong-obovate, to 6 in. long, sharply toothed, shining above, grayish-pubescent beneath; cup en-closing about ⅓ of nut. Korea, China, Japan. Zone 6. Wood used for lumber in Japan.

glauca Thunb. RING-CUPPED O. Evergreen, to 50 ft.; lvs. oblong, to 5 in. long, toothed above middle, silky and glaucous beneath when young; cup enclosing about ⅓ of nut, pubescent. China, Taiwan, Ja-pan. Zone 8.

grosseserrata: *Q. mongolica* var.

guatimalensis A. DC. A doubtful sp. from Cent. Amer.; material so named may belong to *Q. sapotifolia* Liebm. or *Q. polymorpha* Cham. & Schlechtend., but neither of these is known in cult.

Hancei: *Lithocarpus Hancei.*

Harlandii: *Lithocarpus Harlandii.*

Havardii Rydb. [*Q. Andrewsii* Sarg.]. SHINNERY O., HAVARD O. De-ciduous low shrub, to 2½ ft.; lvs. oblong, to 2½ in. long, coarsely lobed or toothed, bright green, pubescent beneath; acorns to 1 in. long, cup enclosing ⅓–½ of nut. Tex., New Mex. Zone 6.

×**heterophylla** Michx.f.: *Q. phellos* × *Q. rubra.* BARTRAM O. De-ciduous, to 80 ft.; lvs. variable in shape, usually oblong to elliptic, to 6 in. long, with 3–5 pairs of bristle-tipped lobes or nearly entire, glabrous beneath except for tufts of hairs in axils of veins. E. U.S.

Ilex L. [*Q. crispa* Hort. ex C. Koch]. HOLLY O., HOLM O. Evergreen, to 60 ft.; lvs. ovate to lanceolate, to 3 in. long, toothed or entire, shining dark green above, yellowish- or whitish-tomentose beneath; cup en-closing about half of nut. Medit. region. Cv. 'Fordii'. Small pyramidal tree; lvs. narrow. Var. **rotundifolia** (Weston) Batt. BALLOTA O., BEL-LOOT O., BELOTE O. Lvs. small, suborbicular, acorns large, edible. Sw. Eur. Zone 8.

ilicifolia Wangenh. SCRUB O., BEAR O. Deciduous, much-branched shrub, to 10 ft. or more; lvs. obovate, to 4½ in. long, with 2 pairs of broad, entire, or bristly-toothed lobes, whitish-tomentose beneath; cup enclosing half of nut. Me. to Va. and Ky. Zone 5.

imbricaria Michx. SHINGLE O., LAUREL O. Deciduous, to 60 ft.; lvs. oblong, to 6 in. long, entire, pale and pubescent beneath; cup enclos-ing ⅓–½ of nut. Penn. to Ga. and Ark. Zone 5. An important hardwood sp.

incana Bartr. BLUEJACK O., TURKEY O., HIGH-GROUND WILLOW O., BLUEJACK, SAND JACK. Deciduous shrub or low tree, to 25 ft.; lvs. lanceolate to oblong, to 4 in. long, entire or coarsely few-toothed, stellate-puberulent above, gray-stellate-tomentose beneath; nuts sub-rotund, cup enclosing about ¼ of nut. Se. U.S.

Kelloggii Newb. CALIFORNIA BLACK O., KELLOGG O. Deciduous, to 80 ft. or more; lvs. oblong, to 6 in. long, divided about halfway into narrow, sharply dentate lobes, pubescent or sometimes becoming glabrous underneath; cup enclosing ⅓ of nut or more. Ore., Calif. Zone 8.

×**kewensis** Osborn: *Q. cerris* × *Q. Wislizenii.* Evergreen, to 50 ft.; lvs. oblong-ovate, to 3½ in. long, with 5–6 triangular, mucronate lobes on each side, dull green above, glossy beneath. Zone 7.

laevis Walt. [*Q. Catesbaei* Michx.]. TURKEY O., CATESBY O. Decid-uous, to 50 ft. and more; related to *Q. falcata*, but having lvs. glabrous and shining underneath, petioles very short; cup deeper, enclosing half of nut, scales curving over edge and down inside. N.C. to Fla., w. to La. Zone 8.

lamellosa Sm. Large evergreen tree; lvs. obovate, to 8 in. or as much as 15 in. long, glossy, glabrous and with deeply impressed lateral veins above, brownish-silky-pubescent, reticulate and with prominent lat-eral veins beneath, leathery; cup nearly enclosing nut, with about 10 lamellate rings. A handsome oak with magnificent foliage and unusual acorns. Himalayas and w. China.

laurifolia Michx. LAUREL O., LAUREL-LEAVED O. Deciduous or semi-evergreen, to 60 ft.; lvs. oblong, to 6 in. long, entire or sometimes slightly lobed, shining dark green above, light green beneath; cup enclosing ¼ of nut. Va. to Fla. and La. Zone 8. The so-called DARLING-TON OAK belongs here.

libani Olivier. LEBANON O. Deciduous tree, to 30 ft.; lvs. oblong-lanceolate, to 4 in. long, with 9–12 pairs of veins terminated at the margin by bristle-tipped teeth, pubescent along veins or thinly pubes-cent all over; cup nearly enclosing nut, prominently scaly. Asia Minor. Zone 7.

lobata Née. VALLEY O., CALIFORNIA WHITE O. Deciduous, to 100 ft.; obovate, to 3 in. long, with 7–11 obtuse lobes, grayish-tomentose beneath; cup enclosing ¼–⅓ of nut. Calif. Zone 9.

lyrata Walt. OVERCUP O., SWAMP POST O. Deciduous, to 100 ft.; lvs. obovate-oblong, to 8 in. long, deeply pinnatifid, with a large terminal lobe, white-tomentose or green and pubescent beneath; cup usually enclosing nut. N.J. to Fla. and Tex. Zone 6.

Macdonaldii Greene. MCDONALD O. Deciduous small tree, to 45 ft.; lvs. oblong to obovate, to 3 in. long, with 2–4 bristle-tipped lobes on each side, glabrous above, pubescent beneath; cup enclosing about half of nut, scales strongly tubercled, pubescent. Coastal Is., s. Calif. Sometimes considered a var. of *Q. dumosa.*

macranthera Fisch. & C. A. Mey. Deciduous, to 60 ft.; lvs. obovate, to 7 in. long, with 8–10 pairs of broad lobes, grayish-tomentose beneath; cup enclosing about half of nut. W. Asia. Zone 6.

macrocarpa Michx. [*Q. macrocarpa* var. *oliviformis* (Michx.f.) A. Gray; *Q. oliviformis* Michx.f.]. BUR O., MOSSY-CUP O. Deciduous, to 80 ft. or more; lvs. obovate, to 10 in. long, pinnatifid with large terminal lobe, grayish-pubescent beneath; cup enclosing half of nut, with fringelike border. Nov. Sc. to Penn. and Tex. Zone 4. Furnishes an important wood.

macrolepis Kotschy [*Q. Aegilops* of auth., not L.]. Semievergreen, to 80 ft.; lvs. elliptic to oblong, to 4 in. long, with 3–7 pairs of triangu-lar, bristle-tipped lobes, often secondarily lobed, glabrous above, tomentose beneath; cup enclosing ⅓–½ of nut, scales large and thick-ened, the upper narrowed and these, or all, reflexed. S. Eur., w. Asia. Zone 7?

marilandica Muenchh. BLACKJACK O., BLACKJACK, JACK O. Decid-uous, to 50 ft., but mostly less; lvs. broader toward apex, to 6 or 8 in. long, shallowly lobed at top, brown-tomentose underneath; cup hemispherical-turbinate, enclosing ⅓ or more of nut, upper scales often recurving. N.Y. to Fla., w. to Nebr. and Tex. Zone 6.

maxima: *Q. rubra.*

minor: *Q. stellata.*

Mirbeckii: *Q. canariensis.*

mongolica Fisch. ex Turcz. MONGOLIAN O. Deciduous, to 100 ft.; lvs. clustered at ends of brs., short-petioled, obovate, to 8 in. long, with 7–10 broad teeth; cup enclosing half of nut, scales keeled, thick, and overlapping. Ne. Asia. Zone 5. Var. **grosseserrata** (Blume) Rehd. & E. H. Wils. [*Q. crispula* Blume; *Q. grosseserrata* Blume]. Lvs. often narrower, more acute, with acute teeth; scales less keeled, strongly appressed. Japan, Kuriles, Sakhalin. An important timber tree.

montana: *Q. prinus.*

Morii Hayata. Evergreen, to 100 ft., bark gray, peeling off; lvs. ovate-oblong, to 4 in. long, serrate in upper half, glabrous except along veins beneath; cup enclosing ¾ of nut, scales united into 7–10 rings, densely tomentose on both surfaces. Mts., Taiwan.

Muehlenbergii Engelm. [*Q. acuminata* (Michx.) Sarg., not Roxb.; *Q. castanea* Muhlenb., not Née.]. YELLOW CHESTNUT O., YELLOW O., CHESTNUT O. Deciduous, to 100 ft. and more; lvs. oblong to lanceolate-oblong, to 6 in. long, with incurved, coarse, marginal teeth, pubescent underneath; cup enclosing nearly half of nut. New Eng. to Fla., w. to Minn. and Tex. Zone 5.

myrsinifolia Blume [*Q. bambusifolia* Fort.]. Evergreen, to 60 ft., brs. purplish-brown, stout; lvs. lanceolate, to 5 in. long, acuminate, toothed, shining above, glaucous beneath; cup enclosing ⅓–½ of nut, scales united into 5–7 glabrous rings; fr. maturing first year. E. Asia. Zone 8.

nigra L. [*Q. aquatica* Walt.]. WATER O., POSSUM O. Mostly deciduous or in some regions evergreen, to 80 ft.; lvs. obovate, to 3 in. long, 3-lobed at apex or entire, bluish-green above; cup enclosing ¼–⅓ of nut. Del. to Fla. and Tex. Zone 6?

oliviformis: *Q. macrocarpa.*

oxyadenia: *Q. agrifolia.*

pagodifolia: *Q. falcata* var.

Palmeri Engelm. Evergreen shrub, to 15 ft.; lvs. elliptic to round-ovate, to 1³⁄₁₆ in. long, wavy-spinose, gray-green above; cup enclosing less than ⅓ of nut. Ariz., Calif., Baja Calif.

palustris Muenchh. PIN O., SPANISH O. Deciduous, to 80 ft. or more; lvs. elliptic, to 5 in. long, with 5–7 oblong, toothed lobes, bright green; cup enclosing about ⅓ of nut. Mass. to Del. and Ark. Zone 5. Planted as a street tree. Furnishes an important commercial wood.

pedunculata: *Q. robur.*

petraea L. ex Liebl. [*Q. sessiliflora* Salisb.]. DURMAST O. Deciduous; very similar to *Q. robur*, differing chiefly in having longer petioles and fr. almost sessile. Eur., w. Asia. Zone 5. Cv. **'Mespilifolia'** [cv. 'Louettii']. Lvs. narrow, nearly entire.

phellos L. WILLOW O. Deciduous, to 60 ft.; lvs. linear-oblong, to 4 in. long, entire, light green and shining above; cup enclosing about ¼ of nut. N.Y. to Fla. and Tex. Zone 6.

phillyraeoides A. Gray. UBAME O. Evergreen, to 30 ft.; lvs. elliptic or obovate, to 2½ in. long, wavy-toothed; cup enclosing about half of nut, thinly scaly. China, Japan. Zone 7?

prinoides Willd. CHINQUAPIN O., DWARF CHESTNUT O. Deciduous shrub, to 6 ft., or rarely small tree; lvs. oblong to 5 in. long, toothed, grayish-pubescent beneath; cup enclosing about half of nut. Me. to Ala. and Tex. Zone 5?

prinus L. [*Q. montana* Willd.]. BASKET O., CHESTNUT O., SWAMP C.O., ROCK C.O. Deciduous, to 100 ft.; lvs. obovate, to 7 in. long, coarsely toothed, shining bright green above, grayish-pubescent beneath; cup enclosing ⅓–½ of nut. Del. to Fla. and Tex. Zone 6. Furnishes an important wood and tanbark.

reticulata Humb. & Bonpl. Evergreen shrub or small tree, to 25 ft.; lvs. obovate, to 5 in. long, leathery, sometimes cordate at base, spiny-dentate toward apex, strongly reticulate beneath; cup enclosing about ¼ of nut, hoary-tomentose. Ariz., New Mex., adjacent Mex.

robur L. [*Q. pedunculata* J. F. Ehrh.]. ENGLISH O., TRUFFLE O. Deciduous, to 80 ft. or more; lvs. obovate, to 5 in. long, with 3–7 pairs of rounded lobes; cup enclosing about ⅓ of nut. Eur., N. Afr., w. Asia. Zone 5. Furnishes an important wood. Some of the cvs. are: **'Atropurpurea'**, lvs. purple; **'Concordia'**, lvs. bright yellow during summer; **'Dauvessei'**: 'Pendula'; **'Fastigiata'**, of columnar habit; **'Filicifolia'**, lvs. deeply cut into linear, crisped lobes; **'Holophylla'** [cv. 'Longifolia'], lvs. entire; **'Longifolia'**: Holophylla'; **'Pectinata'**, lvs. deeply cut into narrow lobes; **'Pendula'** [cv. 'Dauvessei'], brs. pendulous; **'Variegata'**, lvs. margined or variegated white.

rubra L. [*Q. rubra* var. *maxima* Marsh.; *Q. borealis* Michx.f.; *Q. maxima* (Marsh.) Sarg.]. RED O., NORTHERN R.O. Deciduous, to 80 ft.; lvs. oblong, to 9 in. long, 7–11-lobed halfway to middle, pale beneath; cup enclosing ⅓ of nut. E. N. Amer. Zone 5. Wood important for general construction.

Sadlerana R. Br. Campst. DEER O. Evergreen shrub, to 8 ft.; lvs. chestnutlike, elliptic to oblong-ovate, to 5 in. long, prominently pinnate-veined, coarsely and regularly serrate, nearly glabrous; cup enclosing about ¼ of nut, thin-walled. Calif.

salicifolia: a listed name of no botanical standing which may refer to *Q. phellos*, the willow oak.

salicina Blume [*Q. stenophylla* (Blume) Mak.]. Evergreen tree, brs. grayish-brown, slender; lvs. lanceolate, to 4 in. long, waxy-white beneath. Japan. Closely related to *Q. myrsinifolia* in lf. shape and acorns, but fr. maturing second year.

serrata: see *Q. acutissima; Q. glandulifera.*

serrulata Trel. A little-known oak, doubtfully in cult. Mex.

sessiliflora: *Q. petraea.*

Shumardii Buckl. SHUMARD'S RED O. Deciduous, to 75 ft.; lvs. ovate or obovate, to 6 in. long, with 2–4 awn-tipped, deep lobes on each side; cup enclosing ¼ of nut, scales narrow, closely appressed. Se. U.S. Zone 5.

sinensis: a listed name of no botanical standing, perhaps for *Q. chinensis.*

stellata Wangenh. [*Q. minor* (Marsh.) Sarg.]. POST O. Deciduous, to 100 ft. but usually much less; lvs. obovate, 6–8 in. long, with obtuse, strap-shaped lobes, grayish or whitish underneath; cup enclosing ⅓ or more of nut. Mass. to Fla., w. to Kans. and Tex. Zone 5.

stenophylla: *Q. salicina.*

Suber L. CORK O. Evergreen, to 60 ft., bark thick; lvs. ovate, to 3 in. long, toothed, shining dark green above, grayish-tomentose beneath; cup enclosing ⅓–½ of nut. S. Eur., N. Afr. Zone 8. The very thick bark furnishes cork of commerce.

ternaticupula: *Lithocarpus ternaticupula.*

texana Buckl. TEXAS RED O. Deciduous tree, to 35 ft.; lvs. elliptic to obovate, to 3½ in. long, with 5 sharp-pointed lobes, occasionally with minute tufts of hairs in axils of veins beneath; nut to ¾ in. long, cup enclosing ¼–½ of nut. Tex. Similar to *Q. Shumardii*, but of questionable hardiness in the North.

tinctoria: *Q. velutina.*

tomentella Engelm. ISLAND O. Evergreen tree, to 35 ft.; lvs. oblong-lanceolate, to 3 in. long, often revolute, glabrous above, tomentose and prominently reticulate beneath; cup enclosing ¼ of nut, scales embedded in dense tomentum. Coastal Is., Calif. and Baja Calif.

turbinella Greene. Evergreen shrub, related to *Q. dumosa;* lvs. mostly oblong, spinose-dentate, dull and stellate-pubescent above. Calif. and n. Baja Calif., e. to w. Tex.

Turneri Willd. TURNER O. May be a hybrid between *Q. Ilex* and *Q. robur;* semievergreen tree, to 50 ft.; lvs. oblong-obovate, to 4 in. long, 4–6-lobed; cup enclosing half of nut.

undulata Torr. ROCKY MOUNTAIN SCRUB O. Deciduous, to 30 ft.; lvs. elliptic-oblong, to 3 in. long, coarsely toothed or lobed, bluish-green and pubescent; cup enclosing about half of nut. Colo. to Tex. and Mex. Zone 5.

utahensis: *Q. Gambelii.*

vacciniifolia Kellogg. HUCKLEBERRY O. Evergreen, to 4 ft., spreading, often prostrate; lvs. oblong-ovate, to 1¼ in. long, usually entire, glabrous above, pale and more or less pubescent beneath; cup enclosing ¼ of nut, thin-walled, scales white, tomentose. Calif. to Ore. Often considered a var. of *Q. chrysolepis.*

variabilis Blume [*Q. chinensis* Bunge]. Deciduous, to 80 ft.; lvs. oblong, to 6 in. long, with bristlelike teeth, white-tomentose beneath; cup enclosing about half of nut, scales subulate, curved. N. China, Korea, Japan. Zone 6.

velutina Lam. [*Q. tinctoria* Bartr.]. BLACK O., YELLOW-BARKED O., QUERCITRON. Deciduous, to 100 ft. or more; lvs. ovate to oblong, to 10 in. long, with 7–9, broad, toothed lobes, shining dark green above; cup enclosing about half of nut, pubescent, with fringelike border. Me. to Fla. and Tex. Warmer parts of Zone 4. Bark yields tannin and the inner bark the bright yellow dye quercitron.

virginiana Mill. LIVE O., SOUTHERN L.O. Evergreen, to 60 ft.; lvs. elliptic to oblong, to 5 in. long, usually entire, shining dark green above, whitish-tomentose beneath; cup enclosing about ¼ of nut, scales thin, appressed, hoary-tomentose. Va. to Fla. and Mex. Zone 8.

Wislizenii A. DC. INTERIOR LIVE O. Evergreen, to 75 ft.; lvs. usually oblong, to 4 in. long, entire or spiny-toothed, glossy above, yellowish beneath; nut to 1⅝ in. long, cup enclosing ¼–½ of nut. Calif. Var. **frutescens** Engelm. Shrubby, with rigid twigs; lvs. small.

QUESNELIA Gaud.-Beaup. *Bromeliaceae.* Fourteen spp. of terrestrial or epiphytic herbs, native to Brazil; lvs. in basal tubular rosettes, spiny; infl. scapose, unbranched or branched, conelike to spicate; fls. sessile, sepals without spines, separate, petals separate or nearly so, ovary inferior, ovules blunt; fr. a dry berry.

Grown outdoors in warm climates or under glass. Requires bright to filtered light. For culture see *Bromeliaceae.*

arvensis (Vell.) Mez. Lvs. many, to 2½ ft. long, 1⅝ in. wide, strongly spiny; infl. thick, cylindric-ellipsoid, fl. bracts bright pink, membranous, strongly and transversely undulate-crispate; fls. blue, to 1¾ in. long, sepals asymmetrical, to ½ in. long. Brazil.

humilis Mez. Lvs. about 10, to 8 in. long, 1³⁄₁₆ in. wide, green, or sometimes spotted; infl. few-fld., subcorymbose; fls. to 1¾ in. long, blue, turning red, sepals symmetrical, ¾ in. long, villous-floccose at tip. Brazil.

lateralis Wawra [*Billbergia Enderi* Regel]. Lvs. linear, to 2 ft. long, 2⅜ in. wide; infl. slender, interrupted-cylindrical, not conelike; fls. blue, to 1⅝ in. long, sepals asymmetrical. Brazil.

Liboniana (De Jonghe ex Ysab.) Mez. Lvs. few, linear, to 1½ ft. long, 1⅝ in. wide; infl. spicate, loose, few-fld.; fls. dark blue, to 2 in. long or more, sepals symmetrical, glabrous. Brazil.

marmorata (Lem.) Read [*Aechmea marmorata* (Lem.) Mez; *Billbergia marmorata* Lem.]. GRECIAN-VASE. Lvs. in a tubular rosette, 2-ranked, glaucous, with dark green and maroon mottling, to 18 in. long, 2½ in. wide; infl. branched at base, scape bracts pink, fl. bracts minute; fls. blue, to 1 in. long, sepals blue-green. Brazil.

Quesneliana (Brongn.) L. B. Sm. Branching to form mats; lvs. many, to 3 ft. long, 1⅝ in. wide, green; infl. cylindrical, fl. bracts crisped, pink; sepals asymmetrical, petals white, edged lavender-blue, to 9⁄16 in. long. Brazil.

testudo Lindm. Lvs. broadly linear, to 1⅝ in. wide, minutely spinose, green with faint white bands; infl. thick, cylindric-ellipsoid, fl. bracts rose-pink, membranous, entire, not undulate; sepals asymmetrical, minute, petals white, with violet tips, to ⅝ in. long. Brazil.

QUIABENTIA Britt. & Rose. *Cactaceae*. About 4 spp. of trees and shrubs of the Chaco region of Argentina and Paraguay; lvs. ovate to oblong, thick; areoles large, with spines and glochids; fls. red; seeds bony, glabrous. Similar to *Pereskiopsis*, with which this genus should perhaps be united, but fls. terminal and seeds glabrous.

For culture see *Cacti*.

chacoensis Backeb. Shrub, brs. 1 in. thick; lvs. lanceolate, acuminate, nearly cylindrical at the base, white-margined, to 3 in. long; areoles white-woolly, spines about 9, unequal, irregularly disposed, the longest to 2 in. long. N. Argentina.

QUILLAJA Mol. *Rosaceae*. About 4 spp. of glabrous, evergreen trees, native to S. Amer.; lvs. alt., simple, thick and leathery, almost entire; fls. hairy, in clusters of 3–5, the lateral ones male, the central ones female and fertile, sepals 5, persistent, leathery, petals 5, spatulate, stamens 10; frs. 5 leathery follicles.

The bark of some species has soaplike or medicinal properties. Grown outdoors in milder areas. Propagated by cuttings under glass.

Saponaria Mol. SOAP-BARK TREE. To 60 ft.; lvs. oblong-ovate, somewhat remotely and shallowly serrate, shining, to 2 in. long; fls. white, ½ in. across. Chile. Zone 8.

QUINCE. The pomological quinces are several and include the common or true quince, *Cydonia oblonga*, and several species of Oriental quinces of the Asiatic genus *Chaenomeles*. Four of the latter are grown as ornamental flowering quinces and two have some value for their fruit. *Chaenomeles speciosa*, a spreading shrub hardy in Zone 5, produces fruits 3–4 inches in length. Though possessing little flavor, they have a high pectin content and so are often mixed with other fruits to make jelly and preserves. *Cydonia sinensis*, a more tender species (Zone 8), is a small tree with large fruits to 6 inches long used in similar fashion; its foliage turns an attractive brilliant scarlet in autumn. Species of *Chaenomeles* are self-sterile, hence several plants are required to assure fruit production.

The common orchard quince, *Cydonia oblonga*, is a small, crooked-branched tree native to western Asia and grown in temperate climates since ancient times for its fragrant fruit. The hard, golden-yellow flesh is rather unpalatable when fresh, and hence is used mainly in preserves and cooking. It is a slow-growing, shallow-rooted tree, requiring a rather heavy, moist, deep soil for best results, but very heavy lands are likely to produce green fruit of poor quality. The trees may be set about 16 feet apart both ways, which is greater than the usual full height of large specimens. The quince propagates readily from long hardwood cuttings. Nursery practice is to bud named cultivars on rooted 'Angers' quince cuttings, or more rarely on seedlings. Plants are set when one or two years old; the second or third year thereafter a few fruits should be produced and then the crop should be steady for any number of years. The quince is but little hardier than the peach in its wood and may be severely injured at temperatures of −15° to −20° F. In the warmer parts of the country where the humidity is high, fire blight is the limiting factor. Commercial quince culture is therefore largely restricted to the favored fruit regions of California, Ohio, Pennsylvania, New York, and Ontario. In home planting it is worth attention over a much wider area.

The fruit, up to 5 inches in diameter, is hand-picked when mature and well colored. Although a hard fruit, the quince shows bruises very readily and must, therefore, be handled with great care. The fruit may be kept for a relatively short time, as compared with the apple, at 30° to 32° F. Usually, however, the crop is used at once. In some parts of the world quinces of much higher quality have been developed than any grown in North America. Here the cultivar 'Orange' is outstanding for its earliness, quality, and color. Other cultivars sometimes grown are 'Champion', 'Fuller', 'Meech', and 'Smyrna', the latter being one of the best.

Fire blight, the worst disease of the quince, can be kept in check by avoiding over-stimulation of the trees and by cutting out the diseased twigs as with the pear. Borers, often a serious pest, can be dug out as in the case of the apple. Spraying for the codling moth, quince curculio, and Oriental fruit moth is necessary.

QUINCULA: *PHYSALIS*.

QUINTINIA A. DC. *Saxifragaceae*. Eight or more spp. of trees or shrubs in Australia, New Zeal., New Guinea, the Philippine Is.; lvs. alt., leathery, usually with glandular marginal teeth; fls. small, in axillary or terminal racemes, sepals, petals, and stamens 5, calyx tube united to ovary; fr. a caps., obovoid to elliptic, inferior to half-inferior.

serrata A. Cunn. Tree, to 30 ft.; lvs. narrow-lanceolate to oblong, to 5 in. long, margins toothed and more or less wavy; fls. pale lilac, in racemes to 3 in. long; caps. to 3⁄16 in. long. New Zeal.

QUISQUALIS L. *Combretaceae*. About 4 spp. of climbing shrubs, native to tropics of Old World; lvs. opp., simple; fls. in spikes, showy, bisexual, with elongate slender fl. tube, petals 5, stamens 10; fr. dry, 5-angled or 5-winged.

A common vine in tropical gardens; grown outdoors in Zone 10b and sometimes under glass. Propagated by softwood cuttings over heat.

indica L. RANGOON CREEPER. To 30 ft. or more; lvs. to 5 in. long; spikes terminal, drooping; fls. fragrant, fl. tube slender, green, to 3 in. long, petals white, changing to pink or red. Burma, Malay Pen., Philippine Is., New Guinea.

RABIEA N. E. Br. *Aizoaceae*. About 6 spp. of dwarf, stemless, deep-rooting succulents, native to S. Afr., rhizomes fleshy; lvs. opp., in dense rosettes, with each pair more or less dissimilar, ascending to spreading, enclosing the internodes, often roughened by raised, white or reddish-brown dots, upper side flat, lower side rounded or keeled, 3-angled toward apex; fls. solitary, calyx nearly equally or unequally 5-lobed, petals yellow to orange, many, in 3–4 series, stamens many in an erect columnar mass, ovary inferior, 9–10-celled, stigmas 9–10; fr. a caps., expanding keels broadly winged, placental tubercles absent.

Growth occurs chiefly in summer, the plants requiring very tall or tubular pots with a sandy, stony, loamy soil; in winter plants should be grown at relatively cool temperature of about 60° F. See also *Succulents*.

albinota (Haw.) N. E. Br. [*Nananthus albinotus* (Haw.) L. Bolus]. Lvs. 6–8, grayish-green, densely white- or greenish-dotted, to 1³⁄₁₆ in. long, ³⁄₈ in. wide, saber-shaped, narrowed to an acute, recurved-mucronate tip, upper side flat, lower side rounded basally, keeled and laterally compressed apically, keel abruptly rounded to tip; fls. to 1½ in. across, sessile or nearly so, petals yellow. Cape Prov.

albipuncta (Haw.) N. E. Br. Lvs. 6–8, grayish-green, densely white-dotted, to 1⅝ in. long, ¼ in. wide and not as thick, semicylindrical in lower part, flat or slightly concave on upper side, keeled on lower side, laterally compressed toward the acute apex; fls. to 1³⁄₁₆ in. across, solitary, sessile or nearly so, petals pale yellow to flesh-colored and striped with red. Orange Free State.

Jamesii (L. Bolus) L. Bolus [*Nananthus Jamesii* L. Bolus]. Lvs. 4–6, gray-green, conspicuously dotted, to 1³⁄₁₆ in. long, ³⁄₈ in. wide and thick, semicylindrical or nearly cylindrical, upper side more or less rounded, lower side rounded basally, obtusely keeled toward apex; fls. to 2³⁄₁₆ in. across, nearly sessile, petals golden-yellow. Cape Prov.

RADERMACHERA Zoll. & Moritzi. *Bignoniaceae*. About 30 spp. of trees, native from India to China, to Java, Celebes Is., and Philippine Is.; lvs. opp., 1–3-pinnate; fls. in terminal or axillary panicles, calyx truncate or 2–5-lobed, corolla funnelform to tubular-campanulate, slightly 2-lipped, stamens 4 or 5; fr. a linear, 2-valved, often spirally twisted caps.

Grown in subtropical climates; propagated by seeds, cuttings, and air layering.

Fenicis Merrill. Small evergreen tree; lvs. 2-pinnate or the uppermost 1-pinnate, to 8 in. long, lfts. oblong-elliptic or obovate-elliptic, to about 3 in. long; fls. in panicles to 6 in. long, white, to 1½ in. long, stamens 4; fr. to 8 in. long. Celebes Is., Philipine Is.

pentandra Hemsl. [*Oroxylum flavum* Rehd.]. Evergreen tree, to 20 ft.; lvs. 2-pinnate, to 3 ft. long, lfts. oblong, to 7 in. long; fls. in panicles to 1 ft. long, yellow, 2 in. long and 3 in. across, stamens 5; fr. to 3 ft. long. China.

sinica (Hance) Hemsl. Small evergreen tree; lvs. 2-pinnate, lfts. ovate-lanceolate, to 2 in. long; fls. sulphur-yellow, to 3 in. long, stamens 4; fr. to 16 in. long. China.

RADICULA Moench. *Cruciferae*. Not cult. **R. Armoracia:** *Armoracia rusticana*.

RADISH. Radishes have tuberlike roots. The smaller ones are commonly eaten in the United States as a relish or used as a garnish, but the harder, larger, summer and autumn kinds are used freely in Europe, and in the Far East the durable winter radishes are important articles of food. These various cultivars, with roots of many sizes, shapes, and colors, belong to a species *(Raphanus sativus)* that is unknown as an indigenous,plant and is supposedly a development from the weedy charlock, *R. Raphanistrum*.

The small radishes so much used as table delicacies should be grown quickly in order to ensure crispness; seeds may be sown as early in the spring as the ground is workable. Edible

roots of quick-growing cultivars grown in good soil and under the best conditions may be had in four to six weeks. Seeds may be sown every week up to midspring for succession. The seeds, which germinate quickly, are sown in drills 6–12 inches apart, and the plants are thinned to 1–3 inches as they grow. Radishes force readily, in hotbeds or in frames, and certain cultivars are especially adapted for such use.

Another set of cultivars is adapted for summer use, requiring a longer growing period, although the spring kinds may be grown late in ground sufficiently cool and moist. The common spring radishes run to seed the same season, but the winter kinds of the Orient make deep, hard roots, sometimes 2 feet long, and bloom the following year.

The most serious radish pest is the root maggot. Rotation is to be practiced if the maggot is abundant.

RAMONDA L. Rich. ex Pers. *Gesneriaceae*. Three spp. of per., hairy herbs in mts. of Eur.; lvs. in a rosette; fls. 1–6, on ascending scapes, calyx 4–6-lobed, corolla rotate or slightly campanulate, tube very short, glandular in throat, lobes 4–6, elliptic or ovate, longer than tube, stamens 4–5, borne at base of corolla, anthers erect, separate, disc scarcely developed, ovary superior; fr. a septicidal caps.

Propagated by seeds or by leaf cuttings. For cultivation see *Gesneriaceae*.

Heldreichii: *Jankaea Heldreichii*.

Myconi (L.) Rchb. [*R. pyrenaica* L. Rich. ex Pers.]. Lvs. elliptic to ovate, to 2½ in. long, 2 in. wide, crenate, wrinkled, dark green with white hairs above, reddish-hairy at base and beneath; scapes reddish, to 5 in.; corolla violet or deep lilac to pink or white, with yellow center, 5-parted, lobes ½ in. long, anthers yellow, tipped with a short point; caps. ½–¾ in. long. Pyrenees. Cv. 'Alba'. Fls. white. Cvs. 'Carnea' and 'Rosea'. Fls. pink; said to be less hardy. Cvs. 'Alborosea' and 'Pygmaea' are also listed.

Nathaliae Panč. & Petrovič [*R. serbica* var. *Nathaliae* Hort.]. Lvs. nearly elliptic to obovate-elliptic, to 2 in. long and nearly as wide, rounded at apex, more or less regularly toothed; scapes to 4½ in. long, 1–3-fld.; calyx 4–6-lobed, corolla flat, lavender-violet to white, with orange-yellow center, 4–6-lobed, lobes ½ in. long, anthers yellow or tinged with blue, blunt at tip; caps. ⁵⁄₁₆ in. long. Diploid. Yugoslavia. Cv. 'Alba'. Fls. white.

pyrenaica: *R. Myconi*.

serbica Panč. Similar to *R. Nathaliae* in having blunt, bluish anthers, but tetraploid, with lvs. spatulate to obovate, deeply and irregularly lobed, upturned at edges, corolla somewhat campanulate. Balkan Pen. Var. **Nathaliae:** *R. Nathaliae*.

RANDIA L. *Rubiaceae*. About 200–300 spp. of trop. trees or shrubs, often spiny; lvs. opp., stipules small, interpetiolar; fls. solitary or in clusters, axillary or terminal, corolla funnelform or salverform, tube short or elongate, ovary incompletely 2-celled; fr. a berry, seeds many, separating in a single mass from the wall of the fr.

dumetorum: *Xeromphis spinosa*.

formosa (Jacq.) K. Schum. Shrub, without spines; lvs. mostly ovate or elliptic, to 2½ in. long, pubescent beneath; fls. solitary, terminal, corolla white, tube slender, to 2 in. long; fr. ellipsoid, to 2 in. long. Trop. S. Amer.

maculata: *Rothmannia longiflora*.

malabarica: *Xeromphis spinosa*.

RANUNCULACEAE Juss. CROWFOOT or BUTTERCUP FAMILY. Dicot.; about 50 genera and 1,900 spp. of herbs or sometimes shrubs, mostly of the N. Temp. Zone; lvs. alt. or opp.; fls. chiefly bisexual, sepals and petals 2 to many, petals sometimes absent, stamens many, pistil 1 and compound (in *Nigella*) or simple (in *Actaea*) or pistils few to many and spiralled; fr. an achene, follicle, or berry. Genera cult. are:

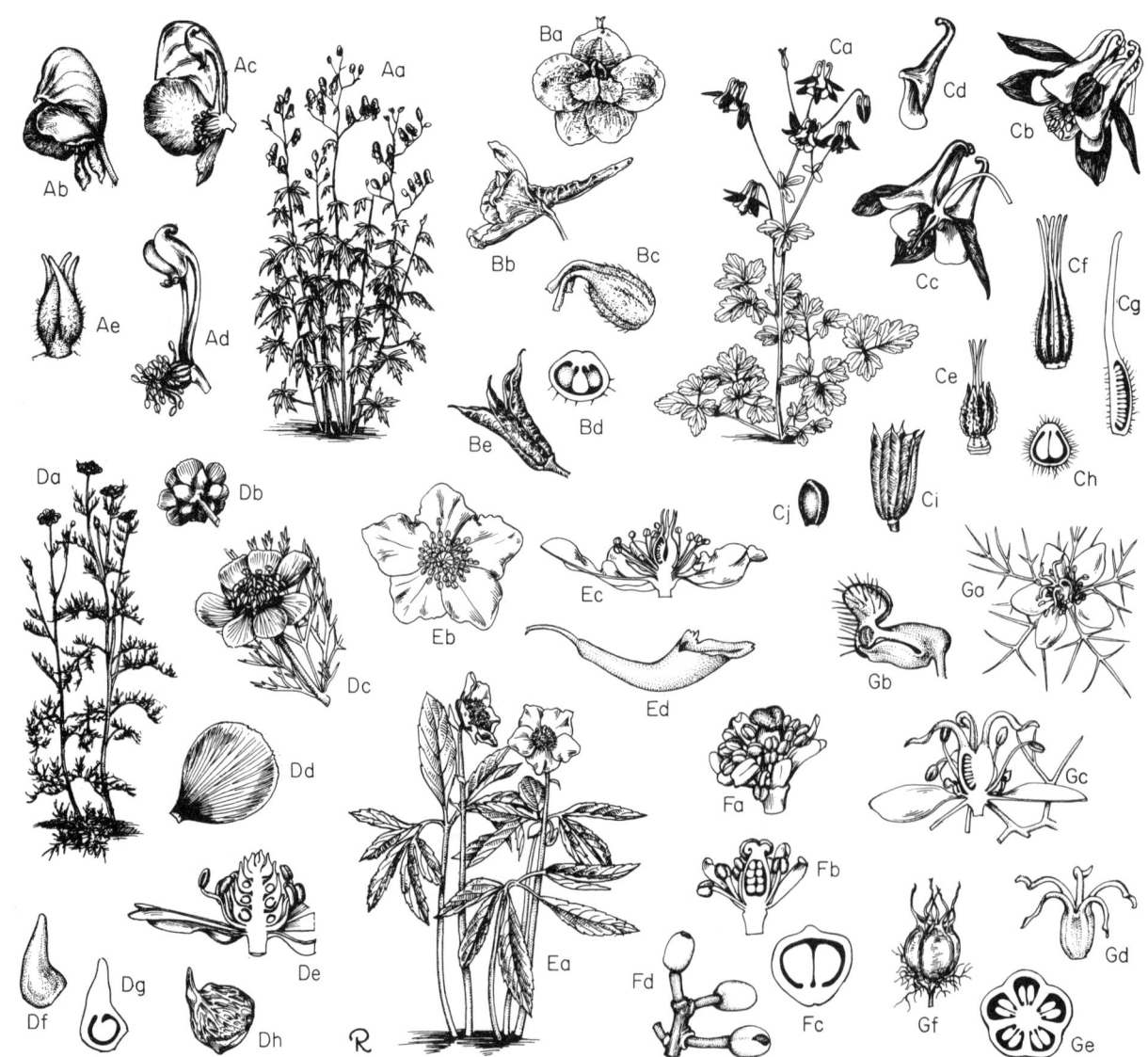

RANUNCULACEAE. **A,** *Aconitum Henryi:* **Aa,** plant, × ¹⁄₁₆; **Ab,** flower, side view, × ¾; **Ac,** flower, vertical section, × ¾; **Ad,** petals and stamens, × 1; **Ae,** pistils, × 3. **B,** *Delphinium elatum:* **Ba,** flower, face view, × ½; **Bb,** flower, side view, × ½; **Bc,** pistils, × 3; **Bd,** ovary, cross section, × 6; **Be,** follicles, × ½. **C,** *Aquilegia vulgaris:* **Ca,** plant, × ⅛; **Cb,** flower, × ½; **Cc,** flower, vertical section, × ½; **Cd,** petal, × ½; **Ce,** staminodes surrounding pistils, × 1; **Cf,** pistils, × 1½; **Cg,** pistil, vertical section, × 2; **Ch,** ovary, cross section, × 6; **Ci,** follicles, × ½; **Cj,** seed, × 3. **D,** *Adonis annua:* **Da,** plants, × ⅙; **Db,** flower, back view, × ½; **Dc,** flower, × 1; **Dd,** petal, × 2; **De,** flower, vertical section, × 2; **Df,** pistil, × 5; **Dg,** pistil, vertical section, × 5; **Dh,** achene, × 4. **E,** *Heleborus niger:* **Ea,** plant, × ⅙; **Eb,** flower, × ⅓; **Ec,** flower, vertical section, × ½; **Ed,** petal, × 3. **F,** *Actaea pachypoda:* **Fa,** flower, × 3; **Fb,** flower, vertical section, × 3; **Fc,** pistil, cross section, × 8; **Fd,** berries, × ½. **G,** *Nigella damascena:* **Ga,** flower surrounded by involucre, × ½; **Gb,** petal, × 4; **Gc,** flower, vertical section, × 1; **Gd,** pistil, × 1; **Ge,** ovary, cross section, × 3; **Gf,** capsule, × 1.

Aconitum, Actaea, Adonis, Anemone, Anemonella, Anemonopsis, Aquilegia, Callianthemum, Caltha, Cimicifuga, Clematis, Consolida, Coptis, Delphinium, Eranthis, Glaucidium, Helleborus, Hepatica, Hydrastis, Isopyrum, Leptopyrum, Nigella, Paraquilegia, Ranunculus, Semiaquilegia, Thalictrum, Trautvetteria, Trollius, and *Xanthorhiza.*

Includes many ornamentals as well as some medicinal plants. Many of the genera are poisonous if eaten. Most of the species are hardy in the northern states and Canada; many are alpine or boreal and are prized in rock gardens.

RANUNCULUS L. [*Batrachium* S. F. Gray]. BUTTERCUP, CROWFOOT. *Ranunculaceae.* About 250 spp. of widely distributed herbs; lvs. alt., simple or compound; fls. yellow, white, or red, sepals and petals mostly 5, petals often falling early, stamens many; fr. a head of achenes.

Only two or three species have been much modified under cultivation into double-flowered and variously colored forms. The florist's ranunculus is *R. asiaticus* (sometimes *R. aconitifolius*), and is propagated by the tuberous roots, which should be taken up and stored in a dry place. It may be grown outdoors in the summer; in the winter it may be grown in the greenhouse or, in a mild climate, as a late winter and spring garden plant.

Other species are grown in the flower garden and borders, and are propagated by seeds or by division of the plants in spring. Most of the species are yellow-flowered, but some are white-flowered, particularly in the section *Batrachium,* which includes aquatic and bog plants useful for colonizing in and about the margins of ponds. Many species are alpine and boreal and well adapted to rock gardens.

acer: a feminine form of the name sometimes used incorrectly instead of *R. acris.*

aconitifolius L. Per., with tuberous roots, to 2 ft., sts. leafy, branched; lvs. 3–7-parted, segms. sometimes 3-lobed and deeply notched; pedicels strigose; fl. buds reddish, fls. white, ¾–1 in. across;

sepals glabrous, petals oblong to round. Mts., cent. Eur. Cv. **'Flore Pleno'**. Fls. double. Cv. **'Luteus Plenus'**. Fls. double, yellow. Subsp. **platanifolius** (L.) Rouy & Foucaud [*R. platanifolius* L.]. Larger, to 3 ft., stiffer; lvs. less divided; pedicels glabrous. Eur.

acriformis A. Gray. Spreading-hirsute per., to 2 ft.; lvs. 2-ternate, ultimate segms. narrow; sepals 5, yellow-green, spreading, less than 3/16 in. long, pubescent, petals mostly 5, yellow, 5/16 in. long, receptacle glabrous; achenes compressed, discoid, 1/8 in. long. S. Wyo., n. Colo. Var. **montanensis** (Rydb.) L. Bens. [*R. montanensis* Rydb.]. Sepals reflexed, petals to 1/2 in. long; achene obovate. Idaho, w. Mont., w. Wyo.

acris L. TALL B., COMMON B. Nonstoloniferous per., to 3 ft., sts. branched, hairy, hollow in lower part; basal lvs. pentagonal or orbicular, palmately 2–7-lobed, lobes cut into 3-toothed segms., terminal lobe not stalked; fls. to 1 in. across, sepals not reflexed, hairy, petals yellow, to 1/2 in. long, receptacle glabrous; achenes with short, hooked beak. Eurasia.; widely introd. elsewhere. Cv. **'Flore Pleno'**. Fls. double.

adoneus A. Gray. Tufted, scapose per., to 10 in., sts. 1–3-fld.; lower lvs. 2–3-ternately parted into linear segms.; fls. golden-yellow, sepals 5, spreading, 5/16 in. long, petals mostly 5, 1/2–5/8 in. long, receptacle glabrous; achenes with somewhat curved beak. Mts., Wyo., Utah, Colo.

alismifolius Geyer ex Benth. Glabrous, erect per., to 2 1/2 ft., lvs. elliptic to lanceolate, to 1 in. wide, entire or toothed; sepals spreading, to 1/8 in. long, petals 5, yellow, obovate, 3/8 in. long, receptacle glabrous; achenes with straight beak. B.C., s. to Mont. and Calif.

alpestris L. Fibrous-rooted per., to 6 in., sts. mostly 1-fld. and 1-lvd.; basal lvs. orbicular, palmately 3–5-lobed, lobes deeply crenate; fls. white, 3/4 in. across, petals 5, obcordate or 3-lobed. Alps.

amplexicaulis L. Per., roots fleshy, sts. to 1 ft.; lvs. simple, elliptic-lanceolate, clasping, entire, glaucous; scapes 3–6-fld.; fls. white, with yellow center, 1 in. across or more, sepals glabrous. Pyrenees, w. Alps.

anemonoides: *Callianthemum rutifolium.*

asiaticus L. PERSIAN B., PERSIAN R. Strigose per., with tuberous roots to 1 1/2 ft., sts. simple or somewhat branched, 1–4-fld.; lvs. 2–3-ternate, segms. toothed or deeply trifid; fls. long-stalked, variously colored, large, to 1 1/2 in. across, sepals reflexed in age, hairy, petals obovate, blunt. Se. Eur. and se. Asia. Usually double in cult. Cv. **'Superbissimus'**. Tall, fls. large.

bilobus Bertol. Per., to 4 in., sts. 1–3-fld., 1–2-lvd.; lower lvs. reniform, almost orbicular, cordate, crenate, glabrous; fls. to 1 in. across, yellow, petals obcordate; achenes with hooked beak. S. Tyrol, n. Lombardy.

bulbosus L. BULBOUS B., BULBOUS C. More or less hairy per., from a cormlike tuber, to 16 in.; lvs. petioled, ovate, 3-lobed to ternate, lobes cleft with toothed segms.; fls. bright yellow, 1/2–1 1/4 in. across, mostly in irregular cymes, sepals 5, strongly reflexed, petals 1/4–3/4 in. long, receptacle hairy. Eur., N. Afr., to Caucasus; introd. into Amer., New Zeal. Cv. **'Flore Pleno'**. Fls. double.

calandrinioides D. Oliver. Per., 4–6 in., sts. 1–3-fld.; lvs. lanceolate or ovate-lanceolate, 1 1/2–2 1/2 in. long, entire, blue-gray, crinkled; fls. 1 1/2–2 1/2 in. across, sepals reddish, ascending, 5/8 in. long, petals white, flushed pink. Morocco.

californicus Benth. Hirsute to subglabrous per., to 2 ft., sts. freely branching; lvs. ternate, segms. linear or lanceolate, lobed or divided; sepals 5, to 5/16 in. long, reflexed at the middle, pilose, petals yellow, 5/16–5/8 in. long, receptacle cylindrical, glabrous; achenes with stout, recurved beak. Ore. and Calif.

crenatus Waldst. & Kit. Slightly hairy per., to 4 in.; lower lvs. orbicular-cordate, round-toothed, dull dark green; fls. white, to 1 in. across, sepals spreading-reflexed, glabrous, petals obovate, nearly entire. Hungary, Macedonia.

creticus L. Slightly hairy per., from fleshy roots, to 1 ft., sts. branched, several-fld.; basal lvs. orbicular, large, shallowly and obtusely palmately lobed, crenate; fls. golden-yellow, to 3 in. across. Greek Is.

delphinifolius: *R. flabellaris.*

Eschscholtzii Schlechtend. Glabrous, scapose per., to 6 in.; lvs. orbicular, about 1 in. across, deeply 3-parted, middle lobe 3-lobed to entire, lateral lobes parted, all sinuses and ultimate segms. obtuse; sepals yellow, to 5/16 in. long, mostly glabrous, petals 5, yellow, to 1/2 in. long, receptacle glabrous; achenes with straight beak. High mts., Alaska to Calif. and New Mex. Var. **eximius** (Greene) L. Bens. [*R. eximius* Greene; *R. saxicola* Rydb.]. Basal lvs. with middle lobes entire, ultimate lobes acute. Mont., Idaho, Utah.

eximius: *R. Eschscholtzii* var.

fascicularis Muhlenb. ex Bigel. EARLY B., EARLY C. Tufted per., to 1 ft., sts. 1–4-fld.; lvs. ternately to pinnately 3–5-parted or only lobed, the lobes oblong or linear; sepals 5, spreading, 5/16 in. long, petals mostly 5, yellow, 1/4–1/2 in. long, receptacle sparsely hispidulous; achenes with slender, straight beak. Ont. to Tex.

Ficaria L. LESSER CELANDINE, SMALL C., PILEWORT. Per., with fleshy, tuberous roots, to 1 ft., sts. branched; lvs. petioled, sheathing, cordate-ovate, to 2 in. long, fleshy; fls. solitary, terminal, 1 in. across, sepals 3, concave, ovate, petals 8–12, golden-yellow, receptacle hairy; achenes with minute beak. Eur., w. Asia; naturalized in N. Amer.

flabellaris Raf. [*R. delphinifolius* Torr.]. YELLOW WATER B., YELLOW WATER C. Amphibious aquatic, submersed or floating sts. stout, hollow, glabrous; submersed lvs. remote, ternately decompound into flaccid, filiform segms., emersed lvs. thicker, with broader segms.; peduncles 1–7-fld.; sepals 5, broad, to 5/16 in. long, petals yellow, 1/4–3/4 in. long; achenes corky-thickened at base, beaked. Me. to B.C., s. to N.C., La., Utah, Calif.

giganteus Wedd. Basal lvs. oblanceolate, toothed, to 2 ft. high; fls. greenish, 4–6 in. across, sepals 3–4 in. long, 2–3 in. broad, petals fleshy, deeply pitted. Peru. Cv. **'Florentinus'** is listed.

glaberrimus Hook. Glabrous per., with fleshy roots, to 6 in.; basal lvs. orbicular to obovate, usually 3–5-lobed; sepals spreading, to 5/16 in. long, slightly pubescent, petals usually 5, yellow, becoming white in age, to 1/2 in. long, receptacle glabrous; achenes with straight beak. B.C. to S. Dak. and n. Calif.

glacialis L. Per., 3–6 in., sts. 1–3-fld.; lvs. usually glabrous, gray-green, deeply 3–5-parted to ternate or nearly 2-ternate, lobes rather blunt; fls. white or tinged pink or purple, to 1 in. across; sepals ovate, very hairy, petals persistent, receptacle glabrous; achenes with straight beak. Mts., Eur., Greenland.

gramineus L. [*R. graminifolius* Salisb.]. Per., to 1 ft., sts. 1–7-fld.; lvs. linear, to several in. long, entire, glabrous; fls. yellow, to 1 in. across, sepals glabrous. Se. Eur.

graminifolius: *R. gramineus.*

Haastii Hook.f. Glabrous, stout fleshy per., to 6 in.; lvs. broad-reniform to orbicular, 2–4 in. across, 5–7-lobed, then irregularly incised; scape thick, 1–5-fld.; fls. yellow, 1–1 1/2 in. across, sepals 5, glabrate, petals 5–15, narrow-cuneate. New Zeal.

hirtellus Royle. Pubescent, erect or decumbent per., to 1 1/2 ft.; lvs. reniform, 3–5-parted, lateral segms. often 2-lobed; fls. few to many, 1/2–5/8 in. across, sepals strigose. W. Himalayas.

illyricus L. White-silky-hairy per., with tuberous roots, sts. to 1 1/2 ft., several-fld.; lvs. deeply 2–3-parted, segms. lanceolate-linear; fls. lemon-yellow, 1–1 1/2 in. across; achenes pitted, with long beak. Cent. Eur. to sw. Asia.

lappaceus Sm. Erect, spreading-hairy per., to 1 1/2 ft.; basal lvs. ovate, to 3 in. long, 3-lobed or with stalked segms. that are again lobed and toothed; sepals spreading, hairy, petals yellow, 1/2–1 in. long, receptacle hairy; achenes with long, recurved beak. Australia.

Lindleyi: a listed name of no botanical standing.

Lingua L. Stoloniferous per., sts. short, stout, lower part creeping in the mud, upper part erect and branched, hollow, mostly glabrous; basal lvs., more or less ovate, to 8 in. long; fls. 1–2 in. across, bright yellow, sepals 5, almost glabrous, petals round-ovate, receptacle glabrous; achenes minutely pitted. Eur., Siberia.

Lyallii Hook.f. Tufted, almost hairless per., with fleshy roots, to 4 1/2 ft.; lvs. long-petioled, peltate, simple, 4–12 in. across, crenate; infl. paniculate; fls. 2–3 in. across, sepals hairy, petals white; achenes with slender beak. New Zeal.

Macauleyi A. Gray. Nearly glabrous per., to 6 in., sts. 1–2-fld.; lvs. oblong to spatulate, to 2 in. long, mostly entire, truncate and toothed at apex; fls. light yellow, sepals spreading, 5/16 in. long, petals 5–8, 1/4–1/2 in. long, receptacle glabrous; achenes with slender, straight or recurved beak. Colo. and New Mex.

macranthus Scheele. Per., to 2 ft., sts. mostly robust, hirsute; larger lvs. to 6 in. long, lfts. usually 3–5 or 7; sepals 5, reflexed, to 5/16 in. long, petals 8–18, yellow, 3/8–3/4 in. long, receptacle hairy; achenes with straight, slender beak. Ariz., adjacent Mex.

macrophyllus Desf. Per., to 1 1/2 ft.; lvs. 3-lobed, lobes rhombic, not deeply divided; fls. yellow, to 1 3/16 in. across; achenes with stout, more or less curved beak. Medit. region. Material cult. under this name is probably misidentified.

millefoliatus Vahl. Per., with fleshy roots, to 1 ft., sts. somewhat branched, 1–2-fld.; lvs. mostly basal, decompound, multifid, ultimate segms. acute; fls. yellow, to 1 in. across, sepals glabrous; achenes with hooked beak. Medit. region.

monspeliacus L. Per., to 16 in.; lvs. mostly basal, ternate or 3-lobed, segms. somewhat incised-dentate; fls. several, yellow, to 1 1/2 in. in diam.; achenes with long beak. Eur.

montanensis: *R. acriformis* var.

montanus Willd. Glabrous per., from creeping rootstocks, to 6 in.; lvs. 3–5-parted, segms. linear-oblong; fls. usually solitary, bright yellow, 1 in. across, sepals hairy; achenes with short, hooked beak. Pyrenees to the Caucasus.

occidentalis Nutt. Suberect, hirsute per., to 1½ ft.; lvs. deeply 3-parted, segms. ovate or cut; sepals 5, greenish-yellow, reflexed at middle, ovate-acute, ⁵⁄₁₆ in. long, pubescent, petals yellow, to ½ in. long, nectary scale 1–2 times as long as broad; achenes with recurved beak. B.C. to Ore.

parnassifolius L. Hairy per., with fleshy roots, to 8 in., sts. 1–6-fld.; basal lvs. somewhat cordate, round-ovate, entire, reddish on margins, woolly underneath along the veins; fls. white, rarely purplish, about 1 in. across, sepals hairy, petals orbicular, overlapping; achenes with slender, short, strongly curved beak. Mts., Pyrenees to Austria.

plantanifolius: *R. aconitifolius* subsp.

pyrenaeus L. Per., to 1 ft., glabrous in the lower part, somewhat woolly above, sts. 1- to few-fld.; lvs. largely basal, linear or lanceolate, entire; fls. white, to 1 in. across, sepals glabrous; achenes with somewhat hooked beak. Pyrenees, Alps.

repens. L. BUTTER DAISY, CREEPING B., CREEPING C., YELLOW GOWAN. Stoloniferous per., to 2 ft., sts. leafy, hairy; basal lvs. petioled, triangular-ovate, 3-lobed or ternate, lobes cut into 3-toothed segms.; fls. about 1 in. across, sepals not reflexed, hairy, petals 5, yellow, ovate, ¼–½ in. long, receptacle hairy; achenes with short, curved beak. Eurasia; naturalized in Amer., and New Zeal. Cv. 'Pleniflorus' [cv. 'Flore Pleno']. Fls. double. Cv. 'Nanus'. Dwarf.

rupestris Guss. [*R. spicatus* Desf.]. Villous per., to 1 ft. or more, sts. simple or few-branched in upper part; 1- or few-fld.; basal lvs. orbicular, 3–5-parted, lobes cuneate-obovate, then incisely dentate; fls. yellow, about 1 in. across, sepals spreading, hairy; achenes with hooked beak. W. Medit. region.

saxicola: *R. Eschscholtzii* var. *eximius.*

Seguieri Vill. Like *R. glacialis,* but sepals glabrous, receptacle hairy; achene with hooked beak. Alps.

spicatus: *R. rupestris.*

Thora L. Glabrous per., with tuberous roots, to 9 in., sts. 1–3-fld.; basal lvs. withering early, st. lf. sessile, reniform, crenate; fls. yellow, ⅜–¾ in. across, sepals spreading; achenes with very short, bent beaks. Pyrenees to Balkans.

RANZANIA T. Ito. *Berberidaceae.* One sp., a per. herb native to Japan; sts. simple; lvs. 2, near apex of st., ternately divided; fls. in terminal fascicles, subtended by 3 deciduous sepal-like bracts, sepals 6, petaloid, petals 6, smaller than sepals, stamens 6, pistil solitary, with many ovules; fr. a berry.

japonica (T. Ito) T. Ito. To 20 in.; lvs. to nearly 5 in. long, lfts. 3-lobed or -incised, glaucous beneath; fls. purple, nodding, about 1 in. across. Suitable for planting in moist, shaded locations. Zone 8.

RAOULIA Hook.f. *Compositae* (Inula Tribe). About 25 spp. of tufted or creeping per. herbs or subshrubs, native chiefly to New Zeal., a few spp. in New Guinea, Australia, and Tasmania; lvs. alt., crowded and overlapping; fl. heads discoid, solitary, terminal, involucre hemispherical, ovoid, or campanulate, involucral bracts imbricate in several rows, scarious to membranous, usually white, receptacle flat or convex, pitted, naked; fls. all tubular, bisexual, the anthers tailed, or the outer fls. female; achenes oblong, glabrous, papillose, or hairy, pappus of 1 or more rows of capillary bristles.

Adapted to the sunny rock garden.

australis Hook.f. [*R. lutescens* Beauverd]. Much-branched, prostrate per., forming mats to 3 ft. across; lvs. densely imbricate, spatulate, about ³⁄₃₂ in. long, 1-nerved, glabrous basally, densely hairy apically; heads ³⁄₁₆ in. across, involucral bracts with bright yellow, radiating tips. New Zeal.

eximia Hook.f. Per., forming cushion 3 ft. across and 20 in. high, sts. woody at base; lvs. densely imbricate, narrowly oblong to obovate- or oblong-spatulate, to ⅛ in. long, 1-nerved, with dense, long hairs on both sides at apex; heads about ⅛ in. across, involucral bracts not white, not radiating. New Zeal.

glabra Hook.f. Loosely branched per., forming mats to 1 ft. across, sts. prostrate, rooting; lvs. loosely imbricate, linear-oblong to ovate-oblong, to ³⁄₁₆ in. long, 3-nerved, nearly glabrous; heads to ⅜ in. across, involucral bracts with white or yellowish, radiating tips. New Zeal.

grandiflora Hook.f. Much-branched per., forming mats or cushions to 6 in. across, sts. woody at base; lvs. densely imbricate, lanceolate, to ⅜ in. long, 3-nerved, silvery-tomentose; heads to ⅝ in. across, involucral bracts with white, radiating tips. New Zeal.

Haastii Hook.f. Per., forming cushions to 3 ft. across and 1 ft. high, sts. creeping and rooting; lvs. densely imbricate, ¹⁄₁₆ in. long, 3-nerved, glabrous basally, silky-hairy apically; heads to ³⁄₁₆ in. across, involucral bracts with creamy-white to dark, nonradiating tips. New Zeal.

lutescens: *R. australis.*

mammillaris Hook.f. Per., forming rounded, dense, woody cushions to 20 in. across; lvs. densely imbricate, obovate-spatulate, to ⅛ in. long, hairy on back apically; heads about ¼ in. across, involucral bracts with white, radiating tips. New Zeal.

subsericea Hook.f. Much-branched per., sts. prostrate, rooting, forming mats; lvs. loosely imbricate, narrowly oblong, to ¼ in. long, 3-nerved, pale green, silvery- to golden-tomentose beneath; heads to ⅜ in. across, involucral bracts with white, radiating tips. New Zeal.

tenuicaulis Hook.f. Per., forming mats to 3 ft. across, sts. creeping and rooting; lvs. loosely imbricate, lanceolate, 1-nerved, whitish-tomentose toward apex; heads to ¼ in. across, involucral bracts with dark, nonradiating tips. New Zeal.

RAPE. In North America rape *(Brassica Napus)* is primarily a forage crop for late autumn and early spring pasturing. The seed is sown late, as for rutabagas, sometimes following a grain crop; if the land is good and rains are sufficient, excellent late forage is secured, and as the plants withstand the winter they also give good spring pasturage if not previously grazed too close; it soon runs to seed. Hogs and lambs, as well as other animals, are sometimes pastured or soiled on rape. 'Dwarf Essex' is the prevailing cultivar. It is sown either broadcast or in drills in June or July or sometimes even in May in the North. Better results are to be expected in drills far enough apart to permit tillage; about three pounds of seed are required for an acre of drills.

Annual or summer races of rape, presumably of the same species, are grown in some countries for the seed, used for oil and as birdseed.

RAPHANUS L. *Cruciferae.* About 10 spp. of ann. to per., tall, branching herbs, from Eur. to e. Asia; lvs. mostly lyrate-lobed or pinnatifid; fls. white to purplish or yellowish, in bractless racemes, sepals 4, petals 4, abruptly clawed; fr. a cross-jointed, indehiscent silique, commonly constricted between the seeds, the lower segm. short, slender, seedless, the upper segm. cylindrical.

caudatus: *R. sativus* cv.

sativus L. RADISH. Root much-thickened, globose to elongate, edible; sts. produced during first or second year from seeds; fls. white, or lilac-veined. Cv. 'Caudatus' [*R. caudatus* L.]. RAT-TAILED RADISH. Root not enlarged; siliques to 12 in. long or more, soft and thick, eaten either raw or used for pickles; has been called "AERIAL RADISH." Cv. 'Longipinnatus'. Root very large, usually long, hard, and durable, usually a winter radish; lvs. to 2 ft. long, deeply pinnatifid. Known as CHINESE RADISH or the "DAIKON" of the Japanese; much grown in the Far East for food. See *Radish.*

RAPHIA Beauvois. *Palmae.* About 20 spp. of unarmed, monoecious palms in Cent. and S. Amer., Afr., and Madagascar; sts. monocarpic, solitary or clustered or scarcely evident; lvs. pinnate, pinnae acute; infls. rarely erect, mostly pendulous, from axils of reduced lvs. at apex of st., thus appearing as a single terminal, branched infl., each infl. with many bracts subtending brs., the brs. again bracted and divided into short rachillae crowded with bracted, unisexual fls.; male fls. in upper part of rachillae, calyx tubular, petals united basally, valvate above, stamens 6–20 or more, filaments erect, female fls. in lower part of rachillae, calyx tubular, petals united basally with a staminodial ring, valvate and acute above, pistil 3-celled; fr. 1-seeded, ovoid to ellipsoid, covered with prominent shining scales, seed with ruminate endosperm and lateral embryo.

The genus is a source of fiber and palm wine, as well as ornamentals; grown in the tropics and subtropics. For culture see *Palms.*

farinifera (Gaertn.) Hyl. [*R. Ruffia* (Jacq.) Mart.]. RAFFIA PALM. Trunk to 30 ft.; lvs. to 65 ft. long, nearly erect, pinnae very numerous, to 5 ft. long, rather rigid, green above, whitish below; male fls. with 6 stamens; fr. shortly top-shaped, to 2⅜ in. long. Trop. Afr., Madagascar. Warmest parts of Zone 9b. Raffia of commerce is obtained from the lvs.

Ruffia: *R. farinifera.*

RAPHIDOPHORA Hassk. (Sometimes but incorrectly spelled *Rhaphidophora*). *Araceae.* About 60 spp. of repent or scandent, often stout climbers, native to se. Asia and Pacific Is.; lvs. pinnatifid or entire, sometimes perforate with small or large holes, petioles long, geniculate; spathe expanded at anthesis, spadix stout, covered with bisexual fls.; perianth absent, stamens 4, ovaries 1-celled, the ovules many, on 2 or 3 parietal placentas, or incompletely 2–3-celled, the ovules borne on margins of the partial partitions.

Strictly tropical, for culture see *Philodendron.*

aurea: *Epipremnum aureum.*

decursiva (Roxb.) Schott. Vigorous climber; lf. blades oblong in outline, to 3 ft. long and 2 ft. wide, leathery, regularly pinnatisect, segms. to 18 on each side, elongate-falcate and somewhat narrowed at base, with a single main nerve and a pair of strong secondary nerves, petioles stout, to 2 ft. long; spathe to 7 in. long, yellowish, spadix gray-green. India to N. Vietnam.

celatocaulis (N. E. Br.) F. Knoll. SHINGLE PLANT. Tall-climbing, sts. of juvenile shoots with short, flattened internodes; lf. blades of juvenile shoots overlapping and covering the petioles and st., elliptic-ovate, basally oblique-cordate, leathery, blue-green, petioles broadly winged, ¼–1¼ in. long; lf. blades of mature shoots pinnatifid, to 16 in. long and 12 in. wide, petioles as long as blades; spathe and spadix yellowish. Borneo.

laciniosa: *Monstera subpinnata.*

pinnata: *Epipremnum pinnatum.*

silvestris (Blume) Engl. Tall-climber; lf. blades elongate-lanceolate, to 5 in. long and 1 in. wide, entire, leathery, petioles short, sheathed up to the blades; spathe to 2 in. long. Indonesia.

RAPHIOLEPIS Lindl. *Rosaceae.* About 14 spp. of evergreen, Asiatic shrubs; lvs. alt., leathery, shining; fls. white or pink, in racemes or panicles, sepals and petals 5, stamens 15–20, pistils 2–3, joined at base; fr. a small, purple or black, drupelike pome.

Grown outdoors in warm climates and sometimes under glass farther north. Propagated by seeds, by cuttings of mature wood late in the summer, by layers, and rare sorts sometimes by grafting on *Crataegus* species.

×**Delacourii** André.: *R. indica* × *R. umbellata.* To 6 ft.; lvs. obovate, crenate in upper half, 1½–3½ in. long; pedicels pubescent; fls. in panicles 3–4 in. high, rosy-pink, ½–¾ in. across.

hybrida: a listed name of no botanical standing.

indica (L.) Lindl. INDIAN HAWTHORN. Shrub, to 5 ft.; lvs. oblong-lanceolate, 2–3 in. long, sharply serrate; fls. white to pinkish, ⅝ in. across, in loose glabrous panicles 2–3 in. high. S. China. Cv. 'Rosea'. Fls. deeper pink.

japonica: *R. umbellata.*

ovata: *R. umbellata* forma.

umbellata (Thunb.) Mak. [*R. japonica* Siebold & Zucc.]. YEDDA HAWTHORN. Rounded shrub, 6–10 ft.; lvs. stout, leathery, ovate-oblong to obovate, 1½–3 in. long, inconspicuously toothed, revolute; fls. white, ¾ in. across, fragrant, in dense, pubescent panicles 3–4 in. high; fr. black, pear-shaped, ⁵⁄₁₆ in. long. Japan, where a brown dye is made from the bark. Zone 8. Forma **ovata** (C. Briot) C. K. Schneid. [*R. ovata* C. Briot]. Lvs. broad, entire or nearly so.

RASPBERRY. The cultivated raspberries of North America are of three groups: (1) red raspberries, *Rubus idaeus,* native to Europe, Asia, and America, and its var. *strigosus,* which is the commonest form of the species in the fields and woodsides of the United States; (2) black raspberries or blackcaps, *Rubus occidentalis,* native to North America east of the Rocky Mountains; (3) purple raspberries, *R.* × *neglectus,* which are hybrids between the two preceding groups. All raspberries have biennial canes; the shoots that bear fruit one year arose from the root the previous year. The canes bear but once (except for the autumn-bearing types), in their second year, and are then cut away at the ground level. New suckers or canes develop in the meantime to take their place.

The red raspberry is one of the hardiest of fruits (Zone 3), growing well in most of the northern United States, in a large part of Canada, and in parts of Alaska. The black and purple raspberries are not so hardy (Zone 4), their range extending little north of the Great Lakes. Raspberries are not tolerant

of heat and drought and consequently are not grown to advantage below the Mason-Dixon line although recent breeding programs have developed some cultivars which extend the growing of raspberries further south. Deep and well-drained soils of good moisture-holding capacity are favorable. Black raspberries thrive better than red raspberries on light soils.

The black and most of the purple cultivars propagate best by means of tip layering. The tips of long, arching canes are inserted vertically behind a spade, with the soil pressed firmly around them. The tips are generally layered in August; that autumn, roots will have formed and the tip or layer may be separated in autumn or spring for planting. Red raspberries are increased from the suckers that naturally arise from the crown or roots.

In the northern states, raspberries are commonly planted in the spring. The red raspberry is planted 2–3 feet apart in rows 7–9 feet apart in commercial plantings, depending upon size of equipment and ability of pickers to move between the rows. Black and purple raspberries are planted 3–4 feet apart in rows of similar width. In the home garden or where land is available, plants may be confined to hills. During the growing season, the new canes of blacks and purples are cut to a height of 24–30 inches depending upon the vigor of the planting. This action will stimulate branching. If the canes are not pruned to this height, a top-heavy plant may develop which is susceptible to wind breakage. The third season from setting, a full crop should be produced.

Raspberries are shallow-rooted plants requiring very little cultivation, only sufficient to keep down weeds, eliminate sucker growth, and break up the hard surface created by pickers. Various mulching materials may be used around raspberries, particularly in the home garden. Mulching material is too expensive to be used on a commercial basis. A good planting of black or purple raspberries may remain productive for five to ten years, while a red raspberry planting may remain productive for 20 years.

Pruning consists of cutting out the fruiting canes immediately after picking, and thinning out the weak canes of the new growth of the previous spring. In the case of red raspberries, the long current season's canes may be pruned back to a height of 5 feet in very early spring. The lateral branches of blacks and purples may be pruned to a length of 8–12 inches, depending upon the vigor and amount of winter injury. For red raspberries, four to six strong canes per linear foot of row should be allowed to remain each year after the planting is established, and the superfluous and weak ones removed. If trained to a hill system, six to eight strong canes per hill are allowed to fruit. For blacks and purples, all strong canes are allowed to grow from the hill.

Insects and diseases can be serious problems to a long-lived raspberry planting. The most serious disease problem in raspberries is viruses. Only virus-free stock should be planted. The new planting should not be located adjacent to an old, established planting and all wild raspberry plants in the surrounding area should be eliminated. The raspberry aphid is the primary vector; however, nematodes are serious vectors, which should be controlled by fumigation before planting. Spur blight, mildew, fruit rot, and anthracnose can be controlled by spraying. The tarnished plant bug, sap beetles, and crown borers are the most serious insect pests. Raspberries can be grown in the home garden with little or no spraying but in order to maintain a profitable commercial planting, various control measures may be required. Plants which become infected with orange rust should be removed from the planting immediately. Sanitation measures greatly reduce insect and disease problems. Old canes should be removed and destroyed. Simazine is the most effective herbicide for use in raspberries; it controls many types of weeds.

Recommended red raspberry cultivars are: for the northeastern United States, 'Amber', 'Hilton', 'Latham', 'Milton', 'Newburgh', 'September', 'Taylor', and the autumn-bearing cultivars 'Augustred', 'Fallgold', 'Fallred', 'Heritage'; for the northwestern United States, 'Canby', 'Fairview',

'Haida', 'Matsqui', 'Meeker', 'Puyallup', 'Summer', 'Willamette'; for Maryland, 'Citadel', 'Reveille', 'Scepter', 'Sentinel'; for Virginia, 'Cherokee', 'Pocahontas', 'Sunrise'; for the southern and central United States, 'Dormanred', 'Southland'; for Ontario, Canada, 'Boyne', 'Comet', 'Festival', 'Gatineau', 'Madawaska', 'Viking'.

Recommended black raspberry cultivars are: for the eastern United States, 'Allegany', 'Allen', 'Bristol', 'Dundee', 'Huron', 'Jewel'; for the western United States, 'Black Hawk', 'Morrison', 'Munger', 'New Logan'.

Recommended purple cultivars are: 'Amethyst', 'Clyde', 'Purple Autumn', 'Sodus'.

Recommended yellow raspberry: 'Amber'.

RATHBUNIA Britt. & Rose. *Cactaceae*. Two spp. of few-ribbed, cylindrical cacti, native to w. Mex.; sts. bushy, branching from base; fls. diurnal, tubular, slightly irregular, tube with few short-tipped, long-decurrent scales, perianth segms. short, spreading, stamens and style exserted, stigma lobes connivent, ovary scaly; fr. spiny, with persistent perianth, seeds black, pitted, hilum oblique, basal.

For culture see *Cacti*.

alamosensis (J. Coult.) Britt. & Rose [*R. sonorensis* (Runge) Britt. & Rose]. Sts. to 10 ft. high and 3 in. thick, ribs 5–8, obtuse, crenate; radial spines 11–18, needle-shaped, whitish, central spines stouter, to 2 in. long; fls. 2–4 in. long; fr. globose, to 1½ in. in diam., with clusters of 5–6 needle-shaped spines. Spring.

sonorensis: *R. alamosensis.*

RATIBIDA Raf. [*Lepachys* Raf.]. PRAIRIE CONEFLOWER. *Compositae* (Helianthus Tribe). Five bien. or per., rough-hairy herbs of N. Amer.; lvs. alt., pinnatifid; fl. heads radiate, solitary, peduncled, involucral bracts in 1 row, green, receptacle globose to columnar, scaly; disc fls. brownish, ray fls. drooping, yellow or purplish; achenes compressed, each one partly enclosed by its subtending receptacular scale, pappus lacking or of 2 awns with or without a crown of smaller scales.

Grown in the flower garden, flowering in early summer to autumn. Propagated by seeds.

columnifera (Nutt.) Woot. & Standl. [*R. columnaris* (Pursh) D. Don; *Lepachys columnaris* (Pursh) Torr. & A. Gray; *L. columnifera* (Nutt.) Macbr.; *Rudbeckia columnaris* Pursh; *Rudbeckia columnifera* Nutt.]. Bien. or per., 1–3½ ft., branching from base; lf. segms. linear to narrowly lanceolate, entire; disc cylindrical, ½–1½ in. long, as long as to much longer than the ½–¾ in.-long, yellow ray fls. Sw. Canada to n. Mex., e. to Minn. and Tex.; also naturalized farther east. Forma **pulcherrima** (DC.) Fern. [*R. pulcherrima* Hort.; *Lepachys pulcherrima* Hort.]. Ray fls. wholly or partly brownish-purple.

columnaris: *R. columnifera.*

pinnata (Venten.) Barnh. [*Lepachys pinnata* (Venten.) Torr. & A. Gray; *Rudbeckia pinnata* Venten.]. Per., coarser than *R. columnifera*, to 4 ft., branched in upper part; lf. segms. narrowly to broadly lanceolate, serrate; disc ellipsoid to oblong, ½–¾ in. long, shorter than the ¾–2 in.-long, yellow ray fls. Ont. to Ga., w. to Minn. and Okla.

pulcherrima: a listed name of no botanical standing for *R. columnifera* forma.

Tagetes (James) Barnh. [*Lepachys Tagetes* (James) A. Gray; *Rudbeckia Tagetes* James]. Per., to 1½ ft., branching from base, very leafy; lf. segms. linear, entire; disc globular to oblong, ⅜–⅝ in. long, ray fls. ¼ in. long or less, inconspicuous, yellow or purple. Kans. and Colo., s. to n. Mex.

RAUVOLFIA L. (sometimes, but not originally, spelled *Rauwolfia*). *Apocynaceae*. Perhaps 70 spp. of pantropical shrubs and small trees with milky sap; brs. whorled; lvs. opp., or often 3–5 at a node, entire; infl. a few- to many-fld. dichasium, terminal or lateral; fls. small, 5-merous, bisexual, corolla salverform or tubular-salverform, mostly greenish or white, stamens borne on corolla, included, anthers free from stigma; fr. of 1 or 2 drupes, each with 1 or 2 seeds.

Rauvolfias are cultivated as ornamentals and for curiosity; in some tropical countries, some species, especially *R. serpentina* Baill., are grown as a source of tranquilizing drugs, which are derived from the roots. Propagated by stem and root cuttings, and by seeds.

canescens: *R. tetraphylla.*

chinensis: *R. verticillata.*

javanica Koord. & Val. Tree, to 100 ft.; lvs. in whorls of 4, oblong-lanceolate to oblanceolate, to 1 ft. long, 2½ in. wide, acute to acuminate, basally attenuate, petioles to 1 in. long; infls. terminal, umbelliform, peduncles 4 together, to 3 in. long; calyx lobes acute, corolla campanulate-funnelform, almost twice as long as calyx, tube ¼ in. long, lobes ⅛ in. long; drupes broadly obcordate to obreniform, ½ in. across, blue-black. Java.

pleiosiadica: *R. vomitoria.*

pseudoclada: a listed name of no botanical standing.

samarensis Merrill. Tree, to 25 ft.; lvs. in whorls of 4, oblong-elliptic, to 8 in. long, acute to acuminate at each end, with 30–35 primary veins on each side, petioles to 1 in. long; peduncles at anthesis 2 in. long, each bearing an umbel of several brs.; fls. white, to ³⁄₁₆ in. long, hirsute in throat, lobes ¹⁄₁₆ in. long; drupes ellipsoid, to ½ in. long, dark purple, rather fleshy. Samar (Philippines). Doubtfully in cult.; material offered under this name may be *R. javanica.*

tetraphylla L. [*R. canescens* L.]. Shrub, to 5 ft.; lvs. 4 in a whorl, very unequal, variable in shape, ovate to ovate-elliptic, to 6 in. long, abruptly tapered at base, with obscure lateral veins, indistinctly petioled; infls. mostly lateral, unbranched, few-fld., much shorter than lvs.; fls. small, calyx lobes acute, corolla urceolate, white or cream-yellow, tube slender, ⅛ in. long, lobes rounded, half as long as tube, ovaries fused; drupe globoid, to ⅜ in. across, becoming red, then black, 2-seeded. Trop. Amer.

verticillata (Lour.) Baill. [*R. chinensis* (K. Spreng.) Hemsl.]. Shrub, to 5 ft.; brs. slender; lvs. in whorls of 3, rarely 4, elliptic to oblanceolate, to 5 in. long, acuminate, basally long-attenuate into slender petiole to ⅜ in. long; peduncles terminal, several together, to 1½ in. long; calyx lobes reflexed at apex, corolla white, scarcely ¼ in. across, tube slender, to ½ in. long, expanded near middle; drupes mostly paired, ellipsoid, to ½ in. long, red. S. China, Indo-China, Taiwan.

vomitoria Afzel. [*R. pleiosiadica* K. Schum.]. Glabrous shrub or small tree, to 20 ft.; lvs. in whorls of 3–4, lanceolate to elliptic, to 7 in. long, acuminate at both ends, thin; infls. pubescent; corolla lobes very short, tube to ¼ in. long, hairy in throat; drupes solitary or paired, ovoid, to ¼ in. long, red. Trop. Afr.

RAVENALA Adans. *Strelitziaceae*. One sp., a large treelike plant of Madagascar, with palmlike trunks; lvs. bananalike, 2-ranked toward apex of st. resulting in a fan-shaped aspect; infl. axillary; fls. many in axils of stiff, boatlike bracts shorter than lvs., bisexual, outer segms. separate, equal, inner with 2 lateral segms. similar to outer, the lower short, stamens 6; fr. a 3-valved caps., seeds many, with arils.

madagascariensis Sonn. TRAVELER'S TREE, TRAVELER'S PALM. Sts. in clumps, to 30 ft. or more; lvs. to about 10 ft. long, long-petioled; fls. white, bracts to 12 in each infl.; caps. to 4 in. long, aril blue. Madagascar. Cult. in tropics. Fl. bracts and lf. sheaths hold rainwater useful for emergency drinking, hence common name; a striking plant when mature.

RAVNIA Ørst. *Rubiaceae*. Four spp. of eiphytic shrubs, native to Cent. Amer.; lvs. opp., somewhat fleshy or leathery when dry, stipules large, oblong; fls. in 3's at the ends of brs., large, red, 5–6-merous, corolla tube slender, stamens 5–6; fr. a slender, cylindrical caps., seeds many.

triflora Ørst. To 3 ft.; lvs. elliptic or lanceolate-oblong, to 4 in. long, stipules to ½ in. long; fls. 2 in. long. An attractive plant, though not floriferous; looks more like a member of the Gesneriaceae.

REBUTIA K. Schum. [*Aylostera* Speg.; *Mediolobivia* Backeb.]. CROWN CACTUS. *Cactaceae*. Perhaps 27 spp. of small, tubercled cacti, native to s. Bolivia and n. Argentina; sts. simple or cespitose, globose to short-cylindrical; fls. from old spiniferous areoles, diurnal, mostly red to orange, funnelform, scales of tube and ovary naked or with axillary hairs, stamens (always?) in 1 series; fr. small, dry. Spp. of this genus formerly assigned to *Aylostera* have a solid column between ovary and style, and the fl. scales have axillary bristles.

For culture see *Cacti*.

aureiflora Backeb. [*Mediolobivia aureiflora* (Backeb.) Backeb.; *M. elegans* Backeb.]. Sts. cespitose, to 1½ in. thick, tubercles ¼ in. in diam.; spines 15–20, bristlelike, white or brownish, mostly to ¼ in. long, 3–4 or more appearing central and to ⅜ in. long; fls. yellow, to 1½ in. long and across. Argentina. Cv. '**Longiseta**'. Spines golden, to 1½ in. long; fls. tinged with orange.

chrysacantha Backeb. Sts. to 2½ in. high and 2 in. thick, tubercles flattened; spines 25–30, bristlelike, white, becoming yellow, to ½ in. long; fls. slender, brick-red with orange-yellow tube, to 2 in. long, scales with short axillary bristles. Argentina. Perhaps only a var. or form of *R. senilis.*

deminuta (A. Web.) Britt. & Rose [*Aylostera deminuta* (A. Web.) Backeb.]. Sts. cespitose, globose, to 2½ in. thick, tubercled, ribs 11–13; spines 10–12, brown-tipped or brown, to ¼ in. long; fls. dark orange-red, 1¼ in. long. Argentina. Forma **pseudominuscula** (Speg.) Buin. & Donald [*R. pseudominuscula* (Speg.) Britt. & Rose; *Aylostera deminuta* var. *pseudominuscula* (Speg.) Backeb.]. Central spines more or less distinguishable, to 4; fls. dark purple, 1 in. long.

Einsteinii: a listed name of no botanical standing.

elegans: a listed name of no botanical standing, probably for *R. aureiflora.*

Fiebrigii (Gürke) Britt. & Rose [*Aylostera Fiebrigii* (Gürke) Backeb.]. Sts. globose, to 2½ in. thick; spines bristlelike, radial spines 25–35, white, to ⅜ in. long, central spines 2–5, brown, to ¾ in. long; fls. yellowish-red, to 1½ in. long. Bolivia.

grandiflora Backeb. SCARLET CROWN CACTUS. Related to *R. minuscula* and perhaps only a var. of it, with fls. to 2½ in. long.

Haagei: *Lobivia pygmaea.*

Knuthiana Backeb. Sts. to 1¾ in. thick, tubercles flattened; spines 30 or more, hairlike, brown, interlacing; fls. carmine, to 2 in. long. Argentina. Perhaps only a var. of *R. violaciflora.*

Krainziana W. Kesselr. Sts. cespitose, depressed-globose, to 2 in. high and 1⅝ in. thick, tubercles small; areoles white-woolly, radial spines 8–12, bristlelike, white, central spines 0; fls. red to crimson, to 1⅝ in. across. Bolivia?

Kupperana Böd. [*Aylostera Kupperana* (Böd.) Backeb.]. Sts. branching, to 1½ in. thick, tubercles ⅛ in. long and wide; spines thin-needle-shaped, brown, radial spines 13–15, to ³⁄₁₆ in. long, central spines 1–3, thicker, to ½ in. long; fls. orange-red, to 1½ in. long. Argentina.

minuscula K. Schum. RED-CROWN. Sts. simple or cespitose, to 2½ in. thick, spines about 30, bristlelike, white, to ⁵⁄₁₆ in. long; fls. crimson, to 1½ in. long. N. Argentina.

pseudodeminuta Backeb. [*Aylostera pseudodeminuta* (Backeb.) Backeb.]. WALLFLOWER-CROWN. Sts. cespitose, to 1½ in. thick; spines slender-needle-shaped, white, brown-tipped, radial spines 11, to ⁵⁄₁₆ in. long, central spines 2–3, to ½ in. long; fls. golden, to 1½ in. long. Argentina. Cv. 'Schumanniana'. Spines thicker, brown.

pseudominuscula: *R. deminuta* forma.

pygmaea: *Lobivia pygmaea.*

senilis Backeb. FIRE-CROWN CACTUS. To about 3 in. high and 2¾ in. thick; spines about 25, bristlelike, white; fls. carmine-red, 1⅜ in. across. N. Argentina.

Spegazziniana Backeb. Sts. cespitose, short-cylindrical; areoles white-woolly, spines yellowish, tipped with brown, radial spines to 14, to ⁵⁄₃₂ in. long, central spines 2, longer; fls. dark red, to 1⅝ in. across. N. Argentina.

spinosissima Backeb. [*Aylostera spinosissima* (Backeb.) Backeb.]. Sts. cespitose, to 1½ in. thick; areoles close-set, spines many, bristlelike, radial spines 5–6, brownish; fls. brick-red, to 1¼ in. long. Argentina.

Steinbachii Werderm. Sts. cespitose, tubercles oblong, projecting below the areole, more or less united into 10–15 ribs; spines 6–12, blue-black, thickened at base, the upper and central spines slender-awl-shaped, to 1 in. long; fls. scarlet, to 1½ in. long, scales naked in axils. Bolivia.

Steinmannii: *Lobivia Steinmannii.*

violaciflora Backeb. Sts. solitary, to 1¼ in. thick, spines about 20, bristlelike, brown, to 1 in. long; fls. rose-violet, about 1½ in. long. N. Argentina.

xanthocarpa Backeb. Sts. cespitose, globose, to 1¾ in. high and 2 in. thick; spines 15–20, glassy, gray or white, about 4 yellowish and to nearly ⁵⁄₁₆ in. long, lower spines shorter; fls. carmine-red, about ¾ in. across. N. Argentina.

RECHSTEINERIA: *SINNINGIA.* R. cyclophylla: *S. macropoda.* R. Douglasii: see *S. Claybergiana.* R. Lindleyi: *S. Claybergiana.* R. lineata: *S. macropoda.* R. macrantha: see *S. cardinalis.* R. purpurea: see *S. verticillata.* R. Sellovii: see *S. Claybergiana.*

REEVESIA Lindl. *Byttneriaceae.* Probably not more than 10 spp. of small trees, native to trop. Asia; lvs. alt., simple, entire; fls. cymose, in terminal corymbs, calyx irregularly 4–6-toothed, petals 5, clawed, the claws channelled and apically biauriculate, androgynophore present, bearing 5 groups of 3 sessile anthers alternating with 5 small staminodes, and a

stalked, 5-carpelled ovary; fr. a loculicidally dehiscent, woody caps., seeds 1–2 in each cell, winged.

thyrsoidea Lindl. To 60 ft.; lvs. ovate to broadly oblong, to 10 in. long, 5 in. wide, leathery, glossy; corymbs shorter than the lvs.; petals white, mostly yellow-spotted above claw, about ½ in. long, spreading or slightly reflexed, androgynophore exserted; fr. obovate, nearly 1 in. long. S. China to Java.

REGISTRATION. Registration, as the word applies to cultivated plants, is the acceptance of a cultivar name (or, in some cases, a collective name) by a registration authority and the inclusion of the name in a register. The registration authority may be a statutory one, i.e., a body established by law by a country or by treaty between countries, or it may be nonstatutory, i.e., any organization or body, national or international in scope, entrusted with registration by agreement of organizations concerned. The aim of registration is to promote uniformity, accuracy, and stability in the naming of agricultural, horticultural, and silvicultural cultivars. Encompassed within this aim is, importantly, the prevention of the use of the same name for more than one cultivar, and, except under specified conditions, of the use of more than one name for a particular cultivar. Registers also serve as integrated sources for certain kinds of information about cultivars.

Especially important to the aim of registration are the nonstatutory International Registration Authorities (IRA's), appointed by the International Society for Horticultural Science (ISHS) and charged with the registration of all known cultivar names in specific genera or other groups of related cultivated plants and, when possible, with the publication of comprehensive check lists of such names. National Registration Authorities (NRA's) function similarly, but on a national level, and cooperate with the IRA concerned with registration in the same plant genus or group. An NRA is usually set up within a national society devoted to the knowledge and culture of a particular plant group.

The principles governing acceptance or rejection of cultivar names for registration are laid down in the International Code of Nomenclature of Cultivated Plants (often referred to as the Horticultural Code). The information required for registration by a registration authority varies somewhat with the organization and the plant group concerned, but ordinarily includes at least the names and addresses of the originator, the namer, and the introducers to cultivation and to commerce of the cultivar, and a description of it. Prepared specimens, photographs, or illustrations of the plant are sometimes required. Registration authorities are not expected to judge the merits or evaluate the distinctness of the cultivars they register, though they may do the latter should their facilities permit. There is no legal requirement that the namer of a cultivar follow the rules laid down in the International Code or that he register the name with the appropriate nonstatutory registration authority, but it is strongly recommended that he do so, in order to further the systematization of information on cultivars and help promote order where chaos and confusion too often exist.

Lists of IRA's are available from the ISHS Commission for Horticultural Nomenclature and Registration; organizations interested in being considered for appointment as IRA's should also apply to this Commission. The addresses of particular registration authorities or of the current Chairman of the ISHS Commission may be had on request from the L. H. Bailey Hortorium, Cornell University, Ithaca, New York 14853.

REHDERODENDRON H. H. Hu. *Styracaceae.* About 9 spp. of deciduous trees, native to s. and w. China; lvs. alt., simple; fls. in axillary racemes or panicles, calyx 5-lobed, petals 5, united only at base, stamens 10, ovary almost inferior; fr. indehiscent, woody, seeds 1–3.

macrophyllum H. H. Hu. Tree, to 30 ft.; lvs. elliptic or elliptic-ovate to oblong-elliptic, to 4¼ in. long, acute to acuminate, broadly cuneate at base, finely toothed, stellate-hairy on veins underneath, petiole to ⅝ in. long; fls. appearing before the lvs., white, in 6–10-fld. racemes to 2 in. long; fr. oblong, to 3 in. long, with 8–10 ribs. W. China. Zone 8.

REHMANNIA Libosch. ex Fisch. & C. A. Mey. *Gesneriaceae* or *Scrophulariaceae.* Eight spp. of hairy, per. herbs in China; lvs. in a basal rosette, alt. on the erect flowering sts., blades crenate to serrate or pinnately lobed; fls. solitary in axils of the lvs. or of bracts in a raceme, calyx 5-lobed, upper lobes longest, corolla obliquely funnelform, slightly swollen on lower side, 2-lipped, the upper lobes shorter than 3 lower lobes, tube with 2 ridges extending inside from sinuses of lower lip, stamens 4, borne near base of corolla, anthers not coherent, disc ringlike, poorly developed, ovary superior, with parietal placentas but sometimes 2-celled at base, stigma 2-lobed; fr. a caps. The genus has been placed in 2 families, and its position is still uncertain.

For cultivation see *Gesneriaceae.*

angulata: see *R. elata.*

elata N. E. Br. [*R. angulata* Hort., not (D. Oliver) Hemsl.]. To 6 ft.; lf. blades ovate or elliptic, to 10 in. long, 4 in. wide, cuneate at base, with 2–6 acute, often toothed lobes on each side; lvs. or bracts of infl. with long-cuneate base not broader than blade near its apex; corolla to 2½ in. long, limb rose-purple, tube yellow dotted with red inside. Originally confused with *R. angulata* and still often grown under this name.

glutinosa (Gaertn.) Libosch. ex Steud. To 10 in.; lvs. obovate, irregularly crenate but not lobed; corolla about 1½ in. long, dull purple-brown and creamy-yellow, densely glandular-pubescent.

REICHARDIA Roth [*Picridium* Desf.]. *Compositae* (Cichorium Tribe). About 8 spp. of ann. or per. herbs with milky sap, native from Canary Is. to e. India; lvs. alt. or basal; fl. heads long-peduncled; fls. all ligulate, yellow; achenes tapering at both ends, 4–5-ribbed, pappus of white bristles united at the base and deciduous as a unit.

tingitana (L.) Roth [*Picridium tingitanum* (L.) Desf.]. Ann., to 18 in.; basal lvs. to 5 in. long, pinnatifid and denticulate or nearly entire, st. lvs. shorter, clasping; heads 1½ in. across; fls. yellow, with dark purple base. Canary Is., Medit. region to e. India.

REINECKIA Kunth. *Liliaceae.* One sp., a rhizomatous, per. herb of China and Japan; sts. forming clumps; lvs. basal, tufted; fls. flesh-pink, in dense, bracted, scapose spikes, perianth segms. 6, united into a tube, stamens 6, filaments arising from the perianth; fr. a berry. Likely to be confused with *Ophiopogon.*

Sometimes grown as a pot plant, and in the open in mild climates. Propagated by division.

carnea (Andr.) Kunth. Lvs. linear to lanceolate, to 1½ ft. long and ¾ in. wide, 2-ranked, arching; fls. fragrant, ½ in. long; fr. red.

REINHARDTIA Liebm. [*Malortiea* H. Wendl.]. *Palmae.* Five spp. of small or dwarf, solitary or cespitose, unarmed, monoecious understory palms, native to wet forests from Mex. to Colombia; sts. slender; lvs. pinnate or pinnately ribbed, sheaths fibrous, blades merely 2-cleft apically with margins coarsely toothed, or pinnate with 1-ribbed, 2-cleft, acuminate pinnae, or with pinnae several-ribbed, coarsely toothed and often fenestrate along the rachis; infl. among lvs., spicate or branched, bracts 2, persistent, tubular, papery, peduncle elongate, brs. few to many, simple or once-branched, rachillae with white fls. in triads (2 male and 1 female); male fls. with sepals 3, broadly rounded, imbricate, petals 3, valvate, stamens 8–40, erect, female fls. with sepals 3, broadly rounded, imbricate, petals 3, imbricate and often partly united basally, valvate above, spreading at flowering, staminodes united and joined basally to petals, with 2–5 teeth at apex, these spreading in flowering, pistil 3-celled, usually 3-ovuled; fr. 1-seeded, with apical stigmatic residue, seed with homogeneous or ruminate endosperm, embryo basal.

Diminutive ornamental palms suited to protected shady gardens in the tropics and subtropics or pot culture in the home or greenhouse. Zone 10a. For culture see *Palms.*

gracilis (H. Wendl.) Drude ex Dammer [*Malortiea gracilis* H. Wendl.]. Sts. solitary or cespitose, to 8 ft.; lvs. with 2–4 several-ribbed, coarsely toothed, perforated pinnae on each side of rachis; infl. with 2–11 or more rachillae; male fls. to ¼ in. long, stamens 8–22,

female fls. to ³⁄₁₆ in. long, staminodes with subulate teeth; fr. black on red rachillae at maturity, ½–⅝ in. long, endosperm homogeneous or minutely ruminate marginally. A variable sp. Var. **gracilis.** The typical var.; lvs. with ribs 14–22 on each side, rachis to nearly 10 in. long; male fls. to ¼ in. long, stamens 16–22. Brit. Honduras, Honduras. Var. **gracilior** (Burret) H. E. Moore. Lvs. with ribs 8–11 on each side, rachis to about 2½ in. long; male fls. about ⅛ in. long, stamens 8–10. S. Mex. to Honduras.

simplex (H. Wendl.) Drude ex Dammer. Mostly cespitose; lvs. to 8 in. long, simple, elliptic, coarsely toothed, 8–12-ribbed, and very briefly 2-cleft at apex or more often with an additional 3–4-ribbed basal pinna on each side; infl. with 3–7 rachillae; male fls. to about ³⁄₁₆ in. long, stamens 14–19; fr. black on red axis at maturity, to ⅝ in. long, seed with homogeneous or minutely marginally ruminate endosperm. Honduras to Panama.

REINWARDTIA Dumort. *Linaceae.* One or 2 spp. of subshrubs, native to mts. of n. India and China; lvs. alt.; fls. yellow, solitary, or in axillary or terminal cymelike clusters, sepals 5, petals 5, falling early, stamens 5, alternating with 5 staminodes; fr. a 3–5-celled caps.

Grown under glass; they require a temperature of 55–60° F. Propagated by cuttings from strong shoots in spring in sandy loam. Stems should be pinched back frequently to induce compact habit. Adapted to outdoor culture in the South and Calif.

indica Dumort. [*R. tetragyna* Planch.; *R. trigyna* (Roxb.) Planch.; *Linum trigynum* Roxb., not L.]. YELLOW FLAX. Glabrous subshrub, to 3 ft.; lvs. elliptic-obovate or oblong-obovate, mucronate, entire to serrulate; fls. 1–2 in. across, petals united into a tube at base, styles 3–5. Sometimes grown erroneously as *Linum flavum.*

tetragyna: *R. indica.*

trigyna: *R. indica.*

RENANTHERA Lour. *Orchidaceae.* About 15 spp. of epiphytes, native to trop. Asia and Malay Arch.; sts. leafy; lvs. 2-ranked; infl. horizontal, branched, many-fld.; fls. small to large, red or red and yellow, sepals and petals spreading, narrow, lip small, not hinged, with shallow conical spur as long as midlobe, oblong callus on each side at junction of midlobe and lateral lobes. For structure of fl. see *Orchidaceae.*

Warm greenhouse. For culture see *Orchids.*

coccinea Lour. St. long-climbing; lvs. to 2½ in. long, light green, 2-lobed at apex; infl. branched nearly in 1 plane; fls. red, upper sepal and the petals mottled, lateral sepals clear red, upper sepal 1 in. long, lateral sepals 1½ in. long, lip 3-lobed, lateral lobes yellow with red stripes, midlobe white at base, red apically, calluses white. Flowering most of the year. Se. Asia.

Imschootiana Rolfe. St. short, never long-climbing; lvs. to 2 in. long; infl. branched on all sides; fls. yellow and red, upper sepal and the petals yellow, petals spotted with red, upper sepal ¾ in. long, lateral sepals 1½ in. long, lip 3-lobed, with 7 calluses. Assam, Indochina.

Lowii: *Arachnis Lowii.*

✕**Maingayi:** *Arachnis* ✕ *Maingayi.*

monachica Ames. St. short; lvs. strap-shaped, to 5 in. long, dark green, 2-lobed at apex; infl. erect, loosely racemose, to 7 in. long, about 6-fld.; fls. 1 in. across, yellow with red spots, lateral sepals ¾ in. long, petals strongly curved, ½ in. long, lip 3-lobed, saccate, lateral lobes triangular, midlobe oblong, 1 in. long. Philippine Is.

Storiei Rchb.f. St. short; lvs. linear-oblong, to 8 in. long, 2-lobed at apex; infl. branched usually in 1 plane, many-fld.; fls. to 3 in. long vertically, deeper red than in *R. coccinea,* lateral sepals wide, with crisped, undulate margins, and with deeper crimson blotches. Philippine Is.

RENEALMIA L.f. *Zingiberaceae.* About 60 spp. of per. herbs in trop. Amer. and W. Afr.; similar to *Alpinia,* infl. often on a separate peduncle from the base; staminodial lip erect and not spreading, stalked, often 3-lobed.

For culture see *Zingiberaceae.*

ventricosa Griseb. Lvs. linear-lanceolate, to slightly more than 1 ft. long, 2 in. wide, acuminate, ligule very short; infl. terminating the leafy st., dense, ellipsoid, bracts lanceolate, 1 in. long or more; fls. 2–4 on short pedicels in axils of tubular fl. bracts, calyx shortly 3-toothed, not much shorter than the small corolla, lip 3-lobed. Cuba. Has been offered as *Alpinia ventricosa,* and some material cult. as *Alpinia vittata* is also this sp.

RESEDA L. MIGNONETTE. *Resedaceae.* About 60 spp. of mostly Medit. herbs; lvs. alt., simple to pinnate; fls. small, in terminal spikelike racemes, usually bisexual, sepals 4–7, petals 4–7, unequal, cleft, stamens 7–40, more or less united, crowded on 1 side of fl., carpels 3–6, united below and open at apex; fr. a 1-celled caps., open at top.

Mignonettes are grown outdoors and under glass, mostly for their very fragrant flowers. They thrive in partly shaded locations with moderately rich soil. In the greenhouse, the night temperature should be about 48° F. Seeds should be sown where plants are to grow, or else in pots since they transplant poorly.

alba L. WHITE UPRIGHT M. Ann. or bien., to 3 ft., sts. hollow; lvs. deeply pinnatifid, with 5–8 pairs of narrow, unequal lobes; racemes dense, conical; fls. greenish-white, not fragrant, sepals and petals usually 5, stamens 11–14; caps. usually 4-lobed, about 7/16 in. long. Summer to autumn. Medit. region to Iran; naturalized in ne. U.S.

complicata Bory. Tender per., to 18 in., much-branched; lvs. linear-oblong, entire, glabrous; racemes slender, loose; fls. subsessile, sepals 6, with white, membranous margins, petals 6, twice as long as sepals; caps. 4-lobed. S. Spain.

lutea L. Ann. to per., to 30 in., sts. solid, roughish; basal lvs. to 3 in. long, entire to 3-parted, st. lvs. variously pinnatifid into oblong segms.; racemes short, compact; fls. greenish-yellow, sepals and petals usually 6, stamens 12–20; caps. ellipsoid, 3-lobed, erect, roughish. Summer to autumn. Medit. region; naturalized in N. Amer.

luteola L. DYER'S ROCKET, WELD. Bien., to 5 ft., sts. hollow, little branched; lvs. entire, basal lvs. narrowly oblanceolate, to 3 in. long, st. lvs. narrowly oblong; racemes dense; sepals and petals usually 4, stamens 20–25; caps. 3-lobed nearly to middle, to ¼ in. long. Medit. region, Canary Is. Formerly cult. as source of a deep yellow dye; occasionally planted in collections of economic plants.

odorata L. COMMON M. Ann., becoming decumbent; lvs. entire and elliptic to spatulate, or 3-lobed, obtuse, to 3 in. long; racemes dense; fls. yellowish-white, very fragrant, sepals and petals 6, anthers orange; caps. 3-lobed, pendent. N. Afr. Cult. abroad for essential oil used in perfumery. Cv. 'Grandiflora'. A large-fld. garden form.

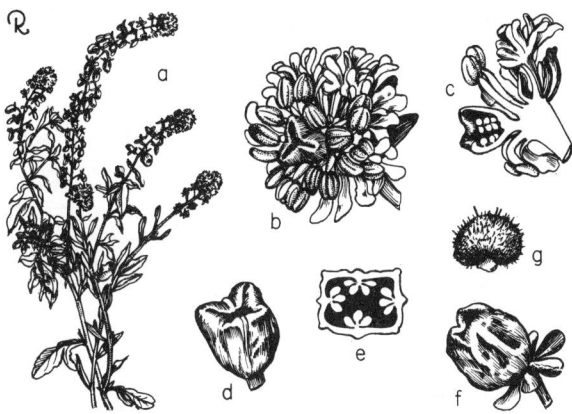

RESEDACEAE. *Reseda lutea*: **a,** flowering stems, × ¼; **b,** flower, × 3; **c,** flower, vertical section, × 3; **d,** pistil, × 3; **e,** ovary, cross section, × 4; **f,** capsule, × 1; **g,** seed, × 5.

RESEDACEAE S. F. Gray. MIGNONETTE FAMILY. Dicot.; 6 genera of herbs, native to Medit. region, ne. Afr., sw. Asia, Calif., and Mex.; lvs. alt., simple to pinnate, stipules small, glandlike; fls. mostly bisexual and irregular, sepals 4–7, petals 4–7 or 0, small, often laciniate, stamens 3–40, not covered by petals in bud, filaments separate or united basally, carpels 2–6, separate or united, each with a separate stigma; fr. a caps. or berry. *Reseda* is grown as an ornamental, a perfume plant, and formerly was grown as source of a dye.

RESTREPIA HBK. *Orchidaceae*. About 20 spp. of epiphytes, native to trop. Cent. and S. Amer.; sts. in tufts, covered by flattened, overlapping sheaths; lf. solitary; infl. 1-fld.; fls. conspicuous, upper sepal separate, with a club-shaped tip, lateral sepals united, petals filiform, with a knob at tip, lip small, commonly with 2 slender appendages at base, column with a foot, pollinia 4. For structure of fl. see *Orchidaceae*.

For culture see *Orchids.*

antennifera HBK [*Pleurothallis Ospinae* R. E. Schult.]. To 1 ft.; lvs. fleshy, ovate, to 5 in. long; peduncle filiform, shorter than lvs.; fls. showy, to 1 in. long, upper sepal and the petals filiform, white, lateral sepals united up to apex, boat-shaped, yellow-brown with maroon-purple stripes, lip fleshy, papillose. Andes, Venezuela and Colombia.

guttulata Lindl. [*R. maculata* Lindl.]. Similar to *R. antennifera;* sts. to 2 in. high; upper sepal and the petals linear-lanceolate, white with crimson line along center, lateral sepals united up to apex, boat-shaped, greenish-yellow with many purple spots, lip fleshy, roughened. Andes, Venezuela to Ecuador.

maculata: *R. guttulata.*

RESTREPIELLA Garay & Dunst. *Orchidaceae*. Eight spp. of tufted epiphytes, native to trop. Cent. and S. Amer.; sts. erect, 1-lvd.; infls. clustered, 1-fld.; fls. sessile, sepals and petals separate, lip jointed to column foot, column arching, pollinia 4. For structure of fl. see *Orchidaceae*.

For culture see *Orchids.*

ophiocephala (Lindl.) Garay & Dunst. [*Pleurothallis ophiocephala* Lindl.]. To 14 in., sts. erect, to 7 in. long, with 1 loose-fitting sheath at the middle; lvs. fleshy, oblong-strap-shaped, short-petioled; fls. ¾ in. long, dull yellowish-brown, spotted with dull purple, upper sepal elliptic-oblong, lateral sepals similar, united up to apex, petals much shorter, oblong-strap-shaped, lip fleshy, tongue-shaped. Mex., Guatemala.

RETINISPORA: *CHAMAECYPARIS.*

REYNOUTRIA: *POLYGONUM.* **R. japonica:** *P. cuspidatum.*

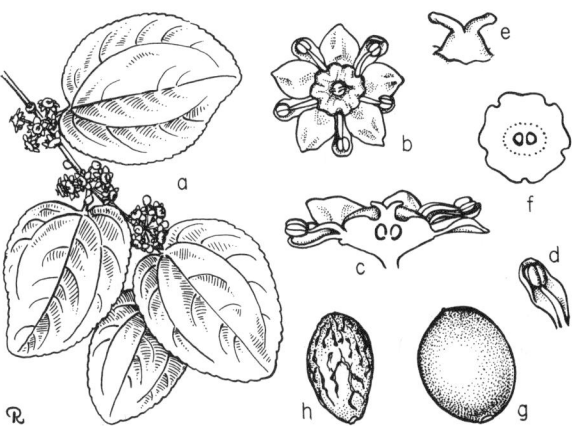

RHAMNACEAE. *Ziziphus mauritiana:* **a,** flowering branch, × ½; **b,** flower, × 3; **c,** flower, vertical section, × 4; **d,** petal and stamen, × 5; **e,** stigmas, × 8; **f,** ovary, cross section, × 4; **g,** fruit, × 1; **h,** stone, × 1.

RHAMNACEAE Juss. BUCKTHORN FAMILY. Dicot.; about 55 genera and 900 spp. in temp. and trop. regions around the world; trees or erect or climbing shrubs, rarely herbs; lvs. mostly alt., simple; fls. mostly in axillary corymbs or cymes, greenish, whitish, or pink to blue, small, regular, bisexual, rarely unisexual, the plants then usually monoecious, sepals 5, petals 5, sometimes 0, usually concave, frequently clawed, stamens 5, opp. the petals, ovary 2–4-celled, superior, disc often present; fr. a drupe or caps., sometimes winged. *Hovenia* and *Zizyphus* are grown for the edible frs., *Rhamnus* as a source of dyes and drugs from the bark, and the following genera as ornamentals: *Adolphia, Alphitonia, Berchemia, Ceanothus, Colletia, Colubrina, Discaria, Emmenosperma, Hovenia, Noltea, Paliurus, Pomaderris, Rhamnus, Sageretia, Spyridium, Trevoa,* and *Zizyphus.*

RHAMNUS L. BUCKTHORN. *Rhamnaceae*. About 150 spp. of mostly deciduous shrubs and small trees, chiefly in temp. regions of N. Hemisphere, a few in Brazil and S. Afr.; lvs. alt. or opp., pinnately nerved, with more or less conspicuous parallel veins; fls. small, greenish, in axillary clusters, umbels, or racemes; fr. a drupe.

Some are grown as ornamentals for their foliage and fruits. A few species yield dyes of economic value, and some have medicinal uses because of the purgative properties of drugs in the bark. Propagated by seeds sown in autumn or stratified, by cuttings and grafting, the evergreen kinds by cuttings of mature wood under glass.

Alaternus L. ITALIAN B. To 20 ft., evergreen or partly so; lvs. ovate, to 2 in. long, toothed, paler beneath, with 3–5 pairs of veins; fls. in short racemes; fr. bluish-black. S. Eur. Zone 7? Cv. 'Argenteo-variegata' [forma *argenteo-variegata* (Weston) Rehd.; var. *variegata* Bean]. Lf. margins creamy-white. Var. **variegata:** cv. 'Argenteo-variegata'.

alnifolia L'Hér. To 3 ft., deciduous; lvs. ovate, to 4 in. long, toothed, with 6–8 pairs of veins; fls. 2–3 together; fr. black. N. Amer. Zone 2.

alpina L. ALPINE B. To 10 ft., deciduous; lvs. elliptic, to 4 in. long, toothed, with 9–12 pairs of veins; fls. in clusters; fr. black. Sw. Eur. Zone 6.

californica Eschsch. COFFEEBERRY. To 6 ft., evergreen; lvs. oblong, to 2½ in. long, finely toothed, with 8–12 pairs of veins; fls. in umbels; fr. red, turning black when ripe. Ore., Calif., Ariz. Zone 7? Subsp. **crassifolia** (Jeps.) C. Wolf. Lvs. broadly elliptic, tomentose beneath. Subsp. **occidentalis** (T. J. Howell) C. Wolf. Lvs. ovate or broadly elliptic, yellowish and glabrous beneath. Subsp. **tomentella** (Benth.) C. Wolf [*R. tomentella* Benth.]. Lvs. narrowly elliptic, tomentose beneath.

canariensis: a listed name of no botanical standing.

caroliniana Walt. INDIAN CHERRY, CAROLINA B. To 30 ft., deciduous; lvs. elliptic or oblong, to 6 in. long, finely toothed or entire, with 8–10 pairs of veins; fls. in umbels; fr. red, turning black when ripe. N.Y. to Fla. and Tex. Zone 6.

cathartica L. COMMON B. To 12 ft., deciduous, often with spines at ends of branchlets; lvs. ovate, to 3 in. long, toothed, with 3–5 pairs of veins; fls. in clusters, unisexual, the plants then polygamodioecious; fr. black. Eur., Asia; escaped in e. U.S. Zone 3. The bark is used medicinally as a cathartic.

Chadwickii: a listed name of no botanical standing for *R. utilis.*

corymbosa: a listed name of no botanical standing.

crenata Siebold & Zucc. To 10 ft., deciduous; lvs. oblong, to 4 in. long, finely toothed, with 7–12 pairs of veins; fls. in umbels; fr. from red to purplish-black. Japan, China. Zone 4.

crenulata Ait. Evergreen shrub; lvs. oblong, to 1¾ in. long, narrowly cuneate at base, crenulate, glabrous; fls. in dense clusters, in the axils of previous year's lvs. Canary Is. Tender.

crocea Nutt. REDBERRY. To 3 ft., evergreen; lvs. elliptic, about ½ in. long, finely toothed; fls. in clusters, sometimes unisexual, petals 0; fr. bright red. Ariz., Calif., and Baja Calif. Zone 8. Subsp. **ilicifolia** (Kellogg) C. Wolf [*R. ilicifolia* Kellogg]. Lvs. glabrous to pubescent, margins mostly serrate to dentate. Subsp. **insula** (Kellogg) C. Wolf [*R. insula* Kellogg; *R. insularis* Greene]. Lvs. glabrous, margins repand-mucronate. Subsp. **pyrifolia** (Greene) C. Wolf. Lvs. glabrous, margins crenate to entire.

davurica Pall. To 30 ft., deciduous; lvs. oblong, to 4 in. long, finely toothed, with 4–6 pairs of veins; fls. in dense clusters; fr. black. Siberia to n. China. Zone 5. Var. **nipponica** Mak. [*R. nipponica* (Mak.) Grubov]. Lvs. narrow-oblong, to 6 in. long, light green beneath. Japan, Korea. Zone 6.

Frangula L. ALDER B. To 12 ft., deciduous; lvs. obovate, to 2½ in. long, entire, with 8–9 pairs of veins; fls. in umbels; fr. red, turning black when ripe. Eur., N. Afr., Asia; escaped in e. U.S. Zone 3. A secondary source of the drug cascara. Cv. 'Asplenifolia' [forma *asplenifolia* (Dipp.) Beissn.]. Lvs. narrow, wavy-margined.

glandulosa Ait. Similar to *R. Alaternus*, but having large bacteria-inhabited nodules or cavities at the base of the lateral veins on the lower lf. surface. Canary Is., Madeira.

ilicifolia: *R. crocea* subsp.

infectoria L. AVIGNON BERRY. To 6 ft., deciduous, spiny; lvs. elliptic, to 1½ in. long, toothed, with 3–4 pairs of veins; fr. black. S. Eur. to Iran. Zone 7. The unripe frs. called "Persian berries" are a source of a natural dyestuff.

insularis: *R. crocea* subsp. *insula.*

insula: *R. crocea* subsp. *insula.*

integrifolia DC. Similar to *R. Alaternus*, but having lvs. entire. Canary Is.

japonica Maxim. To 9 ft., deciduous, brs. often spine-tipped; lvs. obovate to oblong-obovate, to 3 in. long, with 3–5 pairs of veins; fls. in dense, rounded clusters on short spurs; fr. black. Japan. Zone 4.

lanceolata Pursh. To 6 ft., deciduous; lvs. ovate-lanceolate, to 3 in. long, finely toothed, with 7–9 pairs of veins; fr. black. Penn. to Tex. Zone 5b.

nipponica: *R. davurica* var.

ovata: a listed name of no botanical standing.

Pallasii Fisch. & C. A. Mey. Spreading shrub, with spines; lvs. linear to linear-lanceolate, to 1⅜ in. long. W. Asia.

Purshiana DC. CASCARA SAGRADA, BEARBERRY. To 20 ft., deciduous; lvs. oblong, to 8 in. long, finely toothed, with 10–12 pairs of prominent veins; fls. in umbels; fr. black. Wash. to Calif. Zone 7. Probably not hardy n. of Philadelphia. Bark is source of cascara sagrada, an important drug.

rubra Greene. To 4 ft., low, spreading, deciduous shrub; lvs. narrowly elliptic to oblong, to 2½ in. long, with 6–13 pairs of veins; fls. in umbels; fr. black. Mts., n. Calif., Nev. Subsp. **yosemitana** C. Wolf. Lvs. soft-puberulent. N. Calif. Zone 7.

rupestris Scop. To 2½ ft., low spreading shrub, sometimes decumbent; lvs. elliptic to ovate or sometimes nearly orbicular, to 2 in. long, with 5–8 pairs of veins; fls. in 3–8-fld. umbels; fr. red, becoming black. Se. Eur. Zone 6.

saxatilis Jacq. ROCK B. To 2½ ft., low, spreading, spiny, deciduous shrub, branchlets minutely pubescent; lvs. elliptic, ovate, or obovate, to 1 in. long, with 2–4 pairs of veins; fr. black. Cent. and s. Eur. Zone 6.

spathulifolia Fisch. & C. A. Mey. To 6 ft., shrub, branchlets minutely pubescent, sometimes spiny; lvs. elliptic to lanceolate, to 2 in. long; fr. black. W. Asia. Zone 6.

tomentella: *R. californica* subsp.

utilis Decne. [*R. Chadwickii* Hort.]. To 10 ft., deciduous; lvs. oblong, to 5 in. long, finely toothed, yellowish-green, with 5–8 pairs of yellowish, pubescent veins; fr. black. China. Zone 7. Probably not hardy n. of N.Y.

Wilsonii C. K. Schneid. To 6 ft., somewhat spiny; lvs. opp., ovate-lanceolate, to 4 in. long, acuminate, serrate-dentate, glabrous; fr. probably black. China.

RHAPHIDOPHORA: see *RAPHIDOPHORA.*

RHAPIDOPHYLLUM H. Wendl. & Drude. *Palmae.* One sp., a low, polygamodioecious palm mostly in low wet areas, on the coastal plain of U.S. from S.C. to Fla. and Miss., remarkable for the long, sharp, erect needles of the lf. sheaths; lvs. palmate, deeply divided into shallowly 2-cleft segms.; infls. short, condensed, with 5–7 open bracts, buried in the lf. sheaths and needles at base of plant; fls. of two sexes similar, sepals 3, petals 3, imbricate, male fls. with 6 stamens and 3 rudimentary carpels, female fls. with 6 sterile stamens and 3 separate carpels with short styles; fr. ovoid, 1 in. long or less, woolly, seed with homogeneous endosperm.

A slow-growing suckering ornamental palm for temperate areas where most palms cannot be grown. For culture see *Palms.*

hystrix (Pursh) H. Wendl. & Drude. NEEDLE PALM, PORCUPINE P., BLUE PALMETTO. Cespitose, forming large clumps but sts. scarcely evident; lvs. with long, slender, unarmed petioles, blades to 2½ ft. across, divided nearly to base into 5–12 or more spreading, stiffish, 3-ribbed segms. 1½ in. wide or less; fls. wine-red. Cult. in native area and in s. Calif. Probably Zone 7; the hardiest of palms, withstanding temperature to −6° F.

RHAPIS L.f. LADY PALM. *Palmae.* About 9 spp. of low, reedlike or bamboolike, dioecious, cespitose palms in s. China and se. Asia; lvs. palmate, divided nearly to the base into often 2-ribbed segms. shallowly, sharply, and obliquely toothed at apex, sheaths fibrous, persistent; infls. among the lvs., peduncle with several empty bracts, rachis with several brs. bearing short rachillae; fls. yellowish, sessile, the male with calyx 3-toothed, cupular, corolla 3-lobed, stamens 6, and rudiments of carpels, the female similar but the calyx stalked, stamens absent, carpels 3, separate, short-styled; fr. a small, 1-seeded berry with soft exterior and globose seed with homogeneous endosperm.

Two species have long been grown as pot or tub specimens indoors and for clumps or hedges in the open in Zone 9b in southern Calif. and southern Fla. For culture see *Palms.*

excelsa (Thunb.) A. Henry [*R. flabelliformis* L'Hèr. ex Ait.; *Chamaerops excelsa* Thunb.; *Trachycarpus excelsa* (Thunb.) H. Wendl.].

BAMBOO PALM, SLENDER L. P., MINIATURE FAN P., FERN R. Sts. several to many, 5–10 ft., covered with coarse fiber; some or many of the lvs. only 3–7 parted, others to 10-parted, green on both surfaces, segms. uniformly curving or drooping, broad at the apex, 1½–3 in. broad at middle, cross-wrinkled or puckered. Probably native in s. China, but introd. to cult. from Japan, where many cvs., including variegate-lvd. forms, are offered. An excellent house palm.

flabelliformis: *R. excelsa.*

humilis Blume. REED R. Sts. more slender, with finely fibrous sheaths; lf. segms. narrow, mostly 9 or more, the lower ones usually spreading or directed somewhat backward, usually not exceeding 1 in. wide, apex very narrow, surface not puckered. S. China.

RHAZYA Decne. *Apocynaceae.* Two spp. of hardy, rhizomatous, per. herbs, native to s. Eur. and w. Asia; allied to *Amsonia*, but differing in having lvs. always alt., corolla tube widest at middle and constricted at apex, stamens borne at middle of tube, and a disc present at base of ovaries.

Easily grown from seeds.

orientalis (Decne.) A. DC. [*Amsonia orientalis* Decne.]. Erect, hardy, suffrutescent per., to 3 ft.; lvs. sessile, ovate-lanceolate to elliptic, mostly 1–2 in. long, acuminate, rounded at base, thin, pilose at margin and on midrib underneath; infls. dense, many-fld., not longer than upper lvs.; fls. blue to lilac, about ⅝ in. long and ½ in. across; follicles spreading, about 1¼ in. long. Early summer. Greece to Asia Minor.

RHEEDIA L. *Guttiferae.* About 30 spp. of polygamodioecious trees of trop. Amer. and Madagascar, with yellow sap; lvs. lanceolate or elliptic, leathery, petioles with a margined pit on upper side at base; fls. small, yellowish-green, solitary or the male fls. in axillary clusters, sepals 2, petals 4, stamens many in male fls., few and in a single series around the disc in bisexual fls.; fr. a berry with a leathery covering, 1-celled, seeds 1–5, enclosed in an edible, aril-like pulp.

aristata Griseb. To 30 ft.; lvs. elliptic, sharp-pointed; berry ⅜ in. in diam. Cuba.

RHEKTOPHYLLUM N. E. Br. *Araceae.* One or 2 spp. of scandent per. herbs, native to W. Afr.; adult lvs. irregularly perforate or pinnately parted; fls. unisexual, ovaries 1-celled, 1-ovuled.

Strictly tropical; for culture see *Philodendron.*

mirabile N. E. Br. [*Nephthytis picturata* N. E. Br.]. To 30 ft.; adult lf. blades ovate-sagittate, split into 2 or 3 segms. on each side, to 2 ft. long or more, green, petioles as long as blades; peduncle very short, spathe greenish outside, red-purple inside, to 4 in. long; generally seen in juvenile condition with lvs. entire, triangular-hastate, variegated whitish between the veins. Nigeria to Congo.

RHEUM L. RHUBARB. *Polygonaceae.* About 25 spp. of stout, per. herbs, native to Asia; lvs. in basal clumps, large; fls. small, greenish, whitish, or reddish, in panicled clusters or racemes on tall hollow sts., calyx 6-parted, stamens 6–9, styles 3; fr. a winged achene.

One species, *R. Rhabarbarum,* grown for the edible leaf stalks, and others for bold foliage effects.

acuminatum Hook.f. & T. Thoms. SIKKIM RHUBARB. To 3 ft., sts. leafy; lvs. cordate, with deep sinus, tapered, hairy beneath; brs. of panicle few, little-spreading; fls. and fr. dark red. Himalayas.

Alexandrae Batal. Unbranched, 2–5 ft.; lower lvs. ovate-oblong, with prominent sinus, long-petioled; bracts of infl. sessile, greenish-yellow, very large, reflexed and overlapping, scarcely exceeded by the brs. and nearly concealing them. Himalayas.

australe D. Don [*R. emodi* Wallich]. RED-VEINED PIE PLANT. Branched, 6–10 ft., sts. leafy; lvs. more or less cordate, with broad sinus, margins wavy; infl. fastigiate-branched, bracts leafy, small; fls. greenish-white or dark red. Cent. Asia.

emodi: *R. australe.*

giganteum: a listed name of no botanical standing.

nobile Hook.f. & T. Thoms. SIKKIM RHUBARB. To 4 ft., sts. densely covered with bracts, these straw-colored, 6 in. across, concealing short, axillary panicles; lvs. ovate-oblong, 1 ft. across, entire, leathery. Himalayas.

officinale Baill. Sts. to 10 ft.; lvs. round-elliptic, to 3 ft. across, 3–7 lobed, the lobes notched; brs. of panicle spreading; fls. white. W. China and Tibet. Roots and rhizome used medicinally.

palmatum L. Sts. to 6 ft.; lvs. nearly orbicular, cordate at base, deeply palmately lobed, the lobes sometimes again divided. Ne. Asia.

Rhabarbarum L. RHUBARB, GARDEN R., PIE PLANT, WINE PLANT. Sts. to 6 ft.; lvs. ovate, to 1½ ft. long, cordate at base, margins entire but wavy. Manchuria. Widely grown in temp. countries for edible lf. stalks. Cv. 'Victoria', stalks greenish; cvs. 'MacDonald' and 'Cherry', stalks red. For cult. see *Rhubarb.*

Rhaponticum L. A sp. native to Bulgaria, not generally cult. The name has been misapplied to rhubarb, *R. Rhabarbarum.*

Webbianum Royle. To 6 ft., sts. leafy; lvs. orbicular to reniform, with a deep sinus; infl. a branched panicle, the brs. spreading in age, bracts not large; fls. yellow. Himalayas.

RHEXIA L. MEADOW BEAUTY, DEER GRASS. *Melastomataceae.* About 10 spp. of herbaceous or suffrutescent pers., native to N. Amer.; lvs. opp., simple, 3–5-nerved; fls. terminal, solitary or in cymes, petals 4, stamens of equal length, anthers each 1-celled at maturity; fr. a caps.

Cultivated in borders and rock gardens in moist locations. Propagated by tubers and seeds.

mariana L. To 2 ft., sts. cylindrical, glandular-pubescent; lvs. elliptic to lanceolate, to 1½ in. long, serrulate; fls. few to many in open cymes, white or rose-purple, to 1½ in. across. Summer and autumn. Coastal Plain, Mass. to Fla., w. to Okla. and Tex.

virginica L. Sts. to 1½ ft., from tubers, 4-angled, somewhat pubescent; lvs. ovate to lanceolate, to 2 in. long, serrulate-ciliate; fls. in much-branched cymes, rose-purple, to 1½ in. across. Summer. Nov. Sc. to Ont., s. to Fla., Iowa, Tex.

RHIGOZUM Burchell. *Bignoniaceae.* About 9 spp. of erect, much-branched, spiny shrubs, native to trop. and S. Afr.; lvs. fascicled, simple, with 3 lfts., or pinnate; fls. white, yellow, or salmon-colored, solitary, or clustered on short brs., calyx 5-toothed, corolla funnelform to campanulate, slightly 2-lipped, stamens 5; fr. an oblong or elliptic-oblong caps., compressed parallel to partition.

obovatum Burchell. Shrub to 5–8 ft.; lvs. or lfts. obovate to obovate-oblong, to ½ in. long; fls. yellow, to 1 in. long; fr. elliptic-oblong, to 2 in. long. S. Afr.

RHINANTHUS L. YELLOW-RATTLE. *Scrophulariaceae.* Between 40 and 50 spp. of summer-flowering, ann. herbs of the N. Hemisphere, particularly Eur.; lvs. opp., simple; fls. yellow or yellowish to bronze, in one-sided, hairy-bracted, spikelike racemes, calyx 4-lobed, becoming veiny and much inflated in fr., corolla 2-lipped, upper lip helmetlike, lower 3-lobed, stamens 4; fr. a caps.

Sometimes grown in rock gardens or elsewhere.

crista-galli L. [*R. Kyrolliae* Chabert]. RATTLEBOX. Erect, simple or branched ann., to 2 ft. or more; lvs. lanceolate or oblong-lanceolate, to 2 in. long, toothed, sessile; fls. yellow, to ¾ in. long. Circumboreal.

Kyrolliae: *R. crista-galli.*

RHINEPHYLLUM N. E. Br. *Aizoaceae.* About 10–14 spp. of succulents, native to S. Afr.; sts. compact or well developed, showing internodes; lvs. opp., 1–4 pairs on a shoot, thick, clavate to spatulate, roughened by hard, white tubercles, upper surface flat, lower surface rounded or keeled; fls. solitary, terminal, fragrant, bractless, calyx subequally 5-lobed, petals yellow to yellowish-white, in 1 series, stamens many, erect, ovary inferior, 5-celled, stigmas 5; fr. a caps., cell lids absent, expanding keels as long as valves, placental tubercles absent.

Growth occurs in summer, and plants should be placed in a light place under glass with moderate moisture; in winter they should be in a light place, kept dry, at a relatively cool temperature of about 55° F. Propagation easy by seeds or cuttings. See also *Succulents.*

Comptonii L. Bolus. Lvs. with only the edge bearing short soft teeth, to ⅞ in. long, ⅜ in. wide, ⅜ in. thick; fls. medium-sized, nearly sessile, opening at night, petals yellow. Cape Prov.

RHIPOGONUM: *RIPOGONUM.*

RHIPSALIDOPSIS Britt. & Rose. *Cactaceae.* Two spp. of epiphytic cacti, native to Brazil; sts. jointed, the joints short, branching and flowering apically, sometimes (especially the lower ones) 3–6-angled, the upper mostly flattened, oblong, weakly crenate; areoles marginal, spines bristlelike; perianth segms. slightly united, spreading, stamens in 1 series, ovary angled, stigma lobes spreading. Probably allied to *Rhipsalis,* but with rather large fls. terminal on short flattened joints and with angled ovary. Differs from *Schlumbergera* in the short perianth tube, separate stamens, and spreading stigma lobes.

For culture see *Cacti.*

Andreae: a listed name of no botanical standing.

Gaertneri (Regel) Moran [*Schlumbergera Gaertneri* (Regel) Britt. & Rose; *S. Makoyana* Hort.]. EASTER CACTUS. Joints 1½–3 in. long and ¾–1 in. wide, each margin with 4–6 crenations; bristles mostly in the apical areoles, short or to ½ in. long; fls. bright red, 2½–3½ in. across, stigma lobes 5–7; fr. described as dry, apically circumscissile, seeds semiovate. Spring.

rosea (Lagerh.) Britt. & Rose. Joints 1–1½ in. long and to ½ in. wide, each margin with 2–4 crenations; bristles short; fls. rose-pink, fragrant, 1–1½ in. across, stigma lobes 3. Spring. A handsome floriferous plant.

RHIPSALIS Gaertn. [*Lepismium* Pfeiff.]. WICKERWARE CACTUS. *Cactaceae.* Perhaps 60 spp. of mainly epiphytic or rock-dwelling cacti, mostly native to Brazil but widespread in trop. Amer., a few also in Afr. and Ceylon; sts. cylindrical, angled, or flattened (2-winged), often with aerial roots, elongate or jointed, branched laterally or often from the apex of the joints; areoles small, with hairs or bristles, rarely spiny; fls. small, mostly lateral, 1–5 in an areole, perianth segms. few, separate, mostly spreading, ovary mostly cylindrical, sessile or somewhat sunken in the br.; fr. globose, nearly transparent, mucilaginous, with persistent perianth. Diverse in st. structure but apparently not readily divided into natural units.

The species of *Rhipsalis* are interesting pot or basket plants and are easily grown; propagated by cuttings, and by seeds when available. For culture see *Cacti.*

baccifera (Soland. ex J. Mill.) Stearn [*R. Cassutha* Gaertn.; *R. pendula* Hort. ex Pfeiff., not Vöcht.]. MISTLETOE CACTUS. Sts. pendent in large masses, to 30 ft., brs. cylindrical, to ³⁄₁₆ in. in diam., all elongate, pale; areoles bristly only when young; fls. lateral, greenish, to ¼ in. across, ovary naked, not sunken; fr. white, to ³⁄₁₆ in. in diam., seeds about 20. Fla. to Brazil and Peru; Ceylon, Afr.

boliviana (Britt.) Lauterb. Sts. 4-angled, brs. flat, to 1 ft. long and ¾ in. wide, deeply crenate; areoles with 5–10 short bristles; fls. lateral, 1–2 at an areole, yellow, ⅝ in. long, ovary not sunken; fr. ⁵⁄₁₆ in. in diam. Bolivia.

capilliformis A. Web. Sts. slender, cylindrical, elongate, the ultimate joints short, ¹⁄₁₆ in. thick; fls. lateral, many, cream-colored, to ¼ in. across, ovary naked, not sunken; fr. white, ³⁄₁₆ in. in diam., seeds 1–3. E. Brazil.

Cassutha: *R. baccifera.*

Cassytha: incorrect spelling for *Cassutha.*

cereuscula Haw. CORAL CACTUS, POPCORN C. Erect, to 2 ft., sts. cylindrical, elongate, with many short joints, to ⁵⁄₃₂ in. thick, often angled when young; areoles bristly; fls. nearly terminal, almost campanulate, white to pink or yellowish, about ½ in. long, ovary not sunken; fr. white, few-seeded. Cent. Brazil to Uruguay.

clavata: *Hatiora clavata.*

cribrata Lem. [*R. pendula* Vöcht., not Hort. ex Pfeiff.]. Sts. pendent, cylindrical, elongate, with whorled short brs., to ⁵⁄₃₂ in. thick; areoles with few short bristles; fls. terminal, pendulous, nearly campanulate, white with red center, ½ in. long, perianth segms. 5–7, ovary naked, not sunken; fr. red, ⅛ in. in diam., seeds 5–6. Brazil.

crispata (Haw.) Pfeiff. Sts. erect, flat, thin, to 16 in. long, joints elliptic to oblong, crenate, yellow-green, to 5 in. long and 3 in. wide; fls. 1–4 at an areole, pale yellow, ½ in. across, ovary naked, not sunken; fr. white, ¼ in. in diam. Brazil.

crispimarginata Löfgr. Sts. pendent, cylindrical below, bearing clusters of thin, oblong, green or purplish joints to 2½ in. long, margins crisped; fls. 1–3 at an areole, white, ½ in. across, ovary not sunken; fr. white, ¼ in. in diam. Brazil.

cruciformis (Vell.) Castell. [*Lepisium cruciforme* (Vell.) Miq.]. Sts. mostly creeping, brs. flat or 3–5-ribbed or -winged, to 1 ft. long and 1 in. wide but often narrower, obliquely crenate; areoles with bristles to ⅜ in. long; fls. lateral, 1–5 at an areole, white, to ½ in. across, perianth segms. slightly united, ovary sunken; fr. purplish to red, to ½ in. in diam. Brazil.

dissimilis (G. A. Lindb.) K. Schum. Sts. erect or pendent, juvenile brs. with 6–9 low ribs, areoles close-set, bristly, flowering brs. weakly

to strongly 3–5-angled, to ⁵⁄₁₆ in. thick; areoles without bristles; often nearly whorled; fls. solitary, pink, to ¾ in. across, ovary naked, sunken in the brs., surrounded by woolly hairs; fr. red, ½ in. in diam., fewseeded. Brazil.

elliptica G. A. Lindb. Sts. erect or becoming pendent, joints flat, thick and leathery, crenulate to subentire, 1–8 in. long and ¾–3 in. wide; fls. 1–3 at an areole, yellowish, ½ in. across, ovary not sunken; fr. reddish, ¼ in. in diam. Brazil.

grandiflora Haw. Brs. stout, cylindrical, elongate, to ⅜ in. thick; areoles without bristles, often red-ringed; fls. lateral, white or pink, to 1 in. across, ovary naked, not sunken; fr. purplish, ¼ in. in diam. Brazil.

heteroclada Britt. & Rose. Sts. stiff, dark green, cylindrical, brs. slender, to ³⁄₃₂ in. thick; areoles often with 1 bristle; fls. white, small, ovary not sunken; fr. white, ¼ in. in diam. Brazil.

Houlletiana Lem. SNOWDROP CACTUS. Brs. indeterminate, flat, thin, 1–2 in. wide, serrate to obtusely serrate-lobed; fls. campanulate, white, becoming yellow, often with red center, ¾ in. long, ovary angled, not sunken; fr. red, globose, ¼ in. in diam. Brazil.

leucorhaphis K. Schum. Sts. much-branched, cylindrical, ¼ in. in diam., with many aerial roots; areoles with 1–6 appressed bristles to ⁵⁄₃₂ in. long; fls. lateral, white, to ¾ in. across, ovary weakly angled, scaly, not sunken. Paraguay, n. Argentina.

Lindbergiana K. Schum. Sts. pendent, much-branched, brs. cylindrical, elongate, to ³⁄₁₆ in. thick; areoles close-set, with 2 black bristles; fls. lateral, white, ⁵⁄₁₆ in. across, ovary naked, not sunken; fr. red, ⅛ in. in diam., seeds 16–20. Brazil.

lumbricoides Lem. Sts. much-branched, creeping, to 10 ft., brs. cylindrical or faintly angled, elongate, ¼ in. thick, rooting freely; areoles close-set, at first with 5–10 brittle white bristles; fls. lateral, white, ¾ in. across, ovary naked, not sunken; fr. purplish. Brazil to n. Argentina.

mesembryanthoides Haw. Sts. erect, slender, elongate, cylindrical, bristly, to 16 in. long, bearing close-set ellipsoid joints about ⁵⁄₁₆ in. long and ⅛ in. thick, bristly especially at the apex; fls. lateral, white or pink, ½ in. across, ovary naked, not sunken; fr. white, ³⁄₁₆ in. in diam. Brazil. The specific epithet often but not originally spelled *mesembryanthemoides.*

micrantha (HBK) DC. Sts. clambering or pendent, brs. 3–4-angled or flattened, to ⁵⁄₁₆ in. wide, weakly obliquely crenate; areoles remote, with 1–4 bristles; fls. lateral, white, ¼ in. across, ovary naked, not sunken; fr. white to reddish, ⁵⁄₁₆ in. in diam. Ecuador, Peru.

monacantha Griseb. [*Acanthorhipsalis monacantha* (Griseb.) Britt. & Rose]. Sts. flat or 3-winged, obliquely crenate, to 2 ft. long and 1 in. wide; spines 1–3, white, needle-shaped, to ½ in. long; fls. orange, campanulate, ¾ in. long, ovary with few scales, not sunken; fr. 4–5-angled, orange, seeds few. N. Argentina.

Neves-Armondii K. Schum. Sts. pendent, stiff, cylindrical, to 8 in. long and ³⁄₁₆ in. diam., brs. whorled at apex, the ultimate ones to 2 in. long, cylindrical or somewhat angled; areoles small, without bristles, the flowering ones with long hairs; fls. nearly terminal, 1–2 per areole, white, ¾ in. across, ovary naked, sunken; fr. greenish, ⁵⁄₁₆ in. in diam. Brazil.

oblonga Löfgr. Sts. pendent, cylindrical below, flattened above, brs. flat, oblong, obliquely crenate, bright green, 2–6 in. long, ¾ in. wide; fls. solitary, lateral, to ¾ in. across, ovary naked, not sunken; fr. to ⁵⁄₁₆ in. long. Brazil.

pachyptera Pfeiff. Sts. flat or sometimes 3-winged, thickish, nearly round or elongate, crenate, green or purplish, to 8 in. long or more and 3 in. wide or more; fls. 1–4 per areole, white, 1 in. across, stamens many, ovary smooth, not sunken; fr. white. Brazil.

paradoxa Salm-Dyck. CHAIN CACTUS, LINK PLANT. Sts. pendent, to 3 ft. or more, with many aerial roots, brs. about 1 ft. long, ½–¾ in. thick, sharply 3–4-angled, with nearly whorled areoles and with internodes 1–2 in. long, the angles of one internode alternating with those of the next; flowering areoles woolly; fls. white, ¾ in. across, ovary naked, sunken; fr. red, ⁵⁄₁₆ in. in diam. Brazil.

pendula: *R. cribrata;* but see also *R. baccifera.*

pentaptera Pfeiff. Brs. to 6 in. long and ½ in. thick, sharply 5–6-ribbed; areoles often ¾ in. apart, small, sometimes with small bristles; fls. 1–5 at an areole, white, ½ in. across, ovary naked, not sunken; fr. white, ⁵⁄₃₂ in. in diam., seeds subglobose. S. Brazil, Uruguay.

prismatica (Lem.) Rümpler. Sts. much-branched, prostrate, cylindrical, elongate, brs. short, angled, less than ⅛ in. thick; areoles bristly; fls. lateral, white, ⅜ in. across, ovary not sunken; fr. ⅛ in. in diam. Brazil.

pulvinigera G. A. Lindb. Sts. pendent, cylindrical, dark green, to 18 ft. long and ¼ in. in diam., brs. often whorled; areoles woolly, the flowering ones with long hairs; fls. solitary, lateral, white, becoming yellowish, to 1 in. across, ovary sunken; fr. purple, ⁵⁄₁₆ in. in diam. Brazil.

puniceodiscus G. A. Lindb. Sts. pendent, rooting freely, brs. whorled, cylindrical, 3–4 in. long, ⁵⁄₃₂ in. in diam.; areoles small, red-ringed, without bristles, the flowering ones with hairs; fls. lateral, solitary, ⅝ in. across, white with red center, ovary sunken; fr. red, becoming yellow. Brazil.

ramulosa (Salm-Dyck) Pfeiff. Sts. erect, cylindrical, to 1 ft., brs. flat, 3–6 in. long, to 1 in. wide, crenate; fls. solitary, white, small, ovary scaly, not sunken; fr. white, ¼ in. in diam. Peru, Bolivia, w. Brazil.

rhombea (Salm-Dyck) Pfeiff. Sts. cylindrical or angled, to 2 ft. long, joints flat or sometimes 3-winged, oblong to rhombic, obtuse, crenate, green or purplish, 1–5 in. long and ½–2 in. wide; fls. mostly solitary, yellowish or marked with red, ⅜ in. across, ovary naked, not sunken; fr. red, ¼ in. in diam., seeds many. Brazil.

Shaferi Britt. & Rose. Sts. cylindrical, ³⁄₁₆ in. in diam., brs. elongate, the upper mostly without bristles; fls. lateral, mostly solitary, white, to ⅜ in. across, ovary naked, not sunken; fr. white, ⅛ in. in diam. Paraguay, n. Argentina.

teres (Vell.) Steud. Sts. erect, much-branched, cylindrical, to 2 ft. high and ½ in. in diam., brs. whorled, elongate, to ⅛ in. in diam.; bristles few, black; fls. lateral, pale yellow, ½ in. across, ovary not sunken; fr. whitish, ⁵⁄₁₆ in. in diam., seeds about 30. Brazil.

Tonduzii A. Web. Sts. erect or pendent, with many aerial roots, whorled, mostly 4–5-(sometimes 2–7-)ribbed, about 4 in. long and ½ in. thick, ribs thin, obliquely crenate; areoles ¾ in. apart, at first with bristles; fls. lateral, white, ½ in. long, ovary not sunken; fr. white, to ¾ in. long. Costa Rica.

trigona Pfeiff. Sts. pendent, much-branched, to 6 ft. long, brs. 3-ribbed, ½ in. thick, ribs acute, irregularly crenate; fls. solitary, lateral, white, ¾ in. across, ovary sunken; fr. red, ⅜ in. in diam. Brazil. The application of the name to the plant described is uncertain.

tucumanensis A. Web. Brs. sometimes whorled, cylindrical, or becoming somewhat angled, to ⅜ in. thick; fls. lateral, white or rosy, ¾ in. across, ovary sunken; fr. white or reddish, to ⅜ in. in diam., seeds 20–30. N. Argentina.

virgata A. Web. Sts. suberect or pendent, much-branched, stiff, cylindrical, to 3 ft. long, ³⁄₁₆ in. in diam., ultimate brs. ⅛ in. in diam. or less; fls. lateral, white, ⁵⁄₁₆ in. across, ovary not sunken; fr. white, ⅛ in. in diam., seeds 1–5. Brazil.

Warmingiana K. Schum. POPCORN CACTUS. Brs. flat or 3–4-ribbed, 4–10 in. long and to ¾ in. wide, narrowed and often cylindrical below, margins obtusely serrate; fls. lateral, solitary, white, ½ in. across, ovary strongly 4–5-angled, not sunken; fr. globose, black, ¼ in. in diam. Brazil.

RHIZOPHORA L. MANGROVE. *Rhizophoraceae.* About 3 spp. of trop. trees of wide distribution along seashores; lvs. opp., stipules interpetiolar, large, deciduous; peduncles few-fld.; fls. large, leathery, 4-merous, stamens 8–12, ovary conical, 2-celled, exserted beyond calyx; fr. 1-seeded, ovoid or obconical, germinating and producing an elongate radicle before falling from tree.

Mangle L. AMERICAN M. To 40 ft. or more, with thick crown; lvs. petioled, obovate to elliptic, obtuse, to 6 in. long, stipules to 1½ in. long; petals yellow, ⁵⁄₁₆ in. long, villous inside; fr. to 1⁵⁄₁₆ in. long, radicle to 1 ft. long. Tidal shores and marshes, s. Fla. and trop. Amer. The many arching aerial roots form stilts and trunks that make dense, soil-stabilizing tangles. Bark an important source of tannin.

RHIZOPHORACEAE R. Br. MANGROVE FAMILY. Dicot.; about 15 genera of trop. and subtrop. trees and shrubs, mostly of the Old World; lvs. thick, leathery, mostly opp., entire; fls. usually bisexual, regular, sepals and petals 3–14, stamens 2–4 times as many as sepals, ovary 1–6-celled, usually inferior; fr. leathery, indehiscent or tardily splitting. *Anopyxis* and *Rhizophora* are sometimes cult.

RHODANTHE: *HELIPTERUM.*

RHODIOLA: *SEDUM.* R. integrifolia: *S. Rosea* subsp.

RHODODENDRON L. [*Azalea* of auth., not L.; *Azaleastrum* Rydb.; × *Azaleodendron* Rodig.; *Biltia* Small; *Rhodora* L.; *Therorhodion* Small]. AZALEA, RHODODENDRON. *Ericaceae.* Perhaps 800 spp. of evergreen, semievergreen, or deciduous shrubs or rarely small trees or epiphytes, native chiefly in the temp. areas of the N. Hemisphere, most abun-

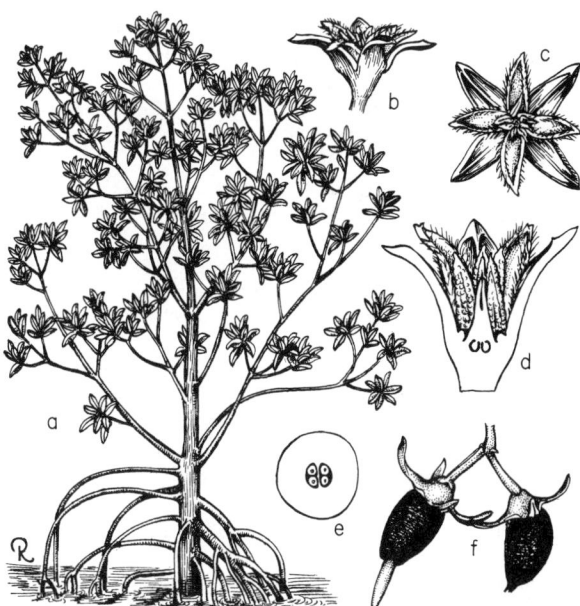

RHIZOPHORACEAE. *Rhizophora Mangle:* **a**, tree, greatly reduced; **b**, flower, side view, × 1; **c**, flower, face view, × 1; **d**, flower, vertical section, × 1¼; **e**, ovary, cross section, × 2; **f**, fruits, × ½.

dant in the Himalayas, se. Asia and mts. of Malaysia, but found on all continents except Afr. and S. Amer.; lvs. simple, alt. or sometimes crowded toward the ends of brs., mostly entire; fls. of various colors, usually in terminal, umbel-like clusters, or sometimes solitary, calyx usually 5-parted, corolla usually irregular, campanulate, funnelform, or sometimes tubular, stamens 5–10 or even –20, anthers without appendages, opening by a terminal pore, ovary superior; fr. a woody caps. As here understood, *Rhododendron* includes the azaleas, even though these are usually considered distinct by gardeners. There are no constant botanical differences between azaleas and rhododendrons; azaleas are largely deciduous and have funnelform fls., whereas rhododendrons are mostly evergreen and have campanulate fls., but there are many exceptions to this generalization. *Azalea* L. emend. Salisb. is a synonym of *Loiseleuria.*

The genus has been divided variously by different authors. The treatment of general horticultural acceptance divides the genus into 43 series, with some of these further divided into subseries. Because these "series" do not represent clearly defined and separable groups, they are not accepted here. The genus does, however, separate rather naturally into 8 subgenera, each with its respective sections.

The species of a section possess the characteristics of that section. These characteristics are not repeated in the brief descriptions of the species; instead, the following two-letter symbols are used to indicate the subgenus and section to which each species belongs, roman type being used to indicate the subgenus and italics to indicate the section: AZ, *AZ Azaleastrum;* BR, *Brachycalyx;* CA, *Candidastrum;* CH, *Chionastrum;* HY, *HY, Hymenanthes;* MU, *Mumeazalea;* PA, *Pseudazalea;* PE, *PE, Pentanthera;* PM, *Pseudorhodorastrum;* PO, *Pogonathum;* RA, *Rhabdorhodion;* RM, *Rhodorastrum;* RN, *RN, Rhododendron;* RO, *Rhodora;* RS, *Rhodobotrys,* TH, *Therorhodion;* TR, *Trachyrhodion;* TS, *Tsusiopsis;* TT, *Tsutsusi;* TU, *Tsutsusi;* VR, *Vireya;* VS, *Viscidula.*

The distinguishing characters of the subgenera and sections follow:

Subgenus **Rhododendron** (RN). Lvs. usually persistent, lepidote (scaly) beneath and sometimes also above; infls. terminal.

Section **Rhododendron** *(RN).* Lf. scales entire-margined, stamens exserted, seeds without marginal appendages.

Section **Pogonanthum** G. Don *(PO)*. Lf. scales lacerate-margined, stamens included, seeds without marginal appendages.

Section **Vireya** (Blume) H. Copel. *(VR)*. Lf. scales entire- or lacerate-margined, seeds with appendages or long tails at each end.

Subgenus **Pseudazalea** Sleum. (PA). Lvs. usually deciduous, lepidote, fls. in terminal infls., appearing before the lvs. in spring.

Subgenus **Hymenanthes** (Blume) Endl. (HY). Lvs. persistent, not lepidote, fls. in terminal infls., arising from terminal buds, the new brs. arising from lf. axils of previous year's growth.

Section **Hymenanthes** (Blume) DC. *(HY)*. With characters of the subgenus.

Subgenus **Pentanthera** (G. Don) Pozhark. (PE). Lvs. deciduous, not lepidote, fls. in terminal infls., arising from terminal buds, the new brs. arising from lf. axils of the previous year's growth.

Section **Pentanthera** G. Don *(PE)*. Corolla funnelform, stamens always 5.

Section **Rhodora** (L.) G. Don. *(RO)*. Corolla rotate-campanulate, lobed almost to the base, fls. appearing in spring, before the lvs. or as the lvs. develop.

Section **Viscidula** Matsum. & Nakai *(VS)*. Corolla tubular-campanulate, fls. appearing as the lvs. develop or after the lvs.

Subgenus **Tsutsutsi** Pozhark. (TT). Lvs. deciduous or persistent, not lepidote, fls. developing from a terminal bud, the new brs. from the axils of terminally whorled lvs.

Section **Brachycalyx** Sweet *(BR)*. Sts. and lvs. pubescent or glabrous, lvs. whorled toward ends of brs.

Section **Tsusiopsis** Sleum. *(TS)*. Lvs. leathery, persistent, in 2 or 3 whorls toward ends of branchlets.

Section **Tsutsusi** Sweet *(TU)* Brs. and lvs. with appressed setose hairs, lvs. scattered, dimorphic, the early lvs. thin, broad, deciduous, the later ones thick, persisting over winter.

Subgenus **Azaleastrum** C. Koch (AZ). Lvs. deciduous or persistent, not lepidote, infls. lateral, new brs. from pseudoterminal buds or from axils of lower lvs.

Section **Azaleastrum** Planch. ex Maxim. *(AZ)*. Lvs. persistent, calyx with large, broad lobes, stamens 5, seeds lacking marginal appendages.

Section **Candidastrum** Sleum. *(CA)*. Lvs. deciduous, stamens 10, all the same length, fls. appearing after the lvs.

Section **Choniastrum** Franch. *(CH)*. Lvs. persistent, calyx with minute lobes, stamens 10, seeds with spindle-shaped appendages at both ends.

Section **Mumeazalea** (Mak.) Sleum. *(MU)*. Lvs. deciduous, stamens 5, two shorter than the other three, fls. appearing after the lvs.

Subgenus **Pseudorhodorastrum** Sleum. (PM). Lvs. persistent, lepidote, infls. lateral, the new brs. from pseudoterminal buds or from axils of lower lvs.

Section **Rhabdorhodion**. Sleum. *(RA)*. Lvs. always glabrous, stamens 10, fls. solitary in lf. axils, seeds with marginal appendages.

Section **Rhodobotrys** Sleum. *(RS)*. Lvs. always glabrous, stamens 10, fls. in a group of 2–5 in lf. axils, seeds with marginal appendages.

Section **Trachyrhodion** Sleum. *(TR)*. Lvs. with at least the upper surface soft-hairy to hispid, seeds lacking marginal appendages.

Subgenus **Rhodorastrum** (Maxim.) C. B. Clarke (RM). Lvs. deciduous or semipersistent, lepidote beneath, infl. lateral, the new brs. arising from foliage beneath infl., fls. appearing before the new growth.

Subgenus **Therorhodion** (Maxim.) Drude (TH). Lvs. deciduous, fls. on leafy-bracted peduncles arising from young leafy shoots, not from special buds.

Rhododendrons do not thrive in clay or limestone soils, but grow best in a well-drained mixture of leaf mold, peat, and sandy loam. They should be protected from strong winds and continuous hot sun, and the soil kept moist. Transplanting of these shallow-rooted plants is easily effected in spring or early autumn if a good ball of earth is kept around the roots. Most of the species require a mulch to conserve soil moisture, improve soil aeration, and decrease frost penetration in colder areas. The evergreen species usually need protection from early spring sun and winds, and are therefore placed where somewhat screened by other plantings. Rhododendrons are adapted to planting within the high shade of deep-rooted deciduous or evergreen trees. Azaleas, especially deciduous azaleas, tend to be more sun-tolerant than large-leaved rhododendrons, but all require some sunlight for flower production.

Azaleas and rhododendrons may be propagated by seeds sown in pans or boxes of sandy peat and only slightly covered with sphagnum or sand. Seedlings should be transplanted as soon as they can be handled. The second year they may be planted out. Plants may be propagated also by layers, which cannot be separated until the second year, and by cuttings of half-ripe wood, hormone-treated and rooted in a well-drained mixture of perlite or vermiculite and peat moss. Named cultivars were formerly increased by grafting, particularly veneer grafting, but, with the advent of the more modern misting and Nearing-frame techniques, are now grown largely from cuttings. Rooted cuttings of deciduous azaleas may require supplemental lighting to encourage shoot growth.

Rhododendrons and azaleas are often forced under glass for the florist trade. They are grown in pots and can be brought into bloom in about 6 weeks with a night temperature of 50–55° F. Plant habit and flower production are subject to regulation through application of plant hormones.

A general range of rhododendrons show preference for moderate temperatures and moist climates, and many species are adapted to cultivation in the coastal Northwest. Severity of climate almost precludes their cultivation in the north-central states, however, and rather drastically limits potentials in the Northeast. The cultivars and hybrids of *R. catawbiense* are the standard and dependable rhododendrons for planting in the Northeast. Some other species also endure colder winters, such as *R. brachycarpum*, *R. campanulatum*, *R. carolinianum*, *R. caucasicum*, *R. dauricum*, *R. ferrugineum*, *R. hirsutum*, *R. Metternichii*, *R. micranthum*, *R. minus*, *R. Przewalskii*, and *R. Smirnowii*. The few far-northern species, such as *R. lapponicum*, *R. maximum*, *R. parvifolium*, and *R. prinophyllum*, are of course very hardy. A surprising number of species and hybrids are being successfully cultivated in southeastern communities from Washington, D.C., to Atlanta, Ga. The Gulf Coast has become noted for its displays of Indian and native azaleas, and many tender species succeed well in San Francisco and other regions of coastal Calif. Climates of the central and south-central states necessitate close attention to cultural details for successful cultivation of a limited range of the more tolerant kinds.

The cultivated rhododendrons and azaleas may be species, but more frequently they are cultivars of well-known hybrid groups or the recombination products of modern breeding of several of these groups. Among the evergreen rhododendrons some of these hybrid groups are: (1) CATAWBA HYBRIDS, derived mainly from *R. catawbiense* crossed with *R. maximum*, *R. caucasicum*, *R. ponticum*, or *R. arboreum;* the primary source of hardy cultivars suitable for northeastern planting. (2) CAUCASICUM HYBRIDS, a group exhibiting the major influence of *R. caucasicum;* represented usually by hardy or semi-hardy plants of rather slow, compact growth and early flowering. (3) FORTUNEI HYBRIDS (including the DEXTER HYBRIDS), incorporating the attractive fragrant flowers and clear color of *R. Fortunei*, one of the hardiest of the Chinese rhododendrons, in hybrids that can often withstand winters characteristic of Zone 7b. (4) GRIFFITHIANUM HYBRIDS, derived from various crosses with the Himalayan *R. Griffithianum*, which possesses a loose inflorescence of large flowers; offering wide variation in color and some of the largest and most attractive flowers, but generally tender and limited in culture to the milder Pacific Coast regions. (5) JAVANICUM HYBRIDS, a group representing crosses of related, often epiphytic, tropical species, with *R. javanicum;* having colors ranging from deep crimson to golden-yellow and pure white, and with salverform to campanulate flowers; outside the wet tropics, suitable only for use in the warm conservatory. (6) THOMSONII HYBRIDS, brilliantly colored tender rhododendrons originating from crosses with the deep blood-red-flowered *R. Thomsonii;* grown mainly in milder areas of the West Coast.

Among the well-known hybrid groups of azaleas are: (1) GABLE HYBRIDS, derived from a number of parents, but largely from *R.*

yedoense var. *poukhanense* and *R. Kaempferi;* among the hardiest evergreen hybrids. (2) GHENT HYBRIDS, known also as *R.* × *gandavense,* derivatives of *R. luteum* and most of the deciduous azaleas; deciduous, including a wide color range, and very hardy and long-lived. (3) GLEN DALE HYBRIDS, derived from a large number of parents, including KAEMPFERI and KURUME HYBRIDS; evergreen azaleas hardy in the Middle Atlantic states, with flowers to 4½ in. across, in a wide range of colors. (4) INDIAN or INDICUM ["INDICA"] HYBRIDS, a group of tender, evergreen hybrids derived mostly from *R. indicum, R. mucronatum,* and *R. Simsii;* much grown under glass for the florist trade and in the open in the South and in Calif. (5) KAEMPFERI HYBRIDS, derived mainly from *R. Kaempferi;* tall, tender plants, with flowers to 2½ in. across, ranging from orange-red to purple. (6) KNAP HILL HYBRIDS, a recent development of the Ghent and Mollis hybrids, with large and flattened flowers in many shades, and with 4 subgroups: Exbury, Ilam, Slocock, and Knap Hill. (7) KURUME HYBRIDS, derived from *R. Kaempferi* and *R. kiusianum;* evergreen, not hardy in our colder areas, but popular there under glass, with flowers to 2½ in. across, white, scarlet, to purple, and sometimes striped or flecked. (8) MOLLE ["MOLLIS"] HYBRIDS, also known as *R.* × *Kosteranum,* hybrids of *R. molle* and *R. japonicum;* deciduous, of varying hardiness, with trumpet-shaped flowers to 2½ in. across, white, yellow, to orange or rose.

It has been common, though not consistent, practice among rhododendron and azalea specialists, even in the International Rhododendron Register, to distinguish Latin-named cultivars of azaleas from Latin-named cultivars of rhododendrons by treating the former as feminine (e.g., cv. 'Alba Grandiflora') and the latter as neuter (e.g., cv. 'Album Grandiflorum'). This practice, however, is inconsistent with that in all other groups of cultivated plants, and is also at variance with the International Code of Nomenclature of Cultivated Plants ("Cultivar names should agree in gender with the generic name concerned"). All names in Latin form are therefore treated here as neuter, in agreement with the gender of the generic name *Rhododendron.*

Publications of The American Rhododendron Society and the American Horticultural Society are sources of further information on the genus, including cultural details and descriptions of the many cultivars.

Aberconwayi Cowan. HY, *HY;* shrub, to 8 ft.; lvs. broadly lanceolate or oblong to oblong-elliptic, to 2¾ in. long, rigid and very brittle, with recurved margins, dark green and glabrous at maturity above, glaucous beneath, petiole to ½ in. long; infl. racemose or an umbel-like raceme; corolla white or tinged with pink, sometimes with pink or red specks on upper lobe, saucer-shaped to flatly campanulate, to 2½ in. across, ovary and style glandular. E. Yunnan. Zone 7.

adenogynum Diels. HY, *HY;* to 9 ft.; lvs. oblong to ovate-oblong, to 4 in. long, and 1¼ in. across, glabrous, felty with reddish-brown hairs beneath; fls. fragrant, corolla white, tinged pink or crimson, to 2½ in. across, ovary glandular. Nw. Yunnan. Zone 6.

adenophorum Balf.f. & W. W. Sm. HY, *HY;* to 8 ft.; lvs. lanceolate to oblong, to 5 in. long, acute, glandular above and on petiole, tawny beneath; corolla rose, to ¾ in. across, tube cylindrical, longer than limb, ovary glandular, style as long as corolla. Yunnan.

adenopodum Franch. HY, *HY;* to 10 ft., branchlets gray-tomentose-glandular; lvs. oblong-lanceolate to oblanceolate, to 8 in. long, acute, cuneate at base, densely tomentose beneath; fls. on glandular pedicels nearly as long as fls., calyx ciliate, about ⁵⁄₃₂ in. long, corolla pale rose, more or less spotted, 1¾ in. long, ovary pubescent, style glabrous. Hupeh and e. Szechwan. Zone 6.

aechmophyllum Balf.f. & Forr. RN, *RN;* to 6 ft.; lvs. oblong to lanceolate, to 2 in. long, acuminate to mucronate, not strongly pubescent; corolla white to rose, to 1¾ in. long, stamens of unequal lengths. Sw. Szechwan. Zone 8.

aeruginosum: *R. campanulatum* var.

alabamense Rehd. [*Azalea alabamensis* (Rehd.) Ashe]. ALABAMA A. PE, *PE;* low stoloniferous shrub, brs. irregularly whorled, strigose when young, winter buds glabrous; lvs. elliptic to obovate, to 2¼ in. long, usually short-villous beneath and on midrib above; fls. fragrant, appearing with lvs., corolla white, usually with yellow blotch, funnelform, about 1 in. long, tube longer than lobes, hairy outside. Ala. Zone 7.

× **albicans** Hort. Waterer: *R. molle* × *R. occidentale.* PE, *PE;* corolla white, tinged yellow, with orange blotch. Zone 7.

albiflorum Hook. [*Azalea albiflora* (Hook.) O. Kuntze; *Azaleastrum albiflorum* (Hook.) Rydb.]. AZ, *CA;* to 6 ft., deciduous; lvs. oblong to elliptic, to 2¾ in. long, rusty-pubescent; fls. nodding, in 1–3-fld., lateral clusters, corolla white, ¾ in. across. Early summer. B.C., s. to Ore. and Colo. Zone 5.

Albrechtii Maxim. [*Azalea Albrechtii* (Maxim.) O. Kuntze]. PE, *RO;* to 5 ft.; lvs. in clusters of 5 toward ends of brs., obovate to oblong-oblanceolate, to 4¾ in. long, pubescent beneath; fls. in 3–6-fld. clusters, corolla magenta, 2 in. across. N. and cent. Japan. Zone 6.

album Blume. RN, *VR;* small evergreen shrub; lvs. lanceolate to narrowly elliptic, to 5 in. long, rusty-lepidote beneath; corolla yellowish-white, campanulate. Java. A greenhouse plant.

× **album elegans:** a listed name of no botanical standing for *Rhododendron* cv. 'Album Elegans'. A hybrid, with *R. catawbiense* as one parent; corolla pale mauve, fading to white. Zone 5.

× **album grandiflorum:** a listed name of no botanical standing for *Rhododendron* cv. 'Album Grandiflorum'. A hybrid, with *R. catawbiense* as one parent; corolla large, very pale mauve, becoming white. Zone 6.

× **album novum:** a listed name of no botanical standing for *Rhododendron* cv. 'Album Novum'. A hybrid, with *R. catawbiense* as one parent; corolla white, tinged lilac, with green spots.

× **altaclerense** Lindl., not *Azalea altaclerensis* Gowen: *R. arboreum* × (*R. catawbiense* × *R. ponticum*). Corolla crimson. The epithet is usually misspelled *altaclarense. Azalea altaclarensis* Gowen is one of the Ghent Hybrid Azaleas (*R.* × *gandavense*).

alutaceum Balf.f. & W. W. Sm. HY, *HY;* to 12 ft.; lvs. oblong or broadly lanceolate, to 6 in. long, leathery; fls. on glandular pedicels, calyx glandular-ciliate, corolla rose, with crimson spots, 1¼ in. long. Nw. Yunnan.

amagianum Mak. MT. AMAGI A. AN, *AN;* to 12 ft.; lvs. in 3's toward ends of brs., to 3 in. long, lustrous; corolla orange-red with red blotch, 1¾ in. long. Japan. Zone 7.

ambiguum Hemsl. RN, *RN;* to 6 ft.; lvs. elliptic-lanceolate, to 3 in. long, lepidote beneath; corolla pale yellow to greenish-yellow, spotted green, to 2 in. across, lepidote outside. W. Szechwan. Zone 7.

Amesiae Rehd. & E. H. Wils. RN, *RN;* to 14 ft.; lvs. elliptic to elliptic-oblong, to 3 in. long, acute, leathery, somewhat villous beneath on midrib, petioles setose; corolla purple-red, funnelform, 2 in. across, glabrous. W. Szechwan. Zone 7.

amoenum: *R. obtusum* cv.

× **Anneliesae** Rehd.: *R. arborescens* × *R. calendulaceum.* Hybrids intermediate in character between the parents. The original cv., 'Anneliesae', differs from *R. arborescens* in having midrib pubescent and strigose beneath, corolla pale pink, with yellow blotch on upper lobe, and from *R. calendulaceum* in having branchlets almost glabrous, and lvs. glabrous and glaucous. Zone 5.

anthopogon D. Don. RN, *PO;* strongly aromatic, to 2 ft.; lvs. elliptic or obovate, to 1¾ in. long, glossy above, rusty-lepidote beneath; corolla white or pink, fading to yellow, tubular, ¾ in. across, stamens glabrous. E. Himalayas of Tibet. Zone 7.

anwheiense E. H. Wils. HY, *HY;* to 12 ft., young brs. sparingly floccose-tomentose; lvs. ovate-lanceolate, to 2½ in. long, glabrous; corolla white, sometimes flushed pink and with purplish-red spots. E. China.

aperantum Balf.f. & Ward. HY, *HY;* dwarf, spreading shrublet, to 1 ft., forming mats to 20 ft. across in the wild; lvs. ovate to obovate, to 1¾ in. long, glabrous above, glaucous beneath; corolla white, rose, to deep crimson, or even orange or yellow, stamens 10, about half as long as corolla, ovary setose-pubescent. Ne. Burma. Zone 7.

apiculatum Rehd. & E. H. Wils. RN, *RN;* to 5 ft.; lvs. ovate, to 2 in. long, acuminate, glabrous above, brown-lepidote beneath; corolla dark purple, 1½ in. across. W. Szechwan.

apodectum Balf.f. & W. W. Sm. HY, *HY;* to 6 ft.; lvs. oblong or elliptic to obovate, to 3 in. long, glabrous above, with matted hairs beneath, revolute; corolla varying from orange to yellowish-scarlet and crimson, to 1¾ in. long. Yunnan. Zone 8.

aralioides: a listed name of no botanical standing, probably for *R.* × *azaleoides.*

arborescens (Pursh) Torr. [*Azalea arborescens* Pursh]. SMOOTH A., SWEET A. PE, *PE;* to 10 ft. or more in the wild, branchlets glabrous; lvs. elliptic or oblong-lanceolate to obovate, to 3 in. long, glabrous; fls. fragrant, corolla white, funnelform, to 2 in. across, stamens much exserted, style glabrous, red. Early spring. Penn. to Ga. and Ala. Zone 5.

arboreum Sm. TREE R. HY, *HY;* to 40 ft.; lvs. oblong-lanceolate, to 8 in. long, green and glossy above, silvery to fawn beneath; corolla scarlet with darker spots, to 2 in. across, stamens white, glabrous. Early spring to late spring. Himalayas. Zone 8b. Cv. 'Album'. Corolla white. Cv. 'Campbelliae' [*R. Campbelliae* Hook.f.]. Lvs. reddish beneath; corolla purplish. Var. **nilagiricum:** *R. nilagiricum.* Var. **roseum:** *R. nilagiricum.* Var. **zeylanicum:** a listed name of no botanical standing for *R. zeylanicum.*

×**arbutifolium** Rehd.: *R. ferrugineum* × *R. minus*. RN, *RN;* evergreen, to 4 ft.; lvs. elliptic, to 3 in. long, lepidote beneath; corolla pink, to ¾ in. across. Early summer. Zone 6.

argenteum: *R. grande.*

argyrophyllum Franch. HY, *HY;* to 20 ft., branchlets gray-pubescent; lvs. oblong-lanceolate, to 5 in. long, acuminate, white-felted beneath; corolla white, often suffused rose, spotted pink or rose, campanulate, narrowed toward base, 1½ in. long, 6–10-lobed, ovary white-floccose. Sw. China. Zone 6. Var. **cupulare** Rehd. & E. H. Wils. Branchlets glabrous; corolla broad-campanulate.

arizelum Balf.f. & Forr. HY, *HY;* to 20 ft.; lvs. obovate, to 9 in. long, leathery, wrinkled above, felty beneath with cinnamon-brown hairs; corolla pale yellow or yellow tinged with rose, with crimson blotch, 1¾ in. across, 8-lobed, stamens 16, ovary hairy but not glandular. Ne. Burma, Tibet, w. China. Zone 8.

×**arnoldianum** [*R. obtusum* var. *arnoldianum* Rehd.]: a listed name of no botanical standing for the hybrid *R. Kaempferi* × *R. obtusum* cv. 'Amoenum'. ARNOLD HYBRID AZALEAS. TT, *TU;* hardy; fls. single, corolla rose to purple, 1–1¼ in. across. Zone 7.

artosquameum Balf.f. & Forr. RN, *RN;* to 8 ft.; lvs. elliptic to broadly elliptic, to 1½ in. long, cordate at base, lepidote beneath; corolla rose to purple, not spotted, to 2 in. across, not lepidote outside. Se. Tibet. Zone 6.

astrocalyx: *R. Wardii.*

atlanticum (Ashe) Rehd. [*Azalea atlantica* Ashe]. COAST A., DWARF A. PE, *PE;* to 2 ft., stoloniferous; lvs. oblong or elliptic to cuneate-obovate, to 2½ in. long, bristly-ciliate; fls. fragrant, generally preceding the lvs., pedicels, calyx lobes, and corolla glandular, corolla white or pinkish, funnelform, 1¾ in. long. Del. to S.C. Zone 6.

×**atrosanguineum:** a listed name of no botanical standing for *Rhododendron* cv. 'Atrosanguineum' [*R. catawbiense* cv. 'Atrosanguineum']. A Catawba Hybrid Rhododendron, involving *R. catawbiense, R. arboreum,* and perhaps other spp.; corolla red. Zone 5.

Aucklandii: *R. Griffithianum.*

Augustinii Hemsl. RN, *RN;* to 10 ft., branchlets downy, becoming glabrous; lvs. lanceolate, to 4 in. long, lepidote, petioles and lower surface of midrib with a fine line of hairs; corolla pink or gray-blue to mauve, with green spots, 2½ in. across, ovary hairy, lepidote. Spring. W. Hupeh and Szechwan. Zone 7.

aureum: see *R. xanthostephanum.*

auriculatum Hemsl. HY, *HY;* to 20 ft.; lvs. oblong, to 1 ft. long, auriculate at base, rusty-tomentose beneath; corolla white to rose-pink, widely funnelform, to 4 in. across, 7-lobed. Summer. Hupeh. Zone 6.

auritum Tagg. RN, *RN;* straggly shrub, to 10 ft.; lvs. elliptic to lanceolate, to 2 in. long, lepidote on both surfaces; corolla creamy-white to yellow, tinged pink, tubular-campanulate, 1 in. long, ovary lepidote. Tibet.

austrinum (Small) Rehd. [*Azalea austrina* Small]. FLORIDA FLAME A. PE, *PE;* to 10 ft.; lvs. elliptic or broadly elliptic to obovate, to 3½ in. long, finely pubescent; fls. slightly fragrant, corolla yellow to orange, funnelform, to 1¼ in. long, stamens exserted. Spring. Fla. and adjacent Ga. and Ala. Zone 6.

×**azaleoides** Dum.-Cours. [*Azaleodendron azaleoides* Hort.]: *R. ponticum* × probably *R. periclymenoides*. Best treated as *Rhododendron* cv. 'Azaleoides'; corolla pale purple, to 2 in. across. Zone 6.

Baileyi Balf.f. RN, *RN;* to 6 ft.; lvs. oblong to elliptic to obovate-oblong, to 3½ in. long, dark green, above, buff to rust-colored beneath; corolla deep red-purple, rotate, to nearly ¾ in. across, stamens 10, as long as corolla tube. S. Tibet. Zone 7.

Bakeri (W. P. Lemm. & McKay) H. Hume [*R. cumberlandense* E. Braun; *Azalea Bakeri* W. P. Lemm. & McKay.]. CUMBERLAND A. PE, *PE;* to 9 ft.; lvs. obovate, to 2 in. long, ciliate; fls. appearing after the lvs., on pedicels without glands, corolla red, orange, or yellow, with yellow-orange blotch, tubular-funnelform, to 2 in. across, filaments and style carmine. Ky. and w. Va. to N.C., Ga., and Ala. Zone 5.

Balfourianum Diels. HY, *HY;* to 8 ft.; lvs. ovate to oblong-elliptic, to 3½ in. long, silky-shining beneath; fls. on glandular pedicels to 1 in. long, corolla pale rose with crimson markings, funnelform-campanulate, to 1¾ in. long, 5-lobed, ovary glandular. W. Yunnan. Zone 6.

balsaminiflorum: *R. indicum* cv.

barbatum Wallich. HY, *HY;* tree, to 60 ft.; lvs. elliptic-lanceolate or oblong, to 9 in. long, glabrous beneath, petiole bristly; corolla deep red, campanulate, 1½ in. across, stamens glabrous, ovary strongly glandular. Spring. Sikkim and Nepal. Zone 8.

×**Barclayi:** a listed name of no botanical standing for *Rhododendron* cv. 'Barclayi'. Hybrid; fls. deep blood-red.

basilicum Balf.f. & W. W. Sm. HY, *HY;* shrub or tree, to 30 ft., young sts. red-tomentose; lvs. obovate, to 10 in. long, pubescent beneath; corolla pale yellow, spotted red, campanulate, to 1½ in. long, 8-lobed, fleshy, stamens 16, ovary tomentose. W. Yunnan. Zone 8.

bathyphyllum Balf.f. & Forr. HY, *HY;* to 5 ft., brs. densely tomentose; lvs. oblong, to 3 in. long, revolute, leathery, rusty-tomentose beneath; corolla white, spotted crimson, campanulate, markedly oblique, to 1½ in. long, stamens hairy, shorter than corolla, ovary tomentose, style glabrous. Sw. Szechwan and se. Tibet.

bauhiniiflorum G. Watt ex Hutch. RN, *RN;* perhaps not distinct from *R. triflorum,* but reported to differ in having infl. 2-fld., and scales of lower surface of lvs. unequal in size and of uniform color. Assam.

Beanianum Cowan. HY, *HY;* to 8 ft., young sts. bristly; lvs. oblong to elliptic-oblong or rarely obovate, to 4 in. long, revolute, green and shining above, felty-brown beneath; calyx fleshy, corolla blood-red to pink, tubular-campanulate, with 5 basal nectar pouches, 1½ in. long. N. Burma and se. Tibet. Zone 8.

Beesianum Diels. HY, *HY;* shrub or small tree, to 20 ft.; lvs. oblong-lanceolate to oblanceolate, to 1 ft. long, green and glabrous above, felty beneath; corolla white to magenta-rose, often with crimson markings, campanulate, 2 in. across, ovary brown-tomentose. Szechwan, Yunnan, Tibet. Zone 7.

×**Blandyanum:** a listed name of no botanical standing for *Rhododendron* cv. 'Blandyanum'. Hybrid, with *R. catawbiense* as one parent; fls. rosy-crimson. Zone 6.

Bodinieri Franch. RN, *RN;* small shrub; lvs. oblong-lanceolate, to 3 in. long, acuminate, glabrous beneath, rarely lepidote above; fls. usually 6–7 in an infl., corolla rose, spotted purple, 1¼ in. long, glabrous outside. Yunnan. Zone 7.

Boothii Nutt. RN, *RN;* straggling epiphytic shrub, to 10 ft.; lvs. ovate to ovate-elliptic, to 5 in. long, short-acuminate, hairy above on margins and midrib, glaucous and densely lepidote beneath; corolla bright lemon-yellow, unspotted, campanulate, to 1 in. across and 1¼ in. long, anthers red, ovary lepidote. Bhutan. Zone 9.

brachyanthum Franch. RN, *RN;* shrub, to 5 ft., brs. stiff, lepidote; lvs. oblong-lanceolate or oblong-elliptic to obovate, 2¼ in. long, glaucous and lepidote beneath; fls. on pedicels to 1½ in. long, calyx leafy, to ⁵⁄₁₆ in. long, corolla pale yellow or greenish-yellow, campanulate, to ¾ in. long. Yunnan. Zone 6. Var. **hypolepidotum** Franch. [*R. charitostreptum* Balf.f. & F. K. Ward; *R. hypolepidotum* (Franch.) Balf.f. & Forr.]. Lvs. densely lepidote beneath.

brachycarpum D. Don ex G. Don. FUJIYAMA R. HY, *HY;* shrub, to 10 ft.; lvs. oblong to oblong-elliptic, to 6 in. long, gray-tomentose beneath; calyx minute, corolla cream-white, flushed pink, spotted brownish-yellow, funnelform, to 2 in. across, ovary hairy, style glabrous. Japan. Zone 6. Cv. 'Rosiflorum'. Corolla pink.

brachysiphon Balf.f. ex Hutch. RN, *RN;* to 8 ft., young brs. lepidote; lvs. obovate or elliptic, to 5 in. long, glabrous above, rusty-lepidote beneath; fls. fragrant, corolla pink, 1¾ in. long, stamens 20, unequal, exserted, ovary rusty-lepidote. Bhutan.

bracteatum Rehd. & E. H. Wills. RN, *RN;* to 6 ft.; lvs. ovate-elliptic, to 2 in. long, lepidote, with the odor of black currants when crushed; corolla white, spotted red, campanulate, ¾ in. long, tube hairy inside, lepidote outside. W. Szechwan. Zone 7.

brevistylum Franch. RN, *RN;* to 10 ft.; lvs. ovate-lanceolate to ovate-oblong, to 4 in. long, lepidote; corolla rose with crimson markings, campanulate, 1½ in. long, lepidote outside, ovary lepidote, pubescent in lower half. Yunnan.

×**Broughtonii aureum:** a listed name of no botanical standing for *Rhododendron* cv. 'Broughtonii Aureum': (*R. maximum* × *R. ponticum*) × *R. molle*. Corolla soft yellow with orange spots. Zone 7.

bullatum Franch. RN, *RN;* to 8 ft., branchlets densely and softly woolly; lvs. ovate-elliptic, to 4 in. long, abruptly acuminate, wrinkled above, brown-tomentose beneath; fls. fragrant, corolla white with yellowish-green blotch, campanulate, to 2½ in. across, wavy-margined. Yunnan. Zone 9.

Bureavii Franch. HY, *HY;* to 6 ft., young branchlets thickly rusty-felty; lvs. ovate or elliptic, to 4½ in. long, rusty-tomentose and glandular beneath; calyx to ⅜ in. long, corolla rose or reddish, spotted crimson, tubular-campanulate, 1 in. across, ovary red-tomentose, glandular. Yunnan. Zone 6

burmanicum Hutch. RN, *RN;* small shrub, to 6 ft., branchlets rusty-brown-lepidote; lvs. oblanceolate to obovate, to 3¼ in. long, lepidote on both surfaces; fls. fragrant, calyx minute, corolla greenish-white to yellowish, funnelform, 2 in. long, lepidote outside, ovary lepidote. Sw. Burma. Zone 9.

caeruleum Lév. RN, *RN;* to 6 ft., branchlets purplish, not lepidote; lvs. elliptic, 1¼ in. long, slightly lepidote beneath; corolla rose-lavender to white, ¾ in. long. Yunnan. Zone 7.

caesium Hutch. RN, *RN;* twiggy shrub, to 4 ft.; lvs. oblong-lanceolate, to 2½ in. long, green and glabrous above, bluish-gray beneath, with glandlike scales; corolla greenish-yellow, lepidote outside, anthers chocolate-brown, ovary with glandular scales. W. Yunnan. Zone 7.

calendulaceum (Michx.) Torr. [*Azalea calendulacea* Michx.]. FLAME A., YELLOW A. PE, *PE;* to 10 ft. or rarely more, young brs. hairy; lvs. elliptic, oblong or obovate, to 3 in. long, pubescent beneath; fls. appearing before or with the lvs., corolla orange-yellow to scarlet, funnelform, 2 in. across, glandular outside, stamens much exserted. Late spring. Sw. Penn. and Ohio to Ga. Zone 5. Cv. 'Croceum', corolla yellow. Cvs. 'Luteum' and 'Roseum' are listed.

californicum: *R. macrophyllum.*

callimorphum Balf.f. & W. W. Sm. [*R. cyclium* Balf.f. & Forr.]. HY, *HY;* to 10 ft.; lvs. elliptic to ovate-orbicular, to 2¾ in. long, cordate at base, green and shiny above, glaucous beneath; corolla rose, campanulate, to 2 in. long, stamens glabrous, ovary glandular. W. Yunnan. Zone 7.

calophytum Franch. HY, *HY;* to 50 ft. in the wild, but mostly to 10 ft. in cult.; lvs. oblong to oblanceolate, to 1 ft. long; corolla white to rose, with a dark basal blotch and spotted, campanulate, to 3 in. across, 5–7-lobed, stamens 15–20, shorter than corolla, ovary glabrous. W. Szechwan. Zone 6.

calostrotum Balf.f. & F. K. Ward [*R. riparium* F. K. Ward]. RN, *RN;* shrublet, to 1 ft., branchlets lepidote; lvs. elliptic to obovate, to 1 in. long, reddish and lepidote beneath; fls. solitary or in pairs, calyx to ¼ in. long, densely lepidote, corolla pink to reddish-purple, rotate, 1½ in. across, pubescent outside. Ne. Burma. Zone 6.

caloxanthum Balf.f. & Farrer. HY, *HY;* to 5 ft., branchlets glandular; lvs. elliptic to orbicular, to 2½ in. long, dark green above, glabrous and glaucous-green beneath; corolla yellow, but scarlet in bud, campanulate, 1¼ in. long, stamens glabrous, ovary densely glandular. Ne. Burma. Zone 7.

camelliiflorum Hook.f. RN, *RN;* straggling epiphytic shrub, to 6 ft.; lvs. narrowly oblong-lanceolate, to 4 in. long, glabrous above, densely lepidote beneath; fls. in terminal pairs, corolla white, tinged pink, campanulate, 1½ in. across, stamens 12–16, ovary glabrous. Bhutan and Sikkim.

campanulatum D. Don. HY, *HY;* to 12 ft.; lvs. oblong-elliptic to elliptic or obovate, to 6 in. long, dark green, glabrous and glossy above, rusty-felty beneath; corolla white to rosy-purple, spotted, campanulate, to 2 in. across, ovary and style glabrous. Early summer. Bhutan to Kashmir. Zone 6. Var. **aeruginosum** (Hook.f.) Hook.f. [*R. aeruginosum* Hook.f.]. Young foliage with metallic luster.

Campbelliae: *R. arboreum* cv.

campylocarpum Hook.f. HONEY-BELL R. HY, *HY;* to 8 ft., branchlets glandular; lvs. ovate to elliptic, to 4 in. long, dark green and glossy above, glaucous beneath; corolla yellow, sometimes with crimson blotch, campanulate, 2 in. across, ovary glandular. Sikkim and e. Nepal. Zone 7.

campylogynum Franch. RN, *RN;* to 6 ft., but usually a compact cushion to 1 or 2 ft.; lvs. obovate, to 1 in. long, glabrous above, at first lepidote beneath, becoming glabrous; corolla rose- to dark purple, glaucous outside, campanulate, ¾ in. across, ovary glandular-lepidote, style abruptly recurved. W. Yunnan. Zone 7. Var. **cremastrum** (Balf.f. & Forr.) Davidian [*R. cremastrum* Balf.f. & Forr.]. Erect shrub, to 4 ft.; lvs. pale green on both sides. Var. **myrtilloides** (Balf.f. & F. K. Ward) Cowan & Davidian [*R. myrtilloides* Balf.f. & F. K. Ward]. Lvs. smaller.

camtschaticum Pall. [*Therorhodion camtschaticum* (Pall.) Small]. TH; small deciduous shrub, to 8 in.; lvs. obovate to spatulate-obovate, to 2½ in. long, sessile, ciliate; fls. solitary or in pairs, corolla rose-purple, spotted, rotate-campanulate, 1½ in. across. Ne. Asia; Alaska to B.C. Zone 6. The epithet sometimes incorrectly spelled kamtschaticum.

canadense (L.) Torr. [*Azalea canadensis* (L.) O. Kuntze; *Rhodora canadensis* L.]. RHODORA. PE, *RO;* deciduous, much-branched shrub, to 3 ft.; lvs. elliptic to oblong, to 2 in. long, gray-pubescent beneath; fls. mostly preceding lvs., rose-purple, to ¾ in. long, 2-lipped, lower two lobes separate to base, ovary pubescent. Spring. Nfld. to Penn. Zone 3. Cv. 'Albiflorum'. Fls. white.

×**candidissimum**: a listed name of no botanical standing for *Rhododendron* cv. 'Candidissimum'. An Indian Hybrid Azalea; corolla large, white.

canescens (Michx.) Sweet [*Azalea canescens* Michx.]. FLORIDA PINXTER, HOARY A. PE, *PE;* deciduous, sparingly branched shrub, to 15 ft.; lvs. oblong-obovate or oblanceolate, to 4 in. long, usually gray-pubescent beneath; corolla pink or white, funnelform, 1½ in. across, glandular outside, tube much longer than lobes, stamens much-exserted. Spring. N.C. to Fla. and Tex. Zone 7. Vars. **album** and **roseum** are listed, but they may be color forms of *R. periclymenoides.*

cantabile: *R. russatum,* but material offered under the name *R. cantabile* may be *Rhododendron* cv. 'Cantabile', one of the Glenn Dale Hybrid Azaleas; corolla white.

capitatum Maxim. RN, *RN;* to 3 ft., branchlets densely lepidote; lvs. elliptic, to ⅝ in. long, lepidote on both surfaces; corolla mauve, funnelform, ovary lepidote, style glabrous. Kansu.

×**cardinale**: a listed name of no botanical standing for *Rhododendron* cv. 'Cardinale'. One of the Kaempferi Hybrid Azaleas; corolla phlox-pink.

cardiobasis Sleum. HY, *HY;* to 10 ft.; lvs. elliptic or ovate-orbicular, to 6½ in. long; corolla white and rose, funnelform-campanulate, to 2¼ in. long, 7-lobed, stamens 14, ovary glandular. Kwangsi. Perhaps not in cult.; material grown under this name seems to be misidentified.

carolinianum Rehd. CAROLINA R. RN, *RN;* compact shrub to 6 ft.; lvs. elliptic, to 3 in. long, acute or short-acuminate, glabrous above, rusty-scaly beneath; corolla pale rose-purple, funnelform, about 1½ in. across, tube shorter than lobes. Late spring. Higher slopes of Blue Ridge Mts., N.C. Zone 6. Its compact habit, lighter corolla color, earlier flowering season, and higher altitudinal range separate this sp. from *R. minus,* with which it is sometimes combined. Cv. 'Album' [cv. 'White Carolinianum']. Corolla white; not to be confused with the following var. Var. **album** Rehd. Lvs. lighter green; corolla pure white, with yellow-green blotch. Comes true from seed; considered superior to the typical var. as a hort. subject.

catawbiense Michx. CATAWBA R., MOUNTAIN ROSEBAY, PURPLE LAUREL. HY, *HY;* shrub, to 10 ft., sometimes a small tree, to 20 ft.; lvs. elliptic to obovate, to 6 in. long, glabrous, shining above; corolla lilac-purple to paler lilac-rose and occasionally white, broadly campanulate, to 2½ in. across, ovary rusty-pubescent. Late spring. Mts., W.Va. and Va. to Ga. and Ala. Zone 5. One of the parents of the Catawba Hybrid Rhododendrons. Var. **compactum** Hort. A dwarf, compact form, to 3 ft. Native to summit of Mt. Mitchell, N.C. Cv. 'Album': better treated as *Rhododendron* cv. 'Catawbiense Album'; possibly of hybrid origin; corolla white, flushed with pale lilac in bud. Cv. 'Atrosanguineum': a hybrid, *Rhododendron* cv. 'Atrosanguineum'; see under *R. atrosanguineum.* Cv. 'Grandiflorum': better treated as *Rhododendron* cv. 'Catawbiense Grandiflorum'; possibly of hybrid origin; corolla lilac.

caucasicum Pall. CAUCASIAN R. HY, *HY;* to 3 ft.; lvs. oblong, ovate, or obovate, to 4 in. long, cuneate at base, brown-tomentose beneath; corolla pink or yellowish-white, spotted, campanulate, 2 in. across, stamens white-hairy at base, ovary white-hairy, style pink, glabrous. Late spring. Caucasus. Zone 7. One of the parents of the Caucasicum Hybrid Rhododendrons. Var. **coriacea** is listed.

cephalanthoides: *R. primuliflorum* var.

cephalanthum Franch. RN, *PO;* to 4 ft., branchlets bristly, densely lepidote, bud scales persistent; lvs. oblong-elliptic, to 1¼ in. long, glabrous above, lepidote beneath; corolla white or pink, tubular, ⅝ in. long, not lepidote, ovary lepidote. W. China. Zone 7. Var. **crebreflorum** (Hutch. & F. K. Ward) Cowan & Davidian [*R. crebreflorum* Hutch. & F. K. Ward]. A dwarf form; corolla pink, stamens 6, filaments glabrous. Assam.

cerasinum Tagg. HY, *HY;* to 12 ft.; lvs. oblong, oblong-elliptic, or oblanceolate, to 4 in. long, glabrous; fls. nodding, corolla creamy-white to cherry-red or scarlet, campanulate, to 2 in. across, stamens glabrous, ovary and style glandular. Burma, Assam, se. Tibet. Zone 7.

chaetomallum Balf.f. & Forr. HY, *HY;* to 5 ft., branchlets bristly; lvs. obovate or elliptic-obovate, to 3½ in. long, glabrous above, tawny-woolly beneath; calyx red, fleshy, to ⅜ in. long, corolla crimson, tubular-campanulate, 1½ in. long, ovary tomentose, style green, glabrous. Nw. Yunnan and se. Tibet. Zone 8.

Chamaecistus: *Rhodothamnus Chamaecistus.*

chamae-Thomsonii (Tagg & Forr.) Cowan & Davidian [*R. repens* Balf.f. & Forr. var. *chamae-Thomsonii* Tagg & Forr.]. HY, *HY;* erect shrub, to 3 ft., branchlets usually glandular; lvs. obovate or oblong-obovate, to 4 in. long, usually glabrous; corolla crimson, tubular-campanulate, to about 2 in. long, ovary glandular, hairy, or glabrous. Yunnan and Tibet. Zone 7. Var. **chamaethauma** (Tagg) Cowan & Davidian [*R. repens* var. *chamaethauma* Tagg]. Lvs. smaller.

chameunum Balf.f. & Forr. [*R. charidotes* Balf.f. & Farrer; *R. cosmetum* Balf.f. & Forr.]. RN, *RN;* low shrub, to 1 ft., branchlets densely bristly, lepidote; lvs. oblong-elliptic, to ½ in. long, glabrous above, lepidote beneath; corolla deep rose-purple, marked crimson, broadly funnelform, to 1 in. long, ovary short-tomentose, style glabrous. W. Yunnan.

Chapmanii A. Gray [*R. minus* var. *Chapmanii* (A. Gray) W. Duncan & Pullen]. CHAPMAN'S R. RN, *RN;* to 6 ft., brs. erect, rigid; lvs. obtuse, petioles to ¼ in. long; corolla rose-pink, to 1½ in. across, with crisped margins. Late spring. Sandy coastal pinelands, nw. Fla. Zone 7. Useful along the Gulf Coast.

charianthum Hutch. RN, *RN;* to 15 ft.; lvs. oblanceolate or elliptic-oblanceolate, to 2 in. long, glabrous except for scales on both surfaces; corolla rose, spotted red, 1 in. long, glabrous, ovary lepidote. Nativity unknown, but probably w. China. Zone 7.

charidotes: *R. chameunum.*

charitopes Balf.f. & Farrer. RN, *RN;* to 1 ft., foliage fragrant; lvs. obovate, to 1½ in. long, glaucous beneath, lepidote on both surfaces; corolla apple-blossom pink, spotted crimson, tubular, 1 in. long, slightly lepidote outside, ovary lepidote. N. Burma. Zone 7.

charitostreptum: *R. brachyanthum* var. *hypolepidotum.*

chartophyllum Franch. RN, *RN;* semideciduous shrub, to 8 ft. or more; lvs. elliptic to oblanceolate, to 2½ in. long, slightly lepidote beneath; corolla pale purple, broadly funnelform, to 2 in. across, glabrous outside, stamens long-exserted. Yunnan. Zone 7.

chasmanthoides: *R. chasmanthum.*

chasmanthum Diels [*R. chasmanthoides* Balf.f. & Forr.]. RN, *RN;* to 20 ft.; lvs. lanceolate or oblong-lanceolate to elliptic-obovate, to 5 in. long, tapered to apex, glabrous above, lepidote beneath; corolla lavender-rose to violet, with olive markings, funnelform, stamens exserted, ovary lepidote. Yunnan and e. Tibet. Zone 8.

chinense: a listed name of no botanical standing, perhaps intended for *R. sinense,* which is *R. molle.*

×**chionoides:** a listed name of no botanical standing for *Rhododendron* cv. 'Chionoides'. Hybrid, derived from *R. ponticum:* corolla white with yellow center.

chloranthum Balf.f. & Forr. PA; deciduous shrub, to 4 ft.; lvs. obovate, to 1 in. long, glabrous above, lepidote beneath and bristly on midrib; fls. preceding the lvs., corolla greenish-yellow, campanulate, 1 in. across, ovary lepidote, style green, curved, glabrous. Nw. Yunnan. Zone 8.

chlorops Cowan. HY, *HY;* shrub, to 10 ft.; lvs. oblong to oblong-elliptic, to 4¾ in. long, leathery, green, smooth, waxy, glossy above, very minutely hairy beneath, petiole to 1⅜ in. long; calyx unequally 6–7-lobed, corolla cream to light yellow, greenish and blotched with purple basally inside, with rows of purple spots in the tube, campanulate, 7-lobed, 1½ in. long, fleshy, stamens 14, hairy at base, ovary and style glandular. Nativity uncertain, probably Yunnan.

chrysanthum Pall. HY, *HY;* dwarf, prostrate or semiprostrate shrublet, to 1 ft.; lvs. oblanceolate or obovate, to 1½ in. long, glabrous and dark green above; corolla pale yellow, campanulate, 1¼ in. long, ovary rusty-tomentose, style glabrous. Siberia to cent. Japan. Zone 2. Var. **nikomontanum** Komatsu [*R. nikomontanum* (Komatsu) Nakai]. Habit erect.

chryseum Balf.f. & F. K. Ward [*R. muliense* Balf.f. & Forr.]. RN, *RN;* much-branched, evergreen shrub, to 2½ ft., branchlets densely lepidote; lvs. ovate-elliptic or obovate-elliptic to oblong, to ½ in. long, densely lepidote; corolla yellow, funnelform, to 1 in. across, lepidote outside, stamens 5, ovary lepidote above, pubescent at base. Nw. Yunnan. Zone 6.

ciliatum Hook.f. FRINGED R. RN, *RN;* to 6 ft., branchlets bristly; lvs. elliptic, to 4 in. long, hairy above on margins, lepidote beneath; corolla rosy-red on bud, opening pink, becoming white, broadly funnelform, 2½ in. across, glabrous, lobes notched, ovary lepidote, style glabrous. Sikkim Himalayas. Zone 8.

ciliicalyx Franch. RN, *RN;* to 10 ft.; lvs. elliptic, obovate-elliptic, or oblong-lanceolate, to 4½ in. long, glaucous and lepidote beneath; fls. fragrant, calyx lobes bristly ciliate, corolla white or tinged rose, funnelform, 4 in. across, ovary and style lepidote. W. Yunnan. Zone 9.

×**cilpinense:** a listed name of no botanical standing for *Rhododendron* cv. 'Cilpinense': *R. ciliatum* × *R. moupinense.* RN, *RN;* corolla pale shell-pink. Zone 8.

cinnabarinum Hook.f. RN, *RN;* to 6 ft.; lvs. elliptic to oblanceolate, to 4 in. long, lepidote beneath; corolla brick-red to cinnabar-red, tubular, to 2 in. long, not lepidote, ovary lepidote. Sikkim Himalayas. Zone 8. Var. **aestivale** Hutch. Corolla cinnabar-red with pale yellow lobes more or less suffused with red. Var. **blandfordiiflorum** Hook.f. Corolla red outside, yellow or greenish-yellow inside. Var. **Roylei** Hook.f. Corolla deep plum-crimson or purple.

citriniflorum Balf.f. & Forr. HY, *HY;* to 4 ft.; lvs. oblong-obovate, to obovate, to 2¼ in. long, woolly beneath with fawn-colored hairs; corolla lemon-yellow, campanulate, 1¾ in. long, ovary glandular-hairy or with tawny hairs, style glabrous. W. Yunnan, se. Tibet. Subsp. **horaeum** (Balf.f. & Forr.) Cowan [*R. horaeum* Balf.f. & Forr.]. To 1 ft.; corolla deep crimson. Tibet. Subsp. **rubens** Cowan [*R. rubens* Hort.]. Corolla red or crimson, ovary glandular. Se. Tibet.

Clementinae Forr. HY, *HY;* to 10 ft., branchlets thick; lvs. elliptic to oblong-elliptic, to 5½ in. long, usually auriculate-cordate at base, woolly beneath with cinnamon hairs; corolla yellowish-white to bright rose with crimson markings, broadly campanulate, to 2½ in. across, 6–7-lobed, stamens 12–14, ovary and style glabrous. Sw. Szechwan and nw. Yunnan.

×**coccineum speciosum:** a listed name of no botanical standing for *Rhododendron* cv. 'Coccineum Speciosum'. One of the Ghent Hybrid Azaleas; corolla brilliant orange-red. Zone 6.

complexum Balf.f. & W. W. Sm. RN, *RN;* matted shrublet, to 2 ft., branchlets short, lepidote; lvs. elliptic or oblong-elliptic, ¼ in. long, lepidote on both sides; corolla deep rose-purple, funnelform, ½ in. long, lepidote outside, stamens 5, ovary lepidote, style glabrous. Yunnan.

concatenans Hutch. RN, *RN;* to 6 ft., branchlets glaucous; lvs. oblong to oblong-elliptic, to 3 in. long, glabrous above, lepidote and glaucous beneath; corolla apricot, faintly tinged with purple outside, campanulate, 2 in. across, ovary lepidote. Se. Tibet. Zone 8.

×**concessum:** a listed name of no botanical standing for *Rhododendron* cv. 'Concessum'. Hybrid of uncertain parentage; corolla bright rose, with a light center.

concinnoides Hutch. & F. K. Ward. RN, *RN;* small shrub; lvs. obovate-elliptic, to 1¾ in. long, cuneate at base, brown-lepidote beneath; corolla pinkish-purple, 1 in. long, ovary lepidote, style glabrous, much longer than stamens. Assam.

concinnum Hemsl. [*R. yanthinum* Bur. & Franch.]. RN, *RN;* twiggy shrub, to 7 ft., branchlets densely lepidote; lvs. oblong-lanceolate, to 2 in. long, lepidote on both sides; corolla purple, spotted, funnelform, 2 in. across, lepidote outside, ovary lepidote, style glabrous. Szechwan. Zone 7.

cosmetum: *R. chameunum.*

crassum Franch. RN, *RN;* shrub or small tree, to 20 ft., branchlets lepidote; lvs. crowded, whorled, lanceolate or obovate-oblanceolate, to 5 in. long, glossy above, rusty-lepidote beneath; fls. fragrant, corolla white, funnelform, to 3½ in. long, lepidote outside, stamens 15–21, ovary and style lepidote. N. Burma, w. Yunnan, se. Tibet. Zone 9.

crebreflorum: *R. cephalanthum* var.

cremastrum: *R. campylogynum* var.

crinigerum Franch. HY, *HY;* to 14 ft., branchlets glandular-bristly; lvs. oblong or oblanceolate, to 7 in. long, densely woolly beneath with cinnamon hairs; corolla pink or flushed rose, spotted, campanulate, to 2 in. across, ovary and style glandular. Nw. Yunnan and se. Tibet. Zone 8.

croceum: *R. Wardii;* however, the name *R. croceum* may sometimes be intended for *R. calendulaceum* cv. 'Croceum'.

cucullatum: *R. Roxieanum.*

cumberlandense: *R. Bakeri.*

cuneatum W. W. Sm. RN, *RN;* to 4 ft., branchlets short and densely lepidote; lvs. elliptic, to 2 in. long, densely rusty-lepidote on both sides; corolla deep rose, funnelform, 1 in. long, stamens 10, exserted, ovary lepidote, style glabrous. Yunnan. Zone 6.

×**Cunninghamii:** a listed name of no botanical standing for *Rhododendron* cv. 'Cunninghamii': *R. arboreum* var. *cinnamomeum* × *R. maximum.* HY, *HY;* lvs. with brownish felt beneath; corolla white with purple spots.

Cuthbertii: *R. minus.*

cyanocarpum (Franch.) W. W. Sm. HY, *HY;* shrub or small tree, to 20 ft.; lvs. elliptic to orbicular, to 4½ in. long, glabrous above, glaucous and finely pubescent beneath; fls. fragrant, corolla white or creamy-white, flushed rose, or rose, campanulate to widely funnelform, to 3½ in. across, stamens 10, glabrous, ovary not glandular, style glabrous. Yunnan.

cyclium: *R. callimorphum.*

dahuricum: *R. dauricum.*

Dalhousiae Hook.f. RN, *RN;* to 8 ft., often epiphytic, branchlets bristly; lvs. obovate to oblanceolate, to 6 in. long, glaucous and densely lepidote beneath; fls. fragrant, corolla pale yellow or white tinged rose, funnelform, 3½ in. across, ovary densely lepidote. Bhutan and Sikkim. Zone 9.

×**daphnoides:** a listed name of no botanical standing for *Rhododendron* cv. 'Daphnoides'. A hybrid of *R. virgatum;* to 6 ft.; corolla rose-purple.

dasycladum Balf.f. & W. W. Sm. HY, *HY;* shrub, to 12 ft., branchlets with glands and hairs; lvs. oblong to oblong-elliptic, to 3⅛ in. long, dark green and glabrous above, paler and with small glands and minute hairs beneath, petiole to ¾ in. long; corolla pinkish, funnelform-campanulate, to 1 in. long, ovary tomentose. Szechwan.

dauricum L. [*R. dahuricum* DC.; *Azalea daurica* (L.) C. Koch]. RM; deciduous or semievergreen, to 6 ft., branchlets pubescent, lepidote; lvs. elliptic to elliptic-ovate or oblong-ovate, to 2 in. long, lepidote on both sides; corolla rosy-purple, rotate-campanulate, ovary densely lepidote, style glabrous. Early spring. Siberia to Japan. Zone 5. Var. **mucronulatum:** *R. mucronulatum.* Var. **sempervirens** Sims. Lvs. dark, persistent.

Davidii Franch. HY, *HY;* to 15 ft.; lvs. oblong-lanceolate or oblong-oblanceolate, to 7 in. long, glabrous; corolla rose or lilac, spotted purple, campanulate, 2 in. long, 7–8-lobed, glandular outside, stamens 14–16, glabrous, ovary densely glandular outside, style glabrous. W. Szechwan. Zone 7.

Davidsonianum Rehd. & E. H. Wils. RN, *RN;* to 10 ft., often leggy; lvs. lanceolate or oblanceolate, to 2½ in. long, dull brown and lepidote beneath; corolla pink, spotted red, campanulate-funnelform, to 1½ in. long, ovary lepidote. W. Szechwan. Zone 7.

×**Daviesii:** a listed name of no botanical standing for *Rhododendron* cv. 'Daviesii': *R. molle* × *R. viscosum.* PE, *PE;* a Ghent Hybrid Azalea; stoloniferous; corolla pale yellow to white, with a yellow blotch, 2¼ in. across. Zone 5.

decorum Franch. HY, *HY;* glabrous shrub, to 20 ft.; lvs. oblong or oblong-ovate to oblong-obovate, to 6 in. long, glabrous; fls. fragrant, corolla white to soft rose, funnelform-campanulate, to 3½ in. across, 7-lobed, stamens 12–16, downy at base, ovary and style glandular. Szechwan and Yunnan. Zone 7.

Degronianum Carrière. HY, *HY;* to 6 ft.; lvs. oblong or elliptic to obovate, to 6 in. long, glossy and glabrous above, rusty-tomentose beneath; corolla soft pink, campanulate, 2½ in. across, stamens white-hairy at base, ovary white-hairy, style glabrous. Japan. Zone 7.

Delavayi Franch. HY, *HY;* to 40 ft.; lvs. oblong-lanceolate to oblong-oblanceolate, to 7 in. long, with a spongy tomentum beneath; corolla crimson, campanulate, 2 in. long, fleshy, ovary tomentose, style glabrous. W. Yunnan and Burma. Probably only a variant of *R. arboreum.*

deleiense: *R. tephropeplum.*

×**delicatissimum:** a listed name of no botanical standing for *Rhododendron* cv. 'Delicatissimum'. Hybrid, developed from *R. catawbiense;* corolla white, tinged pale lilac.

desquamatum Balf.f. & Forr. [*R. stenoplastum* Balf.f. & Forr.]. RN, *RN;* shrub or small tree, to 25 ft., branchlets lepidote; lvs. oblong-lanceolate, to 4 in. long, glabrous above, densely lepidote beneath; corolla mauve, spotted crimson, widely funnelform, 1½ in. long, ovary densely lepidote, style glabrous. W. Yunnan, n. Burma, se. Tibet. Zone 7.

detonsum Balf.f. & Forr. HY, *HY;* to 12 ft., branchlets stout, glabrous; lvs. oblong to oblong-elliptic, to 5 in. long, abruptly mucronate, densely reddish-tomentose; corolla rose-pink, spotted carmine, funnelform-campanulate, to 1¾ in. long, 5–7-lobed, stamens 10–14, ovary and base of style glandular. Yunnan. Zone 7.

diacritum Balf.f. & W. W. Sm. RN, *RN;* mat-forming, procumbent shrublet, to 2 ft., brs. densely lepidote; lvs. broadly elliptic, ¼ in. long, densely lepidote on both sides; corolla dark rose-purple with white throat, broadly funnelform, ⁵⁄₁₆ in. long, ovary lepidote, style glabrous, longer than stamens. Yunnan.

diaprepes Balf.f. & W. W. Sm. HY, *HY;* to 25 ft.; lvs. oblong to oblong-elliptic, to 1 ft. long, dull green above, glaucous-green and glabrous beneath; fls. fragrant, corolla white or flushed rose, widely funnelform, to 5 in. across, fleshy, 7-lobed, stamens 15–20, pubescent at base, ovary and style glandular. Sw. Yunnan and ne. Burma. Zone 8.

dichroanthum Diels. HY, *HY;* to 5 ft., branchlets with white down; lvs. oblong to oblanceolate or obovate, to 4 in. long, glabrous above, white-scurfy beneath; calyx and corolla fleshy, corolla yellow-rose to yellow or purplish-red, tubular-campanulate, 1 in. across, ovary tomentose, style glabrous. Yunnan. Zone 7. Subsp. **herpesticum** (Balf.f. & F. K. Ward) Cowan [*R. herpesticum* Balf.f. & F. K. Ward]. To 2 ft., branchlets and lvs. bristly-glandular; pedicels and ovary glandular. Nw. Yunnan and ne. Burma. Subsp. **scyphocalyx** (Balf.f. & Forr.) Cowan [*R. scyphocalyx* Balf.f. & Forr.]. To 4 or 5 ft.; lvs. broadly obovate, 2½–3½ in. long; pedicels and ovary glandular. Yunnan, ne. Burma. Zone 8.

didymum: *R. sanguineum* subsp.

dilatatum: *R. reticulatum.*

diphrocalyx Balf.f. HY, *HY;* to 15 ft., branchlets setose-glandular; lvs. oblong-ovate to ovate, to 6 in. long, glaucous-green and essentially glabrous beneath; calyx large, one-sided, fleshy, colored like corolla, corolla crimson to bright red, spotted crimson and with blotch at base, tubular-campanulate, to 1½ in. long, fleshy, ovary and style pubescent. W. Yunnan.

discolor Franch. HY, *HY;* robust shrub, to 6 ft. or up to 20 ft. in the wild; lvs. oblong-elliptic to oblong-oblanceolate, to 8 in. long, glabrous, dark green above, paler beneath; corolla white to pale pink, funnelform-campanulate, to 4 in. across, 7-lobed, stamens 14–16, glabrous, ovary and style glandular. Hupeh and Szechwan. Zone 7.

drumonium Balf.f. & F. K. Ward. RN, *RN;* tufted shrub, to 2 ft.; lvs. elliptic, ¼ in. long, lepidote on both sides; corolla mauve, open-funnelform, ½ in. long, lepidote outside on lobes, ovary lepidote, style glabrous. Yunnan. Zone 7.

dryophyllum Balf.f. & Forr. [*R. sigillatum* Balf.f. & Forr.]. HY, *HY;* shrub or small tree, to 25 ft.; lvs. oblong or oblong-elliptic to lanceolate, to 6½ in. long, felty beneath; corolla white, creamy-white, white flushed rose, pink, to pinkish-purple, sometimes crimson-spotted or -blotched, funnelform-campanulate or campanulate, to 1½ in. long. Sw. Szechwan, Yunnan, n. Burma, se. Tibet, Bhutan.

eclecteum Balf.f. & Forr. HY, *HY;* to 10 ft., branchlets usually glandular; lvs. oblong or obovate, to 5 in. long, glabrous except the midrib; corolla yellow or white to deep rose, sometimes spotted, tubular-campanulate, 1¾ in. long, fleshy, ovary glandular. Sw. Szechwan, Yunnan, ne. Burma, se. Tibet. Zone 8. Var. **brachyandrum** (Balf.f. & Forr.) Tagg. Fls. deep rose or crimson.

Edgarianum Rehd. & E. H. Wils. RN, *RN;* to 3 ft.; lvs. broadly elliptic, to ⅜ in. long, lepidote on both sides; corolla rose-purple, open-funnelform, ¾ in. across, not lepidote, ovary lepidote, style glabrous. W. Szechwan and se. Tibet.

Edgeworthii Hook.f. RN, *RN;* straggly shrub, to 10 ft., often epiphytic; lvs. elliptic to ovate-elliptic, to 4½ in. long, dark green and bullate above, rusty-tomentose beneath; fls. fragrant, corolla white or tinged pink, funnelform, to 4 in. long, ovary tomentose. Himalayas of Bhutan and Sikkim. Zone 10.

×**Edmondii:** a listed name of no botanical standing for *Rhododendron* cv. 'Edmondii': *R. arboreum* × *R. barbatum.* HY, *HY;* corolla orange-scarlet.

elaeagnoides: *R. lepidotum.*

elegans: *R. pauciflorum.*

×**elegans superbum:** a listed name of no botanical standing for *Rhododendron* cv. 'Elegans Superbum' [cvs. 'Pride of Mobile', 'Watermelon Pink']. Corolla rose-pink with brownish-purple blotch.

Elliottii G. Watt ex Brandis. HY, *HY;* shrub or much-branched small tree, to 12 ft.; lvs. oblong-elliptic, to 6 in. long, dull green above, paler beneath; corolla scarlet with darker spots, funnelform-campanulate, to 5 in. across and 2 in. long, stamens red, glabrous, ovary and style glandular. India. Zone 9.

×**emasculum** W. Wats.: *Rhododendron* cv. 'Emasculum': *R. ciliatum* × *R. dauricum.* Corolla rosy-lilac to pale purple, stamens lacking. Zone 7.

eriogynum Balf.f. & W. W. Sm. HY, *HY;* shrub or small tree, to 10 ft., branchlets stellate-pubescent, becoming glabrous; lvs. oblong-elliptic, to 8 in. long, blunt at apex, glabrous at maturity; corolla bright red, spotted, campanulate, 2 in. across, ovary stellate-pubescent. Yunnan. Zone 9.

eritimum Balf.f. & W. W. Sm. HY, *HY;* to 18 ft.; lvs. oblong, to 8 in. long; corolla dark crimson or rose-magenta, with basal blotch, tubular-campanulate, 1½ in. long, 7-lobed, stamens 14, glabrous, ovary and style glabrous. Yunnan.

erubescens Hutch. HY, *HY;* shrub, branchlets with smooth purple bark; lvs. oblong-elliptic, to 4 in. long, dark green above, yellowish-green beneath; corolla white, rose-carmine outside, campanulate, 2 in. across, 7-lobed, stamens 12–14, pubescent at base, ovary glandular. China. Zone 7?

euchaites Balf.f. & Forr. HY, *HY;* to 15 or 20 ft.; lvs. oblong or oblong-ovate, to 4 in. long; corolla crimson-scarlet, tubular-campanulate, 1½ in. long, ovary tomentose. Yunnan and Burma. Zone 8. Often regarded as a var. or subsp. of *R. neriiflorum,* from which it differs chiefly in height.

eudoxum Balf.f. & Forr. HY, *HY;* to 6 ft.; lvs. oblong-ovate, to 3 in. long, mealy on lower side; corolla clear crimson-rose, tubular-campanulate, 1¼ in. long, ovary glandular, hairy, style glabrous. Nw. Yunnan and se. Tibet.

×**Everestianum:** a listed name of no botanical standing for *Rhododendron* cv. 'Everestianum'. Hybrid, developed from *R. catawbiense;* corolla rosy-lilac, spotted, with frilled edges. Zone 5.

eximium Nutt. HY, *HY;* tree, to 30 ft.; lvs. obovate-elliptic, to 10 in. long, rusty-tomentose on both sides, becoming glabrous above; corolla tinted rose or pink, oblique-campanulate, 1¾ in. long, 8–10-lobed, stamens 10–14, ovary densely glandular. Bhutan. Zone 8.

×**exoniense:** a listed name of no botanical standing for *Rhododendron* cv. 'Exoniense'. RN, *RN;* hybrid, developed from *R. ciliatum* and *R. Veitchianum;* corolla creamy-white. Zone 8b.

exquisitum Hutch. RN, *RN;* to 5 ft. or more; lvs. elliptic, to 3 in. long, rounded at base, glabrous above, glaucous-green and lepidote beneath; corolla pink to pale lavender, funnelform, 1 in. long, ovary lepidote, style glabrous. Sw. Szechwan. Zone 8.

Falconeri Hook.f. HY, *HY;* tree, to 30 or 50 ft., branchlets stout, woolly; lvs. oblong, elliptic, or obovate, to 1 ft. long, rusty-tomentose beneath; corolla creamy-white to pale yellow, with purple blotch at base, campanulate, 2 in. across, 8-lobed, stamens 12–16, ovary glandular, hairy. Himalayas from Bhutan to Nepal. Zone 9.

Fargesii Franch. HY, *HY;* to 18 ft.; lvs. elliptic to oblong-elliptic, to 3½ in. long, dark green above, glaucous beneath; corolla white to rose or purplish-pink, campanulate, 5–7-lobed, stamens 14, glabrous, ovary densely glandular, style glabrous. Hupeh and Szechwan. Zone 6.

fastigiatum Franch. RN, *RN;* dwarf, evergreen shrub, to 3 ft., branchlets lepidote; lvs. elliptic-oblanceolate, ⅜ in. long, densely lepidote on both sides; corolla light purple, ½ in. long, glabrous, stamens 10, ovary lepidote, style glabrous. Yunnan. Zone 7.

×**fastuosum flore pleno:** a listed name of no botanical standing for *Rhododendron* cv. 'Fastuosum Flore Pleno': *R. catawbiense* × *R. ponticum*. Corolla double, mauve. Zone 6.

Fauriei Franch. HY, *HY;* to 10 ft.; lvs. oblong-elliptic to obovate, to 5 in. long, glabrous; corolla white or cream-colored, flushed pink along midveins of lobes, green-spotted, funnelform-campanulate, 1 in. long, filaments white, ovary tawny-white-tomentose, stigma orange. Japan. Zone 5. Var. **rufescens** Nakai. Lvs. with light brown hairs underneath.

ferrugineum L. ALPINE ROSE. RN, *RN;* to 5 ft.; lvs. lanceolate or elliptic to oblanceolate, to 1¾ in. long, densely rusty-lepidote with overlapping scales beneath; corolla rose, funnelform, ¾ in. long, lepidote outside, pubescent inside, ovary densely lepidote, style glabrous. Summer. Mts. of cent. Eur. Zone 6.

fictolacteum Balf.f. HY, *HY;* tree, to 45 ft.; lvs. elliptic to obovate, to 1 ft. long, dark green above, rusty-tomentose beneath; corolla white or creamy-white tinted rose, blotched crimson, campanulate, 2½ in. across, 7–8-lobed, stamens 14–16, ovary densely tomentose, style glabrous. Yunnan and sw. Szechwan. Zone 7.

fimbriatum Hutch. RN, *RN;* to 2 ft.; lvs. lanceolate to oblong-lanceolate, to 1½ in. long, lepidote on both sides; corolla mauve-purple, campanulate, ⅝ in. long, stamens exserted, ovary densely lepidote. Ne. Yunnan.

flammeum (Michx.) Sarg. [*R. speciosum* (Willd.) Sweet]. OCONEE AZALEA. PE, *PE;* deciduous, to 6 ft., branchlets hairy; lvs. oblong, elliptic, or obovate, to 2½ in. long, ciliate, pubescent beneath; corolla orange to scarlet and bright red, blotched orange, funnelform, to 2 in. across, tube longer than limb, hairy outside but not glandular, stamens 5, exserted, ovary setose. S.C., Ga. Zone 6.

flavantherum Hutch. & F. K. Ward. RN, *RN;* to 10 ft., branchlets sparingly lepidote; lvs. oblong-elliptic, to 2 in. long, glaucous, with widely spaced scales beneath; corolla bright, clear yellow, broadly tubular, ¾ in. long, anthers orange, ovary and base of style lepidote. Tibet.

flavidum Franch. [*R. primulinum* Hemsl.]. RN, *RN;* densely branched, to 2 ft.; lvs. ovate-oblong, to 1 in. long, lepidote on both sides; corolla yellow, open-funnelform, 1¼ in. across, not lepidote, stamens 10, ovary lepidote. W. Szechwan and e. Tibet. Zone 6.

flavum: *R. luteum.*

Fletcheranum Davidian. RN, *RN;* shrub, to 3 ft., sometimes to 4 ft., branchlets bristly; lvs. elliptic to obovate-elliptic, shallowly crenate and bristly-ciliate, dark green above, light green and sparsely lepidote beneath, petioles ¼ in. long; corolla pale greenish-yellow, broadly funnelform, to 1¼ in. long, stamens white-woolly basally, ovary bristly-hairy, lepidote, style glabrous but lepidote. Se. Tibet.

floccigerum Franch. HY, *HY;* to 5 ft., twiggy; lvs. oblong to oblong-elliptic, to 5 in. long, dark green above, rusty-tomentose beneath, becoming glabrous and white-glaucous; corolla crimson, rose, or yellow edged with rose, tubular-campanulate, 1¼ in. long, filaments white, anthers black, ovary white-tomentose. Yunnan. Zone 8.

floribundum Franch. HY, *HY;* to 15 ft.; lvs. oblong-oblanceolate to lanceolate, to 6 in. long, acuminate, dark green, glabrous and bullate above, white-woolly-tomentose beneath; corolla pink, streaked and spotted with crimson, campanulate, 2 in. across, ovary tomentose, style glabrous. E. Yunnan and s. Szechwan. Zone 6.

formosum Wallich. RN, *RN;* to 10 ft.; lvs. oblanceolate to obovate, to 3 in. long, glaucous and lepidote beneath, ciliate on margins and petioles; fls. fragrant, corolla white, tinged yellow and rose, with 5 red stripes outside, funnelform, 2½ in. long, lepidote outside, ovary densely lepidote, style lepidote at base. Assam. Zone 9.

×**Forsteranum:** a listed name of no botanical standing for *Rhododendron* cv. 'Forsteranum': *R. Edgeworthii* × *R. Veitchianum.* RN, *RN;* fls. fragrant, corolla white. Zone 8b.

Forrestii Balf.f. ex Diels. HY, *HY;* prostrate, creeping shrub, to 1½ ft.; lvs. obovate to orbicular, to 1½ in. long, dark green, with impressed veins above, purple-red beneath; fls. solitary or in 2's or 3's, corolla deep crimson, tubular-campanulate, to 1⅜ in. long, ovary glandular, style glabrous. Nw. Yunnan and se. Tibet. Zone 7. Var. **chamaedoxa:** var. *tumescens.* Var. **repens** (Balf.f. & Forr.) Cowan & Davidian [*R. repens* Balf.f. & Forr.]. Lvs. glaucous-green beneath. Yunnan, n. Burma, Tibet. Var. **tumescens** Cowan & Davidian [var. *chamaedoxa* Hort.]. Of dome-shaped habit, outer brs. creeping; lvs. larger. Yunnan, Burma, Tibet.

Fortunei Lindl. FORTUNE'S R. HY, *HY;* to 12 ft.; lvs. oblong to oblong-elliptic, to 8 in. long, glabrous; fls. fragrant, corolla lilac to pink, funnelform-campanulate, 3 in. across, 7-lobed, stamens 14, ovary and style glandular. E. China. Zone 6. One of the parents of the Fortunei Hybrid Rhododendrons.

×**fragrantissimum:** a listed name of no botanical standing for *Rhododendron* cv. 'Fragrantissimum': *R. Edgeworthii* × *R. formosum.* RN, *RN;* fls. fragrant, corolla white, tinged pink. Zone 8b.

×**Fraseri** W. Wats. [*A. Fraseri* Hort.]: *R. canadense* × *R. japonicum.* Corolla rose-lilac, 2-lipped, to 1½ in. across.

fulgens Hook.f. HY, *HY;* to 8 ft.; lvs. obovate, obovate-elliptic, or broadly elliptic, to 4 in. long, glossy and glabrous above, rusty- or tawny-tomentose beneath; corolla blood-red, tubular-campanulate, 1½ in. across, fleshy, ovary and style glabrous. Himalayas, from Bhutan to Nepal. Zone 7.

fulvum Balf.f. & W. W. Sm. HY, *HY;* shrub or small tree, to 20 ft.; lvs. oblanceolate to oblong-obovate, to 8 in. long, glabrous above, downy with tawny to rusty-red hairs beneath; corolla pink, flushed crimson outside, broadly tubular, 1½ in. long, filaments, ovary, and style glabrous; caps. sickle-shaped. W. Yunnan and se. Tibet. Zone 8.

galactinum Balf.f. HY, *HY;* shrub or small tree, to 25 ft.; lvs. oblong-ovate to elliptic-lanceolate or lanceolate, to 10 in. long, pubescent beneath; corolla white or tinged pale rose, with basal crimson blotches, campanulate, 1¼ in. long, 7-lobed, stamens 14, ovary and style glabrous. Szechwan. Zone 6.

×**gandavense** (C. Koch) Rehd. [*Azalea* × *gandavensis* C. Koch]. The GHENT HYBRID AZALEAS. A series of hybrids between *R. luteum* and other spp., probably including *R. calendulaceum, R. molle, R. periclymenoides,* and *R. viscosum.*

giganteum Forr. ex Tagg. HY, *HY;* large tree, to 80 ft.; lvs. elliptic or oblanceolate, to 16 in. long, glabrous above, rusty-brown-woolly beneath or glabrous in young plants; corolla bright rose-purple with basal crimson blotch, campanulate, 2½ in. long, 8-lobed, stamens 16, glabrous, ovary downy, style glabrous. Nw. Yunnan and ne. Burma. Zone 8b. *Rhododendron* cv. 'Giganteum', a hybrid developed from *R. catawbiense,* with corolla light crimson, is sometimes offered under the name *R. giganteum.*

glaucopeplum Balf.f. & Forr. HY, *HY;* to 8 ft.; lvs. ovate or oblong-elliptic, to 4 in. long, grayish-white-pubescent beneath; corolla bright rose, marked crimson, funnelform-campanulate, 1¼ in. long, ovary and style glabrous. Yunnan.

glaucophyllum Rehd. [*R. glaucum* Hook.f., not (Lam.) Sweet or G. Don]. RN, *RN;* to 6 ft., branchlets lepidote; lvs. lanceolate to oblanceolate or elliptic-lanceolate, to 3 in. long, lepidote on both sides; corolla pink, rose, or pinkish-purple, campanulate, 1 in. long, glabrous to densely lepidote outside, ovary densely lepidote, style glabrous. Bhutan and Sikkim. Zone 6. *R. glaucophyllum* Balf.f. is *R. lochmium.*

glaucum: see *R. glaucophyllum.*

glischrum Balf.f. & W. W. Sm. HY, *HY;* shrub or small tree, to 25 ft., young branchlets bristly-glandular; lvs. narrowly oblong to lanceolate or oblanceolate, to 10 in. long, glabrous above, bristly beneath, petiole glandular-setose; corolla deep rose with basal crimson blotch, campanulate, 2 in. across, ovary glandular-setose. Nw. Yunnan and adjacent n. Burma. Zone 7.

globigerum Balf.f. & Forr. HY, *HY;* to 6 ft., young branchlets tomentose; lvs. oblong to obovate, to 3 in. long, dark green above, felty with tawny hairs beneath; slow to flower, corolla white, marked crimson, campanulate, 1 in. long, ovary sparsely woolly, style glabrous. Sw. Szechwan.

glomerulatum Hutch. RN, *RN;* to 3 ft., young branchlets densely lepidote; lvs. ovate or ovate-elliptic, to ⅝ in. long, lepidote on both sides; corolla purple-mauve, widely funnelform, ⅝ in. long, glabrous outside, ovary densely lepidote, style glabrous. W. China? Zone 7.

grande Wight [*R. argenteum* Hook.f.]. SILVERY R. HY, *HY;* tree, to 30 ft.; lvs. oblong to oblanceolate, to 15 in. long, deep green and shining above, silvery-white-hairy beneath, sometimes tawny; corolla pale rose in bud, white to creamy when open, with purple basal blotch, campanulate, to 3 in. across, 8-lobed, stamens 16, ovary glandular, downy, style glabrous. Bhutan and Sikkim. Zone 9. Var. **roseum** Hook.f. Corolla bright rose, 6-lobed.

grandiflorum: a listed name for no botanical standing for *Rhododendron* cv. 'Catawbiense Grandiflorum'. A selection or possibly a hybrid of *R. catawbiense;* corolla lilac. Zone 6.

Griersonianum Balf.f. & Forr. HY, *HY;* to 10 ft., young branchlets bristly and glandular; lvs. lanceolate, to 8 in. long, rusty-woolly beneath, petiole bristly-glandular, woolly; corolla geranium-scarlet with darker spots, funnelform, 2½ in. across, with mealy-woolly hairs outside, ovary and base of style hairy. W. Yunnan. Zone 9.

Griffithianum Wight [*R. Aucklandii* Hook.f.]. HY, *HY;* to 12 ft. or more; lvs. oblong or elliptic-oblong, to 1 ft. long, glabrous; fls. slightly fragrant, corolla white, campanulate, to 6 in. across, stamens 12–18, style glandular. Himalayas of Bhutan and Sikkim. Zone 9. One of the parents of the Griffithianum Hybrid Rhododendrons. Var. **roseum** is listed.

gymnocarpum Balf.f. ex Tagg. HY, *HY;* to 3 ft.; lvs. oblong-elliptic to oblong-oblanceolate, to 2¾ in. long, lower side with fawn-colored pubescence; corolla deep claret-crimson with darker marks, widely campanulate, about 1½ in. long, stamens pubescent, ovary and style glabrous. Se. Tibet. Zone 7.

habrotrichum Balf.f. & W. W. Sm. HY, *HY;* to 10 ft., branchlets glandular-bristly; lvs. elliptic-oblong to oblong-ovate, to 6½ in. long, cordate at base, essentially glabrous but petiole margins glandular-bristly; corolla white or pale rose, funnelform-campanulate, to 2½ in. across, calyx, ovary, and style glandular-bristly. W. Yunnan. Zone 8.

haemaleum: *R. sanguineum* subsp.

haematocheilum: *R. oreodoxa.*

haematodes Franch. HY, *HY;* dwarf shrub, sometimes to 10 ft.; lvs. oblong to obovate, to 3½ in. long, glabrous above, rusty-felty beneath; corolla crimson to scarlet-crimson, tubular-campanulate, 2 in. long, ovary woolly, style glabrous. Yunnan. Zone 7.

Hanceanum Hemsl. RN, *RN;* to 3 ft.; lvs. lanceolate to narrowly obovate, to 4 in. long, stiff, lepidote on both sides; corolla pale yellow, funnelform, to 1 in. long, not lepidote outside, ovary densely lepidote, style glabrous. W. Szechwan. Zone 8. Var. **nanum** Hort. To 1½ ft.; corolla pale yellow.

hedyosmum: *R. trichostomum* var.

heliolepis Franch. RN, *RN;* to 10 ft.; lvs. oblong-elliptic, to 4 in. long, lepidote beneath; corolla red to rose, broadly funnelform, to 1½ in. across, lepidote outside, ovary lepidote, stamens and style pubescent at base. Yunnan. Zone 7.

hemitrichotum Balf.f. & Forr. PM, *TR;* twiggy shrub, to 4 ft.; lvs. oblanceolate, to 1 in. long, pubescent above, lepidote and glaucous beneath; fls. mostly in pairs, corolla white or pale rose, widely funnelform, less than 1 in. across, ovary densely lepidote, style glabrous. Sw. Szechwan. Zone 7.

Hemsleyanum E. H. Wils. HY, *HY;* small tree, to 18 ft.; lvs. oblong to oblong-ovate, to 8 in. long, thick, leathery, dark green, glabrous, and somewhat glossy above, paler and minutely papillose beneath, petiole to 2 in. long; corolla white, broadly campanulate, to 2 in. long, glandular outside, filaments glabrous, ovary and style glandular. Mt. Omei (Szechwan). Zone 7.

herpesticum: *R. dichroanthum* subsp.

×**Hinodegiri:** a listed name of no botanical standing for *Rhododendron* cv. 'Hinodegiri'. One of the Kurume Hybrid Azaleas; corolla crimson-red.

×**Hinomayo:** a listed name of no botanical standing for *Rhododendron* cv. 'Hinomayo'. One of the Kurume Hybrid Azaleas; corolla phlox-pink to pale pink, spotted in the throat.

hippophaeoides Balf.f. & W. W. Sm. RN, *RN;* to 5 ft.; lvs. oblong to narrowly elliptic, to 1½ in. long, lepidote on both sides; corolla lilac to rose, campanulate, 1 in. across, villous inside, not lepidote, stamens 10, exserted, ovary densely lepidote, style glabrous. Yunnan. Zone 6.

hirsutum L. HAIRY ALPINE ROSE. RN, *RN;* to 3 ft.; lvs. oblanceolate to elliptic-oblanceolate, 1¼ in. long, lepidote beneath, margins ciliate with bristly hairs; corolla rose to almost scarlet, funnelform, ½ in. across, ovary densely lepidote. Early summer. Alps of s.-cent. Eur. Zone 6.

Hodgsonii Hook.f. HY, *HY;* shrub or small tree, to 20 ft.; lvs. elliptic to obovate, to 1 ft. or more, glabrous and glossy above, rusty-tomentose beneath; corolla magenta-purple, fading lighter, campanulate, 2 in. across, 7–8-lobed, fleshy, stamens 15–18, ovary tomentose, style glabrous. Himalayas, from Bhutan to Nepal.

Hookeri Nutt. HY, *HY;* erect shrub, to 14 ft., or to 20 ft. when very old; lvs. oblong or elliptic-oblong, to 7 in. long, thick, leathery, glabrous and glaucous above, with hairs in separate tufts on veins beneath, petiole about 1 in. long; corolla blood-red, with darker red blotches at base, funnelform or tubular-campanulate, about 1½ in. long, ovary and style glabrous. Bhutan. Zone 8b.

horaeum: *R. citriniflorum* subsp.

hormophorum Balf.f & Forr. RN, *RN;* to 3 ft., young branchlets lepidote; lvs. lanceolate, to 2 in. long, lepidote, margin and petiole ciliate; corolla rose, marked brown, funnelform, 1¼ in. long, ovary lepidote, style glabrous. Sw. Szechwan. Zone 7?

hortense: *R. lineariifolium* var. *macrosepalum* forma *decandrum.*

Houlstonii Hemsl. & E. H. Wils. HY, *HY;* to 20 ft.; lvs. oblong-oblanceolate to oblong-elliptic, to 6 in. long, glabrous, pale beneath; fls. on glandular pedicels, corolla pink or white, funnelform-campanulate, to 2 in. long, ovary and style glandular. Hupeh and e. Szechwan. Zone 7.

×**hybridum** Ker-Gawl.: *R. maximum* × *R. viscosum.* Fls. fragrant, corolla whitish-yellow, spotted and edged pink.

hyperythrum Hayata. HY, *HY;* shrub, to 10 ft., branchlets stout, glabrous; lvs. oblong-lanceolate to elliptic-lanceolate, to 4 in. long, leathery, glabrous above, with minute brownish dots beneath, petiole to 1 in. long; corolla white, funnelform-campanulate, to 1⅜ in. long, filaments densely hairy at base, ovary hairy or glandular-hairy, style slightly hairy at base. Taiwan. Zone 6.

hypoglaucum Hemsl. HY, *HY;* shrub or small tree, to 20 ft.; lvs. oblong-elliptic to oblanceolate, to 4½ in. long, green and glossy above, white-tomentose beneath; corolla white, flushed rose, spotted deep rose, campanulate, 1½ in. across, ovary glandular, woolly. Hupeh.

hypolepidotum: *R. brachyanthum* var.

×**impeanum** Hort.: *Rhododendron* cv. 'Impeanum': *R. Hanceanum* × *R. impeditum.* RN, *RN;* dense shrub; corolla deep lilac or blue. Zone 7.

impeditum Balf.f. & W. W. Sm. RN, *RN;* dwarf, cushionlike shrub, to 1½ ft.; lvs. elliptic to ovate, to ⅝ in. long, densely lepidote on both sides; fls. slightly fragrant, corolla mauve to purplish-blue, broadly funnelform, ⅝ in. long, stamens long-exserted, ovary lepidote, style glabrous. Yunnan. Zone 6.

imperator Hutch. & F. K. Ward. RN, *RN;* mat-forming dwarf shrub, to 1 ft.; lvs. lanceolate or oblanceolate, to 1½ in. long, glaucous and lepidote beneath, the scales spaced 2–6 times their own diameter apart; corolla bright purple, funnelform, to 1½ in. across, downy outside, ovary lepidote, style glabrous. Burma. Zone 6.

indicum (L.) Sweet [*R. lateritium* ((Lindl.) Planch.; *R. macranthum* (Bunge) G. Don; *Azalea indica* L.; *A. indica* var. *lateritia* Lindl.; *A. lateritia* (Lindl.) André; *A. macrantha* Bunge]. MACRANTHUM A. TT, *TU;* evergreen shrub, to 6 ft.; lvs. lanceolate to oblanceolate, to 1½ in. long, hairy on both sides, margins crenulate; corolla rose to scarlet, broadly funnelform, 2½ in. across, stamens 5, ovary bristly. Early summer. S. Japan. Zone 6. Despite the scientific name, this sp. is native to Japan, not India; one of the parents of, but not to be confused with, the Indian Hybrid Azaleas, or Indian Azaleas, of the florist and s. gardens, which are sometimes offered erroneously as vars. or cvs. of *Azalea indica.* Cv. **'Balsaminiflorum'** [var. *balsaminiflorum* (Carrière) Nichols.; var. *rosiflorum* Rehd.; *Azalea balsaminiflora* Carrière; *A. indica* var. *balsaminiflora* Hort.]. BALSAM A. Corolla double, salmon-red. Cv. **'Iveryanum'** [*Azalea indica* cv. 'Iveryana']. Corolla single, white with rose flecks, 3 in. across. Cv. **'Laciniatum'** [forma *laciniatum* E. H. Wils.; *Azalea indica* cv. 'Laciniata']. Corolla deeply 5-parted, brick-red. Cv. **'Rosiflorum'**: cv. 'Balsaminiflorum'. Var. **sublanceolatum:** perhaps *R. scabrum.*

inopinum Balf.f. ex Tagg. RN, *RN;* shrub, perhaps to 2½ ft.; lvs. oblong to ovate-oblong, to 5 in. long; corolla creamy-white with crimson basal blotch and smaller spots, funnelform-campanulate, 1 in. long, ovary densely tomentose, style glabrous. Szechwan.

insigne Hemsl. & E. H. Wils. HY, *HY;* to 12 ft.; lvs. oblong-lanceolate, to 5 in. long, glossy green and glabrous above, felty beneath with white hairs that become coppery; corolla white to pink, spotted crimson, widely campanulate, ovary white-tomentose, style glabrous. Sw. Szechwan. Zone 8.

intricatum Franch. BLUET R. RN, *RN;* low, intricately branched shrub, to 1 ft., branchlets lepidote; lvs. oblong-elliptic to suborbicular, to ½ in. long, lepidote on both sides; corolla mauve, broadly funnelform, ⁵⁄₁₆ in. long, stamens included, ovary densely lepidote, style glabrous. W. Szechwan. Zone 6.

irroratum Franch. HY, *HY;* shrub or small tree, to 25 ft.; lvs. elliptic to oblanceolate, to 5 in. long, rigid, pale and glabrous beneath; corolla white to creamy, tinged rose, with crimson spots, tubular-campanulate, to 2 in. long, ovary and style glandular. Yunnan. Zone 6.

Iveryanum: *R. indicum* cv.

×**Jacksonii:** a listed name of no botanical standing for *Rhododendron* cv. 'Jacksonii': *R. caucasicum* × *R.* cv. 'Nobleanum'. HY, *HY,* corolla rosy-pink, striped with deeper pink on outside of lobes. Zone 6.

japonicum (A. Gray) Suring. [*Azalea japonica* A. Gray]. JAPANESE A. PE, *PE;* to 6 ft.; lvs. oblanceolate to obovate, to 4 in. long, ciliate, with scattered hairs above and on veins beneath; fls. preceding the lvs., corolla yellow to orange or brick red, broadly funnelform, to 3 in. across, tube much shorter than lobes, stamens 5, ovary villous, style glabrous. N. and cent. Japan. Zone 6. One of the parents of the Molle Hybrid Azaleas. Var. **album:** *R. mucronatum* cv. 'Japonicum Album'.

javanicum (Blume) J. Benn. RN, *VR;* shrub, to 6 ft., epiphytic; lvs. elliptic-lanceolate, to 7 in. long, dark green and glossy, lepidote beneath; corolla orange-yellow, funnelform, to 2½ in. across, ovary and style pubescent, not lepidote. Java. A greenhouse plant. One of the parents of the Javanicum Hybrid Rhododendrons. Var. **atroluteum** is listed.

Johnstoneanum G. Watt ex Hutch. RN, *RN;* to 6 ft.; lvs. elliptic, to 4 in. long, bristly-ciliate when young; lepidote beneath; fls. fragrant, corolla white to pale yellow, spotted red inside, with yellow basal blotch, funnelform, to 2½ in. long, ovary and base of style lepidote. Manipur and Assam. Zone 9.

Kaempferi Planch. [*R. obtusum* var. *Kaempferi* (Planch.) E. H. Wils.; *Azalea Kaempferi* (Planch.) André]. TORCH A. TT, *TU;* loosely branched, deciduous or semievergreen shrub, to 8 ft.; lvs. elliptic or lanceolate to lanceolate-ovate or obovate, to 2½ in. long, ciliate, pubescent on both sides; calyx ciliate, corolla orange-red to pink, rosy-scarlet, or bright red, funnelform, to 2 in. across, ovary densely hairy, style glabrous. Japan. Zone 6. One of the parents of the Gable, Kaempferi, and Kurume Hybrid Azaleas.

kamtschaticum: a misspelling of *R. camtschaticum.*

Keiskei Miq. RN, *RN;* to 5 ft.; lvs. lanceolate to oblong-lanceolate, to 2½ in. long, lepidote beneath; corolla lemon-yellow, not spotted, widely campanulate, to 2 in. across, lepidote outside, ovary lepidote. Cent. Japan. Zone 6.

keleticum Balf.f. & Forr. RN, *RN;* to 1 ft.; lvs. elliptic, ovate, or obovate, to ½ in. long, glabrous above, densely lepidote beneath; corolla purplish-crimson with darker markings, rotate-funnelform, to 1 in. across, ovary lepidote; caps. enclosed in persistent calyx. Se. Tibet. Zone 6.

×**kewense** W. Wats.: *Rhododendron* cv. 'Kewense': *R. Fortunei* × *R. Griffithianum.* HY, *HY;* corolla bluish-white or pink.

Keysii Nutt. RN, *RN;* leggy shrub, to 12 ft.; lvs. oblong-lanceolate, to 4 in. long, densely lepidote on both sides; corolla red or pink, with erect, yellow lobes, ¾ in. long, tube cylindrical, ovary glandular-lepidote. Bhutan.

kiusianum Mak. [*R. obtusum* forma *japonicum* (Maxim.) E. H. Wils.]. KYUSHU A. TT, *TU;* semievergreen, twiggy shrub, to 3 ft.; lvs. elliptic to elliptic-ovate, or summer lvs. oblanceolate to obovate, to 1 in. long, bright green; corolla purple, rarely white or crimson, funnelform, 1 in. across. Japan. One of the parents of the Kurume Hybrid Azaleas.

Komiyamae: *R. tosaense.*

×**Kosteranum** C. K. Schneid. [*Azalea* × *Kosterana* Hort.]: *R. japonicum* × *R. molle.* The MOLLE ["MOLLIS"] HYBRID AZALEAS. A hybrid group, with corollas white, yellow, orange, pink, to red.

Kotschyi Simonk. [*R. myrtifolium* Schott & Kotschy, not Lodd.]. RN, *RN;* low, twiggy shrub, to 2 ft.; lvs. elliptic-oblong or oblanceolate, to ¾ in. long, rusty-lepidote beneath; corolla rose or rarely white, tubular with spreading limb, ½ in. long, stamens 10, included, ovary lepidote, style glabrous. Mts. of cent. Eur. Zone 6.

Kyawii Lace & W. W. Sm. HY, *HY;* shrub or small tree, to 20 ft.; lvs. oblong to elliptic-oblong, to 1 ft. long, floccose-tomentose with stellate hairs beneath, becoming glabrous and shining on both sides; corolla deep crimson, with 5 deeper-colored basal pouches, tubular-campanulate, to 3 in. across, filaments and style crimson, ovary stellate-hairy, glandular. Ne. Burma. Zone 9.

laciniatum: a listed name of no botanical standing for *R. indicum* cv.

lacteum Franch. HY, *HY;* shrub or tree, to 30 ft.; lvs. oblong to ovate, to 8 in. long, tawny-felty beneath; corolla pale or clear yellow, rarely white, widely campanulate, to 2 in. across, ovary white-downy, style glabrous. Yunnan. Zone 8.

×**laetevirens** Rehd.: *R. carolinianum* × *R. ferrugineum.* RN, *RN;* corolla rose, 1¼ in. across.

lanatum Hook.f. HY, *HY;* shrub or small tree, to 15 ft., branchlets woolly; lvs. elliptic to obovate, to 5 in. long, woolly beneath and on petiole; corolla pale yellow, spotted crimson-purple, campanulate, 2 in. across, ovary woolly, style glabrous. Assam, Bhutan, Sikkim, Tibet. Zone 7. Var. **luciferum:** *R. luciferum.*

lanigerum Tagg. HY, *HY;* small tree; lvs. oblong-lanceolate or oblong-oblanceolate, to 9 in. long, glabrous at maturity except for vestiges of hairs on midrib beneath; corolla rose-white, broadly campanulate, with 5 basal pouches, to 2 in. long, ovary with dense, fawn to grayish, branched hairs, style glabrous. Assam. Zone 8.

lapponicum (L.) Wahlenb. [*Azalea lapponica* L.]. LAPLAND R., LAPLAND ROSEBAY. RN, *RN;* dwarf, procumbent shrublet, to 1 ft.; lvs. oblong, to ¾ in. long, rusty-lepidote beneath; corolla purplish, broadly campanulate, ½ in. across, stamens 5–10, ovary lepidote, style glabrous. Early summer. Mts. of n. Eur., n. Asia, and n. N. Amer. Zone 2.

lateritium: *R. indicum.*

Leachianum: *Kalmiopsis Leachiana.*

ledifolium: *R. mucronatum.* Var. **album:** *R. mucronatum.* Var. **purpureum:** *R. pulchrum* var. *calycinum.*

ledoides: *R. trichostomum* var.

lepidostylum Balf.f. & Forr. PA; compact shrub, to 1 ft.; lvs. ovate or obovate, 1½ in. long, bristly on the margins, glaucous, lepidote, and bristly beneath; fls. in 2's, corolla pale yellow, widely funnelform, 1 in. long, pubescent and lepidote outside, ovary densely bristly, lepidote. W. Yunnan. Zone 7.

lepidotum Wallich [*R. elaeagnoides* Hook.f.; *R. obovatum* Hook.f.]. WILLOW-LEAVED R. RN, *RN;* twiggy shrub, to 4 or 5 ft., branchlets warty, lepidote; lvs. lanceolate to obovate, to 1½ in. long, lepidote above, glaucous and lepidote beneath; corolla pink, rose, purple, crimson, white, or yellow, rotate, 1 in. across, densely lepidote outside, stamens 8–10, ovary densely lepidote, style glabrous, short, thick, sharply bent. Szechwan, Yunnan, Burma, Tibet, Nepal. Zone 7.

leptothrium Balf.f. & Forr. AZ, *AZ;* to 20 ft.; lvs. lanceolate, to 3 in. long, glabrous except on midrib, papery, dark glossy green; fls. axillary, corolla deep magenta-rose, marked crimson, subrotate, 1½ in. across, deeply 5-lobed, stamens 5, ovary glandular. Nw. Yunnan and ne. Burma. Zone 8b.

leucaspis Tagg. RN, *RN;* bushy shrub, to 2 ft., branchlets bristly and lepidote; lvs. elliptic to obovate, to 2 in. long, pilose above and on margin, glaucous and lepidote beneath, petioles bristly; corolla white, rotate, 2 in. across, lepidote outside, ovary densely lepidote, style short, stout, sharply bent. Tibet. Zone 7.

lilacinum: *R. mucronatum* cv.

Lindleyi T. Moore. RN, *RN;* often epiphytic, to 15 ft., but usually about 5 ft. in cult., branchlets lepidote; lvs. ovate-elliptic to narrowly elliptic, to 6 in. long, brown-lepidote beneath; fls. fragrant, calyx lobes well developed, white-ciliolate, corolla white, campanulate-funnelform, 3½ in. across, ovary densely lepidote, style lepidote at base. Burma, Sikkim, s. Tibet. Zone 10.

linearifolium Siebold & Zucc. [*Azalea linearifolia* (Siebold & Zucc.) Hook.f.]. SPIDER A. TT, *TU;* evergreen shrub, to 4 ft.; lvs. linear to linear-lanceolate, to 3 in. long; corolla rose-lilac, deeply divided into linear segms., stamens 5. Japan. Zone 7. Var. **macrosepalum** (Maxim.) Mak. [*R. macrosepalum* Maxim.; *Azalea macrosepala* (Maxim.) C. Koch]. To 3 ft., often deciduous; lvs. elliptic-ovate to oblanceolate; fls. fragrant, corolla rose-purple. Forma **decandrum** E. H. Wils. [*R. hortense* Nakai]. Stamens 6–10.

litangense Balf.f. ex Hutch. RN, *RN;* to 2 ft.; lvs. oblong-elliptic, to ½ in. long, loosely lepidote on both sides; corolla dull plum-purple, ½ in. long, not lepidote outside, stamens 10, exserted, ovary lepidote, style glabrous. Sw. Szechwan. Zone 7.

litiense Balf.f. & Forr. HY, *HY;* to 12 ft., branchlets glandular; lvs. oblong, to 4 in. long, truncate to cordate at base, glabrous and glaucous beneath; calyx glandular-ciliate, corolla yellow, unspotted, widely campanulate, 1½ in. long, ovary and style glandular. Yunnan. Zone 7. Differs from *R. Wardii* in having lvs. oblong, waxy-glaucous beneath, and fls. smaller, more campanulate.

lochmium Balf.f. [*R. glaucophyllum* Balf.f., not Rehd.]. RN, *RN;* straggling shrub, to 10 ft.; lvs. oblanceolate, to 2½ in. long, recurved from the midrib, glabrous above, lepidote beneath; corolla pink, spotted red, funnelform, 1½ in. long, glabrous outside, ovary densely lepidote, style glabrous. Probably w. Szechwan; described originally from cult. material passing as *R. Davidsonianum.*

×**Loderi** W. Wats.: *R. Fortunei* × *R. Griffithianum.* HY, *HY;* fls. fragrant, corolla white or shell-pink, to 7 in. across. Zone 8. There are a number of named cvs.

longesquamatum C. K. Schneid. HY, *HY;* to 10 ft. or more, branchlets covered with long, rusty, branched hairs and persistent scales; lvs. oblong-oblanceolate to obovate, to 5 in. long, minutely glandular beneath, midrib beneath and petiole clothed with long hairs; corolla bright pink, with crimson blotch, widely campanulate, 1½ in. long, ovary densely setose-villous, style glabrous. W. Szechwan. Zone 6.

longistylum Rehd. & E. H. Wils. RN, *RN;* to 7 ft.; lvs. narrowly oblanceolate, to 2 in. long, glabrous, with impressed veins above, loosely lepidote beneath; corolla pink or white, funnelform, ½ in. across, ovary densely lepidote, style glabrous, longer than stamens. W. Szechwan. Zone 7.

luciferum (Cowan) Cowan [*R. lanatum* Hook.f. var. *luciferum* Cowan]. HY, *HY;* shrub or small tree, to 24 ft., branchlets densely tomentose; lvs. oblong or elliptic-oblong to elliptic-lanceolate, to 5½ in. long, tawny-woolly beneath; corolla pale yellow or white, sometimes spotted red, funnelform-campanulate, 1¼ in. long, ovary densely woolly, style glabrous. S. Tibet.

×**Luscombei:** a listed name of no botanical standing for *Rhododendron* cv. 'Luscombei' [*R. Luscombeanum* Hort.]: *R. Fortunei* × *R. Thomsonii.* HY, *HY;* corolla rose-red. Zone 7.

Luscombeanum: see *R. Luscombei.*

lutescens Franch. RN, *RN;* to 10 ft. or more; lvs. lanceolate, to 3½ in. long, long-acuminate, lepidote with scattered scales; corolla yellow, spotted light green, funnelform, 1½ in. long, stamens 10, long-exserted, ovary lepidote. W. Szechwan and Yunnan. Zone 7.

luteum Sweet [*R. flavum* (Hoffmanns.) G. Don; *Azalea lutea* Hort., not L.; *A. pontica* L.]. PONTIC A. PE, *PE;* deciduous shrub, to 12 ft.; lvs. linear-oblong to oblanceolate, to 5½ in. long, hairy on margin and midrib; fls. very fragrant, yellow, corolla funnelform, 2 in. across, ovary glandular-pilose. Caucasus of e. Eur. Zone 6. One of the parents of the Ghent Hybrid Azaleas.

lysolepis Hutch. RN, *RN;* dwarf shrub, to 4 ft.; lvs. oblong-elliptic, to ¾ in. long, glossy, glandular-lepidote above, lepidote beneath; corolla purple or deep violet to pinkish-violet, funnelform, 1 in. across, stamens 10, long-exserted, ovary lepidote, style glabrous. Nativity unknown.

Macabeanum G. Watt ex Balf.f. HY, *HY;* large shrub, to 15 ft., or tree to 45 ft.; lvs. oblong-elliptic, to 1 ft. long, grayish-white-woolly beneath; corolla whitish-yellow to lemon-yellow, with purple basal blotch, campanulate, to 2⅜ in. across, 8-lobed, fleshy, stamens 16, ovary tomentose, style glabrous, stigma crimson. Manipur-Burma border and Assam. Zone 8b.

macranthum: *R. indicum.*

macrophyllum D. Don ex G. Don [*R. californicum* Hook.; *R. Washingtonianum* Hort. ex Zab.]. WEST COAST R., CALIFORNIA ROSEBAY. HY, *HY;* to 12 ft. or more; lvs. oblong to elliptic, to 8 in. long, glabrous; corolla rose to rose-purple, spotted brown, broadly campanulate, to 2½ in. across, ovary rusty-tomentose. Near the coast, s. B. C. to cent. Calif. Zone 7.

macrosepalum: *R. linearifolium* var.

macrostemon: *R. obtusum* cv.

Maddenii Hook.f. [*R. Maddenii* var. *calophyllum* Hort.]. RN, *RN;* much-branched shrub, to 8 ft.; lvs. lanceolate to oblong-lanceolate, to 6 in. long, densely rusty-lepidote beneath; fls. very fragrant, corolla white, faintly flushed rose, funnelform, 4 in. across, 5-lobed, fleshy, lepidote outside, stamens 20, ovary lepidote. Bhutan and Sikkim. Zone 9.

magnificum F. K. Ward. HY, *HY;* tree, to 60 ft.; lvs. oblong to oblong-obovate, to 15 in. long, with white-cobwebby pubescence beneath disappearing with age; corolla rosy-purple, tubular-campanulate, 2½ in. long. Burma-Tibet border. A doubtful sp., allied to *R. giganteum.*

Makinoi Tagg. HY, *HY;* to 7 ft., branchlets woolly; lvs. narrowly lanceolate, recurved, to 7 in. long, tawny-woolly beneath; corolla soft pink, often spotted crimson, funnelform-campanulate, 1½ in. long, ovary woolly, style glabrous. Japan. Zone 6.

mallotum Balf.f. & F. K. Ward. HY, *HY;* shrub or small tree, to 15 ft. or more, branchlets densely rusty-tomentose; lvs. elliptic to obovate-elliptic, to 6 in. long, densely red-brown-woolly beneath; corolla crimson, tubular-campanulate, 1¾ in. across, fleshy, ovary densely woolly-tomentose, style glabrous, curved. W. Yunnan and n. Burma. Zone 8b.

×**malvaticum** Hort. ex H. L. Späth: *Rhododendron* cv. 'Malvaticum'. One of the Kurume Hybrid Azaleas; corolla mauve. This hybrid and *R. Kaempferi* are the parents of the Malvaticum ["Malvatica"] Hybrid Azaleas.

×**Manglesii** Hort.: *Rhododendron* cv. 'Manglesii': *R. Griffithianum* × a *R. catawbiense* hybrid. HY, *HY;* corolla white, spotted pink.

Mariae Hance. TT, *TU;* to 10 ft.; lvs. dimorphic, spring lvs. elliptic-lanceolate, to 3½ in. long, summer lvs. elliptic to obovate, to 1¼ in. long; fls. fragrant, corolla lilac, funnelform, ¾ in. across, stamens 5, exserted, ovary densely rusty-brown-hairy, style glabrous, longer than stamens. E. China.

Mariesii Hemsl. & E. H. Wils. MARIES'S A. TT, *BR;* to 10 ft.; lvs. ovate to elliptic, to 3 in. long, glabrous at maturity; corolla pale rose-purple, spotted red-purple, rotate-funnelform, stamens 10, glabrous, ovary densely setose, style glabrous. Se. and cent. China. Zone 6.

maximum L. [*R. maximum* var. *roseum* Pursh]. GREAT LAUREL, ROSEBAY. HY, *HY;* to 15 ft., sometimes a tree to 30 ft.; lvs. oblong or oblong-obovate, to 10 in. long, tomentose beneath; corolla rose-pink with white center, spotted green, campanulate, to 1½ in. across, ovary glandular. Flowering in early summer, after lvs. have developed. N.C. to Ga. and Ala. Zone 4. Forma **album** (Pursh) Fern. Corolla white, spotted green. Forma **purpureum** (Pursh) Fern. Corolla deep pink to purple, spotted green. Vax. **Leachii** Harkness. Dwarfer; lvs. smaller, with deeply waved margins and down-curved tips. W. Va.

Maxwellii L. Gibbs. RN, *VR;* shrub; lvs. oblong-obovate, to 4 in. long, glabrous on both sides, markedly bullate; corolla yellow, funnelform, about 1 in. long, lepidote outside, ovary densely pilose, style hairy at base. Borneo. Probably not in cult. *Rhododendron* cv. 'Maxwellii', a hybrid derived in part from *R. pulchrum,* with dark-blotched carmine corolla, is sometimes offered under the name *R. Maxwellii. Rhododendron* cv. 'Maxwellii Album' is a cv. of *R. mucronatum.*

Meddianum Forr. HY, *HY;* shrub, to 6 ft.; lvs. broadly obovate-elliptic, to 4¾ in. long, abruptly narrowed to petiole, leathery, dark glaucous-green, and glabrous above, paler and glabrous beneath, petiole ¾ in. long; corolla deep crimson-red, with darker lines and spots inside, broadly funnelform, to 2¼ in. long, ovary and style glabrous. Ne. Burma, w. Yunnan.

megacalyx Balf.f. & F. K. Ward. RN, *RN;* shrub or small tree, to 16 ft.; lvs. elliptic to oblong, to 6 in. long, glabrous above, glaucous and densely lepidote beneath; fls. nutmeg-scented, calyx to 1 in. long, persistent and enclosing caps., corolla white, funnelform, to 3½ in. across, stamens 10, ovary white-lepidote, style curved. Ne. Burma and s. Tibet.

megeratum Balf.f. & Forr. RN, *RN;* to 2 ft., branchlets bristly, bud scales persistent; lvs. elliptic, 1½ in. long, glossy above, glaucous and lepidote beneath, petiole bristly; corolla bright yellow, campanulate, 1¼ in. across, lepidote outside, filaments hairy at middle, ovary densely lepidote, style stout, curved. Yunnan, ne. Burma, se. Tibet. Zone 9.

melinanthum Balf.f. & F. K. Ward. PA; deciduous shrub, to 8 ft., branchlets bristly; lvs. oblong to oblong-obovate, 1½ in. long, ciliate, glabrous above, glaucous and lepidote beneath; fls. appearing with the lvs., corolla yellow, broadly campanulate, 1¼ in. across, ovary densely lepidote, style glabrous. Nw. Yunnan and adjacent Tibet. Zone 7.

Metternichii Siebold & Zucc. LEATHERLEAF R. HY, *HY;* to 8 ft.; lvs. oblong to oblong-lanceolate, to 6 in. long, glabrous and glossy above at maturity, rusty-tomentose beneath; corolla rose, spotted deeper rose, campanulate, 7-lobed, stamens 14, ovary rusty-tomentose, style glabrous. Japan. Zone 6.

micranthum Turcz. RN, *RN;* bushy shrub, to 6 ft. or more; lvs. narrowly oblanceolate, to 1½ in. long, rusty-lepidote beneath; fls. inconspicuous, corolla white, campanulate, about ¼ in. long and ⅝ in. across, ovary lepidote, style glabrous, shorter than stamens. Early summer. N. Korea, Manchuria, China. Zone 5; very hardy.

microgynum Balf.f. & Forr. HY, *HY;* to 4 ft., branchlets tawny-floccose, glandular; lvs. lanceolate or oblanceolate, to 3 in. long, felty beneath; corolla soft rose, spotted crimson, campanulate, 1 in. long, ovary glandular, floccose, style glabrous, shorter than stamens. Se. Tibet.

microleucum Hutch. RN, *RN;* much-branched shrublet, to 1½ ft.; lvs. narrowly oblanceolate, ½ in. long, lepidote; corolla mauve to white, broadly funnelform, ½ in. across, ovary and base of style lepidote. Nativity uncertain; described originally from cult. material. Zone 7.

minus Michx. [*R. Cuthbertii* Small; *R. punctatum* Andr.]. PIEDMONT R. RN, *RN;* shrub of loose habit, to 12 ft. or, in the wild, even to 30 ft.; lvs. narrowly elliptic, elliptic, lanceolate, to ovate, to 5 in. long, acute at both ends, lepidote beneath; corolla magenta-pink to bright magenta, broadly funnelform, to 1½ in. across, lepidote outside, ovary densely lepidote, style glabrous. Early summer. Piedmont and lower mountain elevations, Tenn. and N.C. to Ala. Zone 5. The most rapid-growing of native evergreen rhododendrons. Var. **Chapmanii:** *R. Chapmannii.*

×**mixtum** E. H. Wils. [*Azalea rustica flore pleno* Hort.]. The RUSTICUM ["RUSTICA"] AZALEAS OR RUSTICUM FLORE PLENO HYBRID AZALEAS. A group of double-fld. forms derived from *R.* × *gandavense* and *R. molle.*

molle (Blume) G. Don [*R. sinense* (Lodd.) Sweet; *Azalea mollis* Blume; *A. sinensis* Lodd.]. CHINESE A. PE, *PE;* deciduous shrub, to 5 ft.; lvs. oblong, oblong-lanceolate, or oblanceolate, to 6 in. long, ciliate, gray-pubescent beneath; corolla yellow, spotted green, campanulate-funnelform, 2 in. across, ovary pilose, style glabrous. Spring. E. to cent. China. Zone 7. One of the parents of the Molle Hybrid Azaleas.

mollicomum Balf.f. & W. W. Sm. PM, *TR;* evergreen shrub, to 6 ft.; lvs. narrowly elliptic, oblong, or lanceolate, to 1¼ in. long, pubescent on both sides, lepidote beneath; fls. in axillary clusters, corolla rose or crimson, funnelform, to 1 in. across, ovary pubescent, lepidote. Yunnan. Zone 7.

monosematum Hutch. HY, *HY;* compact shrub, to 10 ft., branchlets with gland-tipped bristles; lvs. oblong, 4¼ in. long, glabrous, petiole setose-glandular; corolla white, suffused with pink, with basal purple blotch, campanulate, 2 in. long, ovary covered with long-stalked, glandular hairs. Szechwan.

Morii Hayata. HY, *HY;* shrub or tree, to 25 ft.; lvs. oblong-lanceolate, to 5 in. long, dark green and glossy above, glabrous or glandular-pubescent on midrib; corolla white or flushed rose, spotted or blotched crimson, broadly campanulate, to 1¾ in. long, stamens 10–14, ovary and base of style glandular. Taiwan. Zone 7.

×**Mossieanum:** a listed name of no botanical standing for *Rhododendron* cv. 'Mossieanum'. One of the Kaempferi Hybrid Azaleas; corolla violet-red.

moupinense Franch. RN, *RN;* small shrub, to 4 ft., sometimes epiphytic; lvs. elliptic to ovate-elliptic, to 1½ in. long, glabrous above, lepidote beneath; fls. fragrant, corolla white, pink, or rose, broadly funnelform, 1½ in. long, ovary lepidote, style glabrous. Szechwan and e. Tibet. Zone 8.

mucronatum (Blume) G. Don [*R. ledifolium* (Hook.) G. Don; *R. ledifolium* var. *album* Rehd.; *R. rosmarinifolium* (Burm.f.) Dipp., not S. Vidal; *R. rosmarinifolium* var. *album* C. K. Schneid.; *Azalea indica alba* Lindl.; *A. ledifolia* Hook.; *A. mucronatum* Blume; *A. rosamarinifolia* Burm.f.; *A. rosmarinifolia* var. *alba* Rehd.]. SNOW A. TT, *TU;* evergreen, much-branched, spreading shrub, to 6 ft.; lvs. dimorphic, spring lvs. lanceolate to ovate-lanceolate, to 2¼ in. long, mucronate, summer lvs. oblong-lanceolate or oblong-oblanceolate, to 1½ in. long, tomentose and often glandular; fls. fragrant, corolla white, broadly funnelform, 2 in. across, ovary densely setose, not glandular. Spring. Japan. Zone 8. Perhaps derived from *R. ripense* Mak. or from *R. ripense* × *R. linearifolium* var. *macrosepalum.* One of the parents of the Indian Hybrid Azaleas. Cvs. include: 'Amethystinum' [*Azalea ledifolia* var. *amethystina* Hort.; *A. mucronata* var. *amethystina* Hort.], corolla white, flushed lilac, faintly spotted, petals pointed; 'Japonicum Album' [*R. japonicum* var. *album* Hort.; *Azalea japonica* var. *alba* Hort.], sparse-flowering, corolla pure white; 'Lilacinum' [*Azalea ledifolia* var. *lilacina* Hort.], corolla soft lavender-purple with red blotch; 'Maxwellii Album', corolla white with faint chartreuse throat; 'Magnificum': cv. 'Sekidera'; 'Narcissiflorum' [*R. mucronatum* forma *narcissiflorum* (Planch.) E. H. Wils.], corolla double, white; 'Noordtianum' [*Azalea ledifolia* var. *Noordtiana* Wittm.], corolla large, white; 'Plenum'. fls. double, corolla reddish-violet; 'Roseum' [*Azalea ledifolia* var. *rosea* Hort.] is listed; 'Sekidera' [cv. 'Magnificum'; *R. mucronatum* forma *Sekidera* (Komatsu) E. H. Wils.; *Azalea ledifolia* cv. 'Magnifica'], corolla white, spotted crimson-rose. Var **purpureum:** *R. pulchrum* var. *calycinum.*

mucronulatum Turcz. [*R. dauricum* var. *mucronulatum* (Turcz.) Maxim.; *Azalea mucronulata* Hort.]. RM; deciduous shrub, to 8 ft.; lvs. elliptic-lanceolate or lanceolate, to 3 in. long, acute and mucronate, lepidote on both sides; fls. preceding the lvs., corolla rose-purple, broadly funnelform, 1¾ in. across, stamens 10, ovary lepidote. Ne. Asia and n. Japan. Zone 5. Very early-flowering.

muliense: *R. chryseum.*

×**myrtifolium** Lodd.: *R. hirsutum* × *R. minus.* RN, *RN;* lvs. to 2½ in. long, rusty-lepidote beneath; corolla lilac-pink, 1 in. across. Zone 6. *R. myrtifolium* Schott & Kotschy is *R. Kotschyi.*

myrtilloides: *R. campylogynum* var.

neriiflorum Franch. HY, *HY;* spreading shrub, to 9 ft.; lvs. oblong to narrowly obovate, to 4 in. long, dark green and glabrous above, glaucous-white and floccose beneath; corolla scarlet to crimson or rose, tubular-campanulate, 1¾ in. long, ovary tomentose. Yunnan. Zone 8.

nikoense: *R. pentaphyllum.*

nikomontanum: *R. chrysanthum* var.

nilagiricum Zenk. [*R. arboreum* var. *nilagiricum* (Zenk.) C. B. Clarke and var *roseum* DC.]. HY, *HY;* shrub or tree, to 35 ft.; lvs. oblong to elliptic-oblong, to 5 in. long, bullate above, rusty-tomentose beneath; calyx reduced to a mere rim, densely hairy, corolla scarlet, crimson, to crimson-rose, campanulate, 1½ in. long, ovary densely tomentose. Madras (India).

nitens Hutch. RN, *RN;* dwarf, much-branched shrub, to 1½ ft.; lvs. oblong-elliptic, to ⅝ in. long, glossy and lepidote above, densely lepidote beneath, margins of young lvs. bristly; corolla pinkish-purple to deep pink-magenta, spotted crimson, rotate, to about 1½ in. across, ovary densely gray-lepidote, style crimson, glabrous. Ne. Burma. Zone 6.

niveum Hook.f. HY, *HY;* to 15 ft. or more; lvs. oblong or obovate-lanceolate, to 7 in. long, white-tomentose beneath, becoming brown; corolla purplish-lilac or magenta, campanulate, 1½ in. long, ovary densely tomentose, style glabrous. Sikkim Himalayas. Zone 7.

×**Nobleanum** Hort. ex Lindl.: *Rhododendron* cv. 'Nobleanum': *R. arboreum* × *R. caucasicum.* HY, *HY;* corolla rich rose-pink. Zone 7. Of the same ancestry are: *R.* cv. 'Nobleanum Album', with white corolla; cv. 'Nobleanum Coccineum', with bright scarlet corolla; and cv. 'Nobleanum Venustum', with rose corolla.

nudiflorum: *R. periclymenoides.*

Nuttallii T. J. Booth. RN, *RN;* to 30 ft., sometimes epiphytic; lvs. elliptic, to 1 ft. long, bullate above, lepidote beneath; fls. fragrant, corolla white flushed with yellow, or pale yellow, funnelform, to 5 in. across and long, stamens 10, ovary lepidote. Bhutan. Zone 10. One of the largest-fld. rhododendrons.

oblongifolium (Small) Millais [*Azalea oblongifolia* Small]. PE, *PE;* deciduous shrub, to 6 ft. or less; lvs. oblong or elliptic to obovate, to 4 in. long, usually hairy beneath; corolla white, tubular-funnelform, 1¼ in. across, hairy outside, stamens hairy below middle, ovary hairy, partly glandular. May. Ark. to Okla. and se. Tex. Zone 7.

obovatum: *R. lepidotum.*

obtusum (Lindl.) Planch. [*Azalea obtusa* Lindl.]. HIRYU A., KIRISHIMA A. TT, *TU;* much-branched, evergreen or semievergreen shrub, to 3 ft.; lvs. dimorphic, spring lvs. elliptic to elliptic-lanceolate, to 1 in. long, summer lvs. obovate, obtuse, lustrous above; corolla rose-red to purple, funnelform, to 1 in. across, stamens 5, ovary hairy. Spring. Japan. Zone 7. Cv. 'Album' [forma *album* (Mottet) C. K. Schneid.]. Corolla white. Cv. 'Amoenum' [var. *amoenum* (Lindl.) Rehd.; forma *amoenum* (Lindl.) Komatsu; *R. amoenum* (Lindl.) Planch.]. Corolla purple or magenta, about 1 in. across, hose-in-hose. Cv. 'Hatsugiri'. Corolla purplish-crimson or magenta. Cv. 'Macrostemon' [*R. macrostemon* Maxim.]. Corolla salmon-orange, 1½ in. across, stamens long-exserted. Forma japonicum: *R. kiusianum.* Var. arnoldianum: *R.* ×*arnoldianum.* Var. Kaemperi: *R. Kaemperi.*

occidentale (Torr. & A. Gray) A. Gray. WESTERN A. PE, *PE;* deciduous shrub, to 10 ft. or more; lvs. elliptic to obovate, to 4 in. long, pubescent, ciliate; fls. fragrant, corolla white or pink-tinged, with yellow blotch, funnelform, to 2½ in. across, stamens 5, exserted, ovary pubescent. S. Ore. to s. Calif. Zone 7.

ochraceum Rehd. & E. H. Wils. HY, *HY;* to 9 ft., branchlets glandular; lvs. narrowly oblanceolate, to 4 in. long, pubescent beneath and on petioles; corolla crimson, unspotted, open-campanulate, to 1¼ in. long, stamens 10–12, ovary hairy, often glandular, stamens and style glabrous. W. Szechwan.

×**odoratum:** a listed name of no botanical standing for *Rhododendron* Cv. 'Odoratum': *R. periclymenoides* × *R. ponticum.* Corolla pale pink or pale lilac; an "azaleodendron," a hybrid between a rhododendron and an azalea. Zone 7.

odoriferum Hutch. RN, *RN;* shrub; lvs. elliptic to oblanceolate, to 4 in. long, glabrous above, lepidote beneath; fls. fragrant, corolla white, flushed rose outside, tinged green inside, funnelform, 1½ in. long, stamens 15, glabrous, ovary loosely lepidote. S. Tibet. Zone 9.

Oldhamii Maxim. [*Azalea Oldhamii* (Maxim.) Hort. Veitch ex M. T. Mast.]. OLDHAM'S A. TT, *TU;* twiggy, evergreen shrub, to 10 ft., branchlets glandular, very hairy; lvs. elliptic or oblong-lanceolate to nearly ovate, to 3 in. long, hairy; corolla red with lilac-pink blotch, funnelform, to 2 in. across, stamens 10, ovary glandular-setose, style papillose below, longer than stamens. Taiwan. Zone 8.

oleifolium Franch. PM, *RA;* erect shrub, to 6 ft.; lvs. oblong-lanceolate, to 2¼ in. long, glabrous above, densely lepidote beneath; corolla pink or nearly white, tubular-campanulate, about 1 in. long, pubescent and lepidote outside, ovary densely lepidote, style glandular at base. Yunnan. Zone 9.

oporinum Balf.f. & F. K. Ward. RN, *RN;* shrub, to 10 ft.; lvs. lanceolate to oblong-lanceolate, to about 3 in. long, long-apiculate, aromatic; corolla rose-pink, with dark red basal blotch, campanulate, 1 in. long, lepidote and pubescent outside, ovary lepidote, style pubescent at base. Ne. Burma.

orbiculare Decne. HY, *HY;* rounded, much-branched shrub, to 10 ft.; lvs. broadly ovate to orbicular, to 4 in. long, cordate at base, glaucous beneath; corolla rose-pink, often with bluish tint, widely campanulate, to 2½ in. across, 7-lobed, stamens 14, ovary glandular, style glabrous. W. Szechwan. Zone 6.

oreodoxa Franch. [*R. haematocheilum* Craib]. HY, *HY;* shrub or small tree, to 20 ft. or more; lvs. oblong, elliptic to oblanceolate-elliptic, to 4 in. long, glabrous above, glaucous beneath; corolla pale rose, often purple-spotted, campanulate, 7-lobed, stamens 14, ovary and style glabrous. W. Szechwan. Zone 7.

oreotrephes W. W. Sm. RN, *RN;* shrub, to 10 ft. or more; lvs. oblong to elliptic, to 3 in. long, gray-green above, glaucous and lepidote beneath; corolla mauve or mauve-pink, often spotted crimson, funnelform, 1¼ in. long, not lepidote outside, ovary lepidote. Yunnan and se. Tibet. Zone 7.

orthocladum Balf.f. & Forr. RN, *RN;* twiggy shrub, to 4 ft.; lvs. narrowly oblong or lanceolate, about ½ in. long, lepidote on both sides; corolla mauve to lavender-blue, open-funnelform, ½ in. long, not lepidote outside, ovary densely lepidote. N. Yunnan. Zone 7.

ovatum (Lindl.) Planch. ex Maxim. [*Azalea ovata* Lindl.]. AZ, *AZ;* evergreen shrub or small tree, to 15 ft.; lvs. ovate, to 2½ in. long, glossy above, downy on midrib and petiole; corolla white, pink or purplish, spotted purple, rotate, 1 in. across, stamens 5, ovary bristly. Late spring. E. China. Zone 6.

pachytrichum Franch. HY, *HY;* shrub, to 18 ft., branchlets with shaggy brown hairs; lvs. oblong to obovate, to 6 in. long, bristly on midrib, ciliate, petiole shaggy-hairy; corolla white to rose, with purple blotch, campanulate, 1½ in. across, ovary densely tomentose, style glabrous. W. Szechwan. Zone 7.

pallescens Hutch. RN, *RN;* evergreen, leggy shrub; lvs. oblong-lanceolate or oblanceolate, to 2½ in. long, glabrous and glossy above, glaucous and lepidote beneath; fls. terminal and in upper lf. axils, corolla white, flushed pink and dotted red, broadly funnelform, about ¾ in. long, ovary lepidote. Described originally from cult. plants grown from seeds from Yunnan; perhaps a natural hybrid between *R. Davidsonianum* and *R. racemosum.* Zone 7.

paludosum Hutch. & F. K. Ward. RN, *RN;* intricately branched shrublet, branchlets blackish-lepidote; lvs. oblong-elliptic, to ½ in. long, lepidote on both sides; corolla bright violet, rotate, 1 in. across, stamens long-exserted, ovary lepidote. Tibet.

pankimense Cowan & F. K. Ward. HY, *HY;* shrub or small tree, to 10 ft. or more; lvs. lanceolate, to 4 in. long, becoming glabrous, margins recurved; corolla crimson with darker spots, but not blotched, campanulate, to 1¼ in. long, ovary hairy, not glandular, style glabrous. Assam. Zone 8b.

paradoxum Balf.f. HY, *HY;* compact shrub, to 7 ft.; lvs. oblong, to 5 in. long, glabrous above, pubescent beneath; corolla white with crimson blotch, campanulate, 1½ in. long, glabrous, ovary tomentose, style glabrous. Szechwan.

pauciflorum King & Gamble [*R. elegans* Ridl.]. RN, *VR;* small shrub, often epiphytic; lvs. elliptic-lanceolate or obovate, to 1 in. long; corolla bright red, tubular, 5⁄16 in. long, stamens pubescent. Malay Pen.

pemakoense F. K. Ward. RN, *RN;* compact, cushionlike shrub, to 1½ ft.; lvs. elliptic to obovate, to 1 in. long, glossy, lepidote, aromatic; corolla pinkish-purple, funnelform, to 1½ in. across, ovary lepidote. Tibet. Zone 7.

pendulum Hook.f. RN, *RN;* shrub or straggling epiphyte, to 4 ft., branchlets densely woolly; lvs. elliptic or oblong-elliptic, to 2 in. long, glabrous above, woolly and lepidote beneath; corolla white, tinged yellow inside, broadly tubular, to 1½ in. across, densely lepidote outside, ovary bristly-hairy and lepidote. Sikkim Himalayas.

×**pennsylvanicum** (Gable) Rehd. [*Azalea* × *pennsylvanica* Gable]: *R. atlanticum* × *R. periclymenoides.* PE, *PE;* natural hybrid; lvs. elliptic, glaucous, ciliate; fls. fragrant, early, corolla white, flushed pink. Penn. Zone 5?

pentaphyllum Maxim. [*R. nikoense* (Komatsu) Nakai; *R. quinquefolium* var. *roseum* Rehd.; *Azalea pentaphylla* (Maxim.) H. Copel.]. FIVE-LEAF A. PE, *RO;* deciduous, much-branched shrub or small tree, to 10 ft., sometimes much more; lvs. elliptic to elliptic-lanceolate, to 2½ in. long, in whorls of 5 at ends of branchlets, ciliate; fls. 1–3 in a cluster, preceding the lvs., corolla rose-pink, rotate-campanulate, to 2 in. across, stamens 10, ovary and style glabrous. Cent. and s. Japan. Zone 7.

peregrinum Tagg. HY, *HY;* shrub or small tree; lvs. elliptic to oblong-elliptic, to 7 in. long, pubescent beneath; corolla white, tinged rose, with red spots, blotch, and lines, campanulate, to 2 in. across, 6–7-lobed, stamens 14, ovary and style glabrous. Sw. Szechwan.

periclymenoides (Michx.) Shinn. [*R. nudiflorum* (L.) Torr.; *Azalea nudiflora* L.]. PINXTERBLOOM, PINXTER FLOWER, HONEYSUCKLE, PURPLE H., ELECTION PINK. PE, *PE;* deciduous shrub, to 9 ft., branchlets sparingly strigose-setose, winter buds glabrous; lvs. elliptic to oblong or oblong-obovate, to 3 in. long, green and glabrous except on midrib; fls. only slightly scented, corolla pink or purplish to nearly white, funnelform, 1½ in. across, corolla tube setose, with or without gland-tipped hairs. Spring. Me. to S.C. and Tenn. Zone 4. Var. **roseum:** *R. prinophyllum.*

phoeniceum: *R. pulchrum* var.

pholidotum Balf.f. & W. W. Sm. RN, *RN;* shrub, to 8 ft.; lvs. ovate-elliptic, to 3 in. long, lepidote beneath; corolla rose to rose-purple, spotted, widely funnelform, ovary lepidote, style pubescent at base. N. Yunnan.

planetum Balf.f. HY, *HY;* shrub, to 15 ft., branchlets stout; lvs. oblong or narrowly oblong, to 8 in. long, pale green beneath; corolla pink, often with basal blotch or spots, funnelform-campanulate, to 2 in. long, 6–7-lobed, stamens 12–14, ovary and style glabrous. Szechwan.

pleistanthum Balf.f. ex Hutch. RN, *RN;* shrub, to 6 ft.; lvs. lanceolate or oblanceolate, to 2¼ in. long, not lepidote above, lepidote beneath, with scales spaced 3–4 times their own diam. apart; corolla rose-lavender, spotted crimson, widely funnelform, some stamens glabrous, others pubescent, calyx not lepidote. Yunnan.

polyandrum Hutch. RN, *RN;* shrub, to 10 ft.; lvs. oblong or oblong-lanceolate, to 3 in. long, densely lepidote beneath; corolla white or flushed pink, or pale yellow, funnelform, 2¾ in. long, lepidote outside, stamens 25, exserted, ovary and style lepidote. Bhutan. Zone 8b.

polylepis Franch. RN, *RN;* shrub, to 12 ft.; lvs. oblanceolate or oblong-lanceolate, to 3 in. long, lepidote beneath with overlapping scales; corolla purple or violet-purple, spotted yellow, 1 in. across, ovary lepidote. W. Szechwan and n. Yunnan. Zone 7.

ponticum L. RN, *RN;* shrub or small tree, to 15 ft. or more; lvs. elliptic to oblong, glabrous, dark green and glossy above, pale beneath; corolla purple, spotted brown, campanulate, 2 in. across, ovary and style glabrous. Late spring. Spain, Portugal, Asia Minor. Zone 7. Var. *Daviesiae* is listed.

poukhanense: *R. yedoense* var.

×**praecox** Carrière.: *Rhododendron* cv. 'Praecox': *R. ciliatum* × *R. dauricum.* Corolla purple, rosy-purple, or rosy-lilac, funnelform, 1½ in. across. Early spring. Zone 7.

praestans Balf.f. & W. W. Sm. HY, *HY;* shrub or tree, to 30 ft.; lvs. oblong-lanceolate to oblong-obovate, to 15 in. long, cuneate at base, glabrous above, scurfy beneath; corolla magenta-rose or pink, with crimson blotch, oblique-campanulate, 2 in. long, 8-lobed, stamens 16, ovary tomentose, style glabrous. Yunnan.

praevernum Hutch. HY, *HY;* compact shrub, to 6 ft. or more; lvs. elliptic-oblanceolate, to 8 in. long, glabrous, dark green above, pale gray-green beneath; corolla white, or white flushed rose, with wine-red blotch, campanulate, 2 in. long, stamens 15, ovary and style glabrous. Hupeh. Zone 7.

primuliflorum Bur. & Franch. [*R. tsarongense* Balf.f. & Forr.]. RN, *PO;* shrub, to 6 ft.; lvs. oblong, oblong-elliptic, or ovate-oblong, to 1¼ in. long, glabrous above, lepidote beneath, aromatic; corolla white, yellow, or pale rose, narrowly tubular, ¾ in. long, stamens 5, included, ovary sometimes lepidote. Tibet, Yunnan, Szechwan, Kansu. Var. **cephalanthoides** (Balf.f. & W. W. Sm.) Cowan & Davidian [*R. cephalanthoides* Balf.f. & W. W. Sm.]. Corolla tube densely puberulous outside.

primulinum: *R. flavidum.*

prinophyllum (Small) Millais [*R. roseum* of auth., not (Loisel.) Rehd.; *R. nudiflorum* (L.) Torr. var. *roseum* of auth., not (Loisel.) Wieg.; *Azalea prinophylla* Small; *A. rosea* of auth., not Loisel.]. EARLY A., PIEDMONT A., MAYFLOWER A., ROSE-SHELL A., HONEYSUCKLE, ELECTION PINK. PE, *PE;* deciduous shrub, to 8 ft. or more, branchlets and winter buds gray-pubescent-pilose; lvs. elliptic or obovate to obovate-oblong, to 2¾ in. long, ciliate, grayish-villous beneath; fls. spicy-fragrant, appearing with the lvs., corolla whitish to rosy or deep pink, funnelform, 1½ in. across, stamens twice as long as corolla tube, tube with gland-tipped hairs, ovary glandular-setose, style pubescent below, longer than stamens. S. Que. and Me. to sw. Va., w. to Ohio, s. Ill., Mo., Ark., and Okla. Zone 4.

probum: *R. selense* var.

procumbens: *Loiseleuria procumbens.*

prostratum W. W. Sm. RN, *RN;* prostrate, spreading shrub, to 4 in., branchlets bristly; lvs. oblong-elliptic, to ¾ in. long, ciliate, glossy above, lepidote beneath, petioles bristly; corolla pink-violet, spotted red, widely funnelform, ¾ in. long, ovary lepidote, style glabrous. Yunnan. Zone 7.

proteoides Balf.f. & W. W. Sm. HY, *HY;* much-branched shrub, to 3 ft.; lvs. oblong, to 1½ in. long, with revolute margin, rugose, glabrescent above, with dense, reddish, woolly hairs beneath, petiole to 3/16 in. long; corolla cream-colored to canary-yellow, with crimson markings or sometimes flushed with rose, funnelform, to 1¼ in. long, ovary hairy, glandular, style glabrous. Yunnan. Zone 8.

pruniflorum: *R. tsangpoense* var.

prunifolium (Small) Millais [*Azalea prunifolia* Small]. PLUM-LEAVED A. PE, *PE;* deciduous, glabrous shrub, to 10 ft.; lvs. elliptic to oblong or obovate, to 5 in. long, ciliate, pale beneath; fls. appearing after the lvs., corolla apricot to orange-red, funnelform, 1½ in. across, stamens much-exserted, ovary not glandular, style glabrous, longer than stamens. Summer. Ga. and Ala. Zone 7.

Przewalskii Maxim. HY, *HY;* shrub, to 9 ft.; lvs. elliptic or oblong to ovate, to 5 in. long, mostly glabrous above, hairy beneath; corolla white or rose-pink, sometimes spotted, campanulate or funnelform-campanulate, 1¾ in. long, ovary and style glabrous. Kansu, sw. Szechwan, e. Tibet. Zone 6.

pseudoyanthinum Balf.f. RN, *RN;* often confused with *R. concinnum,* but differing in having lvs. larger, 2½ in. long and 1–1¼ in. wide, and corolla larger, dark purple. W. Szechwan. Zone 7.

pubescens Balf.f. & Forr. PM, *TR;* shrub, to 4 ft., branchlets hairy; lvs. narrowly lanceolate or oblong, ¾ in. long, densely villous on both sides, lepidote beneath; calyx lobes rounded, ciliate, corolla rose to pinkish-white, funnelform, ¾ in. long, ovary lepidote, pubescent, style glabrous. S. Szechwan and nw. Yunnan. Zone 7.

pulchrum Sweet [*Azalea pulchra* (Sweet) Paxt.]. TT, *TU;* loosely branched, evergreen shrub, to 6 ft.; lvs. dimorphic, elliptic to oblong-oblanceolate, to 2¼ in. long, glabrescent above, somewhat hairy beneath; corolla rosy-purple with darker spots, funnelform, to 2½ in. across, stamens 10, ovary densely strigose. Introd. from cult. in China; possibly of hybrid origin. Cv. **'Maxwellii'.** Corolla carmine, with darker spots. Var. **calycinum** (Lindl.) Rehd. [*R. ledifolium* (Hook.) G. Don var. *purpureum* Maxim.; *Azalea ledifolia* Hook. var. *purpurea* Hort.]. Calyx lobes usually acuminate, corolla large, rose-purple. Var. **phoeniceum** (Sweet) Rehd. [*R. phoeniceum* (Sweet) G. Don]. Corolla magenta.

punctatum: *R. minus.*

puralbum Balf.f. & W. W. Sm. HY, *HY;* shrub, to 15 ft., branchlets glandular; lvs. oblong, oblong-elliptic, or oblong-ovate, to 6 in. long, glabrous and dark green above, glaucous beneath; corolla pure white, saucer-shaped, to 1½ in. long, ovary and style glandular. Yunnan. Zone 7.

×**purpureum crispum:** a listed name of no botanical standing for *Rhododendron* cv. 'Purpureum Crispum'. Hybrid derived from *R. catawbiense;* corolla lilac-purple, spotted green. Of the same ancestry, *R.* cv. **'Purpureum Elegans'** has deep purple corollas, and *R.* cv. **'Purpureum Grandiflorum'** has purple corollas.

quinquefolium Bisset & S. Moore [*Azalea quinquefolia* Hort.]. CORK A. TT, *BR;* deciduous shrub or small tree, to 25 ft.; lvs. 4 or 5 together at ends of branchlets, broadly elliptic to obovate, to 2 in. long, ciliate; fls. nodding, corolla white, spotted green, broadly funnelform, 1½ in. across, stamens 10, ovary and style glabrous. Late spring. Japan. Zone 7. Var. **album** is listed, but does not differ from the typical sp. Var. **roseum:** *R. pentaphyllum.*

racemosum Franch. PM, *RA;* leggy, evergreen shrub, to 6 ft. or more, but may also be quite dwarf; lvs. elliptic or oblong-elliptic, to 2 in. long, glaucous and lepidote beneath; corolla white, pink, or rose, campanulate, to 1 in. across, lobes lepidote outside but not pubescent, ovary densely lepidote. Yunnan. Zone 6. Hardiness varies with the cvs.

radicans Balf.f. & Forr. RN, *RN;* prostrate, matted shrub, to 6 in.; lvs. oblanceolate, ½ in. long, dark green, lepidote beneath; corolla purple, tubular, ¾ in. long, pubescent and lepidote outside, ovary lepidote. Tibet. Zone 7. Attractive rock garden plant.

radinum: *R. trichostomum* var.

ravum Balf.f. & W. W. Sm. RN, *RN;* shrub, to 6 ft. or more; lvs. oblong-elliptic, to 2 in. long, lepidote on both sides; corolla deep rose to purple, widely funnelform, 1¼ in. long, stamens 10, villous, ovary lepidote, style pubescent at base. Yunnan. Zone 6.

recurvoides Tagg & F. K. Ward. HY, *HY;* slow-growing, compact shrub, to 3 ft.; lvs. lanceolate, elliptic, or oblanceolate, to 2¾ in. long, cuneate at base, with recurved margin, rugose, glabrous and glossy at maturity above, felty with tawny hairs and with strigose glandular hairs beneath, petiole to ¾ in. long; corolla whitish-rose, with deeper spots, funnelform-campanulate, to 1¼ in. long, ovary with strigose glandular hairs, style glabrous. N. Burma.

repens: *R. Forrestii* var. Var. **chamaethauma:** *R. chamae-Thomsoniae* var. Var. **chamae-Thomsonii:** *R. chamae-Thomsonii.*

reticulatum D. Don ex G. Don [*R. dilatatum* Miq.; *R. rhombicum* Miq.; *Azalea dilatata* (Miq.) O. Kuntze; *A. reticulata* (D. Don ex G. Don) C. Koch]. TT, *BR;* much-branched, deciduous shrub, to 25 ft.; lvs. rhombic to broadly ovate, to 2½ in. long, pubescent beneath; fls. preceding the lvs., corolla purple or rose-purple, rotate-funnelform, to 2 in. across, stamens usually 10, ovary and style hairy. Early spring. Japan. Zone 6.

rex Lév. HY, *HY;* tree, to 20 ft., branchlets gray-white-hairy; lvs. oblanceolate, to 10 in. long, dark green above, with gray to pale buff hairs beneath, petiole to 1¾ in. long; corolla rose, with darker blotch and spots, tubular-campanulate, to 8 in. long, ovary hairy, style glabrous. Ne. Yunnan, sw. Szechwan. Zone 7.

rhabdotum Balf.f. & R. Cooper. RN, *RN;* shrub or small tree, to 12 ft.; lvs. narrowly oblong-elliptic to obovate-oblong, to 7¼ in. long, glabrous above, glaucous-green and lepidote with hairs between scales beneath; corolla cream-white, with crimson stripes in middle of lobes outside, waxy, funnelform with a campanulate base, with basal pouches, to 3 in. long, ovary densely lepidote, style lepidote in lower half. Bhutan. Zone 9.

rhantum: *R. vernicosum.*

rhombicum: *R. reticulatum.*

rigidum Franch. RN, *RN;* shrub, to 7 ft.; lvs. oblanceolate, to 2 in. long, lepidote-glandular on both sides; corolla pale rose with crimson-brown markings, ¾ in. long, ovary lepidote, style glabrous. Yunnan.

riparium: *R. calostrotum.*

Ririei Hemsl. & E. H. Wils. HY, *HY;* to 18 ft.; lvs. lanceolate, oblong-elliptic, to obovate, to 6 in. long, bright green and glabrous above, silvery-tomentose beneath; corolla dull purple, spotted black, campanulate, 2 in. long, ovary densely gray-tomentose, style glabrous. Szechwan. Zone 8.

rosiflorum: *R. indicum* cv. 'Balsaminiflorum'.

roseotinctum: *R. sanguineum* subsp.

roseum: see *R. prinophyllum.*

×**roseum elegans:** a listed name of no botanical standing for *Rhododendron* cv. 'Roseum Elegans'. Of hybrid origin, derived from *R. catawbiense;* corolla rose-lilac. Zone 5. Of similar ancestry, *Rhododendron* cv. **'Roseum Superbum',** has corolla purplish-rose. Zone 6.

rosmarinifolium S. Vidal. RN, *VR;* slender shrub, to 12 ft., branchlets lepidote; lvs. linear-oblanceolate, to ¾ in. long, glandular beneath; corolla red, tubular, 5/16 in. long, lepidote outside, ovary densely lepidote, style glabrous. Philippines. *R. rosmarinifolium* (Burm.f.) Dipp. is *R. mucronatum,* as is *R. rosmarinifolium* var. *album.*

Roxieanum Forr. [*R. cucullatum* Hand.-Mazz.]. HY, *HY;* slow-growing shrub, to 9 ft.; lvs. linear-lanceolate, to 5 in. long, densely crowded around infl., strongly recurved at margin, densely rusty-woolly-tomentose beneath; corolla creamy-white, sometimes flushed rose, with crimson markings, campanulate, to 1¾ in. long, ovary tomentose, style glabrous. Yunnan and se. Tibet. Zone 7.

rubens: a listed name of no botanical standing for *R. citriniflorum* subsp.; but the name *R. rubens* may sometimes be intended for *Rhododendron* cv. 'Rubens', a name that has been applied to an evergreen hybrid rhododendron, as well as to a Ghent Hybrid Azalea, and to two Indian Hybrid Azaleas.

roseotinctum: *R. sanguineum* subsp.

rubiginosum Franch. RN, *RN;* shrub or tree, to 30 ft.; lvs. elliptic-lanceolate, to 3½ in. long, densely rusty-lepidote beneath; corolla mauve, spotted brown, funnelform, 1¼ in. long, lepidote outside, ovary densely lepidote, style glabrous. Yunnan. Zone 6.

rufescens Franch. RN, *PO;* shrub, to 2 ft., branchlets densely lepidote; lvs. oblong-elliptic to oblong-ovate, to 1 in. long, glabrous above, reddish-brown-lepidote beneath; corolla white to rose, narrowly tubular, ¾ in. long, not lepidote or hairy outside, stamens 5, ovary lepidote. Szechwan.

rupicola W. W. Sm. RN, *RN;* shrub, to 2 ft.; lvs. broadly elliptic, to ½ in. long, lepidote on both sides; corolla dark purple-crimson, widely funnelform, to 1 in. across, lobes lepidote outside, ovary densely lepidote, style glabrous. Yunnan. Zone 7.

russatum Balf.f. & Forr. [*R. cantabile* Balf.f. ex Hutch.]. RN, *RN;* shrub, to 4 ft.; lvs. oblong, elliptic, to ovate, to 1 in. long, lepidote on both sides, rusty-brown beneath; corolla blue-purple with white throat, open-funnelform, 1 in. across, not lepidote outside, ovary densely lepidote, style pubescent at base. Nw. Yunnan. Zone 7.

×**Rutherfordianum** a listed name of no botanical standing for the RUTHERFORD HYBRID AZALEAS. A group of Indian Hybrid Azaleas with persistent lvs. and corolla ranging from white through crimson.

saluenense Franch. RN, *RN;* shrub, to 4 ft., branchlets bristly and lepidote; lvs. oblong to elliptic, to 1 in. long, densely lepidote beneath; calyx ciliate, corolla pinkish-purple to purple-crimson, spotted crimson, rotate-funnelform, 1½ in. across, ovary densely lepidote, style glabrous. Nw. Yunnan. Zone 7.

×**Sanderi** E. H. Wils.: *R. obtusum* × *R. Simsii.* The SANDER HYBRID AZALEAS. Fls. in shades of red and pink.

sanguineum Franch. HY, *HY;* shrub, to 3 ft.; lvs. oblong-obovate to elliptic, to 2½ in. long, dark green and glabrous above, gray-white-pubescent beneath; fls. with deciduous bud scales, corolla black-crimson, crimson-scarlet, or carmine, tubular-campanulate, to 1½ in. long, ovary densely tomentose, but not glandular. Nw. Yunnan and se. Tibet. Zone 8. Subsp. **didymum** (Balf.f. & Forr.) Cowan [*R. didymum* Balf.f. & Forr.]. Fls. with persistent bud scales, corolla black-crimson, ovary glandular. Se. Tibet. Zone 8. Subsp. **haemaleum** (Balf.f. & Forr.) Cowan [*R. haemaleum* Balf.f. & Forr.]. Fls. with deciduous bud scales, corolla black-crimson or dark crimson. Yunnan and Se. Tibet. Zone 7. Subsp. **roseotinctum** (Balf.f. & Forr.) Cowan [*R. roseotinctum* Balf.f. & Forr.]. Fls. with deciduous bud scales, corolla rose to yellowish-red or creamy-white, margined deep rose-crimson, ovary tomentose and glandular. Yunnan and se. Tibet.

Sargentianum Rehd. & E. H. Wils. RN, *PO;* twiggy shrub, to 2 ft.; lvs. elliptic, ⅝ in. long, glabrous and glossy above, lepidote beneath, aromatic; corolla lemon-yellow, funnelform, ⅝ in. long, lepidote outside, stamens 5, included, ovary lepidote. W. Szechwan. Zone 7.

scabrum G. Don [*R. sublanceolatum* Miq.; *Azalea sublanceolata* (Miq.) O. Kuntze]. LUCHU A. TT, *TU;* evergreen shrub, to 6 ft. or more; lvs. dimorphic, spring lvs. elliptic-lanceolate to lanceolate, to 4 in. long, summer lvs. oblanceolate; corolla rose-red to scarlet with darker blotch, broadly funnelform, 3 in. across, stamens 10, ovary glandular-bristly, style glabrous. Ryukyu Is. Zone 8.

Schlippenbachii Maxim. [*Azalea Schlippenbachii* (Maxim.) O. Kuntze]. ROYAL A. TT, *BR;* deciduous shrub, to 15 ft., branchlets glandular-pubescent; lvs. in whorls of 5, obovate to rhombic, to 5 in. long; fls. fragrant, corolla pale to rose-pink, occasionally deep pink or white, spotted light reddish-brown, rotate-funnelform, to 3½ in. across, ovary glandular. Late spring. Manchuria, Korea, Japan. Zone 5.

scintillans Balf.f. & W. W. Sm. RN, *RN;* shrub, to 3 ft.; lvs. oblong-lanceolate to oblanceolate, to ¾ in. long, densely lepidote on both surfaces; corolla lavender-blue, broadly funnelform, 1 in. across, not lepidote outside, ovary lepidote. Yunnan. Zone 7.

scyphocalyx: *R. dichroanthum* subsp.

Searsiae Rehd. & E. H. Wils. RN, *RN;* shrub, to 12 ft.; lvs. oblanceolate or lanceolate, to 3½ in. long, acuminate, densely lepidote beneath; corolla white to mauve, widely funnelform, to 2½ in. across, ovary densely lepidote, style glabrous. W. Szechwan. Zone 7.

selense Franch. HY, *HY;* shrub, to 9 ft.; lvs. oblong to elliptic or obovate, to 4½ in. long, glabrous or with a few hairs; corolla pink or rose, often with spots or blotch, funnelform-campanulate, to 1½ in. long, ovary densely glandular, sometimes hairy. Szechwan, Yunnan, Tibet. Zone 7. Var. **probum** (Balf.f. & Forr.) Cowan & Davidian [*R. probum* Balf.f. & Forr.]. Corolla white.

semibarbatum Maxim. AZ, *MU;* deciduous shrub, to 10 ft.; lvs. elliptic-oblong to elliptic or elliptic-ovate, to 2 in. long, serrate, setose on veins beneath, petioles bristly; fls. solitary, corolla white or yellowish-white, flushed pink and spotted red, rotate-campanulate, ¾ in. across, stamens 5, white-bearded, 3 long, 2 short. Cent. and s. Japan. Zone 6.

serpyllifolium (A. Gray) Miq. [*Azalea serpyllifolia* A. Gray]. WILD-THYME A. TT, *TU;* low, much-branched shrub, to 4 ft., branchlets appressed-hairy; lvs. elliptic to oblong-obovate, to ¾ in. long, hairy on midrib beneath; fls. mostly solitary, corolla rosy-pink, funnelform, ¾ in. across, ovary hairy, style glabrous. Cent. and s. Japan. Zone 6. There is a white-fld. form.

serrulatum (Small) Millais [*Azalea serrulata* Small]. PE, *PE;* deciduous shrub, to 20 ft.; lvs. elliptic to obovate or obovate-oblong, to 3¼ in. long, serrulate, ciliate; fls. appearing after lvs., fragrant, corolla white, funnelform, 1½ in. long, stamens exserted, ovary densely glandular-setose. Summer. Ga. and Fla. to La. Zone 7.

setosum D. Don. RN, *RN;* shrub, to 4 ft., branchlets bristly; lvs. oblong-elliptic, to ½ in. long, glandular-lepidote above, lepidote and bristly beneath; corolla bright purple-pink, widely funnelform, to 1 in. long, stamens 10, exserted, ovary densely lepidote. S. Tibet, Sikkim Himalayas.

Sheltoniae: *R. vernicosum.*

×**Sherwoodii:** a listed name of no botanical standing for *Rhododendron* cv. 'Sherwoodii'. A Kurume Hybrid Azalea, derived from *Rhododendron* cv. 'Hinodegiri'; corolla reddish-violet with darker blotch.

×**Shilsonii:** a listed name of no botanical standing for *Rhododendron* cv. 'Shilsonii': *R. barbatum* × *R. Thomsonii.* HY, *HY;* corolla scarlet or crimson. Zone 8.

shweliense Balf.f. & Forr. RN, *RN;* shrub, to 2½ ft., branchlets densely lepidote; lvs. oblong-obovate or obovate, to 2 in. long, lepidote above, glaucous and lepidote beneath, aromatic; corolla pink, tinged yellow, spotted pink, campanulate, ⅝ in. long, lepidote outside, ovary densely lepidote, style stout, sharply bent. Yunnan. Zone 7.

siderophyllum Franch. RN, *RN;* shrub, to 9 ft.; lvs. oblanceolate or elliptic-oblanceolate, to 3½ in. long, lepidote beneath; corolla white, pink, rose, or violet, spotted crimson or dark brown, widely funnelform, to 1 in. across, lepidote outside on lobes only, ovary lepidote. Sw. Yunnan. Zone 7.

sigillatum: *R. dryophyllum.*

silvaticum Cowan. HY, *HY;* large shrub or small tree, to 20 ft., branchlets gray-woolly; lvs. oblong to oblong-lanceolate, to 10 in. long, whitish-gray-pubescent beneath becoming russet-pubescent; corolla magenta to reddish-purple, campanulate, to 1½ in. long, ovary white-tomentose, style glabrous. Se. Tibet.

Simsii Planch. SIMS'S A. TT, *TU;* semievergreen shrub, to 5 ft. or more, branchlets appressed-hairy; lvs. dimorphic, spring lvs. oblong-elliptic to ovate, to 2 in. long, hairy, summer lvs. oblanceolate or obovate, to 1½ in. long; corolla rose-red to bright or dark red, spotted darker, widely funnelform, to 2 in. across, stamens 10, ovary strigose, style glabrous. Late spring. China and Taiwan. Zone 8. A parent of the Indian Hybrid Azaleas. Var. **eriocarpum** (Hayata) E. H. Wils. Corolla pink or white. Cv. 'Vittatum' [var. *vittatum* (Fort.) E. H. Wils.]. Corolla white, striped with lilac-purple.

sinense: *R. molle.*

sinogrande Balf.f. & W. W. Sm. HY, *HY;* tree, to 30 ft.; lvs. elliptic, oblong, or obovate, to 2 ft. long and 1 ft. across, dark glossy green above, white-pubescent beneath; corolla dull creamy-white with crimson blotch, campanulate, to 2½ in. long, 8–10-lobed, stamens 18–20, ovary densely tomentose, style glabrous. W. Yunnan, ne. Burma, se. Tibet. Zone 8.

Smirnowii Trautv. SMIRNOW R. HY, *HY;* shrub or small tree, to 10 ft., branchlets white-felty; lvs. oblong-lanceolate, to 6 in. long, glabrous above, white-felty beneath, becoming brown-felty; corolla pale rose to rose-purple, funnelform-campanulate, to 3 in. across, ovary white-tomentose, style glabrous. Late spring. Caucasus. Zone 6.

Smithii Nutt. ex Hook. HY, *HY;* shrub or small tree, to 15 ft., branchlets bristly; lvs. oblong-lanceolate, to 6 in. long, glossy and glabrous above, gray-white-woolly beneath, petioles bristly; corolla deep scarlet-crimson with crimson nectar pouches at base, tubular-campanulate, 1¾ in. long, ovary glandular, style glabrous. Bhutan and e. Sikkim. Zone 8.

×**Smithii aureum:** a listed name of no botanical standing for *Rhododendron* cv. 'Smithii Aureum'. Hybrid involving *R. maximum, R. ponticum,* and *R. molle;* corolla orange-yellow; an "azaleodendron," a hybrid derived from an azalea and 2 rhododendrons. Zone 7.

sordidum: *R. tsangpoense* var. *pruniflorum.*

Souliei Franch. HY, *HY;* shrub, to 15 ft.; lvs. oblong-elliptic or ovate-elliptic to almost orbicular, to 4 in. long, often cordate at base, usually rounded at apex, metallic-green above, glabrous and pale glaucous-green beneath; corolla white, tinged pink to deep rose, saucer-shaped, 2½ in. wide, ovary and style glandular. W. Szechwan and Tibet. Zone 7.

speciosum: *R. flammeum.*

sperabile Balf.f. & Farrer. HY, *HY;* shrub, to 6 ft., branchlets woolly and glandular; lvs. oblong to lanceolate, to 4 in. long, tawny-pubescent beneath, petioles glandular; corolla scarlet or crimson, tubular-campanulate, 1½ in. long, fleshy, ovary glandular-tomentose. Ne. Burma. Zone 8.

sperabiloides Tagg & Forr. HY, *HY;* shrub, to 4 ft., branchlets white-scurfy but not glandular; lvs. oblong to lanceolate, to 3 in. long, scurfy beneath, petioles white-scurfy but not glandular; corolla crimson, tubular-campanulate, 1 in. long, ovary tomentose. Se. Tibet. Zone 8.

spiciferum Franch. PM, *TR;* shrub, to 3 ft., branchlets bristly and pubescent; lvs. narrowly oblanceolate, 1 in. long, softly pubescent and lepidote beneath; calyx ciliate and lepidote outside, corolla pink, funnelform, ½ in. long, ovary densely hairy, glandular. Yunnan. Zone 8.

spinuliferum Franch. PM, *TR;* shrub, to 8 ft.; lvs. lanceolate to oblanceolate, to 3 in. long, bullate above, downy and lepidote beneath; corolla crimson to brick-red, tubular, to 1 in. long, stamens exserted, ovary tomentose. Yunnan. Zone 8.

stenoplastum: *R. desquamatum.*

stereophyllum Balf.f. & W. W. Sm. RN, *RN;* shrub, to 6 ft., branchlets resinous-glandular; lvs. elliptic to obovate, to 2 in. long, densely lepidote on both sides; corolla mauve-rose, widely funnelform, to 3/4 in. long, stamens hairy at base, ovary lepidote, style glabrous. Yunnan.

Stewartianum Diels. HY, *HY;* shrub, to 10 ft.; lvs. obovate, elliptic, or oblong-obovate, to 5 in. long, glabrous above, thinly hairy to glabrous beneath; corolla white, yellow flushed rose, rose, or crimson, sometimes with markings, tubular-campanulate, 1 3/4 in. long, ovary usually glandular. Yunnan, ne. Burma, se. Tibet, Assam. Zone 7.

×**Stewartsonianum:** a listed name of no botanical standing for *Rhododendron* cv. 'Stewartsonianum' [cv. 'Stewartsonian']. One of the Gable Hybrid Azaleas; foliage changing to wine-red in winter; corolla bright clear red.

strigillosum Franch. HY, *HY;* shrub, to 8 ft., sometimes to 20 ft., branchlets and petioles with long, stiff, glandular bristles; lvs. oblong-lanceolate, to 6 in. long, brown-hairy beneath; corolla crimson-scarlet to white, campanulate, to 2 in. across, fleshy, ovary setose-glandular, style glabrous. Szechwan. Zone 8.

sublanceolatum: *R. scabrum.*

supranubium Hutch. RN, *RN;* shrub, to 12 ft., branchlets lepidote; lvs. oblanceolate, obovate-oblanceolate, or elliptic, to 3 1/2 in. long, glaucous and lepidote beneath; fls. fragrant, corolla white, rose outside, funnelform, 1 1/4 in. long, lepidote outside, ovary and base of style lepidote. Yunnan.

sutchuenense Franch. HY, *HY;* shrub or small tree, to 20 ft.; lvs. oblong-oblanceolate or oblong-elliptic, to 10 in. long, essentially glabrous at maturity; corolla lilac-rose or rosy-pink, spotted purple, campanulate, to 2 1/2 in. across, stamens 12–15, ovary and style glabrous. Hupeh and Szechwan. Zone 6.

sylvaticum: a misspelling of *R. silvaticum.*

Taggianum Hutch. ex L. B. Stewart. RN, *RN;* shrub, to 8 ft., branchlets glandular-lepidote; lvs. oblong, oblong-lanceolate, or oblong-elliptic, to 6 in. long, glaucous and glandular-lepidote beneath; fls. fragrant, corolla white with yellow blotch, funnelform, to 4 in. long and wide, ovary densely lepidote, style lepidote at base. Ne. Burma and se. Tibet. Zone 9.

taliense Franch. HY, *HY;* shrub, to 10 ft., branchlets woolly-tomentose; lvs. lanceolate to oblong-ovate, to 5 in. long, rusty-tomentose beneath, petioles felty-tomentose; corolla creamy-yellow or cream flushed rose, marked with crimson, narrowly campanulate, 1 1/4 in. long, ovary and style glabrous. W. Yunnan.

tapetiforme Balf.f. & F. K. Ward. RN, *RN;* slow-growing, mat-forming shrub, to 2 ft., branchlets lepidote; lvs. broadly elliptic, to 1/2 in. long, densely lepidote on both sides; corolla pink, funnelform, 1/2 in. long, not lepidote, ovary lepidote, style glabrous. Yunnan-Tibet border.

taronense Hutch. RN, *RN;* shrub, to 15 ft., epiphytic; lvs. elliptic to obovate, to 6 in. long, abruptly acuminate, thinly lepidote beneath; fls. fragrant, corolla white, suffused yellow inside, striped pink on lobes outside, campanulate, 2 in. long, slightly fleshy, ovary densely lepidote, style lepidote at base. Nw. Yunnan and n. Burma. Zone 9.

telmateium Balf.f. & W. W. Sm. RN, *RN;* shrub, to 3 ft.; lvs. elliptic-lanceolate, 1/2 in. long, densely lepidote on both sides; corolla rosy-purple with white throat, broadly funnelform, about 1 in. across, lepidote outside, stamens pubescent, ovary lepidote, style glabrous. Yunnan. Zone 7.

telopeum Balf.f. & Forr. HY, *HY;* shrub, to 10 ft., branchlets moderately glandular; lvs. elliptic, ovate or orbicular, to 2 in. long, dark green and glabrous above, pale glaucous-green and glandular or minutely hairy beneath; corolla bright yellow, campanulate, 1 1/2 in. wide, ovary densely glandular. Yunnan and se. Tibet. Zone 7.

tephropeplum Balf.f. & Farrer [*R. deleiense* Hutch. & F. K. Ward]. RN, *RN;* shrub, to 6 ft., branchlets lepidote; lvs. lanceolate to oblong-obovate, to 4 3/4 in. long, glaucous and densely lepidote beneath; corolla pink or rose to purple, rarely white, tubular-campanulate, 1 1/4 in. long, ovary and base of style lepidote. Yunnan, n. Burma, Assam, Tibet. Zone 8.

Thayeranum Rehd. & E. H. Wils. HY, *HY;* shrub, to 15 ft.; lvs. narrowly oblanceolate, to 8 in. long, acuminate, with yellowish-brown felt beneath; corolla white, flushed pink, spotted crimson, funnelform-campanulate, to 1 1/4 in. long, ovary and style glandular. W. Szechwan.

Thomsonii Hook.f. HY, *HY;* shrub or small tree, to 20 ft.; lvs. elliptic, ovate, or orbicular, to 4 in. long, blue-green and glabrous above, whitish-green beneath; corolla deep blood-red, often spotted, campanulate, to 3 in. across, ovary and style not glandular. Sikkim, Bhutan, Tibet. Zone 8. One of the parents of the Thomsonii Hybrid Rhododendrons. Var. **candelabrum** (Hook.f.) C. B. Clarke. Calyx smaller, corolla paler, ovary glandular. Tibet.

timeteum Balf.f. & Forr. RN, *RN;* shrub, to 8 ft., branchlets not lepidote; lvs. elliptic, oblong-elliptic or ovate, to 3 in. long, bright green and glabrous above, brown-lepidote beneath; corolla purplish-rose with darker markings, funnelform, 1 1/2 in. long, hairy but not lepidote outside, ovary densely lepidote. Sw. Szechwan. Zone 8.

tosaense Mak. [*R. Komiyamae* Mak.]. TT, *TU;* semievergreen or deciduous, much-branched shrub, to 7 ft.; lvs. dimorphic, spring lvs. lanceolate to oblanceolate, to 1 1/2 in. long, appressed-hairy, summer lvs. linear to oblanceolate, to 1/2 in. long; corolla lilac-purple, funnelform, 1 1/4 in. across, ovary strigose-pubescent. S. Japan. Zone 7.

Traillianum Forr. & W. W. Sm. HY, *HY;* shrub or small tree, to 30 ft.; lvs. oblong, oblong-lanceolate, oblong-elliptic, or oblong-obovate, to 7 in. long, powdery to felty beneath with fawn to rusty or yellowish hairs; corolla white to rose, funnelform-campanulate, to 1 1/2 in. long, ovary tomentose or glabrous, style glabrous. Sw. Szechwan and nw. Yunnan. Zone 7.

trichanthum Rehd. [*R. villosum* Hemsl. & E. H. Wils., not Roth]. RN, *RN;* shrub, to 20 ft., branchlets densely bristly; lvs. elliptic to oblong-lanceolate, to 4 in. long, lepidote beneath, bristly on the midrib; fls. with bristly pedicels, corolla light or dark purple or rose, widely funnelform, 1 1/2 in. across, lepidote outside, ovary bristly and lepidote. W. Szechwan. Zone 7. The name *R. villosum* Roth is a synonym of *Clerodendrum fragrans.*

trichocladum Franch. PA; deciduous shrub, to 4 ft.; lvs. oblong, to 1 1/2 in. long, pubescent above, minutely lepidote beneath, ciliate; corolla greenish-yellow, spotted dark green, broadly funnelform, to 1 1/2 in. across, ovary lepidote, style glabrous, sharply bent. W. Yunnan and ne. Burma. Zone 8.

trichostomum Franch. RN, *PO;* twiggy shrub, to 4 ft., branchlets bristly and lepidote; lvs. linear-lanceolate, narrowly oblanceolate, or ovate to ovate-oblong, to 1/2 in. long, densely lepidote beneath; corolla rose to white, narrowly tubular, to 3/4 in. long, lepidote outside, stamens 5, ovary lepidote, style glabrous. Szechwan and Yunnan. Zone 7. Var. **hedyosmum** (Balf.f.) Cowan & Davidian [*R. hedyosmum* Balf.f.]. Lvs. elongate-oblong; fls. with longer corolla tube. Szechwan. Var. **ledoides** (Balf.f. & W. W. Sm.) Cowan & Davidian [*R. ledoides* Balf.f. & W. W. Sm.]. Lvs. linear-lanceolate; corolla pale rose, not lepidote. Szechwan and Yunnan. Var. **radinum** (Balf.f. & W. W. Sm.) Cowan & Davidian [*R. radinum* Balf.f. & W. W. Sm.]. Corolla densely lepidote outside. Szechwan and Yunnan.

triflorum Hook.f. RN, *RN;* shrub, to 8 ft.; lvs. lanceolate or oblong-lanceolate, to 2 1/2 in. long, glabrous above, glandular-lepidote beneath; infl. 3-fld., fls. fragrant, corolla yellow, spotted green, funnelform, 1 1/2 in. long, lepidote outside, ovary lepidote, style glabrous. Bhutan and Sikkim Himalayas. Zone 8.

trinerve: *R. Tschonoskii.*

tsangpoense F. K. Ward. RN, *RN;* shrub, to 3 ft.; lvs. obovate or oblong-elliptic, to 2 in. long, glaucous and thinly lepidote beneath, the scales spaced 3–6 times their diam. apart; corolla pink, crimson, or pinkish-purple, campanulate, to 1 in. long, densely lepidote, style glabrous, thick, sharply bent. Tibet. Zone 8. Var. **pruniflorum** (Hutch.) Cowan & Davidian [*R. pruniflorum* Hutch.; *R. sordidum* Hutch.]. Underside of lvs. densely lepidote, the scales slightly overlapping. Burma, Assam, Tibet.

tsarongense: *R. primuliflorum.*

Tschonoskii Maxim. [*R. trinerve* Franch. ex Boiss.; *Azalea Tschonoskii* (Maxim.) O. Kuntze]. TT, *TU;* much-branched, deciduous shrub, to 8 ft., branchlets densely brown-pubescent; lvs. narrowly lanceolate to elliptic-lanceolate or ovate-lanceolate, to 1 in. long, pubescent; corolla white, funnelform, 3/8 in. long, stamens 4 or 5, ovary densely brown-hairy, style glabrous. S. Korea, Japan. Zone 6.

Ungernii Trautv. HY, *HY;* shrub, to 20 ft.; lvs. oblong-lanceolate, to 7 1/2 in. long, dark green and glabrous above, tawny and felty beneath; corolla pink to white, campanulate, 2 in. across, ovary glandular, style glabrous. Caucasus. Zone 6.

uniflorum Hutch. & F. K. Ward. RN, *RN;* procumbent shrub, to about 1 ft.; lvs. oblong-obovate, to 3/4 in. long, glaucous and lepidote beneath; fls. solitary or in pairs, corolla purple, broadly funnelform, 1 in. long, ovary lepidote, style glabrous. S. Tibet. Zone 7.

vaccinioides Hook.f. RN, *VR;* straggling epiphyte; lvs. spatulate-oblanceolate, to about 1 in. long, lepidote beneath; corolla pink or white, shortly and broadly tubular, to 1/2 in. long, fleshy, sparingly glandular-lepidote outside, ovary lepidote, style glabrous, short, stout. N. Burma, se. Tibet, Sikkim.

Valentinianum Forr. RN, *RN;* freely branching shrub, to 3 ft., twigs lepidote, bristly-ciliate; lvs. elliptic to oblong-elliptic, to 1 3/4 in. long, leathery, with ciliate, revolute margins, dark green and with scattered scales and bristles above, tawny-brown and densely lepidote beneath, petiole to 3/4 in. long; corolla bright yellow, lepidote outside, hairy outside and basally inside, funnelform-campanulate, to 1 3/8 in. long, ovary lepidote, style lepidote basally. W. Yunnan. Zone 8b.

Vaseyi A. Gray [*Azalea Vaseyi* (A. Gray) Rehd.; *Biltia Vaseyi* (A. Gray) Small]. PINK-SHELL A. PE, *RO;* deciduous shrub, to 15 ft.; lvs. elliptic to elliptic-oblong, to 5 in. long, ciliate; fls. appearing before the lvs., corolla rose, spotted brown, rotate-campanulate, 2-lipped, 1½ in. across, stamens 5–7, exserted, ovary glandular-pubescent. Spring. N.C. Zone 5. Forma **album** (Bean) Rehd. (var. *album* Bean]. Corolla white.

Veitchianum Hook. RN, *RN;* shrub, to 8 ft., often epiphytic; lvs. obovate, to 4 in. long, glaucous and lepidote beneath; corolla white, broadly funnelform, 5 in. across, with crinkled lobes, ovary and base of style lepidote. Thailand and Burma. Zone 8b.

venator Tagg. HY, *HY;* shrub, to 10 ft., branchlets glandular, white-woolly; lvs. oblong-lanceolate to oblong-oblanceolate, to 5 in. long, cuspidate, bright green above, pale glaucous-green beneath; corolla scarlet, tubular-campanulate, 1½ in. long, fleshy, ovary tomentose, setose-glandular. Se. Tibet. Zone 8.

vernicosum Franch. [*R. rhantum* Balf.f. & W. W. Sm.; *R. Sheltoniae* Hemsl. & E. H. Wils]. HY, *HY;* shrub, to 25 ft.; lvs. oblong-elliptic to oblong-ovate, to 5 in. long, glabrous; corolla white to rose or lavender-rose, often with crimson markings, funnelform-campanulate, to 2½ in. across, 7-lobed, stamens 14, glabrous, ovary and style with dark red glands. W. Szechwan and w. Yunnan. Zone 6.

× **Vervaenianum:** a listed name of no botanical standing for *Rhododendron* cv. 'Vervaenianum'. One of the Indian Hybrid Azaleas; corolla rose, bordered with white. Also of this group of azaleas, cv. **'Vervaenianum Album'** has pure white corollas, and cv. **'Vervaenianum Salmoneum'** has salmon corollas.

villosum: see *R. trichanthum.*

Vilmorinianum Balf.f. RN, *RN;* shrub, to 6 ft., branchlets lepidote, slightly pubescent; lvs. lanceolate or oblanceolate, to 2¼ in. long, lepidote beneath, petiole margins bristly; corolla white or tinged pink, with ochre spots, funnelform, 1¼ in. long, tube glandular-lepidote, ovary lepidote, style glabrous. Probably e. Szechwan. Zone 7.

virgatum Hook.f. PM, *RA;* shrub, to 6 ft.; lvs. oblong to lanceolate, to 3 in. long, thinly lepidote above, densely lepidote beneath; fls. solitary or in pairs, corolla white, pink, or mauve, funnelform, 1¼ in. across, stamens 10, exserted, ovary densely lepidote. Bhutan and Sikkim. Zone 9.

viridescens Hutch. PA; shrub, 4 ft., branchlets bristly; lvs. oblong-elliptic, to 1½ in. long, glaucous and lepidote beneath; calyx lepidote, bristly-pilose on margin, corolla pale yellowish-green, spotted green, funnelform, 1½ in. across, ovary lepidote, style curved, glabrous. Tibet. Zone 7.

viscosum (L.) Torr. [*Azalea viscosa* L.]. SWAMP A., WHITE SWAMP A., SWAMP HONEYSUCKLE, CLAMMY A. PE, *PE;* deciduous shrub, to 8 ft., branchlets hairy; lvs. narrowly ovate or oblong-lanceolate to elliptic-obovate, to 2½ in. long, bristly-ciliate; fls. fragrant, corolla white or pink, funnelform, to 2 in. long, glandular outside, stamens 5, exserted, ovary setose, often glandular, style pubescent below middle. Summer. Swamps, Me. to S.C. Zone 4. Var. **aemulans** Rehd. Fl. heads larger. Late spring. Cent. Ga. to Miss. Var. **montanum** Rehd. Low, densely branched, highly stoloniferous. Higher elevations of the Great Smoky Mts.

vittatum: *R. Simsii* cv.

× **Vuykianum** a listed name of no botanical standing; used for a group of large-fld., evergreen azaleas known as the VUYKIANA HYBRID AZALEAS, developed from *Rhododendron* cv. 'J. C. Van Tol' (a Molle Hybrid Azalea) crossed with a Kaempferi Hybrid or *R. mucronatum* and perhaps with other azaleas. About a dozen cvs. have been named.

Wallichii Hook.f. HY, *HY;* shrub, to 10 ft.; lvs. elliptic, obovate, or oblong, to 6 in. long, dark green above, with scattered tufts of rusty hairs beneath; corolla white, lilac, or pinkish-mauve, spotted rose, broadly campanulate, to 2 in. long, ovary usually glabrous. Sikkim Himalayas. Zone 7?

Wardii W. W. Sm. [*R. astrocalyx* Balf.f. & Forr.; *R. croceum* Balf. & W. W. Sm.]. HY, *HY;* shrub, to 20 ft.; lvs. oblong to ovate or orbicular, to 5 in. long, dark green and glabrous above, pale glaucous-green beneath; corolla bright yellow, sometimes with crimson blotch, saucer-shaped, to 2 in. across, ovary and style glandular. Szechwan, w. Yunnan, se. Tibet. Zone 7.

Washingtonianum: *R. macrophyllum.*

Wattii Cowan. HY, *HY;* tree, to 20 ft.; lvs. oblong or oblong-ovate, to 6 in. long, glabrous above, rusty-tomentose beneath; corolla pink, spotted purple, tubular-campanulate, to 2 in. long, 6-lobed, ovary white-hairy, style glabrous. Manipur.

× **Wellesleyanum:** a listed name of no botanical standing for *Rhododendron* cv. 'Wellesleyanum': *R. catawbiense* × *R. maximum.* HY, *HY;* corolla white, tinged light rose.

Weyrichii Maxim. [*Azalea Weyrichii* (Maxim.) O. Kuntze]. AN, *BR;* deciduous shrub, to 15 ft.; lvs. often in 3's, rhombic-ovate to suborbicular, to 3½ in. long, becoming glabrous; fls. appearing before the lvs., corolla bright brick-red, funnelform, 2½ in. across, stamens 6–10, ovary densely pilose, style glabrous, red. S. Japan, Cheju Is. Zone 7.

Wightii Hook.f. HY, *HY;* shrub or small tree, to 15 ft.; lvs. oblong, elliptic, or obovate, to 8 in. long, felty beneath with fawn to rusty-brown hairs; corolla yellow, often with crimson blotch, campanulate, to 2 in. long, ovary densely tomentose, style glabrous. Sikkim and Bhutan Himalayas. Zone 8.

Williamsianum Rehd. & E. H. Wils. HY, *HY;* shrub, to 5 ft., often low and spreading, branchlets setose-glandular; lvs. elliptic to ovate or orbicular, to 2¼ in. long, essentially glabrous, petioles setose-glandular; corolla pale rose, campanulate, 2¼ in. across, stamens glabrous, ovary and style glandular. Szechwan. Zone 7. Much used as a parent in breeding rhododendrons.

× **Wilsonii:** a listed name of no botanical standing for *Rhododendron* cv. 'Wilsonii': *R. ciliatum* × *R. glaucophyllum.* RN, *RN;* corolla pale rose. Material offered as *R. Wilsonii* may be *R.* × *laetevirens.*

Wiltonii Hemsl. & E. H. Wils. HY, *HY;* shrub, to 10 ft., branchlets brown-woolly; lvs. oblanceolate or oblong-oblanceolate, to 5 in. long, somewhat bullate above, cinnamon-brown-tomentose beneath; corolla white to pink, with red spots or blotch, campanulate, to 2½ in. across, ovary white-tomentose, style glabrous. W. Szechwan.

xanthocodon Hutch. RN, *RN;* shrub, to 25 ft., branchlets lepidote; lvs. elliptic to oblong-elliptic, to 3 in. long, lepidote on both sides; corolla creamy-yellow, campanulate, ¾ in. long, fleshy, ovary lepidote, style glabrous. Tibet. Zone 8.

xanthostephanum Merrill [*R. aureum* Franch., not Georgi]. RN, *RN;* shrub, to 9 ft.; lvs. lanceolate or oblong-lanceolate, to 4 in. long, lepidote above, glaucous and lepidote beneath; corolla bright yellow, tubular-campanulate, 1 in. long, densely lepidote outside, ovary and base of style lepidote. Yunnan, Burma, Tibet. Zone 9.

yakusimanum Nakai. HY, *HY;* compact shrub, to 3 ft.; lvs. linear-oblong or lanceolate to oblanceolate, to 3 in. long, at first densely tomentose beneath, becoming almost glabrous; corolla white or pink, broadly campanulate, to 2½ in. across. Japan. Zone 6.

yanthinum: *R. concinnum.*

× **Yayegiri:** a listed name of no botanical standing for *Rhododendron* cv. 'Yayegiri'. A Kurume Hybrid Azalea; corolla double, salmon-red.

yedoense Maxim. ex Regel [*R. Yodogava* (Hort. Truffaut) Kunert; *Azalea Yodogava* Hort. Truffaut]. YODOGAWA A. AN, *AN;* deciduous or semievergreen shrub; lvs. narrowly elliptic to lanceolate, to 3 in. long, pale and hairy beneath; corolla double, rosy-purple. Late spring. Korea. Zone 6. Var. **poukhanense** (Lév.) Nakai [*R. poukhanense* Lév.; *Azalea poukhanensis* Hort.]. KOREAN A. To 6 ft.; fls. fragrant, corolla single, funnelform, to 2 in. across, pale lilac-purple with deeper spotting, ovary bristly. Cent. and s. Korea, Japan. One of the parents of the Gable Hybrid Azaleas.

Yodogava: *R. yedoense.*

yunnanense Franch. YUNNAN R. RN, *RN;* leggy, free-flowering shrub, to 12 ft.; lvs. elliptic-lanceolate or oblanceolate, to 3 in. long, ciliate, lepidote and hairy above, lepidote beneath; corolla pink to nearly white, spotted red, funnelform, to 2 in. across, stamens long-exserted, ovary densely lepidote, style glabrous. Yunnan. Zone 7.

zaleucum Balf.f. & W. W. Sm. RN, *RN;* shrub or small tree, 20–30 ft.; lvs. lanceolate to oblong-lanceolate, to 3 in. long, dull green above, grayish-white- to white-waxy and red-brown-lepidote beneath; fls. slightly fragrant, corolla mauve or rose to white, broadly funnelform, 1½ in. long, lepidote outside, ovary lepidote, style glabrous. W. Yunnan and ne. Burma.

zeylanicum W. B. Booth ex Cowan [*R. arboreum* var. *zeylanicum* Hort.]. HY, *HY;* shrub or tree, to 60 ft., branchlets glandular; lvs. elliptic or elliptic-oblong, to 5½ in. long, revolute at margins, glabrous and bullate above, glandular and tomentose beneath, calyx 5-lobed, glandular-pilose, corolla pink to deep red, campanulate, 1½ in. long, ovary hairy, style glabrous. Ceylon. Zone 8.

RHODOHYPOXIS Nel. *Hypoxidaceae.* Two spp. of stemless, scapose herbs, native to S. Afr.; lvs. linear, from a short, fibrous-coated rhizome; fls. 1–2, rose, white flushed with rose, or white, perianth segms. 6, united in a short tube, stamens 6, in 2 series, anthers sessile, erect, stigmas 3-lobed; fr. a caps.

Suitable for use in the rock garden when planted in a sandy soil in full sun, though not hardy north. Propagated by offsets or seeds.

Baurii (Bak.) Nel. To 2½ in.; lvs. 5–6, to 2 in. long, ⅜ in. wide, white-hairy, glaucous; fls. rose, to 1 in. across. Var. **platypetala** (Bak.) Nel [*R. platypetala* Hort.]. Fls. paler, white flushed with rose, or white.

platypetala: a listed name of no botanical standing for *R. Baurii* var.

RHODOLEIA Hook. *Hamamelidaceae.* Seven spp. of Asiatic evergreen trees; lvs. alt., entire, leathery, glaucous beneath; infl. of axillary, pendent, 5–10-fld. heads surrounded by colored involucral bracts; petals 2–4, clawed, rose-colored, stamens 7–10, ovary 2-celled; fr. a cluster of 5 radiating caps.

Championii Hook. Small tree; lvs. glabrous, elliptic-obovate, to 3½ in. long; fl. heads 2½ in. across. China, Hongkong.

RHODOMYRTUS (DC.) Rchb. *Myrtaceae.* About 20 spp. of shrubs or trees, native from trop. Asia to New Caledonia and Australia; lvs. opp., simple, 3- or 5-nerved; fls. rather large, axillary, pink or white, calyx lobes usually 5, persistent, petals usually 5, stamens many, ovary inferior, 1–3-celled, but appearing 2–4- or 6-celled because of false partitions; fr. a globose, few-seeded berry. Allied to *Myrtus* but having ovary appearing multicelled with one ovule in each apparent cell.

The following species will withstand several degrees of frost and is not particular as to soil. Propagated by seeds sown in flats.

tomentosa (Ait.) Hassk. DOWNY MYRTLE, HILL GOOSEBERRY, HILL GUAVA. Shrub, to 5 ft.; lvs. elliptic-ovate, sometimes obovate, to 2½ in. long, densely tomentose beneath, 3-nerved from base; fls. rose-pink, to 1 in. across; berry ½ in. across, dark purple, edible. Late spring. India, e. through China, to Philippine Is. Zone 10b. Fleshy pulp of the berry sweet and aromatic; may be eaten raw or made into jam.

RHODOPHIALA: *HIPPEASTRUM.*

RHODORA: *RHODODENDRON.*

RHODORRHIZA: *CONVOLVULUS.*

RHODOSPATHA Poepp. *Araceae.* Fifteen spp. of climbers, native to trop. Amer.; lvs. large, oblong-elliptic, petioles long-sheathing, geniculate; spathe convolute, early deciduous, spadix slender, densely covered with bisexual fls.; perianth absent, stamens 4, ovary 2-celled, ovules many in each cell, superposed. Has sometimes been included in *Stenospermation.*

hastata: a listed name of no botanical standing; material so listed may be a sp. of *Raphidophora* or *Epipremnum.*

costaricensis Engl. Differs from *R. latifolia* in having lf. blades oblong, to 14 in. long and 6½ in. wide, nearly cuneate, petioles shorter, sheathing up to the lf. blade; spathe 4 in. long, spadix sessile, somewhat shorter. Costa Rica. Doubtfully in cult.; material so listed may be *Philodendron inaequilaterum.*

latifolia Poepp. Lf. blades wide-elliptic, to 18 in. long and 10 in. wide, rotund to truncate at base, corrugated by 30 or more pairs of widely spreading lateral veins, petioles as long as blades, sheathing up to geniculum; peduncle 6–8 in. long, spathe rosy, to 7 in. long, spadix nearly as long as spathe, violet. Peru, Brazil.

picta Nichols. To 30 in. or more; lf. blades erect, elliptic, to 26 in. long and 10 in. wide, acute at each end, with about 18 primary lateral veins on each side, glossy dark green above mottled with bright yellow-green, petioles to 16 in. long, sheathing nearly to apex; peduncle 1 ft. long, spathe 11 in. long, yellow, spadix slightly shorter than spathe, rosy. Nativity unknown.

RHODOSPHAERA Engl. *Anacardiaceae.* One sp., a dioecious tree, of ne. Australia; lvs. pinnate, leathery, minutely puberulent above; fls. red, in dense panicles, unisexual, petals 5, stamens 10; fr. a large globose drupe.

rhodanthema (F. J. Muell.) Engl. YELLOWWOOD. Tree, 20–40 ft., bark shedding in thick scales or plates; lfts. 7–9, oblong, mostly 2–4 in. long (longer on young plants), coarsely undulate, petiolules about ¼ in. long; fls. red, nearly ⅛ in. across; fr. ½ in. in diam. The wood prized in its native region for cabinet work. Queensland.

RHODOSTACHYS: *OCHAGAVIA.* **R. andina:** *O. Lindleyana.*

RHODOTHAMNUS Rchb. *Ericaceae.* One sp., an evergreen shrub, native to the Alps; lvs. simple, alt., entire; fls. purple, solitary or in terminal, few-fld. clusters, sepals 5, corolla rotate, 5-lobed, stamens 10; fr. a 5-valved caps.

Does best in peaty, moist soil in partial shade, in the rock garden. Propagated by seeds, layers, and cuttings of ripe wood.

Chamaecistus (L.) Rchb. [*Rhododendron Chamaecistus* L.]. Much-branched, semiprostrate shrub, to 1 ft., brs. glandular-pubescent; lvs. elliptic to oblong-cuneate, to ½ in. long, ciliate; fls. to 1 in. across, anthers dark brown, pedicels glandular-hairy. Late spring. Zone 6?

RHODOTYPOS Siebold & Zucc. JETBEAD, WHITE KERRIA. *Rosaceae.* One sp., a deciduous shrub, native to temp. e. Asia; lvs. opp.; fls. white, petals 4, stamens many; frs. 1–6, mostly 4, achenes.

Much planted as an ornamental; propagated by seeds and cuttings.

kerrioides: *R. scandens.*

scandens (Thunb.) Mak. [*R. kerrioides* Siebold & Zucc.; *R. tetrapetala* (Siebold) Mak.]. Commonly 3–6 ft. in cult., to 15 ft. in the wild, twigs greenish-brown; lvs. ovate, slender-pointed, 1½–3 in. long, glabrous, doubly serrate; fls. solitary, to 2 in. across; achenes shining black, about as large as small peas. Japan, China. Zone 5.

tetrapetala: *R. scandens.*

RHOEO Hance. *Commelinaceae.* One spp., a succulent, per. herb, native to W. Indies, Mex., and Guatemala; sts. erect; infls. axillary, short-peduncled, rarely branched, of dense paired cincinni, each pair nearly concealed by a boat-shaped envelope of 2 bracts; fls. white, sepals 3, hyaline, petals 3, separate, stamens 6, filaments bearded, ovary 3-celled, each cell with 3 ovules; fr. a caps., seeds usually 2, roughened.

discolor: *R. spathacea.*

spathacea (Swartz) Stearn [*R. discolor* (L'Hér.) Hance; *Tradescantia bicolor* Hort., not Kunth; *T. discolor* L'Hér.]. PURPLE-LEAVED SPIDERWORT, OYSTER PLANT, BOAT LILY, MOSES-ON-A-RAFT, MOSES-IN-A-BOAT, MOSES-IN-THE-CRADLE, MOSES-IN-THE-BULRUSHES, MAN-IN-A-BOAT, TWO-MEN-IN-A-BOAT, THREE-MEN-IN-A-BOAT. Sts. to 8 in. long; lvs. crowded, to 1 ft. long, 3 in. wide, dark green above, purple beneath. Attractive foliage plant. Cv. **'Concolor'.** Lvs. uniformly green. Cv. **'Variegata'** [cv. 'Vittata']. Lvs. striped lengthwise with pale yellow above.

RHOICISSUS Planch. AFRICAN GRAPE. *Vitaceae.* Ten spp. of tender, evergreen, tendril-bearing vines or shrubs with simple or palmately compound lvs., native to trop. and S. Afr.; differs from *Cissus* in having fls. 5-merous and from *Vitis* in having disc adnate to ovary.

capensis (Burm.f.) Planch. [*Cissus capensis* (Burm.f.) Willd.; *Vitis capensis* Burm.f.]. CAPE GRAPE, EVERGREEN G. Roots producing globose tubers; lvs. simple to 8 in. across, orbicular to reniform, coarsely crenate, rusty-tomentose beneath; fr. in axillary clusters, an edible, glossy reddish-purple berry, to ¾ in. in diam. S. Afr. Zone 10.

rhomboidea (E. H. Mey.) Planch. Tendrils not forked; lvs. trifoliolate, lateral lfts. very asymmetrical, terminal lft. rhombic. Not in cult.; material offered under this name is *Cissus rhombifolia.*

RHOMBOPHYLLUM (Schwant.) Schwant. *Aizoaceae.* Three spp. of shrubby or tufted succulents, native to S. Afr., roots fleshy; lvs. 4-ranked, densely crowded, semicylindrical, slightly joined at base, keeled toward apex, surface more or less glossy, smooth, green with whitish dots, margin entire or with 1 or 2 short teeth; fls. 3–7 in a group, calyx 5-lobed, petals golden-yellow, many, stamens many, erect, ovary inferior, 5-celled, stigmas 5; fr. a caps., placental tubercles flattish, divided into 2 toward outer side, usually close to the wall.

Growth occurs from late spring to late autumn. In summer, place plants in a sunny, airy greenhouse or window with careful watering; in winter, plants should be in a light place at a relatively cool temperature of about 55° F. and with moderate moisture. Propagation easy by seeds or cuttings. See also *Succulents.*

dolabriforme (L.) Schwant. [*Hereroa dolabriformis* (L.) L. Bolus]. Shrubby when old, to 1 ft. high, much-branched, brs. erect, gray, ¼ in. thick; lvs. spreading, curved, green with translucent dots, to 1¼ in. long, upper side flat, tapered, lower side rounded basally, keeled toward apex, keel wedge-shaped near tip, to ⅝ in. wide in side view, and with a toothlike projecting tip; fls. to 1½ in. across, petals golden-yellow. Cape Prov.

Nelii Schwant. ELKHORNS. Like *R. dolabriforme,* but roots woody, fibrous, st. short, brs. 2–4 without visible internodes; lvs. united at base, pale bluish gray-green covered with dark dots, smaller, keel not wedge-shaped but tip 2-lobed; fls. solitary or several, petals yellow. Cape Prov.

rhomboideum (Salm-Dyck) Schwant. Stemless, forming tufts; lvs. 8–10, slightly unequal, dark gray-green with whitish dots, to 2 in. long, ¾ in. wide, rhombic, upper side flatly grooved, lower side rounded basally, keeled toward tip and laterally compressed, edges whitish, sometimes with 1–2 small teeth; fls. to 1¼ in. across, on pedicels 1¼ in. long, petals golden-yellow, reddish outside. Cape Prov.

RHOPALOBLASTE Scheff. [*Ptychoraphis* Becc.]. *Palmae.* Six or 7 spp. of solitary or cespitose, unarmed, monoecious palms of the wet tropics from the Nicobar Is. and Malay Pen. to New Guinea and the Solomon Is.; lvs. pinnate, sheaths forming a tubular crownshaft, pinnae regularly arranged, with prominent midrib above, acute to acuminate, spreading or often more or less pendulous from the rachis; infl. below lvs., bracts 2, usually deciduous, the upper enclosed by the lower, peduncle short, rachis short to prominent, with lower brs. simple or forked to 1–2 times branched, upper brs. less branched or simple, rachillae with fls. in triads (2 male and 1 female); male fls. symmetrical, sepals 3, broadly rounded, imbricate, petals 3, valvate, stamens 6 or perhaps sometimes 9, filaments inflexed at the apex in bud, pistillode large, club-shaped to ovoid-conic and obsoletely 3-lobed, about as long as filaments, female fls. surrounded by 2 prominent bracteoles, sepals 3, imbricate, rounded, petals 3, imbricate with briefly valvate apices, staminodes 3–6, pistil 1-celled, 1-ovuled; fr. with terminal stigmatic residue, seed with deeply ruminate endosperm and large basal embryo.

Sometimes grown in the tropics as ornamentals, attractive for their often pendent leaflets. For culture see *Palms.*

augusta (Kurz) H. E. Moore [*Ptychoraphis augusta* (Kurz) Becc.]. St. solitary, to 100 ft. or more, 10 in. in diam. at base; lvs. short-petioled, to 10 ft. long, pinnae about 90–100 on each side, drooping, to 30 in. long, 1½ in. wide, rachis minutely puberulous or glabrous above, densely scaly below; infl. large, lower brs. 1–2 times branched into glabrous rachillae to ⅛ in. in diam.; triads with prominent liplike bract and liplike upper margin; male fls. greenish, ³⁄₁₆–¼ in. long, stamens and pistillode yellow; fr. ellipsoid, red, to 1 in. long, ½ in. in diam., with cupular perianth about ¼ in. high. Nicobar Is.

ceramica (Miq.) Burret [*R. hexandra* Scheff.]. St. solitary, to 50 ft. or more; lvs. short-petioled, to 10 ft. long, pinnae 80–90 on each side, drooping, to 3 ft. long, 1¼ in. wide, rachis with many curly brown scales on protected places above; infl. large, lower brs. twice-branched into thick, glabrous rachillae to ¼ in. in diam., triads with low bract and no evident upper margin; male fls. ³⁄₁₆ in. long, green with yellow stamens and orange stamens; fr. about 1¼ in. long, ¾ in. in diam., scarlet. Batjan Is., Ceram (Indonesia).

hexandra: *R. ceramica.*

singaporensis (Becc.) Hook.f. [*Ptychoraphis singaporensis* (Becc.) Becc.]. Sts. usually cespitose, slender, to 8 ft., gray-brown; lvs. long-petioled, pinnae about 40–50 on each side, spreading, to 1 ft. long, ½ in. wide; infl. small, curved downward, with few simple or forked, densely hairy rachillae; male fls. yellowish, ⅛ in. long; fr. orange-yellow, ovoid, ½ in. long, ⅜ in. in diam. Malay Pen., Singapore.

RHOPALOSTYLIS H. Wendl. & Drude. NIKAU PALM. *Palmae.* Three spp. of solitary, unarmed, monoecious palms in New Zeal., Norfolk Is., and Raoul (Sunday) Is.; lvs. pinnate, sheaths forming a short, basally inflated crownshaft, pinnae acute to acuminate, regularly arranged, midrib prominent above; infl. below lvs., bracts 2, deciduous, upper enclosed within lower, peduncle short, rachis with several brs., the lower once-branched into rachillae with fls. in triads (2 male and 1 female); male fls. asymmetrical, sepals 3, narrow, acute, scarcely imbricate, petals 3, valvate, stamens 6, filaments erect in bud, pistillode slender, cylindrical, equalling stamens, female fls. symmetrical, sepals 3, imbricate, acutish, petals 3, imbricate with prominent valvate apices, pistil 1-celled, 1-ovuled; fr. red, with apical stigmatic residue, seed with homogeneous endosperm, embryo basal.

For culture see *Palms.*

Baueri H. Wendl. & Drude. Similar to *R. sapida,* but differing in taller habit; infl. larger, to 3 ft. long; fr. subglobose to ellipsoid, to about ⅝ in. long, ½ in. in diam., seed globose, dull brown. Norfolk Is. Warmest parts of Zone 9b.

Cheesemanii Becc. To 20 ft. or sometimes to 40 ft.; lvs. to about 11 ft. long, sheath about 2½ ft. long, pinnae to 3½ ft. long, 2 in. wide;

infl. to 2 ft. long, male fls. about ¼ in. long; fr. subglobose, ⅝ in. long, ½ in. wide, seed globose, light brown. Raoul Is.

sapida H. Wendl. & Drude [*Areca sapida* Soland. ex Hook.f.]. NIKAU PALM, FEATHER-DUSTER P. To 25 ft., trunk 9 in. in diam., strongly and closely ringed; lvs. ascending, to 8 ft. long, pinnae to 3 ft. long, 2 in. wide; infl. to 2 ft. long; fr. ellipsoid, to ⁹⁄₁₆ in. long, ⁵⁄₁₆ in. diam., seed ellipsoid with tightly adherent fibers. New Zeal. Grown in mild climates, Zone 10a in Calif., not well adapted to Fla.

RHUBARB. *Rheum Rhabarbarum* or rhubarb is a strong, hardy, Old World perennial grown for the thick leaf stalks, which are cooked fresh in early spring for their agreeable acid flavor. It is known also as pie plant (see *Rheum*).

Rhubarb thrives on any good garden soil but is a cool-weather species, which does not thrive where the mean summer temperature is much above 75° F or where the mean winter temperature is above 40° F. As large leaf stalks in abundance are wanted, the land should be rich and kept moist. Select cultivars such as 'MacDonald', 'Ruby', and 'Valentine', having more colorful petioles (strawberry rhubarb), yield more attractive pies and sauces and so should be favored in home plantings over the old, vigorous, green-stalked 'Victoria'.

The plant is usually propagated by division of the fleshy roots, small pieces of which will grow if separated from the old established roots and planted in rich, mellow soil, every piece having a good eye. Planting is usually in spring; roots are planted 2–3 feet apart in rows 4–6 feet apart and covered 3–4 inches deep. It is wise to plant rhubarb where it does not interfere with the annual preparation of the rest of the garden. Because of the ornamental character of its leaves, it is sometimes planted with other perennials in the ornamental border. Clean tillage should be maintained throughout the season. If given good care and heavily fertilized annually with manure or 5–10–5 fertilizer, the plants will yield abundantly for many years. The stalks should not be harvested until the second year. Flowering stems should be removed as quickly as they form, for failure to do so means fewer and less succulent edible stalks. In harvesting, the stalks are pulled (not cut) and the expanded portion of the leaf is cut off. The leaf blades contain toxic quantities of oxalic acid and *should never be eaten.*

Rhubarb may be forced for winter and very early spring, either by placing a temporary glass structure over rows in the field or by digging the roots in autumn and growing them in the cellar or under a greenhouse bench. For the latter kind of forcing, strong roots are employed, allowed to freeze after digging, then planted with earth underneath them and over them in a room or space with diffused light and a temperature of 50° to 75° F. After forcing, the roots are usually discarded. Rhubarb for year-round home use can be had simply by freezing the fresh pulled and chopped stalks when available in spring.

RHUS L. [*Malosma* Nutt. ex Abrams; *Schmaltzia* Desv. ex Small; *Toxicodendron* Mill.]. SUMAC. Anacardiaceae. About 150 spp. of erect, usually dioecious shrubs, trees, or vines supported by clinging roots, native to temp. and subtrop. regions, with milky or resinous juice; lvs. simple, with 3 lfts., or pinnately compound; fls. small, usually unisexual, usually in panicles, stamens 5, ovary 1-celled, styles 3, terminal; fr. small, 1-seeded, drupaceous. *Toxicodendron* has recently been revived for 6 spp. of poison ivies and poison oaks. The following, here included in *Rhus,* are perhaps better considered as spp. of *Toxicodendron: R. diversiloba* [= *T. diversilobum* (Torr. & A. Gray) Greene]; *R. radicans* [= *T. radicans* (L.) O. Kuntze]; *R. Toxicodendron* [= *T. toxicaria* (Salisb.) Gillis].

Grown as ornamentals. The dried leaves of some species yield tannin, while other species produce lacquers; some are poisonous causing dermatitis on contact. Cultivation is simple in any garden soil. Propagated by seeds and root cuttings, some species by layers and by cuttings of mature wood. Planted mostly in shrub borders, some for the effect of the pinnate foliage, the bright red, orange, or yellow autumn color, or the often colorful fruit.

ambigua: see *R. orientalis.*

aromatica Ait. [*R. canadensis* Marsh., not Mill.]. FRAGRANT S., LEMON S., SWEET-SCENTED S., POLECAT BUSH. Shrub, to 8 ft.; lvs. aromatic, compound, lfts. 3, ovate, to 3 in. long, coarsely toothed; fls. yellowish, in clustered spikes, appearing before the lvs.; fr. red, hairy. Early summer. Ont. to Minn., s. to Fla. and Tex. Cv. 'Laciniata'. Lvs. more narrowly and deeply lobed. Var. **serotina** (Greene) Rehd. An upright shrub, to 6 ft.; lfts. sparsely pilose to glabrate beneath, terminal lft. flabelliform-obovate, obtuse; fls. appearing with the lvs. Ind. to Tex.

canadensis: see *R. aromatica.*

chinensis Mill. [*R. javanica* of auth., not L.]. NUTGALL TREE. Shrub or tree, to 25 ft.; lvs. compound, lfts. 7–13, ovate to 5 in. long, commonly toothed, brownish-pubescent beneath, rachis and often the petiole winged; fls. creamy-white, in large terminal panicles; fr. red, hairy. Late summer. Temp. e. Asia. Zone 8.

cismontana: *R. glabra* var.

copallina L. DWARF S., SHINING S., MOUNTAIN S., WING-RIB S. Shrub or tree, to 20 ft.; lvs. compound, lfts. 9–21, to 4 in. long, oblong-lanceolate, usually entire, rachis winged between the lfts.; fls. greenish, in dense terminal panicles; fr. red, hairy. Late summer. E. U.S. A source of tannin.

coriaria L. SICILIAN S., TANNER'S S., ELM-LEAVED S. Shrub, to 20 ft.; lvs. compound, lfts., 9–15, elliptic to oblong, to 2 in. long, toothed, pubescent beneath, petiole winged; fls. greenish, in loose terminal panicles; fr. brownish-purple, hairy. Summer. Medit. region. Cult. as a source of tannin in s. Italy.

cotinoides: *Cotinus obovatus.*

Cotinus: *Cotinus Coggygria;* see also *C. obovatus.*

diversiloba Torr. & A. Gray. POISON OAK. Shrub, to 8 ft., or sometimes climbing, poisonous to touch; lvs. compound, lfts. 3, to 3 in. long, variously toothed or lobed, glabrate on both surfaces; fls. greenish, in axillary panicles; fr. whitish. B.C. to Baja Calif.

glabra L. SMOOTH S., SCARLET S., VINEGAR TREE. Glabrous shrub or tree, to 20 ft., often glaucous; lvs. compound, lfts. 11–31, oblong-lanceolate, to 5 in. long, toothed; fls. green, in dense panicles; fr. scarlet, hairy. Summer. Temp. e. N. Amer. Cv. 'Laciniata'. Lfts. deeply cut. Var. **cismontana** (Greene) Cockerell [*R. cismontana* Greene]. Differs chiefly in having lfts. fewer, smaller, narrower, and the infl. smaller, pyramidal. S. Dak. and Wyo., s. to Mo. and Ariz. Cv. 'Flavescens'. Foliage yellow in autumn.

hirta: *R. typhina.*

hypoleuca Champ. ex Benth. Shrub; lvs. compound, lfts. 11–17, ovate-lanceolate, acute, inequilateral basally, veins tomentose; fls. in pyramidal panicles. China.

integrifolia (Nutt.) Benth. & Hook.f. ex S. Wats. LEMONADE BERRY, SOURBERRY, LEMONADE S. Evergreen shrub or tree, to 30 ft.; lvs. simple, elliptic, to 2 in. long, entire or toothed; fls. white or pinkish, in pubescent panicles; fr. dark red, hairy. Spring. S. Calif., Baja Calif.

javanica: *Brucea javanica,* but the name *R. javanica* has been widely used, but erroneously for *R. chinensis.*

lancea L.f. Small tree, to 25 ft.; lvs. compound, lfts. 3, linear-lanceolate, to 5 in. long, mucronulate; fls. greenish-yellow, in panicles shorter than lvs. Early spring. S. Afr.

laurina Nutt. [*Malosma laurina* (Nutt.) Nutt. ex Abrams. LAUREL S. Shrub 10–20 ft.; lvs. simple, ovate-elliptic or oblong, 1½–4 in. long, mucronulate, reddish above, long-petioled, aromatic; fls. greenish-white, in dense panicles 2–4 in. long; fr. whitish. Early summer. S. Calif., Baja Calif.

microphylla Engelm. DESERT S., SCRUB S., SMALL-LEAVED S., CORREOSA. Shrub, to 7 ft., rarely treelike to 16 ft., brs. glabrous to warty or puberulent; lvs. compound, lfts. 5–9, ovate to lanceolate-ovate, appressed-pilose and dull; fls. white, in heads or spikes; fr. globose, to ¼ in. in diam. orange-red, hispidulous. Sw. U.S. and adjacent Mex.

orientalis (Greene) C. K. Schneid. [*R. ambigua* Lavall. ex Dipp., not Unger]. Shrub, poisonous to touch, brs. stout, angular; lvs. compound, lfts. 3, ovate, to 5 in. long, acute, cuspidate, entire; fls. greenish, large, in short divaricately branched panicles. Japan, Kurile Is., Sakhalin. The Japanese counterpart of the N. Amer. *R. radicans.*

ovata S. Wats. SUGARBUSH, SUGAR S. Evergreen shrub, to 10 ft., rarely to 15 ft.; lvs. simple, ovate, to 3 in. long, usually entire; fls. light yellow, in short dense spikes; fr. dark red, hairy. Spring. Ariz., s. Calif., n. Baja Calif.

radicans L. POISON IVY, POISON OAK, MERCURY, MARKRY, COW-ITCH. Trailing or climbing vine, shrub, or rarely a tree, poisonous to touch; lvs. compound, lfts. 3, to 10 in. long, entire, toothed, or lobed, acute to acuminate, glossy or dull above, glabrous to velvety-hairy beneath; fls. greenish-white; fr. in axillary clusters, berrylike, whitish, waxy, persisting into the winter. Early summer. Temp. N. Amer. from Canada to Guatemala. Often weedy in shaded gardens.

succedanea L. [*Toxicodendron succedaneum* (L.) O. Kuntze]. WAX TREE. Shrub or tree, to 30 ft.; lvs. compound, lfts. 9–15, oblong, to 4 in. long, glossy above, colorful in autumn; fls. yellow-green, in panicles; fr. whitish. E. Asia from s. Japan to India. Zone 8. In Japan cult. for the berries, source of a commercial wax, and exudates from the sts. which yield a natural lacquer.

sylvestris Siebold & Zucc. Tree, to 30 ft.; lvs. compound, lfts. 7–13, ovate, to 4 in. long; fls. brownish-pubescent, in panicles; fr. brownish-yellow, glabrous. Temp. e. Asia. Zone 8.

terebinthifolia Schlechtend. & Cham. TEMAZCAL. Evergreen shrub, to 7 ft.; lvs. compound, lfts. 3–15, oblong to ovate, to 2½ in. long; fls. small, in axillary or terminal panicles; fr. red or orange, hairy. Mex. and Guatemala.

Toxicodendron L. POISON IVY, POISON OAK, HIEDRA. Shrub, to 6½ ft., poisonous to touch; lvs. compound, lfts. 3, velvety-tomentose beneath, pilose above, variously lobed, rounded or blunt; fls. greenish, in panicles; fr. whitish, usually pubescent. Summer. E. N. Amer. Sometimes confused with *R. radicans.*

trichocarpa Miq. Tree, to 25 ft. or more, branchlets hairy when young; lfts. 13–17, ovate to oblong, with terminal lfts. to 4 in. long, acuminate, rounded basally, entire, pubescent beneath on veins, orange to scarlet in autumn; fls. in axillary panicles to 6 in. long; fr. whitish. Temp. e. Asia. Zone 8. A bonsai subject in Japan.

trilobata Nutt. [*Schmaltzia trilobata* (Nutt.) Small]. SKUNKBUSH. Ill-smelling shrub, to 6 ft.; lvs. compound, lfts. ovate, to 1 in. long, usually coarsely toothed; fls. greenish, in clustered spikes, appearing before the lvs.; fr. red, hairy. Spring. Ill. to Calif. Once used by Indians for food, smoking, and for making baskets. Var. **malacophylla** (Greene) Munz. SQUAWBUSH. Diffusely branched shrub, to 4 ft., brs. pubescent, strongly scented when broken; lfts. cuneate-obovate, terminal lft. to 1½ in. long; fls. yellow, in clustered spikes. Calif.

typhina L. [*R. hirta* (L.) Sudw.]. STAGHORN S., VELVET S., VIRGINIAN S. Shrub or tree, to 30 ft., twigs densely pubescent; lvs. compound, lfts. 11–31, oblong-lanceolate, toothed, to 5 in. long, colorful in autumn; fls. greenish, in dense, terminal panicles; fr. crimson, hairy. Summer. Temp. e. N. Amer. Important source of tannin. Easily distinguished from *R. glabra* by the dense pubescence of the sts. and petioles. Cv. 'Dissecta'. Lfts. pinnately dissected. Cv. 'Laciniata'. Densely pubescent; lfts. and bracts laciniately toothed.

verniciflua J. Stokes. VARNISH TREE, LACQUER TREE, JAPANESE L.T. Tree, to 60 ft., poisonous to touch; lvs. compound, lfts. 11–15, ovate-oblong, to 8 in. long, entire; fls. whitish, in loose axillary panicles; fr. yellowish, glabrous. Summer. Temp. e. Asia. Cult. in sw. Japan, where the principal source of lacquer. Zone 9.

Vernix L. POISON S., SWAMP S., POISON ELDER, POISON DOGWOOD. Shrub or small tree, to 20 ft., poisonous to touch; lvs. compound, lfts. 7–13, entire, glabrous, petiole and rachis reddish; fls. greenish, axillary; fr. greenish-white, in pendent, axillary panicles to nearly 8 in. long, pedicels persisting through the winter. Swamps, Me. to Minn., s. to Fla. and La. Foliage brilliant in autumn. Can be distinguished from other native plants with which it may be confused by its alt., pinnately compound lvs., the lfts. with entire margins, and its swamp habitat. Rarely cult.

viminalis Ait. Tree, to 40 ft. or more; lvs. compound, lfts. 3, lanceolate, to 2½ in. long; fls. whitish-green, to ⅛ in. across, in terminal panicles. S. Afr.

virens Lindh. ex A. Gray. EVERGREEN S., TOBACCO S., LENTISCO. Shrub; lvs. compound, lfts. mostly 5–9, rhombic-ovate, to 1½ in. long, dark above, lighter and sparsely pilose beneath; fls. white, to 1½ in. long, in terminal panicles. Sw. U.S.

RHYNCHELYTRUM Nees. *Gramineae.* Perhaps 40 spp. of ann. or per. grasses in Afr.; panicles rather open; spikelets with 1 bisexual terminal floret above a sterile floret, on short capillary pedicels, glumes membranous, the first minute, villous, the second and the sterile lemma equal, swollen below, short-awned, silky-hairy, fertile lemma shorter than the spikelet, cartilaginous, smooth, boat-shaped, obtuse, margin thin, not inrolled, enclosing margins of the palea. For terminology see *Gramineae.*

repens (Willd.) C. E. Hubb. [*R. roseum* (Nees) Stapf & C. E. Hubb.; *Tricholaena rosea* Nees]. NATAL GRASS. Short-lived per. or behaving as ann., sts. to 3 ft., slender; lf. blades flat, to ¼ in. wide; panicle rosy-purple, fading to pink, silvery in age, to 6 in. long, brs. slender, ascending; spikelets about ¼ in. long, on flexuous or recurved capillary pedicels. S. Afr.; naturalized in Fla., Tex., and Ariz. Cult. as a meadow grass in sandy soil. Sometimes used as an ornamental.

roseum: *R. repens.*

RHYNCHOGLOSSUM Blume [*Klugia* Schlechtend.]. *Gesneriaceae.* About 17 spp. of ann. or per., succulent, weak herbs in trop. Amer. and Asia; lvs. alt., asymmetrical; fls. several to many in 1-sided racemes, calyx 5-lobed, tube angled or winged, corolla strongly 2-lipped, tube slender, more or less flattened top and bottom, upper lip short, shortly 3-lobed, lower lip larger, nearly entire, stamens 2 or 4, anthers all coherent or coherent in pairs, disc ringlike, prominent, ovary superior; fr. a thin caps.

For cultivation see *Gesneriaceae.*

Notonianum (Wallich) B. L. Burtt [*Klugia Notoniana* (Wallich) A. DC.]. To 1½ ft.; lvs. asymmetrically elliptic, to 8 in. long, 2⅜ in. wide, strongly nerved; fls. to 1 in. long, calyx to ⁵⁄₁₆ in. long, tube winged or angled basally, lobes triangular, corolla tube cylindrical, white, upper lip white, lower lip deep blue with yellow patches near 2-hooded depression in base, stamens 4. Ceylon and India.

RHYNCHOLAELIA: *BRASSAVOLA.*

RHYNCHOPHORUM: *PEPEROMIA.*

RHYNCHOSPERMUM Reinw. *Compositae.* Not in cult.; material grown under this name is either *Chonemorpha* or *Trachelospermum,* which are in the *Apocynaceae.* **R. asiaticum:** *Trachelospermum asiaticum;* **R. divaricatum:** *Trachelospermum asiaticum;* **R. fragrans:** *Chonemorpha fragrans;* **R. jasminoides:** *Trachelospermum jasminoides.*

RHYNCHOSTYLIS Blume. *Orchidaceae.* About 15 spp. of epiphytes, native to trop. Asia and Malay Arch.; sts. stout, leafy; lvs. leathery, linear-oblong, 2-lobed at apex; infl. a pendent, axillary, many-fld. raceme; fls. brightly colored, sepals and petals spreading, broad, petals narrower than sepals, lip united to column foot, hypochil forming a deep, pubescent sac, without lateral lobes, epichil obovate, concave, column short, dilated at base, with a short foot. For structure of fl. see *Orchidaceae.*

For culture see *Orchids.*

coelestis (Rchb.f.) Rchb.f. et Hort. Veitch [*Saccolabium coeleste* Rchb.f.]. Sts. erect, to 1 ft. or more; lvs. 2-ranked, to 6 in. long, deep green; racemes erect, to 9 in. long; fls. small, sepals and petals cuneate-oblong, white, tipped with sky-blue, lip blue, spur blunt, tinted blue, anther brown with flush of mauve. Summer. Thailand.

densiflora: *Anota densiflora.*

retusa Blume [*Saccolabium Blumei* Lindl.; *S. praemorsum* Lindl.]. Sts. stout, to 8 in. high; lvs. to 16 in. long, curved; racemes longer than lvs., densely many-fld.; fls. ¾ in. across, white or pink with purple or pink markings, sepals ovate to oblong, ½ in. long, petals blunt, widening from narrow base, lip very variable in shape, spur as long as lip, ¼ in. long, pale mauve. Early summer. Trop. Asia from India to Philippine Is. Cv. **'Alba'.** Fls. entirely white. Cv. **'Gigantea'.** More robust than typical form. Cv. **'Holfordiana'.** Fls. waxy, white, spotted with crimson, lip crimson.

violacea: *Anota violacea.*

RHYTICOCOS Becc. *Palmae.* One sp., a tall, slender, unarmed, monoecious coastal palm in the Lesser Antilles; lvs. pinnate, sheath fibrous, petiole not toothed along the margins, pinnae acute; infl. among lvs., long-peduncled, simply branched, bracts 2, the upper woody, deeply sulcate outside, enclosing infl. in bud, rachillae with fls. in a few triads (2 male and 1 female) near the base and above these with many paired male fls.; male fls. with sepals 3, small, petals 3, much wider than thick, acute, valvate, stamens 6, anthers straight, female fls. with sepals and petals imbricate, pistil 3-celled; fr. ovoid, 1-seeded, endocarp thick, with pores near the base, seed with ruminate endosperm.

For culture see *Palms.*

amara (Jacq.) Becc. OVERTOP PALM. To 60 ft. or more; lvs. to more than 10 ft. long, dark green, pinnae 30 or more on each side, to 3 ft. long, 1⅝ in. wide, more or less clustered and in 2 planes; fr. about 2 in. long, orange. Dominica, Guadeloupe, Martinique. Occasionally planted in the tropics of the New World; Zone 10b. Suitable for seaside plantings.

RIBES L. [*Grossularia* Mill.]. CURRANT, GOOSEBERRY. *Saxifragaceae.* About 150 spp. of low shrubs in temp. regions of N. Hemisphere, extending into S. Hemisphere in the Andes of S. Amer.; with or without prickles; lvs. alt., often clustered, usually deciduous, simple, mostly palmately veined and lobed; fls. small, in few- to many-fld. racemes or solitary, usually bisexual, or unisexual and the plants dioecious, 5-merous, ovary inferior, 1-celled, styles 2, separate or united; fr. a berry, glabrous or glandular or with prickles, crowned by calyx remnants. The genus comprises 2 rather distinct groups, the currants and the gooseberries; these are considered by some to be separate genera, *Ribes* and *Grossularia,* respectively. The currants mostly lack nodal spines and are usually otherwise unarmed; the fls. are mostly in racemes on pedicels jointed at summit; the fr. disarticulating at the joints. The gooseberries have nodal spines and are usually prickly; the fls. are solitary or few, the pedicels commonly not jointed at summit, and fr. not disarticulating. The gooseberries are indicated here by their synonyms in *Grossularia.*

Some species are grown for their edible fruit, as *R. uva-crispa, R. hirtellum, R. nigrum, R. odoratum,* and *R. sativum;* and others for their ornamental habit and flowers, as *R. aureum, R. odoratum, R. speciosum,* and *R. viburnifolium.* Propagated by cuttings and mound-layering as well as by seeds. See *Currant and Gooseberry.*

alpestre Decne. [*Grossularia alpestris* (Decne.) A. Berger]. HEDGE G. To 10 ft., with spines about 1 in. long; lvs. roundish, to 2 in. across, 3–5-lobed; fls. greenish or reddish, 1–2 together; fr. purple, glandular-bristly. Himalayas and w. China. Zone 6.

alpinum L. MOUNTAIN C., ALPINE C. To 8 ft., unarmed; plants dioecious, fls. greenish-yellow, in erect racemes; fr. scarlet, glabrous. Eur. Zone 2. Cvs. are: **'Aureum',** foliage yellowish; **'Laciniatum',** lvs. deeply cut; **'Pumilum',** dwarf, less than 3 ft. high, lvs. small. Zone 2.

americanum Mill. [*R. floridum* L'Hér.]. AMERICAN BLACK C., WILD BLACK C. To 5 ft., unarmed; lvs. resinous-dotted beneath; fls. yellowish-white, in many-fld., drooping racemes; fr. black, glabrous. Nov. Sc., s. to Va., w. to Colo. Zone 2.

aureum Pursh [*R. tenuiflorum* Lindl.]. GOLDEN C., BUFFALO C., MISSOURI C. To 6 ft., unarmed; fls. yellow, in 5–15-fld. racemes, with spicy odor, sepals as long as calyx tube; fr. black or purplish, glabrous. Wash. to Mont., s. to Calif. Zone 2. Var. **chrysococcum** Rydb. Fr. yellow. Var. **gracillimum** (Cov. & Britt.) Jeps. [*R. gracillimum* Cov. & Britt.]. Fls. odorless, becoming reddish; fr. yellow. Cent. and s. Calif. See *R. odoratum.*

bracteosum Dougl. ex Hook. STINK C., CALIFORNIAN BLACK C. To 10 ft., unarmed; lvs. resinous-glandular beneath; fls. greenish or purplish, in erect racemes to 10 in. long; fr. black, with whitish bloom. Alaska to Calif. Zone 7. The berry has a disagreeable taste.

californicum Hook. & Arn. [*Grossularia californica* (Hook. & Arn.) Cov. & Britt.]. To 4 ft., spiny; twigs and lvs. glabrous; fls. solitary, sepals greenish, with reddish tips, petals whitish, less than half as long as filaments. Cent. Calif. Zone 7? Var. **hesperium** (McClat.) Jeps. [*R. hesperium* McClat.; *Grossularia hesperia* (McClat.) Cov. & Britt.]. Twigs and lvs. pubescent; petals whitish, tinged with red, almost as long as filaments. S. Calif.

cereum Dougl. SQUAW C., WHITE-FLOWERED C. To 3 ft., unarmed, glandular-pubescent; fls. white or greenish, in few-fld., drooping racemes; fr. bright red. B.C. to Mont., s. to Calif. Zone 5.

curvatum Small [*Grossularia curvata* (Small) Cov. & Britt.]. To 3 ft., with spines to ¼ in. long; fls. white, 1–5 together; fr. greenish, glabrous. Ga. to La., w. to Tex. Zone 6.

cynosbati L. [*Grossularia cynosbati* (L.) Mill.]. DOGBERRY, DOG BRAMBLE, PRICKLY G. To 5 ft., with spines to ½ in. long or lacking; fls. green, 1–3 together; fr. wine-red, prickly. New Bruns. to N.C. and Ala. Zone 2. Forma **inerme** Rehd. Ovary and fr. not prickly.

diacanthum Pall. To 6 ft., with small prickles; plants dioecious, fls. greenish-yellow, in erect racemes; fr. scarlet, glabrous. N. Asia. Zone 2.

echinellum (Cov.) Rehd. [*Grossularia echinella* Cov.]. To 3 ft., with spines about ½ in. long; lvs. less than 1 in. long; fls. green or greenish-white, 1–2 together; fr. green, very prickly. Fla.

fasciculatum Siebold & Zucc. To 5 ft., unarmed; plants dioecious, fls. yellowish, fragrant, male fls. in 4–9-fld. umbels, female fls. in pairs; fr. scarlet, glabrous. Japan, Korea. Zone 5. Var. **chinense** Maxim. More vigorous; lvs. larger. N. China.

floridum: *R. americanum.*

glandulosum Grauer [*R. prostratum* L'Hér.]. FETID C., SKUNK C. Low, sts. prostrate; fls. white or pinkish, in 8–12-fld. racemes; fr. red, bristly. N. Amer. Zone 2. Lvs. turn red in fall. All parts of plant malodorous.

glutinosum: *R. sanguineum* var.

×**Gordonianum** Lem.: *R. odoratum* × *R. sanguineum.* Fls. yellow, tinged red outside. Zone 7.

gracillimum: *R. aureum* var.

Grossularia: *R. uva-crispa.*

hesperium: *R. californicum* var.

hirtellum Michx. [*Grossularia hirtella* (Michx.) Spach]. To 3 ft., brs. bristly; fls. greenish or purplish, 1–3 together; fr. purple or black, commonly glabrous. Nfld. to W.Va. and S.Dak. Zone 4. An important edible gooseberry, which has been used to produce hybrids.

hudsonianum Richardson. NORTHERN BLACK C. Erect, twigs and lower lf. surface resin-dotted; fls. white, tomentose; fr. black, glabrous, somewhat bitter. Canada. Zone 2.

indecorum Eastw. WHITE-FLOWERED C. To 7½ ft., young twigs densely pubescent and glandular; lvs. with stalked glands, rugose above, tomentose beneath; fls. white; fr. viscid-pubescent. S. Calif., n. Baja Calif. Zone 7? Related to *R. malvaceum,* but with fls. smaller, white.

inebrians Lindl. [*R. pumilum* Nutt.]. Branched, erect shrub, to 4 ft.; lvs. 3–5-lobed, glandular beneath; fls. pink, in few-fld. racemes; fr. red, often glandular. Mont. and S. Dak., s. to cent. Calif. and n. Mex. Zone 6.

inerme Rydb. [*Grossularia inermis* (Rydb.) Cov. & Britt.]. To 6 ft., usually with few, small spines; fls. green or purplish, 1–4 together; fr. purplish-red, glabrous. B.C. to New Mex. Zone 6.

japonicum Maxim. To 6 ft., unarmed; fls. greenish or brownish, in erect racemes; fr. black, glabrous. Japan. Zone 6.

lacustre (Pers.) Poir. BRISTLY BLACK C., SWAMP G. To 3 ft., with clustered spines and bristles; lvs. glabrous; fls. greenish or purplish, in 12–20-fld. drooping racemes; fr. purple, bristly. N. Amer. Zone 4.

lasianthum Greene [*R. leptanthum* var. *lasianthum* (Greene) Jeps.; *Grossularia lasiantha* (Greene) Cov. & Britt.]. To 3 ft., stiffly branched, with spines ½ in. long; fls. yellow, 2–4 together; fr. crimson, glabrous. Mts., Calif.

lentum: *R. montigenum.*

leptanthum A. Gray [*Grossularia leptantha* (A. Gray) Cov. & Britt.]. To 6 ft., with spines to ½ in. long; fls. greenish-white, 1–2 together; fr. black, glossy. Colo. to New Mex. Zone 6. Var. **lasianthum:** *R. lasianthum.*

Lobbii A. Gray [*Grossularia Lobbii* (A. Gray) Cov. & Britt.]. GUMMY G. To 6 ft., with spines to ¾ in. long; fls. purple-red, 1–2 together; fr. purple, densely glandular. B.C. to Calif. Zone 7.

malvaceum Sm. CHAPARRAL C. To 6 ft., unarmed; lvs. glandular, gray-pubescent beneath; fls. pink or purple, in drooping racemes; fr. purple-black, sticky-pubescent. Calif. Zone 7. Var. **viridifolium** Abrams. Lvs. scabrous with a coarse pubescence and greenish beneath; fls. larger. Mts., s. Calif.

Menziesii Pursh [*Grossularia Menziesii* (Pursh) Cov. & Britt.]. CANYON G. To 6 ft., young twigs bristly at internodes, nodal spines usually 3; lvs. nearly glabrous to roughish with glandular hairs above, velvety-pubescent with gland-tipped hairs beneath; calyx tube purplish, petals white; fr. glandular-bristly. S. Ore., n. and cent. Calif. Zone 7. The purple and white fls. are attractive.

missouriense Nutt. [*Grossularia missouriensis* (Nutt.) Cov. & Britt.]. MISSOURI G. To 6 ft., more or less bristly, and with spines ¾ in. long or less; fls. greenish-white, 2–3 on a slender peduncle; fr. purplish, glabrous. Tenn., w. to Minn., S.Dak., Kans. Zone 5.

montigenum McClat. [*R. lentum* Cov. & Rose]. To 2 ft., straggling, twigs mostly bristly-prickly, glandular-pubescent, nodal spines 3–5; lvs. 5-cleft almost to base, glandular-pubescent on both surfaces; fls. purplish, in few-fld. racemes; fr. red, glandular-bristly. B.C. to Calif., e. to Rocky Mts. Zone 6. Related to *R. lacustre,* but lvs. glandular-pubescent and fr. red.

nevadense Kellogg. SIERRA C. Unarmed; fls. rose, in 12–20-fld. racemes; fr. blue, glaucous. Ore., Calif., Nev. Zone 7.

nigrum L. BLACK C., EUROPEAN B. C. To 6 ft., unarmed; fls. greenish-white, in 4–10-fld. drooping racemes; fr. black, glabrous. Eur., Asia. Zone 5. Cvs. include: **'Chlorocarpum'**, fr. green; **'Heterophyllum'** [cv. 'Laciniatum'], lvs. deeply cut; **'Reticulatum'**, lvs. mottled with yellow; **'Xanthocarpum'**, fr. yellow or white. The black currants of fr. gardens are of this sp.

niveum Lindl. [*Grossularia nivea* (Lindl.) Spach]. To 10 ft., with spines to ¾ in. long; fls. white, 1–4 together; fr. bluish-black, glabrous. E. Wash. and Ore., e. to Idaho and n. Nev. Zone 6.

odoratum H. Wendl. BUFFALO C., MISSOURI C. To 6 ft., unarmed; fls. yellow, fragrant, in 5–10-fld. racemes; fr. black, glabrous. S. Dak. and Minn., s. to Tex. and Ark. Zone 5. Often cult. for its large, fragrant, yellow fls. Sometimes confused with the related *R. aureum,* but differing in fls. larger, and sepals less than half as long as calyx tube. Cv. **'Crandall'**. Fr. large, edible, the form usually grown.

orientale Desf. [*Ribes resinosum* Pursh ex Sims]. To 6 ft., unarmed; plants dioecious, fls. green, tinged with red, in short racemes; fr. scarlet, pubescent. Eur., Asia. Zone 6.

oxycanthoides L. [*Grossularia oxycanthoides* (L.) Mill.]. HAWTHORN-LEAVED G. Low, bristly, with spines ½ in. long or less; lvs. usually broader than long, rather deeply 5-lobed, slightly pubescent to nearly glabrous; fls. greenish-white, 1–2 together; fr. red, glabrous. B.C. to Nfld., s. to Mich. and N.Dak. Zone 2.

petraeum Wulfen. To 6 ft., unarmed; fls. red or pink, in racemes to 4 in. long; fr. dark red. Mts., Eur. Zone 6. A variable sp., with many botanical vars.

pinetorum Greene [*Grossularia pinetorum* (Greene) Cov.]. To 6 ft., with spines 1 in. long or less; fls. orange-red, 1–2 together; fr. purple, prickly. Ariz., New Mex. Zone 6.

prostratum: *R. glandulosum.*

pumilum: *R. inebrians.*

reclinatum: *R. uva-crispa.*

resinosum: *R. orientale.*

×**robustum** Jancz. [*Grossularia* ×*robusta* (Jancz.) A. Berger]: *R. niveum* × (probably) *R. inerme.* With small spines; fls. white or pinkish; fr. black, glabrous, acidulous, edible.

Roezlii Regel [*Grossularia Roezlii* (Regel) Cov. & Britt.]. SIERRA G. To 6 ft., brs. spreading, tortuous, with spines usually in 3's and to ½ in. long; lvs. orbicular, to 1 in. across, 3–5-lobed, incised-crenate, more densely hairy beneath than above; fls. with white petals; fr. dark red to purplish, about ½ in. in diam., hairy and prickly. Calif. Zone 7.

rotundifolium Michx. [*Grossularia rotundifolia* (Michx.) Cov. & Britt.]. To 3 ft., with few, small spines; fls. greenish-purple, 1–3 together; fr. purplish, glabrous. Mass. to N.C. Zone 6.

rubrum L. RED C., NORTHERN R. C. To 6 ft., unarmed; fls. greenish-brown, in racemes; fr. red. Eur., Asia. Zone 4. Cult. in Eur., but rarely in Amer.

sanguineum Pursh. To 12 ft., unarmed; lvs. tomentose beneath; fls. red, in erect or ascending, many-fld. racemes; fr. bluish-black, bloomy. B.C. to n. Calif. Zone 6. An attractive ornamental shrub. Cvs. are **'Atrorubens'** and **'Splendens'**, both with fls. dark red. Var. **glutinosum** (Benth.) Loud. [*R. glutinosum* Benth.]. Lvs. not tomentose beneath; fls. rose, in drooping racemes.

sativum (Rchb.) Syme [*R. vulgare* C. K. Schneid.]. COMMON C., GARDEN C., RED C. To 5 ft., unarmed; fls. green or purplish, in many-fld., drooping racemes; fr. red or white, juicy. W. Eur. Zone 5. Frequently cult. and sometimes escaping. This sp. is the parent of the more commonly cult. red currants. Cv. **'Macrocarpum'**. CHERRY C. Fr. large, red. Cv. **'Variegatum'**. Lvs. variegated.

setosum Lindl. [*Grossularia setosa* (Lindl.) Cov. & Britt.]. MISSOURI G. To 3 ft., bristly, with spines to about 1 in. long; fls. white, 1–3 together; fr. red or black, glabrous or slightly bristly. Mich. and Minn. to Sask., s. to Nebr. and Wyo. Zone 2.

speciosum Pursh [*Grossularia speciosa* (Pursh) Cov. & Britt.]. FUCHSIA-FLOWERED G. Evergreen, to 12 ft., bristly and spiny; fls. bright red, 2–4 together, drooping, stamens long-exserted; fr. red, glandular-bristly. Calif. Zone 7?

stenocarpum Maxim. [*Grossularia stenocarpa* (Maxim.) A. Berger]. To 6 ft., spiny; fls. reddish, 1–3 together; fr. greenish or reddish, mostly glabrous. China. Zone 6.

tenue Jancz. To 8 ft., unarmed; plants dioecious, fls. brownish-red, in racemes; fr. red. W. Asia. Zone 6.

tenuiflorum: *R. aureum.*

triste Pall. SWAMP RED C. Sts. decumbent; fls. purple, in drooping racemes; fr. red, glabrous. N. N. Amer., n. Asia. Zone 2.

uva-crispa L. [*R. Grossularia* L.; *R. reclinatum* L.; *Grossularia reclinata* (L.) Mill.; *G. uva-crispa* (L.) Mill.]. ENGLISH G., EUROPEAN G. To 4 ft., with stout nodal spines to ½ in. long; fls. 1–3 together, greenish to pinkish-green; fr. red, yellow, or green, pubescent. Eur. Zone 5. Has given rise to the large-fruited cult. gooseberries. Escapes from cult. and becomes naturalized.

viburnifolium A. Gray. Evergreen, to 8 ft., unarmed, sts. straggling; fls. rose, small, inconspicuous, in erect racemes; fr. red. S. Calif., n. Baja

Calif. The sprawling evergreen brs., often rooting, make it adaptable for use as a ground cover. Said to have a turpentinelike odor.

vulgare: *R. sativum.*

RICCIA L. *Ricciaceae.* About 200 spp. of mostly terrestrial, rootless, stemless plants of nearly cosmopolitan distribution; thallus not leathery on upper surface, scales on lower surface small; antheridia scattered or in groups, superficial.

fluitans L. CRYSTALWORT. Plant much-branched, floating near surface, light green or blue-green, brs. of thallus about ¹⁄₁₆ in. wide, widening toward ends, tip of lobes grooved, scales on lower surface lunate, usually purplish, only at tip of brs.

RICCIACEAE Rchb. RICCIA FAMILY. Liverworts; 2 genera and about 201 spp. of aquatic or terrestrial liverworts of nearly cosmopolitan distribution; thallus with diverging forked brs., forming rosettes; archegonia scattered singly and superficially on the thallus or in irregular groups in the thallus. *Riccia* and *Ricciocarpos* are sometimes grown in aquaria. See *Mosses and Liverworts.*

RICCIOCARPOS Corda. *Ricciaceae.* One sp., an aquatic liverwort of cosmopolitan distribution; plants usually floating, thallus 1–3 times parted, upper surface leathery, lower surface with several rows of purplish serrate scales; fertile areas within the thallus but rarely formed.

natans (L.) Corda. Floating plants triangular or cordate, flat, to ⅜ in. wide, 2-lobed, bright green, upper surface with a narrow groove. Sometimes grown in aquaria.

RICHARDIA Kunth, not L.: *ZANTEDESCHIA.* **R. africana:** *Z. aethiopica.*

RICHARDIA L. [*Richardsonia* Kunth]. *Rubiaceae.* About 10 spp. of pubescent or hairy herbs, native to S. Amer., 1 sp. n. to U.S.; lvs. opp., entire; fls. white or pink, in terminal clusters subtended by an involucre, corolla funnelform, 3–5-lobed; fr. of 3–4 indehiscent, 1-seeded cells.

scabra L. [*Richardsonia scabra* (L.) St.-Hil.]. MEXICAN CLOVER. Ann., sts. erect or diffuse, to 4 ft. long; lvs. ovate to lanceolate, to 3 in. long, rough; fls. white, ¼ in. long. S.C. to S. Amer. Grown as a forage, green manure, and cover crop in s. U.S. Thrives on sandy soil; prop. by seeds.

RICHARDSONIA: *RICHARDIA.*

RICINUS L. *Euphorbiaceae.* One monoecious, very variable sp., with watery juice, probably originally from trop. Afr., but widely naturalized in the tropics and warm regions; lvs. alt., simple, palmately veined, peltate, long-petioled; fls. in panicles, male fls. below, female fls. toward the apex; fr. a caps.

Commonly planted for foliage effects; the seeds poisonous if eaten, yield an oil, which is extensively used medicinally and in the manufacture of soap, paints, and varnishes. Castor beans thrive in sandy or clay loams with good drainage, although they grow on any land that is not too wet. Seeds may be sown where the plants are to stand or sown in pots under glass and transplanted about the middle of May.

borboniensis: a listed name of no botanical standing for *R. communis* cv.

cambodgensis: *R. communis* cv.

communis L. CASTOR BEAN, CASTOR-OIL-PLANT, PALMA CHRISTI, WONDER TREE. Ann., to 15 ft., or in the tropics a tree 30–40 ft.; lvs. 5–11-lobed, to 3 ft. across; fls. without petals, stamens many, filaments much-branched, ovary 3-celled; fr. to 1 in. long, smooth or covered with soft, dark brown spines. The many cvs. include: 'Borboniensis', very large and rank, foliage green; 'Borboniensis Arboreus', tall, sts. red, lvs. glaucous; 'Cambodgensis' [*R. cambodgensis* Benary; cv. 'Black Beauty'], sts. black-purplish, foliage very dark; 'Carmineus'; cv. 'Scarlet Queen'; 'Gibsonii' [*R. Gibsonii* Hort.], small form, 4–5 ft., foliage dark red, with metallic luster; 'Gibsonii Mirabilis', compact dwarf plant, 4 ft., with very fine red foliage and sts.; 'Major', lvs. large, green; 'Red Spire', sts. showy, red, foliage bronze-green; 'Sanguineus' [*R. sanguineus* Hort. ex Groenl.], lvs. and sts. blood-red; 'Scarlet Queen' [cv. 'Carmineus'], foliage maroon, fls. orange-scarlet; 'Zanzibarensis' [*R. zanzibarensis* Hort. ex Garn.], lvs. bright green, with white veins; 'Zanzibarensis Enormis', foliage all green; 'Zanzibarensis Viridis', dwarf, to 10 ft., foliage green.

Gibsonii: a listed name of no botanical standing for *R. communis* cv.

sanguineus: *R. communis* cv.

zanzibarensis: *R. communis* cv.

RIMARIA: *GIBBAEUM.* **R. divergens:** *Vanheerdia divergens.* **R. Luckhoffii:** *Gibbaeum Heathii.* **R. Primosii:** *Vanheerdia Primosii.*

RIPOGONUM J. R. Forst. & G. Forst. *Liliaceae.* About 8 spp. of climbing shrubs, native to Australia and New Zeal.; sts. much-branched; lvs. mostly opp., some alt.; fls. small, white or greenish, in racemes or panicles, perianth segms. 6, separate, deciduous, stamens 6, filaments flattened; fr. a 1- to few-seeded berry. Sometimes, but not originally, spelled *Rhipogonum.*

scandens J. R. Forst. & G. Forst. Lvs. ovate-oblong to oblong-lanceolate, to 5 in. long, leathery; fls. greenish, ⁵⁄₁₆ in. across, in axillary racemes to 6 in. long; fr. bright red, ⁵⁄₁₆ in. across. New Zeal.

RITTEROCEREUS: *LEMAIREOCEREUS.* **R. Martinezii:** a listed name of no botanical standing for *L. Martinezii.*

RIVEA Choisy. *Convolvulaceae.* Not. cult. **R. corymobsa:** *Turbina corymbosa.*

RIVINA L. *Phytolaccaceae.* One sp., usually herbaceous; lvs. alt., entire; fls. small, bisexual, in many-fld. racemes, perianth lobes 4, persistent in fr., stamens 4, shorter than perianth, ovary 1-celled; fr. a berry.

Grown outside and in greenhouses for the ornamental fruits. Propagated by seeds or cuttings in the spring with bottom heat.

humilis L. ROUGE PLANT, BLOODBERRY, BABY PEPPER. To 4 ft., sometimes woody at base; lvs. ovate to oblong, thin, to 4 in. long, petioles slender; racemes slender, loose, to 8 in. long; fls. greenish to rosy; fr. bright red, ³⁄₁₆ in. in diam. S. U.S. and trop. Amer. Fr. yields a red dye.

ROBINIA L. LOCUST. *Leguminosae* (subfamily *Faboideae*). Perhaps 20 spp. of deciduous trees and shrubs, native to N. Amer.; lvs. odd-pinnate, usually with pairs of short, stipular spines; fls. in pendent racemes, showy, papilionaceous, white to pink or purple, keel petals united basally; fr. an elongate, flat legume.

Locusts are planted as ornamentals. They are mostly hardy in the North and thrive in any usual soil. Propagated by seeds sown in spring, by suckers, root cuttings, division, and the cultivars by grafting.

×ambigua Poir. [*R.* × *hybrida* Audib. ex DC.]: *R. Pseudoacacia* × *R. viscosa.* Tree, with small spines, branchlets slightly viscid; lfts. in 6–10 pairs; fls. light pink. Var. **bella-rosea** (Nichols.) Rehd. Branchlets very viscid; fls. larger, of deeper color. Cv. **'Decaisneana'** [*R. Decaisneana* Hort.; *R. Pseudoacacia* var. *Decaisneana* Carrière; *R. Pseudoacacia* forma *Decaisneana* (Carrière) Voss]. Fls. light rose-colored. Cv. **'Idahoensis'** [*R. Pseudoacacia* cv. 'Idahoensis']. Fls. pink to lavender.

Boyntonii Ashe. Unarmed shrub, to 10 ft., branchlets glabrous, or at first minutely pubescent; lfts. in 3–6 pairs, elliptic to oblong-obtuse; racemes rather loose, 8–10-fld., peduncles glabrous; fls. pink, or rose-purple and white; fr. glandular-hispid. N.C. and Tenn., s. to Ga. and Ala.

Decaisneana: a listed name of no botanical standing for *R.* × *ambigua* cv.

Elliottii (Chapm.) Ashe [*R. hispida* var. *rosea* Elliott ex Chapm.]. Shrub, to 5 ft., young branchlets tomentose, not hispid; lfts. in 5–7 pairs, elliptic, to 1 in. long, grayish-pubescent beneath; racemes 5–10-fld., peduncles pubescent; fls. rose-purple, or purple and white, to ⅞ in. long; fr. hispid. N.C. to Ga.

fertilis Ashe. Differs from *R. hispida* in having lfts. narrower, elliptic- to oblong-ovate, slightly pubescent beneath, fls. smaller, and frs. freely produced. N.C. to Ga.

globosa: a listed name of no botanical standing for plants resembling *R. Pseudoacacia* cv. 'Rehderi'.

hispida L. MOSS L., ROSE ACACIA, BRISTLY L., MOSSY L. Stoloniferous shrub, to 7 ft., herbage hispid; lfts. in 3–6 pairs, oblong to nearly orbicular, to 1⁵⁄₁₆ in. long, glabrous; fls. rose or pale purple, 1 in. long; fr. hispid, to 3 in. long. Late spring. Se. U.S. Var. **macrophylla** DC. Lfts. and fls. larger, branchlets and petioles nearly destitute of bristles. Var. **rosea:** *R. Elliottii;* but material offered as var. *rosea* is *R. Boyntonii.* Cv. **'Superba'** is listed.

×**Holdtii** Beissn.: *R. luxurians* × *R. Pseudoacacia.* Tree; lfts. to 2 in. long; fls. light pink or rose.

×**hybrida:** *R.* × *ambigua.*

Kelseyi Kelsey ex Hutch. ALLEGHANY MOSS L. Similar to *R. Boyntonii,* but with stipular spines, acute lfts., racemes 5–8-fld., slightly glandular-hairy, and fr. covered with purple glandular hairs. N.C.

leucantha Rehd. Differs from *R. nana* in having glabrous branchlets, and pure white fls. Ga.

luxurians (Dieck) C. K. Schneid. Shrub or tree, to 30 ft., branchlets glandular-pubescent when young; lfts. in 7–10 pairs, oblong, to 1⁵⁄₁₆ in. long; racemes dense; fls. pale rose or nearly white; fr. to 4 in. long, glandular-hairy. Summer. Colo. to Utah. and New Mex.

nana Elliott. Shrub, to 1 ft., usually unarmed, branchlets minutely pubescent; lfts. in 3–5 pairs, elliptic to elliptic-ovate, glabrous; peduncles glandular-hispid, racemes 3–5-fld.; sepals nearly caudate, petals pink; fr. glandular-hispid. S.C.

neomexicana A. Gray. Shrub, to 6 ft.; lfts. in 4–7 pairs, elliptic-lanceolate, to 1½ in. long; infl. pubescent and glandular-hispid; fls. rose; fr. nearly smooth, to 4 in. long. Summer. New Mex.

Pseudoacacia L. BLACK L., FALSE ACACIA, YELLOW L. Open tree, to 80 ft., nearly glabrous, brs. prickly; lfts. to 9 pairs, elliptic to ovate-obtuse, to 1¾ in. long; racemes dense, to 8 in. long; fls. white, fragrant, fr. to 4 in. long, reddish-brown, glabrous, remaining on tree over winter. E. and cent. U.S. Widely planted in temp. regions. Bee plant; wood very durable and with many uses. Var. **Decaisneana:** *R.* × *ambigua* cv. Var. **fastigiata:** cv. 'Pyramidalis'. Forma **Decaisneana:** *R.* × *ambigua* cv. Forma **erecta:** cv. 'Monophylla Fastigiata'. Cv. 'Bessoniana' [forma *Bessoniana* (Nichols.) Voss]. Similar to cv. 'Umbraculifera', but brs. more slender and forming a more open ovoid head. Cv. 'Frisia'. Branchlets orange, with bright red spines, and bright golden lvs. Cv. 'Idahoensis': *R.* × *ambigua* cv. Cv. 'Inermis' [var. *inermis* (Mirb.) DC.; forma *inermis* (Mirb.) Rehd.]. Branchlets unarmed. Cv. 'Monophylla Fastigiata' [forma *erecta* Rehd.]. Tree of columnar habit, with lvs. of 1 to few lfts. Cv. 'Pyramidalis' [var. *fastigiata* Lem.; var. *pyramidalis* Pépin]. Of columnar habit, with spineless branchlets. Cv. 'Rectissima' [var. *rectissima* Raber]. SHIP-MAST L. Trunks very straight and columnar, with narrow, more or less columnar crown; lateral brs. fewer than usual, with fewer racemes; rarely producing fr. Cv. 'Rehderi' [forma *Rehderi* (Otto) C. K. Schneid.]. Of low, globose form. Cv. 'Semperflorens' [forma *semperflorens* (Carrière) Voss] is listed. Cv. 'Spectabilis': cv. 'Inermis'. Cv. 'Tortuosa' [var. *tortuosa* DC.]. Brs. short, twisted, sometimes with tips pendent. Cv. 'Umbraculifera' [var. *umbraculifera* (DC.) DC.]. With dense, somewhat globose head and unarmed brs.; rarely flowering.

×**Slavinii** Rehd.: *R. Kelseyi* × *R. Pseudoacacia.* Shrub; racemes slightly villous, but not glandular; fls. rosy-pink; fr. finely roughened.

viscosa Venten. CLAMMY L. Tree, to 40 ft., young brs. and other parts glandular-viscid; lfts. in 6–12 pairs, ovate; racemes to 3 in. long; calyx dark red, petals pink, the standard yellow-spotted; fr. narrow, to 3½ in. long, glandular-hispid. Late spring. N.C. to Ala.

ROBINSONELLA Rose & Bak.f. *Malvaceae.* Thirteen spp. of shrubs and trees in Mex. and Cent. Amer.; lvs. simple, unlobed or palmately lobed; fls. in panicles or racemose to cymose clusters on short axillary branchlets, involucral bracts 0, petals 5, white to yellowish or lavender, sometimes lavender-veined, style brs. as many as the mericarps, stigmas capitate; fr. a schizocarp, mericarps 8–30, in a single whorl, membranous, inflated, each 1-seeded basally, seeds black.

cordata Rose & Bak.f. Tree, 15–40 ft., with pilose brs. and lvs.; lvs. 3–6 in. long, ovate, scarcely 3-lobed, acuminate, cordate to subtruncate at base; infl. racemose, on short axillary branchlets; calyx less than ½ in. long, petals white to lavender, up to 1 in. long; mericarps 9–12, about ½ in. long. Mex. and Guatemala.

edentula: *R. Lindeniana* subsp. *divergens.*

Lindeniana (Turcz.) Rose & Bak.f. Shrub or small tree, to 30 ft.; lower lvs. to about 9 in. long, deeply to shallowly 3- or 5-lobed, upper lvs. less deeply lobed or even unlobed; infl. leafy, paniculate; calyx about ¼ in. long, petals white, sometimes with lavender veins, to ½ in. long; mericarps 8–15, to about ⅜ in. long. Mex. to Costa Rica. Subsp. **divergens** (Rose & Bak.f.) Fryx. [*R. edentula* Rose & J. D. Sm.]. Differs from the typical var. in being generally treelike and having lvs. moderately 3-lobed or unlobed, infl. more congested, and mericarps 8–12. Mex. to Costa Rica.

ROCHEA DC. *Crassulaceae.* Three spp. of succulent, per. herbs or subshrubs, native to S. Afr.; lvs. opp., sessile, somewhat jointed at base, cartilaginous-ciliate; fls. 5-merous, white, yellow, or red, in showy, dense, terminal clusters, se-

pals separate, ciliate, corolla salverform, tubular at base, the long claws of the lobes scarcely coherent above, stamens 5. Differs from *Crassula* in having corolla tubular.

For culture see *Succulents.*

coccinea (L.) DC. [*Crassula coccinea* L.]. Erect, 1–2 ft.; lvs. obovate or oblong-ovate, 1–1½ in. long, glossy, green; fls. fragrant, corolla brilliant crimson, 1½–2 in. long. Summer.

falcata: *Crassula falcata.*

×**versicolor** (Burchell) DC. Similar to *R. coccinea,* but having lvs. oblong-lanceolate, fls. white or pink, about 1 in. long. Apparently a natural hybrid of *R. coccinea* × *R. subulata* (L.) Adamson.

ROCK GARDENING. This is a type of gardening in which special provision is made for rock-loving or saxicolous plants. It is likely to be confused with alpine gardening, which may be only one phase of it (see *Alpines*).

A rock garden is not primarily a pile of rocks; the rocks and stones are employed for the purpose of providing proper conditions for the growing of plants. The plants, rather than the rocks, are the primary consideration, and the plants should be such as especially thrive in rock crevices and pockets or are at least comparable with them in size and form. A tumulus of rocks in which is grown a miscellaneous collection of plants that do not profit by such conditions is not a rock garden; such plants may be grown with less trouble elsewhere, and are likely to be much more in keeping.

The special appeal of a rock garden lies in the skillful growing of plants that in nature inhabit cliffs, moraines, and mountains. Many such plants are tall, and take much room in the wild, but those kinds most prized in the constructed rock garden are the low, tufted, and spreading species, for the most part perennial. They are likely to have a penetrating root system, often a pronounced taproot, and are therefore able to establish themselves in deep, cool, moist chinks and depressions. The proper preparation for the rock gardener is a keen knowledge of such plants; he then finds or makes conditions for them where they may come to perfection. Having provided a proper place for the plant, he will keep it in place, restricting it to its confines. He will be careful with his labels and his notebook records. He will provide inhabitants for all the pockets or spaces, and this may require a supply of extra plants, sometimes even of temporary annuals if they are conformable and not the usual horticultural subjects of flower gardens and borders.

The exposure of the rock garden must depend on the kinds of plants to be grown in it, and the climate. In general, it should occupy an open free space not overshadowed by trees or buildings; yet in parts of North America it is well if the severity of midday and afternoon sun can be mitigated. The area should be protected from the roots of trees that may forage underneath it.

Knowing the kinds of plants he may wish to grow, the rock gardener will make his rock areas to suit them. If there are rocky cliffs or outcrops on the property, he may utilize them rather than attempt to make a wholly artificial area. Stone walls and old foundations may sometimes be utilized to advantage. Old quarries often yield excellent results. The larger part of any structural rock or stone is below the surface of the ground. In placing the rocks, one must always have in mind the providing of good roothold for plants. All cavities should be firmly filled to avoid covered hollows that dry out. Every part of the construction should be easily accessible from paths and trails. The success or failure of the rock garden may depend on its ability to hold moisture and thereby to carry the plants through dry times, although provisions must be at hand for applying water when needed. On the other hand, good natural drainage is essential, for saxicoles are not bog plants. The soil with which to fill the pockets and leads will depend on the plants to be grown, but in general its main elements should be good garden earth, fine or sifted leaf mold or peat, and gritty sand or fine gravel, all well mixed. Fertilizing is likely to be necessary.

The visible part of the rock construction should be attractive. Rocks from the neighborhood or region are commonly the most desirable. Generally speaking, only about one-third of the mass of any boulder should be exposed to view. There should be harmony in the work, the rocks, and the positions and directions in which they are laid, presenting a pleasing uniformness of character. The growth habit of the plants should be in harmony with the rocks, usually taking the form of tufts, mats, and growths lying close to the rocks. Many of the rock garden mats are evergreen, and at appropriate places very dwarf compact forms of certain conifers may be utilized, as well as various kinds of shrublets.

The kinds of plants suited to rock gardening are legion. Crassulaceous plants of this character, especially in the genera *Sedum* and *Sempervivum*, are many (see *Succulents*), as are ferns; some of the best of those in other families are in the genera *Aethionema, Allium, Alyssum, Androsace, Anemone, Aquilegia, Arabis, Arenaria, Aster* (dwarf), *Aubrieta, Campanula, Cassiope, Corydalis, Cotoneaster, Daboecia, Daphne, Dianthus, Draba, Dryas, Epigaea, Epimedium, Erinus, Gentiana, Heuchera, Iberis, Iris* (dwarf), *Leontopodium, Lewisia, Linaria, Linnaea, Lithodora, Lithospermum, Loiseleuria, Lychnis, Oxalis, Papaver, Petrocallis, Phyllodoce, Phlox, Potentilla, Primula, Ranunculus, Rhododendron, Saxifraga, Shortia, Soldanella, Thymus, Viola,* and *Wahlenbergia.* The attentive rock gardener will observe the saxicolous plants native in his region and find satisfaction in growing them.

A rock garden properly placed, constructed, and maintained, and with a population of well-chosen and skillfully grown plants, constitutes one of the choicest departments of horticulture.

RODGERSIA A. Gray. *Saxifragaceae.* About 5 spp. of per. herbs of e. Asia, with thick rhizomes; lvs. large, peltate or pinnately or palmately compound; fls. white, small, in showy terminal panicles, calyx tube only slightly united to ovary, sepals 5, petals 5, narrowly linear, sometimes 0, stamens 10, ovary nearly superior, 2-celled, styles 2; fr. a caps., dehiscent between the styles, seeds many, small. Closely related to *Astilbe.*

Propagated by division of the plants, also by seeds when obtainable.

aesculifolia Batal. To 6 ft.; lvs. palmately compound, resembling those of the horse chestnut, lfts. usually 7, to 10 in. long, coarsely toothed; fls. white, in flat clusters in an infl. to 2 ft. long. China.

pinnata Franch. To 4 ft.; lvs. pinnate, lfts. 5–9, oblanceolate, to 8 in. long; fls. red outside, white inside, in large, branched panicles with reddish rachis and brs. China. Cv. **'Alba'.** Fls. white, in large, loose panicles.

podophylla A. Gray. To 5 ft.; lvs. palmately compound, the lfts. 5, up to 10 in. long and 5 in. wide or more, long-cuneate, acuminately lobed and many-toothed toward the apex, light green in spring, metallic-bronzy in summer; fls. small, yellowish-white, in panicles to 1 ft. long. China, Japan.

sambucifolia Hemsl. To 3 ft.; lvs. pinnate, lfts. 3–11; fls. white, small, in terminal, flat-topped panicles. China.

tabularis (Hemsl.) Kom. To 3 ft.; lvs. peltate, to 2 ft. across, long-petioled, with many, short toothlike lobes; fls. white, small, in many-fld. panicles. N. China, Korea.

RODRIGUEZIA Ruiz & Pav. *Orchidaceae.* About 30 spp. of epiphytes, native to trop. Cent. and S. Amer.; pseudobulbs 1- or 2-lvd. at apex; lvs. oblong, leathery or fleshy; infl. basal, racemose, several- to many-fld.; fls. conspicuous, upper sepal separate, lateral sepals more or less united, saccate at base, often spreading, petals similar to upper sepal, lip obcordate, basally narrowed and extended into a short horn or spur, disc with 1 or more keels or crests. For structure of fl. see *Orchidaceae.*

Intermediate greenhouse. For culture see *Orchids.*

candida Batem. Pseudobulbs elliptic-ovate, 1-lvd.; lvs. oblong-lanceolate, to 6 in. long; racemes to 5 in. long, loosely 4–7-fld.; fls. pendent, fragrant, white, almost transparent, sepals 1¼ in. long, petals to 1¼ in. long, lip erect, pale yellow, to 1¾ in. long. Autumn. Guyana, Brazil.

compacta Schlechter. Pseudobulbs oblong-elliptic, to 1 in. long, 1-lvd.; lvs. to 5½ in. long; racemes 1–2, to 2 in. long, loosely few-fld.; fls. pale yellow or greenish-yellow, upper sepal oblong, 1 in. long, lateral sepals united entire length, 1 in. long, lip yellow, ovate-spatulate, 1 in. long, united to column, 2-lobed at apex. Costa Rica, Panama.

decora Rchb.f. Pseudobulbs ovoid, 1 in. long, 1-lvd.; lvs. linear-oblong, to 6 in. long; racemes to 14 in. long, loosely 5–15-fld.; fls. nodding, pale rose with reddish-brown spots, sepals to ½ in. long, lateral sepals united, petals to ½ in. long, lip orbicular, white with reddish-brown dots on claw, 2-lobed at apex. Brazil. Cv. **'Picta'** [var. *picta* Hook.]. Racemes to 20-fld.; fls. white with rich deep purple mottling on sepals and petals.

pubescens Rchb.f. Pseudobulbs small, oblong, 1-lvd.; lvs. oblong-strap-shaped, to 5 in. long; racemes nodding, to 6 in. long, many-fld.; fls. fragrant, snow-white, sepals to ½ in. long, lateral sepals united, petals to ½ in. long, lip white with yellow base, ¾ in. long, 2-lobed at apex. Winter–Spring. Brazil.

secunda HBK. CORAL ORCHID. Pseudobulbs oblong-elliptic, to 1½ in. long, 1-lvd.; lvs. linear-strap-shaped, to 9 in. long; racemes 1–6, simple, 1-sided, to 15 in. long; fls. many, small, pink to rose-red, upper sepal ovate, minutely apiculate, ½ in. long, lateral sepals united entire length, petals obovate, lip entire, with 2-auricled claw united to base of column and extended into a very short spur, 2-lobed at apex, margins undulate. Panama and trop. S. Amer.

Strobelii Garay. Pseudobulbs oblong-ovoid, 1-lvd.; lvs. oblong, to 3 in. long; racemes short, few-fld.; fls. white, with lilac striations on lip, upper sepal ovate-oblong, ¾ in. long, lateral sepals united, otherwise similar to upper sepal, petals ovate-oblong, 1¼ in. long, lip oblong, to 1 in. long, truncate and retuse at apex. Ecuador.

venusta Rchb.f. Pseudobulbs ovoid-oblong, to 1 in. long, 1-lvd.; lvs. linear-lanceolate, to 6 in. long, dark green; racemes pendent, many-fld.; fls. white, with center of lip yellow, sepals ½ in. long, lateral sepals united, petals similar to sepals, lip erect, to 1 in. long, 2-lobed at apex. Brazil.

ROEMERIA Medic. *Papaveraceae.* About 5 spp. of slender, ann. herbs, with foetid yellow sap, native from the Medit. region e. to cent. Asia; lvs. pinnately dissected, the lower petioled, the upper sessile; fls. solitary, red or violet, sepals separate, petals 4, stamens many; caps. linear, cylindrical, more than 10 times as long as wide.

Sometimes cultivated for their showy flowers.

hybrida (L.) DC. [*R. violacea* Medic.]. To 1½ ft.; lvs. 2–3-pinnately dissected, segms. linear, terminated by bristle; fls. on short peduncles, petals violet, with a dark spot at base; caps. setose, at least near apex. Medit. region.

refracta DC. Similar to *R. hybrida,* but having petals red with a black blotch at base, and caps. glabrous except for 4 apical setae. Turkey, e. to cent. Asia; reported as a weed in Utah and Calif.

violacea: *R. hybrida.*

ROHDEA Roth. *Liliaceae.* Two or 3 spp. of rhizomatous, per. herbs, native to Japan and sw. China; lvs. tufted, leathery; fls. in a compact, bracted, scapose, terminal spike, perianth campanulate, shortly 6-lobed, stamens 6, arising from perianth; fr. a berry, often with a single seed.

Sometimes grown as a durable plant in the house or outdoors in mild climates; much prized in Japan.

japonica (Thunb.) Roth. LILY-OF-CHINA, SACRED L.-OF-C. Lvs. in basal rosette, lanceolate to oblanceolate, 2-ranked, to 2 ft. long and 3 in. wide; fls. pale yellow, in short spike resembling an aroid infl., concealed by the foliage; fr. red, infrequently yellow. China, Japan. There are many cvs. with striped, variegated, and otherwise modified lvs., such as **'Marginata', 'Multifolia',** and **'Variegata'.**

ROLLINIA St.-Hil. *Annonaceae.* About 50 spp. of trop. Amer. trees and shrubs; lvs. alt., simple; fls. bisexual, 3-merous, solitary or few together, petals 6, valvate in 2 series, united at base, forming a short globose tube, the outer 3 petals with dorsal spur or laterally compressed wing, the inner 3 minute, stamens many, with connectives dilated above the anthers, pistils many; fr. a globoid or ovoid syncarp resembling that of *Annona,* formed by fusion of pistils. For cultivation see *Cherimoya.*

pulchrinervis A. DC. Tree, new branchlets rusty-silky; lvs. oblong to oblong-elliptic, to 11 in. long, pubescent beneath, membranous; fls. axillary, silky, on pedicels to $1\frac{5}{16}$ in. long, corolla about 1 in. across or more, with oblong, winged appendages ½ in. long; fr. subglobose, to 4½ in. in diam. Fr. Guiana, and Pará, Brazil. Fr. edible, but of poor quality.

ROMANZOFFIA Cham. ex Nees. *Hydrophyllaceae.* Four spp. of bulbous or tuberous per. herbs, native to moist areas of w. N. Amer.; lvs. chiefly basal, long-petioled, reniform-orbicular to obovate, toothed or lobed; fls. white, often with a yellow ring in the tube, pedicelled, in racemelike terminal cymes, calyx 5-parted, corolla campanulate or campanulate-funnelform, 5-lobed, stamens 5, included, style undivided; fr. a caps.

sitchensis Bong. To 10 in., with somewhat bulbous base but without tubers; pedicels to 1 in. long in fr. Summer to autumn. Alaska to n. Calif., e. to Alta. and Mont.

Suksdorfii Greene. To 1 ft., from cluster of tomentose tubers; infl. much longer than lvs., pedicels to 1 in. long in fr.; corolla tube longer than calyx. Spring. Mts., w. Wash. to cent. Calif.

Tracyi Jeps. Low succulents, to 4 in., from cluster of tomentose tubers; infl. slightly longer than lvs., pedicels stout, to ¼ in. long in fr.; corolla tube shorter than calyx. Early spring. Rocky ocean bluffs, Wash., Ore., Calif.

unalaschensis Cham. ex Nees. To 6 in., with somewhat bulbous base, but without tubers; pedicels to 5⁄16 in. long in fr. E. Aleutian Is.

ROMNEYA Harv. MATILIJA POPPY. *Papaveraceae.* One sp., an erect, glaucous, per. herb, with woody base and colorless sap, native to s. Calif. and n. Baja Calif.; lvs. irregularly pinnately divided; fls. large, white, sepals 3, petals 6, stamens many; fr. a leathery, oblong to ovoid caps.

Striking in the flower garden and borders where it is hardy. Propagated by suckers and seeds, but seedlings require several years before flowering. Transplants with difficulty.

Coulteri Harv. CALIFORNIA TREE POPPY. To 8 ft.; lvs. pinnately divided, to 4 in. long; fls. fragrant, 6 in. across, petals delicate, crepe-like. Var. **trichocalyx** (Eastw.) Jeps. Buds rounded, not beaked, with appressed setose hairs.

ROMULEA Maratti [*Trichonema* Ker-Gawl.]. *Iridaceae.* Perhaps 75 spp. of cormous herbs, native to the Old World; resembling *Crocus,* but having lvs. without a keel; fls. on an exposed peduncle that raises the ovary above ground at flowering time, perianth tube short, segms. longer than tube.

The Eur. species are generally less hardy than *Crocus* and those of S. Afr. less hardy than *Ixia.* The plants require full sun, and do best in a sand-compost mixture. Best planted in groups and left undisturbed; propagated by seeds or offsets.

bulbocodioides (D. Delar.) Bak. Sts. 2½–4 in.; lvs. 2, the longer one to 12 in. long; inner spathe valve membranous; fls. starlike, bright yellow, perianth segms. about ½ in. long. Spring. Sw. Cape Prov. (S. Afr.). Easily grown and attractive.

Bulbocodium (L.) Sebast. & Mauri. Sts. 2–3 in.; lvs. mostly 4, nearly cylindrical, curved, 2–3 in. long; spathe valves herbaceous; perianth broadly funnelform, lilac, with yellow throat, segms. about 1 in. long, veined purple. Spring. Medit. region. Very variable; in some races the yellow of the throat predominates, and only the tips of the segms. are lilac. Does best if protected from heavy spring rains.

hirsuta Eckl. Sts. 1–2 in.; lvs. 2–4, erect or spreading, filiform, to 4 in. long, setaceous, weakly pilose to glabrous; fls. 1–2, perianth segms. about 1 in. long, lower half bright golden-yellow, upper half red-purple. Spring. Sw. Cape Prov. (S. Afr.). Does best in sandy, well-drained soil, and full sun; not hardy to ground freezes.

rosea (L.) Eckl. [*Ixia rosea* L.]. Sts. 2–3 in.; lvs. mostly 4, flexuous, to 1 ft. long; corm several-fld., each peduncle usually 1-fld., inner spathe valve membranous; perianth funnelform, 1–1½ in. long, reddish-lilac with yellow throat, outer segms. with 3 purple stripes outside. Early spring. S. Afr.

sabulosa Schlechtend. Sts. 2–4 in.; lvs. 2–4, filiform, cylindrical, shorter than st.; inner spathe valve herbaceous; perianth campanulate, 1–1½ in. long, deep rose-pink with brownish-purple blotch in throat, segms. separate to base, not forming a tube, outer segms. veined yellow outside. Late spring. Cape Prov. (S. Afr.). One of the hardier S. Afr. spp.

RONDELETIA L. *Rubiaceae.* More than 100 spp. of evergreen trees or shrubs, native to Amer. tropics; lvs. opp., sessile or petioled, stipules interpetiolar, usually broad and persistent; fls. in terminal or axillary cymes or panicles, red, yellow or white, 4–5-merous, corolla funnelform or salverform, tube slender, elongate; fr. a caps., seeds many, small.

Grown as ornamentals in Calif. and southern U.S., and in the greenhouse, where the temperature should not be allowed to go below 50° F. Propagated by cuttings of half-ripened wood.

amoena (Planch.) Hemsl. [*R. versicolor* Hook.]. Shrub or small tree; lvs. ovate, to 6 in. long, densely pubescent beneath, stipules triangular, reflexed; fls. in densely fld. terminal and axillary panicles 1–6 in. long, as broad as or broader than long, corolla pink, pubescent, yellow-bearded at throat, ½ in. long. S. Mex. to Panama.

cordata Benth. Shrub, to 7 ft.; lvs. ovate-oblong or ovate, to 5 in. long, nearly glabrous; corolla pink or red, yellow-bearded at throat, pubescent. Guatemala. Similar to *R. amoena,* but having lvs. glabrous or sparsely strigose beneath.

odorata Jacq. [*R. speciosa* Lodd.]. Shrub, to 6 ft.; lvs. ovate to oblong, 2 in. long, nearly glabrous, margins often revolute; corolla orange-red, without hairs at throat. Cuba and Panama.

speciosa: *R. odorata.*

splendens: a listed name of no botanical standing.

thyrsoides Swartz. Shrub, to 6 ft.; lvs. ovate or elliptic, to 6 in. long, pubescent beneath; corolla yellow, ¼ in. long, pubescent. Jamaica. The only cult. sp. with small, yellow, axillary fls.

versicolor: *R. amoena.*

RONNBERGIA E. Morr. *Bromeliaceae.* Eight spp. of herbs, native to Colombia and Brazil; lvs. entire and petioled, or spiny and sessile; infl. simple, bracted; fls. sessile, sepals awned, petals separate, without appendages, ovary inferior, ovules many, blunt; fr. a berry, seeds without appendages.

Grown outdoors in warm climates or under glass. Requires filtered light. For culture see *Bromeliaceae.*

columbiana E. Morr. Lvs. to 16 in. long, 2 in. wide, sessile, linear, spiny; scape erect, shorter than lvs.; fls. violet, to 1¾ in. long. Colombia.

ROODIA: *ARGYRODERMA.* R. digitifolia: *A. brevipes.*

RORIPPA Scop. YELLOW CRESS. *Cruciferae.* About 70 spp. of ann. to per. aquatic or terrestrial herbs in the N. Hemisphere, glabrous or with unbranched hairs; lvs. simple to pinnate; fls. small, in racemes, petals yellow; fr. a short silique or silicle, ovoid to oblong or rounded, valves strongly convex, nerveless, seeds more or less in 2 rows in each cell.

amphibia (L.) Bess. Stoloniferous per. herb, to 5 ft., sts. hollow, branched; lvs. variable, lower lvs. elliptic to oblanceolate, entire to pinnatifid, bright green; fls. to ¼ in. across; silicles ovoid, to ¼ in. long, style persistent. N. Afr., Eur., Siberia. Sometimes grown in aquaria.

Armoracia: *Armoracia rusticana.*

Nasturtium-aquaticum: *Nasturtium officinale.*

ROSA L. ROSE, BRIER. *Rosaceae.* More than 100 spp. of prickly shrubs, sometimes climbing and trailing, mostly in the temp. parts of the N. Hemisphere; lvs. alt., mostly odd-pinnate, deciduous or persistent, stipules adnate to the petiole; fls. solitary, corymbose, or panicled, petals 5, these and the many stamens inserted on a disc at the edge of the calyx tube, pistils many, borne on the inside of the deep hypanthium; fr. a fleshy hip containing the hairy achenes.

Important essential oils, used in perfumery, are obtained from several species of roses, but most roses are garden ornamentals. See *Rose.*

acicularis Lindl. To 3 ft., densely bristly; stipules glandular-ciliate; lfts. 3–7, opaque, ovate to elliptic, 1–2 in. long, serrate; fls. solitary, dark red, fragrant, 2 in. across; hip pear-shaped, ½ in. long. Zone 5. Subsp. **acicularis**. The typical subsp.; lfts. mostly 5, simply serrate, rarely glandular; pedicels glandular. Eurasia; Alaska. Subsp. **Sayi** (Schweinitz) W. H. Lewis [var. *Bourgeauiana* Crép.; *R. Sayi* Schweinitz]. Lfts. 5 or 7, usually doubly serrate, often glandular; pedicels rarely glandular. New Bruns. to Alaska, s. to W. Va. and New Mex. Var. **Bourgeauiana**: subsp. *Sayi.*

×**alba** L.: ?*R. canina* × *R. damascena.* To 6 ft., with unequal, hooked prickles; lfts. 5–7, broad-elliptic, pubescent beneath; fls. white to pinkish, double, 2½–3½ in. across. Zone 5. Cv. 'Incarnata'. Fls. double, white, tinged pink. Cv. 'Suaveolens'. Fls. partly double.

alpina: *R. pendulina.*

altaica: *R. spinosissima* var.

Andersonii: a listed name of no botanical standing for *R.* ×*collina* cv.

anemoniflora Fort. ex Lindl. Prickles small, hooked; lfts. mostly 3, lanceolate-ovate, to 3 in. long, simply serrate, glabrous; fls. white, 1–2 in. across, single in wild forms, semidouble in cult. China. Zone 7.

arkansana T. Porter [*R. pratincola* Greene; *R. suffulta* Greene]. Like *R. acicularis*, but smaller; lfts. 9–11, sharply serrate, 1–2 in. long; fls. bright red, 1 in. across; hip globose, ½ in. in diam., red. N.Y. to Alta., s. to D.C., Tex., Colo. Zone 5.

arvensis Huds. FIELD R. Sts. glabrous or nearly so, weak, trailing or climbing over other plants, almost glaucous, often purple-tinted, with hooked, subequal prickles; lfts. 2–3 pairs, ½–1½ in. long, ovate to ovate-elliptic, mostly simply serrate, glabrous, or pubescent beneath on veins, stipules narrow; fls. 1–6, white, 1–2 in. across; hip red, smooth, round to oblong, ¾ in. long. Eur. Zone 6.

Banksiae Ait.f. BANKSIA R. To 20 ft., evergreen, with few prickles; lfts. 3–5, pointed, 1–2½ in. long, finely serrate; fls. white or yellow, 1 in. across, single, many; hip round, red, pea-sized. China. Zone 7. Cvs. include: **'Alba Plena'**, fls. double, white; **'Lutea'**, fls. double, yellow; **'Lutescens'**, fls. single, yellow.

Beggerana Schrenk. To 8 ft., with hooked prickles; lfts. 5–9, elliptic-ovate to obovate, 5/16–1 in. long, simply serrate, mostly bluish-green and pubescent beneath; fls. several to many, in a corymb, white, 1 in. across; hip red, later deep purple, 5/16 in. long. Asia. Zone 4.

bella Rehd. & E. H. Wils. Related to *R. Moyesii*, but bristly; lfts. smaller; fls. rose, 2 in. across, in groups of 1–3. China. Zone 6.

blanda Ait. To 6 ft., often unarmed; lfts. 5–7, elliptic to obovate, finely pubescent beneath, simply serrate, to 2½ in. long; fls. pink, 1 to few, 2 in. across; hip red, round, ⅜ in. in diam. Nfld. to Penn., w. to Mo. Zone 2?

×**borboniana** Desp.: *R. chinensis* × *R. damascena* (or possibly *R. gallica*). BOURBON R. Lfts. 7; fls. dark carmine-rose, medium-sized. HYBRID BOURBON ROSES represent crosses between this hybrid and *R. odorata*, the tea rose, and are the ancestors of the HYBRID PERPETUAL ROSES or REMONTANTS.

bracteata J. C. Wendl. MACARTNEY R. Evergreen, climbing, to 20 ft., with broad-based, paired, infrastipular prickles, twigs densely tomentose; lfts. 5–9, narrow-obovate, crenate-denticulate, shining above, tomentose beneath; fls. solitary, white, fragrant, 2–3 in. across; hip orange, 1 in. in diam. China; naturalized in U.S. Zone 7.

Brunonii Lindl. HIMALAYAN MUSK R. Climbing, mostly pubescent on young growth, with strong, hooked prickles; lfts. 5–7, elliptic-lanceolate, 1–2 in. long, soft-pubescent; fls. white, 1–2 in. across, many, fragrant; hip ovoid, 5/16 in. in diam. Himalayas. Zone 7?

californica Cham. & Schlechtend. To 10 ft., branched, with stout, flattened, usually recurved prickles; lfts. 5–7, elliptic, ½–1½ in. long, simply or doubly serrate, pubescent, often glandular beneath; fls. corymbose, pink, 1½ in. across; hip globose or ovoid, 5/16–⅝ in. long. Ore. to Baja Calif. Zone 6. Ripe fr. after being exposed to frost are edible.

canina L. DOG R., BRIER R., DOG BRIER. Three to 10 ft., with arching sts. and strongly curved or hooked prickles; lfts. 2–3 pairs, ovate to elliptic, ½–1½ in. long, simply to doubly serrate, glabrous or pubescent beneath, acute to acuminate; fls. 1–4, pink to white, long-pedicelled; hip ½ in. long, scarlet. Eur., w. Asia, N. Afr.; naturalized in N. Amer. Zone 4. Fresh fr. used medicinally. Cv. **'Inermis'** is listed.

cantabrigiensis: a listed name of no botanical standing.

carolina L. [*R. humilis* Marsh.]. PASTURE R. To 3 ft. or more, branchlets slender, with many prickles, especially infrastipular ones; lfts. 5–9, elliptic to lanceolate-ovate or narrow-obovate, rather dull above, ½–1½ in. long, coarsely serrate; fls. mostly solitary, 1½–2 in. across, rose; hip red, subglobose, 5/16 in. in diam. Nov. Sc. to Minn., s. to Fla., Nebr., Tex. Zone 5.

cathayensis: *R. multiflora* forma.

caudata Bak. To 12 ft., with scattered, straight, thick prickles; lfts. 7–9, ovate-elliptic, 1–2 in. long, simply serrate, glabrous and bluish beneath; fls. few, in a corymb, 1½–2 in. across, red; hip elongate-ovoid, 1 in. long, with long neck, orange-red. China. Zone 6.

Celsiana: *R. damascena* cv.

centifolia L. CABBAGE R. Differing from *R. gallica* in stouter and taller growth, coarser prickles, thinner and longer lfts., and nodding, double, pink fls. Caucasus. Zone 6. Grown in Eur., especially France, as a source of attar of roses, an essential oil distilled from the fragrant fresh fls. Cvs. are: **'Cristata'**, sepal edges mossy; **'Muscosa'** [*R. muscosa* Mill.], MOSS R., calyx and pedicels mossy; **'Parvifolia'**, BURGUNDY R., lfts. to ¾ in. long, fls. 1 in. across. Cv. **'Alba'** is listed.

chinensis Jacq. [*R. mutabilis* Correv.]. CHINA R. Low, evergreen, with almost no prickles; lfts. 3–5, ovate, pointed, 1–2½ in. long, glabrous; fls. few, in a corymb, 2 in. across, pink to almost white, sepals deciduous in age. China. Zone 7? Cvs. are: **'Minima'** [*R. Roulettii* Correv.], FAIRY R., PYGMY R., to 1½ ft.; fls. single or double, to 1½ in. across, rose-red; **'Semperflorens'**, fls. crimson, usually solitary; **'Viridiflora'** [*R. viridiflora* Lavall.], fls. double, green.

cinnamomea L. CINNAMON R. Spreading by subterranean roots to form dense thickets, up to 6 ft. high, branchlets slender, flexuous, red, with broad-based, infrastipular prickles; lfts. 5–7, to 1½ in. long, pubescent; fls. pinkish-purple, 2 in. across; hip scarlet, ½ in. in diam. Eurasia; escaped in U.S. Zone 5. Cv. **'Plena'**. Fls. double.

clinophylla Thory. Like *R. bracteata*, with straight prickles and lfts. acute, often pubescent beneath, rachis pubescent. India.

×**collina** Jacq.: ?*R. canina* × *R. gallica*. About 5 ft., with strong, hooked prickles; lfts. mostly 5, finely serrate, pubescent on nerves beneath; fls. 1–3, pink, fragrant, sepals persistent. Cv. **'Andersonii'** [*R. Andersonii* Hort.]. Fls. to 3 in. across, rose-red, fading white.

coriifolia: *R. dumalis*.

corymbifera: *R. dumetorum*.

damascena Mill. DAMASK R. To 8 ft., with many, equal, hooked prickles; lfts. usually 5, ovate, simply serrate, pubescent beneath, to 2½ in. long; fls. pink to red, fragrant, double, corymbose. Introd. from Asia Minor. Zone 5. The major source of attar of roses distilled from the fls. in Bulgaria, where most of it is produced. Cvs. **'Celsiana'**, [*R. Celsiana* Hort. ex C. Koch] and **'Semperflorens'** are listed. Cv. **'Trigintipetala'**. Fls. red, semidouble. Cv. **'Versicolor'**. YORK-AND-LANCASTER R. Fls. all white, all pink, or both white and pink on same br. or plant, semi-double. Often confused with *R. gallica* cv. 'Versicolor'.

Davidii Crép. To 10 ft., with straight, thick prickles; lfts. mostly 7–9, narrow-elliptic, simply serrate, to 1½ in. long; fls. pink, to 2 in. across, in corymbs. China. Zone 6.

davurica Pall. Like *R. cinnamomea*, but with straighter prickles and smaller lfts. N. Asia.

devoniensis: a listed name of no botanical standing.

dumalis Bechst. [*R. coriifolia* Fries; *R. glauca* Vill. ex Loisel., not Pourr.]. Close to *R. canina*, but with smaller prickles, shorter pedicels to only 1 in. long, more persistent sepals. Eur., w. Asia.

dumetorum Thuill. [*R. corymbifera* Borkh.]. Like *R. canina*, but with pubescent lvs. Medit. region. Zone 6.

Ecae Aitch. Like *R. Primula*, but to 3 ft., densely prickly; lfts. 5–9, mostly obovate, to 5/16 in. long; fls. ½–¾ in. across, yellow. Afghanistan. Zone 7.

Eglanteria L. [*R. rubiginosa* L.]. EGLANTINE, SWEETBRIER. Three to 6 ft., erect, with unequal, hooked prickles; lfts. 2–3(–4) pairs, orbicular to nearly elliptic, ½–1 in. long, pubescent and very glandular on veins beneath; fls. 1–3, bright pink, 1 in. across, styles pilose; hip scarlet, round to ovoid, ½ in. in diam., sepals persistent. Eur., w. Asia; naturalized in N. Amer. Zone 6. Fls. have been used medicinally. Cv. **'Duplex'**. Fls. pink, double.

elegantula Rolfe [*R. Farreri* Stapf; *R. Farreri* forma *persetosa* Stapf]. To 5 ft., young shoots densely red-bristly; lfts. 7–9, elliptic-ovate, ½–⅝ in. long, bluish, simply serrate; fls. pink, 1 in. across, 1 to several. W. China. Zone 6.

excelsa: a listed name of no botanical standing.

Farreri: *R. elegantula*. Forma **persetosa:** *R. elegantula*.

Fedtschenkoana Regel. To 5 ft., bristly, prickles paired; lfts. 5–7, elliptic, 1 in. long, acute, serrulate, bluish above and beneath; fls. mostly white, 1–4 in a cluster, 2 in. across, with disagreeable odor; hip pear-shaped, red. Turkestan.

filipes Rehd. & E. H. Wils. Climbing, to 15 ft., with small, hooked prickles; lfts. 5–7, lanceolate-ovate, 2–3 in. long, glandular beneath, simply serrate; fls. white, 1 in. across, in many-fld. corymbs; hip ovoid, red. W. China. Zone 6.

foetida J. Herrm. AUSTRIAN B. To 10 ft., with few, unequal, straight prickles; lfts. 5–9, elliptic, 1–1½ in. long, doubly glandular-serrate, pubescent and glandular beneath; fls. 1 or 2, deep yellow, 2 in. across, with unpleasant odor. Asia. Zone 5. Cv. **'Bicolor'**. AUSTRIAN COPPER B. Fls. yellow outside, orange-scarlet inside. Cv. **'Persiana'**. PERSIAN YELLOW R. Fls. double, golden-yellow.

foliolosa Nutt. ex Torr. & A. Gray. To 1½ ft., unarmed or with short prickles; lfts. 7–9, narrow, to 1¼ in. long; fls. bright red, 1 in. across, solitary or few. Ark. to Tex. Zone 6. Cv. **'Alba'**. Fls. white.

×**Fortuniana** Lindl.: *R. Banksiae* × ?*R. laevigata*. Climber resembling *R. Banksiae*; lfts. 3–5; fl. white, double, 2–4 in. across, solitary. Used frequently as an understock for Fla. soils.

fujisanensis Mak. To 10 ft., sts. flexuous; lfts. 3–9, to ¾ in. long; fls. white, corymbose, 1 in. across. Japan.

gallica L. FRENCH R. Sts. solitary, slender, to 5 ft., bristly, stipitate-glandular, and prickly; lfts. 3, 5, or 7, leathery, round-ovate to elliptic, rugose above, pubescent beneath, 1–2 in. long; fls. solitary, pink to red, 2–2½ in. across, fragrant; hip red. Eur., w. Asia; naturalized in e. N.

Amer. Zone 6. Dried petals have been used medicinally. Cvs. are: **'Conditiorum'**, fls. magenta, semidouble; **'Pumila'** [*R. pumila* Jacq.], very low, fls. single, red; **'Rosa Mundi'**: cv. 'Versicolor'; **'Versicolor'** [cv. 'Rosa Mundi'], fls. semidouble, striped white, pink, red. Often confused with *R. damascena* cv. 'Versicolor'. Cvs. **'Bicolor'**, **'Complicata'**, **'Grandiflora'**, **'Marmorata'**, and **'Splendens'** are also listed.

gigantea: *R. odorata* cv.

Giraldii Crép. Slender shrub; lfts. mostly 7, rounded to ovate, to 1 in. long; fls. pink, 1 in. across. China.

glauca: see *R. dumalis* and *R. rubrifolia*.

gymnocarpa Nutt. WOOD R. Slender-stemmed, to 8 ft., mostly with slender, straight prickles; lfts. 5–7, elliptic to roundish, ½–1½ in. long, doubly glandular-serrate, glabrous; fls. usually solitary, rose, 1 in. across; hip ellipsoid to globose, ⁵⁄₁₆ in. long. B.C. to Calif., Mont. Zone 6.

gypsicola: *R. rubrifolia*.

×**Harisonii** Rivers: *R. foetida* × *R. spinosissima*. To 2 ft.; lfts. 5–9, elliptic, doubly serrate; fls. solitary, semidouble, bright yellow, 2 in. across. Cv. **'Vorbergii'** [*R. × Vorbergii* Graebn. ex Späth]. Fls. cream-colored, single, many.

Helenae Rehd. & E. H. Wils. Climbing, to 16 ft., with many hooked prickles; lfts. 7–9, lanceolate-ovate, 1–2 in. long, pubescent beneath, sharply serrate; fls. white, 1 in. across, many, in flat corymbs. China. Zone 6.

Henryi Bouleng. To 12 ft., partly climbing, with hooked prickles; lfts. usually 5, elliptic to elliptic-ovate, 2–3 in. long, acuminate, simply serrate, glabrous; fls. many, in flat corymbs, white, fragrant, to 1½ in. across. China. Zone 7.

×**hibernica** W. Templeton: *R. canina* × *R. spinosissima*. Three to 6 ft., dark red with scattered prickles; lfts. 7–9; fls. 1–3, rose.

×**highdownensis** Hort. Hillier: *R. Moyesii* × ?. Lvs. glaucous beneath; fls. carmine-red with white center, on arching sts.; hip flask-shaped.

×**Hillieri:** *R. × pruhoniciana*.

horrida Fisch. Low, with stiff brs. and short, unequal, strongly hooked prickles; lfts. 5–7, elliptic-ovate, ½ in. long, doubly serrate; fls. solitary, white, 1 in. across. S. Eur., Asia Minor.

Hugonis Hemsl. To 8 ft., with flat, straight prickles, shoots bristly at base; lfts. 7–13, obovate to elliptic, ⁵⁄₁₆–⅝ in. long, pubescent beneath, at least when young; fls. solitary, bright yellow, 2 in. across; hip red or darker. China.

humilis: *R. carolina*.

×**Iwara** Siebold ex Regel: *R. multiflora* × *R. rugosa*. Lfts. 5–7, elliptic, gray-tomentose beneath; fls. many, in a corymb, small, white.

×**kamtchatica** Venten: *R. davurica* × *R. rugosa*. Branchlets thinner than in *R. rugosa*, less prickly; fls. 3–5, smaller.

×**Kordesii:** a listed name of no botanical standing; used for a tetraploid hybrid of *R. rugosa* × *R. Wichuraiana*.

koreana Kom. Close to *R. spinosissima*, but densely bristly, dark red; lfts. 7–11, elliptic, to ¾ in. long, sharply glandular-serrate; pedicels stipitate-glandular; fls. 1 in. across, white flushed with pink; hip orange-red. Korea.

laevigata Michx. CHEROKEE R. Climbing, to 15 ft., evergreen, with many hooked prickles; lfts. mostly 3, lanceolate-ovate, shining, smooth; fls. white, fragrant, to 3½ in. across, solitary; hip orange, pear-shaped. China; naturalized in U.S. Zone 7.

laxa Retz. To 8 ft., with hooked or straight prickles; lfts. 7–9, glabrous or pubescent beneath, to 1½ in. long; fls. several, white, to 2 in. across. Turkestan. Cv. **'Alba'** is listed.

×**Lheritierana** Thory: *R. chinensis* × *R. pendula*. BOURSAULT R. Climbing to 20 ft.; lfts. 3–7; fls. red, in corymbs.

lucida: *R. virginiana*.

Macounii: *R. Woodsii*.

×**macrantha** Desp.: *R. gallica* × ?. To 4 ft.; lfts. 5–7, ovate, 1¼ in. long; fls. light pink, 3 in. across.

macrophylla Lindl. To 12 ft., with few, strong, straight prickles; lfts. 9–11, elliptic-ovate, to 1½ in. long; fls. 1 to few, red, 2 in. across. Himalayas. Zone 7.

Manettii: *R. × Noisettiana* cv.

marginata Wallr. Erect, to 8 ft., close to *R. canina*, but with straight prickles; lvs. doubly glandular-serrate; fls. 1 to several, pink, aging white, to 3 in. across. Eur., Asia Minor.

Marretii Lév. To 6 ft.; branchlets dark purple, with slender prickles; lfts. 7–9, 1 in. long, simply serrate, glabrous; fls. few, pink, 2 in. across. Sakhalin. Zone 2?

Maximowicziana Regel. Climbing, with small, straight and also hooked bristles; lfts. 7–9, elliptic-ovate, 1–2 in. across; hip red, ½ in. in diam. N. Asia. Var. **Jackii** (Rehd.) Rehd. Without bristles; hip ¼ in. long. Korea. Zone 6. Cv. **'Pilosa'** is listed.

micrantha Borrer ex Sm. Close to *R. rubiginosa*, but sts. more arched; prickles subequal; styles glabrous, sepals soon falling. Eur.; naturalized in N. Amer. Zone 6.

microphylla: *R. Roxburghii*.

mirifica: *R. stellata* subsp.

mollis: *R. villosa*.

moschata J. Herrm. MUSK R. Arching or overhanging, with straight or slightly curved prickles; lfts. 5–7, ovate to lanceolate-elliptic, ½–3 in. long, subacuminate, finely serrate, glabrous; fls. white, 1–2 in. across, of musky odor; hip ovoid, small. S. Eur., N. Afr., w. Asia; naturalized in N. Amer. Zone 7? Cv. **'Plena'**. Fls. double. Var. **nastarana** Christ. More robust; fls. over 2 in. across, pinkish. Iran.

Moyesii Hemsl. & E. H. Wils. To 10 ft., brs. brown-red, with straight, paired, yellowish prickles; lfts. 7–13, elliptic-ovate, ½–1½ in. long, serrulate, pubescent on midrib; fls. several, dark wine-red, 2 in. across; hip flask-shaped, dark orange-red. China. Zone 6.

multibracteata Hemsl. & E. H. Wils. To 10 ft., branchlets thin, arched, with paired, straight prickles; lfts. 7–9, ovate, 2–6 in. long, doubly serrate, gray-green beneath, subglabrous; fls. light pink, 1 in. across, 1 to several in a cluster; hip ovoid, ⅝ in. long, orange-red, glandular-bristly. China. Zone 7.

multiflora Thunb. ex J. Murr. [*R. polyantha* Siebold & Zucc., not Carrière]. BABY R. To 10 ft., climbing; lfts. 5–11, obovate to lanceolate, to 1¼ in. long, stipules pectinate; fls. white, many, in large clusters; ¾ in. across, styles glabrous; hip red, pea-sized. Japan, Korea. Cv. **'Carnea'**. Fls. rose, double. Cv. **'Platyphylla'**. SEVEN-SISTERS R. Lvs. large; fls. deep pink. Cvs. **'Japonica'** and **'Nana'** are listed. Var. **cathayensis** Rehd. & E. H. Wils. [*R. cathayensis* (Rehd. & E. H. Wils.) L. H. Bailey]. Fls. rose, ¾–1⅝ in. across, single. China.

muscosa: *R. centifolia* cv.

mutabilis: *R. chinensis*.

nitida Willd. Erect, to 1½ ft., very bristly; lfts. 7 or 9, narrowly elliptic, serrulate, to 1¼ in. long, shining above; fls. 1 to few, pink, 1½–2½ in. across, fragrant; hip dark red, subglobose, ⁵⁄₁₆ in. in diam. Nfld. to Conn. Zone 4.

×**Noisettiana** Thory: *R. chinensis* × *R. moschata*. NOISETTE R., CHAMPNEY R. Climbing, with hooked, red prickles; lfts. 5–7, lanceolate; fls. yellow, white, or pink, fragrant, up to 100 in a cluster. Not hardy north. Cv. **'Manettii'** [*R. Manettii* Criv. ex Rivers]. MANETTI R. To 6 ft., branchlets with white stripes, prickles many, dark; lfts. 7–9, broadly elliptic; fls. pink, semidouble.

nutkana K. Presl. NOOTKA R. Stout, 3–6 ft., mostly with stout, straightish prickles; lfts. 5–9, elliptic to broadly ovate, ½–2 in. long, doubly glandular-serrate; fls. mostly solitary, rose-pink, 1½–2½ in. across; hip globose, ⅝ in. in diam., red. Calif. to Alaska, n. Rocky Mts. Zone 6. Cv. **'Halliana'**. Fls. large, pink.

odorata (Andr.) Sweet. TEA R. More or less evergreen, partly climbing, with scattered, hooked prickles; lfts. 5–7, narrow-elliptic, shining, sharply serrate, 1–3 in. long; fls. 1 to several, white, pink, or yellowish, 2–3 in. across, single or double. China. Zone 7. One of the spp. involved in the parentage of HYBRID TEA ROSES. Cvs. include: **'Erubescens'**, fls. single, bright to dark pink; **'Ochroleuca'**, fls. double, bright yellow; **'Pseudindica'**, GOLD R., OPHIR R., fls. double, salmon-yellow; **'Gigantea'** [*R. gigantea* Collet ex Crép.], fls. cream-colored, to 6 in. across.

omeiensis Rolfe. To 12 ft., prickles many, broad at base; lfts. 9–17, to 1 in. long; fls. white, to 1 in. across, mostly 4-petalled; hip pear-shaped. China. Zone 7. Forma **chrysocarpa** Rehd. Fls. yellow. Forma **pteracantha** (Franch.) Rehd. & E. H. Wils. [*R. sericea* var. *pteracantha* Franch.]. Prickles larger, red and translucent when young.

omissa: *R. Sherardii*.

palustris Marsh. SWAMP R. Up to 7 ft., from stoloniferous rhizomes, prickles largely infrastipular; lfts. mostly 7, broad-elliptic, 1–2 in. long, sharply and finely serrate, pubescent beneath; fls. pink, 2 in. across; hip round, pea-sized, red. Nov. Sc. to Minn., s. to Fla. and Ark. Zone 5.

×**Paulii** Rehd.: *R. arvensis* × *R. rugosa*. Procumbent; fls. large, white, in corymbs.

pendulina L. [*R. alpina* L.]. ALPINE R. To 4 ft., mostly without prickles; lfts. 7–9, doubly glandular-serrate, more or less pubescent on both sides, 1–2½ in. long; fls. 1–5, rose to purple, to 1½ in. across; hip pendent, bright red, pedicel not glandular-bristly. Eur. Zone 6.

×**Penzanceana** Rehd.: *R. Eglanteria* × *R. foetida*. LADY PENZANCE R. Brs. arching, prickles hooked; lfts. 7; fls. pink with yellow center.

×**Pernetiana:** a listed name of no botanical standing for the hybrid *R. borboniana* × *R. foetida* 'Persiana'. Now merged with Hybrid Tea Roses and the source of brilliant yellow color in the group.

pimpinellifolia: *R. spinosissima.*

pisocarpa A. Gray. CLUSTER R. Slender, 3–6 ft., with few straight prickles; lfts. 5–7, ovate to elliptic-oblong, puberulent beneath, to 1½ in. long, finely serrate; fls. pink, 1 in. across; hip globose, ⁵⁄₁₆ in. in diam. B.C. to Calif. Zone 6.

polyantha: see *R. multiflora, R. × Rehderana.*

pomifera: *R. villosa.*

pratincola: *R. arkansana.*

Primula Bouleng. To 6 ft., with stiff broad prickles; lfts. 7–13, elliptic, to ½ in. long, doubly serrate; fls. solitary, pale yellow, 1 in. across, fragrant; hip brown-red, ½ in. in diam. Asia. Zone 7. Confused in cult. with *R. Ecae.*

×**pruhoniciana** Kriechb. ex C. K. Schneid. [*R. × Hillieri* Hort. Hillier]: *R. Moyesii* × *R. Willmottiae.* Like *R. Willmottiae,* but fls. deep red-brown.

×**pteragonis** a listed name of no botanical standing for the hybrid *R. Hugonis* × *R. omeiensis* forma *pteracantha.* To 6 ft., with broad, dark red prickles; fls. yellow, petals 5.

pumila: *R. gallica* cv.

×**Rehderana** Blackb. [*R. × polyantha* Carrière, not *R. polyantha* Siebold & Zucc.]: *R. chinensis* × *R. multiflora.* POLYANTHA R. Like *R. multiflora,* but sts. less than 3 ft., low or spreading.

Richardii Rehd. To 2 ft., very prickly, with short, unequal, hooked prickles; lfts. 3–5, rugose, narrow-elliptic, glandular on margin, pubescent beneath; fls. 2–3 in. across, sepals pinnately incised, leafy at apex, petals bright pink. Ethiopia. Zone 7?

Roulettii: *R. chinensis* cv. 'Minima'.

Roxburghii Tratt. [*R. microphylla* Roxb. ex Lindl.]. CHESTNUT R., CHINQUAPIN R. To 8 ft., with paired infrastipular prickles; lfts. 7–15, narrow-elliptic, somewhat pubescent, ½–1 in. long; fls. double, bright pink, 2 in. across; hip round, green. China, Japan. Forma **normalis** Rehd. & E. H. Wils. Fls. single. China, Japan. Var. **hirtula** (Regel) Rehd. & E. H. Wils. Lvs. pubescent beneath. Japan.

rubiginosa: *R. Eglanteria.*

rubrifolia Vill. [*R. glauca* Pourr., not Vill. ex Loisel.; *R. gypsicola* Blocki]. Upright, 6–7 ft., prickles few, straight or hooked; lfts. 5–9, rather narrow, tinged red, somewhat glaucous, 1–1½ in. long, glabrous, mostly simply serrate; fls. single, red to pink, 1½ in. across; hip red, roundish, ½ in. in diam. Cent. Eur. Zone 2.

rugosa Thunb. TURKESTAN R., JAPANESE R. To 6 ft., densely prickly and bristly, tomentose; lfts. 5–9, rugose, 1–2 in. long, dark green and furrowed above; pedicels bristly; fls. rose to white, 2½–3¼ in. across; hip 1 in. in diam., red, crowned with erect sepals. China, Japan. Zone 2. Cvs. 'Kamtschatica', 'Magnifica', 'Repens Alba', 'Rosea', and 'Rubra' are listed.

Sayi: *R. acicularis* subsp.

sempervirens L. EVERGREEN R. Climbing, to 16 ft., with slender, red thorns; lfts. 5–7, narrow-elliptic, acute, 1–2½ in. long, simply serrate; fls. 1–2 in. across, white, fragrant, sepals deciduous; hip ovoid, ½ in. long, orange-red. N. Afr., s. Eur. Zone 7.

Serafinii Viv. One to 2½ ft., prickles unequal, hooked; lfts. 7–11, ovate to nearly orbicular, ¼–½ in. long, sharply serrate, glandular beneath; fls. 1–3, pale pink, 2 in. across; hip red, ½ in. in diam. Medit. region.

sericea Lindl. To 8 ft., with large, broad prickles; lfts. 7–11, round-elliptic, sharply serrate, silky beneath, to ¾ in. long; fls. solitary, white, to 2 in. across; hip red to orange. Himalayas. Zone 7? Var. **pteracantha:** *R. omeiensis* forma.

setigera Michx. PRAIRIE R., CLIMBING R. Three to 6 ft., climbing or leaning, with remote, broad-based prickles; lfts. 3 or 5, to 4 in. long, serrate, the underside gray-green and hairy on veins; fls. several, rose fading to white, 1½–2 in. across, sepals reflexed, deciduous; hip small, brown-green. Ont. to Kans., s. to Fla. and Tex. Zone 5. Var. **tomentosa** Torr. & A. Gray. Lvs. tomentose beneath.

setipoda Hemsl. & E. H. Wils. Thick-stemmed, to 10 ft., with few prickles; lfts. mostly 3, lanceolate-ovate, 1–3½ in. long, pubescent beneath; fls. pink or rose, corymbose, 2 in. across; hip flask-shaped, 1 in. long. Cent. China. Zone 6.

Sherardii Davies [*R. omissa* Déségel.]. Lower and more compact than *R. tomentosa,* sts. flexuous; lvs. bluish-green; sepals persistent. Eur. Zone 5.

Soulieana Crép. Climbing, to 12 ft., very prickly; lfts. gray-green, 5–9, glabrous, to 1¼ in. long; fls. many, white, 1¼ in. across, somewhat fragrant; hip orange-yellow. W. China. Zone 7.

Spaldingii Crép. Erect, to 3 ft., usually with straight infrastipular prickles; lfts. 5–7, elliptic to ovate, ½–2 in. long, coarsely serrate, puberulent beneath; fls. usually solitary, about 2 in. across; hip globose, ½–¾ in. in diam. B.C. to Ore., Utah, Wyo. Zone 6.

spinosissima L. [*R. pimpinellifolia* L.]. SCOTCH R., BURNET R. Low, to 3 ft., erect, deciduous, forming large patches, prickles many, straight, mixed with stiff bristles; lfts. 3–5 pairs, ¼–¾ in. long, roundish to elliptic, obtuse, mostly simply serrate and glabrous, stipules narrow; fls. cream-white, rarely pink, ¾–1½ in. across; hip roundish, purplish-black, ½ in. in diam. Eur., Asia. Zone 5. Cvs. are: 'Andrewsii', fls. double, bright red; 'Nana', dwarf, with large, white, semidouble fls.; 'Plena', fls. double, white. Also listed are 'Alba', 'Cestiflora', 'Flavescens', 'Fulgens', 'Lutea', and 'Sulphurea'. Var. **altaica** (Willd.) Rehd. [*R. altaica* Willd.]. With few prickles; fls. white. E. Asia. Var. **hispida** (Sims) Koehne. With many bristles and prickles; lfts. 7–9, simply serrate, 1 in. long; fls. pale yellow, 2 in. across. Russia. Forma **luteola** (Andr.) Rehd. Three to 6 ft.; lfts. 7, elliptic, ¾ in. long; fls. pale yellow; hip dark purple. Russia. Var. **myriacantha** (DC.) Koehne. To 2 ft., thickly prickly; lfts. very small; fls. white, tinged pink. Medit. region.

spithamea S. Wats. GROUND R. Low, from creeping rootstocks, with straight, mostly infrastipular prickles; lfts. 3–7, ovate to roundish, ½–1 in. long, doubly glandular-serrate; fls. 1 to few, rose, to 1¼ in. across; hip subglobose. Calif. Var. **sonomensis** (Greene) Jeps. Lfts. ¼–½ in. long, glabrous beneath. Calif.

stellata Woot. One to 4½ ft., hairy, prickly; lfts. 3–5, broad-cuneate, ¼–¾ in. long, incised-toothed, glabrous to pubescent; fls. solitary, dark red, 2 in. across; hip glabrous or puberulent, bristly. Zone 6. Subsp. **stellata.** The typical subsp.; fl. brs. tomentose-woolly, prickles few between nodes. New Mex. Subsp. **mirifica** (Greene) W. H. Lewis [*R. mirifica* Greene]. Fl. brs. glabrous, prickles and bristles many. New Mex., s. Tex.

stylosa Desv. Sts. arching, 3–12 ft., with hooked, stout prickles; lfts. 5–7, ovate to elliptic, ½–2 in. long, serrate; fls. 1–8, white to pink, to 2 in. across, sepals reflexed; hip red, smooth, globose to ovoid, Eur. Zone 6.

suffulta: *R. arkansana.*

Sweginzowii Koehne. To 15 ft., with large 3-angled prickles; lfts. 7–11, elliptic to lanceolate-ovate, 1–2 in. long, doubly serrate, pubescent beneath; fls. bright pink, 1½ in. across, 1–3 in a group; hip flask-shaped, red. China. Zone 6.

tomentosa Sm. To 6 ft., sts. arching, pale green when young, stout, prickles curved or nearly straight; lfts. 2–3 pairs, ½–1½ in. long, ovate to elliptic, pointed, usually densely pubescent or tomentose on both sides; pedicels glandular-hispid; fls. bright rose, to whitish, 1½ in. across, sepals deciduous; hip ovoid, red, ⅜–¾ in. long. Eur., w. Asia. Zone 6. Cv. 'Cuspidata' is listed.

villosa L. [*R. mollis* Sm.; *R. pomifera* J. Herrm.]. Erect, 1½–6 ft., brs. straight with slender, straight, subulate prickles; lfts. 2–3(–4) pairs, oblong to elliptic, ½–1½ in. long, tomentose on both sides; fls. 1–3, pink or almost red, 1–2 in. across, sepals persistent. Eur. to Iran. Zone 6. Fr. eaten and used for making beverages.

virginiana Mill. [*R. lucida* J. F. Ehrh.]. To 6 ft.; prickles straight or curved, slender, bristles on young shoots only; lfts. 2–4 pairs, 1–2½ in. long, more or less elliptic, coarsely serrate; fls. in few-fld. corymbs, pale pink, 2–2½ in. across; hip red, ½ in. in diam. Nfld. to Del. Zone 4. Cv. 'Alba'. Fls. white. Cv. 'Plena'. Fls. double, pink.

viridiflora: *R. chinensis* cv.

×**Vorbergii:** *R. × Harisonii* cv.

×**Waitziana** Tratt.: *R. canina* × *R. gallica.* To 6 ft., unequally armed; lfts. thickish, simply serrate, sometimes pubescent beneath on midrib; fls. mostly solitary, 2½–3 in. across, dark rose.

Watsoniana Crép. To 3 ft.; lfts. 3–5, long, narrow, with entire, wavy margins; fls. many, in a corymb, white or pink, ½ in. across; hip pea-sized, red. Of garden origin. Zone 7.

Webbiana Royle. To 5 ft., branchlets thin, prickles few, straight, in pairs; lfts. 5–9, roundish to broadly elliptic, simply serrate, to ¾ in. long; fls. mostly solitary, light pink, 2 in. across; hip flasklike. Himalayas. Zone 6.

Wichuraiana Crép. MEMORIAL R. Semievergreen trailer and climber, differing from *R. multiflora* in having smaller, rounder, and firmer lfts., jagged-dentate stipules, fewer fls., and pubescent styles. E. Asia; naturalized in N. Amer. Zone 6. Cv. 'Dorothy Perkins' is a derivative.

Willmottiae Hemsl. To about 10 ft., prickles paired, straight; lfts. 7–9, elliptic, to nearly round, to ⅝ in. long, simply or doubly serrate, glabrous; fls. solitary, about 1³⁄₁₆ in. across, sepals deciduous, petals rose-purple; hip nearly globose, ⅜ in. long. W. China. Zone 6.

×**Wintoniensis** Hort. Hillier: *R. Moyesii* × *R. setipoda.* Like *R. Moyesii,* but fls. in clusters, rose-pink.

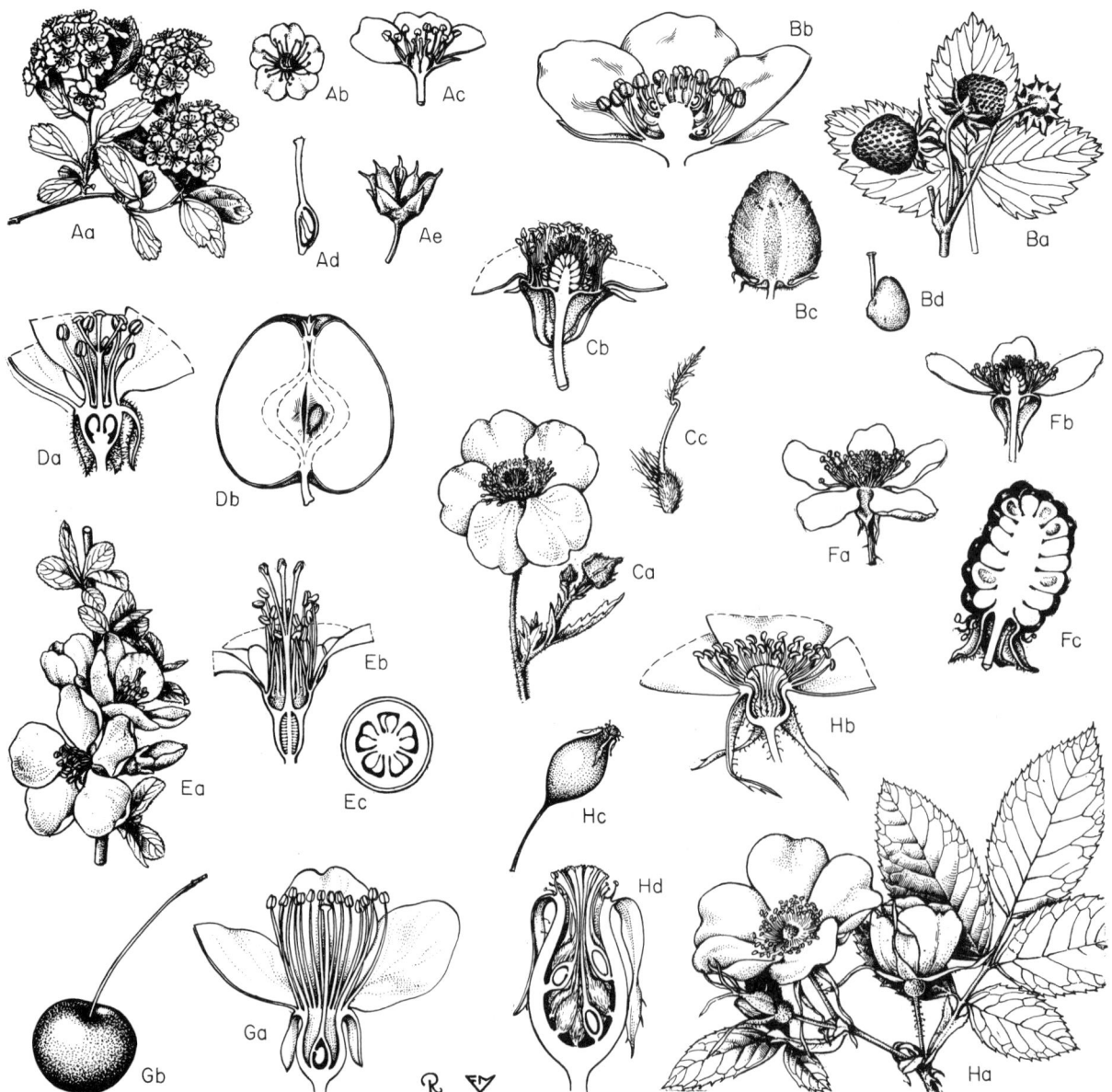

ROSACEAE. **A,** *Spiraea* ×*Vanhouttei:* **Aa,** flowering branch, × ½; **Ab,** flower, × 1; **Ac,** flower, vertical section, × 2; **Ad,** pistil, vertical section, × 6; **Ae,** follicles, × 2. **B,** *Fragaria* ×*Ananassa:* **Ba,** leaf and "fruits," × ¼; **Bb,** flower, vertical section, × 1½; **Bc,** "fruit," × ½; **Bd,** achene with persistent style, × 5. **C,** *Geum* hybrid: **Ca,** flower and bud, × ½; **Cb,** flower, vertical section (petals cut short), × 1; **Cc,** achene, × 2. **D,** *Malus pumila:* **Da,** flower, vertical section (petals cut short), × 1; **Db,** fruit (pome), vertical section, × ⅓. **E,** *Chaenomeles speciosa:* **Ea,** segment of flowering branch, × ½; **Eb,** flower, vertical section (petals cut short), × 1; **Ec,** ovary, cross section, × 4. **F,** *Rubus flagellaris:* **Fa,** flower, × 1; **Fb,** flower, vertical section, × 1; **Fc,** "fruit" (aggregate of drupelets), vertical section, × 1. **G,** *Prunus avium:* **Ga,** flower, vertical section, × 1½; **Gb,** fruit (drupe), × ½. **H,** *Rosa canina:* **Ha,** flowering twig, × ½; **Hb,** flower, vertical section (petals cut short), × 1; **Hc,** "fruit" (hip), × ½; **Hd,** hip, vertical section, × 1. (From Bailey, *Manual of Cultivated Plants,* ed. 2, except for Bb, Ga, Gb, Hd, which are from Lawrence, *An Introduction to Plant Taxonomy.*)

Woodsii Lindl. [*R. Macounii* Greene]. To about 6 ft., sts. sometimes bristly, prickles straight or slightly curved; lfts. 5–7, obovate to oblong-obovate, to 1³⁄₁₆ in. long, simply serrate, glabrous to puberulent beneath; fls. 1–3, to 1¾ in. across, petals pink or sometimes white. Minn. to B.C., s. to Nebr., Ariz., n. Mex. Zone 4.

xanthina Lindl. Resembling *R. Hugonis,* but having a stipular wing along petiole, shoots lacking bristles, prickles stouter and more broadly flattened basally; fls. semidouble. N. China, Korea. Forma **spontanea** Rehd. Fls. single. Zone 6.

ROSACEAE Juss. ROSE FAMILY. Dicot.; about 100 widely distributed genera and 2,000 spp. of herbs, shrubs, and trees; lvs. mostly alt.; fls. bisexual, regular, sepals and petals 4–5, or petals lacking, stamens 5 to many, borne on edge of a calyx tube, pistils 1 to many, ovary superior or inferior; fr. an achene, follicle, berry, pome, or drupe. The family includes many of the most important fr. plants and ornamentals in the N. Temp. Zone, most of them grown outdoors. Genera treated here are: *Acaena, Adenostoma, Agrimonia, Alchemilla, Amelanchier, Aronia, Aruncus, Cercocarpus, Chaenomeles, Chamaebatia, Chamaebatiaria, Cotoneaster, Cowania, Crataegus, Cydonia, Dalibarda, Dendriopoterium, Docynia, Dryas, Duchesnea, Eriobotrya, Exochorda, Fallugia, Filipendula, Frageria, Geum, Gillenia, Heteromeles, Holodiscus, Horkelia, Ivesia, Kageneckia, Kelseya, Kerria, Leutkea, Lyonothamnus, Maddenia, Malus, Marcetella, Margyriacarpus, Mespilus, Neillia, Neviusia, Oemleria, Osteomeles, Petrophytum, Photinia, Physocarpus, Potentilla,*

Poterium, Prinsepia, Prunus, Purshia, Pyrachantha, Pyrus, Quillaja, Raphiolepis, Rhodotypos, Rosa, Rubus, Sanguisorba, Sibbaldia, Sibiraea, Sorbaria, × *Sorbaronia, Sorbus, Spenceria, Spiraea, Stephanandra, Stranvaesia,* and *Waldsteinia.*

ROSCOEA Sm. *Zingiberaceae.* About 17 spp. of per. herbs, native to Himalayas and w. China, with thick fleshy roots as in *Curcuma;* lvs. lanceolate or oblong, parallel-veined; fls. purple, blue, or rarely yellow, in terminal condensed spikes, calyx split down one side, fls. and fr. similar to those of *Cautleya* but the upper corolla lobe broader than the others; fr. elongate, slow to open.

Suitable for the greenhouse or for borders in mild climates. Zone 8. The roots should be planted in sandy loam 4–5 in. deep. Propagated by division. Dormant and in need of rest in winter.

alpina Royle. To 6 in.; lvs. oblong-lanceolate, to 4 in. long, sessile, becoming fully developed after flowering; fls. with dark purple limb and white tube, to 1 in. long. Himalayas to Burma. See also *R. capitata.*

capitata Sm. To 16 in.; lvs. commonly about 7, lanceolate, to 8 in. long or more, ¾ in. wide; fls. blue or purplish, 5–7 in a dense, long-peduncled spike with green bracts, calyx about 1 in. long, corolla half again as long, lip ¾ in. long. Apparently not offered under this name, but plants answering to the description of this sp. have appeared in cult. under the name *R. alpina.* Himalayas.

cautleoides Gagnep. To 1 ft.; lvs. usually sessile, to 6 in. long, 1 in. wide; fls. 2–5, pale primrose-yellow, to 3 in. long or more, in a peduncled spike. China.

Humeana Balf.f. & W. W. Sm. To 8 in.; lvs. 4–6, broadly lanceolate or ovate-lanceolate, to 8 in. long, 2¼ in. wide, broadly sheathing at base, more or less expanded at time of flowering; infl. 2–8-fld., not much longer than lvs.; fls. violet-purple, large and showy, calyx to 4 in. long, corolla lobes to 1¾ in. long, lip to 1 in. long. W. China.

purpurea Sm. To 1 ft.; lvs. lanceolate, undulate, usually 5–6 on a st.; fls. few in a sessile spike, corolla with limb and tube white to purple. Himalayas to Burma and Assam. Var. **capitata** is listed and may be *R. capitata.*

ROSE. Many species of *Rosa* have been modified through selection and hybridization in cultivation, giving rise to some 20,000 cultivars, more than 12,000 of which are recorded in *Modern Roses 7* published by The McFarland Company under the auspices of the American Rose Society, which serves as the International Registration Authority for Roses. Irrespective of the great amount of hybridization carried on over the past 200 years, parental species resemblances are usually apparent to students of the genus on the basis of taxonomic characteristics or chromosome studies. Most of the members of the genus are important to horticulturists for growing as ornamental shrubbery, for landscape use, for garden cut flowers, or as an important greenhouse florist crop.

Rose cultivars can be divided into three groups: (1) the garden-display and cut-flower types that are being hybridized and introduced at the rate of several hundred a year, in other words, the contemporary roses; (2) those that have essentially reached the end of their development and are no longer being hybridized extensively—in general, the old garden rose types, popular before 1900; (3) the species and species hybrids and selected variations.

As hybridization has gone on, the system of cultivar classification has become complicated and inexact. It is now nearly impossible to classify accurately the new introductions on sight because the class specifications are not precise and often overlap. Many inconsistencies have been perpetuated. Sometimes the classification has been based on species origin, sometimes on flowering characteristics, as in the Hybrid Perpetual Roses; at other times, commercial terms have been applied, as in Grandiflora and Floribunda Roses. See *Registration.*

Contemporary Rose Classes

Hybrid Tea Roses (HT) are by far the most popular contemporary class. They were derived from crosses between the older Hybrid Perpetual cultivars and the Teas and Chinas (see below). They are less hardy than most of the Hybrid Perpetuals, but because of their reliably recurrent-blooming habit, refined, high-centered bud and flower form, color range, and rich or spicy fragrance, they predominate as garden roses and for greenhouse production of cut flowers. The first cultivar to be so classified was 'La France', introduced in 1867.

The Hybrid Teas are grown throughout America, with such winter protection as may be required in the colder climates. The color range of the early introductions lacked yellow, but by about 1900 the French hybridizer Joseph Pernet-Ducher succeeded in making a cross with the Austrian brier *(R. foetida),* which introduced brilliant yellow and copper tones into the color range. Today all shades of white, yellow, and red, with many variations of blends and bicolors, are included. Cultivars with distinct lavender and purplish hues are developing as well as some approaching tan or brown. While Hybrid Tea is still used as a class name, it is no longer distinctive, because all classes of modern roses can be traced back to the same basic species.

Floribunda Roses (F) have many of the Hybrid Tea characteristics as far as color and hardiness are concerned, except that the flowers are typically smaller and borne in clusters. Often they lack the high pointed center and refinement usually seen in the Hybrid Teas, although in recent years this has been improved. While they were developed primarily for garden display, they are being used more and more as a greenhouse cut flower. The color range is the same as that of the Hybrid Tea, but, in general, plants are of lower habit.

The Floribunda class was developed by crossing Hybrid Polyantha cultivars with Hybrid Teas, the Hybrid Polyanthas themselves resulting from crosses between Polyanthas and Hybrid Teas, Hybrid Perpetuals, and other classes. The term Floribunda was adopted for commercial purposes and the first cultivar so called was 'Rochester', originated by Dr. J. H. Nicolas. The name Floribunda is credited to E. L. D. Seymour. Later, many other cultivars were included that had formerly been classes as Hybrid Polyanthas. The term Hybrid Polyantha is no longer common in America, although it is used frequently in other parts of the world.

Recently Flora-Tea Roses, a new type, have been promoted. This group is an offshoot of the Floribunda type, selected to combine the characteristics of Hybrid Teas and Floribundas so that it is useful for both landscape purposes and for cutting. The strong main canes branch into six or more individual stems approximately 1 foot long, each bearing one bloom of Hybrid Tea form.

The Grandiflora (Gr) class is based on the cultivar 'Queen Elizabeth', originated by Dr. Walter E. Lammerts about 1950 by crossing 'Charlotte Armstrong' (HT) and 'Floradora' (F). 'Queen Elizabeth' is a tall-growing plant with flowers similar to the Hybrid Tea type but does not fit the accepted specifications of either a Floribunda or a Hybrid Tea, thereby necessitating a new class. In general, the Grandifloras are tall-growing and produce several individual stems on each sturdy cane. The flowers are borne singly or in small clusters and respond favorably to disbudding. Typically, the flowers are smaller than those of the average Hybrid Tea. While most of the cultivars in this class possess these characteristics, there are many exceptions, and they are often difficult to distinguish from the Hybrid Teas.

Miniature Roses (Min) have become popular in the last twenty years for both gardeners and exhibitors. There have been probably 500 cultivars recorded. The older cultivars were derived largely from crosses of *R. chinensis* 'Minima' *(R. Roulettii)* with Hybrid Teas and others. Some have also been selected from seedling populations of various crosses not necessarily descendants of miniatures. To be classed as a miniature, the plant is usually less than 18 inches high, with diminutive stems, foliage, and blooms. Some cultivars that have long, slender, flexible stems with very small leaves and flowers have been introduced as Climbing Miniatures.

Climbing Roses (Cl) include those cultivars that produce long, more or less flexible canes and require some support for best landscape effect. The early ones were derived from *R.*

multiflora, R. setigera, R. Wichuraiana, and a number of other species, and for the most part bloomed only once a year. Climbing roses have also originated as mutations of cultivars of Hybrid Teas, Floribundas, and other classes, and these more or less retained their recurrent-flowering habit. Recurrent-flowering climbers are also selected from seedlings of crosses of bush roses. At the present time almost no climbers are being introduced unless they are reliably recurrent-flowering.

Virtually all the more recent introductions are less rampant than the older types and are better suited to garden use, the exception being the Kordesii Roses, which are highly recurrent but very vigorous growers. With most new cultivars the long canes tend to terminate in an inflorescence and later flowers appear on lateral shoots from the main canes.

Shrub roses are an important class for landscape use, and while most of the cultivars are better considered as old garden roses, new introductions frequently appear. They may be derived from almost any combination of parents. The newer cultivars are predominantly recurrent bloomers, but a few may be valuable because of special growth, foliage, or fruiting characteristics.

It should be recognized that the classification of cultivars as Climbing or Shrub Roses is often a function of cultural practices. This is also true of Tree or Standard Roses, which are produced by budding cultivars on a tall understock 3–6 feet above the ground. Roses are not true climbing plants in the sense that they can support themselves by twining or holdfasts. Almost any rose can be made into a climber by restrictive pruning to prevent it from taking on its natural bush habit. Some climbers grow long, more or less flexible canes up to 30 feet in length in a season, and are referred to as Ramblers. Those in the 8–10-foot group may be referred to as Pillar Roses. For attractive use they need some supporting structure unless used as ground covers. Others produce rather stout, arching canes that may be supported on a fence or trellis or they can be grown as free-standing shrubs. Many of the more rampant climbers can be used as shrubs by proper pruning. This is particularly true of the Kordesii Roses (see below.)

Old Garden Rose Types

Hybrid Perpetual (HP) or Remontant Roses seem, for all practical purposes, to have reached the end of their development, since there have been no introductions in this class for the last 50 years. Some cultivars are still offered by nurserymen but they are no longer in extensive, common use except among collectors. A hundred years ago they were the dominant type grown for both landscape and greenhouse use. The term Hybrid Perpetual was, by present day standards, somewhat of a misnomer because they do not flower as continuously as the name would suggest. Hybrid Perpetuals are of mixed ancestry, with *R. × borboniana* probably prevailing. They produce, in early summer and sparingly in autumn, very large, double, and fragrant flowers limited in color to white through pink to deep purplish-crimson.

Tea Roses (T), derived principally from *R. odorata,* are no longer important in commercial production. Only a few varieties are still available from American nurserymen because they have been superseded by the Hybrid Teas. They were useful primarily in the warmer sections of the country and fine specimens and historic plantings can still be found. Many cultivars are highly prized by fanciers of old garden roses. At one time they were grown quite extensively under glass but have long since disappeared as a florist's cut flower. While they had large, well-shaped flowers, they often lacked substance and strong, stiff stems. Their greatest value came from the good qualities they contributed to the heredity of the Hybrid Teas, such as their continuous-flowering habit, high-centered flower form, and spicy fragrance. The term Tea was applied because the odor of the blooms suggested that of crushed tea leaves.

Polyantha Roses (Pol) are now attributed to *R. × Rehderana* instead of *R. multiflora* 'Nana' because they are

recognized as hybrids. The group includes dwarf roses with small flowers borne in dense clusters or trusses and is sometimes called "bably ramblers." Formerly they were important for garden use but in recent years have been largely superseded by the Floribundas, which owe their origin to crosses between Polyanthas, Hybrid Teas, and other classes. They also were used in quantity for greenhouse forcing as pot plants but this practice has largely disappeared. Only a relatively few cultivars are being produced in quantity for garden use in America. The Polyanthas are floriferous and hardy.

China and Bengal Roses (Ch), attributed to *R. chinensis* and *R. odorata* and their hybrids, were significant in the early development of recurrent-flowering cultivars, especially the Hybrid Perpetuals and the Polyanthas. So conspicuous was their recurrent-flowering habit that they were often called "monthly roses" and "daily roses." Only a very few true Chinas are available today, having been replaced by their hardier and more appealing descendants.

The Gallica (G) or French Roses, derived from *R. gallica,* are important because of their antiquity and because they played a direct part in the ancestry of a majority of our modern cultivars. One form was the Red Rose of Lancaster. They were the dominant roses from the twelfth through the early nineteenth centuries. Many variations and hybrids were discovered and propagated. They ranged in color from pale pink to deep purplish-maroon, and some were striped, mottled, or variegated. They were very hardy and productive. *Rosa gallica* 'Officinalis' was called the "apothecary's rose" because the petals could be dried and powdered and made into conserves and confections that still possessed a delicate perfume. Many Gallicas are still available.

The Damask Roses (D), derived from *R. damascena,* represent another group of great antiquity and seem to have been first generally known during the Crusades. Like the Gallicas, they played a notable role in the heredity of our modern cultivars. *Rosa damascena* is the species from which attar of roses is prepared, and certain cultivars are grown in large quantities for this purpose, especially in Bulgaria. While most cultivars in the group bloom but once a year, some are recurrent, possibly the result of hybridizing with China Roses.

The Centifolias (C), Cabbage, or Province Roses, derived from *R. centifolia,* are similar to the Gallicas except for their taller and stouter growth. Many botanical varieties are recorded and many attractive hybrids were produced. More than likely they entered into the ancestry of the Hybrid Perpetuals. The Moss Roses were a conspicuous variant of the Centifolias and until recently, most of the Moss Roses were referred to this species. Breeding work with this interesting group is continuing, and within the last few years "mossiness" has been introduced into contemporary cultivars. Many Centifolia cultivars still exist and while most are not recurrent bloomers, there are a few that flower about as freely as the Hybrid Perpetuals.

The Bourbon Roses (B), *R. × borboniana,* were an important group in their own right as well as being a parent of the Hybrid Perpetuals. Derived from crosses between *R. chinensis* and *R. damascena,* they were mostly compact, sturdy plants. The first hybrid was apparently a natural one that occurred on L'Île Bourbon (now Réunion) in the Indian Ocean. Virtually all the hybridizers of the nineteenth century made use of them and several hundred cultivars were introduced. A few are still available commercially, and 'Souvenir de la Malmaison' can be found in most catalogues offering old garden roses.

The Portland Roses, being derivatives of *R. damascena,* might be considered a subclass of the Damasks. They bloomed with a degree of recurrence and were the forerunners of the Hybrid Perpetuals. The name was given in honor of the Duchess of Portland. Many cultivars were produced, but by 1850 they began to be replaced by the Hybrid Perpetuals. The most important cultivar was 'Rose du Roi', which is still available along with several others.

The Boursault Roses were popular from about 1820 to 1850. Considered to have been derived from hybridization between *R. chinensis* and *R. pendulina*, they first went under the name of *R.* × *Lheritierana*. They were primarily climbers, but the class soon reached the end of its potential for development. Several cultivars still exist, the most notable being 'Amadis', which at one time was used as an understock.

Noisette (N) or Champney Roses, *R.* × *Noisettiana*, resulted from a hybrid between *R. chinensis* and *R. moschata* produced by John Champney of Charleston, South Carolina. The first cultivar of the group came to be called 'Champney's Pink Cluster'. Plants were given to a friend, Philip S. Noisette, by whom they were sent to France, and Noisette's name became used for the class. Later introductions may have involved *R. odorata* as well as *R. chinensis*. A considerable number of cultivars and derivatives were introduced during the nineteenth century and some are still available and useful, particularly in the warmer parts of the country. Probably the most popular variety was 'Maréchal Niel', which was acclaimed the "finest yellow rose in the world; a model of beauty and fragrance." Another was 'Manettii', which has long been used as an understock for greenhouse roses. Cultivars in the class include extremely vigorous roses useful as shrubs or climbers and some which are dwarf and adapted for bedding. The blooms are produced in large clusters, with as many as 100 buds and flowers in a corymb.

The Musk Roses (Msk) originated in England, largely through the work of Rev. Joseph Pemberton, who crossed *R. moschata* with numerous cultivars. All of his varieties and some others are considered Hybrid Musks (H Msk). Most of them are large shrubs or climbers that produce clusters of small flowers. A few are recurrent-flowering.

The Ayrshire Roses (Ayrs), while not as important genetically as many others, were popular in Europe and a few were introduced in the United States. They are primarily *R. arvensis* hybrids, most of which are rampant climbers.

The Sweetbriers, *R. Eglanteria* (E), are interesting because of their fragrant foliage. They are chiefly used as shrubs. Hybrid derivatives are known as Penzance hybrids, after Lord Penzance, who produced many hybrids. Occasionally new cultivars are introduced. In Europe, the synonym *R. rubiginosa* is commonly used for the species.

The Austrian Brier Roses, *R. foetida*, include a few variations within the species, and many hybrids. The flowers are predominantly of yellow and copper hues and the plants are commonly used as shrubs. The brilliant yellow seen in modern roses comes from this species. The still popular early American hybrid, 'Harison's Yellow', is believed to have been a hybrid involving *R. spinosissima*.

The Scotch of Burnet Roses were derived from *R. spinosissima*, a species with many natural variations and known for hundreds of years. Because of their hardiness, persistence, and abundant delicate flowers, they were used extensively as landscape plants. Great numbers of selections and hybrids were introduced but only a relative few are available today. Occasionally new cultivars are introduced.

The Alba Roses (A) include the White Rose of York. Their origin is somewhat uncertain, but they are now generally believed to be hybrids of *R. canina* and *R. damascena* on the basis of chromosome studies. Typically they bear small, fragrant, white, single or double flowers in small clusters. They were one of the roses described by Pliny and are believed to have been cultivated by the Romans. Some of the roses seen in the paintings of the Italian Renaissance can be identified as Albas. A few cultivars classified as Albas are still obtainable and the group seems to have entered into the ancestry of many early hybrids.

The Multiflora Roses (Mult), *R. multiflora*, are important in the heredity of several cultivar groups. The species and its numerous variants are also valuable as shrubs because of their hardiness and dense clusters of small white blooms followed by fruits borne in great profusion. Their greatest use, however, has been as an understock in the nursery propagation of garden roses. A large proportion of plants produced in the United States are budded on one or more of the varieties of *R. multiflora*, a practice initiated by the Bobbink and Atkins

Company in 1902. Many of the early climbers were hybrids of which *R. multiflora* was one parent; 'Crimson Rambler' was the most famous. Few true Multiflora climbers are available today.

The Wichuraiana Roses (W), *R. Wichuraiana*, are largely climbers, although they are used to some extent as ground covers. They were popular because of their bright, glossy leaves and their long, flexible canes which produced a profusion of dense clusters of small blooms in the early summer. Following the distribution of the species by the Arnold Arboretum in 1890, it was used freely by many hybridizers, notably M. H. Horvath, M. H. Walsh, and Dr. Walter Van Fleet. Many cultivars were introduced; some of the most widely grown were 'Dorothy Perkins', 'Excelsa', 'American Pillar', 'Silver Moon', 'Dr. W. Van Fleet', and 'Glen Dale'. Later hybridizers, particularly Walter D. Brownell, used some of these F_1 hybrids in the development of bush roses by crossing with Hybrid Teas and other types. Even though the Wichuraiana climbers were nonrecurrent, they were used abundantly until the middle of the twentieth century and their influence can be seen in many of the modern recurrent-flowering climbers. A number of the nonrecurrent Wichuraiana climbers are still available.

The Setigera Roses (Set) were derived from *R. setigera*, the prairie rose, a vigorous hardy shrub that has been used as a parent of many hardy climbers and some bush roses. M. H. Horvath and Dr. Walter Van Fleet used it often with *R. Wichuraiana* in producing such cultivars as 'American Pillar', 'Doubloons', and 'Thor'.

The Rugosa Roses (Rug) include numerous variants and hybrids of *R. rugosa*, a very hardy, widespread, Oriental species with bright dark-green, disease-resistant, wrinkled foliage, more or less recurrent bloom, and large red-orange fruits. Rugosas are used abundantly for landscape purposes and while few nurseries now produce many cultivars, most of them offer a few selected ones. The Rugosas have been used frequently as breeding material, but in general the *R. rugosa* characteristics have not blended well with other parents. Consequently, without exception, *R. rugosa* hybrids can easily be distinguished by their foliage and flower characteristics.

The Kordesii Roses are the most recent group to have been developed, since the first cultivars were not introduced until 1954. Their origin stems from a hybrid *R. rugosa* × *R. Wichuraiana* called 'Max Graf'. This cultivar was almost completely sterile, but W. Kordes succeeded in growing a few seedlings which apparently resulted from a chance doubling of the chromosomes in the parent plant. They proved to be fertile and in 1951 were determined by H. D. Wulff to be amphidiploids. The name *Rosa* × *Kordesii* has been used for these hybrids but it appears to have no botanical standing. The cultivars introduced as hybrids of *R.* × *Kordesii* are very vigorous, recurrent-flowering shrubs or climbers with bright, glossy foliage. They are valuable for landscape use and especially for the rose breeder because they make possible many new combinations. Most of the cultivars introduced to date have come from the Kordes firm but the inherent characteristics of the class will undoubtedly encourage further development.

The New Classification System

Because of the inconsistent and imprecise method of classification of contemporary cultivars, the World Federation of Rose Societies is attempting to develop a simplified, internationally accepted classification system based strictly on horticultural characteristics. It applies, however, only to modern cultivars that are being hybridized and introduced in large numbers. The classification of the old garden roses is to remain as established, since they are no longer subjects of intensive hybridization.

The proposed system is based first on habit of growth: I. Climbing vs. II. Nonclimbing. The next division involves flowering habit: A. Recurrent vs. B. Nonrecurrent. Under the nonclimbing recurrent-flowering roses (II A), five classes are recognized: (1) Shrub Roses, with plants large and tall, suitable primarily for landscape use; (2) Large-flowered Roses (to include present Hybrid Teas and most Grandifloras) with flowers of medium to large size with high symmetrical centers (in semidouble and double forms) and capable of being cut as specimens (with or without side buds) on long stems; (3) Cluster-flowered Roses (to include present Floribundas), distinguished by a mass of medium-sized flowers produced in clusters or trusses or on numerous stems; (4) Polyantha Roses, with small flowers, usually of rosette form, borne in large clusters; (5) Miniature Roses, with diminutive flowers, foliage, and growth.

Obviously, this new classification system, which was tentatively approved at the first World Rose Convention in 1971, will take time to refine and become internationally used.

Culture

The garden roses in America include, in order of their importance, the Hybrid Teas, Floribundas, Grandifloras, Miniatures, Climbers, and Shrubs. They are currently available in hundreds of horticultural varieties and represent one of the most useful, most widely grown, and attractive group of garden plants. They do best in an open, sunny location where the soil is fertile, well drained, and well away from invading tree roots. The shrub types are useful for background border plantings and in combination with other plants. Some of the species and shrub roses have, in addition to their abundant flowers, decorative fruits called hips, which in some cases remain in good condition over winter.

Broadly speaking, garden roses need to be planted by themselves, in beds or borders, partly for appearance and partly for ease of culture. The Floribunda Roses are useful for mass display and with care may be grown in herbaceous borders and as low hedges. Climbers are adapted to growing on fences, arbors, posts, and trellises. The shrub roses are used in landscape borders, as hedges, or in other ways to serve as a background against which the lower-growing roses may be displayed.

It is important that the rose garden be so planted that it can be adequately cared for. This means that the beds not be so wide or the plants so close that cultivating, mulching, watering, and disease and insect control cannot be taken care of easily.

Roses do well in any soil that will grow most other garden plants. The addition of peat moss, rotted manure, leaf mold, compost, and other forms of organic matter will improve both light and heavy soils. Roses seem to do best in soils neither strongly acid nor alkaline, and a pH value of about 6.5 is considered optimum. In all cases thorough drainage is essential because roses will not tolerate a waterlogged soil.

Planting methods vary according to the region of the country. Ordinarily, roses in beds in the North can be as close together as 18–20 inches. In warmer climates, where growth is greater, distance must increase to 3 or 4 feet. In general, the rose grower varies his soil composition and his cultural practice according to his own experience or by reading the information constantly supplied by other amateurs through the American Rose Society publications.

Roses are best planted as fully dormant, bare-root plants very early in the spring. Autumn planting is satisfactory, but is less commonly practiced in recent years because rose plants are no longer readily available in the autumn. In most production areas, the plants are not harvested until too late for autumn planting. Plants set out in the autumn require soil mounded around the base for winter protection. Plants are also available in containers during the spring and early summer so that they may be purchased and transplanted to the garden without seriously disturbing the growth cycle. They are especially convenient to fill in where plants may be lost after the spring planting season is over.

Pruning is as necessary to obtain good roses as it is for good fruit. In Cold climates, winter injury usually dictates the procedure that involves removing all the dead wood and small twiggy growth. In milder climates, where the bushes are not killed back to the soil level, the dead and weak wood is removed and the large strong canes cut back, depending on how large one desires his plants, usually 18–24 inches above the ground.

Climbers are pruned in essentially the same way except that the canes are cut back only far enough to make the plants conform to the support and give the desired effect. Periodically, however, it is necessary to thin out the plants by removing some of the oldest canes to keep the plants from becoming overgrown. In the case of the recurrent-flowering climbers, only the flower cluster itself is cut off after the blooms have withered. The species and shrub roses are usually pruned only by removing shoots that have become tangled or are obviously diseased or worn out. Pruning for special regions is best learned by conferring with others who are successful, and in that respect the American Rose Society is prepared to provide important information and put one in touch with other rose gardeners.

Generally speaking, rose pruning should be done in late winter or early spring, though it may be necessary to do some during the summer to keep the plants tidy. Those exhibiting blooms in shows often prune or cut back their plants in order to time the flowers for the date of the show.

Winter protection depends on climate and location of the garden. Throughout the middle states, mounding soil from 6 inches to 1 foot above the base will suffice. Even if the cold is severe, the base of the plants will not be killed. Gardens in exposed, windy locations need more covering than those in protected locations. Usually it is well to cut back tall plants to prevent the canes from whipping in the wind. Placing a mulch of straw, wood chips, or other loose organic matter on top of the soil mound helps to keep it in place and adds further protection. In very cold climates it may be necessary to remove climbers from their supports and weight them to the ground to prevent winter damage. Winter protection should not be given until after the growth has been stopped by hard freezes in the autumn.

Rose plants may be propagated by rooting cuttings, budding, or grafting. For the gardener, propagation by rooting cuttings is the most practical. The simplest method is to make cuttings 5–7 inches long from stems that have just finished flowering. These are then placed in the ground under a glass jar in a shady location and kept moist at all times. Usually the cuttings are left in place until the following spring, when they can be transplanted to their permanent location. Cuttings may also be rooted indoors in water, under mist in a greenhouse, or in cold frames.

The commercial nursery method of propagation is by budding on an understock in the field. This practice permits more rapid buildup of stock, and plants of good quality can be produced more rapidly. Also, many cultivars are more vigorous when budded than on their own roots. The most common understocks used for garden roses are the various forms of *R. multiflora* and an old large-flowered climber named 'Dr. Huey'. In Europe, various forms of *R. canina* are used as the understock. Nursery-grown, budded roses are sold by grades set up by the American Association of Nurserymen. For the garden the No. 1 grade is best. Obviously, there is little economy in buying poor stock simply because it is cheap. Top quality No. 1 grade plants from a reputable nurseryman are recommended. Plants purchased in stores should be carefully examined to make sure that the canes and roots have not dried out and that long, white shoots are not already growing. These will invariably die and the plants will be severely weakened.

The production of roses is an important part of the nursery industry in the United States and annually about 40 million are grown for garden use. Another 20 million are grown for greenhouse cut-flower production. The major production areas in the United States are in Texas, California, Arizona, and Pennsylvania.

ROSELLE. This is an annual species of *Hibiscus, H. Sabdariffa,* sometimes grown in the warmest parts of the United

States and in the tropics for the large, thick, acid calyx and bracts that are prized in the making of jams, sauces, jellies, and acid drinks. It is grown like tomatoes or eggplants. Rows are ordinarily spaced for garden tractor tillage, and plants may be set 18–24 inches apart in the row. The plants reach 4–5 feet or more in height, making a continuous line or hedge. The bolls or heads are picked when immature, before becoming woody, and utilized either fresh or after being dried. There are yellowish forms of roselle, but in the usual kind the bolls are red. The plant is known also as Jamaica sorrel.

ROSEOCACTUS: *ARIOCARPUS.* **R. Lloydii:** *A. fissuratus* var.

ROSEOCEREUS: *TRICHOCEREUS.*

ROSMARINUS L. ROSEMARY. *Labiatae.* Three spp. of evergreen shrubs of the Medit. region; sts. mostly square in cross section; lvs. opp., simple; fls. in few-fld. verticillasters, arranged in short, axillary racemes, calyx campanulate, 2-lipped, upper lip entire, lower lip 2-lobed, corolla longer than calyx, 2-lipped, upper lip strongly concave, 2-lobed, lower lip 3-lobed with concave middle lobe, fertile stamens 2, exserted, style long, incurved, unbranched; fr. of 4 glabrous nutlets.

The fresh flowering tops of *R. officinalis* are used to distill the aromatic oil used in perfumery and medicine; dried leaves are used in seasoning. Rosemary requires a well-drained soil and some winter protection in the North; it is a useful hedge plant in southern Calif., especially along the coast where it is dry and rocky. Propagated by seeds or cuttings; probably as hardy as lavender.

Foresteri: a listed name of no botanical standing for *R. officinalis* cv. 'Lockwood de Forest'.

Lockwoodii: a listed name of no botanical standing for *R. officinalis* cv. 'Lockwood de Forest'.

officinalis L. ROSEMARY. Shrub, 2–4 ft., rarely to 6 ft., young brs. pubescent; lvs. leathery, linear, ½–1½ in. long, obtuse, generally revolute, tomentose beneath; calyx campanulate, corolla about 3 times as long as calyx, to 5/16 in. long, pale blue, rarely pink or white. Spring. Medit. region, Portugal and nw. Spain. Many cvs. have been segregated on the basis of habit, lf. width, or fl. color. These include: **'Albus'**, fls. white; **'Collingwood Ingram'**, brs. curving gracefully, fls. bright blue-violet; **'Lockwood de Forest'**, like 'Prostratus', but foliage lighter, brighter, and fls. bluer; **'Prostratus'** [*R. prostratus* Hort., perhaps not Mazziari], prostrate; **'Tuscan Blue'**, sts. rigid, upright, lvs. green, fls. bright blue-violet.

prostratus: see *R. officinalis* cv.

ROSULARIA (DC.) Stapf. *Crassulaceae.* About 25 spp. of succulent, mostly tuber-bearing, per. rosette plants of Asia Minor and Asia; lvs. flat, broad-based; fl. st. mostly lateral, infl. more or less paniculate; fls. 5–6-merous, corolla tubular basally, stamens 10–12, pistils erect.

For culture see *Succulents.*

pallida (Schott & Kotschy) Stapf [*Cotyledon chrysantha* (Boiss. & Heldr.) Bornm.; *Sedum chrysanthum* (Boiss. & Heldr.) Hamet; *Umbilicus chrysanthus* Boiss. & Heldr.]. Glandular-pubescent, rosettes 1–1½ in. wide, with offsets; lvs. oblong-spatulate, to ¾ in. long, obtuse; fl. st. to 8 in.; fls. erect, ½ in. long, corolla white or yellowish, often striped with red, cleft about to middle. Summer. Asia Minor.

Sempervivum (Bieb.) A. Berger [*Umbilicus Sempervivum* (Bieb.) DC.]. Minutely glandular-villous; lvs. spatulate, ¾ in. long, truncate-rounded, dentate-ciliate; fl. st. 2–6 in.; corolla reddish, ⅜ in. long, cleft to middle, pubescent outside. Late spring. Caucasus to Asia Minor.

ROTALA L. TOOTH-CUP. *Lythraceae.* About 40 spp. of ann. or rarely per. herbs of wet places, native to temp. and trop. regions; lvs. usually opp. or whorled, rarely alt., sessile or subsessile; fls. inconspicuous, axillary, or in terminal or axillary spikes, rarely in axillary umbels, calyx 3–6-lobed, petals 3–6, sometimes 0, stamens 1–6, ovary 2–4-celled; fr. a septicidal caps.

indica (Willd.) Koehne. Sts. to 14 in.; lvs. opp., elliptic to oblanceolate, to 4 in. long; fls. sessile, solitary in axils of reduced upper lvs., calyx teeth pink, petals purplish-violet, stamens 4. Japan to India and Malay Arch. Sometimes grown in aquaria.

ROTHMANNIA Thunb. *Rubiaceae.* About 20 spp. of shrubs or small trees, native to trop. and s. Afr.; lvs. opp., elliptic, stipules ovate, united between lvs., hairy on inner surface; fls. solitary, sessile, corolla 5-lobed, tube cylindrical basally, campanulate above, stamens 5, anthers sessile or nearly so; fr. fleshy, globose.

capensis Thunb. [*Gardenia Rothmannia* L.f.]. Small tree; lvs. to 3 in. long; fls. showy, fragrant, corolla yellowish, spotted in throat, tube to 2 in. long, lobes to 1 in. long, spreading, anthers slender, almost sessile, exserted. S. Afr.

globosa (Hochst.) Keay [*Gardenia globosa* Hochst.]. Shrub or small tree, with dark-colored bark; lvs. lanceolate or oblanceolate, to 6 in. long; fls. showy, 1–3, axillary or terminal, fragrant, corolla campanulate, white with pink lines in throat, tube broad, 2 in. long, lobes spreading, about ½ as long as tube. S. Afr.

longiflora Salisb. [*Randia maculata* DC.]. Shrub or small tree, to 15 ft.; lvs. more or less elliptic, to 5 in. long, acuminate, cuneate; fls. more or less erect, corolla greenish or reddish and hairy outside, lobes white inside, spotted with purple or red, tube to 2 in. long. W. Trop. Afr.

urcelliformis (G. Schweinf. ex Hiern) Bullock ex A. Robyns [*Gardenia urcelliformis* G. Schweinf. ex Hiern]. Shrub or small tree, to 25 ft.; lvs. elliptic, often broadly so, to 5 in. long; fls. axillary, solitary, corolla campanulate, white with purple markings, tube broad, to 2½ in. long; fr. subglobose, to 3 in. long. Trop. Afr.

ROUPALA Aubl. *Proteaceae.* About 50 spp. of trop. Amer. trees or shrubs; lvs. evergreen, alt., simple or pinnate (sometimes both on same plant), leathery; fls. bisexual, in racemes; fr. a hard caps.

corcovadensis: *R. macrophylla.*

macrophylla Pohl [*R. corcovadensis* Hort. ex Meissn.; *R. Pohlii* Meissn., in part]. To 30 ft. or more; young shoots rusty-tomentose; lvs. simple or pinnate, pinnate lvs. about 12 in. long, lfts. 5-8 pairs, ovate, to 5 in. long, acuminate, oblique at base, coarsely toothed, simple lvs. broadly ovate, to 6 in. long, coarsely toothed. Brazil.

Pohlii: *R. macrophylla.*

ROYENA L. *Ebenaceae.* Fifteen spp. of shrubs or trees, native to Old World tropics; lvs. usually alt., entire; fls. mostly solitary, bisexual, 4–8-merous, commonly with 10 stamens; fr. fleshy, ½-1 in. long, with enlarged persistent calyx.

lucida L. Evergreen shrub or tree, to 12 ft., brs. spreading, young growth and calyces tawny-hairy; lvs. elliptic-ovate, to 2¼ in. long, petioles very short; fls. solitary, axillary, on peduncles to 1 in. long, 5-merous, white to yellowish, anthers hispid; fr. ovoid to subglobose, to 1 in. long, red or purple, with firm, whitish flesh. S. Afr.

ROYSTONEA O. F. Cook. [*Oreodoxa* of auth., not Willd.]. ROYAL PALM. *Palmae.* About 14 or probably fewer spp. of solitary, columnar, unarmed, monoecious palms of the Caribbean region and ne. S. Amer.; lvs. pinnate, sheaths forming a prominent crownshaft, pinnae acute, midrib prominent; infl. below the lvs., much-branched, peduncle short, bracts 2, deciduous, the lower short, open, the upper cylindrical, enclosing the infl. in bud, rachillae with fls. in triads (2 male and 1 female); male fls. somewhat asymmetrical, sepals 3, briefly imbricate basally, acute, petals 3, valvate, acute, much exceeding sepals, stamens 6-9, filaments erect in bud or minutely inflexed at apex, pistillode short, globose, female fls. with sepals 3, broadly imbricate, rounded, petals 3, united basally, valvate above, staminodes united in a 6-lobed tube joined to corolla, pistil 1-celled, 1-ovuled, but sometimes with additional cells functional and more than 1 fr. formed; fr. ellipsoid to subglobose, stigmatic residue subbasal, seed with homogeneous endosperm, embryo subbasal. A genus in which spp. are poorly distinguished except for two main types represented by *R. oleracea* and *R. regia.*

The roystoneas are fast-growing, highly ornamental palms of striking appearance, much planted throughout the tropics and particularly effective for avenues or in groups or masses. They require rich, moist, well-drained soil, and are resistant to wind and salt spray. Zone 10. For culture see *Palms.*

borinquena O. F. Cook. PUERTO RICAN R.P. To 50 ft. or more, swollen in upper part and tapered to infl.; lvs. to 10 ft. long, pinnae many, in 2 planes on each side, to 3 ft. long, 2 in. wide; infl. with scurfy rachillae; male fls. dense, with 6-9 stamens, anthers purple; fr. obovoid, to about ⅝ in. long, ½ in. in diam. Puerto Rico.

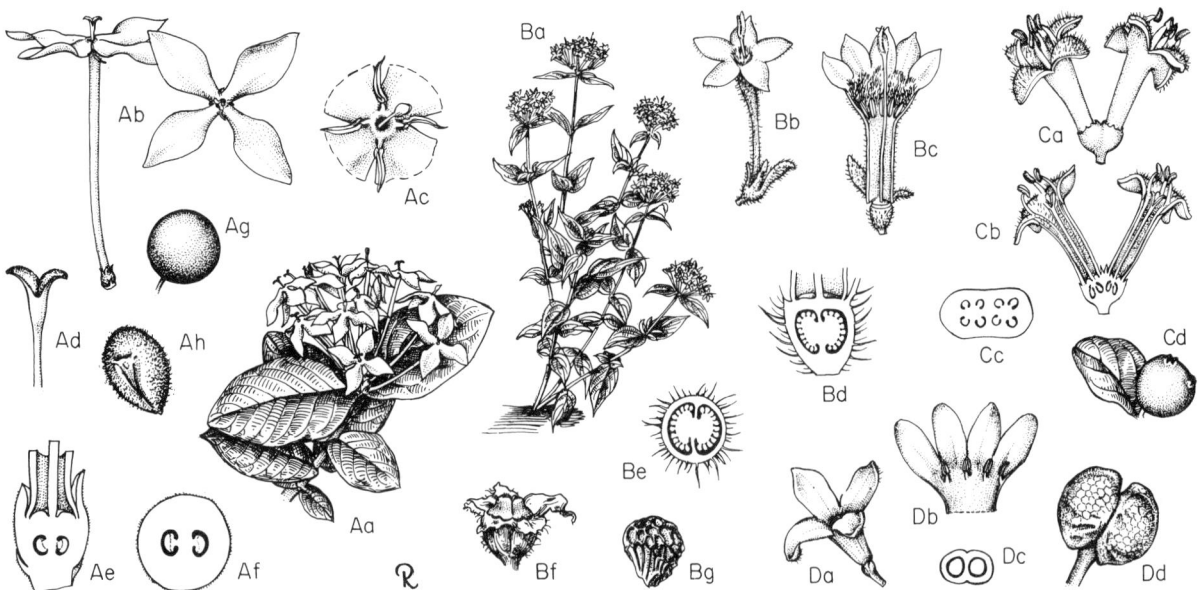

RUBIACEAE. **A,** *Ixora coccinea:* **Aa,** flowering branch, × ½; **Ab,** flower, side and face view, × 1; **Ac,** detail of center of flower (corolla lobes cut short), × 2; **Ad,** stigma and upper part of style, × 4; **Ae,** base of flower, vertical section, × 5; **Af,** ovary, cross section, × 8; **Ag,** berry, × 1; **Ah,** seed, × 1½. **B,** *Pentas lanceolata:* **Ba,** plant, × ⅛; **Bb,** flower, × 1; **Bc,** flower with corolla expanded, × 1; **Bd,** ovary, vertical section, × 5; **Be,** ovary, cross section, × 5; **Bf,** capsule, × 2; **Bg,** seed, × 15. **C,** *Mitchella repens:* **Ca,** paired flowers, × 1½; **Cb,** flowers, vertical section, × 1½; **Cc,** united ovaries, cross section, × 3; **Cd,** berry, × 1. **D,** *Asperula ciliata:* **Da,** flower, × 3; **Db,** corolla, expanded, × 3; **Dc,** ovary, cross section, × 10; **Dd,** fruit, × 5.

elata (Bartr.) F. Harper [*R. floridana* O. F. Cook]. FLORIDA R.P. Similar to *R. regia,* but said to differ in less prominent secondary veins of the pinnae and in the nearly globose fr. S. Fla. Zone 10a.

floridana: *R. elata.*

hispaniolana L. H. Bailey. HISPANIOLAN R.P. Similar to *R. borinquena,* but said to differ in the duller upper surface of lvs.

Jenmanii: *R. regia.*

oleracea (Jacq.) O. F. Cook [*Oreodoxa oleracea* (Jacq.) Mart.; *R. venezuelana* L. H. Bailey]. CARIBBEE R.P., S. AMER. R.P. To 100 ft. or more, trunk swollen at base, then cylindrical; lvs. to 20 ft. long, ascending or spreading, forming a crown usually appearing nearly flat on lower side, pinnae in 1 plane near base and apex of lf. but usually in 2 planes at middle of lf. in mature individuals; infl. with undulate rachillae; male fls. ¼ in. long, stamens 6, filaments usually exceeding the petals and anthers much exserted; fr. oblong-ellipsoid, blackish at maturity, to ¾ in. long, ⅜ in. in diam. Trinidad, Barbados, Venezuela, e. Colombia. Zone 10b.

princeps (Becc.) Burret. MORASS R.P. Similar to *P. regia* but rachillae very slender, male fls. small. In swamps, Jamaica.

regia (HBK) O. F. Cook [*Oreodoxa regia* HBK; *R. Jenmanii* (C. H. Wright) Burret; *R. ventricosa* (C. H. Wright) Burret]. CUBAN R. P. To 75 ft. or more; trunk nearly uniform or often enlarged at base and variously swollen near the middle, tapering upward; lvs. arched and usually the lower drooping to form a nearly globose crown, pinnae to 3 ft. long, 1–1½ in. wide, in several planes along most of the rachis; infl. to 3 ft. long or more, rachillae essentially straight in bud and in fr.; male fls. ³⁄₁₆ in. long, stamens scarcely exserted, often violet, filaments not exceeding petals; fr. dull dark red to purple, variable, from nearly globose to obovoid, to ½ in. long, ⅜ in. in diam. Cuba, where all parts of the plant are used. Widely cult. Zone 10a.

venezuelana: *R. oleracea.*

ventricosa: *R. regia.*

RUBIA L. *Rubiaceae.* About 40 or more spp. of mostly per. herbs, native to Medit. region, s. Afr., trop. Afr. and Amer., and temp. Asia; lvs. whorled or rarely opp., stipules 3-sided or minute; fls. in axillary or terminal cymes, small, 5-merous, corolla rotate or slightly campanulate; fr. fleshy, seeds few.

tinctorum L. MADDER. To 4 ft., erect or decumbent; lvs. in whorls of 4–6, lanceolate, to 4 in. long, prickly on midribs and edges; fls. greenish-yellow, in branching cymes; fr. red, turning black. S. Eur., Asia Minor. Once cult. for the root dye alizarin, now prepared artificially.

RUBIACEAE Juss. MADDER FAMILY. Dicot; nearly 400 genera and 4,800–5,000 spp. of herbs, shrubs, vines, or trees, native chiefly to tropics and subtropics; lvs. opp. or whorled, simple, stipules present, commonly interpetiolar, sometimes leafy; fls. in cymes, these sometimes aggregated into globose heads, usually regular, bisexual, calyx and corolla mostly 4–5-lobed, more rarely 6–9-lobed, stamens 4–5 or more, borne on the corolla, ovary inferior, cells 2 or more; fr. a caps., berry, or drupe. Closely allied to the Caprifoliaceae, but differing in having stipules.

The cult. genera are: *Adina, Alberta, Anthocephalus, Asperula, Bouvardia, Burchellia, Calycophyllum, Canthium, Catesbaea, Cephaelis, Cephalanthus, Chiococca, Cinchona, Coccocypselum, Coffea, Coprosma, Coutarea, Crucianella, Crusea, Damnacanthus, Duggena, Emmenopterys, Faramea, Feretia, Galium, Gardenia, Genipa, Guettarda, Hamelia, Hedyotis, Hoffmannia, Isertia, Ixora, Kraussia, Leptodermis, Luculia, Manettia, Mitchella, Mitragyna, Mitriostigma, Morinda, Mussaenda, Nauclea, Nertera, Oldenlandia, Palicourea, Pavetta, Pentas, Pinckneya, Pogonopus, Portlandia, Posoqueria, Psychotria, Putoria, Randia, Ravnia, Richardia, Rondeletia, Rothmannia, Rubia, Serissa, Tarenna, Vangueria, Warszewiczia, Wendlandia,* and *Xeromphis.*

Besides ornamentals the family includes a number of economic plants producing such products as coffee and quinine, dyes and medicines.

RUBUS. BRAMBLE. *Rosaceae.* More than 250 spp. (and many more apomictic segregates) of shrubs, rarely nearly herbaceous, the woody spp. with bien. canes (fruiting the second year and then dying), most of them prickly, cosmopolitan but mostly in N. Hemisphere; lvs. alt., prevailingly palmately or pinnately compound, but sometimes simple; fls. white or pinkish or rose, mostly clustered in the cult. spp.; fr. an aggregate of small drupes, in raspberries the cone or thimble of cohering drupelets separating from the receptacle when mature, in blackberries or dewberries the drupelets remaining attached to the receptacle, the receptacle being eaten as part of the fr. The new cane, which usually does not flower and fruit the first year, is called a *primocane;* the second year, it bears fls. and frs., may have different foliage, and is called a *floricane.* The characters of the cane at these two stages are important in distinguishing the spp. botanically. Includes the blackberries, dewberries, raspberries; grown for fr. and also a good number of exotic spp. planted for the showy fls. and ornamental foliage. Dewberries differ from blackberries only in being vines, running over the ground, or needing support when planted.

The pomological blackberries and dewberries in N. Amer. are derived from native species, but the cultivars cannot now always be referred to their original sources.

The brambles are of simple culture. The canes of blackberries and raspberries should be removed at the ground after fruiting to allow the new ones to develop. An open exposure and average garden soil are suitable. They grow readily from seeds, but the usual method of propagation is by root cuttings or by suckers; in some of them the new canes take root either at the nodes or at the recurving tip. See *Blackberry, Boysenberry, Dewberry*, and *Raspberry*.

albescens: *R. niveus.*

alleghdeniensis T. C. Porter. SOW-TEAT BLACKBERRY. Sts. glandular, erect or finally somewhat arching, to 10 ft., with hooked prickles; lfts. 3 or 5, ovate or oblong-ovate, long-pointed, soft-pubescent beneath; infl. elongate; fr. mostly long or oblong, sweet and aromatic. Nov. Sc., s. to N.C. and Mo. Zone 4. In dry open lands the plant may remain as low as 1 or 2 ft.

arcticus L. CRIMSON B., ARCTIC B. Herbaceous, 3–15 in., with slender underground rhizomes but lacking aerial stolons; lvs. with 3 lfts., coarsely toothed, central lft. longer than broad, to 2 in. long; fls. solitary, pink; fr. red. Arctic and subarctic Eurasia. The plant so listed in Amer. is probably *R. stellatus.*

argutus Link. Sts. nonglandular, erect or becoming arching, stiff and upright in the open, or more or less decumbent in woods, to 8 ft. or more; lfts. 3 or 5, mostly elliptic to oblong or lanceolate-ovate, commonly soft-pubescent beneath, petioles and infl. essentially glandless; infl. short; fr. black, rather small, short-oblong. Cent. e. states, w. to Miss. R.

australis G. Forst. Lofty tree climber, dioecious, brs. slender and drooping, recurved-prickly; lfts. usually 3 or 5, variable, narrow-ovate to lanceolate, to 5 in. long, glabrous or sometimes tomentose beneath, sharp-serrate; fls. white, to ½ in. across; fr. reddish-orange, ¼ in. in diam. New Zeal. Adapted only to warm regions, sometimes grown under glass.

Chamaemorus L. CLOUDBERRY, MALKA, SALMONBERRY, YELLOW-BERRY, BAKE APPLE, BAKED-APPLE, BAKED-APPLE BERRY. Monoecious or dioecious, sts. nearly or quite herbaceous, 3–10 in. high, from a creeping rhizome; lvs. 2 or 3, rounded in outline and obtusely lobed; fl. solitary, white, to 1 in. across; fr. reddish or yellow. Arctic and subarctic, circumpolar, s. to Me. Zone 2. Suitable for the cool rock garden.

coronarius Sweet. BRIER ROSE. Smaller than *R. rosifolius*, young parts and lvs. glabrous and strongly resin-dotted, prickles much more numerous and stout; lfts. relatively small, not prominently acuminate, mostly narrowed at base; fls. double, white, 1 in. across or more. Probably Asia; cult. in warm regions; hardy as far n. as N.J.

cuneifolius Pursh. SAND BLACKBERRY. Stiff and erect, 1–3 ft., branched, strongly armed; lvs. white-pubescent beneath, lfts. 3 or 5, mostly obovate, dentate, obtuse or short-acute; fls. white or pinkish, few in a cluster; fr. blackish, oblong, small but good. Sand, Conn. to Fla. Useful for cover on poor land.

deliciosus Torr. ROCKY MOUNTAIN FLOWERING RASPBERRY, ROCKY MOUNTAIN R. Upright, to 6 ft. or more, spreading and arching, unarmed; lvs. orbicular-ovate to reniform, with 3 or 5 broad, shallow lobes; fls. white, mostly solitary, to 2 in. across; fr. dark purple or wine-red. Canyons, Colo. Grown for the roselike fls. Zone 6.

dumetorum Weihe. EUROPEAN DEWBERRY. Canes long and slender, often to 25 ft., trailing or half-prostrate, glaucous, densely curved-spiny; lfts. usually 3, mostly broad-ovate, pointed, irregularly sharp-serrate; fls. small, white, calyx white-tomentose; fr. of a few large black drupelets. Useful for covering banks and for its bronzy autumn color.

ellipticus Sm. Clambering, strong, evergreen, to 10 or 15 ft., sts. densely reddish- or brownish-hairy and stout-prickly; lfts. 3, ovate to elliptic or broader, obtuse or short-acute, serrate, gray-tomentose beneath; fls. white, in panicles; fr. yellow. India. Grown in warm climates.

flagellaris Willd. AMERICAN DEWBERRY. Trailing, rooting at tips, not glandular, with recurved prickles; lfts. 3 or 5, ovate to triangular-ovate, acute to acuminate, serrate-dentate; fls. few, in a forking infl.; fr. round to oblong, black, edible. Canada to the Gulf states. Zone 4. Cvs. are: 'Almus', unarmed, fl. clusters usually arising from lateral buds on floricanes rather than on leafy shoots; 'Foster Thornless' dewberry belongs here; 'Geophilus', lvs. very large, cut-toothed, probable origin of the 'Mayes' or 'Austin' and similar dewberries; 'Roribaccus'

[cv. 'Lucretia'], robust, lfts. cuneate-obovate and doubly serrate, pedicels to 6 in. long, fls. and fr. very large.

×**Fraseri** Rehd.: *R. parviflorus* × *R. odoratus.* To 8 ft., less glandular-hairy than *R. odoratus;* fls. rose, fading to pale purple.

Henryi Hemsl. & O. Kuntze. Climbing, evergreen, sts. tomentose when young, with few prickles; lvs. deeply 3–5-parted, white-tomentose beneath, segms. or lfts. long and narrow, to 6 in. long and 1 in. wide; fls. pink, ¾ in. across, in glandular racemes. China. Zone 7. Var. **bambusarum** (Hemsl.) Rehd. Lfts. 3, narrow, short-stalked, to 4 in. long.

hispidus L. SWAMP DEWBERRY, RUNNING BLACKBERRY, SWAMP B. Slender, hispid, often glandular trailer, lying close to the ground, without prickles; foliage glossy, mostly evergreen, lfts. mostly 3, obovate and obtuse; fls. small, few; fr. black at full maturity, sour. Low places, Canada, s. to Ga. and Kans. Zone 4.

idaeus L. RED RASPBERRY, EUROPEAN R., FRAMBOISE. Erect, 3–5 ft. or more, prickles many, or few or none, sometimes bristly but not glandular, propagating by suckers; lfts. 3 or 5, ovate or broader, dentate, grayish, or white-pubescent beneath; fls. whitish, few and small; fr. oblong, conical, or thimble-shaped, mostly dark red, but sometimes yellowish or whitish. Eurasia. Zone 4. The pomological red raspberries belong to this sp. and its vars. Var. **canadensis** Richardson. Young canes ashy-tomentose, not bristly. Lab. to Colo., n. to Alaska. Var. **strigosus** (Michx.) Maxim. [*R. strigosus* Michx.]. AMERICAN RED R. More hardy; infl., and sometimes new canes, bristly and glandular; fr. light red, hemispherical to conical, soft. Nfld. to N.C., w. to Wyo. and B.C.; e. Asia. The purple cane raspberries, frs. mostly purplish, are apparently hybrids of *R. idaeus* or relatives and *R. occidentalis.*

laciniatus Willd. CUT-LEAF BLACKBERRY, CUT-LEAVED B., EVERGREEN B., PARSLEY-LEAVED B. Strong, more or less evergreen, hardy blackberry, canes per., prickly, trailing, becoming glabrous; lfts. 3 or 5, cut into very narrow, acute, toothed segms.; fls. white or pink, in large panicles; fr. small to medium, round or nearly so, black. Eur.; often naturalized in N. Amer. Zone 6. There are a few pomological cvs., such as 'Starr' and 'Wonder'.

laudatus A. Berger. Tall, erect, nonglandular, canes furrowed, becoming glabrous, with straight or retrorse prickles; lfts. 3 or 5, obovate-oblong to oblanceolate to ovate, acuminate, serrate; fls. white, in a short, leafy cluster; fr. ovoid, black, sweet, early. Mo., Kans. 'Bundy' and 'Kenoyer' blackberries belong here.

leucodermis Dougl. ex Torr. & A. Gray. Differs from *R. occidentalis* in yellowish canes, more strongly recurved and flattish prickles; lfts. yellowish-green above, less acuminate, more strongly cut and sharply toothed; fr. reddish or black, edible. B.C. to Calif., e. to Mont. and Utah. Zone 6.

louisianus A. Berger. Erect, nonglandular, with scattered prickles, canes becoming glabrous with age; distinguished by the narrowly lanceolate and long-pointed lfts., to 4 in. long, sharp-serrate; fls. white, in open, leafy clusters; fr. cylindrical, white or nearly so. S. U.S. The pomological cvs. 'Crystal White' and 'Iceberg' are derived from this sp.

macropetalus Dougl. ex Hook. BLACKBERRY, DEWBERRY. At first ascending, becoming procumbent or vinelike, not tomentose, canes slender, glaucous, with weak prickles; lfts. 3, green on both sides, thin, mostly acuminate or pointed, very sharply toothed; fls. unisexual, white, variable in size, in short clusters, pedicels and large calyx with stalked glands; fr. glabrous, black. N. Calif. to B.C. Often confused with *R. ursinus.*

mirus L. H. Bailey. Decumbent or clambering, with stout prickles, but no bristles or glands, prickles on pedicel also long and prominent; lfts. on new shoots ovate or elliptic, more than half as wide as long; fls. white, very large, commonly more than 1 in. across; fr. 1 in. long or more, black, of good quality. Fla. The 'Marvel' dewberry belongs here.

moluccanus L. Robust, raspberrylike, tomentose, red-hairy, with curved prickles; lvs. simple, tomentose beneath, usually broad-ovate and deeply cordate, more or less 3–5-lobed; fls. white, in terminal clusters; fr. edible. India, Malay Pen.

nemorosus Hayne. Related to *R. caesius*, sts. slender, to 25 ft., pruinose, rather thickly set in lower part with small, somewhat curved prickles; lfts. usually broad-ovate, irregularly serrate, bronzy in autumn, pubescent beneath; fls. small, corymbose, calyx greenish-tomentose. Caucasus, Eur. Zone 6.

nivalis Dougl. ex Hook. Woody, prickly vine, to 3 ft. or more; lvs. persistent, mostly simple, more or less 3-lobed, rounded, serrate; fls. red. Idaho, Ore., n. to B.C.

niveus Thunb. [*R. albescens* Roxb.]. HILL RASPBERRY, MYSORE R. Sts. to 6 ft., cylindrical, tomentulose when young or glabrous and bloomy, with hooked prickles; lfts. 5 or 7, elliptic-ovate, 1–2½ in. long, acute or acuminate, broad-cuneate, simply and coarsely serrate; fls. small, rosy-purple, in paniclelike clusters, calyx glabrous; fr. red. India, w. China. Zone 7?

occidentalis L. BLACK RASPBERRY, BLACKCAP, THIMBLEBERRY. Erect, 3–5 ft., canes glaucous, prickly, bending over and rooting at tip; lfts. mostly 3, ovate-acuminate, doubly dentate, white-tomentose beneath; fls. small, whitish, in dense, short, prickly clusters; fr. hemispherical, black, sometimes amber, glaucous, firm. Que. to e. Colo., s. to Ga. and Ark. Zone 4. The source of many cvs. of black raspberry.

odoratus L. FLOWERING RASPBERRY, PURPLE-FLOWERING R., THIMBLEBERRY. To 6 ft., erect, unarmed, with shredding bark, forming colonies; lvs. simple, large, broad-ovate, cordate, 3–5-lobed, finely serrate, pubescent beneath; fls. to 2 in. across, rose-purple to whitish, many, in loose clusters; fr. red, flat, dry, not eaten. Mich., s. to N.C., Ga., Tenn.

parviflorus Nutt. THIMBLEBERRY, SALMONBERRY. Like *R. odoratus*, but fls. fewer and white. Mich. to Alaska, s. to Mex. Zone 4.

parvus J. Buchan. Prostrate, dioecious, sts. to 1½ ft., glabrous; lvs. consisting of single lft., this linear or linear-lanceolate, acute, dentate, to 3 in. long; fls. solitary or panicled, small, white; fr. ½–1 in. long. New Zeal.

pedatus Sm. To 3 ft. or more, more or less herbaceous, very slender vine, without prickles; lfts. 5, small, dentate-serrate; fls. white, solitary, on slender pedicels. Alaska to Ore.

phoenicolasius Maxim. WINEBERRY. Canes long, recurving and rooting at the tip, with weak, nearly straight prickles and red-brown, glandular hairs; lfts. usually 3, broadly cordate-ovate, dentate, purplish-veined, white-tomentose beneath; fls. small, whitish or pink, in close clusters; calyx large, bristly; fr. bright red, small, edible. China, Japan; escaped in U.S. Zone 6.

procerus P. J. Muell. HIMALAYA BERRY. Very vigorous and thorny, canes woody, per., 20–40 ft. long, trailing or clambering, white-tomentose on young parts; lvs. thick, persistent, white-tomentose beneath; lfts. 3 or 5, broadly elliptic-ovate, sharply double-serrate; fls. white, in tomentose panicles; fr. subglobose to elliptic, black, edible. Eur.; now naturalized in many parts of N. Amer., where sometimes grown for the fr.

pubescens Raf. DWARF RASPBERRY. Soft, small, unarmed, herbaceous or somewhat woody; lfts. 3 or 5, rhombic-ovate, acute, serrate, thin, subglabrous; fls. white, to ½ in. across, 1–3 on a peduncle; fr. red-purple. Nfld. to Alaska, s. to N.J. and Nebr.

rosifolius Sm. MAURITIUS RASPBERRY. More or less trailing, canes 5–8 ft. long, pubescent at least on younger parts, with few recurved prickles; lvs. pinnate, thinly hairy, sharply double-serrate; lfts. 5 or 7, lanceolate, long-acuminate, broad at base; fls. white, solitary or in small clusters, long-pedicelled, sepals long-caudate; fr. globose to oblong, red, edible. E. Asia. Zone 7. Often grown in tropics. Roots used medicinally.

spectabilis Pursh. SALMONBERRY. Sts. per., upright, becoming long and prostrate, with few or weak spines, bark shredding, spreading by underground roots; lfts. 3, thin, ovate to oblong-ovate, acuminate, doubly dentate and somewhat lobed, nearly glabrous; fls. 1–4, rose to purplish, about 1 in. across; fr. more or less conical, salmon-colored, edible. Idaho and Calif. to Alaska. Zone 6.

stellatus Sm. NAGOONBERRY, KNESHENEKA. Herbaceous, unarmed, glabrous, decumbent or mat-forming, resembling strawberry; lfts. 3 or lvs. 3-lobed, close to ground; floricanes arising from crown or at ground, with 1 or 2 rose-colored fls.; fr. very small, globular. Alaska.

strigosus: *R. idaeus* var.

ulmifolius Schott. Sts. robust, arching or procumbent, prickles stout, broad-based, hairy; lfts. 3–5, white-tomentose beneath; infl. elongate; fls. pink or white. Eur. Var. **inermis** (Willd.) Focke. EVERGREEN THORNLESS BLACKBERRY. Canes per., very long, clambering, without prickles; lfts. 3 or 5, thick, ovate to elliptic-ovate, serrate, acute; fr. nearly globose, black. Often called 'Burbank Thornless'. Zone 6.

ursinus Cham. & Schlechtend. PACIFIC DEWBERRY, PACIFIC BLACKBERRY. Mostly strongly ascending at first, but becoming decumbent or vinelike, primocanes with hairs among the prickles; foliage dull green, felted or tomentose beneath, at least when young; lvs. usually having 3 lfts. except sometimes in the fl. clusters; fls. often functionally unisexual, white, pedicels and calyx usually glandless. Ore. to Baja Calif. Zone 6. Cvs. of the following are much grown for the frs. Var. **loganobaccus** (L. H. Bailey) L. H. Bailey. Fr. to 1¼ in. long, dark red, acid; includes cvs. 'Boysen', BOYSENBERRY and 'Logan', LOGANBERRY. Cv. 'Young', YOUNGBERRY, is also a derivative of *R. ursinus*. See *Boysenberry*.

vitifolius Cham. & Schlechtend. Differs from *R. ursinus* in having foliage thinner, green, glabrous or only pubescent beneath, not tomentose; middle lvs. of flowering shoots mostly 3-lobed rather than

having 3 lfts. W.-cent. Calif. The 'Mammoth' and 'Cory' blackberries are probably derived from this sp.

RUDBECKIA L. CONEFLOWER. *Compositae* (Helianthus Tribe). About 25 spp. of coarse, ann., bien., or per. herbs in N. Amer.; lvs. alt., simple, pinnatifid, or compound; fl. heads usually radiate and showy, terminal, receptacle hemispherical to columnar, scaly, the scales shorter than or just equalling the disc fls.; disc fls. fertile, ray fls. sterile, yellow to redbrown, not subtended by receptacular scales; achenes 4-angled, pappus a short crown or lacking. Of the closely related genera, *Dracopis* differs in its cylindrical achenes, *Echinacea* in its purplish ray fls. and the spinescent receptacular scales surpassing the disc fls., and *Ratibida* in its compressed achenes and scales subtending the ray fls.

Coneflowers thrive in almost any soil and location. Propagated by seeds, cuttings, or division. They are useful for yellow border effects in summer and autumn; some of the annuals are adapted to the flower garden.

amplexicaulis: *Dracopis amplexicaulis*.

bicolor: *R. hirta* var. *pulcherrima*.

californica A. Gray. CALIFORNIA C. Per., to 5 ft.; lvs. simple, slightly hairy, the lower broadly lanceolate to oblanceolate, toothed, petioled, the upper entire, clasping; heads large, receptacle conic-columnar in age, 1–2 in. long; disc fls. greenish-yellow, ray fls. yellow, spreading. Sierra Nevada of Calif. Var. **glauca** S. F. Blake. Lvs. glabrous, glaucous. Coastal forests, n. Calif., s. Ore.

columnaris: *Ratibida columnifera*.

columnifera: *Ratibida columnifera*.

Deamii: *R. fulgida* var.

flava: *R. hirta* var. *pulcherrima*.

fulgida Ait. Hairy, rhizomatous per., to 3 ft.; lvs. simple, basal lvs. long-petioled, lanceolate to ovate, entire, serrate, or crenate, uppermost st. lvs. sessile; heads many, medium-sized, receptacle shortconic; disc fls. brown-purple, with erect lobes, ray fls. orange-yellow, spreading; pappus a short crown. Var. **fulgida**. The typical var.; basal lvs. narrowly lanceolate to oblanceolate, ⅓ as broad as long. N.J. to Ill., s. to n. Ala. Var. **Deamii** (S. F. Blake) Perdue [*R. Deamii* S. F. Blake; *R. speciosa* var. *Deamii* Hort.]. Basal lvs. broadly elliptic to ovate, ½–⅜ as broad as long, coarsely crenate or serrate, upper st. lvs. about as large as lower st. lvs., with small, distant teeth; receptacular scales not ciliate at apex. Ind. Var. **speciosa** (Wender.) Perdue [*R. Newmanii* Hort.; *R. speciosa* Wender.; *R. speciosa* var. *Newmanii* Hort.]. Similar to var. *Deamii*, but basal lvs. entire or obscurely crenate, st. lvs. coarsely serrate or lacerate. N.J. to Ill., s. to Ala. Var. **Sullivantii** (Beadle & Boynt.) Cronq. [*R. speciosa* var. *Sullivantii* (Beadle & Boynt.) B. L. Robinson; *R. Sullivantii* Beadle & Boynt.]. Like var. *Deamii*, but st. lvs. successively reduced upward, the uppermost merely large bracts; ray fls. 1–2 in. long. Conn. to W.Va., w. to Mich. and Mo. Showiest and most frequently cult. of the vars.; improved cvs. are 'Oreile' and 'Goldsturm' [cv. 'Goldstorm'].

grandiflora (Sweet) DC. Rhizomatous per., to 3 ft.; lower lvs. ovate, long-petioled, upper lvs. sessile; heads 1 or few, long-peduncled, receptacle conic; disc fls. brown-purple, with reflexed lobes, ray fls. yellow, drooping, 1½–2½ in. long; pappus a short crown. Mo. and Okla. to La. and Tex.

hirta L. BLACK-EYED SUSAN. Hairy, nonrhizomatous ann., bien., or short-lived per., to 3 ft.; lvs. simple, the lower petioled, the upper sessile; receptacle conical; disc fls. brown-purple, ray fls. spreading; pappus lacking. Var. **hirta** [var. *monticola* (Small) Fern.; *R. monticola* Small]. The typical var.; lvs. coarsely toothed, blades of basal lvs. broadly elliptic to ovate, twice as long as wide, the upper ovate to ovate-lanceolate; ray fls. orange-yellow. Appalachian highlands, Penn. to Ga., and to n. Me., w. to Ill. Var. **pulcherrima** [*R. bicolor* Nutt.; *R. flava* T. V. Moore; *R. serotina* Nutt.]. Lvs. entire or finely serrate, blades of basal lvs. broadly oblanceolate, 3–5 times as long as wide, the upper oblanceolate to linear. Originally of the midwestern states; now naturalized in s. Canada, throughout the U.S., and n. Mex. Variable, and the more commonly cult. var., with many cvs., dwarfer or larger-headed or with ray fls. banded or suffused with maroon or multiplied in number. The cvs. 'Gloriosa Daisy' and 'Double Gloriosa Daisy' are tetraploid strains, tending to be per. but blooming first year from seed, coarser, with heads 6 in. across or more.

laciniata L. Per., to 9 ft.; lvs. pinnate, nearly glabrous, lfts. deeply lobed; receptacle hemispherical, becoming conic-oblong in age; disc fls. greenish-yellow, ray fls. yellow, 1½–2½ in. long, drooping. Que. to n. Fla., w. to Rocky Mts. and beyond. Cv. 'Soleil d'Or'. Ligules broader, showier. "Double-fld." cvs. include: 'Hortensia', GOLDEN-GLOW, 6–8 ft., the commonest form in cult., but invasive, weak-stemmed, and subject to aphids; 'Golden Globe', similar, but only about 4 ft.; 'Goldquelle' [*R. nitida* Hort. cv. 'Goldquelle'], with stronger sts., under 3 ft., and heads more symmetrically doubled.

maxima Nutt. Very coarse, glabrous per., sts. stiff, erect, 3–9 ft.; lvs. simple, glaucous, blades of basal lvs. elliptic, to 14 in. long, petioled, uppermost st. lvs. smaller, ovate, clasping; receptacle conic, becoming conic-cylindric and 2–3 in. long in age; ray fls. yellow, drooping, to 2 in. long. Mo., s. to La. and Tex.

monticola: *R. hirta* var. *hirta*.

Newmanii: *R. fulgida* var. *speciosa*.

nitida Nutt. Glabrous per., to 3 ft.; lvs. simple, leathery, ovate to lanceolate, upper st. lvs. tapering to a sessile base; receptacle conic-cylindric; disc fls. green-yellow, ray fls. yellow. Ga. and Fla. to Tex. Not reliably hardy north, and not in cult. Material grown under this name is *R. laciniata*. Cv. 'Goldquelle': *R. laciniata* cv.

occidentalis Nutt. Coarse per., to 6 ft.; lvs. large, simple, ovate; receptacle broadly conic-cylindric; disc fls. brown-purple, ray fls. lacking. Mont. to Colo., w. to Pacific states.

pallida: *Echinacea pallida*.

pinnata: *Ratibida pinnata*.

purpurea: *Echinacea purpurea*.

serotina: *R. hirta* var. *pulcherrima*.

speciosa: *R. fulgida* var. Var. **Deamii:** *R. fulgida* var. Var. **Newmanii:** *R. fulgida* var. *speciosa*. Var. **Sullivantii:** *R. fulgida* var.

subtomentosa Pursh. Nonrhizomatous per., to 4½ ft.; lvs. scabrous above, velvety-pubescent beneath, the lower deeply 3-lobed, the upper lanceolate to ovate, toothed; receptacle conic, scales of the receptacle inconspicuous, shorter than the disc fls., with pubescent, blunt tips; disc fls. brown-purple, ray fls. yellow, spreading. Wisc., s. to La. and Tex.

Sullivantii: *R. fulgida* var.

Tagetes: *Ratibida Tagetes*.

triloba L. Weedy bien. or per., to 4½ ft.; lvs. toothed, thinly hairy to nearly glabrous, lower lvs. ovate to cordate-ovate, often 3-lobed, long-petioled, upper lvs. narrower, sessile; receptacle hemispherical, scales of receptacle with conspicuous, acuminate, glabrous tips; disc fls. brown-purple, ray fls. uniformly yellow or with orange base, spreading. S. New Eng. to Minn., s. to Ga. and Okla.

RUELLIA L. *Acanthaceae*. About 250 spp. of per. herbs or shrubs, mostly in trop. Amer., Afr., and Asia, a few spp. in temp. regions of N. Amer.; lvs. opp., sessile or petioled, mostly entire; fls. usually large and showy, or small and cleistogamous, solitary or in axillary cymes or terminal panicles, calyx deeply 5-parted or -cleft, corolla with funnelform throat, lobes 5, spreading, nearly equal, stamens 4, didynamous, filaments of each pair united at base and decurrent on corolla tube, anther sacs parallel, oblong, symmetrical; fr. a cylindrical or clavate caps., seeds 4–20, often apparently glabrous when dry, but mucilaginous-pubescent when moist. *Ruellia* is a taxonomically difficult genus because of its size and diversity, and has been divided by different workers into smaller but not easily differentiated segregate genera.

Grown under glass and outdoors in the South for the ornamental flowers. Propagated by cuttings, seeds and division.

amoena: see *R. graecizans*.

affinis (Schrad.) Lindau. Shrub, to 3 ft., glabrous; lvs. elliptic, to 5 in. long, short-petioled; fls. axillary, solitary, corolla 3½ in. long, scarlet or pale red, broadly funnelform, lobes spreading. Brazil.

Blumei Steud. Stemless; lvs. narrow-oblong, to 4 in. long, crenulate; fls. small, in few-fld. axillary spikes shorter than lvs., corolla ¾ in. long, white, narrow-tubular in lower half, abruptly funnelform above. Supposedly native to Java, but perhaps only introd. there.

Brittoniana E. Leonard. Somewhat woody, to 3 ft.; lvs. elongate-linear, to 12 in. long and ¾ in. wide, entire to undulate, petioles to ¾ in. long; fls. terminal on elongated, axillary peduncles, corolla to 1½ in. long, lavender, tube about ½ in. long, expanded above, lobes rounded, spreading. Mex.; escaped from cult. in se. U.S. Sometimes confused with *R. malacosperma*.

caroliniensis (J. F. Gmel.) Steud. [*R. hybrida* Pursh]. To 2½ ft., sts. mostly simple; lvs. lanceolate to ovate, to 5 in. long, petioled; fls. subsessile or on short peduncles in axils of upper lvs., corolla to 2 in. long, lilac to lavender-blue, tube slender, about equalling expanded throat. S. N.J. and Penn., w. to s. Ind., s. to e. Tex. and Fla. A variable sp., closely related to *R. humilis*. Var. **dentata** (Nees) Fern. Lvs. often

undulate-dentate, the uppermost reduced in size and smaller than the lower. S. Penn., w. to s. Ind., s. to Tenn. and S.C.

ciliosa Pursh. Per. herb, forming a rosette, pubescent, sts. several from the base, to 12 in.; lvs. oblong to obovate, to 3 in. long, petioled; fls. in dense, sessile or subsessile, axillary glomerules, corolla 1–2 in. long, bluish to lavender, tube slender, not greatly expanded into throat. Se. U.S. Closely related to *R. caroliniensis* and perhaps only a form of it.

coccinea (L.) Vahl. Per. herb or somewhat woody, to 6 ft.; lvs. ovate, to 4 in. long, crenate, pubescent or glabrate, petioled; fls. solitary or few, axillary, sessile or peduncled, corolla to 1 in. long, red, tube somewhat curved, lobes about half as long as tube, rounded. W. Indies.

Devosiana Hort. Makoy ex E. Morr. Shrubby, to 1½ ft., pubescent; lvs. elliptic, to 3 in. long, entire, purple beneath, green and white-veined above, short-petioled; fls. solitary, sessile, axillary, calyx lobes linear, ciliate, corolla to 1¾ in. long, white and lavender, tube slender, abruptly expanded into throat, lobes about as long as throat with lavender lines, emarginate. Brazil. Foliage plant for the greenhouse or warm areas.

elegans Poir. [*R. formosa* Andr., not HBK]. Per., sts. pubescent, 4-angled; lvs. ovate, to 4 in. long, tapering to winged petiole; fls. 2 or 3 on long peduncles in axils of uppermost lvs., corolla to 1¾ in. long, scarlet, lobes spreading, upper two united halfway, stamens and style exserted. Brazil.

formosa: see *R. elegans*.

graecizans Backer [*R. amoena* Nees, not Sessé & Moç.; *R. longifolia* (Pohl) Griseb. ex Lindau, not L. Rich.]. Subshrub, to 2 ft.; lvs. ovate to oblong-lanceolate, to 5 in. long; fls. several on long axillary peduncles, corolla to 1 in. long, red. S. Amer. Used as a house plant, or outside in warm areas.

heteromorpha Fern. Per. herb, sts. dimorphic, those of spring, simple and erect, followed by trailing, elongate sts.; lvs. obovate or elliptic, to 2 in. long, strigose above, glabrous beneath, petioled; spring fls. solitary, axillary, corolla 2 in. long, blue-purple or pale, tube gradually expanded upward, summer fls. many, small, mostly remaining closed. Fla. The 2 flowering phases might be mistaken for different spp. May be only a local variant of *R. caroliniensis*.

humilis Nutt. Pubescent per., sts. to 2 ft., usually branched near base; lvs. ovate to lanceolate, to 3 in. long, sessile or subsessile; fls. in sessile or subsessile cymose clusters in axils of upper lvs., corolla to 2 in. long, lavender to bluish, tube about equalling throat. S. Penn., w. to Nebr., s. to nw. Fla. and Tex. A wide-ranging variable sp., with several vars. recognized, and closely related to *R. caroliniensis*. Var. **expansa** Fern. Lvs. broad; fls. longer.

hybrida: *R. caroliniensis*.

lilacina: *R. Schauerana*.

longifolia: see *R. graecizans*.

Lorentziana Griseb. Sts. simple or branched, to 3 ft., 4-angled; lvs. ovate, to 4 in. long; fls. in a narrow, terminal panicle, corolla to 1½ in. long, mauve. Colombia, Peru, Argentina; naturalized in s. Fla. Resembles *R. tuberosa* but has infl. glandular-hairy and caps. puberulous.

macrantha Mart. ex Nees. Shrub, to 6 ft.; lvs. ovate-lanceolate, to 6 in. long; fls. large, showy, solitary in uppermost lf. axils, corolla to 3 in. long, rose-purple, with prominent veins, tube slender below, gradually expanded upward, lobes rounded, broadly spreading. Brazil.

Makoyana Hort. Makoy ex Closon. MONKEY PLANT, TRAILING VELVET PLANT. To 2 ft.; lvs. ovate, to 3 in. long, marked with white above, purple beneath; fls. red-purple, 2 in. long. Brazil.

malacosperma Greenm. To 3 ft., sts. 4-angled, glabrous or sparsely pilose; lvs. lanceolate, to 6 in. long, narrowed to petiole about ¾ in. long, sparingly long-pilose; fls. axillary, peduncles forking, corolla to 2 in. long, lavender. Mex.; rarely escaped from cult. in se. U.S. Confused with *R. Brittoniana*, which has longer, narrower lvs., and with *Strobilanthes isophyllus*.

nudiflora (A. Gray) Urb. To 1 ft. or more, woody at base; lvs. elliptic to oblong-lanceolate, to 2 in. or more long, gray-green, pubescent, strongly reticulate beneath, margins crisped and with callosities on vein tips; fls. in terminal panicles, corolla about 2 in. long, purplish-blue, conspicuously curved, cleistogamous fls. smaller, produced in spring; caps. finely puberulent. Tex. and adjacent n. Mex.

occidentalis: a listed name of no botanical standing.

pedunculata Torr. To 2 ft., puberulent, brs. ascending to spreading; lvs. ovate-oblong, to 4 in. long, short-petioled; fls. solitary or cymose, on axillary peduncles to 2¾ in. long, corolla to 2 in. long, purple to lavender; caps. puberulent. Ill. and Ind., s. to Tex. and La.

Portellae Hook.f. Ann. or per., about 1 ft., much-branched, pubescent; lvs. ovate-acute, to 3 in. long, reddish-purple beneath, marked with white on veins above, narrowed to a slender petiole; fls. solitary, axillary, sessile, corolla about 1½ in. long, rose-pink, tube long, gradually expanded above middle, lobes abruptly spreading. Brazil.

Purshiana Fern. Related to *R. pedunculata*, but having sts. usually simple, petioles to ⅜ in. long, and fls. usually solitary, on peduncles to 1½ in. long. Appalachian region.

rosea (Nees) Hemsl. Per. herb, to 3 ft., hirsute-pubescent, sts. angled; fls. few, on long axillary pendundes, corolla to 2 in. long, rose. S. Mex.

Schauerana (Nees) Voss [*R. lilacina* Hook.]. Subshrub, to 2 ft., glabrous; lvs. ovate, about 2 in. long, entire or crenate, glossy above; fls. 1 or 2, axillary, corolla lavender, veined darker purple, funnelform, tube bent about middle, lobes rounded, spreading. Peru and Brazil. Related to *R. Devosiana*, but glabrous, with lvs. somewhat glossy above and paler beneath and fls. sometimes in 2's, lilac or purple.

squarrosa: a listed name of no botanical standing, used for a plant with bright blue fls., grown in s. Fla. as a ground cover or rock garden plant.

strepens L. Per., to 3 ft., pubescent; lvs. ovate to ovate-lanceolate, to 6 in. long, petioled; fls. usually several, axillary, calyx lobes lanceolate, to ½ in. long, glandular-pubescent, corolla to 2 in. long, pale blue or violet, throat broad, tube slightly longer than throat. N.J. to Ill., s. to S.C. and Tex.

tuberosa L. MEADOW-WEED, MENOW WEED. Roots tuberous-thickened, plant more or less hairy but not glandular, sts. erect, to 2 ft.; lvs. ovate or oblong, to 4 in. long, undulate, abruptly narrowed to a short petiole; fls. showy, 1 to several in axillary cymes, corolla to 2 in. long, mauve; caps. glabrous. W. Indies and n. S. Amer.

RUFACER: *ACER*. **R. carolinianum:** *A. rubrum* var. *trilobum*.

RUMEX L. DOCK, SORREL, DOCK S. *Polygonaceae*. More than 100 spp. of per. herbs, widely distributed in temp. regions; sts. leafy, usually grooved; lvs. usually conspicuous, basal; fls. many, small, greenish or reddish, unisexual or bisexual, in close or spreading panicles, sepals 6, 3 of them winged, and often one or all bearing a grainlike tubercle at base or center, stamens 6; fr. an achene, 3-angled.

Many of the species are weeds of Eurasian origin; some are grown for greens and one as a source of tannin. The dried inflorescences of weedy species native to Eur. and S. Amer. as well as N. Amer. are used for materials in dried flower arrangements; for example, *R. occidentalis* S. Wats., WESTERN DOCK; *R. crispus* L., SOUR DOCK; *R. conglomeratus* A. Murray, GREEN DOCK; *R. maritimus* L., GOLDEN DOCK. Of easy cultivation in any garden soil. Propagated by seeds which yield plants for cutting in 1 or 2 years.

abyssinicus Jacq. SPINACH RHUBARB. Per., to 9 ft.; lvs. broadly ovate to arrow-shaped or lanceolate, to 7 in. long, entire or somewhat 3-lobed; fls. unisexual, Ethiopia. The lvs. are eaten like spinach and the stalks like rhubarb.

Acetosa L. GARDEN S., SOUR D. Per., to 3 ft.; lvs. oblong or oblong-elliptic, to 5 in. long, arrow-shaped at base; fls. unisexual. Eur., Asia; naturalized in N. Amer. Lvs. are edible. Cv. **'Large Belleville'**. One of the principal cvs.

Acetosella L. SHEEP S., RED S., COMMON S. About 1 ft., spreading by slender rootstocks; lvs. petioled, sessile in upper part, 1 in. long, entire or with spreading triangular lobes at base; fls. unisexual, usually red, in open panicles. Meadows and grassy slopes, N. Amer. and Eurasia; attractive but invasive weed.

alpinus L. MONK'S RHUBARB, MOUNTAIN R. Per. to 3½ ft.; basal lvs. ovate-cordate, very large; panicles showy. Mts., Eur. Young lvs. eaten as greens or as salad.

flexuosus Soland. ex Hook.f. Per., to 18 in., sts. slender, flexuous; lvs. spreading, linear to lanceolate, reddish-brown; fls. in distant clusters, sepals with spines. New Zeal.

hydrolapathum Huds. GIANT WATER D. Per., to 6 ft.; lvs. oblong-lanceolate, to 2 ft. long, wavy-margined; fls. bisexual, in very large panicles. Eur. Planted along ponds and streams.

hymenosepalus Torr. CANAIGRE, TANNER'S D., WILD RHUBARB. Per., to 3 ft.; lvs. oblong to oblong-lanceolate, to 1 ft. long; fls. bisexual, in panicles to 1 ft. long, sepals rose-colored, nearly ½ in. wide. W. N. Amer. Grown for the thick roots, which yield tannin and also a minor yellow dye; lvs. eaten as greens and the petioles like rhubarb.

Patientia L. MONK'S RHUBARB, SPINACH D., PATIENCE D., PATIENCE, HERB P., GARDEN P. Per., to 6 ft.; lvs. elliptic-ovate to lanceolate, to 1 ft. long; fls. bisexual, in panicles to 2 ft. long. Eur.; naturalized in N. Amer.

roseus L. Ann., to 2 ft.; lvs. triangular-ovate; fls. unisexual, in short racemes, inner sepals veined with rose in fr. Egypt to Iran.

scutatus L. FRENCH S., GARDEN S. Low per., sts. prostrate or ascending; lvs. cordate-ovate, st. lvs. arrow- or fiddle-shaped; fls. unisexual. Eur. and Asia.

venosus Pursh. WILD BEGONIA, WILD HYDRANGEA, SOUR GREENS. Per., to 1½ ft.; lvs. ovate to oblong, to 5 in. long; sepals red, fr. with large wings to 1½ in. across. Sask., s. to Wash. and Nev. Sometimes grown for its showy frs.

RUMOHRA Raddi. *Polypodiaceae*. One sp. of terrestrial or sometimes epiphytic ferns of trop. and temp. regions in the S. Hemisphere; rhizomes stout, densely covered with brown, papery scales; lvs. borne at intervals, 3–4-pinnate at base, petioles stout, scaly; sori large, on the under surface of segms., indusia peltate, leathery.

Much used for cut foliage in the florist trade. For culture see *Ferns*.

adiantiformis (G. Forst.) Ching [*Polystichum adiantiforme* (G. Forst.) John Sm.; *P. capense* (Willd.) John Sm.; *P. coriaceum* (Swartz) Schott]. LEATHER FERN, LEATHERLEAF F., IRON F. Lvs. leathery, broadly triangular, to 3 ft. long, 2½ ft. wide, or smaller and more ovate, 3–4-pinnate at base, basal pinnae triangular, pinnules oblong to narrowly ovate, cuneate at base, acute to acuminate at apex, coarsely toothed, glabrous.

RUNYONIA: *MANFREDA*.

RUPICAPNOS Pomel. *Fumariaceae*. Perhaps 32 spp. of very variable, nearly stemless, evergreen, per. herbs, native to cliffs in N. Afr. and Spain; lvs. pinnate, lfts. pinnatisect; fls. in subcorymbose racemes, pedicels becoming very long and spreading-deflexed, sepals 2, very small, petals 4, lower petal separated from the other 3, uppermost petal spurred; fr. a slightly flattened, 1-seeded caps.

africana (Lam.) Pomel. Variable; lvs. glaucescent or glaucous, segms. ovate, oblong, or linear; fls. about ½ in. long, rose-purple with dark purple tips, rarely white, spur often downcurved; fr. obovate-suborbicular, rugose. Shady places on calcareous cliffs and rocky places, N. Afr.

RUPPIA L. DITCH GRASS. *Ruppiaceae*. Two or more spp. of submersed herbs with characters of the family.

Sometimes introduced into saline waters for duck food.

maritima L. Very variable, sts. elongate, slender, much-branched; lvs. alt., scattered, very narrow, ¾–4 in. long, sheaths to ½ in. long; peduncles 2–4 in. long; fls. green, raised above water at flowering; drupes less than ⅛ in. long, beaked, on stalks to ⅝ in. long. Saline marshes, nearly cosmopolitan.

occidentalis S. Wats. WIDGEON GRASS. Distinguished from *R. maritima* in having lvs. more clustered into fan-shaped groups, blades 4–8 in. long, sheaths ¾-2¾ in. long, and fr. slightly larger. Alkaline waters, Alaska, s. to B.C., Sask., Minn., and Nebr.

RUPPIACEAE Hutch. DITCH GRASS FAMILY. Monocot.; 1 genus, *Ruppia*, of submersed herbs of saline waters, native to temp. and subtrop. regions; lvs. alt., linear or bristlelike, basally sheathing; fls. bisexual, 2 on a slender spike, perianth absent, stamens 2, sessile, opp. each other, with separate anther cells, pistils 4 or more, sessile, with solitary pendulous ovules, each pistil becoming long-stalked and developing into a small, ovoid drupe. Sometimes included in Zosteraceae or Najadaceae.

RUPRECHTIA C. A. Mey. *Polygonaceae*. About 30 spp. of dioecious shrubs or trees, native to trop. and subtrop. regions from Mex. to S. Amer.; lvs. alt., simple, tubular sheaths deciduous; female fls. clustered, calyx red, sepals winged, falling with fr., stamens 9; fr. an achene, 3-angled.

One species recently introduced into cultivation in Fla.

coriacea (Karst.) S. F. Blake. BISCOCHITO. Evergreen shrub or small tree, to 20 ft.; female fls. in close panicles among lvs. Like *Triplaris* in having winged calyx. Venezuela.

RUSCHIA Schwant. *Aizoaceae*. About 350 spp. of succulent shrubs, native to S. Afr. and widely distributed there; sts. prostrate to erect, sometimes tufted, the older sts. often bearing dry lf. sheaths or remains of old lvs.; lvs. opp., half-clasping, the sheath usually with an impressed, longitudinal line, blades 3-angled, stiff, bluish-green, usually with dark transparent dots, keel entire or toothed; fls. solitary or in an infl., calyx deeply 4–5-lobed, petals pink, red, violet, or white, many, in 1 to many series, stamens many, united to form a cone, filaments hairy at base, staminodes few, ovary inferior, 4–5-celled, stigmas 4–5; fr. a caps., cell lids appendaged, wings absent, placental tubercles present.

Taller, shrubby kinds are generally free-flowering and can be grown outdoors in a sunny place or in an airy greenhouse or window. The tufted kinds should be grown under glass away from excessive moisture, and in winter in a sunny spot at a relatively cool temperature of about 50–55° F. Propagation easy by seeds or cuttings. See also *Succulents.*

acuminata L. Bolus [*Mesembryanthemum exacutum* N. E. Br.]. Shrub, herbaceous parts bluish, covered with dull green dots, later finely roughened by small papillae, sts. robust, wandlike, 8 in. long, ascending to prostrate, with erect fl. brs.; lvs. ascending, ⅝ in. long, ¼ in. wide at base, sheath ⅞ in. long, ½ in. wide above, bluntly keeled, keel entire, rarely indistinctly 1-toothed, upper side flat to slightly convex, sides convex, apex acute to acuminate, with a mucro; fls. 1¼ in. across, pedicels 1¼ in. long, petals white to pale pink. Cape Prov.

crassa (L. Bolus) Schwant. [*Mesembryanthemum crassum* L. Bolus]. Robust shrub, the herbaceous parts pale glaucous-green with transparent dots and short, soft, white hairs, fl. brs. densely crowded, internodes enclosed by lf. sheaths; lvs. inflated, to ¾ in. long and almost as wide, upper side flat, apex blunt, mucronate, lower side keeled, keel with 1 indistinct tooth; fls. ⅞ in. across, pedicels ¼–⅜ in. long, petals white. Cape Prov.

Derenbergiana (Dinter) L. Bolus [*Ebracteola Derenbergiana* (Dinter) Dinter & Schwant.; *Mesembryanthemum Derenbergianum* Dinter]. Plants forming cushions to 8 in. across, with a thick taproot to 8 in. long, and each shoot bearing 2–3 pairs of lvs.; lvs. bluish-green, with barely visible dots, 1⅛–1¼ in. long, bluntly 3-angled, wedge-shaped toward apex and expanded to ⅜ in., apex blunt; fls. ¾–1 in. across, on pedicels ⅜ in. long petals light pink. S.-W. Afr.

edentula (Haw.) L. Bolus [*Braunsia edentula* (Haw.) N. E. Br.; *Echinus edentulus* (Haw.) N. E. Br.; *Mesembryanthemum edentulum* Haw.]. Plants shrubby, brs. glabrous; lvs. 3-angled, thick, contiguous, obtuse, marginal teeth more or less developed. S. Afr.

impressa L. Bolus. Compact, glabrous shrub, 2½ in. high, with spreading brs. and erect fl. branchlets to ¾ in. long; lvs. pale blue-green, ⅝ in. long, ¼ in. thick at tip, laterally convex, bluntly keeled, margins obscurely transparent, apex blunt; fls. ⅜ in. across, petals pink. Cape Prov.

karrooica (L. Bolus) L. Bolus [*Mesembryanthemum karrooicum* L. Bolus]. Robust, erect, stiff, glabrous shrub to 1 ft.; lvs. blue, dotted with green, ascending to spreading, with a recurved spiny tip, to ⅞ in. long and ¼ in. wide, ⅜ in. thick at apex, upper side slightly convex, lower side rounded, tapering toward apex, sheaths enclosing internodes; fls. solitary, 2 in. across, on pedicels to 1¾ in. long, petals purplish with a darker purple stripe. Cape Prov.

rostella (Haw.) Schwant. [*Mesembryanthemum rostellum* Haw.]. Brs. prostrate, fl. branchlets many, brown, covered with withered lvs.; lvs. gray-green, covered with fine prominent dots, to ¾ in. long and ⅛ in. wide, sheath elongate, the youngest lvs. adpressed, curved upward and beaklike, older lvs. spreading, semicylindrical, 3-angled below apex; fls. 1 in. across, solitary, terminal, nearly sessile, petals white. Cape Prov.

Steingroeveri (Pax ex Engl.) Schwant. [*Mesembryanthemum Steingroeveri* Pax ex Engl.]. Erect, minutely pubescent, much-branched shrub; lvs. spreading, to ⅝ in. long and ⅛ in. across, upper side flat, lower side keeled, apex blunt. S.-W. Afr.

RUSCUS L. *Liliaceae.* Three spp. of dioecious, evergreen shrubs, native from Azores and Madeira through w. Eur. and Medit. region to Iran; lvs. minute, bractlike, the apparent lvs. being leaflike branchlets or cladophylls; fls. unisexual, solitary or clustered, attached on midrib of cladophylls, perianth segms. 6, separate, stamens 3, filaments united; fr. a red or yellow berry.

Grown outdoors in southern U.S. (Zone 8). Dried, artificially colored sprays of *R. aculeatus* are frequently used in florists' winter decorations.

aculeatus L. BUTCHER'S-BROOM, BOX HOLLY, JEW'S MYRTLE. To 3 ft.; cladophylls ovate, to 1½ in. long and 1 in. wide, stiff and spiny-pointed; fls. 1–2, greenish; fr. red or yellow, to ½ in. wide. Azores and w. Eur., through Medit. region to Iran.

Hypoglossum L. To 1½ ft.; cladophylls elliptic to oblanceolate, to 4½ in. long and 1½ in. wide; fls. 3–5, yellow; fr. red, ⅜ in. wide. S. Eur.

Hypophyllum L. To 1 ft.; cladophylls elliptic to ovate, to 3 in. long and 1½ in. wide; fls. mostly 5 or 6, white; fr. red, ⁵⁄₁₆ in. wide. Madeira to Caucasus.

racemosus: *Danae racemosa.*

RUSPOLIA Lindau. *Acanthaceae.* Four spp. of Afr. shrubs; lvs. opp., short-petioled, ovate; fls. red, in spikes or panicles, calyx 5-parted almost to base, corolla tubular, tube long, cylindrical, much longer than calyx, lobes much shorter than tube, stamens 2, shortly exserted, anther sac 1, ovary 2-celled, each cell with 2 ovules, style filiform, stigma slightly 2-lobed; fr. a caps., seeds nearly round, flat, with margin somewhat thickened, outer surface smooth, inner surface smooth or irregularly ridged. Differs from *Pseuderanthemum* in having fls. always red, anther sac 1, and seeds with smooth outer surface and horny rim.

hypocrateriformis (Vahl) Milne-Redh. Small, glabrous, straggling shrub, brs. 4-angled; lvs. to 3 in. long; fls. in showy terminal heads, corolla tube yellow, lobes crimson on outer surface, yellow on inner surface; both surfaces of seeds smooth. Trop. Afr.

seticalyx (C. B. Clarke) Milne-Redh. [*Pseuderanthemum seticalyx* (C. B. Clarke) Stapf]. Differs from preceding in having brs. cylindrical, sts. and lvs. somewhat hirsute; fls. less intensely colored, corolla lobes cinnabar-red above and paler beneath; one surface of seeds marked with irregular ridges. Trop. Afr.

RUSSELIA Jacq. CORALBLOW, CORAL PLANT. *Scrophulariaceae.* About 50 spp. of shrubs and subshrubs, native to Cuba, and from Mex. to Colombia; sts. erect, pendent or scandent, angled or cylindrical; lvs. opp. or whorled, simple, sometimes reduced to scales, sometimes resinous-dotted; fls. red, or mottled red, pink, or white, in axillary cymes, calyx 5-parted, corolla tubular or funnelform, slightly 2-lipped, stamens 4; fr. a caps.

Russelias are often grown in the greenhouse and in the open far south; also good as basket plants since they flower nearly continuously. Of easy culture; propagated by cuttings.

equisetiformis Schlechtend. & Cham. [*R. juncea* Zucc.]. CORAL PLANT, FOUNTAIN P., FOUNTAIN BUSH. Glabrous, much-branched shrub, to 4 ft., brs. whorled, rushlike, nodding or drooping, sts. 4–12-angled, prominently ridged; lvs. 3–6 in a whorl, ovate or elliptic, to ⅝ in. long, dentate, falling early, but mostly reduced to scales on the brs.; fls. red, in 1–3-fld. clusters. Mex.; naturalized in Fla., W. Indies, and other warm parts of the world.

juncea: *R. equisetiformis.*

sarmentosa Jacq. Glabrous or slightly pubescent shrub, to 6 ft., sts. 4–6-angled; lvs. ovate, to 3 in. long, toothed, resinous-dotted; fls. red, in many-fld. clusters. Cuba and Mex. to Colombia.

RUTA L. RUE. *Rutaceae.* About 40 spp. of aromatic or pungent, per. herbs and subshrubs, native from Medit. region to w. Asia; lvs. alt., 2–3-pinnately dissected, glandular-dotted; fls. yellow, in terminal corymbs or panicles, sepals 4, petals 4, usually denticulate or fimbriate, stamens 8 or 10, ovary sessile; fr. a 4- or 5-lobed caps.

Grown for medicinal properties and in herb gardens. Hardy; propagated by division and seeds.

chalepensis L. Puberulent, glaucous per., to 2½ ft.; lf. segms. elliptic, about ½ in. long; infl. corymbose; petals fringed with long cilia; caps. lobes pointed. Medit. region.

divaricata: *R. graveolens* var.

graveolens L. COMMON R., HERB-OF-GRACE. Glabrous, glaucous subshrub, to 3 ft.; lf. segms. oblong or spatulate, to ½ in. long; infl. corymbose; petals concave, toothed; caps. lobes obtuse. S. Eur. Grown in herb gardens; causes dermatitis in some persons. Used medicinally and as a condiment. Cv. 'Variegata'. Lvs. variegated. Var. **divaricata** (Ten.) Willk. [*R. divaricata* Ten.]. Lvs. yellow-green, segms. linear-lanceolate. S. Eur.

montana Mill. Glabrous, glaucous per., to 1½ ft.; lf. segms. linear; petals entire; caps. longer than the stalks, lobes rounded. Medit. region to Caucasus and n. Iran.

RUTABAGA. The rutabaga (*Brassica Napus*, Napobrassica Group) is a hardier plant than the turnip and requires a longer season of growth. The edible root has a long leafy

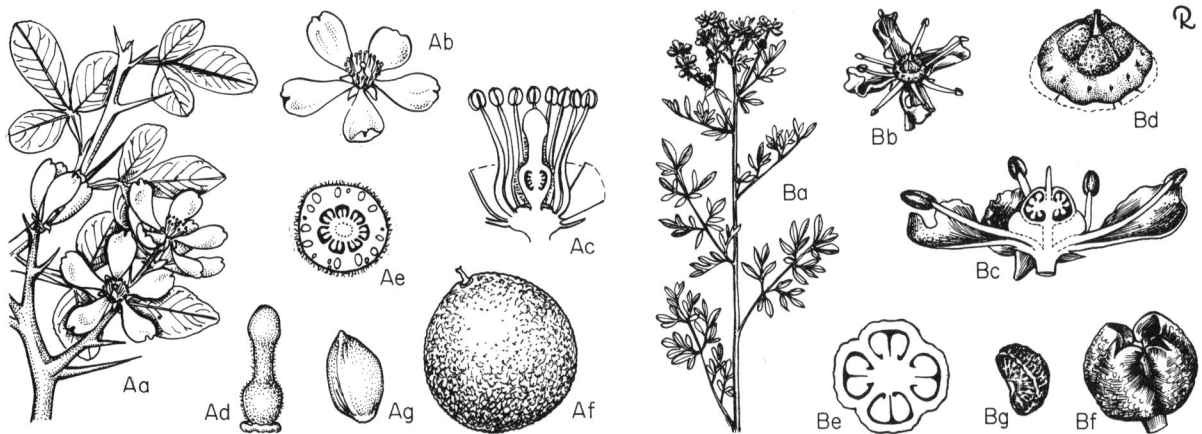

RUTACEAE. **A,** *Poncirus trifoliata:* **Aa,** flowering branch (below) and leafy branch (above), × ⅓; **Ab,** flower, × ½; **Ac,** flower, vertical section (petals cut short), × 2; **Ad,** pistil, × 2; **Ae,** ovary, cross section, × 5; **Af,** fruit, × ½; **Ag,** seed, × 1. **B,** *Ruta graveolens:* **Ba,** flowering stem, × ⅙; **Bb,** flower, × 1; **Bc,** flower, vertical section, × 2; **Bd,** pistil surrounded by gland, × 3; **Be,** ovary, cross section, × 4; **Bf,** fruit, × 2; **Bg,** seed, × 4.

neck, and the foliage is glaucous-blue-green, smooth, very different from that of the turnip. Roots left in the ground may survive the winter and go to seed the following year, becoming more or less spontaneous.

Seeds of rutabagas are sown in the northern parts of the country in June or very early July, usually in drills about 18 inches apart. Rutabagas are not grown as an early-summer vegetable.

RUTACEAE Juss. RUE FAMILY. Dicot.; about 150 genera and 1,600 spp. of mostly evergreen or deciduous, armed or unarmed trees or shrubs, native to trop. and temp. regions, but rare in Eur.; lvs. alt. or opp., simple or compound and sometimes reduced to 1 lft., glandular-dotted; fls. sometimes unisexual, mostly regular, in various types of infl., sepals 3–5, petals 3–5, rarely 0, stamens 3–10, sometimes 20–60, arising from a disc, filaments separate, sometimes united into bundles, ovary superior, usually 4–5-celled, with axile placentation, rarely 1-celled; fr. a caps., leathery-skinned berry (hesperidium), drupe, samara, follicle, or sometimes separating into individual sections. The cult. genera are: *Acradenia, Acronychia, Adenandra, Aegle, Aeglopsis, Afraegle, Agathosma, Balfourodendron, Balsamocitrus, Boenninghausenia, Boronia, Calodendrum, Casimiroa, Chloroxylon, Choisya,* × *Citrofortunella,* × *Citroncirus, Citropsis, Citrus,* *Clausena, Cneoridium, Coleonema, Correa, Dictamnus, Diosma, Eremocitrus, Esenbeckia, Evodia, Feronia, Flindersia, Fortunella, Geijera, Glycosmis, Melicope, Microcitrus, Murraya, Orixa, Paramignya, Phellodendron, Poncirus, Ptelea, Ruta, Severinia, Skimmia, Swinglea, Thamnosma, Toddalia, Triphasia,* and *Zanthoxylum.*

The family is commonly known in cultivation through citrus fruits; most of the genera yield essential oils, many have medicinal properties, and some provide fine cabinet wood.

RUTTYA Harv. *Acanthaceae.* Three spp. of Afr. shrubs; lvs. opp., short-petioled, ovate, entire; fls. in short cymes, bracts and bracteoles linear, scarcely ¼ in. long, calyx deeply 5-parted, segms. equal, narrowly lanceolate, corolla 2-lipped, upper lip emarginate, lower lip 3-lobed, stamens 2, anther sac 1, ovary glabrous; fr. a caps., seeds 4, nearly smooth, without hairs.

fruticosa Lindau. Evergreen shrub, to 12 ft.; lvs. narrowed at both ends, to 2¼ in. long; fls. several, on short lateral shoots, calyx to ¼ in. long, corolla to 2 in. long, variable in color, bright yellow, orange-red, or scarlet, with an irregular, dark reddish to brown to black blotch at base of middle lobe of lower lip. E. Trop. Afr.

Scholesei: a listed name of no botanical standing, applied to a plant said to have yellow fls.; may refer to one of the color variants of *R. fruticosa.*

SABAL Adans. PALMETTO. *Palmae.* Fewer than 20 spp. of dwarf to mostly stout, unarmed palms with bisexual fls., native from Bermuda and se. U.S. to n. S. Amer. and W. Indies; lvs. costapalmate, either regularly divided ½ to ¾ to the base into 1-ribbed segms., or deeply and irregularly divided into less deeply divided pairs of segms. which appear 3-ribbed, petiole unarmed, the base split centrally and often long-persistent; infls. among lvs., with tubular sheathing bracts on peduncle and subtending each of several primary brs., these simply branched *(S. minor)* or 2–3 times branched into slender rachillae, each br. except the rachillae usually bearing a keeled bract; fls. creamy-white, borne singly, sepals united in a 3-lobed calyx, petals 3, joined basally to filaments and there united by their margins *(S. Yapa)* or separated by a filament, lobes imbricate in bud, stamens 6, carpels 3, united; fr. globose to pear-shaped with basal stigmatic residue, seed somewhat dorso-ventrally compressed, slightly hollowed, with homogeneous endosperm intruded by seed coat basally, embryo lateral.

The leaves of palmettoes are much used in thatching and the buds of some supply an edible palm cabbage. Palmettoes are simple in cultural requirements, thriving both in nature and in gardens in both moist and fairly dry lands. Fresh seeds germinate readily and can be transplanted in the following year, but are subsequently slow-growing so that mature plants are often transplanted from the wild. Whether the leaves on mature trees shed from the trunks when a year or two old or persist when dead depends on vigor of tree, protection from wind, and perhaps to some extent on the particular plant. The petioles usually break midway and the old bases or boots may persist for years. When the grounds are extensive enough to afford distance, these trunk coverings may be highly attractive. Most species are fully hardy or half-hardy in Zone 9b. See also *Palms*.

Adansonii: *S. minor.*

Beccariana: *S. princeps.*

bermudana L. H. Bailey. BERMUDA P. To 40 ft.; lf. blades 6–9 ft. across, green on both surfaces but with a yellowish area along the main axis at the base, central undivided portion about 1 ft. wide on each side of main axis, segms. 1-ribbed, often with filaments in the sinuses between them; infl. shorter than lvs., with several primary brs. again mostly twice-branched into rachillae to 6 in. long; fls. about ⅛ in. long; fr. black, glossy, top-shaped or pear-shaped, ⅝ in. in diam., about as long, seed brown. Bermuda, where much planted as an ornamental. At one time confused with *S. Blackburniana* and some material so identified may be *S. bermudana.*

Blackburniana Glazebr. ex Schult. & Schult.f. [*S. umbraculifera* (Jacq.) Mart.]. Lvs. to 6½ ft. long, divided halfway to the base into 1-ribbed segms. with filaments in the sinuses between them; infl. shorter than lvs., primary brs. again mostly twice-branched; fls. white, anthers orange; fr. globose, ¾ in. in diam. Described from cult. material of unknown origin, this sp. is imperfectly understood. The name has been applied to *S. bermudana* and to *S. domingensis.*

causiarum (O. F. Cook) Becc. PUERTO RICAN HAT PALM. Trunk thick, columnar, to 50 ft.; lvs. green to glaucous, strongly costapalmate, about 6 ft. long and wide, divided about ⅔ to the main axis into 50–60 segms., these 1-ribbed with prominent filaments in the sinuses between them; infl. longer than lvs., primary brs. twice-branched into rachillae mostly less than 6 in. long; fls. about ¼ in. long; fr. nearly globose with slightly tapered base, about ½ in. in diam. Puerto Rico.

Deeringiana: *S. minor.*

domingensis Becc. Trunk columnar, to 60 ft. or more; lvs. grayish-green, blade to 6 ft. long, divided about halfway to the main axis into 1-ribbed segms. often with filaments in the sinuses between them; infl. shorter than lvs.; fls. about ¼ in. long; fr. globose-pear-shaped, to ¾ in. in diam. Hispaniola. May be grown under the names *S. Blackburniana* or *S. umbraculifera.*

Etonia Swingle ex Nash. SCRUB P. Trunk mostly subterranean, sometimes prostrate or even erect and to 6 ft. high; lvs. green, costapalmate, blade 3 ft. across or more, divided ¾ to the main axis into as many as 60 or more 1-ribbed segms. with prominent filaments in

the sinuses between them; infl. shorter than lvs., primary brs. twice-branched into rachillae to 6 in. long; fls. ³⁄₁₆ in. long; fr. black, variable, ½–¾ in. wide. Fla.

glaucescens: *S. mauritiiformis.*

guatemalensis: *S. mexicana.*

jamaicensis Becc. JAMAICAN P., BULL THATCH. Trunk to 40 ft., usually bare; lvs. green, 3 ft. long or more, regularly divided beyond middle into 80 or more 1-ribbed segms. with prominent filaments in the sinuses between them; infl. shorter than to slightly exceeding lvs., primary brs. twice-branched into rachillae to 4 in. long; fls. to ³⁄₁₆ in. long; fr. depressed-globose, about ½ in. in diam. Jamaica.

Japa: an erroneous spelling sometimes used for *S. Yapa.*

louisiana: *S. minor.*

mauritiiformis (Karst.) Griseb. & H. Wendl. [*S. glaucescens* Lodd. ex H. E. Moore]. Trunk slender, to 75 ft., usually bare; lvs. green above, glaucous to silvery beneath, irregularly divided to or nearly to the main axis into pairs of 2-cleft segms., filaments lacking in the sinuses; infl. equalling or exceeding lvs., primary brs. mostly 3 times branched into very slender rachillae to 5 in. long; fls. about ⅛ in. long; fr. black, about ⅜ in. in diam. Mex. to Venezuela, Trinidad.

mayarum: *S. Yapa.*

mexicana Mart. [*S. guatemalensis* Becc.; *S. texana* (O. F. Cook) Becc.]. TEXAS P. Trunk to 60 ft. or more, rough and bare in age; lvs. green with yellowish patch along main axis at base when living, to 3 ft. long or more, strongly costapalmate, regularly divided ½ to ¾ to the main axis into 1-ribbed segms. with filaments in the sinuses between them; infl. equalling or slightly exceeding lvs., primary brs. twice-branched into rachillae to 5 in. long; fls. white, fragrant, about ¼ in. long, petals separated basally by stamens, lobes inrolled when dry, broadest near middle; fr. black, ½–¾ in. in diam. Tex., Mex., Guatemala.

minor (Jacq.) Pers. [*S. Adansonii* Guers.; *S. Deeringiana* Small; *S. louisiana* Bomh.]. DWARF P., SCRUB P., BUSH P. Sts. subterranean or rarely erect but short; lvs. green or bluish, stiff and nearly flat, briefly costapalmate, regularly divided ⅔ or more to the base into 16–40 entire or very briefly 2-cleft, 1-ribbed segms.; infl. erect, usually exceeding lvs., primary brs. once- or rarely twice-branched into short rachillae; fls. whitish, about ⅛ in. long; fr. black, glossy, ⁵⁄₁₆–½ in. in diam. N.C. to Fla., Tex., and Mo. The hardiest sabal and, along with *Rhapidophyllum* and spp. of *Trachycarpus*, among the hardiest palms.

Palmetto (Walt.) Lodd. ex Schult. & Schult.f. [*S. viatoris* L. H. Bailey]. CABBAGE P., CABBAGE TREE, BLUE P. Trunk to 90 ft., rough and bare at maturity; lvs. green, to 6 ft. long, strongly costapalmate, regularly divided about ⅔ to the main axis or rarely more into 1-ribbed, deeply 2-cleft segms. with filaments in the sinuses between them; infl. usually exceeding the lvs., primary brs. twice-branched into rachillae to 4 in. long or more; fls. whitish, ³⁄₁₆ in. long, calyx lobes dark-tipped, margins of petals inrolled when dry; fr. black, to ½ in. in diam. N.C. to Fla., Bahama Is. Zone 9a.

parviflora Becc. Trunk stout, to 50 ft., bare in age; lvs. green, strongly costapalmate, 3 ft. long or more, regularly divided up to ¾ to the main axis into 1-ribbed, deeply 2-cleft segms. with prominent filaments in the sinuses between them; infl. shorter than to equalling lvs., primary brs. twice-branched into stoutish rachillae to 6 in. long; fls. about ¼ in. long, margins of petals inrolled when dry; fr. globose, brown-black, to ⅝ in. in diam. Cuba.

peregrina: *S. Yapa.*

princeps Hort. ex Becc. [*S. Beccariana* L. H. Bailey]. Trunk large, with long-persistent petiole bases; lvs. large, to 5 ft. long, divided about halfway to the base into about 100 1-ribbed segms. with filaments in the sinuses between them; infl. usually shorter than lvs., primary brs. twice-branched; fr. black, shining, broadest near apex, tapered to base, about ⅝ in. in diam. Described from cult., origin not known; the name has been variously applied in hort.

texana: *S. mexicana.*

umbraculifera: *S. Blackburniana,* but the name has been universally misapplied to *S. domingensis.*

uresana Trel. SONORAN P. Trunk to 30 ft., obscurely ringed; lvs. glaucous-blue, to 6 ft. long, strongly costapalmate, regularly divided about halfway to the main axis into 1-ribbed, deeply 2-cleft segms. with filaments in the sinuses between them; infl. about equalling lvs., primary brs. twice-branched into thickened rachillae; fls. ¼ in. long, petals more or less reflexed, not strongly nerved when dry nor the margins much inrolled; fr. to ¾ in. wide. Nw. Mex.

viatoris: *S. Palmetto.*

Yapa Wright ex Becc. [*S. mayarum* Bartlett; *S. peregrina* L. H. Bailey]. Trunk to 20 ft. or sometimes much higher, roughly ringed in age; lvs. green on both surfaces, unequally divided nearly to the main axis into pairs of 2-cleft segms., filaments lacking in the sinuses; infl. equal to or exceeding lvs., primary brs. mostly twice-branched into slender rachillae to 4 in. long; fls. to ³⁄₁₆ in. long, calyx 3-angled with solid base, petals united basally in a tube outside the stamens, free lobes broadest at the base, not inrolled but usually reflexed when dry; fr. often 2–3-seeded, ⁵⁄₁₆–½ in. in diam. W. Cuba, Yucatan, Brit. Honduras. The name is sometimes written *S. Japa* but was published as *S. Yapa.*

SABATIA Adans. (sometimes, but not originally spelled *Sabbatia*). *Gentianaceae.* About 17 spp. of ann. or per., glabrous, erect herbs, with opp. or alt. brs., mostly in the se. U.S. but extending n. to Nov. Sc., w. to prairies of Okla. and Tex., s. to W. Indies and cent. plateau of Mex.; lvs. opp., sessile or clasping, entire, sometimes thick and turgid; fls. in terminal cymes, rose or white, calyx and corolla deeply divided, their lobes 5 or more, longer than their tubes, stamens as many as calyx and corolla lobes, anthers twisted or coiled after discharge of pollen, ovary subglobose, style deeply 2-lobed; fr. a 2-valved, many-seeded caps. Something like *Centaurium*, but having corolla lobes much longer than tube and style deeply 2-lobed.

angularis (L.) Pursh. ROSE PINK, BITTER-BLOOM. Ann., to 3 ft., brs. opp.; lvs. ovate or oblong, to 1½ in. long; fls. usually solitary at ends of brs., corolla rose-pink with greenish eye, to 1½ in. across. N.Y., s. to Fla. and La.

campestris Nutt. Ann., to 15 in., sts. 4-angled, brs. usually alt.; lvs. ovate-oblong, to 1 in. long; fls. solitary, corolla lilac, 1 in. long, as long as calyx. Mo. and Kans., s. to Tex.

paniculata: see *S. quadrangula.*

quadrangula Wilb. [*S. paniculata* of auth., not (Michx.) Pursh]. Ann., to 1½ ft., sometimes more, usually branched above, sts. 4-angled; lvs. lanceolate, 1½ in. long, occasionally longer; corolla white, about 1 in. across. Va. to Fla.

stellaris Pursh. SEA PINK, MARSH P. Ann., to 2 ft., brs. alt.; lvs. lanceolate-oblong to linear, to 2 in. long; fls. solitary at ends of brs., corolla pink, rarely white, with yellow eye bordered with red, to 1½ in. across. Coastal Mass. to Fla.

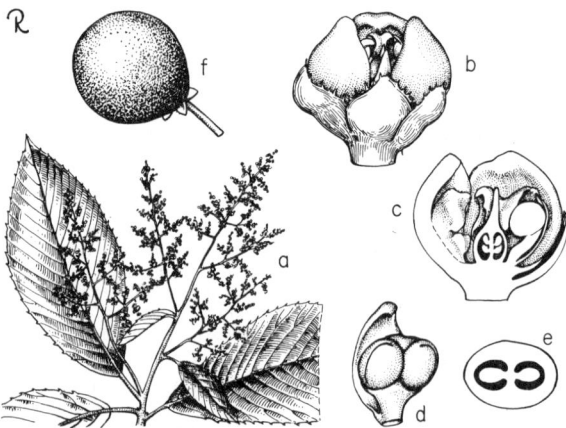

SABIACEAE. *Meliosma myriantha:* **a,** flowering branch, × ¼; **b,** flower, × 12; **c,** flower, vertical section, × 12; **d,** stamen, × 15; **e,** ovary, cross section, × 25; **f,** fruit, × 5. (From Lawrence, *Taxonomy of Vascular Plants.*)

SABIACEAE Blume. SABIA FAMILY. Dicot.; 4 genera of trees, shrubs, and vines, native to trop. and warm temp. Asia and Amer.; lvs. alt., simple or pinnate; fls. usually bisexual, irregular, sepals 3–5, petals 4–5, the inner 2 much-reduced,

stamens 3–5, opp. the petals, sometimes only 2 fertile, ovary superior, 2-celled; fr. berrylike. *Meliosma* is sometimes grown as an ornamental.

SABINEA DC. *Leguminosae* (subfamily *Faboideae*). Three spp. of shrubs and small trees, native to W. Indies; lvs. alt., even-pinnate, deciduous; lfts. small, with petiolules; fls. large, axillary, papilionaceous, pink to red, calyx nearly truncate, stamens 10, 9 united and 1 separate; fr. a linear, flat, dehiscent legume.

One species is planted in tropics and subtropics for its showy flowers, which appear before the new foliage. Propagated by seeds.

carinalis Griseb. CARIB WOOD. Small tree; lfts. in 6–8 pairs, distant, oblong, to ¾ in. long, blunt; fls. scarlet to deep crimson, to 1½ in. long, in clusters of 3–5; fr. long-stalked. Dry coastal scrub, Dominica. Zone 10b.

SACCHARUM L. *Gramineae.* About 12 spp. of robust, per. grasses, mostly in trop. Old World; infl. of panicled racemes; spikelets in pairs, one sessile, the other pedicelled, both bisexual, awnless, deciduous, glumes somewhat hard, sterile lemma similar but hyaline, fertile lemma hyaline, or sometimes absent. For terminology see *Gramineae.*

bengalense Retz. MUNJ. St. tall; lf. blades glaucous, very scabrous; panicle to 32 in. long, narrow, dense, silvery; spikelets to ¼ in. long, longer than the joints of the rachis. Iran to ne. and n. India. Sometimes cult. for ornament.

officinarum L. SUGARCANE. Sts. to 15 ft. high and 2 in. thick, solid, juicy, the lower internodes short, swollen; lf. sheaths overlapping, blades elongate, mostly to 2½ in. wide; panicle plumelike, to 24 in. long, the racemes slender, drooping; spikelets about ⅛ in. long, obscured by a basal tuft of long, silky hairs. Trop. se. Asia. Widely cult. in warm parts of the world as the major source of sugar. Cult. in Hawaii and the s. states, especially La. Prop. by st. cuttings, but seeds produced in the tropics assist in the production of cvs. through hybridization.

sinense Roxb. CHINESE SWEET CANE. Distinguished from *S. officinarum* by long hairs on the axis of the infl. China. Cult. for syrup.

SACCOLABIUM Blume. *Orchidaceae.* Six spp. of epiphytes, native to Malay Arch. and trop. Asia; sts. leafy; lvs. leathery, flat or folded lengthwise; infl. an erect, axillary, many-fld. raceme, corymb, or panicle; fls. usually small, sepals and petals similar, spreading or reflexed, united to base of column, lip sessile on footless column, 3-lobed, lateral lobes triangular, midlobe tongue-shaped, with a spur shorter than ovary and pedicel, without keels, column short. For structure of fl. see *Orchidaceae.*

For culture see *Orchids.*

ampullaceum: *Ascocentrum ampullaceum.*

Blumei: *Rhynchostylis retusa.*

coeleste: *Rhynchostylis coelestis.*

curvifolium: *Ascocentrum curvifolium.*

giganteum: *Anota densiflora.*

Hendersonianum: *Ascocentrum Hendersonianum.*

miniatum: *Ascocentrum miniatum.*

praemorsum: *Rhynchostylis retusa.*

trichromum Rchb.f. Sts. pendent, to 3 ft. long; lvs. oblong, to 6 in. long, 2-lobed at apex; infl. half as long as lvs., few-fld.; fls. 1 in. long, pale straw-color with stripes of pale pink, sepals and petals oblong, lip with rose-colored spur divided into 2 chambers by a horizontal plate, column white. Summer. Assam.

violaceum: *Anota violacea.*

SACCOLOMA Kaulf. [*Orthiopteris* E. Copel.]. *Polypodiaceae.* Perhaps 3 spp. of ferns of widespread trop. distribution; rhizomes short, erect, scaly; lvs. 2–4-pinnate, not jointed to rhizome; sori marginal or terminal, each served by a single veinlet, indusia open at the end but attached only along basal part of 1 side, obconical.

Grown in the greenhouse or in open in subtropical regions. See also *Ferns.*

brasiliensis: *S. inaequalis.*

inaequalis (Kunze) Mett. [*S. brasiliensis* (K. Presl) Mett.; *Davallia brasiliensis* (K. Presl) Hook.; *Orthiopteris inaequalis* (Kunze) E. Copel.]. A large plant; lvs. 4–6 ft. long, pinnules oblong, usually 2–9 in.

long, apically serrate; sori broader than long at apex, mostly marginal at sinus of pinnules. Tropics, Amer.

SADLERIA Kaulf. *Polypodiaceae.* Six spp. of low tree ferns of Hawaii; lvs. tufted, 2-pinnate; sori linear, in rows on each side of midrib.

Planted in Hawaiian gardens and sometimes grown elsewhere outdoors or under glass. For culture see *Ferns.*

cyatheoides Kaulf. Trunk 5 ft. or more; lvs. leathery, to 3 ft. long, dark green, pinnules linear, to ½ in. long, with revolute margins, lateral veins not visible on glaucous under surface, petioles to 2 ft. long, scaly basally. Hawaii. Zone 10, in s. Calif.

Hillebrandii W. J. Robinson. Like *S. cyatheoides,* but lateral veins visible on under surface of pinnules, base and upper part of petiole covered with scales. Hawaii. Zone 10.

SAGERETIA Brongn. *Rhamnaceae.* Perhaps as many as 35 spp. of deciduous or evergreen, usually spiny shrubs, sometimes scandent, native to e. and s. Asia and to N. Amer.; lvs. opp.; fls. small, whitish, bisexual, in clusters or spikes; fr. a berrylike drupe.

Sometimes planted as ornamentals in Calif.; propagated by seeds and cuttings.

Thea (Osbeck) M. C. Johnst. [*S. theezans* (L.) Brongn.]. Lvs. ovate or broad-elliptic, to 1 in. long; spikes villous, usually paniculate; fls. fragrant; fr. purplish-black, to ⅜ in. across. Cent. and e. China. Zone 7.

theezans: *S. Thea.*

SAGINA L. Pearlwort. *Caryophyllaceae.* About 25 spp. of small, often tufted, ann. or per. herbs, native to n. temp. regions and cool mts.; lvs. opp., often united at base, subulate to linear-lanceolate; fls. white, in a dichasial cyme, or solitary and terminal, sepals 4–5, separate, petals 4–5, sometimes none, entire, stamens as many as sepals or twice as many, ovary 1-celled, styles 4–5; fr. a caps., 4–5-valved, splitting to base; seeds many.

Suited to wall or rock gardens. Propagated by seeds and division.

×**Normaniana** Lagerh.: *S. procumbens* L. × *S. saginoides* (L.) Karst. Per.; lvs. in a rosette, to 1 in. long; fls. solitary or paired, pedicels to 1½ in. long, sepals ⅛ in. long; caps. ⅛ in. long, seed usually not viable. Mts., Scandinavia, Scotland, Austria.

pilifera (DC.) Fenzl. Cespitose per., to 1 in.; lvs. long-aristate; petals more than twice as long as sepals. Mts., Corsica and Sardinia. Material offered under this name is probably *S. subulata.*

subulata (Swartz) K. Presl [*Spergula pilifera* Hort. ex Vilm., not DC.]. Mat-forming per., flowering sts. to 5 in.; st. lvs. aristate, to ¼ in.; fls. mostly solitary, 5-merous, pedicels about 1 in. long, glandular-hairy, sepals ovate, glandular, petals as long as sepals, stamens 10; caps. ⅛ in. long. Dry, sandy, rocky places, w. and cent. Eur. Cv. **'Aurea'.** Lvs. yellow-green.

SAGITTARIA L. [*Lophotocarpus* T. Durand]. Arrowhead, swamp potato. *Alismataceae.* Twenty spp. of monoecious, stoloniferous, often tuber-bearing, mostly per. herbs, native to bogs and aquatic habitats, chiefly of temp. and trop. Amer.; lvs. tufted, submersed and reduced to linear phyllodes without blades, or emersed and with blades linear to elliptic, lanceolate, or ovate, often sagittate; infl. racemose or paniculate, scapose, with female fls. in lower part; sepals 3, green, petals 3, white, deciduous, stamens 7 to many, anthers attached near base, carpels many, 1-ovuled, spirally arranged on receptacle; fr. a head of flattened, winged, beaked achenes.

Tubers, when present, are edible and *S. sagittifolia* is widely grown in the Orient for this food. Arrowheads are planted on pool or pond margins and submersed in aquaria. Propagated by division, seeds, and underground tubers when produced.

cuneata E. P. Sheld. Wapato. Similar to *S. latifolia,* but somewhat smaller, to 2½ ft., lf. blades to 11 in. long, fl. bracts lanceolate-attenuate and somewhat membranous, and beak of achene apical. Canada, U.S.

Engelmanniana J. G. Sm. Lvs. emersed, blades linear to lanceolate, to 8 in. long, 4¾ in. wide, base commonly sagittate, petioles to 2 ft. long; scapes to 2½ ft.; fls. white, to 1 in. across, sepals reflexed. E. U.S.

filiformis: *S. subulata.*

gigantea: *S. lancifolia* cv.

graminea Michx. [*S. isoetiformis* J. G. Sm.; *S. sinensis* Sims]. Ann. or per., to 3 ft. or more, often cormous; emersed lvs. with blades very variable, linear to ovate, usually without basal lobes; scapes erect, bracts more or less united, membranous; fls. to ½ in. across, female fls. obviously stalked, sepals reflexed, filaments dilated, pubescent; beak of achene less than $^1/_{32}$ in. long. Nfld. to S. Dak., s. to Fla., Tex., and Cuba; naturalized in Panama Canal Zone. Var. **platyphylla** Engelm. [*S. platyphylla* (Engelm.) J. G. Sm.]. Pedicels of female fls. recurved; achenes with longer beaks. Se. Mo. to Kans., s. to Tex. and Ala. Var. **teres** (S. Wats.) Bogin [*S. teres* S. Wats.]. Submersed lvs. reduced to spongy, cylindrical phyllodes; fl. bracts completely united. Coastal, Mass. to Long Is. and N.J.

guyanensis HBK [*Lophotocarpus guyanensis* (HBK) J. G. Sm.]. Lvs. mostly floating, blades thin, broadly ovate, obtuse, cordate at base, to about 4 in. long; fls. submersed or floating, inconspicuous, female fls. with appressed or spreading sepals, often with a ring of functional stamens, pedicels recurved and thickened in fr.; wing of achene usually crenate. Pantrop.

isoetiformis: *S. graminea.*

japonica: a listed name of no botanical standing for *S. sagittifolia* cv. 'Flore Pleno'.

lancifolia L. Per., to 6 ft.; lvs. mostly emersed, blades elliptic to linear or ovate, to 14 in. long, pale green, leathery; pedicels ascending, bracts thickened, papillose or ridged, nearly separate, lanceolate-attenuate, to 1¼ in. long; fls. to 2 in. across, filaments linear, pubescent; achene obovate to sword-shaped. N.C. to Fla. and W. Indies; Cent. Amer. to n. S. Amer. Cv. **'Gigantea'** [*S. gigantea* Hort. Vilm.-Andr.]. A larger plant.

latifolia Willd. Wapato, duck potato. Per., to 4 ft., with large tubers; emersed lf. blades variable, to 20 in. long, mostly triangular in outline and sagittate, or the upper half of blade linear to ovate with basal lobes about as long, often flaring, acute-tipped; fl. bracts boat-shaped and somewhat firm in texture, pedicels ascending; fls. white, to 1½ in. across, filaments glabrous; wing of achene entire, beak horizontal to incurved, about 4 times as long as body of achene. N. Amer. Tubers formerly used for food by Amer. Indians.

longiloba Engelm. ex Torr. Lvs. emersed, blades linear to triangular-ovate, to 6 in. long and 4 in. wide, sagittate, basal lobes to twice as long as blade, petioles to 30 in. long; scapes to 4½ ft., pedicels to 1¼ in. long; fls. white, to ⅜ in. across. Nebr. and Calif. to s. Mex.

lorata: see *S. subulata* vars. *gracillima* and *subulata.*

macrophylla Zucc. Lvs. emersed, blades lanceolate to ovate, to 8 in. long, 2¾ in. wide, somewhat leathery, base obtuse to hastate; scape to 3 ft.; fls. white, to 1½ in. across. Vicinity of Mex. City.

microfolia: a listed name of no botanical standing.

montevidensis Cham. & Schlechtend. Giant a. To 2½ ft.; lvs. commonly emersed, very variable, blades linear to broad-ovate, sagittate, to 16 in. long, basal lobes divergent, nearly as long as rest of blade; pedicels thickened and recurved, bracts membranous; fls. with sepals closely appressed to mature receptacle, petals ovate, to ⅞ in. long, sometimes with purple spot at base; achenes narrowly winged. Warm-temp. N. and S. Amer.

natans: *S. sagittifolia* or *S. subulata* var. *subulata.*

papillosa Buchenau. Lvs. emersed, blades linear to linear-lanceolate, to 10 in. long, ¾ in. wide, leathery, base not sagittate, petioles to 16 in. long; scape to 3 ft., bracts densely papillate; fls. whitish, on pedicels to ⅝ in. long, petals about ½ in. long, filaments glabrous. Ark. to se. Tex.

platyphylla: *S. graminea* var.

pusilla: *S. subulata* var. *subulata.*

rigida Pursh. Similar to *S. graminea,* but scape geniculate and bending at lowest whorl of fls., female fls. subsessile, filaments subulate, achenes larger, with stoutish, recurved beak $^1/_{32}$ in. long or more; lf. blades to 16 in. long. Que. and Ont., s. to Va., Mo., Minn.

sagittifolia L. [*S. natans* Pall., not Michx.]. Old World a., swamp potato, swan p. Differs from *S. latifolia* in having fls. smaller, about 1 in. across, petals spotted purple at base, achenes with beak erect, shorter than the body; foliage very variable. Eurasia. Tubers used for food in Orient where grown in paddies. Cv. **'Flore Pleno'** [*S. japonica* Hort.]. Fls. double.

sinensis: *S. graminea.*

subulata (L.) Buchenau. [*S. filiformis* J. G. Sm.]. Awl-leaf a. Submersed or tidal; lvs. very variable, all reduced to phyllodes, mostly linear or narrowly oblanceolate, to 3–4 ft. long, ½ in. wide, rarely terminated by a blade to 2 in. long, 1 in. wide; fls. few, to ¾ in. across, filaments glabrous and subulate, female fls. with sepals loosely appressed to mature receptacle or spreading, pedicels recurved in fr. Coastal regions, Mass. to Fla. and Ala. A common aquarium plant. Var.

subulata [*S. lorata* (Chapm.) Small, in part; *S. natans* Michx., not Pall.; *S. pusilla* Nutt.]. The typical var.; plant usually tidal and dwarf; phyllodes less than ¼ in. wide, rarely submersed, to 1 ft. long, floating ends often bladelike. Var. **gracillima** (S. Wats.) J. G. Sm. [*S. lorata* (Chapm.) Small, in part]. Plant submersed, commonly elongate; phyllodes less than ¼ in. wide, more than 1 ft. long, floating, rarely with bladelike ends. Mass. to N.J., and S.C. to Ala.

teres: *S. graminea* var.

SAINTPAULIA H. Wendl. AFRICAN VIOLET. *Gesneriaceae.* About 21 spp. of terrestrial, per., hairy herbs in E. Afr.; sts. varying from scarcely evident to well developed and repent; lvs. opp. or, in caulescent spp., sometimes nearly opp. to alt., petioled, blades nearly orbicular to elliptic, often fleshy; fls. 1 or several on axillary peduncles, calyx 5-parted, corolla tube short-cylindrical, limb usually spreading at right angles, 2-lipped, upper lip 2-lobed, lower lip 3-lobed, stamens 2, borne in corolla tube, anthers yellow, cohering face to face, cells dehiscent by confluent slits, disc ringlike, ovary superior; fr. a caps.

For cultivation see *Gesneriaceae.*

amaniensis: *S. magungensis.*

bicolor: a listed name of no botanical standing, perhaps for *S. orbicularis.*

brevipilosa B. L. Burtt. Lvs. in a rosette, blades nearly orbicular, to 1⅝ in. long and wide, rounded at apex, cordate at base, crenate, with very dense, short, erect, even hairs above, pilose beneath; fls. 2–6 on peduncles to 2⅜ in. long, corolla purple, lobes glandular-ciliate, upper lip to ⅜ in. long, ½ in. wide, lower lip to ⅝ in. long, ⅞ in. wide. Nguru Mts. (Tanzania).

confusa B. L. Burtt. Lvs. in a rosette or on a very short st., petioles to 3 in. long, blades elliptic to ovate, to 1½ in. long, 1¼ in. wide, crenate, rounded at apex, sparsely to densely hairy, with long and short appressed hairs intermixed, medium green above, paler and glistening beneath; fls. about 4 on peduncles shorter than lvs., corolla to 1¼ in. across, blue-violet; caps. cylindrical, to ½ in. long, with more or less appressed hairs. E. Usambara Mts. (Tanzania). Material formerly cult. as *S. kewensis* belongs here, as may some plants called *S. diplotricha.*

difficilis B. L. Burtt. Similar to *S. confusa,* but more robust, petioles to 4¾ in. long, blades elliptic, with the long hairs not appressed but more or less spreading. E. Usambara Mts. (Tanzania).

diplotricha B. L. Burtt. Similar to *S. confusa* in having the hairs on upper surface of lf. of 2 lengths, but the long hairs more or less erect and the much denser short hairs erect; blades purplish above, reddish-purple beneath, margins slightly recurved; corolla about 1 in. across, very pale violet, lower lip at an angle to the tube. Usambara Mts. (Tanzania). *S. confusa* was once grown under this name.

Goetzeana Engl. Sts. to 6 in. long, creeping, branched, white-hairy; lvs. orbicular, to 1⅛ in. long and wide, nearly or quite entire, green with pale veins and with more or less uniform hairs above, purplish beneath; corolla white, with rosy-lilac markings on lower 2 lobes. Uluguru Mts. (Tanzania).

grandifolia B. L. Burtt. Lvs. in a rosette, large, petiole to 4 in. long, blade broadly ovate-elliptic, to 4 in. long, 3¼ in. wide, rounded at apex, cordate at base, crenate-serrate, clear green, with erect uniform hairs above; corolla 1 in. across, deep violet, margins glandular-ciliate. W. Usambara Mts. (Tanzania).

Grotei Engl. Sts. procumbent, branched; lvs. with petioles to 10 in. long, blades orbicular, to 3½ in. long, coarsely crenate, thin, conspicuously veined, with long and short hairs intermixed above; fls. 2–4 on peduncles shorter than lvs., corolla to 1¼ in. across, pale mauve, shading to violet in throat; caps. 1 in. long or more. E. Usambara Mts. (Tanzania).

intermedia B. L. Burtt. Sts. prostrate and rooting, with short internodes; lvs. with petioles to 3⅝ in. long, blades ovate or ovate-orbicular, to 2 in. long, 1⅝ in. wide, rounded or subcordate at base, crenate-serrate, dark green with long, curved, silvery hairs above, red-purple and short-pilose beneath; fls. several on a peduncle, corolla 1 in. across, deep violet. E. Usambara Mts. (Tanzania).

ionantha H. Wendl. [*S. kewensis* C. B. Clarke]. COMMON A. V. Lvs. in a rosette, blades nearly orbicular to ovate, to 2⅜ in. long, green and with long and short, appressed hairs intermixed above, paler beneath; fls. 8–10 on peduncles longer than lvs., corolla ⅞ in. across, light blue to violet, or white with violaceous center, but of many colors in cvs.; caps. cylindrical, ½ in. long. Coastal Tanzania. Cvs. are numerous and are registered by the African Violet Society of America, Inc.

kewensis: *S. ionantha,* but most material formerly cult. as *S. kewensis* is *S. confusa.*

magungensis E. P. Roberts [*S. amaniensis* E. P. Roberts]. Sts. procumbent, branched, to 6 in. long; lvs. with petioles to 2 in. long or rarely more, blades broadly ovate to orbicular, to 2¾ in. long, blunt, rather obscurely crenate, inconspicuously veined, with long and short, appressed hairs above; fls. 2–4 on peduncles slightly longer than lvs., corolla ¾ in. across, purple; caps. ½ in. long. Var. **magungensis.** The typical var.; lvs. thin, to 2¾ in. long. E. Usambara Mts. (Tanzania). Var. **minima** B. L. Burtt. More slender; lvs. to 1⅜ in. long; fls. smaller. E. Usambara Mts. (Tanzania). Var. **occidentalis** B. L. Burtt. Robust, sts. purplish; lvs. thicker, glossy, less hairy above. W. Usambara Mts. (Tanzania).

nitida B. L. Burtt. Lvs. in a rosette, petiole to 3⅝ in. long, blade broadly ovate or nearly orbicular, rounded at apex, cordate, shallowly crenate, dark green and glossy with appressed, inconspicuous hairs above; fls. several on peduncles shorter than lvs., corolla ¾ in. across, deep violet; caps. ⅝ in. long. Nguru Mts. (Tanzania).

orbicularis B. L. Burtt. Sts. very short; lvs. with petioles to 3 in. long, blades orbicular to ovate, to 2½ in. long, coarsely toothed, medium green with long and short, appressed hairs above; fls. 8–10 on peduncles longer than lvs., corolla ⅞ in. across, light blue or violet, to white with blue center. Var. **orbicularis.** The typical var.; fls. pale, with deeper center. E. Usambara Mts. (Tanzania). Var. **purpurea** B. L. Burtt. Fls. deep purple. W. Usambara Mts. (Tanzania).

pendula B. L. Burtt. Sts. prostrate and rooting; lvs. with petioles to 1⅜ in. long, blade broadly ovate or nearly orbicular, obtuse at apex, somewhat cordate at base, crenate-serrate, green with long, erect hairs above, short-pilose and green beneath; fls. mostly solitary, on peduncles to 2 in. long, corolla 1 in. across, blue-purple, with darker throat. E. Usambara Mts. (Tanzania).

rupicola B. L. Burtt. Lvs. in a rosette, petioles to 3⅝ in. long, blades ovate, to 2⅝ in. long, 1¾ in. wide, cordate, crenate-serrate, green, with erect and somewhat uneven hairs above; fls. to 6 on peduncles about as long as petioles, corolla purple, to ⅞ in. across; caps. to ¾ in. long. Kenya.

shumensis B. L. Burtt. Compact, lvs. many, ovate or ovate-orbicular, small, to 1⅜ in. long, toothed, pale to dark olive-green with many erect conspicuous hairs above, pale or reddish along veins beneath; fls. about 5 on peduncles to 2⅜ in. long, corolla ¾ in. across, pale blue-lilac, splotched violet beneath middle of lower lip; caps. cylindrical, ½ in. long. W. Usambara Mts. (Tanzania).

teitensis B. L. Burtt. Lvs. in a rosette on sts. to 4 in., petioles to 6 in. long, blades ovate or nearly orbicular, to 3 in. long, 2¼ in. wide, obscurely crenate-dentate, with hairs erect at first but becoming appressed in age, older blades subpeltate; fls. in an infl. shorter than lvs., on peduncles to 2 in. long, corolla 1 in. across, violet; caps. cylindrical, 1 in. long. Kenya.

tongwensis B. L. Burtt. Lvs. in a rosette, sometimes on a thick, basal st., petioles to 3½ in. long, blades thickish, elliptic or ovate-elliptic, to 3¼ in. long, 2 in. wide, coarsely crenate, dark green with pale central vein and more or less uniform erect or spreading hairs above, pale green or purplish-red beneath; fls. 4–6 on peduncles longer than lvs., corolla 1⅛ in. across, lavender; caps. cylindrical, to ¾ in. long. E. Usambara Mts. (Tanzania).

velutina B. L. Burtt. Lvs. in a rosette, petioles to 3⅝ in. long, blades nearly orbicular, cordate at base, with incurved, inconspicuously crenate-serrate margins, dark green with long, erect hairs and dense, short, erect hairs above, rose-purple beneath; fls. on a peduncle to 2 in. long, corolla violet. W. Usambara Mts. (Tanzania).

SALACCA Reinw. (often but incorrectly spelled *Zalacca*). *Palmae.* About 11 spp. of cespitose, nearly stemless, spiny, dioecious palms of trop. Asia, islands of the Sunda Shelf in the Malay Arch., and the Philippine Is.; lvs. pinnate or pinnately ribbed, pinnae acute and often curved, 1-ribbed except the compound terminal pinna, or rarely the blade only 2-cleft at the apex and pinnately ribbed; infls. among the lvs., unlike, peduncle and brs. sheathed by tubular bracts, the male bearing several catkinlike brs. sheathed by bractlets, the female with fewer and larger brs.; male fls. in pairs, calyx deeply 3-parted, corolla longer, 3-lobed, stamens 6, female fls. larger, sepals 3, corolla 3-lobed, staminodes 6 in throat of corolla, pistil 3-celled; fr. covered with appressed or rough, imbricate scales, 1–3-seeded, seed with homogeneous endosperm and fleshy seed coat.

One species is widely cultivated within its natural range for the edible fruit and is occasionally grown for interest in collections in the tropics of the New World. Zone 10b. For culture see *Palms.*

conferta: *Eleiodoxa conferta.*

edulis Reinw. Lvs. irregularly or sometimes regularly pinnate, viciously prickly, pinnae many, green above, grayish beneath; female infl. short, with few brs.; fr. top-shaped or pear-shaped, to 3 in. long, with succulent, edible flesh, seeds usually 3. Malay Arch., but cult. elsewhere.

SALAZARIA Torr. BLADDER SAGE. *Labiatae.* One sp., a desert shrub of sw. U.S. and adjacent n. Mex.; brs. broadly spreading, mostly square in cross section, spiny; lvs. opp., short-petioled; fls. in axillary, 1–3-fld. verticillasters arranged in interrupted racemes, calyx inflated in fr., 2-lipped, lips equal, entire, corolla 2-lipped, upper lip arched, lower lip broad, margins recurved, stamens 4, in 2 pairs; fr. of 4 tuberculed nutlets.

mexicana Torr. To 3 ft., branchlets spine-tipped, pale green, gray-pubescent; lvs. ovate to oblong, to 1 in. long, rounded at base, entire or rarely toothed; calyx ¼ in. long, corolla to ¾ in. long, violet, pubescent outside. Winter–spring. Deserts, sw. U.S. and nw. Mex. Well-suited to arid climates.

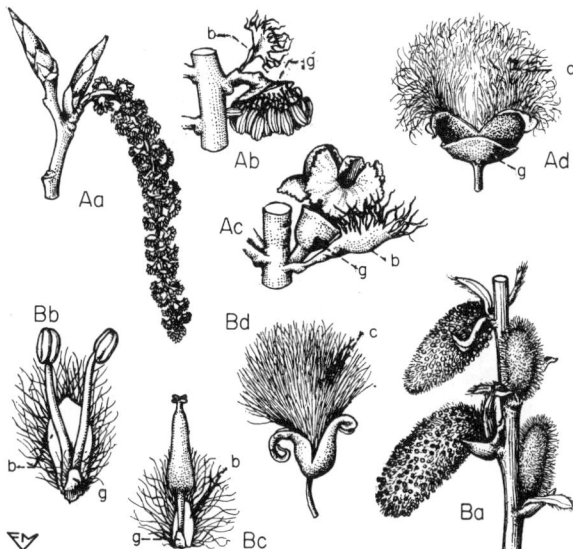

SALICACEAE. **A,** *Populus balsamifera:* **Aa,** twig with male catkin, × ½; **Ab,** part of axis of male catkin with flower, × 2; **Ac,** part of axis of female catkin with flower, × 4; **Ad,** capsule, × 2. **B,** *Salix fragilis:* **Ba,** twig with male catkins (those on left of twig in flower, others less mature), × 1; **Bb,** male flower, × 6; **Bc,** female flower, × 6; **Bd,** capsule, × 2. (b bract, c coma of seeds, g gland.) (From Bailey, *Manual of Cultivated Plants,* ed. 2.)

SALICACEAE Mirb. WILLOW FAMILY. Dicot; 3 genera and about 500 spp. of dioecious trees and shrubs, of almost worldwide distribution; lvs. alt., simple, deciduous, generally petioled; fls. unisexual, borne in more or less silky-hairy catkins, perianth 0, stamens 1 or many, ovary 1-celled; fr. a small caps., seeds with tuft of hairs. *Populus* and *Salix* are cult.

Both genera include ornamentals; several species of *Salix* with slender stems are used in basketry and *Populus* produces important commercial wood.

SALICORNIA L. GLASSWORT, SAMPHIRE. *Chenopodiaceae.* About 10 spp. of cosmopolitan, small, erect, fleshy herbs of saline places; sts. succulent, jointed, brs. opp.; lvs. reduced to scales; fls. very small, bisexual, in 3's sunken in tissue in axils of lvs., forming terminal spikes to 4 in. long, calyx 4-lobed, corolla none, stamens 1–2, exserted, ovary 1-celled, with 2–4 style brs.; fr. a utricle, surrounded by the calyx, which becomes corky in age.

europaea L. SAMPHIRE, CHICKEN-CLAWS, PIGEON-FOOT. Ann., to 2 ft., turning yellow to bright red in autumn; spikes to 4 in. long, with st. joints longer than thick. Eur., Asia, N. Amer.

SALISBURIA: *GINKGO.* **S. adiantifolia:** *G. biloba.*

SALIX L. WILLOW, OSIER. *Salicaceae.* About 300 spp. of dioecious shrubs and trees, or the alpine spp. nearly herbaceous, native to the colder and temp. regions of the N. Hemisphere, a few in the S. Hemisphere except Australia; lvs. mostly lanceolate; fls. small, borne in dense catkins appearing before or after the lvs.; fr. a small caps., seeds covered with hair or down. The taxonomy of the genus is difficult, and hybrids are many.

Many willows are grown as ornamentals, and for screens, shelter, holding banks, and some of the species for the tough flexible branches from which baskets are made. They are well adapted to moist locations and along stream banks, but most of them succeed also in almost any soil; a few species are plants of dry soil. They grow rapidly. Propagated by ripe wood cuttings taken in the autumn and planted at once or kept in the cellar until spring; also by seeds sown in pans on moss as soon as the capsules are ripe. Weeping or special forms may be top-grafted on upright stock. They are soft-wooded plants.

acutifolia Willd. Similar to *S. daphnoides,* but smaller, lvs. narrower, and catkins more slender. Russia to e. Asia. Zone 5. Twigs used in basketry.

adenophylla: *S. cordata.*

aegyptiaca L. [*S. Medemii* Boiss.]. Tall shrub or low tree, to about 12 ft.; lvs. obovate to elliptic, to 6 in. long, toothed, glabrous above at maturity, sparingly pubescent and glaucous beneath; catkins sessile, thick, male to 1½ in. long, female to 3 in. long when mature. E. Turkey, Iran, sw. Asiatic U.S.S.R. Zone 6. One of earliest to flower.

alba L. WHITE W. To 75 ft.; lvs. lanceolate, to 4 in. long, finely toothed, white-silky beneath; catkins appearing with the lvs. Eur., N. Afr., Asia; escaped in N. Amer. Zone 2. Twigs used for wicker work and basketry, wood useful. Var. **calva** G. F. Mey. [*S. coerulea* Sm.]. CRICKET-BAT W. Brs. upright, branchlets dark brown; lvs. slightly silky, finally glabrous. Var. **chermesina** T. Hartig. Branchlets bright red. Var. **sericea** Gaudin [*S. regalis* Hort. ex Dipp.]. Lvs. densely silky beneath. Var. **tristis** (Ser.) Gaudin [var. *vitellina* 'Pendula']. Brs. bright yellow, drooping. Var. **vitellina** (L.) J. Stokes [*S. vitellina* L.]. YELLOW W., GOLDEN W. Branchlets yellow; lvs. glaucous beneath. Var. *vitellina* 'Pendula'; var. *tristis.*

× **ambigua** J. F. Ehrh. [*S. mutabilis* Schleich.]: *S. aurita* × *S. repens.* PUZZLE W. Common wherever the parents grow together; shrub, to 3 ft., erect or procumbent; lvs. variable, oblong, ovate, obovate, or oblanceolate, to 1 in. long, usually glaucous and silky beneath.

amygdalina: *S. triandra.*

amygdaloides Anderss. PEACH-LEAVED W. Differs from *S. triandra* chiefly in having petioles slender, glandless, and lvs. cuspidate-acuminate. N. Amer. Zone 5.

anglorum: *S. arctica.*

annularis: *S. babylonica* cv. 'Crispa'.

arctica Pall. [*S. anglorum* Cham.; *S. petrophila* Rydb.]. ARCTIC W. Prostrate, to 4 in. high, more or less creeping, tending to form mats; lvs. elliptic to obovate, ¾–2 in. long, entire, hairy when young, later glabrous, usually paler beneath; female catkins with 25–50 fls. Arctic N. Amer., s. to mts. of w. N. Amer. Zone 1. Resembles *S. cascadensis.*

aurita L. Shrub, to 6 ft.; lvs. obovate or oblanceolate, to 3 in. long, obscurely toothed, gray-tomentose beneath but becoming glabrous, stipules conspicuous, persistent; catkins appearing before the lvs. Eur., w. Asia. Zone 6.

babylonica L. [cv. 'Pendula'; *S. elegantissima* C. Koch; *S. pendula* Gater.; ?*S. Sieboldii* C. Koch]. WEEPING W. To 30 ft., brs. long, drooping; lvs. narrow-lanceolate, to 6 in. long, finely toothed, grayish-green beneath; catkins appearing with the lvs. Nativity uncertain, may be China. Zone 5. Sometimes confused with *S.* × *blanda,* but may be distinguished by its narrow-lanceolate lvs. usually ⅜–⅝ in. wide. Cvs. are : 'Aurea', brs. golden-yellow; 'Crispa', [var. *crispa* Hort. ex Loud.; *S. annularis* J. Forbes], lvs. curled into a ring; 'Ramulis Aureis', brs. yellowish, perhaps not distinct from cv. 'Aurea'.

× **blanda** Anderss. [*S. pendula* Hort., not Gater.; *S. Petzoldii* Hort. ex Schelle; *S. Petzoldii* var. *pendula* Hort. ex Rehd.]: probably *S. babylonica* × *S. fragilis.* WISCONSIN WEEPING W., NIOBE W. Brs. pendulous, green to brown; lvs. lanceolate, to 6 in. long, finely toothed, blue-green and glabrous beneath. Zone 4. Sometimes confused with *S. babylonica.*

Bockii Seemen. Shrub, to 9 ft.; lvs. oblong or obovate, to ½ in. long, entire or slightly toothed, deep green above, bluish-white and silky beneath; catkins appearing with the lvs. Autumn. China. Zone 6.

brachycarpa Nutt. Shrub, to 3 ft.; lvs. elliptic-oblong to oblanceolate, to 1 in. long, entire, hairy on both sides; catkins appearing with the lvs. Alaska to Que., s. to mts. of Wash., Ore., Colo., Utah. Zone 6.

caprea L. GOAT W., PUSSY W., FLORIST'S W., SALLOW. To 25 ft.; lvs. broad-ovate to oblong, to 4 in. long, slightly toothed or entire, gray-pubescent beneath; catkins appearing before the lvs. Eur. Zone 5. Cv. 'Pendula' [var. *pendula* T. Lang]. KILMARNOCK W. Brs. crooked, drooping. Cv. 'Variegata' [var. *variegata* Weston]. Lvs. variegated with white.

cascadensis Cockerell. Similar to *S. arctica*, but having lvs. smaller, ¾ in., rarely 1 in. long, catkins smaller, fewer-fld., female catkins with 12–25 fls. W. N. Amer.

chilensis Mol. [*S. Humboldtiana* Willd.; *S. Humboldtiana* var. *stipulacea* (M. Martens & Galeotti) C. K. Schneid.]. Shrub or small tree, branchlets slender, often drooping or sometimes fastigiate; lvs. linear or linear-lanceolate, to 6 in. long, bright green, glabrous, petioles short. Mex., s. to Cent. and S. Amer. Differs from other willows in keeping its lvs. for all or most of the year so that it is always green and attractive. The tough, slender, flexible brs. are used for making baskets and wicker furniture. A fastigiate columnar form has a habit much like the Lombardy poplar.

chlorolepis Fern. GREEN-SCALED W. Low shrub, to 3 ft., glabrous throughout, brs. ascending; lvs. crowded, broadly elliptic to narrowly obovate, to 1¼ in. long; catkins few, shorter than lvs. Gaspé Pen. (Que.).

chlorophylla: *S. planifolia*.

cinerea L. GRAY W. Shrub, to 15 ft.; lvs. elliptic to obovate-lanceolate, to 3½ in. long, wavy-margined, gray-pubescent beneath; catkins appearing before or with the lvs. Eur., Asia. Zone 2. Cv. 'Variegata' [forma *tricolor* Dipp.; forma *variegata* (Ser.) Rehd.]. Lvs. variegated with yellow and white, sometimes also with red.

coerulea: *S. alba* var. *calva*.

commutata Bebb. Shrub, to 9 ft., twigs dark colored beneath hairy covering; lvs. elliptic to elliptic-ovate, to 3 in. long, woolly-hairy when young, especially beneath, becoming glabrate in age; catkins appearing with the lvs., the female mostly to 2¼ in. long, the male to 1¼ in. long. Wet places, in mts., w. N. Amer.

cordata Michx. [*S. adenophylla* Hook.]. HEART-LEAVED W. Shrub, to 12 ft., branchlets gray-puberulous at first, later glabrous; lvs. lanceolate, to ovate, to 5½ in. long, rounded or cordate at base, glandular-serrate; catkins appearing with the lvs., to 3 in. long, male catkins conspicuous. E. N. Amer. Zone 2?

daphnoides Vill. To 30 ft.; lvs. oblong- to narrow-lanceolate, to 4 in. long, finely toothed or nearly entire, glaucous beneath; catkins appearing before or with the lvs. Eur., Asia. Zone 5. Its pruinose brs. make it conspicuous in winter. Var. **pomeranica** (Willd.) W. D. J. Koch. Usually shrubby; lvs. narrower; catkins more slender.

× **dasyclados** Wimm.: probably *S. caprea* × *S. cinerea* × *S. viminalis*. To 18 ft.; lvs. lanceolate, to 8 in. long, gray-pubescent beneath; catkins appearing before the lvs.

discolor Muhlenb. PUSSY W., LARGE P. W. Large shrub or small tree, to 20 ft.; lvs. oblong, to 4 in. long, wavy-toothed or nearly entire, glaucous beneath; catkins appearing before the lvs. Wet ground, e. N. Amer. Zone 2.

dolorosa: a listed name of no botanical standing for *S.* × *blanda*.

× **Doniana** Sm.: *S. purpurea* × *S. repens*. Branchlets thinly pubescent when young; lvs. oblong to lanceolate, sparsely silky-hairy when young, later glabrous above, glaucous and glabrescent beneath.

Drummondiana Barratt ex Hook. Shrub, to 9 ft., branchlets glabrous or puberulent, becoming conspicuously glaucous; lvs. lanceolate to oblanceolate, to 4 in. long or more, entire, somewhat revolute, glabrous above, white-silky-hairy beneath; catkins appearing before or with the lvs. B.C. and Alta., s. to Calif., Utah, New Mex. Zone 3.

Elaeagnos Scop. [*S. incana* Schrank, not Michx.]. Shrub or tree, to 45 ft.; lvs. narrow-lanceolate, to 6 in. long, revolute, white-tomentose beneath; catkins appearing before the lvs. Mts. of cent. and s. Eur., Asia Minor. Zone 4. Its slender, grayish lvs. turn yellow in autumn.

elegantissima: *S. babylonica*.

× **Erdingeri** J. Kern.: *S. caprea* × *S. daphnoides*. Young branchlets pubescent; lvs. obovate to oblong, silky when young, later glabrous above, and gray-green and glabrate beneath.

eriocephala Michx. [*S. missouriensis* Bebb]. Large shrub or tree, to 45 ft., branchlets pubescent; lvs. usually lanceolate to ovate-oblong, to 6 in. long, glaucous beneath. Iowa and Nebr., s. to Ky. and Mo. Zone 6. Closely related to *S. rigida* and perhaps only a form of it, having lvs. longer, more glaucous, and branchlets more densely white-hairy.

fragilis L. BRITTLE W., CRACK W. To 60 ft.; twigs brittle at base; lvs. lanceolate, to 7 in. long, toothed, light green beneath; catkins appearing with the lvs. Eur., Asia; sometimes escapes in e. U.S. Zone 5. Cv. 'Bullata' [var. *bullata* Rehd.]. Compact, subglobose shrub. Cv. 'Repandens' is listed.

franciscana: *S. lasiolepis*.

glabra Scop. Shrub, to 4 ft.; lvs. broad-elliptic to oblong, to 3 in. long, wavy-toothed, glaucescent beneath; catkins appearing with the lvs. Mts. of cent. and se. Eur. Zone 6.

glacialis Anderss. Prostrate shrub; lvs. ovate to obovate, to ½ in. long, obtuse, entire or with few teeth at base, glabrous at maturity; female catkins ovoid to globose, the scales black and nearly glabrous. Arctic coast, w. N. Amer., from Mackenzie R., n. to Pt. Barrow.

glauca L. [*S. glaucops* Anderss.]. Shrub, to 3 ft., young branchlets dark or reddish under the villous hairs; lvs. lanceolate to obovate, to 2½ in. long, entire, glaucous beneath, more or less hairy, especially when young, later glabrate; catkins appearing with the lvs. N. and cent. Eur., n. Asia, nw. N. Amer. Zone 2?

glaucophylla: see *S. glaucophylloides* var. *glaucophylla*.

glaucophylloides Fern. To 15 ft.; lvs. elliptic to oblong-lanceolate, to 5 in. long, finely toothed, glaucous beneath; catkins appearing with the lvs. New Bruns. to Me. Zone 4. Var. **glaucophylla** (Bebb) C. K. Schneid. [*S. glaucophylla* Bebb, not Schleich., or Bess., or Anderss.]. Lvs. firmer and thicker.

glaucops: *S. glauca*.

gracilistyla Miq. Shrub, young branchlets with whitish pubescence; lvs. oblong, to 4 in. long, finely toothed, grayish-pubescent beneath; catkins appearing before the lvs. Manchuria, China, Korea, Japan. Zone 6.

hastata L. HALBERD-LEAVED W. Shrub, to 7 ft., branchlets greenish or brownish, glossy, glabrous; lvs. ovate to obovate, to 3 in. long, sometimes cordate, finely toothed, glaucous beneath; catkins appearing with the lvs. Eur., Asia. Zone 6.

herbacea L. Dwarf shrub, to 1 ft., sts. creeping, often underground, angled; lvs. suborbicular, to ¾ in. long, rounded or notched at apex, crenate-serrate, bright glossy green; catkins few-fld. Arctic N. Amer., s. to New Hamp.; mts. of Eur. and n. Asia. Zone 2.

Humboldtiana: *S. chilensis*.

humilis Marsh. PRAIRIE W., SMALL PUSSY W., GRAY W. Shrub, to 8 ft.; lvs. oblong-lanceolate, to 4 in. long, slightly toothed, glaucous and tomentose beneath; catkins appearing before the lvs. Nfld. and s. Que., s. to Fla., e. to N. Dak. and e. Tex. Zone 4.

incana: see *S. Elaeagnos*.

interior Rowlee [*S. longifolia* Muhlenb., not Lam.]. SANDBAR W. Stoloniferous shrub with many sts., to 15 ft., branchlets reddish-brown, usually glabrous; lvs. linear or linear-oblanceolate, to 5½ in. long, remotely and irregularly serrate, paler beneath; catkins appearing after the lvs. Sandbars, mudbars, and moist alluvial soil, Alaska and Yukon to Que., s. to Va., W. Va., La., Tex. Zone 2.

irrorata Anderss. Shrub, to 10 ft., branchlets with white bloom; lvs. oblong to linear-lanceolate, to 4 in. long, entire or slightly toothed, glossy above, glaucous beneath; catkins appearing before the lvs. Colo., s. to Ariz., New Mex., w. Tex. Zone 5.

japonica Thunb. Shrub, to 6 ft.; lvs. elliptic-oblong, to 5 in. long, sharply toothed, silky-pubescent, becoming glabrous; catkins appearing with the lvs. Mts. of cent. Japan. Zone 6?

jessoensis Seemen. Tree, to 90 ft., branchlets light brown, glabrous; lvs. narrowly lanceolate, to 3½ in. long, finely toothed, very silky when young, less so above at maturity, petioles to nearly 2 in. long; catkins appearing with the lvs., to 2 in. long, on short peduncles. Japan. Zone 6.

laevigata Bebb. RED W., POLISHED W. To 45 ft., branchlets glabrous, reddish-brown to yellow; lvs. lanceolate, to 6 in. long, nearly entire, glaucous beneath; catkins appearing with the lvs. Along streams, Calif., e. to Utah and Ariz.

Lambertiana: *S. purpurea* var.

lanata L. WOOLLY W. Shrub, to 5 ft., twigs mostly woolly; lvs. elliptic-orbicular to oblong-ovate, to nearly 3 in. long, entire to undulate, glaucous and silky-hairy beneath, silky above, becoming glabrescent; catkins appearing with the lvs., 2 in. long or more. Arctic and subarctic Eur. and Asia. Zone 1.

lapponum L. Dense, much-branched shrub, to 5 ft., branchlets pubescent, later glabrous, dark brown and glossy; lvs. elliptic-oblong to lanceolate, to 2¼ in. long, entire, pubescent above, tomentose beneath; catkins appearing before or with the lvs. Mts. of Eur., e. to cent. Asia. Zone 4.

lasiandra Benth. Shrub or small tree, rarely to 40 ft., branchlets reddish, glossy, glabrous; lvs. lanceolate, to 4 in. long, acuminate, closely glandular-serrulate, glaucous beneath, dark green and glossy above; catkins appearing with the lvs. Alaska to Calif., e. to Ariz., Colo., New Mex. Similar to *S. laevigata*, but having lvs. acuminate, margin glandular-serrulate, and upper surface glossy.

lasiolepis Benth. [*S. franciscana* Seemen; *S. lasiolepis* var. *Bigelovii* (Torr.) Bebb]. ARROYO W. Shrub or small tree, to 35 ft., branchlets yellowish to dark brown, usually pubescent; lvs. oblanceolate, to 4 in. long, nearly entire, glaucous beneath; catkins appearing before the lvs. B.C. to Calif.

laurifolia: *S. pentandra.*

Lemoinei: a listed name of no botanical standing.

longifolia: *S. interior.*

lucida Muhlenb. SHINING W. Shrub or small tree, to 18 ft., branchlets chestnut-brown, glossy, glabrous; lvs. ovate-lanceolate or lanceolate, to 5 in. long, finely toothed, glossy on both sides, paler beneath; catkins appearing with the lvs. Nfld. to Sask., s. to Va. and Nebr. Zone 2.

lutea: *S. rigida.*

magnifica Hemsl. Shrub or small tree, to 18 ft., branchlets glabrous, purplish; lvs. elliptic to obovate, to 8 in. long, entire, dull gray-green above, glaucous beneath; catkins appearing with the lvs., male catkins to 7 in. long, female to 12 in. China. Zone 7. Remarkable for its large, broad lvs. and long catkins.

mandshurica: a listed name of no botanical standing.

Matsudana G. Koidz. PEKIN W. To 40 ft. or more, branchlets slender, at first downy and yellowish, becoming brownish-gray; lvs. narrow-lanceolate, to 3 in. long, sharply toothed, whitish beneath; catkins appearing with the lvs. N. Asia. Zone 5. Resembles *S. babylonica*, but having lvs. shorter, not more than 3 in. long, glandular-serrate. Cv. 'Pendula' [forma *pendula* C. K. Schneid.]. Having a weeping habit. Cv. 'Tortuosa' [forma *tortuosa* Rehd.]. DRAGON-CLAW W. Branchlets spirally twisted, giving the tree a bizarre appearance. Cv. 'Umbraculifera' [forma *umbraculifera* Rehd.]. Having broad, umbrella-shaped crown.

Medemii: *S. aegyptiaca.*

missouriensis: *S. eriocephala.*

×**mollissima** J. F. Ehrh., not Sm.: *S. triandra* × *S. viminalis.* Lvs. lanceolate, serrate or undulate-denticulate, gray-tomentose beneath.

×**multinervis** Döll, not Franch. & Sav.: *S. aurita* × *S. cinerea.* Branchlets densely pubescent; lvs. obovate to oblong-obovate, gray-pubescent, later usually glabrate above.

mutabilis: *S. ambigua.*

×**myricoides** Muhlenb.: *S. rigida* × *S. sericea.* Branchlets pubescent; lvs. lanceolate, somewhat silky beneath, stipules small.

myrsinifolia: *S. nigricans.*

myrsinites L. Shrub, to 1½ ft.; lvs. elliptic to lanceolate, to 2 in. long, serrate, glossy green on both sides, glandular, dead lvs. persist until end of following growing season; catkins appearing with the lvs. Mts. of n. and e. Eur., and w. Asia. Zone 5.

myrtilloides L. Low shrub, to 1½ ft., with underground creeping st., young branchlets brown, with short pubescence, soon glabrous; lvs. elliptic, entire, light green beneath; catkins appearing before or with the lvs. Cent. and n. Eur., w. Asia. Zone 2.

nigra Marsh. BLACK W. To 35 ft., bark dark brown to blackish, branchlets yellowish, slightly pubescent when young; lvs. lanceolate, to 5 in. long, finely toothed, pale green beneath; catkins appearing with the lvs. Cent. and e. U.S., n. Mex. Zone 4.

nigricans Sm. [*S. myrsinifolia* Salisb.]. Shrub, to 12 ft., young branchlets whitish-pubescent, often glabrescent; lvs. orbicular-ovate to oblong-lanceolate, to 4 in. long, toothed, gray-green and glabrous or pubescent beneath; catkins appearing before or with the lvs. Cent. and n. Eur. Zone 5.

Niobe: a listed name of no botanical standing; probably from the common name Niobe willow, *S.* × *blanda.*

·**nivalis** Hook. [*S. saximontana* Rydb.]. Tufted, creeping shrub; lvs. oblong to ovate, to nearly ½ in. long, acute, entire, smooth, dark green above, glaucous beneath; catkins appearing after the lvs., terminating the principal vegetative shoots of the season. B.C. and Sask., s. to Calif., Utah and New Mex.

×**patula** Ser.: *S. aurita* × *S. Elaeagnos.* Branchlets gray-pubescent; lvs. oblong to lanceolate, pubescent above, gray-tomentulose beneath.

×**Peasei** Fern.: *S. herbacea* × *S. Uva-ursi.* Prostrate shrub, brs. flexuous or decumbent, to 2 ft. long, very dark brown, glossy; lvs. elliptic to narrowly obovate, to nearly 1 in. long and ¾ in. wide, crenate-dentate, dark green and glossy above and beneath; catkins to 1¼ in. long. Wet, shaded, mountainous ravines, New Hamp.

pendula: *S. babylonica;* see also *S.* × *blanda.*

pentandra L. [*S. laurifolia* Wesm.]. BAY W., BAY-LEAVED W., LAUREL W. Shrub or small tree, to 25 ft., branchlets glabrous, glossy; lvs. elliptic, to 5 in. long, finely toothed, glossy dark green above, paler

beneath; catkins appearing with the lvs. Eur.; sparingly escaped in e. U.S. Zone 5.

petiolaris Sm. Shrub, to 4 ft., branchlets purple; lvs. lanceolate, to 3 in. long, tapering at base, acuminate, serrulate, glabrous; catkins appearing with the lvs. New Bruns. to Man., s. to Wisc. and Tenn. Zone 2.

petrophila: *S. arctica.*

Petzoldii: *S.* × *blanda.*

phylicifolia L. Shrub, to 3 ft. or more; lvs. elliptic to lanceolate, to 3 in. long, with short glandular teeth, glossy above, grayish-green beneath; catkins appearing before or with the lvs. N. Eur. Zone 4.

planifolia Pursh [*S. chlorophylla* Anderss.]. Shrub, to 10 ft., branchlets purplish; lvs. to 2 in. long, elliptic to lanceolate, glabrous, somewhat glaucous beneath; catkins small, appearing with or before the lvs. Rocky Mts., e. to ne. U.S. and adjacent Canada. Zone 1. Closely related to *S. phylicifolia* and perhaps conspecific with it.

×**Pontederana** Willd.: *S. cinerea* × *S. purpurea.* Branchlets becoming glabrous; lvs. obovate-lanceolate to lanceolate, glabrous or nearly so above at maturity, silky and glaucous beneath.

purpurea L. PURPLE O., BASKET W. Shrub, to 9 ft., branchlets slender, tough, purple at first, later grayish, glabrous; lvs. often opp., mostly oblanceolate, to 4 in. long, serrate only above the middle, dull green above, pale or glaucous beneath, turning black on drying; catkins appearing before the lvs. Eur. and N. Afr., e. to cent. Asia and Japan. Zone 5. Source of salicin, used medicinally, and twigs used in basketry. Cv. 'Gracilis' [forma *gracilis* (Gren. & Godr.) C. K. Schneid.; *S. uralensis* Hort. ex C. Koch]. Brs. slender; lvs. narrow. Cv. 'Nana'. Listed as dwarf form. Cv. 'Pendula' [var. *pendula* Regel]. Brs. slender, drooping. Var. **Lambertiana** (Sm.) W. D. J. Koch [*S. Lambertiana* Sm.]. Lvs. obovate or oblong, serrate for almost entire length, at least some opp. Mainly in lowlands, Eur. Var. **pendula:** cv. 'Pendula'.

regalis: *S. alba* var. *sericea.*

repens L. CREEPING W. Low shrub, brs. more or less procumbent, branchlets slender, pale, glabrous; lvs. ovate-elliptic, usually to 1¼ in. long, rarely longer, with flat, glandular margins, silky beneath, becoming glabrous, at least above; catkins cylindrical, appearing with or shortly before the lvs. Wet places, Eur. and Asia. Zone 5. Var. **argentea** (Sm.) Ser. Upper lf. surface remaining hairy.

reticulata L. Depressed shrub; lvs. elliptic to orbicular, green, reticulate, rugulose above, whitish beneath; catkins slender, on long peduncles. Arctic and Antarctic regions. Zone 1.

retusa L. Low shrub, sts. procumbent; lvs. small, rarely to ½ in. wide, obtuse to retuse at apex, entire, seemingly parallel-veined; catkins cylindrical. Mts. of cent. Eur. Zone 1.

rigida Muhlenb. [*S. lutea* Nutt.]. Shrub, to 12 ft., rarely more, branchlets yellowish to dark brown, pubescent when young; lvs. lanceolate to oblanceolate, to 4½ in. long, rounded to nearly cordate at base, dark green above, somewhat glaucous beneath, rigid and veiny in age; catkins appearing with or before the lvs. Nov. Sc. to Sask. and Mont., s. to Ga., Ark., Nebr. Zone 4.

rosmarinifolia L. Low shrub, with creeping sts., closely related to *S. repens*, but having lvs. linear, with 10–12 pairs of lateral veins; catkins globose. Wet places, cent. and e. Eur.

×**rubens** Schrank: *S. alba* × *S. fragilis.* Intermediate between parents, but variable; lvs. usually silky when young, later glabrous, and usually glaucous beneath.

×**rubra** Huds.: *S. purpurea* × *S. viminalis.* Shrub, to 9 ft., brs. slender, pubescent at first, later glabrous and yellow; lvs. lanceolate, to 5½ in. long, glaucescent and glabrescent or sometimes pubescent beneath. Brs. used in basket making.

sachalinensis Friedr. Schmidt. Tree, to 30 ft., branchlets thinly pubescent, becoming glabrous; lvs. lanceolate, to 6 in. long, dark green above, glaucous and slightly pubescent beneath. Sakhalin Is. and Japan. Zone 5. Cv. 'Sekka' [var. 'Setsuka']. A male clone, branchlets flattened, sometimes as much as 2 in. wide; lvs. to 2 in. long, green above, silvery beneath. The flattened branchlets are sometimes twisted and curled; often used in fl. arrangements.

Salamonii: *S.* × *sepulcralis.*

saximontana: *S. nivalis.*

Scoulerana Barratt ex Hook. SCOULER W. Large shrub or tree, to 30 ft.; lvs. oblong-obovate, to 4 in. long, usually entire, but sometimes more or less toothed, hairy on both surfaces when young, at maturity dark green and glabrous or puberulent above, densely villous or glabrescent beneath; catkins appearing before or with the lvs. Alaska, s. to s. Calif. and New Mex. Zone 6.

×**sepulcralis** Simonk. [*S. Salamonii* Carrière]: *S. alba* × *S. babylonica.* Habit similar to *S. babylonica*, but less weeping and a more vigorous grower, young growth silky-hairy; lvs. silky-pubescent or glabrous, bluish or whitish beneath. Zone 5.

sericea Marsh. SILKY W. Shrub, to 12 ft., branchlets slender, brown, puberulent to glabrous; lvs. lanceolate, to 4 in. long, finely toothed, silky beneath; catkins appearing before the lvs. Nov. Sc. and New Bruns. to Mich., s. to Mo. and Ga. Zone 4.

serpyllifolia Scop. Closely related to *S. retusa,* but having more compact habit, lvs. smaller, ⅜ in. long or less, and catkins globose. Mts. of cent. Eur.

×**sesquitertia** F. White: *S. aurita* × *S. phylicifolia* × *S. purpurea.* Shrub, to 6 ft., brs. slender, pubescent when young; lvs. oblong-obovate, crenate-serrate, rugulose above, glaucous beneath; catkins with both male and female fls.

sibirica Pall. Shrub, to 3 ft., brs. red-brown; lvs. elliptic to oblong, ½ in. long; catkins appearing with the lvs. Siberia.

Sieboldii: *S. babylonica.*

×**Smithiana** Willd.: *S. caprea* × *S. viminalis.* Tall shrub, to 18 ft., branchlets becoming glabrescent; lvs. oblong-lanceolate, to 5 in. long, soon glabrous above, gray-pubescent beneath.

Tominii Dode. Related to *S. jessoensis,* with branchlets dark brown, glabrous; lvs. lanceolate, to 4 in. long, remotely serrulate, glabrate above, appressed silky and bluish-white beneath. Caucasus.

triandra L. [*S. amygdalina* L.]. Shrub or small tree, to 30 ft., branchlets glabrous, greenish or reddish-brown; lvs. oblong-ovate or oblong-lanceolate, to 4 in. long, short-acuminate, serrate, glabrous and somewhat glossy above, glaucous or pale green beneath, petioles with 2–3 small glands; catkins appearing with the lvs. Eur. Zone 5. Twigs used in basketry.

tristis Ait. Low, many-stemmed, leafy shrub, to 3 ft.; lvs. crowded toward ends of twigs, oblanceolate, to 2 in. long, entire, white-tomentose beneath; catkins appearing before the lvs. Me. to Fla., w. to Minn. and Tenn. Zone 2.

×**tsugaluensis** G. Koidz.: supposedly *S. integra* Thunb. × *S. vulpina* Anderss. Shrub, branchlets yellowish-green; lvs. lanceolate, to 4 in. long, silvery beneath; catkins silvery, appearing before the lvs. Cv. **'Ginme'.** A female clone with reddish branchlets.

umbraculifera: a listed name of no botanical standing for *S. Matsudana* cv.

uralensis: *S. purpurea* cv. 'Gracilis'.

Uva-ursi Pursh. BEARBERRY W. Prostrate, matted shrub, with stoutish, leafy, brown twigs; lvs. obovate, to 1 in. long, entire or slightly toothed, shining above, glaucous beneath; catkins appearing with the lvs. Alaska to Lab., s. to mts. of N.Y. Zone 1.

viminalis L. OSIER, BASKET W. Shrub or small tree, to 30 ft., branchlets gray-pubescent; lvs. lanceolate, to 10 in. long, entire, silvery-white and silky-tomentose beneath; catkins appearing before the lvs. Cent. Eur., Asia; escaped from cult. in e. U.S. Zone 4. Much used for basketry, and also grown as an ornamental.

vitellina: *S. alba* var.

Wentworthii: a listed name of no botanical standing.

Wolfii Bebb ex Rothr. Much-branched shrub, to 2½ ft., young branchlets thinly villous-puberulent; lvs. more or less elliptic, to 1¾ in. long, entire, usually gray-pubescent, more so beneath than above. Streambanks and moist low ground, Mont., Idaho, e. Ore., s. to Utah and Colo.

SALMALIA: *BOMBAX.* **S. malabarica:** *B. Ceiba.*

SALPICHROA Miers. *Solanaceae.* About 25 spp. of herbs and shrubs of temp. S. Amer. and sw. U.S.; sts. divergent to flexuous, glabrous or pubescent; lvs. alt. or nearly opp., simple, entire, often hairy, narrowed to long petioles; fls. solitary in lf. axils or cymose, calyx tubular, 5-cleft, hardly enlarged in fr., corolla white or yellow, tubular to urceolate, lobes 5, recurved, stamens 5, borne on the corolla; fr. a 2-celled, ovoid or oblong berry, seeds many, compressed.

One species sometimes grown as a ground cover in southern Calif. (Zone 10), thriving in dry and alkaline places. Propagated by cuttings of half-ripened wood under glass, also by seeds when obtainable.

origanifolia (Lam.) Baill. [*S. rhomboidea* (Gillies & Hook.) Miers]. COCK'S-EGGS. Ann., or per. in mild climates, from a fleshy root, somewhat woody, with green flexuous brs. and strong odor; lvs. nearly opp., ovate-rhombic, to 1½ in. long and wide, ciliate; fls. solitary, rarely in pairs, nodding, on filiform pedicels, corolla white, urceolate, short, to 5/16 in. long; berry oblong, yellow or white, edible but of poor flavor. Argentina; an occasional escape in Zone 9 on the West Coast and Tex. A bee plant.

rhomboidea: *S. origanifolia.*

SALPIGLOSSIS Ruiz & Pav. *Solanaceae.* About 5 spp. of erect, viscid-pubescent ann., bien., or per. herbs, native in Chile; lvs. alt., simple, entire to sinuate-dentate or pinnatifid; fls. axillary or opp. lvs., solitary, mostly large and relatively few, long-pedicelled, calyx tubular, 5-lobed, corolla funnelform, with wide throat and 5-lobed limb, often colorfully veined, striped, or marked, stamens 4, in 2 pairs, staminode 1; fr. an oblong or ovoid, 2-valved caps., seeds minute.

One species grown as a tall, erect annual for the flower garden. Salpiglossis requires the usual treatment given half-hardy annuals, but young plants should not be allowed to become stunted before transplanting to the garden. For winter greenhouse bloom, seeds should be sown in later summer.

gloxiniiflora: see under *S. sinuata.*

grandiflora: see under *S. sinuata.*

sinuata Ruiz & Pav. PAINTED-TONGUE. Half-hardy, branching, to 2½ ft.; lvs. elliptic or narrowly oblong, to 4 in. long, sinuate-toothed or pinnatifid; corolla to 2½ in. long, to 2 in. across, dull to bright yellow or dark purple to scarlet or nearly blue, with much variation in venation and markings. This sp. is offered under a variety of hort. names, *S. gloxiniiflora, S. grandiflora, S. superbissima,* and *S. variabilis* Hort. Vilm.-Andr., all except the last apparently of no botanical standing.

superbissima: see under *S. sinuata.*

variabilis: see under *S. sinuata.*

SALPINGOSTYLIS: *SPHENOSTIGMA.*

SALVIA L. SAGE, RAMONA. *Labiatae.* More than 750 spp. of herbs, subshrubs, and shrubs, of wide distribution throughout the world, usually growing in dry or stony sites; sts. mostly square in cross section; lvs. opp., simple to pinnatisect or sometimes pinnate, the upper ones reduced to bracts; fls. in axillary, 2- to many-fld. verticillasters, calyx 2-lipped, teeth unequal, lower lip deeply 2-toothed, upper lip 3-toothed, corolla 2-lipped, stamens 2, each with 1 fertile cell; fr. of 4 ovoid, 3-angled nutlets.

Some salvias are cultivated as ornamentals in the garden or conservatory, others, such as *S. officinalis* and *S. Sclarea,* for perfumery or medicinal purposes. Scarlet sage, *S. splendens,* is the most widely cultivated of the ornamental sages. It is treated as an annual, grown preferably in full sun. It will bloom continuously from early summer to frost. The other salvias require only simple treatment as flower garden and border plants. The sweet herb, *S. officinalis,* persists for years once established.

ambigens: *S. guaranitica.*

apiana Jeps. WHITE S., GREASEWOOD. Subshrub, 3–8 ft., appressed-white-hairy; lvs. lanceolate-oblong, to 3½ in. long, obtuse, crenulate, mostly crowded near base of brs.; infl. spicate or a loose panicle; corolla ½–⅞ in. long, white to very pale lavender. S. Calif., n. Baja Calif.

argentea L. SILVER S. Erect, much-branched per., 2–4 ft., densely villous; lvs. ovate or oblong, to 6 in. long, irregularly lobed to toothed, woolly when young; verticillasters 4–8-fld.; calyx glandular-viscid, teeth spinose; corolla white, tinged with pink or yellow, upper lip curved. S. Eur., e. to Bulgaria.

aurea L. Much-branched shrub, 3–8 ft., white-tomentose; lvs. obovate, to 2½ in. long, entire to basally lobed, undulate; fls. in upper lf. axils, calyx enlarging in fr., corolla to 1¾ in. long, yellow, soon turning rusty-orange to russet-brown, lower lip broadly 3-lobed, spreading. Sw. Cape Prov. (S. Afr.). Tender shrub requiring sandy, well-drained soil.

azurea Lam. BLUE S. Erect per., 1½–6 ft., sts. glabrous to glabrescent; lower lvs. lanceolate or oblong, 2–3 in. long, serrate, tapering to petioles, upper lvs. narrower, often linear; infl. spicate; calyx with upper lip entire, corolla ⅝–¾ in. long, deep blue, rarely white. Minn. and Nebr., s. to Ky., Ark., Tex.; naturalized in the East. Subsp. **Pitcheri:** var. *grandiflora.* Var. **grandiflora** Benth. [*S. Pitcheri* Torr. ex Benth.; *S. azurea* subsp. *Pitcheri* (Torr. ex Benth.) Epl.]. Sts. with appressed and retrorse hairs; fls. often larger. Minn. and Nebr., s. to Ark. and Tex.

Barrelieri Etling. [*S. bicolor* Desf.]. SPANISH S. Erect bien. or per., to 3 ft.; lvs. simple, broadly ovate, serrate, or pinnatifid with broad lobes, sticky-pubescent; infl. branched, loose, verticillasters 4–6-fld.; calyx to ⅜ in. long, corolla 1¼ in. long, upper lip curved, bluish-violet, lower lip white. Sw. Spain, nw. Afr.

Bertolonii: *S. pratensis.*

bicolor: *S. Barrelieri.*

bracteata Banks & Soland. Subshrub, 1½–2½ ft., sts. much-branched basally, viscid-glandular-hairy; lvs. pinnatisect, lobes often crenate;

infl. paniculate, bracts boat-shaped, pinkish at base; corolla scarcely ½ in. long, purplish. Asia Minor. Cv. **'Rosea'.** Fls. rose-pink.

Brandegei Munz. Much-branched shrub, 3–8 ft., sts. with branching hairs; lvs. linear-oblong, ¾–2½ in. long, obtuse, revolute, rugose above, white-tomentose beneath; infl. an interrupted spike; corolla ½ in. long, lavender. Channel Is. (Calif.), n. Baja Calif.

Broussonetii Benth. Per. herb or subshrub, to 3 ft., sts. viscid, villous; lvs. broad-ovate, obtuse at apex, cordate at base, sinuate-crenate, green and subglabrous above, white-tomentose beneath; infl. paniculate; corolla scarcely ½ in. long, white. Canary Is.

canariensis L. Shrub, 3–6 ft., sts. white-woolly; lvs. lanceolate, hastate at base, rugose; infl. racemose to paniculate, bracts membranous, tinged or colored rose-purple; corolla purplish. Canary Is.

carduacea Benth. THISTLE S. Thistlelike ann., 1–2 ft., tomentose, sts. stout, scapelike; lvs. oblong, 3–6 in. long, sinuate-pinnatifid, spiny-toothed; fls. in 1–4 dense headlike verticillasters, bracts spiny-toothed, calyx densely woolly, half as long as corolla, corolla 1–1⅜ in. long, lavender, lower lip with middle lobe fringed. Calif., n. Baja Calif.

carnosa: *S. Dorrii* subsp. Var. **pilosa:** *S. Dorrii.*

clandestina: *S. verbenaca* var. *vernalis.*

Clevelandii (A. Gray) Greene. BLUE S. Aromatic shrub, about 3 ft., gray-hairy; lvs. elliptic-oblong, to 1¼ in. long, crenulate, rugose, tomentose beneath; verticillasters usually solitary, forming a head at the ends of the brs., but sometimes 2 or rarely 3 in an interrupted spike; corolla about ¾ in. long, blue. S. Calif., Baja Calif. Recommended as substitute for *S. officinalis* in cookery.

coccinea Juss. ex J. Murr. TEXAS S., SCARLET S. Per. or subshrub, sts. 1–2 ft., with spreading hirsute hairs basally; lvs. ovate to triangular, 1–2 in. long, acute, crenate, on long slender petioles; infl. racemose; calyx purplish, corolla mostly ¾–1 in. long, deep scarlet. S.C. to Fla., w. to Tex. and Mex.; W. Indies, and trop. Amer. Cult. as an ann. Cvs. include: **'Bicolor'**, corolla with upper lip white, lower lip rose-pink; **'Lactea'**, fls. white; **'Punicea'** [cv. 'Splendens'], taller, later blooming, more slender, fls. brighter red, more velvety; **'Splendens'**: 'Punicea'.

columbariae Benth. CHIA. Ann., 4–20 in.; lvs. mostly basal, oblong-ovate, 1–4 in. long, pinnatifid; verticillasters forming heads at ends of sts. and brs.; corolla slightly longer than the calyx, ½–⅝ in. long, blue. Calif. to cent. Baja Calif., e. to Utah and Ariz.

costaricensis Ørst. Probably per., sts. 1–2 ft., villous, becoming glabrous; lvs. broadly triangular, to 6 in. long, acute or obtuse, crenate-serrate, sagittate-cordate; infl. interrupted, racemose to paniculate, verticillasters few-fld.; corolla scarcely ½ in. long, lavender-blue. Costa Rica.

dichroa Hook.f. Allied to *S. Barrelieri*, but basal lvs. oblong, cuneate at the base, with irregular obtuse lobes. Atlas Mts. (Morocco). Cv. **'Magnifica'.** Fls. larger, more showy.

Dorisiana Standl. Per., to 4 ft., villous with intermixed gland-tipped hairs; lvs. thin-papery, ovate, 3–7 in. long, acuminate, deeply cordate, toothed; infl. racemose, bracts early deciduous; corolla 2¼ in. long, magenta, upper lip longer than lower. Honduras. Cult. as an ann.

Dorrii (Kellogg) Abrams [*S. carnosa* var. *pilosa* (Merriam) Jeps.]. GRAY BALL S. Low, much-branched shrub, 1–2½ ft.; lvs. obovate to spatulate, about ½ in. long, obtuse to emarginate, entire; infl. mostly densely spicate, bracts ciliate; corolla about ½ in. long, blue, tube generally hairy inside, upper lip half as long as tube or longer. S. Calif., Nev. Subsp. **carnosa** (Dougl. ex Jeps.) Abrams [*S. carnosa* Dougl. ex Jeps.]. Lvs. mostly ovate to elliptic, ⅝–1¼ in. long. E. Wash. and Idaho, s. to Calif.

elegans Vahl. [*S. rutilans* Carrière]. PINEAPPLE-SCENTED S. Per. or subshrub, to 3½ ft.; lvs. ovate, mostly 2–4 in. long, serrate, pubescent to tomentose; infl. racemose to paniculate, verticillasters mostly 4-fld.; calyx teeth triangular-aristate, corolla 1½ in. long, scarlet, lobes of lower lip reflexed. Mex. Cult. as an ann.

eremostachya Jeps. DESERT S. Much-branched shrub, 2–2½ ft., sts. with simple, spreading, gray, glandular hairs; lvs. lanceolate-oblong, ⅝–1½ in. long, obtuse, crenulate, green and rugose above, hispidulous beneath; infl. spicate, interrupted, bracts purplish-green, weakly spine-tipped; corolla barely 1 in. long, violet-blue to rose. Deserts, s. Calif.

farinacea Benth. MEALY-CUP S. Branched per., 2–3 ft., puberulent; lvs. ovate-lanceolate to ovate, 1½–3 in. long, obtuse to acute at apex, coarsely and irregularly serrate, uppermost lvs. linear-lanceolate; infl. interrupted, spicate, bracts small, green, early deciduous; calyx densely white- to purplish-tomentose, corolla ½–⅝ in. long, violet-blue. New Mex., Tex. Cv. **'Alba'.** Fls. white.

fruticosa Mill. [*S. triloba* L.f.]. Shrub, 2–4½ ft., sts. much-branched, appressed-white-tomentose; lvs. simple, or pinnate with 1–2 pairs of ovate lateral lfts. and a large oblong-elliptic terminal lft., rugose, greenish above, gray-white beneath, petioled; verticillasters 2–6-fld.; calyx campanulate, toothed, often purple, glandular- or nonglandular-pubescent, corolla about ½ in. long, lilac or pink, rarely white. Sicily to Syria.

glutinosa L. JUPITER'S-DISTAFF. Erect per., to 3 ft., sts. hairy in lower part, glandular-viscid above; lvs. simple, ovate, to 8 in. long, cordate or hastate at base, serrate or crenate, pubescent, petioled; verticillasters 2–6-fld.; calyx tubular-campanulate, to ⅝ in. long, corolla 1½ in. long, yellow, with red-brown markings. Mt. woods, cent. and s. Eur., Asia.

grandiflora Etling. Erect herb or small shrub, to 40 in.; lvs. simple, ovate to oblong, to 2½ in. wide, rounded or cordate at base, rugose, not glandular-pubescent, long-petioled; verticillasters 4–10-fld.; calyx about ½ in. long, glandular-viscid, often reddish-purple, corolla to 1⅜ in. long, lilac, pink, or violet-blue, rarely white. Cent. and s. Balkan Pen., Asia Minor.

Greggii A. Gray. AUTUMN S. Subshrub, to 3 ft., sts. with recurved hairs; lvs. oblong to spatulate, about ½–1 in. long, obtuse or mucronate, entire; infl. racemose, bracts early deciduous; corolla about 1 in. long, red to purplish-red, lower lip large and showy. Tex. and Mex. Cv. **'Alba'.** Fls. white. Cv. **'Rosea'.** Fls. pale red. Autumn.

guaranitica St.-Hil. ex Benth. [*S. ambigens* Briq.]. Per. or subshrub, sts. to 3½ ft., with recurved, often gland-tipped hairs; lvs. ovate, 2–5 in. long, coarsely crenate, dark green and rugose above, paler and pubescent beneath; infl. racemose; fls. mostly 1½–2 in. long, dark blue to violet-blue, often whitish basally, rarely bluish-rose. Se. Brazil to e. Paraguay and n. Argentina. Often cult. as an ann.

haematodes: *S. pratensis.*

hians Royle ex Benth. Per., 2–3 ft.; lvs. triangular-ovate, 3–5 in. long, cordate-hastate at base, serrate, rugose, pubescent; infl. racemose, 8–12 in. long, villous; corolla about 1½ in. long, sapphire-blue, tube inflated, lips large and spreading, lower lip spotted white. Kashmir.

hierosolymitana Boiss. JERUSALEM S. Allied to *S. pratensis*, but sts. retrorse-scabrous on the angles, lvs. narrower and more nearly ovate-oblong, calyx teeth long-stiff-awned, and upper lip of corolla not markedly curved. Lebanon, Syria, Israel.

hispanica L. Ann., to 2 ft.; lvs. ovate, 2–3 in. long, crenate-serrate, glabrous; infl. racemose, dense, 2–4 in. long; corolla pale blue, tube as long as calyx. Mex. to Peru; naturalized in W. Indies.

Horminum: *S. viridis.*

interrupta Schousb. Hardy, subshrub, sts. woolly, to 4 ft.; lvs. broadly ovate, 6–10 in. long, cordate to obtuse, white-tomentose beneath, pinnatisect, lobes crenate, terminal lobe oblong-ovate, 2–3 in. long; infl. racemose, to 2 ft. long, verticillasters 5–10-fld., 2–3 in. apart; calyx campanulate, viscid, corolla about 1½ in. long, dark violet-purple, with white throat. Morocco.

involucrata Cav. ROSY-LEAF S. Per. herb to 4 ft., sts. woody at base; lvs. ovate, to 4 in. long, acuminate, entire to crenate, glabrous on both sides, petioles to 2 in. long; bracts pink to red, deciduous when fls. appear; calyx to ½ in. long, pink to red, prominently veined, corolla to 2 in. long, pink, rose, or red. Late summer and autumn. Mex. and Cent. Amer.

judaica Boiss. Per., to 3½ ft.; lvs. puckered, crenate-dentate, basal lvs. lyrate-pinnatifid, segms. ovate-oblong, obtuse, st. lvs. cordate, sessile; infl. paniculate; corolla ⅝ in. long, violet. Lebanon, Israel.

Jurisicii Kosanin. Per., 8–24 in., sts. densely hairy; lvs. pinnate, lfts. 4–6 pairs, narrow-linear; infl. loose, much-branched, verticillasters 4–6-fld.; calyx about ⅛ in. long, villous, glandular-punctate, corolla about ½ in. long, violet-blue, resupinate. S. Yugoslavia.

lavandulifolia Vahl. SPANISH S. Small shrub or herb, to 20 in., sts. erect, pubescent; lvs. simple, narrowly oblong or oblong-linear, to 2 in. long, crenulate, tomentose, petioled; verticillasters 6–8-fld.; calyx about ⅜ in. long, often red-purple, pubescent, glandular-punctate, corolla ¾–1 in. long, blue or violet-blue. Spain, s. France.

leucantha Cav. MEXICAN BUSH S. Shrub, to 2 ft., sts. deciduously white-woolly; lvs. linear-lanceolate, 2–6 in. long, acute, crenate, rugose, tomentose beneath; infl. racemose, 6–10 in. long; calyx funnelform, densely violet-purple, woolly, corolla ⅝–¾ in. long, white. Mex.

leucophylla Greene. GRAY S., PURPLE S. Shrub, to 5 ft., whitish-gray-tomentose; lvs. oblong-lanceolate, ¾–2½ in. long, nearly cordate at base, obtuse at apex, crenulate, rugose; infl. spicate, interrupted, bracts often purplish; corolla about ¾ in. long, bluish-lavender. S. Calif.

lyrata L. CANCERWEED. Per., 8–24 in., forming rosettes; lvs. basal, obovate, spring lvs. lyrate-pinnatifid to sinuate, later summer lvs. nearly entire; infl. mostly scapose, simple or branched; corolla ¾–1½ in. long, violet, upper lip straight, much shorter than the lower. E. U.S.

mellifera Greene. BLACK S. Shrub, to 7 ft., sts. often glandular-pubescent; lvs. oblong-elliptic, ¾–2½ in. long, crenulate, green and rugose above, white-tomentose beneath; infl. an interrupted spike; corolla about ½ in. long, lavender-blue. Calif., n. Baja Calif.

mexicana L. Per., to 3 ft.; lvs. ovate to oblong, to 3 in. long, crenate-serrate, tomentose beneath; infl. racemose, dense, 8–16 in. long, bracts gray-pubescent; corolla about ¾ in. long, deep blue. Mex. Var. **minor** Benth. Infl. 3–8 in. long; calyx pubescent.

microphylla HBK. BABY S. Shrub, to 3 ft.; lvs. ½–¾ in. long, triangular-ovate to elliptic, obtuse, mostly crenulate-serrate, pubescent beneath; infl. racemose, 1 ft. long or more; fls. 1 in. long, red. Mex.

Munzii Epl. Like *S. mellifera*, but young sts. more slender; lvs. oblong-obovate, to ¾ in. long, ashy, hirtellous above, with minute appressed hairs beneath; corolla about ⅜ in. long, clear blue. S. Calif., n. Baja Calif.

nemorosa L. Not in cult.; material cult. under this name is usually *S.* × *sylvestris;* some of it may be *S.* × *sylvestris.*

officinalis L. COMMON S., GARDEN S. Erect shrub, to 2 ft., sts. more or less white-woolly; lvs. oblong, 1–2½ in. long, entire or crenulate, rugose; verticillasters 5–10-fld.; calyx ⅜–½ in. long, pubescent, corolla to 1⅜ in. long, violet-blue, pink, or white. N. and cent. Spain to w. Balkan Pen. and Asia Minor. Much grown as a potherb or spice. Cvs. include: 'Albiflora', fls. white; 'Purpurascens' and 'Purpurea', lvs. reddish-purple; 'Tricolor', lvs. variegated white, often margined or tipped purple.

pachyphylla Epl. ex Munz. ROSE S. Similar to *S. Dorrii,* but of more sprawling habit, and having corolla about ⅝ in. long, the tube with a distinct inner band of hairs, the upper lip to ¼ as long as tube. Deserts, s. Calif. to Baja Calif.

patens Cav. GENTIAN S. Per., 1–3½ ft., sts. stiffly viscid-hairy; lvs. ovate to oblong-ovate, 2–5 in. long, nearly cordate to hastate, obtuse, crenulate; infl. spicate, 8–16 in. long, bracts longer than calyx; corolla 2–2¾ in. long, bright blue. Mts., Mex. Cv. 'Alba'. Fls. white.

Pitcheri: *S. azurea* var. *grandiflora.*

pratensis L. [*S. Bertolonii* Vis.; *S. haematodes* L.]. MEADOW CLARY. Aromatic per., 1–3½ ft., pubescent, the upper parts glandular; lvs. ovate to oblong, 3–6 in. long, cordate, doubly crenate or lobed, rugose; infl. spicate, verticillasters 4–6-fld., bracts green, shorter than calyx; calyx teeth acute or mucronate, corolla ⅝–1 in. long, strongly curved, typically violet-blue, rarely pink or white, but in cult. varying from rose-pink to dark violet-purple. Extremely variable, especially in shape and size of corolla. Eur., Morocco. Some material grown under this name may be the hybrid, *S.* × *sylvestris.* Cvs. include: 'Alba', 'Atroviolacea', and 'Rosea'.

purpurea Cav. Per., to 9 ft., sts. woody at base, mostly glabrous; lvs. broadly ovate, 2¼–5 in. long, rounded basally, acuminate, serrate-crenate; infl. spicate to paniculate; corolla mostly ⅝–¾ in. long, rose-purple. Mex., Cent. Amer.

reflexa Hornem. Ann., to 2 ft.; lvs. spreading or reflexed, lanceolate to linear-lanceolate, to 2 in. long. irregularly serrate to entire; infl. spicate, interrupted; calyx deeply 2-lipped, corolla about ⁵⁄₁₆ in. long, slightly exserted, blue. Wisc. to Mont., s. to Ark. and Mex.; adventive east.

ringens Sibth. & Sm. Erect per., to 2 ft., woody at base; lvs. rugose, appressed-hairy, pinnatisect or pinnate with 3–6 pairs of small lfts., terminal lft. ovate to elliptic; infl. cymose, verticillasters 2–4-fld.; calyx ⅜–⅝ in. long, glandular-pubescent, corolla to 1¾ in. long, violet-blue or blue. S. and e. Balkans to se. Romania.

rutilans: *S. elegans.*

scabiosifolia Lam. Per., 1–1½ ft., sts. woody and woolly at base; lvs. pinnate or pinnatisect, with many pairs of linear or oblong segms., petioled; verticillasters 6–10-fld.; calyx deeply 2-lipped, ⅓ as long as corolla, corolla about 1½ in. long, violet-blue or violet. Crimea.

Sclarea L. CLARY. Erect bien. or per., to 3 ft., sts. glandular above; lvs. simple, broad-ovate, 6–9 in. long, cordate, pubescent, petioled; verticillasters 4–6-fld., bracts longer than calyx, white or lilac; calyx about ⅜ in. long, pubescent, teeth spinose, corolla about 1 in. long, lilac or pale blue, upper lip curved. S. Eur. Source of an aromatic oil used in medicine and for flavoring. Var. **turkestaniana** Mottet. Bracts twice as long as calyx or longer, corolla white, tinged with pink. Turkestan.

sonomensis Greene. CREEPING S. Per., 4–16 in., sts. creeping, matted, and leafy at base, the tips ascending and leafless; lvs. elliptic-obovate, ¾–2 in. long, crenulate, rugulose, white-tomentose beneath; infl. spicate, verticillasters 4–6-fld.; corolla about ¾ in. long, blue-violet. Calif. Useful as a ground cover.

spathacea Greene. PITCHER S. Coarse per., with creeping rhizomes, sts. ann., glandular-villous; lvs. oblong, 4–8 in. long, hastate at base, rugose; infl. spicate, rather dense, bracts purplish, as long as calyx; corolla 1¼–1⅝ in. long, purplish-red. Calif.

splendens F. Sellow ex Roem. & Schult. SCARLET S. Per. subshrub, to 8 ft., glabrous; lvs. ovate, to 3½ in. long, acuminate, crenate-serrate; infl. racemose, bracts red, deciduous; calyx campanulate, scarlet, corolla to 1½ in. long, scarlet, lower lip much reduced. S. Brazil. Often cult. as an ann. Many cvs., including: 'Alba', fls. white; 'Atropurpurea', fls. dark violet-purple; 'Atrosanguinea', fls. dark crimson; 'Bruantii', of dwarf habit, fls. brilliant scarlet; 'Compacta', dwarf, infl. dense, fls. bright scarlet; 'Grandiflora', growing to 3½ ft. first season, corolla to 2¼ in. long; 'Souchetii', dwarf, fls. white.

× **superba** Stapf [*S. nemorosa* Mottet and auth., not L.; *S. virgata* Hort., not Jacq.; *S. virgata nemorosa* Hort.]: *S.* × *sylvestris* × *S. villicaulis* Borb. A sterile hybrid; per., to 4½ ft., sts. woody at base; lvs. ovate-oblong to oblong, 1–3 in. long, obtuse to truncate at base, crenulate, rugulose, gray-green, puberulent beneath, the lower st. lvs. mostly sessile; infl. densely spicate, 4–8 in. long, bracts red-purple; corolla nearly ½ in. long, violet-purple, anthers without pollen. Known only in cult.

× **sylvestris** L.: *S. nemorosa* × *S. pratensis.* Per., 6–30 in.; similar to *S. pratensis* but st. lvs. more numerous and oblong-lanceolate, the bracts purple, fls. more numerous, scarcely more than ½ in. long. Eur. to w. Asia. Some material of *S. pratensis* may belong here.

tiliifolia Vahl. Ann., to 4 ft. or more; lvs. broadly ovate, 1½–4 in. long, acuminate, sparsely crenate-serrate, mostly appressed-pilose; infl. an interrupted spike or a panicle of interrupted spikes, to 10 in. long; corolla to ⁵⁄₁₆ in. long, bluish. Mex. to Ecuador.

tricolor Lem. Per.; lvs. ovate, mostly to 1¼ in. long, abruptly acuminate, crenulate-serrate; infl. racemose, verticillasters mostly 2–4-fld., spaced apart, bracts early deciduous; calyx campanulate, green, corolla about 1½ in. long, white, lower lip salmon-red, upper lip hoodlike, straight, with reddish hairs at apex. Known only from cult. Cult. as an ann. Some material labeled *S. tricolor* may be *S. officinalis* cv. 'Tricolor'.

triloba: *S. fruticosa.*

turkestanica: a listed name of no botanical standing for *S. Sclarea* var. *turkestaniana.*

uliginosa Benth. BOG S. Per., to 6 ft.; lvs. oblong-lanceolate, to 4 in. long, acute, cuneate, serrate; infl. racemose to paniculate, long-peduncled, bracts broad-ovate; corolla about ¾ in. long, blue, with white markings. S. Brazil, Uruguay, Argentina.

Vaseyi (T. C. Porter) S. Parish. Shrub, to 4½ ft.; lvs. oblong-lanceolate to ovate, to 1½ in. long, obtuse, cuneate, crenate, white-tomentose; infl. spicate, interrupted, long-peduncled, verticillasters headlike; bracts and calyx teeth long-aristate to spinescent, corolla about ¾ in. long, white. Deserts, s. Calif., n. Baja Calif.

Verbenaca L. VERVAIN S., WILD CLARY. Erect per., to 2 ft.; lvs. oblong to ovate, 3–4 in. long, more or less pinnatifid with wide lobes; infl. dense or loose, verticillasters 6–10-fld.; calyx about ¼ in. long, enlarging slightly in fr., corolla about ½ in. long, lilac-blue, rarely white. S. and w. Eur., w. Asia. Var. **vernalis** Boiss. [*S. clandestina* L.]. Sts. low and scapelike; corolla twice as long as calyx, blue. Bulgaria to Israel and Syria.

verticillata L. LILAC S. Erect per., to 3 ft., sts. pilose-hispid; lvs. broad-ovate, to 3 in. long, simple or lyrate with 1–2 pairs of small lateral segms., acute at apex, cordate to truncate at base, petioled; verticillasters (8–)15–30-fld.; calyx about ³⁄₁₆ in. long, corolla ⁵⁄₁₆ in. long, lilac-blue, tube slightly exserted. S. and e. Eur. to Asia Minor.

villosa Fern. Per., to 15 in., more or less procumbent, sts. densely glandular-pilose; lvs. triangular, to 1½ in. long, obtuse, serrate-crenate; infl. spicate, interrupted; fls. nearly ¾ in. long. Mex.

virgata: see *S.* × *superba.* [Var.] *nemorosa: S.* × *superba.*

viridis L. [*S. viridis* var. *comata* Heldr.; *S. Horminum* L.]. Villous ann., to 1½ ft.; lvs. oblong to ovate, 1–2½ in. long, obtuse or cuneate, crenulate; infl. racemose, bracts usually white or rose to deep purple, the terminal ones sometimes leaflike, sterile, forming a tuftlike crown; calyx tubular, shortly 2-lipped, corolla about ½ in. long, pale lilac to reddish-violet or purple. S. Eur. Cv. 'Alba'. Bracts white. Cv. 'Violacea'. Bracts violet, veined darker.

Wagnerana Polak. Per., 3–10 ft., sts. and lvs. glabrous; lvs. ovate, 2–4 in. long, mostly cuneate, acuminate, serrulate; infl. racemose, densely red-viscid-tomentose, bracts nearly orbicular; calyx red-pilose, glandular-viscid, corolla 1½–3 in. long, scarlet. Guatemala and Costa Rica.

SALVINIA Séguier. *Salviniaceae.* About 10 spp. of free-floating, rootless, aquatic ferns, widely distributed in trop. and warm-temp. regions; lvs. small, dimorphic, in whorls of 3, 2 entire, flat, and floating, the 3rd finely pinnately dissected, completely submerged, and functioning as a stabilizer and absorption organ; lvs. hairy or papillose; sporangia in sporocarps on the lower side of the floating lvs. and produced infrequently in cult. material.

Often a troublesome pest of lakes in the tropics. Grown in pools (not hardy) or in aquaria or greenhouse tanks, reproducing asexually to form colonies on the surface of the water. See also *Ferns.*

auriculata Aubl. [*S. natans* Kunth, not (L.) All.]. Plants to 10 in. long; floating lvs. boat-shaped, 1 in. long, 1¾ in. wide, upper surface with even rows of papillae, each with a tuft of 4 hairs, the hairs joined by a dark-colored body, lower surface with many hairs. Cuba, Mex. to Argentina.

cucullata Roxb. ex Bory. Plants to 2¾ in. long; floating lvs. to ⅝ in. long and about ⅜ in. wide, the edges curved upward and inward, upper surface covered with irregular rows of papillae, each with a tuft of hairs, lower surface with short brown hairs. India, Malay Pen., Sumatra, w. Australia.

natans (L.) All., not Kunth. Plants to 6 in. long; floating lvs. flat, broadly elliptic, to ⅝ in. long and ⅜ in. wide, upper surface covered with rows of papillae, each with a tuft of 3 or 4 hairs, lower surface with brown hairs. Eur., Asia, N. Afr.; naturalized in Java. Not cult. in N. Amer.; material grown under this name is *S. rotundifolia. S. natans* Kunth is *S. auriculata.*

oblongifolia Mart. Plants to 1 ft. long; floating lvs. oblong, to 1¾ in. long and ⅝ in. wide, upper surface covered with rows of papillae, each with a tuft of hairs, lower surface with brown hairs. Brazil.

rotundifolia Willd. FLOATING MOSS. Plants to 2¾ in. long; floating lvs. nearly orbicular, to ⅝ in. long and ¾ in. wide, upper surface covered with rows of papillae, each with a tuft of 4 hairs, the hairs separate from one another, lower surface with brown hairs. Trop. Amer.; introd. locally in e. U.S.

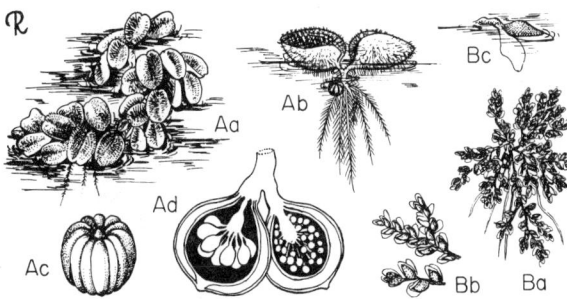

SALVINIACEAE. **A,** *Salvinia rotundifolia:* **Aa,** plants, × ½; **Ab,** single plant with sporocarp and submerged pinnately dissected leaves, × 1; **Ac,** sporocarp, × 5; **Ad,** sporocarps, vertical section, with megasporangia (left) and microsporangia (right), × 10. **B,** *Azolla filiculoides:* **Ba,** plant viewed from above, × 1; **Bb,** sterile branches, × 2; **Bc,** single leaf, with floating upper lobe and submerged lower lobe, × 8. (From Bailey, *Manual of Cultivated Plants,* ed. 2.)

SALVINIACEAE Dumort. Ferns; 2 genera and about 18 spp. of free-floating, aquatic ferns widely distributed in tropics and warm-temp. regions; lvs. small, simple, entire or 2-lobed, lacking circinate vernation; sporangia in soft, spore-bearing structures (sporocarps) under the lvs., bearing small spores (microspores) or large spores (megaspores). *Azolla* and *Salvinia* are grown in aquaria or pools.

SAMANEA (Benth.) Merrill. *Leguminosae* (subfamily *Mimosoideae).* Perhaps 20 spp. of unarmed trees or shrubs, native to trop. Amer. and Afr.; lvs. alt., 2-pinnate; fls. in globose heads, 5-merous, stamens many, united basally; fr. an indehiscent, straight, or somewhat curved legume, with partitions, seeds embedded in pulp.

Propagated by seeds.

Saman (Jacq.) Merrill [*Pithecellobium Saman* (Jacq.) Benth.]. RAIN TREE, SAMAN, SAMAN TREE, MONKEYPOD, ZAMANG. To 80 ft., with short, thick trunk, and spineless brs., spreading to 100 ft.; lvs. large, with 2–6 pairs of pinnae, lfts. to 8 pairs, oblong-rhombic to obovate, velvety beneath, terminal lft. largest, to 2½ in. long; fls. in dense umbel-like heads, yellowish, stamens long, pink; fr. to 8 in. long. Trop. Amer. A fast-growing, ornamental shade tree, suitable for parks or large gardens in the tropics. Very well suited for use as a host for ornamental epiphytes.

SAMBUCUS L. ELDER, ELDERBERRY. *Caprifoliaceae.* About 20 spp. of shrubs or small trees with pithy sts., rarely herbs, of wide distribution in temp. and subtrop. regions; lvs. opp., odd-pinnate, lfts. toothed; fls. in compound terminal cymes, small, white, usually 5-merous, corolla rotate, ovary inferior, 3–5-celled; fr. a small berrylike drupe, with 3–5 nutlets. The spp. in *Sambucus* are difficult to delimit, and there is no agreement among various treatments in regional floras.

Elders are ornamental when planted in mass; some species are also grown for the edible fruit, although in other species the fruit is poisonous. Most of the elders are hardy north and thrive in rich, rather moist soil. Propagated by seeds, cuttings, and some kinds by suckers. See also *Elderberry.*

acutiloba: a listed name of no botanical standing for *S. canadensis.*

aurea: a listed name of no botanical standing; has been used for yellow-lvd. forms of *S. canadensis* and *S. nigra.*

caerulea Raf. [*S. glauca* Nutt.]. BLUE E. To 50 ft.; lfts. 5–7, oblong, to 6 in. long; fls. yellowish-white, in umbel-like cymes 6 in. across; fr. blue-black, glaucous, edible. Early summer. Fr. has culinary uses similar to *S. canadensis.* B. C. to Calif. and Utah. Var. **neomexicana** (Woot.) Rehd. [*S. neomexicana* Woot.]. Lfts. 3–5, lanceolate, grayish-green. Ariz. and New Mex. Var. **velutina** (E. Durand) Schwer. [*S. californica* Hort. ex C. Koch]. Lfts. large, pubescent. Calif.

californica: *S. caerulea* var. *velutina.*

callicarpa Greene. PACIFIC COAST RED E. To 20 ft., sometimes treelike; lfts. 5–7, oblong to obovate, pubescent underneath particularly on rib, sharp-toothed to apex; fr. scarlet, in showy clusters. Calif. to Wash.

canadensis L. AMERICAN E., SWEET E. To 8 ft., stoloniferous, pith white; lfts. usually 7, elliptic or lanceolate, to 6 in. long; fls. white, in umbel-like cymes to 10 in. across; fr. purple-black, edible. Early summer. Nov. Sc. to Fla. and Tex. Zone 4. Fr. is used for making wines, sauces, jellies, and pies. Cvs. include: 'Acutiloba', lvs. much-dissected; 'Aurea', lvs. golden-yellow, fr. red; 'Chlorocarpa', fr. greenish; 'Dissecta', listed; 'Laciniata', listed; 'Maxima', larger form, cymes to 15 in. across. Pomological cvs. with large clusters and berries include: 'Adams No. 1', 'Ezyoff', 'Johns', 'Kent', 'Nova', 'Scotia', 'York'. Var. **submollis** Rehd. Lfts. grayish-green, soft pubescent beneath. Ill. to Iowa, s. to Okla. and Tex.

chinensis: *S. javanica.*

Ebulus L. DWARF E., DANEWORT, WALLWORT. Herbaceous per., to 4 ft., with many sts.; lfts. narrow-oblong, long-pointed, sharp-serrate; fls. white tinged pink, in broad cymes; fr. small, black. Fr. yields a blue dye. Eur., N. Afr., Asia.

glauca: *S. caerulea.*

javanica Reinw. ex Blume [*S. chinensis* Lindl.]. Sparsely branched, erect shrub, to 9 ft., pith white; lfts. in 2–6 pairs, short-stalked to sessile, oblong to linear-lanceolate, to 8½ in. long, 2½ in. broad, pubescent along veins above and below, or glabrous below; fls. white or creamy in flat-topped infl., some fls. aborted into turbinate, mostly yellow, persistent nectaries; fr. black. Japan, Taiwan, se. Asia, Malay Arch.

melanocarpa A. Gray. To 6 ft.; lfts. 5–7, oblong-lanceolate, to 6 in. long, somewhat pubescent beneath, especially when young, or glabrous; fls. yellowish-white, in an ovoid cyme to 3 in. across; fr. black. Summer. B. C. to Calif. and n. Rocky Mts. Zone 6.

microbotrys Rydb. To 6 ft., sts. light brown, pith of young sts. white; lfts. 5–7, ovate-lanceolate, to 4 in. long, sharply toothed, essentially glabrous; fls. nearly white, in pyramidal cymes; fr. scarlet. Colo. to Calif. Zone 6.

Miquelii: *S. racemosa.*

neomexicana: *S. caerulea* var.

nigra L. EUROPEAN E. To 30 ft.; lfts. usually 5, elliptic, to 5 in. long, of disagreeable odor when bruised; fls. yellowish-white, in umbel-like cymes to 8 in. across, of heavy odor; fr. shining black, edible. Late spring. Eur., N. Afr., w. Asia. Zone 6. Some of the cvs. are: 'Albovariegata', lvs. variegated with white; 'Argentea', lvs. predominantly white; 'Aurea', lvs. golden-yellow; 'Aureo-variegata', lvs. variegated with yellow; 'Laciniata', lfts. regularly and deeply dissected; 'Variegata', lvs. variegated.

pubens Michx. AMERICAN RED E., RED-BERRIED E., STINKING E. To 15 ft., pubescent when young, pith brownish-red; lfts. 5–7, oblong, to 4 in. long; infl. a rather loose pyramidal cyme to 4 in. long, lower brs. spreading; fr. scarlet, not edible. Late spring. Widespread in e. N. Amer., extending w. to Rocky Mts. Zone 5. Cvs. include: 'Leucocarpa', fr. white; 'Maxima', cymes large; 'Xanthocarpa', fr. amber-yellow.

racemosa L. [*S. Miquelii* (Nakai) Kom. & Klob.-Alis.]. EUROPEAN RED E. To 12 ft., glabrous, pith brown; lfts. 5–7, ovate or elliptic, to

3 in. long; fls. yellowish-white, in dense, ovoid, paniculate cymes to 3 in. long, the lower brs. usually reflexed; fr. scarlet. Spring. Eur., w. Asia. Zone 5. Cvs. include: 'Aurea', lfts. yellowish; 'Laciniata', lfts. regularly and deeply dissected, green when unfolding; 'Plumosa', lfts. toothed to about middle with long and narrow teeth, purplish when unfolding.

Sieboldiana (Miq.) Graebn. To 20 ft.; lfts. usually 7, oblong, to 8 in. long; fls. yellowish-white, in ovoid, panicled cymes to 3 in. long; fr. scarlet. Spring. China, Japan. Zone 6?

SAMOLUS L. WATER PIMPERNEL, BROOKWEED. *Primulaceae*. About 10 spp. of small per. herbs, represented on all continents; lvs. simple, alt. or sometimes in basal rosettes, entire; fls. small, white, in terminal racemes or panicles, calyx 5-cleft, corolla somewhat campanulate, 5-cleft, stamens 5; fr. a 5-valved caps.

Sometimes used as aquarium plants, or planted in moist places.

floribundus: *S. parviflorus.*

parviflorus Raf. [*S. floribundus* HBK]. UNDERWATER ROSE. Glabrous, to 2 ft.; lvs. obovate or spatulate, to 3 in. long; fls. $\frac{1}{16}$ in. across, in racemes. N. Amer.

Valerandi L. Glabrous, to 1 ft., sometimes more; lvs. obovate to oblong, to 3 in. long; fls. to $\frac{1}{8}$ in. across, in racemes. Eur., Asia. Smaller than *S. parviflorus*, but with fls. larger.

SANCHEZIA Ruiz & Pav. *Acanthaceae*. About 60 spp. of erect or climbing, usually glabrous herbs or shrubs of Cent. and S. Amer.; lvs. opp., large; fls. in heads, spikes, or racemes, subtended by small or large bracts, corolla tubular, with 5 equal lobes, stamens 2, exserted, anther sacs 2, staminodes 2; fr. a caps., oblong, 6–8-seeded.

glaucophylla Hort. A name, probably referring originally to *S. nobilis;* material cult. as *S. glaucophylla* in the U.S., however, is *S. speciosa.*

nobilis Hook. Differs from *S. speciosa* chiefly in having lvs. broadest near apex, and staminodes only $\frac{3}{16}$ in. long. Ecuador. Apparently not now in cult.; material grown as *S. nobilis* is *S. speciosa.*

speciosa J. Léonard. Shrub, to 5 ft.; lvs. oblong-ovate, broadest near the middle, to 1 ft. long, abruptly acuminate, narrowed at base, the midrib and veins usually white to yellow; fls. in spikes, bracts red, to 1½ in. long, corolla 2 in. long, yellow, glabrous, staminodes ¾–1 in. long. Perhaps Ecuador or Peru; known only as a cult. plant. Commonly but incorrectly grown as *S. nobilis.* Cvs. with the midrib and veins of lvs. more broadly marked with white or yellow are known.

spectabilis: a listed name of no botanical standing, probably referring to *S. speciosa.*

SANDERSONIA Hook. *Liliaceae*. One sp., a tuberous-rooted, per. herb, native to S. Afr.; sts. erect, leafy; lvs. alt.; fls. axillary, perianth globose-campanulate, shortly 6-lobed, saccate at base, stamens 6, anthers versatile, style 3-parted; fr. a loculicidal, 3-valved caps.

Adapted to greenhouse culture.

aurantiaca Hook. CHINESE-LANTERN LILY, CHRISTMAS-BELLS. To 2 ft.; lvs. linear or lanceolate, to 4 in. long, sessile; fls. orange, to 1 in. long, on slender, drooping pedicels.

SANGUINARIA L. BLOODROOT. *Papaveraceae*. One sp., a woodland per. herb, native to e. N. Amer., with red sap and stout prominent rhizome; lf. solitary, petioled, lobed; fl. terminating a scape, sepals 2, falling early, petals 8–16, stamens many; fr. an ellipsoidal caps.

Often and easily transplanted to the wild garden where it flowers very early in the spring.

canadensis L. RED PUCCOON. Lvs. basal, palmately lobed, to 1 ft. across; fls. white, sometimes tinged with pink, to 1½ in. across, solitary, on scapes about 8 in. high; caps. to 1 in. long. Dried rhizomes used medicinally. Cv. 'Multiplex' [var. *plena* Barcl.; cv. 'Flore Pleno']. Fls. double, without stamens or carpels.

SANGUISORBA L. BURNET. *Rosaceae*. Two or 3 spp. of erect, per. herbs from N. Temp. Zone; lvs. pinnate; fls. bracted, in dense terminal spikes or heads, bisexual, sepals 4, colored, petals none, stamens 4, pistils 1–3, stigma simple; fr. an achene.

Propagated by seeds and division.

canadensis L. CANADIAN B. Sts. 1–6 ft., simple or branched; lfts. of lower lvs. 7–17, lanceolate-oblong to ovate, obtuse, coarsely serrate-

dentate, 1–4 in. long; spikes whitish, cylindrical, 2–8 in. long; filaments spatulate to club-shaped, exserted. Lab. to Mich., s. to Ga., Ind., Ill. Dried rhizomes have been used medicinally.

minor: *Poterium Sanguisorba.*

obtusa Maxim. [*Poterium obtusatum* Hort.; *P. obtusum* (Maxim.) Franch. & Sav.]. To about 4 ft.; basal lvs. 5–20 in. long; lfts. 5–16, bluntly ovate to elliptic, 1½–2½ in. long, somewhat glaucous beneath, toothed, petiolulate; spikes cylindrical, 2–3½ in. long, rose-purple; stamens exserted. Japan.

officinalis L. GREAT B., BURNET BLOODWORT. Like *S. canadensis* in habit; spikes deep red or purplish, ovoid to oblong, to 1½ in. long; filaments filiform, included or barely exserted. Eurasia; naturalized in N. Amer. Young lvs. sometimes eaten.

sitchensis C. A. Mey. Close to *S. canadensis*, but lfts. broadly elliptic; bracts narrower, more long-acuminate; sepals larger, broader, thicker. Alaska to Ore., Idaho; e. Asia.

tenuifolia Fisch. ex Link. To 4 ft. or more; lvs. mostly basal, lfts. 13–21, linear-oblong, to 3 in. long, deeply toothed; fls. white, varying to purple, in spikes to 2 in. long. N. Asia. Cvs. 'Alba' and 'Rosea' are listed.

SANICULA L. SNAKEROOT, BLACK S., SANICLE. *Umbelliferae*. About 37 spp. of nearly cosmopolitan per. or or rarely bien., often leafy-stemmed herbs; lvs. palmately or pinnately divided, to pinnately or ternate-pinnately decompound, or rarely entire; fls. white, greenish, yellow, or purple, in irregular, few-rayed, compound umbels with leafy involucres, involucels of small to large bractlets; fr. oblong-ovoid to subglobose or ellipsoid, covered with hooked bristles or tubercles.

arctopoides Hook. & Arn. FOOTSTEPS-OF-SPRING. Prostrate or decumbent, to 1 ft. across; basal lvs. palmately 3-parted, divisions toothed; involucels of 8–17 prominent bractlets longer than heads; fls. yellow; upper part of fr. bristly. Ore., Calif.

bipinnatifida Dougl. PURPLE SANICLE. To 2½ ft., glabrous except at nodes, sts. purplish; lvs. variable, entire to 5-lobed in young plants, pinnate in old plants, segms. 5–7, subovate, pinnatifid; involucels of short, lanceolate bractlets; fls. yellow or purple; fr. with conspicuous bristles. At low elevations, Vancouver Is. (B.C.), s. to Baja Calif.

SANSEVIERIA Thunb. BOWSTRING HEMP, DEVIL'S TONGUE, GOOD-LUCK PLANT, LUCKY P., HEMP. P. *Agavaceae*. About 60 spp. of stiff, erect, per. herbs in arid Afr. and s. Asia, with short, thick rhizomes; lvs. basal, elongate, very thick, erect, flat or cylindrical, often variegated and mottled; infl. a panicle, raceme, or spike; fls. whitish or yellowish, narrow, perianth segms. united into a tube, stamens 6, ovary superior, 3-celled, each cell with 1 ovule; fr. a berry.

Sansevierias are commonly grown as durable porch and house plants in the North and out of doors in the South; some kinds have become naturalized in warm countries where they may also be grown commercially for their strong white leaf fibers, known as bowstring hemp. Of easy culture in a rather heavy soil. Propagated by division; also by cuttings of the leaf, about 3 in. long, placed upright in sand, which produce a rhizome at the base.

aethiopica Thunb. Stemless; lvs. linear-lanceolate, to 16 in. long, ¾ in. wide, sometimes with dark green cross bands, more or less glaucous, tips white, awl-like, to 3 in. long, margins red or white; fls. white, in racemose infl. to 30 in. S. Afr.

Craigii: a listed name of no botanical standing for *S. trifasciata* cv.

cylindrica Bojer. St. very short or lacking; lvs. 3–4, cylindrical or slightly flattened, to 5 ft. long, 1¼ in. in diam., with dark green stripes and cross bands; fls. white or tinged with pink, 1½ in. long, in a raceme to 3 ft. long. Afr.

Ehrenbergii G. Schweinf. ex Bak. SELEB S., BLUE S. St. to 9 in.; lvs. 5–9, 2-ranked, to 6 ft. long, 1¼ in. wide, a little thicker than wide, margins flattened; fls. in clusters of 4–7 in a paniculately branched infl. to 6½ ft. long, perianth tube ¼ in. long. Trop. Afr.

guineensis: *S. hyacinthoides.*

Hahnii: a listed name of no botanical standing for *S. trifasciata* cv.

hyacinthoides (L.) Druce [*S. guineensis* (L.) Willd.; *S. spicata* Haw.; *S. thyrsiflora* Thunb.]. AFRICAN B.H. Stemless; lvs. nearly flat, but narrowing into a channeled petiole, to 1½ ft. long, 3½ in. wide, with pale green cross bands, margins yellow; fls. greenish-white, 1½ in. long, fragrant, in a raceme to 2½ ft. long. S. Afr. Important for fibers of lvs.

Laurentii: *S. trifasciata* cv.

liberica Gérôme & Labroy. Stemless; lvs. 1–3, flat, lanceolate, to 3½ ft. long, 2–5 in. wide, deep green, often with paler cross bands, margins reddish-brown. Liberia.

parva N. E. Br. St. to 5 in.; lvs. recurved and spreading, stiff, very concave above, narrowly lanceolate, to 18 in. long, variegated, tip awnlike, to 3 in. long; fls. pale pinkish-white inside, much darker outside, in pairs in a raceme to 1 ft. long. E. Afr.

Roxburghiana Schult. INDIAN B.H. Stemless; lvs. 6–24, not 2-ranked, ascending-recurved, stiff, concave above, to 2 ft. long, 1 in. wide, ⁵⁄₁₆ in. thick; fls. about 4 in each cluster, in a raceme to 2½ ft. long, perianth tube ¼ in. long, lobes to ⅜ in. long. India. Important as a fiber plant.

spicata: *S. hyacinthoides.*

subspicata Bak. RED-EDGE S. St. to 1½ ft.; lvs. with slender petiole, lanceolate, to 2 ft. long, dark green, mature lvs. not variegated; fls. white, solitary or in pairs in a raceme to 1½ ft. long. S. Afr.

suffruticosa N. E. Br. St. to 1 ft., branching; lvs. 7–18, cylindrical, slightly furrowed in age, to 2 ft. long, ¾ in. wide, slightly cross-banded with pale green and streaked with darker green; fls. whitish or greenish-white, ½ in. long, in a raceme to 1½ ft. long. E. Afr.

thyrsiflora: *S. hyacinthoides.*

trifasciata Prain. SNAKE PLANT, MOTHER-IN-LAW'S TONGUE. Stemless; lvs. 1–2 (-6), erect, stiff, linear-lanceolate, to 4 ft. long, 2¾ in. wide, with light green to whitish-green and black-green cross bands; fls. greenish-white, to ⁹⁄₁₆ in. long, 3–8 in solitary or grouped clusters in a racemose infl. to 2½ ft. long. Cv. 'Craigii'. Lvs. with broad, whitish-yellow, longitudinal stripes. Cv. 'Hahnii'. HAHN'S S., BIRD'S-NEST S. Dwarf; lvs. short, forming a funnel-shaped rosette. Cv. 'Laurentii' [var. *Laurentii* (De Wild.) N. E. Br.; *S. Laurentii* De Wild.]. Lvs. with golden-yellow marginal stripes. Var. **Laurentii:** cv. 'Laurentii'.

zeylanica (L.) Willd. CEYLON B.H. Stemless; lvs. concave at middle, to 2½ ft. long, ¾ in. wide, with light green cross bands and lines down outer side. Ceylon. A poorly known sp.; most material cult. under this name is probably *S. aethiopica* or *S. Roxburghiana.*

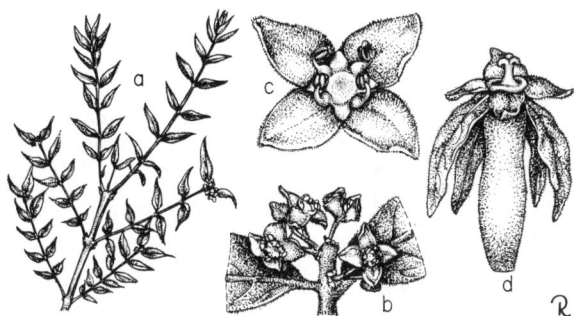

SANTALACEAE. *Buckleya distichophylla:* **a,** flowering branch, × ⅙; **b,** male inflorescence, × 2; **c,** male flower, × 8; **d,** female flower, × 3. (From Lawrence, *Taxonomy of Vascular Plants.*)

SANTALACEAE R. Br. SANDALWOOD FAMILY. Dicot.; 27 genera of semiparasitic herbs, trees, and shrubs, of wide distribution; lvs. entire; fls. bisexual or unisexual, perianth 3–6-lobed, stamens 3–6, ovary usually inferior, 1-celled; fr. a nut or drupe. *Buckleya* and *Comandra* are sometimes cult.; sandalwood and sandalwood oil of commerce are obtained from *Santalum.*

SANTALUM L. SANDALWOOD. *Santalaceae.* About 8 or 9 spp. of glabrous, evergreen trees and shrubs, native from India to Australia and Hawaii; lvs. opp., simple; fls. in panicles, bisexual, perianth 4–5-lobed, stamens 4–5, ovary half-inferior; fr. a subglobose drupe.

The fragrant wood is much used in making chests, and the oil extracted from the wood is an important fixative for perfumes.

album L. WHITE SANDALWOOD. Small tree; lvs. ovate to ovate-lanceolate, to 2 in. long, glaucous beneath; panicles much shorter than lvs.; fls. yellowish, turning red; fr. black, the size of a cherry. India. Cult. in tropics including Hawaii. One of the important commercial sources of sandalwood and sandalwood oil.

SANTOLINA L. *Compositae* (Anthemis Tribe). About 8 spp. of grayish, aromatic shrubs, subshrubs, or herbs, native to Medit. region; lvs. alt., pinnately toothed to pinnately divided; fl. heads solitary, on long peduncles, discoid, involucral bracts imbricate in 2–3 rows, scarious or with scarious margins, receptacle convex, with chaffy scales; fls. all tubular, bisexual, white or yellow; achenes 3-angled, glabrous, pappus absent.

Santolinas are used as low border or edging plants. Mostly not hardy north. Propagated by cuttings taken in spring from plants overwintered in a frame, or from the plants in the autumn before frost.

Chamaecyparissus L. [*S. incana* Lam.; *S. tomentosa* Pers.]. LAVENDER COTTON. Much-branched, evergreen shrub, to 2 ft.; lvs. to 1⅜ in. long, pinnately divided into narrow segms., tomentose, silvery-gray; heads globular, to ¾ in. across; fls. yellow. Summer. Spain and N. Afr.; escaped locally in U.S. Cv. 'Nana'. A dwarf form. Cv. 'Plumosus'. Foliage lacy, silvery-gray.

ericoides Poir. Shrub, to 2 ft., brs. pubescent; lvs. linear, tomentose, finely dentate; fls. yellow. S. Eur. Perhaps not specifically distinct from *S. Chamaecyparissus;* however, material offered in the trade as *S. ericoides* has glabrous, green lvs. and cream-colored fls., and may be referable to *S. virens.*

incana: *S. Chamaecyparissus.*

neapolitana Jord. & Fourr. Felty-white, evergreen shrub, to 2½ ft.; lvs. to 3 in. long, pinnately divided; heads to ¾ in. across; fls. bright yellow. S. Italy.

pinnata Viv. Evergreen, essentially glabrous, bushy shrub, to 2½ ft., brs. very leafy; lvs. to 1½ in. long, pinnately divided, green; heads globular, to ⅝ in. across; fls. dull white. Italy.

rosmarinifolia L. Shrub, to 2 ft., brs. erect; lvs. fleshy, narrowly linear, with inrolled margins, green, mostly glabrous, lower lvs. tessellated on the surface by the crowded flattened segms., upper lvs. sometimes entire or finely toothed; heads globular; fls. yellow. S. Eur.

tomentosa: *S. Chamaecyparissus.*

virens Mill. [*S. viridis* Willd.]. Green, spreading subshrub, to 2 ft.; lvs. linear, 1–2 in. long, dark green, glabrous; heads globular, to ¾ in. across; fls. yellow. Medit region.

viridis: *S. virens.*

SANVITALIA Lam. *Compositae* (Helianthus Tribe). Seven spp. of ann. or per. herbs or shrubs, native to sw. U.S., Mex., and Cent. Amer., 1 sp. endemic to s. Bolivia and n. Argentina; lvs. opp., simple, pubescent, the lower petioled, the upper sessile, their bases then united and sheathing the st., margins entire to lobed; fl. heads radiate, terminal, peduncled or sessile, involucral bracts imbricate in 2–3 rows, rarely in 1 row and valvate, often leaflike and hairy, becoming scarious, receptacle hemispherical to conical, scaly, the scales acuminate-cuspidate or rounded at apex; disc fls. bisexual, fertile, brown to purple, ray fls. female, fertile, white to pale yellow or orange; central achenes compressed and winged, outer disc achenes 3–4-angled, ray achenes 3-angled, pappus lacking or of 3–4 awns.

One species is grown as an annual in the flower garden, thriving in light or open soil and full sunlight. Propagated by seeds.

procumbens Lam. Procumbent, much-branched ann., to about 6 in., with a well-developed taproot; lvs. broadly lanceolate to broadly ovate, to 2½ in. long, strigose, entire; heads ¾ in. across; disc fls. mostly dark purple, ray fls. yellow to orange. Mex., Guatemala.

SAPINDACEAE Juss. SOAPBERRY FAMILY. Dicot.; about 150 genera and 2,000 spp., primarily of pantrop. distribution; evergreen or deciduous shrubs or trees, sometimes herbaceous, tendril-bearing vines, usually monoecious; lvs. usually alt., mostly pinnate, sometimes 3-foliolate or 2-ternate, rarely simple; fls. unisexual or bisexual, regular or irregular, in axillary or terminal racemes or panicles, sepals 4 or 5, petals 4 or 5, sometimes 0, stamens 5–10, pistil 1, ovary superior, usually 3-celled; fr. berrylike, drupaceous, or a caps., sometimes inflated, sometimes winged and a samara, seeds often with an aril. Genera grown for the edible fr. or as ornamentals are: *Aitonia, Alectryon, Allophylus, Aphania, Atalaya, Blighia, Cardiospermum, Cupaniopsis, Dodonaea, Erioglossum, Euphoria, Harpullia, Koelreuteria, Litchi, Melicoccus, Sapindus, Schleichera, Serjania, Trigonachras, Ungnadia,* and *Xanthoceras.*

SAPINDUS L. SOAPBERRY. *Sapindaceae.* About 12 spp. of polygamous, deciduous or evergreen shrubs and trees, native

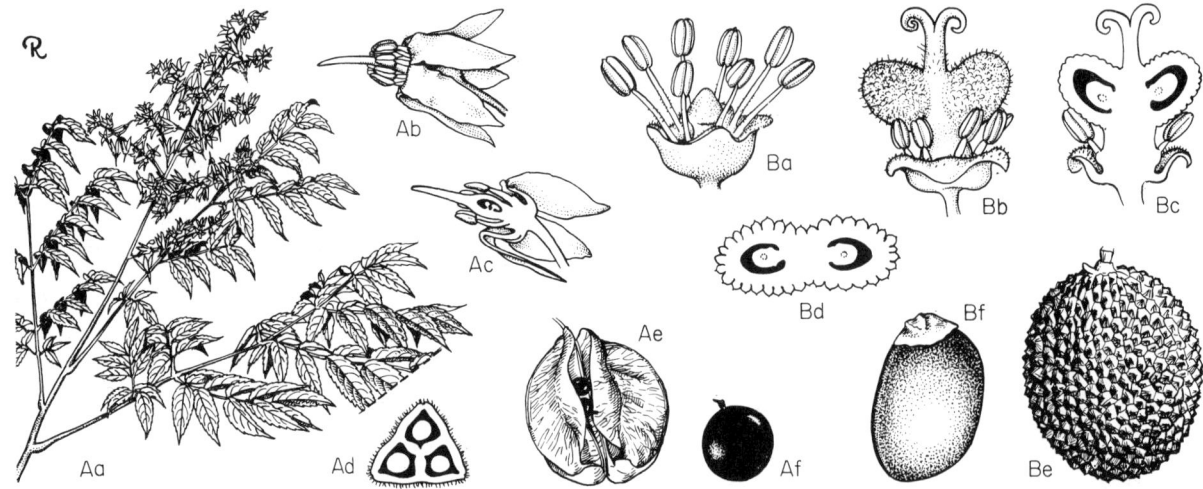

SAPINDACEAE. **A,** *Koelreuteria elegans:* **Aa,** flowering branch, greatly reduced; **Ab,** flower, × 2; **Ac,** flower, vertical section, × 2; **Ad,** ovary, cross section, × 8; **Ae,** capsule, × ½; **Af,** seed, × 2. **B,** *Litchi chinensis:* **Ba,** male flower, × 5; **Bb,** female flower, × 4; **Bc,** female flower, vertical section, × 4; **Bd,** ovary, cross section, × 5; **Be,** fruit, × ¾; **Bf,** seed, × 1.

to the tropics and subtropics of the New and Old World; lvs. alt., pinnate, occasionally with a single lft.; fls. small, in axillary or terminal racemes or panicles, regular, sepals and petals 4 or 5, stamens 8–10, filaments usually pubescent; fr. a fleshy or leathery berry.

The saponin-rich fruits are used like soap in some countries. The species thrive in sandy or dry and rocky soil; propagated by seeds and cuttings in spring. Grown in the South as ornamentals.

attenuatus: *Aphania rubra.*

detergens: *S. Mukorossi.*

Drummondii Hook. & Arn. Deciduous tree, to 50 ft.; lvs. to 8 in. long, lfts. 8–18, lanceolate, to 3 in. long; panicles to 10 in. long; fls. yellowish-white; fr. round, yellow, turning black, to ½ in. in diam. Mo. to Ariz. and Mex. Zone 6.

emarginatus: *S. trifoliatus.*

indicus: *S. Saponaria.*

marginatus Willd. WILD CHINA. Evergreen tree, to 40 ft.; lvs. to 14 in. long, lfts. 7–13, lanceolate to elliptic-lanceolate, to 6 in. long, acuminate; infl. to 8 in. long; petals long-clawed. Coastal, S.C. to Fla.

Mukorossi Gaertn. [*S. detergens* Roxb.]. CHINESE S. Evergreen, brittle tree, to 45 ft.; lvs. to 16 in. long, lfts. 8–13, oblong-lanceolate to oblong-ovate, to 6 in. long, rachis narrowly winged; fr. yellow or orange-brown, ¾ in. in diam., seeds black. India to cent. Japan. Zone 9. The fr. has a high saponin content and is used like soap. Planted in Fla. Seeds are used for beads.

Rarak DC. Evergreen tree, to 60 ft.; lvs. to 1½ ft. long, lfts. 12–24, oblong-lanceolate, 3–4 in. long; infl. to 6 in. long; fr. ¾ in. in diam. Se. Asia and Java.

Saponaria L. [*S. indicus* Poir.]. SOAPBERRY, FALSE DOGWOOD, JABONCILLO. Evergreen tree, to 30 ft.; lvs. to 1 ft. long, lfts. usually 7–9, elliptic to oblong-lanceolate, to 4 in. long, rachis usually broadly winged; panicles to 10 in. long; fls. white; fr. round, orange-brown, ¾ in. in diam., glossy. Trop. Amer., where fr. used locally like soap.

trifoliatus L. [*S. emarginatus* Vahl]. Small, evergreen tree; lvs. to 10 in. long, lfts. 4–6, elliptic-lanceolate, to 4 in. long, acuminate, leathery, glabrous; panicles terminal, to 8 in. long, pubescent; fls. white; fr. 2–3-lobed, to ¾ in. long. Tropics, Old World.

SAPIUM P. Br. [*Triadica* Lour.]. *Euphorbiaceae.* Over 100 spp. of monoecious or seldom dioecious trees and few shrubs, with milky juice, native to the tropics; lvs. alt., simple, petioled; fls. in spikes, sepals present, petals absent, ovary 2–3-celled; fr. a caps.

The latex of several species furnishes rubber, the fatty seed covering of *S. sebiferum* is used in making candles and soap, and the seeds yield a drying oil. Propagated by seeds or cuttings, or varieties are top-grafted on seedling stocks; not easily transplanted.

japonicum (Siebold & Zucc.) Pax & K. Hoffm. Small tree; lvs. elliptic, ovate to obovate, to 6 in. long, acuminate; spike to 3–4 in. long;

fr. to ¾ in. in diam., seeds spotted dark brown. China, Korea, Japan. Zone 8.

rubrum: a listed name of no botanical standing.

sebiferum (L.) Roxb. [*Triadica sebifera* (L.) Small]. CHINESE TALLOW TREE, VEGETABLE-TALLOW. Tree, to 40 ft.; lvs. rhombic-ovate, abruptly acuminate, to 3 in. long, becoming yellow or red in autumn; spike to 4 in. long; fr. ½ in. in diam., the 3 large white seeds adhering to the central column. China, Japan; naturalized in s. U.S. Zone 4. Cult. in Japan and elsewhere as an ornamental. Grown as a shade or ornamental tree; it has the aspect of a poplar and is a good street tree.

SAPONARIA L. SOAPWORT. *Caryophyllaceae.* About 30 spp. of ann., bien., or per. herbs, native to Eurasia, but chiefly to Medit. region; lvs. opp.; infl. cymose, capitate, or paniculate, calyx cylindrical or oblong, 5-toothed, not scarious, not subtended by an epicalyx, petals 5, white, pink, or red, clawed, with coronal scales at juncture of claw and blade, entire or emarginate, stamens 10, ovary 1-celled, styles 2, rarely 3; fr. a 4-toothed caps., seeds flat, reniform.

Cultivation easy, as plants are tolerant of poor soils; some species tend to be weedy. Propagated by seeds or perennials by division.

bellidifolia Sm. Cespitose, sts. to 16 in., unbranched, glabrous, with 1 pair of lvs.; basal lvs. spatulate; infl. capitate, bracts linear-lanceolate; fls. sessile, calyx hairy at apex, teeth triangular, petals yellow, blade about ⅛ in. long, filaments yellow, exserted. Mts., s. Eur.

caespitosa DC. Densely cespitose, sts. to 6 in., unbranched, glabrous, hairy towards apex; lvs. linear-lanceolate, to 1 in. long; infl. capitate; calyx purplish, hairy, teeth triangular, petals rosy-purplish. Pyrenees.

calabrica Guss. [*S. multiflora* Regel]. Ann., sts. much-branched, glandular-hairy at apex; basal lvs. spatulate, st. lvs. oblong-ovate; infl. a loose panicle, pedicels glandular-hispid; calyx to ⅜ in. long, glandular-hispid, teeth obtuse, petals pale rosy-purplish, rarely white, to ¼ in. long. Italy to w. Turkey.

lutea L. Cespitose, sts. to 6 in., erect, unbranched, hairy; basal lvs. linear-lanceolate, st. lvs. linear; infl. capitate, pedicels hairy; calyx densely hairy, teeth triangular, petals yellow, less than ³⁄₁₆ in. long, filaments violet, exserted. Sw. and cent. Alps.

multiflora: *S. calabrica.*

nana: *S. pumila.*

Ocymoides L. Per., to 10 in., sts. procumbent to ascending, much-branched; lvs. nearly spatulate or elliptic to ovate-lanceolate, usually less than 1 in. long, lower lvs. short-petioled, upper lvs. sessile; infl. a broad, loose cyme; calyx cylindrical, to ½ in. long, glandular-hairy, petals purplish. Sw. and s.-cent. Eur. Cvs. are: 'Rosea' [var. *rosea* Hort.], fls. bright rose; 'Rubra' [var. *rubra* Hort.], fls. deep red; 'Splendens' [var. *splendens* Hort.], fls. larger, deeper rose.

officinalis L. BOUNCING BET. Stout, rhizomatous per., to 3 ft., forming colonies, sts. sparingly branched, usually glabrous; lvs. ovate-lanceolate to elliptic or ovate, to 4 in. long, 3-veined; infl. terminal, condensed; calyx cylindrical, to 1 in. long, usually glabrous, petals entire to slightly emarginate, white or pink. Eur., Asia; naturalized in N. Amer. Roots have been used medicinally and juice can be used for forming a lather with water.

×**olivana** Wocke: *S. caespitosa* × *S. pumila*. Forming a cushion; fls. many, nearly sessile, to ¾ in. across, petals rose-red.

pulvinaris: *S. pumilio.*

pumila (St.-Lag.) Janch. [*S. nana* Fritsch; *S. pumilio* (L.) Fenzl ex A. Braun, not Boiss.; *Silene pumilio* (L.) Wulfen]. Cespitose per., to about 3 in.; lvs. linear, to 1 in. long; fls. solitary, to 1 in. across, calyx to ¾ in. long, rather inflated, hairy, petals rose or white, styles 3. E. Alps, se. Carpathians.

pumilio Boiss., not (L.) Fenzl ex A. Braun [*S. pulvinaris* Boiss.]. Densely cespitose per., forming tufts to 16 in. across; basal lvs. linear, to ¼ in. long, st. lvs. few and sessile, or absent; infl. glandular-hairy, the brs. 3–10-fld.; calyx oblong-cylindrical, to ⁵⁄₁₆ in. long, glandular, petals crimson or purple, styles less than ¹⁄₁₆ in. long. W. Turkey. See also *S. pumila.*

Vaccaria: *Vaccaria pyramidata.*

SAPOTA: *MANILKARA.* **S. Achras:** *M. Zapota.*

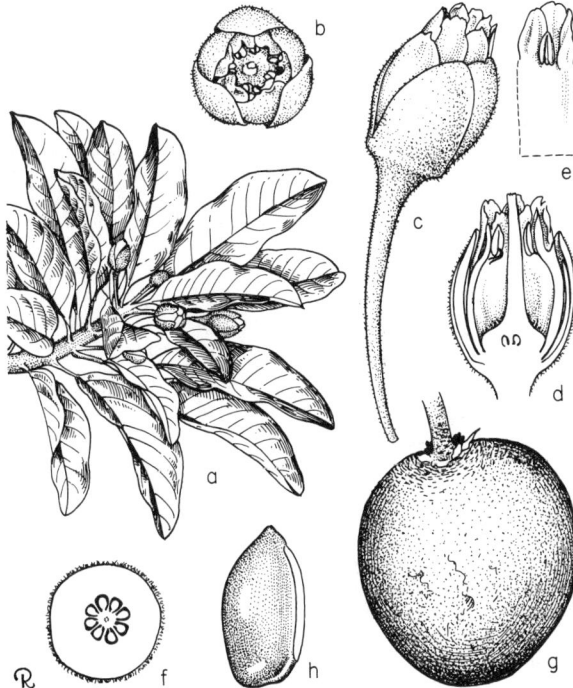

SAPOTACEAE. *Manilkara Zapota:* **a,** flowering branch, × ³⁄₈; **b,** flower, face view, × 2; **c,** flower, side view, × 2; **d,** flower, vertical section, × 2; **e,** segment of corolla with stamen, × 2; **f,** ovary, cross section, × 4; **g,** fruit, × ½; **h,** seed, × 1.

SAPOTACEAE Juss. SAPODILLA FAMILY. Dicot.; about 40 genera and 800 spp. of mostly trop. and subtrop. trees and shrubs with milky latex, native to both hemispheres; lvs. alt. to nearly opp., simple, entire; fls. regular, bisexual, sepals 4–12, rarely united, corolla lobed, sometimes with petal-like appendages, stamens as many as corolla lobes, or rarely twice as many, staminodes often present, ovary superior; fr. a 1- to several-seeded berry. *Argania, Bumelia, Chrysophyllum, Manilkara, Mastichodendron, Mimusops, Payena, Planchonella, Pouteria,* and *Synsepalum* are cult., primarily in the tropics.

Several genera have edible fruit, the seeds of several (*Butyrospermum* Kotschy, *Madhuca* J. F. Gmel.) supply vegetable fats, two (*Palaquium* Blanco, *Payena*) provide gutta-percha, and one *(Manilkara)* chicle.

SARACA L. *Leguminosae* (subfamily *Caesalpinioideae*). Twenty spp. or more of usually smallish, understory forest trees, native to se. Asia; lvs. alt., even-pinnate, lfts. rigid,

young lvs. limp, appearing in colorful flushes; fls. in panicled corymbs, usually with somewhat petal-like, reddish bracts, calyx with tube and 4 unequal, brightly colored, or petal-like lobes, petals 0, stamens 3–8 in. long, exserted; fr. a tough, narrowly oblong, dehiscent legume.

Grown as ornamentals in the wet lowland tropics (and Zone 10b) for the masses of beautiful flowers produced among the leaves on the older branches. Require shade and moist, well-drained soil; best grown under shade of taller trees. Sometimes grown in the warm greenhouse. Propagated by seeds; slow-growing when young.

cauliflora Bak. To about 20 ft.; lfts. in 5–6 pairs, strongly veined, the upper lfts. oblanceolate-oblong, larger, to 1 ft. long or more, acute; corymbs dense, 4–6 in. across; fls. opening orange-yellow, later turning red; fr. to 1 ft. long. Malay Pen. Closely resembling *S. declinata* Miq., a much taller Malayan sp. apparently not cult. in the U.S.

indica L. ASOKA, SORROWLESS TREE. To 30 ft.; lfts. in 3–6 pairs, oblong or oblong-lanceolate, to 9 in. long, often blunt; corymbs to 4 in. across; fls. orange-red, deepening in color with age, fragrant at night; fr. to 10 in. long. India to Malay Pen. Favorite ornamental in India, where fls. used as offerings at temples.

thaipingensis Cantley. To 30 ft.; lfts. in 5–8 pairs, oblong-lanceolate, to 16 in. long, 5 in. wide, acuminate, thick; corymbs to 12 in. across, from old wood, with yellow bracts; fls. yellow, becoming red at mouth of calyx tube; fr. to 18 in. long. Malay Pen.

SARCANTHUS Lindl. *Orchidaceae.* About 80 spp. of epiphytes, native to trop. se. Asia; sts. elongate, leafy, erect or pendent; lvs. fleshy, cylindrical or flat; infl. axillary, racemose or paniculate; fls. small, fleshy, sepals spreading, upper sepal concave and arching over column, petals smaller, spreading, lip 3-lobed, united to column, spurred, the spur funnelform, having a conspicuous callus at its entrance, lateral lobes of lip triangular, small, midlobe triangular or hastate. For structure of fl. see *Orchidaceae.*

For culture see *Orchids.*

pallidus Lindl. [*Aerides racemifera* Wallich ex Hook.]. St. stout, to 6 in. high, leafy at base; lvs. leathery, flat, to 1 ft. long; infl. ascending, to 18 in. long, much-branched, many-fld.; fls. to ½ in. across, sepals and petals elliptic, dirty greenish-white with faint purple central streak, lip longer than sepals, with a blunt, cylindrical spur basally, midlobe fleshy, ovate, with an incurved apical beak and with a fleshy 2-lobed callus protruding from under column. Vietnam.

teretifolius Lindl. St. 1 ft. high or more, jointed, with many fibrous aerial roots; lvs. cylindrical, to 4 in. long; infl. horizontal, directed to other side of st., 7–8-fld.; fls. to ¾ in. across, dull green with red lines, sepals and petals elliptic, lip pendent, longer than sepals, ovate, slipper-shaped, white with 2 incurved lobes at base edged with red. China.

Williamsonii Rchb.f. Lvs. light green, cylindrical; infl. paniculate, longer than lvs., few-fld.; sepals and petals oblong to strap-shaped, amethyst-colored, lip 3-lobed, lateral lobes and midlobe triangular, midlobe with median grooved line. Assam.

SARCOBATUS Nees. GREASEWOOD. *Chenopodiaceae.* One sp., a monoecious or dioecious, spiny, much-branched shrub of w. N. Amer.; lvs. simple; fls. without bracts, male fls. in catkinlike terminal spikes, perianth none, stamens 2–3, covered by a peltate, scarious scale, female fls. 1 or 2 in lf. axils, with calyx united to ovary and enlarging and forming a broad horizontal wing around middle of fr., ovary 1-celled, stigmas 2.

vermiculatus (Hook.) Torr. To 10 ft., brs. whitish, some branchlets leafless and spinelike; lvs. linear, sessile, fleshy, to 1¾ in. long, obtuse or subacute; male spikes to 1¼ in. long; wings of fr. to ½ in. across. Alkaline areas, N. Dak. to Tex., w. to Alta., e. Wash., Calif. The wood is yellow, very hard, and used for fuel.

SARCOCAULON (DC.) Sweet. *Geraniaceae.* A few spp. of much-branched, fleshy, spiny, suffrutescent shrubs, native to S. and cent. Afr., distinguished technically from other genera of the family in having fls. with 15 united stamens; spines represent persistent, hardened lf. petioles which may bear lf. blades when very young, but normal lvs. occur also, in axils of the thorns.

Burmannii: *S. spinosum.*

rigidum Schinz. To 20 in., sts. irregularly slightly constricted, to 1¼ in. in diam.; spines about 1¼ in. long, lvs. obcordate, to ⅝ in.

long, mucronate, entire, glabrous; fls. rose-pink, to 2 in. across, solitary. Cent. Afr.

spinosum (Burm.f.) O. Kuntze [*S. Burmannii* (DC.) Sweet]. To 20 in., sts. cylindrical, to 1¼ in. in diam.; lvs. obovate-cuneate, to ¾ in. long, incised-crenate, fleshy, tomentose; fls. white with rose-pink center, to 2 in. across, solitary. S. Afr.

SARCOCEPHALUS: *NAUCLEA*. **S. esculenta:** *N. latifolia*.

SARCOCHILUS R. Br. *Orchidaceae.* About 20 spp. of epiphytes, native to trop. Asia, Malay Arch., and Australia; sts. short or absent; lvs. oblong or absent; infl. a pendent raceme; sepals and petals separate, spreading, lateral sepals united to foot of column, lip jointed or united to column foot, without a spur, 3-lobed, lateral lobes large, erect, midlobe minute, toothlike, disc with hairy ridges and calluses. For structure of fl. see *Orchidaceae.*

For culture see *Orchids.*

Ceciliae F. J. Muell. [*Thrixspermum Ceciliae* (F. J. Muell.) Rchb.f.]. St. to 4 in. high, leafy; lvs. linear, to 3 in. long; racemes erect, slender, few-fld.; fls. campanulate, bright pink, sepals and petals similar, convergent, to ¼ in. long, lip 3-lobed, lateral lobes sickle-shaped, midlobe fleshy, pubescent, column with a long foot. Autumn–early winter. Australia.

Hartmannii F. J. Muell. [*Thrixspermum Hartmannii* (F. J. Muell.) Rchb.f.]. Robust, st. erect, leafy; lvs. fleshy, deeply channelled; racemes on long peduncles, densely many-fld.; fls. white with deep maroon spots in center, sepals and petals convergent, lip very small, conical, red-striated inside, column short and stout. Australia.

lilacinus: *Thrixspermum lilacinum.*

Mannii Hook.f. [*Camarotis Mannii* (Hook.f.) King. & Pantl.]. St. pendent, to 1 ft. long, leafy, sometimes branched; lvs. leathery, linear, to 4 in. long, bifid at apex; racemes rigid, shorter than lvs.; fls. ¼ in. across, pale pink, segms. spotted with crimson at base, sepals and petals obovate, reflexed, petals curved, lip an elongated sac at right angle to ovary, lateral lobes truncate, midlobe triangular, with callus or scale projecting into cavity of spur. Early summer. Sikkim.

SARCOCOCCA Lindl. SWEET BOX. *Buxaceae.* About 14 spp. of monoecious, evergreen shrubs, native to w. China, the Himalayas, and se. Asia; distinguished from *Buxus* in having lvs. alt., fls. in axillary clusters with imbricate bracts, the male fls. borne above the female fls., and fr. drupaceous.

Autumn- and winter-flowering shrubs with attractive foliage and black or red fruits ripening in autumn; hardy north in sheltered places, but most useful on the Pacific Coast and in southern states. Zone 8. Propagated by cuttings and seeds.

confusa Sealy. Dense, much-branched, to 6 ft., branchlets finely hairy when young; lvs. elliptic-lanceolate to elliptic, to 2½ in. long, 1 in. wide, acute or acuminate, thin-leathery, dark green above; male fls. without bracts, sepals 4, to ⅛ in. long, shorter than stamens, anthers cream-colored, female fls. subtended by 4–6 bracts, stigmas 2–3; fr. ellipsoid, to ⅜ in. long, black. Known only from cult.

Hookerana Baill. Rhizomatous, erect shrubs, to 6 ft., branchlets finely hairy when young; lvs. lanceolate, narrow-elliptic to elliptic, 1½–4 in. long, acute to long-attenuate, thin-leathery; fls. small, in short racemes, anthers cream-colored or bright pink, stigmas 2–3; fr. globose, about ⅜ in. long, black or purplish-black. Se. Tibet to e. Himalayas. Var. **digyna** Franch. Anthers cream-colored, stigmas 2; fr. purplish-black. One form has purplish sts., petioles, and midribs. China. Var. **humilis** Rehd. & E. H. Wils. [*S. humilis* (Rehd. & E. H. Wils.) Stapf]. Rarely over 2 ft.; lvs. broader, anthers bright pink, stigmas 2. China.

humilis: *S. Hookerana* var.

ruscifolia Stapf. FRAGRANT S., SWEET BOX. Similar to *S. confusa,* but differing in having lvs. mostly ovate, male fls. bracted, female fls. subtended by 6–12 bracts, stigmas 3, and fr. bright red or scarlet. S. China.

saligna (D. Don) Müll. Arg. WILLOW-LEAF S. Rhizomatous, distinguished from all other cult. spp. by its completely glabrous branchlets; lvs. lanceolate, to 6 in. long, 1 in. wide, acuminate to caudate; fr. dark purple. W. Himalayas.

SARCOPODIUM: *EPIGENIUM.*

SARCOSTEMMA R. Br. *Asclepiadaceae.* About 10 spp. of more or less leafless, trailing or twining, succulent shrubs with jointed brs., native to Old World tropics and subtropics; fls. small, in sessile, terminal or lateral umbels, 5-merous, corolla rotate or rotate-campanulate, corona of 2 whorls, the outer annular or cup-shaped, the inner of 5 erect, fleshy, compressed or keeled lobes; fr. a follicle.

For culture see *Succulents.*

andongense Hiern. Similar to *S. viminale,* but having corolla about ⅝ in. across, and seeds glabrous. Angola.

viminale (L.) R. Br. Sts. slender, trailing or twining, sometimes erect, appearing dichotomously branched, becoming woody with age; lvs. minute, scalelike; umbels lateral and terminal, many-fld., corolla greenish or sulphur-colored, to ½ in. across; seeds puberulous. Ethiopia to S. Afr. May be offered as *Euphorbia pendula.*

SARITAEA Dug. *Bignoniaceae.* Two spp. of climbing shrubs or vines, native to S. Amer.; lvs. opp., with 2 lfts.; fls. showy, rose to rose-purple, in a few-fld., terminal or axillary, cymose panicle, calyx cupular-campanulate, membranous, entire, corolla tubular-funnelform, stamens 4, included; fr. a linear, leathery caps.

magnifica (T. Sprague ex Steenis) Dug. [*Arrabidaea magnifica* T. Sprague ex Steenis; *Bignonia magnifica* Hort.]. Vine, to 10 ft.; lvs. opp., short-petioled, leathery, lfts. 2, obovate or obovate-oblong, to 4¾ in. long, glabrous; corolla rose-pink to pale purple, funnelform, to 3 in. long; caps. about 13 in. long, ⅝ in. wide. Colombia.

SARMIENTA Ruiz & Pav. *Gesneriaceae.* One sp., a per. vine in s. Chile, with slender, woody sts.; lvs. opp.; fls. solitary in lf. axils, on peduncles with 2 bracts at apex, sepals 5, spreading, recurved at apex, the upper 2 shortly united basally, corolla tubular, strongly narrowed above base, then urceolate-inflated and narrowed to throat, limb 5-lobed, lobes short, rounded, stamens 2, borne on corolla tube, filaments short, disc ringlike, poorly developed, ovary superior, 2-celled at base; fr. a berry.

For cultivation see *Gesneriaceae.*

repens: *S. scandens.*

scandens (Brandis) Pers. [*S. repens* Ruiz & Pav.]. Lvs. very short-petioled, blades elliptic to obovate, briefly to deeply 3–5-toothed at tip, minutely glandular on both surfaces, to 1 in. long, ½ in. wide; peduncle to 1¼ in. long, pedicel to ³⁄₁₆ in. long, deflexed; corolla coral-pink with deeper rose limb, ¾ in. long; fr. ⅜ in. long.

SAROTHRA: *HYPERICUM.*

SARRACENIA L. PITCHER PLANT. *Sarraceniaceae.* Eight spp. of rhizomatous, carnivorous per. herbs of e. N. Amer.; lvs. clustered in rosettes, erect, tubular or trumpet-shaped, with a keel or wing on 1 side and terminated by a lid; fls. nodding, solitary on erect, naked scapes, regular, bisexual, sepals and petals 5, stamens many, style expanded at the apex into an umbrellalike cap, ovary superior, 5-celled; fr. a caps.

Sometimes grown as curiosities, pitcher plants are native to moist or swampy places, mostly on the southeastern and Gulf coastal plain, and should be grown in a humid atmosphere in pots of fine-sandy, acid muck or live sphagnum standing in about 1 in. of water. They withstand temperatures to nearly freezing (below freezing in native places when dormant), except *S. purpurea* which is hardy through Zone 3. Propagated by seeds. Many natural hybrids are known, and many artificial hybrids also have been produced.

alata (A. Wood) A. Wood [*S. Sledgei* Macfarl.]. YELLOW-TRUMPETS. Lvs. erect, trumpet-shaped, to 2½ ft. long, yellow-green, reddish in the upper part and on the nearly erect lid; fls. pale cream-yellow, to 2½ in. across. Ala. to Tex.

×**Catesbaei** Elliot: *S. flava* × *S. purpurea.* Intermediate between parents; lvs. erect, to 2½ ft. long, green to dark purple, lid nearly erect, maroon-veined; fls. yellow and purple. Sporadic, Va. to Fla. This name has been applied mistakenly to several spp. and forms of the genus.

Drummondii: *S. leucophylla.*

flava L. YELLOW P.P., TRUMPETS, TRUMPETLEAF, UMBRELLA-TRUMPETS, HUNTSMAN'S-HORN, WATCHES. Lvs. erect, trumpet-shaped, to 4 ft. long, yellowish-green with crimson throat or sometimes entirely crimson, the lid erect with reflexed margins; fls. yellow, to 4 in. across. Va. to Fla. and Ala.

Jonesii: *S. rubra.*

leucophylla Raf. [*S. Drummondii* Croom]. Lvs. erect, trumpet-shaped, to 4 ft. long, green, the upper part and lid nearly erect, wavy-margined, white, veined with red-purple; fls. red-purple, to 4 in. across. Ga. to Fla. and Miss.

minor Walt. HOODED P.P., RAINHAT-TRUMPET. Lvs. erect, to 2 ft. long, expanded upward, the upper part and the overarching lid with purple veins and translucent-white blotches; fls. clear-yellow, to 2½ in. across. N.C. to Fla.

×**Mooreana** Hort. Veitch.: *S. flava* × *S. leucophylla*. Lvs. erect, trumpet-shaped, to 2 ft. long, green, lid about 3 in. across, suborbicular, wavy-margined, with crimson veins; fls. about 4 in. across, fragrant, sepals greenish, tinted rose outside, petals rose-pink outside, paler inside.

oreophila (Kearney) Wherry. Lvs. erect, green, trumpet-shaped, 1–2½ ft. long, lid more or less erect; scape about as long as lvs.; sepals green, to 2 in. long, petals yellowish-green, slightly exceeding sepals. Ne. Ala. to w.-cent. Ga.

psittacina Michx. Lvs. evergreen, decumbent, about 8 in. long, narrowly tubular and slightly sigmoid-curved, green variegated with red and having opaque pale blotches in upper part, opening laterally; fls. red-purple, to 2 in. across. Ga. and Fla. to La.

purpurea L. [*S. purpurea* forma *heterophylla* (Eat.) Fern.; *S. purpurea* subspp. *gibbosa* (Raf.) Wherry and *venosa* (Raf.) Wherry]. COMMON P.P., SWEET P.P., SOUTHERN P.P., SIDE-SADDLE FLOWER, HUNTSMAN'S-CUP, INDIAN-CUP. Lvs. evergreen, decumbent, to 12 in. long, slender below, swollen above, green, variegated or suffused with red-purple, rarely only green, lid erect; scape shorter than to about as long as lvs.; fls. purple or greenish-purple, to 2½ in. across. A variable sp. of acid bogs, widely distributed in e. N. Amer.

rubra Walt. [*S. Jonesii* Wherry]. SWEET P.P. Lvs. erect, many, tubular, 1–4 in. long, dull green, reticulated with dark purple on inside of opening and small overarching lid; scape usually longer than lvs.; fls. maroon, to 1½ in. across. N.C. to Fla. and Miss.

Sledgei: *S. alata.*

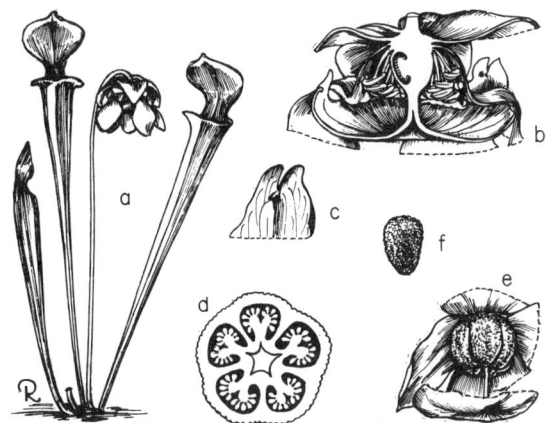

SARRACENIACEAE. *Sarracenia flava:* **a,** plant, × ⅛; **b,** flower, vertical section, × ½; **c,** a stigma, × 1; **d,** ovary, cross section, × 2; **e,** fruit, × ½; **f,** seed, × 3.

SARRACENIACEAE Dumort. PITCHER PLANT FAMILY. Dicot.; 3 genera with about 15 spp. of carnivorous, rhizomatous, per. herbs of N. and S. Amer.; lvs. clustered, erect, tubular or trumpet-shaped, bearing a ridge on the inner side and terminated by an expanded hood or lid; fls. usually solitary, on erect, naked, terminal scapes; fls. regular, bisexual, sepals 4–5, subtended by 3 appressed bracts, petals 5 or 0, early deciduous, stamens many, style 3–5-lobed, ovary superior, 3–5-celled; fr. a caps. The N. Amer. genera *Darlingtonia* and *Sarracenia* are sometimes cult. as fancier's plants or for botanical demonstrations.

SASA Mak. & Shib. BAMBOO. *Gramineae*. More than 150 spp. of rhizomatous woody grasses in temp. e. Asia, especially Japan, plants dwarf or seldom very tall, sts. cylindrical, fistulose, not spotted, with 1 or rarely 2 brs. at each node; st. sheaths persistent, appendaged; lf. blades crowded at the ends of branchlets, sheaths with or without rigid, scabrid bristles; infl. a lax panicle; spikelets 2–9-fld., glumes 2, small, lemma acuminate, palea shorter, keeled, bifid, stamens 6. For terminology see *Gramineae*.

Propagated by division. See *Bamboos*.

bicolor G. Koidz. Sts. to 2 ft. high and ⅝ in. in diam., simple to branched, nodes swollen, pilose, internodes to 3 in. long; st. sheath gray-striate; lf. blades at the end of brs., linear-lanceolate, to 7 in. long and 1⅛ in. wide, abruptly acuminate, lower blades more ovate and smaller, margin with minute bristles, white-and-yellow-zoned, petiole to 1 in. long, ligule very short, truncate. Japan. Zone 8.

chrysantha (Mitf.) E. Camus. Sts. to 7 ft. high, hollow, nodes to 4½ in. apart, brs. several at each node; st. sheaths ciliate on one margin; lf. blades to 4½ in. long and ¾ in. wide, 8–12-nerved, rather abruptly long-pointed, rounded at base, bright green above or often more or less variegated with yellow, glabrous. Japan. Zone 8.

disticha: *Arundinaria disticha.*

Fortunei: a listed name of no botanical standing for *Arundinaria variegata.*

humilis: *Arundinaria humilis.*

japonica: *Pseudosasa japonica.*

Kumasasa: a listed name of no botanical standing; the colloquial name "Kumazasa" is applied by the Japanese to *Sasa Veitchii;* see also *Shibataea Kumasaca.*

palmata E. Camus [*Bambusa palmata* Burb.]. Sts. to 8 ft. high, ⁵⁄₁₆ in. in diam., waxy, hollow, the nodes to 6 in. apart; st. sheaths terminated by a deciduous, lanceolate, strongly tessellated, ciliate tongue; lf. blades to 13 in. long, 4½ in. wide, bright green above, glaucous beneath, many-nerved, broadly wedge-shaped at the base, long-pointed, minutely tessellate. Japan, Sakhalin. Cult. in Eur. and elsewhere. Zone 7. Tends to spread rapidly. The name *Sasa senanensis* (Franch. & Sav.) Rehd. has been applied erroneously to this sp. in cult.

pumila: *Arundinaria pumila.*

pygmaea: a listed name of no botanical standing for *Arundinaria pygmaea.*

senanensis: see *S. palmata.*

tessellata (Munro) Mak. & Shib. Sts. to 5 ft., slightly fistulose, soon arching, nodes to 3¼ in. apart; st. sheaths persistent, ciliate, each also clasping parts of the 2–3 sheaths above it; lf. blades to 2 ft. long and 4 in. wide, 30–36-nerved, tessellate, long-pointed, abruptly contracted at the base, sharply serrate, light green above, glaucous beneath and minutely pubescent, hairy on one side of the yellow midrib toward the base. Japan. Zone 8.

Veitchii (Carrière) Rehd. [*Bambusa Veitchii* Carrière]. KUMA BAMBOO GRASS. Sts. to 2 or rarely 3 ft. high in sun, taller in partial shade, green, narrow-fistulose, nodes to 4½ in. apart; st. sheaths persistent, pubescent at first; lf. sheaths with tufts of bristles at the apex, blades to 8 in. long and 2⅜ in. wide, 12–18-nerved, rather abruptly long-pointed, abruptly contracted at the base, dark green above, glaucous and minutely pubescent beneath. Japan, where popular in gardens. Cult. in Eur. Zone 8. Spreads rapidly, so useful as ground cover; in the autumn the lf. margins turn a straw color and provide interest for the winter garden.

SASSAFRAS Trew. *Lauraceae*. Three spp. of deciduous trees, 1 in e. N. Amer., 2 in e. Asia; all parts spicy-aromatic; lvs. alt., entire or lobed; fls. in clustered involucrate racemes, unisexual or bisexual, greenish-yellow, naked, appearing with the lvs.; fr. a drupe, ovoid, having a fleshy pedicel.

Of easy culture; propagated by seeds, suckers, and root-cuttings.

albidum (Nutt.) Nees [*S. officinale* Nees & Eberm.; *S. variifolium* (Salisb.) O. Kuntze]. SASSAFRAS. To 60 ft. or more; lvs. ovate, to 5 in. long, entire, sometimes 1–3-lobed at apex, pale beneath; infl. to 2 in. long; fr. dark blue, with red stalks. Me. to Fla. and Tex. Foliage colors brilliant in autumn. The bark yields oil of sassafras, an important flavoring.

officinale: *S. albidum.*

Tzumu (Hemsl.) Hemsl. Differs from *S. albidum* in having lvs. longer, to 8 in., more pointed; and racemes to 3 in. long. Cent. China.

variifolium: *S. albidum.*

SATAKENTIA H. E. Moore. *Palmae*. One sp., a monoecious, solitary palm, native to Ryukyu Is.; trunk stout, enlarged basally; lvs. pinnate, sheaths tubular, forming a crownshaft, blades evenly pinnate, pinnae 1-ribbed, acute; infl. a panicle below lvs., with 2 (rarely 3) deciduous, papery, enclosing bracts, twice-branched basally, peduncle shorter than rachis, rachillae with fls. in triads (2 male and 1 female) in lower ¼–⅓ and above these with paired male fls.; male fls. about as large as female, sepals 3, imbricate, petals 3, valvate, stamens 6, filaments inflexed at apex in bud, pistillode as long as stamens, cylindrical, nearly capitate at apex, female fls. ovoid, sepals 3, imbricate, petals 3, imbricate with short valvate apices, staminodes 3, very small, pistil 1-celled, stigmas 3; fr. ovoid-ellipsoid with apical stigmatic residue, endocarp operculate, seed ellipsoid with homogeneous endosperm.

For culture see *Palms.*

liukiuensis (Hatus.) H. E. Moore. To 60 ft., trunk 1 ft. in diam.; lvs. to 10 ft. long or more, petiole short, pinnae more than 90 on each side, to 28 in. long, 1⅝ in. wide; infls. several, stiffly branched, about 3 ft. long; male fls. cream-colored, ³⁄₁₆ in. long; fr. black, ½ in. long, ¼ in. in diam. Iriomote and Ishigaki Is.

SATUREJA L. SAVORY, CALAMINT. *Labiatae.* About 30 spp. of herbs of temp. and warm regions; sts. mostly square in cross section; lvs. opp.; fls. in verticillasters or loose axillary cymes, calyx tubular to campanulate, 10–13-nerved, 5-toothed, not 2-lipped, corolla tube straight, inflated at throat, limb 2-lipped, upper lip erect, lower lip spreading, 3-lobed, stamens 4, in 2 pairs; fr. of 4 glabrous nutlets.

Several species are cultivated as condiments. Savories are propagated by seeds sown where they are to grow, and perennials also by division and cuttings of the new growth.

Acinos: *Acinos thymoides.*

alpina: *Acinos alpinus.*

Calamintha: *Calamintha Nepeta.*

chinensis: *Clinopodium chinense.*

Douglasii (Benth.) Briq. [*Micromeria Chamissonis* (Benth.) Greene; *M. Douglasii* (Benth.) Benth.]. YERBA BUENA. Per., sts. trailing, and rooting, to 2 ft. long; lvs. ovate, to 1¼ in. long, 1 in. wide, obtuse, crenate or crenate-serrate, glabrous to glabrescent, petioled; fls. solitary in the axils on large pedicels, calyx to ³⁄₁₆ in. long, corolla to ⅜ in. long, white or purplish. Spring, autumn. W. U.S.

georgiana (R. M. Harper) Ahles [*Calamintha georgiana* (R. M. Harper) Shinn.; *Clinopodium carolinianum* Hort., not (Michx.) A. Heller; *Clinopodium georgiananum* R. M. Harper]. Woody shrub, to 2 ft., slightly pubescent; lvs. elliptic, to 1 in. long, ½ in. long, obtuse, weakly crenate, glabrous above, short-petioled; infl. of 3–9-fld. verticillasters; calyx to ¼ in. long, corolla about twice as long as calyx, pink to lavender. Summer. N.C. to Fla. and Miss.

glabella (Michx.) Briq. [*S. glabra* Hort., not Thell.; *Calamintha glabella* (Michx.) Benth.]. Per., to 12 in., glabrous except at nodes; lvs. oblanceolate, mostly ¾–1½ in. long, to ¾ in. wide, obtuse, with 2–4 teeth on each side; fls. 2–8 at node, calyx to ½ in. long, corolla 2–2½ times as long as calyx, pale purple. Summer. Ky. to Ark.

glabra: see *S. glabella.*

graeca: *Micromeria graeca.*

grandiflora: *Calamintha grandiflora.*

hortensis L. SUMMER S. Ann., 12–18 in., lightly pubescent; lvs. linear to oblanceolate, to ⅞ in. long, acute, entire, more or less revolute; fls. in few-fld. verticillasters spaced apart, calyx to ⅜ in. long, corolla to ⁵⁄₁₆ in. long, pale lavender or white. Summer. Medit. region.

illyrica: *S. montana.*

intricata: *S. montana.*

Juliana: *Micromeria Juliana.*

Kitaibelii: *S. montana.*

montana L. [*S. illyrica* Host; *S. intricata* J. Lange; *S. Kitaibelii* Wierzb. ex Heuff.; *S. pygmaea* Sieber ex Vis.; *S. subspicata* Bartl. ex Vis.]. WINTER S. Per., 6–12 in., glabrous or glabrescent; lvs. linear or linear-lanceolate, to 1 in. long, ³⁄₁₆ in. wide, acute, entire; fls. in few-fld. verticillasters, calyx ¹⁄₁₆–³⁄₁₆ in. long, corolla more than twice as long as calyx, white or pink. Summer. Medit. region.

Nepeta: *Calamintha Nepeta.*

pygmaea: *S. montana.*

rupestris: *Micromeria thymifolia.*

subspicata: *S. montana.*

thymifolia: *Micromeria thymifolia.*

vulgaris: *Clinopodium vulgare.*

SAUROMATUM Schott. *Araceae.* Four spp. of tuberous stemless per. herbs, native to Old World; lvs. solitary, pedate, petioles long; infl. appearing before the lvs., peduncle short, spathe elongate, tubular basally, with margins united, expanded above into an oblong blade, spadix terminated by a long, slender, sterile appendage emitting a disagreeable odor, with zones of female and male fls. below, separated by zone of sterile, rudimentary fls.

For culture see *Amorphophallus.*

guttatum (Wallich) Schott [*Arum cornutum* Hort.]. VOODOO LILY, RED CALLA, MONARCH-OF-THE-EAST. Lvs. with 7–15 lanceolate to oblong segms., median one to 18 in. long and 5 in. wide, lateral ones progressively smaller, petiole stout, to 2 ft. long; spathe to 30 in. long and 4 in. wide, greenish outside, spotted red-purple and yellow inside, spadix with sterile appendage tail-like, to 14 in. long, grayish-purple. Nw. India. Var. **venosum** (Ait.) Engl. [*S. venosum* (Ait.) Kunth]. Lf. segms. 7–11, petioles with oblong, dark purple spots.

nubicum Schott. Differs from *S. guttatum* in having lf. segms. wider, to 1 ft. long and 5 in. wide, spathe with narrower blade and fewer sterile rudimentary fls. Ethiopia to Cameroon, s. to Nyasaland and Angola.

venosum: *S. guttatum* var.

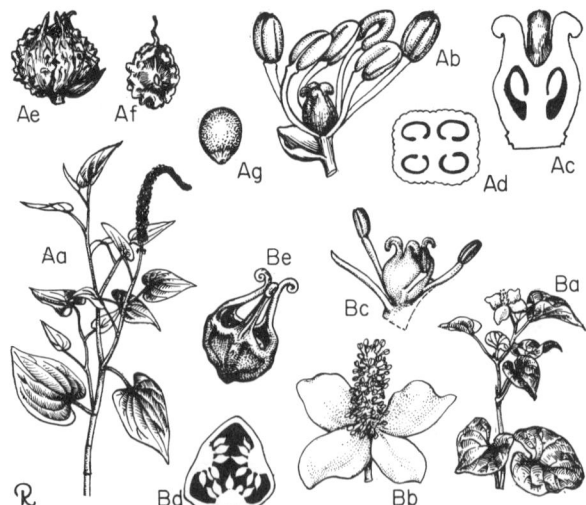

SAURURACEAE. **A,** *Saururus cernuus:* **Aa,** flowering stem, × ⅛; **Ab,** flower, × 4; **Ac,** pistil, vertical section, × 12; **Ad,** ovary, cross section, × 12; **Ae,** fruit, × 4; **Af,** single mature carpel, × 4; **Ag,** seed, × 6. **B,** *Houttuynia cordata:* **Ba,** flowering stem, × ¼; **Bb,** spike and subtending bracts, × 1; **Bc,** flower, × 5; **Bd,** ovary, cross section, × 10; **Be,** fruit, × 6.

SAURURACEAE E. H. Mey. LIZARD'S-TAIL FAMILY. Dicot.; 4 genera of per. herbs, native to N. Amer. and Asia; lvs. alt., entire, stipules united to petioles; fls. small, in racemes or spikes sometimes subtended by petal-like bracts, bisexual, perianth none, stamens 3–8, carpels 3–4, separate or united basally into a 3–4-celled or 1-celled compound pistil; fr. dry, dehiscing at top, or indehiscent when carpels separate. *Anemopsis, Houttuynia,* and *Saururus* are cult.

SAURURUS L. LIZARD'S-TAIL. *Saururaceae.* Two spp., per. herbs of swampy locations of temp. e. N. Amer. and e. Asia; lvs. alt., entire, petioles sheathing; fls. in lateral, slender racemes, perianth none, stamens 6–8, carpels 3–4, united only at base, styles separate; fr. depressed-globose, dry, indehiscent, carpels 1-seeded.

Propagated by division or by seeds.

cernuus L. [*S. lucidus* J. Donn]. WATER-DRAGON, SWAMP LILY. To 3–5 ft., from long, aromatic, creeping rhizome; lvs. broadly to narrowly ovate, to 6 in. long, more or less palmately veined; racemes spikelike, to 12 in. long, nodding at apex; fls. white, fragrant; fr. rugose-warty. Swamps, e. N. Amer.

lucidus: *S. cernuus.*

SAUSSUREA DC. *Compositae* (Carduus Tribe). About 130 spp. of nonspiny herbs of diverse aspect, in Eur., Asia, and N. Amer., 1 sp. in Australia; lvs. alt., entire, toothed, or pinnate; fl. heads small to large, solitary to corymbose, involucre cylindrical to globose, inner involucral bracts often purplish, receptacle usually scaly; fls. all tubular, purple to bluish; pappus of 1–2 rows of bristles, the inner plumose, or pappus rarely absent. Similar to *Centaurea,* but involucral bracts without scarious or spiny appendages; and to *Serratula,* but anthers long-tailed and pappus plumose.

albescens (DC.) Hook.f. & T. Thoms. ex C. B. Clarke. Coarse per., sts. 3–10 ft., erect, leafy; lvs. entire to sinuate-lobed, white-tomentose beneath, the lowermost oblong, to 12 in. long, petioled, the st. lvs. smaller, ovate to linear, sessile; heads to ⅝ in. long, cylindrical, many in open corymbs; fls. purple. Himalayas.

alpina (L.) DC. Per., rhizomatous, 2–18 in.; lvs. mostly toothed, glabrate above, white-cottony beneath, basal lvs. ovate to lanceolate, to 7 in. long, petioled, st. lvs. shorter and narrower, sessile; heads to ¾ in. long, ovoid-cylindrical, sessile, few in a dense corymb; fls. purple. Eur., Siberia, N. Amer.

angustifolia (L.) DC. Differs from *S. alpina* in having lvs. linear, entire, green and nearly glabrous on both sides; perhaps not specifically distinct. Siberia.

discolor (Willd.) DC. Per., sts. 2–14 in., leafy mostly in lower half; lvs. glabrous above, white-tomentose beneath, basal lvs. narrow-triangular, often cordate, toothed, petioled, uppermost lvs. lanceolate, entire, sessile; heads ¾ in. long, ovoid-cylindrical, short-peduncled, 3–8 in a dense corymb; fls. pale violet to rose-red. Mts., cent. Eur., the Urals, and Himalayas.

gossipiphora D. Don. Per., st. solitary, 6–12 in., hollow, enlarged above, woolly; lvs. oblong, sinuate-toothed, leathery, the lower glabrous above, tomentose beneath, the upper lvs., infl. bracts, and infl. largely hidden in a broad mass of whitish wool; heads to 1 in. long, cylindrical, sessile, many in a capitate corymb, each at the base of a tubular opening in the woolly mass. Alpine Himalayas. A very curious plant, very difficult to cult. at lower elevations.

pygmaea (Jacq.) K.Spreng. Per., st. solitary, 1½–8 in., densely hirsute, leafy especially toward base; lvs. sessile, linear to linear-lanceolate, to 3 in. long, entire or toothed, revolute, hirsute; head solitary, large, to 1½ in. long, 1¼ in. across; fls. blue-violet. Mts., cent. Eur.

stella Maxim. Bien., stemless, glabrous; lvs. many in a rosette, linear, 3–8 in. long, attenuate from an expanded, ovate base to a fine point, entire, bases of inner lvs. purple; heads ¾–1⅛ in. long, to ⅜ in. across, cylindrical, few to 30, sessile; fls. purple, anthers exserted, blue. Alpine meadows, China, Tibet, Sikkim Himalayas.

triptera Maxim. Per., rhizomatous, sts. to 2 ft., winged, puberulent; lvs. green and pubescent on both sides, basal lvs. ovate to ovate-oblong, to 5 in. long, cordate or truncate, toothed or lobed, petioled, upper st. lvs. smaller, sessile, decurrent; heads ⅜ in. long, cylindrical, short-peduncled, many, corymbose; fls. purplish. Mts., Japan. Var. **minor** (Takeda) Kitam. Sts. to 8 in., prominently winged; heads only 3–5. Alpine.

wernerioides Schultz-Bip. ex Hook.f. Dwarf, almost stemless per.; lvs. in a rosette, lanceolate, to ½ in. long, leathery, glabrous above, tomentose beneath, margins toothed and revolute; heads to ½ in. across, solitary, sessile among lvs. Sikkim Himalayas.

SAVIA Willd. *Euphorbiaceae*. Not in cult. **S. phyllanthoides:** *Andrachne phyllanthoides.*

SAXEGOTHAEA Lindl. *Podocarpaceae*. One sp., a monoecious, coniferous, evergreen tree, native to Chile; lvs. spirally arranged or 2-ranked, linear, curved; male cones short-stalked, cylindrical, spikelike, ¼ in. long, clustered near ends of twigs, female cones solitary, terminal, globose, about ½ in. long, consisting of broad, flattened, spine-tipped scales, each usually bearing 2 seeds and eventually becoming fleshy. Differing from other genera of Podocarpaceae in the characters of the female cone.

Cultivated in Fla. and Calif. Zone 8. Propagated by cuttings with bottom heat. For culture see *Conifers*.

conspicua Lindl. PRINCE ALBERT YEW. Erect, yewlike tree or shrub, to 40 ft., bark on mature trees peeling; lvs. linear-oblong, ½–1⅛ in. long, spinescent-acute, dark green above, with 2 white bands beneath. N. Chile.

SAXIFRAGA L. [*Micranthes* Small]. SAXIFRAGE, ROCKFOIL. *Saxifragaceae*. About 300 spp. of varied per. herbs, a few ann. or bien., native to mts. and rocky places in temp., subarctic, and alpine regions of Eur., Asia, N. Afr., and N. and S. Amer.; lvs. usually basal and clustered, st. lvs. commonly smaller and alt.; fls. white, pink, purple, or yellow, in racemose, paniculate, or cymose clusters, appearing commonly in late spring and early summer, 5-merous, calyx either free or adhering to base of ovary, 5-cleft or -parted, petals entire, commonly deciduous, carpels 2, fused except for beaks, or sometimes almost quite separate, ovary 2-celled, superior to inferior. Assigned to several genera by some authors.

Many adapted to the rock garden, a few to the border or to the wild or bog garden, while one *(S. stolonifera)* is often grown as a window and basket plant.

The species of *Saxifraga* are grouped into sections to show natural relationships and to facilitate identification. The species of a given section possess in common the characteristics of that section. These characteristics are not repeated in the brief descriptions given; instead, a 3-letter symbol in parentheses is used to indicate the section to which each species belongs: (BOR) *Boraphila;* (CYM) *Cymbalaria;* (DAC) *Dactyloides;* (DIP) *Diptera;* (EUA) *Euaizoonia;* (HIR) *Hirculus;* (KAB) *Kabschia* (including *Engleria*, which is sometimes made a segregate from *Kabschia*); (MIS) *Miscopetalum;* (POR) *Porphyrion;* (ROB) *Robertsonia;* (SAX) *Saxifraga;* (TET) *Tetrameridium;* (TRA) *Trachyphyllum;* (TRI) *Tridactylites;* (XAN) *Xanthizoon.* The sections of the genus and their distinguishing characters follow:

Diptera (Borkh.) Rchb. (DIP). Per.; fls. irregular, petals markedly unequal; plants generally hairy, usually with runners.

Tetrameridium Engl. (TET). Per.; fls. regular, 4-merous, perhaps without petals; lvs. opp., with an apical pit.

All the other sections (following) have regular, 5-merous fls. with petals normally present:

Boraphila Engl. (BOR). Per., rhizomes usually subterranean, secondary shoots permanently attached; lvs. not pitted, not lime-secreting, usually toothed; petals white or purplish, rarely yellow, seeds oblong.

Hirculus (Haw.) Tausch (HIR). As in *Boraphila*, but lvs. usually entire, rarely dentate toward apex; petals usually yellow.

Robertsonia (Haw.) Engl. (ROB). Per., rhizomes usually above ground, secondary shoots permanently attached; lvs. not pitted, not lime-secreting, obovate or orbicular, usually toothed; petals white or purple-spotted.

Miscopetalum (Haw.) Sternb. (MIS). Per., rhizomes above ground, secondary shoots permanently attached; lvs. not pitted, not lime-secreting, reniform, toothed or lobed; petals white, sometimes spotted with purple or yellow.

Cymbalaria Griseb. (CYM). Ann. or bien.; lvs. not pitted, not lime-secreting, usually reniform, usually toothed; petals yellow or white.

Tridactylites (Haw.) Engl. (TRI). Ann. or bien.; lvs. not pitted, not lime-secreting, usually cuneate, toothed, or entire; petals usually white, rarely yellow.

Saxifraga [*Nephrophyllum* Gaudin] (SAX). Bien. or rarely per. or ann., secondary shoots usually bulbous, eventually separating from rhizomes; lvs. not pitted, not lime-secreting, reniform or ovate, toothed to parted; petals usually white, sometimes yellow or pink.

Dactyloides Tausch (DAC). Per., rhizomes above ground, secondary shoots not bulbous, remaining permanently attached to rhizomes; lvs. not lime-secreting, linear to usually 3-lobed and toothed; petals usually white, rarely purple.

Trachyphyllum Gaudin (TRA). As in *Dactyloides*, but lvs. lanceolate or cuneate, ciliate, apically aristate, or 3-toothed; petals white or yellowish, sometimes red-spotted.

Xanthizoon Griseb. (XAN). Per., rhizomes above ground, elongate; lvs. alt., with a single apical pit but not lime-secreting, linear to oblong, entire, ciliate or slightly toothed; petals yellow, orange, or purple, sometimes spotted.

Euaizoonia (Schott) Engl. (EUA). Per., rhizomes above ground, secondary shoots usually separating from rhizomes; lvs. alt., pitted along margins, lime-secreting, rigid, linear to obovate, entire or toothed; petals usually white, rarely rose or yellow, sometimes purple-spotted.

Kabschia Engl. (KAB). As in *Euaizoonia*, but secondary shoots remaining attached to rhizomes; petals white, yellow, rose, or purple.

Porphyrion Tausch (POR). Per.; lvs. usually opp., arranged in 4 vertical rows, orbicular to oblong-lanceolate, with 1–5 apical, usually lime-secreting pits, ciliate; petals rose or purple.

The section *Engleria*, encountered in trade publications, is a segregate from *Kabschia* and is not considered botanically distinct by the more recent monographers of the genus. Many horticultural and natural hybrids whose parents belong in different sections are in cultivation. These are sometimes difficult to identify, but as complete descriptions as are practical are given here.

Saxifrages are prized by fanciers, but are relatively little grown in N. Amer. They require the usual treatment for rock garden or border perennials. Propagated by seeds, by division, and in some species, by runners, also by the bulbils which some kinds produce.

adscendens L. TRI; lvs. in a basal rosette, sessile, to ⅜ in. long, 3–5-lobed, cuneate; fl. st. to 5 in. long; petals white, emarginate, to ⅜ in. long. Eur.

aemula: probably *Bergenia* × *media*.

aestivalis: *S. Nelsoniana*.

affinis: *S. rosacea*.

aizoides L. YELLOW MOUNTAIN S. XAN; loosely cespitose; lvs. linear-oblong, to 1 in. long, thick; fl. sts. leafy, to 6 in. or more, fls. in a terminal, somewhat leafy cyme, to ⅜ in. long, petals yellow or orange, often spotted with red. A polymorphic sp. Eur., Asia, arctic N. Amer. Cv. 'Atrorubens' is listed.

aizoon: *S. paniculata*.

Albertii Regel & Schmalh. KAB; densely cespitose; lvs. narrow-oblong to linear-lanceolate, concave above; fl. st. to 1 in., fls. in panicles, petals yellow. Turkestan.

Allionii: *S. moschata*.

altissima: *S. Hostii*.

×**Andrewsii** Harv.: *S.* × *Geum* × *S. paniculata*. To 6 in.; petals white, spotted with red.

androsacea L. DAC; lvs. nearly all basal, in loose rosettes, spatulate, to ¾ in. long; fl. sts. to 3 in. long, fls. 1–3, petals white, to ¼ in. long. Eur.

apennina: *S. cuneifolia*.

×**apiculata** Engl.: *S. juniperifolia* subsp. *sancta* × *S. marginata* var. *Rocheliana*. KAB; loosely tufted; basal lvs. linear-oblong, to ½ in. long, sharp-pointed, lower surface pitted, st. lvs. spatulate, to ¼ in. long; fl. sts. to 3½ in., fls. 5–9, terminal, petals yellow, ⁵⁄₁₆ in. long, spreading.

aquatica Lapeyr. DAC; loosely cespitose; leafy shoots ascending, to 2 ft.; lvs. orbicular, about 1 in. wide, 3-lobed; petals white, to ⅜ in. long. Pyrenees.

arachnoidea Sternb. SAX; decumbent, densely covered with viscid, webby hairs; lvs. to ¾ in. long, variable in shape, mostly rhombic, 3–7-lobed; fls. on long pedicels, in terminal cymes, petals yellowish, ⅛ in. long. Alps, cent. Eur.

×**arco-valleyi** Sünderm. *S. lilacina* × *S. marginata* var. *Rocheliana*. KAB; lvs. in rosettes to ⅜ in. across, silver-gray; fl. sts. to 1 in. high, petals bright red.

×**Arendsii** Engl. Hybrid of mixed parentage, probably including *S. exarata* Vill. and *S. rosacea*; to 4 in.; lvs. in dense tufts, dissected, light green; fls. to ¾ in. across, petals rose to blood-red. Cv. 'Splendens'. Fls. larger, deeper red.

aretioides Lapeyr. KAB; to 2 in., densely tufted; lvs. linear, to ¼ in. long, leathery, stiff, margins cartilaginous; fls. ½ in. across, petals golden-yellow. S. Eur.

arguta: *S. Nelsoniana*.

austromontana: *S. bronchialis* subsp.

balcana: a listed name of no botanical standing for *S. paniculata* cv.

baldensis: a listed name of no botanical standing for *S. paniculata* cv.

Beesiana: a listed name of no botanical standing; probably used for a sp. of *Bergenia*.

×**Bertolonii** Sünderm. Hybrid, the parentage including *S. porophylla*; to 3 in.; petals red.

×**Biasolettii** Sünderm. Hybrid, supposedly *S. Grisebachii* × *S. porophylla*; sts. red; lvs. narrow-spatulate, acute; petals reddish-purple.

biflora All. POR; lvs. broadly obovate to suborbicular, to ⅜ in. long, not lime-encrusted, often reddish beneath; fls. several in terminal corymbose cymes, petals reddish-purple or dull white, to ⅜ in. long. Alps, cent. Eur.

×**Boeckeleri** Sünderm.: *S. Ferdinandi-Coburgi* × *S. Stribrnyi*. KAB; tufted, lf. rosettes less than 1 in. across; basal lvs. linear-spatulate,

to ⅜ in. long, fleshy, white-pitted; fl. sts. to 3 in., petals yellow, tinged red.

×**Borisii** Kellerer: *S. Ferdinandi-Coburgi* × *S. marginata*. KAB; to 3 in.; petals yellow.

bronchialis L. subsp. **austromontana** (Wieg.) Piper [*S. austromontana* Wieg.]. TRA; to 8 in., tufted; lvs. stiff, linear, to ½ in. long, ciliate; petals yellowish-white, spotted with red. Asia, N. Amer. Subsp. **Funstonii** (Small) Hult. [*S. nitida* Ledeb.]. Petals clawed, with yellow spots. Alaska.

Brunoniana Wallich. HIR; loosely tufted, with many slender rhizomes producing new plants; basal lvs. linear-lanceolate, to ⅝ in. long, bristle-margined, st. lvs. scattered, smaller than basal lvs., sometimes with bulbils in the axils; fl. sts. branched, slender, to 4 in., fls. to ¾ in. across, petals yellow. Himalayas.

Bucklandii: a listed name of no botanical standing for *S. cuneifolia*.

Burserana L. KAB; to 4 in., tufted; lvs. stiff, linear-subulate, to ½ in. long, margins cartilaginous; fls. usually solitary, 1 in. across, petals white. Cv. 'Crenata'. Petals crenate. Cv. 'Major' [cvs. 'Grandiflora', 'Magna', 'Tridentina']. Fls. larger.

caesia L. KAB; to 3 in., densely tufted; lvs. linear-oblong, ³⁄₁₆ in. long; fls. 1–2 together, about ½ in. across, petals white. Mts., cent. Eur.

caespitosa L. DAC; to 6 in., tufted; lvs. 3-lobed, about ½ in. long; fls. ½ in. across or less, petals white. N. N. Amer., n. Eur., n. Asia. Similar to *S. rosacea*.

calabrica: a listed name of no botanical standing.

californica Greene. Probably not in cult.; material grown under this name is a cv. of *S. paniculata*.

callosa Sm. [*S. lantoscana* Boiss. & Reut.; *S. lingulata* Bellardi]. EUA; lf. rosettes dense, with central fl. st., basal and st. lvs. linear, to 5 in. long, reddish near base, with many lime-encrusted marginal pits; fls. many in much-branched panicles, petals to ⅜ in. long, spreading, white, often with reddish spots toward base. S. Eur. Cvs. are: 'Leichtlinii', petals rose-red; 'Rosea', perhaps not distinct from 'Leichtlinii', petals rose-red; 'Superba', fls. large, in arching, plumelike infls., petals creamy-white.

cartilaginea: *S. paniculata*.

caucasica Somm. & Levier. KAB; basal lvs. lanceolate, to 1¼ in. long; fls. in corymbs, to ⅜ in. across, petals yellow. Caucasus. Var. **Desoulavyi** (Oetting.) Engl. & Irmsch. [*S. Desoulavyi* Oetting.]. Lvs. smaller, strongly ciliate.

cebennensis Rouy & E. Camus. DAC; basal lvs. usually 3-lobed, forming mossy cushions, st. lvs. usually not lobed; fl. sts. slender, branched, to 2 in., petals white. S. France.

ceratophylla: *S. trifurcata*.

cernua L. [*S. simulata* Small]. SAX; to 9 in.; basal lvs. petioled, reniform, 5–7-lobed, st. lvs. with bright red bulbils in axils; fls. solitary, terminal, petals white. Arctic and subarctic, Eur. and N. Amer. Similar to *S. granulata*, but smaller.

chrysantha A. Gray. HIR; low, tufted, to 2 in., sts. creeping; lvs. basal, imbricated in a rosette, oblong, glabrous, fleshy; fls. large, usually 1–3 in terminal infl. on slender, glandular-pubescent peduncles, petals yellow. Mts., Colo. and New Mex.

×**Churchillii** Huter: *S. Hostii* × *S. paniculata*. EUA; rosettes large; lvs. stiff, with silvery marginal glands; fls. many, petals white.

×**Clarkei** Sünderm.: *S. media* × *S. Vandellii*. KAB; to 2½ in.; lvs. linear-oblong to linear-subulate, to 4 in. long, glandular-hairy; infl. usually 1–2-fld., fls. to ⅜ in. across, petals rose.

cochlearis Rchb. EUA; densely tufted; basal lvs. linear-spatulate, to 1½ in. long, apex suborbicular; fl. st. to 18 in., branched, petals white. Alps. Cvs. are: 'Major', fls. larger; 'Minor', lvs. silvery, in minute rosettes; and 'Longifolia'.

cordifolia: *Bergenia cordifolia*.

coriophylla: *S. marginata*.

cortusifolia Siebold & Zucc. DIP; to 1½ ft.; lvs. roundish, to 3 in. long, 5–11-lobed, fleshy; fls. to ¾ in. long, in loose panicles, petals white. E. Asia. Autumn. Var. **Fortunei** (Hook.f.) Maxim. [*S. Fortunei* Hook.f.]. Lvs. reniform, to 2 in. long and 4 in. wide, usually 9-lobed; fls. smaller, petals toothed. Japan.

corymbosa: see *S. luteoviridis*.

Cotyledon L. [*S. Cotyledon* var. *pyramidalis* (Lapeyr.) Ser.; *S. nepalensis* Hort.; *S. pyramidalis* Lapeyr.]. EUA; to 2 ft. or more; lvs. in rosettes, tongue-shaped, to 3 in. long, toothed; fls. to ¾ in. across, fragrant, petals white, veined with pink. Mts., Eur. Cv. 'Caterhamensis'. To 3 ft.; petals white, spotted with red. Cv. 'Icelandica'. To 4 ft., the largest form of the sp.; rosettes large, flat, lvs. bronzy, leathery.

crassifolia: *Bergenia crassifolia*.

crustata Vest [*S. crustata* var. *vochinensis* Hort.; *S. incrustata* Vest]. DAC; to 1 ft., densely tufted; lvs. linear, to 1½ in. long, encrusted with lime; fls. ⅜ in. across, petals white, sometimes marked with purple at base. E. Alps, s. to Yugoslavia.

cultrata: *S. paniculata.*

cuneata Willd. DAC; to 6 in., loosely tufted; lvs. cuneate, ½ in. long, 3-lobed, leathery, glossy; fls. ¼ in. long, in loose panicles, petals white. S. Eur.

cuneifolia L. [*S. cuneifolia* var. *subintegra* Ser.; *S. apennina* Bertol.; *S. Bucklandii* Hort.; *S. capillaris* Host]. ROB; to 1 ft.; lvs. in rosettes, broad-spatulate, to 1½ in. long, rounded and toothed at apex; fls. ¼ in. across, petals white, yellowish at base. Mts., cent. and s. Eur. Cv. **'Infundibuliformis'**. Lvs. spatulate.

cuscutiformis Lodd. DIP; to 6 in., with threadlike stolons; lvs. basal, elliptic, to 2 in. long, coarsely toothed or wavy, veined with white; fls. 1 in. across, petals white, very unequal. Resembles *S. stolonifera.* Nativity uncertain.

Cymbalaria L. CYM; weak-stemmed ann.; lvs. petioled, reniform, fleshy, glossy; sepals spreading, petals yellow.. Se. Eur., sw. Asia, n. Afr.; self-sows and becomes naturalized. Similar to *S. Sibthorpii.*

dalmatica: a listed name of no botanical standing, for a plant in the *Kabschia* section with "minute, spiny cushions, fls. white, in trusses."

decipiens: *S. rosacea.*

Delavayi: *Bergenia purpurascens.*

Desoulavyi: *S. caucasica* var.

diapensioides Bellardi. KAB; forming cushions, sts. many, leafy, to 4 in.; lvs. crowded at base of st., scattered above, oblong, to ¼ in. long, grayish; fls. 2–6, terminal, petals white. Mts., cent. Eur. Cv. **'Lutea'**. Petals yellow.

diversifolia Wallich. HIP; to 12 in.; basal lvs. long-petioled, cordate, 1–2 in. long, st. lvs. smaller, sessile, scattered; fls. in panicles, petals yellow. Himalayas, w. China. Resembles *Parnassia* in habit.

elatior: *S. Hostii.*

×**Elizabethae** Sünderm. [*S.* ×*Godseffiana* Hort.]: *S. Burserana* × *S. juniperifolia* subsp. *sancta.* KAB; forming blue-green mats; fl. sts. to 3 in., fls. in heads, small, petals yellow. Early spring.

×**Engleri** Huter: *S. crustata* × *S. Hostii.* EUA; forming rosette; lvs. narrow, silvery; fl. sts. branching, petals white. A natural hybrid. Mts., cent. Eur. This name has been also, but incorrectly, used for other hybrids involving *S. paniculata, S. cuneifolia,* and probably *S. longifolia.*

Eschscholtzii Sternb. HIP; forming dense cushions, sts. erect, to about 1 in., covered with overlapping, obovate lvs. with hairy margins; fls. small, terminal, sessile, petals yellow. Arctic N. Amer. Of interesting and unusual habit.

Ferdinandi-Coburgi Kellerer & Sünderm. KAB; low-growing, densely tufted; lvs. oblong, to ½ in. long, ciliate; fls. about ½ in. across, petals yellow. Macedonia.

ferruginea R. C. Grah. BOR; to 6 in., covered with reddish hairs; lvs. spatulate or oblanceolate, to 2½ in. long, toothed; fls. ⅛ in. long, in cymes, petals white. Alaska to B.C. and Mont.

flagellaris Willd. HIP; erect, stoloniferous, to 8 in.; lvs. obovate to lanceolate; fls. to nearly 1 in. across, almost sessile, in corymbs of 1–10, petals golden-yellow. N. Eur., Asia, and N. Amer. in Rocky Mts. s. to Ariz. A bog plant, requiring moist soil.

Fortunei: *S. cortusifolia* var.

Friderici-Augusti: *S. porophylla.*

fusca Maxim. BOR; to 12 in.; st. lvs. long-petioled, reniform-orbicular, to 2½ in. long; fls. in terminal panicles, on slender, glandular-hairy pedicels, petals reddish or greenish-brown. Japan. Var. **Kikubuki** Ohwi. Pubescent, but the hairs not glandular.

×**Geum** L.: *S. hirsuta* L. × *S. umbrosa.* ROB; intermediate between the parents; the usually broadly oblong, crenate, conspicuously cartilaginous-margined lf. blades resemble those of *S. umbrosa,* while the long, hairy, fairly narrow petioles are like those of *S. hirsuta.*

globulifera Desf. [*S. oranensis* Munby]. DAC; to 4 in., tufted; lvs. spatulate, ½ in. long, usually 3-lobed, petioles dilated at base; fls. ⅜ in. across, petals white. S. Spain, N. Afr.

×**Godseffiana:** a listed name of no botanical standing for *S.* ×*Elizabethae.*

granulata L. MEADOW S., FAIR-MAIDS-OF-FRANCE. SAX; to 20 in., bulbous at base, with many bulbils in axils of basal lvs.; lvs. reniform, to 1 in. long and 1½ in. wide, lobed; fls. 1 in. across, petals white. Eur. Cv. **'Flore Pleno'**. Fls. double.

Grisebachii Degen & Dörfl. [*S. montenegrina* Halácsy & Bald.]. KAB; to 8 in., tufted; lvs. spatulate, to 1½ in. long, margins cartilaginous; infl. spicate, fls. 5/16 in. across or less, petals purple. Balkan Pen. to n. Greece.

×**Gusmusii** Sünderm.: *S. luteoviridis* Schott & Kotschy × *S. porophylla.* KAB; to 6 in.; fls. in short spikes, petals reddish.

×**Haagii** Sünderm.: *S. juniperifolia* × *S. Ferdinandi-Coburgi.* KAB; to 3 in., with loose rosettes forming dark green mats; petals yellow.

×**Haussmannii** A. Kern.: *S. aizoides* × *S. mutata.* Resembles *S. mutata* in appearance; fl. sts. to 8 in.; petals copper-orange. Occurring naturally where the parent spp. meet.

hibernica: *S. rosacea.*

Hostii Tausch [*S. altissima* A. Kern.; *S. elatior* Mert. & W. D. J. Koch]. EUA; to 2 ft.; lvs. in rosettes, tongue-shaped, to 4 in. long, wavy-margined; fls. in many-fld. panicles, ½ in. across, petals white, sometimes dotted with purple. Alps.

hypnoides L. [*S. sponhemica* of auth., not C. C. Gmel.]. DAC; to 6 in., with many sterile shoots; lvs. linear, about 1/16 in. long, sometimes 3–5-lobed and ½ in. long; fls. to 1 in. across, petals white. Eur. Cv. **'Gemmifera'**. Of compact habit.

icelandica: a listed name of no botanical standing for *S. Cotyledon* cv.

incrustata: *S. crustata.*

integrifolia: see *S. oregana.*

intermedia: a name used in various senses; in hort., a name of no botanical standing for the hybrid *S. Grisebachii* × *S. Stribrnyi.* KAB; differs from *S. Grisebachii* in having infl. racemose, pedicels longer, petals red.

irrigua Bieb. SAX; to 1 ft.; lvs. in rosettes, reniform, ½ in. long, deeply 3-parted to base, the lobes toothed, petioles to 2 in. long; fls. to 1 in. across, in many-fld. panicles, petals white. S. Eur.

Irvingiana: *S. Sundermannii.*

×**Irvingii:** a listed name of no botanical standing for the hybrid *S. Burserana* × (perhaps) *S. porophylla* or *S. lilacina.* Forming cushions, to 1½ in.; lvs. of rosettes blue-gray, spiny; petals lilac-pink.

Jenkinsii: a listed name of no botanical standing.

juniperifolia Adams [*S. juniperina* Bieb.; *S. pseudosancta* Janka]. KAB; to 3 in., tufted; basal lvs. stiff, lanceolate, to ¾ in. long, ciliate, st. lvs. to ¾ in. long; infl. ovoid to somewhat globose; fls. 5/16 in. across, petals yellow. Bulgaria. Subsp. **sancta** (Griseb.) D. A. Webb [*S. sancta* Griseb.]. Fls. in nearly globose infl.

juniperina: *S. juniperifolia.*

×**Kellereri** Sünderm.: *S. Sempervivum* C. Koch × (probably) a form of *S. Burserana.* With habit of *S. Sempervivum,* rosettes to 2 in. across, lvs. longer, narrower, pitted with white dots; fl. sts. to 5 in., fls. cylindrical, petals pink, darker in center, not reflexed.

×**kestonensis** Hort. ex Farrer. Hybrid, probably of *S. Burserana;* to 3 in.; fl. sts. bright red, petals white. Early spring.

×**kewensis** Hort. ex: W. Irving *S. Burserana* × *S. Sempervivum* C. Koch. Cushion-forming; lvs. linear-lanceolate; fl. sts. glandular-hairy, bracts red, tipped green, sepals deep red, petals rose.

Kolenatiana: *S. paniculata.*

×**Kyrillii** Kellerer: *S. Ferdinandi-Coburgi* × *S. marginata.* KAB; lf. rosettes in clusters; fl. sts. to 4 in.; lvs. gray-green, spiny; petals lemon-yellow.

lagraveana: a listed name of no botanical standing for *S. paniculata* cv.

lantoscana: *S. callosa.*

lasiophylla: *S. rotundifolia.*

latepetiolata Willk. SAX; to 10 in., densely tufted; lvs. reniform, to 1¾ in. long, 3-parted into lobed segms., glandular-hairy, petiole broadly winged; fls. small, petals white. Medit. region.

×**Leichtlinii:** a listed name of no botanical standing for *Bergenia* ×*Schmidtii.*

leucanthemifolia: *S. Michauxii.*

ligulata: *Bergenia ciliata.* Var. **speciosa:** *Bergenia* ×*Schmidtii.*

lilacina Duthie. KAB; to 1 in., tufted; lvs. oblong, to 3/16 in. long, margins cartilaginous; fls. solitary, ½ in. across, petals pale lilac with purple streaks. Himalayas.

lingulata: *S. callosa.*

longifolia Lapeyr. EUA; to 2 ft.; lvs. in rosettes, linear-spatulate, to 3 in. long; fls. ½ in. across, in many-fld. panicles, petals white, rarely purple-spotted. Pyrenees. Cv. **'Magnifica'**. Rosettes to 1 ft. across; panicles large.

lutea: a listed name of no botanical standing for *S. paniculata* cv.

luteoviridis Schott & Kotschy [*S. corymbosa* Boiss., not Lucé]. KAB; to 6 in., densely tufted; lvs. spatulate, to 1 in. long, entire, glaucous, often purple beneath; fls. 1/4 in. across, in many-fld. panicles, petals pale yellow. E. Eur.

Lyallii Engl. [*Micranthes Lyallii* (Engl.) Small]. BOR; to 1 ft.; lvs. obovate, coarsely toothed, to 2½ in. long; fls. in few-fld. panicles, petals white with yellow spots. Alaska to Mont.

×**Macnabiana** R. Lindsay.: *S. callosa* × *S. Cotyledon.* Some plants are more like *S. callosa,* with petals spotted with red; others are more like *S. Cotyledon,* with petals not spotted.

marginata Sternb. [*S. coriophylla* Griseb.]. KAB; to 3 in., tufted; lvs. variable, from linear-oblong to obovate-spatulate, to ½ in. long, margins translucent; fls. to ½ in. across, usually 2–8 in a corymbose infl., petals white or pale pink. Se. Eur. Var. **Rocheliana** (Sternb.) Engl. & Irmsch. [*S. Rocheliana* Sternb.]. Lvs. in a flat rosette.

media Gouan. KAB; to 3 in., tufted; lvs. oblong- or linear-spatulate, to 1 in. long, margins cartilaginous; fls. 3/16 in. long, in branched panicles, petals purple. Similar to *S. Stribrnyi,* but with lvs. narrower, fls. usually in a raceme, fewer and smaller. S. Eur.

Megasea: a listed name of no botanical standing; sometimes used for spp. of *Bergenia.*

Merkii Fisch. HIR; to 4 in., tufted; lvs. somewhat fleshy, broadly lanceolate to obovate, to ¾ in. long; fls. to ½ in. across, 1–8 in a cymose infl., petals white. Kamchatka, Kurile Is., Japan. Var. **Idsuroei** (Franch. & Sav.) Engl. Lvs. 3-lobed at apex; infl. 1–4-fld.

Mertensiana Bong. BOR; to 1 ft.; lvs. long-petioled, cordate-orbicular, to 3 in. across, toothed; petals white, with yellow spots at base. Alaska to Calif.

Michauxii Britt. [*S. leucanthemifolia* Michx., not Lapeyr.]. BOR; to 1½ in.; lvs. oblong or lanceolate, to 7 in. long, coarsely toothed; fls. 1/4 in. across, petals white. Se. U.S.

microlepis: a listed name of no botanical standing.

montanensis: *S. oregana.*

montenegrina: *S. Grisebachii.*

moschata Wulfen [*S. Allionii* Gaud.-Beaup.; *S. Rhei* Schott]. DAC; to 5 in.; leafy shoots forming fairly dense but sometimes rather flat cushions; lvs. variable, broadly linear or obovate, to ¾ in. long, entire or 3-lobed; petals yellowish, less often purplish or white. Cent. and s. Eur. Similar to *S. muscoides.* Cvs. are: **'Acaulis'**, densely tufted and low-growing, petals white; **'Alba'**, petals white; **'Atropurpurea'**, petals purple; **'Pygmaea'**, densely tufted.

muscoides All. DAC; to 2 in., densely tufted; lvs. linear, 1/4 in. long; fls. 1/4 in. across, petals white or yellowish. Mts., cent. Eur. Similar to *S. moschata* but sts. shorter, more densely tufted, and lvs. narrower, entire. Cv **'Alba'**. Petals white. Cv. **'Atropurpurea'**. Petals dark red; may be of hybrid origin.

mutata L. EUA; to 1 ft., with thick rhizome; lvs. in rosettes, thick, spatulate, to 3 in. long, very obtuse, margins cartilaginous; fls. about ½ in. across, petals yellow or orange. Mts., cent. Eur.

Nelsoniana D. Don [*S. aestivalis* Fisch.; *S. arguta* D. Don; *S. punctata* of auth., not L.]. BOR; to 1½ ft.; lvs. basal, long-petioled, reniform, coarsely crenate; fls. small, usually in loose panicles, petals white or pale pink. Eur., n. Asia, w. N. Amer.

nepalensis: a listed name of no botanical standing for *S. Cotyledon.*

nitida: *S. bronchialis* subsp. *Funstonii.*

nivalis L. BOR; to 6 in., usually less; lvs. ovate, thick, leathery, dark green above, purplish-red beneath; fl. sts. erect, glandular-viscid, fls. in cymules, petals white. Arctic and subarctic regions, circumboreal.

×**Obristii** Sünderm.: *S. Burserana* × *S. marginata.* KAB; to 4 in.; fls. to 1 in. across, petals ivory-white.

obscura: *S. pubescens.*

occidentalis S. Wats. [*Micranthes occidentalis* (S. Wats.) Small]. BOR; to 8 in.; lvs. ovate or oblong, to 2½ in. long, toothed, often red-pubescent beneath; fls. small, in cymes, petals white. Alta. to Mont.

oppositifolia L. PURPLE MOUNTAIN S. POR; to 2 in., densely matted; lvs. obovate to 3/8 in. long, keeled, ciliate; fls. to ½ in. across, petals rose or purple. Arctic and subarctic regions, circumboreal. Cv. **'Splendens'**. Fls. large, petals purplish-crimson.

oranensis: *S. globulifera.*

oregana T. J. Howell [*S. integrifolia* of auth., not Hook.f.; *S. montanensis* Small]. BOR; st. stout, to 1½ ft. or even 3 ft., glandular-pubescent; lvs. basal, obovate to elliptic, to 6 in. long, narrowed to a short petiole, somewhat glandular-toothed; fls. small, in open panicles, petals white. W. N. Amer.

paniculata Mill. [*S. aizoon* Jacq.; *S. cartilaginea* Willd.; *S. cultrata* Schott; *S. Kolenatiana* Regel; *S. pectinata* Schott, Nym., & Kotschy, not Pursh]. EUA; to 12 in., sometimes more; lvs. in dense, basal rosettes, narrow-spatulate, to 1¼ in. long; fl. sts. branched above, forming a panicle, fls. to ½ in. across, petals creamy-white, marked with purple. Arctic N. Amer., Eur., and Asia. Variable in size of plant and in lf. shape. Cvs. include: **'Alba'**, petals white; **'Atropurpurea'**, petals rose-purple; **'Balcana'**, petals white, with red spots; **'Baldensis'**, lvs. ashy-gray, short, thick; **'Brevifolia'**, petals white; **'Californica'** petals white; **'Churchillii'**, lvs. in stiff rosettes, pointed, gray; **'Cristata'**, lvs. narrow, silvery, petals cream-colored; **'Cultrata'**, to 14 in., basal lvs. narrow, obtuse, serrate, petals cream-colored; **'Densa'**, rosettes small, very silvery; **'Emarginata'**, to 10 in., fls. in loose corymbs, petals creamy; **'Flavescens'**, petals lemon-yellow; **'Hainoldii'**, to 1 ft., rosettes large, petals rose; **'Labradorica'**, rosettes very small, to ¾ in. across, fl. sts. to 3 in., petals white; **'Lagraveana'**, to 6 in., rosettes small, silvery, petals creamy, thick, waxlike; **'Lambertii'**, perhaps a hybrid; **'Lutea'**, petals yellow; **'Major'**, lvs. oblong-linear, not widening much at apex; **'Minima'** [cv. 'Minor'], small, petals white; **'Notata'**, lvs. silver-margined; **'Paradoxa'**, lvs. bluish, petals white; **'Pectinata'**, lvs. margined with silver, petals white, spotted red; **'Rex'**, to 10 in., fls. large, petals cream-colored; **'Rosea'**, petals bright pink; **'Rosularis'**, lvs. of rosettes incurved, petals white; **'Stabiana'**, to 8 in., lvs. to 1 in. long.

paradoxa Sternb. Probably not cult.; material grown under this name is *S. paniculata* cv.

×**Paulinae** Sünderm.: *S. Burserana* × *S. Ferdinandi-Coburgi.* KAB; to 2 in.; fls. pale yellow, to ¾ in. across.

pectinata: see *Luetkea pectinata* and *L. paniculata;* however, material offered as *S. pectinata* may be either *S. paniculata* cv. 'Pectinata' or a hybrid between *S. paniculata* and *S. crustata.*

pedemontana All. DAC; to 4 in., tufted; lvs. petioled, obovate, palmately divided into 5–11 segms.; fls. 3–7 in a corymbose cyme, petals white. Mts., cent. and s. Eur.

peltata: *Peltiphyllum peltatum.*

pensylvanica L. [*Micranthes pensylvanica* (L.) Haw.]. SWAMP S., WILD BEET. BOR; to 3 ft., with thick rhizome; lvs. basal, oblong to spatulate, to 1 ft. long, ciliate; fls. greenish, to 1/4 in. across. Me., s. to Va. and Mo. Suited to the bog garden.

pentadactylis Lapeyr. DAC; to 3 in., mat-forming; lvs. palmately lobed or cleft, glabrous, viscid-clammy, aromatic; fls. 3–30 in a terminal, compact, usually corymbose cyme, star-shaped, petals white. Spain.

petiolaris: *S. rivularis.*

petraea L. TRI; to 8 in., sts. weak, often decumbent; lvs. of basal rosette petioled, semicircular or rhombic in outline, divided almost to base into many toothed segms., st. lvs. less deeply divided; petals white. Alps.

×**Petraschii** Sünderm.: *S. marginata* × *S. tombeanensis.* KAB; to 2 in.; fls. 1 in. across, petals white.

Polodae: a listed name of no botanical standing.

porophylla Bertol. [*S. Friderici-Augusti* N.Terracc.; *S. thessalica* Schott]. KAB; to 5 in., tufted; lvs. oblong-spatulate to linear, to ½ in. long, margins cartilaginous; fls. 3/16 in. across, petals pink or purple. S. Eur.

Portiae: a listed name of no botanical standing, which has been applied to several cvs.

primuloides: a listed name of no botanical standing for *S. umbrosa* cv.

pseudosancta: *S. juniperifolia.*

pubescens: Pourr. [*S. obscura* Gren. & Godr.]. DAC; cespitose to loose and spreading; basal lvs. 3–5-cleft, densely glandular-hairy, st. lvs. divided into entire segms.; fl. sts. 1–4 in. high, petals white, sometimes veined. Pyrenees.

punctata: see *S. Nelsoniana.*

purpurascens: *Bergenia purpurascens.*

pyramidalis: *S. Cotyledon.*

repanda: *S. rotundifolia.*

retusa Gouan. POR; tufted, to 2 in.; lower lvs. imbricate, oblong-lanceolate, thick, keeled beneath; fls. in 1–4-fld. clusters, petals ruby- or purple-red. High mts., s. Eur.

Rhei: *S. moschata.*

rhomboidea Greene [*Micranthes rhomboidea* (Greene) Small]. BOR; to 1 ft.; lvs. ovate, to 2½ in. long, toothed; infl. cymose-paniculate, compact, fls. 3/16 in. long, petals white. S. B.C. and Alta. to Idaho, Colo., and Utah.

rivularis L. [*S. petiolaris* R. Br.]. ALPINE BROOK S. SAX; tufted, to 3 in.; basal lvs. reniform, palmately 3–7-lobed, with petioles 3–5 times longer than blades, upper lvs. 3-lobed, short-petioled; fls. usually 1–5 on axillary peduncles to 3 in. long, petals white, sometimes tinged purple. Circumboreal; in N. Amer., s. to White Mts. and in Rocky Mts. to Mont.

Rocheliana: *S. marginata* var.

rosacea Moench [*S. affinis* D. Don; *S. decipiens* J. F. Ehrh.; *S. hibernica* Haw.; *S. Sternbergii* Willd.]. DAC; variable in habit and foliage, low and tufted, cushions large or small, loose or compact; lvs. obovate-cuneate, usually cut into 5 linear segms.; fls. ½ in. or more across, opening flat, petals white or pink to red. Eur. Similar to *S. caespitosa*, but lvs. usually 5-lobed, with rather long nonglandular hairs, and petals nearly ½ in. long. Subsp. **sponhemica** (C. C. Gmel.) D. A. Webb [*S. sponhemica* C. C. Gmel.]. Leafy shoots more or less erect; lf. lobes narrow, strongly mucronate or apiculate. Cent. Eur.

rotundifolia L. [*S. rotundifolia* var. *repanda* (Willd.) Engl.; *S. lasiophylla* Schott; *S. repanda* Willd.]. MIS; to 2 ft.; lvs. in rosettes, reniform, to 2 in. across, coarsely toothed, petioles much longer than blades; fls. to ¾ in. across, petals white, spotted with red or purple. Eur., Asia.

rubicunda: a listed name of no botanical standing.

sachalinensis Friedr. Schmidt. BOR; to 18 in.; basal lvs. short-petioled, ovate to oblong, to 4 in. long, rather fleshy, often purplish beneath; fls. many in a loose panicle, petals white. Sakhalin, s. Kurile Is., n. Japan.

sancta: *S. juniperifolia* subsp. *sancta.*

sarmentosa: *S. stolonifera.*

scardica Griseb. KAB; to 4 in., tufted; lvs. stiff, oblong to lanceolate, to ½ in. long, keeled beneath, margins cartilaginous and ciliate at least in part, with 5–15 pits; fls. 5/16 in. long, in corymbs, petals white or rose. Medit. region.

×**Schmidtii:** *Bergenia* ×Schmidtii.

serratifolia: *S. umbrosa.*

sibirica L. SAX; to 8 in.; lvs. petioled, reniform, palmately 5–9-lobed, the basal ones with bulbils in axils; fls. few in terminal cymes, petals white. Se. Eur.

Sibthorpii Boiss. CYM; weak-stemmed ann., related to *S. Cymbalaria*, but sepals and fr. deflexed. Greece.

simulata: *S. cernua.*

speciosa (Dörfl. & Hayek) Dörfl. & Hayek. POR; closely related to *S. oppositifolia*, but lvs. without cilia and cartilaginous near apex. Eur. *S.* ×*speciosa* Leichtl. is *Bergenia* ×*Schmidtii.*

sponhemica: *S. rosacea* subsp., but the name has been commonly missapplied to *S. hypnoides.*

Spruneri Boiss. KAB; similar to *S. marginata*, but lvs. smaller, glandular-hairy beneath and fls. in a close corymb. Mts., Balkan Pen.

squarrosa Sieber. KAB; to 3 in., densely tufted; lvs. linear or linear-lanceolate, ⅛ in. long, margin narrow, cartilaginous; fls. to 5/16 in. long, petals white. Mts., Eur.

Sternbergii: *S. rosacea.*

stolonifera Meerb. [*S. sarmentosa* L.]. STRAWBERRY GERANIUM, BEEFSTEAK G., STRAWBERRY BEGONIA, CREEPING-SAILOR, MOTHER-OF-THOUSANDS. DIP; to 2 ft., with threadlike stolons like those of strawberry; lvs. long-petioled, orbicular-cordate, to 4 in. across, coarsely toothed, reddish beneath, veined with silver above; fls. to 1 in. across, petals white, 2 much longer than others. E. Asia. Used as a pot or basket plant, but hardy outdoors rather far north, especially with protection. Cv. **'Tricolor'**. MAGIC-CARPET S. Lvs. variegated dark green, gray-green, and ivory-white, and flushed with pink or rose.

Stracheyi: *Bergenia Stracheyi.*

Stribrnyi (Velen.) Podp. KAB; sts. branching, to 5 in., terminating in flat, silver-gray lf. rosettes; lvs. oblong-spatulate, to 1 in. long; pedicels to ½ in. long, fls. to 5/16 in. across, in 10–30-fld. panicles, calyx inflated, densely covered with deep-red glandular hairs, petals purplish-pink. Bulgaria, Greece. Parent of several garden hybrids.

×**Stuartii** Sünderm. Hybrid, with *S. Stribrnyi* as one parent; to 4 in.; fls. 5/16 in. across, petals pale yellow or purple.

×**Sundermannii** W. Irving [*S. Irvingiana* Engl. & Irmsch.]: *S. Burserana* × *S. marginata.* KAB; tufted, lf. rosettes to ⅝ in. across; lvs. triangular, to ¼ in. long, upper surface concave, margins chalky-white; fl. sts. 1–2-fld., green, fls. to ¾ in. across, petals white, wavy-margined, twice as long as sepals. Cv. **'Major'** is listed.

taygetea Boiss. & Heldr. ROB; to 6 in.; lvs. reniform, ½ in. long, slightly 5–9-lobed; fls. in panicles, 5/16 in. long, petals white, spotted purple. Greece.

tellimoides: *Peltoboykinia tellimoides.*

tenella Wulfen. DAC; to 4 in., tufted; lvs. linear-subulate, to ½ in. long; fls. very small, petals white or yellowish. Mts., cent. Eur.

tennesseensis Small [*Micranthes tennesseensis* (Small) Small]. GOLDEN-EYE S. BOR; to 1 ft.; lvs. elliptic-ovate to orbicular-reniform, to 5 in. long; fls. in open cymules, petals white with yellow eye, to 3/16 in. long. Tenn.

thessalica: *S. porophylla.*

×**tirolensis** A. Kern.: *S. caesia* × *S. squarrosa.* KAB; very small, to 3½ in.; petals white. Alps.

Tolmiei Torr. & A. Gray. BOR; to 5 in.; lvs. imbricate on the short sts., linear, ⅜ in. long; fls. very small, petals white. B.C. to Calif.

tombeanensis Boiss. ex Engl. KAB; to 2 in.; lvs. ovate- to linear-lanceolate, ⅛ in. long, thick, keeled beneath; fls. ½ in. long, petals white. Alps, s. Eur.

tricuspidata Rottb. DAC; to 8 in.; lvs. linear, to ¾ in. long, with 3 spine-tipped lobes at apex; fls. small, petals white. N. N. Amer.

trifurcata Schrad. [*S. ceratophylla* Dryand.]. DAC; to 8 in.; lvs. reniform, to ¾ in. across, palmately 3-parted, segms. toothed or lobed, petioles very long; fls. to ¾ in. across, petals milk-white. Pyrenees.

umbrosa L. [*S. serratifolia* Mackay]. LONDON-PRIDE. ROB; to 18 in.; lvs. petioled, thick, ovate to oblong, to 2½ in. long, often reddish beneath, margins cartilaginous; fls. to 5/16 in. across, petals white or pink. Eur. Cv. **'Covillei'**. To about 6 in.; fls. many, petals pink and white. Cv. **'Primuloides'**. To 6 in.; lvs. primroselike; petals rose-pink. Plants offered as London-pride or as cvs. of *S. umbrosa* may be *S.* ×*urbium.*

×**urbium** D. A. Webb: *S. spathularis* Brot. × *S. umbrosa.* LONDON-PRIDE. Similar to *S. umbrosa* but differs in having longer, less densely ciliate petioles, larger lf. blades with more pointed and numerous crenations, and larger fls.

valdensis DC. EUA; to 3 in., densely tufted; lvs. spatulate-linear, to ⅜ in. long, keeled, purplish beneath; fls. in corymbs, 3/16 in. long, petals white. Mts., cent. Eur.

Vandellii Sternb. KAB; differs from *S. Burserana* in having fls. several to many, not solitary. Alps, cent. Eur.

vespertina (Small) Fedde. EUA; to 5 in.; lvs. oblong, to ⅜ in. long, spine-tipped; fls. small, petals white, often spotted yellow. Alaska to Ore.

virginiensis Michx. [*Micranthes virginiensis* (Michx.) Small]. EARLY S. BOR; to 1 ft.; lvs. in rosettes, ovate to oblong, to 3 in. long, toothed; fls. about 5/16 in. across, petals white. New Bruns. to Ga. and Tenn., w. to Ark.

vochinensis: a listed name of no botanical standing for *S. crustata.*

×**Wildiana** Kunze: *S.* ×*Geum* × *S. paniculata.* To 8 in.; fls. to 5/16 in. across, petals white.

Zolikoferi: a listed name of no botanical standing.

SAXIFRAGACEAE. SAXIFRAGE FAMILY. Dicot.; about 80 genera and 1,200 spp. of herbs or shrubs, occasionally small trees, rarely woody climbers, mostly of temp. regions; lvs. alt., or sometimes opp.; fls. in few-fld. cymes or in many-fld. clusters, racemes, or panicles, or solitary, usually bisexual and regular, sepals and petals usually 4 or 5, sometimes partly united to form a calyx tube, stamens as many or twice as many as sepals and petals, carpels 2–5, united, or partly separate; fr. a caps. or berry. Several genera are grown as ornamentals and the currant and gooseberry *(Ribes)* for their edible frs. The cult. genera are: *Anopterus, Astilbe, Bauera, Bensoniella, Bergenia, Bolandra, Boykinia, Brexia, Cardiandra, Carpenteria, Carpodetus, Chrysosplenium, Decumaria, Deinanthe, Deutzia, Elmera, Escallonia, Fendlera, Francoa, Heuchera,* ×*Heucherella, Hydrangea, Itea, Jamesia, Jepsonia, Kirengeshoma, Leptarrhena, Lithophragma, Mitella, Parnassia, Peltiphyllum, Peltoboykinia, Philadelphus, Pileostegia, Quintinia, Ribes, Rodgersia, Saxifraga, Schizophragma, Suksdorfia, Sullivantia, Tanakaea, Telesonix, Tellima, Tiarella, Tolmiea,* and *Whipplea.*

SCABIOSA L. SCABIOUS, PINCUSHION FLOWER. *Dipsacaceae.* About 80 or more spp. of ann. or per. herbs, or rarely subshrubs, native to Eur., Asia, and Afr., but mainly the Medit. region; lvs. opp., entire to dissected; fls. in long-stalked, involucrate heads, white, yellowish, rose, or blue, subtended by nonspiny receptacular bracts, calyx cup-shaped, with 5 bristly teeth, enveloped by a cup-shaped involucel, corolla with 4–5 nearly equal lobes, or sometimes 2-lipped, marginal corollas usually larger, stamens 4 or rarely 2; fr. an achene, crowned with persistent calyx.

Scabiosas are popular for flower gardens and thrive in any good soil and sunny exposure. Propagated by seeds, and the perennials also by division.

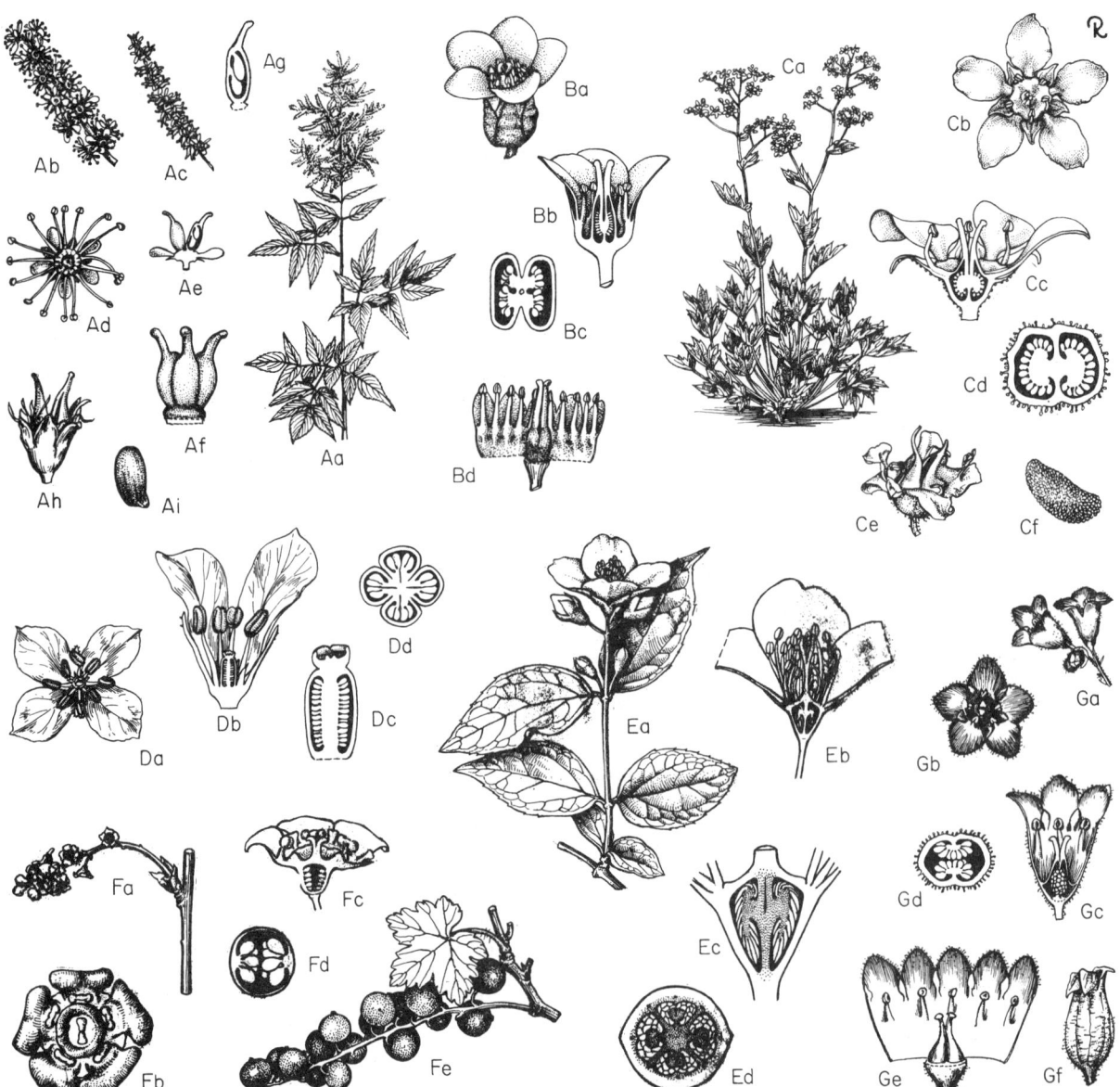

SAXIFRAGACEAE. **A,** *Astilbe chinensis:* **Aa,** part of flowering (male) stem, × ¹⁄₁₆; **Ab,** branch of male inflorescence, × 1; **Ac,** branch of female inflorescence, × 1; **Ad,** male flower, × 4; **Ae,** female flower, vertical section, × 4; **Af,** pistils, × 8; **Ag,** pistil, vertical section, × 8; **Ah,** follicles, × 5; **Ai,** seed, × 10. **B,** *Bergenia crassifolia:* **Ba,** flower, × 1; **Bb,** flower, vertical section, × 1; **Bc,** ovary, cross section, × 3; **Bd,** flower, calyx tube expanded (petals removed), × 1. **C,** *Boykinia major:* **Ca,** plant, × ¹⁄₁₀; **Cb,** flower, × 1½; **Cc,** flower, vertical section, × 2½; **Cd,** ovary, cross section, × 6; **Ce,** capsule, × 3; **Cf,** seed, × 15. **D,** *Francoa sonchifolia:* **Da,** flower, face view, × 1½; **Db,** flower, vertical section, × 2½; **Dc,** pistil, vertical section, × 8; **Dd,** ovary, cross section, × 10. **E,** *Philadelphus inodorus:* **Ea,** flowering twig, × ½; **Eb,** flower, vertical section, × 1; **Ec,** ovary, vertical section, × 3; **Ed,** ovary, cross section, × 3. **F,** *Ribes sativum:* **Fa,** inflorescence, × ½; **Fb,** flower, face view, × 3; **Fc,** flower, vertical section, × 3; **Fd,** ovary, cross section, × 8; **Fe,** fruit, × ½. **G,** *Heuchera sanguinea:* **Ga,** flowers, × 1; **Gb,** flower, face view, × 2; **Gc,** flower, vertical section, × 2; **Gd,** ovary, cross section, × 5; **Ge,** flower, calyx tube expanded, × 2; **Gf,** capsule, × 2. (Ea-Ed, Fa-Fe from Bailey, *Manual of Cultivated Plants,* ed. 2.)

africana L. Per., sts. to 3 ft., softly hairy; lvs. obovate or oblong, to 6 in. long, upper lvs. undivided or pinnatifid, soft-tomentose; heads to 1¾ in. across; fls. mauve. S. Afr.

alpina: *Cephalaria alpina.*

anthemifolia Ecklon & Zeyh. [*S. columbaria* var. *anthemifolia* Hort.]. Short-lived per., sts. decumbent, to 2½ ft.; lvs. obovate to obovate-spatulate or oblong-oblanceolate, toothed to 2–3-pinnatifid; heads to 2½ in. across; fls. mauve or rose to violet, silky-hairy outside. S. Afr.

atropurpurea L. PINCUSHIONS, SWEET SCABIOUS, MOURNING-BRIDE. Erect ann., to 2 ft.; basal lvs. oblong-spatulate to lyrate, coarsely toothed, st. lvs. pinnatifid; heads ovate to oblong, to 2 in. across; fls. dark purple, rose, lilac, or white. S. Eur.; naturalized in Calif. Variable

in habit and fl. color. Cv. **'Grandiflora'** [*S. grandiflora* Scop.]. Fl. heads large. Cv. **'Nana'** [*S. nana* Hort.]. Plant shorter, much-branched.

caucasica Bieb. Per., to 2 ft., or sometimes taller; basal lvs. lanceolate-linear, glaucous, st. lvs. divided; heads flattish, to 3 in. across, involucre gray-tomentose; fls. light blue. Caucasus. Cvs. are: **'Alba'**, fls. white; **'Goldingensis'** [*S. goldingensis* Hort.], fls. large, deep lavender; **'Perfecta'**, fls. large, fringed.

columbaria L. Bien. or per., to 2 ft.; basal lvs. oblanceolate or obovate to lyrate, st. lvs. pinnately cut, segms. linear; heads to 1½ in. across; fls. blue, pink, or white. Eur., Afr., Asia. Var. **anthemifolia:** *S. anthemifolia.*

drymeia: a listed name of no botanical standing; material offered may be *Knautia drymeia.*

Fischeri DC. Much-branched per., sts. to 2 ft.; lvs. pinnately cut, segms. linear, entire; heads to 2½ in. across, on stiff peduncles; fls. blue-purple, corolla 5-lobed. Se. Siberia.

goldingensis: a listed name of no botanical standing for *S. caucasica* cv.

graminifolia L. Woody-based per., to 1 ft.; lvs. linear, entire, silvery-pubescent; heads to 2 in. across; fls. pale blue or lilac. S. Eur.

grandiflora: *S. atropurpurea* cv.

japonica Miq. Bien., sts. to 2½ ft., soft-hairy; lvs. pinnatifid to 2-pinnatifid; heads to 2 in. across; fls. blue, corolla 4-lobed. Japan.

limoniifolia Vahl. Per.; basal lvs. obovate, glabrous above, white-hairy underneath, entire; fls. blue, corolla 6-lobed. Sicily.

lucida Vill. Per., to 2 ft.; basal lvs. ovate or rhombic, coarsely toothed to somewhat lyrate, st. lvs. pinnatifid, segms. lanceolate; heads dense, hemispherical, to 1½ in. across; fls. rose-lilac. Cent. Eur. Cv. **'Rosea'.** Fls. rose-pink.

lyrophylla: *Knautia lyrophylla.*

macedonica: *Knautia macedonica.*

nana: a listed name of no botanical standing for *S. atropurpurea* cv.

ochroleuca L. Bien. or per., to 2½ ft.; basal lvs. lyrate or sometimes undivided, st. lvs. pinnatifid to 2-pinnatifid, whitish-pubescent, segms. oblong or linear; heads to 1½ in. across; fls. pale yellow. Eur., w. Asia. Var. **Webbiana** (D. Don) Boiss. [*S. Webbiana* D. Don]. Lower lvs. usually dissected, white-villous. Se. Eur. to Asia Minor.

palaestina L. Erect, branched ann., sts. to 1½ ft., pubescent; lvs. oblong to oblong-spatulate, or sometimes lyrate-pinnatifid, entire or toothed; heads to 1¼ in. across, involucral bracts oblong-lanceolate; fls. pale yellow, rarely lilac. Balkan region to Iraq.

parnassi: *Pterocephalus parnassi.*

pennsylvanica: a listed name of no botanical standing; material grown under this name is *Knautia tatarica.*

prolifera L. CARMEL DAISY. Ann., to 2 ft.; lvs. oblong to oblong-lanceolate to linear; heads nearly sessile, to 2 in. across; fls. cream-colored. N. Afr. to Asia Minor.

pterocephala: *Pterocephalus parnassi.*

pyrenaica All. [*Pterocephalus pyrenaicus* Hort.]. Per., to 1½ ft., white-tomentose; basal lvs. elliptic, crenate to incised, st. lvs. pinnately divided; fls. blue-lilac. S. Eur.

rotata Bieb. Ann., to 1 ft.; lvs. oblong-lanceolate or linear-lanceolate, entire, upper lvs. linear, with 1 or 2 basal lobes; fls. reddish. Asia Minor to cent. Asia and Afghanistan.

scabra: *Cephalaria scabra.*

silenifolia Waldst. & Kit. Per., to 1 ft.; basal lvs. spatulate, entire, st. lvs. lanceolate to pinnatifid, segms. linear; heads to 1¼ in. across; fls. blue-violet. S.-cent. Eur.

Sosnowskyi Sulak. Per., to 2½ ft.; st. lvs. pinnate to lyrate-pinnatifid, segms. entire or dentate; heads to ⅝ in. across; fls. pale yellow. Caucasus.

speciosa Royle. Tufted per., to 2 ft., sts. downy; lvs. oblong or pinnatifid, to 2 in. long, pubescent; heads nearly flat, to 2 in. across; fls. lavender to mauve, corolla hairy on exterior. Himalayas.

stellata L. Ann., to about 1½ ft., sts. and lvs. with short and long hairs; lvs. dentate or incised to pinnatisect; heads hemispherical, to 1¼ in. across; fls. blue or rose-violet, hirsute outside. W. Medit. region.

Succisa: *Succisa protensis.*

sylvatica: *Knautia sylvatica.*

ucranica L. Bien. or per., to about 2½ ft.; lvs. entire to pinnatisect, segms. linear, entire; heads to 1 in. across; fls. white, pale yellow, or pale blue. S. Eur., w. Asia.

variifolia Boiss. Woody-based per.; lvs. oblong or oblong-lanceolate, to 3 in. long, entire or with a few teeth or 3-lobed, glabrous; fls. pale blue. Is. of Karpathos and Rhodes (Greece).

Webbiana: *S. ochroleuca* var.

SCAEVOLA L. *Goodeniaceae.* About 80 or more spp. of herbs and shrubs, pantrop. but mostly Australian; lvs. simple; infls. axillary; calyx very small, corolla 5-lobed, slit to base on upper side; fr. drupaceous, dry or fleshy.

frutescens (Mill.) Kurt Krause. BEACH NAUPAKA. Spreading shrub, to 10 ft. high; lvs. clustered at br. tips, obovate, to 6 in. long, fleshy, entire, glabrous; corolla white, with purple streaks, ¾ in. long; fr. white, fleshy. Islands and coasts of Indian and Pacific Oceans. Zone 10. Occasionally planted in s. Fla.; useful for hedges and soil-binding on coastal sands. Var. **sericea** (G. Forst.) Merrill. Lvs. and infls. silky-downy.

SCAPHYGLOTTIS Poepp. & Endl. *Orchidaceae.* About 40 spp. of epiphytes, native to trop. Amer.; sts. hard or pseudobulbous, simple or branched; lvs. 1–3, grasslike, or flat and leathery; infl. a terminal cluster or raceme; fls. small, sepals ovate, petals similar but smaller, lip jointed to apex of column foot, clawed or clawless, entire or 3-lobed, column short, wingless or winged, with a distinct foot, pollinia 4. For structure of fl. see *Orchidaceae.*

For culture see *Orchids.*

amethystina (Rchb.f.) Schlechter. To 10 in., sts. cylindrical to spindle-shaped, 1–2-lvd. at apex; lvs. linear, to 4½ in. long; infl. a few-fld. cluster at apex of st. segms.; sepals and petals lanceolate, to ¼ in. long, amethyst, lip ⅜ in. long, 3-lobed, lateral lobes large, rounded, midlobe squarish, longer than lateral lobes, column with 2 arms. Costa Rica, Panama.

Lindeniana (A. Rich. & Galeotti) L. O. Williams. To 20 in., sts. slender below, spindle-shaped and pseudobulbous above, 2-lvd.; lvs. leathery, oblong-elliptic, to 10 in. long; infl. a cluster at apex of pseudobulb; fls. greenish-white to purplish-green with white lip, sepals and petals lanceolate, to ⅜ in. long, lip oblanceolate, obscurely 3-lobed, apiculate. Early winter–late winter. Cent. Amer.

livida (Lindl.) Schlechter. Sts. pseudobulbous, spindle-shaped, to 6 in. long, 1-lvd.; lvs. linear, to 6 in. long; infl. a cluster; fls. nodding, pale yellow-green to purplish, semitransparent, sepals and petals ovate, to ¼ in. long, concave, lip cordate. Winter–late spring. Mex., Guatemala, Honduras.

mesocopis (Endres & Rchb.f.) Benth. & Hook.f. ex Hemsl. Erect or creeping, sts. cylindrical or spindle-shaped, 1–2-lvd. at apex; lvs. linear, to 6 in. long; infl. a few-fld. cluster or short raceme; fls. white, tinged with purple, sepals and petals ¼ in. long, lip oblong-fiddle-shaped, obscurely toothed, disc with 1 or more raised and papillose central lines. Costa Rica, Panama.

SCHAUERIA Nees. *Acanthaceae.* About 8 spp. of herbs or shrubs of trop. Brazil; lvs. opp., entire; fls. yellow or red, in terminal spikes, calyx lobes and bracts very long and narrowly linear, giving a shaggy appearance to the fl. cluster, corolla tubular, 2-lipped, stamens 2, anther sacs 2, parallel; fr. a caps.

Propagated by cuttings.

flavicoma (Lindl.) N.E.Br. To 4 ft.; lvs. ovate or ovate-lanceolate, to 6 in. long, glossy; fls. pale yellow, 1½ in. long. Brazil.

SCHEELEA Karst. *Palmae.* About 40 spp. of often large, solitary, unarmed, monoecious palms of trop. Amer.; lvs. very large, ascending-erect on young plants, pinnate, pinnae many, 1-ribbed, acute; infls. long-peduncled, among the lvs., often pendulous, at least in fr., bracts 2, the upper very thick, woody, deeply sulcate outside, often beaked, enclosing the infl. in bud, rachillae simple, with fls. of one sex only or with fls. of both sexes; male fls. with sepals very small, petals 3, elongate, nearly cylindrical or not more than twice as wide as thick, stamens 6, shorter than petals, anthers straight, female fls. with sepals and petals imbricate, pistil 3–7-celled, stigmas 3–7; fr. usually beaked, 1- to several-seeded, mesocarp fleshy-fibrous, endocarp bony, with 3 pores near base, seed with homogeneous endosperm.

Slow-growing palms requiring many years to produce an emergent trunk. Sometimes planted in the tropics. For culture see *Palms.*

Lauromullerana Barb.-Rodr. Sts. not produced above ground; lvs. 20–24, elongate, arcuately twisted at apex, 15 ft. long or more, pinnae spreading, regularly arranged, recurved at apex; infl. more than 3 ft. long, rachillae slender, reflexed; male fls. purple; fr. oblong, yellow-green. Brazil.

Leandroana Barb.-Rodr. To 12 ft. or more, sts. with persistent petiole bases in 8 vertical rows; lvs. 26–30, erect-spreading, more than 20 ft. long, pinnae in groups and in more than 1 plane; infl. to 4½ ft. long; male fls. rose-colored, ¼ in. long, female fls. 2–4 on rachillae; fr. 1–2-seeded, to 1⅝ in. long. Cult., origin not certain.

Liebmannii Becc. To 100 ft., trunk to 2 ft. in diam.; lvs. to 20 ft. long or more, often curved at the apex, pinnae many, regularly arranged, to 4½ ft. long, nearly 3 in. wide; infl. to 4 ft. long or more; fls. cream-colored, male fls. ½ in. long, female fls. ¾ in. long; fr. ovoid or ellipsoid, to 2⅜ in. long, 1⅜ in. in diam. E. Mex.

zonensis L. H. Bailey. Sts. massive, roughened, 30 ft. high or more, 1½ ft. in diam.; lvs. to 20 ft. long or more, ascending, twisted at apex, pinnae many, regularly arranged, to 4 ft. long, 2½ in. wide; infls. to 9 ft. long, rachillae many, to 1 ft. long; fls. cream-colored, male to ⁹⁄₁₆ in. long; fr. dull orange, to 2⅝ in. long. Panama.

SCHEFFLERA J. R. Forst. & G. Forst. UMBRELLA TREE, RUBBER TREE, STARLEAF. *Araliaceae.* About 150 spp. of trop., dioecious, unarmed, evergreen shrubs or small trees; lvs. palmately compound, rarely simple, lfts. arranged in whorls at the end of the petiole; fls. mostly unisexual, in umbels arranged in racemes or panicles, petals 5–7, valvate, ovary mostly 5-celled, styles united basally; fr. a drupe, pyrenes 5 or more.

Grown as foliage plants indoors, or outdoors in subtropical or warm temperate areas.

actinophylla: *Brassaia actinophylla.*

Delavayi (Franch.) Harms. Tree, to 20 ft.; lfts. 4–7, to 9 in. long, 4½ in. wide, dentate or lobed, leathery, glabrous, dark green above, densely white-tomentose beneath; infl. terminal; fr. globose. China. Zone 9.

digitata J. R. Forst. & G. Forst. Small tree, to 25 ft.; lfts. 7–10, obovate-cuneate, to 7 in. long, sharply toothed, membranous; umbels many, in panicles to 1 ft. long; fls. small, greenish; fr. purple, globose, to ⅛ in. across. New Zeal. Zone 10.

octophylla (Lour.) Harms. Tree or shrub; lfts. 6–8, elliptic, 3–7 in. long, 1–2 in. wide, petioles glabrescent, 3–10 in. long; panicles 10 in. long; fls. small, white; fr. ⅛ in. long. S. China, Taiwan, Vietnam, Japan, Ryukyu Is. Zone 9.

SCHIMA Reinw. ex Blume. *Theaceae.* One extremely polymorphic sp. (previously interpreted as many spp.) of evergreen trees of trop. and subtrop. Asia; lvs. alt., simple; fls. showy, solitary, axillary, bisexual, sepals and petals 5–6, petals unequal, stamens many, in 3–5 series, anthers versatile, ovary superior, 5(–7)-celled; fr. a globose woody caps., separating into individual carpels, each with 3 winged seeds.

Suitable for greenhouse culture or outdoors in Zone 10. Thrives in peaty soils; propagated by cuttings under glass.

arborea: a listed name of no botanical standing for *S. Wallichii.*

kankaoensis: *S. Wallichii.*

Noronhae: *S. Wallichii.*

oblata: *S. Wallichii.*

superba: *S. Wallichii.*

Wallichii (DC.) Korth. [*S. arborea* Hort.; *S. kankaoensis* Hayata; *S. Noronhae* Reinw. ex Blume; *S. oblata* (Roxb.) Kurz; *S. superba* G. Gardn. & Champ.] To 120 ft. or more, very variable; lvs. short-petioled, mostly elliptic, rarely broadly so, to 7 in. long (to 11 in. in suckers), acuminate, entire to serrate, glossy, reddish when young; fls. scarlet in bud, opening purplish-cream to white, to 2½ in. across, fragrant, stamens golden; fr. turning whitish to red to violet, finally drying black, to 1 in. across. India, e. to Indonesia and Taiwan. Wood useful for contruction.

SCHINUS L. *Anacardiaceae.* About 28 spp. of usually dioecious trees, native mostly to S. Amer.; lvs. simple or compound; fls. small, in racemes or panicles, calyx 5-parted, petals 5, stamens 10, inserted on a disc; fr. drupaceous, round, 1-seeded.

Planted as lawn and avenue trees, but *S. Molle* harbors black scale, a pest of citrus; a few grown in subtropical regions, and in greenhouses north. Propagated by seeds or cuttings.

dependens: *S. polygamus.*

latifolius (Gillies) Engl. Small tree; lvs. simple, oblong-ovate, to 3 in. long, irregularly sinuate-dentate; fls. white, in short racemes; fr. lavender. Chile.

lentiscifolius Marchand. Shrub, to 8 ft.; lvs. compound, lfts. in 4–7 pairs, elliptic or lanceolate, nearly entire, to 1 in. long; fls. white, in loose panicles to 3 in. long; fr. pinkish or whitish. Summer. Brazil.

longifolius (Lindl.) Speg. Small tree; lvs. simple, spatulate, to 2 in. long, entire; fls. white, in axillary racemes; fr. lavender. Spring. Argentina.

Molle L. PEPPER TREE, CALIFORNIA P.T., PERUVIAN P.T., PERUVIAN MASTIC TREE, AUSTRALIAN PEPPER, MOLLE, PIRUL. Evergreen tree, 20–50 ft., with graceful hanging brs. and foliage; lvs. compound, lfts. 15–41, linear-lanceolate, to 2½ in. long, entire or toothed; fls. yellowish-white, in much-branched terminal panicles; fr. rose-colored. Summer. Andes of Peru; introd. widely elsewhere into the drier tropics and subtropics. Zone 9. Cult. in Calif.

polygamus (Cav.) Cabr. [*S. dependens* Ort.]. Shrub or small tree, to 15 ft.; lvs. simple, oblong, usually entire; fls. yellow, in short axillary racemes; fr. red to deep purple. Late spring. W. S. Amer. Hardier than other cult. spp.

terebinthifolius Raddi. BRAZILIAN PEPPER TREE, CHRISTMAS-BERRY TREE. Shrub or tree, to 20 ft., less graceful in habit than *S. Molle,* the brs. not pendent; lvs. compound, lfts. 5–13, oblong, to 2½ in. long, dark green above, lighter beneath; fr. bright red. Late summer. Brazil. Very ornamental. Weedy. Widely naturalized in peninsular Fla. and Hawaii. Much used for wreaths at Christmas.

SCHIPPIA Burret. *Palmae.* One sp., a small, unarmed palm of Brit. Honduras with bisexual fls., st. solitary; lvs. palmate, sheath fibrous, split basally below the petiole, blades divided to below middle into 1-ribbed segms. with 2-cleft apices; infl. among lvs., bearing several bracts, brs. several, rachillae with bisexual fls. near the base and above these the similar but functionally male fls.; fls. with elongate pedicel-like base, calyx 3-lobed, petals 3, valvate, stamens 6, pistil 1, 1-celled, 1-ovuled; fr. glōbose with nearly apical stigmatic residue, endosperm homogeneous, embryo near the apex.

For culture see *Palms.*

concolor Burret. To 30 ft., trunk 4 in. in diam.; lvs. long-petioled, blades to about 2½ ft. wide, segms, about 32; fls. cream-colored, about ¼ in. long; fr. white, about 1 in. in diam.

SCHISANDRA Michx. *Schisandraceae* (previously included in *Magnoliaceae).* MAGNOLIA VINE. Twenty-five spp. of twining, dioecious or monoecious shrubs, native to e. Asia and e. N. Amer.; lvs. simple, alt., congested on the short shoots, usually finely toothed; fls. axillary, red or white, perianth segms. 5–20, elliptic to obovate, male fls. with 40–60 stamens variously arranged, female fls. with 12–20 pistils in several series on receptacle, which in fr. is greatly elongated and drooping, and bears mostly red, ellipsoid to obovoid berries.

Both male and female plants should be planted to obtain the decorative fruits. *Schisandra chinensis* is hardy north. Propagated by seeds, greenwood cuttings, root cuttings, layering, and suckers.

chinensis (Turcz.) Baill. To 25 ft.; lvs. oblong-elliptic to obovate, to 4 in. long, glossy above, denticulate or serrate; fls. fragrant, on pedicels to 1½ in. long, perianth segms. 6–8, white or pinkish, anthers 4–5, sessile on short column, pistils 17–40; receptacle to 3 in. long in fr.; berries 6–23, red, to ⅜ in. long. Temp. e. Asia. Zone 5.

coccinea Michx. [*S. glabra* (Brickell) Rehd.]. BAY STAR VINE, WILD SARSAPARILLA. High-climbing; lvs. ovate to elliptic, fleshy, to 5 in. long, entire to remotely undulate-denticulate; peduncles slender, to 2 in. long; perianth segms. 9–12, crimson, to ⁵⁄₁₆ in. long, stamens 5, united into a disc ⅛ in. in diam., pistils 12–30; receptacle to 1⁵⁄₁₆ in. long in fr.; berries 7–12, red. S.C., Tenn., and Ark., s. to Fla. and La. Zone 7.

glabra: *S. coccinea.*

Henryi C. B. Clarke. Lvs. ovate to ovate-elliptic, 4–5 in. long, denticulate, glaucous underneath; peduncles 2½–4½ in. long; perianth segms. mostly 6–10, white, broad, to ½ in. long, stamens 14–40, united only at base, on a conical or clavate column in several series, pistils 50–60, in a globose head; receptacle to 5½ in. long in fr.; berries many, to ⅜ in. long. Cent. and s. China.

propinqua (Wallich) Baill. Lvs. ovate to oblong-lanceolate, to 4½ in. long, remotely denticulate or entire, petioles to ¾ in. long; peduncles to ⅜ in. long; fls. orange, petals 6–16, ⁵⁄₁₆–⅝ in. long, stamens 6–16 in a globose head, pistils 25–45 in a head; receptacle to 6 in. long in fr.; berries 10–45, red. Cent. and w. China.

SCHISANDRACEAE Blume. SCHISANDRA FAMILY. Dicot.; 2 genera of monoecious or dioecious woody vines, native to e. Asia and e. N. Amer.; lvs. alt. or congested, simple, petioled, without stipules; fls. axillary, often solitary, perianth parts few to many, all similar, male fls. with stamens 4–80, filaments fused at least basally, female fls. with many pistils borne on the elongated or rounded receptacle, ovary superior, 1-celled, 2–5-ovuled; fr. an aggregate of many berries. Related to Magnoliaceae. Both *Kadsura* and *Schisandra* are cult. as ornamentals.

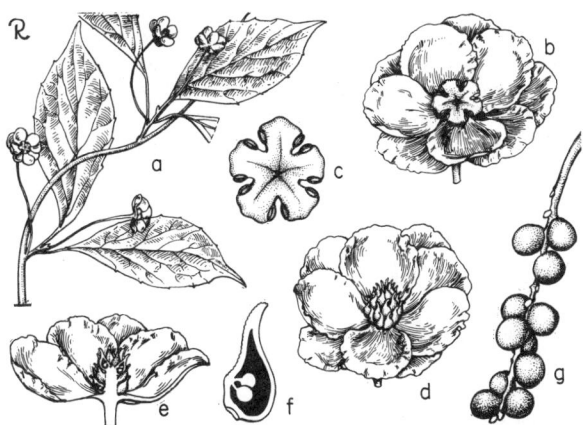

SCHISANDRACEAE. *Schisandra coccinea:* **a,** flowering branch, × ½; **b,** male flower, × 2; **c,** united stamens, top view, × 4; **d,** female flower, × 2; **e,** female flower, vertical section, × 2; **f,** pistil, vertical section, × 6; **g,** fruits on elongated receptacle, × ½. (From Lawrence, *Taxonomy of Vascular Plants.*)

SCHISMATOGLOTTIS Zoll. & Moritzi. DROP-TONGUE. *Araceae.* Perhaps 100 spp. of herbs with erect or rhizomatous sts., native to trop. Asia and Amer.; lvs. lanceolate to ovate-sagittate, petioles long, sheathing only toward base; peduncle shorter than petiole, fls. unisexual, spathe tube persistent around female fls., the blade early dehiscent, exposing the male fls. and terminal sterile appendage of spadix; ovary 1-celled, ovules many, parietal, superposed.

Strictly tropical, for culture see *Dieffenbachia.*

calyptrata (Roxb.) Zoll. & Moritzi. Plants 10–30 in. tall, sts. creeping; lf. blades rather thick, elongate-triangular, cordate-subsagittate, 6–11 in. long or more, and half as wide, petioles as long as blades to twice as long, dark green with rosy sheaths; peduncle 2–4 in. long at anthesis becoming 6–7 in. long in fr., spathe to 4¼ in. long, tube green, blade whitish. Burma and Philippine Is., s. to Malay Arch. and Indonesia.

neoguineensis (Linden) N. E. Br. Differs from *S. calyptrata* in having lf. blades ovate, cordate, thin, bright green, irregularly blotched with pale green or yellow, and peduncle and spathe shorter. New Guinea.

ornata Alderw. To 6–8 in.; lvs. nodding, blades lanceolate, to 6 in. long and 1½ in. wide, acute, velvety dark green with a gray-green central strip with feathery margins, petioles as long as blades; peduncle ¾ in. long, spathe green, 1 in. long. Borneo. Material with ovate-cordate lf. blades has been offered under this name, but is doubtfully of this sp.

picta Schott. PAINTED-TONGUE. Questionably distinct from *S. calyptrata,* from which it has been separated by its proportionally broader, ovate lf. blades to 8 in. long and 5 in. wide, or sometimes twice as large, somber green marked grayish or white between the primary veins, or the markings confluent, or with 3 longitudinal grayish bands, rarely solid pale green. Indonesia.

Roebelinii: *Aglaonema crispum.*

Rutteri Alderw. To 20 in.; lf. blades oblong, to 12 in. long and 7 in. wide, sagittate with triangular lobes, bright green, petioles as long as blades; peduncle and spathe each 3–4 in. long, spadix to 2 in. long, female zone bearing a few clavate staminodes up to twice as long as pistils. Molucca Is.

SCHIVERECKIA Andrz. *Cruciferae.* About 5 spp. of per. herbs of Eur., with minute stellate hairs; fls. white, sepals and petals 4; fr. a silicle, with convex valves. Similar to *Draba* and *Alyssum,* but differing in technical characters.

Bornmuelleri: *S. Doerfleri.*

Doerfleri (Wettst.) Bornm. [*S. Bornmuelleri* Prantl; *S. podolica* Boiss., not (Bess.) Andrz.; *Draba Doerfleri* Wettst.]. Loosely cespitose, fl. sts. to 6 in.; basal lvs. in a rosette, oblanceolate, usually entire, st. lvs. attenuate at base, entire; racemes up to 15-fld. Se. Eur.

podolica (Bess.) Andrz. [*Alyssum podolicum* Bess.]. Densely cespitose, fl. sts. to 10 in.; basal lvs. oblanceolate to oblong-spatulate, usually with 2–5 teeth on each side, st. lvs. sessile, with 1–4 teeth on each side; racemes up to 30-fld. Se. Eur. See also *S. Doerfleri.*

SCHIZACHYRIUM Nees. *Gramineae.* Fewer than 100 spp., cosmopolitan in distribution, distinguished from *Andropogon* in having racemes solitary at the ends of the sts. and their brs., rachis joints oblique, hollow at the summit, rachis and pedicels often somewhat stout, pedicelled spikelets male, neuter, or absent. For terminology see *Gramineae.*

littorale: *S. scoparium* var.

scoparium (Michx.) Nash [*Andropogon scoparius* Michx.]. BLUE-STEM, LITTLE B., BROOM BEARD GRASS, PRARIE B.G., BROOM, WIRE GRASS, BUNCHGRASS. Per., green or glaucous, often purplish, sts. to 5 ft., clustered, compressed, slender to robust, erect, the upper half branching freely; lf. sheaths and flat blades commonly glabrous or nearly so, frequently sparsely pilose at their junction, rarely hairy throughout, blades to ¼ in. wide; racemes to 2⅜ in. long, peduncles filiform, wholly or partly included in the sheaths, commonly spreading, rachis slender, flexuous, pilose; sessile spikelet mostly ¼–⁵⁄₁₆ in. long, scabrous, awn to ⅝ in. long, pedicelled spikelet usually reduced, short-awned, spreading, on pilose pedicel. Que. to Alta., s. to Fla. and Ariz. Var. **littorale** (Nash) Gould [*S. littorale* (Nash) Bickn.; *Andropogon littoralis* Nash]. Sts. more compressed, the tufts crowded on a slender rhizome, decumbent or bent at base; lower lf. sheaths broad, keeled, overlapping, often bluish-glaucous, lf. blades ⅛–¼ in. wide; rachis joints and pedicels copiously long-villous. Mass. to Ont., s. to N.C., also s. Tex.

SCHIZAEA Sm. *Schizaeaceae.* About 30 spp. of small, mostly trop. ferns; lvs. simple or dichotomously divided; sporangia in rows along the segms. of fertile lvs.

For culture see *Ferns.*

pusilla Pursh. CURLY GRASS. Forming dense tufts; sterile lvs. linear, grasslike, curled, fertile lvs. erect, longer, 3–5 in. long, terminated by pinnately disposed fertile lobes. Coast, Nfld. to N.J., well-known in the pine barrens. Sometimes planted as a curiosity, resembling a little grass more than a fern.

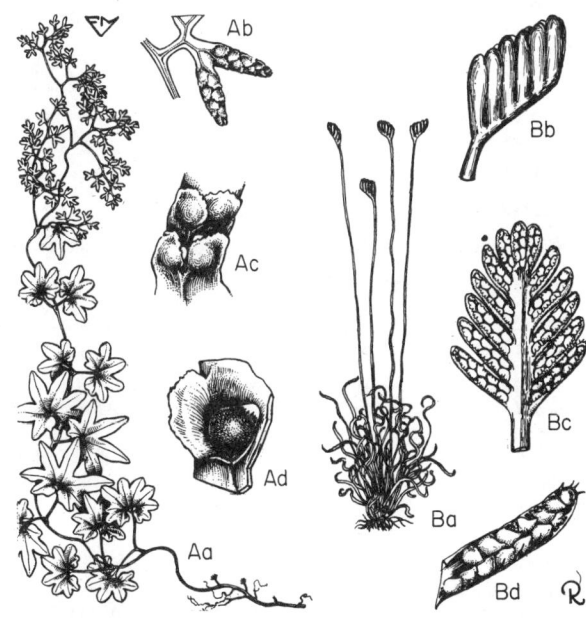

SCHIZAEACEAE. **A,** *Lygodium palmatum:* **Aa,** plant with sterile (below) and fertile (above) pinnae, × ¼; **Ab,** fertile lobes, × 2; **Ac,** sporangia covered by indusia, × 5; **Ad,** sporangium with indusium cut and opened back, × 10. **B,** *Schizaea pusilla:* **Ba,** plant, × ½; **Bb,** blade of fertile leaf, × 3; **Bc,** blade of fertile leaf, expanded, × 3; **Bd,** fertile lobe, × 6. (Aa-Ad from Bailey, *Manual of Cultivated Plants,* ed. 2.)

SCHIZAEACEAE Kaulf. CURLY-GRASS FAMILY. Ferns; 4 genera and about 150 spp. of widely distributed, mainly trop. ferns, sts. upright or creeping; lvs. simple or dichotomously or pinnately cleft, sometimes very elongate and climbing, some lvs. or some pinnae fertile; sori in rows on specialized segms., sporangia solitary, stalked, annulus complete, apical. *Anemia, Lygodium,* and *Schizaea* are cult.

SCHIZANTHUS Ruiz & Pav. BUTTERFLY FLOWER, POOR-MAN'S ORCHID. *Solanaceae.* About 10 spp. of erect, often glandular-viscid, ann. or bien. herbs, native in Chile; lvs. alt., often pinnately dissected or even pinnate, segms. incised or dentate; fls. in terminal cymes or panicles, calyx tubular, deeply 5-parted, segms. linear, corolla variously colored, tube long or short, limb spreading, more or less 2-lipped, lobes laciniate, fertile stamens 2, staminodes 3 (1 minute); fr. a 2-valved caps., seeds many, small.

Grown outdoors or in the cool greenhouse for the profusion of showy flowers. Of easy cultivation; propagated by seeds sown indoors in autumn for flowering plants in early spring or later winter; sown in the garden in May for midsummer and autumn bloom.

excelsior: a listed name of no botanical standing for *S. pinnatus* cv.

Grahamii: *S. retusus* cv.

grandiflorus: a listed name of no botanical standing for *S. pinnatus* cv.

hybridus: a listed name of no botanical standing, variously applied, often in combination with the words *grandiflorus* and *maximus,* to large fld. plants.

pinnatus Ruiz & Pav. Ann. to 4 ft., pelucid-glandular; lvs. pinnate to 2-pinnatifid, lanceolate to oblanceolate in outline, to 5 in. long; fls. long-pedicelled, in cymes, corolla variously colored, lower lip usually lilac or violet, lateral lobes linear, longer than the retuse midlobe, upper lip paler, its middle lobe with a yellow blotch near the base and spotted with purple or violet, stamens prominently exserted. Cvs. include: '**Candidissimus**', corolla white; '**Carmineus**', corolla carmine; '**Excelsior**', plant tall; '**Grandiflorus**', fls. large; '**Lilacinus**', corolla lilac; and '**Roseus**', corolla rose-pink.

retusus Hook. Vegetatively similar to *S. pinnatus,* but corolla tube as long as calyx or longer, the lower lip short, with lateral lobes linear-subulate and shorter than the elliptic, retuse midlobe. Cvs. include: '**Albus**', corolla white, middle lobe of upper lip yellowish; '**Grahamii**' [*S. Grahamii* Gillies ex Hook.], corolla lavender, middle lobe of upper lip yellow; '**Roseus**', corolla rose-pink; '**Trimaculatus**', corolla purplish-red, with 3 golden-yellow, purple-bordered spots.

× **wisetonensis** Hort. A name applied to an alleged hybrid of *S. pinnatus* × *S. retusus* cv. 'Grahamii'; intermediate between the parents; fls. from white to bluish, or from pinkish to carmine-brown, with middle lobe of upper lip mostly suffused with yellow, corolla tube shorter than calyx, stamens slightly exserted. Cv. '**Compactus**'. More dense, low-growing.

SCHIZOBASOPSIS: *BOWIEA.*

SCHIZOCAPSA: *TACCA.*

SCHIZOCASIA: *XENOPHYA.* **S. Portei:** *Alocasia Portei.*

SCHIZOCENTRON: *HETEROCENTRON.*

SCHIZOCODON: *SHORTIA.* Schizocodon macrophyllus: *Shortia soldanelloides* var. *magna.*

SCHIZOLOBIUM Vogel. *Leguminosae* (subfamily *Caesalpinioideae*). A few spp. of trees of lowland trop. Amer.; lvs. alt., very large, 2-pinnate, lfts. many, small; fls. in axillary racemes or terminal panicles, large, showy, almost regular, 5-merous, stamens 10, separate; fr. a 1-seeded, flat, spatulate legume.

Cultivated as an ornamental in warm regions.

excelsum: *S. parahybum.*

parahybum (Vell.) S. F. Blake [*S. excelsum* Vogel]. To 100 ft. or more, with buttressed trunks, young plants resembling a tree fern; lvs. to 3 ft. long, sometimes with 10 pairs of pinnae, lfts. in 15–20 pairs, narrow, oblong, silky-pubescent beneath, petioles viscid; fls. light yellow, mostly in large, erect, terminal panicles, petals ¾ in. long; fr. to 4¾ in. long, 2 in. wide. Tropics, s. Mex. to s. Brazil.

SCHIZOPETALON Sims. *Cruciferae.* About 5 spp. of erect, gray-hairy herbs of Chile; lvs. sinuately-lobed or pinnatifid; fls. purple or white, in terminal racemes, sepals 4, petals 4, pinnatifid; fr. a silique.

Walkeri Sims. Small, delicate, erect ann., to 1 ft. or more; lower lvs. 4–5 in. long, scabrid-pubescent; fls. fragrant, petals white, fringed. Sometimes grown in the fl. garden for the attractive fls. Seeds sown in the open in early May produce flowering plants late in June and through the summer. Sometimes seeds are sown in autumn and the plants carried over in a cool greenhouse, for bloom in early spring.

SCHIZOPHRAGMA Siebold & Zucc. *Saxifragaceae.* Four spp. of deciduous climbers of e. Asia, climbing by aerial rootlets; lvs. opp., entire or toothed, long-petioled; fls. white, in loose, terminal, corymbose clusters, of 2 kinds, the marginal, sterile fls. long-pedicelled, showy, consisting of a single, enlarged, petal-like calyx lobe, the fertile fls. almost sessile, small, calyx tube united to ovary, sepals and petals 4–5, stamens 10, ovary inferior, style short, stigma lobed; caps. 10-ribbed, dehiscing between the ribs.

As in *Hydrangea anomala,* young plants produce small leaves and little growth if unsupported and allowed to trail over the ground. Propagation is by seeds, greenwood cuttings struck under glass, and by layers.

hydrangeoides Siebold & Zucc. JAPANESE HYDRANGEA VINE. Climbing to 30 ft. or more; lvs. broadly ovate, to 4 in. long, rounded or cordate at base, coarsely dentate, pale beneath; infl. to 4 in. across, the enlarged calyx lobe of sterile fls. ovate to narrowly elliptic, to 1½ in. long. Japan, Korea. Zone 5. Sometimes mistaken in cult. for *Hydrangea anomala,* but readily distinguished by the sterile fls. having only 1, not 4, showy calyx lobes.

integrifolium (Franch.) D. Oliver [*S. integrifolium* vars. *denticulatum* Rehd. and *molle* Rehd.]. Climbing to 12 ft. or more; lvs. ovate or broad-ovate, to 6 in. long, entire or sparingly denticulate, pubescent beneath; infl. to 10 in. or more across, enlarged calyx lobe of sterile fls. variable in shape, from mostly elliptic to ovate, to as much as 3½ in. long. Cent. and s. China, Taiwan. Zone 7. Not as hardy as *S. hydrangeoides,* but desirable in warmer areas for its larger sterile fls. and infl.

SCHIZOSTYLIS Backh. & Harv. CRIMSON FLAG, KAFFIR LILY. *Iridaceae.* Two spp. of herbs with fibrous fleshy roots, native to S. Afr.; lvs. 2-ranked, with definite midrib; infl. a spikelike raceme; fls. red, each subtended by a green spathe, perianth tube short, segms. nearly equal, ligulate, style short, style brs. 3, long, subulate; fr. a caps.

Grown under glass to limited extent for winter bloom and cut flowers, and in the open along Pacific coast and Hawaii. Propagated by division, less commonly by seeds.

coccinea Backh. & Harv. Sts. 15–24 in.; lvs. erect, sword-shaped, 1 ft. long, ¼–½ in. wide; infl. a 4–8-fld. spike; fls. crimson-red, erect, perianth campanulate, tube 1 in. long, segms. ovate, about 1 in. long, acute; caps. obovoid-oblong, obtuse, ⅝ in. long, seeds small, angled. Cv. '**Mrs. Hegarty**'. Fls. clear pink.

SCHLEICHERA Willd. *Sapindaceae.* One sp., a deciduous, polygamodioecious tree, native to se. Asia; lvs. alt., pinnate; fls. small, clustered in interrupted spikelike racemes, regular, calyx 4–6-lobed, petals 0, stamens 5–8, filaments pubescent; fr. dry and indehiscent, seeds with a fleshy, edible aril.

oleosa (Lour.) Merrill [*S. trijugata* Willd.]. GUM-LAC, LAC TREE, CEYLON OAK. Large tree, to 60 ft.; lvs. to 14 in. long, bright red when young, lfts. usually 6, elliptic, lower ones 2–3½ in. long, terminal one 4–9 in. long; infl. to 6 in. long; fls. yellowish-green. Timber useful; an important host tree for lac insect.

trijugata: *S. oleosa.*

SCHLUMBERGERA Lem. [*Zygocactus* K. Schum.]. *Cactaceae.* Three spp. of epiphytic cacti with flat-jointed sts., native to Brazil; joints thin, obovate-truncate, crenate to serrate, with marginal areoles bearing short bristles, new joints and fls. produced apically; fls. regular or irregular, inner perianth segms. united in a tube, inner stamens united by their bases in a tube around the style, stigma lobes erect, appressed; fr. umbilicate by abcission of the perianth.

Commonly grown as window or conservatory plants for their abundant flowers in winter. For culture see *Cacti.*

Bridgesii (Lem.) Löfgr. CHRISTMAS CACTUS. Brs. arching, to 1 ft. long, joints ¾–2 in. long and ½–1 in. wide, margins 2–3-crenate; fls. nearly regular, cerise, 2½–3 in. long, ovary 4–5-angled. Winter. The common sp., often confused with *S. Russelliana* (G. Gardn.) Britt. & Rose, which is not cult., and with *S. truncata.*

Gaertneri: *Rhipsalidopsis Gaertneri.*

Makoyana: a listed name of no botanical standing for *Rhipsalidopsis Gaertneri.*

Russelliana: see *S. Bridgesii.*

truncata (Haw.) Moran [*Epiphyllum truncatum* Haw.; *Zygocactus truncatus* (Haw.) K. Schum.]. CRAB CACTUS, CLAW C., YOKE C., THANKSGIVING C., LINKLEAF. Similar to *S. Bridgesii*, but margins of joints sharply 2–4-serrate; fls. irregular, ovary cylindrical. Autumn. Var. **delicata** (N. E. Br.) Moran [*Zygocactus delicatus* (N. E. Br.) Britt. & Rose; *Z. truncatus* var. *delicatus* (N. E. Br.) Borg]. More erect, joints to nearly 3 in. long, with acuminate teeth; fls. white or becoming pink, with a carmine ring at the throat. Many hybrids and cvs. are grown, including: 'Bicolor', fls. early, white with rose; 'Salmonea', fls. salmon-pink; 'Violacea', fls. bright violet.

SCHMALTZIA: RHUS.

SCHOMBURGKIA Lindl. COW-HORN ORCHID. *Orchidaceae*. About 15 spp. of epiphytes, native to trop. Amer.; pseudobulbs 2-lvd. at apex; lvs. thick, leathery, oblong; infl. a simple raceme, on a terminal, elongated, sheathed peduncle; sepals and petals separate, spreading, undulate, lip erect, shortly united with base of column, 3-lobed, margins undulate, column winged, pollinia 8. For structure of fl. see *Orchidaceae*.

Cultivation as for *Cattleya*. For general culture see *Orchids*.

crispa Lindl. Pseudobulbs spindle-shaped, to 6 in. long; lvs. lanceolate, to 9 in. long; racemes to 3 ft. long; fls. 2½ in. across, sepals and petals similar, linear-oblong, 1 in. long, bright yellow, margins very crisped and undulate, lip pink, darker at apex, lateral lobes flat, midlobe sessile, very crisped. Guyana.

Humboldtii (Lindl.) Rchb.f. [*Laelia Humboldtii* (Lindl.) L. O. Williams]. Pseudobulbs pear-shaped, to 5½ in. long, dull light green, 2- or sometimes 3-lvd.; lvs. rigid, ovate, to 6 in. long, light green; racemes to 3 ft. long, to 20-fld., fls. opening successively upward; fls. lilac, sepals and petals elliptic, to 1½ in. long, lip obscurely 3-lobed, white with lilac venation on midlobe and margins of lateral lobes, the disc yellow, dark purple in center. Venezuela.

Lyonsii Lindl. [*Laelia Lyonsii* (Lindl.) L. O. Williams]. To 3 ft. pseudobulbs spindle-shaped, jointed, to 15 in. long; lvs. to 1 ft. long; racemes to 3 ft. long, sheaths to 2½ in. long, with purplish-brown spot; fls. 2 in. across, white, spotted with purple, sepals and petals ovate-oblong, to 1 in. long, margins crisped, lip with prominent, sometimes ridgelike veins and with undulate, crisped margins, lip sometimes dull violet with crimson veins. Late summer–late autumn. Jamaica.

superbiens (Lindl.) Rolfe [*Laelia superbiens* Lindl.]. Pseudobulbs spindle-shaped, to 1 ft. long; lvs. elliptic-oblong, as long as pseudobulbs; racemes to 6 ft. long, jointed, to 20-fld.; fls. to 5 in. across, sepals and petals lanceolate, rosy-mauve, paler at base, lip shorter, lateral lobes convolute over column, yellow, streaked with purple inside, midlobe depressed, bright rosy-purple with darker venation, the disc yellow, with 5 toothed platelike keels. Early winter–late winter. Mex. and Guatemala.

Thomsoniana Rchb.f. [*Laelia Thomsoniana* (Rchb.f.) L. O. Williams]. Pseudobulbs ovoid, to 3 in. long; lvs. elliptic, to 3 in. long, pale green; racemes to 10 in. long, 6- to many-fld., streaked with brown; fls. 2½ in. across, sepals and petals linear-oblong, lemon-colored, lip longer than sepals, lateral lobes oblong, yellow, streaked with red, midlobe orbicular, 2-lobed, crisped, bright rose-purple. W. Indies.

tibicinis Batem. ex Lindl. [*Laelia tibicinis* (Batem. ex Lindl.) L. O. Williams]. To 9 ft., pseudobulbs hollow, elongate-spindle-shaped, to 20 in. long, several-lvd. at apex; lvs. oblong-elliptic, to 14 in. long; racemes many-fld.; fls. brownish-orange to bright purple-magenta, sepals oblong-elliptic, to 2 in. long, petals linear-spatulate, to 2 in. long, margins undulate-crisped, lip whitish-yellow to purplish, lateral lobes semiorbicular, enclosing column, midlobe small, nearly orbicular, 1 in. across, margins erose-crisped. Late spring. Mex. to Panama.

undulata Lindl. [*Laelia undulata* (Lindl.) L. O. Williams]. Pseudobulbs spindle-shaped, to 1 ft. long; lvs. to 8 in. long; racemes to 5 ft. long, densely fld. at top of scape; sepals and petals linear-oblong, to 2 in. long, purplish-brown, very undulate and twisted, lateral lobes of lip oblong, rosy-purple, midlobe cordate, purple, the disc with 5 raised white ridges. Early spring. Venezuela, Colombia.

SCHONLANDIA: DELOSPERMA. S. algoense: a listed name of no botanical standing; see *Delosperma algoense*.

SCHOTIA Jacq. *Leguminosae* (subfamily *Caesalpinioideae*.) Perhaps 20 spp. of unarmed trees and shrubs, native to trop. and subtrop. Afr.; lvs. alt., even-pinnate; fls. showy, in panicles, heads, or racemes, calyx lobes 4, deciduous, petals 5, stamens 10, of 2 lengths, generally united at the base; fr. flat, oblong, leathery, thickened or winged along 1 or both sutures.

Grown as ornamentals in the greenhouse or in the open in warm regions. Propagated by seeds or half-ripened cuttings.

afra (L.) Bodin [*S. speciosa* Jacq.]. KAFFIR BEAN. Small, much-branched, shrubby tree, to 12 ft.; lfts. in 4-16 pairs, linear to oblong or obovate, to ¾ in. long; fls. pedicelled, bright red, in terminal panicles, petals much longer than calyx; fr. to 3½ in. long, green, rust, and pink while developing. Sw. S. Afr., where called HOTTENTOT'S BEAN. Seeds edible.

brachypetala Sond. TREE FUCHSIA. Large shrub or wide-spreading tree, to 40 ft.; lfts. in 4–5 pairs, obtuse to emarginate, ¾–1½ in. long; fls. pedicelled, crimson, petals minute, linear, hidden by calyx; fr. to 4 in. long, and 1 in. across. Rhodesia, Mozambique, ne. S. Afr.

capitata C. Bolle [*S. transvaalensis* Rolfe]. Slender shrub, to 20 ft., differing from *S. brachypetala* in having lf. rachis narrowly winged, and fls. with petals normally developed, narrowly obovate, exserted, more than ½ in. long. E. S. Afr., Mozambique.

latifolia Jacq. Differs from *S. brachypetala* in having fls. almost sessile, pale pink or flesh-colored, with normally developed petals. E. S. Afr.

speciosa: *S. afra*.

transvaalensis: *S. capitata*.

SCHRANKIA Willd. SENSITIVE BRIER. *Leguminosae* (subfamily *Mimosoideae*). About 20–30 spp. of per. herbs, with prickly sts. and petioles, native to N. Amer.; lvs. alt., 2-pinnate, sensitive; fls. in axillary heads or short spikes, pink or purple, 5–4-merous, with stamens as many as or twice as many as the petals, separate, exserted; fr. a linear, prickly, dehiscent legume.

Sometimes planted as ornamentals.

angustata: *S. microphylla*.

microphylla (Dryand. ex Sm.) Macbr. [*S. angustata* Torr. & A. Gray; *S. uncinata* Willd.]. Differs from *S. Nuttallii* in having more slender, prostrate or decumbent sts., oblong-linear lfts. with faint or obsolete veins, and fr. with a shorter beak, finely puberulent beneath prickles. Va. and Ky., s. to Fla. and Tex.

Nuttallii (DC.) Standl. [*S. uncinata* Torr. & A. Gray, not Willd.]. CATCLAW. Sts. decumbent, rather stout, 2–4 ft. long, very prickly throughout; lvs. with 4–8 pairs of pinnae, lfts. in 8–15 pairs, elliptic, small, strongly reticulate-veined beneath; fr. cylindrical, 2–4 in. long, beaked, the beak ⅜–¾ in. long, glabrous under the prickles. Ill. to S. Dak., s. to S.C. and Tex.

uncinata: see *S. microphylla* and *S. Nuttallii*.

SCHREBERA Roxb. *Oleaceae*. Mostly trop. trees or shrubs, about 8 spp. in Afr., 1 in Peru, and 1 in India; lvs. opp., pinnate or simple; fls. in terminal panicles, corolla white, with a dark eye, with well-developed tube and 6 lobes; fr. a woody, 2-valved caps., usually pear-shaped, seeds winged.

alata (Hochst.) Welw. [*S. Saundersiae* Harv.]. Evergreen shrub or tree, to 25 ft. or more; lvs. compound, lateral lfts. 2 pairs, elliptic, to 3½ in. long, terminal lft. to 4½ in. long, rachis more or less winged; corolla white with dark center, tube to ½ in. long; caps. to 1½ in. long. Trop. and s. Afr.

Saundersiae: *S. alata*.

tomentosa: a listed name of no botanical standing.

trichoclada Welw. Shrub or small tree, to 20 ft. or more, deciduous; lvs. simple, elliptic, to 4 in. long, nearly leathery; corolla white, with dark center, tube to ¾ in. long; caps. to 2½ in. long. Trop. E. Afr.

SCHUBERTIA Mart. *Asclepiadaceae*. Not cult. **S. albens:** a listed name of no botanical standing; material so offered may be *Araujia sericifera*.

SCHWALBEA L. CHAFFSEED. *Scrophulariaceae*. One sp., a per. herb, native to e. U.S.; lvs. alt., simple, sessile; fls. dull purplish-yellow, subtended by 2 bracteoles, in terminal spikelike racemes, calyx tubular, 5-lobed, 10–12-ribbed, corolla tubular, 2-lipped, stamens 4; fr. a septicidal caps.

americana L. [*S. australis* Penn.]. Sts. simple, pubescent, to 2 ft.; lvs. ovate or oblong, to 1½ in. long, acute, 3-nerved, upper lvs. becoming bractlike; fls. to 1½ in. long. Late spring to summer. Wet sandy soil, e. Mass. to Fla., e. to La.

australis: *S. americana*.

SCHWANTESIA Dinter. *Aizoaceae*. About 11 spp. of dwarf succulents, native to S. Afr., with lf. sheaths enclosing internodes, drying and remaining on sts.; lvs. opp., the pair unequal in size, erect or ascending, glabrous or velvety, upper side flat or slightly convex, more or less oblique, lower side rounded, usually keeled toward apex, keel eccentric, often bearing papillae (pearls) terminating in a minute hair; fls. solitary, terminal on an axillary shoot of previous year, opening in the afternoon, pedicelled, calyx 5-lobed, petals yellow or rarely orange, many, stamens many, ovary inferior, 5-celled, stigmas 5; fr. a caps., cell lids rudimentary, expanding keels narrow, with broad wings, placental tubercles absent.

Growth occurs from spring to autumn. Cultivate in sandy soil in greenhouse or window with maximum light, keeping the soil moderately moist in summer, but dry in winter and the plants at a relatively cool temperature of about 60° F. Propagated by seeds or by carefully dividing old plants. See also *Succulents*.

Pillansii L. Bolus. To 2$\frac{3}{16}$ in. high; lvs. 2 on a br., erect, glaucous-green, to 2$\frac{1}{8}$ in. long, $\frac{3}{16}$ in. thick, acute in side view but apex often oblique, upper side flat, lower side acutely keeled, keel eccentric and one side convex, the other side flat, margins and keel with dull red lines; fls. to 1$\frac{1}{4}$ in. across, solitary, diurnal, on peduncles to $\frac{5}{8}$ in. long, petals yellow. Cape Prov.

Triebneri L. Bolus. Lvs. minutely papillate and nearly velvety, glaucous-green, often spotted with dull red, to 2$\frac{3}{8}$ in. long, to about $\frac{3}{8}$ in. wide, one side rounded and widened above middle, then contracted and attenuate, thicker than the other side, tip acute to obtuse, margins entire; fls. on peduncles $\frac{5}{8}$ in. long, petals golden or orangish in age, to $\frac{3}{4}$ in. long. Cape Prov.

SCIADOPITYS Siebold & Zucc. *Taxodiaceae*. One sp., a slow-growing, monoecious, pyramidal, coniferous, evergreen tree, native to cent. and sw. Japan, brs. horizontal, ascending at tips; lvs. of 2 kinds, one small, scalelike, spirally arranged on twigs and crowded near the tips, the other large, linear, glossy dark green, grooved on upper and lower surfaces, in whorls of 20–30; male cones globose, clustered terminally on brs., female cones ovoid-globose, scales broad, subtended by a bract; seeds 5–9 to each scale, maturing in 2 years.

Propagated by seeds; thrives in fertile, moist, shady, protected sites; not tolerant of air pollution. For culture see *Conifers*.

verticillata (Thunb.) Siebold & Zucc. UMBRELLA PINE, JAPANESE U.P. Occasionally to 100 ft. or more, usually much less in cult.; scale lvs. $\frac{3}{16}$ in. long, linear lvs. 3–5 in. long, emarginate, with 2 white bands beneath; female cones 2–4 in. long. Zone 6.

SCIAPHYLLUM Bremek. *Acanthaceae*. One sp., known only in cult.; lvs. opp., purplish; fls. in terminal spikes, corolla with cylindrical tube, 2-lipped, lower lip of 3 nearly equal lobes, the lateral 2 spreading, the middle reflexed, stamens 2; fr. a stalked caps., seeds 4.

amoenum Bremek. To 2 ft., per., more or less woody at base; lvs. long-petioled, ovate, to 6 in. long, glabrous, purple beneath; fls. purple, in stiff spikes to 5 in. long. Grown in Fla.

SCILLA L. SQUILL. *Liliaceae*. Between 80 and 90 spp. of bulbous, scapose, per. herbs, native to Afr., Eur., and Asia; bulbs tunicate, lasting for several years, scales not tubular; lvs. basal; fls. blue to purple or white, subtended by a bract, or bractless, in few- to many-fld., terminal racemes, perianth segms. 6, prominently 1-nerved, stamens 6, filaments arising from segms., anthers dorsifixed; fr. a 3-lobed or 3-angled, loculicidal caps., seeds few in each cell, black, sometimes angled.

Squills are of easy culture outdoors and may be left undisturbed for many years, with an occasional top dressing. They may also be grown in pots in a cool greenhouse. Propagated by offsets planted early in autumn. The usual kinds are hardy and flower in early spring.

amethystina: *S. Litardierei* or *Brimeura amethystina*. Material offered at present as *S. amethystina* is a vigorous form of *S. Litardierei*.

amoena L. [*S. siberica* var. *amoena* Hort.]. STAR HYACINTH. To 6 in.; lvs. 4–7, strap-shaped, to 9 in. long and $\frac{5}{8}$ in. wide, flaccid; fls. rotate, blue, to $\frac{3}{4}$ in. across, in a bracted, scapes several. Nativity uncertain, probably s. Eur. or Asia Minor.

autumnalis L. AUTUMN S., STARRY HYACINTH. To 6 in.; lvs. 5–10, linear, to 6 in. long, channelled, partly cylindrical; fls. rotate, purple, to $\frac{1}{4}$ in. across, in a bractless, open, 4–20-fld. raceme on a scabrous scape, anthers purple. Autumn. Eur. and N. Afr.

bifolia L. To 6 in.; lvs. 2, seldom 3, linear to linear-lanceolate, to 8 in. long and $\frac{1}{2}$ in. wide, hooded at apex; fls. rotate, blue, to $\frac{1}{2}$ in. across, mostly nodding, in loose 3–8-fld. racemes, anthers blue. Eur. and sw. Asia. Cv. 'Alba'. Fls. white. Cv. 'Rosea'. Fls. rose.

campanulata: *Endymion hispanicus*.

chinensis: *S. scilloides*.

hispanica: *Endymion hispanicus*.

Hughii: *S. peruviana*.

hyacinthoides L. HYACINTH S. To 3 ft.; lvs. 8–12, to 1$\frac{1}{2}$ ft. long and 1$\frac{1}{4}$ in. wide, tapering to both ends, ciliate; fls. campanulate, violet-blue, $\frac{3}{4}$ in. across, long-pedicelled, in a bracted, loose, many-fld. raceme, anthers greenish. Medit. region.

italica: *Endymion italicus*.

liliohyacinthus L. Bulb with yellowish, imbricate scales, sts. to 1$\frac{1}{2}$ ft.; lvs. 5–6, linear, to about 1 ft. long and 1 in. wide; fls. campanulate, blue, to $\frac{3}{8}$ in. long, in a bracted, 6–20-fld. raceme, anthers blue-violet. N. Spain, w. France.

Litardierei Breistr. [*S. amethystina* Vis., not Salisb.; *S. pratensis* Waldst. & Kit.]. To 10 in.; lvs. 3–6, linear, to 1 ft. long and $\frac{5}{16}$ in. wide; fls. campanulate, blue, to $\frac{3}{16}$ in. long, in a bracted, dense, 12–35-fld. raceme on a glabrous scape. Yugoslavia.

maritima: *Urginea maritima*.

monophyllos Link. DWARF S. To 10 in.; lf. usually 1, strap-shaped, to about 10 in. long and $\frac{1}{2}$ in. wide; fls. campanulate, lilac-blue, to $\frac{5}{16}$ in. long, in a bracted, loose, 2–12-fld. raceme on a flexuous scape, filaments blue, anthers violet. Spain, Portugal.

natalensis Planch. To about 3 ft.; lvs. 4–9, strap-shaped-lanceolate, to 1 ft. long and 4 in. wide, acuminate; fls. rotate, blue, to $\frac{3}{4}$ in. across, in a bracted, dense, 50–100-fld. raceme on a stout scape, filaments white, anthers yellow. S. Afr.

non-scripta: *Endymion non-scriptus*.

nutans: *Endymion non-scriptus*.

peruviana L. [*S. Hughii* Bertol.]. CUBAN LILY, PERUVIAN JACINTH, HYACINTH-OF-PERU. To 1$\frac{1}{2}$ ft. or more; lvs. 5–15, strap-shaped, to 1 ft. long, margins bristly-ciliate; fls. rotate, blue-violet, purple, or white, to 1 in. across, in a bracted, dense, 50–100-fld. raceme on a stout scape, pedicels several times longer than fls., the lower ones much longer than the upper, anthers bluish. Medit. region (the specific epithet is a misnomer). Cv. 'Alba'. Fls. white.

pratensis: *S. Litardierei*.

scilloides (Lindl.) Druce [*S. chinensis* Benth.; *S. sinensis* (Lour.) Merrill]. CHINESE S., JAPANESE JACINTH. To about 1$\frac{1}{4}$ ft.; lvs. 2, linear, to 10 in. long, channelled; fls. rotate, rose-purple. to $\frac{1}{8}$ in. long, in a bracted, dense, 20–60-fld. raceme, filaments pubescent on edges, anthers yellow; fr. with cells 1-seeded. E. Asia.

siberica Andr. SIBERIAN S. To 6 in.; lvs. 2–5, strap-shaped, to 6 in. long and $\frac{1}{4}$ in. wide, ascending; scapes 1–6; fls. rotate, deep blue, to $\frac{1}{2}$ in. across, in bracted, 1–3-fld. racemes, anthers violet. Russia. Cvs. include: 'Alba', fls. white; 'Azurea', fls. bright blue; 'Taurica', earlier-blooming; fls. light blue, with dark midveins. Var. amoena: *S. amoena*.

sinensis: *S. scilloides*.

socialis: *Ledebouria socialis*.

Tubergeniana J. M. C. Hoog ex Stearn. To 5 in.; lvs. 3–5, linear-oblanceolate, to 4 in. long; fls. open-campanulate, almost white, tinged with blue, with a blue dorsal stripe on each segm., to 1$\frac{1}{2}$ in. across, in a bracted, 1–3-fld. raceme, filaments white, anthers grayish-blue. Nw. Iran.

verna Huds. SEA ONION, SPRING S. To 6 in.; lvs. 3–6, linear, to 8 in. long and $\frac{1}{8}$ in. wide, channelled; fls. violet-blue, to $\frac{1}{2}$ in. across, in a bracted, dense, 2–12-fld. corymbose raceme, anthers violet-blue. W. Eur.

violacea: *Ledebouria socialis*.

SCINDAPSUS Schott. *Araceae*. About 20 spp. of climbers, mostly in Malay Arch.; lvs. simple, petioles long-sheathing, geniculate; spathe early deciduous, spadix covered with bisexual fls.; perianth absent, ovaries 1-celled, 1-ovuled.

Strictly tropical, for culture see *Philodendron*.

aureus: *Epipremnum aureum*.

pictus Hassk. Climbing, to 40 ft.; lf. blades obliquely ovate to oblong, to 6 in. long, cordate, dark green splotched gray-green above, very pale beneath, petioles much shorter; spathe white, about 3 in. long. Malay Arch., Indonesia. Cv. 'Argyraeus' [var. *argyraeus* Engl.; *Pothos argyraeus* Hort.]. Lvs. deeply cordate, spotted silvery-gray above. The commonly cult. form.

tricolor: a listed name of no botanical standing, used for *Epipremnum aureum* cv. 'Tricolor'.

Wilcoxii: a listed name of no botanical standing, used for *Epipremnum aureum* cv. 'Wilcoxii'.

SCLERANTHUS L. KNAWE. *Caryophyllaceae.* About 10 spp. of ann. or per. herbs, widely distributed in the Old World; lvs. opp., scarious, united at base; fls. solitary, in pairs, or in terminal or axillary cymes, sepals 4 or 5, persistent in fr., petals absent, stamens 1–10, ovary 1-celled, styles 2; fr. an indehiscent, usually 1-seeded nutlet.

Not commonly cultivated, but can be used in the rock garden. Propagated by seeds or division.

biflorus (J. R. Forst. & G. Forst.) Hook.f. Closely branched per., yellowish, mat-forming; lvs. subulate, to ⅜ in. long, nearly mucronate; fls. in sessile pairs, terminal on axillary peduncle, each fl. subtended by 2 bracts, sepals 4, acute, stamen 1; fr. with sepals persistent. New Zeal., Tasmania, Victoria, New S. Wales.

Brockiei Williamson. Loosely tufted per.; lvs. linear, to ¼ in. long, not leathery; fls. sessile, in pairs, sepals 5, stamen 1. New Zeal.

uniflorus Williamson. Compact, tufted per.; lvs. linear, about ³⁄₁₆ in. long, appressed to st., slightly curved, rather leathery and rigid; fls. solitary, sessile, sepals 4, stamen 1. New Zeal.

SCLEROCACTUS Britt. & Rose. *Cactaceae.* Six spp. of small, ovoid, undulate-ribbed cacti of the sw. U.S.; sts. mostly solitary, globose to short-cylindrical, ribs 10–18, undulate to tubercled; spines smooth, usually 1 or more central spines hooked; fls. subapical, funnelform, scales of ovary few, erose, slightly woolly in axils; fr. thin-walled, opening by a basal pore or by 2–3 short, vertical lines, seeds tubercled, black, hilum lateral, large.

For culture see *Cacti.*

intermedius: *S. Whipplei* var.

polyancistrus (Engelm. & Bigel.) Britt. & Rose [*Echinocactus polyancistrus* Engelm. & Bigel.]. Sts. globose to oblong, to 16 in. high and 5 in. thick, ribs 10–17, undulate; radial spines 15–20, needle-shaped, flat, white, to 2 in. long, central spines 6–11, the upper one curved, 4-angled, white, to 5 in. long, the others nearly cylindrical, purplish, mostly hooked, to 3½ in. long; fls. purple to red, to 3 in. long, style glabrous; fr. 1¼ in. long. Spring. Sw. Utah, s. Nev., nw. Ariz., se. Calif.

Whipplei (Engelm. & Bigel.) Britt. & Rose. Sts. globose to oblong, to 8 in. high and 4 in. thick, ribs 13–15, somewhat tubercled; radial spines 7–11, flattened, white, ¾ in. long, central spines 2–5, the upper flat, white, ascending, to 1½ in. long, hooked spines 1–2; fls. greenish-yellow to pink, purple, or white, to 2 in. long, style puberulent. Late spring to summer. Sw. Colo., s. Utah, ne. Ariz. Var. **Whipplei.** The typical var.; sts. depressed-globose to short-ovoid, to 3 in. high and 3½ in. long and thick; lower hooked central spine purplish-pink, to 1½ in. long; fls. yellow, to 1 in across. Ariz. Var. **intermedius** (Peebles) L. Bens. [*S. intermedius* Peebles]. Sts. elongate, to 8 in. long and 4 in. thick; lower hooked central spine reddish, ; fls. purple, pink, or rarely white. Utah, Colo., Ariz., New Mex.

SCOLOPENDRIUM: *PHYLLITIS.*

SCOLOPIA Schreb. *Flacourtiaceae.* About 45 spp. of Old World shrubs or small trees; lvs. simple, alt.; fls. small, usually in axillary racemes, sepals and petals 4–6, stamens many; fr. fleshy, berrylike.

Ecklonii (Arn.) Harv. Small, unarmed tree, to 20 ft.; lvs. rhombic, entire or repand-dentate, to 3 in. long; racemes few-fld. S. Afr. Zone 10.

SCOLYMUS L. *Compositae* (Cichorium Tribe). Three spp. of stout, erect or wide-branching, thistlelike herbs with milky sap, native in the Medit. region, sts. spiny-winged; lvs. alt., spiny-toothed or -lobed; fl. heads sessile, involucral bracts spine-tipped, receptacle scaly; fls. all ligulate, yellow; achenes compressed, each enclosed by a winged receptacle scale, pappus a low ring or a few deciduous bristles.

The Spanish oyster plant is occasionally grown for its edible taproot; it is milder in flavor than the root of the true oyster plant *(Tragopogon).* Cultivation as for parsnips and the oyster plant; grown from seed.

hispanicus L. SPANISH OYSTER PLANT, GOLDEN THISTLE. Bien., much-branched, to 4 ft., usually pubescent; heads about 1 in. long, terminal and axillary, subtended by leafy bracts; pappus of 2–3 bristles. S. Eur.

SCORZONERA L. *Compositae* (Cichorium Tribe). About 150 spp. of per., rarely ann. herbs with milky sap, native to Eur., and cent. Asia; lvs. more or less grasslike, sometimes lobed or dissected; fl. heads long-peduncled, involucre cylindrical or campanulate, the outer involucral bracts short, the inner long, receptacle naked; fls. all ligulate, yellow, purple, or rose; achenes ribbed, pappus of plumose bristles with interwoven lateral hairs.

One species is cultivated as a root vegetable, like parsnips and salsify. It is treated as an annual or biennial, grown from seeds. The leaves are also eaten in salads.

hispanica L. BLACK SALSIFY, SPANISH S., VIPER'S GRASS, BLACK OYSTER PLANT. Per., to 3 ft., usually somewhat pubescent, the long, fleshy taproot with a black skin; lvs. oblanceolate to linear, to 16 in. long, undulate, the basal ones long-petioled; heads to 2 in. across, expanded only in the morning; fls. yellow. Eur.

SCROPHULARIA L. FIGWORT. *Scrophulariaceae.* About 200 spp. of strong-scented, coarse, bien. or per. herbs, or subshrubs, native to the N. Hemisphere; sts. 4-angled; lvs. opp. or the upper sometimes alt., simple or compound; fls. greenish, purple, red, or yellow, small, not showy, in terminal cymes arranged in panicles, calyx 5-parted, corolla tubular, irregularly 5-lobed, stamens 4; fr. a septicidal caps.

Rarely planted in the flower border or for medicinal purposes.

californica Cham. & Schlechtend. Per., to 5 ft.; lvs. ovate, to 6 in. long, cordate to truncate, serrate to doubly serrate; infl. often sticky-hairy; fls. dull red, to ⅝ in. long. Winter to summer. Vancouver Is. to s. Calif.

chrysantha Jaub. & Spach. Glandular-hairy per. or bien., to 2 ft.; lvs. ovate or orbicular, cordate, doubly serrate, lower lvs. long-petioled, upper lvs. sessile; fls. yellow, to ½ in. long, stamens long-exserted. Caucasus.

marilandica L. CARPENTER'S-SQUARE. Glabrous per., to 10 ft., sts. with rounded angles and sunken, grooved sides; lvs. ovate to ovate-lanceolate, to 5 in. long or more, cordate or rounded, serrate or serrate-dentate, slender-petioled; fls. dull greenish-purple outside, ⁵⁄₁₆ in. long. Summer, autumn. Me. to Minn., s. to S.C., Ga., La., Okla.

SCROPHULARIACEAE Juss. FIGWORT FAMILY. Dicot.; about 210 genera and nearly 3,000 spp., mostly ann. or per. herbs or shrubs, rarely trees, of cosmopolitan distribution; lvs. alt. or opp., rarely whorled or clustered, entire or lobed to pinnatifid; infl. various; fls. bisexual, typically irregular, calyx 4–5-lobed or -parted, corolla 4–5-lobed, often 2-lipped, sometimes personate, sometimes nearly regular, stamens usually 4, sometimes 2 or 5, ovary superior, 2-celled; fr. typically a caps., rarely a berry or indehiscent. Plants of many genera are grown as ornamentals and some for medicinal purposes. The cult. genera are: *Agalinis, Alonsoa, Anarrhinum, Angelonia, Antirrhinum, Asarina, Aureolaria, Bacopa, Bartsia, Besseya, Bowkeria, Buchnera, Calceolaria, Campylanthus, Castilleja, Celsia, Chaenorrhinum, Chelone, Chionophila, Collinsia, Cymbalaria, Diascia, Digitalis, Erinus, Galvezia, Halleria, Hebe, Hebenstretia, Isoplexis, Jovellana, Leucocarpus, Leucophyllum, Leucospora, Limnophila, Linaria, Lindenbergia, Mazus, Micranthemum, Mimulus, Mohavea, Nemesia, Orthocarpus, Ourisia, Parahebe, Pedicularis, Penstemon, Phygelius, Rhinanthus, Russelia, Schwalbea, Scrophularia, Selago, Sopubia, Sutera, Synthyris, Tetranema, Tonella, Torenia, Verbascum, Veronica, Veronicastrum, Walafrida, Wulfenia,* and *Zaluzianskya.*

SCUTELLARIA L. SKULLCAP. *Labiatae.* About 300 spp. of cosmopolitan, rhizomatous, per. herbs, bitter, not aromatic; sts. mostly square in cross section; lvs. opp., simple; fls. in pairs., remote or in dense, oblong, sometimes paniculate racemes, calyx campanulate, 2-lipped, lips entire, with crest-like projection on back of upper lip, closed in fr., corolla tube long, curved upwards from base, glabrous inside, limb 2-lipped, stamens 4, anthers hairy; fr. of 4 nutlets.

albescens: a listed name of no botanical standing.

albida L., Per., 1½–2½ ft.; lvs. triangular, 1½ in. long, crenate, more or less pubescent; fls. in a dense, 1-sided raceme, bracts green, corolla about ½ in. long, white. Se. Eur. to cent. Asia.

SCROPHULARIACEAE. **A,** *Veronica latifolia:* **Aa,** flowering stems, × ⅛; **Ab,** flower, × 2; **Ac,** flower, longitudinal section, × 2; **Ad,** corolla expanded, × 2; **Ae,** ovary, cross section, × 8; **Af,** capsule, × 5. **B,** *Mazus reptans:* **Ba,** plant, × ½; **Bb,** flower, × 1; **Bc,** flower, longtudinal section, × 2; **Bd,** flower, corolla expanded (apical half cut off), × 2; **Be,** ovary, cross section, × 8. **C,** *Penstemon barbatus:* **Ca,** flowering stems, × ⅒; **Cb,** flower, × ¾; **Cc,** corolla expanded, × ¾; **Cd,** flower, longitudinal section, × 1; **Ce,** ovary, cross section, × 10; **Cf,** capsule, × 1. **D,** *Verbascum Blattaria:* **Da,** plant, × ⅛; **Db,** flower, back and face views, × ½; **Dc,** corolla expanded (lobes cut off), × 1½; **Dd,** pistil, × 3; **De,** ovary, vertical section, × 5; **Df,** ovary, cross section, × 5. **E,** *Antirrhinum majus:* **Ea,** plant, × ⅒; **Eb,** flower, × ½; **Ec,** flower with lower lip cut off, × ½; **Ed,** capsule, × 1. **F,** *Digitalis purpurea:* flower, × ½. **G,** *Chelone glabra:* flower, × 1. **H,** *Diascia Barbarae:* flower, back view, × 1. **I,** *Pedicularis canadensis:* flower, × 1. **J,** *Calceolaria tripartita:* flower, face and side views, × 1.

alpina L. Spreading, to 10 in.; lvs. ovate, to 1 in. long, minutely crenate-serrate, glabrous to pubescent, subsessile; fls. in dense, terminal racemes, bracts purplish; corolla 1 in. long, purple. Mts. of s. Eur. to Siberia.

baicalensis Georgi. To 15 in., sts. basally decumbent; lvs. lanceolate, obtuse, entire, ciliate, subsessile; fls. in a 1-sided raceme, corolla bluish-purple, upper lip incurved. E. Asia. Cv. 'Coelestina'. Fls. bright blue, in spicate racemes.

Brittonii T. C. Porter. Rhizomatous, 6–10 in.; lvs. ovate-elliptic, to 1¼ in. long, entire, uppermost lvs. sessile; corolla 1–1⅜ in. long, deep violet-blue. Wyo. to Colo., n. New Mex.

californica A. Gray. Per., 6–10 in.; lvs. ovate to oblong-elliptic, to 1¼ in. long, pubescent, lower lvs. crenate-serrate, upper lvs. entire; corolla to ¾ in. long, yellowish-white. Ore., Calif.

canescens: *S. incana.*

coelestina: a listed name of no botanical standing for *S. baicalensis* cv.

Columnae All. Per., 2–3 ft.; lvs. ovate, to 2 in. long, cordate at base, crenate-serrate; fls. in a raceme to 8 in. long, corolla to 1 in. long, strongly curved, purplish, lower lip whitish. Se. Eur.

costaricana H. Wendl. Slender, per., 1½–3 ft., rarely to 6 ft.; lvs. elliptic to ovate-elliptic, 3–5½ in. long, acuminate, petioled; fls. in a 1-sided raceme, calyx purple, corolla 2½ in. long, erect, orange-scarlet, lips deep yellow inside. Costa Rica. Tender.

epilobiifolia: *S. galericulata.*

galericulata L. [*S. epilobiifolia* A. Hamilt.]. Per., 1–2 ft.; lvs. ovate-oblong, to 2½ in. long, nearly truncate at base, acute, crenate-serrate; fls. in remote axillary pairs, corolla ½–¾ in. long, violet-blue, with white markings, tube curved. Cosmopolitan in n. temp. regions.

hirta Sibth. & Sm. Sts. erect, to 10 in., densely pubescent; lvs. ovate, to ¾ in. long, truncate to cordate at base, coarsely crenate, petioled; fls. in few-fld. infl., corolla cream, about ⅜ in. long, upper lip reddish. Mts., Crete.

incana K. Spreng. [*S. canescens* Nutt.]. To 4 ft., robust; lvs. ovate, 2½–5 in. long, crenate-serrate, petioled; fls. in showy, more or less corymbose panicle, corolla to ¾ in. long, blue, gray-pubescent. Ont., s. to Va. and Mo.

indica L. To 1 ft., basally procumbent; lvs. ovate, to 1 in. long, crenate-serrate, petioled; fls. in dense raceme to 4 in. long, corolla to ¾ in. long, bluish. China, Japan. Cvs. include: 'Alba', fls. white; 'Humilis', semiprostrate, to 6 in., may belong to *S. laetiviolacea* G. Koidz., a sp. not otherwise known in cult. Var. **parvifolia** (Mak.) Mak. [*S. japonica* Hort., not Burm.f.]. Plant 4–7 in.; fls. lilac to blue; may belong to *S. abbreviata* Hara, a sp. not otherwise known in cult.

integrifolia L. Per., 1–2 ft.; lvs. ovate to narrowly elliptic, 1–2½ in. long, mostly entire, appressed-hairy on both sides, petioled; fls. in raceme 2–4 in. long, sometimes branched at base, corolla 1 in. long, blue to whitish. Conn., s. to Fla. and Mo.

japonica: see *S. indica* var. *parvifolia.*

longifolia Benth. To 20 in.; lvs. ovate to ovate-lanceolate, mostly 3–4 in. long, acuminate, sinuate-serrate, petioled; fls. in racemose to paniculate infl. 4–12 in. long, corolla 1¼ in. long, scarlet. Mex. to El Salvador.

orientalis L. Decumbent, woody; lvs. ovate to oblong, to ¾ in. long, incised-dentate, white-tomentose beneath, long-petioled; fls. in racemose infl., corolla yellow, rarely pink, lower lip often reddish. Mts. of se. Spain, and se. Eur. to Siberia. Varies greatly in dissection of lvs. and in size and shape of bracts. Var. **pinnatifida** Boiss. Lower lvs. deeply pinnatifid, upper lvs. less so. Greece to Iran.

ovata subsp. **versicolor:** *S. versicolor.*

parvula Michx. Densely glandular-hairy, 4–12 in.; lvs. triangular-ovate, mostly ⁵⁄₁₆–⅝ in. long, capitate-glandular-hairy, erosely dentate; fls. axillary, corolla scarcely ½ in. long, blue. Que. to Va., w. to Minn. and Tex.

resinosa Torr. Much-branched, to 9 in., from woody root crown; lvs. ovate to nearly orbicular, to ⅝ in. long, obtuse, short-petioled; corolla to ¾ in. long, deep blue-violet. Kans. to Tex. and Ariz.

scordiifolia Fisch. ex Schrank. Ann. or per., to 18 in.; lvs. oblong, mostly 1 in. long, obtuse to acutish, crenate-serrate; fls. axillary, calyx purplish, corolla ½ in. long, blue. E. Eur. and Asia.

tuberosa Benth. To 5 in., sometimes mat-forming, tuberous; lvs. ovate, to ½ in. long, coarsely dentate, viscid-villous; fls. axillary, corolla to ¾ in. long, violet-purple. Ore., Calif., Baja Calif.

versicolor Nutt. [*S. ovata* J. Hill subsp. *versicolor* (Nutt.) Epl.]. To 3 ft., soft-hairy; lvs. ovate to orbicular, 2¼–4½ in. long, cordate, crenate-serrate, rugose; fls. in a panicle 4–6 in. long, corolla about 1 in. long, bright blue, with whitish lower lip. Ind. to Minn., s. to S.C. and Tex.

SCUTICARIA Lindl. *Orchidaceae.* Three spp. of epiphytes, native to trop. Amer.; pseudobulbs small; lvs. cylindrical, long; infl. lateral, 1- to several-fld.; fls. conspicuous, sepals and petals spreading, similar, lip 3-lobed, jointed to long column foot, pollinia 2. For structure of fl. see *Orchidaceae.*

For culture see *Orchids.*

Steelei Lindl. Pseudobulbs oblong, with solitary, pendent lvs. 2–5 ft. long; infl. a 1–3-fld. raceme; fls. 2½ in. across, fragrant, primrose-yellow, blotched with reddish-brown, sepals and petals 1½ in. long, lip pale yellow with brownish-crimson striations, the crest with orange teeth in front. Flowering throughout the year. Guyana.

SEAFORTHIA: *PTYCHOSPERMA,* but for plants cult. as *Seaforthia* see *Archontophoenix Cunninghamiana.*

SEA KALE. The sea kale is *Crambe maritima,* a heavy, hardy, succulent, perennial herb of the coasts of western Europe, grown for the young shoots, which, when blanched, are used as a pot herb like asparagus. The great, thick, glaucous-blue leaves are conspicuous and showy and may be used to advantage even in ornamental borders (see *Crambe*).

The young spring shoots (leaf stalks) of sea kale are blanched by growing into loose fine earth with which the crown has been covered to the depth of 1 foot or more; or a light-tight box or other receptacle may be inverted over the plant. If the growth is not cut for the kitchen until late in the season, it is well to allow a part of the plant to go naturally into leaf in order to maintain the vigor of the root; and in any case, after the cutting is over, the plant should be stimulated into good growth for the remainder of the season, as with asparagus and rhubarb. Sea kale should give good yields for eight to ten years.

Sea kale comes readily from seeds, sown in their globular seedlike pods. It is well to carry the seedlings in a bed the first year, and then to transplant to permanent quarters. The field distance is ordinarily about 3 × 3 feet. A good harvest from seedlings should be had the third year from seed. The plant is also propagated by means of root cuttings, and a good crop may then be taken the second year. Cuttings 4 or 5 inches long are made of vigorous roots, and these cuttings are usually planted directly in the field.

SEAWEEDS: see *Algae.*

SECALE L. RYE. *Gramineae.* Five spp. of ann. or per. grasses in Eurasia, sts. erect; lf. blades flat; spikes dense; spikelets usually 2-fld., compressed, solitary, placed flatwise against and on opp. sides of the terminal rachis, rachilla disarticulating above the glumes, glumes subulate, 1-nerved, rigid, lemma broader, sharply keeled, 5-nerved, ciliate on the keel and exposed margins, tapering into a long awn. For terminology see *Gramineae.*

cereale L. COMMON R. Ann., glaucous, sts. to 5 ft., slender, glabrous to pubescent near the spike; lf. blades soft, smooth or slightly scabrous, to ½ in. wide, sheaths long and loose; spike to 6 in. long, curved, narrow; spikelets with 2 fertile florets, lemma long and narrow, keel prominently set with stiff points or teeth; fr. oblong, about ⁵⁄₁₆ in. long. A cultigen without well-marked races, supposedly developed from *S. montanum* Guss., a per. in the mts. of sw. Asia. An important cereal and fodder crop, cult. principally in n. Eur.

SECHIUM P. Br. *Cucurbitaceae.* One sp., a tendril-bearing, monoecious, herbaceous vine with tuberous per. root, native to trop. Amer.; fls. small and whitish, male fls. racemose, filaments united, anthers separate, flexuous, female fls. 1 or 2, axillary; fr. large, thick, fleshy, with 1 large seed.

edule (Jacq.) Swartz. CHAYOTE, CHOYOTE, CHRISTOPHINE. Tall-climbing or running; lvs. broad-ovate to triangular-ovate, to 10 in. across, angled or shallowly lobed; fr. of various sizes and shapes in the cult. vars., mostly somewhat pear-shaped, 3–4 in. long, furrowed, green or whitish, the apex puckered over the seed, which is 1–2 in. long. Much grown in the tropics and warm-temp. regions for the edible frs. and tubers, cooked as vegetables. For cult. see *Chayote.*

SECURIDACA L. *Polygalaceae.* About 70 spp. of trees or often scandent shrubs of tropics of New and Old World, except Australia; lvs. alt., simple, entire, with stipular glands; fls. in axillary and terminal, often panicled racemes, irregular, sepals 5, the inner 2 petal-like (wings), petals 3, the lower petal usually keeled, clawed, with a fringed crest, stamens 8, filaments united into a sheath split on upper side; fr. a samara with a dorsal wing.

diversifolia (L.) S. F. Blake [*Polygala diversifolia* L.]. Trailing or climbing shrub; lvs. elliptic-oblong to ovate or elliptic, to 5 in. long, thick, pubescent, shining and prominently reticulate above, petioles short; fls. pink to purplish, keel with a yellow tip; samara puberulous. W. Indies and Mex., s. to Ecuador.

longipedunculata Fresen. Shrub or small tree, 10–25 ft.; lvs. oblong to linear-lanceolate or oblong-ovate, to 2 in long, glabrous or glabrescent, petioles short; fls. in terminal racemes, red or purple, fragrant; samara glabrous. Trop. Afr.

SECURINEGA Comm. ex Juss. *Euphorbiaceae.* About 20 spp. of monoecious or dioecious, deciduous shrubs of temp. and subtrop. regions; lvs. alt., simple, entire, short-petioled; fls. without petals, axillary, male fls. in clusters, female fls. solitary, ovary 3-celled; fr. a caps.

flueggeoides: *S. suffruticosa.*

ramiflora: *S. suffruticosa.*

suffruticosa (Pall.) Rehd. [*S. fleuggeoides* Müll. Arg.; *S. ramiflora* (Ait.) Müll. Arg.]. Shrub, with spreading sts., to 6 ft.; lvs. elliptic to lanceolate-ovate, to 2½ in. long, wedge-shaped at base, mostly bright green; fls. greenish; caps. ¼ in. in diam., on long peduncles. Ne. Asia.

×SEDADIA Moran. *Sedum* × *Villadia. Crassulaceae.*

amecamecana (Praeg.) Moran [*Sedum* × *amecamecanum* Praeg.]: *S. dendroideum* × *V. Batesii.* Glabrous, sts. branching, decumbent, to 1 ft.; lvs. alt., crowded to somewhat scattered, oblanceolate, ¾ in. long, flat, acute, green; infl. terminal, roundish; fls. pale yellow, ⅝ in. wide. Late spring. Mex.

SEDASTRUM: *SEDUM.*

SEDUM L. [*Clementsia* Rose; *Corynephyllum* Rose; *Gormania* Britt.; *Rhodiola* L.; *Sedastrum* Rose; *Sinocrassula* A. Berger]. STONECROP, ORPINE. *Crassulaceae.* Perhaps 600 spp. of succulent, mostly per. herbs and subshrubs of the N. Temp. Zone and mts. of the tropics; lvs. commonly alt., often small and overlapping, mostly sessile; infl. commonly terminal, mostly a cyme of 2 or more cincinni; fls. mostly 5-merous, sepals separate or nearly so, equal or unequal, sometimes spurred, petals separate or shortly united, commonly yellow or white, mostly spreading, stamens usually twice as many, rarely as many, carpels usually separate or nearly so; fr. of follicles. The largest genus of the family, difficult to separate on technical characters from some other genera.

The genus has been divided into 8 informal groups; in effect, 7 peripheral groups are removed, leaving most species in the ill-defined and unwieldy Sedum (Eusedum) group which is not readily further divided into large natural units. The species of a group possess the characteristics of that group. These characteristics are not repeated in the brief descriptions of the species; instead, the following symbols are used to indicate the group to which each species belongs: A, Aizoon; E, Sedum (Eusedum); G, Gormania; P, Pachysedum; R, Rhodiola; S, Sedastrum; Sin, Sinocrassula; T, Telephium.

The distinguishing characters of the groups follow:

Aizoon group (A). Hardy per. herbs, with woody rhizomes and mostly ann. shoots; lvs. mostly alt., flat and thin, mostly toothed or crenate; fls. nearly sessile, 5-merous, yellow, petals separate, carpels slightly united, divergent at maturity. Ne. Asia.

Gormania group (G). Hardy per. herbs, with horizontal sts. and evergreen rosettes; lvs. alt. or especially on the offsets opp., glabrous, spatulate; infl. terminal; petals erect at least in the lower $\frac{1}{10}$, and often united in the lower $\frac{1}{4}$. Calif. to B.C.

Pachysedum group (P). Tender, glabrous shrubs or subshrubs; lvs. alt., mostly turgid, entire or retuse; fl. sts. often axillary; fls. 5-merous, yellow or white, petals separate or nearly so. Mex. Not clearly delimited from the Sedum group and probably not a natural group.

Rhodiola group (R). Hardy, glabrous, per. herbs, dioecious or with bisexual fls., root crown with broad-based lvs. often reduced to scales; fl. sts. axillary, strictly ann., mostly simple and erect, their lvs. mostly alt., flat, often toothed; fls. 4–5-merous, petals nearly separate. N. temp. and subarctic regions.

Sedastrum group (S). Tender per. herbs, with thick rhizomes and bien. shoots that remain as rosettes until flowering time; lvs. alt., thick, usually pubescent; infl. paniculate; fls. sessile, 5-merous, white, petals separate, carpels erect, concave behind the nectar glands. Mex.

Sedum (Eusedum) group (E). Hardy or tender, mostly per. herbs, sts. commonly decumbent basally and low, dying back after flowering; lvs. mostly evergreen; fl. sts. usually terminal; petals mostly separate or nearly so. N. Hemisphere.

Sinocrassula group (Sin). Hardy, bien. or per. herbs, with dense basal rosettes; lvs. alt., turgid, red-flecked; infl. terminal; fls. 5-merous, petals white or reddish, erect, S-shaped, urceolate-connivent, stamens 5. Himalayas to w. China.

Telephium group (T). Hardy, glabrous, per. herbs, with short, thick or slender rhizomes, often with tuberous roots; fl. sts. strictly ann. or lower part persisting; lvs. alt. or whorled, flat and thin, mostly crenate or dentate; infl. corymbose; fls. mostly 5-merous, white to red or purple, petals nearly separate, carpels erect, narrowed below. Eur., Asia, e. N. Amer.

Some of the species are grown under glass for the interesting habit and more or less showy bloom. The low, hardy kinds are popular in rock gardens and edgings. The stonecrops are of easy cultivation, even in thin poor soils. Propagated by seeds or offsets or pieces planted as cuttings. See also *Succulents.*

acre L. GOLDEN-CARPET, GOLD MOSS. E; glabrous, creeping, mat-forming, evergreen, to 5 in.; lvs. alt., overlapping, triangular-ovoid, to $\frac{3}{16}$ in. long; fls. bright yellow, to $\frac{1}{2}$ in. wide, on 2–3 short brs., petals lanceolate, acute, longer than stamens; follicles wide-spreading. Early summer. The common stonecrop of walls, rocky places, and yards, naturalized in the North and often colonized as a mosslike cover plant. N. Afr., Eur., w. Asia. Cvs. are: **'Aureum'**, foliage yellow; **'Majus'**, larger; **'Minus'**, smaller.

Adolphi Hamet. GOLDEN SEDUM. P; loosely bushy, to 1 ft.; lvs. somewhat scattered, elliptic-lanceolate, to 2 in. long and $\frac{3}{8}$ in. thick, nearly acute, keeled beneath, flattened above; fl. sts. axillary but similar to sterile sts., with lvs. about half as long, infl. paniculate, pedicels $\frac{5}{16}$–$\frac{1}{2}$ in. long; petals white, ovate-lanceolate, stamens $\frac{3}{16}$ in. long or more. Mex. Plants offered under this name are likely to be *S. Nussbaumeranum.*

Aizoon L. [*S. Maximowiczii* Regel; *S. Woodwardii* N. E. Br.]. A; glabrous, leafless in winter, rhizome short, ann. sts. few, erect, 1–2 ft.; lvs. alt, linear-lanceolate to oblong-lanceolate, 2–3 in. long, acute, toothed from below middle; infl. corymbose, many-fld.; fls. yellow to orange, $\frac{1}{2}$ in. wide. Summer. Siberia to Japan. Commonly cult. in the North. Cvs. are: **'Atrosanguineum'**, listed; **'Floribundum'**, very tall, narrow-lvd.; **'Major'**, listed.

alamosanum S. Wats. E; glabrous, tufted, to 5 in.; lvs. alt., crowded, linear-oblong, $\frac{1}{4}$ in. long, blunt, glaucous, papillose; fls. few, white or greenish, pinkish at center, $\frac{3}{8}$ in. wide. Spring. Nw. Mex.

Albertii Regel. E; glabrous; sts. many, to 6 in.; lvs. alt., crowded, linear-oblong, $\frac{1}{4}$ in. long, nearly cylindrical, obtuse, tubercled; fls. nearly sessile, white, $\frac{3}{8}$ in. wide. Late spring, early summer. W. Siberia. See also *S. gracile.*

$\times$ **alboroseum:** *S.* $\times$ *erythrostictum.*

album L. [*S. balticum* Hartm.]. E; glabrous, mat-forming, 3–8 in.; lvs. alt., linear-oblong to ovate or even globose, $\frac{1}{8}$–$\frac{5}{8}$ in. long, obtuse, cylindrical or nearly so; infl. paniculate, pedicels to $\frac{3}{16}$ in. long; fls. white, $\frac{3}{8}$ in. wide, petals obtuse, pistils erect. Early summer. Eur., w. Asia, N. Afr. Commonly cult., variable. Cvs. are: **'Athoum'** [*S. athoum* DC.], lvs. smaller, infl. fewer-fld.; **'Brevifolium'**, lvs. very short; **'Chloroticum'**, yellowish-green, fls. greenish-white; **'Murale'** [*S. murale* Hort., not Sessé & Moç.], and **'Purpureum'**, lvs. purple, fls. pinkish; cvs. **'Bathoniense'**, **'Minus'**, **'Pallens'**, **'Roseum'**, and **'Tenuifolium'** are also listed. Var. **micranthum** (Bast.) DC. [*S. micranthum* Bast.]. Fls. half as large. Pyrenees, N. Afr.

allantoides Rose. P; glabrous, odorous, branching below, to 1 ft.; lvs. alt., scattered, club-shaped to triangular-obovate, 1–2 in. long, $\frac{1}{4}$–1 in. wide, glaucous; infl. a terminal, open panicle; fls. $\frac{3}{4}$ in. wide, petals white, red-marked near tip. Winter, spring. S. Mex.

alpestre Vill. E; glabrous, creeping; lvs. alt., crowded, oblong-obovate, to $\frac{3}{8}$ in. long, obtuse, turgid but flattened; fl. sts. to 3 in., loosely leafy; fls. few, $\frac{3}{16}$ in. long, sepals like lvs., petals erect, greenish-yellow. Early summer. Mts., Eur., Asia Minor.

altissimum: *S. sediforme.*

$\times$ **amecamecanum:** $\times$ *Sedadia amecamecana.*

amplexicaule: *S. tenuifolium.*

Anacampseros L. EVERGREEN O. T; sterile sts. creeping, with terminal rosettes; lvs. obovate to orbicular, $\frac{1}{4}$–1 in. long, obtuse, or retuse, or minutely pointed, entire, spurred, glaucous; fl. sts. 6–10 in.; fls. densely clustered, $\frac{1}{4}$ in. wide, dull purple. Summer. S. Eur.

anglicum Huds. E; glabrous, mat-forming; lvs. alt., crowded, elliptic, to $\frac{3}{16}$ in. long, nearly cylindrical, obtuse; fl. sts. 1–6 in., with 2–3 cincinni; fls. white or pink, $\frac{1}{2}$ in. wide, pistils erect, red in fr. Early summer. W. Eur. Cv. **'Minus'**. Smaller; fls. pinker.

annuum L. E; much-branched, glabrous, ann. or bien., to 3 in.; lvs. alt., linear-oblong, $\frac{1}{4}$ in. long, obtuse, pale green; fls. yellow, $\frac{1}{4}$ in. wide; follicles spreading. Early summer. Greenland, Eur., Asia Minor.

anomalum: *S. spathulifolium* subsp.

anopetalum: *S. ochroleucum.*

aoikon Ulbr. P; sts. to 3 in.; lvs. scattered for 3–6 in. from the st. tips in alt. zones of shorter and longer lvs., obovate, to spatulate, to 2 in. long and 1 in. wide, flat, rounded to nearly minutely pointed; infl. terminal, dense; fls. yellow, $\frac{3}{8}$ in. wide. Winter, early spring. Presumably Mex.

arboreum M. T. Mast. Not cult.; but the name has been applied to material of *S. sediforme.*

arcticum (A. Boris.) Rønning. R; root crown short, sometimes branching, with acuminate scale lvs., ann. sts. many, 3–4 in.; lvs. crowded, round-ovate, $\frac{3}{8}$ in. long, acuminate, clasping, entire or serrate near apex, glaucous-green; fls. unisexual, 4-merous, yellow, $\frac{1}{8}$ in. long. Summer. N. Russia.

asiaticum (D. Don) A. Spreng. Not cult.; but the name has been used for *S. crassipes.*

athoum: *S. album* cv.

atlanticum (J. Ball) Maire [*Monanthes atlantica* J. Ball]. E; glabrous; lvs. in dense rosettes, spatulate, to $\frac{1}{4}$ in. long, flattened, gray-green; fl. sts. to 1 in.; fls. 3–5, on pedicels to $\frac{3}{8}$ in. long, 6–7-merous, to $\frac{5}{16}$ in. wide, nectar glands spatulate, conspicuous. N. Afr.

atropurpureum: *S. Rosea* var.

aureum Wirtg. ex F. W. Schultz. Not cult.; but the name has been used for *S. mexicanum.*

australe Rose. E; glabrous, sts. decumbent, brown, roughened, lacking aerial roots; lvs. alt., flat, obovate, $\frac{1}{4}$–$\frac{3}{8}$ in. long, obtuse, gray-green; fls. 1–4, yellow, $\frac{5}{16}$ in. wide. Mex. Often grown as *S. oaxacanum.*

azureum: *S. caeruleum;* see also *S. Ewersii.*

balticum: *S. album.*

bellum Rose. E; glabrous, sts. arising one spring and flowering the next, 3–6 in.; lvs. alt., spatulate, to 1 in. long, glaucous; fls. white, ½ in. wide. Winter, spring. W. Mex.

Beyrichianum: *S. Nevii.*

bithynicum Boiss. [*S. hispanicum* var. *minus* Praeg.]. E; per., glabrous or sts. villous; lvs. alt., crowded on nearly globose sterile shoots, linear to oblong, to ¼ in. long, almost obtuse, nearly cylindrical; fls. mostly 5-merous, rose to purplish. Early summer. Asia Minor, Balkans. Cv. **'Minus'** is listed. Sometimes grown as *S. glaucum* or *S. lydium* var. *glaucum.*

boloniense: *S. sexangulare.*

Borderi: *S. Telephium* var.

brevifolium DC. E; glabrous, sts. creeping; lvs. opp. or alt., crowded, 4- or 5-ranked, ovoid or nearly globose, ⅛ in. long, chalky-gray, often suffused with red; fl. sts. to 5 in.; fls. few, white, ⁵⁄₁₆ in. wide. Early summer. Sw. Eur., nw. Afr. Sometimes grown as *S. Pittonii.* Cv. **'Album'**, with bronzy foliage, listed but probably does not belong here.

bupleuroides Wallich ex Hook.f. & T. Thoms. R; root crown massive, mostly below ground, with scale lvs., ann. sts. erect to 1 ft.; lvs. triangular-ovate to ovate-lanceolate, ½–1 in. long, entire, cordate, acute to rounded; infl. loose; fls. unisexual, 5-merous, red-purple, ¼ in. wide. Early summer. Himalayas.

caeruleum Vahl [*S. azureum* Desf., not Royle]. E; ann. to 6 in.; lvs. alt., ovoid to oblong, to ¾ in. long, nearly cylindrical; infl. loose, sparsely fine-hairy; fls. 6–9-merous, blue, ¼ in. wide. Summer. S. Eur., N. Afr.

calcareum: a listed name of no botanical standing.

callichroum Boiss. E; glabrous ann., to 1½ in.; lvs. few, alt., oblong to ovate, obtuse, to ⅛ in. long, half-cylindrical; fls. pink, ³⁄₁₆ in. wide; follicles erect. Iran.

carpaticum: *S. Telephium.*

caucasicum: *S. maximum* var.

cauticola Praeg. T; close to *S. Sieboldii,* but lvs. short-petioled, mostly opp.; infl. looser and leafy; carpels more gradually tapered below. Early autumn. N. Japan.

Cepaea L. E; hairy, usually ann., to 1 ft.; lvs. alt. to whorled and 4-lvd., oblanceolate to spatulate, to 1 in. long, red-spotted; infl. a loose raceme of cymes; fls. white, ⅜ in. wide, on pedicels to ¼ in. Early summer. Cent. and s. Eur.

Chanetii: *Orostachys Chanetii.*

chrysanthum: *Rosularia pallida.*

coccineum Royle. Not cult.; plants grown under this name are usually *S. spurium.*

Cockerellii Britt. E; glabrous, tufted; lvs. alt., those on sterile shoots crowded, obovate to spatulate, ¼ in. long, acute to truncate, papillose; fl. sts. to 8 in., the lvs. oblanceolate, to ¾ in. long; fls. white, to ½ in. wide. Late summer. S. Colo. to n. Mex.

cockscombianum: a listed name of no botanical standing.

coloniense: a listed name of no botanical standing for *S. hispanicum.*

compressum: *S. Palmeri.*

confusum Hemsl. P; sts. to 1 ft., woody below; lvs. in rosettes, within 2½ in. of st. apex, obovate-spatulate, nearly emarginate, glossy green, ⅝–1½ in. long, ⁵⁄₁₆–⅝ in. wide, the lowermost largest; infl. terminal, rather dense; fls. yellow, ½–⅝ in. wide, petals ovate-lanceolate. Winter, spring. Presumably Mex.

corsicum: *S. dasyphyllum* var. *glanduliferum.*

Corynephyllum Fröd. [*S. viride* (Rose) A. Berger, not Mak.; *Corynephyllum viride* Rose]. P; shrub, erect, to 2 ft. or trailing to 3 ft. or more; lvs. 15–30, club-shaped, 1–2½ in. long, ⅜–⅝ in. wide and nearly as thick, obtuse to rounded, often upcurved, green or glaucous; fl. sts. lateral, below rosette, 4–7 in., with 6–10 cincinni, each of 2–8 nearly sessile fls.; sepals erect, unequal, ¼ in. long, corolla pentagonal-urceolate, whitish, ¼ in. long, petals separate. Winter. E. Mex.

Craigii R. T. Clausen. P; sts. thick, erect, to 6 in. or more; lvs. scattered, oblong-elliptic, 1–2 in. long, turgid but slightly flattened, glaucous, somewhat purplish, apex and margins rounded; fl. sts. axillary, slender, to 2 in.; fls. few, ¼ in. long, petals yellowish-white, erect and narrowed below, apex recurved. Autumn. Nw. Mex.

crassipes Wallich ex Hook.f. & T. Thoms. [*S. Wallichianum* Hook.]. R; root crown thick, branched, aerial, with scale lvs. at first green, ann. shoots simple, erect, to 1 ft.; lvs. linear to lanceolate, to ¾ in. long, acute, with 1–3 remote teeth on each side in upper half; fls. 5-merous, bisexual, yellowish-white to greenish, ½ in. wide. Early summer and often again later. Himalayas, China. The name *S. asiaticum* has been used for this sp. in error.

Cremnophila: *Cremnophila nutans.*

cremnophylla: a listed name of no botanical standing; evidently a misspelling of *Cremnophila.*

crista-galli: a listed name of no botanical standing, for plants perhaps allied to *S. rupestre.*

cristatum: *S. rupestre.*

cupressoides Hemsl. E; glabrous, sts. slender, weak, branching, to 6 in.; lvs. alt., closely crowded, spreading, triangular, to ⅛ in. long, obtuse, withering-persistent and whitish or gray; fls. 1–3, nearly sessile, 5–7-merous, white, red-marked outside, ½ in. wide. Often described as yellow-fld. Summer. S. Mex.

cyaneum J. H. Rudolph. T; sts. creeping or ascending, to 4 in.; lvs. alt. or opp., oblong-lanceolate, to ¾ in. long, flat, bluish-glaucous; fls. lilac-pink, ½ in. wide. Summer. E. Siberia.

dasyphyllum L. E; glandular-pubescent, tufted, to 3 in.; lvs. opp., ovoid to obovoid, ⅛–³⁄₁₆ in. long; fls. 5–6-merous, ¼ in. wide, petals white, pink on the back. Early summer. S. Eur., N. Afr. Var. **glanduliferum** (Guss.) Moris [*S. corsicum* Duby; *S. glanduliferum* Guss.]. Very densely glandular-pubescent. Var. **macrophyllum** Rouy & E. Camus. Lvs. to ⅜ in. long.

debile S. Wats. [*Gormania debilis* (S. Wats.) Britt.]. E; glabrous, to 5 in.; lvs. opp., obovate to orbicular, to ³⁄₁₆ in. long, flattened, obtuse; fls. yellow, ⅜ in. wide; follicles erect. Summer. Nev. to Wyo.

decipiens grandiflorum: a listed name of no botanical standing.

dendroideum Moç. & Sessé ex DC. P; shrub, to 7 ft. high or trailing to 18 ft., trunk to 4 in. in diam.; lvs. nearly in a rosette within 2–4 in. of st. tip, spatulate, 1¼–2 in. long, ⅝–¾ in. wide, ³⁄₁₆ in. thick, rounded at apex, glossy green, with marginal red or dark green glandular dots; fl. sts. lateral, to 1 ft., nearly as thick as sterile sts., cincinni several; fls. yellow, ½–¾ in. wide. Winter, spring. Mex. Subsp. **praealtum** (DC.) R. T. Clausen [*S. praealtum* DC.]. Lvs. oblong-elliptic, 1½–3 in. long, to 1 in. wide, lacking marginal dots. Mex. Cv. **'Cristatum'**. GREEN COCKSCOMB. Lvs. crested.

Derenbergii: a listed name of no botanical standing.

diffusum S. Wats. E; glabrous, sts. long-creeping; lvs. alt., oblong, ⅛–½ in. long, nearly cylindrical, obtuse, papillose at apex, pale green with pink tips; fl. sts. to 3 in., infl. of 1–2 ascending cincinni; fls. white, ⅜–½ in. wide; follicles divergent. Spring. Ne. Mex.

divergens S. Wats. E; glabrous; lvs. opp., nearly globose, ⅛–⅜ in. long, green or reddish; fl. sts. to 6 in.; fls. yellow, ⅜ in. wide; follicles divergent. Summer. N. Calif. to B.C.

diversifolium: *S. Greggii.*

Douglasii: *S. stenopetalum.*

dumulosum Franch. R; root crown aerial, branching, with old st. bases, ann. sts. 4–8 in.; lvs. alt., linear, acute, ½–1 in. long; infl. compact, few-fld.; fls. bisexual, 5-merous, campanulate, white, ⅜ in. long, petals acuminate, fringed. Early summer. N. China.

ebracteatum Moç. & Sessé ex DC. [*S. rubricaule* (Rose) Praeg.]. S; more or less pubescent; rosette lvs. obovate to oblong-oblanceolate, acute, yellow-green, to 1½ in. long; fl. sts. ½–2 ft., infl. paniculate; fls. ½ in. wide. Late summer, autumn. Mex.

elegans: *S. rupestre.*

Ellacombianum: *S. kamtschaticum* subsp.

elongatum: a listed name of no botanical standing which may apply to *S. bupleuroides* or *S. Rosea.*

×**erythrostictum** Miq. [*S.* ×*alboroseum* Bak.]: *S. spectabile* × *S. viridenscens* Nakai. T; ann., sts. erect, 1–2 ft.; lvs. mostly opp., ovate to obovate-cuneate, 2–4 in. long, half as wide, obtusely toothed, light green; fls. ½ in. wide, petals white, about as long as stamens, pistils pinkish. Early autumn. The fls. are irregular in numbers of parts, and most of the pollen is abortive. Grown under the misapplied names *S. japonicum* and *S. macrophyllum.*

euphorbioides Schlechtend. ex Ledeb. Of doubtful status; the name has been applied to *S. Aizoon.*

Ewersii Ledeb. [*S. azureum* Royle, not Desf.]. T; sts. decumbent, 6–12 in. high, their lower parts persisting and branching; lvs. opp., ovate-cordate, mostly entire, glaucous, ¼–1 in. long; fls. ⁵⁄₁₆ in. wide, pink. Early summer to early autumn. Himalayas to Mongolia. What seems a small garden form has been offered as *S. Hayesii.* Var **homophyllum** Praeg. A dwarf form, 2–3 in., more glaucous.

Fabaria: *S. Telephium* var.

farinosum Lowe. E; glabrous, sts. woody at base, to 3 in.; lvs. alt., oblong to obovoid, to ¼ in. long, cylindrical, blunt, spurred; fls. white. Madeira Is.

fimbriatum: *Orostachys fimbriata.*

floriferum Praeg. A; glabrous ann., sts. ascending or decumbent, much-branched, to 6 in.; lvs. alt., spatulate-oblanceolate, to 1½ in. long, toothed in upper ⅓; fls. yellow, ½ in. wide, sepals linear to oblanceolate. Summer. China. Intermediate between *S. hybridum* and *S. kamtschaticum* and perhaps a hybrid.

Forsteranum: *S. rupestre* cv.

friseum: a listed name of no botanical standing.

frutescens Rose. P; like *S. oxypetalum,* but lvs. elliptic-linear to elliptic-oblong, acute, ¾–2 in. long; fls. white. Mex.

furfuraceum Moran. E; glabrous, sts. creeping, ¼ in. in diam.; lvs. alt., crowded, ovoid, ¼–⅜ in. long, obtuse, obtusely margined and keeled near apex, dark green and frosted; fl. shoots 1½ in., infl. sessile, compact, 1–8-fld.; fls. white or pinkish, ⅜ in. wide. Early spring. Mex.

fusiforme Lowe. E; Glabrous, much-branched subshrub, to 6 in.; lvs. alt., fusiform, to ¾ in. long, glaucous; fls. yellow, 5/16 in. wide, in small terminal cymes. Spring and autumn. Madeira Is.

glabrum (Rose) Praeg. S; close to *S. ebracteatum* and perhaps not distinct, but less than 1 ft., usually glabrous except for the glandular carpels. Summer, autumn. Ne. Mex.

glanduliferum: *S. dasyphyllum* var.; see also *S. Moranii.*

glaucophyllum R. T. Clausen. E; glabrous; lvs. of sterile sts. in dense rosettes, obovate to spatulate, to ⅝ in. long and ⅜ in. wide, obtuse or nearly acute, papillose-crenulate at apex, glaucous; fl. sts. to 8 in., lvs. 30–50, oblanceolate, to 1 in. long and ¼ in. wide; fls. mostly 4-merous, white, to ½ in. wide. Late spring, summer. Va., W. Va. Formerly included with *S. Nevii* which has fewer, narrower, nonglaucous lvs.

glaucum: *S. hispanicum;* also see *S. bithynicum.*

globosum: a listed name of no botanical standing.

Gormanii: a listed name of no botanical standing.

gracile C. A. Mey. E; glabrous, sts. procumbent; lvs. alt., linear-lanceolate, nearly cylindrical, ⅛–¼ in. long, obtuse, minutely papillose; fl. sts. to 2½ in., with mostly 2 spreading brs.; fls. white, ¼ in. wide, sepals ovate, acute. Early summer. Caucasus. Has been grown under the hort. name *S. Albertii.*

Greggii Hemsl. [*S. diversifolium* Rose]. E; glabrous; lvs. alt., densely overlapping on sterile shoots, scattered and easily detached on fl. shoots, elliptic to obovate-oblong, to ¼ in. long or more, obtuse, papillose; fl. sts. weak, to 6 in.; fls. yellow, ⅜ in. wide, nearly sessile in small cymes. Winter. Mex.

griseum Praeg. E; glabrous subshrub, to 1½ ft., with peeling bark; lvs. alt., linear-fusiform, ¼–1 in. long, nearly cylindrical, obtuse, finely papillose, glaucous; cyme terminal, compact, 1–2 in. wide; fls. white, ½ in. wide. Winter. Mex.

guatemalense Hemsl. Not cult.; the name has been used in error for *S. × rubrotinctum.*

gypsicola Boiss. & Reut. E; like *S. album,* but lvs. rhomboid-ovate, gray-puberulous, ¼ in. long, closely overlapping in 5 rows on sterile shoots. Early summer. Spain.

Hayesii: a listed name of no botanical standing; probably a form of *S. Ewersii.*

Heckneri: *S. laxum* subsp.

Hemsleyanum Rose. S; like *S. ebracteatum* but smaller; lvs. linear or oblanceolate, to ¾ in. long and ⅛ in. wide; fl. sts. to 12 in.; fls. to ⅜ in. wide. Autumn, early winter. S. Mex.

Hillebrandtii: *S. Sartorianum* subsp.

himalense D. Don. R; root crown elongate, with conspicuous scale lvs., ann. sts. reddish, 6–12 in.; lvs. lanceolate to obovate, ⅝–1 in. long, acute to obtuse, rough; fls. unisexual, 4–5-merous, purple, ¼ in. wide. Late spring. Himalayas.

hirsutum All. E; glandular-pubescent and spicy-aromatic; lvs. alt., in dense rosettes at ends of runnerlike shoots, oblanceolate, to ⅜ in. long, blunt, nearly cylindrical, lustrous green; fl. sts. 2–6 in., with usually 2 cincinni; fls. white, often red-veined, about ½ in. wide, petals united 1/16 in. or less. Late winter to summer. Sw. Eur. Subsp. **baeticum** Rouy [*S. Winkleri* (Willk.) Wolley-Dod.]. Lvs. paler, to ¾ in. long; fls. white or green-veined, to ¾ in. wide, petals united to ⅛ in. S. Spain, Morocco.

hispanicum L. [*S. glaucum* Waldst. & Kit.]. E; mostly ann. or bien., mostly glandular-pubescent above; lvs. alt., linear to oblong-lanceolate, 3/16–⅝ in. long, acute, cylindrical or nearly so, glaucous; fl. sts. to 7 in.; fls. mostly 6-merous, white, ¼–½ in. wide, petals lanceolate, acuminate, carpels erect to somewhat divergent, stellate in fr. Early summer. Se. Eur., sw. Asia. Plants listed as *S. coloniense* are a small form allied to this sp. Cv. **'Aureum'** is listed. Var. **bithynicum:** a listed name apparently of no botanical standing for *S. bithynicum.* Var. **minus:** *S. bithynicum.*

Hobsonii Prain ex Hamet. R; root crown short, with tuberous roots, ann. sts. decumbent, 2–6 in.; lvs. on root crown oblanceolate to obovate, ⅜ in. long, nearly acute, entire, attenuate to long petioles, on ann. sts. to 1 in. long, oblanceolate to oblong; fls. few, 5-merous, white, ⅜ in. long. Summer. China.

humifusum Rose. E; mat-forming per., ½ in. high; rosettes globular, to 3/16 in. wide, lvs. obovate, to 3/16 in. long, ciliate; fls. yellow, to ⅜ in. wide, solitary, terminal. Winter, early spring. Mex.

hybridum L. A; evergreen, glabrous, sts. creeping and branching; lvs. alt., oblong-lanceolate to spatulate, about 1 in. long, coarsely toothed toward apex, teeth often red-tipped; fl. sts. 3–12 in.; fls. yellow, ½–¾ in. wide, sepals linear, stamens about ⅔ length of petals. Late spring, summer. E. Eur., Siberia, Mongolia.

hyperaizoon Kom. To nearly 3 ft.; lvs. to 4 in. long, 1½ in. wide. E. Siberia. Probably only an extreme phase of *S. Aizoon.*

ibericum: *S. stoloniferum.*

indicum (Decne.) Hamet. Sin; glabrous; rosette lvs. turgid, spatulate to oblanceolate, 1½–2½ in. long, ¼–⅝ in. wide, acuminate to minutely pointed, red-blotched; fl. sts. 6–18 in., with scattered lvs. easily falling and rooting; infl. paniculate or corymbose; fls. white with red tips, ⅛ in. long. Autumn. Himalayas, w. China. Has been grown under the name *Echeveria maculata.*

integrifolium: *S. Rosea* subsp.

intermedium: a listed name of no botanical standing.

involucratum: *S. spurium* var.

Jaccardianum Maire & Wilcz. E; pubescent, sterile sts. to 2½ in.; lvs. in dense rosettes, spatulate, to ⅝ in. long; fl. sts. to 4 in.; fls. long-pedicelled, 7–10-merous, ⅜ in. wide, petals ascending, yellow. Morocco.

japonicum Siebold. Not cult.; material cult. under this name is *S. × erythrostictum.* Var. **senanense:** *S. senanense.*

Jepsonii: a listed name of no botanical standing for *S. laxum.*

kamtschaticum Fisch. & C. A. Mey. A; glabrous, rhizome elongate, ann. sts. several, often weak, 6–12 in.; lvs. alt., linear to mostly spatulate, ½–2 in. long, toothed toward the apex, margins papillose; fls. yellow, ⅝–¾ in. wide, stamens as long as petals; follicles widely spreading. Summer. E. Asia. Cv. **'Variegatum'.** Lvs. variegated. Cv. **'Nanum'.** A listed name. Subsp. **Ellacombianum** (Praeg.) R. T. Clausen [*S. Ellacombianum* Praeg.]. Lvs. light green, spatulate, crenate; fls. about ½ in. wide. N. Japan. Subsp. **Middendorffianum** (Maxim.) R. T. Clausen [*S. Middendorffianum* Maxim.]. Lvs. linear or linear-oblanceolate, crenate-dentate above, with 1–4 teeth on each side; stamens shorter than petals. N.-cent. Asia.

Kirilowii Regel & Tiling. R; root crown thick, branching, with scale lvs., ann. sts. erect, 1 ft. or more; lvs. alt., oblong, 1–1½ in. long, ¼ in. wide, widest at base, mostly toothed; fls. unisexual, mostly 5-merous, mostly brownish-red. Spring. Himalayas to n. China.

laconicum Boiss. & Heldr. E; glabrous; lvs. alt., oblanceolate, to ¼ in. long, long-spurred, spotted, mammillate at tips; infl. often with few-fld. lateral brs. below the terminal cyme; fls. sessile, yellow, to ½ in. wide. Greece, Asia Minor.

laetivirens: a listed name of no botanical standing.

Laggeri: a listed name of no botanical standing; applied to *S. Aizoon* and also to *S. maximum.*

lanceolatum Torr. [*S. stenopetalum* of auth., not Pursh]. E; glabrous, tufted, sterile shoots ascending; lvs. alt., linear-lanceolate, ½–¾ in. long, minutely papillose; fl. sts. to 8 in.; fls. yellow, ½ in. wide; follicles erect. Early summer. W. temp. N. Amer.

lanceratum: a listed name of no botanical standing.

latifolium: *S. maximum.*

laxum (Britt.) A. Berger. G; glabrous; lvs. opp., especially on the offsets, or alt., spatulate, ½–2 in. long, ¼–1 in. wide, rounded to retuse; fl. sts. 4–16 in., infl. paniculate; fls. to ⅜ in. long, white to pink, sepals to 3/16 in., petals united in the lower ⅓, often spreading above. Early summer. S. Ore., n. Calif. Variable, including about 5 divergent but intergrading subspp.; also intergrading with the yellow-fld. *S. obtusatum.* Subsp. *Heckneri* (Peck) R. T. Clausen [*S. Heckneri* Peck]. Fl. sts. 4–8 in.; lvs. cordate to nearly cordate, about as wide as long. Sw. Ore.

Leibergii Britt. E; glabrous, with few sterile shoots at flowering time; basal lvs. narrow-spatulate or oblanceolate, ½–1 in. long, petioles slender; fl. sts. to 10 in., their lvs. lanceolate or oblong; fls. sessile, greenish-yellow to bright yellow, ⅜ in. wide; follicles widely spreading. Nw. U.S. Var. **Borschii** R. T. Clausen. With more sterile shoots at flowering time; basal lvs. oblong-spatulate to oblong-obovate, sessile, to ⅜ in. long, st. lvs. oblong-spatulate to oblong-elliptic; fls. deep yellow. Mont.

lidakense: a listed name of no botanical standing.

Liebmannianum Hemsl. E; glabrous, to 6 in. high, sts. procumbent, branching, woody below, covered by persistent silvery bases of old lvs.; lvs. alt., oblong, to ¼ in. long, obtuse, broad-spurred; fls. few, terminal, sessile, white, ⅜ in. wide. Summer, autumn. S. Mex. Differs from *S. moranense* in its larger lvs. with the dried bases covering the sts. more densely and conspicuously.

lineare Thunb. E; glabrous, sts. erect or decumbent, to 1 ft.; lvs. in 3's, linear to linear-lanceolate, ¾–1¼ in. long, flat, nearly acute; cyme of 2–3 simple or forked brs.; fls. sessile, yellow, ⅝ in. wide. Late spring, early summer. E. Asia. Cv. **'Robustum'**. Stouter, more branched, gray-green. Cv. **'Variegatum'**. Lvs. white-margined.

littorale Kom. A; glabrous, rhizome creeping, ann. sts. erect, to 1 ft.; lvs. in 3's, obovate to ovate-lanceolate, to 2½ in. long, obtuse, white-dotted, with hooked teeth; fls. golden, ⅜ in. wide. Summer. E. Siberia.

lucidum R. T. Clausen. P; subshrub, branched from base, to 1½ ft.; lvs. scattered, elliptic to oblanceolate, 1–2 in. long, ½–¾ in. wide, acute to obtuse, lustrous dark green; fl. sts. axillary, 3–6 in., pedicels to ¼ in. long; fls. white, ½ in. wide, with musky odor, stamens to ³⁄₁₆ in. long. Late autumn to early spring. Mex. Has been grown under the name of *S. tortuosum.*

×**luteoviride** R. T. Clausen: ?*S. dendroideum* × *S. Greggii.* P × E; subshrub, sts. procumbent at base; lvs. somewhat scattered for 2–6 in. from st. apex in alt. zones of shorter and longer lvs., oblong-elliptic to nearly spatulate, ³⁄₁₆–⅝ in. long, obtuse, yellow-green; infl. terminal, open; fls. nearly sessile, yellow, to ½ in. wide. Winter, spring. Mex., probably a natural hybrid.

lydium Boiss. E; glabrous, sterile shoots 1 in. high, densely leafy above; lvs. alt., linear, ¼ in. long, cylindrical, obtuse, green or red-tinged; fl. sts. 2–5 in., cymes dense, flat-topped; fls. white, ¼ in. wide, sepals oblong, obtuse. Early summer. Asia Minor. Cvs. **'Purpurascens'** and **'Roseum'** are listed. Var. **glaucum:** a listed name, apparently of no botanical standing, used for *S. bithynicum.*

macrophyllum: *S. maximum;* see also *S. erythrostictum.*

magellense Ten. [*S. olympicum* Boiss.]. E; glabrous; lvs. mostly alt., obovate to elliptic-oblong, to ⅜ in. long, flat, obtuse, bright green; fl. sts. 3–6 in., infl. a raceme of short cymes; fls. white, ¼ in. wide, carpels oblong, widest near tip, abruptly tapered. Late spring. Italy, Greece, Asia Minor.

Makinoi Maxim. E; glabrous, forming mats, sts. prostrate, ring-grooved and rooting at nodes; lvs. opp., spatulate, ¼–¾ in. long, bright green; fl. sts. to 3 in., cymes to 5 in. wide, the 2–3 brs. forked 1–4 times; fls. nearly sessile except the lowest, yellow, ⅜–½ in. wide, sepals unequal, spatulate. Early summer. Japan.

Maximowiczii: *S. Aizoon.*

maximum Suter [*S. latifolium* Bertol.; *S. macrophyllum* Hort. ex Vilm.]. T; roots tuberous, ann. sts. erect, 1–3 ft.; lvs. mostly opp., broadly ovate, 2–5 in. long, 1–2 in. wide, obtuse, truncate or cordate-clasping, slightly and irregularly toothed, mostly dark green; fls. greenish, less than ⅜ in. wide, petals ovate-lanceolate, stamens as long as petals or longer. Late summer. Eur., Caucasus. Cvs. are: **'Atropurpureum'**, lvs. and sts. dark purple; **'Haematodes'**, purple but smaller; **'Variegatum'**, variegated with yellow. Var. **caucasicum** Grossh. [*S. caucasicum* (Grossh.) A. Boris.]. Lvs. to 2 in. long and 3 in. wide, clasping with large auricles. Caucasus. A variable sp. intergrading with *S. Telephium.*

Meddempium: a listed name of no botanical standing.

mexicanum Britt. E; glabrous, sts. decumbent, to 6 in. high; lvs. in whorls of 3 or 5 or alt. above, linear, ¼–¾ in. long, nearly cylindrical, obtuse; cyme of about 3 forked, spreading brs.; fls. nearly sessile, yellow, ⅜–½ in. wide. Spring. S. Mex. A floriferous and showy plant, sometimes grown as *S. aureum.*

micranthum: *S. album* var.

Middendorffianum: *S. kamtschaticum* subsp.

minus: *S. rupestre* cv.

monregalense Balb. E; sts. decumbent, slender, to 6 in. high; lvs. opp. below, in 4's above, oblong-spatulate, ⅛–⅜ in. long, obtuse, mostly glabrous, cymes paniculate, glandular-puberulent; fls. white, ⅜ in. wide, on pedicels to ¼ in. long. Summer. S. Eur.

montanum: *S. ochroleucum* subsp.

moranense HBK. E; glabrous, to 6 in., sts. much-branched, decumbent, woody below; lvs. alt., close-set, ovate to ovate-lanceolate, ³⁄₁₆ in. long, obtuse, the dried bases persisting but not densely and conspicuously covering the sts.; fls. few, terminal, sessile, white, ⅜ in. wide. Spring, early summer. Mex. Cv. **'Arboreum'**. Stouter, more branched, to 1 ft.

Moranii R. T. Clausen [*S. glanduliferum* (L. F. Henders.) Peck, not Guss.]. G; rosette lvs. 15–20, oblong-spatulate, 1–1½ in. long, ⅜–½ in. wide, emarginate to minutely pointed, glabrous, margins horny-denticulate toward tip; fl. sts. 7–10 in., cyme 2–5-branched, glandular; petals erect, united ⅛ in., greenish-yellow, to ⅝ in. long. Late spring. Sw. Ore.

Morganianum Walth. BURRO'S-TAIL, BURRO-TAIL, DONKEY'S-TAIL, HORSE'S-TAIL, LAMB'S-TAIL. P; sts. branching at base, trailing or hanging to 3 ft., persistent-leafy; lvs. oblong-lanceolate, to 1 in. long and ⅜ in. thick, acute, nearly cylindrical, curved forward, glaucous, readily detached and rooting; infl. terminal, corymbose, 6–12-fld., pedicels 1 in. long; fls. deep rose, ½ in. long, sepals nearly as long. Spring. Presumably Mex. Handsome basket plant readily prop. by the lvs.

multiceps Coss. & Durieu. JOSHUA TREE, MINIATURE J. T., LITTLE J. T., BABY J. T. E; glabrous subshrub, to 6 in., sts. shaggy with old lvs.; lvs. alt., crowded, linear-oblong, ¼ in. long, obtuse, papillose; fl. sts. 1–3 in., with more scattered lvs., cymes 3-branched; fls. sessile, yellow, ½ in. wide; follicles spreading. Early summer. Algeria.

murale: *S. album* cv.

nevadense Coss. E; glabrous ann., to 4 in., simple or branching from base; lvs. alt., linear to oblong, ¼ in. long, nearly cylindrical; pedicels ¼ in. long; fls. reddish, ¼ in. wide, stamens 5. Mts., Spain, N. Afr.

Nevii A. Gray [*S. Beyrichianum* M. T. Mast.]. E; glabrous; lvs. of sterile sts. in loose rosettes, spatulate, to ³⁄₁₆ in. wide, smooth at tip, not glaucous, lvs. of fl. sts. 12–40, oblanceolate or linear-oblanceolate, to ¾ in. long and ⅛ in. wide, mostly nearly cylindrical; fl. sts. to 6 in.; fls. mostly 4-merous, to ½ in. wide, white. Spring. Ala., Tenn. Plants grown under this name are likely to be *S. glaucophyllum.*

nicaeense: *S. sediforme.*

niveum A. Davids. E; glabrous, forming mats, sts. trailing and rooting; lvs. alt., cuneate-obovate or oblanceolate, ⅛–½ in. long, mostly obtuse, papillose, often red-dotted; fl. sts. 1–3 in.; fls. 1–12, nearly sessile, ⅜–¾ in. wide, petals white or with 2 red dots near base. Summer. S. Calif., n. Baja Calif.

Nussbaumeranum Bitter. P; close to *S. Adolphii,* for which it is often mistaken, but lvs. yellow-green, obtusely convex on the back, not more than ⅜ in. thick; cymes corymbose, pedicels ¼–¾ in. long; petals linear-lanceolate. Winter. Mex.

nutans: see *Cremnophila nutans.*

Nuttallianum Raf. E; glabrous ann., to 5 in., branching from base; lvs. alt., oblong, to ⅝ in. long, obtuse; cyme leafy, 2–5-branched; fls. nearly sessile, yellow, ¼ in. wide; follicles spreading. Late spring. Mo to Tex.

oaxacanum Rose. E; glabrous, sts. decumbent, reddish, roughened, often bearing many aerial roots; lvs. alt., oblong-elliptic, ¼ in. long, obtuse, green; fls. 1–4, sessile, yellow, ⁵⁄₁₆ in. wide; follicles spreading. Mex. Plants offered under this name are likely to be *S. australe.*

obtusatum A. Gray. G; glabrous; lvs. alt. or, especially on the offsets, nearly opp., spatulate, ½–1 in. long, to ½ in. wide, obtuse to retuse, often glaucous and in age orange-red; fl. sts. 4–8 in., infl. thyrsoid; fls. to ⅜ in. long, petals yellow, united in lower ⅓, somewhat spreading above. Summer. Mts., Calif.

obtusifolium C. A. Mey. E; rhizome short, with bulblets ¼ in. thick, sts. villous, 4–10 in.; lvs. opp., obovate, ¼–1¼ in. long, flat, obtuse, crenulate; infl. loosely corymbose; fls. pink, ⅜ in. wide. Late spring, summer. Caucasus.

ochroleucum Chaix [*S. anopetalum* DC.]. E; glabrous, creeping and mat-forming, sterile sts. densely leafy; lvs. alt., linear to linear-lanceolate, ⅜ in. long, spinulose-tipped, nearly cylindrical, green or glaucous; fl. sts. 6–12 in., lvs. to ¾ in. long, cymes round-topped; sepals lanceolate to ovate-lanceolate, petals erect, white, ⅜ in. long, carpels erect. Early summer. S. Eur., w. Asia. Subsp. **montanum** (Song. & Perr.) D. A. Webb [*S. montanum* Song. & Perr.]. Petals spreading, yellow, ⁵⁄₁₆ in. long. Mts., Eur.

olympicum: *S. magellense.*

oppositifolium: *S. spurium* var. *album.*

opsinifolium: a listed name of no botanical standing; plants grown under this name have been *S. sexangulare.*

oreganum Nutt. E; glabrous, sterile sts. to 6 in.; lvs. alt., nearly in a rosette, spatulate, ½–¾ in. long, obtuse, glossy green, often suffused with red; fl. sts. to 10 in.; petals yellow, ascending, narrowly lanceolate, acuminate, to ⅝ in. long, united ⅛. Summer. Ore. to Alaska. Cv. **'Glaucum'** is listed.

oregonense (S. Wats.) Peck [*S. Watsonii* (Britt.) Tidestr.; *Gormania Watsonii* Britt.]. G; glabrous; lvs. alt. or, especially on the offsets, opp., spatulate, about 1 in. long, yellow-green; fl. sts. to 11 in., cyme paniculate; fls. white or creamy, ⁵⁄₁₆ in. long, petals united in lower ⅓, somewhat spreading above. Summer. Ore. Close to *S. obtusatum,* which is smaller, with yellow fls.

oxypetalum HBK. P; glabrous, much-branched shrub, to 5 ft., trunk to 4 in. in diam., bark papery, peeling; lvs. spatulate, ½–2 in. long, flat, retuse, deciduous; cymes terminal, of about 3 forked brs.; fls. reddish, especially at center, ½ in. wide, musty-scented, sepals narrow-acute, petals spreading from near base; follicles spreading. Summer, early autumn. Mex. Larger than *S. retusum*, with more entire lvs., acute sepals, and more spreading petals.

pachyphyllum Rose. MANY-FINGERS, JELLY-BEANS, JELLY-BEAN PLANT. P; subshrub, to 1 ft.; lvs. somewhat scattered, curved-club-shaped, ½–1½ in. long, ¼ in. thick, cylindrical, obtuse, glaucous and often red-tipped; fl. sts. axillary, 4–5 in., with flattish cyme; fls. nearly sessile, yellow, ⅝ in. wide. Winter, spring. S. Mex.

pallescens: *S. Telephium* var.

Palmeri S. Wats. [*S. compressum* Rose]. P; subshrub, to 1 ft., branching near base, sts. each with a flattish terminal rosette; lvs. obovate-spatulate, 1–2 in. long, ½–⅞ in. wide, obtuse, glaucous; fl. sts. lateral, 2–4 in., cyme of several spreading cincinni; fls. yellow to orange-yellow, ⁵⁄₁₆–⅝ in. wide. Winter, spring. Mex.

paraguayense: *Graptopetalum paraguayense.*

pendulum: a listed name of no botanical standing.

pilosum Bieb. E; glandular-pubescent, bien., the first year making a dense *Sempervivum*-like rosette of incurved, linear-spatulate, obtuse lvs. ½ in. long; fl. sts. to 4 in. in spring or early summer of second year, infl. corymbose; fls. pink, ⅜ in. long. Late spring. Asia Minor, Caucasus.

Pinus: a listed name of no botanical standing.

Pittonii: a listed name of no botanical standing; sometimes used for *S. brevifolium.*

platyphyllum Alexand. P; subshrub, to 1 ft.; lvs. spatulate to triangular-obovate, 1–3 in. long, ¾–2 in. wide, mucronate to retuse, glaucous; infl. terminal, open-paniculate, to 1 ft. long; fls. ½–¾ in. wide, petals white with red marks near tip. Winter, early spring. S. Mex. Close to *S. allantoides*, differing in the broader, flattened lvs., with margins acute to obtuse and not rounded.

pluricaule (Maxim.) Kudo. T; cespitose, sts. creeping; lvs. mostly opp., united at base, ovate to orbicular, to ⅜ in. long, obtuse, entire; fl. sts. 2–3 in.; fls. many, in rounded cluster, purple, to ³⁄₁₆ in. long, on pedicels to ³⁄₁₆ in. long. Summer. Sakhalin Is.

populifolium Pall. E; glabrous, deciduous subshrub, with fibrous roots, per. sts. short, branched; fl. sts. to 1 ft.; lvs. alt., ovate or oblong, ½–1 in. long, cordate or truncate at base, coarsely and irregularly dentate, petioled; fls. pink or white, to ⅜ in. wide. Summer. W. Siberia.

potosinum Rose. E; glabrous, to 6 in.; lvs. alt., linear, ⅜–½ in. long, cylindrical, obtuse, glaucous; cyme loose, 2–3-branched; fls. nearly sessile, white, ⅝ in. wide; follicles erect. Summer. Mex.

praealtum: *S. dendroideum* subsp.

pruinatum Link ex Brot. Not cult.; material grown under this name is *S. rupestre.*

pruinosum: *S. spathulifolium* subsp.

pulchellum Michx. E; glabrous, mostly bien.; lvs. alt., linear, mostly ⅜–1 in. long, cylindrical, obtuse, 2-spurred, glaucous; fl. sts. mostly 4–12 in., cyme of 3–6 often elongate, spreading brs.; fls. sessile, 4-merous, rosy-purple, nearly ½ in. wide. Spring, early summer. E. U.S.

pulvinatum R. T. Clausen. P; subshrub, sts. procumbent, bearing aerial roots; lvs. scattered, oblong-elliptic, ³⁄₁₆–⅜ in. long, spurred and thickened at base; fls. solitary, axillary or terminal, white, to ½ in. wide. Late spring, summer. S. Mex.

Purdyi Jeps. G; similar to *S. spathulifolium*, but lvs. green, more closely compacted in rosettes, prominently papillate on margins, to ¾ in. long. Spring. N. Calif.

purpurascens: a listed name of no botanical standing; perhaps applying to a form of *S. Telephium.*

purpureum: *S. Telephium.*

radiatum: *S. stenopetalum* subsp.

reflexum L. E; glabrous, sts. decumbent; lvs. alt., crowded, linear, ¼–½ in. long, acute, cylindrical, short-spurred; fl. sts. erect, simple, 6–13 in., cyme nearly globose and drooping when young, cup-shaped in age; fls. 5–7-merous, golden-yellow, ½ in. wide. Summer. Eur. Lvs. sometimes eaten in soups or salads. Cv. **'Cristatum'**. Crested. Cv. **'Minus'**. A small form.

replesianum: a listed name of no botanical standing.

retusum Hemsl. P; subshrub, to 1 ft.; lvs. scattered, spatulate, ½–1 in. long, flat, mostly retuse to obcordate, margins papillose; cymes terminal; fls. nearly sessile, white or reddish at center, ⅜ in. wide, sepals obtuse, petals erect below, spreading from near middle. Summer, autumn. Mex.

rhodanthum A. Gray [*Clementsia rhodantha* (A. Gray) Rose]. R; root crown thick, branching, with persistent st. bases, ann. sts. simple, erect, to 1 ft. or more; lvs. alt., linear-oblanceolate, about 1 in. long and ¼ in. wide, flat, acute, entire or obscurely toothed toward tip; infl. spikelike or nearly capitate; fls. 5-merous, rose, ½ in. long. Summer. Mont. to Ariz.

Rhodiola: *S. Rosea.*

rigidum: a listed name of no botanical standing.

roanense: *S. Rosea.*

Rollianum: a listed name of no botanical standing.

Rosea (L.) Scop. emended by T. Sprague [*S. Rhodiola* DC.; *S. roanense* Small; *Rhodiola Rosea* L.]. ROSEROOT. R; root crown thick, branching, aerial, with reduced scale lvs., ann. sts. simple, erect, 6–16 in.; lvs. alt., lanceolate to obovate, ½–1½ in. long, acute, somewhat toothed toward tip, glaucous; fls. mostly unisexual, 4-merous, yellow, greenish-yellow, or purplish, ¼ in. wide. Late spring, early summer. Circumboreal, polymorphic. Commonly but erroneously listed as *S. roseum.* Var. **atropurpureum** (Turcz.) Fröd. [*S. atropurpureum* Turcz.]. Petals dark purple. Siberia. Perhaps belonging to the following subsp. Subsp. **integrifolium** (Raf.) Hult. [*S. integrifolium* (Raf.) A. Nels.; *Rhodiola integrifolia* Raf.; *R. Rosea* var. *integrifolia* (Raf.) Jeps.]. R; sts. commonly less then 6 in.; lvs. obovate, to 1 in. long but commonly ½ in.; fls. purple. Early summer. Alaska to Calif. and Colo.

roseum: see *S. Rosea.*

rubens L. E; glandular-pubescent, sticky ann., 2–4 in.; lvs. alt., oblong-linear, ½ in. long, obtuse, nearly cylindrical, becoming red; cyme of 3–4 ascending, leafy brs.; fls. sessile, white or reddish, ½ in. wide, stamens mostly 5; follicles divergent. Spring, early summer. Eur., N. Afr.

rubricaule: *S. ebracteatum.*

×**rubrotinctum** R. T. Clausen. CHRISTMAS-CHEER. P; glabrous subshrub, to 1 ft., branching from near base; lvs. crowded, club-shaped, ½–¾ in. long, ¼ in. thick, lustrous green, often suffused with red; cyme terminal; fls. yellow, ½ in. wide. Winter. Apparently a garden hybrid. Often grown under the misapplied name *S. guatemalense.*

rupestre L. [*S. cristatum* Schrad.; *S. elegans* Lej.; *S. virens* Ait.]. E; glabrous, sts. decumbent at base, shaggy below with old lvs., the sterile sts. densely leafy; lvs. alt., linear to linear-oblanceolate, to ⅝ in. long, acute, spurred, flattened above, mostly glaucous; fl. sts. 6–12 in., cymes nearly globose and nodding when young; fls. 5-(or 6–8-)merous, golden-yellow, nearly ½ in. wide. Late spring, early summer. W. Eur. Differs from *S. reflexum* in having lvs. in dense sterile rosettes, flattened above. Sometimes listed under the misapplied name *S. pruinatum.* Cv. **'Forsteranum'** [*S. Forsteranum* Sm.]. Smaller, green. Cv. **'Minus'** [*S. minus* Haw.]. Smaller, glaucous. Cvs. **'Lutea'** and **'Prostrata'** are also listed.

sarmentosum Bunge. E; glabrous, prostrate; lvs. in 3's, broad-lanceolate, ½–1 in. long, ¼ in. wide, flat, acute, spurred; cymes loose, leafy, of 3 often forked brs.; fls. nearly sessile, yellow, to ⅝ in. wide. Late spring, early summer. Japan, n. China.

sartorianum Boiss. subsp. **Hillebrandtii** (Fenzl) D. A. Webb [*S. Hillebrandtii* Fenzl]. E; glabrous; sts. 3–5 in., white below with dead lf. bases; lvs. alt., crowded, narrow-ovoid or oblong, ³⁄₁₆ in. long, spurred, glaucous; cymes of 1–2 nearly erect brs. each with 7–15 remote fls.; corolla yellow, ½ in. wide. Summer. E. Eur. Subsp. **Stribrnyi** (Velen.) D. A. Webb [*S. Stribrnyi* Velen.]. Sts. 3–8 in.; lvs. linear-oblong, ⅜–⅝ in. long; cyme brs. spreading, with 4–8 fls. Early summer. Bulgaria, Greece.

Scopolii: a listed name of no botanical standing.

sediforme (Jacq.) Pau [*S. altissimum* Poir.; *S. nicaeense* All.]. E; glabrous, glaucous, sts. decumbent at base; lvs. alt., elliptic-lanceolate, ½–¾ in. long, cuspidate, flattened above, fl. sts. simple, erect, ½–2 ft., cymes nearly globose; fls. almost sessile, whitish, rarely yellow, ½ in. wide, sepals ovate, petals oblanceolate. Summer. Asia Minor, s. Eur., N. Afr. Cvs. **'Latifolium'** and **'Latifrons'** are listed. Plants of this sp. have been grown under the misapplied name *S. arboreum.*

Selskianum Regel & Maack. A; grayish-pubescent, ann. sts. many, erect, 1–1½ ft.; lvs. alt., lanceolate to linear-oblong, 2 in. long, toothed; fls. glabrous, yellow, ⅜ in. wide. Summer. Manchuria. Plants grown under this name may be *S. Aizoon* or *S. kamtschaticum* subsp. *Ellacombianum*, both of which differ in being glabrous.

Semenovii (Regel & Herder) M. T. Mast. R; root crown thick, branched, with triangular scale lvs., ann. sts. simple, erect, 1–2 ft.; lvs. alt., linear, 1–2½ in. long, obtuse, entire or remotely toothed; infl. nearly capitate to spikelike; fls. 4–5-merous, greenish-white or pink, ⅜ in. long. Early summer. Turkestan.

sempervivoides Fisch. [*S. Sempervivum* Ledeb. ex K. Spreng.]. E; pubescent bien., the first year making a loose rosette of fleshy, oblong-spatulate, acute, purplish lvs. to 1¼ in. long and ½ in. wide; fl. sts. formed the following summer, 6–10 in., with scattered, similar lvs.; infl. paniculate; fls. crimson, ½ in. wide; follicles spreading. Asia Minor, Caucasus.

Sempervivum: *S. sempervivoides.*

senanense Mak. [*S. japonicum* var. *senanense* (Mak.) Mak.]. E; glabrous, to 4 in.; lvs. alt., those on sterile sts. crowded, narrowly oblong, to ⅜ in. long, obtuse, often reddish; cyme 1–3-branched; fls. yellow, nearly sessile, ⁵⁄₁₆ in. wide. Summer. Alpine, cent. Japan.

sexangulare L. [*S. boloniense* Loisel.]. E; glabrous, sts. decumbent at base; lvs. alt., commonly in 6 spiral rows, linear, ⅛–¼ in. long, cylindrical, obtuse, spurred, green; fl. sts. 3–6 in., cymes 3-branched; fls. yellow, ⅜ in. wide; follicles spreading. Early summer. Eur., sw. Asia. Plants of this sp. have been grown under the name *S. opsinifolium*.

Sieboldii Sweet. OCTOBER DAPHNE, OCTOBER PLANT. T; ann., sts. simple, low-arching, 6–9 in.; lvs. in 3's, suborbicular-cuneate, ½–1 in. long, sessile, sinuate or obscurely toothed toward apex, blue-glaucous; fls. pink, nearly ½ in. wide, in dense rounded cluster. Early autumn. Japan. Cvs. '**Medio-variegatum**' and '**Variegatum**' have variegated lvs.

sordidum Maxim. T; roots tuberous, ann. sts. 8–16 in.; lvs. alt. or opp., ovate or orbicular, 1½–2½ in. long, 1–1½ in. wide, obtuse, rounded to cuneate at base, green or purplish or on back wine-red, petiole widened above, ³⁄₁₆–⅜ in. long; fls. 30–120, in rounded cymes, petals erect, white, ³⁄₁₆ in. long. Summer, early autumn. Cent. Japan.

spathulatum: a listed name of no botanical standing; perhaps intended for *S. spathulifolium*.

spathulifolium Hook. [*S. Woodii* Britt.]. G; glabrous; lvs. alt., in mostly flat rosettes, spatulate, ½–1¼ in. long, obtuse, mostly glaucous; fl. sts. mostly 3–6 in., cymes of 3 often forked brs.; fls. yellow, to ⅝ in. wide, petals separate, erect in the lower ¹⁄₁₀, then wide-spreading; follicles spreading. Late spring. Calif. to B.C. Cv. '**Purpureum**'. Lvs. purple. Cvs. '**Aureum**' and '**Roseum**' are listed. Subsp. **anomalum** (Britt.) R. T. Clausen & Uhl [*S. anomalum* Britt.; *S. yosemitense* Britt.]. Usually smaller and less glaucous. Cent. and s. Calif. Subsp. **pruinosum** (Britt.) R. T. Clausen & Uhl [*S. pruinosum* Britt.]. Usually larger and more glaucous, sometimes with sts. of offsets leafy throughout rather than with only a terminal rosette. Coastal, B.C. to n. Calif.

spectabile Boreau. T; roots tuberous, ann. sts. simple, erect, 12–22 in.; lvs. opp. or in 3's or 4's, obovate, to about 3 in. long and 2 in. wide, somewhat toothed, glaucous; fls. many, in a flat cluster, pink, ½ in. wide, stamens longer than petals. Early autumn. China, Korea. A showy plant, well known in cult. Cvs. are: '**Album**', fls. white; '**Atropurpureum**', '**Rubrum**', and '**Brilliant**', fls. deeper-colored; '**Variegatum**', foliage variegated. Cvs. '**Brilliantissima**', '**Purpurea**', and '**Rubrifolia**' are also listed.

spinosum: *Orostachys spinosa*.

spurium Bieb. E; glabrous but somewhat papillose, sts. decumbent at base; lvs. opp., obovate-cuneate, ½–1 in. long, crenate-serrate toward apex, papillose-ciliate, dark green; fl. sts. ascending, reddish, to 9 in., cyme dense, of about 4 forked brs.; fls. pink to purple, ½ in. long, petals lanceolate, acute, entire, twice as long as the calyx. Summer. Caucasus. Cv. '**Album**'. Fls. white. Cvs. '**Coccineum**' and '**Splendens**'. Fls. deep pink. Cvs. '**Roseum**', '**Salmoneum**', and '**Splendidissimum**' are also listed. Var. **album** Trautv. [*S. oppositifolium* Sims]. Fls. white or cream, petals linear-lanceolate, acuminate. Var. **involucratum** (Bieb.) Fröd. [*S. involucratum* Bieb.]. Upper lvs. surpassing infl.; fls. white or yellowish, petals narrow-lanceolate, acuminate, erose, 1½ times as long as calyx. Var. **roseum**: a listed name of no botanical standing, apparently for the typical form. Plants in the trade as *S. coccineum* are mostly *S. spurium*.

Stahlii Solms-Laub. CORAL-BEADS. E; puberulent, sts. decumbent at base, to 15 in. high; lvs. opp., ovoid-oblong to globose, ¼–½ in. long, often red, cyme terminal, of 2–3 forked brs.; fls. nearly sessile, yellow, ½ in. wide; follicles spreading. Early spring and late summer. Mex.

stellaris: a listed name of no botanical standing.

stellatum L. E; glabrous ann., sts. simple or branching below, to 6 in.; lvs. alt., or the lower opp., spatulate, to 1 in. long, cuneate, entire or crenate, somewhat papillose; cyme of 1 to several brs.; fls. sessile, sepals nearly erect, often unequal, ¼ in. long or more, becoming longer than petals, petals erect, purplish; follicles horizontally spreading. Spring. Crete to Portugal.

stenopetalum Pursh [*S. Douglasii* Hook.]. E; glabrous, sts. decumbent at base and branching, often with axillary shoots throughout; lvs. alt., linear-lanceolate, ½–1 in. long, flat, acute, bases broad-spurred, sometimes silvery-persistent; fl. sts. to 16 in., infl. about 3-branched; fls. sessile, yellow, ½–¾ in. wide; follicles horizontally spreading. Calif. to B.C., and Mont. See also *S. lanceolatum*. Subsp. **radiatum** (S. Wats.) R. T. Clausen [*S. radiatum* S. Wats.]. Sts. 3–7 in.; lvs. to ½ in. long, not broad-spurred. N. Calif.

stoloniferum S. G. Gmel. [*S. ibericum* Bieb.]. E; glabrous or somewhat papillose, sts. decumbent at base; lvs. opp., broadly or rhomboidally spatulate, ½–1 in. long, entire or obscurely crenate above, slightly papillose on margins, dark green; fl. sts. 6–12 in., cyme loose, of 3 often forked brs.; fls. nearly sessile, pink, ½ in. wide. August. Asia Minor, Caucasus. Confused with *S. spurium*, which differs in the coarsely crenate, papillose-ciliate lvs. and longer, nearly erect petals.

Cv. '**Coccineum**'. Foliage deep bronze. Cvs. '**Album**' and '**Roseum**' are listed.

Stribrnyi: *S. Sartorianum* subsp.

subulatum (C. A. Mey.) Boiss. E; glabrous; lvs. alt., crowded, linear-subulate, to ⅝ in. long, acuminate, spurred, glaucous; fl. sts. 5–9 in., cymes dense, corymbose; fls. nearly sessile, white, ½ in. wide; follicles erect, long-beaked. Asia Minor to Iran.

Tatarinowii Maxim. T; roots tuberous, ann. sts. erect or arching, 4–8 in.; lvs. alt., oblanceolate, nearly obtuse, coarsely toothed toward apex, ½–1 in. long; fls. pinkish-white, ½ in. wide. Summer. China.

telephioides Michx. T; glabrous, ann. sts. erect or slightly decumbent, 6–20 in.; lvs. mostly alt., usually elliptic-spatulate, 1–2½ in. long, not markedly smaller upward, obtuse, cuneate, entire or remotely dentate, petioled; cymes many-fld.; fls. white to pink, ⅜ in. wide, stamens slightly shorter than petals. Summer, early autumn. N.C. to Ill.

Telephium L. [*S. carpaticum* G. Reuss; *S. purpureum* (L.) Link]. ORPINE, LIVE-FOREVER. T; roots tuberous, ann. sts. erect, 1–2 ft.; lvs. alt., ascending, oblong to ovate-oblong, 1–3 in. long, half as wide, toothed toward apex, sessile, truncate at base, upper lvs. smaller; fls. mostly red-purple, ⅜ in. wide, stamens nearly as long as petals, carpels grooved on outer side. Late summer. E. Eur. to Japan. A variable and difficult sp., intergrading with *S. maximum* but generally distinguished by alt. lvs. and purple fls. Var. **Borderi** (Jord. & Fourr.) Rouy & E. Camus [*S. Borderi* (Jord. & Fourr.) A. Cheval.]. Lvs. deeply and irregularly toothed and distinctly stalked. France. Var. **pallescens** (Freyn) Kom. [*S. pallescens* Freyn]. Roots slender; lvs. cuneate; fls. pink. E. Siberia. Subsp. **Fabaria** (W. D. J. Koch) Kirschl. [*S. Fabaria* W. D. J. Koch]. Lvs. cuneate, sometimes stalked; carpels not grooved. W. and cent. Eur.

tenellum Bieb. E; glabrous, sterile sts. 1 in.; lvs. crowded, oblong to nearly orbicular, ⅛ in. long; fl. sts. 2–4 in., lvs. alt., linear-oblong, ¼ in. long, cylindrical, obtuse, spurred; fls. few, pedicelled, reddish, ¼ in. wide; follicles erect. Iran, Armenia, Caucasus.

tenuifolium (Sibth. & Sm.) Strobl [*S. amplexicaule* DC.]. E; glabrous, sterile sts. 1–3 in., covered in summer with broad scarious lf. bases; lvs. linear, ¼–¾ in. long, minutely pointed, glaucous, with 3-lobed spur; fl. sts. 2–8 in., sparsely leafy, lvs. narrow-spurred, cymes 2-branched; fls. 6–10-merous, yellow, ⅝ in. wide, sepals grooved; follicles erect. Late spring, early summer. Asia Minor, s. Eur., N. Afr.

ternatum Michx. E; smooth or finely papillose, sts. decumbent below; lvs. in 3's, obovate or round-spatulate, ½–1 in. long; fls. sts. 3–6 in., cymes mostly 3-branched; fls. 4-merous, sessile, white, ½ in. wide; follicles spreading. Spring. E. U.S.

tortuosum Hemsl. Not cult.; material grown under this name is *S. lucidum*.

torulosum R. T. Clausen. P; branching shrub, to 3 ft., sts. irregularly thickened, to 4 in. in diam. at base; lvs. in rosettes at br. tips, 1–3 in. long, spatulate, acute, glaucous, deciduous; cyme terminal, corymbose; fls. nearly sessile, yellow, ½ in. wide. S. Mex.

Treleasii Rose. SILVER S. P; subshrub, to 1½ ft., sts. erect or decumbent, branching below; lvs. scattered, oblong-obovate, 1–1½ in. long, obtuse, turgid but flattened above, glaucous; fl. sts. axillary, to 1 ft., with lvs. ¼–½ in. long, cyme nearly globose; fls. almost sessile, yellow, ½ in. wide. Late autumn to early spring. S. Mex.

undulatum aureo-variegatum: a listed name of no botanical standing.

ussuriense Kom. T; root crown short, with slender roots, ann. sts. 8–24 in.; lvs. opp. except the lower, orbicular or broadly elliptic, 1¼–2 in. long and wide, clasping, sinuate-dentate; fls. many, mostly 4-merous, purple, ⁵⁄₁₆ in. wide. Late summer. E. Siberia.

variegatum: *Dudleya variegata* (S. Wats.) Moran, which is not cult.; but the name *S. variegatum* as used in the trade is probably a variegated form of some sp. of *Sedum*.

villosum L. E; glandular-pubescent, bien. or mostly per. by small offsets, 2–6 in.; lvs. alt., linear-oblong, ¼–½ in. long, obtuse, flattened above; cymes loose; fls. pale purple, ¼ in. wide. Early summer. Eur., N. Afr.

virens: *S. rupestre*.

viride Mak. T; very close to *S. sordidum*, but having lvs. mostly opp., sometimes in 3's, bright green, paler on back, with clearly delimited petioles to 1 in. long; petals to ³⁄₁₆ in. long. Summer, early autumn. Sw. Japan. For *S. viride* (Rose) A. Berger, see *S. Corynephyllum*.

Wallichianum: *S. crassipes*.

Watsonii: *S. oregonense*.

Weinbergii: *Graptopetalum paraguayense*.

Winkleri: *S. hirsutum* subsp. *baeticum*.

Woodii: *S. spathulifolium.*

Woodwardii: *S. Aizoon.*

Wrightii A. Gray. E; glabrous; lvs. of sterile sts. in rosettes, elliptic to ovate or obovate, ⅜ in. long, turgid but flattened, yellow-green; fl. sts. 3–8 in. or more, the lvs. easily falling and rooting, cymes 2–5-branched; fls. nearly sessile, white, ⅜ in. wide, petals spreading from near middle. Summer, early autumn. Tex., New Mex., n. Mex.

yosemitense: *S. spathulifolium* subsp. *anomalum.*

yunnanense Franch. R; root crown short and thick, ann. sts. 1–3 ft.; lvs. of root crown reniform, petioled, lvs. of ann. sts. mostly in 3's, ovate to lanceolate, 1–4 in. long, acute, serrate; thyrse 2–6 in. long; fls. unisexual, 4-merous, yellow-green or purplish, to ⅛ in. long. Summer. China.

SEEMANNIA Regel. *Gesneriaceae.* A few spp. of per., terrestrial herbs with scaly rhizomes, native to S. Amer.; lvs. opp. or mostly whorled; fls. solitary, or a few clustered in axils or from a short peduncle, calyx 5-lobed, corolla tubular-campanulate, lobes spreading, very short, stamens 4, borne at base of corolla tube, anthers coherent, disc ringlike, low, indistinctly 5-lobed, ovary half-inferior; fr. a caps.

Propagated by the scaly rhizomes. For cultivation see *Gesneriaceae.*

sylvatica (HBK) Hanst. To 2 ft. or more; lvs. opp. or in whorls of 3–5, ovate-elliptic, to 5¼ in. long, 1¼ in. wide; fls. 1–2, pedicels to 2⅜ in. long, calyx lobes linear to narrowly ovate, to ⅛ in. long, corolla tube ½ in. long, orange-red, red, or sometimes yellow, lobes bright yellow, margined with maroon. Peru, Bolivia.

SELAGINELLA Beauvois. LITTLE CLUB MOSS, SPIKE M. *Selaginellaceae.* About 700 spp. of spore-bearing mosslike plants with dichotomous branching, of cosmopolitan distribution, but chiefly trop. and subtrop. Characteristics of the family.

Selaginellas are of easy culture. They are grown for their ornamental foliage outdoors and in greenhouses in the North. Certain of the tropical species make excellent ground covers in moist shady sites; others are good subjects for hanging baskets. Propagated by spores or cuttings in the spring. Cuttings of some of the greenhouse kinds can be scattered over the soil of the propagating bench, covered with glass and kept at a temperature of 70° F., until they form roots. See also *Ferns.*

amoena: *S. pulcherrima.*

apoda (L.) Spring [*S. densa* Hort., not Rydb.]. MEADOW S. M., BASKET S. Sts. delicate, weak, prostrate, forming mats to 16 in. across; lvs. dimorphic, 4-ranked, minute, pale green; strobili sessile, to ½ in. long. E. N. Amer.

Braunii Bak. TREELET S. M. Sts. erect, to 1½ ft. long, straw-colored, triangular and flexuous in the upper half, unbranched below; lvs. dimorphic, 4-ranked, very small; strobili 4-angled. W. China.

caulescens Wallich. ex Spring: *S. bryopteris* Bak., which is not known to be cult.; material cult. as *S. caulescens* is *S. involvens.*

cuspidata: *S. pallescens.*

densa Rydb. [*S. Engelmannii* Hieron.]. Sts. much-branched, mat-forming, to 4 in. long; lvs. all alike, in several ranks, strap-shaped to more triangular, imbricate, glaucous when young, becoming dark gray, terminated by a white bristle; strobili to 1 in. long. W. N. Amer. Material cult. under the name *S. densa* is usually *S. apoda.*

denticulata (L.) Link. Sts. much-branched, matted, creeping, to 6 in. long; lvs. dimorphic, 4-ranked, minute, imbricate, firm, flat, toothed; strobili sessile, 4-angled, about ½ in. long. Medit. region, from Madeira and Canary Is. to Syria.

Douglasii (Hook. & Grev.) Spring. DOUGLAS'S S. M. Sts. prostrate, rooting and creeping, to 16 in. long; lvs. dimorphic, 4-ranked, firm, spreading, to ⅛ in. long, yellowish-green. Ore. and n. Calif. to B.C. and Idaho.

Emmeliana: *S. pallescens.*

Engelmannii: *S. densa.*

erythropus (Mart.) Spring. Sts. erect, to 1 ft., crimson, branched above, unbranched in lower ⅓–½; lvs. dimorphic, 4-ranked, firm, dark green, ascending; strobili 4-angled, ⅜–½ in. long. Trop. Amer. Var. **major:** *S. umbrosa.*

haematodes (Kunze) Spring. Sts. erect, to 2 ft., much-branched above, unbranched below, bright crimson; lvs. dimorphic, 4-ranked, bright green; strobili 4-angled, to 1½ in. long. Panama to Bolivia.

involvens (Swartz) Spring. Sts. erect, stiff, to 1 ft. or sometimes more, much-branched above, unbranched in lower half, greenish; lvs. dimorphic, 4-ranked, crowded, bright green, lvs. of inner rows smaller, overlapping, their bases covered or obscured; strobili 4-angled, to ½ in. long. Malay Pen., Indonesia, China, Japan. Sometimes cult. under the name *S. caulescens.*

Kraussiana (Kunze) A. Braun. TRAILING S., MAT S. M. Sts. mosslike, creeping, jointed, rooting, much-branched, to 1 ft. long; lvs. dimorphic, 4-ranked, bright green, ciliate; strobili 4-angled, short. S. Afr. CV. **'Brownii'** [var. *Brownii* Hort.]. DWARF CLUB MOSS, CUSHION M., IRISH M., SCOTCH M. More dwarf. Cvs. **'Aurea'** and **'Variegata'.** Lvs. variegated.

lepidophylla (Hook. & Grev.) Spring. RESURRECTION PLANT, ROSE-OF-JERICHO. Sts. stiff, densely tufted, to 4 in. long, branched to base, curling up into a ball when dry but expanding in water; lvs. dimorphic, 4-ranked, flat, imbricate, obtuse, ciliate; strobili 4-angled, to ½ in. long. Tex. and Ariz., s. to El Salvador.

Martensii Spring. Sts. ascending in upper half, trailing and rooting in lower half, to 1 ft. long, branched to base; lvs. dimorphic, 4-ranked, green, with unequal sides, serrulate; strobili 4-angled, to ½ in. long. Mex. Forma **albolineata** (T. Moore) Alston [var. *Watsoniana* Hort. ex Hort. Sander]. Some lvs. white or partly white. Forma **albovariegata** (Bull) Alston [var. *variegata* E. Morr.]. Brs. white-tipped. Var. **variegata:** forma *albovariegata.* Var. **Watsoniana:** forma *albolineata.*

pallescens (K. Presl) Spring [*S. cuspidata* (Link) Link; *S. Emmeliana* Van Geert]. MOSS FERN, SWEAT PLANT. Sts. densely tufted, erect, to 1 ft., branched nearly to base; lvs. dimorphic, 4-ranked, pale green, white-margined, upper lvs. cuspidate; strobili 4-angled, to ½ in. long, bracts cuspidate, strongly keeled. N. Amer., s. to n. Colombia and Venezuela. Cv. **'Aurea'.** Lvs. golden-green.

pulcherrima Liebm. ex Bak. [*S. amoena* Bull]. Sts. erect, to 1 ft., yellowish, 3–4 times branched above, unbranched below; lvs. dimorphic, 4-ranked, light green; strobili 4-angled, to ½ in. long. Mex.

rupestris (L.) Spring. ROCK S., DWARF LYCOPOD. Sts. tufted, to 5 in. long, forming open, spreading mats; lvs. dimorphic, 4-ranked, imbricate, ciliate, tipped with white or tawny awns ½–¾ as long as blade; strobili 4-angled, to 1 in. long. E. N. Amer.

serpens (Desv. ex Poir.) Spring. Sts. trailing and matted, to 9 in. long, with many spreading-erect brs.; lvs. dimorphic, 4-ranked, 1/16 in long, bright green in the morning, becoming pale and silvery in late afternoon, ciliate toward base; strobili 4-angled, to ½ in. long. W. Indies.

umbrosa Lem. ex Hiern [*S. erythropus* var. *major* Spring]. Similar to *S. erythropus,* but with longer sts., and all lvs. appressed. Yucatan to Colombia.

uncinata (Desv. ex Poir.) Spring. PEACOCK MOSS, RAINBOW FERN, BLUE S., TRAILING S. Sts. weak, trailing, rooting, to 2 ft. long, yellowish; lvs. dimorphic, 4-ranked, bright blue-green; strobili 4-angled, to ½ in. long. China.

Willdenovii (Desv. ex Poir.) J. G. Bak. PEACOCK FERN, WILLDENOW'S S. M. Sts. climbing, to 20 ft. or more, branched to base; lvs. dimorphic, 4-ranked, green, tinted blue, crowded; strobili 4-angled, to 1 in. long. Old World tropics.

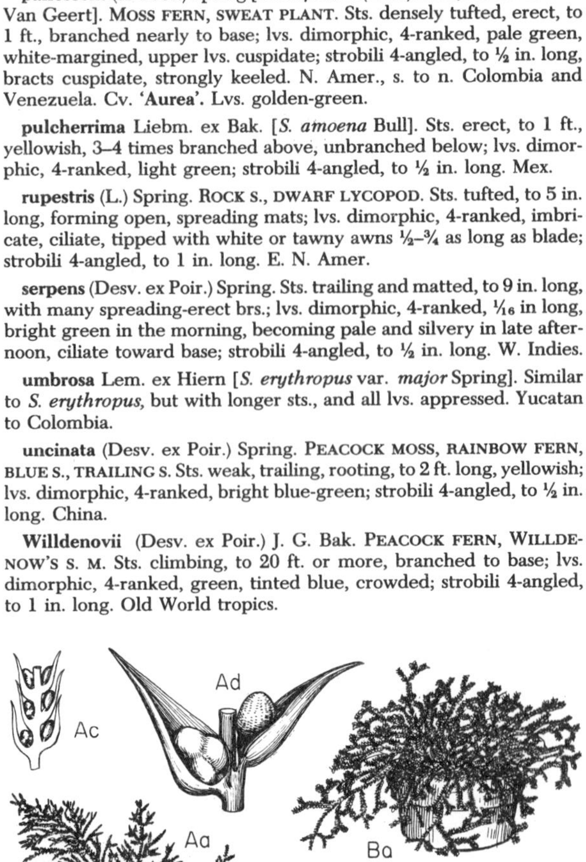

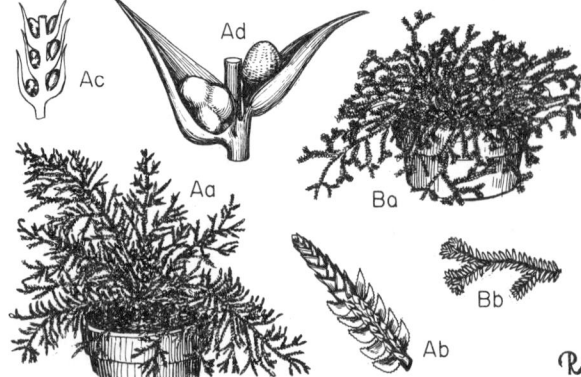

SELAGINELLACEAE. **A,** *Selaginella pallescens:* **Aa,** plant, × 1/10; **Ab,** underside of branch with terminal strobilus, × 3; **Ac,** part of strobilus, vertical section, × 6; **Ad,** part of strobilus, showing megasporangium (left) and microsporangium (right), × 20. **B,** *S. Kraussiana:* **Ba,** plant, × 10; **Bb,** branch tip, × ½. (From Bailey, *Manual of Cultivated Plants,* ed. 2.)

SELAGINELLACEAE Wilk. SPIKE MOSS or SELAGINELLA FAMILY. Fern allies; 1 genus, *Selaginella,* of about 700 spp. of primitive, spore-bearing, vascular plants of cosmopolitan distribution; sts. prostrate to erect, sometimes climbing, often rooting, branching dichotomously, the br. systems sometimes frondlike; lvs. scalelike, many, all alike and spirally arranged, or dimorphic and 4-ranked; sporophylls in a terminal, spikelike cone (strobilus) bearing microsporangia with many microspores, and megasporangia with usually 4 megaspores.

SELAGO L. *Scrophulariaceae.* About 140 spp. of evergreen shrubs or subshrubs, rarely ann. herbs, native mostly to S. Afr., but a few to trop. Afr.; lvs. solitary at the nodes or in clusters, alt., or the lower opp. or subopp., simple, often heathlike; fls. white, pink, blue, or purple, tiny, in spikes or heads often arranged in corymbs or panicles, calyx 5-lobed, corolla nearly equally 5-lobed or somewhat 2-lipped, stamens 4, exserted; fr. indehiscent, often separating into 2 halves.

Galpinii Schlechter. Much-branched, bushy per., to 9 in., becoming glabrous; lvs. somewhat clustered, linear, to ½ in. long, entire; fls. pink to purple, in panicles of dense heads. S. Afr.

serrata Bergius. Glabrous subshrub, to 2 ft., sts. erect or decumbent; lvs. solitary at the nodes, but crowded, sessile, obovate or oblong, to 1 in. long, toothed; fls. pale blue to purple, in compact corymbs of heads. S. Afr.

spuria L. Ann. or per., to 2 ft., sts. glabrous or finely hairy; lvs. mostly solitary at nodes, linear or linear-lanceolate, to 1¼ in. long, toothed; heads of white, pink, or purple fls. becoming corymbose in fr. S. Afr.

Thunbergii Choisy. Much-branched per., to 2 ft. or more, sts. hairy; lvs. clustered, linear, to ⅜ in. long; fls. blue in panicles of heads. S. Afr.

SELENICEREUS (A. Berger) Britt. & Rose [*Mediocactus* Britt. & Rose]. NIGHT-BLOOMING CEREUS, MOON C., MOON CACTUS. *Cactaceae.* About 20 spp. of cacti climbing by aerial roots, native to trop. Amer.; sts. slender, 3–11-angled or -ribbed; spines small or rarely 0; fls. nocturnal, large, 5–16 in. long, perianth tube usually longer than the limb, scales with axillary hairs, bristles, or spines, outer perianth segms. narrow, yellow to brown, inner segms. mostly twice as wide or more, white or rarely red, upper stamens in a distinct close circle; fr. with deciduous clusters of spines or hairs. Tex. to Venezuela and perhaps to Argentina.

These plants are among those known as night-blooming cereus; raised under glass in cold countries and in the open in frost-free places. They are readily grown, and old plants bloom freely. For culture see *Cacti.*

brevispinus Britt. & Rose. Sts. about 1 in. thick, ribs 8–10, low; areoles tawny, at first with white hairs, spines about 12, conical, ³⁄₆₄ in. long, radial spines curved, central spines thicker; fls. 10 in. long, areoles of perianth tube with long white hairs. Cuba. Cv. **'Spinulosus'** is listed.

coniflorus (Weing.) Britt. & Rose [*S. Pringlei* Rose]. Sts. about 1 in. thick, ribs 5–6, rather prominent; spines needle-shaped, pale yellow, radial spines 4–6, central spine 1, to ½ in. long; fls. 9–10 in. long, areoles of perianth tube with white hairs and spines; fr. globose, 2½ in. in diam. E. Mex.

Donkelaarii (Salm-Dyck) Britt. & Rose. Sts. elongate, ⅜ in. thick, ribs 9–10, low; spines 10–15, radial spines bristlelike, appressed, to ⁵⁄₃₂ in. long, central spines to ³⁄₃₂ in. long; fls. 7 in. long, areoles of perianth tube with long hairs. Yucatan.

grandiflorus (L.) Britt. & Rose [*Cereus grandiflorus* (L.) Mill.]. QUEEN-OF-THE-NIGHT. Sts. to 1 in. thick, ribs 5–8, low; areoles with whitish hairs, spines various, needle-shaped, to ⅜ in. long; fls. 7–10 in. long, areoles of perianth tube with tawny hairs; fr. 3 in. long. Jamaica, Cuba. Widely planted; naturalized in trop. Amer. Cv. **'Armatus'**. Said to have longer spines. Cv. **'Tellii'**. Sts. ⅜ in. thick, ribs mostly 4; fls. small.

hamatus (Scheidw.) Britt. & Rose. Sts. about ½ in. thick, ribs 3–5, with remote, deflexed spurs about ¼ in. high, each with an areole on its upper side; spines few, stout, short; fls. 8–10 in. long, scales of perianth tube with long axillary hairs. S. and e. Mex.

hondurensis (K. Schum.) Britt. & Rose. Sts. about ½ in. thick, ribs 7–10, low; areoles with long white bristles, spines needle-shaped, ¼ in. long; fls. 8 in. long or more, areoles of perianth tube with bristly hairs. Honduras, Guatemala.

Macdonaldiae (Hook.) Britt. & Rose. QUEEN-OF-THE-NIGHT. Sts. about ½ in. thick, becoming cylindrical, ribs 5–7, low, with prominent tubercles ½–2 in. apart; spines conical, to ³⁄₃₂ in. long; fls. 12–14 in. long, areoles of perianth tube with brown hairs and spines; fr. 3 in. long. Cent. Amer.; doubtfully reported from Uruguay and Argentina.

Maxonii: *S. Urbanianus.*

megalanthus (K. Schum.) Moran [*Mediocactus megalanthus* (K. Schum.) Britt. & Rose]. Sts. 3-angled, pendent; areoles to 3 in. apart, spines 0–3, to ⅛ in. long; fls. white, to 15 in. long, areoles with wool and 1 or more slender spines to ⁵⁄₁₆ in. long. Ne. Peru.

Murrillii Britt. & Rose. Sts. ⁵⁄₁₆ in. thick, ribs 7–8, low; areoles to 1 in. apart, spines 5–6, conical, to ³⁄₃₂ in. long; fls. 6 in. long and across, perianth tube with a few minute spines, areoles of the ovary with 1–3 short spines but without hairs. Mex.

Pringlei: *S. coniflorus.*

pteranthus (Link & Otto) Britt. & Rose. PRINCESS-OF-THE-NIGHT, KING-OF-THE-NIGHT. Sts. 1–2 in. thick, ribs 4–6, prominent; spines 1–4, conical, to ⅛ in. long; fls. 10–12 in. long, fragrant, areoles of ovary with long white hairs and bristles; fr. globose, red, 2½ in. in diam. Mex.

setaceus (Salm-Dyck) Werderm. [*Mediocactus coccineus* (Salm-Dyck) Britt. & Rose]. Sts. ½–1(–3) in. wide, mostly 3-, sometimes 4–6-winged; areoles with 10–15 deciduous white bristles, later with mostly 2–3 conical spines to ⅛ in. long; fls. 10–12 in. long, ovary and perianth tube with hairs and weak spines; fr. ovoid, red, 3 in. long, with spines to ¾ in. long. Brazil to Argentina.

spinulosus (DC.) Britt. & Rose. Sts. to ¾ in. thick, ribs mostly 4–6; spines short, radial spines 5–6, central spines 1–2; fls. 5–6 in. long, ovary and perianth tube with clusters of small spines. Tex., e. Mex.

Urbanianus (Gürke & Weing.) Britt. [*S. Maxonii* Rose]. Sts. to 1¼ in. thick, often purple, ribs mostly 4–5, at first prominent; areoles with reflexed white bristles, spines about 4–7, needle-shaped, to nearly ½ in. long; fls. 8–12 in. long, areoles of ovary and perianth tube with long white hairs, ovary strongly tubercled. Cuba, Hispaniola.

vagans (K. Brandeg.) Britt. & Rose. Sts. about ½ in. thick, ribs about 10, low; spines many, needle-shaped, ¼ in. long; fls. 6 in. long, ovary and tube with clusters of 5–8 needle-shaped spines. Mex.

Wercklei (A. Web.) Britt. & Rose. Sts. ¼–½ in. thick, ribs 6–12, low, spineless; fls. red, 6 in. long, ovary spiny; fr. ovoid, yellow. Costa Rica.

SEMECARPUS L.f. *Anacardiaceae.* About 40 spp. of trees of trop. Asia, Micronesia, Solomon Is., and Australia; lvs. simple, alt.; fls. in terminal or axillary panicles, calyx 5-lobed, petals 5, stamens 5, inserted around the disc, ovary 1-celled, styles 3; fr. a fleshy drupe.

Anacardium L.f. MARKING-NUT TREE, VARNISH TREE. To 15 ft.; lvs. oblong or ovate-oblong, to 1 ft. or longer, brown above, minutely pubescent beneath, poisonous to touch; fls. greenish-white, to ¼ in. across; fr. oblong or nearly globose, 1 in. in diam., set in a fleshy, orange cup, the thickened disc and calyx base. Trop. Asia, n. Australia. Sap of the young fr. hardens to a black resin used as an ink or dye when mixed with lime water.

SEMEIANDRA Hook. & Arn. *Onagraceae.* One sp., an openly branched pubescent shrub of Mex.; lvs. alt. or opp.; fls. crimson, in large drooping panicles, sepals and petals 4, stamens 2, united at base with the style, ovary inferior; fr. a caps.

grandiflora Hook. & Arn. To 10 ft.; lvs. 2–6 in. long; calyx tube ½–¾ in. long, sepals 1 in. long, petals ½ in. long. Mex. Semihardy.

SEMELE Kunth. CLIMBING BUTCHER'S-BROOM. *Liliaceae.* One sp., a dioecious, shrubby vine, native to the Canary Is.; lvs. reduced to scales, the apparent lvs. being leaflike brs. or cladophylls; fls. unisexual, borne in umbels, usually on margins of cladophylls, perianth segms. 6, united into a very short tube, stamens 6, filaments united; fr. a 3-celled, 1–2-seeded berry. The name has three syllables.

Suitable for greenhouse culture, or outdoors in the South; sometimes mistakenly cultivated as a species of *Asparagus.*

androgyna (L.) Kunth. To 60 ft.; cladophylls alt., ovate to lanceolate-ovate, to 4 in. long and 2 in. wide, leathery, acuminate; fls. small, yellow; fr. yellowish-white.

SEMIAQUILEGIA Mak. *Ranunculaceae.* About 7 spp. of per. herbs of the N. Temp. Zone resembling *Aquilegia,* but practically spurless, the petals gibbous at the base, stamens surrounded by a whorl of membranous staminodes; follicles 3–10.

adoxoides (DC.) Mak. To 1 ft., sts. slender, ribbed, pubescent; lvs. small, ternate; fls. cup-shaped, cream- and chocolate-colored, sepals reddish-brown, narrow, petals about ³⁄₁₆ in. long. Japan, Korea, e. China. Cult. material listed as *S. ecalcarata* may belong here.

ecalcarata: *Aquilegia ecalcarata,* but cult. material listed as *S. ecalcarata* may be *S. adoxoides.*

simulatrix: *Aquilegia ecalcarata.*

SEMIARUNDINARIA Mak. ex Nakai. BAMBOO. *Gramineae.* Three spp. of erect, running, rhizomatous bamboos in Japan and e. Asia; sts. woody, brs. few at each node; st. sheaths deciduous, bearing a small blade; lf. sheaths with rigid, smooth bristles; spikelets 1–3 in spicate fascicles on branchlets, 3–4-fld., lemma 9–10-nerved, stamens 3, style short, with 3 stigmas. For terminology see *Gramineae.*

Propagation by division in late winter or early spring. See *Bamboos.*

fastuosa (Marliac ex Mitf.) Mak. ex Nakai [*Phyllostachys fastuosa* (Marliac ex Mitf.) Houz. de Leh.]. NARIHIRA B. Sts. erect, rather distant, to 25 ft. high, thin-walled, to 1⅜ in. in diam., cylindrical, but the upper internodes flattened, dark green, marked with purplish-brown, brs. erect; st. sheaths to 9 in. long, thick, green becoming purplish, glossy inside, many tardily deciduous; lf. blades to 7¼ in. long and 1 in. wide, 10–12-nerved, long-pointed, gradually narrowed into a rather long petiole, shiny dark green above, glaucous on one side beneath, puberulous; spikelets to 1½ in. long. Japan, where frequently cult. as a garden ornamental and for the useful sts. Zone 8. Less rampant than many running bamboos.

SEMNANTHE N. E. Br. *Aizoaceae.* One spp., a succulent shrub with 2-angled brs., native to S. Afr.; lvs. with transparent dots, spreading, incurved, keeled, 3-angled, in section the keels irregularly lacerately toothed; fls. solitary or in pairs, calyx 5-lobed, petals many, stamens many, concealed by inflexed petals and staminodes, ovary inferior, 10-celled, stigmas 10; fr. a caps., expanding keels awn-tipped, placental tubercles absent.

The shrubs may be planted outdoors in summer, but at a relatively cool winter temperature of about 45–50° F. Propagation easy by seeds or cuttings. See also *Succulents.*

lacera (Haw.) N. E. Br. To 32 in. high, brs. stout, green, sometimes becoming reddish and gray-skinned; lvs. light green with transparent dots, gray-pruinose, to 2 in. long, ½ in. wide, nearly saber-shaped, upper side flat, sides much compressed; fls. to 2 in. across, petals bright rose-red. Cape Prov.

SEMPERVIVUM L. [*Jovibarba* Opiz]. HOUSELEEK, LIVE-FOREVER. *Crassulaceae.* About 40 spp. of succulent per. herbs, native to Eur., Morocco, and w. Asia, mostly cespitose, spreading by offsets; lvs. in dense basal rosettes, alt., oblong to obovate, broad-based, ciliate; fl. sts. terminal, leafy, with usually compact cymes; fls. 6–20-merous, red, purple, yellow, or white, petals separate, either 6–7, erect, fringed (section *Jovisbarba* Mert. & W. J. D. Koch), or 9–20, spreading, not fringed though variously ciliate (section *Sempervivum*), stamens twice as many as petals.

Many names are known in cultivation, but many of them represent variants or hybrids of a few species, particularly of *S. tectorum.* The species entered here are presumably hardy in the northern states. The tender plants of Madeira and the Canary Is. formerly included in *Sempervivum* are placed in *Aeonium, Aichryson, Greenovia,* and *Monanthes.* One houseleek, *S. tectorum,* is an old-fashioned plant about houses and in borders, prized for its durable rosettes and the progeny of smaller ones. In European countries it often grows on roofs, therefore the Latin name; it has also escaped somewhat in this country. Other kinds are useful in rock gardens, spreading slowly. Propagation is naturally by the small rosettes or offsets; plants grow readily from seeds when available, but some of them seldom bloom. See also *Succulents.*

acuminatum: *S. tectorum* var. *glaucum.*

admontense: a listed name of no botanical standing.

Albertii: a listed name of no botanical standing for *Sedum gracile.*

albidum Schnittsp. & C. B. Lehm. Similar to *S. tectorum* and perhaps a form or hybrid derivative of it; petals whitish.

Allionii (Jord. & Fourr.) Nym. [*S. austriacum* Nym; *S. hirsutum* Pollini; *Jovibarba Allionii* (Jord. & Fourr.) D. A. Webb]. Rosettes mostly closed, pale green, to 1 in. wide; lvs. ½ in. long, glandular-pubescent; fl. sts. to 6 in.; fls. 6–7-merous, greenish-white, ½ in. long. Summer S. Alps.

alpestre: *S. montanum.*

alpinum: *S. tectorum* var.

arachnoideum L. COBWEB H., SPIDERWEB H. Rosettes ½–¾ in. wide, offsets crowded and sessile; lvs. about 50, cuspidate, to ⅜ in. long, the tips connected by cobwebby strands; fl. sts. 3–5 in.; fls. 9–12-merous, bright red, ½–1 in. wide. Summer. S. Eur. Var. **glabrescens** Willk. [*S. Doellianum* C. B. Lehm.; *S. Moggridgei* De Smet ex Hook.f.]. Rosettes ovoid, with sparse cobwebby hairs. Var. **tomentosum** (C. B. Lehm. & Schnittsp.) Hayek [*S. Laggeri* Schott; *S. tomentosum* C. B. Lehm. & Schnittsp.; *S. Webbianum* C. B. Lehm. & Schnittsp.]. Rosettes flattish, almost concealed by cobwebby hairs. Cvs. **'Collettii'**, **'Fimbriatum'**, **'Hastipetalum'**, **'Major'**, **'Minus'**, and **'Rubrum'** are listed.

arenarium W. D. J. Koch [*S. cornutum* Hort.; *S. Kochii* Facch.; *Jovibarba arenaria* (W. D. J. Koch) Opiz]. Rosettes ⅛–¾ in. wide, offsets minute on slender horizontal sts.; lvs. 60–80, pale green, glabrous, to ¾ in. long; fls. sts. 3–5 in.; fls. 6-merous, corolla pale yellow, about ¾ in. long, 3 times as long as the calyx. Summer. E. Alps. Plants grown under this name are likely to be a form or hybrid of *S. montanum.*

arvernense: *S. tectorum.*

assimile: *S. marmoreum;* but plants grown under the name *S. assimile* are likely to be *S. tectorum.*

atlanticum J. Ball. Rosettes not widely open, 2–3 in. wide, offsets on short and weak sts.; lvs. pale green, finely pubescent on both faces, to 1½ in. long; fl. sts. to 1 ft.; fls. 12-merous, about 1¼ in. wide, petals white with broad red-purple band. Early summer. Morocco.

atropurpureum: a listed name of no botanical standing; at least some plants offered under this name are *S. tectorum.*

atroviolaceum: a listed name of no botanical standing for *S. tectorum.*

austriacum: *S. Allionii.*

×**barbatulum:** *S.* × *barbulatum.*

×**barbulatum** Schott [*S.* × *barbatulum* Bak.; *S.* × *elegans* Lagger; *S.* × *fimbriatum* Schnittsp. & C. B. Lehm.]: *S. arachnoideum* × *S. montanum.* More or less intermediate between the parents; a variable complex of hybrids; rosettes mostly about ⅜ in. across; fl. sts. to 2 in.; petals intermediate in shape and color. Some material grown as *S.* × *Hausmannii* may belong here.

blandum: *S. marmoreum.*

Boissieri: *S. tectorum.*

Borisii: *S. ciliosum.*

Boutignyanum: *S. tectorum* var. *alpinum.*

Braunii: *S. montanum* var.

Brownii: a listed name of no botanical standing; probably a misspelling of *S. Braunii.*

caespitosum: *Aeonium Simsii.*

calcareum: *S. tectorum* var.

cantalicum: *S. tectorum.*

ciliatum: *Aeonium ciliatum.*

ciliosum Craib [*S. Borisii* Degen & Urum.]. Rosettes 1–2 in. wide, usually closed or half-closed; lvs. many, about 1 in. long, densely glandular-pilose on both surfaces and with longer, hyaline, eglandular hairs on back and edges interwoven across the rosette; fl. sts. 4 in.; fls. 10–12-merous, greenish-yellow, 1 in. wide. Summer. Bulgaria.

cinerascens: *S. erythraeum.*

Clusianum Ten. A poorly known sp.; probably a synonym of *S. tectorum.*

×**Comollii** Rota. Probably *S. tectorum* × *S. Wulfenii.*

Cooperi: a listed name of no botanical standing.

cornutum: a listed name of no botanical standing for *S. arenarium.*

crassicaule: a listed name of no botanical standing.

crystallinum: a listed name of no botanical standing.

cuspidatum: *Orostachys spinosa.*

Doellianum: *S. arachnoideum* var. *glabrescens.*

dolmiticum Facch. Rosettes dense, ½–2 in. wide; lvs. ½–1 in. long, glandular-pubescent on both sides, ciliate with hairs of irregular length, with longer hairs at apex; fl. sts. 3–5 in.; fls. 10–14-merous, ¾ in. wide, petals broadly lanceolate, ⅜ in. long, rose-red with darker purple stripe and white dots. Summer. E. Alps.

×**elegans:** *S.* × *barbulatum.*

erythraeum Velen. [*S. cinerascens* Panč.]. Rosettes open, 1–2½ in. wide; lvs. 80 or more, ½–1½ in. long. about ½ in. wide, usually purplish, glandular-pubescent with white hairs, unequally ciliate; fl. sts. 6–8 in., infl. very hairy with unequal white hairs; fls. 11–12-merous, red-purple, ¾ in. wide. Summer. Bulgaria.

Farreri: a listed name of no botanical standing.

×**Fauconnettii** Reut. [*S.* × *Hausmannii* Schnittsp. & C. B. Lehm.; *S.* × *piliferum* Jord.; *S.* × *Pilosella* C. B. Lehm. & Schnittsp.; *S.* × *Pomelii* Lamotte; *S.* × *pseudoarachnoideum* Lamotte; *S.* × *Schnittspahnii* Lagger; *S.* × *Thomayeri* Correv.]: *S. arachnoideum* × *S. tec-*

torum. Rosettes smaller and denser than in *S. tectorum;* lvs. slightly hairy; infl. larger than in *S. arachnoideum;* fls. intermediate.

×**fimbriatum:** *S.* × *barbulatum;* but the name *S. fimbriatum* has also been used for *S.* × *roseum.*

flagelliforme: *S. montanum;* but plants grown as *S. flagelliforme* may be *S. tectorum.*

×**Funckii** F. Braun: ?*S. arachnoideum* × *S. montanum* × *S. tectorum.* Rosettes dense, open, 1–1½ in. wide; lvs. about ½ in. long, glandular-pubescent on both sides, conspicuously and unequally ciliate; fl. sts. 8 in.; fls. 11–12-merous, purple-rose, ¾ in. across. Summer. Alps. A plant often grown under this name is *S. tectorum* var. *calcareum.*

Gaudinii: *S. grandiflorum.*

giganteum: a listed name of no botanical standing.

glaucum: *S. tectorum* var.

globiferum: botanically a confused name applied to several spp.; the plant grown under this name apparently is a form or hybrid of *S. montanum.*

grandiflorum Haw. [*S. Gaudinii* Christ]. Rosettes loose, 2–4 in. wide or more, strongly scented, sts. of offsets leafy. 3–9 in. long; lvs. dull green, glandular-hairy on both sides, 1–3 in. long; fl. sts. 6–12 in.; fls. 10–15-merous, yellow with purple center. 1–2 in. wide. Summer. S. Switzerland.

Greenei: *S. tectorum* var. *calcareum.*

×**Hausemannii:** *S.* × *Fauconnettii;* but the name *S.* × *Hausmannii* has also been used for *S.* × *barbulatum.*

Heuffelii Schott [*S. patens* Griseb. & Schenk; *Jovibarba Heuffelii* (Schott) Á.Löve & D. Löve]. Rhizome thick, short-branched, rosettes open, 2–3 in. wide, new ones arising by division of the old and not by offsets; lvs. 30–40, finely pubescent or glabrous, 1–2½ in. long; fl. sts. 4–8 in.; fls. 6–7-merous, pale yellow, about ½ in. long. Summer. Se. Eur.

Hillebrandtii: *S. hirtum.*

hirsutum: *S. Allionii.*

hirtum L. [*S. Hillebrandtii* Schott; *S. Neilreichii* Schott; *S. Simonkaianum* Degen; *Jovibarba hirta* (L.) Opiz]. Rosettes open, 1–2 in. wide, offsets many, small, globular, easily detached; lvs. broadest below middle, glabrous, ½–1 in. long; fl. sts. 4–8 in., mostly glandular-hairy; fls. 6-merous, pale yellow to greenish-white, ⅝ in. long. Summer. Se. Eur. Cv. 'Purpureum' is listed. *S. Hillebrandtii*, with gray-green rosette lvs. to ½ in. wide and broad glabrous st. lvs., and *S. Neilreichii*, with rosette lvs. ⅛ in. wide and glabrous st. lvs., are extreme forms intergrading with the typical form.

Histonii: a listed name of no botanical standing.

Hookeri: a listed name of no botanical standing for *S.* × *barbulatum.*

hougifolium: a listed name of no botanical standing.

×**Huteri:** *S.* × *rupicola.*

juratense: *S. tectorum.*

kanswansii: a listed name of no botanical standing.

Kindingeri Adamovič. Rosettes open. 1½–2½ in. wide; lvs. about 1 in. long, glandular-pubescent on both sides and somewhat villous toward apex, unequally long-ciliate; fl. sts. very leafy, glandular-villous, to 10 in.; fls. 12–14-merous, ivory with red center, 1 in. wide. Macedonia.

Kochii: *S. arenarium.*

Laggeri: *S. arachnoideum* var. *tomentosum.*

LeHarpei: a listed name of no botanical standing for *S. tectorum.*

Lamottei: *S. tectorum.*

latifolium: a listed name of no botanical standing.

lesurinum: *S. tectorum.*

leucanthum Panč. Rosettes 1½–3 in. wide, offsets long-stemmed; lvs. 70–80, 1 in. long, erect, glandular-pubescent on both sides, unequally ciliate; fl. sts. 4–8 in.; fls. 11–13-merous, 1 in. wide, pale- or greenish-yellow. Summer. Bulgaria.

longifolium: a listed name of no botanical standing.

longobardum: a listed name of no botanical standing; at least some plants under this name are *S. tectorum.*

Lowei: *Monanthes brachycaulon;* but probably for some sp. of *Sempervivum.*

magnificum: a listed name of no botanical standing.

Malbyi: a listed name of no botanical standing.

marmoreum Griseb. [*S. assimile* Schott; *S. blandum* Schott; *S. Reginae-Amaliae* Heldr. & Sartori; *S. rubicundum* Schur; *S. Schlehanii* Schott]. Rosettes open, flattish, 2–4 in. across; lvs. 60–80, 1–2 in. long,

hairy when young, green or mostly red with green margins and tip; fl. sts. 4–6 in.; fls. 12–13-merous, 1 in. wide, petals crimson with white margins. Summer. Hungary to Greece. Cv. 'Brunneifolium' [*S. ornatum* Duruz]. Lvs. glabrous, uniformly brown or in winter red.

Mettenianum: *S. tectorum.*

Moggridgei: *S. arachnoideum* var. *glabrescens.*

montanum L. [*S. alpestre* Lamotte; *S. flagelliforme* Fisch.]. Rosettes dense, mostly open, 1–1½ in. wide; lvs. 40–50, ½–1 in. long, glandular-pubescent, the hairs mostly longer at the tip and on the edges; fl. sts. 2–4 in. or more; fls. 10–15-merous, 1½ in. wide, violet-purple, petals linear-lanceolate, ⅜–¾ in. long. Summer. Eur. Var. **Braunii** (Funck) Wettst. ex Hayek [*S. Braunii* Funck]. Petals white or yellowish-white. Var. **stiriacum** (Wettst.) Praeg. Larger, rosettes to 2 in. wide; lvs. red-tipped; fl. sts. to 7 in.; fls. to 2 in. E. Alps.

×**Morelianum** Viviand-Morel: a hybrid of uncertain status; probably derived from *S. arachnoideum.*

Neilreichii: *S. hirtum.*

nigrum: a listed name of no botanical standing.

Ollonii: a listed name of no botanical standing.

ornatum: *S. marmoreum* cv. 'Brunneifolium'.

pallidum: *S. tectorum.*

patens: *S. Heuffelii.*

Pedoyanum or **Piedoyanum:** a listed name of no botanical standing.

×**piliferum:** *S.* × *Fauconnettii.*

×**Pilosella:** *S.* × *Fauconnettii.*

Pittonii Schott. Rosettes dense, 1–2 in. wide; lvs. ½–1 in. long, glandular-hairy on both sides, purple-tipped; fl. sts. 2–4 in. or more; fls. about 11-merous, 1 in. wide, pale yellow without purple. Summer. Syria.

×**Pomelii:** *S.* × *Fauconnettii.*

Potsii: a listed name of no botanical standing for *S. tectorum.*

Powellii: a listed name of no botanical standing.

×**pseudoarachnoideum:** *S.* × *Fauconnettii.*

pumilum Bieb. Rosettes open, ½–¾ in. wide; lvs. ⅜ in. long, glandular-pubescent with hairs of unequal length, unequally glandular-ciliate; fl. sts. 1½–4 in.; fls. 10–12-merous, ¾ in. wide, rosy-purple, petals lanceolate to oblanceolate. Summer. Caucasus.

purpureum: a listed name of no botanical standing. Cv. 'Acutifolium' is also listed.

pyrenaicum: *S. tectorum.*

Rangeri: a listed name of no botanical standing.

Reginae-Amaliae: *S. marmoreum.*

rhodanicum: *S. tectorum.*

robustum: *S. tectorum.*

Rosaninii: a listed name of no botanical standing.

×**roseum** Huter ex Nym. [*S.* × *fimbriatum* Schott ex Hegi]: *S. arachnoideum* × *S. Wulfenii.* Like *S. Wulfenii*, but smaller; lvs. with a tuft of woolly hairs at apex; fls. yellow and red or reddish with yellow edge or intermediate.

royanum: *S. tectorum.*

rubicundum: *S. marmoreum.* Cv. 'Hybridum' is also listed.

rubrum: a listed name of no botanical standing; at least some plants under this name are *S. tectorum.*

rupestre: *S. tectorum;* but plants grown as *S. rupestre* are likely to be a form or hybrid of *S. montanum.*

×**rupicola** A. Kern. [*S.* × *Huteri* Hausm. ex F. Graf; *S.* × *Theobaldii* Brügg.]: *S. montanum* × *S. Wulfenii.* More or less intermediate between the parents and variable.

ruthenicum Schnittsp. & C. B. Lehm. [*S. Zeleborii* Schott]. Rosettes dense, 1½–2½ in. wide; lvs. to 1¼ in. long, rarely purple-tipped, densely puberulous on both sides; fl. sts. 4–6 in.; fls. 11–12-merous, ¾–1 in. wide, pale green or light yellow with purple center. Summer. Se. Eur., Asia Minor.

Sanfordii: a listed name of no botanical standing.

Scherzianum: a listed name of no botanical standing.

Schlehanii: *S. marmoreum.*

×**Schnittspahnii:** *S.* × *Fauconnettii.*

×**Schottii** C. B. Lehm. & Schnittsp. [*S.* × *Verlotii* Lamotte]: *S. montanum* × *S. tectorum.* Intermediate between parents or some more like *S. montanum*, others more like *S. tectorum.* The name has also been used for *S. tectorum* var. *glaucum.*

Seguieri DC. A name of dubious application; material cult. under this name is probably referable to *Sedum dasyphyllum.*

Simonkaianum: *S. hirtum.*

soboliferum Sims [*Jovibarba sobolifera* (Sims) Opiz]. HEN-AND-CHICKENS. Rosettes flattened-globose, ½–1¼ in. wide, offsets many, globose, slender-stemmed, borne among outer and middle lvs.; lvs. 60–80, glabrous, light green or red-tipped, to 1 in. long, broadest above middle; fl. sts. 4–8 in.; fls. 6-merous, greenish-yellow, ⅝ in. long. Summer. N. Eurasia.

speciosum: *S. tectorum.*

spinosum: a listed name of no botanical standing; perhaps referring to *Orostachys spinosa.*

spinulifolium: a listed name of no botanical standing.

spinulosum: a listed name of no botanical standing.

Stansfieldii: a listed name of no botanical standing.

Syleri: a listed name of no botanical standing.

tectorum L. [*S. arvernense* Lecoq. & Lamotte; *S. Boissieri* Bak.; *S. cantalicum* Jord. & Fourr.; *S. juratense* Jord. & Fourr.; *S. Lamottei* Boreau; *S. lesurinum* Lamotte; *S. Mettenianum* C. B. Lehm. & Schnittsp.; *S. pallidum* Jord. & Fourr.; *S. pyrenaicum* Jord. & Fourr.; *S. rhodanicum* Jord. & Fourr.; *S. royanum* Correv.; *S. robustum* Jord. & Fourr.; *S. rupestre* Rouy & E. Camus; *S. speciosum* Lamotte; *S. triste* Bak.; *S. violascens* Jord. & Fourr.]. COMMON H., ROOF H., HEN-AND-CHICKENS, OLD-MAN-AND-WOMAN. Rosettes open, flattish, 3–4 in. wide or more; lvs. 50–60, glabrous, green, often purple-tipped, 1½–3 in. long; fl. sts. 8–18 in., shaggy with white hairs; fls. about 13-merous, ¾–1 in. wide, purplish-red. Summer. Eur. This most variable sp. is the most widely grown, appearing in many forms and under many names. It is the only red-fld. sp. with lvs. glabrous even when young. It may be listed as *S. atropurpureum, S. atroviolaceum, S. LaHarpei, S. longobardum, S. Potsii,* and *S. rubrum.* Cv. **'Robustum'**. Rosettes to 6 in. wide; lvs. purple-tipped. Cvs. **'Atroviolaceum'**, **'Bicolor'**, **'Majus'**, **'Rubrum'**, and **'Violaceum'** are listed. Var. **alpinum** (Griseb. & Schenk) Praeg. [*S. alpinum* Griseb. & Schenk; *S. Boutignyanum* Billot & Gren.]. Smaller, rosettes 1–2½ in. wide; lf. bases red. Var. **calcareum** (Jord.) Cariot & St.-Léger [*S. calcareum* Jord.; *S. Greenei* Bak.]. Lvs. very glaucous, with conspicuous brown-purple tips. Var. **glaucum** (Ten.) Praeg. [*S. acuminatum* Schott; *S. glaucum* Ten.; *S. Schottii* Bak., not C. B. Lehm. & Schnittsp.]. Lvs. glaucous, whitish at base.

tenellum: a listed name of no botanical standing.

ternatum: a listed name of no botanical standing.

×**Theobaldii:** *S.* × *rupicola.*

×**Thomayeri:** *S.* × *Fauconnettii.*

tomentosum: *S. arachnoideum* var.

×**tortuosum:** *Aichryson* × *domesticum.*

triste: *S. tectorum.*

Tuscanii: a listed name of no botanical standing.

×**Verlotii:** *S.* × *Schottii.*

violaceum: a listed name of no botanical standing; perhaps referring to *S. tectorum.*

violascens: *S. tectorum.*

Webbianum: *S. arachnoideum* var. *tomentosum.*

Wulfenii Hoppe. Rosettes 2–3½ in. wide, open but with young lvs. mostly in a compact bud; lvs. ¾–1½ in. long, glaucous, gray-green, rosy-purple at base but not at tip; fl. sts. 4–12 in.; fls. 12–15-merous, 1 in. wide, petals yellow or greenish-yellow, purple at base. Summer. Alps.

Zeleborii: *S. ruthenicum.*

SENECIO L. [*Cineraria* L.; *Jacobaea* Mill.; *Kleinia* L.; *Notonia* DC.]. GROUNDSEL. *Compositae* (Senecio Tribe). One of the largest genera of flowering plants, variously estimated at 2,000–3,000 spp., in all parts of the world; ann. or per. herbs, or shrubs, sometimes climbing, many xerophytes with fleshy to succulent lvs. and sts., a few, in the region of the E. Afr. volcanos, treelike; lvs. alt., sometimes all basal; fl. heads usually radiate, sometimes discoid, solitary or clustered, involucral bracts in 1 row, usually with shorter bracts at base, these not overlapping and calyxlike in appearance; fls. commonly yellow, but sometimes shades of orange, red, blue, or purple; achenes mostly cylindrical, ribbed, pappus of soft, whitish, often copious bristles.

A number of species are cultivated for their attractive flowers or foliage, and some in collections of succulents. They are of easy culture. Practically all can be propagated by seeds and the perennials by division, or by stem or root cuttings. A few species are known to be poisonous to livestock and human beings, because of the presence of one or more alkaloids.

abrotanifolius L. [*S. carpathicus* Herbich; *S. tiroliensis* A. Kern.]. Per., with creeping rhizome, sts. to 18 in., glabrous or slightly pubescent; lower lvs. 2-pinnate, upper lvs. pinnate into linear-lanceolate acute segms.; heads to 2 in. across, in corymbs; ray fls. 10–13, orange-yellow or orange-red. Eur. Has been confused with *S. adonidifolius.*

acaulis (L.f.) Schultz-Bip. [*Kleinia acaulis* (L.f.) DC.]. Succulent, with tuberous rhizome, sts. to 3 in., densely leafy; lvs. nearly cylindrical, to 6 in. long, somewhat incurved, mucronate, reddish at apex and at base; peduncle erect, simple, to 8 in., with a single, terminal head. S. Afr.

adonidifolius Loisel. Glabrous per., to 18 in.; lvs. finely pinnately divided; heads small, in a compound corymb; fls. orange-yellow. Mts., s. Eur. Useful in rock garden. Resembles *S. abrotanifolius,* with which it has been confused.

alatus Wallich. Per., to 2 ft.; lvs. membranous, ovate-cordate or lanceolate, to 12 in. long, serrate, petiole short or long, with broad, toothed wing and broadly auricled at base; heads to ½ in. long, in a large, branched panicle. Himalayas.

altaicus: *Ligularia altaica.*

ambraceus Turcz. ex DC. Per., sts. erect, branched in upper part; lower st. lvs. pinnately divided nearly to midrib, to 3 in. long, sessile or auriculate-clasping, upper st. lvs. reduced, mostly entire; heads to 1 in. across, terminal on peduncles to 2 in. long, few in a panicle; ray fls. yellow, 8–10, to ½ in. long. Moist areas, n. China, w. Siberia, Mongolia.

angulatus L.f. Glabrous, scandent subshrub, sts. several ft. long; lvs. ovate, to 2½ in. long, waxy, somewhat fleshy, more or less angularly lobed, lobes few, short and broad, or toothlike, petioles to 1½ in. long; heads many in a corymb; fls. yellow, disc fls. about 20, ray fls. 4–6. S. Afr. Resembles *S. mikanioides,* but has ray fls. and a greater number of disc fls.

alpinus (L.) Scop. [*Cineraria alpina* L.]. Per., to 3 ft.; lvs. ovate, unequally toothed or pinnatifid, the lower petioled, the upper lanceolate, auriculate at base; heads to 1½ in. across, in terminal corymbs; fls. yellow, ray fls. spreading. Alps, Eur.

amaniensis (Engl.) Jacobsen [*Kleinia amaniensis* (Engl.) A. Berger; *Notonia amaniensis* Engl.]. Succulent subshrub, leafy st. to 18 in., simple and erect, later procumbent and sparingly branched; lvs. obovate to spatulate, to 4 in. long, narrowed to short petiole, 3-nerved from base, bloomy when young; heads many in a panicle, to 2½ ft. high; fls. red-yellow. E. Trop. Afr.

antennariifolius Britt. Per., to 1½ ft., white-woolly; lvs. mostly basal, elliptic to spatulate, to 2½ in. long, green above, densely white-woolly beneath, upper lvs. linear; heads to 1 in. across, corymbose; ray fls. yellow. Shale barrens, Md., Va., W. Va.

Anteuphorbium (L.) Schultz-Bip. [*Kleinia Anteuphorbium* (L.) DC.]. Succulent shrub, sts. many, cylindrical, erect, to about 4 ft.; lvs. scattered along sts., narrow-oblong, to 1 in. long or more, entire, thick and fleshy, midrib prominent; heads discoid, cylindrical, solitary or 2–3, terminal; disc fls. yellow, ray fls. lacking. S. Afr., sw. Morocco.

arenarius Thunb. Ann., sticky-pubescent; lvs. pinnately lobed, lobes usually toothed; heads showy, several in a corymb; disc fls. yellow, ray fls. purple, rarely white. S. Afr.

argyreus Phil. Subshrub, to 18 in., sts. and lvs. densely silvery-hairy; lvs. linear-oblanceolate, to 1½ in. long, attenuate at base, entire; heads solitary, terminal; fls. yellow, ray fls. about 8, to ½ in. long. S. Argentina, adjacent Chile.

articulatus (L.f.) Schultz-Bip. [*Kleinia articulata* (L.f.) Haw.]. CANDLE PLANT, HOT-DOG CACTUS, SAUSAGE CRASSULA. Succulent per., sts. to 2 ft., brs. jointed, the joints cylindrical, swollen; lvs. to 2 in. long, deeply 3–5-lobed, petiole as long as blade or longer; heads about ½ in. across, in corymbs on peduncles to 10 in. long; fls. white. S. Afr. Forma **globosa** Jacobsen. Joints nearly globose.

aurantiacus (Hoppe) DC. [*Cineraria aurantiaca* Hoppe]. Per., to 18 in., erect; basal lvs. elliptic, petioled, st. lvs. few, linear; heads about ¾ in. across; fls. orange-red. Mts., cent. Eur.

aureus L. GOLDEN G., GOLDEN RAGWORT. Per., to 30 in., often with leafy basal offsets, lightly tomentose when young, later glabrous; basal lvs. cordate-ovate, to 6 in. long, toothed, sometimes tinged purple beneath, st. lvs. pinnately cut; heads ¾ in. across, in corymbs; ray fls. 8–12, yellow. Nfld. to Fla. and Tex.

australis: see *S. linearifolius.*

balsamitae: *S. pauperculus.*

barbertonensis Klatt. Succulent subshrub, brs. short, somewhat fleshy; lvs. in tufts crowded at ends of brs., linear, to 3½ in. long, flattened and grooved above; heads solitary, terminal; disc fls. golden-yellow, ray fls. lacking. S. Afr.

blitoides: *S. Fremontii.*

Bolanderi A. Gray [*S. Harfordii* Greenm.]. Per., to 2 ft., sts. slender, glabrous or nearly so; basal lvs. orbicular-cordate, to 1¼ in. wide, mostly palmately lobed, rather firm, on long, slender petioles, st. lvs. successively much-reduced; heads several in a cyme; ray fls. 5–10, yellow. N. Calif., sw. Ore.

calamifolius: *S. scaposus* var. *caulescens.*

canus Hook. [*S. Purshianus* Nutt.]. Per., from a branched root crown, more or less white-tomentose, sts. several, slender, to 18 in.; basal and lowermost st. lvs. in a loose rosette, blades oblong-oblanceolate, to 2 in. long, entire or toothed, on petioles as long as blades or shorter, upper st. lvs. few, reduced; heads several in a flat-topped terminal cluster; fls. yellow, ray fls. 5–13, about ½ in. long. Mostly dry, rocky places in mts., w. N. Amer.

capitatus (Wahlenb.) DC. Per., to 12 in., rhizome fibrous, st. simple, somewhat stout, cobwebby-pubescent; basal lvs. in a rosette, obovate to oblanceolate, toothed, narrowed to a short petiole, upper st. lvs. reduced; heads 2–10, about 1 in. across; fls. yellow or orange, ray fls. about 10, to ½ in. long, rarely lacking. Mts., cent. Eur.

carniolicus: *S. incanus* subsp.

carpathicus: *S. abrotanifolius.*

Cineraria DC. [*Centaurea maritima* cv. 'Diamond'; *Cineraria maritima* L.]. DUSTY-MILLER. Per., to 2½ ft., stiff, white-woolly; lvs. pinnately cut into oblong blunt segms., becoming green on upper surface; heads 1½ in. across, in compound terminal corymbs several in. across; ray fls. yellow or cream. Medit. region. Sometimes confused with *S. Vira-vira* when not in fl., but differs in its stiff habit, broader, narrow-oblong lf. segms. rounded at apex, yellow fls., and the presence of ray fls.

cinerascens Ait. Subshrub, to 2 ft., sts. slender, wandlike, erect, thinly white-woolly; lvs. to 5 in. long, white-tomentose beneath, pinnately lobed, lobes 2–4 on each side, linear or lanceolate-oblong, margins revolute; heads 5–8 in a corymb; fls. yellow, disc fls. 60–80, ray fls. few or none. S. Afr.

citriformis Rowley. Succulent subshrub, densely tufted, brs. short, nearly erect, arising from a fleshy rhizome; lvs. many, irregularly arranged around st., somewhat lemon-shaped, to ¾ in. long, short-pointed, blue-gray with narrow, vertical, translucent lines, narrowed to short petiole; fls. creamy-white. S. Afr.

clivorum: *Ligularia dentata.*

compactus T. Kirk. Evergreen shrub, compactly branched, to 2 ft. or more, sts. white-tomentose; lvs. obovate to oblong, to 2 in. long, rounded at apex, more or less crenate and wavy-margined, with prominent midrib, white-tomentose when young, later becoming glabrous above; heads to 1¼ in. across, solitary or in few-fld. racemes; fls. yellow, ray fls. 10 or more. New Zeal. Most material of this sp. in cult. has been erroneously called *S. Greyi*, which has longer lvs. and glandular-pubescent involucral bracts.

confusus (DC.) Britten. MEXICAN FLAME VINE, ORANGEGLOW VINE. Glabrous vine or scandent shrub; lvs. thickish, narrowly ovate-acuminate, to 2 in. long or more, remotely dentate; heads ½ in. across or more, in terminal clusters; ray fls. orange or orange-red. Mex.

crassissimus Humbert. VERTICAL LEAF. Succulent, glabrous shrub, to 2½ ft.; lvs. flat, thick, and fleshy, obovate, to 2¼ in. long, rounded and abruptly mucronate at apex, cuneate at base, glaucous-green, more or less red-margined, soon withering and falling leaving prominent scars on st.; heads several in corymbs terminal on an elongate scape; fls. yellow, ray fls. several. Madagascar.

cruentus (Masson) DC. [*Cineraria cruenta* Masson]. Per. herb, 2–3 ft.; lvs. ovate or ovate-lanceolate, to 2 in. long, purplish beneath, margins crenate-ciliate, base of blade confluent with winged petiole; heads 1–1½ in. across, many in an open, cymosely branched infl.; disc and ray fls. purple. Canary Is. Possibly no longer in cult. in the U.S., but one of the supposed parents of the hybrid complex, *S.* × *hybridus*, the florist's cineraria.

cuneatus: see *S. kleiniiformis.*

Descoingsii (Humbert) Jacobsen [*Notonia Descoingsii* Humbert]. Succulent per., st. erect, slender, cylindrical, simple or sparingly branched, to 1 ft. or more, grooved; lvs. scattered, small, linear, early-deciduous leaving conspicuous scars; heads 1–3, terminal or sometimes axillary, shortly peduncled; disc fls. 40–50, pale yellow or white, ray fls. lacking. Madagascar.

Desmondii: a listed name of no botanical standing.

diversifolius: *S. scapiflorus.*

Doria L. Per., to 4 ft., erect, glabrous; lvs. lanceolate to oblong-elliptic, to 5 in. long, glabrous, glaucous, entire or toothed, the lowermost narrowed to a short, winged petiole, the upper sessile, more or less decurrent on st.; heads to ¾ in. across, many in terminal compound corymbs; fls. yellow, ray fls. 6–9, showy. Cent. and s. Eur., N. Afr.

Doronicum L. LEOPARD'S-BANE. Per., to 2 ft., more or less cottony-pubescent to nearly glabrous; lvs. ovate to lanceolate, to 5 in. long, irregularly toothed, the lowermost narrowed to a somewhat winged petiole, the uppermost sessile; heads to 2 in. across, solitary or 2–4; ray fls. yellow, 10–20, showy. Cent. and s. Eur., N. Afr.

Douglasii DC. BUSH S. Subshrub, to 5 ft., sts. erect, woody at base, leafy, striate, white-tomentose when young; lvs. to 3 in. long, mostly pinnately lobed, lobes usually 5–9, linear, revolute; heads several to many in a terminal compound corymb; fls. yellow, ray fls. 10–13, to ½ in. long, showy. Sw. U.S.

dryadeus: see *S. linearifolius.*

elaeagnifolius Hook.f. Evergreen shrub, to 10 ft., gray-tomentose; lvs. obovate to oblong-lanceolate, to 4 in. long, leathery, dark green above, gray-woolly beneath; heads to ½ in. across, many in a pyramidal infl.; disc fls. yellow, ray fls. lacking. New Zeal.

elegans L. [*Jacobaea elegans* (L.) Moench]. PURPLE RAGWORT. Pubescent ann., to 2 ft.; lvs. clasping or auriculate at base, to 3 in. long, pinnately lobed, lobing variable; heads to 1 in. across, showy, in loose corymbs; disc fls. yellow, ray fls. purple or rarely white. S. Afr.; escaped in Calif.

ficoides (L.) Schultz-Bip. [*Kleinia ficoides* (L.) Haw.]. Succulent subshrub, to 3 ft., white-pruinose, sts. green, white-dotted; lvs. flattened-cylindrical, to 6 in. long, sessile; heads in terminal cymes; fls. white. S. Afr.

flammeus Turcz. ex DC. Per., with slender rhizome, sts. simple, to 18 in., cobwebby and puberulent; basal lvs. oblong, long-petioled, withering before fls. open, lower st. lvs. oblanceolate-oblong, to 3½ in. long, narrowed to a winged petiole, upper lvs. successively reduced upward; heads 2–7 in false umbels; ray fls. orange-red, to about 1 in. long. Mts., e. Asia. Var. **glabrifolius** Cuf. Sts. somewhat taller; fl. heads more numerous.

Flettii Wieg. Per., to 12 in., glabrous or nearly so; basal lvs. ovate to obovate in outline, pinnatifid or lyrate-pinnatifid, lobes toothed, petiole often as long as blade, st. lvs. few, successively reduced upward; heads 2–10 in a terminal, umbel-like cluster; fls. yellow, ray fls. 5–10. Mts., Wash.

Fremontii Torr. & A. Gray [*S. blitoides* Greene]. Per., to 8 in., glabrous; lvs. scattered along st., obovate to spatulate, to 1¾ in. long, somewhat fleshy, variously toothed, narrowed at base to short petiole; heads terminal on short naked peduncles; fls. yellow, ray fls. several, to ⅜ in. long. Mts., w. N. Amer.

fulgens (Hook.f.) Nichols. [*Kleinia fulgens* Hook.f.]. Succulent, branched subshrub, to 3 ft., pale green and glaucous throughout; lvs. mostly basal, spatulate to obovate, to 4 in. long, indistinctly veined, remotely toothed; narrowed at base to a broadly winged decurrent petiole; heads 1–2 on peduncles 4–8 in. long; disc fls. red or orange, ray fls. lacking. S. Afr.

Galpinii Hook.f. [*Kleinia Galpinii* (Hook.f.) A. Berger]. Succulent, branched subshrub, to 1½ ft., gray-green thoughout; lvs. oblanceolate, to 6 in. long, with distinct midrib, tapering to semiclasping base; heads 3–4 in a loose terminal corymb; disc fls. orange-red, ray fls. lacking. S. Afr.

glastifolius L.f. Branched shrub, to 5 ft.; lvs. linear to lanceolate, to 3 in. long, unequally toothed, glabrous, the lowermost strongly decurrent on st.; heads to 2½ in. across, in corymbose panicles; disc fls. yellow, ray fls. about 13, purple to pink. S. Afr. Showy and attractive in fl. See also *S. Kirkii.*

gnaphalodes Sieber. Sts. erect, woody at base, white-tomentose; lvs. linear, entire or sparsely lobed, silky-tomentose beneath; heads to ¾ in. across, in dense corymbs; fls. yellow, ray fls. present. Crete and Is. of Karpathos.

Graberi: a listed name of no botanical standing.

grandifolius Less. Large, evergreen, leafy shrub, to 15 ft.; lvs. ovate or ovate-oblong, to 18 in. long, cordate to rounded at base, sinuate-dentate, pinnately veined, glabrous or nearly so above, tawny-tomentose beneath, petioles stout, to 5 in. long; heads many in terminal, nearly corymbose cymes; fls. yellow, ray fls. usually 5. S. Mex. Differs from *S. Petasitis* in its larger, pinnately veined lvs.

Gregorii: *S. stapeliiformis.*

Greyi Hook.f. Evergreen shrub, to 6 ft., brs. stout, white-tomentose; lvs. oblong to ovate-oblong, to 3½ in. long, entire or shallowly sinuate, leathery, very young lvs. densely white-tomentose above and beneath, petioles to 1¾ in. long; heads to 1 in. across, in large corymbs, involucral bracts glandular-pubescent; fls. yellow, ray fls. about 15. New Zeal. Perhaps not in cult.; plants grown under this name are mostly *S. compactus.*

Hallianus Rowley. Succulent, sts. short, viscid, prostrate, with wiry aerial roots that produce fusiform tubers on contact with soil, tubers to 4 in. long, ½ in. in diam.; lvs. cylindric-fusiform, to 1 in. long, 1–1¾ in. in diam., glaucous, the upper side with a broad longitudinal translucent stripe and about 10 narrower inconspicuous stripes; fls. whitish. S. Afr.

Harfordii: *S. Bolanderi.*

Haworthii Schultz-Bip. [*Kleinia tomentosa* (Haw.) Haw.]. COCOON PLANT. Succulent subshrub, to 12 in. or more, covered with soft, white, feltlike tomentum; lvs. spirally arranged, cylindrical to fusiform, to 2 in. long; heads discoid, terminal on stout sts. 8–10 in. long; disc fls. orange-yellow, ray fls. lacking. S. Afr.

× **Hessei:** *Ligularia* × *Hessei.*

Herreianus Dinter [*Kleinia gomphophylla* Dinter]. GOOSEBERRY KLEINIA. Succulent, sts. slender, cylindrical, prostrate, rooting, 1–2 ft. long; lvs. fleshy, elliptic, to ½ in. long, attenuate at both ends, green, with many translucent lines; heads small, on peduncles about 3 in. high. Sw. Afr. Suitable for hanging baskets.

× **hybridus** (Willd.) Regel [*Cineraria* ×*hybrida* Willd.]. CINERARIA, FLORIST'S C. Per., or often grown as an ann., ranging in size from compact cushionlike plants about 1 ft. high or more to openly branched plants to 3 ft. high; heads single or double, to 2 in. across, in corymbs; fls. varying from white to pink, red, reddish-purple, deep purple, violet, and blue, never yellow, ray fls. sometimes bicolored, with white base and colored apex. A variable complex of forms, which appears to have originated in England as hybrids between *S. cruentus* and *S. Heritieri* and possibly other spp. of the section *Pericallis* from the Canary Is. They self-sow in damp places in areas with mild climates, as in coastal Calif. For cult. see *Cineraria.*

incanus L. Per., 3–4 in., appressed-white-hairy; lvs. in basal tuft, lowermost obovate, petioled, with toothed lobes, the uppermost reduced; heads many in a terminal crowded corymb; fls. yellow, ray fls. 3–10. Alps, Eur. Subsp. **carniolicus** (Willd.) Br.-Bl. [*S. carniolicus* Willd.]. Lvs. with cobwebby hairs or glabrous; heads larger.

integrifolius (L.) Clairv. Per., sts. erect, more or less cottony, to 2½ ft., mostly branched only in the infl.; basal lvs. in a rosette, ovate to ovate-oblong, to 4 in. long, entire or toothed, narrowed to a winged petiole as long as to shorter than blade, st. lvs. few, reduced, sessile; heads to 12 in a corymb; fls. yellow, ray fls. about 13. Eur.

Jacobaea L. RAGWORT, TANSY R. Bien. or per., to 4 ft., sts. erect, branched above the middle, glabrous or cottony; lvs. more or less deeply pinnatifid or pinnately dissected, glabrous or sparsely cottony beneath, basal lvs. in a rosette, lyrate-pinnatifid, petioled, upper st. lvs. semiclasping; heads to 1 in. across, in a large umbellate corymb; fls. yellow, ray fls. to 15. Eur., s. Asia, N. Afr.; naturalized in N. Amer. in disturbed soil. Poisonous to livestock.

Jacobsenii Rowley [*S. petraeus* Muschl., not Klatt; *Notonia petraea* (Muschl.) R. E. Fries]. Succulent, glabrous per., sts. creeping, to 18 in. long, sparingly branched, rooting at nodes; lvs. obovate, to 3 in. long, narrowed to sessile base; heads 1–3; fls. orange. E. Afr.

japonicus: see *Ligularia japonica.*

Kaempferi: *Ligularia tussilaginea.*

Kirkii Hook.f. [*S. glastifolius* Hook.f., not L.f.]. Evergreen shrub, to 15 ft., brs. stout, erect, glabrous; lvs. obovate to linear-lanceolate, to 5 in. long, sparingly toothed, narrowed to short petiole; heads to 2 in. across, in terminal, much-branched, somewhat flattened clusters to 12 in. across; disc fls. yellow, ray fls. about 10, white. New Zeal. A handsome plant in fl.

Kleinia (L.) Less. [*S. neriifolius* (Haw.) Baill.; *Kleinia neriifolia* Haw.]. Succulent shrub, to 3 ft., sts. thick, with forked or whorled branching, covered with old lf. bases; lvs. linear-lanceolate, to 6 in. long, thickish, gray-green, with prominent midvein, terminating young brs. in winter, later falling; heads cylindrical, in corymbs; fls. yellow-white. Canary Is.

kleiniiformis Suess. [*S. cuneatus* Jacobsen, not Hook.; *Kleinia kleiniiformis* (Suess.) Boom]. SPEARHEAD. Succulent, glabrous, white-pruinose subshrub, sts. prostrate but not creeping, brs. erect, to 12 in. tall; lvs. somewhat boat-shaped with margins curved upward, to 4 in. long, with 1 to few large teeth, narrowed toward petiole; heads 10–30 in the infl.; fls. white or yellow. S. Afr. Broken sts. give off a pungent odor.

lagopus Raoul. Per., lvs. in basal rosettes, round or elliptic to ovate-oblong, to 6 in. long, cordate basally, leathery, netted-veined, hispid above, white-woolly-tomentose beneath, petiole stout, hairy, to 2 in. long; heads to 1¾ in. across, on a simple or branched scape to 15 in. tall; fls. yellow, ray fls. several. Alpine rocky places, New Zeal. Suitable for the rock garden.

latifolius: see *S. rufiglandulosus* var. *Solandri.*

lautus Soland, ex Willd. Ann. or short-lived per., fleshy, sts. erect or prostrate, to about 15 in., simple to much-branched, leafy throughout; lvs. entire to pinnatifid, to 2½ in. long, successively reduced upward; heads cylindrical, in loose corymbs, involucral bracts brown- or black-tipped; fls. yellow, ray fls. about 13. New Zeal. Related Australian plants also included under this name in the past have recently been shown to be distinct.

laxifolius J. Buchan. Evergreen shrub, to 4 ft., branchlets tomentose when young; lvs. elliptic to lanceolate, to 3 in. long, to ¾ in. wide, obscurely toothed to entire, somewhat leathery, grayish-tomentose beneath; heads to ¾ in. across, in loose panicles; fls. yellow, ray fls. 10–15, showy; achenes glabrous. Mts., New Zeal. Confused with *S. Greyi* and *S. compactus*, but differing from *S. Greyi* in its narrower lvs., not more than ¾ in. wide, from *S. compactus* in its entire or only obscurely crenate-sinuate lvs., and from both in its glabrous achenes.

Ledebourii: *Ligularia macrophylla.*

leucophyllus DC. Per., with creeping rhizome and basal rosette of lvs., sts. simple, to 8 in., white-cobwebby; basal lvs. pinnatifid, lyrate, rounded at apex, petioled, upper lvs. reduced, sessile; heads in terminal corymbs; fls. yellow, ray fls. 5–7. Mts., France.

leucostachys: *S. Vira-vira.*

linearifolius A. Rich. [*S. australis* A. Rich., not K. Spreng. or Willd.; *S. dryadeus* F. J. Muell., not Sieber]. Per., to 3 ft., glabrous or nearly so; lvs. narrow-lanceolate to elliptic, to 5 in. long, toothed, narrowed to base or sometimes with clasping auricles; heads in corymbose panicles; fls. yellow, ray fls. about 12. Se. Australia.

longiflorus (DC.) Schultz-Bip. [*Kleinia longiflora* DC.]. Succulent shrub, to 2 ft., sts. cylindrical, striped, branched, with prominent lf. scars; lvs. scattered, subulate, ¼ in. long, early-deciduous; heads 3–5, terminal on short peduncles. S. Afr.

macroglossus DC. NATAL IVY, WAX VINE. Glabrous, slender, evergreen climber; lvs. petioled, triangular-hastate, about 2½ in. long, usually shallowly 3–5-lobed, lobes acuminate or acute; heads 2½ in. across, solitary on axillary or terminal peduncles; fls. yellow, ray fls. 8 or more, elliptic, to 1 in. long. S. Afr. Useful as a trailing plant or ground cover; the heads are unusually large and showy. Cv. 'Variegatum'. VARIEGATED WAX VINE. Lvs. variegated green and yellow.

magellanicus Hook. & Arn. Cespitose per., to 10 in., lower part of sts. densely covered with old dry lvs.; lvs. silvery-hairy, the basal ones linear-lanceolate, to 3 in. long, narrowed to sheathing petiolar base, st. lvs. successively reduced upward, sessile; heads terminal, solitary; disc fls. many, yellow, ray fls. lacking. S. tip of S. Amer. (Straits of Magellan).

Mandraliscae (Tineo) Jacobsen [*Kleinia Mandraliscae* Tineo]. Succulent subshrub, to 12 in.; lvs. semicylindrical, to 4 in. long, ⁵⁄₁₆ in. wide, somewhat flattened on upper surface, sharp-pointed, glaucous; heads 10–13 in a forking cyme on peduncles longer than lvs.; fls. whitish. S. Afr.

mikanioides Otto [*S. scandens* DC., not Buch.-Ham.]. GERMAN IVY, PARLOR I., WATER I. Glabrous, tall-twining per.; lvs. ovate, mostly with a deep basal sinus, sharply 5–7-angled; heads about ⁵⁄₁₆ in. across, in close clusters on axillary and terminal brs.; disc fls. 8–10, yellow, ray fls. lacking. S. Afr.; naturalized in England and Calif. Sometimes confused with *S. scandens* Buch.-Ham. ex D. Don, but lacking ray fls. Easily increased by sts. cuttings.

Monroi Hook.f. Evergreen shrub, to 6 ft., white-tomentose; lvs. obovate-oblong, to 1½ in. long, leathery, crenate-undulate, dull green above, white-tomentose beneath; heads to ⅝ in. across, in terminal compound clusters; ray fls. 10–15, yellow. Mts., New Zeal.

multiflorus (L'Hér.) DC. [*Cineraria multiflora* L'Hér.]. Erect per., st. hairy in lower half, glabrous and glaucous above; lvs. broadly ovate to nearly orbicular, acute at apex, cordate at base, glabrous above, cobwebby-pubescent beneath, petioles auriculate, those of lower lvs. longer than blade, winged only at base, those of upper lvs. winged their full length; heads large, showy, in an openly much-branched infl.; disc fls. dark purple, ray fls. lilac. Canary Is. Related to *S. cruentus*, one of the ancestors of the florist's cineraria. Vars. **maxima** and **nana** are listed.

neriifolius: *S. Kleinia.*

obovatus Muhlenb. ex Willd. Per., to 2 ft., usually with abundant and conspicuous stolons; basal lvs. mostly obovate, obtuse or rounded at base, toothed, petiole 1–2 times as long as blade, st. lvs. often pinnatifid, successively reduced upward; heads 3–10 or more in a corymbose cyme; fls. yellow, ray fls. 8–13 or sometimes lacking. Mass., s. to n. Fla. and e. Tex.

× **palmatilobus:** a listed name of no botanical standing for a hybrid *Ligularia* known as *Ligularia* × *palmatiloba.*

pauciflorus Pursh. Per., to 2 ft., from a stout, horizontal to nearly erect root crown; lvs. thickish and somewhat succulent, basal lvs.

elliptic-ovate, to 1¾ in. long, crenate-dentate, petiole 1–2 times as long as blade, st. lvs. successively reduced upward, lowermost variously dissected; heads to 6 or more in a somewhat umbellate cyme; fls. orange, ray fls. usually lacking. Alpine and subalpine, Lab. and Nfld., w. to Pacific Northwest and Calif.

pauperculus Michx. [*S. balsamitae* Muhlenb. ex Willd.]. BALSAM G. Per., to 2 ft., from a root crown; basal lvs. lanceolate to oblong, to 3 in. long, crenate-dentate to nearly entire, petiole about as long as blade, st. lvs. successively reduced upward, variously dissected, the uppermost sessile; heads 10 or more in a corymbose cyme; ray fls. 8–13 or lacking. Lab. to Ga., w. to Alaska and Ore.

pendulus (Forssk.) Schultz-Bip. [*Kleinia pendula* (Forssk.) DC.; *Notonia pendula* (Forssk.) Chiov.]. INCHWORM, TAPEWORM. Succulent shrub, sts. cylindrical, decumbent, snakelike, about ¾ in. in diam.; lvs. subulate, ¼ in. long, eventually becoming hard, recurved spines; heads to 1¼ in. across, solitary, terminal on peduncles 8–10 in. long; fls. red to orange. S. Arabia, Yemen, Ethiopia, Somaliland.

Petasitis (Sims) DC. [*Cineraria Petasitis* Sims]. VELVET G., CALIFORNIA GERANIUM. Tall shrub, to 8 ft. or more, branched from base, sts. and lvs. velvety-pubescent; lvs. ovate or nearly orbicular, to 8 in. long, 9–13-lobed, grayish-tomentose beneath; heads in terminal, many-headed panicles; fls. yellow, ray fls. about 5. Mex.

petraeus: see *S. Jacobsenii* and *S. werneriifolius.*

petrocallis: *S. werneriifolius.*

praecox (Cav.) DC. [*Cineraria praecox* Cav.]. Shrub or small tree, to 15 ft., sts. somewhat fleshy or soft-woody, glabrous; ovate-cordate, to 7 in. long, glabrous, palmately veined, 5–7-angled, lobes acuminate; heads in terminal, compound, corymbose cymes; fls. yellow, ray fls. 5 or 6. Mex. Small plants are sometimes included in succulent collections.

Przewalskii: *Ligularia Przewalskii.*

pseudaureus Rydb. Per. herb, to 2½ ft. or more, more or less floccose-tomentose when young; basal lvs. ovate or broadly lanceolate, 2 or sometimes 4 in. long, somewhat hastate or truncate to cordate or obtuse at base, variously toothed, petiole to twice as long as blade, st. lvs. somewhat lyrate or laciniate to entire, successively reduced upward; heads 5–20 in a corymbose cyme; fls. yellow, ray fls. 8–13, sometimes lacking W. N. Amer.

pseudoarnica Less. Rhizomatous, fleshy per., sts. stout, usually simple, to 18 in., cobwebby, densely leafy; middle st. lvs. oblong or ovate-oblong, to 6 in. long, mucronate-toothed, slightly narrowed at base and semiclasping, cobwebby beneath, the basal, lowermost, and uppermost lvs. smaller; heads about 1½ in. across, few, or sometimes as many as 30 in peduncled corymbs; ray fls. yellow, to 1 in. long. Near seashores, e. Asia and N. Amer.

pulcher Hook. & Arn. Per., to 2 ft., young parts cobwebby-hairy; lvs. elliptic or lanceolate, leathery, irregularly toothed, basal lvs. narrowed to petiole, st. lvs. successively reduced upward, sessile; heads 2–3 in. across, solitary, or few in an open, terminal corymb; disc fls. yellow, ray fls. many, purple. Brazil, Uruguay, Argentina. Handsome plant, with large, attractive heads.

Purshianus: *S. canus.*

pusillus: a listed name of no botanical standing, used for *S. citriformis.*

radicans (L.f.) Schultz-Bip. [*Kleinia radicans* (L.f.) Haw.]. CREEPING BERRIES. Succulent, sts. slender, glabrous, prostrate, rooting at nodes, forming mats; lvs. ovate, to 1 in. long, fleshy, acute at apex, short-petioled, glaucous-green, with a longitudinal stripe; heads 1–2 on long scapes; disc fls. white, ray fls. lacking. S. Afr. Lvs. have strong, pungent, turpentine taste and are edible; fls. are sweet-scented. Grown in succulent collections, rock gardens, and hanging baskets.

repens: see *S. serpens.*

resedifolius Less. Per., to 8 in., glabrous or nearly so, sts. 1 or more from a stout rhizome; basal lvs. ovate to orbicular-ovate, to 1 in. long, toothed to somewhat lobed, narrowed to petiole, st. lvs. successively reduced upward and sessile; heads 1 or sometimes 2 on long peduncles; fls. yellow, ray fls. variously developed, sometimes lacking. Mts., w. N. Amer.

Riddellii Torr. & A. Gray. Per., to 3 ft., glabrous, sts. several from a stout, woody root crown; lvs. irregularly pinnately divided, segms. flattened, linear-filiform, to 3 in. long; heads 5–20 in a corymbose cyme; fls. yellow, ray fls. often early deciduous. W. U.S.

Rowleyanus Jacobsen. STRING-OF-BEADS S. Succulent per., sts. slender, prostrate, rooting at nodes, forming mats; lvs. almost globose, about ¼ in. in diam., with narrow translucent band ¹⁄₁₆ in. wide; heads about ⅜ in. high, solitary, terminal on peduncle to 1½ in. long; disc fls. about 20, white, ray fls. lacking. Sw. Afr. Related to *S. citriformis* and other spp. with similar form and habit but distinguished by the

single, narrow, longitudinal "window" seen when leaf is held to the light. Used in hanging baskets.

rufiglandulosus Colenso. Shrub, to 3 ft., sts. flexuous, grooved; lvs. broadly ovate to ovate-oblong, to 8 in. long, sometimes lobed, margins sinuate, toothed, lower lvs. with winged petioles, upper lvs. sessile, clasping; heads in corymbs; fls. yellow. New Zeal. Var. **rufiglandulosus.** The typical var.; sts. about ⅝ in. in diam.; lvs. not lobed, densely glandular-hairy; heads to 1⅛ in. across, in large corymbs; achenes densely hairy. Var. **Solandri** (Allan) Allan [*S. latifolius* Banks & Soland. ex Hook.f., not DC.; *S. Solandri* Allan]. Sts. not stout; lvs. lobed, sparsely glandular-hairy; heads to ¾ in. across, in smaller corymbs; achenes glabrous to pubescent.

scandens Buch.-Ham. ex D. Don. Per., woody at base, sts. climbing to several ft., densely pubescent when young, later only sparsely so; lvs. ovate or elongate-triangular, to 4 in. long, toothed, subentire, or often lobed with 2 or more divisions, finely pubescent on both sides, petiole to ¾ in. long; heads ½ in. across, in terminal or axillary clusters; fls. yellow, ray fls. usually 8. Near seashore, e. Asia. *S. scandens* DC. is *S. mikanioides*, which is distinguished by the presence of ray fls.

scapiflorus (L'Hér.) C. A. Sm. [*S. diversifolius* Harv.]. Per., to about 18 in., white-woolly when young; lvs. mostly basal, long-petioled, usually simple, triangular, toothed, occasionally with a few lateral lobes along upper part of petiole; heads solitary, terminal on long peduncle; fls. white, ray fls. lacking. S. Afr.

scaposus DC. Succulent subshrub, st. short; lvs. in a basal rosette, cylindrical, to 3 in. long, silvery-white, covered with cobwebby feltlike pubescence when young, later green and glabrous; heads usually 3–5 on peduncle to 18 in.; fls. yellow, ray fls. about 12. S. Afr. Var. **caulescens** Haw. [*S. calamifolius* Hook.]. St. short, branched; lvs. flattened at ends.

scorzoneroides Hook.f. Per., to about 20 in., st. stout, covered with old lf. bases. glandular-pubescent above; lvs. entire or obscurely toothed, rather fleshy, glandular-pubescent, basal lvs. linear to ovate-lanceolate, to 4 in. long, st. lvs. reduced, the uppermost sessile; heads to 2½ in. across, many, on glandular-pubescent peduncles; ray fls. white. New Zeal.

serpens Rowley [*S. repens* (L.) Muschl., not J. Stokes or DC. or Dulac or Baill.; *S. succulentus* Schultz-Bip.; *Kleinia repens* Haw.]. BLUE-CHALKSTICKS. Succulent shrub, to 12 in., branching from base, glaucous-blue; lvs. linear-lanceolate, nearly cylindrical, obtuse, grooved above; heads few in a corymb; fls. white. S. Afr.

sibiricus: see *Ligularia sibirica.*

Solandella A. Gray. Per., with stout rhizome, sts. purplish, glabrous, to 6 in.; lvs. few, mostly basal, nearly orbicular to oblong-obovate, to 1½ in. long, entire or denticulate, usually truncate to broadly cuneate at base, attenuate to a long petiole; heads solitary, erect or somewhat nodding; fls. yellow, ray fls. 6–18. High mts., Colo.

Solandri: *S. rufiglandulosus* var.

speciosus Willd. Per., to 1 ft. or more; basal lvs. obovate-lanceolate to spatulate, to 7 in. long, toothed or sinuately-lobed, glandular-hairy, narrowed to petioled, st. lvs. reduced upward; heads to 1½ in. across, few in terminal corymbs; disc fls. yellow, ray fls. 6–20, purple, S. Afr.

sphaerocephalus Greene. Robust per., fibrous-rooted, to 3 ft., sparsely hairy; lvs. entire or slightly toothed, lowermost oblanceolate or elliptic, petioled, blade and petiole to 10 in. long, upper lvs. successively reduced upward, the uppermost sessile; fls. yellow, ray fls. present. Wet places in mts., Mont. and Idaho, s. to Colo. and Nev.

stapeliiformis E. P. Phillips [*Kleinia Gregorii* (S. L. Moore) Jacobsen; *K. stapeliiformis* (E. P. Phillips) Stapf]. Succulent shrub, branched from base, sts. several, erect, 4–6-angled, to 8 in. or longer; lvs. borne along angles of st., subulate to somewhat spinelike, to ¼ in. long; heads to 1½ in. across, solitary on erect peduncles to 6 in. long; fls. red, ray fls. lacking. S. Afr.

stenocephalus: *Ligularia stenocephala.*

subalpinus C. Koch. Per., rhizomatous, to 30 in., sts. erect, glabrous or somewhat cobwebby, corymbosely branched above; lvs. ovate, often broadly so, glabrous or sparsely hairy beneath along veins, rarely somewhat cobwebby, basal lvs. few, in a rosette, long-petioled, coarsely toothed, upper lvs. successively reduced upward, more deeply toothed to weakly pinnately lobed; heads about 1½ in. across, several in a loose corymb; fls. yellow, ray fls. about 21. Mts., cent. Eur.

succulentus: *S. serpens.*

sylvaticus L. Ann., to 2½ ft., leafy throughout, sparsely pubescent to nearly glabrous; lvs. pinnatifid and irregularly toothed, to 4½ in. long, successively reduced upward; heads several to many in a terminal panicle; ray fls. small, inconspicuous. Eur.; naturalized in U.S. More weedy than ornamental. Somewhat resembling *S. vulgaris* L., the weedy, common groundsel, but readily distinguished by the presence of ray fls.

Takedanus Kit. Rhizomatous per., to 18 in., sts. and lvs. cobwebby, sometimes short-pubescent; basal and lower st. lvs. spatulate-oblong, to 2 in. long, irregularly toothed, clasping at base, upper lvs. successively reduced upward and more broadly clasping; heads to 1 in. across, several in umbels; ray fls. dark orange-red, about ½ in. long. Mts., Honshu (Japan). Related to *S. flammeus,* but heads smaller and ray fls. shorter.

tanguticus Maxim. [*Ligularia tangutica* (Maxim.) Bergmans]. Rhizomatous per., to 4 ft. or more, sts. erect, stout, leafy; lvs. petioled, broad-ovate in outline, the lowest to 8 in. long, deeply pinnately lobed, lobes lanceolate, acuminate, toothed, glabrous above, puberulent on veins beneath; heads small, ⅜ in. long, narrow-cylindrical, many in a panicle of racemes; fls. yellow, disc fls. 4, ray fls. 3. China.

tiroliensis. *S. abrotanifolius.*

tomentosus Michx. E. U.S. Not known to be in cult.; material grown under this name is probably *S. Haworthii.*

triangularis Hook. Per., to 3 ft. or more, sts. several from base, glabrous or slightly puberulent; lvs. many, only gradually reduced upward, lower lvs. triangular-ovate to lanceolate, to 8 in. long, long-petioled, uppermost lvs. sessile; heads several to many in a flat-topped infl.; fls. yellow, ray fls. 6–12, about ½ in, long. Wet places in mts., w. N. Amer.

tropaeolifolius MacOwan. Somewhat fleshy per. with tuberous root and trailing sts.; lvs. irregularly orbicular, peltate, more or less fleshy; heads few in a long-peduncled corymb; fls. all tubular, whitish-yellow, ray fls. lacking. S. Afr. Lvs. resemble those of the garden nasturtium *(Tropaeolum majus)* in shape and petiole-attachment.

Veitchianus: *Ligularia Veitchiana.*

Vira-vira Hieron. [*S. leucostachys* Bak.; *Cineraria candidissima* Hort.; *C. maritima* var. *candidissima* Hort.]. DUSTY-MILLER. Subshrub, to 2 ft., branched from base, densely white-tomentose; lvs. to 2½ in. long, deeply pinnately dissected into 2–4 pairs of linear, entire segms.; heads few, in corymbs; fls. white, ray fls. lacking. Argentina. Sometimes confused with *S. Cineraria,* but distinguished by its looser habit and linear lf. segms.

Websteri Greenm. Per., to 8 in., with well-developed short rhizome, more or less cobwebby hairy at least when young; basal and lower st. lvs. broadly oblanceolate to nearly round, to 3 in. long, toothed, petioled, uppermost lvs. reduced, short-petioled; heads 1 or rarely 2, large, usually nodding; ray fls. several, about ½ in. long. Olympic Mts. (Wash.).

werneriifolius A. Gray [*S. petraeus* Klatt; *S. petrocallis* Greene]. Per., sts. several, thinly hairy, to 6 in.; lvs. mostly basal, spatulate or elliptic or orbicular-obovate, to 1 in. long, petioled, st. lvs. successively reduced upward; heads 1–6, usually long-peduncled; ray fls. 9–13, yellow, to ⅜ in. long. Mts., w. N. Amer.

Wilsonianus: *Ligularia Wilsoniana.*

SEQUOIA Endl. *Taxodiaceae.* One sp., a gigantic, monoecious, coniferous, evergreen tree, native to w. N. Amer., often becoming 300 ft. high or more and with immense trunks; buds scaly, lvs. of 2 kinds, those on terminal and fertile shoots scalelike, those on other brs. spreading, linear, and more or less curved, to 1 in. long; female cones ovoid or globose, scales 15–20, obliquely peltate, woody, each bearing 3–7 ovules; seeds many, minute, maturing in 1 year.

Propagated by seeds. For culture see *Conifers.*

gigantea: *Sequoiadendron giganteum;* but if retained in *Sequoia,* the correct name of this sp. is *S. Wellingtonia.*

sempervirens (D. Don) Endl. REDWOOD, COAST R. Scalelike lvs. to ½ in. long, linear lvs. to 1 in. long, mostly spreading in 2 ranks; female cones broadly oblong in outline, to 1⅜ in. long. Coast Ranges, s. Ore., n. and cent. Calif. Zone 7. One of the world's largest trees, yielding a durable timber. Cvs. are: **'Adpressa'** [cv. 'Albospica'], young lvs. and tips of branchlets creamy; **'Glauca'**, lvs. bluish; **'Nana Pendula'**, brs. spreading or pendulous but producing some vigorous, erect shoots, lvs. glaucous; **'Pendula'**, brs. drooping; **'Prostrata'**, prostrate but producing some vigorous, erect shoots, lvs. to ⅝ in. long.

Wellingtonia: *Sequoiadendron giganteum.*

SEQUOIADENDRON Buchh. *Taxodiaceae.* One sp., a monoecious, gigantic, coniferous tree, native on w. slopes of the Sierra Nevadas in Calif., formerly treated as belonging to the genus *Sequoia,* but differing in having ovate to lanceolate, appressed or slightly spreading lvs. of 1 kind, buds not scaly, female cones larger, scales 30–40, seeds maturing in 2 years, and in other technical characters of the reproductive structures.

Propagated by seeds. For culture see *Conifers.*

giganteum (Lindl.) Buchh. [*Sequoia gigantea* (Lindl.) Decne., not Endl.; *Sequoia Wellingtonia* Seem.]. GIANT SEQUOIA, BIG TREE, GIANT REDWOOD. To 250 ft. or more, narrowly pyramidal when young, trunk many ft. in diam., bark to 20 in. thick; female cones ellipsoid, to 3½ in. long, very hard and woody, remaining on the tree many seasons. Zone 7. Cv. **'Pendulum'**. Narrowly columnar, brs. strongly deflexed. Cv. **'Pygmaeum'**. Dwarf, shrubby.

SERAPIAS L. *Orchidaceae.* Not in general cult. **S. gigantea:** *Epipactis gigantea.*

SERENOA Hook.f. *Palmae.* One sp., a small colonial stemless or short-stemmed palm with bisexual fls., native to coastal regions from S.C. to Fla. and Tex., unarmed except for closely toothed petiole margins; lvs. palmate, blades divided more than halfway to the base into 1-ribbed, briefly 2-cleft segms.; infl. among the lvs., usually surpassing the petiole, with tubular bracts sheathing peduncle and subtending several primary brs., these 1–2 times branched; fls. creamy-white, fragrant, arranged in pairs or singly along the rachillae, sepals united in a 3-lobed calyx, petals 3, united nearly half their length, valvate above, stamens 6, carpels 3, separate except united styles; fr. 1-seeded, ellipsoid to subglobose, seed with homogeneous endosperm slightly intruded by seed coat on one side, embryo lateral.

repens (Bartr.) Small [*S. serrulata* (Michx.) Nichols.]. SAW PALMETTO, SCRUB P. Sts. mostly prostrate or creeping and branching, forming great colonies in the wild, rarely erect and several ft. tall; lf. blades 2–2½ ft. across, green or blue, segms. 20 or more, stiff; fr. black, to ⅝ in. long. Zone 9.

serrulata: *S. repens.*

SERICOCARPUS: *ASTER.* **S. asteroides:** *A. paternus.*

SERICOGRAPHIS: *JUSTICIA.* **S. incana:** *J. Leonardii.* **S. pauciflora:** *J. Rizzinii.* **S. Mohintli:** *J. spicigera.*

SERISSA Comm. ex Juss. *Rubiaceae.* One or perhaps 3 spp. of shrubs, of se. Asia; sts. and lvs. fetid when bruised; lvs. opp., stipules persistent; fls. axillary or terminal, solitary or clustered, small, 4–6-merous, corolla funnelform; fr. a 2-seeded berry.

Grown in the open in warm areas or in the greenhouse. Propagated by cuttings over heat.

foetida (L.f.) Lam. [*S. japonica* Thunb.]. To 2 ft.; lvs. ovate, to ½ in. long; fls. white, to ½ in. long. Se. Asia.

japonica: *S. foetida.*

SERJANIA Schumach. *Sapindaceae.* About 200 spp. of large or small, woody, polygamous vines, native to trop. and subtrop. Amer.; lvs. alt., pinnate, 3-foliolate, or 2-ternate; fls. small, in axillary or terminal, often tendril-bearing racemes or panicles, irregular, sepals 5 or 4, with 2 sepals united, petals 4, stamens 8; fr. of 3, indehiscent, winged sections.

communis Camb. Sts. triangular, hairy; lvs. 2-ternate, to 5½ in. long, lfts. lanceolate, elliptic to ovate, 2–3 in. long, serrate-dentate; fr. cordate-ovate, about 1 in. long. E. Brazil to Peru. Var. **glabra** Radlk. Sts. glabrous or hairy only on the angles.

glabrata HBK. Lvs. 2-ternate, to 11 in. long, lfts. ovate, to 6 in. long, cuneate at base, crenate, serrate, or repand-dentate, glabrous above, softly pubescent beneath; fr. cordate-ovate, to 1½ in. long. Paraguay to Ecuador.

SERRASTYLIS: *MACRADENIA.*

SERRATULA L. *Compositae* (Carduus Tribe). About 70 spp. of herbs, seldom spiny, in Eur., N. Afr., and temp. Asia; lvs. alt., toothed or cut; fl. heads large and solitary, or smaller and in corymbs, involucral bracts imbricate in many rows, receptacle scaly; fls. all tubular, various shades of purple; pappus of many rows of simple, unequal bristles. Allied to *Centaurea,* but involucral bracts without scarious or spiny appendages; and to *Saussurea,* but anthers not long-tailed and pappus hairs simple.

Sometimes planted in the border, flowering in summer and autumn.

centauroides L. Per., 1–2½ ft.; lvs. pinnately parted, scabrous, segms. linear-lanceolate, entire or few-toothed; heads few, ovoid, ¾–1¼ in. across, involucral bracts glabrous or nearly so, the outer appressed, ovate-lanceolate, mucronate, the inner elongated to a scarious, obtuse tip; fls. all bisexual. Siberia.

coronata L. Per., to 5 ft.; lvs. glabrous, pinnately dissected into oblanceolate, serrate segms.; heads few, corymbose, ovoid, to 1¼ in. long, involucral bracts slightly tomentose, the outer ovate, appressed, somewhat sharp-tipped, the inner long-acuminate, scarious-tipped; fls. wine-red, the marginal ones female, with sterile stamens, longer than the inner bisexual fls. E. Eur., Siberia.

Gmelinii Tausch. Per., 2–3 ft.; lvs. deeply pinnately cut or divided, glabrous, glaucous, the segms. linear, coarsely toothed, lower lvs. long-petioled, the upper sessile; heads solitary, ¾–1 in. across, nearly globose, involucral bracts yellow-green, glabrous, mucronate; fls. all bisexual. E. Eur., w. Siberia. *S. Gmelinii* Ledeb. ex DC. is *S. marginata*.

macrocephala: *S. tinctoria* subsp.

marginata Tausch [*S. Gmelinii* Ledeb. ex DC., not Tausch]. Per., to 2½ ft.; lvs. glabrous, slightly glaucous, the lower subcordate-ovate to oblong, pinnately lobed or toothed, petioled, the upper pinnately dissected, with oblong, entire, mucronate segms., sessile; heads solitary, ovoid, involucral bracts slightly cobwebby-pubescent, the outer appressed, ovate, spiny-mucronate, dark brown marginally, the inner longer, scarious; fls. all bisexual. Siberia.

monticola: *S. tinctoria* subsp. *macrocephala.*

pinnatifida (Cav.) Poir. Per., sts. woolly, 3–10 in.; lvs. ovate to oblong, irregularly lyrate or merely dentate, tomentose at least on veins, petioled; heads terminal, solitary, 1½ in. high, oblong-cylindrical, involucral bracts ovate-oblong, with spreading spinulose tips; fls. all bisexual. Spain.

Shawii: a listed name of no botanical standing, applied to a dwarf plant to 9 in. high, with small heads of mauve-purple fls. in an open corymb.

tinctoria L. SAWWORT, CENTAURY. Per., to 3 ft., glabrous, more or less dioecious; lvs. very variable, ovate-lanceolate to lanceolate, simple, lobed, or pinnately divided into narrow segms., the lvs. or segms. with very small bristle-tipped teeth, lower lvs. petioled, upper lvs. sessile; heads to ¾ in. long, ⅜ in. across, corymbose, 2–3 at end of each br., female heads ovoid-cylindrical, male heads smaller, oblong-cylindrical; fls. red-purple. Eur., N. Afr., Siberia. Subsp. **macrocephala** (Bertol.) Rouy [*S. macrocephala* Bertol.; *S. monticola* Boreau]. To 2 ft.; lf. segms. broader, the terminal one much longer than the lateral; heads larger, ⅝–¾ in. long, to ½ in. across, only 2–5 clustered on a st. Mts., Eur.

SERRURIA Salisb. *Proteaceae.* About 50 spp. of erect or prostrate shrubs, restricted to sw. Cape Prov., S. Afr.; lvs. linear, often pinnately divided; fls. bisexual, regular, solitary in axils of bracts, in terminal heads, surrounded by involucral bracts shorter than fls.; fr. an ovoid or subglobose drupe.

aemula R. Br. Shrub, to 2 ft., brs. usually pubescent; lvs. to 2 in. long, linear, 1–2 pinnately divided; fl. heads several at end of each shoot, bracts pinkish, lanceolate, spreading away from fls.

florida J. Knight. BLUSHING-BRIDE. Shrub, to 5 ft. or more, differs from *S. aemula* in having fl. heads larger and more showy, because of larger, papery, petal-like bracts.

SESAMUM L. *Pedaliaceae.* About 16 spp. of erect or prostrate herbs, native to trop. and s. Afr. and Asia; herbage often scabrous; lower lvs. opp., upper lvs. alt. or subopp.; fls. white to violet, solitary, axillary, calyx 5-parted, corolla 2-lipped, stamens 4, included; fr. a caps.

One species, *S. indicum,* widely grown for the seeds, which yield an important edible oil called sesame oil or gingelly oil; it is a specialty crop in some parts of the U.S., grown as an annual from seeds.

alatum Thonn. Erect, branched, to 3 ft., sts. 4-angled; lower lvs. long-petioled, blades palmately divided into 3–5 segms. or lfts., the segms. and lfts. linear-lanceolate, to 3 in. long, acute, entire, mealy-glandular beneath, upper lvs. entire, linear to lanceolate, short-petioled; fls. to 1 in. long, pink to bright red, with dark spots in throat; caps. 1½–2 in. long, finely pubescent, seeds winged at each end. Trop. Afr.

capense Burm.f. Erect, to 6 ft.; lvs. all palmate with 3–5 lfts., lfts. to 2½ in. long, obovate-oblong to linear, obtuse, entire, mealy-glandular on both sides; fls. to 1½ in. long, violet outside, darker inside; caps. to 1¾ in. long, seeds broadly winged. S. Afr.

indicum L. [*S. orientale* L.]. SESAME. Erect, to 3 ft., sparingly and finely pubescent; lvs. oblong to ovate, sometimes 3-lobed, to 5 in. long; fls. 1 in. long, pale rose or white; caps. 1 in. long or more, with 4 grooves, seeds not winged. Tropics; naturalized from Fla. to Tex.

orientale: *S. indicum.*

SESBANIA Scop. [*Agati* Adans.; *Daubentonia* DC.]. *Leguminosae* (subfamily *Faboideae*). Perhaps 50 spp. or more of herbs and shrubs, native mostly to warm regions; lvs. even-pinnate, with many lfts.; fls. in axillary racemes, yellow to red, papilionaceous, standards reflexed, stamens 10, 9 united and 1 separate; fr. an elongate, dehiscent legume, slightly compressed to 4-angled or 4-winged.

Grown outdoors for ornament in warm climates and one species as a cover crop. Propagated by seeds.

aegyptiaca: *S. Sesban.*

Drummondii (Rydb.) V. L. Cory [*Daubentonia Drummondii* Rydb.]. Shrub, to 20 ft.; lvs. to 8 in. long, lfts. in 10–25 pairs, oblong, about 1 in. long, apically rounded and mucronate, to 5 in. long; fls. yellow, standard ⅝ in. across; fr. to 2¼ in. long, scarcely ½ in. wide, abruptly acuminate, prominently 4-winged. W. Fla. to Ark. and Tex.

Emerus (Aubl.) Urb. Shrubby, to 16 ft., sts. somewhat angled; lfts. in 12–25 pairs, linear-oblong, to 1½ in. long, mostly obtuse, glaucous beneath; racemes shorter than lvs., 2–6-fld.; fls. yellow, standard spotted dark purple on back, ¾ in. wide or more; fr. linear, to 8 in. long. Trop. Amer.

exaltata (Raf.) V. L. Cory. COLORADO RIVER HEMP. Doubtfully distinct from *S. Emerus,* from which it differs in having lfts. in 35 pairs, mucronate, and corolla slightly smaller. N.Y. to Fla., w. to s. Calif. Formerly an important fiber plant of the Indians of w. U.S.

grandiflora (L.) Poir. [*Agati grandiflora* (L.) Desv.]. SCARLET WISTARIA TREE, VEGETABLE-HUMMING-BIRD. Short-lived, soft-wooded tree, to 40 ft.; lvs. to 1 ft. long, lfts. in 10–30 pairs, to 2 in. long; fls. 2–4 together, to 4 in. long, red to white; fr. slender, flat, to 20 in. long. Trop. Asia; naturalized in s. Fla. and W. Indies. Bark and lvs. have been used medicinally.

macrocarpa Muhlenb. ex Raf.: a botanically illegitimate name that has been used for *S. exaltata.*

macrophylla: a listed name of no botanical standing.

punicea (Cav.) Benth. [*Daubentonia punicea* (Cav.) DC.]. Shrub, to 6 ft. or more; lfts. in 6–20 pairs, to 1 in. long; racemes to 4 in. long; fls. vermilion, to ¾ in. long; fr. to 4 in. long, 4-winged. S. Brazil, Uruguay, ne. Argentina; naturalized from Fla. to La.

Sesban (L.) Merrill [*S. aegyptiaca* Poir.]. Much-branched shrub, or small tree to 20 ft.; lfts. in 10–27 pairs, oblong, 1 in. long, glaucous; racemes axillary, 6–10-fld.; fls. yellow, standard often tinged or spotted red-purplish; fr. narrow, nearly cylindrical and irregularly swollen, 6–9 in. long and less than ³⁄₁₆ in. wide. Old World tropics, where important for fodder and green manure. Var. **zambesiaca** J. B. Gillett. Sts. and lf. rachises pubescent; fr. broader. N. Rhodesia, Bechuanaland, S.-W. Afr.

Tripetii (Poit.) Hort. ex F. T. Hubb. [*Daubentonia Tripetii* Poit.]. SCARLET WISTARIA TREE. Distinguished from *S. punicea* in having drooping racemes, and standard with basal, yellow spot. N. Argentina and Brazil.

zambesiaca: a listed name of no botanical standing for *S. Sesban* var.

SESELI L. *Umbelliferae.* About 80 spp. of per., bien., or ann. herbs of the Old World with erect, branching sts.; lvs. in rosettes, 1–3-pinnate or pinnately decompound into entire to toothed lfts.; infl. of loose, compound umbels, involucre inconspicuous or absent, involucels usually of many linear, entire bractlets; fls. usually white; fr. ovoid to oblong, slightly compressed to cylindrical.

caespitosum Sibth. & Sm. Cespitose, glabrous, to 6 in.; lvs. 1–2-pinnate, lfts. oblong; umbels 1 to few, 3–5-rayed, bracts of involucre and bractlets of involucels linear. Greece.

glaucum: *S. montanum* var. *peucedanifolium.*

Libanotis (L.) W. D. J. Koch. Bien. or per., monocarpic, to 3 ft., st. angled, often pubescent; lvs. 1–2-pinnate with pinnately lobed lfts.; bractlets of involucels numerous; calyx with elongate teeth; fr. ovoid, to ³⁄₁₆ in. long, pubescent or glabrous. Eur. to Asia. Var. **daucifolium:** var. *pyrenaicum.* Var. **pyrenaicum** (L.) Briq. [var. *daucifolium* Gren. & Godr.]. Lfts. more deeply divided than in the typical var. Eur.

montanum L. Bien. or ann., st. rounded, unbranched, to 2 ft. or more; lvs. 2-pinnate or decompound, lfts. linear; involucre usually absent, bractlets of involucels numerous, narrow, as long as the rays of the umbellets. Eur., as far e. as Russia. Var. **peucedanifolium** (Mérat) DC. [*S. glaucum* L.]. Taller, lower lvs. longer and wider, blades mostly not longer than petiole. Spain to Italy.

SETARIA Beauvois. BRISTLE GRASS. *Gramineae.* About 125 spp. of ann. or per. grasses in warm countries; panicles narrow, terminal, dense and spikelike or somewhat loose and open; spikelets with 1 bisexual terminal floret above a sterile floret and 2 glumes, subtended by 1 to several bristles, falling free from the bristles, awnless, first glume broad, usually less than half the length of the spikelet, 3–5-nerved, second glume and sterile lemma equal, or the glume shorter and several-nerved, fertile lemma hard, transversely roughened or smooth. For terminology see *Gramineae.*

italica (L.) Beauvois [*Panicum germanicum* Mill.]. FOXTAIL MILLET, JAPANESE M., ITALIAN M., HUNGARIAN GRASS, BENGAL G. Ann., sts, to 3 ft. high or more, branching at base; lf. blades flat, to 6 in. long and over ⅜ in. wide; panicles erect or somewhat nodding, dense, yellow or purple, cylindrical but tapering a little at the summit, to 1 ft. long and 1¼ in. thick; bristles from scarcely longer than the spikelets to 3–4 times as long; fr. tawny to red, brown or black, smooth or nearly so, glossy at maturity, falling away from the remainder of the spikelet. Eurasia. A cultigen, perhaps derived from *S. viridis* (L.) Beauvois, a widespread weed. Foxtail millet is cult. in many forms in this country for hay and forage and elsewhere as a cereal grain; the smaller forms are known as Hungarian grass.

macrostachya HBK. PLAINS B. G. Per., sts. to 4 ft., densely clustered, usually pale or glaucous; lf. blades flat or folded, scabrous above or rarely pubescent on both surfaces, to 16 in. long and ⅜ in. wide; panicle spikelike, to 10 in. long, mostly ¼–⅜ in. thick, somewhat tapering but not attenuate, more or less interrupted or lobed; spikelets ⅛ in. long or less, very turgid, bristles to ⅝ in. long. Tex. to Colo. and Ariz., s. to Mex.

palmifolia (J. König) Stapf [*Panicum palmifolium* J. König]. PALM GRASS. Per., sts. tall; lf. blades plicate, to 20 in. long and 2⅜ in. wide; panicle loose, to 16 in. long, brs. usually 2⅜–10 in. long; bristles inconspicuous, below only part of the spikelets. India. Cult. in frost-free areas and in greenhouses for ornament. There is also a striped-lvd. form.

Poiretiana (Schult.) Kunth. POIRET B. G. Distinguished from *S. palmifolia* by narrower panicle about 1 ft. long, with many ascending brs. usually less than 2⅜ in. long. Trop. Amer. Occasionally cult. for ornament.

SETCREASEA K. Schum. & Sydow. *Commelinaceae.* About 6 spp. of per. herbs, native to Mex. and s. Tex.; roots ropy to tuberous-thickened, sts. succulent or swollen, erect or clambering, brs. emerging through the orifice of lf. sheaths; lvs. linear to ovate or oblong; infls. terminal, or both terminal and axillary, of paired cincinni, each pair subtended by 2 large leaflike bracts at the end of a usually long peduncle; fls. white to purple, pedicels villous in upper part, petals separate but their bases clawed and connivent in a tube with spreading limb, stamens 6, two inserted on each petal, filaments often bearded, ovary 3-celled, each cell with 2 ovules; fr. a caps., each cell with usually 2 roughened seeds.

Cultivated under glass or indoors in the North, and useful as a bedding plant or ground cover in the extreme South. Propagated by seeds and cuttings.

pallida Rose. Plants green to intense violet-purple, sts. erect to sprawling, to 16 in. high, glabrous; lvs. oblong, somewhat trough-shaped, to 7 in. long, 1 in. wide, glabrous or often with a few deciduous, long, soft hairs on both surfaces, with cobwebby hairs at margin toward the base and at orifice of lf. sheath; infls. terminal, or sometimes terminal and axillary; sepals glabrous, petals pale purplish-white or lavender-pink to rose-purple. Ne. Mex. Cv. **'Purple Heart'** [*S. purpurea* Boom; *S. tampicana* Hort.]. PURPLE-HEART. Fls. violet-purple; the most frequently cult. form.

purpurea: *S. pallida* cv. 'Purple Heart'.

striata: a listed name of no botanical standing, used for plants referable to *Callisia elegans.*

tampicana: a listed name of no botanical standing, used for deeply colored plants referable to *S. pallida* cv. 'Purple Heart'.

tumida (Lindl.) K. Schum. & Sydow. Sts. pilose, with swollen internodes; lvs. oblong, recurved, to 5 in. long, purplish beneath, more or less pubescent; fls. pink, sepals pilose or nearly glabrous, petals ridged in center. W.-cent. Mex.

SETICEREUS: *BORZICACTUS.* **S. Humboldtii:** *B. icosagonus.* **S. Roezlii:** *B. sepium;* but the name *S. Roezlii* has been used in cult. for a different sp. not yet identified.

SETIECHINOPSIS (Backeb.) Backeb. *Cactaceae.* One sp., a small, oblong, ribbed cactus of Argentina; resembling *Echinopsis* but differing in the slender floral tube with narrow scarious scales, stamens in 1 series, and the slender dry fr.; fls. subapical, inodorous, scales with wool and bristles in axils. Perhaps better referred to *Arthrocereus.*

For culture see *Cacti.*

mirabilis (Speg.) De Haas ex Backeb. [*Arthrocereus mirabilis* (Speg.) W. T. Marsh.; *Echinopsis mirabilis* Speg.]. Sts. simple, to 6 in. high and 1 in. thick, ribs 11, weakly cross-furrowed; radial spines 9–14, bristlelike, glabrous, to $^{3}/_{16}$ in. long, central spines 1, needle-shaped, villous, brown, to ⅝ in. long; fls. white, to 5 in. long; fr. to 1½ in. long and ¼ in. in diam. N. Argentina.

SEVERINIA Ten. *Rutaceae.* About 5–6 spp. of spiny shrubs or small trees, native in se. Asia, Philippine Is., Kai Is., and New Guinea; lvs. alt., simple, conspicuously parallel-veined, glandular-dotted; fls. small, in clusters, corymbs, or panicles, sepals 3–5-lobed, petals 3–5, stamens 6–10, separate; fr. a small berry, with rudimentary pulp vesicles.

One species planted as an ornamental, suitable for hedges, and perhaps of value as a stock for citrus.

buxifolia (Poir.) Ten. [*Atalantia buxifolia* (Poir.) D. Oliver]. CHINESE BOX ORANGE. Small tree; lvs. obovate, to 1½ in. long, retuse, leathery, dark green; fls. white, in clusters; fr. black, 2–3-celled, about $^{5}/_{16}$ in. in diam. Taiwan and s. China. Hardy in Gulf Coast region.

SHADE (PLANTS FOR). No green plant can thrive in the absence of light but some kinds are tolerant of shade, living in their native haunts in shady sites, usually in woodlands and forests where the light levels may be as much as one-tenth of the light in full sun. Ornamental shade plants are much used in horticulture. Many shade-tolerant plants of tropical forests—such as Araceae, *Begonia,* Bromeliaceae, *Dracaena,* ferns, *Hoya,* Orchidaceae, *Peperomia, Saintpaulia ionatha* and other Gesneriaceae—thrive outdoors in shaded tropical gardens or in our homes, where lack of sufficient sun is the general rule. The plants of our shaded outdoor gardens in temperate North America are species native mainly to woodlands and forests of the whole temperate world.

Shade in the outdoor garden ranges from the open shade with unobstructed overhead sky found on the north side of buildings or tall trees to the partial or rather complete shade found under trees. The latter kind of shade may vary greatly depending upon the character of the tree and its canopy. Species of many evergreen coniferous genera, such as *Tsuga,* have a heavy unrelenting shade not very conducive to underplanting, whereas many deciduous trees provide abundant light that is filtered through a high canopy. Most shade plants favor such high, filtered sunlight provided that the trees are deep-rooted and thus not competitive for water and nutrients with the species planted underneath in their shade. *Fagus* and most species of *Acer* exemplify canopy trees having extensive, shallow, fibrous surface roots, which make it almost completely impossible to grow shade-loving plants beneath them.

Plants suited to shaded gardens have shade tolerances ranging from that of very deep shade (very few species) to light shade (many species). Plants for shady sites vary widely in form and habit and are available to suit the gardener's needs in all seasons. They include herbs and woody species, annuals and perennials, evergreens and deciduous plants, vines, bulbs, and ground covers.

Among genera herein described having species that are suitable for shaded sites are the following, listed alphabetically by habit: bamboos—*Arundinaria, Bambusa, Phyllostachys, Pseudosasa, Sasa, Shibataea;* bulbs or tubers (hardy)—*Anemone, Chionodoxa, Colchicum, Cyclamen, Eranthis, Erythronium, Galanthus, Leucoium, Lilium, Lycoris, Narcissus, Ornithogalum, Puschkinia, Scilla;* bulbs, tubers, or rhizomes (tender)—*Achimenes, Begonia* (tuberous), *Caladium, Colocasia, Zantedeschia, Zephyranthes;* ferns and fern allies—most temperate kinds are suitable for temperate gardens and many tropical kinds for warm climates or shade indoors (see *Ferns*); herbs (annual)—*Begonia, Coleus, Impatiens;* herbs (perennial)—*Aconitum, Adonis, Ajuga, Anemone, Aquilegia, Arisaema, Aruncus, Asarum, Asperula, Astilbe, Aubrieta, Bergenia, Brunnera, Campanula, Ceratostigma, Chelone, Chimaphila, Chrysogonum, Cimicifuga, Convallaria, Cornus, Dicentra, Digitalis, Dodecatheon, Doronicum, Epigaea, Epimedium, Eupatorium, Filipendula, Galax, Gaultheria, Geranium, Glaucidium, Helleborus, Hemerocallis, Hepatica, Hesperis, Heuchera,* × *Heucherella, Hosta, Iris, Kirengeshoma, Liriope, Lobelia, Lysimachia, Maianthemum, Mazus, Mertensia, Mitchella, Monarda, Myosotis, Pachysandra, Phlox, Podophyllum, Polemonium, Polygonatum, Primula, Pulmonaria, Ranunculus, Sanguinaria, Saxifraga, Shortia, Smilacina, Symplocarpus, Thalictrum, Tiarella, Trientalis, Trillium, Trollius, Vancouveria, Vinca, Viola, Waldsteinia;* shrubs (deciduous)—*Abelia, Abeliophyllum, Aronia, Berberis, Callicarpa, Ceanothus, Chamaedaphne, Clethra, Corylopsis, Cotoneaster, Diervilla, Dirca, Edgeworthia, Enkianthus, Euonymus, Fothergilla, Hamamelis, Hydrangea, Hypericum, Ilex, Kerria, Ligustrum, Menziesia, Rhododendron, Rhodotypos, Stephanandra, Symphoricarpos, Vaccinum, Viburnum;* shrubs (evergreen)—*Abelia, Aucuba, Berberis, Camellia, Cyrilla, Gaultheria, Ilex, Kalmia, Leucothoe, Ligustrum, Mahonia, Nandina, Osmanthus, Paxistima, Pieris, Prunus, Rhododendron, Skimmia, Taxus;* trees (small hardy undertrees)—*Acer, Amelanchier, Cercis, Cornus, Ilex;* vines (hardy)—*Celastrus, Clematis, Euonymus, Hedera, Hydrangea, Lonicera, Parthenocissus, Polygonum, Schizophragma.*

SHALLOT: see *Onions.*

SHEPHERDIA Nutt. *Elaeagnaceae.* Three spp. of dioecious shrubs or small trees with brown or silvery scales, native to N. Amer.; lvs. opp., simple; fls. small, yellowish; fr. drupelike.

The 2 deciduous species are grown as ornamentals, and *S. argentea* for the fruits. Adapted to dry rocky soils. Propagated by seeds sown in autumn or stratified.

argentea (Pursh) Nutt. [*Elaeagnus utilis* A. Nels.]. BUFFALO BERRY, SILVER B. B. To 18 ft., thorny; lvs. oblong, silvery on both sides; fr. ovoid, about ¼ in. across, red or yellow. Man. to Minn. and Kans. Sometimes grown for its edible frs., which are made into jelly and as a hedge plant in the Northwest; valuable for its great hardiness. Zone 2. Cv. 'Xanthocarpa'. Fr. yellow.

canadensis (L.) Nutt. BUFFALO BERRY, SOAPBERRY. To 8 ft., thornless; lvs. ovate or elliptic, differing from *S. canadensis* in having lvs. green and nearly glabrous above, silvery and scurfy with brown scales beneath, and fr. insipid. Temp. N. Amer. Cv. 'Rubra'. Fr. red. Cv. 'Xanthocarpa'. Fr. yellow.

utilis: a listed name of no botanical standing for *S. argentea.*

SHIBATAEA Mak. ex Nakai. BAMBOO. *Gramineae.* Two spp. of small bamboos, 1 in China and 1 in Japan, with elongate rhizomes, sts. zigzag, much flattened, nearly solid, grooved on one side; st. sheaths papery, with short blades, brs. very short, 3–5 at each node; lf. blades terminal on brs., short-petioled, sheaths without bristles; flowering brs. leafless, indeterminate; spikelets 1–2-fld., stamens 3, style long, stigmas 3. For terminology see *Gramineae.*

Kumasaca (Zoll. ex Steud.) Nakai. Sts. slender, to 6 ft. high or more, erect, narrowly fistulose, green, with prominent nodes, internodes short, to 3¼ in. long; lf. blades distinctly petioled, ovate-oblong to ovate-lanceolate, broad, to 4¾ in. long and 1 in. wide, 12–14-nerved, long-pointed, broadly cuneate at the base, shining dark green above, puberulous beneath at first. Japan, where a common garden subject. Zone 8. A useful ground cover. See *Bamboos.* Has been offered under the erroneous name *Sasa Kumasaca.*

SHORTIA Torr. & A. Gray [*Schizocodon* Siebold & Zucc.]. *Diapensiaceae.* About 8 spp. of evergreen, stemless herbs with creeping roots, native to temp. e. N. Amer. and Asia; lvs. basal, simple, glossy; fls. white, pink, or blue, nodding, on slender scapes, calyx deeply 5-lobed, corolla campanulate, 5-lobed, stamens 5, alternating with 5 staminodes; fr. a caps.

Shortias are grown in rock gardens and wild gardens. They should be planted in shady locations, and require abundant leaf mold and humus; propagated by division and runners.

galacifolia Torr. & A. Gray. OCONEE-BELLS. To 8 in.; lvs. orbicular to ovate, to 3 in. across, glossy, crenate-dentate, teeth often spine-tipped, petioles to 5 in. long; fls. solitary, white, pink, or blue, 1 in. across. Mts., Va. to Ga.

ilicifolia: *S. soldanelloides* var.

macrophylla: a listed name of no botanical standing for *S. soldanelloides* var. *magna.*

soldanelloides (Siebold & Zucc.) Mak. [*Schizocodon soldanelloides* Siebold & Zucc.]. FRINGED GALAX, FRINGE-BELL. Alpine, to 9 in.; lvs. orbicular, cordate, coarsely toothed; fls. deep rose, white, or bluish toward edge, to 1 in. across, in 4–6-fld. scapose racemes, corolla lobes fringed. Japan. Forma **alpina** (Maxim.) Mak. [*Schizocodon soldanelloides* forma *alpinus* Maxim.]. Plant smaller, more compact. Var. **ilicifolia** (Maxim.) Mak. [*Shortia ilicifolia* (Maxim.) H. L. Li; *Schizocodon ilicifolius* Maxim.; *Schizocodon soldanelloides* var. *ilicifolius* (Maxim.) Mak.]. Lf. margins with coarser and fewer teeth. Var. **magna** Mak. [*Shortia macrophylla* Hort.; *Schizocodon macrophyllus* Hort.; *Schizocodon soldanelloides* var. *macrophyllus* Hort. and var. *magnus* (Mak.) Hara]. Lvs. larger, margins crenate-dentate with many small teeth.

uniflora (Maxim.) Maxim. [*Schizocodon uniflorus* Maxim.]. NIPPON-BELLS. Differs from *S. galacifolia* in having lvs. more cordate and deeply wavy-margined. Japan. Cv. 'Grandiflora'. Fls. larger than in typical form.

SIBBALDIA L. *Rosaceae.* About 8 spp. of low, tufted per. herbs of the colder parts of the N. Hemisphere, allied to *Potentilla;* lvs. alt., of 3 lfts.; fls. small, yellow, in cymes, 5-merous, stamens 5(4 or 10), pistils 5–12, style deciduous in fr.; frs. achenes.

Adapted to alpine gardens, hardy.

maxima: Kesselr. ex Murav.: *S. cuneata* Hort. ex Kunze, not in general cult. Material cult. as *S. maxima* is usually *Potentilla ambigua.*

parviflora Willd. Larger and less cespitose than *S. procumbens,* to 10 in. tall; lfts. broader, cuneate-obovate, with almost parallel sides, ⅜–¾ in. long, ½–⅝ in. wide, mostly with 3, broad, terminal teeth. Eurasia.

procumbens L. To 4 in.; lfts. narrowly wedge-shaped, to ¾ in. long, 3–5-toothed at apex; fls. less than 3/16 in. across. N. Amer., Eurasia. Cv. 'Grandiflora' is listed.

SIBIRAEA Maxim. *Rosaceae.* Two spp. of deciduous, polygamodioecious shrubs from Asia and se. Eur. once included in *Spiraea;* lvs. alt., entire; fls. small, in terminal panicles, sepals and petals 5; frs. 2-seeded follicles united at base.

Propagated by seeds or layers.

laevigata (L.) Maxim. To 5 ft., bark scaly, cracked, twigs glabrous; lvs. oblong, to 4 in. long, bluish-green; fls. greenish-white, in panicles to 5 in. long. Siberia. Hardy north. Subsp. **croatica** (Degen) C. K. Schneid. Lower, to 3 ft., more intricately branched; lvs. to 3 in. long, scarcely if at all glaucescent; sepals wider. Balkans. Zone 5.

SICANA Naud. *Cucurbitaceae.* One sp., a tendril-bearing, monoecious, per. Amer. vine; fls. solitary, yellowish, corolla campanulate, 1 in. long or less, male fls. with separate, flexuous anthers, female fls. with inferior ovary, placentas 3; fr. fleshy, indehiscent, seeds many, horizontal.

odorifera (Vell.) Naud. CURUBÁ, CURUA, COROA, CASSABANANA. To 40 ft. and more; lvs. nearly orbicular and several-angled or -lobed, to 1 ft. across; fr. long-oblong, nearly cylindrical, to 2 ft. long, orange-crimson, scented. S. Amer. Grown to some extent in the Gulf region. Grown as an ann., for its ornamental, fragrant fr., which is also edible. The name cassabanana is sometimes mistakenly applied to *Benincasa hispida.*

SICYOS L. *Cucurbitaceae.* More than 30 spp. of ann., tendril-bearing, monoecious vines, native to Amer. and Australasia; fls. small, white or greenish, mostly in clusters, male fls. with united filaments and anthers; fr. small, indehiscent, usually spiny.

angulatus L. BUR CUCUMBER, STAR C. To 20 ft. or more; petioles and peduncles hairy; lvs. cordate-orbicular, sharply angled or lobed; fr. about ½ in. long, spiny, 1-seeded, in clusters. E. Canada and U.S. Sometimes grown as a screen, but may become a weed.

SIDA L. *Malvaceae.* Perhaps 150 spp. of ann. or per. herbs or small shrubs in warm-temp. and trop. regions; lvs. simple, mostly unlobed; fls. solitary or in axillary clusters, spikes, racemes, or panicles, involucral bracts usually 0, petals white, yellow, or lavender, often inconspicuous, stamens united in a tubular column, style brs. as many as the mericarps, stigmas capitate; fr. a schizocarp, mericarps mostly 5–10, in a single whorl, each 1-seeded, the apical part dehiscent and beaked or awned on inner edge, the basal part indehiscent, laterally rugose to fenestrate.

Abutilon: *Abutilon Theophrasti.*

dioica: *Napaea dioica.*

hermaphrodita (L.) Rusby [*S. Napaea* Cav.]. VIRGINIA MALLOW. Per. herb, to 10 ft.; lvs. large, lower lvs., to 10 in. long or more, 3-, 5-, or 7-lobed, lobes lacerate-serrate, long-acuminate; fls. in loose, peduncled, axillary cymes, white, to 1 in. across; mericarps 10. Rare along stream banks and in woods. Del., w. to Ohio and Tenn.

Napaea: *S. hermaphrodita.*

SIDALCEA A. Gray. *Malvaceae.* About 22 spp. of ann. or per. herbs in w. N. Amer.; lvs. mostly rounded, usually palmately lobed or parted; fls. in terminal racemes, bisexual or sometimes female by the abortion of the anthers, involucral bracts usually 0, petals 5, white, pink, or purple, stamens united in a tubular column, filaments more or less terminal, in 2 whorls, style brs. slender, stigmatic along the inner edge, as many as the mericarps; fr. a schizocarp, mericarps 5–9, in a single whorl, each 1-seeded.

The cultivated species are all perennial; propagated by seeds or the named cultivars by division.

californica: *S. malviflora* subsp.

candida A. Gray. More or less glaucous, glabrate herb, 2–3 ft., usually simple-stemmed from spreading rhizomes; lower lvs. to 8 in. wide, 5- or 7-lobed, coarsely crenate, upper lvs. divided into 3, 5, or 7 segms.; fls. congested in spikelike racemes 2–5 in. long, petals white drying yellowish, to ¾ in. long, anthers bluish-pink. Summer. Wyo., Colo., New Mex., Utah.

Hendersonii S. Wats. Sts. mostly several, from a heavy taproot or short rhizome, 2–6 ft., glabrous or glabrate; lower lvs. to 6 in. wide, shallowly 5-lobed, upper lvs. cut to near the base in 3 or 5 laciniate segms.; fls. ¾–1¼ in. across, congested in spikelike racemes, petals pinkish-lavender to deep rose; mericarps 7–8, about 3/16 in. long. Early summer. B.C., Wash., and Ore.

hybrida: a listed name of no botanical standing; plants so offered are probably selections of *S. malviflora.*

Listeri: a listed name for *S. malviflora* cv.

malviflora (DC.) A. Gray. CHECKERBLOOM. Glabrous or pubescent, erect-stemmed herb, to 3 ft., roots fibrous; lvs. to 3 in. wide, sometimes fleshy, lower lvs. unlobed or shallowly 7- or 9-lobed, upper lvs. more deeply divided; fls. in simple or compound, rather loose racemes, petals pinkish-rose or watermelon-pink, ½–1 in. long; mericarps about ⅛ in. long, slightly or prominently reticulate laterally. Ore., Calif., and n. Baja Calif. Cv. **'Listeri'**. Fls. satiny-pink. A number of subspp. are recognized of which one is offered. Subsp. **californica** (Nutt. ex Torr. & A. Gray) C. L. Hitchc. [*S. californica* Nutt. ex Torr. & A. Gray]. More densely pubescent.

neomexicana A. Gray. Herb, usually hirsute, with simple or forked hairs, sts. erect, to 3 ft., roots fleshy, single or clustered; lvs. to about 3 in. wide, lower lvs. shallowly lobed, upper lvs. mostly 5-parted; fls. in simple or compound, many-fld. racemes, corolla white to pinkish, about ¾ in. across; mericarps about ⅛ in. long with mostly smooth lateral walls. Ore. to Wyo., s. to Mex.

nervata: *S. oregana.*

oregana (Nutt. ex Torr. & A. Gray) A. Gray. [*S. nervata* A. Nels.]. Glabrous or pubescent, 1–6 ft., with a heavy taproot and branching root crown, usually producing rhizomes; lower lvs. to 6 in. wide, crenate, shallowly 5- or 7-lobed, upper lvs. divided to near the base; fls. in spicate racemes, petals pinkish or deep pink, to ¾ in. long; mericarps about ⅛ in. long, smooth or reticulate. Early spring–summer. Idaho to Wash., s. to Utah and Calif. Subsp. **spicata** (Regel) C. L. Hitchc. [*S. spicata* Regel]. Sts. hirsute, spikes more densely fld., mericarps usually smooth. Ore., Calif., and Nev.

rosea: a listed name of no botanical standing; plants so offered are probably *S. malviflora.*

spicata: *S. oregana* subsp.

SIDERANTHUS: *HAPLOPAPPUS.*

SIDERASIS Raf. [*Pyrrheima* Hassk.]. *Commelinaceae.* One sp., a per. herb, native to Brazil; sts. short, underground; lvs. in a rosette, covered with dense rust-colored hairs; fls. in unpaired cincinni, subtended by small bracts, on short hairy peduncles from the crown, sepals and petals separate, stamens 6, filaments glabrous, ovary hairy, 3-celled, each cell with 2 ovules.

fuscata (Lodd.) H. E. Moore [*Pyrrheima fuscata* (Lodd.) Backer; *Tradescantia fuscata* Lodd.]. Lvs. elliptic, to 8 in. long, 3 in. wide, dark green above with whitish center, purplish-red beneath; fls. nearly violet to rose-purple, about 1 in. across. Cult. under glass or as a houseplant.

SIDERITIS L. [*Leucophae* Webb & Berth.]. *Labiatae.* About 100 spp. of herbs or small shrubs of the Canary Is., Madeira, and n. temp. Eur. and Asia; sts. mostly square in cross section; lvs. opp., entire or toothed; fls. in 2- to many-fld. verticillasters arranged in spikes or racemes, calyx campanulate, 10-nerved, 5-toothed, corolla yellow, tube not longer than calyx, limb 2-lipped, upper lip nearly concave, lower lip 3-lobed, stamens 4, in 2 pairs, included; fr. of 4 nutlets rounded at apex.

Thrives on sunny, rocky, dry hillsides in the wild. Sometimes grown in the perennial border; propagated by seeds, division, and cuttings.

argosphacelus (Webb & Berth.) Clos [*Leucophae argosphacelus* Webb & Berth.]. Low shrub, mostly 6–18 in., felty-tomentose; lvs. ovate, 2–4 in. long, crenate, greenish above, white-felty beneath; spike dense, somewhat flexuous, with sessile fls., verticillasters densely white-tomentose, the lower ones sometimes distant, bracts shorter than calyx; corolla exserted. Canary Is.

candicans Ait. [*Leucophae candicans* (Ait.) Webb & Berth.]. Shrub, to 3 ft., lvs. and young sts. densely long-white-hairy; lvs. triangular, to 2 in. long, obtuse, cordate; spike to 12 in. long or more, the lower 2 or 3 verticillasters frequently distant, bracts linear-lanceolate, about 3 times as long as calyx, obtuse; calyx 5-toothed, corolla longer than calyx, yellow. Summer. Canary Is. Cv. **'Stricta'**. A listed name.

hyssopifolia L. Glabrescent to villous per., to 15 in.; lvs. linear to ovate, obovate, or oblanceolate, to 1½ in. long, entire or coarsely toothed; spike dense, verticillasters 5–15, 6-fld., bracts ovate, ¼–½ in. long, with several short-pointed teeth; calyx about ¼ in. long, with a ring of hairs inside, corolla yellow. Mts. of se. Eur. to Switzerland.

libanotica Labill. Per., to 1½ ft., glabrescent to densely white-woolly; lvs. oblanceolate to spatulate, to 2½ in. long, serrate; spike with verticillasters more or less distant, bracts ovate, to ½ in. long; calyx to 5/16 in. long, 5-toothed; corolla as long as calyx, yellow. Syria, Israel.

macrostachys Poir. [*Leucophae macrostachys* (Poir.) Webb & Berth.]. Shrub, to 3 ft.; lvs. nearly orbicular to ovate, crenate, bright green above, white-tomentose beneath; spike stiff, dense, 2–3 in. long, lower bracts much longer than calyx; corolla scarcely longer than calyx. Canary Is.

Massoniana Benth. [*Leucophae Massoniana* (Benth.) Webb & Berth.]. Shrub, 2–3 ft., sts. glabrescent; lvs. oblong-ovate, 1½–2 in. long, bluntly acute, weakly crenate, greenish-pubescent above, gray-tomentose beneath, young growth ashy-gray; racemes on slender sts., in panicles, verticillasters somewhat distant, only lowest bracts longer than calyx; corolla about twice as long as calyx. Madeira, Canary Is. Var. **albida** Pit. Less pubescent throughout; lvs. more ovate and acute.

montana L. Ann., to 15 in., sparsely to densely villous-woolly; lvs. oblanceolate to elliptic, to ¾ in. long, dentate; verticillasters 6-fld., distant or more or less crowded; calyx weakly 2-lipped, to ¼ in. long, pubescent, teeth aristate, corolla yellow, nearly as long as calyx. Medit. region.

scariosa: a listed name of no botanical standing.

syriaca L. Per., to 20 in., densely white-tomentose; lower lvs. oblong or oblong-lanceolate, obtuse, crenate, middle and upper lvs. linear-lanceolate or oblong, entire; spike loose, verticillasters 5–20, mostly distant, 6–10-fld., bracts cordate, short-acute; calyx woolly, teeth short-acuminate, corolla slightly longer than calyx, yellow. On mt. rocks, s. Eur.

SIDEROXYLON L. *Sapotaceae.* An Afr. genus not represented in cult. in U.S. Spp. listed under this name are referred as follows: **S. foetidissimum** and **S. Mastichodendron:** *Mastichodendron foetidissimum;* **S. novozeylandicum:** *Planchonella costata.*

SIEVERSIA: *GEUM.*

SIGMATOSTALIX Rchb.f. *Orchidaceae.* About 20 spp. of epiphytes, native to Cent. and trop. S. Amer.; short-rhizomatous, pseudobulbs 1- or 2-lvd.; lvs. leathery; infl. basal, longer than lvs., racemose or paniculate; fls. small, membranous, sepals and petals separate, spreading or reflexed, lip sessile or with long claw, entire or variously lobed, column slender, somewhat dilated at apex, arching, without a foot, pollinia 2. For structure of fl. see *Orchidaceae.*

For culture see *Orchids.*

bicornuta: *S. graminea.*

graminea (Poepp. & Endl.) Rchb.f. [*S. bicornuta* Rolfe; *S. peruviana* Rolfe]. To 2½ in., pseudobulbs ovoid, close together, to ½ in. long, 1-lvd.; lvs. linear, to 2 in. long; racemes loosely few-fld.; sepals and petals light yellow, upper sepal and the petals with deep purple band or stripe, oblong-lanceolate, to ⅛ in. long, petals with a hornlike projection on back, lip sessile, triangular-kidney-shaped, less then ¼ in. long, undulate, the disc with lobed callus at base. Peru.

peruviana: *S. graminea.*

SILENE L. [*Heliosperma* (Rchb.) Rchb.; *Melandrium* Röhling]. CAMPION, CATCHFLY. *Caryophyllaceae.* About 500 spp. of ann., bien., or per. herbs or sometimes subshrubs, widespread in the N. Hemisphere; lvs. opp., stipules absent; fls. white, pink, or red, solitary, cymose or panicled, not subtended by epicalyx, bisexual or rarely unisexual, calyx tubular, 5-toothed, 10–60-veined, petals 5, mostly 2-lobed or emarginate, coronal scales usually present at juncture of blade and claw, stamens 10, ovary 1-celled above but often 3–5-celled at base, styles usually 3, sometimes 4 or 5, alt. with calyx teeth; fr. a caps., dehiscent by teeth twice as many as the styles, usually borne on a stalk, seeds many, reniform. The name has 3 syllables.

Cultivated in rock gardens, rock walls, and in borders. Of easy culture. If seeds of annuals are sown in the autumn, flowering occurs much earlier the following spring. Perennials propagated from seeds, division, or cuttings.

acaulis (L.) Jacq. [*S. bryoides* Jord.]. CUSHION PINK, MOSS CAMPION. Per., mosslike, cespitose, mat-forming, to 2 in., flowering sts. to 4 in.; lvs. linear-subulate, ¼–½ in. long, ciliate; fls. ½ in. across, calyx to ⁵⁄₁₆ in. long, 10-veined, glabrous, petals 2-lobed, deep pink to purplish; caps. to ⅝ in. long. Arctic Eurasia, mts. of w. N. Amer., and cent. Eur. A showy alpine suitable for the rock garden, but commonly not free-flowering under cult. Cv. **'Alba'.** Fls. white. Cv. **'Cenisia'.** Fls. double. Subsp. **longiscapa:** var. *elongata.* Var. **elongata** DC. [subsp. *longiscapa* (A. Kern. ex Vierh.) Hayek; var. *pedicularis* Hort. and var. *pedunculata* Hort.; *S. longiscapa* A. Kern. ex Vierh.]. Fl. sts. to 4 in.; caps. up to twice as long as calyx. Var. **exscapa** (All.) DC. Fl. sts. to ³⁄₁₆ in.; lvs. ⅛–¼ in. long; calyx ¼ in. long; caps. scarcely longer than calyx. Circumpolar. Var. **pedicularis:** var. *elongata.* Var. **pedunculata:** var. *elongata.*

alba (Mill.) E. H. L. Krause [*Lychnis alba* Mill.]. WHITE CAMPION, EVENING C., EVENING LYCHNIS, WHITE COCKLE. Dioecious ann., bien., or short-lived per., to 3 ft., with a stout root, sts. glandular-hairy above; lower lvs. oblanceolate or elliptic, narrowed to the petiole, upper lvs. lanceolate to elliptic, to 4 in. long, sessile, hairy; infl. a few-fld., terminal, leafy-bracted dichasial cyme; fls. opening in the evening, slightly scented, calyx of male fls. to ⅞ in. long, 10-veined, calyx of female fls. to 1¼ in. long, 20-veined, more or less inflated, petals white, styles 5; caps. with 10 erect teeth. N. Afr., Eur., w. Asia; naturalized in N. Amer. as a weed of disturbed ground.

alpestris: *S. quadrifida.*

alpina: *S. vulgaris* subsp. *prostrata;* but the name *S. alpina* has been applied to several spp.

amoena: a confused name, applied to several spp.

antirrhina L. SLEEPY CATCHFLY. Ann., sts. to 3 ft., retrorsely scabrous towards the base, glabrous towards apex; basal lvs. oblanceolate, to 3 in. long, to ½ in. wide, st. lvs. oblanceolate to linear, glabrous to scabrous; infl. an open cyme, many-fld., pedicels 1–2 in.; calyx ⁵⁄₁₆ in. long, 10-nerved, glabrous, teeth triangular, tipped purple, petals to ½ in., 2-lobed, white to pink. N. Amer., Mex., S. Amer.; naturalized in Eur.

Armeria L. [*S. glauca* Salisb.]. SWEET WILLIAM CATCHFLY, GARDEN C., NONE-SO-PRETTY. Ann. or bien., glabrous, glaucous, sts. to 16 in., erect, viscid at apex; basal lvs. oblanceolate, to 3 in. long, withering early, st. lvs. united-perfoliate, ovate-cordate; infl. of flat-topped cymes; calyx ½ in. long, petals emarginate, pink. Eur.; naturalized in N. Amer.

Baldwynii Nutt. Per., to 16 in.; lvs. spatulate, to 3 in. long; calyx to 1 in. long, petals white or pink, blade fan-shaped, to 1 in. long; caps. ovoid, to ⁵⁄₁₆ in. long. Fla., Ga.

brahuica Boiss. Bushy per., to 14 in., slightly woody at base, sts. recurved-hairy; lvs. linear to linear-lanceolate, about 1 in. long, hairy; infl. paniculate; calyx about ⅝ in. long, with simple and glandular hairs, petals cleft to middle, white; caps. scarcely longer than stalk. Iran to cent. Asia.

bryoides: *S. acaulis.*

californica E. Durand. CALIFORNIA INDIAN PINK. Stout per., sts. 2–4 ft., retrorsely pubescent; lvs. ovate, 3–4 in. long, to 1½ in. wide, crenate, pubescent; infl. few- to many-fld., pedicels glandular-hairy; calyx to 1 in. long, puberulent-glandular, petals showy, to 1 in. long, crimson, claws ciliate, lobes dissected. Sw. Ore. to s. Calif.

caramanica Boiss. & Heldr. Erect per., sts. to 20 in., puberulent at base; lvs. linear-lanceolate, puberulent; infl. racemose to 1-fld., bracts linear-lanceolate; calyx to 1 in. long, petals whitish. Mts., Turkey.

caroliniana Walt. WILD PINK. Per., to 8 in., brs. many from base, scaly, sts. glabrous to pubescent; basal lvs. ovate-oblanceolate, to 5 in. long, 1 in. wide, pilose to glabrous; infl. 5–13-fld., pedicels to ⅝ in., glandular-hairy; calyx to 1 in. long glandular-pubescent, petals to ⅝ in. long, showy, white to dark pink. New Hamp., s. to Ala., w. to Mo. Subsp. **pensylvanica** (Michx.) R. T. Clausen [*S. pensylvanica* Michx.; *S. caroliniana* var. *pensylvanica* (Michx.) Fern.]. Calyx glandular, narrow. Subsp. **Wherryi** (Small) R. T. Clausen [*S. Wherryi* Small]. Calyx without glands, broad. Especially attractive, thrives on dry, sandy, acid soil.

caryophylloides (Poir.) Otth ex DC. Cespitose per., sts. to 16 in., pilose-glandular; basal lvs. 3-angled, to ¾ in. long, acute, st. lvs. lanceolate to linear, pubescent to glandular; infl. 1–2-fld.; calyx over 1 in. long, hairy, petals emarginate, white to pink. Lebanon, Turkey, Iran. Subsp. **Echinus** (Boiss. & Heldr.) Coode & Cullen [*S. Echinus* Boiss. & Heldr.]. Lvs. of basal rosette bristly-ciliate; calyx without glands, petals bright pink. Turkey.

caucasica (Bunge) Boiss. Per., sts. to 8 in., erect, puberulous; lvs. oblong-lanceolate, to 1 in. long, puberulous; cyme dichasial, 3–5-fld.; calyx inflated, ¾ in. long, puberulous, petals 2-lobed. Caucasus to Mt. Ararat.

ciliata Pourr. Cespitose per., sts. to 12 in., pubescent; lvs. of rosettes linear-lanceolate; infl. 1–7-fld.; calyx to ¾ in. long, pubescent, petals white or pink, green to red below. Mts., Portugal to Greece.

colorata Poir. [*S. pyrenaica* Pourr. ex Rohrb.]. Ann., diffusely branched, sts. whitish-pilose; basal lvs. spatulate, st. lvs. obovate to linear, puberulent to glabrescent; infl. a 1-sided cyme; calyx ¾ in. long, puberulent, petals 2-lobed, pink or whitish. Nw. Afr., s. Eur., sw. Asia.

compacta Fisch. ex Hornem. [*S. orientalis* Hort., not Mill.]. Bien., or a short-lived per., to 4 ft., glabrous, sts. erect; lvs. in basal rosettes, lanceolate-spatulate, st. lvs. many, united-perfoliate, ovate; infl. capitate, with uppermost lvs. forming an involucre; calyx ¾ in. long, glabrous, petals entire, bright pink. Se. Eur. and sw. Asia.

cretica L. Ann., sts. to 12 in., puberulent to viscid; basal lvs. oblong to lanceolate to spatulate, puberulent, st. lvs. lanceolate, glabrous; infl. a loose dichasial cyme; calyx ½ in. long, glabrous, petals 2-lobed, pink. Nw. Afr., s. Eur., Turkey, Palestine.

Cserei Baumg. Per., sts. to 3 ft., glabrous; basal lvs. broadly spatulate, st. lvs. ovate to cordate, glabrous; infl. dichasial; calyx ½ in. long, 15–20-nerved, greenish-white, petals 2-lobed, white. Se. Eur. to Turkey.

Cucubalus: *S. vulgaris.*

dalmatica: *S. multicaulis.*

Delavayi Franch. Cespitose per., sts. glabrous to glandular-pubescent; lvs. oblong-lanceolate to linear-lanceolate, minutely ciliate, glabrous, often purplish; infl. a racemose cyme, 1–6-fld., bracts glandular, pedicels purple, glandular; calyx glandular, petals intense purple. Yunnan (sw. China).

dinarica K. Spreng. Related to *S. acaulis;* mat-forming per., sts. pubescent; lvs. linear-subulate, to ½ in. long, st. lvs. in 2–4 pairs; infl. 2–4-fld.; calyx oblong-campanulate, ½ in. long, lateral veins reticulate, petals pink. Mts., Romania.

dioica (L.) Clairv. [*Lychnis dioica* L.; *L. silvestris* Schkuhr; *Melandrium diurnum* (Sibth.) Fries; *M. rubrum* (Weigel) Garcke]. RED CAMPION, MORNING C. Dioecious bien. or per. herb, to 3 ft., sts. pilose; lvs. hairy, basal lvs. obovate, to 8 in. long including winged petiole, st. lvs. ovate, to 4 in. long, short-petioled to sessile; fls. red-purple to rose, in a leafy-bracted dichasial cyme, blooming in the day, scentless, calyx inflated, hairy, teeth triangular, 10-veined in male fls., 20-veined in female fls., styles 5; caps. with 10 recurved teeth. Eur.; naturalized in e. N. Amer.

Douglasii Hook. [*S. Lyallii* S. Wats.]. Per., sts. 4–30 in., pubescent; lvs. many at base, linear-oblanceolate, 1–3 in. long, to ½ in. wide, puberulent to glabrous, long-petioled, the opp. petioles united at base, st. lvs. nearly sessile; infl. 1–3-fld., pubescent; calyx ½ in. long, 10-nerved, ciliate, puberulent, petals creamy-white often tinged green, brown, pink, or purple, blade ¼ in. long. Mts., B.C., s. to Calif., w. to Idaho and Nev.

Echinus: *S. caryophylloides* subsp.

Elisabethae Jan [*Melandrium Elisabethae* (Jan) Rohrb.]. Cespitose per., sts. to 12 in.; lvs. glabrous to sparsely ciliate, basal lvs. lanceolate, to 5 in. long, st. lvs. in 3–5 pairs; fls. very large, often solitary, calyx ¾ in. long, glandular-hairy, petals dark red or reddish-purple, blade ⅝ in. long, coronal scales laciniate. S. Alps.

falcata Sibth. & Sm. Plant forming dense cushion, densely glandular-pubescent; lvs. rigid, subulate, curved, st. lvs. in 1–2 pairs; fls. solitary, calyx ¾ in. long, petals white, coronal scales small. Mts., n. Greece.

fimbriata: *S. multifida.*

flavescens Waldst. & Kit. Per., sts. to 12 in., stiffly erect, woody and pubescent at base, viscid towards apex; basal lvs. spatulate, densely hairy, st. lvs. linear-lanceolate; fls. solitary or paired, pedicels long, calyx ⅜ in. long, hairy, petals yellow. Mts. of Hungary to Balkan Pen.

Fortunei Vis. Per., erect, woody at base, scabrous-puberulent; lvs. linear-lanceolate, glabrous, petioles ciliate; infl. 1-fld. to a racemose cyme, pedicels short; calyx glabrous, teeth ovate, margin white, ciliate, petals 2-lobed, rose. Cent. and e. China.

Frivaldszkyana Hampe. Per., glabrous, sts. erect, to 3 ft.; basal lvs. linear, st. lvs. linear-lanceolate, to ⅛ in. wide; infl. racemose, with 2–3 fls. in axil of bract; calyx ½ in. long, petals 2-lobed, whitish. Balkan Pen. and nw. Turkey.

gallica L. Ann., sts. to 18 in., erect, much-branched, pubescent to viscid; lvs. pubescent, basal lvs. petioled, spatulate, st. lvs. sessile, lanceolate, to 2 in. long; infl. a nearly 1-sided cyme; calyx ovoid, ⅜ in. long, hispid, petals white or pink, often spotted crimson, blade to ¼ in. long. Much of Eur., Turkey to India; naturalized in N. Amer. A cosmopolitan weed.

glauca: a name applied to several spp., among them *S. Armeria* and *S. vulgaris.*

gracillima Rohrb. [*Lychnis gracillima* (Rohrb.) Mak.]. Per., to 3 ft., sts. white-pubescent; lvs. sessile, ovate-lanceolate, to 5 in. long, 1⁵⁄₁₆ in. wide, glabrescent; infl. glabrous, pedicels to 2 in. long; calyx to ½ in. long, glabrous, teeth ciliate, petals white, blade ½ in. long, 2-lobed, toothed. Mts., cent. Japan.

Hitchguirei Bocquet [*Lychnis montana* S. Wats.]. Dwarf, cespitose per., sts. glandular-pubescent toward apex, glabrous at base; lvs. linear to oblanceolate; fls. solitary, calyx inflated, 5-toothed, petals included within calyx, emarginate. In Rocky Mts., s. Canada, Wyo., Utah, Colo.

Hookeri Nutt. ex Torr. & A. Gray [*S. Ingramii* Tidestr. & Dayt.]. Per., sts. many, grayish-hairy; lvs. oblanceolate, 2–4 in. long, grayish, pubescent; infl. a dichasial cyme, bracts linear-lanceolate, ½ in. long; calyx to ¾ in. long, grayish-villous, petals white to pink, purple, or violet, blade fimbriate. Sw. Ore. and nw. Calif.

inflata: *S. vulgaris.*

Ingramii: *S. Hookeri.*

japonica: a listed name of no botanical standing.

Keiskei Miq. [*S. Keiskei* var. *major* Hort.; *Melandrium Keiskei* (Miq.) Ohwi]. Cespitose per., sts. glabrous to pubescent; lvs. sessile, linear-lanceolate, to about 2 in. long; cymes few-fld.; calyx ½ in. long, nearly glabrous, petals ½ in. long, 2-lobed. Cent. Japan. Var. **minor** Takeda. Lvs., pedicels, and calyx soft-hairy.

Kitaibelii: *S. multicaulis.*

laciniata Cav. INDIAN PINK, FRINGED I.P., MEXICAN CAMPION. Per., pubescent to glandular, sts. to 3 ft.; lvs. sessile, linear-lanceolate to obovate, 1–5 in. long; infl. 1- to few-fld.; calyx to ¾ in. long, petals crimson, 4-cleft, showy. Mts., Calif. to New Mex. and Mex. Subsp. **Greggii** (A. Gray) C. L. Hitchc. & Maguire. Lvs. elliptic to broadly lanceolate or oblanceolate, to 3 in. long, all but uppermost narrowed abruptly to petiole; calyx to 1 in. long. Se. Ariz., s. New Mex., sw. Tex. and adjacent Mex. Subsp. **major** C. L. Hitchc. & Maguire. Fls. larger, more showy.

latifolia: *S. vulgaris.*

legionensis Lag. Related to *S. ciliate;* fl. sts. 6–16 in., arising laterally from below lf. rosettes; lvs. linear-lanceolate to spatulate; infl. simple, 3–9-fld.; calyx to 1 in. long, petals white or pink. Ne. Portugal, Spain.

Lerchenfeldiana Baumg. Related to *S. rupestris;* sts. lateral, curving-ascending, from axils of longer basal lvs.; fls. few, large, short-pedicelled, calyx ½ in. long, petals red to purple. Balkan Mts. and s. Carpathians.

longiscapa: *S. acaulis* var. *elongata.*

Lyallii: *S. Douglasii.*

Macounii: *S. Parryi.*

macrantha (Panč.) Neumay. [*Heliosperma macranthum* Panč.]. Related to *S. quadridentata;* per., sts. to 6 in., glandular-hairy; lvs. obovate-lanceolate; fls. relatively large, calyx ⁵⁄₁₆ in. long, slightly hairy, petals pink, blade exserted. Mts., Albania and sw. Yugoslavia.

macropoda Velen. Densely cespitose per., sts. erect, to 10 in.; lvs. crowded, linear; infl. 1–5-fld.; calyx to 1 in. long, teeth acute, petals white, the claws exserted. Mts., Bulgaria.

maritima: *S. vulgaris* subsp.

mollissima (L.) Pers. Robust per., densely tomentose, sts. to 2 ft.; lvs. lanceolate to spatulate; infl. more or less flat-topped; calyx nearly 1 in. long, densely tomentose, without glands, petals whitish, the claws ciliate, coronal scales small. Balearic Is. and Gibraltar.

multicaulis Guss. [*S. dalmatica* Scheele; *S. Kitaibelii* Vis.]. Cespitose per., sts. to 16 in.; lvs. linear to linear-lanceolate; infl. 1–8-fld.; calyx ¾ in. long, petals purplish or greenish, the claws exserted. Mts., Italy to Greece and Albania.

multifida (Adams) Rohrb. [*S. fimbriata* Sims]. Per., sts. to 5 ft., puberulent; lvs. ovate-lanceolate, 3–5-nerved, basal lvs. petioled; infl. a dichasial cyme; calyx ¾ in. long, inflated, puberulous to glabrescent, petals white, blade fimbriate. Caucasus and ne. Turkey.

nana Kar. & Kir. Pubescent ann., sts. to 2 in., forked at base, densely leafy; lvs. oblong-lanceolate to linear-subulate; fls. axillary and terminal, calyx glabrescent, enlarged in fr., petals entire, white. Se. Iran and Baluchistan.

noctiflora L. [*Melandrium noctiflorum* (L.) Fries]. NIGHT-FLOWERING CATCHFLY, STICKY COCKLE. Coarse ann. herb, to 3 ft., sts. viscid with glandular hairs above, densely pubescent below; lvs. obovate to ovate-lanceolate, to 4¾ in. long, lower lvs. petioled, upper ones sessile; fls. in a loose dichasial cyme, white or pink, opening at night, scented, calyx ⅝ in. long, enlarging to 1–2 in. in fr., 10-veined, glandular-hairy, petals 2-lobed. Eur., sw. Asia; naturalized as a weed in N. Amer.

nutans L. NOTTINGHAM CATCHFLY. Per., sts. to 2 ft., pubescent at base; lvs. oblong-spatulate to linear-lanceolate, to 4 in. long; infl. paniculate, 1-sided; calyx ½ in. long, glandular-pubescent, petals 2-lobed, whitish to greenish or reddish beneath. Most of Eur.; naturalized in ne. N. Amer.

odontopetala Fenzl. Per., to 1 ft., woody at base, herbage hairy, densely papillose; basal lvs. oblanceolate to obovate, to 4 in. long, including petiole, st. lvs. smaller, lanceolate or oblong to narrowly ovate; fls. solitary or in a few-fld. cyme, calyx to ¾ in. long, becoming inflated in fr., petals deeply 2-lobed, white to pinkish; caps. to ⅜ in. long. E. Turkey to n. Iran, s. to Lebanon and Arabia.

orientalis: see *S. compacta.*

Otites (L.) Wibel. SPANISH CATCHFLY. Dioecious bien. or short-lived per., sts. 4–20 in., occasionally to 4 ft.; lvs. spatulate to linear-lanceolate, to 3 in. long, ciliate, softly hairy; infl. a narrow panicle; calyx ¼ in. long, glabrous, petals entire, greenish, without coronal scales. Eur., Turkey to cent. Asia and Siberia.

paradoxa L. Per. or bien., sts. to 2 ft.; lvs. lanceolate to obovate to linear; infl. loose; calyx to 1 in. long, glandular, petals creamy-white above, yellowish beneath, coronal scales acute. Se. France, Corsica, Italy, Yugoslavia to Greece.

Parryi (S. Wats.) C. L. Hitchc. & Maguire [*S. Macounii* S. Wats.]. Per., sts. to 2 ft., pubescent to glandular; lvs. petioled, linear-oblanceolate, to 3 in. long; infl. 3–7-fld.; calyx to ¾ in. long, glandular-pubescent, purplish-veined, petals white, tinged green or purple, 2-lobed, lobes toothed, claws ½ in. long. Rocky Mts., n. Wyo., n. to se. Alaska.

pendula L. NODDING CATCHFLY. Ann., sts. to 16 in., pubescent; lvs. ovate-lanceolate, to 2 in. long, pubescent; infl. a racemose cyme; calyx ¾ in. long, inflated, petals ⅜ in. long, pink, rarely white. S. Medit. region, s. Russia, Caucasus, Turkey. Cv. 'Compacta'. Plant forming cushion to 4 in. high. Cv. 'Ruberrima Bonnettii'. Plant glabrous, purplish; fls. bright carmine-pink.

pensylvanica: *S. caroliniana* subsp.

Petersonii Maguire. Per., sts. to 6 in., glandular-pubescent; lvs. oblanceolate, 1–2 in. long, glandular-puberulent; infl. 1–7-fld., pedicels to 1 in. long; calyx ¾ in. long, glandular, petals pink to rose-purple, 1 in. long, with 3 purple nerves, toothed. S. Utah.

petraea: *S. Saxifraga.*

pindicola Hausskn. Dwarf, cespitose per., sts. to 4 in., 1-fld., pubescent at base, viscid at apex; lvs. linear, to ½ in. long; calyx to 1 in. long, glabrous, petals brownish, the claws exserted, coronal scales minute. Serpentine rock, mts. of n. Greece.

pudibunda: *S. quadrifida.*

pumilio: *Saponaria pumila.*

pusilla: *S. quadridentata.*

pygmaea Adams [*S. spathulata* Bieb.]. Sts. densely pubescent, to 8 in.; basal lvs. in a rosette, long-petioled, orbicular, ciliate, pubescent, st. lvs. spatulate, sessile toward apex; infl. a dichasial cyme; calyx puberulous, teeth ciliate, margins white, petals 2-lobed, rose, claws glabrous. Alpine regions, Caucasus.

pyrenaica: *S. colorata.*

quadridentata (A. Murr.) Pers. [*S. pusilla* Waldst. & Kit.; *Heliosperma albanicum* K. Malý; *H. monachorum* Vis. & Panč.]. Per., sts. to 12 in., subglabrous to glandular-hairy; lvs. linear-lanceolate, ⅛ in. wide; infl. a dichasial cyme; calyx ¼ in. long, glabrous to glandular-hairy, petals white, rarely pink or lilac, claws glabrous. Mts., s. and cent. Eur.

quadrifida (L.) L. [*S. alpestris* Jacq.; *S. pudibunda* Hoffmanns. ex Rchb.; *Heliosperma alpestre* (Jacq.) Rchb.; *H. quadrifidum* (L.) Rchb.]. Robust per., sts. to 12 in., subglabrous to hairy; lvs. obovate-lanceolate to linear-lanceolate, to 5/16 in. wide; infl. viscid; fls. large, calyx ¼ in. long, scabrid, glandular-puberulent, petals 4–6-toothed, white, claw ciliate. E. Alps, n. Balkan Pen.

regia Sims. ROYAL CATCHFLY. Per., sts. 2–5 ft., glabrous to glandular-puberulent; lvs. lanceolate, to 5 in. long, ½ in wide, glabrous to puberulent; infl. many-fld., 6–12 in. long; fls. showy, calyx to 1 in. long, glandular, petals crimson. Ohio to Mo., s. to Ala. and Ga.

Regis-Ferdinandi Degen & Urum. Densely cespitose per., sts. to 1 ft.; lvs. crowded, linear; fls. very large, usually solitary, 1 5/16 in. across, calyx 1 5/16 in. long, petals showy, white. Mts., Bulgaria.

Reichenbachii Vis. Cespitose per., sts. 6–24 in., glabrous to hairy; lvs. spatulate to linear-lanceolate; infl. 5–20-fld., the brs. 1–3-fld.; calyx to ½ in. long, petals white, coronal scales small. W. Yugoslavia.

repens Patr. ex Pers. Stoloniferous per., sts. to 2 ft., scabrous-pubescent; lvs. linear, to 2 in. long, lower lvs. withering; infl. few-fld.; calyx ½ in. long, scabrid, petals white, claws glabrous. Russia to Siberia, Alaska, Yukon, Mackenzie Delta.

Roemeri Friv. Per., to 20 in., densely puberulent; lvs. oblong-spatulate to linear, petiole ciliate; fls. in whorls, calyx ⅛ in. long, nearly glabrous, petals broad, emarginate, white. Mts., Italy and Balkan Pen.

rubella L. Slender, erect ann., to 1½ ft.; lvs. oblong to oblong-spatulate, to 1½ in. long, undulate, pubescent; infl. a 2–4-fld. dichasial cyme; calyx to ½ in. long, the veins hairy, petals emarginate, pink; caps. to 5/16 in. long. Portugal to se. Italy.

rupestris L. Glabrous per., sts. to 10 in.; lvs. oblanceolate to lanceolate; infl. a dichasial cyme; fls. small, pedicels long, calyx ¼ in. long, glabrous, petals emarginate, white or pink. Mts. of Eur., widespread.

sachalinensis Friedr. Schmidt. Mat-forming, sts. to 4 in.; basal lvs. petioled, spatulate, to 2 in. long, ⅜ in. wide, middle st. lvs. sessile, ovate-lanceolate, to 1 in. long and ⅜ in. wide, upper st. lvs. short-pointed, pubescent; pedicel solitary, terminal, rusty-pubescent, to 1 5/16 in. long, calyx 5/16 in. long, pubescent, petals longer than calyx, white; caps. to ⅜ in. long. E. Siberia, Sakhalin Is.

saxatilis Sims. Per., generally glabrous, to 20 in.; basal lvs. oblanceolate, linear, or spatulate, papillose; infl. racemose-paniculate, pedicels glabrous; calyx ⅜ in. long, petals 2-lobed, greenish, yellowish, or whitish. Turkey, Caucasus, n. Iran.

Saxifraga L. [*S. petraea* Waldst. & Kit.]. Densely cespitose per., sts. many, to 8 in., pubescent at base, viscid at apex; lvs. linear-spatulate to linear, ciliate; infl. 1–2-fld.; calyx ½ in. long, glabrous, petals whitish to greenish, often reddish beneath. Mts. of s. Eur.

Schafta C. C. Gmel. ex Hohen. Per.; basal lvs. in a rosette, ovate, ½ in. long, ¼ in. wide; infl. 1–2-fld.; calyx hairy, 1 in. long, petals ½ in. long, emarginate, pink or purple. Caucasus.

Sendtneri Boiss. Related to *S. Roemeri;* dioecious per., sts. to 20 in.; lvs. oblanceolate to linear; infl. nearly capitate; calyx ⅛ in. long, nearly glabrous, petals nearly entire, white. Albania, Yugoslavia.

serpentinicola: a listed name of no botanical standing.

sibirica (L.) Pers. Monoecious per., to 2 ft., nearly glabrous; lvs. oblong to linear to linear-lanceolate, st. lvs. clustered; fls. in whorls, mostly unisexual, calyx ¼ in. long, petals yellowish-green. Russia, cent. Asia, Siberia.

spathulata: *S. pygmaea.*

stellata (L.) Ait.f. STARRY CAMPION, WIDOW'S-FRILL. Per., to 3 ft., puberulent to glabrous; lvs. 4 at a node, linear-lanceolate, to 4 in. long, 1½ in. wide, pubescent; infl. paniculate, pubescent; calyx ½ in. long, pubescent, petals laciniate, white, lanate at base. Mass. to Minn., s. to Ga. and Tex.

taimyrense (Tolm.) Bocquet [*Lychnis taimyrense* (Tolm.) Polun.]. Frequently tufted, to 14 in., sts. hoary-villous to pubescent; lvs. linear to oblanceolate, to 2⅜ in. long; fls. 2–4 or rarely solitary, calyx elliptic-campanulate, to 7/16 in. long, viscid-pubescent, petals emarginate, white to purplish. Siberia, Alaska, arctic of w. Canada.

tetraquetra: a listed name of no botanical standing, used for *Arenaria tetraquetra.*

turkestanica Regel [*Melandrium turkestanicum* (Regel) Vved.]. Sts. to 3 ft.; lvs. pubescent, basal lvs. lanceolate, middle lvs. ovate, upper lvs. subulate; infl. to 2 in. long, densely rusty-hairy; calyx to 1 in. long, petals to 1–1½ in. long, white, rarely violet; fr. stalk hairy. Mts. of Turkestan to Pamirs and Tian-Shan.

uralensis (Rupr.) Bocquet. Per. to 1 ft., sts. 1 to several, hairy, glandular-hairy toward apex; lvs. linear-lanceolate or narrowly oblanceolate, to 1¾ in. long; fls. solitary or rarely 2, nodding, calyx about ¾ in. long, inflated, veins dark purple, with coarse, glandular hairs, petals shorter than calyx, 2-lobed, lilac; caps. erect. Canada, Alaska, Siberia. Subsp. **apetala** (L.) Bocquet [*S. Wahlbergella* Chowdh.; *Lychnis apetala* L.]. Sts. 2–8 in.; lower lvs. linear-spatulate, upper lvs. linear-oblong. Mts., Scandinavia and is. in Bering Sea.

vallesia L. Mat-forming per., sts. to 6 in., glandular-pubescent; lvs. lanceolate to linear, pubescent; infl. 1–3-fld.; calyx ½–1 in. long, petals showy, pale pink above, red beneath; caps. scabrous. W. Alps, Appennines, Balkan Mts.

virginica L. FIRE PINK. Showy per., sts. to 2–3 ft., puberulent to glandular to glabrous at base; lvs. oblanceolate, to 4 in. long, ¾ in. wide, glabrous to puberulent, petioles ciliate, st. lvs. nearly sessile; infl. 7–11-fld., pedicels glandular, to 1 in. long; calyx ¾ in. long, pubescent, petals 2-lobed, scarlet. N.J. to Minn., s. to Ga. and Okla.

viridiflora L. Vigorous, sts. to 3 ft.; lvs. spatulate to ovate-lanceolate; infl. loose, peduncle long; fls. inclined, calyx ¾ in. long, pubescent, petals whitish, tinged green, lobes linear. S. and cent. Eur.

vulgaris (Moench) Garcke [*S. Cucubalus* Wibel; *S. glauca* Sm. ex Steud., not Salisb.; *S. inflata* (Salisb.) Sm.; *S. latifolia* (Mill.) Britten & Rendle; *S. Wallichiana* Klotzsch]. BLADDER CAMPION, MAIDEN'S-TEARS. Per., sts. to 2 ft., glabrous to pubescent to glaucous; lvs. ovate to linear; fls. solitary or cymose; calyx inflated, 20-veined, petals 2-lobed, large, white, rarely red, clawed, coronal scales present. Throughout Eur., nw. Afr., temp. Asia. Subsp. **maritima** (With.) Á. Löve & D. Löve [*S. maritima* With.]. Sts. diffuse, nearly cespitose; lvs. linear-lanceolate to spatulate. Coasts of w. Eur. Subsp. **prostrata** (Gaudin) Chater & Walters [*S. alpina* (Lam.) E. Thomas]. Cespitose, sts. to 10 in.; lvs. ovate to ovate-lanceolate; infl. 1–3-fld. Alps and mts. of s. Eur.

Wahlbergella: *S. uralensis* subsp. *apetala.*

Waldsteinii Griseb. Cespitose per., to 10 in., woody at base; lvs. crowded, linear, scabrous and hairy beneath; fls. solitary, or in a 2–5-fld. cyme, calyx to 1⅛ in. long, petals white; caps. longer than calyx. Mts., Balkan Pen.

Wallichiana: *S. vulgaris.*

Wherryi: *S. caroliniana* subsp.

Zawadskii Herbich [*Melandrium Zawadskii* (Herbich) A. Braun]. Cespitose per., sts. to 1 ft.; lvs. elliptic, to 5 in. long, ciliate; calyx ⅝ in. long, hairy, petals ⅜ in. long or more. E. Carpathian Mts., Romania, w. Ukraine.

SILPHIUM L. ROSINWEED. *Compositae* (Helianthus Tribe). About 20 spp. of coarse, per. herbs, native to e. N. Amer.; sts. usually sparingly branched, scabrous-hispid at least above; lvs. usually opp. on lower part of st., mostly alt. above, coarse, usually scabrous; fl. heads radiate, in racemes or corymbose panicles, involucre shallowly campanulate, involucral bracts nearly equal or imbricate in 2 to several rows, coarse, usually scabrous, receptacle flat to convex, scaly; disc fls. appearing bisexual but sterile, yellow, ray fls. in 2–3 rows, female, fertile, yellow or rarely white; achenes compressed, broadly winged on the edges, pappus lacking or of 2 minute awns confluent with the marginal wings.

Silphiums thrive in any good soil and in full sunlight, and are useful for rear borders. Propagated by seeds or division.

integrifolium Michx. Sts. to 5 ft.; lvs. essentially all opp., sessile, lanceolate to ovate or elliptic, to 6 in. long, entire to slightly toothed, scabrous; heads to 2 in. across, in a broad corymb. Ohio to Minn., s. to Miss. and Okla.

laciniatum L. COMPASS PLANT. Sts. stout, to 6 ft., very hispid; lvs. alt., deeply pinnatifid to 2-pinnatifid, lower lvs. to 20 in. long, upper lvs. successively reduced; heads to 5 in. across, racemose. Ohio to S. Dak., s. to Ala. and Tex.

perfoliatum L. Cup plant. Sts. 4-angled, to 8 ft., essentially glabrous; lvs. connate-perfoliate, the blade triangular to ovate, to 14 in. long, coarsely toothed, scabrous; heads to 3 in. across, corymbose. S. Ont. to S. Dak., s. to Ga., Miss., and Okla; occasionally naturalized elsewhere in the Northeast.

terebinthinaceum Jacq. Prairie dock. Taprooted, sts. to 10 ft., essentially glabrous; lvs. mostly basal, but alt. on sts. above, long-petioled, ovate to oblong or elliptic, to 2 ft. long, usually cordate, thick, sharply serrate to pinnatifid, scabrous; heads to 3 in. across, in corymbiform panicles. Prairies, s. Ont. and Ohio to Minn., s. to Ga., La., and Mo.

SILYBUM Vaill. ex Adans. *Compositae* (Carduus Tribe). Two spp. of thistlelike herbs of Medit. region; lvs. large, pinnately lobed, spiny-toothed; fl. heads large, solitary, terminal, involucral bracts large, spiny-margined and -tipped; fls. all tubular, purple; pappus of minutely barbed bristles, deciduous.

Of simple culture; propagated by seeds.

Marianum (L.) Gaertn. [*Carduus Marianus* L.]. St. Mary's thistle, blessed t., milk t., holy t. Ann. or bien., to 4 ft., glabrous, st. simple or little-branched; lvs. to 2½ ft. long, 6–12 in. across, clasping, green marbled with white, glossy; heads 2–2½ in. across, involucral bracts spreading to reflexed, acuminate; achenes smooth, mottled with brown. Medit. region; naturalized and a weed in Calif. and elsewhere in U.S.

SIMAROUBA Aubl. *Simaroubaceae*. Six spp. of polygamodioecious or dioecious trees and shrubs of trop. Amer.; lvs. alt., usually even-pinnate; fls. small, in complex panicles, calyx 5-lobed, petals 5, stamens 10, with basal appendages, carpels 5, weakly cohering, borne on a disc, united by the single style; fr. a drupe.

glauca DC. Paradise tree, bitterwood, aceituno. Tree, to 50 ft.; lvs. to 16 in. long. lfts. 6–19, oblong to elliptic-oblong or narrowly obovate, to 4 in. long; drupes ellipsoid to broadly ellipsoid, scarlet or purple. Spring. S. Fla., W. Indies, Mex. to Costa Rica. Cult. in El Salvador for the valuable edible oil expressed from the seeds.

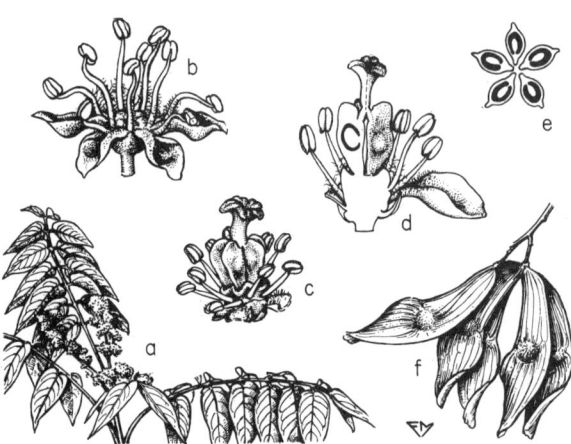

Simaroubaceae. *Ailanthus altissima:* **a,** branch with male flowers, × ¹⁄₁₂; **b,** male flower, × 3; **c,** female flower, × 4: **d,** female flower, vertical section, × 5; **e,** ovaries, cross section, × 6; **f,** fruits, × ½. (a, b, f from Bailey, *Manual of Cultivated Plants,* ed. 2; c-e from Lawrence, *Taxonomy of Vascular Plants.*)

SIMAROUBACEAE DC. Quassia family. Dicot.; about 30 genera and 200 spp. of trees and shrubs, mostly trop., a few extending into the temp. regions., often dioecious or polygamodioecious, usually with bitter bark; lvs. alt., pinnate, rarely simple or rudimentary, stipules present or absent; fls. regular, in axillary or terminal racemes, cymose spikes, or compound panicles, bisexual or unisexual, usually 5-merous, but calyx 3–8-lobed, petals 3–8, rarely 0, stamens 1 or 2 times as many as petals, ovary deeply 2–8-lobed or with carpels separate, borne on a disc, with axile placentas, styles 1–8, united or separate; fr. a caps., samara, drupe, or berry. Cult.

genera are: *Ailanthus, Brucea, Holacantha, Kirkia, Quassia,* and *Simarouba.*

Some members of the family produce bitter substances useful in insecticides, medicines, and dyes; one is the source of a vegetable seed oil.

SIMMONDSIA Nutt. *Buxaceae.* One sp., a dioecious shrub, native to the arid frost free sw. U.S. and n. Mex.; lvs. opp., leathery; fls. on short, axillary peduncles, male fls. clustered, female fls. solitary, sepals 5 or 6, petals 0, stamens 10–12; fr. a nutlike, leathery-walled caps., partly enclosed by the sepals.

A horticultural substitute for *Buxus* in arid sites.

californica: *S. chinensis.*

chinensis (Link) C. K. Schneid. [*S. californica* (Link) Nutt.]. Goat nut, jojoba. Stiff-branched, to 7 ft.; lvs. nearly sessile, oblong-ovate, to 1½ in. long, mostly dull green; sepals of male fls. less than ¼ in. long, of the female fls. to ¾ in. long; caps. ovoid, 3-angled, about as long as the sepals. Early spring. Grown in s. Calif. Zone 10. Frs. yield jojoba oil, a substitute for sperm oil.

SIMSIA Pers. *Compositae* (Helianthus Tribe). About 22 spp. of ann. and per. herbs, in arid sw. U.S. to Argentina, also Jamaica; lvs., at least the lower ones, opp.; fl. heads radiate or discoid, solitary or in panicles, involucral bracts imbricate, receptacle with rigid, persistent scales; disc and ray fls. usually yellow, rarely purple, ray fls. sometimes lacking; achenes compressed, pappus of 2 awns or lacking.

calva (A. Gray & Engelm.) A. Gray [*Encelia calva* (A. Gray & Engelm.) A. Gray]. Erect, much-branched, harshly pubescent ann. from a thick, tuberlike root; lvs. lanceolate-ovate, serrate, often 3-lobed, petioled, the bases of the opp. lvs. expanded and united into a disc; heads 1¼ in. across, solitary on long peduncles; fls. yellow, ray fls. ⁵⁄₁₆ in. long. Tex., n. Mex.

SINAPIS: *BRASSICA.* S. alba: *B. hirta.* S. arvensis: *B. Kaber.*

SINNINGIA Nees [*Corytholoma* (Benth.) Decne.; × *Gloxinera* Weathers; *Rechsteineria* Regel]. *Gesneriaceae.* More than 75 spp. of per., hairy herbs or shrubs from Mex. to Argentina and Brazil; small to large woody tuber usually present, rarely lacking, rhizomes in 2 spp.; lvs. opp. or whorled or congested basally on short sts. or direct from the tuber; fls. 1 or more in lf. axils or in axillary cymes, peduncles often elongate; calyx 5-lobed, tubular, rounded or angled or winged in lower part, lobes slender to broad, corolla nearly campanulate to cylindrical, limb spreading, 5-lobed, flat or 2-lipped, stamens 4, borne at base of corolla tube, anthers coherent by sides and tips, disc of 2–5 separate glands, ovary half-inferior; fr. a caps., dehiscent by 2–4 valves, seeds many, very small.

For cultivation see *Gesneriaceae.*

barbata (Nees & Mart.) Nichols. Small shrub, sts. to 1 ft. or more, red-brown; lf. blades oblong-lanceolate, to 6 in. long, acute, sharply toothed, dark bluish-green and glossy above, red-purple, hairy, and prominently veined beneath; fls. 1–2 in axils on pedicels to 1½ in. long, calyx lobes triangular, large, wavy-margined, leafy, green, corolla 1½ in. long, white, hairy, curved to a pouch on lower side below the narrowed throat, lobes short, disc glands 2. Brazil.

cardinalis (Lehm.) H. E. Moore [*Gesneria cardinalis* Lehm.; *G. macrantha* Hort., not K. Spreng.; *Rechsteineria cardinalis* (Lehm.) O. Kuntze]. Cardinal flower, helmet f. Sts. less than 1 ft., bearing 4–5 pairs of lvs.; lf. blades cordate-ovate, to 6 in. long, 4½ in. wide, crenate, densely short-hairy, green, variegated with dark green about the veins; fls. solitary or several on short peduncles in axils of upper lvs., calyx lobes erect, lanceolate, ¼ in. long, corolla to 2 in. long, scarlet, hairy, strongly 2-lipped, disc glands 2. Brazil.

Claybergiana H. E. Moore [*Rechsteineria Lindleyi* (Hook.) Fritsch]. Sts. to 4½ ft., green flecked with lighter green, sometimes red-purple with green lines; lvs. opp. or whorled, short-petioled, blades elliptic, to 5½ in. long, 2½ in. wide, crenate, densely and shortly hairy above, pale hairy beneath; fls. in clusters in axils of small lvs. or bracts, forming an erect terminal raceme to 18 in. long, calyx lobes triangular, to ⅜ in. long, corolla to 1½ in. long, pale red, hairy, spurred on upper side at base, then narrowed and gradually expanded to a spreading, slightly 2-lipped limb, lobes nearly equal, the 2 upper smallest, the lowermost longest, disc of a large, 2-lobed gland and 1–3 smaller ones. Brazil. This sp. has been misidentified in cult. as *Rechsteineria Sellovii* (Mart.) O. Kuntze and as a variety of *R. Douglasii* Lindl.

coerulea: a listed name of no botanical standing, apparently used for *S. speciosa* cv. 'Speciosa'.

concinna (Hook.f.) Nichols. Sts. short; lvs. with slender petioles, blades ovate, to ¾ in. wide, crenate, red-veined, green, hairs on upper surface erect, of one length; fls. ¾ in. long, solitary in axils, on slender pedicels longer than lvs., calyx lobes lanceolate, 1/16 in. long, corolla obliquely funnelform with flaring limb, lilac on upper side, paler or yellowish on under side, purple-spotted in tube, the 2 upper lobes deeper lilac than the lower, disc glands 5. Brazil.

eumorpha H. E. Moore. Sts. short, reddish, hairy, fleshy; lvs. with minutely hairy petioles to 2½ in. long, blades cordate-ovate, to 4 in. long, 3½ in. wide, crenate, minutely hairy, green; fls. 1 or several in lf. axils, peduncles to 4½ in. long, calyx reddish-green, lobes ovate-lanceolate, to ½ in. long, corolla oblique in the calyx, to 1½ in. long, curved on under side, white or faintly lavender-flushed, lobes to ⅜ in. long, inside of tube with a red-spotted yellow band, often bordered with pale violet, disc glands 2. Brazil.

×**gesnerioides** (Lem.) H. E. Moore [× *Gloxinera gesnerioides* (Lem.) H. E. Moore]: "*Rechsteineria Cooperi* (Paxt.) O. Kuntze" × *S. tubiflora.* Fls. much resembling those of *S. tubiflora,* but rose.

hirsuta (Lindl.) Nichols. Sts. short; lf. blades broadly ovate, to 6 in. long, 4 in. wide, or sometimes longer, crenate, long-hairy; fls. many, on long-hairy pedicels above lvs., calyx lobes 3/16 in. long, corolla lavender outside, medium purple inside, with a white stripe and red-purple dots on inner lower surface of tube, tube short, ½ in. long, limb flared, ¾ in. across, disc glands 5. Brazil.

leucotricha (Hoehne) H. E. Moore [*Rechsteineria leucotricha* Hoehne]. BRAZILIAN EDELWEISS. Sts. to 10 in. long, densely white-woolly; lvs. whorled, blades nearly obovate, to 6 in. long, 4 in. wide, densely white-hairy; fls. 3–5 on peduncles in lf. axils or at end of st., calyx lobes tapering from a triangular base, corolla cylindrical, 1¼ in. long, salmon-red or rose, hairy, lobes nearly equal, short, rounded, dark purple with chestnut lines at the throat, disc glands 2. Brazil.

macropoda (T. Sprague) H. E. Moore [*Corytholoma macropodum* T. Sprague; *Rechsteineria cyclophylla* Hjelmqv.; *R. lineata* Hjelmqv.; *R. macropoda* (T. Sprague) C. H. Curtis]. Sts. fleshy, to 2 ft., flecked with dark red lines; lvs. often only 2 pairs on young plants, but 4–5 pairs on old plants, blades broadly ovate, to 8 in. long, 6 in. wide, cordate at base, crenate, softly short-hairy; fls. 6–18, nodding, on elongate, axillary, glandular-hairy, red-spotted peduncles to 6 in. long, calyx hairy, lobes triangular, to ⅜ in. long, slender-tipped, corolla tube nearly cylindrical but enlarged upward, to 1½ in. long, glandular-hairy, red, lobes 5, spreading, nearly equal, ¼ in. long, the 3 lower with purple spots or lines, disc of 2 prominent glands or 1 large 2-lobed gland, sometimes also with 3 smaller ones. Brazil.

Maximiliana (Hanst.) Benth. & Hook.f. ex Fritsch. Not in cult.; material of *S. eumorpha* was originally introd. under the name *S. Maximiliana.*

pusilla (Mart.) Baill. Similar to *S. concinna* but smaller, the lvs. with erect hairs of 2 lengths and with prominent raised bases, corolla tube spurred at base, lilac on upper side, white on under side, lobes lilac with violet lines, disc of 2 large and 1–3 vestigial glands. Brazil.

regina T. Sprague. VIOLET SLIPPER GLOXINIA, CINDERELLA-SLIPPERS. Similar to *S. speciosa* cv. 'Speciosa' but lvs. deep green, veined with white above, deep red beneath, calyx lobes ½ in. long or less, with slender tip, corolla trumpet-shaped, very gradually expanded toward the throat, glandular-hairy outside. Brazil.

Richii Clayb. Sts. semierect, to nearly 4 in., from small tubers and slender rhizomes; lvs. in 2–3 pairs, blades ovate, to 10¾ in. long, 4¾ in. wide, crenate, short-hairy; fls. 1–2 in lf. axils, pedicels to 3¼ in. long, short-hairy, calyx lobes triangular, to ¼ in. long, reflexed, corolla to 1⅜ in. long, obliquely inflated on under side, white with short red-purple lines, short-hairy, disc glands 5. Mex.

×**rosea** (H. E. Moore & R. G. Wils.) H. E. Moore [× *Gloxinera rosea* H. E. Moore & R. G. Wils.]: *S. eumorpha* × *S. macropoda.* Intermediate between the parents in many respects, but fls. pink resembling those of *S. eumorpha* in form and borne on axillary infl. as in *S. macropoda.*

Schiffneri Fritsch. Suffruticose, to 18 in. or more, without tubers; lvs. with petioles to 1½ in. long, hairy, blades ovate, to 6 in. long. 2½ in. wide, toothed, hairy, green; fls. 1–3 in axils, on hairy pedicels shorter than petioles, calyx lobes linear-lanceolate, to ½ in. long, green, corolla obliquely funnelform, about 1 in. long, creamy-white, spotted with red in the tube. Brazil.

speciosa (Lodd.) Hiern. GLOXINIA, BRAZILIAN G., VIOLET SLIPPER G. Sts. short, rarely to 1 ft.; lvs. short-petioled, blades ovate to oblong, to 8 in. long, 6 in. wide or more in cult., crenate, finely hairy on both surfaces, green above, green or flushed with red beneath; fls. 1–3 or more in axils on long pedicels, calyx lobes ovate, to ⅞ in. long, slender-tipped, corolla oblique in the calyx, 1½ in. long or more in cult., flattened at the back with a hairy central ridge and prominently swollen on the lower side, or erect and campanulate, violet to red or white in the wild, with other colors in cult., stamens 4 or sometimes more in cult. forms, disc of 5 glands. Brazil. The sp. may be divided into 3 groups: the Speciosa Group includes only the wild forms, with small, nodding, violet or rarely red or white, oblique fls. The Maxima Group, NODDING G., SLIPPER G., has fls. similar to those of the Speciosa Group but larger and in a greater range of color. The Fyfiana Group [*Gloxinia crassifolia* Hort.; *G.* × *hybrida* Hort.; *G. macrophylla* Hort.; *G. tigrina* Hort.; *G. violacea* Hort.], GLOXINIA of florists, has erect, campanulate, regular fls. with violet, rose, red, white, yellowish, spotted, or banded corolla with limb 5–12-lobed. Many cvs. are listed for the last group.

tuberosa (Mart.) H. E. Moore [*Rechsteineria tuberosa* (Mart.) O. Kuntze]. St. not developed, lvs. and infl. arising from tuber; lf. blades ovate or oblong, to 18 in. long, 12 in. wide, crenate, slightly hairy, green; fls. 1–6 or more in infl. to 6 in. long, calyx lobes triangular, to ¼ in. long, reddish, puberulent, corolla cylindrical, 1½ in. long, tomato-red, yellowish in throat, lobes about ¼ in. long, upper 2 directed forward, lower 3 spreading, disc glands 5, equal, yellowish. Brazil.

tubiflora (Hook.) Fritsch [*Achimenes tubiflora* (Hook.) Britt.]. Sts. to 2 ft. or more, hairy; lvs. short-petioled, blades oblong-elliptic, to 5 in. long, 1½ in. wide, crenate, green, finely hairy; fls. in a 1-sided terminal raceme, fragrant, calyx lobes lanceolate, ⅜ in. long, corolla white, tube nearly cylindrical, oblique, slightly curved on under side to the somewhat 2-lipped limb, lobes spreading, to ½ in. long, disc glands 4. Argentina, Paraguay, Uruguay.

verticillata (Vell.) H. E. Moore [*Rechsteineria purpurea* Hort.; *R. verticillata* (Vell.) L. B. Sm.]. Sts. to nearly 2 ft., reddish, soft-hairy; lvs. in a false whorl of 2–6, petioles to 2½ in. long, blades cordate-ovate, to 7½ in. long, 4 in. wide, sharply toothed, softly hairy; fls. many in axils of reduced lvs. or bracts in 1–2 whorls above normal lvs., pedicels to 3 in. long, calyx lobes narrowly triangular, 3/16 in. long, corolla cylindrical, 1½ in. long, red with purple splotches, limb oblique, 5-lobed, with 4 of the lobes nearly equal, smaller than the lowermost one, disc glands 2. Brazil.

Warscewiczii (Bouché & Hanst.) H. E. Moore [*Corytholoma Warscewiczii* (Bouché & Hanst.) Standl.; *Rechsteineria Warscewiczii* (Bouché & Hanst.) O. Kuntze]. Sts. to 3 ft. or more; lvs. opp., long-petioled, blades elliptic-ovate, to 6 in. long, 2¾ in. wide, cuneate, crenate, rough-hairy above, velvety beneath; fls. 1–3 in axils of small lvs. or bracts in a terminal raceme, calyx lobes triangular, ¼ in. long, corolla to 1¾ in. long, orange-red, evenly inflated above a narrowed and spurred base, upper lip nearly square, to ⅜ in. long, lower lip oblique, of small lobes, disc glands 5. Mex.

SINOCALAMUS McClure. *Gramineae.* A genus that has been abandoned, with spp. now placed in *Bambusa* and *Dendrocalamus.* **S. Beecheyanus:** *Bambusa Beecheyana.* **S. Oldhamii:** *Bambusa Oldhamii.*

SINOCRASSULA: *SEDUM.*

SINOFRANCHETIA (Diels) Hemsl. *Lardizabalaceae.* One sp., a deciduous, twining shrub, native to cent. and w. China; lvs. of 3 lfts., rather papery; fls. unisexual, in a bractless raceme, with 6 sepals and 6 nectaries, male fls. with 6 stamens, female fls. with 3 pistils; fr. a berry, seeds many.

chinensis (Franch.) Hemsl. Sts. to 30 ft., glabrous; lfts. 3, the central one rhombic-obovate to broadly ovate, on petiolule to 1¼ in. long, the lateral ones obliquely ovate, on shorter petiolules; racemes drooping; fls. white, to ¼ in. across; berries lavender-purple, seeds black.

SINOJACKIA H. H. Hu. *Styracaceae.* Three spp. of deciduous shrubs or trees, native to s. China; lvs. alt., simple, finely serrate; fls. in lateral racemes, calyx 5–7-lobed, petals 5–7, united only at base, stamens 10–14, ovary almost inferior; fr. indehiscent, woody.

Rehderana H. H. Hu. Shrub, to 15 ft., youngest brs. stellate-hairy; lvs. elliptic to obovate, to 4 in. long, essentially glabrous, margins glandular-toothed, petiole to ¼ in. long; fls. white, stellate-hairy, in 2–4-fld. racemes; fr. spindle-shaped, to 1 in. long, long-beaked, seed 1. Zone 8.

SINOWILSONIA Hemsl. *Hamamelidaceae.* One sp., a deciduous, monoecious, stellate-pubescent tree, native to cent. and w. China; lvs. alt., entire; fls. unisexual, without petals, in pendulous racemes, male racemes catkinlike, female racemes shorter, fl. tube urceolate, enclosing the ovary, styles exserted; fr. a caps.

Henryi Hemsl. To 25 ft.; lvs. elliptic to broad-ovate, to 6 in. long; male racemes to 2½ in. long, female racemes to 1¼ in. long.

SIPHOKENTIA Burret. *Palmae.* Two spp. of solitary, slender, unarmed, monoecious palms in the Molucca Is.; lvs. pinnate, sheaths forming a prominent crownshaft, pinnae linear, curved and coarsely toothed at apex, the basal and apical several-ribbed, the intermediate mostly 1-ribbed; infl. below lvs., bracts 2, thin, deciduous, peduncle short, rachis short, rachillae 9–15, arcuate-pendulous, with fls. in triads (2 male and 1 female); male fls. with calyx short, 3-lobed, petals 3, lanceolate-acuminate, stamens 9, female fls. with calyx cupular, 3-lobed, petals 3, triangular-acuminate, markedly valvate above the imbricate base, pistil 1-celled, 1-ovuled; fr. narrowly cylindrical with terminal, conic, stigmatic residue, seed oblong-ovoid, with ruminate endosperm.

Occasionally planted in tropical gardens. For culture see *Palms.*

Beguinii Burret. To 30 ft.; lvs. to 3 ft. long or more, glossy green above, pinnae about 20 on each side, to 2 ft. long, mostly 2 in. wide; fls. creamy-white on slender rachillae to 20 in. long; fr. red, about ⅝ in. long, ³⁄₁₆ in. in diam., with persistent cupular perianth. Zone 10b in Fla.

SIPHONANTHUS: see *CLERODENDRUM.*

SIPHONIA: *HEVEA.*

SIPHONOSMANTHUS: *OSMANTHUS.*

SISYMBRIUM L. *Cruciferae.* About 90 spp. of ann., bien., or per. herbs, mainly of temp. Eurasia but also in the New World and S. Afr., sts. glabrous or with coarse simple hairs; st. lvs. alt., entire to pinnatisect; fls. yellow, in elongate racemes, calyx open, petals entire, often with slender claw at base; fr. a linear, cylindrical or angled silique, valves 3-nerved, style short, bifid; seeds small, in 1 series.

Many species are weedy and widely naturalized.

luteum (Maxim.) O. E. Schulz [*Hesperis lutea* Maxim.]. Coarsely pilose, branched per., 2–4 ft.; lvs. petioled, lower lvs. pinnate; racemes elongating after flowering, pedicels ⅜–⅝ in., sepals about ⁵⁄₁₆ in. long, coarsely pilose, petals yellow, about 1½ in. long; siliques narrowly linear, 3–4 in. long. Late spring. Japan, Korea, Manchuria.

Thalianum: *Arabidopsis Thaliana.*

SISYRINCHIUM L. [*Hydastylus* Salisb. ex Bickn.; *Olsynium* Raf.]. BLUE-EYED GRASS. *Iridaceae.* About 75 spp. of clump-forming herbs, native to W. Hemisphere; rhizomes very short or none; lvs. grasslike, linear or cylindrical; fls. blue, yellow, or white, in terminal, solitary or fascicled clusters, each cluster subtended by a spathe, perianth rotate or campanulate, segms. 6, nearly equal, oblong, spreading, stamens 3, filaments united at base, style brs. 3, subulate; fr. a 3-valved caps., seeds many, small.

Mostly of easy cultivation in any garden soil, but not all species are hardy at ground-freezing temperatures. Propagated by seeds and division.

anceps: *S. angustifolium.*

alatum Hook. Sts. erect, to 1 ft. or more, unbranched or little-branched, flattened, broadly winged, flexuous; lvs. sword-shaped, to 2 in. long or more, ¼–⁵⁄₁₆ in. wide; spathes 2, terminal; fls. 2–4 in each spathe, perianth segms. yellow with purple lines. Surinam, s. to Argentina. Some material offered as *S. alatum* may be *S. convolutum.*

albidum Raf. Sts. 6–18 in., flattened, slightly winged; lvs. flat, ⅛ in. wide, persisting or withering; spathes sessile, subtended by an erect leaflike bract, perianth ½ in. across, whitish or pale violet. Dry sandy soils, e. N. Amer.

angustifolium Mill. [*S. anceps* Cav.; *S. gramineum* Lam.; *S. graminoides* Bickn.]. Sts. 4–20 in., usually forking, broadly winged; lvs. basal, deep green, old lf. bases deciduous or shredding; spathes on stout, flattened or winged peduncles; perianth about ½ in. across, pale blue to violet. Moist situations, e. N. Amer. Cv. 'Album'. Fls. white. *S. angustifolium* Bickn., not Mill. is *S. montanum* var. *crebrum.*

atlanticum Bickn. Related to *S. angustifolium,* occupying the same area and differing in having peduncles slender and wiry and lvs. pale green or glaucous.

bellum S. Wats. [*S. Eastwoodiae* Bickn]. CALIFORNIA B.-E.G. Sts. 4–20 in., branched 1–3 times, narrowly winged; lvs. basal, old bases

shredding; spathes on slender, slightly winged, but cylindrical peduncles; perianth about ¾ in. across, amethyst-violet, veined purple. Calif. Zone 8. Cv. 'Album'. Fls. white.

Bermudiana L. [*S. iridioides* Curtis]. Sts. 12–24 in., stout, flattened, broadly winged; lvs. basal, flat, about as long as sts., ¼ in. wide; peduncles 1–4 in. long, stout, flattened-winged, bearing 2–3 stalked clusters of pedicelled nodding fls., spathes 3–8-fld., the valves nearly equal, green with white edge; perianth to ¾ in. across, violet-blue with yellow eye, segms. obovate, mucronate. Bermuda. Zone 8. Tender to severe frost. The epithet *Bermudiana* was an early substantive name for the plant.

birameum Piper. Sts. 12–20 in., loosely tufted, slender, 2-branched, cylindrical, with narrow wings; lvs. basal, about half as long as sts., to ⅛ in. wide; spathes on long, slender, winged peduncles, reddish, the outer valve about ¼ in. longer than inner, not markedly white-margined, pedicels 2–5, slender, flexuous; perianth to ⅝ in. long, dark blue, with yellow eye. Swamps, sw. Wash.

bogotense HBK. Sts. 3–6 in., simple, very slender, winged; lvs. basal, less than ⅛ in. wide, mostly 2–3½ in. long; spathes 2–4-fld., subequal, pedicels wiry, cylindrical, somewhat exserted beyond the spathes; perianth yellow, campanulate. Moist areas, cent. Colombia. Zone 9. A tender sp.

boreale: see under *S. californicum.*

brachypus: see under *S. californicum.*

californicum (Ker-Gawl.) Dryand. [*Hydastylis californicus* (Ker-Gawl.) Salisb.]. GOLDEN-EYED GRASS. Sts. 6–24 in., clump-forming, simple, flat, broadly winged, dull green, glaucescent; lvs. basal, flat, mostly half as long as sts., to ¼ in. wide; outer spathe valve longer than the inner, pedicels slender and very weakly winged, not much exserted beyond spathe; perianth yellow, about 1 in. across, rotate, facing upward, segms. elliptic, bluntly acute, style deeply cleft. Late spring, summer. Moist coastal meadows, Ore., Calif. Zone 8. A good garden subject; fls. from May–July if given abundant moisture in full sun, though it is not hardy in colder parts of the country. Two closely related yellow-fld. spp., considered by some auth. to be conspecific with this sp. are *S. boreale* (Bickn.) J. Henry and *S. brachypus* (Bickn.) J. Henry. *S. boreale* is said to differ from *S. californicum* in having anthers and perianth segms. shorter; and *S. brachypus* in having pedicels shorter than spathe valves and smaller seeds. These 2 elements extend the range n. to Vancouver Is.

campestre Bickn. Sts. 4–20 in., tufted, slender, flat, winged, glaucous; lvs. about ⅔ as long as sts., about ⅛ in. wide; spathe sessile, solitary, half as long as its subtending bract, pedicels wiry, ascending, slightly exserted; perianth about ½ in. across, light blue to white. Dry sandy loam, Ill. to Man., s. to La. and Tex. Forma *flaviflorum* (Bickn.) Steyerm. Fls. yellow.

coeleste: a listed name of no botanical standing.

convolutum Nocca. Sts. 6–12 in., usually forked, flat, broadly winged; lvs. basal and cauline, basal lvs. linear, shorter than sts., to ¼ in. wide; spathes sessile, basally enlarged, valves about equal; perianth about ¾ in. across, segms. oblong, yellow, veined brown; caps. oblong. Temp. highlands, Mex. to Ecuador. Material cult. under the names *S. alatum* and *S. iridifolium* may be this sp.

cuspidatum Poepp. Roots fleshy, cylindrical, sts. 1–2 ft., nearly cylindrical; basal lvs. linear, 6–12 in. long, st. lvs. 2–3; infl. spicate, rarely forked, flexuous, with many-fld. clusters, each subtended by a bract about 1 in. long; perianth about ¾ in. across, yellow. Chile.

Douglasii A. Dietr. [*S. grandiflorum* Dougl., not Cav.; *Olsynium Douglasii* (A. Dietr.) Bickn.]. GRASS-WIDOW, PURPLE-EYED GRASS. Sts. 6–12 in., leafy at base, flexuous, cylindrical; lvs. 2–3, cauline, nearly cylindrical, bractlike; spathes 2–3-fld., solitary, terminal, pedicels slender, flexuous; fls. nodding, perianth campanulate, about ¾ in. long, dark reddish-purple; caps. ⁵⁄₁₆–½ in. long. B.C. to n. Calif.

Eastwoodiae: *S. bellum.*

ensigerum Bickn. Sts. 6–15 in., branched, winged, herbage pale green and glaucous; basal lvs. often curved, more than half as long as plant, to ³⁄₁₆ in. wide, st. lvs. about as long as peduncles; spathe with serrulate keel, peduncles 2–4, flattened, pedicels slender; perianth about ¾ in. across, pale violet-blue. Tex.

gramineum: *S. angustifolium.*

graminoides: *S. angustifolium.*

grandiflorum: *S. Douglasii.*

idahoense Bickn. Sts. 8–20 in., simple, winged, pale glaucous-green, often twisted, leafless; spathe sessile, the outer 1¼–2½ in. long; perianth 1 in. long, dark violet-blue with yellow eye. Mont. to B.C., Idaho, Ore. By some auth. included in *S. sarmentosum.*

inalatum A. Nels. Sts. 12–18 in., simple, not winged, each with 1 basal lf.; lvs. about ¼ in. wide; spathes sessile, the outer valve twice as long as the inner; fls. purple. Idaho.

inflatum (Suksd.) St. John. Differs from *S. Douglasii* in having staminal tube inflated at base, perianth segms. pinkish-purple, each with a green basal blotch, and caps. 3/16–5/16 in. long. Wash.

iridifolium: *S. micranthum;* but material grown under the name *S. iridifolium* may be *S. convolutum* and *S. laxum.*

iridioides: *S. Bermudiana.*

juncifolium Herb. Robust, sts. 18–28 in., about ⅜ in. in diam., winged; lvs. shorter than sts., about ½ in. wide, green with very narrow purplish edge; infl. branched, 30–50-fld., becoming loosely diffuse, spathes about 1 in. long, purplish; perianth about 1 in. across, rose-colored, filaments united along basal half. Chile. Sometimes included in the Chilean *S. junceum* E. H. Mey., which is not cult., and is a delicate, smaller plant with infl. of usually only 10–25 small fls.

laxum Otto. A variable ann. sp., allied to, and often mistaken for *S. micranthum,* but differing in having spathe valves subequal; perianth mostly about ½ in. long, white or bluish, ovary often glandular-pubescent and the plant not blackening on drying. Temp. S. Amer.; an adventive weed in Eur. and potentially so in parts of N. Amer. Sometimes cult. as *S. iridifolium.*

littorale Greene. Allied to *S. idahoense,* said to differ in having sts. and lvs. thinner, broader, fls. smaller, and fr. larger. B.C. to Alaska.

Macounii Bickn. Sts. 12–20 in., slender, very weakly winged; lvs. 1–2 in. long; spathes sessile, the outer valve 1½–3 in. long; fls. 2–4, purple, segms. ¾ in. long. B.C.

macrocephalum R. C. Grah. Clump-forming, robust, sts. 2½–3½ ft., weakly winged, sts. and lvs. ⅛–½ in. wide; infl. appearing lateral, overtopping the lvs., occasionally unbranched, but usually of several open, forked cymes, each cyme about 4 in. long; perianth about ½ in. long, yellow. N. Argentina, Bolivia, e. Brazil, Uruguay. United with *S. palmifolium,* by some auth.

Marchio (Vell.) Steud. Per., sts. mostly 8–16 in., simple or branched, broadly flattened, winged, basal lvs. none, lvs. many, to ¾ in. long; perianth about 1 in. across, yellow, filaments united more than halfway; caps. about ⅜ in. long. Bolivia.

micranthum Cav. [*S. iridifolium* HBK]. Slender weedy ann., herbage blackening on drying, sts. 3–8 in., branching at base, flattened, narrowly winged; spathes peduncled, subequal, 2–6-fld., green; perianth white, suffused with yellow at base, with reddish-purple eye, segms. about ¼ in. long, ovary mostly glabrous. Cent. Amer. to nw. Argentina. Some material cult. as *S. iridifolium* may be *S. laxum.*

montanum Greene. Sts. 4–24 in., simple, flattened, winged, pale green; lvs. shorter than sts., to ⅛ in. wide; spathe sessile, pedicels erect, scarcely longer than the spathe; fls. blue-violet. Que. to B.C., s. to n. N.Y. and Colo. Var. **crebrum** Fern. [*S. angustifolium* Bickn., not Mill.]. Foliage darker green, often tinged purple. Nfld. to Ont., s. to W.Va. Distinguished from *S. angustifolium* Mill. in having spathes sessile, not peduncled.

mucronatum Michx. Differs from *S. montanum* in having sts. more slender and scarcely winged, sometimes 2-ridged; lvs. usually not more than 1/16 in. wide; pedicels becoming spreading or recurving and much exceeding the inner spathe valve. Me. to Wisc., s. to S.C. Cv. **'Album'.** Fls. white.

pachyrhizum Bak. Roots fleshy, cylindrical, sts. 1–2 ft., much-branched in upper ⅓, leafy, flattened, narrowly winged; lvs. linear, shorter than sts.; infl. of cymose clusters, spathes 3–6-fld.; perianth ¼ in. long, yellow, filaments united to apex, ovary and pedicels glandular-puberulent. Brazil, Paraguay, Argentina. Material cult. as *S. Sellowii* belongs here.

palmifolium L. A name of uncertain application, but probably of a Brazilian sp. related to *S. macrocephalum.* By some auth. it is accepted as the valid name for the sp. complex represented by *S. macrocephalum, S. nidulare* (Hand.-Mazz.) I. M. Johnst., and *S. Wettsteinii* Hand.-Mazz.

sarmentosum Suksd. Sts. 6–12 in., ascending, very slender; lvs. linear, ⅛ in. wide or less; spathe valves narrowly linear, very unequal in length, even the inner ones longer than the fls.; perianth to ¼ in. long, light blue, segms. acuminate, ovary and perianth puberulent. Wash. Some auth. include *S. idahoense* and related spp. of nw. U.S. in this sp.

Sellowii: a listed name of no botanical standing, material so listed may be *S. pachyrhizum.*

striatum Sm. Sts. 15–30 in., stout, narrowly winged; basal lvs. lanceolate, 8–14 in. long, to ¾ in. wide, cauline lvs. 1–2; infl. spicate, the sessile cymules 8–20, spaced apart, each subtended by a thin, broadly ovate to ovate-lanceolate, acuminate bract about ¾ in. long; perianth about ⅝ in. long, greenish-yellow with brown veins, filaments united at base. Late summer. Argentina, Chile. Not hardy at low temperatures and requires well-drained situations in full sun.

vaginatum K. Spreng. Densely tufted, sts. 12–18 in., much-branched, winged; lvs. all cauline, well-developed or reduced and scalelike, sheathing; spathes 2–6-fld.; perianth to ½ in. long, yellow, filaments united at base. Brazil and Bolivia, s. to Uruguay and Paraguay. Zone 8. Not hardy to severe cold.

SIUM L. *Umbelliferae.* About 10 spp. of per. aromatic herbs of N. Hemisphere and Afr.; lvs. pinnate; fls. small, white, usually in involucrate compound umbels; fr. ovate.

cicutifolium: *S. suave.*

latifolium L. WATER PARSNIP. To 3 ft.; lfts. 11–17, oblong-lanceolate, to 1¼ in. long, margins evenly and closely serrulate; involucral bracts lanceolate, reflexed, involucels of small bractlets. Eur.

Sisarum L. SKIRRET. To 3 ft., with clustered tuberous roots; lfts. 3–11, lanceolate, toothed; involucral bracts and bractlets of involucels slender. E. Asia. Grown for the edible root. Does best in rich soil. Seeds may be sown in autumn or spring. Roots may be dug and stored in sand over winter or left in the ground.

suave Walt. [*S. cicutifolium* Schrank]. WATER PARSNIP. To 4 ft.; lfts. 7–17, to 5 in. long, acutely and distantly serrate; involucral bracts 6–10, reflexed, lanceolate, bractlets of involucels 4–8, linear-lanceolate. U.S., s. Canada, e. Asia.

SKIMMIA Thunb. *Rutaceae.* About 9 spp. of evergreen shrubs, native to the Himalayas, China, and Japan; lvs. alt., simple, glandular-dotted; fls. small, white, in compact, terminal panicles, bisexual and unisexual, calyx 4- or 5-lobed, petals and stamens 4 or 5; fr. with 2–4 1-seeded stones.

Skimmias are grown in warm temperate areas as ornamentals for the fragrant flowers and attractive fruits; where not hardy they are sometimes grown under glass. Plants may be grown in pots in a mixture of sand, peat, and loam, or set out in partly shaded locations. With the dioecious species, both female and male plants are required to ensure fruit. Propagated by seeds or by cuttings over heat.

×**Foremanii** H. Knight: *S. japonica* × *S. Reevesiana.* To 20 in.; lvs. lanceolate to oblanceolate, yellow-green; fr. scarlet, globose or pear-shaped in the same infructescence.

Fortunei: *S. Reevesiana.*

fragrans: *S. japonica.*

japonica Thunb. [*S. fragrans* Carrière]. To 5 ft., glabrous except for infl.; lvs. elliptic to oblong-obovate, to 5 in. long; fls. yellowish-white, in panicles to 3 in. long, mostly unisexual, 4-merous; fr. bright red, globose, to 5/16 in. in diam. Japan. Zone 8, and farther north on the coast in sheltered places.

Reevesiana Fort. [*S. Fortunei* M. T. Mast.]. Glabrous, to 6 ft.; lvs. lanceolate to oblong-lanceolate, to 4 in. long, dark green above; fls. bisexual, 5-merous; fr. dull red. China, Luzon (Philippine Is.), Taiwan. Zone 9.

repens Nakai. To 1 ft., with creeping, rooting sts.; lvs. crowded, oblong to oblanceolate, to 3 in. long, dark green; fr. red, globose. Japan. Zone 8. Sometimes treated as a form [forma *repens* (Nakai) Hara] of *S. japonica.*

SMELOWSKIA C. A. Mey. *Cruciferae.* Two spp. of tufted, gray-tomentose, per. herbs, in arctic-alpine regions of w. N. Amer. and e. Asia; basal lvs. entire to pinnate or pinnatifid; fls. showy, in racemes, sepals 4, petals 4, white or cream to purplish, spatulate; fr. an ovoid to linear, dehiscent silique, valves prominently 1-nerved or keeled, seeds several.

Used in rock gardens, but do not persist in nonalpine sites.

americana: *S. calycina.*

calycina (Steph.) C. A. Mey. [*S. americana* Rydb.]. Sts. several to many, simple, to 6 in.; basal lvs. deeply lobed, rarely dissected to midrib, strongly ciliate at base with long acicular hairs; petals to ⅜ in. long; mature silicles linear to oblong, to ½ in. long, tapering at both ends. Arctic-alpine regions, w. N. Amer. and e. Asia.

ovalis M. E. Jones. Sts. often branched, to 6 in.; basal lvs. dissected to midrib, not strongly ciliate at base; petals to ¼ in. long; mature silicles ovate to slightly oblong, to ¼ in. long, truncate at base. Cascade Mts., n. Calif. to Wash.; said to grow at highest elevations at which fl. plants are found on Mt. Rainier and other high peaks.

SMILACINA Desf. [*Vagnera* Adans.]. FALSE SOLOMON'S-SEAL, SOLOMON'S-FEATHER, SOLOMON'S-PLUMES. *Liliaceae.* About 25 spp. of rhizomatous, per. herbs, native to N. Amer. and Asia; sts. unbranched, leafy; lvs. alt.; fls. sometimes unisexual, white, pink, or purplish, in terminal racemes or panicles; perianth segms. 6, separate, persistent, stamens 6; fr. a few-seeded berry.

Of easy culture in moist, partly shady places; useful for colonizing. Propagated by division.

amplexicaulis: *S. racemosa* var.

bifolia: *Maianthemum bifolium.*

racemosa (L.) Desf. [*Vagnera racemosa* (L.) Morong]. FALSE SPIKE-NARD, SOLOMON'S-ZIGZAG, TREACLEBERRY. Sts. to 3 ft., arching to ascending, finely pubescent; lvs. short-petioled, elliptic to lanceolate-ovate, to 6 in. long and 3 in. wide, acuminate, pubescent beneath; fls. white, many, in panicles to 6 in. long with pubescent axes; fr. red, sometimes spotted purple. N. Amer. Var. **amplexicaulis** (Nutt.) S. Wats. [*S. amplexicaulis* Nutt.; *Vagnera amplexicaulis* (Nutt.) Greene]. FAT SOLOMON. Lvs. ovate, clasping, often sessile. S. B.C. and s. Alta. to Calif., Ariz., and New Mex.

sessilifolia (Bak.) Nutt. ex S. Wats. [*Vagnera sessilifolia* (Bak.) Greene]. SLIM SOLOMON. Sts. to 2 ft., usually flexuous above; lvs. ovate-lanceolate, to 6 in. long, flat, spreading; fls. few, in racemes to 2 in. long; fr. dark red. S. Calif. to B.C. and Mont.

spicata: a listed name of no botanical standing.

stellata (L.) Desf. [*Vagnera stellata* (L.) Morong]. STARFLOWER, STAR-FLOWERED LILY-OF-THE-VALLEY. Sts. to 2 ft.; lvs. lanceolate to oblong-lanceolate, to 6 in. long and 2 in. wide, usually folded length-wise, finely pubescent beneath; fls. whitish, in almost sessile racemes to 2 in. long; fr. at first green with black stripes, then dark red.

trifolia (L.) Desf. Sts. to 15 in.; lvs. elliptic to oblanceolate, to 5 in. long and 2 in. wide, sessile, glabrous; fls. few, in long-peduncled racemes; fr. dark red. Bogs and peaty soils, N. Amer. and Siberia.

SMILAX L. GREENBRIER, CATBRIER. *Liliaceae.* About 200 spp. of dioecious, woody or herbaceous vines, climbing by paired stipular tendrils, widely distributed in temp. areas and tropics around the world; rootstock rhizomatous or tuberous, sts. climbing or straggling, sometimes prickly; lvs. alt., the lower reduced to scales; fls. unisexual, greenish, whitish or yellowish, in axillary umbels, perianth segms. 6, separate, stamens 6, arising from base of perianth segms., anthers basi-fixed; fr. a 1–6-seeded berry.

The dried roots of several tropical Amer. species yield sarsaparilla, used medicinally and as a flavoring; other temperate species are gathered for winter greens from the wild. The latter are sometimes transferred to wild gardens; the tropical species are sometimes seen in greenhouses. The smilax of florists is *Asparagus asparagoides.*

asparagoides: *Asparagus asparagoides.*

glauca Walt. SAWBRIER, WILD SARSAPARILLA. Widely climbing deciduous shrub, sts. cylindrical, with scattered prickles; lvs. ovate or elliptic to reniform, to 6 in. long, glaucous beneath, entire; fr. glaucous, blue to black, on peduncles longer than subtending petioles. N.J. to s. Ill., s. to Fla. and e. Tex.

herbacea L. CARRION FLOWER, JACOB'S-LADDER. Herbaceous, climbing to 6 ft., unarmed; lvs. oblong-ovate to round, to 5 in. long, the base variable, glabrous beneath; fr. bluish-black. Que. and New Bruns., s. to Ala.

hispida Muhlenb. [*S. tamnoides* L. var. *hispida* (Muhlenb.) Fern.]. BRISTLY G., HAGBRIER, HELLFETTER. High-climbing, deciduous shrub, sts. usually conspicuously prickly; lvs. ovate to round, to 4¾ in. long and 4¼ in. wide, serrulate; fr. black, on peduncles longer than subtending petioles. Sw. Conn. to Minn., s. to Fla., Ala., and e. Tex.

Kraussiana Meissn. Climbing shrub, sts. prickly; lvs. elliptic-ovate to ovate, to 6 in. long and 4 in. wide; fr. nearly globose, purple, about ½ in. long. Afr.

lanceolata L. JACKSON BRIER. Climbing, evergreen, woody vine, older sts. merely sparsely prickly; lvs. lanceolate-ovate to ovate, to 3½ in. long and 2 in. wide, glossy above, entire; fr. globose, dull red to brown, to ⅜ in. in diam., on peduncles longer than subtending petioles. N. Fla. s. to W. Indies, Mex., and Panama.

laurifolia L. LAUREL-LEAVED G., BLASPHEME VINE, BAMBOO VINE. High-climbing, evergreen vine, sts. thorny; lvs. oblong, elliptic, or lanceolate, to 4 in. long, wedge-shaped at base; fr. black, 1-seeded. N.J. to Fla. and Tex.

myrtifolia: *Asparagus asparagoides* cv.

rotundifolia L. COMMON G., COMMON C., BULLBRIER, HORSE BRIER. High-climbing, deciduous, woody vine, sts. often 4-angled and thorny; lvs. ovate to nearly circular, to 6 in. long, glossy, base round to cordate; fr. blue-black to black. Nov. Sc. to Mich., s. to Fla. and e. Tex.

Walteri Pursh. RED-BERRIED G., RED-BERRIED BAMBOO. Slender, climbing, deciduous, woody vine, older sts. often prickly; lvs. ovate

to oblong-ovate, to 4¾ in. long, glossy; fr. bright red. N.J. to Fla. and e. Tex.

SMITHIANTHA O. Kuntze [*Naegelia* Regel]. TEMPLE-BELLS. *Gesneriaceae.* Four spp. of terrestrial, per., hairy, herbs with scaly rhizomes, native to Mex.; lvs. opp., petioled, broadly ovate, cordate at base, toothed; fls. nodding, alt. in a terminal raceme, calyx lobes 5, corolla tubular-campanu-late, neither spurred nor swollen at base, lobes spreading, stamens 4, borne at base of corolla tube, anthers united in pairs by their tips, disc ringlike or 5-lobed, ovary half-inferior; fr. a caps.

Propagated by the scaly rhizomes. For cultivation see *Gesneriaceae.*

cinnabarina (Linden) O. Kuntze [*Naegelia cinnabarina* Linden]. Sts. to 2 ft.; lvs. with red-hairy petioles, blades to 6 in. long, 5 in. wide, deep green variegated with purple along the veins and densely red- or purplish-hairy above, paler green variegated with red beneath; fls. to 1½ in. long, calyx red-glandular-hairy, lobes ⅛ in. long, corolla tube brick-red outside, banded with pale yellow or white on lower side and inside, limb red with pale spots and lines.

exoniensis Hort.: presumably a hybrid, parentage unknown; fls. orange.

fulgida (Ortg.) Voss. Similar to *S. cinnabarina,* but lvs. green, fls. scarlet.

×**hybrida** Voss: *S. multiflora* × *S. zebrina.* A variable hybrid, with several cvs.

multiflora (M. Martens & Galeotti) Fritsch. NAEGELIA. To 2½ ft.; lf. blades to 6 in. long, 4 in. wide, velvety-hairy, dark green; fls. to 1½ in. long, corolla white or cream-colored, yellowish at throat.

zebrina (Paxt.) O. Kuntze [*Naegelia zebrina* (Paxt.) Regel]. To 2½ ft.; lvs. velvety-hairy, blades to 7 in. long, 6½ in. wide, dark green, variegated with purple or brown about veins; fls. to 1½ in. long, corolla tube scarlet above with broad yellow band on lower side, yellow and spotted with red inside, upper lobes orange-yellow, lower lobes yellow.

SMODINGIUM E. H. Mey. ex Sond. *Anacardiaceae.* One sp., a S. Afr. polygamous shrub; lvs. palmate with 3 lfts.; fls. smaller, in terminal panicles, calyx 5-lobed, petals 5, stamens 5, opp. the calyx lobes; fr. a samara. Differs from *Rhus* in having styles 3, fr. winged, with seeds adhering, and from *Laurophyllus* in having lvs. with 3 lfts. and fr. oblique, with larger wings.

argutum E. H. Mey. ex Sond. Erect shrub, with striate brs.; lf. rachis, and panicle thinly pubescent, lfts. lanceolate, to 5 in. long, mucronate, green above, paler beneath.

SMYRNIUM L. *Umbelliferae.* About 7 spp. of erect, bien. herbs, of the Old World; lvs. biternately or triternately com-pound, glabrous; fls. greenish-yellow, in compound umbels, usually without involucres; fr. ovate, laterally flattened.

Olusatrum L. ALEXANDERS, HORSE PARSLEY. To 4 ft., stout; lower lvs. to 1½ ft. long, segms. broadly ovate, to 2½ in. long, coarsely serrate, crenate, or occasionally lobed; umbels to 4 in. across; fr. to ¼ in. long. Medit. region and w. Eur.; naturalized in Bermuda.

SOBRALIA Ruiz & Pav. *Orchidaceae.* About 90 spp. of terrestrial or epiphytic herbs, native to Cent. and S. Amer.; sts. leafy; lvs. leathery, blades jointed to long sheaths; fls. showy, in a terminal or axillary raceme, sepals spreading, united to base, petals similar, lip united to base of column, the apex reflexed, spreading, undulate or fringed, the disc smooth or crested, column elongated, without a foot, winged, 3-lobed at apex. For structure of fl. see *Orchidaceae.*

In culture treated much like *Coelogyne.* For general culture see *Orchids.*

Cattleya Rchb.f. Sts. canelike, to 5 ft. high; lvs. ovate-lanceolate, to 10 in. long, acuminate; infls. several, axillary, shorter than lvs., few-fld.; fls. fleshy, rose, to 3 in. across, sepals oblong-strap-shaped, petals ovate, lip 3-lobed, lateral lobes enveloping column, midlobe horizontal, the disc crested. Colombia.

decora Batem. [*S. panamensis* Schlechter]. Sts. to 30 in. high, leafy, sts., lower surface of lvs., and lf. sheaths black-warty; lvs. oblong-lanceolate, to 9 in. long; fls. 1–2, terminal, sessile, subtended by scar-ious sheaths, pale lavender and white, lasting only 1 day, sepals linear-oblong, to 2 in. long, apiculate, recurved, petals oblong-elliptic, to 1½ in. long, lip tubular-involute, to 1¾ in. long, hooded at base, undu-late-crisped, flared on front margin, rose-lavender or lavender, disc streaked with yellow and brown, with many sinuately anastomosing veins, column white. Highlands, Mex. and Cent. Amer.

fragrans Lindl. Sts. to 14 in. high, 1-lvd., sts. and peduncles flattened, 2-edged; lvs. oblong-lanceolate, to 9 in. long; fls. 1–2, small, yellowish-white, tinged with pink, fragrant, bracts elliptic-lanceolate, to 2 in. long, with whitish, scarious margins, sepals and petals linear, to 1½ in. long, lip obovate-cuneate, entire and involute at base, crisped or deeply fringed at apex, the disc with 9 elevated, fringed keels. Cent. Amer. to Venezuela.

leucoxantha Rchb.f. Sts. to 4½ ft. high; lvs. elliptic, to 9 in. long, lf. sheaths warty or punctate; fls. solitary, large, yellowish-white, sepals and petals oblong, to 2¾ in. long, lip obovate, 2¾ in. long, with yellow throat, undulate margins, and short callus at base. Costa Rica and Panama.

Lowii Rolfe. Sts. to 1½ ft. high; lvs. lanceolate, to 6 in. long, sheaths covered with minute black hairs; fls. solitary, deep purple, sepals and petals lanceolate, 2 in. long, lip shorter than sepals, elliptic, crisped-undulate, the disc smooth, with a pair of linear, white, fleshy calluses. Colombia.

macrantha Lindl. Sts. to 7 ft. high, leafy; lvs. rigid, lanceolate, to 1 ft. long; fls. solitary, rose-purple, subtended by large leaflike bracts, sepals linear-oblong, to 4 in. long, petals oblong-ovate, to 3½ in. long, margins undulate-crisped, lip large, to 4½ in. long, basal half a laterally compressed tube around column, deeply 2-lobed at apex, margins undulate-crisped above middle. Mex. to Costa Rica. Cv. 'Alba'. Fls. white. Cv. 'Splendens'. Fls. darker than in typical form.

macrophylla Rchb.f. Sts. 3–5 ft. high; lvs. 2–3, oblong, to 6 in. long; fl. solitary, terminal, sessile, pale sulphur-yeilow, sepals 4 in. long, meeting, petals similar, lip erect, enclosed within, but longer than other perianth segms., obovate, undulate, the disc striated, column deep yellow. Brazil.

panamensis: *S. decora*.

xantholeuca Rchb.f. Sts. to 2 ft. high; lf. sheaths pale greenish, speckled with red-brown, lvs. spreading, drooping, sessile, lanceolate, to 7 in. long; fls. solitary, terminal, lemon-yellow with golden throat streaked with darker yellow, sepals and petals linear-lanceolate, to 4½ in. long, lip not longer than sepals, tube cylindrical, blade orbicular, margins crisped-undulate, crenate. Cent. Amer.

SOEHRENSIA: *LOBIVIA*. **S. famatimensis:** a listed name of no botanical standing for *L. famatimensis*. **S. polycephala:** a listed name of no botanical standing for *L. polycephala*.

SOILLESS GARDENING: see *Hydroponics*.

SOILS. Good gardening starts with an understanding of the soil, for plants and the soil influence each other and both respond to the prevailing climate. Soil serves to anchor roots and thus supports plants; it is also the storehouse of raw materials, minerals, and water, taken in by root hairs and transported within the plant to be used for nutrition and growth. The soil is the home of living organisms of many sorts, which in life, death, and decay modify the soil characteristics. Thus the soil environment is not stable but changes continuously and the gardener must continually be aware of this.

The gardening environment mainly involves the usually organic-rich topsoil; subsoil, though rich in mineral elements, appears sterile because of the lack of incorporation of much organic material and must be improved before it can be used as a growing medium. The main elements of topsoil are solid (inorganic and organic), liquid (water with soil minerals in solution), and gaseous (air), roughly in the proportion of 50–25–25; most plants require all of these elements in acceptable proportions for successful growth.

Soil is particulate and the major characteristic or class of a soil depends on the size of its major particles, the progression being from large particles of gravel decreasing through sand to silt and finally clay, in which soil particles are exceedingly fine. Good garden soils, known as loams, are composed of mixes of at least two particulate sizes and take their names from the dominant particle size. Thus there are gravelly, sand, silty, or clay loams.

The nature of the major soil particles determines the soil structure and the nature of the latter is important in managing the garden. Sandy soils are porous, permitting free movement of water and air but having low capacity for holding either water or the important nutrients dissolved in water.

Sandy soils thus have low fertility as garden soils, requiring abundant fertilizers; but in the greenhouse the porosity of sand makes it ideal, so long as it is kept moist, for such horticultural practices as the temporary rooting of cuttings, where good aeration and control of disease are needed. For gardening, soils of medium rather than sandy or fine texture are best, for they hold moisture and nutrients better than sandy soils and provide better aeration for roots than is furnished by clay soils. Soils of medium texture also can be cultivated over a reasonable range of soil-moisture levels, whereas fine-textured soils, such as clay loams, cannot be tilled when wet and are easily overwatered with consequent poor growth of roots.

Poor soils can be improved by good management. The periodic addition of organic matter is the best treatment for substandard soils. It is equally effective on soils that are sandy, making them more retentive of water and nutrients, or on heavy clay, separating the compacted particles to make a more granular texture that permits better drainage and aeration. Valuable organic material includes compost, well-rotted manure, peat moss, lawn clippings, deciduous leaves, pine needles, wood chips, seaweed, spent hay, and any locally available industrial wastes such as sawdust, ground corncobs, etc. Certain of these materials, especially compost and leaf mold, are obtainable free by developing a compost pile on the home property. Ideally, organic material needs to be incorporated thoroughly into the soil with plough or rototiller, or dug in by hand with garden fork, but in areas of permanent ornamental plantings it may be added annually as a mulch. In vegetable gardens, additions are made preferably at the beginning and end of the gardening season, and temporary green manure or cover crops may also be planted to be turned under later.

In some areas, owners of new homes find that developers have stripped away topsoil, leaving only barren subsoil for lawn and garden use. Such subsoil may be converted to an adequate soil for plants first by deep-ploughing the subsoil, then by ploughing under, for each 1,000 square feet of the ploughed area, 2½ cubic yards of rotted manure or compost, 1 cubic yard of coarse sand, 100 pounds of ground limestone, and 100 pounds of high-nitrogen fertilizer. The area may be planted in about two weeks after the soil has settled, preferably first to a cover crop, which can be followed in proper season by lawn or garden plants.

Soil reaction, its relative acidity or alkalinity as measured by the pH scale, is also an important element in horticulture, especially when growing plants that require a more or less specific soil reaction. Soils are termed neutral (pH of 7), acid (below pH of 7), or alkaline or basic (above pH of 7). Some plants thrive only under rather specific pH ranges. Most vegetables and some lawn grasses grow poorly on soils that are very acid (below pH 5) or very alkaline (above pH 8) and do best in the range of pH 5.8–pH 7.4. On the other hand, numerous ornamentals and nearly all ericaceous species, such as *Rhododendron* and *Vaccinium*, thrive only on very acid soils (pH 5–4). Generally speaking, soils in temperate North America are acid where rainfall is high (the eastern United States and coastal Pacific Northwest) and normally neutral or alkaline in the arid western and intermontane areas. There may be local exceptions to this general rule and so the wise home owner should invest in some soil tests. Soil-testing services are commonly available at state agricultural extension offices or local garden centers or the gardener may purchase a soil-testing kit. Agricultural limestone, spread evenly over the lawn or rototilled into the vegetable garden every two or three years at the rate of 5 pounds per 100 square feet is the best and cheapest way to improve acid or sub-acid soils. Limestone not only reduces soil acidity but improves the texture of clay soils through separation of the fine particles. Where ornamentals only are to be grown, it is sometimes simpler to select plants suited to the pH of one's garden. Lists of plants appended to this account separate some common horticultural species into four classes according to preference for the following types of soil as determined by studies of E. T. Wherry, Wiggin and Gourley, G. M. Shear, and others.

Circumneutral . . . . . Soils in which neither acid nor alkaline
(pH 8 to 6)   influences are markedly dominant. The soils of the Mediterranean region, where so many of our garden plants are native, are of this class.

Minimacid . . . . Humus-rich meadows, swamps, and
(pH 7 to 6)   woods, in calcareous regions. Fields and gardens under standard types of cultivation.

Subacid . . . . Many sorts of marshes, meadows,
(pH 6 to 5)   swamps, and upland woods. Long-abandoned fields and gardens in noncalcareous regions.

Mediacid . . . . Various kinds of peat bogs. Swamps
(pH 5 to 4)   where the water is lacking in calcium bicarbonate. Thickets of *Rhododendron, Kalmia,* and other ericaceous plants. Woods where such plants as hemlock *(Tsuga),* pine *(Pinus),* spruce *(Picea),* or oak *(Quercus)* are dominant. Accumulations of upland peat, rotting wood, and similar materials. Mountain peaks and sandhills where the substrata are noncalcareous.

The gardener who desires to grow plants demanding high acidity on circumneutral or minimacid soils may prepare special beds of acid soil by incorporating such organic materials as sphagnum-derived peat moss, upland peat from beneath such conifers as pine, spruce, and hemlock, or from composted oak leaves, pine needles, bark, rotted wood, or well-weathered sawdust in well-washed, clay- and lime-free sand to obtain a porous and open-textured soil. Regular annual mulching with oak leaves or pine needles is required to keep such soil acid, or acidifying chemicals, like aluminum sulfate, may also be applied but with caution and as directed. Annual pH tests should be made to make certain that a proper level of acidity is maintained.

In the home or greenhouse, where plants are usually grown in pots, soil mixes may be tailored to each species being grown. Satisfactory soil mixes for greenhouse use will vary with the parent soil used. On a volume base, two parts of virgin field soil, one part sphagnum peat moss, and one part coarse builder's sand or horticultural Perlite will make a soil satisfactory for most greenhouse plants. If the field soil is a heavy clay loam, then a 1–1–1 mix of the above is appropriate; with sandy loam, the ratio should be 3–1–1. Since field soils contain living organisms such as damping-off fungi, nematodes, insects, and weed seeds, all such soil should be pasteurized before being used in a greenhouse mix. One way of accomplishing this is by cooking it in an oven at 250° F for an hour. Garden soil is not recommended for starting seed or for certain pot plants grown in home or greenhouse, such as tropical species with ornamental foliage or epiphytes. Special soilless mixes are easily prepared for these. A recommended seed-starting mix to make 1 bushel of medium texture includes ½ bushel shredded sphagnum peat moss, ½ bushel fine (# 4) horticultural vermiculite, 5 level tablespoons of ground limestone, 3 level tablespoons of 20 percent powdered superphosphate, and two level tablespoons of ammonium nitrate. Germination in this medium is rapid, the seedlings developing quickly to transplanting size.

The following formulas, each sufficient to make approximately one bushel of a growing mix, are recommended for potted foliage plants and epiphytes.

Foliage Plant Mix

Recommended for plants requiring a growing medium with high moisture-retaining characteristics, such as *Aphelandra squarrosa, Begonia, Buxus, Caladium, Cissus, Citrus, Coleus,* ferns, *Ficus, Hedera Helix, Hippeastrum, Justicia Brandegeana, Maranta, Oxalis,* Palmae, *Pilea, Sansevieria, Soleirolia Soleirolii,* and *Tolmiea Menziesii.*

Material	Amount
Sphagnum peat moss (screened ½ inch mesh)	½ bushel
Horticultural vermiculite (No. 2)	¼ bushel
Perlite (medium grade)	¼ bushel
Ground dolomitic limestone	8 tablespoons *
20 percent powdered superphosphate	2 tablespoons
10–10–10 fertilizer	3 tablespoons
Iron sulfate	1 tablespoon
Potassium nitrate (14–0–44)	1 tablespoon
Granular wetting agent (such as Aqua-gro, etc.)	3 tablespoons

* All tablespoon measurements in formula are level.

Epiphytic Plant Mix

Recommended for plants such as epiphytes, which require good drainage, aeration, and have the ability to withstand drying between waterings. Such plants include *Aeschynanthus, Aglaonema, Aloe,* Bromeliaceae, Cactaceae (epiphytic), *Columnea, Crassula, Dieffenbachia, Drymonia, Episcia, Gloxinia, Hoya, Kohleria, Monstera, Nephthytis, Peperomia, Philodendron, Pothos, Saintpaulia,* and *Syngonium.*

Material	Amount
Sphagnum peat moss (screened ½ inch mesh)	⅓ bushel
Firbark (Douglas, red, or white fir) ⅛–¼ inch size (finely ground)	⅓ bushel
Perlite (medium grade)	⅓ bushel
Ground dolomitic limestone	8 tablespoons *
20 percent powdered superphosphate	6 tablespoons
10–10–10 fertilizer	3 tablespoons
Iron sulphate	1 tablespoon
Potassium nitrate (14–0–44)	1 tablespoon
Granular wetting agent (such as Aqua-Gro)	3 tablespoon

* All tablespoon measurements in formula are level.

List of garden plants by pH preference

Note that reactions given are considered to represent optimum values for the individual species, but many plants will grow nearly as well in soils of a pH class adjoining that in which a plant is listed. Common garden plants not included in this listing appear to thrive equally well in soils of all degrees of acidity usually encountered.

1. Circumneutral-soil plants (pH 8–6): many, though not necessarily all, species of the genera *Abelia, Acer, Actaea, Adiantum, Aesculus, Alyssum, Ampelopsis, Anemone, Antirrhinum, Apium, Asparagus, Aster, Astilbe, Berberis, Beta, Brassica, Bromus, Buddleia, Buxus, Calendula, Callicarpa, Callistephus, Campanula, Canna, Celastrus, Clematis, Coleus, Convolvulus, Cosmos, Cotoneaster, Crataegus, Crocus, Cucumis, Cucurbita, Dahlia, Daucus, Delphinium, Deutzia, Dianthus, Euonymus, Fagus, Forsythia, Fraxinus, Gaillardia, Gladiolus, Hedera, Helianthus, Hibiscus, Hyacinthus, Impatiens, Iris, Juniperus, Lactuca, Lespedeza, Ligustrum, Lonicera, Lychnis, Lycopersicon, Malus, Medicago, Melilotus, Mertensia, Narcissus, Oenothera, Paeonia, Papaver, Pastinaca, Pelargonium, Phaseolus, Philadelphus, Pisum, Poa, Polygonum, Portulaca, Primula, Prunus, Pyrus, Ranunculus, Rhamnus, Ribes, Rosa, Salvia, Scabiosa, Secale, Spinacia, Spiraea, Syringa, Tagetes, Taxodium, Taxus, Thuja, Trifolium, Triticum, Tropaeolum, Tulipa, Ulmus, Viola, Wisteria, Yucca, Zinnia.*

2. Minimacid-soil plants (pH 7–6): *Acanthus mollis, Adlumia fungosa, Aesculus Pavia, Agrostis stolonifera* var. *palustris, Allium Schoenoprasum, Amelanchier, Apocynum androsaemifolium, Aquilegia caerulea* and hybrids, *A. chrysantha, Aralia hispida, A. spinosa, Aster undulatus, Avena sativa, Brassica Rapa, Calypso bulbosa, Cardamine pratensis, Centaurea Cyanus, Cerastium arvense, Cheilanthes lanosa, Chrysogonum virginianum, Coreopsis* species, *Cornus florida, Corylus cornuta, Delphinium nudicaule,*

Dryopteris austriaca var. *intermedia, D. austriaca* var. *spinulosa, Epilobium angustifolium, Fagopyrum esculentum, Filipendula vulgaris, Fuchsia* × *hybrida, Garcinia Mangostana, Gillenia trifoliata, Gymnocarpium Dryopteris, Helianthemum nummularium, Hedyotis caerulea, Iberis sempervirens, Linum usitatissimum, Litchi chinensis, Lonicera Periclymenum, Lotus corniculatus, Lupinus hirsutus, Miscanthus sinensis, Monarda didyma, Orchis rotundifolia, Petunia* × *hybrida, Phaseolus lunatus, Phlox Drummondii, Poa nemoralis, Prunus Persica, Rubus occidentalis, Rumex scutatus, Selaginella rupestris, Silene compacta, S. caroliniana, Stizolobium Deeringianum, Trillium Catesbaei, Vigna unguiculata* subsp. *sesquipedalis, Vitis* species, *Zea Mays.*

3. Subacid-soil plants (pH 6–5): *Abies, Acer pensylvanicum, A. spicatum, Agrostis capillaris, A. stolonifera, Aletris farinosa, Aleurites Fordii, Anaphalis margaritacea, Antennaria, Arachis hypogaea, Aronia, Asarum virginicum, Aster linearifolius, A. macrophyllus, A. patens, A. spectabilis, Athyrium Filix-femina, Baptisia tinctoria, Betula lenta, Botrychium dissectum, B. dissectum* var. *obliquum, B. matricariifolium, Calluna vulgaris, Campanula divaricata, Castanea dentata, C. pumila, Ceanothus americanus, Chamaedaphne calyculata, Chamaelirium luteum, Cheilanthes lanosa, Chelone Lyonii, C. obliqua, Chimaphila, Chionanthus virginicus, Chrysopsis mariana, Cimicifuga americana, Citrullus lanatus, Claytonia caroliniana, Clematis crispa, Clethra, Clintonia umbellulata, Clitoria mariana, Comptonia peregrina* var. *asplenifolia, Convallaria majalis, Coreopsis rosea, C. verticillata, Corydalis sempervirens, Cuthbertia rosea, Cyclamen persicum, Cymophyllus Fraseri, Cypripedium arietinum, Cytisus scoparius, Dalibarda repens, Dennstaedtia punctilobula, Dentaria diphylla, Dicentra eximia, Diphylleia cymosa, Disporum lanuginosum, Dryopteris* × *Boottii, D. cristata* var. *Clintoniana, Erica, Eryngium aquaticum, Fothergilla Gardenii, Franklinia Alatamaha, Galium boreale, Gaultheria procumbens, Gaylussacia, Gelsemium sempervirens, Goodyera pubescens, G. repens, G. tesselata, Gordonia Lasianthus, Habenaria viridis* var. *bracteata, H. ciliaris, H. psychodes* var. *grandiflora, H. Hookeri, H. lacera, H. obtusata, H. peramoena, Halesia carolina, Hedyotis Michauxii, Heuchera villosa, Hydrangea macrophylla, Hypoxis hirsuta, Ilex Cassine, I. glabra, I. opaca, Ipomoea Batatas, Iris virginica, I. Kaempferi, I. tenax, Juniperus communis* var. *montana, J. horizontalis, Kalmia angustifolia, K. latifolia, Krigia montana, Leucothoe, Liatris graminifolia, L. squarrosa, Lilium Grayi, L. philadelphicum, L. superbum, Listera cordata, Lupinus Hartwegii, L. perennis, Lycopodium clavatum, L. complanatum* var. *flabelliforme, L. lucidulum, L. obscurum, Lyonia ligustrina, Magnolia* (excepting *M. virginiana*), *Maianthemum bifolium, M. canadense, Medeola virginica, Melanthium virginicum, Menyanthes trifoliata, Mitchella repens, Mitella nuda, Monotropa uniflora, Myrica, Nemopanthus mucronatus, Oenothera tetragona* var. *Fraseri, Opuntia compressa, Parnassia asarifolia, Paronychia virginica, Phlox amoena, P. ovata, P. stolonifera, Picea, Pinus* (many though not all species), *Polygala paucifolia, Pteridium aquilinum* var. *latiusculum, Pyrola, Quercus falcata, Q. laevis, Q. marilandica, Q. Phellos, Q. stellata, Rhododendron* (including azaleas), *R. canadense, Rubus idaeus, Salix repens, Sedum anglicum, Senecio cruentus, Shortia galacifolia, Smilax laurifolia, S. Walteri, Solanum Melongena, S. tuberosum, Solidago bicolor, S. odora, Spiraea tomentosa, Spiranthes gracilis, S. cernua* var. *odorata, Stellaria Holostea, Stewartia ovata, Styrax americana, Tsuga caroliniana, Ulex europaeus, Vaccinium* (many species), *Veronica spicata, Viburnum alnifolium, V. nudum, Viola pedata, Woodsia ilvensis, Zenobia pulverulenta, Zephyranthes Atamasco, Zigadenus.*

4. Mediacid-soil plants (pH 5–4): *Andromeda, Arenaria groenlandica, Arethusa bulbosa, Arnica, Asarum Shuttleworthii, Asclepias rubra, Asplenium montanum, A. pinnatifidum, Calla palustris, Calopogon tuberosus, Chamaecyparis thyoides, Cleistes divaricata, Clintonia borealis,*

Coptis, Corema Conradii, Cornus canadensis, Cypripedium acaule, Darlingtonia californica, Dionaea muscipula, Drosera, Empetrum nigrum, Epigaea repens, Galax urceolata, Habenaria blephariglottis, H. cristata, H. orbiculata, Helonias bullata, Iris prismatica, I. verna, Kalmia polifolia, Ledum groenlandicum, Leiophyllum, Lilium Catesbaei, Linnaea borealis var. *americana, Loiseleuria procumbens, Lygodium palmatum, Magnolia virginiana, Menziesia pilosa, Molinia caerulea, Paronychia argyrocoma, Pieris, Pogonia ophioglossoides, Polypodium aureum, Potentilla tridentata, Quercus ilicifolia, Rhexia, Rubus hispidus, Sarracenia, Sorbus americana, Stenanthium gramineum* var. *robustum, Streptopus roseus, Trientalis borealis, Trillium undulatum, Vaccinium Vitis-idaea* var. *minus, Woodwardia areolata, Xerophyllum asphodeloides.*

SOLANACEAE Juss. NIGHTSHADE FAMILY. Dicot.; about 90 genera and 2,000 spp. of herbs, shrubs, trees, and vines of trop. and temp. regions, chiefly Cent. and S. Amer.; sts. often prickly; lvs. usually alt., simple or pinnate; fls. bisexual, calyx 5-lobed, persistent, corolla usually rotate, funnelform, or salverform, 5-lobed, rarely 2-lipped, stamens usually 5, borne on the corolla, 1 or more of these sometimes sterile, ovary superior, mostly 2-celled, ovules 1 to many in each cell, stigma 2-lobed; fr. a berry or caps. Distinguished from related families in having the corolla usually plicate in bud. Genera treated here are: *Anthocercis, Atropa, Browallia, Brugmansia, Brunfelsia, Capsicum, Cestrum, Cyphomandra, Datura, Fabiana, Hyoscyamus, Iochroma, Lycium, Lycopersicon, Mandragora, Nicandra, Nicotiana, Nierembergia, Petunia, Physalis, Salpichroa, Salpiglossis, Schizanthus, Solandra, Solanum, Streptosolen,* and *Vestia.*

Besides having many ornamentals, the family abounds in plants with medicinal or poisonous properties, and the potato, tomato, eggplant, red pepper, tobacco, and others are of great economic importance.

SOLANDRA Swartz [*Swartzia* J. F. Gmel.]. CHALICE VINE. Solanaceae. About 10 spp. of climbing, woody shrubs or vines of trop. Amer.; lvs. alt., simple, entire, mostly leathery and glossy; fls. solitary, axillary, on thick but short pedicels, calyx long-tubular, 2–5-parted at apex, persistent, corolla white to yellow, sometimes marked purple, funnelform with cylindrical tube and campanulate throat, lobes 5, overlapping in bud, reflexed in fl., stamens 5, borne on the corolla; fr. a fleshy, globose, 2-celled berry, more or less included in the calyx.

Planted in the tropics and subtropics, or under glass, for the showy flowers, which are fragrant at night. Solandras grown under glass require a temperature of at least 50° F., full sun, and abundant water from early autumn to late spring. They should be kept dry in summer, during the rest period. Propagated by cuttings of firm young shoots taken with a heel, with moderate bottom heat.

grandiflora Swartz [*Swartzia grandiflora* (Swartz) J. F. Gmel.]. Coarse, glabrous, woody vine, to 30 ft. or more; lvs. elliptic to obovate, to 7 in. long, acute, petioles less than 1 in. long; calyx tubular, to 3 in. long, 2-lobed, as long as the narrow portion of the corolla tube, corolla white, turning yellow to brownish-yellow on the second day, 4–6 in. long, expanded above the calyx and slightly contracted at the mouth. Jamaica, Puerto Rico, Lesser Antilles.

guttata D. Don ex Lindl. [*Swartzia guttata* (D. Don ex Lindl.) Standl.]. GOLDCUP, CUP-OF-GOLD, TRUMPET PLANT. Pubescent, climbing shrub; lvs. elliptic-oblong, 3–6 in. long, acute or acuminate, petioles to 2 in. long, calyx to 3 in. long, 3-lobed, corolla rich yellow, spotted or feathered with purple, chalicelike, to 9 in. long. Mex. Most material offered as this sp. is *S. maxima.*

Hartwegii: *S. maxima.*

longiflora Tussac. Very similar to *S. grandiflora* and differing from it in the calyx being only half as long as the narrow tube of the corolla. Cuba, Hispaniola.

maxima (Sessé & Moç.) P. S. Green [*S. Hartwegii* N. E. Br.; *S. nitida* Zuccagni]. Similar to *S. guttata,* but entirely glabrous; lvs. elliptic, to 6½ in. long, obtuse to shortly acuminate, petioles to 3 in. long; calyx to 2¾ in. long, 3–4-lobed, corolla yellow, with 5 purple lines, chalicelike, to 9 in. long. Mex.

nitida: *S. maxima.*

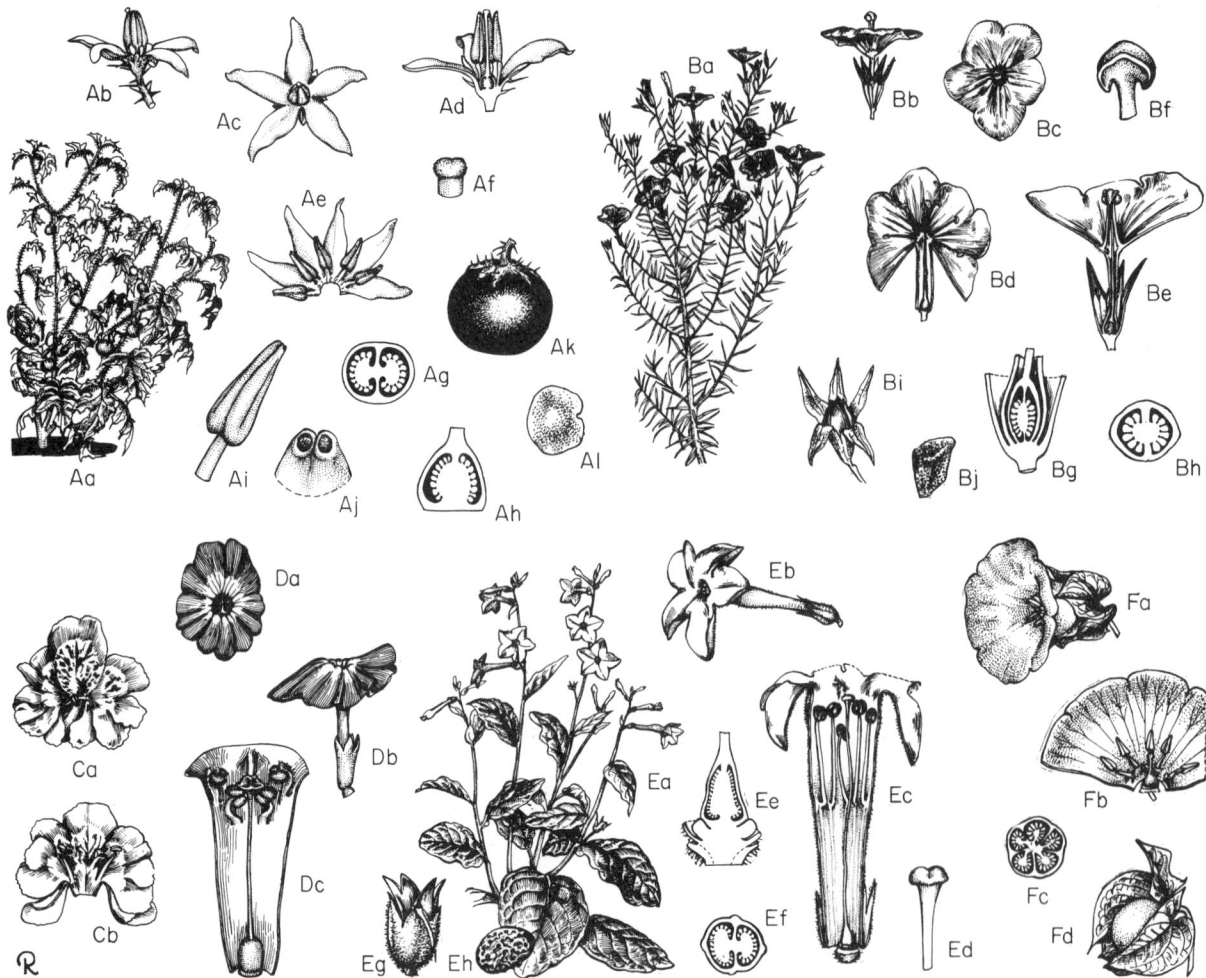

SOLANACEAE. **A,** *Solanum aculeatissimum:* **Aa,** plant, × ¹⁄₁₂; **Ab,** flower, side view, × ³⁄₄; **Ac,** flower, face view, × ³⁄₄; **Ad,** flower, vertical section, × ³⁄₄; **Ae,** corolla, expanded, × ³⁄₄; **Af,** stigma, × 6; **Ag,** ovary, cross section, × 5; **Ah,** ovary, vertical section, × 5; **Ai,** stamen, × 3; **Aj,** apex of anther, × 10; **Ak,** berry, × ¹⁄₂; **Al,** seed, × 2. **B,** *Nierembergia hippomanica* var. *violacea:* **Ba,** flowering stem, × ¹⁄₆; **Bb,** flower, side view, × ¹⁄₂; **Bc,** flower, face view, × ¹⁄₂; **Bd,** flower, corolla expanded, × ¹⁄₂; **Be,** flower, vertical section, × 1; **Bf,** stigma, × 4; **Bg,** base of flower, vertical section, × 5; **Bh,** ovary, cross section, × 8; **Bi,** capsule, × 1¹⁄₂; **Bj,** seed, × 6. **C,** *Schizanthus pinnatus:* **Ca,** flower, face view, × ¹⁄₂; **Cb,** corolla expanded, × ¹⁄₂. **D.** *Browallia viscosa:* **Da,** flower, face view, × 1; **Db,** flower, side view, × 1; **Dc,** corolla tube, expanded, and pistil, × 2. **E,** *Nicotiana alata* cv. 'Grandiflora': **Ea,** plant, × ¹⁄₁₀; **Eb,** flower, × ¹⁄₃; **Ec,** flower, corolla expanded, × ¹⁄₂; **Ed,** apex of style and stigma, × 2; **Ee,** ovary, vertical section, × 2; **Ef,** ovary, cross section, × 3; **Eg,** capsule, × 1; **Eh,** seed, × 8. **F,** *Nicandra Physalodes:* **Fa,** flower, × ¹⁄₂; **Fb,** flower, corolla expanded, × ¹⁄₂; **Fc,** ovary, cross section, × 3; **Fd,** berry in calyx, × ¹⁄₂.

SOLANUM L. *Solanaceae.* Perhaps 1,700 spp. of cosmopolitan herbs, shrubs, rarely trees, sometimes climbing, sometimes strongly spiny, often stellate-pubescent; lvs. alt., simple or compound; infl. axillary or opp. the lvs., few- to many-fld. or fls. solitary; calyx 4–10- but mostly 5-toothed, corolla rotate to campanulate, 5-lobed, plicate in bud, showy, white, yellow, bluish, or purple, stamens usually 5, borne on the corolla, anthers connivent in a cone around style, usually opening by apical pores; fr. a 2-celled, rarely 3–4-celled berry, seeds many, more or less reniform. A taxonomically difficult genus that requires much further study.

Solanum includes important food plants, such as, the white potato, eggplant, pepino, and naranjilla; a few medicinal plants; and many ornamental species for the garden or conservatory. Most solanums are propagated by seeds, sown where the plants are to stand in the case of the annuals, but indoors for the tender greenhouse kinds. The shrubby forms for greenhouse or tropical plantings are also increased by softwood cuttings. The tuberous species are usually grown from the tubers, or from divisions of them, including at least one "eye" or bud.

aculeatissimum Jacq. [*S. ciliatum* Lam.]. LOVE APPLE, COCKROACH BERRY, SODA-APPLE NIGHTSHADE. Tender per. or shrub, to 3 ft. or more, sts. and lvs. with long, yellowish-brown prickles, to ³⁄₄ in. long,

interspersed with smaller prickles and long, deciduous, simple hairs; lvs. broadly ovate, to 6 in. long, 5–7-lobed, prickly on veins beneath; fls. in few-fld. cymes, corolla white, star-shaped, to 1 in. across; fr. burnt-orange to brownish-red, globose, to 2 in. in diam., corrugated, the skin parchmentlike when ripe. Widespread in s. U.S., trop. Amer.; introd. early into Old World tropics.

aviculare G. Forst. [*S. laciniatum* Ait.]. KANGAROO APPLE. Shrub, to 10 ft., unarmed, glabrous; lvs. lanceolate to ovate, to 12 in. long, entire to irregularly lobed; infl. a many-fld. cyme; corolla violet-blue, 1–1¹⁄₂ in. across, lobes about as long as tube, acute; fr. yellow, ovoid, with inconspicuous stone cells. New Zeal., Australia. The name *S. laciniatum* is applied to a tetraploid form with larger fls. and more abundant stone cells in the fr.

Burbankii Bitter. SUNBERRY, WONDERBERRY. Ann., to 2 ft., puberulent; lvs. ovate, 1¹⁄₂ in. long, weakly and irregularly toothed; fls. in many, few-fld., axillary cymes, corolla white, about ¹⁄₄ in. across, anthers orange-yellow; fr. black or orange, nearly ¹⁄₂ in. in diam. Of uncertain origin, introd. by Luther Burbank as "Sunberry" and "Orange Sunberry," and said to be a cross between *S. guineense* Lam., not L. and *S. villosum* Dunal, although this is now believed doubtful.

Capsicastrum Link ex Schauer. FALSE JERUSALEM CHERRY. Shrub, to 2 ft., unarmed, stellate-hairy; lvs. ovate-lanceolate, to 3 in. long, undulate; fls. in 1–3-fld. cymes, corolla white, to ¹⁄₂ in. across; fr. scarlet to orange-red, ovoid, pointed, ½ in. in diam. Brazil. Cvs. are: **'Craigii'**, fr. white or red; **'Melvinii'**, of compact form, about 1 ft. high; **'Nanum'**, dwarf; **'Pattersonii'**, probably S. *Pseudocapsicum* cv.; **'Variegatum'**, lvs. variegated.

carolinense L. HORSE NETTLE, BALL NIGHTSHADE. Rhizomatous per., to 3 ft., prickly, pubescent with stellate hairs; lvs. elliptic to ovate, to 5 in. long, sinuately toothed, prickly on veins beneath; fls. in few-fld. cymes, corolla violet to white, to ¾ in. across; fr. yellow, to ⅝ in. in diam. New Eng. to Nebr., s. to Fla. and Tex.

ciliatum: *S. aculeatissimum.*

citrullifolium A. Braun. MELON-LEAF NIGHTSHADE. Ann., to 3 ft., prickly, pubescent; lvs. 1–2-pinnatifid, to 6 in. long; fls. in racemes, corolla violet, to 1½ in. across, stamens purple, 1 longer than the others; fr. small, enclosed in a prickly calyx. Iowa and Kans., s. to Mex.

Clevelandii: a listed name of no botanical standing, probably for a cv. of *S. Pseudocapsicum,* perhaps the same as 'Cleveland Red'.

coccineum: *S. tomentosum.*

Craigii: a listed name of no botanical standing for *S. Capsicastrum* cv.

dimidiatum Raf. [*S. Torreyi* A. Gray]. WESTERN HORSE NETTLE. Per., to 3 ft., somewhat prickly, felty-hairy; lvs. ovate, to 6 in. long, 5–7-lobed; fls. in cymes, corolla violet, to 1½ in. across; fr. pale yellow, globose, 1 in. in diam. Kans. to Tex.

Donnell-Smithii J. Coult. Large woody vine, sts. with stout recurved prickles, densely spiny-hairy, the hairs tufted-stellate at tips; lvs. oblong to elliptic, usually angularly lobed, with prickles on midrib beneath; fls. in few-fld., axillary cymes, corolla white; fr. orange, ¾ in. in diam. Mex. to Salvador.

Douglasii Dunal. Suffrutescent per., 3–7 ft.; lvs. grayish-pubescent to pilose, ovate, to 4 in. long, entire to sinuate-dentate; corolla white, purple tinged, to ¾ in. across, lobes deeply cleft; fr. black, about 5/16 in. in diam. S. Calif. to Mex.

Dulcamara L. BITTERSWEET, NIGHTSHADE, POISONOUS N., DEADLY N. Shrubby climber, to 15 ft.; lvs. ovate, to 4 in. long, entire or with 2 or more basal lobes; fls. in long-stalked cymes, corolla violet, spotted green, to ½ in. across, lobes reflexed, stamens yellow; fr. scarlet, ovoid, to ½ in. long. Eurasia; naturalized and weedy in Amer. All parts of the plant are considered poisonous if eaten raw.

erianthum D. Don [*S. verbascifolium* of auth., not L.]. Shrub or tree, to 30 ft., unarmed, tomentose; lvs. ovate or elliptic, to 1 ft. long, entire, often slightly undulate; fls. in cymes, corolla white, ½ in. across; fr. yellow, globose, to ¾ in. in diam. Tropics.

galeatum André. Shrub, 6 ft. or more, stoutly spiny, velvety-pubescent; lvs. broadly ovate, to 18 in. long, sinuately toothed, purplish, with greenish, reticulate veins beneath; fls. in short-peduncled cymes, corolla pale violet, to 1½ in. across. Brazil.

giganteum Jacq. AFRICAN HOLLY. Shrub, 4–10 ft. or more in the wild, with stout prickles; lvs. oblong-lanceolate, mostly 4–8 in. long, white-tomentose beneath; fls. in many-fld. cymes, corolla pale violet to blue, to ¾ in. across; fr. bright red, globose, 5/16 in. in diam. India, Ceylon. Cult. occasionally in s. Calif. (Zone 10) for showy fr.

havanense Jacq. Shrub, 6 ft. or more, glabrous; lvs. oblong-lanceolate, to 2½ in. long, acute; fls. in 2–3-fld. cymes, corolla blue; fr. blue, ovoid. Cuba, Jamaica, Martinique.

Hendersonii Hort. ex L. H. Bailey. Allied to *S. pseudocapsicum,* possibly a hybrid, having many white fls. and orange-red fr.

hispidum Pers. [*S. Warszewiczii* Hort. Weick ex Lambertye]. DEVIL'S FIG. Shrub, to 6 ft., with short stout spines, rusty-stellate-hairy; lvs. to 1 ft. long or more, lobed; fls. in racemes, corolla white, 1½ in. across; fr. pale yellow, ½ in. across, glossy. Mex.; naturalized in Amer. and Afr. tropics.

integrifolium Poir. [*S. texanum* Dunal]. TOMATO-FRUITED EGGPLANT. Ann., to 3 ft., spiny, pubescent; lvs. ovate to oblong-ovate, to 10 in. long, sinuately toothed, often prickly along midrib above; fls. in few-fld. clusters, corolla white, to ¾ in. across; fr. scarlet or yellow, globose, to 2 in. in diam., ribbed. Tropics. May be confused with *S. aculeatissimum.*

intrusum: *S. melanocerasum.*

jasminoides Paxt. POTATO VINE. Shrubby climber, to 15 ft. or more, unarmed, glabrous; lvs. ovate-lanceolate, 1–3 in. long, entire or lower ones irregularly pinnately divided; fls. in branched cymes, corolla bluish-white, star-shaped, to 1 in. across. Brazil. Zone 10b. Cv. **'Grandiflorum'.** Fl. clusters large.

khasianum C. B. Clarke. Stout per., 2–4 ft., prickly, densely yellow-hirsute; lvs. ovate, to 8 in. long, deeply triangularly lobed, prickly on both sides; corolla ⅝ in. across, glabrous, lobes lanceolate, acuminate; fr. globose, 1 in. in diam., glabrous, the persistent calyx hirsute, not prickly. W. Assam.

laciniatum: *S. aviculare.*

lanceolatum Cav. Shrub, to 8 ft. or more, sparingly prickly, pubescent; lvs. linear-lanceolate to narrowly lanceolate, to 9 in. long, acute or obtuse; infl. many-fld., densely pubescent, corolla lavender-blue, to 1 in. across; fr. orange, globose, small. Mex.

laurifolium: *S. subinerme.*

macranthum Dunal. POTATO TREE, BRAZILIAN P.T. Often a shrub, to 6 ft. or more in cult., but a tree to 30 ft. in the tropics, spiny, pubescent; lvs. broadly ovate, to 15 in. long, sinuately toothed or lobed; infl. axillary, to 5 in. long; corolla usually dark bluish-violet, fading to nearly white, to 2 in. across. Brazil. Zone 10b.

mammosum L. NIPPLEFRUIT. Small shrub, usually cult. as an ann., to 3 ft., prickly, downy-pubescent; lvs. broadly ovate, 4–6 in. long, irregularly cut into short blunt lobes; fls. solitary or few in axillary cymes, corolla violet, about 1½ in. across; fr. yellow or orange, bluntly conical, about 2 in. long, frequently with nipplelike basal lobes. Lowland, trop. Amer. Cult. widely in trop. and warm temp. regions for its ornamental fr., which is considered poisonous to eat.

marginatum L.f. Shrub, to 8 ft., prickly, pubescent; lvs. ovate, to 8 in. long, sinuately lobed or toothed, densely white-stellate-pubescent, becoming glabrous above; calyx spiny, persistent, corolla white, veined with violet, to 1¼ in. across; fr. yellow, to 1¾ in. in diam. N. Afr.

melanocerasum All. [*S. intrusum* Soria; *S. nigrum* var. *guineense* L.]. GARDEN HUCKLEBERRY. Ann., to 2½ ft.; lvs. broadly ovate, 3–7 in. long, entire to subentire, petioles 1–3 in. long; corolla white, thick, about ⅜ in. across, anthers brown; fr. black, ½–⅝ in. in diam. Perhaps of garden origin; cult. widely in W. Trop. Afr. Ripe berries edible, with flavor of a bitter tomato; cooked as a vegetable or used in preserves and pies.

Melongena L. Tender per. herb or shrub, often cult. as ann., to 3 ft., spiny, pubescent; lvs. ovate, to 9 in. long, angled or lobed; fls. usually solitary, corolla violet-purple, to 1½ in. across; fr. blackish-purple, to 6 in. long. Afr., Asia. Many cvs. are known in the Old World but only a few are cult. in this country. Prop. by seeds, requiring a long growing season. For cult. see *Eggplant.* Var. **esculentum** Nees. EGGPLANT, JEW'S APPLE, MAD A., MELONGENE, AUBERGINE. Bushy, erect per., cult. as an ann., rarely spiny, more or less scurfy-tomentose; fr. usually purplish-black but white, yellowish, or striped, in some cvs., ovoid, oblong, or obovoid, 2–12 in. long, glossy. Var. **serpentinum** L. H. Bailey. SNAKE EGGPLANT. Fr. about 10–15 in. long, elongate, curled at one end.

muricatum Ait. PEPINO, MELON SHRUB, PEAR MELON, MELON PEAR. Erect per. or subshrub, 2–3 ft., spiny, young growth gray- to white-hairy; lvs. oblong to ovate-lanceolate, 2–3 in. long, entire, often undulate, finely pubescent or silky, long-petioled; corolla bright blue, ½–¾ in. across; fr. violet-purple, ovoid, 4–6 in. long, flesh firm, yellow, acid, aromatic. Andes. Eaten fresh.

muticum N. E. Br. Shrub, to 5 ft., sts. angular, unarmed, pilose; lvs. lanceolate-undulate, 1½–3½ in. long, softly pubescent with simple hairs; infls. axillary, cymose; corolla violet, broadly funnelform, 1–1½ in. across, lobes reduced to apiculate tips projecting beyond the broad spreading limb; fr. reddish, ½ in. in diam. Paraguay.

nigrum L. COMMON NIGHTSHADE, BLACK N., POISONBERRY. Prostrate or erect ann., to 2½ ft.; lvs. ovate to ovate-lanceolate, mostly 4–7 in. long, entire or angularly lobed, undulate, glossy above; fls. white, ¼ in. across, usually in axillary cymes; fr. dull black, rarely greenish, ¼ in. in diam. Eur.; now cosmopolitan. Often reported as a poisonous plant, but cooked locally as a potherb and ripe berries made into pies and preserves. Var. **guineense:** *S. melanocerasum.*

Pattersonii: a listed name of no botanical standing for *C. Pseudocapsicum* cv.

Pseudocapsicum L. JERUSALEM CHERRY. Erect shrub, to 4 ft., glabrous; lvs. oblong to oblanceolate, 2–4 in. long, undulate, glossy above; fls. solitary or few at a node, corolla white, ⅝ in. across; fr. scarlet or yellow, globose, ½ in. in diam., long-persistent. Old World; naturalized in tropics and subtropics, and Zone 9 in U.S. Pot plant popular for showy fr., which is poisonous if eaten. Cv. **'Pattersonii'.** Spreading, dwarf habit, very heavily fruiting. Other cvs. are **'Clevelandii'**, **'Nanum'**, and **'Tom Thumb'.**

pseudolycioides Rusby. Much-branched shrub, to 10 ft., unarmed, glabrous; lvs. oblong to oblanceolate, to 1 in. long, obtuse, entire, somewhat fleshy; corolla blue, ¾ in. across; fr. depressed-globose, 5/16 in. in diam. Peru.

quitoense Lam. NARANJILLA, LULO. Coarse per. subshrub, to 6–8 ft., densely stellate-pubescent when young, sts. and lvs. with or without spines, with strong purple color; lvs. broadly ovate, 8–20 in. long, angular-sinuate, veins bright purple, especially when young; fls. in axillary cymes, more or less hidden by foliage, corolla white, about ¼ in. across; fr. orange, tomato-shaped, to 1½ in. in diam. or more, with deciduous hairs, flesh greenish. N. Andes. Planted locally in tropics of New World, particularly Colombia, Ecuador, and Costa Rica, for a refreshing juice extracted from the fresh fr. Heavy feeder, requiring partial shade and high humidity. Grows best at elevations of 3,000-5,800 ft. where native. Sometimes grown as an ornamental foliage plant in conservatories or outdoors in Zone 10b where subject to nematodes.

Rantonnetii Carrière. BLUE POTATO BUSH. Shrub, to 6 ft., unarmed, nearly glabrous; lvs. ovate, to 4 in. long, mostly acuminate, undulate; fls. in axillary cymes, corolla dark blue or violet, with paler eye, scarcely ½ in. across; fr. red, cordate, to 1 in. long, drooping. Argentina to Paraguay. Cv. **'Grandiflorum'.** Corolla to 1 in. across; most frequent in cult.

Seaforthianum Andr. Slender vine, to 20 ft. high, glabrous; lvs. 4–8 in. long, thin, usually pinnate, lfts. 3–9, mostly unequal or lvs. unequally pinnatifid; fls. in many-fld. axillary cymes, showy, corolla blue to purple, star-shaped, about 1 in. across; fr. scarlet, globose, to 5/16 in. in diam. Trop. Amer.

sisymbriifolium Lam. STICKY NIGHTSHADE. Ann., to 4 ft., spiny, sticky-pubescent; lvs. pinnately lobed, sinuate or toothed; fls. pale blue to white, 1¼ in. across; fr. red, globose, about ½ in. in diam. Trop. Amer.; adventive in e. U.S.

sodomeum L. APPLE OF SODOM, YELLOW POPOLO, DEAD SEA APPLE. Shrub, to 6 ft., spiny, pubescent; lvs. pinnate, lfts. entire, undulate; fls. in cymes, corolla violet, about 1 in. across; fr. yellow, globose, about 1½ in. in diam., glossy. Medit. region. Somewhat weedy.

subinerme Jacq. [*S. laurifolium* Mill.]. Shrub, to 6 ft., with a few prickles, pubescent; lvs. ovate to oblong, to 4 in. long, acuminate, more or less heavily pubescent beneath, glabrous above; infl. axillary, many-fld.; corolla blue; fr. yellow. Caribbean region.

texanum: *S. integrifolium.*

tomentosum L. [*S. coccineum* Jacq.]. Ann., prickly, densely felty-pubescent, mostly tawny; lvs. orbicular to broadly ovate, mostly 1–3 in. long, obtuse, angularly to sinuately shallow-lobed; fls. in small axillary cymes, corolla pale blue, ½ in. across; fr. dull orange, about ⅝ in. in diam., densely tomentose, becoming glabrous at maturity. Trop. Amer.

Torreyi: *S. dimidiatum.*

tuberosum L. POTATO, WHITE P., IRISH P. Plants with edible underground tubers, sts. weak, to 3 ft. long, unarmed; lvs. pinnate, to 10 in. long, lfts. ovate, with smaller ones between; fls. in clusters, corolla white or bluish, about 1 in. across; fr. yellowish or green, globose, to ¾ in. in diam. Probably Andes. Widely cult. in temp. regions as one of the world's most important food plants. Many cvs. are grown. For culture see *Potato.*

umbelliferum Eschsch. Spreading subshrub, to 3½ ft., broader than high; lvs. elliptic-ovate, entire or weakly lobed at base, pubescent; corolla mostly blue, about ¾ in. across, shallowly angular-lobed; fr. whitish, about ⅝ in. in diam. Calif.

verbascifolium L.: a name for a prickly plant, but of otherwise uncertain application; the sp. long known by this name is *S. erianthum.*

Wallacei (A. Gray) S. Parish. Spreading subshrub, 3–7 ft., tawny-villous, somewhat viscid; lvs. oblong-ovate, 1½–5 in. long, acute, thickish; fls. in cymes, corolla purplish-blue, to 1½ in. across; fr. dark purple, globose, to 1 in. in diam. Santa Catalina and Guadalupe Is.

Warszewiczii: *S. hispidum.*

Wendlandii Hook.f. POTATO VINE, GIANT POTATO CREEPER, PARADISE FLOWER. Shrubby climber, prickly, glabrous; lvs. usually pinnate, 4–10 in. long, with a large terminal lft., or upper lvs. simple; fls. in branched clusters, corolla lilac-blue, to 2½ in. across; fr. globose to ovoid, 3–4 in. in diam. Costa Rica. Cult. in tropics, in Zone 10, or under glass. CV. **'Albescens'.** Fls. whitish.

Xantii A. Gray. Pubescent shrub, with erect or decumbent sts. to 2 ft. long; lvs. ovate, to 1¾ in. long, entire or lobed; fls. in cymes, corolla violet, to 1 in. across; fr. green or purplish, globose. Calif. Occasionally cult.

SOLDANELLA L. *Primulaceae.* About 6 or 8 spp. of scapose per. herbs, native in the mts. of Eur.; lvs. simple, basal, long-petioled, entire; fls. blue, violet, or rarely white, nodding, solitary, or in umbels; calyx 5-parted, corolla campanulate, 5-parted, corolla lobes fringed, stamens 5; fr. a caps.

Sometimes grown in rock gardens; propagated by division or seeds.

alpina L. To 6 in.; lvs. reniform, to 1½ in. across; fls. pale blue, ½ in. long, in 1–3-fld. umbels. Spring. Pyrenees, Alps. Cv. **'Alba'.** Fls. white.

carpatica: *S. hungarica.*

hungarica Simonk. [*S. carpatica* Vierh.]. To 4 in.; lvs. orbicular-reniform, to 1 in. across; fls. bluish, to ¾ in. long, in 1–3-fld. umbels. Spring. Carpathian Mts. to Balkans.

minima Hoppe ex Sturm. To 4 in.; lvs. orbicular-ovate, ⅜ in. across; fls. pale bluish-purple, with darker markings, corolla to ½ in. long, fringed about ⅓ its length, pedicels hairy. Spring. S. Alps.

montana Willd. To 6 in.; lvs. orbicular, to 2½ in. across, deeply cordate at base, petiole glandular-hairy; fls. blue to bluish-lilac, to ¾ in. long, in 3–10-fld. umbels. Spring–summer. Alps.

pindicola Hausskn. To 3½ in.; lvs. orbicular, to 1½ in. across, sky-blue beneath, petiole glabrous; fls. rose-lilac, in 1–3-fld. umbels, pedicels minutely glandular-hairy. Albania, Greece.

pusilla Baumg. To 6 in.; lvs. orbicular, to ½ in. across; fls. blue to violet, ½ in. long, solitary. Spring–late spring. Alps. Differs from *S. minima* in having pedicels rough, but nonhairy.

villosa Darracq. Lvs. orbicular, petioles hairy; fls. blue, in 1–4-fld. umbels. Pyrenees.

SOLEIROLIA Gaud.-Beaup. [*Helxine* Req., not L.]. *Urticaceae.* One sp., a creeping, monoecious herb, native to w. Medit. Is. and Italy; lvs. small, alt.; fls. minute, solitary, axillary, male fls. with calyx 4-parted, stamens 4, female fls. with calyx tubular, 4-lobed; fr. an achene enclosed by the calyx and 1–2 bracts.

Useful as a ground cover in greenhouses and in mild climates, though apt to become a weed. Propagated by cuttings of rooting stems.

Soleirolii (Req.) Dandy [*Helxine Soleirolii* Req.]. BABY'S-TEARS, POLLYANNA VINE, ANGEL'S-TEARS, IRISH MOSS, JAPANESE M., CORSICAN-CURSE, CORSICAN CARPET PLANT, PEACE-IN-THE-HOME, MIND-YOUR-OWN-BUSINESS. Delicate, sparsely hairy, mat-forming per.; lvs. nearly orbicular, about ¼ in. across, very shortly petioled.

SOLENANTHUS Ledeb. *Boraginaceae.* About 12 spp. of hairy, bien. and per. herbs, native to s. and e. Eur. and w. Asia; lvs. simple, alt., basal and cauline; fls. rose to blue, in axillary panicled cymes, calyx deeply 5-lobed, corolla with 5 erect lobes, throat with scales, stamens 5, exserted; fr. of 4 spiny, horizontal nutlets.

Propagated by division or seeds. Useful in the hardy border or among shrubbery.

apenninus (L.) Hohen. Sts. hollow, to 3 ft.; basal lvs. oblong-ovate or elliptic, st. lvs. linear, sessile; fls. blue to purple, 5/16 in. long, scales hairy. Italy.

SOLENOMELUS Miers. *Iridaceae.* Three spp. of herbs, native to Chile, allied to *Sisyrinchium,* but having fls. with a perianth tube, and style not divided, with a single capitate stigma.

chilensis Miers. GOLD-FLOWER-OF-CHILE. Per., with short rhizomes, sts. nearly cylindrical, 1–1½ ft. with 1–3 long-peduncled infls.; lvs. grasslike, 6–12 in. long; fls. yellow, perianth 1 in. long, segms. narrowly oblanceolate, ½ in. long, filaments united into a tube, pubescent; caps. enclosed by spathe.

SOLENOSTEMON Schumach. & Thonn. *Labiatae.* About 10 spp. of erect herbs of trop. Afr.; sts. mostly square in cross section; lvs. opp., often toothed, petioled; fls. small, in 6- to many-fld. verticillasters arranged in elongate racemes, calyx ovoid-campanulate, nearly equally 2-lipped, corolla tube exserted, limb 2-lipped, upper lip 4-toothed, lower lip elongate-concave, stamens 4, in 2 pairs, filaments united at base, anthers 1-celled; fr. of 4 glabrous nutlets. Similar to *Coleus* and *Plectranthus,* but calyx nearly equally 2-lipped.

zambesiacus Bak. Stout, pubescent per.; lvs. ovate-cordate, to 5 in. long, crenate, glabrescent to pubescent, petioled; racemes in panicles; calyx campanulate, to nearly 3/16 in. long, corolla to 5/16 in. long. Trop. Afr.

SOLIDAGO L. GOLDENROD. *Compositae* (Aster Tribe). About 130 spp. of summer- and autumn-flowering per. herbs, native chiefly to N. Amer., with a few spp. in Eur., Asia, the Azores, and S. Amer., sts. from a rhizome or root crown; lvs. alt., simple, entire or toothed; fl. heads radiate, small, many in racemes, corymbs, panicles, or sometimes thyrses, involucre nearly cylindrical to campanulate, involucral bracts in few rows, nearly equal or imbricate, receptacle flat or slightly convex, naked, pitted; disc fls. bisexual, fertile, yellow, ray fls. female, fertile, usually yellow; achenes angled or nearly cylindrical, several-nerved, pappus of many, usually equal, capillary bristles.

The goldenrods improve under cultivation, but some of them become weedy if the soil is too rich. They are easily grown from seeds, blooming the second year; mature plants may be divided in spring or in autumn. Any number of species may occasionally be transferred to home grounds. They are often mistakenly considered a cause of hayfever.

algida: *S. multiradiata.*

altissima L. Rhizomatous per., to 6½ ft., sts. gray with short hairs; lvs. many, lanceolate to elliptic-lanceolate, to 6 in. long, long-acuminate, scabrous above, gray-hairy beneath, 3-nerved, remotely serrate; heads many in a dense pyramidal panicle with 1-sided, spreading brs. Que. to Fla., w. to N. Dak., Kans., and Ariz.

bicolor L. SILVERROD, WHITE G. Fibrous-rooted per., to 4 ft., sts. gray with soft hairs; basal lvs. oblanceolate to elliptic, to 8 in. long including the petiole, thickish, serrate to crenate, st. lvs. reduced upward, sessile, elliptic to lanceolate-elliptic or rhombic; heads in an elongated, interrupted, spikelike panicle; ray fls. whitish or cream-colored. Nov. Sc. to Wisc., s. to N.C. and Ark.

brachystachys: a listed name of no botanical standing for *S. Virgaurea.*

caesia L. WREATH G., BLUE-STEM G. Slender per., to 3 ft., sts. glabrous and glaucous, simple to paniculately branched, arching; basal and lowest st. lvs. deciduous, upper lvs. many, lanceolate to lanceolate-elliptic or oblong, to 4¾ in. long, tapering to sessile base, sharply serrate; heads in loose, axillary clusters sometimes in loose, leafy panicles. Nov. Sc. to Wisc., s. to Fla. and Tex.

californica Nutt. CALIFORNIA G. Rhizomatous per., to 4 ft., densely ashy-gray-pubescent; basal and lowest st. lvs. spatulate to obovate or elliptic, to 4¾ in. long, firm, serrate to crenate, upper st. lvs. much-reduced, sessile, elliptic, entire; heads in a dense, narrow thyrse or sometimes in a pyramidal panicle with spreading brs. Sw. Ore. to Baja Calif.

canadensis L. Rhizomatous per., to 5 ft., without a root crown, sts. hairy at least above middle; basal and lowest st. lvs. deciduous, upper lvs. many, lanceolate-linear to elliptic-lanceolate or narrowly elliptic, to 6 in. long, long-attenuate, 3-nerved, glabrous or scabrous above, pubescent beneath, sharply serrate, upper lvs. only slightly reduced upward; heads in panicles with 1-sided, recurved brs. Nfld. to Man., s. to Va., Ill., and Colo. Subsp. **elongata** (Nutt.) Keck [*S. elongata* Nutt.]. Sts. hairy, including infl.; lvs. lanceolate to oblong-lanceolate, to 4¾ in. long; heads in a dense, usually rhombic panicle, the lower brs. not 1-sided or recurved. B.C. to cent. Calif., e. to Rocky Mts.; Baja Calif.

Cutleri Fern. [*S. Virgaurea* var. *alpina* Bigel.]. Commonly tufted per., to 14 in.; basal lvs. oblanceolate to spatulate-obovate, to 6 in. long including petiole, glabrous except for the ciliate petiole, margins crenate to serrate, st. lvs. few, successively reduced upward, the uppermost sessile; heads in a racemose to corymbose, often leafy thyrse or panicle. Alpine, Me. to n. N.Y.

Drummondii Torr. & A. Gray. Per., to 3¼ ft., with a branched root crown, sts. with short, spreading hairs; basal and lowest st. lvs. deciduous, other lvs. ovate to elliptic-ovate, to 3½ in. long, finely velvety-hairy, serrate; heads in panicles with 1-sided, recurved brs. Ill., Mo., Ark., La.

elongata: *S. canadensis* subsp.

flexicaulis L. [*S. latifolia* A. Gray]. Rhizomatous per., to 4 ft., sts. zigzag, striate-angled and grooved, glabrous in lower part; basal and lowest st. lvs. usually deciduous, other lvs. elliptic to ovate, to 6 in. long, abruptly contracted to winged petiole, acuminate, glabrous or sparsely hairy above, hirsute beneath, sharply toothed; heads in axillary clusters. Nov. Sc. to N. Dak., s. to Ga. and Ark.

glaberrima: *S. missouriensis* var. *fasciculata.*

hispida Muhlenb. Per., to 3½ ft., with a stout, branched root crown, usually spreading-hirsute; basal and lowest st. lvs. persistent, oblanceolate to obovate or elliptic, to 8 in. long including petiole, entire to toothed, st. lvs. successively reduced upward, the uppermost sessile; heads in a leafy-bracted, simple or paniculate thyrse. Nfld. to N. Dak., s. to Ga. and Ark.

latifolia: *S. flexicaulis.*

microcephala (Greene) Bush [*S. minor* (Michx.) Fern., not Mill.]. Slender, rhizomatous per., to 3 ft., sts. glabrous or sometimes puberulent; basal and lowest st. lvs. deciduous, other lvs. nearly needlelike to filiform-subulate, to 2⅜ in. long, glabrous or with spreading hairs beneath, often with clusters of lvs. in their axils; heads in many small corymbs. N.J. to Fla. and Miss.

minor: see *S. microcephala.*

missouriensis Nutt. Rhizomatous per., to 2½ ft., glabrous; lowest lvs. oblanceolate, petioled, to 8 in. long, scabrid-ciliate, soon deciduous, upper lvs. reduced, lanceolate to linear, tapering to an essentially sessile base, often bearing reduced lf. clusters in their axils; heads in panicles with 1-sided, recurved brs. B.C. to Calif., e. to Great Plains and Ariz. Var. **fasciculata** Holzing. [*S. glaberrima* M. Martens]. Plants to 3½ ft.; brs. of infl. arched-recurving. Mich. to Idaho, s. to New Mex., Tex., and Tenn. See also × *Solidaster luteus.*

mollis Bartl. Stout, rhizomatous per., to 2 ft., gray-pubescent; basal lvs. absent, lower lvs. oblanceolate, to 4 in. long, lvs. successively reduced upward, the uppermost elliptic, sessile, all firm, 3-nerved; heads in a compact thyrse or panicle, with lower brs. often 1-sided and recurved. Man. and w. Minn., w. to Mont., s. to Okla. and New Mex.

multiradiata Ait. [*S. algida* Piper; *S. scopulorum* (A. Gray) A. Nels.]. Tufted per., to 1½ ft., with a branched root crown or short, woody rhizome; basal lvs. oblanceolate to elliptic, to 4 in. long, tapering to petiole, glabrous, margins serrate to serrate-crenate, scabrous, st. lvs. lanceolate to spatulate, sessile, entire; heads usually in a dense corymb. Alaska and adjacent Siberia to Lab., s. to Calif. and s. in the Rocky Mts. to Ariz. and New Mex.

nemoralis Ait. [*S. pulcherrima* A. Nels.]. Clump-forming per., to 3½ ft., with a branched root crown, pubescent with minute, dense, spreading hairs; basal lvs. persistent, oblanceolate to spatulate-obovate, to 9 in. long including petiole, toothed, st. lvs. successively reduced upward; heads in panicles with 1-sided, recurved brs. Nov. Sc. to Alta., s. to Fla., Ga., and Tex. Var. **decemflora** (DC.) Fern. [var. *longipetiolata* (Mackenz. & Bush) Palmer & Steyerm.]. Basal lvs. linear-lanceolate to narrowly lanceolate, entire to shallowly toothed, st. lvs. linear to linear-oblanceolate. Ont. to Alta., s. to Ky., Ark., Tex., and Ariz. Var. **longipetiolata:** var. *decemflora.*

odora Ait. SWEET G. Per., to 5 ft., with stout root crown, sts. glabrous or with lines of hairs; basal lvs. and lowest st. lvs. reduced and deciduous, other lvs. sessile, many, linear-lanceolate to oblong-lanceolate or lanceolate, to 4 in. long, successively reduced upward, glabrous, scabrous on margins, usually with the odor of anise when bruised; heads in large panicles with 1-sided, recurved brs. New Hamp. to Fla., Okla., and Tex. Lvs. have been used as a tea.

pallida (T. C. Porter) Rydb. Glabrous per., to 2½ ft.; basal lvs. obovate to lanceolate, to 6 in. long, pale, entire, upper lvs. successively reduced; heads in a dense, elongated panicle. S. Dak., Nebr., and Colo.

petiolaris Ait. [*S. Wardii* Britt.]. Rhizomatous per., to 5 ft., sts. stiff, erect, minutely gray-pubescent; basal and lowest st. lvs. soon deciduous, other lvs. essentially sessile, linear-lanceolate to lanceolate, elliptic, or ovate, to 6 in. long, firm, glutinous, glabrous or scabrous, entire or with few teeth; heads usually in a narrow, elongate, spicate infl., less commonly panicled. N.C., cent. Mo., and Nebr., s. to Fla. and Tex.

puberula Nutt. Per., to 3½ ft., with a branched root crown, minutely puberulent; basal and lowest st. lvs. usually persistent, oblanceolate to elliptic or obovate, to 6 in. long including petiole, margins mostly serrate-dentate, upper lvs. successively reduced upward, the uppermost linear-lanceolate and sessile; heads in a dense, often leafy-bracted thyrse. Nov. Sc. and Que., s. to Fla. and Miss.

pulcherrima: *S. nemoralis.*

rigida L. Coarse, rhizomatous per., to 5 ft., usually densely pubescent with spreading hairs; basal lvs. elliptic to lanceolate or ovate, the blades to 1 ft. long on petioles as long as blade or sometimes longer, st. lvs. reduced, ovate, to 4 in. long, all lvs. entire or slightly serrate; heads in dense corymbs. Mass. to Sask., s. to Ga., La., and Tex.

rugosa Mill. Rhizomatous per., to 6 ft., sometimes taller, sts. very leafy, usually with spreading hairs; basal and lowest st. lvs. reduced and deciduous, other lvs. many, crowded, lanceolate to elliptic or ovate, to 5 in. long, rugose-veiny, not 3-nerved, glabrous or scabrous above, hairy beneath especially on veins, usually serrate to dentate; heads in large panicles with 1-sided, recurved brs. Nfld. to Ont., s. to W. Va. and Ky.

scopulorum: *S. multiradiata.*

sempervirens L. SEASIDE G. Somewhat succulent per., to 8 ft., essentially glabrous; basal lvs. persistent, oblanceolate to spatulate-oblong, to 16 in. long, petioled, st. lvs. oblong-lanceolate to lanceolate, the uppermost sessile; heads in large panicles with 1-sided, recurved brs. Coastal, w. Nfld. to N.J., locally in Va.

spathulata DC. Stout per., to 2 ft., with a root crown or woody rhizome, glabrous, strongly aromatic; basal lvs. spatulate-oblanceolate to obovate, to 6 in. long including petiole, crenate-serrate, st. lvs. successively reduced upward, the uppermost almost sessile; heads in simple or compound thyrses, the thyrses sometimes racemose. Coastal, cent. Calif. to s. Ore. Var. **nana** (A. Gray) Cronq. To 6 in., less aromatic; basal lvs. mostly spatulate or obovate; infl. short, compact. Wash. and n. Ore., and in Rocky Mts. from Sask. to Utah and New Mex.

Var. **neomexicana** (A. Gray) Cronq. Plants to 2½ ft., not very aromatic; basal lvs. mostly oblanceolate; infl. elongate, mostly spicate-thyrsoid to subracemose. Wash. and Sask. to New Mex.

spectabilis (D. C. Eat.) A. Gray. Rather stout, glabrous per., to 4 ft., with short woody rhizome or root crown; basal lvs. oblanceolate, to 11 in. long including the tapering, winged, clasping petiole, st. lvs. reduced upward, linear-lanceolate, all entire or upper lvs. scabrid-ciliate; heads in a dense, oblong panicle usually less than 4 in. long. Se. Ore., s. to Death Valley (Calif.), e. to Utah.

stricta Ait. Glabrous per., to 3 ft., with rhizomes producing slender stolons, sts. simple, wandlike, straight; basal lvs. spatulate to oblanceolate, to 1 ft. long including petiole, entire to obscurely serrate, st. lvs. abruptly reduced upward, sessile; heads in spikelike panicles, the panicle tip sometimes nodding, the lower brs. sometimes 1-sided and recurved. Coastal, N.J. to Fla., e. to Tex.; also W. Indies.

Virgaurea L. [*S. brachystachys* Hort.]. EUROPEAN G. Per., to 3 ft., sts. erect, often little-branched; basal lvs. oblanceolate to obovate or elliptic, to 4 in. long, usually toothed, on petioles as long as or longer than the blades, st. lvs. successively reduced and becoming short-petioled, the uppermost sessile; heads to ⅜ in. across, in a dense terminal thyrse. Eur., Asia, N. Afr. Subsp. **alpestris** (Waldst. & Kit.) Gaudin. Per., to 8 in.; lvs. lanceolate; heads to ¾ in. across, in a loose raceme or little-branched panicle. Mts., Eur. Sometimes used medicinally. Var. **alpina**: *S. Cutleri.*

Wardii: *S. petiolaris.*

×**SOLIDASTER** Wehrh. [×*Asterago* T. H. Everett]: *Aster* × *Solidago. Compositae* (Aster Tribe). Bigeneric hybrids intermediate in character between the parent genera. Only 1 sp., of hort. origin, is known at present.

hybridus: ×*S. luteus.*

luteus M. L. Green ex Dress [×*S. hybridus.* Wehrh. (not validly publ.); *Aster hybridus luteus* Hort.; *A. luteus* Hort.; ×*Asterago lutea* T. H. Everett (not validly publ.)]: *Aster ptarmicoides* × unknown sp. of *Solidago.* Per., to 2½ ft., scabrous; lvs. lanceolate, to 6 in. long, remotely serrate; heads ⁵⁄₁₆ in. across, many, in a much-branched corymbose panicle, disc fls. golden-yellow, ray fls. canary-yellow. Originated in nurseries of Leonard Lille, Lyon, France, 1910. In the past has sometimes been mistakenly listed as *Solidago missouriensis.*

SOLISIA: *MAMMILLARIA* subgenus *Solisia.* **S. pectinata**: *M. pectinifera.*

SOLLYA Lindl. *Pittosporaceae.* Three spp. of evergreen, climbing shrubs, native to Australia; lvs. alt., simple; fls. small, blue, nodding, in terminal cymes, anthers coming together around style, longer than filaments, ovary 2-celled; fr. a berry.

One species, *S. heterophylla*, is grown in the greenhouse in the North and outdoors in the South where it makes a good cover for banks or fences. Propagated by seeds and cuttings under glass.

fusiformis: *S. heterophylla.*

heterophylla Lindl. [*S. fusiformis* Payer; *S. fusiformis* (Labill.) Briq.]. BLUEBELL CREEPER, AUSTRALIAN B.C., AUSTRALIAN BLUE-BELLS. To 6 ft. or more, twining; lvs. variable, from narrow-lanceolate to oblong, to 2 in. long, much paler beneath; fls. to ½ in. long.

SONERILA Roxb. *Melastomataceae.* Over 100 spp. of herbs or subshrubs, native to trop. Asia; lvs. simple, 3–5-nerved, often ornamental; fls. showy, in racemes or spikes, 3-merous, ovary 3-sided or 3-winged; fr. a caps.

Grown under glass with high humidity and at a temperature of about 75° F. Propagated by well-ripened cuttings, division, and seeds.

margaritacea Lindl. Herb; lvs. ovate-lanceolate, purplish beneath, with rows of puckered, pearly spots between the nerves; fls. rose-lavender, to ½ in. across. Java to Burma. Cv. 'Argentea'. Lvs. wine-red, densely overlaid with silver. Cv. 'Hendersonii'. Lvs. coppery-red, speckled with silver dots above, uniformly purple beneath.

SOPHORA L. *Leguminosae* (subfamily *Faboideae).* About 50 spp. or more of mostly woody plants of wide distribution; lvs. alt., odd-pinnate; fls. in terminal panicles or racemes, papilionaceous, stamens 10, separate; fr. a cylindrical or 4-winged legume constricted between seeds, tardily or not at all dehiscent.

Sophoras, often showy in bloom, are planted as ornamentals; the evergreen species are hardy only in the South. Propagated by seeds, greenwood cuttings, layers, and grafts.

affinis Torr. & A. Gray. Round-headed tree, to 20 ft.; lfts. in 6–9 pairs, elliptic, to 1½ in. long, blunt; fls. white, tinged pinkish, ½ in.

long, in slender racemes to 6 in. long; fr. to 3 in. long, black, pubescent. Ark. and Tex. Zone 8.

chrysophylla (Salisb.) Seem. MAMANE. Densely leafy, deciduous shrub, to 10 ft., pubescent; lfts. in 7–9 pairs, obovate, to 1¼ in. long, retuse; fls. bright yellow, ¾ in. long, in short axillary racemes, stamens exserted; fr. to 5 in. long, strongly 4-winged. Hawaii. Zone 10b. Wood hard and durable.

Davidii (Franch.) Skeels [*S. viciifolia* Hance]. Deciduous shrub, to 8 ft.; lfts. in 6–9 pairs, elliptic, to ⅜ in. long, blunt; fls. bluish-violet to nearly white, to ¾ in. long, in 6–12-fld. racemes; fr. to 2 in. long. China. Zone 5.

grandiflora: *S. tetraptera;* but material offered as *S. grandiflora* may be misidentified.

japonica L. JAPANESE PAGODA TREE, CHINESE SCHOLAR TREE. Round-headed, deciduous tree, to 80 ft.; lfts. in 3–8 pairs, ovate to lanceolate-ovate, glaucous beneath, to 2 in. long, acute; fls. yellowish-white, ½ in. long, in loose panicles to 15 in. long; fr. to 3 in. long. Late summer. China and Korea. Zone 5. Wood, bark, and fr. yield yellow dye. Cv. 'Pendula' [var. *pendula* Loud.]. WEEPING PAGODA TREE. Brs. pendent. Cv. 'Tortuosa'. Brs. twisted. Cv. 'Violacea' [var. *violacea* Carrière; *S. violacea* Hort. ex Koehne, not Thwaites]. Very late-flowering, fls. with wings and keel petals tinged purplish.

microphylla Ait. [*S. tetraptera* var. *microphylla* (Ait.) Hook.f.]. Similar to *S. tetraptera*, but lfts. less than ⁵⁄₁₆ in. long, fls. to 1¾ in. long with standard almost as long as wings. New Zeal. Zone 8, where summers are cool. Var. **longicarinata** (Simps.) Allan [*S. Treadwellii* Hort.]. To 16 ft.; lfts. smaller, about ⅛ in. long; fls. to 2 in. long, lemon-yellow.

mollis (R. C. Grah. ex Royle) Bak. Low, deciduous shrub, brs., lfts., and calyces gray-downy; lfts. in 10–12 pairs, stiff, to ¾ in. long, emarginate, pale gray-green; fls. before lvs., yellow, to ¾ in. long, in abundant racemes to 3 in. long; fr. to 4 in. long, glabrous, each segm. 4-winged. Himalayas.

prostrata J. Buchan. Prostrate or ascending shrub, to 6 ft. high; lvs. to 1 in. long, lfts. in 8 pairs, oblong, ³⁄₁₆ in. long; fls. orange to brownish-yellow, rarely bright yellow, to ¾ in. long, 1–3 together on slender silky-hairy peduncles; fr. very narrowly winged, 1–2 in. long. New Zeal. Zone 8, where summers are cool.

secundiflora (Ort.) Lag. ex DC. MESCAL BEAN, FRIJOLITO. To 50 ft., evergreen; lfts. in 3–5 pairs, to 2 in. long, silky-hairy beneath; fls. violet-blue, 1 in. long, fragrant; fr. woody, to 8 in. long, seeds bright red. Tex., New Mex., n. Mex. Seeds used in making necklaces.

tetraptera J. F. Mill. [*S. grandiflora* (Salisb.) Skottsb.]. KOWHAI. Tree, to 40 ft., young branchlets yellowish-tomentose; lvs. 6 in. long or more, lfts. in 10–20 pairs, to 1⁵⁄₁₆ in. long, silky-hairy; fls. golden-yellow, to 2 in. long, in 4–10-fld. racemes, standard shorter than wings; fr. broadly winged, to 8 in. long. New Zeal., Chile. Zone 8, where summers are cool. Var. **microphylla**: *S. microphylla.*

tomentosa L. SILVERBUSH. Tall shrub or small tree, white-pubescent throughout; lfts. to 9 pairs, broadly ovate to obovate, 1–2 in. long, obtuse or retuse; fls. pale yellow, in loose racemes 6 in. long, standard reflexed, ¾ in. across; fr. to 6 in. long, indehiscent. Seashores, Old World tropics. Zone 10b.

Treadwellii: a listed name of no botanical standing for *S. microphylla* var. *longicarinata.*

viciifolia: *S. Davidii.*

violacea: see *S. japonica* cv.

×**SOPHROCATTLEYA** Rolfe: *Cattleya* × *Sophronitis. Orchidaceae.* Bigeneric hybrids, intermediate in character between the parents.

×**SOPHROLAELIOCATTLEYA** Hurst. *Orchidaceae.* Trigeneric hybrids involving *Cattleya, Laelia,* and *Sophronitis.*

SOPHRONITIS Lindl. *Orchidaceae.* Six spp. of dwarf epiphytes, native to Brazil; pseudobulbs close together, 1-lvd.; lvs. leathery; peduncle slender, terminal, usually 1-fld.; sepals and petals similar, lip erect, sessile on base of column, column short, with petal-like wing on each side of stigmatic cavity, pollinia 8. For structure of fl. see *Orchidaceae.*

Grown mostly in shallow pans close to the greenhouse roof. For culture see *Orchids.*

cernua Lindl. Pseudobulbs nearly cylindrical, ½ in. long; lvs. elliptic-oblong, 1 in. long; peduncles 2–3-fld.; fls. small, ¼ in. across, bright cinnabar-red, with base of lip and column orange-yellow, sepals elliptic, petals ovate, lip ovate, convolute over column at base. Brazil.

coccinea Rchb.f. [*S. grandiflora* Lindl.]. Pseudobulbs oblong-ovoid, to 1½ in. long; lvs. elliptic, to 2¼ in. long; fls. solitary, to 3 in. across, crimson-scarlet to bright cinnabar, sepals oblong-lanceolate, to 1 in.

long, petals elliptic, lip 3-lobed, midlobe acuminate, yellow, streaked with red. Early spring. Brazil.

grandiflora: *S. coccinea.*

violacea Lindl. Pseudobulbs to 1 in. long, oblong-spindle-shaped; lvs. to 2½ in. long; peduncle ½ in. long; fls. violet-purple, sepals and petals oblong-lanceolate, ¾ in. long, lip 3-lobed, to ¾ in. long. Brazil.

SOPUBIA Buch.-Ham. ex D. Don. *Scrophulariaceae.* About 40 spp. of ann. herbs or subshrubs, native mostly to trop. Afr., a few in S. Afr., India, and se. Asia; lvs. opp. or whorled, or the upper alt., entire or pinnatifid; fls. variously colored, in bracted terminal spikes or racemes, calyx 5-toothed or -lobed, corolla subequally 5-lobed, stamens 4; fr. a loculicidal caps.

Propagated by cuttings or seeds.

angolensis Engl. White-hairy, erect herb or subshrub, to 2 ft.; lvs. in false whorls of 4, linear, to 1¾ in. long, entire; fls. reddish-purple or bluish-purple. Trop. Afr.

leprosa S. L. Moore. Sts. minutely scaly-tomentose when young, glabrous at maturity; lvs. linear, mostly opp., to 1 in. long, entire; fls. in racemes. Trop. Afr.

SORBARIA (Ser.) A. Braun. FALSE SPIRAEA. *Rosaceae.* Several spp. of rather large deciduous shrubs of e. Asia; lvs. alt., pinnate, bright green, serrate; fls. small, white, in large terminal panicles, calyx tube cup-shaped, sepals 5, short, reflexed, petals 5, broad, stamens 20–50, carpels 5, united at base; frs. several-seeded follicles.

Sorbarias are cultivated as ornamentals. They sucker freely and thrive in moist rich soil; propagated by seeds, suckers, cuttings of ripe wood, or root cuttings.

Aitchisonii (Hemsl.) Hemsl. ex Rehd. [*Spiraea Aitchisonii* Hemsl.]. To 10 ft., glabrous and red on young growth; lfts. 15–21, lanceolate, 1½–3 in. long, to ½ in. wide; panicles 8–10 in. long, leafy at base, upright. W. Asia. Zone 6.

arborea C. K. Schneid. [*Spiraea arborea* (C. K. Schneid.) Bean]. Spreading shrub, to 18 ft. high, usually stellate-pubescent on young growth; lfts. 13–17, lanceolate to ovate-oblong, 2–4 in. long, more than ½ in. wide, stellate-pubescent to nearly glabrous beneath; panicles to 1 ft. long, spreading. China. Zone 6. Var. **glabrata** Rehd. Lfts. glabrous.

sorbifolia (L.) A. Braun [*Spiraea sorbifolia* L.]. To 6 ft., stout; lfts. 13–23, lanceolate to lanceolate-ovate, 2–4 in. long, more than ½ in. wide, long-acuminate, doubly serrate, almost glabrous; panicles 4–10 in. long, puberulous, dense, upright. Asia. Zone 2. Var. **stellipila** Maxim. [*S. stellipila* (Maxim.) C. K. Schneid.]. Lvs. more or less stellate-pubescent beneath. E. Asia.

stellipila: *S. sorbifolia* var.

tomentosa (Lindl.) Rehd. To 18 ft., wide-spreading, almost glabrous; lfts. 15–21, lanceolate, 2–4 in. long, over ½ in. wide, pubescent on veins beneath when young; panicles 8–12 in. long, with spreading brs. Himalayas. Zone 7.

×SORBARONIA C. K. Schneid.: *Aronia* × *Sorbus. Rosaceae.* Deciduous shrubs; lvs. simple or partly pinnate; infl. rather small, dense; styles 3–4; fr. red to nearly black.

Hardy north.

×hybrida (Moench) C. K. Schneid. [*Sorbus* × *spuria* Pers.]: *Aronia arbutifolia* × *Sorbus Aucuparia.* Shrub or small tree, with slender, somewhat pendulous brs., young branchlets tomentulose; lvs. ovate to oblong-ovate, obtuse, 1–3 in. long, with 2–3 pairs of lobes or lfts. near the base, pubescent beneath; infl. about 1¼ in. across, pubescent or nearly glabrous; fls. white or pinkish-white; fr. subglobose or pear-shaped, 5/16 in. long, dark purple.

SORBUS L. [*Micromeles* Decne.]. MOUNTAIN ASH. *Rosaceae.* Perhaps 85 spp. of deciduous trees or shrubs of the N. Hemisphere; lvs. alt., simple or pinnate; fls. in late spring, white, in terminal corymbs, mostly bisexual, sepals and petals 5, stamens 15–20, carpels 2–5, more or less united, each 2-ovuled; fr. usually a small pome, cells 2–5, with cartilaginous walls.

Hardy north; grown as ornamentals. Most species thrive even in dry soil. Propagated by seeds sown when ripe or stratified, by layering, or rare kinds by budding on *S. americana* and *S. Aucuparia.*

alnifolia (Siebold & Zucc.) C. Koch [*Micromeles alnifolia* (Siebold & Zucc.) Koehne]. Tree, to 60 ft., with thick rounded crown; twigs red-brown, pubescent only when young; lvs. simple, ovate to nearly elliptic, abruptly pointed, 2–4 in. long, unequally serrate, with 6–10 pairs of veins, mostly glabrous beneath; fls. ½ in. across, mostly 6–10 in a cluster; fr. pea-sized, red and yellow. Temp. e. Asia. Zone 6.

americana Marsh. [*Pyrus americana* (Marsh.) DC.]. AMERICAN M.A., DOGBERRY, MISSEY-MOOSEY, ROUNDWOOD. Shrubby, or to 30 ft.; lvs. to 10 in. long, lfts. 11–17, narrow-lanceolate, 1½–4 in. long, sharply serrate, gray-green beneath, more or less hairy when young; infl. of dense corymbs to 6 in. across, axis glabrous; fls. ¼ in. across; fr. ¼ in. in diam., bright red. E. N. Amer. Zone 2.

amurensis Koehne. Resembling *S. Aucuparia;* lfts. acuminate, incisely serrate above the middle, slightly pubescent beneath when young; fr. ¼–5/16 in. in diam., orange-red. Ne. Asia. Zone 5.

Aria (L.) Crantz. WHITE BEAM, CHESS APPLE. To 50 ft., twigs tomentose when young; lvs. simple, elliptic, to 5 in. long, doubly crenate-serrate or shallowly lobed, white-tomentose beneath, with 10–14 pairs of veins; fls. ½ in. across, in a large, broad, tomentose infl.; fr. 5/16–⅝ in. in diam., more or less ellipsoid, scarlet. Eur. Zone 6. Cvs. are **'Aurea'**, lvs. yellow; **'Lutetiana'**, new growth yellow-green; **'Majestica'** [var. **Decaisneana** Rehd.], lvs. to 6 in. long, snow-white beneath.

Aucuparia L. [*Pyrus Aucuparia* (L.) Gaertn.]. ROWAN, EUROPEAN M.A., QUICKBEAM. Narrow-crowned tree, to 60 ft., twigs pubescent when young, later glabrous, gray-brown; lvs. 4–10 in. long, lfts. mostly 13–15, oblong, 1–2½ in. long, acute, serrate, sometimes doubly so, slightly glaucous beneath, at first pubescent; infl. dense, many-fld., woolly-pubescent; fls. 5/16 in. across; fr. subglobose, scarlet. Eur., Asia Minor. Zone 2. Cvs. are: **'Asplenifolia'**, lfts. deeply serrate, occasionally with 1–2 small lobes, densely pubescent beneath; **'Edulis'**, lvs. almost glabrous, lfts. 1½–3 in. long, fr. acid, used for preserves; **'Fastigiata'**, habit narrow, twigs stiff, thick, fr. large; **'Luteo-variegata'**, lvs. variegated with yellow; **'Rossica'**, lfts. blunt, not toothed in the lower third; **'Xanthocarpa'**, fr. orange-yellow.

californica Greene. Doubtfully distinct from *S. cascadensis;* plant 3–6 ft., young twigs more glabrous; lfts. 1–1½ in. long; fls. ¼ in. across. Calif.

cascadensis G. N. Jones. Shrub, 6–15 ft., young twigs pubescent; lfts. 9–11, oblong-elliptic, abruptly acute, glabrous, glossy above, 2–3 in. long, coarsely and sharply serrate except toward base; fls. 5/16 in. across; fr. scarlet, globose, 5/16 in. in diam. N. Calif. to B.C.

Chamaemespilus (L.) Crantz. Three to 10 ft., hairy on young growth, later glabrous; lvs. simple, elliptic, 1–3 in. long, pointed to blunt, finely serrate, somewhat leathery, yellow-green beneath, glabrous to somewhat tomentose, with 6–9 pairs of veins; fls. pink, in dense clusters; fr. ovoid, red. Cent. Eur. Zone 6.

commixta Hedl. Tree, to over 20 ft.; lfts. 11–15, lanceolate-elliptic, acuminate, 1½–3 in. long, bluish beneath; infl. 3–6 in. across, glabrous; fls. 5/16 in. across, white; fr. subglobose, pea-sized, scarlet. Japan, e. Asia. Zone 6.

cuspidata (Spach) Hedl. [*S. vestita* Hort.]. Tree, with purple-brown twigs; lvs. simple, elliptic, 3–6 in. long, doubly serrate, closely white-tomentose beneath, leathery; fls. many, in clusters to 4 in. across; fr. subglobose, orange-red, ¾ in. in diam. Himalayas. Zone 7.

decora (Sarg.) C. K. Schneid. Shrub or tree, to 30 ft.; lfts. 11–17, elliptic to lanceolate-ovate, to 3 in. long, blunt or sharp-pointed, dark blue-green, glabrous, or pubescent beneath when young; infl. pubescent, 2–4 in. across; fls. ⅜ in. across; fr. red. Lab. to N.Y., w. to Minn. Zone 2.

discolor (Maxim.) Maxim. To 30 ft., young twigs red, glabrous to pubescent; lfts. 11–15, lanceolate, sharp-pointed, sharply serrate, 1–3 in. long, blue-green beneath, glabrous; infl. 4–6 in. across; fls. ⅜ in. across; fr. ovoid, white or yellowish, ¼ in. in diam. N. China. Zone 6.

domestica L. SERVICE TREE. Differing from *S. Aucuparia;* larger, to 60 ft.; fls. ⅝ in. across; fr. 1 in. in diam., green or brown. Medit. region. Zone 6. Bark used for tanning leather, wood for various purposes, and fr. after frost as food.

dumosa Greene. Shrub, 6–9 ft., young twigs pubescent; lfts. 9–11, thin, 1–1½ in. long, lanceolate-oblong, evenly serrate, sharply acute, glabrous except for few hairs on midveins beneath; infl. narrow; fls. 40–60, 5/16 in. across; fr. red, glossy, 5/16 in. in diam. Ariz., New Mex.

Folgneri (C. K. Schneid.) Rehd. Large shrub or small tree, shoots arched, at first white-tomentose; lvs. simple, lanceolate to lanceolate-ovate, 2–4 in. long, pointed, serrate, white-tomentose beneath, with 8–9 pairs of veins; infl. to 4 in. across; fls. 5/16 in. across, many, white; fr. red, ½ in. in diam. China. Zone 6.

×Hostii (Jacq.f.) C. Koch: *S. Chamaemespilus* × *S. Mougeotii.* To 10 ft.; lvs. elliptic, sharply serrate, loosely tomentose beneath; fls. whitish-pink, in corymbs to 6 in. across.

hybrida L. Robust, to 35 ft., older brs. spreading, young parts tomentose; lvs. 3–4 in. long, bluish-green above, white-tomentose beneath, mostly with 1–2 pairs of basal pinnules; fls. ⅝ in. across; fr. globose, red, ½ in. in diam. Scandinavia, Finland. Zone 5.

intermedia (J. F. Ehrh.) Pers. Tree, to 35 ft., sometimes shrubby, young twigs woolly; lvs. simple, broadly ovate, 2½–4 in. long, lobed, with 7–9 pairs of lateral veins, gray-tomentose beneath; infl. 3–4 in. across; fls. ½ in. across; fr. ellipsoid, to ½ in. in diam., orange-red. N. Eur. Zone 6.

japonica (Decne.) Hedl. Tree, to 60 ft., tomentose on young growth; lvs. simple, ovate to oblong, 3–4 in. long, short-pointed, cuneate at base, doubly serrate and shallowly lobed, with 10–12 pairs of veins, whitish-tomentose beneath; fls. in dense, woolly infl.; fr. ellipsoid, bright red, ½ in. long. Japan, Korea. Zone 6.

latifolia (Lam.) Pers. Tree, to 45 ft. or more; lvs. round-ovate, 3–4 in. long, simple, lobed and sharply serrate, gray-yellow-tomentose beneath; fl. clusters 4 in. across, with tomentose brs.; fls. cream-white, ⅝ in. across; fr. ellipsoid, ⅝ in. long. Eur. Zone 5. Apomictic, probably of hybrid origin.

Mougeotii Soy.-Willem. & Godr. Close to *S. latifolia;* lvs. light gray beneath, lateral veins 9–12 pairs; fr. red, ⅜ in. in diam. Alps, Pyrenees. Zone 6. Apomictic, probably of hybrid origin.

occidentalis (S. Wats.) Greene. Shrub, 3–9 ft., young twigs finely pubescent; lfts. 7–11, thin, glabrous at maturity, oblong to elliptic, 1–2½ in. long, obtuse, entire except near apex; fls. 15–40, about ⅜ in. across; fr. red, glaucescent, ellipsoid, 5/16 in. long. B.C. to Ore. Zone 6?

pohuashanensis (Hance) Hedl. Small tree, with pubescent young shoots; lfts. 11–13, oblong to elliptic, pointed, 1–2½ in. long, gray-green and soft-pubescent beneath, upper half sharply serrate, stipules very large; infl. to 4 in. across; fls. ⅜ in. across; fr. orange-red, ¼ in. in diam. N. China. Zone 6.

Prattii Koehne. To 25 ft., young shoots glabrous; lfts. 21–27, entire in lower third or half, 1 in. long, blue-green beneath, mostly pubescent, at least on midrib; infl. 2–3 in. across, glabrous or pubescent; fls. scarcely ½ in. across; fr. white, 5/16 in. in diam. W. China.

quercifolia: *S.* × *thuringiaca* cv.

rufoferruginea (C. K. Schneid.) C. K. Schneid. Small tree resembling *S. commixta,* pedicels and midveins of under surface of lvs. rusty-pubescent. Japan. Zone 6.

sambucifolia (Cham. & Schlechtend.) M. J. Roem. Shrub, 3–8 ft., young shoots somewhat pubescent; lfts. 9–11, lanceolate-ovate, pointed, 1–3 in. long, asymmetrical at base, shining above, soon glabrous beneath; infl. 1½–2 in. across; fls. ⅝ in. across, sepals glabrous; fr. roundish, to ½ in. in diam. Ne. Asia, Japan. Zone 2.

Sargentiana Koehne. Tree, 20–30 ft., young growth somewhat pubescent; lfts. 7–11, narrow-lanceolate, 3–4½ in. long, 1 in. wide, finely serrate, greenish-tomentose beneath; infl. about 6 in. across, densely hairy; fr. ¼ in. in diam., scarlet. W. China. Zone 7.

scalaris Koehne. To 18 ft., young growth soft hairy; lvs. 4–8 in. long, lfts. 21–37, narrow, 1 in. long, toothed toward apex only, grayish-arachnoid beneath, furrowed above; infl. 5–6 in. across, hairy; fls. ¼ in. across; fr. red, ¼ in. in diam. W. China. Zone 6?

scopulina Greene. Shrubby, 3–12 ft.; lfts. 11–13, oblong, 1–2½ in. long, subacuminate, simply or doubly acutely serrate, glabrous; fls. ⅜ in. across, sepals pilose; fr. orange to scarlet, round, 5/16 in. in diam. Rocky Mts., Calif. To B.C. Zone 6.

sitchensis M. J. Roem. Shrub, 4–15 ft., with rust-colored pubescence on young growth; lfts. 9–13, thick, ovate to ovate-lanceolate, rounded at apex, strongly serrate to below the middle, glabrous; fls. 5/16 in. across; fr. bright red. to ⅜ in. in diam. Alaska to B.C. and Idaho. Zone 5.

×**spuria:** × *Sorbaronia hybrida.*

×**thuringiaca** (Ilse) Fritsch: *S. Aria* × *S. Aucuparia.* Like *S. hybrida,* but lvs. of fertile spurs narrowed toward the tip, finely serrate; fls. ½ in. across; fr. small, red. Cvs. are: **'Meinichii'**, like *S. Aucuparia,* lvs. darker green, larger, with 4–6 pairs of lfts.; **'Neuillyensis'**, stipules large, lfts. 4–5 pairs, 1–2 in. long; **'Quercifolia'** [*S. quercifolia* Hedl.: *S. Aria* var. *longifolia* Pers. × *S. Aucuparia*], tree with narrow crown, lvs. lanceolate-ovate, obtuse, with 1–4 lfts. at base, fr. dark red.

tianshanica Rupr. Shrub or small tree, to 16 ft., young growth mostly glabrous; lfts. 9–15, lanceolate, pointed, 1–2 in. long, finely serrate, entire toward the base, shining above, paler and glabrous beneath; infl. 3–5 in. long; fls. ¾ in. long; fr. red, 5/16 in. in diam. Cent. Asia. Zone 6.

torminalis (L.) Crantz. WILD SERVICE TREE. Round-crowned tree, 30–45 ft., twigs at first tomentose, later glabrous and olive-brown; lvs. simple, ovate, deeply and acutely lobed, to 4 in. long, sharply serrate, soon glabrous; infl. to 5 in. across; fls. white, ½ in. across; fr. ellipsoid, brown, to ⅝ in. long. Eur., N. Afr., Asia Minor. Zone 6.

vestita: a listed name of no botanical standing for *S. cuspidata.*

Vilmorinii C. K. Schneid. Shrub or small tree, 10–18 ft., glabrous or reddish-pubescent; lfts. 19–25, elliptic, sharply serrate in upper half, ⅝–1 in. long, gray-green beneath, mostly winged on rachis; infl. to 4 in. across; fls. ¼ in. across; fr. 5/16 in. in diam., round, red. China. Zone 6.

SORGHASTRUM Nash. *Gramineae.* About 15 spp. of per. grasses in Amer. and Afr., sts. erect; lf. sheaths auricled, blades narrow, flat; panicles narrow, terminal, of 1- to few-jointed racemes; spikelets with 1 bisexual terminal floret above a sterile floret, pedicel articulate below the spikelet, glumes leathery, brown or yellowish, the first hirsute, the edges inflexed over the second, sterile and fertile lemmas thin and hyaline, the latter extending into a usually well-developed bent and twisted awn. For terminology see *Gramineae.*

avenaceum (Michx.) Nash [*S. nutans* of auth., not (L.) Nash]. WOOD GRASS, INDIAN G. Sts. to 5 ft., from short, scaly rhizomes; lf. blades elongate, mostly ¼–⅜ in. wide; panicle yellowish, rather dense, to 1 ft. long, contracted and darker at maturity; spikelets to 5/16 in. long, lanceolate, hirsute, awn ⅜–⅝ in. long, once-bent. Que. to Man., s. to Fla., Ariz., and Mex. Important as a forage grass.

nutans: see *S. avenaceum.*

SORGHUM Moench. *Gramineae.* About 35 spp. of ann. or per. grasses in the Old World, 2 in trop. Amer.; lf. blades flat; infl. terminal, of 1–5-jointed racemes tardily disarticulating below the spikelets; spikelets in pairs, 1 sessile and fertile with a terminal bisexual floret above a sterile floret, the other pedicelled, sterile but well-developed, usually male, the terminal sessile spikelets in groups of 3, 2 of them pedicelled and sterile or male, glumes hard, fertile and sterile lemmas and palea hyaline. For terminology see *Gramineae.*

The genus is complex and its interpretation is difficult. Some taxonomists recognize more spp. than are given here; for convenience, all cult. sorghums except the grass sorghums (*S. halepense* and *S. sudanense*) are referred to a polymorphic sp., *S. bicolor,* in which the different kinds are recognized as groups.

Grown for grain and forage and as a source of syrup, brushes, and paper. Under certain circumstances, the forage sorghums may cause prussic-acid poisoning when grazed by stock.

bicolor (L.) Moench [*S. vulgare* Pers.]. SORGHUM. Distinguished from *S. halepense* by ann., more robust sts., to 12 ft. or more, sometimes producing prop roots; panicle variable; spikelets large and broad, hairy, the lemmas awned or awnless. Probably Afr. Three types of sorghum are grown; for the grain (nonsaccharine sorghums), for the sweet juice or for forage (sorgos or saccharine sorghums), and for manufacture of brushes (broom corns).

Caffrorum Group [*S. vulgare* var. *caffrorum* (Retz.) F. T. Hubb. & Rehd.]. KAFIR CORN, KAFIR, HEGARI. Sts. stout, to 7 ft., the pith dry or almost acid; panicle slender, oblong or cylindrical, dense, erect; spikelets elliptic-ovate, loosely hairy, short-acute but not awned, glumes about half as long as grain; grain large, broad, obovoid or subglobose, white or colored. Late-maturing. Trop. Afr. Important for grain and forage; grown in s. Great Plains.

Caudatum Group [*S. vulgare* var. *caudatum* (Hack.) A. F. Hill]. FETERITA. Sts. to 14 ft., dry; panicles erect, very dense, oblong; grains very large, soft, white, yellow, or red. Sudan. Cult. for grain in s. Great Plains.

Cernuum Group [*S. vulgare* var. *cernuum* (Ard.) Fiori & Paol.]. WHITE DURRA. Like the Durra Group, but grains white. Cult. in Calif. as feed for poultry.

Durra Group [*S. vulgare* var. *Durra* (Forssk.) F. T. Hubb. & Rehd.]. BROWN DURRA. Sts. medium or stout, pith dry or not sweet; panicle compact, ovate or broad-elliptic, erect or inclined but mostly recurved; spikelets very broad, rhombic-ovate when in bloom, awned or awnless, hairy, lower glume with greenish, usually strongly nerved tip; grain large, brown, nearly globose to lens-shaped, with a rounded top. Early-maturing. Nile region. The principal grain sorghum of n. Afr. and s. Asia. Cult. in Calif.

Roxburghii Group [*S. vulgare* var. *Roxburghii* (Stapf) H. Haines]. SHALLU. Sts. stout and tall, often somewhat waxy; panicle oblong or ovoid-oblong, erect, mostly contracted and dense, or becoming loose at maturity, the slender brs. whorled; spikelets ovate and acute, tawny, glumes equal, lower 10–13-nerved, upper 7–9-nerved; grain small, elliptic, often exposed, white. Late-maturing. Afr. and India. Grown for grain in Gulf states.

Saccharatum Group [var. *saccharatum* of auth., not (L.) Boerl.], SWEET S., SUGAR S., SORGO. Sts. to 12 ft., pith juicy, sweet; panicle dense or loose, mostly erect but sometimes recurved, ovate to cylindrical in outline; spikelets ovate to obovate, awned or awnless. China, S. Afr. Cult. for syrup, forage, and silage in Great Plains and Gulf states.

Subglabrescens Group [*S. vulgare* var. *subglabrescens* (Steud.) A. F. Hill]. MILO. Sts. to 6 ft., freely suckering, slightly juicy; panicles compact, usually bearded, recurved; grains large, soft, white or yellow. Maturing late (but earlier than the Caffrorum Group). Trop. Afr. An important grain sorghum of s. Great Plains.

Technicum Group [var. *technicum* (Körn.) Stapf ex Holland; *S. vulgare* var. *technicum* (Körn.) Fiori & Paol.]. BROOMCORN. Sts. 10–15 ft.; panicle long and loose, to 30 in. long, rays of the panicle naked below, stiff, arising from nearly a common point but branching toward the end; spikelets usually awned. Probably derived from a sweet sorghum; elongate panicle brs. are the principal source of domestic brooms and brushes. Cult. in Great Plains.

halepense (L.) Pers. JOHNSON GRASS, ALEPPO G., MEANS-GRASS, GRASS S., EGYPTIAN MILLET. Per., rhizomatous, sts. to 5 ft.; lf. blades mostly less than ¾ in. wide; panicle open, to 18 in. long; sessile spikelet about ¼ in. long, ovate, appressed-silky, the awn deciduous, to ⅝ in. long, spikelet pedicelled, ¼ in. long, lanceolate. Medit. region, but now found in the trop. and warmer regions of both hemispheres. Cult. for forage and naturalized in many parts of the U.S.; often a troublesome weed.

sudanense (Piper) Stapf [*S. vulgare* var. *sudanense* (Piper) A. S. Hitchc.; *Holcus sudanensis* (Piper) L. H. Bailey]. SUDAN GRASS, GRASS S. Ann., sts. to 9 ft., branching from the base; lf. blades to 1 ft. long and ½ in. wide; panicle erect, loose, to 1 ft. long, about half as wide, brs. nearly whorled; sessile spikelet ¼ in. long, lanceolate-ovate, with a ring of hairs at base, sparsely appressed-silky toward the apex, awn persistent, to ⅝ in. long, pedicelled spikelet narrow, about as long as the sessile spikelet, strongly nerved. Sudan. Extensively cult. for forage, and escaped in the s. and midwestern states, and in Ariz. and Calif.

vulgare: *S. bicolor*. Var. **sudanense**: *S. sudanense*.

SOYBEAN. The soybean, *Glycine Max*, a native cultigen of southeastern Asia, is now one of the most important industrial crops of the United States. The species has long been cultivated in the Orient as a garden vegetable and is now similarly used in some parts of the United States, being handled like bush or snapbeans. The soybean requires a growing season of 80 to 100 days but cannot be planted until all danger of frost is past and the soil has warmed. Pods are picked when nearly full grown (before starting to turn yellow) and can be more easily shelled if placed in boiling water for a few minutes. In Japan, green pods are placed in salted boiling water for ten to 20 minutes, the length of time depending on how firm or tender the end product is preferred. The cooked beans, high in oil content, are eaten directly and individually by squeezing them out of the boiled pods. Shelled dry soybeans are used as needed to produce bean sprouts, a common fresh winter vegetable of the Orient, which can also be produced here.

SOYMIDA A. Juss. *Meliaceae*. One sp., a large timber tree with hard, red wood, native to India and Ceylon; lvs. crowded toward tips of brs., even-pinnate; fls. in axillary and terminal panicles, sepals and petals 5, stamens 10, filaments united in a cup-shaped tube, ovary 5-celled; caps. woody, 5-valved, seeds many, winged at each end.

febrifuga (Roxb.) A. Juss. Tall glabrous tree; lvs. 9–18 in. long, lfts. 6–12, elliptic or oblong, 2–5 in. long, base asymmetrical; lobes of staminal tube bifid, anthers attached in the notch, stigma discoid; caps. black when mature. India and Ceylon. Wood used for houses and furniture, bark for tannin.

SPARAXIS Ker-Gawl. WANDFLOWER. *Iridaceae*. About 6 spp. of per. herbs, with tunicate corms, native to S. Afr.; sts. usually unbranched; lvs. mostly basal, 2-ranked, linear to sword-shaped, soft; spathe valves membranous, lacerate; fls. essentially regular, perianth tube funnelform, short, stamens 3, filaments not united, style brs. 3; fr. a 3-valved caps.

Cultivation and treatment as for *Ixia*.

grandiflora (D. Delar.) Ker-Gawl. To 2 ft.; lvs. to 1 ft. long; fls. yellow or purple, to about 1 in. long, perianth segms. oblong, obtuse, stamens whitish or yellow.

pendula: *Dierama pendula*.

Pillansii L. Bolus. To 2 ft.; fls. rose, with a dark yellow center, filaments whitish, contiguous anthers dark purple.

pulcherrima: *Dierama pulcherrima*.

tricolor (Curtis) Ker-Gawl. To 1½ ft.; lvs. linear to lanceolate, to 1 ft. long; fls. dark purple or yellow tinged with brown-purple, or white with purple, yellow at throat, and with dark blotch at base of each perianth segm., 1 in. long, or more, anthers yellow. Cv. 'Alba'. Fls. white.

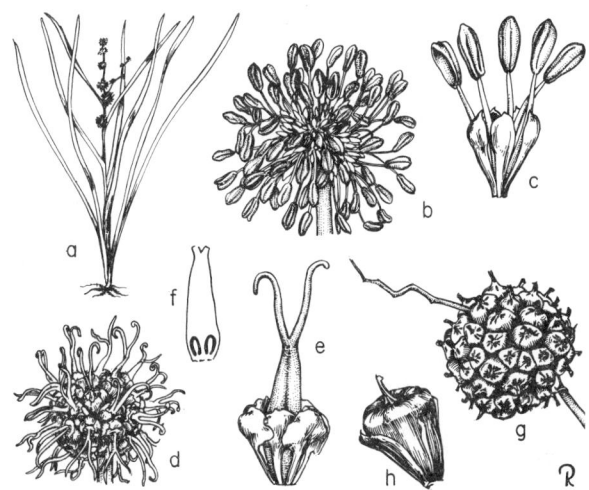

SPARGANIACEAE. *Sparganium eurycarpum:* **a,** flowering plant, much reduced; **b,** male flower head, × 3; **c,** male flower, × 5; **d,** female flower head, × 1½; **e,** female flower, × 4; **f,** ovary, vertical section, × 4; **g,** fruit cluster, × ¾; **h,** fruit, × 1½. (From Lawrence, *Taxonomy of Vascular Plants*.)

SPARGANIACEAE F. Rudolphi. BUR REED FAMILY. Monocot.; 1 genus, *Sparganium*, of monoecious, aquatic, per. herbs with creeping rhizomes, native to N. Temp. Zone, Australia, and New Zeal.; lvs. sessile, alt., linear; fls. in heads, those in upper heads male, those in lower ones female, stamens 3–6, ovary superior, 1–2-celled; fr. an indehiscent nutlet.

SPARGANIUM L. BUR REED. *Sparganiaceae*. About 20 spp. of colony-forming herbs; characteristics those of the family.

Of easy culture, thriving in wet habitats and full sun.

erectum L. [*S. ramosum* Huds.]. Erect per., to 5 ft., or sometimes higher; lvs. linear, triangular in cross section; infl. usually branched; perianth black-tipped. Eur. to cent. Siberia.

eurycarpum Engelm. Plants 1½–4½ ft.; lvs. stiff, ascending, flat; infl. forking. N. N. Amer.

minimum (Hartm.) Fries. Sts. mostly floating, 2–30 in. long; lvs. floating, filiform, about ⅛ in. wide, thin and flat. Eurasia, n. N. Amer. Sometimes cult. in aquaria.

ramosum: *S. erectum*.

SPARMANNIA L.f. INDOOR LINDEN. *Tiliaceae*. Three spp. of large, pubescent or glabrescent shrubs, native to Afr. and Madagascar; lvs. alt., simple, unlobed or palmately 3–7-lobed, toothed; fls. in long-peduncled, axillary or subterminal umbels, sepals 4, deciduous, petals 4, oblanceolate, glandless, stamens many, outer ones sometimes sterile, beadlike; fr. a caps., spiny, 4–5-celled, many-seeded.

Suitable for cultivation outdoors in Zone 9, and in the greenhouse where they require moderate temperatures and plenty of light and air. Propagated by cuttings of young shoots.

africana L.f. AFRICAN HEMP. Mostly many-stemmed, soft-woody, 10–20 ft.; lvs. cordate-ovate, to 9 in. long, acuminate, unlobed, or palmately angled or lobed; petals white, ¾ in. long or more, inner stamens fertile, mostly purple, outer stamens sterile, yellow at base, purple at apex; fr. globose. S. Afr. Cv. 'Flore Pleno'. Fls. double.

palmata: *S. ricinicarpa*.

ricinicarpa (Eckl. & Zeyh.) O. Kuntze [*S. palmata* E. H. Mey. ex Harv.]. To 9 ft.; lvs. variable, angularly to deeply 3–5–7-lobed, lobes mostly narrow, acuminate; petals white to pinkish, less than ½ in. long, about as long as sepals; caps. ellipsoid. Ethiopia to S. Afr.

SPARTINA Schreb. CORDGRASS, MARSH GRASS. *Gramineae.* Perhaps 16 spp. of erect, often stout, rhizomatous, per. grasses in coastal regions of N. and S. Amer., Eur., N. Afr.; lf. blades long, tough; spikes 2 to many, usually appressed-racemose on the main axis; spikelets 1-fld., much flattened laterally, sessile and usually closely imbricate on one side of a continuous rachis, disarticulating below the glumes, glumes unequal, narrow, keeled, usually 1-nerved, acute or short-awned, lemma firm, keeled, narrowed to a rather obscure point, palea 2-nerved, keeled and flattened. For terminology see *Gramineae.*

Michauxiana: *S. pectinata.*

pectinata Link [*S. Michauxiana* A. S. Hitchc.]. PRAIRIE C., FRESH WATER C., SLOUGH GRASS. Sts. to 7 ft., firm or wiry; lf. blades elongate, flat when fresh but involute when dry, as much as ⅝ in. wide, margins very scabrous; spikes mostly 10–20, to 3¼ in. long, peduncles slender; glumes hispid-scabrous on the keel, the first acuminate, the second with an awn to ¼ in. long, lemma to 5/16 in. long. Cool-temp. N. Amer.

SPARTIUM L. *Leguminosae* (subfamily *Faboideae*). One sp., a shrub, native to Medit. Eur.; lvs. alt., with 1 lft.; fls. yellow, in terminal racemes, papilionaceous, calyx spathelike, stamens 10, united, alternately of 2 lengths; fr. a flat, linear legume.

Widely planted and naturalized in parts of the world with Mediterranean type of climate. Propagated by seeds, and greenwood cuttings under glass.

junceum L. [*Genista juncea* (L.) Scop.]. SPANISH BROOM, WEAVERS' B. To 10 ft., brs. cylindrical, nearly leafless, rushlike; lfts. oblanceolate to linear, 1 in. long or more, blue-green; racemes to 18 in. long; fls. fragrant, 1 in. long; fr. to 3 in. long. Naturalized in Calif. Zone 8. Fls. yield yellow dye and the plant a fiber.

SPATHICARPA Hook. *Araceae.* About 6 spp. of tuberous or rhizomatous herbs, native to S. Amer.; lvs. lanceolate to ovate-sagittate or 3-parted, membranous, petioles slender, channelled; peduncle long and slender, spathe open, green, spadix united to spathe, loosely covered with male and female fls.

For culture see *Callopsis.*

sagittifolia Schott. To 12 in.; lf. blades mostly ovate-lanceolate, to 4–5 in. long, sagittate, cordate, or nearly hastate, petioles to 10 in. long; peduncle exceeding foliage, spathe oblong-lanceolate, recurved, 2 in. long and ¾ in. wide, spadix shorter than spathe, male and female fls. intermixed. Brazil, Paraguay, Argentina.

SPATHIPHYLLUM Schott. SPATHE FLOWER. *Araceae.* About 35 spp. of trop. per. herbs with short rhizomes; lvs. in clusters, oblong or elliptic, petioles long-sheathing; spathe white or green, spadix usually white, fragrant, densely covered with bisexual fls.; perianth present.

Grown in warm greenhouses for their blossoms and as foliage plants for interior decoration. Require soil high in organic matter with abundant water, and partial shade. There are several fancy-named cultivars, probably of hybrid origin.

blandum Schott. To 2 ft.; lf. blades elliptic, equally acute at each end; spathe erect-hooded, elliptic, to 10 in. long, broadly decurrent on peduncle, spadix nearly sessile, roughened by exserted conical pistils. Brit. Honduras to Honduras.

candidum: *S. Patinii.* Material so listed may be *Spathiphyllum* cv. 'Clevelandii'; see *S. Clevelandii.*

cannifolium (Dryand.) Schott. To 2½ ft.; lf. blades oblanceolate to elliptic, basally acute, petiolar sheaths early becoming dry and fibrous; spathe lanceolate, to 10 in. long, reflexed, not decurrent on the peduncles, white inside, greenish outside, spadix stalked, smooth; perianth thick, cuplike, pistils truncate, not exserted. N. S. Amer., Trinidad.

Clevelandii: WHITE ANTHURIUM, a listed name of no botanical standing, treated as *Spathiphyllum* cv. 'Clevelandii', a free-flowering form of uncertain origin; lf. blades narrow, to 1 ft. long and 2½ in. wide, acuminate at both ends, glossy, petioles slender, longer than blades; peduncle slender, spathe borne well above foliage, erect, ovate, to 6 in. long, long-acuminate, decurrent, white, spadix stalked, to 2 in. long; pistils exserted. Flowering plants and cut infls. sometimes offered for sale by florists; good foliage plants for interior decoration.

cochlearispathum (Liebm.) Engl. To 5 ft. or more; lf. blades oblong, rounded at base, petiolar sheaths crinkled-crisped; spathe erect-hooded, oblanceolate to elliptic, to 13 in. long, broadly decurrent on peduncle, spadix nearly sessile, long, roughened by exserted, attenuate pistils. Se. Mex.

commutatum Schott. Distinguished from *S. cannifolium* in having lvs. broadly elliptic, and spathe broader, obtuse at base and sometimes narrowly decurrent on peduncle. Molucca Is., Philippine Is.

cordatum: a listed name of no botanical standing; see *Anthurium fraternum.*

floribundum (Linden & André) N. E. Br. SNOWFLOWER. About 1 ft.; lf. blades elliptic to broadly oblanceolate, dark green above with a velvety luster, petiolar sheaths often expanded and winglike; spathe to 3 in. long, reflexed, clasping but not decurrent on peduncles, spadix smooth; perianth green, pistils truncate, scarcely longer than perianth, white. Colombia.

Friedrichsthalii Schott. To 3 ft.; distinguished from *S. cochlearispathum* in having lf. blades elliptic to oblanceolate, acute basally, and spadix stout, shorter, very densely fld. Nicaragua to Colombia. Doubtfully in cult.; material so listed may be *S. phryniifolium.*

grandiflorum: a listed name of no botanical standing; material so listed may be *S. cochlearispathum.*

×hybridum N. E. Br.: *S. cannifolium* × *S. Patinii.* Intermediate between parents; lvs. similar to *S. cannifolium,* but blades narrower, petioles more slender; spathe much larger than in *S. Patinii,* white, with midrib green beneath. Doubtfully in cult.; material so listed probably represents a selection from among the many recent hybrids.

Kochii Engl. & Kurt Krause. Distinguished from *S. blandum* in having lf. blades obtuse at the base, spadix shorter, peduncle slender, nearly half as long as the spadix. Venezuela. Doubtfully in cult.; material so listed is probably *Spathiphyllum* cv. 'Clevelandii'.

Patinii (Hogg) N. E. Br. [*S. candidum* (Bull) N. E. Br.]. To 1½ ft.; lf. blades 4 times longer than wide, petioles very slender; spathe reflexed, obtuse and clasping basally, but not decurrent on peduncle, spadix smooth; perianth green, pistils truncate, as long as perianth, white. Known only in cult.

phryniifolium Schott. Closely allied to *S. Kochii,* but having spadix only short-peduncled. Nicaragua to Panama.

SPATHODEA Beauvois. *Bignoniaceae.* Two or 3 spp. of handsome evergreen trees, native to trop. Afr.; lvs. opp. or sometimes in 3's, odd-pinnate; fls. orange-red or scarlet, in terminal corymbose racemes, calyx spathelike, split on one side exposing corolla to base, tomentose, corolla campanulate and ventricose, slightly 2-lipped, stamens 4; fr. an oblong-lanceolate caps., acuminate at both ends.

One species *(S. campanulata)* is grown as a showy street or specimen tree in the tropics and in Zone 10b. in Fla. It grows under many conditions, but does best in fertile, well-drained soil. Propagated by seeds or cuttings.

campanulata Beauvois. TULIP TREE, AFRICAN T.T., FLAME-OF-THE-FOREST. Showy tree, to 70 ft.; lvs. to 1½ ft. long, lfts. 9–19, ovate-lanceolate, to 4 in. long, entire, nearly glabrous; calyx 2½ in. long, leathery, corolla scarlet, to 5 in. long, ovary papillose; fr. 8 in. long and 2 in. across. There is a yellow-fld. form.

nilotica Seem. Much-branched bushy tree, to 20 ft. or more, branchlets pubescent; lvs. to 16 in. long, lfts. 9–15, ovate-oblong, to 4 in. long, entire, leathery, densely pubescent beneath; calyx 2½ in. long, corolla crimson or flame-colored, edged yellow, to 5 in. long, ovary hairy; fr. 6–10 in. long.

SPATHOGLOTTIS Blume. *Orchidaceae.* About 40 spp. of terrestrial herbs, native to trop. Asia, Malay Arch., n. Australia; pseudobulbs ovoid, several-lvd.; lvs. plicate; infl. in axil of basal lf., racemose, rachis with a succession of many fls.; sepals and petals about equal, spreading, lip 3-lobed, lateral lobes narrow-oblong, midlobe with narrow claw, and with 2 small ovoid calluses and 2 small teeth at base. For structure of fl. see *Orchidaceae.*

Warm greenhouse. For culture see *Orchids.*

aurea Lindl. Pseudobulbs to 8 in. long; lvs. to 3 ft. long, tinged with purple; fls. 3 in. across, rich golden-yellow, sepals and petals similar, lip marked with streaks of small crimson spots at base, lateral lobes spotted with crimson, midlobe narrow. Malay Pen.

plicata Blume. Pseudobulbs 3–4-lvd. at apex; lvs. lanceolate; racemes 8–10-fld.; fls. 1½ in. across, purple, sepals elliptic, petals ovate, lip white with purple spots, lateral lobes spreading, midlobe narrow, widened at apex, with 2 round, fleshy, spotted, yellow calluses at its junction with lateral lobes. Malay Arch.

SPATHYEMA: *SYMPLOCARPUS.*

SPECIES (the word is either singular or plural). The species is the primary or fundamental concept in the understanding of the forms of life. It is the basic unit in classification. Species are combined into genera (see *Genus*), and variations or subordinate forms of them may be distinguished as subspecies, variety (varietas), and form (forma) in descending order of the botanical hierarchy (see *Classification*). Botanical binomial nomenclature of higher plants begins with *Species Plantarum* (Species of Plants) of Linnaeus, published in 1753. The name of a species consists of two words, the first (the generic name) representing the genus or group, the second (the specific epithet) identifying the particular kind or member of the group. The two together provide the species name. Thus there are some 300 species of violets, all of the genus *Viola;* the florist's violet is named *Viola odorata,* the horned violet *V. cornuta,* the birds-foot violet *V. pedata; odorata, cornuta, pedata* are the *specific* epithets. Unlike the generic name, and except under certain circumstances, specific epithets are decapitalized. Today it is recommended that all specific epithets be decapitalized, but capitalization is permitted for epithets derived from personal names *(Crocus Kotschyanus),* from old generic names *(Cercis Siliquastrum),* or from barbaric (non-Latin) names *(Dolichos Lablab).* Capitalization is followed in *Hortus Third* as a guide to those who still prefer to use it.

Authors differ on the limits or definition of genera, and thus it happens that a species may be placed in different genera by different writers, but the original specific epithet normally follows it in whatever genus it may rest; thus the peach was *Amygdalus Persica* to Linnaeus and this disposition of it is followed by some contemporary authors; other authors prefer to place it in the genus with the other orchard stone fruits, and it is then *Prunus Persica.* Some authors keep the genus *Thea* separate, other unite it with *Camellia;* the tea plant may therefore bear the name *Camellia sinensis* or *Thea sinensis.*

The number of species of plants is unknown. Of course, the count depends to some extent on the varying definitions by different authors. The earth is as yet only partially explored for the species of plants and animals. Among the seed plants, probably more than a million specific names have been published; many of these names are duplicates or synonyms, but it is probably fair to assume that at least one-fourth of them represent separate species in nature. Some species are known only from cultivation (see *Cultigen* and *Indigen*).

SPECULARIA: *LEGOUSIA.* **S. perfoliata.** *Triodanis perfoliata.*

SPENCERIA Trimen. *Rosaceae.* Two spp. of per. herbs from China, differing from *Agrimonia* in having 30–40 stamens, a spineless but pilose calyx tube, a funnel-shaped involucre of 2 united bracts, and filiform, not capitate, stigmas.

ramalana Trimen. To 1 ft., sts. many, erect, from branched rhizomes, silvery-pilose throughout; basal lvs. pinnate, lfts. about 12, broadly elliptic, to ⅝ in. long, with 2 large lobelike teeth at apex, st. lvs. of 1–2 pairs of lfts. or simple, acute; fls. bright golden- to reddish-yellow, about 1 in. across, on pedicels to 1¾ in. long, and in stiff racemes; fr. a subglobose, hairy-tufted achene to ⅛ in. long. W. China.

SPERGULA L. SPURRY or SPURREY. *Caryophyllaceae.* About 5 spp. of cosmopolitan ann. or rarely per., often weedy herbs, sts. much-branched, with very short internodes on lateral brs.; lvs. linear, stipules scarious; fls. 5-merous, sepals green with scarious margins, petals white, entire, stamens 5–10, ovary 1-celled, styles 5; caps. ovoid, dehiscent by 5 valves opp. sepals, seeds often winged.

Spurrey is cultivated for forage as a green manure crop on poor sandy soil.

arvensis L. [*S. sativa* Boenn.]. CORN SPURRY, TOADFLAX. Ann., sts. to 2 ft., glandular-hairy; lvs. mostly to 1 in. long, rarely to 3 in., linear; calyx ¼ in., petals white, slightly longer than calyx. Eur.; naturalized as a weed in many temp. regions of the world.

pilifera: see *Sagina subulata.*

sativa: *S. arvensis.*

SPERGULARIA (Pers.) J. Presl & K. Presl. SAND SPURRY or SAND SPURREY. *Caryophyllaceae.* About 40 spp. of mostly salt-loving, cosmopolitan ann. or per. herbs; lvs. 4-ranked, stipules scarious, surrounding the node; fls. in terminal cymose panicles, bisexual or unisexual, sepals 5, petals 5, white or pink, entire, stamens 2–10, ovary 1-celled, styles 3; fr. a caps., dehiscent by 3 valves, seeds orbicular-reniform or spherical, the margin often winged.

rubra (L.) J. Presl & K. Presl. Ann. or bien. herb, sts. prostrate to ascending, to 1 ft., glabrous in lower part, glandular above; lvs. linear-filiform, ½–1 in. long, awned; cymes few- to many-fld.; sepals lanceolate, to $^3/_{16}$ in. long, glandular, with scarious margins, petals pink. Eur.; naturalized in N. Amer.

SPHACELE Benth. *Labiatae.* Not in cult. **S. calycina:** *Lepechinia calycina.*

SPHAERALCEA St.-Hil. GLOBE MALLOW, FALSE M. *Malvaceae.* About 50 spp. of ann., suffrutescent per. herbs, or small shrubs in arid N. and S. Amer.; lvs. linear-lanceolate to orbicular, scarcely 3-lobed to deeply palmately parted or divided, the lobes or divisions serrate, often lobed; infl. racemose to thyrsoid- or open-paniculate; involucral bracts 3, rarely 0, but usually falling early, corolla yellowish, orange, lavender, or whitish, cuplike, stamens united in a tubular column, style brs. as many as the mericarps, stigmas capitate or very slightly decurrent; fr. a densely pubescent, suborbicular to depressed-conical schizocarp, mericarps usually 10–20 in a single whorl, upper part smooth-walled, dehiscent, basal part indehiscent, laterally reticulate, 1–3 seeded.

Propagated by seeds, division, or softwood cuttings.

acerifolia: *Iliamna rivularis.*

ambigua A. Gray. Per., to 3 ft., sts. many, erect, from a woody root crown; lvs. ovate to orbicular, to about 2½ in. long, more or less 3-lobed; infl. usually open-paniculate; petals orange, ½–1¼ in. long; mericarps 12–16, about ¼ in. long and up to ⅔ as broad, strongly reticulate in the lower ⅓, 2-seeded. Utah, Ariz., Nev., Calif., and Mex.

angustifolia (Cav.) G. Don. Gray-pubescent per., to 6 ft., sts. from a woody root crown; lvs. lanceolate to oblong-lanceolate, to 4½ in. long, unlobed or scarcely lobed; infl. a narrow, interrupted thyrse, leafy to near the apex; petals usually mauve or lavender, less than 1 in. long; mericarps mostly 10–16, usually somewhat united at maturity, to about ¼ in. long, reticulate in the lower ⅓ or less, 1–3-seeded. Tex. and Mex. Var. **cuspidata** (Britt.) A. Gray [*S. cuspidata* Britt.]. Lvs. linear-lanceolate; petals orange, about ½ in. long; mericarps less united at maturity. Kans. to Colo., s. to Tex., Calif. and Mex.

bonariensis (Cav.) Griseb. [*S. cisplatina* St.-Hil.]. Erect, suffrutescent per., to 3 ft.; lvs. ovate, moderately 3-lobed, lobes acute or rounded; fls. up to 10 in dense axillary clusters, petals apricot, salmon-pink to brick-red, usually darker spotted on the claw, to ¾ in. long; fr. truncate-conical, mericarps 11–18, oblong, short-beaked, less than ¼ in. long, reticulate in lower ⅓, 3-seeded. S. Amer.

cisplatina: *S. bonariensis.*

coccinea (Pursh) Rydb. [*Malvastrum coccineum* (Pursh) A. Gray]. PRAIRIE MALLOW, RED F.M. Decumbent, grayish- or whitish-pubescent per., sts. mostly less than 2 ft. long, from a taproot or small root crown; lvs. pedately parted or divided, usually broader than long; fls. in short racemes, involucral bracts mostly 0, petals orange to red, less than ¾ in. long; mericarps 10–14, suborbicular, about ⅛ in. long, reticulate in lower ¾, 1-seeded. Man., s. to Tex. and Ariz.

cuspidata: *S. angustifolia* var.

fasciculata: *Malacothamnus fasciculatus.*

hastulata A. Gray. Per., with usually few decumbent brs. less than 2½ ft. long, from a root crown or as root shoots; lvs. oblong- to lanceolate-ovate, about 2 in. long, hastately toothed or shallowly lobed near the base, bright green; fls. mostly solitary in the upper axils, seldom more than 8 on a st., petals orange, to 1 in. long; mericarps 14–20, less than ¼ in. long, reticulate in lower ½–¾, distinctly broader in reticulate part than in smooth part, 1–2-seeded. Tex. and Mex.

Munroana (Dougl.) Spach. Several stemmed per., to about 3 ft., from a woody root crown; lvs. ovate to subrhombic, about 2 in. long, shallowly 3- or 5-lobed, cuneate to cordate; fls. in many-fld., narrowly thyrsoid-glomerate infl., petals orange, about ¾ in. long; mericarps 10–12, suborbicular, about ⅛ in. long, reticulate in lower half, 1–

2-seeded. B.C. to Utah and Nev. Var. **subrhomboidea** (Rydb.) Kearn. [*S. subrhomboidea* Rydb.]. Lvs. cleft beyond the middle or 3-parted, divisions cleft or parted, cuneate. Wyo., Utah, and Nev.

Philippiana Krapov. [*Malvastrum prostratum* (Phil.) Hieron.]. TRAILING MALLOW. Trailing, gray-pubescent, per. herb, sts. to 18 in., from a loose root crown; lvs. small, 3- or 5-lobed, serrate-crisped; fls. 1–3 in the axils, petals rose, about 1 in. across; mericarps short-beaked, reticulate in the lower half, 1-seeded. Argentina.

    remota: *Iliamna remota.*

    rivularis: *Iliamna rivularis.*

    rosea: *Phymosia rosea.*

    subhastata J. Coult. Per., sts. decumbent or erect, to 1½ ft. long, from a root crown or as root shoots; lvs. oblong-lanceolate to ovate, somewhat hastately toothed near the cuneate base; fls. 1–3 in the upper lf. axils, petals orange; mericarps 10–17, often united, about ¼ in. long, reticulate in lower half, 1–2-seeded. Tex., New Mex., Ariz., Mex.

    subrhomboidea: *S. Munroana* var.

    umbellata: *Phymosia umbellata.*

    vitifolia: *Phymosia rosea.*

SPHAEROPTERIS Bernh. TREE FERN. *Cyatheaceae.* About 120 spp. of trop., sometimes very large tree ferns; lvs. to 20 ft. long, usually 2–3-pinnate, petioles lacking spines, and petiolar scales lacking a differentiated margin, with or without a black terminal bristle; sori on lower surface of pinnules between margin and midrib, indusia absent, or a small scale or saucer-shaped to globose.

    For culture see *Ferns.*

    Cooperi (F. J. Muell.) Tryon [*Alsophila Cooperi* F. J. Muell.; *Cyathea Cooperi* (F. J. Muell.) Domin]. AUSTRALIAN T.F. Very much like *Alsophila australis*, but differs in having scales on the petiole with an undifferentiated margin, scales on midribs of pinnules nearly stellate. Australia. Zone 10. Most of the plants offered as *Alsophila australis* belong here. Cv. 'Brentwood'. A rapid-growing, vigorous variant.

    insignis (D. C. Eat.) Tryon [*Cyathea insignis* D. C. Eat.]. Trunk to 18 ft., clothed with linear, spinulose-ciliate, cinnamon-brown, matted scales; lvs. 3-pinnate, ultimate pinnules oblong-obtuse, ¼ in. long, rachis finely scabrous. Jamaica.

    medullaris (G. Forst.) Bernh. [*Cyathea medullaris* (G. Forst.) Swartz]. BLACK T.F., BLACK-STEMMED T.F., SAGO F. Trunk to 50 ft.; petioles black at base in mature plants, with scales mostly linear, dark brown, minutely spinescent-serrate, lvs. 3-pinnate, pinnules crenate-dentate, lower surface of midrib clothed with broad, whitish, puffy scales usually with reddish marginal spinules. New Zeal. Cult in warmer temp. countries; outdoors in Calif., where it thrives in moist, shaded sites. Zone 10. Pith of st. yields an edible sago.

SPHAGNUM: see *Mosses and Liverworts,* and *Soils.*

SPHEDAMNOCARPUS Planch. ex Benth. & Hook.f. *Malpighiaceae.* About 10 spp. of scandent shrubs, native to S. Afr. and Madagascar; lvs. opp., simple, entire; calyx 5-parted, without glands, petals yellow, unequal in length, short-clawed, glabrous, stamens 10, all fertile; fr. of 3 samaras, each with a vertical dorsal wing.

    pruriens (A. Juss.) Szysz. Scandent shrub; lvs. ovate or ovate-lanceolate, to 1½ in. long; infl. of 4-fld. umbels. S. Afr.

SPHENOMERIS Maxon. *Polypodiaceae.* Eighteen pantrop., terrestrial ferns formerly included in *Odontosoria* Fée, but differing in pinnules wedge-shaped, sori terminal on the veins at apex of pinnules, and indusia about as broad as lobe and attached at base and usually along sides.

    Easily grown under glass. See also *Ferns.*

    chinensis (L.) Maxon [*S. chusana* (L.) E. Copel.; *Davallia tenuifolia* Swartz]. Rhizomes short-creeping; lvs. evergreen, to 1½ ft. long and 9 in. wide, lanceolate to ovate, 3–4-pinnatifid into fine pinnules about ⅛ in. long. Temp. e. Asia to trop. Asia, Polynesia. Zone 9. A sun-loving sp.

    chusana: *S. chinensis.*

SPHENOSTIGMA Bak. [*Salpingostylis* Small]. *Iridaceae.* About 13 spp. of trop., bulbous herbs, native to Fla., s. to Argentina; allied to *Cipura,* but having inner perianth segms. not cohering, and style brs. cuneate or reniform, usually erose or ciliate.

    Culture as for *Cipura* or *Nemastylis.*

    coelestinum (Bartr.) R. Foster [*Ixia coelestina* Bartr.; *Nemastylis coelestina* (Bartr.) Nutt.; *Salpingostylis coelestina* (Bartr.) Small]. Sts. 12–24 in.; lvs. narrowly linear, 4–12 in. long; fls. to 2½ in. across, violet with small white eye, blooming from sunrise to about 8 A.M. Early autumn. Grassy pinelands and prairie, n. Fla.

SPHENOSTYLIS E. H. Mey. *Leguminosae* (subfamily *Faboideae*). About 16–18 spp. of scandent herbs and erect shrubs, sometimes with underground tubers, native to Afr.; lvs. alt., pinnate with 3 lfts., lfts. with petiolules; fls. in axillary racemes, papilionaceous, standard eared at base, the uppermost stamen separate; fr. a tough, linear, flat, dehiscent legume.

    marginata E. H. Mey. Sts. slender, procumbent or twining, woody at base; lfts. elliptic-oblong, to 2½ in. long, thick-margined; peduncles to 10 in. long, racemes short, 4–6-fld.; petals red to yellow, standard ½ in. wide; fr. 3–4 in. long. Trop. Afr.

SPIGELIA L. PINKROOT, WORM GRASS. *Loganiaceae.* About 30 spp. of herbs, native from se. U.S. to S. Amer.; lvs. opp., entire; fls. 5-merous, red, yellow, or purplish, in 1-sided cymes, 5-merous, corolla tubular, stamens inserted in corolla tube, ovary 2-celled; fr. a 2-lobed caps., circumscissile at base.

    marilandica L. INDIAN PINK, PINKROOT, WORM GRASS. Per. herb, to 2 ft.; lvs. ovate, to 4 in. long, sessile; fls. red outside, yellow inside, to 2 in. long. S.C., s. to Fla. and Tex. Dried roots and rhizomes used medicinally.

SPILANTHES Jacq. *Compositae* (Helianthus Tribe). About 60 spp. of mostly creeping or spreading herbs of New and Old World tropics; lvs. opp., serrate; fl. heads radiate or discoid, solitary on long peduncles, involucral bracts in 2 rows, receptacle conical, scaly; disc fls. bisexual, fertile, yellow; ray fls. female, yellow or whitish, sometimes lacking; achenes compressed, pappus of 2–3 awns.

    oleracea L. Diffusely branched; lvs. broadly ovate, to 3 in. long, wavy-toothed; heads ovoid, to 1 in. long, involucral bracts oblong; fls. greenish-yellow, ray fls. lacking. Tropics. Occasionally grown for the lvs., which give a pungent flavor to salads.

SPINACH. Spinach, *Spinacia oleracea,* is essentially a cool-season crop. The plants run quickly to seed at high temperatures and under a long daily light period (photoperiod). Close crowding in the row contributes to the early development of the seed stalks.

Culture of spinach is possible during the winter where the weather is mild; elsewhere it is grown as a spring and fall crop. The seed is sown in drills 10–15 inches apart. Large scale commercial plantings are seldom thinned, the stand being adjusted by the rate of seeding. Stocky plants are obtained when they are thinned to a spacing of 4–5 inches in the row. The plants are harvested by cutting the stem near the ground level, before seed-stalk elongation commences. See *Spinacia.*

The unrelated New Zealand spinach *(Tetragonia tetragonioides)* does well in hot weather. The seed should be soaked before planting. When the plants are spaced 1–2 feet in rows 3–4 feet apart, the much-branched growth spreads out to form a mat over the ground. The apical 3–4 inches of the branches are cut off and cooked like true spinach.

SPINACIA L. *Chenopodiaceae.* Three or 4 spp. of mostly dioecious, erect ann. herbs of sw. Asia; lvs. alt., simple; fls. small, male fls. in terminal spikes or panicles, with 4–5-lobed calyx and 4–5 stamens, female fls. usually axillary, subtended by 2 bracts that grow together and enclose the utricle, ovary 1-celled, stigmas 4–5, exserted.

    oleracea L. SPINACH. To 2 ft.; basal lvs. in a rosette, narrowly oblong to ovate or subcircular, lobed at base and sometimes on sides, st. lvs. narrower, becoming progressively smaller toward apex of st. Sw. Asia. Var. **oleracea.** PRICKLY-SEEDED S. The typical var.; fr. (the "seeds" of commerce) enclosed in capsulelike body with 2–4 spines. Var. **inermis** (Moench) Peterm. ROUND-SEEDED S. Fr. spineless. For cult. see *Spinach.*

SPIRAEA L. SPIREA or SPIRAEA, BRIDAL-WREATH. *Rosaceae.* Almost 100 spp. of deciduous shrubs in the N. Hemisphere; lvs. alt., simple, sometimes pinnately lobed, lacking stipules; fls. mostly bisexual, white, pink, or reddish, not large but conspicuous by being aggregated into umbel-like racemes, corymbs, or panicles, sepals and petals usually 5, stamens many, pistils commonly 5, distinct; frs. dehiscent, uninflated follicles.

Spiraeas thrive in any good soil, but require plenty of moisture and sunny exposure. Propagated by seeds sown as soon as ripe or stratified, by cuttings of green wood in summer under glass, by cuttings of mature wood, and some species by layers. There are many horticultural forms and hybrids. The species are hardy to Zone 6 unless stated otherwise.

Many spiraeas are planted as ornamentals. They have a wide range of adaptable white-flowered and pink-flowered forms. If allowed to take their natural form without shearing, they soon make attractive masses with side branches arching or drooping to the ground. Some may be injured at the tips in winter, and these parts may be cut back. The spring-flowering kinds, as *S. prunifolia, S. × Vanhouttei, S. trilobata, S. crenata,* may be pruned after blooming; the summer-flowering kinds, as *S. × Bumalda, S. × Billiardii, S. japonica, S. salicifolia, S. tomentosa,* may be pruned in spring (if at all) to stimulate summer-flowering shoots.

Aitchisonii: *Sorbaria Aitchisonii.*

alba Du Roi MEADOWSWEET. Erect, 1–4 ft., sts. tough, yellowish-brown; lvs. finely serrate, lanceolate-oblong, 2–3 in. long; infl. thyrsoid, tomentulose; fls. white, 5/16 in. across. Que. to Sask., s. to N.C., Ill., Mo. Zone 5.

albiflora (Miq.) Zab. [*S. japonica* var. *alba* (Clemenc.) Nichols.]. To 2 ft., shoots puberulent; lvs. lanceolate, acuminate, glabrous, glandular-serrate to entire, 2½–3 in. long; fls. white, small, in dense corymbs 1½–2 in. across; follicles glabrous. Japan; known only in cult. Zone 5.

arborea: *Sorbaria arborea.*

×arguta Zab.: *S. × multiflora × S. Thunbergii.* Three to 6 ft., rounded; lvs. oblong-obovate, acute, 1–1½ in. long, acutely and often doubly serrate, finally glabrous; fls. white, 5/16 in. across, in small umbels along the whole br. Zone 5. Cvs. **'Compacta'**, **'Graciosa'**, **'Multiflora'** are listed.

Aruncus: *Aruncus sylvester.*

aurea: A listed name of no botanical standing; applied to golden-foliaged cvs. of several spp.

bella Sims. Dioecious, to 3 ft., brs. slender, spreading, angled, somewhat pubescent; lvs. elliptic to ovate, 1–2 in. long, doubly serrate in upper half, glabrous or pubescent beneath on veins; fls. white to pink, ¼ in. across, in loose clusters ¾–1½ in. across. Himalayas. Zone 7.

bethlehemensis: a listed name of no botanical standing; used for *S. latifolia.*

betulifolia Pall. Dense, 2–3 ft., shoots red-brown, glabrous, striped; lvs. elliptic to broadly ovate, mostly rounded at apex, ¾–1¾ in. long, doubly or singly bluntish-serrate, mostly glabrous, gray-green beneath; fls. white, in dense corymbs 1–2½ in. across. Ne. Asia, Japan. Zone 5?

×Billiardii Hérincq: *S. Douglasii × S. salicifolia.* To 6 ft., like *S. Douglasii,* but lvs. acute, grayish-tomentose beneath when young, 2–3 in. long, sharply serrate; fls. bright pink, in narrow panicles, 4–8 in. long. Zone 5. Cvs. include: **'Lenneana'**, shoots glabrous, lvs. lanceolate-elliptic to obovate, 2½–3 in. long; **'Macrothyrsa'** [*S. Menziesii* forma *macrothyrsa* Zab.; *S. macrothyrsa* Dipp.], lvs. broadly obovate, 2 in. long, green beneath; **'Triumphans'** [*S. Menziesii* cv. 'Triumphans'], lvs. elliptic-lanceolate, 1–2½ in. long, green and somewhat pubescent beneath. Cvs. **'Alba'** and **'Rosea'** are listed.

bullata Maxim. [*S. crispifolia* Hort.]. To 1½ ft., dense, compact, rusty-pubescent; lvs. roundish-ovate, leathery, ½–1¼ in. long, coarsely serrate, crisped; fls. at first deep rose, in corymbs 2–3½ in. across, stamens pinkish. Japan; known only in cult. Zone 6.

×Bumalda Burv.: *S. albiflora × S. japonica.* To 2 ft., much like *S. japonica,* but shorter, strongly striped on the shoots; fls. white to deep pink. Cvs. are: **'Atrorosea'**, almost glabrous, of round form, lvs. to 3 in. long, fls. dark pink; **'Crispa'**, weak grower, lvs. red when young, deeply toothed; **'Froebelii'** [*S. Froebelii* Hort.], to 3 ft., with bright crimson fls.; **'Wallufii'**, compact, young lvs. red, fls. pale red. Cvs. **'Alpina'**, **'Coccinea'**, and **'Superba'**, are listed.

caespitosa: *Petrophytum caespitosum.*

callosa: *S. japonica.*

camtschatica: *Filipendula camtschatica.*

cantoniensis Lour. [*S. Reevesiana* Lindl.]. REEVES S. Glabrous, of graceful spreading growth, to 5 ft. high; lvs. lanceolate-ovate, 1–2 in. long, coarsely serrate to 3-lobed, dark green above, blue-green beneath; fls. in hemispherical corymbs 2 in. across, white. China. Long cult in Japan. Zone 7. Cv. **'Lanceata'**. Fls. double.

chamaedryfolia L. [*S. flexuosa* Fisch. ex Camb.]. Suckering shrub, to 5 ft. high, shoots angled, zigzag, glabrous; lvs. ovate, elliptic to lanceolate, 1½–3 in. long, incised-serrate, mostly glabrous; fls. white, many, in somewhat convex glabrous corymbs. Ne. Asia. Zone 5. Var. **ulmifolia** (Scop.) Maxim. Taller, stiffer; lvs. ovate, doubly serrate; infl. larger. Se. Eur. to Japan.

chinensis Maxim. To 5 ft., yellowish-pubescent on the arched shoots; lvs. rhombic-ovate to obovate, 1–2 in. long, incised-serrate, sometimes 3-lobed, deep green and finely pubescent above, yellowish-tomentose beneath; fls. white, 5/16 in. across, in dense, pubescent corymbs. E. China. Zone 7.

corymbosa Raf. One to 3 ft., sts. glabrous on young parts or somewhat pubescent, dark purple; lvs. 1–3 in. long, ovate or broadly oblong, obtuse or rounded at apex, coarsely toothed from near the middle to the apex; fls. white, in corymbs 2–4 in. across. N.J. and Penn. to Ga. and Ky. Zone 6.

crenata L. Tree to 5 ft., shoots cylindrical, slender, at first finely pubescent; lvs. obovate to oblanceolate, 3-nerved, 1–1 5/16 in. long, grayish-green, becoming glabrous, entire, or toothed at apex; fls. in dense pubescent umbels, white, ¼ in. across. Se. Eur., Asia. Zone 6.

crispifolia: a listed name of no botanical standing for *S. bullata.*

decumbens W. D. J. Koch. Glabrous, often almost prostrate, to 8 or 10 in. high; lvs. elliptic-oblong, acute at both ends, ½–1¼ in. long, simply or doubly serrate; fls. white, in corymbs 1–2 in. across. S. Eur. Zone 6.

densiflora Nutt. ex Rydb. One to 3 ft., glabrous or lvs. ciliate; lvs. ovate to elliptic, ½–1¼ in. long, crenate or serrate in upper half; infl. 1–1½ in. broad; fls. small, rose, sepals not reflexed. Mts., Calif. to B.C. Zone 6. Subsp. **splendens** (E. Baumann ex C. Koch) Abrams [*S. rosea* Koehne, not Raf.; *S. splendens* E. Baumann ex C. Koch]. Twigs, petioles, infl., and veins on under side of lvs. finely puberulent. Ore. to Calif.

digitata nana: a listed name of no botanical standing for *Filipendula purpurea* cv. 'Nana'.

Douglasii Hook. Erect, 3–6 ft., young growth and under surface of lvs. more or less white-tomentose; lvs. elliptic to oblong, serrate above the middle, 1–3½ in. long, obtuse to roundish at apex; fls. rose, in elongate panicles. B.C. to Calif. Zone 5. Cv. **'Rosea'** is listed.

eximia: a listed name of no botanical standing; probably *S. × Billiardii.*

Filipendula: *Filipendula vulgaris.*

flexuosa: *S. chamaedryfolia.*

×Fontenaysii Lebas: *S. canescens × S. salicifolia.* Erect, to 6 ft., pubescent on young growth, twigs slender, angled; lvs. elliptic, 1–2 in. long, crenate-serrate in their upper part, obtuse at both ends, blue-green and almost glabrous beneath; fls. white, in pubescent panicles.

Froebelii: a listed name of no botanical standing for *S. × Bumalda* cv.

gemmata Zab. [*S. mongolica* Koehne, not Maxim.]. Six to 9 ft., glabrous, brs. arched; lvs. narrow-elliptic to linear, entire, gray-green beneath, ½–1 in. long; fls. white, 5/16 in. across, 2–6 in sessile umbels. China. Zone 5.

Hacquetii: *S. lancifolia.*

Hendersonii: *Petrophytum Hendersonii.*

Henryi Hemsl. Six to 8 ft., shoots pubescent only when young, cylindrical; lvs. elliptic to oblanceolate, pointed or rounded, 1–3 in. long, margin coarsely toothed at apex, or entire in smaller lvs., glabrous or somewhat pubescent above, pubescent beneath; fls. white, ¼ in. across, in loose, pubescent corymbs. China. Zone 6.

hypericifolia L. Bushy, to 6 ft., brs. arched, pubescent when young; lvs. nearly sessile, broadly oblanceolate to lanceolate, to 1½ in. long, entire or few-toothed near apex, gray-green, slightly pubescent beneath, 3-nerved at base; fls. before the lvs., small, white, in sessile umbels. Se. Eur. to Siberia. Zone 5. Cv. **'Nana'**. A compact form. Cv. **'Obovata'**. Lvs. broader.

japonica L.f. [*S. callosa* Thunb.]. JAPANESE S. To 6 ft., shoots stiffly erect, little-branched, glabrous or pubescent when young, sometimes angled; lvs. lanceolate-ovate, more or less acuminate, coarsely and sharply toothed, 1–4 in. long, gray-green beneath and pubescent on veins; fls. pink, in large, terminal corymbs, leafy at base. Temp. e. Asia. Zone 6. Cvs. are: **'Atrosanguinea'**, fls. dark red, infl. densely pubescent; **'Macrophylla'**, lvs. ovate, to 6 in. long and 3 in. wide; **'Ruberrima'**, shorter, to 3 ft., fls. dark pink. Cvs. **'Alpina'**, **'Coccinea'**, and **'Rosea'** are also listed. Var. **alba:** *S. albiflora.* Var. **Fortunei** (Planch.) Rehd. Taller, shoots cylindrical; lvs. narrow-lanceolate, 2–4 in. long, glabrous beneath. China. Var. **ovalifolia** Franch. Lvs. elliptic, glabrous and bluish beneath; fls. white. W. China.

lancifolia Hoffmanns. [*S. Hacquetii* Fenzl & C. Koch]. Low, to 1 ft., shoots often prostrate, gray-hairy; lvs. elliptic, toothed apically, ½–1 in. long; fls. white, in small clusters. Austria, n. Italy. Zone 6.

latifolia (Ait.) Borkh. [*S. bethlehemensis* Hort.]. MEADOWSWEET. Like *S. alba*, but infl. glabrous; brs. red to purplish-brown; lvs. coarsely toothed; fls. white to pale pink. Nfld. to Mich., s. to N.C. Zone 2.

×**Lemoinei** Zab.: *S. bullata* × *S.* ×*Bumalda*. Habit of *S. albiflora;* lvs. ovate, somewhat bullate; fls. rose-pink. Cv. **'Alpestris'** is offered.

lobata: *Filipendula rubra.*

lucida Dougl. ex Greene. To 3 ft. high, sts. from a creeping rootstock, glabrous; lvs. ovate or obovate, 1–2½ in. long, glabrous, shining above, coarsely and irregularly serrate; fls. white, in flat-topped corymbs 1–4 in. across. B.C. to Ore., Wyo., Mont. Zone 6.

macrothyrsa: *S.* ×*Billiardii* cv.

×**Margaritae** Zab.: *S. japonica* × *S. superba*. To 5 ft., shoots finely hairy, dark brown, nearly cylindrical; lvs. ovate to elliptic-ovate, 2–3½ in. long, acute, coarsely simply or doubly serrate, somewhat pubescent beneath; fls. in open infl. to 6 in. across, pink, 5/16 in. across.

media Franz Schmidt. Resembling *S. chamaedryfolia*, but stiffer, more erect, brs. straw-colored to brown; lvs. lanceolate to oblanceolate, 1–2 in. long, incised-serrate above the middle, dark green above, lighter and more or less pubescent beneath; fls. white, 5/16 in. across, in clusters at the ends of the leafy lateral shoots. E. Eur. to ne. Asia. Zone 5. Cvs. **'Mollis'** and **'Sericea'** are listed.

Menziesii Hook. Much like *S. Douglasii*, but lvs. green and nearly or quite glabrous beneath, 1–2 in. long; calyx tube glabrous. Alaska to Ore., Idaho. Zone 6. Forma **macrothyrsa:** *S.* ×*Billiardii*. Cv. **Triumphans:** *S.* ×*Billiardii* cv.

mongolica: see *S. gemmata.*

×**multiflora** Zab.: *S. crenata* × *S. hypericifolia*. About 5 ft., shoots slender, brown, finely pubescent; lvs. obovate, long-cuneate at base, gray-green, about 1 in. long, crenate-serrate in the upper half, rounded at apex; fls. white, many, in sessile umbels.

Newmannii: a listed name of no botanical standing; a dwarf form.

nipponica Maxim. TOSA S. Five to 8 ft., shoots glabrous, arching; lvs. obovate to elliptic, ½–1¼ in. long, round and few-toothed at apex, cuneate at base, dark green above, bluish-green beneath; fls. 5/16 in. across, white, in many-fld., hemispherical corymbs. Mts., Japan. Zone 5. Var. **rotundifolia** (Nichols.) Mak. Lvs. larger, broader. Var. **tosaensis** (Yatabe) Mak. Lvs. oblanceolate; fls. smaller. Shikoku (Japan).

Normandii: a listed name of no botanical standing; said to be a dwarf form of *S.* ×*Bumalda* turning scarlet in autumn.

opulifolia: *Physocarpus opulifolius.*

palmata: see *Filipendula palmata, F. purpurea*, and *F. rubra;* material cult. as *S. palmata* is usually *F. purpurea.*

×**pikoviensis** Bess.: *S. crenata* × *S. media*. Like *S. crenata*, but shoots almost glabrous, cylindrical; lvs. 1–2 in. long, very slightly pubescent beneath; fls. many.

prunifolia Siebold & Zucc. [*S. prunifolia* cv. 'Plena']. BRIDAL-WREATH. Erect shrub, to 6 ft., twigs slender, arching, finely pubescent at first; lvs. ovate-elliptic, 1–1½ in. long, finely toothed, soft-pubescent beneath; fls. white, double, about 5/16 in. across, few in sessile umbels. Garden form from China. Zone 5. Forma **simpliciflora** Nakai. The wild form with single fls. Temp. e. Asia.

pubescens Turcz. Three to 6 ft., brs. arched, cylindrical, pubescent when young; lvs. rhombic-ovate to elliptic, ½–1½ in. long, incised-serrate to weakly 3-lobed, pubescent above, gray-tomentose beneath; fls. white, to 5/16 in. across, in hemispherical, glabrous corymbs. N. China. Zone 6.

×**pyramidata** Greene: *S. lucida* × *S. Menziesii*. Upright, to 3 ft., mostly glabrous; lvs. elliptic to oblong, 1–3 in. long, coarsely and sometimes doubly serrate above the middle; fls. white or pinkish, in dense pyramidal panicles. B.C. to Ore. and Idaho. Zone 6.

Reevesiana: *S. cantoniensis.*

richmensis, richmonensis: listed names of no botanical standing; used for *Spiraea* cv. 'Richmensis', perhaps derived from *S. Douglasii*, with elliptic lvs. and long, dense, terminal panicles of rose fls.

rosea: see *S. densiflora; S. tomentosa.*

salicifolia L. Three to 6 ft., sts. many, erect, suckering, puberulous when young; lvs. 1–3 in. long, oblanceolate-oblong, to elliptic-oblong, cuneate at base, acute, sharply and sometimes doubly serrate, glabrous; infl. a many-fld., narrow panicle, 1–4 in. long, pubescent; fls. pink, ¾ in. across, stamens twice as long as petals; follicles parallel. Eur. to ne. Asia. Zone 5. Cvs. **'Alba'** and **'Rosea'** are listed.

×**sanssouciana** C. Koch: *S. Douglasii* × *S. japonica*. To 5 ft., twigs angled, finely pubescent when young; lvs. lanceolate to narrow-elliptic, doubly serrate, 2–3½ in. long, pale and pubescent beneath; fls. rose, in dense, pyramidal, pubescent panicles.

Sargentiana Rehd. To 6 ft., new shoots divaricate, pubescent when young; lvs. narrow-elliptic to narrow-obovate, ½–1 in. long, finely toothed near apex, slightly pubescent above, more so beneath; fls. cream-white, ¼ in. across, in dense, pubescent corymbs. W. China. Zone 6.

×**Schinabeckii** Zab.: *S. chamaedryfolia* × *S. trilobata*. Resembling *S. chamaedryfolia*, but the twigs zigzag, angled toward their base; lvs. ovate to oblong, 1–2 in. long, incised-serrate, glabrous, bluish beneath; fls. white, umbellate.

sorbifolia: *Sorbaria sorbifolia.*

splendens: *S. densiflora* subsp.

×**superba** (Froeb.) Zab. ex Dieck: *S. albiflora* × *S. corymbosa*. Low, almost glabrous; lvs. narrow-elliptic to oblong, short-pointed, 1½–3 in. long, entire to doubly serrate; fls. light pink, in terminal corymbs.

Thunbergii Siebold ex Blume. To 5 ft., twigs wiry, more or less puberulent; lvs. linear-lanceolate, ½–1¼ in. long, pointed, sharply and finely toothed, especially toward apex; fls. white, 5/16 in. across, in small sessile umbels. Japan, China. Zone 5.

tomentosa L. [*S. rosea* Raf., not Koehne]. HARDHACK, STEEPLEBUSH. To 4 ft., shoots brown-tomentose; lvs. yellow-tomentose beneath, ovate or oblong, serrate, to 3 in. long; fls. purple-rose, crowded in short, spikelike racemes. Que. to N.C. Zone 5. Cvs. **'Alba'** and **'Rosea'** are listed.

trichocarpa Nakai. Spreading, 3–5 ft. high, shoots angled, glabrous; lvs. oblanceolate to elliptic-lanceolate, grass-green above, pale beneath, 1½–2½ in. long, few-toothed toward apex; fls. white, 5/16 in. across, in rounded clusters at the ends of the short, lateral brs. Korea. Zone 6.

trilobata L. To 4 ft., twigs wiry, glabrous, spreading; lvs. roundish, ½–1 in. wide, coarsely toothed or obscurely 3–5-lobed, bluish-green, especially beneath; fls. white, crowded in small umbels on ends of short lateral branchlets. Cent. and e. Asia. Zone 5.

Ulmaria: *Filipendula Ulmaria.*

×**Vanhouttei** (C. Briot) Zab.: *S. cantoniensis* × *S. trilobata*. BRIDAL-WREATH. To 6 ft., sts. arching, glabrous; lvs. rhombic to obovate, weakly 3–5-lobed, 1–1½ in. long, coarsely serrate, dark green above, bluish and glabrous beneath; fls. white, 5/16 in. across, in flat corymbs 1–2 in. across. Zone 5.

Veitchii Hemsl. Close to *S. Wilsonii*, but taller, 9–12 ft., young twigs reddish, pubescent; lvs. elliptic to oblong, ¾–1½ in. long, cuneate at base, entire, glabrous above, bluish and finely pubescent beneath; fls. white, less than 3/16 in. across, in finely pubescent corymbs 1–2½ in. across. China. Zone 6.

venusta: *Filipendula rubra* cv.

Wilsonii Duthie. To 8 ft., brs. reddish, arched, soft-pubescent when young; lvs. elliptic to obovate, 1–2 in. long, coarsely toothed at apex, cuneate at base, pubescent on both sides; fls. white, ¼ in. across, in dense glabrous, hemispherical, leafy corymbs borne at ends of short, lateral twigs. China. Zone 6.

SPIRANTHES L. Rich. *Orchidaceae.* LADIES'-TRESSES, PEARL-TWIST. About 200 spp. of cosmopolitan terrestrial herbs with tuberous roots; sts. concealed by lf. sheaths or bracts; lvs. basal or on the sts.; infl. a terminal spike or raceme, short or long, often spirally twisted, loosely or densely few- to many-fld.; fls. small, glabrous or pubescent, upper sepal narrow, with petals adherent to it, lateral sepals united below and more or less saccate or extended into a spur at bases, lip sessile or clawed, 1–3-lobed, column with or without a foot. For structure of fl. see *Orchidaceae.*

Grown in shady locations in the wild garden. For culture see *Orchids.*

cernua (L.) L. Rich. COMMON L.-T., SCREW-AUGUR, NODDING L.-T. Erect, to 20 in.; lvs. basal or on lower part of st., linear, to 10 in. long; spike densely fld., spirally twisted; fls. usually in 2 spiral ranks, small, nodding, white, fragrant, upper sepal oblong-lanceolate, to ⅜ in. long, lateral sepals separate, lanceolate, petals linear, to ⅜ in. long, lip ovate-oblong, constricted in middle, dilated at apex, to ⅜ in. long, margins crisp, erose, basal calluses prominent, pubescent. Early summer–early autumn. U.S., Canada. Var. **odorata** (Nutt.) Correll [*S. odorata* Nutt.]. FRAGRANT L.-T., SWEET L.-T., SWAMP L.-T., WATER ORCHID. Lvs. often extending up st.; lip of fl. larger, broadly rhombic-ovate, dilated at base, tapering to an obtuse or acutish apex. Frequent in the s. part of the range of the sp., especially in swamps and other wet places. Sometimes offered as an aquarium plant.

gracilis (Bigel.) L. Beck. SOUTHERN L.-T., SLENDER L.-T., GREEN P.-T., LONG-TRESSES. Slender, to about 2½ ft.; lvs. basal, ovate, blade 2½ in. long; infl. slender, densely or loosely fld., spirally twisted, to 10 in. long; fls. in a single spiral rank, small, white with green stripe in center of lip, to ¼ in. long, sepals and petals similar, elliptic-oblong, lip squarish-oblong, to ¼ in. long, apical margins crenulate to fringed-erose, calluses short and erect. Early summer–autumn. U.S. and Canada.

Grayi Ames. LITTLE L.-T., LITTLE P.-T. To 2 ft.; lvs. basal, ovate, to 2½ in. long; infl. loosely or densely fld. spirally twisted, to 6 in. long; fls. in a single spiral rank, small, white, sepals and petals less than ¼ in. long, sepals lanceolate, petals linear-oblong, lip white, ovate, to ¼ in. long, margins crisped-erose at apex. Early spring–autumn. E. U.S.

odorata: *S. cernua* var.

praecox S. Wats. GRASS-LEAVED L.-T., GIANT L.-T., WATER-TRESSES. To 2½ ft.; lvs. to 7, linear, to 10 in. long; infl. loosely or densely fld., spirally twisted, pubescent with ball-tipped hairs; fls. white with green venation, sepals lanceolate, to ⅜ in. long, petals linear, to ⅜ in. long, lip oblong, with short claw, with green veins on disc, margins undulate, crenulate, or toothed. E. U.S.

Romanzoffiana Cham. & Schlechtend. HOODED L.-T., ROMAN-ZOFF'S L.-T. To nearly 2 ft.; lvs. basal, linear, to 10 in. long; infl. densely fld., spirally twisted, to 5 in. long; fls. in 3 ranks, white, tubular, dilated and gaping above middle, sepals and petals convergent, forming hood over column, to ½ in. long, lip fiddle-shaped, prominently veined, to ½ in. long. Summer–autumn. U.S. and Canada.

sinensis (Pers.) Ames. To 10 in.; lvs. few, basal, linear, to 3½ in. long; infl. many-fld., to 4 in. long; fls. sessile, white, tinged with mauve, sepals less than ¼ in. long, petals close to dorsal sepal, spatulate, lip as long as sepals, white, flushed with mauve at apex, with 2 spherical glands at base, column green. Asia to Australia and New Zeal.

speciosa (J. F. Gmel.) A. Rich. To 20 in.; lvs. basal, orbicular-ovate, to 8 in. long; infl. short, densely few- to many-fld., to 4 in. long; fls. bright red to purple-red, sepals and petals lanceolate, to ¾ in. long, with involute margins, lip sessile, cuneate-lanceolate, to ½ in. long, 3-lobed, disc pubescent, with 2 flat calluses on each side. Trop. Amer.

SPIRODELA Schleid. DUCKWEED. *Lemnaceae.* Four spp. of cosmopolitan, minute, floating, per. herbs; plant body or thallus disc-shaped, leaflike, with several rootlets, proliferating, the offshoots remaining connected for a short time; infl. similar to that of *Lemna.*

polyrhiza (L.) Schleid. GREAT D., WATER FLAXSEED. Plant bodies solitary, or 2–5 and connected, roundish-ovate, ⅜ in. long, flat, purplish beneath.

SPIRONEMA: *CALLISIA.* S. Warscewiczianum: *Hadrodemas Warscewiczianum.*

SPONDIAS L. *Anacardiaceae.* About 12 spp. of polygamous trees of trop. Amer. and Asia; lvs. compound; fls. small, in racemes or panicles, calyx 4–5-cleft, petals 4–5, stamens 8–10, inserted below the disc, ovary 4–5-celled, styles 4–5; fr. fleshy, drupaceous.

Grown in frost-free regions for the edible fr., to make live fences, and sometimes as ornamentals; almost any soil is suitable, although good loams give best results. Propagated by cuttings of mature wood, and *S. cytherea* by shield budding. Much selection of superior fruit forms is possible.

axillaris: *S. Mombin.*

cytherea Sonn. [*S. dulcis* G. Forst.]. AMBARELLA, WI TREE, GOLDEN APPLE, OTAHEITE A. Erect, semideciduous tree, to 60 ft., bark smooth, gray; lfts. 11–23, elliptic to oblong, to 3½ in. long, entire or slightly toothed; fls. small, whitish, in large terminal panicles; fr. with tough orange-yellow skin, ovoid or obovoid, 1–3 in. long, flesh pale yellow, firm, very juicy, nearly acid, seeds 1–5. Spring. Society Is. Widely cult. in tropics. Zone 10b in Fla. Fr. eaten fresh or used for preserves and pickles.

dulcis: *S. cytherea.*

lutea: *S. Mombin.*

Mombin L. [*S. axillaris* Roxb.; *S. lutea* L.]. HOG PLUM, YELLOW MOMBIN, JOBO. Tree, to 60 ft., bark furrowed; lfts. 7–17, ovate-lanceolate, to 4 in. long, nearly entire; panicles large, loose, terminal; fls. yellowish-white; fr. bright yellow, ovoid, with thin skin, about 1 in. long, flesh yellow, soft, juicy, subacid, seed large. Trop. Amer. Occasional, Zone 10b in Fla.

purpurea L. SPANISH PLUM, RED MOMBIN, PURPLE M., JOCOTE. Tree, to 30 ft., semideciduous; lfts. 7–23, oblong, to 1½ in. long, entire or slightly toothed; fls. purple or greenish, in small axillary panicles; fr. dark red or yellow, obovoid, flesh spicy, nearly acid, seed large. Trop. Amer. Widely cult. especially in W. Indies., Mex. and Cent. Amer., also elsewhere in tropics. Zone 10b in Fla. Fr. eaten fresh or boiled, sometimes dried.

Solandri: *Pleiogynium cerasiferum.*

SPOROBOLUS R. Br. DROPSEED, RUSH GRASS. *Gramineae.* About 100 spp. of ann. or per. grasses in N. and S. Amer., Asia, and Afr.; panicles open or contracted; spikelets small, 1-fld., pedicelled, rachilla disarticulating above the glumes, glumes 1-nerved, not longer than the membranous, 1-nerved, awnless lemma, palea usually prominent, as long as or longer than the lemma; caryopsis free from the lemma and palea, pericarp free from seed, slipping away when moist. For terminology see *Gramineae.*

cryptandrus (Torr.) A. Gray. SAND D. Per., usually in small clumps, sts. to 3 ft., erect or spreading to prostrate; lf. sheaths with a tuft of long white hairs at summit, blades to ¼ in. wide, flat or becoming involute when dry; panicles usually included at base, panicle well-developed, terminal, open, to 10 in. long, brs usually spreading, naked at base, to 3¼ in. long or more; spikelets crowded on the upper part of the main brs., pale to lead-colored, ⅛ in. long. Widespread in N. Amer.

pulchellus R. Br. [*Agrostis pulchella* (R. Br.) Roth]. Sts. clustered, to 1 ft.; lf. blades chiefly at base of st., flat or keeled, rather stiff, margins ciliate; panicle loosely pyramidal, to 5 in. long, brs. many, capillary, spreading, whorled; spikelets pedicelled, to ⅛ in. long, glossy, glumes almost hyaline, rather obtuse, slightly keeled, nearly equal, palea very readily splitting in half. Australia.

SPRAGUEA: *CALYPTRIDIUM.*

SPREKELIA Heist. *Amaryllidaceae.* One sp., a bulbous herb, native to Mex.; bulb tunicate; lvs. linear; fl. solitary, pedicelled, on a scape and subtended by a tubular spathe bifid at apex and splitting along one side; perianth irregular, tube barely perceptible, stamens 6, of 4 lengths, stigma trifid, ovary inferior, ovules many; fr. a caps., seeds flat, black, winged.

Grown in the greenhouse and outdoors in warm climates. For cultivation see *Hippeastrum.*

formosissima (L.) Herb. [*Amaryllis formosissima* L.]. JACOBEAN LILY, ST. JAMES'S L., AZTEC L., ORCHID AMARYLLIS. To 1 ft.; lvs. linear, developing at same time as fls.; fls. bright crimson, to 4 in. long, the 3 upper segms. erect and narrow, the 3 lower ones rolled together into a horizontal cylinder for part of their length. Spring and summer. Cv. 'Superba' is listed.

SPYRIDIUM Fenzl. *Rhamnaceae.* About 30 spp. of shrubs of Australia; lvs. alt., simple, more or less pubescent; fls. mostly in small, sessile heads, surrounded by imbricate, dry, brown bracts.

globulosum (Labill.) Benth. Tall, evergreen shrub; lvs. ovate to oblong, to 1½ in. long, leathery, white-tomentose beneath; heads almost globular, many in dense axillary corymbs. W. Australia. Introd. in Calif.

SQUASH: see *PUMPKIN.*

STACHYS L. [*Betonica* L.]. BETONY, HEDGE NETTLE, WOUNDWORT. *Labiatae.* About 300 spp. of herbs and subshrubs of temp. and subtrop. regions and trop. mts.; sts. mostly square in cross section; lvs. opp., entire or toothed; fls. small, sessile to short-pedicelled, in 2- to many-fld. verticillasters arranged in terminal spikelike to headlike infl., calyx tubular-campanulate, 5–10-nerved, 5-toothed, teeth bristly, corolla purple, red, pink, yellow, or white, tube cylindrical, shorter or longer than calyx, often hairy inside, limb 2-lipped, upper lip often concave, often 2-lobed, lower lip 3-lobed, middle lobe often 2-lobed, stamens 4, in 2 pairs, anthers 2-celled; fr. of 4 ovoid nutlets.

A few species are grown as ornamentals in borders and one, *S. affinis,* is cultivated in eastern Asia for its edible tubers. Propagated readily by seeds or division.

affinis Bunge [*S. Sieboldii* Miq.]. CHOROGI, CHINESE ARTICHOKE, JAPANESE A., KNOTROOT, CROSNES-DU-JAPON. Erect herb, to 1½ ft., hairy, with slender, knotty, white tubers abundantly produced just beneath the soil surface; lvs. ovate to ovate-lanceolate; fls. white or light red. China. Much cult. in Japan for the edible tubers; sometimes grown in U.S. in garden collections of economic plants.

Alopecuros (L.) Benth. Erect per., to 2 ft., hirsute; lvs. triangular-ovate-cordate, to 3½ in. long, coarsely crenate or crenate-dentate; spikes dense, the lower verticillasters sometimes spaced apart; calyx to ⅜ in. long, teeth up to half as long as the tube, corolla to 7/16 in. long, pale yellow. Limestone mts., s. and cent. Eur.

Betonica: *S. officinalis.*

bullata Benth. Procumbent per., sts. 1½–3 ft. long; lvs. ovate to oblong-ovate, 1½–8 in. long, mostly obtuse, crenate-serrate, upper lvs. mostly sessile; spikes interrupted, verticillasters 6-fld.; calyx 5/16 in. long, pilose, teeth spine-tipped, corolla nearly ⅝ in. long, purple, stamens exserted. Calif.

byzantina C. Koch [*S. lanata* Jacq., not Crantz; *S. olympica* of auth., not Poir.]. WOOLLY B., LAMB'S-EARS. Erect per., to 32 in., sts. and lvs. densely white-tomentose; lvs. to 4 in. long, cuneate to attenuate at base, lower lvs. oblong-spatulate, upper lvs. elliptic; calyx to ½ in. long, teeth ⅓ as long as tube, corolla to 1 in. long, pink or purple, densely white-woolly. Turkey, sw. Asia. A much cult. ornamental.

ciliata Dougl. ex Benth. Erect per., 3–4 ft., glabrescent to pubescent; lvs. petioled, ovate, to 3½ in. long, cordate, acute, dentate; infl. racemose, verticillasters few-fld., spaced apart; calyx to ½ in. long, teeth triangular, spinescent, corolla 3 times as long as calyx, reddish-purple. B.C. to Ore.

cordata: see *S. Riddellii.*

corsica Pers. Per., to 6 in., procumbent, carpet-forming, short-lived, sparsely hairy; lvs. petioled, broadly ovate, to ½ in. long, obtuse, nearly cordate, broadly crenate; fls. solitary or in 2-fld. verticillasters spaced apart; calyx campanulate, to ⅛ in. long, densely hairy, corolla to ½ in. long, white to purple. Mts., Corsica and Sardinia. Often cult. as an ann.

germanicsa L. DOWNY W. Per., to 4 ft., densely white-woolly; lvs. petioled, ovate or ovate-lanceolate, 4 in. long, acute or obtuse at apex, cordate at base, more or less serrate, green above, gray-tomentose beneath, lower lvs. largest and long-petioled; infl. more or less spicate, verticillasters many-fld., usually spaced apart; calyx to ⅜ in. long, nearly equally toothed, corolla about twice as long as calyx, usually pink or purple, densely hairy. Eur., N. Afr., cent. Asia.

grandiflora (Willd.) Benth. [*Betonica grandiflora* Willd.; *B. macrantha* C. Koch]. Rosette-forming per., sts. to 18 in., villous; lvs. ovate, to 2¾ in. long, obtuse, coarsely crenate-serrate, the lower ones largest and long-petioled; verticillasters several, more or less spaced apart; calyx tubular, to ⅜ in. long, teeth subulate, nearly equal, corolla to 1½ in. long, violet. Summer. Caucasus. Cvs. include: **'Alba'**, **'Robusta'**, **'Superba'**.

hyssopifolia Michx. Stoloniferous per., to 30 in., glabrous or glabrescent; lvs. sessile or nearly so, linear to linear-oblong, to 1½ in. long, obtuse to bluntly acute; infl. of several verticillasters spaced apart; calyx campanulate, to 3/16 in. long, teeth lanceolate-attenuate, corolla 2–3 times as long as calyx, pinkish. Shores of ponds and in bogs, Mass. to Ga.

lanata: see *S. byzantina.*

lavandulifolia Vahl. Stoloniferous subshrub, brs. ascending, to 6 in., densely gray-pubescent; lvs. petioled, narrowly elliptic-lanceolate, to 2 in. long, entire; verticillasters several, few-fld.; calyx narrowly campanulate, to ⅜ in. long, rose-purple, teeth narrowly triangular, nearly equal, about twice as long as tube, caudate, corolla rose-purple, tube shorter than calyx teeth. Asia Minor.

nivea Labill. [*Betonica nivea* (Labill.) Steven]. Woody at base, 6–12 in., densely pubescent; lvs. nearly sessile, obovate to oblong, to 1½ in. long, obtuse, entire; verticillasters several, few-fld.; calyx 5/16 in. long, teeth short-triangular, corolla white, tube as long as calyx teeth. Syria. Doubtfully in cult.

officinalis (L.) Trevisan [*S. Betonica* Benth.; *Betonica officinalis* L.]. BETONY. Erect, rosette-forming per., sts. to 3 ft., nearly glabrous to densely hirsute; lvs. oblong to ovate-oblong, to 5 in. long, cordate at base, crenate or crenate-dentate, the lower long-petioled, the upper nearly sessile; infl. a dense spike; calyx to ¼ in. long, corolla red-purple, rarely pink or white, tube longer than calyx. Spring. Eur. and Asia. Cv. **'Alba'**. Fls. white.

olympica: see *S. byzantina.*

pubescens Ten. Erect per., to 12 in., with persistent rosettes, pubescent; lvs. petioled, oblong to oblong-ovate, to 1 in. long, obtuse, entire; verticillasters 4–6-fld., spaced apart; calyx to ¼ in. long, villous, teeth triangular-acuminate, corolla about ½ in. long, pale yellow, pubescent. Maritime sands, Medit. region.

Riddellii House [*S. cordata* Ridd., not Gilib.]. Tuberous per., 1½–4½ ft.; lvs. petioled, membranous, ovate, to 3½ in. long, cordate, acuminate, crenate-dentate; spike slender, interrupted; calyx minutely pilose, teeth triangular, much shorter than tube, corolla ½ in. long, purplish, with darker spots. Rich soils and shaded locations, Md. to Ill, s. to N.C. and Tenn.

Sieboldii: *S. affinis.*

tenuifolia Willd. Creeping per., sts. erect, to 40 in. high, glabrous or glabrescent; lvs. short-petioled, narrowly lanceolate to ovate, to 3½ in. long, acute, dentate; verticillasters several, spaced apart, few-fld.; calyx campanulate, to 3/16 in. long, glabrous, teeth sharply acute, corolla to ⅜ in. long, purplish. N.Y. to Minn., s. to Ala. and Tex. A variable sp. Var. **platyphylla** Fern. Lvs. broadly oblong, to 6 in. long and 2½ in. wide.

STACHYTARPHETA Vahl. *Verbenaceae.* About 65 spp. of shrubs, subshrubs, or per. or ann. herbs, native to trop. and subtrop. N. and S. Amer., 1 or 2 spp. in trop. Asia and Afr.; lvs. opp. or alt., simple, toothed, often rugose; fls. red, purple, blue, or white, in terminal spikes, calyx 5-toothed, corolla 5-lobed, stamens 2; fr. dry, enclosed in the calyx, separating into 2 nutlets at maturity.

Frantzii Polak. Subshrub, to 6 ft., brs. densely pilose; lvs. elliptic to ovate, to 4 in. long, coarsely serrate, scabrous and pilose above, pilose and tomentose beneath; spikes stout, to 1 ft. long; fls. purple. Costa Rica.

indica: *S. jamaicensis.*

jamaicensis (L.) Vahl [*S. indica* Vahl]. Ann. or per. herb, to 4 ft.; lvs. oblong or elliptic, to 3 in. long, coarsely serrate, almost glabrous; spikes stiff or flexuous, to 1½ ft. long; fls. blue, ¼ in. across. Widely dispersed in tropics.

urticifolia (Salisb.) Sims. Subshrub, to 2 ft.; lvs. ovate or ovate-oblong, to 4 in. long, toothed, glabrous or with few hairs on veins beneath; spikes slender, to 1½ ft. long; fls. blue. S. Amer.

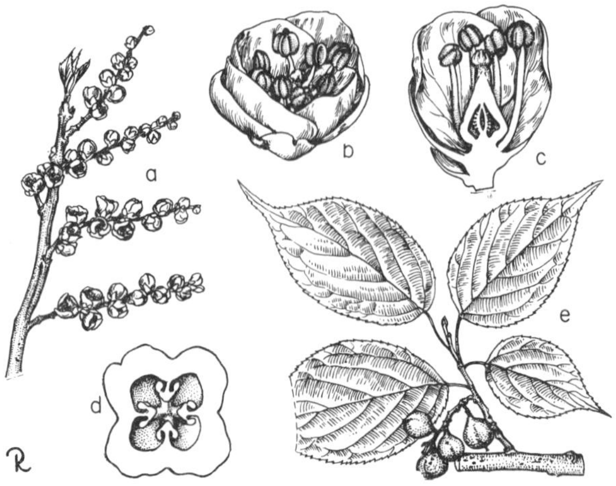

STACHYURACEAE. *Stachyurus praecox:* **a,** flowering branch, × ½; **b,** flower, × 3; **c,** flower, vertical section, × 3; **d,** ovary, cross section, × 8; **e,** fruiting branch, × ½. (From Lawrence, *Taxonomy of Vascular Plants.*)

STACHYURACEAE J. Agardh. STACHYURUS FAMILY. Dicot.; 1 genus, *Stachyurus,* of shrubs and small trees, native to e. Asia; lvs. alt., simple, without stipules; fls. in axillary, drooping racemes or spikes, small, 4-merous, petals separate, stamens 8, not united, ovary 4-celled, superior; fr. 4-celled, berrylike, seeds many.

STACHYURUS Siebold & Zucc. *Stachyuraceae.* Five or 6 spp. of shrubs or small trees of e. Asia with characters of the family; flowering in early spring before the lvs.

chinensis Franch. Very similar to *S. praecox,* but with more acuminate lvs., spreading fls., longer styles, and smaller frs. China.

praecox Siebold & Zucc. Shrub, to 12 ft.; lvs. ovate or ovate-lanceolate, to 5½ in. long, serrate; racemes to 3 in. long; fls. yellow, campanulate, 5/16 in. long; fr. globose, greenish-yellow, 5/16 in. in diam. Japan. Zone 8. Cv. **'Gracilis'** is listed.

STAHLIA Bello. *Leguminosae* (subfamily *Caesalpinioideae*). One sp., a large tree, native to Puerto Rico; lvs. alt., even-pinnate, lfts. gland-dotted; fls. in racemes, 5-merous, nearly regular, stamens 10, separate, with woolly filaments; fr. an ovoid, leathery legume, indehiscent or tardily dehiscent.

Sometimes planted as an ornamental in warm regions.

monosperma (Tulasne) Urb. COBANA, POLISANDRO. To 65 ft.; lfts. in 3–6 pairs, ovate to ovate-lanceolate, to 3½ in. long, acute-acuminate, entire to irregularly crenulate; racemes to 6 in. long; petals yellow, papillose, ⁵⁄₁₆ in. long, stamens deflexed; fr. purple, to 2 in. long, 1 in. wide and ⁵⁄₁₆ in. thick, 1-seeded. Puerto Rico. Zone 10b.

STANDARD. In horticultural rather than botanical language, a standard is a nonarborescent, usually woody plant trained over a period of several years to simulate a slender tree form. The leafy branches are produced at the top of a single upright unbranched stem, the standard, which may be from three to six feet high depending upon the proportions desired. So-called tree roses *(Rosa),* tree azaleas *(Rhododendron),* and tree fuchsias *(Fuchsia)* are examples of such trained plants.

Vigorous plants produced from cuttings or grafts and with strong-growing shoots or leaders are usually selected for training as standards. They are normally grown in pots or other containers. The main stem is trained to a stake, with all lateral branches kept pinched back (but not cut off completely) so as to encourage growth of the main stem and to assist in its more rapid thickening. Regular fertilizing, frequent but light, is essential. Once a predetermined height is reached, the growing tip is pinched out so as to allow development of an attractive and symmetrical head, which may be either bushy or pendent, as determined by the natural habit of the subject.

Among genera supplying species useful as standards are: *Allamanda, Aucuba, Bougainvillea, Bouvardia, Callistemon, Camellia, Cytisus, Fuchsia, Hedera, Heliotropium, Justicia, Lantana, Leptospermum, Pelargonium, Rhododendron* (Indian Hybrid Azaleas), *Rosa, Streptosolen,* and *Wisteria.*

STANGERIA T. Moore. *Stangeriaceae.* One sp., a dioecious, fernlike, per. cycad, native to S. Afr.; sts. underground, branched or unbranched, each br. bearing 1–4 apical lvs.; lvs. pinnate, pinnae lanceolate, in opp. or subopp. pairs, the uppermost united; cones solitary, stalked, silvery-pubescent, the male more or less cylindrical, the female ovoid-elliptic.

Rarely cultivated under glass or outdoors in Zone 10. For culture see *Cycads.*

eriopus (Kunze) Nash [*S. paradoxa* T. Moore]. Lvs. to 6 ft. long, pinnae to 16 in. long, 2½ in. wide; male cones 4–6 in. long, female cones to 7 in. long.

paradoxa: *S. eriopus.*

STANGERIACEAE L. A. S. Johnson. STANGERIA FAMILY, CYCADS. Gymnosperms; 1 genus, *Stangeria,* native to S. Afr.; differs from the Zamiaceae in having lvs. convolute, not imbricate in bud, and pinnae with a well-developed midvein and many transverse, parallel, dichotomously branched, lateral veins, and from the Cycadaceae in having pinnae with lateral venation and female sporophylls (cone scales) in determinate cones.

STANHOPEA Frost ex Hook. *Orchidaceae.* About 200 spp. of epiphytes, native to trop. Amer.; pseudobulbs 1-lvd.; lvs. petioled, plicate; infl. lateral, pendent, racemose, 1- to several-fld.; fls. showy, sepals membranous, the lateral ones united at base and reflexed, petals membranous, often reflexed, lip fleshy, either saccate and simple or divided into a saccate hypochil, hornlike mesochil, and a somewhat lengthwise-folded epichil, column slender, with prominent wings. For structure of fl. see *Orchidaceae.*

Grown in hanging containers which will permit the lateral inflorescences to emerge at bottom after passing through the planting medium. For general culture see *Orchids.*

costaricensis Rchb.f. Pseudobulbs to 2 in. long; lvs. ovate-elliptic, to 14 in. long; infl. 2–4-fld.; fls. large, to 6 in. across, pale yellow with reddish-brown spots, sepals ovate, reflexed, petals strap-shaped, undulate, reflexed, lip to 3 in. long, hypochil ovate-fiddle-shaped, invagi-

nate below, mesochil with sickle-shaped arms, epichil nearly orbicular or elliptic, column with broadly triangular wings. Costa Rica.

eburnea: *S. grandiflora.*

ecornuta Lem. Pseudobulbs ovoid, to 1½ in. long; lvs. broadly ovate-elliptic, to 20 in. long, 6 in. wide; infl. 2–3-fld.; fls. fleshy, 4–5 in. across, sepals and petals spreading, ovate, white, lip somewhat slipper-shaped, entire and undivided, column short, fleshy. Guatemala, Honduras.

grandiflora (Lodd.) Lindl. [*S. eburnea* Lindl.]. Pseudobulbs ovoid; lvs. ovate-elliptic, to 1 ft. long; infl. 1–2-fld.; fls. to 5 in. across, white, sepals ovate, semireflexed or spreading, petals narrower, oblong-linear, lip lanceolate in outline, entire, white with purple markings inside, basally swollen and with a pair of short curved teeth on both sides, sides erect, triangular, column long, winged toward apex. Colombia, Venezuela, Guyana.

graveolens Lindl. Pseudobulbs conical, to 1½ in. long; lvs. elliptic-lanceolate, to 2 ft. long; infl. several-fld.; fls. large, to 4 in. across, fragrant, yellow with reddish spots, sepals ovate-lanceolate, lateral ones reflexed, petals semireflexed, strap-shaped, undulate, lip with hypochil deep orange, swollen, mesochil sickle-shaped, white with purple dots, epichil elliptic-ovate, white with purplish dots on upper surface, column broadly winged in upper part. Mex., Guatemala, Honduras.

insignis Frost ex Hook. Pseudobulbs conical, grooved, to 2 in. long; lvs. oblong-elliptic, to 20 in. long; infl. 2–3-fld.; fls. large, to 5 in. across, sepals and petals ovate, yellow with purple spots, petals narrower, lip with hypochil subglobose, purple with dark maroon spots, mesochil sickle-shaped, white with a few purple spots, epichil white with a few purple spots, column purple, winged in upper part. Brazil.

Martiana Batem. ex Lindl. Pseudobulbs conical, grooved, to 2 in. long; lvs. oblong-lanceolate, to 1 ft. long; infl. 1–2-fld.; fls. large, to 6 in. across, sepals and petals spreading, ovate or ovate-elliptic, white or cream, with reddish spots, lip with hypochil saccate, mesochil filiform, epichil 3-toothed, column hardly winged. Mex.

oculata (Lodd.) Lindl. Pseudobulbs ovoid; lvs. elliptic-lanceolate, to 20 in. long; infl. 2–4-fld.; fls. to 5 in. across, sepals elliptic-lanceolate, cream-white, reflexed, petals linear-lanceolate, lip with hypochil boat-shaped, mesochil short, slender, sickle-shaped, epichil obovate, apiculate, column winged in upper part. Mex. to Panama.

platyceras Rchb.f. Pseudobulbs pear-shaped, to 2 in. long; lvs. elliptic, to 18 in. long; infl. 2-fld.; fls. large, to 6 in. across, sepals and petals ovate, reflexed, yellow with red-purple blotches, petals narrower, lip with hypochil boat-shaped, maroon with red-purple spots, mesochil sickle-shaped, flat, yellow with red-purple spots, epichil ovate, column arching, prominently winged. Colombia.

Shuttleworthii Rchb.f. Lvs. relatively small, to 15 in. long; infl. many-fld.; fls. large, to 5 in. across, pale yellow with large purple blotches, sepals and petals ovate, reflexed, lip with hypochil boat-shaped, mesochil sickle-shaped, linear, epichil ovate, apiculate. Colombia.

tigrina Batem. ex Lindl. Large, pseudobulbs to 2 in. long; lvs. to 20 in. long; infl. 2-fld.; fls. to 8 in. across, sepals and petals spreading, yellow with large maroon blotches, sepals ovate, petals strap-shaped, lip with hypochil saccate, globular, yellow, mesochil linear-curved, white, epichil cuneate-fan-shaped, white, column arching, prominently winged. E. Mex.

tricornis Lindl. Pseudobulbs pear-shaped, to 2 in. long; lvs. oblong-elliptic, to 1 ft. long; infl. 2-fld.; fls. large, to 5 in. across, sepals spreading or reflexed, ovate, yellow, petals oblong, remaining parallel with column, yellow, lip with hypochil globose, mesochil strap-shaped, epichil squarish, apiculate, column fleshy, short, with broad wings. Colombia, Ecuador.

Wardii Lodd. ex Lindl. Pseudobulbs ovoid; lvs. elliptic-oblong; infl. several-fld.; fls. yellow with dark puce spots, sepals spreading, ovate, petals lanceolate, undulate, lip with hypochil squarish, with a dark eye on both sides, mesochil linear-curved, epichil ovate-apiculate, column winged. Nicaragua to Venezuela.

STANLEYA Nutt. PRINCE'S-PLUME. *Cruciferae.* About 6 spp. of ann. or per. herbs of w. N. Amer., glaucous, usually glabrous, sts. simple or branched; lvs. lobed, entire, or divided; fls. white to yellow, in racemes, sepals and petals 4, very narrow; fr. an elongated silique on a long stalk, seeds many, oblong.

Sometimes grown as ornamentals in regions like those to which they are native.

elata M. E. Jones. To 2 ft.; lvs. lanceolate-ovate, to 8 in. long, entire or with a few small basal lobes; fls. lemon-yellow to nearly white, in racemes becoming 4–20 in. long. Desert washes and slopes, Calif., Nev., Ariz.

pinnata (Pursh) Britt. Subshrubby per., to 5 ft.; lower lvs. lanceolate in outline, to 6 in. long, pinnatifid or sometimes 2-pinnate, upper lvs. lanceolate to ovate, to 4 in. long, entire to pinnatifid, glabrous or sparsely hairy; racemes congested, to 1 ft. long, fls. golden-yellow. S. Calif. and nw. Nev., e. to Tex., Kans., and N. and S. Dak.

STAPELIA L. CARRION FLOWER, STARFISH FLOWER, STARFISH PLANT. *Asclepiadaceae.* About 90 spp. of low, succulent, per. herbs, native to trop. and s. Afr.; sts. thick, fleshy, branched from the base, 4- (rarely 5–6-) angled, the angles toothed; lvs. small, if present; fls. often large, solitary or several together along sts., pedicelled, usually fetid, corolla usually yellowish, purplish, or brownish, often barred and mottled with darker colors, rotate to open-campanulate, with or without a raised ring, the annulus, at the center surrouding the corona, staminal column bearing a corona of 2 whorls, the lobes of the outer whorl mostly 5, separate, entire or divided, the lobes of the inner whorl 5, simple, bifid or 2-horned, dorsally winged or crested, united to the base of the anthers, anthers without terminal appendages; fr. a narrow or stout, spindle-shaped follicle, seeds with tuft of hair at apex. The spp. are distinguished technically chiefly on the basis of the characters of the complex coronas.

Stapelias are grown in light shade under glass or out of doors in southern Calif. and similar climatic areas. They require open, porous, well-drained sandy soil, and should remain dormant in winter. Propagated by seeds, or by cuttings when pure lines are desired. For additional information on culture, see *Succulents.* Many forms are known, some perhaps interspecific hybrids, others only garden selections. Many have been given varietal or even specific ranking, but in most instances, with their origin unknown, it is difficult or impossible to determine whether they should be recognized as hybrids, botanical varieties, or cultivars.

acuminata Masson. Sts. to 6 in., puberulous, tinted purplish-brown; fls. mostly in clusters of 2–5 at about the middle of the st., corolla rotate, to 1¾ in. across, glabrous, dark purple-brown, with yellow, transverse ridges, lobes acuminate to a short tail-like point, fringed with white hairs, lobes of outer whorl of corona bifid or 3-toothed, mottled purple-brown and yellow, lobes of inner whorl 2-horned. S. Afr.

albocastanea Marloth [*S. Caroli-Schmidtii* Dinter & Berger]. Sts. tufted, curving upwards, about 3 in.; fls. 3–6 at middle of st., corolla 1–1½ in. across, nearly white, spotted all over with purple-brown. S.-W. and S. Afr.

ambigua Masson. Sts. to 9 in., soft-pubescent; fls. 3–5 at base of st., corolla 4–5 in. across, brownish-purple with darker transverse ridges, purple-pubescent, lobes lanceolate, recurved, lobes of outer whorl of corona dull red, ⁵⁄₁₆ in. long, reflexed at apex, lobes of the inner whorl diverging. S. Afr. Var. **fulva** Sweet. Central area of corolla and lower part of lobes yellow-green with purple-brown ridges, apex of lobes purple-brown.

×**angulata** Tod. Reportedly a hybrid, with one parent probably *S. mutabilis,* from which it may be distinguished by its small, yellow, inconspicuously marked annulus. Known only in cult.

Arnotii N. E. Br. Sts. to 8 in.; fls. 2–3 at base of st., corolla about 4 in. across, bright purple, without markings, smooth, purplish-pubescent, lobes lanceolate, acute, reflexed, slightly ridged, black at apex. S. Afr.

asterias Masson. Sts. to 10 in., nearly flat-sided, not prominently toothed; fls. 1–5 at base of st., corolla mostly starlike, 3–4 in. across, glossy, dark purple-brown with whitish or yellowish transverse ridges not reaching the margins, corolla lobes spreading, lobes of outer whorl of corona ascending-spreading, 3-toothed or apiculate, blackish-purple, lobes of inner whorl nearly as long, minutely dotted at apex. S. Afr. Var. **lucida** (DC.) N. E. Br. Corolla entirely purplish-red or -brown without transverse markings, sometimes dull greenish at apex of lobes. S. Afr.

×**bella** A. Berger. Sts. to 7 in., minutely puberulent; fls. 3–4 on a very short peduncle near base of st., corolla about 2 in. across, deep purplish-red, browner towards the tips of lobes, paler near center, glabrous on both surfaces, but the lobes fringed, lobes of corona about ⅛ in. long. Believed to be a garden hybrid of *S. revoluta,* and perhaps involving *S. deflexa.*

berlinensis: a listed name of no botanical standing, applied to a plant with large, purple-black fls.

cantabrigiensis A. Berger. Reported as a hybrid, but perhaps only a form of *S. grandiflora,* and distinguished from it by its bell-shaped

corolla, with more narrowly lanceolate lobes, shorter red-brown pubescence, and linear, awn-tipped outer corona lobes. Known only in cult.

Caroli-Schmidtii: *S. albocastanea.*

×**comparabilis** A. C. White & Sloane. Sts. erect, to about 8 in.; fls. several at base of st., corolla 3½–4½ in. across, dull reddish-purple inside, sometimes with yellowish or whitish transverse ridges, annulus purple-pubescent, corolla lobes spreading or reflexed, lobes of outer whorl of corona to ³⁄₁₆ in. long, those of inner whorl 2-horned, the horns laterally compressed, up to ⁵⁄₁₆ in. long. Origin unknown, but probably a garden hybrid.

Cooperi: *Stultitia Cooperi.*

deflexa Jacq. Sts. erect, decumbent at the base, loosely branched, 4–7 in.; fls. 3–6 at base of st., corolla 2–3½ in. across, entirely dark, livid purple-red or with greenish-white or -yellowish shallow ridges, lobes strongly reflexed and revolute, lobes of outer whorl of corona about ⅛ in. long. S. Afr. Var. **atropurpurea** Jacq. Corolla darker-colored, with faint white lines and fringe of white and red hairs. Perhaps a hybrid rather than a var.

Desmetiana N. E. Br. Sts. erect, 6–12 in., conspicuously velvety-pubescent; fls. 3–10 on a peduncle near base of st., corolla 4½–6½ in. across, pale to dark purple-red with transverse yellow ridges and pale purple pubescence, tips of lobes entirely dark purple, fringed with pale purple hairs. S. Afr.

×**discolor** Tod. A hybrid of *S. mutabilis,* from which it differs in having corolla dark purple-brown with inconspicuous, yellowish, transverse lines on the disc and lower part of lobes, and annulus yellowish, with irregular purple lines. Material offered under this name is likely to be a variant of *S. variegata.*

divaricata Masson. Sts. spreading to erect, very loosely branched, 3–4 in.; fls. 1–6 near base of st., corolla 1–2 in. across, varying from pale flesh-color to dull purple, lobes greenish-tipped. S. Afr.

Dummeri N. E. Br. Sts. to 4 in., long-toothed; fls. 4–6 in a cluster near base of st., corolla about 1½ in. across, olive-greenish-ochre, lobes ascending, pointed, papillate-pubescent, lobes of corona (apparently) yellow. Tanzania, Kenya.

Englerana Schlechter. Sts. procumbent or decumbent, sparingly branched, to 1 ft. long; fls. solitary near middle or apex of st., corolla orbicular, about 1 in. across, dark purple, with or without yellow transverse ridges, tube 5-angled at throat, whitish and spotted purple-brown, lobes reflexed against exterior of tube. S. Afr.

flavirostris N. E. Br. Similar to *S. grandiflora,* but corolla less hairy and with more prominent transverse ridges, and lobes of inner whorl of corona yellow at apex. S. Afr.

fulva: *S. ambigua* var.

Gettleffii R. Pott. Sts. to 10 in., the teeth tipped with rudimentary lvs. to ½ in. long; fls. 1–3 together near base of st., corolla rotate, to 6½ in. across, yellowish, with purple transverse ridges, densely pubescent with pale purplish hairs, lobes purple at apex, fringed with hairs. S. Afr.

gigantea N. E. Br. GIANT S., ZULU-GIANT, GIANT TOAD PLANT. Sts. erect, 4–8 in.; fls. 1–2 together at base or middle of st., corolla very large, 11–16 in. across, light ochreous-yellow, with crimson transverse ridges, finely purple-pubescent. Trop. and S. Afr. Var. **pallida** E. P. Phillips. Corolla lighter colored, with depressed, more or less cup-shaped center.

glabricaulis N. E. Br. Sts. erect, to 8 in., glabrous; fls. 2–5 together at base of st., corolla 2½–3½ in. across, reddish-purple, without markings but becoming somewhat yellowish centrally, finely silky-pubescent toward center, corona dark purple-brown. S. Afr.

glandulifera: *S. glanduliflora.*

glanduliflora Masson [*S. glandulifera* Willd.]. Sts. erect, to 6½ in., sometimes 5–6-angled; fls. 3–9 at base of st., corolla 1–1½ in. across, pale sulphur-yellow, marked with fine purple-red dots and transverse lines, lobes with long, dense, clavate, white hairs on lower half and along entire margin, lobes of inner whorl of corona subulate, dull yellow, red-spotted. S. Afr.

grandiflora Masson. Sts. to 1 ft., deeply troughed, angles very compressed; fls. 1–3 at base of st., corolla flat, 5–6 in. across, uniformly dark purple-brown, slightly rugose, lobes densely soft-villous with long, erect, purple hairs on the surface of lower half, fringed to their tips with whitish hairs, corona dark purple-brown, lobes of inner whorl gracefully horned. S. Afr. Material offered under this name may be one of various hybrids or other spp.

Hanburyana: *S. variegata.*

hirsuta L. HAIRY TOAD PLANT, HAIRY S. F., SHAGGY S. Sts. erect, to 8 or more in.; fls. 1–3 near base of st., corolla 4–5 in. across, lobes dark purple-brown, marked with transverse cream or yellowish lines except at apex, passing below into yellowish with purple-brown lines, center and the base of lobes densely soft purple-pubescent, lobes of inner whorl of corona ascending, to ⅜ in. long, blackish. S. Afr. Var. **unguipetala** (N. E. Br.) N. E. Br. Corolla to 4½ in. across, the upper part of the lobes strongly revolute with upcurved tips. Known only in cult.

kwebensis N. E. Br. About 6 in.; fls. few in nearly sessile cymes at base of st., corolla to 1⁵⁄₁₆ in. across, chocolate-colored to maroon or ochre, with transverse ridges, lobes pubescent at tips, lobes of corona less than ¹⁄₁₆ in. long. S. Afr., Botswana.

Leendertziae N. E. Br. Sts. somewhat loosely branched, to 4 in.; fls. mostly solitary at middle of st., corolla cup-shaped, to 3 in. long, 3–4 in. across at the mouth, dark purple-brown or purple-black, transversely ridged, lobes slightly spreading, to 2½ in. long, glabrous. S. Afr.

lepida Jacq. Plants glabrous throughout, sts. 2–3 in.; fls. 1–2 at base of st., corolla about 1½ in. across, sulphur-yellow, purple-brown-spotted, ridged, annulus prominent, lighter colored than lobes. Known only in cult.

Longii Lückh. Sts. slender, procumbent, to 9 in.; fls. solitary at middle of st., corolla about 1 in. across, glabrous, light brown with a few ridges and yellow lines at center, lobes fringed at the base with clavate, purple hairs, lobes of corona terminated by round, fleshy, papillate knobs. S. Afr.

luxurians: *S. variegata.*

maculata: *S. maculosa.*

maculosa J. Donn [*S. maculata* Poir.]. Sts. 3–4 in.; fls. solitary or in 2's or 3's at base of st., corolla 3–4 in. across, with a distinct annulus, greenish-yellow, transversely streaked or spotted purple-brown, deep purple-brown at the tips and margins of lobes, glabrous, except for purplish hairs on the margin and on the annulus. Of garden origin, probably a hybrid.

maculosoides N. E. Br. Sts. erect, to about 3 in.; corolla up to 3 in. across, violet-purple with yellowish ridges, lobes fringed with purple hairs, otherwise glabrous. Of garden origin, probably a hybrid.

margarita Sloane. Sts. to 6 in.; fls. 1 or 2 at base of st., corolla to 4½ in. across, inner surface and lower part of lobes cream-colored with pale purple, transverse ridges, densely covered with fine, soft, pink hairs, lobes reddish-purple at apex, glabrous except for fringe of long, white hairs. S. Afr.

marientalensis Nel. Sts. erect, distinctly grooved; fls. solitary near middle of st., corolla 1¾ in. across, inner surface yellowish, white-papillate, lobes yellow- and purple-mottled at base, deep blackish-purple in upper part, fringed with long, white, clavate hairs. S. Afr.

Molonyae A. C. White & Sloane. Sts. 2–4 in. long, very strongly toothed; fls. mostly 1–2 together, corolla 1¾–2½ in. across, deep maroon, lobes with 4–5 irregular, golden-yellow markings toward apex, fringed with purple, clavate hairs. Kenya.

mutabilis Jacq. Sts. 3–18 in., glabrous; fls. 1–3 near base of young sts. or higher on older sts., corolla about 3 in. across, yellow banded with purple-brown, the bands becoming fainter on the raised, pentagonal annulus, lobes purple-brown at apex, strongly reflexed, glabrous except for a fringe of purple, clavate hairs. Of garden origin, presumably a hybrid.

namaquensis N. E. Br. Sts. 2–3 in., glabrous; fls. 1–4 at base of st., corolla 3–4 in. across, papillate-rugose, yellow with wide, transverse, purple-brown markings, annulus prominent, with recurved outer margin, densely purple-pubescent inside the cup, lobes flat, recurved, lobes of outer whorl of corona yellow, dotted brown. S. Afr.

nobilis N. E. Br. Differing from *S. gigantea* in having a more compact habit, and corolla usually smaller, open-campanulate, more prominently purple-pubescent. S. Afr., Mozambique.

parvipuncta N. E. Br. Sts. erect, 2–5 in., glabrous; fls. several near base or middle of st., corolla 1–1¼ in. across, flat, pale sulphur-yellow, purple-brown-dotted, glabrous except for fringe of purple, clavate hairs, lobes of outer whorl of corona deep purple-brown, shiny, deeply bifid. S. Afr.

pasadenensis A. C. White & Sloane. Name applied to a supposed garden hybrid, but perhaps only a form of *S. grandiflora,* from which it differs in having corolla slightly smaller, to 5 in. across, wine-red, with strongly reflexed lobes and deep central cup.

Peglerae N. E. Br. Sts. erect, to 5 or 6 in., glabrous; fls. 3 or 4 together, corolla to 3 in. across, shiny, dark purple-brown, transversely ridged, pubescent in lines below the sinuses of the lobes and fringed with purple hairs, corona dark purple-brown. S. Afr.

Pillansii N. E. Br. Sts. erect, to 7 in., velvety-pubescent; fls. 2–5 near base of st., corolla 4–5 in. across, nearly smooth, shiny purple-brown without markings, glabrous, lobes lanceolate, attenuate, fringed with light purple hairs, lobes of outer corona 5 or 10, black, shiny. S. Afr. Var. **attenuata** N. E. Br. Corolla 6–8 in. across, lobes very long-tapering.

Plantii Hook.f. Rather compact, to 8 in; fls. 1–3 at base of st., corolla to 5 in. across, dark purple-brown, with narrow, yellowish transverse ridges, lobes reflexed, fringed with long, purple hairs, lobes of outer whorl of corona blackish-purple, passing to dull orange basally. S. Afr.

pulchella Masson. Sts. thick, to 4 in.; fls. 2 or 3 at base of st., corolla 1¼–2½ in. across, glabrous, not fringed, sulphur-yellow, purple-brown-dotted, the dots more minute and dense on annulus. S. Afr.

pulvinata Masson. Sts. erect, to 4 in.; fls. solitary at base of st., corolla to 4½ in. across, inner surface and lower part of lobes densely covered with a thick cushion of soft, purple hairs, lobes dark purple-brown, with yellow transverse ridges centrally on lower half, densely fringed with purple hairs. S. Afr.

revoluta Masson. Sts. 6–15 or more in.; fls. 1–3 on upper part of st., corolla 1¼–1¾ in. across, glabrous, smooth, pale purple to dull purple or purple-brown, lobes very strongly recurved, fringed with long, purple, clavate hairs, corona enclosed in a tubelike depression. S. Afr. Var. **tigridia** (Decne.) N. E. Br. Inner surface of corolla and lower part of lobes marked with yellow dots and transverse lines.

rufa Masson. Sts. erect, to 9 in.; fls. 3–5 at base or near middle of st., corolla to 2 in. across, transversely ridged all over, dull red or chocolate-red or with fine, dull green lines between the ridges, upper parts and margins of lobes puberulous, lobes of inner whorl of corona obtuse to bifid. S. Afr. Material offered under this name may be *S. hirsuta.*

Schinzii A. Berger & Schlechter. Sts. to about 3 in.; fls. solitary near base of st., corolla nearly 5 in. across, with shallow tube, dull green with dense, red, transverse ridges, lobes long, delicate, attenuate, fringed with clavate hairs, lobes of outer whorl of corona wine-red, lobes of inner whorl with red, filiform horns tipped with white. Botswana, S.-W. Afr.

semota N. E. Br. Similar to *S. Molonyae,* but the corolla smaller, to 1½ in. across, yellow, with dark chocolate-brown markings. Tanzania.

senilis N. E. Br. Sts. erect, to 1 ft.; corolla 4–5 in. across, transversely ridged, thickly white-pubescent, the disc and lower part of lobes light purple with narrow yellowish lines, the lobes dull purple-brown at apex, fringed with long, white hairs, most of them pointing inward. S. Afr.

tsomoensis N. E. Br. Similar to *S. Peglerae,* but the fls. 4–9 together at base of st., corolla dull smoky-purple with yellowish or greenish ridges, the inner surface more generally pubescent. S. Afr.

Uspenskyi: *S. variegata.*

variegata L. [*S. Hanburyana* A. Berger & Rüst; *S. luxurians* Hort. Dammann; *S. Uspenskyi* Rüst]. TOAD CACTUS, TOAD PLANT, STARFISH CACTUS. STARFISH PLANT. Sts. to 6 in., glabrous; fls. 1–5 at base of st., corolla 2–3 in. across, transversely ridged, pale greenish-yellow with dark purple-brown spots mostly in 6–7 rows or sometimes irregularly scattered, annulus pentagonal, ⅞ in. across, pale yellow with small dots, lobes of corona yellow, dusted or dotted purple. S. Afr. Many forms of this very variable sp. have been given varietal names or have been recognized as distinct spp. These variants, differing principally in corolla size and color pattern, are best treated as cvs. if one wishes to name them.

verrucosa Masson. Sts. erect, decumbent at base, to 3 in.; fls. 1–3 at base of st., corolla campanulate, to 2½ in. across, very rugose with papillate, irregular, transverse ridges, pale yellow, spotted blood-red, glabrous or with a few hairs between the annulus and the corona. S. Afr. Var. **conspicua** N. E. Br. Corolla about 1¾ in. across, with large spots. Var. **pulchra** (Haw.) N. E. Br. Annulus with center uniformly purple.

Wilmaniae Lückh. Similar to *S. Leendertziae,* but corolla violet-crimson, the transverse ridges nearly black, lobes fringed with purple hairs in basal third. S. Afr.

Youngii N. E. Br. Sts. crowded, erect, to 6 in.; corolla to 5 in. across, yellow or greenish-yellow, with transverse, purple ridges, sparsely purple-pubescent except at apex of lobes. S. Rhodesia.

STAPELIANTHUS Choux. *Asclepiadaceae.* Five spp. of small succulents, native to Madagascar; similar to *Huernia* in having pointed teeth in the sinuses between the corolla lobes, and in other respects, but differing in having the outer whorl of the corona arising in a diverging-erect crown, with the lobes free to the base and deeply cleft.

For culture see *Succulents.*

Decaryi Choux. Densely tufted, sts. mostly 6-angled, to 4 in.; fls. in cluster at base of st., corolla tubular, to 1 in. long, the interior mottled dark purple above but almost uniformly purple at base, papillate, the papillae tipped with triangular hairs, outer corona lobes about ¼ in. long.

madagascariensis (Choux) Choux. Similar to *S. Decaryi*, but the corolla broadly campanulate, to ⅝ in. long, mottled dark purple, the papillae without hairs, corona lobes about ⅛ in. long.

Montagnacii (Boiteau) Boiteau & A. Bertrand. Similar to *S. madagascariensis*, but the corolla white, streaked purple.

STAPHYLEA L. BLADDERNUT. *Staphyleaceae*. About 11 spp. of shrubs or small trees, native to temp. regions of N. Hemisphere; lvs. opp., compound, serrulate; fls. white, in terminal panicles, bisexual, sepals, petals, and stamens 5; fr. an inflated caps.

Most bladdernuts are hardy and thrive in partial shade and moist rich soil. Propagated by seeds sown when ripe or stratified till spring, by suckers, layers, and cuttings. Greenwood cuttings taken from forced plants will root readily.

Bumalda DC. To 6 ft.; lfts. 3, elliptic to elliptic-ovate, to 3 in. long; panicles erect, to 3 in. long; fls. about ⁵⁄₁₆ in. long; fr. 2-lobed, flat, to 1 in. long. Japan. Zone 5.

colchica Steven. To 12 ft.; lfts. mostly 5, sometimes 3, oblong-ovate, to 3½ in. long, acuminate; panicles erect or nodding, to 4 in. long; fls. ¾ in. long; fr. 2–3-lobed, to 4 in. long. Caucasus. Forma **grandiflora** Zab. Fls. larger.

holocarpa Hemsl. Shrub or tree, to 25 ft. or more; lfts. 3, elliptic to oblong, to 4 in. long, acuminate; fls. before the lvs.; fr. ellipsoid or pear-shaped, not lobed, to 2 in. long. China. Var. **rosea** Rehd. & E. H. Wils. Young lvs. white-tomentose beneath; fls. pink.

pinnata L. EUROPEAN B. To 15 ft.; lfts. 5–7, oblong-ovate, to 4 in. long, acuminate; panicles nodding, to 5 in. long; fls. ½ in. long; fr. subglobose, 2–3-lobed, to 1½ in. long. Eur.

trifolia L. AMERICAN B. To 15 ft.; lfts. 3, elliptic or ovate, to 3 in. long, acuminate, pubescent beneath at least when young; panicles nodding, to 2 in. long; fls. about ⁵⁄₁₆ in. long; fr. 3-lobed, to 2 in. long. E. U.S. Zone 5.

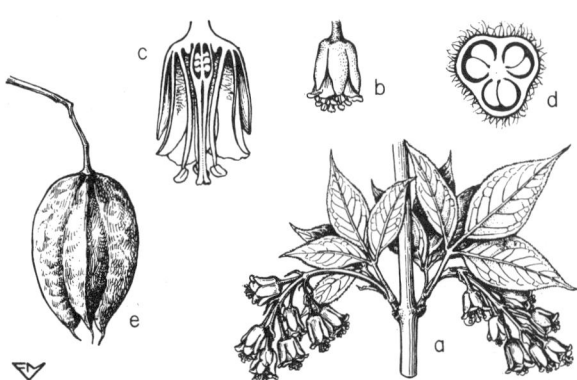

STAPHYLEACEAE. *Staphylea trifolia*: **a,** flowering branch, × ½; **b,** flower, × 1; **c,** flower, vertical section, × 2; **d,** ovary, cross section, × 6; **e,** fruit, × ½. (From Bailey, *Manual of Cultivated Plants*, ed. 2.)

STAPHYLEACEAE Lindl. BLADDERNUT FAMILY. Dicot.; 5 genera and about 60 spp. of widely distributed trees and shrubs, native to N. Hemisphere, with a few in n. S. Amer.; lvs. opp., pinnate, stipuled; fls. in racemes or panicles, regular, bisexual, sepals, petals and stamens 5, pistil 1, compound, 2–3-celled, ovary superior, or pistils 2–3(–4), 1-celled, separate, styles 2 or 3(–4); fr. an inflated caps., rarely a berry. *Euscaphis* and *Staphylea* are planted as ornamentals.

STATICE L. When Linnaeus published the genus *Statice* in 1753, he included in it both the thrifts (now known as *Armeria*) and the sea lavenders (now known as *Limonium*), as well as a few other spp. In 1768, P. Miller separated them, using the name *Statice* for the thrifts and *Limonium* for the sea lavenders. In 1809 Willdenow, ignoring Miller's names, used a new name, *Armeria*, for the thrifts, and *Statice* for the sea lavenders. Finally, by action of an International Botanical Congress, the name *Armeria* was conserved for the thrifts, and *Statice* was rejected entirely, as a confused name.

altaica G. Don. A name of uncertain application.

Armeria: see *Armeria maritima*.

auriculifolia: see *Limonium binervosum*.

bellidifolia: *Limonium bellidifolium*.

binervosa: *Limonium binervosum*.

Bonduellii: *Limonium Bonduellii*.

brasiliensis: see *Limonium carolinianum*.

brassicifolia: *Limonium brassicifolium*.

caesia: *Limonium caesium*.

caespitosa: *Armeria juniperifolia*.

callicoma: *Goniolimon callicomum*.

caroliniana: *Limonium carolinianum*.

caspia: *Limonium bellidifolium*.

cosyrensis: *Limonium cosyrense*.

delicatula: *Limonium delicatulum*.

Dregeanum: *Limonium Dregeanum*.

dumosa: a listed name of no botanical standing.

formosa: a listed name of no botanical standing, perhaps used for an *Armeria*.

globulariifolia: *Limonium ramosissimum*.

Gmelinii: *Limonium Gmelinii*.

Gougetiana: *Limonium Gougetianum*.

incana: *Goniolimon callicomum*. Vars. **nana** and **rosea** are listed.

latifolia: *Limonium latifolium*.

Limonium: *Limonium vulgare*.

macrophylla: *Limonium macrophyllum*.

minima: a listed name of no botanical standing.

minuta: *Limonium minutum*.

Mouretii: *Limonium Mouretii*.

otolepis: *Limonium otolepis*.

peregrina: *Limonium peregrinum*.

Perezii: *Limonium Perezii*.

Preauxii: *Limonium Preauxii*.

pseudarmeria: *Armeria pseudarmeria*.

puberula: *Limonium puberulum*.

ramosissima: *Limonium ramosissimum*.

reticulata: see *Limonium bellidifolium*.

rhytidophylla: *Limonium peregrinum*.

rosea: *Limonium peregrinum*.

sibirica: a listed name of no botanical standing, probably for *Armeria maritima* var.

Sieberi: *Limonium Sieberi*.

sinensis: *Limonium sinense*.

sinuata: *Limonium sinuatum*. Vars. **alba, albocaerulea, candidissima,** and **rosea-superba** have been listed.

spathulata: *Limonium spathulatum*.

spicata: *Psylliostachys spicata*.

speciosa: *Goniolimon speciosum*.

Suworowii: *Psylliostachys Suworowii*.

tatarica: *Goniolimon tataricum*.

tetragona: see *Limonium Dregeanum*.

Thouinii: *Limonium Thouinii*.

virgata: *Limonium virgatum*.

Zimmermannii: a listed name of no botanical standing.

STAUNTONIA DC. *Lardizabalaceae*. Six or more spp. of evergreen, monoecious, woody climbers, native to e. Asia; lvs. alt., palmately compound; fls. in few-fld. axillary racemes; sepals 6, acuminate, stamens 6, united into a column, or pistils 3; fr. ellipsoid berries.

Hardy in Zone 8, thriving in moist, shady locations in soil rich in humus. Propagated by cuttings of half-ripened wood.

hexaphylla (Thunb.) Decne. To 40 ft.; lfts. 3–7, ovate to elliptic, acute to acuminate, to 4 in. long; fls. white, tinged violet, fragrant, about ¾ in. long; fr. purple, 2 in. long, edible. Japan, China.

STAUROPSIS: *VANDOPSIS*.

STEIRODISCUS: *GAMOLEPIS*.

STEIRONEMA: *LYSIMACHIA.*

STELIS Swartz. *Orchidaceae.* About 300 spp. of epiphytic or rock-dwelling, rhizomatous or tufted herbs, native to trop. Amer.; sts. erect, 1-lvd.; lvs. leathery; infls. 1 to many, racemose, many-fld.; fls. small, greenish or dark purple, sepals spreading or fls. seemingly 2-lipped, petals much smaller, fleshy, lip minute, fleshy, column without a foot, stigmas commonly 2, pollinia 2. For structure of fl. see *Orchidaceae.*

For culture see *Orchids.*

aprica Lindl. Epiphytic, tufted, to 10 in., commonly shorter, sts. close together; lvs. fleshy, linear-oblong, to 4 in. long; infls. 1–3, slender, arching, densely fld., as long as lvs. or longer; sepals ovate or ovate-elliptic, 1/16 in. long, petals cuneate-obovate, truncate, much smaller than sepals, lip 3-lobed, midlobe triangular, with a very swollen disc, column short. Trop. Amer.

STELLARIA L. CHICKWEED, STARWORT. *Caryophyllaceae.* About 120 spp. of cosmopolitan, often tufted, ann. or per. herbs; lvs. opp., stipules absent; fls. solitary or in a dichasial cyme, sepals 4–5, petals 4–5, sometimes absent, white, deeply 2-lobed, stamens 8, 10, sometimes fewer, ovary 1-celled, styles 3, rarely 4; fr. a caps., dehiscent by 6 or 8 valves, seeds several to many, rough or smooth.

alaskana Hult. Glabrous per., sts. solitary or loosely tufted; lvs. sessile, ovate-elliptic, to 5/8 in. long, moderately thick; fls. solitary, rarely 2, bracts scarious or with broad scarious margins, sepals triangular-lanceolate, to 5/16 in. long, with scarious margins, petals cleft almost to the base. Alaska.

Holostea L. GREATER STITCHWORT. Per. herb, to 2 ft., sts. 4-angled, weak, brittle, pubescent to almost glabrous; lower lvs. oblong or narrowly lanceolate, to 1 1/8 in. long, upper lvs. lanceolate, to 2 1/4 in. long, acuminate, margins and midrib beneath very rough; fls. in a loose infl., sepals to 3/8 in. long, petals 3/4 in. long, deeply 2-cleft. N. Afr., Eur., the Near East.

media (L.) Cyr. CHICKWEED, STITCHWORT. Ann., sts. to 18 in., rarely to 3 ft.; lvs. ovate, to 1 1/2 in. long, glabrous to pubescent, basal lvs. with petioles ciliate, upper lvs. sessile; fls. in a few- to many-fld. infl., sepals 1/4 in. long, pilose, petals white, shorter than sepals or absent, stamens 0–3–10. Probably s. Eur.; naturalized in many parts of the world, often a serious weed.

pubera Michx. STAR C., GREAT C. Showy per., to 1 ft., sts. puberulent in lower part; lvs. elliptic, 1–4 in. long; pedicels puberulent; fls. large, starry, conspicuous, sepals 1/4 in. long, petals white, very deeply cleft, seemingly 10, stamens 10. N.J. to Ill., s. to Fla. Attractive for the wild garden.

ruscifolia Willd. Glabrous, glaucous per., sts. to 6 in.; lvs. ovate to linear, to 1 in. long, 1/2 in. wide, basally cordate or united to opp. lf., 1-nerved; fls. few, solitary in axils, pedicels 1/4 in. long, sepals 1/4 in. long, petals bifid, to 1/2 in. long. Alpine regions, cent. and n. Japan, Kurile Is.

STENANDRIUM Nees. *Acanthaceae.* More than 60 spp. of usually stemless herbs, widely distributed in trop. and subtrop. Amer.; lvs. basal, entire; fls. small, in spikes, corolla tube slender, lobes 5, spreading, subequal, stamens 4, didynamous; fr. a caps., seeds 4.

igneum: see *Aphelandra ignea.*

Lindenii N. E. Br. Lvs. broad-elliptic, dark green, veined with white or yellow above, purplish beneath; fls. yellow, in spikes to 3 in. long. Peru.

STENANTHIUM (A. Gray) Kunth. *Liliaceae.* About 4 spp. of grasslike, per. herbs, native to N. Amer. and e. Asia; sts. with tunicate, somewhat bulbous base, leafy; lvs. long, linear; fls. bisexual or unisexual, greenish, whitish, or purplish, in diffuse, terminal racemes or panicles; perianth segms. 6, united basally into a short tube, persistent, stamens 6, filaments arising from perianth segms., styles 3; fr. a septicidal, 3-beaked caps.

Occasionally planted in the border or wild garden.

gramineum (Ker-Gawl.) Morong. FEATHER-BELLS. To 4 ft.; lvs. to 1 ft. long and 5/8 in. wide; fls. to 1/2 in. across, in panicles to 2 ft. long; fr. on reflexed pedicels. S. U.S. Var. **robustum** (S. Wats.) Fern. [*S. robustum* S. Wats.]. FEATHER-FLEECE. To 5 ft.; lvs. to 1 in. wide; fr. often erect. Md. and se. Penn. to Ind.

occidentale A. Gray. To 2 ft.; lvs. to 1 ft. long and 3/4 in. wide; fls. purplish-green, to 3/4 in. long, in racemes to 8 in. long. B.C. and Alta., s. to n. Calif.

robustum: *S. gramineum* var.

STENOCACTUS: *ECHINOFOSSULOCACTUS.* The following are listed names of no botanical standing: S. bicolor, S. carneus, S. debilispinus, S. densispinus, S. esperanzensis, S. flavispinus, S. grisacanthus, S. longispinus, S. Malmsianus, S. oxygonus, S. polylophus, S. rectispinus, S. robustus, S. sphacelatus, S. stenogonus, S. undulatus.

STENOCARPUS R. Br. *Proteaceae.* About 22 spp. of shrubs or trees, native to Australia, Malay Arch., and New Caledonia; lvs. alt., simple or pinnatifid, with few lobes; fls. bisexual, slightly irregular, yellow or red, in umbels, perianth tube opening along lower side, limb nearly globose and recurved, anthers sessile; fr. a leathery follicle.

Cunninghamii R. Br. Tall, bushy shrub or small tree; lvs. oblong-lanceolate, to 4 in. long; fls. yellowish, ovary glabrous. N. Australia.

salignus R. Br. REEFWOOD. Lvs. ovate-lanceolate, to 4 in. long; fls. yellowish, 1/2 in. long, in 10–30-fld. umbels, ovary usually pubescent. Queensland, New S. Wales. Produces an important furniture wood.

sinuatus (A. Cunn.) Endl. FIREWHEEL TREE, WHEEL-OF-FIRE. Lvs. to 1 ft. long, oblong-lanceolate or pinnately cut, segms. 1–4 pairs, oblong; fls. bright red, 1 in. long, in 12–20-fld. umbels. Queensland and New S. Wales.

STENOCEREUS: *LEMAIREOCEREUS.*

STENOCHLAENA John Sm. *Polypodiaceae.* About 5 spp. of climbing, epiphytic ferns, native from Afr. to the Pacific; lvs. leathery, dimorphic, 1–2-pinnate, fertile with contracted pinnae covered with sporangia beneath.

Sometimes grown in warm, humid greenhouses on stems of tree ferns or other supports. For culture see *Ferns.*

palustris (Burm.f.) Beddome. CLIMBING FERN. Lvs. to 4 ft. long, glossy, pinnae of sterile lvs. to 10 in. long and 1 1/2 in. wide, toothed toward tip, the fertile lvs. 1-pinnate. India, s. China, Australia.

tenuifolia (Desv.) T. Moore. Lvs. 3–6 ft. long, pale green, glossy, pinnae of sterile lvs. short-stalked, the margins finely and densely serrulate, the fertile lvs. 2-pinnate. Afr. Zone 10. Cult. outdoors in s. Calif.

STENODRABA O. E. Schulz. *Cruciferae.* Fewer than 10 spp. of dwarf per. herbs in S. Amer. in the s. Andes; lvs. narrow-spatulate to obovate, slightly fleshy or somewhat leathery; fls. minute, sepals and petals 4; fr. a linear silique with filiform pedicels. Similar to *Draba,* differing chiefly in fr. larger and nearly linear.

andina: *S. colchaguensis.*

colchaguensis (Barnéoud) O. E. Schulz [*S. andina* (Phil.) O. E. Schulz; *Draba andina* Phil., not Nutt.]. Tufted per. to 3 in., sts. many, short, ascending; basal lvs. in rosettes, fleshy, oblong-elliptic to obovate, to 3/4 in. long, obtuse and usually 1–3-toothed at apex, remotely ciliate. st. lvs. narrower, entire, to 3/16 in. long; fls. in compact racemes, white, often obscurely blue-spotted; siliques to 3/8 in. long, usually without persistent style. Chile.

STENOGLOTTIS Lindl. *Orchidaceae.* Three or 4 spp. of terrestrial herbs, native to subtrop. S. Afr.; sts. short, roots tuberous; lvs. basal, in rosettes; infl. erect, racemose, many-fld.; fls. small, sepals separate, spreading, petals nearly erect, lip continuous with base of column, 3–5-lobed at apex, column short and broad, stigmas 2. For structure of fl. see *Orchidaceae.*

Temperate greenhouse. For culture see *Orchids.*

fimbriata Lindl. Tubers oblong; lvs. many, spreading horizontally, linear-oblong, to 2 in. long, undulate, deep green with many transverse, black blotches; infl. to 1 ft. long; fls. 5/16 in. across, rose-pink with a few purple blotches on lip, sepals ovate, finely erose-toothed, petals smaller, converging, deeply erose-toothed, lip twice as long as sepals, oblong-obovate, 3-lobed, midlobe narrow, entire. Natal.

longifolia Hook.f. Lvs. many, linear-oblong, to 2 in. long, undulate, green, sparsely spotted with dark brown; infl. to 2 ft. long, with many purple-spotted bracts; fls. 3/8 in. across, rose-pink with purple spots on lip, sepals prominent, petals smaller, enveloping column, lip 5-lobed. S. Afr.

STENOLOBIUM: *TECOMA*.

STENOMESSON Herb. *Amaryllidaceae*. Twenty or more spp. of bulbous herbs, native to the Andes; bulbs tunicate; lvs. linear to lanceolate; infl. a 1- to several-fld. umbel on a solid or hollow scape and subtended by separate spathe valves; fls. variously colored but not white, funnelform, tube long, lobes short, ascending, stamens inserted at throat of tube, filaments united at base in a distinct, often toothed cup or corona, ovary inferior, 3-celled, ovules many; fr. a caps., seeds small, flat, black.

luteum (Herb.) Bak. Lvs. linear, to 8 in. long, about as long as scape; umbel 2-fld.; fls. ascending, yellow, to 2 in. long, filaments broadly winged at base, corona without teeth between filaments. Peru.

variegatum (Ruiz & Pav.) Macbr. Lvs. to 1 in. wide; umbel 2–4-fld., scape to 2 ft.; fls. pale to bright red, tube curved, to 3 in. long, lobes to 1 in. long, keeled with green, corona toothed between filaments. Peru.

STENOSPERMATION Schott (sometimes but not originally spelled *Stenospermatium*). *Araceae*. About 300 spp. of suberect, herbaceous climbers of trop. Amer., with usually short internodes; lvs. 2-ranked, oblong-elliptic to lanceolate with many, almost parallel lateral veins, petioles long-sheathing, geniculate; peduncle elongate, infl. nodding or erect, spathe convolute, white or maroon, early deciduous, spadix white, stalked, covered with bisexual fls.; perianth absent, stamens 4, ovaries 2-celled, ovules 4 to many in each cell, basal.

For culture see *Philodendron*.

popayanense Schott. To 3 ft.; lf. blades to 1 ft. long and 2¾ in. wide, leathery, petioles 6–7 in. long; peduncle as long as petiole, infl. nodding, spathe white, to 4 in. long, partly opening. Colombia, Ecuador.

STENOTAPHRUM Trin. *Gramineae*. About 6 spp. of creeping, stoloniferous per. grasses in subtropics and tropics of New and Old World, flowering sts. short; lf. blades rather broad and short, obtuse; racemes terminal and axillary; spikelets with a bisexual terminal floret above a sterile or male floret, embedded in one side of an enlarged and flattened corky rachis which disarticulates toward the tip at maturity, the spikelets remaining attached to the joints, first glume small, second glume and sterile lemma about equal, fertile lemma papery. For terminology see *Gramineae*.

americanum: *S. secundatum.*

secundatum (Walt.) O. Kuntze [*S. americanum* Schrank]. ST. AUGUSTINE GRASS, BUFFALO G. Sts. branching, compressed, flowering shoots 4–14 in. high; lf. blades mostly less than 6 in. long, to ⅜ in. wide; racemes 2–4 in. long; spikelets solitary or paired, rarely in 3's, ⅛–¼ in. long. S.C. to Fla. and Tex.; trop. Amer. Cult. as a lawn grass along the coast, also in Calif., and escaping. Propagated by cuttings. Cv. 'Variegatum' [*S. secundatum* var. *variegatum* A. S. Hitchc.; *S. americanum* cv. 'Variegatum']. Lvs. striped with white. Cult. as a basket plant.

STEPHANANDRA Siebold & Zucc. *Rosaceae*. Four spp. of deciduous shrubs of temp. e. Asia; lvs. alt., toothed or lobed; fls. small, white or greenish, in terminal panicles or corymbs, sepals and petals 5, stamens 10–20, pistil usually 1; fr. dehiscent only at base.

The following species are hardy in Zone 5, although requiring protection in severe winters. Propagated by seeds, by cuttings of green wood under glass, by division, and sometimes by root cuttings.

chinensis Hance. Sts. flexuous; lvs. ovate-lanceolate to oblong-ovate, to 2½ in. long, acute, doubly serrate, remotely or not at all incised; fls. white, in racemose panicles. E. China.

flexuosa: *S. incisa.*

incisa (Thunb.) Zab. [*S. flexuosa* Siebold & Zucc.]. LACE SHRUB. To 8 ft., with long drooping brs.; lvs. ovate, 1½–2½ in. long, long-pointed, deeply lobed, sometimes halfway to the midrib; stamens 10. Japan, Korea. Zone 5.

Tanakae (Franch. & Sav.) Franch. & Sav. To 6 ft.; lvs. 2–4 in. long, pubescent beneath, shallowly 3-lobed, finely toothed; stamens 15–20. Japan. Zone 6.

STEPHANOCEREUS: *CEPHALOCEREUS*.

STEPHANOTIS Thouars. *Asclepiadaceae*. About 15 spp. of climbing, glabrous shrubs, native from Malaya to Madagas-car; lvs. opp., simple, leathery; fls. in short-peduncled, axillary cymes, calyx leafy, 5-parted, without glands, corolla funnelform or salverform, the tube expanded at base; fr. a thick, fleshy, obtuse or acuminate follicle.

One species is a popular greenhouse plant, but may be grown outdoors in the South in a loamy soil at a temperature of about 65° F. Propagated by cuttings of half-matured wood over bottom heat.

floribunda Brongn. MADAGASCAR JASMINE, FLORADORA, WAX-FLOWER. Twining, to 15 ft. or more; lvs. elliptic, 2–4 in. long, abruptly pointed at apex, obtuse or subcordate, thick, shining; fls. white, waxy, fragrant, 1–2 in. long; follicles 3–4 in. long. Madagascar.

jasminoides: a listed name of no botanical standing; material so offered is probably *S. floribunda*.

STEPHEGYNE: *MITRAGYNA*.

STERCULIA L. *Sterculiaceae*. About 100 spp. of monoecious or polygamous trees, rarely shrubs, native to the Old and New World tropics; lvs. alt., unlobed or palmately lobed or compound; fls. mostly in axillary panicles, petals none, calyx usually 5-lobed and colored, male fls. with 5–20 anthers clustered near the apex of the slender column terminated by vestigial carpels, female and bisexual fls. with carpels 3–6, coherent, 2- to many-ovuled, longer than the whorl of sterile or fertile anthers; fr. of up to 5 separate, woody or leathery follicles with 1 to many seeds.

Planted for shade and ornament in tropical climates; propagated by seeds and cuttings of ripened wood.

acerifolia: *Brachychiton acerifolius.*

alata: *Pterygota alata.*

apetala (Jacq.) Karst. [*S. carthaginensis* Cav.]. To 45 ft. or more, with a densely leafy crown and naked trunk; lvs. up to 20 in. long and wide, 5-lobed, deeply cordate; calyx about 1 in. long, yellow inside, spotted pink or purple; follicles about 4 in. long, tomentose, seeds about ¾ in. long, lustrous. Trop. Amer. Timber tree.

Bidwillii: *Brachychiton Bidwillii.*

carthaginensis: *S. apetala.*

colorata: *Firmiana colorata.*

discolor: *Brachychiton discolor.*

diversifolia: *Brachychiton populneus.*

Fairchildii: a listed name of no botanical standing, perhaps a sp. of *Brachychiton.*

foetida L. INDIAN ALMOND. To 60 ft.; lvs. 4–12 in. long, divided into 5–7 (15 in young plants) lanceolate lfts.; panicles clustered below lvs.; fls. with putrid odor, calyx red or purplish and yellow, about ½ in. long; follicles dark red, to 4 in. long. Old World tropics.

lurida: *Brachychiton discolor.*

platanifolia: *Firmiana simplex.*

rubiginosa Venten. Shrub or small tree, to about 20 ft.; lvs. simple, obovate to lanceolate, acute to acuminate, 4–12 in. long, stellate-tomentose beneath; fls. in drooping panicles, calyx red to ¾ in. long, the lobes longer than tube; follicles 3–6-seeded, oblong, to 4 in. long. India to Java.

rupestris: *Brachychiton rupestris.*

Sextonii: a listed name of no botanical standing; trees cult. under this name are *Brachychiton* × *hybridus.*

Trichosiphon: *Brachychiton australis.*

villosa Roxb. White-barked, few-branched tree; lvs. up to 18 in. long and wide, 5–7-lobed, lobes sometimes trifid velvety-pubescent beneath; panicles pendulous, many-branched and -fld.; calyx about ½ in. across, downy-pubescent outside, pink inside; follicles 1½–2 in. long, rusty-villous. India.

STERCULIACEAE Bartl. STERCULIA FAMILY. Dicot.; about 12 genera of monoecious or sometimes polygamous, large shrubs and trees, native principally to the Old World tropics; lvs. alt., stipitate, unlobed, palmately lobed, or digitately compound; fls. generally in axillary panicles, regular, petals 0, calyx mostly 5-lobed, corollalike, male fls. with 5–15 anthers clustered apically on a usually long, slender staminal column, female and bisexual fls. with carpels mostly 3–6, generally stalked, coherent, longer than anthers, mature carpels separate, often borne on stipes, mostly follicles or samaralike. The family furnishes the cola nuts of commerce, timber, and

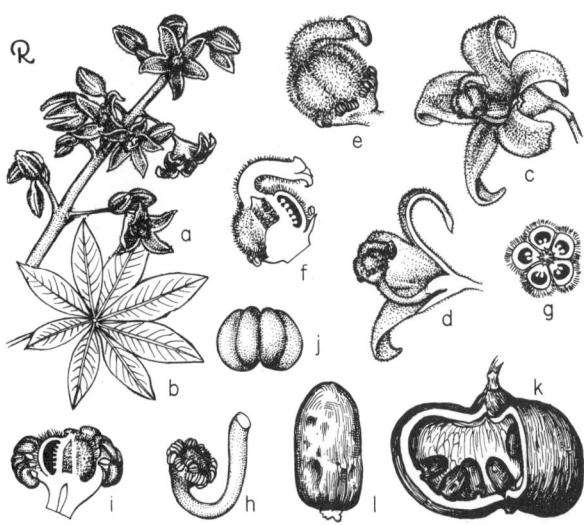

STERCULIACEAE. *Sterculia foetida:* **a,** branch of inflorescence, × ½; **b,** leaf, × ¹/₁₂; **c,** female flower, × 1; **d,** female flower, vertical section except for pistil, × 1; **e,** pistil and staminodes, × 2½; **f,** pistil, vertical section, × 2½; **g,** ovaries, cross section, × 2½; **h,** column of male flower, bearing anthers and vestigial pistil, × 2; **i,** apex of same, vertical section, × 4; **j,** anther, × 8; **k,** mature carpel, × ⅓; **l,** seed, × 1½.

several ornamentals suitable for cult. in trop. and subtrop. areas, as: *Brachychiton, Cola, Firmiana, Heritiera, Hildegardia, Pterygota,* and *Sterculia.*

STEREOSPERMUM Cham. *Bignoniaceae.* About 20 spp. of trees, native to Afr., and from se. Asia to the Malay Pen.; lvs. opp., 1–2-pinnate; fls. white, pink, lilac, or yellow, in large, terminal or lateral panicles, calyx irregularly 2–5-lobed, corolla funnelform to campanulate-funnelform or tubular, slightly 2-lipped, stamens 4; fr. an elongate, 2-valved caps., seeds immersed in partition.

chelonoides DC. To 60 ft.; lvs. to 16 in. long, lfts. 7–11, elliptic, to 4¾ in. long, caudate; fls. rose with yellow or pink lobes, to 1 in. long; fr. to 20 in. long. India to Malay Pen.

Kunthianum Cham. To 30 ft.; lvs. to 14 in. long, lfts. 5–9, oblong to oblong-elliptic, mostly 2–4 in. long; fls. pale pink or lilac, rarely almost white, to 2 in. long; fr. to 2 ft. long, spirally twisted. Afr.

STERNBERGIA Waldst. & Kit. *Amaryllidaceae.* Five spp. of bulbous herbs, native to se. Eur. and se. Asia; bulbs tunicate; lvs. basal, narrow; fls. solitary, erect, on a short scape subtended by a more or less tubular spathe split down one side, perianth yellow, funnelform, tube short, stamens inserted at throat, anthers versatile, ovary inferior, ovules many; fr. a berry, seeds nearly globose.

The following species are fairly hardy and succeed in a dry sunny location in rather heavy soil. Bulbs should be planted about 6 in. deep.

Fischerana (Herb.) Rupr. Differs from *S. lutea* in having ovary and caps. stalked, and lvs. and fls. appearing in spring. E. Transcaucasia, Iran.

lutea (L.) Roem. & Schult. WINTER DAFFODIL, LILY-OF-THE-FIELD. Lvs. to 1 ft. long and ¾ in. wide; fls. developing with or before lvs., 1½ in. long, tube very short. Autumn. S. Eur. to Asia Minor and cent. Asia. Cv. 'Major'. Fls. larger.

STETSONIA Britt. & Rose. *Cactaceae.* One sp., a treelike cactus of Argentina; sts. erect, much-branched, strongly ribbed; fls. nocturnal, funnelform, white, perianth segms. about half as long as tube, ovary densely covered with ovate, mucronate, ciliate scales naked in the axils, scales of perianth tube similar but scattered; fr. (probably) umbilicate. Perhaps better placed in *Cereus,* but the ovary scaly.

For culture see *Cacti.*

coryne (Salm-Dyck) Britt. & Rose. TOOTHPICK CACTUS. To 30 ft. high and nearly as broad as high, trunk short, to 2 ft. thick, brs. about 4 in. thick, ribs 8–9; spines 7–9, the longest to 2 in. long, awl-shaped; fls. 5–6 in. long.

STEUDNERA C. Koch. *Araceae.* About 8 spp. of herbs of Asia with sts.; lvs. peltate, ovate, usually emarginate at base, petioles long; peduncle short, spathe expanded, yellow or purple, at length reflexed or revolute, spadix short, densely fld., the lower (female) part mostly united to the spathe, unisexual; perianth absent, female fls. with 5–8 staminodes, ovary 2-celled.

For culture see *Caladium.*

discolor Bull. To 14 in.; st. to 2 in. long or more; lf. blades 10–12 in. long, glaucous and blotched with purple-brown between veins beneath; spathe ovate, to 4½ in. long, golden-yellow on both sides, purple basally inside, spadix 1½ in. long. India?

STEVENSONIA: *PHOENICOPHORIUM.* **S. grandifolia:** *P. Borsigianum.*

STEVIA Cav. *Compositae* (Eupatorium Tribe). Perhaps 150 spp. of per. herbs and shrubs, native to subtrop. and trop. N. and S. Amer.; lvs. opp. or alt.; heads discoid, 5–8-fld., corymbose-paniculate, involucral bracts 5–8; fls. all tubular, bisexual, purple to white; achenes usually 5-ribbed, pappus of scales or awns or a mixture of both, or sometimes reduced to a toothed crown.

serrata Cav. Erect per. herb, to 3½ ft., sts. hairy, usually wandlike, very leafy; lvs. alt., mostly oblanceolate or linear-spatulate, to 2 in. long, usually toothed; heads in dense corymbs; fls. essentially white. S. Ariz. and New Mex. to Cent. Amer. Probably not in cult. *S. serrata* Hort., the florist's "stevia," is *Piqueria trinervia.*

STEWARTIA L. [*Malachodendron* Cav.]. *Theaceae.* About 6 spp. of deciduous shrubs and small trees of temp. e. Asia and e. N. Amer.; lvs. alt., simple, toothed; fls. showy, white, axillary, solitary, bisexual, sepals 5(–6), persistent, petals 5(–8), stamens many, anthers versatile, ovary superior, 5-celled; fr. a woody caps., without columella, dehiscent from apex, seeds 1–4 in each cell, wingless (except in *S. ovata*).

Stewartias are planted as ornamentals and are moderately hardy north. Zone 7b. A mixture of peat and loam is the best soil. Propagated by seeds, layering, and cuttings in late summer under glass.

koreana Nakai ex Rehd. Tree, to 50 ft., branchlets zigzag; lvs. elliptic, to 4 in. long, somewhat serrulate, usually pubescent beneath, turning orange-red in autumn; fls. terminal or nearly so, styles united. Korea. Zone 6.

Malacodendron L. [*S. virginica* Cav.]. SILKY CAMELLIA. Shrub, to 12 ft.; lvs. very short-petioled, ovate to elliptic, fls. to 4 in. across, filaments purple, anthers bluish, styles united. Se. U.S. Zone 7b.

monadelpha Siebold & Zucc. Tree, to 80 ft.; lvs. long-petioled, elliptic, less than 1½ in. wide, densely silky-pubescent along veins beneath; bracts beneath calyx large and leaflike, fls. to 1⅜ in. across, anthers violet, styles united. Cent. and s. Japan. Zone 8.

ovata (Cav.) Weatherby [*S. pentagyna* L'Hér.; *Malachodendron pentagynum* (L'Hér.) Small]. MOUNTAIN CAMELLIA. Shrub, to 15 ft.; lvs. ovate, to 5 in. long, broadly rounded at base; fls. to 3 in. across, filaments white, anthers orange, styles 5, separate; seeds winged. Ky. and Va., s. to Ga. Zone 7b. Forma **grandiflora** (Bean) Kobuski [var. *grandiflora* (Bean) Weatherby]. Fls. to 4 in. across, filaments purple.

pentagyna: *S. ovata.*

Pseudocamellia Maxim. JAPANESE S. Shrub or tree, to 50 ft., branchlets straight, glabrous; lvs. to 3 in. long, acuminate, glabrous beneath, turning dark purple in autumn; bracts beneath calyx small, fls. to 2½ in. across, petals furry on outside, stamens small, anthers orange, filaments white, united below, styles united. Japan. Zone 8.

serrata Maxim. Shrub or tree, to 40 ft., differing from *S. Pseudocamellia* in having branchlets pilose, lvs. somewhat longer, serrulate with incurved teeth, fls. slightly smaller, petals reddish at base, filaments separate. Cent. China.

sinensis Rehd. & E. H. Wils. Shrub or tree, to 30 ft., young branchlets pubescent; lvs. elliptic-obovate, to 4 in. long, serrate with spreading teeth; bracts beneath calyx longer than calyx, fls. 2 in. across, filaments joined in basal ⅓, styles united. China.

virginica: *S. Malacodendron.*

STICTOCARDIA H. G. Hallier. *Convolvulaceae.* Perhaps 12 spp. of herbaceous or woody twiners, 1 pantrop., the others in trop. Afr. and Asia; lvs. mostly ovate, cordate at base, densely covered with minute, black glands beneath; fls. large, red or purple, corolla funnelform, stigma divided into 2 rounded lobes; fr. completely enclosed by much-enlarged calyx and dehiscing irregularly, exposing the seeds. Very similar to *Ipomoea* in vegetative and floral characters, but differing in the black glandular lower lf. surface and the unusual dehiscence of the fr.

beraviensis (Vatke) H. G. Hallier [*Ipomoea beraviensis* Vatke]. Strong, woody twiner, more or less pubescent; lvs. ovate, to 6 in., or even 9 in. long, lateral veins nearly parallel, prominent at least beneath; fls. bright crimson, several together in the axils. Trop. Afr.

STIGMAPHYLLON A. Juss. *Malpighiaceae.* About 70 spp. of mostly twining, woody vines, native to trop. Amer.; lvs. opp., simple, entire, toothed or rarely lobed; fls. yellow, in umbel-like corymbs, calyx 5-parted, with glands on exterior, petals 5, clawed, stamens 10, only 6 fertile, filaments united at base; fr. of 1–3 samaras.

Grown outdoors in warm regions, also sometimes in the greenhouse, where propagated by cuttings with heat.

ciliatum (Lam.) A. Juss. BRAZILIAN GOLDEN VINE, ORCHID VINE, BUTTERFLY VINE, AMAZON VINE, GOLDEN CREEPER. Slender, twining vine; lf. blades ovate, 2–3 in. long, strongly cordate, margins pectinate, with very narrow, attenuate teeth, petioles long; fls. in clusters of 3–6. Trop. Amer.

littorale A. Juss. Tall, leafy vine; lf. blades ovate, usually slightly lobed, 2–5 in. long, glabrous above, pubescent beneath, petioles long; fls. in 10–20-fld. clusters. Brazil, Paraguay, Uruguay, Argentina.

STILBOCARPA (Hook.f.) Decne. & Planch. *Araliaceae.* Three spp. of stoutly branched, somewhat fleshy, per. herbs, native to islands off s. New Zeal. and adjacent islands; lvs. alt., orbicular to reniform, dentate or slightly lobed; fls. unisexual or bisexual, in compound umbels subtended by large leafy bracts, mostly 5-merous, petals imbricate, ovary 2–4-celled; fr. a depressed-globose drupe, pyrenes 2–4.

Lyallii J. B. Armstr. Prostrate or somewhat ascending, more or less pilose, stoloniferous herb; lvs. to 12 in. wide, shallowly lobed, crenate-serrate with awned teeth, glabrous above, pubescent below; petals reddish-purple, ovary 2-celled; fr. black, ³⁄₁₆ in. in diam. Stewart Is. and adjacent islands. Cooler parts of Zone 10 in Calif.

STILLINGIA Gard. *Euphorbiaceae.* About 30 spp. of monoecious, glabrous herbs, shrubs, and trees, with milky juice, native to Fiji Is., Madagascar, N. and S. Amer.; lvs. alt., opp., or verticillate, simple, pinnately veined, with 2 or 3 glands at base of blades, entire to serrate; fls. without petals, in spikelike panicle, male fls. in clusters, female fls. solitary and near the base of the infl., ovary 2–3-celled; fr. a caps. Very closely allied to *Sapium,* but gynobase persisting after the caps. dehisces, and sepals absent or not united.

sylvatica Gard. QUEEN'S-DELIGHT, QUEEN'S ROOT. Subshrub, to 2 ft., from a woody rhizome; lvs. alt., sessile or short-petioled, elliptic to obovate or spatulate, 1–4½ in. long, toothed, green or sometimes red; fls. yellow, in spikes to 5 in. long. Va. to Fla. and Tex. Rhizome contains medicinal substances.

STIPA L. NEEDLEGRASS, FEATHER GRASS, SPEAR G. *Gramineae.* A widely distributed genus of about 150 spp. of tufted per. grasses; lf. blades usually convolute; panicles mostly narrow; spikelets 1-fld., pedicelled, disarticulating above the glumes, the articulation oblique, leaving a bearded, sharp-pointed callus attached to the base of the floret, glumes membranous, often papery, usually long and narrow, acute to aristate, lemma narrow, cylindrical, strongly convolute, terminating in a prominent awn several to many times as long as the hardened fr., the awn twisted below, geniculate, usually persistent, palea enclosed in the convolute lemma. For terminology see *Gramineae.*

capillata L. Sts. to 3 ft., erect, clustered; lf. blades glaucous, stiffly erect, filiform; panicle lax, the brs. unequal; glumes about ¾ in. long, short-pointed, lemma with scaberulous awn 4–6 in. long. Eurasia.

Caragana Trin. Sts. to 3 ft., lax, clustered; lf. blades linear, involute, glaucous, to 8 in. long, less than ⅛ in. wide; panicle elongate, narrow, loose, to 18 in. long, brs. to 4 in. long or more, naked in lower half; glumes lanceolate, acute, equal, 3-nerved, lemma short-pubescent, 2-toothed, with stiff awn about ½ in. long, articulate at base, deciduous. Sw. Eur., se. Asia.

comata Trin. & Rupr. NEEDLE-AND-THREAD. Sts. to 2 ft. or more; lf. blades to 1 ft. long and nearly ⅛ in. wide; panicle commonly in-

cluded at base, to 8 in. long; glumes to ¾ in. long, the attenuate tips nearly hyaline, lemma ⁵⁄₁₆–½ in. long, pale to brownish, sparsely pubescent or glabrate toward the summit, awn to 6 in. long, very slender, often deciduous. Ind. to Yukon, s. to Tex. and Calif. Cult. as a forage grass.

dasyphylla: *S. pennata* var. *Grafiana.*

elegantissima Labill. AUSTRALIAN F.G. Foliage scant; panicle loose and open, brs. filiform, spreading, conspicuously feathery; spikelets purple, long-awned. Australia. Sometimes cult. for ornament.

gigantea Link. Sts. to 7 ft., fistulose, in clusters; lf. sheaths glabrous, blades involute when dry, to 28 in. long and nearly ⅛ in. wide; panicle to 20 in. long, loose, lower brs. clustered; spikelets yellow, glumes nearly equal, 3-nerved, attenuate, to 1¼ in. long, lemma to ⅝ in. long, hairy on back, awn ⁵⁄₁₆ in. long. Portugal, Spain, Morocco.

Ichu (Ruiz & Pav.) Kunth. Blades all similar, filiform, bristly, convolute; panicle compact, spikelike, 6–8 in. long. Highlands, Mex. to Argentina.

Joannis: *S. pennata* var.

leucotricha Trin. & Rupr. TEXAS N., TEXAS WINTER GRASS. Sts. to 2 ft., nodes pubescent; lf. blades to 1 ft. long and ⅛ in. wide, minutely hispid beneath; panicle narrow, mostly not more than 4 in. long; glumes to ¾ in. long, lemma about ⅜ in. long, brownish, appressed-pubescent on the lower part, the upper part smooth, cylindrical, whitish, forming a ciliate crown, awn 2⅜–4 in. long, rather stout, twice-bent. Okla. and Tex. to cent. Mex.

pennata L. EUROPEAN F.G. Sts. 2–3 ft.; lf. blades elongate, involute; panicle few-fld.; spikelets large, yellow, glumes ½ in. long or more, with awns twice as long, awns of lemma 10–14 in. long, conspicuously feathery above the bend; fr. ⅝ in. long. Eurasia. Sometimes cult. for ornament. Var. **Grafiana** (Steven) Lindem. [*S. dasyphylla* Czerniak. ex Komarov]. Lf. blades flat when fresh, involute in drying; fr. to 1 in. long. Russia. Var. **Joannis** (Čelak.) Asch. & Graebn. [*S. Joannis* Čelak.]. Lf. blades involute, broader, smooth, variable in width. Cent. Eur.

Redowskii Trin. Per., sts. to 2 ft., smooth, clustered; lf. sheaths glabrous, purplish, bearded at top, blades to 1 ft. long, flat, linear, or the upper ones involute; panicle contracted, erect, brs. purplish; glumes 3-nerved, lemma white-hairy at base, awn twice as long, reflexed, hispid. Siberia. An obscure, incompletely known sp.

semibarbata R. Br. Sts. to 3 ft.; lf. blades narrow, convolute, glabrous or short-pubescent; panicle oblong, rather dense, to 10 in. long, the brs. erect; glumes to ¾ in. long, long-pointed, lemma silky-hairy, to ¼ in. long, awn 2–4 in. long, shortly plumose-hairy below the bend or to the end. Australia.

splendens Trin. CHEE GRASS. Per., sts. to 7 ft., stout, clustered; foliage scabrous; panicle 12–20 in. long, many-fld., loose; spikelets ¼ in. long, lemma as long as the glumes, silky, awn weakly geniculate, to ⅝ in. long. Eurasia.

tenacissima L. ESPARTO, ESPARTO GRASS. Sts. with a tough, branching base; lf. blades elongate, involute, tomentose at base, with erect auricles; panicle narrow, dense; awns 1⅝–2½ in. long, feathery below the bend. W. Medit. Sts. utilized in Eur. to make fine paper. Sometimes cult. for ornament.

viridula Trin. GREEN N., FEATHER BUNCHGRASS. Sts. to 3 ft.; lf. sheaths glabrous but villous at throat, blades to 1 ft. long, and ¼ in. wide; panicle 4–8 in. long, rather closely fld., greenish or tawny at maturity; glumes to ⅜ in. long, thin, papery, lemma ¼ in. long, over ¹⁄₁₆ in. wide, brownish, appressed-pubescent, awn to 1¼ in. long, twice-bent. Alta. to Wisc., s. to Ill. and Ariz.; adventive in N.Y.

STIPAGROSTIS Nees. *Gramineae.* About 50 spp. of ann. or per. grasses in desert or semidesert areas of Afr. and Eurasia, sts. erect, often clustered; lf. blades narrow, elongate, often convolute, ligule a fringe of hairs; panicles narrow and spikelike or open; spikelets solitary, pedicelled, rachilla disarticulating above the glumes, floret 1, bisexual, as long as or shorter than glumes, glumes narrow, acuminate to obtuse, lemma cylindrical, hard, 3-nerved, awned, awns 1–3, at least the central plumose or hairy. For terminology see *Gramineae.*

pennata (Trin.) De Winter [*Aristida pennata* Trin.]. Per.; sts. to 20 in., erect, robust, branched, smooth and glabrous; lf. blades linear-acuminate, flat to involute, scabrous on both surfaces; panicle very diffuse, to 8 in. long and 6 in. wide, brs. feathery; spikelets straw-colored, glumes unequal, lemma glabrous, awn attached obliquely to the tip. Se. Eur. and Asia.

STIZOLOBIUM: *MUCUNA.*

STOKESIA L'Hér. STOKES' ASTER. *Compositae* (Vernonia Tribe). One sp., a stout per. herb of N. Amer.; lvs. alt.; fl. heads large, many-fld., involucral bracts in several rows, the intermediate ones spinulose-pectinate, receptacle naked; inner fls. tubular, outer fls. with 5-lobed ligules; achenes 3–4-angled, pappus of 4–5 early-deciduous awns.

Propagated by seeds and division.

cyanea: *S. laevis.*

laevis (J. Hill) Greene [*S. cyanea* L'Hér.]. Sts. to 2 ft., woolly or floccose in upper part; lvs. oblong-lanceolate, to 8 in. long, spiny-toothed toward base, the upper ones clasping; heads to 4 in. across, solitary or few in a corymb; fls. lavender-blue. Summer–autumn. S.C., s. to La. and Fla. Cvs. are: **'Alba'**, fls. white; **'Caerulea'**, fls. blue; **'Lilacina'**, fls. lilac; **'Purpurea'**, fls. purplish; **'Rosea'**, fls. rosy. Cvs. **'Praecox'** and **'Superba'** have also been listed.

STOMATIUM Schwant. [*Agnirictus* Schwant.]. *Aizoaceae.* About 40 spp. of glabrous, short-stemmed, tufted succulents, native to S. Afr.; lvs. 4-ranked, crowded, members of a pair unequal in length, shortly triangular, broadly spatulate or elongate-lanceolate in outline, semicylindrical at base, more or less keeled toward apex, soft, surface dull, usually with transparent tubercles, lower side sometimes drawn forward like a chin, margins and keel often armed with few broad, short teeth; fls. nocturnal, fragrant, bractless, calyx 4–6-lobed, forming a tube, petals yellow, rarely white, or pinkish, many, in several series, united into a short tube, stamens many, ovary inferior, 5-celled, stigmas 5–6; fr. a caps., cell lids absent, expanding keels winged.

Growth occurs in summer. The plants should be given a light location under glass with moderate moisture; in winter they should be in a light, dry place at a relatively cool temperature of about 55° F. Propagation easy by seeds or cuttings. See also *Succulents.*

agninum (Haw.) Schwant. [*Agnirictus agninus* (Haw.) Schwant.; *Mesembryanthemum agninum* Haw.]. LAMB'S-TONGUE, SHEEP'S-TONGUE. Lvs. dull gray-green, roughened, green-dotted, inclined, to 2 in. long and ⅝ in. wide, oblong, bluntish, 3-angled in section, upper side flat, lower side strongly rounded and keeled, margins entire or armed with 3–5 short and blunt teeth; fls. 1 in. across, on pedicels ¾ in. long, petals light yellow. Cape Prov.

Comptonii: a listed name of no botanical standing.

Fulleri L. Bolus. Lvs. 6–8, green, roughened by light gray dots, to 1¼ in. long, ½ in. wide at base, somewhat expanded toward apex and blunt, upper side flat, lower side rounded, obliquely keeled toward apex, margins with 3–7 blunt to acute teeth at apex; fls. ¾ in. across, petals yellowish-white. Cape Prov.

murinum (Haw.) Schwant. Much-branched; lvs. gray-green, covered with many white dots, spreading, slightly incurved, to 1¼ in. long, ⅜ in. wide, thickened toward apex, keel raised, margins and usually keel armed with 3 teeth; fls. to 1 in. across, solitary, nearly sessile, petals yellow. Cape Prov.

STOVE PLANTS: see *Greenhouse.*

STRANVAESIA Lindl. *Rosaceae.* Four or 5 spp. of evergreen trees and shrubs of se. and e. Asia; lvs. alt., simple; fls. white, in terminal corymbs, sepals and petals 5, stamens about 20; fr. a small pome.

Grown in southern U. S. Propagated by seeds or cuttings of half-ripe wood under glass.

Davidiana Decne. To 20 ft. or more, silky-pubescent on young twigs, later glabrous; lvs. oblong-lanceolate, cuneate at base, entire, to about 5 in. long, 1 in. wide, glabrous; fls. $^5/_{16}$ in. across; infl. 2–3 in. across; fr. red, pea-sized. Zone 8. Var. **salicifolia** (Hutch.) Rehd. [*S. salicifolia* Hutch.]. Lvs. narrow-lanceolate; infl. densely pubescent. W. China. Var. **undulata** (Decne.) Rehd. [*S. undulata* Decne.]. Shorter; lvs. 1–3 in. long, wavy at margin.

glaucescens: *S. Nussia.*

Nussia Decne. [*S. glaucescens* Lindl.]. To 15 ft.; lvs. leathery, lanceolate to obovate, 3–5 in. long, finely toothed; fls. ½ in. across, in corymbs 4–6 in. across; fr. orange, pubescent. Himalayas.

salicifolia: *S. Davidiana* var.

undulata: *S. Davidiana* var.

STRATIFICATION: see *Propagation.*

STRATIOTES L. WATER-SOLDIER, WATER ALOE. *Hydrocharitaceae.* One sp., a dioecious, stoloniferous, per. aquatic herb, native to Eur.; lvs. spirally arranged in rosettes, submersed or projecting above water; fls. borne in a 2-valved, peduncled spathe, sepals and petals 3, male fls. long-stalked, stamens in 3 rings, female fls. short-stalked, ovary with 6 stigmas.

Occasionally grown in aquaria, pools, or ponds. Propagated by side shoots from base of leaves.

aloides L. Lvs. to 1 ft. long, stiff, linear-lanceolate, margins spiny-toothed; fls. white, to 2 in. across.

STRAWBERRY. The common cultivated strawberry, *Fragaria* × *Ananassa*, is a perennial herb derived from the hybridization of *Fragaria chiloensis* with *F. virginiana.* It is grown for its large red "fruit," which is structurally an enlarged fleshy receptacle with many "seeds" embedded in its surface; these "seeds," however, are really achenes (the true fruits in a botanical sense), and there is a true seed inside the thin, dry wall of each achene (see *Fragaria*). In some species of *Fragaria* the flowers are usually or often unisexual. In *F. moschata* Duchesne, the hautbois strawberry of Europe, for example, pistillate (female), staminate (male), and perfect-flowered (bisexual) types are found. All present-day commercial cultivars of the common strawberry, however, are perfect-flowered.

As a results of strawberry-breeding programs throughout the United States, strawberries can be grown in nearly all the states, including parts of Alaska, and in most of Canada. It thus has a wider distribution than any other Temperate Zone fruit. Strawberries need full sun all day to bear fruit abundantly. Most cultivars perform best on sandy soils; a few, however, are productive on heavier silt and clay loams. Generally, soils that are suitable for vegetables are also suitable for strawberries. Good drainage is essential in order to prevent or reduce serious soil-borne diseases. Planting in a fertile soil with a good moisture supply throughout the growing season is also essential. Although perennial, strawberries do not bear good crops indefinitely. With good care, a planting may fruit profitably for two to six years. To maintain a continuous good supply of fruit, new plantings should be made every year or two.

Propagation is by new plants formed on runners, which are produced abundantly during the growing season. In the nursery, where plants are grown for propagation only, rows are 4–6 feet apart with plants 2 feet apart in the row; the blossoms are removed as they develop. In the home garden, new plantings can be set with young plants from the old bed, although commercial growers usually set nursery-grown plants. Planting time may vary depending upon different climates. In the northern states, early spring is the usual time, but in California and in the South, autumn planting is advantageous, being governed by the time of the desired fruiting season. The plants are set so that the crowns are just level with the soil surface, and the soil is well firmed about the roots. Frost pockets should be avoided, for damage to the flowers by spring frosts may greatly reduce the crop.

As to the methods of culture, so much depends on the size of the plot, the purpose for which the fruit is wanted, and the amount of care one is willing to give, that no set rules can be stated. In most commercial plantings, other than in California and Florida, the matted row system of culture is used. The plants are set 15–30 inches apart in rows spaced at 3½–5 foot intervals. All of the runner plants are allowed to grow but are confined in a strip 15–24 inches wide. Extremely late-rooting runner plants are often removed by a disclike colter.

High yields and fancy fruits can be obtained from hill or special plant-spacing systems. In the hill system, all runner plants are removed as they develop. Such plants become large, with multiple crowns, and are extremely productive; plants can be placed 12–18 inches apart in single or multiple rows or used in garden-border plantings.

Many commercial growers fumigate the soil before planting. Fumigation controls nematodes, reduces to some extent potential weed problems, and reduces some soil diseases.

Plantings should not be made in fields where perennial weeds are a problem. Fumigation of home gardens is not practical since land is generally limiting. To improve the soil structure, a cover crop is frequently grown the previous year. In many areas of California, with heavy fumigation, strawberries are being planted successively on the same land for many years.

In the northern states, the winter treatment of a strawberry bed consists of covering the plants with a straw or hay mulch in late autumn after several light freezes. A wheat straw is preferred; however, salt-marsh hay can be used. One should avoid using a mulch containing weed seeds. The plants should be covered to a depth of 2–3 inches when the straw has settled. When growth begins in the spring, the mulch should be raked off lightly so that a small quantity remains around the plants while most of it is placed between the rows. A light mulch around the plants will keep the fruit clean. For local or home use, the berries are allowed to ripen on the plants.

Cultivars should be chosen with reference to soil, climate, and latitude. No single cultivar possesses all of the desired horticultural characteristics. Some cultivars are of extremely high quality, others are disease and insect resistant. They also differ in firmness, suitability for freezing, color, productivity, runner development, season of ripening, and fruit size.

Cultivars recommended are: for the northeastern United States and New England, 'Catskill', 'Earlidawn', 'Fletcher', 'Gala', 'Garnet', 'Holiday', 'Midway', 'Raritan', 'Redchief', 'Redglow', and 'Surecrop'; for the mid-Atlantic states, 'Apollo', 'Atlas', 'Darrow', 'Guardian', 'Marlate', 'Pocahontas', 'Raritan', 'Redchief', 'Sunrise', 'Surecrop', and 'Titan'; for Florida and the Gulf states, 'Albritton', 'Dabreak', 'Earlibelle', 'Florida Ninety', and 'Headliner'; for the central United States, 'Atlas', 'Delite', 'Guardian', 'Midway', 'Redchief', and 'Surecrop'; for Oregon and Washington, 'Hood', 'Northwest', 'Olympus', 'Rainier', and 'Shuksan'; for California, 'Aliso', 'Heidi', 'Salinas', 'Sequoia', 'Tioga', and 'Tufts'.

Cultivars for the northern states are: 'Badgerbelle', 'Catskill', 'Earlimore', 'Midway', 'Redcoat', 'Robinson', 'Sparkle', 'Stoplight', 'Surecrop', 'Trumpeter', 'Veestar', and 'Viking'. Those recommended for Canadian areas are: for Nova Scotia, 'Acadia' and 'Bounty'; for Ontario, 'Veestar' and 'Vibrant'; for British Columbia, 'Cheam', 'Northwest', and 'Totem'.

Everbearing cultivars are: for the Northwest, 'Nisqually' and 'Quinalt'; for the East, 'Gem', 'Geneva', 'Ozark Beauty', 'Streamliner', and 'Superfection Brilliant'; for the Midwest, 'Arapahoe', 'Gem', and 'Ogallala'.

The hautbois, alpine, and perpetual strawberries are forms of *Fragaria moschata* and *F. vesca* of Europe and are seldom grown in North America, though sometimes seen in gardens of amateurs.

Although many pests and diseases may cause serious damage, it is usually possible to grow strawberries for home use without spraying, particularly if the rotation is short. The commercial grower should spray to meet his special problems. It is important from the standpoint of disease and pest control to keep the plants vigorous by good cultural practices, obtain virus-free and disease-free plants, and avoid such problems as verticillium wilt, which is common in garden areas where tomatoes, peppers, potatoes, and eggplants have been grown. For the latest in insect, disease, and weed control measures, local agricultural extension agents should be consulted.

STREET TREES. Trees are the most common plants used along streets, avenues, and parkways for shade, ornament, or general landscape use. When properly selected and maintained, such streetside plantings can create a desirable parklike atmosphere and improve the environment of the community; when improper plantings are made, the result can be continuing trouble and expense. Most street-tree plantings, together with their care, fall under the jurisdiction of local public authorities, who are not always familiar with

trees and their cultural requirements. Common faults have been the selection of species that are too large and out-of-scale for the planting site, and the setting of trees too close together. Large street trees often interfere with overhead or underground utilities and their beauty is then marred by essential but unaesthetic pruning; those that are shallow-rooted often lift up the adjacent pavement of roads and walkways. Some trees are naturally untidy, shedding bark, branches, or undesirable fruits; they should not be selected for street plantings. Moreover, a diversity of species is desirable to avoid such devastation of single species as has been caused by the Dutch elm disease affecting *Ulmus americana*, once a popular street tree. As much care must be given to the testing, planning, and maintenance of trees for street plantings as with any other horticultural or gardening operation.

The proper embellishment of streets with trees requires not only adequate horticultural knowledge but imagination as well. The variety of available materials is increasing and information about trees most suitable for a given area is usually available from local or regional botanical gardens, arboreta, and some horticultural experiment stations. Smaller species often more appropriate for street plantings are now being used and some cultivars are almost tailor-made for specific sites. The custom, long-established in tropical and subtropical areas, of using showy flowering species along streets, is gradually spreading to temperate parts of the country, with increasing use of such ornamental trees as *Catalpa*, flowering cherries *(Prunus)*, crabapples *(Malus)*, and dogwoods *(Cornus)*.

Among trees most commonly used in street plantings are the following. Many others are useful for, but often limited to, parts of the West Coast and southern Florida. Hardiness zones for some trees are indicated within parentheses in the following lists.

Deciduous trees: species of *Acer, Aesculus, Albizia, Amelanchier, Betula, Carpinus, Celtis, Cladrastis, Fraxinus, Ginkgo, Gleditsia, Koelreuteria, Liquidambar, Liriodendron, Morus, Nyssa, Ostrya, Oxydendrum, Phellodendron, Pistacia, Platanus, Pyrus, Quercus, Sophora, Sorbus, Tilia,* and *Zelkova.*

Broadleaf evergreen trees (mostly Zones 8–10): *Ceratonia, Cinnamomum, Ficus, Harpephyllum, Magnolia, Melaleuca, Olea, Pittosporum, Podocarpus, Pyrus, Quercus, Schinus,* and *Tristania.*

Flowering trees: *Aesculus carnea* (3–6), *Callistemon viminalis* (9–10), *Catalpa bignonioides* (4–6), *Cercis canadensis* (4–7), *Cornus florida* (4–9), *C. Kousa* (5–9), *C. mas* (4–7), *Crataegus* × *Lavallei* (4–7), *C. Phaenopyrum* (4–7), *Halesia carolina* (4–9), *Koelreuteria paniculata* (5–9), *Lagerstroemia indica* (7–9), *Liriodendron Tulipifera* (4–9), *Magnolia grandiflora* (7–9), *Malus* species (2–9), *Nerium Oleander* (9–10), *Prunus* × *blireiana* (5–7), *P. cerasifera* (4–7), *P. Sargentii* (4–7), *P. serrulata* (5–7), *P. subhirtella* (5–7), and *P. yedoensis* (5–7).

Trees for cities: *Acer platanoides* (3–9), *Albizia Julibrissin* (7–9), *Crataegus Phaenopyrum* (4–7), *Ficus retusa* (9–10), *Fraxinus pennsylvanica* (3–9), *Ginkgo biloba* (4–9), *Gleditsia triacanthos* var. *inermis* (4–10), *Koelreuteria paniculata* (5–9), *Magnolia grandiflora* (7–9), *Phellodendron amurense* (3–6), *Platanus* × *acerifolia* (5–9), *Podocarpus macrophyllus* (7–9), *Pyrus Calleryana* 'Bradford' (5–9), *Sophora japonica* (4–7), and *Zelkova serrata* (5–9).

Small trees: species of *Acer* and *Ilex, Laurus nobilis, Ligustrum lucidum, Pittosporum,* and *Prunus.*

STRELITZIA Ait. BIRD-OF-PARADISE. *Strelitziaceae.* Four spp. of herbs lacking evident sts. or with woody, palmlike trunks, native to subtrop. S. Afr.; lvs. bananalike, 2-ranked; fls. in a rigid, boatlike bract on lateral, simple or compound infl., bisexual, irregular, sepals 3, narrow, petals 3, 1 small and 2 united in an often arrow-shaped organ (the tongue) in the groove of which lie the 5 stamens and style; fr. a 3-celled caps., seeds many, with filamentous aril.

The species are suitable for warm climates or for growing under glass in tubs with a night temperature of 50° F. Propagated by suckers, division, and seeds.

alba (L.f.) Skeels [*S. augusta* Thunb.]. Trunk solitary, to 18 ft.; lvs. to 4 ft. long, 2 ft. wide, petiole deeply wing-channelled; infl. simple, bracts deep purple, to 15 in. long; fls. white, margins of tongue not hastate but sometimes turned inward and overlapping at base.

augusta: *S. alba.*

juncea: *S. reginae* var.

Nicolai Regel & Körn. BIRD-OF-PARADISE TREE. Resembling *S. alba* but much larger and treelike; infl. compound, bracts reddish-brown; petals light mauve or blue to nearly white, tongue boat-shaped, hastate at base, margins turned inward and meeting over the center.

parvifolia: *S. reginae.*

reginae Ait. [*S. parvifolia* Ait.f.]. BIRD-OF-PARADISE, BIRD-OF-PARADISE FLOWER, QUEEN'S BIRD-OF-PARADISE, CRANE FLOWER, CRANE LILY. To 3 ft., trunkless, clump-forming; lvs. oblong-lanceolate, to 1½ ft. long, 6 in. wide, acute, glaucescent beneath, the blade sometimes reduced; bracts green, edged with purple or red, to 8 in. long; fls. orange or yellow with dark blue tongue. Var. **juncea** (Ker-Gawl.) H. E. Moore [*S. juncea* Link; *S. parvifolia* var. *juncea* Ker-Gawl.]. Lvs. bladeless or nearly so.

royallii: a listed name of no botanical standing.

STRELITZIACEAE. *Strelitzia reginae.* **a,** flowering plant, × 1/20; **b,** inflorescence, × 1/8; **c,** flower, × 1/6; **d,** flower, vertical section (sepals cut away), × 1/4; **e,** stamens and style, × 1/2; **f,** stigma, × 1½; **g,** ovary, cross section, × 1; **h,** capsule, dehisced, × 1/2; **i,** seed, × 1.

STRELITZIACEAE (K. Schum.) Hutch. STRELITZIA FAMILY. Moncot.; 3 genera of per. or monocarpic herbs, sometimes treelike, native to tropics and subtropics of S. Amer., S. Afr., and Madagascar; lf. blades rolled in bud, pinnately veined; fls. in axils of large bracts in a terminal or lateral infl., bisexual, irregular, sepals 3, petals 3, nearly equal or 1 small and 2 united and enclosing stamens, stamens 5 or 6, separate, ovary inferior, 3-celled; fr. a caps., seeds with colored, lacerate or filamentous arils. *Ravenala* and *Strelitzia* are widely cult. as ornamentals in warm regions or under glass.

STREPTANTHERA Sweet. *Iridaceae.* Two spp. of cormous herbs, native to the Cape Prov., S. Afr.; resembling *Ixia* and *Sparaxis;* lvs. basal, 2-ranked, forming a fan; fls. 2–4 in a spike, rotate, perianth tube short, funnelform, stamens radially disposed, anthers spirally twisted, style brs. club- or wedge-shaped; fr. a caps.

cuprea Sweet. Corm with reticulate fibers, roots fleshy; lvs. mostly 8–12, about 3–5 in. long and 5/16 in. wide; sts. simple, not longer than lvs.; fls. 2–4, 2 in. across, copper-pink, with purple throat cross-banded black, perianth segms. obtuse, obovate. Cv. **'Coccinea'.** Fls. bright orange, with purple-black eye.

elegans Sweet. Differs from *S. cuprea* in having sts. slightly longer than lvs., usually forked at base; fls. 1–2, white or nearly so, with pale yellow throat, cross-banded purple.

STREPTOCALYX Beer. *Bromeliaceae.* About 16 spp. of mostly epiphytic herbs, native to S. Amer.; lvs. in a rosette, spiny; infl. scapose or nearly sessile, paniculate; fls. sessile, blue or white, sepals and petals separate or nearly so, petals without appendages, ovary inferior; fr. a dry berry, seeds without appendages.

Grown outdoors in warm climates or under glass. Requires bright light. For culture see *Bromeliaceae.*

floribundus (Mart. ex Schult.) Mez. To 9 ft.; lvs. to 5 ft. long, 6 in. wide, strongly spiny; scape 4½ ft. or more, infl. a 3-pinnate panicle, fl. bracts conspicuous; fls. white, to 1 5/16 in. long. Brazil.

Poeppigii Beer. Lvs. to 2 ft. long, 1⅜–2 in. wide, spiny-margined and spine-tipped; infl. nodding from short scape, 2-pinnately paniculate, primary bracts large, fl. bracts minute; fls. to 1½ in. long, petals blue. Brazil.

STREPTOCARPUS Lindl. CAPE PRIMROSE. *Gesneriaceae.* About 132 spp. of often hairy, ann., per., or monocarpic (the plant dying after fruiting) herbs or subshrubs, native in Afr., Madagascar, and Asia; sts. erect or creeping; lvs. opp. or whorled, or several and basal, or only the leaflike cotyledon developed; fls. in axillary cymes or 1–2 to many on a scapose infl. from the crown, calyx deeply 5-parted, rarely with a tube, corolla cylindrical or funnelform, 5-lobed, lobes orbicular, often unequal, fertile stamens 2, borne on corolla tube, staminodes 2–3, anthers often coherent face to face, with confluent cells, disc ringlike, ovary superior; fr. a spirally twisted, 2-valved caps., seeds minute. Spp. with a single lf. (actually a cotyledon) are usually monocarpic.

For cultivation see *Gesneriaceae.*

×**achimeniflorus** Hort. A hybrid between *S. polyanthus* and a hybrid strain.

candidus Hilliard. Lvs. in a basal rosette from a vertical rhizome, to 2 ft. long, 8 in. wide, crenate; infl. to 25-fld., with many fls. open at one time, peduncle to 1 ft.; fls. honey-scented, corolla 1⅝ in. long, white or suffused with pale violet, tube nearly cylindrical, straight, with yellow stripe on floor of tube streaked and spotted violet-blue, lobes to ⅝ in. long, lower lip with 2 violet-blue chevrons at base; caps. to 2⅝ in. long. Natal.

caulescens Vatke. To 30 in.; lvs. opp., petioled, blades narrowly to broadly elliptic or ovate, to 2⅝ in. long, 1¼ in. wide, with 10–12 pairs of nerves, dark green, velvety-hairy; infl. cymose, 6–12-fld., axillary, peduncles long; corolla to ¾ in. long, violet, or white striped with violet, tube slender, limb nearly closed at throat, lower lip prominent, upper lobes short, ovary glabrous; fr. to 1¾ in. long. E. Afr. Var. **caulescens.** The typical var.; corolla violet, essentially straight on lower side. Var. **pallescens** Engl. Corolla violet, or white striped with violet, swollen on lower side.

confusus Hilliard. Monocarpic, lf. solitary, to 1 ft. long, 6¾ in. wide, usually red-purple beneath, dark green above; infl. to 36-fld., peduncle to 1 ft.; corolla to 2¼ in. long, tube laterally compressed at throat, pale violet to whitish, limb oblique, pale to medium violet, throat white or pale yellow; caps. to 3⅜ in. long. S. Afr. Subsp. **confusus.** The typical subsp.; fls. less than 1 in. long, stigma nearly capitate. Subsp. **lebomboensis** Hilliard & B. L. Burtt. Fls. 1⅜–2¼ in. long, stigma more nearly 2-lobed.

Cooksonii B. L. Burtt. Monocarpic, lf. solitary, to 16 in. long, 1 ft. wide, crenate, pilose; infl. crowded, with many fls. open at one time; corolla to 1½ in. long, tube broadly cylindrical, abruptly widened upward, to ¾ in. long, ½ in. across mouth, deep violet with white streak on under side, lobes deep violet grading to deep blue and a white patch in throat, with 2 violet ellipses at apex of patch; caps. to 1⅝ in. long. S. Afr.

Cooperi C. B. Clarke. Monocarpic, lf. solitary, to 28 in. long and wide, cordate at base, crenate; infl. many-fld., peduncles to 20 in.; corolla to 2¾ in. long, medium violet, tube narrowly funnelform, white on lower side, base of lower lip marked with white wedges; caps. to 6 in. long. S. Afr.

cyanandrus B. L. Burtt. Plants deep purple-red; lvs. several in a tuft, linear-oblong to lanceolate, to 6 in. long, 2 in. wide, pilose; infls. 1–2, few-fld., peduncles to 18 in.; corolla to 1⅜ in. long, magenta-pink on upper side, paler on under side, tube funnelform, with magenta-pink spots, lobes on the floor, each with 3 magenta-pink stripes extending inside tube as lines of dots; caps. to ¾ in. long. Rhodesia.

cyaneus S. L. Moore. Lvs. suberect, to 16 in. long, 4 in. wide, crenate; infl. 1–2 or 4–6(–12)-fld., to 8 in. long; corolla 1–3 in. long, pale to deep purple or bright pink, rarely white, tube funnelform, with a central yellow stripe on floor of tube flanked by deep violet or reddish-violet streaks extending onto lobes of lower lip, lobes to 1 in. long; caps. to 4⅜ in. long. S. Afr.

Daviesii N. E. Br. ex C. B. Clarke. Lvs. 1 each year, superimposed, the fl.-bearing lf. often cordate, to 9½ in. long, 7 in. wide, green or purplish beneath; infl. to 20-fld., peduncle to 4 in.; corolla to 1¾ in. long, tube compressed toward throat, about ¾ in. long, greenish, flushed with violet, limb oblique, pale to medium violet, throat white, with yellow blotch; caps. to 2⅛ in. long. S. Afr.

dracomontanus: a listed name for *S. polyanthus* subsp. *dracomontanus.*

Dunnii M. T. Mast. ex Hook.f. Monocarpic or per., with orange-red granules on all parts except upper surface of lf.; lvs. 1 or several, to 1 ft. long, 8 in. wide, crenate, gray-green above; infl. with many fls. open at one time, to 1 ft. long, corolla 2 in. long, pink to reddish, tube cylindrical, widening upward, white and striped red on floor, limb nearly regular, lobes to ¼ in. long; caps. to 1¼ in. long. S. Afr.

erubescens Hilliard & B. L. Burtt. Monocarpic, pubescent with spreading hairs; lf. solitary, to 6 in. long, 4¾ in. wide, crenate, dark green above, sometimes purple beneath; infls. 2–3, few-fld., peduncle to 4 in. long; corolla to 1⅝ in. long, white, flushed pink on upper side and on outside of upper lobes, tube bearded on roof, grooved on floor, lobes with 3 magenta-pink stripes inside, lower lobes with a central magenta-pink stripe; caps. to 2 in. long. Malawi and Mozambique.

Eylesii S. L. Moore. Monocarpic; lf. solitary, to 1 ft. long, 8 in. wide, crenate-dentate, pilose; infl. to 1 ft.; corolla to 2⅝ in. long, pale or whitish outside, tube funnelform, curved downward, throat white, rarely with yellow patch, limb pale to medium violet, with 2 darker patches at mouth of tube; caps. to 3 in. long. Tanzania to Rhodesia.

Fanniniae Harv. ex C. B. Clarke. Per., creeping; lvs. to 3 ft. long, 8¾ in. wide, crenate; infls. 1–2, just below blade, many-fld., to 1 ft. long; fls. honey-scented, corolla pale blue to whitish, tube nearly cylindrical, with 2 often yellow keels on floor, spotted or striped violet, and usually a yellow stripe, limb straight, lower lobes to 1 in. long; caps. to 2½ in. long. Natal.

Galpinii Hook.f. Monocarpic or per.; lvs. 1 or several, to 6 in. long, 4¾ in. wide, cordate to cuneate at base, appressed-hairy above, green or red beneath; infl. from crown, to 24-fld., peduncle to 6⅜ in. long; corolla to 1¼ in. long, tube widening toward throat, violet, limb medium violet with white triangular blotch in center; caps. to 1 in. long. S. Afr.

Gardenii Hook. Lvs. basal, ovate-elliptic, to 1 ft. long, 2⅜ in. wide, rugose; infl. 1–2–6-fld.; corolla to 2 in. long, tube green or greenish-white, limb 2-lipped, pale violet, upper lobes often with solid violet lines at base, lower lobes with deep violet dots and streaks. S. Afr.

glandulosissimus Engl. [*S. ruwenzoriensis* Bak.]. Sts. weak, straggling; lvs. opp., variable, blade ovate to elliptic or elliptic-obovate, to 5¼ in. long, 2 in. wide, asymmetrical at base; infl. axillary, peduncle to 6 in. long, pedicels glandular; corolla to 1¼ in. long, deep violet to violet-blue, tube nearly closed at mouth, ovary pubescent. Cent. Afr.

gracilis: *S. prolixus.*

grandis N. E. Br. Monocarpic; lf. solitary, to 3½ ft. long, 2¼ ft. wide, harshly hairy; infls. several, peduncles to 3½ ft. long; corolla 1–1¾ in. long, light blue, tube cylindrical, slightly curved, white inside with 2 broad violet stripes in throat; caps. to 4¼ in. long. S. Afr.

Haygarthii N. E. Br. ex C. B. Clarke [*S. Reynoldsii* Verd.]. Monocarpic; lvs. 1–2, ovate, to 16 in. long or more, 14 in. wide, cordate at base, softly hairy on both sides; infl. cymose, to nearly 15 in.; corolla tubular, to 1¾ in. long, laterally compressed at mouth, pale blue, lobes small; caps. to 3⅜ in. long. S. Afr.

Hilsenbergii R. Br. Sts. to 2 ft., straggling at base; lvs. opp., blades ovate to elliptic or elliptic-lanceolate, to 2⅜ in. long, 1⅜ in. wide, crenate-serrate to dentate-serrate; infl. axillary, 1- to many-fld., peduncle to 4 in. long; corolla to 1¾ in. long, pale violet to vivid red, usually darker or white-marked in throat, filaments slender, arising well above base of tube; caps. to 2¼ in. long. Madagascar.

Holstii Engl. To 2 ft., sts. glabrescent, glossy; lvs. opp., long-petioled, blades ovate or ovate-elliptic, to 1¾ in. long, with 7–9 pairs of veins, slightly hairy; infl. cymose, axillary, 2–6-fld., sparsely glandular, peduncle long; corolla to 1¼ in. long, mauve-purple, throat white, upper lip very short; caps. to 2¼ in. long. E. Afr.

×**hybridus** Voss. CAPE PRIMROSE. A complex hybrid derived from several spp., with the compact habit of *S. Rexii* but with large fls. in many colors. Several cvs. and strains, such as the Wiesmoor Hybrids, probably belong here.

insignis: *S. primulifolius* subsp. *formosus.*

johannis L. L. Britten. Per.; lvs. many in a rosette, to 14 in. long, 4 in. wide; infl. 1–12-fld., peduncle to 1 ft. long; corolla to 1¾ in. long, whitish to pale violet, throat white or yellowish, tube cylindrical, curved, laterally compressed at mouth, limb oblique, stigma 2-lobed; caps. to 2⅜ in. long. S. Afr.

kentaniensis L. L. Britten & Story. Per., lvs. many in a rosette, lanceolate, to 8 in. long, ¾ in. wide, crenate; infl. 2–5-fld., peduncle to 4¾ in. long; corolla to 1¼ in. long, tube cylindrical, pale violet, 2-keeled and with pale yellow stripe spotted with violet on floor, limb oblique; caps. to 2 in. long. S. Afr.

×**kewensis** N. E. Br.: *S. Dunnii* × *S. Rexii*. Lvs. 2–3, basal, oblong or elongate-ovate, large, bright green; infls. several from crown, 6–8-fld.; corolla 2 in. long, to 1½ in. across, bright mauve-purple, throat striped with dark brownish-purple.

Kirkii Hook.f. Sts. to 16 in., slender, often branched, hairy, becoming woody at base; lvs. opp., short-petioled, blades obovate-oblong to nearly orbicular, to 2¼ in. long, finely hairy, bright green; infl. to 10-fld., peduncles axillary; corolla to ¾ in. long, blue or lilac, throat sometimes purple-spotted; caps. 1⅝ in. long. E. Afr.

Michelmorei B. L. Burtt. Monocarpic; lf. solitary, to 14 in. long, 12 in. wide; infls. 1 or several, many-fld., peduncles short; corolla to 2 in. long, medium violet with deep violet patch inside throat on lower surface, and with yellow deeper within the tube, mouth open, limb nearly regular; caps. to 5¼ in. long. Rhodesia.

micranthus C. B. Clarke. Monocarpic; lf. solitary, to 6 in. long, 5⅝ in. wide; infl. many-fld., peduncle to 6 in. long; corolla small, about ¼ in. long, white or tinged pale green at base, tube cylindrical, limb straight; caps. to ¾ in. long. S. Afr.

molweniensis Hilliard. Similar to *S. Wendlandii*, but corolla tube to 1 in. long, lower lip ⅜–¾ in. long, lf. usually green beneath, occasionally red; and to *S. Saundersii*, but corolla with a white stripe on floor of tube. Natal.

montanus D. Oliver. Lvs. 3–5, basal, lanceolate to obovate, to 1 ft. long, 6 in. wide, toothed, with 18 pairs of nerves, hairy; infl. several-to many-fld., peduncles to 1 ft. long; corolla ⅝ in. long, pale to medium violet, tube with 7–9 violet stripes on lower side; caps. to 1 in. long. E. Afr.

montigena L. L. Britten. Per.; lvs. many, to 1 ft. long, 4 in. wide, crenate; infl. 2–12-fld., peduncles to 8 in. long; corolla to 2⅛ in. long, tube slightly curved, widening upward, pale violet on upper side, creamy-white on underside, limb oblique, lobes pale violet, lower lip cream at base, with 2 elliptic yellow patches. S. Afr.

nobilis C. B. Clarke. Sts. to 3 ft., branched; lvs. opp., sparsely hairy, blades cordate-ovate, to 6 in. long, with 10 pairs of nerves; infl. axillary, short-peduncled; fls. several, to 1 in. long, purple, cleistogamous fls. usually also present, smaller, paler; caps. hairy, to 2⅜ in. long. W. Afr. Plants grown under this name have often proved to be *S. Rexii.*

parviflorus Hook.f. Per.; lvs. many, strap-shaped, to 18 in. long, 2¾ in. wide, crenate; infl. to 20-fld., peduncle to 10 in. long; corolla to 1¼ in. long, white or suffused with pale violet, tube straight, with a yellow stripe on floor of throat, usually with 3–7 violet streaks extending onto lower lip, limb slightly oblique; caps. to 2½ in. long. S. Afr.

polyanthus Hook. Monocarpic or per.; lvs. 1–3, to 9⅝ in. long, 6¾ in. wide; infl. from base of midrib, to 36-fld., peduncles to 10 in. long; corolla ⅝–1¾ in. long, pale violet or rarely greenish-white, tube cylindrical, sharply deflexed, then directed forward, laterally compressed at mouth, limb flat, oblique, usually pale to medium violet, throat white, greenish, or yellow; caps. to 2⅝ in. long. S. Afr. Subsp. **polyanthus.** The typical subsp.; per., with 2–3 lvs.; infl. often many-fld., peduncles stout; corolla limb usually 1 in. wide or more, upper 2 lobes strongly reflexed. Subsp. **dracomontanus** Hilliard. Per., with 2–3 lvs.; infl. usually few-fld., short, stout; corolla limb less than ¾ in. wide, upper 2 lobes not strongly reflexed.

primulifolius Gand. Lvs. in a basal rosette, to 18 in. long, 4⅜ in. wide; infl. 1–2–4-fld., to 10 in. long; calyx lobes to 5/16 in. long, corolla narrowly funnelform, 2⅝–4¼ in. long, pale blue-violet to whitish outside, limb and inside varied. S. Afr. Subsp. **primulifolius.** The typical subsp.; lower surface of tube and base of lower lip deep violet, marked with 5 red-purple lines, lobes pale bluish-violet inside. Subsp. **formosus** Hilliard & B. L. Burtt [*S. insignis* B. L. Burtt]. Tube spotted violet-purple, with yellow zone on floor extending onto lower lip, lobes whitish, with medium violet margin, lower lip with purple-spotted veins.

prolixus C. B. Clarke [*S. gracilis* B. L. Burtt]. Per.; lvs. 2–3, to 9¼ in. long, 6 in. wide, cordate at base, crenate, pilose; infl. erect, to

36-fld., peduncle to 8 in. long; corolla to 1⅛ in. long, pale to medium violet, often marked with a yellow blotch in throat, tube nearly cylindrical, sharply bent downward, then directed forward, laterally compressed at mouth, limb flat, oblique; caps. to nearly 2 in. long. Natal.

pusillus Harv. ex C. B. Clarke. Monocarpic; lf. solitary, elliptic, to 8¾ in. long, 5½ in. across, hairy; infls. 10–30-fld., short, to 4¾ in. long; corolla less than 1 in. long, white. S. Afr.

Rexii (Bowie ex Hook.) Lindl. Lvs. in a basal rosette, ovate-oblong, to 1 ft. long, 2⅝ in. wide, scalloped, rugose, hairy; infls. 1–2- or rarely to 6-fld., to 8 in. long; corolla to 3 in. long, finely hairy, tube white, bluish or mauve, widening to oblique limb, lobes orbicular, nearly equal, the lower striped with purple toward base; caps. to 5¼ in. long. S. Afr.

Reynoldsii: *S. Haygarthii.*

rimicola Story. Monocarpic; lf. solitary, broadly ovate to narrowly oblong, to 2⅝ in. long, 2 in. wide, slightly serrate, hairy; infls. 1–4, 2–3(–9–20)-fld., to 2¾ in. long; corolla ⅜ in. long, white; caps. to ⅜ in. long. S. Afr.

ruwenzoriensis: *S. glandulosissimus.*

Saundersii Hook. Similar to *S. Wendlandii,* but corolla tube usually with a yellow stripe on the floor, with 2 deep violet blotches on each side in the throat. Natal.

saxorum Engl. Sts. branched, densely hairy; lvs. opp. or whorled, elliptic to ovate, to 1¼ in. long, with 4–6 pairs of veins, paler beneath; infl. 1–2-fld., peduncles slender, to 3 in. long; corolla white, tube slender, ⅝ in. long, laterally compressed at mouth, glandular, limb spreading, 1½ in. across, lilac with white around mouth; caps. 2½ in. long. E. Afr.

silvaticus Hilliard. Lvs. 2–5 in a rosette, to 4¾ in. long, 2¾ in. wide; infl. about 10-fld., to 6¼ in. long; corolla about 1¼ in. long, tube sharply bent downward, then directed forward, laterally compressed at throat, greenish, limb oblique, pale violet with impressed lines and 2 small keels, throat yellow-green; caps. to 2⅛ in. long. S. Afr.

solenanthus Mansf. Monocarpic; lf. solitary, ovate to oblong, to 6 in. long, 4¾ in. wide, rarely to 14 in. long and 6¾ in. wide; infls. 1–4, peduncles to 6 in. long; fls. at one level, corolla to 1½ in. long, wholly white or light violet, or the tube and outside of limb whitish and inside of limb light to medium violet, often with darker patches at throat, stamens arising in upper ⅓ of tube; caps. to 3¼ in. long. Tanzania.

Sutherlandii: a listed name of no botanical standing.

tubiflos C. B. Clarke. A confused name, to be rejected; identity of plants cult. under this name is not known.

Vandeleurii Bak.f. & S. L. Moore. Monocarpic; lf. solitary, to 1 ft. long and wide; infl. to 36-fld., peduncle to 1 ft. long; corolla to 2¼ in. long, white with yellow blotch at base of lower lip, tube funnelform, curved downward, sometimes with 3 red-violet V's in mouth; caps. to 2 in. long. S. Afr.

viscosus: a listed name of no botanical standing.

Wendlandii Sprenger ex Hort. Dammann. Monocarpic; lf. solitary, large, to 3 ft. long, 2 ft. wide, hairy, prominently nerved, wine-red or beet-red beneath; infls. several, to 30 in. long; fls. nodding, corolla to 2 in. long, tube about ¾ in. long, whitish, suffused medium violet on upper side, limb oblique, medium violet, with 2 deep violet blotches in throat on each side of a white stripe on floor of tube, lower lobes with violet lines; caps. 3 in. long. S. Afr.

Wilmsii Engl. Monocarpic or per.; lf. usually 1, to 10 in. long, 7¼ in. wide, crenate; infl. to 25-fld., peduncle to 10 in. long; fls. honey-scented, corolla to 1½ in. long, white or pale blue-violet, tube with yellow stripes, streaked and spotted blue-violet on floor of tube and extending onto base of lower lip, tube cylindrical, straight, limb slightly oblique; caps. to 3⅝ in. long. S. Afr.

×STREPTOGLOXINIA Rodig. *Gesneriaceae.* A name used for a purported hybrid between *Streptocarpus* and *Sinningia,* which has not been reproducible; plants listed under this name are generally slipper forms of *Sinningia speciosa.* If the cross is ever made and clearly documented, this name will not apply, since it is not of proper form. Also known as ×*Stroxinia* Hort.

STREPTOPUS Michx. TWISTED-STALK. *Liliaceae.* About 7 spp. of rhizomatous, per. herbs native to N. Amer., Eur., and Asia; st. simple or branched, leafy; lvs. alt., sessile or clasping; fls. white, pink, rose, or purple, nodding, solitary or in pairs, supra-axillary, on twisted pedicels, perianth segms. 6, separate, stamens 6, filaments dilated; fr. a berry.

Of easy culture in the wild garden.

amplexifolius (L.) DC. WHITE MANDARIN. Sts. to 3 ft., glabrous to hispid; lvs. lanceolate-ovate to ovate or oblong-ovate, to 5 in. long and 2 in. wide, glaucous beneath, clasping; fls. greenish-white, ½ in. long, in pairs; fr. red, ellipsoid, to ¾ in. long. Eurasia, N. Amer. Amer. plants, in the broad sense, have been distinguished as var. **americanus** Schult., LIVERBERRY, SCOOTBERRY.

curvipes: *S. roseus* var.

japonicus: *S. streptopoides* var.

roseus Michx. ROSE MANDARIN. Sts. to 2½ ft., finely pubescent; lvs. lanceolate to ovate-lanceolate, to 3½ in. long and 1½ in. wide, sessile, not clasping, ciliate; fls. solitary, on glabrous pedicels, rose to purple, ½ in. long, with perianth lobes recurved; fr. red, ⅜ in. in diam. E. U.S. Var. **curvipes** (Vail) Fassett [*S. curvipes* Vail]. Fls. campanulate. N. Ore. to Alaska. Var. **perspectus** Fassett. Pedicels ciliate. S. Labrador and s. Nfld., s. to Penn. and w. to Mich.

streptopoides (Ledeb.) Frye & Rigg. Sts. to 1 ft.; lvs. oblong to ovate-oblong, to 3⅛ in. long and 1⅛ in. wide, sessile; fls. solitary, rotate, pink, perianth lobes yellowish-green toward apex; fr. red, globose. Japan. Var. **japonicus** (Maxim.) Fassett [*S. japonicus* (Maxim.) Ohwi]. Stouter, taller; lvs. lanceolate to ovate, to 4 in. long. Japan.

STREPTOSOLEN Miers. *Solanaceae.* One sp., a scabrous-pubescent, evergreen shrub of Andean Colombia and Ecuador; lvs. alt., entire; fls. pedicelled, in terminal, paniculate corymbs, calyx tubular-campanulate, shortly 5-lobed, corolla funnelform, 4–5-lobed, tube elongate, spirally twisted, limb 2-lipped, fertile stamens 4, in 2 pairs; caps. 2-valved, seeds minute.

A popular greenhouse plant, also grown outdoors in Zone 9. Propagated by cuttings.

Jamesonii (Benth.) Miers. FIREBUSH, ORANGE BROWALLIA, MARMALADE BUSH, YELLOW HELIOTROPE. To 6 ft.; lvs. ovate, to 1¼ in. long, obtuse; fl. clusters at the ends of flexuous brs.; corolla orange-red, to 1¼ in. long.

STROBILANTHES Blume [*Goldfussia* Nees; *Perilepta* Bremek.]. MEXICAN PETUNIA. *Acanthaceae.* About 200–300 spp. of herbs or shrubs of trop. Asia; lvs. opp., the members of a pair sometimes unlike; fls. in spikes or panicles or solitary, corolla tubular, the tube constricted at base and swollen above, lobes 5, unequal, stamens usually 4, didynamous; fr. an oblong or linear caps., seeds 4. A large genus, variable and difficult to define.

Grown for flowers and foliage. The following are grown under glass and require high temperatures and abundant moisture. Care must be taken or the plants may become weedy. Propagated by cuttings.

anisophyllus (Wallich ex Lodd.) T. Anderson [*Goldfussia anisophylla* (Wallich ex Lodd.) Nees]. Differs from *S. isophyllus* chiefly in having lvs. broader, those of each pair unequal in size. Assam.

Dyeranus M. T. Mast. [*Perilepta Dyerana* (M. T. Mast.) Bremek.]. PERSIAN-SHIELD. Shrub; lvs. ovate-lanceolate, to 8 in. long, toothed, purple beneath, iridescent above; fls. in spikes, corolla violet, 1½ in. long. Burma. An attractive foliage plant.

isophyllus (Nees) T. Anderson [*Goldfussia isophylla* Nees]. BEDDING CONEHEAD. Shrub, to 3 ft.; lvs. willowlike, to 4 in. long, toothed; fls. in axillary clusters, corolla 1 in. long, pinkish or blue and white. Probably Assam. Sometimes confused with *Ruellia malacosperma.*

STROMANTHE Sond. *Marantaceae.* About 10 spp. of per., rhizomatous, caulescent herbs, native to trop. S. Amer.; basal lvs. 2-ranked, long-petioled; flowering shoots leafy, the racemes or panicles with deciduous colored bracts and zigzag rachises; fls. with sepals 3, corolla 3-parted, tube very short, fertile stamen 1, staminodes small, 4, or rarely the outer 2 absent, ovary inferior, 1-celled; fr. a caps.

For culture see *Calathea.*

amabilis (Linden) E. Morr. [*Calathea amabilis* Hort.; *Maranta amabilis* Linden]. Compact; lf. blades elliptic-oblong, subtruncate and abruptly acuminate at both ends, green and with broad gray bands between lateral veins above, gray-green beneath. Brazil.

Porteana Gris [*Maranta Porteana* (Gris) Körn.]. To 6 ft.; lvs. to 1 ft. long and 6 in. wide, bright green with silvery-white along lateral veins above, purple beneath; bracts blood-red.

sanguinea Sond. To 5 ft.; lvs. elliptic-oblong, to 20 in. long and 6 in. wide, shining dark green above, wine-purple or striped with green beneath; peduncle 1 ft. longer than petiole, infl. branched; fls. white, calyx and bracts cherry-red. Brazil.

STROMBOCACTUS Britt. & Rose [*Turbinicarpus* (Backeb.) Buxb. & Backeb.]. *Cactaceae.* Five to 10 spp. of small, depressed-globose to cylindrical cacti, native to Mex.; sts. with close-set, irregularly rhombic, hard tubercles; spines cylindrical or flattened; fls. subapical, from the spiniferous areoles, diurnal, campanulate or short-funnelform, tube naked or nearly so, ovary naked or with a few scales near the apex; fr. dry, splitting, seeds dustlike, tubercled, arillate.

For culture see *Cacti.*

disciformis (DC.) Britt. & Rose. Sts. simple, to 2½ in. thick; tubercles to ¾ in. wide, spines 1–4, bristlelike, white, to ⅝ in. long; fls. white, to 1½ in. long; fr. ¼ in. long. Cent. Mex.

Klinkeranus (Backeb. & Jacobsen) Buin. [*Turbinicarpus Klinkeranus* Backeb & Jacobsen]. Sts. simple or branched, to 1¼ in. high and 1⅝ in. thick, tubercles broader than high; spines 3, flattened basally, rounded apically, the lower longer, to about ⅜ in. long; fls. white, about ½ in. long and across. N. Mex. Probably only a var. of *S. Schmiedickianus.*

macrochele (Werderm.) Backeb. [*Turbinicarpus macrochele* (Werderm.) Buxb. & Backeb.]. Sts. to 1½ in. high and 2 in. thick, tubercles low, to ¾ in. wide; areoles elongate, spines 3–5, mostly 4, flat, channelled, somewhat papery, yellowish, becoming gray, nearly equal, to 1½ in. long; fls. white or pinkish. Cent. Mex. The specific epithet often misspelled *macrohele.*

pseudomacrochele Backeb. [*Turbinicarpus pseudomacrochele* (Backeb.) Buxb. & Backeb.]. Root elongate, sts. to 2½ in. high and 1¼ in. thick, tubercles in 5 oblique rows, polygonal, low, rounded, to ½ in. wide; areoles elongate, spines about 8, slender, yellow, becoming gray, twisted, stiff, to ⅝ in. long; fls. white, 1 in. long; fr. almost naked. Cent. Mex.

Schmiedickeanus (Böd.) J. West [*Turbinicarpus Schmiedickeanus* (Böd.) Buxb. & Backeb.]. Sts. to 2 in. high and 1¼ in. thick, tubercles in 8 oblique rows, rhombic, nearly conical; areoles circular, spines 3–4, ascending, semicylindrical, channelled, brown, curved, the lowest to 1 in. long, the others shorter and narrower; fls. rose, ¾ in. across. Ne. Mex.

STRONGYLOCARYUM: *PTYCHOSPERMA.* **S. latius:** *P. salomonense.*

STRONGYLODON Vogel. *Leguminosae* (subfamily *Faboideae*). About 20 spp. of shrubs or climbers, native to trop. Old World; lvs. of 3 lfts.; fls. in axillary, long-peduncled clusters or racemes, papilionaceous, showy, standard recurved, with appendages above claw, keel petals nearly as long as standard, stamens 10, 9 united and 1 separate; fr. an ovate-oblong, stalked legume.

macrobotrys A. Gray. JADE VINE. Liana, to 60 ft. long, sts. more than 1 in. in diam.; lvs. pale green or nearly reddish when young, becoming dark green, lfts. to 5 in. long, 2½ in. wide; raceme to 3 ft.; fls. bluish-green, to 3 in. long; fr. large, indehiscent, 3–10-seeded. Philippine Is.

STROPHANTHUS DC. *Apocynaceae.* About 40 spp., mostly shrubs, often climbing, native to trop. S. Afr. and Asia, brs. mostly brown with many pale lenticels; lvs. opp. or whorled; fls. in terminal, usually corymbose clusters, 5-merous, bisexual, mostly showy, corolla funnelform or campanulate, tube cylindrical at base, lobes mostly acuminate to extremely long-caudate, with a pair of appendages in each sinus, stamens borne at apex of cylindrical part of corolla tube, connivent into a cone around stigma; fr. a pair of cylindrical, spindle-shaped, spreading follicles, seeds generally hairy, with a large apical, plumose awn and basal, deciduous tuft of hairs.

A few species are grown as ornamentals. The seeds of several species yield strophanthus, an important cardiac drug. Propagated by seeds and softwood cuttings.

capensis: *S. speciosus.*

caudatus (Burm.f.) Kurz. Shrub, to 18 ft., sometimes climbing; lvs. elliptic-oblong to elliptic-obovate, to 6½ in. long, abruptly acute, somewhat leathery; corolla tube whitish, about 1 in. long, basal cylindrical part longer than expanded part, lobes purple, caudate, 5–7 in. long; follicles widely divergent, 5–6 in. long. Java to Burma.

divaricatus (Lour.) Hook. & Arn. [*S. divergens* R. C. Grah.]. Scandent shrub, to 10 ft.; lvs. oblong-elliptic, to 3 in. or more long, acute at both ends; fls. ill-scented, corolla greenish-yellow marked with crimson in throat, tube to about ½ in. long, angular, velutinous, espe-

cially inside, lobes caudate, to 1¾ in. long, appendages in sinuses short and blunt; follicles acuminate to an obtuse apex, to 8 in. long. Se. China.

divergens: *S. divaricatus.*

gratus (Wallich & Hook. ex Benth.) Baill. Scandent shrub, to 25 ft. or more, glabrous; lvs. oblong, to 6 in. long, short-acuminate, veins spreading at right angles to midrib; sepals broad, scarious, corolla white or tinged with pink, tube 1½ in. long, lobes obovate, to 1 in. long, obtuse, never caudate, with crisped margins, appendages in sinuses lanceolate-subulate, rose-colored, exserted about ⁵⁄₁₆ in.; follicles obtusely acuminate, to 15 in. long, seeds glabrous. Trop. W. Afr.

Preussii Engl. & Pax. Climbing shrub, to 12 ft. or more; lvs. elliptic to obovate or ovate, to 5 in. long, bluntly short-acuminate, truncate to cuneate, glabrous; fls. fragrant, sepals foliaceous, corolla white but darkening to dull lemon-yellow, strongly marked with yellow and purple in throat, tube about ⅝ in. long, basal cylindrical part purplish, as long as campanulate part, lobes very long-caudate, to 1 ft. long, tails maroon, appendages in sinuses very short, obtuse, golden with purplish tips; follicles lanceolate, to 10 in. long. Trop. W. Afr.

sarmentosus DC. Tall-climbing shrub; lvs. ovate to oblong, to ⅜ in. long, acuminate, petioles nearly equal; cymes few- to 1-fld., generally on short, lateral, leafless brs.; corolla funnelform, to 4 in. long including the lobes, white with 10 purple streaks in throat, tube 1 in. long or more, basal cylindrical part much shorter than expanded upper part, lobes with caudate tips 2½ in. long, appendages in sinuses subulate, purple; follicles spindle-shaped, to 1 ft. long, spreading horizontally. Senegal to Congo region.

speciosus (Ward & Harv.) Reber [*S. capensis* A. DC.]. Rambling shrub, brs. olive-green; lvs. in whorls of 3–4, oblong-lanceolate, to 3½ in. long, acute, leathery; corolla cream to yellow or orange, spotted with red, tube ½ in. long, basal cylindrical part much shorter than expanded part, lobes long-caudate, tails to 1½ in. long, appendages in sinuses subulate, very short; follicles very slender, to 6 in. long, seeds glabrous. S. Afr.

STROPHOLIRION: *DICHELOSTEMMA.* **S. californicum:** *D. volubile.*

×**STROXINIA:** see × *STREPTOGLOXINIA.*

STRUTHIOPTERIS: see *BLECHNUM* and *MATTEUCCIA.* **S. Spicant:** *B. Spicant.*

STRYCHNOS L. *Loganiaceae.* About 150 or more spp. of trop. and subtrop. trees, shrubs, and vines; lvs. opp., 3–5-nerved from near base; fls. small, white to yellowish, in cymes, corolla 4–5-cleft, stamens 5; fr. berrylike but often with a hard shell.

Many species contain drug alkaloids. Grown as drug plants and one species for curiosity and the edible fruit.

Nux-vomica L. STRYCHNINE, NUX-VOMICA TREE. Tree, to 40 ft.; lvs. ovate, to 3½ in. long; fls. in terminal cymes 2 in. across; berry 1½ in. in diam., seeds several, disc-shaped. S. Asia. Seeds yield the drug nux vomica, containing the poison strychnine.

potatorum L.f. CLEARING NUT, WATER-FILTER N. Tree; lvs. ovate, leathery, to 3 in. long; fls. small, white, fragrant, in cymes; berry black when ripe. E. Burma, e. India.

spinosa Lam. NATAL ORANGE. Shrub, to 10 ft., with spines ½ in. long or more; lvs. nearly orbicular to obovate, to 2 in. long; fls. in terminal compound cymes; berry 4 in. in diam., becoming yellow, seeds embedded in sweet, edible pulp. Trop. and s. Afr.

STULTITIA E. P. Phillips. *Asclepiadaceae.* Four spp. of small, leafless, succulent, per. herbs, native to S. Afr., intermediate between *Stapelia* and *Caralluma;* distinguished from *Stapelia* by the union basally of the outer whorl of corona lobes to form a cup, and from *Caralluma* by the broad, cushionlike annulus at the center of the corolla.

For culture see *Succulents.*

Cooperi (N. E. Br.) E. P. Phillips [*Stapelia Cooperi* N. E. Br.]. Sts. to 2 in., 4-angled, the angles with large, spreading, acute, conical teeth; fls. clustered at base of st., corolla flat, about 1½ in. across, ridged, tubercled, narrowly banded dull yellow and purple-brown, annulus pinkish with purple-brown spots, outer corona 10-toothed or with 5 bifid lobes, deep maroon, inner corona with apex of lobes erect-connivent and purple-spotted.

STYLIDIACEAE R. Br. STYLIDIUM FAMILY. Dicot.; 3 or more genera of herbs, native to S. Hemisphere; lvs. alt. or

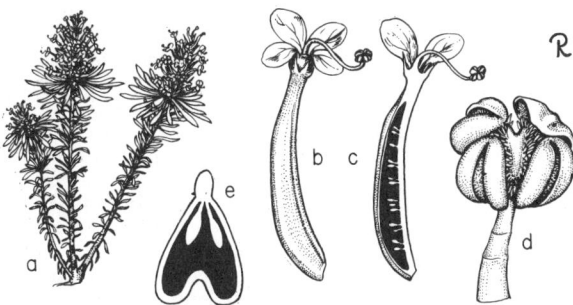

STYLIDIACEAE. *Stylidium adnatum* R. Br.: **a,** flowering branch, × ¼; **b,** flower, × 3; **c,** flower, vertical section, × 3; **d,** apex of gynandrium, with two stamens and bilobed stigma, × 18; **e,** ovary, cross section, × 12. (Species representative, but not in general cultivation; from Lawrence, *Taxonomy of Vascular Plants*.)

basal, simple; fls. bisexual or unisexual, irregular, calyx 3–7-lobed, corolla 5-lobed, stamens 2–3, united around the style, ovary inferior, 1–3-celled; fr. a caps. *Forstera* and *Stylidium* are sometimes cult.

STYLIDIUM Swartz ex Willd. TRIGGER PLANT. *Stylidiaceae*. About 90 spp. of herbs, mostly native to Australia; lvs. basal or tufted, usually linear; fls. usually in terminal racemes, spikes, or corymbs, irregular, bisexual, sepals 5, petals 5, one much smaller than the others, stamens 2, united around the style, forming a deflexed column that springs up when touched, ovary inferior, 1(–2)-celled.

Propagated by seeds.

graminifolium Swartz ex Willd. Per., to 3 ft.; lvs. grasslike, in basal rosettes, to 1 ft. long, acute; fls. in a glandular-pubescent raceme on long scape, calyx 2-lipped, corolla pink, to ½ in. long; caps. spindle-shaped, to ½ in. long. Se. Australia. Zone 8.

STYLOMECON G. Tayl. *Papaveraceae*. One sp., an erect, ann. herb with yellow sap, native to w. N. Amer.; lvs. alt., pinnately lobed; fls. axillary, on elongate peduncles. Distinguished from *Papaver* in having a distinct slender style at the apex of the somewhat flattened ovary; caps. dehiscing by 8 pores at summit.

heterophylla (Benth.) G. Tayl. [*Meconopsis heterophylla* Benth.; *Papaver heterophyllum* (Benth.) Greene]. FLAMING POPPY, WIND P. Sts. leafy, erect, to 2 ft., glabrous or only sparsely pubescent; lvs. irregularly pinnately divided, rarely sessile, somewhat fleshy; fls. brick-red with purple center, to 2 in. across, on slender peduncles; caps. obovate. Calif. and Baja Calif. Requires shade and good drainage.

STYLOPHORUM Nutt. *Papaveraceae*. About 3–6 spp. of per. herbs with yellow sap, native to e. Asia and 1 in e. N. Amer.; lvs. mostly basal, pinnately lobed; fls. yellow, few in a terminal umbel, sepals 2, petals 4, stamens many; caps. bristly, 2–4-valved.

Sometimes transplanted from the wild; of easy culture in rich soil and partial shade.

diphyllum (Michx.) Nutt. CELANDINE POPPY, WOOD P. To 20 in.; basal lvs. usually 2, sometimes 1 or 3, petioled, 5–7-lobed; fls. 2 in. across, closely resembling those of *Chelidonium*. Spring. Rich, moist woods, e. U.S.

STYLOPHYLLUM: *DUDLEYA.* S. Orcuttii: *D. attenuata* subsp.

STYPHELIA Sm. *Epacridaceae*. About 15 spp. of shrubs, native to Australia; lvs. alt., sessile or subsessile; fls. solitary in lf. axils, with several imbricate bracts, 5-merous, corolla tubular, hairy inside, lobes narrow, revolute, stamens inserted at rim of tube and exserted, ovary 5-celled, each 1-ovuled; fr. a drupe.

Cultivation as for *Erica.*

viridis Andr. To 6 ft., straggly; lvs. narrowly oblong to oblanceolate, to 1¼ in. long, with stiff awn; fls. greenish-yellow or pink with yellow, longer than lvs., calyx ½ in. long; fr. ovoid, ⁵⁄₁₆ in. long. Near sea, e. Australia. Zone 10 in Calif.

STYRACACEAE Dumort. STORAX FAMILY. Dicot.; 6 genera of trees or shrubs of wide distribution; lvs. alt., simple; fls. regular, bisexual, calyx 4–5-lobed, petals 4–8, united at base, stamens 4–16, ovary superior or almost inferior; fr. drupaceous or dry and dehiscent, sometimes winged. *Halesia, Pterostyrax, Rehderodendron, Sinojackia,* and *Styrax* are grown as ornamentals.

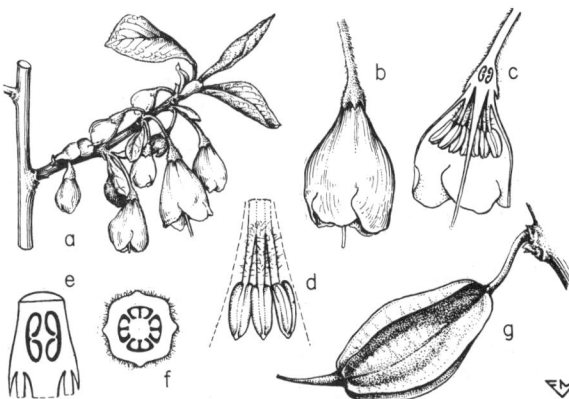

STYRACACEAE. *Halesia carolina:* **a,** flowering branch, × ½; **b.** flower, × 1; **c,** flower, vertical section, × 1; **d,** stamens, × 2; **e,** ovary, vertical section, × 3; **f,** ovary, cross section, × 4; **g,** fruit, × 1. (From Bailey, *Manual of Cultivated Plants,* ed. 2.)

STYRAX L. SNOWBELL, STORAX. *Styracaceae*. About 100 spp. of shrubs or trees of trop. and warm-temp. regions in the N. Hemisphere; lvs. alt., simple; fls. showy, white, calyx campanulate, corolla deeply 5(–8)-lobed, stamens 10(–16), ovary superior, 3-celled below and 1-celled above; fr. dry or drupaceous.

The genus is the source of balsamic resin, benzoin, obtained from tropical species of southeastern Asia. Storaxes succeed in light porous soil. Few of the species are hardy north without winter protection. Propagated by seeds, layering, cuttings (with difficulty), and by grafting on seedlings of available species or on *Halesia carolina.*

americanus Lam. MOCK ORANGE. To 10 ft.; lvs. ovate to oblong, to 3½ in. long, pubescent; fls. in 1–4-fld. racemes, pedicels to ½ in. long; fr. ⁵⁄₁₆ in. long. Va. to Fla. and La. Zone 7.

californicus: *S. officinalis* var.

dasyanthus Perkins. To 25 ft.; lvs. to 4 in. long, lightly pubescent beneath, finally glabrous; fls. about ½ in. long, in many-fld. racemes or panicles to 4 in. long. Cent. China.

grandiflorus: see *S. grandifolius.*

grandifolius Ait. [*S. grandiflorus* J. F. Gmel., not Griff.]. To 12 ft.; lvs. ovate to obovate, to 7 in. long, gray-pubescent beneath, base of petiole not enlarged; fls. fragrant, in 7–12-fld. racemes to 5 in. long, calyx evenly dentate; fr. ½ in. in diam. Va. to Fla. Zone 8.

Hemsleyana Diels. To 30 ft.; lvs. obliquely ovate to obovate, to 5¼ in. long, acuminate, cuneate to rounded at base, glabrous above, sparsely stellate-hairy beneath; fls. to 1 in. across, in racemes to 6 in. long; fr. obovoid, to ⅝ in. long. Cent. and w. China.

japonicus Siebold & Zucc. JAPANESE SNOWBELL. To 30 ft.; lvs. elliptic, to 3 in. long, becoming glabrous; fls. fragrant, in 3–6-fld. racemes, drooping, on pedicels to 1 in. long or more; fr. ½ in. long. Japan, China. Zone 5. Seeds yield an oil.

Obassia Siebold & Zucc. FRAGRANT SNOWBELL. To 30 ft.; lvs. nearly orbicular to ovate, to 10 in. long, tomentose or densely pubescent beneath, base of petiole enlarged and enclosing the axillary bud; fls. fragrant, in many-fld. racemes to 8 in. long; fr. ¾ in. long. Early summer. Japan. Zone 5. Fast growing, does best in sun and good drainage.

officinalis L. To 20 ft.; lvs. elliptic to ovate or nearly orbicular, apically blunt, to 3 in. long, entire or slightly denticulate; infl. 3–8-fld., pedicels to ½ in. long; fls. ¾ in. long, calyx truncate, only indistinctly denticulate, corolla 5–7(–10)-lobed, stamens usually 10; fr. subglobose, to ⅝ in. in diam. Balkans to Israel; Calif. Var. **officinalis.** The typical var.; lvs. mostly densely stellate-pubescent beneath. Var. **californicus** (Torr.) Rehd. [*S. californicus* Torr.]. SNOWDROP BUSH. Lvs. glabrous or lightly tomentose beneath. N. Calif. Var. **flavescens:** a listed name;

perhaps intended for var. *fulvescens.* Var. **fulvescens** (Eastw.) Munz & I. M. Johnst. Lvs. broader, usually subcordate, generally pubescent above as well as beneath, hairs longer, characteristically tawny; calyx teeth more prominent. S. Calif.

philadelphoides Perkins. Shrub, to 7 ft.; lvs. narrowly oblong, to 3¼ in. long, sparsely hairy when young; fls. to ¾ in. long, in 4–6-fld. racemes, calyx covered with yellow hairs. E. China.

Shiraiana Mak. Small tree, brs. becoming glabrous; lvs. broadly rhombic to rhombic-orbicular, to about 4 in. long, with irregular large teeth above the middle, becoming nearly glabrous; fls. ¾ in. long, in racemes to about 2½ in. long; fr. ellipsoid, to ⅝ in. long, stellate-hairy. Japan.

Wilsonii Rehd. Differs from *S. americana* in having denser habit, and smaller lvs., ⅜–1 in. long. China. Zone 8.

SUBMATUCANA: *BORZICACTUS.* S. **calvescens:** *B. aurantiacus.*

SUBPILOCEREUS: *CEREUS.*

SUBSPECIES: see *Species.*

SUBULARIA L. AWLWORT. *Cruciferae.* Two dwarf, stemless, per. spp. of aquatic or littoral herbs with short rhizome, native to N. Amer., Eur., n. Asia, and e. Afr.; lvs. in a basal rosette, awl-shaped; infl. a scapose, few-fld. raceme; fls. minute, sepals and petals 4, stamens 6, ovary surrounded basally by a glandular ring, style absent; fr. a few-seeded, ovoid or globular silicle.

aquatica L. Glabrous, aquatic per.; lvs. many, to 2¾ in. long; scape to 4 in. high; fls. white. In sands or gravels of lakes or slow streams, circumboreal. Sometimes grown in the unheated aquarium.

SUCCISA Haller. DEVIL'S-BIT. *Dipsacaceae.* About 3 spp. of per. herbs, native to Eur., w. Asia, and Afr.; lvs. basal and opp. on sts.; fls. in long-stalked, involucrate heads, calyx cup-shaped, with 4–5 teeth, enveloped by a 4-angled, 4-toothed involucel, corolla 4-lobed, stamens 4; fr. an achene.

pratensis Moench [*Scabiosa Succisa* L.]. Per., to 3 ft.; basal lvs. narrowly elliptic to obovate-lanceolate, to 1 ft. long, usually entire, st. lvs. narrower, sometimes toothed; heads to 1½ in. across; fls. violet-blue, rarely pink or white. N. Afr., Eur., w. Siberia; naturalized in ne. U.S. Cv. 'Alba'. Fls. white.

SUCCULENTS. A succulent plant or a succulent in horticultural usage is a thick, fleshy plant, commonly with abundant sap.

Most succulent plants are native to regions that are arid or semiarid for at least part of the year, and the succulence has relation to water storage. However, others, like many epiphytic or rock-inhabiting species, occupy sites where the microclimates may be seasonally or otherwise dry. It is in the study of habitats, therefore, that the gardener obtains the initial clue to the cultivation and handling of succulents.

The succulents are of many genera in many natural families. The regions they inhabit have widely different temperature characteristics. Some of the succulents, as a few species of *Sedum,* are indigenous in regions of severe winter cold, with temperatures far below 0° F. Mostly, however, they are natives in mild-temperate and tropical climates. Succulents abound in the Aizoaceae, Crassulaceae, African members of *Euphorbia,* Asclepiadaceae such as *Stapelia* and its relatives, Liliaceae, Amaryllidaceae, some species of *Senecio* and a few other Compositae, Bromeliaceae, Gesneriaceae, Orchidaceae, Piperaceae, and Portulacaceae. Cactaceae, though treated separately (see *Cacti*), may also be classed with succulents. In the following remarks, succulents of all kinds are in mind.

Many succulents and associates are prized for their oddity, since they are given to condensed and often grotesque forms. Many of them have a slow-growing, more or less durable body, changing little from year to year. Often the flowers are brilliant and large. All these characteristics make them interesting to fanciers. Succulents, as a class, are special horticultural subjects prized by collectors and enthusiasts; they are therefore notable and worth the particular care they may require.

As a class these plants are not difficult to grow. Most need

a full-sun exposure, also a soil that is porous and gritty yet sufficiently compact and retentive to hold the moisture the plant requires. Good drainage is essential. Much fresh organic material is to be avoided in the soil. Sand, pulverized brick, or rock may be added to soil to give it the proper porosity. The trouble in growing succulents is mostly in trying to raise them in moist, cloudy climates, to which most of them are not adapted; it is then that particular attention is required to make sure that they do not rot at the root from soggy and sour soil. These succulents may thrive with a minimum of attention in a region naturally adapted to them, as in central and southern California or the arid Southwest. Diminutive species are ideal house plants for windows with sunny southern exposures; most homes have arid, desertlike climates perfect for small succulents when sun is adequate. Yet many kinds are naturally at home in humid climates, as some species of *Sedum, Kalanchoe, Rochea,* and other Crassulaceae. In their growing season, the succulents require plenty of moisture, as they do where most of them grow naturally; usually there is a semidormant period corresponding to the dry or the cold season of their native places, and at this time they may easily be injured by thoughtless soaking. On the other hand, it is a mistake to suppose that succulents, more than other plants, can withstand dessication of the roots for any length of time. In North America, their native home, the leading succulents will always be cacti; one has but to observe the conditions under which they grow to apprehend the proper treatments (see *Cacti*).

The softer nonwoody kinds (to which the term succulents is sometimes incorrectly restricted), such as *Cotyledon, Gasteria,* and *Stapelia,* are readily grown in pots in a sunny greenhouse or conservatory, the essentials being the gritty or porous soil that disposes of excess moisture, care in watering to suit the needs of the plant, and patience to allow them to come slowly and naturally to their full stature. The gardener soon learns when to keep them "slow" and when to repot and stimulate new growth. All succulents in pots make interesting subjects in the open in summer; they are not turned out of the pots but are plunged to the rims. Sometimes the roots of succulents are ruined by nematodes, which are nearly or quite microscopic worms. The preventive is sterilized soil.

As succulents do not belong to one class or type of plant, so there is no single method of propagating them. Many of them make natural offsets, and multiplication is then very simple. Seeds commonly grow readily; care must be taken to prevent damping off of the seedlings from too-wet soil; sterilized earth or clean sand or other sterile medium is advisable. In the cacti, one kind may be grafted on another with ease. Many kinds grow readily from stem cuttings, and many of the Crassulaceae can be propagated by single leaves placed on the soil.

Because succulents are striking subjects, there is the temptation to make either permanent or summer plantings where they are quite out of harmony. A miscellaneous mess of succulents in the front yard may be anything but desirable or attractive; and yet the same plants placed at one side or in the rear with relationship to banks, boundaries, and buildings, and properly harmonized among themselves, may be worthy of all admiration. Some of the low and tufted kinds lend themselves well to rock gardening. The imitation of an arid or desert landscape is worthwhile in a dry or desert country when area is sufficient and surroundings are in keeping: this kind of landscaping is far more suitable than the introduction of material from more humid regions.

The kinds of plants known as succulents are so many and so peculiar, and the records of them have been so imperfect in herbaria, that the amateur finds a special satisfaction in making living collections and in trying to understand them. In regions like California and the Southwest, succulent gardening has become an important enterprise, and is adding many plants to the North American cultivated flora. The interest in succulents is represented by the Cactus and Succulent Society of America, Inc.

SUKSDORFIA A. Gray. *Saxifragaceae.* Two spp. of small per. herbs of w. N. Amer., with short, bulbiferous rootstock; basal lvs. cordate to reniform, long-petioled, st. lvs. smaller, with stipules; fl. sts. pubescent at least in upper part, fls. few in terminal panicles, calyx tube campanulate, united to ovary, calyx lobes 5, triangular, petals 5, entire and obovate, or sometimes 2-lobed, stamens 5, ovary slightly to nearly completely inferior, prolonged into 2 beaklike styles; fr. a dehiscent caps., seeds many.

Growing on damp, shady cliffs and rocky places. Useful in the shaded rock garden.

ranunculifolia (Hook.) Engl. [*Hemieva ranunculifolia* (Hook.) Raf.]. Sts. simple or occasionally branched from base, to 15 in.; basal lvs. several, blades lobed, to 1½ in. across, petioles to 4½ in. long; calyx tube lined with a disc partially covering ovary, calyx lobes to ⅛ in. long, recurved at apex, petals usually white, obovate, to ¼ in. long, entire, ovary partly inferior. B.C., Alta., Mont., s. to n. Calif.

violacea A. Gray [*Hemieva violacea* (A. Gray) Wheelock]. Differs from *S. ranunculifolia* in sts. more slender, shorter; blades of basal lvs. smaller, usually withering before flowering; and calyx tube without a disc. Mont. to e. Wash., nw. Ore.

SULLIVANTIA Torr. & A. Gray. *Saxifragaceae.* Six spp. of stoloniferous, per. herbs in cent. U.S.; lvs. reniform, incisedly lobed, cordate at base, petioles slender; fl. sts. leafy, fls. in terminal, compound cymes, calyx tube campanulate, united to ovary, calyx lobes 5, triangular, petals 5, entire, stamens 5, ovary partly inferior, the upper sterile part divided into 2 attenuated, beaklike projections, true styles lacking; fr. a caps., dehiscent along inner side of the 2 projections.

oregana S. Wats. Delicate per., glabrous except for infl., fl. sts. to 8 in. or more; lvs. to 4 in. across, reduced in size upward, incisedly lobed ⅓–½ their length, lobes 7–9, somewhat cuneate, serrate; fls. erect, becoming reflexed in fr., calyx 3/16 in. long, petals slightly longer, stamens shorter than calyx lobes; projections of caps. longer than calyx in fr. Moist cliffs and banks, nw. Ore. Useful in rock garden.

SUTERA Roth [*Chaenostoma* Benth.]. *Scrophulariaceae.* About 140 spp. of ann. or per. herbs, subshrubs, or small shrubs, native mostly to S. Afr., few to trop. Afr.; lvs. mostly opp., sometimes in clusters, entire, lobed or pinnatifid; fls. of various colors, axillary or in terminal racemes, simple or compound spikes, or cymes, calyx 5-parted or -lobed, corolla with 5 subequal lobes or slightly 2-lipped, tube cylindrical or funnelform, nearly straight or curved upwards, stamens 4 or 2; fr. a septicidal caps.

Certain low kinds are grown out of doors in southern U.S. and in the greenhouse for the profuse small flowers and compact habit; useful for edgings. Propagated by seeds or cuttings.

Burkeana (Wettst. ex Diels) Hiern [*Chaenostoma Burkeanum* Wettst. ex Diels]. Erect, sticky shrub, to 4 ft.; lvs. usually clustered, obovate or cuneate-oblong, to ⅜ in. long, toothed to pinnatifid; fls. in racemes, corolla to 1 in. long, white, yellow or reddish. Trop. and S. Afr.

caerulea (L.f.) Hiern. Sticky ann., to 1½ ft.; lvs. linear or oblong, to 1½ in. long, entire or toothed; fls. in racemes, corolla blue or mauve, with yellow throat. S. Afr.

cephalotes: *S. fastigiata.*

fastigiata (Benth.) Druce [*S. cephalotes* O. Kuntze; *Chaenostoma fastigiatum* Benth.]. LITTLE STARS. Densely branched, hairy subshrub, to 1 ft.; lvs. oblong or oblanceolate, to ½ in. long, with few teeth toward apex; fls. in headlike racemes, corolla ½ in. long. S. Afr.

grandiflora (Galpin) Hiern. PURPLE GLORY PLANT. Erect, sticky-pubescent subshrub or small shrub, to 4 ft.; lvs. mostly alt., ovate-oblong, to 1½ in. long, cuneate, crenate-serrate, hispid; fls. in racemes to 1 ft. long, corolla deep purple, to 1¼ in. long; limb broad, tube very slender. S. Afr.

hispida (Thunb.) Druce [*Chaenostoma hispidum* Benth.]. Hispid subshrub, to 2 ft.; lvs. usually opp., elliptic or obovate, to 1¼ in. long; fls. in leafy racemes, corolla to ½ in. long, white, occasionally pink, throat yellow. S. Afr.

microphylla (Benth.) Hiern [*Chaenostoma microphyllum* (Benth.) Wettst. ex Diels]. Low bush, to 1 ft., with wiry, glandular-hairy branchlets; lvs. clustered, or 4-ranked and overlapping, lanceolate, to 3/16 in. long, fleshy; fls. axillary, corolla purple, to ½ in. long. S. Afr.

phlogiflora (Benth.) Hiern [*Chaenostoma phlogiflorum* (Benth.) Wettst. ex Diels]. Glandular-hispidulous, decumbent or suberect subshrub, to 2 ft.; lvs. somewhat clustered, ovate to obovate or oblong, to ½ in. long, incised-dentate or pinnatifid; fls. in loose racemes, corolla bright purple to white, to ½ in. long. S. Afr.

stenophylla Hiern. Subshrub, to 1 ft., usually branched at or near infl.; lvs. sublinear, to 1¼ in. long, entire, revolute, thick; fls. in corymbosely arranged racemes, corolla to 3/16 in. long. S. Afr.

SUTHERLANDIA R. Br. *Leguminosae* (subfamily *Faboideae*). One or a few spp. of shrubs, native to S. Afr.; lvs. alt., odd-pinnate; fls. showy, red, in axillary racemes, the standard folded, shorter than the keel, stamens 10, 9 united and 1 separate; fr. a large, bladderlike legume.

Grown in the greenhouse or outdoors in the South. Propagated by seeds and cuttings.

frutescens (L.) R. Br. Erect, grayish-pubescent shrub, 2–3 ft., or procumbent; lfts. in 8–10 pairs, small; racemes short; fls. scarlet, to 1 in. long; fr. papery, 2 in. long and 1 in. in diam. Zone 10.

SUTTONIA A. Rich. *Myrsinaceae.* Perhaps 15 spp. of shrubs or small trees, native to New Zeal.; lvs. simple, alt. or fascicled on short brs., entire; fls. small, in axillary clusters, calyx deeply 5-toothed, corolla with 4 or 5 separate petals, stamens 4 or 5; fr. a 1-seeded drupe. Differs from *Myrsine,* chiefly in having petals separate or nearly so.

Occasionally cultivated in Calif. in Zone 10.

australis A. Rich. Small tree, to 20 ft.; lvs. oblong, to 2 in. long, wavy-margined; fls. whitish, unisexual; fr. black.

divaricata (A. Cunn.) Hook.f. Much-branched shrub, to 12 ft.; lvs. obovate or obcordate, to ½ in. long; fls. minute; fr. purplish.

SVIDA: a rejected variant of *SWIDA.*

SWAINSONA Salisb. *Leguminosae* (subfamily *Faboideae*). About 55–60 spp. of herbs and subshrubs, native to Australia and New Zeal.; lvs. alt., odd-pinnate; fls. in axillary, long-peduncled racemes, papilionaceous, stamens 10, 9 united and 1 separate; fr. a swollen legume.

Grown under glass or outdoors in warm regions (Zone 10). Propagated by cuttings when seeds are not available.

galegifolia (Andr.) R. Br. SWAN FLOWER, WINTER SWEET PEA, DARLING P. Glabrous per., to 4 ft.; lfts. in 5–10 pairs, oblong, to ⅝ in. long, blunt; fls. typically deep red, calyx nearly glabrous, standard with yellow spot at base; fr. membranous, to 2 in. long. Cv. **'Albiflora'.** Fls. white. Cv. **'Violacea'.** Fls. rose-violet. E. Australia.

grandiflora: *S. Greyana.*

Greyana Lindl. [*S. grandiflora* R. Br.]. Differs from *S. galegifolia* in having calyx densely white-tomentose, and sometimes larger lfts. to 1½ in. long. Se. Australia.

SWARTZIA J. F. Gmel., not Schreb.: *SOLANDRA.*

SWARTZIA Schreb. *Leguminosae* (subfamily *Caesalpinioideae*). About 129 spp. of unarmed trees or shrubs, mostly of trop. Amer., 2 spp. in trop. Afr.; lvs. alt., odd-pinnate, of 1 lft.; fls. in short racemes, sometimes solitary, with a solitary yellow or white petal, stamens many; fr. a legume, seeds 1 or several of various shapes.

Showy-flowered trees sometimes planted as ornamentals in warm regions. Propagated by seeds.

Langsdorffii Raddi. Differs from *S. panamensis* in having lfts. 7–11, 2–4 in. long, the rachis winged, racemes shorter, to 6 in. long, and petals orbicular, 1½–2 in. across. Se. Brazil.

madagascariensis Desv. Shrub or tree, to 30 ft.; lvs. to 8 in. long, densely rusty-yellow pubescent, lfts. alt., 5–13, oblong to elliptic, to 3 in. long, apically rounded to emarginate, with petiolules; fls. solitary or in few-fld. racemes to 4 in. long, petals orbicular, to 1 in. long, silky-red-pubescent outside; fr. linear-cylindrical, to 14 in. long, indehiscent. Trop. Afr.

panamensis Benth. To 60 ft.; lfts. 5, elliptic or ovate-lanceolate, acuminate, to 7 in. long, with petiolules; racemes axillary, many-fld., pendent, to 16 in. long; petals cream-yellow, almost square, more than 1 in. across; fr. leathery, flat, to 1 ft. long, 4 in. wide. Panama.

SWEET POTATO. The sweet potato, *Ipomoea Batatas,* is a warm-season root vegetable, grown in most tropical, subtropical, and warmer temperate regions for use as food or stock feed and for industrial purposes. It is a perennial that flowers during short days, but is generally cultured as an annual. The sweet potato is highly nutritious, making it an important food item in many tropical and subtropical countries where the white potato cannot be grown. Production in the United States is confined largely to the warmer regions, with southern New Jersey and central California being the northern boundaries for commercial production.

Cultivars may be classified as food or industrial types. In the food type, there are dry-flesh and moist- or soft-flesh cultivars. The latter are often referred to in the trade as "yams," a misnomer, for true yams are species of the genus *Dioscorea* and are mainly planted and used in the tropics. Roots of sweet potatoes also vary in skin color (from purplish-red to light yellow), in flesh color (from white to deep orange), and in shape. Plant habit is generally one of long trailing vines, though there is also a short-vined or bunch type. 'Centennial', the current leading cultivar, has soft flesh, as do other important cultivars such as 'Georgia Red', 'Gold Rush', 'Porto Rico', and 'Velvet'. 'Orlis' and 'Yellow Jersey' are in the dry-flesh group, with 'Nemagold' and 'Nugget' classed as intermediate. 'Pelican Processor' and 'Whitestar' are industrial types with a high starch content. Resistance to several diseases and to nematodes has been incorporated into some cultivars.

Although many soil types are used for sweet potatoes, the preferred soils are deep, friable, sandy loams, as the general overall appearance of the roots develops best on these. A minimum of four months of warm, frost-free weather is necessary to produce satisfactory yields.

Propagation is asexual, using transplants or vine cuttings. The transplants or slips arise from "seed" roots placed in either heated or unheated beds and covered by about 2 inches of sterilized sand. At a temperature of 75–80° F, plants are ready in about six weeks. Two or three pullings of slips are often practiced. Maintaining a supply of healthy seed-stock and using clean plant beds are critical factors in holding diseases and pests in control. In areas of long growing seasons, after early plantings are established with transplants, later plantings may be established with vine cuttings obtained by cutting 8–10 inches of tips of growing vines. This involves considerable labor and tends to reduce yields of the "mother" plantings, but has the advantages of requiring less seed stock and of reducing danger of spreading diseases and pests.

Sweet potatos are grown on ridges 6–10 inches high. Providing adequate nutrients by fertilizing, controlling weeds by cultivation and with herbicides, and irrigating when rainfall is deficient are important growing practices. Sweet potatoes are very tender, so much care in harvesting and handling is needed to avoid serious skinning and bruising. The roots are sensitive to chilling and should be protected from temperatures below 55° F at all times. Curing at 75–80° F for ten to 15 days after harvest speeds healing of wounds and often results in better keeping in storage. With good storage conditions sweet potatoes will remain usable for six to seven months. Chilling by exposure to temperatures below 50–55° F can result in rotting, increase of storage disorders, and poor eating quality.

The crop is susceptible to a large number of field and storage diseases and to nematodes. Clean planting stock, field rotation, and proper storage conditions are the chief control measures. In areas where nematodes are troublesome, soil fumigation is practiced and certain newer cultivars with resistance to one or more species of nematodes are being used.

SWERTIA L. (sometimes, but not originally, spelled *Sweertia*). *Gentianaceae.* About 50 spp. of glabrous ann. or per. herbs, in N. Amer., Eurasia, and Afr., but mostly in e. Asia; lvs. usually opp., entire; fls. usually blue, rarely white, in a thyrsoid infl., 5-merous, sometimes 4-merous, corolla rotate, each lobe with a pair of nectar-bearing pits basally, stamens borne at base of corolla, style very short or 0, stigma 2-lobed. Closely related to *Frasera* and sometimes combined with it, but having style short, thick, and fls. 5-merous.

albicaulis: *Frasera albicaulis.*

Aucheri Boiss. Per.; lower lvs. oblong, tapering to a petiole; fls. yellowish. Armenia and Iran.

bimaculata Hook.f. & T. Thoms. Much-branched ann., to 6 ft.; lvs. elliptic, to 6 in. long, 3-nerved, tapering to a petiole; fls. in many-fld. corymbs, 4–5-parted, corolla whitish or yellow-green, black-spotted on upper half. E. Himalayas.

multicaulis D. Don. Per., to 8 in., much-branched; lvs. narrowly spatulate-oblong, to 2 in. long; corolla 5-parted, lobes to ½ in. long, minutely fringed at base. Himalayas.

Parryi: *Frasera Parryi.*

perennis L. Per., to 1 ft.; basal lvs. oblong-elliptic, long-petioled, st. lvs. ovate-oblong; corolla usually 5-parted, blue to white. Alpine regions, Eur., Asia, Alaska to Calif., e. to Rocky Mts.

perfoliata Royle ex G. Don [*S. speciosa* Wallich ex D. Don, not G. Don]. Glabrous per., to 4 ft., st. hollow; lvs. opp., 7-nerved, basal lvs. long-petioled, elliptic-lanceolate, to 8 in. long, st. lvs. to 5 in. long, united at base into a sheath to ½ in. long; fls. in cymes forming a narrow panicle, corolla white with dark blue irregular blotches, lobes about ¾ in. long; seeds compressed, not winged. Himalayas.

petiolata Royle ex D. Don, [*S. speciosa* G. Don, not Wallich ex D. Don]. Similar to *S. perfoliata*, but having lvs. 5-nerved, and seeds several-sided and not winged. Himalayas.

radiata: *Frasera speciosa.*

speciosa: see *S. perfoliata* and *S. petiolata.*

SWIDA [SVIDA]: *CORNUS. S. microcarpa:* *C. asperifolia.*

SWIETENIA Jacq. MAHOGANY. *Meliaceae.* Between 3 and 6 spp. of large evergreen trees with reddish, hard wood, native to trop. N. and S. Amer.; lvs. alt., even-pinnate, glabrous, shiny; fls. in axillary and terminal panicles, calyx 5-lobed, petals 5, spreading, stamens 10, united in an urceolate tube, ovary 5-celled; fr. a very large woody caps. dehiscing from the base, usually into 5 parts, seeds winged at apex.

Two species produce the true mahogany of commerce, premier cabinet wood and most important export timber of tropical Amer.

Candollea Pitt. VENEZUELAN M. To 120 ft.; lvs. 6–9 in. long, lfts. opp., 6–8, ovate to elliptic-lanceolate, oblique at base, petioluled; fr. to 5½ in. long, obpyriform, seeds winged, to 3½ in. long, rich brown. Venezuela. Often considered to be only a form of *S. macrophylla.* Wood used for interior work and furniture.

humilis Zucc. Tree, 20–30 ft.; lvs. 3–8 in. long, lfts. 6–12, narrowly lanceolate to lanceolate, more or less oblique at base, sessile to subsessile; fr. 6–8 in. long, seeds winged, to 3 in. long, light brown. W. and s. Mex. to Costa Rica. Wood used in construction work and for cabinet making.

macrophylla King. HONDURAS M., BIG-LEAF M. To 150 ft.; lvs. 6–14 in. long, lfts. 8–12, lanceolate, long-acuminate, oblique at base, petioluled; fr. 5–6 in. long, seeds winged, 3–3¾₁₆ in. long, chestnut-brown. Widespread in lowland continental trop. Amer., sometimes planted for timber. The major source of true mahogany timber. Strictly trop.

Mahagoni (L.) Jacq. WEST INDIAN M., SPANISH M., MADEIRA RED-WOOD. To 75 ft., bark scaly; lvs. 4–8 in. long, lfts. 4–10, ovate to lanceolate, oblique at base, entire, petioluled; fr. to 5 in. long, seeds winged, 2 in. long or more. Fla., W. Indies. Zone 10. Sometimes planted for shade and as street trees; the original mahogany of commerce, now largely replaced as a source of timber by *S. macrophylla.*

SWINGLEA Merrill. TABOG. *Rutaceae.* One sp., a spiny, evergreen tree, native to Luzon, Philippine Is.; lvs. alt., with 3 lfts., glandular-dotted; fls. white, solitary or in axillary clusters, calyx 5-lobed, petals 5, stamens 10, separate; fr. with thick, leathery skin, seeds woolly.

glutinosa (Blanco) Merrill. Small to medium-sized tree; terminal lft. elliptic to ovate, to 4¾ in. long, cuneate, lateral lfts. elliptic to obovate, to 2 in. long; fr. oblong-ovoid, about 1½ in. in diam., longitudinally ribbed, 8–10-celled.

SYAGRUS Mart. *Palmae.* More than 30 spp. of solitary, monoecious palms in S. Amer.; lvs. pinnate, sheath fibrous, open, petioles not or rarely toothed along the margin, pinnae acute, briefly 2-cleft, or obtuse at apex, regularly arranged or irregularly arranged and then in groups of mostly 2–5 along the rachis and borne in several planes, midrib prominent; infl. among the lvs., simply branched, long-peduncled, bracts 2, the upper woody, beaked, deeply sulcate externally, rachillae with fls. in triads (2 male and 1 female) nearly throughout or in lower part and above these with paired or solitary male fls.; male fls. usually asymmetrical, sometimes pedicelled, sepals 3, mostly small, imbricate, acute, petals 3, much broader than thick, valvate, stamens 6, pistillode small, 3-cleft, female fls. with sepals 3, broadly imbricate, petals 3, broadly imbricate except briefly valvate apices, staminodes united in a low, membranous, often 6-lobed ring, pistil 3-celled, 3-ovuled; fr. mostly ovoid or ellipsoid and 1-seeded, smooth, mesocarp fleshy-fibrous, endocarp acute at both ends, with 3 shining streaks (vittae) inside, pores 3 near the base, operculum not sunken, seed cylindrical, more or less angled, or (when more than 1) partly flattened in cross section, embryo basal on abaxial side, endosperm homogeneous.

Species of the genus are a source of palm kernel oil and some species are planted in the tropics and subtropics as ornamentals. For culture see *Palms.*

campestris (Mart.) H. Wendl. [*Cocos campestris* Mart.]. To 10 ft. or more; lvs. spreading-recurved, to 6 ft. long, pinnae to 1 ft. long, ½ in. wide, in groups of 4–5 along the rachis; infl. 1½ in. long, gray-tomentose beneath, rachillae about 12, 3–10 in. long; male fls. about ¼ in. long, female fls. 5/16–⅝ in. long. Brazil.

comosa (Mart.) Mart. To about 10 ft.; lvs. to 4 ft. long, spreading, pinnae to 1 ft. long, ½ in. wide or more, mostly arranged in pairs along the rachis; infl. 1 ft. long or more, rachillae 5–6 or more; male fls. about 5/16 in. long, longer than the female; fr. to 1 9/16 in. long, oblong-obovoid. Brazil. Warmer parts of Zone 9b.

coronata (Mart.) Becc. [*S. quinquefaria* (Barb.-Rodr.) Becc.]. LICURI PALM, OURICURI P. To 30 ft.; lvs. to 8 ft. long, pinnae to 16 in. long or more, nearly 1 in. wide, arranged in groups of 2–4 along the rachis; infl. 2 ft. long, rachillae 10 or more; male fls. 5/16–⅝ in. long, female fls. shorter than the male; fr. scarcely 1 in. long, ovoid. Arid regions, e. Brazil. Source of licuri oil, a palm kernel oil.

flexuosa (Mart.) Becc. [*Cocos flexuosa* Mart.]. To 15 ft.; lvs. about 6 ft. long, pinnae about 1 ft. long, ½ in. wide, arranged in groups along the rachis; infl. to 2 ft. long, rachillae about 10, somewhat flexuous apically, to 16 in. long; male fls. to ½ in. long, female fls. larger, to ⅞ in. long; fr. ovoid. Brazil. Warmer parts of Zone 9b.

orinocensis (Spruce) Burret. To 60 ft.; lvs. yellow-green, to 6½ ft. long, pinnae to 2 ft. long, ⅜ in. wide, in groups of 2–3 along the rachis; infl. 1½ ft. long, rachillae to 12 in. long, with female fls. in lower ⅓; fr. 1 in. long, yellow when mature. Venezuela.

quinquefaria: *S. coronata.*

Weddelliana: *Microcoelum Weddellianum.*

SYCOPSIS D. Oliver. *Hamamelidaceae.* Six spp. of evergreen, monoecious trees or shrubs, native to China, the Himalayas, and Philippine Is.; lvs. pinnately nerved, entire, short-petioled; fls. unisexual, without petals, in terminal or axillary short racemes or heads surrounded by pubescent bracts, male fls. with minute sepals and 8–10 stamens, female fls. with fl. tube urceolate, 5-lobed, ovary superior, enclosed by the fl. tube; fr. a caps., with 2 shining brown seeds.

sinensis D. Oliver. Shrub or small tree, to 20 ft.; lvs. leathery, elliptic-lanceolate, to 4 in. long, glabrous, entire or remotely toothed toward apex; male fls. with stamens 10, filaments slender, conspicuous, yellow, anthers reddish. Spring. Cent. and w. China. Male plants, with their showy stamens, are the more ornamental.

SYMINGTONIA: *EXBUCKLANDIA.*

SYMPHORICARPOS Duh. [*Symphoria* Pers.]. SNOWBERRY. *Caprifoliaceae.* Sixteen spp. of deciduous shrubs, native to N. Amer., 1 to China; lvs. opp., simple; fls. white or pink, usually borne in clusters or spikes, calyx 4–5-toothed, corolla campanulate or tubular, 4–5-lobed, ovary with 2 fertile and 2 sterile cells; fr. a 2-seeded, white or colored berry.

These shrubs are grown for the ornamental fruits as well as the foliage. They are variously hardy in the North except *S. microphyllus,* and are not particular as to soil. Propagated by seeds, cuttings, suckers, and division.

albus (L.) S. F. Blake [*S. racemosus* Michx.]. SNOWBERRY, WAXBERRY. To 3 ft.; lvs. elliptic, to 2 in. long, sometimes lobed on young brs., pubescent beneath; fls. pinkish, campanulate, ¼ in. long; fr. snow-white. Summer to early autumn. N. Amer. e. of Continental Divide. Zone 3. Var. **laevigatus:** *S. rivularis.*

×**Chenaultii** Rehd. Probably a hybrid between *S. microphyllus* HBK and *S. orbiculatus.* Erect, to 3 ft.; lvs. elliptic, to ¾ in. long, pubescent beneath; fls. in spikes; fr. purplish-red, with minute pale dots. Not as high as either presumed parent; attractive in fr.

Hancockii: a listed name of no botanical standing for plants having prostrate, rooting sts. to 18 in. long.

mollis Nutt. Procumbent or diffuse; lvs. nearly orbicular to elliptic, to 2½ in. long, pubescent on both sides; fls. pinkish or white, campanulate, less than 3/16 in. long; fr. white. Early summer. Calif.

occidentalis Hook. [*S. occidentalis* var. *Heyeri* Dieck]. WOLFBERRY. To 5 ft.; lvs. elliptic or ovate, to 3 in. long, grayish and pubescent beneath; fls. pinkish, campanulate, ¼ in. long, stamens and style exserted; fr. white. Early summer. B.C. to New Mex., e. to Ill. and Mich. Zone 3.

orbiculatus Moench [*S. vulgaris* Michx.]. INDIAN CURRANT, CORALBERRY. To 7 ft.; lvs. elliptic or ovate, to 2½ in. long, glaucous and usually pubescent beneath; fls. white, campanulate, less than 3/16 in. long; fr. ¼ in. long, coral-red. N.Y. to Colo., s. to Fla. and Tex., n. Mex. Zone 3. Cv. **'Leucocarpus'.** Fr. white. Cv. **'Variegatus'.** Lvs. variegated with yellow.

oreophilus A. Gray. To 5 ft.; lvs. elliptic, to 1 in. long, glabrous; fls. pinkish, tubular, ½ in. long; fr. white. Early summer. Colo., Utah, Nev., s. to New Mex., Ariz., and Sonora (Mex.). Zone 6.

ovatus: *S. rivularis.*

racemosus: *S. albus.*

rivularis Suksd. [*S. albus* var. *laevigatus* S. F. Blake; *S. ovatus* Hort. ex C. K. Schneid.]. To 10 ft.; lvs. elliptic, to 1¼ in. long; fls. in short racemes, often many, rosy-pink to white, to ¼ in. long; fr. white, rounded, about ½ in. across. Se. Alaska to Mont. and Calif. Zone 2. Cv. **'Nanus'.** Dwarf.

rotundifolius A. Gray. To 3½ ft.; lvs. suborbicular to ovate, to 1 in. long, pubescent, grayish beneath; fls. pink, in dense clusters, tubular-funnelform, to 5/16 in. long; fr. white, ellipsoid, about ½ in. long. S. Colo., Ariz., New Mex. Zone 7.

vulgaris: *S. orbiculatus.*

SYMPHYANDRA A. DC. RING BELLFLOWER. *Campanulaceae.* About 8 spp. of bien. or per. herbs, native to the E. Medit. region, 1 to Asia; resembling *Campanula* but differing in having anthers united into a tube around style, stigmas 3; fr. a 3-celled caps.

Culture as for *Campanula.*

armena (Steven) A. DC. Erect or sprawling per., 1–2 ft.; lvs. ovate, cordate to cuneate, deeply and irregularly serrate, petioles of lowermost lvs. to 6 in. long and much longer than the blades; fls. terminal, erect, calyx lobes narrow-triangular, with a reflexed appendage in each sinus, corolla blue or white, to ¾ in. long, velvety-pubescent. Caucasus.

cretica A. DC. [*Campanula cretica* (A. DC.) D. Dietr.]. Erect per., to about 20 in., sts. rather sparsely leafy; lvs. cordate-ovate, crenate, glabrous, lower lvs. mostly with blades 3–4 in. long and petioles of equal length, upper lvs. sessile; fls. drooping, few, in terminal racemes, calyx without appendages in the sinuses, corolla blue, glabrous. Crete, Greece.

Hoffmannii Pant. Hairy per., 1–2 ft.; lvs. obovate, coarsely and irregularly serrate, lower lvs. to 7 in. long including the winged petiole; fls. drooping, in terminal leafy panicles or racemes, calyx lobes ovate to oblong, ½–¾ in. long, obtuse or acute, veiny, with a broad, reflexed appendage in each sinus, corolla white to cream, to 1½ in. long and broad. W. Yugoslavia. This sp. may be offered under the name *Campanula planiflora.*

pendula (Bieb.) A. DC. Similar to *S. Hoffmannii,* but lvs. cordate-ovate to oblong, velvety-pubescent, petioles not winged; fls. in racemes, calyx lobes narrow-triangular with an acute-triangular appendage in each sinus, corolla yellowish-white, to 1½ in. long. Caucasus.

Wanneri (Rochel) Heuff. [*Campanula Wanneri* Rochel]. Bien., to 18 in., sparsely pilose throughout; lvs. in rosettes and on the sts., lanceolate to oblanceolate, acute, long-cuneate to a winged petiole or sessile, deeply toothed to nearly laciniate; fls. nodding in paniculate infls., calyx without appendages in the sinuses, corolla violet-blue, 1–2 in. long. Alps.

SYMPHYTUM L. COMFREY. *Boraginaceae.* About 25 spp. of per. herbs, native to Eur. and w. Asia; plants coarse, erect, often hispid, sometimes with tuberous roots; lvs. simple, alt., basal and cauline, upper lvs. sometimes nearly opp.; fls. blue, white, rose, purple, or yellow, in scorpioid, racemose cymes, calyx usually deeply 5-lobed, corolla tubular, expanded above, 5-lobed, with scales in the throat, stamens 5, included; fr. of 1–4 nutlets, the base of nutlet with a tumid annular ring.

Comfreys are sometimes planted in the border. Of easy cultivation; propagated by seeds, division, and root cuttings.

asperum Lepech. PRICKLY C. Per., to 5 ft., with thick roots; lvs. ovate or elliptic, petioled, covered with prickly hairs; fls. rose, changing to clear blue, about ½ in. long, calyx lobes blunt, tips of corolla lobes erect, anthers much shorter than their filaments. Russia to Iran; naturalized in N. Amer. Sometimes cult. for fodder.

caucasicum Bieb. Softly hairy, branched per., to 2 ft.; lvs. ovate-lanceolate to ovate-oblong, shortly decurrent at the base, hairy on both sides; fls. first red-purple then changing to azure, to ¾ in. long, in terminal, paired, scorpioid cymes, calyx not lobed below middle. Caucasus.

grandiflorum DC. Unbranched, to 16 in., sterile shoot decumbent; lvs. ovate or oblong-ovate, sometimes cordate, hairy on both sides; fls. pale yellow, to ¾ in. long, corolla 2 or 3 times longer than calyx. Caucasus.

officinale L. COMMON C., HEALING HERB, BONESET. Per., to 3 ft., with thick roots; lvs. oblong-ovate to oblong-lanceolate, decurrent at base, covered with stiff hairs; fls. white, yellowish, purple, or rose, about ½ in. long, long-pedicelled, anthers longer than their filaments. Eur., Asia; naturalized in N. Amer. Can be used as a potherb. Cv. 'Variegatum'. Lvs. margined with white.

orientale L. Branched per., to 2 ft., with thick roots; lvs. lanceolate to oblong, base rounded but not cordate, hairy, the margin undulate; fls. white, ¾ in. long, calyx not lobed below middle. Asia Minor.

peregrinum: S. × *uplandicum*.

tauricum Willd. Branched per., to 1½ ft.; lvs. ovate, with a broad, often cordate base, undulate; fls. yellowish-white to white, to about ½ in. long, in terminal, nodding, paired, helicoid cymes. S.-cent. Eur., to s. Russia.

×**uplandicum** Nym. [*S. peregrinum* Ledeb.]; *S. asperum* × *S. officinale*. RUSSIAN C. Coarse, hispid per., to 6 ft., with thick roots; lvs. oblong, elliptic-lanceolate or ovate, often somewhat decurrent at base, hairy on both sides, base cordate or rounded, st. lvs. sessile; fls. rose, changing to purple, to ¾ in. long, anthers and their filaments about equal, calyx lobes acuminate. Caucasus.

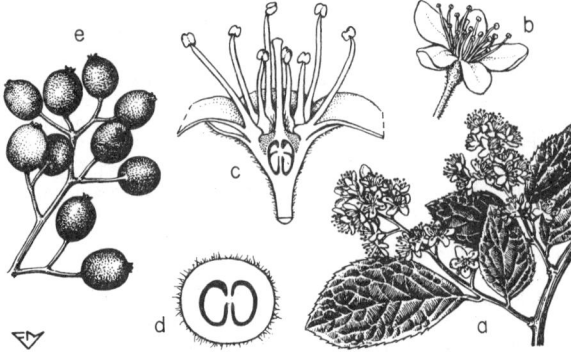

SYMPLOCACEAE. *Symplocos paniculata:* **a,** flowering branch, × ½; **b,** flower, × 2; **c,** flower, vertical section (corolla partially cut away), × 4; **d,** ovary, cross section, × 10; **e,** fruit, × 1. (From Bailey, *Manual of Cultivated Plants,* ed. 2.)

SYMPLOCACEAE Desf. SYMPLOCOS or SWEETLEAF FAMILY. Dicot.; 1 genus, *Symplocos,* of trees and shrubs of wide distribution, sometimes evergreen; lvs. alt., simple, without stipules; fls. in axillary clusters, or in racemes or panicles, mostly bisexual, regular, calyx 4(–5)-lobed, corolla 5–10-lobed, stamens usually 15 to many, separate or united in fascicles, ovary inferior or half-inferior, 2–5-celled, each cell 2-ovuled; fr. drupaceous.

SYMPLOCARPUS Salisb. [*Spathyema* Raf.]. *Araceae.* One sp., a hardy, per. herb of swamps and wet woods, with disagreeable skunklike odor when bruised; lvs. large, arising from stout vertical rhizomes; spathe inflated, spadix spherical, enveloped by the spathe; fls. bisexual, perianth 4-parted, stamens 4, ovaries 1-celled, 1-ovuled.

Of easy culture in moist locations in partial shade; propagated by seeds or division.

foetidus (L.) Salisb. [*Spathyema foetida* (L.) Raf.]. SKUNK CABBAGE, POLECAT WEED. Lf. blades ovate-cordate, to 18 in. long and 12 in.

wide, entire, petioles to 10 in. long; infl. appearing before lvs., peduncle subterranean, spathe fleshy, ovoid, to 6 in. long with pointed, inflexed tips, purple-brown mottled with greenish-yellow, spadix stout, black and 3–6 in. long in fr. Late winter to spring. Ne. N. Amer. and ne. Asia.

SYMPLOCOS Jacq. SWEETLEAF. *Symplocaceae.* About 290 spp. of trees and shrubs, native from trop. to warm-temp. areas of Eurasia, Australia, and Amer.; with characters of the family.

A few species are grown as ornamentals. Only *S. paniculata* is hardy north. Propagated by seeds, which are slow to germinate, by layering, and by cuttings of young wood.

coreana (Lév.) Ohwi. Differs from *S. paniculata* in having lvs. ovate, to 3 in. long and 2 in. wide, hairy on both sides, denticulate, and often with hooked teeth. S. Korea and w. Japan. Zone 9.

crataegoides: *S. paniculata.*

japonica: *S. lucida.*

koreana: a misspelling for *S. coreana.*

lucida Siebold & Zucc. [*S. japonica* A. DC.]. Small, evergreen tree; lvs. elliptic to oblong, to 2¾ in. long, leathery, petioles to ⅝ in. long; fls. in dense, axillary heads, pale yellow, to ⅝ in. across; fr. oblong, black, ⅝ in. long. Japan. Zone 8.

paniculata (Thunb.) Miq. [*S. crataegoides* Buch.-Ham. ex D. Don]. SAPPHIRE BERRY, ASIATIC SWEETLEAF. To 40 ft.; lvs. deciduous, very variable, elliptic to obovate, to 4 in. long, serrulate, tawny-pubescent underneath, short-petioled; fls. in panicles to 3 in. long, white, fragrant, ⁵⁄₁₆ in. across, stamens about 30; fr. blue, globose, ⁵⁄₁₆ in. long. Late spring. Himalayas to China, s. Korea, and sw. Japan. Zone 5.

theifolia D. Don. Shrub; lvs. oblong to lanceolate, to 5 in. long, denticulate or nearly entire; fls. yellow, stamens 12–20; fr. ovate, red-brown. Himalayas.

SYNADENIUM Boiss. *Euphorbiaceae.* About 13 spp. of monoecious, succulent shrubs or small trees with fleshy brs. and milky juice, native to cent., e., and s. Afr.; lvs. simple, alt., fleshy; fls. in cyathia (see *Euphorbiaceae*), arranged in axillary cymes, or terminal or axillary umbels, involucre saucerlike, entire-margined, with a spreading or erect rimlike gland surrounding an inner series of 5 membranous, fringe-toothed lobes, ovary 3-celled; fr. a caps.

Sometimes planted as ornamental in tropics and warm regions. For culture see *Succulents.*

cupulare (Boiss.) Wheeler. shrub, 3–5 ft.; lvs. obovate, 2–4 in. long, cuneate, tapering to a short petiole, entire; cyathia in axillary and terminal umbels, gland greenish-yellow. S. Afr.

Grantii Hook.f. AFRICAN MILKBUSH. Shrub, 8–12 ft.; lvs. somewhat fleshy, tapering to a stout petiole to about ⁵⁄₁₆ in. long, oblanceolate to obovate, 3–7 in. long, margins entire, wavy to slightly toothed; cyathia in much-branched axillary cymes. Cent. E. Afr. Cv. 'Rubra'. Lvs. red.

SYNCARPIA Ten. *Myrtaceae.* About 4–5 spp. of evergreen trees with fibrous bark, endemic in e. Australia; lvs. opp., pinnately veined; fls. in dense, globose heads, either solitary on axillary peduncles or in terminal panicles, calyx tube united at base to ovary, calyx lobes and petals usually 5, stamens many, ovary inferior; fr. a caps., enclosed in and adnate to the calyx tube, 2–3-valved, dehiscing loculicidally.

Grown in the South as a shade tree; the wood is used for building purposes.

glomulifera (Sm.) Niedenzu [*S. laurifolia* Ten.]. TURPENTINE TREE. To 30 ft., the young shoots and underside of lvs. more or less hoary-pubescent; lvs. elliptic-oblong, to 3 in. long; heads 6–10-fld., on peduncles about 1 in. long, produced at the base of new shoots; fls. white, calyx hairy. New S. Wales and Queensland. Zone 9.

Hillii F. M. Bailey. Similar to *S. glomulifera,* but having lvs. larger, 4½–6 in. long, and calyx glabrous. N. Queensland.

laurifolia: *S. glomulifera.*

SYNECHANTHUS H. Wendl. *Palmae.* Two variable spp. of solitary or cespitose, slender, unarmed, monoecious palms from Mex. to n. S. Amer.; lvs. pinnate or rarely only pinnately ribbed, pinnae 1-ribbed or often several-ribbed; infl. interfoliar or infrafoliar, long-peduncled, with 5–6 tubular bracts on the peduncle, brs. simple or once-branched, rachillae flexuous; fls. very small, green in bud, yellowish at flowering, borne in lines (acervuli) of a basal female and several male, male fls. with sepals united in a low 3-lobed cupule, petals valvate, stamens 3 or 6, pistillode small or lacking, female fls. with sepals united, petals imbricate, staminodes 6 or 0, pistil 3-celled, 3-ovuled; fr. fleshy, red, 1-seeded, seed with homogeneous or ruminate endosperm, embryo lateral near the apex.

Sometimes planted in Zone 10a in Fla. For culture see *Palms.*

angustifolius: *H. Warscewiczianus.*

fibrosus (H. Wendl.) H. Wendl. St. solitary, to 18 ft. high, 1³⁄₁₆ in. in diam. but plants sometimes flowering before st. emerges; lvs. long-petioled, blades to more than 3 ft. long, pinnae, except broader terminal pair, with 1 midrib and 2 lateral veins elevated on the upper surface and dull yellow-brown beneath, rarely regularly arranged, usually in 2 to several groups of 2–4 or more along the rachis; infl. with lower brs. once-branched, rachillae minutely scaberulous; male fls. with stamens 6, erect; fr. globose to ellipsoid, to nearly ⅞ in. long, ⅝ in. in diam., seed with endosperm homogeneous or minutely ruminate marginally. Mex. to Costa Rica.

Warscewiczianus H. Wendl. [*S. angustifolius* H. Wendl.]. Sts. usually cespitose, very rarely solitary, to 18 ft. high, 2 in. in diam.; lvs. long-petioled, blades variable, to more than 5 ft. long, rarely undivided, usually with pinnae, except broader terminal pair, regularly arranged, all with 1 midrib and 2 lateral veins elevated on the upper surface and straw-colored beneath, or pinnae irregularly arranged, some 1-ribbed, others broad and many-ribbed; infl. with rachillae unbranched, not scaberulous; male fls. with stamens 3, horizontally exserted; fr. globose to ellipsoid, to 1¼ in. long, ⅝ or rarely to nearly 1¼ in. in diam., seed with conspicuously ruminate endosperm. Costa Rica to Ecuador.

SYNGONIUM Schott [*Nephthytis* Hort., not Schott]. *Araceae.* About 20 spp. of mostly stout, per., climbing vines of trop. Amer., with milky juice; lvs. of adult phase rarely entire, usually 3-parted or pedate, segms. 3–13, inequilateral, the middle one largest, the lateral ones progressively smaller toward outside, petioles long, sheathing in lower half; lvs. of juvenile phase simple; fls. unisexual, perianth absent, spathe tube inflated, persistent around lower (female) part of spadix, often orange or red in fr., blade expanded, mostly hooded, early deciduous, spadix shorter than spathe; fr. a berry, these fused together, brownish.

Identification of young plants is difficult, since their leaves are usually simple and scarcely resemble those of adult phase. For culture see *Philodendron.*

albolineatum: *S. angustatum* cv.

angustatum Schott [*S. Oerstedianum* Schott; *S. podophyllum* var. *Oerstedianum* (Schott) Engl.]. Similar to *S. podophyllum,* but lf. segms. of adult phase generally narrower, with median one largest and usually elliptic, juvenile phase very early producing 3–5-parted lvs. Cent. Amer. Cv. 'Albolineatum' [*?S. albolineatum* Hort. ex Bull; *?Nephthytis liberica* var. *variegata* Hort.]. A juvenile phase, with first lvs. white-variegated along midribs and lateral veins, sometimes only the margins green, but soon lvs. dissected into 3–5 segms. variegated only along midribs.

auritum (L.) Schott [*Philodendron auritum* Hort., not Lindl.; *P. trifoliatum* Hort.]. FIVE-FINGERS. Lf. blades 3–5-parted, very glossy, dark green, outermost segms. each with a small earlike lobe at base, middle segm. to 15 in. long and half as wide, primary lateral veins nearly perpendicular to midrib; spathe to 11 in. long, tube cylindrical, green, blade twice as long as tube, reflexed, yellowish, red-purple in throat. Jamaica and Hispaniola.

erythrophyllum Birdsey ex Bunt. Adult lf. blades deeply 3-parted, red-purple or green beneath, middle segms. oblong-elliptic, to 8 in. long and 3 in. wide, with 2–3 pairs of strongly ascending primary lateral veins, lateral segms. half as large as middle one, petioles slightly shorter than blades, seen mostly in juvenile phase with lf. blades to 5 in. long and 1¾ in. wide, obtuse, sagittate, entire, red-purple or green beneath, petioles 2 in. long, sheathing to blade; spathe 7 in. long, tube green, blade expanded, twice as long as tube, white. Panama.

Hoffmannii Schott [*Nephthytis Hoffmannii* Hort.]. Differs from *S. Wendlandii* in having lf. blades medium green, dull, of firmer texture, with lateral lobes basally hastate-lobate on outer side, petioles with wider sheaths, spathe with blade white, pale purplish in throat. Costa Rica.

lingulatum: a listed name of no botanical standing; used for *S. macrophyllum.*

macrophyllum Engl. [*S. lingulatum* Hort.]. Suggestive of *S. auritum,* but lf. blades dull above, lvs. of juvenile phase simple, lanceolate-elliptic, cordate to sagittate-subhastate, middle lobe of adult lvs. with lower primary lateral veins arched-ascending, connecting above with the more spreading upper lateral veins, spathe with tube ellipsoid. Mex. to Panama.

Mauroanum Birdsey ex Bunt. Lf. blades deeply 3-parted, middle lobe elliptic, to 6 in. long and half as wide, attenuate at each end, with a satin sheen and many deeply impressed lateral veins above, lateral lobes slightly shorter than middle one, asymmetrical, 2¼ in. wide from midvein to outer margin, ¾ in. from midvein to inner margin, basally rounded to angular or lobed, petioles to 9 in. long, lvs. of juvenile phase silvery along midrib; spathe to 5 in. long, tube green, blade scarcely longer than tube, white. Costa Rica.

Oerstedianum: *S. angustatum.*

peliocladum Schott. Sts. dark, finely prickly; lf. blades of adult phase 3-parted, middle segm. oblong-elliptic, 6–8 in. long, 2–2½ in. wide, with about 3 pairs of primary lateral veins, lateral segms. oblique, somewhat curved, to 6 in. long and 1¾ in. wide, basally lobed, petiole to 1 ft. long, lvs. of juvenile phase ovate-triangular, sagittate; spathe about 5 in. long, green, blade twice as long as tube. Nicaragua, Costa Rica.

podophyllum Schott. NEPHTHYTIS, AFRICAN EVERGREEN, ARROW-HEAD VINE. Lf. blades of adult phase pedate, glossy, medium green, segms. 7(5–9), distant from each other, middle segm. elliptic-oblanceolate to obovate, to 1 ft. long and ⅓ as wide, often narrower than adjacent lateral segms., petioles to 2 ft. long, often seen in juvenile phase with lf. blades oblong to ovate, sagittate to subhastate or hastate, entire, sometimes variegated with silver, cream, or white; infl. 6–9 together, spathe less than 4 in. long, tube oblong-ovoid, green, blade scarcely longer than spadix, whitish. Mex. to Panama. Commonly incorrectly offered as *Nephthytis Afzelii, N. liberica,* and *N. triphylla* Hort. Cv. 'Albovirens' and 'Atrovirens'. Juvenile phases with lvs. variously variegated white or yellowish. Var. **Oerstedianum:** *S. angustatum.*

salvadorense Schott. Lf. blades 3-parted, middle lobe narrowly to broadly ovate, to 9 in. long and 5 in. wide, lateral segms. elliptic to lanceolate, 5 in. long and half as wide, petioles to 1 ft. long, wide-winged; spathe less than 6 in. long, tube wine-red inside. S. Mex. to El Salvador.

Seemanii: a listed name of no botanical standing.

Standleyanum Bunt. [*S. triphyllum* Hort. cv. 'Lancetilla']. Lf. blades of adult phase deeply 3-parted, not glossy, with many pairs of prominent lateral veins, middle segm. elliptic to oblong, to 11 in. long and 4¾ in. wide, long-acuminate, the lateral segms. oblique-lanceolate, to 9 in. long and 3 in. wide, acute, rounded at base on outside, petioles to 14 in. long, lvs. of juvenile phase elliptic, entire; spathe 4½ in. long. Honduras to Costa Rica.

tripartitum: a listed name of no botanical standing.

triphyllum: a listed name of no botanical standing. Cv. 'Lancetilla': *S. Standleyanum.*

Wendlandii Schott [*Nephthytis Wendlandii* Hort.]. Lf. blades of adult phase 3-parted, dark green with a velvety sheen, thin-textured, middle lobe elliptic, to 7 in. long and 3 in. wide, with an ash-gray zone along midrib, lateral segms. slightly smaller, basally rounded to subhastate on outside, petioles to 10 in. long, angled, the angles narrowly winged, lvs. of juvenile phase simple, sagittate to hastate; spathe to 5 in. long, tube fusiform, green outside, purple inside, blade yellowish outside, white inside. Costa Rica.

xanthophilum Schott. Juvenile phase of undetermined sp., with midrib and lateral veins fading yellow; possibly a variant of *S. podophyllum.* Mex.

xanthosomifolium: a listed name no botanical standing.

SYNNEMA: *HYGROPHILA.* S. **triflorum:** *H. difformis.*

SYNNOTIA Sweet. *Iridaceae.* About 7 spp. of per. herbs with tunicate corms, native to S. Afr.; st. sometimes branched; lvs. 2-ranked, linear to sword-shaped, soft; spathe valves membranous, lacerate; fls. irregular, perianth tube long, funnelform toward apex, stamens 3, grouped together and arching in the upper part of the perianth, filaments not united, style brs. 3; fr. a 3-valved caps.

Propagated by seeds or by cormlet offsets; cultivation as for *Gladiolus,* succeeding best in a light soil.

bicolor: *S. villosa.*

Metelerkampiae L.Bolus. Sts. to 10 in.; lvs. linear, to 3 in. long; infl. loose, branched, 2–12-fld.; fls. deep violet, perianth tube filiform, to 1½ in. long, segms. about ½ in. long, pollen purple.

villosa (Burm.f.) N. E. Br. [*S. bicolor* Sweet]. Sts. to 1½ ft.; lvs. linear-oblong, to 6 in. long; infl. loose, sometimes branched, 2–6-fld.; fls. yellow, tinged violet, perianth tube to ½ in. long, segms. about 1 in. long, the upper one erect and broadly oblong, the others reflexed and much narrower, pollen yellow.

SYNSEPALUM (A. DC.) Baill. *Sapotaceae.* Three or 4 spp. of trees or shrubs with slender, leafy-tipped brs., native to trop. Afr.; lvs. lanceolate, with up to 20 pairs of lateral veins, somewhat leathery; fls. small, clustered in axils, sepals 5, united above middle, corolla 5-lobed, staminodes 5, ovary superior; fr. an ovoid, fleshy berry, 1-seeded.

dulcificum (Schumach. & Thonn.) Daniell ex S. Bell. MIRACULOUS FRUIT. Shrub, to 12 ft.; lvs. broadly lanceolate, 4–6 in. long, obtuse, with about 8 pairs of lateral veins; fls. whitish; fr. red, oblong to ovoid, ¾ in. long, ⅜ in. in diam., succulent. W. Afr. Acid citrus frs. are said to taste sweet after chewing frs. of this plant, whence the common name.

SYNTHERISMA: *DIGITARIA.*

SYNTHYRIS Benth. *Scrophulariaceae.* About 14 or 15 spp. of rhizomatous, per. herbs, native to w. N. Amer.; lvs. basal, long-petioled, toothed to pinnatisect; fls. blue to violet-blue, or white, in scapose racemes, calyx 4-parted, corolla campanulate or rotate, 4-lobed, not obviously 2-lipped, stamens 2; fr. a flattened loculicidal caps.

alpina: *Besseya alpina.*

cinerea: *Besseya cinerea.*

columbiana: a listed name of no botanical standing; plants offered under this name are probably *S. stellata.*

cordata: *S. reniformis* var.

cymopteroides Penn. Erect, to 6 in., white-tomentose, usually becoming glabrate; lvs. finely bipinnatifid, to 2 in. long and 1¾ in. wide, ultimate segms. linear-attenuate; fls. violet-blue, to ¼ in. long; caps. to 5⁄16 in. long, becoming glabrous. Spring, summer. Sw. Mont. to cent. Idaho.

Hendersonii Penn. To 3 in., white-tomentose, becoming glabrate; lvs. coarsely bipinnatifid, to 2 in. long and ⅝ in. wide, ultimate segms. ovate-acuminate, callose-tipped; fls. sky-blue, to ¼ in. long; caps. white-tomentose. Summer. Idaho.

laciniata (A. Gray) Rydb. To 6 in.; lvs. orbicular to reniform, lacinately cleft to the middle or less; fls. pale violet, to ¼ in. long. Spring, summer. Mts., cent. Utah.

lanuginosa: *S. pinnatifida* var.

major: *S. missurica* var.

missurica (Raf.) Penn. To 16 in., glabrous, or rachis and pedicels with brownish hairs; lvs. orbicular-cordate to reniform, to 2¾ in. across, shallowly lobed or toothed; fls. bright bluish-purple. Ne. Wash. and n. Idaho to ne. Calif. and s.-cent. Idaho. Var. **major** (Hook.) Penn. [*S. major* (Hook.) A. Heller]. Plants taller; fls. in denser racemes, rachis and pedicels with white hairs.

Paysonii Penn. & L. O. Williams. With simple or clustered rosettes, to 8 in., white-tomentose, becoming glabrate; lvs. 2-pinnatifid, to 5½ in. long, ultimate segms. linear-attenuate; fls. violet-blue, to ⅜ in. long, in stout racemes; caps. glabrous. Summer. W. Wyo. and adjacent Idaho.

pinnatifida S. Wats. To 6 in.; lvs. to 4 in. long, 2–3-pinnate, lfts. linear, pubescent; fls. to ⅛ in. long, in slender racemes, corolla to ⅝ in. long, violet-blue. Summer. Mts., n. Utah. Var. **lanuginosa** (Piper) Cronq. [*S. lanuginosa* (Piper) Penn. & J. W. Thomps.]. Herbage permanently white-tomentose; caps. tomentulose. Wash.

plantaginea: *Besseya plantaginea.*

platycarpa Gail & Penn. Closely allied to *S. schizantha,* but having lvs. less sharply toothed, corolla to ⅛ in. long, slightly longer than sepals, and caps. to ⅛ in. wide. Idaho.

reniformis (Dougl. ex Benth.) Benth. [*S. rotundifolia* A. Gray]. To 9 in.; lvs. orbicular-cordate to reniform, to 2 in. across, doubly crenate, glabrous or hairy; fls. blue or purple, to ¼ in. long, on pedicels more than twice as long as bracts, corolla campanulate. Wash., Ore., n. Calif. Cv. 'Alba'. Fls. white. Var. **cordata** A. Gray [*S. cordata* (A. Gray) A. Heller; *S. rotundifolia* A. Gray var. *Sweetseri* L. F. Henders.; *S. Sweetseri* Hort.]. Lvs. ovate-cordate, more deeply cut, fls. deeper blue.

Ritterana: *Besseya Ritterana.*

rotundifolia: *S. reniformis.* Var. **Sweetseri:** *S. reniformis* var. *cordata.*

rubra: *Besseya rubra.*

schizantha Piper. To 1 ft.; lvs. cordate-orbicular to reniform, to 6 in. across, doubly dentate-lobed, glabrous above, hairy on veins below; fls. blue, to ¼ in. long, corolla rotate, much longer than sepals, lobes laciniately cut; caps. ¼ in. wide. Early summer. Mts., Wash., nw. Ore.

stellata Penn. To 10 in.; lvs. cordate-orbicular, to 3½ in. wide, doubly dentate-toothed; fls. violet-blue, to ⅜ in. long, on pedicels about as long as bracts. Ore. Cv. 'Alba' is listed.

Sweetseri: a listed name of no botanical standing; used for *S. reniformis* var. *cordata.*

wyomingensis: *Besseya cinerea.*

SYRINGA L. LILAC. *Oleaceae.* About 30 spp. of deciduous shrubs or small trees in e. Asia, the Himalayas, and se. Eur.; lvs. opp., mostly simple; fls. small, white, lilac, pink, red, or purple, in showy panicles or thyrses, often very fragrant, corolla tubular; fr. a leathery caps. As a common name, syringa is sometimes applied to mock-orange (*Philadelphus*).

Lilacs are among the most popular ornamental shrubs and most of them are hardy north. They thrive in fertile, rather moist soil, although growing readily in most soils. Transplanting is easily effected in autumn or spring. Best propagated by softwood cuttings and by grafting onto lilac seedlings or privet; seed stratified and sown in spring, root cuttings, ripe to hardwood cuttings, layers, and suckers may also be used in particular cases.

Adamiana: *S. tomentella.*

afghanica C. K. Schneid. Low shrub; lvs. linear-lanceolate to ovate-lanceolate, to 3 in. long, glabrous, somewhat leathery; fls. lilac, in small, dense, lateral and terminal panicles to 1½ in. long, corolla tube slender, ⅜ in. long. Afghanistan.

amurensis: *S. reticulata* var. **mandshurica.** Var. **japonica:** *S. reticulata.*

×**chinensis** Willd. [*S. rothomagensis* Hort. ex Mord. de Laun.]: *S. persica* × *S. vulgaris.* CHINESE L. To 15 ft.; lvs. ovate-lanceolate, to 3 in. long, glabrous; fls. lilac or purple. Zone 3. Cvs. include: 'Alba', fls. white; 'Duplex', fls. double, purplish-lilac; 'Metensis', fls. rosy-lilac; 'Nana', dwarf; 'Rubra': 'Saugeana'; 'Saugeana' [cv. 'Rubra'], fls. lilac-red.

dilatata: *S. oblata* var.

emodi Wallich ex Royle HIMALAYAN L. To 15 ft.; lvs. elliptic or oblong, to 8 in. long, glabrous, glaucous beneath; fls. lilac or whitish, in dense terminal panicles to 6 in. long, corolla tube 5⁄16 in. long. W. Asia. Zone 7. Cvs. 'Aurea' and 'Superba' are listed.

×**Henryi** C. K. Schneid.: *S. Josikaea* × *S. villosa.* Lvs. pubescent on midrib beneath; fls. pale violet-purple, in panicles to 10 in. long. Zone 2. Cv. 'Lutece'. The typical cv. of this hybrid, but material offered under this name is not uniform. Var. **eximia:** *S. Josikaea* cv.

×**hyacinthiflora** (Hort. Lemoine) Rehd.: *S. oblata* × *S. vulgaris.* Lvs. broad-ovate. Cv. 'Plena'. Fls. double; the original cv. of this hybrid. There are many other cvs.

japonica: *S. reticulata.*

×**josiflexa** Preston: *S. Josikaea* × *S. reflexa.* Shrub; infl. pendulous.

Josikaea Jacq.f. ex Rchb. HUNGARIAN L. To 12 ft.; lvs. elliptic, to 5 in. long, glossy above, glaucous and nearly glabrous beneath; fls. lilac, in terminal panicles to 7 in. long, corolla tube ½ in. long. Hungary. Zone 4. Cv. 'Eximia' [*S.* × *Henryi* var. *eximia* Rehd.]. Fls. rose-red, in large panicles. Cv. 'Pallida'. Fls. pale violet. Cv. 'Rosea' is listed.

Julianae C. K. Schneid. To 6 ft.; lvs. ovate, to 2½ in. long, pubescent on both sides; fls. lilac, in lateral panicles to 4 in. long, fragrant, corolla tube 5⁄16 in. long, anthers purple or bluish. China. Zone 6. Distinguished by pubescent lvs., fragrant fls., and purple peduncles and pedicels.

Komarowii C. K. Schneid. To 15 ft.; lvs. ovate-oblong to oblong-lanceolate, to 6 in. long, pubescent beneath; fls. lilac, in nodding terminal panicles to 6 in. long. China. Zone 6.

laciniata Mill. [*S.* × *persica* var. *laciniata* (Mill.) Weston]. CUT-LEAF L. To 6 ft.; lvs. to 2½ in. long, glabrous, pinnately cut to midrib into 3–9 lobes, or some sometimes entire; fls. lilac, in loose lateral panicles to 3 in. long, fragrant, corolla tube 5⁄16 in. long. Nw. China. Zone 5.

macrostachya: a listed name of no botanical standing; used for *S. vulgaris* cv. 'Macrostachya', with single pink fls.

marlyensis: a listed name of no botanical standing; used for *S. vulgaris* cv. 'Marlyensis', with single deep purple fls.

Maximowiczii: a listed name of no botanical standing; used for *S. vulgaris* cv. 'Maximowicz', with semidouble fls. purplish-lilac inside, paler outside.

Meyeri C. K. Schneid. Small shrub; lvs. elliptic, to 1½ in. long, pubescent on veins beneath; fls. purple-lilac, in dense lateral panicles to 3 in. long, corolla tube ½ in. long. China. Zone 6.

microphylla Diels. Small shrub; lvs. ovate, to 1½ in. long, pubescent beneath; fls. lilac, in lateral panicles to 3 in. long, corolla tube ⁵⁄₁₆ in. long. China. Zone 4. Cv. 'Superba'. Fls. pinkish.

×**nanceiana** McKelv.: *S.* × *Henryi* × *S. Sweginzowii.* Fls. mauve-lilac.

nigricans: a listed name of no botanical standing; used for *S. vulgaris* cv. 'Nigricans', with dark foliage and dark purple fls.

oblata Lindl. To 12 ft.; lvs. ovate or reniform, to 4 in. long, cordate at base, glabrous; fls. lilac, in dense lateral panicles to 5 in. long, corolla tube ½ in. long. China. Zone 4. The earliest-blooming sp., and the only one with autumn foliage color. Var. **alba** Rehd. Lvs. smaller; fls. white. Var. **dilatata** (Nakai) Rehd. [*S. dilatata* Nakai]. Lvs. long-acuminate. Var. **Giraldii** (Hort. Lemoine) Rehd. Lvs. often pubescent beneath; panicles 6 in. long.

Palibiniana: *S. patula.*

patula (Palib.) Nakai [*S. Palibiniana* Nakai; *S. velutina* Kom.]. To 10 ft.; lvs. elliptic or ovate-oblong, to 4 in. long, pubescent on both sides; fls. lilac, in pubescent panicles to 5 in. long, corolla tube ⁵⁄₁₆ in. long. China, Korea. Zone 4. Cv. 'Excellens' is listed.

pekinensis Rupr. To 15 ft.; lvs. ovate or ovate-lanceolate, to 4 in. long, glabrous; fls. yellowish-white, in panicles to 6 in. long, corolla tube short. China. Zone 5. Cv. 'Pendula'. Brs. drooping.

×**persica** L.: *S. afghanica* × *S. laciniata.* PERSIAN L. To 6 or rarely 10 ft.; lvs. lanceolate, to 2½ in. long, glabrous; fls. similar to those of *S. laciniata.* Zone 5. Cvs. include: 'Alba', fls. white; 'Rosea' and 'Rubra', fls. red. Var. **laciniata:** *S. laciniata.*

pinetorum W. W. Sm. Differs from *S. Julianae* in having lvs. not more than 1½ in. long, pilose beneath only on veins; anthers yellow. Sw. China. Zone 7.

pinnatifolia Hemsl. To 10 ft.; lvs. unequally pinnate, lfts. 7–11, ovate or ovate-lanceolate, to 1 in. long; fls. white or pale lilac, in lateral panicles to 3 in. long, corolla tube ⁵⁄₁₆ in. long. China. Zone 5.

Potaninii C. K. Schneid. Graceful shrub, to 12 ft., shoots and lvs. pubescent; lvs. elliptic, to 3 in. long; fls. white to rose-purple, in loose erect panicles, fragrant. China.

×**Prestoniae** McKelv.: *S. reflexa* × *S. villosa.* Lvs. resembling those of *S. villosa;* fls. pale pink to pinkish-lilac. Very hardy Zone 2. Devloped in Canada.

pubescens Turcz. To 6 ft.; lvs. broad-ovate, to 3 in. long, pubescent beneath; fls. pale lilac, in dense lateral panicles to 5 in. long, fragrant, corolla tube ½ in. long. China. Zone 6.

reflexa C. K. Schneid. to 12 ft.; lvs. oblong, to 6 in. long, pubescent beneath; fls. pinkish, white inside, in terminal, drooping racemes to 7 in. long, not fragrant, corolla tube ⁵⁄₁₆ in. long. China. Zone 5. The bicolored corollas and cylindrical, drooping racemes are distinctive. Cvs. 'Alba' and 'Pallens' are listed.

reticulata (Blume) Hara [*S. amurensis* Rupr. var. *japonica* (Maxim.) Franch. & Sav.; *S. japonica* (Maxim.) Decne.]. JAPANESE TREE L. To 30 ft.; lvs. broad-ovate to ovate-oblong, to 5 in. long, pubescent beneath; fls. yellowish-white, in loose panicles to 12 in. long, with privetlike odor, corolla tube very short, stamens exserted. Japan. Zone 4. Var. **mandshurica** (Maxim.) Hara [*S. amurensis* Rupr.]. To 12 ft.; lvs. ovate, glabrous; panicles to 6 in. long. Manchuria. Zone 4.

rothomagensis: *S. chinensis.*

Saugeana: a listed name of no botanical standing for *S. chinensis* cv.

×**Skinneri** F. Skinner: *S. patula* × *S. pubescens.* Generally intermediate between the parents; fls. pale mauve, opening white, in large panicles to 9 in. across, fragrant.

×**swegiflexa** Hesse: *S. reflexa* × *S. Sweginzowii.* Fls. coral-pink, in long panicles.

Sweginzowii Koehne & Lingelsh. To 10 ft.; lvs. oblong or ovate, to 4 in. long, pubescent on veins beneath; fls. lilac, in terminal panicles to 8 in. long, fragrant, corolla tube ⁵⁄₁₆ in. long. China. Zone 6. Cv. 'Albida'. Fls. paler. Cvs. 'Densiflora' and 'Superba' are listed.

Thunbergii: a listed name of no botanical standing, perhaps for *S. vulgaris* cv. 'Thunberg', with double purplish-lilac fls.

tomentella Bur. & Franch. [*S. Adamiana* Balf. & W. W. Sm.]. To 10 ft.; lvs. elliptic to oblong-lanceolate, to 4 in. long, pubescent beneath; fls. lilac and whitish, in loose terminal panicles to 7 in. long, corolla tube ½ in. long. China. Zone 6.

velutina: *S. patula.*

villosa Vahl. LATE L. To 10 ft.; lvs. elliptic to oblong, to 7 in. long, pubescent on veins beneath; fls. lilac or pinkish-white, in terminal panicles to 1 ft. long, corolla tube ½ in. long. China. Zone 2. Cvs. 'Aurea', 'Rosea', and 'Superba' are listed.

vulgaris L. COMMON L. To 20 ft.; lvs. ovate, to 5 in. long, glabrous; fls. lilac or white, in lateral panicles to 10 in. long, fragrant, corolla tube ⁵⁄₁₆ in. long. Se. Eur. Zone 4. Cv. 'Alba'. Taller, more slender, more upright in habit; lvs. white, single; this is the old, common white-flowered lilac. There are hundreds of other named cvs. (often mistakenly termed hybrids) of this much cult. sp.; among those generally available, the following have been especially highly recommended. Fls. white, single: 'Jan Van Tol', 'Maud Notcutt', 'Mont Blanc', 'Vestale'; fls. white, double: 'Edith Cavell', 'Ellen Willmott', 'Madame Lemoine', 'Monique Lemoine', 'Saint Joan'; fls. violet, single: 'Cavour', 'De Miribel'; fls. violet, double: 'Maréchal Lannes', 'Violetta'; fls. blue, single: 'Decaisne', 'Firmament', 'President Lincoln'; fls. blue, double: 'Ami Schott', 'Olivier de Serres', 'Président Grévy'; fls. lilac, single: 'Cristophe Colomb', 'Jacques Callot'; fls. lilac, double: 'Alphonse Lavallée', 'Henri Martin', 'Léon Gambetta', 'Victor Lemoine'; fls. pink, single: 'Charm', 'Lucie Baltet', 'Macrostachya', 'Mrs. Harry Bickle'; fls. pink, double: 'Belle de Nancy', 'Katherine Havemeyer', 'Madame Antoine Buchner', 'Montaigne'; fls. magenta, single: 'Capitaine Baltet', 'Congo', 'Madame F. Morel'; fls. magenta, double: 'Charles Joly'. 'My Favorite', 'Paul Thirion', 'Président Poincaré'; fls. purple, single: 'Ludwig Spaeth', 'Monge', 'Mrs. W. E. Marshall', 'Night', 'Sensation'; fls. purple, double: 'Adelaide Dunbar', 'Anne Tighe', 'Paul Hariot'.

Wolfii C. K. Schneid. To 20 ft.; lvs. elliptic-oblong, to 6 in. long, pubescent on veins beneath; fls. lilac, in terminal panicles to 1 ft. long, fragrant, corolla tube ½ in. long. Manchuria, Korea. Zone 4. Var. **hirsuta** (C. K. Schneid.) Hatus. Twigs, lvs., and infl. more densely pilose.

yunnanensis Franch. To 10 ft.; lvs. elliptic to elliptic-lanceolate, to 3 in. long, glaucous beneath; fls. pink, in terminal panicles to 6 in. long, corolla tube ¼ in. long. China. Zone 6. Cv. 'Rosea'. Fls. darker.

SYZYGIUM Gaertn. [*Jambosa* DC.]. *Myrtaceae.* About 400–500 spp. of evergreen trees, mostly in tropics of Old World; lvs. opp., simple, pinnately veined; fls. in terminal or axillary cymes or panicles, calyx tube produced beyond the ovary, calyx lobes 4–5, petals 4–5, separate or united into a cap, often falling early, stamens many, anther sacs opening by lateral valves, ovary inferior, 2–4-celled, ovules many; fr. a berry, usually 1-seeded. These Old World spp. have been removed from *Eugenia.* Differs from *Eugenia* in having cotyledons of the embryo free (not coherent), the seed coat roughish, adhering loosely or closely to the pericarp, and the infl. mostly paniculate-cymose.

For culture see *Eugenia.*

aqueum (Burm.f.) Alston [*Jambosa aquea* (Burm.f.) DC.]. WATER ROSE-APPLE. Tree, to 30 ft.; lvs. ovate, to 6 in. long or longer, cordate, leathery, nearly sessile; fls. white, red, or pale purple, about 1 in. across, in terminal or axillary, 3–7-fld. clusters; berry light red or white, top-shaped, to 1 in. across, several-seeded. Malay Pen. and Borneo. Cult. in Fla.

aromaticum (L.) Merrill & L. M. Perry [*Eugenia aromatica* (L.) Baill.; *E. caryophyllata* Thunb.; *Jambosa Caryophyllus* (K. Spreng.) Niedenzu]. CLOVE. Tree, to 30 ft.; lvs. elliptic, glandular-dotted; fls. yellow, to ¼ in. across, in terminal, few-fld. panicles. Moluccas. Widely cult. in warm regions. Cloves, the commercial spice, are the sun-dried fl. buds. The lvs. smell strongly of cloves when crushed.

australe: a listed name of no botanical standing; used for *S. paniculatum.*

coolminianum (C. Moore) L. A. S. Johnson [*Eugenia cyanocarpa* F. J. Muell. ex Maiden & Betche]. BLUE LILLY-PILLY. Shrub or small tree, to 18 ft., bark white; lvs. elliptic-lanceolate, to 4 in. long, tapering at both ends, closely glandular-dotted, finely nerved; fls. cream-colored, in few-fld., open panicles, petals almost round, ⅛ in. across; berry pale to dark violet, globose, to ½ in. across, crowned by persistent calyx lobes. Se. Australia. Attractive for the unusual coloring of the frs., similar to those of *Acmena Smithii.*

cumini (L.) Skeels [*S. Jambolana* (Lam.) DC.; *Eugenia cumini* (L.) Druce; *E. Jambolana* Lam.]. JAVA PLUM, BLACK P., JAMBOLAN, JAMBOLAN PLUM, JAMBOOL, JAMBOO, JAMBU. Tree, 50–80 ft., branchlets white or gray; lvs. elliptic or obovate, to 5 in. long, lateral veins close together; fls. in few-fld. panicle, petals white, united into a cap; berry purplish-red, ovoid, to ½ in. long, edible. India and Ceylon, e. to Malay Arch. Cult. in trop. regions for edible fr.

densiflorum: see *S. pycnanthum.*

grande (Wight) Walp. [*Eugenia grandis* Wight]. SEA APPLE. Large tree; lvs. broadly obovate to suborbicular, to 9 in. long, glossy; fls. white, to 1½ in. across, in terminal and axillary panicles, petals separate; berries globose or pear-shaped, to 1 in. across, crowned by persistent calyx lobes, covered with a green leathery rind, dry but edible. Burma, s. to Thailand and Malay Pen. Cult. in Fla.

Jambolana: *S. cumini.*

Jambos (L.) Alston [*Eugenia Jambos* L.; *E. malaccensis* Lour., not L.; *Jambosa Jambosa* Millsp.; *J. vulgaris* DC.]. ROSE APPLE, MALABAR PLUM. Tree, 30–40 ft.; lvs. lanceolate, to 8 in. long, dark green, glossy; fls. greenish-white, 2–3 in. across, in terminal, few-fld. clusters, stamens long and showy; fr. cream-yellow, ovoid, to 1½ in. long, fragrant. Se. Asia. Widely cult. and often naturalized in trop. regions. Cult. for the showy fls. and fragrant frs., which are dry, crisp, rather insipid when raw, but prized for jellies and confections.

javanicum: see *S. samarangense.*

malaccense (L.) Merrill & L. M. Perry [*Eugenia malaccensis* L., not Lour.; *Jambosa malaccensis* (L.) DC.]. MALAY APPLE, ROSE APPLE, LARGE-FRUITED R.A., POMERAC JAMBOS. Tree, 15–40 ft.; lvs. ovate-oblong, 6–12 in. long, leathery, dark green, glossy; fls. from old wood, showy, purplish-red, in few-fld. cymes; fr. pear-shaped, about 2 in. long, seed large, brown. Malay Pen. Cult. widely as an ornamental and for the frs., which are eaten raw or cooked, and used as preserves, or for wine. One of the most beautiful of trop. trees.

oblatum (Roxb.) Wallich [*Eugenia oblata* Roxb.]. Tree; lvs. oblong or broadly lanceolate, 3–4 in. long, acuminate, finely nerved; fls. rather large, in terminal and axillary panicles, petals united into a cap; berries globose, about the size of a cherry. N. India, Burma, China.

paniculatum Gaertn. [*S. australe* Hort.; *Eugenia australis* J. C. Wendl. ex Link; *E. Hookerana* Hort.; *E. Hookeri* Hort.; *E. myrtifolia* Sims; *E. paniculata* (Gaertn.) Britten; *E. paniculata* var. *australis* (J. C. Wendl. ex Link) L. H. Bailey; *Jambosa australis* (J. C. Wendl. ex Link) DC.]. BRUSH CHERRY, AUSTRALIAN B. C. Tree, to 40 ft.; lvs. oblong-lanceolate, to 3 in. long, dark green, glossy, tinged with red when young; fls. cream-white, ½–1 in. across, in terminal and axillary, few-fld. panicles; berry rose-purple, ovoid, to ¾ in. across. Australia. Cult. in Calif. and Fla. as a background hedge, which may be kept clipped. Variable in habit, lf. and fl. size. The fragrant fr. is sometimes used in jelly.

polycephalum (Miq.) Merrill & L. M. Perry [*Eugenia polycephala* Miq.]. Tree; lvs. oblong, oblong-lanceolate, or nearly obovate, to 4 in. long, acuminate, subcordate; fls. white, in many-fld. panicles; berry dark purple, 1½ in. across. Java. Sometimes cult. for the fr.

pycnanthum Merrill & L. M. Perry [*S. densiflorum* Hort., not Brongn. & Gris; *Eugenia densiflora* (Blume) Duthie; *Jambosa densiflora* (Blume) DC.]. WILD ROSE APPLE. Shrub or small tree; lvs. ovate-oblong to lanceolate, to 12 in. long, glossy above, often dotted beneath; fls. white or pinkish, 1½–2 in. across, in 2–3-fld. showy clusters; berry dark red-purple, nearly globose, ½ in. across, crowned with persistent calyx lobes. Malay Pen., Sumatra, Java. Cult. in Fla., handsome tree when in fl.

samarangense (Blume) Merrill & L. M. Perry [*S. javanicum* Hort., not Miq.; *Eugenia javanica* Lam.; *Jambosa alba* Blume; *J. samarangense* (Blume) DC.]. JAVA APPLE, WAX A., JAMBOSA, JUMROOL. Tree, 20–30 ft.; lvs. elliptic-oblong, to 6 in. long or more, obtuse, rounded or subcordate, nearly sessile; fls. white, 1½ in. across, in many-fld. clusters; berry white or red, pear-shaped, to 1½ in. long, edible but insipid. Malay Arch. Handsome ornamental tree for warm regions.

TABEBUIA Gomes ex DC. TRUMPET TREE. *Bignoniaceae.* About 100 spp. of shrubs or trees, native to trop. Amer.; lvs. opp., palmately compound or rarely simple; fls. showy, yellow, white, pink, red, or purple, in terminal spikelike racemes, panicles, dense heads, or umbels, calyx unequally 2- or 5-lobed, corolla funnelform or funnelform-campanulate, straight or partly curved, slightly 2-lipped, stamens 4; fr. a pendent caps., linear or oblong-linear, smooth.

Several species yield excellent timber. Tabebuias are among the most common and showy flowering trees in the New World tropics and subtropics and are particularly useful as specimen trees or street trees. In the U.S. tabebuias are mostly grown in Zone 10b in Fla., where they thrive in rich soil. Some may be grown in tubs under glass. Propagated by cuttings and air layering, as well as by seeds, flowering at an early age.

argentea (Bur. & K. Schum.) Britt. [*Tecoma argentea* Bur. & K. Schum.]. SILVER T. T., PARAGUAYAN S. T. T., TREE-OF-GOLD. Tree, to 25 ft.; lfts. 5–7, oblong, to 6 in. long, with dense silvery scales; fls. yellow, to 2½ in. long; fr. to 4 in. long, gray, with black lines. Paraguay, Argentina. Zone 9b, in Fla.

Avellanedae Lorentz ex Griseb. [*T. Ipe* (Mart.) Standl.]. To 60 ft.; lfts. 5, to 6 in. long; fls. red or pink, to 1½ in. long; fr. to 1 ft. long. Paraguay, Argentina. Zone 10b in Fla. A good cabinet wood.

chrysantha (Jacq.) Nichols. Tree; lfts. 5–7 in. long, lanceolate, elliptic-oblong to somewhat obovate, acuminate; fls. in dense headlike clusters, bright yellow, to 2¾ in. long, not all blooming at the same time; fr. to 1 ft. long. Mex. to Venezuela. Zone 10b in Fla.

chrysea: *Cybistax chrysea.*

chrysotricha (Mart. ex DC.) Standl. [*Tecoma chrysotricha* Mart. ex DC.]. to 50 ft.; lfts. 5, obovate-oblong, oblong, or ovate, to 4 in. long; fls. in umbellate clusters, bright yellow, to 2½ in. long; fr. to 8 in. long, densely hairy. Colombia, Brazil. Zone 10b in Fla.

crassifolia: *T. dubia.*

Donnell-Smithii: *Cybistax Donnell-Smithii.*

dubia (C. H. Wright) Britt. ex Seib. [*T. crassifolia* Britt.]. Tree, to 15 ft.; lvs. simple, oblong-elliptic, to about 4¾ in. long, leathery, old lvs. scaly beneath, shining above; fls. light purple, to 2 in. long. Cuba.

Gaudichaudii: a listed name of no botanical standing; used for *Tecoma castanifolia.*

glomerata: *T. rufescens.*

Guayacan (Seem.) Hemsl. To 100 ft.; lfts. 5, ovate, minutely glandular-scaly beneath; fls. to 3¾ in. long, all blooming at the same time, corolla golden-yellow, with stellate hairs in the sinuses. S. Mex. to Panama, Zone 10b in Fla. Produces a good timber.

haemantha (Bertol.) DC. Shrub or small tree, to 25 ft.; lfts. 3–5, elliptic, oblong-elliptic, or ovate, to 6 in. long; fls. red or crimson, to 2 in. long; fr. to 4¼ in. long. Puerto Rico.

heptaphylla (Vell.) Toledo [*Tecoma heptaphylla* (Vell.) Mart.]. To 50 ft.; lfts. oblong to oblong-obovate, to 2½ in. long; fls. pink to rose-purple, to 2 in. long. Brazil.

heterophylla (DC.) Britt. [*T. triphylla* DC.]. Shrub to 12 ft., or tree to 30 ft.; lfts. 1–5, elliptic to oblong or obovate, to 2¾ in. long, densely scaly; fls. pink or white, to 2¾ in. long; fr. to 4¼ in. long. W. Indies.

impetiginosa (Mart. ex DC.) Toledo. Tree, to 20 ft.; lfts. 5, oblong to oblong-ovate, to 5 in. long; fls. purple, to 2 in. long. Brazil.

Ipe: *T. Avellanedae.*

leucoxyla (Vell.) DC. [*T. obtusifolia* (Cham.) Bur.]. Large shrub or tree; lvs. simple, oblong, oblong-lanceolate, or oblong-obovate, to 7 in. long; fls. to 3⅜ in. long, calyx scaly on outside; fr. to 9 in. long. Brazil.

leucoxylon: a listed name of no botanical standing; used for *T. riparia.*

longiflora: see *T. Vellosoi.*

obtusifolia: *T. leucoxyla.*

odontodiscus: *T. roseoalba.*

pallida (Lindl.) Miers. WHITE CEDAR, CUBAN PINK T. T. Tree; lfts. usually 1–3, sometimes 4 or 5, oblong or narrowly obovate, to 4½ in. long, obtuse; fls. solitary or in few-fld. cymes, to 2 in. long, corolla lilac-white with yellow tube; fr. to 8 in. long. W. Indies. Zone 10b in Fla.

Palmeri Rose. Large tree, to 25 ft.; lfts. usually 5, elliptic-oblong to elliptic-lanceolate or sometimes lanceolate-obovate, 2–5 in. long, glandular-scaly; fls. 2¾ in. long, corolla mauve with white and yellow patches; fr. to 15 in. long. Mex., Guatemala. Zone 10b in Fla.

pentaphylla: *T. riparia;* but *T. pentaphylla* has been misapplied to *T. rosea.*

riparia (Raf.) Sandw. [*T. leucoxylon* Hort.; *T. pentaphylla* (L.) Hemsl.; *Bignonia leucoxylon* L.; *B. pentaphylla* L.]. WHITEWOOD. Shrub or small tree, to 20 ft.; lfts. 1–5, elliptic to oblanceolate, to 3 in. long, scaly; fls. to 2½ in. long, corolla white, with yellow throat; fr. to 5 in. long. Jamaica.

rosea (Bertol.) DC. PINK POUI, ROSY T. T. To 80 ft.; lfts. 3–5, elliptic-oblong to sometimes elliptic-ovate, acuminate, fls. purplish-pink or nearly white, to 3¼ in. long, calyx and ovary glandular-scaly; fr. to 14 in. long. Mex., s. to Venezuela and Ecuador. Zone 10b in Fla. Sometimes erroneously called *T. pentaphylla.*

roseoalba (Ridl.) Sandw. [*T. odontodiscus* (Bur. & K. Schum.) Toledo]. Tree, to 25 or 30 ft., scaly on vegetative parts and calyx; lfts. 3, ovate to ovate-lanceolate, to 5 in. long; fls. to 2 in. long, corolla white to pink or purple, blotched with yellow on lower lip, lobes ciliate; fr. to 14 in. long. Brazil, Bolivia, Paraguay.

rufescens J. R. Johnst. [*T. glomerata* Urb.]. To 45 ft.; lfts. 5, obovate to elliptic, 2–6 in. long, acuminate, lower surface densely scaly, with stellate hairs on veins; fls. yellow, to 2¾ in. long; fr. to 10 in. long. S. Lesser Antilles to n. S. Amer.

serratifolia (Vahl) Nichols. YELLOW POUI. Tree; lfts. 5, oblong to lanceolate or ovate, to 6 in. long, toothed; fls. to 3 in. long, corolla yellow, hairy inside, ovary glandular; fr. to 1½ ft. long. W. Indies, n. S. Amer. to Bolivia. Zone 10b in Fla.

spectabilis (Planch. & Lindl. ex Planch.) Nichols. Small tree; lfts. 5, oblong, to 4 in. long, toothed; fls. orange-yellow, to 3 in. long. Venezuela, Colombia.

triphylla: *T. heterophylla.*

umbellata (Sond.) Sandw. Small tree, to 15 ft.; lfts. 3–5, oblong, elliptic, or obovate-oblong, to 3 in. long; fls. yellow, to 2¾ in. long; fr. to 1½ ft. long. Brazil.

Vellosoi Toledo [*T. longiflora* Hort., not (Griseb.) Greenm. ex Combs; *Tecoma longiflora* (Vell.) Bur. & K. Schum.]. Tree; lfts. 5–7, lanceolate or ovate-oblong, to 3½ in. long; fls. yellow, to 4 in. long. Brazil.

TABERNAEMONTANA L. [*Conopharyngia* G. Don; *Ervatamia* Stapf]. RED BAY. *Apocynaceae.* About 140 spp. of trop. trees and shrubs with milky sap; brs. sometimes spiny; lvs. opp., entire, leathery, those of a pair sometimes unequal; fls. in compound, cymose clusters, 5-merous, bisexual, calyx lobes obtuse, corolla yellow or white, salverform, the tube widening at point of stamen attachment, stamens borne at apex of corolla tube, anthers sagittate at base, free from stigma, mostly included; fr. a pair of globoid to ovoid or cylindrical follicles, seeds 1 to many, deeply grooved, embedded in fleshy aril.

Planted outdoors in frost-free areas as ornamentals. Propagated by seeds and cuttings.

coronaria: *T. divaricata.*

divaricata (L.) R. Br. [*T. coronaria* (Jacq.) Willd.; *Ervatamia coronaria* (Jacq.) Stapf; *E. divaricata* (L.) Burkill]. CRAPE JASMINE, CRAPE GARDENIA, PINWHEEL FLOWER, EAST INDIAN ROSEBAY, BROAD-LEAVED R., FLOWERS-OF-LOVE, ADAM'S APPLE. Much-branched, glabrous shrub, to 8 ft. or more; lvs. of each pair unequal, oblong-lanceolate to obovate, to 6 in. long or more, acuminate to subcaudate, thin; infls. few-fld.; corolla waxy, white, to 1½ in. across, fragrant at night, tube to 1 in. long; follicles oblong with recurved beak, to 3 in. long. India; widespread in trop. and warm regions. Cv. **'Flore Pleno'.** FLEUR-D'AMOUR, BUTTERFLY GARDENIA. Fls. double. Cv. **'Grandifolia'** [*T. grandifolia* Hort.]. Lvs. larger; fls. double. Cv. **'Cashmere'** appears to belong to this sp.

grandiflora Jacq. Shrub, to 8 ft.; lvs. elliptic to oblong-ovate, 3–5 in. long, sharply acuminate; cymes few-fld.; fls. inodorous, calyx lobes unequal, outer 2 cordate and foliaceous, half as long as corolla tube, inner 3 narrower, corolla bright yellow, 1½–2 in. across, tube 2 in. long, lobes elliptic, obtuse, stamens borne at middle of tube, included; follicles broadly ovoid, acuminate, reflexed. N. Colombia to Guianas. Doubtfully in the trade; material offered under this name is probably *T. divaricata.*

grandifolia: a listed name of no botanical standing for *T. divaricata* cv.

Holstii K. Schum. [*Conopharyngia Holstii* (K. Schum.) Stapf]. Shrub or tree, to 20 (–35) ft.; lvs. broadly elliptic, mostly 7–12 in. long, sometimes much larger, acute, cuneate; fls. very fragrant, corolla white with yellow throat, 1½ in. across, tube 1¼ in. long, ⅜ in. in diam., densely tomentose inside; follicles drupelike, globose, to 4 in. in diam., green, Uganda, Kenya, Mozambique.

TACCA J. R. Forst. & G. Forst. [*Schizocapsa* Hance]. *Taccaceae.* Ten spp. of rhizomatous or tuberous per. herbs of trop. Asia, Afr., Australia, the Pacific Is., and S. Amer.; lvs. entire or much-lobed; infl. scapose, umbel-like, subtended by an involucre of leaflike bracts and, in at least the cult. spp., with long, filiform bracts among the fls.; fls. 3-merous, brownish or greenish; fr. a berry, seeds many.

Suitable for greenhouse cultivation in rich, well-drained soil; should be rested in winter. Propagated by division or seeds.

aspera: *T. integrifolia.*

Chantrieri André. DEVIL FLOWER, BAT FLOWER, MAGICIAN'S FLOWER, DEVIL'S-TONGUE, CAT'S-WHISKERS, JEW'S-BEARD. Differs from *T. integrifolia* chiefly in having the 4 involucral bracts in 2 pairs more or less at right angles to each other, and the seeds reniform, laterally flattened. Se. Asia.

cristata: *T. integrifolia.*

integrifolia Ker.-Gawl. [*T. aspera* Roxb.; *T. cristata* Jack; *T. laevis* Roxb.]. BAT PLANT, BAT FLOWER. Rhizomatous; lf. blades entire, oblong-ovate to linear-lanceolate, to 2 ft. long and 10 in. wide, rounded to attenuate at base but not decurrent on petiole, petiole to 16 in. long; scape to 2 ft. or more, violet to brownish, involucral bracts 4, variable in shape, usually acuminate, the outer 2 opp., green to brown-purple, the inner 2 in the axil of one of the outer 2 bracts, thinner, whitish or greenish, shaded purple and veined with black, the filiform bracts white- or yellow-green; fls. up to 30, green to brown-purple; fr. ¾–2 in. long, seeds ovoid, concave on one side, convex on the other. Se. Asia.

laevis: *T. integrifolia.*

Leontopetaloides (L.) O. Kuntze [*T. pinnatifida* J. R. Forst. & G. Forst.]. TAHITI ARROWROOT, FIJI A., SOUTH SEA A., EAST INDIAN A., POLYNESIAN A., PIA, SALEP. Tuberous, tubers globose, 1–3 in. in diam.; lf. blades to 3½ ft. across, 3-lobed, the lobes again parted and ultimately coarsely pinnatifid, petiole to 6 ft. long; scape 1–5 ft., involucral bracts 4–12, ovate to lanceolate, acuminate, green, filiform bracts purple to dark brown; fls. 20–40, about ½ in. across, yellowish-green to blackish-purple; fr. globose, seeds ovoid to ellipsoid, flattened. Widespread in tropics of Old World. Once widely grown in tropics for its starchy tubers, a source of arrowroot starch. Becoming dormant, with lvs. deciduous, in winter.

pinnatifida: *T. Leontopetaloides.*

plantaginea (Hance) Drenth [*Schizocapsa plataginea* Hance]. Differs from *T. integrifolia* chiefly in having base of lf. blade attenuate, decurrent along petiole, and fr. ⅜ in. long, seeds oblong-ovoid to ellipsoid, round in cross section. S. China to Thailand and Laos.

TACCACEAE Dumort. TACCA FAMILY. Monocot.; 1 genus, *Tacca*, with 10 spp. of rhizomatous or tuberous per. herbs of tropics of Old World and S. Amer.; lvs. basal, large, entire or lobed; infl. umbel-like, subtended by an involucre of bracts, borne on a scape; perianth campanulate, 6-lobed, stamens 6, inserted on the perianth ovary inferior, 1-celled; fr. a berry, seeds many.

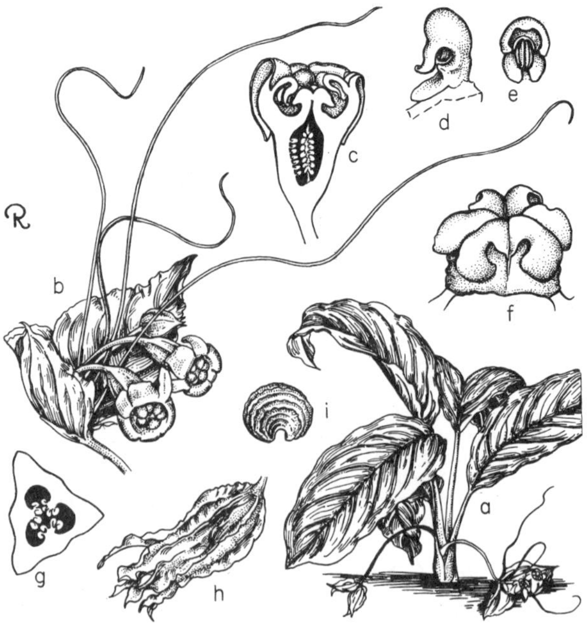

TACCACEAE. *Tacca Chantrieri:* **a,** flowering plant, × 1/10; **b,** inflorescence, × ½; **c,** flower, vertical section, × 1; **d,** stamen, side view, × 2; **e,** stamen, face view of upper part, × 2; **f,** stigma, × 3; **g,** ovary, cross section, × 2; **h,** fruit, dehisced, × ¾; **i,** seed, × 3.

TACCARUM Brongn. ex Schott. *Araceae.* Four spp. of tuberous herbs of trop. Amer.; lvs. solitary, 3-parted, each segm. irregularly 2–3-pinnatifid, median segm. larger than laterals, petioles long; infl. appearing with the lvs., solitary, peduncle much shorter than petiole, spathe broad, very loosely convolute, expanded above, fls. unisexual, spadix loosely covered with fls., the female fls. at base with 4–6 staminodes and long styles.

For propagation see *Amorphophallus.*

Weddellianum Brongn. ex Schott. Tuber large; lf. blade to 16 in. long, lateral lobes to 12 in. long, ultimate blade segms. small, petiole to 3 ft.; peduncle 2–6 in. long, spathe 4½–6 in. long and prominently longitudinally veined, yellow-gray-green, fls. unisexual, spadix 10–16 in. long, the zone of male fls. exceeding spathe, male fls. yellow, on white, clavate stalks ¾ in. long. S. Brazil, Bolivia, Paraguay.

TACINGA Britt. & Rose. *Cactaceae.* One sp., a scrambling cactus of Brazil; sts. slender, cylindrical; lvs. small, early deciduous; glochids easily shed; fls. lateral, floral tube extending well above the ovary, perianth segms. recurved, staminodes present between perianth and stamens, stamens erect, not sensitive, long-exserted; fr. narrow, deeply umbilicate, seeds few, bony, white. Allied to *Opuntia*, but with long-exserted stamens.

For culture see *Cacti.*

funalis Britt. & Rose. Sts. erect, then clambering, to 40 ft. long, slender; spines 2–3, to ⅛ in. long, recurved; fls. 3 in. long including ovary, petals greenish, 1½ in. long.

TACITUS Moran. *Crassulaceae.* One sp., a glabrous, succulent, per. herb of w. Mex.; lvs. in a rosette, withering but persistent; fl. st. axillary, with 1 to a few cymes; fls. long-pedicelled, 5-merous, sepals equal, reflexed, corolla segms. overlapping in bud, spreading from top of short tube, uniformly colored, narrowed to base, with basal outgrowths closing opening, stamens 10, pistils erect but separating, long-styled. Like *Echeveria* but with large open fls.

For culture see *Succulents.*

bellus Moran & Meyrán. Rosettes 1 to several, sessile, compact, 1–3 in. wide, lvs. 25–50, obovate-cuneate, obtuse, mucronate; fls. 1–10, deep pink, 1¼–1½ in. wide. Late spring, early summer.

TACSONIA: *PASSIFLORA.* **T. Van-Volxemii:** *P. antioquiensis.*

TAENIDIA (Torr. & A. Gray) Drude. *Umbelliferae.* One sp., a per. herb of e. N. Amer., sometimes transplanted from the wild.

integerrima (L.) Drude. YELLOW PIMPERNEL. To 3 ft.; lvs. biternately to triternately compound, segms. ovate to lanceolate, entire, to 1 in. long; umbels compound, without involucre or involucels; fls. yellow; fr. elliptic, 3/16 in. long. Que. to Ga., w. to Minn., Kans., and Ark.

TAGETES L. MARIGOLD. *Compositae* (Helenium Tribe). Perhaps 30 spp. of strongly scented ann. or per. herbs, native from Ariz. and New Mex. to Argentina; lvs. usually opp., simple or more often pinnatifid or pinnate, gland-dotted; fl. heads usually radiate, solitary or in cymose clusters, involucre campanulate or cylindrical, involucral bracts in 1 row, united nearly to apex; fls. yellow, orange, or red-brown, ray fls. usually present; achenes elongate, club-shaped, pappus of 3–10 scales, with 1 or 2 of these usually bristlelike.

Marigolds are popular as cut flowers and are of simple cultivation. Propagated by seeds sown where plants are to stand or started early in the house.

erecta L. AFRICAN M., BIG M., AZTEC M. Stout, glabrous ann., erect, to 3 ft.; lvs. pinnate; heads solitary, 2–5 in. across, the long peduncle much-enlarged upwards; involucre campanulate; ray fls. 5–8 in. the wild form, many and often 2-lipped or quilled in cvs., light yellow to orange; pappus of scales united basally, one longer than the rest. Mex., Cent. Amer.; now naturalized in many warm regions.

ficifolia: a listed name; perhaps in error for *filifolia.*

filifolia Lag. IRISH-LACE. Much-branched, nearly glabrous ann., to 1 ft.; lvs. pinnatifid, segms. linear-filiform; heads few-fld., solitary in lf. axils, but numerous, peduncles filiform, ½–1 in. long, involucre fusiform, 5/16 in. long; ray fls. 1–3, inconspicuous, 1/16 in. long, white; pappus of both bristlelike and short, broad scales. Mex., Costa Rica. Grown for its mass of finely cut foliage, useful as an edging in the fl. garden.

lucida Cav. SWEET-SCENTED M., SWEET MACE. Glabrous per., usually cult. as an ann., st. usually simple and unbranched, to 2½ ft.; lvs. sessile, simple, linear to oblong, serrulate; heads ⅜ in. across, many in terminal cymes, short-peduncled, involucre cylindrical, ⅜ in. long; ray fls. mostly 3, yellow, ligules 3/16 in. long; pappus of bristlelike and also shorter, broad scales. Mex., Guatemala.

minuta L. MUSTER-JOHN-HENRY. Glabrous, branched ann., to 3 ft. or more; lvs. pinnate; heads about 3/16 in. across, many in dense cymes, peduncles less than ¼ in. long, involucre cylindrical, ⅜ in. long; ray fls. usually 3, light yellow, ligules about 1/16 in. long; pappus of a few short and 1 or 2 much longer scales. Peru and Brazil to Chile and Argentina; naturalized in e. U.S. and S. Afr. Occasionally cult. for seasoning or for medicinal uses.

patula L. FRENCH M. Bushy, glabrous ann., ½–1½ ft.; lvs. pinnate; heads to 2 in. across, solitary, peduncles long, slightly enlarged upward, involucre campanulate; ray fls. few to many, yellow, orange, red-brown, or parti-colored; pappus of basally united scales, one twice as long as the rest. Mex., Guatemala.

signata: *T. tenuifolia.*

tenuifolia Cav. [*T. signata* Bartl.]. SIGNET M. Slender, glabrous ann., to 2 ft.; lvs. pinnate, lfts. small, narrowly linear-lanceolate; heads 1 in. across, solitary but numerous, peduncles slender, usually 1–2 in. long, involucre cylindric-campanulate; ray fls. few, ½ in. long, yellow; pappus scales all elongate. Mex., Cent. Amer. **"Pumila"** is a group name covering various cvs. of low, dwarf, compact habit, 1 ft. or less.

TAINIA Blume. *Orchidaceae.* Not in general cult. **T. viridifusca:** *Ascotainia viridifusca.*

TAINIOPSIS Schlechter. *Orchidaceae.* One sp., an epiphyte native to India, Burma, Thailand; roots villous, pseudobulbs 2-lvd.; lvs. plicate; infl. lateral, erect, loosely many-fld.; lateral sepals reflexed, all minutely puberulent on exterior, petals filiform, lip S-shaped, movable, column curved, with a large foot, pollinia 8. For structure of fl. see *Orchidaceae.*

For culture see *Orchids.*

barbata (Lindl.) Schlechter [*Eria barbata* (Lindl.) Rchb.f.]. Pseudobulbs to 2 in. long, 2–3-lvd.; lvs. oblong, to 14 in. long, acuminate; infl. axillary, from sheath beneath pseudobulb, racemose or paniculate, to 3 ft. long, rachis dark purple, hairy; fls. yellow, to 1 in. across, sepals and petals with 2–3 brownish-purple stripes, lip yellow with purple stripes. Autumn. India.

TAIWANIA Hayata. *Taxodiaceae.* Perhaps 3 spp. of tall, monoecious, coniferous, evergreen trees, native to temp e. Asia; allied to *Cryptomeria,* but differing in having lvs. of 2 kinds, adult lvs. scalelike, juvenile lvs. awl-shaped, sharp-pointed; female cones subglobose, scales many; seeds 2 to each scale.

Cultivated as an ornamental in mild climates. Propagated by seeds. For culture see *Conifers.*

cryptomerioides Hayata. To 175 ft. or more in native habitats, but mostly 20–50 ft. in cult.; juvenile lvs. ½–¾ in. long, pungent, curved, keeled, adult lvs. triangular, imbricate, to 3/16 in. long; female cones terminal, subglobose, about ½ in. long, scales 12–16, leathery, obovate; seeds with narrow wing about ¼ in. long. Mts., Taiwan. Zone 9.

TALAUMA Juss. *Magnoliaceae.* About 40 spp. of tender, evergreen, large-lvd. trees, native to trop. Amer. and Asia; closely allied and similar to *Magnolia,* but having indehiscent, deciduous carpels.

Propagated by fresh seeds or cuttings.

Hodgsonii Hook.f. & T. Thoms. To 60 ft.; lvs. obovate-oblong, to 20 in. long and 9 in. wide, glabrous, leathery; fls. terminal, to 6 in. across and 4 in. deep, cup-shaped, with spicelike odor, sepals 3, purplish-blue, petals usually 6, ivory-white and fleshy; fr. to 6 in. long. Himalayas.

TALINUM Adans. FAMEFLOWER. *Portulacaceae.* About 50 spp. of ann. or per. herbs, more or less succulent, sometimes woody at base, native mostly to N. Amer., a few in S. Amer., Asia, and Afr.; lvs. basal, alt., or nearly opp., linear, the midribs sometimes persisting and becoming spiny; fls. showy, ephemeral, mostly in erect terminal cymes or panicles, sepals 2, deciduous, petals 5 or more, stamens few to many; fr. a 3-valved caps., seeds many.

Some are useful in borders and rock gardens, and sometimes as tub plants for the foliage.

calycinum Engelm. Per., to 8 in., with thick root; lvs. to 2 in. long; fls. pink, 1 in. across or more. Ark. to Mex.

guadalupense W. Dudl. Compact, succulent shrub, to 2 ft., with a fleshy globose or cylindrical root and thickened, knotted sts.; lvs. ovate-spatulate or spatulate, to 2 in. long, fleshy, blue-green, edged with red; fls. pink, in panicles. Guadalupe Is. (Baja Calif).

Mengesii W. Wolf. Similar to *T. teretifolium,* differing in its somewhat taller habit and in having fls. to 1 in. across, stamens 40 or more, much shorter than style. Tenn., s. to Ga. and Ala.

okanoganense English. Low, cushion-forming per.; lvs. somewhat cylindrical, to ⅜ in. long, fleshy, grayish-green, deciduous; fls. usually solitary, white, saucer-shaped, to ¾ in. across, on short peduncles to 1½ in. long, stamens yellow. Wash. Fls. short-lived, but produced in succession for several weeks. Requires drainage and withstands drought conditions.

paniculatum (Jacq.) Gaertn. [*T. patens* (L.) Willd.]. JEWELS-OF-OPAR, FAMEFLOWER. Per., to 2 ft. or more, with tuberous roots; lvs. elliptic or obovate, to 3 in. long; fls. red to yellowish, in a panicle to 10 in. long. S. U.S., s. to Cent. Amer. A form with white-edged lvs. is a tub or pot plant.

parviflorum Nutt. Per., to 8 in., with fleshy roots; lvs. cylindrical or nearly so, linear, to 2 in. long; fls. pink, about 5/16 in. across. Minn., s. to Tex. and Ariz.

patens: *T. paniculatum.*

rugospermum Holzing. Per., to 10 in., with deep root; lvs. basal, cylindrical, linear, to 2 in. long; fls. pink, ½ in. across. Ind. to Minn. and Wisc.

spinescens Torr. Low per., forming tight cushions as much as 6 in. across, lower sts. covered with small spines; lvs. cylindrical, ½ in. long; fls. rose. Mts., Wash.

teretifolium Pursh. Per., with fleshy root, sts. short, tufted, to 1 ft.; lvs. cylindrical, linear, to 2 in. long; fls. pink, ½ in. across, stamens 20 or fewer, as long as the style or longer. Penn., s. to Ga. and Tex.

triangulare (Jacq.) Willd. Per., to 1½ or 2 ft., stout and fleshy; lvs. obovate or narrower, about 3 in. long; fls. red to whitish or yellowish, in racemes. Trop. Amer. Widely used as an ornamental, especially in collections of succulents. Sometimes eaten as a vegetable.

TAMARICACEAE Link. TAMARISK FAMILY. Dicot.; 4 genera and about 100 spp. of shrubs or trees, native mostly to Medit. region and cent. Asia; lvs. alt., mostly small and scale-

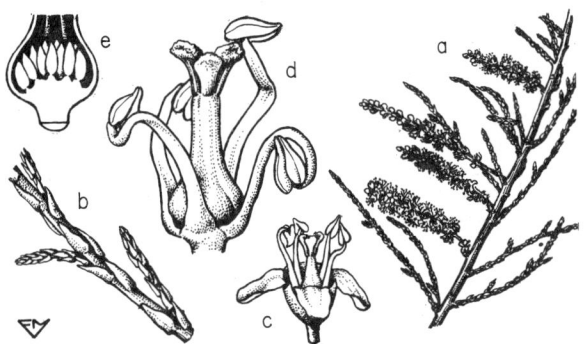

TAMARICACEAE. *Tamarix parviflora:* **a,** flowering branch, × ½; **b,** leafy twig, × 2; **c,** flower, × 4; **d,** flower, perianth removed, × 10; **e,** ovary, vertical section, × 10. (From Bailey, *Manual of Cultivated Plants,* ed. 2.)

like; fls. regular, bisexual, sepals and petals 4–5, stamens 8–10, ovary superior, 1-celled; fr. a caps. *Myricaria* and *Tamarix* are planted as ornamentals.

TAMARINDUS L. *Leguminosae* (subfamily *Caesalpinioideae*). One sp., a trop. evergreen tree, native to Asia; lvs. alt., even-pinnate, lfts. small, many; fls. in terminal racemes, small, sepals 4, petals 3, nearly equal, stamens 3, united; fr. a thick, oblong, indehiscent legume, usually slightly constricted between seeds.

Besides being important as a fruit tree, the tamarind, with a good form and graceful foliage, is one of the best ornamentals for tropical planting, thriving even in semiarid areas when irrigated. Prefers deep soil with abundant moisture. Propagated by seeds planted ½ in. deep in light sandy loam and by shield budding. Young seedlings are subject to damping off and seedling trees are slow to bear.

indica L. TAMARIND, TAMARINDO. To 80 ft., making a handsome tree; lfts. in 10–18 pairs, oblong, to 1 in. long, apically rounded or retuse; racemes few-fld., shorter than lvs.; fls. pale yellow, 1 in. across; fr. cinnamon-brown, 2–6 in. long. Possibly India. Widely naturalized and cult. in the tropics as an ornamental and for the frs., the acid pulp of which is eaten as fresh fr., as an ingredient of chutneys and curries, or made into cooling drinks, or used medicinally. Warmest parts of Zone 10b in Fla.

TAMARIX L. TAMARISK, SALT CEDAR. *Tamaricaceae.* About 54 spp. of deep-rooted shrubs or small trees with green brs., native to Eur., Afr., and Asia, often in dry desert regions; lvs. small, scalelike, with salt-secreting glands; infl. of simple or compound racemes, usually on twigs of the current year's growth or on the woody brs. of the previous year; fls. white, pink, or rose, 4- or 5-merous, stamens 4–5, rarely 8–12, filaments separate or united only basally; fr. a caps., seeds many, with apical tuft of hairs. A few spp. are widely naturalized in N. Amer. The spp. are not easily identified, being usually distinguished by technical characters of the fls., fr., and lvs., not readily seen with the naked eye.

Tamarisks are grown as ornamentals and as windbreaks. They are useful along the coast, since they withstand salt spray. Propagated by seeds, hardwood cuttings, or greenwood cuttings under glass.

aestivalis: a listed name of no botanical standing; plants cult. under this name may be *T. ramosissima.*

africana Poir. Shrub or bushy tree, bark black to dark purple; lvs. sessile; racemes to 2½ in. long, mostly on brs. of previous year; fls. 5-merous. Spring. W. Eur., Canary Is., nw. Afr.

algeriensis: a listed name of no botanical standing; used for *T. gallica.*

amurensis: *T. chinensis.*

anglica: *T. gallica.*

aphylla (L.) Karst. [*T. articulata* Vahl]. ATHEL. Tall shrub or tree, to 30 ft., bark reddish-brown to gray, branchlets grayish, appearing jointed like those of *Casuarina;* lvs. sheathing; racemes to 2½ in. long, on current year's growth; fls. pale pink to whitish, 5-merous, petals falling early. Summer–autumn. N. Afr. and e. Medit. region.

aralensis Bunge. Shrub or tree, bark reddish-brown to brown; lvs. sessile; racemes densely fld., to 2½ in. long; fls. 5-merous. Spring–summer. S.-cent. Russia and Iran.

articulata: *T. aphylla.*

canariensis Willd. Bushy tree, bark reddish-brown; lvs. sessile; racemes densely fld., to 2 in. long; fls. 5-merous. Spring–summer. Medit. region.

caspica: *T. chinensis.*

chinensis Lour. [*T. amurensis* Hort. ex Chow; *T. caspica* Hort. ex Dipp.; *T. elegans* Spach; *T. japonica* Hort. ex Dipp.; *T. juniperina* Bunge; *T. libanotica* Hort. ex C. Koch; *T. plumosa* Hort. ex Carrière]. Tree, bark brown to black; lvs. sessile; racemes on current year's growth, those of spring many and dense, those of summer loose and slender; fls. pinkish, 5-merous, sepals entire, petals ovate to elliptic, persistent. Temp. e. Asia; extensively cult. and naturalized in sw. U.S., where it is often invasive and weedy.

dioica Roxb. ex Roth. Dioecious, small tree, to 9 ft., bark reddish-brown; lvs. sheathing; infl. simple or loosely compound; fls. 5-merous, petals persistent. India, Pakistan, Afghanistan, Iran.

elegans: *T. chinensis.*

gallica L. [*T. algeriensis* Hort.; *T. anglica* Webb]. MANNA PLANT, FRENCH T. Shrub or small tree, to 12 ft., bark reddish-brown to deep purple; lvs. sessile; racemes to 2 in. long, mostly on current year's growth; fls. 5-merous, pinkish, petals falling early. S. Eur. Rarely grown in the U.S., although formerly believed to be the commonly cult. sp.

germanica: *Myricaria germanica.*

hispida Willd. Shrub or small tree, to 15 ft., usually hairy throughout, bark reddish-brown; lvs. sessile, cordate-auriculate at base; fls. 5-merous, in racemes on current year's growth, petals falling early. Summer through autumn. Cent. Asia.

indica Willd. Not known to be cult.; plants offered under this name are probably *T. chinensis* or *T. ramosissima.*

japonica: *T. chinensis.*

juniperina: *T. chinensis.*

libanotica: *T. chinensis.*

odessana: *T. ramosissima.*

parviflora DC. Shrub or small tree, to 9 ft., bark dark brown to deep purple; lvs. sessile; fls. rose-pink, 4-merous, in racemes to 1½ in. long, on brs. of previous year. Spring. Turkey, Greece, Crete, Yugoslavia, Albania; occasionally naturalized in sw. U.S. Plants cult. as *T. tetrandra* are this sp.

pentandra: *T. ramosissima.*

plumosa: *T. chinensis.*

ramosissima Ledeb. [*T. odessana* Steven ex Bunge; *T. pentandra* Pall.]. Shrub or small tree, to 18 ft., bark reddish-brown; lvs. sessile; racemes on current year's growth; fls. 5-merous, pinkish, sepals unevenly toothed, petals obovate, persistent. Spring and summer. E. Eur. to cent. and e. Asia; naturalized and frequently cult. in the U.S., especially in the arid Southwest.

tetrandra Pall. Not cult. in U.S.; cult. plants so named are *T. parviflora.*

TANACETUM L. TANSY. *Compositae* (Anthemis Tribe). About 50 spp. of mostly aromatic, ann. or per. herbs or sometimes subshrubs, native to N. Hemisphere, chiefly of the Old World; lvs. alt., entire to 1–3-pinnatifid; fl. heads solitary and terminal or more commonly in corymbs or heads, radiate or discoid, involucral bracts imbricate in 2–3 rows, usually more or less scarious, receptacle flat to low-conical, naked; disc fls. tubular, bisexual, yellow, ray fls., if present, female, yellow; achenes usually 5-angled or 5-ribbed, often glandular, pappus absent or a short crown. Sometimes considered a subgenus of *Chrysanthemum.*

Tansy is grown in the garden as an ornamental and for medicinal purposes. It thrives in all common situations and in soils that are not too wet. Propagated usually by division of old clumps, also by seeds.

Balsamita: *Chrysanthemum Balsamita.*

camphoratum Less. Stout, villous-tomentose, rhizomatous per., to about 2½ ft.; lvs. 2-pinnatifid, to 10 in. long, expanded and clasping at base; heads to ⅝ in. across, in corymbs, ray fls. few, inconspicuous. Coastal, around San Francisco.

compactum H. M. Hall. Silvery-silky, cespitose per., to 1½ in. high; lvs. pinnately parted, to ¾ in. long; heads solitary, to ¾ in. across; fls. pale yellow. S. Nev.

Douglasii DC. Stout, more or less villous, rhizomatous per., to 2 ft., sts. sometimes reddish; lvs. 2–3-pinnatifid, basal lvs. to 8 in. long, st. lvs. shorter, expanded and clasping at base; heads to ⅝ in. across, in corymbs, ray fls. usually conspicuous. Coastal, n. Calif.

Herderi Regel & Schmalh. Gray-hairy, cespitose per., to 1 ft.; lvs. 2–3-pinnatifid; heads hemispherical, in corymbs; fls. all tubular, bright yellow. Turkestan.

macrophyllum: *Chrysanthemum macrophyllum.*

vulgare L. [*Chrysanthemum vulgare* (L.) Bernh.]. COMMON TANSY, GOLDEN-BUTTONS. Coarse, aromatic, subglabrous, rhizomatous per., to 3 ft.; lvs. pinnate, to 4¾ in. long, lfts. toothed or incised, punctate; heads many, to ⁵/₁₆ in. across, in corymbs; fls. all tubular, golden-yellow; pappus minute, a 5-lobed crown. Eur., Asia; widely naturalized in N. Amer. Dried lvs. used medicinally. Var. **crispum** DC. Foliage more luxuriant, lf. divisions larger and more finely cut.

TANAKAEA Franch. & Sav. *Saxifragaceae.* One sp., an evergreen, dioecious stoloniferous, per. herb of e. Asia; lvs. basal, long-petioled; scape usually leafless, infl. paniculate; fls. small, greenish-white, calyx tube short, shallow, united basally to ovary, calyx lobes usually 5, petals 0, stamens 10, ovary nearly superior, styles short; fr. a dehiscent caps.

radicans Franch. & Sav. Scapes to 12 in.; lf. blades thickish, almost fleshy, oblong to ovate-lanceolate, to 3 in. long, petioles of about the same length, coarsely hairy; infl. densely fld.; caps. to ⅛ in. long. China and Japan.

TANK FARMING: see *Hydroponics.*

TARAKTOGENOS: *HYDNOCARPUS.*

TARAXACUM Wiggers. DANDELION, BLOWBALLS. *Compositae* (Cichorium Tribe). Between 50 and 60 spp. (although hundreds of forms, mostly apomictic, have been described as spp.) of scapose, bien. or per. herbs with milky sap, mostly native to the N. Hemisphere; lvs. in a basal rosette, entire to pinnatifid and runcinate; scapes hollow, fl. heads solitary, involucral bracts in 2 rows, the inner erect, the outer shorter, often reflexed, receptacle flat, pitted, naked; fls. all ligulate, bisexual, yellow or rarely white; achenes cylindrical or 4–5-angled, ribbed, beakless or with a short beak, pappus persistent, of several rows of simple, white hairs.

Occasionally grown as ornamentals. One species is used for salad greens or as a pot herb, and another as a source of rubber.

albidum Dahlst. Per.; lvs. lanceolate to oblanceolate, to 1 ft. long, pinnatifid; heads to 1¾ in. across, on scapes to 1 ft. high, involucral bracts bright to pale green; fls. usually white; achenes pale yellow-brown. Japan, Korea.

alpicola Kitam. Per.; lvs. tongue-shaped, to 1 ft. long, usually incised; heads to 1½ in. across, on scapes to 15 in. high, involucral bracts dark green; fls. orange-yellow; achenes pale yellow-brown. Japan.

alpinum (Hoppe) Hegetschw. Per.; lvs. oblanceolate to oblong-obovate, sinuate-dentate to runcinate-pinnatifid; heads to 1¼ in. across, on scapes to 8 in. high, outer involucral bracts often dark green, recurved; fls. golden-yellow. Pyrenees, Alps, Apennines.

Kok-saghyz Rodin. RUSSIAN D. Similar to *T. officinale*, differing in lvs. not so deeply lobed, often nearly entire, heads smaller, involucral bracts not reflexed and with well-developed hornlike appendages. Turkestan. Has been cult. in the U.S.S.R. and elsewhere for rubber, obtained from the latex. Sometimes seen in collections of economic plants.

Leontodon: *T. officinale.*

officinale Wiggers [*T. Leontodon* Gueldenst.; *Leontodon Taraxacum* L.]. COMMON D. Per.; lvs. oblong, spatulate, or oblanceolate, to 1 ft. long, nearly entire to sinuate-pinnatifid, the terminal segm. largest; heads to 2¼ in. across, on scapes to 1½ ft. high, outer involucral bracts reflexed; fls. deep yellow; achenes beaked, gray-brown to olive-brown. Eur. and Asia; a cosmopolitan weed. Sometimes grown for greens. See *Dandelion.*

TARENNA Gaertn. [*Webera* Schreb.]. *Rubiaceae.* About 370 spp. of shrubs or small trees, native to Madagascar, trop. Afr., Asia, and Australia; lvs. opp.; fls. in terminal panicles or compact cymes, 5-merous, corolla cylindrical or funnelform; fr. a berry, seeds 2.

zeylanica Gaertn. [*Webera corymbosa* Willd.]. Small tree or shrub, buds exuding waxy secretion; lvs. oblong-lanceolate, to 6 in. long, glossy above, lateral veins prominent beneath with small pits in their axils; fls. white, in panicles, faintly odorous, corolla tube about ⁵/₁₆ in. long, lobes somewhat longer, reflexed, exposing stamens and style. India, Ceylon, Malay Arch.

TARO. *Colocasia esculenta* or taro is a large, perennial, herbaceous aroid, long cultivated in the Old World tropics

and subtropics (especially in eastern Asia and the Pacific Islands) as an important food plant. Once an acrid principle (calcium oxalate) is destroyed by heat, all parts of the plant may be eaten, but the tuberous roots are the main food source. From the latter is made poi, the fermented, pastelike but palatable and very digestible food of the native Hawaiians. Many cultivars exist but they are generally of two kinds, wetland (wet) taros and upland (dry) taros. Wetland taro is the source of poi; upland taro is not suitable for making poi, but its side tubers or corms are used in the same ways as the tubers of the white potato, *Solanum tuberosum.* Upland taros are the more widely grown in the world, being common food plants in China, Japan, the West Indies, and occasionally in the continental United States (Zone 10), where it is called by the West Indian name dasheen.

Propagation is simple, a few inches of the top of a corm serving as "seed." Wetland taro is planted in plots flooded with a few inches of water; it requires eight to 12 months or more to mature. Upland taro (dasheen) requires only moist, rich soil, in which it is hilled up like potatoes; mature corms are produced in six to eight months. Dasheen corms must be dug soon after the leaves start to yellow; if left longer, corms start to sprout, causing deterioration in their flavor and consistency.

The dasheen is sometimes grown as an ornamental foliage plant, and the top of a corm, sliced off and placed in a shallow dish of water, produces an attractive, if temporary, display of small leaves for the sunny window sill indoors.

TARRIETA: *HERITIERA.* **T. argyrodendron:** *H. trifoliolata.*

TAVARESIA Welw. *Asclepiadaceae.* Three or 4 spp. of leafless, *Stapelia*-like plants, native to s. Afr.; sts. strongly angled, tubercled, each tubercle bearing 3 bristles; fls. funnelform, large, borne mostly at base of young sts.

For culture see *Succulents.*

grandiflora (K. Schum.) A. Berger. Sts. clustered, to 8 or sometimes 12 in., 14-angled, the central bristle on each tubercle longer than the lateral ones; corolla yellowish-green and covered with longitudinal purple-red lines outside, yellow and spotted maroon inside, the tube densely papillate, to 4 in. long or more, 1½ in. across, the lobes 1¼ in. long. S.-W. Afr.

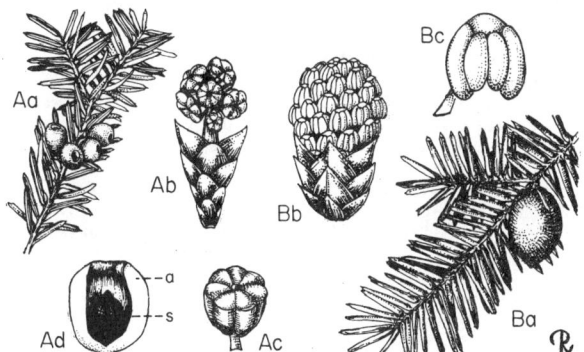

TAXACEAE. **A,** *Taxus cuspidata:* **Aa,** branch bearing seeds, × ¼; **Ab,** male cone, × 4; **Ac,** microsporophyll from male cone, × 8; **Ad,** aril (a), vertical section to show seed (s), × 1. **B,** *Torreya taxifolia:* **Ba,** branch bearing seed, × ¼; **Bb,** male cone, × 8; **Bc,** microsporophyll from male cone, × 16. (From Bailey, *Manual of Cultivated Plants,* ed. 2.)

TAXACEAE S. F. Gray. YEW FAMILY. Gymnosperms; 5 genera of dioecious or sometimes monoecious, evergreen trees and shrubs, native mostly to the N. Hemisphere but extending s. to New Caledonia; lvs. needlelike, linear, or scalelike, often appearing to be 2-ranked; male cones catkinlike, axillary, solitary or in spikes, scales peltate or apically thickened; female reproductive structures solitary or paired in axils, consisting of a single, erect ovule terminal on short scaly stalks; seed with a hard coat, partly or completely surrounded by a fleshy aril. *Taxus* and *Torreya* are cult.

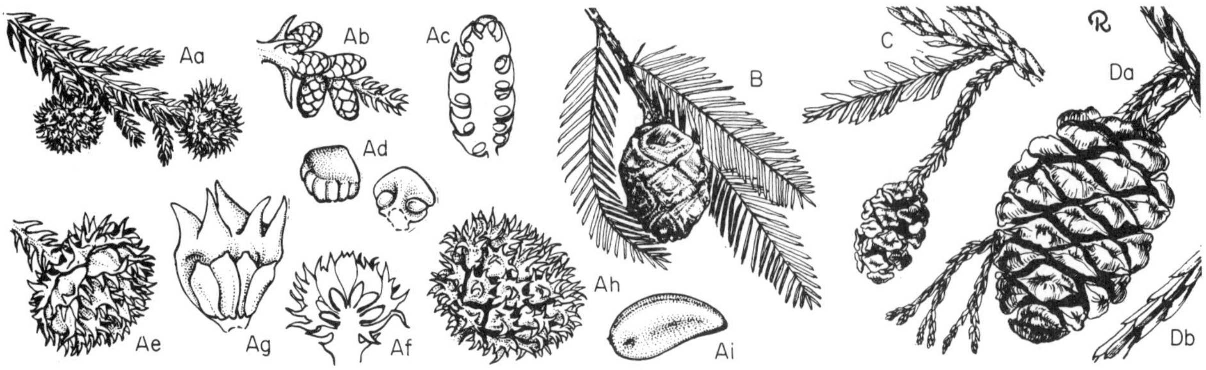

TAXODIACEAE. **A,** *Cryptomeria japonica:* **Aa,** coning branch, × ½; **Ab,** male cones, × 1; **Ac,** male cone, vertical section, × 2; **Ad,** scale from male cone, two views, × 4; **Ae,** young female cone, × 1; **Af,** young female cone, vertical section, × 1; **Ag,** scale from female cone, × 3; **Ah,** mature cone, × ¾; **Ai,** seed, × 3. **B,** *Taxodium distichum* var. *distichum:* coning branch, × ½. **C,** *Sequoia sempervirens:* coning branch, × ½. **D,** *Sequoiadendron giganteum:* **Da,** coning branch, × ½; **Db,** part of leafy twig, × 1. (B, C, Da, Db from Bailey, *Manual of Cultivated Plants,* ed. 2.)

TAXODIACEAE Warm. TAXODIUM FAMILY. Gymnosperms; 10 genera of monoecious, resinous, coniferous, evergreen or deciduous trees of temp. N. Amer., e. Asia, and Tasmania; lvs. linear, needlelike, or awl-shaped, arranged in spirals, or sometimes apparently 2-ranked, solitary, not clustered; cones woody, globose or subglobose, scales spirally arranged, more or less fused with the bracts; seeds 2–9 on each scale, winged or wingless. The Taxodiaceae have been treated as a subfamily of the Pinaceae, but differ in having cone scales lacking separate bracts and bearing 2–6 seeds. The family includes many valuable timber trees and ornamentals. The cult. genera are: *Athrotaxis, Cryptomeria, Cunninghamia, Glyptostrobus, Metasequoia, Sciadopitys, Sequoia, Sequoiadendron, Taiwania,* and *Taxodium.*

TAXODIUM L. Rich. CYPRESS. *Taxodiaceae.* Two spp. of coniferous, monoecious trees of river and lake margins in e. N. Amer. and highland Mex.; lvs. short, appearing 2-ranked, linear, deciduous or evergreen, on deciduous brs.; male cones many, very small, in catkinlike clusters at ends of brs., female cones globose, scales many, thick, shield-shaped; seeds irregularly 3-angled, 2 to each scale.

The species are important for their strong durable timber, but are also planted as ornamentals. For culture see *Conifers.*

ascendens: *T. distichum* var. *nutans.*

distichum (L.) L. Rich. Trees of swamps and streamsides, occasionally to 150 ft., with buttressed trunks, and in wet places, with aerating projections or "knees" growing up from the roots, usually extending above the water; lvs. deciduous, of 2 types, one spirally arranged, awl-shaped, to ½ in. long, incurved or appressed, the other flat, linear, to ¾ in. long, spreading and 2-ranked, both types sometimes on the same tree; cones to 1 in. across. Zone 5, but often remains small in northern states; suited to pond or streamside planting. Wood valuable for construction around water. Var. **distichum.** BALD CYPRESS. The typical var.; large tree; lvs. flat, spreading, 2-ranked, on horizontal branchlets. Del. to Fla., w. to Ark. and Tex. Several cvs. have been described, but only **'Pendens'** [var. *pendulum* Horsey], with drooping branchlets and large cones is much offered. Var. **nutans** (Ait.) Sweet [*T. ascendens* Brongn.]. POND CYPRESS. Smaller; lvs. awl-shaped, usually appressed and spirally arranged, on ascending or sometimes pendulous branchlets. Va. to Fla. and Ala.

mexicanum: *T. mucronatum.*

mucronatum Ten. [*T. mexicanum* Carrière]. MONTEZUMA CYPRESS. Differs from *T. distichum* in having lvs. persistent, shorter, and cones larger. Cent. plateau, Mex. Zone 8, on Pacific Coast; reported to be deciduous in colder climates.

TAXUS L. YEW. *Taxaceae.* Eight spp. of dioecious, evergreen trees and shrubs with alt. branchlets, native to the N. Hemisphere; lvs. spirally arranged or 2-ranked or nearly so, linear, dark green above, paler or yellowish beneath; microsporophylls stamenlike, in small globose heads solitary in lf. axils, female reproductive structures consisting of a single terminal ovule with several bracts at base; seed bony, nearly enclosed by a fleshy, scarlet aril.

Foliage poisonous if eaten. For culture see *Conifers.*

baccata L. ENGLISH Y. Densely branched tree, to 60 ft. or more; winter buds obtuse, the scales persistent at base of brs.; lvs. to 1¼ in. long, gradually acuminate, glossy dark green above, pale beneath; aril nearly globose, to ½ in. in diam. Eur., N. Afr., W. Asia. Zone 7, but some cvs. hardier than the typical form. Valuable for wood carving and as a source of bows. There are many named cvs., including: **'Adpressa'** [cv. 'Tardiva'], shrub or small tree, lvs. obtusely mucronulate, to ½ in. long, with color or habit forms including **'Adpressa Aurea'** and **'Adpressa Erecta'; 'Argentea'**: 'Variegata'; **'Aurea'**, GOLDEN Y., compact, lvs. golden-yellow changing to green; **'Brevifolia'**, small dense shrub, lvs. to ½ in. long, not to be confused with *T. brevifolia;* **'Cavendishii'**, low, spreading, with curved, pendulous branchlet tips; **'Chestnutensis'**, more broadly spreading than cv. 'Stricta', lvs. bluish-green; **'Columnaris'**, dense, columnar; **'Compacta'**, dwarf, compact, conical, lvs. curved, about ½ in. long; **'Decora'**, dwarf, dense, prostrate; **'Dovastoniana'**, brs. spreading, branchlets pendulous; **'Dovastonii Aurea'** [cv. 'Dovastonii Aureo-variegata'], branchlets pendulous, lvs. variegated yellow; **'Elegantissima'**, compact, young lvs. striped pale yellow; **'Erecta'** [cv. 'Pyramidalis'], upright, bushy; **'Erecta Aurea'**, golden form of 'Erecta'; **'Ericoides'**, dwarf, low, spreading, lvs. small, bronze in winter; **'Expansa'**, procumbent, lvs. to 1⅛ in. long; **'Fastigiata'**: 'Stricta'; **'Fructu Luteo'**: 'Lutea'; **'Glauca'**, lvs. bluish-green beneath; **'Gracilis Pendula'**: 'Pendula'; **'Hibernica'**: 'Stricta'; **'Horizontalis'**, brs. horizontal in several series, wide-spreading, without leader; **'Imperialis'**, upright, dense; **'Jacksonii'**, brs. spreading, pendulous at tips; **'Lutea'** [cv. 'Fructu Luteo'], fr. yellow; **'Nana'**, dwarf, dense; **'Nidpathensis'**, vigorous, much-branched tree; **'Pendula'** [cv. 'Gracilis Pendula'], spreading, brs. slender, pendulous; **'Procumbens'**, prostrate, much-branched, material so listed is often cv. 'Expansa'; **'Prostrata'**, dwarf, spreading, lvs. dark green above; **'Pygmaea'**, very dwarf, forming a small, ovoid shrub; **'Pyramidalis'**: 'Erecta'; **'Repandens'**, nearly prostrate, lvs. bluish-green; **'Semperaurea'**, lvs. golden-yellow with color persisting through the second year; **'Standishii'**, columnar, slow-growing, lvs. yellow; **'Stricta'** [cvs. 'Fastigiata' and 'Hibernica'] IRISH Y., columnar, lvs. very dark green, with color variations including **'Stricta Aurea'** and **'Stricta Variegata'; 'Tardiva'**: 'Adpressa'; **'Variegata'** [cv. 'Argentea'], lvs. variegated with white or whitish; **'Washingtonii'**, wide-spreading, lvs. golden-yellow.

×**brevicata:** a listed name of no botanical standing; reported to be a garden hybrid of *T. brevifolia* × *T. cuspidata.*

brevifolia Nutt. WESTERN Y. Tree, 15–45 ft. or more, brs. somewhat pendent; lvs. more or less in the same plane, to 1 in. long, abruptly narrowed to a bristly point, dark yellowish-green; aril ovoid, to ½ in. long. Mont. to B.C. and Calif. Zone 6. Most material offered as *T. brevifolia* is *T. baccata* cv. 'Adpressa' or *T. cuspidata* cv. 'Nana'. Should not be confused with *T. baccata* cv. 'Brevifolia'. Cvs. offered are: **'Erecta'**, columnar; **'Nana'**, dwarf; **'Nuttallii'**, brs. drooping.

canadensis Marsh. GROUND HEMLOCK, AMERICAN Y. Straggling shrub, sometimes 6 ft. high; lvs. 1 in. long, abruptly pointed, dark yellowish-green above; aril nearly globose, to ½ in. in diam. Nfld. to Va. and Iowa. Zone 3. Cvs. include: **'Aurea'**, lvs. slightly variegated yellow; **'Compacta'**, more densely branched; **'Fastigiata'** and **'Stricta'**, dwarf, brs. erect.

chinensis (Pilg.) Rehd. CHINESE Y. Shrub or tree, to 50 ft., winter buds obtuse, the scales deciduous; lvs. distinctly 2-ranked to 1¾ in. long, curved, abruptly pointed, glossy green above, grayish-green beneath; fr. to about ⅝ in. long. China. Zone 6. Allied to *T. baccata* and differing in having winter bud scales deciduous and lvs. abruptly pointed.

cuspidata Siebold & Zucc. [*T. Sieboldii* Hort.]. JAPANESE Y. Shrub or tree to 50 ft., brs. spreading or upright; winter buds ovoid-oblong; lvs. 2-ranked with the ranks often upright and forming a V-shaped trough, to 1 in. long, abruptly mucronate, dull green above, with 2 yellowish bands beneath; aril ellipsoid, about ½ in. long. Japan, Korea, Manchuria. Zone 5. Wood used for furniture, turnery, and various other articles. Cvs. are many and some listed below may not be distinct from others: **'Andersonii'**, reported to have larger lvs. than typical form, but most material offered under this name is *T.* × *media* cv. 'Andersonii'; **'Aurea'**, lvs. slightly variegated yellow; **'Aurescens'**, low, new lvs. deep yellow, requiring sheltered place; **'Brevifolia'**: 'Nana'; **'Brownii'**: *T.* × *media* cv. 'Brownii'; **'Buffumii'**, compact, spreading; **'Bulkii'**, erect, lvs. dark green; **'Capitata'**, the typical form of *T. cuspidata;* **'Columnaris'**, erect, cylindrical; **'Compacta'**: 'Nana'; **'Densa'**, low, dense bush; **'Densiformis'**, dense, compact, spreading to 6 ft. or more; **'Depressa'**, very prostrate; **'Erecta'**, erect, more or less columnar; **'Expansa'**, low, broadly spreading; **'Fastigiata'**, dwarf, columnar, lvs. yellowish; **'Fieldsii'**, compact, low, spreading, lvs. small; **'Hicksii'**: *T.* × *media* cv. 'Hicksii'; **'Hillii'**, pyramidal, lvs. dark green; **'Hoytii'**, compact, upright-spreading, lvs. dense, dark green; **'Intermedia'**, dense, subglobose, moderately slow-growing; **'Minima'**, dwarf, to 1½ ft.; **'Nana'** [cvs. 'Brevifolia' and 'Compacta'], dense, ascending, to 6 ft.; **'Nigra'**, lvs. very dark green; **'Ovata'** lvs. wider than usual; **'Prostrata'**, wide-spreading, low; **'Pyramidalis'**, erect, columnar; **'Robusta'**: *T.* × *media* cv. 'Robusta'; **'Stovekenii'**, broadly columnar, strong-growing; **'Tardiva'**: *T. baccata* cv. 'Adpressa'; **'Thayerae'**, wide-spreading, brs. horizontal or slightly ascending, plumose; **'Vermueleri'**, upright, vase-shaped, of slow growth; **'Visseri'**, dense, spreading, slow-growing; **'Wilsonii'**, compact, vase-shaped, lvs. dark green.

floridana Nutt. ex Chapm. FLORIDA Y. Shrub or tree, to 25 ft., brs. many, stout, spreading; lvs. very narrow, dark green, curved, to 1 in. long, ¹⁄₁₆ in. wide. Fla.

hibernica: a listed name of no botanical standing for *T. baccata* cv. 'Stricta'.

×**Hunnewelliana** Rehd.: *T. canadensis* × *T. cuspidata.* Resembling *T. cuspidata,* but more slender and becoming reddish in winter.

intermedia: a listed name of no botanical standing for *T. cuspidata* cv. 'Intermedia'; it may also be used in error for *T.* × *media.*

×**media** Rehd.: *T. baccata* × *T. cuspidata.* Similar to *T. cuspidata,* but with mature brs. olive-green, lvs. more distinctly 2-ranked and spreading. Of garden origin in the U.S. Zone 5. An increasing number of cvs. are being introd. under this name. Some of these may belong to *T. cuspidata* and in other instances the same name may be applied to cvs. of both *T. cuspidata* and *T.* × *media.* Cvs. listed under *T.* × *media* include: **'Amherstii'**, spreading; **'Andersonii'**, erect, free-branching; **'Brevifolia'**: *T. cuspidata* cv. 'Nana'; **'Brevimedia'**, reported to be very hardy, spreading-upright, lvs. dark green; **'Brownii'**, erect, conical, lvs. short, dense; **'Cliftonii'**, erect, growth dense, irregular, lvs. dark green; **'Columnaris'**, broadly columnar, lvs. dark green; **'Densiformis'**, dense, spreading, lvs. dark green, similar to *T. cuspidata* cv. 'Nana', but faster growing, may be confused with *T. cuspidata* cv. 'Densiformis'; **'Devermannii'**, dense, compact, to 10 ft., lvs. waxy, dark green; **'Dovastonii'**, a listed name, perhaps for *T. baccata* cv. 'Dovastoniana'; **'Erecta'**, tall, more or less columnar; **'Fieldsii'**: *T. cuspidata* cv.; **'Grandifolia'**, compact, upright, lvs. large, dark green; **'Halloriana'**, erect, conical, perhaps not distinct from cv. 'Brownii'; **'Hatfieldii'**, conical, brs. ascending, lvs. wide-spreading; **'Heasleyi'**, dwarf; **'Helleri'**, erect, to 15 ft., rapid-growing, brs. ascending, lvs. bright green, **'Henryi'**, dense, spreading, with ascending brs., similar to cv. 'Densiformis'; **'Hicksii'**, columnar, brs. upright, lvs. radially spreading; **'Kelseyi'**, upright dense, reported to fr. heavily; **'Kohlii'**, upright, globose, lvs. very dark green; **'Microphylla'**, a name variously applied to dwarf or upright forms with small lvs., may also be a form of *T. baccata;* **'Moonii'**, more or less upright, with dense, ascending brs.; **'Nana-grand'**, globose, compact; **'Ovata'**, broad, upright, lvs. large, dark green, reported to fr. heavily; **'Pilaris'**, narrow, columnar, lvs. medium green; **'Pyramidalis'**, columnar, loosely branched, to 15 ft.; **'Repandens'**: *T. baccata* cv.; **'Robusta'**, columnar, compact, to 20 ft.; **'Sentinalis'**, narrow-columnar, with few lateral brs. and open foliage; **'Stovekenii'**: *T. cuspidata* cv.; **'Stricta'**, erect, compact, lvs. medium green; **'Tauntonii'**, globose, dense; **'Thayerae'**: *T. cuspidata* cv.; **'Vermuelenii'**: *T. cuspidata* cv.; **'Viridis'**, narrow-columnar, dense, lvs. bright green, twisted; **'Wardii'**, erect, compact, to 8 ft., lvs. dark green; **'Wellesleyana'**, broadly erect; **'Wymanii'**, broad, vase-shaped, densely branched to the center.

Sieboldii: a listed name of no botanical standing for *T. cuspidata.*

Standishii: a listed name of no botanical standing for *T. baccata* cv.

Tauntonii: a listed name of no botanical standing for *T. media* cv.

TECOMA Juss. [*Stenolobium* D. Don]. TRUMPET BUSH, YELLOWBELLS. *Bignoniaceae.* About 16 spp. of shrubs or small trees, native from s. Fla. and Mex. to Argentina; lvs. opp., simple or mostly odd-pinnate; fls. yellow to orange, in racemes or panicles, calyx 5-lobed, corolla campanulate-funnelform or tubular-funnelform, stamens 4; fr. a smooth, linear caps.

Tecomas are grown in southern U.S. and will stand only a few degrees of frost. Propagated by seeds and by cuttings of green wood under glass.

alata DC. [*T. Smithii* W. Wats.; *Stenolobium alatum* (DC.) T. Sprague]. Erect shrub; lfts. 11–17, oblong, to 2 in. long, serrate; fls. yellow, tinged orange, to 2 in. long, tubular-funnelform, gradually narrowed to base. Supposedly a hybrid between *T. stans* var. *velutina (T. mollis)* and *Tecomaria capensis.*

argentea: *Tabebuia argentea.*

australis: *Pandorea pandorana.*

Brycei: *Podranea Brycei.*

capensis: *Tecomaria capensis.*

castanifolia (D. Don) Melchior [*T. Gaudichaudii* DC.; *Tabebuia Gaudichaudii* Hort.]. Shrub or small tree; lvs. simple, elliptic-oblong, to 6 in. long, acuminate, serrate; fls. in terminal panicles, yellow, to 2 in. long; fr. to 5 in. long. Ecuador.

chinensis: *Campsis grandiflora.*

chrysotricha: *Tabebuia chrysotricha.*

Garrocha Hieron. [*Stenolobium Garrocha* (Hieron.) R. E. Fries]. Shrub, to 5 ft. or more; lfts. 7–11, oblong-ovate, to 2 in. long, acuminate, serrate, glabrous; fls. 2 in. long, and 1 in. across, corolla yellow or salmon, tube scarlet; fr. to 4 in. long. Argentina.

Gaudichaudii: *T. castanifolia.*

grandiflora: *Campsis grandiflora.*

heptaphylla: *Tabebuia heptaphylla.*

incisum: *T. stans* var. *angustata.*

jasminoides: *Pandorea jasminoides.*

longiflora: *Tabebuia Vellosoi.*

Mackenii: *Podranea Ricasoliana.*

mollis: *T. stans* var. *velutina.*

nyassae: *Tecomaria nyassae.*

radicans: *Campsis radicans.*

Reginae-Sabae: *Podranea Brycei.*

Ricasoliana: *Podranea Ricasoliana.*

shirensis: *Tecomaria shirensis.*

Smithii: *T. alata.*

stans (L.) HBK [*Bignonia stans* L.; *Stenolobium stans* (L.) Seem.]. YELLOWBELLS, YELLOW ELDER, YELLOW BIGNONIA. Shrub or small tree, to 20 ft.; lfts. 5–13, lanceolate to oblong-ovate, to 4 in. long, serrate; fls. bright yellow, to 2 in. long, corolla funnelform-campanulate, abruptly contracted toward base; fr. to 8 in. long. Fla. and Mex., s. to S. Amer. Var. *angustata* Rehd. [*T. incisum* (Rose & Standl. ex Woot. & Standl.) I. M. Johnst.; *Stenolobium incisum* Rose & Standl. ex Woot. & Standl.]. Lfts. narrower, incised-toothed. Var. **velutina** DC. [*T. mollis* HBK]. Lfts. pubescent beneath.

velutina: *T. stans* var.

TECOMARIA Spach. *Bignoniaceae.* Three spp. of erect or scandent shrubs, native to trop. and s. Afr. and introd. throughout the tropics; lvs. opp. or in 3's, odd-pinnate; fls. yellow, orange, or scarlet, in terminal racemes, calyx 5-lobed, corolla funnelform, curved, 2-lipped, stamens 4, exserted; fr. an oblong-linear caps.

capensis (Thunb.) Spach [*Bignonia capensis* Thunb.; *Tecoma capensis* (Thunb.) Lindl.]. CAPE HONEYSUCKLE. Rambling shrub, to 6 ft. or more; lvs. to 6 in. long, lfts. 5–9, elliptic to ovate, orbicular, or rhomboidal, to 2 in. long, serrate; fls. orange-red to scarlet, 2 in. long, calyx ⁵⁄₁₆ in. long; fr. to 2 in. long. S. Afr. Cv. **'Aurea'**. YELLOW CAPE HONEYSUCKLE. Fls. yellow. Cv. **'Lutea'**: perhaps 'Aurea'. Grown in the South as a hedge plant and sometimes under glass; prop. by seeds and cuttings under glass.

nyassae (D. Oliver) K. Schum. [*Tecoma nyassae* D. Oliver]. Shrub; lvs. to 5 in. long, lfts. 5–7, elliptic, to 1⅝ in. long, obtuse, crenate-serrate; fls. to 1½ in. long, calyx to ½ in. long, corolla orange, striped red. Trop. Afr.

shirensis (Bak.) K. Schum. [*Tecoma shirensis* Bak.]. Shrub, to 10 ft.; lvs. to 9 in. long, lfts. 9–13, ovate, to 3 in. long, serrate; fls. orange, to 1½ in. long, calyx ½ in. long; fr. to 4½ in. long. Trop. Afr.

TECOMELLA Seem. *Bignoniaceae.* One sp., a shrub or small tree, native from Arabia to w. India; lvs. usually opp., simple; fls. in terminal corymbose racemes, calyx nearly equally 5-toothed, corolla tubular-campanulate and ventricose, stamens 4, exserted; fr. a linear-oblong caps.

Planted in southern Fla.; propagated by seeds and cuttings.

undulata (Sm.) Seem. Large shrub or tree, brs. drooping, gray; lvs. narrowly oblong, to 5 in. long, nearly or quite obtuse, entire, wavy, glaucous; fls. orange-yellow, to 2½ in. long; fr. to 8 in. long.

TECOPHILAEA Bertero ex Colla. *Tecophilaeaceae.* Two spp. of small tender herbs with fibrous-coated corms, native to Andes of Chile; lvs. linear-lanceolate, few, enclosed in scarious sheath; scape arising from sheath at base of lvs.; fls. usually solitary, blue, perianth regular, campanulate, with a short tube, stamens 3, staminodes 3, ovary half-inferior, 3-celled; fr. a conical caps.

Propagated by seeds and offsets.

cyanocrocus Leyb. CHILEAN CROCUS. To 6 in.; lvs. 2–3, somewhat undulate, to 5 in. long, bright green, glabrous; pedicels about ¾ in. long, often weakly arching; perianth deep blue, veined or suffused with white in throat, perianth segms. to 1½ in. long, lateral ones sometimes white-margined. Zone 8. Soil should be moist during flowering in early spring, but dry throughout remainder of season.

TECOPHILAEACEAE Leyb. TECOPHILAEA FAMILY. Monocot.; 6 genera and 22 spp. of herbs with fibrous-tunicate corms or thick tubers, native to Calif., w. S. Amer., cent. and s. Afr.; lvs. parallel-veined, basal or on lower part of st., linear to ovate-orbicular; fls. bisexual, regular, solitary or in a racemose or paniculate infl., perianth tube short or none, perianth segms. 6, stamens 6, fertile, or 3 fertile and 3 staminodes, ovary half-inferior, 3-celled, ovules many; fr. a loculicidal caps., seeds many. *Cyanella* and *Tecophilaea* are cult.

TECTARIA Cav. *Polypodiaceae.* Some 200 spp. of often large, coarse, terrestrial ferns of the New and Old World tropics; rhizomes stout, short-creeping to erect, with many thin, entire scales; petioles clustered, lvs. wide at base, 1–3-pinnate, coarsely divided, pinnules never spinulose or spine-tipped, veins irregularly netted, often with separate included veinlet; sori round, indusia absent, or if present, round-peltate, or reniform and fastened at sinus.

Grown under glass. For culture see *Ferns.*

cicutaria (L.) E. Copel. BUTTON FERN. Lvs. to about 2½ ft. long, 1½ ft. wide, triangular, 2-pinnate-pinnatifid at base, with buds on rachis, upper ⅔ or more with pinnae pinnatifid, with the lobes coarsely dentate-crenate, lower ⅓ with sessile or stalked, lobed pinnules; indusia round-reniform. S. Amer.

heracleifolia (Willd.) Underw. HALBERD FERN. Lvs. to about 3 ft. long, triangular-ovate, 3–5(–7)-pinnate-pinnatifid, pinnae triangular-ovate to oblong-lanceolate, to 1 ft. long, terminal pinna symmetrical, lateral pinnae more or less curved, deeply lobed, or margin wavy-crenate to lobed; indusia orbicular. W. Indies, Fla., s.-cent. Tex., and Mex. to Costa Rica and Venezuela.

TECTONA L.f. *Verbenaceae.* Four spp. of tall, deciduous trees, native in se. Asia, Philippine Is., and Malay Arch.; lvs. opp. or whorled, entire; fls. white or blue, in cymes arranged in panicles, calyx 5–7-lobed, corolla salverform, 5–7-lobed, stamens 5 or 6; fr. a weakly 4-lobed drupe.

grandis L.f. TEAK. To 150 ft., brs. tomentose; lvs. drooping, ovate or broadly elliptic, to 1 ft. long or more, tomentose beneath; fr. globose, 1 in. across. India, Burma, Malay Pen. and Arch. Furnishes teak-wood of commerce. Sometimes planted far south and in the tropics for timber or as an ornamental; tends to naturalize in favorable climates. Zone 10.

TELANTHERA: *ALTERNANTHERA.*

TELEKIA Baumg. *Compositae* (Inula Tribe). Two spp. of per. herbs, native from cent. Eur. to Caucasus and s. Russia; lvs. alt.; fl. heads radiate, solitary, involucral bracts imbricate in 3–4 rows, receptacle flat to convex, scaly; disc fls. bisexual,

anthers tailed, ray fls. female, fertile; disc achenes many-ribbed, ray achenes slightly 3-angled, pappus a short crown.

Of easy culture in the border, and mostly hardy north. Propagated by division; also by seeds, and sometimes blooming the first year.

speciosa (Schreb.) Baumg. [*Buphthalmum speciosum* Schreb.]. Strongly scented, robust per., to 6 ft.; lvs. alt., glabrous above, hairy beneath, lower lvs. triangular-cordate, to 10 in. long, doubly-serrate, petioled, upper lvs. ovate, serrate, sessile; heads to 3¼ in. across; disc fls. yellow, ray fls. filiform, orange-yellow. Se. Eur. to Asia Minor, Caucasus, and s. Russia.

TELEPHIUM L. *Caryophyllaceae.* Six spp. of woody-based per. herbs, chiefly in the Medit. region, 1 sp. in Madagascar; herbage glabrous and glaucous; lvs. alt., stipules scarious; fls. white, in capitate-corymbose cymes, sepals 5, white-margined, petals 5, opp. sepals, ovary 3–4-celled toward base, styles 3; fr. a 3-angled caps., dehiscent by 3–4 valves, seeds many, spherical-reniform.

One species cultivated in rock gardens.

Imperati L. Glabrous, dwarf shrub, sts. to 16 in., cylindrical; lvs. alt., to ½ in. long, fleshy, glaucous, secund; cymes 5–50-fld.; sepals green, margin scarious, petals white, longer than calyx. W. Medit. region.

TELESONIX Raf. *Saxifragaceae.* One sp., a per. herb native to mts. of w. N. Amer., with short, thick rhizome; lvs. basal, reniform, long-petioled; fls. showy, in compact, few-fld., short-branched panicles, calyx tube partly united to base of ovary, calyx lobes and petals 5, stamens 10, ovary half-inferior, prolonged into 2 beaklike styles. Closely related to *Boykinia,* but with 10 stamens.

Jamesii (Torr.) Raf. [*Boykinia Jamesii* (Torr.) Engl.; *Telesonix heucheriformis* (Rydb.) Rydb.]. Lf. blades to 2 in. across, crenate, petioles slender, to 5 in. long; fl. sts. several, to 8 in. long; fls. reddish-purple. Alta. to Nev., e. to S. Dak. and Colo.

heucheriformis: *T. Jamesii.*

TELLIMA R. Br. *Saxifragaceae.* One sp., a rhizomatous, hirsute and more or less glandular, per. herb of w. N. Amer.; lvs. cordate-ovate, on long petioles; fl. sts. sparsely leafy, calyx tube campanulate-tubular, united to base of ovary, calyx lobes 5, erect, triangular, petals 5, reflexed, pectinately fringed, stamens 10, included within calyx tube, ovary partly inferior, tapered above into 2 sterile, beaklike projections with short styles; fr. a caps., dehiscent along inner sides of the 2 projections.

affinis: *Lithophragma affine.*

grandiflora (Pursh) Dougl. [*T. odorata* T. J. Howell]. FRINGECUPS. Basal lvs. to 4 in. across, petioles hirsute, to 8 in. long; fl. sts. to 24 in., racemes loosely fld., calyx greenish, to ¼ in. long, petals greenish-white, becoming reddish in age; caps. not extending beyond calyx tube. Useful in the rock garden.

odorata: *T. grandiflora.*

parviflora: *Lithophragma parviflorum.*

TELOPEA R. Br. *Proteaceae.* Four spp. of evergreen shrubs, native to Australia; lvs. alt., leathery; fls. red, bisexual, irregular, in dense, terminal, headlike racemes surrounded by an involucre of colored bracts, perianth tube open on lower side, anthers sessile; fr. a leathery follicle, seeds winged.

speciosissima (Sm.) R. Br. WARATAH. Stout shrub, to 8 ft.; lvs. oblanceolate to obovate, to 10 in. long, toothed in upper part, venation prominent; fls. in dense ovoid or globose heads to 4 in. across, bracts to 3 in. long; follicles to 4 in. long. New S. Wales.

truncata (Labill.) R. Br. TASMANIAN WARATAH. Differs from *T. speciosissima* in having lvs. shorter, always entire; fl. heads shorter, more flattened, and involucral bracts to ¾ in. long, covered with appressed hairs. Tasmania.

TEMPLETONIA R. Br. *Leguminosae* (subfamily *Faboideae*). About 7 spp. of shrubs, native to Australia; lvs. absent or of 1 lft., alt.; fls. solitary or few, axillary, papilionaceous, stamens united, alternately of 2 lengths; fr. a flat, leathery, dehiscent legume.

Propagated by cuttings.

retusa (Venten.) R. Br. CORALBUSH. Glabrous, to 10 ft.; lfts. rigid-leathery, oblanceolate to obovate, to 1½ in. long, blunt, glaucous;

petals nearly equal, red or rarely yellow, longer than 1 in.; fr. linear-oblong, to 2 in. long. S. and w. Australia. Zone 10.

TEPHROCACTUS: *OPUNTIA* section *Tephrocactus*. **T. diadematus:** *O. articulata* cv. **T. Turpinii:** *O. articulata* cv. 'Syringacantha'.

TEPHROSIA Pers. HOARY PEA. *Leguminosae* (subfamily *Faboideae*). Perhaps 300–400 spp. of herbs or shrubs of wide distribution, but mostly trop. and subtrop.; lvs. alt., odd-pinnate; infl. a raceme; fls. papilionaceous, standard silky-hairy outside, the uppermost stamen separate to middle or base; fr. a flat, dehiscent legume.

Some species are important in the tropics for green manure, others as sources of fish poisons; a few are planted as ornamentals. Propagated by seeds planted where they are to grow.

candida DC. Shrub, to 10 ft.; lfts. in 8–12 pairs, lanceolate, 2 in. long, acute, silky-pubescent beneath; racemes terminal and in upper axils; fls. white, 1 in. long; fr. to 4 in. long. India; naturalized in W. Indies. Cult. in the tropics (Zone 10b) and there grown as a green-manure crop or as low windbreaks.

glomeruliflora Meissn. Similar to *T. grandiflora,* but white-pubescent, fls. smaller, to ½ in. long, calyx lobes short, ovate, nearly acute, and fr. nearly glabrous. S. Afr. Zone 10.

grandiflora Pers. shrub, to 2 ft., variably pubescent; lfts. in 5–7 pairs, cuneate-oblong; fls. red, in clustered corymbs, ¾ in. long, calyx lobes awl-shaped; fr. linear. S. Afr. Zone 10.

pubescens Ewart & A. Morrison. Subshrub, sts. unbranched, sts., petioles, and infl. rusty-pubescent; lfts. 3, ovate to obovate, about 1 in. long, with very prominent veins, densely gray-pubescent; racemes ⅝ in. long, on long peduncles in uppermost axils, standard yellowish, with purple veins, ⅝ in. long. N. Australia. Zone 10b.

virginiana (L.) Pers. GOAT'S RUE, CATGUT, RABBIT'S PEA. Per., to 2 ft., young growth white-silky-pubescent; lfts. in 8–14 pairs, linear-oblong to -elliptic, nearly glabrous above; racemes dense, terminal; fls. yellowish and pink-purple, to ¾ in. long; fr. to 2 in. long. Me., s. to Fla. and New Mex. Zone 5.

Vogelii Hook.f. Shrub, to 10 ft., densely tawny-hairy; lfts. in 8–12 pairs, oblanceolate, to 2½ in. long, blunt, densely silky-hairy beneath; racemes dense, terminal, to 6 in. long; fls. violet-purple or rarely white, standard 1 in. across; fr. to 5 in. long, ½ in. wide. Trop. Afr. Yields a fish poison; cult. as a cover crop and green manure.

TERMINALIA L. *Combretaceae*. About 200 spp. of polygamodioecious trees widely distributed in the tropics; lvs. simple, crowded toward ends of branchlets; infl. a spike or raceme; fls. small, 4–5-merous, calyx tubular below and campanulate above, petals 0, stamens 10, exserted; fr. dry or drupaceous, 1-seeded, angular or winged.

Planted in tropical climates as ornamentals or for the bark and fruits of several species, which yield dyes and tannins. Propagated by seeds.

Arjuna (Roxb.) Beddome. To 80 ft.; lvs. nearly opp., oblong, to 6 in. long, suddenly narrowed or often cordate at base; fls. in short spikes or panicles, green or white; fr. dark brown, to 2 in. long, narrowly 5-winged. India and Ceylon where a valuable timber tree. Grown in Fla. Zone 10b.

bellirica (Gaertn.) Roxb. MYROBALAN. To 80 ft.; lvs. alt., broadly elliptic, to 6 in. long, glabrous and punctate on upper surface when mature, deciduous in cold season, petioles to 3 in. long; spikes axillary, with bisexual fls. below and male fls. above; fls. grayish, with offensive odor; fr. drupaceous, globose, to ¾ in. long, pubescent. India to Malay Pen. Cult. in India for timber and the unripe frs., an important tannin source.

Calamansanai (Blanco) Rolfe. To 90 ft.; lvs. lanceolate, glabrous, petioles short; spikes axillary; fls. bisexual, calyx tomentose, with revolute lobes; fr. nutlike, subglobose, flattish, to 2½ in. across and half as long, with 3 or more ribs and 2 wings. Philippine Is.

Catappa L. TROPICAL ALMOND, INDIAN A., KAMANI, MYROBALAN. To 80 ft., brs. long, horizontal; lvs. stiff, obovate, to 1 ft. long, becoming rich red before falling in dry season; spikes to 6 in. long; fls. greenish-white; fr. flattened, to 2 in. long, greenish or reddish, the 2 angles winged, seeds edible, oily. Malay Pen. Widely planted and naturalized in trop. areas, and in Fla. as a street tree; thrives along seashores. Zone 10b. Unripe frs. a source of tannin.

Chebula Retz. MYROBALAN. To 100 ft.; lvs. not clustered, often nearly opp., ovate to elliptic, to 5 in. long, acute, basally rounded, deciduous in cold season; infl. a terminal spike, often a panicle; fls. all bisexual; fr. ellipsoid or obovoid, to 1¼ in. long, somewhat 5-ribbed

when dry. Ceylon and India to Malay Pen. Unripe frs. a source of tannin.

Muelleri Benth. Small tree; lvs. rather narrowly obovate, to 4 in. long, obtuse or abruptly pointed, leathery, sparsely short-hairy beneath; spikes axillary; fls. small; fr. bluish, to ¾ in. long. Queensland.

tomentosa Beddome. To 100 ft.; lvs. nearly opp., elliptic, to 8 in. long, variable, mostly thinly tomentose beneath; spikes terminal; fls. bisexual, dull yellow; fr. to 2 in. long, with 5 broad wings. India, Ceylon, Burma.

TERNSTROEMIA Mutis ex L.f. *Theaceae*. Perhaps 85 spp. of evergreen trees and shrubs widely distributed in tropics; lvs. spirally arranged, crowded at tips of season's growth, simple, mostly entire, usually leathery; fls. axillary, solitary, bisexual or unisexual, sepals 5, petals 5, separate or united in lower part, stamens 15 to many (–300), in 2 or several series, anthers glabrous, apiculate, basifixed, ovary superior, 2–3-celled; fr. indehiscent, seeds usually few, large.

One slow-growing species cultivated in the greenhouse, or outdoors in well-drained, moist soils. Propagated by cuttings, transplants easily.

gymnanthera (Wight & Arn.) T. Sprague [*T. japonica* of auth., not Thunb.]. Glabrous tree, to 30 ft., branchlets reddish-brown; lvs. elliptic to oblanceolate or obovate, to 3½ in. long and 1¾ in. wide, obtuse to rounded or rarely acuminate, entire, short-petioled; peduncles ½–¾ in. long in axils of fallen lvs., fls. yellow-white, to ¾ in. across; fr. globose, about ½ in. across. India to Malay Pen. and cent. Japan Zone 7. Wood useful in construction.

japonica: see *T. gymnanthera.*

TERRARIUM. A terrarium is an unheated enclosure, usually of glass, in which a collection of small, usually shade-loving plants can be grown in the home or elsewhere. The glass enclosure functions as a kind of diminutive greenhouse, displaying the plants while it protects them from the drying effects of the arid atmosphere typical of the usual American home. The Wardian case, a glass box with typical greenhouse shape, invented by an early English botanist, was the original terrarium. It was used to house and protect plants collected in distant lands during the long sea voyages necessary to get them back to Europe or America.

Modern terrariums use the same principle if not always the same design. Almost any kind of glass or other transparent container can be used so long as its dimensions are sizeable enough to maintain the plant population desired. The only requirements are that the terrarium glass be clear (colored or cloudy glass filters out essential daylight) and that there be a cover (to maintain ample moisture and humidity). Plain or decorative glass jars or bottles of all kinds, aquariums and fish bowls, goblets or carboys are all fitting terrarium containers so long as the opening is large enough for planting and maintaining the plants.

A special soil mix rather than regular garden soil, which becomes too soggy, is preferred for terrariums. The mix is one part sand, one part peat moss or humus, and one part garden loam. To this should be added 1 level teaspoon of 5–10–5 fertilizer for each 6-inch potful of mix. Special provision is also needed for drainage, since terrariums lack the drainage hole normally found in flower pots. In smaller containers, thin moss sheets collected from woodland stones or fallen logs, laid bottom up on the terrarium bottom, may serve as the drainage layer. In larger terrariums, small pieces of broken pot or charcoal or sand are placed on top of the basal mossy sheet. A minimum of soil is required, only sufficient to anchor the plants. The end product is to simulate the naturalistic greenery of a woodland or forest floor, temperate or tropical, and bare soil should not be seen.

A variety of plants are suitable for terrarium culture. Originally, appropriate native materials usually collected in the autumn from nearby woodlands constituted the bulk of terrarium plantings. Familiar terrarium plants in the northern states include *Chimaphila umbellata, Coptis, Gaultheria procumbens, Goodyera, Hepatica,* various species of *Lycopodium, Mitchella repens,* terrestrial lichens, mosses, small ferns, and the like. However, any woodsy woodland area wherever located will produce similarly appropriate material. The variety of tropical houseplants now available makes it also possible to make a terrarium exclusively of such species (temperate and tropical species should not be mixed), which usually thrive much better under humid terrarium conditions than under those of a normal dry home. Among suitable plants are *Saintpaulia ionantha* and other Gesneriaceae, *Fittonia, Dracaena, Zebrina pendula, Selaginella,* miniature species of *Peperomia, Maranta leuconeura,* ferns, *Soleirolia Soleirolii,* seedling palms, especially of the genus *Chamaedorea,* and juvenile material of such Araceae as *Philodendron* and *Syngonium.* Cacti and other succulents typical of arid regions are not appropriate subjects for usual terrariums, for the humidity of the container causes them to rot.

In setting the plants, make a logical design just as in a regular landscape planting. If the terrarium is to be viewed from one side, the smaller plants should be in the front and the larger ones as background. Plants should not be crowded nor should they press against the container walls. Once installed, plants are wetted down with a sprayer with only enough water added to seep through the bottom liner of moss. No excess water should stand on the terrarium bottom. Terrariums need little care besides periodic watering, about once a month. They are kept where there is light but not in direct sunlight. Plants may need pinching back if they grow too tall or crowd others.

TESTUDINARIA: *DIOSCOREA.*

TETRACLINIS M. T. Mast. *Cupressaceae.* One sp., a monoecious, coniferous, evergreen tree, native to somewhat arid areas of Medit. region; branchlets flattened, jointed; lvs. scalelike, 4-ranked, of 2 kinds, decurrent at bases; female cones globose, scales 4, woody, with small spine near apex; seeds 2–9 to each scale, 2-winged. Allied to *Callitris* and *Widdringtonia* but differing from the former in having 4 nearly equal cone scales, and the latter in having flattened, jointed brs. and lvs. 4-ranked.

Sometimes cultivated as an ornamental in warmer, drier parts of the U.S. For culture see *Conifers.*

articulata (Vahl) M. T. Mast. [*Callitris quadrivalvis* Venten. ex L. Rich.]. ARAR TREE. Small tree, to 20 ft., brs. spreading, slender; lvs. in whorls of 4, scalelike, minute, triangular, glandular; female cones 4-sided, 1/2 in. across, scales ovate, fertile ones usually 2–3-seeded. S. Spain, Malta, N. Afr. Zone 10. A source of sandarac, a hard resin used in industry.

TETRACOCCUS Engelm. *Euphorbiaceae.* Five spp. of dioecious shrubs, native to sw. U.S. and Mex.; lvs. simple, petioled, alt., opp., or in 3's, often fascicled; fls. without petals, male fls. in axillary panicles, racemes, or in cluster on spur brs., female fls. solitary and axillary, or clustered on spur brs., ovary usually 3–4-celled; fr. a caps.

dioicus Parry. Shrub, 5–6 ft., sts. slender, reddish; lvs. oblong-strap-shaped to lanceolate, sometimes nearly linear, to 1 in. long; male fls. in racemes, 1 in. long, female fls. solitary, ovary 4-celled, tomentose; fr. 3/8 in. wide. S. Calif., n. Baja Calif.

TETRAGONIA L. *Tetragoniaceae.* Over 50 spp. of herbs or small shrubs, native to Afr., e. Asia, Australia, New Zeal., and s. temp. Amer.; sts. prostrate or subscandent, glabrous, pilose, or papillose; lvs. alt., entire, sometimes fleshy, without stipules; fls. axillary, 1 or a few together, bisexual or unisexual, calyx tube angled, winged, or horned, the lobes 3–7, petals 0, stamens 1 or more, ovary inferior, rarely half-inferior, 3–8-, rarely 1–2-celled, ovules 1 in each cell; fr. nutlike or drupaceous.

Unlike true spinach, New Zeal. spinach does well in hot weather. The seeds should be soaked before planting. When plants are spaced 1–2 ft. in rows 3–4 ft. apart, the much-branched growth spreads out to form a mat over the ground. The apical 3–4 in. of the brs. are cut off and cooked like spinach.

expansa: *T. tetragonioides.*

tetragonioides (Pall.) O. Kuntze [*T. expansa* J. Murr.]. NEW ZEALAND SPINACH. Herb, sts. decumbent, branching, soft-woody toward base, up to 2 ft. long; lvs. ovate-rhombic to triangular, obtuse to subacute, entire to slightly sinuate or shallowly lobed, papillose, petioled; fls. 1–2 together, sessile or subsessile, 1/4 in. across, yellowish, sometimes unisexual, stamens 10–20, ovary 3–8-celled, styles 3–8; fr. 5/16–3/8 in. long, turbinate, angled, with 2–4 horns, seeds 4–10. Summer. Japan, Pacific Is., Australia, Tasmania, New Zeal., S. Amer. Cult. as a vegetable.

trigyna Banks & Soland. ex Hook.f. Trailing herb or small shrub, sts. cylindrical, branching, soft-woody, up to 10 ft. long; lvs. triangular to broad-ovate to ovate-rhombic, obtuse, 3/8–2 in. long, 1/2 in. wide, fleshy, papillose, petioles flattened; fls. on slender pedicels, 1–2 together, yellow, sometimes unisexual, calyx tube subglobose, stamens 10–20, ovary 2–3-celled, styles 2–3; fr. 1/4 in. in diam., subglobose, succulent, bright to dark red, not horned, seeds 1–3. Summer. New Zeal.

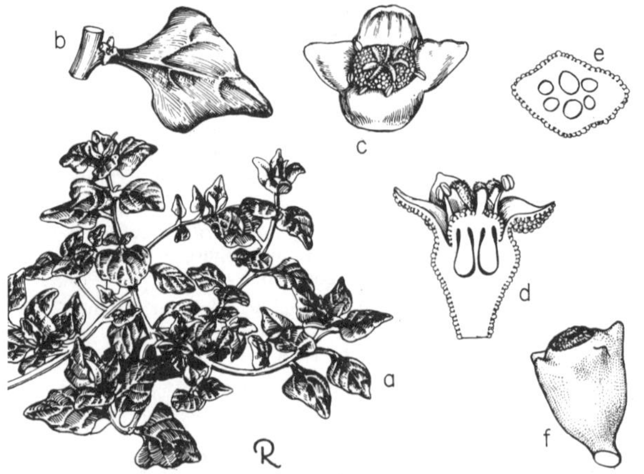

TETRAGONIACEAE. *Tetragonia tetragonioides:* **a,** plant, × 1/8; **b,** leaf with axillary flower, × 1/2; **c,** flower, × 3; **d,** flower, vertical section, × 4; **e,** ovary, cross section, × 4; **f,** fruit, × 1 1/2.

TETRAGONIACEAE Nakai. NEW ZEALAND SPINACH FAMILY. Dicot.; 3 genera, of prostrate or subscandent herbs or small fleshy shrubs, 2 native to S. Afr., each with 1 sp., and *Tetragonia,* widely distributed, but mostly in the S. Hemisphere; lvs. alt., entire; fls. with 4–5 sepal-like perianth segms., stamens 3–15, inserted on perianth tube, ovary inferior, 3–8-celled, each cell 1-ovuled, stigmas 3–8; fr. indehiscent, nutlike or drupaceous.

TETRAMICRA Lindl. *Orchidaceae.* Ten spp. of terrestrial herbs, native to W. Indies; sts. leafy, pseudobulbs lacking; lvs. 1–4, from rhizome, fleshy, semicylindrical; peduncle terminal, rigid, raceme simple, loosely fld.; fls. small, sepals equal, spreading, petals similar, narrower, lip attached to base of column, lateral lobes spreading, entire, contracted at base, short-clawed, column erect, 2-winged. For structure of fl. see *Orchidaceae.*

For culture see *Orchids.*

bicolor: *Leptotes bicolor.*

canaliculata (Aubl.) Urb. To 2 ft.; lvs. 2–4, leathery, linear-subulate, to 7 in. long; peduncle rarely branched, raceme many-fld., to 2 ft. long; sepals oblong, 3/8 in. long, petals oblong-spatulate, as long as sepals, lip 1/2 in. long, lateral lobes somewhat cordate, midlobe obovate, 3/8 in. long, column 1/4 in. long. W. Indies.

TETRANEMA Benth. ex Lindl [*Allophyton* Brandeg.]. *Scrophulariaceae.* Two spp. of small, suffrutescent per. herbs, native to Mex. and Guatemala; lvs. seemingly basal but opp. on short woody st., simple; fls. in terminal, bracted, umbel-like clusters on long peduncles, calyx 5-parted, corolla 2-lipped, stamens 4; fr. a caps.

Generally grown under glass for attractive bloom, but uncommon in cultivation.

mexicanum: *T. roseum.*

roseum (M. Martens & Galeotti) Standl. & Steyerm. [*T. mexicanum* Benth. ex Lindl.; *Allophyton mexicanum* (Benth. ex Lindl.) Brandeg.]. MEXICAN VIOLET, MEXICAN FOXGLOVE. Fl. sts. 4–8 in., well above the foliage; lvs. obovate, 3–6 in. long, bluntly acute, weakly serrulate, somewhat leathery, glaucous beneath; corolla about 1/2 in. long, purple, throat and tube pale, with darker mottling, lobes about 5/16 as long as tube.

TETRANEURIS: *HYMENOXYS.* **T. stenophylla:** *H. scaposa* var. *linearis.*

TETRAPANAX C. Koch. *Araliaceae.* One sp., a stoloniferous, unarmed, evergreen shrub or small tree, native to s. China and Taiwan; lvs. more or less whorled, large, long-petioled, palmately lobed, densely tomentose beneath; fls. in small, globose umbels arranged in large, terminal, woolly panicles, petals 4, valvate, stamens 4, ovary 2-celled, styles 2, separate; fr. a drupe, pyrenes 2.

papyriferus (Hook.) C. Koch [*Aralia papyrifera* Hook.; *Fatsia papyrifera* (Hook.) Benth & Hook.f.]. RICE-PAPER PLANT, CHINESE R.-P. P. Lvs. orbicular, 10–15 in. across, deeply cut into 5–14 toothed lobes, white-felty when young; rusty with age; panicles to 3 ft. long, white, standing out beyond the lvs. Cv. **'Variegata'.** Lvs. variegated with cream to white and shades of bright to dark green. The white pith of the st. is a source of rice paper in China. A root-hardy ornamental in Zone 8.

TETRAPATHAEA Rchb. NEW ZEALAND PASSION-FLOWER, NEW ZEALAND PASSION FRUIT. *Passifloraceae.* One sp., a tendril-bearing vine, endemic to New Zeal.; differing from *Passiflora* in being dioecious, the infl. a few-fld. axillary cyme without bracts (the female fls. sometimes solitary), the fls. 4-merous, not 5-merous.

tetrandra (Banks & Soland. ex DC.) Cheesem. Very high-climbing vine, glabrous, sts. woody, becoming 3–4 in. in diam.; lvs. simple, ovate-lanceolate to oblong, acuminate, entire; fls. unisexual, greenish, about ¾ in. across, corona white to yellow; fr. nearly globose, 1–1½ in. in diam., orange. Cult. for its showy frs.

TETRAPLASANDRA A. Gray. *Araliaceae.* About 20 spp. of small unarmed, sticky trees of Hawaii, 4 spp. from Celebes, New Guinea, and Philippine Is.; lvs. pinnate, lfts. mostly entire, glabrous; fls. in terminal or axillary umbels sometimes arranged in panicles, petals 5–9, stamens as many as petals or more, ovary 2–13(–16)-celled; fr. drupaceous, usually dry.

meiandra (Hillebr.) Harms. Shrub or tree, to about 20 ft., branching from near the base; lvs. to 18 in. long, lfts. 7–13, ovate or oblong, leathery; infl. a compound umbel; fls. small, greenish, petals 5–8, stamens as many as petals, ovary 2–3-celled; fr. conical, to ½ in. long, angled when dry. Is. of Oahu, Hawaii. Zone 10.

TETRAPLEURA Benth. *Leguminosae* (subfamily *Mimosoideae*). Two spp. of unarmed trees, native to trop. Afr.; lvs. alt., 2-pinnate; fls. in axillary, spikelike racemes, small, 5-merous, stamens 10, separate; fr. an oblong, woody, indehiscent legume, with valves longitudinally winged or keeled.

tetraptera (Schumach. & Thonn.) Taub. To 100 ft.; lvs. to 1 ft. long, lfts. in 6–13 pairs, elliptic-oblong, ½–¾ in. long, obtuse or emarginate; racemes to 4½ in. long; fls. rose-yellowish to orange; fr. winged, 6–10 in. long, 1½–2½ in. wide, the wing ¾–1¼ in. wide. Senegal to Congo region, e. to Tanzania.

TETRASTIGMA Planch. JAVAN GRAPE. *Vitaceae.* About 90 spp. of climbing, woody, deciduous or evergreen, dioecious vines, with or without tendrils, native to subtrop. and trop. Asia; lvs. alt., palmately compound, lfts. 3–5(–7); infl. of axillary umbels or cymes; fls. unisexual, petals 4, expanding, disc adnate to base of ovary, stigma 4-lobed, broader than the style is long; fr. a 2–4-seeded berry.

Harmandii Planch. AYO. High-climbing vine, with tendrils; lfts. 3–5, rarely 7, narrowly lanceolate, cuspidate, serrate, glabrous; fls. in short-stalked cymes; fr. edible. Philippine Is., w. to Cambodia.

Voinieranum (Baltet) Pierre ex Gagnep. [*Cissus Voinierana* (Baltet) Viala; *Vitis Voinierana* Baltet]. CHESTNUT VINE, LIZARD PLANT. Coarse, stout, rampant vine, young sts. and petioles often densely tawny-pilose to woolly; lfts. mostly 5, 4–8 in. long, usually rhombic, weakly serrate to crenate-serrate, puberulent to tomentose beneath, petioles 4–12 in. long; sepals lacking or very short. Laos. Cult. as lattice cover and for screening in s. Calif., usually as *Cissus Voinierana* or *C. vomerensis.*

TETRATHECA Sm. *Tremandraceae.* About 20 spp. of heathlike shrubs and subshrubs, native to nontrop. Australia and Tasmania; lvs. simple, alt., opp., or whorled; fls. showy, solitary, axillary, sepals and petals 4–5, rarely 3, stamens 8–10, filaments short; fr. a caps.

Grown under glass or in the open in warmer regions. A soil of fibrous peat and silver sand is desirable.

ericifolia Sm. Shrub, to 1 ft., sts. and foliage hairy; lvs. sessile, linear, in whorls of 4–6, to ½ in. long, revolute; fls. pink, drooping, to 5/16 in. long, anthers purplish-brown with whitish tips; caps. pendulous. New S. Wales. Zone 10.

TETRAZYGIA L. Rich. ex DC. *Melastomataceae.* About 15 spp. of trees or shrubs, native to Fla. and W. Indies; lvs. entire or toothed, often scurfy; infl. terminal, panicled or corymbose; fls. small, stamens 8 or 10, all similar, ovary half-inferior; fr. a fleshy berry.

bicolor (Mill.) Cogn. Shrub or small tree, to 15 ft.; lvs. 3–8 in. long, lanceolate to oblong-lanceolate, acuminate, strongly 3-nerved, green above, whitish-scurfy beneath; panicles 3–6 in. long; fls. ⅝ in. across, white, stamens showy, yellow. S. Fla., Bahama Is., Cuba, Jamaica, Dominica.

TEUCRIUM L. GERMANDER. *Labiatae.* About 300 spp. of herbs or shrubs of wide distribution, especially in the Medit. region; sts. mostly square in cross section; lvs. opp., entire or toothed; fls. rather showy, in 2- to many-fld. verticillasters arranged in terminal spikes or racemes or heads, calyx tubular or campanulate, 5-toothed, 2-lipped or regular, corolla with one 5-lobed lip, tube often shorter than calyx, without ring of hairs inside, stamens 4, in 2 pairs; fr. of 4 smooth or reticulate nutlets.

Variously used as ornamentals, often as edging plants or as dwarf hedges; propagated by seeds, cuttings, or division.

aroanium Orph. ex Boiss. [*T. arvanicum* of auth.]. Evergreen shrub, sts. to 1 ft., procumbent, rooting, much-branched; lvs. obovate to ovate-oblong, ¼–⅝ in. long, entire, densely white-tomentose beneath, sparsely so above; fls. in racemes, corolla much longer than calyx, ⅝ in. long, bluish. Mts., Greece.

arvanicum: a misspelling of *T. aroanium.*

aureum: *T. Polium.*

bicolor Sm. [*T. heterophyllum* Cav., not L'Hér.]. Shrub, 3–6 ft.; lvs. lanceolate to obovate, ⅜–½ in. long, entire, mostly with 2 lateral lobes near middle, usually glossy above; fls. axillary, ½–¾ in. long, white, with lavender streaks. Chile.

canadense L. AMERICAN G., WOOD SAGE. Rhizomatous per., to 3 ft., glabrescent; lvs. ovate-lanceolate, 1¼–3 in. long, acute, serrate, thick-hoary beneath; fls. in a spikelike raceme 4–8 in. long, verticillasters 6-fld., calyx gray-pubescent, corolla to ¾ in. long, pinkish-purple. E. N. Amer.

Chamaedrys L. Dwarf rhizomatous shrub, sts. to 1–2 ft., hairy; lvs. oblong to obovate-oblong, ½–¾ in. long, often deeply serrate- to crenate-toothed; infl. loose to dense, always longer than wide; calyx about ¼ in. long, corolla to ⅝ in. long, pale to deep purple, rarely white, hairy. Eur. and sw. Asia. Cv. **'Prostratum'.** Dwarf, sts. conspicuously procumbent.

flavum L. Per., to 2 ft., sts. woody at base; lvs. leathery, ovate, crenate-serrate; fls. in a long, interrupted spike, bracts lanceolate, entire, corolla yellow. Rocky slopes, Medit. region.

fruticans L. TREE G. Evergreen shrub, to 4 ft., twigs 4-angled, white-tomentose; lvs. ovate to lanceolate, to 1¼ in. long, obtuse, entire, revolute, glabrous above; fls. in axils, bracts leaflike, calyx campanulate, white-tomentose outside, corolla to 1 in. long, blue or lilac, stamens long-exserted. Sunny places, w. Medit.

heterophyllum L'Hér. Shrub, 4–6 ft., new growth densely appressed-yellowish-tomentose; lvs. dimorphic, lvs. of young shoots ovate, crenate-dentate, nearly truncate at base, lvs. of older growth oblong, cuneate at base, usually entire, densely white- to yellowish-pubescent; corolla to ½ in. long, rose-purple, stamens long-exserted. Canary Is. Tender. Cult. material of Chilean origin, called *T. heterophyllum* is *T. bicolor.*

hircanicum L. Erect per., to 2½ ft., pubescent; lvs. ovate, ¾–1¼ in. long, mostly obtuse at apex, cordate to truncate at base, crenate; spikes dense, 4–12 in. long; fls. about ¾ in. long, red to purple. Caucasus to Iran.

hircanum: a listed name, probably in error for *T. hircanicum.*

krymense Juz. Per., to 1½ ft., sts. nearly erect, densely pilose; lvs. ovate-oblong, 1–1½ in. long, obtuse, attenuately cuneate, finely and deeply crenate-serrate, pilose; calyx hispidulous, corolla about ⅝ in. long, red-purple. Crimea.

lucidum L. Similar to *T. Chamaedrys,* but larger and almost glabrous; sts. erect, to 2 ft.; lvs. ovate-oblong, to 1½ in. long, deeply toothed or shallowly lobed; infl. loose, verticillasters mostly 2–4-fld. Sw. Alps. Rare in cult. in U.S.

Marum L. Small shrub, 12–18 in., much-branched, sts. white-tomentose; lvs. linear-lanceolate to rhombic, to 5/16 in. long, entire, often revolute; infl. cylindrical, dense; corolla 1–3 in. long, purplish. W. Medit. Is.

massiliense L. Per., to 1 ft., gray-tomentose; lvs. oblong-ovate, to ½ in. long, crenate; calyx glandular-pubescent, corolla pink, tube included in calyx. W. Medit., Crete.

montanum L. Dwarf shrub, sts. to 1 ft. long, decumbent, white-appressed-hairy; lvs. narrowly elliptic, to ¾ in. long, entire, densely hairy beneath, sessile; fls. in a terminal head, corolla cream. S. and cent. Eur. to w. Asia.

occidentale A. Gray. Stoloniferous per., sts. to 3 ft., villous; lvs. lanceolate- to ovate-oblong, white-villous beneath; bracts and calyx villous with viscid hairs, upper calyx lobes acute, corolla to ½ in. long. Alluvial soils, n. U.S. to New Mex. and Calif.

orientale L. Shrub or subshrub, to 18 in.; lvs. to 2 in. long, 1–2-pinnatifid, segms. linear; racemes corymbose to panicled; corolla blue-violet. Sw. Asia.

Polium L. [*T. aureum* Schreb.]. Dwarf shrub, sts. to 18 in. long, covered with white, greenish, or golden, branched hairs; lvs. narrowly oblong to narrowly obovate, to 1 in. long, crenate; fls. in a simple or compound head, calyx densely hairy, corolla white or red. S. Eur. and w. Asia.

pyrenaicum L. Per., sts. to 8 in. long, woody at base, creeping, slender, villous; lvs. nearly orbicular, ½–¾ in. wide, to 1 in. long, crenate, green; fls. in a terminal head, calyx campanulate, to 5/16 in. long, sparsely hairy, corolla to ¾ in. long, white, or white with purple, upper lobes spatulate. Summer. Pyrenees, Dauphiné Alps.

Scorodonia L. WOOD SAGE, WOOD G. Dwarf shrub, rhizomatous, sts. to 8–20 in., pubescent; lvs. triangular-ovate, cordate to truncate at base, crenate, rugose; infl. to 6 in., simple or branched; calyx villous, glandular, corolla 5/16 in. long, pale yellow, stamens long-exserted. Eur.; naturalized in Ont. and Ohio.

subspinosum Pourr. ex Willd. Small shrub, to about 1 ft. across, with stout main brs., hemispherical, dense, spiny; lvs. very narrow, almost triangular, to ¼ in. long; infl. loose, verticillasters few-fld.; corolla to ¼ in. long, purple. Summer. Balearic Is.

TEYSMANNIA: see *JOHANNESTEIJSMANNIA*.

THALIA L. *Marantaceae*. About 7 spp. of tall, aquatic or marsh herbs, native to warm and trop. Amer.; lvs. basal, long-petioled; fls. purplish, in axils of deciduous or persistent bracts, in spikes or panicles, sepals 3, small, corolla 3-lobed, outer staminode longer than petals, ovary inferior, 1-celled. Fls. with explosive mechanisms for pollination.

Plants should be grown in wet soil or preferably shallow water; propagated by division.

dealbata J. Fraser. Plant white-powdery; scapes to 10 ft. or more; lf. blades oblong-ovate to lanceolate-elliptic, to 20 in. long and 10 in. wide, petioles much longer; fls. small, crowded in narrow panicles, bracts pale blue. S.C. to Fla., w. to Mo. and Tex.

divaricata: *T. geniculata.*

geniculata L. [*T. divaricata* Chapm.]. Differs from *T. dealbata* in not being white-powdery, and in having lf. blades larger, lanceolate, to 32 in. long, panicles loosely branched, with fls. separated on the rachis, and bracts leaflike, red or purple beneath. Trop. Amer.

THALICTRUM L. MEADOW RUE. *Ranunculaceae*. About 100 spp. of per. herbs, chiefly of the N. Temp. Zone; lvs. ternately compound or decompound; fls. small, unisexual or bisexual, borne in panicles, racemes, or corymbs, sepals 4–5, deciduous, petals 0, stamens many, sometimes colored and showy, pistils few; fr. of stalked or sessile, ribbed, angled, or winged achenes.

Thalictrums are of easy culture in well-drained loamy soil. Propagated by division in early spring, also by seeds. In most species, the flowers are not striking except for the many stamens, but the large open panicles make showy mass effect. In some species, as *T. dipterocarpum* and *T. Delavayi*, the sepals are very large and showy, and violet or mauve. The native Amer. species which have foliage like that of *Aquilegia*, are excellent in the wild garden.

adiantifolium: see *T. minus;* material cult. as *T. adiantifolium* may be some other sp.

alpinum L. ALPINE M. R. Cespitose or somewhat stoloniferous, sts. simple, to 10 in., glabrous; lvs. few, 2–4-ternate, to 4½ in. long, lfts. fanlike, thick, glaucous, revolute; scape with terminal, nodding raceme; fls. bisexual, sepals to 1/16 in. long, stamens 8–15; achenes 3–6, sessile, obliquely oblanceolate to obovate, ⅛ in. long, 5–6-ribbed. Circumpolar, s. to Calif., Rocky Mts. Var. **stipitatum** Yabe. Achenes long-stipitate. Japan.

anemonoides: *Anemonella thalictroides.*

angustifolium: *T. simplex.*

aquilegifolium L. Dioecious, sts. 2–3 ft., glaucous; lvs. 2–3-pinnate, lfts. orbicular or oblong, with few, broad teeth at apex; male fls. with erect purple or pink stamens much longer than the white sepals; achenes 3-winged, stipitate, pendulous. Eur., Asia. Cvs. with stamens of other colors are: **'Album'**, white; **'Atropurpureum'**, dark purple; **'Aurantiacum'**, orangish; **'Purpureum'**, purple; **'Roseum'**, lilac-rose.

baicalense Turcz. Sts. to 1½ ft.; lfts. large, orbicular, toothed at apex; fls. few, erect, with long stamens; achenes ribbed, flattened, very short-stalked. Siberia to Korea, Japan.

calabricum K. Spreng. Sts. 1–3 ft.; lvs. ternately or pinnately decompound, lfts. entire or 3-lobed, lobes small, entire or few-toothed; fls. bisexual, few, sepals to 3/16 in. long, stamens to ⅜ in. long, filaments clavate, purple; achenes short-stalked, ribbed. S. Italy.

Chelidonii DC. Sts. 1½–3 ft. or more; lvs. decompound, lfts. ovate, 7–13-lobed or -toothed, glabrous, to 1 in. wide; fls. bisexual, ⅝ in. across, in loose glabrous panicle, sepals mauve, 5/16 in. long, stamens about as long, drooping, filaments threadlike; achenes flattened, stalked. Himalayas.

clavatum DC. LADY RUE. Roots fleshy, fusiform, sts. to 3 ft., very slender, glabrous, 1–3-lvd.; basal lvs. 2-ternate; fls. few, bisexual, sepals white, obovate, filaments expanded above into petal-like blade, anthers blunt; achenes stipitate, scimitar-shaped. Va. to Ky., Ga., Ala.

dasycarpum Fisch. & Avé-Lall. Mostly dioecious, crown short, thick, erect, sts. to 6 ft., often purple; upper lvs. subsessile, lfts. firm, veins prominent and pubescent on under surface; fls. corymbose-paniculate, sepals acuminate, filaments filiform, soon drooping, anthers subulate at apex. Ont. to Alta., s. to Ohio, and Ariz. Most of the material cult. as *T. purpurascens* belongs here.

Delavayi Franch. Sts. 2–3 ft., slender; lvs. ternately or pinnately decompound, lfts. long-stalked, 3–5-lobed; fls. bisexual, to 1 in. across, sepals reddish or lilac, about as long as stamens, filaments threadlike, anthers yellow; achenes flattened, long-stalked, ⅜ in. long. W. China. Commonly cult. under the name of *T. dipterocarpum*, but that sp. has slightly smaller fls. and broader, shorter anthers.

dioicum L. EARLY M. R., QUICKSILVER WEED. Dioecious, crown erect, sts. to 30 in.; lvs. 1–3, decompound, petioled, the upper with semiovate to lunate stipules, lfts. reniform to obovate with blunt lobes or teeth; panicles terminal and axillary; sepals green or purple, filaments filiform, anthers mucronate-acuminate. Que. to N. Dak., s. to Ga. and Mo.

dipterocarpum Franch. Sometimes polygamous, sts. to 3 ft., angled in upper part; lvs. decompound, lfts. nearly orbicular, notched at apex; fls. all bisexual or both bisexual and unisexual, nodding, in a large loose panicle, sepals rose-violet, 5/16 in. long, filaments threadlike; achenes sessile, flattened, 2-winged. W. China. Material so named may be *T. Delavayi*. Cvs. **'Album'**, **'Magnificum'**, and **'Minus'** are listed.

Fendleri Engelm. ex A. Gray. Dioecious, sts. to 3½ ft., slender, erect, branched in upper part; lvs. 2–4-ternate, lfts. round or cordate at base; fls. in panicles, filaments filiform; achenes glandular-puberulent, compressed, 3–5-ribbed on each side, the nerves not anastomosing. Ore. and Wyo. to Baja Calif. and Tex.

flavum L. Rhizome creeping, stoloniferous, sts. to 4 ft., usually simple, robust; lvs. 2–3-pinnate, lfts. obovate-cuneate, 3–4-lobed; fls. in panicles, bisexual, fragrant, sepals whitish, stamens yellow; achenes 6-ribbed, glaucous. Eurasia.

foetidum L. To 2½ ft., covered with minute odorous glands; st. lvs. 3–4-pinnate, lfts. small, notched at apex; fls. bisexual, nodding, greenish-red, in a loose panicle, sepals shorter than the yellow stamens; achenes sessile, many-ribbed. Mts., cent. Eur.

glaucum: *T. speciosissimum.*

kiusianum Nakai. Stoloniferous, sts. slender, to 5 in.; lvs. 1–2-ternate, lfts. ovate, toothed, purplish; fls. purplish, 5/16 in. across, sepals purple, shorter than the pinkish or purplish stamens; achenes stalked, ribbed. Japan.

minus L. Cespitose to stoloniferous, sts. to 1½ ft., branched, often flexuous, leafy, often glandular in upper part; lvs. 3–4-pinnate, lfts. rounded-cuneate to cordate at base, green or glaucous, more or less glabrous; panicle usually branching from above the middle of the st.; fls. bisexual, stamens many, with apiculate anthers; achenes 8–10-ribbed. Eur., n. Asia. *T. adiantifolium* Bess. and *T. purpureum* Shang. are also said to belong to the *T. minus* complex.

occidentale A. Gray. Dioecious, glabrous, to 4 ft.; lvs. 3–4-ternate, lfts. orbicular to cuneate-obovate, 3-lobed, thin; infl. paniculate, to 2 ft., leafy; filaments purplish, filiform; achenes reflexed to divaricate, stipitate, ¼–⁵⁄₁₆ in. long, 8–12-ribbed, with shallow nonreticulate intervals. Wash., Ore.; and, in several vars., to B.C., Utah, and Calif.

petaloideum L. Sts. to 20 in.; lvs. 3-ternate, lfts. entire, or 2–3-lobed; fls. bisexual, to ½ in. wide, few or many, corymbose, sepals less than ⅛ in. long, filaments clavate, white; achenes sessile, ribbed. E. Asia.

polycarpum (Torr.) S. Wats. Like *T. Fendleri*, but pistils and lvs. glabrous; achenes obovate, 1-nerved to reticulate, more or less reflexed, turgid when fresh. Wash. to Calif.

polygamum Muhlenb. TALL M. R., MUSKRAT WEED, KING-OF-THE-MEADOW. Polygamous, to 8 ft., glabrous or puBescent, but not glandular; st. lvs. sessile, lfts. rather firm; panicles very compound; fls. mostly white, filaments clavate, anthers blunt; achenes nearly sessile. Nfld. to Ont., s. to Ga. and Tenn.

purpurascens L. A name of doubtful application. Most plants grown under this name are *T. dasycarpum*.

purpureum: see *T. minus*.

Rochebrunianum Franch. & Sav. Glabrous; upper lvs. 2-pinnate, leathery, lfts. obtuse, entire or the terminal ones 3-lobed; fls. few, in panicles, bisexual, sepals white, oblong, ¼ in. long, stamens as long, somewhat clavate; achenes many, fusiform, stipitate, 10–12-nerved. Japan.

simplex L. [*T. angustifolium* L., not of auth.]. Sts. 1–3 ft., leafy; lvs. ternate, divisions pinnate, lfts. more or less lanceolate, 3-lobed or entire; fls. bisexual, small, many, in narrow panicles, sepals greenish, less than ⅛ in. long, stamens longer, pendulous; achenes sessile, ribbed. Eur.

speciosissimum L. [*T. glaucum* Desf.]. Sts. 2–5 ft., stout, glaucous; lvs. 2–3-pinnate, lfts. 3-lobed or entire, to 1½ in. wide; fls. bisexual or unisexual, small, many, crowded in panicles, sepals pale yellow, less than ⅛ in. long, stamens bright yellow, ¼ in. long; achenes sessile, ribbed. W. Medit. region.

sulphureum: a listed name of no botanical standing.

venulosum Trel. Dioecious; rhizome horizontal, cordlike, sts. to 2½ ft.; st. lvs. 1–3, lfts. leathery, strongly veiny on under surface, with small closed reticulations; fls. in narrow, dense panicles, filaments filiform; achenes turgid, to ⅛ in. long, with thick corky ribs. B.C. to Wyo., S. Dak., Wisc.

THAMNOSMA Torr. & Frém. *Rutaceae*. About 6 spp. of strong-scented shrubs or subshrubs of sw. N. Amer., S. Afr., and Socotra Is.; lvs. alt., simple, glandular-dotted; fls. in racemose corymbs, calyx 4-lobed, petals 4, stamens 8, ovary 2-celled, stalked; fr. a leathery, glandular, 2-lobed caps.

montana Torr. & Frém. TURPENTINE BROOM. To 2 ft., sts. like broom, yellowish-green, glandular; lvs. oblanceolate-linear, to ⅝ in. long, obtuse, early-deciduous; fls. purplish, petals ½ in. long. Dry slopes and deserts, Colo., Utah, New Mex., to Calif. and n. Mex.

THEA: *CAMELLIA*.

THEACEAE. *Camellia sinensis:* **a,** flowering branch, × ½; **b,** flower bud, × 1; **c,** flower, exterior view, × 1; **d,** flower, vertical section, × 1; **e,** anther, × 6; **f,** pistil, × 4; **g,** ovary, vertical section, × 6; **h,** ovary, cross section, × 6; **i,** fruit, × 1; **j,** seed, × 1.

THEACEAE D. Don [*Ternstroemiaceae* R. Br.]. TEA FAMILY. Dicot.; about 25 genera of mostly trop. and subtrop. trees and shrubs; lvs. alt., simple, often leathery and persistent, sometimes crowded at tips of current season's growth; fls. axillary, solitary or in clusters, bisexual or rarely unisexual, sepals and petals mostly 5, stamens many, ovary superior, 2–10-celled; fr. a caps., berrylike, or dry and indehiscent. The genus *Camellia* is a source of tea of commerce as well as seed oils, and the following genera are grown as ornamentals: *Camellia, Cleyera, Eurya, Franklinia, Gordonia, Schima, Stewartia, Ternstroemia,* and *Tutcheria.*

THELESPERMA Less. [*Cosmidium* Nutt.]. *Compositae* (Helianthus Tribe). About 12 spp. of ann., bien., or per. herbs of w. N. Amer. and s. S. Amer.; lvs. opp. or alt., simple or pinnately dissected; fl. heads radiate or discoid, solitary on long peduncles, involucral bracts in 2 rows, the inner united in lower ⅓ or more; ray fls., when present, yellow or brown-red; achenes cylindrical, warty, pappus of 2 retrorsely barbed awns.

Burridgeanum (Regel, Körn., & Rach) S. F. Blake [*T. hybridum* Voss.; *Cosmidium Burridgeanum* Regel, Körn., & Rach]. Erect ann., to 1½ ft., branching; lvs. to 4 in. long, divided into filiform lobes; heads to 1½ in. across; ray fls. orange-yellow or dark red with yellow apex. Tex.

hybridum: *T. Burridgeanum.*

THELOCACTUS (K. Schum.) Britt. & Rose. *Cactaceae.* Perhaps 20 spp. of small, ovoid cacti, native to Mex.; sts. simple or cespitose, globose to oblong, tubercles grooved on upper side, separate or somewhat united into ribs; spines not hooked; fls. subapical, from the groove, diurnal, campanulate, scales of ovary few, with naked axils; fr. opening by a basal pore, seeds warty, black, hilum large, basal, surrounded by a large smooth collar. Resembling *Coryphantha* but with different fr. and seeds. Related to *Neolloydia.*

For culture see *Cacti.*

bicolor (Galeotti) Britt. & Rose. GLORY-OF-TEXAS. Sts. solitary, globose to conical, to 8 in. high and 3 in. thick, ribs mostly 8, tubercles twice as wide as high; spines somewhat curved, radial spines needle-shaped, to 1¼ in. long, the upper 4 often flat, central spines 4, spreading, to 2 in. long; fls. purple, to 2½ in. long; fr. to ½ in. long. S. Tex., n. Mex. Var. **bicolor.** The typical var.; spines red and yellow, radial spines 4–18, to 1¼ in. long, central spines to 2 in. long. Mex. Var. **bolansis** (Runge) Backeb. & F. M. Knuth. Spines stouter, white. Var. **Schottii** (Engelm.) L. Bens. Spines tinged with pink, radial spines 15–17, the upper ones straw-colored or white, central spines to 1⅝ in. long. Tex., n. Mex. Var. **tricolor** (K. Schum.) Backeb. & F. M. Knuth. Densely spiny, spines red. N. Mex.

bolensis: a listed name of no botanical standing, doubtless for *T. bicolor* var. *bolansis.*

Buekii (Klein) Britt. & Rose. Sts. solitary, tubercles distinct, angled; spines about 7, reddish, unequal, curved; fls. dark red. Mex. Smaller than *T. tulensis.*

conothelos (Regel & Klein) F. M. Knuth. Sts. to 4 in. high and 3 in. thick, ribs oblique, tubercles to ¾ in. long; radial spines 14–16, white, spreading or recurved, ⁵⁄₁₆ in. long, central spines 2–4, erect or spreading, stouter, to 1½ in. long; fls. purple. Ne. Mex.

Ehrenbergii (Pfeiff.) Borg. Closely resembling *T. leucacanthus* and perhaps a var. of it with pink fls.

fossulatus (Scheidw.) Britt. & Rose. Sts. globose, to 6 in. thick, ribs usually 13, tubercles large, flabby; spines awl-shaped, radial spines 4–5, unequal, the lowest to 1½ in. long, central spine 1, cross-ringed, to 1¾ in. long; fls. white or pink. Cent. Mex.

Gielsdorfianus (Werderm.) Bravo [*Gymnocactus Gielsdorfianus* (Werderm.) Backeb.]. Sts. simple, to 3 in. high and 2 in. thick, tubercles in about 12 spiral rows, scarcely united, conical to pyramidal, the base irregularly hexagonal; spines 6–7, radial, awl-shaped, straight or curved, to ¾ in. long; fls. ivory-white, 1 in. long. Ne. Mex.

hastifer (Werderm. & Böd.) F. M. Knuth. Sts. simple, to 6 in. high and 2½ in. thick, ribs 18–20, to ⁵⁄₁₆ in. high; radial spines 20–25, needle-shaped, glassy-white, ½ in. long, central spines about 4, white, to 1¼ in. long, upcurved; fls. violet-pink, 1¾ in. long. Mex.

heterochromus (A. Web.) Van Ooststr. Sts. simple, to 6 in. high and thick, ribs 8–9, slightly oblique, broad, obtuse; radial spines 7–10, needle-shaped, straight or incurved, to 1¼ in. long, central spines several, awl-shaped, stiff, somewhat flattened, mostly incurved; fls. pale purple, to 2½ in. long; fr. globose, ⅝ in. in diam. N. Mex. The name *T. Pottsii* (Salm-Dyck) Britt. & Rose has been applied in error to this sp.

hexaedrophorus (Lem.) Britt. & Rose. Sts. globose or depressed, to 6 in. thick, tubercles scarcely united, somewhat hexagonal, 1 in. wide; radial spines 6–9, awl-shaped, cross-ringed, unequal, to ¾ in. long, central spine 1, stouter, to 1¼ in. long; fls. purplish, 2¼ in. long. Cent. Mex.

Knuthianus (Böd.) Bravo [*Gymnocactus Knuthianus* (Böd.) Backeb.]. Sts. cespitose, globose, to 2½ in. thick, tubercles in about 13 spiral rows, scarcely united, conic-truncate, 5/16 in. long; spines needle-shaped, white, radial spines 18–20, appressed, 5/16 in. long, central spine 1, ascending, slightly larger; fls. rose, 1 in. long. Cent. Mex.

leucacanthus (Zucc.) Britt. & Rose. Sts. cespitose, to 6 in. high and 3 in. thick, ribs 8–13, spiralled, tubercles ovoid, ½ in. long; radial spines 7–20, minutely pubescent, yellow, becoming gray, unequal, the longest cross-ringed, to 1½ in. long, central spine 1, directed outward, to 2 in. long; fls. yellow, 2 in. long. Mex.

lophothele (Salm-Dyck) Britt. & Rose. Sts. cespitose, to 10 in. high, tubercles in 15–20 oblique rows, scarcely united, conical, ¾ in. high and wide; radial spines 3–5, stout, purplish-brown, to 1¼ in. long, central spine 0–1, longer, directed outward or deflexed; fls. salmon to yellow, 2½ in. long. N. Mex.

nidulans (Quehl) Britt. & Rose. Sts. simple, to 4 in. high and 8 in. thick, ribs 20–25, oblique, tubercles conical, angled, ¾ in. long and wide; spines 13–15, brown, channelled, the lower to ⅜ in. long, the central to 2½ in. long, mostly disappearing, 4–6 of the largest remaining but disintegrating into wool and fibers; fls. yellowish-white, 1½ in. long. Mex.

phymatothele (Poselg.) Britt. & Rose. Sts. simple, to 2 in. high and 4 in. thick, tubercles scarcely united, in about 13 oblique rows, low, irregular; spines 0–3, awl-shaped, spreading, black, becoming gray, ¾ in. long; fls. rose-purple to pink, 2½ in. across. Mex.

porrectus (Lem.) F. M. Knuth. Closely resembling *T. leucacanthus* and perhaps a var. of it with 4 central spines.

Pottsii: see. *T. heterochromus.*

pseudopectinatus (Backeb.) E. F. Anderson & Boke [*Pelecyphora pseudopectinata* Backeb.]. Sts. simple, to 2½ in. high and 1¾ in. thick; spines glassy-white, yellowish at base, less than 1/16 in. long; fls. next to spine cluster, rosy-white, ¾ in. long, perianth segms. ascending, acute. N. Mex.

rectispinus: a listed name of no botanical standing.

rinconensis (Poselg.) Britt. & Rose. Sts. simple, to 3 in. high and 5 in. thick, tubercles scarcely connected, in about 13 oblique rows, conical, angled above and below; spines 0–3, awl-shaped, straight, yellow-brown, becoming gray, to ½ in. long; fls. white, 1½ in. long. Ne. Mex. Sometimes, but not originally spelled *T. rinconadensis.*

Roseanus: *Coryphantha Roseana.*

Saussieri (A. Web.) Bravo. Sts. simple, depressed-globose, to 8 in. thick, tubercles scarcely united, conical, angled at base; radial spines 9–15, stellate, needle-shaped, white, ⅝ in. long, central spines 4, needle-shaped, spreading, to 1½ in. long; fls. purple, 1½ in. across. Cent. Mex.

Schottii: a listed name of no botanical standing, probably for *T. bicolor* var.

tricolor: a listed name of no botanical standing, probably for *T. bicolor* var.

tulensis (Poselg.) Britt. & Rose. Sts. cespitose, to 5 in. high and thick, ribs about 8, oblique, tubercles conical or pyramidal, to ¾ in. high; radial spines 6–8, the upper and lower needle-shaped, to ⅝ in. long, the lateral spines stouter and longer, central spines 1–2, stouter, to 1¼ in. long; fls. rose, 1 in. long. Ne. Mex.

uncinatus: *Ancistracanthus uncinatus.*

Valdezianus (A. F. Moell.) Bravo [*Pelecyphora Valdeziana* A. F. Moell.]. Sts. simple, to 1 in. thick, tubercles ⅛ in. long; spines about 30, fine, white, velvety-feathery, 3/32 in. long; fls. next to spine cluster, violet-rose, ¾ in. long, perianth segms. ascending, obtuse; fr. globose. N. Mex.

Wagneranus (A. Berger) F. M. Knuth. Sts. cespitose, to 8 in. high and 2½ in. thick, ribs 13, obtuse; radial spines about 20, somewhat spreading, nearly comblike, stout, central spines 1–4, stout, cylindrical, to ¾ in. long. E. Mex.

THELYCRANIA: *CORNUS.*

THELYPODIUM Endl. *Cruciferae.* About 16 spp. of ann. to per., essentially glabrous herbs of w. N. Amer.; sts. erect, simple or branched; lvs. simple, entire or toothed, sometimes pinnatifid; fls. white or purplish, in racemes, sepals and petals 4; fr. a linear silique.

laciniatum (Hook.) Endl. Stout, glabrous, glaucous bien., sts. often hollow, irregularly branched in upper part, 1 ft. to as much as 6 ft.; basal lvs. triangular-lanceolate, irregularly and deeply lobed, st. lvs. subpinnatifid to subentire; fls. white, in dense, spikelike racemes. W. N. Amer.

THELYPTERIS Schmidel. [*Cyclosorus* Link; *Lastrea* Bory; *Phegopteris* (K. Presl) Fée]. *Polypodiaceae.* About 500 spp. of ferns, primarily pantrop., a few boreal; lvs. mostly 1-pinnate-pinnatifid, frequently narrowed at the base, with sparse to dense, simple (or sometimes branched) hairs, scales few; indusia absent, or reniform.

For culture see *Ferns.*

acuminata (Houtt.) C. V. Mort. [*Dryopteris acuminata* Houtt.]. Rhizomes wide-creeping, to 2½ ft.; lvs. glabrous, 2-pinnatifid, abruptly narrowed and long-tapering at apex, pinnae 4–6 in. long, acuminate, pinnules obtuse, mucronate, petioles pale, pubescent; sori close together. Temp. Asia.

decursive-pinnata (Van Hall) Ching [*Dryopteris decursive-pinnata* (Van Hall) O. Kuntze]. Lvs. 1-pinnate to 2-pinnatifid, the rachis winged, wings triangular between pinnae; indusia absent. China.

dentata (Forssk.) E. St. John [*Aspidium violascens* Link; *Dryopteris dentata* (Forssk.) C. Chr.; *D. mollis* (Jacq.) Hieron.]. DOWNY WOOD FERN. Rhizomes very short-creeping to erect; lvs. to 3 ft. long and 1 ft. wide, 2-pinnatifid, decidedly narrowed below to short pinnae, pinnae 2–25 pairs, segms. rounded, hairy, petioles dark. Pantrop. Confused with *T. parasitica.*

hexagonoptera (Michx.) Weatherby [*Dryopteris hexagonoptera* (Michx.) C. Chr.; *Phegopteris hexagonoptera* (Michx.) Fée; *Polypodium hexagonopterum* Michx.]. BEECH FERN, BROAD B.F. Lvs. triangular, to 15 in. long and wide, 1-pinnate, pinnae pinnatifid, wavy-toothed; indusia absent. E. N. Amer.

nevadensis (Bak.) C. V. Mort. [*Dryopteris nevadensis* (Bak.) Underw.; *D. oregana* C. Chr.]. SIERRA WATER FERN. Lvs. lanceolate, 1½–3 ft. long and 4–6 in. wide, 1-pinnate, the pinnae linear-lanceolate, from a broad base, deeply pinnatifid, the lower ones distant and greatly reduced. B.C. to Nev. and Calif.

normalis (C. Chr.) Moxl. [*Dryopteris normalis* C. Chr.]. Rhizomes horizontal, slender; lvs. usually in 2 ranks, 2–3 ft. long, pinnatifid, somewhat pubescent beneath on the midribs, scales linear, ciliate, hairy. Coastal, s. U.S., Bahama Is., W. Indies, Bermuda.

noveboracensis (L.) Nieuwl. [*Aspidium noveboracense* (L.) Swartz; *Dryopteris noveboracensis* (L.) A. Gray]. NEW YORK FERN. Lvs. to 2 ft. long and 7 in. wide, pale green, 1-pinnate, pinnae deeply pinnatifid. E. N. Amer.

octhodes (Kunze) Ching [*Dryopteris octhodes* (Kunze) C. Chr.]. Lvs. 2–4 ft. long, to 1 ft. wide, pinnate-pinnatifid, pinnae with entire bluntish lobes, bearing a gland at base beneath, lower pinnae gradually reduced; indusia hirsute. China, India, Ceylon.

Oreopteris (J. F. Ehrh.) Sloss. [*Dryopteris Oreopteris* (J. F. Ehrh.) Maxon; *Polystichum montanum* (Vogl.) Roth]. MOUNTAIN WOOD FERN. Lvs. to 3 ft. long and 8 in. wide, lanceolate, 1-pinnate to pinnatifid, pinnae oblong-lanceolate, to triangular-ovate at base. Wash. to Alaska, Japan, Eur.

palustris Schott [*Aspidium Thelypteris* (L.) Swartz; *Dryopteris Thelypteris* (L.) A. Gray]. MARSH FERN. Rhizomes creeping; lvs. to 2½ ft. long and 6 in. wide, 1-pinnate, pinnae deeply pinnatifid, margins revolute; indusia typically glandular-toothed or glandular-ciliate. Temp. N. Hemisphere. The more hairy American plants (SNUFFBOX FERN, MEADOW F.) with nonglandular indusia are distinguished by some authors as var. **pubescens** (G. Laws.) Fern. [*Dryopteris Thelypteris* var. *pubescens* (G. Laws.) Nakai].

parasitica (L.) C. V. Mort. [*Dryopteris parasitica* (L.) O. Kuntze]. Like *T. dentata* except rhizomes wider-creeping, petioles tan to green, and lvs. not narrowed basally, with orange glands present on lower surface. Tropics and subtropics.

patens (Swartz) Small [*Aspidium patens* Swartz; *Dryopteris patens* (Swartz) O. Kuntze]. Rhizomes erect, stout; lvs. clustered, with ovate scales, 2–4 ft. long, 2-pinnatifid, with the main divisions linear-acuminate and the ultimate segms. acutish. Trop. Amer. Cv. '**Lepida**'. A skeletonized variant.

pennigera (G. Forst.) Allan [*Dryopteris pennigera* (G. Forst.) C. Chr.; *Polypodium pennigerum* G. Forst.]. Rhizomes erect, trunklike; lvs. to 2 ft. long, 1 ft. wide, 1-pinnate, pinnae pinnatifid, cut into blunt, curved, slightly crenate lobes about ³/₁₆ in. wide, lower pinnae gradually reduced; sori in a row near midrib, indusia absent. New Zeal.

Phegopteris (L.) Sloss. [*Dryopteris Phegopteris* (L.) C. Chr.; *Polypodium Phegopteris* L.]. LONG BEECH FERN, NARROW B. F. Lvs. triangular, to 9 in. long and 8 in. wide, 1-pinnate, the pinnae deeply pinnatifid, ultimate segms. entire; indusia absent. Temp. N. Hemisphere.

reticulata (L.) Proctor [*Dryopteris reticulata* (L.) Urb.; *Meniscium reticulatum* (L.) Swartz]. Lvs. 2–4 ft. long, 1 ft. wide or more, 1-pinnate, pinnae 6–12 in. long, 1–4 in. wide, acuminate, entire, round or cuneate at base, veins with 8–12 areoles between midrib and edge; indusia absent. Trop. Amer.

setigera (Blume) Ching [*Dryopteris setigera* (Blume) O. Kuntze]. Rhizomes almost erect, very stout, with dark brown scales; lvs. large, broad-triangular, 3–6 ft. long, 3-pinnatifid and finely dissected, white-hairy beneath on veins and veinlets; indusia inconspicuous. Trop. Amer. Frequently confused with *T. uliginosa*.

uliginosa (Kunze) C. Chr. [*Dryopteris uliginosa* (Kunze) Ching]. Confused with *T. setigera*, from which it differs in having petioles and older rachis free of hairs. E. Asia to Australia.

THEMEDA Forssk. *Gramineae*. About 50 spp. of ann. or per. grasses in Asia and Australia; infl. of several short racemes, each subtended by a spathe and consisting of 2 approximate pairs of sessile, awnless male or neuter spikelets, which form an involucre around a short rachis that bears a single fertile, awned spikelet and a pair of sterile pedicelled ones, the rachis disjointing above the pairs of sessile male spikelets and forming a pointed callus below the bisexual one. For terminology see *Gramineae*.

australis (R. Br.) Stapf. Per., sts. to 3 ft., in tussocks to 9 in. wide, smooth, often powdery near nodes; lf. blades flat or folded, with rough edges; infl. about 1 ft. long, interrupted, nodding; involucral spikelets to about ⅝ in. long, bisexual, pedicelled spikelets ¼–⅜ in. long, awn of bisexual spikelets 2–2¾ in. long, brown, hairy, bent. Australia.

THENARDIA HBK. *Apocynaceae*. Four trop. spp. of woody climbers with milky sap, native to Mex.; lvs. opp., entire, petioled; fls. in 3-forked, umbel-like cymes, 5-merous, bisexual, calyx small, corolla rotate, stamens borne on corolla, conspicuously exserted, anthers sagittate, with appendages at base, coherent and adhering to stigma; fr. a pair of elongate, cylindrical follicles, seeds many, with tuft of hairs.

floribunda HBK. Tall, glabrous climber, brs. slender; lvs. lanceolate-elliptic to oblong-ovate, 2–5 in. long, acuminate, membranous; primary peduncles lateral, to 3 in. long, cymes many-fld., to 4 in. across; corolla starlike, to 1¼ in. across, purple inside with pale center, greenish-white and tinged with purple outside, tube scarcely ⅛ in. long, lobes ovate, acuminate, stamens with elongate filaments twisted together around style; fr. unknown. S. Mex.

THEOBROMA L. *Byttneriaceae*. Perhaps 20 spp. of trees, native to lowland trop. Amer.; lvs. alt., simple, or in 1 sp. palmately compound; fls. small, in axillary clusters or borne directly on brs. and trunk, calyx 2–5-lobed, petals 5, clawed, hooded, with a spatulate to strap-shaped blade above the hood, stamens 5, opp. the petals, united in a short tube with the 5 staminodes; fr. usually very large, woody, 5-celled, seeds many.

Several species are cultivated in tropical Amer. and one, *T. Cacao*, the principal source of cacao, is grown throughout the wet, lowland tropics. Usually grown under shade of taller trees. Propagated by seeds; trees bear in about 4 years.

Cacao L. CACAO. To 25 ft. or more, evergreen; lvs. leathery, oblong, to 12 in. long, young lvs. red, pendent; fls. borne on trunk and brs., long-pedicelled, calyx pinkish, petals yellowish, about ⅜ in. long; fr. yellowish, purple, or brown, 10-ribbed, to 1 ft. long, seeds ellipsoid, to 1 in. long, borne within a mucilaginous pulp. Cent. and S. Amer. The seeds, cacao, yield the cocoa and chocolate of commerce, after fermentation and roasting.

THEOCOPHYLLUM: *VRIESEA*.

THEOPHRASTACEAE D. Don. THEOPHRASTA FAMILY. Dicot.; 4 genera and about 60 spp. of evergreen, sometimes

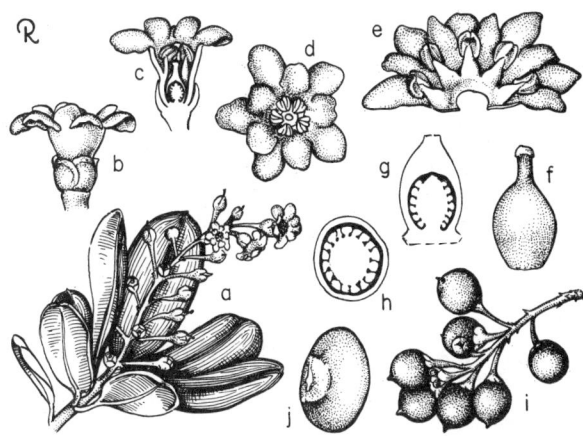

THEOPHRASTACEAE. *Jacquinia Barbasco:* **a,** flowering branch, × ½; **b,** flower, side view, × 1½; **c,** flower, vertical section, × 1½; **d,** flower, face view, × 1½; **e,** corolla, expanded, × 2; **f,** pistil, × 5; **g,** ovary, vertical section, × 5; **h,** ovary, cross section, × 6; **i,** fruit, × ½; **j,** seed, × 2.

dioecious, shrubs and trees, native to trop. Amer. and the Hawaiian Is.; lvs. alt., opp., or whorled, simple, sometimes spine-tipped; fls. bisexual or unisexual, regular, in racemes, corymbs, or panicles, sepals 5, corolla 5-lobed, stamens 5, borne on corolla, staminodes 5, petal-like, pistil 1, ovary superior, 5-carpelled, 1-celled, with free-central placentation; fr. a leathery or fleshy berry or drupe. *Jacquinia* is planted as an ornamental in Zone 10.

THERMOPSIS R. Br. ex Ait.f. FALSE LUPINE. *Leguminosae* (subfamily *Faboideae*). About 20 spp. of herbs of N. Amer. and ne. Asia; lvs. of 3 lfts. palmately arranged, stipules leaf-like; fls. in racemes, papilionaceous, stamens 10, separate; fr. a narrow, flat legume.

Planted as ornamentals; suited to deep, well-drained soils. Propagated by seeds sown in autumn or spring over heat, or outdoors, also by division of dormant plants.

caroliniana M. A. Curtis. CAROLINA LUPINE. To 5 ft., little-branched; lfts. ovate to obovate, to 3 in. long, pubescent and glaucous beneath; racemes terminal, dense, to 10 in. long; fls. yellow; fr. erect, to 2 in. long, densely villous. N.C. to Ga.

fabacea (Pall.) DC. To 3 ft.; lfts. broadly elliptic to obovate; racemes axillary, erect; fls. yellow; fr. flat, to 3 in. long and more. Kamchatka, Kurile Is.

gracilis T. J. Howell. To 2½ ft., sts. nearly glabrous, purplish, semi-glaucous; lfts. oblanceolate or obovate, to 2 in. long; racemes rather loose, to 6 in. long; calyx silky-villous with broadly triangular teeth; fr. spreading, to 2¾ in. long, villous. Calif. to B.C. and Mont.

lanceolata: *T. lupinoides*.

lupinoides (L.) Link [*T. lanceolata* R. Br. ex Ait.f.]. To 1 ft.; lfts. ovate-lanceolate, to 1½ in. long, narrowly cuneate; racemes compact; fls. yellow; fr. strongly recurved, to 2 in. long. Siberia, Alaska.

macrophylla Hook. & Arn. Sts. stout, to 2½ ft., hairy throughout; lfts. obovate, to 3 in. long; racemes dense, 6–10 in. long; fls. yellow; calyx teeth lanceolate; fr. erect, to 3 in. long. Calif.

montana Nutt. To 2 ft., sts. glabrous, usually stout; lfts. to 2 in. long; racemes terminal, to 8 in. long; fls. yellow; fr. linear, 2 in. long or more, pubescent. Wash. to Mont., s. to Nev. and Colo.

rhombifolia Nutt. ex Richardson. To 1 ft.; lfts. ovate-rhombic, to 1 in. long or more, broadly cuneate; racemes terminal or axillary; fls. yellow; fr. recurved, to 2½ in. long, pubescent to glabrous. N.Dak. to Alta., s. to Nebr. and Colo.

THERORHODION: *RHODODENDRON*.

THESPESIA Soland. ex Corrêa. *Malvaceae*. About 15 spp. of trop. trees or shrubs; lvs. simple, triangular to elliptic, unlobed or palmately lobed, usually cordate, entire; fls. 1 or few in the axils, sometimes in racemes, involucral bracts 3–6(–15), often falling early, calyx usually cup-shaped, entire or minutely 5-toothed, persistent, petals large, yellowish to reddish or reddish-purple, usually with a dark purple-red center, stamens united in a tubular column usually much shorter than the petals, style unbranched, stigma 5-grooved or furrowed, ovary 5- or 10-celled, each cell with 1 or more ovules; fr. woody or leathery, dehiscent or indehiscent.

Propagated by seeds.

Garckeana F. Hoffm. Shrub or small tree, to 35 ft.; lvs. to 8 in. long and wide, 3- or 5-lobed; fls. solitary in the axils, involucral bracts united with the calyx, cup-shaped at base, with 5–10(–15) linear, early falling teeth above, calyx about ⅜ in. long, 5-toothed, petals yellow to purplish-red, dark red at the center, to 2½ in. long; fr. about 1½ in. long, subglobose to ellipsoid, loculicidally dehiscent by 5 valves. E. and s. Afr.

grandiflora: *Montezuma speciosissima.*

lampas (Cav.) Dalzell ex Dalzell & A. Gibs. [*Hibiscus lampas* Cav.]. Shrub, to about 8 ft.; lower lvs. deeply 3- or 5-lobed, to 8 in. long and wide or more, upper lvs. smaller, often unlobed; fls. solitary or few in the upper lf. axils, involucral bracts 4–6, subulate, to ⅜ in. long, falling early, calyx about ⅜ in. long, 5-toothed, petals yellow, with a dark purple center, to 3 in. long; fr. globose to ovoid, ¾–1¼ in. long, dehiscent or indehiscent. E. Afr., s. and se. Asia to the Philippines.

populnea (L.) Soland. ex Corrêa. PORTIA TREE. Tree, to 60 ft.; young brs. covered with minute scales; lvs. cordate-ovate, to 6 in. long or more, unlobed, acuminate; fls. solitary, involucral bracts 3, oblong-lanceolate, to ½ in. long, falling early, calyx to ½ in. long, entire or 5-toothed, corolla yellow, with a red center, fading to orange-yellow, to 2½ in. long; fr. depressed-globose, obscurely 5-angled, about 1⅝ in. in diam., indehiscent. Shores, pantrop.

THEVETIA L. *Apocynaceae.* About 8 spp. of shrubs and trees with milky sap, native to trop. Amer.; lvs. alt., entire; fls. in terminal cymes, large, 5-merous, bisexual, corolla funnelform, with 5 hairy scales in throat, stamens 5, alternating with the scales, borne on corolla, included, anthers separate, without enlarged connective, ovary 2-lobed, 2-celled, with 2 ovules in each cell; fr. drupelike, broader than long.

Thrives in rich sandy soil and will tolerate a few degrees of frost if banked with dry sand. Propagated by cuttings and seeds.

neriifolia: *T. peruviana.*

peruviana (Pers.) K. Schum. [*T. neriifolia* A. Juss. ex Steud.]. BE-STILL TREE, YELLOW OLEANDER, LUCKY NUT. To 30 ft., evergreen; lvs. nearly sessile, linear to linear-lanceolate, to 6 in. long and ¼ in. wide, narrowly acuminate, dark green, glossy, secondary veins, obscure; fls. fragrant, orange or yellow, to 2 in. across; fr. hard, angled, to 1 in. across, red turning black. Trop. Amer. Widely planted in trop. of both hemispheres. Cv. **'Alba'** is offered.

thevetioides (HBK) K. Schum. Small tree, to 15 ft.; lvs. linear-lanceolate, to 4 in. long and ½ in. wide, acuminate to an acute apex, secondary veins conspicuous on both surfaces; fls. orange or pinkish-yellow, to 2 in. across or more; fr. to 2½ in. across. Mex.

THLADIANTHA Bunge. *Cucurbitaceae.* Seven or 8 spp. of per., tuberous-rooted, tendril-climbing, dioecious herbs, native to cent. and e. Asia and the Philippine Is.; fls. yellow, campanulate, male fls. mostly clustered, sometimes solitary, stamens 5, separate, female fls. often solitary; fr. small, seeds small, horizontal.

dubia Bunge. Tall climber, pubescent; lvs. cordate-ovate, hairy, not lobed, but toothed; fls. 1 in. across or less, male and female fls. solitary; fr. oblong, 10-ribbed, mostly less than 1 in. long. N. China. Little planted in the U.S., but naturalized in some areas.

THLASPI L. PENNY CRESS, PENNY GRASS. *Cruciferae.* About 60 spp. of erect ann. to per. herbs in the N. Hemisphere, mostly glabrous and glaucous; lvs. oblong to broad-ovate, entire or toothed, basal lvs. forming a rosette, st. lvs. auricled; fls. white, rose, or purplish, in racemes, sepals and petals 4; fr. mostly a flat, short, winged silicle.

A few species are grown in the rock garden and others for the large, flat, ornamental pods often used in dry arrangements.

alpestre L. Bien. or per., to 1½ ft. in fr., glabrous, often glaucous; basal lvs. obovate, petioled; fls. white, mostly reddish-tinged, in rather open infl. High mts., Eur.

alpinum Crantz. Per., to 6 in., mat-forming to cespitose, glabrous; basal lvs. spatulate, entire or dentate, st. lvs. ovate-cordate; petals white, twice as long as sepals; silicles oblong-obovate. Mts., cent. Eur.

arvense L. PENNY CRESS, FIELD P. C., FRENCH WEED, FANWEED, STINKWEED, MITHRIDATE MUSTARD. Rather weedy ann., erect, glabrous, somewhat fetid, branching above; st. lvs. oblong to lanceolate, dentate, only the upper ones clasping; silicles flat, nearly orbicular, to ½ in. across. Eur.; naturalized in N. Amer. Of interest for its pods.

bellidifolium Griseb. Tufted per. allied to *T. rotundifolium,* but lvs. oblong-spatulate and fls. violet; differs from *T. stylosum* in silicles retuse at apex. Albania, Yugoslavia.

bulbosum Sprun. ex Boiss. Cespitose per., to 4 in.; basal lvs. ovate-orbicular, petioled; fls. deep violet, racemes to 4 in. long in fr. Greece.

cepiifolium: *T. rotundifolium* subsp.

densiflorum Boiss. & Kotschy. Glaucescent bien., to 4 in., sts. several, simple; basal lvs. ovate-oblong, mostly entire, petioled, st. lvs. oblong, auricled, clasping; fls. white, in compact headlike-corymbose infl. Turkey.

Jankae: *T. praecox.*

limosellifolium: *T. rotundifolium.*

praecox Wulfen [*T. Jankae* A. Kern.]. Per., to 8 in. or more, glabrous, more or less glaucous; basal lvs. in rosettes, petioled, oblong or orbicular, entire or nearly so, often purplish beneath; calyx purplish, edged with white, petals white. S. Eur.

rotundifolium (L.) Gaud.-Beaup. [*T. limosellifolium* Reut.]. Stoloniferous per., to 8 in.; lvs. thick, entire or dentate, basal lvs. roundish to obovate, st. lvs. elliptic; fls. purple. Mts., cent. Eur. Subsp. **cepiifolium** (Wulfen) Rouy & Foucaud [*T. cepiifolium* (Wulfen) C.Koch]. Basal lvs. smaller, notched, st. lvs. more numerous.

stylosum (Ten.) Mutel. Dwarf, cespitose per., lvs. tufted, spatulate, ¼ in. long, entire; fls. rose, in dense racemes about 1 in. long. Italy.

THOMSONIA Wallich. *Araceae.* One sp., a tuberous, stemless herb in the trop. Himalayas; similar to *Amorphophallus* but having the terminal part of spadix covered with tuberculate, rudimentary fls.

napalensis Wallich. Lf. solitary, blade 3-parted, to 4 ft. long, 2 ft. across, petiole stout, pale greenish, mottled dark green; infl. solitary, appearing before the lf., peduncle to 2½ ft., mottled, spathe convolute at base, expanded above, to 18 in. long, bright green outside, paler inside, spadix nearly as long as spathe. Nepal to Assam.

THRINAX Swartz. THATCH, THATCH PALM, PEABERRY P. *Palmae.* About 10 or perhaps only 4 spp. of slender, small or moderate, unarmed palms with bisexual fls., native to s. Fla., W. Indies, Mex. to Brit. Honduras; st. solitary, naked or clothed with persistent lf. bases; lvs. palmate, petiole splitting at back basally in the sheath, sheath fibrous; infl. often longer than lvs., peduncle with several sheathing bracts, primary brs. several, each subtended by a bract, 1, rarely 2 times branched into slender rachillae; fls. solitary, sessile or pedicelled, perianth usually a 6-lobed cupule, stamens (5–)6–15, carpel solitary, 1-celled, 1-ovuled; fr. globose, pealike, white or ivory, pulpy, seed globose but with a central intrusion of seed coat extending partly or wholly through it.

Where native the species are often used as sources of thatch; also grown as ornamentals. For culture see *Palms.*

altissima: a listed name of no botanical standing, material so named in cult. is probably *Coccothrinax alta.*

argentea: *Coccothrinax argentea,* but material cult. as *T. argentea* is often misidentified.

Ekmanii: *T. Morrisii.*

excelsa Lodd. ex Griseb. [*T. rex* Britt. & W. Harris]. To 30 ft. or more, trunk 6 in. in diam. or more; lvs. large, sheath to 3 ft. long with tonguelike projection opp. petiole, petiole to 6 ft. long or more, velvet-hairy beneath at first, becoming tan, blades with densely interlocked, pale scales beneath, segms. 55–65, to 5 ft. long or more; infl. to 5 ft. long; fls. pink to purple; fr. to ⅜ in. in diam. Jamaica. Most material under this name in hort. is *T. radiata.*

floridana: *T. radiata.*

keyensis: *T. Morrisii.*

microcarpa: *T. Morrisii.*

Morrisii H. Wendl. [*T. Ekmanii* Burret; *T. keyensis* Sarg.; *T. microcarpa* Sarg.]. KEY PALM. To 30 ft. or more; lvs. nearly orbicular, to 3½ ft. wide, glaucescent to silver-white beneath, deeply cleft into about 30 segms.; infl. with hairy to glabrescent bracts; fls. sessile or short-pedicelled; fr. spherical, about $^{3}/_{16}$ in. in diam., central cavity extending only part way through seed. S. Fla., W. Indies. Zone 10a in Fla.

multiflora Mart.: a name of uncertain application in the genus *Coccothrinax;* material grown as *T. multiflora* may be *T. radiata.*

parviflora Swartz. FLORIDA T. P., PALMETTO THATCH. To 30 ft. or more, trunk to 6 in. in diam.; lvs. moderately large, sheath with tonguelike projection opp. petiole, becoming fibrous in age, petiole to 4½ ft. long, blades with 37–57 segms., to 3 ft. long, lacking perceptible scales below; infl. to 5 ft. long or more; fls. ivory to yellowish, stamens 5–15; fr. to nearly 5/16 in. in diam. on pedicels to ⅛ in. long. Jamaica. Most or all material cult. under this name is *T. radiata.*

radiata Lodd. ex Schult. & Schult.f. [*T. floridana* Sarg.; *T. Wendlandiana* Becc.; *Coccothrinax radiata* (Lodd. ex Schult. & Schult.f.) Sarg.]. To 36 ft. or more; sheath to 2 ft. long, with oblique, downward opening opp. petiole, becoming coarsely fibrous, petiole to 3 ft. long, segms. 51–63, with perceptible but scattered scales below; fls. white, stamens 5–10; fr. to 5/16 in. in diam. on pedicels to 3/16 in. long. At low elevations near the sea, Fla., W. Indies, Mex. and Brit. Honduras. Zone 10a in Fla.

rex: *T. excelsa.*

Wendlandiana: *T. radiata.*

THRIXANTHOCEREUS: *ESPOSTOA.*

THRIXSPERMUM Lour. *Orchidaceae.* About 100 spp. native to trop. Asia and Malay Arch.; sts. short and with few lvs., or long, climbing, and with many, spaced lvs.; infls. short or long, several from a node; fls. in 2 alt. ranks or facing in all directions, close together, opening in succession, 1 to few at a time, short-lived, sepals and petals equal, short or long, narrow, lip united to column foot, saccate, with a callus in front of sac, 3-lobed, lateral lobes erect, midlobe fleshy, short or long, column short, with broad foot, pollinia unequal, on short stalks. For structure of fl. see *Orchidaceae.*

For culture see *Orchids.*

Ceciliae: *Sarcochilus Ceciliae.*

Hartmannii: *Sarcochilus Hartmannii.*

lilacinum (Griff.) Rchb.f. [*Sarcochilus lilacinus* Griff.]. Epiphytic, sts. to 6 ft. long, leafy; lvs. ovate, clasping the st., to 1 in. long; infl. racemose, to 1 ft. long, few-fld.; fls. 1 in. across, white or pale lilac, sepals and petals ovate, lateral lobes of lip strongly curved, midlobe conical. Malay Arch.

THRYALLIS: see *GALPHIMIA.*

THRYPTOMENE Endl. *Myrtaceae.* Perhaps more than 20 spp. of heathlike, evergreen shrubs, in Australia; lvs. opp., entire; fls. 1–3, small, white, axillary, 5-merous, sepals petal-like, stamens 5 or 10, staminodes 0; fr. nutlike, formed by ovary and the enlarged base of the calyx, crowned by the persistent calyx lobes and petals. Resembling *Baeckea*, but having sepals scarious and petal-like.

Grown in Zone 10 in Calif.

australis Endl. To 4 ft., or more, brs. slender, erect; lvs. oblong, to ¼ in. long, usually with a short recurved point at apex; fls. white, axillary, solitary, petals and sepals about same length, stamens 10. W. Australia.

calycina (Lindl.) Stapf [*T. Mitchelliana* (Schauer) F. J. Muell.]. To 10 ft., brs. slender, wandlike; lvs. oblong or slightly cuneate at base, obtuse or mucronate, to ½ in. long; fls. white or pink, 1–3 in axils of upper lvs., pedicelled, stamens 5. Victoria.

Mitchelliana: *T. calycina.*

saxicola (A. Cunn.) Schauer. To 4 ft.; lvs. oblong or obovate, to 5/16 in. long; fls. white, 1–2 in upper lf. axils, stamens 10. W. Australia.

THUJA L. ARBORVITAE. *Cupressaceae.* Five spp. of coniferous, evergreen, monoecious trees, native to N. Amer. and e. Asia; branchlets flattened, in a horizontal plane; lvs. scale-like or, when young, needlelike, 4-ranked, dimorphic; female cones erect, ovoid-oblong, small, scales in 4–10 pairs, thin, leathery, the innermost pair often united, the middle pairs bearing 2–3 small, 2-winged seeds.

Although thujas may become tall, important timber trees in nature, in plantations they are often prized for their slow compact growth and the many dwarf garden forms. For culture see *Conifers.*

beverleyensis: *Platycladus orientalis* cv.

bonita: *Platycladus orientalis* cv.

elegantissima: plants so listed may be *T. occidentalis* cv. 'Lutea' or *Platycladus orientalis* cv. 'Elegantissimus'.

japonica: *T. Standishii.*

koraiensis Nakai. Spreading shrub or rarely tree, to 35 ft., horizontal brs. much flattened; lvs. concave or grooved, glaucous beneath, glandular; female cones 5/16 in. long. Korea. Differs from the related *T. Standishii* in having coarser lvs. wholly glaucous beneath.

Lobbii: *T. plicata.*

obtusa: *Chamaecyparis obtusa.*

occidentalis L. AMERICAN A., WHITE CEDAR. To 60 ft.; lvs. dark green above, yellowish-green beneath, glandular; female cones ½ in. long, scales in 4–5 pairs. Nov. Sc. to N.C. and Ill. Zone 3. Important commercially for its soft, light, easily worked wood. There are many cvs. including: **'Alba'** [cvs. 'Albospica'; 'Albospicata'], tips of young branchlets white; **'Aurea'**, bushy, lvs. deep yellow; **'Aureo-variegata'**, lvs. variegated with golden-yellow; **'Bodmeri'**, monstrous form with thick clumpy growth; **'Boothii'**, low, compact, lvs. rather large; **'Brubakeri'**, a listed name; **'Buchananii'**, narrow-pyramidal, lvs. grayish-green; **'Burrowii'**, lvs. yellow; **'Columbia'**, lvs. variegated with silver; **'Columnaris'**: 'Fastigiata'; **'Compacta'**, brs. dense; **'Conica'**, cone-shaped; **'Cristata'**, dwarf, with stout, crowded branchlets; **'Douglasii Aurea'**, lvs. bronzy-yellow; **'Douglasii Pyramidalis'**, dense, pyramidal, brs. fernlike; **'Elegantissima'**, narrowly conical, lvs. glossy green; **'Ellwangerana'**, low, with both adult and juvenile lvs.; **'Ellwangerana Aurea'**, lvs. yellow; **'Ericoides'**, dwarf or bushy, lvs. needle-shaped; **'Fastigiata'** [cv. 'Columnaris'], columnar, brs. short; **'Filicoides'**, narrowly pyramidal, branchlets pinnately arranged; **'Froebelii'**, dwarf; **'George Peabody'**: 'Lutea'; **'Globosa'**, [cv. 'Tom Thumb'], globose, dwarf, lvs. bright green; **'Hollandica'**, subglobose, lvs. green; **'Hoveyi'**, globose, dwarf, lvs. bright green; **'Intermedia'**, compact, dwarf; **'Little Gem'**: 'Pumila'; **'Lutea'** [cv. 'George Peabody'], pyramidal, branchlets much flattened; **'Martinii'** and **'Minima'**, listed names; **'Nigra'**, compact, lvs. dark green **'Ohlendorfii'** [cv. 'Spaethii'], bushy; **'Pendula'**, brs. bending downward; **'Pumila'** [cv. 'Little Gem'], dense, dwarf, lvs. dark green; **'Pygmaea'**, dwarf; **'Pyramidalis'**, dense, pyramidal; **'Recurva Nana'**, dwarf, branchlets recurved; **'Reidii'**, dwarf, spreading; **'Riversii'**, compact, pyramidal, lvs. yellowish-green; **'Rosenthalii'**, columnar, lvs. glossy dark green; **'Semper-aurea'**, lvs. golden-yellow; **'Shermanii'**, a listed name; **'Smithiana'**, low, compact, lvs. nearly purple in autumn; **'Spaethii'**: 'Ohlendorfii'; **'Spiralis'**, branchlets appearing as if spirally arranged; **'Tom Thumb'**: 'Globosa'; **'Umbraculifera'**, dwarf, with umbrellalike top; **'Vervaeneana'**, smaller, denser, branchlets bronzy in winter; **'Viridis'**, narrowly pyramidal, lvs. glossy dark green; **'Wagneri'** [cv. 'Wagnerana'], globose, lvs. dark green; **'Woodwardii'**, dense, globose, lvs. dark green.

orientalis: *Platycladus orientalis.*

plicata J.Donn ex D. Don [*T. Lobbii* Gord.]. GIANT A., GIANT CEDAR, WESTERN RED C. To 200 ft.; lvs. glossy green above, paler with distinct whitish marks beneath, often with a small gland; female cones ½ in. long, scales in 5–6 pairs. Alaska to Calif. Zone 5, but needs protection from strong winter winds. The soft, durable wood is an important product in the Pacific Northwest. Cvs. are: **'Atrovirens'**, lvs. dark green; **'Aurea'** [cv. 'Zebrina'], lvs. yellowish; **'Cuprea'**, dwarf, lvs. bronze to yellowish; **'Fastigiata'**, columnar; **'Hogan'**, tightly compact; **'Pendula'**, brs. drooping; **'Rogersii'**, dwarf, very compact, lvs. small, yellow; **'Zebrina'**: 'Aurea'.

pyramidalis: *T. occidentalis* cv. or *Platycladus orientalis* cv. 'Strictus'.

Standishii (Gord.) Carrière [*T. japonica* Maxim.]. JAPANESE A. To 50 ft.; lvs. with triangular white marks beneath, not glandular; female cones to ½ in. long, scales in 4–5 pairs. Japan. Zone 6.

torulosa: a listed name of no botanical standing.

THUJOPSIS (L.f.) Siebold & Zucc. *Cupressaceae.* One sp., a monoecious, coniferous, evergreen, pyramidal tree, native to Japan; allied to *Thuja* but differing in having branchlets broad, very flat; lvs. broader than wide, white beneath; female cones nearly flat-topped, globose, scales 6–8, thickly wedge-shaped; seeds 3–5 to each scale, winged.

Propagated easily by cuttings. Adapted to shade and rich moist soil. Difficult to transplant and slow-growing when young. For culture see *Conifers.*

dolabrata (L.f.) Siebold & Zucc. HIBA ARBORVITAE, FALSE A. To 100 ft., but usually a large shrub in cult., brs. spreading horizontally, often nodding at ends, branchlets nearly ¼ in. wide; lvs. bright glossy green above, with a broad white band beneath; female cones ½–¾ in. long, seeds winged. Zone 7. The durable wood is used in Japan. Var. **dolabrata.** The typical var.; to 50 ft., female cones about ½ in. long, scales thickened at apex and bluntly triangular. S. to cent. Japan. Commonly cult. Var. **Hondae** Mak. To 75 ft. or more, lvs. smaller and whiter beneath, female cones to ¾ in. across, scales thin, with a much reduced point. N. Japan. Cv. **'Nana'.** Erect, dwarf, branchlets more slender, lighter green. Cv. **'Variegata'.** Tips of branchlets creamy-white.

THUNBERGIA Retz. *Acanthaceae.* Perhaps more than 100 spp. of erect or climbing herbs or shrubs, native to the warm parts of Cent. and s. Afr., Madagascar, and Asia; lvs. opp.; fls. conspicuous, blue, yellow, orange, or white, usually solitary, subtended by 2 large bracts, calyx small, ringlike, corolla large, lobes 5, rounded, equal or nearly so, tube curved, swollen on one side, stamens 4, didynamous, borne near base of tube; fr. a spherical caps., lower part fertile, upper part beaked, sterile.

Thunbergias are popular ornamentals in the tropics and in the southern U.S. for covering porches, trellises and arbors, and are also grown in the North under glass. Propagated by seeds, cuttings of young growth, and by layers in summer.

alata Bojer. BLACK-EYED SUSAN VINE. Twining, per. herb, sometimes grown as an ann.; lvs. triangular-ovate, to 3 in. long, toothed, petiole winged; fls. 1½ in. long, solitary on long peduncles, corolla creamy, with dark purple throat, or white with dark center, or pure white, or orange-yellow with dark center. Trop. Afr.; widely naturalized in tropics. Cvs. include: 'Alba', fls. white, with dark center; 'Bakeri', fls. pure white; 'Aurantiaca', fls. orange-yellow, with dark center.

Battiscombei Turrill. Tall herb, often climbing or scrambling; lvs. ovate-elliptic, to 4 in. long, palmately 3–5-nerved; fls. blue, in axillary racemes. Trop. Afr.

coccinea Wallich. Woody twiner; lvs. ovate, to 5 in. long, thick, toothed, 3–5-nerved from base; fls. in drooping racemes, corolla scarlet, with yellow throat, 1 in. long, lobes reflexed over tips of bracts. India.

erecta (Benth.) T. Anderson [*Meyenia erecta* Benth.]. KING'S-MANTLE, BUSH CLOCK VINE. Erect or sometimes scandent shrub, to 6 ft.; lvs. ovate, to 3 in. long, nearly entire; fls. solitary, corolla blue-purple, the tube yellowish-white or white, to 2¾ in. long. Trop. Afr. Cv. 'Alba'. Fls. white.

fragrans Roxb. Woody twiner; lvs. lanceolate to triangular-ovate, to 3 in. long, nearly entire; fls. solitary, fragrant, corolla white, 1¼ in. long, 2 in. across. India and Ceylon.

Gibsonii: *T. Gregorii.*

grandiflora (Roxb. ex Rottl.) Roxb. BLUE TRUMPET VINE, CLOCK VINE, BENGAL C.V., SKY VINE, SKYFLOWER, BLUE S. Woody twiner; lvs. ovate, to 8 in. long, usually 3–5-nerved from base, very rough, angular-toothed; fls. usually in drooping racemes, pedicels usually 1½–2 in. long, corolla blue, somewhat 2-lipped, to 3 in. long and broad. India; naturalized in the tropics. Common in cult. for arbors and porches. Cv. 'Alba'. Fls. white. Closely related to *T. laurifolia*, but differs in lf. shape and length of pedicels.

Gregorii S. L. Moore [*T. Gibsonii* S. L. Moore]. Twining per. herb; lvs. ovate, to 3 in. long, toothed, petioles winged; fls. solitary on long, hairy peduncles, corolla orange, 1¾ in. long and broad. Trop. Afr. Readily grown as an ann. from seeds.

Harrisii: *T. laurifolia.*

laurifolia Lindl. [*T. Harrisii* Hook.]. Woody twiner; lvs. lanceolate or ovate-lanceolate, leathery, to 5 in. long, nearly entire, usually 3-nerved from base; fls. in racemes, pedicels usually ¾ in. long, corolla light blue, with white or yellowish throat, 3 in. across. India.

primulina Hemsl. Weak per., silky-hairy; lvs. rhomboid-ovate with small lobe on each side, to 2½ in. long, 3–5-nerved; fls. axillary, solitary, corolla 1½ in. across, pale yellow, lobes spreading. Trop. Afr.

THUNIA Rchb.f. *Orchidaceae.* Six spp. native to Himalayas, India, Burma; sts. not pseudobulbous, many-lvd.; lvs. close together, thin, deciduous, to 8 in. long, covered with waxy bloom; infl. a terminal, densely fld. raceme, bracts large, pale green or white; sepals and petals similar, lip broad, with 5–7 fringed keels and a short, obtuse spur, column with 2 small wings at apex, pollinia 4, 2-parted. For structure of fl. see *Orchidaceae.*

Intermediate greenhouse; plants require warmth and frequent watering during growth, but need a decided period of rest after flowering, when the leaves have fallen, and should then be kept cool and dry. For general culture see *Orchids.*

alba Rchb.f. Sts. to 3½ ft. long; lvs. oblong-lanceolate, to 8 in. long, light green, glaucous beneath; racemes 5–9-fld., pedicels white, sheathed by white, boat-shaped bracts; fls. to 3 in. across, white, sepals and petals similar, oblong-lanceolate, lip oblong, fringed on front margin, with 5 fringed purple keels on disc and sometimes additional purple or citron-yellow markings. Summer. N. India, Burma. Cv. 'Nivalis'. Lip pure white. Var. **Marshalliana** (Rchb.f.) Hook. [*T. Marshal-*

liana Rchb.f.]. Lvs. and infl. as in typical var.; sts. taller; lip shorter, apical half yellow, with orange-yellow, fringed keels, the hairs of the fringe longer and more numerous, column shorter and stouter.

Marshalliana: *T. alba* var.

THURBERIA: *GOSSYPIUM.* **T. thespesioides:** *G. Thurberi.*

THYMBRA L. *Labiatae.* Two spp. of small shrubs of se. Eur. and sw. Asia; sts. mostly square in cross section; lvs. opp.; fls. in 6–10-fld. verticillasters arranged in dense, narrow, spikes, bracts leaflike, imbricate, calyx flattened, 13-nerved, 2-lipped, corolla tube straight, limb 2-lipped, stamens 4, in 2 pairs, included; fr. of 4 glabrous nutlets.

Propagated by seeds or cuttings.

spicata L. Low, stout shrub, sts. to 22 in.; lvs. sessile, linear, ¼–⅝ in. long, entire, glabrous, densely glandular-dotted; infl. headlike to spicate, 1–4 in. long, bracts densely white-ciliate; corolla to ⅝ in. long, pink, tube twice as long as calyx, upper lip longer than lower. Sunny slopes, Greece to Israel.

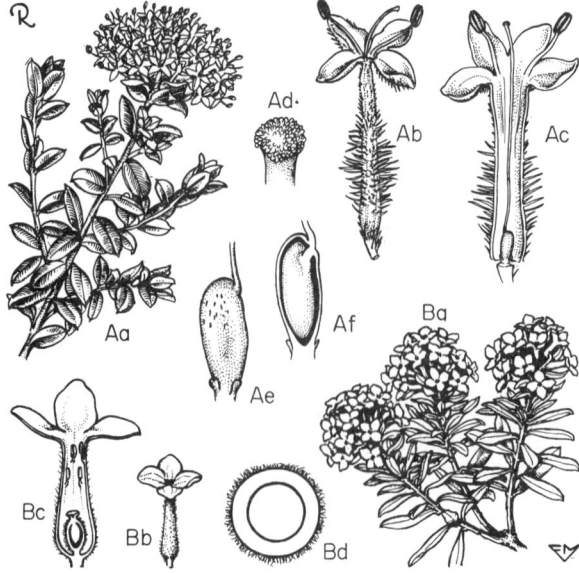

THYMELAEACEAE. **A,** *Pimelea ferruginea:* **Aa,** flowering branch, × ½; **Ab,** flower, × 2; **Ac,** flower, perianth expanded, × 2; **Ad,** stigma, × 20; **Ae,** ovary, × 8; **Af,** ovary, vertical section, × 8. **B,** *Daphne Cneorum:* **Ba,** flowering branch, × ½; **Bb,** flower, × 1; **Bc,** flower, vertical section, × 2; **Bd,** ovary, cross section, × 10. (Ba-Bd from Bailey, *Manual of Cultivated Plants,* ed. 2.)

THYMELAEACEAE Juss. MEZEREUM FAMILY. Dicot.; about 40 genera and 50 spp. of deciduous or evergreen trees or shrubs, rarely herbs, native to temp. and trop. regions of both hemispheres; lvs. alt. or opp., simple, entire; fls. few to many in racemes or umbels, bisexual, or unisexual and the plants then usually dioecious, calyx tubular, lobes 4–5, spreading, petals 0 or scalelike, at mouth of calyx tube, stamens 4 or 8, sometimes 2, inserted in the calyx tube, pistil 1, ovary superior, 1- or 2-celled; fr. usually a drupe, rarely a caps. or berry. *Daphne* and *Edgeworthia* are sources of fine hand-crafted paper, and *Dais, Daphne, Dirca, Edgeworthia, Gnidia,* and *Pimelea* are cult. as ornamentals.

THYMOPHYLLA: *DYSSODIA.*

THYMUS L. THYME. *Labiatae.* About 300–400 spp. of aromatic small shrubs or per. herbs of Eur. and Asia; sts. usually prostrate or creeping, woody at least at base, mostly square in cross section; lvs. opp., small, entire; fls. in 1- to many-fld. verticillasters often crowded in a terminal head, calyx cylindrical to campanulate, 10–13-nerved, usually 2-lipped, tube straight, hairy in throat, corolla tube straight, limb 2-lipped, stamens 4, usually exserted; fr. of 4 glabrous nutlets. Most thymes grown in American gardens appear to be of confused identity and often erroneously named.

Grown as ornamentals in rock gardens, borders, walks and paths, and *T. vulgaris* in the kitchen garden as a sweet herb for seasoning. Propagated by cuttings or division.

Adamovicii Velen. Prostrate creeper, densely velvety, fl. sts. 2–4 in.; lvs. somewhat fleshy, elliptic, red-glandular on both surfaces; infl. headlike; corolla rose-red, densely red-glandular-hairy. Cent. Yugoslavia.

albus (Waldst. & Kit.) Link. Not cuet. The name is used in hort. for a white-fld. form or forms of uncertain identity.

augustifolius: *T. Serpyllum.*

arcticus: *T. praecox* subsp.

argenteus: a listed name of no botanical standing for *T. vulgaris* cv.

aureus Hort. ex E. Morr. Probably *T. Serpyllum,* but the name variously applied in hort. to yellow-lvd. forms.

azoricus: *T. caespititius.*

balticus: a listed name of no botanical standing.

britannicus: *T. praecox* subsp. *arcticus.*

brittoniensis: a listed name of no botanical standing for *T. praecox* subsp. *arcticus.*

Broussonetii Boiss. Erect, much-branched shrub, 5–12 in., sts. hairy on 4 sides or 2 opp. sides almost glabrous; lvs. narrowly ovate to elliptic, sometimes rhombic, to ¾ in. long, flat, glabrous, ciliate; infl. ovoid, to ¾ in. across, bracts ovate, to ¾ in. long, purplish-red, mostly ciliate; corolla to ¾ in. long, rose-red. Morocco.

caespititius Brot. [*T. azoricus* Lodd.; *T. micans* Soland. ex Lowe]. Mat-forming subshrub, brs. prostrate, fl. sts. erect, ¾–2½ in., hairy on 4 sides; lvs. in dense tufts, linear to narrowly oblanceolate, to 5/16 in. long, glabrous, ciliate at base, glandular-dotted on both sides, sessile; infl. loose; fls. solitary in axils, calyx glabrescent, corolla about 3/16 in. long, purplish-pink or whitish. Nw. Iberian Pen., Canary Is., Azores.

camphoratus Hoffmanns. & Link. Shrub, 6–12 in., brs. densely white-puberulent on 4 sides; lvs. triangular-ovate, ⅛ in. long, bluntly acute, revolute, densely white-tomentose beneath, petiole nearly as long as blade; infl. terminal, about ½ in. long, bracts nearly orbicular, ¼ in. long, often purplish; corolla rose. S. Portugal.

carnosus Boiss. Stiffly erect, fastigiate shrub, 5–9 in.; lvs. elliptic, to 3/16 in. long, revolute, glabrous above, tomentose beneath, petioled; infl. nearly globose, about 5/16 in. across; corolla about ¼ in. long, whitish. S. Portugal. Some material offered as *T. nitidus* belongs here.

Chamaedrys: *T. pulegioides.*

cimicinus Blum ex Ledeb. Sts. procumbent, woody, much-branched; lvs. oblong, to ¼ in. long, obtuse, entire, glabrous, ciliate at base; fls. axillary, shorter than the leaflike bracts, corolla scarcely longer than calyx, reddish. S. Russia.

×**citriodorus** (Pers.) Schreb. ex Schweigg. & Körte: *T. pulegioides* × *T. vulgaris.* Much-branched, lemon-scented shrub, sts. 4–12 in., mostly erect; lvs. narrowly rhombic-ovate to lanceolate, to ⅜ in. long, revolute, glabrous; infl. of oblong heads about 5/16 in. in diam.; fls. pale lilac. Cvs. are: **'Argenteus'**, **'Aureus'**, and **'Silver Queen'**.

coccineus: a listed name of no botanical standing; applied to reddish-fld. forms of *T. praecox, T. Serpyllum,* and *T. vulgaris.*

comosus Heuff. ex Griseb. & Schenk. Brs. procumbent to nearly erect, woody at base, fl. sts. to 6 in. high, hairy on 4 sides; lvs. ovate to suborbicular, to ⅝ in. long, with distinct marginal veins, glabrous to slightly hairy, petioled; infl. globose to cylindrical, to 2¾ in. long; corolla about ⅜ in. long, purple. Mts., Romania.

comptus Friv. Procumbent, woody at base, sts. densely hairy on 4 sides, fl. sts. ascending, 2–6 in. long; lvs. stiff, linear to lanceolate, to ½ in. long, glabrous, ciliate at base, sessile; infl. to 4 in. long, verticillasters many-fld., spaced apart; corolla scarcely longer than calyx, 3/16 in. long, rose. E. Balkan Pen.

Doerfleri Ronn. Of uncertain taxonomic status, resembling *T. praecox;* sts. hairy on 4 sides, fl. sts. to 3½ in.; lvs. linear, twice as wide as lvs. of nonflowering sts., cuneate, densely covered with long and short hairs. Albania.

Drucei: *T. praecox* subsp. *arcticus.*

erectus: a listed name of no botanical standing.

ericifolius: *Micromeria ericifolia.*

fragrantissimus: a listed name of no botanical standing, perhaps for *T.* × *citriodorus.*

glaber: *T. pulegioides.*

glabrescens Willd. [*T. glabrescens* var. *Loevyanus* (Opiz) Ronn.]. Low, mat-forming, fl. sts. erect, to 6–12 in., essentially herbaceous, usually hairy on 4 sides; lvs. elliptic-lanceolate to obovate, 5/16–⅞ in. long, mostly obtuse, glabrous, ciliate at base; infl. globose, lowest verticillasters often spaced apart; corolla purple. Cent. and se. Eur. A variable sp. Some material grown as *T. odoratissimus* belongs here.

Herba-barona Loisel. CARAWAY T. Procumbent subshrub, fl. sts. often ascending, 2–5 in. high; lvs. ovate-lanceolate, to 5/16 in. long, acute, ciliate, glabrous and glandular-dotted above; infl. oblong, lower verticillasters sometimes spaced apart; corolla about ¼ in. long, rose. Corsica, Sardinia. Foliage has scent of caraway when crushed.

hyemalis J. Lange. Erect shrub, to 1 ft., sts. gray, hairy; lvs. linear-lanceolate, to ¼ in. long, ciliate, revolute; infl. a dense, nearly globose head; calyx glandular-dotted, corolla to ¼ in. long, deep rose. Se. Spain.

Jankae: *T. praecox* subsp. *Skorpilii.*

lanicaulis: *T. thracicus.*

lanuginosus Mill. Closely allied to *T. Serpyllum;* not known to be cult.; material listed under this name is *T. pseudolanuginosus.*

Marschallianus: *T. pannonicus.*

Marshallii: a listed name of no botanical standing; possibly a mistake for *Marschallianus.*

Mastichina L. Erect shrub, 6–12 in., sts. hairy on all sides; lvs. elliptic, to ⅝ in. long, glandular-dotted; infl. nearly globose, 5/16–⅝ in. across, bracts similar to the lvs., greenish; calyx with upper lip very deeply divided, teeth long-ciliate, corolla about 5/16 in. long, white. Iberian Pen., N. Afr.

membranaceus Boiss. Nearly globose shrub, 4–8 in., brs. spreading or ascending, sts. hairy on all sides; lvs. linear to rhombic-lanceolate, to ⅝ in. long, revolute, appressed-hairy on both sides; infl. ovoid, about ⅝ in. long, bracts showy, membranous, ovate, to ⅝ in. long, greenish-white, flushed pink; corolla about ½ in. long, white. Se. Spain.

micans: *T. caespititius.*

montanus: *T. pulegioides.*

nitidus: *T. Richardii* subsp.; but some material offered as *T. nitidus* is *T. carnosus.*

nummularius Bieb. Spreading, woody at base, per., fl. sts. 8–12 in., hairy on 2 sides; lvs. broadly ovate to broadly elliptic, sometimes spatulate, to ¾ in. long, obtuse, ciliate at base, usually glabrous; infl. oblong to hemispherical, to 1 in. in diam.; corolla 5/16 in. long, rose-pink to mauve. Caucasus to Asia Minor.

odoratissimus: *T. Pallasianus;* but some material grown as *T. odoratissimus* is *T. glabrescens.*

Pallasianus H. Braun [*T. odoratissimus* Bieb.]. Sts. erect or procumbent, woody, creeping nonflowering brs. absent, fl. sts. to 6 in., short-hairy on 4 sides; lvs. linear to lanceolate, to ¾ in. long, glabrous, with prominent midrib, sessile; infl. headlike, bracts similar to lvs.; calyx tube campanulate, hirsute, corolla pale pink. S. U.S.S.R.

pannonicus All. [*T. Marschallianus* Willd.]. Per. herb with ascending brs., sts. woody at base, fl. sts. 4–8 in., hairy on 4 sides; lvs. lanceolate, ½–¾ in. long, sparsely glandular-punctate, herbaceous, with indistinct veins, nearly sessile; infl. rarely branched; corolla about ¼ in. long, rose. E.-cent. Eur. to the Caucasus.

pectinatus Fisch. & C. A. Mey. Not in cult.; material offered under this name is *T. Pallasianus,* to which it is closely related.

praecox Opiz. Per., sts. creeping, long, somewhat woody, fl. sts. slender, to 4 in., with basal cluster of small lvs., hairy on 4 sides or on 2 opp. sides; lvs. nearly leathery, obovate to nearly orbicular, with prominent lateral veins; bracts similar to lvs.; calyx campanulate, about ⅛ in. long, corolla purple. Eur. Represented in cult. by the following 2 subsp. Subsp. **arcticus** (E. Durand) Jalas [*T. arcticus* (E. Durand) Ronn.; *T. britannicus* Ronn.; *T. brittoniensis* Hort.; *T. Drucei* Ronn.; *T. Serpyllum* of auth., not L.]. MOTHER-OF-THYME. Sts. hairy, mostly on 2 sides only; lvs. mostly obovate, about ¼ in. long, densely glandular-dotted; infl. hemispherical, about ½ in. across; calyx to ⅛ in. long, corolla rose-purple. Greenland and Scandinavia to nw. Spain. Cvs. include: **'Albus'**, fls. white; **'Coccineus'**, fls. crimson; **'Splendens'**, fls. red. Subsp. **Skorpilii** (Velen.) Jalas [*T. Jankae* Čelak.]. Sts. hairy on 4 sides; basal lvs. on fl. sts. sessile; corolla to 5/16 in. long, purplish. N. and cent. Balkan Pen.

pseudolanuginosus Ronn. [*T. lanuginosus* of auth., not Mill.]. Mat-forming, creeping per., scarcely ½ in. high, sts. woody at base; lvs. broadly elliptic, about ⅛ in. long, obtuse, hairy on both sides; fls. few in lf. axils, corolla pale pink, about 3/16 in. long. Nativity unknown. Long cult. erroneously as *T. lanuginosus.* Often planted in flagstone walks and terraces.

pulegioides L. [*T. Chamaedrys* Fries; *T. glaber* Mill.; *T. montanus* Waldst. & Kit.]. Spreading, bushy shrub, 4–12 in., sts. hairy only on the angles and sometimes also on 2 opp. sides; lvs. ovate, lanceolate, or elliptic, mostly 5/16 in. long, cuneate, obtuse, glabrous and glandular-dotted above, with veins not much raised beneath, petioled; infl. interrupted, oblong; corolla typically mauve. Eur. Cv. **'Alba'**. Corolla white. Cvs. **'Coccineus'** and **'Kermesinus'**. Corolla crimson.

quinquecostatus Čelak. Prostrate desert shrub, to 4 in., sts. creeping, wiry, cylindrical, white-pilose; lvs. narrowly to broadly ovate, 1/4–5/16 in. long, obtuse, entire, ciliate at base, glabrous, glandular-dotted on both sides; infl. a terminal spike; corolla rose-purple. Mongolia to Japan.

Richardii Pers. Prostrate per., sts. woody at base, fl. sts. ascending, to 4½ in. high; lvs. rhombic-ovate, to 7/16 in. long, bluntly acute, with few or no glandular dots above but many beneath; infl. headlike, cymes 3- to many-fld.; corolla nearly 5/16 in. long, pale lilac. Balearic Is., Sicily, w. Yugoslavia. Subsp. **nitidus** (Guss.) Jalas [*T. nitidus* Guss.]. Lvs. more than twice as long as wide; calyx hirsute, densely covered with stalked glands. Marettimo Is. (w. Sicily). Material cult. as *T. nitidus* may be *T. carnosus.*

roseus Shipch. Not in cult.; material so listed usually represents a cv. of either *T., praecox* subsp. *arcticus* or *T. vulgaris.*

Serpyllum L. [*T. angustifolius* Pers.]. LEMON T., WILD T. Mat-forming, per., rooting at nodes, sts. woody at base, fl. sts. erect, to 4 in., hairy on 4 sides; lvs. linear to elliptic, to 5/16 in. long, nearly sessile; infl. usually headlike; corolla 3/16 in. long, purple. Nw. Eur. Apparently rarely cult. in U.S. and much material offered as *T. Serpyllum* represents other spp., such as, *T. nummularius, T. pannonicus, T. praecox, T. pseudolanuginosus,* or *T. pulegioides.*

thracicus Velen. [*T. lanicaulis* Ronn.]. Procumbent, sts. woody, fl. sts. to 4 in., hairy on 4 sides or on 2 opp. sides; lvs. elliptic-spatulate, about 5/16 in. long, nearly obtuse; calyx to 3/16 in. long, tinged purple, upper lip somewhat longer than lower, corolla to 5/16 in. long, purple. Cent. Balkan Pen. and n. Aegean region.

vulgaris L. GARDEN T., COMMON T. Shrub, 6–15 in., sts. woody, erect; lvs. linear to elliptic, 3/16–5/8 in. long, revolute, tomentose, not ciliate, petioled; infl. many-fld., dense and headlike or interrupted; corolla about 3/16 in. long, whitish to lilac. W. Medit. region to se. Italy. A very variable sp. Cult. as a potherb. Cvs. include **'Argenteus'**, **'Aureus'**, **'Fragrantissimus'**, **'Roseus'**.

Zygis L. Stout, erect shrub, 4–7 in., rarely to 12 in.; lvs. clustered at nodes, linear, 3/16–5/16 in. long, revolute, tomentose, glandular-dotted, sessile; infl. to 4 in. long, verticillasters in upper lf. axils; corolla about 1/8 in. long, scarcely exserted from calyx, white. Iberian Pen.

THYRSACANTHUS: *ODONTONEMA.* **T. rutilans:** *O. Schomburgkianum.*

THYSANOCARPUS Hook. LACEPOD, FRINGEPOD. *Cruciferae.* About 5 spp. of erect, slender, ann. herbs of w. N. Amer.; sts. simple or branched; lvs. simple; fls. in slender racemes, minute, white to purplish, sepals and petals 4; fr. an indehiscent, flattened, 1-celled, 1-seeded silicle, with an entire to crenate, often perforate winged margin.

curvipes Hook. [*T. elegans* Fisch. & C. A. Mey.]. To 20 in., pubescent or hirsute at base, branched above; basal lvs. in rosettes, oblong, to 2 in. long or more, sinuate-dentate to entire, st. lvs. lanceolate, sagittate, clasping, entire or nearly so; fls. about 1/16 in. long; silicles round-obovate, to 1/4 in. long, the wing sometimes perforate. W. N. Amer.

elegans: *T. curvipes.*

THYSANOLAENA Nees. *Gramineae.* About 10 spp. of per. grasses in Asia; sts. solid, reedlike; lf. blades very broad, firm, long; infl. a very large, much-branched panicle; spikelets pedicelled on the brs. of the panicle, all similar, minute, 2- or rarely 3-fld., with the lower floret reduced to the lemma, the upper complete, and the third, if present, male or much reduced, rachilla tough, tardily disarticulating above the glumes and between the florets, prolonged, pedicels fragile, glumes about half as long as the lemmas, obtuse, nerveless, or obscurely 1-nerved, delicate, lower lemma thinly membranous, 3-nerved, acuminate, the palea absent, upper lemma ovate, acute or mucronate, 3-nerved, ciliate on the margins, the palea short, hyaline, truncate. For terminology see *Gramineae.*

Agrostis: *T. maxima.*

maxima (Roxb.) O.Kuntze [*T. Agrostis* Nees]. Robust per., sts. to 10 ft.; lf. blades to 2¾ in. wide; panicle 1 ft. long or more, brs. slender, flat, densely fld., drooping; spikelets less than 1/8 in. long, pointed, fertile lemma long-ciliate. Se. Asia. Cult. as an ornamental in s. Fla. and Calif.

TIARELLA L. FALSE MITERWORT. *Saxifragaceae.* Six spp. of rhizomatous, mostly spring-flowering, per. herbs in e. and w. N. Amer., 1 sp. in Asia; lvs. basal and on the sts., blades cordate and palmately lobed, or of 3 lfts.; fls. small, white or reddish, in simple or branched racemes, calyx tube campanulate, united to base of ovary, calyx lobes 5, triangular, petals 5, stamens 10, ovary superior, with 2 unequal, beaklike projections; caps. of 2 unequal parts.

Useful in the wild garden or rock garden in shady locations; especially attractive in autumn for the brilliant color of the foliage. Propagated by division, and by seeds when obtainable.

cordifolia L. FOAMFLOWER. Stolons sometimes present; fl. sts. to 12 in.; lvs. ovate-cordate, to 4 in. long, dentate, petioles to 4 in.; fls. whitish or reddish. Nov. Sc., Appalachian Mts. to Ga. and Ala. Cvs. include: **'Lilacina'**, a listed name; **'Major'**, fls. salmon-rose or wine-red; **'Marmorata'**, foliage bronze, turning blackish-green, marbled with purple, fls. many, maroon; **'Purpurea'**, fls. purple. Var. **collina:** *T. Wherryi.*

laciniata Hook. Rhizomes slender; fl. sts. to 15 in.; lvs. of 3 lfts., lfts. divided nearly their full length into irregularly toothed segms.; fls. in panicles, white. S. Alaska to n. Ore.

polyphylla D. Don. Stoloniferous; fl. sts. to 18 in.; basal lvs. cordate-orbicular, to 2½ in. across, petioles to 4 in. Himalayas, China, Japan, Taiwan.

purpurea: *T. cordifolia* cv.

trifoliata L. Related to *T. laciniata,* but differing chiefly in having the 3 lfts. shallowly lobed to middle or less. Alaska to Ore., e. to Rocky Mts.

unifoliata Hook. SUGAR-SCOOP. Differs from *T. trifoliata* in having lvs. usually simple, palmately 3–5-lobed. S. Alaska, s. to w. Mont. and cent. Calif.

Wherryi Lakela [*T. cordifolia* var. *collina* Wherry]. Related to *T. cordifolia,* but differing in lacking stolons, in having more slender racemes and narrower petals, and in other, technical characters. Summer-flowering. Va. and Tenn. to Ga., Ala., Miss.

TIBOUCHINA Aubl. [*Pleroma* D. Don]. GLORY BUSH. *Melastomataceae.* About 350 spp. of shrubs or subshrubs, native to trop. Amer.; lvs. simple, 3–7-nerved; fls. large, solitary or in terminal, branched panicles, 5-merous, stamens 10; fr. a caps., seeds resembling minute spiral shells.

Grown under glass or outdoors in the South or Calif., where they will withstand a few degrees of frost. Propagated by cuttings under glass.

alba Cogn. Not in cult.; but plants offered under this name are probably *Melastoma candidum.*

bicolor (Naud.) Cogn. Shrub, brs. densely velvety; lvs. stiff, oblong-lanceolate, 1½–3 in. long, 5-nerved, densely strigose above, pilose beneath; fls. 1½ in. across, petals bicolored red and orange. Bolivia.

elegans (Naud.) Cogn. Shrub, to 6 ft., brs. obscurely 4-angled, hairy; lvs. oblong-ovate, 2–3 in. long, 1–1½ in. wide, 3-nerved, petioles short; petals purple, about 1 in. long, ½ in. wide, stamens purple. Brazil.

grandiflora: a listed name of no botanical standing for *T. Urvilleana.*

grandifolia Cogn. Shrub, to 10 ft., brs. obtusely 4-angled, scabrous to pilose; lvs. oblong-ovate, 5–9 in. long, 3–6 in. wide, 5–7-nerved, densely pubescent beneath; panicles 8–16 in. long, 3-branched, setose; fls. about 1 in. across, petals violet. Brazil.

granulosa (Desr.) Cogn. Tree, to 40 ft., brs. 4-angled, the angles winged; lvs. oblong-lanceolate, 5–8 in. long 1–3 in. wide, entire, 5-nerved, sparsely hairy above, pubescent beneath; panicles terminal, 2–12 in. long; fls. to 2 in. across, petals rose-purple to purplish-violet; caps. 5/16 in. long. Brazil.

Langsdorffiana (Bonpl.) Baill. Shrub, brs. 4-angled to 4-winged, bristly; lvs. ovate-oblong, 4–6 in. long, about 2 in. wide, membranous, 5–7-nerved, minutely setose above, silky beneath; fls. 2–3 in. across, petals purplish-violet. Brazil.

Langsdorffii: a listed name of no botanical standing for *T. Langsdorffiana.*

laxa (Desr.) Cogn. Scandent shrub, to 7 ft., brs. hirsute; lvs. ovate, to 2 in. long, somewhat cordate, 7-nerved, sparsely setulose; fls. few in a cluster, about 2 in. across, petals violet-purple. Peru.

multiflora (G. Gardn.) Cogn. Shrub, to 6 ft., brs. 4-angled-winged; lvs. ovate, to 6 in. long, to about 3 in. wide, 5–7-nerved, densely villous-velvety above, densely tomentose and ashy-gray beneath; panicle to 20 in. long; fls. violet, petals to 5/8 in. long. Brazil.

mutabilis (Vell.) Cogn. Tree, to 20 ft., brs. cylindrical, reddish to ashy-gray; lvs. oblong-lanceolate, 3–4 in. long, about 1 in. wide, entire, 5-nerved; petals white, reddish, or red-violet, 1–1½ in. long, stamens purplish-violet. Brazil.

rosea: a listed name of no botanical standing.

semidecandra: see *T. Urvilleana.*

sericea: a listed name of no botanical standing.

Urvilleana (DC.) Cogn. [T. *grandiflora* Hort.; *T. semidecandra* Hort., not (DC.) Cogn.; *Pleroma grandiflora* Hort.; *P. splendens* Hort.]. GLORY BUSH, LASIANDRA, PLEROMA, PRINCESS FLOWER, PURPLE GLORY TREE. Shrub, to 15 ft., brs. 4-angled, reddish-pilose; lvs. ovate or oblong-ovate, 2–4 in. long, 1–1½ in. wide, serrulate, 5-nerved, setose above, pilose beneath; fls. showy, with petals rosy-purple to violet, 2 in. long, stamens purple; caps. ½ in. across. Brazil.

TIGRIDIA Juss. TIGER FLOWER, SHELL FLOWER, ONE-DAY LILY. *Iridaceae.* About 27 spp. of bulbous, per. herbs, native to temp. Mex., Guatemala, and the Andes of Peru and Chile; sts. simple or forked, cylindrical; lvs. few, linear to linear-lanceolate or sword-shaped, pleated; fls. in many colors, ephemeral, produced in succession, erect or nodding, perianth campanulate or cup-shaped, spreading or reflexed, segms. 6, in 2 dissimilar series, stamens 3, filaments united into a tube, anthers erect or spreading, style long, filiform, style brs. 3, bifid; fr. a 3-valved caps.

Bulbs should be planted 2–3 in. deep in late spring and will bloom in July or Aug. They should be lifted before frost and stored in a dry place over winter. Tigridias are easily grown from seeds in a warm climate; when sown in the ground in spring they will bloom the following season. Also propagated by offsets.

Pavonia (L.f.) DC. [*T. Pringlei* S. Wats.]. TIGER FLOWER. Sts. erect, to 2 ft., sometimes branched; lvs. to 1½ ft., rather rigid; fls. 3–6 in. across, perianth red, spotted with yellow and purple in the cuplike center, inner segms. lanceolate-oblong, pinched in the middle, ½ as long as the outer. Mex., Guatemala. Bulbs used as food by local people. Cvs. in many color combinations include: **'Alba'** ['Alba Grandiflora'], fls. pearly white, with red spots in center; **'Alba Grandiflora':** cv. 'Alba'; **'Alba Immaculata'**, fls. pure white; **'Aurea'**, fls. yellow and red; **'Canariensis'**, fls. pale yellow, spotted red in the center; **'Carminea'**, fls. salmon-red, with darker spots; **'Grandiflora'**, fls. large, variously colored; **'Liliacea'**, fls. crimson-carmine, with bold blotch at center; **'Liliacea Immaculata'**, fls. crimson-carmine, with a white ring at center; **'Lutea'**, a listed name; **'Lutea Immaculata'**, fls. pure yellow; **'Rosea'**, fls. rose, with yellow-variegated center; **'Speciosa'**, fls. scarlet, with golden-yellow center spotted deep red; **'Watkinsonii'** [*T. Watkinsonii* Hort.], fls. deep orange-yellow, often streaked and spotted red; **'Wheeleri'** [*T. Wheeleri* Hort.], fls. vermilion-red, with brightly spotted, clear yellow center.

Pringlei: *T. Pavonia.*

Watkinsonii: a listed name of no botanical standing for *T. Pavonia* cv.

Wheeleri: a listed name of no botanical standing for *T. Pavonia* cv.

TILIA L. LINDEN, BASSWOOD, LIME TREE, WHITEWOOD. *Tiliaceae.* About 30 spp. of large, deciduous trees in the temp. N. Hemisphere; lvs. alt., 2-ranked, slender-petioled, usually abruptly acuminate, cordate to truncate, with or without tufts of hair in the axils of the veins beneath; fls. yellowish or white, fragrant, mostly in drooping cymes, peduncle united for about half its length to large ligulate bract, sepals and petals 5, stamens many, separate or in fascicles opp. the petals, staminodes present or absent, ovary 5-celled, cells 2-ovuled; fr. nutlike, globose, 1–3-seeded.

Lindens are valuable ornamentals, an important source of nectar for bees, and also furnish fiber from the inner bark and wood. They are hardy in the North, and not particular as to soil, but do not stand drought well. Propagation is by seeds sown in the autumn or stratified and sown in the spring, by layers, mound layering, and cuttings. The named kinds are commonly grafted in spring or budded in summer on available common stocks.

americana L. [*T. glabra* Venten.]. AMERICAN L., BASSWOOD, WHITEWOOD. To 130 ft., bark deeply furrowed, young brs. green, glabrous; lvs. broadly ovate, 4–8 in. long, coarsely serrate, glabrous beneath except for axillary tufts; cymes 6–15-fld., pendulous, the bract stalked; staminodes present; fr. smooth, tomentose. New Bruns., s. to Va. and Tex. Zone 3. Bee plant; wood used for making inexpensive furniture and excelsior; inner bark used for fabric. Cvs. are: **'Dentata'**, lvs. coarsely, often nearly doubly dentate; **'Fastigiata'**, narrowly pyramidal, with ascending brs.; **'Macrophylla'**, lvs. large; **'Pyramidalis'**, narrowly pyramidal.

amurensis Rupr. Similar to *T. cordata,* but having thin scaly bark; lvs. broadly ovate, coarsely serrate, with acuminate teeth; cymes 5–20-fld.; staminodes sometimes present. Manchuria and Korea.

argentea: *T. tomentosa.*

cordata Mill. [*T. parviflora* J. F. Ehrh. ex Hoffm.]. SMALL-LEAVED EUROPEAN L. To 100 ft.; lvs. nearly orbicular, often broader than long, to 2½ in. long, sharply and finely serrate, glaucous and glabrous beneath except for axillary tufts; cymes 5–7-fld., pendulous or nearly erect; staminodes lacking; fr. globose, sometimes slightly ribbed. Eur. Zone 4. Widely planted as a street tree. Cv. **'Cordifolia'** is listed. Cv. **'Pyramidalis'**. Habit narrow, pyramidal.

dasystyla Steven. To 100 ft., young brs. red, glabrous; lvs. broadly ovate, to 6 in. long, obliquely cordate, serrate, with aristate teeth, glabrous except for whitish axillary tufts beneath; cymes 3–7-fld.; staminodes lacking; fr. globose, obtuse at the ends, slightly 5-ribbed. Se. Eur. and w. Asia. Zone 6.

×**euchlora** C. Koch: *T. cordata* (probably) × *T. dasystyla.* CRIMEAN L. To 65 ft.; young brs. glabrous, often slightly pendent; lvs. rounded-ovate, to 4 in. long, serrate, with acuminate teeth, with brownish axillary tufts beneath; cymes 3–7-fld. pendulous; fr. short-ellipsoid, narrowed at ends. Zone 6.

×**europaea** L. [*T.* × *intermedia* DC.; *T.* × *vulgaris* Hayne]: *T. cordata* × *T. platyphyllos.* To 120 ft.; lvs. broadly ovate, to 4 in. long, obliquely cordate or truncate, sharply serrate, dull dark green above, with axillary tufts beneath; cymes 5–10-fld.; staminodes present; fr. faintly 5-ribbed. Cv. **'Pallida'**. Lvs. larger, yellowish- to bluish-green beneath. Zone 4. Var. **grandiflora:** *T. platyphyllos.*

glabra: *T. americana.*

Henryana Szysz. To about 50 ft., brs. pubescent, then glabrous; lvs. broadly ovate, 2–5 in. long, obliquely cordate or truncate, denticulate with bristlelike teeth, pubescent along veins above, brownish-stellate with axillary tufts beneath; cymes 20-fld. or more, pendulous; staminodes present; fr. short-ellipsoid, 5-ribbed. Cent. China. Zone 6.

heterophylla Venten. WHITE B. Large tree, young brs. glabrous, reddish- or yellow-brown; lvs. ovate, to 5 in. long, obliquely truncate or rarely subcordate, finely serrate with aristate teeth, glabrous and lustrous above, white- or sometimes brownish-tomentose and with axillary tufts beneath; cymes 10–20-fld.; staminodes present; fr. short-beaked, rusty-tomentose. W. Va. to Fla., w. to Ind. and Ala. Zone 6.

×**intermedia:** *T.* × *europaea.*

japonica (Miq.) Simonk. JAPANESE L. Similar to *T. cordata,* but shorter, to 65 ft.; lvs. to 3¼ in. long, light bluish-green and pubescent on the veins beneath when young, with brownish axillary tufts; cymes 7–40-fld., pendulous; staminodes present; fr. ellipsoid, not ribbed. Japan. Zone 6.

mandshurica Rupr. & Maxim. MANCHURIAN L. To about 65 ft., brs. and buds brown-tomentose; lvs. orbicular-ovate, to 6 in. long, usually cordate, sometimes indistinctly lobed, serrate, with long-pointed teeth, sparsely pubescent above, grayish- or whitish-tomentose beneath, without axillary tufts; cymes 7–10-fld.; staminodes present; fr. globose, 5-ribbed basally. Ne. Asia. Zone 5.

Maximowicziana Shiras. [*T. Miyabei* J. Jack]. To 100 ft.; similar to *T. mandshurica,* but lvs. obliquely cordate, more coarsely serrate, mucronate-toothed, with brownish, axillary tufts beneath; cymes 10–18-fld.; fr. distinctly 5-ribbed. Japan. Zone 6.

Miqueliana Maxim. To 45 ft., young brs. tomentulose; lvs. triangular-ovate, acute or acuminate, obliquely cordate, coarsely serrate, grayish-tomentose beneath, without axillary tufts; cymes 10–20-fld.; staminodes present; fr. 5-ribbed basally. E. China. Zone 6.

Miyabei: *T. Maximowicziana.*

×**Moltkei** F. L. Späth. [*T.* × *spectabilis* Dipp., not Host]: presumably *T. americana* × *T. petiolaris.* Vigorous tree, brs. more or less pendent, puberulent at first; lvs. similar to those of *T. americana,* slightly grayish-tomentose beneath, often pilose on the veins, without axillary tufts; cymes densely 5–8-fld.; staminodes present; fr. ribbed.

mongolica Maxim. MONGOLIAN L. To about 35 ft., brs. reddish, glabrous; lvs. reddish when unfolding, suborbicular to ovate, to 2¾ in. long, often 3-lobed, coarsely serrate, glaucescent, glabrous beneath, with or without axillary tufts; cymes 6–20-fld.; staminodes present; fr. globose, thick-walled. Mongolia and China. Zone 5. A small, graceful tree.

neglecta Spach. To 100 ft., brs. red, glabrous; lvs. broadly ovate, to 8 in. long, obliquely cordate or truncate, coarsely serrate with forward-pointing teeth, openly stellate-pubescent beneath with scattered, usually simple hairs on the veins; cymes loosely 5–15-fld.; staminodes present; fr. subglobose or ellipsoid, rarely angled. E. Canada to Ga., w. to Ohio and Tex. Zone 5.

Oliveri Szysz. To 45 ft., brs. glabrous, reddish-brown; lvs. ovate to suborbicular, to 4 in. long, obliquely cordate or truncate, sinuate-serrate with short, gland-tipped teeth, white-tomentose beneath; cymes 15–20-fld.; fls. small, staminodes present; fr. globose, beaked, warty, thick-shelled. Cent. China. Zone 6.

parviflora: *T. cordata.*

petiolaris DC. PENDENT SILVER L. To about 75 ft., brs. pendent, tomentose when young; lvs. ovate-orbicular, about 4 in. long, obliquely cordate or truncate, regularly serrate, slightly pubescent above, white-tomentose beneath, petioles over half as long as blade; cymes 3–10-fld., brownish-tomentose; staminodes present; fr. 5-grooved, warty. Doubtfully native to Se. Eur., w. Asia. Zone 6.

platyphyllos Scop. [*T.* × *europaea* var. *grandiflora* Hort.]. LARGE-LEAVED L. To 130 ft., young brs. usually pubescent; lvs. roundish-ovate, to 5 in. long, obliquely cordate, regularly serrate, dull, glabrous or short-pubescent above, pubescent beneath, especially on the veins; cymes 3- to rarely 4–6-fld.; fr. globose or pear-shaped, 5-ribbed. Eur. Zone 4. Cvs. are: **'Aurea'**, bracts yellow; **'Corallina'**, bracts red; **'Fastigiata'**, of narrow, pyramidal habit; **'Lacinia'**, smaller tree, lvs. irregularly cut into narrow divisions; **'Pyramidalis'**, of narrow pyramidal habit; **'Rubra'**, bracts red.

×spectabilis: see *T.* × *Moltkei.*

tomentosa Moench [*T. argentea* DC.]. SILVER L. Broadly pyramidal tree, to 90 ft.; differing from *T. petiolaris* in having brs. upright; lvs. sharply and sometimes doubly serrate, petioles less than half as long as blade; fr. slightly 5-angled. Se. Eur., Asia. Zone 4.

×vulgaris: *T.* × *europaea.*

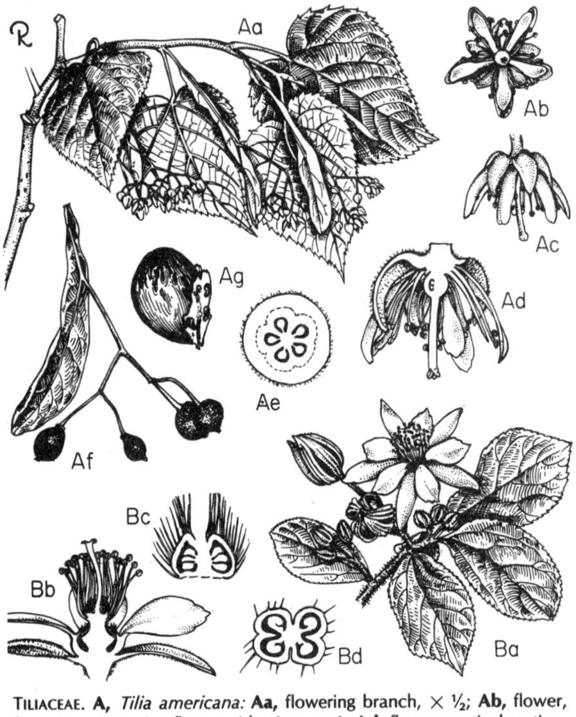

TILIACEAE. **A,** *Tilia americana:* **Aa,** flowering branch, × $\frac{1}{2}$; **Ab,** flower, face view, × 1; **Ac,** flower, side view, × 1; **Ad,** flower, vertical section, × $1\frac{1}{2}$; **Ae,** ovary, cross section, × 5; **Af,** fruit, × $\frac{1}{2}$; **Ag,** seed, × $2\frac{1}{2}$. **B,** *Grewia tiliifolia:* **Ba,** flowering branch, × $\frac{1}{2}$; **Bb,** flower, vertical section, × $\frac{3}{4}$; **Bc,** ovary, vertical section, × 5; **Bd,** ovary, cross section, × 6.

TILIACEAE Juss. LINDEN OR BASSWOOD FAMILY. Dicot.; about 50 genera of trees, shrubs, or, rarely, herbs of wide distribution; lvs. usually alt., simple; fls. regular, usually bisexual, mostly in cymes in lf. axils or opp. lvs., or in cymose panicles, sepals and petals commonly 5, sometimes fewer, or petals 0, stamens generally many, separate or short-connate into 5–10 fascicles, all fertile or the outer ones staminodes, often on an androgynophore, ovary superior, 2–10-celled, each cell 1- to many-ovuled; fr. a caps. or drupe, cells 1–10, sometimes horizontally septate between seeds. The following genera are cult. as ornamentals, and for timber and fiber: *Belotia, Berrya, Carpodiptera, Clappertonia, Corchorus, Entelea, Grewia, Heliocarpus, Luehea, Sparmannia,* and *Tilia.*

TILLANDSIA L. *Bromeliaceae.* About 374 spp. of mostly epiphytic herbs, native to W. Hemisphere; lvs. crowded in basal rosettes or sometimes along a st., entire; fls. blue, green, purple, red, orange, or white, in spikes, heads, panicles, or rarely solitary, petals separate, without appendages, stamens in the cult. spp. usually exserted, ovary superior; fr. a caps., seeds with a straight, basal, plumose tail.

Most species are ornamentals, but one species, *T. usneoides,* of the southern U.S. is processed commercially for use as a horsehair substitute in stuffing upholstery. Grown in greenhouses or outdoors in warm climates. Most species thrive in bright light. For culture see *Bromeliaceae.*

aeranthos (Loisel.) L. B. Sm. St. long, to $1\frac{1}{2}$ ft.; lvs. along st., to $1\frac{3}{4}$ in. long; scape short, infl. simple, few-fld.; fls. to $\frac{3}{4}$ in. long, sepals symmetrical, unequally united, petals dark blue, longer than stamens, which are visible in corolla throat. Brazil to Argentina.

albida Mez & J. Purpus. St. to 16 in., branched; lvs. in several ranks, to $4\frac{3}{4}$ in. long, whitish; infl. terminal, erect, short, bright red; fls. pedicelled, greenish-white, $1\frac{3}{8}$ in. long. Mex.

aloifolia: *T. flexuosa.*

anceps Lodd. Lvs. many in a rosette, to 16 in. long, recurving and narrowly triangular, pale scurfy; infl. erect, stout, short, nearly hidden by lvs., unbranched, elliptic in outline, fl. bracts imbricate, green, or pale rose with greenish margins; fls. blue or rarely white. Cent. Amer., n. S. Amer.

Andrieuxii (Mez) L. B. Sm. Stemless or short-stemmed, to 4 in., forming clusters; lvs. to 6 in. long, $\frac{3}{8}$ in. wide, recurving, ashy; infl. erect or somewhat curved, largely obscured by lvs., scape bracts and infl. bracts rosy; fls. violet, to 2 in. long or more. Mex., Costa Rica.

argentea Griseb. To 10 in.; st. curved, short, but often branched; lvs. many in a rosette, blades linear-subulate, whitish; scape erect or ascending, longer than lvs., infl. simple, about 6-fld.; sepals $\frac{3}{4}$ in. long, petals $1\frac{3}{16}$ in. long, bright red. Mex., W. Indies.

Balbisiana Schult.f. To 2 ft.; lvs. many in a dense rosette, sheaths inflated, forming a pseudobulb to 5 in. high, blades linear-triangular, scurfy, often purple-margined; scape erect, infl. unbranched to densely pinnate, fl. bracts leathery, scarcely nerved, often bright red, longer than sepals and internodes; petals violet, to $1\frac{3}{4}$ in. long. Fla. to n. S. Amer.

brachycaulos Schlechtend. Lvs. many, linear, longer than infl.; scape short or none, infl. branched or appearing unbranched, few-fld.; sepals to $\frac{5}{8}$ in. long, petals violet, to $2\frac{3}{4}$ in. long. Mex., Cent. Amer.

bulbosa Hook. Stemless, usually clustered, to 9 in.; lvs. with sheaths inflated, forming a pseudobulb, often red- or purple-margined, blades slender, contorted; scape erect, with leafy bracts, infl. unbranched or digitate, bracts red or green, spikes 2–8-fld., fl. bracts longer than sepals; sepals $\frac{1}{2}$ in. long, petals blue or violet, to $1\frac{5}{8}$ in. long, stamens longer than petals. Mex., Cent. Amer., W. Indies, S. Amer.

Butzii Mez. To 1 ft.; lvs. few in a rosette, to 20 in. long, pale, sheaths inflated, variegated; infl. unbranched or digitate; fl. bracts twice as long as internodes, prominently nerved, somewhat papery, pale scurfy; fls. violet, stamens exserted. Mex., Cent. Amer.

capitata Griseb. To 20 in.; lvs. many in a rosette, blades narrowly triangular, sheaths darker; scape erect, infl. seemingly unbranched to few-branched, capitate, 1–5-fld., sheaths of primary bracts longer than the axillary spikes; petals blue, to 2 in. Cuba, Mex.

caput-Medusae E. Morr. To 10 or rarely 16 in.; lvs. pale, sheaths uniformly colored, inflated into a pseudobulb; infl. unbranched or digitate; fl. bracts twice as long as internodes, prominently nerved, glabrous or nearly so; fls. violet, to $1\frac{3}{8}$ in. long, stamens exserted. Mex., Cent. Amer.

circinnata Schlechtend. POT-BELLIED T. To 18 in.; lvs. many in a rosette, sheaths inflated, forming a pseudobulb to 6 in. high, blades subulate, pale scurfy, often curved or coiled; scape erect, infl. unbranched or rarely branched, 2–10-fld., fl. bracts much longer than internodes, with appressed, pale scales; petals violet, to $1\frac{3}{4}$ in. long. Fla., W. Indies, Mex., Cent. Amer., Colombia.

cyanea Linden ex C. Koch [*T. Lindenii* E. Morr., not Regel]. Stemless, to 10 in.; lvs. suberect and recurved, to 14 in. long, $\frac{5}{8}$ in. wide; scape short, hidden by lvs., infl. unbranched, broad, up to 20-fld., bracts rose or red, smooth; petal blades orbicular, spreading, deep violet, to 1 in. long, petal claws much longer than stamens, style short and stout. Ecuador.

excelsa Griseb. To 3 ft. or more; lvs. many in a rosette, to 1½ ft. long, to 2¼ in. wide, light green or with red or purplish markings; infl. branched, sheaths of primary bracts shorter than the axillary brs.; petals violet, to 1 3/16 in. long, stamens shorter than petals but exserted from throat of corolla, style longer than ovary. W. Indies, Cent. Amer.

fasciculata Swartz. WILD PINEAPPLE. To 3½ ft.; lvs. many in basal rosette, blades narrowly triangular, pale scurfy, sheaths darker; scape erect, shorter than lvs., bracts usually red or red-tinged, infl. unbranched or branched, usually of dense, somewhat flattened spikes, fl. bracts thin, much longer than the internodes and concealing them; petals white to purple, to 2⅜ in. long. A variable sp. of trop. Amer., with several vars.

filifolia Schlechtend. & Cham. Stemless; lvs. many, filiform; scape erect, infl. branched, loose, many-fld.; petals pale lilac, ⅜ in. long. Mex., Cent. Amer.

flabellata Bak. To 1 ft.; lvs. in dense rosette, narrowly triangular, to ⅝ in. wide; scape erect, short, concealed, infl. digitate, the basal ½–⅔ of spikes sterile, fl. bracts thin, reddish, much longer than the internodes; petals violet, to 1⅝ in. long. S. Mex. to El Salvador.

flexuosa Swartz [*T. aloifolia* Hook.]. To 5 ft.; lvs. to 20 in. long, 1 in. wide, densely pale scurfy, often white-barred; scape erect, infl. unbranched to 2-pinnate, open, fl. bracts as long as internodes, spreading with the fls.; petals white, rose, or purple, to 1⅝ in. long. S. Fla. to n. S. Amer.

geminiflora Brongn. Stemless; lvs. to 7 in. long, narrowly triangular; scape to 3½ in. long, erect, infl. compact, paniculate, the spikes loose, few-fld.; fls. 11/16 in. long, sepals symmetrical, longer than fl. bracts, stamens shorter than petals, visible in throat of corolla. Brazil to Argentina.

grandis Schlechtend. [*T. viridiflora* Bak.]. Lvs. strap-shaped, to 2½ ft. long, 3 in. wide, glaucous beneath; infl. candelabralike, to 11 ft. high, bracts green; fls. greenish-white, to 5 in. long. On rocks, Mex., Brit. Honduras.

ionantha Planch. Dwarf, to 2½ in.; lvs. dense, the outer green, the inner often pink or red; scape lacking, infl. nearly concealed at base by the lvs.; fls. few, violet. Mex. to Nicaragua.

juncea (Ruiz & Pav.) Poir. To 16 in.; lvs. linear-subulate and filiform-acuminate; infl. as long as or longer than lvs., densely digitate, bracts broad, massed on scape below infl., fl. bracts often red; fls. violet, to 1⅝ in. long. S. Fla. to n. S. Amer.

Karwinskyana Schult. To 2 ft.; lvs. in a rosette, to 8 in. long, blades linear-triangular, ⅜ in. wide at base, ashy-scurfy; scape erect, about as long as lvs., bracts bright red, infl. simple or few-branched, very loose, fl. bracts spreading, to ¾ in. long, with often blackish margins; sepals ⅞ in. long, petals greenish-yellow, 1¼ in. long. Mex.

Lindeniana: *T. Lindenii.*

Lindenii Regel [*T. Lindeniana* Regel]. To 2½ ft.; lvs. arching, to 16 in. long, ½ in. wide; scape erect, infl. unbranched, narrow, to 20-fld., bracts green- or rose-nerved; petals deep blue, blades orbicular, to 2 in. long or more, claws much longer than stamens, style short and stout. Peru. May be confused with *T. cyanea.*

loliacea Mart. ex Schult. Short-stemmed; lvs. to 1⅝ in. long, 3/16 in. wide, white-bloomy; scape slender, to 4 in., infl. unbranched, flexuous; fls. erect, distant, petals pale violet, to ⅜ in. long. Brazil.

Mallemontii Glaziou ex Mez. Long-stemmed; lvs. mostly 2-ranked, nearly cylindrical, to 4⅜ in. long; scape very slender, usually naked, infl. unbranched, 2–4-fld.; fls. to 1 1/16 in. long, sepals symmetrical, petals blue or purple, blades broad, claws longer than the deeply included stamens. Brazil.

melanocrater: *T. tricolor* var.

narthecioides K. Presl. Short-stemmed or stemless; lvs. to 8 in. long, slender; scape thin, erect, shorter than lvs., infl. unbranched, loose, to 30-fld.; fls. spreading, to ¾ in. long, petals white. Ecuador.

paraensis Mez. Lvs. forming a pseudobulb, narrow, erect; scape shorter than lvs., infl. unbranched, erect, 6–8-fld.; fls. 1⅜ in. long. Brazil.

plumosa Bak. Stemless, to 7 in., densely clustered; lvs. many in a dense rosette, blades filiform; scape nearly absent or to about 4 in., usually curved, bracts rosy, imbricate, infl. headlike, branched or appearing unbranched, spikes few-fld.; sepals 9/16 in. long, petals 11/16 in. long, yellow-green. Mex., Cent. Amer.

polystachya L. To 2 ft.; lvs. many, narrowly triangular, arching, pale scurfy, often purple-margined, sheath darker than blade; infl. longer than lvs., spikes linear-lanceolate, ½ in. wide or less, fl. bracts leathery, longer than internodes; petals violet, to 1¼ in. long. Mex. to n. S. Amer.

pruinosa Swartz. Stemless, to 8 in.; lvs. forming an elongate pseudobulb, ashy- or reddish-scurfy, blades very slender, recurved or contorted; infl. sessile, unbranched or digitate, spikes flattened, fl. bracts erect, elongate, densely scaly, pink; fls. sessile, sepals to ¾ in. long, petals violet, to 1¼ in. long. Mex., Cent. Amer., and W. Indies to Brazil.

pulchella: *T. tenuifolia.*

punctulata Schlechtend. & Cham. MEXICAN BLACK-TORCH. To 18 in.; lvs. many in a dense rosette, recurving, gray-scurfy; infl. erect, red-brown, unbranched or digitately branched, fl. bracts imbricate; petals white above a violet base. Mex. to Costa Rica, Surinam.

recurvata (L.) L. BALL MOSS, BUNCH M. Plants pendent, branching; lvs. 2-ranked, filiform, to 2 in. long, ashy- or reddish-scaly; infl. reduced to few fls. or a single fl. with pale green or blue petals. S. U.S. to Argentina.

Schiedeana Steud. St. well developed, simple or branched; lvs. ashy- or rusty-scaly, sheaths large, blades narrow; scape shorter than lvs., infl. unbranched, to 2¾ in. long; sepals ¾ in. long, petals yellow. Mex., Cent. Amer., W. Indies, n. S. Amer.

Selerana Mez. Lvs. forming a bulbous base, to 10 in. long; scape erect, infl. subdigitate, spikes 3–6, compressed; sepals ⅝ in. long, petals violet, 1⅜ in. long. Mex., Guatemala.

setacea Swartz [*T. tenuifolia* of auth., not L.]. Stemless; lvs. many, threadlike; infl. shorter than lvs., unbranched to 2-pinnate, scape bracts not massed below infl.; petals violet, to ¾ in. long. S.C. to n. S. Amer.

spiculosa Griseb. To 32 in.; lvs. in a rosette, to 1 ft. long, 1⅝ in. wide, inflated at base; infl. branched, primary bracts shorter than or longer than sterile bases of spikes, spreading, fl. bracts less or more than twice as long as the internodes; fls. erect, sepals broadly elliptic, rounded, glabrous, petals yellowish, much longer than sepals. Cent. Amer., n. S. Amer., Trinidad. Var. **spiculosa.** The typical var.; lvs. green or spotted; infl. 3-pinnate, fl. bracts mostly more than twice as long as internodes. Cent. Amer., n. S. Amer., Trinidad. Var. **ustulata** (Reitz) L. B. Sm. [*T. triticea* Burchell ex Bak.]. Lf. blades irregularly cross-banded with dark purple; infl. usually 2-pinnate; fl. bracts mostly more than twice as long as internodes. Trinidad, s. to Brazil, w. to Peru.

streptophylla Scheidw. To 18 in. or more; lvs. many, scurfy, sheaths somewhat inflated, forming a dense pseudobulb, blades narrowly triangular; scape erect, infl. pinnate, with bright red axes, fl. bracts papery, strongly nerved, densely covered with pale spreading scales, much longer than internodes; petals purple, to 1⅝ in. long. W. Indies, Mex., Cent. Amer.

stricta Soland. Stemless or short-stemmed; lvs. to 6 in. long, ¼ in. wide, flexible, not much curved, green; scape short, infl. unbranched, dense; fls. in more than 2 rows, sepals symmetrical, to ¾ in. long, shortly united, petals blue, stamens in throat of corolla. Trinidad, Venezuela to Argentina.

tenuifolia L. [*T. pulchella* Hook.]. Somewhat stemmed, sts. to 10 in. long, branching to form mats; lvs. narrowly triangular; scape mostly erect, short, infl. unbranched, about as long as lvs.; fls. in more than 2 rows, petals blue, white, or rose, to ¾ in. long, stamens included but longer than throat of corolla, style slender and long. Cuba to n. Argentina. Var. **surinamensis** (Miq.) L. B. Sm. [*T. pulchella* var. *surinamensis* (Miq.) Mez]. Stemless or nearly so; lvs. broader, mostly curved to one side, shorter than infl. Surinam and Brazil. This sp. has been confused with *T. setacea.*

tricholepis Bak. Small, mosslike; lvs. in many ranks, subulate, to ⅜ in. long, rarely ¾ in. long; scape evident, bracted, infl. a dense spike, 1–5-fld.; sepals symmetrical, small, petals narrow, yellow or green, stamens shorter than petals, deeply included. Brazil to Argentina.

tricolor Schlechtend. & Cham. To 18 in.; lvs. many, recurved, sheaths dark, blades narrowly triangular; scape erect, infl. unbranched or digitate, spikes flat-sided, fl. bracts leathery, much longer than internodes; petals violet, to 2¾ in. long. Mex. to Costa Rica. Var. **tricolor.** The typical var.; spikes linear-lanceolate; petals to 2¾ in. long. Mex. to Costa Rica. Var. **melanocrater** (L. B. Sm.) L. B. Sm. [*T. melanocrater* L. B. Sm.]. Spikes of infl. linear-oblong to broadly elliptic; petals to 1⅜ in. long. Cent. Amer.

triticea: *T. spiculosa* var. *ustulata.*

usneoides L. SPANISH MOSS, GRAYBEARD. Sts. slender, branching, leafy, hanging, often 20 ft. long or more, hoary-gray, festooned in masses over trees; lvs. scattered, very narrowly linear, to 2 in. long; fls. small, pale green or blue, solitary in axils of lvs. Fla. to Tex., s. to Argentina. Common on trees in se. U.S., where it is collected for use as a packing and stuffing material.

utriculata L. To 6 ft.; lvs. many in a rosette, broad at base, forming water-holding pockets, linear-triangular, acuminate above, light green; scape erect, infl. unbranched or more usually 2–3-pinnate, with loose spikes, bracts often violet, fl. bracts purple-margined, appressed to and about as long as internodes; fls. white, erect, to 1⅜ in. long. S. U.S. to n. S. Amer.

Valenzuelana A. Rich. To 2 ft.; lvs. many, in a rosette, forming basal water-holding pocket, linear-triangular, to 16 in. long, 1 in. wide; scape erect, bracts pink or red, infl. unbranched or pinnate, fl. bracts thin, prominently nerved, red or pink, longer than internodes but narrower and exposing them in flowering; petals lilac or violet, to 1¼ in. long. S. Fla. to n. S. Amer.

viridiflora: *T. grandis.*

TINANTIA Scheidw. *Commelinaceae.* Two spp. of erect herbs, native to trop. Amer.; lvs. alt.; fls. in terminal, simple or compound cincinni, sepals 3, petals 3, unequal, the lower shortest, stamens 6, the upper bearded, the lower glabrous, ovary 3-celled.

Occasionally grown under glass or planted out in summer; they have something of the habit of *Tradescantia.*

anomala: *Commelinantia anomala.*

erecta (Jacq.) Schlechtend. [*T. fugax* Scheidw.]. To 1½ ft.; lvs. ovate-lanceolate, to 4 in. long; fls. pink to blue, about ½ in. long, calyx glandular-puberulent. Summer. Mex. to S. Amer.

fugax: *T. erecta.*

TINNEA Kotschy & Peyr. *Labiatae.* About 30 spp. of herbs and shrubs of trop. and s. Afr., often pubescent; sts. mostly square in cross section; lvs. opp., entire; fls. fragrant, usually solitary in the axils, in terminal racemes, pedicels with 2 bractlets, calyx ovoid, 2-lipped, inflated in fr., corolla violet to purplish-brown, tube short, wide, limb 2-lipped, upper lip emarginate, lower lip spreading, lobes rounded, stamens 4, in 2 pairs, anthers 2-celled; fr. of 4 densely bristly nutlets.

Propagated by seeds or cuttings.

abyssinica: a listed name of no botanical standing, perhaps referable to *T. aethiopica.*

aethiopica Kotschy & Peyr. Shrub, to 6 ft., pubescent; lvs. ovate, to 2 in. long, entire, glabrous; fls. violet-scented, calyx deeply 2-lipped, ⅜ in. long, enlarged in fr. Trop. Afr.

TIPUANA Benth. TIPU TREE. *Leguminosae* (subfamily *Faboideae*). One sp., a tree, native to S. Amer.; lvs. odd-pinnate; fls. in axillary racemes, showy, papilionaceous, stamens united; fr. a samaralike, winged legume, 1–3-seeded.

Planted as a fast-growing ornamental shade, park, or street tree in subtropical regions.

Tipu (Benth.) O. Kuntze. ROSEWOOD, PRIDE-OF-BOLIVIA. Tall tree; all but early lvs. opp. or nearly so., lfts. in 6–11 pairs, to 1½ in. long and ¾ in. wide, emarginate; racemes shorter than lvs.; fls. golden, standard reflexed, reddish centrally; fr. to 2½ in. long. S. Brazil to Bolivia. Zone 10. A source of rosewood.

TIPULARIA Nutt. *Orchidaceae.* Six spp. of terrestrial herbs, native to N. Amer. and Asia; lf. solitary from a corm, cordate-ovate, green above, purplish beneath, produced in autumn and withering in spring; infl. a slender, scapose, loose raceme in summer; fls. greenish-yellow to purplish, sepals and petals similar, lip 3-lobed, with slender spur at base. For structure of fl. see *Orchidaceae.*

Sometimes planted in the shaded woodland garden. For culture see *Orchids.*

discolor (Pursh) Nutt. [*T. unifolia* (Muhlenb.) BSP]. CRANEFLY ORCHID, ELFIN-SPUR, CRIPPLED-CRANEFLY, MOTTLED-CRANEFLY. To 2 ft., scape naked except for tubular sheath at base; lf. slender-petioled, cordate, to 4 in. long, dull green and blotched with purple above, purplish beneath; raceme many-fld., to 10 in. long; fls. pendent, greenish, yellow, rust-bronze, or purplish, sepals oblong-elliptic, to ¼ in. long, lateral sepals sometimes spatulate, petals linear-oblong, ¼ in. long, lateral lobes of lip short, with broadly rounded, erose or crenulate margins, midlobe linear-oblong, with undulate and erose margins, spur horizontal, to ¾ in. long. N.J. to S.C.

unifolia: *T. discolor.*

TISSERANTODENDRON Sillans. *Bignoniaceae.* Two spp. of trees, native to cent. Afr.; lvs. opp., odd-pinnate; fls. yellow, in few-fld. corymbose cymes in fascicles on old wood, calyx unequally 2–3-lobed, corolla campanulate-funnelform, stamens 4; fr. a linear caps.

Chevalieri Sillans. To 60 ft.; lvs. to 1 ft. long, lfts. 7–9, lanceolate, to 7 or 8 in. long; fls. yellow, to 2⅜ in. long and 1½ in. across; fr. to 2 ft. long.

TITANOPSIS Schwant. *Aizoaceae.* About 6 spp. of stemless, tufted or clump-forming succulents from fleshy roots, native to S. Afr.; lvs. in rosettes, 4-ranked, 3 or more pairs on a br., spatulate with a triangular apex, surface bluish-green to reddish- or yellowish-white, with many raised tubercles; fls. solitary, sessile or pedicelled, calyx unequally and deeply 6-lobed, petals yellow or orange, many, in 1–2 series, stamens many, ovary inferior to half-superior, 5–6-celled, stigmas 5–6; fr. a caps., with valves as broad as long, cell lids transparent, expanding keels minutely toothed, awned, placental tubercles absent.

Growth occurs in summer. Plants grow best in very sandy soil with old marble rubble added and in an airy place under glass with moderate water; in winter should be grown at a relatively cool temperature of about 60° F. with fairly dry soil. Careless watering can cause decay between the leaves. Propagated by seeds or by careful division of plants; seedlings usually flower during the second year. See also *Succulents.*

calcarea (Marloth) Schwant. JEWEL PLANT. Rosettes to 3¼ in. across; lvs. spreading, to 1 in. long, ½ in. wide below tip, spatulate, apex truncate, more or less triangular in outline and somewhat rounded, densely covered with reddish-gray-white tubercles; fls. ¾ in. across, nearly sessile, petals golden-yellow to nearly orange. Cape Prov.

Luckhoffii: *Aloinopsis Luckhoffii.*

Primosii: a listed name of no botanical standing; used for plants similar to *T. Schwantesii,* but fls. slightly larger, petals yellow with flesh-colored tips.

Schwantesii (Dinter ex Schwant.) Schwant. WHITE-JEWEL. Lvs. ascending, light gray-glaucous, to 1¼ in. long, to ¼ in. wide at base, ½ in. thick at the suddenly expanded and rounded-triangular apex, upper side flat or slightly concave, lower side rounded, tip and upper part of sides covered with roundish, yellow-brown tubercles; fls. to ¾ in. across, nearly sessile, petals light yellow. S.-W. Afr.

setifera: *Aloinopsis setifera.*

TITANOTRICHUM Solereder. *Gesneriaceae.* One sp., a terrestrial, per., hairy herb in China and Taiwan, with scaly rhizomes; sts. erect, sometimes branched at base; lower lvs. opp., upper lvs. alt.; fls. in a terminal raceme, nodding, subtended by lvs. or bracts, calyx lobes usually 5, triangular-lanceolate, unequal, corolla tubular, constricted above base, then expanded to the spreading limb, yellow, lobes and interior of tube blotched or dotted with dark crimson, stamens 4, borne at base of corolla tube, disc ringlike, ovary superior; fr. a caps.

For cultivation see *Gesneriaceae.*

Oldhamii (Hemsl.) Solereder. To 5 ft.; lvs. ovate, to 7 in. long, 4 in. wide, toothed; calyx lobes to ½ in. long, corolla 1¾ in. long, minutely hairy outside, lobes nearly ½ in. long; fls. sometimes replaced by brs. bearing green, scalelike reproductive bodies.

TITHONIA Desf. MEXICAN SUNFLOWER. *Compositae* (Helianthus Tribe). Ten spp. of stout, ann. or per. herbs or shrubs, native to Mex. and Cent. Amer.; lvs. alt. or occasionally opp. on lower part of st., 3-nerved, coarsely toothed to deeply lobed; fl. heads radiate, usually solitary on long, hollow peduncles, involucre broadly campanulate to hemispherical, involucral bracts in 2–5 rows, nearly equal or graduated in length, receptacle hollow, scaly; disc fls. bisexual, fertile, yellow, ray fls. neutral, golden-yellow to orange; achenes oblong, thickened or 4-angled, pubescent or glabrous, pappus of 1 or 2 persistent, scalelike awns and several separate to united scales, or sometimes lacking.

diversifolia (Hemsl.) A. Gray. Robust per. or straggling shrub, to 15 ft.; lvs. ovate to ovate-oblong or triangular-ovate, the blade to about 1 ft. long, narrowing to a petiole to 4 in. long, usually 3–5-lobed, crenate-serrate, pubescent; heads 2½–6 in. across; ray fls. orange-yellow. Mex. and Cent. Amer.; naturalized in tropics of New and Old World.

rotundifolia (Mill.) S. F. Blake [*T. speciosa* Hook.]. Robust, erect ann., to 6 ft.; lvs. ovate to triangular-ovate, to 1 ft. long, cordate basally, narrowing to a petiole to 5½ in. long, undivided to 3-lobed, serrate to crenate, hairy on the veins; heads to 3 in. across; ray fls. orange-scarlet. Mex. and Cent. Amer.; naturalized in W. Indies. Cv. 'Grandiflora'. An improved strain.

speciosa: *T. rotundifolia.*

TITHYMALOPSIS: *EUPHORBIA.*

TITHYMALUS: see *EUPHORBIA.*

TODDALIA Juss. *Rutaceae.* One sp., an evergreen, scandent shrub, native to trop. Afr. and Asia; lvs. alt., with 3 lfts., glandular-dotted; fls. unisexual, in axillary or terminal, cymose panicles, calyx 5-lobed, petals 5, stamens 5; fr. 4–6-celled and grooved, fleshy.

asiatica (L.) Lam. Sts. usually prickly; lfts. elliptic to elliptic-oblanceolate, to 3½ in. long; fls. white; fr. orange.

TODEA Willd. *Osmundaceae.* One sp. of the s. temp. Old World, with massive, erect rhizome; lvs. leathery, 2-pinnate; sporangia closely placed along the veins of normal or slightly contracted pinnules.

Occasionally cultivated where native, in the U.S. in Zone 10, or as a greenhouse ornamental. Propagated by spores. For culture see *Ferns.*

barbara (L.) T. Moore. Lvs. leathery, 3–4 ft. long, about 1 ft. wide, 2-pinnate, pinnules toothed; sporangia on lower pinnules. Australia, New Zeal., S. Afr.

hymenophylloides: *Leptopteris hymenophylloides.*

superba: *Leptopteris superba.*

TOFIELDIA Huds. [*Triantha* (Nutt.) Bak.]. FALSE ASPHODEL. *Liliaceae.* Fourteen or more spp. of tufted, rhizomatous, per. herbs, native to acid wet grounds in N. Amer., S. Amer., Eur., and Asia; roots fibrous; lvs. mostly basal, 2-ranked, linear, grasslike; fls. white, greenish-white, yellowish, or brown, in terminal racemes or spikes, perianth segms. 6, separate, glandless, persistent, stamens 6, anthers basifixed, styles 3; fr. a septicidal, 3-celled caps.

calyculata (L.) Wahl. To 1 ft.; basal lvs. to 6 in. long, st. lvs. 2 or 3, much shorter; fls. greenish-yellow; seeds not appendaged. Eur.

coccinea Richardson [*T. nutans* Willd. ex Schult. & Schult.f.]. To 5½ in.; basal lvs. to 2 in. long, margin rough, st. lvs. 1 or 2, short; fls. white to brownish, nodding, anthers yellow; seeds not appendaged. Japan. Var. **fusca** (Miyabe & Kudo) Hara [*T. fusca* Miyabe & Kudo]. Perianth and fr. dark brown. Japan.

fusca: *T. coccinea* var.

glutinosa (Michx.) Pers. [*Tofieldia intermedia* Rydb., in part; *Triantha glutinosa* (Michx.) Bak.]. To 20 in., scapes with many dark brown glands; basal lvs. to 8 in. long, the st. lf. much shorter, usually solitary; fls. white, perianth segms. longer than the mature, thin-walled caps.; seeds brownish, appendaged at both ends. N. Amer. Subsp. *montana* C. L. Hitchc. [var. *montana* (C. L. Hitchc.) R. J. Davis; *T. intermedia* Rydb., in part]. Scapes with short, viscid hairs; fruiting pedicels about ³⁄₁₆ in. long, seeds whitish. Mts., Idaho, Mont., Wyo., and adjacent Canada.

intermedia: see *T. glutinosa* and *T. glutinosa* subsp. *montana.*

japonica Miq. To 20 in., scapes viscid-glandular above; basal lvs. to 16 in. long and ⁵⁄₁₆ in. wide, margin rough, st. lvs. 1 or 2, much shorter; fls. white, anthers dark purple, pedicels glandular; seeds appendaged. Japan.

nuda Maxim. To 14 in., scape glabrous; basal lvs. to 5 in. long or more, arcuate, st. lvs. 2 or 3, much shorter; fls. white, on spreading pedicels; seeds not appendaged. Japan.

nutans: *T. coccinea.*

TOLMIEA Torr. & A. Gray. *Saxifragaceae.* One sp., a per. herb of w. N. Amer.; a rhizome well developed; lvs. cordate, shallowly lobed, palmately veined, long-petioled, stipules well developed; fl. st. sparingly leafy, with terminal raceme; fls. irregular, calyx tube cylindrical, separate from ovary, split on one side nearly to base, calyx with 3 large and 2 smaller lobes, petals usually 4, persistent, stamens 3, ovary superior, tapering above into 2 beaklike projections; fr. a caps., dehiscent along inner side of projections.

Menziesii (Pursh) Torr. & A. Gray. PICKABACK PLANT, PIGGYBACK PLANT, THOUSAND-MOTHERS, YOUTH-ON-AGE. Fl. sts. to 24 in., st. and lvs. hirsute; lvs. to 4 in. across, petioles to 8 in. long; calyx greenish-

purple, tube to ³⁄₈ in. long, lobes to ¼ in., petals purplish, about twice as long as calyx lobes, stamens unequal in length, shorter than petals; caps. slender, to ⁵⁄₈ in. long, extending beyond calyx. Reproduces vegetatively by buds that develop and form new plants at base of lf. blades. Useful in the shaded rock garden but also grown as a house plant.

TOLPIS Adans. *Compositae* (Cichorium Tribe). About 20 spp. of herbs with milky sap, in the Azores, Canary Is., Medit. region, and ne. Afr.; lvs. mostly basal, some on the sts.; fl. heads with involucral bracts in 1–2 rows, the inner narrow, erect, the several outer rows spreading, filiform; fls. all ligulate, yellow; pappus of a row of minute scales and a few bristles.

Propagated by seeds.

barbata (L.) Gaertn. [*Crepis barbata* L.]. Ann., to 2½ ft.; lvs. oblanceolate, coarsely toothed; heads to 1¼ in. across, the bracts of the sts. grading into the outer involucral bracts; outer fls. sulphur-yellow, inner fls. red-brown with yellow tips. S. Eur.

TOMATO. The cultivated tomatoes belong to the species *Lycopersicon lycopersicum* and *L. pimpinellifolium,* and are tender perennial herbs grown as annuals for their fruits, both outdoors and under glass. The fruits of most tomatoes are round and red, but some are plum- or pear-shaped, their colors range from greenish-white and yellow through orange to red, and they vary in size from less than an ounce to a pound or more. Unusual combinations of size, shape, and color may be of interest in the home garden for salads and conserves. The currant tomato, *L. pimpinellifolium,* is grown mostly for curiosity and ornament because the fruits are so small. The husk tomato and strawberry tomato are species of *Physalis* and the tree tomato is *Cyphomandra betacea.* The true tomatoes are closely allied to the white potato *(Solanum tuberosum),* and it is possible to graft one on the other.

Tomatoes are warm-season plants and susceptible to frost injury, hence should not be set out until after the last killing frost. They are strong feeders, with a large root system, and grow best on fertile, deep soils. From 2–5 pounds of fertilizer such as 5–10–5 should be incorporated in the soil for each 100 square feet of garden space before planting, the lower rate being used if the garden has been well fertilized in previous years. Lime may be needed if the pH is below 5.8–6.0.

The choice of a tomato cultivar for the home garden is much less crucial than for many other vegetables, and can be based to a great extent on personal preference. One common mistake, however, is to plant only one late variety. A few plants each of an early, a midseason, and a late variety will provide ripe tomatoes for a longer period. Varieties with resistance to verticillium and fusarium wilts should be chosen if one suspects that fungi causing those diseases might be present in the soil. Gardeners should be aware that many of the newer varieties are determinate or self-pruning in growth habit and are not as suitable for staking or trellising as the indeterminate types. The indeterminate tomatoes generally have a longer bearing period and their fruit is somewhat higher in sugar. For aid in selection of the best cultivars for a local area, the gardener should consult the nearest agricultural extension office.

Most home gardeners buy started tomato plants because there is seldom enough light in the house to grow good transplants. For this, a greenhouse or hot bed is almost essential, but reasonably good transplants can be grown under fluorescent lights if the lights are kept close to the tops of the plants. Some of the prepared commercial mixes, which usually contain vermiculite and peat moss with fertilizer added, are useful in reducing losses from damping off and the need for soil sterilization. In general, seeds are sown about 5–6 weeks before the average date of last killing frost. They can be sown directly in flats or other containers, dropping 2–3 seeds in holes ½ inch deep and thinning to 1 seedling at the time first leaves appear. Plants should be in a vigorous growing condition when set out, but should not have any open blossoms, especially in the case of varieties with small vines. Fruit which sets before the plants have become fully established in the field is likely to stunt the plant and result in a low total yield.

Tomato plants may be set in rows 4–5 feet apart, with plants 2–4 feet apart in the rows. Early-bearing and small-vined varieties can be planted closer. To conserve space and improve fruit quality, home gardeners frequently stake or trellis and prune their tomatoes, in which case plants may be spaced 18 inches apart in the row. Stakes ¾ inches in diameter and 4–5 feet long are appropriate, and plants should be tied to them with soft twine or strips of cloth several times during the early season.

Mulching tomato plants will help reduce loss of water from the soil and control weeds. Appropriate mulches include two or more inches of organic material such as straw or hay. Black polyethylene plastic can also be used, in which case all fertilizer must be applied before the plastic is laid down.

Green or turning fruits may be picked just before the first frost and ripened indoors in order to extend the tomato season. Such tomatoes will ripen most rapidly at 70–75° F, but for prolonged storage they should be held at 55° F. Lower temperatures will cause chilling injury and subsequent ripening will not be normal.

TONELLA Nutt. ex A. Gray. *Scrophulariaceae.* Two spp. of ann. herbs, native to w. N. Amer.; allied to *Collinsia,* but having some st. lvs. divided into 3's or 3-parted, and corolla lobes rotately spreading, not 2-lipped.

tenella (Benth.) A. Heller [*T. collinsioides* Nutt. ex A. Gray]. Sts. loosely ascending, to 1 ft.; lower lvs. orbicular to ovate, to ⅜ in. long, entire or apically notched, upper lvs. 3-parted or divided into oblong segms.; fls. minute, corolla white or pale blue, scarcely longer than calyx, lobes sometimes purple-dotted. Sw. Wash. to cent. Calif.

collinsioides: *T. tenella.*

TOONA: *CEDRELA.*

TOPIARY. The sculpturing, through pruning, of shrubs to produce formal geometrical shapes or often whimsical animal subjects constitutes the horticultural practice of topiary. Originally a development in formal gardens of the Old World, it is sometimes met with in American horticulture. Topiary requires good design, artful execution, and a proper place in the landscape. Special gardens featuring topiary work are sometimes developed. Some plant subjects popular for use in topiary may be found under the genera *Buxus, Cupressus, Eugenia, Juniperus, Ligustrum, Taxus,* and *Tsuga.*

TORENIA L. WISHBONE FLOWER, WISHBONE PLANT. *Scrophulariaceae.* About 40 spp. of ann. or per. herbs, of trop. and subtrop. Asia and Afr.; sts. freely branching, prostrate, decumbent, or erect, 4-angled; lvs. opp., simple; fls. of various colors, axillary or in few-fld. terminal racemes, calyx tubular, pleated or 3–5-winged, enlarging in fr., corolla cylindrical, 2-lipped, stamens 4; fr. a septicidal caps.

Produced freely from spring to frost; a few species grown in the greenhouse for winter bloom but usually in the garden as annuals; in Fla. they are successfully used as a substitute for pansies. Torenias require no special culture but do well in some shade with plenty of moisture. They are easily propagated by seeds sown either inside or in the open early in the spring, or from cuttings.

asiatica L. Ann. with prostrate sts.; lvs. ovate-deltoid, to 1 in., toothed; fls, axillary, corolla to 1½ in. long, violet-purple, lower lip white. S. India.

Baillonii Godefr. Ann. or grown as such, erect or decumbent; lvs. ovate, to 2¼ in. long, toothed; fls. axillary or terminal, corolla to 1½ in. long, tube yellow, red-purple above. Indochina. Often confused with *T. flava.*

flava Buch.-Ham. Often confused with *T. Baillonii,* but having lvs. almost sessile, pedicels shorter, and fls. much smaller. N. India, Malay Pen., Vietnam, China. Not known to be in cult.

Fournieri Linden ex E. Fourn. BLUEWINGS. Much-branched, glabrous ann., to 1 ft.; lvs. to 2 in. long, toothed; calyx 5-winged, corolla tube pale violet, yellow on the back, upper lip pale blue, lower lip with 3 purplish-blue lobes and yellow blotch at base of middle lobe. Vietnam. Cvs. include: **'Alba'**, corolla white with yellow blotch at base of middle lobe of lower lip; **'Bicolor'**, a listed name; **'Compacta'**, of dense habit; **'Grandiflora'**, fls. larger.

peduncularis: *T. violacea.*

violacea (Azaola) Penn. [*T. peduncularis* Benth.]. Decumbent ann., to 1 ft.; lvs. ovate-deltoid, to 2½ in. long, toothed; corolla tube yellow, limb pale blue with purple and yellow blotches. India.

TORREYA Arn. [*Tumion* Raf.]. *Taxaceae.* Six spp. of dioecious or monoecious, evergreen trees, native to N. Amer. and Asia, with opp. or subopp. brs.; lvs. linear, yewlike, spirally arranged but sometimes appearing 2-ranked, linear, with 2 glaucous bands beneath; microsporophylls in 6–8 whorls surrounded by scales at the base; female reproductive structures consisting of a single terminal ovule; seeds drupelike, completely covered by a fleshy aril.

Propagated by seeds or cuttings of side shoots. Mostly hardy through Zone 7. See *Conifers.*

californica Torr. CALIFORNIA NUTMEG. To 70 ft. and more, branchlets reddish-brown; lvs. linear, to 2½ in. long, glossy dark green above; aril ellipsoid or obovoid, to 1¾ in. long, green, streaked purple. Calif. Zone 7. Sometimes grown in sheltered areas in Zone 6 but there may be deciduous.

Fargesii Franch. Differs from *T. grandis* in having lvs. darker green and more gradually pointed. China.

grandis Fort. Tree, to 75 ft., but often remaining a shrub, branchlets yellow-green; lvs. linear, to 1 in. long, yellow-green above; aril ellipsoid to 1 in. long, brownish. China. Zone 7?

nucifera (L.) Siebold & Zucc. KAYA, JAPANESE T. To 75 ft., branchlets reddish-brown; lvs. lanceolate, to 1¼ in. long, glossy dark green above; aril narrowly obovoid, ¾–1 in. long, green, tinged purple. Japan. Hardy in sheltered places in Zone 6. Seed rich in oil, edible; wood valuable.

taxifolia Arn. [*Tumion taxifolium* (Arn.) Greene]. STINKING CEDAR. To 40 ft., branchlets yellow-green; lvs. linear, to 1½ in. long, glossy dark green above; aril obovoid, to 1½ in. long, purple, of fetid odor when bruised. Fla. Zone 8.

TOUMEYA: *PEDIOCACTUS.*

TOWNSENDIA Hook. *Compositae* (Aster Tribe). About 20 spp. of low, ann., bien., or per., mostly taprooted herbs of w. N. Amer.; lvs. alt., spatulate to linear, entire; fl. heads radiate, solitary, sessile or peduncled, many-fld.; disc fls. yellow, ray fls. white, pink, or purple; achenes glabrate or pubescent with hairs usually shortly forked or shortly 2-hooked at their apex, pappus of bristles.

A few species may be grown in the wild or rock garden.

alpina (A. Gray) Rydb. [*T. Parryi* var. *alpina* A. Gray]. Thought to be a hybrid of *T. Parryi* and *T. spathulata* Nutt. Wyo. to Alta.

exscapa (Richardson) T. C. Porter [*T. sericea* Hook.; *T. Wilcoxiana* A. Wood]. EASTER DAISY. Short-branched, cespitose per., 2–3 in. high; lvs. narrowly oblanceolate, to 2 in. long, strigose-pubescent; heads sessile or short-peduncled, to 2 in. across; ray fls. white or pinkish. Man. to n. Mex.

florifera (Hook.) A. Gray. Winter ann. or bien., with several often branching sts. to 10 in. high; lvs. narrowly spatulate, 1–2 in. long, strigose; heads to 1½ in. across; ray fls. white to pink. Nw. U.S.

formosa Greene. Fibrous-rooted, rhizomatous per., sts. several, erect, leafy, 1-headed, 1–2 ft. high; lvs. oblanceolate or spatulate, to 3 in. long, glabrous except on margins and midrib; heads 2 in. across; ray fls. white, purple underneath. Ariz., n. New Mex.

grandiflora Nutt. Bien., 2–3 in. high, sts. few, slender, spreading, branching; lvs. spatulate to oblanceolate, to 2 in. long, strigose; heads subtended by lvs., involucral bracts bristly-tipped; ray fls. white, often pink-striped on underneath. S. Dak. to New Mex.

Hookeri Beaman. EASTER DAISY. Densely cespitose per., 2–3 in. high, sts. branched, short, thick, woody; lvs. linear to narrowly oblanceolate, to 2 in. long, strigose-silky; heads sessile or very short-peduncled, about 1 in. across; ray fls. white, pinkish underneath. S. B.C., Alta., Sask., s. to Utah and Wyo.

Parryi D. C. Eat. Bien. or short-lived per., sts. 1 or few, to 1 ft. or more, scapelike, erect; basal lvs. in a rosette, spatulate, 1½–4 in. long, strigose or glabrous; heads to 2½ in. across; ray fls. violet-blue. Alta. to Idaho and Wyo.

Rothrockii A. Gray ex Rothr. Cespitose per., 2–3 in. high, brs. short, becoming woody; lvs. spatulate-oblanceolate, to 1½ in. long, thick, glabrous; heads sessile or on short peduncles, 1½ in. across; ray fls. blue-purple. Colo.

sericea: *T. exscapa.*

Wilcoxiana: *T. exscapa.*

TOXICODENDRON: see *RHUS.*

TOXICOSCORDION: *ZIGADENUS.*

TRACHELIUM L. [*Diosphaera* Buser]. THROATWORT. *Campanulaceae.* About 7–10 spp. of usually erect per. herbs, often woody at the base, native to the Medit. region; lvs. alt., simple; fls. small, purplish, blue, or white, in dense, terminal, corymbose clusters, corolla salverform or nearly so the tube 3–4 times as long as lobes, stamens separate, style usually much exserted.

Propagated by seeds or cuttings.

caeruleum L. Erect, 2–4 ft., similar in aspect to *Centranthus ruber;* lvs. ovate, to about 3 in. long, acute, sharply double-serrate; fls. many, corolla deep blue to white, ¼–½ in. across, tube very slender. W. and cent. Medit. region. Hardy only in the far South, but flowering in 1 yr. from seed and treated as an ann. in the North.

rumelianum Hampe [*Diosphaera dubia* Buser]. Sprawling, 6–12 in.; lvs. ovate to oblong, to about 1 in. long, acute, sparsely toothed, all but the lowermost sessile; fls. many in corymbose heads, corolla blue, to ½ in. long, stamens and style long-exserted. Bulgaria, Greece. A rock garden subject requiring limestone soil.

TRACHELOSPERMUM Lem. [*Rhynchospermum* Hort., not Reinw. or DC.]. *Apocynaceae.* More than 10 spp. of twining or clambering shrubby vines with milky sap, native to trop. and subtrop. e. Asia, with 1 in N. Amer.; lvs. opp., entire, petioled; infl. loose, thyrsiform, terminal and lateral; fls. rather small, 5-merous, bisexual, corolla white, sometimes becoming yellow or purplish, salverform, slightly inflated above insertion of stamens, lobes oblong, stamens borne on corolla, anthers basally spurred, united, adhering to stigma, included or with tips barely exserted; fr. a pair of slender, cylindrical follicles, seeds linear, with tufts of hairs.

Often grown in greenhouses, and outdoors in mild climates, as ornamentals and for the fragrance of the fls.; propagated by cuttings in spring.

asiaticum (Siebold & Zucc.) Nakai [*T. divaricatum* (Thunb.) Kanitz; *Rhynchospermum asiaticum* Hort.; *R. divaricatum* Hort.]. Differs from *T. jasminoides* in being hardier, and in having fls. with calyx to ⅛ in. long, calyx lobes erect, shorter than the narrow part of corolla tube, corolla yellowish-white, darker and glabrous in throat, stamens borne on upper part of corolla tube, anthers slightly exserted. Korea, Japan. Zone 8.

divaricatum: *T. asiaticum.*

fragrans: *T. lucidum;* however, material cult. as *T. fragrans* and as *T. fragrans* var. *grandiflorum* is *Chonemorpha fragrans.*

grandiflorum: *Chonemorpha fragrans.*

japonicum: a listed name of no botanical standing for *T. jasminoides* cv.

jasminoides (Lindl.) Lem. [*Rhynchospermum jasminoides* Lindl.]. STAR JASMINE, CONFEDERATE J. To 30 ft. or more, evergreen, brs. with holdfast roots; lvs. elliptic to oblong or oblanceolate, to 4 in. long; peduncles slender, longer than lvs.; fls. fragrant, calyx somewhat foliaceous, to ³⁄₁₆ in. long, calyx lobes longer than narrow part of corolla tube, strongly recurved, corolla white, to 1 in. across, tube ⁵⁄₁₆ in. long, lobes obliquely truncate at apex, stamens borne on middle of corolla tube or slightly below, anthers included; follicles to 6 in. long. China. Zone 9. Cv. **'Japonicum'.** Lvs. white-veined, turning bronze in autumn. Cv. **'Variegatum'.** Lvs. variegated green and white, often tinged red; said to be hardier. Cv. **'Wilsonii'**, is listed.

longifolium: a listed name of no botanical standing.

lucidum (D. Don) K. Schum. [*T. fragrans* Wallich ex Hook.f., not Hort.]. Tall climber; lvs. elliptic to obovate-elliptic, acuminate, basally broadly cuneate; peduncles in upper axils only, about as long as subtending lvs., very slender, many-fld.; calyx lobes ovate to lanceolate, erect, ¼ to ½ the length of corolla tube, corolla white, ⅝ in. across, tube slender, about ⅜ in. long, conspicuously puberulent in throat, stamens borns above middle of corolla tube, anthers included; follicles incurved, 8–12 in. long. Ne. India and Nepal. Probably not cult. in Amer. Plants grown as *T. fragrans* are *Chonemorpha fragrans.*

miniatum: a listed name of no botanical standing.

TRACHYCARPUS H. Wendl. FAN PALM. *Palmae.* Six spp. of dioecious, rarely monoecious or polygamous, small or moderate palms, native to the Himalayan region of Asia; trunks solitary or cespitose, often covered with persistent, fibrous lf. sheaths; lvs. palmate, divided into 1-ribbed segms.; infls. among lvs., with several thin bracts on peduncle, paniculate, 2–3 times branched, brs. not subtended by sheathing bracts; fls. in clusters of 2–4, sepals 3, basally imbricate, petals 3, imbricate, male fls. with 6 stamens, 3 small pistillodes, female fls. with 6 staminodes, 3 carpels, bisexual fls. with 6 stamens and 3 carpels; fr. globose-reniform to oblong-ovoid, stigmatic residue apical, seed with homogeneous endosperm intruded by seed coat below the raphe, embryo lateral.

Widely planted in warm-temperate regions; one species among the hardiest of palms. For culture see *Palms.*

excelsus: *Rhapis excelsa,* but material offered as *T. excelsus* is *T. Fortunei.*

Fortunei (Hook.) H. Wendl. [*Chamaerops Fortunei* Hook.]. WINDMILL PALM, CHINESE W.P., HEMP P. Trunk solitary, slender, to 40 ft., conspicuously covered with black hairlike fiber from old lf. sheaths; lvs. orbicular, 2–4 ft. wide, dull green and sometimes slightly glaucous, variously divided to middle or almost to base into stiffish horizontal or drooping segms., petiole elongate, finely toothed along margins; fr. globose-reniform, bluish, ½ in. wide, seed depressed in the center. N. Burma, cent. and e. China, and perhaps Kyushu (s. Japan). Zone 8b. In the Orient the fibers of the lf. sheaths are made into a decorative hemplike rope. Often cult. under names *Chamaerops excelsa* or *T. excelsus.*

Martianus (Wallich) H. Wendl. Trunk slender, usually naked and ringed with lf. scars; lvs. nearly orbicular, very regularly divided to middle into many segms.; fr. glossy blue, oblong-ovoid, ½ in. long or less; seed deeply sulcate. Cent. and e. Himalayas, Assam, n. Burma.

Takil Becc. Very similar to *T. Fortunei,* distinguished by tendency of young plants to grow obliquely and in conical shape, and by fibers on trunk tightly clasping, not ruffled. W. Himalayas. Zone 10.

TRACHYLOBIUM: *HYMENAEA.*

TRACHYMENE Rudge [*Didiscus* DC.]. *Umbelliferae.* More than 12 spp. of herbs of Australia and S. Pacific Is.; lvs. mostly ternately compound; fls. white or blue, in simple umbels subtended by lanceolate bracts; fr. flattened laterally.

A few are grown as ornamentals. For summer bloom, seeds should be sown in spring where plants are to stand. Seeds may be sown in autumn under glass for spring bloom.

coerulea R. C. Grah. [*Didiscus coeruleus* (R. C. Grah.) DC.]. BLUE LACE FLOWER. Ann., to 2 ft.; lvs. ternately to biternately compound into narrow lobes; fls. light blue, umbels long-peduncled, to 3 in. across. Australia.

pilosa Sm. [*Didiscus pusillus* F. J. Muell.]. Ann., to 6 in.; lvs. divided into linear lobes; fls. white, tinged with purple, in small, short-peduncled umbels; fr. hairy on one half, smooth or ridged on the other. Australia.

TRADESCANTIA L. SPIDERWORT. *Commelinaceae.* Twenty or more spp. of per. herbs, native to N. and S. Amer.; sts. erect to trailing; infls. terminal, or terminal and axillary, of paired sessile cincinni, each pair subtended by usually paired leaflike or spathelike bracts when terminal, or by one bract when axillary; fls. blue, rose, purple, or white, sepals and petals separate, equal, stamens 6, filaments usually hairy, equal, ovary 3-celled, each cell with 2 ovules.

Spiderworts are grown under glass, in baskets, or in the open, depending on their hardiness. Of easy culture; propagated by cuttings of the growing shoots, seeds, or division. Some species hybridize readily and many garden plants (see *T. ×Andersoniana*) are hybrids involving two or more species.

albiflora Kunth [*T. tricolor* Hort. ex C. B. Clarke; *T. viridis* Hort.]. WANDERING JEW. Sts. decumbent to erect, rooting at nodes, with a line of hairs on one side; lvs. oblong-acuminate, to 2 in. or rarely 3 in. long, 1 in. wide, green above and beneath, glabrous except for ciliate margin; fls. white, to ¼ in. long, sepals pilose along the green keel, anthers with triangular connectives. S. Amer.; naturalized in s. U.S. Common under benches in greenhouses. Has been confused with *T. fluminensis.* Cvs. are: **'Albovittata'**, GIANT WHITE INCH PLANT, lvs. white-striped; **'Aurea'**, lvs. yellow; **'Laekenensis'** [*T. laekenensis* Hort. ex L. H. Bailey], lvs. pale green, striped with white and banded with purple; **'Variegata'** [*T. striata* Hort.], lvs. striped with yellow and white.

×**Andersoniana** W. Ludw. & Rohw. [*T. virginiana* of many auth., not L.]: *T. ohiensis* × *T. subaspera* × *T. virginiana*. A complex series of garden hybrids, with erect sts. and bright fls. often 1 in. across. Grown as an outdoor garden plant. Cvs. (offered mostly under *T. virginiana*) include: **'Alba'**, fls. white; **'Caerulea'**, fls. bright blue; **'Carnea'**, fls. pinkish; **'Coccinea'**, fls. reddish; **'Hutchinsonii'**, fls. pale blue; **'Lilacina'**, fls. pale lilac; **'Major'**, fls. double; **'Nana'**, of dwarf habit; **'Purpurea'**, fls. purple; **'Rosea'**, fls. rose-pink; **'Rubra'**, fls. purplish-red; **'Violacea'**, fls. violet.

azurea: a listed name of no botanical standing.

bicolor Kunth. Not known in cult.; the name is sometimes, but incorrectly, applied to *Rhoeo spathacea*.

Blossfeldiana Mildb. FLOWERING INCH PLANT. Sts. trailing or ascending, purplish, densely white-villous; lvs. oblong-elliptic, green and glabrous above, purplish and pilose beneath, to 4 in. long, 1¾ in. wide; fls. clustered in axils of leaflike paired bracts, on lateral or terminal peduncles to 1½ in. long, pedicels and sepals purplish, pilose, petals equal, ¼ in. long, white below middle, pink above, stamens equal, white, hairy, anthers yellow. Argentina. Cv. **'Variegata'**. Lvs. variegated.

bracteata Small. To 1½ ft.; lvs. linear-lanceolate, bright-, often yellow-green, to 12 in. long, ¾ in. wide; fls. rose, or rarely blue, sepals densely sticky-pubescent. Minn. to Iowa, s. to Tex. Cv. **'Rosea'**. Fls. rose-colored.

brevicaulis Raf. An old name of somewhat ambiguous application, sometimes used for plants that are now considered to be diminutive forms of *T. virginiana*.

canaliculata: *T. ohiensis*.

discolor: *Rhoeo spathacea*.

dracaenoides: *Callisia fragrans*.

fluminensis Vell. WANDERING JEW. Similar to *T. albiflora*, but differing in having lvs. ovate-acuminate, to 1⅝ in. long, ¾ in. wide, deep purple-violet beneath, anthers with rectangular connectives. Sometimes confused with *Zebrina pendula*, but differs in having fls. white.

fuscata: *Siderasis fuscata*.

gigantea Rose. To 2 ft.; lvs. linear-lanceolate, to 12 in. long, 1³⁄₁₆ in. wide; infl. subtended by inflated bracts with reduced, soft-velvety blades; fls. magenta-pink to blue, sepals not glandular-velvety. E. Tex.

hirsuticaulis Small. Forming large clumps, sts. to 12 in., mostly simple, long-hairy; lvs. elongate, to 12 in. long, attenuate, hirsute; fls. deep blue, violet, rose, or pink, sepals green or purple-margined, hirsute. Ga. and Fla. to Ark. and Tex. Hardy north; plants become dormant and die back in midsummer, but basal lvs. reappear in autumn and remain green over winter.

hirsutiflora Bush. To 1½ ft., sts. hairy; lvs. firm, linear-lanceolate, to 12 in. long, ¾ in. wide, deep green, usually edged with pink or purple; fls. blue or rarely pink, sepals dull green or sometimes flushed with rose, pubescent with glandless or both glandular and glandless hairs. W. Fla. to Ark. and Tex.

humilis Rose. To 1 ft. or a little more, sts. diffuse, branched, puberulent; lvs. linear-lanceolate, to 7 in. long, ½ in. wide; fls. blue, sepals dull green or suffused with rose, pubescent with glandular and glandless hairs. Se. Tex.

hybrida: a listed name of no botanical standing, for plants probably referable to *T.* ×*Andersoniana*.

laekenensis: *T. albiflora* cv.

micrantha Torr. Small creeper or prostrate; lvs. narrow, flat, 1½ in. or less long; fls. many, small, rose-purple. Tex. and adjacent Mex. Sometimes cult. in greenhouses and gardens of the region.

moluccana: a listed name of no botanical standing, used for *Cyanotis moluccana*.

montana: *T. subaspera* var.

multicolor: a listed name of no botanical standing: used for *Zebrina pendula* cv. *quadricolor*.

multiflora: *Tripogandra multiflora*.

navicularis Ortg. CHAIN PLANT. Small creeper; lvs. fleshy, narrow, folded together, mostly 1 in. long or less; fls. rose-purple. Mex. and (questionably) Peru.

occidentalis (Britt.) Smyth. To 2 ft., sts. glabrous, branching, glaucous; lvs. linear-lanceolate, to 18 in. long, ¾ in. wide, glaucous; fls. blue to rose or magenta, sepals with glandular hairs or rarely glabrous. Minn. to La. and Ariz. Cv. **'Rubra'**. Fls. red.

ohiensis Raf. [*T. canaliculata* Raf.; *T. reflexa* Raf.]. To 3 ft.; lvs. linear-lanceolate, to 1½ ft. long, 1¾ in. wide, glaucous; fls. blue to rose or nearly white, sepals glabrous or with a tuft of glandless hairs at apex. S. New Eng. to Fla., w. to Minn. and Tex. Cult. in the open. Cv. **'Alba'**. Fls. white, stamens blue.

pexata: *T. sillamontana*.

pilosa: *T. subaspera*.

quadricolor: a listed name of no botanical standing for *Zebrina pendula* cv.

reflexa: *T. ohiensis*.

reginae: *Dichorisandra reginae*.

rosea: *Cuthbertia rosea*. Var. **graminea:** *Cuthbertia graminea*.

sillamontana Matuda [*T. pexata* H. E. Moore]. WHITE-VELVET, WHITE-GOSSAMER. Plants white-villous throughout, sts. from stout rhizome with fibrous roots, branched, loose, to 8 in. long, brs. breaking through lf. sheaths at lower nodes; lvs. at base of st. reduced, those above elliptic-ovate, to 2½ in. long, 1 in. wide; fls. rose-magenta, filaments glabrous. Ne. Mex Originally grown under the erroneous names *Cyanotis veldthoutiana* and *Tradescantia velutina;* also known as *Tradescantia* cv. 'White Velvet' or 'White Gossamer'.

striata: a listed name of no botanical standing, referable to *T. albiflora* cv. 'Variegata'.

subaspera Ker-Gawl. [*T. pilosa* Lehm.]. To 3 ft.; sts. zigzag and shaggy-pilose to glabrate; lvs. elliptic-lanceolate, to 10 in. long, 2 in. wide, blade much broader than sheath and conspicuously narrowed at base, dark green; fls. light to deep blue, rarely white, about 1 in. across, sepals hairy and often glandular. S. Penn. to Fla. and Mo. Var. **montana** (Shuttl.) E. Anderson & Woodson. Sts. straight; uppermost cymes peduncled, not sessile. From s. W. Va. to n. Fla. and Ala.

tampicana: a listed name of no botanical standing; plants so named are *Setcreasea pallida* cv. 'Purple Heart'.

tricolor: *T. albiflora*.

velutina: see *T. sillamontana*.

virginiana L. COMMON S., WIDOW'S-TEARS. To 3 ft.; lvs. delicate, linear-lanceolate, to 1 ft. long, 1 in. wide; fls. violet-purple, rarely rose or white, sepals bright green, somewhat turgid and inflated, pubescent but without glands. Conn. to Ga., w. to Mo. Most plants so named in gardens are *T.* ×*Andersoniana*.

viridis: a listed name of no botanical standing; used for *T. albiflora*.

Warszewicziana: *Hadrodemas Warszewiczianum*.

zebrina: *Zebrina pendula*.

TRAGOPOGON L. GOATSBEARD. *Compositae* (Cichorium Tribe). About 50 spp. of erect, taprooted bien. and per. herbs with milky sap, native to s. Eur., N. Afr., and Asia; lvs. narrow, grasslike; fl. heads solitary, expanding only in early morning, involucre of 1 row of equal, narrow bracts; fls. all ligulate, bisexual, yellow or purple; achenes narrow, slender-beaked, pappus of 1 row of plumose bristles with interlaced brs.

Seeds of salsify are sown in spring where plants are to stand. The roots may remain in the ground during the winter.

porrifolius L. SALSIFY, VEGETABLE-OYSTER, OYSTER PLANT. Hardy bien., to 4 ft., roots to 1 ft. long; heads to 4 in. across; fls. purple, shorter than involucral bracts; pappus brownish. S. Eur.; naturalized as a weed in N. Amer. Widely cult. for its edible root.

pratensis L. JACK (or JOHN)-GO-TO-BED-AT-NOON. Hardy bien., to 3 ft.; heads to 2½ in. across; fls. yellow, longer than involucral bracts; pappus whitish. Eur.; naturalized as a weed in N. Amer. Rarely cult.

TRAPA L. WATERNUT, WATER CHESTNUT. *Trapaceae*. Three or 4 spp., native to Eur., Asia, and Afr., with characters of the family; blades of floating lvs. glossy above, dentate toward the apex, more or less hairy underneath.

Grown in ponds and aquaria as ornamentals, but can be weedy. Propagated by seeds which must be kept moist to remain viable. The seeds are edible and are used as food in various parts of the world.

bicornis Osbeck. Fls. white; fr. to 3 in. across, with 2 straight or slightly curved horns. E. Asia.

Maximowiczii Korsh. Fls. light purple; fr. with 4 thin, straight or slightly curved horns. Se. Asia, Indonesia.

natans L. TRAPA NUT, JESUIT N., WATER CALTROP, LING, SALIGOT. Fls. white; fr. to 1½ in. across, with 4 stout horns. Eurasia, Afr.; naturalized and a weed in several rivers in e. U.S. Seeds edible; eaten in the Orient; also used for making rosaries.

TRAPACEAE Dumort. WATER CHESTNUT FAMILY. Dicot.; 1 genus, with 3–4 spp., native to warm parts of Eur., Asia, and Afr.; ann., aquatic herbs; sts. long, slender, rooting in lower part, submerged nodes with deciduous, linear lvs. and plumelike roots, floating lvs. alt., forming a terminal rosette, blades ovate-rhombic, petioles inflated; fls. solitary in axils of floating lvs., bisexual, sepals, petals, and stamens 4, ovary half-inferior; fr. a 1-seeded, top-shaped drupe, the thin, fleshy outer wall disintegrating and exposing a hard, indehiscent nut with sculptured walls and 2–4 horns. *Trapa* is cult. in water gardens.

TRAPACEAE. *Trapa natans:* **a,** flowering plant, × ¼; **b,** flower, × 2; **c,** flower, vertical section, × 3; **d,** ovary, cross section, × 5; **e,** nut, × ½.

TRAUTVETTERIA Fisch. & C. A. Mey. FALSE BUGBANE. *Ranunculaceae.* A few spp. of per. herbs, native to N. Amer. and Asia, lvs. palmately lobed, broad; fls. small, white, in corymbs, sepals, 3–5, falling early, petal-like, petals 0, stamens many.

Grown in the wild garden; propagated by division.

carolinensis (Walt.) Vail [*T. palmata* (Michx.) Fisch. & C. A. Mey.]. To 3 ft.; lvs. to 16 in. across, lobes 5–11, toothed; fls. about ½ in. across. Penn. to Fla. and Mo.

grandis Nutt. ex Torr. & A. Gray. Differs from *T. carolinensis* in having lvs. more deeply lobed, and styles longer, somewhat curled. B.C. to Mont., s. to n. Calif. and New Mex.

palmata: *T. carolinensis.*

TRECULIA Decne. ex Trécul. *Moraceae.* Perhaps 12 spp. of dioecious shrubs and trees, native to trop. Afr. and Madagascar; lvs. alt., short-petioled; fls. axillary, unisexual; fr. a syncarp. Related to *Artocarpus* from which it differs in the stamens 2–4 (commonly 3) instead of 1.

Prefers rich soil with much organic matter and moisture. For tropical plantings.

africana Decne. ex Trécul. AFRICAN BREAD TREE. Evergreen tree, to 120 ft.; lvs. 3–8 in. long, glabrous, oblong-ovate to lanceolate, obtuse-pointed, leathery; male fls. green, in globose heads to 2¾ in. in diam.; fr. globose, to 1 ft. in diam. or more, yellowish when ripe, roughened by the knoblike tops of perianth segms., weighing 18–30 pounds, seeds abundant, about ¼ in. long. Trop. Afr. Zone 10b. Var. **mollis** (Engl.) J. Léonard [*T. mollis* Engl.]. Lvs. soft-pubescent beneath; fr. 8–10 in. in diam.

mollis: *T. africana* var.

TREMA Lour. *Ulmaceae.* About 20 spp. of trees or shrubs, often pubescent, native to trop. and warm regions of both hemispheres; lvs. alt., toothed, often 3-nerved from base; fls. small, in axillary clusters, unisexual and bisexual; fr. an ovoid drupe.

guineensis (Schumach. & Thonn.) Ficalho. To 15 ft.; lvs. ovate, to 6 in. long, attenuate to apex, variously pubescent; fr. round, to ⅜ in. across, black. Trop. Afr. Wood useful.

TREMANDRACEAE R. Br. ex DC. TREMANDRA FAMILY. Dicot.; 3 genera and about 30 spp. of heathlike shrubs or suffrutescent herbs, native to Tasmania and s. and w. Australia, often with glandular hairs; lvs. small, simple, alt., opp., or whorled, without stipules; fls. bisexual, solitary, axillary, sepals and petals 4 or 5, rarely 3, stamens 8–10, usually in 2 whorls, pistil 1, ovary superior; fr. a caps., seeds often hairy. *Tetratheca* is occasionally cult. as an ornamental in warmer regions.

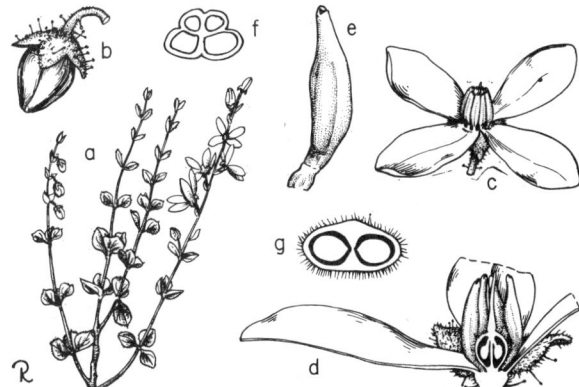

TREMANDRACEAE. *Tetratheca ciliata* Lindl.: **a,** flowering branch, × ½; **b,** flower bud, showing calyx, × 2; **c,** flower, × 1½; **d,** flower, vertical section (part of petals cut off), × 3; **e,** stamen, × 7; **f,** anther, cross section, × 10; **g,** ovary, cross section, × 10. (Species representative, but not in general cultivation; from Lawrence, *Taxonomy of Vascular Plants.*)

TREVESIA Vis. *Araliaceae.* Four spp. of prickly, glabrous or pubescent, evergreen shrubs or small trees, native from India to Malay Pen. and Polynesia; lvs. large and palmately lobed, sometimes compound except for blade uniting bases of petiolules; fls. in umbels arranged in panicles or racemes, petals 7–12, valvate, often united, stamens as many as petals, styles united in a grooved column, ovary 7–12-celled; fr. a fleshy, ovoid drupe, pyrenes 7–12.

Grown in the greenhouse in a moist atmosphere. Propagated by cuttings.

Burckii Boerl. [*T. Sanderi* Hort.]. Shrub, to 5 ft., with thick, prickly sts.; lvs. to 2 ft. across, palmately lobed, the lobes irregularly pinnatifid, petiolules united basally in a wing nearly to the lobes; fls. small, on long, slender pedicels, in reddish-tomentose, racemose infls. Sumatra and Borneo.

Micholitzii: a listed name of no botanical standing for *T. palmata* cv.

palmata (Roxb.) Vis. Small tree, to 20 ft.; brs. mostly simple, prickly, tomentose; lvs. palmately 7–11-lobed, or in young plants compound, about 2 ft. across or more; infl. paniculate, erect, at first reddish-tomentose. N. India to sw. China. Cv. 'Micholitzii' [*T. Micholitzii* Hort.]. SNOWFLAKE PLANT, TROPICAL SNOWFLAKE, SNOWFLAKE ARALIA, SNOWFLAKE TREE. Lvs. dotted silvery-white on glossy green.

Sanderi: a listed name of no botanical standing: used for *T. Burckii.*

sundaica Miq. Shrub or small tree, to 25 ft., with prickly brs.; lvs. deeply palmately lobed, serrate, glossy dark green above, lighter beneath, reddish-tomentose when young; infl. racemose, axillary, becoming reflexed; fls. greenish-white, large, pedicels thick. Java, Sumatra.

TREVOA Miers. *Rhamnaceae.* About 6 spp. of small, much-branched, spiny trees or shrubs of Chile, Argentina, and Bolivia; lvs. opp., 3-nerved; fls. in axillary clusters; fr. small, drupaceous.

trinervis Miers. Spines about ½ in. long; lvs. to 1 in. long, toothed. Chile. Sometimes cult. in Calif.

TRIADICA: *SAPIUM.*

TRIANTHA: *TOFIELDIA.*

TRIBULUS L. CALTROP. *Zygophyllaceae.* About 12 spp. of trop. and subtrop. herbs, native to both the New and Old Worlds; sts. ascending or mostly prostrate, radiating from a tap root; lvs. opp., pinnate; fls. usually white or yellow, solitary on axillary peduncles, sepals 5, early-deciduous, petals 5, stamens 10; fr. with 3–5 carpels separating at maturity into spinose, bony nutlets.

Propagated by seeds or cuttings.

terrestris L. PUNCTURE VINE, BURNUT. Prostrate or decumbent ann. or per., sts. to 3 ft., hairy; lvs. of each node unequal, the larger to 2½ in. long, lfts. 5–8 pairs, oblong to linear-oblong, to nearly ½ in. long, acutish, sessile, villous beneath; fls. usually yellow, petals to ¼ in. long;

fr. to ¾ in. across, separating into 5 woody nutlets, each armed with 2 sharp, stout, divergent spines to ¼ in. long and several smaller spines. Old World tropics; naturalized in warmer regions of the world, a troublesome weed in Calif., sw. U.S., and Mex., extending n. to S. Dak. and to s. N.Y.

TRICALYSIA A. Rich. ex DC. *Rubiaceae.* Not cult. **T. floribunda** and **T. Kraussiana:** *Kraussia floribunda.*

TRICHANTHA: *COLUMNEA.*

TRICHILIA P. Br. *Meliaceae.* About 240 spp. of trees and shrubs, native to trop. Amer. and Afr.; lvs. alt., with 3 lfts. or odd-pinnate (1 sp. has 1 lft.); fls. not showy, in axillary or terminal panicles or cymes, calyx 4–5-lobed or -toothed, petals 4–5, stamens 4–10, usually more or less united in a tube, ovary 2–3-celled; fr. a dry, mostly leathery caps., opening and exposing the seeds and their orange or red aril.

emetica Vahl. Tree, to 30 ft., young parts pubescent; lfts. 7–11, usually oblong-elliptic, to 6 in. long, leathery, pubescent beneath; fls. white, calyx 5-lobed. Afr., Arabia. Seeds contain a useful oil.

hirta L. Tree, to 25 ft. and more, young parts hairy; lfts. 9–21 (sometimes 3–7), oblong-lanceolate to ovate-lanceolate, to 5 in. long, membranous, hairy or glabrous beneath; infl. long-peduncled; fls. white, calyx usually 5-lobed, ovary hairy. Trop. N. and S. Amer.

pallida Swartz. Shrub or small tree, to 15 ft. or sometimes much taller, young parts hairy, twigs often scarred with lenticels; lfts. 3–7, oblong-elliptic to elliptic, oblanceolate, or obovate, lateral lft. to 6 in. long, terminal lft. longer; infl. sessile or subsessile; fls. white, calyx usually 4-lobed, ovary hairy. W. Indies.

Zenkeri Harms. Tree, young parts glabrous or slightly pubescent; lfts. 7–11, oblong, to 9 in. long, short-acuminate, glabrous or nearly so beneath; infl. half as long as lvs.; fls. yellow or yellowish-green, very fragrant. W. Afr.

TRICHOCENTRUM Poepp. & Endl. *Orchidaceae.* About 30 spp. of epiphytes, native to Cent. and trop. S. Amer.; sts. short, pseudobulbs fleshy, 1-lvd.; lvs. leathery, oblong; infl. basal, 1- to few-fld.; fls. small to large, perianth segms. spreading, sepals similar, lip united to base of column, simple to 3-lobed, fiddle-shaped, prolonged at base into a spur, column short, with a pair of erect, spreading wings. For structure of fl. see *Orchidaceae.*

For culture see *Orchids.*

albopurpureum Linden & Rchb.f. To 4 in., pseudobulbs ovoid; lvs. fleshy, elliptic, to 3½ in. long; infl. solitary, 1-fld.; fls. variable, sepals and petals oblong, brown with reddish tint, lip larger than sepals and petals, 1 in. long, 2-lobed at apex, purple or white with 2 large purple blotches at base. N. S. Amer.

Pfavii Rchb.f. Short, stemless; lvs. sessile, cuneate-strap-shaped, to 5 in. long; infl. short, 2-fld.; fls. 1¼ in. across, sepals and petals spatulate, white with brown basal blotch, lip narrowly fan-shaped, 2-lobed, crisped, white with a reddish basal blotch. Cent. Amer.

tigrinum Linden & Rchb.f. Short, stemless; lvs. sessile, oblong, to 3½ in. long, dull green, speckled with red; infl. to 3 in. long, 1-fld.; fls. pendent, to 3 in. across, sepals and petals linear, yellow, spotted with red, lip larger, cuneately obovate, 2-lobed at apex, white, streaked with rose toward base, disc with 3 calluses at base, calluses elongate, laterally compressed, triangular, acute, yellow, with 2 erect teeth behind them. Costa Rica, Ecuador.

TRICHOCEREUS (A. Berger) Riccob. [*Helianthocereus* Backeb.; *Roseocereus* Backeb.; *Weberbauerocereus* Backeb.]. *Cactaceae.* Perhaps 25 spp. of ribbed cylindrical cacti, native to S. Amer.; sts. prostrate or cespitose to treelike, ribs 4–38; fls. nocturnal, funnelform, white, scales bearing hairs in axils, stamens many, the upper ones in a distinct close circle at the mouth, perianth persisting or deciduous. Apparently intergrading with *Echinopsis.*

For culture see *Cacti.*

auricolor: *T. Huascha.*

Bertramianus Backeb. [*Helianthocereus Bertramianus* (Backeb.) Backeb.]. Sts. solitary or branching from base, erect, club-shaped, to 5 ft. high and 10 in. thick, ribs 20, to ¾ in. high; spines needle-shaped, pale yellow, radial spines 12, to 1 in. long, central spines 4, the longest deflexed, to 3 in. long; fls. subapical, diurnal, yellowish-white, 4–5 in. long. N. Bolivia.

Bridgesii (Salm-Dyck) Britt. & Rose. To 18 ft., brs. pale green, 4–6 in. thick, ribs 4–8, the sinuses broad, shallow; areoles large, ¾ in. apart, spines 2–6, unequal, needle-shaped to awl-shaped, yellow, to 4 in. long; fls. 7 in. long, scales scattered; fr. long-hairy, to 2½ in. long. Bolivia.

candicans (Gillies) Britt. & Rose. Sts. cespitose, erect or spreading, to 2 ft. high and 6 in. thick, forming clumps to 10 ft. wide, ribs 9–11, low; areoles large, about 1 in. apart, spines awl-shaped, yellowish, mottled, radial spines 10 or more, to 1½ in. long, central spines several, to 4 in. long; fls. white, 6 in. long; fr. globose or ellipsoid, splitting. N. Argentina. Var. **gladiatus** (Lem.) A. Berger [*T. gladiatus* (Lem.) Backeb.]. Sts. to 3 ft. high and 8 in. thick; spines red at base. Paraguay.

chiloensis (Colla) Britt. & Rose. To 25 ft. high, mostly with fastigiate brs., ribs 16–17, low, cross-furrowed; spines needle-shaped, yellow, becoming gray, radial spines 8–12, to 1½ in. long, central spine 1, to 5 in. long; fls. white, to 6 in. long; fr. globose. Chile. Although the original spelling is *chiloensis,* the plant is not known in Chiloe.

coquimbanus (Mol.) Britt. & Rose. Sts. erect, to 4 ft., or prostrate, 3 in. thick, ribs 12–13; areoles large, spines about 20, the larger awl-shaped, to 3 in. long; fls. white, 4 in. long. Chile.

cuzcoensis Britt. & Rose. Much-branched, to 20 ft., ribs 7–8, low; areoles ½ in. apart, spines about 12, stout, swollen at base, to 3 in. long; fls. white, fragrant, 5 in. long, stamens declined. Peru.

fascicularis (Meyen) Britt. & Rose [*Weberbauerocereus fascicularis* (Meyen) Backeb.]. To 15 ft., branching from base, ribs 16, low; areoles close-set, spines many, yellowish to brown, radial spines needle-shaped, to ½ in. long, central spines stouter, to 1½ in. long; fls. greenish or brownish, to 4½ in. long, tube slender, curved, segms. short; fr. globose, umbilicate, reddish, splitting, 1½ in. in diam. S. Peru. Cv. **'Montanus'** is listed.

gladiatus: *T. candicans* var.

huancayensis: a listed name of no botanical standing; said to apply to a form of *T. peruvianus.*

Huascha (A. Web.) Britt. & Rose [*T. auricolor* Backeb.; *Lobivia Huascha* (A. Web.) W. T. Marsh.]. Sts. cespitose, to 5 ft. high and 2½ in. thick, ribs 12–18, low, rounded; spines needle-shaped, yellowish to brownish, radial spines 8–13, to $^5/_8$ in. long, central spine 1, longer; fls. yellow to red, to 4 in. long. Argentina.

Knuthianus Backeb. Treelike, to 10 ft., brs. to 4 in. thick, glaucescent, ribs 7, rounded; radial spines 7, awl-shaped, yellowish, becoming gray, to 1¼ in. long, central spine 1, stout, to 5 in. long; fls. large, white. Cent. Peru.

lamprochlorus (Lem.) Britt. & Rose. Sts. simple or branching at base, to 7 ft. high and 3 in. thick, ribs 10–17, low, the sinuses undulate, scarcely acute; spines stout, yellowish, becoming brown, radial spines 11–15, to $^5/_{16}$ in. long, central spines 4, to 1 in. long; fls. white, to 10 in. long. N. Argentina. The name may not be correctly applied.

litoralis (Johow) Looser. Sts. erect or sprawling, to 3 ft. high and 5 in. thick; areoles to ½ in. apart, spines yellowish, becoming gray, radial spines 20, thin-awl-shaped, central spines 5–8, stouter, longer; fls. white, to 6 in. long. Chile.

macrogonus (Salm-Dyck) Riccob. Sts. bluish, slender in cult., ribs 7, rounded, ⅝ in. high; areoles large, ¾ in. apart, radial spines 8–10, brown, to ¾ in. long, central spine 1, 1½–4 in. long; fls. white, odorless, 4 in. long; fr. 2 in. in diam. S. Amer.

Pachanoi Britt. & Rose. To 20 ft., fastigiately branched, ribs 6–8, broad; spines 0 or 3–7, yellow to brown, to ¾ in. long; fls. white, fragrant, to 9 in. long, with long black hairs. Ecuador.

Pasacana (A. Web.) Britt. & Rose. Low or to 35 ft., few-branched, sts. club-shaped, to 1 ft. thick, ribs 20–38, ¾ in. high; areoles close-set, spines many, brown to yellow, awl-shaped in lower areoles, to 6 in. long, bristlelike in upper areoles, 4–5 in. long; fls. 4 in. long, brown-hairy; fr. globose, to 1½ in. in diam. Bolivia, N. Argentina. Cv. **'Albicephala'** is listed.

peruvianus Britt. & Rose. PERUVIAN TORCH CACTUS. Sts. much-branched, to 15 ft. high and 6–8 in. thick, glaucous, ribs 6–8, rounded; areoles large, to 1 in. apart, spines 10, stout, brown, to 1½ in. long; fls. large. Peru. Perhaps referable to *T. macrogonus.*

Poco Backeb. [*Helianthocereus Poco* (Backeb.) Backeb.]. Sts. much lower and thinner than in *T. Pasacana;* spines yellow, slender; fls. diurnal, red. Bolivia.

purpureopilosus (Weing.) Backeb. & F. M. Knuth. Sts. simple or branching at base, 2½ in. thick, ribs 12, low; areoles ¼ in. apart, spines many, needle-shaped, yellowish, ¼ in. long, hiding the st., radial spines 20, central spines 4; fls. white, 8½ in. long. Argentina.

santiaguensis (Speg.) Backeb. Treelike, to 25 ft., brs. fastigiate, 2½–4 in. thick, ribs 14 or more, low; areoles ½ in. apart, spines nearly bristlelike, yellowish, becoming white, radial spines 8–11, the lower to ⅜ in. long, central spine 1, stouter, to ¾ in. long; fls. white, to 8 in. long. Argentina.

Schickendantzii (A. Web.) Britt. & Rose. Sts. simple or cespitose, to 1 ft. high and 2½ in. thick, ribs 14–18, low; areoles close-set, spines yellowish, slender, to ⅜ in. long, radial spines at first 9, central spines 2–8; fls. white, to 9 in. long; fr. edible. N. Argentina.

Shaferi Britt. & Rose. Sts. cespitose, 12–20 in. high and 4–5 in. thick, ribs 14, to ⅝ in. high; areoles ¼ in. apart, spines about 10, needle-shaped, yellow, ½ in. long; fls. subapical, white, 6–7 in. long, tube slender. N. Argentina.

Spachianus (Lem.) Riccob. TORCH CACTUS, WHITE T. C., GOLDEN-COLUMN. Sts. erect, branching at base, to 3 ft. high and 2½ in. thick, ribs 10–15, obtuse; areoles ⅜ in. apart, spines needle-shaped, yellow to brown, to ½ in. long, radial spines 8–10, central spine 1, stronger; fls. white, 8 in. long. Argentina.

strigosus (Salm-Dyck) Britt. & Rose. Sts. cespitose, to 2 ft. high and 2½ in. thick, forming clumps to 3 ft. across, ribs 15–18, obtuse, 3/16 in. high; areoles to 5/16 in. apart, spines many, needle-shaped, variable in color and length, ½–2 in. long; fls. white, 8 in. long. W. Argentina.

tephracanthus (Labour.) Borg [*Eriocereus tephracanthus* (Labour.) Riccob.; *Roseocereus tephracanthus* (Labour.) Backeb.]. Sts. erect, to 3 in. thick, ribs 8, rounded; areoles large, to 1 in. apart, spines brown, becoming gray, at first 8, finally 13, radial spines in 2 concentric arcs in lower half of areole, mostly to ¼ in. long, 1 nearly central, to ¾ in. long. Bolivia. Perhaps referable to *T. macrogonus;* both spp. poorly known.

Terscheckii (Parm.) Britt. & Rose. Treelike, to 40 ft., brs. erect, 4–10 in. thick, ribs 8–14, obtuse, to 1½ in. high; areoles ½ in. wide, 1 in. apart, spines 8–15, awl-shaped, yellow, 3 in. long; fls. white, 6–8 in. long. N. Argentina. Var. **montanus** Backeb. Brs. fewer and thicker.

thelegonoides (Speg.) Britt. & Rose. Treelike, to 20 ft., brs. fastigiate, 2–3 in. thick, ribs 15, low, obtuse, cross-furrowed; areoles ⅜ in. apart, spines bristlelike, yellow or brownish, to 5/16 in. long, radial spines 7–9, central spine 1; fls. white, 8–10 in. long. Argentina.

thelegonus (A. Web.) Britt. & Rose. Sts. erect, to 7 ft., or procumbent, 2–3 in. thick, ribs 12–13, divided into low, hexagonal tubercles; areoles to ⅜ in. apart, spines needle-shaped, yellow or brown, radial spines 6–8, to ¾ in. long, central spine 1, to 1½ in. long; fls. white, 8 in. long.

uyupamensis Backeb. Sts. scandent, to 7 ft. long and 1½ in. thick, ribs 9, flat, narrow; spines 8–10, thickened at base, the longest 2 dark, to ¼ in. long; fls. white, 6 in. long. S. Peru.

Vollianus Backeb. Sts. erect, to 4 in. thick, ribs 13, rounded, 3/16 in. high; spines yellow, radial spines 8–11, slender, ¼ in. long, central spine 1, to 1 in. long; fls. white, to 5 in. long. Bolivia.

Werdermannianus Backeb. Treelike, trunk to 2 ft. thick, brs. to 6 in. thick, ribs many; radial spines 8, pale yellow, central spine 1, awl-shaped, longer; fls. white. S. Bolivia. Perhaps a form of *T. Pasacana.*

TRICHODIADEMA Schwant. *Aizoaceae.* About 36 spp. of shrubby or short-stemmed, more or less tufted succulents, native to S. Afr., 1 in. Ethiopia, roots fleshy to woody; lvs. opp., semicylindrical to cylindrical, surface glistening with papillae, apex with a diadem of spreading bristles; fls. solitary, nearly sessile, calyx lobes 5–8, each with an apical tuft of hairs, petals red or white, many, in 1 to several series, stamens many, staminodes many, ovary inferior, 5–8-celled, stigmas 5–8; fr. a caps., cell lids present, expanding keels lying close to each other, placental tubercles absent.

Growth occurs most of the year except for a short resting period in winter. The plants can be grown outdoors in full sun with plenty of water in summer, but in winter should be kept rather dry and at a relatively cool temperature of about 50° F. in an airy greenhouse. Propagation easy by seeds, but faster from cuttings for larger plantings outdoors. See also *Succulents.*

album: a listed name of no botanical standing.

barbatum (L.) Schwant. [*Mesembryanthemum barbatum* L.]. PICKLE PLANT. Roots turniplike, brs. prostrate; lvs. not congested, gray-green with acute papillae, stiffly ascending, to ½ in. long, ⅛ in. wide, semicylindrical, slightly recurved, tip with 8–10 black bristles; fls. to 1¼ in. across, petals deep red. Cape Prov.

densum (Haw.) Schwant. DESERT ROSE. Roots fleshy, thick, sts. short, tuft-forming; lvs. green, with acute papillae, crowded, to ¾ in. long and ¼ in. thick, tip with a tuft of 20–25 prominent white bristles; fls. to 2 in. across, petals carmine. Cape Prov.

TRICHOGLOTTIS Blume. *Orchidaceae.* About 60 spp. of epiphytes, native to trop. Asia and Malay Arch.; sts. long, climbing or pendent; lvs. oblong; infl. short, often 1-fld.; fls. small to large, sepals and petals usually yellowish with red-brown markings, lateral sepals united to short column foot, sometimes decurrent on spur of lip, lip saccate or spurred at base, with tongue-shaped, often hairy structure on back wall of sac or spur, lateral lobes erect, midlobe simple or 3-lobed, column short, with horn on each side. For structure of fl. see *Orchidaceae.*

For culture see *Orchids.*

brachiata: *T. philippinensis* var.

luzonensis Ames. Sts. short; lvs. leathery, to 8 in. long; infl. paniculate, to 30 in. long; fls. 1¼ in. across, cream with small red-brown spots, lateral sepals spatulate, clawed, to ½ in. long, upper sepal spatulate, petals similar, lip ½ in. long, pubescent, lateral lobes erect, triangular, midlobe oblong, with papillaelike calluses at base. Philippine Is. Var. **brachiata** (Ames) L. O. Williams [*T. brachiata* Ames.]. BLACK ORCHID. Sts. longer than in typical *T. luzonensis;* lvs. broader, shorter; fls. solitary, large, sepals and petals deep crimson-purple, margined with cream, lip white, midlobe 3-lobed. Philippine Is.

TRICHOLAENA Schrad. ex Schult. & Schult.f. *Gramineae.* Not cult. **T. repens** and **T. rosea:** *Rhynchelytrum repens.*

TRICHONEMA: *ROMULEA.*

TRICHOPETALUM Lindl. [*Bottionea* Colla]. *Liliaceae.* One or 2 spp. of per. herbs, native to Chile; roots clustered, fleshy; lvs. mostly basal, grasslike; fls. white to greenish-white, in loose racemes, perianth segms. 6, separate, inner ones fringed with many white hairs, stamens 6; fr. a 3-valved, loculicidal caps.

plumosum (Ruiz & Pav.) Macbr. [*Anthericum plumosum* Ruiz & Pav.; *Bottionea thysanthoides* Colla]. To 3 ft.; lvs. linear-subulate, to 1 ft. long, glabrous; fls. greenish-white, to ⅝ in. across.

TRICHOPILIA Lindl. *Orchidaceae.* About 30 spp. of epiphytes, native to trop. Amer.; pseudobulbs conspicuous, 1-lvd.; lvs. leathery, linear and nearly cylindrical or broad and flat; infl. basal, short, loosely 1- to many-fld; fls. showy, perianth segms. spreading, often twisted, upper sepal narrow, separate, lateral sepals united, petals similar to upper sepal, lip sessile to deeply united to column, 3–4-lobed, concave, disc often keeled, column elongated, with fringed hood over anther. For structure of fl. see *Orchidaceae.*

For culture see *Orchids.*

coccinea: *T. marginata.*

fragrans (Lindl.) Rchb.f. Pseudobulbs oblong-cylindric, to 5 in. long; lvs. elliptic, to 1 ft. long; infl. erect to pendent, racemose, 1–4-fld.; fls. large, fragrant, sepals green to white, linear-lanceolate, to 1¾ in. long, undulate on margins, petals similar but broader, lip rhombic-ovate, to 1½ in. long, 3-lobed, white with yellow spot near base, midlobe suborbicular, disc with central keel. W. Indies, Venezuela to Peru.

leucoxantha L. O. Williams. Pseudobulbs oblong-elliptic, 2 in. long; lvs. elliptic, to 8 in. long; infl. pendent, 1–4-fld.; fls. 2 in. across, white, with pale yellow markings on lip, sepals and petals oblanceolate, lip nearly orbicular, 1½ in. long, 3-lobed, midlobe deeply emarginate, margins undulate, disc with 1 elongated raised callus, column with membranous fringed hood over anther. Late summer. Panama.

maculata Rchb.f. [*T. Powellii* Schlechter]. Pseudobulbs elliptic-oblong, to 2 in. long; lvs. elliptic-lanceolate, to 5 in. long; infl. solitary, arching, 1-fld.; fls. 2 in. across, sepals and petals lanceolate, often twisted, to 1½ in. long, pale yellow or greenish-yellow, lip obovate, 1¼ in. long, 3-lobed, united to base of column, white, with many fine orange-red lines at base, midlobe emarginate, disc with short, inconspicuous central keel. Panama.

marginata Henfr. [*T. coccinea* Warsz. ex Lindl.]. Pseudobulbs oblong, to 4½ in. long; lvs. lanceolate, 1 ft. long; infl. pendent, 2–3-fld.; fls. to 4 in. across, conspicuous, sepals and petals lanceolate, reddish, with lighter, undulate margins, lip 3-lobed, to 3 in. long, white, rarely red, lateral lobes convolute, forming a tube, tube deep rose-red inside, midlobe deeply emarginate, margin reflexed, undulate, white, disc with prominent keel, column with obscurely 3-lobed fringed hood over anther. Cent. Amer. and Colombia.

Powellii: *T. maculata.*

suavis Lindl. & Paxt. Pseudobulbs oblong-ovoid, to 3 in. long; lvs. elliptic-lanceolate, to 1 ft. long; infl. arching, 2–5-fld.; fls. large, fragrant, sepals and petals lanceolate, to 2 in. long, undulate, white, spotted with pale rose-pink or red, lip tubular, 3-lobed, white, heavily spotted with rose-pink, lateral lobes convolute, forming a tube, margins crisped and undulate, midlobe emarginate, crisped, reflexed, disc with prominent, erect central keel longer than column, column with 4-lobed hood over anther. Early spring. Costa Rica to Colombia.

tortilis Lindl. Pseudobulbs ovoid, 2½ in. long; lvs. elliptic-lanceolate, to 7 in. long; infl. shorter than lvs., solitary pendent; sepals and petals linear-oblong, 2½ in. long, spirally twisted, pale rose with light yellow-green margins, lip 4-lobed, white, blotched and spotted with red-brown, apical lobes with crisped, undulate margins, column cylindrical, with 3-lobed fringed hood over anther. Mex.

turialbae Rchb.f. Pseudobulbs to 4 in. long; lvs. elliptic-lanceolate, to 8 in. long; infl. arching, 1–3-fld.; fls. white, sepals lanceolate, to 1¼ in. long, lateral sepals united to middle, lip tubular, to 1½ in. long, 3-lobed, white with pale orange lines in throat, united to base of column, margins undulate, disc with elongate central keel, column with denticulate hood over anther. Costa Rica, Panama.

TRICHOSANTHES L. *Cucurbitaceae.* Forty or more spp. of tendril-bearing, ann. or per., monoecious or dioecious herbs, native to trop. Asia, Australia, and Polynesia; fls. white, corolla rotate, petals fringed, male fls. usually racemose, stamens 3, filaments separate, anthers flexuous, female fls. usually solitary; fr. fleshy, indehiscent, of various shapes.

Anguina L. [*T. colubrina* Jacq.f.]. SERPENT CUCUMBER, SERPENT GOURD, SNAKE G., CLUB G., VIPER'S G. Climbing or long-running, monoecious ann.; lvs. broad-ovate to triangular-ovate, to 9 in. long, sometimes shallowly 3-lobed; petals deeply and finely laciniate, raceme of male fls. long-stalked, with minute bracts; fr. 1–6 ft. long, very slender, mostly curved or coiled unless hanging from a support, seeds flat, without longitudinal band on each face. India; there and in other countries much grown for the edible fr.; grown in U.S. as a curiosity.

colubrina: *T. Anguina.*

cucumeroides Maxim. ex Franch. & Sav. SNAKE GOURD. Dioecious; sts. 10–15 ft. long, from a tuberous root; lvs. ovate, 3–5-lobed or sometimes nearly entire, villous at least underneath, undulate or crenulate; male fls. in racemes with caducous subulate bracts to ⅛ in. long, female fls. on very short, slender pedicels; fr. ovoid, 2–3 in. long, cinnabar-red, seeds turgid, broader than long, with broad longitudinal band on each face. Japan. Dried fr. may be used as a soap substitute.

japonica Regel. Sts. slender, long, branching, plant glabrous; lvs. ovate, shallowly 3–5-lobed, entire or denticulate; male fls. few, in racemes with large bracts, female fls. on pedicels 1–2 in. long; fr. ovoid but tapering to each end, about 3 in. long, yellowish-green, seeds flat, without longitudinal band on each face. Japan.

TRICHOSMA: *ERIA.* **T. suavis:** *E. coronaria.*

TRICHOSPORUM: *AESCHYNANTHUS.*

TRICHOSTEMA Gronov. ex L. BLUE-CURLS. *Labiatae.* About 16 spp. of herbs or shrubs of N. Amer.; sts. mostly square in cross section; lvs. opp., mostly entire; fls. in densely many-fld. verticillasters, calyx campanulate, 10-nerved, 5-toothed, corolla bluish or purplish, nearly regular, 5-lobed, stamens 4, in 2 pairs, anthers 2-celled, ovary 4-lobed, not deeply cleft; fr. of 4 reticulate-rugose nutlets.

Cultivated in the wild garden or the rock garden.

dichotomum L. BASTARD PENNYROYAL. Ann., 4–30 in., much-branched, viscid-hairy; lvs. oblong to rhombic-lanceolate; fls. about ⁵⁄₁₆ in. long, blue, pink, or white. Autumn. Me. to Mich., s. to N.C. and Mo.

lanatum Benth. ROMERO, WOOLLY B.-C. Erect shrub, 1½–3½ ft., densely floccose-tomentose when young; lvs. narrowly linear, mostly 1½–2½ in. long, revolute, glabrous above, tomentose beneath; fls. in dense, violet- to purplish-woolly, interrupted spikes, corolla about ⅝ in. long, stamens exserted 1 in. or more. Spring. Calif.

lanceolatum Benth. VINEGAR WEED. Glandular-villous ann., to 2 ft., strongly scented; lvs. sessile, lanceolate, to 1¼ in. long, acuminate, crenate, not revolute; fls. in axillary racemes, calyx villous-tomentose, corolla about ½ in. long, light blue. Ore. to Calif.

ovatum Curran. SAN JOAQUIN B.-C. Similar to *T. lanceolatum,* but lvs. ovate to nearly orbicular, rounded to cordate at base. Calif.

Parishii Vasey. SAN JOAQUIN B.-C. Similar to *T. lanatum,* but verticillasters and spikes usually gray-woolly, the verticillasters open, showing peduncles and pedicels, stamens ⅝–¾ in. long, exserted. Calif.

TRICHOSTIGMA A. Rich. *Phytolaccaceae.* Three spp. of glabrous shrubs, native to trop. Amer.; lvs. alt., entire; fls.

unisexual, small, in loose, many-fld. racemes, petals lacking, sepals 4, concave, persistent in fr., stamens 8–25, pistil 1-carpelled, carpel 1-celled; fr. drupaceous, globose.

peruvianum (Moq.) H. Walt. [*Ledenbergia roseo-aenea* Lem.]. Shrub, to 6 ft., branchlets pubescent; lvs. thin, elliptic to rhomboid-elliptic, to 12 in. long and 5 in. wide, acuminate, slightly auriculate at base, purple beneath, petioles hairy, to 1 in. long; racemes axillary, solitary, slender and eventually nodding, to 20 in. long; fls. ³⁄₁₆ in. long, sepals broad, concave, reflexed, stamens 12. Andes of Peru.

TRICUSPIDARIA: *CRINODENDRON.* **T. dependens:** *C. Patagua.*

TRICYRTIS Wallich. TOAD LILY. *Liliaceae.* Between 10 and 15 spp. of rhizomatous, per. herbs, native from Himalayas to Japan and Taiwan; sts. leafy; lvs. alt., sometimes clasping; fls. white or yellow, spotted with purple, axillary or terminal, solitary or in clusters or cymes, perianth segms. 6, separate, the outer ones basally saccate or, less frequently, short-spurred, the inner ones flat, stamens 6, styles 3, each bifurcate; fr. a many-seeded, septicidal caps., seeds flat.

Grown in pots or in the rock garden or shade garden, though not reliably hardy outdoors in the North (Zone 7). Propagated by division or seeds.

affinis Mak. To 2 ft.; lvs. oblong to oblong-ovate or oblanceolate, to 7 in. long and 2 in. wide, pubescent; fls. axillary, white, spotted dark purple inside, ¾ in. long. Japan.

flava Maxim. To 20 in., slightly hairy; lvs. elliptic to oblanceolate, to 6 in. long, occasionally spotted above; fls. axillary and terminal, yellow, spotted dark purple inside, 1 in. long. Japan.

formosana Bak. [*T. formosana* var. *stolonifera* (Matsum.) Masam.; *T. stolonifera* Matsum.]. To 2 ft.; lvs. oblanceolate, to 5 in. long or more; fls. in a loose terminal cyme, white, spotted purple, to 1 in. long. Taiwan.

hirta (Thunb.) Hook. To 3 ft., hairy all over; lvs. oblong to ovate, to 6 in. long; fls. axillary or terminal, solitary or in clusters, white, spotted purple inside, to 1 in. long. Japan. Cv. 'Variegata'. Lvs. variegated.

latifolia Maxim. To 2½ ft., glabrous; lvs. oblong to obovate, to 6 in. long, abruptly acuminate; fls. in distinct peduncled terminal cymes, or in upper lf. axils, yellow, spotted purple inside, to 1 in. long. Japan.

macrantha Maxim. To 2½ ft., with coarse brown hairs; lvs. ovate-oblong to ovate-lanceolate, to 4 in. long; fls. axillary, pendulous, on long pedicels, yellow, spotted chocolate inside, outer perianth segms. short-spurred. Japan.

macropoda Miq. To 2½ ft.; lvs. oblong to ovate, to 5 in. long; fls. in axillary or terminal 1–2-fld. cymes, white, spotted purple, ¾ in. long. Japan.

stolonifera: *T. formosana.*

TRIDAX L. *Compositae* (Helianthus Tribe). Twenty-six spp. of ann. or per. herbs of Mex. to trop. S. Amer.; lvs. opp., toothed or lobed; fl. heads radiate, long-peduncled, involucre of 2–3 rows of similar bracts; disc fls. yellow, ray fls. white, pink, or yellow; achenes turbinate, silky-hairy, pappus of ciliate scales or plumose bristles.

trilobata Hemsl. Ann., to 1½ ft.; lvs. ovate to oblong, coarsely toothed, sometimes 3-lobed; heads about 1 in. across; fls. orange-yellow. Mex.

TRIENTALIS L. STARFLOWER, CHICKWEED WINTERGREEN. *Primulaceae.* Four spp. of per. herbs, native to Eur., Asia, and N. Amer.; lvs. mostly clustered at top of st., frequently with a few lvs. or scale lvs. below; fls. white or pink, solitary, axillary on slender pedicels, calyx 5-parted, corolla rotate, stamens 5; fr. a caps.

americana: *T. borealis.*

arctica Fisch. ex Hook. [*T. europaea* var. *arctica* (Fisch. ex Hook.) Lehm.]. To 8 in.; lvs. somewhat scattered, oblanceolate to obovate, to 1½ in. long, obtuse; fls. white, rarely pink, to ¾ in. across. E. Siberia and Aleutians to Ore.

borealis Raf. [*T. americana* Pursh]. STARFLOWER. To 9 in.; lvs. in a whorl of 5–10, lanceolate, to 4 in. long, acuminate; fls. white, ½ in. across, on pedicels to 2 in. long. Lab. to Va. and Ill.

europaea L. To 10 in.; lvs. somewhat scattered, obovate to obovate-lanceolate, to 2½ in. long, stiff and glossy, acute or obtuse; fls. white, to ¾ in. across. Eur., Asia. Var. **arctica:** *T. arctica.* Var. **latifolia:** *T. latifolia.*

latifolia Hook. [*T. europaea* var. *latifolia* (Hook.) Torr.]. To 8 in.; lvs. in a whorl of 4–8, ovate or somewhat obovate, to 3 in. long, acute or acuminate; fls. rose-pink or white, to ¾ in. across. S. Alta. and B.C., s. to cent. Calif.

TRIFOLIUM L. CLOVER, TREFOIL. *Leguminosae* (subfamily *Faboideae*). Perhaps 300 spp. of herbs of wide distribution in temp. and subtrop. regions; lvs. alt., mostly of 3 lfts., but rarely more, stipules united to petioles; fls. in dense heads or spikes, small, papilionaceous, fragrant, petals persistent, more or less united to stamen tube, the uppermost stamen separate or partly united with the others; fr. a small, mostly indehiscent legume, nearly or quite enclosed by calyx.

Some species are valuable forage and cover-crop plants, some are constituents of lawns, and a few are grown as ornamentals. Propagated by seeds sown broadcast in early spring.

agrarium L. HOP C., YELLOW C. To 18 in.; differing from *T. procumbens* in having terminal lfts. sessile, stipules mostly equal to petioles or longer, and fls. many, in dense heads to ⅝ in. across, the standard conspicuously furrowed in age. Eur. and Asia Minor; naturalized in N. Amer.

alpinum L. Glabrous per., to 6 in.; lfts. lanceolate-linear; fls. large, red, rarely yellowish-white, in loose heads; fr. beaked. Mts., Eur. Cv. 'Album' [forma *albiflorum* Gaudin]. Fls. whitish.

ambiguum Bieb. KURA C. Rhizomatous per., to 18 in., glabrous; lfts. wide, elliptic, to 3 in. long, serrulate; fls. white, becoming reddish, in 1–3 axillary, peduncled, globose to ovate heads; fr. glabrous. E. Eur., Caucasus.

badium Schreb. Per., sts. ascending, to 8 in. high; upper lvs. nearly opp., lfts. obovate to oblong, minutely toothed; fls. golden, in rather large, globose heads. Mts., Eur.

caeruleomontanum: a listed name of no botanical standing for *T. macrocephalum*.

campestre Schreb. LOW C., LARGE HOP C. Differs from *T. procumbens* in having fls. in many-fld., dense heads to ⅝ in. across, the standard conspicuously furrowed in age. Medit. region; naturalized in N. Amer.

dubium: *T. procumbens*.

fragiferum L. STRAWBERRY C., STRAWBERRY-HEADED C. Per., sts. creeping, to 1 ft. long, rooting at nodes; lfts. cuneate-obovate, to ½ in. long; fls. pink to white, in dense, globose, long-peduncled heads ½ in. across. Medit. region.

hybridum L. ALSIKE C. Per., sts. erect or hanging down, to 2 ft. high, or prostrate in age, not rooting at nodes; lfts. ovate, to 1 in. long, minutely toothed; fls. pink, in globose heads to 1 in. across on rather short peduncles. Eur.; naturalized in U.S. Used as forage and in crop rotation.

incarnatum L. CRIMSON C., ITALIAN C. Hairy, erect ann., to 3 ft.; lfts. broadly obovate, to 1¼ in. long; fls. showy, crimson, in spikelike heads to 2½ in. long. Eur. Used as forage and in crop rotation.

macrocephalum (Pursh) Poir. [var. *caeruleomontanum* St. John; *T. caeruleomontanum* Hort.]. Rhizomatous, pubescent, erect per., to 1 ft.; lvs. palmately compound, lfts. 5–9, oblanceolate to obcordate, to 1 in. long; fls. pink, 1 in. long, in mostly terminal heads to 2 in. across. Wash., Ore., Nev., Idaho. Useful rock garden plant.

nanum Torr. Tufted per., to 3 in.; lfts. linear-oblanceolate, to ⅜ in. long, minutely denticulate; fls. rose to reddish-purple, in usually 1–3-fld. heads on peduncles to 1¼ in. long. Mont., Colo., Utah.

pannonicum L. HUNGARIAN C. Erect per., with short rhizomes; lfts. of lower lvs. small and obovate, of upper lvs. oblong-lanceolate, stipules narrow, apex long-linear; fls. yellowish, in large heads to 2 in. long. E. Eur.

Parryi A. Gray. Low, tufted per.; lfts. elliptic to obovate, to 1¾ in. long, entire to sharply and minutely toothed; fls. purple, bracts conspicuous, peduncles 2–6 in. long. Wyo., Colo., Utah.

pratense L. RED C. Short-lived per., to 2 ft.; lfts. ovate to obovate, to 2½ in. long, often hairy and with white blotch, stipules broad at base, awned apically; fls. rose-purple or rarely white, in dense, globose heads 1 in. long, calyx hairy outside. Eur.; naturalized in N. Amer. Used as forage and in crop rotation. Var. **perenne** Host. MAMMOTH C. Similar to var. *sativum*. Var. **sativum** Schreb. Coarser, to 2½ ft.; lfts. and fl. heads larger. The commonly cult. var.

procumbens L. [*T. dubium* Sibth.]. SMALL HOP C., COW H.C., YELLOW C., SHAMROCK, IRISH S. Sts. procumbent or ascending, to 1 ft. high; lfts. obovate, terminal lfts. stalked, stipules ovate, acute, shorter than petiole, rounded at base; fls. yellow, 3–15 in loose heads less than ⁵⁄₁₆ in. across on peduncles longer than the lvs. S. Eur.; naturalized in N. Amer. Material offered under this name may be *T. campestre*.

repens L. WHITE C., WHITE DUTCH C. Prostrate per., sts. creeping, to 1 ft. long; lfts. obcordate, to ¾ in. long, petioles long and slender; fls. white, in rather loose, globose heads to ¾ in. across on slender peduncles to 1 ft. long. Eur.; naturalized in N. Amer. Used as forage and in crop rotation. Cv. 'Atropurpureum'. Dwarf form; lfts. deep bronzy-red with green margins. Var. **latum**: a listed name of no botanical standing for forma *lodigense*. Forma **lodigense** Hort. ex Gams. LADINO C. A giant form used especially for pastures. Italy. Forma **minus** (Gibelli & Belli ex Bald.) Bald. ex Rohlena. SHAMROCK, IRISH S. Lfts. very small; peduncles shorter; fls. small, rose-colored.

resupinatum L. PERSIAN C., REVERSED C. Ann., sts. to 18 in. high or diffuse; lfts. obovate, stipules lanceolate; fls. pink-purple, in globose heads, calyces whitish-tomentose. Greece to Iran.

subterraneum L. SUBTERRANEAN C., SUBCLOVER. Soft-hairy ann., sts. procumbent; lfts. wide, obcordate; fls. fertile, 2–5 in loose heads, petals white, standard striped rose, peduncles deflexed in fr.; fr. subterranean, 1-seeded. England to Medit. region. Used as forage.

TRIGLOCHIN L. ARROW GRASS. *Juncaginaceae*. About 15 spp. of herbs of cosmopolitan distribution in freshwater and salt marshes; lvs. basal, semicylindrical, somewhat fleshy, with a prominent sheath, ligule present between sheath and blade; fls. in bractless terminal spikes and racemes on long scapes; perianth segms. and stamens 3 or 6, ovary of 3 or 6 carpels, which separate at maturity.

Sometimes grown in bog gardens or aquaria.

maritima L. Plants tufted; lvs. linear, to 20 in. long and ⅛ in. wide, not furrowed, ligule entire; scape to 2½ ft. high; perianth segms. 6, fertile carpels and stigmas 6. Salt or freshwater marshes, N. Amer., Eurasia.

palustris L. Lvs. linear, to 1 ft. long, deeply furrowed, ligule 2-parted; scape to 2 ft. high; perianth segms. 6, fertile carpels and stigmas 3. Cosmopolitan.

striata Ruiz & Pav. Lvs. linear, to 10 in. long and ⅛ in. wide, ligule entire; scape to 8 in. high, often angled; perianth segms. 3, fertile carpels and stigmas 3. N. and S. Amer., Afr., Australia.

TRIGONACHRAS Radlk. *Sapindaceae*. Nine spp. of polygamous trees, native mostly to the Philippine Is., one in Malay Pen.; lvs. alt., pinnate; fls. in axillary and terminal panicles, regular, calyx 5-lobed, petals 5, each with 2 basal, ciliate scales, stamens 8; fr. drupaceous, 3-angled, 3-celled.

acuta (Hiern) Radlk. Lvs. 6–12 in. long, lfts. 11–15, oblong-lanceolate, to 4½ in. long; fr. orange, pear-shaped, to about 2 in. long, densely tomentose. Malay Pen.

TRIGONELLA L. *Leguminosae* (subfamily *Faboideae*). About 70 spp. of temp. herbs, native to Old World; lvs. of 3 lfts.; fls. solitary or in racemes or heads, papilionaceous, petals separate, deciduous after flowering, standard scarcely clawed, stamens 10, 9 united and 1 separate; fr. a beaked, sometimes indehiscent legume.

Occasionally grown for forage or as ornamentals; propagated by seeds.

caerulea (L.) Ser. Slender ann., to 2 ft.; fls. blue and white, in long-stalked, globose heads; fr. rhombic-ovate, long-beaked. S. Eur.

Foenum-graecum L. FENUGREEK. Ann., to 2 ft.; lfts. obovate, toothed at apex; fls. 1–2 together in axils, whitish; fr. linear, with long beak. S. Eur., Asia. Used in Medit. region for forage; in India the seeds are used for curries, dyes, and medicine.

TRIGONIDIUM Lindl. *Orchidaceae*. Ten spp. of epiphytes, native to Cent. and S. Amer.; pseudobulbs ovoid, ridged, 1–3-lvd. at apex; lvs. leathery, linear; infl. basal, 1-fld.; fls. relatively large, sepals nearly equal, their bases forming a tube, their apices reflexed, petals smaller, lip very small, shorter than petals, 3-lobed, lateral lobes parallel to column, midlobe spreading, often tubercled, recurved at apex, the disc with fleshy, strap-shaped callus. For structure of fl. see *Orchidaceae*.

For culture see *Orchids*.

Egertonianum Batem. ex Lindl. Pseudobulbs to 2¾ in. long, 2-lvd.; lvs. linear-lanceolate, to 2 ft. long; infls. 1 to several, to 16 in. long; fls. greenish-yellow to pinkish-tan with brown or purple stripes, upper sepal elliptic-lanceolate, recurved at apex, petals lanceolate, to 1 in. long, lip ⅓ as long as petals, yellowish-tan, striped with brown or red, lateral lobes parallel to column, midlobe ovate, ⅓ as long as lip, pale yellow with darker center, warty, column purple, footless. Cent. Amer., Colombia.

monophyllum: *Neocogniauxia monophylla.*

TRILLIUM L. WAKE-ROBIN, BIRTHROOT. *Liliaceae.* About 30 spp. of low, per., spring-flowering, woodland herbs with short, thick rootstocks, native to N. Amer., the Himalayas, and e. Asia; st. simple; lvs. 3, in a terminal whorl subtending a solitary, sessile or peduncled fl.; sepals 3, usually green, petals 3, white, yellow, green, pink, or purple, separate, stamens 6, anthers basifixed; fr. a 3-celled berry. Many aberrant forms occur in nature.

Trilliums require fertile moist soil and partial shade. Roots may be transplanted from the wild, preferably after flowering. Propagated by division, and also by seeds.

apetalon: *T. Smallii.*

californicum: *T. ovatum.*

Catesbaei Elliott [*T. declinatum* Raf.; *T. stylosum* Nutt.]. ROSY W.-R. To 1½ ft.; lvs. elliptic to ovate; fls. pink or rose, sometimes white, on nodding peduncles to 2 in. long. N.C. to Ga. and Ala.

cernuum L. NODDING T. To 1½ ft.; lvs. broadly rhombic-ovate, to 4 in. long or more, narrowed to an obscure petiole; fls. white or pinkish, nodding, on peduncles to 1¼ in. long. Nfld. to Ga.

chloropetalum (Torr.) T. J. Howell [*T. sessile* var. *californicum* Torr.]. St. stout, to 2½ ft.; lvs. rhombic-ovate, to 6 in. long, often mottled, sessile; fls. maroon to greenish-yellow or white, to 3½ in. long, sessile; fr. winged. Wash. to cent. Calif.

cuneatum Raf. [*T. Hugeri* Small]. WHIPPOORWILL FLOWER. St. coarse, to 10 in.; lvs. circular-ovate, to about 6 in. long, often faintly mottled; fls. faintly ill-scented, dark maroon or brown, to 4½ in. long, sessile, stamens only ⅓ as long as petals. N.C. to nw. Fla. and Miss.

declinatum: see *T. Catesbaei* and *T. flexipes.*

erectum L. [*T. flavum* Raf.]. PURPLE T., STINKING BENJAMIN, SQUAWROOT, BROWN BETH. To 2 ft.; lvs. broadly rhombic-ovate, to 7 in. long, sessile; fls. ill-scented, brownish-purple or purple, less commonly white, yellow, or green, to 2 in. long, nearly erect, on peduncles to 4 in. long, petals spreading from the base, ovary purple; fr. dark red, 6-angled. Ont. and Que., s. to ne. Ill., Ga., and N.C. Forma **albiflorum** R. Hoffm. [var. *album* (Michx.) Pursh]. Fls. white. Var. **album:** forma *albiflorum.*

flavum: *T. erectum.*

flexipes Raf. [*T. declinatum* (A. Gray) Gleason, not Raf.; *T. Gleasonii* Fern.]. To 16 in.; lvs. broadly rhombic, to 6 in. long, abruptly acuminate, sessile; fls. white, to 2 in. long, on declined or spreading peduncles to 4¾ in. long, filaments about half as long as anthers, ovary pink or white, 6-angled. N.Y. to s. Minn. and Mo.

Gleasonii: *T. flexipes.*

grandiflorum (Michx.) Salisb. WHITE W.-R. St. stout, to 1½ ft.; lvs. broadly ovate to rhombic or subcircular, to 5 in. long or more, acuminate, base cuneate and usually sessile; fls. white, fading to rosy-pink, to 3 in. long, on peduncles to 3 in. long, petals spreading at their tips, wavy-margined, filaments as long as anthers; fr. 6-angled, greenish-white. Minn. to Que., s. to Mo., Ga., and S.C. Abnormal forms are frequent, usually appearing as individual plants with long-petioled lvs. or with various bizarre forms of fls., including several double-fld. forms; many of these have been given botanical names as formae.

Hugeri: *T. cuneatum.*

luteum: *T. viride* var.

nivale Ridd. SNOW T., DWARF WHITE T. To 6 in.; lvs. elliptic to ovate, to 2 in. long, obtuse, definitely petioled; fls. erect, white, marked with purple, to 1½ in. long, peduncles to 1 in. long, recurved in fr. Early spring. W. Penn. to Minn., s. to Mo. and Nebr.

ovatum Pursh [*T. californicum* Kellogg]. COAST T. To 20 in.; lvs. rhombic-ovate, to 6 in. long, abruptly acuminate, subsessile; fls. white, fading to rose, to 2 in. long, on peduncles to 2¾ in. long; ovary winged. B.C. to cent. Calif.

ozarkanum: *T. pusillum* var.

petiolatum Pursh. To 6 in., st. scarcely rising above the ground; lvs. broadly ovate to circular, to 6 in. long, on stout petioles to 4½ in. long; fls. maroon, to 1¾ in. long, sessile. Ore., Wash., Idaho.

pusillum Michx. St. slender, to 1 ft.; lvs. oblong to lanceolate-ovate, to 3¼ in. long, 3-nerved, sessile; fls. white, fading to pink and purple, to 1¼ in. long, on erect peduncles to 1¼ in. long, style straight; fr. 3-angled. Ky., se. Va., S.C., N.C. Var. **ozarkanum** (Palmer & Steyerm.) Steyerm. [*T. ozarkanum* Palmer & Steyerm.]. Lvs. 5-nerved; fls. larger, on longer peduncles. S. Mo. and nw. Ark.

recurvatum L. Beck. PURPLE T., PURPLE W.-R., BLOODY-BUTCHER. To 1½ ft.; lvs. elliptic to obovate, to 4¼ in. long, spotted with purple, on petioles to 1 in. long; fls. brown-purple, to 1¾ in. long, sepals reflexed, petals clawed. Mich. to Iowa, s. to Ala. and Miss.

rivale S. Wats. St. to 10 in.; lvs. ovate-lanceolate, to 2 in. long, on petioles to 1 in. long; fls. white, marked with rose-carmine, to 2 in. long, erect or eventually nodding, on pedicels to 3⅛ in. long. Sw. Ore. and adjacent Calif.

sessile L. TOADSHADE, WAKE-ROBIN. St. stout, to 1 ft.; lvs. ovate to subcircular, to 4 in. long, often mottled; fls. brown-purple, maroon, or yellow-green, to 1½ in. long, sessile, stamens half as long as petals; fr. 6-angled. W. N.Y. to Mo., s. to Ga., Miss., Ark. Var. **californicum:** *T. chloropetalum.* Var. **luteum:** *T. viride* var. Cv. 'Rubrum'. Fls. red-purple.

Smallii Maxim. [*T. apetalon* Mak.]. St. to 16 in.; lvs. rhombic-circular, to 6¾ in. long, abruptly acuminate; fls. to ¾ in. long, peduncles to 1½ in. long, erect in fr., petals usually lacking, or, when present, shorter than sepals. Japan.

stylosum: *T. Catesbaei.*

Tschonoskii Maxim. To about 1½ ft.; lvs. rhombic-circular to subcircular, to 6¾ in. long; fls. white, to 1 in. long, on peduncles to 1½ in. long. Japan and Korea.

undulatum Willd. PAINTED T. To 20 in.; lvs. ovate, to 7 in. long at maturity, acuminate, definitely petioled; fls. white, veined purple at base, to 1½ in. long, erect to somewhat nodding, on peduncles to 2½ in. long, petals wavy. Que. to e. Man., s. to S.C., Tenn., Ga.

viride L. Beck. WOOD T. St. stout, to 20 in., often hairy toward top; lvs. lanceolate to subcircular, to 4 in. long, often mottled, finely pubescent on veins beneath, sessile; fls. greenish, 2 in. long, sessile, stamens ¼–⅓ as long as petals. Se. Kans. to sw. Ill., s. to e. Okla. and n. Ark. Var. **luteum** (Muhlenb.) Gleason [*T. luteum* (Muhlenb.) Harb.; *T. sessile* var. *luteum* Muhlenb.]. St. and lvs. glabrous; fls. yellow, said to be lemon-scented. Mts., Ky. to Ga., and lowlands, S.C. and Fla.

TRIMEZIA Salisb. ex Herb. *Iridaceae.* About 9 spp. of cormous, per. herbs native to trop. Amer.; lvs. linear to linear-lanceolate, not pleated; fls. yellow, perianth tube absent, segms. in 2 dissimilar series, stamens 3, filaments not united; fr. a caps.

martinicensis (Jacq.) Herb. [*Cipura martinicensis* (Jacq.) HBK]. Sts. nearly cylindrical, to 2½ ft., sometimes branched; lvs. to 1 ft. long; fls. yellow, with purple-brown spots at base, ¾ in. long. Trop. Amer.

TRIODANIS Raf. *Campanulaceae.* Eight spp. of ann. herbs, native to the New World, 1 to the Medit. region; lvs. alt., simple, toothed; fls. sessile or nearly so, 1 to several in the axils, forming a spicate infl., lower fls. usually cleistogamous with reduced corollas, upper fls. opening, the corolla deeply divided, anthers separate, filaments ciliate, mostly abruptly expanded at base; fr. a linear, ellipsoid, or obovate caps., opening by pores usually above the middle.

Cultivated to a limited extent in the flower garden; easily propagated.

biflora (Ruiz & Pav.) Greene. Differing from *T. perfoliata* in having narrower lvs. and bracts, the main st. and brs. usually with only 1 fl. opening, and pores of caps. usually reaching the caps. apex. Va. to Mo. and sw. Ore., s. to Mex. and S. Amer.

perfoliata (L.) Nieuwl. [*Specularia perfoliata* (L.) A. DC.]. To 3 ft., simple or usually with several strongly ascending brs. from near the base; lvs. and bracts sessile, clasping, rounded-cordate, ¼–1¼ in. long, nearly as broad or broader; fls. deep purple to lavender, about ½ in. long; fr. oblong to obovoid, ¼–½ in. long, with pore opening from the middle. New Eng. to B.C., s. to trop. Amer.

TRIOLENA Naud. *Melastomataceae.* About 50 spp. of subshrubs of w. trop. Amer.; lvs. very asymmetrical; fls. in racemes, showy, petals 5, stamens dimorphic; distinguished from *Bertolonia* by 3 threadlike appendages on connectives of the 3 larger stamens, and fr. a 3-winged caps.

Cultivation as for *Bertolonia.*

pustulata Triana [*Bertolonia pubescens* Hort.]. Herb; lvs. 3–7 in. long, 1–4 in. wide, warty-setose above, red-brown in a longitudinal central strip; infl. scorpioid; petals white, small. Ecuador.

TRIOSTEUM L. HORSE GENTIAN, FEVERWORT. *Caprifoliaceae.* About 5–6 spp. of per. herbs of weedy habit, native to e. Asia and e. N. Amer.; lvs. opp., simple, entire, sessile, fiddle-shaped or obovate; fls. usually axillary, sessile, solitary or clustered, yellowish or purplish, not showy, calyx lobes leafy, corolla tubular, 5-lobed, ovary inferior, 3-celled; fr. a leathery drupe with 3 nutlets.

aurantiacum Bickn. WILD COFFEE. To 4 ft.; lvs. ovate to oblong-lanceolate, to 10 in. long; fls. dull red, ¾ in. long; fr. orange-red. New Bruns. to N.C. and Mo. Zone 5.

perfoliatum L. WILD COFFEE, FEVERROOT, TINKER'S WEED. To 4 ft.; lvs. ovate or elliptic, to 9 in. long, often united at base; fls. purplish, ¾ in. long; fr. orange-yellow. Mass. to Ky. and Kans. Zone 6.

TRIPETALEIA Siebold & Zucc. *Ericaceae*. Two spp. of deciduous shrubs, native to Japan; lvs. simple, alt., entire; fls. white or pink, in terminal racemes or panicles, sepals 3–5, petals 3, stamens 6, anthers opening by slits; fr. a many-seeded caps.

bracteata Maxim. To 6 ft.; lvs. obovate, to 2 in. long, rounded to obtuse; racemes few-fld., to 6 in. long; fls. to ⅜ in. long, sepals separate. Zone 6?

paniculata Siebold & Zucc. To 7 ft.; lvs. rhombic to rhombic-ovate, to 2½ in. long, usually acute with an obtuse tip, tapering toward base; panicles many-fld., to 6 in. long; fls. to ⅜ in. long, sepals united. Zone 6.

TRIPHASIA Lour. *Rutaceae*. Three spp. of spiny, evergreen shrubs or trees, native from se. Asia and Philippine Is. to New Guinea; lvs. alt., simple or with 3 lfts., glandular-dotted; fls. 1–3 in axils of lvs., calyx 3–5-toothed, petals 3–5, stamens 6–10; fr. a thick-skinned, 3–5-celled berry.

Widely cultivated in the warmer parts of the world. Grown far south as an ornamental and a hedge. Propagated by seeds.

Aurantiola: *T. trifolia.*

trifolia (Burm.f.) P. Wils. [*T. Aurantiola* Lour.]. LIMEBERRY. To 15 ft.; lvs. nearly sessile, lfts. 3, emarginate, more or less finely crenate, terminal lft. ovate, to 1½ in. long, cuneate, lateral lfts. to ¾ in. long; fls. white, solitary, fragrant; fr. dull red, ½ in. in diam., with mucilaginous pulp. Nativity unknown, probably Malay Pen. Zone 9.

TRIPLARIS Loefl. HORMIGO, VOLADOR. *Polygonaceae*. About 25 spp. of dioecious trees or large shrubs, native to trop. S. Amer.; lvs. alt., simple, entire, veiny; fls. in clusters of spikelike racemes, female fls. showy, in shades of red, calyx lobes 6, 3 of them developing into conspicuous wings, stamens 9; fr. an achene, sharply 3-angled.

Tender, grown only in the tropics and subtropics (Zone 10b in Fla.).

americana L. LONG JOHN, ANT TREE, PALO SANTO. Tree, to 30 ft. or more; lvs. oblong to elliptic, to 15 in. long, acuminate; fls. in great panicles, female fls. red; fr. falling with a spinning motion. Probably n. S. Amer. Planted in s. Fla.

Cumingiana Fisch. & C. A. Mey. Habit like *T. americana;* lvs. petioled, blade oblong, to 9 in. or more; calyx wings to 2 in. long, 2–3 times as long as tube. Costa Rica to Ecuador.

guanaiensis Rusby. Described as having very densely hairy infl. Nw. S. Amer.

surinamensis Cham. GUAYABO HORMIGUERO, LONG JOHN. Similar to *T. Cumingiana*, but female fls. creamy-white, becoming red in age; brs. of infl. less hairy. Ne. S. Amer. Planted in s. Fla.

TRIPLEUROSPERMUM Schultz-Bip. *Compositae* (Anthemis Tribe). About 25 spp. of ann. or per. herbs, native to Eur. and w. Asia; lvs. alt., finely pinnately dissected; fl. heads solitary and terminal on scapose brs., radiate or discoid, involucral bracts imbricate in 2–3 rows, receptacle hemispherical to conical, solid, naked; fls. white or yellow, disc fls. tubular, ray fls. present or absent; achenes 3-ribbed on inner surface, with 2 conspicuous oil glands toward apex on outer surface, scar of point of attachment to receptacle strictly basal, pappus a membranous rim or absent.

Cultural requirements as for *Chrysanthemum*.

inodorum: *T. maritimum* subsp.

maritimum (L.) W. D. J. Koch [*Matricaria maritima* L.]. Short-lived per., brs. usually decumbent or prostrate, to about 1 ft.; lvs. to about 3 in. long, 2-pinnatifid into linear or filiform, fleshy segms.; heads to about 1¾ in. across; disc fls. yellow, ray fls. white; achenes with much elongated oil glands. Seashores, Eur.; naturalized in e. N. Amer. and Pacific Northwest. Subsp. **inodorum** (L.) Hyl. ex Vaar. [*T. inodorum* (L.) Schultz-Bip.; *Chrysanthemum inodorum* L.; *Matricaria Chamo-*

milla L.; *M. inodora* L.]. BRIDAL ROBE. Ann., brs. usually erect, to 2 ft.; ultimate lf. segms. acute or bristle-pointed; heads to about 1⅝ in. across; achenes with orbicular oil glands. Waste places, Eur.; naturalized in e. U.S.

oreades (Boiss.) Rech.f. [*Matricaria oreades* Boiss.]. Much-branched per., to 1½ ft.; sts. ascending, pubescent; lvs. oblong in outline, to ¾ in. long, 2-pinnately dissected into acute, linear segms.; heads to 1½ in. across, involucral bracts with rusty, scarious margins; ray fls. white. Syria, Lebanon.

Tchihatchewii (Boiss.) Bornm. [*Chrysanthemum Tchihatchewii* Hort.; *Matricaria Tchihatchewii* Boiss.; *Pyrethrum Tchihatchewii* Hort. ex W. Robinson]. TURFING DAISY. Nearly scentless, mat-forming, glabrous per.; lvs. 1–2-pinnately dissected; heads to about 1 in. across, on scapes to 1 ft. high; disc fls. yellow, ray fls. white. Asia Minor.

TRIPLOCHITON K. Schum. *Byttneriaceae*. Three spp. of trees, native to trop. Afr.; lvs. alt., palmately lobed and veined; fls. in axillary or terminal cymes or cymose panicles, each fl. subtended by 2–3 early-deciduous involucral bracts, calyx campanulate, the lobes 5, valvate, petals 5, tomentose, clawed at base, androgynophore present, stamens many, staminodes 5, carpels 5, separate or coherent, each with 6–12 ovules in 2 series; fr. of 5 single-seeded samaras, each with a large wing on one side.

scleroxylon K. Schum. To 100 ft. or more, buttressed; lvs. 5–7-lobed to about the middle, to 6½ in. long and 10 in. wide; fls. in panicled cymes, involucral bracts 2, about ⅛ in. long, petals nearly ½ in. long, white, with a reddish center, early deciduous; samaras pubescent or glabrous, about 2 in. long, of which ⅘ is the oblong wing. Spring. W. and cent. Afr.

zambeziacum Milne-Redh. To 60 ft.; lvs. 5–9-lobed, to 4½ in. long and 6 in. wide; fls. in reduced 1–4-fld. cymes, involucral bracts 3, over ¼ in. long, petals nearly 1½ in. long, about twice as long as calyx, white or yellowish, deep rose at base, androgynophore to ⅜ in. long; samara to 2¾ in. long, the wing stiffish, obovoid-oblong. Zambia and Rhodesia.

TRIPLOCHLAMYS Ulbr. *Malvaceae*. Six or more spp. of shrubs from Brazil; lvs. simple, unlobed, lanceolate-ovate to elliptic or oblong, entire to dentate, stipules large, appressed, linear; fls. solitary in the lf. axils, but forming racemose to corymbose or headlike infls. at the end of brs., involucral bracts mostly 10–24 in 2 series, but sometimes 4–5 in a single whorl, linear to cordate-ovate, usually as long as or longer than the calyx, often bright red, calyx tubular, 5-lobed, corolla tubular, stamens united in a tubular column, filamentous over most of its length and 5-toothed apically, style brs. 10, filiform, stigmas discoid; fr. a schizocarp, mericarps 5, smooth, elongate, apiculate, 1-seeded.

multiflora (Juss.) Ulbr. [*Pavonia multiflora* Juss.]. Shrub, to 6 ft.; lvs. lanceolate-ovate to oblong, to 10 in. long, subentire to dentate; fls. solitary in the upper axils and terminal in a naked corymb, involucral bracts 10–24, in 1 or 2 whorls, those of the outer whorl sometimes falling early, ascending, linear, shorter, to 1½ in. long, all bright red, calyx shorter than the bracts, red, petals purple-red, to 1½ in. long, staminal column exserted, slightly deflexed, reddish, with blue anthers.

TRIPOGANDRA Raf. [*Neodonnellia* Rose]. *Commelinaceae*. Perhaps 20 or more spp. of per. herbs, native mostly to warmer areas of N. and S. Amer.; sts. procumbent to erect; lvs. alt.; fls. white or pink, in paired, sessile cincinni with small subtending bracts on elongate, terminal and axillary peduncles, sepals 3, soft, green or colored, petals 3, separate, stamens 6, in 2 dissimilar rows, those opp. the petals the longest and with bright anthers, usually sterile pollen, and often bearded filaments, twisting to stand in front of the upper petal at flowering, those opp. the sepals much shorter and with less conspicuous anthers, fertile, ovary 3-celled, each cell with 1–2 ovules; fr. a loculicidal caps.

Mostly cultivated indoors or under glass. Propagated by seeds or cuttings.

cumanensis (Kunth) Woodson. Sts. creeping at base, with ascending brs.; lvs. narrowly ovate-oblong to lanceolate, to 2½ in. long, ½ in. wide; peduncles shorter than subtending lvs., pedicels to about 1 in. long, glandular; fls. small, white or pink, the longer stamens with filaments erect, bearded, the shorter glabrous, with narrow, pale anthers; seeds gray, reticulate. Mex. to n. S. Amer.

grandiflora (J. D. Sm.) Woodson [*Neodonnellia grandiflora* (J. D. Sm.) Rose]. Sts. smooth, scandent, to 9 ft.; lvs. lanceolate, to 3⅜ in.

long, 1 in. wide, glossy, dark green; peduncles to 1¾ in. long, pedicels glabrous; fls. fragrant, sepals ⅜ in. long, petals 7/16 in. long, white, reflexed, acute, the longer stamens with bearded filaments and brilliant orange connectives, the shorter glabrous. S. Mex., Brit. Honduras, Guatemala.

multiflora (Swartz) Raf. [*Tradescantia multiflora* Swartz]. FERN-LEAF INCH PLANT. Sts. creeping, with ascending brs.; lvs. cordate-ovate, 1–2 in. long; peduncles shorter than subtending lvs.; fls. small, white, sepals ⅛ in. long, hairy, the longer stamens with bearded filaments thickened and deflexed at apex, the shorter glabrous; seeds black, pitted. W. Indies, n. S. Amer.

rosea: *Cuthbertia rosea.*

Warszewicziana: *Hadrodemas Warszewiczianum.*

TRIPTERIS: *OSTEOSPERMUM.*

TRIPTEROCALYX: *ABRONIA.*

TRIPTEROSPERMUM Blume. *Gentianaceae.* About 10 spp. of per. herbs of e. Asia with climbing, spirally twisted sts.; lvs. opp.; fls. 5-merous, calyx tubular, 5-winged, corolla tubular or tubular-campanulate, stamens bent downward, filaments unequal in length, the free part uniform; fr. a berry or caps., seeds winged.

japonicum (Siebold & Zucc.) Maxim. [*Crawfurdia Blumei* G. Don may belong here; *C. japonica* Siebold & Zucc.; *C. trinervis* (Thunb.) Mak.; *Gentiana trinervis* (Thunb.) Marq.]. Lvs. deltoid-ovate to lanceolate, to 3 in. long, gradually acuminate, 3-nerved; fls. 1–3, terminal and axillary, calyx tube to ½ in. long, lobes lanceolate, as long as tube, corolla reddish-purple, to 1¼ in. long, pleated; fr. a stalked, ellipsoid-globose berry, to ⅜ in. across, red-purple, slightly exserted from corolla. Japan, Kurile Is., Sakhalin, Korea, Taiwan, Java.

TRIPTERYGIUM Hook.f. *Celastraceae.* Two spp. of polygamous, deciduous, scandent shrubs of e. Asia; lvs. alt., simple, large; fls. white, in large terminal panicles, calyx 5-lobed, petals 5, stamens 5; fr. a 1-seeded, 3-winged samara.

Occasionally cultivated as ornamentals.

Regelii T. Sprague & Takeda. Shrub, 6–30 ft.; lvs. broadly elliptic to ovate, to 6 in. long, crenate-serrate; panicles to 10 in. long; fr. nearly orbicular, ¾ in. in diam. or more, greenish-white. Manchuria to Japan. Zone 5.

Wilfordii Hook.f. Climbing shrub, 30–40 ft.; lvs. oblong-elliptic to ovate, to 6 in. long, finely crenate, often glaucous beneath; panicles 1 ft. long; fr. about ½ in. in diam., purplish-red to brown. Taiwan and e. China. Zone 9. An insecticidal plant.

TRISTANIA R. Br. *Myrtaceae.* About 20 spp. of evergreen trees and shrubs, 12–14 endemic in Australia, several in se. Asia and New Caledonia; lvs. alt., or irregularly whorled at the ends of branchlets, simple; fls. small, yellow or white, in peduncled, axillary clusters, calyx tube adnate to ovary, calyx lobes 5, petals 5, stamens many, more or less united in bundles opp. petals, ovary inferior or half-inferior; fr. a 3-valved caps., loculicidally dehiscent.

Grown as ornamentals in warm-temperate and subtropical areas. Propagated by seeds or cuttings under glass.

conferta R. Br. BRISBANE BOX. Tree, to 150 ft. where native, but mostly 20–50 ft. in Calif.; lvs. ovate or ovate-lanceolate, to 6 in. long; fls. white, 1 in. across, in cymes of 3–7, usually on young wood below the cluster of lvs.; fr. to ½ in. across. Australia. The outer bark is deciduous, leaving an attractive, smooth, reddish-brown trunk.

lactiflua F. J. Muell. Tree, to 30 ft.; lvs. ovate or broadly ovate-lanceolate, to 6 in. long; fls. white, small, and very abundant in axillary cymes. Australia.

laurina (Sm.) R. Br. Small tree or shrub; lvs. lanceolate, elliptic, or obovate, to 4 in. long, acuminate, narrowed into a petiole; fls. yellow, in short axillary cymes; fr. ¼ in. across. Australia.

TRISTELLATEIA Thouars. *Malpighiaceae.* About 30 spp. of woody vines, native to trop. e. Afr., Madagascar, se. Asia, and Pacific Is.; lvs. opp., simple; fls. yellow, in axillary or terminal infls., sepals rarely with glands, petals clawed, stamens 10, all fertile; fr. of 3 samaras.

australasiae A. Rich. [*T. australis* A. Rich.]. Lvs. ovate to lanceolate-ovate, to 6 in. long, obtuse or cordate; racemes terminal, loose, to 30-fld. Se. Asia to New Caledonia.

australis: *T. australasiae.*

TRITELEIA Dougl. [*Calliprora* Lindl.]. *Amaryllidaceae.* About 14 spp. of per. herbs, native to w. N. Amer.; corms with straw-colored, fibrous-reticulate coat; lvs. 1–2, narrowly linear and elongate, flattened, keeled on underside, grooved on upper side; scape slender, retrorsely scabrous or hairy toward the base, umbel subtended by an involucre of scarious, green, or rarely purplish spathe valves; fls. jointed to the pedicel, perianth tube various, lobes spreading, stamens 6, all fertile, filaments equal, unequal, or unequally inserted, ovary superior, stalked, stigma small, 3-lobed; fr. a loculicidal caps., seeds black, rounded, ridged on one side, their surface coarsely and irregularly pitted, minutely granular or granular-reticulate.

Culture as for *Brodiaea.*

Bridgesii (S. Wats.) Greene [*Brodiaea Bridgesii* S. Wats.]. Scape to 1½ ft. high; lvs. to ⅜ in. wide; perianth lilac or blue, to 1¾ in. long, tube gradually expanded, slender-based, lobes longer than tube, spreading, stamens inserted at mouth of tube, more or less equal. Coastal mts., Ore to cent. Calif.

crocea (A. Wood) Greene [*Brodiaea crocea* (A. Wood) S. Wats.]. Scape to 1 ft.; lvs. about as long as scape, to ⅜ in. wide; pedicels not quite twice as long as fls., perianth bright yellow, to ¾ in. long, stamens in 2 series, filaments of the lower series about half as long as the upper, stalk of ovary about equal to body of ovary or longer. Ore., Calif.

grandiflora Lindl. [*Brodiaea Douglasii* S. Wats.; *B. grandiflora* Macbr., not Sm.]. Scape to 2 ft.; lvs. to ⅜ in. wide; pedicels mostly shorter than fls., elongating somewhat in fr.; perianth bright blue to white, to 1¼ in. long, tube rounded at base, stamens in 2 series, filaments slender, but dilated toward base, stalk of ovary about half as long as body of ovary. N. Utah to e. Ore. and e. B.C. Var. **Howellii** (S. Wats.) Hoover [*Brodiaea bicolor* Suksd.]. Differs in having the filaments broad, rounded at the apex, and the anthers and filaments sometimes longer. Vancouver Is. to n. Calif.

Hendersonii Greene [*Brodiaea Hendersonii* (Greene) S. Wats.]. Scape to 1 ft.; lvs. to ½ in. wide; spathe valves long and narrow; perianth yellow, to ⅞ in. long, lobes about twice as long as tube, with dark purple midvein, stamens attached at mouth of tube, more or less equal. Ore. Var. **Leachiae** (Peck) Hoover [*Brodiaea Leachiae* Peck]. Differs in having fls. white, often suffused with blue. Ore.

hyacinthina (Lindl.) Greene [*Brodiaea hyacinthina* (Lindl.) Bak.; *B. lactea* (Lindl.) S. Wats.; *Hookera hyacinthina* (Lindl.) O. Kuntze]. WILD HYACINTH. Scape to 2½ ft.; lvs. to ⅞ in. wide; perianth usually white, sometimes blue or lilac, bowl-shaped, lobes twice as long as tube or longer, stamens inserted in throat, more or less equal, stalk of ovary very short in fl. B.C. to Idaho, s. to s. Calif. and Nev.

ixioides (Ait.f.) Greene [*Brodiaea ixioides* (Ait.f.) S. Wats., not Hook.; *Calliprora ixioides* (Ait.f.) Greene]. PRETTY-FACE, GOLDEN BRODIAEA. Scape to 2 ft.; lvs. to ½ in. wide; perianth golden-yellow, with dark midribs, to 1 in. long, tube ¼ in. or longer, lobes spreading but not rotate, about twice as long as tube, stamens inserted in throat, alternately long and short, filaments with wings extending as teeth beyond the anthers. Calif. Var. **scabra** (Greene) Hoover [var. *splendens* Hort.; *Calliprora scabra* Greene]. Scape usually hairy at base; fls. cream- or straw-colored to deep golden-yellow, perianth tube ¼ in. long or less, lobes rotate.

laxa Benth. [*Brodiaea candida* (Greene) Bak.; *B. laxa* (Benth.) S. Wats.]. GRASS NUT, TRIPLET LILY. Scape to 2½ ft.; lvs. about ⅔ as long as scape, to 1 in. wide; pedicels shorter than fls. or to twice as long; perianth violet-purple, blue, or rarely white, 1¼–1¾ in. long, funnelform, tube attenuate at base, lobes shorter than tube, stamens inserted in 2 series, filaments about equal, stalk of ovary 2–3 times as long as body of ovary in fl. Sw. Ore. to s. Calif.

lugens Greene [*Brodiaea ixioides* (Ait.f.) S. Wats. var. *lugens* (Greene) Jeps.]. Scape to 1½ ft.; lvs. to ⅜ in. wide; perianth dull yellow or brownish-purple, to ½ in. long, tube funnelform, lobes about twice as long as tube, stamens inserted in throat, alternately long and short, filaments very broad, the rounded apex not extending as teeth beyond anthers. Calif., Baja Calif.

peduncularis Lindl. [*Brodiaea peduncularis* (Lindl.) S. Wats.]. LONG-RAYED T. Scape to 3 ft.; lvs. often longer than scape, to ⅜ in. wide; umbels 3–15-fld.; pedicels 2–5 times as long as fls., perianth white or tinged with lilac, to 1 in. long, tube funnelform-campanulate, lobes longer than tube, stamens inserted at 2 levels, ovary yellow, its stalk about as long as its body in fl. Wet places, coast ranges of Calif. Plants grown under the name *Brodiaea Eastwoodiae* may be this sp.

TRITHRINAX Mart. *Palmae.* About 5 spp. of low or middle-sized palms with bisexual fls., native to trop. and s. Brazil, Bolivia, Paraguay, and Argentina; st. solitary or cespitose, usually covered with persistent fibrous lf. sheaths armed at margin with long, stout spines; lvs. palmate, more or less orbicular in outline, firm, cut into many 1-ribbed segms., petiole not toothed; infl. among lvs., paniculate, twice-branched, with several thin bracts on peduncle; sepals 3, united in a low cupule, petals 3, imbricate, stamens 6, filaments separate, carpels 3, styles slender; fr. globose, smooth, 1 in. in diam. or less, seed with homogeneous endosperm deeply intruded by seed coat.

For culture see *Palms.*

acanthocoma Drude. Trunk single, to 15 ft., densely clothed with deflexed, slender but stiff spines 3–6 in. long; lvs. to 3 ft. wide, deeply divided into about 40 segms. 2-cleft for 1–2 in. at apex; fr. about ¾ in. in diam. S. Brazil. Zone 9b.

TRITICUM L. WHEAT. *Gramineae.* About 30 spp. of ann. grasses in the Medit. region and sw. Asia; lf. blades flat; spikes thick; spikelets 2–5-fld., solitary, compressed, placed flatwise at each joint of a continuous or articulate rachis, the rachilla continuous or in cult. forms disarticulating above the glumes and between the florets, glumes ovate, rigid, keeled, 3- to several-nerved, the apex abruptly mucronate or toothed or with one to several awns, lemmas broad, keeled, many-nerved, abruptly pointed or awned; fr. free or remaining in the glumes. For terminology see *Gramineae.*

The cultivated kinds of wheat, which are the most important cereals of temperate regions, may be divided into 3 groups: diploid (see *ploidy*) species, allopolyploids (of hybrid origin), and other artificial and natural interspecific hybrids; of these only the first 2 groups are represented below. The primitive diploid group with 7 pairs of chromosomes includes einkorn, *T. monococcum,* a wild species which has been a source of genes in the hybridization of wheat cultivars. Among allopolyploids are the allotetraploid wheats, cultivars with 14 pairs of chromosomes, including emmer, and the durum, poulard, and Polish wheats; and the allohexaploid wheats, cultivars with 21 pairs of chromosomes, represented by *T. aestivum,* a complex of cultivars, including spelt, club wheat, and most of the common bread wheats. The allohexaploid cultivars are presumed to represent hybrids arising from various crossings of allotetraploid wheats with *T. aegilops* Beauvois ex Roem. & Schult. [*Aegilops squarrosa* L.].

aestivum L. Sts. erect, freely branching at base, to 4 ft.; lf. blades to ¾ in. wide; spikes awned or awnless, somewhat compressed; spikelets imbricate, crowded or more remotely spaced, glumes with 1 winged keel, the wing indistinct towards base of glume, lemma awned or awnless. Six groups of cvs. are recognized of which 3 are represented in our area.

Aestivum Group [*T. aestivum* L.]. COMMON WHEAT. Spikes awned, glumes white, glabrous, awns white, grains reddish, the bread and flour wheats, with many cvs. including the common winter and spring grain wheats; escaping occasionally but not established anywhere.

Compactum Group [*T. compactum* Host]. CLUB WHEAT, DWARF W., HEDGEHOG W. Plants small, sts. stiff, strong; spikes short, only several times taller than broad; spikelets densely compacted; grains small, elliptic-oblong, about ¼ in. long, ⅛ in. broad. These are wheats adapted to poorer, arid, mountain soils and are grown mainly in sw. Asia but also locally in the U.S. in the Pacific and Rocky Mt. states. The grains are soft, low in protein, and are mainly used for pastry flour.

Spelta Group [*T. spelta* L.]. SPELT. Spikes slender, loose, 5–8 in. long, somewhat 4-sided, with a slender, brittle, exposed rachis; spikelets well separated, grains 2 in a spikelet, pale red, long, laterally compressed, enclosed in the glumes after threshing. These are ancient cvs. and are very hardy, enduring poorest soils. Cult. in Medit. area and sometimes in the U.S. for stock feed or forage.

compactum: *T. aestivum,* Compactum Group.

dicoccon: *T. turgidum,* Dicoccon Group.

durum: *T. turgidum,* Durum Group.

monococcum L. EINKORN, ONE-GRAINED W. Sts. rigid, to 3½ ft. tall, graceful; spike slender, laterally compressed, long-awned; spikelets 1-seeded, glumes 2-keeled, with lateral tooth pointed, the second floret not fertile, palea splitting into 2 parts at maturity; grains remaining in spikelets after threshing, pale red, slender, much-compressed with almost no crease. E. Medit. Cult. in mts. in Eur. and sw. Asia. Often grown in economic gardens and breeding collections. A diploid fodder wheat of the Stone Age.

polonicum: *T. turgidum,* Polonicum Group.

spleta: *T. aestivum,* Spelta Group.

turgidum L. Spikes usually awned and compressed, narrow across the faces, much broader across the 2-rowed profiles; spikelets usually compressed, crowded, imbricate in the lateral rows, glume 1-keeled,

lemma usually long-awned. The sp. includes 8 groups of cvs. of allotetraploid wheats of which 4 are grown in our area.

Dicoccon Group [*T. dicoccon* Schrank]. EMMER, TWO-GRAINED W., GERMAN W., STARCH W., RICE W., TWO-GRAINED SPELT. Winter or spring wheats. Cult. by Babylonians and Swiss Lake dwellers and now grown in mts. of Eur. on dry soils; grown for livestock and for breakfast foods in the U.S.

Durum Group [*T. durum* Desf.]. DURUM W. Hardy, drought-resistant, spring wheats, the plants tall with pithy peduncle in upper part of st.; spikes with long, coarse, stiff awns; grains white or red, long, pointed with short apical tuft, very flinty. These are gluten-rich wheats of arid regions of the Old World, especially in Spain, India, and the U.S.S.R., grown in our Great Plains states, where important for stock feed and the flour, used for macaroni and similar foods.

Polonicum Group [*T. polonicum* L.]. POLISH W., GIANT RYE. Spring wheats with tall, pithy sts. spikes large, lax, awned; glumes lanceolate, 1 in. long, as long or longer than the spikelet, membranous in texture; grains nearly ½ in. long, narrow, hard, resembling a grain of rye. These are grown in Medit. Eur. and occasionally in U.S. and yield poorly.

Turgidum Group [*T. turgidum* L.]. POULARD W., ENGLISH W., RIVER W., MEDITERRANEAN W., ALASKA W. Tall winter or spring wheats, sts. thick, solid, lvs. very broad, hairy; spikes short, thick, to 4½ in. long, to ½ in. broad; glumes shorter than lemma, awns brittle, longer than spike, attached to convex glume, grain short, thick, humped, very starchy. Cvs. grown in the U.S. are not of major commercial importance.

TRITOMA: *KNIPHOFIA.*

TRITONIA Ker-Gawl. [*Montbretia* DC.]. *Iridaceae.* Perhaps 50 spp. of cormous herbs, native to S. Afr.; lvs. usually linear; infl. simple or branched, spathe valves brown, emarginate; perianth tube tapering basally, but dilated toward mouth into a broad throat, usually shorter than perianth segms.; fr. an ovoid or oblong caps., seeds 1–2 in each cell.

Grown for showy summer flowers. Culture as for *Gladiolus;* hardy except in the far North, and may be left permanently in the ground or replanted annually from well-ripened corms that have been stored dry after foliage dies.

aurantiaca: *T. crocata.*

crocata (L.) Ker-Gawl. [*T. aurantiaca* Eckl.; *Montbretia crocata* (L.) Voigt]. Sts. 12–18 in.; lvs. 4–6, mostly 4–8 in. long, to ½ in. wide; spike loose, 1-sided; perianth bright tawny-yellow, about 1¼ in. long, segms. broadly cuneate to obovate, more than twice as long as tube. Var. **miniata** (Jacq.) Bak. [*T. miniata* (Jacq.) Ker-Gawl.; *Montbretia miniata* (Jacq.) Voigt]. Lvs. darker green; fls. smaller, bright red.

×**crocosmiiflora:** *Crocosmia* × *crocosmiiflora.*

hyalina (L.f.) Bak. Differs from *T. crocata* in having perianth segms. tapering below the middle, becoming spatulate, claws narrowed, and margins inflexed, hyaline.

lineata (Salisb.) Ker-Gawl. [*Montbretia lineata* (Salisb.) Voigt]. Sts. to 18 in., simple or forked; lvs. 4–6, linear, mostly 6–12 in. long, ¼–½ in. wide; perianth white to pale pink, 1–1¼ in. long, tube broadly funnelform, segms. about as long as tube.

Masoniorum: *Crocosmia Masoniorum.*

miniata: *T. crocata* var.

rosea: see *T. rubrolucens.*

rubrolucens R. Foster [*T. rosea* Klatt, not (Jacq.) Ait.; *Montbretia rosea* (Klatt) Bak., not (Jacq.) Voigt]. Sts. to 2 ft.; lvs. few, linear, to 12 in. long; spike branched, loose, mostly 4–12-fld.; fls. 2-ranked, rose, perianth 1 in. long, tube broadly funnelform, segms. as long as tube.

squalida (Ait.) Ker-Gawl. Similar to *T. crocata,* but having perianth whitish, flushed or veined rose-pink, some or all segms. often with obscure yellowish blotch at base.

TRIZEUXIS Lindl. *Orchidaceae.* One sp., an epiphyte, native to trop. Amer.; pseudobulbs very small or lacking; lvs. 2-ranked, laterally compressed, sickle-shaped; infl. slender, paniculate, with short, many-fld. brs.; fls. minute, greenish with yellow lip, sepals and petals similar, united basally, campanulate, lip parallel with column, column footless, pollinia 2, on slender elliptic stalk. For structure of fl. see *Orchidaceae.*

For culture see *Orchids.*

falcata Lindl. Pseudobulbs very small, to ³⁄₁₆ in. long, or lacking; lvs. in irregular fan-shaped sprays, to 2½ in. long; infl. to 4 in. long; fls. pale, translucent green, few opening at a time, upper sepal boat-shaped, united for half its length to petals, lateral sepals united for ⅔ their length, petals very small, lip ¹⁄₁₆ in. long, pale greenish-yellow, to orange-yellow at apex. Trop. Amer.

TROCHODENDRACEAE. *Trochodendron aralioides:* **a,** flowering branch, × ⅜; **b,** flower, × 1½; **c,** flower, vertical section, × 2; **d,** anther, × 6; **e,** anther, cross section, × 6; **f,** fruit, × 1½. (From Lawrence, *Taxonomy of Vascular Plants.*)

TROCHODENDRACEAE Prantl. TROCHODENDRON FAMILY. Dicot.; 1 genus, *Trochodendron*, of evergreen trees, native to e. Asia; lvs. simple, alt., in clusters at ends of brs., without stipules; fls. clustered in racemose infls., bisexual, perianth none, stamens many, in several series, carpels 5–11, in a single series, laterally united, 1-celled; fr. a ring of follicles.

TROCHODENDRON Siebold & Zucc. *Trochodendraceae*. One sp.; characteristics those of the family.

aralioides Siebold & Zucc. WHEEL TREE. To 60 ft.; lvs. obovate to lanceolate, to 5 in. long, crenulate-serrulate, petioles to 3½ in. long; infls. to 5 in. long; fls. many, bright green, ½ in. across, stamens 40–70; follicles brown, in a cluster ½ in. across. Mts., Japan and s. S. Korea to Taiwan. Zone 8.

TROLLIUS L. GLOBEFLOWER. *Ranunculaceae*. About 20 spp. of per. herbs with thick, fibrous roots, native mostly to swampy or low places of the N. Temp. Zone; lvs. palmately lobed or divided; fls. usually solitary, terminal, sepals 5–15, petal-like, petals 5 or more, often small, stamens many; fr. of many follicles.

Trolliuses require moist soil. They bloom in the spring; useful for borders and rock gardens. Propagated by seeds or division.

acaulis Lindl. Sts. 3–10 in.; lvs. palmately 5–7-parted, divisions 3-lobed; fls. solitary, stellate, overtopped by lvs., 2 in. across, sepals 9, deep yellow, lanceolate, petals 12–16, deep orange, linear-cuneate, rounded at apex, shorter than stamens; follicles 15. Himalayas.

albiflorus: *T. laxus* var.

asiaticus L. Like *T. europaeus*, but smaller, bronzy-green; lf. lobes finely toothed; sepals 10, orange, slightly longer than petals, petals 10, longer than stamens. Cv. 'Fortunei' [*T. japonicus* cv. 'Flore Pleno']. Sepals many, fls. double. Cv. 'Giganteus'. Robust form.

caucasicus: *T. ranunculinus*.

chinensis Bunge. Sts. stout, grooved, to 3 ft.; lower lvs. reniform, upper lvs. more rounded, up to 7 in. across, 5-parted, segms. broad-lanceolate, to 3 in. long, sharply toothed; fls. on peduncles to 1 ft. long, globular, golden-yellow, sepals 12–13, the outer wide-ovate, ¾ in. long, petals 20, linear, over 1 in. long. N. China. Most plants cult. as *T. Ledebourii* seem to belong here.

dschungaricus Regel. Like *D. europaeus*, but fls. open, not globose, golden-yellow inside, reddish outside, sepals about 15, rounded, mucronate. Turkestan.

europaeus L. GLOBEFLOWER. To 2 ft., usually simple, leafy; lvs. dark green above, paler beneath, basal lvs. stalked, 3–5-lobed, st. lvs. sessile, 3-lobed; fls. more or less globular, 1 in. across or more, sepals 5–15, pale or greenish-yellow, incurved, petals yellow, equalling stamens;

follicles ½ in. long, transversely wrinkled, beaked. Eur., arctic Amer. Cvs. include: 'Giganteus', of robust form; 'Grandiflorus', a listed name; 'Loddigesii', fls. deep yellow; 'Superbus', a listed name.

giganteus: a listed name of no botanical standing; sometimes applied to large forms of *T. asiaticus* and *T. europaeus*.

hybridus: a listed name of no botanical standing; applied in hort. to many desirable seedling forms intermediate between various spp.

japonicus Miq. Four to 8 in.; lvs. radical and cauline, sometimes forming an involucre; fls. yellow, sepals 5–6, about 1 in. long, spreading, petals longer than stamens. Japan. Cv. 'Flore Pleno': *T. asiaticus* cv. 'Fortunei'.

laxus Salisb. SPREADING G. Sts. more or less ascending, ½–2 ft.; lower lvs. petioled, 5–7-parted, lf. segms. cuneate, much cleft and toothed; fls. solitary, greenish-yellow, 1–2 in. across, sepals 5–7, spreading, entire to toothed at tip, petals many, short. Swamps and bogs, e. U.S. Var. **albiflorus** A. Gray [*T. albiflorus* (A. Gray) Rydb.]. To 1 ft.; lf. segms. 5; fls. pale or white, petals almost as long as stamens. High montane, B.C., s. to Wash. and Colo.

Ledebourii Rchb.f. Sts. 2–3 ft.; lvs. cleft to base, segms. lobed and toothed; fls. deep orange, cup-shaped, 2–2½ in. across, sepals 5, petals 10–12, narrow-linear, stamens dark orange, shorter than petals. E. Siberia. Most plants offered under this name seem to be *T. chinensis*.

orientalis: a listed name of no botanical standing.

patulus: *T. ranunculinus*.

pumilus D. Don. Sts. glabrous, simple, 3–8 in.; lvs. mostly basal, ½–2 in. wide, 5–7-lobed, lobes laciniate; fls. yellow, 1 in. across, sepals 5–7, spreading, broadly elliptic, petals and stamens about equal in length, shorter than sepals. Himalayas.

ranunculinus (Sm.) Stearn [*T. caucasicus* Steven; *T. patulus* Salisb.]. Sts. scapelike, 3–12 in.; lvs. palmately cleft, then cut and toothed; fls. golden-yellow, 1½–1¾ in. across, sepals 5–10, spreading, deciduous, petals 1–10, linear-spatulate, about as long as stamens. Caucasus, Armenia.

yunnanensis (Franch.) Ulbr. Glabrous, to 2 ft.; lvs. more or less pentagonal, 1½–4 in. across, deeply 3–5-cleft, segms. broadly ovate to obovate, with broad, acute teeth; fls. golden-yellow, 1½–2 in. across, sepals usually 5, spreading, petals about 12, orange-tipped, linear-spatulate, ⁵⁄₁₆ in. long. W. China.

TROPAEOLACEAE A. DC. NASTURTIUM FAMILY. Dicot.; 2 genera, with over 50 spp. of somewhat succulent herbs, native to mountainous regions from Mex. to cent. Chile and Argentina; plants prostrate or climbing by the sensitive petioles; lvs. mostly simple, entire or palmately lobed or parted, peltate, often long-petioled; fls. bisexual, irregular, solitary, rarely in an umbel, calyx 2-lobed, spurred, petals 5, often clawed, entire, or emarginate or fimbriate, stamens 10, ovary superior, 3-celled; fr. separating at maturity into 3 1-seeded indehiscent sections. *Tropaeolum* is cult.

TROPAEOLUM L. NASTURTIUM, BITTER INDIAN. *Tropaeolaceae*. Over 50 spp. in the cool highlands, ranging from Mex. to cent. Argentina and Chile; ann. or per. herbs with acrid watery sap, spreading or climbing by means of coiling petioles, roots sometimes tuberous; lvs. alt., simple, rarely compound, entire, or lobed or parted, peltate, usually long-petioled; fls. showy, mostly yellow, orange, or red, irregular, solitary on long axillary peduncles, rarely in umbels, sepals 5, the upper one lengthened into a nectar-bearing spur, petals 5, clawed, the upper 2 differing from the lower 3, stamens 8, in 2 whorls; fr. wrinkled, 3-lobed, separating into 3 1-seeded, indehiscent sections.

One species, *T. tuberosum*, is of local importance as a vegetable tuber crop in the high Andes. Nasturtiums contain mustard oil, so that the flower buds and young fruits are used for seasoning and are sometimes pickled. The leaves are used in salads. They are grown as cool-temperate annuals thriving in sunny locations. Seeds may be sown where plants are to stand, or in boxes and pots in early spring and transplanted in May. The plants are frost tender.

canariense: *T. peregrinum*.

Lobbianum: *T. peltophorum*.

majus L. GARDEN N., TALL N., INDIAN CRESS. Ann., usually climbing, glabrous and somewhat succulent; lvs. orbicular or somewhat reniform, 2–7 in. across, mostly entire; fls. to 2½ in. across, of various shades of yellow, orange, or red, sometimes striped and spotted. Andean S. Amer. Double-fld. and dwarf cvs. are offered. Cv. 'Burpeei'. Fls. very double, not producing seeds, prop. vegetatively.

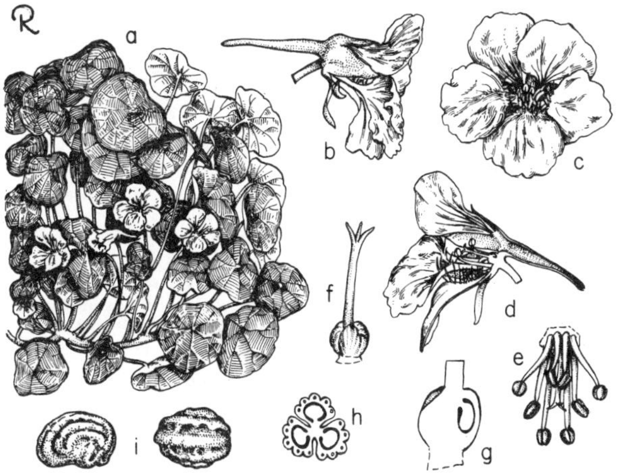

TROPAEOLACEAE. *Tropaeolum majus:* **a,** flowering plant, × ⅛; **b,** flower, side view, × ½; **c,** flower, face view, × ½; **d,** flower, vertical section, × ½; **e,** stamens surrounding pistil, viewed from in front and above, × 1; **f,** pistil, × 1½; **g,** ovary, vertical section, × 3; **h,** ovary, cross section, × 4; **i,** one section of fruit, two views, × 1.

minus L. DWARF N. Differs from *T. majus* in being dwarf, sts. not climbing but more or less scrambling; lvs. with each vein ending in a point; fls. 1½ in. across or less, the lower 3 petals with a dark central spot. Andean S. Amer.

peltophorum Benth. [*T. Lobbianum* Hort. Veitch]. Sts. climbing, hairy; lvs. orbicular, long-petioled, hairy beneath, sinuate; fls. 1 in. long, orange-red, the 3 lower petals long-clawed, margins toothed. Andean S. Amer.

peregrinum L. [*T. canariense* Hort. ex Lindl. & T. Moore]. CANARY-BIRD FLOWER, CANARY-BIRD VINE, CANARY CREEPER. Sts. climbing; lvs. deeply 5-lobed, petioles longer than peduncles; fls. to 1 in. across, canary-yellow, the upper petals erect and fimbriate, the spur curved, green. Probably Andes of Peru and Ecuador.

polyphyllum Cav. Small, glabrous, glaucous per., sts. prostrate; lvs. deeply 5–7-lobed, lobes obovate, entire or toothed, petioles longer than peduncles; fls. yellow or orange, upper petals emarginate. Chile.

speciosum Poepp. & Endl. High-climbing per., from a more or less fleshy rhizome; lvs. usually 6-parted, segms. obovate to spatulate, hairy beneath, petioles shorter than flexuous peduncles; fls. to 1½ in. long, vermilion-red, petals clawed and emarginate. Chile.

tuberosum Ruiz & Pav. ANYU. Sts. high-climbing, glabrous, from large elongate, underground tubers; lvs. 5–6-lobed, lobes mucronate; fls. to ¾ in. long, petals yellow, spur red. Andean S. Amer. Tubers edible.

TSUGA Carrière. HEMLOCK, HEMLOCK SPRUCE. *Pinaceae.* About 10 spp. of coniferous, evergreen, monoecious trees, native to temp. N. Amer. and e. Asia; brs. slender, horizontal; lvs. linear, usually flattened, with 2 white bands beneath, leaving projecting base on falling; male cones axillary, female cones small, scales woody, persistent; seeds 2 to each scale, winged, maturing in 1 year.

Hemlocks yield valuable timber, pulpwood, tanbark, and ornamentals with delicate foliage. They are valuable lawn trees, particularly as young specimens, doing best when not too much exposed to winter winds and winter sun. *T. canadensis* is the hardiest, but most of the others are hardy in Zone 6. For culture see *Conifers.*

canadensis (L.) Carrière. CANADA H. To 80 ft. or more; lvs. to ⅜ in. long, finely toothed, obtuse or acutish; cones to ¾ in. long, stalked. Nov. Sc. to Ala. Zone 3. Cvs. are : **'Albospica'**, tips of young branchlets white; **'Atrovirens'**, lvs. very dark green; **'Aurea'**, lvs. tinged yellow; **'Brandleyi'** and **'Cinnamomea'**, listed names; **'Compacta'**, dwarf, conical; **'Contorta'**, a listed name; **'Dawsoniana'**, slow-growing, compact, lvs. dark green; **'Fastigiata'**, narrow or columnar; **'Fremdii'**, conical, slow-growing, lvs. dark green; **'Globosa'**, rounded, compact; **'Gracilis'**, brs. drooping at ends, lvs. very small; **'Hortordii'**, a listed name; **'Hussii'**, very dwarf, brs. short, twiggy; **'Lutea'**, a listed name; **'Macrophylla'**, lvs. larger; **'Microphylla'**, lvs. ¼ in. long or less; **'Minima'**, a listed name; **'Nana'**, DWARF H., dwarf, to 7 ft., broader than high; **'Outpost'**, a listed name; **'Pendula'** [*T. Sargentii* Hort.], brs. drooping, forming a dense broad bush; **'Pomfret'**, **'Pyramidalis'**, **'Ruggii'**, listed names; **'Sargentii'**: 'Pendula'; **'Stranger'**, **'Taxifolia'**, **'Westonigra'**, **'Wolfii'**, listed names.

caroliniana Engelm. CAROLINA H. To 70 ft.; lvs. to ¾ in. long, entire, obtuse or slightly notched at apex, dark green above; cones to 1½ in. long. Mts., Va. to Ga. Zone 5. Cv. **'Compacta'**, dense, round-topped.

diversifolia (Maxim.) M. T. Mast. JAPANESE H., NORTHERN J.H. From 50–80 ft., branchlets pubescent, reddish-brown; lvs. to ½ in. long, entire, obtuse or notched; cones to ¾ in. long. High mts., Japan. Zone 6. Smaller and hardier than *T. Sieboldii.* Cv. **'Nana'** is listed.

heterophylla (Raf.) Sarg. WESTERN H. To 200 ft. or more, branchlets hairy; lvs. to ¾ in. long, flat, grooved above, finely toothed, obtuse or acutish; cones to 1 in. long, scales longer than broad. Alaska to Calif. Zone 7. Wood valued for timber and pulp. This sp., long known as *T. Mertensiana,* may sometimes still be offered under that name.

macrophylla: a listed name of no botanical standing for *T. canadensis* cv.

Mertensiana (Bong.) Carrière. MOUNTAIN H. To 150 ft., branchlets pubescent; lvs. to 1 in. long, rounded or keeled above, bluish-green, acutish; cones to 3 in. long. Alaska to Calif. Zone 6. This name was formerly misapplied in hort. to *T. heterophylla.* Cv. **'Argentea'.** Lvs. bluish-white. Cv. **'Microphylla'** is listed.

microphylla: a listed name of no botanical standing for *T. canadensis* cv. or *T. Mertensiana* cv.

Sargentii: a listed name of no botanical standing for *T. canadensis* cv. 'Pendula'.

Sieboldii Carrière. JAPANESE H., SIEBOLD H. To 100 ft., branchlets glabrous; lvs. entire, notched at apex, white bands beneath very narrow; cones to 1¼ in. long. Japan. Zone 6.

TSUSIOPHYLLUM Maxim. *Ericaceae.* One sp., a semi-evergreen shrub, native to Japan; lvs. simple, alt., entire; fls. white or pinkish, 1–6 in terminal clusters, calyx 5-parted, corolla tubular, stamens 5, included, anthers opening by slits; fr. a caps. Distinguished from *Rhododendron* in having corolla tubular and stamens included.

Tanakae Maxim. Prostrate, to 1½ ft.; lvs. elliptic to obovate, to ¾ in. long, setose above, glabrous and glaucous beneath except on midrib; fls. to ½ in. long, corolla pubescent, with short, spreading lobes. Interesting for the rock garden. Zone 6.

TUBERARIA (Dunal) Spach. *Cistaceae.* About 12 spp. of ann. or per. herbs, with basal lf. rosette; lvs. 3-veined; fl. sts. erect; fls. yellow, terminal, sepals 5, the outer 2 usually smaller, stigma more or less sessile; fr. a 3-valved caps. Sometimes considered a section of *Helianthemum,* but distinguished by its basal lf. rosette and sessile stigma.

guttata (L.) Fourr. [*Helianthemum guttatum* (L.) Mill.]. Villous ann., to 12 in.; lvs. obovate to lanceolate, flat, uppermost lvs. linear, more or less revolute; fls. to ¾ in. across, long-pedicelled, in short terminal racemes, petals usually with dark spot at base. Eur.

lignosa (Sweet) Sampaio [*T. vulgaris* Willk.; *Helianthemum Tuberaria* (L.) Mill.]. Per., to 15 in.; lvs. obovate-lanceolate to elliptic, to 2 in. long, narrowed to short petiole; fl. sts. unbranched; fls. about 1¼ in. across, 3–7 in bracted cymes, petals unspotted. W. Medit. region.

praecox Grosser [*Helianthemum praecox* Hort.]. Slender, unbranched, gray-villous ann.; uppermost lvs. with stipules ⅓ as long as lvs.; petals unspotted, scarcely longer than sepals. Cent. Medit. region.

vulgaris: *T. lignosa.*

TULBAGHIA L. *Amaryllidaceae.* About 24 spp. of per., tuberous or cormous herbs, native to trop. and s. Afr.; fls. many, in a terminal umbel subtended by 2 spathe valves, perianth urceolate or salverform, tube long, often cylindrical, lobes short, corona present, ringlike or consisting of 3 distinct scales opp. inner lobes, stamens included in tube, ovary superior; fr. a caps. Plants, at least the tuber or corm, usually with an onionlike odor.

Adapted to pot culture in the North, or may be grown in the open in the South in a light sandy soil. Propagated by seeds and offsets.

cepacea L.f. To 1½ ft.; lvs. usually 4–8, sometimes to 12, linear, to 8 in. long and ½ in. wide; umbel 6–12-fld.; fls. bright lilac, to ½ in. long, pedicels slightly shorter. S. Afr.

fragrans Verd. SWEET GARLIC, PINK AGAPANTHUS. To 1½ ft.; lvs. 5–7, 10–12 in. long, ¾ in. wide; umbel 30–40-fld.; fls. sweet-scented, bright lilac, ½ in. long, pedicels to 1¾ in. long. S. Afr.

violacea Harv. SOCIETY GARLIC. To 2½ ft.; lvs. usually 4–8, erect, linear, to 1 ft. long, acute, channelled at base; umbel 7–16 (or to 20)-fld.; fls. bright lilac, about ¾ in. long, lobes lanceolate, with deeper colored median stripe, pedicels violet, to 1½ in. long. S. Afr.

TULIPA L. TULIP. *Liliaceae.* Between 50 and 150 spp. of hardy spring-blooming, bulbous, per. herbs, native to temp. areas of the Old World, particularly in cent. Asia; bulb tunicate, tunics of various textures and variously hairy to glabrous inside; lvs. basal or borne on the st.; fls. basal or borne on the st.; fls. campanulate to rotate, in most colors except blue, usually solitary, perianth segms. 6, separate, without nectaries, stamens 6, anthers basifixed, stigma 3-lobed and sessile in garden kinds; fr. a 3-valved, loculicidal caps., seeds many, flat.

Most modern garden tulips are the result of extensive horticultural breeding and selection, begun by European gardeners during the latter half of the sixteenth century following the introduction of the first tulips from the gardens of Turkey. It is thought that they had their ultimate origin, however, in *T. Gesnerana* or, in some cases, in the dwarf *T. suaveolens* of southern Russia.

In addition to these complex hybrids, many tulip species are cultivated, especially in rock gardens and other specialized plantings. They and their immediate derivatives form a horticultural group known as species or botanical tulips. They have furnished such outstanding cultivars as *T. Fosterana* cv. 'Madam Lefeber' ['Red Emperor'], and many hybrids, such as the Peacock Tulips [*T. Greigii* × *T. Kaufmanniana*]. Many of this group are among the first tulips to flower each spring.

The *Classified List*, revised 1971, uses the following scheme for the classification of cultivated tulips:

Early
1. SINGLE EARLY TULIPS.
2. DOUBLE EARLY TULIPS.

Midseason
3. MENDEL TULIPS. Chiefly the result of crosses between the old Duc van Tol and Darwin Tulips. Single; plants seldom more than 20 in. high.
4. TRIUMPH TULIPS. Chiefly the result of crosses between Single Early Tulips and Late (May-flowering) Tulips. Single; plants generally of stouter build than Mendel Tulips and seldom more than 20 in. high.
5. DARWIN HYBRID TULIPS. Chiefly the result of crossing Darwin Tulips with *Tulipa Fosterana* and the result of crossing other tulips with tulip species when the offspring have the same habit and show little evidence of the wild species; single.

Late or May-flowering
6. DARWIN TULIPS. Single; tall; lower part of flower usually rectangular in outline.
7. LILY-FLOWERED TULIPS. Single; flowers with pointed, reflexed segments.
8. COTTAGE TULIPS (SINGLE LATE TULIPS). Tulips which do not belong to division 6 or 7. Single; flowers often long or egg-shaped.
9. REMBRANDT TULIPS. Broken Tulips, striped or marked brown, bronze, black, red, pink, or purple on red, white, or yellow ground.
10. PARROT TULIPS. Tulips with laciniate petals.
11. DOUBLE LATE TULIPS (PEONY-FLOWERED TULIPS).

Species (Wild plants and their cultivars, and those hybrids in which the wild plant is evident.)
12. KAUFMANNIANA, varieties and hybrids. Very early-flowering, sometimes with mottled foliage.
13. FOSTERANA, varieties and hybrids. Large, early-flowering, sometimes with mottled or striped foliage.
14. GREIGII, varieties and hybrids. Flowering later than Kaufmanniana Tulips, always with mottled or striped foliage.
15. OTHER SPECIES, and their varieties and hybrids.

Cultivar names of tulips may be found in the latest edition of the *Classified List and International Register of Tulip Names*, an alphabetical listing of all names that have been published for cultivated tulips, including specific epithets as well as cultivar names, and synonyms of those.

Tulips are planted in autumn, usually in Oct. in the North. The soil should be deep, fertile, and well-drained. The bulbs may sit 4–6 in. below the surface, depending somewhat on size and soil, and 4–6 or 8 in. apart, depending on the size and variety. For uniform results in height and blooming season, the bulbs should be graded to one size and set in one kind of soil at the same depth; in making pattern beds, it is well to remove the soil, firm the undersoil, place the bulbs carefully, then cover with soil without disturbing them. Mulch freely for winter. After 2 or 3 years, the tulip planting becomes crowded, and it is well to take up the bulbs after the leaves have ripened and replant only the best ones. For pattern beds, new bulbs are set each year.

Tulips force readily. Strong bulbs are placed in pots or boxes in autumn, set in a frame or other outdoor area, and covered a few in. with a mulch of leaves, litter, or even light earth until the pots are well filled with roots, in 4–6 weeks. Five or 6 bulbs of the usual single forcing kinds may be placed in a 6 in. pot or pan, and 6–8 in a 7 in. pot, and the bulbs covered to the tip. When the bulbs are well rooted, pots may be brought to a fairly warm building until growth is well started, when they may be placed in the conservatory or living room; it is well to have a sufficient supply so that pots may be brought in every 10 days or 2 weeks for succession. The best season for bloom is from the beginning of the year till spring. Early tulips are sometimes forced in water glasses, like hyacinths. After blooming in the house, the bulbs are usually discarded, although they may be transferred to the border, where they may flower after a year or two.

Propagation of tulips is usually effected by the natural increase of the bulbs by means of offsets or young bulbs; these, planted by themselves, produce a blooming bulb in 1 or 2 years. Expert propagators stimulate the formation of offsets by cutting the bulb. Seeds may be used if one desires to produce new kinds, or for rare species; 3 or more years are required to bring seedlings to blooming size;

acuminata Vahl ex Hornem. [*T. cornuta* Delile; *T. cornuta* var. *stenopetala* (Mord. de Laun. ex Loisel.) Hort.]. TURKISH T. Tunic papery, with hairs inside near base and apex, st. 1–1½ ft.; lvs. 3–5, rather narrow, undulate; fls. to 4 in. long, perianth segms. light yellow or pink, slender, very long-acuminate. Midseason. Probably of garden origin; perhaps only a variant of *T. Gesnerana.*

alpestris: *T. australis.*

Aucherana Bak. Tunic with a few hairs inside, st. to 8 in.; lvs. 2–5, basal, linear, to 6 in. long, undulate; fls. star-shaped when open, to 1¼ in. long, perianth segms. pink, with yellow-brown basal blotch inside, striped green or brown outside, stamens yellow, filaments hairy at base. Syria and Iran.

australis Link [*T. alpestris* Jord. & Fourr.]. Tunic hairy inside, st. to 10 in. high; lvs. 3–5, linear, folded, to 8 in. long or more; fls. fragrant, erect, nodding and urn-shaped in bud, star-shaped when open, to 2 in. long, perianth segms. yellow inside, reddish outside, pointed, stamens yellow, filaments hairy at base. Midseason. Medit. region.

Batalinii Regel. Tunic hairy inside at apex, st. to 6 in.; lvs. linear, to 7 in. long, glaucous; fls. to 2 in. long, perianth segms. pale yellow, with darker basal blotch inside, obtuse or nearly so, stamens yellow. Early. Uzbek S.S.R. Perhaps only a pale form of *T. linifolia.*

biflora Pall. Tunic silky inside at apex, st. 5 in., hairy; lvs. strap-shaped, 4–5 in. long, hairy; fls. 1–5, star-shaped when open, to ¾ in. long, perianth segms. white, with yellow basal blotch inside, stained red and green outside, inner segms. with green median line, stamens yellow with purple-tipped anthers, filaments hairy at base. S. Russia. Var. turkestanica: *T. turkestanica.*

Burpeeana: *T. Fosterana* cv.

Celsiana: *T. patens.*

chrysantha Boiss. ex Bak. Tunic firm, woolly inside, st. to 6 in.; lvs. 3 or 4, lanceolate to linear, to 6 in. long, glaucous, undulate; fls. to 1 in. long, perianth segms. bright yellow, stained red outside, outer segms. acuminate. Iran and nw. India. Material offered under this name is probably *T. Clusiana* var. *chrysantha.*

Clusiana DC. LADY T. Tunic leathery, woolly inside near apex, st. to 1 ft.; lvs. about 4, linear, folded lengthwise, to 10 in. long; open fls. almost starlike, to 2 in. long, perianth segms. pointed, white or yellowish, with carmine basal blotch inside, exterior of outer segms. red, margined white, stamens purple. Midseason. Iran to Afghanistan; naturalized in s. Eur. Var. **chrysantha** (A. D. Hall) Sealy. Perianth segms. yellow within, blotchless, stamens yellow. India. Var. **stellata** (Hook.) Regel [*T. stellata* Hook.]. Fls. with yellow blotch inside, stamens yellow. Afghanistan and nw. India.

cornuta: *T. acuminata.* Var. **stenopetala:** *T. acuminata.*

cretica Boiss. & Heldr. Stoloniferous, tunic with a few hairs inside at base and apex, st. to 8 in.; lvs. 2 or 3, lanceolate, almost flat, glabrous; fls. 1–3 per st., to 1¼ in. long, perianth segms. white, tinged pink, with yellow basal blotch inside, outer segms. spreading, inner erect, stamens yellow, filaments hairy at base. Crete.

dasyantha: a listed name of no botanical standing.

dasystemon (Regel) Regel. Tunic papery, hairy inside, st. to 7 in.; lvs. 2, lanceolate to almost linear; fls. solitary, perianth segms. acute, to 1¼ in. long, yellow, outer segms. sordid violet outside, stamens yellow, filaments hairy at base; caps. short-beaked. Cent. Asia. Material offered under this name is probably *T. tarda.*

Didieri Jord. Tunic with a few long hairs inside, st. to 1 ft.; lvs. 4, to 8 in. long, undulate, ciliate; fls. large, perianth segms. bright crimson, with faintly yellow-margined olive or black basal blotch inside, filaments black, with yellow at both ends, anthers yellow. S. Eur.

Eichleri Regel. Tunic hairy at base inside, st. to 8 in., slightly pubescent; lvs. 4 or 5, broadly strap-shaped, to 8 in. long, glaucous; fls. to 4 in. long, perianth segms. brilliant glossy scarlet, with yellow-margined black basal blotch inside, light buff outside, stamens deep violet. Turkestan. Cv. '**Excelsa**'. Fls. large, bright scarlet. Cv. '**Maxima**'. Fls. later, larger, crimson-scarlet.

elegans Hort. ex Bak. Tunic glabrous inside, st. to 1½ ft., pubescent; lvs. strap-shaped-lanceolate, to 10 in. long, arising from lower half of st.; fls. to 3½ in. long, perianth segms. scarlet, with yellow base, gradually narrowed to acute point, stamens purple, glabrous. A garden plant not known from the wild; perhaps not distinct from *T. Gesnerana*. Cv. '**Alba**'. Fls. white.

florentina: *T. sylvestris*. Var. **odorata**: *T. sylvestris*.

formosa: *Tulipa* cv. 'Formosa', one of the Cottage Tulips, with yellow and green fls.

Fosterana W. Irving. Tunic silky-hairy inside, st. to 10 in., slightly hairy; lvs. 3 or 4, broadly ovate, to 8 in. long; fls. opening flat, to 4 in. long, perianth segms. brilliant scarlet, with yellow-margined black basal blotch inside, stamens black. Turkestan. Cvs. include: '**Princeps**', fls. large, brilliant orange-red, with yellow blotch inside; '**Purissima**' [*T. purissima* Hort.], fls. large, milky-white; '**Burpeeana**' [*T. Burpeeana* Hort.], to 16 in., fls. bright vermilion, flushed fiery orange, with a yellow base.

fulgens: *T. Gesnerana*.

galatica Freyn. Tunic silver-hairy inside, st. to 8 in.; lvs. 4, linear-lanceolate, to 5 in. long, acuminate; fls. campanulate, to about 3 in. long, perianth segms. pale yellow, with a smoky yellow basal blotch inside, stamens golden-yellow. Asia Minor.

Gesnerana L. [*T. fulgens* Hort. ex Bak.]. Tunic papery, with a few hairs inside, st. to 2 ft.; lvs. 3–5, lanceolate to nearly ovate, to 6 in. long, glaucous; fls. to 3 in. long, cup-shaped, opening widely, perianth segms. dull crimson-scarlet, with yellow-margined olive or black basal blotch inside, stamens deep purple. E. Eur. and Asia Minor. Most of the cvs. of the common tall late-flowering garden tulips are derived chiefly from this sp., and this name has been frequently used in a broad sense to include them also.

Greigii Regel. Tunic membranous, with a few silky hairs inside toward apex, st. to 8 in. or more, downy; lvs. 3 or 4, lanceolate, to 8 in. long, usually streaked with purple-brown; fls. to 3 in. long, perianth segms. orange-scarlet, with yellow-margined black basal blotch inside, stamens black. Early. Turkestan.

Grullemansii: a group of tulips derived from crossing *T. Kaufmanniana* with Darwin Tulips.

Hageri Heldr. Tunic membranous, with long silky hairs inside at apex, st. to 1 ft.; lvs. 4 or 5, strap-shaped, to 8 in. long, green with red margins; fls. 1–4, to 2 in. long, perianth segms. coppery to scarlet, with olive basal blotch inside, outer segms. buff to green outside, inner segms. coppery with green midrib outside, stamens brown to olive, filaments hairy at base. Early. Greece, w. Asia Minor. Cv. '**Splendens**'. Fls. several, globular, coppery-red inside, dark crimson-scarlet outside.

Hoogiana B. Fedtsch. Tunic papery, woolly inside, st. to 1 ft., glabrous; lvs. up to 8, to 8 in. long, folded, glaucous; fls. to 6 in. long, perianth segms. bright scarlet, with yellow-margined olive-black basal blotch inside, stamens black, filaments half as long as anthers. Cent. Asia.

humilis Herb. Tunic sparingly hairy inside toward apex, st. to 4 in.; lvs. 2–4, linear, to 4 in. long; fls. 2½ in. long, perianth segms. acute, pale purple, with yellow basal blotch inside, reddish-green outside, filaments hairy at base. Iran.

ingens J. M. C. Hoog. Tunic papery, brown, with long silky hairs inside, st. to 10 in., red, slightly hairy; lvs. 3–5, lanceolate, to 10 in. long, glaucous; fls. to 4½ in. long, perianth segms. brilliant glossy vermilion, with black basal blotch inside to ⅓ length of segm., stamens deep purple. Early. Cent. Asia.

Kaufmanniana Regel. WATER-LILY T. Tunic papery, sparsely hairy inside, st. to 8 in. long, slightly hairy; lvs. 3–5, broadly oblong, to 10 in. long; fls. to 3 in. long, opening flat and starlike, perianth segms. varying from white to pink or scarlet or yellow, with yellow basal blotch and carmine nerves inside, stamens yellow. Turkestan. Cv. '**Aurea**'. Fls. golden-yellow, banded with crimson, segms. long-acuminate. Cv. '**Coccinea**'. Fls. scarlet.

Kolpakowskiana Regel. Tunic thick, with a few hairs inside near base and apex, st. to 6 in.; lvs. 2–4, to 8 in. long, nearly flat; fls. 1 or 2, to 2¼ in. long, opening flat, then reflexed, perianth segms. yellow, not blotched, reddish or olive outside, stamens yellow. Turkestan.

kuschkensis B. Fedtsch. ex Sealy. Tunic woolly inside, st. to about 9 in.; lvs. 4, narrowly lanceolate, to 8 in. long, glaucous; fls. to 3 in. long, opening flat, perianth segms. vermilion-scarlet, with yellow-margined basal blotch inside, duller outside, stamens black. Turkestan and Afghanistan.

lanata Regel. Stoloniferous, tunic papery, woolly inside, st. to 20 in., downy; lvs. 4 or 5, lanceolate, to 10 in. long; fls. to 3 in. long, perianth segms. rich vermilion, not glossy, with yellow-margined dark olive basal blotch inside, filaments black, anthers purple. Turkestan, nw. Iran, Afghanistan.

linifolia Regel. Tunic leathery, with yellowish-woolly hairs inside, st. to 6 in.; lvs. in a basal rosette, linear, to 5 in. long, with red margins; fls. to 2 in. long, perianth segms. scarlet, glossy, with black basal blotch inside, stamens black. Uzbek S.S.R.

lutea Freyn. St. to 1 ft. or more, glabrous; lvs. somewhat falcate, to 14 in. long, erect, pale green, margins undulate and somewhat ciliate; fls. campanulate, perianth segms. yellow, oblong-ovate, erect. Cent. Asia Minor. Var. **major** is listed.

Marjolettii Perr. & Song. Tunic papery, with a few hairs inside, st. to 2 ft.; lvs. 3–5, narrow, acuminate; fls. over 1½ in. long, perianth segms. yellow, becoming white, tinted purple outside, filaments blue-black, anthers yellow. Midseason. Savoy (se. France). Doubtfully distinct botanically from *T. Gesnerana*.

Maximowiczii Regel. Tunic leathery, with woolly, somewhat bristly hairs inside, st. to 6 in.; lvs. scattered on st., erect, linear, to 5 in. long, margins flat; fls. to 2 in. long, perianth segms. scarlet, glossy, with white-margined black basal blotch inside, stamens black. Uzbek S.S.R. and Afghanistan. Perhaps not specifically distinct from *T. linifolia*.

mauriana: *T. mauritiana*.

mauritiana Jord. [*T. mauriana* Jord. & Fourr.]. Tunic glabrous, st. to 1 ft.; lvs. about 4, broadly lanceolate, undulate; perianth segms. red, with yellow basal blotch inside, filaments yellow, anthers dark violet. Savoy (se. France).

Micheliana J. M. C. Hoog. Tunic brown, papery, with a few silky hairs inside at base, st. to 1 ft.; lvs. 3, lanceolate to linear-lanceolate, to 6 in. long, glaucous, undulate, often striped brown; fls. to 2¼ in. long, perianth segms. vermilion-scarlet, tinged lilac outside, with yellow-margined black basal blotch half the length of segm. inside, stamens black. Turkmen S.S.R. and Iran.

montana Lindl. Tunic leathery, purplish, hairy inside toward apex, st. 8 in.; lvs. 3 or 4, oblong-lanceolate to linear, to 4 in. long, long-acuminate, glaucous; fls. to 2 in. long, perianth segms. deep crimson, with black basal blotch inside, paler outside, filaments scarlet, anthers yellow. Turkmen S.S.R. and Iran.

oculus-solis St. Amans. Stoloniferous, tunic papery, brown, felty with silky hairs inside, st. to 8 in., glabrous; lvs. 4, oblong, to 10 in. long, erect, glabrous; fls. to 3 in. long, campanulate, perianth segms. dull scarlet, with yellow-margined black basal blotch inside, dull green and brown outside, stamens black. Early. S. Eur.

Orphanidea Boiss. ex Heldr. Tunic tough, brown, with silky hairs inside toward apex, st. to 8 in.; lvs. 3 or 4, linear, to 8 in. long, folded; fls. to 2 in. long, opening flat, perianth segms. orange to brown, with poorly defined basal blotch inside, tinged with purple or green outside, filaments olive-brown. Early. Greece.

Ostrowskiana Regel. Tunic with a few hairs inside near base and apex, st. to 8 in.; lvs. 2–4, oblong, to 1 ft. long; fls. to 3 in. long, perianth segms. bright scarlet, with olive basal blotch inside, filaments yellow, stained olive, anthers purple. E. Turkestan.

patens Agardh ex Schult. & Schult.f. [*T. Celsiana* DC.; *T. persica* Willd. ex Kunth]. Tunic brown, st. to 1 ft.; lvs. 2 or 3, to 5½ in. long; fls. to 1¾ in. long, fragrant, perianth segms. whitish or yellowish, with yellow basal blotch, stamens yellow, filaments hairy at base. Siberia. Probably not in cult.

persica: *T. patens*.

polychroma Stapf. Stoloniferous, tunic felty with silky hairs inside, st. to 6 in.; lvs. 2–4, linear, to 6 in. long, erect, glaucous; fls. 1–5, to 1¾ in. long, cup-shaped, spreading, perianth segms. white, tinged pink or purple, with yellow basal blotch ⅓ length of segm. inside, stamens yellow, with black apex, filaments hairy at base. Iran and Afghanistan.

praecox Ten. Stoloniferous, tunic papery, felty with woolly hairs inside, st. stout, to 20 in., slightly pubescent; lvs. 3–5, oblong-ovate to oblong-lanceolate, to 1 ft. long, very glaucous; fls. to 3½ in. long, perianth segms. dull scarlet, with yellow-margined olive basal blotch inside, outer segms. dull orange or green outside, reflexing, inner segms. with median yellow stripe outside, stamens deep olive to black, filaments half as long as anthers. N. Italy.

praestans Hort. van Tuberg. Tunic leathery, with few silky hairs inside, st. to 1 ft., slightly hairy; lvs. 5 or 6, narrowly lanceolate, to 10 in. long, long-acuminate, slightly hairy, channelled; fls. 1–4, to 2½ in. long, cup-shaped, perianth segms. brick-red, without a blotch, filaments vermilion, anthers purple. Cent. Asia.

primulina Bak. Tunic thick, hairs few near apex inside, st. to 8 in.; lvs. 4 or 5, strap-shaped, to 8 in. long, glabrous; fls. 1 or 2, about 2 in. long, on long, drooping pedicels, opening in afternoon, fragrant, perianth segms. creamy-white, becoming pale yellow toward base, green and lavender outside, filaments greenish-yellow with hairy base, anthers yellow. Algeria.

princeps: *T. Fosterana* cv.

pulchella (Regel) Fenzl ex Bak. Tunic rough, hairy inside at base and apex, st. to 4 in.; lvs. 2 or 3, strap-shaped, to 6 in. long; fls. 1–3, to 1¼ in. long, opening flat, perianth segms. crimson to purple, with white-margined bluish basal blotch inside, outer segms. gray or green outside, filaments white, apically white or blue, basally yellow and hairy, anthers deep purple. Asia Minor. Cvs. are: 'Humilis', fls. violet-pink; 'Pallida', fls. white, with deep blue blotch inside; 'Violacea', fls. violet.

purissima: *T. Fosterana* cv.

rubra maxima: *Tulipa* cv. 'Rubra Maxima', one of the Double Early Tulips, with scarlet fls.

saxatilis Sieber ex K. Spreng. Stoloniferous, tunic with a few hairs inside at base and apex, st. to 1 ft.; lvs. basal, to 8 in. long, shining, flat, glabrous; fls. 1–3, to 2 in. long, opening almost to a flat cup, fragrant, perianth segms. pale lilac, with yellow basal blotch inside, hairy on edges near base, filaments orange-yellow, hairy at base, anthers purple or chocolate-brown. Early. Crete.

Schrenkii: *T. suaveolens.*

sharonensis Dinsm. Tunic papery, woolly inside, st. to 6 in., mostly underground; lvs. 3 or 4, narrowly linear to lanceolate, to 6 in. long, often overtopping the fls., margins wavy and ciliate, circinate at tip; fls. to 1¼ in. long, perianth segms. dark scarlet, with yellow-margined dark olive basal blotch inside, paler outside, stamens black. Israel.

Sprengeri Bak. Tunic papery, with a few silky hairs inside, st. to 1 ft.; lvs. 4–6, basal, narrow, to 10 in. long, shining, glabrous; fls. to 2½ in. long, perianth segms. light brownish-crimson, without a blotch, lighter outside, outer segms. recurving, filaments scarlet, anthers yellow. Very late. Asia Minor.

stellata: *T. Clusiana* var.

suaveolens Roth [*T. Schrenkii* Regel]. Tunic brown, papery, with a few hairs inside at base and apex, st. to 6 in.; lvs. 3 or 4, elliptic-lanceolate; fls. fragrant, to 2 in. long, perianth segms. crimson-scarlet, with yellow, black, or olive basal blotch, stamens yellow. S. U.S.S.R. to Iraq. Most of the cvs. of the common short early garden tulips are derived chiefly from this sp.

sylvestris L. [*T. florentina* Hort. ex Bak.; *T. florentina* var. *odorata* Hort.]. Stoloniferous, tunic bright yellow, tinged with red, with a few hairs inside at base and apex, st. to 1 ft.; lvs. 2 or 3, to 10 in. long, glaucous; fls. 1 or 2, erect, but nodding in bud, fragrant, perianth segms. clear yellow, somewhat green and red outside, to 2 in. long, stamens yellow or orange, filaments hairy at base. Midseason to late. Eur., N. Afr., Iran. Spreading and forming large colonies, but frequently rather shy-flowering. Cv. 'Major', free-flowering, each st. with 2 or 3 golden-yellow fls. Cv. 'Tabriz'. Taller, larger-fld., more free-flowering than the usual form. Iran.

tarda Stapf [*T. dasystemon* Hort., not Regel]. Stoloniferous, tunic thin, yellow, with a few hairs inside at base and tip, st. to 3 in.; lvs. 4–7, in a rosette, linear to lanceolate, to 9 in. long; fls. 1–7, to 2 in. long, buds erect, opening to a flat star, perianth segms. white with yellow base, outer segms. tinged green and red outside, filaments yellow, hairy at base, anthers yellow. Turkestan.

Tubergeniana Hort. van Tuberg. Tunic papery, with silky-brown hairs inside, st. to 1 ft., pubescent; lvs. 4 or 5, to 1 ft. long, erect, long-acuminate, glaucous, hairy; fls. to 3½ in. long, perianth segms. bright glossy vermilion, with yellow-margined olive basal blotch inside, filaments black, anthers dark purple. Cent. Asia.

turkestanica (Regel) Regel [*T. biflora* var. *turkestanica* (Regel) Hort.]. Stoloniferous, tunic purple or bright crimson, densely lined with silky hairs above, st. to 8 in.; fls. 1–7, ivory-white, with orange basal blotch, about 1¼ in. long, outer segms. reddish outside, filaments orange, hairy, anthers purple or chocolate-brown. Turkestan.

urumiensis Stapf. Tunic dark brown, with a few hairs toward base inside, st. mostly underground, to 2 in. high above the ground; lvs. 2–4, linear, to 5 in. long, channelled; buds nodding, but fls. erect, 1 or 2, urn-shaped, opening widely in sunlight, golden-yellow, to 1½ in. long,

outer segms. red and olive outside, stamens yellow, filaments hairy at base. Nw. Iran.

Urumoffii T. Hay. Tunic dark, hairy at base inside, st. to 10 in.; lvs. 3 or 4, broadly lanceolate, to 10 in. long, glaucous, margins wavy; fls. yellow, somewhat grayish outside, to 2 in. long. Bulgaria.

violacea Boiss. & Buhse. Tunic tough, yellow or reddish, with a few hairs at base and tip inside, st. to 1 ft.; lvs. 3–5, lanceolate or linear, to 6 in. long; fls. starlike when fully open, crimson, violet, or purple, with a yellow-margined blue or olive basal blotch, to 2 in. long, stamens purple, filaments hairy at base, ovary deep purple to nearly black. N. Iran and Kurdistan.

viridiflora: *Tulipa* cv. 'Viridiflora', one of the Cottage Tulips, with yellow and green fls.

Whittallii A. D. Hall. Tunic tough, slightly hairy inside, st. to 1 ft.; lvs. 3 or 4, to 8 in. long; fls. bright orange, with dark olive basal blotch, to 2½ in. long, filaments dark green to olive, hairy at base, alternately long and short, anthers nearly black. Izmir (W. Turkey).

Wilsoniana J. M. C. Hoog. Tunic thick, brown, woolly toward apex inside, st. to 8 in.; lvs. about 5, linear-lanceolate, to 4¾ in. long, glaucous, undulate, with narrow red cartilaginous margin; fls. vermilion-scarlet, with black basal blotch, to 2 in. long, filaments black below, red above, anthers yellow. Turkmen S.S.R.

TUMION: *TORREYA.*

TUNICA: see *Petrorhagia.* **T. rhodopea:** *Petrorhagia illyrica* subsp. *Haynaldiana.*

TUPIDANTHUS Hook.f. & T. Thoms. *Araliaceae.* One sp., native to trop. Asia; in cult. a glabrous shrub, in nature a high-climbing scandent woody vine; lvs. palmately compound, lfts. 7–9, whorled at the end of the petiole, entire; fls. few, large, in simple or compound umbels or in umbels arranged in panicles, pedicels green, thick, petals fleshy, united, stamens many, in 2 or more series around the central disc, ovary many-celled, stigmas sessile; fr. a drupe, pyrenes many.

calyptratus Hook.f. & T. Thoms. Four to 12 ft.; lfts. drooping, leathery, to 12 in. long, petioles cylindrical, to 14 in. long; fls. greenish, ¾–1¼ in. in diam.; fr. globose. India to Cambodia. Zone 10.

TURBINA Raf. *Convolvulaceae.* Perhaps more than 10 spp. of herbaceous or nearly woody twiners of trop. Amer. and Afr., extending into S. Afr.; lvs. ovate, cordate at base, entire; calyx lobes ovate to oblong, obtuse, enlarging in fr.; corolla campanulate, white; fr. woody or leathery. Closely related to *Ipomoea* but differing in having fr. indehiscent, mostly woody, enclosed in enlarged calyx. Differs from the Asiatic *Argyreia* in having fr. ovoid-oblong, hard and woody or thin-walled and leathery, and the corolla glabrous or only sparsely hairy outside.

corymbosa (L.) Raf. [*Ipomoea sidifolia* (HBK) Choisy; *Rivea corymbosa* (L.) H. G. Hallier]. Lvs. ovate, to 4 in. long; corolla to 1¼ in. long, white with yellowish center, glabrous or sparsely hairy outside along stripes. Trop. Amer.; introd. and naturalized locally in the Old World. Known in Mex. as OLOLIUQUI and used by Indians as a hallucinogen in religious ceremonies and in medicine.

TURBINICARPUS: *STROMBOCACTUS.*

TURNERA L. *Turneraceae.* About 60 spp. of herbs and low shrubs, pubescent with simple hairs, native to trop. Amer. and Afr.; lvs. simple, petioled, with 1 or 2 pairs of glands at base; fls. mostly solitary, axillary, often showy, petals yellow, white, or mauve, stamens attached to fl. tube below petals, stigmas fimbriate; fr. a many-seeded caps.

Propagated by seeds, cuttings, and division.

ulmifolia L. YELLOW ALDER. Shrubby, to 2 ft. or more, densely pubescent; lvs. lanceolate to oblong-ovate, to 4 in. long, serrate to crenate-serrate, acute to acuminate, basally cuneate, with 2 glands near apex of petiole, petiole and peduncle united; fls. yellow, sometimes violet at base, to 2 in. across, opening only in the morning. Trop. Amer. Zone 10b.

TURNERACEAE A. DC. TURNERA FAMILY. Dicot.; 8 genera of herbs, shrubs, and trees of trop. and warm regions; lvs.

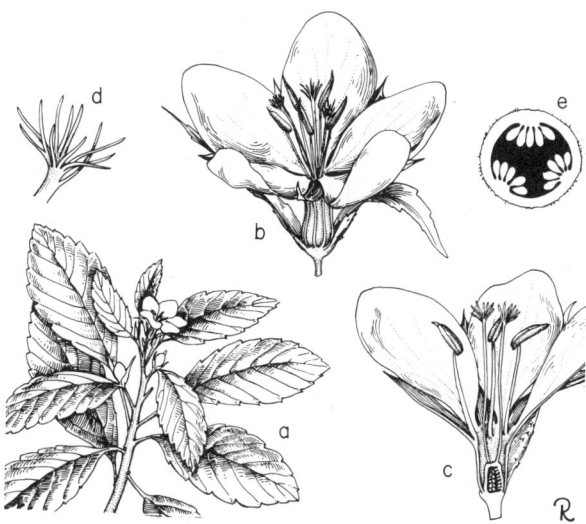

TURNERACEAE. *Turnera ulmifolia*: **a**, flowering branch, × ¼; **b**, flower, × 1; **c**, flower, vertical section, × 1; **d**, stigma, × 5; **e**, ovary, cross section, × 10. (From Lawrence, *Taxonomy of Vascular Plants*.)

alt., petioled, simple; peduncles sometimes united with petioles, fls. axillary, regular, sepals, petals, and stamens 5, on fl. tube, ovary superior, 1-celled, styles 3; fr. a caps. *Turnera* is occasionally cult.

TURNIP. The common turnip, grown for its edible underground fleshy stem and root, is *Brassica Rapa*, Rapifera Group. Turnips are hardy cool-season plants of Old World origin, but they will not withstand as much frost as rutabagas (see *Rutabaga*). They have been grown for several thousand years, the fine-textured sorts for man and the coarser types for his animals. Turnip tops are also used for greens and forage.

The true turnips are mostly "flat," that is, without a long neck and with the root broad rather than long, although there are exceptions in the shape; most of those grown in this country have white or light flesh; the substance is less firm and durable than in the rutabaga. All the usual turnips are short-season plants; the supply for late autumn and winter use in the northern states is grown from seeds sown in July—"on the twenty-fifth of July sow your turnips wet or dry" is an old saw. Seed is produced from roots planted out after the winter or that may be left in the ground in very mild climates; the early cultivars often run to seed the first year if sown very early and not gathered at the maturity of the root. The seeds are broadcast or sown in drills that are 10–20 inches apart; it is necessary to thin the plants well if the best roots are desired. For late spring or summer use, seeds of early cultivars are sown as soon as the ground is fit. The commonest pest of turnips is aphis, which is controlled (as on cabbage) by thorough spraying or dusting.

TURRAEA L. *Meliaceae*. About 90 spp. of small trees or shrubs, of the Old World tropics; lvs. alt., simple, entire or obtusely lobed; fls. white, reddish, or yellowish, in axillary clusters or racemes, calyx 4–5-lobed or -toothed, petals 4 or 5, very long, strap-shaped, stamens 8–10, filaments united in a long cylinder, ovary 4–20-celled; caps. woody or leathery.

Grown outdoors in southern Calif. and sometimes under glass.

obtusifolia Hochst. SOUTH AFRICAN HONEYSUCKLE. Shrub, to 3 ft., brs. glabrous, leafy; lvs. often crowded on short shoots, obovate or oblanceolate, to rhomboid-oblanceolate, to 2 in. long, entire, often 3-lobed at the apex; fls. 1–4, in axillary clusters, white, petals 1 in. long or more, style exserted, longer than petals. S. Afr. Zone 10.

TURRICULA Macbr. *Hydrophyllaceae*. One sp., a per. herb of s. Calif. and Baja Calif.; lvs. alt., sessile, simple; fls. purple, in panicled scorpioid cymes, calyx 5-parted, corolla

funnelform, 5-lobed, stamens 5, styles divided to base; fr. dehiscent into 4 valves. Differs from *Eriodictyon* in being nonwoody.

Parryi (A. Gray) Macbr. [*Eriodictyon Parryi* (A. Gray) Greene; *Nama Parryi* A. Gray]. Coarse, erect, ill-smelling, sticky-hairy, sometimes woody-based herb, to 8 ft.; lvs. crowded, lanceolate, to 1 ft. long, dentate or entire; fls. to ¾ in. long, in densely glandular-hairy infls. Summer. May be planted in its native region.

TUSSACA, TUSSACIA: *CHRYSOTHEMIS*.

TUSSILAGO L. COLTSFOOT. *Compositae* (Senecio Tribe). One sp., a stoloniferous per. herb of the Old World; lvs. basal, appearing after fls.; fl. heads solitary, scapose; disc fls. bisexual but sterile, ray fls. many, fertile; achenes linear, ribbed, pappus of white hairs.

Propagated by division, root cuttings, or seeds.

Farfara L. COLTSFOOT. Lvs. long-petioled, blades orbicular-cordate, 4–8 in. wide or more, sinuately lobed, shallowly dentate, white-floccose-tomentose, upper surface becoming glabrous; scapes scaly, purplish, woolly, to 6 in. in fl., elongating in fr.; heads to 1⅜ in. across; fls. light yellow, ray fls. narrowly linear. Eur., w. and n. Asia, N. Afr.; widely naturalized in e. N. Amer. Occasionally cult. as one of the earliest fls. of spring, but capable of becoming a pernicious weed. Fresh foliage sometimes eaten as a vegetable, dried lvs. used medicinally.

TUTCHERIA S. T. Dunn. *Theaceae*. Perhaps 8 subtrop. spp. of evergreen trees of e. Asia; lvs. alt., simple, leathery; fls. axillary, bracteoles many, imbricate, sepals and petals 5, stamens many, anthers versatile, ovary 3–6-celled; caps. with valves falling away separately from the persistent columella, seeds 2–5 in each cell, laterally compressed.

Suitable for greenhouse cultivation or outside in Zone 10. For culture see *Camellia*.

spectabilis (Champ. ex Benth.) S. T. Dunn [*Camellia spectabilis* Champ. ex Benth.]. Small tree; lvs. ovate-lanceolate, to 6 in. long, acuminate, slightly crenate, glossy above, short-petioled; peduncles short, fls. white, about 3 in. across, sepals 2, petal-like, densely tawny-tomentose on back, petals broadly obovate, emarginate; caps. 2–3 in. in diam. Se. China.

TWEEDIA Hook. & Arn. *Asclepiadaceae*. Not cult. **T. caerulea:** *Oxypetalum caeruleum*.

TYDAEA: *Kohleria*. **T. grandiflora:** see *K. gigantea*. **T. hybrida:** see *K. gigantea*.

TYPHA L. CATTAIL, CATTAIL FLAG, REED-MACE, BULRUSH. *Typhaceae*. About 15 spp. of widely distributed per. herbs of swamps, marshes, and watercourses; characters those of the family.

The leaves are used in basketry and for making woven chair seats, while the floss is a good kapok substitute. Cattails are sometimes used in bog gardens and on the margins of pools, but can be weedy unless

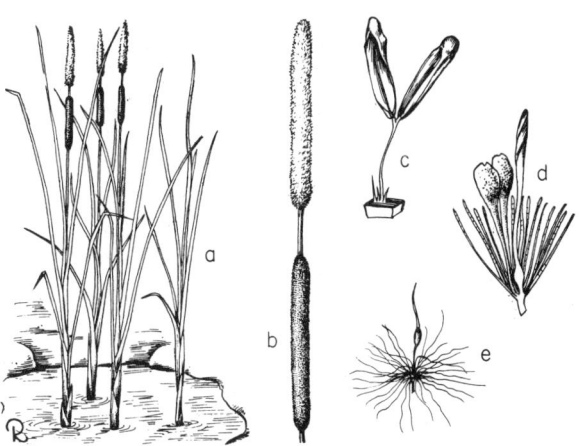

TYPHACEAE. *Typha angustifolia*: **a**, flowering plants, × ¹⁄₂₀; **b**, inflorescence, × ⅙; **c**, male flower, × 4; **d**, female flower, × 8; **e**, fruit, × 2.

restrained. Propagated usually by division, sometimes by seeds planted in pots in water.

angustifolia L. NARROW-LEAVED C., SOFT FLAG, SMALL B. To 6 ft.; lvs. to ⁵⁄₁₆ in. across; spikes ⅜–1¼ in. in diam. in fr., light brown, male and female zones usually separated by naked segm. of axis. Amer., Eur., Asia.

latifolia L. COMMON C., NAIL-ROD, BULRUSH, COSSACK ASPARAGUS. To 10 ft.; lvs. ½–1 in. across; spikes ⁵⁄₁₆–⅝ in. in diam. in fr., dark brown to black, male and female zones usually contiguous. N. Amer., Eur., Asia.

minima Hoppe. To 2½ ft.; lvs. to ⅛ in. wide; spikes to ⅜ in. in diam. in fr., to 5 in. long, brown, the male and female zones separated by a naked segm. of axis 1 in. long. Eur.

TYPHACEAE Juss. CATTAIL FAMILY. Monocot; 1 cosmopolitan genus, *Typha*, of about 10–15 spp. of widely distributed, monoecious, per. herbs of wet places, with creeping rootstocks and tall, erect, unbranched sts.; lvs. long, linear, flat, erect, parallel-veined; fls. in a dense terminal spike, male above, female below, male fls. with 2–5 united stamens, female fls. with ovary superior, 1-celled, 1-ovuled, style and stigma 1; fr. an achene, subtended by capillary bristles.

UGNI Turcz. *Myrtaceae.* About 5–15 spp. of evergreen, densely leafy shrubs, native from s. Mex. to Peru, Venezuela, and Chile; lvs. opp., simple, small, leathery; fls. solitary, axillary, 4–5-merous, stamens many, unequal, filaments somewhat flattened, short, anthers basifixed, ovary 3–5-celled, ovules several in each cell; fr. a several-seeded, round berry. Has been included in the larger genus *Myrtus*, but differs in its characteristic stamens.

Molinae Turcz. [*Eugenia Ugni* (Mol.) Hook. & Arn.; *Myrtus Ugni* Mol.]. CHILEAN GUAVA. Shrub, to 6 ft., rarely a small tree; lvs. ovate, usually broadly so, to 1 in. long, rarely longer, smooth and glossy above, paler beneath; pedicels to 1½ in. long, becoming reflexed, petals pink-tinged, erect, to ¼ in. long, concave and forming a globe enclosing the stamens and style; berry blue-black, about ¼ in. across, fragrant, edible. Chile and Bolivia. Zone 9. The fr. is sometimes used to make jam.

ULEX L. *Leguminosae* (subfamily *Faboideae*). About 25 spp. of very spiny shrubs, native to w. Eur. and N. Afr.; lvs. alt., very small, spine-tipped, often scalelike; fls. axillary, yellow, papilionaceous, stamens all united, alternately of 2 lengths; fr. a small, ovoid, dehiscent legume.

Grown as ornamentals and as cover on poor and sandy soils; propagated by seeds.

europaeus L. GORSE, FURZE, WHIN. To 6 ft., glaucous, spines to 1 in. long, deeply furrowed; fls. fragrant, ¾ in. long; fr. hairy, black, ½ in. long. Spring or all year in warm climates. W. Eur.; sometimes naturalized and often weedy. Widely cult.

hispanicus: see *Genista hispanica.*

minor Roth [*U. nanus* T. F. Forst.]. DWARF FURZE. Differs from *U. europaeus* in its smaller stature, to 3 ft.; shorter, faintly-furrowed spines, to ⅜ in. long; smaller fls., to ⅜ in. long in late summer and autumn; and persistent fr. only half as long. W. Eur.

nanus: *U. minor.*

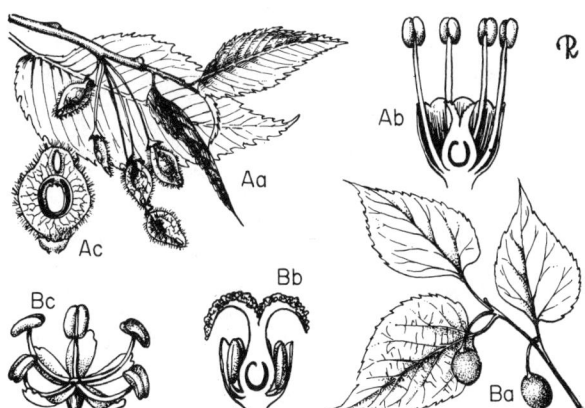

ULMACEAE. **A,** *Ulmus americana:* **Aa,** fruiting branch, × ½; **Ab,** flower, vertical section, × 4; **Ac,** fruit, vertical section, × 1. **B,** *Celtis occidentalis:* **Ba,** fruiting branch, × 1; **Bb,** bisexual flower, vertical section, × 4; **Bc,** male flower, × 6. (From Bailey, *Manual of Cultivated Plants,* ed. 2.)

ULMACEAE Mirb. ELM FAMILY. Dicot; about 15 genera and 150 spp. of usually deciduous trees and shrubs, native throughout the N. Hemisphere; lvs. alt., simple, often asymmetrical at base, petioled, stipules early deciduous; fls. small, bisexual or unisexual, calyx 3–9-parted, petals 0, stamens as many or twice as many, ovary superior, 1-celled; fr. a samara, nut, or drupe. Genera cult. as ornamentals are: *Aphananthe,*

Celtis, Hemiptelea, Holoptelea, Planera, Trema, Ulmus, and *Zelkova.*

ULMUS L. ELM. *Ulmaceae.* About 18 spp. of deciduous or rarely partly evergreen trees, native to N. Temp. Zone, in N. Amer. from Rocky Mts. to n. Mex. and in Eur. and Asia; lvs. alt., simple, toothed, usually asymmetrical at base; fls. inconspicuous, in clusters or racemes, bisexual, usually appearing before lvs. in spring, or in autumn in axils of lvs.; fr. a flat, 1-celled, 1-seeded samara with the wing surrounding the nutlet and usually notched at apex, maturing a few weeks after flowering, often conspicuous.

Elms are favorite shade and avenue trees and of easy cultivation. Practically all the species here listed are hardy in the North, some of them being among the hardiest lawn and street trees. However, they are attacked by several insects and in such case should be sprayed every year for best results. *Ulmus americana* is highly susceptible to the Dutch elm disease and should not be planted where the disease is rampant. Elms bear transplanting well. Propagated by seeds sown as soon as ripe, by layers in autumn, and some species by greenwood cuttings under glass. Cultivars may be grafted on common stocks.

alata Michx. WAHOO E., WINGED E., SMALL-LEAVED E. To 50 ft., branchlets with 2 broad, corky wings; lvs. small, to 2½ in. long, oblong; fr. about ⁵⁄₁₆ in. long, with incurved beaks, covered with long white hairs. Va. to Fla., w. to Tex. Zone 5. Wood useful.

americana L. AMERICAN E., WHITE E., WATER E. To 120 ft.; lvs. to 6 in. long; fls. on slender drooping stalks; fr. deeply notched, with densely ciliate margins. Nfld. to Fla., w. to Rocky Mts. Zone 2. Very commonly planted. Wood useful. Cvs are: 'Ascendens', lateral brs. small, fastigiate, forming a narrow, oval crown; 'Aurea', foliage yellow; 'Columnaris', of columnar form; 'Incisa', lvs. rather small, deeply serrate; 'Littleford', upright branching, with a rather narrow vase-shaped form, foliage larger and somewhat heavier than usual; 'Moline', MO-LINE E., narrow tree with upright trunk, but older brs. eventually horizontal; 'Nigricans', lvs. deep dark green; 'Pendula', vase-shaped in form, brs. pendulous at ends; 'Pyramidata' [cv. 'Pyramidalis'], pyramidal in form; 'Urnii' 'Vase'; 'Vase' [cv. 'Urnii'], VASE E., vase-shaped in form.

angustifolia (Weston) Weston var. **cornubiensis** (Weston) Melv. [*U. carpinifolia* var. *cornubiensis* (Weston) Rehd.]. CORNISH E. Tree, with narrow crown and erect brs.; lvs. elliptic or broadly obovate, more or less tufted-pubescent beneath. Less pyramidal than *U. sarniensis.* S. England.

campestris: see *U. carpinifolia* and *U. procera.* Var. **Wheatleyi:** *U. sarniensis.*

carpinifolia Ruppius ex Suckow [*U. campestris* L., in part; *U. carpinifolia* var. *suberosa* (Moench) Rehd.]. SMOOTH-LEAF E. Pyramidal or upright tree, commonly suckering, brs. often corky, young brs. mostly glabrous; lvs. not large, ovate to obovate, doubly serrate, glossy and smooth above and nearly glabrous beneath, lateral veins 7–12 pairs; fr. obovate, seed close to notch. Brs. sometimes corky-winged in juvenile state, therefore clonal or cv. names should not be given to young trees. Eur., n. Afr., w. Asia. Zone 5. A variable sp. with many cvs.: 'Koopmanii', brs. often corky, lvs. small, grayish-puberulent beneath; 'Pendula', brs. slender, drooping; 'Prependens', brs. stiff but drooping, corky, lvs. rather small; 'Purpurascens', lvs. small, usually 1 in. long or less, purplish; 'Purpurea', lvs. dark purple, of ordinary size, this and cv. 'Purpurascens' possibly belong here, though have been considered cvs. of *U. procera;* 'Umbraculifera' [*U. procera* cv. 'Umbraculifera'], GLOBE E., crown dense and broad, lvs. 2–3 in. long, elliptic to broad-ovate, somewhat rough above; 'Webbiana': *U.* × *hollandica* cv.; 'Wheatleyi': *U. sarniensis* cv.; 'Wredei': *U.* × *hollandica* cv. Var. **cornubiensis:** *U. angustifolia* var. Var. **Dampieri:** *U.* × *hollandica* cv. Var. **sarniensis:** *U. sarniensis.* Var. **suberosa:** *U. carpinifolia.*

crassifolia Nutt. CEDAR E. Medium-sized tree, brs. stiff, corky or scaly; lvs. stiffish, 1–2 in. long, oblong to ovate-oblong, obtuse or nearly so, closely serrate, rough above, somewhat pubescent beneath. Autumn. Miss. to Tex. and n. Mex. Sometimes planted in its region.

1137

Davidiana Planch. Tree, to 90 ft., brs. usually with 2 corky wings; lvs. broadly ovate to elliptic-ovate, to 4 in. long; fr. elliptic, pubescent centrally. N. China. Zone 6. Var. **japonica** (Rehd.) Nakai [*U. japonica* (Rehd.) Sarg. JAPANESE E. Large tree, to 90 ft., with broad crown, young brs. often somewhat drooping, pubescent; lvs. 3–5 in. long, obovate or oblong, acuminate, roughish above and pubescent beneath, lateral veins 12–16 pairs; seed near apex of fr. Ne. Asia. Zone 6.

fulva: *U. rubra.*

glabra Huds. WYCH E., SCOTCH E. Wide-spreading, large tree, not suckering; lvs. large, 4–8 in. long, mostly obovate, coarsely double-serrate, rough above, pubescent beneath, dull green, lateral veins 12–18 pairs; fr. large, abundant, seed in center of samara. Gr. Brit. to Siberia. Zone 5. The following cvs. much planted in N. Amer.: 'Aspleniifolia': 'Crispa'; 'Atropurpurea', lvs. dark purple, folded; 'Camperdownii': *U. vegeta* cv.; 'Cornuta', HORNED E., with 3 or 5 long projections or lobes at apex of larger lvs.; 'Crispa' [cvs. 'Aspleniifolia', 'Urticifolia'], FERN-LEAF E., slow-growing tree, brs. sometimes pendulous, lvs. narrow. 1–2 in. wide, crispate-serrate, thick, heavily veined; 'Exoniensis' [cvs. 'Fastigiata', 'Pyramidalis'], EXETER E., brs. erect, forming a narrow crown; 'Fastigiata': 'Exoniensis'; 'Horizontalis' [cv. 'Pendula'], TABLETOP E., brs. stiffly drooping, more or less elbowed, making a spreading crown worked on erect stocks; 'Lutescens', lvs. yellow; 'Nana': a hybrid, possibly of *U. × hollandica;* 'Pendula': 'Horizontalis'; 'Pyramidalis': 'Exoniensis'; 'Urticifolia': 'Crispa'; 'Variegata', lvs. variegated.

× hollandica Mill.: *U. carpinifolia × U. glabra × U. Plotii* Druce. HOLLAND E., DUTCH E. Large, broad tree, often with drooping brs., suckering from the trunk, young parts glabrous or nearly so; lvs. rather prominently petioled, mostly large, ovate or broadly elliptic, asymmetrical, nearly smooth and usually dark green, little pubescent beneath, lateral veins 14 pairs or less; fr. with seed near notch. Zone 5. Cvs. include: 'Belgica' ['Latifolia' may be a synonym], BELGIAN E., twigs becoming smooth, lvs. 4–5 or –6 in. long, mostly rather narrowly obovate, soft-pubescent beneath, lateral veins 14–18 pairs; 'Clemmeri': 'Klemmer'; 'Dampieri' [*U. carpinifolia* var. *Dampieri* (Wesm.) Rehd.], a narrow pyramidal tree, lvs. crowded on short branchlets, broadly ovate, deeply and doubly toothed; 'Dauvessei', with broad pyramidal crown and hairy branchlets, lvs. to 4 or 5 in. long, very asymmetrical at base, soft-pubescent beneath; 'Dumont', similar to 'Belgica', with straight trunk and narrow, regular pyramidal crown, but lvs. somewhat smaller; 'Klemmer' [cvs. Clemmeri, 'Klehmii', 'Klemmeri'], probably belongs here, a rapid-growing tall tree, with root suckers, brs. ascending, forming a narrow pyramidal crown that widens later; 'Latifolia': see 'Belgica'; 'Nana', BUSH E., a dwarf form, not growing above 2 ft. in 10–12 years, of uncertain origin, but possibly belonging here; 'Pitteursii', strong-growing, lvs. large, to 5 in. long, broadly ovate to obovate, more or less rough and pubescent; 'Superba', narrow-pyramidal, lvs. to 5 in. long, very asymmetrical at base, glabrous except for axillary tufts beneath; 'Vegeta': *U. vegeta;* 'Webbiana' [*U. carpinifolia* cv. 'Webbiana'; *U. Webbiana* C. Koch], probably belongs here, tree with narrow crown, lvs. to 3 in. long, ovate to obovate, roughish above, folded lengthwise; 'Wredei' [*U. carpinifolia* cv. 'Wredei'], probably belongs here, resembles cv. 'Dampieri', with narrow crown, lvs. crowded, broad, deeply toothed, yellowish.

japonica: *U. Davidiana* var.

laevis Pall. EUROPEAN WHITE E. Tall, with open crown, branchlets at first pubescent; lvs. to 4 or 5 in. long, oblong or obovate, usually broadest above middle, acuminate, mostly glabrous and smooth above, pubescent beneath. Cent. Eur. to w. Asia. Zone 5.

parvifolia Jacq. [*U. parvifolia* var. *sempervirens* Hort.]. CHINESE E. Tree, with open crown, partly evergreen in mild climates, branchlets thinly pubescent; lvs. small, 1–2 or –3 in. long, elliptic to ovate, shining and mostly smooth above, becoming nearly or quite smooth beneath, firm or thick; fr. about 5/16 in. long. Late summer–autumn. Zone 6. China, Japan. Cv. 'Drake' [cv. 'Brea']. Brs. sweeping upright.

procera Salisb. [*U. campestris* L., in part]. ENGLISH E. To 90 ft., suckering, twigs more or less pubescent; lvs. mostly relatively small, 2–4 in. long, broadly elliptic or ovate, acuminate, roughish above, pubescent beneath, lateral veins 10–12 pairs; seed above middle of samara. W. and s. Eur. Zone 6. Popular tree in ne. states; rarely produces seeds; prop. by suckers. Cvs. listed are: 'Argenteo-variegata', lvs. striped and spotted with white; 'Berardii': possibly a cv. of *U. pumila;* 'Dampieri': *U. × hollandica* cv.; 'Louis Van Houtte' [cv. 'Van Houttei'], lvs. entirely yellow, remaining so through the summer; 'Monumentalis': *U. sarniensis;* 'Nigrescens': probably *U. carpinifolia;* 'Purpurascens', 'Purpurea': probably cvs. of *U. carpinifolia;* 'Superba': *U. × hollandica* cv.; 'Umbraculifera': *U. carpinifolia* cv.; 'Van Houttei': 'Louis Van Houtte'; 'Vegeta': *U. vegeta;* 'Wheatleyi': *U. sarniensis.*

pumila L. DWARF E., SIBERIAN E. Small tree, sometimes shrublike, brs. slender, often drooping, branchlets glabrous or pubescent only when young; lvs. 2–3 in. long, elliptic to oblong, long- or short-pointed, not deeply serrate, smooth above, mostly glabrous beneath or with axillary tufts, not lustrous or leathery; fr. about ½ in. long. Early spring. E. Siberia, n. China to Turkestan. Zone 3. Cvs. are: 'Berardii', often referred to *U. procera* but possibly belonging here, bushy tree, brs. slender, upright; 'Pendula', brs. pendulous, lvs. small, equally toothed. Var. **arborea** Litv. Lvs. narrowly ovate or ovate-lanceolate, shining above.

racemosa: *U. Thomasii.*

rubra Muhlenb. [*U. fulva* Michx.]. SLIPPERY E., RED E. Small or medium-sized tree, with broad, open crown and spreading brs., branchlets pubescent; lvs. large, to 6 or 8 in. long, obovate or broadly oblong, acuminate, coarsely serrate, very rough above, pubescent beneath, turning dull yellow in autumn. Se. Canada, s. to Fla. and Tex. Zone 4. Inner bark used medicinally, wood used for utilitarian articles.

× sarniensis (Loudon) H. H. Bancroft [*U. campestris* var. *Wheatleyi* Hort. Simon-Louis; *U. carpinifolia* var. *sarniensis* (Lodd.) Lodd.; *U. carpinifolia* cv. 'Wheatleyi'; *U. procera* cv. 'Monumentalis'; *U. procera* cv. 'Wheatleyi'; *U. angustifolia × U. × hollandica*. JERSEY E., GUERNSEY E., WHEATLEY E. Tree, narrow and tapering due to primary brs. arising from main trunk at about a 45° angle; resembles Cornish elm, *U. angustifolia* var. *cornubiensis,* but more stiffly erect, and lvs. broader, less tufted-pubescent beneath.

sempervirens: a listed name of no botanical standing; has been used for *U. parvifolia.*

serotina Sarg. SEPTEMBER E., RED E. Medium-sized tree, brs. pendulous, often corky; lvs. small, 2–3 in. long, oblong or somewhat obovate, acuminate, smooth and shining above, pubescent on veins beneath, lateral veins about 20 pairs. Autumn. S. Ky. and Ill., to Ga., Ala., Ark. Zone 6. Planted in its region.

Thomasii Sarg. [*U. racemosa* D. Thomas, not Borkh.]. ROCK E., CORK E. Large tree, irregularly columnar in habit, brs. very corky, buds pubescent; lvs. large, to 4 or 6 in. long, elliptic to oblong-obovate, rather short-pointed, coarsely serrate, glabrous or nearly so above, pubescent beneath; fr. ½ in. long or more, notched, pubescent. Que. to Tenn. and Nebr. Zone 2. Wood used for utilitarian articles.

vaseyi: a listed name of no botanical standing for the VASE E., *U. americana* cv. 'Vase'.

× vegeta (Loud.) Lindl. [*U. × hollandica* cv. 'Vegeta'; *U. procera* cv. 'Vegeta']: *U. carpinifolia × U. glabra.* HUNTINGDON E., CHICHESTER E. Vigorous large tree, brs. ascending; lvs. elliptic, to 5–6 in. long, mostly smooth above, pubescent beneath only in axils, lateral veins 14–18 pairs. Cv. 'Camperdownii' [*U. glabra* cv. 'Camperdownii']. CAMPERDOWN E., brs. gracefully drooping, forming a globose head, grown as a topworked head on an erect elm stock.

Webbiana: *U. × hollandica* cv.

UMBELLIFERAE Juss. or, alternatively, APIACEAE

Lindl. PARSLEY or CARROT FAMILY. Dicot.; about 250 genera and 2,800 spp., commonly herbs, rarely somewhat shrubby, widely distributed, mostly in temp. and boreal regions; lvs. alt., mostly compound; fls. in simple or compound umbels, or sometimes heads, small, bisexual or rarely unisexual, calyx 5-lobed, petals and stamens 5, ovary inferior, 2-celled; fr. dry, of 2 ribbed or winged carpels, which contain oil tubes in the pericarp and separate at maturity. The cult. genera are: *Aciphylla, Actinotus, Aegopodium, Aletes, Ammi, Anethum, Angelica, Anthriscus, Apium, Arracacia, Astrantia, Bupleurum, Carum, Chaerophyllum, Cicuta, Conium, Coriandrum, Crithmum, Cryptotaenia, Cuminum, Daucus, Erigenia, Eryngium, Ferula, Foeniculum, Hacquetia, Heracleum, Hydrocotyle, Levisticum, Ligusticum, Lomatium, Meum, Musineon, Myrrhis, Oenanthe, Oreoxis, Osmorhiza, Pastinaca, Perideridia, Petroselinum, Pimpinella, Sanicula, Seseli, Sium, Smyrnium, Taenidia, Trachymene,* and *Zizia.*

Plants often of strong or pungent odor, some poisonous, many grown for food, flavoring, and medicinal purposes, and some as ornamentals.

UMBELLULARIA Nutt. *Lauraceae.*

One sp., an aromatic evergreen tree of Calif. and Ore.; lvs. alt., entire, leathery; fls. several in peduncled umbels clustered in the terminal axils, bisexual, calyx 6-parted, deciduous, petals 0, stamens 9, those of whorl 3 with 2 orange glands at base; fr. a drupe.

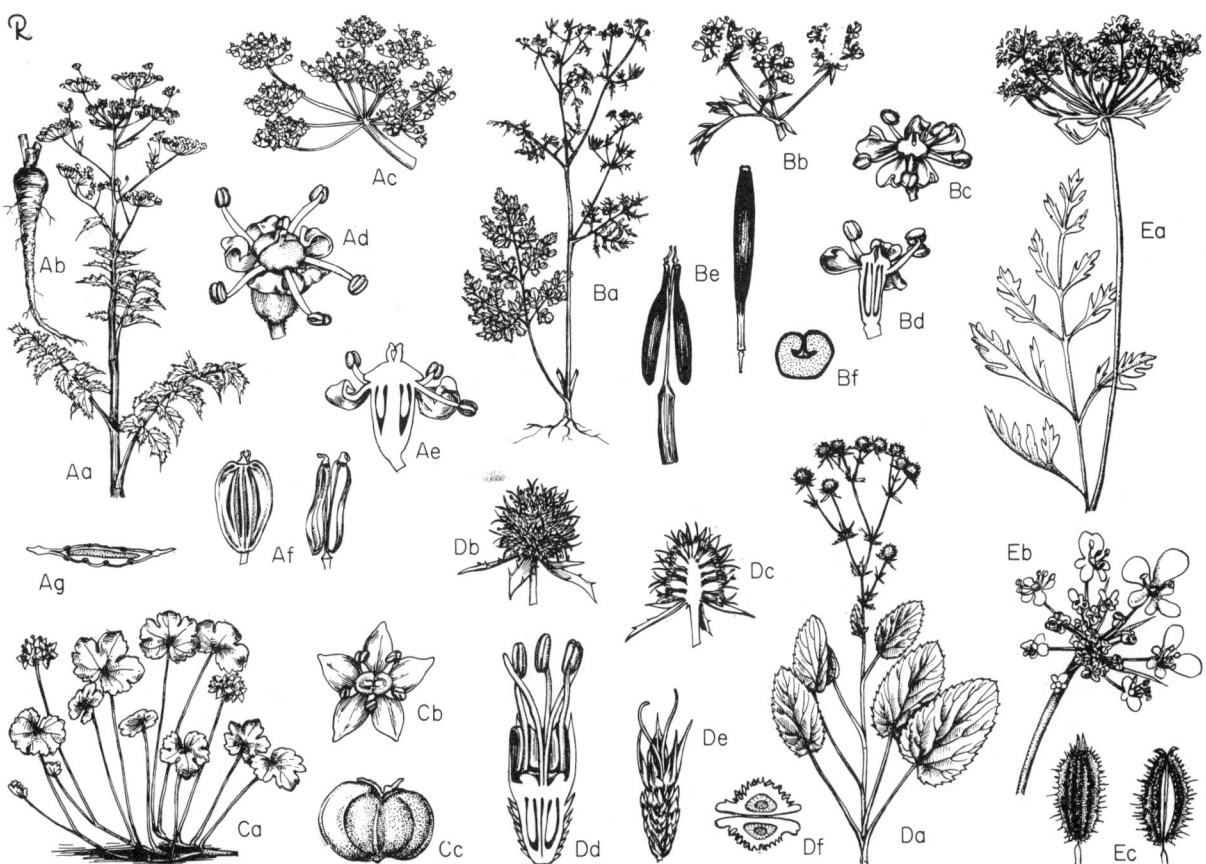

UMBELLIFERAE. **A,** *Pastinaca sativa:* **Aa,** upper part of flowering stem, $\times \frac{1}{12}$; **Ab,** root, $\times \frac{1}{8}$; **Ac,** compound umbel, $\times \frac{1}{2}$; **Ad,** flower, $\times 5$; **Ae,** flower, vertical section, $\times 5$; **Af,** fruit, two views, $\times 1\frac{1}{2}$; **Ag,** single carpel, cross section, $\times 4$. **B,** *Anthriscus Cerefolium:* **Ba,** plant, $\times \frac{1}{6}$; **Bd,** compound umbel, $\times 1\frac{1}{2}$; **Bc,** flower, $\times 5$; **Bd,** flower, vertical section, $\times 5$; **Be,** fruit, two views, $\times 3$; **Bf,** single carpel, cross section, $\times 10$. **C,** *Hydrocotyle sibthorpioides:* **Ca,** plant, $\times 1$; **Cb,** flower, $\times 1\frac{1}{2}$; **Cc,** fruit, $\times 6$. **D,** *Eryngium planum:* **Da,** plant, $\times \frac{1}{8}$; **Db,** flower head, $\times \frac{1}{2}$; **Dc,** flower head, vertical section, $\times \frac{1}{2}$; **Dd,** flower, vertical section, $\times 4$; **De,** fruit, $\times 2$; **Df,** fruit, cross section $\times 4$. **E,** *Daucus Carota:* **Ea,** compound umbel and leaf, $\times \frac{1}{2}$; **Eb,** an umbellet, $\times 2$; **Ec,** fruit, two views, $\times 4$. (Ea-Ec from Bailey, *Manual of Cultivated Plants,* ed. 2.)

californica (Hook. & Arn.) Nutt. CALIFORNIA BAY, CALIFORNIA LAUREL, CALIFORNIA OLIVE, MYRTLE, OREGON M., PEPPERWOOD. Handsome tree, to 80 ft.; lvs. ovate-oblong to lanceolate, to 5 in. long, glossy above, with strong pungent odor when bruised; infl. many-fld.; fls. yellowish-green; fr. to 1 in. long, dark purple. Sometimes grown as an ornamental tree. Thrives in fairly moist soils. Prop. by seeds. The wood is valued for fine woodworking.

UMBILICUS DC. *Crassulaceae.* About 15 spp. of succulent, per. herbs, native to s. Eur., n. and cent. Afr., and w. Asia, glabrous, rhizomes with ann. shoots; lvs. alt., cordate to mostly peltate, the lower petioled, the upper reduced; fl. sts. terminal, infl. of 1 or more racemes; fls. 5-merous, sepals separate, corolla yellowish or greenish, tubular, lobes often shorter than tube, stamens 10, rarely 5.

For culture see *Succulents.*

chrysanthus: *Rosularia pallida.*

horizontalis (Guss.) DC. Similar to *U. rupestris,* but fls. horizontal, pedicels shorter than bracts, corolla lobes lanceolate, acuminate. Spring. S. Medit. region.

oppositifolius: *Chiastophyllum oppositifolium.*

pendulinus: *U. rupestris.*

rupestris (Salisb.) Dandy [*U. pendulinus* DC.; *Cotyledon Umbilicus* L.]. NAVELWORT, PENNYWORT. Basal lvs. peltate, orbicular, 1–3 in. wide, sinuate-crenate; fl. st. 6–20 in.; fls. pendent, pedicels longer than bracts, corolla to ⅜ in. long, lobes ovate, much shorter than tube, mucronate. Spring. Asia Minor to Gr. Brit. and Canary Is.

Sempervivum: *Rosularia Sempervivum.*

spinosus: *Orostachys spinosa.*

UNGNADIA Endl. *Sapindaceae.* One sp., a deciduous, polygamous, shrubby tree, native to Tex., New Mex., and n. Mex.; lvs. alt., pinnate; fls. in clusters, irregular, calyx 5-parted, petals usually 4, clawed, stamens 7–10, unequal, exserted; fr. a leathery, stalked, 3-valved caps.

speciosa Endl. TEXAN BUCKEYE, MEXICAN B., SPANISH B., FALSE B. To 30 ft.; lvs. 5–12 in. long, lfts. 5–7, lanceolate to ovate, to 5 in. long, crenate-serrate; fls. before the lvs., rose, 1 in. across, fragrant; caps. 2 in. in diam., seeds brown or black, usually only one developing. Spring. Occasionally planted in Zone 8.

UNIOLA L. *Gramineae.* Two spp. of rhizomatous and stoloniferous per. grasses from e. N. Amer. to S. Amer., sts. glabrous; lf. blades involute when dry; infl. a contracted, stiffly erect panicle with imbricate, appressed-ascending or spreading brs.; spikelets 5- to many-fld., straw-colored or violet-tinged, compressed, disarticulating below the glumes, falling entire; glumes 2, shorter than lemmas, 3-nerved, keeled, lemmas 3–9-nerved, keeled, lower 2–6 empty, keel serrate to minutely serrate, florets bisexual, stamens 3. For terminology see *Gramineae.*

latifolia: *Chasmanthium latifolium.*

paniculata L. SEA OATS, SPIKE-GRASS. Sts. erect, to nearly 8 ft.; lf. sheaths with tufts of hairs at collar, blades to 27 in. long, ⅜ in. wide; panicles to about 2 ft. long, brs. drooping or nodding in age, densely fld.; spikelets mostly 5–20-fld., long-pedicelled, to 1³⁄₁₆ or 2 in. long. On coastal dunes from Va. to Tex. and e. Mex., also n. W. Indies.

URBINIA: *Echeveria.* U. *Purpusii: E. Purpusiorum.*

URCEOLINA Rchb. *Amaryllidaceae.* A few spp. of herbs with tunicate bulbs, native to the Andes of S. Amer.; lvs. thin, oblong or lanceolate; fls. many in an umbel on a scape and subtended by separate spathe valves, perianth tube cylindrical at the base, abruptly dilated near the middle, lobes shorter than tube, equal, spreading, stamens 6, inserted at the throat, filaments indistinctly appendaged at base, ovary inferior, ovules many; fr. a caps., seeds many, small.

miniata: *U. peruviana.*

peruviana (K. Presl) Macbr. [*U. miniata* (Herb.) Benth. & Hook.f.]. To 1½ ft.; lvs. lanceolate, to 1 ft. long, 1½ in. wide, developing after fls.; umbel 2–6-fld.; fls. pendulous, bright scarlet, to 1½ in. long. Peru, Bolivia.

URGINEA Steinh. *Liliaceae.* Between 30 and 40 spp. of bulbous, per. herbs, native to Afr., Eur., Medit, region, and India; bulb tunicate; lvs. basal; fls. whitish, yellowish, or rose, in racemes terminating leafless scapes, perianth segms. 6, separate, 1-nerved, stamens 6, anthers versatile; fr. a 3-valved, loculicidal caps., seeds often winged.

Occasionally grown as ornamentals, but only moderately hardy. Propagated by division or by seeds.

maritima (L.) Bak. [*Scilla maritima* L.]. SEA ONION, SQUILL, RED S. To 4 or 5 ft.; lvs. to 1½ ft. long and 4 in. wide, glaucous, rather fleshy; fls. whitish, ½ in. long, in dense *Eremurus*-like racemes to 2 ft. long. Produces lvs. in spring, is dormant during the summer, and blooms in autumn. Canary Is., Medit. region, e. to Syria; also in S. Afr. The bulbs are collected from the wild for their medicinal properties and as the source of squill or red squill, a rat poison.

URSINIA Gaertn. *Compositae* (Anthemis Tribe; until recently included in the Arctotis Tribe). About 40 spp. of ann. and per. herbs, subshrubs, and shrubs, native to S. Afr., herbage strongly scented and gland-dotted; lvs. alt., rarely in clusters, usually deeply pinnately parted, rarely entire; fl. heads solitary, on long peduncles, radiate, involucral bracts imbricate in 3–7 rows, the inner bracts membranous at apex; disc fls. tubular, bisexual, each subtended by a scale, ray fls. ligulate, neutral, rarely female or sterile; achenes cylindrical or pear-shaped, sometimes with a basal tuft of hairs, pappus of 1 row of scales, or of 1 row of scales and 1 row of bristles, rarely absent.

The annual ursinias of the flower garden are grown from seeds planted indoors or directly in the open.

anethoides (DC.) N. E. Br. Glabrous or thinly cobwebby shrub, to 2 ft.; lvs. lanceolate or obovate in outline, to 1½ in. long, pinnately dissected into filiform, semicylindrical segms.; heads to 1 in. across, on peduncles to 8 in. long; fls. golden-yellow; achenes with a basal tuft of hairs, pappus of 1 row of scales. Perhaps best treated culturally as an ann.

anthemoides (L.) Poir. [*U. pulchra* N. E. Br.]. Ann., to 1½ ft.; lvs. ovate in outline, to 2¼ in. long, pinnately to 2-pinnately parted into flat, linear, acute lobes; heads to 2½ in. across, on peduncles to 8 in. long; ray fls. entirely yellow or the underside purple; achenes with basal tuft of hairs, pappus of 1 row of scales.

cakilifolia DC. Ann., to 1½ ft.; lvs. obovate in outline, to 2 in. long, 2-pinnately parted; heads to 2 in. across, on peduncles to 8 in. long; disc fls. yellow toward base, purple toward apex, ray fls. deep yellow or orange; pappus in 2 rows.

calenduliflora (DC.) N. E. Br. Ann. to about 14 in.; lvs. ovate in outline, to 2½ in. long, pinnately parted, glabrous; heads to 2½ in. across, on peduncles to 8 in. long; disc fls. deep yellow, purple toward apex, ray fls. deep yellow, frequently with dark purple basal spot; achenes usually with a basal tuft of hairs, pappus of 1 row of scales.

chrysanthemoides (Less.) Harv. Ann. or per. herb, to 3 ft.; lvs. alt. or in clusters, lanceolate to ovate in outline, to 2 in. long, 1–2-pinnately parted, glabrous or pubescent; heads to 1½ in. across, on peduncles to 7 in. long; disc fls. yellow or yellow at base and purple at apex, ray fls. entirely yellow, or yellow or more rarely white on upper surface and coppery underneath; pappus in 2 rows.

pulchra: *U. anthemoides.*

sericea (Thunb.) N. E. Br. Subshrub, to about 2½ ft.; lvs. lanceolate or obovate in outline, to 3 in. long, pinnately parted, pubescent; heads to about 1¼ in. across, on peduncles to 2 ft. long; fls. yellow; achenes with basal tuft of hairs, pappus of 1 row of scales.

speciosa DC. Glabrous ann., to 16 in.; lvs. ovate in outline, to 2 in. long, 2-pinnately parted; heads to 2 in. across, on peduncles to 5 in. long; disc fls. usually deep yellow or sometimes with purple apex, ray fls. deep yellow, orange, rarely white; pappus in 2 rows.

URTICA L. NETTLE. *Urticaceae.* About 50 spp. of monoecious or sometimes dioecious ann. or per. herbs with mostly stinging hairs, widely distributed in both hemispheres; lvs. opp., stipuled, mostly lobed or deeply toothed; fls. minute, in clusters, the clusters in axillary racemes, panicles or loose heads, sepals 4, paired in the female fls., the outer 2 smaller, the inner 2 membranous in fr. and enclosing the achene.

One species sometimes grown for medicinal uses and another as an ornamental; young tops sometimes cooked like spinach. Propagated by seeds and cuttings.

dioica L. STINGING N. Per., 2–6 ft., little-branched, bristly, generally dioecious; lvs. mostly ovate, to 6 in. long, acuminate, cordate to truncate at base, deeply serrate; fl. clusters in loose racemes or panicles generally longer than subtending petioles. Eur. and Asia; widely naturalized.

pilulifera L. ROMAN N. Ann., to 3 ft., monoecious; lvs. ovate, 1–3 in. long, serrate, petioles of the lower lvs. nearly as long as blades; male infl. spicate; female fls. with inflated calyx, in loose heads terminating long, naked peduncles. S. Eur. Sometimes grown under glass as an ornamental.

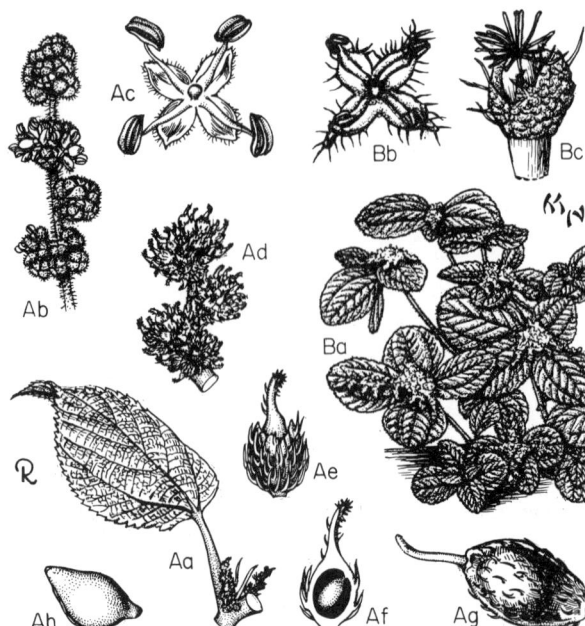

URTICACEAE. **A,** *Boehmeria nivea:* **Aa,** leaf with axillary female inflorescences, × ¼; **Ab,** segment of male inflorescence, × 2; **Ac,** male flower, × 5; **Ad,** segment of female inflorescence, × 4; **Ae,** female flower, × 16; **Af,** pistil, vertical section, × 16; **Ag,** fruit enclosed by calyx, × 15; **Ah,** achene, × 15. **B,** *Pilea involucrata:* **Ba,** flowering plant, × ⅓; **Bb,** male flower, × 4; **Bc,** female flower, × 20.

URTICACEAE Juss. NETTLE FAMILY. Dicot.; more than 40 genera and about 500 spp. of widely distributed herbs, shrubs, trees, or sometimes vines, some with stinging hairs; lvs. alt. or opp., mostly stipuled; fls. small and inconspicuous, in cymes or clusters, or rarely on a fleshy receptacle, generally unisexual, calyx mostly 4–5-parted or -lobed, petals 0, stamens as many as calyx segms. and opp. them, ovary superior, 1-celled, 1-ovuled; fr. an achene, more or less enclosed in the dry or succulent calyx. The cult. genera are: *Boehmeria, Debregeasia, Gesnouinia, Pellionia, Pilea, Soleirolia, Urtica,* and *Villebrunea.*

Grown principally for their foliage, but of minor importance horticulturally; one species, *Boehmeria nivea,* is an important source of fiber.

UTAHIA: *PEDIOCACTUS.*

UTRICULARIA L. BLADDERWORT. *Lentibulariaceae.* Cosmopolitan genus of about 200 spp. of herbs, growing in water or wet places, with mostly submersed sts. and lvs., some trop. spp. epiphytic; lvs. simple, usually becoming dissected into hairlike segms. bearing many small bladders; peduncles aerial, 1- to several-fld.; calyx 2-parted, corolla 2-lipped, lower lip spurred, stamens 2, inserted on corolla; caps. 1-celled.

exoleta R. Br. Sts. floating, capillary; lvs. to 3 in. long, with filiform segms., bearing bladders; peduncles to 4 in. high; corolla yellow, to ¼ in. long, lips nearly equal. Se. Asia to n. Australia. Sometimes grown in aquaria.

minor L. Sts. threadlike, to 1 ft. long, leafy; lvs. submersed, to ⅜ in. long, forked 1–3 times into hairlike segms., with few bladders; peduncles to 8 in. long, 2–9-fld.; corolla yellow, to ⁵⁄₁₆ in. long, lower lip very much longer than the upper, with short blunt saccate spur. N. Eurasia, N. Amer. Often grown in aquaria.

vulgaris L. Sts. coarse, submersed, to 6 ft. long; lvs. many, to 1½ in. long, mostly 3-pinnately divided, with many bladders; peduncles to 1 ft. high, 4–20-fld.; corolla yellow, lower lip much broader than upper, with elevated palate and long spur. Eurasia, N. Amer.

UVARIA L. *Annonaceae.* Over 100 spp. of climbing shrubs, native to Old World tropics; lvs. alt., entire; fls. in cymose fascicles or solitary, bisexual; petals 6, broad, imbricate in 2 series, stamens and pistils many; fr. dry or fleshy, many-seeded, often sweet and edible.

lancifolia Merrill. Differs from *U. scandens* in being nearly glabrous at maturity, and in having lvs. prominently nerved, lanceolate, to 6 in. long and 1¾ in. wide; pedicels longer, to ¾ in.; petals ⁵⁄₁₆ in. long; fr. glabrous, globose to ellipsoid, ⅜ in. long. Luzon (Philippine Is.).

scandens C. B. Robinson. Sts. to 2¼ in. in diam., young branchlets rusty-tomentose; lvs. elliptic to obovate, to 10 in. long, 3¾ in. wide, bluish-green above, with pubescent veins, petioles to ¼ in. long; fls.

in rusty-tomentose, short, axillary cymes, or rarely solitary, petals subequal, dark red, to ⅝ in. long. Mindanao (Philippine Is.).

UVA-URSI: *ARCTOSTAPHYLOS.*

UVULARIA L. [*Oakesia* S. Wats.; *Oakesiella* Small]. BELLWORT, MERRYBELLS, HAYBELLS, COWBELLS. *Liliaceae.* Five spp. of rhizomatous, per. herbs, native to e. N. Amer.; sts. simple or branched, leafy; lvs. alt., sessile or perfoliate; fls. campanulate, yellow, pendulous, usually solitary at ends of brs., perianth segms. 6, separate, stamens 6, style 3-parted; fr. a 3-lobed or 3-winged, loculicidal caps.

Bellworts are sometimes grown in the wild garden. Of easy cultivation in rich soil and shady locations; propagated by division.

caroliniana (J. F. Gmel.) Wilb. [*U. puberula* Michx.; *U. pudica* (Walt.) Fern.; *Oakesiella puberula* (Michx.) Small]. To 20 in.; lvs. sessile, elliptic, to 3 in. long, bright green and glossy, minutely serrulate; fls. greenish-yellow, style parted to below the middle, ovary and caps. not stipitate. N.J. and W.Va., s. to Ala. and Ga.

grandiflora Sm. To 2½ ft. at maturity; lvs. perfoliate, oblong to lanceolate-ovate, to 5 in. long, pubescent beneath; fls. lemon-yellow, to 2 in. long, perianth segms. smooth inside. Sw. Que. to Minn., s. to Tenn. and Okla.

perfoliata L. STRAWBELL. To 2 ft.; lvs. perfoliate, oblong to lanceolate-ovate, to 3½ in. long, glabrous; fls. pale yellow, 1¼ in. long, perianth segms. glandular-papillose on inside. Que. to Ohio, s. to n. Fla. and n. La.

puberula: *U. caroliniana.*

pudica: *U. caroliniana.*

sessilifolia L. [*Oakesiella sessilifolia* (L.) Small]. WILD OATS. To 16 in.; lvs. sessile, oblong-lanceolate, to 3 in. long; fls. greenish-yellow, 1¼ in. long, style parted only ⅓ its length; ovary and caps. stipitate. New Bruns. to S.Dak., s. to S.C., Ala., and Ark.

VACCARIA N. M. Wolf. *Caryophyllaceae.* About 4 spp. of ann. herbs, native in e. and cent. Eur., temp. Asia, and Medit. region; sts. forked; lvs. opp.; fls. in an open, dichasial cyme, epicalyx absent, calyx 5-lobed, 5-winged, inflated, petals 5, coronal scales at juncture of claw and blade, ovary 1-celled, styles 2; fr. a caps., dehiscent by 4 teeth, seeds nearly globose.

pyramidata Medic. [*V. segetalis* Garcke; *Saponaria Vaccaria* L.]. COW HERB, COCKLE, DAIRY PINK. Erect, glabrous ann., to 2 ft.; lvs. sessile, lanceolate to ovate, to 2¾ in. long, cordate; calyx to ⅝ in. long, petals pink to dark purplish, long-clawed, entire or emarginate. Eur. and Asia; adventive in N. Amer. as a weed in grain fields.

segetalis: *V. pyramidata.*

VACCINIUM L. [*Cyanococcus* (A. Gray) Rydb.; *Herpothamnus* Small; *Oxycoccus* Hill; *Polycodium* Raf.]. BLUE-BERRY, HUCKLEBERRY, CRANBERRY, BILBERRY. *Ericaceae.* Perhaps 150 spp. of deciduous or evergreen shrubs, rarely small trees or vines, native to the N. Hemisphere, with the greatest number of spp. in N. Amer. and e. Asia; plants often stoloniferous; lvs. simple, alt., often brilliantly colored in autumn; fls. solitary, or in racemes or clusters, white, or greenish to red or purple, calyx mostly 4–5-lobed, corolla urceolate, campanulate, or cylindrical, stamens 8 or 10, anthers with or without spurs, opening by a terminal pore, ovary inferior; fr. a many-seeded berry with persistent calyx. Sometimes divided into several large genera, but usually more conservatively treated as a large genus comprising several subgenera.

Some of the vacciniums are grown as ornamentals in borders or are colonized in wild areas; others are managed in the wild or grown for the edible fruits. Most of them require peaty or sandy, acidic soils and do not thrive in limy soils. For culture see *Blueberry* and *Cranberry.*

angustifolium Ait. LOWBUSH BLUEBERRY, LOW SWEET B., LATE SWEET B., SWEET-HURTS. Deciduous shrub, to 1 ft.; lvs. lanceolate, to ¾ in. long, serrulate with bristle-tipped teeth, bright green, glabrous; fls. in small clusters, white or tinged pink, to ¼ in. long; fr. blue, heavily glaucous, to ½ in. in diam., sweet. Spring. Arctic Amer., s. to Minn. and mts. of N.Y. and New Hamp. Zone 2. Var. **laevifolium** House [*V. pensilvanicum* Lam., not Mill.]. To 2 ft.; lvs. narrowly elliptic to oblong-lanceolate, to 1½ in. long. Nfld. to Wisc., s. to Va. Fr. much collected from wild plants managed for commercial production. See *Blueberry.* Cv. **'Leucocarpum'** [forma *leucocarpum* (W. Deane) Rehd.; Cv. 'Album']. Fr. white.

Arctostaphylos L. Deciduous shrub, to 12 ft.; lvs. ovate-oblong, to 4 in. long, finely serrate; fls. in racemes to 2 in. long, greenish-white, corolla campanulate, to ⁵⁄₁₆ in. long; fr. purple. Late spring. Caucasus. Zone 6.

Ashei Reade. RABBIT-EYE BLUEBERRY. Crown-forming or suckering, erect, deciduous to semievergreen shrub, 4–18 ft.; lvs. elliptic, 1–2½ in. long, acute to obtuse, entire or serrate, dark to pale green, usually glandular and pubescent beneath; corolla mostly pale to bright pink, sometimes white or red, urceolate, to ⅜ in. long; fr. black, often dull, sometimes glaucous, to ¾ in. in diam., insipid or of excellent quality. Ga. to n. Fla. and s. Ala. A source of some highbush blueberry cvs. grown in the se. U.S.

atrococcum (A. Gray) A. Heller [*Cyanococcus atrococcus* (A. Gray) Small]. BLACK HIGHBUSH BLUEBERRY. Deciduous shrub, to 10 ft.; lvs. elliptic to ovate or oblong, to 3 in. long, entire, downy or woolly beneath; fls. preceding the lvs., yellowish-white or pink; fr. polished black, sweet. Late spring. Se. Va. to e. S.C. Zone 4. Often sought out in the wild for its fr.

australe: *V. corymbosum.*

buxifolium: *V. Stapfianum;* but material offered as *V. buxifolium* is probably *V. Vitis-idaea.*

caesium Greene [*Polycodium caesium* (Greene) Greene]. DEER-BERRY, SQUAW H. Deciduous shrub, 2–3 ft., or rarely more; lvs. ovate to elliptic, to 2 in. long, white-glaucous beneath; fls. in bracted racemes, stamens long-exserted; fr. dark blue, glaucous. Penn. and W. Va., s. to Fla. and La.

caespitosum Michx. DWARF BILBERRY. Deciduous tufted shrub, to 1 ft.; lvs. obovate to spatulate, to 1½ in. long, crenate-serrate, shining above; fls. solitary, white or pink, ³⁄₁₆ in. long; fr. dark blue, glaucous, ¼ in. in diam., sweet. N. Amer. Zone 2.

canadense: *V. myrtilloides.*

candicans Michx. [*Polycodium candicans* (Michx.) Small]. Deciduous shrub, to 6 ft.; lvs. elliptic to ovate or obovate, to 4 in. long, white beneath; fls. in bracted racemes, white, stamens exserted; fr. blue, glaucous. Ga. to Ala.

corymbosum L. [*V. australe* Small; *Cyanococcus corymbosus* (L.) Rydb.]. HIGHBUSH BLUEBERRY, SWAMP B., WHORTLEBERRY. Deciduous shrub, to 15 ft.; lvs. elliptic-lanceolate to ovate, to 3 in. long, entire, green on both sides, glabrous to pubescent; fls. in clusters, white to pinkish, ⁵⁄₁₆ in. long; fr. blue to blue-black, glaucous, to ⁵⁄₁₆ in. in diam., sweet. Late spring. Me. to Fla. and La. Zone 4. Fr. much collected from wild plants. Parent of a number of cvs. grown as sources of commercial fr. or for planting in the home garden. See *Blueberry.*

crassifolium Andr. [*Herpothamnus crassifolius* (Andr.) Small]. CREEPING BLUEBERRY. Evergreen, prostrate shrub, forming mats to 6 ft. across; lvs. elliptic to ovate, to ½ in. long, margin revolute, minutely and distantly glandular-serrulate; fls. in small, axillary clusters, pink, ⅛ in. long; fr. black, ⅛ in. in diam., sweet. Se. Va. to S.C.

cylindraceum Sm. Deciduous shrub, to 10 ft. or more; lvs. elliptic to obovate, to 3 in. long, toothed; fls. in loose racemes, greenish-white, tubular, to ½ in. long. Azores.

Delavayi Franch. Compact evergreen shrub, to 2½ ft., branchlets short-hispid; lvs. ovate to cuneate-obovate, to ½ in. long, notched at apex, entire, glabrous; fls. in racemes, cream-white; fr. crimson, less than ³⁄₁₆ in. in diam. W. China. Zone 7.

deliciosum Piper. Deciduous, glabrous, densely branched shrub, to 1 ft.; lvs. elliptic to obovate, to 2⅜ in. long, glaucescent beneath; fls. axillary, pink, ¼ in. long; fr. blue-black, glaucous, ¼ in. in diam., sweet. Wash. to n. Ore.

Donnianum: *V. Sprengelii.*

Dunalianum Wight. Evergreen glabrous shrub or small tree, to 20 ft.; lvs. elliptic to oblong-lanceolate, to 5 in. long, caudate-acuminate, leathery; fls. in racemes to 3 in. long, white, ³⁄₁₆ in. long; fr. black. Himalayas.

Elliottii Chapm. [*Cyanococcus Elliottii* (Chapm.) Small]. ELLIOTT'S BLUEBERRY. Deciduous, straggling shrub, to 10 ft.; lvs. elliptic, to 1⅜ in. long, crenate to serrate, glossy green on both sides; fls. in racemes, pink to white, ¼ in. long; fr. black to purple-black, to ⁵⁄₁₆ in. in diam. Va. to Fla., w. to Ark. and La.

fuscatum Ait. [*Cyanococcus fuscatus* (Ait.) Small]. Evergreen or semideciduous shrub, to 10 ft.; lvs. lanceolate to elliptic, to 2 in. long, entire, leathery; fls. in racemes, pink to almost red, to ⅜ in. long; fr. dark, to ⅜ in. in diam. S. Ga., Fla.

glaucalbum Hook.f. ex C. B. Clarke. Evergreen, much-branched shrub, to 4 ft.; lvs. lanceolate, elliptic, to oblong-obovate, to 2½ in. long, finely toothed, leathery, green above, white-glaucous beneath; fls. in racemes, pink, to ¼ in. long; fr. black, glaucous, ⁵⁄₁₆ in. in diam. Himalayas.

hirsutum Buckl. [*Cyanococcus hirsutus* (Buckl.) Small]. HAIRY H. Deciduous shrub, to 3 ft.; lvs. elliptic to ovate, to 2¼ in. long, entire, pubescent; fls. in racemes, white or pinkish, to ⅜ in. long, glandular-pubescent; fr. black, glandular-pubescent, ¼ in. in diam. Tenn., N.C. Zone 6.

macrocarpon Ait. [*Oxycoccus macrocarpos* (Ait.) Pers.]. CRAN-BERRY, LARGE C., AMERICAN C. Evergreen, to 3 ft. across, sts. creeping, mat-forming; lvs. oblong-elliptic, to ¾ in. long, whitish beneath; fls. in lateral clusters, pink, corolla 4-parted, ⁵⁄₁₆ in. long; fr. red, to ¾ in. in diam. Summer. In acid bogs and swamps, Nfld. to Minn., s. to N.C. Zone 2. A number of cvs. are grown commercially. See *Cranberry.*

membranaceum Dougl. THIN-LEAF H., BLUE H., MOUNTAIN BLUE-BERRY. Deciduous shrub, to 4½ ft., branchlets 4-angled, with exfoliating bark; lvs. ovate to obovate, to 3 in. long, serrulate, thin, glabrous, bright green; fls. pink, solitary, on drooping pedicels to ⅝ in. long; fr. black. Ont. and Mich. to B.C., s. to n. Calif. Zone 6. Fr. aromatic, delicious, and much collected in wild.

Mortinia Hook.f. MORTINIA. Evergreen procumbent shrub, to 4 ft.; lvs. oblong-lanceolate to ovate, to ¾ in. long, leathery; fls. in compact, drooping racemes, rose-pink or pinkish-white, ¼ in. long; fr. purple, glaucous, $^3/_{16}$ in. in diam. Ecuador.

Myrsinites Lam. [*V. nitidum* Andr.; *Cyanococcus Myrsinites* (Lam.) Small]. Evergreen, much-branched shrub, to 2 ft.; lvs. elliptic, ovate to obovate, to ¾ in. long; fls. in umbel-like clusters, white to pink, ¼ in. long; fr. black, often glaucous, to $^5/_{16}$ in. in diam. N.C. to Fla. and La. Zone 7.

myrtilloides Michx. [*V. canadense* Kalm ex Richardson]. SOURTOP BLUEBERRY, VELVET-LEAF B. Deciduous, twiggy shrub, usually 1–2 ft., forming colonies, branchlets velvety; lvs. oblong-lanceolate to elliptic, to 2 in. long, entire, soft-pubescent on both sides; fls. greenish or tinged purple, about ¼ in. long; fr. blue, more or less glaucous, ⅜ in. in diam., sour. Lab. to Va., w. to B.C. Zone 2. Fr. much collected from wild plants often managed for commercial production. See *Blueberry.*

Myrtillus L. WHORTLEBERRY, BILBERRY, WHINBERRY. Deciduous, glabrous shrub, to 2 ft.; lvs. ovate, to 1¼ in. long, serrulate, bright green; fls. solitary, greenish-pink, ¼ in. long; fr. black, glaucous, $^5/_{16}$ in. in diam. Eur., n. Asia. Zone 5.

neglectum: *V. stamineum* var.

nitidum: *V. Myrsinites.*

Nummularia Hook.f. & T. Thoms. ex C. B. Clarke. Evergreen, rigid shrub, to 1½ ft., branchlets bristly; lvs. ovate or orbicular, to 1 in. long, bristly-serrate, leathery; fls. in racemes, pink, $^3/_{16}$ in. long; fr. black. Himalayas. Zone 7.

occidentalis A. Gray. WESTERN BLUEBERRY. Deciduous, compact, glabrous shrub, to 2½ ft.; lvs. oblanceolate to obovate, to ¾ in. long, entire, glaucous; fls. solitary or in 2's, white or pinkish, $^3/_{16}$ in. long; fr. blue-black, glaucous, ¼ in. in diam. B.C. to cent. Calif., e. to Rocky Mts.

Oldhamii Miq. Deciduous shrub, to 12 ft., branchlets pubescent; lvs. elliptic to ovate, to 3¼ in. long, toothed; fls. in loose racemes to 3⅜ in. long, corolla reddish, campanulate; fr. black, $^5/_{16}$ in. in diam. Early summer. Korea, Japan. Zone 6.

ovalifolium Sm. MATHERS. Deciduous, straggly shrub, to 15 ft., branchlets 4-angled; lvs. ovate to oblong, to 2 in. long, entire to undulate, glabrous, glaucescent beneath; fls. solitary, preceding the lvs., pink, $^5/_{16}$ in. long; fr. blue to black or purplish, glaucous, ⅜ in. in diam. N. Amer. Zone 5.

ovatum Pursh. CALIFORNIA H., EVERGREEN H., SHOT H. Evergreen, much-branched shrub, to 10 ft. or more; lvs. ovate to lanceolate-oblong, to 1¼ in. long, serrate, leathery, glabrous and shining above; fls. in short racemes, corolla white to pink, campanulate, ¼ in. long; fr. black, sometimes glaucous, $^5/_{16}$ in. in diam., edible. Early to late spring. B.C. to Calif. Zone 7. An important source of florists' greens, called "HUCKLEBERRY" or "LEATHERLEAF."

Oxycoccos L. SMALL CRANBERRY, EUROPEAN C. Evergreen, sts. creeping, to 1 ft. long; lvs. oblong-ovate to ovate, $^5/_{16}$ in. long, glaucous beneath, revolute; fls. 1–4 in terminal clusters, corolla pink, 4-parted, ¼ in. long, stamens exserted; fr. red, $^5/_{16}$ in. in diam., edible. Late spring, early summer. N. Asia, n. Eur., N. Amer. Zone 2.

padifolium Sm. Evergreen shrub, to 9 ft., but a small tree in the wild; lvs. oblong to ovate, to 2 in. long, serrulate; fls. in racemes, corolla yellowish, with red stripes, campanulate, to ½ in. long; fr. black, ⅜ in. in diam., sweet. Madeira.

pallidum Ait. [*Cyanococcus pallidus* (Ait.) Small]. Deciduous shrub, to 3 ft., brs. yellow-green, hairy in lines; lvs. elliptic to ovate, to 2 in. long, serrate, glabrous, glaucous beneath; fls. in dense clusters, white, often tinged pink, ¼ in. long; fr. blue, glaucous, to $^5/_{16}$ in. in diam. N.Y. to Ga. and Ala., also Mo. and Ark. Zone 4.

parvifolium Sm. RED H. Deciduous shrub, to 10 ft., branchlets and twigs with decurrent ridges; lvs. nearly sessile, oblong to ovate, to ½ in. long, entire; fls. solitary, pinkish-white, ¼ in. long; fr. bright red, ⅜ in. in diam. Alaska to Calif.

pensilvanicum: see *V. angustifolium* var. *laevifolium.*

praestans Lamb. KAMCHATKA BILBERRY. Deciduous, low shrub, to 6 in., with creeping rootstocks; lvs. elliptic to obovate, to 2 in. long, finely toothed, green on both sides, glabrous; fls. solitary or 2 or 3 in a cluster, corolla white, tinged pink, campanulate, ¼ in. long; fr. shiny red, ½ in. in diam., sweet, fragrant. Early summer. Ne. Asia. Zone 4.

scoparium Leib. GROUSEBERRY, LITTLE-LEAF H. Deciduous, tufted, glabrous shrub, to 16 in., sts. yellow-green, resembling broom, strongly angled; lvs. elliptic-oblong to ovate, to ½ in. long, serrulate; fls. solitary, pink, ⅛ in. long; fr. red, about ¼ in. in diam., sweet and palatable. Alta. to B.C., s. to Colo. and n. Calif.

Sprengelii (G. Don) Sleum. [*V. Donnianum* Wight]. Evergreen shrub, to 10 ft.; lvs. almost sessile, oblong-ovate to lanceolate, to 3 in. long, acuminate, toothed, glabrous; fls. white, in racemes, corolla tubular, ¼ in. long; fr. black-purple, $^3/_{16}$ in. in diam. Himalayas, China, se. Asia. Zone 7.

stamineum L. [*Polycodium stamineum* (L.) Greene]. DEERBERRY, SQUAW H. Deciduous shrub, to 10 ft., branchlets pubescent; lvs. oblong, elliptic to ovate, to 4 in. long, glaucous beneath; fls. in loose-bracted racemes to 2½ in. long, corolla white or purplish, open-campanulate, to ¼ in. long, stamens exserted; fr. greenish to blue or purple, $^5/_{16}$ in. in diam. Mass. to Mo., s. to Fla. and La. Zone 6. Var. **neglectum** (Small) Deam [*V. neglectum* (Small) Fern.; *Polycodium neglectum* Small]. Branchlets and lvs. glabrous. N.J. to e. Kans.

Stapfianum Sleum. [*V. buxifolium* Hook.f.]. Erect shrub, 1½–4 ft., glabrous; lvs. oblong, to ⅜ in. long, obtuse, very thick and leathery, black-dotted beneath; fls. in dense racemes, white or pink, about ⅛ in. long. Borneo.

uliginosum L. BOG BILBERRY, MOORBERRY. Deciduous, erect, glabrous, much-branched shrub, to 2 ft.; lvs. roundish or oblong to obovate, to 1 in. long, entire, prominently veined; fls. solitary, or in 2's or 4's, pink, ¼ in. long; fr. dark blue, glaucous, to ⅜ in. in diam. N. Eur., n. Asia, N. Amer. Zone 2.

vacillans Torr. SUGAR H., LOW BILBERRY, EARLY SWEET B., LOW BLUEBERRY, LOW SWEET B. Deciduous, glabrous shrub, to 3 ft., brs. stiff; lvs. obovate, ovate, or elliptic, to 2 in. long, becoming almost leathery, pale or dull; fls. in racemes, greenish to purplish, ⅜ in. long; fr. dark blue, slightly glaucous, ⅜ in. in diam., very sweet. W. Nov. Sc. to Mich., s. to Ga. and Mo. A source of edible wild blueberries.

virgatum Ait. [*Cyanococcus virgatus* (Ait.) Small]. Deciduous shrub, to 10 ft.; lvs. elliptic to ovate or obovate, to 2 in. long, serrate, pale and glandular beneath; fls. in racemes, white to pink, $^5/_{16}$ in. long; fr. black, shiny, to ⅜ in. in diam. Ga. to n. Fla., w. to Ark. and Tex. Zone 7.

Vitis-idaea L. COWBERRY, FOXBERRY, CRANBERRY. Evergreen shrub, to 1 ft., with creeping rhizome; lvs. obovate, to 1¼ in. long, leathery, dark green and glossy above, gland-dotted beneath; fls. in drooping racemes, corolla white or pink, campanulate, ¼ in. long; fr. red, to ⅜ in. in diam., sour. Late spring. Eur., n. Asia. Fr. sometimes marketed from collections from wild plants, especially in n. Eur. Var. **majus** Lodd. Lvs. and fr. larger. Var. **minus** Lodd. MOUNTAIN CRANBERRY, ROCK C., LINGBERRY, LINGEN, LINGENBERRY, LINGONBERRY. Dwarf, forming dense mats; lvs. to ¾ in. long; fls. pink to red. Mass. to Alaska. Zone 6.

VAGNERA: *SMILACINA.*

VALERIANA L. VALERIAN. *Valerianaceae.* About 200 spp. of per. herbs, subshrubs, or shrubs, with thickened, strong-smelling taproots or rhizomes, native to all continents except Australia; lvs. opp., simple, pinnatifid, or compound, often in a basal rosette; fls. small, white, pink, rose, or yellowish, in clustered or paniculate cymes, bisexual or unisexual, calyx inrolled at first, becoming pappuslike in fr., corolla rotate, funnelform, or somewhat campanulate, stamens usually 3, ovary inferior, 3-celled at base; fr. an achene with 1 fertile and 2 sterile cells, crowned by persistent calyx.

One species yields the drug valerian. Valerians are of easy culture in the flower garden or border. Propagated by seeds or division.

acutiloba: *V. capitata* subsp.

alba: a listed name of no botanical standing; some material so labeled is *Centranthus ruber* cv. 'Alba'.

arizonica A. Gray. Sts. to 1 ft.; basal lvs. simple and ovate to nearly orbicular, or sometimes pinnately divided, to 2½ in. long, petioles to 2¼ in. long, st. lvs. pinnate or pinnatifid; fls. bisexual, corolla whitish or pinkish, funnelform, ½ in. long. Se. Colo. to sw. Utah, s. to Sonora (Mex.).

capitata Pall. ex Link. Sts. to 2 ft.; lvs. mostly cauline, ovate to obovate, to 2¼ in. long, petioles to ⅝ in. long; fls. bisexual, corolla white to pinkish, funnelform, ¼ in. long. Arctic Alaska and Siberia to Kola Pen. Subsp. **acutiloba** (Rydb.) F. G. Mey. [*V. acutiloba* Rydb.]. Glabrous; lvs. mostly basal and simple, oblong-spatulate to obovate-spatulate, to 3 in. long; fls. to $^5/_{16}$ in. long. Se. Wyo., s. to Ariz. and New Mex.

celtica L. Cespitose, glabrous, very fragrant, sts. to 6 in.; lvs. mostly basal, narrowly lanceolate to oblong, to 1½ in. long, obtuse, entire; fls. yellowish, corolla rotate. Alps.

coccinea: a listed name of no botanical standing for *Centranthus ruber*.

excelsa: *V. officinalis.*

montana L. Sts. to 1 ft.; lvs. ovate or elliptic-ovate to lanceolate, to 1½ in. long, acuminate, petioles to ¾ in. long; fls. pink to white, unisexual and bisexual, corolla funnelform, slightly saccate at base. Eur. Var. **rotundifolia** (Vill.) Sims [*V. rotundifolia* Vill.]. Sts. shorter; lvs. more rounded.

officinalis L. [*V. excelsa* Poir.]. COMMON V., GARDEN HELIOTROPE. Sts. to 3½ ft. or sometimes to 5 ft.; lvs. mostly cauline, pinnatifid to pinnate, with 7–10 pairs of oblong-ovate to lanceolate segms., entire or toothed; fls. white, pink, or lavender, very fragrant, bisexual, corolla funnelform, slightly saccate near base, to ³⁄₁₆ in. long. Eur., w. Asia; naturalized locally in Canada and n. U.S. Dried rhizomes yield an official drug, valerian. Cvs. are: **'Alba'**, fls. white; **'Coccinea'**, fls. deep red; **'Rubra'**, fls. red.

rosea: a listed name of no botanical standing for *Centranthus ruber* cv.

rotundifolia: *V. montana* var.

rubra: *Centranthus ruber.*

saliunca All. Cespitose, glabrous, sts. to 6 in.; lvs. mostly basal, elliptic to oblong, to 1¼ in. long including petiole, entire, dark green; fls. pink, fragrant, corolla funnelform. S. Eur.

sitchensis Bong. Robust per., to 4 ft.; lvs. mostly cauline, pinnatifid to pinnate, with mostly 1–3 pairs of lateral lobes, to 8 in. long including petiole, membranous, basal lvs. simple to pinnate, to 16 in. long including petiole; fls. white, fragrant, to ¼ in. long, corolla funnelform. Mts., Alaska to Mont., Idaho, n. Calif. Subsp. **uliginosa** (Torr. & A. Gray) F. G. Mey. [*V. uliginosa* Torr. & A. Gray]. Slender per., to 3½ ft.; st. lvs. with 4–6 pairs of lateral lobes. Wet areas, ne. U.S. and adjacent Canada.

supina L. Cespitose, sts. to 6 in.; lvs. simple, obovate to lanceolate, to ¾ in. long including petiole, essentially entire, dark shiny green, ciliate; fls. pink, fragrant, corolla funnelform. Cent. Eur.

uliginosa: *V. sitchensis* var.

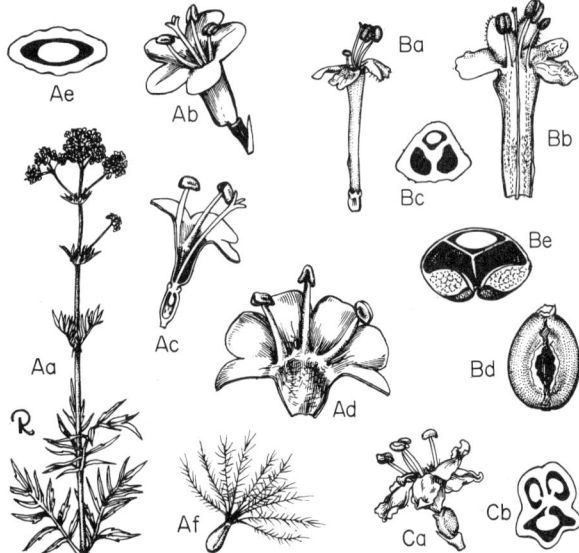

VALERIANACEAE. **A,** *Valeriana officinalis:* **Aa,** upper part of flowering stem, × ⅙; **Ab,** flower, × 3; **Ac,** flower, vertical section, × 3; **Ad,** upper part of corolla, expanded, × 4; **Ae,** ovary, cross section, × 16; **Af,** fruit, × 2. **B,** *Fedia cornucopiae:* **Ba,** flower, × 1½; **Bb,** corolla, expanded, × 2; **Bc,** ovary, cross section, × 6; **Bd,** fruit, × 3; **Be,** fruit, cross section, × 5. **C,** *Patrinia scabiosifolia:* **Ca,** flower, × 3; **Cb,** ovary, cross section, × 10.

VALERIANACEAE Batsch. VALERIAN FAMILY. Dicot.; about 10 genera and 400 spp. of per. herbs, rarely shrubs, often with a rank odor when dried, widespread, but native mostly to N. Hemisphere, and absent in Australia except as introduced weeds; lvs. opp., simple, pinnatifid, or compound; infl. cymose or headlike; fls. small, bisexual or unisexual, calyx obsolete or variously toothed, or inrolled in fl. and becoming pappuslike in fr., corolla 5-lobed, often 2-lipped, saccate or

spurred at base, stamens 1–4, arising from corolla tube, ovary inferior, usually 3-celled; fr. indehiscent, dry, usually with 1 fertile and 2 sterile cells, often crowned with the persistent calyx. *Centranthus, Fedia, Nardostachys, Patrinia, Plectritis, Valeriana,* and *Valerianella* are grown as ornamentals, and a few spp. rarely as vegetables or for medicinal use.

VALERIANELLA Mill. CORN-SALAD, LAMB'S LETTUCE. *Valerianaceae.* Between 50 and 60 spp. of ann. and bien. herbs, native to N. Amer., Eur., N. Afr., and Asia; lvs. simple, opp., rather succulent; fls. white, rose, or blue, in headlike cymes, calyx minute or obsolete, corolla funnelform, salverform, or tubular, 5-lobed, stamens 3 or 2, ovary inferior, 3-celled; fr. dry, indehiscent, with 1 fertile and 2 sterile cells.

Two species are grown as pot herbs or salad plants and others as ornamentals. Corn-salad of easy cultivation in spring and autumn.

eriocarpa Desv. ITALIAN C.-S. Ann., sts. to 16 in., hairy; lvs. linear to spatulate, to 5 in. long; fls. in very dense cymes; fr. flattened, crowned with a distinct, deeply 5–6-toothed calyx. N. Afr., Portugal to Greece; naturalized in Brit. Is.

Locusta (L.) Betcke [*V. Locusta* var. *olitoria* L.; *V. olitoria* (L.) Pollich]. COMMON C.-S., LAMB'S LETTUCE. Ann., sts. to 1½ ft., almost glabrous; lvs. spatulate or oblong-ovate, to 3 in. long, toothed or entire; fls. light blue; fr. nearly spherical, crowned with small, inconspicuous calyx. N. Afr. and Eur., w. to w. Asia; introd. in N. Amer.

olitoria: *V. Locusta.*

VALLARIS Burm.f. *Apocynaceae.* About 6 spp. of woody, twining vines with milky sap, native to trop. Asia; lvs. opp., entire, minutely dotted; fls. in lateral forked cymes, 5-merous, bisexual, corolla white, salverform, lobes broad, longer than tube, stamens borne at top of corolla tube, anthers spurred at base, connivent, adhering to stigma, exserted, carpels 2, united at first, developing into an oblong follicular fr. and finally separating, seeds many, with tuft of hairs.

One species grown in warm regions as a veranda and arbor cover.

dichotoma: *V. solanacea.*

Heynei: *V. solanacea.*

solanacea (Roth) O. Kuntze [*V. dichotoma* (Roxb.) Wallich ex Wight; *V. Heynei* K. Spreng.]. Tall-climbing; lvs. elliptic to linear-oblong, to 4 in. long, petioles to ⅝ in. long; cymes 3–10-fld., pubescent; fls. fragrant, ⅝ in. across, filaments villous, anthers woolly, styles pubescent; fr. woody, to 6 in. long and 2 in. wide, seeds ovate, 1 in. long, with very long tuft of hairs. India and Ceylon. Zone 10b.

VALLESIA Ruiz & Pav. *Apocynaceae.* About 8 spp. of shrubs and small trees, native to trop. Amer.; lvs. alt., entire, petioled; fls. small, in cymes opp. the lvs., 5-merous, bisexual, calyx without glands, corolla white, salverform, tube slightly inflated at base and apex, puberulent in lower part, lobes shorter than tube, stamens borne on corolla, included, anthers ovate, apically acuminate, basally cordate; fr. of 1 or 2 obovoid, divergent, 1–2-seeded drupes, seeds obovoid, grooved.

flexuosa Woodson. To 30 ft.; lvs. oblong-ovate, to 6 in. long, acute to acuminate, obtuse at base; fls. greenish-white, star-shaped; fr. to ¾ in. across, pale cream-colored when mature. Costa Rica.

VALLISNERIA L. EEL GRASS, TAPE G. *Hydrocharitaceae.* About 8–10 spp. of submersed, dioecious, grasslike aquatic herbs, native to trop. and temp. regions; lvs. ribbonlike; male fls. in a head subtended by an ovoid 3-valved spathe on a short scape, female fls. solitary and sessile in a tubular spathe on a long scape coiled or spiralling in fr.

Occasionally grown in aquaria or pools; propagated by stolons.

americana Michx. WILD CELERY, WATER C. Lvs. to 6 ft. long, ¾ in. wide; male spathe to ⅝ in. long, tapered to short stout scape, female spathe on a stout scape that curves or spirals in fr.; fr. curved. Quiet water, New. Bruns. to N.Dak., s. to Gulf Coast states. Becomes dormant in winter, even in aquaria.

asiatica Miki. Lvs. linear, to ¼ in. wide, 5-veined, slightly serrate toward apex; female spathe to ¾ in. long, enclosing fl.; fr. to 8 in. long. Japan and China to Taiwan and se. Asia.

gigantea Graebn. Coarse per.; lvs. linear, to 3 ft. long and ¾ in. wide, 5–9-veined, with longitudinal black and brown stripes, indistinctly dentate; fr. greenish-yellow, striped with black or red-brown, to 8 in. long. S. and e. Asia and Philippine Is. to e. Australia and Tasmania.

rubra Hort. Name applied to a plant which has lvs. bronzy-red when grown in good light; probably a cv. of *V. gigantea* or *V. spiralis*.

spiralis L. Similar to *V. americana*, but lvs. generally more slender; male spathe rounded basally, on a longer, filiform scape, female scape larger, filiform, becoming coiled in fr.; fr. straight. S. Eur., w. Asia. This is the plant known in the trade as "Italian Type"; although not winter-hardy north, it grows all year long in aquaria, while *V. americana* does not. Cv. **'Torta'**. Lvs. shorter and broader, twisted in close spirals for their whole length.

VALLOTA Herb. *Amaryllidaceae.* One sp., a bulbous herb, native to S. Afr.; bulb tunicate; lvs. strap-shaped; infl. a 6–9-fld. umbel terminal on a hollow scape and subtended by 2 free spathe valves; fls. erect, funnelform, tube prominent, lobes equal, connected at base by a callus, stamens borne below throat of tube, anthers dorsifixed, stigma headlike, ovary inferior, ovules many; fr. a caps., seeds black, flat, winged at base.

Grown in the greenhouse; the bulbs should be kept somewhat moist even during the resting period. The roots should be interfered with as little as possible, and plants may be kept in the same pots several years if liquid manure is applied. Repotting should be done after flowering is over.

purpurea: *V. speciosa.*

speciosa (L.f.) T. Durand & Schinz [*V. purpurea* (Ait.) Herb.; *Amaryllis purpurea* Ait.]. SCARBOROUGH LILY. Lvs. to 2 ft. long and 1 in. wide, developing at same time as the scarlet fls. Summer and autumn. Cv. **'Alba'**. Fls. white.

VANCOUVERIA C. Morr. & Decne. *Berberidaceae.* Three spp. of rhizomatous per. herbs, native to w. N. Amer.; lvs. usually basal, twice ternate, lfts. cordate, somewhat 3-lobed; fls. small, drooping, in panicles on leafless scapes, 3-merous, the outer sepals 6–9, small, the inner 6 petaloid, petals 6, narrow, with apical nectary, stamens 6, ovary with 2 to several ovules.

chrysantha Greene. To 1 ft., evergreen; lfts. to 1 in. long, somewhat leathery, pubescent beneath; fls. golden-yellow, about ½ in. long. Ore.

hexandra (Hook.) C. Morr. & Decne. [*Epimedium hexandrum* Hook.]. To 1½ ft., deciduous; lfts. to 1½ in. long, thin, nearly glabrous beneath; fls. white, ½ in. long. Wash. to Calif.

parviflora: *V. planipetala.*

planipetala Calloni [*V. parviflora* Greene]. INSIDE-OUT FLOWER. To 1½ ft., evergreen; lfts. to 1½ in. long, with cartilaginous margins, nearly glabrous beneath; fls. white or tinged lavender, 5/16 in. long. Ore. and Calif.

VANDA R. Br. [*Euanthe* Schlechter]. *Orchidaceae.* About 60 spp. of epiphytes, native to trop. Asia and Malay Arch.; sts. stout, enveloped by bases of lf. sheaths; lvs. leathery or fleshy, flat, keeled, or cylindrical; infls. 1 to several, lateral, axillary, racemose; fls. usually large, showy, sepals and petals nearly equal, spreading or converging, narrowed at base, lip large, 3-lobed, saccate or spurred at base, the lateral lobes united to short foot of column or to sides of sac or spur, midlobe fleshy, variable in shape, disc usually ridged, column short. For structure of fl. see *Orchidaceae.*

For culture see *Orchids.*

alpina Lindl. St. and lvs. as in *V. cristata;* racemes shorter than lvs., 1–2-fld.; fls. nodding, about 1 in. across, sepals and petals converging, oblong, with coloring of fls. of *V. cristata;* lip united to column, swollen but not saccate or spurred, lateral lobes rounded, midlobe retuse, upper surface with shallow ridges. Winter–summer. Himalayas.

Amesiana Rchb.f. Lvs. strap-shaped, 2-ranked, fleshy; racemes 1 ft. long or more, 10–12-fld., rachis dotted with brown; fls. fragrant, 1½ in. across, sepals and petals cuneate-oblong, cream-white, faintly tinged with pink, becoming yellow with age, lateral lobes of lip nearly square, erect, cream-white, midlobe kidney-shaped, rich rosy-magenta, with 3 thickened lines and small round callosity on disc, margin denticulate, spur short, conical. Late spring. India.

Batemannii: *Vandopsis lissochiloides.*

Bensonii Batem. To 1 ft. or more; lvs. 2-ranked, strap-shaped, leathery, to 6 in. long; racemes erect, many-fld., to 1½ ft. long; fls. 2½ in. across, white on outside, yellowish-green dotted with reddish-brown inside, sepals and petals clawed, obovate, lip as long as sepals, lateral lobes white, triangular, midlobe violet, ovate, with 3 ridges, apex bifid, kidney-shaped. Burma.

Boxallii: *V. lamellata* cv.

coerulea Griff. ex Lindl. BLUE ORCHID. St. to 3 ft. high; lvs. 2-ranked, strap-shaped, leathery, to 8 in. long; racemes erect, many-fld.; fls. to 5 in. across, light to deep blue, checkered with darker blue, sepals and petals clawed, obovate, lateral sepals longer than other segms., lip shorter, lateral lobes with short, incurved cusp at apex, midlobe deep blue, with 2 small tubercles at apex, each with 2–3 thickened ridges, spur short, conical, with 2-parted callus at mouth, column white with violet stain. Himalayas and mts. of Burma and Thailand.

coerulescens Griff. Lvs. 2-ranked, leathery, to 8 in. long, apices with spiny tip; racemes as long as lvs., many-fld.; fls. to 1½ in. across, on twisted pedicels, pale blue, sepals and petals obovate-spatulate, lip deep blue, lateral lobes oblong, midlobe obovate, with thickened median ridges, margins deflexed, spur short, incurved, column blue. Early spring. Burma.

Cathcartii: *Arachnis Cathcartii.*

Clarkei: *Arachnis Clarkei.*

cristata Lindl. St. to 3 ft. long; lvs. 2-ranked, narrowly oblong, to 4 in. long, 2-lobed at apex; racemes 2–5-fld., not longer than lvs.; fls. to 2 in. across, sepals and petals olive-green or yellowish, oblong, lip longer than sepals, united to base of column, green, blotched with dull purplish-brown, midlobe oblong, with divaricate lobules and hornlike fleshy beak pointing downward from under apex, upper surface with 5 warty ridges. Late spring. Himalayas.

Denisoniana R. Bens. & Rchb.f. Lvs. to 1 ft. long or more, strap-shaped, 2-lobed at apex; racemes shorter than lvs., few-fld.; fls. 2½ in. high, white tinged with green, sepals and petals obovate to oblong-spatulate, lateral lobes of lip white, erect, round, concave, midlobe greenish-white, contracted in middle, with angular sinus in forward margin and 4–5 raised lines, spur conical, callus 2-lobed, with a semilunate orange-yellow blotch on each side. Burma. Cv. **'Hebraica'** [var. *hebraica* Rchb.f.]. Sepals and petals sulphur-yellow, covered inside with many spots and transverse bars, spur orange inside, forward part of blade of lip olive-green.

densiflora: *Anota densiflora.*

gigantea: *Vandopsis gigantea.*

Hookerana Rchb.f. St. to 7 ft. high; lvs. stemlike, to 3 in. long, mucronate at apex; racemes 2–5-fld.; fls. 2½ in. across, sepals white, obovate-oblong, dorsal sepal undulate, white, flushed with light purple, petals broadly elliptic, undulate, white, flushed with light purple and dotted with deeper purple, lateral lobes of lip triangular-curved, amethyst-purple with paler striations, midlobe fan-shaped, 3-lobed, white-spotted and marked with amethyst-purple, margins crenulate, spur short, column cylindrical, purple above, anther beaked. Borneo.

insignis Blume. St. nearly erect; lvs. 2-ranked, linear-strap-shaped, to 1 ft. long; racemes scarcely longer than lvs., 4–7-fld.; fls. to 2½ in. across, sepals and petals white externally, tawny-yellow inside with dark brown oblong spots, sepals obovate-spatulate, petals similar but narrower, lip more or less fiddle-shaped, with 2 short white basal auricles and 2 white ridges, midlobe broadly clawed, semilunar at apex, concave, bright rose-purple, spur conical, column stained with pale rose. Late spring. Moluccas, Timor. Cv. **'Schroederana'**. Fls. yellow and white, forward part of midlobe of lip large, concave, pure white.

lamellata Lindl. Lvs. strap-shaped, to 15 in. long, 2-toothed at apex; racemes erect, as long as lvs., many-fld.; fls. to 2 in. across. light yellow, blotched with chestnut-brown, sepals and petals oblong, lip prolonged at base into spur, lateral lobes white, auricled, midlobe oblong, retuse at apex, with 2 raised transverse ridges. Late autumn. Philippine Is. Cv. **'Boxallii'** [var. *Boxallii* Rchb.f.; *V. Boxallii* (Rchb.f) Rchb.f.]. Racemes longer, with more fls.; fls. brightly colored, sepals and petals cream-white, lower half of lateral sepals red-brown, basal auricles of lip white, spotted with light purple, midlobe rose-purple.

limbata Blume. St. robust; lvs. leathery, channelled, to 8 in. long; racemes erect, as long as lvs., 10–12-fld.; fls. 2 in. across, sepals and petals similar, spatulate, bright cinnamon-colored and checkered, with golden margin, suffused with lilac externally, lip pale lilac, with short, conical spur, lateral lobes small, rounded, midlobe rosy-lilac, squarish, disc convex, with 5–7 parallel grooves, margins reflexed, claw with prominent callus. Early summer. Java.

Lowii: *Arachnis Lowii.*

luzonica Loher ex Rolfe. St. to 1 ft. high, stout; lvs. oblong, leathery, to 14 in. long; racemes erect, to 8 in. long, many-fld.; fls. 2 in. across, sepals and petals obovate, to 1 in. long, white with spot of purple toward apex, lip to 1 in. long, with saccate base, lateral lobes erect, auricled, midlobe oblong-fiddle-shaped, deep magenta-purple, column broad. Philippine Is.

Merrillii Ames & Quisumb. To 3 ft., st. cylindrical; lvs. 2-ranked, linear-oblong, to 1 ft. long; racemes 1–3, to 10 in. long, 7–11-fld.; fls. fragrant, fleshy, to 1½ in. across, sepals obovate, undulate, petals similar, sepals and petals light yellow, washed and stained with carmine or red and with striations of same color in center, lip shortly spurred, lateral lobes erect, squarish, white with purple dots, midlobe fiddle-shaped, ½ in. long, yellow washed with blood-red, with 2 raised papillae at throat of spur. Philippine Is.

Parishii Rchb.f. [*Vandopsis Parishii* (Rchb.f.) Schlechter]. St. stout; lvs. elliptic-oblong, to 9 in. long; racemes erect, longer than lvs., many-fld.; fls. fleshy, scented, 2 in. across, sepals elliptic-oblong, greenish-yellow, spotted with red-brown, petals nearly orbicular, of same color as sepals, lateral lobes of lip auricled, midlobe rhomboidal, with raised median line and conical protuberance at base, magenta-purple with pale margins, spur short, swollen, with orange-striped auricles, column short, white. Summer. Burma. Cv. **'Marrottiana'** [var. *Marrottiana* Rchb.f.]. Fls. unscented, sepals and petals bronzy-brown, richly suffused with magenta, lip with white basal auricles and magenta midlobe.

parviflora Lindl. St. to 1 ft. high; lvs. linear-oblong, to 4 in. long, 2-lobed at apex; racemes as long as lvs., few-fld.; fls. yellow, ½ in. across, sepals spatulate, lateral sepals shorter than dorsal, petals similar, spreading, lip united to column foot, spurred, lateral lobes oblong, erect, midlobe decurved, fleshy, oblong, upper surface blue, warty and grooved in center, spur slender, conical, half as long as lip. Late spring. Himalayas.

pumila Hook.f. St. and lvs. as in *V. cristata* and *V. alpina;* racemes shorter than lvs., 2-fld.; fls. cream-colored, 1 in. across, fragrant, pendent, sepals and petals nearly equal, oblong, lateral sepals convergent, lip shorter than sepals, base with funnel-shaped sac, lateral lobes triangular, midlobe ovate, with 2 small knobs at apex and 4–6 short ridges in center. Late spring. Sikkim.

×**Rothschildiana** Hort.: *V. coerulea* × *V. Sanderana.* Similar to *V. coerulea;* racemes 1 to several, many-fld.; fls. blue to purple-blue, checkered, to 5 in. across, lip 1 in. long.

Roxburghii: *V. tesselata.*

Sanderana Rchb.f. [*Esmeralda Sanderana* Rchb.f.; *Euanthe Sanderana* (Rchb.f.) Schlechter]. Similar to *V. coerulea;* lvs. strap-shaped, leathery, to 1 ft. long; racemes many-fld.; fls. flat, 4 in. across, sepals and petals obovate, blush-pink, stained with buff-yellow, reticulated and checkered with dull crimson, especially on lateral sepals, lip small, concave, pale purplish-red at base, strongly recurved and chocolate-purple at apex, with 3 prominent keels from base to apex. Autumn. Philippine Is.

spathulata K. Spreng. Sts. to 2 ft. high; lvs. to 4 in. long, obtusely 2-lobed; racemes to 18 in. long, few-fld.; fls. 1¼ in. across, golden-yellow, sepals and petals oblong-spatulate, flat, lip as long as sepals, clawed, lateral lobes small, obovate, midlobe nearly orbicular, 3-lobed. Ceylon, India.

suavis: *V. tricolor* var.

teres Lindl. St. cylindrical, to several ft. high; lvs. similar to st., to 5 in. long; racemes to 10 in. long, few-fld.; fls. to 4 in. across, sepals white, tinged with rose, spreading vertically, petals deep rose, spreading horizontally, dorsal sepal obovate, lateral sepals rhomboidal, lip yellow, spotted with crimson, midlobe kidney-shaped, purple or rose, spur funnel-shaped, anther beaked. Late spring–early autumn. Cv. **'Alba'**. Fls. white. Cv. **'Andersonii'** [var. *Andersonii* L. O. Williams]. Fls. larger and more brightly colored.

tesselata Hook. ex G. Don [*V. Roxburghii* R. Br.]. St. to 2 ft. high; lvs. 2-ranked, narrow, crowded, to 8 in. long; racemes longer than lvs., 3–10-fld.; fls. to 2 in. across, sepals and petals obovate, spreading, undulate, yellowish-green or bluish, checkered with brown, claws and outer surfaces white, lip half as long as sepals, lateral lobes small, midlobe fiddle-shaped, with a purple, dilated, truncate, 2-lobed apex and deflexed margins, disc convex, with fleshy ridges, spur conical, hairy inside. India, Ceylon, Burma.

tricolor Lindl. Robust; lvs. strap-shaped, curved, to 18 in. long; racemes shorter than lvs., 7–10- or more-fld.; fls. fragrant, fleshy, to 3 in. across, on twisted pedicels, sepals and petals similar, obovate-oblong, undulate, leathery, light yellow, densely spotted with red-brown in longitudinal rows, white on exterior, lateral lobes of lip squarish, white, midlobe somewhat fiddle-shaped, deeply emarginate, with 3 ridges, whitish at base with red-brown streaks, elsewhere magenta-purple, spur short, white. Java. Cv. **'Patersonii'**. Sepals and petals cream-white, heavily spotted with brown, lip magenta-crimson. Cv. **'Planilabris'** [var. *planilabris* Lindl.]. Fls. larger and brighter in color than in the typical form, citron-yellow, densely marked with brown spots, lip large, flat, rose, margined with purplish-mauve and striped with chocolate-purple on disc. Var. **suavis** (Lindl.) Rchb.f. [*V. suavis* Lindl.]. Fls. large, white, sepals and petals spotted with purple, lip deep purple. E. Java, Bali.

undulata: *Vandopsis undulata.*

violacea: *Anota violacea.*

VANDOPSIS Pfitz. *Orchidaceae.* About 20 spp., native to trop. Asia and Malay Arch.; sts. erect, with short internodes; lvs. broad, strap-shaped, fleshy; infl. an erect or arching, axillary, many-fld. raceme; fls. large, fleshy, sepals and petals equal, spreading, lip 3-lobed, midlobe long, fleshy, keeled, glabrous, lateral lobes united to base of column and joined by a fleshy flap arching over basal keel of midlobe, column short, with a projection in front at its base. For structure of fl. see *Orchidaceae.*

For culture see *Orchids.*

gigantea (Lindl.) Pfitz. [*Vanda gigantea* Lindl.]. St. to 1 ft. high; lvs. to 14 in. long, 2-lobed at apex; racemes to 14 in. long, to 15-fld.; fls. 3 in. across, sepals and petals to 1¼ in. long, dull yellow with red-brown blotches, petals spatulate-obovate, lip straight, ¾ in. long, white, lateral lobes suffused with purple, midlobe yellow. Burma, Thailand.

lissochiloides (Gaud.-Beaup.) Pfitz. [*Stauropsis lissochiloides* (Gaud.-Beaup.) Benth. ex Pfitz.; *Vanda Batemannii* Lindl.]. St. taller and lvs. straighter than in *V. gigantea;* racemes to 6 ft. long, with few fls. open simultaneously; sepals and petals obovate, bright purple or yellowish on exterior, bright yellow with purple spots on interior, lip crimson-purple or yellowish. Summer–early autumn. Philippine Is.

Lowii: *Arachnis Lowii.*

Parishii: *Vanda Parishii.*

undulata (Lindl.) J. J. Sm. [*Stauropsis undulata* (Lindl.) Benth. ex Hook.f.; *Vanda undulata* Lindl.]. St. leafy, to 2 ft. high; lvs. 2-lobed apically; racemes to 10 in. long; fls. 1½ in. across, sepals and petals similar, oblanceolate, undulate, white with pink suffusion, lateral lobes of lip squarish, midlobe spatulate, truncate, the disc with a pair of purple keels. China, Sikkim, Burma.

VANGUERIA Juss. *Rubiaceae.* About 27 spp. of shrubs or trees, native to trop. Afr. and Madagascar; lvs. opp., stipules interpetiolar, frequently united in a ring; fls. in axillary clusters, white or greenish, small, mostly 4–5-merous, corolla cylindrical or campanulate, tube short, lobes spreading or reflexed; fr. fleshy, often edible, seeds few.

Sometimes grown in warm areas.

edulis Vahl [*V. madagascariensis* J. F. Gmel.]. TAMARIND-OF-THE-INDIES. Shrub, to 15 ft.; lvs. ovate or broadly elliptic, to 8 in. long; fls. greenish, to ¼ in. long; fr. apple-shaped, to 1½ in. across, edible, seeds 5. Madagascar.

infausta Burchell. Shrub, to 10 ft., or small tree, rusty-tomentose; lvs. ovate or nearly orbicular, to 3 in. long; fls. greenish, ¼ in. long; fr. globose, brownish, to ¾ in. across. S. Afr.

madagascariensis: *V. edulis.*

VANHEERDIA L. Bolus. *Aizoaceae.* Four spp. of dwarf, stemless, clump-forming succulents, native to S. Afr.; lvs. opp., symmetrical, paired, united ½–⅔ their length to form a subglobose or compressed-ovoid body (growth) without dots, keel usually distinct, it and the margins usually finely toothed, apex of lf. in 1 sp. with transparent areas (windows); fls. 1–3, expanding in the afternoon, calyx subequally 5–9-parted, petals yellow to orange-yellow, many, in about 3 series, stamens many, erect, staminodes absent, ovary inferior, 7–15-celled, stigmas 7–15; fr. a caps., expanding keels with broad, membranous, marginal wings, placental tubercles absent.

Growth occurs in spring. These plants require good illumination, limy soil, and moderate watering, but need to be dry during the resting period. Propagated by seeds. See also *Succulents.*

divergens (L. Bolus) L. Bolus [*Rimaria divergens* L. Bolus]. Growths reddish during resting period; lvs. gray-green, the pairs to 2½ in. long, united for ¾–1 in., to 1¼ in. wide, to 1 in. across, upper side of each lf. flat, more or less appressed, apex broad, angled, margins and keel of the lower side finely dentate; fls. to 1½ in. across, on pedicels to ⅝ in. long, petals yellow. Cape Prov.

Primosii (L. Bolus) L. Bolus [*Rimaria Primosii* L. Bolus]. Growths 1⅜ in. long, ⅞ in. across; lvs. pale violet, upper sides of free portion separated about ¼ in., 1½ in. long, apex rounded to slightly truncate with a window marbled with pale green; fls. 1 in. across, petals golden-yellow. Cape Prov.

VANILLA Swartz. *Orchidaceae.* About 90 spp. of pantrop., epiphytic, scandent, leafy or leafless, branching vines; lvs. leathery or fleshy, sessile or short-petioled; infl. an axillary raceme; sepals and petals similar, spreading, separate, lip 3-lobed, with claw united to column and enveloping it, column elongate, toothless, wingless, pollinia granular. For structure of fl. see *Orchidaceae.*

Grown for ornament and in the hot, wet tropics chiefly for the elongated seed pods ("vanilla beans") which, in some species, after curing, yield the vanilla extract of commerce. The vanilla orchid is grown commercially in many tropical areas, principally in Mex. and Madagascar, where temperature and humidity are high, the soil is rich in organic matter, and constant shade is present. The vines are supported on poles or the trunks of shade trees. Plants are increased by stem cuttings. Outside its area of nativity, vanilla requires hand-pollination in order to set fruits. The fully grown but unripe capsules are gathered and cured by a sweating process, which develops the flavor and aroma required for commerce. For general culture see *Orchids.*

articulata: *V. barbellata.*

barbellata Rchb.f. [*V. articulata* Northr.]. LINK VINE, WORM VINE, WORMWOOD. Sts. with bracts or abortive lvs. and aerial roots at nodes, internodes to 1 ft. long; lvs. abortive, linear-lanceolate, to 1½ in. long; racemes short, to 12-fld.; sepals and petals green, sepals oblong-elliptic, to 1½ in. long, petals elliptic-oblanceolate, to 1½ in. long, lip greenish basally, deep red fading to white at margins, midlobe reflexed, 1½ in. long, the disc with retrorse tuft of hairs in center. Late spring–summer. W. Indies and Fla.

Chamissonis Klotzsch. Sts. cylindrical; lvs. leathery, short-petioled, elongate-lanceolate, to 8 in. long; racemes 20-fld.; fls. yellow, sepals oblong, to 2¼ in. long, petals elongate-oblong to somewhat spatulate, lip as long as sepals and petals, with undulate margins, disc with longitudinal keel and central mat of hairs. Brazil.

fragrans: *V. planifolia.*

grandiflora: *V. pompona.*

planifolia Andr. [*V. fragrans* Ames]. VANILLA. Sts. stout; lvs. short-petioled, oblong-lanceolate, to 8 in. long; racemes to 20- or more-fld.; fls. yellowish, sepals and petals oblanceolate, to 2½ in. long, lip to 2 in. long, yellow with intense orange keel; fr. aromatic, to 8 in. long. Late autumn. Trop. Amer. The chief source of commercial vanilla.

pompona Schiede [*V. grandiflora* Lindl.]. WEST INDIAN VANILLA, POMPONA V. Sts. stout; lvs. leathery, oblong, to 1 ft. long; racemes short, to 7 in. long, many-fld.; fls. white to greenish-yellow, sepals oblanceolate, to 3¾ in. long, petals similar, smaller, lip white or orange-yellow, longer than sepals and petals, obscurely 3-lobed, with undulate and crenulate margins, disc smooth except for crest of retrorse, cuneate, imbricate appendages beneath column. Trop. Amer. A secondary source of commercial vanilla, producing shorter, thicker capsules.

VARIETY: see *Species.*

VEGETABLE GARDENING. This is the branch or department of horticulture that is concerned with the growing of oleraceous or esculent herbs, or of the class of cultivated plants known by custom and traditions as "vegetables." Its formal or Latin equivalent is the term olericulture. The terms are impossible of close definition because the plants that fall within their scope are so various. The best definition is an enumeration of the plants. These plants are prevailingly annual or treated as such, the marked exceptions being asparagus *(Asparagus officinalis)* and rhubarb *(Rheum Rhabarbarum)* and also some of the horticultural herbs. There are several kinds of vegetable gardening, as home or kitchen gardening, market gardening, and truck gardening.

VEITCHIA H. Wendl. [*Adonidia* Becc.]. *Palmae.* About 18 spp. of solitary, unarmed, monoecious palms in the Fiji Is., New Hebrides Is., and Palawan (Philippine Is.); trunk closely or distantly ringed; lvs. pinnate, sheath tubular, forming a prominent crownshaft, petiole short or long, pinnae many, slender, obliquely toothed at apex and sometimes appearing acute, with a prominent midrib and thick marginal veins; infl. below lvs., bracts 2, deciduous, the lower enclosing the upper, peduncle short to somewhat elongate, lower brs. 1–2 times branched, rachillae with fls. in triads (2 male and 1 female) near the base and above these with paired or solitary male fls.; male fls. symmetrical, sepals 3, imbricate, petals 3, valvate, stamens many, filaments erect in bud, anthers attached by back, pistillode ovoid-attenuate, about as long as stamens, female fls. with sepals 3, imbricate, petals 3, imbricate, staminodes 3–6, toothlike, pistil 1-celled, 1-ovuled; fr. orange or orange-red to crimson, ovoid, stigmatic residue apical, seed with homogeneous or ruminate endosperm, embryo basal.

The cultivated species are highly ornamental; primarily for tropical plantings, Zone 10b in Fla. For culture see *Palms.*

arecina Becc. To 40 ft. or more, trunk to 7 in. in diam.; lvs. spreading, sheath to 3½ ft. long, green with silvery scales, pinnae about 60 on each side, not minutely brown-dotted beneath, to 2 ft. long, 1 in. wide; female fls. borne only on lowermost part of rachillae, male fls. greenish; fr. bright crimson, to 1¾ in. long, 1 in. in diam., endosperm homogeneous. New Hebrides Is.; described from cult. in New Caledonia.

Joannis H. Wendl. To 100 ft., trunk to 10 in. in diam.; lvs. becoming horizontal, pinnae 70–80 on each side, drooping, glabrous; infl. stout; female fls. only 2–3(–6) at base of rachillae, male fls. to about ¾ in. long, stamens 100–110; fr. orange-red, 2–2⅜ in. long, seed pointed, endosperm homogenous. Fiji Is.

Merrillii (Becc.) H. E. Moore [*Adonidia Merrillii* (Becc.) Becc.]. MANILA PALM, CHRISTMAS P. Trunk to 15 ft. or more, with narrow internodes when grown in sun; lvs. to 6 ft. long, ascending, with arched apex, pinnae 48–63 on each side, ascending, pale-scaly beneath; infl. with female fls. along most of rachillae; male fls. about ½ in. long, stamens 47–62; fr. 1–1⁵⁄₁₆ in. long, crimson, endosperm ruminate. Palawan Is.

Montgomeryana H. E. Moore. To nearly 40 ft. or perhaps more, trunk to 8 in. in diam.; lvs. to nearly 9 ft. long, arching, pinnae 50–60 on each side, spreading, minutely scaly beneath; infl. with female fls. along most of rachillae; male fls. ½ in. long, stamens 130–140; fr. about 1¾ in. long, red, seed rounded at apex, endosperm homogeneous. Cult., origin unknown, but probably from New Hebrides Is.

Winin H. E. Moore. Similar in habit to *V. Montgomeryana* but male fls. about ½ in. long, stamens about 50; fr. ¾ in. long or less, seed with homogeneous endosperm. New Hebrides is.

VELTHEIMIA Gled. *Liliaceae.* Five spp. of bulbous, per. herbs, native to S. Afr.; bulb tunicate; lvs. basal; fls. tubular, pendulous, in a dense terminal raceme, perianth segms. united into a tube with 6 short lobes, stamens 6, filaments arising from perianth; fr. a 3-valved, loculicidal caps.

Of easy culture in the cool greenhouse; planted and started into growth in early autumn, and allowed to rest in summer after the leaves have died down. Propagated by seeds.

capensis (L.) DC. Lvs. lanceolate, to 1 ft. long and 1 in. wide, somewhat fleshy, glaucous-green, margins undulate; scape to 1 ft., stout, glaucous, mottled with purple; perianth tubular, to 1 in. long, pale pink with greenish tips; caps. inflated.

viridifolia Jacq. Lvs. strap-shaped to oblong, to 15 in. long and 4 in. wide, green and glossy on both sides, margins undulate; scape to 2 ft., stout, dark purple with yellow spots; perianth tubular, to 1½ in. long, pinkish-purple with yellow spots; caps. conspicuously 3-winged.

VENIDIUM Less. NAMAQUALAND DAISY. *Compositae* (Arctotis Tribe). Between 20 and 30 spp. of ann. or per. herbs, native to S. Afr.; lvs. alt., lobed to lyrately pinnatifid, usually woolly; fl. heads solitary, involucral bracts imbricate in several rows, receptacle pitted, essentially naked; disc fls. tubular, bisexual, ray fls. ligulate, female; achenes 3–5-winged or -ridged, essentially glabrous, pappus absent, or of 4 minute scales.

Venidiums are usually treated as annuals in the garden, but are sometimes grown as perennials under glass. Propagated by seeds sown under glass and transplanted.

calendulaceum: *V. decurrens.*

decurrens Less. [*V. calendulaceum* Less.]. Spreading, tomentose per., to 2 ft.; lvs. mostly lyrate, with terminal lobe to 1½ in. long, glabrate above in age, white-hairy beneath; heads to 2½ in. across; disc fls. yellowish-brown, ray fls. golden-yellow, with paler basal zone.

fastuosum (Jacq.) Stapf. CAPE DAISY. Hoary ann., to 2–3 ft.; lvs. lanceolate to oblanceolate, to 5–6 in. long, irregularly lobed to almost lyrate, gray-hairy; heads to 4–6 in. across; disc fls. brownish-purple to black, ray fls. bright orange, with dark purple-brown base.

VERATRUM L. FALSE HELLEBORE. *Liliaceae.* About 45 spp. of coarse, rhizomatous, per. herbs, native to N. Amer., Eur., and Asia in wet ground; plants polygamous, sts. stout, leafy; lvs. alt., pleated; fls. white, green, brown, maroon, or purple, in terminal panicles, perianth segms. 6, many-nerved, separate, stamens 6, anthers sacs confluent, styles 3; fr. a 3-lobed, septicidal caps.

Sometimes planted in the border or wild garden. Of easy culture and hardy. Propagated by division and seeds. The species yield poisonous substances of medicinal and insecticidal value.

album L. EUROPEAN WHITE HELLEBORE. To 4 ft., downy; lvs. oblong to elliptic, to 1 ft. long and 6 in. wide; fls. greenish outside, whitish inside, wavy-toothed, in downy panicles to 2 ft. long. Eur., n. Asia.

californicum E. Durand. CORN LILY, SKUNK CABBAGE. To 6 ft.; lvs. broadly elliptic to ovate, to 16 in. long and 8 in. wide, those toward top of plant lanceolate; fls. dull white, to ¾ in. long, in tomentose panicles to 1½ ft. long, with lower brs. erect. Wash. to Baja Calif., e. to Mont., Colo., and New Mex.

Eschscholtzii: *V. viride.*

insolitum Jeps. To 5 ft.; lvs. elliptic, to 10 in. long, those toward top of plant lanceolate; fls. white, ⁵⁄₁₆ in. long, irregularly fringed, in lanate-tomentose panicles to 20 in. long, ovary densely woolly. Sw. Ore. and adjacent Calif.

japonicum: *V. Maackii* var.

Maackii Regel. Sts. slender, to 2 ft.; lvs. only on lower part of st., broadly linear, to 16 in. long; fls. dark purple, to ¼ in. long, perianth reflexed in fr., in pubescent panicles to 12 in. long. E. Asia, Japan. Var. **japonicum** (Bak.) T. Shim. [*V. japonicum* (Bak.) O. Loes.]. Lvs. oblong to linear-lanceolate; fls. brown-purple, in panicles to 1 ft. long. Japan.

nigrum L. To 4 ft.; lvs. broadly elliptic to linear-lanceolate, to 1 ft. long and 8 in. wide; fls. blackish-purple, about ⅜ in. across, in pubescent, narrow panicles. Eur., Asia.

stamineum Maxim. To 3 ft.; lvs. broadly elliptic, to 8 in. long, those toward top of plant shorter and oblong, essentially glabrous; fls. white, about ¼ in. long, in pilose panicles to 10 in. long. Japan. Var. **lasiophyllum** Nakai. Lvs. hairy beneath, particularly on veins. Japan.

viride Ait. [*V. Eschscholtzii* A. Gray]. WHITE HELLEBORE, AMERICAN W.H., ITCHWEED, INDIAN POKE. Sts. to 7 ft., leafy to the top; lvs. elliptic to ovate, to 1 ft. long; fls. yellow-green, to 1 in. across, in 2 ft. hairy panicles with drooping lower brs. N. Amer.

Woodii J. W. Robbins. Sts. slender, to 5 ft.; lvs. elliptic to oblanceolate, to 1 ft. long, upper lvs. becoming linear; fls. dark maroon, to ⁵⁄₁₆ in. long, in slender, hairy panicles to 2 ft. long. Ohio to Iowa and Mo., s. to Okla.

VERBASCUM L. MULLEIN. *Scrophulariaceae.* About 250 spp. of hardy, mostly bien. herbs, rarely annuals or subshrubs, native to Asia and Eur., chiefly the Medit. region, but several naturalized or escaped in N. Amer.; sts. erect, from a rosette; lvs. alt., simple, sometimes pinnatifid; fls. mostly yellow, sometimes tawny, red, blue, or purple, rarely white, in spikes, racemes, or panicles, calyx deeply 5-parted, corolla rotate, deeply 5-lobed, tube short, stamens 5, some of the filaments hairy; fr. a caps.

Several kinds are grown in the sunny border, where their columnar habit and gray-green foliage give a pleasing contrast. There are named garden kinds, said to be hybrids. *Verbascum* also hybridizes with *Celsia.* Mulleins grow well in any soil except a cold, wet one. Propagated by cuttings, division, or by seeds; they often self-sow freely, blooming the following year.

Baldaccii Degen. Bien., to 7 ft. or more, green and sticky-glandular throughout; basal lvs. obovate to oblong-elliptic, st. lvs. ovate-oblong to ovate, truncate to cordate at base, toothed; corolla yellow, 1¼–2 in. across, tomentose outside, filaments woolly. Greece, Yugolsavia. A parent of both wild and hort. hybrids.

Blattaria L. MOTH M. Bien. or rarely ann., to 6 ft., green and glabrous or sparingly glandular-pubescent in upper part; st. lvs. elliptic to ovate, to 2½ in. long or more, doubly serrate-crenate; corolla yellow with lilac base, 1 in. across, filaments violet-pubescent. Eur., Asia; naturalized in N. Amer. A parent of several hort. hybrids. Forma **albiflorum** House. Fls. white.

bombyciferum Boiss. [*V. broussa* Hort.]. Bien., to 5 ft. or more, felty-white-tomentose, especially the infl.; basal lvs. ovate-oblong or obovate, to 16 in. long, st. lvs. ovate; fls. in clusters in a spike, corolla yellow, to 1½ in. across, filaments whitish-pubescent. Asia Minor.

broussa: *V. bombyciferum.*

Chaixii Vill. Mostly per., to 3 ft., sts. white-tomentose; lvs. to 6 in. long, coarsely toothed; fls. in panicled racemes, corolla yellow, filaments purple-woolly. S. Eur. A parent of several hort. hybrids. Cv. 'Album'. Fls. white.

densiflorum: *V. thapsiforme.*

Hinkei: *V. lanatum.*

×**hybridum** Brot. Botanically a hybrid between *V. pulverulentum* Vill. and *V. sinuatum* L., but material offered as *V. hybridum* may not be of this parentage.

lanatum Schrad. [*V. Hinkei* Friv.]. White-woolly per. or bien., to 4 ft.; lvs. broadly ovate to elliptic, densely white-woolly beneath, less so above; corolla dull yellow, to ¾ in. across, filaments purple-woolly. Cent. Eur.

longifolium Ten. White- or yellowish-tomentose per. or bien., to 4 ft.; lvs. to 2 ft. long, wavy; fls. pedicelled, in densely fld. racemes 1 ft. long, corolla golden-yellow, 1 in. across, longer filaments glabrous. S. Eur. Var. **pannosum** (Vis.) Murb. [*V. pannosum* Vis.]. More woolly; fls. larger.

lychnitis L. WHITE M. Bien., to 3 ft., sts. angled; lvs. ovate to lanceolate, entire, white-hairy beneath; corolla bright yellow, about ½ in. across, filaments white-woolly. Cent. and w. Eur.; naturalized in e. N. Amer. A sp. with several botanical vars. and a parent of hort. hybrids.

olympicum Boiss. Densely white-hairy bien., to 5 ft.; lvs. entire, to 6 in. long; fls. clustered in very long, many-fld. racemes, corolla bright yellow, 1 in. across, filaments white-woolly. Greece.

paniculatum Vul'f. Bien., to 3½ ft., with gray-stellate hairs; basal lvs. oblong, to 8 in. long, crenate-sinuate, st. lvs. oblong or ovate-lanceolate, nearly entire; corolla yellow, ½ in. across, stellate-hairy outside, 3 filaments with violet-purple hairs. S. Caucasus. Cv. 'Album' is listed.

pannosum: *V. longifolium* var.

phlomoides L. Gray- to yellowish-hairy bien., to 4 ft.; lvs. oblong-elliptic or obovate-oblong, crenate or crenate-dentate, hairy beneath, subglabrous above; fls. in racemes, corolla yellow, 2 in. across, stellate-hairy outside, 3 shorter filaments white-woolly. Cent. and s. Eur.; naturalized in e. U.S.

phoeniceum L. PURPLE M. Per., to 5 ft.; lvs. glabrous above, pubescent beneath, toothed; fls. in a simple, slender, glandular raceme, corolla purple or red, nearly glabrous, filaments purple-woolly. Se. Eur., Asia. A parent of many hort. hybrids.

speciosum Schrad. Densely stellate-hairy bien., to 6 ft.; basal lvs. oblong-lanceolate, entire, st. lvs. ovate, cordate-clasping, not decurrent; fls. in panicles, corolla yellow, 1 in. across, stellate-hairy outside, filaments white-woolly. Se. Eur., Asia Minor, Caucasus; naturalized in Ore.

thapsiforme Schrad. [*V. densiflorum* Vis.]. Densely yellowish-tomentose bien., to 5 ft.; basal lvs. oblong-elliptic to elliptic-lanceolate, crenate, st. lvs. narrowly decurrent; fls. sessile, in clusters in a long spike, corolla yellow, to 2 in. across, 3 filaments densely white-bearded. Eur.

Thapsus L. COMMON M., FLANNEL PLANT, VELVET PLANT. Bien., to 6 ft., yellowish-tomentose with stellate hairs; lvs. to 1 ft. long, toothed, soft; fls. sessile in clusters, in dense erect spikes, corolla yellow, 1 in. across, 2 lower filaments glabrous, anthers all basifixed. Eur. and Asia; extensively naturalized in N. Amer. in old dry fields.

virgatum J. Stokes. Bien., to 4 ft., stellate-glandular-hairy; lvs. to 3 in. long or the lower to 1 ft., toothed or lobed, pubescent and green; fls. short-pedicelled in clusters, corolla yellow or white, 1 in. across, filaments purple-woolly. Eur.; naturalized in w. N. Amer.

Wiedemannianum Fisch. & C. A. Mey. Cobwebby bien., to 3 ft.; lvs. to 5 in. long, toothed; fls. in long racemes, pedicels solitary, corolla blue or purplish-lilac, to 1¼ in. across, filaments purple-woolly. Asia Minor.

Wilmottiae: a listed name of no botanical standing.

Wilsonii: a listed name of no botanical standing.

VERBENA L. [*Glandularia* J. F. Gmel.]. VERVAIN. *Verbenaceae.* About 200 spp. of usually hairy, erect or decumbent to prostrate, ann. or per. herbs or subshrubs, native mostly to trop. and subtrop. N. and S. Amer.; sts. often 4-angled; lvs. opp., rarely whorled or alt., toothed, parted, or dissected, rarely entire; fls. of various colors, spicate, the spikes terminal or rarely axillary, solitary or sometimes arranged in corymbs or broad panicles, mostly bracted, calyx 5-toothed, 5-ribbed, corolla salverform or funnelform, somewhat 2-lipped, stamens 4, rarely 2; fr. dry, enclosed in the persistent calyx, separating into 4 nutlets at maturity.

Garden verbenas are treated as annuals in the North, the seeds being started under glass in the window and planted out to 1 ft. or so apart; or they may be propagated by cuttings from over-wintered plants. They are hardy in the open in the southernmost states and give early and brilliant bloom in spring. They do best in an open sunny exposure.

The wild verbenas native in many parts of the U.S. and Canada are rarely cultivated, except forms of *V. canadensis.* Many of them are erect, weedy plants, and the flowers are small, not showy, in dense, mostly long spikes. These are generally known as VERVAIN.

abyssinica: a listed name of no botanical standing.

alpina: *V. tenera* var. *Maonettii.*

Aubletia: *V. canadensis.*

bipinnatifida Nutt. DAKOTA VERVAIN. More or less prostrate per. with ascending sts. to 15 in.; lvs. triangular in outline, to 2 in. long, 3-parted or 2-pinnate, segms. oblong or linear; spikes dense, headlike, elongating in fr., bracts shorter than or as long as the calyx; fls. lilac-purple, ½ in. across. S. Dak. to Ala., w. to Ariz. and adjacent Mex.

bonariensis L. Rough-pubescent ann. or per., to 4 ft.; lvs. clasping, elliptic to elliptic-lanceolate, to 4 in. long, toothed; spikes dense, to 1½ in. long, in clusters that are often panicled; fls. lilac. S. Amer.; naturalized in Calif., s. U.S., W. Indies.

bracteata Lag. & Rodr. [*V. bracteosa* Michx.]. PROSTRATE VERVAIN. Ann. or per., sts. diffusely branched, decumbent or ascending; lvs. usually 3-lobed, or pinnatifid, to 2½ in. long; spikes terminal, bracts large; fls. small, purplish, obscured by bracts. Ont. to B.C., s. to Fla. and Mex.

bracteosa: *V. bracteata.*

canadensis (L.) Britt. [*V. Aubletia* Jacq.; *Glandularia canadensis* (L.) Small]. ROSE VERBENA, CLUMP VERBENA, CREEPING VERVAIN, ROSE VERVAIN. Branching per. to 1½ ft., sts. creeping, ascending or decumbent; lvs. ovate or ovate-oblong, to 4 in. long, truncate or broadly cuneate at base, toothed and cut or 3-cleft; spikes elongating, bracts shorter than calyx; fls. reddish-purple, lilac, rose, or white, to ⅝ in. across. Va. to Fla., w. to Iowa, Colo., Mex. Grown as an ann. in the North. Cvs. are: **'Candidissima'**, fls. white; **'Compacta'**, offered as more dense and shorter; **'Grandiflora'**, a listed name; **'Rosea'**, offered as low, continuously blooming, and having fls. rose-purple and fragrant.

candidissima: a listed name of no botanical standing for *V. canadensis* cv.

chamaedryfolia: *V. peruviana.*

citriodora: *Aloysia triphylla.*

compacta: a listed name of no botanical standing; see *V. canadensis* cv. and *V. × hybrida* cv.

corymbosa Ruiz & Pav. Per., to 3 ft., spreading by undergound shoots; lvs. ovate, to 1¼ in. long, coarsely serrate to pinnately lobed, hispidulous on both surfaces; spikes dense, to ¾ in. long, in a terminal, corymbose panicle; fls. reddish-purple to lavender, about ¼ in. across. Chile. Does best in moist, sunny location. Distinguished from *V. rigida* in being larger and in having lvs. with 2 small, toothed or entire basal lobes.

erinoides: *V. laciniata,* but material offered as *V. erinoides* is *V. tenuisecta.*

gigantea: a listed name of no botanical standing for *V. × hybrida* cv.

Gooddingii Briq. Per. to 1½ ft., sts. several, erect or decumbent-ascending, hairy, often glandular; lvs. ovate, to 2 in. long, 3-cleft, segms. toothed or incised; spikes headlike, elongating in fr.; fls. pink, lavender, or blue. Calif. to Utah, s. to Ariz. and n. Mex.

grandiflora: a name used by several authors; in hort., probably for *V. canadensis* cv. or *V. × hybrida* cv.

hastata L. BLUE VERVAIN, SIMPLER'S-JOY. Per., to 4–5 ft. or more, sts. stiff and erect; lvs. lanceolate or oblong-lanceolate, to 6 in. long, serrate or dentate; spikes narrow, in a panicle; fls. small, blue. B.C. to Nov. Sc., s. to Calif., Ariz., Fla. Dried plant used medicinally.×

×hortensis: *V. × hybrida.*

×hybrida Voss [*V. × hortensis* Hort. Vilm.-Andr.]. GARDEN VERBENA. Gray-hairy per., mostly grown as an ann., sts. decumbent, commonly creeping, 1–2 ft.; lvs. oblong to oblong-ovate, 2–4 in. long, broadened and truncate or truncate-cuneate at base, obtusely dentate or somewhat lobed basally, with short-margined petiole; spikes flattish, headlike, elongating in fr. to 2–3 in. ; fls. pink, red, white, yellowish, blue, purple, or variegated. A variable sp.; probably a hybrid of *V. peruviana* with other spp. Cvs. include: **'Compacta'**, **'Gigantea'**, **'Grandiflora'**, **'Luminosa'**, **'Multiflora'**, **'Rosea Stellata'**, **'Violacea Stellata'**.

laciniata (L.) Briq. [*V. erinoides* Lam.]. Per. in mild climates, but grown as an ann., sts. more or less stiff and erect, much-branched,

decumbent, rooting at nodes; lvs. ovate in outline, deeply 3-parted or pinnatifid-laciniate, to ¾ in. long; spikes headlike; fls. red-violet, lavender, or blue. Argentina, Chile.

lasiostachys Link. VERVAIN. Per., to 1½ ft. or more, often diffuse, sts. prostrate to erect, villous; lvs. elliptic to oblong, to 2½ in. long, often 3-cleft, coarsely and irregularly serrate; spikes in a panicle, 18–20 in. long; fls. purple or rarely white. W. Ore. to n. Baja Calif.

luminosa: a listed name of no botanical standing for *V. × hybrida* cv.

multiflora: a listed name of no botanical standing for *V. × hybrida* cv.

officinalis L. Glabrous or nearly glabrous, loosely branched ann., 1–3 ft.; lvs. narrowly ovate to obovate, lowermost 1–3 in. long, pinnatifid or cleft; spikes loosely paniculate; calyx to ⅛ in. long, longer than bract, corolla violet, less than ¼ in. long. Mass., s. to Fla. and La.

peruviana (L.) Britt. [*V. chamaedryfolia* Juss.; *Glandularia peruviana* (L.) Small]. Per., but grown as an ann., sts. procumbent, forking and rooting at nodes; lvs. oblong-lanceolate to ovate, to 2 in. long, tapering at base, rather sharply serrate or dentate, very scabrous; spikes long-peduncled, solitary, densely headlike; fls. scarlet or crimson. Argentina to s. Brazil.

platensis K. Spreng. [*V. teucrioides* Gillies & Hook.]. Tufted per., rooting at base, but sts. ascending; lvs. nearly sessile, ovate or oblong-triangular, to 2 in. long, serrate, pubescent; spikes terminal, elongating; fls. yellowish-white or pinkish, fragrant at night. Peru to Chile, s. Brazil and southward.

pulchella: *V. tenera.*

rigida K. Spreng. [*V. venosa* Gillies & Hook.]. VERVAIN. Stiff per. herb, 1–2 ft., sts. ascending to erect, roots tuberous; lvs. sessile, clasping, oblong, 2–3 in. long, irregularly toothed, rigid; spikes often in 3's; fls. purple or magenta. S. Brazil, Argentina; naturalized from N.C. to Fla., w. to Tex. Blooms first year from seed. Cv. **'Alba'**. Fls. white. Cv. **'Lilacina'**. Fls. lilac.

rosea stellata: a listed name of no botanical standing for *V. × hybrida* cv.

stricta Venten. HOARY VERVAIN. Soft-pubescent per., sts. erect and stiff, leafy, to 1½ ft.; lvs. nearly sessile, oblong, elliptic to broadly ovate, to 4 in. long, sharply serrate; spikes solitary, dense, elongate; fls. purple or blue. Mass. to Mont., s. to n. Mex.

tenera K. Spreng. [*V. pulchella* Sweet]. Somewhat shrubby per., sts. cespitose, decumbent, rooting at nodes; lvs. laciniate-pinnatifid, to 1 in. long, hairy; spikes elongating; fls. rose-violet, calyx twice as long as bracts, with spreading hairs. S. Brazil and La Plata region. Cv. **'Albiflora'**. Fls. white. Var. **Maonettii** Regel [*V. alpina* Hort.; *V. pulchella* var. *Maonettii* (Regel) Regel]. Fls. white-margined.

tenuisecta Briq. [*Glandularia tenuisecta* (Briq.) Small]. MOSS VERBENA. Per., to 1 ft., sts. decumbent or ascending; lvs. triangular in outline, to 1½ in. long, 3-pinnatifid, segms. linear, entire or toothed; spikes dense, headlike, elongating to 2 in. in fr.; fls. blue, purple, violet, or lilac. S. Amer.; naturalized from Ga. to La. This sp. has been cult. as *V. erinoides*. Cv. **'Alba'**. Fls. white.

teucrioides: *V. platensis.*

triphylla: *Aloysia triphylla.*

urticifolia L. WHITE VERVAIN. Erect per., to 5 ft.; lvs. ovate, oblong, or oblong-lanceolate, to 8 in. long, coarsely toothed, glabrous or with scattered hairs on veins beneath; spikes many in a panicle, stiff, strigose; fls. white. Que. and Me. to S. Dak., s. to Fla. and Tex.

venosa: *V. rigida.*

violacea stellata: a listed name of no botanical standing for *V. × hybrida* cv.

VERBENACEAE Jaume St.-Hil. VERVAIN or VERBENA FAMILY. Dicot.; 75–98 genera and 2,600–3,000 spp. of herbs, subshrubs, shrubs, or trees, often with quadrangular twigs, predominantly trop. and subtrop., a few in temp. regions; lvs. usually opp. or whorled, mostly simple, rarely compound; fls. typically bisexual, irregular or rarely regular, in spikes, racemes, or modified cymes, calyx usually 4–5-lobed or -toothed, corolla usually with as many lobes as calyx, mostly salverform, sometimes campanulate or 2-lipped, stamens usually 4, sometimes 2 or 5, pistil 1, ovary superior, mostly with 2 carpels; fr. typically a drupe, or dry and separating into nutlets. The cult. genera are: *Aloysia, Callicarpa, Caryopteris, Citharexylum, Clerodendrum, Congea, Cornutia, Diostea, Duranta, Gmelina, Holmskioldia, Lantana, Nyctanthes, Oxera, Petrea, Phyla, Stachytarpheta, Tectona, Verbena, Vitex,* and *Viticipremna.*

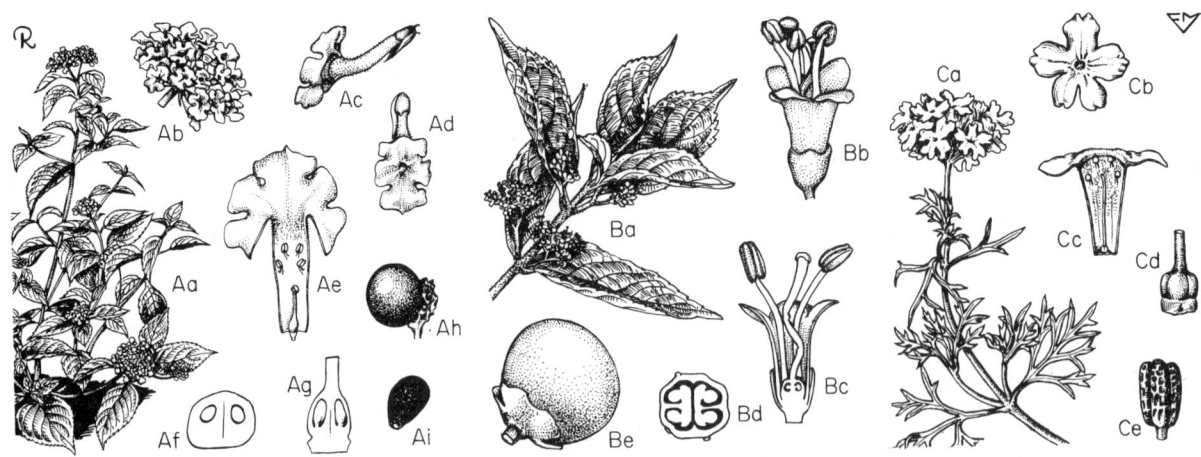

VERBENACEAE. **A,** *Lantana Camara:* **Aa,** plant, × ⅛; **Ab,** inflorescence, × ½; **Ac,** flower, side view, × 1; **Ad,** flower, face view, × 1; **Ae,** pistil and expanded corolla, × 1½; **Af,** ovary, cross section, × 10; **Ag,** ovary, vertical section, × 6; **Ah,** fruit, × 1½; **Ai,** seed, × 1½. **B,** *Callicarpa dichotoma:* **Ba,** flowering branch, × ½; **Bb,** flower, × 5; **Bc,** flower, vertical section, × 5; **Bd,** ovary, cross section, × 15; **Be,** fruit, × 5. **C,** *Verbena bipinnatifida:* **Ca,** flowering stem, × ½; **Cb,** flower, face view, × 1; **Cc,** pistil and expanded corolla, × 1; **Cd,** ovary and base of style, × 8; **Ce,** fruit, × 3. (Ca-Ce from Bailey, *Manual of Cultivated Plants,* ed. 2.)

The family includes many showy garden and greenhouse plants, and *Tectona,* the source of teakwood.

VERBESINA L. [*Actinomeris* Nutt.]. CROWN-BEARD. *Compositae* (Helianthus Tribe). About 200 spp. of herbs, shrubs, and trees in N. and S. Amer.; lvs. opp. or alt.; fl. heads radiate or discoid, small to large, receptacle scaly, the scales enfolding the achenes; fls. usually yellow, disc fls. bisexual, fertile, ray fls. female or neutral, sometimes lacking; achenes compressed, 2-winged, pappus of 2 awns, rarely lacking.

alternifolia (L.) Britt. ex C. Mohr [*Actinomeris alternifolia* (L.) DC.; *A. squarrosa* Nutt.]. WINGSTEM, YELLOW IRONWEED. Per., to 9 ft., sts. winged; lvs. alt., lanceolate-oblong, to 10 in. long, serrate, narrowed to a petiolar base; heads 1–2 in. across, many, corymbose; fls. yellow; achenes spreading in all directions to form a globose head when mature. E. U.S.

encelioides (Cav.) Benth. & Hook.f. BUTTER DAISY, GOLDEN C.-B. Ann., to 3 ft., sts. not winged; lvs. ovate to lanceolate, to 4 in. long, irregularly toothed, green above, white-strigose beneath, petioled; heads to 2 in. across, paniculed; fls. deep yellow; achenes spreading. W. U.S. and Mex.; also naturalized eastward.

helianthoides Michx. Per., to 3 ft., sts. winged; lvs. alt., ovate-lanceolate, 2–6 in. long, serrate, sessile; heads 1½ in. across, few, compactly cymose; fls. yellow; achenes spreading. Iowa and Ohio, s. to Tex. and Ga.

VERNONIA Schreb. IRONWEED. *Compositae* (Vernonia Tribe). Between 500 and 1,000 spp. of per. herbs, subshrubs, shrubs, trees, or sometimes even woody climbers, native to warmer regions of N. and S. Amer., Asia, Afr., and Australia; lvs. alt., rarely opp.; fl. heads solitary, or in corymbose or panicled cymes, involucre cylindrical, nearly globose, urceolate, campanulate, or turbinate, involucral bracts imbricate in few to several rows, receptacle flat or convex, naked, pitted; fls. all tubular, bisexual, fertile; achenes columnar or turbinate, ribbed, often resin-dotted between the ribs, glabrous or hairy, pappus usually of 2 rows of bristles, the inner capillary, the outer scalelike.

Vernonias are sometimes grown in the border or wild garden, flowering in late summer and autumn. They are easily cultivated in any good rich soil. Propagated usually by division, also by seeds and cuttings.

altissima Nutt. Per. herb, to 10 ft., sts. glabrous, leafy; lvs. lanceolate to lanceolate-oblong or lanceolate-ovate, to 10 in. long, long-acuminate, essentially glabrous above, thinly hairy beneath, entire to sharply but irregularly serrate; heads ½ in. across, in a loose, corymbose cyme; fls. purple. W. N.Y. to Mo., s. to Ga. and La.

angustifolia Michx. Per. herb, to 4 ft., sts. glabrous or pubescent, leafy; lvs. linear to narrowly elliptic, to 6 in. long, margins revolute; heads to about ⅝ in. across, in compact corymbs; fls. purple. N.C. to Fla., e. to Miss.

Baldwinii Torr. WESTERN I. Per. herb, to 6 ft., sts. pubescent to tomentose, leafy; lvs. elliptic or elliptic-lanceolate to ovate-lanceolate, to 6 in. long or more, acuminate, puberulent above, tomentose beneath, sharply serrate; heads ½ in. across, in loose, corymbose cymes; fls. purple. Minn. to Ill., s. to Tex. and La.

crinita Raf. Per. herb, to 10 ft., sts. nearly glabrous, more or less glaucous, leafy; lvs. linear or linear-lanceolate, to 7¼ in. long, usually glabrous, nearly entire to denticulate; heads about 1 in. across, in loose corymbose cymes; fls. purple. E. Ill. to e. Kans., s. to Ark. and Okla.

flexuosa Sims. Per., to 2½ ft., sts. from a woody tuber, pubescent; lvs. basal and on sts., lanceolate, to 5½ in. long, acute, attenuate at base, glabrous or loosely pubescent, entire; heads to 1 in. across, in a cyme with flexuous brs.; fls. purple. S. Brazil to Paraguay, ne. Argentina, and Uruguay.

gerberiformis D. Oliver & Hiern. Dwarf per., from a woody rhizome; lvs. in basal rosettes, oblanceolate, to 6 in. long, rounded at apex, thin, glabrous, margins repand-denticulate; heads to 1 in. long, solitary on scapose peduncles to 8 in. long; fls. purplish-blue. Sudan.

glabra (Steetz) Vatke. Glabrous herb, to 3 ft., sts. leafy; lvs. nearly sessile, oblong, to 4 in. long, membranous, serrate; heads about ¾ in. across, in terminal, compact, corymbose panicles; fls. purple. Ethiopia to Rhodesia and Mozambique.

karaguensis D. Oliver & Hiern. Coarse, erect herb, to 3 ft., sts. with crisp hairs, leafy; lvs. nearly sessile, narrowly elliptic or lanceolate, to 1½ in. long, scabrous above, pubescent with dense short hairs beneath, serrulate; heads about ¼ in. across, in terminal corymbose cymes; fls. purple. Trop Afr.

Melleri D. Oliver & Hiern. Erect shrub, brs. ascending, scabrous above; lvs. clasping and sessile, oblong to linear, to 6 in. long, coarsely scabrous, denticulate; heads to 1 in. across or more, in corymbose or elongated panicles. E. Trop. Afr.

noveboracensis (L.) Michx. Per. herb, to 6 ft., sts. glabrous or sparsely hairy, leafy; lvs. linear-lanceolate to lanceolate, to 8 in. long, long-acuminate, rather scabrous above, glabrous or sparsely hairy beneath, almost entire to sharply serrate; heads ½ in. across, in a loose cyme; fls. purple. Mass. to Miss., occasionally to s. Ohio.

VERONICA L. SPEEDWELL, BROOKLIME. *Scrophulariaceae.* About 250 spp. of ann. or per. herbs of the N. Temp. Zone; plants prostrate to erect; lvs. opp., at least in lower part of plant, rarely whorled, sometimes alt. above, simple, entire or toothed; fls. small, white, rose, purple, or blue, in axillary or terminal spikes, racemes, or corymbs, sometimes solitary, calyx 4- or 5-parted, corolla rotate, stamens 2; fr. a flattened, notched, loculicidal caps. The New Zeal. shrubby, evergreen spp., much planted on the Pacific Coast, are now referred to the genus *Hebe.*

Speedwells are grown in the flower garden and border, the low or dwarf kinds in the rock garden. They are of easy culture in good soil. Propagated by seeds and division.

albicans: *Hebe albicans.*

Allionii Vill. [*Hebe Allionii* Hort.]. Mat-forming per., sts. to 1 ft.; lvs. elliptic to oblong, entire to serrulate, almost glabrous; fls. in spicate racemes, corolla violet. Sw. Alps.

alpestris: *V. serpyllifolia.*

alpina L. Per., to 6 in.; lvs. oblong, elliptic, or rounded, to 1 in. long, entire to toothed; fls. in dense racemes, corolla dark blue or violet. Eur., Asia, nw. Amer. Cv. 'Rosea'. Fls. pink.

altissima: a listed name of no botanical standing.

americana (Raf.) Schweinitz ex Benth. AMERICAN B. Fleshy, creeping, prostrate to ascending per.; lvs. elliptic, oblong to suborbicular, serrate to crenate, glabrous; fls. in loose racemes, corolla violet to blue. Swamps and marshes, N. Amer.

amethystina: *V. spuria.*

amplexicaulis: *Hebe amplexicaulis.*

Andersonii: *Hebe Andersonii.*

armena Boiss. & Huet. Tufted per., sts. decumbent or ascending, to 4 in.; lvs. pinnate, lfts. linear, ¼ in. long; fls. in few-fld. racemes, corolla deep blue or violet-blue. Armenia.

Astonii: *Hebe subsimilis* var.

australis: *V. spicata.*

austriaca L. Per., to 2 ft.; lvs. simple, serrate or pinnately cut into oblong or linear segms.; fls. in long racemes, calyx unequally lobed, corolla deep blue, to ½ in. across. Eur., Asia Minor. Subsp. **Jacquinii** (Baumg.) K. Malý. Lvs. deeply divided.

Bachofenii: *V. grandis.*

Balfouriana: *Hebe Balfouriana.*

Beccabunga L. EUROPEAN B. Glabrous per., to 2 ft.; lvs. oblong to ovate, to 2¼ in. long, crenate-serrate, rather fleshy; fls. in loose, 10–30-fld. racemes, corolla blue, to ⁵⁄₁₆ in. across. Wet areas, Eur., N. Afr., Asia.

bellidioides L. Prostrate per., fl. sts. erect, to 6 in.; lvs. in a rosette, obovate, slightly toothed, gray-pubescent; fls. in short, few-fld. racemes, corolla bluish. S. Eur.

Bidwillii: see *Parahebe Bidwillii* and *P. decora.*

Bollonsii: *Hebe Bollonsii.*

bombycina Boiss. & Kotschy. Tufted, matted, white-silky, dwarf per.; lvs. ovate to oblong-spatulate, ⅛ in. long, sessile; fls. solitary, or in few-fld. terminal racemes, corolla reddish. Lebanon.

Bonarota: *Paederota Bonarota.*

buxifolia: *Hebe buxifolia.*

caespitosa Boiss. Tufted, dwarf per., to 3 in.; lvs. linear, ⅜ in. long, entire, revolute, hairy; fls. in few-fld. racemes, corolla rose. Greece and Asia Minor.

canadensis: a listed name of no botanical standing.

candida: *V. incana.*

canescens: see *Parahebe canescens.*

carnea: see *Hebe* × *carnea.*

catarractae: *Parahebe catarractae.*

caucasica Bieb. Pubescent per., sts. erect or ascending, to 6 in.; lvs. ovate or oblong, or once or twice pinnately cut into oblong or linear segms.; fls. in loose racemes, corolla white, veined with violet. Caucasus.

Chamaedrys L. [*V. pulchella* Salisb.]. GERMANDER S., ANGEL'S-EYE, BIRD'S-EYE. Hairy per., to 1½ ft., from a creeping base; lvs. broad-ovate to 1½ in. long, toothed; fls. in racemes to 6 in. long, corolla blue, ⁵⁄₁₆ in. across. Eur., Asia; naturalized in N. Amer. Cv. 'Alba'. Fls. white.

chathamica: *Hebe chathamica.*

corymbosa: a listed name of no botanical standing, probably used for *V. spicata* cv.

cupressoides: *Hebe cupressoides.*

Cusickii A. Gray. Erect, unbranched per., to 9 in.; lvs. oblong, ovate, to suborbicular, to ¾ in. long, entire, sessile; fls. in few-fld. racemes, corolla blue or violet, ⁵⁄₁₆ in. across. Calif. and Ore.

decumbens: *Hebe decumbens.*

decussata: *Hebe elliptica.*

elegans: *V. spuria* cv.

elegantissima: a listed name of uncertain application.

elliptica: *Hebe elliptica.*

epacridea: *Hebe epacridea.*

Erica: a listed name of no botanical standing for *V. spicata* cv.

ericoides: a listed name of no botanical standing.

exaltata: *V. longifolia.*

filiformis Sm. Ann. or per.; sts. prostrate, rooting; lvs. ovate to reniform, to ⅜ in. long and ¼ in. wide, crenate; fls. on long threadlike pedicels, corolla blue, ⅜ in. across. Asia Minor. Pernicious weed in lawns of cent. N.Y.

flexuosa: *V. longifolia.*

fruticans Jacq. [*V. saxatilis* Scop.]. Much-branched, pubescent or glabrous subshrub, to 6 in.; lvs. obovate or oblong, entire to slightly crenate; fls. in short, few-fld. racemes, corolla deep blue, to ⅜ in. across. Eur.

fruticulosa L. Differs from *V. fruticans* in having lvs. larger, always petioled, fls. pink or white, pedicels, calyx, and caps. glandular-pubescent. S. Eur.

gentianoides Vahl. Tufted per., sts. erect, simple, 6 in. to 2 ft. or more; basal lvs. in a rosette, oblong-lanceolate, to 3 in. long or more, entire or slightly toothed; fls. in long, loose, terminal racemes, corolla pale blue with darker veins, to ⅜ in. across. Asia Minor, Caucasus, Crimea. Cv. 'Variegata' is listed.

glauca Sibth. & Sm. Nearly erect ann., to 8 in.; lvs. broadly ovate, to ¾ in. long, dentate, pubescent; corolla bright blue with white base, to ¾ in. across. Greece. Plants grown under this name may sometimes be glaucous-lvd. forms of *V. incana* or *V. latifolia*, or even of *Hebe glaucophylla.*

glaucophylla: *Hebe glaucophylla.*

grandis Fisch. ex K. Spreng. [*V. Bachofenii* Heuff.; *V. Koenitzeri* Hort.]. Per., to 2 ft., sts. erect or ascending; lvs. oblong-lanceolate to oblong, to 3 in. long, subcordate, incised-dentate to serrate, petioled; fls. in terminal racemes to 6 in. long. Siberia. Var. **holophylla** Nakai [*V. holophylla* (Nakai) Nakai]. Lvs. cordate, glossy, leathery.

× **Guthrieana** Hort. A garden hybrid, said to be 9 in. tall; fls. blue.

Hectorii: *Hebe Hectorii.*

holophylla: *V. grandis* var.

Hulkeana: *Hebe Hulkeana.*

imperialis: a listed name of no botanical standing for *Hebe speciosa* cv.

incana L. [*V. candida* Hort.]. White-pubescent per., to 2 ft.; lvs. oblong or lanceolate, to 3 in. long. obtusely crenate, petioled; fls. in one or several terminal racemes to 6 in. long, corolla blue. N. Asia, Russia. Cvs. 'Nana', 'Rosea', and 'Rubra' are listed.

irrigans: *Parahebe catarractae.*

Kellereri Degen & Urum. Rhizomatous per., with many sts.; lower lvs. ovate, upper lvs. suborbicular, thick, margin entire, thickened and hairy; fls. in dense, terminal racemes, corolla blue. Macedonia.

Koenitzeri: *V. grandis.*

latifolia L. [*V. Teucrium* L.]. Pubescent per., to 2 ft., sts. erect or ascending; lvs. lanceolate to ovate, crenate or toothed; fls. blue, rose, or white, ½ in. across, in racemes from upper lf. axils. Eur. Subsp. **pseudochamaedrys** (Jacq.) DeWolf [*V. pseudochamaedrys* Jacq.]. Lvs. ¾–2½ in. long; racemes elongate. Subsp. **Orsiniana** (Ten.) DeWolf [*V. Orsiniana* Ten.]. Lvs. to 1⅛ in. long; caps. hairy.

Lavaudiana: *Hebe Lavaudiana.*

Lewisii: *Hebe Lewisii.*

linifolia: *Parahebe linifolia.*

longifolia L. [*V. exaltata* Maund; *V. flexuosa* Host & Moretti; *V. maritima* L.]. Per., 2–4 ft.; lvs. sometimes in 3's, lanceolate or oblong, to 4 in. long, toothed, short-petioled; fls. many, in dense racemes, corolla lilac. Eur., Asia; naturalized in e. N. Amer. Cvs. 'Alba', 'Hendersonii', 'Nana', and 'Rosea' are listed. Var. **subsessilis** Miq. Lvs. very short-petioled; fls. larger, deep blue.

Lyallii: *Parahebe Lyallii.*

lycopodioides: *Hebe lycopodioides.*

macrantha: *Hebe macrantha.*

maritima: *V. longifolia.*

Menziesii: *Hebe Menziesii.*

Michauxii Lam. Glandular-pubescent per., to 1½ ft.; sts. ascending; lvs. ovate, crenate-toothed; fls. in few dense racemes from upper lf. axils, corolla pale blue. Iran.

multifida L. Hairy, diffuse per., to 1 ft., sts. decumbent; lvs. to ¾ in. long, pinnately cut into linear segms.; fls. in axillary racemes, corolla pale pink or blue. Asia.

Nummularia Gouan. Small per., to 6 in., sts. creeping; lvs. somewhat imbricate, ovate-orbicular, ⅛ in. long, rather thick, the lowest scale-like; fls. in short, terminal heads, corolla blue or pink. Pyrenees.

officinalis L. COMMON S., GYPSYWEED. Matted, pubescent per., sts. prostrate or ascending, to 1½ ft. long; lvs. ovate-elliptic to oblong, to 2 in. long, serrate; fls. in dense, many-fld. racemes much longer than lvs., corolla pale blue, to ¼ in. across. Eur., Asia, N. Amer.

Onoei Franch. & Sav. Pubescent, prostrate per., fl. sts. erect; lvs. elliptic, to 1¼ in. long, finely serrate, short-petioled; fls. in racemes to 2¼ in. long, corolla blue, ⅜ in. across. Japan.

orchidea: *V. spicata* var.

orientalis Mill. Decumbent or prostrate per., sts. to 8 in. long; lvs. cuneate-oblong, linear, or lanceolate, toothed; fls. in axillary racemes, corolla pink or pale blue. Asia Minor, s. Russia, e. Medit. region.

Orsiniana: *V. latifolia* var.

Pageana: *Hebe pinguifolia* cv. 'Pagei'.

paniculata: *V. spuria.*

parviflora: *Hebe parviflora.*

pectinata L. White-pubescent, prostrate per.; lvs. obovate or elliptic-lanceolate, ½ in. long, toothed or sometimes cut; fls. in many-fld. racemes, corolla deep blue with white center. Asia Minor. Cv. **'Alba'.** Fls. white. Cv. **'Rosea'.** Fls. rose.

peduncularis Bieb. Per., sts. prostrate or ascending, to 1 ft.; lvs. ovate or oblong, coarsely toothed or cut, petioled; fls. in axillary racemes to 5 in., corolla white, veined with pink. Caucasus and Asia Minor. Cv. **'Alba'.** Fls. white.

petraea Steven. Cespitose per., to 1 ft.; lvs. lanceolate, oblong, or elliptic, to ¾ in. long, toothed, sessile or short-petioled; fls. in 10–20-fld. axillary racemes, corolla blue or pink. Caucasus.

pimeleoides: *Hebe pimeleoides.*

pinguifolia: *Hebe pinguifolia.*

pinnata L. [*V. pinnatifida* Salisb.]. Erect per., to 3 ft.; lvs. pinnate, to 2½ in. long, glossy, rather thick; fls. in many-fld. racemes, corolla blue. Cent. Asia.

pinnatifida: *V. pinnata.*

poliifolia Benth. Tufted per., sts. ascending, to 4 in.; lvs. lanceolate, oblong, to linear-spatulate, pectinate-crenate, revolute, sessile; fls. in short, dense racemes, corolla pink; caps. minute, shorter than calyx, woolly. Syria.

prostrata L. [*V. rupestris* Hort., not Aitch. & Hemsl., or Salisb., or Tardent]. Prostrate per., fl. sts. erect or ascending, to 10 in.; lvs. linear to ovate, to 1⅜ in. long, entire to toothed; fls. in many-fld., terminal racemes, corolla deep blue, to ⅜ in. across. Eur. Cvs. **'Alba', 'Aurea', 'Coelestina', 'Flexuosa', 'Heavenly Blue', 'Nana', 'Purpurea', 'Rosea',** and **'Trehanii'** are listed.

pseudochamaedrys: *V. latifolia* subsp.

pulchella: *V. Chamaedrys.*

repens Loisel. Creeping, mat-forming, mosslike per.; lvs. ovate, to ½ in. long, slightly crenate, glossy, glabrous; fls. in few-fld. racemes, corolla pale blue, to ¼ in. across. Corsica and Spain. Cv. **'Alba'.** Fls. white. Cv. **'Rosea'.** Fls. pink.

rosea Desf. Pubescent per., to 1 ft., sts. ascending; lvs. oblanceolate, to 1¼ in. long, toothed or cut; fls. in terminal racemes, corolla pink, rarely blue. Algeria and s. Spain.

rotundata: *Hebe rotundata.*

rupestris: see *V. prostrata.*

salicifolia: *Hebe salicifolia.*

saturejoides Vis. Prostrate, tufted per., sts. creeping; lvs. densely imbricate, elliptic to obovate, ⅜ in. long, entire or slightly toothed; fls. in dense terminal racemes ½ in. long, corolla blue. Dalmatia.

saxatilis: *V. fruticans.*

Saxifraga: a listed name of no botanical standing.

scutellata L. MARSH S. Stoloniferous, glabrous per., sts. simple or branching, to 2½ ft.; lvs. linear to lanceolate, to 3½ in. long, entire or remotely toothed, sessile; fls. in loose axillary racemes, corolla white, bluish, or pinkish. Wet places, N. Amer., Eur., Asia.

senanensis Maxim. Erect, per. herb, to 1 ft.; lvs. lanceolate to ovate, to 1 in. long, cuneate, sharply toothed, petioled; fls. to ⅜ in. across, in loose, terminal racemes, corolla lilac. Japan.

serpyllifolia L. [*V. alpestris* Schur]. THYME-LEAVED S. Much-branched, creeping per., fl. sts. ascending, to 1 ft.; lvs. ovate or oblong, to ½ in. long, entire or obscurely toothed; fls. on pedicels about as long as bracts, in few-fld., terminal racemes, corolla pale blue with darker stripes, 5/16 in. across. Asia, Eur.; naturalized in N. and S. Amer.

speciosa: *Hebe speciosa.*

speciosissima: a listed name of no botanical standing.

spicata L. [*V. australis* Schrad.]. To 1½ ft., sts. erect or ascending; lvs. oblong to lanceolate, to 2 in. long, toothed; fls. sessile, in long, dense racemes, corolla blue or pink. N. Eur. and Asia. Cvs. **"Alba', 'Alpina', 'Caerulea', 'Corymbosa', 'Erica', 'Eugiana', 'Nana', 'Rosea',** and **'Rubra'** are listed. Var. **orchidea** (Crantz) Fiori [*V. orchidea* Crantz]. Corolla convolute in the bud.

spuria L.[*V. amethystina* Willd.; *V. paniculata* L.]. Densely pubescent, erect per., to 2 ft.; lvs. sometimes in whorls of 3, oblong-lanceolate or lanceolate, to 1 in. long, cuneate, toothed; fls. in loose, terminal, panicled racemes, corolla blue, to ½ in. across. Se. Eur. Cv. **'Elegans'** [*V. elegans* DC.]. More branched and pubescent.

subalpina: *Hebe speciosa.*

Teucrium: *V. latifolia.*

thymifolia Sibth. & Sm. Cespitose, hairy per.; lvs. linear-spatulate, entire, revolute, sessile; fls. in short, headlike racemes, corolla blue or pink. Greece, Crete, Asia Minor.

Tournefortii C. C. Gmel. Hairy ann., sts. decumbent or ascending, to 1½ ft.; lvs. widely ovate, to 1¼ in. long and ⅜ in. wide, crenate-serrate; fls. on long, axillary pedicels, corolla bright blue, with lower lobes paler, to ½ in. across. Eur., w. Asia.

Traversii: *Hebe Traversii.*

Trehanii: a listed name for *V. prostrata* cv.

virginica: *Veronicastrum virginicum.*

Wormskjoldii Roem. & Schult. Rhizomatous per., to 1 ft.; lvs. ovate or elliptic, to 1 in. long, entire or slightly toothed; fls. in terminal racemes, corolla dark blue, 3/16 in. across. Mts., N. Amer.

VERONICASTRUM Fabr. [*Leptandra* Nutt.]. CULVER'S-PHYSIC. *Scrophulariaceae.* Two spp. of tall, slender, per. herbs with a single st., of e. N. Amer. and e. Asia; lvs. whorled, simple; fls. in terminal, spicate racemes, calyx 4- or 5-parted, corolla salverform, the tube much longer than the lobes, stamens 2; fr. an ovoid caps.

virginicum (L.) Farw. [*Leptandra virginica* (L.) Nutt.; *Veronica virginica* L.]. CULVER'S ROOT, BOWMAN'S-ROOT, BLACKROOT. To 7 ft.; lvs. mostly 5, lanceolate to oblong-lanceolate, to 6 in., toothed; fls. in racemes to 9 in. long, corolla pale blue or white, to ⅛ in. long. Mass. to Man., s. to Fla. and Tex.

VERSCHAFFELTIA H. Wendl. *Palmae.* One sp. a solitary, monoecious palm with black-spiny trunk and stilt roots, in the Seychelles; lvs. pinnate, sheaths not forming a crownshaft, petiole short, rounded below, blade irregularly divided into 1- or several-ribbed pinnae with toothed, obcuneate, truncate or shallowly 2-cleft apices; infl. interfoliar, long-peduncled, bracts 2, the lower persistent, paniculate, 1–2 times branched, rachillae with fls. in triads (2 male and 1 female); male fls. symmetrical, sepals 3, imbricate, petals 3, valvate, stamens 6, filaments erect in bud, pistillode large, angled, truncate, about as long as petals, female fls. with sepals and petals nearly equal, broadly imbricate, staminodes 6, minute, pistil 1-celled, 1-ovuled; fr. globose, with basal stigmatic residue, seed irregularly ridged, endosperm ruminate, embryo basal.

For culture see *Palms.*

splendida H. Wendl. To 75 ft. or more, trunk to 1 ft. in diam.; lvs. to 9 ft. long or more, short petiole and the sheath spiny on young plants but not on mature plants; infl. to 6 ft. long, scurfy; fr. to 1 in. in diam. Zone 10b.

VERTICORDIA DC. FEATHER FLOWER. *Myrtaceae.* About 50 spp. of evergreen, heathlike shrubs, endemic in Australia; lvs. opp., rarely alt., small, entire; fls. white, pink, or yellow, showy, usually pedicelled in the upper lf. axils, often forming broad, terminal, leafy corymbs, spikes, or racemes, calyx lobes 5, often colored, plumose, spreading, petals 5, entire, fringed, or digitate, stamens 10, alternating with staminodes, ovary inferior, 1-celled; fr. formed by the hardened base of the slightly enlarged, persistent calyx.

Grown in Zone 10 in Calif.

densiflora Lindl. To 3 ft.; lvs. linear, semicylindrical, or 3-angled, to ½ in. long; fls. white or pink, in dense leafy corymbs, each calyx lobe palmately divided into 3–5 pectinate-ciliate lobes, petals nearly orbicular, fringed with many cilia. W. Australia.

nitens Schauer. Erect, much-branched shrub; lvs. linear, to ¾ in. long, mucronulate; fls. golden-yellow, in broad terminal corymbs, each calyx lobe divided into 7–11 subulate, pectinate-plumose lobes, petals obovate, fringed with short irregular teeth. W. Australia.

VESICARIA: *ALYSSOIDES.*

VESTIA Willd. *Solanaceae.* One sp., an erect, much-branched, glabrous shrub of Chile; lvs. alt., persistent, entire, glossy; fls. solitary or few in rather long-peduncled, open, drooping, axillary cymes at ends of brs., calyx tubular-campanulate, 5-lobed, corolla 5-lobed, tube elongate, hairy inside, stamens 5, borne on the corolla, exserted; fr. a 2-valved caps., seeds many.

Cultivated as an ornamental in Zone 10 on the West Coast and elsewhere.

lycioides Willd. Evergreen, to 12 ft., ill-scented; lvs. elliptic to somewhat oblong, 1–2½ in. long, entire, glabrous; calyx about ¼ in. long, with 5 apiculate lobes, corolla nodding, greenish-yellow, tube about 1¼ in. long, ¼ in. in diam., lobes narrowly triangular, spreading and about ¾ in. across; fr. somewhat urceolate, nearly 1 in. long, ⅝ in. in diam. at base. Summer.

VETIVERIA Bory. *Gramineae.* Two spp. of per. grasses in Old World tropics; panicles long, narrow; spikelets in pairs, narrow, acute, mostly appressed, one sessile and bisexual, one pedicelled and male, the bisexual spikelet bearing short, sharp spines and somewhat flattened laterally. For terminology see *Gramineae.*

zizanioides (L.) Nash. VETIVER, KHUS-KHUS, KHAS-KHAS. Sts. robust, to 8 ft., unbranched, densely clustered; lf. sheaths glabrous, blades stiff, long, ⁵⁄₁₆ in. wide or less, glabrous but rough on edges, odorless; panicles large, erect, to 12 in. long, slender, the brs. whorled, ascending, naked at base; spikelets awnless, muricate. Trop. India. Cult. widely in tropics for the sweet-scented roots, made into woven handicrafts, or distilled for oil of vetiver used in perfumery. Sometimes used as a hedge plant and escaped in La.

VIBURNUM L. ARROWWOOD. *Caprifoliaceae.* About 225 spp. of upright shrubs or occasionally small trees native to Amer., Eur., and Asia; lvs. opp., simple, deciduous or persistent; fls. small, white or pinkish, in showy terminal panicles or umbel-like cymes, calyx 5-toothed, corolla rotate to campanulate or tubular, 5-lobed, in a few spp. marginal fls. of infl. sterile and with corolla lobes enlarged, stamens 5, ovary inferior, 1-celled; fr. a 1-seeded drupe, often persisting into winter. Those spp. having sterile marginal fls., often called snowballs, are sometimes confused with the spp. of *Hydrangea* having sterile fls.; however, the conspicuous part of the sterile fl. consists of enlarged corolla lobes in *Viburnum* and enlarged, petal-like sepals in *Hydrangea.*

Viburnums are among the most popular ornamental shrubs; many of them develop attractive autumn colors, and they make good bird refuges because of their autumn and winter fruits. Most of the deciduous species are hardy as far north as New Eng. (Zone 5), grow in ordinary soil, and are propagated by stratified seeds, by hardwood cuttings or cuttings of green wood under glass, by layers, and by grafting. A few of the snowballs are forced in the greenhouse for early flowering.

acerifolium L. MAPLE-LEAVED V., DOCKMACKIE, ARROWWOOD, POSSUM HAW. Deciduous, to 6 ft.; lvs. 3-lobed, like those of maple, to 5 in. long, coarsely toothed, turning red in autumn; fls. white, in long-stalked cymes to 3 in. across, corolla rotate; fr. purple-black. Late spring. New Bruns. to N.C. and Minn. Zone 4.

affine: *V. Rafinesquianum* var.

alnifolium Marsh. HOBBLEBUSH, AMERICAN WAYFARING TREE, DEVIL'S-SHOESTRINGS, DOGBERRY, DOG-HOBBLE, MOOSEWOOD, MOOSE BUSH, MOOSEBERRY, TANGLEFOOT, TANGLE-LEGS, TRIP-TOE, WHITE MOUNTAIN DOGWOOD, WITCH-HOBBLE, WITCH-HOPPLE. Deciduous, to 10 ft.; lvs. nearly orbicular, to 8 in. long, cordate, irregularly denticulate, turning deep claret in autumn; fls. white, in sessile cymes 5 in. across, corolla of fertile fls. rotate, corolla of marginal sterile fls. 1 in. across, stamens as long as corolla lobes; fr. red, becoming purple-black. Late spring. New Bruns. to N.C. and Mich. Zone 4.

americanum Mill. A name based on a mixture; see *V. trilobum.*

Awabuki: *V. odoratissimum* var.

betulifolium Batal. Deciduous, to 12 ft.; lvs. ovate, to 3 in. long, toothed; fls. in short-stalked cymes 4 in. across, corolla rotate; fr. red. Summer. China. Zone 6.

bitchiuense Mak. Deciduous, to 10 ft., loosely branched; lvs. ovate, to 3½ in. long, stellate-pubescent, especially beneath; fls. white, in flat or slightly convex cymes to 2½ in. across, fragrant, corolla tube ¼ in. long; fr. black. Japan. Related to *V. Carlesii.*

×**bodnantense** Aberc.: *V. Farreri* × *V. grandiflorum.* Deciduous, to 11 ft.; lvs. variable, from lanceolate or ovate to oblanceolate or obovate, to 4 in. long, glabrous except for tufts of hairs in the axils of the

veins beneath; fls. deep rose in bud, later almost white, in dense clusters to 3 in. across, terminal on main shoots or short lateral spurs, fragrant, corolla tube slender, to ⅜ in. long; fr. red. Late autumn to early winter. Of the several selections of this hybrid, cv. 'Dawn' is the best.

bracteatum Rehd. Deciduous, to 10 ft.; lvs. orbicular or ovate, to 5 in. long, cordate, wavy-toothed; fls. in cymes to 3 in. across, conspicuously bracted, corolla rotate; fr. bluish-black. Late spring. Ga. Zone 6.

buddleifolium C. H. Wright. Deciduous, to 6 ft.; lvs. oblong-lanceolate, to 6 in. long, slightly toothed, gray-tomentose beneath; fls. in dense cymes 3 in. across, corolla funnelform; fr. black. China.

burejaeticum Regel & Herder. Deciduous, to 15 ft.; lvs. ovate or elliptic, to 4 in. long, wavy-toothed; fls. white, in dense cymes 2 in. across; fr. bluish-black. Late spring. Manchuria and China.

×**Burkwoodii** Hort. Burkw. & Skipw. *V. Carlesii* × *V. utile.* Evergreen, to 6 ft.; lvs. ovate, to 4 in. long, cuneate to cordate, slightly serrate, lustrous green above, tomentose beneath; fls. pinkish, becoming white, in clusters 3½ in. wide, fragrant, corolla funnelform. Spring. Zone 5. Cv. 'Chenault' [*V. × Chenaultii* Hort.]. Early-flowering, fls. pale rose, later white; autumn foliage bronze-brown.

×**carlcephalum** Hort.: *V. Carlesii* × *V. macrocephalum.* Resembling *V. Carlesii* in habit and lvs.; fls. white with a little red, in large globular heads to 5 in. across, fragrant, corolla tube less than ⁵⁄₁₆ in. Spring. Zone 5. Autumn foliage brilliant.

Carlesii Hemsl. Deciduous, to 5 ft.; lvs. ovate or elliptic, to 4 in. long, toothed, pubescent on both sides; fls. white, fragrant, in dense cymes to 3 in. across, corolla tube ⁵⁄₁₆ in. long; fr. blue-black. Korea. Zone 5. Cv. 'Compactum'. Of more compact habit and with more fls., at least when plants are older.

cassinoides L. WITHE-ROD, APPALACHIAN TEA, SWAMP HAW, TEA-BERRY, WILD RAISIN. Deciduous, to 12 ft.; lvs. ovate or elliptic, to 4 in. long, finely toothed; fls. white, in short-peduncled cymes to 5 in. across; fr. blue-black, edible. Summer. Nfld. to N.C. and Minn. Zone 4. Cv. 'Nanum' is listed.

×**Chenaultii:** a listed name of no botanical standing for *V. × Burkwoodii* cv. 'Chenault'.

cinnamomifolium Rehd. Evergreen, to 20 ft.; lvs. elliptic-oblong, to 5 in. long, nearly entire, conspicuously 3-veined; fls. whitish, in loosely spreading cymose clusters to 7 in. across, corolla rotate; fr. blue-black. China. Zone 7.

confertum: a listed name of no botanical standing.

coriaceum: *V. cylindricum.*

corylifolium Hook.f. & T. Thoms. Deciduous, similar to *V. dilatatum*, but distinguished by the long, yellowish-brown pubescence of petioles, infl., and young branchlets. China and Himalayas.

cylindricum D. Don [*V. coriaceum* Blume]. Evergreen, to 40 ft.; lvs. elliptic or oblong, to 7 in. long, entire or slightly toothed, waxy above; fls. white, in peduncled cymes to 4½ in. across, corolla tubular, lobes very short; fr. black. Late summer. China and Himalayas. Zone 7.

dasyanthum Rehd. Deciduous, to 8 ft., shoots glabrous; lvs. ovate to oblong, to 4½ in. long, sparsely and shallowly toothed, glabrous and shining above, pubescent only in axils of veins beneath; fls. white, in several, small, peduncled, terminal clusters, corolla rotate, hairy outside; fr. red. Early summer. China. Zone 7.

Davidii Franch. Evergreen, to 3 ft.; lvs. elliptic, to 5½ in. long, sometimes slightly toothed, conspicuously 3-nerved from base, pale beneath; fls. white, in dense, peduncled cymes to 3 in. across, corolla rotate; fr. bright blue. Early summer. China. Zone 7.

dentatum L. [*V. pubescens* Pursh; *V. pubescens* var. *Canbyi* S. F. Blake]. ARROWWOOD, SOUTHERN A. Deciduous, to 15 ft.; lvs. orbicular or ovate, to 3 in. long, coarsely toothed; fls. white, in long-peduncled cymes 3 in. across, corolla rotate; fr. blue-black. Late spring. New Bruns., s. to Fla. and Tex. Zone 3. Var. **scabrellum** Torr. & A. Gray [*V. scabrellum* (Torr. & A. Gray) Chapm.]. Fls. densely hairy. —A widespread polymorphic sp. varying in shape, texture, and pubescence of lvs., and the presence or absence of stipules. The variants tend to intergrade, although some have been proposed as spp.

dilatatum Thunb. Deciduous, to 10 ft.; lvs. orbicular or ovate, to 5 in. long, coarsely toothed, hairy on both sides; fls. white, in peduncled, pubescent cymes to 5 in. across, corolla rotate; fr. scarlet. Late spring. Japan. Zone 5. Cv. 'Xanthocarpum'. Fr. yellow.

ellipticum Hook. Deciduous, to 8 ft.; lvs. elliptic, to 3 in. long, coarsely toothed above middle; fls. in long-peduncled cymes 2 in. across, corolla rotate; fr. black. Wash. to Calif. Zone 6.

erubescens Wallich. Deciduous, shrub or small tree, to 15 ft.; lvs. elliptic or ovate to oblong, to 4 in. long, glabrous or pubescent beneath, veins and petioles reddish; fls. white, tinged pink, in loose pendulous panicles to 3 in. across, corolla tubular; fr. red, becoming black. Early summer. Himalayas and w. China. Zone 6. Var. **gracilipes** Rehd. Infl. more pendulous, to 4½ in. across.

Farreri Stearn [*V. fragrans* Bunge, not Loisel.]. Deciduous, to 10 ft.; lvs. elliptic, to 3 in. long, toothed, slightly pubescent above and on veins below, veins and petioles reddish; fls. white or pinkish, in panicled cymes 2 in. long, fragrant, preceding lvs., corolla tubular; fr. scarlet. Spring. China. Zone 6. Cvs. are :'Album', fls. pure white; 'Candidissimum', a listed name; 'Nanum', to 1½ ft. tall, lvs. small; 'Roseum', a listed name.

foetens Decne. Deciduous, to 10 ft., brs. glabrous; lvs. ovate, to 5 in. long, serrate, pubescent only in axils of veins beneath; fls. white or pinkish, in loose, sparsely hairy clusters to 2 in. across, fragrant, corolla tube ½ in. long; fr. red, becoming black. Late winter. Zone 6. Himalayas. Closely related to *V. grandiflorum* and perhaps not distinct from it.

fragrans Loisel. Not cult. See *V. Farreri*.

furcatum Blume ex Maxim. Deciduous, closely resembling *V. alnifolium*, but having lvs. narrower and serrate, stamens half as long as corolla. Japan. Zone 6.

grandiflorum Wallich [*V. nervosum* Hook.f. & T. Thoms., not D. Don, or Hook. & Arn.]. Deciduous, to 6 ft.; lvs. elliptic-oblong, to 4 in. long; fls. white, flushed rose, in short, dense, panicled cymes, corolla tube ⁵⁄₁₆ in. long; fr. blue-black or purple. Himalayas. Zone 6. Related to *V. Farreri*.

Henryi Hemsl. Evergreen, to 10 ft., lvs. oblong, to 5 in. long, toothed, shining above; fls. in broad panicles to 4 in. long, corolla rotate; fr. red, becoming black. Late summer. China. Zone 7.

hirsutulum: a listed name of no botanical standing.

hupehense Rehd. Deciduous, to 6 ft.; lvs. ovate, to 3 in. long, coarsely toothed, pubescent; fls. in cymes 2 in. across, corolla rotate, pubescent on exterior; fr. red. Early summer. China. Zone 6. Related to *V. dasyanthum*, but having lvs. pubescent on both surfaces.

ichangense (Hemsl.) Rehd. Deciduous, to 6 ft.; lvs. ovate to ovate-lanceolate, to 2½ in. long, pubescent beneath; fls. in cymes to 1½ in. across, corolla rotate; fr. scarlet-red, showy. Cent. and w. China. Zone 7.

japonicum (Thunb.) K. Spreng. [*V. macrophyllum* Blume]. Evergreen, to 6 ft.; lvs. ovate, to 6 in. long, slightly toothed above middle, somewhat leathery, shining above; fls. white, in short-peduncled, umbel-like cymes to 4 in. across, fragrant, corolla rotate; fr. red. Early summer. Japan. Zone 7. Sometimes confused in nursery trade with *V. odoratissimum*.

×**Juddii** Rehd.: *V. bitchiuense* × *V. Carlesii*. Deciduous, spreading shrub, to 8 ft.; lvs. ovate to ovate-oblong or elliptic, to 3½ in. long, shallowly toothed; fls. pink, turning white, in clusters to 3 in. across, fragrant, corolla tube ⅜ in. long. Spring. Zone 5.

kansuense Batal. Deciduous, to 9 ft.; lvs. broad-ovate, to 2 in. long, deeply 3–5-lobed, coarsely toothed; fls. pinkish-white, in small cymose clusters; fr. red. W. China. Zone 5?

Lantana L. WAYFARING TREE, TWISTWOOD. Deciduous, to 15 ft.; lvs. ovate, to 5 in. long, finely toothed, pubescent on both sides; fls. white, in cymes to 4 in. across; fr. red, becoming black. Late spring. Eur., w. Asia. Zone 3. Cv. **'Rugosum'**. Lvs. larger, more wrinkled, cymes larger.

lantanophyllum: a listed name of no botanical standing, but has been used for the hybrid *V.* × *rhytidophylloides*.

Lentago L. SHEEPBERRY, NANNYBERRY, BLACK HAW, COWBERRY, NANNY PLUM, SWEETBERRY, TEA PLANT, WILD RAISIN, SWEET V. Deciduous, to 30 ft.; lvs. ovate, to 4 in. long, finely toothed; fls. white, in sessile cymes to 5 in. across; fr. blue-black, with a bloom. Late spring. Hudson Bay, s. to Ga. and Miss. Zone 3.

lobophyllum Graebn. Deciduous, to 15 ft.; lvs. broad-ovate or obovate, to 4½ in. long, toothed, pubescent only on veins, fls. in long-peduncled cymes to 4 in. across, corolla rotate; fr. bright red. Early summer. China. Zone 6.

lucidum: *V. Tinus* cv.

macrocephalum Fort. Semievergreen, to 12 ft.; lvs. ovate or elliptic, to 4 in. long, finely toothed, pubescent on both sides; fls. white, in peduncled cymes to 5 in. across. Var. **Keteleeri:** forma *Keteleeri*. Forma **macrocephalum** [cv. 'Sterile']. CHINESE SNOWBALL. The typical form; all fls. sterile, forming a large globose head. Late spring. Of cult. origin. Forma **Keteleeri** (Carrière) Rehd. [var. *Keteleeri* (Carrière) Nichols.; cv. 'Keteleeri']. Infl. with a few sterile fls. 1 in. across surrounding the fertile fls. China. Zone 6. The wild form. Cv. 'Keteleeri': forma *Keteleeri*. Cv. 'Sterile': forma *macrocephalum*.

macrophyllum: *V. japonicum*.

Mariesii: a listed name of no botanical standing for *V. plicatum* cv.

molle Michx. POISON HAW, BLACK ALDER. Deciduous, to 12 ft.; lvs. nearly orbicular, to 5 in. long, cordate, coarsely toothed, pale and pubescent beneath; fls. white, in long-peduncled cymes to 3 in. across, corolla rotate; fr. blue-black. Iowa to Ky. and Mo. Zone 6.

mongolicum (Pall.) Rehd. Deciduous, to 7 ft., twigs stellate-pubescent; lvs. broadly ovate to elliptic, to 2¼ in. long, rounded at base, usually obtuse, slightly toothed, somewhat hairy; fls. in flat, umbel-like cymes, corolla tubular-campanulate; fr. black. Ne. Asia. Zone 6.

nervosum: see *V. grandiflorum*.

nudum L. SMOOTH WITHE-ROD, NANNYBERRY HAW, POSSUM H., SWAMP H., BLACK ALDER, NAKED V. Deciduous, to 15 ft.; lvs. ovate to elliptic-lanceolate, to 5 in. long, nearly entire, pubescent beneath; fls. white or yellowish, in long-peduncled cymes to 5 in. across, corolla rotate; fr. blue-black. Summer. Conn., s. to Fla. and La. Zone 7.

odoratissimum Ker-Gawl. SWEET V. Evergreen, shrub or small tree, to 20 ft.; lvs. elliptic, to 6 in. long, nearly entire, thick-leathery, shining above; fls. white, in panicles 4 in. high, fragrant, corolla tubular-campanulate; fr. red, becoming black. Late spring. Himalayas to Japan. Zone 8. Confused with *V. japonicum*. The sp. is variable in habit, and in texture and shape of lvs. Cv. 'Nanum'. Dwarf. Var. **Awabuki** (C. Koch) Zab. [*V. Awabuki* C. Koch]. About 12 ft. high, lvs. large, very glossy on upper surface, infl. large, paniculate. Japan.

Opulus L. CRANBERRY BUSH, EUROPEAN C.B., GUELDER ROSE, WHITTEN TREE. Deciduous, to 12 ft.; lvs. 3–5-lobed, maplelike, to 4 in. long, pubescent beneath, petioles with narrow groove and large disc glands; fls. white, in peduncled cymes to 4 in. across, marginal fls. sterile, ¾ in. across; fr. scarlet. Late spring. Eur., N. Afr., n. Asia. Zone 3. Fr. edible; bark used medicinally. Cvs. are: 'Aureum', shoots bronze-colored, turning dark yellow, bright yellow, and finally green; 'Compactum', compact; 'Nanum', dwarf form, lvs. small; 'Roseum' [cv. 'Sterile'] SNOWBALL, SNOWBALL BUSH, fls. all sterile, in globose head; 'Sterile': 'Roseum'; 'Xanthocarpum', fr. yellow.

orientale Pall. Deciduous, to 8 ft.; lvs. nearly orbicular, 3-lobed, to 5 in. long, cordate, nearly glabrous except for tufts of hairs in axils of veins beneath; fls. white, in cymose clusters to 2 in. across, corolla rotate; fr. red, becoming black. Caucasus and Asia Minor. Zone 6.

ovatifolium Rehd. Deciduous; lvs. ovate or oblong-ovate, to 3 in. long, toothed; fls. in cymes 3 in. across. China.

pauciflorum Raf. MOOSEBERRY. Deciduous, to 5 ft.; lvs. nearly orbicular, to 3 in. long, 3-lobed at apex, toothed; fls. in heads 1 in. across, corolla rotate; fr. red. Late spring. N. N. Amer. and ne. Asia. Zone 2.

phlebotrichum Siebold & Zucc. Deciduous, to 6 ft.; lvs. ovate to elliptic-ovate, to 2 in. long, toothed; fls. white, tinged pink, in few-fld., cymose, nodding clusters, corolla rotate; fr. red. Late spring. Japan. Zone 7?

plicatum Thunb. Deciduous, to 10 ft., brs. spreading horizontally; lvs. ovate, to 4 in. long, toothed, pubescent beneath; fl. clusters in 2 rows on the brs.; fls. white, corolla rotate. Var. **sterile**: forma *plicatum*. Var. **tomentosum**: forma *tomentosum*. Forma **plicatum** [var. *sterile* C. Koch; cv. 'Plicatum']. JAPANESE SNOWBALL. The typical form; fls. sterile, in globose cluster. Of cult. origin. Forma **tomentosum** (Thunb.) Rehd. [var. *tomentosum* (Thunb.) Miq.; cv. 'Tomentosum'; *V. tomentosum* Thunb.]. DOUBLE FILE V. Fls. forming a flat cluster, inner fls. fertile, marginal fls. sterile; fr. red, becoming black. China, Japan. Zone 5. The wild form. Cv. **'Mariesii'**. Graceful; clusters and sterile fls. larger.

×**pragense** Hort.: *V. rhytidophyllum* × *V. utile*. Shrub with arching brs.; lvs. 2–4 in. long, upper surface rugose, lower feltlike.

propinquum Hemsl. Evergreen, branchlets shining red-brown; lvs. elliptic to ovate-lanceolate, to 3½ in. long, slightly toothed, shining above; fls. greenish-white, in peduncled cymes to 2½ in. across, corolla rotate; fr. black. China. Zone 7.

prunifolium L. BLACK HAW, SWEET H., SHEEPBERRY, NANNY-BERRY, STAGBUSH. Deciduous, to 15 ft.; lvs. ovate or broad-elliptic, to 3 in. long, finely toothed; fls. white, in sessile cymes to 4 in. across; fr. blue-black, with a bloom, edible after frost. Early spring. Conn., s. to Fla. and Tex. Zone 3. Root used medicinally.

pubescens: *V. dentatum*. Var. Canbyi: *V. dentatum*.

Rafinesquianum Schult. DOWNY-LEAVED A., DOWNY A. Deciduous, to 6 ft.; lvs. to 3 in. long, coarsely toothed, densely pubescent beneath; fls. white, in dense, short-peduncled cymes to 3 in. across, corolla rotate; fr. bluish-black. Late spring. Zone 2. E. N. Amer. Var. **affine** (Bush) House [*V. affine* Bush]. Lvs. glabrous beneath or nearly so.

×**rhytidocarpum** Hort. Lemoine: *V. buddleifolium* × *V. rhytidophyllum*. Evergreen or deciduous shrub, intermediate between parents; fr. black, rugose.

×**rhytidophylloides** Suring.: *V. Lantana* × *V. rhytidophyllum.* Lvs. similar to those of *V. rhytidophyllum*, but broader and less rugose.

rhytidophyllum Hemsl. Evergreen, to 10 ft.; lvs. ovate-oblong, to 7 in. long, nearly entire, shining and deeply wrinkled above, gray- or yellow-tomentose beneath; fls. yellowish-white, in cymes to 8 in. across, corolla rotate; fr. red, becoming black. Late spring. China. Zone 6. Grown particularly for its unusual foliage.

robustum: a listed name of no botanical standing.

rotundifolium Raf. A name of uncertain application; material so listed may be a variant of *V. plicatum.*

rufidulum Raf. SOUTHERN BLACK HAW, BLUE H., RUSTY NANNY-BERRY. Deciduous, to 30 ft.; lvs. elliptic, to 4 in. long, finely toothed, shining above, rusty-tomentose beneath; fls. white, in cymes 5 in. across, corolla rotate; fr. dark blue, with a bloom. Late spring. Va. to Fla. and Tex. Zone 6.

Sargentii Koehne. Deciduous, to 12 ft.; lvs. 3-lobed or sometimes oblong-lanceolate and not lobed, 4 in. long or more; fls. in long-peduncled cymes to 4 in. across, corolla of fertile fls. cupulate-rotate, anthers usually purple, marginal fls. sterile, 1 in. across; fr. scarlet. Late spring. Ne. Asia. Zone 6. Cv. 'Flavum'. Lvs. pubescent beneath, anthers and fr. yellow.

scabrellum: *V. dentatum* var.

schensianum Maxim. Deciduous, young branchlets stellate-pubescent; lvs. ovate-elliptic, to 2 in. long, denticulate, glabrous or nearly so above, stellate-pubescent beneath; fls. white, in cymes to 3 in. across, corolla rotate-campanulate, to ¼ in. long; fr. blue-black. Late spring. Nw. China. Zone 6.

setigerum Hance [*V. theiferum* Rehd.]. Deciduous, to 12 ft.; lvs. ovate-oblong, to 5 in. long, slightly toothed, dark green above; fls. in peduncled cymes 2 in. across, corolla rotate; fr. red. Late spring. China. Cv. 'Aurantiacum'. Fr. orange-yellow. Zone 6.

Sieboldii Miq. Deciduous, to 10 ft.; lvs. elliptic or obovate, to 6 in. long, coarsely toothed, shining above, paler and pubescent beneath; fls. creamy-white, in panicled cymes 4 in. long, corolla rotate-campanulate; fr. pink, becoming blue-black. Late spring. Japan. Zone 5.

suspensum Lindl. Evergreen, to 6 ft.; lvs. elliptic, to 4 in. long, toothed toward apex, shining above, paler beneath; fls. pinkish, in dense panicles 1½ in. across, corolla tubular; fr. red. Summer. Ryukyu Is. Zone 8.

theiferum: *V. setigerum.*

Tinus L. LAURUSTINUS. Evergreen, to 10 ft.; lvs. ovate-oblong or oblong, to 3 in. long, entire, dark green above; fls. white or pinkish, in cymes 3 in. across, corolla rotate; fr. black. Summer. Medit. region. Zone 7. Often flowered in the greenhouse. Cvs. are: 'Lucidum' [*V. lucidum* Mill.], lvs. large; 'Robustum', a listed name; 'Strictum', of upright habit; 'Variegatum', lvs. variegated.

trilobum Marsh. [*V. americanum* of auth., not Mill.]. CRANBERRY BUSH, CRANBERRY TREE, HIGHBUSH CRANBERRY, TREE C., CRAMP-BARK, GROUSEBERRY, SQUAWBUSH, SUMMERBERRY, PIMBINA. Deciduous, to 12 ft.; lvs. broad-ovate, to 5 in. long, 3-lobed and coarsely toothed, petioles with broad groove and small glands; fls. white. in short-peduncled cymes to 4 in. across, marginal fls. sterile, corolla of fertile fls. rotate, anthers yellow; fr. scarlet. Late spring. N. N. Amer. Zone 2. Cvs. 'Compactum' and 'Wentworth' are listed. The American representative of *V. Opulus*, and not segregated from it by all auths.; it differs only in the petioles.

urceolatum Siebold & Zucc. Rather straggling, deciduous shrub, to 3 ft., sts. procumbent and rooting; lvs. ovate to ovate-lanceolate, to 5 in. long, acuminate, crenate-serrate, glabrous above, veins scurfy beneath; fls. pinkish-white, in few-fld., flat, umbel-like cymes to 2½ in. across, corolla tubular; fr. black. Japan. Zone 6.

utile Hemsl. Evergreen, to 6 ft.; lvs. ovate to oblong, to 3 in. long, entire, shining above, whitish-tomentose beneath; fls. white, in dense cymes to 3 in. across, corolla rotate-campanulate; fr. bluish-black. Late spring. China. Zone 7.

Veitchii C. H. Wright. Deciduous, to 6 ft.; lvs. ovate, to 5 in. long, slightly toothed, densely pubescent beneath; fls. white, in dense cymes to 5 in. across, corolla rotate; fr. red, becoming black. Late spring. China. Zone 6.

Wilsonii Rehd. Deciduous, upright shrub, to 9 ft.; lvs. ovate to oblong-ovate, to 3 in. long, serrate, pubescent on both sides or glabrous beneath; fls. in yellow-hairy cymes to 2 in. across; fr. red. China. Zone 7.

Wrightii Miq. LEATHERLEAF. Deciduous, to 10 ft.; lvs. broad-ovate, to 6 in. long, coarsely toothed; fls. white, in short-peduncled, glabrous cymes 4 in. across, corolla rotate; fr. red. Late spring. Japan. Zone 5.

Rarely cult. Cv. 'Hessei' [var. *Hessei* (Koehne) Rehd.]. Of dwarf habit; lvs. with few teeth; cymes small.

VICIA L. VETCH, TARE. *Leguminosae* (subfamily *Faboideae*). Perhaps 150 spp. of mostly scandent herbs of wide distribution in temp. regions; lvs. alt., even-pinnate, terminating in tendrils, except in erect spp.; fls. papilionaceous, stamens 10, 9 united and 1 separate; differing from *Lathyrus* in having wing petals united to the keel, and the style filiform, with a tuft or ring of hairs toward tip; fr. a flat, dehiscent legume, mostly oblong.

Several species of vetch are grown for food, forage, and green-manure crops, and a few as ornamentals. They are not particular as to soil. Seeds of species used for cover crops, such as *V. sativa* and *V. villosa*, are sown broadcast. Seeds of *V. Faba* are sown in drills; this species will not thrive under hot dry conditions.

angustifolia L. COMMON V. Ann. or bien., sts. to 2 ft. long; lfts. in 2–5 pairs, linear-oblong, to 1 in. long; fls. purplish to white, usually paired in axils; fr. cylindrical, to 3 in. long, blackish. Eur.; naturalized in U.S.

articulata Hornem. Slender ann.; lfts. in 5–8 pairs, to ⅝ in. long, 1 stipule of each pair much larger and digitately divided into 3–9 slender teeth; peduncles elongate, 1-fld.; petals bluish, keel tipped purple-black; fr. yellow-brown, 1 in. long. S. Eur. Green-manure crop in regions having mild winters.

atropurpurea: *V. benghalensis.*

benghalensis L. [*V. atropurpurea* Desf.]. PURPLE V. Ann. or bien., white-hairy; sts. to 6 ft. long; lfts. linear-oblong, in 5–8 pairs, about 1 in. long; fls. purple, whitish at base, in 1-sided racemes; fr. to 1½ in. long, pubescent. S. Eur.

Cracca L. BIRD V., COW V., TUFTED V., CANADA PEA. Per., sts. to 6 ft. long, glabrous or appressed-hairy; lfts. in 4–6 pairs, linear to oblong, to 1 in. long; fls. small, purplish, varying to white, in peduncled, 1-sided, many-fld. racemes, lower teeth of calyx about as long as tube; fr. to 1 in. long. Eurasia, N. Amer. Subsp. **Gerardii:** *V. incana.*

dasycarpa Ten. WOOLLY-POD V. Separated from *V. villosa* in having sts. appressed-pubescent or glabrate, racemes only 5–15-fld., with appressed rather than spreading pubescence, lowest calyx lobe much shorter and glabrescent. Eur.; naturalized in U.S. Var. **glabrescens** (C. Koch) L. Beck. SMOOTH V. Lfts. commonly acute rather than obtuse, scarcely wider than ⅛ in.; racemes many-fld.

Ervilia (L.) Willd. BITTER V., ERVIL. Erect ann., to 28 in., without tendrils; lfts. in 7–15 pairs, linear-oblong, to about ½ in. long; racemes 2–4-fld., much shorter than lvs.; fls. rose to whitish with purple veins; fr. to 1 in. long, knobby. S. Eur.

Faba L. BROAD BEAN, HORSE B., ENGLISH B., EUROPEAN B., WINDSOR B., FIELD B., TICK B. Coarse, erect ann., to 6 ft., without tendrils, sts. angular; lfts. mostly alt., or in 1–3 pairs, elliptic to oblong, to 4 in. long, blunt, glaucous; fls. solitary or several in axils, white with dark purple or violet blotch, about 1 in. long; fr. plump, sometimes to 1 ft. long and more than 1 in. wide. N. Afr., sw. Asia. Widely grown in cool climates as a cover crop, for forage, and the seeds for human food; the bean of antiquity.

Gerardii: *V. incana.*

gigantea Hook. SITKA V. Per., climbing to several ft.; lvs. to 1 ft. long, lfts. in 7–16 pairs, ovate-oblong, to 2 in. long; fls. reddish-purple or yellow-white, in racemes; fr. 1¾ in. long, glaucous. Calif. to Alaska.

incana Gouan [*V. Cracca* subsp. *Gerardii* (All.) Gaudin; *V. Gerardii* All.]. Similar to *V. Cracca*, but sts. densely spreading-hairy; lower teeth of calyx about 1½ times as long as tube. Mts., cent. and s. Eur.

monantha Retz. BARD V. Slender, glabrous ann., sts. to 16 in. long; lfts. in 4–8 pairs; peduncles shorter than lvs., 1–2-fld.; petals blue; fr. to 1¾ in. long. S. Eur., w. Asia.

narbonensis L. NARBONNE V. Ann., sts. to 2 ft. long; lfts. in 1–3 pairs, obovate to elliptic-oblong, to 2¼ in. long, entire or serrate; fls. purplish, to 1 in. long, solitary or few in axils; fr. to 2½ in. long, minutely ciliate-toothed along sutures. S. Eur.

pannonica Crantz. HUNGARIAN V. Hairy ann., sts. to 30 in. long; lfts. in 5–10 pairs, usually oblong-elliptic, to ¾ in. long; peduncles very short, 2–4-fld.; fls. yellow-white or purplish-tinged, standard streaked red-purple and hairy on the back; fr. purplish, oblong, about 1 in. long, silky-pubescent. Cent. Eur.

sativa L. SPRING V., TARE. Ann. or bien., glabrescent, sts. to 3 ft. long; lfts. in 4–8 pairs, oblong to obovate, to 1⁵⁄₁₆ in. long, truncate to emarginate; fls. purplish, usually paired in axils; fr. plump, to 3 in. long. Eur.; naturalized in N. Amer.

unijuga A. Braun. Per., sts. erect, to 3 ft., without tendrils; lfts. in 1 pair, lanceolate to ovate, to 3 in. long; racemes 1-sided, many-fld.;

petals purple; fr. about 1 in. long, pale brown, glabrous. E. Siberia to China and Japan.

villosa Roth. HAIRY V., WINTER V., LARGE RUSSIAN V. Ann. or bien., pilose throughout; lfts. in 5–10 pairs, linear-oblong, to 1 in. long; racemes 10–40 fld., 1-sided; fls. violet-blue and white, varying to rose or white, calyx swollen at base on upper side, lower lobes longer than tube, villous, to ³⁄₁₆ in. long; fr. about 1 in. long. Eur., Asia; naturalized in U.S.

VICTORIA Lindl. GIANT WATER LILY, WATER-PLATTER.
Nymphaeaceae. Two spp. of very large, aquatic herbs of trop. S. Amer., rooted in mud, prickly except on upper lf. surfaces; lvs. large, circular, floating, peltate, long-petioled, prominently reticulate-rugose, margins turned up vertically 3–8 in.; fls. fragrant, floating, opening white, late in afternoon, remaining open until second day and changing to pink or red; fr. a large berrylike structure.

In temperate regions, victorias are treated as annuals, and require the same treatment as tender nympheas. They are raised from seeds, those of *V. amazonica* requiring a water temperature of 85–90° F for germination, those of *V. Cruziana* 65–70°F. Sown in pots set in shallow water indoors in Feb. or Mar., the young seedlings should be transferred to small pots, and shifted to larger ones as necessary until transferred to permanent positions in pools. If planted outdoors in early summer, the correct water temperature must be maintained with heat until the weather is warm enough.

amazonica (Poepp.) J. DeC. Sowerby [*V. regia* Lindl.; *V. regia* var. *Randii* (Tricker) L. H. Bailey]. AMAZON WATER LILY, ROYAL W.L., WATER MAIZE, AMAZON W.-P. Lvs. 3–6 ft. across, reddish beneath, the larger ones having turned-up margins 2–4, sometimes to 6, in. high; sepals prickly. Guyana and Amazon region.

Cruziana Orb. [*V. Trickeri* Tricker]. SANTA CRUZ WATER LILY, SANTA CRUZ W.-P. Lvs. densely soft-hairy beneath, the upturned margins green and 6–8 in. high; sepals prickly only at base. N. Argentina, Paraguay, Bolivia. The sp. usually grown in this country (sometimes incorrectly as *V. regia*), since it does not require as high temperatures as *V. amazonica.*

regia: *V. amazonica;* material cult. as *V. regia,* however, may be *V. Cruziana.*

Trickeri: *V. Cruziana.*

VIGNA Savi. *Leguminosae* (subfamily *Faboideae*). More than 200 spp. of erect, scandent, or twining herbs, native to warm regions of both the Old and the New World; lvs. of 3 lfts., stipules often prolonged or appendaged at base; fls. clustered or racemose, often on long peduncles, papilionaceous, mostly yellowish-white to purplish, standard orbicular, sometimes basally auricled, keel and upper part of style sometimes strongly twisted, lower, thickened part of style usually twisted not more than 180°, uppermost stamen separate; fr. a flat to cylindrical, sometimes septate, dehiscent legume. Closely related to *Phaseolus,* from which it differs in having stipules often appendaged and the thickened part of the style less strongly twisted, and in characters of the pollen and biochemistry.

Grown for food, forage, and as green manure and cover crop. *Vigna unguiculata* is one of the staple crops of the South. Tender, grown as annuals from seeds planted as soon as soil is warm in spring.

aconitifolia (Jacq.) Maréchal [*Phaseolus aconitifolius* Jacq.]. MOTH BEAN. Sts. slender, erect to diffuse, moderately brownish-hairy; lfts. mostly deeply 3-lobed, to about 2 in. long, thin, stipules lanceolate; racemes more or less headlike, on elongate peduncles, exceeding the lvs., bracteoles longer than the calyx, stiffly ciliate; corolla less than ¼ in. long; fr. cylindrical, 1–2 in. long. S. Asia.

angularis (Willd.) Ohwi & Ohashi [*Phaseolus angularis* (Willd.) W. F. Wight]. AZUKI BEAN. Erect or twining ann., to 2½ ft.; lvs. pilose, lfts. ovate, terminal lft. usually 3-lobed, to 4 in. long; fls. to ¾ in. across; fr. pendent, to 4 in. long. Asia.

Caracalla (L.) Verdc. [*Phaseolus Caracalla* L.]. SNAIL FLOWER, CORKSCREW FLOWER, SNAIL BEAN, SNAIL VINE, CARACOL. Twining per., to 20 ft.; lfts. ovate, to 5 in. long and 4 in. wide, pointed, pubescent on both sides; fls. fragrant, white or yellow with pink-purple wings, to 2 in. long, keel coiled like a snail shell; fr. linear, to 7 in. long, seeds nearly globose. Trop. S. Amer. Sometimes offered under the name *Phaseolus giganteus.*

Catjang: *V. unguiculata* subsp. *cylindrica.*

cylindrica: *V. unguiculata* subsp.

Mungo (L.) Hepper [*Phaseolus Mungo* L.]. URD, BLACK GRAM. Spreading ann., to 3 ft., brownish-silky-hairy; lfts. ovate, to 4 in. long, rarely faintly lobed; fls. in headlike racemes, yellow, to ½ in. long; fr. slender, to 2½ in. long, seeds small, oblong. Trop. Asia, where much cult.

radiata (L.) R. Wilcz. [*Phaseolus aureus* Roxb.; *P. radiatus* L.; *P. sublobatus* Roxb.]. MUNG BEAN, GREEN GRAM, GOLDEN G. Hairy ann., sts. erect, to 3 ft. or more; lfts. ovate to rhomboidal, to 4 in. long or more, acuminate, stipules prominent; fls. yellow, few near tips of peduncles as long as petioles; fr. slender, to 4 in. long, short-hairy, seeds small, globose. Probably Indonesia. Much grown in Orient for highly nutritious seeds, edible green pods, and young sprouts ("bean sprouts"). Sometimes grown for forage in U.S.

sesquipedalis: *V. unguiculata* subsp.

sinensis: *V. unguiculata.* Subsp. **sesquipedalis:** *V. unguiculata* subsp. *sesquipedalis.*

umbellata (Thunb.) Ohwi & Ohashi [*Phaseolus calcaratus* Roxb.]. RICE BEAN. Sts. slender, twining, pubescent; lfts. thin, lanceolate to ovate, mostly entire, to 5 in. long; fls. in elongate, long-peduncled racemes, corolla yellow, to ½ in. long; fr. slender, curved, to 3 in. long, seeds oblong-cylindrical. S. Asia.

unguiculata (L.) Walp. COWPEA. Nearly glabrous, sts. erect or scandent, to 12 ft. long; lfts. to 6 in. long; peduncles to 10 in. long; standard to ¾ in. long; fr. pendent, 8–12 in. long or more, seeds usually with a dark "eye." Widely planted in warm regions for forage or green manure, the seeds for human or stock food. Subsp. **unguiculata** [*V. sinensis* (L.) Savi ex Hassk.]. BLACK-EYED PEA. The typical subsp.; lfts. ovate to lanceolate; fr. pendent, 8–12 in. long, seeds often with a dark "eye." Cent. Afr. Subsp. **cylindrica** (L.) Van Eselt. ex Verdc. [*V. Catjang* (Burm.f.) Walp.; *V. cylindrica* (L.) Skeels]. CATJANG, JERUSALEM PEA, MARBLE P. Fr. shorter, erect or spreading, 3–5 in. long. Cent. Afr. or India. Subsp. **sesquipedalis** (L.) Verdc. [*V. sesquipedalis* (L.) Fruw.; *V. sinensis* subsp. *sesquipedalis* (L.) Van Eselt.]. ASPARAGUS BEAN, YARD-LONG B. Lfts. rhombic-ovate; fr. pendent, 1–3 ft. long, flaccid or somewhat inflated when green. S. Asia.

VIGUIERA HBK. *Compositae* (Helianthus Tribe). About 150 spp. of pubescent herbs and shrubs from U.S. to S. Amer.; lvs. entire, toothed, or pinnatifid; heads radiate, solitary or in cymes; fls. yellow, only the disc fls. fertile; achenes thickened, 4-angled, pappus of 2 awns and several short scales, or lacking.

laciniata A. Gray. Slender-twigged shrub, to 4 ft., resinous; lvs. alt., triangular-lanceolate, to 1½ in. long, toothed, hastately lobed at base; heads 1½ in. across, cymose; disc and ray fls. yellow; achenes strigose, pappus of 2 deciduous awns and several shorter, persistent scales. S. Calif. and adjacent Mex.

multiflora (Nutt.) S. F. Blake [*Gymnolomia multiflora* (Nutt.) Hemsl.]. Slender, branching, per. herb to 3½ ft.; lvs. opp. in lower part, alt. above, lanceolate to ovate-lanceolate, to 1 in. wide, entire or few-toothed; heads to 2 in. across, loosely panicled; disc and ray fls. yellow; achenes glabrous, pappus lacking. Mont. to New Mex. and Ariz. Blooming freely first year from seed. Var. **nevadensis** (A. Nels.) S. F. Blake. Lvs. narrowly linear, less than ¼ in. wide, with revolute margins. Colo. and Utah to Ariz. and Calif.

VILLADIA Rose [*Altamiranoa* Rose]. *Crassulaceae.* About 30 spp. of succulent, per. herbs, native from Tex. to Peru, sts. simple or mostly branching, sometimes woody at base; lvs. alt., mostly cylindrical or nearly so, small; fl. sts. terminal, leafy, infl. a spike, raceme, or thyrse in section *Villadia* or a flat cyme of several cincinni in section *Altamiranoa* (Rose) R. T. Clausen; fls. small, 5-merous, sepals equal, erect, petals more or less united, stamens 10.

For culture see *Succulents.*

Batesii (Hemsl.) Baehni & Macbr. [*Altamiranoa Batesii* (Hemsl.) Rose]. Glabrous, roots thick, sts. several from base, erect or decumbent, 6–10 in.; lvs. linear-lanceolate, ½ in. long, ⅛ in. wide; infl. of 2–5 cincinni; corolla white or pinkish, ⁵⁄₁₆ in. wide. Summer, autumn. Mex.

cucullata Rose. Glabrous, roots tuberous, sts. wandlike, to 15 in.; lvs. acuminate, to 1 in. long; infl. a spike or narrow thyrse, to 8 in. long; corolla reddish or orange, ⅛ in. long, petals hooded, minutely toothed. Autumn. Ne. Mex.

guatemalensis Rose [*V. levis* Rose]. Glabrous, much-branched, to 20 in.; lvs. linear, ¼–1 in. long, acute; infl. a narrow thyrse; corolla yellowish or greenish, ¼ in. wide. Autumn, early winter. S. Mex., Guatemala.

Jurgensenii (Hemsl.) Jacobsen. Puberulent, sts. erect or trailing, to 1½ ft., branching near base; lvs. spreading, lanceolate, ¼ in. long, acute; infl. of 2–5 cincinni, each with 2–13 nearly sessile fls.; corolla white or purplish, $\frac{5}{16}$ in. wide. Summer, autumn. E. Mex.

levis: *V. guatemalensis.*

VILLEBRUNEA Gaud.-Beaup. *Urticaceae.* About 8 spp. of monoecious or dioecious, erect or climbing trees or shrubs, native to s. and e. Asia; lvs. alt., simple; fls. clustered in spikes or panicles, male fls. with a 4–5-parted calyx and as many stamens, female fls. with a tubular, apically constricted calyx, stigma peltate; fr. an achene, adherent to calyx and partly enclosed in fleshy-thickened involucre.

pedunculata Shirai. Small, slender-branched tree; lvs. oblong-lanceolate to lanceolate, to 5 in. long, 1½ in. wide, acuminate, cuneate, serrate, white-tomentose beneath; male fl. clusters sessile, female fl. clusters peduncled. Taiwan and Japan.

pedunculosa: a listed name, probably in error for *V. pedunculata.*

VIMINARIA Sm. *Leguminosae* (subfamily *Faboideae*). One sp., a shrub, native to Australia; lvs. alt., mostly reduced to threadlike petioles; fls. in terminal racemes, small, papilionaceous, stamens separate; fr. an ovoid-oblong, usually indehiscent legume.

denudata Sm. Erect, to 20 ft., with long pendent brs., sometimes decumbent; petioles to 8–9 in. long, lfts. 1–3 when present, lanceolate, to 1½ in. long; fls. orange-yellow, in long racemes; fr. ¼ in. long, slightly longer than calyx. Se. Australia. Zone 10.

VINCA L. PERIWINKLE. *Apocynaceae.* About 12 spp. of trailing evergreen subshrubs, native to the Old World; lvs. opp., entire; fls. solitary, axillary, 5-merous, bisexual, corolla more or less funnelform, stamens borne at middle of tube, anthers short, with prominent, spreading appendages, style broadened toward apex; fr. a pair of erect or spreading, cylindrical follicles, each 6–8-seeded.

Planted as ground cover and in window boxes, thriving in shady locations. Propagated by division and cuttings.

alba Noronha. A sp. of *Tabernaemontana* not in cult.; material listed as *V. alba* in hort. is *V. minor* cv.

alpina: a listed name of no botanical standing for *V. minor* cv. 'Flore Pleno'.

aureo-variegata: a listed name of no botanical standing for *V. minor* cv. 'Variegata'.

Bowlesii: a listed name of no botanical standing for *V. minor* cv.

florepleno: a listed name of no botanical standing for *V. minor* cv.

herbacea Waldst. & Kit. Sts. herbaceous; lvs. elliptic or lanceolate, short-hairy on margin; fls. sessile or essentially so, 1 in. across; follicles to 1 in. long. Late spring. E. Eur., Asia Minor.

major L. GREATER P., BLUE-BUTTONS, BAND PLANT. Sts. to several ft. long; lvs. ovate, to 2 in. long, obtuse or acute, truncate or subcordate at base, ciliate, short-petioled; corolla blue, to 2 in. across, tube about ½ in. long; follicles to 2 in. long. Early spring. Eur. Cv. 'Variegata' [cv. 'Elegantissima']. Lvs. margined with yellowish-white.

minor L. COMMON P., LESSER P., MYRTLE, RUNNING M. Sts. very slender; lvs. oblong to ovate, to 2 in. long, attenuate at both ends; corolla usually lilac-blue, to ¾ in. across, tube ½ in. long or less, lobes obtuse-truncate; follicles to 3 in. long. Early spring. Eur.; long-persistent after cult. Cvs. are: 'Alba', fls. white; 'Bowlesii', fls. darker blue and said to be more freely produced; 'Flore Pleno' [cv. 'Alpina'; cv. 'Multiplex'], fls. double, purplish-blue; 'Variegata' [cv. 'Aureo-variegata'], lvs. variegated.

multiplex: a listed name of no botanical standing for *V. minor* cv. 'Flore Pleno'.

rosea: *Catharanthus roseus.*

variegata: a listed name of no botanical standing for *V. minor* cv.

VINCETOXICUM: see *CYNANCHUM* and *GONOLOBUS.* V. **carolinense:** *Matelea carolinensis.* V. **gonocarpos:** *Gonolobus gonocarpos.* V. **officinale:** *Cynanchum Vincetoxicum.*

VINES. As ornamentals, vines can be used in many ways in landscape or home plantings and some as conservatory subjects or even as house plants. The more vigorous species are suitable for covering wall areas, for screening, and for special decorative effects in which use of foliage is a prime concern. In addition, vines may produce showy flowers, col-

orful fruits that may also serve to attract birds, or attractive autumn colors.

Vines climb in various ways, by stems, tendrils, or leaf petioles that twist around supports, or by aerial roots, hooked thorns, or tiny adhesive discs. A knowledge of how a particular species climbs is often necessary in the selection of an appropriate vine for a special place or purpose in the garden or conservatory. For example, large wall surfaces of stone or masonry (but not wood) and tree trunks are natural climbing areas for ivys (*Hedera* and *Parthenocissus*), which clamber by aerial roots or adhesive discs. On the other hand, open fences, arbors, and trellises are better covered by twining genera requiring such special supports and exemplified by species of *Bignonia, Bougainvillea, Clematis, Jasminum,* and *Wisteria.*

Before choosing a vine for a specific use, it is well to see a representative specimen grown in one's general area, to judge whether the habit and performance are suitable. One should also be aware that some exotic species can be noxious weeds in some areas as, for example, *Lonicera japonica* cv. 'Halliana' and *Pueraria lobata* have become in Zones 7 and 8 in the Southeast. Also, rampant woody plants of certain genera like *Wisteria* may need to be kept within bounds so as not to damage home roofs or siding.

Like most plants, vines thrive best in well-prepared, fertile soil. Propagation is easy but may vary with the species. Seed is satisfactory when available, but where selections or cultivars are grown, vegetative propagation by cuttings is essential.

A sampling of some vining taxa from *Hortus Third* for select parts of the United States follows. The hardiest woody vines (Zone 4): *Ampelopsis brevipedunculata, Aristolochia durior, Celastrus orbiculatus, C. scandens, Clematis dioscoreifolia* var. *robusta, C.* × *Jackmanii, Lonicera sempervirens, Menispermum canadense, Parthenocissus quinquefolia.* Hardy woody vines (Zones 5 and 6): *Actinidia arguta, Akebia quinata, Campsis radicans, Clematis montana* 'Rubens', *C. tangutica,* cultivars of *Euonymus Fortunei, Hedera Helix, Hydrangea anomola* subsp. *petiolaris, Lonicera Heckrottii, L. japonica* 'Halliana', *Parthenocissus tricuspidata, Polygonum Aubertii, Tripterygium Regelii, Vitis Coignetiae, Wisteria floribunda, W. sinensis.* Woody vines for warm-temperate areas (Zones 7, 8, and 9): any of the preceding, plus other *Actinidia* species, *Akebia trifoliata, Campsis grandiflora, Clematis Armandii, Eccremocarpus scaber, Hedera canariensis, Macfadyena Unguis-cati, Gelsemium sempervirens, Passiflora caerulea, Rosa Banksiae, Stauntonia hexaphylla.*

Vines for the tropics (Hawaii), subtropics (Zone 10), and warm conservatories are very numerous and will be found listed in part under the genera *Allamanda, Antigonon, Araujia, Aristolochia, Arrabidaea, Asparagus, Bauhinia, Beaumontia, Bignonia, Bougainvillea, Camoensia, Cereus, Cissus, Clematis, Clerodendrum, Clitoria, Clytostoma, Combretum, Cryptostegia, Dioscorea, Distictis, Epipremnum, Ficus, Gloriosa, Hardenbergia, Hibbertia, Hoya, Hylocereus, Ipomoea, Jacquemontia, Jasminum, Lonicera, Lygodium, Mandevilla, Monstera, Mucuna, Pandorea, Passiflora, Petrea, Philodendron, Plumbago, Podranea, Pyrostegia, Quisqualis, Rhoicissus, Scindapsus, Senecio, Solandra, Solanum, Stephanotis, Stigmaphyllon, Strongylodon, Strophanthus, Syngonium, Tecomaria, Thunbergia,* and *Trachelospermum.*

Herbaceous perennial vines hardy in the North (Zone 5) but dying to the ground each winter: *Adlumia fungosa* (biennial), *Apios tuberosa* (weedy), *Asparagus verticillatus, Clematis texensis, Dioscorea Batatas, Humulus Lupulus, Lathyrus latifolius, Lygodium palmatum, Pueraria lobata.*

Annual vines, including some that are grown as annuals in the North but are perennial in milder climatic zones: *Asarina erubescens* (perennial), *Cardiospermum Halicacabum, Centrosema virginianum* (perennial), *Clitoria Ternatea, Cobaea scandens* (perennial), *Cucurbita* species, especially *C. Pepo* var. *ovifera, Cucumis* species, especially *C. Anguria* and *C. dipsaceus, Diplocyclos palmatus, Dolichos Lablab, Eccremocarpus scaber* (perennial), *Echinocystis lobata, Humu-*

lus japonicus, Ipomoea species, especially *I. alba* (perennial), *I.* × *multifida, I. purpurea, I. Quamoclit,* and *I. tricolor, Lagenaria siceraria, Lathyrus odoratus, Luffa acutangula, L. aegyptiaca, Momordica Balsamina, M. Charantia, Phaseolus coccineus, Sicyos angulatus, Thunbergia alata, Tropaeolum majus, T. peregrinum.*

VIOLA L. [*Erpetion* DC. ex Sweet]. VIOLET. *Violaceae.* About 500 spp. of per. or ann. herbs, or rarely subshrubs, of wide distribution in temp. regions, stemless or with leafy sts.; stipules persistent and often leafy; fls. in many spp. of 2 kinds, those in early spring showy and sterile, those in summer cleistogamous, without petals, and producing many seeds, showy fls. nodding, the lower petal spurred, the other 4 in 2 unlike pairs; fr. a caps., dehiscing into 3 boat-shaped, keeled valves.

Many species are suitable for the rock and wild garden and as edging plants in the semishady border. Nearly all species thrive best in partial shade and fairly rich soil. They require plenty of moisture and a winter covering of leaves or evergreen boughs. The violets may be grown from seeds sown in autumn in boxes and exposed to freezing, germination then taking place in spring. A quicker method of propagation is by division or by runners when these are produced. The florist's violet, *V. odorata,* is usually increased by offsets removed in late winter or early spring and rooted in sand. Sometimes old plants are divided when they are lifted in spring, but one should not save hard or weak material.

Pansy, *V.* × *Wittrockiana,* is a viola. In this country the pansy is usually propagated by seeds, which should be sown from the middle of July to the middle of Aug. for the next spring bloom. The plants may be wintered over in coldframes or in milder sections may be planted in permanent quarters if covered with a mulch. If desired, the seeds may be sown indoors in late winter. For cultivars or special colors, cuttings or layers should be used. Pansies are usually treated as annuals or biennials since they give their best flowers when relatively young, although plants may persist and with care flower for a number of years. They thrive in a cool, rather moist soil, and although they may benefit from protection from the noonday sun, they should not be planted in shade. Spring and autumn give the best flowers, but by mulching the bed to retain moisture and exclude heat, and by careful watering and not allowing seeds to form, one may have pansies all summer; pruning will keep plants stocky and compact. Seeds sown in boxes in Jan. or Feb. make flowering plants by Apr., taking the place of those flowering earlier from overwintered stock.

adunca Sm. [*V. bellidifolia* Greene; *V. montanensis* Rydb.]. WESTERN DOG V., HOOK-SPUR V. Puberulent, sts. leafy, to 4 in.; lvs. ovate to round-ovate, to 1½ in. long, finely crenulate, petioles to 2½ in. long; fls. violet, turning red-purple, peduncles shorter to longer than lvs. W. N. Amer., e. to Atlantic Coast.

aetolica Boiss. & Heldr. [*V. saxatilis* var. *aetolica* (Boiss. & Heldr.) Hayek]. Sts. to 16 in.; lvs. ovate to lanceolate, crenate, to ¾ in. long, stipules pinnately divided; fls. to ¾ in. long, petals yellow or the upper ones sometimes violet, spur ¼ in. long. Mts., Balkan Pen.

affinis Le Conte. Rhizomes moderately stout, branched; lvs. cordate-ovate, wavy-toothed, long-petioled; petals violet, white at base. Vt., s. to Ga. and Ala., w. to Wisc. A form of this with reddish-purple petals, found in s. Miss. and La., has been called *V. rosacea* Brainerd.

alba Bess. To 5 in.; lvs. lying close to ground, cordate-acuminate to ovate, to 4 in. long, entire, ciliate, pubescent beneath; fls. white, with violet center and veins, to 1 in. across, peduncles erect. Cent. Eur. and Medit. region. Sweet-scented.

allchariensis G. Beck. Cespitose per., to 10 in., sts. woody at base; lvs. elliptic-oblong and remotely toothed (lower) to linear (upper), gray, densely pubescent; fls. violet or yellow, to 1 in. long. Balkan Pen.

alpina Jacq. Sts. leafy, to 4 in. in fl.; lvs. all basal, broadly ovate to oblong-ovate, wavy-toothed, long-petioled; fls. bright violet, rarely white. Mts., se. Eur.

altaica Ker-Gawl. Creeping, sts. leafy, to 5 in.; lvs. elliptic to broadly ovate, shallowly crenate, long-petioled; fls. large, corolla yellow or sometimes violet, to 1½ in. long, spur to 3/16 in. long. Asia Minor.

appalachiensis L. K. Henry. Stoloniferous, forming mats, sts. prostrate, to 2½ in. long; lvs. round to ovate, to ⅝ in. long at flowering, 1 in. long when mature, cordate, crenate, somewhat leathery; fls. to ½ in. long, petals pale to deep violet, 3 lower petals white at base and veined with violet. Penn. to W. Va.

arborescens L. Sts. leafy, to 8 in., woody at base; lvs. ovate to linear-lanceolate; fls. to ⅝ in. long, petals white or pale violet, spur curved. Medit. region. Plants cult. under this name are usually *V. elatior.*

arenaria: *V. rupestris.*

Arkwrightii: a listed name of no botanical standing for a crimson-fld. *V. cornuta* hybrid, cv. 'Arkwright Ruby'.

arvensis J. Murr. Ann., to 16 in., sts. branched, short-hairy; lvs. oblong-spatulate, to 2 in. long, acute or obtuse, crenate, stipules pinnately parted; fls. to ⅝ in. long, sepals lanceolate, petals cream to yellow or bluish-violet, as long as or shorter than sepals. Eur.

Bakeri: *V. Nuttallii* var.

Beckwithii Torr. & A. Gray. GREAT BASIN V. Sts. leafy, to 4 in., from stout rhizome with fibrous roots; lvs. palmately 3 times 3-parted into linear segms.; upper 2 petals purple, lower 3 pale violet. Ore., s. to Calif. and Nev.

bellidifolia: *V. adunca.*

Bertolonii Pio. Sts. to 1 ft., leafy; lvs. variable, lower ones different from upper, lower usually orbicular, upper narrower; fls. violet or yellow, more or less square in face view. S. Eur.

biflora L. Sts. leafy, weak, to 6 in., from short rhizome; lvs. reniform, toothed, glabrous; fls. small, petals yellow, the lowermost streaked with blackish-purple, spur very short. Eur. to n. Asia; Alaska and Rocky Mts.

blanda Willd. SWEET WHITE V. Stemless, stoloniferous; lvs. ovate, acute, somewhat hairy on the upper surface; fls. white, petals narrow, strongly reflexed. Que., s. to Ga. and La.

bosniaca: *V. elegantula.*

Brittoniana Pollard. COAST V. Stemless, to 8 in.; lvs. reniform in outline, glabrous beneath, each of the 3 lobes divided into 2–4 linear, remotely serrulate segms., middle lobe widest; fls. large, petals dark violet, with white throat. Me. to Va.

calcarata L. Almost stemless, to 4 in., with underground stolons; lvs. ovate to lanceolate, wavy-toothed; petals violet, the spur as long as petals. Mts., s. Eur.

canadensis L. CANADA V., TALL WHITE V. Sts. leafy, to 1 ft. or more, from thick rhizome; lvs. broad-ovate, cordate, acute, toothed, nearly glabrous beneath; petals white inside with yellow base, often tinged violet outside, spur very short. New Bruns. to Ala., w. to Rocky Mts., Ariz., Ore., Wash. Cv. **'Alba'** is listed. Var. **rugulosa** (Greene) C. L. Hitchc. [*V. rugulosa* Greene]. Rhizome slender, stoloniferous; lvs. often wider than long, ciliate-margined, pubescent beneath.

canina L. DOG V. Sts. leafy, to 3 in., rhizome short, creeping; lvs. ovate-cordate, toothed; petals bluish-purple, spur yellow. N. Eur. and Asia. Cv. **'Alba'** is listed.

cenisia L. Branching from root crown into slender stolons to 9 in. long, each ending in a short st. to 6 in. long; lvs. small, ovate; petals light violet, to 1 in. long, spur slender, to ¼ in. long. Alps, Eur.

chrysantha: *V. Douglasii.*

conspersa Rchb. AMERICAN DOG V. Sts. leafy, to 8 in. when in fl., from a branched rhizome; lower lvs. cordate-orbicular, toothed; fls. many, petals pale violet, varying to white, spur short. Que. to Minn., s. to Ga.

cornuta L. HORNED V., VIOLA. More or less tufted, to 12 in.; lvs. ovate, wavy-toothed, stipules large, triangular, coarsely toothed; petals violet, spur slender, as long as sepals. Spain and Pyrenees. The tufted or bedding pansies, with shorter spurs, are probably derived from this sp. Some cvs. are: **'Alba'**, petals white; **'Atropurpurea'**, petals dark purple, with small yellow center; **'Papilio'**, fls. very large, petals violet, with purple center; **'Purpurea'**, petals purple.

corsica Nym. Sts. leafy, ascending, glabrous; basal lvs. ovate-orbicular, st. lvs. oblong to lanceolate, entire or nearly so, stipules entire, the lower ones with 2 linear lateral lobes; sepals lanceolate, petals violet-blue, acute, spur twice as long as sepals. Corsica and Sardinia.

crassa Mak. Sts. leafy, to 4 in., from short creeping rhizomes; lvs. reniform-cordate, to ¾ in. long and twice as wide, wavy-toothed; fls. small, petals deep yellow. Japan, Kurile Is., Kamchatka.

cucullata Ait. MARSH BLUE V. Stemless, from scaly rhizome; lvs. broad-ovate to reniform, to 3½ in. wide, acute, crenate; petals violet with darker throat and white at base, peduncles to 6 in. long. Wet places, Nfld. to Ga., w. to Ark. Cvs. are: **'Alba'**, petals white; **'Bicolor'**, petals white, with violet center and veins; **'Rubra'**, a listed name.

cuneata S. Wats. Sts. leafy, slender, to 8 in., glabrous; lvs. ovate, toothed; fls. with 2 upper petals purple, lower violet or whitish-veined or spotted with purple, spur yellowish. Ore. and Calif.

Cunninghamii Hook.f. Tufted, sts. to 6 in. when in fl., glabrous; lvs. ovate or broadly ovate, almost triangular, to 1 in. wide, shallowly crenate or almost entire, long-petioled; fls. small, petals white or pale violet, about ½ in. long, spur very short. New Zeal.

Curtisii: *V. tricolor.*

dissecta Ledeb. var. **chaerophylloides** (Regel) Mak. [*V. dissecta* var. *eizanensis* Mak.; *V. eizanensis* (Mak.) Mak.]. Stemless, to 4 in. when in fl.; lvs. divided into 3 segms., each further divided; fls. fragrant, petals pale rose or purplish, about 1 in. long, spur about ³⁄₁₆ in. long. Japan.

Douglasii Steud. [*V. chrysantha* Hook.]. Sts. leafy, to 6 in., from deep rhizome; lvs. 2-pinnate into linear or oblong segms.; petals orange-yellow, veined with purple, the 2 upper brownish-purple outside. Calif.

Dubyana Burnat ex Gremli. Sts. to 1 ft.; lower lvs. orbicular, to 1⅝ in. across, upper lvs. narrowly lanceolate to linear, stipules pinnately divided; fls. to 1 in. long, petals violet, the lowermost with a yellow spot, spur curved, to ¼ in. long. Mts., n. Italy.

eizanensis: *V. dissecta* var. *chaerophylloides.*

elatior Fries. Sts. leafy, robust, erect, to 16 in.; lvs. lanceolate to lanceolate-ovate, to 3 in. long, glabrous; petals bright blue with darker veins, spur short, blunt, less than ⅛ in. long. Marshy places, Eur., w. Asia.

elegantula Schott [*V. bosniaca* Form.]. Per., but better treated as bien., sts. leafy, prostrate to ascending, to 12 in.; lvs. ovate, wavy-toothed, stipules conspicuous, palmately divided into irregular segms.; petals rose-purple, the lowermost with yellow, striped spot at base, spur slender, about ¼ in. long. Sw. Eur.

×**emarginata** (Nutt.) Le Conte. TRIANGLE-LEAVED V. Naturally occurring series of hybrids between *V. affinis* and *V. sagittata.*

eriocarpa: *V. pubescens* var.

fimbriatula Sm. NORTHERN DOWNY V. Stemless, to 4 in.; lvs. ovate to oblong-ovate, acute, cordate, serrulate, pubescent beneath; fls. to ¾ in. across, petals violet-purple. Nov. Sc. to Wisc., s. to n. Ga.

Flettii Piper. ROCK V., OLYMPIC V. Sts. leafy, to 6 in., glabrous, from deep-seated rhizome; lvs. reniform, toothed; petals violet with yellow base, about ¾ in. long, spur short, blunt, yellow. Mts., Wash.

×**florariensis** Correv.: *V. cornuta* × *V. tricolor.* Fls. purple, but lower petal yellow at base, striped purple, spur short. Long flowering season.

glabella Nutt. STREAM V. Sts. leafy, to 1 ft., sometimes pubescent; lvs. cordate; petals bright yellow, veined with purple, spur short. Mts., w. N. Amer.; ne. Asia.

gracilis Sibth. & Sm. Sts. leafy, to 6 in., hairy; lvs. oblong to broad-ovate, somewhat toothed, stipules pinnately parted; petals violet, spur longer than sepals. Balkan Pen. to Asia Minor. Cvs. listed are: 'Alba', fls. white; 'Lutea', fls. yellow; 'Major', 'Minor', and 'Purpurea'.

grandiflora: a listed name of no botanical standing; has been used for various hort. forms.

Hallii A. Gray. Sts. leafy, to 6 in.; lvs. palmately 2–3-parted into narrow segms.; fls. with 2 upper petals dark violet and 3 lower yellow or white. Ore. and Calif.

hastata Michx. HALBERD-LEAVED V. Sts. leafy, elongate, with 2–4 lvs. near top, to 10 in.; lvs. hastate, toothed; petals yellow, tinged violet outside, about ⁵⁄₁₆ in. long, spur very short, broad. Penn. to Fla.

hederacea Labill. [*Erpetion reniforme* Sweet]. AUSTRALIAN V., IVY-LEAVED V., TRAILING V. Stemless, tufted, stoloniferous; lvs. reniform to spatulate, entire or toothed; petals blue varying to white, to ½ in. long, scarcely spurred. Australia.

hiemalis: a listed name of no botanical standing.

hispida Lam. Sts. leafy, branched, to 8 in., with spreading hairs; lower lvs. ovate, subcordate, upper lvs. lanceolate, cuneate, all lvs. crenate, long-petioled; petals light violet with darker veining, about ¾ in. long, spur blunt, to ³⁄₁₆ in. long. France.

hybrida Wulfen ex Roem. & Schult.: *V. uliginosa* Bess., a plant not known in cult., but the name *V. hybrida*, is used incorrectly in the trade for various forms of uncertain lineage.

incognita Brainerd [*V. incognita* var. *Forbesii* Brainerd]. LARGE-LEAVED WHITE V. Stemless, to 3 in., from creeping rhizome, with slender stolons in summer; lvs. orbicular-reniform, abruptly acuminate, serrulate, glabrous above, pubescent beneath and on petioles; fls. white. Que. to Wisc., s. to Mass. and Tenn.

japonica Langsd. Rhizome short; spring lvs. ovate to triangular-ovate, to 2 in. long, obtusely toothed, summer lvs. elongate-triangular, to 3¼ in. long; fls. purple, to ⅝ in. long, on peduncles to 6 in. long. Japan, s. Korea, Ryukyu Is.

Jooi Janka. Stemless, to 3½ in., from creeping rhizome, lacking stolons; lvs. ovate to oblong, to 1¼ in. wide, subtruncate to cordate, crenulate, glabrous; fls. to ¾ in. across, sepals oblong-lanceolate, petals pinkish-violet, lateral petals bearded at base. Se. Eur. Sometimes distributed as *V. missouriensis.*

labradorica Schrank. LABRADOR V. Diminutive, sts. leafy, to 3 in., closely related to *V. adunca*, differing chiefly in being essentially glabrous. Nfld. to Alaska, s. to New Hamp. and Minn.

lanceolata L. LANCE-LEAVED V., EASTERN WATER V. Stemless, to 9 in., glabrous, from creeping rhizome, profusely stoloniferous in summer; lvs. lanceolate, slightly toothed, tapering to margined petioles; fls. white. Moist soil, Nov. Sc. to Fla., w. to Tex.

Langsdorfii Fisch. ALASKA V. Sts. leafy, to 8 in.; lvs. ovate-cordate, wavy-toothed; petals blue or violet, varying to white, spur broad. Alaska, s. to Ore.; Siberia.

lobata Benth. YELLOW WOOD V. Sts. leafy, to 1 ft.; lvs. palmately 3–7-parted into nearly entire lobes; petals yellow, veined at base, purple outside. Ore. and Calif.

lutea Huds. Sts. leafy, to 10 in., with slender rhizomes; lvs. ovate to lanceolate, wavy-toothed, stipules pinnatifid; petals yellow, the upper 2 sometimes purple, or all purple, spur as long as sepals. Eur. Cvs. listed are: 'Elegans', 'Grandiflora', and 'Splendens'.

macedonica: *V. tricolor* subsp.

Macloskeyi F. Lloyd. WESTERN SWEET WHITE V. Stemless, to 6 in. or less; lvs. in tufts at ends of leafy stolons, cordate to orbicular, remotely crenulate; fls. white. Alta. to B.C., s. to Calif. Var. **pallens** (Banks) C. L. Hitchc. [*V. pallens* (Banks) Brainerd]. Lvs. prominently crenate, often over 1 in. wide. E. and w. U.S.

mandshurica W. Becker. Stemless, to 8 in. or more; lvs. triangular-lanceolate to broadly oblong-lanceolate, to 3 in. long, petioles as long as to shorter than blades; petals dark purple or rarely white with purple striations, spur to ¼ in. long. E. Asia.

missouriensis Greene. MISSOURI V. Stemless, to 6 in., glabrous; lvs. ovate-cordate, toothed; petals pale violet marked with purple around white center. Ill. to Nebr., s. to Mo. and Tex. Some material grown under this name may be *V. Jooi.*

montanensis: *V. adunca.*

Munbyana Boiss. & Reut. Sts. leafy, ascending from a prostrate base, to 18 in.; lvs. cordate-ovate, toothed, glabrous, stipules pinnate', cut; fls. large, 1–3 from the lower axils, petals violet or yellow, spur straight, about ½ in. long. N. Afr.

nana: a listed name of no botanical standing.

nephrophylla Greene. NORTHERN BOG V. Stemless; lvs. cordate-ovate or reniform, wavy-toothed, petioles longer than blades; petals deep violet, to 1 in. long or more, spur to ⅛ in. long. Wet and boggy places, N. Amer.

nigra: a listed name of no botanical standing.

Nuttallii Pursh. YELLOW PRAIRIE V. Sts. leafy, to 5 in. in fl.; lvs. lanceolate, tapering to margined petioles, entire or nearly so; petals yellow, with brown veins on 3 lower ones, about ½ in. long, spur very short. B.C. to Calif., e. to cent. U.S. Var. **Nuttallii.** The typical var.; lvs. narrowly lanceolate to elliptic-lanceolate, 3 times as long as wide or more, tapered at base to long petioles. Mo., w. to Alta. and Ariz. Var **Bakeri** (Greene) C. L. Hitchc. [*V. Bakeri* Greene]. Lvs. less than 3 times as long as wide, to 2 in. long; fls. to ½ in. long, upper petals yellow on back. Wash., s. to Calif. Var. **praemorsa** (Dougl. ex Lindl.) S. Wats. [*V. praemorsa* Dougl. ex Lindl.]. Lvs. less than 3 times as long as wide, 2 in. long, cuneate, mostly densely hairy. B.C. to n. Calif. Var. **vallicola** (A. Nels.) St. John [*V. vallicola* A. Nels.]. Lvs. less than 3 times as long as wide, generally less than 2 in. long, usually truncate or subcordate at base, glabrous to sparsely hairy. B.C. to Ore., e. to Rocky Mts.

ocellata Torr. & A. Gray. TWO-EYED V. Sts. leafy, to 1 ft.; lvs. cordate-ovate, wavy-toothed; petals to ¾ in. long, the 2 upper ones white, violet on outside, the 3 lower white or yellow, spotted or veined with purple, spur rather conspicuous. Ore. and Calif.

odorata L. SWEET V., GARDEN V., FLORIST'S V., ENGLISH V. Tufted, stemless, with long stolons; lvs. cordate-ovate to reniform, toothed; fls. fragrant, about ¾ in. across, petals deep violet, rarely rose or white, spur short, nearly straight. Eur., Afr., Asia. Best known sp., since it has long been important as a source of perfume and is in the florist trade; it has a number of garden forms. The many hort. forms vary in stature, size and color of fls., and some have double fls.

orbiculata Geyer ex Hook. WESTERN ROUND-LEAVED V. Sts. leafy, to 3 in.; lvs. orbicular, wavy-toothed; fls. yellow, to ⅝ in. long. B.C. to Ore., e. to Mont. and Idaho.

pallens: *V. Macloskeyi* var. *pallens.*

palmata L. WILD OKRA, EARLY BLUE V. Stemless, hairy, from short, stout rhizome; lvs. palmately 5–11-lobed or -parted, toothed or cut, middle segms. largest; petals violet-purple, to ¾ in. long, spur short, blunt. Mass. to Minn., s. to n. Ga.

palustris L. MARSH V., ALPINE M. V. Stemless, glabrous, from creeping rhizome; lvs. cordate-ovate or reniform, wavy-toothed; fls. to ½ in. across, petals pale lilac with darker veins, varying to nearly white, spur short, blunt. Moist places, n. N. Amer., Eur., Asia.

Papilio: a listed name of no botanical standing for *V. cornuta* cv.

papilionacea: *V. sororia.*

parviflora: a confused name; material so listed may be referable to *V. tricolor.*

Patrinii DC. Stemless, to 5 in., not stoloniferous; lvs. triangular-ovate to linear, to 4 in. long, hastate or cordate, to cuneate at base, crenate or serrate; fls. to ½ in. across, petals lilac. Siberia, e. to Japan.

pedata L. [*V. pedata* vars. **concolor** H. T. Holm and *lineariloba* DC.]. BIRD-FOOT V., PANSY V., CROWFOOT V. Stemless, to 6 in. in fl., glabrous; lvs. 3–5-divided, segms. 2–4-cleft or -toothed near apex; fls. to nearly 1 in. across, with 2 upper petals dark violet, 3 lower pale lilac. E. U.S. Distinguished by a short, thick, vertical rhizome, deeply palmately cut lvs., the large petals spread in one plane giving the fls. a flattened appearance. Fl. color varies; in some plants all petals are light blue, in others the upper 2 are dark purple and the lower light blue, and there are white- and pinkish-fld. forms. See *V. pedatifida.* Vars. **concolor** and **lineariloba:** *V. pedata.*

pedatifida G. Don. LARKSPUR V., PURPLE PRAIRIE V. Stemless, to 3 in. in fl., glabrous or sparsely hairy; lvs. palmately many-parted, the ultimate segms. linear; petals violet, to ¾ in. long, spur short, blunt, peduncles longer than lvs. Alta. and Sask., s. to Okla. and Ark. Cv. 'Alba'. A listed name. This sp. is sometimes confused with *V. pedata,* from which it differs in having the petals forming a papilionaceous or pea-flowerlike corolla, not flattened.

pedunculata Torr. & A. Gray. CALIFORNIA GOLDEN V. Sts. leafy, ascending, often 2 ft. long, from a stout, deep rhizome; lvs. round-ovate, coarsely toothed; petals orange-yellow, veined purple on the inside. Calif. and Baja Calif. In Calif. also called JOHNNY-JUMP-UP and WILD PANSY.

pensylvanica: *V. pubescens* var. *eriocarpa.*

pinnata L. Stemless, to 4 in. in fl.; lvs. palmately divided into many narrow segms.; fls. fragrant, petals blue-violet, to ½ in. long, spur stout, about ³⁄₁₆ in. long. Mts., cent. Eur., n. Asia. Remarkable for its much-divided lvs.

praemorsa: *V. Nuttallii* var.

Priceana: *V. sororia.*

primulifolia L. PRIMROSE-LEAVED V. Stemless, to 10 in. in fl., producing leafy stolons after flowering; lvs. oblong to ovate or obovate, obtuse or rounded at apex, rounded to cuneate at base; petals small, white, with purplish veins. New Bruns. to Minn., s. to Fla. and Tex.

pubescens Ait. DOWNY YELLOW V. Sts. leafy, to 16 in., more or less pubescent, from a short, stout rhizome; lvs. ovate-cordate, usually wider than long, crenate-dentate, stipules broadly ovate; petals yellow, with purple-brown markings near base. Nov. Sc. to N.Dak., s. to N.C., Ga., Miss., Okla. Var. **eriocarpa** (Schweinitz) N. H. Russell [*V. eriocarpa* Schweinitz; *V. pensylvanica* Michx.; *V. scabriuscula* Schweinitz ex Torr. & A. Gray may belong here]. SMOOTH YELLOW v. Of small stature, often 6 in. or less; lvs. finely pubescent to nearly glabrous.

purpurea Kellogg. PINE V. Sts. leafy, to 8 in.; lvs. ovate, longer than broad, cuneate; petals deep yellow with purple-brown markings, upper 2 petals purple-brown on back, spur short, saccate. Mts., Calif. and Ore.

Rafinesquii Greene [*V. Kitaibeliana* Roem. & Schult. var. *Rafinesquii* (Greene) Fern.]. FIELD PANSY. Ann., sts. leafy, often branched from base, to 15 in., glabrous; lvs. variable, spatulate to obovate, irregularly toothed, stipules conspicuous, leafy, pectinately cut; petals bluish-white to cream-colored, peduncles slender. E. U.S., w. to Colo. and Ariz.

Reichenbachiana Jord. ex Boreau [*V. sylvestris* Lam., in part]. Closely related to *V. Riviniana,* but of smaller stature, petals pale violet, spur dark purple, slender. Eur., N. Afr., Asia.

renifolia A. Gray. NORTHERN WHITE V., KIDNEY-LEAVED V. Stemless, to 4 in., glabrous to pubescent; lvs. broadly reniform, rarely acute, remotely crenate-serrate; petals white, lower 3 with brown veins, spur short, rounded. Swamps, Nfld. to Minn., s. to Penn., also Rocky Mts. in Colo.

Riviniana Rchb. DOG V., WOOD V. Sts. leafy, to 8 in., with short erect rhizome; lvs. broadly ovate, almost orbicular, to 3 in. wide, deeply cordate, crenate; petals blue-violet, to 1 in. long, spur paler, to ³⁄₁₆ in. long. Eur., N. Afr. See *V. Reichenbachiana.*

rosacea: see *V. affinis.*

rosea: a listed name of no botanical standing.

rostrata Pursh. LONG-SPURRED V. Sts. leafy, to 15 in., glabrous; lvs. cordate-ovate or orbicular, toothed, stipules conspicuous, with spiny

teeth on each side; petals lilac with darker spots, spur to ½ in. long. Que. to Mich., s. to Ga.

rotundifolia Michx. ROUND-LEAVED YELLOW V., EARLY Y. V. Stemless, to 4 in., rhizome elongate, covered with persistent lf. bases; lvs. elliptic, obtuse, crenate, thick and prostrate; petals bright yellow, lower 3 with brown lines. Me. to Ga.

rugulosa: *V. canadensis* var.

rupestris F. W. Schmidt [*V. arenaria* DC.]. Fl. sts. axillary, to 4 in.; lvs. in a rosette, cordate-reniform, to 1¼ in. long; fls. reddish-violet, pale blue, or white, to ⅝ in. long. Eur. Cv. 'Rosea' is listed.

sagittata Ait. ARROW-LEAVED V. Stemless, to 4 in. in fl.; lvs. lanceolate or oblong-lanceolate, more or less saggitate and toothed at base; fls. violet-purple, to 1 in. across, peduncles erect, standing above lvs. Me. to Minn., s. to Ga., La., and e. Tex.

sarmentosa: *V. sempervirens.*

saxatilis: *V. tricolor* subsp. *subalpina.* Var. **aetolica:** *V. aetolica.*

scabriuscula: perhaps *V. pubescens* var. *eriocarpa.*

Selkirkii Pursh ex J. Goldie. GREAT-SPURRED V. Stemless, to 4 in. in fl.; lvs. broadly ovate-cordate, to 1¼ in. across or more, crenate; fls. ½ in. across, petals pale violet, spur large, blunt, to ¼ in. long. New Bruns. to Minn. and Alta., s. to Me. and n. Penn.

sempervirens Greene [*V. sarmentosa* Dougl. ex Hook.]. REDWOOD V., EVERGREEN V. Sts. leafy, to 3 in., from rhizomes producing stolons; lvs. round-cordate, toothed, dark-spotted; fls. to ¾ in. across, petals yellow, spur very short. B.C. to Calif.

septemloba Le Conte. SOUTHERN COAST V. Stemless, to 6 in. in fl., glabrous; lvs. ovate-cordate, early spring lvs. entire, later lvs. pedately cut into 7–9 somewhat oblanceolate lobes; fls. to 1½ in. across, petals bright violet, spur short, broad. Va. to Fla., w. to Miss.

septentrionalis Greene. NORTHERN BLUE V. Stemless, to 5 in. in fl., pubescent; lvs. ovate to reniform, toothed, ciliate; fls. large, petals violet-purple, rarely white. Me., s. to Appalachian Mts., w. to Mich. and Wisc.

Sheltonii Torr. Sts. leafy, to 6 in., glabrous to sparsely pubescent; lvs. orbicular in outline, deeply cleft into 3 main lobes, each further dissected into linear segms.; petals yellow, marked with purple, about ½ in. long. Wash. to Baja Calif.

sororia Willd. [*V. papilionacea* Pursh; *V. papilionacea* var. *Priceana* (Pollard) Alexand.; *V. Priceana* Pollard]. WOOLLY BLUE V. Stemless, from thick fleshy rhizome, not stoloniferous; lvs. ovate-cordate, large, broader than long, not lobed or divided, equally pubescent on both surfaces, petioles as long as peduncles or longer; petals usually dark blue or purple but may be red, light blue, white, or gray-blue. E. U.S. The most widespread sp. in e. U.S. Plants in n. part of range are smaller than those in s. part; pubescence varies from densely villous to almost glabrous. The plant known as *V. papilionacea* Pursh is a glabrous form of this sp. The color of the fls. is also variable, and the name *V. Priceana* Pollard has been used for the so-called CONFEDERATE VIOLET, a form with gray-blue fls.

striata Ait. CREAM V., PALE V., STRIPED V. Sts. leafy, to 12 in. in fl., later elongating to 24 in.; lvs. ovate to orbicular, crenate-toothed, stipules conspicuous, fimbriate-margined; fls. small, petals cream-white, veined with purple, spur blunt, less than ¼ in. long. N.Y. to s. Ill., s. to n. Ga. and Ark.

sylvestris: see *V. Reichenbachiana.*

tricolor L. [*V. Curtisii* E. Forst.; *V. tricolor* var. *hortensis* DC.; *V. variegata* Vuk. may belong here.]. EUROPEAN WILD PANSY, MINIATURE P., FIELD P., JOHNNY-JUMP-UP. Ann. or short-lived per., often branched, to 12 in.; lvs. ovate to lanceolate, cuneate at base, crenate, stipules large, leafy, deeply lobed; fls. about ¾ in. long, variously colored, petals yellow to purple-red, violet-blue, or white, or various combinations. Eur.; naturalized in N. Amer., particularly purple-fld. forms, known as WILD or FIELD PANSY. One of the parents of the GARDEN PANSY, *V.* × *Wittrockiana.* Subsp. **tricolor.** The typical subsp.; ann., to 16 in.; fls. usually blue-violet. Subsp. **macedonica** (Boiss. & Heldr.) A. Schmidt [*V. macedonica* Boiss. & Heldr.]. Usually per., to 8 in.; upper petals bright violet, lateral and lower petals yellowish, without veins or the lower with a few veins. Balkan Pen. Subsp. **subalpina** Gaudin [*V. saxatilis* F. W. Schmidt]. Per. or bien., to about 1 ft.; fls. to 1⅜ in. long, petals all yellow or the upper violet, lateral and lower petals veined. Mts., s. and cent. Eur.

triloba Schweinitz. Stemless, variously hairy; lvs. variable, the earliest and latest lvs. uncut, those at flowering time lobed or divided; fls. dark to pale blue-violet. Vt., s. to Mass., and Ga., w. to Mo. and Tex. Resembles *V. sororia* except for lobing of lvs.

trinervata T. J. Howell. SAGEBRUSH V. Tufted, sts. leafy, to 6 in.; lvs. dissected, firm and thick, segms. lanceolate or ovate-lanceolate, strongly 3-nerved; fls. with upper petals dark blue, and lower pale blue to white with yellow base. Wash. and Ore.

vallicola: *V. Nuttallii* var.

variegata: see *V. tricolor.*

verecunda A. Gray var. **yakusimana** (Nakai) Ohwi [*V. yakusimana* Nakai]. Dwarf, sts. leafy, to 1 in. in fl.; lvs. reniform-cordate, to ¼ in. wide, shallowly toothed, glabrous; petals white, about ⁵⁄₁₆ in. long. Yakushima (s. Japan).

viarum Pollard. PLAINS V. Stemless, to 5 in., glabrous; lvs. simple or 3–7-lobed, incised or serrate; fls. deep violet. Ill. to e. Nebr., s. to Ark.

Vilmoriniana: a listed name of no botanical standing.

Walteri House. Sts. leafy, to 8 in., eventually lying flat on ground, rooting at nodes, and developing new crowns; lvs. orbicular or ovate, mottled with dark green; fls. violet-blue. S.C. to Fla., w. to Tex.

Wellsiana: a listed name of no botanical standing.

×**Wittrockiana** Gams. PANSY, GARDEN P., LADIES-DELIGHT, HEARTSEASE, STEPMOTHER'S FLOWER. Hybrid between *V. tricolor* and apparently *V. lutea,* together with *V. altaica.* Ann. or short-lived per., sts. leafy, much-branched, to 9 in.; lvs. ovate and subcordate or lanceolate-elliptic and cuneate; fls. to 2–5 in. across, rounded in outline, flattened, variously colored.

yakusimana: *V. verecunda* var.

yesoensis Maxim. Stemless; lvs. ovate-cordate, to 2 in. long, white-hairy, petioles longer than blade; petals white with purple lines, lateral petals bearded, spur slender, to ¼ in. long. Japan.

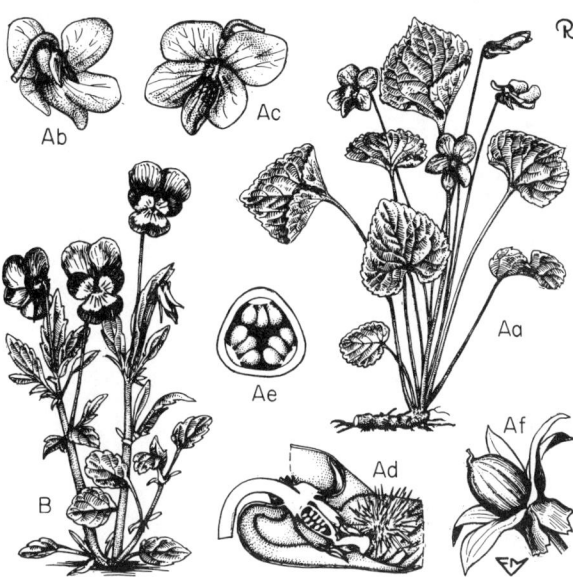

VIOLACEAE. **A,** *Viola sororia:* **Aa,** plant, × ¼; **Ab,** flower, back view, × ¾; **Ac,** flower, face view, × ¾; **Ad,** flower, vertical section (apices of corolla lobes cut off), × 2; **Ae,** ovary, cross section, × 8; **Af,** capsule, × 1. **B,** *Viola tricolor:* plant, × ½. (Af from Bailey, *Manual of Cultivated Plants,* ed. 2.)

VIOLACEAE Batsch. VIOLET FAMILY. Dicot; about 18 genera and 800 spp. of herbs, usually per., or shrubs, rarely trees or climbers, widely distributed and occuring on all continents; lvs. alt., rarely opp. (in *Hybanthus* Jacq.), usually simple, sometimes lobed or divided, with minute or leafy stipules; fls. bisexual or rarely unisexual, regular or irregular, sometimes cleistogamous, sepals and petals 5, the lower petal often spurred or saccate, stamens 5, ovary superior, 1-celled; fr. a caps. or berry, seeds 1–2, or many, sometimes winged. *Hymenanthera, Melicytus,* and *Viola* are cult. as ornamentals.

VIORNA: *CLEMATIS.*

VIRGILIA Poir. *Leguminosae* (subfamily *Faboideae).* Perhaps 2 spp. of trees, native to S. Afr.; lvs. alt., odd-pinnate; fls. in axillary racemes, showy, papilionaceous, standard reflexed, stamens 10, separate; fr. a leathery, flat, dehiscent legume.

Grown as ornamentals, Zone 10. Propagated by seeds soaked in hot water, or scarified, before sowing.

capensis (L.) Poir. [*V. oroboides* (Bergius) Salter]. Shrubby tree, to 30 ft.; lvs. to 8 in. long, lfts. in 6–10 pairs, leathery, linear-oblong, to 1 in. long, pale and tomentose beneath; fls. fragrant, mauve-pink, ½ in. long; fr. 2–3 in. long. Early summer to autumn.

divaricata Adamson. Differs from *V. capensis* in having a more compact habit, with horizontal brs., deep pink fls. in infls. aggregated at tips of brs., and flowering during a short, definite period in spring.

oroboides: *V. capensis.*

VISCARIA: *LYCHNIS.* **V. atropurpurea:** *L. Viscaria* subsp. **V. cardinalis:** *L. Coeli-rosa* cv. 'Kermesina'. **V. viscosa** and **V. vulgaris:** *L. Viscaria.*

VISCUM: see *LORANTHACEAE.*

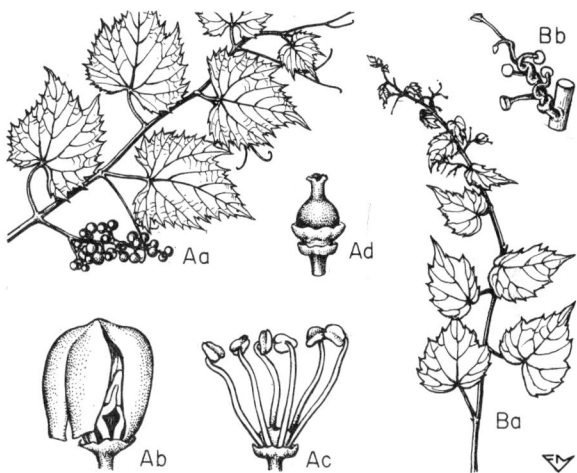

VITACEAE. **A,** *Vitis vulpina:* **Aa,** fruiting branch, × ⅙; **Ab,** flower bud with corolla dehiscing, × 8; **Ac,** male flower (after loss of corolla), × 5; **Ad,** female flower (after loss of corolla), × 5. **B,** *Parthenocissus tricuspidata:* **Ba,** leafy branch, × ¼; **Bb,** segment of stem with disc-bearing tendrils, × 1. (From Bailey, *Manual of Cultivated Plants,* ed. 2.)

VITACEAE Juss. GRAPE or VINE FAMILY. Dicot.; 12 widely distributed genera of woody vines climbing by tendrils, sometimes ending in discoid suckers, rarely shrubby; lvs. alt., simple or compound, stipuled; fls. usually in lf.-opposed, compound-cymose or paniculate infls., small, bisexual or unisexual, sepals, petals, and stamens 4–5, ovary superior, 2–6-celled, subtended or partially enveloped by a glandular disc; fr. a berry. The cult. genera are: *Ampelopsis, Cissus, Parthenocissus, Rhoicissus, Tetrastigma,* and *Vitis.* The genus *Leea* is here treated as in the Leeaceae.

Several genera are grown as ornamentals and screens, covering arbors and walls; *Vitis* is grown primarily for the edible fruit and wine fermented from it. The plants are of easy cultivation and many of them are hardy in the northern states.

VITEX L. *Verbenaceae.* About 270 spp. of trees and shrubs, native mostly to trop. and subtrop. regions, a few in temp. regions; lvs. opp., palmately compound, lfts. 3–7, rarely 1, often darker above than beneath; fls. white, yellow, red, or blue to purple, cymose, the cymes axillary, or terminal and in panicles, calyx 5-toothed or entire, corolla tubular-funnelform, 5-lobed, slightly 2-lipped, stamens 4; fr. a small drupe.

Vitexes do well in any good soil. Propagated by seeds in spring, layers, and greenwood cuttings under glass. *V. Negundo* var. *incisa* is usually root-hardy in some of the northern parts of the country, and *V. Agnus-castus* sometimes to Zone 6; other species are limited to Zone 10 and the warmer parts of Zone 9. When the roots survive, the young shoots produce flowers.

Agnus-castus L. CHASTE TREE, HEMP TREE, MONK'S PEPPER TREE, SAGE TREE, INDIAN-SPICE, WILD PEPPER. Aromatic shrub or small tree, to 10–20 ft.; lfts. 5–7, lanceolate or elliptic, to 4 in. long, acuminate, nearly entire, very dark green above, grayish-tomentose beneath; cymes dense, sessile or subsessile, in panicles to 1 ft. long; fls. lilac to lavender. S. Eur.; naturalized in s. U.S. and warm parts of the world. Zone 7. Cv. **'Alba'** [var. *alba* Weston.]. Fls. white. Cv. **'Latifolia'** [var. *latifolia* (Mill.) Loud.; *V. latifolia* Mill.; *V. macrophylla* Hort.]. Lvs. shorter, broader. Cv. **'Variegata'** is listed. Used medicinally and in basketry.

altissima L.f. Tree, to 100 ft.; lfts. 3, elliptic or obovate-elliptic, to 8 in. long, entire, dark green above, lighter beneath; cymes in panicles to 9 in. long; fls. cream-colored with white lip. Pakistan, India, Ceylon. Valuable timber tree used in cabinet work and building construction.

divaricata Swartz. Shrub or tree, to 60 ft.; lfts. 3, rarely 1 or 5, oblong, oblong-elliptic, or elliptic, to 8½ in. long, entire, glabrous or sometimes with a few hairs on midrib; cymes axillary; fls. violet or blue, to ¼ in. across. W. Indies, Venezuela. Wood used for making shingles, and lvs. yield tannin.

incisa: *V. Negundo* var. *heterophylla*.

keniensis Turrill. Tree, to 90 ft.; lfts. 5, oblong-elliptic, to 8 in. long, pubescent; cymes terminal in panicles; corolla rusty-brown-tomentose outside. Trop. e. Afr.

kewensis: probably a misspelling for *V. keniensis*.

laciniata: *V. Negundo* var. *heterophylla*.

latifolia: *V. Agnus-castus* var.

lucens T. Kirk. PURURI. Tree, to 60 ft.; lfts. 3–5, obovate or elliptic, to 5 in. long, entire, glabrous, glossy; cymes axillary, many-fld.; fls. red or pink, to 1 in. long; fr. bright red. New Zeal.

macrophylla: *V. Agnus-castus* var. *latifolia*.

Negundo L. Shrub or small tree, to 15–25 ft.; lfts. 3–5, oblong, elliptic, lanceolate, or ovate, to 4 in. long, entire or toothed, dark green above, grayish-tomentose beneath; cymes peduncled, in loose panicles to 8 in. long; fls. lilac or lavender, ¼ in. long, fragrant. Se. Afr., Madagascar, e. and se. Asia, Philippine Is., Guam; naturalized in Fla. Var. **heterophylla** (Franch.) Rehd. [var. *incisa* (Lam.) C. B. Clarke; *V. incisa* Lam.; *V. laciniata* Hort. ex Schauer]. Lfts. smaller, deeply toothed or cut. N. China, Mongolia. Zone 6. Cv. **'Variegata'** is listed.

parviflora Juss. Tree, to 50 ft.; lfts. 3, oblong-elliptic or elliptic, to 6 in. long, entire, undulate; cymes in panicles to 8 in. long; fls. blue to purplish. Malay Arch., Philippine Is., Hawaii. Wood utilitarian.

quinata (Lour.) F. N. Williams. Shrub or large, tall tree; lfts. 3–5, oblong-elliptic to obovate, to 4 in. long, long-acuminate or caudate, entire, nearly glabrous, gland-dotted; cymes in panicles to 8 in. long; fls. fragrant. Se. Asia, Philippine Is. Fls. of various colors have been reported.

trifolia L. Shrub or shrubby tree, to 20 ft.; lfts. 1 or 3, oblong-elliptic to oblanceolate or obovate, to 3 in. long, entire, white-tomentose beneath; cymes many-fld., in panicles to 9 in. long; corolla blue to purple, 2-lipped. Asia to Australia. Cv. **'Variegata'**. Lvs. variegated. Var. **simplicifolia** Cham. Prostrate, creeping or sprawling; lfts. mostly 1.

Zeyheri Sond. ex Schauer. Tree, to 10 ft., with black, rough bark; lfts. 3–5, nearly sessile, oblong or oblong-lanceolate, to 3 in. long, entire, hoary and densely glandular; cymes axillary. S. Afr.

VITICELLA: *CLEMATIS*.

VITICIPREMNA H. J. Lam. Verbenaceae.
Two spp. of shrubs or trees, native to Philippine Is., New Guinea, New Britain, and New Ireland; lvs. opp., palmately compound; fls. yellow, in narrow terminal panicles, calyx truncate or 4–5-toothed, corolla 2-lipped, stamens 4, in 2 pairs; fr. drupaceous.

novae-pommeraniae (Warb.) H. J. Lam. Shrub or large tree; lfts. 3–5, ovate or obovate-oblong, to 3¼ in. long, acuminate, entire; fls. yellow-green, in panicles to 7 in. long. New Guinea, New Britain, New Ireland.

VITIS L. GRAPE. Vitaceae.
Tendril-climbing, woody, deciduous vines, or in arid regions sometimes almost erect shrubs, of the N. Hemisphere, with brown pith and usually shreddy bark, tendrils simple or branched, often coiled, slender-tipped; lvs. simple, more or less palmately lobed; fls. in narrow panicles, often unisexual, petals 5, united at apex and falling as a cap in one piece, disc separate from ovary; fr. a globose to ovoid berry, seeds mostly pear-shaped, in soft pulp.

Grown for their fruit and also on trellises and as screens and ornamentals. Most of the cultivated species are hardy in the middle or northern states; propagated readily by seeds, or ripe dormant wood cuttings. For culture see *Grape*.

acerifolia Raf. [*V. Longii* W. Prince]. BUSH G., PANHANDLE G. Low and sprawling, rarely climbing, young parts floccose, bark exfoliating only on older wood, tendrils only at tips of fertile brs.; lvs. leathery, triangular-ovate to suborbicular, to 5 in. long, indistinctly lobed, very coarsely dentate, remaining somewhat pilose beneath to maturity, becoming glossy above; fr. clusters to 3 in. long, berry ½ in. in diam. or less, black, glaucous, sweet, soon falling. Okla., n. Tex. to s. Colo. and New Mex. Zone 6.

aestivalis Michx. SUMMER G., PIGEON G., BUNCH G. Tall, vigorous climber; lvs. soft, broadly ovate, 2–8 in. long, unlobed to deeply 3–5-lobed, irregularly toothed, rusty-tomentose or cobwebby beneath; fr. clusters 2–7 in. long, berry ¼–⅜ in. in diam., glaucous, black, persistent. New Eng. to Fla., Kans., and e. Tex. Zone 5. Var. **argentifolia** (Munson) Fern. [*V. argentifolia* Munson]. SILVER-LEAF G., BLUE G. Brs. and petioles glabrous or glabrate; lvs. whitish beneath and hairy only on veins beneath.

amurensis Rupr. AMUR G. Strong vine, similar to *V. cordifolia*, but brs. and petioles red or reddish, lvs. more or less 3-lobed, with basal sinus very broad and shallow; fr. about ⅜ in. in diam., black, 2–3-seeded. Manchuria. Zone 5. Grown mostly for its highly colored autumn foliage.

antarctica: *Cissus antarctica*.

argentifolia: *V. aestivalis* var.

arizonica Engelm. CANYON G. Low, shrubby, scarcely climbing, gray-tomentose to glabrous, tendrils mostly perishing if not attached to support, internodes short; lvs. rather small, broadly ovate, 2–4 in. long, unlobed or scarcely to rarely deeply 3–5-lobed, broadly cordate at base, cobwebby beneath when young; fr. clusters 2–4 in. long, berry about ⅜ in. in diam., black, sometimes slightly glaucous, sweet. W. Tex. to Calif. and Mex. Zone 7.

Baileyana Munson. POSSUM G. Slender, high climber, brs. angled or striate, pubescent when young; lvs. mostly 3-lobed, petioles and veins of lower side persistently pilose; fr. ¼ in. in diam. or less, glossy black. Va. to Mo., s. to Ga. and Ark. Zone 6. Perhaps not distinct from *V. vulpina*.

Berlandieri Planch. SPANISH G. Stout, moderately climbing, cottony-pubescent when young; lvs. cordate-ovate, 3–6 in. long, mostly 3-lobed toward apex, glossy above, remaining pubescent on veins beneath; fr. clusters 3–8 in. long, berry up to ⅜ in. in diam., purple, reddish, or black, glaucous. Tex., New Mex. Zone 7.

californica Benth. Tall climber; lvs. orbicular to reniform, 3–5 in. long, sometimes 3–5-lobed, cordate, cobwebby beneath; fls. very fragrant; fr. clusters 2–6 in. long, berry about ⅜ in. in diam., purple with whitish bloom. Calif. to s. Ore. Zone 7.

capensis: *Rhoicissus capensis*.

Coignetiae Pulliat. CRIMSON GLORY VINE. Stout vine, with heavy foliage, brightly colored in autumn; lvs. cordate-orbicular, to 1 ft. across, sometimes shallowly lobed, gray- or rusty-tomentose beneath, dull above; fr. clusters to 8 in. long, berry about ⅜ in. in diam., black, glaucous, scarcely edible. Japan. Zone 5.

cordifolia: *V. vulpina*.

Davidii (Roman.) Foëx. Vigorous, prickly climber; lvs. broadly ovate, 4–8 in. long, often obscurely lobed towards apex, dull above, glaucous beneath, glandular, bristly on veins and petioles; fr. clusters exceeding the lvs., berry about ½ in. in diam., black, edible. China. Zone 7.

Doaniana Munson ex Viala. Vigorous climber; lvs. broadly ovate, to 3 in. long, coarsely dentate, blue-green and somewhat floccose above when young, tomentose beneath; berry ½ in. in diam., black with whitish bloom, sweet. Okla. to New Mex. Zone 6. Perhaps only a form of *V. acerifolia*.

flexuosa Thunb. Slender climber, reddish-tomentose when young; lvs. broadly ovate, sometimes 3-lobed, 2–3 in. across, glossy above and pubescent on veins beneath at maturity; fr. clusters to 3 in. long, berry about ¼ in. in diam., bluish-black. Japan, Korea, China. Zone 6. Material offered under this name is sometimes *Ampelopsis brevipedunculata*.

Girdiana Munson. High climber, differing from *V. californica* in having young growth densely white-tomentose, persistently so on underside of lvs., fr. black, lightly or not at all glaucous. S. Calif., Baja Calif. Zone 8.

Henryana: *Parthenocissus Henryana*.

Henryi: a listed name of no botanical standing, perhaps for *Parthenocissus Henryana*.

heterophylla: *Ampelopsis brevipedunculata* var. *Maximowiczii*.

himalayana: *Cissus himalayana*.

hypoglauca: *Cissus hypoglauca.*

Labrusca L. [*V. Labruscana* L. H. Bailey]. FOX G., SKUNK G. Strong, high climber, with white to rusty tomentum on young parts; lvs. cordate-ovate to triangular-ovate, 4–8 in. wide, mostly obscurely 3-lobed, nearly entire to scallop-toothed, dull above, persistently pubescent beneath; fr. clusters short, often nearly as broad as long, berry ½–¾ in. in diam., purple-black to reddish-brown, sweet or astringent with a strong musky or "foxy" flavor. New Eng. to Ind. and Ga. Zone 5. The source of the Labruscan vineyard grapes, sometimes offered under the cultigen name *V. Labruscana,* including the cvs. 'Concord', 'Warden', and 'Hartford', and the dominant parent in the ancestry of such cvs. as 'Niagara', 'Catawba', 'Isabella', 'Iona', and 'Brighton'.

Labruscana: *V. Labrusca.*

Longii: *V. acerifolia.*

Mandranum: a listed name of no botanical standing for *Cissus rhombifolia* cv. 'Mandaiana'.

monticola Buckl. MOUNTAIN G., SWEET M.G. Slender climber, young growth gray- or white-tomentose; lvs. suborbicular to reniform, 2–3 in. across, somewhat 3-lobed, glossy light green; fr. clusters to 3 in. long, berry ¼–½ in. in diam., black, not glaucous or only slightly so. Tex. Zone 7.

Pagnuccii: *V. Piasezkii* var.

palmata Vahl. RED G., CAT G., CATBIRD G. High, glabrous climber, with reddish brs. and petioles; lvs. ovate, about 3 in. wide, 3–5-lobed, acuminate, sharply toothed, glossy dark green, mostly glabrous above; fr. clusters 2–6 in. long, berry about ⅜ in. in diam., black or bluish-black, not glaucous. Ill. to Tex. Zone 5.

Piasezkii Maxim. Climber, young sts. often glandular; lvs. tomentose beneath, mostly palmately compound, lfts. 3–5, lanceolate to ovate; fr. ⅜ in. in diam., black, glaucous. China. Zone 7. Rarely cult. but sometimes represented by the hardier var. **Pagnuccii** (Planch.) Rehd. [*V. Pagnuccii* Planch.], which is glabrous throughout.

quinquefolia: *Parthenocissus quinquefolia.*

rhombifolia: *Cissus rhombifolia.*

rhomboidea: a listed name of no botanical standing, probably for *Cissus rhombifolia;* see also *Rhoicissus rhomboidea.*

riparia Michx. RIVER-BANK G., FROST G. Vigorous climber, fragrant in bloom, glabrous except for veins on underside of lvs.; most lvs. on fertile brs. 3–7 in. long, with tapering lobes ½–1½ in. long, margins ciliolate; fr. clusters to 6 in. long, berry ¼–½ in. in diam., glaucous, black, acid. Nov. Sc. to Man., s. to Tenn. and Tex. Zone 3. See also *V. vulpina.*

rotundifolia Michx. MUSCADINE G., SCUPPERNONG, BULLACE, BULLACE G., SOUTHERN FOX G. Large, vigorous climber, bark of brs. and sts. dotted with lenticels, not exfoliating, pith continuous and lacking diaphragms at nodes, tendrils unbranched; lvs. firm, orbicular to triangular-ovate, to 5 in. long, rarely slightly lobed, glossy above; fr. in small clusters, to 1½ in. long, berry to 1 in. in diam., dull purple, thick-skinned, with strongly musky-flavored pulp. Del. to Fla., w. to Kans. and Mex. Zone 6.

rupestris Scheele. SAND G., SUGAR G., BUSH G., MOUNTAIN G., ROCK G. Shrubby, scarcely climbing, glabrous, tendrils often absent; lvs. thick, mostly reniform, to 4 in. long, 8 in. wide, folded upward showing light-colored undersurface, coarsely toothed or infrequently irregularly lobed; fr. clusters to 2 in. long, berry ½ in. in diam. or less, purple-black and lightly glaucous, early deciduous, sweet. S. Penn. to Mo., s. to Tenn. and Tex. Zone 6.

striata: *Cissus striata.*

vinifera L. WINE G., EUROPEAN G. More or less climbing, tendrils intermittent, young growth glabrous or cottony; lvs. thin, broadly cordate-ovate to suborbicular, 4–9 in. wide, 3–5-lobed, with deep, narrow basal sinus, coarsely toothed, glabrous or sometimes tomentose beneath; fr. clusters large, variable in size, form, and color, skin adhering to pulp. Probably of the Caucasian region. Zone 5b. Widely dispersed and cult. in many forms; in the U.S. grown principally in Calif. Cvs. grown as ornamentals include: 'Apiifolia', lvs. deeply cut; 'Ciotat', a sport of 'Chasselas Doré', lvs. cut so deeply as to be often compound, some material so listed may be *Ampelopsis aconitifolia;* 'Incana', MILLER G., lvs. densely white-cobwebby; 'Purpurea', young lvs. claret-red, becoming purplish.

Voinierana: *Tetrastigma Voinieranum.*

vulpina L. [*V. cordifolia* Michx.]. WINTER G., FROST G., CHICKEN G. High-climbing vine, sometimes confused with *V. riparia,* from which it differs in having lvs. of fertile brs. unlobed or with short, abrupt, and shoulderlike lobes; fr. black and glossy, very acid but becoming sweet after frost. Penn. to Fla., w. to Kans. and Tex. Zone 5.

VITTADINIA A. Rich. *Compositae* (Aster Tribe). Eight or more spp. of per. herbs or subshrubs, native to Australia, Tasmania, New Zeal., New Guinea, New Caledonia, and s. S. Amer.; lvs. alt.; fl. heads radiate, solitary or in loose, leafy corymbs, involucre hemispherical or campanulate, involucral bracts imbricate in several rows, scarious-margined, receptacle pitted, naked; disc fls. bisexual, yellow, ray fls. female, white, blue, or pink; achenes more or less compressed, sometimes ribbed, pappus of many, unequal, capillary bristles.

australis A. Rich. Bushy subshrub, to 1 ft., brs. glandular, hispid; lvs. spatulate-cuneate to obovate-cuneate, to ⅝ in. long, glandular-pubescent, entire to 3-toothed or 3-lobed at apex, minutely ciliate; heads solitary, to ⅝ in. across; ray fls. white. Australia, Tasmania, New Zeal.

VITTARIA Sm. GRASS FERN. *Polypodiaceae.* About 50 spp. of epiphytic trop. and subtrop. ferns of Old and New Worlds, rhizomes clustered, branched; lvs. in tufts, pendent, simple, linear, grasslike, veins weak, forming a single row of areoles along each side of midrib; sori linear, in 2 or more parallel rows, indusia lacking.

For culture see *Ferns.*

lineata (L.) Swartz. SHOESTRING FERN, BEARD F., FLORIDA RIBBON F., OLD-MAN'S-BEARD. Lvs. densely clustered, drooping, to 3 ft. long or more and ¼ in. wide, often revolute, glossy above, glabrous. Ga., Fla., trop. Amer. Zone 9. Easily grown as an epiphyte either under glass or outdoors.

VOANDZEIA Thouars. *Leguminosae* (subfamily *Faboideae*). One sp., a creeping, ann. herb of W. Afr.; lvs. of 3 lfts.; infl. axillary, few-fld., bending downward after flowering; fls. small, unisexual, calyx 2-lipped, male fls. with pale yellow petals, stamens 10, 9 united and 1 separate, female fls. without petals; fr. developing underground, oblong-obovoid, beaked.

Widely cultivated in the tropics for the edible seeds.

subterranea (L.) Thouars. BAMBARA GROUNDNUT. Sts. sparsely pubescent, densely leafy; lvs. erect, lfts. elliptic to oblanceolate, to about 3 in. long, 1⅝ in. wide; fr. to ⅞ in. long, seeds variously colored, to ⅝ in. long.

VOLKAMERIA: see *CLERODENDRUM.*

VONITRA Becc. *Palmae.* A few spp. of solitary or mostly cespitose, unarmed, monoecious palms of Madagascar, with sts. often forked once or repeatedly; lvs. pinnate, sheaths with elongate ligule which breaks into masses of pendulous fibers, pinnae acute; infl. interfoliar, long-peduncled, paniculate, lower brs. twice-branched, bracts 2, the upper longer than the lower and deciduous, rachillae with fls. in triads (2 male and 1 female); male fls. with sepals 3, imbricate, petals 3, valvate, stamens 6, filaments in 2 series, thickened, not inflexed at apex, anther cells nearly separate, pistillode columnar, as long as stamens, female fls. with sepals and petals imbricate, pistil 1-celled with 2 abortive cells; fr. globose, with basal stigmatic residue, seed with pointed base, lateral embryo, and ruminate endosperm.

One of the sources of the vegetable fibers known in commerce as piassava. For culture see *Palms.*

fibrosa (C. H. Wright) Becc. [*V. Thouarsiana* (Baill.) Becc.; *Dictyosperma fibrosum* C. H. Wright]. Sts. clustered, slender, to 25 ft., unbranched or forked; lvs. to about 8 ft. long, regularly pinnate with about 30 pinnae on each side, these to 2 ft. long, 1⅜₆ in. wide, petiole with reddish hairs underneath toward the base; infl. to 5 ft. long including peduncle to 3 ft. long; fls. green; fr. to nearly 1 in. in diam.

Thouarsiana: *V. fibrosa.*

VRIESEA Lindl. [*Thecophyllum* André]. *Bromeliaceae.* About 246 spp. of mostly large and showy epiphytic herbs, native to trop. Amer.; lvs. stiff, entire, in dense rosettes; fls. yellow, green, or rarely white, arranged in 2 or more ranks in spikes, subtended by conspicuous bracts; petals separate or united in a short tube, bearing 1 or 2 scales on inner surface, ovary superior; fr. a caps., seeds with a basal tuft of long, straight hairs.

Grown outdoors in warm climates or under glass for the often brilliant, long-lasting inflorescences, and also for the foliage, which is frequently banded or variegated. Most species thrive best in subdued light. For culture see *Bromeliaceae.*

One of the most hybridized genera of the family, especially in the past century. *Vriesea* ×*Mariae* (PAINTED-FEATHER) and *V.* ×*Chantrieri* are currently offered. Others that may still be grown or have only recently been introduced are *V.* × *Capperi, V.* × *Duchartrei, V.* × *elegans, V.* × *gemma, V.* × *illustris, V.* × *Magnisiana, V.* × *rex,* and *V.* × *Vigeri,* which are mostly of unknown or complex parentage.

Barilletii E. Morr. Lvs. linear, 1½ ft. long, 2 in. wide, not spotted; infl. unbranched, erect, slightly shorter than the lvs., bracts densely imbricate, spotted with purplish-brown; fls. 2 in. long, stamens exserted. Brazil.

bituminosa Wawra. To 3 ft.; lvs. to 2 ft. long, 3 in. wide, green, tipped with maroon; infl. unbranched, loose; fls. dirty-yellow-green, to 2½ in. long, stamens included. Brazil.

Blokii: *V. regina.*

botafogensis: *V. Saundersii.*

carinata Wawra. LOBSTER-CLAWS. To 1 ft.; lvs. to 8 in. long, ⅝ in. wide, green; scape obliquely erect, infl. longer than lvs., bracts imbricate; fls. yellow, to 2¼ in. long, stamens exserted. Brazil. This is one parent of *V.* × *Mariae.*

conferta: *V. ensiformis;* however, plants listed as *V. conferta* are probably hybrids.

×**elegans** E. Morr. A complex hybrid involving *V. Barilletii, V. carinata, V. fulgida,* and *V. psittacina.*

ensiformis (Vell.) Beer [*V. conferta* Gaud.-Beaup.]. To 3 ft. or more; lvs. sword-shaped, pointed, streaked and dotted with red near base when young, to 2¼ ft. long, 1⅝ in. wide; infl. many-fld., unbranched or pinnately branched, bracts yellow; fls. spreading, petals yellow, to 4 in. long. Brazil.

erythrodactylon E. Morr. ex Mez. To 16 in.; lvs. deep violet, to 1 ft. long, ⅞ in. wide; scape erect, infl. unbranched; fls. 2-ranked, imbricate, fl. bracts red, to 1¾ in. long, longer than sepals; petals yellow. Brazil.

favorita: a listed name of no botanical standing, for plants with large green rosettes, wine-red flat infl., and yellow fls.

fenestralis Linden & André. To 3 ft.; lvs. broadly linear, to 16 in. long, nearly 1 in. wide, pale green with dark green longitudinal veins and irregular horizontal lines, spotted with red toward base; infl. to 1½ ft., unbranched, bracts green; petals pale golden-yellow, 2–2½ in. long, longer than stamens. Brazil.

flammea L. B. Sm. To 20 in., stoloniferous; lvs. to 11 in. long, sheaths dark brown, blades narrowly triangular; scape erect, infl. unbranched, fls. in about 4 ranks, mostly suberect, fl. bracts red, or red with yellow above, inflated; fls. spreading, petals yellow. Brazil.

Fosterana L. B. Sm. To 6 ft.; lvs. to 2¼ ft. long, 2¾ in. wide, blue-green with maroon pencilling; infl. unbranched; petals green with purplish tips, to 1⅛ in. long or more, longer than stamens. Brazil.

×**gemma:** a listed name of no botanical standing; used for a complex hybrid involving 5 spp.

gigantea Gaud.-Beaup. [*V. tessellata* (Linden) E. Morr.]. To 3 ft. or more; lvs. broadly linear, to 2¼ ft. long, 2½ in. wide, green or with darker green crossbands; infl. to 1½ ft., paniculate, bracts green; fls. to 1½ in. long, sepals pale yellow, petals white, about as long as stamens. Brazil. Other spp., such as *V. amazonica* (Bak.) Mez and *V. geniculata* (Wawra) Wawra, have at various times gone under the name *V. gigantea* in botany and hort.

gladioliflora (H. Wendl.) Ant. To 3 ft.; lvs. to 2 ft. long, 3¼ in. wide, deep green or purplish; scape erect, infl. unbranched, fl. bracts imbricate, 2-ranked, not keeled, 3–4 times as long as internodes; petals greenish-white, to 2¾ in. long. Cent. Amer.

glutinosa: see *V. neoglutinosa.*

guttata Linden & André. To 16 in.; lvs. to 10 in. long, 1 in. wide, green, spotted and mottled with maroon or brown; scape pendulous, infl. unbranched, white-mealy, bracts pink, imbricate; petals yellow, stamens exserted. Brazil.

heliconioides (HBK) Hook. ex Walp. To 16 in.; lvs. 8 in. long, 1¼ in. wide, green suffused with red or spotted beneath, but not banded; scape erect, infl. unbranched, fl. bracts imbricate, 2-ranked, keeled toward apex, bright red above middle, greenish-yellow at tip; petals white. Cent. Amer. to Brazil.

hieroglyphica (Carrière) E. Morr. BROMELIAD-KING, KING-OF-BROMELIADS. To 6 ft.; lvs. to 1½ ft. long, 3¾ in. wide, green, with very dark bars and spots; infl. paniculate; fls. dirty-yellow, to 1⅜ in. long, stamens included. Brazil.

hybrida: a listed name of no botanical standing.

×**illustris:** a listed name of no botanical standing, for an undetermined hybrid.

imperialis E. Morr. ex Bak. To 15 ft.; lvs. to 4½ ft. long, 4¾ in. wide, pointed and recurved at tip, forming very large rosettes, green; infl. much-branched, brs. 10–50-fld.; fls. erect, yellow, 6½ in. long or more. Brazil.

incurvata Gaud.-Beaup. To 16 in.; lvs. to 1 ft. long, 1¼ in. wide, green; scape erect, infl. unbranched, barely as long as lvs., fl. bracts imbricate, to 2⅜ in. long, red with broad, yellow, obtusely angled margins; petals yellow with green-spotted tips, to 2 in. long, shorter than stamens. Brazil. Has been grown under the name *V. Poelmanii.* Var. **inflata:** *V. inflata.*

inflata (Wawra) Wawra [*V. incurvata* var. *inflata* (Wawra) Mez]. Similar to *V. incurvata,* but fl. bracts red with narrow, yellow or green, evenly curved margins, to 2 in. long. Brazil.

Jonghii (Libon ex C. Koch) E. Morr. To 2½ ft.; lvs. linear, recurved at apex, sometimes banded with dark green lines; scape erect, infl. unbranched, fl. bracts green, with decurrent bases and dark margins; fls. spreading, sepals broad, petals red-spotted. Brazil.

×**Kitteliana** Wittm.: *V. Barilletii* × *V. Saundersii.* To 4 ft.; lvs. to 2¾ ft. long, green and glossy, 4 in. wide and red-spotted at base; infl. to 3 ft. high, few-branched, bracts spotted with wine-red, fl. bracts tipped with wine-red; fls. golden yellow.

longibracteata: *V. splendens* var.

longicaulis (Bak.) Mez. To 3 ft.; lvs. linear, to 20 in. long, 1⅜ in. wide; scape erect, infl. branched, brs. densely fld., fl. bracts drying dark brown; fls. 2-ranked; sepals acute. Brazil.

×**magnifica:** × *Guzvriesea magnifica.*

Malzinei E. Morr. To 2½ ft.; lvs. to 1 ft. long, 2 in. wide, upper surface green or with red spots, lower surface dark red or sheaths green with red spots; scape erect, infl. unbranched, fls. in 2 to several ranks, fl. bracts shorter than sepals, red-brown or pale green with dark green border; petals greenish-white. Mex.

×**Mariae** André: *V. Barilletii* × *V. carinata.* PAINTED FEATHER.

×**Morreniana** Hort. ex E. Morr.: *V. carinata* × *V. psittacina.* Very similar to *V. carinata,* but infl. with longer rachis.

neoglutinosa Mez [*V. glutinosa* (Mart. ex Schult.) Wawra, not *V. glutinosa* Lindl.]. To 6 ft.; lvs. nearly linear, to 28 in. long, 2¾ in. wide; scape thick, erect, bracts leafy, longer than internodes, infl. 2-pinnately paniculate, to 3 ft.; fls. to 1½ in. long, petals yellow. Brazil, Paraguay. Plants in the trade listed as *V. glutinosa* belong here.

paraibica Wawra. Similar to *V. carinata,* but infl. longer than broad, barely longer than lvs., 4½ in. long, fl. bracts 1½ in. long. Brazil.

petropolitana L. B. Sm. To 14 in., stoloniferous; lvs. to 15 in. long; scape erect, infl. unbranched, fls. 2-ranked, erect, fl. bracts orangish, imbricate until after flowering, with strongly curved keel; petals yellow with green tip. Brazil.

Philippocoburgii Wawra. To 3 ft., rhizomes short; lvs. broadly linear, to 2 ft. long, 3¼ in. wide, red-spotted near apex; infl. paniculate, loose, to 2¼ ft. high; fls. to 1½ in. long, dirty-yellow. Brazil. Var. **vagans:** *V. vagans.*

platynema Gaud.-Beaup. To 3 ft.; lvs. broadly linear, to 1½ ft. long, 2¼ in. wide; scape erect, infl. unbranched, fls. 2-ranked, usually reflexed at flowering; sepals longer than broad, petals green. Brazil. Cv. **'Vaginata'** is listed.

Platzmannii E. Morr. To 1½ ft.; lvs. linear, spotted above; scape erect, bracts shorter than internodes, infl. unbranched, loose, 1-sided, fl., bracts acute, keeled; petals yellow. Brazil.

×**Poelmanii** Hort. A complex hybrid, probably not in cult. in the U.S.; material offered under this name is *V. incurvata.*

×**polonia:** a listed name of no botanical standing for a hybrid, perhaps in error for *V.* × *Poelmanii.*

procera (Mart. ex Schult.) Wittm. To 3 ft. or more; lvs. broadly sublinear, to 16 in. long, 2¼ in. wide, green; scape erect, infl. branched, brs. slender, subtended by bracts not reaching to lowermost fls.; fls. 2-ranked, 1⅛ in. long, petals yellow, stamens included. Guyana, Brazil.

psittacina (Hook.) Lindl. To 1½ ft.; lvs. sword-shaped, to 16 in. long, ⅞ in. wide; scape erect, infl. unbranched, with spreading, 2-ranked fls., fl. bracts truncate at base, green to red, or red and yellow, to twice as long as internodes; sepals to 1½ in. long, petals yellow, tipped with green, stamens exserted. Brazil.

recurvata Gaud.-Beaup. Lvs. nearly sword-shaped, not spotted, 1½ ft. long, 1¼ in. wide; infl. unbranched, erect, bracts loosely arranged, not imbricate, not spotted; fls. about 2 in. long, stamens exserted. Brazil.

regina (Vell.) Beer [*V. Blokii* (Hemsl.) Mez]. To 6 ft.; lvs. thick, leathery, linear-oblong, to 3 ft. long, ³⁄₁₆ in. wide below middle, abruptly long-acuminate, recurved, red-purple-spotted; infl. paniculate, to 4½ ft. long, bracts red, brs. recurved; fls. to 4 in. long, yellow, petals soon flaccid and drooping. Brazil.

×**retroflexa** E. Morr.: *V. psittacina* × *V. scalaris.*

×**rex** Hort. Duval. A complex hybrid involving *V. Barilletii, V.* ×*Morreniana, V. carinata,* and *V. psittacina* as parents.

ringens (Griseb.) Harms. To 3 ft.; lvs. linear, to 3 ft. long, 2½ in. wide, sometimes banded; scape erect, stout, bracts imbricate, infl. unbranched or branched, rachis roughened below nodes, fls. 2-ranked, becoming 1-ranked, fl. bracts green or brownish; fls. erect, to 3¼ in. long, petals white or yellow, coiled backwards, stamens exserted. W. Indies, Cent. Amer., Colombia.

Rodigasiana E. Morr. To 1½ ft. or more; lvs. linear, brown-spotted on back; scape erect, bracts as long as internodes, infl. branched, loose, broad, fls. 2-ranked but ranks not borne on 1 side, to 1⅜ in. long, fl. bracts yellow, ⅜ in. long, shorter than sepals; fls. nearly erect, sepals ⅝ in. long, petals pale yellow, shorter than stamens. Brazil.

Saundersii (Carrière) E. Morr. ex Mez [*V. botafogensis* Mez]. To 1½ ft.; lvs. broadly linear, gray-green, spotted purple-brown at base; scape erect, infl. loosely paniculate, to 1 ft. long; fls. to 1⅞ in. long. Brazil.

scalaris E. Morr. To 8 in.; lvs. to 6 in. long, ¾ in. wide, green; scape pendulous, infl. unbranched, bracts spreading, red and yellow; petals yellow with green tips, to 1½ in. long, shorter than stamens. Brazil.

Schwackeana Mez. To 3 ft. or more; lvs. to 16 in. long, 1¾ in. wide, dull green with maroon flecks; infl. paniculate; fls. pale yellow, to 1¼ in. long, stamens exserted. Brazil.

simplex (Vell.) Beer. To 1½ ft.; lvs. linear, to 16 in. long, 1¼ in. wide, minutely toothed, green or red-purple beneath; scape pendulous, infl.

loosely pinnate, bracts red, with upper half yellow; fls. to 1½ in. long, yellow. Brazil.

Sintenisii (Bak.) L. B. Sm. & Pittendr. [*Thecophyllum Sintenisii* (Bak.) Mez]. Stemless, to 2 ft.; lvs. in a dense rosette, nearly or quite erect, 10–18 in. long, often red at tip at time of flowering; scape red, erect, infl. several-ranked on spikes above lvs., bracts of rachis red; fls. light yellow, 1³⁄₁₆ in. long. Cuba, Jamaica, Puerto Rico.

speciosa: *V. splendens.*

splendens (Brongn.) Lem. [*V. speciosa* Hook.]. FLAMING-SWORD. To 3 ft.; lvs. to 16 in. long and 2¼ in. wide, green with brown crossbands; scape erect, infl. unbranched, bracts imbricate, red; fls. yellow, to 2⅝ in. long, stamens exserted. Fr. Guiana. Var. **longibracteata** (Bak.) L. B. Sm. [*V. longibracteata* Bak.]. Differs from typical var. in lacking irregular crossbands on lvs. Cv. '**Major**' is also listed.

tessellata: *V. gigantea.*

unilateralis (Bak.) Mez. To 1½ ft.; lvs. linear, to 1 ft. long, 1 in. wide; scape erect, infl. unbranched, 5–10-fld., fls. 2-ranked, but secund, fl. bracts green, not secund sepals to 1 in. long. Brazil.

vagans (L. B. Sm.) L. B. Sm. [*V. Philippocoburgii* var. *vagans* L. B. Sm.]. VAGABOND PLANT. Similar to *V. Philippocoburgii,* but rhizomes elongate, lvs. much narrower. Brazil.

×**versaliensis** A. Truff. ex Rodig.: *V. carinata* × *V. Duvaliana* E. Morr. Lvs. green, recurved at tip; infl. unbranched, bracts red, tipped with yellow; fls. yellow.

×**Vigeri** Hort. Duval: *V.* ×*rex* × *V. Rodigasiana.*

viridiflora (Regel) Wittm. To nearly 3 ft.; lvs. linear, to 14 in. long, 1½ in. wide, green; scape erect, bracts straw-colored, infl. unbranched, 6 in. long, flattened; fls. pedicelled, to 1⅜ in. long, petals white. Costa Rica.

VULPIA: *FESTUCA.*

WACHENDORFIA L. *Haemodoraceae.* A few spp. of herbs with tuberous roots, native to S. Afr.; lvs. plicate; fls. in panicles, usually bright yellow, pilose, funnelform, stamens 3, ovary superior.

thyrsiflora L. To 2 ft.; lvs. to 3 ft. long and 3 in. wide; fls. ¾ in. long, in dense, cylindrical panicles 1 ft. long.

WAHLENBERGIA Schrad. ex Roth. *Campanulaceae.* Over 100 spp. of ann. or per. herbs, widely distributed especially in the S. Hemisphere; lvs. alt. or opp., simple; fls. blue, white, or red, solitary on bractless pedicels or in cymes, perianth 3–4-merous or rarely 6–10-merous, calyx tube united to ovary, lobed above, corolla campanulate to rotate, stamens mostly 5, filaments more or less dilated basally, ovary 2–5-celled; fr. a caps., dehiscing by apical pores, generally between the calyx lobes. Distinguished from both *Campanula* and *Edraianthus* by the caps. dehiscing by apical pores.

Cultivation as for *Campanula;* propagated by seeds and the perennial species sometimes by cuttings.

albomarginata Hook.f. Tufted per., with slender, branching rhizome, each rhizome br. bearing a rosette of lvs.; lvs. lanceolate to spatulate, to about 1 in. long, denticulate; peduncles up to 5 from each rosette, naked, 2–8 in. high; fls. erect, calyx deeply and acutely 5-lobed, lobes as long as corolla tube; corolla white to light blue, campanulate, ¾–1¼ in. across; fr. obconical, glabrous. New Zeal. Material offered as *W. saxicola* is sometimes this sp.

congesta (Cheesem.) N. E. Br. Low, mat-forming per., sts. much-branched and interlaced; lvs. orbicular to elliptic-spatulate, to about 1 in. long, petioles slender, ciliate, 2–3 times as long as blade, peduncles erect, to 2 in. long; corolla white or blue, less than ½ in. across; fr. globose. New Zeal.

dalmatica: *Edraianthus dalmaticus.*

gracilis (G. Forst.) A. DC. [*W. vinciflora* (Venten.) Decne.]. Erect, usually branched, short-lived per., to about 12 in., sts. woody, leafy, mostly hispid-pilose near the base; lower lvs. mostly oblanceolate to lanceolate, denticulate, the upper narrower; corolla white to dark blue, campanulate or nearly rotate, to ¾ in. across but usually smaller; fr. obconical, usually ribbed. New Zeal. Apparently not cult.; probably all material offered as *W. gracilis* or its synonym, *W. vinciflora,* is *W. trichogyna.*

hederacea (L.) Rchb. Ann. or per., sts. slender, creeping; lvs. petioled, suborbicular, to about ½ in. across, usually angled or lobed; fls. more or less nodding, on peduncles to 1½ in. long, corolla pale blue, about 5/16 in. long. W. Eur.

Kitaibelii: *Edraianthus graminifolius.*

lobelioides (L.f.) Link [*W. pendula* Schrad.]. Erect ann., 1–15 in., branching, smooth-stemmed; lvs. confined to lower parts of sts. and brs., lanceolate to oblanceolate, 1–3 in. long, denticulate; fls. small, many, mostly nodding, corolla tinged blue, funnelform, 3–5-lobed, about ¼ in. long; fr. obconical, glabrous. Madeira and Canary Is.

Matthewsii Cockayne. Glabrous, tufted per., with woody or fleshy rhizome; lvs. in rosettes, leathery, linear, to about 1½ in. long, entire or denticulate; peduncles many, slender, simple or branched, to about 8 in. high; fls. erect, corolla campanulate, whitish to pale lilac, ¾–1¼ in. across; fr. obconical, to ½ in. long, glabrous. New Zeal.

pendula: *W. lobelioides.*

pumilio: *Edraianthus pumilio.*

saxicola (R. Br.) A. DC. Small per., to 4 in.; lvs. in rosettes, oblanceolate to lanceolate, to about 1 in. long, entire, usually somewhat undulate; peduncles erect, 1-fld.; fls. erect, calyx 5-lobed, lobes much shorter than corolla tube, corolla light blue, open-campanulate, ½–¾ in. across; fr. nearly globose. Tasmania. This sp. is usually offered under the name *W. tasmanica;* material offered as *W. saxicola* may be *W. albomarginata.*

serpyllifolia: *Edraianthus serpyllifolius.*

tasmanica: a listed name of no botanical standing; material so offered is *W. saxicola.*

tenuifolia: *Edraianthus tenuifolius.*

trichogyna Stearn. Erect, many-stemmed per., mostly 10–24 in.; lvs. opp. or alt., on lower half of st., lanceolate to oblanceolate, to about 2 in. long, denticulate, hairy; fls. many, terminal and lateral, corolla blue with yellowish center, funnelform, to about 1¼ in. across; fr. globose, ribbed, to about 3/16 in. in diam., pilose. New Zeal., Australia. This sp. has generally been cult. under the names *W. gracilis* and *W. vinciflora,* or sometimes as *Campanula polymorpha.*

vinciflora: *W. gracilis;* but material listed as *W. vinciflora* is generally *W. trichogyna.*

WALAFRIDA E. H. Mey. *Scrophulariaceae.* About 40 spp. of subshrubs or shrubs, rarely ann. herbs, native mostly to S. Afr., a few to trop. Afr.; dwarf, much-branched, often heathlike; lvs. alt. or clustered, entire; fls. white, pink, or purple, in terminal spikes or heads often arranged in corymbs or panicles, calyx 2- or 3-lobed, corolla unequally 5-lobed or 2-lipped, stamens 4; fr. indehiscent, often separating into 2 halves when mature. Allied to *Selago* but having calyx 2- or 3-lobed.

nitida E. H. Mey. Much-branched per., to 2 ft.; lvs. solitary at nodes, ovate or ovate-oblong, to ½ in. long, glabrous; fls. in dense spikes to 1 in. long, corolla rose-purple. S. Afr.

WALDSTEINIA Willd. *Rosaceae.* A few spp. of strawberrylike herbs of the N. Temp. Zone, with creeping rhizomes near the surface of the ground; lvs. mostly basal, 3–5-lobed or -divided; fls. small, yellow, on bracted scapes about as tall as the lvs., sepals 5, alternating with 5 bracteoles, petals 5, stamens many; frs. 2–6 achenes, each with terminal, slender, deciduous style.

Sometimes planted in the rock garden; of easy culture.

fragarioides (Michx.) Tratt. BARREN STRAWBERRY. Lfts. 3, to 2 in. long, broadly cuneate, toothed at apex; scapes several-fld., to about 8 in. high; fls. ¾ in. across. Woods, New Bruns. to Minn., s. to Ga., Tenn., Mo.

geoides Willd. Lvs. 3–10 in. long, more or less deeply 5-lobed, cordate-reniform in outline, incised-dentate; fls. 5–9, about ¾ in. across. Hungary to the Balkans.

sibirica: *W. ternata.*

ternata (Steph.) Fritsch [*W. sibirica* Tratt.; *W. trifolia* Rochel ex W. D. J. Koch]. Lfts. 3, short-stalked, ½–1¼ in. long, evergreen, irregularly toothed to lobed; fls. 1–7, to ¾ in. across. Cent. Eur. to Siberia, Japan.

trifolia: *W. ternata.*

WALLACEODENDRON Koord. *Leguminosae* (subfamily *Mimosoideae*). One sp., a tree, native to Indonesia; lvs. 2-pinnate, with rather large lfts.; fls. in axillary racemes, regular, bisexual, 5-merous, petals valvate, stamens many, united basally into a tube; fr. an oblong, thick, flat legume.

celebicum Koord. To 125 ft., unarmed; lvs. of adult shoots with 2–3 pairs of pinnae (6–7 in juvenile shoots), lfts. in 6 pairs, nearly sessile, oblong to obovate or nearly rhomboidal, to 3½ in. long; peduncles solitary or 2 together, to 6 in. long, racemes pyramidal, to 2 in. long; fls. about 1½ in. long, corolla brown outside, whitish inside, stamens yellowish-white. Celebes.

WALLICHIA Roxb. *Palmae.* Six spp. of dwarf to moderate, monocarpic, monoecious palms with solitary or clustered sts., native in India, se. Asia, s. China; lvs. pinnate, pinnae linear to cuneate, irregularly toothed and lobed along margin; fls. in triads (2 male and 1 female) in the same infl. or male and female in separate infls., then the male infl. with slender, often pendulous brs., female infl. shorter, with mostly spreading brs.; male fls. symmetrical, calyx 3-lobed, corolla tubular, with valvate lobes, stamens 6 or rarely 9–15, female fls. with sepals imbricate, petals united at base, valvate above, pistil 2–3-celled; fr. 1–3-seeded, fleshy, seeds with homogeneous endosperm.

Sometimes grown as ornamentals in the tropics and subtropics and in the warmest parts of Zone 9b. Many palms called *Wallichia* in U.S. are species of *Arenga*. Individual stems die after fruiting. Propagated by suckers or seeds. See also *Palms*.

caryotoides Roxb. Sts. very short, clustered; lvs. to 9 ft. long, pinnae oblong, deeply lobed and sharply toothed; stamens 6; fr. oblong-ovoid, 2-seeded. India, Burma.

densiflora (Mart.) Mart. Sts. very short, clustered; lvs. to 10 ft. long, pinnae to 2 ft. long, linear-oblong or oblong, sinuately lobed; stamens 6; fr. ½ in. long, 2-seeded. India.

disticha T. Anderson [*Didymosperma distichum* (T. Anderson) Hook.f.]. Sts. solitary, to 20 ft.; lvs. 2-ranked, to 10 ft. long, pinnae in clusters, 1–2 ft. long, linear-lanceolate, toothed near apex, pale beneath; stamens 6; fr. ¾ in. long, 2–3-seeded. India, Burma.

WALNUT. Walnuts are species of the genus *Juglans*. Most important is the commercial Persian walnut *(J. regia)*, or English walnut as it is often erroneously called, whose nuts have shells that are easy to crack and excellent meats used in many ways. Of native walnuts, the black walnut *(J. nigra)* and butternut *(J. cinerea)* produce hard-shelled nuts and small meats having a pronounced, distinctive flavor. The Japanese walnut *(J. ailanthifolia)*, sometimes planted, is related to the butternut and has somewhat similar fruits. Nuts of the tropical *J. neotropica* of the central Andes resemble those of *J. nigra;* this species brings the possibility of walnut-growing to the cooler tropics.

Various cultivars of Persian walnuts thrive over a wide territory in North America. They have been grown somewhat in Zone 6 in the East but in most localities have been severely damaged or killed outright by occasional cold winters with temperatures ranging to −20° to −30° F. Selections from a strain introduced from the Carpathian Mountains have withstood temperatures as low as −40° F and are promising throughout the eastern United States. The commercial acreage, however, is in California, with the northernmost limit in the West in the low valleys of western Oregon and Washington. 'Franquette' is an excellent Persian walnut cultivar for the Pacific Northwest since it flowers late and the tree is cold-resistant. It does well in California along with 'Concord', 'Eureka', 'Hartley', 'Serr', and 'Vina'; 'Payne' and 'Placentia' are suitable for southern California. Among better cultivars for the East are 'Broadview', 'Colby', 'Hansen', 'Jacobs', 'Lake', 'McKinster', 'Metcalfe', and 'Schafer'. In northern California, black walnut seedlings are the usual stocks used, for they are resistant to oak-root fungus.

Fertile, deep, and well-drained loams are desired, with dependable irrigation water. Trees may be set as close as 40 × 50 feet, but this is too close together for trees at maturity, 60 or 65 feet being preferable. Clean tillage is given from the first, with a good cover crop for winter or following fruiting; this crop is plowed under in spring. The trees are strong, free growers on good land. The young tree may be pruned to the desired height for a trunk, but thereafter little regular pruning is undertaken except to thin out the poor, weak, and crowding branches. Persian walnut trees are 50 to 70 feet high at maturity.

Formerly, trees were grown directly from seed, but with the coming of improved named cultivars grafting must be employed. The desired cultivar may be worked on common seedling stocks, or on seedlings of the wild California walnut or of the black walnut. The year-old seedling is grafted at the crown in the nursery in spring, the whip-graft method being usual, the parts being covered with wax. At one year from the graft the tree should be 6 feet tall or more, if the soil is good and it has been staked to prevent injury. This one-year-old tree (with a two-year-old root) is set in the orchard or grove. The tree is cut back to four or five buds above the graft union and one shoot is tied to a stake to form the tree trunk; any other growth above the union is left on, but pinched back the first year to shade and strengthen the lower trunk. The walnut tree is long-lived.

Insects and diseases are usually not particularly damaging, but the grower should keep informed by the latest extension service bulletins and reports.

Like the Persian walnut, the hardier black walnut also grows rapidly to a large size and so requires plenty of room. It can be used as a lawn tree, for its shade is high and will not kill off the lawn; a good cultivar will also provide plenty of nuts for the average family. Black walnuts, however, should not be planted close to vegetable gardens because their roots are apparently toxic to tomatoes and certain other home-garden crops. Hardier cultivars of black walnuts for more northern plantings include 'Michigan', 'Patterson', 'Snyder', 'Sparrow', and 'Thomas', while cultivars requiring 180 days or more for nut maturity are 'Elmer Meyers', 'Ohio', 'Stabler', and 'Stambaugh'.

The hardiest species in the genus is the butternut (Zone 4). Again, grafted cultivars are far superior and include 'Ayers', 'Craxeasy', 'Johnson', 'Thill', and 'Van Syckle'.

WALTHERIA L. *Byttneriaceae*. About 40 spp. of herbs or shrubs, native mostly to trop. Amer.; lvs. alt., toothed; fls. small, in axillary cymose clusters or in terminal racemes or panicled cymes, calyx 5-lobed, petals 5, persistent when withered, stamens 5, all fertile, united at base into a short tube, ovary 1-celled, 2-ovuled; fr. a 2-valved caps., seeds 1–2.

One species sometimes grown in Fla.

americana L. Per. herb or shrub, to about 4 ft.; lvs. short-petioled, ovate to oblong, to 2 in. long, densely tomentose; fls. yellow, about ¼ in. across, in dense clusters. Pantrop.

WARREA Lindl. *Orchidaceae*. Three spp. of terrestrial herbs, native to Cent. and S. Amer.; sts. short, leafy, thickened into short, ovoid pseudobulbs; lvs. few, 2-ranked, lanceolate-elliptic, plicate; infl. basal, simple, often longer than lvs.; racemose, loosely few- to several-fld.; fls. large, showy, sepals and petals similar, lateral sepals united to column foot, lip attached to column foot, simple or 3-lobed, rounded or 2-lobed at apex, the disc with keels or elevated lines in middle. For structure of fl. see *Orchidaceae*.

For culture see *Orchids*.

bidentata: *W. tricolor*.

costaricensis Schlechter. Erect, to nearly 2½ ft.; lvs. to 2 ft. long, with sheathing petiole at base; racemes from base of plant, erect, as long as lvs.; fls. reddish-bronze, the lip lighter, with reddish-bronze markings, sepals oblong-ovate, to 1¼ in. long, lateral sepals forming a short mentum basally with column foot, petals obovate, to 1¼ in. long, lip to 1¼ in. long, nearly orbicular, entire, with narrow callus basally. Costa Rica, Panama.

discolor: *Cochleanthes discolor*.

tricolor Lindl. [*W. bidentata* Lindl.]. Pseudobulbs erect, cylindrical, to 4¾ in. long; lvs. 4–5, oblong-lanceolate, to 20 in. long; infl. to 3 ft. long, 7–10-fld.; fls. nodding, white, pale yellow on exterior, sepals nearly orbicular, to 1 in. long, petals similar, lip erect, rigid, to 1 in. long, white, marked with yellow and dotted with red-purple. Late winter. Venezuela, Colombia.

WARSCEWICZELLA: *COCHLEANTHES*. W. Wendlandii: *C. aromatica*.

WARSZEWICZIA Klotzsch. *Rubiaceae*. About 4 spp. of trees or shrubs, native to Amer. tropics; lvs. opp., large, stipules united between lvs., glandular at base on inner surface; fls. in cymes borne in terminal panicles, small, 5-merous, calyx lobes unequal, one lobe often large, colored, leaflike, corolla funnelform; fr. a small caps., seeds many, minute.

One species sometimes seen in greenhouses or in tropical or subtropical gardens.

coccinea (Vahl) Klotzsch. To 20 ft. or more; lvs. obovate, to 2 ft. long or more and 1 ft. across; infl. 1 ft. long or more; fls. yellow or orange, ¼ in. long, leaflike calyx lobe red, elliptic or oblong, to 2½ in. long. Trinidad, Cent. Amer. to Brazil.

WASHINGTONIA H. Wendl. [*Neowashingtonia* Sudw.]. WASHINGTON PALM. *Palmae*. Two spp. of massive palms with bisexual fls., native in arid regions of Sonora and Baja Calif. (Mex.) and in the interior of s. Calif. and sw. Ariz.; lvs. costapalmate, divided into 1-ribbed segms., petioles armed with spinose teeth along the margins; infls. among lvs. and exceeding them, with several bracts on the peduncle and woody, sword-shaped, open bracts subtending each of several pendulous brs. bearing slender rachillae; fls. with calyx tubular, petals tardily deciduous, stamens 6, carpels 3, separate except united styles; fr. 1-seeded, small, ellipsoid to globose, to ⁵⁄₁₆ in. long, seed with homogeneous endosperm.

Washingtonias are extensively grown in Calif., often for street plantings, and are common along the Gulf Coast, and in Fla., as well as in other parts of the world, particularly those with Mediterranean type of climate. For culture see *Palms*.

filamentosa: *W. filifera.*

filifera (L. Linden) H. Wendl. [*W. filamentosa* (Fenzi) O. Kuntze; *Pritchardia filifera* L. Linden]. DESERT FAN PALM, PETTICOAT P. To more than 80 ft., trunk not tapered, clothed in nature with a dense, evenly thatched "petticoat" or shag of hanging old lvs. that usually tapers inward somewhat at the base when the lower trunk is bare; lower lvs. displaying the long, flat, mostly green (except at base) petioles, upper lvs. standing well separated so that the crown is open and very broad, blades gray-green, lacking a tawny patch beneath about the hastula, filiferous, the long, limp, narrowly attenuate segms. hanging gracefully. Native about streams and springs on borders of Colorado Desert, Calif. and in sw. Ariz. Zone 9a. Not so well adapted as the next for planting near the coast.

gracilis: *W. robusta.*

robusta H. Wendl. [*W. gracilis* S. Parish; *W. sonorae* S. Wats.; *Pritchardia robusta* (H. Wendl.) Hort. ex Schroet.]. THREAD PALM, MEXICAN W.P. A taller and more slender tree than *W. filifera*, trunk tapered from a stout base, clothed in nature with a long, cylindrical, uneven or ragged shag; lf. blades brilliant green, with a large tawny patch beneath about the hastula, segms. stiffer and mostly less deeply cut and less slender-pointed, bearing few or no fibers except on very young trees, very variable aº to their drooping habit and the number of filaments. Mex. Zone 9b. The shag or thatch sometimes falls from the upper part of the trunk of tall trees, leaving the st. bare. Faster-growing but less hardy than *W. filifera.*

sonorae: *W. robusta.*

WATER CULTURE: see *Hydroponics.*

WATERING: see *House Plants.*

WATER LILY. This name is used for several genera of perennial aquatic herbs of the family Nymphaeaceae, grown outdoors or indoors in ponds and pools for their ornamental leaves and showy, colorful flowers. The more familiar water lilies belong to the genus *Nymphaea*, but other closely related genera are also grown as water lilies, including: *Euryale* and *Victoria*, whose species have giant leaves; *Nelumbo* (usually called lotus, though species of *Nymphaea* also pass under this name), with peltate leaves mostly standing above the water; and the less showy *Nuphar* (cow lily or spatter-dock).

Water lily culture is simple and essentially similar for most species. Full sun throughout the day and warm water of an even temperature are required for most kinds, hence pools intended for water lilies must not be shaded and are preferably shallow, usually about 2 feet deep. Most plants need no more than a foot of water above their crowns and the container (a bushel box, tub, or half barrel) in which they are grown is also about a foot deep. Water lilies may be planted in pools having a complete covering of soil on the bottom, but the water in such pools easily discolors and more rampant water lily species (especially in *Nelumbo* and *Nuphar*) may cover more pool area than is desired. Although certain pygmy species of *Nymphaea*, such as *N. tetragona*, may be grown in a tub, or even potted in a large aquarium, the typical tropical *Nymphaea* cultivar requires pool culture, since each of its numerous leaves may measure as much as 18 inches in diameter and the plant may occupy a water surface area measuring about 6–8 feet in diameter. The dozen or more giant platter leaves of the tropical *Victoria*, each up to 6 feet in diameter, require proportionately a much greater water surface area and can only be grown satisfactorily in large pools in which the water temperature does not fall below 80° F. Thus they are best suited to the tropics and subtropics, or to heated pools elsewhere. Outside the tropics, *Victoria Cruziana*, which can be grown with water temperatures of 75° F and above, is more adaptable than *V.*

amazonica, which requires minimum water temperatures of 85° F; both species are usually propagated by seed and can be expected to reach flowering size about five months from planting.

Most species of water lilies may be raised from seed, but this is usually impossible or inconvenient for the casual home gardener. Occasionally divisions of plants of the hardy native species of *Nelumbo, Nuphar*, and *Nymphaea* are transplanted to pools from the wild, usually in the spring, as soon as the first leaves appear, but most water lilies are obtained as young seedlings, as plantlets (in the case of those tropical cultivars which are viviparous, producing plantlets at the junction of leaf blade and petiole), or, most commonly, as divisions of rhizomatous or tuberous plants grown by and shipped from nurseries specializing in aquatics. The time to plant tropical water lilies outdoors depends upon the climate. They should not be set out until both night and day temperatures range above 70° F. Lower temperatures make such plants become dormant, a condition from which they are slow to recover.

Water lilies are gross feeders and should be planted in soil sufficiently rich to carry them through the full growing season. A bushel of soil is satisfactory for an average *Nymphaea* plant and should consist of a mix of three parts fibrous loam and one part well-decayed cow manure, enriched with four ounces of a 4–8–5 or similar fertilizer. The young water lily is planted firmly, with the crown slightly above the soil level. The soil surface needs to be fully covered with about a half inch of washed sand or gravel to prevent soil from floating in the pool or from having it disturbed by fish; however, the crown of the plant must remain uncovered by this extra sand layer. After planting, no more than a foot of water should stand above the crown, at least until after the plants have become established.

Water lily care during the growing season is simple. Besides controlling the few insect pests which may attack the plants, discolored leaves, faded flowers, and seed pods should be removed. Some kind of fish is usually required in a pool to dispose of mosquito larvae, but with a fish population the gardener should use care with insecticides such as rotenones, which are toxic to fish. Water lily genera and species that are hardy can be left in deep ponds or pools over winter, provided that roots are below the level of freezing. Roots and rhizomes of most kinds may also be overwintered at about 50° F in a cellar if kept in moist sand that is not permitted to dry out, but usually it is easier to purchase fresh propagations in the spring.

There are hardy and tender tropical kinds of *Nymphaea*. The latter only thrive in water about 70° F, but some of the former are native even in Zone 4. The native, fragrant, white-flowered *Nymphaea odorata*, a hardy species common in the eastern United States, is often transplanted to pools. Hardy species of *Nymphaea* start flowering in late spring only a few weeks after planting, much earlier in the season than the tender ones, and continue into the summer. Their flowers open in the morning and close about midafternoon. Their color range includes white, yellow, pinks, and reds. Among recommended hardy cultivars are 'Attraction', 'Gloriosa', 'Chromatella', 'Marliacea Albida', 'Marliacea Rosea', and 'Rose Arey', mainly hybrids between varieties of *N. odorata* and *N. alba*. Tropical species of *Nymphaea* flower either in the day or at night. The former have blossoms that open early in the morning and remain open until afternoon, like the hardy waterlilies, while the night-flowering cultivars open in the later afternoon and bloom throughout the night. With both day- and night-blooming types available, the gardener can have continuous flowering. Among the day-flowering tropical cultivars are: (blue) 'Bagdad', 'Bob Trickett', *N. colorata*, 'Director George T. Moore', *N. gigantea*, 'Henry Shaw', 'Joe Cutak', 'Judge Hitchcock', 'Midnight', 'Mrs. Edward Whitaker'; (pink) 'American Beauty', 'General Pershing', 'Peach Blow', 'Pink Platter', 'Rio Rita'; (yellow) 'Aviator Pring', 'St. Louis', 'St. Louis Gold', 'Sunbeam'; (white) 'Daisy', 'Isabella Pring', 'Mrs. George H. Pring', *N. gigantea*

'Alba'. Among night-blooming tropicals are: (red) 'B. C. Berry', 'Frank Trelease', 'H. C. Haarstick'; (pink) 'Emily Grant Hutchings', 'James Gurney', 'Mrs. George C. Hitchcock'; (white) 'Missouri'.

WATERMELON. The watermelon, *Citrullus lanatus*, a native of tropical Africa, is a frost-tender, vining, annual fruit that requires a fairly long growing season of high temperatures. It thrives in the southern, southwestern, and central states, but only fast-maturing cultivars are suitable for the northern states. It is normally served cool as a dessert and is relished mostly during warm weather.

Watermelon cultivars vary in size and shape and in color of skin, flesh, and seed, as well as in maturing time. Generally red-fleshed, small-seeded, medium to large melons are preferred, though recently some small "icebox" cultivars of fairly good quality have become available. Hybrids, including some seedless types, also have been developed. Presently important cultivars are 'Charleston Gray', 'Crimson Sweet', 'Jubilee', 'Klondike', and 'Sugar Baby'. The citron or preserving melon (var. *citroides*) is a small-fruited type with hard white flesh, occasionally grown for watermelon-rind preserves; it should not be confused with the true citron, which is a species of *Citrus*.

Culture is relatively simple. Deep, fertile, sandy loams are preferred, though other well-drained soils can be used. Planting dates range from late autumn in southern Florida to early June in the northern states. Seed is usually planted in hills spaced 6–10 feet apart in rows 8–12 feet apart. In cooler regions, where temperatures are borderline, the plants often are started in the greenhouse, using peat pots or plant bands, and in two to three weeks transplanted into the field. Hot caps or hot tents are often used on early plantings. Black plastic mulch helps to hold weeds in check and sometimes speeds maturity by a week or more. Herbicides are available for weed control. Since the watermelon is monoecious and insect-pollinated, it often helps to place hives of bees around commercial plantings.

Watermelons are susceptible to a number of diseases and pests. Rotation of fields, selection of disease-resistant cultivars, sanitation, and chemical sprays are means for control. Cucumber beetles can be a serious pest early in the season and must be controlled immediately as they can destroy young seedlings.

Picking mature watermelons at the correct time takes experience. The fruits must be ripe and sweet but not overripe, and there are few reliable, easy signs for indicating proper maturity. Size of fruit, a change in color of the ground spot, a slight bumpiness, and a hollow sound when thumped are helpful signs.

WATSONIA Mill. [*Meriana* Trew]. BUGLE LILY. *Iridaceae.* About 60 spp. of summer-blooming herbs with fibrous, tunicate corms, native to S. Afr., 1 sp. in Madagascar; lvs. sword-shaped, usually rigid; fls. red or white, in simple or branched spikes, spathe valves entire, green or brownish, perianth tube curved, segms. nearly equal, usually spreading, style brs. 3, bifid, subulate. Differs from *Gladiolus* in having style brs. bifid, perianth tube widening at or below the middle, and spathe valves more rigid.

Cultivated as for *Gladiolus* in loamy soil and full sun; requiring abundant moisture during blooming period. Most kinds bloom in three years from seeds, soon forming clumps.

angusta: *W. fulgens.*

Ardernei Hort. Sander. Sts. 3–5 ft.; basal lvs. 4, to 2 ft. long and 1¼ in. wide; spikes branched, many-fld., bracts green; fls. pure white, perianth tube 1½ in. long, slightly curved, broadly funnelform at apex, segms. about ¾ in. long, elliptic, flaring, anthers yellow. Early summer. Perhaps a white-fld. variant of *W. Wordsworthiana.*

Beatricis Mathews & L.Bolus. Sts. 3–4 ft.; basal lvs. 3, to 30 in. long and 1¼ in. wide, subglaucous, margins thickened; spikes congested, many-fld., bracts conspicuously pink-tipped; fls. apricot-red, tube about 2 in. long, segms. 1 in. long, mucronate, spreading and recurved, anthers white, becoming blue-purple after dehiscence. Many fls. open at one time. Late summer.

bulbillifera Mathews & L. Bolus. Sts. 5–6 ft., producing clusters of brown cormlets in axils of upper st. lvs.; basal lvs. 5–6, about 2 ft. long and 2¼ in. wide; spikes branched, open, few-fld.; fls. orange to brick-red, paler outside, suberect, perianth tube about 2 in. long, bent about ½ in. from base, segms. about 1 in. long, ascending to spreading, outer segms. oblong, inner ones obovate, anthers purple-blue, with pale purple pollen. Early summer.

densiflora Bak. Sts. 2–3 ft.; basal lvs. several, 2–3 ft. long, ½–¾ in. wide; spikes congested, 40–50-fld. or more, bracts overlapping for half their length, membranous; fls. rose-red, perianth tube about 1¼ in. long, curved, segms. nearly ¾ in. long, oblong, cuspidate, anthers red. Late summer. Cv. 'Alba'. Fls. white.

Fourcadei Mathews & L. Bolus. Sts. 3½–5 ft.; basal lvs. about 8, to 2 ft. long, 1½ in. wide, deep green; spikes branched, open, many-fld., bracts about ½ in. long; fls. coral-red, perianth tube about 2 in. long, curved, segms. about 1⅛ in. long, oblong, ascending-spreading, anthers purple, on pale pink filaments. Early summer.

fulgens (Andr.) Pers. [*W. angusta* Ker-Gawl.]. Sts. about 3 ft.; basal lvs. several, 1–2 ft. long, ¾–1 in. wide; spikes branched, loose, many-fld.; fls. scarlet, perianth tube 1½–2 in. long, sharply bent basally, segms. ¾–1 in. long, oblanceolate, cuspidate, spreading, anthers deep violet, style brs. yellowish-red. Early summer.

Galpinii L. Bolus. Sts. 2½ ft.; basal lvs. 4–8, 12–15 in. long, ¼–½ in. wide, stiffly erect, margins thickened; spikes simple, dense, 8–10-fld.; fls. orange-red, perianth tube about ¾ in. long, curved, segms. ½ in. long, obovate, mucronulate, anthers white, with white pollen. Late summer.

marginata (Eckl.) Ker-Gawl. Sts. 4–5 ft., stout; basal lvs. several, mostly 18–30 in. long, margins thickened, brown; spikes branched, many-fld., bracts longer than internodes; fls. rose-pink, fragrant, perianth tube about ¾ in. long, curved, segms. nearly 1 in. long, ovate-oblong, spreading, anthers yellow. Early summer.

Meriana (L.) Mill. Sts. 2–3 ft.; basal lvs. several, 1–2 ft. long, ³⁄₁₆–½ in. wide, rigidly erect; spikes usually simple, loose, few- to several-fld.; fls. rose-red to salmon or pink, perianth tube about 2 in. long, curved, segms. 1 in. long, oblong, cuspidate, spreading, anthers blackish. Early summer.

pyramidata (Andr.) Stapf [*W. rosea* Ker-Gawl.]. Sts. 4–5½ ft.; basal lvs. 5, linear, to 2½ ft. long and 1 in. wide; spikes usually branched, open, many-fld.; fls. rose-pink, perianth tube about 1¼ in. long, bent, broadly funnelform at apex, segms. 1½–1¾ in. long, elliptic, often narrowly so, cuspidate, flaring, anthers brownish-purple, 6–12-lobed. Early summer.

rosea: *W. pyramidata.*

tabularis Mathews & L. Bolus. Sts. 5–6 ft., stout, rigid; basal lvs. 4–5, mostly 3–3½ ft. long, 1¾–2 in. wide, margins hyaline; spikes simple, with purple rachis, several-fld.; fls. deep coral-red outside, pale salmon or rose-pink inside, horizontal or nodding, perianth tube 1¾ in. long, curved, segms. 1¼ in. long, oblong-obovate, obtuse, spreading, outer segms. darker than the inner, anthers dark purplish-blue, with whitish pollen. Early summer.

Vanderspuyae L. Bolus. Sts. to 3½ ft., stout; basal lvs. 3–4, 12–24 in. long, 1½ in. wide, margins thickened; spikes branched, dense, many-fld., 2-ranked; fls. bright coral-rose to scarlet, very large, perianth tube about 2 in. long, slightly curved at throat, segms. 1 in. long, oblong-obovate, acute, spreading, anthers deep purple.

Wilmaniae Mathews & L. Bolus. Sts. about 4 ft.; basal lvs. 6, to 20 in. long and ¾–1 in. wide, margins pale yellow; spikes usually branched, open, many-fld.; fls. rose-purple, striped darker, perianth tube 2–2½ in. long, abruptly bent in middle, segms. ¾ in. long, obovate, anthers purple. Late summer.

Wordsworthiana Mathews & L. Bolus. Sts. 5–5½ ft.; basal lvs. 4, about 2 ft. long, to 1½ in. wide; spikes branched, open, many fld.; fls. purplish-lilac, funnelform, perianth tube about 2 in. long, curved, segms. 1½ in. long, obovate-oblong, obtuse, anthers rich purple, with very pale purple pollen.

WEBERA: *TARENNA.* **W. corymbosa:** *T. zeylanica.*

WEBERBAUEROCEREUS: *TRICHOCEREUS.*

WEBEROCEREUS Britt. & Rose. *Cactaceae.* About 3 spp. of cacti climbing by aerial roots, native to Cent. Amer.; sts. 2–5-angled or cylindrical; fls. nocturnal, small, white, perianth tube shorter than the limb, ovary and fr. with close-set tubercles, each with an apical areole bearing bristles.

For culture see *Cacti.*

Biolleyi (A. Web.) Britt. & Rose. Sts. much-branched, cylindrical or slightly angled, to ¼ in. thick; areoles remote, spineless or occasionally with 1–3 yellow spines; fls. to 2 in. long, pink, perianth segms. oblong, obtuse, tubercles of ovary elongate and crowded, without terminal scales. Costa Rica.

trichophorus J. H. Johnson & Kimnach. Sts. cylindrical or obtusely 6–7-angled, to ½ in. thick; spines white, radial spines 30–40, hairlike, to ¾ in. long, central spines 10, rigid, to ½ in. long; fls. funnelform-campanulate, dark pink, to 1⅜ in. across, tubercles of ovary with long hairs. Costa Rica.

trichotus: a listed name of no botanical standing; used for *W. trichophorus.*

WEDELIA Jacq. *Compositae* (Helianthus Tribe). About 70 spp. of ann. or per. herbs, subshrubs, or shrubs, of cosmopolitan distribution in the tropics and subtropics, sts. erect to prostrate and often rooting at nodes, sometimes climbing; lvs. opp. or the uppermost occasionally alt.; fl. heads radiate, axillary or terminal, solitary or in small clusters, long-peduncled, involucre nearly globose to campanulate, involucral bracts in 2–3 rows, the outer herbaceous, the inner scarious, receptacle flat to convex, scaly; disc fls. bisexual, fertile, yellow; ray fls. female, fertile, yellow; achenes cuneate-oblong to obovoid, the outer 4-angled, the inner 3-angled, glabrous or pubescent, smooth or tubercled, pappus cup-shaped and of 1–2 awns, or lacking.

trilobata (L.) A. S. Hitchc. Sts. creeping and rooting, to 6 ft. long or more; lvs. elliptic or oblong-obovate to obovate, to 5 in. long, 3-lobed at apex but sometimes entire to weakly lobed, or even serrate-dentate; heads to ¾ in. across, solitary on erect peduncles to 6 in. long; fls. yellow to orange-yellow. S. Fla. and trop. Amer. Often used as a ground cover. Zone 10.

WEED. A weed is a plant not wanted and therefore to be destroyed. A plant desired under one circumstance, as horseradish or vegetable-garden dandelion, may be a weed under other circumstances. Some plants are naturally weedy, that is, they invade habitable and cultivated grounds and make trouble, and are therefore not wanted. Plants that do not make trouble excite no opposition and are not weeds even though they may have no "uses" in cooking, commerce, ornament, or medicine.

The primary remedy for weeds is to grow well the plants that one wants; the better they are grown, the less will be the opportunity for invaders. If naturally weedy places are kept clean, most of their breeding grounds will be eliminated. For some situations, chemical weed killers are now available. Aside from this, special practices may be necessary to circumvent and control some kinds of weeds under given conditions. The gardener and grower will find these means by consulting current books and bulletins and persons with experience and knowledge in weed control.

WEIGELA Thunb. *Caprifoliaceae.* Ten to 12 spp. of deciduous shrubs, native to Asia, formerly included in *Diervilla,* not stoloniferous; lvs. opp., simple; fls. showy, pink, purplish, to carmine, or white, to 1½ in. long, on short leafy shoots of the season, often in more or less compound clusters, sepals 5, sometimes partly united, corolla 5-lobed, often unequally lobed, but not 2-lipped, stamens 5, ovary inferior, 2-celled; fr. an oblong, woody, 2-valved caps., dehiscing from the top, leaving a central column.

The kinds are much confused by variation, probably by hybridization, so that some of the horticultural names applied to plants which cannot be referred exactly to species are here treated as cultivars.

Weigelas are hardy shrubs adapted to any good garden soil if it is not too dry, although they benefit by winter protection of the ground. They require no special attention. Since flowers are borne on twigs of the preceding year, the shrubs should not be trimmed before flowering. Propagated by greenwood cuttings in frames in summer.

amabilis: *W. coraeensis.*

arborea: a listed name of no botanical standing, used for both *W. coraeensis* and *W. florida.*

argenteomarginata: a listed name of no botanical standing, probably used for plants with variegated foliage.

biformis: *Weigela* cv. 'Biformis'. Fls. dark rose and purple, with yellow markings; may be a cv. of *W. florida.*

candida Carrière: *Weigela* cv. 'Candida'. Fls. white; may be a cv. of *W. florida.*

candidissima: a listed name of no botanical standing, probably used for more than one white-fld. kind.

coraeensis Thunb. [*W. amabilis* Planch.; *W. grandiflora* C. Koch]. Large, stout shrub, to 15 ft., distinguished from other spp. in having brs. and lvs. nearly glabrous; lvs. broad; fls. sessile, sepals separate to base, narrow, corolla pale rose to carmine or whitish, abruptly narrowed below the middle. Japan. Zone 6. Cv. **'Alba'.** Fls. whitish.

decora (Nakai) Nakai. Related to *W. japonica,* but lvs. somewhat villous underneath and fls. very short-pedicelled, changing in color from green to white to rose-red. Japan. Zone 6?

Desboisii Carrière: *Weigela* cv. 'Desboisii'. Small shrub, fls. early; may be a cv. of *W. floribunda..*

Feerei: a listed name of no botanical standing for *Weigela* cv. 'Feerei'. Medium-sized shrub; fls. bright rose-colored.

floribunda (Siebold & Zucc.) C. Koch. To 10 ft.; lvs. somewhat pubescent above, more so underneath; characterized by the narrowly funnelform, dark crimson, sessile fls. crowded on short lateral branchlets, the projecting style, and sometimes short-exserted anthers; sepals separate to base, narrow, corolla pubescent on exterior. Late spring. Japan. Zone 6. Cv. **'Grandiflora'.** Fls. large, brownish-red. Other cvs. that probably belong to this sp. are **'Abel Carrière', 'Desboisii', 'Hendersonii',** and **'Versicolor'.**

florida (Bunge) A. DC. [*W. rosea* Lindl.]. Diffuse, nearly glabrous shrub, to 8 or 10 ft.; lvs. short-petioled, elliptic or obovate, to 4 in. long, acuminate, pubescent on veins underneath; sepals united basally, broad, corolla rose-colored, broadly funnelform, lobes blunt, spreading. Late spring. N. China, Korea. Zone 5. The commonest weigela in old yards; very variable. Cv. **'Alba'.** Fls. white. Cv. **'Variegata'.** Lvs. margined with yellowish-white. Other cvs. apparently associated with this sp. are: **'Biformis', 'Eva Rathke', 'Glorieux', 'Gustave', 'Intermedia', 'Madame Tellier', 'Mallet', 'Mont Blanc', 'Vanhouttei', 'Venosa',** and **'Verschaffeltii'.** Var. **venusta** (Rehd.) Nakai [*W. venusta* Rehd.]. To 6 ft.; calyx small, 2-lipped, corolla rose-purple, gradually contracted into a slender tube, lobes short. Korea.

gigantiflora: a listed name of no botanical standing.

grandiflora: *W. coraeensis;* but see also *W. floribunda* cv.

gratissima: a listed name of no botanical standing, may refer to a hybrid between *W. hortensis* and *W. florida.*

Groenewegenii Carrière: *Weigela* cv. 'Groenewegenii'. Fls. like those of *Weigela* cv. 'Biformis', but darker red, corolla dark red outside, rose-red inside.

Hendersonii: a listed name of no botanical standing for *Weigela* cv. 'Hendersonii'. Probably a cv. of *W. floribunda.*

hortensis (Siebold & Zucc.) C. Koch. To 10 ft., young brs. hairy; lvs. ovate or oblong-acuminate, 3–4 in. long, densely tomentose underneath, pubescent above when young; fls. carmine or white, 3 together on slender peduncle, sepals separate to base, narrow, corolla narrow-campanulate, style sometimes slightly exserted. Japan. Zone 7.

hybrida: a listed name of no botanical standing for horticultural forms of uncertain origin.

japonica Thunb. To 10 ft., branchlets glabrous or nearly so; lvs. elliptic to long-obovate, to 4 in. long, acuminate, densely pubescent underneath, particularly on veins; fls. pedicelled, mostly in 3's on short shoots, sepals separate to base, very narrow, corolla whitish changing to carmine, narrowly campanulate. Late spring. Japan. Zone 6. Var. **sinica** (Rehd.) L. H. Bailey. Lvs. soft-pubescent underneath; corolla pale rose-colored, abruptly narrowed toward base. China. Zone 7.

Kosterana variegata: a listed name of no botanical standing for *Weigela* cv. 'Kosterana Variegata'. Lvs. variegated.

Looymansii: a listed name of no botanical standing for *Weigela* cv. 'Looymansii'. Slow-growing; lvs. yellowish; fls. red.

lutea: a listed name of no botanical standing.

Maximowiczii (S. L. Moore) Rehd. To 5 ft., branchlets with 2 rows of hairs; lvs. elliptic-ovate or obovate, to 3 in. long, acuminate, broad-cuneate, with scattered hairs above, pilose on veins beneath; fls. usually 2, sessile, calyx 2-lipped, corolla greenish-yellow, about 1¼ in. long, tube longer than calyx, anthers connivent; fr. with valves separating at apex from central column. Japan. Zone 6.

Middendorffiana (Trautv. & C. A. Mey.) C. Koch. To 5 ft., related to *W. Maximowiczii,* but differing in having the valves of the caps. cohering at apex to central column. Manchuria, n. China, Japan. Zone 5.

nana variegata: a listed name of no botanical standing.

praecox (Hort. Lemoine) L. H. Bailey. To 6 ft.; related to *W. florida,* but differing in being the earliest-flowering sp.; lvs. soft-pubescent underneath; fls. on very short lateral branchlets, sepals united at base, broad, corolla rose-colored or pink with yellow in throat, narrowly campanulate, much narrowed below the middle, pubescent outside.

Korea. Zone 5. Cvs. apparently associated with this sp. are: 'Avalanche', 'Bouquet Rose', 'Conquerant', 'Daubenton', 'Esperance', 'Floreal', 'Girondin', 'Gracieux', 'Le Printemps', 'Seduction', 'Variegata', 'Vestale'.

purpurata, purpurea: listed names of no botanical standing.

rosea: *W. florida.*

sessilifolia: a listed name of no botanical standing, perhaps refers to *Diervilla sessilifolia.*

Sieboldii: a listed name of no botanical standing.

splendens: *Diervilla splendens.*

Stelzneri Van Houtte: *Weigela* cv. 'Stelzneri'. A hybrid involving *W. florida*, fls. many, large, dark red, in clusters to 8 in. long.

styriaca Klenert: *Weigela* cv. 'Styriaca'. Lvs. bright green; fls. many, carmine-rose to carmine-red.

Vanhouttei: a listed name of no botanical standing for *Weigela* cv. 'Vanhouttei'. A hybrid, probably *W. florida* × *W. hortensis.*

Vanicekii: a listed name of no botanical standing for *Weigela* cv. 'Vanicekii'. Upright shrub; fls. large, light red, borne on young wood.

venosa: a listed name of no botanical standing for *Weigela* cv. 'Venosa'. Supposed hybrid between *W. coraeensis* and *W. florida.*

venusta: *W. florida* var.

Verschaffeltii: a listed name of no botanical standing for *Weigela* cv. 'Verschaffeltii'. Probably a cv. of *W. florida.*

versicolor: *Weigela* cv. 'Versicolor'. Probably a cv. of *W. floribunda.*

×**Wagneri** (N. Kusn.) L. H. Bailey: *W. florida* × *W. Middendorffiana.* Fls. showy, pinkish.

WEINGARTIA: *GYMNOCALYCIUM.*

WEINMANNIA L. *Cunoniaceae.* About 100 spp. of evergreen shrubs or trees, mostly of the S. Hemisphere except Afr.; lvs. opp., simple or odd-pinnate, rachis often winged, stipules deciduous; fls. small, in terminal or axillary, erect racemes, sepals and petals 4 or 5, stamens 8 or 10, ovary superior, styles 2; fr. a 2-celled caps. Related to *Ackama,* which differs in having fls. in panicles and sepals imbricate.

Benthamii: *Geissois Benthamii.*

racemosa L.f. To 80 ft.; lvs. simple, oblong-lanceolate to ovate, and to 4 in. long, on adult trees, or of 3–5 lfts. on young trees, very leathery, coarsely toothed; racemes to 4 in. long; fls. white or pink. New Zeal.

sylvicola Soland. ex A. Cunn. To 50 ft.; lvs. of 3 lfts. on adult trees, of about 11 lfts. on young trees, lfts. oblong to lanceolate, to 2 in. long, leathery, coarsely toothed; racemes to 4 in. long; fls. white or pink. New Zeal.

WELDENIA Schult.f. *Commelinaceae.* One sp., a per. herb, native to high mts. of Mex. and Guatemala; roots deep-seated, tuberous, st. underground; lvs. in a basal rosette, linear-lanceolate; fls. 10–40 from lf. axils but appearing as if from the crown, bractless, in paired cincinni, sepals united into an oblique, membranous tube, petals united into a long tube, the lobes 3, ovate, spreading, stamens 6.

candida Schult.f. Lvs. to 6 in. long, ¾ in. wide; fls. white, corolla tube to 5 in. long, lobes to ¾ in. long.

WELWITSCHIA Hook.f. *Welwitschiaceae.* One sp., native to desert areas of s. Angola and S.-W. Afr., with characters of the family.

Welwitschia is very slow growing and difficult to cultivate, requiring desert conditions and room to accommodate the long taproot. Propagated by seeds.

mirabilis Hook.f. Sts. 1–1½ ft. high or more, to 2(–5) ft. in diam.; lvs. leathery, to 6(–8) ft. long and 3 ft. wide, twisting and splitting into many segms. in age; female cones up to 20, on stalks nearly 1 ft. long, scarlet, 4-angled, 1 in. long, each scale bearing 1 broadly winged seed, male cones smaller.

WELWITSCHIACEAE Markgr. WELWITSCHIA FAMILY. Gymnosperms; 1 genus of bizarre, dioecious plants, native to deserts of sw. Afr.; sts. very short, tuberous, woody, obconical, with a 2-lobed, disclike apex; lvs. 2, opp., arising from the circumference of the apex, straplike, persisting and continuing to grow throughout the life of the plant, splitting lengthwise into many segms. in age; male or female cones borne around the inner margin of disc on short, branched stalks. *Welwitschia* is rarely cult., as a curiosity.

WENDLANDIA Bartl. *Rubiaceae.* About 56 spp. of shrubs or trees, native to trop. and subtrop. Asia; lvs. opp. or whorled, stipules entire or 2-parted; fls. in terminal panicles, small, white, pink, or yellow, 4–5-merous, corolla salverform or funnelform; fr. a small, globose caps., seeds many, minute.

exserta DC. Small tree; lvs. ovate-lanceolate, to 9 in. long, leathery; panicles to 10 in. long and broad; fls. fragrant, corolla white, ³⁄₁₆ in. across, tube shorter than lobes. India.

WERCKLEA Pitt. & Standl. *Malvaceae.* About 2–4 spp. of shrubs or small trees in Costa Rica and Panama; lvs. simple, orbicular to ovate, unlobed or slightly angled; fls. solitary or paired in the lf. axils, involucre of 3–10 bracts joined to the middle or separate nearly to base, persistent or deciduous, calyx 5-lobed, sometimes deciduous, petals 5, yellow to rose-red, stamens united in a tubular column, more or less included in corolla or exserted, style brs. 5, stigmas discoid; fr. a 5-celled, 5-angled caps.

insignis Pitt. & Standl. Tree, 15–60 ft., with pale bark and rounded crown; lvs. orbicular to reniform-orbicular, to 16 in. across, cordate, entire to sinuate or undulate-dentate; fls. solitary or paired, on pedicels to 3 in. long (to 8 in. in fr.), involucre about ½ in. long, 3–4-lobed to near the base, calyx about 1½ in. long, enlarging in fr., petals lilac-rose or pink, to 5 in. long, staminal column included; caps. oblong-obovoid, 5-angled, 2–3 in. long, hispid. Costa Rica.

WERCKLEOCEREUS Britt. & Rose. *Cactaceae.* Two spp. of cacti climbing by aerial roots, native to Cent. Amer.; sts. mostly 3-angled, with bristles or a few short spines; fls. nocturnal, short-funnelform, white, the ovary and tube with clusters of needle-shaped, dark spines.

For culture see *Cacti.*

glaber (Eichlam) Britt. & Rose. Sts. pale green, slightly glaucous, ¾ in. wide; spines 2–4, to ⅛ in. long, swollen at the base; fls. 4 in. long, spines yellow to brown. Guatemala.

imitans: *Eccremocactus imitans.*

Tonduzii (A. Web.) Britt. & Rose. Sts. deep green; areoles spineless but sometimes with bristles; fls. 3 in. long, spines black; fr. globose, yellow, flesh white. Costa Rica.

WESTRINGIA Sm. *Labiatae.* About 20 spp. of Australian shrubs, often pubescent; sts. mostly square in cross section; lvs. 3–4 in a whorl, small, stiff, narrow, entire; fls. axillary or in terminal leafy heads, calyx campanulate, 10-nerved, 5-toothed, corolla showy, longer than calyx, limb 2-lipped, upper lip erect, 2-lobed, lower lip 3-lobed, fertile stamens 2, anthers 1-celled, staminodes 2, with appendages at apex; fr. of 4 reticulate-rugose nutlets.

Propagated by seeds or cuttings. One species cultivated in Calif.

rosmariniformis Sm. To 6 ft., pubescent; lvs. 4 in a whorl, nearly sessile, narrowly lanceolate to elliptic, to 1 in. long, generally revolute, densely white-pubescent beneath; fls. axillary, to ½ in. long, corolla white with brownish spots. Spring and summer. Se. Australia.

WHIPPLEA Torr. *Saxifragaceae.* One sp., a deciduous, trailing subshrub, of w. N. Amer.; lvs. opp.; fls. white, small, in dense, terminal clusters, calyx tube top-shaped, partly united to ovary, calyx lobes 5–6, petals 5–6, spreading, stamens 10–12, styles 4–5, separate; fr. a globose caps.

modesta Torr. YERBA-DE-SELVA. Sts. to 2 ft. long, pubescent, rooting freely; lvs. nearly sessile, ovate, to 1¼ in. long, sparsely toothed; peduncles to 3 in. long, more or less erect; fls. to ¼ in. across. Shaded woods, Coast ranges of n. Calif. to Ore. Zone 7? Useful in the rock garden.

WHITFIELDIA Hook. *Acanthaceae.* About 10 spp. of trop. Afr. shrubs; lvs. opp., ovate, entire, short-petioled; fls. white or red, in terminal racemes, calyx 5-parted, segms. colored, petaloid, subequal, corolla 2-lipped, lobes 5, subequal, stamens 4, didynamous, shortly exserted or included, anther sacs 2, opp. each other; fr. a glabrous caps., seeds 2–4, round, without hairs, nearly smooth.

Grown in greenhouses or outdoors in extreme south; propagated by cuttings or seeds.

lateritia Hook. Evergreen, to 3 ft., brs. cylindrical, loose; calyx lobes broadly lanceolate, brick-red, half as long as corolla tube, corolla brick-red, narrowly campanulate, upper 2 lobes erect, lower 3 spreading.

WHITFORDIODENDRON Elmer [*Adinobotrys* S. T. Dunn]. *Leguminosae* (subfamily *Faboideae*). Nine spp. of lianas and trees of trop. Asia; lvs. alt., odd-pinnate, lfts. 5-toothed; racemes axillary, often in terminal panicles; fls. papilionaceous; differs from *Millettia* in having fr. ovoid, nearly indehiscent, seed usually 1, large, not flattened.

atropurpureum (Wallich) Merrill [*Adinobotrys atropurpureus* (Wallich) S. T. Dunn; *Millettia atropurpurea* (Wallich) Benth.]. Tree, to 80 ft., with thick brs.; lfts. in 3–4 pairs, rigidly leathery, narrowly oblong-acute, to 6 in. long, glabrous; panicles dense; fls. dark purple, 1 in. long; fr. 4 in. long, 2 in. wide. Burma to Indonesia. Planted in trop. regions.

WHITLAVIA: *PHACELIA*. **W. grandiflora:** *P. minor*.

WIDDRINGTONIA Endl. AFRICAN CYPRESS. *Cupressaceae*. Five spp. of monoecious or sometimes dioecious, coniferous, evergreen trees, native to Afr. and Madagascar; lvs. opp., scalelike or linear; female cones subglobose; seeds 5 or more to each scale, 2-winged. Allied to *Callitris*, with which it is sometimes united, but differs in having cone scales 4, of about equal size.

Suitable for warm climates; mostly grown in the greenhouse, and infrequently in the open in localities that are nearly frost-free. Zone 10. For culture see *Conifers*.

cupressoides (L.) Endl. [*Callitris cupressoides* (L.) Schrad. ex E. H. Mey.]. BERG CYPRESS. Shrub or small tree, to 12 ft.; lvs. scalelike, imbricate, 4-ranked; female cones ¾ in. in diam. or less, about 3 together, smooth. Mts., S. Afr.

juniperoides (L.) Endl. CLANWILLIAM CEDAR. To 60 ft.; lvs. scalelike, imbricate, juvenile lvs. awl-shaped, to ¾ in. long, spirally arranged; female cones ¾ in. in diam., solitary or several together. S. Afr.

Schwarzii M. T. Mast. WILLOWMORE CEDAR. Similar to *W. juniperoides*, but lvs. smaller, 4-ranked, female cones smaller, scales warty or tubercled. S. Afr.

Whytei Rendle. MLANJE CEDAR. To 140 ft.; lvs. imbricate, scalelike, but linear and to 1 in. long on young plants; female cones ¾ in. in diam., about 1 in. long, 4–6 together. E. Afr.

WIGANDIA HBK. *Hydrophyllaceae*. About 5 spp. of large, per. herbs, subshrubs, or small trees, native to trop. Amer.; lvs. alt., simple, large, dentate, covered with glistening irritating hairs; fls. in terminal scorpioid cymes often arranged in panicles, calyx 5-parted, corolla campanulate, 5-lobed, stamens 5, styles 2; fr. a 2-valved caps.

Wigandias are grown as foliage plants in subtropical plantings. Propagated by seeds sown under glass in winter or by cuttings of the roots in spring.

caracasana HBK. Robust subshrub, to 10 ft., yellow- or silky-pubescent; lvs. ovate, to 1½ ft. long, subcordate at base, long-petioled; corolla violet, with white tube, filaments hairy in lower part. S. Mex., s. to Venezuela and Colombia. Var. **macrophylla:** *W. macrophylla*.

macrophylla Cham. & Schlechtend. [*W. caracasana* var. *macrophylla* (Cham. & Schlechtend.) Brand]. Similar to *W. caracasana* but lvs. larger, infl. with white pubescence. Mex.

urens (Ruiz & Pav.) HBK. To 12 ft.; lvs. to 1 ft. long, cordate at base; fls. violet. Peru.

WIGGINSIA D. M. Porter [*Malacocarpus* Salm-Dyck, not Fisch. & C. A. Mey.]. *Cactaceae*. About 13 spp. of globose to oblong, ribbed cacti, native to S. Amer.; sts. woolly at apex; fls. subapical, funnelform to nearly rotate, mostly yellow, diurnal, bearing wool and often bristles in the scale axils, lasting several days, stamens many, included, mostly in 1 series, stigmas mostly red; fr. fleshy, perianth persistent, seeds black or brown, tubercled, with broad truncate base.

For culture see *Cacti*.

corynodes (Pfeiff.) D. M. Porter [*Malacocarpus corynodes* (Pfeiff.) Salm-Dyck]. Sts. to 8 in. high and 4 in. thick, ribs 13–16, acute; spines to ¾ in. long, radial spines 7–12, brownish, central spine 1, erect, awl-shaped; fls. yellow, 2 in. long. S. Brazil, Uruguay, n. Argentina.

erinacea (Haw.) D. M. Porter [*Malacocarpus erinaceus* (Haw.) Rümpler]. Sts. to 6 in. high and thick, ribs 15–20, obtuse; radial spines 6–8, needle-shaped, yellowish, to ¾ in. long, the upper shorter, central spine 1, deflexed, dark, longer; fls. yellow, to 2 in. long. S. Brazil, Uruguay, n. Argentina.

Kovaricii: a listed name of no botanical standing, perhaps applying to a form of *W. corynodes*.

Sellowii: a listed name of no botanical standing for *W. tephracantha*.

sessiliflorus (Hort. Mackie ex Hook.) D. M. Porter [*Malacocarpus pauciareolatus* (Arech.) A. Berger ex Backeb. & F. M. Knuth]. Sts. simple, discoid, to 4 in. thick, ribs about 15–21, acute; areoles 2 on each rib, spines 4, radial, awl-shaped, whitish, to ½ in. long; fls. yellow, to 1½ in. long. Uruguay.

tephracantha (Link & Otto) D. M. Porter [*Malacocarpus Sellowii* (Link & Otto) K. Schum.; *M. tephracanthus* (Link & Otto) K. Schum.]. Sts. simple, subglobose, to 6 in. thick, ribs 18–22, acute; areoles to ¾ in. apart, spines 4–6, needle-shaped, straight or recurved, to ¾ in. long; fls. yellow, to 2 in. long; fr. purple, ⅜ in. long. S. Brazil, Uruguay, n. Argentina.

Vorwerkiana (Werderm.) D. M. Porter [*Malacocarpus Vorwerkianus* (Werderm.) Backeb.]. COLOMBIAN BALL CACTUS. Sts. depressed-globose, to 3½ in. thick, ribs about 20, acute, to 5/16 in. high; areoles 2–3 on each rib, radial spines 5–6, awl-shaped, yellowish-white, 5/16 in. long, central spine 0–1, upcurved; fls. red; fr. rose, ⅝ in. long. Colombia.

WILCOXIA Britt. & Rose. *Cactaceae*. About 6 spp. of cacti, native to Tex. and Mex.; roots tuberous, sts. slender, ribs low, mostly 8–10, rarely 3–5; spines slender, often bristlelike and appressed; fls. opening several days, campanulate-funnelform, purple or red, tube shorter or longer than the limb, stigma green; fr. spiny.

For culture see *Cacti*.

australis: a listed name of no botanical standing.

Diguetii: *W. striata*.

Poselgeri (Lem.) Britt. & Rose. Tubers clustered, to 1½ in. thick, sts. to 2 ft. long and ⅝ in. thick, ribs 8–10; radial spines 9–12, bristlelike, appressed, to 5/32 in. long, central spine 1, erect, appressed, rigid, black-tipped, to ⅜ in. long; fls. purple to pink, fragrant, 2 in. long. Tex., n. Mex.

Schmollii (Weing.) F. M. Knuth. LAMB'S-TAIL CACTUS. Tubers to 3 in. thick, sts. to 10 in. high and ⅝ in. thick, ribs 9–10, low, tubercled; areoles 3/32 in. apart, with about 35 spreading, whitish, hairlike spines and sometimes 1 glandspine; fls. rose-purple, 1¼ in. long. Cent. Mex.

senilis: a listed name of no botanical standing, probably for *W. Schmollii*.

striata (Brandeg.) Britt. & Rose. [*W. Diguetii* (A. Web.) Peebles; *Peniocereus Diguetii* (A. Web.) Backeb.]. Tubers clustered, to 3 in. thick, sts. to 3 ft. long and ⅜ in. thick, ribs 8–9, low, flattened, the sinuses narrow; areoles to ½ in. apart, spines bristlelike, thickened at base, black, often appressed, to ⅛ in. long, radial spines 8–10, central spines 1–2; fls. purple, to 5 in. long; fr. red, 1½ in. long. Baja Calif.

tamaulipensis Werderm. Sts. to 8 in. long and ½ in. thick, ribs about 10, to ⅛ in. high; areoles ¼ in. apart, radial spines 15–20, bristlelike, to nearly ⅛ in. long, central spines 5–10, shorter, thicker, thickened at base; fls. rose, 2 in. long. Ne. Mex.

viperina (A. Web.) Britt. & Rose. Sts. much-branched, to 7 ft. long and ¾ in. thick, minutely pubescent, ribs 8–10, low, the sinuses narrow; areoles to ¾ in. apart, radial spines 8–9, appressed, dark, to 3/16 in. long, central spines 3–4, conical; fls. dark red, to 2½ in. long; fr. red, to ½ in. in diam. Cent. Mex.

WILLARDIA Rose. *Leguminosae* (subfamily *Faboideae*). Six spp. of shrubs and small trees, native to Mex.; lvs. alt., odd-pinnate; fls. in axillary racemes, papilionaceous, calyx truncate, the upper stamen united with others except at base; fr. a thin, flat, linear-oblong, dehiscent legume.

mexicana (S. Wats.) Rose. Tree, to 40 ft.; lfts. in 4–7 pairs, oblong-elliptic, to 1¼ in. long, blunt, pubescent, especially beneath; fls. many, lilac, less than ½ in. long; fr. to 5 in. long. Nw. Mex.

WILMATTEA: *HYLOCEREUS*.

WINDBREAK: see *Hedge*.

WINTERACEAE Lindl. WINTER'S BARK FAMILY. Dicot.; 8 genera and about 70 spp. of monoecious or sometimes polygamodioecious evergreen trees and shrubs, native mostly to the S. Hemisphere; lvs. alt., aromatic, with pellucid dots, without stipules; fls. rather small, fl. parts arranged more or less in whorls on a short axis, calyx 2–6-parted, petals 5–6 or more, in 2 series or more, stamens mostly many, carpels

1 to several, in a single whorl; fr. berrylike or a caps. Related to Magnoliaceae. *Drimys* and *Pseudowintera* are grown as ornamentals.

WISTERIA Nutt. WISTARIA, WISTERIA. *Leguminosae* (subfamily *Faboideae*). Nine or 10 spp. of woody lianas with twining sts., native to temp. e. Asia and e. U.S.; lvs. alt., odd-pinnate, lfts. alt.; fls. in pendent, mostly terminal racemes, papilionaceous, petals blue to purplish, pink, or white, standard reflexed, stamens 10, 9 united, and 1 separate; fr. an elongate, thick, flat, knobby legume, tardily dehiscent.

Two species, *W. floribunda* and *W. sinensis*, are the commonly planted species and are hardy north (Zone 5). They thrive in deep rich soil, and do not transplant readily. Propagated by seeds, division, layering, cuttings of ripened wood under glass, root cuttings over bottom heat, and the cultivars by grafting.

chinensis: *W. sinensis.*

floribunda (Willd.) DC. JAPANESE W. Sts. to 35 ft. or more; lfts. 13–19, ovate-elliptic, usually to 3 in. long; racemes 8–18(–48) in. long, produced with lvs.; fls. violet to violet-blue, pink, red, or white, to ¾ in. long, fragrant, standard basally eared; fr. velvety, to 6 in. long. Japan. Cvs. include: 'Alba' [forma *alba* (Carrière) Rehd. & E. H. Wils.; *W. multijuga* vars. *alba* Carrière and *albiflora* Hort.], fls. white; 'Carnea', fls. flesh-pink; 'Issai': 'Praecox'; 'Longissima' [*W. multijuga* var. *longissima* Hort.], racemes very long, fls. light purple; 'Longissima Alba', racemes very long, fls. white; 'Macrobotrys' [forma *macrobotrys* (Neub.) Rehd. & E. H. Wils.; *W. multijuga* Van Houtte], lfts. to 4 in. long, racemes to 3 ft. long or more; 'Praecox' [cv. 'Issai'; *W. multijuga* var. *praecox* Hort.], more dwarf, fls. blue-purple; 'Purpurea' [*W. multijuga* var. *purpurea* Hort.], fls. purple; 'Rosea' [forma *rosea* (Bean) Rehd. & E. H. Wils.; *W. multijuga rosea* Hort.], PINK W., fls. rose-pink; 'Rubra', fls. deep pink to red; 'Violacea Plena' [var. *violaceo-plena* (C. K. Schneid.) L. H. Bailey; *W. violaceo-plena* Hort.], fls. reddish-violet, double.

frutescens (L.) Poir. Lfts. 9–15, ovate to oblong-lanceolate; racemes villous, dense, 2–5 in. long; fls. lilac-purple, ½ in. long, standard basally eared; fr. to 4 in. long, glabrous. Va. to Fla., w. to Tex. Zone 5.

japonica Siebold & Zucc. Slender; lfts. 9–13, ovate-lanceolate, to 2¼ in. long; racemes axillary, solitary or two together, slender, loose, to 1 ft. long; fls. greenish-white, ½ in. long, standard not basally eared; fr. glabrous. Japan, Korea. Zone 8.

macrostachya (Torr. & A. Gray) Nutt. ex Torr. & A. Gray [*W. magnifica* Hort.]. Slender; lfts. usually 9, ovate; racemes to 1 ft. long; fls. lilac-purple or light blue; fr. to 4½ in. long, glabrous. Latest to flower. Swamps, Ill. to Ark. Zone 6.

magnifica: a listed name of no botanical standing for *W. macrostachya.*

multijuga: *W. floribunda* cv. 'Macrobotrys'. Var. **alba:** *W. floribunda* cv. Var. **albiflora:** a listed name of no botanical standing for *W. floribunda* cv. 'Alba'. Var. **longissima:** a listed name of no botanical standing for *W. floribunda* cv. Var. **praecox:** a listed name of no botanical standing for *W. floribunda* cv. Var. **purpurea:** *W. floribunda* cv. Var. **rosea:** a listed name of no botanical standing for *W. floribunda* cv.

sinensis (Sims) Sweet [*W. chinensis* DC.]. CHINESE W. Lfts. usually 11, ovate to ovate-lanceolate, to 3 in. long; racemes to 1 ft. long, all fls. of a raceme opening together; fls. appearing before lvs., bluish-violet, 1 in. long, not fragrant; fr. to 6 in. long, velvety. China. Zone 5. Cv. 'Alba' [var. *alba* Lindl.]. Fls. white, very fragrant. Cv. 'Purpurea'. Fls. purplish-violet.

venusta Rehd. & E. H. Wils. SILKY W. Lfts. 9–13, oblong-lanceolate or broader, to 4 in. long, velvety-pubescent; racemes open, to 6 in. long; fls. white, 1 in. long, fragrant, standard basally eared; fr. to 8 in. long, velvety. Earliest to flower. China. Zone 5. Cv. 'Alba' is listed, but may not differ from typical cv. Cv. 'Violacea'. Fls. lavender-blue, standard whitish.

violaceo-plena: a listed name of no botanical standing for *W. floribunda* cv.

WITTMACKIA: *AECHMEA.*

WITTROCKIA Lindm. *Bromeliaceae.* Seven spp. of epiphytic herbs, native to Brazil; similar to *Canistrum* and sometimes included in it, but differing in having petals united and bracts of scape and rachis leaflike.

Grown in warm climates or under glass. Prefer bright light. For culture see *Bromeliaceae.*

amazonica (Bak.) L. B. Sm. [*Canistrum amazonicum* (Bak.) Mez; *Nidularium amazonicum* (Bak.) Lindm.]. Lvs. to 20 in. long, 2 in. wide, finely toothed, purplish-maroon and green; bracts brick-red; fls.

waxy-white, to 1¾ in. long, petals rounded at apex. Plants in cult. bearing this name, or one of its synonyms, may be *Nidularium Innocentii* var. *Innocentii.*

superba Lindm. Lvs. to 3 ft. long, 3 in. wide, glossy green, tipped with stout red spines; fls. bluish, to 2⅜ in. long, petals acute at apex.

WOLFFIA Horkel. WATER-MEAL. *Lemnaceae.* About 8 spp. of very minute floating herbs, widely distributed in warm and trop. regions; plant body or thallus fleshy, more or less globular, rootless, proliferating, but the offshoots soon detached and the plant bodies usually solitary; fls. extremely rare, bursting through the upper surface, the 1 stamen or 1 pistil usually considered to represent a fl. The smallest of flowering plants.

arrhiza (L.) Wimm. Plant bodies ellipsoid, to ¹⁄₁₆ in. long, not dotted, upper surface convex or slightly arched, lacking pigmented cells. Eur., Asia, Afr., Australia.

columbiana Karst. COMMON WOLFFIA. Plant bodies globose, to ¹⁄₁₆ in. long, not dotted, with 3 papillae on upper surface, floating just beneath water surface. N. and S. Amer.

microscopica (Griff.) Kurz. Plant bodies elongate-octagonal, to ¹⁄₃₂ in. long, upper surface flat, lacking pigmented cells, lower surface with elongated protuberance. India.

punctata Griseb. Plant bodies ellipsoid, with acutish apex, less than ¹⁄₁₆ in. long, upper surface smooth, flattened, emersed, brown-dotted and gibbous beneath. N. Amer., W. Indies.

WOLFFIELLA Hegelm. *Lemnaceae.* Six spp. of minute, floating herbs, native to Afr., N. Amer., and S. Amer.; plant bodies thin, flat, rootless; proliferating, the offshoots solitary, or remaining attached; fls. extremely rare, in cavities on upper surface or marginal, the 1 stamen or 1 pistil usually considered to represent a fl.

floridana (J. D. Sm.) C. H. Thomps. MUD-MIDGET, BOGMAT. Plant bodies tongue-shaped, to ⅜ in. long, brown-dotted, remaining connected and forming large mats floating beneath water surface. Fla.

WOODFORDIA Salisb. *Lythraceae.* Two spp. of shrubs, native to Afr., Madagascar, and s. Asia; lvs. opp., black-dotted beneath; fls. red, in axillary clusters, regular, 5–6-merous, calyx tube with short calyx lobes, petals small, stamens 12; fr. an indehiscent caps., not longer than calyx tube.

fruticosa (L.) Kurz. To 15 ft. or more; lvs. sessile, lanceolate, to 5½ in. long; fls. 2–15 in short racemes, to ⅝ in. long, petals deep rose, as long as calyx lobes, narrow, sharply pointed. Madagascar and s. Asia. Cult. in Fla.

WOODSIA R. Br. *Polypodiaceae.* About 40 spp. of small rock-loving ferns, native in temp. and cool-temp. areas of the N. and S. Hemispheres, plants tufted; lvs. pinnately divided; sori on veins, indusia attached beneath and splitting into star-like lobes or slender filiform segms.

Sometimes transplanted to rock gardens or alpine gardens. See also *Ferns.*

alpina (Bolton) S. F. Gray. NORTHERN W. Lvs. linear to narrowly oblong-lanceolate, to 5 in. long, 1-pinnate, pinnae ovate, obtuse, pinnately lobed, smooth above, hairy but not scaly on midrib, petioles scaly, hairy, jointed at base. Eur., Asia, N. Amer.

Cathcartiana B. L. Robinson. CATHCART'S W. Lvs. lanceolate, to 1 ft. long and 2 in. wide, 1-pinnate, pinnae oblong, pinnatifid, pinnules oblong, separated by wide sinuses, denticulate, glandular beneath. W. N.Y. and n. Mich. to n. Minn.

glabella R. Br. SMOOTH W. Lvs. linear or linear-lanceolate, to 6 in. long, 1-pinnate, pinnae triangular or ovate, crenately lobed, glabrous above, petioles straw-colored, articulate near base, glabrous above joint. N. N. Amer., Eur.

ilvensis (L.) R. Br. RUSTY W., FRAGRANT W. Lvs. lanceolate, to 10 in. long and 1½ in. wide, 1-pinnate, pinnae pinnatifid into oblong, wavy-toothed pinnules, midrib with rusty chaff beneath, petioles jointed at base, stoutish, reddish-tan. Eur., Asia, n. N. Amer.

mexicana Fée. MEXICAN W. Lvs. leathery, lanceolate, to 1 ft. long, pinnate-pinnatifid or sometimes 2-pinnate, segms. finely toothed, with semitransparent or whitish margins. Tex. to Mex.

obtusa (K. Spreng.) Torr. BLUNT-LOBED W., COMMON W., LARGE W. Lvs. elliptic-lanceolate to broadly lanceolate, to 15 in. long and 4 in. wide, pinnate-pinnatifid to 2-pinnate, pinnae toothed or cut, glandular, rachis scaly; indusia broad-lobed. Cent. U.S., to Fla.

oregana D. C. Eat. OREGON W. Lvs. narrowly lanceolate-oblong to linear, to 8 in. long and 1 in. wide, 1-pinnate, pinnate-pinnatifid, pinnae oblong-ovate, crenate-serrulate, bright green, with minute stalked glands, otherwise glabrous, petioles not jointed basally, glabrous; indusia segms. short and hidden by sporangia. Que. to B.C., s. to New Mex. and Baja Calif.

scopulina D. C. Eat. ROCKY MOUNTAIN W. Lvs. to 10 in. long and 2 in. wide, 1-pinnate, pinnae pinnatifid, glandular and covered with fine, white hairs beneath, petioles not jointed, puberulent; indusia obscured by sporangia. Mts., N. Amer.

WOODWARDIA Sm. CHAIN FERN. *Polypodiaceae.* About 12 spp. of large, terrestrial ferns, native to Eur., Asia, and N. Amer.; lvs. usually 2-pinnatifid; sori in rows parallel to the midrib, indusia introrse.

Sometimes transplanted to the woodland garden; of easy culture, requiring mostly a moist location, a few grown under glass. See also *Ferns.*

angustifolia: *W. areolata.*

areolata (L.) T. Moore [*W. angustifolia* Sm.]. NETTED C.F. Lvs. dimorphic, pinnatifid, to 15 in. long, sterile lvs. with slender green petioles, pinnae lanceolate and toothed, fertile lvs. with darker petioles, the fertile pinnae linear, entire. Me. to Fla. and La.

Chamissoi: *W. fimbriata.*

fimbriata Sm. [*W. Chamissoi* Brackenr.]. GRANT C.F. Lvs. to 9 ft. long and 1½ ft. wide, 1-pinnate, pinnae pinnatifid, glabrous beneath. B.C. to Calif.

orientalis Swartz. Differs from *W. radicans* in having many small buds scattered over the lf., pinnae lanceolate, pinnules sinuate. Temp. e. Asia.

radicans (L.) Sm. EUROPEAN C.F. Lvs. producing large buds at end of rachis, triangular to ovate-lanceolate, to 7 ft. long, 1-pinnate, pinnae lanceolate-ovate, to 1 ft. long, pinnules curved, to 3 in. long, finely serrate; sori oblong. Sw. Eur. to sw. Italy. Asiatic material formerly included in *W. radicans* is *W. unigemmata.*

simplex: a listed name of uncertain application.

spinulosa M. Martens & Galeotti. Differs from *W. fimbriata* in having filamentous scales and stalked glands beneath. Mex., Guatemala.

unigemmata (Mak.) Nakai. Rhizomes and stipes stout, to 20 in. long, straw-colored to pale brown, basal scales membranous, linear to linear-lanceolate, to 1⅛ in. long, acuminate, entire; lvs. broadly ovate-lanceolate, to 40 in. long, to 20 in. wide, pinnae pinnately cleft to parted, equilateral, thinly leathery, ovate-lanceolate or triangular-lanceolate, to 12 in. long, 3½ in. wide, with large densely scaly vegetative buds in axils of upper pinnae; sori along midveins of pinnules. E. and se. Asia.

virginica (L.) Sm. [*Blechnum virginicum* L.]. VIRGINIA C.F. Rhizomes long and creeping; lvs. oblong-lanceolate, to 2 ft. long and 9 in. wide, 1-pinnate, pinnae oblong or ovate, pinnatifid, pinnules fine-toothed; sori oblong, confluent when mature. Nov. Sc. to Fla. and La., Bermuda.

WORMIA: *DILLENIA.* W. Burbidgei: *D. suffruticosa.*

WORSLEYA Traub. *Amaryllidaceae.* One sp., a bulbous herb, native to Brazil; bulb slender, tunicate, with a long aerial neck; lvs. 2-ranked, falcate; fls. 4–14, in an umbel terminal on a hollow scape and subtended by 4 spathe valves, perianth tube very short, lobes acute, ovary inferior, ovules many; fr. a caps., seeds black, D-shaped.

Rayneri (Hook.) Traub [*Amaryllis procera* Duchartre; *Hippeastrum procerum* (Duchartre) Lem.]. BLUE AMARYLLIS. To 16 in.; lvs. 12–14, to 3 ft. long, 3 in. wide at the middle; pedicels about 3 in. long; fls. lilac with white base, 5½–6½ in. long, tube very short, lobes to 6 in. long, dark-spotted, much longer than stamens, stigma headlike.

WRIGHTIA R. Br. *Apocynaceae.* About 15 spp. of trees and shrubs, native to Old World tropics; brs. often slender, cordlike; lvs. opp., entire; fls. in sessile, forked cymes, 5-merous, bisexual, corolla salverform, with 1–2 rows of usually fringed scales in throat, stamens borne on the corolla, anthers sagittate-spurred, connivent, adhering to stigma, exserted; fr. a pair of linear, erect follicles, seeds many, linear, with deciduous tuft of hairs.

Propagated by seeds or by cuttings.

coccinea (Roxb.) Sims. Tree, shoots with white bark; lvs. elliptic to elliptic-lanceolate, to 5 in. long, caudate-acuminate at base, thin, petioles very short; cymes 3–4-fld.; corolla dark red, about 1 in. across, somewhat fleshy, scales crimson, entire, broad and rounded, anthers very hairy on outer side. India.

tinctoria (Roxb.) R. Br. Small tree; lvs. very variable, elliptic-ovate to obovate-oblong, bluntly acuminate or caudate, to 5 in. long, short-petioled; cymes to 5 in. across; corolla white, to ¾ in. in diam., scales scattered, fringed, lobes linear-oblong, stamens large; follicles 18 in. long or more, united at apex, seeds linear, ⅝ in. long, glabrous except for tuft of hairs. Cent. India, e. to Burma and Timor.

WULFENIA Jacq. *Scrophulariaceae.* Five spp. of tufted, nearly glabrous per. herbs, with thick rhizomes, native to se. Eur., w. Asia, and the Himalayas; lvs. basal, petioled, crenate or toothed to nearly lobed; fls. blue or purple, in scapose racemes, calyx 5-parted, corolla with cylindrical tube and 4-lobed limb, stamens 2; fr. a caps.

Suitable for the rock garden or the border. Wulfenias need rich moist soil, but prevention of excessive moisture in winter, as they decay easily. Propagated by seeds or division.

Amherstiana Benth. Lvs. obovate-oblong, to 6 in. long, coarsely crenate; fls. in one-sided raceme to 1 ft.; corolla blue-purple, to ⁵⁄₁₆ in. long, lobes acuminate. Summer. W. Himalayas and Afghanistan.

Baldaccii Degen. Lvs. elliptic to broadly ovate, to 4 in. long, deeply crenate or toothed to nearly lobed; fls. in a loose raceme to 6 in. long, corolla lilac-blue, to ⅜ in. long, lobes rounded. Summer. Albania.

carinthiaca Jacq. Lvs. oblong to oblanceolate, to 8 in. long, shallowly or deeply crenate; fls. in dense, spicate raceme to 2 ft., corolla blue-violet, to ½ in. long, lobes rounded. Summer. E. Alps, Balkan Pen. Cv. 'Alba'. Fls. white.

WYETHIA Nutt. *Compositae* (Helianthus Tribe). About 14 spp. of coarse, taprooted, per. herbs in w. U.S., sts. leafy; lvs. alt., linear to ovate, entire or serrate; fl. heads usually radiate, mostly large, solitary or few, involucral bracts imbricate, herbaceous, receptacle scaly; disc fls. bisexual, fertile, yellow; ray fls. usually present, female, fertile, yellow to white; pappus a crown of short scales, rarely lacking.

Slow-growing, long-lived plants, taking several years to come to flowering when grown from seeds.

amplexicaulis (Nutt.) Nutt. To 2½ ft., glabrous; lvs. green, glossy, varnished, basal lvs. oblong-lanceolate, 8–18 in. long, short-petioled, st. lvs. smaller, sessile; heads 3–4 in. across, several, more rarely solitary, involucral bracts glabrous; ray fls. yellow. Wash. and Mont., s. to Nev. and Colo.

angustifolia (DC.) Nutt. To 3 ft., hirsute; lvs. variable, basal lvs. mostly narrowly oblanceolate, 6–20 in. long, st. lvs. smaller, petioled to sessile; heads 3–4 in. across, usually solitary, involucral bracts ciliate; ray fls. yellow. S. Wash. to Calif.

helenioides (DC.) Nutt. To 2 ft., white-tomentose at first, becoming nearly glabrous with age; basal lvs. lanceolate to elliptic-ovate, about 1 ft. long, short-petioled, st. lvs. similar but smaller; heads to 5 in. across, usually solitary, involucral bracts tomentose; ray fls. yellow. Mts., cent. Calif.

XANTHERANTHEMUM Lindau. *Acanthaceae*. One sp., a per. herb in the Andes of Peru; lvs. opp.; fls. in terminal spikes, bracts elliptic, acute, serrate, overlapping, calyx deeply 5-parted, corolla yellow, tube long, lobes 5, subequal, stamens 4, included, anthers with a few apical hairs; fr. a caps.

igneum (Linden) Lindau [*Eranthemum igneum* Linden; *Chamaeranthemum igneum* (Linden) Regel]. Prostrate; lvs. dark green above with veins marked with yellow, purplish beneath. Grown indoors for its attractive foliage.

XANTHISMA DC. SLEEPY DAISY. *Compositae* (Aster Tribe). One sp., an ann., in N. Amer.; lvs. alt.; fl. heads radiate, solitary on the brs., involucre hemispherical, involucral bracts thick, scarious-margined, receptacle bristly; disc and ray fls. yellow; achenes with pappus of 3 rows of scales, the innermost longest and slender-tipped.

texana DC. Sts. to 3 ft., slender, branching; lvs. mostly sessile, narrow-lanceolate, the lower pinnatifid, to 2½ in. long, the upper much smaller, entire; heads to 2½ in. across, closing at night, the long ray fls. expanding only in middle of day. Spring, summer. Tex.

XANTHOCERAS Bunge. *Sapindaceae*. Two spp. of deciduous, polygamous shrubs or small trees, native to n. China; lvs. alt., pinnate; fls. in axillary or terminal racemes, regular, sepals and petals 5, stamens 8, disc with 5 horns about half as long as stamens; fr. a hard, green caps. resembling a horse chestnut.

Thrives in any good soil; hardy north. Propagated by seeds stratified and sown in spring, or by root cuttings over heat.

sorbifolium Bunge. To 15 ft., occasionally more; lvs. to 1 ft. long, lfts. 9–17, narrow-elliptic to lanceolate, to 2 in. long, sharply serrate, dark green above, paler beneath; fls. nearly 1 in. across, petals white, with yellow or red blotch at base; fr. 2½ in. long. Spring. Zone 6.

XANTHORHIZA Marsh. [*Zanthorhiza* L'Hér.]. SHRUB YELLOW-ROOT. *Ranunculaceae*. One sp., a deciduous, polygamous shrub with bitter yellow roots, native to e. N. Amer.

Thrives in damp shaded places; propagated by division and by seeds.

apiifolia: *X. simplicissima*.

simplicissima Marsh. [*X. apiifolia* (L'Hér.) Guimpel, Otto, & Hayne; *Z. apiifolia* L'Hér.]. To 2 ft.; lvs. 1–2-pinnate, lfts. usually 5-toothed or 5-lobed; fls. brownish-purple, about ³⁄₁₆ in. across, in drooping racemes to 4 in. long, sepals 5, petal-like, petals 5, small. N.Y. to W. Va., Fla., Ala.

XANTHORRHOEA Sm. GRASS TREE, BLACKBOY. *Liliaceae*. About 12 spp. of slow-growing, long-lived, woody perennials of Australia; sts. thick, woody, palmlike; lvs. linear, in tuft at top of trunk; scape arising from the tuft of lvs., bearing a dense spike of white fls., perianth segms. 6, separate, persistent, stamens 6; fr. a leathery, 3-valved, loculicidal caps., seeds dull black, flat.

Acaroid resins, produced at the base of the old leaves of some species, have industrial importance. Grass trees have the habit of *Dasylirion* and are similarly suited to dry climates. Propagated by offsets.

arborea R. Br. Arborescent at maturity; lvs. flat, to 4 ft. long; scape 5–6 ft. long, bearing a spike 3–4 ft. long and to 1½ in. in diam., fls. ¼ in. long; fr. ⅝ in. long. Queensland and New S. Wales.

quadrangulata F. J. Muell. To 10 ft.; lvs. quadrangular, to 3 ft. long; scape 2½–5 ft. long, bearing a spike 2½–3 ft. long and 2¼ in. in diam., fls. ⅜ in. long; fr. to ¾ in. long. S. Australia.

XANTHOSOMA Schott. YAUTIA, MALANGA, TANNIA, TANIER, TANYAH, OCUMO. *Araceae*. About 40 spp. of nearly stemless or caulescent, often large, herbs with thick rhizomes or tubers and milky sap, native to trop. Amer.; lvs. entire and sagittate or hastate, or pedately dissected, with 3–13 segms., petioles long, succulent; peduncle short, spathe convolute,

constricted between the inflated tube and expanded, early-deciduous blade; fls. unisexual, the upper part of spadix clavate, bearing male fls. quite to its apex, perianth absent, ovaries 2–4-celled, ovules many in each cell, axile. Closely related to *Caladium* but having pistil constricted between the ovary and the dilated annular style.

Grown in this country mostly as ornamentals, though some are cultivated in the South, but principally in tropical America, for their edible tubers. Several species of entire-leaved xanthosomas produce cylindrical to obovoid tubers with white to orange, rose, or purplish flesh. Many cultivars are recognized. For culture see *Colocasia*.

atrovirens C. Koch & Bouché. Differs from *X. sagittifolium* in having lf. blades ovate, sagittate, with 4–6 pairs of primary lateral veins, dark green, glaucous gray-green beneath, petioles dark green, bluish-glaucous, especially in sheathing part; spathe green, violet at apex, red-nerved outside. Trop. Amer. Cv. 'Albomarginatum'. Lf. blades variously contorted, marginally blotched with white.

bataviense: a listed name of no botanical standing; applied to at least 2 different plants.

daguense Engl. Aerial sts. to 4 ft.; lf. blades to 1 ft. long or more, elongate-ovate, saggittate with attenuate, oblong-triangular basal lobes; spathe 4 in. long, tube green, blade white. Colombia.

Lindenii (André) Engl. INDIAN KALE, SPOON FLOWER. Tuberous; lf. blades oblong to ovate, hastate or sagittate, to 19 in. long, glossy green, marked with white along midribs and main lateral veins, green and rusty-pilose beneath, petioles to 4 ft. long, glaucous; spathe to 5½ in. long, tube green, blade white. Colombia. Cv. 'Magnificum'. Lvs. more heavily variegated, the veinlets also white.

sagittifolium (L.) Schott. Aerial sts. developing with age; lf. blades broadly ovate, sagittate with broad basal lobes, to 3 ft. long, with 8–9 pairs of primary lateral veins, glaucous when young, petioles longer than blade, green; spathe to 10 in. long, tube green, blade greenish-white. W. Indies. Widely grown in the tropics for its edible tubers.

violaceum Schott [*Alocasia violacea* Hort.]. BLUE TARO, VIOLET-STEMMED T., BLUE APE. Differs from *X. sagittifolium* in having lf. blades oblong-ovate, sagittate, with violet margins and primary lateral veins, especially on lower side, petioles to 6 ft. long, violet, prominently gray-glaucous; spathe to 1 ft. long, tube pale violet, glaucous, blade yellowish. W. Indies. Produces tubers of excellent table quality.

XANTHOXALIS: *OXALIS*.

XANTHOXYLUM: *ZANTHOXYLUM*.

XENOPHYA Schott [*Schizocasia* Engl.]. *Araceae*. Two spp. of erect herbs, native to the Molucca Is. and New Guinea, with milky sap; lvs. in a crown, long-petioled, lobed or pinnatifid; infls. many, axillary, short-peduncled, spathe convolute, persistent, tube inflated, blade long, very slender, scarcely expanded, spadix slender, terminated by a long sterile appendage; fls. unisexual, perianth absent; fr. a berry with 2–5 seeds.

For culture see *Callopsis*.

Lauterbachiana (Engl.) Nicols. [*Alocasia Wavriniana* M. T. Mast.; *Schizocasia Lauterbachiana* Engl.]. To 4 ft. or more; lf. blades narrow-lanceolate, to 20 in. long, basally truncate to subhastate, sinuate, with a lobe over each primary lateral vein, glossy, dark blue-green above, silver-purple beneath, petioles a little shorter than blades, winged nearly to apex, with black-green markings; spathe 6 in. long, tube marked with a few blackish stripes. New Guinea to New Ireland.

XERANTHEMUM L. *Compositae* (Carduus Tribe). About 6 spp. of nonspiny ann. herbs, native from Medit. region to Iran; sts. erect, branching, leafy; lvs. alt., entire; heads solitary, long-stalked, involucre hemispherical or cylindrical, involucral bracts imbricate in several rows, the inner elongate, scarious, petal-like, persistent, lilac, rose, purple, or white, receptacle scaly; fls. all tubular, the outer few, sterile, the inner bisexual, anthers tailed; achenes silky-hairy, pappus of 1 row of pointed scales.

One of the oldest-known and most satisfactory of the immortelles or everlastings. Propagated by seeds.

annuum L. IMMORTELLE. White-tomentose herb, to 2 ft., sometimes taller; lvs. oblong to oblong-lanceolate, to 2 in. long; heads to 1½ in. across, involucral bracts purple or rose, the inner glossy, much longer than the outer; fls. purple or white. S. Eur. Cv. 'Ligulosum' [*X. imperiale* Hort.]. Heads double or semidouble.

imperiale: *X. annuum* cv. 'Ligulosum'.

XERODERRIS Roberty. *Leguminosae* (subfamily *Faboideae*).

One sp., a deciduous tree of trop. Afr.; lvs. alt., odd-pinnate; fls. papilionaceous, stamens 10, 9 united and 1 separate; fr. an indehiscent, hardened, elongate legume, narrowly winged on each side.

Stuhlmannii (Taub.) Mendonça & E. P Sousa [*Ostryoderris Stuhlmannii* (Taub.) Harms]. Tree, to 40 ft. or more, herbage rusty-pubescent; lfts. in 4–9 pairs, oblong-ovate, nearly cordate and retuse, to 4 in. long, glabrous and glossy above, only the midrib impressed; corolla white, to ⅝ in. long; fr. oblong, to 6 in. long, glabrous, wings ⅛ in. wide, 1(–3)-seeded. Savannas, Trop. Afr.

XEROMPHIS Raf. *Rubiaceae*.

About 7 spp. of shrubs or small trees, native to trop. Afr. and Asia; brs. usually armed with spines representing modified lateral branchlets; lvs. opp., often in unequal pairs, stipules interpetiolar; fls. 1–2, or sometimes 3, terminal on leafy lateral shoots, corolla tube broad, with a distinct band of long hairs inside; fr. a berry. Related to *Randia* but having band of hairs inside corolla tube, and ovary and fr. distinctly 2-celled.

spinosa (Thunb.) Keay [*Randia dumetorum* (Retz.) Lam.; *R. malabarica* Wallich, not Lam.]. Small tree or rigid shrub, with stout straight spines; lvs. obovate, to 2 in. long; fls. usually solitary, greenish-yellow or white, corolla hairy outside; fr. globose or ovoid, to 1½ in. long. Trop. Asia.

uliginosa (Retz.) Maheshw. [*Randia uliginosa* (Retz.) DC.]. Small, usually rigid tree, with short, straight, stout spines; lvs. obovate or ovate, to 8 in. long; fls. solitary, white, corolla glabrous on outside; fr. ellipsoid, to 2 in. long, yellow, edible. India.

XEROPHYLLUM Michx. *Liliaceae*.

Two spp. of tall, per. herbs with woody rootstocks, native to N. Amer.; sts. simple, leafy; lvs. mostly basal, linear, grasslike; fls. white, in dense terminal racemes, perianth segms. 6, separate, 5–7-nerved, persistent, stamens 6, styles 3; fr. a 3-lobed, loculicidal caps., seeds 3-angled.

asphodeloides (L.) Nutt. TURKEYBEARD, MOUNTAIN ASPHODEL. To 5 ft.; basal lvs. to 1½ ft. long and ³⁄₃₂ in. wide, st. lvs. reduced in size toward top of plant; fls. ⅜ in. across, in racemes to 1 ft. long at maturity. N.J. to Tenn. and Ga.

tenax (Pursh) Nutt. ELK GRASS, BEAR G., INDIAN BASKET G., SQUAW G., FIRE LILY. To 6 ft.; basal lvs. to 3 ft. long and ¼ in. wide, reduced in size toward top of plant; fls. ⅝ in. across, in racemes to 2 ft. long. B.C., s. to Wyo. and cent. Calif.

XIPHIDIUM Aubl. *Haemodoraceae*.

Two spp. of per. herbs with horizontal rhizomes, native to trop. Amer.; lvs. alt., in 2 ranks, sword-shaped; infl. terminal, paniculate-cymose; fls. small, white, bisexual, regular, perianth segms. 6, equal, stamens 3, ovary nearly inferior, 3-celled; fr. a berry, seeds many.

caeruleum Aubl. To 2½ ft.; lvs. to 20 in. long, 1¾ in. wide; panicle to 1 ft. long, 5 in. wide, scurfy-puberulent; perianth segms. to ¼ in. long. Mex., W. Indies, S. Amer.

speciosum: a listed name of no botanical standing.

XOLISMA: *LYONIA*.

XYLOBIUM Lindl. *Orchidaceae*.

About 30 spp. of epiphytes, native to trop. Amer.; pseudobulbs ovoid, 1–2-lvd. at apex; lvs. somewhat leathery, lanceolate, plicate; infl. a basal, short-elongate, erect or arching, few- to many-fld. raceme; upper sepal separate, lateral sepals broader, united to foot of column and forming a short mentum, petals nearly equal to upper sepal, lip entire or 3-lobed, jointed to column foot at base, disc smooth or with calluses or with prominent keel,

column narrowly winged at apex. For structure of fl. see *Orchidaceae*.

For culture see *Orchids*.

brachystachyum: *X. Colleyi*.

bractescens (Lindl.) Kränzl. Pseudobulbs oblong-conical, 1½ in. long, 1-lvd.; lvs. oblong-elliptic, to 10 in. long; racemes longer than lvs., flexuous and arching; fls. dull yellow with reddish-brown lip, upper sepal oblong-lanceolate, with revolute margins, lateral sepals triangular-lanceolate, as long as upper sepal, petals similar but smaller, lip oblong-elliptic, 3-lobed above middle, lateral lobes triangular-ovate, midlobe larger, ovate, with oblong, apically 3-lobed callus and covered with lines of warts over the veins. Amazonian Brazil, Ecuador.

Colleyi (Batem. ex Lindl.) Rolfe [*X. brachystachyum* Kränzl.; *Maxillaria Colleyi* Batem. ex Lindl.]. Pseudobulbs globose, small for size of plant, to 1 in. long, 1-lvd.; lvs. obovate, to 16 in. long; racemes much shorter than lvs., pendent, capitate, 4–5-fld.; sepals and petals fleshy, pale brown with pinkish flush and maroon spots, sepals ¾ in. long, petals smaller, lip ¾ in. long, with fleshy, very dark red, sticky-lustrous apex, pinkish-maroon, tubercled, undulate margins, and pale brown base overlaid with dark reddish-maroon, column and anther pale brown. Trinidad, Venezuela, Guyana, Brazil.

decolor: *X. palmifolium*.

elongatum (Lindl. & Paxt.) Hemsl. Pseudobulbs cylindrical, 2-lvd.; lvs. elliptic, to 16 in. long; racemes shorter than pseudobulbs, loosely or densely several- to many-fld.; fls. large, fleshy, whitish to yellow or pinkish, marked with dull red, brown, or violet, upper sepal oblong-lanceolate, to 1 in. long, mentum conical, almost as long as upper sepal, petals similar, margins involute, lip erect, ovate-lanceolate, 3-lobed, lateral lobes erect, triangular-ovate, midlobe lanceolate, with upcurved lateral margins, disc covered with papillose ridges above veins, studded with papillae or short tubercles. Costa Rica, Panama.

foveatum (Lindl.) Nichols. [*X. stachyobiorum* (Rchb.f.) Hemsl.]. Pseudobulbs ovoid, to 3½ in. long, 2–3-lvd. at apex; lvs. elliptic, to 16 in. long; racemes arching, to 13 in. long; fls. small, yellowish, lip white, rarely striped with red, sepals and petals oblong-lanceolate, to ½ in. long, mentum conical, as long as upper sepal, lip erect, obovate-oblong, to ½ in. long, with upcurved lateral margins, 3-lobed near apex, with 3–5 thickened central lines below disc. Cent. Amer., n. S. Amer.

palmifolium (Swartz) Fawc. [*X. decolor* (Lindl.) Nichols.]. Over 1 ft., pseudobulbs cylindric-ovate, to 3 in. long, 1-lvd.; lvs. lanceolate, to 16 in. long; racemes 4 in. long, loosely few-fld.; fls. yellowish-white, fragrant, upper sepal oblong, ¾ in. long, lateral sepals triangular-lanceolate, ¾ in. long, petals linear-oblong, ½ in. long, lip obovate-oblong, ½ in. long, white, fleshy and warty at apex, margins incurved, crisped, disc with 4–5 central lines. W. Indies.

Powellii Schlechter. Pseudobulbs cylindrical, to 2½ in. long, 1–2-lvd.; lvs. lanceolate, to 2 ft. long; racemes erect, to 6 in. long, few-to many-fld.; fls. yellow or tan, sometimes suffused with light green, sepals membranous, elliptic-lanceolate, to ½ in. long, petals similar, lip 3-lobed, ½ in. long, disc with 3 keels. Summer. Costa Rica, Panama.

stachyobiorum: *X. foveatum*.

XYLOCOCCUS Nutt. *Ericaceae*.

One sp., a densely branched, evergreen shrub, native in scattered localities in s. Calif. and Baja Calif.; lvs. simple, alt. or opp., leathery; fls. white or pink, in terminal, simple or branched panicles, calyx 5-lobed, corolla urceolate, stamens 10, ovary superior; fr. a smooth drupe.

Culture as for *Arbutus*.

bicolor Nutt. [*Arctostaphylos bicolor* (Nutt.) A. Gray]. Arborescent shrub, to 6 ft., branchlets ash-colored; lvs. ovate to oblong, to 2 in. long, dark green and glabrous above, gray-tomentose beneath, with revolute margins; fr. red to nearly black. Winter. Zone 7.

XYLOPHYLLA: *PHYLLANTHUS*. X. speciosa. *Phyllanthus arbuscula*.

XYLOSMA G. Forst. [*Myroxylon* J. R. Forst. & G. Forst.]. *Flacourtiaceae*.

About 100 spp. of dioecious, evergreen trees or shrubs, native to trop. and subtrop. regions, except Afr.; lvs. alt., simple; fls. small, in axillary racemes, sepals 4–5, mostly united at base, petals none, stamens many, surrounded by a disc; fr. a small, 2–8-seeded berry.

congestum (Lour.) Merrill [*X. racemosum* (Miq.) Siebold & Zucc.; *X. senticosum* Hance; *Myroxylon senticosum* (Hance) Warb.]. Shrub or small tree, to 15 ft., with sharp slender axillary spines; lvs. ovate-acuminate, to 3½ in. long, serrate, shining above, petioles slender, to ¼ in. long; berry black, globose, to ³⁄₁₆ in. in diam. China.

flexuosum (HBK) Hemsl. Spiny shrub or small tree, to 18 ft.; lvs. elliptic-oblong to obovate, to 2½ in. long, leathery, serrate; berry red, subglobose, to ¼ in. in diam. Mex., Cent. Amer.

heterophyllum (Karst.) Gilg. Shrub, without spines; lvs. ovate-acute, to 2½ in. long, leathery, serrate, dull above, petioles short, thick, to ⅛ in. long; berry globose, to ¼ in. in diam. Colombia.

racemosum: *X. congestum.*

senticosum: *X. congestum.*

XYLOTHECA: *ONCOBA.*

XYRIDACEAE Agardh. YELLOW-EYED GRASS FAMILY.
Monocot.; 2 genera and perhaps 50 spp. of rushlike herbs, chiefly trop., of worldwide distribution, except Eur.; lvs. basal, 2-ranked, sheathing; fls. in dense, bracted heads terminal on leafless scapes, sepals 3, unequal, petals 3, fertile stamens 3, ovary superior, 3-carpelled, many-ovuled; fr. a caps. Only *Xyris* is cult.

XYRIS L. YELLOW-EYED GRASS. *Xyridaceae.* About 240
spp. of tufted herbs, native chiefly to warmer regions of world, except Eur.; lvs. erect, narrow, basal; fls. yellow, borne in heads, in axils of leathery, imbricate bracts, on leafless scapes, sepals, petals, fertile stamens, and staminodes 3; fr. a caps.

Yellow-eyed grasses are of little horticultural interest except in wild gardens. Propagated by seeds or division.

Congdonii Small. To 2¼ ft., without bulbous base; lvs. to 2 ft. long, ½ in. wide, concave; heads ovoid, to ¾ in. long; sepals projecting beyond bracts, keeled, not fringed. Me. to N.J. Less ornamental than the following spp.

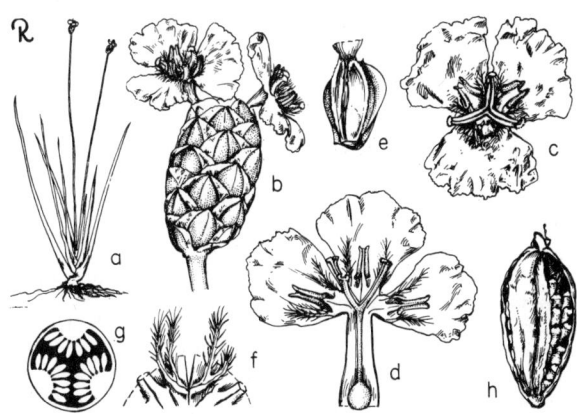

XYRIDACEAE. *Xyris Congdonii:* **a,** plant in flower, × ¹⁄₂₀; **b,** inflorescence, × 1½; **c,** flower, face view, × 2; **d,** flower, perianth expanded, × 2; **e,** sepals and subtending bract, × 2; **f,** staminode between bases of two filaments, × 4; **g,** ovary, cross section, × 10; **h,** fruit, × 5. (From Lawrence, *Taxonomy of Vascular Plants.*)

flexuosa Muhlenb. To 1½ ft., with glossy, chestnut-colored bulbous base; lvs. rigid, often spiralled, to 18 in. long, ⅛ in. wide; heads globose, to 1 in. in diam.; fls. ¼ in. across, sepals projecting beyond bracts, keeled, long-fringed. Summer to early autumn. N.J., s. to Fla., w. to e. Tex.

montana Ries. To 1½ ft., tufted or matted, without bulbous base; lvs. to 6 in. long, less than ⅛ in. wide; heads narrowly to broadly ovoid, to ½ in. long, ¼ in. wide; sepals projecting slightly beyond bracts, keeled, not fringed. Early autumn. Wet places, Nfld. to Ont., s. to N.J. and Mich.

YAM. The true yams are vining species of the monocotyledonous genus *Dioscorea* (see *Dioscorea*). In some parts of the United States the soft-fleshed types of the sweet potato (*Ipomoea Batatas*) are erroneously called "yams." The majority of the cultivated dioscoreas are grown in the tropics or subtropics, where, in some regions, their large and variously shaped storage roots constitute a major starchy-food source. The roots are baked in the skin like potatoes, boiled, or ground into flour; they are also fed to livestock, especially hogs. Among cultigens with edible roots sometimes planted in Hawaii and Puerto Rico or in the South (Zone 9) are *Dioscorea alata* (white or water yam), *D. Batatas* (Chinese yam), *D. bulbifera* (air potato), *D. cayenensis* (Negro yam), and *D. trifida* (cush-cush). Some of these, as well as others, may also be grown as ornamental foliage vines, the fast growth making them useful for screening purposes.

Yams are of easy culture in good soil. In the vegetable garden they are usually planted 2–3 feet apart in rows 4–5 feet apart, the rows being hilled up to provide ample growing room for the often very large roots. Some species, like *D. Batatas*, are best grown on poles or stakes arranged as temporary tripods as for pole beans. Propagation is by seed, root sections, or basal stem cuttings, the latter considered best.

YOUNGBERRY: see *Boysenberry*.

YUCCA L. [*Hesperoyucca* (Engelm.) Bak.]. *Agavaceae.* About 40 spp. in warmer regions of N. Amer.; stemless or with erect woody trunks; lvs. stiff, sword-shaped or rarely stilettolike; infl. racemose or paniculate; fls. white or violet, perianth cup- or saucer-shaped, segms. 6, separate or partly united, stamens 6, ovary superior, 3-celled, each cell with many ovules; fr. indehiscent and fleshy or sometimes dry, or dehiscent and capsular, seeds usually black, either rough and thickened, or smooth, thin, and winged or wingless.

Cultivated in the South, and a few species are hardy in the North. Good drainage, sandy loam, and open exposure are preferred. Propagated by seeds, offsets, and cuttings of stems, rhizomes, or roots.

aloifolia L. SPANISH-BAYONET, DAGGER PLANT. To 25 ft., trunk simple or branched; lvs. to 2½ ft. long, 2½ in. wide, very sharp-pointed, margins denticulate but not thread-bearing; infl. paniculate, to 2 ft. long; fls. white, often tinged with purple, to 4 in. across; fr. indehiscent, with purple pulp and no core, seeds thick. S. U.S., W. Indies, Mex. Cvs. include: 'Marginata', lvs. yellow-margined; 'Quadricolor', probably not distinct from cv. 'Tricolor'; 'Tricolor', lvs. yellow or white in center; 'Variegata', a listed name. Var. **draconis** (L.) Engelm. Trunk branched above; lvs. to 2 in. across, more flexuous, recurved and not rigid.

angustifolia: *Y. glauca.*

angustissima Engelm. ex Trel. Stemless or rarely with short prostrate or procumbent st.; lvs. linear, to 18 in. long, ¼ in. wide, margins white when young, with separated fibers massed at base; infl. racemose, to nearly 7 ft.; fls. pale green tinged with rose or rose-purple, to 2¼ in. long, segms. only shortly united at base; fr. dehiscent, usually deeply constricted. Ariz. and Utah.

arborescens: *Y. brevifolia.*

arizonica McKelv. St. to 8 ft.; lvs. somewhat flexuous, sword-shaped, to 26 in. long, to 1³⁄₁₆ in. wide, blue-green, margin thin, with few, fine, straight fibers; infl. above lvs., erect, to 5 ft., narrow, with about 35 brs.; fls. campanulate, white or cream, often tinged with purple, to 5 in. long, segms. essentially separate, pistil to 3 in. long; fr. fleshy, indehiscent, to 6 in. long, seeds wingless. Ariz. and Sonora (Mex.).

baccata Torr. SPANISH-BAYONET, BLUE Y., BANANA Y., DATIL. Sts. short, prostrate; lvs. sword-shaped, to 28 in. long, 2¼ in. wide, margin with coarse, often curly fibers; infl. paniculate, to 2 ft. long; fls. campanulate, white or cream, often tinged with purple, segms. essentially separate, pistil to 3 in. long; fr. fleshy, indehiscent, to nearly 10 in. long, seeds thick, rough, wingless. Sw. U.S.

brevifolia Engelm. [*Y. arborescens* (Torr.) Trel.]. JOSHUA TREE. St. to 40 ft., simple or branched; lvs. stilettolike, to 14 in. long, ⅝ in. wide, margin minutely toothed; infl. paniculate, to 20 in. long; fls. greenish-yellow to green, rarely cream, to 2¾ in. long; fr. dry and spongy, indehiscent, seeds smooth, thin, wingless. Calif. to Utah. Var. **brevifolia.** The typical var.; sts. solitary or 2–3, to nearly 40 ft., branched 6–10 ft. above the ground. Var. **Herbertii** (Webber) Munz. Sts. many, clumped, to about 15 ft. Var. **Jaegerana** McKelv. Differs in smaller habit, to 20 ft., brs. shorter, rarely spreading, developing at about 3 ft. above the ground or less; lvs. shorter, to 8 in. long.

carnerosana (Trel.) McKelv. SPANISH-DAGGER. Arborescent, sts. solitary or clumped, to 15 ft. or more; lvs. in a terminal rosette, rigid, sword-shaped, to 40 in. long, 3 in. wide, margins entire; infl. densely branched, longer than foliage, bracts white, persistent; fls. white, to 3¾ in. long, segms. united into a slender tube to 1³⁄₁₆ in. long, pistil to 2½ in. long; fr. fleshy, indehiscent. Tex. and n. Mex.

constricta Buckl. [*Y. tenuistyla* Trel.]. Stemless or with short, prostrate sts.; lvs. linear, to 26 in. long, ⅝ in. wide, flat to 3-angled, pale to dark green, striate, margin white or green, thread-bearing; infl. paniculate, to about 10 ft.; fls. greenish-white, to 2 in. long, segms. united basally; fr. dehiscent, usually constricted. Tex.

elata Engelm. SOAP TREE, SOAPWEED, PALMELLA. St. to 20 ft., trunk simple or branched; lvs. flexuous, linear, to 38 in. long, 1 in. wide, striate, pale green, margins white or greenish, finely thread-bearing; infl. paniculate, to nearly 10 ft.; fls. white to green or tinged with pink, to 2¼ in. long, segms. shortly united basally; fr. dehiscent, to nearly 3 in. long, seeds thin, winged. W. Tex., Ariz., Mex.

elephantipes Regel [*Y. gigantea* Lem.; *Y. guatemalensis* Bak.]. SPINELESS Y. Arborescent, st. to 30 ft., branched, trunk often thickened and rough; lvs. to 4 ft. long, 3 in. wide, margins rough; infl. paniculate; fls. white or creamy-white. Mex. Cult. in Guatemala.

filamentosa L. ADAM'S-NEEDLE, NEEDLE PALM. Nearly stemless; lvs. to 2½ ft. long, 1 in. wide, spatulate, abruptly narrowed to a stout terminal spine, margins with long curly threads; infl. paniculate, to 15 ft.; fls. nearly white, to 2 in. long; fr. dry, dehiscent. N.C., s. to Fla. and Miss. Hardy. Much material distributed under this name is actually *Y. flaccida* or *Y. Smalliana.*

flaccida Haw. Often grown as *Y. filamentosa*, but differing in having lvs. less rigid, attenuate from base to apex, and with straight marginal fibers. N.C. to Ala.

gigantea: *Y. elephantipes.*

Gilbertiana (Trel.) Rydb. Stemless, forming dense small clumps; lvs. lanceolate to spatulate-lanceolate, to 20 in. long, 1¾ in. wide, pale green, margins white or brown, eventually with curly fibers; infl. a raceme, sometimes with a few basal brs., to about 30 in. long, peduncle seldom longer than lvs.; fls. yellow or greenish-yellow, often tinged with purple, to 2¼ in. long; fr. dehiscent, to 1¾ in. long, seeds narrowly winged. Utah.

glauca Nutt. ex J. Fraser [*Y. angustifolia* Pursh]. SOAPWEED, SOAPWELL. Sts. short, prostrate, forming clumps; lvs. linear, to 28 in. long, ½ in. wide, pale green, margins white or greenish-white, thread-bearing; infl. racemose, sometimes with a few abortive basal branchlets, to 3 ft.; fls. fragrant, greenish-cream, often tinged rosy-brown, segms. separate or briefly united basally, to 2½ in. long, style dark green, swollen; fr. dehiscent, scarcely constricted, to 2¼ in. long. S. Dak. to New Mex. Hardy. Cv. 'Rosea'. Fls. tinted rose outside.

gloriosa L. SPANISH-DAGGER, PALM LILY, ROMAN-CANDLE, LORD'S-CANDLESTICK. Sts. to 8 ft., trunk short; lvs. to 2½ ft. long, 2 in. wide, with stiff terminal point; fls. greenish-white to reddish, 4 in. across; fr. indehiscent but scarcely fleshy, 6-ribbed, seeds thin, shining. N.C. to Fla.

guatemalensis: *Y. elephantipes.*

Harrimaniae Trel. Thought to represent a hybrid between *Y. Gilbertiana* and *Y. neomexicana*; some material cult. as *Y. Harrimaniae* may be one or the other of these spp.

intermedia McKelv. Variable and now thought to represent hybrids, chiefly among spp. of the *Y. glauca* alliance.

Jaegerana: see *Y. brevifolia* var.

louisianensis Trel. Stemless or nearly so; lvs. flexuous but wiry, to 1½ ft. long or rarely more, to ¾ in. wide, margins white; infl paniculate, to about 9 ft.; fls. greenish-white, style green and swollen; fr. dehiscent, erect. La. Most material bearing this name probably does not represent the true sp., which may be of hybrid origin.

macrocarpa: a name confused in its application; material so listed may be referable to *Y. Torreyi, Y. Schottii,* or *Y. schidigera.*

mohavensis: *Y. schidigera.*

neomexicana Woot. & Standl. Similar to *Y. Gilbertiana,* but differing in having lvs. linear to lanceolate, peduncle usually longer than foliage, and fls. white. Colo., s. to New Mex. and Okla.

pallida McKelv. Differs from *Y. rupicola* in having 10–30 rosettes in a clump, lvs. flat, margins bright yellow; infl. with wide-spreading brs.; fls. with stoutish style and erect or only slightly spreading stigmas. Ne. Tex.

parviflora: a listed name, perhaps for small-fld. forms of *Y. Torreyi,* which were once separated as *Y. Torreyi* forma *parviflora* McKelv.

recurvifolia Salisb. St. to 6 ft., trunk branching; lvs. sword-shaped, 2 in. wide, recurving; fr. indehiscent but dry, 6-winged, seeds thin. Ga. to Miss. Var. **variegata** (Carrière) Trel. Lvs. with central yellow stripe.

Reverchonii Trel. SAN ANGELO Y. Similar to *Y. rupicola,* but plants forming a dense clump; lvs. not twisted, to ¾ in. wide, light glaucous-green. S. Tex.

rigida (Engelm.) Trel. St. to about 15 ft., simple or with few brs.; lvs. rigidly spreading, mostly concave, to 2 ft. long, 1¼ in. wide, glaucous, margins yellow, minutely denticulate; infl. paniculate; fls. not very large; fr. dehiscent, mucronate, the valves flat on the back. Mex.

rostrata Engelm. ex Trel. Aborescent, sts. 1–5, to nearly 15 ft.; lvs. in a symmetrical rosette, slender, to 2 ft. long, ⅝ in. wide, glaucous, margins yellow, minutely denticulate; infl. paniculate, to 28 in. long; fls. white, to 2 in. long; fr. dehiscent, to nearly 3 in. long. Tex. and n. Mex.

rupicola Scheele. TWISTED-LEAF Y. Stemless, forming an open clump of scattered rosettes; lvs. twisted, concave, to nearly 2 ft. long, 1⅝ in. wide, dark green, margins reddish-brown to yellow, minutely denticulate; infl. paniculate, to 3 ft. long; fls. white or greenish-white, to 2¾ in. long, stigma 3-lobed; fr. dehiscent, to 2⅛ in. long. S.-cent. Tex.

schidigera Roezl ex Ortg. [*Y. mohavensis* Sarg.]. Shrubby or with sts. to 8 ft., forming clumps; lvs. sword-shaped, broadest at middle, to 2½ ft. long, 2 in. wide, yellow-green, margins thick, with coarse fibers; infl. paniculate, scarcely longer than lvs.; fls. white or cream, commonly tinged with lavender or purple, to 1¾ in. long, ovary abruptly tapered at apex, style to 1/16 in. long; fr. indehiscent, to nearly 4 in. long, seeds thick, rough, wingless. S. Calif. and Nev., s. to n. Baja Calif. and Ariz.

Schottii Engelm. St. to about 15 ft.; lvs. in terminal rosettes or along st., rather thin and flexuous, to 3 ft. long, 2¼ in. wide, margins without

fibers or with very fine fibers; infl. paniculate, puberulent, somewhat longer than lvs.; fls. small, white, to 1⅜ in. long; fr. indehiscent, to 4¼ in. long, seeds rough, wingless. Sw. New Mex., se. Ariz., and n. Mex.

Smalliana Fern. [*Y. filamentosa* of many auths., not L.]. ADAM'S-NEEDLE, BEAR GRASS. Stemless; lvs. firm, erect and spreading, tapered to both ends, to 2 ft. long, margins with curly fibers; infl. paniculate, tall; fls. white, style pale, stigma lobes spreading; fr. dehiscent. S.C., s. to Fla. and Miss. Cvs. include: 'Maxima', very large, with leafy bracts on scape; 'Rosea', fls. tinged with pink outside; 'Variegata', lvs. variegated.

tenuistyla: *Y. constricta.*

Thompsoniana Trel. Arborescent, to about 10 ft.; lvs. in asymmetrical rosettes, thin and flexuous, linear or broader at middle, to 1 ft. long, ½ in. wide, margins yellow or brownish, minutely denticulate; infl. paniculate, longer than lvs.; fls. white, to 2⅝ in. long, stigma 3-lobed; fr. dehiscent, to 2¾ in. long, seeds flat, wingless. S. Tex.

Torreyi Shafer. To 18 ft., with few brs.; lvs. to 3 ft. long, with short, stout terminal spine, margins thread-bearing; infl. paniculate, glabrous; fls. creamy-white; fr. indehiscent. New Mex., Tex., and n. Mex. Differs from *Y. schidigera* in having the ovary gradually tapered from base to style, which is ⅛–5/16 in. long.

Treculeana Carrière. SPANISH-DAGGER, PALMA PITA. Arborescent, to more than 10 ft.; lvs. in a large, symmetrical rosette, rigid, sword-shaped, to 39 in. long, 3¼ in. wide, margins entire or with few, fine, straight fibers; infl. paniculate, glabrous, longer than lvs.; fls. white or tinged with purple, to 1⅝ in. long; fr. indehiscent, to 4 in. long, seeds thick, rough, wingless. S.-cent. Tex. and w. Mex.

utahensis McKelv. Apparently a hybrid between spp. of the *Y. glauca* and *Y. elata* alliances.

verdiensis McKelv. Apparently a hybrid between spp. of the *Y. glauca* and *Y. elata* alliances.

Whipplei Torr. [*Hesperoyucca Whipplei* (Torr.) Trel.]. OUR-LORD'S-CANDLE. Stemless or nearly so; lvs. rigid, to 1¾ ft. long, ¾ in. wide, with terminal spine, often glaucous, margins yellow to brown, finely toothed; infl. paniculate, on scapes to 12 ft.; fls. fragrant, creamy-white, sometimes tinged with purple, to 2⅝ in. long, stigma capitate, bright green, with long white papillae; fr. dehiscent, to 2 in. long, obovoid or nearly cylindrical, tipped with an abrupt short point. Calif., Baja Calif. Var. **Whipplei.** The typical var.; st. solitary, plant dying after flowering. Var. **caespitosa** M. E. Jones. Cespitose, dense, compact, secondary rosettes formed in seedling stage and in axils of lvs., usually many rosettes in a large clump and with several fl. stalks each spring. Var. **intermedia** (Haines) Webber. Secondary rosettes formed after flowering near base of old fl. stalks, clump rather small, with only one fl. stalk each spring. Var. **percursa** (Haines) Webber. Forming large, rather open clump, with secondary rosettes developed chiefly from rhizomes.

ZALACCA: *SALACCA.*

ZALUZIANSKYA F. W. Schmidt [*Nycterinia* D. Don]. *Scrophulariaceae.* About 40 spp. of more or less viscid ann. or per. herbs, or subshrubs, native to S. Afr.; lvs. simple, entire or toothed, lower lvs. opp., upper lvs. often alt.; fls. of various colors, in terminal spikes, calyx ovoid-tubular, 5-toothed, 2-lipped or 2-parted, corolla tubular, limb 5-lobed, nearly regular to 2-lipped, stamens 4 or 2; fr. a septicidal, 2-valved caps. Flowers especially fragrant toward evening.

Zaluzianskyas are grown as ornamentals and for their fragrance, usually from seeds sown indoors in early spring or in the autumn and the plants wintered in a cold frame.

capensis Walp. [*Nycterinia capensis* (Walp.) Benth.]. NIGHT PHLOX. Erect or ascending ann., to 1½ ft.; lvs. linear, to 2 in. long; fls. white inside, purple-black outside and pubescent, to 1¾ in. long, stamens 4.

selaginoides: *Z. villosa.*

villosa F. W. Schmidt [*Z. selaginoides* Walp.; *Nycterinia villosa* (F. W. Schmidt) Benth.]. Ann., to 1 ft., sts. decumbent; lower lvs. obovate, to 1 in. long, upper lvs. linear-spatulate; fls. white or lilac inside, purple outside and nearly glabrous, to 1 in. long, stamens 2.

ZAMIA L. *Zamiaceae.* About 40 spp. of somewhat palm-like, dioecious, mostly low plants, native to trop. and subtrop. Amer., with trunk normally short, or underground and tuberous; lvs. pinnate; cones with sporophylls (cone scales) borne in vertical rows. The spp. are difficult to distinguish; the width and size of pinnae vary with age and growing conditions, and cones are essential for identification.

Several of the species yield a starchy sago. Sometimes planted under glass or outdoors in Zone 10. Viable seeds often produced. For culture see *Cycads.*

Altensteinii: *Encephalartos Altensteinii.*

angustifolia Jacq. Trunk small; lvs. with smooth petioles, pinnae in 4–60 pairs, narrowly linear, to 10 in. long, denticulate at tip; cones to 2¼ in. long, with tomentose scales. Cuba.

debilis Ait. [*Z. media* Jacq.]. Trunk bulbous or cylindrical, to 6 in. high; lvs. glabrous, to 28 in. long, pinnae in 12–27 pairs, narrowly linear-lanceolate, rusty-tomentose beneath when young, nearly smooth in age; male cones to 3¼ in. long, female cones to 3¾ in. long, 1–2 in. wide, the exterior faces of ends of scales hexagonal, horizontally elongate, brown-tomentose. W. Indies.

Fischeri Miq. Trunk eventually thick; lvs. to 16 in. long, pinnae in 9–17 pairs, narrowly lanceolate, serrulate above the middle, petioles cylindrical; cones 1–2¾ in. long, with tomentose scales. Mex.

floridana A. DC. COONTIE, COMPTIE, SEMINOLE-BREAD. Trunk short, sometimes underground, tuberlike; pinnae to 6 in. long and ¼ in. wide, margins revolute. Fla.

furfuracea: *Z. pumila.*

integrifolia Ait. SAGO CYCAS, COMPTIE, COONTIE, SEMINOLE-BREAD. Trunk to 1½ ft. high; lvs. with angled petioles, pinnae in 6–18 pairs, entire or only slightly toothed toward tip. Fla. and W. Indies.

Loddigesii Miq. [*Z. mexicana* Miq.]. Trunk to 8 in. high; lvs. with prickly petiole, pinnae in 3–27 pairs, variable, linear-lanceolate to obovate-oblong, puberulous below, finely spiny-toothed above the middle. Mex.

media: *Z. debilis.*

mexicana: *Z. Loddigesii.*

pumila L. [*Z. furfuracea* L.f.; *Z. silvicola* Small; *Z. umbrosa* Small]. FLORIDA ARROWROOT, SAGO CYCAS, COMPTIE, COONTIE, SEMINOLE-BREAD. Trunk to 6 in. high or wholly underground; lvs. 2–4 ft. long, pinnae in 2–13 pairs, linear to lanceolate or oblong-obovate, margins toothed above the middle, often revolute, petioles prickly; male cones cylindrical, to 4 in. long, often clustered, female cones elongate-ovoid, to 5 in. long, the exterior faces of the ends of the scales hexagonal, horizontally elongated. Fla., W. Indies, Mex.

Skinneri Warsz. Trunk to 3 ft. high or more; lvs. with petiole cylindrical, glabrous, pinnae in 2–11 pairs, 8–12 in. long, oblong-lanceolate to broadly ovate; male cones long-cylindrical, in clusters of 3–4. Wet forests, Guatemala to Panama.

umbrosa: *Z. pumila.*

villosa: *Encephalartos villosus.*

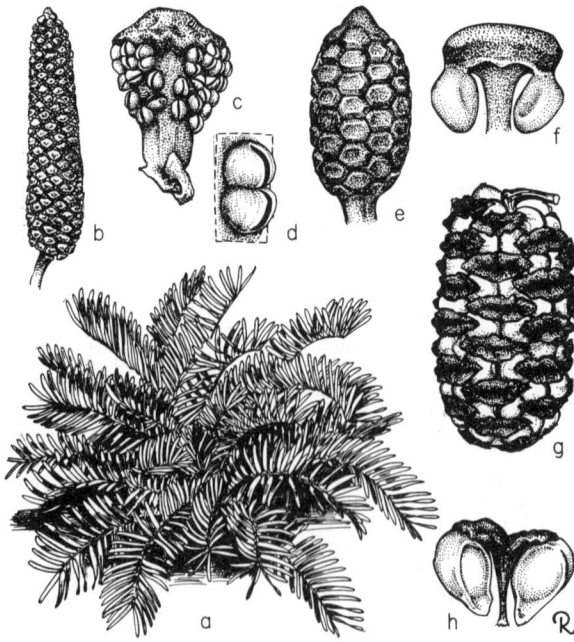

ZAMIACEAE. *Zamia floridana:* **a,** plant, much reduced; **b,** male cone, × ³⁄₈; **c,** male sporophyll, × 2; **d,** portion of male sporophyll with two sporangia, × 6; **e,** female cone, × ³⁄₈; **f,** female sporophyll with two ovules, × 1; **g,** mature female cone, × ⅓; **h,** mature female sporophyll with two seeds, × ½.

ZAMIACEAE Rchb. ZAMIA FAMILY, CYCADS. Gymnosperms; 8 genera and perhaps 80 spp. of palmlike, dioecious plants, native to trop. or warm-temp. Afr., Australia, and Amer.; lvs. pinnate or 2-pinnate, in a rosette or crown. Sometimes included in the Cycadaceae, but differing in having pinnae with more numerous, more or less parallel longitudinal veins but no midrib; both male and female sporophylls (cone scales) in determinate cones; and scales of female cones more or less peltate, with thickened and laterally expanded end, and 2 ovules or rarely more attached on the inner side. Juvenile plants are difficult to identify. Cult. genera are: *Bowenia, Ceratozamia, Dioon, Encephalartos, Lepidozamia, Macrozamia, Microcycas,* and *Zamia.*

ZAMIOCULCAS Schott. *Araceae.* One sp., a stemless herb of S. Afr.; lvs. arising directly from thick horizontal rhizomes, large, pinnately compound; fls. functionally unisexual, perianth 4-parted.

For culture see *Callopsis.* Propagation by division or leaflet cuttings.

zamiifolia (Lodd.) Engl. To 3 ft.; lfts. 6–8 pairs, elliptic, to 6 in. long and 2 in. wide, petioles cylindrical, inflated toward base, narrowed above; peduncle 1½ in. long, spathe green, to 2½ in. long, convolute below, blade reflexed, spadix shorter, white, the upper part clavate, male, exposed. Tanzania.

ZANNICHELLIA L. HORNED PONDWEED. *Zannichelliaceae.* One sp., a cosmopolitan, monoecious herb of fresh or brackish water; male and female fls. usually in same axil, the male of a single stamen, female of usually 4 distinct carpels; fr. an oblong, beaked nutlet.

palustris L. Slender, branched herb; lvs. linear-filiform; fr. to ⅛ in. long, beak slender, about half as long. Sometimes cult. in aquaria.

ZANNICHELLIACEAE Dumort. HORNED PONDWEED FAMILY. Monocot.; 6 genera of monoecious or dioecious, rhizomatous, aquatic herbs mainly of saline or brackish waters, of wide distribution; lvs. linear, with usually strap-shaped sheaths; fls. minute, axillary, solitary or in cymes, perianth of 3 small scales or none, stamens 1–3, carpels 1–9, separate, ovules solitary, pendulous. *Zannichellia* is sometimes cult. in aquaria.

ZANTEDESCHIA K. Spreng. [*Richardia* Kunth]. CALLA, CALLA LILY. *Araceae.* Six spp. of stemless herbs with thick rhizomes, native to S. Afr.; lvs. entire, petioles long, stout; spathe showy, expanded above and convolute basally about the shorter spadix; fls. unisexual, perianth absent. (The wild calla, *Calla palustris,* is a small herb of n. temp. regions.)

Popular greenhouse or indoor plants, grown outdoors in mild regions; winter-hardy in Zone 8. Indoors, callas do best if they are rested throughout the summer. Rhizomes should be planted in rich fibrous soil in 6 in. pots and kept fairly cool until the roots have formed. They may then be given heat, strong light, and plenty of water. After blossoms appear, applications of liquid fertilizer may be beneficial. Propagated by division or offsets; seeds of the species and of mixed hybrids are also available.

aethiopica (L.) K. Spreng. [*Z. africana* Hort.; *Richardia africana* Kunth; *R. aethiopica* Hort.]. FLORIST'S C., GARDEN C., ARUM LILY, CALLA L., PIG L., TRUMPET L., COMMON C. To 3 ft. or more; lf. blades sagittate, to 18 in. long and 10 in. wide, glossy, green; peduncle longer than lvs., spathe 5–10 in. long, milky-white, blade flaring, recurved, cuspidate, spadix yellow, fragrant. Transvaal; naturalized in many frost-free areas of the world. Cv. **'Childsiana'.** Very floriferous dwarf form.

africana: *Z. aethiopica.*

albomaculata (Hook.) Baill. [*Z. melanoleuca* (Hook.f.) Engl.; *Richardia albomaculata* Hook.; *R. melanoleuca* Hook.f.]. SPOTTED C., BLACK-THROATED C. Lf. blades very elongate-triangular, to 18 in. long, with short, subhastate basal lobes, white-spotted, petioles to 3 ft. long; spathe to 4½ in. long, convolute or tube open to the base, whitish to pale yellow or rarely pink, basally marked with purple on the inside, blade relatively narrow. S. Afr. to Angola and Zambia.

Childsiana: a listed name of no botanical standing, used for *Z. aethiopica* cv. 'Childsiana'.

Elliottiana (W. Wats.) Engl. [*Richardia Elliottiana* W. Wats.]. GOLDEN C., YELLOW C. Lf. blades ovate, to 11 in. long and nearly as wide, cordate or sagittate, white-spotted, petioles to 2 ft.; spathe to 6 in. long, bright yellow inside, greenish-yellow outside, blade flaring and recurved. S. Afr.

hygrophila: *Arum hygrophilum.*

melanoleuca: *Z. albomaculata.*

Rehmannii Engl. [*Richardia Rehmannii* (Engl.) N. E. Br. ex W. Harrow]. PINK C., RED C. To 2 ft.; lf. blades narrowly elliptic-lanceolate, to 12 in. long and 2 in. wide, tapering at each end and decurrent on the petioles, sometimes white-spotted; spathe about 5 in. long, rosy-purplish varying to white with pink margins. S. Afr.

ZANTHORHIZA: *XANTHORHIZA:* **Z. apiifolia:** *X. simplicissima.*

ZANTHOXYLUM L. (Incorrectly spelled *Xanthoxylum*). [*Fagara* L.]. PRICKLY ASH. *Rutaceae.* About 200 spp. of prickly, deciduous or evergreen shrubs or trees with aromatic bark, native to N. and S. Amer., Afr., Asia, and Australia; lvs. alt., mostly pinnate, sometimes of 1 lft., glandular-dotted; fls. small, in spikes, cymes, or panicles, unisexual or bisexual, sepals, petals, and stamens 3–5, petals sometimes 0; fr. a 2-valved follicle.

Zanthoxylum americanum is very hardy and most of the other species thrive in the middle latitudes. Several species have medicinal properties and others, like the WEST INDIAN SATINWOOD (*Z. flavum* Vahl), provide a fine cabinetwood. Propagated by seeds, suckers, and root cuttings.

ailanthoides Siebold & Zucc. [*Fagara ailanthoides* (Siebold & Zucc.) Engl.]. Deciduous tree, to 60 ft.; lvs. to 1½ ft. long, lfts. 11–23, ovate-lanceolate to ovate, to 5 in. long; fls. in cymes to 5 in. across or more. Japan and China. Zone 8.

americanum Mill. NORTHERN P. A., TOOTHACHE TREE. Aromatic shrub or tree, to 25 ft.; lvs. to 1 ft. long, lfts. 5–11, oblong to elliptic or ovate, to 2½ in. long; fls. greenish-yellow, in axillary cymes, appearing before the lvs. Que. to N.Dak., s. to Fla., Ala., and Okla. Zone 4. Dried bark has medicinal uses.

clava-Herculis L. SOUTHERN P. A., HERCULES'-CLUB, SEA ASH, PEPPERWOOD. Tall shrub or small tree; lvs. 1 ft. long, lfts. 5–19, lanceolate to ovate, to 2 in. long, oblique, closely serrate, petiole and rachis prickly; fls. in terminal panicles. Se. Va. to Fla., w. to Tex. and Okla. Zone 8. Var. **fruticosum** (A. Gray) S. Wats. [*Z. hirsutum* Buckl.; *Fagara fruticosa* (A. Gray) Small]. Lvs. shorter, 1–5 in. long, lfts. smaller, blunter, to 1⅜ in. long. Tex. Dried bark has medicinal uses.

Fagara (L.) Sarg. WILD LIME. Evergreen shrub or tree, to 30 ft.; lvs. to 4 in. long, lfts. 5–13, elliptic, obovate, or suborbicular, to 1 in. long, crenulate, petiole and rachis winged; fls. 4-merous, in cylindrical axillary cymes. Sw. Tex. and Fla., s. to S. Amer. and W. Indies. Zone 9.

fruticosum: *Z. clava-Herculis* var.

hirsutum: *Z. clava-Herculis* var. *fruticosum.*

piperitum DC. JAPAN PEPPER. Compact shrub or small tree, to 20 ft., with paired spines; lvs. to 6 in. long, lfts. 11–23, ovate, to 1½ in. long; fls. green, in cymes to 2 in. across. N. China, Korea, Japan. Cult. in Japan and elsewhere. Zone 7.

schinifolium Siebold & Zucc. [*Fagara schinifolia* (Siebold & Zucc.) Engl.]. Deciduous shrub or small tree, with spines not paired; lvs. to 7 in. long, lfts. 11–21, lanceolate, to 1½ in. long; fls. greenish, in cymes 4 in. across. China, Korea, Japan. Zone 7.

simulans Hance. Shrub or tree, to 25 ft., with flattened spines; lvs. mostly to 5 in. long, lfts. 7–11, ovate, to 2 in. long, crenate-serrulate; fls. in cymes 2½ in. across. China.

ZAUSCHNERIA K. Presl. CALIFORNIA FUCHSIA. *Onagraceae.* Four spp. of per. herbs, sometimes woody at base, with shredding epidermis on lower sts., usually much-branched and leafy; lvs. alt. or the lower opp.; fls. in spikes, fuchsialike, horizontal, large, day-flowering, calyx tube elongate, sepals and petals 4, red, stamens 8, ovary inferior; fr. a caps., seeds with tuft of hairs.

Propagated by seeds, cuttings, or division; only *Z. californica* subsp. *latifolia* is really hardy in the North.

arizonica: *Z. californica* subsp. *latifolia.*

californica K. Presl [*Z. californica* subsp. *angustifolia* Keck]. Sts. 1–2 ft., woody at base, pubescent; lvs. linear, tomentose-canescent; fls. 1–1½ in. long. Coast, Calif. Subsp. *latifolia* (Hook.) Keck [*Z. arizonica* A. Davids.; *Z. californica* var. *latifolia* Hook.; *Z. latifolia* Greene]. Herbaceous, sts. shorter; lvs. ovate to lanceolate-ovate, often glandular. Montane, w. U.S. Subsp. **mexicana** (K. Presl) Raven [*Z. californica* var. *villosa* (Greene) Jeps.; *Z. mexicana* K. Presl]. Lvs. lanceolate, green to gray-pilose. Calif. Var. **Etteri:** a listed name of no botanical standing. Var. **microphylla:** *Z. cana.* Var. **splendens:** a listed name of no botanical standing. Var. **villosa:** *Z. californica* subsp. *mexicana.*

cana Greene [*Z. californica* var. *microphylla* A. Gray; *Z. microphylla* (A. Gray) Moxl.]. Lvs. much fascicled, gray, less than ⅛ in. wide. Coastal, Calif.

latifolia: *Z. californica* subsp.

macrophylla: a listed name, probably an error for *Z. microphylla.*

microphylla: *Z. cana.*

ZEA L. [*Euchlaena* Schrad.]. *Gramineae.* Two or perhaps 3 spp. of robust ann. or per. grasses, native in trop. Amer.; male spikelets 2-fld., in 2's or 3's along one side of racemes usually in a terminal panicle (tassel), one sessile, the other pedicelled, glumes membranous, lemma and palea hyaline, female spikelets paired, of 1 fertile and 1 usually sterile floret, borne in 2 to many rows along a usually lateral spike (ear) enclosed by 1 to several bracts (husks), glumes broad, rounded or emarginate at apex, lemma hyaline, styles elongate, protruding from the husks. For terminology see *Gramineae.*

Curagua: *Z. Mays* var.

gracillima: a listed name of no botanical standing for *Z. Mays* var.

japonica: *Z. Mays* var.

Mays L. CORN, INDIAN C., MAIZE. Tall, robust ann., to 15 ft., suckering at base; lf. sheaths overlapping, blades broad, conspicuously

2-ranked, to 3 ft. long, 4 in. wide; male spikelets in many long, spike-like racemes, which form large spreading terminal panicles, female infl. in lf. axils, enclosed in large foliaceous bracts, spikelets in 8–16 or even as many as 30 rows on a thickened, almost woody axis (cob), the long styles (silks) protruding; grains at maturity greatly exceeding the glumes, flattened, white, yellow, red, or black. Cultigen of trop. Amer. origin, the wild parent sp. long extinct. One of the world's 3 most important cereal crops; widely cult. for food for man and domestic animals. Var. **Curagua** (Mol.) Alef. [*Z. Curagua* Mol.]. Sts. very robust; lvs. green; endosperm as in var. *praecox*. Var. **dentata**: a name of no botanical standing used for var. *indentata*. Var. **everta**: var. *praecox*. Var. **gracillima** Körn. [*Z. gracillima* Hort.]. Very dwarf; lvs. narrow, green. Cult. for ornament. Cv. 'Variegata'. Lvs. variegated. Var. **indentata** (Sturtev.) L. H. Bailey [var. *dentata* Hort.]. DENT C., DENT M. Sts. usually tall; ears usually relatively thick, thick, and heavy; grains yellow or white, falling in or becoming indented at the top. The principal commercial corn cult.; grown for grain, fodder, and silage. Var. **indurata** (Sturtev.) L. H. Bailey. FLINT C., FLINT M. Plants early-maturing, with tendency to produce 2 ears; ears long, cylindrical; grains hard, smooth, in 8–10 rows. An old var. Var. **japonica** (Van Houtte) A. Wood [*Z. japonica* Van Houtte; cvs. 'Variegata' and 'Quadricolor']. Lvs. striped longitudinally with yellow and nearly white, and sometimes with pink. Cult. for ornament. Cv. 'Quadricolor': var. *japonica*. Cv. 'Variegata': var. *japonica*. Var. **praecox** Bonaf. [Var. *everta* (Sturtev.) L. H. Bailey]. POPCORN, POP M. Plant and ear small; grains small, usually much pointed at base and sometimes at apex, containing a very hard endosperm that explodes or pops when heated. Var. **rugosa** Bonaf. [var. *saccharata* (Sturtev.) L. H. Bailey]. SWEET C., SUGAR C., SWEET M., SUGAR M. Sts. small or of medium size; grains much wrinkled when mature and dried, the horny endosperm more or less translucent, sweet. The common table and canning corn, usually used in the tender, somewhat immature state. Var. **saccharata**: var. *rugosa*. Var. **tunicata** Larrañ. ex St.-Hil. POD C., POD M. Glumes elongated and enveloping each kernel. A primitive var. of corn, grown as a curiosity. For culture see *Corn*.

mexicana (Schrad.) Reeves & Manglesd. [*Euchlaena mexicana* Schrad.]. TEOSINTE. Ann., sts. to 10 or rarely 15 ft., coarse, branching at base, flattened on one side between the dark-colored fruiting nodes; lf. blades sword-shaped, long-pointed, to 3¼ in. wide, midrib prominent, sheaths expanded, very strongly veined; female spikelets solitary on opp. sides of an obliquely articulate rachis, first glume hard, covering the cavity, second glume membranous, lemma hyaline; grains about ¼ in. long, glossy, with a marking resembling an insect pupa on the face. Mex. Planted in southernmost states for forage. Closely related to and resembling *Z. Mays*, with which it readily hybridizes.

quadricolor: a listed name of no botanical standing. See *Z. Mays* var. *japonica*.

ZEBRINA Schnizl. *Commelinaceae*.
Two spp. of trailing succulent herbs, native to Mex. and Guatemala; brs. breaking through the lf. sheaths; lvs. alt.; infl. of paired cincinni, each pair subtended by 2 leafy bracts on a peduncle; sepals united into a hyaline, unequally lobed tube, petals united into a tube with spreading lobes, stamens 6, filaments bearded, ovary 3-celled, each cell with 2 ovules; fr. a caps.

Useful as a ground cover in the extreme South, and grown under benches or in baskets in the greenhouse and in the home. Propagated by stem cuttings.

pendula Schnizl. [*Tradescantia zebrina* Hort.]. WANDERING JEW, INCH PLANT. Decumbent per., rooting at nodes; lvs. ovate-oblong, striped with whitish above, purple beneath in the typical form, or variously variegated or solid dark red or red-green; infl. bracts nearly glabrous to villous at base or throughout; fls. rose-pink. Mex. Cv. 'Purpusii' [*Z. Purpusii* Brückn.]. Lvs. dark red or red-green, not striped, lvs. and bracts villous throughout. Cv. 'Quadricolor' [*Tradescantia multicolor* Hort.; *T. quadricolor* Hort.]. Lvs. metallic-green, striped with green, red, and white.

Purpusii: *Z. pendula* cv.

ZELKOVA Spach. *Ulmaceae*.
About 5 spp. of deciduous, elmlike trees or shrubs, native to w. and e. Asia; lvs. alt., toothed, pinnately veined; fls. unisexual and bisexual, small and inconspicuous, appearing in spring with lvs.; fr. a small, asymmetrical drupe.

Of easy culture, propagated by seeds, layers, and grafting on elms; transplants easily when young. Zone 5.

carpinifolia (Pall.) C. Koch. To 80 ft.; lvs. elliptic to oblong, to 2 in. long, acute, wavy-toothed, with 6–8 pairs of veins, pubescent on veins beneath. Caucasus.

Keakii: *Z. serrata*.

serrata (Thunb.) Mak. [*Z. Keakii* (Siebold) Maxim.]. JAPANESE Z., SAW-LEAF Z. To 100 ft.; lvs. ovate or oblong-ovate, 2–5 in. long, acuminate, sharply toothed, with 8–14 pairs of veins, glabrous beneath. Japan, where an important timber tree and a favorite bonsai subject.

sinica C. K. Schneid. To 60 ft.; lvs. ovate-oblong, to 2 in. long, wavy-toothed, with usually 7–10 pairs of veins. China.

ZENOBIA D. Don. *Ericaceae*.
One sp., a deciduous to semievergreen shrub, native in se. U.S.; lvs. simple, alt.; fls. white, in axillary clusters, calyx 5-lobed, corolla campanulate, stamens 10, anthers 4-awned; fr. a 5-valved caps., seeds not winged.

Does best in sandy or peaty soil and is also adapted for forcing in the greenhouse. Propagated by seeds, by layers, by cuttings of half-ripened wood or green wood from forced plants.

pulverulenta (Bartr. ex Willd.) Pollard [*Z. speciosa* (Michx.) D. Don; *Andromeda speciosa* Michx.]. Glabrous shrub, to 6 ft., sts. often glaucous; lvs. oblong to elliptic, to 3 in. long, entire to serrulate-crenate, glaucous beneath; fls. to ½ in. across, fragrant. Late spring. Coastal plain, se. Va. to ne. S.C. Zone 6. Forma **nitida** (Michx.) Fern. [var. *nuda* (Venten.) Rehd.; *Andromeda cassinifolia* Venten.]. Lvs. green, without bloom.

speciosa: *Z. pulverulenta*.

ZEPHYRANTHES Herb. [*Atamosco* Adans.; *Cooperia* Herb.; *Pyrolirion* Herb.].
ZEPHYR LILY, RAIN L., FAIRY L. *Amaryllidaceae*. About 40 spp. of small bulbous herbs, native to warm regions of W. Hemisphere; lvs. basal, grasslike, mostly ann.; fls. sessile or pedicelled, solitary on a hollow scape and subtended by 2 spathe valves united at base but separating at apex along 1 or both sides; perianth white, yellow, pink, or red, funnelform, tube short or long, lobes 6, stamens equal or in 2 series, erect or declinate, stigma mostly trifid; fr. a loculicidal caps.

Hardy outdoors fairly far north, with winter protection, but in regions of heavy frosts the bulbs should be stored in winter.

×**Ajax** Hort. A hybrid of uncertain parentage; lvs. linear, to 8 in. long; scape 6–8 in. long; fls. 1½ in. across, light yellow.

alba: a listed name of no botanical standing, possibly referable to *Z. candida*.

Andersonii: *Habranthus Andersonii*.

Atamasco (L.) Herb. [*Amaryllis Atamasco* L.]. ATAMASCO LILY. To 1 ft.; lvs. narrowly linear, to 1 ft. long, sharp-edged, acute to acuminate; spathe ¼–⅓ as long as fl., pedicel shorter than the spathe or rarely nearly absent; perianth white, sometimes tinged with purple, to 3 in. long, lobes with spreading tips, stigma trifid. Spring. Se. Va. to Fla. and Ala. Plants offered under this name are sometimes *Z. candida*.

aurea: *Z. tubiflora*.

bifolia (Aubl.) M. Roem. [*Habranthus cardinalis* (C. H. Wright) Sealy]. Lvs. linear, broader than in most other spp.; scape 6–8 in., spathe splitting apically along both sides; fl. on a pedicel longer than the spathe, large, declinate, cardinal-red. Hispaniola.

brasiliensis (Traub) Traub [*Cooperia brasiliensis* Traub]. Bulb with long neck; lvs. linear, to 2 ft. long, 3/16 in. wide; scape to 5 in.; fl. sessile, white, tinged with red outside, to 3½ in. long, tube to ¾ in. long, lobes spreading, about 1 in. long, ½ in. wide, stamens erect; caps. to ¾ in. high, ¾ in. wide. Brazil.

brazosensis (Traub) Traub [*Cooperia Drummondii* Herb., not *Z. Drummondii* D. Don]. Bulb large, nearly globose; lvs. linear, gray-green, upright or curved downward; scape 4–10 in.; fl. sessile, fragrant, white, tinged with red outside, tube to 5 in. long, lobes 1 in. long or less, overlapping below the middle; caps. to ⅜ in. long, ¾ in. wide. Night-blooming. Tex., New Mex., Mex.

californica: a listed name of uncertain application.

candida (Lindl.) Herb. Lvs. per., rushlike, thick, with blunt edges, stiff, to 1 ft. long; fl. white, sometimes tinged with rose outside, 2 in. long, stigmas not markedly cleft. Summer and autumn. La Plata region of S. Amer. Sometimes grown mistakenly as *Z. Atamasco*. Cv. 'Major' is listed.

carinata: *Z. grandiflora*.

citrina Bak. To 10 in.; lvs. to 1 ft. long, 3/16 in. wide, channelled; spathe splitting along 1 side, 2-toothed at apex; fl. on a pedicel about as long as spathe, bright yellow, 2 in. long, tube very short or absent, stigma headlike, 3-lobed. S. Amer.

Drummondii D. Don [*Cooperia pedunculata* Herb.]. Bulb flattened-globose, deeply buried at maturity; lvs. linear, ¼ in. wide or slightly more, twisted, decumbent, glaucous-green; scape 5–8 in.; fl. pedicelled, white, tinged red outside, fragrant, to 3 in. long, tube to 1½ in. long. Night-blooming. Tex., Mex.

gracilifolia: *Habranthus gracilifolius.*

grandiflora Lindl. [*Z. carinata* Herb.]. Lvs. linear, to 1 ft. long, flat; fl. on a pedicel about as long as spathe, rose or pink, to 4 in. across. Spring and summer. S. Mex. to Guatemala. Widely known in cult.; sometimes mistakenly grown under the name *Z. rosea.*

insularum: a listed name of no botanical standing for plants referable to *Z. tubispatha.*

longifolia Hemsl. To 6 in.; lvs. narrowly linear, to 9 in. long; spathe splitting along 1 side, 2-toothed at apex; fl. on a pedicel shorter than the spathe, bright yellow, coppery outside, to 1 in. long, tube short, stigma trifid. W. Tex. to Mex.

macrosiphon Bak. To 1 ft.; lvs. linear, bright green, to 1 ft. long; fl. on a pedicel about as long as spathe or a little longer, bright red, to 2¼ in. long, tube as long as lobes, stigma headlike, 3-lobed. Mex.

mesochloa Herb. Lvs. linear, to 10 in. long; scape 6–8 in.; fl. on a pedicel about as long as spathe, erect, 1¾ in. long, not opening widely, white or pinkish with green base, tube not developed. Argentina.

pseudocolchicum Kränzl. Flowering when leafless; fl. red, tube to 3¾ in. long, slender, lobes spotted, 1¼ in. long, stamens equal in length, erect, stigma headlike. Bolivia.

pulchella J. G. Sm. Lvs. linear, at first erect, twisted, later curved downward, to 10 in. long; spathe splitting along 1 side, the apex entire; fl. on a pedicel about as long as spathe, 1 in. long, buttercup-yellow, stigma headlike, 3-lobed. Se. Tex.

robusta: *Habranthus tubispathus.*

rosea Lindl. Lvs. flat, spreading, very obtuse at apex; fl. on a pedicel much longer than spathe, rose-red, about 1 in. long. Autumn. Cuba. Plants grown under this name are likely to be *Z. grandiflora.*

Simpsonii Chapm. Differs from *Z. Atamasco* in perianth tube more narrow, lobes erect or ascending, often red-margined. Fla.

Smallii (Alexand.) Traub [*Cooperia Smallii* Alexand.]. Bulb globose, to 1 in. in diam.; lvs. linear, to 6 in. long, bright green, more or less erect; scape to 6 in.; fl. on a pedicel ⅛–¼ in. long, yellow, tube green, ¾ in. long, lobes about as long as tube, often flushed with red over yellow and with green lines on the outside. Night-blooming. Tex.

sulphurea: a listed name of uncertain application.

texana: *Habranthus texanus.*

Traubii (Hayw.) Traub [*Cooperia Traubii* Hayw.]. Bulb globose, to ¾ in. in diam.; lvs. linear, reclining, to 10 in. long, glaucous; fl. sessile, starlike, white tinted with pink outside, tube long, slender, lobes narrow, separated. Night-blooming. Tex.

Treatiae S. Wats. Distinguished from *Z. Atamasco* in having lvs. nearly cylindrical, with blunt edges, and mostly obtuse. Fla., se. Ga. Cv. **'Rosea'** is listed.

tubiflora (L'Hér.) Schinz [*Z. aurea* (Ruiz & Pav.) Bak.; *Pyrolirion aureum* (Ruiz & Pav.) Herb.]. FIRE LILY. Lvs. linear, somewhat sickle-shaped, green; scape stout at base, tapering upward, spathe splitting along 2 sides; fl. deep orange, erect, opening flat, 1½–2 in. across, stigma trifid, with spatulate lobes. Peru.

tubispatha Herb. Lvs. narrow-linear, longer than the slender scape; spathe splitting along 1 side, 2-toothed at apex; fl. on a pedicel much longer than spathe, white, 2 in. long or less. Spring and summer. W. Indies. Plants grown as *Z. insularum* are this sp.

verecunda Herb. To 8 in.; lvs. narrow-linear, to 1 ft. long, becoming recurved-spreading; spathe splitting along 1 side, 2 toothed at apex; fl. sessile or nearly so, white, tinged pink outside, 1½–2 in. long, tube to ¾ in. long, Mex.

ZIGADENUS Michx. (Commonly, but not originally, spelled *Zygadenus.*) [*Anticlea* Kunth; *Toxicoscordion* Rydb.]. DEATH CAMAS, ZYGADENE. *Liliaceae.* About 15 spp. of bulbous or rhizomatous per. herbs, native to N. Amer., 1 sp. in e. Asia; sts. simple; lvs. mostly basal, linear; fls. bisexual or unisexual, greenish-white, yellowish-green, or purplish, in terminal racemes or panicles, perianth segms. 6, often joined at base, sometimes with 1 or 2 glands, persistent, stamens 6, anther sacs confluent, styles 3; fr. a 3-lobed, septicidal caps., seeds angled.

Some species of *Zigadenus* are poisonous to livestock. Occasionally grown in the wild garden. Propagated by division or seeds.

brevibracteatus (M. E. Jones) H. M. Hall. Bulbous, st. to 20 in.; basal lvs. to 1 ft. long, margins rough; fls. yellowish, ¼ in. long, in panicles, inner perianth segms. clawed. S. Calif.

elegans Pursh [*Anticlea elegans* (Pursh) Rydb.]. WHITE CAMAS, ALKALI GRASS. Bulbous, st. to 3 ft.; lvs. to 1 ft. long, keeled, glaucous, sharp-pointed; fls. to ½ in. long, in racemes, rarely in panicles, each perianth segm. with a solitary, 2-lobed gland; caps. twice as long as perianth. Minn. and Mo., w. to Alaska and Ariz.

Fremontii (Torr.) Torr. ex S. Wats. STAR Z., STAR LILY. Bulbous, st. to 3 ft.; basal lvs. to 2 ft. long and 1 in. wide, margin rough; fls. yellowish-white, ½ in. long, in racemes or panicles, perianth segms. glandular, clawed. S. Ore. to n. Baja Calif.

glaucus Nutt. WHITE CAMAS. Bulbous, st. to 3 ft.; basal lvs. to 16 in. long and ½ in. wide, leathery, keeled, glaucous; fls. white to greenish, suffused brownish or purplish, to ½ in. long, in panicles, perianth segms. with a solitary, 2-lobed, greenish or bronze gland; caps. only slightly longer than perianth. Minn. to Que. and New Bruns., s. to Ill., Va., and N.C.

gramineus: *Z. venenosus* var.

muscitoxicum: *Amianthium muscitoxicum.*

Nuttallii A. Gray [*Toxicoscordion Nuttallii* (A. Gray) Rydb.]. DEATH CAMAS, POISON C., MERRYHEARTS. Bulbous, st. stout, to 2½ ft.; basal lvs. to 1½ ft. long and ½ in. wide, leathery, sickle-shaped; fls. yellowish-white, ½ in. across, in racemes or rarely in panicles, perianth segms. each with a solitary basal gland. Tenn. to Kans. and Tex.

paniculatus (Nutt.) S. Wats. [*Toxicoscordion paniculatum* (Nutt.) Rydb.]. SAND CORN. Bulbous, st. to 2 ft.; basal lvs. to 20 in. long and ¾ in. wide, folded, margin rough; fls. yellowish-white, ⅛ in. long, in panicles, inner perianth segms. clawed, segms. with green glands, anthers yellow. Wash. to Mont., s. to n. Calif., Ariz., and New Mex.

venenosus S. Wats. [*Toxicoscordion venenosum* (S. Wats.) Rydb.]. DEATH CAMAS. Bulbous, st. slender, to 2 ft.; basal lvs. to 1 ft. long and ⅜ in. wide; fls. whitish, ⅛ in. long, in narrow racemes, perianth segms. clawed, each with a gland, anthers white. B.C. to s. Calif., e. to Mont. and Utah. Var. **gramineus** (Rydb.) Walsh ex Peck [*Z. gramineus* Rydb.; *Toxicoscordion gramineum* (Rydb.) Rydb.]. GRASSY D.C. Fls. to $^{3}/_{16}$ in. long, scarcely clawed, perianth segms. with poorly defined glands. Alta. and Sask. to Utah and New Mex.

ZINGIBER Boehmer. GINGER. *Zingiberaceae.* About 85 spp. or more of herbs in trop. Asia, with tuberous, aromatic rhizomes; sts. leafy; lvs. 2-ranked, with sheaths open opp. the blade; infl. a spike terminal on the leafy st. or more usually on a separate lateral st.; fls. solitary in axils of imbricate bracts, calyx thin, tubular, corolla tube slender, corolla lobes 3, upper lobe often broader than 2 lateral lobes, staminodial lip petal-like, 3-lobed, connective of fertile stamen crested, ovary inferior; fr. a 3-valved caps.

Some of the species are the source of commercial ginger. Gingers should have fertile soil and partial shade and require warm temperatures. Of easy cultivation in the greenhouse, but should be rested in winter. Propagated by division of rhizomes in spring.

Darceyi Hort. VARIEGATED G. A listed name of no botanical standing, applied to plants not yet placed taxonomically; sts. to 3 ft.; lvs. to 8 in. long, 2½ in. wide, bright green with creamy-white or pink margins and oblique stripes; fls. deep red.

Fairchildii: a listed name of no botanical standing.

humile: a listed name of no botanical standing.

officinale Roscoe. COMMON G., TRUE G., CANTON G. Leafy sts. to 20 in.; lvs. to 7 in. long, ¾ in. wide; infl. on a separate st., a dense spike, to 3 in. long, bracts green with translucent margin; fls. yellow-green, lip purple with cream blotches and base. Trop. se. Asia. Cvs. are sterile but widely cult. in trop. and warm temp. lands for the rhizomes, from which ginger is obtained.

Zerumbet (L.) Sm. Leafy sts. to 6 ft.; lvs. to 1 ft. long, 3 in. wide; infl. on a separate st., bracts to 1⅜ in. long, green when young, red when old; fls. white or yellowish, lip pale yellow, tinted with deeper yellow toward base. India and Malay Pen. Uses similar to *Z. officinale.*

ZINGIBERACEAE Lindl. GINGER FAMILY. Monocot.; about 40 genera of per., rhizomatous herbs, throughout the tropics; sts. often erect, canelike, in clumps; lvs. elongate, entire, with parallel or pinnate nerves, the base partly or completely tubular and sheathing the st.; infl. a spike, head, or panicle, on separate st. or terminating a leafy st.; fls. irregular, bisexual, subtended by bracts, calyx and corolla tubular, each 3-lobed, fertile stamen 1, enfolding the style, the connective often extended at the tip into an anther crest, staminodes 1 or more, one of these large and petal-like (the staminodial lip), ovary inferior, 1–3-celled, with axile or parietal placentas; fr. a 3-valved caps. or fleshy, indehiscent, and

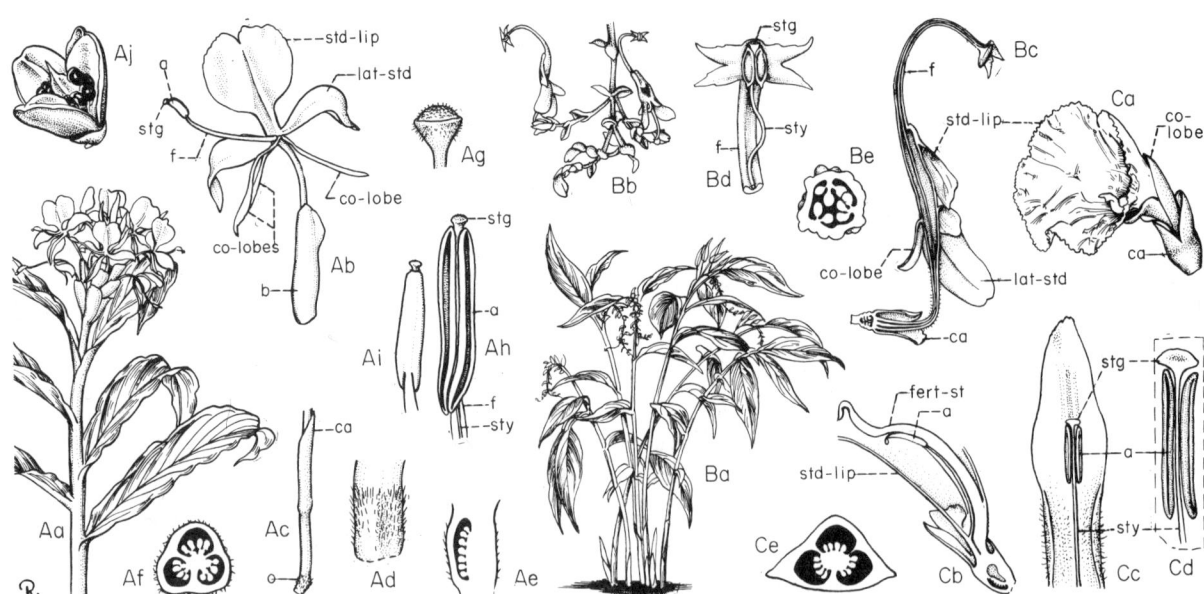

ZINGIBERACEAE. **A**, *Hedychium flavum:* **Aa**, upper part of flowering stem, × ⅙; **Ab**, flower with subtending bract, × ⅜; **Ac**, base of flower, × ½; **Ad**, ovary, × 2; **Ae**, ovary, vertical section, × 2; **Af**, ovary, cross section, × 3; **Ag**, stigma, × 3; **Ah**, anther enfolding style, front view, × 3; **Ai**, same, back view, × 2; **Aj**, fruit, × ½. **B**, *Globba bulbifera* Roxb.: **Ba**, plant, × 1/12; **Bb**, apex of inflorescence, × ½; **Bc**, flower, vertical section, × 1½; **Bd**, apex of stamen and style, × 3; **Be**, ovary, cross section, × 5. **C**, *Costus speciosus:* **Ca**, flower, × ⅜; **Cb**, lower half of flower, vertical section, × ½; **Cc**, upper part of fertile petal-like stamen, with anther enfolding style, × 1; **Cd**, same, enlarged detail, × 2; **Ce**, ovary, cross section, × 2. (a anther, b bract, ca calyx, co-lobe corolla lobe, f filament, fert-st fertile stamen, lat-std lateral staminode, o ovary, std-lip staminodial lip, stg stigma, sty style; *Globba bulbifera* representative of genus but not in general cultivation.)

berrylike. The cult. genera are: *Alpinia, Amomum, Brachychilum, Cautleya, Costus, Curcuma, Elettaria, Globba, Hedychium, Kaempferia, Nicolaia, Renealmia, Roscoea,* and *Zingiber.*

Species of several genera are grown for the ornamental flowers or foliage and others furnish dyes, perfumes, spices, condiments, and medicinal products. Culture is simple in the open in tropical and semitropical regions; members of this family commonly thrive in lowish ground. Under glass they are mostly planted in the ground or grown in tubs or very large pots. Propagation is by division of the thick rhizomes or subterranean tubers. Plants of a few genera, *Cautleya, Curcuma, Kaempferia, Roscoea,* and *Zingiber,* have a dormant stage and should be kept in a warm place over winter.

ZINNIA L. [*Crassina* Scepin]. *Compositae* (Helianthus Tribe). About 17 spp. of pubescent ann. or per. herbs or low shrubs in sw. U.S., Cent. and S. Amer., chiefly Mex.; lvs. opp., entire, usually sessile; fl. heads radiate, showy, on hollow peduncles, solitary and terminal on the brs., receptacle scaly; disc and ray fls. fertile, ray fls. often brightly colored, persistent on the achenes; achenes compressed, pappus of awns or lacking.

Zinnias are popular in the flower garden and as cut flowers. The usual garden soil is satisfactory, preferably in full sun. Propagated by seeds started indoors, or sown outdoors in spring when the ground is warm enough.

acerosa (DC.) A. Gray [*Z. pumila* A. Gray]. Low, cespitose subshrub, to 6 in.; lvs. linear, to ¾ in. long, 1/16 in. wide; heads ½–¾ in. across, receptacle scaly, the scales obtuse, erose; disc fls. 8–13, yellow, ray fls. 4–6, oblong to suborbicular, white; disc achenes oblanceolate, with 2–3 awns. Ariz., New Mex. Cv. 'Apache Plumes'. A selected cv.

angustifolia HBK [*Z. linearis* Benth.]. Erect, ann. herb, to 15 in.; lvs. linear or linear-lanceolate, to 2½ in. long; heads 1½ in. across, receptacle scaly, scales acute or obtuse, nearly entire, yellow; disc fls. black-purple, ray fls. 7–9, ½ in. long, bright orange with central yellow stripe; disc achenes obovate, with a single long awn. Mex. The name has long been misapplied to *Z. Haageana.*

dahliiflora: a name of uncertain application, but probably referring to a cv. of *Z. elegans.*

elegans Jacq. COMMON Z., YOUTH-AND-OLD-AGE. Ann., to 3 ft.; lvs. lanceolate, ovate, or oblong, to 5 in. long; heads large, to 6 in. across

in many cvs., receptacle scaly, scales fimbriate-tipped; disc fls. yellow to purple when present, ray fls. 8–20, spatulate, and usually red in the wild type, but in the cvs. often several times as many and elongated or broader, often twisted or tubular, and of every color but blue, sometimes particolored; disc achenes obovate, emarginate, awnless. Mex. There are many races and cvs. available, differing in stature, size of heads, length of peduncles, and color, form, and number of ray fls. Cvs. 'Gracillima', 'Pumila', 'Scabiosiflora', 'Striata' have been listed, among others.

gracillima: a listed name of no botanical standing for *Z. elegans* cv.

grandiflora Nutt. [*Crassina grandiflora* (Nutt.) O. Kuntze]. Small, cespitose subshrub, 4–10 in.; lvs. linear, to 1 in. long, ⅛ in. wide, strigose; heads 1–1½ in. across, many, borne at one level; disc fls. red or green, ray fls. 3–6, orbicular, yellow; disc achenes oblanceolate, with 0–4 but mostly 2 unequal awns. Colo. and Kans. s. to Mex. and sw. U.S.

Haageana Regel [*Z. angustifolia* of auth., not HBK; *Z. mexicana* Hort. ex Vilm.]. MEXICAN Z. Ann., to 2 ft.; lvs. lanceolate, to 3 in. long, sessile; heads to 2 in. across, receptacle scaly, scales entire, cuspidate, yellow with black tips; disc fls. orange, ray fls. 8–9 and orange in the wild type, but more numerous and usually bicolored red-and-yellow or -orange in cvs.; disc achenes oblong-obovate, emarginate, with 2 unequal awns. Mex. The cvs. 'Old Mexico' and 'Persian Carpet' are offered.

linearis: *Z. angustifolia.*

mexicana: *Z. Haageana.*

multiflora: *Z. peruviana.*

pauciflora: *Z. peruviana.*

peruviana (L.) L. [*Z. multiflora* L.; *Z. pauciflora* L.; *Z. tenuiflora* Jacq.; *Z. verticillata* Andr.]. Differs from *Z. Haageana* in its yellow to scarlet ray fls., erose, rounded, often red-tipped receptacle scales, and linear-oblanceolate disc achenes with a single awn. Ariz. and Mex. to Argentina; also W. Indies.

pumila: *Z. acerosa;* but the name *Z. pumila* is often used for dwarf cvs. of *Z. elegans.*

scabiosiflora: a listed name of no botanical standing for *Z. elegans* cv.

striata: a listed name of no botanical standing for *Z. elegans* cv.

tenuiflora: *Z. peruviana.*

verticillata: *Z. peruviana.*

ZIZANIA L. WILD RICE, WATER OATS. *Gramineae.* Two or 3 spp. of tall, aquatic, ann. or per. grasses in N. Amer. and e. Asia; lf. blades flat; panicles large, terminal; spikelets unisexual, 1-fld., cylindrical or nearly so, disarticulating from the pedicel, glumes obsolete, female spikelet angled at maturity, lemma 3-nerved, palea 2-nerved, male spikelet soon falling, lemma 5-nerved, palea 3-nerved, stamens 6. For terminology see *Gramineae.*

aquatica L. ANNUAL W.R., INDIAN R. Ann.; sts. to 10 ft.; lf. blades to 1⅝ in. wide, minutely scabrous, ligules ⅜–⅝ in. long; panicles to more than 1 ft. long; female spikelet with thin, hispid lemma and palea about ¾ in. long. In shallow water, Me. to Mich., s. to Fla. and La., Idaho. An aboriginal food plant still used for human food; also planted as a food and shelter for waterfowl. Var. **angustifolia** A. S. Hitchc. [*Z. palustris* L.]. Sts. to 5 ft.; lf. blades to ⅜ in. wide, ligule ⅛–⅜ in. long; lemma and palea of female spikelet mostly larger. Que. to N. Dak., s. to N.Y. and Nebr. Var. **brevis** Fassett. Sts. to 3 ft.; lf. blades to ½ in. wide, ligule ⅛ in. long; lemma and palea of female spikelet ¼–⅜ in. long. S. Que. and e. Ont.

palustris: *Z. aquatica* var. *angustifolia.*

ZIZIA W. D. J. Koch. *Umbelliferae.* Four spp. of per. herbs of N. Amer.; lvs. simple to ternately compound; fls. small, yellow, in compound umbels, involucre lacking, involucels of few small bractlets.

aurea (L.) W. D. J. Koch. GOLDEN ALEXANDERS. To 2½ ft.; lvs. ternately compound, lower ones 2–3-compound, segms. ovate or ovate-lanceolate, toothed, to 2 in. long; fls. yellow. Spring, early summer. New Bruns. to Fla. and Tex.

ZIZIPHUS Mill. (Sometimes, but not originally, spelled *Zizyphus*). *Rhamnaceae.* More than 40 spp. of deciduous or evergreen shrubs and trees, in trop. and warmer regions of both hemispheres, mostly with stipular spines; lvs. alt., simple, strongly mostly 3-nerved from the base; fls. small, greenish, whitish, or yellow, in axillary clusters; fr. a fleshy drupe, sometimes edible.

The genus is known in horticulture mostly for the jujubes, *Z. Jujuba* and *Z. mauritiana*, the fleshy fruits of which are preserved, dried, sweet-pickled, stewed, and used in confections. The common Chinese jujube thrives in hot and dry regions, in strongly alkaline soils. Its flowers appear late and thereby usually escape late spring frosts. Irrigation contributes to the production of abundant large fruits. Propagation is simple by means of cleaned and stratified seeds, but the seedlings are utilized only as stocks if the best fruit is desired. The jujube may also be propagated by means of root cuttings. Improved cultivated varieties are whip-grafted on seedlings, usually dormant scions being used. See also *Jujube.*

Jujuba Mill. [*Z. vulgaris* Lam.]. COMMON JUJUBE, CHINESE J., CHINESE DATE. Deciduous tree, to 40 ft., sometimes a large bush; lvs. ovate to oblong-elliptic or nearly lanceolate, 1–2 in. long, obtusely serrate, green on both sides, stipular spines usually 2, slender, one of them usually recurved; fr. oblong to ovoid or subglobose, 1¼ in. long or less. Se. Eur. to China. Zone 5b. Winter-hardy as far north as w. N.Y., with protection. There are many pomological cvs., particularly in the Orient. Var. **inermis** (Bunge) Rehd. Brs. unarmed.

mauritiana Lam. [*Z. Jujuba* (L.) Lam., not Mill.]. INDIAN JUJUBE, COTTONY J. Shrub or small tree, commonly evergreen, twigs and lower lf. surface white- or rusty-tomentose; lvs. broad-elliptic, rounded, to 2½ in. long, stipular spines stout; fr. globose or short-oblong, 1 in. in diam. or less, acid. India; now widespread in warm countries, where it is cult. for its edible fr. Zone 10. Less developed pomologically than *Z. Jujuba.*

mucronata Willd. To 25 ft., deciduous; lvs. ovate, to 3 in. long, 3-nerved from base, markedly asymmetric at base; fr. yellow-brown to reddish-brown, round, to ¾ in. in diam. Trop. Afr. Fr. said to be edible but not palatable. Various parts of the plant are used medicinally, and the seeds made into rosaries.

obtusifolia (Hook. ex Torr. & A. Gray) A. Gray. [*Condalia lycioides* (A. Gray) Weberb.]. Much-branched, stiff shrub; lvs. with stipular spines, ovate or rarely oblong, to 1¼ in. long, entire or slightly toothed, glabrous; fr. black, ⅜ in. long. Var. **obtusifolia.** The typical var.; infl. 1–6-fld., peduncle shorter than to nearly as long as pedicels. Tex. to Ariz., n. Mex. Zone 7. Var. **canescens** (A. Gray) M. C. Johnst. [*C. lycioides* var. *canescens* (A. Gray) Trel.]. Infl. 5–30-fld., peduncle longer than to nearly as long as pedicels. Ariz. to s. Calif., s. to Baja Calif., and Sonora (Mex.).

Parryi Torr. [*Condalia Parryi* (Torr.) Weberb.]. Shrub, to 12 ft., deciduous, main brs. flexuous, secondary brs. shorter, spine-tipped;

lvs. elliptic to obovate, to 1 in. long; fr. brownish to purplish-brown, ovoid, to 1 in. long. S. Calif. and Baja Calif. Zone 9.

vulgaris: *Z. Jujuba.*

ZOMBIA L. H. Bailey. ZOMBI PALM. Palmae. One sp., a cespitose palm with bisexual fls., native in Haiti; trunk clothed with persistent fibrous sheaths margined with long, stout, sharp, spinelike fibers; lvs. palmate, divided into 1-ribbed segms.; infl. among lvs., with bracts on peduncle and subtending each of several brs., brs. divided into slender rachillae; fls. solitary, perianth of short acute lobes, stamens about 12, carpel solitary, 1-celled, 1-ovuled; fr. white, seed 2-lobed nearly to middle with central columnar intrusion.

A cluster palm grown for its unusual sheathed trunks. For culture see *Palms.*

antillarum (Descourt. ex B. D. Jacks.) L. H. Bailey [*Coccothrinax anomala* Becc.]. Trunks 8–10 ft.; lvs. silvery beneath, divided nearly to base; fr. about ¾ in. in diam. Warmer parts of Zone 9b in Fla.

ZOYSIA Willd. *Gramineae.* About 5 spp. of low, per. grasses with creeping rhizomes in se. Asia and New Zeal.; lf. blades short, pungently pointed; racemes terminal, spikelike; spikelets 1-fld., on short, appressed pedicels, articulate below the glumes, falling entire, first glume absent, second glume mucronate or short-awned, firmer than and enclosing palea and lemma. For terminology see *Gramineae.*

Several species important as lawn grasses. Propagated vegetatively by cuttings or plugs.

japonica Steud. KOREAN GRASS, KOREAN LAWN G., JAPANESE L.G. Creeping by underground rhizomes; lf. blades flat, obtuse, usually 5–9 in. long, about ⅛ in. wide or more; racemes spikelike, usually 1 in. long, spikelets about ⅛ in. long, pale purplish-brown. Japan. A common lawn grass requiring full sun. Hardy to Zone 7.

Matrella (L.) Merrill [*Z. pungens* Willd.]. JAPANESE CARPET GRASS, MANILA G., ZOYSIA G., FLAWN. Distinguished from *Z. japonica* in forming a shade-tolerant, drought-resistant and durable, dense close turf; lf. blades to 4 in. long, filiform, erect or ascending; spike 1½ in. long; spikelets slightly smaller, usually greenish. Trop. Asia. Used as a lawn grass in the southernmost states. Zone 9.

pungens: *Z. Matrella.*

tenuifolia Willd. ex Trin. MASCARENE GRASS, KOREAN VELVET G. Distinguished from *Z. japonica* by more shallow roots, lf. blades threadlike and capillary, acute, 1–2 in. long, strongly involute, florets in narrow, compressed spikelets. Asia; introd. for lawns in s. Fla. and s. Calif. Zone 10.

ZYGADENUS: see *ZIGADENUS.*

ZYGOCACTUS: *SCHLUMBERGERA.* Z. **delicatus:** *S. truncata.* var.

×**ZYGOCOLAX:** × *ZYGOPABSTIA.*

× **ZYGOPABSTIA** Garay [× *Zygocolax* Rolfe]: *Pabstia* Garay [*Colax* Lindl.] × *Zygopetalum.* Orchidaceae. Bigeneric hybrids, intermediate in character between the parents.

For culture see *Orchids.*

Veitchii (Rolfe) Dress [× *Zygocolax Veitchii* Rolfe]: *Pabstia jugosa* (Lindl.) Garay [*Colax jugosa* Lindl.] × *Zygopetalum crinitum.* A natural hybrid; fls. about 3 in. across, sepals and petals light yellow-green, spotted and blotched with brown-purple, lip whitish with radiating violet-purple lines. Brazil.

ZYGOPETALUM Hook. *Orchidaceae.* About 20 spp. of epiphytes, native to Cent. and S. Amer.; pseudobulbs ovoid, 1–2-lvd. at apex; lvs. lanceolate, plicate; infl. basal, erect, racemose, few- to many-fld.; fls. small to large, conspicuous, sepals separate, nearly equal, spreading, lateral sepals united to column foot, forming a short, broad mentum, petals resembling the sepals, lip 3-lobed, fused or jointed to column foot at base, lateral lobes spreading or erect, midlobe spreading, recurved at apex, disc with prominent lunate, tubercled or crested callus, column short, stout. For structure of fl. see *Orchidaceae.*

Warm greenhouse. For culture see *Orchids*.

aromaticum: *Cochleanthes aromatica.*

Burkei Rchb.f. Pseudobulbs to 4 in. long, 2-lvd.; lvs. linear-lanceolate, to 14 in. long; racemes 5–6-fld.; fls. 2 in. across, sepals and petals to 1¼ in. long, pale brown with chestnut-brown marks, lip 1 in. long, 3-lobed, with central white callus between 2 groups of 3 pink-veined teeth, with smaller ones behind, column yellow. Guyana, Venezuela, Peru.

cerinum: *Pescatorea cerina.*

coeleste: *Bollea coelestis.*

crinitum Lodd. Similar to *Z. Mackayi* in plant habit, and in color and shape of fls., but lip obovate, puberulent. Brazil.

discolor: *Cochleanthes discolor.*

grandiflorum: *Mendoncella grandiflora.*

intermedium Lodd. Pseudobulbs narrowly ovoid, to 3 in. long, 3–5-lvd.; lvs. lanceolate-strap-shaped, to 18 in. long; racemes longer than lvs., 5–6-fld.; fls. nodding, 3 in. across, sepals and petals oblong-strapshaped, to 1½ in. long, lip flat, to 1½ in. long, whitish, with many radiating purple-violet lines. Late winter–spring. Brazil.

Lalindei: *Bollea Lalindei.*

Mackayi Hook. Pseudobulbs to 3 in. long, 2–3-lvd.; lvs. linear-lanceolate, to 20 in. long; racemes to 30 in. long, 5- or more-fld.; fls. 3 in. high, sepals and petals similar, lanceolate-strap-shaped, yellow-green, blotched with purplish-brown, lip auricled at base, abruptly enlarged into a fan-shaped blade, white, spotted and streaked with violet-purple, with a ridged crest, toothed along front margins, column yellow-green spotted with red-brown, glabrous. Brazil. Cv. 'Charlesworthii'. Sepal and petals emerald-green, without purple markings.

rostratum: *Zygosepalum labiosum.*

Wendlandii: *Cochleanthes aromatica.*

ZYGOPHYLLACEAE R. Br. CALTROP FAMILY. Dicot.; about 27 genera and 200 spp. of herbs and shrubs, rarely trees, chiefly pantrop. but with some spp. in temp. regions of both N. and S. Hemispheres; sts. often swollen at nodes; lvs. mostly opp. and pinnate, rarely simple or reduced to 2 lfts., stipuled; fls. mostly bisexual, regular, solitary or paired, sepals and petals 5, stamens usually twice as many as petals, glandular disc usually present, ovary superior, 2–12-celled, styles united, stigma usually 1; fr. a caps., rarely a drupaceous berry, variously angled or spinescent. Of little hort. importance in this country. *Bulnesia, Guaiacum, Larrea,* and

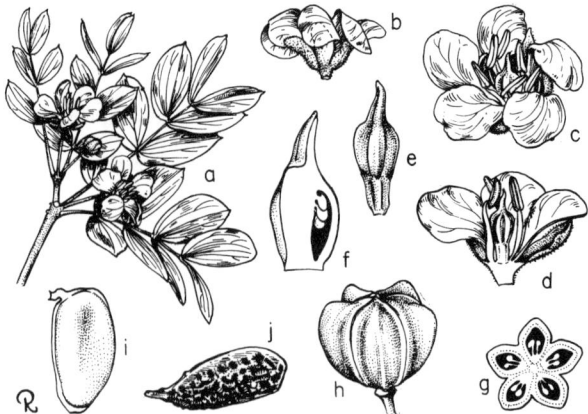

ZYGOPHYLLACEAE. *Guaiacum sanctum:* **a,** flowering twig, × ½; **b,** flower, side view, × 1; **c,** flower, face view, × 1½; **d,** flower, vertical section except for pistil, × 1½; **e,** pistil, × 3; **f,** pistil, vertical section, × 5; **g,** ovary, cross section, × 8; **h,** fruit, × 1; **i,** seed covered by aril, × 1½; **j,** seed, × 3.

Tribulus are cult.; *Guaiacum* furnishes the lignum-vitae of commerce.

ZYGOSEPALUM Rchb.f. *Orchidaceae.* Five spp. of epiphytes, native to trop. S. Amer.; rhizome ascendent, pseudobulbs remote, 1–2-lvd.; lvs. plicate; infl. lateral, few-fld.; fls. large, showy, sepals and petals separate, similar, lip conspicuous, flat, much larger than other perianth segms., column fleshy, winged, hooded over the anther, anther beaked, pollinia 4, on large stalk. For structure of fl. see *Orchidaceae.*

For culture see *Orchids.*

labiosum (L. Rich.) Garay [*Zygopetalum rostratum* Hook.]. Pseudobulbs ovoid, to 2¼ in. long, 2-lvd.; lvs. oblanceolate, to 10 in. long; scape 1-fld.; fls. to 2 in. across, sepals to 2 in. long, greenish, suffused with maroon in center, petals to 1¾ in. long, similar to sepals but suffused with violet at base, lip 1½ in. long, white with violet stripes radiating from a transverse violet callus near base, bright green on underside at extreme base, column white, suffused with violet. Guyana, Venezuela, Amazonian Brazil.

AUTHORS CITED

Note: When the years of birth and death have not been ascertained, the abbreviation "fl." (floruit) preceding a year or period indicates when an author is known to have been working and publishing.

Aarons. Aaron Aaronsohn (1876 or 77–1919)
Aase Hannah Caroline Aase (1883–)
Abbott, G. George Abbott (fl. 1927)
Abel Clarke Abel (1780 [1789?]–1826)
Aberc. Henry Duncan McLaren, Lord Aberconway (1879–1953)
Abrams LeRoy Abrams (1874–1956)
Adamovič Lujo Adamovič (1864–1935)
Adams Johannes Michael Friedrich Adams [J. F. Adam] (1780–1838)
Adams, J. E. Joseph Edison Adams (1903–)
Adams, J. W. Joseph William Adams (1906–)
Adams, W. P. William Preston Adams (1930–)
Adamson Robert Stephen Adamson (1885–)
Adans. Michel Adanson (1727–1806)
Aellen Paul Aellen (1896–1973)
Afzel. Adam Afzelius (1750–1837)
Agardh Carl Adolf Agardh (1785–1859)
Agardh, J. Jacob George Agardh (1813–1901)
Ahles Harry. E. Ahles (1924–)
Ahrendt Leslie Walter Allan Ahrendt (1903–)
Aichele Dietmar Ernst Aichele (1928–)
Airy-Shaw Herbert Kenneth Airy Shaw (1902–)
Ait. William Aiton (1731–1793)
Ait. f. William Townsend Aiton (1766–1849)
Aitch. James Edward Tierney Aitchison (1836–1898)
Akers John F. Akers (1906–)
Akhv. Agazi Asaturovich Akhverdov (1907–)
Alain (Brother) Alain [Henri Eugène (Enrique Eugenio) Liogier]; later, Alain Henri Liogier (1916–)
Albov Nikolaï Mikhaïlovich Albov [Alboff, Albow] (1866–1897)
Alderw. Cornelis Rugier Willem Karel van Alderwerelt van Rosenburgh (1863–1936)
Alef. Friedrich Georg Christoph Alefeld (1820–1872)
Alexand. Edward Johnston Alexander (1901–)
All. Carlo Allioni (1728–1804)
Allan Harry [Henry] Howard Barton Allan (1882–1957)
Allen, P. Paul Hamilton Allen (1911–1963)
Alph. Jean Charles Adolphe Alphand (1817–1891)
Alston Arthur Hugh Garfit Alston (1902–1958)
Alstr. Clas Alströmer (1736–1794)
Altschul Siri Sylvia Patricia von Reis Altschul (1931–)
Ambrosi Francesco Ambrosi (1821–1897)
Ames Oakes Ames (1874–1950)
Ames, L. Lawrence Marion Ames (1900–1966)
Amo Mariano del Amo y Mora (1820–1896 [1809–1894?])
Amsh. Gerda Jane Hildegonda Amshoff (1913–)
Andersen Johannes Carl Andersen (1873–1962)
Anderson, A. Alexander Anderson (?–1811)
Anderson, E. Edgar Shannon Anderson (1897–1969)
Anderson, E. F. Edward Frederick Anderson (1932–)
Anderson, G. George Anderson (?–1817)
Anderson, H. W. Harry Warren Anderson (1885–1971)
Anderson, J. J. Anderson (fl. 1868)
Anderson, P. J. Paul Johnson Anderson (1884–1971)
Anderson, T. Thomas Anderson (1832–1870)
Anderss. Nils Johan Andersson (1821–1880)
Andr. Henry C. Andrews (ca. 1794–1830)
Andr., C. Cecil Rollo Payton Andrews (1870–1951)
Andr., D. Darwin Maxson Andrews (1869–1938)
André Édouard François André (1840–1911)
Andresen John William Andresen (1926–)
Andrz. Antoni Lukianowicz Andrzejowski [Andrzeiovski, Andrejouski] (1785–1868)
Ångstr. Johan Ångström (1813–1879)
Ant. Franz Antoine (1815–1886)
Anth. John Anthony (1891–1972)

Anzi Martino Anzi (1812–1883)
Appleg. Elmer Ivan Applegate (1867–1949)
Arcang. Giovanni Arcangeli (1840–1921)
Ard. Pietro Arduino (1728–1805)
Ardoino Honoré Jean Baptiste Ardoino (1819–1874)
Arech. José Arechavaleta (1838–1912)
Arends Georg Arends (1862–1952)
Armitage (Dr.) Armitage (fl. 1856)
Armstr., C. W. C. W. [C. A. in error] Armstrong (?–1950)
Armstr., J. B. Joseph Beattie Armstrong (1850–1926)
Armstr., J. F. John Francis Armstrong (1820–1902)
Arn. George Arnott Walker-Arnott (1799–1868)
Arn., S. Samuel Arnott (1852–1930)
Arnold Johann Franz Xaver Arnold (fl. 1785)
Arr. Cam. Manoel Arruda da Camara (1752–1810)
Arrh. Johan Petter Arrhenius (1811–1889)
Arth. Joseph Charles Arthur (1850–1942)
Arv.-Touv. Jean Maurice Casimir Arvet-Touvet (1841–1913)
Asami Yoshichi Asami (1894–)
Asch. Paul Friedrich August Ascherson (1834–1913)
Ashby Edwin Ashby (1861–1941)
Ashe William Willard Ashe (1872–1932)
Ashw. Margot Bernice Ashwin (later Forde) (1935–)
Asso Ignacio Jordan de Asso y del Río (1742–1814)
Aubl. Jean Baptiste Christophe Fusée Aublet (1720–1778)
Auch. Pierre Martin Rémi Aucher-Éloy (1792–1838)
Audib. Urbain Audibert (1789–1846)
Audot N. Audot (fl. 1845)
Audub. John James Laforest Audubon (1785–1851)
Augustin Augustin (fl. 1854)
of auth. Of authors; referring to use by various or many authors.
Avé-Lall. Julius Léopold Eduard Avé-Lallemant (1803–1867)
Azaola Iñigo [Ignatius] Gonzalez y Azaola (fl. 1845)
Bab. Charles Cardale Babington (1808–1895)
Babc. Ernest Brown Babcock (1877–1955)
Bacig. Rimo Charles Bacigalupi (1901–)
Backeb. Curt Backeberg (1894–1966)
Backer Cornellis Andries Backer (1874–1963)
Backh. James Backhouse (1825–1890)
Badoux Henri Badoux (1871–?)
Baehni Charles Baehni (1906–1964)
Baenitz Carl Gabriel Baenitz (1837–1913)
Bailey, C. Charles Bailey (1838–1924)
Bailey, E. Z. Ethel Zoe Bailey (1889–)
Bailey, F. M. Frederick Manson Bailey (1827–1915)
Bailey, J. F. John Frederick Bailey (1866–1938)
Bailey, L. H. Liberty Hyde Bailey (1858–1954)
Bailey, V. Virginia Edith Bailey (later Long) (1908–)
Baill. Henri Ernest Baillon (1827–1895)
Baird, R. O. Ralph O. Baird (fl. 1931)
Bak. John Gilbert Baker (1834–1920)
Bak., C. F. Charles Fuller Baker (1872–1927)
Bak., M. S. Milo Samuel Baker (1868–1961)
Bak., R. T. Richard Thomas Baker (1854–1941)
Bak. f. Edmund Gilbert Baker (1864–1949)
Bakh. Reinier Cornelis Bakhuizen van den Brink (1881–1945)
Bal. Benedict Balansa (1825–1891)
Balb. Giovanni Battista Balbis (1765–1831)
Bald. Antonio Baldacci (1867–1950)
Balf. John Hutton Balfour (1808–1884)
Balf. f. Isaac Bayley Balfour (1853–1922)
Ball, C. R. Carleton Roy Ball (1873–1958)
Ball, J. John Ball (1818–1889)
Ball, P. W. Peter William Ball (1932–)
Ballant. Henry Ballantine (1833–1929)

Bally Peter René Oscar Bally (1895–)
Baltet L. Charles Baltet (1830–1908)
Bancr., E. N. Edward Nathaniel Bancroft (1772–1842)
Bancr., H. H. Helen Holme Bancroft (1887–)
Banks Joseph Banks (1743–1820)
Barb. William Barbey-Boissier (1842–1914)
Barb.-Rodr. João Barbosa Rodrigues (1842–1909)
Barcl. Frederic White Barclay (1874–1943)
Barcl., A. S. Arthur S. Barclay (1932–)
Barker, F. Frank Barker (fl. 1934)
Barker, G. George Barker (1776–1845)
Barker, W. F. Winsome Fanny Barker (1907–)
Barkoud. Youssef Ibrahim Barkoudah (1933–)
Barneby Rupert Charles Barneby (1911–)
Barnéoud François Marius Barnéoud (1821–)
Barnh. John Hendley Barnhart (1871–1949)
Baroni Eugenio Baroni (1865–1943)
Barr Peter Barr (1826–1909)
Barr f. Peter Rudolph Barr (1862–1944)
Barratt Joseph Barratt (1796–1882)
Barrett Mary Franklin Barrett (1879–)
Barron William Barron (fl. 1852–1880)
Barroso, G. Graziela Maciel Barroso (1912–)
Barry Patrick Barry (1816–1890)
Bartal. Biagio Bartalini (1746–1822)
Bartik A. Bartik (fl. 1885)
Bartl. Friedrich Gottlieb Bartling (1798–1875)
Bartlett Harley Harris Bartlett (1886–1960)
Barton, B. Benjamin Smith Barton (1766–1815)
Barton, W. William Paul Crillon Barton (1786–1856)
Bartr. William Bartram (1739–1823)
Bartsch Gustav Bartsch (fl. 1903)
Barua P. K. Barua (fl. 1956)
Bast. Toussaint Bastard (1784–1846)
Batal. Aleksandr Fedorovich Batalin (1847–1896[1898?])
Batem. James Bateman (1811–1897)
Bates David Martin Bates (1934–)
Batsch August Johann Georg Karl Batsch (1761–1802)
Batt. Jules Aimé Battandier (1848–1922)
Baudo Firmin Baudo (fl. 1843)
Baum, H. Hugo Baum (1866–1950)
Baumann, C. Charles A. Baumann (fl. 1830)
Baumann, C. A. N. Constantin Auguste Napoléon Baumann (1804–1884)
Baumann, É. Émile Napoléon Baumann (1835–1910)
Baumg. Johann Christian Gottlob Baumgarten (1765–1843)
Bausch Jan Bausch (1917–)
Baxter Edgar Martin Baxter (1903–1967)
Bayer Johann Nepomuk Bayer (1802–1870)
Beadle Chauncey Delos Beadle (1866–1950)
Beal William James Beal (1833–1924)
Beaman John Homer Beaman (1929–)
Bean William Jackson Bean (1863–1947)
Beane Lawrence Beane (1901–)
Beauverd Gustave Beauverd (1867–1942)
Beauvois Ambroise Marie François Joseph Palisot de Beauvois (1752–1820)
Bebb Michael Schuck Bebb (1833–1895)
Becc. Odoardo Beccari (1843–1920)
Becherer Alfred Becherer (1897–)
Bechst. Johann Matthäus Bechstein (1757–1822)
Beck, G. Günther Beck von Mannagetta und Larchenau (1856–1931)
Beck, L. Lewis Caleb Beck (1798–1853)
Becker, A. Alexander Becker (1818–1901)
Becker, J. Johannes Becker (1769–1833)
Becker, W. Wilhelm Becker (1874–1928)
Beckm. Johan Beckmann (1739–1811)
Beddome Richard Henry Beddome (1830–1911)
Beer Johann Georg Beer (1803–1873)
Beetle, A. Alan Ackerman Beetle (1913–)
Beetle, D. Dorothy Erna (née Schoof) Beetle (1916–)
Béguinot Augusto Béguinot (1875–1940)
Behr Hans Hermann Behr (1818–1904)
Beij. Willem Beijerinck (1881–)
Beissn. Ludwig Beissner (1843–1927)
Bell, C. R. Clyde Ritchie Bell (1921–)
Bell, S. S. Bell (fl. 1852)
Bellair Georges Adolphe Bellair (1860–?)
Bellardi Carlo Antonio Ludovico Bellardi (1741–1826)
Belli Saverio Carlo Belli (1852–1919)
Bello Domingo Bello y Espinosa (1817–1884)
Benary Ernst Benary (1819–1892)
Bened. Ralph Curtiss Benedict (1883–)

Benn., A. Arthur Bennett (1843–1929)
Benn., A. W. Alfred William Bennet (1833–1902)
Benn., J. John Joseph Bennett (1801–1876)
Bens., B. W. Bernard W. Benson (fl. 1957)
Bens., G. Gilbert Thereon Benson (1896–1928)
Bens., L. Lyman David Benson (1909–)
Bens., R. Robson Benson (1822–1894)
Benth. George Bentham (1800–1884)
Bercht. Friedrich von Berchtold (1781–1876)
Berckm. Prosper Jules Alphonse Berckmans (1830–1910)
Berg, A. Alexander Berg (fl. 1840)
Berg, E. Ernst von Berg (1782–1855)
Berg, O. Otto Karl Berg (1815–1866)
Berge Ernst Berge (1836–1897)
Berger, A. Alwin Berger (1871–1931)
Bergeret Jean Pierre Bergeret (1751–1813)
Berggr., S. Swen Berggren (1837–1917)
Bergius Peter Jonas Bergius (1730–1790)
Bergman Ferdinand Bergman (1826–1899)
Bergmans Johannes Baptista Bergmans (1892–)
Berk. Miles Joseph Berkeley (1803–1889)
Berland. Jean Louis Berlandier (1805–1851)
Bernh. Johann Jacob Bernhardi (1774–1850)
Bernis Francisco Bernis (fl. 1955)
Bernstiel Otto Bernstiel (fl. 1912)
Bertero Carlo Guiseppe Bertero (1789–1831)
Berth. Sabin Berthelot (1794–1880)
Berthault François Berthault (1857–1916)
Bertin Pierre Bertin (1800–1891)
Bertol. Antonio Bertoloni (1775–1869)
Bertrand, A. André Bertrand (fl. 1950–1956)
Bertrand, C. Charles Eugène Bertrand (1851–1917)
Besant John William Besant (1878–1944)
Bess. Wilibald Swibert Joseph Gottlieb von Besser (1784–1842)
Best George Newton Best (1846–1926)
Betche Ernst Betche (1851–1913)
Betcke Ernst Friedrich Betcke (?–1865)
Bhand. Madar Mal Bhandari (1929–)
Bickn. Eugene Pintard Bicknell (1859–1925)
Bidw. John Carne Bidwill (1815–1853)
Bieb. Friedrich August Marschall von Bieberstein (1768–1826)
Biedenf. Ferdinand Leopold Karl von Biedenfeld (1788–1862)
Biehler Johann Friedrich Theodor Biehler (ca. 1785–?)
Bienert Theophil Bienert (?–1873)
Bigel. Jacob Bigelow (1787–1879)
Billiard L. C. Billiard (fl. 1861–1870)
Billot Paul Constant Billot (1796–1863)
Binn. Simon Binnendijk (1821–1883)
Birdsey Monroe Roberts Birdsey (1922–)
Bisch. Gottlieb Wilhelm Bischoff (1797–1854)
Bissell Charles Humphrey Bissell (1857–1925)
Bisset James Bisset (1843–1911)
Bitter Friedrich August Georg Bitter (1873–1927)
Biv. Antonio de Bivona-Bernardi (1774–1837)
Black John McConnell Black (1855–1951)
Blackb. Benjamin Coleman Blackburn (1908–)
Blake, S. F. Sidney Fay Blake (1892–1959)
Blake, S. T. Stanley Thatcher Blake (1910–1973)
Blakelock Ralph Antony Blakelock (1915–1963)
Blakely William Faris Blakely (1875–1941)
Blanchard, W. William Henry Blanchard (1850–1922)
Blanche Charles Isadore Blanche (1823–1887)
Blanco Francisco Manuel Blanco (1788–1845)
Blankinsh. Joseph William Blankinship (1862–1938)
Blocki Bronislaw Blocki (1857–1919)
Bluff Matthias Joseph Bluff (1805–1837)
Blum Friedrich Blum (fl. 1813–1815)
Blume Carl Ludwig von Blume (1796–1862)
Blytt Mathias Numsen Blytt (1789–1862)
Bobrov Evgenii Grigor'evich Bobrov (1902–)
Bock Thor Methven Bock (fl. 1941)
Bocquill. Henri Bocquillon (1834–1883)
Böd. Friedrich Bödeker (1867–1937)
Bodin Nils Gustaf Bodin (fl. 1798)
Boeck. Johann Otto Boeckeler (1803–1899)
Boehmer Georg Rudolph Boehmer (1723–1803)
Boehmer, L. Louis Boehmer (?–1896)
Boenn. Clemens Maria Friedrich Boenninghausen (1785–1864)
Boerl. Jacob Gijsbert Boerlage (1849–1900)
Bogin Clifford Bogin (1920–)
Böhme Olga Böhme (fl. 1931–1942)
Bois Désiré Georges Jean Maris Bois (1856–1946)

Boiss. Pierre Edmond Boissier (1810–1885)
Boissev. Charles Hercules Boissevin (1893–)
Boissieu Henri de Boissieu (1871–1912)
Boiteau Pierre L. Boiteau (1911–)
Boivin Joseph Robert Bernard Boivin (1916–)
Boivin, L. H. Louis Hyacinthe Boivin (1808–1852)
Bojer Wenzel [Wenceslas] Bojer (1797[1800?]–1856)
Boke Norman Hill Boke (1913–)
Bolander Henry Nicholas Bolander (1831–1897)
Bolle, C. Carl August Bolle (1821–1909)
Bolle, F. Friedrich Bolle (1905–)
Bolós, A. Antoni de Bolós i Vayreda (1889–)
Bolós, O. Oriol de Bolós i Capdevila (1924–)
Bolton James Bolton (1758–1799)
Bolus, F. Frank Bolus (fl. 1896)
Bolus, H. Harry Bolus (1834–1911)
Bolus, L. Harriet Margaret Louisa (née Kensit) Bolus (1877–1970)
Bolz. Pio Bolzon (1867–?)
Bomh. Miriam Lucile Bomhard (1898–1952)
Bonaf. Matthieu Bonafous (1793–1842)
Bonamy François Bonamy (1710–1786)
Bonap. Roland Napoléon Bonaparte (1858–1924)
Bong. August Heinrich Gustav von Bongard (1786–1839)
Bonker Frances Bonker (1895–)
Bonnier Gaston Eugène Marie Bonnier (1853–1922)
Bonpl. Aimé Jacques Alexandre Bonpland (1773–1858)
Boom Boudewijn Karel Boom (1903–)
Booth, J. John Booth (1836–1908)
Booth, J. R. John Richmond Booth (1799–1847)
Booth, T. J. Thomas Jonas Booth (1829–post 1861)
Booth, W. B. William Beattie Booth (1804–1874)
Boothm. H. Stuart Boothman (fl. 1934)
Boott, F. Francis Boott (1792–1863)
Boott, W. William Boott (1805–1887)
Borb. Vinczé von Borbás (1844–1905)
Boreau Alexandre Boreau (1803–1875)
Borg John Borg (1873–1945)
Boris., A. Antonina Georgievna Borisova [Borissova]-Bekrjaseva (1903–1970)
Borkh. Moritz Balthasar Borkhausen (1760–1806)
Börner Carl Julius Bernhard Börner (1880–)
Bornet Jean Baptiste Édouard Bornet (1828–1911)
Bornm. Joseph Friedrich Nicolaus Bornmüller (1862–1948)
Borrer William Borrer (1781–1862)
Bort Katherine Stephens Bort (1870–)
Bory Jean Baptiste Geneviève Marcellin Bory de St. Vincent (1778–1846)
Borza Alexander Borza (1887–1971)
Borzi Antonino Borzi (1852–1921)
Bosc Louis Augustin Guillaume Bosc (1759–1828)
Bosse Julius Friedrich Wilhelm Bosse (1788–1864)
Boucharlat Boucharlat (1807–1893)
Bouché Carl David Bouché (1809–1881)
Bouleng. George Albert Boulenger (1858–1937)
Boullu Antoine Étienne Boullu (1813–1904)
Boutelje Julius B. Boutelje (fl. 1954)
Boutigny Jean François Désiré Boutigny (1820–1884)
Bowden Wray Merrill Bowden (1914–)
Bower Frederick Orpen Bower (1855–1948)
Bowers Clement Gray Bowers (1893–1973)
Bowie James Bowie (1789–1869)
Bowles Edward Augustus Bowles (1865–1954)
Boynt. Frank Ellis Boynton (1859–?)
Boynt., K. R. Kenneth Rowland Boynton (1891–)
Boxall Richard Boxall (fl. 1880)
Br., A. Addison Brown (1830–1913)
Br., Alex. Alexander Carl Heinrich Braun (1805–1877)
Br., J. E. John Ednie Brown (1848–1899)
Br., N. E. Nicholas Edward Brown (1849–1934)
Br., P. Patrick Browne (1720–1790)
Br., R. Robert Brown (1773–1858)
Br., R. W. Roland Wilbur Brown (1893–1961)
Br., S. Stewardson Brown (1867–1921)
Br., S. W. Spencer Wharton Brown (1918–)
Br. Campst., R. Robert Brown, of Campster (1842–1895)
Brackenr. William Dunlop Brackenridge (1810–1893)
Brade Alexandre Curt Brade (1881–1971)
Bradf. Edward Bradford (fl. 1845)
Brads., R. Robert Vernon Bradshaw (1896–)
Brainerd Ezra Brainerd (1844–1924)
Bramw. David Bramwell (fl. 1942)
Brand August Brand (1863–1931)
Brandeg. Townshend Stith Brandegee (1843–1925)

Brandeg., K. Mary Katherine (née Layne) (Curran) Brandegee (1844–1920)
Brandis Dietrich Brandis (1824–1907)
Brandt, M. Max Brandt (1884–1914)
Braun, A. Alexander Carl Heinrich Braun (1805–1877)
Braun, E. Emma Lucy Braun (1889–)
Braun, F. Karl Friedrich Wilhelm Braun (1800–1864)
Braun, H. Heinrich Braun (1851–1920)
Braun, J. Josias Braun (later Braun-Blanquet) (1884–)
Bravo Helia Bravo (later Hollis) (1903–)
Br.-Bl. Josias Braun-Blanquet (earlier Braun) (1884–)
Br. Campst., R. Robert Brown, of Campster (1842–1895)
Breistr. Maurice Breistroffer (1906–)
Breit. August Julius Breitung (1913–)
Bremek. Cornelis Eliza Bertus Bremekamp (1888–)
Brenan John Patrick Micklethwait Brenan (1917–)
Bresl. Moritz Bresler (1802–ca. 1851)
Brewer William Henry Brewer (1828–1910)
Brickell John Brickell (1749–1801)
Bridw. A. W. Bridwell (fl. 1925)
Briot, C. Charles Briot (1804–1888)
Briq. John Isaac Briquet (1870–1931)
Britt. Nathaniel Lord Britton (1859–1934)
Britten James Britten (1846–1924)
Britten, L. L. (Miss) L. L. Britten (fl. 1940–1954)
Broadw. Walter Elias Broadway (1863–1935)
Bromf. William Arnold Bromfield (1801–1851)
Brongn. Adolphe Théodore Brongniart (1801–1876)
Brot. Felix da Silva Avellar Brotero (1744–1828)
Broun Maurice Broun (1906–)
Brouss. Pierre Marie Auguste Broussonet (1761–1807)
Bruant Georges Bruant (1842–1912)
Bruce, E. A. Eileen Adelaide Bruce (1905–1955)
Brückn. Gerhard Brückner (1902–)
Brügg. Christian Georg Brügger (1833–1899)
Brühl Paul Johannes Brühl (1855–?)
Brumh. Philipp Brumhard (1879–?)
Brumm. Richard Kenneth Brummitt (1937–)
BSG Philipp Bruch (1781–1847), Wilhelm Philipp Schimper (1808–1880), & Wilhelm Theodor von Gümpel (1812–1858)
BSP Nathaniel Lord Britton (1859–1934), Emerson Ellick Sterns (1846–1926), & Justus Ferdinand Poggenburg (1840–1893)
Bubani Pietro Bubani (1806–1888)
Buchan., J. John Buchanan (1819–1898)
Buchenau Franz Georg Philipp Buchenau (1831–1906)
Buchh. John Theodore Buchholz (1888–1951)
Buch.-Ham. C. Francis Buchanan, later Lord Hamilton (1762–1829)
Buchinger J. D. Buchinger (1803–1888)
Buc'hoz Pierre Joseph Buc'hoz (1731–1807)
Buchw. Johannes Buchwald (1869–1927)
Buckl. Samuel Botsford Buckley (1809–1884)
Buek Heinrich Wilhelm Buek (1796–1879)
Buhse Friedrich Alexander Buhse (1821–1898)
Buin. Albert Frederick Buining (1901–)
Buist Robert Buist (1805–1880)
Bull William Bull (1828–1902)
Bulley A. K. Bulley (1861?–1942)
Bullock Arthur Allman Bullock (1906–)
Bunge Aleksandr Andreevich von Bunge (1803–1890)
Bunt. George Sydney Bunting (1927–)
Bur. Louis Édouard Bureau (1830–1918)
Burb. Frederick William Thomas Burbidge (1847–1905)
Burchard Oscar Burchard (fl. 1909–1931)
Burchell William John Burchell (1781–1863)
Burck William Burck (1848–1910)
Burgersd. Leendert Alexander Johannes Burgersdijk [Burgersdyk] (1828–1900)
Burgess Edward Sandford Burgess (1855–1928)
Burgsd. Friedrich August Ludwig von Burgsdorf (1747–1802)
Burkart Arturo Erhardo Burkart (1908–1975)
Burkholder Walter Hagemeyer Burkholder (1891–)
Burkill Isaac Henry Burkill (1870–1965)
Burle Marx Roberto Burle Marx (1909–)
Burm. Johannes Burman (1706–1779)
Burm. f. Nicolaas Laurens Burman (1733–1793)
Burnat Émile Burnat (1828–1920)
Burnett Gilbert Thomas Burnett (1800–1835)
Burnh. Stewart Henry Burnham (1870–1943)
Burret Karl Ewald Maximilian Burret (1883–1964)
Burtt, B. L. Brian Lawrence Burtt (1913–)
Burv. Fréderic Burvenich (1857–1917)
Bury Priscilla Susan (Falkner) Bury (fl. 1830)
Buscal. Luigi Buscalioni (1863–?)

Busch, E. Elizabeta Aleksandrovna Busch (1886–1960)
Busch, N. Nikolaï Adol'fovich Busch (1869–1941)
Buse L. H. Buse (1819–1888)
Buser Robert Buser (1857–1931)
Bush Benjamin Franklin Bush (1858–1937)
Butch. Roger William Butcher (1897–1971)
Butler Bertram Theodore Butler (1872–?)
Butters Frederic King Butters (1878–1945)
Butz George C. Butz (1863–1907)
Buxb. Franz Buxbaum (1900–)
Buxt. Bertram Henry Buxton (1852–1934)
Byhouwer Jan Tijs Pieter Byhouwer [Bijhouwer] (1898–1938)
Byles Ronald Stewart Byles (fl. 1957)
Cabr. Angel Lulio Cabrera (1908–)
Caldas Francisco José de Caldas y Tenorio (1771–1816)
Callier Alfons Callier (1866–1927)
Calloni Silvio Calloni (1851–1931)
Calv. Mario Calvino (1875–?)
Camargo, F. Felisberto Cardoso de Carmargo (1896–)
Camb. Jacques Cambessèdes (1799–1863)
Cambage Richard Hind Cambage (1859–1928)
Camus, A. Aimée Antoinette Camus (1879–1965)
Camus, E. Edmond Gustave Camus (1852–1915)
Camp Wendell Holmes Camp (1904–1963)
Canby, M. Margaret Leslie Canby (later Ries, later Funai) (1904–)
Canby, W. William Marriott Canby (1831–1904)
Cantley Nathaniel Cantley (?–1888)
Card Hamilton Hye Card (1877–1953)
Cardenas Martin Cardenas Hermosa (1899–1973)
Carey, J. John Carey (1797–1880)
Carey, W. William Carey (1761–1834)
Cariot Antoine Cariot (1820–1883)
Carlson Margery Claire Carlson (1892–)
Carrière Elie Abel Carrière (1818–1896)
Carruth. William Carruthers (1830–1922)
Carse Harry Carse (1857–1930)
Carter, A. Annetta Mary Carter (1907–)
Carter, W. William R. Carter (fl. 1921)
Caruel Teodoro Caruel (1830–1898)
Casar. Giovanni Casaretto (1812–1879)
Casp. Johann Xaver Robert Caspary (1818–1887)
Cass. Alexandre Henri Gabriel Cassini (1781–1832)
Castagne Jean Louis Martin Castagne (1785–1858)
Castañeda M. Castañeda (fl. 1941)
Castell. Alberto Castellanos (1896–1968)
Castigl. Luigi Castiglioni (1757–1832)
Cav. Antonio José Cavanilles (1745–1804)
Cave George H. Cave (1870–1965)
Cavillier François Georges Cavillier (1868–1953)
Cayeux F. Cayeux (fl. 1921)
Čelak. Ladislav Josep Čelakovsky (1834–1902)
Cels, J. F. Jean François Cels (1810–1888)
Cerv. Vicente Cervantes (1759?–1829)
Chabanne Charles Gabriel Chabanne (1862–1906)
Chabaud J. B. Chabaud (1833–1915)
Chabert Alfred Chabert (1836–1916)
Chadw. Lewis Charles Chadwick (1902–)
Chaix Dominique Chaix (1730–1799)
Chall. Richard Westman Challinor (1871–1951)
Cham. Ludolf Adalbert von Chamisso (1781–1838)
Chamberl. Charles Joseph Chamberlain (1863–1943)
Chambr. Georges de Chambray (1783–1849)
Champ. John George Champion (1815–1854)
Chandl. Harley Pierce Chandler (1875–1918)
Chapm. Alvan Wentworth Chapman (1809–1899)
Charadze Anna Charadze (1905–)
Chase Mary Agnes (Merrill) Chase (1869–1963)
Chatel. Jean Jacques Chatelain (fl. 1760)
Chater Arthur Oliver Chater (1933–)
Chatterj. Debabarta Chatterjee (1911–1960)
Chaub. Louis Anastase Chaubard (1785–1854)
Chav. Édouard Louis Chavannes (1805–1861)
Chaz. Laurent Marie Chazelles de Prizy (fl. 1790)
Cheel Edwin Cheel (1872–1951)
Cheesem. Thomas Frederick Cheeseman (1846–1923)
Cheesm., E. E. Ernest Entwisle Cheesman (1888–)
Chenault Léon Chenault (1853–1930)
Chenev. Paul Chenevard (1839–1919)
Cheng Wan-Chun Cheng (1903–)
Cheval., A. Auguste Jean Baptiste Chevalier (1873–1956)
Cheval., C. Charles Chevalier (fl. 1933–1955)
Chevall. François Fulgis Chevallier (1796–1840)
Chicker. John White Chickering (1831–1913)

Ching Ren-Chang Ching (1899–)
Chiov. Emilio Chiovenda (1871–1940)
Chipp Thomas Ford Chipp (1886–1931)
Chitt. Frederick James Chittenden (1873–1950)
Chodat Robert Hippolyte Chodat (1865–1934)
Choisy Jacques Denis Choisy (1799–1859)
Chouard Pierre Chouard (1903–)
Choux Pierre Choux (1890–)
Chow Hang-fan Chow [Han-fan Chou] (fl. 1934)
Chowdh. Pranatha Kanta Chowdhuri (1923–)
Chr., C. Carl Frederik Albert Christensen (1872–1942)
Christ Konrad Hermann Heinrich Christ (1833–1933)
Christm. Gottlieb Friedrich Christmann (1752–?)
Chun Woon Young Chun (1894–)
Ciferri Raffaele Ciferri (1897–1964)
Clairv. Joseph Philippe de Clairville (1742–1830)
Clapham Arthur Roy Clapham (1904–)
Clapp. Bain Hugh Clapperton (1788–1827)
Clarke, C. B. Charles Baron Clarke (1832–1906)
Clarke, E. D. Edward Daniel Clarke (1779–1822)
Clarke, W. Walter Bosworth Clarke (1879–)
Clarkson, E. Edward Hale Clarkson (1866–1934)
Clarkson, Q. Quentin Deane Clarkson (1925–)
Claus Carl Ernst Claus (1796–1864)
Clausen, J. Jens Christian Clausen (1891–1969)
Clausen, R. T. Robert Theodore Clausen (1911–)
Clayb. Carl Dudley Clayberg (1931–)
Clayt. John Clayton (1685–1773)
Clayt., W. D. William Derek Clayton (1926–)
Clemenc. Clemenceau (fl. 1866–1872)
Clemente Simón de Rojas Clemente y Rubio (1777–1827)
Clementi Giuseppe C. Clementi (1812–1873)
Clements Frederic Edward Clements (1874–1945)
Clokey Ira Waddell Clokey (1878–1950)
Clos Dominique Clos (1821–1908)
Closon Jules Closon (fl. 1897)
Clover Elzada Urseba Clover (1897–)
Clute Willard Nelson Clute (1869–1950)
Cobbold Arthur Cobbold (fl. 1903)
Cochet Charles Cochet (of Montpellier) (fl. 1912)
Cockayne Leonard C. Cockayne (1855–1934)
Cockerell Theodore Dru Alison Cockerell (1866–1948)
Codd Leslie Edward Wastell Codd (1908–)
Coe, E. F. Ernest F. Coe (1867–1951)
Coe, H. S. Howard Sheldon Coe (1888–1918)
Coëm. Henri Eugène Lucien Gaëtan Coëmans (1825–1871)
Cogn. Célestin Alfred Cogniaux (1841–1916)
Cohen-Stuart Combertus Pieter Cohen Stuart (1889–)
Coker William Chambers Coker (1872–1953)
Colebr. Henry Thomas Colebrooke (1765–1837)
Colenso William Colenso (1811–1899)
Colla Luigi Aloysius Colla (1766–1848)
Collad. Louis Théodore Frédéric Colladon (1792–1862)
Collett Henry Collett (1836–1901)
Comber Harold Frederick Comber (1897–)
Combs Robert Combs (1872–1899)
Comes Orazio Comes (1848–1923)
Comm. Philibert Commerson (1727–1773)
Compt. Robert Harold Compton (1886–)
Conard Henry Shoemaker Conard (1874–?)
Conert Hans Joachim Conert (1929–)
Console Michelangelo Console (1812–1897)
Const. Lincoln Constance (1909–)
Coode Mark J. E. Coode (1937–)
Cook, O. F. Orator Fuller Cook (1867–1949)
Coombs Frank Andrew Coombs (1877–1964)
Cooper, J. James Graham Cooper (1830–1902)
Cooper, R. Rowland Edgar Cooper (1891–1962)
Copel., E. Edwin Bingham Copeland (1873–1964)
Copel., H. Herbert Faulkner Copeland (1902–)
Corb. Louis Corbière (1850–1941)
Corda August Carl Joseph Corda (1809–1849)
Cordem. Philippe Eugène Jacob de Cordemoy (1837–1911)
Cornaz Charles Auguste Édouard Cornaz (1825–1911)
Cornelissen Égide Norbert Cornelissen (1769–1849)
Corner Edred John Henry Corner (1906–)
Cornm. John Farnsworth Cornman (1913–)
Cornu Marie Maxime Cornu (1843–1901)
Corr. Carl Franz Joseph Erich Correns (1864–1933)
Corrêa José Francisco Corrêa da Serra (1751–1823)
Correll Donovan Stewart Correll (1908–)
Correv. Louis Henry Correvon (1854–1939)
Cortés Santiago Cortés (1854–1924)

Cory, V. L. Victor Louis Cory (1880–1964)
Coss. Ernest Saint-Charles Cosson (1819–1889)
Costa Antonio Cipriano Costa y Cuxart (1817–1886)
Costantin Julien Noël Costantin (1857–1936)
Coste Hippolyte Jacques Coste (1858–1924)
Cotton Arthur Disbrowe Cotton (1879–1962)
Coult., J. John Merle Coulter (1851–1928)
Coult., T. Thomas Coulter (1793–1843)
Court Arthur Bertram Court (1927–)
Courtin Albert Courtin (fl. 1850–1858)
Courtois Richard Joseph Courtois (1806–1835)
Coutinho António Xavier Pereira Coutinho (1851–1939)
Coutts John Coutts (1872–1952)
Cov. Frederick Vernon Coville (1867–1937)
Cov., J. James Coville (fl. ca. 1820)
Cowan John Macqueen Cowan (1891–1960)
Cowell John Francis Cowell (1852–1915)
Cox Euan Hillhouse Methven Cox (1893–)
Craib William Grant Craib (1882–1933)
Craig, R. T. Robert T. Craig (fl. 1945)
Craig. T. T. Thomas Theodore Craig (1907–)
Craig, W. N. William Nicol Craig (contemp.)
Crantz Heinrich Johann Nepomuk von Crantz (1722–1797)
Crép. François Crépin (1830–1903)
Crevost Charles Crevost (1858–?)
Cripps Cripps (fl. 1876–1880)
Criv. Giuseppe Gabriel Balsamo-Crivelli (1800–1874)
Croiz. Léon Camille Marius Croizat (1894–)
Cronq. Arthur John Cronquist (1919–)
Croom Hardy Bryan Croom (1797–1837)
Crouch. George Croucher (1833–1905)
Crov. Raul Martinez Crovetto (1921–)
Crüger Hermann Crüger (1818–1864)
Cuf. Georg [Giorgio] Cufodontis (1896–)
Cullen James Cullen (1936–)
Cunn., A. Allan Cunningham (1791–1839)
Cunn., A. M. Alida Mabel Cunningham (1868–?)
Cunn., R. Richard Cunningham (1793–1835)
Curran Mary Katharine Curran (later Layne, later Brandegee) (1844–1920)
Curtis William Curtis (1746–1799)
Curtis, C. H. Charles Henry Curtis (1869–1958)
Curtis, M. A. Moses Ashley Curtis (1808–1872)
Cutak Ladislaus Cutak (1908–)
Cutler Hugh Carson Cutler (1912–)
Cyr. Domenico Maria Leone Cyrillo [Cirillo] (1739–1799)
Czerniak. Ekaterina Georgiewna Czerniakowska (1892–)
Dahlgr. Bror Eric Dahlgren (1877–1961)
Dahlst. Hugo Gustaf Adolf Dahlstedt (1856–1934)
Dalla Torre Karl Wilhelm von Dalla Torre (1850–1928)
Dallière Alexis Dallière (1823–1901)
Dallim. William Dallimore (1871–1959)
Dalz. John McEwen Dalziel (1872–1948)
Dalzell Nicol Alexander Dalzell (1817–1878)
Dammer Carl Lebrecht Udo Dammer (1860–1920)
Dams Erich Dams (fl. 1904)
Dandy James Edgar Dandy (1903–)
Danert Siegfried Danert (1926–1973)
Daniel Lucien Louis Daniel (1856–1940)
Daniell William Freeman Daniell (1818–1865)
Daniels Francis Potter Daniels (1869–1947)
Däniker Albert Ulrich Däniker (1894–1957)
Dansereau Pierre Dansereau (1911–)
Darby John Darby (1804–1877)
Darl. Cyril Dean Darlington (1903–)
Darl., J. Josephine Darlington (1905–)
Darn. Anthony William Darnell (1880–)
Darracq Ulysse Darracq (?–1872)
Dauvesse Dauvesse (fl. 1880)
Daveau Jules Alexandre Daveau (1852–1929)
Davenp. George Edward Davenport (1833–1907)
David, A. Armand David (1826–1900)
David, I. Irenée David (1791–1862)
Davidian Hagop Haroutune Davidian (1907–)
Davids., A. Anstruther Davidson (1860–1932)
Davids., J. F. John Fraser Davidson (1911–)
Davies Hugh Davies (1739–1821)
Davis, G. L. Gwenda Louise Rodway Davis (1911–)
Davis, K. C. Kary Cadmus Davis (1867–1936)
Davis, L. D. L. D. Davis (fl. 1878)
Davis, P. H. Peter Hadland Davis (1918–)
Davis, R. J. Ray Joseph Davis (1895–)
Davis, W. T. William Thompson Davis (1862–1945)

Davy Joseph Burtt-Davy (1870–1940)
Dawson Elmer Yale Dawson (1918–1966)
Day John Day (1824–1888)
Dayt. William Adams Dayton (1885–)
DC. Augustin Pyramus de Candolle (1778–1841)
DC., A. Alphonse Louis Pierre Pyramus de Candolle (1806–1893)
DC., C. Anne Casimir Pyramus de Candolle (1836–1918)
Deam Charles Clemon Deam (1865–1953)
Dean Richard Dean (1830–1905)
Deane, H. Henry Deane (1847–1924)
Deane, W. Walter Deane (1848–1930)
Debeaux Jean Odon Debeaux (1826–1910)
De Boer H. W. de Boer (1885–1970)
Debras Édouard Henri Alfred Debras (1889–)
Decary Raymond Decary (ca. 1890–1973)
Decne. Joseph Decaisne (1807–1882)
De Corte C. de Corte (fl. 1909)
Deflers Albert Deflers (1841–1921)
De France Jesse Allison De France (1899–)
Degen Árpád von Degen (1866–1934)
Degener Otto Degener (1899–)
De Haas Th. de Haas (1888–)
Dehnh. Friedrich Dehnhardt (1787–1870)
De Jonghe Jean de Jonghe (1804–1876)
De Lannoy De Lannoy (fl. 1863)
Delar., D. Daniel Delaroche (1743–1813)
Delar., F. François Delaroche (1780–1813)
Delarbre Antoine Delarbre (1724–1813)
De la Sota Elías Ramón de la Sota (1932–)
Delav. Pierre Jean Marie Delavay (1834–1895)
Deleuil J. B. A. Deleuil (fl. 1874)
Delile Alire Raffeneau Delile (1778–1850)
Dematra Dematra (1742–1824)
Denh. Dixon Denham (1786–1828)
Denh., D. L. Dale Lee Denham (1922–)
Denis, T. Thomas Denis (1830–?)
Dennst. August Wilhelm Dennstedt (1776–1826)
De Nob. L. De Nobele (fl. 1893)
De Not. Giuseppe de Notaris (1805–1877)
Deppe Ferdinand Deppe (?–1861)
Derenb. Julius(?) Derenberg (1873–1928)
Derg. Leo Derganc (fl. 1904)
Desb. François Desbois (1827–1902)
Descourt. Michel Étienne Descourtilz (1775–1836)
Déségl. Pierre Alfred Déséglise (1823–1883)
Desf. Réné Louiche Desfontaines (1750–1833)
Desmarais Yves Desmarais (1918–)
De Smet Louis De Smet–Duvivier (1813–1887)
Desmoul. Charles Robert Alexandre Desmoulins (1797–1875)
Desp. Narcisse Henri François Desportes (1776–1856)
Desr. Louis Auguste Joseph Desrousseaux (1753–1838)
Desv. Auguste Nicaise Desvaux (1784–1856)
Detl. LeRoy Ellsworth Detling (1898–)
Devans. Alphonse de la Devansaye (1845–1900)
De Vos Cornelis de Vos (1806–1895)
De Vries Hugo de Vries (1848–1935)
De Vriese Willem Hendrik de Vriese (1806–1862)
De Wild. Émile August Joseph de Wildeman (1866–1947)
De Winter Bernard de Winter (1924–)
De Wit Hendrik Cornelis de Wit (1909–)
DeWolf Gordon Parker DeWolf (1927–)
Dexter Raymond Dexter (fl. 1935)
Dickson, E. Edward Dalzell Dickson (?–1900)
Dickson, G. George Frederick Dickson (fl. 1839)
Didr. Didrik Ferdinand Didrichsen (1814–1887)
Dieck Georg Dieck (1847–1925)
Diels Friedrich Ludwig Emil Diels (1874–1945)
Dierb. Johann Heinrich Dierbach (1788–1845)
Dietr., A. Albert Gottfried Dietrich (1795–1856)
Dietr., D. David Nathanael Friedrich Dietrich ([1799?] 1800–1888)
Dietr., F. Friedrich Gottlieb Dietrich (1765[1768?]–1850)
Dill. Johann Jacob Dillenius [Dillen] (1684–1747)
Dinsm. John Edward Dinsmore (1862–?)
Dinter Moritz Kurt Dinter (1868–1945)
Dipp. Leopold Dippel (1827–1914)
Dixon, W. E. William E. Dixon (fl. 1888)
Dochn. Friedrich Jakob Dochnahl (1820–1904)
Dodds Lionel Dodds (fl. 1937)
Dode Louis Albert Dode (1875–1943)
Dole Eleazor Johnson Dole (1888–)
Döll Johann Christoph Döll (1808–1885)
Dölz Bruno Dölz (?–1945)
Dombey Joseph Dombey (1742–1796)

Dombr. Henry Honywood·Dombrain [D'Ombrain] (1818–1905)
Domin Karel Domin (1882-1953)
Don, D. David Don (1799-1841)
Don, G. George Don (1764-1814)
Don f., G. George Don, the son (1798-1856)
Don, P. P. N. Don (fl. 1845)
Donald John Donald Donald (1923–)
Donck. André Donckelaar [Donkelaar] (1783-1858)
Donn, J. James Donn (1758-1813)
Doorenb., J. J. Doorenbos (1921–)
Dop Paul Louis Dop (1876-?)
Dore William George Dore (1912–)
Dörfl. Ignaz Dörfler (1866-1950)
Dougl. David Douglas (1798-1834)
Dowell Philip Dowell (1864-1936)
Drake Emmanuel Drake del Castillo (1855-1904)
Drap. Pierre Auguste Joseph Drapiez (1778-1856)
Dreer Henry A. Dreer (1818-1873)
Drège Johann Franz Drège (1794-1881)
Drenth Engbert Drenth (1945–)
Drescher Aubrey A. Drescher (1910–)
Dress William John Dress (1918–)
Dressl. Robert Louis Dressler (1927–)
Drew, E. Elmer Reginald Drew (1865-1930)
Drew, W. William Brooks Drew (1908–)
Druce George Claridge Druce (1850-1932)
Drude Carl Georg Oskar Drude (1852-1933)
Drumm., J. James Drummond (1784?-1863)
Drumm., J. R. James Ramsay Drummond (1851-1921)
Drumm., T. Thomas Drummond (1780-1835)
Dryand. Jonas Carlsson Dryander (1748-1810)
Dubard Marcel Marie Maurice Dubard (died ca. 1914-1918)
Duby Jean Étienne Duby (1798-1885)
Duchartre Pierre Étienne Simon Duchartre (1811-1894)
Duchass. Édouard Placide Duchassaing de Fontbressin ([1815?]1818-1873)
Duchesne Antoine Nicolas Duchesne (1747-1827)
Ducke Walter Adolpho Ducke (1876-1959)
Dudl., M. Margaret Gertrude Dudley (1888–)
Dudl., T. Theodore Robert Dudley (1936–)
Dudl., W. William Russel Dudley (1849-1911)
Düesb. Walter Düesberg (fl. 1890)
Dufour Jean Marie Léon Dufour (1780-1865)
Dufr. Pierre Dufresne (1786-1836)
Dug. Armando Dugand (1906-1971)
Duh. Henri Louis Duhamel de Monceau (1700-1781)
Dulac Joseph Dulac (fl. 1867)
Dum.-Cours. George Louis Marie Dumont de Courset (1746-1824)
Dümmer Richard Arnold Dummer (né Dümmer) (1887-1922)
Dumort. Barthélemy Charles Joseph Dumortier (1797-1878)
Dunal Michel Felix Dunal (1789-1856)
Duncan, J. James Duncan (1802-1876)
Duncan, W. Wilbur Howard Duncan (1910–)
Dunkle Meryl Byron Dunkle (1888–)
Dunn, D. David Baxter Dunn (1917–)
Dunn, S. T. Stephen Troyte Dunn (1868-1938)
Dunst. Galfrid Clement Keyworth Dunsterville (1905–)
Dup.-Jam. F. N. Dupuy-Jamain (1817-1888)
Durand, E. Elias Magloire Durand (1794-1873)
Durand, T. Theophile Alexis Durand (1855-1912)
Durande Jean François Durande (1730-1794)
Durazz. Antonio Durazzini (fl. ca. 1772)
Durieu Michel Charles Durieu de Maisonneuve (1796-1878)
Du Roi Johann Philipp Du Roi (1741-1785)
D'Urv. Jules Sébastien César Dumont D'Urville (1790-1842)
Dusén Per Karl Hjalmar Dusén (1855-1926)
Duthie John Firminger Duthie (1845-1922)
Dutrie Louis Dutrie (fl. 1939)
Duval, C. Charles Jeunet Duval (1751-1828)
Duval, H. Henri Auguste Duval (1777-1814)
Dyb. Jean Dybowski [Dybowsky] (1855-1928)
Dyer William Turner Thiselton-Dyer (1843-1928)
Dyer, R. A. Robert Allen Dyer (1900–)
Dykes William Rickatson Dykes (1877-1925)
Eade George William Eade (1905–)
Eames, A. J. Arthur Johnson Eames (1881-1969)
Eames, E. A. Edward Ashley Eames (1872-?)
Eastw. Alice Eastwood (1859-1953)
Eat. Amos Eaton (1776-1842)
Eat., A. A. Alvah Augustus Eaton (1865-1908)
Eat., D. C. Daniel Cady Eaton (1834-1895)
Ebel Paul Wilhelm Sosistheus Eugen Ebel (1815-1884)
Eberm. Carl Heinrich Ebermaier (1802-1870)

Ebing. John Edwin Ebinger (1933–)
Eckl. Christian Friedrich Ecklon (1795-1868)
Eddy Caspar Wistar Eddy (1790-1828)
Edgew. Michael Pakenham Edgeworth (1812-1881)
Edw., A. Alexander Edwards (1904–)
Edw., S. T. Sydenham Teast Edwards (1769-1819)
Eggl. Willard Webster Eggleston (1863-1935)
Ehrenb., C. A. Carl August Ehrenberg (1801-1849)
Ehrenb., C. G. Christian Gottfried Ehrenberg (1795-1876)
Ehrend. Friedrich [Fritz von] Ehrendorfer (1927–)
Ehrh., B. Johann Balthasar Ehrhart (1700-1756)
Ehrh., J. F. J. Friedrich Ehrhart (1742-1795)
Eichl. August Wilhelm Eichler (1839-1887)
Eichlam Friedrich [Federico] Eichlam (?-1911)
Ekm. Erik Leonard Ekman (1883-1931)
Elkan Louis Elkan (1815-1850)
Elliott Stephen Elliott (1771-1830)
Ellis John Ellis (ca. 1710-1776)
Ellw. George Ellwanger (1816-1906)
Elmer Adolph Daniel Edward Elmer (1870-1942)
Elmig. Joseph Elmiger (1790-1859)
Elwes Henry John Elwes (1846-1922)
Emberger Marie Louis Emberger (1897-1969)
Emeric Emeric (fl. ca. 1828)
Encke Fritz Encke (1861-1931)
Endl. Stephen Friedrich Ladislaus Endlicher (1804-1849)
Endres A. R. Endres (?-1877)
Engelm. George Engelmann (1809-1884)
Engl. Heinrich Gustav Adolph Engler (1844-1930)
Engl., V. Victor Engler (1885-1917)
English Carl Schurz English (1904–)
Epl. Carl Clawson Epling (1894-1968)
Epple Paul Epple (fl. 1951)
Erickson Ralph Orlando Erickson (1914–)
Eschsch. Johann Friedrich Eschscholtz (1793-1831)
Espinosa Marcial Ramon Espinosa-Bustos (1874-1959)
Essig Frederick Burt Essig (1947–)
Etling. Andreas Ernst Etlinger (fl. 1777)
Evans, M. Maurice Smethurst Evans (1854-?)
Evans, W. E. William Edgar Evans (ca. 1897-1940)
Evans, W. H. Walter Harrison Evans (1863-1941)
Everett, T. H. Thomas Henry Everett (1903–)
Eversm. Eduard Friedrich Eversmann (1794-1860)
Ewan Joseph Andorfer Ewan (1909–)
Ewart Alfred James Ewart (1872-1937)
Exell Arthur Wallis Exell (1901–)
Eyst. William Henry Eyster (1889–)
Fabr. Philipp Conrad Fabricius (1714-1774)
Facch. Francesco Facchini (1788-1852)
Farden, R. Richard S. Farden (?-1950)
Farq. John Keith Marshall Lang Farquhar (1858-1921)
Farr Edith May Farr (1864-1956)
Farrer Reginald John Farrer (1880-1920)
Farringt. Edward Irving Farrington (1876-?)
Farw. Oliver Atkins Farwell (1867-1944)
Fassett Norman Carter Fassett (1900-1954)
Favrat Louis Favrat (1827-1893)
Fawc. William Fawcett (1851-1926)
Fedde Friedrich Karl Georg Fedde (1873-1942)
Fedorov Andreĭ Aleksandrovich Fedorov (1908–)
Fedtsch., B. Boris Alekseevich Fedtschenko [Fedchenko] (1872 [1873?]-1947)
Fedtsch., O. Ol'ga Aleksandrovna (née Armfeld) Fedtschenko [Fedchenko] (1845-1921)
Fée Antoine Laurent Apollinaire Fée (1789-1874)
Feer Heinrich Feer (1857-1892)
Fenzi Emanuele Orazio Fenzi [same as Francesco Franceschi] (1843-1924)
Fenzl Eduard Fenzl (1808-1879)
Fern. Merritt Lyndon Fernald (1873-1950)
Fernand., A. Abílio Fernandes (1906–)
Fern.-Vill. Celestino Fernandez-Villar (1838-1907)
Ferrero Ferrero (fl. ca. 1821)
Ferris Roxana Judkins (née Stinchfield) Ferris (1895–)
Ferriss James Henry Ferriss (1849-1926)
Fiala Franz Fiala (1861-1898)
Ficalho Francisco Manoel Carlos de Mello de Ficalho (1837-1903)
Fielding Henry Barron Fielding (1805-1851)
Finet Achille Eugène Finet (1863-1913)
Fingerh. Karl Anton Fingerhuth (1802-1876)
Fiori Adriano Fiori (1865-1950)
Fisch. Friedrich Ernst Ludwig von Fischer (1782-1854)
Fisch., C. E. Cecil Ernest Claude Fischer (1874-1950)

Fisch., G. Gustav Fischer (1889–)
Fisher, E. Elmon McLean Fisher (1861–1938)
Fisher, T. R. Tharl Richard Fisher (1921–)
Fitschen Jost Fitschen (1869–1947)
Fitzg., R. Robert Desmond Fitzgerald (1830–1892)
Fitzg., W. William Vincent Fitzgerald (?–1929)
Fitzh. S. Wyndham Fitzherbert (?–1916)
Flem. John Fleming (?–1815)
Fletch., H. R. Harold Roy Fletcher (1907–)
Floerke Heinrich Gustav Floerke (1764–1835)
Florin Carl Rudolf Florin (1894–1965)
Floto Ernst Vilhelm Floto (1902–)
Flügge Johann Flügge (1775–1816)
Focke Wilhelm Olbers Focke (1834–1922)
Foëx Gustave Louis Foëx (1844–1906)
Fomin Aleksandr Vasil'evich Fomin (1869–1935)
Font Quer Pio Font Quer (1888–1964)
Forbes, F. Francis Blackwell Forbes (1839–1908)
Forbes, J. James Forbes (1773–1861)
Ford Neridah Clifton Ford (fl. 1950)
Foret James Aloysius Foret (1921–)
Form. Eduard Formánek (1845–1900)
Forr. George Forrest (1873–1932)
Fors N. S. Fors (fl. before 1828)
Forssk. Petrus [Pehr] Forsskål [Forskål] (1732–1763)
Först., C. F. Carl Friedrich Förster (fl. 1846–1861)
Forst., E. Edward Forster (1765–1849)
Forst., G. Johann Georg Adam Forster (1754–1794)
Forst., J. R. Johann Reinhold Forster (1729–1798)
Först., K. Karl Förster (1874–?)
Forst., T. F. Thomas Furley Forster (1761–1825)
Fort. Robert Fortune (1812–1880)
Fosb. Francis Raymond Fosberg (1908–)
Foster, M. Michael Foster (1836–1907)
Foster, M. B. Mulford Bateman Foster (1888–)
Foster, R. Robert Crichton Foster (1904–)
Fotsch Karl Albert Fotsch (?–1940)
Foucaud Julien Foucaud (1847–1904)
Foucault Emmanuel de Foucault (fl. 1813)
Foug. Auguste Denis Fougeroux de Bondaroy (1732–1789)
Fourc. Henri Georges [Henry George] Fourcade (?–1948)
Fourn., E. Eugène Pierre Nicolas Fournier (1834–1884)
Fourr. Pierre Jules Fourreau (1844–1871)
Foxw. Frederick William Foxworthy (1877–1950)
Frahm G. Frahm (fl. 1898)
Franceschi Francesco Franceschi [same as Emanuele Orazio Fenzi] (1843–1924)
Franch. Adrien René Franchet (1834–1900)
Franco João Manuel Antonio Paes do Amaral Franco (1921–)
Frapp. Charles Frappier (fl. 1853–1883)
Fraser, C. Charles Fraser (ca. 1788–1831)
Fraser, G. George Fraser (1854–?)
Fraser, H. Hugh Fraser (1834–1904)
Fraser, J. John Fraser (1750–1811)
Fraser, S. Samuel Victorian Fraser (1890–)
Freem., G. George Fouché Freeman (1876–1930)
Freem., O. Oliver Myles Freeman (1891–)
Frém. John Charles Frémont (1813–1890)
Fresen. Johann Baptist Georg Wolfgang Fresenius (1808–1866)
Freyer Heinrich Freyer (1802–1866)
Freyn Josef Franz Freyn (1845–1903)
Frič Alberto V. Frič (1882–1944)
Frick Gustav Adolph Frick (1878–?)
Fries Elias Magnus Fries (1794–1878)
Fries, R. E. Klas Robert Elias Fries (1876–1966)
Fries, T. C. E. Thore Christian Elias Fries (1886–1930)
Fries, Th. Theodor Magnus Fries (1832–1913)
Frikart Carl Ludwig Frikart (1879–1964)
Fritsch Karl Fritsch (1864–1934)
Friv. Emmerich Frivaldszky von Frivald (1799–1870)
Fröd. Harold August Fröderström (1876–1944)
Froeb. Karl Otto Froebel (1844–1906)
Froehn. Albrecht Froehner (fl. 1897)
Froel. Joseph Aloys Froelich (1766–1841)
Frost John Frost (1803–1840)
Fruw. Karl Fruwirth (1862–1930)
Frye Theodore Christian Frye (1869–1962)
Fryx. Paul Arnold Fryxell (1927–)
Fuchs, H. P. Hans Peter Fuchs (1928–)
Fuller Albert Morse Fuller (1899–)
Funck Heinrich Christian Funck (1771–1839)
Furtado Caetano Xavier Dos Remedios Furtado (1897–)
Fuss Johann Michael Fuss (1814–1883)

Gable Joseph Benson Gable (1886–1972)
Gabr. Ira Noel Gabrielson (1889–)
Gaertn. Joseph Gaertner (1732–1791)
Gaertn., C. F. Carl Friederich von Gaertner (1772–1850)
Gaertn., P. Philipp Gottfried Gaertner (1754–1825)
Gagnep. François Gagnepain (1866–1952)
Gail Floyd Whitney Gail (1884–)
Gaillardot Charles Gaillardot (1814–1883)
Gaiser Lulu Odell Gaiser (1896–1965)
Galeotti Henri Guillaume Galeotti (1814–1858)
Gallerand R. Gallerand (fl. 1904)
Galpin Ernest Edward Galpin (1858–1941)
Gamble James Sykes Gamble (1847–1925)
Gams Helmut Gams (1893–)
Gand. Michel Gandoger (1850–1926)
Garay Leslie Andrew Garay (1924–)
Garcke Friedrich August Garcke (1819–1904)
Gard. Alexander Garden (1730–1791)
Gard., J. Joy Garden (1923–)
Gardn., C. Charles Austin Gardner (1896–)
Gardn., G. George Gardner (1812–1849)
Garn. Max Garnier (fl. 1895–1918)
Garrett Albert Osbun Garrett (1870–1948)
Gars. François Alexandre Pierre de Garsault (1691–1778)
Gasparr. Gulielmo Gasparrini (1804–1866)
Gastony Gerald Joseph Gastony (1940–)
Gater. Gaterau (fl. 1789)
Gates, H. E. Howard Elliott Gates (1889–1957)
Gates, R. R. Reginald Ruggles Gates (1882–1962)
Gatt. August Gattinger (1825–1903)
Gaud.-Beaup. Charles Gaudichaud-Beaupré (1789–1854)
Gaudin Jean François Aimé Gottlieb Philippe Gaudin (1766–1833)
Gay, C. Claude Gay (1800–1873)
Gay, J. Jacques Étienne Gay (1786–1864)
Gáyer Gyula Gáyer (1883–1932)
Gentil Louis Gentil (1874–1949)
Gentry Howard Scott Gentry (1903–)
Gentry, A. Alwyn Howard Gentry (1945–)
Georgi Johann Gottlieb Georgi (1729–1802)
Germ. Jacques Nicolas Ernest Germain de Saint-Pierre (1815–1882)
Gérôme Joseph Gérôme (1863–1928)
Gerr. William Tyrer Gerrard (?–1866)
Geyer Carl Andreas Geyer (1809–1853)
Gheld. Constantin Gheldolf (fl. 1845)
Ghiesbr. August Boniface Ghiesbreght (1810–1893)
Ghose Birendra Nath Ghose (1885–)
Gaicom. Valerio Giacomini (1914–)
Gibbs, L. Lilian Suzette Gibbs (1870–1925)
Gibbs, V. Vicary Gibbs (1853–1932)
Gibelli Giuseppe Gibelli (1831–1898)
Gibs., A. Alexander Gibson (1800–1867)
Gibs., D. Dorothy Nash Gibson (1921–)
Gibs., F. Frederick Gibson (1892–1953)
Gilb. Benjamin Davis Gilbert (1835–1907)
Gilg Ernst Friedrich Gilg (1867–1933)
Gilib. Jean Emmanuel Gilibert (1741–1814)
Gillek. Leopold Guillaume Gillekens (1833–1905)
Gillett, G. W. George Willson Gillett (1917–1976)
Gillett, J. B. Jan Bevington Gillett (1911–)
Gillett, J. M. John Montague Gillett (1918–)
Gillies John Gillies (1747–1836)
Gillis William Thomas Gillis (1933–)
Gilly Charles Louis Gilly (1911–1970)
Gilm. John Scott Lennox Gilmour (1906–)
Ging. Frédéric Charles Jean Gingins de Lassaraz (1790–1863)
Giord. Ferdinando Giordano (fl. early 19th cent.)
Girard Frédéric de Girard (1810–1851)
Giseke Paul Dietrich Giseke (1741[1745?]–1796)
Glazebr. Thomas Kirkland Glazebrook (1780–1885)
Glaziou Auguste François Marie Glaziou (1828–1906)
Gleason Henry Allan Gleason (1882–1975)
Gled. Johann Gottlieb Gleditsch (1714–1786)
Glogau Arthur Glogau (fl. 1928)
Glox. Benjamin Peter Gloxin (fl. 1785)
Gmel., C. C. Carl Christian Gmelin (1762–1837)
Gmel., J. F. Johann Friedrich Gmelin (1748–1804)
Gmel., J. G. Johann Georg Gmelin (1709–1755)
Gmel., S. G. Samuel Gottlieb Gmelin (1744 or 1745–1774)
Godefr. Alexandre Godefroy-Lebeuf (1852–1903)
Godet Charlet Henry Godet (1797–1879)
Godfr., C. C. Charles Cartlidge Godfrey (1855–1927)
Godfr., R. K. Robert Kenneth Godfrey (1911–)
Godr. Dominique Alexandre Godron (1807–1880)

Goeb. Karl Christian Traugott Goebel (1794–1851)
Goeschke Franz Goeschke (1844–1912)
Goeze Edmund Goeze (1838–1929)
Goldb. Karl Ludwig Goldbach (1793–1824)
Goldie, J. John Goldie (1793–1886)
Goldr. William Goldring (1854–1919)
Gomb. Endré Gombócz (1822–1945)
Gomes Bernardino Antonio Gomes [Gomez] (1769–1823)
Good, R. Ronald D'Oyley Good (1896–)
Goodd., C. Charlotte Olive Goodding (later Reeder) (1916–)
Goodd., L. Leslie Newton Goodding (1880–)
Goodsp. Thomas Harper Goodspeed (1887–)
Göpp. [Johann] Heinrich Robert Göppert (1800–1884)
Gord. George Gordon (1806–1879)
Gorshchk. Sofiâ Gennad'evna Gorshchkova [Gorschkova] (1889–)
Gosse Philip Henry Gosse (1810–1888)
Gouan Antoine Gouan (1733–1821)
Gouas Léon Gouas (fl. 1858)
Goujon Joseph Goujon (1858–?)
Gould Frank W. Gould (1913–)
Gouws Jozef Benjamin Gouws (1909–)
Gowen James Robert Gowen (?–1862)
Gower William Hugh Gower (1835–1894)
Grab. Heinrich Emanuel Grabowski [Grabowsky] (1792–1842)
Graebener Leopold Graebener (1849–?)
Graebn. Karl Otto Robert Peter Paul Graebner (1871–1933)
Graf, F. Ferdinand Graf (1833–1877)
Grah., R. C. Robert C. Graham (1786–1845)
Grant, A. D. Alva (née Day) (Hansen) Grant (later Whittingham) (1920–)
Grant, A. L. Adele Gerard (née Lewis) Grant (1881–)
Grant, G. B. George Bernard Grant (1849–1917)
Grant, V. E. Verne Edwin Grant (1917–)
Grau Hans Rudolph Jürke Grau (1937–)
Grauer Sebastian Grauer (1758–1820)
Gray, A. Asa Gray (1810–1888)
Gray, S. F. Samuel Frederick Gray (1776–1828)
Greb. Igor Segeevich Grebenshchikov [Grebenščikov] (1912–)
Grec. Demetrius Grecescu (1841–1910)
Green, M. L. Mary Letitia Green (later Sprague) (1886–)
Green, P. S. Peter Shaw Green (1920–)
Greene Edward Lee Greene (1843–1915)
Greenm. Jesse More Greenman (1867–1951)
Grembl. P. Julius Gremblich (1851–1905)
Gremli August Gremli (1833–1899)
Gren. Jean Charles Marie Grenier (1808–1875)
Grev. Robert Kaye Greville (1794–1866)
Grey Charles Hervey Grey (1875–?)
Grierson Andrew J. C. Grierson (1929–)
Griff. William Griffith (1810–1845)
Griffiths David Griffiths (1867–1935)
Griggs Robert Fiske Griggs (1881–1962)
Grign. G. T. Grignan (fl. 1900)
Grimm Johann Friedrich Carl Grimm (1737–1821)
Gris Jean Antoine Arthur Gris (1829–1872)
Grisc. Ludlow Griscom (1890–1959)
Griseb. August Heinrich Rudolf Grisebach (1814–1879)
Groenl. Johannes Groenland (1824–1891)
Gronov. Jan Fredrik [Joannes Fridericus] Gronovius (1690–1762)
Grootend. Herman Johannes Grootendorst (1911–)
Grosd. Charles Grosdemange (fl. 1893–1897)
Grosser Wilhelm Carl Heinrich Grosser (1869–?)
Grossh. Aleksandr Al'fonsovich Grossheim (1888–1948)
Grove Arthur Grove (1865–1942)
Grubov Valerii Ivanovich Grubov (1917–)
Gueldenst. Johann Anton von Gueldenstaedt (1745–1781)
Guers. L. B. Guersent (1776–1848)
Guillaum. André Guillaumin (1855–1952)
Guillem. Jean Baptiste Antoine Guillemin (1796–1842)
Guillon Pierre Anatole Guillon (1819–1908)
Guilm. Gustave Guilmot (1818–1885)
Guimpel Friedrich Guimpel (1774–1839)
Guinea Emilio Guinea-López (1907–)
Gumbl. William Edward Gumbleton (1830–1911)
Gunnarss. Johan Gottfrid Gunnarsson (1866–1944)
Gunnerus Johann Ernst Gunnerus (1718–1773)
Gürke Robert Louis August Max Gürke (1854–1911)
Gusmus Hermann Gusmus (1843–?)
Guss. Giovanni Gussone (1787–1866)
Haage Johann Nicolaus Haage (1826–1872)
Haage, jr., F. A. Friedrich Adolph Haage, jr. (1796–1866)
Haage, Ferd. Ferdinand Haage (1859–1930)
Hack. Eduard Hackel (1850–1926)

Hacq. Balthasar Hacquet (1739–1815)
Haenke Thaddaeus Haenke (1761–1817)
Hagerup Olaf Hagerup (1889–1961)
Hahne August Hermann Hahne (1873–?)
Haines, A. A. Adelbert Lee Haines (1915–)
Haines, H. Henry Haselfoot Haines (1867–1943)
Halácsy Eugen von Halácsy (1842–1913)
Hall, A. D. Alfred Daniel Hall (1864– ?)
Hall, C. Edwin Cuthbert Hall (1874–1953)
Hall, C. C. Carlotta Case Hall (1880–1949)
Hall, H. M. Harvey Monroe Hall (1874–1932)
Hall, W. William Hall (1743–1800)
Haller Albrecht [Albert] von Haller (1708–1777)
Haller f. Albrecht von Haller (1758–1823)
Hallier, E. Ernst Hallier (1831–1904)
Hallier, H. G. Hans Gottfried Hallier (1868–1932)
Hamet Raymond Hamet (1890–)
Hamilt., A. Arthur Hamilton (fl. 1832)
Hamilt., W. S. W. S. Hamilton (fl. 1885)
Hampe Georg Ernst Ludwig Hampe (1795–1880)
Hanb., F. J. Fredrick Janson Hanbury (1851–1938)
Hance Henry Fletcher Hance (1827–1886)
Hand.-Mazz. Heinrich von Handel-Mazzetti (1862–1940)
Handro Oswaldo Handro (1908–)
Hanks Lenda Tracy Hanks (1879–1944)
Hann. Lester Stuart Hannibal (1906–)
Hansen, C. Carl Hansen (1848–1903)
Hansen, N. E. Niels Ebbesen Hansen (1866– ?)
Hanson Peter Hanson (ca. 1824–1887)
Hanst. Johannes Ludwig Emil Robert von Hanstein (1822–1880)
Hao Kin-shen Hao [Ching-shêng Ho] (fl. 1931–1936)
Hara Hiroshi Hara (1911–)
Harb. Thomas Grant Harbison (1862–1936)
Hardin James Walker Hardin (1929–)
Hardw. Thomas Hardwicke (1757–1833)
Hare Raleigh Frederick Hare (1870–1934)
Hariot Paul Auguste Hariot (1854–1917)
Harkn. Bernard Emerson Harkness (1907–)
Harling Gunnar Wilhelm Harling (1920–)
Harms Hermann August Theodor Harms (1870–1942)
Harms, V. L. Vernon Lee Harms (1930–)
Harper, F. Francis Harper (1886–)
Harper, R. M. Roland Macmillan Harper (1878–1966)
Harris, W. William Harris (1860–1920)
Harrison, S. G. Sydney Gerald Harrison (1924–)
Harrow, R. Robert Lewis Harrow (1867–1954)
Harrow, W. William Harrow (1861–1945)
Hartig, T. Theodor Hartig (1805–1880)
Hartinger Anton Hartinger (1806–1890)
Hartland W. Baylor Hartland (fl. 1903)
Hartm. Carl Johan Hartman (1790–1849)
Hartm., E. E. Hartmann (fl. 1904)
Hartweg Karl Theodor Hartweg (1812–1871)
Hartwig August Karl Julius Hartwig (1823–1913)
Hartwiss Nicolai von Hartwiss (1791–1860)
Harv. William Henry Harvey (1811–1866)
Harv., M. Margaret Harvey (later Dildine) (1919–)
Hassk. Justus Carl Hasskarl (1811–1894)
Hassl. Emil [Emilio] Hassler (1864–1937)
Hatus. Sumihiko Hatusima (1906–)
Haum. Lucien Hauman (1880–1965)
Hausm. Franz von Hausmann (1810–1878)
Hausskn. Heinrich Karl Haussknecht (1838–1903)
Haw. Adrian Hardy Haworth (1768–1833)
Hawkes Alex Drum Hawkes (1927–)
Hay, T. Thomas Hay (1875–1953)
Hayata Bunzo Hayata (1874–1934)
Hayek August von Hayek (1871–1928)
Hayne Friedrich Gottlob Hayne (1763–1832)
Hayw. Wyndham Hayward (ca. 1903–)
HBK Friedrich Wilhelm Heinrich Alexander von Humboldt, Aimé Jacques Alexandre Bonpland, & Carl Sigismund Kunth
Hedl. Johan Theodor Hedlund (1861–1953)
Hedr. Ulysses Prentiss Hedrick (1870–1951)
Hedw., J. Johann Hedwig (1730–1799)
Hedw., R. Romanus Adolf Hedwig (1772–1806)
Heer Oswald Heer (1809–1883)
Heese Emil Heese (1862–1914)
Hegelm. Christoph Friedrich Hegelmaier (1833–1906)
Hegetschw. Johannes Jacob Hegetschweiler-Bodmer (1789–1839)
Hegi Gustav Hegi (1876–1932)
Heimerl Anton Heimerl (1857–1942)
Heiser Charles Bixler Heiser (1920–)

Heist. Lorenz Heister (1683–1758)
Heldr. Theodor von Heldreich (1822–1902)
Heller Franz Xaver Heller (1775–1840)
Heller, A. Amos Arthur Heller (1867–1944)
Helm, J. Hermann Wilhelm Johannes Helm (1906–)
Hemsl. William Botting Hemsley (1843–1924)
Henckel Leo Victor Felix Henckel von Donnersmarck (1785–1861)
Henders., A. Andrew Henderson (fl. 1857–1864)
Henders., E. G. Edward George Henderson (fl. 1857–1864)
Henders., L. F. Louis Forniquet Henderson (1853–1942)
Henders., M. D. Mayda D. Henderson (1928–)
Henders., M. R. Murray Ross Henderson (1899–)
Henfr. Arthur Henfrey (1819–1859)
Henkel Johann Baptist Henkel (1815–1871)
Henkel, H. Heinrich Henkel (fl. 1897–1914)
Hennings Paul Christoph Hennings (1841–1908)
Hénon Jacques-Louis Hénon (1802–1872)
Henriq. Julio Augusto Henriques (1838–1928)
Henry, A. Augustine Henry (1857–1930)
Henry, J. Joseph Kaye Henry (1866–1930)
Henry, L. Louis Henry (1853–1903)
Henry, L. K. LeRoy Kershaw Henry (1905–)
Henry, M. Mary Gibson Henry (1884–1967)
Henschel August Wilhelm Eduard Theodor Henschel (1790–1856)
Henschen Salomon Eberhard Henschen (1847–1930)
Hensl. John Stevens Henslow (1796–1861)
Hentze Wilhelm Hentze (1793–1874)
Hepper Frank Nigel Hepper (1929–)
Herb. William Herbert (1778–1847)
Herb., D. A. Desmond Andrew Herbert (fl. 1921–1963)
Herbich Franz Herbich (1791–1865)
Herder Ferdinand Godfried Theobald Maximilian von Herder (1828–1896)
Hérincq François Hérincq (1820–1891)
Herm., F. Friedrich Hermann (1873– ?)
Herm., F. J. Frederick Joseph Hermann (1906–)
Hernández Xoloc. Efraim Ildefonso Hernández-Xolocotzi Guzman (1913–)
Herrera Fortunato Luciano Herrera y Garmendia (1875–1945)
Herrm., J. Johann Herrmann (1738–1800)
Herter Wilhelm Gustav Herter (1884–1958)
Hesl.-Harr. John William Heslop Harrison (1881–1967)
Hesse Hermann Albrecht Hesse (1852–1937)
Hester J. Pinkney Hester (fl. 1943)
Heuff. Johann Heuffel (1800–1857)
Heydt Adam Heydt (fl. 1932)
Heyne, B. Benjamin Heyne (? –1819)
Heyne, K. Karel Heyne (1877–1944)
Heynh. Gustav Heynhold (fl. 1828–1850)
Heyw. Vernon Hilton Heywood (1927–)
Hibb. James Shirley Hibberd (1825–1890)
Hickel Paul Robert Hickel (1865–1935)
Hicken Cristóbal Maria Hicken (1875–1933)
Hiern William Philip Hiern (1839–1925)
Hieron. Georg Hans Emo Wolfgang Hieronymus (1846–1921)
Higgins Vera Higgins (1892–1968)
Hiit. Henrik Ilmari Augustus Hiitonen (earlier Hidén) (1898–)
Hildebrand Friedrich Hermann Gustav Hildebrand (1835–1915)
Hildebrandt Johann Maria Hildebrandt (1847–1881)
Hildm. H. Hildmann (? –1895)
Hilg. Theodore Charles Hilgard (1828–1875)
Hill, A. F. Albert Frederick Hill (1889–)
Hill, A. W. Arthur William Hill (1875–1941)
Hill, E. J. Ellsworth Jerome Hill (1833–1917)
Hill, J. John Hill (1716–1775)
Hill, W. Walter Hill (1820–1904)
Hillebr. Wilhelm Hillebrand (1821–1886)
Hilliard Olive Mary Hilliard (1925–)
Hilsenb. Carl Theodor Hilsenberg (1802–1824)
Hitchc., A. S. Albert Spear Hitchcock (1865–1935)
Hitchc., C. L. Charles Leo Hitchcock (1902–)
Hitchc., E. Edward Hitchcock (1793–1864)
Hjelmqv. Karl Jesper Hakon Hjelmqvist (1905–)
Hochr. Bénédict Pierre Georges Hochreutiner (1873–1959)
Hochst. Christian Ferdinand Hochstetter (1787–1860)
Hochst., W. Wilhelm Christian Hochstetter (1825–1881)
Hodge Walter Henricks Hodge (1912–)
Hoefk. Hinrich Hoefker (1859–1945)
Hoehne Frederico Carlos Hoehne (1882–1959)
Hoess Franz Hoess (1756–1840)
Hoffm. Georg Franz Hoffmann (1761–1826)
Hoffm., F. Ferdinand Hoffmann (1860–1914)
Hoffm., J. Johann Joseph Hoffmann (1805–1878)

Hoffm., K. Käthe Hoffmann (fl. 1910–1931)
Hoffm., O. Karl August Otto Hoffmann (1853–1909)
Hoffm., R. Ralph Hoffman (1870–1932)
Hoffmanns. Johann Centurius von Hoffmansegg (1766–1849)
Hoffmeister Werner Hoffmeister (1819–1845)
Hogg Robert Hogg (1818–1897)
Hohen. Rudolph Friedrich Hohenacker (1798–1874)
Holland John Henry Holland (1869–1950)
Holm, H. T. Herman Theodor Holm (1854–1932)
Holm, R. W. Richard William Holm (1925–)
Holm, T. T. Holm (1880–1943)
Holmb. Jens Holmboe (1880–1943)
Holmes Edward Morell Holmes (1843–1930)
Holmsk. Theodor Holmskjold (1732–1794)
Holtt. Richard Eric Holttum (1895–)
Holub, J. Josef Holub (1930–)
Holzing. John Michael Holzinger (1853–1929)
Honck. Gerhard August Honckeny (1724–1805)
Honda Masaji Honda (1897–)
Hoog, J. M. C. Johannes Marius Cornelis [John] Hoog (1865–1950)
Hoog, T. Thomas Hoog (1899–)
Hooibr. Danield Hooibrenk (fl. 1848–1861)
Hook. William Jackson Hooker (1785–1865)
Hook. f. Joseph Dalton Hooker (1817–1911)
Hoover Robert Francis Hoover (1913–1970)
Hoopes Josiah Hoopes (1832–1904)
Hope John Hope (1725–1786)
Hopffer Carl Hopffer (1810–)
Hopk., L. S. Lewis Sylvester Hopkins (1872–1945)
Hopk., M. Milton Hopkins (1906–)
Hoppe David Heinrich Hoppe (1760–1846)
Horan. Pavel Fedorovich Horaninov [Horaninow, Ghorfaninov, Gorianinow] (1796–1865)
Horkel Johann Horkel (1769–1846)
Hornem. Jens Wilken Hornemann (1770–1841)
Hornibr. Murray Hornibrook (1874–1949)
Hornst. Claës [Claudius] Frederic Hornstedt (1758–1809)
Horsey Richard Edgar Horsey (1883–1972)
Hort. *Hortorum* (of gardens) or *hortulanorum* (of gardeners). Indicates a plant name that is used by horticulturists but has no botanical standing. When followed by a personal name, it stands for *horti* (of the garden of) and usually indicates a plant name published in a catalogue of a nursery firm.
Hort. A. Blanc A. Blanc & Co. Philadelphia, Penn. Late 19th century.
Hort. Allw. Allwood Bros. Haywards Heath, Eng. First half 20th century.
Hort. Backh. James Backhouse & Son, later Backhouse Nurseries Ltd. York, Eng. 19th and early 20th centuries.
Hort. Barbier Barbier & Cie. Orleans, France. Late 19th to early 20th century.
Hort. Barr & Sugden Barr & Sugden, later Barr & Son, later Barr & Sons. London, Eng. Latter half 19th to first half 20th century.
Hort. Bobbink & Atkins Bobbink & Atkins. Rutherford, N.J. Established 1898, to first half 20th century.
Hort. Booth James Booth, later James Booth & Söhne. Flottbeck (Hamburg), Germany. Late 18th to 19th century.
Hort. Burkw. & Skipw. Burkwood and Skipwith Ltd. Kingston-on-Thames, Eng. Mid-20th century.
Hort. Cayeux & Le Clerc Cayeux & Le Clerc. Paris, France. Early 20th century.
Hort. Cels Cels Frères. Paris, France. Late 18th to late 19th century.
Hort. Charlesworth Charlesworth & Co. Ltd. Haywards Heath, Sussex, Eng. Late 19th to early 20th century.
Hort. Croux Croux et Fils, later Croux Fils. Châtenay-Malabry, France. 19th to first half 20th century.
Hort. Dammann Dammann & Co. San Giovanni a Teduccio (Naples), Italy. Established 1877, to early 20th century.
Hort. De Smet De Smet Frères. Ghent, Belgium. Late 19th century.
Hort. Dicksons Dicksons Ltd., later Dicksons Nurseries Ltd. Chester, Eng. 19th and 20th centuries.
Hort. Duval Duval et Fils. Versailles, France. Late 19th century.
Hort. Haage Friedrich Adolph Haage, jr. Erfurt, Germany. Established 1822, to early 20th century.
Hort. Haage & Schmidt Haage & Schmidt. Erfurt, Germany. Established 1862, to mid-20th century.
Hort. Henders. Perhaps E. G. Henderson & Son. London, Eng. Latter half 19th century.
Hort. Hillier Hillier & Sons. Winchester, Eng. Established 1864, to present.
Hort. Hoog [Same as **Hort. van Tuberg.**]
Hort. Lemoine V. Lemoine et Fils. Nancy, France. Established 1850, to 20th century.

Hort. Linden J. Linden, later Compagnie Continentale d'Horticulture. Brussels and Ghent, Belgium. Latter half 19th century.

Hort. Makoy Jacob-Makoy & Cie. Liège, Belgium. Established 1810, to late 19th century.

Hort. Nicolai Johannes Nicolai. Blasewitz (Dresden), Austria. Late 19th century.

Hort. Ottol. J. W. Ottolander & Son, later Ottolander & Hooftman. Boskoop, Netherlands. Latter half 19th to early 20th century.

Hort. P. Henders. Peter Henderson & Co. New York, N.Y. Established 1847, to early 20th century.

Hort. Pitcher & Manda Pitcher & Manda (The United States Nurseries). Short Hills, N.J. 1889–1897.

Hort. Pynaert-van Geert Éd. Pynaert-van Geert. Ghent, Belgium. Established 1816, to late 19th century.

Hort. Rivoire Rivoire Père & Fils. Lyon, France. Established 1859, to early 20th century.

Hort. Rollisson William Rollisson & Sons. Tooting, England. Late 19th century.

Hort. R. Smith Richard Smith, later Richard Smith & Co. Worcester, Eng. Late 19th century.

Hort. Sakata T. Sakata & Co. Yokohama, Japan. Early 20th century.

Hort. Sander F. Sander & Co., later Sander & Sons. St. Albans, Eng. Late 19th to early 20th century.

Hort. Simon-Louis Simon Louis Frères & Cie. Bruyères-le-Chatel, France. Established (at Metz) 1666, to early 20th century.

Hort. Späth L. Späth. Berlin, Germany. Established 1720, to 20th century.

Hort. Teutschel Teutschel and Co. Colchester, England. Late 19th century.

Hort. Truffaut Albert Truffaut et Fils. Versailles, France. Established 1824, to early 20th century.

Hort. van Tuberg. C. G. van Tubergen Ltd. Haarlem, Netherlands. Established 1869, to present.

Hort. van Waveren & Kruijff Gt. van Waveren & Kruijff [Kruyff]. Sassenheim, Netherlands. Established 1866, to early 20th century.

Hort. Veitch James Veitch & Sons. Chelsea (London), Eng. Early 19th century to 1914.

Hort. Versch. Ambroise Verschaffelt. Ghent, Belgium. Mid-19th century to 1870.

Hort. Vilm.-Andr. Vilmorin-Andrieux et Cie. Paris, France. Established before 1745, to present.

Hort. Wallace Wallace & Co., later R. Wallace & Co. Colchester, later Tunbridge Wells, Eng. Established 1860, to mid-20th century.

Hort. Waterer Anthony Waterer, later Knap Hill Nursery. Woking, Eng. Established about 1790, to present.

Hort. Watkins & Simpson Watkins & Simpson Ltd. London, Eng. Established 1876, to mid-20th century.

Hort. Weick Adolphe Weick. Strasbourg, France. Mid-19th century.

Horvat, I. Ivo Horvat (1897–1963)

Horvat, M. Marija Dvoržak Horvat (fl. 1947)

Hosseus Carl Curt Hosseus (1878–1950)

Host Nicolaus Thomas Host (1761–1834)

Hottes Alfred Carl Hottes (1891–1955)

Houghton Arthur Duvernoix Houghton (1870–1938)

Houll. B. Houllet (1811[1815?]–1890)

House Homer Doliver House (1878–1949)

Houst. William Houstoun (1695–1733)

Houtt. Maarten Houttuyn (1720–1798)

Houtz. Gijbertus Houtzagers (1888–1957)

Houx. de Leh. Jean Auguste-Hippolyte Houzeau de Lehaie (1867–1959)

Hovey Charles Mason Hovey (1810–1887)

Howell, J. T. John Thomas Howell (1903–)

Howell, S. R. S. R. Howell (fl. 1934)

Howell, T. J. Thomas Jefferson Howell (1842–1912)

Howitt Alfred William Howitt (1830–1908)

Hu, H. H. Hsen-Hsu Hu (1894–)

Hu, S. Y. Shiu-ying Hu (1910–)

Hubb., C. E. Charles Edward Hubbard (1900–)

Hubb., F. T. Frederic Tracy Hubbard (1875–1962)

Hubeny Joseph Hubeny (fl. 1830–1843)

Huber, H. Herbert Franz Josef Huber (1931–)

Huber, J. Jacob [Jacques] E. Huber (1867–1914)

Hübner Wolfgang Hübner (fl. 1933)

Huds. William Hudson (1730–1793)

Huds., J. James Hudson (fl. 1892)

Huet Alfred Huet du Pavillon (1829–1907)

Huet, A. L. P. Augustin Louis Pierre Huet (1814–1888)

Hügel Carl Alexander Anselm von Hügel (1794–1870)

Hughes Dorothy Kate Hughes (later Popenoe) (1899–1932)

Hull John H. Hull (1761–1843)

Hult. Eric Oskar Gunnar Hultén (1894–)

Humb. Friedrich Wilhelm Heinrich Alexander von Humboldt (1769–1859)

Humbert Jean Henri Humbert (1887–1967)

Hume, H. Hardrada Harold Hume (1875–1965)

Hummelinck P. Wagenaar Hummelinck (fl. 1938)

Hunz. Armando Teodoro Hunziker (1919–)

Hurst Charles Chamberlain Hurst (1870– ?)

Hutch. John Hutchinson (1884–1972)

Hutch., J. B. Joseph Burtt Hutchinson (1902–)

Hutchison, P. C. Paul Clifford Hutchison (1924–)

Huter Rupert Huter (1834–1919)

Huth Ernst Huth (1845–1897)

Huttl. Donald Grunert Huttleston (1920–)

Hy Félix Charles Hy (1853–1918)

Hyl. Nils Hylander (1904–1970)

Idrobo Jésus Medardo Idrobo-Muñoz (1917–)

Iinuma Yokusai Iinuma (1782–1865)

Iljin Modest Mihailovicz [Mikhailovič, Mikhaylovich] Iljin [Ilyin] (1889–1967)

Ilse Hugo Ilse (1835–1900)

Iltis Hugh Helmut Iltis (1925–)

Imbach Emil J. Imbach (1897–1970)

Ingham Norman D. Ingham (fl. 1908)

Ingram, C. Collingwood Ingram (1880–)

Ingram, J. John William Ingram (1924–)

Ingw. Walter Edward Theodore Ingwersen (1885–1960)

Irish Henry Clay Irish (1868– ?)

Irmsch. Edgar Irmscher (1887–1968)

Irving, E. E. G. Irving (1816–1855)

Irving, W. Walter Irving (1867– ?)

Ito, T. Tokutaro Ito (1868–1941)

Ito, Y. Yoshio Ito (1907–)

Ivanina L. I. Ivanina (1917–)

Jack William Jack (1795–1822)

Jack, J. John George Jack (1861–1949)

Jackm. George Jackman (1837–1887)

Jacks., A. B. Albert Bruce Jackson (1876–1947)

Jacks., A. K. Arthur Keith Jackson (1914–)

Jacks., B. D. Benjamin Daydon Jackson (1846–1927)

Jacks., G. George Jackson (1790–1811)

Jacks., R. C. Raymond Carl Jackson (1928–)

Jacobi G. Albano von Jacobi (1805–1874)

Jacobs, M. Maxwell Ralph Jacobs (1904–)

Jacobsen Hermann Johannes Heinrich Jacobsen (1898–)

Jacq. Nickolaus Joseph von Jacquin (1727–1817)

Jacq. f. Joseph Franz von Jacquin (1766–1839)

Jacquem. Victor Jacquemont (1801–1832)

Jacques Henri Antoine Jacques (1782–1866)

Jaeg., G. Georg Friedrich von Jaeger (1785–1866)

Jaeg., H. Hermann Jaeger (1815–1890)

Jaenn. Johann Friedrich Jaennicke (1831–1907)

Jalas Arvo Jaakko Juhani Jalas (1920–)

James Edwin James (1797–1861)

Jameson William Jameson (of Quito) (1796–1873)

Jameson, W. William Jameson (of India) (1815–1882)

Jan Georg Jan (1791–1866)

Janch. Erwin Janchen (1882–1970)

Jancz. Edward Janczewski von Glinka (1846–1918)

Janka Victor Janka von Bules (1837–1890)

Jankó Johan Jankó (fl. 1890)

Jaub. Hippolyte François Jaubert (1798–1874)

Jaume St.-Hil. Jean Henri Jaume Saint-Hilaire (1772–1845)

Jáv. Sándor Jávorka (1883–1961)

Jeanb. Ernest Jules Marie Jeanbernat (1835–1888)

Jeffr., C. Charles Jeffrey (1934–)

Jeffr., J. John Jeffrey (?-ca. 1853)

Jeffr., J. F. John Frederick Jeffrey (?–1943)

Jeffs Royal Edgar Jeffs (1879–1933)

Jenk. Edmund Howard Jenkins (1856–1921)

Jennings Otto Emery Jennings (1877–1964)

Jennison Harry Milliken Jennison (1885–1940)

Jeps. Willis Linn Jepson (1867–1946)

Jesson [Miss] E. M. Jesson (fl. 1915–1916)

Jessop John Peter Jessop (1939–)

Johans. Donald Alexander Johansen (1901–)

Johnson, A. M. Arthur Monrad Johnson (1878–1943)

Johnson, J. H. Joseph Harry Johnson (1894–)

Johnson, L. A. S. Lawrence Alexander Sidney Johnson (1925–)

Johnst., I. M. Ivan Murray Johnston (1898–1960)

Johnst., J. R. John Robert Johnston (1880–)

Johnst., M. C. Marshall Conring Johnston (1930–)

Johnstone George Henry Johnstone (1881–1960)

Johow Friedrich [Federico] Richard Adalbert Johow (1859–1933?)

Jones, B. M. G. Brian Michael Glyn Jones (1933–)
Jones, F. Florence Lucinda (née Freeman) Jones (1912–)
Jones, G. N. George Neville Jones (1903–1970)
Jones, M. E. Marcus Eugene Jones (1852–1934)
Jones, Q. Quentin Jones (1920–)
Jonker, A. Anni Margriet Emma Jonker-Verhoef (1920–)
Jonker, F. Frederik Pieter Jonker (1912–)
Jord. Alexis Jordan (1814–1897)
Jotter Mary Lois Jotter (later Cutter) (1914–)
Juehlke Ferdinand Juehlke (1815–1893)
Jumelle Henri Jumelle (1866–1935)
Jungh. Friedrich Franz Wilhelm Junghuhn (1809–1864)
Jusl. Abraham D. Juslenius (fl. 1755)
Juss. Antoine Laurent de Jussieu (1748–1836)
Juss., A. Adrien Henri Laurent de Jussieu (1797–1853)
Juss., B. Bernard de Jussieu (1699–1776)
Juz. Sergei Vasil'evich Juzepczuk [Ĭuzepchuk] (1893–1959)
Kache Paul Kache (1882–1945)
Kalenich. Ivan [Johann] Osipovich Kalenichenko [Kaleniczenko] (1805–1876)
Kalm Pehr [Peter] Kalm (1715–1779)
Kalmb. George Anthony Kalmbacher (1897–)
Kamb. Toyoaki Kambayashi (?–1939)
Kamib. Keijiro Kamibayashi (fl. 1915.)
Kaneh. Ryozo Kanehira (1882–1947)
Kanitz Agost Kanitz (1843–1896)
Kantsch., Z. Zachary Alekseevich Kantschaweli [Kanchaveli] (1894–1932)
Kar. Grigoriĭ Silich [Silovich] Karelin (1801–1872)
Karrer S. Karrer (fl. 1912)
Karst. Gustav Karl Wilhelm Hermann Karsten (1817–1908)
Karw. Wilhelm Friedrich Karwinski von Karwin (1780–1855)
Kaulf. Georg Friedrich Kaulfuss (1786–1830)
Kausel Eberhard Maximilano Leopoldo Otto Kausel (1910–1972)
Kaw. Takiya Kawakami (1871–1915)
Kayser Konrad Kayser (fl. 1932)
Kearn. Thomas Henry Kearney (1874–1956)
Keay Ronald William John Keay (1920–)
Keck David Daniels Keck (1903–)
Keenan James Keenan (1924–)
Keller, A. C. Allan Charles Keller (1914–)
Keller, J. B. J. B. Keller (fl. 1900)
Keller, J. C. Johann Christoph Keller (1737–1796)
Keller, R. Robert Keller (1854–1939)
Kellerer Johann Kellerer (1859–?)
Kellerm. Maude Kellerman (later Swingle) (1888–)
Kellogg Albert Kellogg (1813–1887)
Kelsey Harlan Page Kelsey (1872–1958)
Kemmler Carl Albert Kemmler (1813–1888)
Kem.-Nat. [Mrs.] Lĭubov Kemularia-Natadze (fl. 1928–1949)
Keng Yi Li Keng (1898–)
Kennedy Patrick Beveridge Kennedy (1874–1930)
Kensit Harriet Margaret Louisa Kensit (later Bolus) (1877–1970)
Kent, A. Adolphus Henry Kent (1828–1913)
Kerch. Oswald Charles Eugène Kerchove de Denterghem (1844–1906)
Ker-Gawl. John Bellenden Ker or John Ker Bellenden, or (before 1804) John Gawler (1764–1842)
Kern., A. Anton Josef Kerner von Marilaun (1831–1898)
Kern., J. Josef Kerner (1829–1906)
Kesselr. Jakob Kesselring (1835–1909)
Kesselr., W. Friedrich Wilhelm Kesselring (1876–1966)
Keyserl. Alexander Friedrich Michael Leberecht Keyserling (1815–1891)
Kiaersk. Hjalmar Frederik Christian Kiaerskou (1835–1900)
Kikuchi Akio Kikuchi (1883–1951)
Killick Donald Joseph Boomer Killick (1926–)
Killip Ellsworth Paine Killip (1890–1968)
Kimnach Myron William Kimnach (1922–)
King George King (1840–1909)
Kinney Abbot Kinney (1850–1920)
Kipp. Richard Kippist (1812–1882)
Kir. Ivan Petrovich Kirilov [Kirilow] (1821–1842)
Kirchn. Georg Kirchner (1837–1885)
Kirk, J. John Kirk (1832–1922)
Kirk, T. Thomas Kirk (1828–1898)
Kirschl. Frédéric [Friedrich R.] Kirschleger (1804–1869)
Kit. Paul Kitaibel (1757–1817)
Kitag. Masao Kitagawa (1909–)
Kitam. Siro [Shiro] Kitamura (1906–)
Kittel Martin Balduin Kittel (1798–1885)
Klatt Friedrich Wilhelm Klatt (1825–1897)
Klein Klein (fl. 1859)

Klein, W. William McKinley Klein (1933–)
Kleinh. Anthonia Kleinhoonte (1887–)
Klenert Wilhelm Klenert (fl. 1912)
Klob.-Alis. Evgeniĭa Nikolaevna Klobukova-Alisova [Alisova-Klobukova] (1889–1962)
Klotz, G. Gerhard Klotz (1928–)
Klotzsch Johann Friedrich Klotzsch (1805–1860)
Kmet Andreas Kmet (1841–1908)
Knerr Elsworth Brownell Knerr (1861–1942)
Knight, G. M. G. M. Knight (fl. 1890)
Knight, H. Henry Knight (1834–1896)
Knight, J. Joseph Knight (1781–1855)
Knight, O. W. Ora Willis Knight (1874–1913)
Knoll, F. Fritz Friedrich Knoll (1883–)
Knoop Johann Hermann Knoop (ca. 1700–1769)
Knowles George Beauchamp Knowles (?–1852)
Knuth, F. M. Frederik Marcus Knuth-Knuthenborg (1904–)
Knuth, P. Paul Erich Otto Wilhelm Knuth (1854–1899)
Knuth, R. Reinhard Gustav Paul Knuth (1874–1957)
Kobuski Clarence Emmeren Kobuski (1900–1963)
Koch, C. Carl [Karl] Heinrich Emil Koch (1809–1879)
Koch, W. D. J. Wilhelm Danield Joseph Koch (1771–1849)
Kochs Julius Kochs (fl. 1900)
Koehne Bernhard Adalbert Emil Koehne (1848–1918)
Koelle Johann Ludwig Christian Koelle (1763–1797)
Koidz., G. Gen'ichi Koidzumi (1883–1953)
Koidz., H. Hideo Koidzumi (1886–1945)
Kom. Vladimir Leont'evich Komarov (1869–1945)
Komatsu Shunzo Komatsu (1879–1932)
König, D. D. König (1909–)
König, J. Johann Gerhard [John Gerard] Koenig (1728–1785)
König, K. Karl [Carl] Dietrich Eberhard König [Charles Konig] (1774–1851)
Koopm. Karl Koopmann (fl. 1879–1900)
Koord. Sijfert Hendrik Koorders (1863–1919)
Körn. Friedrich August Körnicke [Koernicke] (1828–1908)
Korovin Evgeniĭ Petrovich Korovin [Korowin] (1891–)
Korsh. Sergei Ivanovich Korshinskiĭ [Korshinsky, Korzhinsky] (1861–1900)
Kort Antoine Kort (1874–1951)
Körte Franz Körte [Koerte] (1782–1845)
Korth. Pieter Willem Korthals (1807–1892)
Košanin Nedelyko Košanin (1874–1934)
Koso-Pol. Boris Mikhaĭlovich Koso-Polĭanskiĭ [Kozo-Poliansky] (1890–1957)
Kostel. Vincenz Franz Kosteletzky (1801–1887)
Kosterm. André Joseph Guillaume Henri Kostermans (1907–)
Kotschy Karl Georg Theodor Kotschy (1813–1866)
Kováts Julius von Kováts von Szentlelek (1815–1873)
Koyama Mitsuo Koyama (1885–1935)
Kraetzl Franz Kraetzl (1852–?)
Krainz Hans Krainz (1906–)
Kraj. Vladimir Joseph Krajina (1905–)
Kral. Jean Louis Kralik (1813–1892)
Kränzl. Friedrich Wilhelm Ludwig Kränzlin (1847–1934)
Krapov. Antonio Krapovickas (1922–)
Krasn. Andreĭ Nikolaevich Krasnov [Krassnov] (1862–1914)
Krause, E. H. L. Ernst Hans Ludwig Krause (1859–1942)
Krause, Karin Karin Krause (later Zimmermann) (1927–)
Krause, Kurt Kurt Krause (1883–1963)
Krausk. Englebert Krauskopf (1820–1881)
Krauss, C. F. Christian Ferdinand Friedrich von Krauss (1812–1890)
Krautter Louis Krautter (1880–1909)
Kriechb. Wilhelm Kriechbaum (fl. 1925)
Krug Carl Wilhelm Leopold Krug (1833–1898)
Krüssm. Gerd Krüssmann (1910–)
Kryl. Porfiriĭ Nikitich Krylov [Kr'ilov, Kriloff] (1850–1931)
Kudo Yushun Kudo (1887–1932)
Kuhn Maximilian Friedrich Adalbert Kuhn (1842–1894)
Kunert F. Kunert (1863–?)
Kunth Carl Sigismund Kunth (1788–1850)
Kuntze, O. Carl Ernst Otto Kuntze (1843–1907)
Kunze Gustav Kunze (1793–1851)
Kupper Walter Kupper (1874–1953)
Kurz Wilhelm Sulpiz Kurz (1834–1878)
Kütz. Friedrich Traugott Kützing [Kuetzing] (1807–1893)
Kuzen. Ol'ga Ĭakinfovna (née Prochorova) Kuzeneva (1887–)
Kuzn. Nikolaĭ Ivanovich Kuznetsov [Kusnezow, Kusnetzov, Kuznetzov, Kuznezov] (1864–1932)
L. Carolus Linnaeus [Carl von Linné] (1707–1778)
L. f. Carl von Linné, the son (1741–1783)
Labill. Jacques Julien Houtton de La Billardière (1755–1834)
Labour. J. Labouret (fl. 1853–1858)

Labroy Oscar Labroy (1877–1953)
Lacaita Charles Carmichael Lacaita (1853–1933)
Lace John Henry Lace (1857–1918)
Lag. Mariano Lagasca y Segura (1776–1839)
Lagerh. Nils Gustav Lagerheim (1860–1926)
Lagger François Joseph Lagger (1802–1870)
Lahm. Bertha Marion (née Sherwood) Lahman (1872–?)
Laínz, M. Manuel Laínz (1923–)
Lakela Olga Lakela (1890–)
Lam. Jean Baptiste Antoine Pierre Monnet de Lamarck (1744–1829)
Lam, H. J. Herman Johannes Lam (1892–)
Lamb. Aylmer Bourke Lambert (1761–1842)
Lambertye Léonce de Lambertye (1810–1877)
Lami Robert Lami (fl. 1935)
Lamotte Martial Lamotte (1820–1883)
Láng, A. Adolph Franz Láng (1795–1863)
Lang, T. Thomas Lang (fl. ca. 1853)
Lange, A. Axel Lange (1871–?)
Lange, J. Johan Martin Christian Lange (1818–1898)
Lange, J. E. Jakob Emanuel Lange (1864–1941)
Langsd. Georg Heinrich von Langsdorff (1774–1852)
Lanza Domenico Lanza (1868–?)
Lapeyr. Philippe Picot de Lapeyrouse (1744–1818)
Lapierre Jean Marie Lapierre (1754–1834)
Larrañ. Dámaso Antonio Larrañaga (1771–1848)
Larreat. José Dionisio Larreategui (fl. 1805)
Lauche Friedrich Wilhelm Georg Lauche (1827–1883)
Lauman George Nieman Lauman (1874–1944)
Lauterb. Carl Adolf Georg Lauterbach (1864–1937)
Lauth Thomas Lauth (1758–1826)
Lavall. Pierre Alphonse Martin Lavallée (1836–1884)
Lavis Mary Gwendolen Lavis (later O'Connor-Fenton) (1902–)
Lavr. John J. Lavranos (1926–)
Lawrance Mary Lawrance (fl. 1790–1831)
Lawr., G. George Lawrence (fl. 1841)
Lawr., G. H. M. George Hill Mathewson Lawrence (1910–)
Lawr., W. E. William Evans Lawrence (1883–1950?)
Laws., C. Charles Lawson (1794–1873)
Laws., G. George Lawson (1827–1895)
Laws., M. Marmaduke Alexander Lawson (1840–1896)
Laws., P. Peter Lawson (?–1820)
Laxm. Erich Laxmann (1737–1796)
Layens Georges de Layens (1834–1897)
Leandri Jacques Leandri (1903–)
Leavenw. Melines Conklin Leavenworth (1796–1862)
Lebas E. Lebas (19th century)
Lechl. Willibald Lechler (1814–1856)
Le Conte John Eaton Le Conte (1784–1860)
Lecoq Henri Lecoq (1802–1871)
Ledeb. Carl Friedrich von Ledebour (1785–1851)
Lee Lee (fl. before 1858)
Lee, H. A. Henry Atherton Lee (1894–)
Lee, R. E. Robert Edwin Lee (1911–)
Leers Johann Danield Leers (1727–1774)
Lees Edwin Lees (1800–1887)
Leeuw. Antonius Josephus Maria Leeuwenberg (1930–)
Le Grand, A. Antoine Le Grand (1839–1905)
Legrand, D. Carlos Maria Diego Enrique Legrand (1901–)
Le Grand, O. O. Le Grand (fl. 1895)
Lehm. Johann Georg Christian Lehmann (1792–1860)
Lehm., C. B. Carl B. Lehmann (fl. 1850–1856)
Leib. John Bernhard Leiberg (1853–1913)
Leichtl. Max Leichtlin (1831–1910)
Leighton Frances M. Leighton (1909–)
Leitn. Edward F. Leitner (?–1838)
Lej. Alexandre Louis Simon Lejeune (1779–1858)
Le Jolis Auguste François Le Jolis (1823–1904)
Lem. Charles Antoine Lemaire (1800–1871)
Léman Dominique Sebastian Léman (1781–1829)
Lemm. John Gill [Gibbs?] Lemmon (1832–1908)
Lemm., W. P. W. P. Lemmon (fl. 1938)
Lemoine, É. Émile Lemoine (1862–1943)
Lemoine, V. Pierre Louis Victor Lemoine (1823–1911)
Lenné Peter Joseph Lenné (1789–1866)
Lenz Lee Wayne Lenz (1915–)
Leon Hermano [i.e. Brother] Leon [Joseph Sylvestre Sauget] (1871–1955)
Leonard, E. Emery Clarence Leonard (1892–1968)
Léonard, J. Jean Joseph Gustavo Léonard (1920–)
Lepech. Ivan Lepechin (1737–1802)
Lepr. F. R. M. Leprieur (1799–1869)
Leresche Louis François Jules Rudolphe Leresche (1808–1885)
Lesc. O. Lescuyer (fl. 1855–1872)

Lesch. Jean Baptiste Louis Théodore Leschenault de la Tour (1773–1826)
Leske Nathanael Gottfried Leske (1751–1786)
Lesq. Charles Leo Lesquereux (1806–1889)
Less. Christian Friedrich Lessing (1810–1862)
Lestib. Gaspard Thémistocle Lestiboudois (1797–1876)
Letourn. Aristide Horace Letourneux (1820–1890)
Lév. Augustin Abel Hector Léveillé (1863–1918)
Levier Emile [Emilio] Levier (1839–1911)
Levyns Margaret R. Levyns (1890–)
Lewis, F. H. Frank Harlan Lewis (1919–)
Lewis, G. J. Gwendoline Joyce Lewis (1909–1967)
Lewis, M. E. Margaret Ensign Lewis (1919–)
Lewis, W. H. Walter Hepworth Lewis (1930–)
Lewt. Frederick Lewis Lewton (1874–?)
Lex. Juan Martinez de Lexarza (1785–1824)
Ley, A. Augustin Ley (1842–1911)
Leyb. Friedrich Leybold (1827–1879)
Leyss. Friedrich Wilhelm von Leysser (1731–1815)
L'Hér. Charles Louis L'Héritier de Brutelle (1746–1800)
Li, H. L. Hui-Lin Li (1911–)
Libon Joseph Libon (1821–1861)
Libosch. Joseph L. Liboschitz (1783–1824)
Liebl. Franz Kaspar Lieblein (1744–1810)
Liebm. Frederik Michael Liebmann (1813–1856)
Liebn. C. Liebner (fl. 1895)
Liegel Georg Liegel (1777–1861)
Lightf. John Lightfoot (1735–1788)
Lilja Nils Lilja (1808–1870)
Liljeblad Samuel Liljeblad (1761–1815)
Lillo Miguel Lillo (1862–1931)
Linchevskiĭ Igor Aleksandrovich Linchevskiĭ [Linczevski] (1908–)
Lindau Gustav Lindau (1866–1923)
Lindb., G. A. Gustaf Anders Lindberg (1832–1900)
Lindb., H. Harald Lindberg (1871–1963)
Lindl., S. Sextus Otto Lindberg (1835–1889)
Lindbl. Alexis Eduard Lindblom (1807–1853)
Lindeb. Carl Johan Lindeberg (1815–1900)
Lindem. Eduard von Lindemann [or Éduard Émanuilovich] (1825–1900)
Linden Jean Jules Linden (1817–1898)
Linden, L. Lucien Linden (fl. 1881–1896)
Lindh. Ferdinand Jacob Lindheimer (1801–1879)
Lindinger L. Lindinger (fl. 1942)
Lindl. John Lindley (1799–1865)
Lindm. Carl Axel Magnus Lindman (1856–1928)
Lindsay, G. George Edmund Lindsay (1916–)
Lindsay, R. Robert Lindsay (1846–1913)
Lingelsh. Alexander von Lingelsheim (1874–1937)
Link Johann Heinrich Friedrich Link (1767–1851)
Linke August Linke (fl. 1853–1857)
Lint Harold LeRoy Lint (1917–)
Linton Edward Francis Linton (1848–1928)
Liou Ho Liou (fl. 1932)
Lipskiĭ Vladimir Ippolitovich Lispskiĭ [Lipsky] (1863–1937)
Litard. René V. de Litardière (1888–1957)
Little Elbert Luther Little (1907–)
Litv. Dimitriĭ Ivanovich Litvinov [Litwinow] (1854–1929)
Llave Canónigo Pablo de La Llave (1773–1833)
Lloyd, F. Francis Ernst Lloyd (1868–1947)
Lloyd, J. James Lloyd (1810–1896)
Lockw. Tommie Earl Lockwood (1941–1975)
Lodd. Conrad Loddiges (1732–1826) & George Loddiges (1784–1846)
Loefl. Pehr [Peter] Loefling (1729–1756)
Loes. Ludwig Eduard Theodor Loesener (1865–1941)
Loes., O. Otto Loesener (fl. 1926)
Loesch Alfred Loesch (1865–1946)
Löfgr. Alberto Löfgren [Loefgren] (1854–1918)
Loher August Loher (fl. 1910)
Loisel. Jean Louis Auguste Loiseleur-Deslongchamps (1774–1849)
Lojac. Michele Lojacono-Pojero (1853–1919)
Lomak. Aleksandr Aleksandrovich Lomakin (1863–1903)
Lönnr. Knut Johan Lönnroth (1826–1885)
Looser Gualterio Looser (1898–)
Lord, E. Ernest E. Lord (1899–)
Lorentz Paul Günther Lorentz (1835–1881)
Lotsy Johannes Paulus Lotsy (1867–1931)
Loud. John Claudius Loudon (1783–1843)
Lour. João de [Juan] Loureiro (1710[1717?]–1791[1796?])
Löve, Á. Áskell Löve (1916–)
Löve, D. Doris Benta Maria (née Wahlen) Löve (1918–)
Lowe Richard Thomas Lowe (1802–1874)
Lucé J. Wilhelm Ludwig von Lucé (fl. 1823)

Miki Shigeru Miki (1901–)
Mildbr. Gottfried Wilhelm Johannes Mildbraed (1879–1954)
Milde Carl August Julius Milde (1824–1871)
Milkuhn F. G. Milkuhn (fl. 1949)
Mill. Philip Miller (1691–1771)
Mill., G. N. Gertrude Nevada Miller (1919–)
Mill., J. John Miller [Johann Sebastian Müller] (1715–1780)
Mill., J. F. John Frederick Miller (fl. 1772–1794)
Mill., P. W. Paul William Miller (1901–)
Mill., W. Wilhelm [William Tyler] Miller (1869–1938)
Millais John Guille Millais (1865–1931)
Millán Aníbal Roberto Millán (1892–)
Milliken Jessie Milliken (later Brown) (1877–1951)
Millsp. Charles Frederick Millspaugh (1854–1923)
Milne-Redh. Edgar Wolston Bertram Handsley Milne-Redhead (1906–)
Miq. Friedrich Anton Wilhelm Miquel (1811–1871)
Miranda Faustino Miranda González (1905–1964)
Mirb. Charles François Brisseau Mirbel (1776–1854)
Mirov Nicholas Tiho Mirov (1893–)
Mirz. Nina Vasil'evna Mirzoeva (1908–)
Misch. Pavel Ivanovich Mischenko [Miščenko, Mischenko, Misczenko, Mishchenko, Mistschenko] (1869–1938)
Misonne Th. Misonne (fl. 1893)
Mitch. John Mitchell (1676–1768)
Mitf. Algernon Bertram Freeman-Mitford, Lord Redesdale (1837–1916)
Miyabe Kingo Miyabe (1860–1951)
Miyoshi Manabu Miyoshi (1861–1939)
Moç. José Mariano Moçiño Suares Losada (1757–182–)
Moehl Heinrich Moehl (fl. 1861–1890)
Moell., A. F. Arturo F. Moeller (fl. 1922–1930)
Moell., H. Henry Moeller (fl. 1927)
Moench Conrad Moench (1744–1805)
Moens Moens (fl. 1881)
Moggr. John Traherne Moggridge (1842–1874)
Mohr, C. Charles Theodore Mohr (1824–1901)
Mohr, D. Daniel Matthias Heinrich Mohr (1780–1808)
Mol. Juan Ignacio (later Giovanni Ignazio) Molina (1737[1740?]–1829)
Moldenke Harold Norman Moldenke (1909–)
Möller Ludwig Möller (1847–1910)
Monn. Jean Pierre Monnard (1791–?)
Montin Lars Jonasson Montin (1723–1785)
Monv. (Chevalier de) Monville (fl. 1838)
Moon Alexander Moon (?–1825)
Moore, A. H. Albert Hanford Moore (1883–)
Moore, C. Charles Moore (1820–1905)
Moore, D. D. T. Daniel David Tompkins Moore (1820–1892)
Moore, F. W. Frederick William Moore (1857–1949)
Moore, H. E. Harold Emery Moore, Jr. (1917–)
Moore, J. W. John William Moore (1901–)
Moore, L. B. Lucy Beatrice Moore (1906–)
Moore, R. J. Raymond John Moore (1918–)
Moore, S. L. Spencer le Marchant Moore (1851–1931)
Moore, T. Thomas Moore (1821–1887)
Moore, T. V. Thomas Verner Moore (1877–1969)
Moq. Christian Horace Bénédict Alfred Moquin-Tandon (1804–1863)
Morales Sebastián Alfredo de Morales (1823–1900)
Moran Reid Venable Moran (1916–)
Mord. de Laun. Jean Claude Mien Mordant de Launay (ca. 1750–1816)
Morel Francisque Morel (fl. 1920)
Morelet Pierre Marie Arthur Morelet (1809–1892)
Moretti Giuseppe Moretti (1782–1853)
Moric. Moïse Étienne (Stefano) Moricand (1779–1854)
Moris Giuseppe Giacinto Moris (1796–1869)
Moritzi Alexander Moritzi (1806–1850)
Morong Thomas Morong (1827–1894)
Morr., C. Charles François Antoine Morren (1807–1858)
Morr., E. Charles Jacques Édouard Morren (1833–1886)
Morris, E. Edward Lyman Morris (1870–1913)
Morrison, A. Alexander Morrison (1849–1913)
Morrison, J. L. John Laurence Morrison (1911–)
Mort., C. V. Conrad Vernon Morton (1905–1972)
Moser Jean Jacques Moser (1846–1934)
Moss Charles Edward Moss (1872–1930)
Mottet Séraphin Joseph Mottet (1861–1930)
Mouill. Pierre Mouillefert (1846–1903)
Moxl. George Loucks Moxley (1871–?)
Mudie Robert Mudie (1777–1842)
Muell., F. J. Ferdinand Jacob Heinrich von Mueller (1825–1896)
Muell., P. J. Philipp Jakob Mueller (1832–1889)
Muenchh. Otto von Muenchhausen (1716–1774)

Muhlenb. Gotthilf Henry Ernest Muhlenberg (formerly Gotthilf Heinrich Ernst Mühlenberg, also Heinrich Ludwig Mühlenberg) (1753–1815)
Mühlenpf. F. Mühlenpfordt (19th century)
Mulf. A. Isabel Mulford (fl. 1894)
Müll., C. Carl [Karl] Müller (of Stuttgart) (1820–1889)
Müll., Fritz [Johann Friedrich Theodor] Fritz Müller (?–1897)
Müll., O. F. Otto Friedrich Müller (1730–1784)
Müll. Arg. Jean Müller ("Argoviensis"–of Aargau) (1828–1896)
Muller, F. G. F. G. Muller (fl. 1889)
Müll. Hal., K. Karl [Carl] August Friedrich Wilhelm Müller (of Halle) (1818–1899)
Mullig. Brian Orson Mulligan (1907–)
Munby Giles Munby (1813–1876)
Mundt Walter Mundt (1853–1927)
Munro William Munro (1818–1880)
Munson Thomas Volney Munson (1843–1913)
Munz Philip Alexander Munz (1892–1974)
Murata Gen Murata [Gen Nakai] (1927–)
Murav. O. A. Muravjova [Muravjeva] (fl. 1936)
Murb. Svante Samuel Murbeck (1859–1946)
Murith Laurent Joseph Murith (1742–1816)
Murr., A. Andrew Murray (1812–1878)
Murr., E. Albert Edward Murray (1935–)
Murr., J. John Andreas Murray (1740–1791)
Murr., R. P. Richard Paget Murray (1842–1908)
Murrill William Alphonso Murrill (1869–1957)
Muschl. Reno Muschler (1883–)
Musil Albina Frances Musil (1894–)
Mutel Pierre Auguste Victor Mutel (1795–1847)
Mutis José Celestino Mutis (1732–1808)
Nadeaud Jean Nadeaud (1834–1898)
Nakai Takenoshin Nakai (1882–1952)
Nannf. Johan Axel Frithiof Nannfeldt (1904–)
Nash George Valentine Nash (1864–1921)
Naud. Charles Victor Naudin (1815–1899)
Naves Andrés Naves (1839–1910)
Neck. Noel Martin Joseph de Necker (1730–1793)
Née Luis Née (fl. 1791)
Nees Christian Gottfried Daniel Nees von Esenbeck (1776–1858)
Neger Franz Wilhelm Neger (1868–1923)
Nehrl. Henry Nehrling (1853–1929)
Neill Patrick Neill (1776–1851)
Neilr. August Neilreich (1803–1871)
Nel Gert Cornelius Nel (1885–1960)
Nels., A. Aven Nelson (1859–1952)
Nels., E. E. Elias Emanuel Nelson (1876–?)
Nels., I. S. Ira Schrieber Nelson (1911–1965)
Nels., J. [E.?] John Nelson (pseudonym "Johannes Senilis") (fl. 1866)
Nels., J. C. James Carlton Nelson (1867–1944)
Nels., J. G. John Gudgeon Nelson (1818–1882)
Nemoto Kwanji Nemoto (1860–1936)
Nestl. Christian Gottfried Nestler (1778–1832)
Neub. Wilhelm Neubert (1808–1905)
Neuman Leopold Martin Neuman (1852–1922)
Neumann, J. Joseph Henri François Neumann (1800–1858)
Neumann, L. Louis Neumann (1827–1903)
Neumay. Hans Neumayer (1887–1945)
Nevskii Sergeï Arsen'evich Nevskiï [Nevsky] (1908–1938)
Newb. John Strong Newberry (1822–1892)
Newm. Edward Newman (1801–1876)
Nicholls William Henry Nicholls (1885–)
Nichols. George Nicholson (1874–1908)
Nicols. Dan Henry Nicolson (1938–)
Niedenzu Franz Josef Niedenzu (1857–1937)
Niemetz W. F. Niemetz (fl. 1898–1922)
Nieuwl. Julius Aloysius Arthur Nieuwland (1878–1936)
Nisbet Gladys T. Nisbet (1895–)
Nitsche Walter Nitsche (1883–)
Nobs Malcolm A. Nobs (1916–)
Nocca Domenico Nocca (1758–1841)
Noë Friedrich Wilhelm Noë (?–1858)
Noerdl. Hermann Noerdlinger (1818–1897)
Nois. Louis Claude Noisette (1772–1849)
Norl. Nils Tycho Norlindh (1906–)
Noronha François Noronha [Francisco Noroña] (ca. 1748–1788)
Northr. Alice Bell (née Rich) Northrop (1864–1922)
Norton Jesse Baker Norton (1877–1938)
Norton, J. B. S. John Bitting Smith Norton (1872–?)
Novák František A. Novák (1892–1964)
Novopokr. Ivan Vasil'evich Novopokrovskiï (1880–)
Nutt. Thomas Nuttall (1786–1859)
Nyár., E. Erasmus Julius Nyárády (1881–1966)

Nym. Carl Fredrik Nyman (1820–1893)
Oakes William Oakes (1799–1848)
Oberm. Anna Amelia Obermeyer [Obermeijer] (later Mauve) (1907–)
O'Brien James O'Brien (1842–1930)
Obrist Johann Obrist (fl. 1879)
Ochot. Isaac Ochoterena (1885–1950)
Ockend. David Jeffery Ockendon (1940–)
O'Don. Carlos Alberto O'Donell (1912–1954)
Oed. Georg Christian van Oeder (1728–1791)
Oehme Hanns Oehme (fl. 1940)
Ørst. Anders Sandøe Ørsted (1816–1872)
Oetting. Heinrich von Oettingen (fl. 1910)
Ohashi Hiroyoshi Ohashi (1936–)
Ohlend. J. H. Ohlendorff (fl. 1819–1840)
Ohwi Jisaburo Ohwi (1905–)
Oken Lorenz (né Okenfuss) Oken (1779–1851)
Olin Johan Henrik Olin (1769–1824)
Oliver, D. Daniel Oliver (1830–1916)
Oliver, W. Walter Reginald Brook Oliver (1883–1957)
Olivier Guillaume Antoine Olivier (1756–1814)
Onno Max Onno (1903–)
Opiz Philipp Maximilian Opiz (1787–1858)
Orb. Alcide Charles Victor Marie Dessalines d'Orbigny (1802–1857)
Orcutt Charles Russell Orcutt (1864–1929)
Ornd. Robert Ornduff (1932–)
Orph. Theodoros Georgios Orphanides (1817–1886)
Ort. Casimiro Gómez [de] Ortega (1740–1818)
Ortg. Karl Eduard Ortgies (1829–1916)
Osbeck Pehr Osbeck (1723–1805)
Osborn Arthur Osborn (1878–)
Ostenf. Carl Emil Hansen Ostenfeld (1873–1931)
Osterh. George Everett Osterhout (1858–1937)
Otth Carl Adolph Otth (1803–1839)
Otto Christoph Friedrich Otto (1783–1856)
Oudem. Cornelis Antoon Jan Abraham Oudemans (1825–1906)
Ovchinn. Pavel Nikolaevich Ovchinnikov [Ovczinnikov] (1903–)
Ownb., G. Gerald Bruce Ownbey (1916–)
Ownb., M. Francis Marion Ownbey (1910–1974)
Pabst Guido Francisco Guillumin Pabst (1914–)
Paine John Alsop Paine (1840–1912)
Painter Joseph Hannum Painter (1879–1908)
Paiva Antonio da Costa Paiva [Castello de Paiva] (1806–1879)
Palacký Jan (Johann Baptist) Palacký (1830–1908)
Palanza Alfonso Palanza (1851–1899)
Palib. Ivan Vladimirovich Palibin (1872–1949)
Pall. Peter Simon Pallas (1741–1811)
Palmer Ernest Jesse Palmer (1875–1962)
Palmer, F. Frédéric Palmer (fl. 1865)
Pamp. Renato Pampanini (1875–1949)
Panč. Josef Pančić (1814–1888)
Pang. Konstantin Ivanovich Pangalo (1883–1965)
Pant. József Pantocsek (1846–1916)
Pantl. Robert Pantling (1856–1910)
Panz. Georg Wolfgang Franz Panzer (1755–1829)
Paol. Giulio Paoletti (1865–1941)
Pappe Carl Wilhelm Ludwig Pappe (1803–1862)
Pardé Léon Gabriel Charles Pardé (1865–1943)
Parish C. Charles Samuel Pollock Parish (1822–1897)
Parish, S. Samuel Bonsall Parish (1838–1928)
Parker, C. S. Charles Sandbach Parker (?–1869)
Parker, K. Kittie Lucille (née Fenley) Parker (1910–)
Parker, R. Richard Neville Parker (1884–1958)
Parkins. Sydney C. Parkinson (1745–1771)
Parl. Filippo Parlatore (1816–1877)
Parm. (Chevalier de) Parmentier (fl. 1840)
Parn. Richard Parnell (1810–1882)
Parodi Lorenzo Raimondo Parodi (1895–1966)
Parry Charles Christopher Parry (1823–1890)
Parsons Samuel Bowne Parsons (1819–1906)
Pasq. Giuseppe Antonio Pasquale (1820–1893)
Patr. Eugène Louis Melchior Patrin (1742–1815)
Patschke Wilhelm Patschke (1888–)
Pau Carlos Pau y Español (1857–1937)
Paul William Paul (1822–1905)
Pav. José Antonio Pavón (1750–1844)
Pavlov Nikolaĭ Vasil'evich Pavlov (1893–)
Pawl. Bogumil Pawlowski (1898–)
Pax Ferdinand Albin Pax (1858–1942)
Paxt. Joseph Paxton (1803–1865)
Payer Jean Baptiste Payer (1818–1860)
Payson Edwin Blake Payson (1893–1927)
Pearce Sydney Albert Pearce (1906–)

Pearson, H. Henry Harold Welch Pearson (1870–1916)
Pearson, R. Robert Hooper Pearson (1866–1918)
Peck Morton Eaton Peck (1871–1958)
Peck, C. H. Charles Horton Peck (1833–1917)
Peebles Robert Hibbs Peebles (1900–1956)
P'ei Chien P'ei (1903–)
Pellegr. François Pellegrin (1881–1965)
Penf. Arthur Raymond Penfold (1890–)
Penh. David Pearce Penhallow (1854–1910)
Penn. Francis Whittier Pennell (1886–1952)
Pépin Pierre Denis Pépin (ca. 1802–1876)
Pérard Alexandre Jules César Pérard (1834[1835?]–1887)
Perdue Robert Edward Perdue (1924–)
Perkins Janet Russell Perkins (1853–1933)
Perp. Candida Leni Perpenti (1764–1846)
Perr. Pierre Eugène Perrier de la Bathie (1825–1916)
Perrine Henry Perrine (1797–1840)
Perrottet Georges Samuel Perrottet (1793–1870)
Perry, L. M. Lily May Perry (1895–)
Perry, T. A. Thomas A. Perry (fl. 1850)
Pers. Christiaan Hendrik Persoon (1761–1836)
Peter Gustav Albert Peter (1853–1937)
Peterm. Wilhelm Ludwig Petermann (1806–1855)
Petersen Otto Georg Petersen (1847–1937)
Petit Ernest Marie Antoine Petit (1927–)
Petitm. Marcel Georges Charles Petitmengin (1881–1908)
Petrak Franz Petrak (1886–1973)
Petrie Donald Petrie (1846–1925)
Petrovič Sava Petrović [Petrovich] (1839–1889)
Peyr. Johann Joseph Peyritsch (1835–1889)
Pfeiff. Ludwig Georg Karl Pfeiffer (1805–1877)
Pfitz. Ernst Hugo Heinrich Pfitzer (1846–1906)
Phil. Rudolf Amandus [Rudolfo Amando] Philippi (1808–1904)
Phil. f. Federico [Friedrich Heinrich Eunom] Philippi (1838–1910)
Philippe Xavier Philippe (1802–1866)
Phillips, E. P. Edwin Percy Phillips (1884–1967)
Phillips, L. L. Lyle Llewellyn Phillips (1923–)
Pich. Marcel Pichon (1921–1954)
Pickersg. Barbara Pickersgill (1940–)
Pierce, N. B. Newton Barris Pierce (1856–1916)
Pierce, W. Wright Pierce (fl. 1933)
Pierre Jean Baptiste Louis Pierre (1833–1905)
Pike A. V. Pike (fl. 1946)
Pilg. Robert Knud Friedrich Pilger (1876–1953)
Pillans Neville Stuart Pillans (1884–1964)
Pio Giovanni Battista Pio (fl. 1800)
Piper Charles Vancouver Piper (1867–1926)
Pirotta Pietro Romualdo Pirotta (1853–1936)
Pit. Joseph Charles Marie [Charles Joseph] Pitard (1873–1927)
Pitt. Henri François Pittier De Fábrega (1857–1950)
Pittendr. Colin Stephenson Pittendrigh (1918–)
Planch. Jules Émile Planchon (1923–1888)
Playne (Dr.) Playne (fl. 1856)
Plenck Joseph Jakob von Plenck (1738–1807)
Plowm. Timothy Charles Plowman (1944–)
Pobed. E. G. Pobedimova (1898–)
Podp. Josef Podpěra (1878–1954)
Poech Joseph Poech (1816–1846)
Poederlé Eugène Joseph Charles Gilain Hubert d'Olmen, Baron de Poederlé (1742–1813)
Poelln. Karl von Poellnitz (1896–1945)
Poepp. Eduard Friedrich Poeppig (1798–1868)
Pohl Johann Baptist Emmanuel Pohl (1782–1834)
Pohl, R. W. Richard Walter Pohl (1916–)
Pohle Richard Richardovich Pohle (1869–1926)
Poir. Jean Louis Marie Poiret (1755–1834)
Poiss. Henri-Louis Poisson (1877–1963)
Poit. Pierre Antoine Poiteau (1766–1854)
Polak. Hellmuth Polakowsky (1847–1917)
Polatsch. Adolf Polatschek (1932–)
Pole-Evans Illtyd Buller Pole Evans (1879–1968)
Polhill Roger M. Polhill (1937–)
Pollard Charles Louis Pollard (1872–1945)
Pollich Johann Adam Pollich (1740–1780)
Pollini Ciro Pollini (1782–1833)
Polun. Nicholas Vladimir Polunin (1909–)
Pomel Auguste Nicolas Pomel (1821–1898)
Popov, M. Mikhaïl Grigor'evich Popov (1893–1955)
Porcher Felix Porcher (fl. 1848–1879)
Porsild Alf Erling Porsild (1901–)
Portenschl. Franz Edler von Portenschlag-Ledermayer (1772–1822)
Porter, C. L. Cedric Lambert Porter (1905–)
Porter, D. M. Duncan MacNair Porter (1937–)

Porter, T. C. Thomas Conrad Porter (1822–1901)
Poselg. Heinrich Poselger (?–1883)
Posth. Oene Posthumus (1898–1945)
Pott, J. F. Johann Friedrich Pott (1738–1805)
Pott, R. Reino (née Leendertz) Pott (1869–1965)
Potzt. Eva Hedwig Ingeborg Potztal (1924–   )
Pourr. Pierre André Pourret de Figeac (1754–1818)
Powell, C. B. C. Baden Powell (fl. 1893)
Pozhark. Antonina Ivanovna Pozharkova [Pojarkova] (1897–   )
Praeg. Robert Lloyd Praeger (1865–1953)
Prain David Prain (1857–1944)
Prantl Karl Anton Eugen Prantl (1849–1893)
Presl, J. Jan Swatopluk Presl (1791–1849)
Presl, K. Karel [Carel] Boriwog Presl (1794–1852)
Preston Isabella Preston (1881–1965)
Prév. Honoré Albert Prévost (1822–1883)
Prince, A. Arthur Reginald Prince (1900–   )
Prince, W. William Robert Prince (1795–1869)
Pring George Harry Pring (1885–1974)
Pringle James Scott Pringle (1937–   )
Pritz., E. Ernst Georg Pritzel (1875–1946)
Pritz., G. Georg August Pritzel (1815–1874)
Prodan Iuliu [Julius] Prodan (1875–1959)
Proust Louis Proust (1878–   )
Puel Timothée Puel (1812–1890)
Pugsl. Herbert William Pugsley (1868–1947)
Puiss. Pierre A. Puissant (1831–1911)
Pullen Thomas Marion Pullen (1919–   )
Pulliat Victor Pulliat (1827–1866)
Purd. William Purdom (1880–1921)
Purdy Carlton [Carl] Elmer Purdy (1861–1945)
Purk. Emanuel (Ritter von) Purkyně (1831–1882)
Purpus, C. Carl Anton Purpus (1853–1914)
Purpus, J. Joseph Anton Purpus (1860–1932)
Pursh Frederick Traugott Pursh (1774–1820)
Pushk. Apollos Apollosovich Musin-Pushkin [Mussin-Puschkin] (?–1805)
Putterl. Aloys Putterlick (1810–1845)
Putz. Jules Antoine Adolphe Henri Putzeys (1809–1882)
Puvill. Puvilland (fl. 1879)
Pynaert Édouard-Christophe Pynaert (later Pynaert-van Geert) (1835–1900)
Quehl Leopold Quehl (1849–1923)
Quer José Quer y Martinez (1695–1764)
Quisumb. Eduardo Quisumbing y Argüelles (1895–   )
Raab W. Raab (?–1835)
Rabenh. Gottlob Ludwig Rabenhorst (1806–1881)
Raber Oran Lee Raber (1893–1940)
Rach Louis [Ludwig] Theodor Rach (1821–1859)
Racib. Marian [Marjan] Raciborski (1863–1917)
Radde Gustav Ferdinand Richard Johannes Radde (1831–1903)
Raddi Giuseppe Raddi (1770–1829)
Radius Justus Wilhelm Martin Radius (1797–1884)
Radl Florian Radl (fl. 1896)
Radlk. Ludwig Adolph Timotheus Radlkofer (1829–1927)
Raf. Constantine Samuel Rafinesque [Rafinesque-Schmaltz] (1783–1840)
Rafarin Rafarin (fl. 1866)
Raffill Charles Percival Raffill (1876–1951)
Rafn Carl Gottlob Rafn (1769–1808)
Ragion. Attilio Ragionieri (1856–1933)
Raim. Rudolf Raimann (1863–1896)
Ramat. Thomas Albin Joseph d'Audibert de Ramatuelle (1750–1794)
Ramond Louis François Élisabeth Ramond de Carbonnières (1753–1827)
Rand, E. L. Edward Lothrop Rand (1859–1924)
Rand, E. S. Edward Sprague Rand (1834–1897)
Randolph Lowell Fitz Randolph (1894–   )
Raoul Étienne Fiacre Louis Raoul (1815–1852)
Raoul, É. F. A. Édouard François Armand Raoul (1845–1898)
Rau Ambrosius Rau (1784–1830)
Rauh Werner Rauh (1913–   )
Raup Hugh Miller Raup (1901–   )
Räuschel Ernst Adolf Räuschel (fl. 1772–1797)
Raven Peter Hamilton Raven (1936–   )
Raym. Joseph Louis Florent Marcel Raymond (1915–1972)
Rchb. Heinrich Gottlieb Ludwig Reichenbach (1793–1879)
Rchb. f. Heinrich Gustav Reichenbach (1823–1889)
Rchb., F. F. Reichenbach (fl. 1896)
Read Robert William Read (1931–   )
Reade John Moore Reade (1876–1937)
Reader Felix Maximillian Reader (1850–1911)
Reaub. Gaston Reaubourg (fl. 1906)

Reber Burkhard Reber (1848–1926)
Rebut P. Rebut (fl. 1886–1896)
Rech. f. Karl Heinz Rechinger (1906–   )
Redf. John Howard Redfield (1815–1895)
Redouté Pierre Joseph Redouté (1761–1840)
Reed, C. A. Clarence Arthur Reed (1880–   )
Reed, C. F. Clyde Franklin Reed (1918–   )
Reeves Robert Gatlin Reeves (1898–   )
Regel Eduard August von Regel (1815–1892)
Rehd. Alfred Rehder (1863–1949)
Rehn. F. Rehnelt (1861–?)
Reichard Johann Jakob Reichard (1743–1782)
Reiche Karl Friedrich [Carlos Federico] Reiche (1860–1929)
Reinw. Caspar Georg Carl Reinwardt (1773–1854)
Reiss. Siegfried Reisseck [Reissek] (1819–1871)
Reitz Raulino Reitz (1919–   )
Rémy Jules Rémy (1826–?)
Rendle Alfred Barton Rendle (1865–1938)
Req. Esprit Requien (1788–1851)
Resende Flávio de Resende (1907–1967)
Retz. Anders Jahan Retzius (1742–1821)
Reuss, G. Gustav Reuss (1818–1861)
Reut. Georges François Reuter (1805–1872)
Reuthe G. Reuthe (fl. 1880)
Reynier Alfred Reynier (1845–1932)
Reynolds Gilbert Westacott Reynolds (1895–1967)
Riccob. Vincenzo Riccobono (1861–1943)
Rich., A. Achille Richard (1794–1852)
Rich., L. Louis Claude Marie Richard (1754–1821)
Richardson John Richardson (1787–1865)
Richardson, I. B. K. Ian Bertram Kay Richardson (1940–   )
Richt., Al. Aladár Richter (fl. 1894–1912)
Richt., H. Hermann Eberhard Friedrich Richter (1808–1876)
Richt., K. Karl [Carl] Richter (1855–1891)
Ricker Percy Leroy Ricker (1878–   )
Rickett Harold William Rickett (1896–   )
Ridd. John Leonard Riddell (1808–1865)
Ridl. Henry Nicholas Ridley (1855–1956)
Riedel Ludwig Riedel (1790–1861)
Ries Heinrich Ries (1871–1951)
Rigg George Burton Rigg (1872–1961)
Righter Frances Irving Righter (1897–   )
Riley Laurence Athelstan Molesworth Riley (1888–1928)
Risso Joseph Antoine Risso (1777–1845)
Ritter, F. Friedrich Ritter (fl. 1929–1959)
Rivers Thomas Rivers (1798–1877)
Riv.-God. Salvador Rivas-Goday (1905–   )
Rivière, A. Marie Auguste Rivière (1821–1877)
Rivière, C. Charles Marie Rivière (1845–?)
Rivoire Antoine Rivoire (fl. 1921)
Robbins, G. T. Guy Thomas Robbins (1916–1960)
Robbins, J. W. James Watson Robbins (1801–1879)
Roberts, E. P. Evan Paul Roberts (1914–   )
Roberty Guy Édouard Roberty (1907–1971)
Robinson, B. L. Benjamin Lincoln Robinson (1864–1935)
Robinson, C. B. Charles Budd Robinson (1871–1913)
Robinson, W. William Robinson (1838–1935)
Robinson, W. J. Winifred Josephine Robinson (1867–?)
Robs., E. Edward Robson (1763–1813)
Robs., N. Norman Keith Bonner Robson (1928–   )
Robyns, A. André Georges Marie Walter Albert Robyns (1935–   )
Rochebr. Alphonse Trémeau de Rochebrune (1834–1912)
Rochel Anton Rochel (1770–1847)
Rock Joseph Francis Charles Rock (1884–1962)
Rodig. Émile Rodigas (1831–1902)
Rodin Leonid Efimovich Rodin (1907–   )
Rodr. José Demetrio Rodriguez (1780–1846)
Rodw. Leonard Rodway (1853–1936)
Roem. Johann Jacob Roemer (1763–1819)
Roem., M. J. Max J. Roemer (fl. 1846–1847)
Roessler Helmut Roessler (1926–   )
Roezl Benedikt [Benito] Roezl (1824–1885)
Rohlena Josef Rohlena (1874–1944)
Röhling Johann Christoph Röhling (1757–1813)
Rohrb. Paul Rohrbach (1847–1871)
Rohw. Otto Rohweder (1919–   )
Rolfe Robert Allen Rolfe (1855–1921)
Rol.-Goss. Robert Roland-Gosselin (1854–1925)
Rollins Reed Clark Rollins (1911–   )
Roman. Frédéric Romanet du Caillaud (fl. 1881–1888)
Ronn. Karl Ronniger (1871–1954)
Roscoe William Roscoe (1753–1831)
Rose Joseph Nelson Rose (1862–1928)

Rosend. Carl Otto Rosendahl (1875–1956)
Rosenth., K. Käthe Rosenthal (fl. 1919)
Rosenth., R. C. R. C. Rosenthal (fl. 1882–1888)
Roshk. Olga Ivanovna Roshkova [Rozhkova] (1909–)
Rossb., G. George Bowyer Rossbach (1910–)
Rossb., R. Ruth (née Peabody) Rossbach (1912–)
Rössig Karl Gottlieb Rössig (1752–1806)
Rost Ernest C. Rost (fl. 1932)
Roster Giorgio Roster (?–1968)
Rostk. Friedrich Wilhelm Gottlieb Rostkovius (1770–1848)
Rota Lorenzo Rota (1819–1855)
Roth Albrecht Wilhelm Roth (1757–1834)
Rothe Heinrich August Rothe (fl. 1890)
Rothm. Werner Hugo Paul Rothmaler (1908–1962)
Rothr. Joseph Trimble Rothrock (1839–1922)
Rottb. Christen Friis Rottboell (1727–1797)
Rottl. Johann Peter Rottler (1749–1836)
Rouhier Alexandre Rouhier (fl. 1926)
Rouleau Joseph Albert Ernest Rouleau (1916–)
Roush Eva Myrtelle (née Fling) Roush (1886–1965)
Rouy Georges C. Ch. Rouy (1851–1924)
Rowlee Willard Winfield Rowlee (1861–1923)
Rowley Gordon Douglas Rowley (1921–)
Roxb. William Roxburgh (1751–1815)
Royen Adrian van Royen (1704–1779)
Royle John Forbes Royle (1799–1858)
Rozeira Arnaldo D. F. Rozeira (1912–)
Rudge Edward Rudge (1763–1846)
Rudolph, J. H. Johann Heinrich Rudolph (1744–1809)
Rudolphi, F. Friedrich Karl Ludwig Rudolphi (1801–1849)
Rudolphi, K. Karl Asmund Rudolphi (1771–1832)
Ruiz Hipólito Ruiz Lopez (1754–1815)
Rümpler Karl Theodor Rümpler (1817–1891)
Runge Carl Runge (fl. 1898)
Ruppius Heinrich Bernhard Ruppius (1688–1719)
Rupr. Franz Joseph Ruprecht (1814–1870)
Rusby Henry Hurd Rusby (1855–1940)
Russell, N. H. Norman Hudson Russell (1921–)
Russell, P. G. Paul George Russell (1889–)
Rüst Rüst (fl. 1889–1899)
Ruthe Johann Friedrich Ruthe (1788–1859)
Rydb. Per Axel Rydberg (1860–1931)
Ryl. Thomas Glazebrook Rylands (1818–1900)
Ruys Jan Daniel Ruys (1897–1931)
Sab. Joseph Sabine (1770–1837)
Sacc. Pier Andrea Saccardo (1845–1920)
Saff. William Edwin Safford (1859–1926)
Sagorski Ernst Sagorski (1847–1929)
Sagot Paul Antoine Sagot (1821–1888)
Salisb. Richard Anthony Salisbury (1761–1829)
Salm-Dyck Joseph Maria Franz Anton Hubert Ignaz Fürst zu Salm-Reifferscheid-Dyck (1773–1861)
Salmon Charles Edgar Salmon (1872–1930)
Salomon Carl Salomon (1829–1899)
Salter Terence Macleane Salter (1883–1969)
Salzm. Philipp Salzmann (1781–1851)
Sam. Gunnar Samuelsson (1885–1944)
Samp. Gonçalo Antonio da Silva Ferreira Sampaio (1865–1937)
Sander Henry Frederick Conrad Sander (1847–1920)
Sandw. Noel Yvri Sandwith (1901–1965)
Santi Giorgio Santi (1746–1822)
Sarg. Charles Sprague Sargent (1841–1927)
Sarg., H. W. Henry Winthrop Sargent (1810–1882)
Sars. Thomas Dixon Sarsons (1880–1951)
Sartorelli Giovanni Battista Sartorelli (1780–1853)
Sartori Josef Sartori (1809–1880)
Sasaki Syun'iti Sasaki (1888–1960)
Satow Ernest Mason Satow (1843–1929)
Saut. Anton Eleutherius Sauter (1800–1881)
Sauv. Camille Sauvageau (1861–1936)
Sav. Paul Amadée Ludovic Savatier (1830–1891)
Savi Gaetano Savi (1769–1844)
Savigny Marie Jules César Lelorgne de Savigny (1777–1851)
Scepin Constantin Scepin (1727–?)
Schaeff. Jacob Christian Schaeffer (1718–1790)
Schaffn., J. H. John Henry Schaffner (1866–1939)
Schaffn., W. Wilhelm Schaffner (?–1882)
Schall. Paul Otto Schallert (1879–)
Schauer Johann Konrad Schauer (1813–1848)
Scheele Georg Heinrich Adolf Scheele (1808–1864)
Scheer Frederick [Friedrich] Scheer (1792?–1868)
Scheff. Rudolph Herman Christiaan Carel Scheffer (1844–1880)
Scheidw. Michel Joseph François Scheidweiler (1799–1861)

Schelle Ernst Schelle (1864–1929)
Schenk Joseph August von Schenk (1815–1891)
Scherb. Johannes Scherbius (1769–1813)
Schery Robert Walter Schery (1917–)
Schick Carl Schick (1881–1953)
Schiede Christian Julius Wilhelm Schiede (1798–1836)
Schiffn. Victor Felix Schiffner (1862–1944)
Schiman-Czeika Helene Schiman-Czeika (1933–)
Schimp., W. Wilhelm Philipp Schimper (1808–1880)
Schindl., A. Anton Karl Schindler (1879–1964)
Schindl., J. Johann Schindler (1881–)
Schinz Hans Schinz (1858–1941)
Schipp William August Schipp (1891–1967)
Schkuhr Christian Schkuhr (1741–1811)
Schlachter Schlachter (fl. ca. 1857)
Schlechtend. Diederich Franz Leonhard von Schlechtendal (1794–1866)
Schlechter Friedrich Richard Rudolf Schlechter (1872–1925)
Schleich. Johann Christoph Schleicher (1768–1834)
Schleid. Matthias Jacob Schleiden (1804–1881)
Schloss. Joseph Calasenz Schlosser von Klekovski (1808–1882)
Schmalh. Ivan Federovich [Johannes Theodor] Schmalhausen (1849–1894)
Schmarse Helmut Schmarse (fl. 1933)
Schmeiss Oskar Schmeiss (fl. 1906)
Schmidel Casimir Christoph Schmidel (1718–1792)
Schmidt, A. Alexander Friedrich Wolfgang Schmidt (1932–)
Schmidt, E. Ernst Schmidt (1834–1902)
Schmidt, Franz Franz Schmidt (1751–1834)
Schmidt, Friedr. Friedrich Schmidt (1832–1908)
Schmidt, F. W. Franz Wilibald Schmidt (1764–1796)
Schmidt, J. A. Johann Anton Schmidt (1823–1905)
Schmidt, W. L. Wilhelm Ludwig Ewald Schmidt (1804–1843)
Schmoll Hazel Marguerite Schmoll (1890–)
Schneev. George Voorhelm Schneevoogt (1755–1850)
Schneid., C. K. Camillo Karl Schneider (1876–1951)
Schnittsp. Georg Friedrich Schnittspahn (1810–1865)
Schnizl. Adalbert Carl Friedrich Hellwig Conrad Schnizlein (1814–1868)
Schoch Gottlieb Schoch (1853–1905)
Scholl. F. A. Scholler (1718–1785)
Schomb. Robert Hermann Schomburgk (1804–1865), or Moritz Richard Schomburgk (1811–1890)
Schönl. Selmar Schönland (1860–1940)
Schott Heinrich Wilhelm Schott (1794–1865)
Schottky Ernst Max Schottky (1888–1915)
Schousb. Peder Kofod Anker Schousboe (1766–1832)
Schrad. Heinrich Adolph Schrader (1767–1836)
Schrank Franz von Paula von Schrank (1747–1835)
Schreb. Johann Christian Daniel von Schreber (1739–1810)
Schreib. Beryl Olive Schreiber (later Jesperson) (1911–)
Schrein. Ernst Jefferson Schreiner (1902–)
Schrenk Alexander Gustav von Schrenk (1816–1876)
Schrödinger R. Schrödinger (1857–1919)
Schroet. Carl Joseph Schroeter (1855–1939)
Schub. Bernice Giduz Schubert (1913–)
Schübl. Gustav Schübler (1787–1834)
Schuldt H. Schuldt (fl. 1937)
Schult. Joseph August Schultes (1773–1831)
Schult. f. Julius Hermann Schultes (1804–1840)
Schult., H. H. Schultes (fl. 1852)
Schult., R. E. Richard Evans Schultes (1915–)
Schultz Karl [Carl] Heinrich Schultz "Schultzenstein" (1798–1871)
Schultz-Bip. Carl [Karl] Heinrich Schultz "Bipontinus" (1805–1867)
Schultz, F. W. Friedrich Wilhelm Schultz (1804–1876)
Schultz, K. F. Karl [Carl] Friedrich Schultz (1765–1837)
Schulz, E. D. Ellen Dorothy Schulz (later Quillin) (1892–)
Schulz, O. E. Otto Eugen Schulz (1874–1936)
Schulz, R. Richard Schulz (fl. 1904)
Schulze, A. E. Arnold Edward Schulze (1914–)
Schum., K. Karl Moritz Schumann (1851–1904)
Schumach. Heinrich Christian Friederich Schumacher (1757–1830)
Schur Philipp Johann Ferdinand Schur (1799–1878)
Schuster, J. Julius Schuster (1886–)
Schwant. Georg Schwantes (1891–1960)
Schwarz, F. Fritz Schwarz (fl. 1949)
Schwarz, O. Otto Schwarz (1900–)
Schwegl. Heinz-Werner Schwegler (1929–)
Schweick. Herold Georg Wilhelm Johannes Schweickerdt (1903–)
Schweigg. August Friedrich Schweigger (1783–1821)
Schweinf., C. Charles Schweinfurth (1890–1970)
Schweinf., G. Georg August Schweinfurth (1836–1925)
Schweinitz Lewis David von Schweinitz (1780–1834)

Schwencke Martin Wilhelm Schwencke (1707–1785)
Schwer. Fritz Kurt Alexander von Schwerin (1856–1934)
Scop. Giovanni Antonio [Johann Anton] Scopoli (1723–1788)
Scott-Ell. George Francis Scott Elliot (1862–1934)
Scribn. Frank Lamson Scribner (1851–1938)
Sealy Joseph Robert Sealy (1907–   )
Seat. Henry Eliason Seaton (1869–1893)
Sebast. Francesco Antonio Sebastiani (1782–1821)
Seem. Berthold Carl Seemann (1825–1871)
Seemen Karl Otto von Seemen (1838–1910)
Séguier Jean François Séguier (1703–1784)
Sello, H. Herman Ludwig Sello (1800–1876)
Sellow, F. Friedrich Sello (later Sellow) (1789–1831)
Selys-Longch. Michel Edmond de Selys-Longchamps (1813–1900)
Sencke Ferdinand Sencke (fl. 1830–1866)
Sendtn. Otto Sendtner (1813–1859)
Sennen (Frère) Sennen [Étienne Marcellin Grenier-Blanc] (1861–1937)
Senoner Adolf Senoner (1806–1895)
Ser. Nicolas Charles Seringe (1776–1858)
Serv. Camille Servettaz (1870–1947)
Sesl. Lionardo Sesler (?–1785)
Sessé Martin de Sessé y Lacasta (?–1809)
Seub. Moritz August Seubert (1818–1878)
Shafer John Adolph Shafer (1863–1918)
Shang. Petr Ivanovich Shangin [Schangin] (1741–1816)
Sharp Ward McClintic Sharp (1904–   )
Sharsm., C. W. Carl William Sharsmith (1903–   )
Sharsm., H. K. Helen Katherine (née Myers) Sharsmith (1905–   )
Shaw George Russell Shaw (1848–1937)
Shchegl. S. Shchegleev [Stschegleew] (fl. 1851)
Sheld., E. P. Edmund Perry Sheldon (1869–?)
Sheld., J. L. John Lewis Sheldon (1865–?)
Sherff Earl Edward Sherff (1886–1966)
Shib. Keita Shibata (1877–1949)
Shim., T. Tatemi Shimizu (1932–   )
Shimadzu Tadashige Shimadzu (fl. 1921)
Shinn. Lloyd Herbert Shinners (1918–1971)
Shipch. Nikolaĭ Valerianovich Shipchinskiĭ [Schipczinsky] (1886–1955)
Shirai Mitsutaro Shirai (1863–1932)
Shiras. Homi Shirasawa (1868–1947)
Shishk. Boris Konstantinovich Shishkin [Schischkin] (1886–1963)
Shreve Forrest Shreve (1878–1950)
Shull, C. Charles Albert Shull (1879–1962)
Shuttl. Robert James Shuttleworth (1810–1874)
Sibth. John Sibthorp (1758–1796)
Sieb. Russell Jacob Siebert (1914–   )
Sieber Franz Wilhelm Sieber (1789–1844)
Siebert August Siebert (1854–1923)
Siebold Philipp Franz von Siebold (1796–1866)
Siegfr. Hans Siegfried (1837–1903)
Siehe Walter Siehe (1859–1928)
Sillans Roger Sillans (fl. 1952)
Silow Ronald Alfred Silow (1908–   )
Silva, P. Antonio Rodrigo Pinto da Silva (1912–   )
Silva-Tar. Ernst Emanuel Silva Tarouca (1860–1936)
Sim, R. Robert Sim (1791–1878)
Sim, T. R. Thomas Robertson Sim (1856–1938)
Simmonds, A. Arthur Simmonds (1892–1968)
Simonk. Lajos tól Simonkai [né Simkowicz] (1851–1910)
Simps. George Simpson (1880–1952)
Sims John Sims (1749–1831)
Sincl. George Sinclair (1786–1834)
Sint. Paul Ernst Emil Sintenis (1847–1907)
Skan Sidney Alfred Skan (1870–1939)
Skeels Homer Collar Skeels (1873–1934)
Skinner, F. Frank Leith Skinner (1882–1967)
Skog Laurence Edgar Skog (1943–   )
Skottsb. Carl Johan Fredrik Skottsberg (1880–1963)
Slav. Arthur Daniel Slavin (1903–   )
Sleum. Hermann Otto Sleumer (1906–   )
Sloane Boyd Lincoln Sloane (1885–   )
Sloss. Margaret Slosson (1872–?)
Sm. James Edward Smith (1759–1828)
Sm., A. C. Albert Charles Smith (1906–   )
Sm., C. A. Christo Albertyn Smith (1898–   )
Sm., C. P. Charles Piper Smith (1877–1955)
Sm., E. B. Edwin Burnell Smith (1936–   )
Sm., Erw. Erwin Frink Smith (1854–1927)
Sm., G. E. Gerard Edwards Smith (1805–1881)
Sm., G. G. G. G. Smith (fl. 1950)
Sm., H. G. Henry George Smith (1852–1924)

Sm., James James Smith (1760–1840)
Sm., J. D. John Donnell Smith (1829–1928)
Sm., J. G. Jared Gage Smith (1866–?)
Sm., J. J. Joannes Jacobus Smith (1867–1947)
Sm., John John Smith (1798–1888)
Sm., L. B. Lyman Bradford Smith (1904–   )
Sm., R. M. Rosemary Margaret Smith (1933–   )
Sm., T. Thomas Smith (fl. 1911)
Sm., W. G. Worthington George Smith (1835–1917)
Sm., W. W. William Wright Smith (1875–1956)
Small John Kunkel Small (1869–1938)
Smiley Frank Jason Smiley (1880–   )
Smirn., M. Mikhaïl Smirnov (fl. 1887)
Smyth Bernard Bryan Smyth (1843–1913)
Sodiro Luis [Luigi, Aloysius] Sodiro (1836–1909)
Söhrens Johannes Söhrens (fl. 1900)
Soland. Daniel Carl Solander (1733–1782)
Sole William Sole (1739–1802)
Soleir. Soleirol (1791–?)
Solem. J. V. L. A. G. Solemacher-Antweiler (1889–   )
Solereder Hans Solereder (1860–1920)
Solms-Laub. Hermann Maximilian Carl Ludwig Friedrich Solms-Laubach (1842–1915)
Solym. Sigmond L. Solymosy (1906–   )
Somm. Carlo Pietro Stefano Sommier (1848–1922)
Sond. Otto Wilhelm Sonder (1812–1881)
Song. André Songeon (1826–1905)
Sonn. Pierre Sonnerat (1748–1814)
Soó Károly Rezsö Soó von Bere (1903–   )
Soul.-Bod. Étienne Soulange-Bodin (1774–1846)
Soulié Joseph Auguste Soulié (1868–1930)
Sousa, E. P. Ester P. de Sousa (fl. 1968)
Sowerby James Sowerby (1757–1822)
Sowerby, J. De C. James De Carle Sowerby (1787–1871)
Soy.-Willem. Hubert Félix Soyer-Willemet (1791–1867)
Spach Édouard Spach (1801–1879)
Spae Dieudonné Spae (1819–1858[1879?])
Sparrm. Anders Sparrman (1748–1820)
Späth, F. L. Franz Ludwig Späth (1839–1913)
Späth, H. L. Hellmut Ludwig Späth (1885–1945)
Speg. Carlos [Carlo Luigi] Spegazzini (1858–1926)
Spenn. Fridolin Karl Leopold Spenner (1798–1841)
Sping. Joel Elias Spingarn (1875–1939)
Splitg. Frederik Louis [Friedrich Ludwig] Splitberger (1801–1845)
Sprague, E. Elizabeth Fern Sprague (1911–   )
Sprague, T. Thomas Archibald Sprague (1877–1958)
Spreng., A. Anton Sprengel (1803–1851)
Spreng., K. Kurt [Curt] Polycarp Joachim Sprengel (1766–1833)
Sprenger Carl [Charles] Ludwig Sprenger (1846–1917)
Spring Anton Friedrich [Frédéric Antoine] Spring (1814–1872)
Spruce Richard Spruce (1817–1893)
Sprun. Wilhelm von Spruner (1805–1874)
Stadtm. Jean Frédéric Stadtmann (1762–1807)
St. Amans Jean Florimond Boudon de Saint Amans (1748–1831)
Standish John Standish (fl. 1850–1871)
Standl. Paul Carpenter Standley (1884–1963)
Stansb. Howard Stansbury (1806–1863)
Stapf Otto Stapf (1857–1933)
Starker Thurman James Starker (1890–   )
Starr, M. P. Mortimer Paul Starr (1917–   )
Stearn William Thomas Stearn (1911–   )
Stechm. Johannes Paul Stechmann (fl. 1775)
Steck Abraham Steck (fl. 1757)
Steedm. Henry Steedman (1866–1953)
Steenis Cornelis Gijsbert Gerrit Jan van Steenis (1901–   )
Steetz Joachim Steetz (1804–1862)
Stefanov Boris Stefanov [Stefanoff] (1894–   )
Stein Berthold Stein (1847–1899)
Steinh. Adolphe Steinheil (1810–1839)
Stellf. Carlos Stellfeld (1900–   )
Stent Sydney Margaret Stent (1875–1942)
Steph. Christian Friedrich Stephan (1757–1814)
Steph., P. Paul Stephen (fl. 1930–1938)
Stern, F. C. Frederick Claude Stern (1884–1967)
Sternb. Kaspar Maria von Sternberg (1761–1838)
Steud. Ernst Gottlieb von Steudel (1783–1856)
Steven Christian von Steven (1781–1863)
Stevens, F. Frank Lincoln Stevens (1871–1934)
Stevens, G. George Walter Stevens (1868–?)
Stevens, O. Orin Alva Stevens (1885–   )
Stewart, J. L. John Lindsay Stewart (1832–1873)
Stewart, L. B. Laurence Baxter Stewart (?–1934)
Stewart, M. G. Margaret Gaylord Stewart (later Grover) (1911–   )

Stewart, S. R. Sara R. Stewart (later Hinckley) (1913–)
Stewart, W. S. William Sheldon Stewart (1914–)
Steyaert René Léopold Alix Ghislain Jules Steyaert (1905–)
Steyerm. Julian Alfred Steyermark (1909–)
St.-Hil. Augustin François César Prouvençal de Saint-Hilaire (1779–1853)
St. John Harold St. John (1892–)
St. John, E. Edward Porter St. John (1866–?)
St.-Lag. Jean Baptiste Saint-Lager (1825–1912)
St.-Léger Léon Saint-Léger (fl. 1899)
Stockw. William Palmer Stockwell (1898–1950)
Stoîanov Nikolaï Andreev Stoîanov [Stojanov, Stoyanoff] (1883–1968)
Stoker Fred Stoker (1878–1943)
Stokes, J. Jonathan Stokes (1755–1831)
Stokes, S. Susan Gabriella Stokes (1868–1954)
Störck Anton von Störck [Störk, Störcke] (Anthony Storck) (1731 [1741?]–1803)
Story Robert Story (1913–)
Stout Arlow Burdette Stout (1876–1957)
Strauss Heinrich Christian Strauss (1850–1922)
Strobl P. Gabriel Strobl (1846–1910)
Stuchlík Jaroslav Stuchlík (1890–1967)
Stuntz Stephen Conrad Stuntz (1875–1918)
Stur Dionys Stur (1827–1893)
Sturm Jacob Sturm (1771–1848)
Sturtev. Edward Lewis Sturtevant (1842–1898)
Suckow Georg Adolph Suckow (1751–1813)
Sudw. George Bishop Sudworth (1864–1927)
Suess. Karl Suessenguth (1893–1955)
Sukachev Vladimir Nikolaevich Sukachev [Sukaczev, Sukatschew] (1880–1967)
Suksd. Wilhelm [William] Nikolaus Suksdorf (1850–1932)
Sulak. Tamara Sulakadze (fl. 1927)
Summerh. Victor Samuel Summerhayes (1897–)
Sünderm. Franz Sündermann (1864–1946)
Suring. Jan Valckenier Suringar (1864–1932)
Suter Johann Rudolf Suter (1766–1827)
Svens. Henry Knute Svenson (1897–)
Svent. Eric R. Sventenius (1910–)
Swartz Olof Peter Swartz (1760–1818)
Sweet Robert Sweet (1783–1835)
Swingle Walter Tennyson Swingle (1871–1952)
Sydow Paul Sydow (1851–1925)
Syme John Thomas Irvine Boswell (né Syme) (afterwards Boswell-Syme) (1822–1888)
Symons Jelinger Symons (1778–1851)
Symons-Jeune Bertram Hanmer Bunbury Symons-Jeune (fl. 1907–1953)
Syrach Carl Syrach-Larsen (1898–)
Szabó Zoltán von Szabó (1882–1944)
Szysz. Ignaz von Szyszylowicz (1857–1910)
Tagawa Motoji Tagawa (1908–)
Tagg Harry Frank Tagg (1874–1933)
Takeda Hisayoshi Takeda (1883–)
Talou A. de Talou (fl. 1858–1866)
Tanaka Yoshio [Ushio] Tanaka (1838–1916)
Tanaka, T. Tyozaburo [Chozaburo] Tanaka (1885–)
Tanaka, Y. Yuichiro Tanaka (1900–)
Tanfani Enrico Tanfani (1848–1892)
Tardent Charles Tardent (fl. 1841)
Tardieu Marie Laure Tardieu-Blot (1902–)
Targ.-Tozz., A. Antonio Targioni-Tozzetti (1785–1856)
Targ.-Tozz., O. Ottaviano Targioni-Tozzetti (1755–1829)
Tatar Mathias Tatar (fl. 1878)
Tatew. Misao Tatewaki (1899–)
Taub. Paul Hermann Wilhelm Taubert (1862–1897)
Tausch Ignaz Friedrich Tausch (1793–1848)
Tayl., G. George Taylor (1904–)
Tayl., N. Norman Taylor (1883–)
Tayl., T. Thomas Mayne Cuninghame Taylor (1904–)
Temple F. L. Temple (fl. 1885)
Templeton Bonnie Carolyn Templeton (1906–)
Templeton, W. William Templeton (fl. 1802)
Ten. Michele Tenore (1780–1861)
Terán Manuel de Mier y Terán (1789–1832)
Terracc., A. Achille Terracciano (1862–1917)
Terracc., N. Nicola Terracciano (1837–1921)
Tersch. Terscheck (fl. ca. 1840)
Teusch. Henry Teuscher (1891–)
Teysm. Johannes Elias Teysmann [Teijsmann] (1809–1882)
Tharp Benjamin Carroll Tharp (1885–1964)
Thell. Albert Thellung (1881–1928)
Theobald William Louis Theobald (1936–)

Thiel Hugo Thiel (1839–1918)
Thomas, D. David Thomas (1776–1859)
Thomas, E. Emmanuel Thomas (1788–1859)
Thomas, F. Friedrich August Wilhelm Thomas (1840–1918)
Thomas, J. H. John Hunter Thomas (1928–)
Thomas, O. Owen Thomas (1843–1923)
Thomps., C. H. Charles Henry Thompson (1870–1931)
Thomps., H. J. Henry Joseph Thompson (1921–)
Thomps., J. John Thompson (fl. 1798)
Thomps., J. V. John Vaughan Thompson (1779–1847)
Thomps., J. W. John William Thompson (1890–)
Thomps., W. William Thompson (1823–1903)
Thoms., J. S. John Scott Thomson (1882–1943)
Thoms., T. Thomas Thomson (1817–1878)
Thonn. Peter Thonning (1775–1848)
Thornb. John James Thornber (1872–1962)
Thory Claude Antoine Thory (1759–1827)
Thouars Louis-Marie Aubert Aubert Du Petit-Thouars (1758–1831)
Thouin André Thouin (1747–1824)
Thuill. Jean Louis Thuillier (1757–1822)
Thunb. Carl Pehr [Peter, Petter] Thunberg (1743–1828)
Thurb. George Thurber (1821–1890)
Thurst. Edgar Thurston (1855–1935)
Thwaites George Henry Kendrick Thwaites (1812–1882)
Tidestr. Ivar Frederick Tidestrom (1864–1956)
Tiegel E. Tiegel (?–1936)
Tiling Heinrich Sylvester Theodor Tiling (1818–1871)
Timb.-Lag. Pierre Marguerite Édouard Timbal-Lagrave (1819–1888)
Timm Joachim Christian Timm (1734–1805)
Tindale Mary D. Tindale (fl. 1970)
Tineo Vincenzo Tineo (1791–1856)
Tisch. Arthur Tischer (1895–)
Tobl. Friedrich Tobler (1879–1957)
Tod. Agostino Todaro (1818–1892)
Toepff. Adolph Toepffer (1853–1931)
Toledo Joaquim Franco de Toledo (1905–1952)
Tolm. Aleksandr Innokent'evich Tolmachev [Tolmatchev] (1903–)
Tomm. Muzio Giuseppe Spirito de Tommasini [Mutius von Tommasini] (1794–1879)
Topf Alfred Topf (fl. 1850)
Torr. John Torrey (1796–1873)
Torr., G. George Safford Torrey (1891–)
Torre Antonio Roche da Torre (1904–)
Toumey James William Toumey (1864–1932)
Tourn. Joseph Pitton de Tournefort (1656–1708)
Trab. Louis Charles Trabut (1853–1929)
Tracy Samuel Mills Tracy (1847–1920)
Trafv. Eric Carl Trafvenfeldt (1774–1835)
Traill, J. James Traill (fl. 1830)
Tratt. Leopold Trattinick (1764–1849)
Traub Hamilton Paul Traub (1890–)
Trautv. Ernst Rudolph von Trautvetter (1809–1889)
Trécul Auguste Adolphe Lucien Trécul (1818–1896)
Trel. William Trelease (1857–1945)
Trevir. Ludolph Christian Treviranus (1779–1864)
Trevisan Count Vittore Benedetto Antonio Trevisan di San Leon [de Saint-Léon] (1818–1897)
Trew Christoph Jakob Trew (1695–1769)
Triana José Jerónimo Triana (1834–1890)
Tricker Charles William Bret Tricker (1852–1916)
Triebn. W. Triebner (fl. 1939)
Trimen Henry Trimen (1843–1896)
Trin. Carl Bernhard von Trinius (1778–1844)
Trott. Alessandro Trotter (1874–?)
Truff., A. Albert Truffaut (1844–1925)
Tryon Rolla Milton Tryon (1916–)
Tseng Charles Chiao Tseng (1932–)
Tub. Carl von Tubeuf (1862–1941)
Tuckerm. Edward Tuckerman (1817–1886)
Tulasne Edmond Louis René Tulasne (1815–1885)
Turcz. Nikolaï Stepanovich Turchaninov [Turczaninow] (1796–1864)
Turner, B. L. Billie Lee Turner (1925–)
Turp. Pierre Jean François Turpin (1775–1840)
Turra Antonio Turra (1730–1796)
Turrill William Bertram Turrill (1890–1961)
Tussac François Richard de Tussac (1751–1837)
Tutin Thomas Gaskell Tutin (1908–)
Ucria Bernardino da Ucria (Michelangelo Aurifici) (1739–1796)
Uhl Charles Harrison Uhl (1918–)
Uitew. Antonius Josephus Adrianus Uitewaal (1899–1963)
Ulbr. Oskar Eberhard Ulbrich (1879–1952)
Ule Ernst Heinrich Georg Ule (1854–1915)
Underw. Lucien Marcus Underwood (1853–1907)

Unger Franz Joseph Andreas Nicolaus Unger (1800–1870)
Uphof Johannes Cornelis Theodorus Uphof (1886–)
Urb. Ignatz Urban (1848–1931)
Ursch Eugène Ursch (1882–1962)
Urum. Ivan Kirov Urumov [Urumoff] (1856–1937)
Usteri, A. Alfred Usteri (1869–?)
Usteri, P. Paul Usteri (1768–1831)
Uyeki Homiki Uyeki (1882–)
Vaar. Otto Antero Vaarama (1912–1975)
Vacc. Lino Vaccari (1873–1951)
Vahl Martin Hendriksen Vahl (1749–1804)
Vail Anna Murray Vail (1863–?)
Vaill. Sébastien Vaillant (1669–1722)
Val. Theodoric Valeton (1855–1929)
Valdés Benito Valdés Castrillón (1942–)
Van Brugg. Heinrich Wilhelm Eduard van Bruggen (1927–)
Vand. Domenico [Domingos] Vandelli (1735–1816)
Vandas Karel Vandas (1861–1923)
Van den Heede Adolphe van den Heede (1841–1928)
Van Eselt. Glen Parker Van Eseltine (1888–1938)
Van Geert Auguste Van Geert (1818–1886)
Van Hall Herman Christiaan van Hall (1801–1874)
Van Houtte Louis B. van Houtte (1810–1876)
Vaniot Eugène Vaniot (?–1913)
Van Keppel J. C. van Keppel (1922–)
Van Kleef C. van Kleef (fl. 1877)
Van Noot. Bertha Hoola van Nooten (fl. 1866)
Van Ooststr. Simon Jan van Ooststroom (1906–)
Van Royen Pieter van Royen (1923–)
Van Tiegh. Philippe Édouard Léon van Tieghem (1839–1914)
Van Tuberg. Cornelis Gerrit van Tubergen, jr. (fl. 1913)
Vanucci Vanucci (fl. 1838)
Vasey George Vasey (1822–1893)
Vatke Georg Carl Wilhelm Vatke (1849–1889)
Vaup. Friedrich Johann Vaupel (1876–1927)
Vauv. Léopold Eugène Vauvel (1848–1915)
Vayr. Estanislao Vayreda y Vila (1848–1901)
Veitch, H. J. Harry James Veitch (1840–1924)
Veitch, J. G. John Gould Veitch (1839–1870)
Veitch f., James James Veitch, jr. (1815–1869)
Velarde M. Octavio Velarde Nuñez (fl. 1949)
Velen. Josef Velenovsky (1858–1949)
Vell. José Marianno da Conceição Velloso [Vellozo] (1742–1811)
Venten. Étienne Pierre Ventenat (1757–1808)
Verd. Inez Clare Verdoorn (1896–)
Verdc. Bernard Verdcourt (1925–)
Verg. Louis Verguin (1866–1936)
Verhoek-Williams Susan Elizabeth Verhoek-Williams (1942–)
Verl., B. Pierre Bernard Lazare Verlot (1836–1897)
Verl., J. Jean Baptiste Verlot (1825–1891)
Versch. Ambroise Colette Alexandre Verschaffelt (1825–1886)
Vest Lorenz Chrysanth von Vest (1776–1840)
Viala Pierre Viala (1859–1936)
Vicioso Carlos Vicioso Martínez (1887–)
Vickery Joyce Winifred Vickery (1908–)
Vict. (Frère) Marie-Victorin [Conrad Kirouac] (1885–1944)
Vidal, S. Sebastian Vidal y Soler (1842–1889)
Vieill. Eugène Vieillard (1819–1896)
Vierh. Friedrich [Fritz] Karl Max Vierhapper (1876–1932)
Vig. Alexandre L. G. Viguier (1790–1867)
Vig., R. René Viguier (1880–1931)
Vign. A. von Vignet (fl. 1795)
Vill. Dominique Villars [Villar] (1745–1814)
Vilm. Pierre Louis François Levêque de Vilmorin (1816–1860)
Vilm., M. L. Maurice [August Louis Maurice] Levêque de Vilmorin (1849–1918)
Vilm., P. L. Philippe [Joseph Marie Philippe] Levêque de Vilmorin (1872–1917)
Vilm., R. Roger de Vilmorin (1905–)
Vines Sydney Howard Vines (1849–1934)
Vis. Roberto de Visiani (1800–1878)
Vischer Wilhelm Vischer (1890–)
Vitm. Fulgenzio Vitman (1728–1806)
Viv. Domenico Viviani (1772–1840)
Viviand-Morel Joseph Victor Viviand-Morel (1843–1915)
Vöcht. Hermann [von] Vöchting (1847–1917)
Vogel Julius Rudolph Theodor Vogel (1812–1841)
Vogl. Johannes Andreas Vogler (fl. 1781)
Voigt Johann [Joachim?] Otto Voigt (1798–1843)
Voll O. Voll (?–1959)
Vollmann Franz Vollmann (1858–1917)
Vollmer Albert Michael Vollmer (1896–)
Von Post Tom Erik von Post (1858–1912)

Voronov Georgiĭ Iuriĭ Nikolaevich Voronov [Woronow] (1874–1931)
Vorosh. F. N. Voroshilov [Voroschilov, Woroschilow] (1908–)
Vos Cornelis de Vos (1806–1895)
Voss Andreas Voss (1857–1924)
Voss, J. John William Voss (1907–)
Vrugtm. Freek Vrugtman (1927–)
Vuk. Ludwig von Farkaš-Vukotinović (1813–1893)
Vul'f Evgeniĭ Vladimirovich Vul'f [Wulf, Wulff] (1885–1941)
Vved. Alekseĭ Ivanovich Vvedenskiĭ [Vvedensky, Wedensky] (1898–)
Wahl Herbert Alexander Wahl (1900–1975)
Wahlb. Peter Fredrik Wahlberg (1800–1877)
Wahlenb. Göran [Georg] Wahlenberg (1780–1851)
Waitz Karl Friedrich Waitz (1774–1848)
Wakef. N. A. Wakefield (1918–)
Waldst. Franz de Paula Adam von Waldstein-Wartemberg (1759–1823)
Walker, J. John Walker (1731–1804)
Walkington David Leo Walkington (1930–)
Wall, A. Arnold Wall (1869–1966)
Wallace, A. Alexander Wallace (1829–1899)
Wallace, R. W. Robert Whistler Wallace (1867–1955)
Wallich Nathaniel Wallich [Nathan Wolff] (1786–1854)
Wallis Gustav Wallis (1830–1878)
Wallr. Carl Friedrich Wilhelm Wallroth (1792–1857)
Walp. Wilhelm Gerhard Walpers (1816–1853)
Walsh Walsh (fl. before 1941)
Walsh, R. Robert Walsh (1772–1852)
Walt. Thomas Walter (1740–1789)
Walt., H. Hans Walter (fl. 1909)
Walters Stuart Max Walters (1920–)
Walth. Edward Eric Walther (1892–1959)
Walton Frederick Arthur Walton (fl. 1890–1905)
Wangenh. Friedrich Adam Julius von Wangenheim (1747–1800)
Wanger. Walther Leonhard Wangerin (1884–1938)
Warb. Otto Warburg (1859–1938)
Warb., E. F. Edmund Fredric Warburg (1908–1966)
Warb., O. E. Oscar Emanuel Warburg (1876–1937)
Ward Nathaniel Bagshaw Ward (1791–1868)
Ward, F. K. Francis Kingdon Ward (1885–1958)
Ward, G. H. George Henry Ward (1916–)
Ward, H. W. Henry William Ward (1840–1916)
Warder John Aston Warder (1812–1883)
Warm. Johannes Eugenius Bülow Warming (1841–1924)
Warner Robert Warner (1814[1815?]–1896)
Warsz. Josef Warszewicz [Warscewicz] (1812–1866)
Wassh. Dieter Carl Wasshausen (1938–)
Wats., H. Hewett Cottrell Watson (1804–1881)
Wats., P. Peter William Watson (1761–1830)
Wats., S. Sereno Watson (1826–1892)
Wats., W. William Watson (1858–1925)
Watt, D. David Allan Poe Watt (1830–1917)
Watt, G. George Watt (1851–1930)
Waugh Frank Albert Waugh (1869–1947)
Wawra Heinrich Wawra Ritter von Fernsee (1831–1887)
Weatherby Charles Alfred Weatherby (1875–1949)
Weathers John Weathers (1867–1928)
Web., A. Frédéric Albert Constantin Weber (1830–1903)
Web., C. Claude [Jeanne-Germaine] Weber (1922–)
Web., G. H. Georg Heinrich Weber (1752–1828)
Web., J. B. J. B. Weber (fl. 1874)
Web., W. A. William Alfred Weber (1918–)
Webb Philip Barker Webb (1793–1854)
Webb, D. A. David Allardice Webb (1912–)
Webber John Milton Webber (1897–)
Weberb. August Weberbauer (1871–1948)
Webst. Angus Duncan Webster (fl. 1893–1920)
Wedd. Hugh Algernon Weddell (1819–1877)
Wedem. Wedemeyer (fl. before 1803)
Wehrh. Heinrich Rudolf Wehrhahn (1887–1940)
Weick Alphonse Weick (fl. 1863)
Weidl. Weidlich (fl. 1928)
Weigel Christian Ehrenfried von Weigel (1748–1831)
Weihe Carl Ernst August Weihe (1779–1834)
Weiller Marc Weiller (1880–1945)
Wein Kurt Wein (1883–1968)
Weing. Wilhelm Weingart (1856–1936)
Weiss Friedrich Wilhelm Weiss [Weis] (1744–1826)
Welch Marcus Baldwin Welch (1895–1942)
Wells Bertram Whittier Wells (1884–)
Welw. Friedrich Martin Josef Welwitsch (1806–1872)
Wender. Georg Wilhelm Franz Wenderoth (1774–1861)
Wendl., H. Hermann Wendland (1825–1903)

Wendl., **H. L.** Heinrich Ludolph Wendland (1791–1869)
Wendl., **J. C.** Johann Christoph Wendland (1755–1828)
Wenz. Theodor Wenzig (1824–1892)
Werderm. Erich Werdermann (1892–1959)
Werneck Ludwig Friedrich Franz von Werneck (fl. 1791)
Werner Klaus Werner (1928–   )
Wesm. Alfred Wesmael (1832–1905)
Wessn. Wilhelm Wessner (fl. 1938–1940)
West Hans West (1758–1811)
West, **J.** James West [Egon Viktor Moritz Karl Maria von Ratibor, Prinz zu Hohenlohe-Schillingsfürst] (1875–1939)
Westc. Frederic Westcott (?–1861)
Weston Richard Weston (1733–1806)
Wettst. Richard Wettstein, Ritter von Westersheim (1863–1931)
Weyer W. van de Weyer (fl. 1920)
Wheeler Louis Cutter Wheeler (1910–   )
Wheelock William Efner Wheelock (1852–1926)
Wherry Edgar Theodore Wherry (1885–   )
White, **A. C.** Alain Campbell White (1880–   )
White, **C. T.** Cyril Tenison White (1890–1950)
White, **F.** Francis Buchanan White (1842–1894)
White, **T. G.** Theodore Greeley White (1872–1901)
Whitehead Jack Whitehead (fl. 1943)
Wibel August Wilhelm Eberhard Christoph Wibel (1775–1814)
Widm. Elisabeth Widmer (1862–1952)
Wieg. Karl McKay Wiegand (1873–1942)
Wiehl. Hans-Joachim Wiehler (1930–   )
Wiem. Heinrich August Wiemann (1860–?)
Wier D. B. Wier (fl. 1877)
Wierzb. Peter Wierzbicki (1794–1847)
Wiesb. Johann Baptist Wiesbaur (1836–1906)
Wiesl. Albert Everett Wieslander (1890–   )
Wiggers Friedrich Heinrich Wiggers (1746–1811)
Wiggins Ira Loren Wiggins (1899–   )
Wight Robert Wight (1796–1872)
Wight, **W. F.** William Franklin Wight (1874–1954)
Wigm. H. J. Wigman (fl. 1894)
Wikstr. Johan Emanuel Wikström (1789–1856)
Wilb. Robert Lynch Wilbur (1925–   )
Wilcz., **E.** Ernst Wilczek (1867–1948)
Wilcz., **R.** Rudolf Wilczek (1903–   )
Wilh. Karl Adolf Wilhelm (1848–1933)
Willd. Carl Ludwig Willdenow (1765–1812)
Willem. Pierre Remi François de Paule Willemet (1762–1790)
Williams, **B. S.** Benjamin Samuel Williams (1824–1890)
Williams, **F. N.** Frederic Newton Williams (1862–1923)
Williams, **L. O.** Louis Otho Williams (1908–   )
Williamson Phyllis Alison Williamson (1925–   )
Willis James Hamlyn Willis (1910–   )
Willk. Heinrich Moritz Willkomm (1821–1895)
Willm., **E.** Ellen Ann Willmott (1860–1934)
Wilm., **A.** Alfred James Wilmott (1888–1950)
Wils., **E. H.** Ernest Henry Wilson (1876–1930)
Wils., **K. A.** Kenneth Allen Wilson (1928–   )
Wils., **P.** Percy Wilson (1879–1944)
Wils., **R. G.** Robert Gardner Wilson (1911–   )
Wimm. Christian Friedrich Heinrich Wimmer (1803–1868)
Wimm., **F. E.** Franz Elfried Wimmer (1881–1961)
Winkl., **C.** Constantin [Alexander] Winkler (1848–1900)
Winkl., **H. J.** Hubert J. P. Winkler (1875–1941)
Winkl., **H. K.** Hans Karl Albert Winkler (1877–1945)
Wirtg. Philipp Wilhelm Wirtgen (1806–1870)
Wisl. Friedrich Adolph Wislizenus (1810–1889)
Witasek Johanna Witasek (1865–1910)

With. William Withering (1741–1799)
Witte Heinrich Witte (1825–1917)
Wittm. Max Carl Ludwig Wittmack (1839–1929)
Wittr. Veit Brecher Wittrock (1839–1914)
Wocke Erich Wocke (1863–1941)
Wohlf. Rudolf Wohlfahrt (1830–1888)
Wolf, **C.** Carl Brandt Wolf (1905–   )
Wolf, **E.** Egbert Liûdvigovich Wolf (1860–1931)
Wolf, **N. M.** Nathanael Mattaeus von Wolf (1724–1784)
Wolf, **T.** Franz Theodor Wolf (1841–1921)
Wolf, **W.** Wolfgang Wolf (1875–1950)
Wolff, **C. F.** Caspar Friedrich Wolff (1733–1794)
Wolley-Dod Anthony Hurt Wolley-Dod (1861–1948)
Wood, **A.** Alphonso Wood (1810–1881)
Wood, **J. M.** John Medley Wood (1827–1915)
Wood, **W.** William Wood (1745–1808)
Woodall Edward H. W. Woodall (1843–1937)
Woodcock Hubert Bayley Drysdale Woodcock (1867–1957)
Woods, **J.** Joseph Woods (1776–1864)
Woodson Robert Everard Woodson (1904–1963)
Woodv. William Woodville (1752–1805)
Woolley Robert Vernon Giffard Woolley (fl. 1921–1926)
Woolls William Woolls (1814–1893)
Woot. Elmer Ottis Wooton (1865–1945)
Wormsk. Morten Wormskjöld (1783–1845)
Worsl. Arthington Worsley (1861–?)
Woyn. Heinrich K. Woynar (1865–1917)
Wright Charles Wright (1811–1885)
Wright, **C. H.** Charles Henry Wright (1864–1941)
Wright, **J.** John Wright (1811–1846)
Wright, **W.** William Wright (1735–1819)
Wu, **C.** Chung-lwen Wu (fl. 1938–1956)
Wu, **Y. C.** Y. C. Wu (fl. 1940)
Wulfen Franz Xaver von Wulfen (1728–1805)
Wurmb Fredrik van Wurmb (?–1783)
Württemb. Friedrich Paul Wilhelm von Württemberg (1797–1860)
Wydl. Heinrich Wydler (1800–1883)
Wyman, **A. P.** A. Phelps Wyman (1870–1947)
Yabe Yoshitada Yabe (1876–1931)
Yatabe Ryokichi Yatabe (1851–1899)
Yates Harris Oliver Yates (1934–   )
Yeo Peter Frederick Yeo (1929–   )
Young, **M.** Maurice Young (fl. 1872)
Young, **R. A.** Robert Armstrong Young (1876–?)
Ysab. Alexandre Victor Frédéric Ysabeau (1793–1873)
Yunck. Truman George Yuncker (1891–1963)
Zab. Hermann Zabel (1832–1912)
Zagar. Pavel Petrovich Zagareli (1897–1937)
Zahlbr. Johann Baptist Zahlbruckner (1782–1851)
Zamels Aleksandrs Zamels [Zamelis] (1897–1943)
Zawadzski Aleksandr Zavadskiĭ [Zawadski, Zawadzki] (1798–1868)
Zdárek Robert Zdárek (fl. 1881–1900)
Zederb. Emerich Zederbaur (1877–   )
Zenari Silvia Zenari (1895–1956)
Zenk. Jonathan Carl Zenker (1799–1837)
Zeyh. Carl Ludwig Philipp Zeyher (1799–1858)
Ziesenh. Rudolf Christian Ziesenhenne (1911–   )
Zimm., **F.** Friedrich Zimmerman (fl. 1914)
Zinn Johann Gottfried Zinn (1727–1750)
Zipp. Alexander Zippelius (1797–1828)
Zoll. Heinrich Zollinger (1818–1859)
Zotov Victor Dmitrievich Zotov (1908–   )
Zucc. Joseph Gerhard Zuccarini (1797–1848)
Zuccagni Attilio Zuccagni (1754–1807)

GLOSSARY of BOTANICAL TERMS

Although *Hortus Third* uses, for precision and universality of comprehension, the most commonly used and familiar technical terms of descriptive botany, an attempt has been made to avoid the less familiar, more technical terms since this work will be consulted by many who are not taxonomists. Not every term listed in this glossary has actually been used in this work, but it is felt that the additional terms and definitions will increase the glossary's usefulness to nontaxonomists whose interest may lead them to consult botanical works such as floras and monographs. This present glossary, with modifications, is based to considerable extent on the Illustrated Glossary of Taxonomic Terms in George H. M. Lawrence's *Taxonomy of Vascular Plants,* Macmillan Publishing Co., Inc., New York (1951).

The plural of nouns of Latin formation that end in *-a, -us,* or *-um* are usually easily derived by replacing terminal *-a* with *-ae* (e.g., *pinna,* pl. *pinnae*), *-us* with *-i* (e.g., *coccus,* pl. *cocci*), and *-um* with *-a* (e.g., *androecium,* pl. *androecia*), and so are mostly not specifically indicated in this glossary. There are also alternative plural forms of English formation for many such terms, made by adding terminal *-s* or *-es* (e.g., *corona,* pl. *coronae* or *coronas*), and these are sometimes preferable.

Abaxial. Away from or facing away from the axis, dorsal; said of the surface or a part of a lateral organ. The lower surface of a leaf is abaxial, for example.

Abortive. Scarcely or imperfectly developed.

Abrupt. 1) Terminating suddenly, as a pinnate leaf that has no terminal leaflet; 2) produced suddenly rather than gradually, as an abrupt point.

Abscissing. Said of a plant part separating and falling away from its point of attachment because of the disintegration of a layer of parenchyma (the abscission layer) at the base of the part.

Acaulescent. Stemless or apparently so; a stem is usually actually present, but subterranean or very short; a descriptive rather than a morphological term.

Accessory fruit. A fruit or assemblage of fruits in which the conspicuous, fleshy parts are not derived from the pistil—as in the strawberry *(Fragaria),* where the soft, red, edible flesh is the enlarged receptacle, the true fruits (achenes) being embedded in its surface.

Accumbent. Lying against another organ. Accumbent cotyledons (in the seed) lie face to face, with their edges on one side lying against the radicle, as in *Alyssum* and *Lunaria* (Cruciferae). **Double-accumbent** cotyledons are folded lengthwise individually and lie side by side, with the two folds lying against the radicle, as in *Cakile* (Cruciferae). Compare *Conduplicate, Incumbent.*

Achene, akene. A small, dry, indehiscent, one-seeded fruit with tight, thin outer wall.

Acicular. Needle-shaped or somewhat so.

Acorn. The fruit of the oak *(Quercus),* composed of a nut and its basal cup or cupule.

Acropetal. Arising or developing sequentially from a lower position toward a more apical one.

Actinomorphic. Regular, radially symmetrical, capable of being divided vertically and in more than one plane into two essentially equal halves, as the flower of *Tulipa* or *Rosa.*

Acuminate. Tapering with somewhat concave sides to a protracted, acute point. **Abruptly acuminate.** Tapering suddenly rather than gradually to such a point.

Acute. Sharp, tapering with essentially straight or only slightly convex sides to a point.

Acyclic. Arranged spirally, not in whorls.

Adaxial. Toward or facing the axis, ventral; said of the surface or a part of a lateral organ. The upper surface of a leaf is *adaxial.*

Adherent, adhering. United, fused; sometimes, clinging together but not actually fused; usually referring to the joining of dissimiliar parts or organs. Compare *Coherent.*

Adnate. Completely or nearly completely united or fused; referring to the union in early development of dissimilar parts or organs, as a filament adnate to the corolla. Compare *Connate.*

Adpressed. See *Appressed.*

Adventitious. Occurring in other than the usual location, as roots on aerial stems, or buds on leaves.

Adventive. Introduced from another region or country and not yet fully naturalized.

Aestivation. The arrangement of the perianth or its parts in the bud.

Aggregate fruit. A "fruit" comprising the several separate ripened ovaries of a single flower, as in blackberry (Rubus).

Alate. Winged.

Albumen. Starchy or other nutritive material in the seed, stored either inside the embryo sac (and then called endosperm) or in the surrounding nucellar cells (and then called perisperm).

Allohexaploid. Having six genomes or basic sets of chromosomes, with one or more sets derived from a species different from that of the other sets. In common wheat *(Triticum aestivum),* for instance, two each of three different chromosome sets are present, derived from three different parent species.

Allopolyploid. Having three or more genomes or basic sets of chromosomes, with one or more sets derived from a species different from that of the other sets.

Allotetraploid. Having four genomes or basic sets of chromosomes, with one or two sets (usually two) derived from a species different from that of the other sets. See *Ploidy* in text.

Alternate. Arranged singly at different heights and on different sides of the axis or stem, as alternate leaves or branches.

Alulate. With a very narrow or small wing.

Ament. A catkin.

Amphibious. Growing equally well on land or in the water.

Amphidiploid, amphiploid. Tetraploid, with two genomes or basic sets of chromosomes from each of two parent species.

Amphitropous. Descriptive of an ovule that is curved back along its supporting stalk (funiculus) so that its base and its micropyle are brought near each other.

Amplexicaul. Clasping the stem, with the base partially surrounding it, as in certain leaves.

Ampulla. A flasklike or bladderlike organ, as those borne on

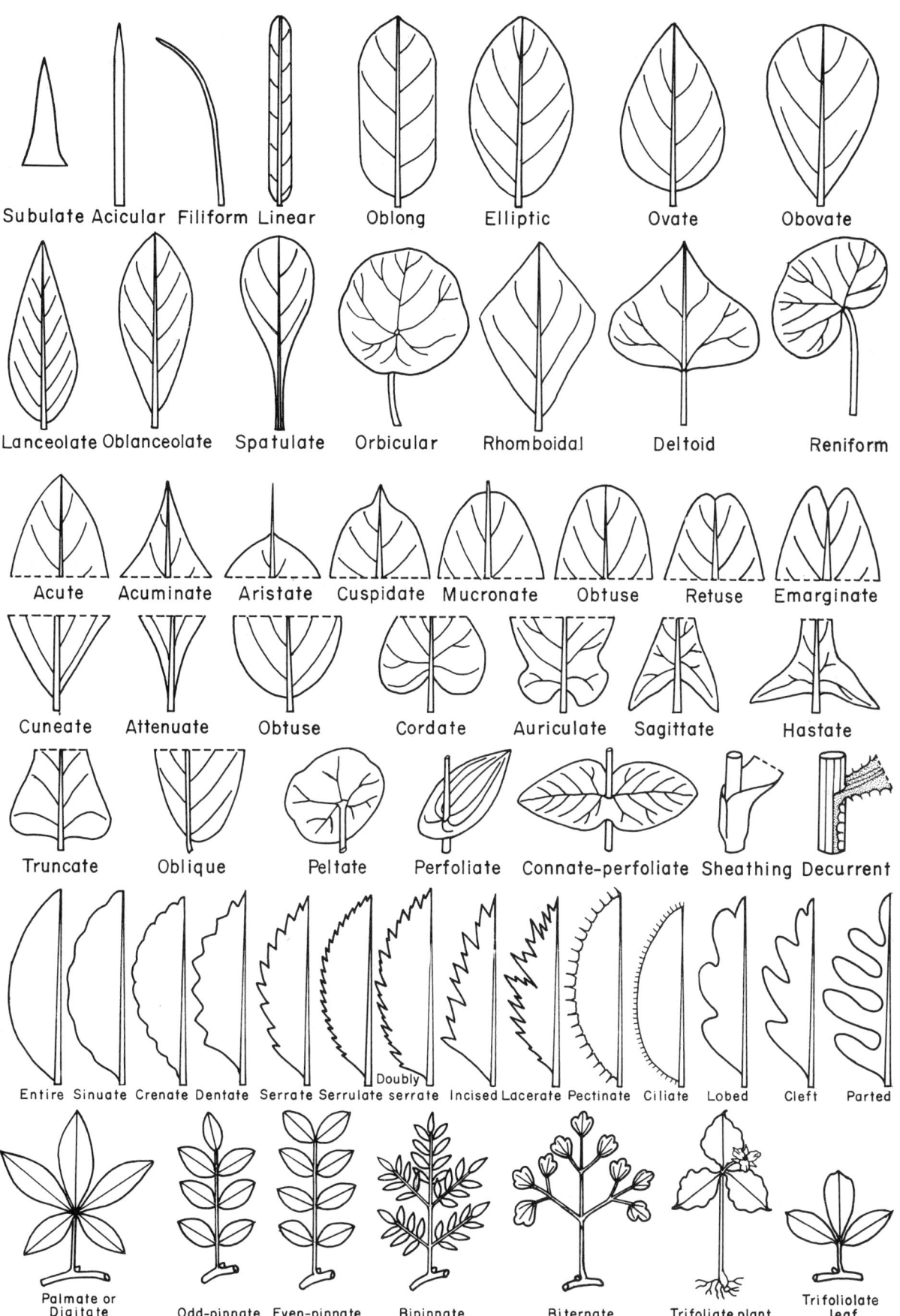

Subulate   Acicular   Filiform   Linear   Oblong   Elliptic   Ovate   Obovate

Lanceolate   Oblanceolate   Spatulate   Orbicular   Rhomboidal   Deltoid   Reniform

Acute   Acuminate   Aristate   Cuspidate   Mucronate   Obtuse   Retuse   Emarginate

Cuneate   Attenuate   Obtuse   Cordate   Auriculate   Sagittate   Hastate

Truncate   Oblique   Peltate   Perfoliate   Connate-perfoliate   Sheathing   Decurrent

Entire   Sinuate   Crenate   Dentate   Serrate   Serrulate   Doubly serrate   Incised   Lacerate   Pectinate   Ciliate   Lobed   Cleft   Parted

Palmate or Digitate   Odd-pinnate   Even-pinnate   Bipinnate   Biternate   Trifoliate plant   Trifoliolate leaf

Terms of Vegetative Structures

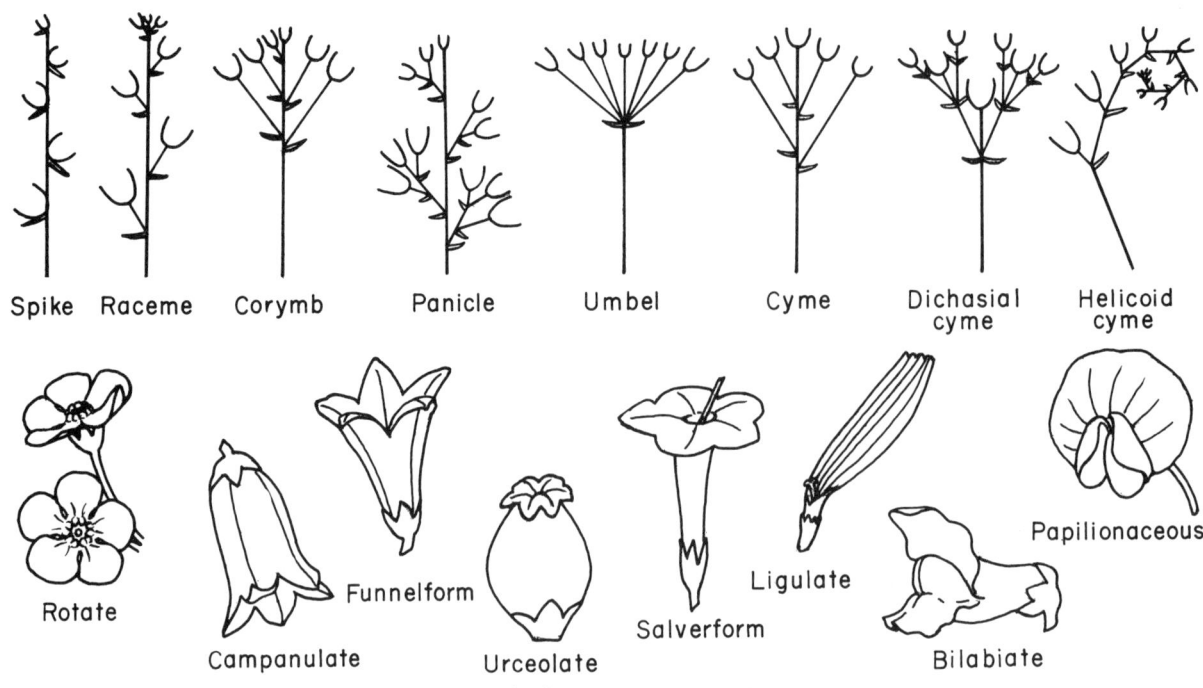

Spike Raceme Corymb Panicle Umbel Cyme Dichasial cyme Helicoid cyme

Rotate Funnelform Campanulate Urceolate Salverform Ligulate Bilabiate Papilionaceous

Terms of Inflorescences and Corollas

the leaves of *Nepenthes* or *Utricularia*.

Analogous. Of similar function, but not of similar evolutionary descent. Compare *Homologous*.

Anastomosing. Forming a network; said of venation in which the veins are interconnected by cross veins.

Anatropous. Descriptive of an ovule that is reversed, one whose opening (micropyle) is close to the point of attachment of its supporting stalk (funiculus).

Androecium. The male element, the stamens, whether one or many, as a unit of the flower.

Androgynophore. An axis or stalk above the point of perianth attachment, bearing both stamens and pistil.

Androphore. A stalk bearing the androecium.

Anemophilous. Wind-pollinated.

Angiosperm. A plant that has its seeds enclosed in an ovary, as any of the flowering plants. Compare *Gymnosperm*.

Annual. Of one season's duration, from germination to maturity and death.

Annular. In the form of a ring.

Annulate. Provided with or composed of rings.

Annulus. Literally, a ring: 1) the fleshy corona or rim of the corolla in some Asclepiadaceae, as in *Stapelia;* 2) a ring of specialized, thin- or thick-walled cells around the rim of the capsule in mosses, involved in dehiscence of the operculum; 3) a ring or sometimes only a group of specialized cells on the sporangium of a fern, involved in its dehiscence.

Antemarginal. Within or not extending quite as far as the margin.

Anterior. On the front side, away from the axis, abaxial, toward the subtending bract; in a bilabiate corolla, for example, the lower lip is anterior, the upper lip posterior. Compare *Posterior*.

Anther. The pollen-bearing part of the stamen, borne at the top of the filament or sometimes sessile.

Anther sac. A saclike unit of the anther, containing the pollen; most commonly, each anther is composed of four pollen sacs, two in each lobe or half of the anther, the tissues that separate them disintegrating before anthesis and the anther then seemingly biloculate (two-celled).

Anther tube. The tube formed by connivent or connate anthers.

Antheridium. The male organ in cryptogams, producing male gametes (sperms), and corresponding to the anther in flowering plants.

Antheriferous. Anther-bearing.

Anthesis. The expansion, or the period of expansion or opening, of a flower, associated with the anthers' and stigmas' becoming functional.

Antrorse. Directed upward or forward.

Apetalous. Without petals.

Apex (pl. **apices**). The tip, the distal end.

Aphyllous. Leafless.

Apical placentation. See *Placentation*.

Apicula. A short, sharp, flexible point.

Apiculate. Terminated by an apicula.

Apocarpous. With carpels separate, not united; frequently applied to a gynoecium of separate simple pistils. Compare *Syncarpous*.

Apomictic. Reproduced or reproducing asexually, without fertilization.

Apomixis. Reproduction, of many types, in which a nonsexual process has replaced the sexual, and no fusion of male and female gametes is involved. In many plants, seeds regularly develop from unfertilized egg cells or from cells other than egg cells; the resultant plants, termed apomicts, are genetically identical with the mother plant.

Aposepalous. Having the sepals distinct from one another, the calyx being composed of separate elements, polysepalous.

Appendage. An attached subsidiary or secondary part, as a projecting or hanging part.

Appressed, adpressed. Closely and flatly pressed against.

Arachnoid. Cobwebby with soft and slender entangled hairs.

Arborescent. Of treelike habit.

Archegonium. In higher cryptogams and gymnosperms, the usually flask-shaped female organ producing the female gamete (egg).

Arcuate. Curved or bowed.

Areole. 1) A small area, especially the open space between anastomosing veins; 2) a spine-bearing sunken or raised spot on the stem in cacti.

Aril. A usually fleshy appendage of the funiculus, sometimes partially or completely covering the seed.

Arillate. Provided with an aril.

Aristate. 1) Bearing a stiff, bristlelike awn or seta; 2) tapered to a very narrow, much-elongated apex.

Armature. Any covering or occurrence of spines, barbs, hooks, or prickles on any part of the plant.

Armed. Provided with any kind of strong or sharp defense, as of thorns, spines, prickles, barbs.

Articulate. Jointed, provided with nodes or joints, or places where separation may naturally take place.

Arundinaceous. Reedlike.

Ascending. Rising up, extending somewhat obliquely or indirectly upward.

Asexual. Nonsexual, without sex.

Assurgent. Ascending, rising.

Asymmetrical. Not symmetrical. **Asymmetrical flower.** A flower having some parts different in form, size, or degree of connation from others of the same whorl (as in the corolla) so that it is incapable of division in any plane into two equal, similar halves.

Atavistic. Reverting to a form characteristic of remote ancestors.

Attenuate. Gradually long-tapering; applied to bases or apices of parts.

Auricle. An ear-shaped lobe or appendage, as the projections at the base of some leaves and petals.

Auriculate. Having an auricle or auricles.

Autopolyploid. Polyploid, with all of the three or more basic chromosome sets derived from the same species.

Awl-shaped. Slender and sharp-pointed, gradually tapering from base to a slender or stiff point, subulate.

Awn. A bristlelike appendage.

Axil. The upper angle that a lateral organ, such as a petiole or peduncle, makes with the axis or stem that bears it.

Axile. See *Placentation.*

Axillary. In an axil.

Axis (pl. **axes**). The main or central line of development of a plant or organ, from which lateral organs or parts arise radially, as a stem or branch.

Baccate. Berrylike, pulpy or fleshy.

Banner. See *Standard.*

Barbed. Said of bristles or awns having short, stiff, terminal or lateral hairs sharply slanted downward or backward.

Basal. At the base. **Basal placentation.** See *Placentation.*

Basifixed. Attached or fixed by the base, as an ovule or anther that is affixed to its support by its bottom.

Basipetal. Developing from an apical or distal point toward the base; the opposite of *acropetal.*

Beak. A long, prominent, substantial point; applied particularly to prolongations of fruits and pistils.

Beard. 1) A long awn or bristlelike hair, as in the inflorescence of some grasses; 2) a tuft, line, or zone of pubescence, as on the falls of the bearded irises.

Berry. A pulpy, indehiscent, few- or many-seeded fruit; technically, the pulpy fruit developing from a single compound pistil, containing one or more seeds but no true stone, as the tomato *(Lycopersicon)* or grape *(Vitis).*

Bi-. A prefix meaning two, as *bilocular,* having two locules.

Biauriculate. With two auricles.

Biennial. Of two seasons' duration, from germination to maturity and death, usually developing vegetative growth the first year, and flowering, fruiting, and dying the second.

Bifid. Forked or cleft, with two points, as the apices of some leaves or petals.

Bifoliate. Having two leaves.

Bifoliolate. Consisting of two leaflets, said of leaves.

Bifurcate. Forked, with two branches, as some Y-shaped hairs, stigmas, or styles.

Bilabiate. Two-lipped, divided into an upper and a lower part, as the corolla and calyx in most Labiatae.

Biovulate. Containing two ovules.

Bipinnate. Twice pinnate, the primary pinnae or leaflets being again divided into secondary leaflets; often written *2-pinnate.*

Bipinnatisect. Twice pinnatisect, the primary divisions being again pinnatisect; often written *2-pinnatisect.*

Biseriate. In two whorls or cycles, as a perianth composed of a calyx and a corolla.

Bisexual. Having both sexes present and functional in the same flower.

Biternate. See *Ternate.*

Bladdery. Inflated, with the walls thin as in the bladder of an animal.

Blade. The expanded part of a leaf or petal.

Bloom. 1) A very fine, often waxy, powdery coating on the surface of certain leaves, stems, fruits, or other organs, usually whitish, grayish, or bluish, and easily rubbed off, as the bloom on a plum; 2) A flower.

Bole. A strong, unbranched caudex, trunk.

Bostryx (pl. **bostryces**). See *Helicoid cyme.*

Bract. A much-reduced leaf, particularly one of the small or scalelike leaves in a flower cluster or associated with the flowers; morphologically a foliar organ.

Bracteate, bracted. Bearing or subtended by bracts.

Bracteolate, bracteoled. Having bracteoles, as the bracteolate pedicel of a flower.

Bracteole. A secondary or very small bract, a bractlet.

Bractlet. A bracteole.

Bristly. Bearing stiff, strong hairs or bristles.

Bulb. A usually subterranean modified leaf bud, consisting of a short, thick stem and crowded, fleshy scales or leaf bases, and serving as a storage organ.

Bulbiferous. Bearing bulbs.

Bulbil, bulblet. A small bulb or bulblike structure, usually borne in leaf axils, or among or in the place of flowers, or in other unusual places.

Bullate. Blistered or puckered, as the leaf of a Savoy cabbage.

Bush. A low and thick shrub, without distinct trunk.

Caducous. Falling very early, as the sepals in the Papaveraceae or the stipules in many plants.

Caespitose. See *Cespitose.*

Calcarate. With a spur.

Caliciform. Calyxlike.

Callosity. A leathery or hard thickening or protuberance, a callus.

Callose. Bearing callosities.

Callus. A callosity; in cuttings or on injuries, the thick new tissue that develops and covers the injury.

Calyculate. 1) Having a calyculus; 2) resembling a calyx.

Calyculus. A whorl of small bracts or bractlets, resembling a calyx and usually subtending a true calyx or an involucre.

Calyptra. A caplike or lidlike structure, particularly the cap or hood of a moss capsule, the united and circumscissile calyx lobes and petals of a *Eucalyptus* flower, or the circumscissile calyx of some Papaveraceae.

Calyx. The outer whorl of floral envelopes, composed of separate or united sepals.

Calyx tube. 1) Strictly, the tube or united part of a gamosepalous calyx as distinguished from the calyx lobes; 2) loosely, and as used in this work, a *hypanthium.*

Campanulate. Bell-shaped.

Campylotropous. Descriptive of an ovule that is curved by uneven growth so that its axis is approximately at right angles to its supporting stalk (funiculus).

Canaliculate. With a longitudinal channel or groove.

Canescent. Grayish-white-pubescent, hoary, densely covered with short, fine, whitish or gray hairs.

Cap. A calyptra.

Capillary. Hairlike, very slender.

Capitate. 1) Headlike, formed like a head; 2) in heads, aggregated into a very dense or compact cluster.

Capitellate. Diminutive of *capitate;* 1) formed like or 2) clustered in a small head.

Capitulum. A head, an inflorescence composed of a dense cluster of usually sessile flowers, as in clover *(Trifolium)* and the Compositae.

Capsule. 1) In angiosperms, a dry, dehiscent fruit composed of two or more united carpels; 2) in cryptogams, a stalked, thin-walled structure containing the spores.

Carinate. Keeled, provided with a projecting central longitudinal line or ridge.

Carnivorous. Literally, meat-eating; in plants, usually equivalent to *insectivorous.*

Carpel. One of the units composing a pistil or ovary. A simple pistil has one carpel, a compound pistil has two or more united carpels.

Carpellate, carpelled. Possessing or composed of carpels; when written *2-carpellate* or *3-carpellate,* meaning composed of two or three carpels respectively.

Carpophore. A wiry stalk that supports each half of the dehiscing fruit in the Umbelliferae.

Cartilaginous. Tough and hard but flexible, like cartilage.

Caryopsis. An achene derived from a superior ovary, with the pericarp united to the seed; a term usually restricted to the grasses (Gramineae).

Catkin. An ament, a scaly-bracted, usually flexuous spike or spikelike inflorescence of cymules, characteristic of *Salix, Betula, Quercus.*

Caudate. Bearing a tail-like appendage or appendages, as the apex of some leaves, the spadix of some Araceae, or the base of the anther in some Compositae.

Caudex. 1) The stout, persistent, usually underground stem base of a perennial herb, from which the annual stems arise; 2) the trunk of a palm.

Caulescent. Having an evident, well-developed stem above ground.

Cauline. Pertaining to or attached to a stem.

Cell. 1) A small, usually microscopic, mass of protoplasm, in the form of cytoplasm and one or more nuclei and usually some nonliving material, enclosed in a membrane; the basic functional and structural unit of living matter; 2) a locule.

Centrifugal. Developing or progressing from the center toward the periphery or margin. Compare *Centripetal.*

Centripetal. Developing or progressing from the periphery or margin toward the center. Compare *Centrifugal.*

Cephalium. A woody outgrowth at the apex of the stem of some Cactaceae, on which the flowers are borne, as in *Melocactus.*

Cernuous. Drooping.

Cespitose, caespitose. Growing in tufts or dense little clumps, forming mats.

Chaff. A small, thin, dry, membranous scale or bract; in particular, the bracts among the florets on the surface of the receptacle, in flowerheads of the Compositae.

Chaffy. Like chaff in texture.

Chalaza. The basal part of an ovule, where it is attached to the funiculus.

Chartaceous. Of papery or tissuelike texture, and not usually green in color.

Chasmogamous. With pollination effected in the expanded flower. Compare *Cleistogamous.*

Chimaera, chimera. Botanically, a plant or plant organ consisting of tissues of more than one genetic composition and origin.

Choripetalous. Having separate and distinct petals, polypetalous.

Cilia (the plural of seldom-used **cilium**). 1) Marginal hairs on a leaf or other flattened organ; 2) whiplike filaments of protoplasm which give locomotion to spores of some algae and sperms of ferns, cycads, ginkgo, et al.

Ciliate. Bearing cilia, fringed with hairs, bearing hairs on the margin.

Ciliolate. Diminutive of *ciliate;* fringed marginally with minute hairs.

Cilium. See *Cilia.*

Cincinnus. See *Scorpioid cyme.*

Cinereous. Ash-colored, light gray.

Circinate. Rolled or coiled from the top downward, with the apex nearest the center of the coil, as an unexpanded fern frond.

Circumscissile. See *Dehiscence.*

Cirrhous. Tendril-like, as the slender, coiled apex of certain leaves.

Cladode. A cladophyll.

Cladophyll. A flattened branch having the form and function of a leaf, but arising in the axil of a minute, bractlike, often caducous, true leaf, as in *Ruscus.*

Clambering. Vinelike, climbing, often without the aid of tendrils or twining stems.

Clasping. Partially or completely surrounding the stem, as the bases of some leaves.

Class. See *Classification* in text.

Clavate. Club-shaped, with a long body thickened toward the top, like a baseball bat.

Clavellate. Diminutive of *clavate;* shaped like a small club.

Claw. The long, narrow, petiolelike base of a petal or a sepal in some flowers.

Cleft. Divided to or nearly to the middle into lobes, as a palmately or pinnately cleft leaf.

Cleistogamous. With pollination (self-pollination) effected in the unexpanded, closed flower. Compare *Chasmogamous.*

Clon, clone. See *Clone* in text.

Coccus. One of the separable parts of a lobed, sometimes leathery or dry fruit with one (rarely two)-seeded cells.

Cochleate. Coiled like a snail shell.

Coherent, cohering. United, fused; sometimes, clinging together but not actually fused; usually referring to the joining of similar parts or organs. Compare *Adherent.*

Columella. The persistent axis of a fruit composed of several carpels.

Column. The structure formed by the union of the style and stamens in the Orchidaceae, or of staminal filaments, as in the Malvaceae.

Column foot. In some orchids, a forward extension at the base of the column, to which the lip is attached.

Coma. 1) A tuft of soft hairs on a seed, as in milkweeds *(Asclepias);* 2) a tuft of leaves or bracts at the apex of an inflorescence, as in pineapple *(Ananas);* 3) a leafy crown or head, as in many Palmae.

Combination. The name of a taxon below the rank of genus, consisting of the name of the genus combined with one or more epithets, as *Cyrtanthus Mackenii* or *Cyrtanthus Mackenii* var. *Cooperi.* See *Epithet.*

Commissure. The place or surface where two bodies or parts meet, as the face along which one carpel is united with another.

Comose. Bearing a coma in any sense of the term.

Complex. As a noun, a group of similar and obviously related plants whose taxonomic relationship to one another is imperfectly understood.

Composite. 1) Compound (said of an apparently simple or homogeneous organ or structure made up of several really distinct parts); 2) any member of the family Compositae.

Compound. Composed of two or more similar parts.

Compound leaf. A leaf composed, usually, of two or more leaflets, but sometimes (as in *Citrus*) of only one, when the lateral leaflets have been lost in the course of evolution and only the terminal one remains (a joint between leaflet and petiole then revealing the compound condition of the leaf). A leaf is **digitately** or **palmately compound** when three or more leaflets arise from a common point at the end of the petiole; **pinnately compound** when one or more pairs of leaflets are arranged along the sides of the axis, with (odd-pinnate) or without (even-pinnate) a terminal leaflet; **ternately compound** when the leaflets or the divisions of the leaf occur in threes.

Compound pistil (or **ovary**). A pistil produced by the partial or complete union of two or more carpels. The number of cells or locules within the ovary may or may not indicate the number of carpels. A pistil in which the ovary has more than one cell or locule is almost always compound. A pistil having a one-celled ovary, but more than one placenta or style or stigma, or with a combination of these duplications, may be presumed to be compound.

Compressed. Flattened, especially flattened laterally.

Concolorous. Of a single uniform color.

Conduplicate. Folded once lengthwise, as the leaves in *Vanda, Paphiopedilum,* and many other Orchidaceae. Conduplicate cotyledons (in the seed) are folded thus with one enfolded within the other, the radicle lying in the fold of the inner one, as in *Brassica* and *Raphanus* (Cruciferae). Compare *Accumbent, Incumbent.*

Cone. A dense and usually elongated collection of sporophylls (cone scales) and usually bracts on a central axis, the whole forming a detachable, homogeneous body; some cones are of short duration, as the male cones of *Pinus,* others may become dry and woody, as the female cones of *Pinus.*

Confluent. Merging or blending together.

Congeneric. Belonging to the same genus.

Connate. United or joined; said, in particular, of like or similar structures joined as one body or organ.

Connate-perfoliate. Said of opposite, sessile leaves that are connate by their bases, the axis seemingly passing through the joined bases.

Connective. The tissue connecting the two cells of an anther, particularly when the cells are separated.

Connivent. Coming in contact or converging, but not fused.

Conoid. Conelike, cone-shaped.

Conspecific. Belonging to the same species.

Contiguous. Touching or in contact, without fusion.

Contorted. Twisted, convolute (in aestivation).

Convariety. A group of similar cultivars within a variable species or interspecific hybrid; formerly used, but now replaced by the term *group.*

Convolute. Rolled up or twisted together lengthwise; said especially of organs, such as leaves or petals, in the bud.

Cordate. Heart-shaped, ovate in general outline but with a sinus between rounded lobes at the base; often applied only to the basal portion of an organ with such a shape.

Coriaceous. Of leathery texture, as a leaf of boxwood *(Buxus).*

Corm. A solid, swollen part of a stem, usually subterranean, as the so-called "bulb" of *Crocus* and *Gladiolus.*

Cormel. A small corm arising from a mother corm.

Corniculate. Bearing or terminating in a small hornlike protuberance or process.

Corolla. The inner circle or second whorl of floral envelopes; if the parts are separate, they are petals and the corolla is said to be choripetalous or polypetalous; if they are to any degree united, the corolla is said to be gamopetalous or sympetalous, and the parts are evident only as teeth or lobes, or may be undifferentiated.

Corolliform. Like a corolla in appearance, as the calyx in Nyctaginaceae.

Corona. A crown, a circular appendage, or a circle of appendages; in a flower, an outgrowth of the perianth, as in *Narcissus,* or of the staminal circle, as in *Asclepias* and *Hymenocallis;* in the Characeae, a cluster of small cells crowning the oogonium.

Corymb. A short and broad, more or less flat-topped, indeterminate inflorescence, the outer flowers opening first.

Costa. 1) A rib (when there is only one), the midvein of a simple leaf or other organ; 2) less commonly, the rachis of a pinnately compound leaf.

Costapalmate. With the petiole continuing through the blade as a distinct, prominent midrib; said of some palmate leaves in the Palmae, as in most species of *Sabal.*

Costate. With a strongly pronounced midrib.

Cotyledon. A seed leaf, a primary leaf in the embryo. In some plants the cotyledons always remain within the seed coats and in others they emerge on germination.

Creeping. Trailing or running along on or under the ground and rooting at intervals.

Cremocarp. A dry, two-seeded fruit of the Umbelliferae, separating at maturity into two mericarps borne on hair-like carpophores; a schizocarp.

Crenate. With shallow, obtuse or rounded teeth, scalloped.

Crenulate. Diminutive of *crenate;* with very small teeth of the crenate type.

Crested. With elevated and irregular or toothed ridge or ridges.

Crispate, crisped. Curled or ruffled on the margin, an extreme form of *undulate.*

Crown. 1) Corona; 2) the base of a plant, where stem and root meet; 3) part of a rhizome with a large bud, suitable for propagation.

Crownshaft. An apparent extension of the bole in some Palmae, as in *Roystonea,* formed by the long, broad, overlapping, and sheathing bases of the leaves.

Crustaceous. Hard and brittle in texture.

Cryptogam. A plant reproducing by spores instead of by seeds, as ferns, mosses, algae, fungi.

Cucullate. Hooded or hood-shaped.

Culm. The stem of the Gramineae (grasses and bamboos), usually hollow except at the swollen nodes; applied often also to the Cyperaceae (sedges), though there usually solid.

Cultigen. See *Cultigen* in text.

Cultivar. See *Cultivar* in text.

Cuneate. Wedged-shaped, narrowly triangular with the narrow end at point of attachment, as the bases of some leaves or petals.

Cupulate. With a cupule at the base.

Cupule. A small cuplike structure, especially one at the base of some fruits, formed by fused bracts, as the cupule of an acorn, or by dry, enlarged floral envelopes, as in some palms.

Cupuliform. Shaped like a small cup.

Cusp. An abrupt, sharp, rigid point.

Cuspidate. With an apical cusp.

Cyathium. A type of inflorescence characteristic of *Euphorbia.* Congested within a small cuplike involucre are several male flowers (each reduced to a single stamen) and a single female flower (reduced to a stalked, three-carpelled pistil); in dioecious species, each involucre contains only several male flowers or a single female flower. The involucre is provided on the exterior with one or more glands and often with more or less petaloid appendages.

Cyclic. Arranged in whorls or circles.

Cylindric, cylindrical. Elongated and circular in cross section.

Cyme. A determinate inflorescence, usually broad and more or less flat-topped, the central or terminal flower opening first. Cymes have many forms, however. See *Dichasial, Monochasial, Helicoid,* and *Scorpioid cymes.*

Cymose. 1) Cymelike, as a cymose inflorescence; 2) borne in cymes, as cymose flowers.

Cymule. Diminutive of *cyme;* a small cyme, usually few-flowered.

Cystolith. A microscopic mineral concretion, usually of calcium carbonate, occurring in some cells of leaves or other organs in certain groups of plants, as *Ficus* and many Acanthaceae.

Deciduous. 1) Not persistent, falling off at the end of a functional period, as leaves of nonevergreen trees, or petals of many flowers. 2) shedding all or nearly all the foliage each year, not evergreen, as *deciduous* trees.

Declinate, declined. Bent downward or forward, as the stamens in *Hippeastrum.*

Decompound. Compound, with the divisions once to several times again compound.

Decumbent. Reclining or lying down, but with the apex ascending.

Decurrent. Extending down along and adnate to the stem, as the leaf base in *Verbascum.*

Decussate. Arranged in pairs alternately at right angles, resulting in four vertical rows along the axis.

Deflexed. *Reflexed.*

Dehiscence. The method or process of opening of a seed capsule or anther. The organ has **circumscissile dehiscence**

when it splits open around the circumference and the top comes off like a lid; **loculicidal dehiscence** when it splits open on the back, directly into a locule; **poricidal dehiscence** when it opens by pores or small holes, which often have flaplike valves; **septicidal dehiscence** when it splits into the interior septa or partitioning walls and not directly into a locule.

Deliquescent. Melting away or dissolving: 1) literally, as when a corolla in aging becomes semiliquid, as in *Tradescantia;* 2) figuratively, as when a stem through repeated branching loses its identity, as in elms *(Ulmus)* or *Eucalyptus.* Compare *Excurrent.*

Deltoid. Shaped like the Greek letter delta, equilaterally triangular, with the broad end at the point of attachment.

Dentate. With sharp, spreading, rather coarse teeth that are perpendicular to the margin.

Denticulate. Diminutive of *dentate;* with small teeth of the dentate type.

Depauperate. As if starved, poorly developed because of unfavorable conditions.

Depressed. 1) More or less flattened endwise or from above; 2) sunken.

Determinate. Said of an inflorescence in which the terminal or central flower opens first and prolongation of the main axis is thereby arrested, as in a cyme.

Diadelphous. Applied to stamens when they are arranged in two distinct groups or clusters, as in many legumes that have nine stamens more or less united in one bundle and a solitary stamen by itself.

Dialypetalous. Polypetalous, the corolla being composed of separate and distinct petals.

Diandrous. Having two stamens, as *Veronica.*

Dichasial cyme. A falsely dichotomous cyme, in which the axis bears a terminal flower between two more or less equal branches, the branches repeating the process one or more times (in a compound dichasial cyme) or bearing each only a terminal flower (in a simple dichasial cyme). The lowermost flower, terminating the primary axis, opens first.

Dichotomous. Forking regularly and repeatedly, the two branches of each fork usually essentially equal.

Dicot, dicotyledon. See *Dicotyledon* in text.

Didynamous. With four stamens in two pairs, the pairs of unequal length, as in most Labiatae.

Diffuse. Loosely branching or spreading, of open growth.

Digitate. Resembling a hand, that is, compound, with the parts arising from one point, as the leaf of horse chestnut *(Aesculus).*

Dilated. More or less flattened and expanded into a blade, as the filaments in *Ornithogalum.*

Dimorphic. Occurring in two different forms, as the leaves of those ferns in which the fertile fronds or segments have a form different from that of the sterile ones, or as the juvenile and adult forms of foliage in *Hedera* and some *Eucalyptus* and *Juniperus.*

Dioecious. With flowers unisexual, the staminate and pistillate flowers (or, in nonflowering plants, the male and female organs) on separate plants. Variously applied to species or other taxa, to plants, or to flowers. Compare *Monoecious.*

Diploid. Having two genomes or basic sets of chromosomes, the condition usual in most organisms.

Diplostemonous. With the stamens in two whorls, those of the outer whorl alternate with the petals, those of the inner whorl opposite the petals. Compare *Obdiplostemonous.*

Disc, disk. 1) A more or less fleshy or elevated development of the receptacle or of coalesced nectaries or staminodes about the pistil; 2) in the Compositae, the central area of the flower head, bearing the florets; 3) in the Orchidaceae, the central area of the lip of the flower; 4) any circular, flattened organ, as an adhesive *disc* at the end of a tendril in *Parthenocissus quinquefolia.*

Disc (disk) flower. One of the tubular flowers in the central area of the flower head in most Compositae, as distinguished from a ray flower.

Discoid. 1) Disc-shaped, circular and flattened, as some stigmas; 2) in the Compositae, having only disc flowers.

Disk. See *Disc.*

Dissected. Deeply divided into many slender segments.

Distal. At or toward the apex, away from the point of attachment.

Distichous. Arranged in two vertical rows.

Distinct. 1) Separate, not united (applied to similar parts of the same whorl, as petals distinct, i.e., not united to one another); 2) (in a nontechnical sense) obvious, evident, distinguishable.

Diurnal. Opening only during the day.

Divaricate. Spreading far apart, extremely divergent.

Divergent. Spreading broadly, but less so than when divaricate.

Divided. Separated to or very nearly to the base or to the midrib.

Division. See *Classification* in text.

Dorsal. Relating to, or attached to, the back or outer surface of a part or organ, facing away from the axis, abaxial; the opposite of *ventral.* In the Orchidaceae, the dorsal sepal is the sepal opposite the lip, the usually uppermost, unpaired sepal.

Dorsifixed. Attached at a point on the back; often, but not necessarily, versatile, as anthers in *Lilium.*

Dorsiventral. Flattened and provided with a definite dorsal and ventral surface, laminate, as a leaf blade.

Double. Said of flowers that have or appear to have more than the usual or normal number of floral envelopes, particularly of petals; the supernumerary "petals" are often petaloid stamens. When applied to flower heads in the Compositae, indicates the conversion of most or all of the normally tubular flowers of the disc to ligulate flowers.

Doubly. When used with terms denoting toothing of the margin (e.g., doubly serrate), indicates that the primary teeth bear smaller secondary teeth.

Downy. Covered with very short, weak, soft hairs.

Drupe. A stone fruit, a one-(rarely two-)seeded indehiscent fruit with a seed enclosed in a stony endocarp (a pyrene) that is in turn enclosed in the fleshy or fibrous outer layers of the pericarp, as a peach, almond, or walnut.

Drupelet. Diminutive of *drupe;* a small drupe, especially a component of an aggregate "fruit," as the blackberry *(Rubus).*

E- or Ex-. A prefix meaning: 1) *not,* as *edentate,* not dentate, *exindusiate,* not indusiate; or 2) *out, outward, beyond,* as *explanate,* flattened out.

Ebracteate. Without bracts.

Eccentric. One-sided.

Echinate. With stout, bluntish prickles.

Eciliate. Without cilia.

Egg. A female gamete or reproductive cell.

Eglandular. Without glands.

Elliptic, elliptical. Oblong, but narrowed to rounded ends and widest at or about the middle.

Elongate. Lengthened, stretched out.

Emarginate. With a shallow notch at the apex.

Embryo. The rudimentary plant formed in the seed of phanerogams and in the archegonium in higher cryptogams.

Embryotega. A disclike callosity on the seed coat near the hilum, in species of Commelinaceae, Flagellariaceae, and Mayacaceae.

Emersed. Raised above the water.

Enation. An outgrowth.

Endemic. Native to or confined naturally to a particular and usually restricted area or region.

Endocarp. See *Pericarp.*

Endosperm. The starch- and oil-containing tissue of many seeds; often referred to as the albumen.

Ensiform. Sword-shaped.

Entire. With a continuous unbroken margin, not in any way toothed or indented.

Entomophilous. Insect-pollinated.

Ephemeral. Lasting for only a day or less, as flowers of *Hemerocallis* and *Tradescantia*.

Epicalyx. A calyxlike involucre of bracts outside and below a true calyx.

Epichil, epichile, epichilium. The terminal part of the lip in some orchids, as in *Stanhopea*, when distinct in form from the basal part.

Epigynous. Literally, borne on or arising from the ovary; referring to calyx, corolla, and stamens that seem to be attached at or near the top of the ovary but which in actuality have their basal parts adnate to the ovary and are separate (free) above it.

Epipetalous. Borne on or arising from the petals or corolla.

Epiphyte. A plant growing on another plant but not deriving its nourishment from it, as most Bromeliaceae and Orchidaceae.

Epithet. Any word (in the name of a taxon below the rank of genus) following the name of the genus and not denoting rank. E.g., in the name *Cyrtanthus Mackenii* var. *Cooperi*, the words *Mackenii* and *Cooperi* are, respectively, specific and varietal epithets.

Equitant. Used of conduplicate leaves that overlap one another in two ranks, forming a fan, as in many species of *Iris*.

Erose. Irregularly jagged, appearing eroded or gnawed; said of margins or apices.

Estipulate, exstipulate. Without stipules.

Even-pinnate. See *Compound leaf*.

Evergreen. Having foliage that remains green and functional through more than one growing season (properly applied to plants, not to leaves).

Ex-. See *E-*.

Excurrent. 1) Projecting or extending beyond a margin or apex, as a midrib extended into a mucro or awn; 2) referring to a growth habit in which the axis is prolonged and identifiable throughout its length, with the branches obviously secondary to it, as in *Picea* and *Araucaria*. Compare *Deliquescent*.

Exfoliate. To peel off in shreds, thin layers, or plates, as the bark in *Platanus* and *Acer griseum*.

Exine, extine. The outer coat of a pollen grain.

Exocarp. See *Pericarp*.

Exserted. Sticking out, projecting, not included, as stamens exserted from the corolla.

Exstipulate. See *Estipulate*.

Extine. See *Exine*.

Extrorse. Facing or directed outward, as the dehiscence of an anther. Compare *Introrse*.

Eye. 1) The differently colored center of a flower; 2) a bud on a tuber, as on a potato; 3) a single-bud cutting.

Falcate. Sickle-shaped, strongly curved.

Fall. One of the parts of the outer whorl of the perianth in *Iris* and related genera, often broader than those of the inner whorl and often drooping or deflexed.

Family. See *Family* in text.

Farinaceous. 1) Starchlike or containing starch; 2) farinose.

Farinose. Covered with a mealy or granular coating, as the leaves of *Primula farinosa* and some other species.

Fasciate, fasciated. Said of two or more stems or other axes abnormally grown together lengthwise, or of a single stem abnormally flattened and malformed as if several stems were thus joined, as in certain teratological forms of cacti.

Fascicle. A close bundle or cluster of stems, leaves, flowers, or other organs.

Fascicled, fasciculate. Grouped in a fascicle or in fascicles.

Fastigiate. With branches erect and more or less appressed, as in Lombardy poplar (*Populus nigra* cv. 'Italica').

Fenestrate. Perforated with windowlike openings or translucent areas.

Fertile. Said of stamens bearing functional pollen, of flowers with functional pistils, or of fruits containing seeds.

Fertilization. The union of two gametes, resulting in the formation of a new individual cell (zygote).

Fetid. Having a disagreeable odor.

Filament. A thread or threadlike organ, particularly the stalk that bears the anther in a stamen.

Filiferous. Bearing threadlike appendages.

Filiform. Threadlike, long and very slender.

Fimbriate. Fringed.

Fistulose. Cylindrical and hollow.

Flabellate, flabelliform. Fan-shaped, very broadly wedge-shaped, as the leaf of *Gingko* or *Rhapis*.

Flaccid. Weak and limp.

Flexuose, flexuous. Zigzag, bent or curved alternately in opposite directions.

Floccose. Covered with tufts of soft, woolly hairs that usually rub off readily.

Flocculent, flocculose. Diminutive of *floccose*.

Floral tube. A tube formed by the union of perianth parts and sometimes other organs; sometimes used in the sense of *hypanthium*.

Floret. 1) A very small flower, especially when part of a dense inflorescence, used especially for the flowers of Compositae; 2) in the Gramineae, comprising the lemma, palea, lodicules, and the flower proper (stamens and pistil).

Floricane. A biennial shoot or cane, particularly of a bramble (*Rubus*), during its second year, when producing flowers and fruits.

Floriferous. Flower-bearing.

Floury. Covered with a flourlike coating.

Flower. An axis bearing one or more pistils or one or more stamens or both; when only the former, it is a *pistillate* (female) *flower*, when only the latter, a *staminate* (male) *flower*, when both, a *perfect* (bisexual or hermaphroditic) *flower*. When a perfect flower is surrounded by a perianth representing two floral envelopes (the inner envelope the corolla, the outer the calyx), it is a *complete flower*.

Foliaceous. Leaflike; said particularly of sepals, calyx lobes, or bracts that in texture, size, and color resemble leaves.

Follicle. A dry, dehiscent, one-carpelled fruit with usually more than one seed and opening only along the ventral suture.

Foot; Footless. See *Column foot*.

Form; officially, **forma** (pl. **formae**). A subdivision of a species, ranking after variety. It is the lowest rank ordinarily employed by botanists, and designates a trivial variation, such as a difference in flower color or leaf lobing. See also *Species* in text.

Forma. See *Form*.

Foveolate. Marked with one or more small pits.

Free. Separate, not fused or adnate to other organs; usually referring to the separateness of dissimilar parts or organs, as filaments free from the corolla, but sometimes used in the sense of *distinct*.

Free-central. See *Placentation*.

Frond. Leaf of a fern; sometimes used in the general sense of a large compound leaf, especially of palms.

Fruit. The ripened ovary with its adnate parts (if any), the seed-bearing organ.

Frutescent. Shrubby or eventually becoming so.

Fruticose. Shrubby, with woody stems and branches but no single main trunk.

Fugacious. Falling or withering away very early.

Funicle, funiculus. The stalk by which an ovule is attached to the placenta in the ovary.

Funnelform. With a tube gradually widening upward and passing insensibly into the limb, as in flowers of *Convolvulus*.

Furcate. Forked.

Furfuraceous. Scurfy, covered with soft, branlike scales.

Furrowed. With longitudinal channels or grooves.

Fusiform. Spindle-shaped, tapering to both ends from a swollen middle.

Galea. A helmet-shaped organ, as the uppermost petaloid sepal of a flower in *Aconitum*.

Galeate. Helmetlike, helmet-shaped.

Gamete. A "sex cell," capable of uniting with another gamete to produce a cell (fertilized egg, or zygote) that in turn is capable of developing into a new individual.

Gametophyte. That generation or stage in the life history of a plant that produces gametes; in ferns, it is a minute thalluslike body bearing archegonia and antheridia, which produce female and male gametes respectively; in angiosperms, it is the pollen tube, which develops from a pollen grain and produces male gametes, and the embryo sac, which develops within the ovule and produces a female gamete.

Gamopetalous. With petals united to one another marginally, at least basally.

Gamophyllous. With leaves or leaflike organs (as bracts, petals, or sepals) united to one another by their margins.

Gamosepalous. With sepals united to one another marginally, at least basally.

Gemma. An asexual budlike reproductive body, in some cryptogams.

Geniculate. Abruptly bent, like a knee.

Geniculum. A kneelike, often thickened joint at which an organ is bent, as the joint in the petiole of some Araceae, or a node in the stem of some Gramineae.

Genus (pl. **genera**). See *Genus* in text.

Gibbous. Swollen on one side, usually basally.

Glabrate, glabrescent. Nearly glabrous, or becoming glabrous with maturity or age.

Glabrous. Without hairs of any kind, not pubescent.

Gland. Properly, a secreting part or prominence or appendage, but often used in the sense of a glandlike body.

Glandular. 1) Bearing glands; 2) glandlike.

Glandular-pubescent. 1) With glands and hairs intermixed; 2) with hairs terminated by pinheadlike glands.

Glandular-punctate. See *Punctate.*

Glandulose. Glandular.

Glandspine. In *Ferocactus* and other Cactaceae, a short spine in the upper part of an areole that acts as a nectary during its first year.

Glaucescent. Slightly glaucous.

Glaucous. Covered with a bloom (a fine whitish, grayish, or pale bluish powder), which is often waxy in nature and easily rubbed off.

Glochid. A minute barbed spine or bristle, often occurring in tufts on the areoles in many Cactaceae.

Glomerate. In a dense or compact cluster or in clusters.

Glumaceous. Resembling a glume in texture, dry and chaffy.

Glume. A small chafflike bract, especially in the Gramineae and related plants; in particular, an empty glume. An *empty glume* is one of two sterile bracts at the base of a grass spikelet, which are usually referred to merely as *the glumes.* A *fertile* or *flowering glume* in another term for a lemma. A *sterile flowering gl..me* is a lemma whose flower is staminate or obsolete.

Glutinous. Sticky.

Granular, granulose. 1) In the form of granules or small particles; 2) covered with small grains, minutely mealy.

Grex. A collective term for cultivars of the same hybrid origin, in some cases further divisible into groups.

Group. As used semitechnically in the nomenclature of cultivated plants, an assemblage of similar cultivars within a species or interspecific hybrid, as the Cepa, Aggregatum, and Proliferum Groups in onion *(Allium Cepa).*

Gymnosperm. A plant that has its seeds naked on a sporophyll, not enclosed in an ovary, as any of the cycads or conifers.

Gynandrium. A structure formed by adnation of the stamens to the pistil, as in the Orchidaceae.

Gynandrous. With the stamens adnate to the pistil.

Gynobase. An elongation or enlargement of the receptacle in a flower, on which the pistil (or pistils) is raised.

Gynobasic. Referring to a style that is attached at its base to an elongation of the receptacle between the carpels, as in the Labiatae.

Gynodioecious. With perfect (bisexual) flowers on some plants, and only pistillate (female) flowers on others.

Gynoecium. The female element of a flower; a collective term employed for the several pistils of a single flower when referred to as a unit; when only one pistil is present, pistil and gynoecium are synonymous.

Gynophore. A stalk raising a pistil above the general level of the receptacle.

Gynostemium. Gynandrium.

Habit. The general appearance of a plant.

Habitat. The kind of locality in which a plant grows wild.

Haft. The narrow, constricted base of an organ, as the haft of a fall (sepal) in an *Iris* flower.

Halophyte. A plant tolerant of salt (sodium chloride) in the soil.

Halophytic. Growing in saline soil.

Hastate. Having the shape of an arrowhead, but with the basal lobes turned outward.

Head. A short, dense cluster of flowers.

Helicoid. Coiled spirally like a spring or most snail shells.

Helicoid cyme or **bostryx.** An inflorescence coiled in bud and superficially resembling a raceme, the lowermost flower opening first and flowers all developing on the same side of the apparent axis. In reality, however, the inflorescence is determinate, since the lowermost flower terminates the main axis, and each succeeding flower similarly terminates a branch that arises from the axil of the next lower flower, the branching being always in the same direction. Compare *Scorpioid cyme.*

Herb. 1) A plant without woody, persistent stems above ground; 2) a plant valued for its savory, medicinal, or aromatic qualities.

Herbaceous. 1) Not woody, dying back to the ground each year (applied to a plant or stems); 2) leaflike in color and texture (applied to plant parts).

Hermaphroditic. Bisexual.

Heterogeneous. Not uniform in kind.

Heterosporous. Producing two kinds of spores, representing two sexes, as in *Isoetes* and *Salvinia.* Compare *Homosporous.*

Hilum. In the seed, the scar or mark indicating the point of attachment.

Hip. The "fruit" of a rose *(Rosa)*, consisting of the fleshy, hollow floral cup and the achenes (the true fruits) enclosed within it.

Hippocrepiform. Horseshoe-shaped.

Hirsute. With rather rough, coarse hairs.

Hirsutulous. Diminutive of *hirsute;* slightly hirsute.

Hirtellous. Softly or minutely hirsute.

Hispid. With stiff or bristly hairs.

Hispidulous. Diminutive of *hispid;* somewhat or minutely hispid.

Hoary. With a close white or whitish pubescence.

Homochlamydeous. With a perianth of tepals, undifferentiated into calyx and corolla.

Homogeneous. 1) Of the same or similar kind; 2) of uniform structure throughout, as the homogeneous endosperm in some palms.

Homologous. Of similar basic structure and of common evolutionary descent. Compare *Analogous.*

Homosporous. Producing spores of only one kind, as in the Polypodiaceae, Osmundaceae. Compare *Heterosporous.*

Husk. An outer covering of some fruits, as *Physalis* or *Juglans,* usually derived from the perianth or involucre.

Hyaline. Translucent or transparent.

Hybrid. A plant resulting from a cross between parents that are genetically unlike; more commonly, in descriptive taxonomy, the offspring of two different species or their infraspecific units.

Hygroscopic. Capable of expanding in the presence or contracting in the absence of moisture.

Hypanthium. A ringlike, cuplike, or tubular structure on which seemingly are borne the sepals, petals, and stamens, but which is formed, usually, by the fusion of the lower parts of these organs, as in many Rosaceae and Saxifragaceae; sometimes known as floral cup or, as in this work, *calyx tube.*

Hypochil, hypochile, hypochilium. The often fleshy basal part of the lip in some orchids, as in *Stanhopea,* when distinct in form from the terminal part.

Hypocotyl. The axis of an embryo below the cotyledons, which on germination of the seed develops into the radicle.

Hypocrateriform. See *Salverform.*

Hypogynous. Borne on the receptacle, or under the ovary; said of the calyx, corolla, and stamens when the ovary is superior.

Illegitimate name. A scientific name validly published but in some way contrary to the rules of the International Code of Botanical nomenclature, and therefore not acceptable.

Imbricate. Overlapping, as shingles on a roof.

Imparipinnate. Odd-pinnate, with leaflets in pairs along the axis and with a single terminal leaflet also.

Incised. Cut, slashed irregularly and more or less deeply and sharply, a condition intermediate between toothed and lobed.

Included. Not projecting, not exserted, as stamens included in the corolla.

Incumbent. Lying or leaning upon another organ. An incumbent anther is turned inward and lies against the inner face of its filament; incumbent cotyledons (in the seed) are face to face, with the back of one lying upon the radicle, as in *Aethionema* and *Erysimum* (Cruciferae). Compare *Accumbent, Conduplicate.*

Indehiscent. Not opening, or not opening by valves or along regular lines, as some fruits or anthers.

Indeterminate. Said of an inflorescence, such as a panicle, raceme, or corymb, in which the prolongation of the main axes is not arrested by the opening on the first flowers.

Indigenous. Native.

Indument, indumentum. A covering, especially of hairs.

Induplicate. Rolled or folded inwards.

Indurate. Hardened.

Indusiate. With an indusium.

Indusium. A small flap of epidermal tissue that, in most ferns, more or less covers a sorus.

Inferior. Beneath, lower, below.

Inferior ovary. See *Ovary.*

Inflated. Blown up, bladdery.

Inflorescence. 1) The mode of arrangement of the flowers on a plant; 2) the flowering part of a plant; 3) the coming into flower of a plant.

Infra-. A prefix meaning below, as *infraspecific,* below the rank of species, *infrapetiolar,* below the petiole.

Infrafoliar. Below the leaves.

Infraspecific. Referring to any unit or units of classification below the rank of species.

Infundibular. Funnel-shaped.

Insectivorous. Literally, insect-eating; applied to plants, such as *Dionaea* and *Sarracenia,* that are adapted to entrapping insects and other small animals.

Inserted. Attached, as a stamen inserted on the corolla.

Integument. The covering of an organ, especially the outer envelope of an ovule, which becomes the seed coat.

Inter-. A prefix meaning *between* or *among,* as *interspecific,* between species, *interstaminal,* between the stamens.

Interfoliar. Among the leaves, as inflorescences in some palms.

Internode. The part of an axis between two nodes.

Interpetiolar. Between petioles, as *interpetiolar* stipules that occur on the stem between the bases of the petioles of opposite leaves, such stipules being the result of connation of stipules of both leaves.

Interrupted. Not continuous; in particular, referring to the interposition of small leaflets or segments between others.

Intra-. A prefix meaning *within, inside,* as *intrastaminal,* inside the [ring of] stamens, *intraspecific,* within a species.

Introrse. Turned or facing inward or toward the axis, as an anther whose line of dehiscence faces toward the center of the flower.

Inverted. Turned over, upside-down.

Involucel. Diminutive of *involucre;* a secondary involucre, subtending an umbellet in a compound umbel.

Involucre. One or more whorls or close spirals of small leaves or bracts standing close beneath a flower or an inflorescence.

Involute. Rolled inward or toward the upper side; said of a flat organ, as a leaf. Compare *Revolute.*

Irregular flower. 1) Usually a zygomorphic flower; 2) an asymmetrical flower.

Jointed. With nodes, or with points of real or apparent articulation.

Jugum. A pair, as of leaflets.

Keel. 1) a central, dorsal ridge, like the keel of a boat; 2) the two united lowermost petals of a papilionaceous flower.

Keeled. Ridged, like the bottom of a boat.

Labellum. The lip, particularly the lip of a flower of the Orchidaceae.

Labiate. 1) With two lips, as a calyx or corolla with the parts segregated by form or position into opposed upper and lower groups; 2) any member of the family Labiatae.

Lacerate. Torn, irregularly cleft or cut.

Laciniate. Slashed into narrow, pointed lobes.

Lacuna. A cavity, hole, gap.

Lamellate. 1) Composed of or having thin plates; 2) with many cross partitions, as a lamellate pith. For *lamellate placentation,* see *Placentation.*

Lamina. A blade or expanded portion, as of a leaf or petal.

Lanate. Woolly, with long, intertwined, curly hairs.

Lanceolate. Lance-shaped, several times longer than broad and widest below the middle, tapering with convex sides upward to the apex.

Lanuginose. Woolly or cottony, downy, the hairs somewhat shorter than in lanate.

Lanulose. Very short-woolly.

Lateral. On or at the side.

Latex. A colorless or colored, usually white or yellowish, fluid produced by the cells of some plants, as *Asclepias* and *Euphorbia;* often referred to as milky sap.

Laticiferous. Producing or containing latex (milky sap).

Lax. Loose, widely spaced; the opposite of *congested.*

Leaf stalk. The stalk of a leaf, a petiole.

Leaflet. One of the ultimate units of a compound leaf.

Legume. A simple, one-carpelled fruit dehiscing along both sutures, typical of most Leguminosae.

Lemma. In the Gramineae, the flowering glume, the lower of the two bracts immediately enclosing the flower. See *Floret* (2).

Lenticular. Lens-shaped, more or less circular and flattened but convex on both surfaces.

Lepidote. Covered with small scurfy scales.

Liana. A vigorous, woody, usually tropical vine.

Ligneous. Woody.

Ligule. A strap-shaped organ or body: 1) particularly, a strap-shaped corolla, as in the ray flowers of the Compositae; 2) also, a projection from the top of the sheath in the Gramineae, Palmae, and some other plants.

Ligulate. Strap-shaped, as a leaf, petal, or corolla.

Ligulate flower. See *Ray flower.*

Limb. The expanded, flat part of an organ, as of a petal, or the expanding part of a gamopetalous corolla.

Linear. Long and narrow, the sides parallel or nearly so, as blades of most grasses.

Lineate. Bearing or marked with thin parallel lines.

Lingulate. Tongue-shaped.

Lip. 1) One of the two opposed (upper and lower) divisions of a bilabiate corolla or calyx; 2) a petal or staminode differentiated from others of its kind, as the highly modified lip (a petal) in the Orchidaceae or the lip (a staminode) in the Zingiberaceae.

Lithophyte. A plant which grows on rocks in little or no soil, deriving its nourishment chiefly from the atmosphere, as some Orchidaceae.

Lobe. A usually major segment of an organ, representing a division halfway to the middle of the organ, or less.

Lobule. Diminutive of *lobe;* a small lobe.

Locule. A chamber, cavity, cell of an anther, ovary, or fruit.

Loculicidal. See *Dehiscence.*

Lodicule. One of two or three minute scales below the stamens and appressed to the base of the ovary in most Gramineae, believed to be rudiments of ancestral perianth parts.

Loment. A leguminous fruit that is contracted between the seeds, the one-seeded segments separating at fruit maturity.

Lorate. Strap-shaped.

Lunate. Crescent-shaped.

Lyrate. Pinnatifid, but with an enlarged, rounded, terminal lobe and smaller lateral lobes.

Marginal placentation. See *Placentation.*

Macrospore. Megaspore.

Mamillate, mammillate. Having nipplelike protuberances.

Marcescent. Withering but persisting.

Marcot. A branch that, for purposes of propagation, is air-layered by having a rooting medium bound to it.

Megasporangium. A sporangium containing only megaspores.

Megaspore. The larger of the two kinds of spores produced by heterosporous plants, developing into a female gametophyte; also called macrospore.

Megasporophyll. A sporophyll that bears megaspores; in angiosperms, a carpel.

Membranaceous, membranous. Thin, soft, and translucent, like a membrane.

Mentum. A chinlike forward extension of the base of the flower in association with the foot of the column in some orchids, as in certain species of *Dendrobium.*

Mericarp. See *Schizocarp.*

Meristem. Undifferentiated tissue that is capable of developing into various organs or tissues.

-merous. A suffix signifying having (a certain number of) parts, as a *tetramerous* or *4-merous* flower, in which the sepals, petals, and stamens (whether separate or connate in each whorl) are each four or in multiples of four.

Mesocarp. See *Pericarp.*

Mesochil, mesochile, mesochilium. The middle part of the lip in some orchids, as in *Stanhopea,* when distinct in form from the basal and terminal parts.

Micropyle. The opening in the integument of an ovule, through which the pollen tube enters.

Microspore. The smaller of the two kinds of spores produced by heterosporous plants, developing into a male gametophyte.

Microsporangium. A sporangium containing only microspores; in angiosperms, usually called an anther sac.

Microsporophyll. A sporophyll bearing microsporangia; in angiosperms, a stamen.

Midrib. The main rib of a leaf or leaflet or leaflike part, a continuation of the petiole.

Monadelphous. Said of stamens united in one group by connation of their filaments, as in the Malvaceae and some Leguminosae.

Moniliform. Constricted at intervals and appearing like a string of beads, as the fruit of some species of *Acacia.*

Monocarpic. Fruiting only once and then dying.

Monocephalic. Bearing one flower head, as the scape of *Taraxacum.*

Monochasial cyme. Similar to a dichasial cyme, but with one (always on the same side) of each pair of lateral branches missing, so that the branching is in one direction only.

Monochlamydeous. Having a perianth of only a single whorl or series, as in Phytolaccaceae.

Monocolpate. Said of pollen grains with a single groove.

Monocot, monocotyledon. See *Monocotyledon* in text.

Monoecious. With flowers unisexual, the staminate and pistillate flowers (or, in nonflowering plants, the male and female organs) on the same plant. Variously applied to species or other taxa, to plants, or to flowers. Compare *Dioecious.*

Monogeneric. Said of a family or category of higher rank composed of a single genus.

Monopetalous. 1) Literally, with a single petal; 2) gamopetalous.

Monophyletic. Derived from a single ancestral line. Compare *Polyphyletic.*

Monopodial. Having growth and prolongation of the stem or rhizome continuing indefinitely, usually without branching, as in the orchid genera *Vanda* and *Phalaenopsis.* Compare *Sympodial.*

Monotypic. In reference to a genus, comprising a single species.

Motile. Self-propelling, as spores or sperms, by means of cilia or elaters.

Mucro. A short, sharp, abrupt spur or spiny tip.

Mucronate. Terminated by a mucro.

Mucronulate. Diminutive of *mucronate;* terminated by a small mucro.

Multi-. A prefix meaning many, as *multiovulate,* many-ovuled.

Multicarpellate. Referring to a compound pistal or ovary, formed by the union of several carpels.

Multiciliate. With many cilia.

Multiple fruit. A "fruit" formed by the connation of the individual fruits of several flowers in a cluster, as the pineapple *(Ananas)* or mulberry *(Morus).*

Muricate. Rough because of the presence of many minute spiculate excrescences on the epidermis.

Mutant, mutation. A variant, differing genetically and often visibly from its parent or parents and arising rather suddenly or abruptly.

Navicular. Boat-shaped, as the glumes of most Gramineae.

Nectary. A nectar-secreting gland, often appearing as a protuberance, scale, or pit.

Neuter, neutral. Without sex or sex organs, sterile. A neuter flower lacks both pistils and stamens.

Nocturnal. Said of flowers that open at night and close during the day.

Node. The place on a stem where, at a single level, one or more leaves are attached.

Nodose. With many close nodes, knobby, knotty.

Nonvascular. Without vascular tissue. Nonvascular plants include the algae, lichens, fungi, mosses, and liverworts. Compare *Vascular.*

Novirame. A flowering or fruiting shoot arising from a primocane, sometimes encountered in *Rubus.*

Nucellar embryo. An embryo developing from a cell in the nucellus rather than from a fertilized egg, and therefore having a genetic constitution wholly like that of the mother plant.

Nucellus. The central part of an ovule, in which the embryo sac develops; megasporangium.

Nut. 1) An indehiscent, one-celled and one-seeded, hard and bony fruit, as the acorn of *Quercus;* 2) as frequently and loosely used, a drupe with relatively thin fleshy exocarp and a large stone (pyrene), or the pyrene itself, as the walnut *(Juglans)* and hickory nut *(Carya).*

Nutlet. A small or diminutive nut, similar to an achene but with harder and thicker wall.

Ob-. A prefix signifying inversion or reversed position, as *oblanceolate,* inversely lanceolate, with the broadest part above the middle *(below the middle in lanceolate).*

Obcompressed. Flattened from front to back rather than from side to side, flattened at right angles to the primary plane or axis, as achenes of some Compositae that are flattened at right angles to the radius of the receptacle.

Obconic, obconical. More or less conical but attached at the narrow end.

Obcordate. Inversely heart-shaped, with the notch at the apex, the reverse of *cordate.*

Obcuneate. Wedge-shaped with the broad end at the point of attachment, inversely cuneate.

Obdeltoid. Inversely deltoid, with the narrow end at the point of attachment.

Obdiplostemonous. With the stamens in two whorls, those of the outer whorl opposite the petals, those of the inner whorl opposite the sepals. Compare *Diplostemonous.*

Oblanceolate. Inversely lanceolate, with the broadest width above the middle, and tapering to the base.

Oblate. Nearly spherical, but somewhat flattened at the poles.

Oblique. Slanting, with unequal sides, as the leaves in *Begonia.*

Oblong. Longer than broad, and with the sides nearly or quite parallel most of their length.

Obovate. Inversely ovate, broader above rather than below the middle.

Obovoid. Inversely ovoid, with the point of attachment at the narrower end.

Obpyriform. Pear-shaped and attached at the narrower end, inversely pyriform.

Obsolescent. Nearly obsolete; applied to a part or organ still evident but much reduced and nonfunctional.

Obsolete. Not evident or apparent, rudimentary, vestigial.

Obtuse. Blunt, rounded.

Ocrea, ochrea. A tubular sheath formed at the node of stem by the fusion of two stipules (as in *Polygonum*) or by an extension of the leaf sheath (as in some Palmae).

Odd-pinnate. See *Compound leaf.*

Oligo-. A prefix meaning *few,* as *oligospermous,* few-seeded.

Ontogenetic. Related to or appearing in the course of ontogeny.

Ontogeny. The development of an individual tissue, organ, or organism.

Oogonium. The female organ in thallus plants (thallophytes), producing eggs (female gametes).

Operculate. With a cap or lid.

Operculum. A lid or cover produced by circumscissile dehiscence.

Opposite. Two at a node, on opposite sides of an axis.

Orbicular, orbiculate. Circular or nearly so.

Order. See *Classification* in text.

Ovary. The basal, ovule-bearing part of a pistil. When borne above the point of attachment of perianth and stamens, or surrounded by a hypanthium that is not adnate to it, it is a *superior ovary;* when below the apparent point of attachment of these floral envelopes, it is an *inferior ovary;* when intermediate, it is a *half-inferior* or *subinferior ovary.*

Ovate. With an outline like that of a hen's egg, more or less rounded at both ends and broadest below the middle.

Ovoid. Referring to a solid body with the shape of a hen's egg, the point of attachment, if any, at the broader end.

Ovulate. Bearing ovules; said of gymnospermous megasporophylls, where the ovules are naked and not enclosed in a pistil.

Ovule. The body that, after fertilization, becomes the seed; the egg-containing unit of the ovary.

Palate. In personate corollas, a rounded prominence on the lower lip, closing or nearly closing the throat.

Palea. A small, chaffy bract, especially: 1) one of the chaffy scales on the surface of the receptacle of the flower head in many Compositae; or 2) (also **palet**) the inner of the two bracts or glumes enclosing a flower in the Gramineae, the outer being the lemma.

Paleaceous. 1) Chaffy or chafflike in texture; 2) bearing paleae.

Palmate. With three or more nerves, lobes, or leaflets radiating fanwise from a common basal point of attachment.

Palmatifid. Cut in palmate fashion about halfway to the base.

Palmatisect. Cut in a palmate fashion, usually more than halfway to the base.

Pandurate, panduriform. Fiddle-shaped, rounded at both ends and somewhat contracted at or about the middle.

Panicle. An indeterminate, branching inflorescence, the branches usually being racemes or corymbs.

Paniculate. Resembling or borne in a panicle.

Pannose. Feltlike.

Papilionaceous. Literally, butterflylike; applied to a type of corolla characteristic of the subfamily Faboideae of the Leguminosae (or to one resembling such a corolla), having five petals, with the uppermost one (the standard, banner, or vexillum) outside and usually largest, the two laterals (the wings) paired and usually clawed, and the two lowermost united along their lower margin and forming a sheath (the keel) enclosing the stamens and pistil.

Papilla. A minute, pimplelike protuberance.

Papillate, papillose. Bearing papillae.

Pappus. A modified perianth whorl in the flowers of the Compositae, borne at the top of the ovary in the position occupied (in other families) by the calyx and usually persisting in fruit; it consists of distinct or united small scales, bristles, barbed or plumose hairs, or other modifications.

Parenchyma. A plant tissue made up of undifferentiated and usually unspecialized cells.

Parietal. See *Placentation.*

Paripinnate. Evenly pinnate, with leaflets in pairs along the axis but without a terminal leaflet.

Parted. Cut or cleft not quite to the base.

Parthenocarpic. Producing fruits without fertilization.

Parthenogenesis. The development of offspring from an unfertilized egg cell.

Patent. Spreading.

Pectinate. Comblike or arranged like the teeth of a comb, or pinnatifid with very close narrow divisions.

Pedate. Said of a palmately lobed or divided leaf in which the two outer side lobes are again divided or cleft.

Pedicel. The stalk of an individual flower.

Pedicellate, pedicelled. Borne on a pedicel

Peduncle. The stalk of a flower cluster, or of a solitary flower when the inflorescence consists of only one flower.

Pellucid. Transparent or nearly so.

Peltate. Said of an organ more or less circular in outline and attached near its center or at least inside its margin, as the solitary leaf of *Podophyllum* or *Nelumbo.*

Pendent, pendulous. Drooping, hanging downward.

Penicillate. Like a small brush or tuft of hairs.

Penninerved. Pinnately nerved.

Pentamerous. Five-merous, with parts in fives or multiples of five; often written *5-merous.*

Pepo. A gourd fruit, one-celled and many-seeded, with fleshy pulp and hard rind, typified by such members of the Cucurbitaceae as pumpkins, squashes, and gourds.

Perennate. To live over from one year to another.

Perennial. Of three or more seasons' duration.

Perforate. Pierced with holes or openings.

Perfoliate. Descriptive of a sessile leaf or bract the base of which completely surrounds the stem, the latter seemingly passing through the blade.

Pergamentaceous. Parchmentlike.

Perianth. A collective term for the floral envelopes, the calyx, corolla, or both.

Pericarp. The wall of a ripened ovary, that is, of a fruit, sometimes differentiated into an outer layer (exocarp), a middle layer (mesocarp), and an inner layer (endocarp).

Perigone. Perianth, more commonly used when the parts are not or scarcely differentiated into calyx and corolla and are then termed tepals.

Perigynium. The papery sheath that envelops the ovary (later the achene) in *Carex.*

Perigynous. Literally, borne or arising around the ovary; used of sepals, petals, and stamens that arise from the upper edge of a hypanthium that is itself attached below the ovary.

Perisperm. See *Albumen.*

Peristome. The fringe around the mouth of a capsule in mosses and other lower plants.

Persistent. Remaining attached, not falling off.

Personate. Said of a two-lipped corolla of which the throat is closed by a palate, as in *Antirrhinum.*

Petal. A unit of the corolla or inner floral envelope of a polypetalous flower, usually colored and more or less showy.

Petaloid. 1) As an adjective, petal-like, in color and shape resembling a petal; 2) as a noun, an organ that is petal-like.

Petiolate, petioled. Having a petiole.

Petiole. The stalk of a leaf.

Petiolule. The stalk of a leaflet in a compound leaf.

Phanerogam. A seed plant, a spermatophyte, as opposed to a cryptogam.

Phyllary. A bract, especially of the involucre of the flowerhead in the Compositae.

Phylloclad, phylloclade. A flattened stem or branch, functioning as a leaf, as in Christmas cactus *(Schlumbergera Bridgesii).*

Phyllode, phyllodium. An expanded, leaflike petiole with no true blade, as in some species of *Acacia.*

Phyllotaxy. The arrangement of leaves or floral parts on their axis; generally expressed numerically by a fraction, the numerator representing the number of revolutions of a spiral made in passing from one leaf past each successive leaf to reach the leaf directly above the initial leaf, and the denominator representing the number of leaves passed in the spiral thus made.

Phylogenetic. Related to or appearing in the course of phylogeny.

Phylogeny. The evolutionary development of a taxon (a genus, species, etc.) or of parts or organs of members of a given taxon.

Pileus. The cap of a mushroom, bearing the spore-bearing tissues (hymenium) on its underside.

Pilose. Beset, but not densely so, with distinct, spreading, soft, straight hairs.

Pilosulous. Diminutive of *pilose.*

Pinna. A primary division or primary leaflet of a pinnately compound leaf. If a leaf is decompound, the primary divisions are pinnae, and the ultimate leaflets are pinnules.

Pinnate. Constructed somewhat like a feather, with the parts (e.g., veins, lobes, branches) arranged along both sides of an axis, as in pinnate venation. A pinnate leaf is compound, with the leaflets arranged on both sides of the rachis.

Pinnately. In a pinnate manner, though not necessarily compound, as pinnately lobed, pinnately divided, pinnately veined.

Pinnatifid. Cleft or parted in a pinnate manner.

Pinnatisect. Cut down to the midrib in a pinnate manner.

Pinnule. A segment of a pinna, a leaflet that is the ultimate and finest division of a (usually pinnately) decompound leaf.

Pistil. A unit of the gynoecium, composed of ovary, style (when present), and stigma. It may consist of one or more carpels; when of one carpel, it is a *simple pistil;* when of two or more carpels, it is a *compound pistil.* See *Carpel* and *Ovary.*

Pistillate. Female, having functional pistils but no functional stamens.

Pistillode, pistillodium. A rudimentary or vestigial pistil present in some staminate flowers.

Pith. The soft, spongy, central cylinder of most angiosperm stems, composed mostly of parenchyma tissue.

Pitted. Having little depressions or cavities.

Placenta. A zone of tissue to which the ovules are attached within the ovary.

Placentation. The arrangement of the placentae within the ovary. Several types are recognized: **apical placentation,** in which the ovules are reduced to a few or one and are borne at the top of a simple or compound ovary, as in *Acorus;* **axile,** in which the ovules are borne at or near the center of a compound ovary on the central axis formed by the meeting of the septa (partitions), as in most Liliaceae and Scrophulariaceae; **basal,** in which the ovules are reduced to few or one and are borne at the base of a simple or compound ovary, as in *Arisaema;* **free central,** in which the ovules are borne on a central column in a compound ovary without septa or with septa confined to the base, as in *Primula* and *Dianthus;* **lamellate** (a modification of *parietal*), in which the ovules are borne on platelike extensions of the placentae into a compound ovary, as in *Nuphar;* **marginal** or **ventral,** in which the ovules are borne on the wall along the ventral suture in a simple ovary, as in *Aquilegia* and *Phaseolus;* **parietal,** in which the ovules are borne on the wall or on slight intrusions of the wall that form incomplete partitions within a compound ovary, as in the Cactaceae and Gesneriaceae (sometimes also used in the sense of *marginal* or *ventral*).

Plane. Flat.

Pleated. Folded lengthwise several times (at least in bud).

Plicate. Pleated.

Plumose. Plumy, featherlike, with fine secondary hairs, as the pappus of some Compositae.

Pneumatophore. A modified root functioning as a respiratory organ, as in many aquatic plants or plants of wet situations.

Pod. A dehiscent, dry fruit; a rather general uncritical term, sometimes used when no other more specific term is applicable.

Pollen. The spores or grains borne by the anther, containing the male element (gametophyte).

Pollen sac. The microsporangium containing the pollen; in angiosperms, an *anther sac.*

Pollination. The transfer of pollen from an anther to a receptive stigma.

Pollinium. A more or less coherent mass of pollen grains, as in the Orchidaceae and Asclepiadaceae.

Poly-. A prefix meaning many, as *polycarpic,* fruiting many times (as opposed to monocarpic).

Polyandrous. With a large, indefinite number of stamens.

Polygamodioecious. Essentially dioecious, but with some bisexual flowers present also on some or all plants.

Polygamomonoecious. Essentially monoecious, but with some bisexual flowers present also.

Polygamous. With both unisexual and bisexual flowers, either on the same plant or on separate plants of the same species.

Polygonal. Many-angled.

Polymorphic. Occurring in several different forms, as a species of many closely related infraspecific taxa, or as leaves of different shapes on one plant; very variable as to habit or some morphological feature.

Polypetalous. With a corolla of separate petals, as opposed to *gamopetalous.*

Polyphyletic. Derived from several ancestral lines. Compare *Monophyletic.*

Polyploid. Having more than the usual two basic sets of chromosomes. See *Ploidy* in text.

Polysepalous. Having a calyx of separate sepals, as opposed to *gamosepalous.*

Pome. The fleshy fruit typical of *Malus, Pyrus, Crataegus,* and related Rosaceae, with several locules and formed by the fusion of an inferior ovary with the hypanthium, the flesh largely derived from the latter.

Pore. A small more or less circular aperture.

Poricidal. See *Dehiscence.*

Porrect. Extending upward and forward.

Posterior. On or at the back, toward the axis, adaxial, away from the subtending bract; in a bilabiate corolla, for example, the upper lip is posterior, the lower lip anterior. Compare *Anterior.*

Praemorse, premorse. Appearing as if bitten off at the end, coarsely erose.

Prickle. A small, weak, spinelike outgrowth of the bark or epidermis rather than of the wood. Compare *Thorn.*

Primocane. A biennial shoot or cane, particularly of a bramble *(Rubus),* during its first year of growth and before flowering.

Procumbent. Trailing or lying flat but not rooting.

Proliferating, proliferous. Producing buds or offshoots, especially in an unusual or abnormal way, as plantlets on leaves, shoots from flowers or flower heads, or fruits on fruits (as in some *Opuntia* species).

Prophyll, prophyllum. 1) A bracteole on a flower stalk, especially one of two subtending the perianth in *Juncus;* 2) a two-edged first bract on the peduncle and sometimes on the branches of an inflorescence, as in the Palmae.

Prop root. A stiff aerial root that arises from the stem, reaches the ground, and helps to support the stem.

Prostrate. A general term for lying flat on the ground.

Protandrous, proterandrous. Said of a flower in which the anthers mature and release their pollen before the stigma of the same flower is receptive.

Prothallium, prothallus. The gametophyte stage or generation of ferns and some other cryptogams, a usually small, delicate, flattened, thalluslike structure growing on the ground, bearing the sexual organs, the antheridia and archegonia.

Protogynous, proterogynous. Said of a flower in which the stigma is receptive before the anthers of the same flower are mature.

Pruinose. Having a bloom on the surface. See *Bloom.*

Pseud- or **Pseudo-.** A prefix meaning *false, not true or typical,* as *pseudoterminal bud,* a bud apparently but not actually terminal.

Pseudobulb. A thickened or bulbiform above-ground stem in certain orchids, varying from globose through clavate to long-cylindrical according to species.

Pseudoterminal bud. The seemingly terminal bud of a twig, but actually the uppermost lateral bud with its subtending leaf scar on one side and the scar of the terminal bud often visible on the opposite side, as in *Castanea.*

Puberulent, puberulous. Minutely pubescent, clothed with minute, soft, erect hairs.

Pubescent. Strictly, this means covered with soft, short, fine hairs; as commonly used, however, the term means hairy, bearing hairs, in a generalized sense, without reference to the type of hair.

Pulvinate. Cushionlike, cushion-shaped, forming a dense, low tuft.

Pulviniform. Having the shape of a *pulvinus;* pad- or cushion-shaped.

Pulvinus. A cushion of tissue, especially: 1) a minute gland or the swollen base of a petiole or petiolule responsive to vibrations and heat, as in leaves of the sensitive plant *(Mimosa pudica);* or 2) a cartilaginous swelling at the base of the pinnae in some Palmae, probably functioning in the expansion of the leaf.

Punctate. Marked with translucent or colored dots, depressions, or pits.

Puncticulate. Diminutive of *punctate;* minutely punctate.

Pungent. 1) Ending in a stiff, sharp point or tip; 2) acrid in taste or odor.

Pustular, pustulate. With many low elevations, as though blistered.

Pustule. A blister or blisterlike elevation.

Pyrene. The nutlet in a drupe; a seed and the surrounding bony endocarp, as a cherry or peach pit or the "seed" of a raspberry drupelet.

Pyriform. Pear-shaped.

Pyxis. A capsule dehiscing circumscissilely, the top coming off as a lid.

Raceme. An unbranched, elongated, indeterminate inflorescence with pedicelled flowers.

Racemose. 1) Racemelike, having flowers in racemelike inflorescences that may or may not be true racemes; 2) borne in a raceme or a racemelike inflorescence, as racemose flowers.

Rachilla, rhachilla. A diminutive or secondary axis or rachis; in particular, in the Gramineae and Cyperaceae, the axis (above the two empty glumes) that bears the florets; in the Palmae, the ultimate flower-bearing axis of a branched inflorescence.

Rachis, rhachis (pl. **rachises** or **rachides**). The axis of an inflorescence or of a compound leaf.

Radiate. 1) Standing on and spreading from a common center; 2) having ray flowers, as in the Compositae.

Radical. Arising from the root or its crown; said of leaves that are basal or rosulate.

Radicle. The rudimentary root of the embryo.

Ramifying. Branching.

Ramose. With many branches.

Rank. 1) A vertical row—leaves that are two-ranked are in two vertical rows, and may be alternate or opposite; 2) in nomenclature, the position of a taxon in the taxonomic hierarchy.

Raphe. That portion of the funiculus of an ovule that is adnate to the integument, usually represented by a ridge, present in most anatropous ovules.

Raphide. A minute, needlelike crystal of calcium oxalate, as in the tuber of *Arisaema* and vegetative parts of many plants.

Ray. 1) A branch of an umbel or an umbel-like inflorescence; 2) a ray flower, or the corolla of a ray flower, or a circle of ray flowers.

Ray flower. A ligulate flower, with corolla flattened and straplike above a very short tube, in the Compositae. In many species, ray flowers are present on the margin of the flower head; in the tribe Cichorieae, ray flowers occupy the whole head.

Receptacle. The more or less enlarged or elongated end of the stem or flower axis on which some or all of the flower parts are borne; sometimes the receptacle is greatly expanded, as in the Compositae, where it bears many flowers. Also called *thalamus* and *torus.*

Reclinate, reclining. Bent down or falling back from the perpendicular.

Recurved. Curved downward or backward.

Reflexed. Abruptly recurved or bent downward or backward.

Regular. Actinomorphic.

Reniform. Kidney-shaped.

Repand. Weakly sinuate.

Repand-denticulate. Weakly sinuate and minutely or finely dentate.

Replum. The framelike placenta that remains when the valves fall away, in certain fruits; in the Cruciferae, this includes the septum joining the two placentae.

Resinous. Containing or producing resin, said of bud scales when coated with a sticky exudate of resin, as in *Aesculus.*

Resupinate. Inverted, turned upside down, as the leaves sometimes in *Alstroemeria,* and the flowers in most Orchidaceae (through a 180° twist in the ovary).

Reticulate. Netted, netlike.

Retrorse. Turned backward or downward.

Retuse. Notched slightly at a usually obtuse apex.

Reversion shoots. Shoots, on a mature plant, that bear the juvenile form of foliage.

Revolute. Rolled backward or toward the lower side.

Rhachilla. See *Rachilla.*

Rhachis. see *Rachis.*

Rhizoid. A structure rootlike in function and general appearance but not so in anatomy.

Rhizomatous. Producing or possessing rhizomes.

Rhizome. Rootstock, a usually horizontal stem on or under the ground that sends up a succession of leaves or stems at the apex.

Rhizophore. A leafless stem that produces roots, as in *Selaginella.*

Rhomboid, rhomboidal. Shaped somewhat like a rhombus or rhomboid, i.e., like a parallelogram with two opposite acute and two opposite obtuse angles.

Rib. In a leaf or similar organ, the primary vein; also, any prominent vein or nerve.

Rootstock. Subterranean stem, rhizome.

Rosette. An arrangement of leaves radiating from a crown or center and usually at or close to the earth, as in the dandelion, *Taraxacum.*

Rosulate. In a rosette or in rosettes.

Rostellum. Literally, a small beak; the tissue, often beaklike in shape, that separates the anther from the functional stigma on the column in single-anthered Orchidaceae; it is often specialized to function in the transfer of pollen by insects or hummingbirds.

Rostrate. Having a beak or beaklike projection.

Rotate. Wheel-shaped; said of a gamopetalous corolla with a flat, circular limb at right angles to the short or obsolete tube.

Rotund. Rounded, nearly circular.

Rudimentary. Imperfectly developed and nonfunctional.

Rugose. Wrinkled, usually covered with wrinkles, the venation seeming impressed into the surface.

Rugulose. Diminutive of *rugose;* finely wrinkled.

Ruminate. Appearing as though chewed; mottled, as the endosperm of some Palmae in which the dark inner layer of the seed coat is infolded into the paler endosperm.

Runcinate. Coarsely serrate to sharply incised, with the teeth pointing toward the base of the organ, as in leaves of *Taraxacum.*

Runner. A slender, trailing shoot taking root at the nodes.

Saccate. Bag-shaped, pouched.

Sagittate. Like an arrowhead in shape, triangular, with the basal lobes pointing downward or concavely toward the stalk.

Salverform. Said of a gamopetalous corolla with a slender tube and an abruptly expanded flat limb, as that of *Phlox;* hypocrateriform.

Samara. An indehiscent winged fruit, as of *Acer* and *Fraxinus.*

Saprophyte. A plant (usually lacking chlorophyll) living on dead organic matter, as *Monotropa.*

Sarmentose. Producing long, flexuous runners or stolons.

Scaberulous. Diminutive of *scabrous;* minutely scabrous.

Scabrid. Somewhat scabrous.

Scabridulous. Diminutive of *scabrid;* slightly or minutely scabrid.

Scabrous. Rough to the touch, with small rough projections.

Scale. 1) A small, mostly dry, mostly appressed leaf or bract, often only vestigial; 2) a minute, flattened trichome, of epidermal origin, as the scales on the lower surface of some leaves.

Scandent. Climbing.

Scape. A leafless peduncle arising from the ground; it may bear scales or bracts but no foliage leaves, and may be one- or many-flowered.

Scapose. Bearing flowers or an inflorescence on a scape.

Scarious. Not green but thin, dry, and membranous, often more or less translucent.

Schizocarp. A dry, dehiscent fruit that splits into two halves, each half called a mericarp, as in most Umbelliferae or in *Acer.*

Scorpioid cyme or **cincinnus.** A coiled, determinate inflorescence similar to a helicoid cyme but the flowers or branches developing alternately to left and right rather than only in one direction. Compare *Helicoid cyme.*

Scurfy. Covered with minute scales or branlike particles.

Scutate. Like a small shield.

Section. See *Genus* in text.

Secund. Having the parts apparently or actually arranged along one side only; said especially of an inflorescence in which the flowers appear to be borne along only one side of the axis.

Seed. A ripened (and usually fertilized) ovule, containing the embryonic plant.

Segment. One of the parts of a leaf, petal, calyx, corolla, or perianth that is deeply divided but not truly compound.

Sepal. One of the separate units of a calyx, usually green and foliaceous.

Sepaloid. Resembling a sepal.

Sept. A small hollow or depression, as those between the carpels on the exterior of the ovary, in which nectaries are developed, in some species of *Allium.*

Septate. Partitioned, divided by partitions or septa.

Septicidal. See *Dehiscence.*

Septum. A partition or cross wall.

Seriate. In series, usually in whorls or apparent whorls.

Sericeous. Silky.

Serrate. Saw-toothed, with the teeth pointing forward toward the apex of the organ.

Serrulate. Diminutive of *serrate;* minutely serrate.

Sessile. Without a stalk.

Seta. 1) A bristle; 2) in mosses, the stalk bearing the spore-containing capsule.

Setaceous. 1) Setiform; 2) setiferous.

Setiferous, setigerous. Bearing bristles.

Setiform. Bristle-shaped or bristlelike.

Setose. Bristly, covered with bristles.

Setulose. Diminutive of *setose;* minutely setose.

Sheath. Any more or less tubular structure surrounding an organ or part, as the basal part of a grass leaf or of a palm leaf, which surrounds the stem.

Shrub. A woody plant that remains relatively low and produces shoots or trunks from the base, not treelike or with a single trunk; a descriptive term not subject to strict circumscription.

Sigmoid, sigmoidal. S-shaped, with a double curve in opposite directions.

Siliceous. Containing minute particles of silica, as the stems of *Equisetum.*

Silicle, silicula, silicule. A short silique, usually not more than twice as long as wide.

Siliqua, silique. The two-carpelled fruit peculiar to the Cruciferae, in which two valves fall away, leaving a longitudinal central replum; the term is usually restricted to long fruits of this type, three or more times longer than wide. Compare *Silicle.*

Silky. Having a covering of soft, appressed, fine hairs.

Silvery. With a whitish, more or less shining, sometimes metallic luster.

Simple. Not compound, not divided into secondary units, as a simple leaf (not compounded into leaflets), or a simple inflorescence (not branched).

Sinus. An indentation or recess in a margin, between two lobes or divisions of a leaf or other expanded organ.

Smooth. 1) Without roughness, not scabrous; 2) also sometimes used in the sense of glabrous, without hairs.

Soboliferous. Bearing or producing lateral shoots from the ground, clump-forming; usually applied to shrubs or small trees, as species of *Syringa, Rhus,* and some Palmae.

Solitary. Occurring or borne singly or alone.

Sorus. A "fruit dot" or cluster of sporangia in ferns, usually located on the underside of the leaf.

Spadix. The thick or fleshy flower spike of certain plants, usually surrounded or subtended by a spathe, as in members of the Araceae.

Spathaceous. Spathelike.

Spathe. A bract or leaf surrounding or subtending a flower cluster or a spadix; it is sometimes colored, as in *Zantedeschia,* or otherwise modified, as in *Arisaema* or the Palmae.

Spathe valve. One of two or more herbaceous or scarious bracts that subtend an inflorescence or flower and generally envelop the subtended unit when in bud.

Spathulate, spatulate. Spatula-shaped, oblong with the basal end narrowed and the apical end rounded.

Species (pl. **species**). See *Species* in text.

Sperm. A male gamete or reproductive cell.

Spermatophyte. A seed-producing plant, such as a flowering plant or conifer.

Spicate. 1) Spikelike; 2) borne in a spike, as spicate flowers.

Spike. A usually unbranched, elongated, indeterminate inflorescence in which the flowers are sessile, the flowers either congested or remote; used also for a similar-appearing inflorescence bearing sessile composite heads, as in *Liatris,* or otherwise condensed flower clusters, as in *Phleum.*

Spikelet. A secondary spike, one spicate part of a compound inflorescence, especially the floral unit, or ultimate cluster, of a grass inflorescence, composed of flowers and their subtending bracts.

Spine. A strong, stiff, sharp-pointed outgrowth on a stem, leaf, or other organ.

Spinescent. 1) Terminated by a spine or sharp tip; 2) with spines, spiny.

Spinule. Diminutive of *spine;* a small spine.

Spinulose. With small spines.

Sporangiophore. The stalk of a sporangium; a sporangium-bearing organ.

Sporangium. A spore case, a sac or body producing spores.

Spore. A simple reproductive body, usually composed of a single detached cell, and containing a nucleated mass of protoplasm (but no embryo) and capable of developing into a gametophyte; used particularly in reference to the ferns, fern allies, and lower plants.

Sporocarp. A firm receptacle containing sporangia, as in *Salvinia, Marsilea.*

Sporophyll. A leaflike organ which bears spores, as in *Selaginella;* in angiosperms, the homologous organ is a carpel or stamen.

Sporophyte. In ferns and seed plants, the foliaceous vegetative plant, which produces spores, as opposed to the gametophyte. Compare *Gametophyte.*

Spreading. Extending outward or horizontally.

Spur. A tubular or saclike projection from a flower, as of a petal or sepal; it usually contains a nectar-secreting gland.

Squama. A scale.

Squamate. Having or covered with scales.

Squamella. Diminutive of *squama;* a small scale, as in the pappus of some Compositae.

Squamellate. With, composed of, or like small scales.

Squamose, squamous. Covered with or consisting of scales.

Squamulose. Covered with small scales.

Stalk. A nontechnical term for the more or less elongate support of any organ, as a petiole, peduncle, pedicel, filament, stipe.

Stalked bud. A bud in which the outer scales are attached above the base of the bud axis.

Stamen. The pollen-bearing organ of a seed plant, a unit of the androecium, typically consisting of anther and filament but sometimes reduced to only an anther.

Staminate. Male, having stamens but no pistils.

Staminode, staminodium. A sterile stamen, or a structure resembling such and borne in the staminal region of the flower; in some flowers, as in *Canna* or the Aizoceae, the staminodes are petal-like and showy.

Staminodial lip. A lip (in a flower) that is a large petaloid staminode.

Standard. 1) The uppermost, usually broad, more or less erect petal in a papilionaceous corolla, also called *banner* or *vexillum;* 2) one of the usually erect or ascending units of the inner whorl or series of the perianth of an *Iris* flower, as opposed to the usually spreading or drooping falls of the outer whorl.

Stellate. Starlike; stellate hairs have radiating branches, though hairs once or twice forked are often treated as stellate.

Stem. The main leaf-bearing and flower-bearing axis of a plant.

Sterile. 1) Nonfunctional, as sterile stamens, or without functional sex organs, as sterile flowers; 2) Not bearing flowers, as sterile specimens or shoots, or not subtending flowers, as sterile bracts; 3) not producing fruit, as sterile plants.

Stigma. The apical part of the pistil, which receives the pollen grains and provides conditions necessary for their germination.

Stigmatic. Pertaining to the stigma.

Stipe. 1) The stalk of a pistil or other small organ when axile in origin; 2) also, the petiole of a fern leaf.

Stipel. A stipule of a leaflet.

Stipitate. Borne on a stipe.

Stipule. A basal appendage of a petiole; usually occurring in pairs when present, and varying in form from foliaceous to glandlike.

Stolon. A shoot that bends to, or runs along, the ground and takes root, giving rise to new plants at the nodes or apex.

Stoloniferous. Producing stolons.

Stoma (pl. **stomata**), **stomate.** A minute pore in the epidermis of a leaf or stem, through which gases are exchanged.

Stone. A large pyrene.

Stone fruit. A drupe or drupelet, especially in the Rosaceae.

Striate. With fine longitudinal lines, channels, or ridges.

Strict. Straight and upright.

Strigose. With sharp, stiff, straight, appressed hairs often basally swollen.

Strobile, strobilus. A conelike structure consisting of sporophylls more or less densely arranged on a central axis, as in *Equiseum, Lycopodium, Cycas,* and the conifers; often synonymous with cone, but less restrictive.

Stylar. Pertaining to the style.

Style. The more or less elongated part of the pistil between the ovary and the stigma.

Stylopodium. A disclike enlargement at the base of the style in some Umbelliferae.

Sub-. A prefix meaning either: 1) *nearly, somewhat, slightly,* as *subcordate,* nearly cordate, or 2) *below, under,* as *subaxillary,* below the axil.

Subclass. See *Classification* in text.

Subfamily. See *Family* in text.

Subgenus (pl. **subgenera**). See *Genus* in text.

Subherbaceous. Herbaceous, but becoming woody as the season progresses.

Subinferior. Somewhat or partly inferior.

Subinferior ovary. See *Ovary.*

Submerged, submersed. Under the water.

Subpetiolar. Under the petiole and usually enveloped by it, as a winter bud in *Platanus.*

Subshrub. A suffrutescent perennial with basally woody stems, or a very low shrub often loosely treated as a perennial herb.

Subspecies (pl. **subspecies**). A major subdivision of a species, ranking between species and variety. It has somewhat varying connatations, depending on the user of the term, and often implies a distinct geographic distribution for the taxon. See also *Species* in text.

Substrate. The material on which a plant lives, as soil or rock.

Subtend. To stand below and close to, as a bract just below a flower, particularly when the bract is prominent or persistent.

Subtribe. See *Family* in text.

Subulate. Awl-shaped, linear and tapering from the base to a sharp apex, as the juvenile leaves of *Juniperus.*

Succulent. Juicy, fleshy, and usually also rather thick.

Suffrutescent. Somewhat or slightly shrubby, perennial with stems woody only at the base.

Suffruticose. Very low and shrubby and with persistent woody stems, as *Epigaea.*

Sulcate. Grooved or furrowed lengthwise.

Superficial. On the surface.

Superior. Above, upper.

Superior ovary. See *Ovary.*

Supine. Prostrate.

Suppressed. Vestigial to the extent of not being evident superficially or macroscopically, but with its existence in ancestral forms indicated by anatomy or otherwise.

Suprafoliar. Borne above a leaf or leaves.

Suture. A seam or groove indicating the line of union of parts or the line along which dehiscence occurs, or both.

Syconium. The "fruit" of a fig *(Ficus),* composed of a hollow, globose receptacle open at the apex and thickly beset inside with reduced flowers.

Symmetrical. 1) Capable of division into similar halves; 2) often used, somewhat inaccurately, in the more restricted sense of radially symmetrical or actinomorphic; 3) said of flowers that have similar numbers of parts in the calyx, corolla, and androecium.

Sympetalous. Gamopetalous.

Sympodial. Having growth of the stem or rhizome periodically terminated, with prolongation of the axis continued by a lateral branch, as in the orchid genera *Cattleya* and *Cymbidium.* Compare *Monopodial.*

Synandrium. An androecium in which the anthers are connate to one another, as in some Araceae.

Synangium. An aggregation of connate sporangia, as in *Marattia.*

Syncarp. A compound "fruit" composed of the massed, often more or less coalescent, fruits either of a single flower (an aggregate "fruit"), as in *Magnolia,* or of several flowers (a multiple "fruit"), as in pineapple *(Ananas)* or *Pandanus.*

Syncarpous. Having carpels united; applied to an ovary of two or more carpels; sometimes used when separate pistils within one flower are partially united. Compare *Apocarpous.*

Syngenesious. With anthers connate in a ring around the style, as stamens in the Compositae.

Synsepalous. Gamosepalous.

Tailed. Said of anthers having spurlike appendages on their back, as in some Ericaceae, or at their base, as in some Compositae.

Tapering. Not abrupt, gradually becoming smaller or diminishing in diameter or width toward one end.

Taxon (pl. taxa). A general term used for a taxonomic group of any rank without being specific, and in the plural (taxa) to refer to more than one such group collectively even if of different ranks.

Tendril. A twisting threadlike process or extension by which a plant grasps and clings to a support; morphologically it may be part of a branch or a leaf.

Tepal. A segment or unit of a perianth not clearly differentiated into typical corolla and calyx, as in *Tulipa, Allium, Begonia.*

Teratological. Abnormal in growth or structure, as a cristate cactus or a *Cattleya* flower with three lips.

Terete. Circular in cross section, cylindrical but usually tapering.

Terminal. Apical, at the tip.

Ternate. 1) In threes, as the leaves in *Trillium;* 2) also, divided into three parts, as a ternate leaf. In a **biternate** (twice ternate) **leaf,** the primary divisions are again divided into three parts; in a **triternate** (thrice ternate) **leaf,** the secondary divisions are still further divided into three parts.

Ternate-pinnate. Compound, with three primary divisions that are themselves pinnate.

Terrestrial. 1) Of or on the ground; 2) a land plant, as opposed to an aquatic or epiphyte.

Tessellate. Checkered.

Testa. The outer coat of a seed.

Tetrad. A group of four, especially a group of four pollen grains or spores.

Tetradynamous. Having four long and two short stamens, as most Cruciferae.

Tetrahedral. Having the form of a solid body with four sides or surfaces, as a pyramid with a base and three sides.

Tetramerous. Four-merous, with parts in fours; often written *4-merous.*

Tetrandrous. With four stamens.

Tetraploid. Having four (rather than the usual two) genomes or basic sets of chromosomes. See *Ploidy* in text.

Thalamus. See *Receptacle.*

Thallophyte, thallus plant. A cryptogam in which the plant body is a thallus, as the bacteria, algae, and fungi.

Thallus. A vegetative body undifferentiated into true roots, stems, or leaves. For *thallus plant,* see *Thallophyte.*

Theca. A small case: 1) in flowering plants, a pollen sac of an anther; 2) in mosses and related plants, a capsule.

Thorn. A sharp, woody, spinelike outgrowth from the wood of a stem; usually a reduced, modified branch. Compare *Prickle.*

Throat. The opening or orifice of the tubular part of a gamophyllous corolla, calyx, or perianth, the place where the tube joins or expands into the spreading limb.

Thyrse, thyrsus. A dense, paniclelike inflorescence in which the main axis is indeterminate and the lateral axes are determinate, i.e., cymose, as usually in *Buddleia, Syringa.*

Thyrsiform. Shaped like a thyrse.

Thyrsoid. Resembling a thyrse.

Tomentose. With tomentum.

Tomentulose. Diminutive of *tomentose;* somewhat or finely tomentose.

Tomentum. A covering of densely matted, short, woolly hairs.

Torulose. More or less cylindrical but irregularly swollen and contracted at close intervals, coarsely and irregularly moniliform.

Torus. See *Receptacle.*

Trapeziform. Unsymmetrically four-sided, like a trapezium.

Tree. A woody plant that produces one main trunk and a more or less distinct and elevated crown.

Tri-. A prefix meaning *three,* as *trilocular,* having three locules.

Triad. A group of three.

Tribe. See *Family* in text.

Trichoma, trichome. A hair or bristle.

Trichotomous. Forking regularly and repeatedly into three branches or divisions.

Tricolpate. Three-grooved, said of pollen grains.

Trifid. Cleft into three divisions.

Trifoliate. Having three leaves, as *Trillium.*

Trifoliolate. Having three leaflets, as the leaves of most species of *Trifolium.*

Trigonal. Three-angled.

Trimerous. Three-merous, with parts in threes; often written *3-merous.*

Trimorphic. Occurring in three different forms.

Triploid. Having three (rather than the usual two) genomes or basic chromosome sets. See *Ploidy* in text.

Triquetrous. Three-angled in cross section.

Triternate. See *Ternate.*

Truncate. Appearing as if cut off nearly or quite straight across at the end, as the leaf of *Liriodendron.*

Tuber. A short, thick, usually but not always subterranean stem or branch bearing buds or "eyes" and serving as a storage organ, as in the potato, *Solanum tuberosum.*

Tubercle. A small, rounded excrescence or projection on an organ.

Tuberculate. Beset with tubercles.

Tuberous. 1) Bearing or producing tubers; 2) tuberlike.

Tumid. Swollen, inflated.

Tunic. A loose, membranous, outer skin not the epidermis, especially the loose membrane about a corm or bulb.

Tunicated. 1) Provided with a tunic as defined above; 2) having concentric or enwrapping coats or layers, as the bulb of an onion *(Allium).*

Turbinate. Inversely conical, shaped like a top.

Turgid. Swollen or distended with fluid contents, tumid.

Turion. A young shoot or sucker, as an emerging stem of *Asparagus.*

Twig. A shoot of a woody plant representing the growth of the current season.

Type, also nomenclatural type. The element of a taxon to which the name of that taxon is permanently attached. The type of a name of a species or of any taxon of lower rank (i. e., subspecies, variety or forma) is ordinarily a specimen, which serves as the standard or criterion for application of the name. The type of a name of a genus or of any taxon between genus and species is a species; that of a family or of any taxon between family and genus is a genus.

Typical. Including the nomenclatural type (see *Type*) of a taxon of higher rank. In a variable species with more than one variety, for example, the typical variety is that which includes the original type of (i. e., has the same type as) the species itself, and therefore has the varietally distinguishing characteristics of the species as it was originally typified. In this sense, "typical" does not necessarily mean the "commonest" or "most representative."

Umbel. An indeterminate, usually flat-topped or convex inflorescence in which the pedicels of the flowers arise from approximately the same point. In a **compound umbel,** the peduncles (rays) supporting the secondary umbels (umbellets) also arise from a common point.

Umbellate. 1) In the form of an umbel or resembling an umbel, as an umbellate cyme; 2) borne in an umbel, as umbellate flowers.

Umbellet. A secondary umbel in a compound umbel.

Umbelliform. Umbel-like, resembling an umbel.

Umbilicate. With a navel-like, usually central, depression.

Umbo. A conical projection arising from a surface, usually centrally.

Unarmed. Without spines, prickles, or other sharp appendages.

Uncinate. Hooked, bearing a hook.

Undulate. 1) Having a wavy surface, i.e., wavy up and down; 2) having a wavy edge, i.e., wavy in and out. Since a margin of a leaf or other organ may be wavy up and down, or in and out, or both at once, in this work *undulate* is used in the first 1) sense, and *sinuate* for the second 2) sense.

Unguiculate. Narrowed into a petiolelike base, clawed.

Unifoliolate. With one leaflet; said of a compound leaf reduced to a single (usually the terminal) leaflet.

Unigeneric. Monogeneric.

Unijugate. Applied to a compound leaf composed of one pair of leaflets.

Unilateral. One-sided.

Unilocular. Containing a single chamber or cell.

Unisexual. Of one sex, staminate only or pistillate only.

Urceolate. Urn- or pitcher-shaped, i.e., ovoid or short-tubular and contracted at or just below the mouth, as the corolla of most species of *Vaccinum* and *Gautheria*.

Utricle. A small bladder; more commonly, a bladdery, 1-seeded, usually indehiscent fruit, as in some Amaranthaceae.

Vaginate. Sheathed, with a sheath.

Valvate. 1) Opening by valves or pertaining to valves; 2) meeting at the edges without overlapping, as leaves or petals in the bud.

Valve. 1) One of the sections into which the wall of a capsule or legume splits at maturity; 2) a flap over a pore in a poricidal anther or capsule.

Varietas. See *Variety.*

Variety; officially, **varietas** (pl. **varietates**). A subdivision of a species, officially ranking between subspecies and forma when these are also used. However, especially as used in the past, it has had varying connotations. It is often used for a major subdivision of a species (sometimes in the sense of subspecies), and has also frequently been used in the sense of form (forma). Before the term cultivar was coined, variety could also have the sense of that term, designating a variant of horticultural origin or importance.

Vascular. Pertaining to or having specialized conducting tissues, in which the xylem elements transport water and mineral salts, and phloem elements transport sugar and other organic substances. Vascular plants include the ferns, fern allies, gymnosperms, and angiosperms. Compare *Nonvascular.*

Velamen. The thick, corky covering of aerial roots in epiphytic orchids, serving to absorb moisture from the atmosphere.

Velutinous. Velvety, with erect, straight, moderately firm hairs.

Venation. Veining, the arrangement or disposition of veins.

Ventral. Relating to, or attached to, the front or inner surface of a part or organ, facing toward the axis, adaxial; the opposite of *dorsal.*

Ventral placentation. See *Placentation.*

Ventricose. Swollen or inflated on one side, more pronounced than *gibbous.*

Vernation. The disposition or arrangement of leaves in the bud. Compare *Aestivation.*

Verrucose. Warty, covered with wartlike protusions.

Verruculose. Diminutive of *verrucose;* covered with small warts.

Versatile. Hung or attached near the middle and capable of moving freely, as an anther attached near its middle on the apex of a filament and capable of being turned.

Verticil. A whorl, a ring of three or more; often used, loosely, in the sense of *verticillaster.*

Verticillaster, verticillastrum. A false whorl, applied to a pair of opposite cymes that are more or less confluent and seem to surround the stem, as in the Labiatae.

Verticillate. Arranged in whorls, or seemingly so.

Vesicle. A small bladdery sac or cavity filled with air or fluid.

Vestigial. Imperfectly developed, said of a part or organ that was fully developed and functional in ancestral forms but is now a degenerate relic, usually smaller and less complex than its prototype.

Vestiture, vesture. Pubescence, any covering of a surface causing it to be other than glabrous.

Vexillum. See *Standard.*

Villous. With long, soft, shaggy, not matted hairs.

Virgate. Long, straight, and slender, wandlike.

Viscid. Sticky.

Viviparous. 1) Said of seeds that germinate or buds that sprout and form plantlets while still on the parent plant; 2) sometimes, bearing such seeds or buds.

Volubile, voluble. Twining.

Whorl. A circle of three or more leaves, flowers, or other organs at one node.

Wing. 1) A thin, dry or membranaceous expansion or flat extension or appendage of an organ, as the wing of a seed of *Acer;* 2) also, one of the two lateral petals of a papilionaceous flower.

Woolly. With long, soft, more or less matted hairs, lanate.

Xerophyte. A plant of an arid habitat, such as the desert.

Zygomorphic. Bilaterally symmetrical, capable of being divided into two equal halves in one plane only, as a flower of *Antirrhinum* or *Cattleya.*

INDEX TO COMMON NAMES

Aloe—*Continued*
  Medicinal: *A. barbadensis.*
  Pearl: ×*Gastrolea Beguinii.*
  Socotrine: *Aloe Perryi.*
  Spider: *A. humilis, A. spinosissima.*
  Spiny: *A. africana.*
  Tiger: *A. variegata.*
  Water: *Stratiotes.*
  Warty: *Gasteria verrucosa.*
  Zanzibar: *Aloe Perryi.*
Alternanthera, copper: *Alternanthera ficoidea* cv. 'Versicolor'.
Althaea: *Hibiscus syriacus.*
  Shrub: *H. syriacus.*
Aluminum plant: *Pilea Cadierei.*
  Alumroot: *Geranium maculatum, Heuchera.*
  Alyssum, sweet: *Lobularia maritima.*
Amaranth: *Amaranthus.*
  Feathered: *Celosia cristata,* Plumosa Group.
  Globe: *Gomphrena globosa.*
  Green: *Amaranthus hybridus, A. retroflexus.*
  Purple: *A. cruentus.*
  Red: *A. cruentus.*
Amarelle: *Prunus Cerasus* var. *Caproniana.*
Amaryllis: *Amaryllis, Hippeastrum.*
  Blue: *Worsleya Rayneri.*
  Orchid: *Sprekelia formosissima.*
Amatungulu: *Carissa grandiflora.*
Amazon nut: *Bertholletia excelsa.*
Amazon vine: *Stigmaphyllon ciliatum.*
Ambarella: *Spondias cytherea.*
Amberbell: *Erythronium americanum.*
Amole: *Chlorogalum.*
Anacahuita: *Cordia Boissieri.*
Anaqua: *Ehretia Anacua.*
Anchor plant: *Colletia cruciata.*
Anemone: *Anemone.*
  European wood: *Anemone nemorosa.*
  False: *Anemonopsis macrophylla.*
  Japanese: *Anemone hupehensis, A.* ×*hybrida.*
  Long-headed: *Anemone cylindrica.*
  Rue: *Anemonella thalictroides.*
  Tree: *Carpenteria californica.*
Angelica: *Angelica Archangelica.*
  Five-leaf: *Acanthopanax.*
  Great: *Angelica atropurpurea.*
  Japanese: *Aralia elata.*
Angelica tree: *Aralia spinosa.*
Angelin: *Andira inermis.*
Angel's-eye: *Veronica Chamaedrys.*
Angel's-fishing-rods: *Dierama pendulum.*
Angel's-tears: *Datura sanguinea, Narcissus triandrus, Soleirolia Soleirolii.*
Angel's-trumpet: *Brugmansia, Datura inoxia.*
  Red: *Brugmansia sanguinea.*
Angel-wings: *Caladium.*
Anglepod: *Gonolobus.*
Anise: *Foeniculum vulgare* var. *azoricum, Myrrhis odorata, Pimpinella Anisum.*
  Chinese: *Illicium anisatum.*
  Common: *Pimpinella Anisum.*
  Purple: *Illicium floridanum.*
  Star: *I. verum.*
Aniseroot: *Osmorhiza longistylis.*
Anise tree: *Illicium.*
  Japanese: *I. anisatum.*
Annatto: *Bixa Orellana.*
Anona blanca: *Annona diversifolia.*
Antelope bush: *Purshia.*
Antelope-ears: *Platycerium.*
Anthericum, walking: *Chlorophytum comosum.*
Ant tree: *Triplaris americana.*
Anthurium: *Anthurium.*
  Crystal: *A. crystallinum.*
  Pigtail: *A. Scherzeranum.*
  White: *Spathiphyllum Clevelandii.*
Anyu: *Tropaeolum tuberosum.*
Apache-plume: *Fallugia.*
Ape: *Alocasia macrorhiza.*
  Blue: *Xanthosoma violaceum.*
  Chinese: *Alocasia cucullata.*
Apio: *Arracacia xanthorrhiza.*
Apostle plant: *Neomarica Northiana.*

Apple: *Malus, M. sylvestris.*
  Adam's: *Tabernaemontana divaricata.*
  American crab: *Malus angustifolia, M. coronaria.*
  Bake: *Rubus Chamaemorus.*
  Baked: *R. Chamaemorus.*
  Balsam: *Clusia rosea, Echinocystis lobata, Momordica Balsamina.*
  Bechtel's crab: *Malus ioensis* cv. 'Plena'.
  Belle: *Passiflora laurifolia.*
  Blade: *Pereskia.*
  Bloomless: *Malus pumila* cv. 'Apetala'.
  Cane: *Arbutus Unedo.*
  Chess: *Sorbus Aria.*
  Chinese: *Malus prunifolia.*
  Chinese flowering: *M. spectabilis.*
  Common: *M. pumila.*
  Common thorn: *Datura Stramonium.*
  Conch: *Passiflora maliformis.*
  Crab: any small-fruited sp. of *Malus.*
  Custard: *Annona Cherimola, A. reticulata, A. squamosa.*
  Dead Sea: *Solanum sodomeum.*
  Downy thorn: *Datura inoxia.*
  Elephant: *Feronia Limonia.*
  Flowering crab: many spp. of *Malus.*
  Garland crab: *Malus coronaria.*
  Gold: *Lycopersicon Lycopersicum.*
  Golden: *Aegle Marmelos, Spondias cytherea.*
  Indian: *Datura inoxia.*
  Indian wood: *Feronia Limonia.*
  Java: *Syzygium samarangense.*
  Jew's: *Solanum Melongena* var. *esculentum.*
  Kai: *Dovyalis caffra.*
  Kangaroo: *Solanum aviculare.*
  Kau: *Dovyalis caffra.*
  Large-fruited rose: *Syzygium malaccense.*
  Long-leaved Argyle: *Eucalyptus cephalocarpa.*
  Love: *Lycopersicon Lycopersicum, Solanum aculeatissimum.*
  Mad: *Solanum Melongena* var. *esculentum.*
  Malay: *Syzygium malaccense.*
  Mammee: *Mammea americana.*
  Melon: *Cucumis Melo,* Chito Group.
  Mexican: *Casimiroa edulis.*
  Oregon crab: *Malus fusca.*
  Otaheite: *Spondias cytherea.*
  Paradise: *Malus pumila* var. *paradisiaca.*
  Peruvian: *Cereus peruvianus.*
  Plum-leaved: *Malus prunifolia.*
  Pond: *Annona glabra.*
  Possum: *Diospyros virginiana.*
  Prairie crab: *Malus ioensis.*
  Prickly custard: *Annona muricata.*
  Rose: *Syzygium Jambos, S. malaccense.*
  Sea: *Syzygium grande.*
  Showy crab: *Malus floribunda.*
  Siberian crab: *M. baccata.*
  Soulard crab: *M. Soulardii.*
  Southern wild crab: *M. angustifolia.*
  Star: *Chrysophyllum Cainito.*
  Sugar: *Annona squamosa.*
  Sweet-scented crab: *Malus coronaria.*
  Thorn: *Crataegus, Datura, D. Stramonium.*
  Toringo crab: *Malus Sieboldii.*
  Water rose: *Syzygium aqueum.*
  Wax: *Syzygium samarangense.*
  Wi: *Spondias cytherea.*
  Wild balsam: *Echinocystis lobata.*
  Wild crab: *Malus angustifolia, M. coronaria, M. ioensis.*
  Wild custard: *Annona senegalensis.*
  Wild rose: *Syzygium pycnanthum.*
  Wild sweet crab: *Malus coronaria.*
  Wood: *Feronia Limonia.*
Apple-of-Peru: *Nicandra Physalodes.*
Apple-of-Sodom: *Solanum sodomeum.*
Apricot: *Prunus Armeniaca.*
  Desert: *P. Fremontii.*
  Japanese: *P. Mume.*
  Japanese flowering: *P. Mume.*
  South American: *Mammea americana.*
Apricot vine: *Passiflora incarnata.*
Arab's-turban: *Crassula hemisphaerica.*
Aralia: *Aralia.*
  Balfour: *Polyscias Balfouriana.*
  False: *Dizygotheca.*
  Fern-leaf: *Polyscias filicifolia.*

Aralia—*Continued*
  Finger: *Dizygotheca elegantissima.*
  Geranium-leaf: *Polyscias Guilfoylei.*
  Snowflake: *Trevesia palmata* cv. 'Micholitzii'.
Arar tree: *Tetraclinis articulata.*
Arborvitae: *Thuja.*
  American: *Thuja occidentalis.*
  False: *Thujopsis dolabrata.*
  Giant: *Thuja plicata.*
  Hiba: *Thujopsis dolabrata.*
  Japanese: *Thuja Standishii.*
  Oriental: *Platycladus orientalis.*
Arbutus, trailing: *Epigaea repens.*
Archangel: *Angelica Archangelica, Lamium album.*
  Yellow: *Lamiastrum Galeobdolon.*
Areca nut: *Areca Catechu.*
Argan tree: *Argania spinosa.*
Argemony: *Argemone.*
Aristocrat plant: *Haworthia Chalwinii.*
Arizona-giant: *Carnegiea gigantea.*
Arracacha: *Arracacia xanthorrhiza.*
Arrowhead: *Sagittaria.*
  Awl-leaf: *S. subulata.*
  Giant: *S. montevidensis.*
  Old-World: *S. sagittifolia.*
Arrowhead vine: *Syngonium podophyllum.*
Arrowroot: *Maranta arundinacea.*
  East Indian: *Tacca Leontopetaloides.*
  Fiji: *T. Leontopetaloides.*
  Polynesian: *T. Leontopetaloides.*
  Queensland: *Canna edulis.*
  South Sea: *Tacca Leontopetaloides.*
  Tahiti: *T. Leontopetaloides.*
Arrowwood: *Viburnum, V. acerifolium, V. dentatum.*
  Downy: *V. Rafinesquianum.*
  Downy-leaved: *V. Rafinesquianum.*
  Southern: *V. dentatum.*
Artemisia, silver-king: *Artemisia ludoviciana* var. *albula.*
Artichoke: *Cynara Scolymus.*
  Chinese: *Stachys affinis.*
  Globe: *Cynara Scolymus.*
  Japanese: *Stachys affinis.*
  Jerusalem: *Helianthus tuberosus.*
  White Jerusalem: *Bomarea edulis.*
Artillery plant: *Pilea microphylla.*
Arum
  Arrow: *Peltandra, P. virginica.*
  Italian: *Arum italicum.*
  Ivy: *Epipremnum aureum.*
  Titan: *Amorphophallus Titanum.*
  Twist: *Helicodiceros muscivorus.*
  Umbrella: *Amorphophallus Rivieri.*
  Water: *Calla palustris.*
Asarabacca: *Asarum.*
Ash: *Fraxinus.*
  Alpine: *Eucalyptus delegatensis.*
  American mountain: *Sorbus americana.*
  Arizona: *Fraxinus velutina* var. *glabra.*
  Black: *F. nigra.*
  Black mountain: *Eucalyptus Sieberi.*
  Blue: *Fraxinus quadrangulata.*
  Carolina: *F. caroliniana.*
  European: *F. excelsior.*
  European mountain: *Sorbus Aucuparia.*
  Evergreen: *Fraxinus Uhdei.*
  Flowering: *F. dipetala, F. Ornus.*
  Green: *F. pennsylvanica.*
  Ground: *Aegopodium Podagraria.*
  Manchurian: *Fraxinus mandshurica.*
  Manna: *F. Ornus.*
  Modesto: see *F. velutina* var. *glabra.*
  Montebello: see *F. velutina* var. *coriacea.*
  Mountain: *Eucalyptus regnans, Sorbus.*
  Northern prickly: *Zanthoxylum americanum.*
  Pop: *Fraxinus caroliniana.*
  Prickly: *Aralia spinosa, Zanthoxylum.*
  Red: *Fraxinus pennsylvanica.*
  Sea: *Zanthoxylum clava-Herculis.*
  Shamel: *Fraxinus Uhdei.*
  Single-leaf: *F. anomala.*
  Southern prickly: *Zanthoxylum clava-Herculis.*
  Stinking: *Ptelea trifoliata.*
  Syrian: *Fraxinus syriaca.*

Ash—*Continued*
  Texas: *F. texensis.*
  Velvet: *F. velutina.*
  Wafer: *Ptelea trifoliata.*
  Water: *Fraxinus caroliniana.*
  White: *Eucalyptus fraxinoides, Fraxinus americana.*
  Yellow-topped mallee: *Eucalyptus Luehmanniana.*
Ashweed: *Aegopodium Podagraria.*
Asoka: *Saraca indica.*
Asparagus: *Asparagus.*
  Cape: *Aponogeton distachyum.*
  Common: *Asparagus officinalis.*
  Cossack: *Typha latifolia.*
  Garden: *Asparagus officinalis.*
  Prussian: *Ornithogalum pyrenaicum.*
  Smilax: *Asparagus asparagoides.*
  Sprenger: *A. densiflorus* cv. 'Sprengeri'.
Aspen: *Populus.*
  Chinese: *P. adenopoda.*
  European: *P. tremula.*
  Japanese: *P. Sieboldii.*
  Large-toothed: *P. grandidentata.*
  Quaking: *P. tremuloides* var. *aurea.*
  Trembling: *P. tremuloides.*
Asphodel: *Asphodelus, Asphodeline lutea.*
  Bog: *Narthecium.*
  False: *Tofieldia.*
  Mountain: *Xerophyllum asphodeloides.*
  Yellow: *Narthecium americanum.*
Aster: *Aster, Callistephus.*
  Annual: *Callistephus chinensis.*
  Beach: *Erigeron glaucus.*
  Blue wood: *Aster cordifolius.*
  China: *Callistephus chinensis.*
  Golden: *Chrysopsis.*
  Heath: *Aster ericoides.*
  Italian: *A. Amellus.*
  Mojave: *Machaeranthera tortifolia.*
  New England: *Aster novae-angliae.*
  Stoke's: *Stokesia.*
  Tartarian: *Aster tataricus.*
  Tree: *Olearia.*
  White upland: *Aster ptarmicoides.*
  White wood: *A. divaricatus.*
Athel: *Tamarix aphylla.*
Aubergine: *Solanum Melongena* var. *esculentum.*
Aucuba, Japanese: *Aucuba japonica.*
Auricula: *Primula Auricula.*
Australian nut: *Macadamia integrifolia, M. tetraphylla.*
Autograph tree: *Clusia rosea.*
Avaram: *Cassia auriculata.*
Avens: *Geum.*
  Mountain: *Dryas octopetala.*
  Purple: *Geum rivale.*
  Water: *G. rivale.*
Avignon berry: *Rhamnus infectoria.*
Avocado: *Persea americana.*
  Trapp: *P. leiogyna.*
Awl tree: *Morinda citrifolia.*
Awlwort: *Subularia.*
Ayo: *Tetrastigma Harmandii.*
Azalea: *Rhododendron.*
  Alabama: *R. alabamense.*
  Alpine: *Loiseleuria procumbens.*
  Arnold Hybrid: *Rhododendron ×arnoldianum.*
  Balsam: *R. indicum* cv. 'Balsaminiflorum'.
  Chinese: *R. molle.*
  Clammy: *R. viscosum.*
  Coast: *R. atlanticum.*
  Cork: *R. quinquefolium.*
  Cumberland: *R. Bakeri.*
  Dwarf: *R. atlanticum.*
  Early: *R. prinophyllum.*
  Five-leaf: *R. pentaphyllum.*
  Flame: *R. calendulaceum.*
  Florida flame: *R. austrinum.*
  Gable Hybrid: see under *Rhododendron.*
  Ghent Hybrid: see under *Rhododendron.*
  Glenn Dale Hybrid: see under *Rhododendron.*
  Hiryu: *R. obtusum.*
  Hoary: *R. canescens.*
  Indian: see under *Rhododendron.*
  Indicum Hybrid: see under *R. indicum.*

Azalea—*Continued*
 Japanese: *R. japonicum.*
 Kaempferi Hybrid: see under *Rhododendron.*
 Kirishima: *R. obtusum.*
 Knapp Hill Hybrid: see under *Rhododendron.*
 Korean: *R. yedoense* var. *poukhanense.*
 Kurume: *R. obtusum.*
 Kurume Hybrid: see under *Rhododendron.*
 Kyushu: *R. kiusianum.*
 Luchu: *R. scabrum.*
 Macranthum: *R. indicum.*
 Maries's: *R. Mariesii.*
 Mayflower: *R. prinophyllum.*
 Mock: *Menziesia.*
 Molle Hybrid: *Rhododendron* ×*Kosteranum,* see also under *Rhododendron.*
 Mt. Amagi: *R. amagianum.*
 Oconee: *R. flammeum.*
 Oldham's: *R. Oldhamii.*
 Piedmont: *R. prinophyllum.*
 Pink-shell: *R. Vaseyi.*
 Plum-leaved: *R. prunifolium.*
 Pontic: *R. luteum.*
 Rose-shell: *R. prinophyllum.*
 Royal: *R. Schlippenbachii.*
 Rusticum: *R.* ×*mixtum.*
 Rusticum Flore Pleno Hybrid: *R.* ×*mixtum.*
 Rutherford Hybrid: *R. Rutherfordianum.*
 Sander Hybrid: *R.* ×*Sanderi.*
 Sims's: *R. Simsii.*
 Smooth: *R. arborescens.*
 Snow: *R. mucronatum.*
 Spider: *R. linearifolium.*
 Summer: *Pelargonium domesticum.*
 Swamp: *Rhodendron viscosum.*
 Sweet: *R. arborescens.*
 Torch: *R. Kaempferi.*
 Western: *R. occidentale.*
 White swamp: *R. viscosum.*
 Wild-thyme: *R. serpyllifolium.*
 Yellow: *R. calendulaceum.*
 Yodogawa: *R. yedoense.*
Azarole: *Crataegus Azarolus.*

Babassú: *Orbignya Barbosiana.*
Baboon flower: *Babiana.*
Baboonroot: *Babiana.*
Babul: *Acacia nilotica.*
Baby-blue-eyes: *Nemophila Menziesii.*
Baby jade: *Crassula argentea.*
Baby-pine-of-China: *Crassula tetragona.*
Baby's-breath: *Gypsophila elegans, G. paniculata.*
 False: *Galium aristatum.*
Baby's-tears: *Hypoestes phyllostachya, Soleirolia Soleirolii.*
 English: *Nertera granadensis.*
Baby's-toes: *Fenestraria rhopalophylla.*
 Purple: *Frithia pulchra.*
Baby-toes: *Fenestraria rhopalophylla.*
Baccharis: *Baccharis.*
 Dwarf: *B. pilularis.*
 Sticky: *G. glutinosa.*
Bachelor's-button: *Centaurea Cyanus.*
 Yellow: *Polygala lutea.*
Bael, Indian: *Aegle Marmelos.*
Bael fruit: *Aegle Marmelos.*
Bael tree: *Aegle Marmelos.*
Bagflower: *Clerodendrum Thomsoniae.*
Baked-apple berry: *Rubus Chamaemorus.*
Balata: *Manilkara bidentata.*
Balisier: *Heliconia Bihai, H. caribaea.*
Ball tree: *Aegle Marmelos.*
Balloon flower: *Platycodon.*
 Dwarf: *P. grandiflorus* var. *Mariesii.*
Balloon vine: *Cardiospermum, C. Halicacabum.*
Balm: *Melissa.*
 Bee: *Melissa officinalis, Monarda didyma.*
 Canary: *Cedronella canariensis.*
 Common: *Melissa officinalis.*
 Field: *Glecoma hederacea.*
 Horse: *Collinsonia.*
 Lemon: *Melissa officinalis.*
 Molucca: *Molucella laevis.*
 Sweet: *Melissa officinalis.*

Balm-of-Gilead: *Cedronella canariensis, Populus gileadensis.*
 Hoary: *Agastache cana.*
Balm-of-Heaven: *Umbellularia californica.*
Balmony: *Chelone glabra.*
Balsa: *Ochroma pyramidale.*
Balsam: *Impatiens.*
 Fir: *Abies balsamea.*
 Garden: *Impatiens Balsamina.*
 He: *Picea rubens.*
 Rose: *Impatiens Balsamina.*
 She: *Abies Fraseri.*
 Wild: *Ibervillea Lindheimeri.*
 Zanzibar: *Impatiens Wallerana.*
Balsamroot: *Balsamorhiza.*
Bamboo: *Arundinaria, Bambusa, Chimonobambusa, Phyllostachys, Pseudosasa, Sasa, Semiarundinaria, Shibataea.*
 Allgold: *Phyllostachys bambusoides* cv. 'Allgold'.
 Alphonse Karr: *Bambusa glaucescens* cv. 'Alphonse Karr'.
 Arrow: *Pseudosasa japonica.*
 Beechey: *Bambusa Beecheyana.*
 Black: *Phyllostachys nigra.*
 Buddha: *Bambusa ventricosa.*
 Calcutta: *Dendrocalamus strictus.*
 Canebrake: *Arundinaria gigantea.*
 Castillon: *Phyllostachys bambusoides* cv. 'Castillon'.
 Chinese-goddess: *Bambusa glaucescens* var. *Riviereorum.*
 Common: *Bambusa vulgaris.*
 Dwarf: *Arundinaria pumila.*
 Dwarf fern-leaf: *A. disticha.*
 Dwarf white-stripe: *A. variegata.*
 Feathery: *Bambusa vulgaris.*
 Fern-leaf hedge: *B. glaucescens* cv. 'Fernleaf'.
 Forage: *Phyllostachys aureosulcata.*
 Giant: *Dendrocalamus.*
 Giant thorny: *Bambusa arundinacea.*
 Hardy: *Pseudosasa japonica.*
 Heavenly: *Nandina domestica.*
 Hedge: *Bambusa glaucescens.*
 Henon: *Phyllostachys nigra* cv. 'Henon'.
 Male: *Dendrocalamus strictus.*
 Mexican: *Polygonum cuspidatum.*
 Meyer: *Phyllostachys Meyeri.*
 Moso: *P. pubescens.*
 Narihira: *Semiarundinaria fastuosa.*
 Oldham: *Bambusa Oldhamii.*
 Oriental hedge: *B. glaucescens.*
 Punting-pole: *B. tuldoides.*
 Pygmy: *Arundinaria pygmaea.*
 Red-berried: *Smilax Walteri.*
 Sacred: *Nandina domestica.*
 Sickle: *Chimonobambusa falcata.*
 Silver-stripe hedge: *Bambusa glaucescens* cv. 'Silverstripe'.
 Simon: *Arundinaria Simonii.*
 Square: *Chimonobambusa quadrangularis.*
 Square-stem: *C. quadrangularis.*
 Stake: *Phyllostachys aureosulcata.*
 Stripe-stem fern-leaf: *Bambusa glaucescens* cv. 'Silverstem Fernleaf'.
 Tonkin: *Arundinaria amabilis.*
 Yellow-groove: *Phyllostachys aureosulcata.*
Bamboo vine: *Smilax laurifolia.*
Banana: *Musa.*
 Abyssinian: *Ensete ventricosum.*
 Canary Island: *Musa acuminata* cv. 'Dwarf Cavendish'.
 Chinese: *M. acuminata* cv. 'Dwarf Cavendish'.
 Chinese dwarf: *M. acuminata* cv. 'Dwarf Cavendish'.
 Dwarf: *M. acuminata* cv. 'Dwarf Cavendish'.
 Edible: *M. acuminata, M.* ×*paradisiaca.*
 Fehi: see *M. Fehi.*
 Fe'i: see *M. Fehi.*
 Flowering: *M. ornata.*
 Governor: *M. acuminata* cv. 'Dwarf Cavendish'.
 Koae: see *M.* ×*paradisiaca* cv. 'Aeae'.
 Ladyfinger: *M. acuminata* cv. 'Dwarf Cavendish'.
Banana plant (of aquarists): *Nymphoides aquatica.*
 Aquatic: *N. aquatica.*
Banana shrub: *Michelia Figo.*
Band plant: *Vinca major.*
Baneberry: *Actaea.*
 Red: *A. rubra.*
 White: *A. pachypoda.*

Banyan: *Ficus.*
  Australian: *F. macrophylla.*
  Chinese: *F. retusa.*
  Indian: *F. benghalensis.*
  Malay: *F. retusa.*
Banyan tree: *Ficus benghalensis.*
Baobab: *Adansonia digitata.*
Barbados nut: *Jatropha Curcas.*
Barbados-pride: *Adenanthera pavonina, Caesalpinia pulcherrima.*
Barbasco: *Jacquinia Barbasco.*
Barbe-de-capuchin: *Cichorium Intybus.*
Barberry: *Berberis.*
  Alleghany: *B. canadensis.*
  American: *B. canadensis.*
  Blue: *Mahonia pinnata.*
  Common: *B. vulgaris.*
  Darwin's: *B. Darwinii.*
  Holly: *B. ilicifolia, Mahonia Aquifolium.*
  Japanese: *B. Thunbergii.*
  Magellan: *B. buxifolia.*
  Salmon: *B. aggregata.*
  Truehedge: *B. Thunbergii* cv. 'Erecta'.
  Violet-bead: *B. hypokerina.*
  Wintergreen: *B. Julianae.*
Barley: *Hordeum.*
  Bulbous: *H. bulbosum.*
  Common: *H. vulgare.*
  Nepal: *H. vulgare.*
  Short-awned: *H. brevisubulatum.*
  Squirreltail: *H. jubatum.*
Barometer bush: *Leucophyllum frutescens.*
Barrel
  Blue: *Echinocactus ingens.*
  Mexican giant: *E. ingens.*
Barroom plant: *Aspidistra elatior.*
Bartsia, alpine: *Bartsia alpina.*
Barwood: *Pterocarpus erinaceus.*
Basil: *Ocimum, Clinopodium vulgare.*
  Common: *O. Basilicum.*
  Hoary: *O. canum.*
  Sweet: *O. Basilicum.*
  Wild: *Clinopodium vulgare.*
Basilweed: *Clinopodium vulgare.*
Basket flower: *Centaurea americana, Hymenocallis, H. narcissiflora.*
Basket-of-gold: *Aurinia saxatilis.*
Basket plant: *Aeschynanthus.*
Basket vine, scarlet: *Aeschynanthus pulcher.*
Basswood: *Tilia, T. americana.*
  White: *T. heterophylla.*
Batflower: *Tacca Chantrieri, T. integrifolia.*
Bat plant: *Tacca integrifolia.*
Bauhinia: *Bauhinia.*
  Bell: *B. tomentosa.*
  Dwarf white: *B. acuminata.*
  Malabar: *B. malabarica.*
  Nasturtium: *B. punctata.*
  Railway-fence: *B. Pauletia.*
  Red: *B. punctata.*
  Yellow: *B. tomentosa.*
Bay: *Gordonia Lasianthus, Laurus nobilis, Pimenta racemosa.*
  Bull: *Magnolia grandiflora.*
  California: *Umbellularia californica.*
  Loblolly: *Gordonia Lasianthus.*
  Red: *Persea Borbonia, Tabernaemontana.*
  Swamp red: *Persea Borbonia.*
  Sweet: *Laurus, L. nobilis, Magnolia virginiana, Persea Borbonia.*
  Willow-leaf: *Laurus nobilis* cv 'Angustifolia'.
Bayberry: *Myrica pensylvanica.*
  California: *M. californica.*
Bay-rum tree: *Pimenta racemosa.*
Bead plant: *Nertera granadensis.*
Bead tree: *Adenanthera, Melia, M. Azedarach.*
  Japanese: *Melia Azedarach.*
  Syrian: *M. Azedarach.*
Bead vine: *Crassula rupestris.*
Beam, white: *Sorbus Aria.*
Bean: *Phaseolus.*
  African locust: *Parkia filicoidea.*
  Algarroba: *Ceratonia Siliqua.*
  Asparagus: *Vigna unguiculata* subsp. *sesquipedalis.*
  Azuki: *V. angularis.*
  Black: *Castanospermum australe.*
  Bonavista: *Dolichos Lablab.*

Bean—*Continued*
  Bovanist: *D. Lablab.*
  Broad: *Vicia Faba.*
  Bush lima: *Phaseolus limensis* var. *limenanus.*
  Butter: *P. lunatus.*
  Carolina: *P. lunatus.*
  Castor: *Ricinus communis.*
  Cherokee: *Erythrina herbacea.*
  Civet: *Phaseolus lunatus.*
  Cluster: *Cyamopsis tetragonolobus.*
  Common: *Phaseolus vulgaris.*
  Coral: *Erythrina herbacea.*
  Dutch case-knife: *Phaseolus coccineus.*
  Dwarf lima: *P. limensis* var. *limenanus.*
  Dwarf sieva: *P. lunatus* var. *lunonanus.*
  Egyptian: *Dolichos Lablab.*
  English: *Vicia Faba.*
  European: *V. Faba.*
  Field: *V. Faba.*
  Florida velvet: *Mucuna Deeringiana.*
  French: *Phaseolus vulgaris.*
  Giant stock: *Canavalia ensiformis.*
  Goa: *Psophocarpus tetragonolobus.*
  Green: *Phaseolus vulgaris.*
  Horse: *Vicia Faba, Canavalia ensiformis.*
  Hottentot's: *Schotia afra.*
  Hyacinth: *Dolichos Lablab.*
  Indian: *Catalpa, C. bignonioides, C. speciosa, Dolichos Lablab.*
  Italian green: *Phaseolus vulgaris.*
  Jack: *Canavalia ensiformis.*
  Java glory: *Clerodendrum speciosissimum.*
  Kaffir: *Schotia afra.*
  Kidney: *Phaseolus vulgaris.*
  Lablab: *Dolichos Lablab.*
  Lima: *Phaseolus limensis, P. lunatus.*
  Locust: *Ceratonia Siliqua.*
  Lubia: *Dolichos Lablab.*
  Manila: *Psophocarpus tetragonolobus.*
  Mescal: *Sophora secundiflora.*
  Moth: *Vigna aconitifolia.*
  Mung: *V. radiata.*
  Nicker: *Entada gigas.*
  Pea: *Phaseolus vulgaris.*
  Pinto: *P. vulgaris.*
  Potato: *Apios americana, Pachyrrhizus tuberosus.*
  Rice: *Vigna umbellata.*
  Romano: *Phaseolus vulgaris.*
  Runner: *P. vulgaris.*
  Sacred: *Nelumbo.*
  Salad: *Phaseolus vulgaris.*
  Sarawak: *Dolichos Hosei.*
  Scarlet flame: *Brownea coccinea.*
  Scarlet runner: *Phaseolus coccineus.*
  Screw: *Prosopis pubescens.*
  Seim: *Dolichos Lablab.*
  Sewee: *Phaseolus lunatus.*
  Sieva: *P. lunatus.*
  Snail: *Vigna Caracalla.*
  Snap: *Phaseolus vulgaris.*
  Soja: *Glycine Max.*
  Soy, Soya: *G. Max.*
  String: *Phaseolus vulgaris.*
  Sword: *Entada gigas, Canavalia ensiformis, C. gladiata.*
  Tepary: *Phaseolus acutifolius* var. *latifolius.*
  Tick: *Vicia Faba.*
  Tonka: *Dipteryx odorata.*
  Velvet: *Mucuna Deeringiana.*
  Wax: *Phaseolus vulgaris.*
  White Dutch runner: *P. coccineus* cv. 'Albus'.
  Wild: *Apios americana.*
  Windsor: *Vicia Faba.*
  Winged: *Psophocarpus tetragonolobus.*
  Wonder: *Canavalia ensiformis.*
  Yam: *Pachyrrhizus erosus, P. tuberosus.*
  Yard-long: *Vigna unguiculata* subsp. *sesquipedalis.*
Bean tree: *Laburnum.*
Bearberry: *Arctostaphylos, Rhamnus Purshiana.*
  Alpine: *Arctostaphylos alpina.*
  Black: *A. alpina.*
  Common: *A. Uva-ursi.*
Beardflower: *Pogonia ophioglossoides.*
Beard-tongue: *Penstemon.*
Bear's-breech: *Acanthus, A. montanus.*

Bear's-foot: *Aconitum Napellus.*
Bear's-tail, Cretan: *Celsia Arcturus.*
Beautyberry: *Callicarpa americana.*
Beautybush: *Kolkwitzia amabilis.*
Beauty-of-the-night: *Mirabilis Jalapa.*
Beaver-poison: *Cicuta maculata.*
Beaver-tail: *Opuntia basilaris.*
Bedstraw: *Galium.*
  Northern: *G. boreale.*
  White: *G. Mollugo.*
  Yellow: *G. verum.*
Beech: *Fagus.*
  American: *F. grandifolia.*
  Blue: *Carpinus caroliniana.*
  Copper: *Fagus sylvatica* cv. 'Atropunicea'.
  Cut-leaf: *F. sylvatica* cv. 'Laciniata'.
  European: *F. sylvatica.*
  Fern-leaf: *F. sylvatica* cv. 'Laciniata'.
  Japanese: *F. crenata.*
  Purple: *F. sylvatica* cv. 'Atropunicea'.
  Water: *Carpinus caroliniana.*
  Weeping: *Fagus sylvatica* cv. 'Pendula'.
Beef plant: *Iresine Herbstii.*
Beefsteak plant: *Acalypha Wilkesiana, Iresine Herbstii.*
Beefwood: *Casuarina.*
Bee plant
  Rocky Mountain: *Cleome serrulata.*
  Yellow: *C. lutea.*
Beet: *Beta vulgaris.*
  Garden: *B. vulgaris,* Crassa Group.
  Leaf: *B. vulgaris,* Cicla Group.
  Red: *B. vulgaris,* Crassa Group.
  Sea: *B. vulgaris.*
  Spinach: *B. vulgaris,* Cicla Group.
  Sugar: *B. vulgaris,* Crassa Group.
  Wild: *Amaranthus hybridus, A. retroflexus, Saxifraga pensylvanica.*
  Yellow: *Beta vulgaris,* Crassa Group.
Beetleweed: *Galax urceolata.*
Beetroot: *Beta vulgaris,* Crassa Group.
Beggar's-lice: *Cynoglossum, Hackelia.*
Beggar-ticks, beggar's-ticks: *Bidens, Desmodium.*
  Fern-leaved: *Bidens ferulifolia.*
Beggarweed: *Desmodium tortuosum.*
Begonia: *Begonia.*
  Alder-leaf: *B. alnifolia.*
  Angel-wing: *B.* ×*argenteo-guttata, B. coccinea, B. corallina* cv. 'Lucerna', *B. stipulacea* cv. 'Acutangula'; see also under *B. rubra.*
  Bamboo: *B. rubra* Hybrids or Angel-wing Hybrids; see under *B. rubra.*
  Bedding: *B.* Semperflorens-Cultorum Hybrids; see *B.* ×*semperflorens-cultorum.*
  Beefsteak: *B. erythrophylla.*
  Blooming-fool: *B.* ×*cheimantha.*
  Bronze-leaf: *B.* ×*ricinifolia.*
  Calla-lily: *B.* Semperflorens-Cultorum cvs.; see under *B.* ×*semperflorens-cultorum.*
  Castor-bean: *B.* ×*ricinifolia.*
  Christmas: *B.* ×*cheimantha.*
  Christmas-flowering: *B.* ×*cheimantha.*
  Climbing: *Cissus discolor.*
  Crazy-leaf: *Begonia phyllomaniaca.*
  Dewdrop: *B. Dregei* cv. 'Macbethii'.
  Elephant's-ear: *B. albo-coccinea.*
  Elm-leaf: *B. ulmifolia.*
  Eyelash: *B. Boweri.*
  Fairy-carpet: *B. versicolor.*
  Fern: *B. foliosa* var. *foliosa.*
  Fern-leaf: *B. foliosa* var. *foliosa.*
  Fern-leaved: *B. foliosa* var. *foliosa.*
  Finger-leaf: *B.* ×*ricinifolia* cv. 'Sunderbruckii'.
  Fire-king: *B. goegoensis.*
  Fuchsia: *B. foliosa* var. *miniata.*
  Grape-leaf: *B. Dregei, B.* Rex-Cultorum Hybrid cv. 'Speculata' (see *B.* ×*speculata*), *B. Sartorii.*
  Grapevine: *B.* ×*weltoniensis.*
  Guinea-wing: *B. albo-picta.*
  Hardy: *B. grandis.*
  Hollyhock: *B. gracilis, B. Martiana.*
  Holly-leaf: *B. acutifolia, B. cubensis.*
  Holly-leaved: *B. cubensis.*
  Honey-bear: *B. lobata.*
  Hybrid tuberous: *B.* Tuberhybrida Hybrids; see *B.* ×*tuberhybrida.*
  Iron-cross: *B. Masoniana.*

Begonia—*Continued*
  Kidney: *B. dichotoma, B. erythrophylla.*
  King: *B. rex.*
  Leopard: *B. manicata* cv. 'Aureo-maculata'.
  Lettuce-leaf: *B. erythrophylla* cv. 'Bunchii', *B.* cv. 'Crestabruchii'; see *B.* ×*crestabruchii.*
  Lily-pad: *B. nelumbiifolia, B. peltata.*
  Lorraine: *B.* ×*cheimantha.*
  Manda's woolly-bear: *B. leptotricha.*
  Maple-leaf: *B. Dregei, B. Dregei* cv. 'Macbethii', *B. olbia, B. suffruticosa, B.* ×*weltoniensis.*
  Metallic-leaf: *B. metallica.*
  Miniature: *B. Boweri.*
  Miniature pond-lily: *B. hydrocotylifolia.*
  Nasturtium-leaf: *B. Francisii.*
  Painted-leaf: *B. rex.*
  Palm-leaf: *B. luxurians.*
  Peanut-brittle: *B. domingensis.*
  Pennywort: *B. hydrocotylifolia.*
  Philodendron-leaf: *B. valdensium.*
  Pond-lily: *B.* ×*erythrophylla* cv. 'Helix', *B. nelumbiifolia.*
  Rex: *B.* Rex-Cultorum Hybrids; see *B.* ×*rex-cultorum.*
  Seersucker: *B. spinibarbis.*
  Shrimp: *B.* ×*Limmingheiana.*
  Star: *B. heracleifolia, B.* ×*ricinifolia.*
  Star-leaf: *B. heracleifolia.*
  Strawberry: *Saxifraga stolonifera.*
  Swedish: *Plectranthus.*
  Trailing: *Cissus discolor.*
  Trailing watermelon: *Pellionia Daveauana.*
  Trout: *B.* ×*argenteo-guttata.*
  Trout-leaf: *B.* ×*argenteo-guttata.*
  Wax: *B.* Semperflorens-Cultorum Hybrids; see *B.* ×*semperflorens-cultorum.*
  Whirlpool: *B. erythrophylla* cv. 'Helix'.
  Wild: *Rumex venosus.*
  Winter: *Bergenia ciliata.*
  Winter-flowering: *Begonia* Elatior Hybrids; see *B.* ×*hiemalis.*
  Youth-and-old-age: *B.* Semperflorens-Cultorum cvs.; see under *B.* ×*semperflorens-cultorum.*
  Zigzag: *B. parilis.*
Bel fruit: *Aegle Marmelos.*
Bela tree: *Aegle Marmelos.*
Belgian evergreen: *Dracaena Sanderana.*
Belladonna: *Atropa Belladonna.*
  Cape: *Amaryllis Belladonna.*
Bellflower: *Campanula.*
  Adriatic: *C. Elatines.*
  Bonnet: *Codonopsis.*
  Canary: *Canarina.*
  Chilean: *Lapageria.*
  Chimney: *Campanula pyramidalis.*
  Clustered: *C. glomerata.*
  Creeping: *C. rapunculoides.*
  Giant: *Ostrowskia, O. magnifica.*
  Italian: *Campanula isophylla.*
  Marsh: *C. aparinoides.*
  Nettle-leaved: *C. Trachelium.*
  Ring: *Symphyandra.*
  Rover: *Campanula rapunculoides.*
  Tall: *C. americana.*
  Trailing: *Cyananthus.*
  Tussock: *Campanula carpatica.*
  Willow: *C. persicifolia.*
Bells-of-Ireland: *Molucella laevis.*
Bellwort: *Uvularia.*
Belvedere: *Kochia scoparia.*
Benjamin bush: *Lindera Benzoin.*
Benjamin tree: *Ficus benjamina.*
Bent: *Agrostis.*
  Autumn: *A. perennans.*
  Brown: *A. canina.*
  Colonial: *A. tenuis.*
  Creeping: *A. stolonifera.*
  Velvet: *A. canina.*
Bergamot: *Citrus Aurantium* subsp. *Bergamia.*
  Wild: *Monarda.*
Be-still tree: *Thevetia peruviana.*
Betel: *Piper Betle.*
Betony: *Stachys, S. officinalis.*
  Wood: *Pedicularis, P. canadensis.*
  Woolly: *Stachys byzantina, S. olympica.*
Bigarade: *Citrus Aurantium.*

Bignay: *Antidesma Bunius.*
Bignonia, yellow: *Tecoma stans.*
Bigroot: *Marah.*
Big tree: *Sequoiadendron giganteum.*
Bilberry: *Vaccinium, V. Myrtillus.*
  Bog: *V. uliginosum.*
  Dwarf: *V. caespitosum.*
  Early sweet: *V. vacillans.*
  Kamchatka: *V. praestans.*
  Low: *V. vacillans.*
  Mountain: *V. membranceum.*
Bilimbi: *Averrhoa Bilimbi.*
Bilsted: *Liquidambar Styraciflua.*
Bindweed: *Calystegia, C. sepium, Convolvulus.*
  Field: *Convolvulus arvensis.*
  Hedge: *Calystegia sepium.*
  Japanese: *C. hederacea.*
  Low: *C. spithamaea.*
  Sea: *C. Soldanella.*
Bine: *Humulus Lupulus.*
Birch: *Betula.*
  Black: *B. lenta, B. nigra.*
  Canoe: *B. papyrifera.*
  Cherry: *B. lenta.*
  Dwarf: *B. glandulosa.*
  European white: *B. pendula.*
  Fire: *B. populifolia.*
  Gray: *B. alleghaniensis, B. populifolia.*
  Japanese cherry: *B. grossa.*
  Japanese white: *B. platyphylla* var. *japonica.*
  Low: *B. pumila.*
  Mahogany: *B. lenta.*
  Monarch: *B. Maximowicziana.*
  Old-field: *B. populifolia.*
  Paper: *B. papyrifera.*
  Red: *B. nigra.*
  River: *B. nigra.*
  Swamp: *B. pumila.*
  Sweet: *B. lenta.*
  Water: *B. occidentalis.*
  West Indian: *Bursera Simaruba.*
  White: *Betula papyrifera, B. pendula, B. populifolia.*
  Yellow: *B. lutea.*
  Young's weeping: *B. pendula* cv. 'Youngii'.
Bird-catcher tree: *Pisonia umbellifera.*
Bird-of-paradise: *Caesalpinia Gilliesii, Strelitzia, S. reginae.*
  False: *Heliconia.*
  Queen's: *Strelitzia reginae.*
Bird-of-paradise flower: *Strelitzia reginae.*
Bird-of-paradise shrub: *Caesalpinia Gilliesii.*
Bird-of-paradise tree: *Strelitzia Nicolai.*
Bird-on-the-wing: *Polygala paucifolia.*
Bird's-eye: *Veronica Chamaedrys.*
Bird's-eye bush: *Ochna.*
Bird's-eyes: *Gilia tricolor.*
Bird's-nest, giant: *Pterospora andromedea.*
Birthroot: *Trillium.*
Birthwort: *Aristolochia.*
Biscochito: *Ruprechtia coriacea.*
Bishop's-cap: *Astrophytum myriostigma, A. ornatum, Mitella.*
Bishop's-hood: *Astrophytum myriostigma.*
Bishop's weed: *Aegopodium Podagraria, Ammi majus.*
Bisnaga: *Ammi Visnaga.*
Bistort: *Polygonum Bistorta.*
  Alpine: *P. viviparum.*
Bitter-bloom: *Sabatia angularis.*
Bitter Indian: *Tropaeolum.*
Bitternut: *Carya cordiformis.*
Bitterroot: *Lewisia rediviva.*
Bittersweet: *Celastrus, Solanum Dulcamara.*
  American: *Celastrus scandens.*
  Climbing: *C. scandens.*
  False: *C. scandens.*
  Oriental: *C. orbiculatus.*
  Shrubby: *C. scandens.*
Bitterweed: *Helenium amarum, Picris.*
Bitterwood: *Quassia amara, Simarouba glauca.*
Blackbead: *Pithecellobium guadalupense, P. Unguis-cati.*
Blackberry: *Rubus.*
  Cut-leaf: *R. laciniatus.*
  Cut-leaved: *R. laciniatus.*
  Evergreen: *R. laciniatus.*
  Evergreen thornless: *R. ulmifolius* var. *inermis.*

Blackberry—*Continued*
  Pacific: *R. ursinus.*
  Parsley-leaved: *R. laciniatus.*
  Running: *R. hispidus.*
  Sand: *R. cuneifolius.*
  Sow-teat: *R. allegheniensis.*
  Swamp: *R. hispidus.*
Blackboys: *Xanthorrhoea.*
  Blackbutt: *Eucalyptus pilularis.*
  Woodward's: *E. Woodwardii.*
Blackcap: *Rubus occidentalis.*
Black-eyed Susan: *Rudbeckia hirta.*
Black-eyed Susan vine: *Thunbergia alata.*
Black-fingers: *Opuntia clavarioides.*
Blacking plant: *Hibiscus Rosa-sinensis.*
Blackjack: *Quercus marilandica.*
Blackroot: *Veronicastrum virginicum.*
Blackthorn: *Crataegus Calpodendron, Prunus spinosa.*
  West Indian: *Acacia Farnesiana.*
Black-torch, Mexican: *Tillandsia punctulata.*
Blackwood: *Acacia penninervis.*
  Australian: *A. melanoxylon.*
Bladderbush: *Cleome Isomeris.*
Bladdernut: *Staphylea.*
  American: *S. trifolia.*
  European: *S. pinnata.*
Bladderpod: *Alyssoides, Lesquerella.*
Bladderwort: *Utricularia.*
Blanketflower: *Gaillardia.*
Blaspheme vine: *Smilax laurifolia.*
Blazing-star: *Chamaelirium luteum, Liatris, Mentzelia laevicaulis.*
Bleeding-heart: *Dicentra spectabilis.*
  Tropical: *Clerodendrum Thomsoniae.*
  Western: *Dicentra formosa.*
  Wild: *D. eximia.*
Bleeding-heart vine: *Clerodendrum Thomsoniae.*
Blimbing: *Averrhoa Bilimbi, A. Carambola.*
Blite, strawberry: *Chenopodium capitatum.*
Blond Lilian: *Erythronium albidum.*
Bloodberry: *Rivina humilis.*
Bloodflower: *Asclepias curassavica.*
Bloodleaf: *Iresine.*
Bloodroot: *Sanguinaria.*
Blood-trumpet: *Distictis buccinatoria.*
Bloodwood
  Red: *Eucalyptus gummifera, E. ptychocarpa.*
  Swamp: *E. ptychocarpa.*
  Yellow: *E. eximia.*
Bloodwood tree: *Haematoxylum campechianum.*
Bloodwort, burnet: *Sanguisorba officinalis.*
Bloody-butcher: *Trillium recurvatum.*
Blow-balls: *Taraxacum.*
Bluebeard: *Caryopteris.*
Bluebell: *Campanula rotundifolia;* see also Bluebells.
  California: *Phacelia campanularia.*
  Clanwilliam: *Ixia incarnata.*
  English: *Endymion non-scriptus.*
  Spanish: *Endymion hispanicus.*
Bluebell creeper: *Sollya heterophylla.*
  Australian: *S. heterophylla.*
Bluebells: *Mertensia, M. virginica.*
  Australian: *Sollya heterophylla.*
  Virginia: *Mertensia virginica.*
Blueberry: *Vaccinium.*
  Black highbush: *V. atrococcum.*
  Creeping: *V. crassifolium.*
  Elliott's: *V. Elliottii.*
  Highbush: *V. corymbosum.*
  Late sweet: *V. angustifolium.*
  Low: *V. vacillans.*
  Lowbush: *V. angustifolium.*
  Low sweet: *V. angustifolium, V. vacillans.*
  Male: *Lyonia ligustrina.*
  Rabbit-eye: *Vaccinium Ashei.*
  Sourtop: *V. myrtilloides.*
  Swamp: *V. corymbosum.*
  Velvet-leaf: *V. myrtilloides.*
  Western: *V. occidentale.*
Bluebird vine: *Petrea.*
Blue-blade: *Opuntia violacea* var. *santa-rita.*
Blueblossom: *Ceanothus thyrsiflorus.*
  Creeping: *C. thyrsiflorus* var. *repens.*
Bluebonnet, Texas: *Lupinus subcarnosus, L. texensis.*

Bluebottle: *Centaurea Cyanus.*
Bluebush: *Eucalyptus macrocarpa.*
Blue-buttons: *Knautia arvensis, Vinca major.*
Blue-candle: *Myrtillocactus geometrizans.*
Blue-chalksticks: *Senecio serpens.*
Blue-curls: *Trichostema, Phacelia congesta.*
  San Joaquin: *Trichostema ovatum, T. Parishii.*
  Woolly: *T. lanatum.*
Blue-devil: *Echium vulgare.*
Blue-dicks: *Dichelostemma pulchellum.*
Blue-eyed Mary: *Collinsia verna.*
Blue-flame: *Myrtillocactus geometrizans.*
Bluegrass: *Poa.*
  Annual: *P. annua.*
  Big: *P. ampla.*
  Bulbous: *P. bulbosa.*
  Canada: *P. compressa.*
  English: *Festuca elatior.*
  Kentucky: *Poa pratensis.*
  Rough: *P. trivialis.*
  Rough-stalk: *P. trivialis.*
  Sandberg: *P. secunda.*
  Texas: *P. arachnifera.*
  Wood: *P. nemoralis.*
Bluehearts: *Buchnera.*
Bluejack: *Quercus incana.*
Blue-sailors: *Cichorium Intybus.*
Bluestar: *Amsonia.*
Bluestem: *Andropogon.*
  Angleton: *Dichanthium aristatum.*
  Australian: *Bothriochloa intermedia.*
  Big: *Andropogon Gerardii.*
  Caucasion: *Bothriochloa caucasica.*
  Diaz: *Dichanthium annulatum.*
  Little: *Schizachyrium scoparium.*
  Sand: *Andropogon Hallii.*
  Turkestan: *Bothriochloa Ischaemum.*
  Yellow: *B. Ischaemum.*
Bluet: see also Bluets.
  Mountain: *Centaurea montana.*
Blue-tangle: *Gaylussacia frondosa.*
Bluets: *Hedyotis, H. caerulea.*
  Creeping: *H. Michauxii.*
Blueweed: *Echium vulgare.*
Bluewings: *Torenia Fournieri.*
Blushing-bride: *Serruria florida.*
Blushwort: *Aeschynanthus.*
Bogbean: *Menyanthes.*
Bog-candle: *Habenaria dilatata.*
Bogmat: *Wolffiella floridana.*
Bog-stars: *Parnassia.*
Bog-torch: *Habenaria nivea.*
Bolbonac: *Lunaria annua.*
Boldo: *Peumus Boldus.*
Bombax, Gold Coast: *Bombax buonopozense.*
Bommara, hairy: *Bommeria hispida.*
Boneset: *Eupatorium, E. perfoliatum, Symphytum officinale.*
  Blue: *Eupatorium coelestinum.*
  Common: *E. perfoliatum.*
Boobyalla: *Myoporum insulare.*
Boojum tree: *Idria columnaris.*
Borage: *Borago.*
  Country: *Coleus amboinicus.*
  Indian: *C. amboinicus.*
Borecole: *Brassica oleracea,* Acephala Group.
Boree, weeping: *Acacia vestita.*
Boronia, scented: *Boronia megastigma.*
Botanical-wonder: ×*Fatshedera.*
Bo tree: *Ficus religiosa.*
Botterboom: *Cotyledon paniculata.*
Bottlebrush: *Callistemon, Melaleuca, Metrosideros.*
  Crimson: *Callistemon citrinus.*
  Natal: *Greyia.*
  One-sided: *Calothamnus.*
  Weeping: *Callistemon viminalis.*
Bottle plant, Australian: *Jatropha podagrica.*
Bottle tree: *Brachychiton.*
  Broad-leaved: *B. australis.*
  Chinese: *Firmiana simplex.*
  Flame: *Brachychiton acerifolius.*
  Narrow-leaved *B. rupestris.*
  Queensland: *B. rupestris.*
  Scrub: *B. discolor.*

Bouncing Bet: *Saponaria officinalis.*
Bower plant: *Pandorea jasminoides.*
Bowman's-root: *Gillenia trifoliata, Veronicastrum virginicum.*
Bowwood: *Maclura pomifera.*
Box: *Buxus;* see also Boxwood.
  Apple: *Eucalyptus Bridgesiana.*
  Bimble: *E. populnea.*
  Black: *E. largiflorens, E. rariflora.*
  Bosisto's: *E. Bosistoana.*
  Brisbane: *Tristania conferta.*
  Chinese: *Murraya paniculata.*
  Common: *Buxus sempervirens.*
  Crimson mallee: *Eucalyptus Lansdowneana.*
  Edging: *Buxus sempervirens* cv. 'Suffruticosa'.
  Flooded: *Eucalyptus microtheca.*
  Gray: *E. moluccana.*
  Kimberley gray: *E. argillacea.*
  Marmalade: *Genipa americana.*
  Mountain: *Arctostaphylos Uva-ursi.*
  Running: *Mitchella repens.*
  Sweet: *Sarcococca, S. ruscifolia.*
  Victorian: *Pittosporum undulatum.*
  White: *Eucalyptus albens.*
  Yellow: *E. melliodora.*
Boxing-glove: *Opuntia fulgida* var. *mamillata.*
Boxwood: *Buxus;* see also Box.
  African: *Myrsine africana.*
  Japanese: *Buxus microphylla* var. *japonica.*
  Korean: *B. microphylla* var. *koreana.*
  Oregon: *Paxistima Myrsinites.*
Boxwood tree, African: *Treculia africana.*
Boysenberry: *Rubus ursinus* var. *loganobaccus* cv. 'Boysen'.
Bracken: *Pteridium, P. aquilinum.*
  Australian: *Pteris tremula.*
  Giant: *P. tripartita.*
Brain plant: *Calathea Makoyana.*
Brake: *Pteridium, P. aquilinum, Pteris.*
  Australian: *Pteris tremula.*
  Australian cliff: *Pellaea falcata.*
  Bird's-foot cliff: *Pellaea mucronata.*
  Brewer's cliff: *Pellaea Breweri.*
  Bridges' cliff: *Pellaea Bridgesii.*
  Canker: *Polystichum acrostichoides.*
  Chinese: *Pteris multifida.*
  Cliff: *Pellaea.*
  Cretan: *Pteris cretica.*
  Fragile cliff: *Cryptogramma Stelleri.*
  Green cliff: *Pellaea viridis.*
  Hog-pasture: *Pteridium aquilinum.*
  Ladder: *Pteris vittata.*
  New Zealand cliff: *Pellaea rotundifolia.*
  Pasture: *Pteridium aquilinum.*
  Purple cliff: *Pellaea atropurpurea.*
  Rock: *Cryptogramma.*
  Sierra cliff: *Pellaea brachyptera.*
  Slender cliff: *Cryptogramma Stelleri.*
  Smooth cliff: *Pellaea glabella.*
  Spider: *Pteris multifida.*
  Striped: *Pteris quadriaurita* cv. 'Agyraea'.
  Sword: *Pteris ensiformis.*
  Toothed: *Pteris dentata.*
  Victoria: *Pteris ensiformis* cv. 'Victoriae'.
Bramble: *Rubus.*
  Arctic: *R. arcticus.*
  Crimson: *R. arcticus.*
  Dog: *Ribes cynosbati.*
Brank: *Fagopyrum esculentum.*
Braschette: *Brassica oleracea,* Acephala Group.
Brass-buttons: *Cotula coronopifolia.*
Brazilian-firecracker: *Manettia inflata.*
Brazilian-plume: *Justicia carnea.*
Brazil nut: *Bertholletia excelsa.*
Brazilwood: *Caesalpinia echinata, C. Sappan.*
  False: *C. peltophoroides.*
Breadfruit: *Artocarpus altilis, Pandanus odoratissimus.*
  African: *Treculia africana.*
  Mexican: *Monstera deliciosa.*
Breadfruit tree: *Treculia africana.*
Breadfruit vine: *Monstera deliciosa.*
Breadnut: *Artocarpus altilis, Brosimum Alicastrum.*
Breadroot: *Psoralea esculenta.*
  Indian: *P. esculenta.*

Bread tree: *Encephalartos Altensteinii.*
  African: *Treculia africana.*
Breath-of-Heaven: *Diosma ericoides.*
Briar: see Brier.
Bridal-bouquet: *Porana paniculata.*
Bridal-robe: *Tripleurospermum maritimum* subsp. *inodorum.*
Bridal-wreath: *Francoa ramosa, Spiraea, S. prunifolia, S. ×Vanhout-tei.*
Bride's-bonnet: *Clintonia uniflora.*
Brier, Briar: *Rosa, Rubus, Smilax.*
  Austrian: *Rosa foetida.*
  Austrian copper: *Rosa foetida.*
  Bull: see Bullbrier.
  Cat: see Catbrier.
  Dog: *Rosa canina.*
  Green: see Greenbrier.
  Hag: see Hagbrier.
  Horse: *Smilax rotundifolia.*
  Jackson: *S. lanceolata.*
  Saw: *S. glauca.*
  Sensitive: *Schrankia.*
  Sweet: see Sweetbrier.
Brittlebush: *Encelia farinosa.*
Broccoli: *Brassica oleracea,* Botrytis Group; *B. septiceps;* see also *B. Rapa,* Rapifera Group.
  Asparagus: *B. oleracea,* Italica Group.
  Italian: *B. oleracea,* Italica Group.
  Sprouting: *B. oleracea,* Italica Group.
  Turnip: *B. Rapa,* Ruvo Group.
Brodiaea
  Golden: *Triteleia ixioides.*
  Harvest: *Brodiaea coronaria, B. elegans.*
  Twining: *Dichelostemma volubile.*
Brome: *Bromus.*
  California: *B. carinatus.*
  Erect: *B. erectus.*
  Fringed: *B. ciliatus.*
  Mediterranean: *B. lanceolatus.*
  Mountain: *B. marginatus.*
  Prairie: *B. unioloides.*
  Rescue: *B. unioloides.*
  Smooth: *B. inermis.*
Bromeliad: any of the Bromeliaceae.
  Blushing: *Neoregelia Carolinae, Nidularium fulgens.*
Bromeliad-king: *Vriesia hieroglyphica.*
Brooklime: *Veronica.*
  American: *V. americana.*
  European: *V. Beccabunga.*
Brookweed: *Samolus.*
Broom: *Cytisus, Genista.*
  Chaparral: *Baccharis pilularis.*
  Dyer's: *Genista tinctoria.*
  Mount Etna: *G. aethnensis.*
  Normandy: *Cytisus scoparius* cv. 'Andreanus'.
  Pink: *Notospartium.*
  Portuguese: *Cytisus albus.*
  Scotch: *C. scoparius.*
  Southern: *Notospartium.*
  Spanish: *Genista hispanica, Spartium junceum.*
  Turpentine: *Thamnosma montana.*
  Warminster: *Cytisus ×praecox.*
  Weaver's: *Spartium junceum.*
  White Spanish: *Cytisus multiflorus.*
Broombrush: *Hypericum prolificum.*
Broomcorn: *Panicum miliaceum; Sorghum bicolor,* Technicum Group.
Broomweed: *Gutierrezia.*
Bronze-shower: *Cassia moschata.*
Browallia: *Streptosolen Jamesonii.*
Brown-barrel: *Eucalyptus fastigiata.*
Brown Beth: *Trillium erectum.*
Brussels sprouts: *Brassica oleracea,* Gemmifera Group.
Bryony: *Bryonia.*
  Red: *B. dioica.*
  White: *B. alba.*
Buchu: *Agathosma betulina, A. crenulata, Diosma ericoides.*
Buckbean: *Menyanthes.*
Buckbrush: *Ceanothus cuneatus.*
Buckeye: *Aesculus, A. parviflora.*
  Bottlebrush: *A. parviflora.*
  California: *A. californica.*
  False: *Ungnadia speciosa.*
  Mexican: *U. speciosa.*

Buckeye—*Continued*
  Ohio: *Aesculus glabra.*
  Red: *A. Pavia.*
  Spanish: *Ungnadia speciosa.*
  Sweet: *Aesculus octandra.*
  Texan: *Ungnadia speciosa.*
  Yellow: *Aesculus octandra.*
Buckhorn: *Osmunda cinnamomea, Plantago lanceolata.*
Buckrams: *Allium ursinum.*
Buckthorn: *Rhamnus, Bumelia lycioides.*
  Alder: *Rhamnus Frangula.*
  Alpine: *R. alpina.*
  Carniolan: *R. fallax.*
  Carolina: *R. caroliniana.*
  Common: *R. cathartica.*
  False: *Bumelia lanuginosa.*
  Italian: *Rhamnus Alaternus.*
  Rock: *R. saxatilis.*
  Sea: *Hippophae.*
  Southern: *Bumelia lycioides.*
Buckwheat: *Fagopyrum, F. esculentum.*
  California: *Eriogonum fasciculatum.*
  Kangra: *Fagopyrum tataricum.*
  Notch-seeded: *F. esculentum.*
  Saffron: *Eriogonum crocatum.*
  Tartarian: *Fagopyrum tataricum.*
  Wild: *Eriogonum.*
Buckwheat brush: *Cliftonia monophylla.*
Buckwheat tree: *Cliftonia monophylla.*
Buddha's-belly: *Bambusa ventricosa.*
Buddleia, orange-eye: *Buddleia Davidii.*
Buffalo berry: *Shepherdia argentea, S. canadensis.*
  Silver: *S. argentea.*
Buffalo-horn: *Burchellia bubalina.*
Bugbane: *Cimicifuga.*
  American: *C. americana.*
  False: *Trautvetteria.*
  Mountain: *Cimicifuga americana.*
Bugler, royal-red: *Aeschynanthus pulcher.*
Bugleweed: *Ajuga, Lycopus.*
  Carpet: *A. reptans.*
Bugloss: *Anchusa, A. officinalis.*
  Siberian: *Brunnera macrophylla.*
  Viper's: *Echium.*
Bullace: *Prunus insititia, Vitis rotundifolia.*
Bullbrier: *Smilax rotundifolia.*
Bullick: *Eucalyptus megacarpa.*
Bullock's-heart: *Annona reticulata.*
Bulrush: *Scirpus, Typha, T. latifolia.*
  Great: *Scirpus validus.*
  (of the Bible): *Cyperus Papyrus.*
  Small: *Typha angustifolia.*
  Soft-stem: *Scirpus validus.*
Bumelia, gum: *Bumelia lanuginosa.*
Bunchberry: *Cornus canadensis.*
Bunchflower: *Melanthium virginicum.*
Bundy: *Eucalyptus goniocalyx.*
Bunny-ears: *Opuntia microdasys.*
  Red: *O. microdasys* var. *rufida.*
  Yellow: *O. microdasys.*
Bunya-bunya: *Araucaria Bidwillii.*
Burdock: *Arctium.*
  Common: *A. minus.*
  Great: *A. Lappa.*
Burhead: *Echinodorus.*
Burnet: *Sanguisorba, Poterium Sanguisorba.*
  Canadian: *Sanguisorba canadensis.*
  Garden: *Poterium Sanguisorba.*
  Great: *Sanguisorba officinalis.*
Bur, New Zealand: *Acaena anserinifolia.*
Burning bush: *Combretum microphyllum, Dictamnus albus, Euonymus atropurpurea, Kochia scoparia* var. *culta.*
  Western: *Euonymus occidentalis.*
Burnut: *Tribulus terrestris.*
Burro-fat: *Cleome Isomeris.*
Bursting-heart: *Euonymus americana.*
Burstwort: *Herniaria.*
Bush fruit, Chinese: *Prunus tomentosa.*
Bushman's-poison: *Acokanthera.*
Busy Lizzy: *Impatiens Wallerana.*
Butcher's-broom: *Ruscus aculeatus.*
  Climbing: *Semele.*
Butter-and-eggs: *Linaria vulgaris.*

Butterbur: *Petasites.*
  White: *P. albus.*
Buttercup: *Ranunculus.*
  Bermuda: *Oxalis Pes-caprae.*
  Bulbous: *Ranunculus bulbosus.*
  Colombia: *Oncidium cheirophorum.*
  Common: *Ranunculus acris.*
  Creeping: *R. repens.*
  Early: *R. fascicularis.*
  Persian: *Ranunculus asiaticus.*
  Tall: *R. acris.*
  Yellow water: *R. flabellaris.*
Butter-cup, Krishna's: *Ficus benghalensis* cv. 'Krishnae'.
Butterfly bush: *Buddleia.*
Butterfly flower: *Asclepias, Bauhinia monandra, Schizanthus.*
Butterfly tree: *Bauhinia purpurea.*
Butterfly vine: *Stigmaphyllon ciliatum.*
Butterfly weed: *Asclepias tuberosa.*
Butternut: *Bertholletia excelsa, Cucurbita moschata, Juglans cinerea.*
  Chinese: *Juglans cathayensis.*
Butter-print: *Abutilon Theophrasti.*
Butterwort: *Pinguicula.*
Buttonball: *Platanus occidentalis.*
Buttonbush: *Cephalanthus.*
Button flower: *Hibbertia.*
Buttons-on-a-string: *Crassula rupestris.*
Buttonwood: *Conocarpus erectus, Platanus, P. occidentalis.*
  Silver: *Conocarpus erectus* var. *sericeus.*

Cabbage: *Brassica oleracea,* Capitata Group.
  Celery: *B. Rapa,* Pekinensis Group.
  Chinese: *B. Rapa,* Pekinensis Group.
  Cow: *B. oleracea,* Acephala Group.
  Deer: *Fauria Crista-galli.*
  Flowering: *Brassica oleracea,* Acephala Group.
  Head: *B. oleracea,* Capitata Group.
  John's: *Hydrophyllum virginianum.*
  Portuguese: *Brassica oleracea,* Tronchuda Group.
  Savoy: see *B. oleracea,* Capitata Group.
  Skunk: *Lysichiton americanum, Symplocarpus foetidus, Veratrum californicum.*
  Tronchuda: *Brassica oleracea,* Tronchuda Group.
  Western skunk: *Lysichiton americanum.*
  Wild: *Brassica oleracea.*
  Yellow skunk: *Lysichiton americanum.*
Cabbage bark: *Andira inermis.*
Cabbage tree: *Andira inermis, Cordyline australis, Cussonia paniculata, C. spicata, Sabal Palmetto.*
  Little: *Cussonia paniculata.*
Cacao: *Theobroma Cacao.*
Cactus
  Agave: *Leuchtenbergia principis.*
  Apple: *Cereus peruvianus.*
  Ball: *Notocactus.*
  Barrel: *Echinocactus Grusonii, Echinopsis multiplex, Ferocactus.*
  Bird's-nest cactus: *Mammillaria camptotricha.*
  Blue barrel: *Ferocactus glaucescens.*
  Brain: *Echinofossulocactus.*
  Burbank's spineless: see *Opuntia Ficus-indica.*
  Button: *Epithelantha, E. micromeris.*
  Candelabra: *Euphorbia lactea, Lemaireocereus Weberi.*
  Cane: *Opuntia cylindrica.*
  Chain: *Rhipsalis paradoxa.*
  Chain-link: *Opuntia imbricata.*
  Chin: *Gymnocalycium.*
  Cholla: *Opuntia.*
  Christmas: *Schlumbergera Bridgesii.*
  Cinnamon: *Opuntia microdasys* var. *rufida.*
  Claw: *Schlumbergera truncata.*
  Club: *Opuntia fulgida* var. *mamillata.*
  Cob: *Lobivia.*
  Colombian ball: *Wigginsia Vorwerkiana.*
  Comb: *Pachycereus pecten-aboriginum.*
  Coral: *Mammillaria Heyderi, Rhipsalis cereuscula.*
  Cotton-pole: *Opuntia vestita.*
  Cow-tongue: *Gasteria.*
  Crab: *Schlumbergera truncata.*
  Creeping-devil: *Lemaireocereus Eruca.*
  Crown: *Rebutia.*
  Cushion: *Opuntia floccosa.*
  Dagger: *Lemaireocereus gummosus.*
  Dancing-bones: *Hatiora salicornioides.*
  Devil: *Opuntia Schottii.*

Cactus—*Continued*
  Dollar: *O. violacea* var. *santa-rita.*
  Dumpling: *Lophophora Williamsii.*
  Dutchman's-pipe: *Epiphyllum oxypetalum.*
  Easter: *Rhipsalidopsis Gaertneri.*
  Easter-lily: *Echinopsis multiplex.*
  Electrode: *Ferocactus histrix.*
  Eve's-pin: *Opuntia subulata.*
  False: *Euphorbia lactea.*
  Feather: *Mammillaria plumosa.*
  Fire-crown: *Rebutia senilis.*
  Fishbone: *Epiphyllum anguliger.*
  Fishhook: *Ancistrocactus Scheeri, Ferocactus, F. Wislizenii, Mammillaria.*
  Fishhook pincushion: *Mammillaria Wildii.*
  Flapjack: *Opuntia chlorotica, O. Gosseliana.*
  Frilled lace: *Echinocereus Reichenbachii* var. *Fitchii.*
  Giant: *Carnegiea gigantea.*
  Golden ball: *Notocactus Leninghousii.*
  Golden barrrel: *Echinocactus Grusonii.*
  Golden bird's-nest: *Mammillaria camptotricha.*
  Golden-star: *M. elongata.*
  Gold lace: *M. elongata.*
  Golf-ball: *Coryphantha vivipara* var. *bisbeeana.*
  Grizzly-bear: *Opuntia erinacea* var. *ursina.*
  Hairbrush: *Pachycereus pecten-aboriginum.*
  Hatchet: *Pelecyphora.*
  Hatpin: *Ferocactus rectispinus.*
  Hat-rack: *Euphorbia lactea.*
  Hedgehog: *Echinocereus.*
  Hook: *Ancistrocactus.*
  Hot-dog: *Senecio articulatus.*
  Joseph's-coat: *Opuntia vulgaris* cv. 'Variegata'.
  Jumping: *O. fulgida.*
  Lace: *Echinocereus Reichenbachii, Mammillaria elongata.*
  Lamb's-tail: *Wilcoxia Schmollii.*
  Large barrel: *Echinocactus ingens.*
  Leaf: *Pereskia.*
  Leafy: *P. aculeata.*
  Living-rock: *Ariocarpus, Pleiospilos Bolusii.*
  Melon: *Melocactus communis.*
  Mexican dwarf tree: *Opuntia vilis.*
  Mistletoe: *Rhipsalis Cassutha.*
  Moon: *Harrisia Jusbertii, Selenicereus.*
  Mule-crippler: *Echinocactus horizonthalonius.*
  Myrtle: *Myrtillocactus.*
  New old-man: *Espostoa lanata.*
  Nipple: *Mammillaria longimamma* var. *uberiformis.*
  Old-lady: *M. Hahniana.*
  Old-man: *Cephalocereus senilis.*
  Old-woman: *Mammillaria Hahniana.*
  Orchid: *Epiphyllum.*
  Organ-pipe: *Lemaireocereus marginatus, L. Thurberi.*
  Paper: *Opuntia articulata* cv. 'Syringacantha'.
  Peanut: *Chamaecereus Sylvestri.*
  Pencil: *Opuntia ramosissima.*
  Peruvian apple: *Cereus peruvianus.*
  Peruvian torch: *Trichocereus peruvianus.*
  Plain: *Gymnocalycium Mihanovichii.*
  Polka-dot: *Opuntia microdasys* cv. 'Albispina'.
  Pond-lily: *Epiphyllum, Nopalxochia phyllanthoides.*
  Popcorn: *Rhipsalis cereuscula, R. Warmingiana.*
  Porcupine: *Opuntia erinacea* var. *hystricina.*
  Powder-puff: *Mammillaria bocasana.*
  Prism: *Leuchtenbergia principis.*
  Rainbow: *Echinocereus pectinatus* var. *neomexicanus.*
  Rattail: *Aporocactus flagelliformis.*
  Redbird: *Pedilanthus tithymaloides.*
  Red orchid: *Nopalxochia Ackermannii.*
  Ribbon: *Pedilanthus tithymaloides.*
  Rose: *Pereskia grandifolia.*
  Scarlet ball: *Notocactus Haselbergii.*
  Scarlet crown: *Rebutia grandiflora.*
  Sea-urchin: *Astrophytum asterias, Echinopsis.*
  Serpent: *Nyctocereus serpentinus.*
  Silver ball; *Notocactus Scopa.*
  Silver cluster: *Mammillaria prolifera.*
  Snake: *Nyctocereus serpentinus.*
  Snowball; *Espostoa lanata, Mammillaria bocasana, Pediocactus Simpsonii.*
  Snowdrop: *Rhipsalis Houlletiana.*
  Spice: *Hatiora salicornioides.*
  Spider: *Gymnocalycium denudatum.*

Cactus—*Continued*
Spineless: *Opuntia Ficus-indica.*
Star: *Ariocarpus fissuratus* var. *fissuratus, Astrophytum, A. ornatum, Haworthia.*
Starfish: *Stapelia variegata.*
Strawberry: *Echinocereus enneacanthus, Ferocactus setispinus, Mammillaria.*
Sun: *Heliocereus speciosus.*
Teddy-bear: *Opuntia Bigelovii.*
Thanksgiving: *Schlumbergera truncata.*
Thimble: *Mammillaria fragilis.*
Toad: *Stapelia variegata.*
Toothpick: *Stetsonia coryne.*
Torch: *Trichocereus Spachianus.*
Tortoise: *Deamia testudo.*
Totem-pole: *Lophocereus Schottii* cv. 'Monstrosus'.
Turk's-cap: *Melocactus communis, M. intortus.*
Turk's-head: *M. communis.*
Unguentine: *Aloe barbadensis.*
Vine: *Fouquieria splendens.*
Whisker: *Lophocereus Schottii.*
White chin: *Gymnocalycium Schickendantzii.*
White torch: *Trichocereus Spachianus.*
Wickerware: *Rhipsalis.*
Woolly torch: *Cephalocereus Palmeri.*
Yoke: *Schlumbergera truncata.*
Cafta: *Catha edulis.*
Caimito: *Chrysophyllum Cainito.*
Cajan: *Cajanus Cajan.*
Cajeput tree: *Umbellularia californica.*
Calabash: *Crescentia Cujete.*
Black: *Enallagma latifolia.*
Sweet: *Passiflora maliformis.*
Calabash tree: *Crescentia Cujete.*
Calabazilla: *Cucurbita foetidissima.*
Calabur: *Muntingia Calabura.*
Caladium
Black: *Colocasia esculenta* var. *illustris.*
Fancy-leaved: *Caladium ×hortulanum.*
Giant: *Alocasia cuprea.*
Calamint: *Calamintha.*
Calamondin: *×Citrofortunella mitis.*
Calamus: *Acorus Calamus.*
Calico bush: *Kalmia latifolia.*
Calico flower: *Aristolochia elegans.*
Calico-hearts: *Adromischus maculatus.*
Calico plant: *Alternanthera ficoides* cv. 'Bettzickiana'.
Calisaya: *Cinchona Calisaya.*
Calla: *Zantedeschia.*
Black: *Arum pictum, A. palaestinum.*
Black-throated: *Zantedeschia albomaculata, Z. melanoleuca.*
Common: *Z. aethiopica.*
Florist's: *Z. aethiopica.*
Garden: *Z. aethiopica.*
Golden: *Z. Elliottiana.*
Miniature: *Callopsis Volkensii.*
Pink: *Zantedeschia Rehmannii.*
Red: *Sauromatum guttatum.*
Spotted: *Zantedeschia albo-maculata.*
Wild: *Calla palustris.*
Yellow: *Zantedeschia Elliottiana.*
Calliopsis: *Coreopsis tinctoria.*
Caltrop: *Tribulus.*
Water; *Trapa natans.*
Camas, Camass: *Camassia.*
Common: *C. Quamash.*
Death: *Zigadenus, Z. Nuttallii, Z. venenosus.*
Eastern: *Camassia scilloides.*
Grassy death: *Zigadenus venenosus* var. *gramineus.*
Poison: *Z. Nuttallii.*
White: *Z. elegans, Z. glaucus.*
Camosh: *Camassia Quamash.*
Camellia: *Camellia.*
Common: *C. japonica.*
Mountain: *Stewartia ovata.*
Sasanqua: *Camellia Sasanqua.*
Silky: *Stewartia Malacodendron.*
Camphor tree: *Cinnamomum Camphora.*
Campion: *Lychnis, Silene.*
Bladder: *Silene vulgaris.*
Evening: *S. alba.*
Mexican: *S. laciniata.*
Morning: *S. dioica.*

Campion—*Continued*
Moss: *S. acaulis.*
Red: *S. dioica.*
Rose: *Lychnis Coronaria.*
Starry: *Silene stellata.*
White: *S. alba.*
Camwood: *Baphia racemosa.*
Caña brava: *Arundo Donax.*
Canaigre: *Rumex hymenosepalus.*
Canary-bird bush: *Crotolaria agatiflora.*
Canary-bird flower: *Tropaeolum peregrinum.*
Canary-bird vine: *Tropaeolum peregrinum.*
Canary creeper: *Tropaeolum peregrinum.*
Cancerweed: *Salvia lyrata.*
Candelabra plant: *Aloe arborescens.*
Candelilla: *Euphorbia antisyphilitica.*
Candleberry: *Myrica cerifera, M. pensylvanica.*
Swamp: *M. pensylvanica.*
Candleberry tree: *Aleurites moluccana.*
Candlenut: *Aleurites moluccana.*
Candlenut tree: *Aleurites moluccana.*
Candle plant: *Plectranthus Oertendahlii, Senecio articulatus.*
Empress: *Cassia alata.*
Candle tree: *Parmentiera cereifera.*
Candytuft: *Iberis.*
Edging: *I. sempervirens.*
Gibraltar: *I. gibraltarica.*
Globe: *I. umbellata.*
Rocket: *I. amara.*
Candyweed: *Polygala lutea.*
Cane: *Arundinaria.*
Arrow: *Gynerium sagittatum.*
Chinese sweet: *Saccharum sinense.*
Dumb: *Dieffenbachia.*
Rattan: *Calamus Rotang.*
Southern: *Arundinaria gigantea.*
Spotted dumb: *Dieffenbachia maculata.*
Sugar: see Sugarcane.
Switch: *Arundinaria tecta.*
Tobago: *Bactris guineensis.*
Tonkin: *Arundinaria amabilis.*
Tsingli: *A. amabilis.*
Wild: *Gynerium sagittatum.*
Yellow-leaf dumb: *Dieffenbachia maculata* cv. 'Rudolf Roehrs'.
Canistel: *Pouteria campechiana.*
Cankerroot: *Coptis groenlandica.*
Canna: *Canna.*
Common garden: *C. ×generalis.*
Edible: *C. edulis.*
Orchid-flowered: *C. ×orchiodes.*
Cannonball tree: *Couroupita guianensis.*
Cantaloupe: *Cucumis Melo,* Cantalupensis Group.
Canterbury-bells: *Campanula Medium.*
Caoutchouc tree: *Hevea brasiliensis.*
Caper: *Capparis spinosa.*
Caper bush: *Capparis, C. spinosa.*
Caper tree, Jamaica: *Capparis cynophallophora.*
Capeweed: *Phyla nodiflora.*
Caracol: *Vigna Caracalla.*
Caramba: *Averrhoa Carambola.*
Carambola: *Averrhoa Carambola.*
Caraway: *Carum Carvi.*
Edible-rooted: *Perideridia Gairdneri.*
False: *P. Gairdneri.*
Indian: *P. Gairdneri.*
Cardamom: *Elettaria Cardamomum.*
Ceylon: *E. Cardamomum.*
Malabar: *E. Cardamomum.*
Round: *Amomum compactum, A. Kepulaga.*
Cardinal climber: *Ipomoea ×multifida, I. Quamoclit.*
Cardinal flower: *Lobelia Cardinalis, Sinningia cardinalis.*
Blue: *Lobelia siphilitica.*
Cardinal's-guard: *Pachystachys coccinea.*
Cardinal-spear: *Erythrina herbacea.*
Cardo-del-valle: *Centaurea americana.*
Cardoon: *Cynara cardunculus.*
Carib wood: *Sabinea carinalis.*
Caricature plant: *Graptophyllum pictum.*
Carmel creeper: *Ceanothus griseus* var. *horizontalis.*
Carnation: *Dianthus Caryophyllus.*
Carnaval: *Cassia Carnaval.*
Caroá: *Neoglaziovia variegata.*
Carob: *Ceratonia Siliqua.*

Carpenter's-square: *Scrophularia marilandica.*
Carpet plant: *Episcia.*
  Corsican: *Soleirolia Soleirolii.*
Carrion flower: *Smilax herbacea, Stapelia.*
Carrizo: *Arundo Donax, Phragmites australis.*
Carrot: *Daucus Carota* var. *sativus.*
  Peruvian: *Arracacia xanthorrhiza.*
  Wild: *Daucus Carota* var. *Carota.*
Cart-track plant: *Plantago major.*
Cascara sagrada: *Rhamnus Purshiana.*
Cashew: *Anacardium occidentale.*
Cashew nut: *Anacardium occidentale.*
Cassabanana: *Benincasa hispida, Sicana odorifera.*
Cassandra: *Chamaedaphne calyculata.*
Cassava: *Manihot esculenta.*
  Bitter: *M. esculenta.*
  Sweet: *M. dulcis.*
Cassena: *Ilex Cassine, I. vomitoria.*
Cassia: *Cassia, Cinnamomum Cassia.*
  Apple-blossom: *Cassia javanica.*
  Desert: *C. nemophila.*
  Feathery: *C. artemisioides.*
  Golden: *C. fasciculata.*
  Horse: *C. grandis.*
  Ringworm: *C. alata.*
  Tanner's: *C. auriculata.*
Cassia-bark tree: *Cinnamomum Cassia.*
Cassia-flower tree: *Cinnamomum Loureirii.*
Cassie: *Acacia Farnesiana.*
Cassie-oil plant: *Acacia Farnesiana.*
Cassina, Cassine: *Ilex Cassine, I. vomitoria.*
Cast-iron plant: *Aspidistra elatior.*
Castor-oil plant: *Ricinus communis.*
Catalpa: *Catalpa.*
  Chinese: *C. ovata.*
  Common: *C. bignonioides.*
  Hybrid: *C. ×hybrida.*
  Western: *C. speciosa.*
Catawba: *Catalpa, C. speciosa.*
Catberry: *Nemopanthus mucronatus.*
Catbrier: *Smilax.*
  Common: *S. Rotundifolia.*
Catchfly: *Lychnis, Silene.*
  Berry: *Cucubalus.*
  Garden: *Silene Armeria.*
  German: *Lychnis Viscaria.*
  Night-flowering: *Silene noctiflora.*
  Nodding: *S. pendula.*
  Nottingham: *S. nutans.*
  Royal: *S. regia.*
  Sleepy: *S. antirrhina.*
  Spanish: *S. Otites.*
  Sweet William: *S. Armeria.*
Catclaw: *Schrankia Nuttallii.*
Catechu: *Acacia Catechu, Areca Catechu.*
Catgut: *Tephrosia virginiana.*
Cathedral-windows: *Calathea Makoyana.*
Catherine-wheel: *Haemanthus Katharinae.*
Catjang: *Vigna unguiculata* subsp. *cylindrica.*
Catmint: *Nepeta, N. Cataria.*
Catnip: *Nepeta Cataria.*
Cat's-breeches: *Hydrophyllum capitatum.*
Cat's-claw: *Macfadyena Unguis-cati, Pithecellobium Unguis-cati.*
Cat's-claw creeper: *Macfadyena Unguis-cati.*
Cat's-claw-trumpet: *Macfadyena Unguis-cati.*
Cat's-ear: *Calochortus coeruleus, Hypochoeris.*
  Spotted: *Hypochoeris radicata.*
Cat's-whiskers: *Tacca Chantrieri.*
Cattail: *Typha.*
  Common: *T. latifolia.*
  Narrow-leaved: *T. angustifolia.*
  Red: *Acalypha hispida.*
  Red-hot: *Acalypha hispida.*
Cattleya: *Cattleya.*
  Autumn: *C. labiata.*
  Christmas: *C. Percivaliana.*
  Queen: *C. Dowiana.*
  Spring: *C. Mossiae.*
  Summer: *C. Gaskelliana.*
  Tulip: *C. citrina.*
  Virgin's: *C. Mendelii.*
  Winter: *C. Trianaei.*
Cauassú: *Calathea lutea.*

Cauliflower: *Brassica oleracea,* Botrytis Group.
Cauliflower-ears: *Crassula argentea.*
Ceanothus: *Ceanothus.*
  Bolinas Ridge: *C. Masonii.*
  Carmel: *C. griseus* var. *griseus.*
  Catalina: *C. arboreus.*
  Coast: *C. ramulosus.*
  Cup-leaf: *C. Greggii* var. *perplexans.*
  Felt-leaf: *C. arboreus.*
  Green-bark: *C. spinosus.*
  Hoary-leaf: *C. crassifolius.*
  Holly-leaf: *C. purpureus.*
  Lompoc: *C. ramulosus* var. *fascicularis.*
  Monterey: *C. rigidus.*
  Mount Vision: *C. gloriosus* var. *porrectus.*
  Navarro: *C. gloriosus* var. *exaltatus.*
  Nipomo: *C. impressus* var. *nipomensis.*
  Point Reyes: *C. gloriosus.*
  Rincon: *C. confusus.*
  San Diego: *C. cyaneus.*
  Santa Barbara: *C. impressus.*
  Vine Hill: *C. foliosus* var. *vineatus.*
  Wart-leaf: *C. papillosus.*
  Wavy-leaf: *C. foliosus.*
  Woolly-leaf: *C. tomentosus.*
  Yankee Point: *C. griseus* var. *griseus.*
Cedar: *Cedrus.*
  Alaska: *Chamaecyparis nootkatensis.*
  Atlantic white: *Chamaecyparis thyoides.*
  Atlas: *Cedrus atlantica.*
  Barbados: *Cedrela odorata.*
  Bermuda: *Juniperus bermudiana.*
  California incense: *Calocedrus decurrens.*
  Chilean incense: *Austrocedrus chilensis.*
  Cigar-box: *Cedrela odorata.*
  Clanwilliam: *Widdringtonia juniperoides.*
  Colorado red: *Juniperus scopulorum.*
  Creeping: *J. horizontalis.*
  Cyprus: *Cedrus brevifolia.*
  Formosa incense: *Calocedrus formosana.*
  Giant: *Thuja plicata.*
  Ground: *Lycopodium complanatum, L. tristachyum.*
  Incense: *Calocedrus, Libocedrus.*
  Japanese: *Cryptomeria japonica.*
  Mlanje: *Widdringtonia Whytei.*
  Ozark white: *Juniperus Ashei.*
  Pink: *Acrocarpus fraxinifolius.*
  Port Orford: *Chamaecyparis Lawsoniana.*
  Red: *Acrocarpus fraxinifolius, Juniperus virginiana.*
  Russian: *Pinus Cembra.*
  Salt: *Tamarix.*
  Southern red: *Juniperus silicicola.*
  Southern white: *Chamaecyparis thyoides.*
  Spanish: *Cedrela odorata.*
  Stinking: *Torreya taxifolia.*
  Swamp white: *Chamaecyparis thyoides.*
  Western red: *Thuja plicata.*
  West Indian: *Cedrela odorata.*
  White: *Chamaecyparis thyoides, Tabebuia pallida, Thuja occidentalis.*
  Willowmore: *Widdringtonia Schwarzii.*
Cedar-of-Goa: *Cupressus lusitanica.*
Cedar-of-Lebanon: *Cedrus libani.*
Celandine: *Chelidonium.*
  Lesser: *Ranunculus Ficaria.*
  Small: *R. Ficaria.*
  Tree: *Macleaya cordata.*
Celeriac: *Apium graveolens* var. *rapaceum.*
Celery: *Apium graveolens* var. *dulce.*
  Turnip-rooted: *A. graveolens* var. *rapaceum.*
  Water: *Vallisneria americana.*
  Wild: *V. americana.*
Ceniza: *Leucophyllum.*
Cenizo: *Atriplex canescens.*
Centaury: *Centaurium, C. Erythraea, Serratula.*
Centranth: *Centranthus.*
Centipede plant: *Homalocladium platycladum.*
Century plant: *Agave americana.*
  Dwarf: *A. Desmettiana.*
Cereus
  Giant Mexican: *Pachycereus Pringlei.*
  Hedgehog: *Echinocereus.*
  Moon: *Harrisia Martinii, Selenicereus.*

Cereus—*Continued*
 Mountain: *Borzicactus fossulatus.*
 Night-blooming: *Hylocereus undatus, Nyctocereus serpentinus, Peniocereus Greggii, Selenicereus.*
 Powder-blue: *Lemaireocereus pruinosus.*
 Purple hedgehog: *Echinocereus sarissophorus.*
Ceriman: *Monstera deliciosa.*
Cestrum, day-blooming: *Cestrum diurnum.*
Ceylon creeper, golden: *Epipremnum aureum.*
Chaffseed: *Schwalbea.*
Chain-of-love: *Antigonon leptopus.*
Chain plant: *Tradescantia navicularis.*
Chalice vine: *Solandra.*
Chamise: *Adenostoma fasciculatum.*
Chamiso: *Atriplex canescens.*
Chamiza: *Atriplex canescens.*
Chamomile: *Anthemis, Chamaemelum nobile.*
 Garden: *Chamaemelum nobile.*
 Russian: *C. nobile.*
 Stinking: *Anthemis Cotula.*
 Sweet false: *Matricaria recutita.*
Champaca: *Michelia Champaca.*
 Fragrant: *M. Champaca.*
Chanal, Chanar: *Gourliea decorticans.*
Chandelier plant: *Kalanchoe tubiflora.*
Chard: *Beta vulgaris,* Cicla Group.
 Swiss: *B. vulgaris,* Cicla Group.
Charity: *Polemonium caeruleum.*
Charlock: *Brassica Kaber.*
Chaste tree: *Vitex Agnus-castus.*
Chatterbox: *Epipactis gigantea.*
Chayote: *Sechium edule.*
Checkerberry: *Gaultheria procumbens.*
Checkerbloom: *Sidalcea malviflora.*
Cheeses: *Malva sylvestris.*
Chenille plant: *Acalypha hispida, Echeveria leucotricha, E. pulvinata.*
Cherimalla: *Annona Cherimola.*
Cherimoya: *Annona Cherimola.*
Cherry
 Australian brush: *Syzygium paniculatum.*
 Barbados: *Eugenia uniflora;* see also *Malpighia glabra.*
 Bastard: *Ehretia tinifolia.*
 Bird: *Prunus avium, P. pensylvanica, P. Padus.*
 Bitter: *P. emarginata.*
 Black: *P. serotina.*
 Brazil: *Eugenia brasiliensis, E. uniflora.*
 Brush: *Syzygium paniculatum.*
 Catalina: *Prunus Lyonii.*
 Cayenne: *Eugenia uniflora.*
 Choke: see Chokecherry.
 Christmas: *Solanum Pseudocapsicum.*
 Clammy ground: *Physalis heterophylla.*
 Cornelian: *Cornus mas.*
 Downy ground: *Physalis pubescens.*
 Duke: *Prunus* ✕*effusus.*
 Dwarf: *P. pumila.*
 European bird: *P. Padus.*
 European dwarf: *P. fruticosa.*
 European ground: *P. fruticosa.*
 Evergreen: *P. ilicifolia.*
 False Jerusalem: *Solanum Capsicastrum.*
 Fire: *Prunus pensylvanica.*
 Ground: *Physalis, P. peruviana, P. pubescens.*
 Hansen's bush: *Prunus tomentosa.*
 Higan: *P. subhirtella.*
 Holly-leaved: *P. ilicifolia.*
 Indian: *Rhamnus caroliniana.*
 Japanese bush: *Prunus japonica.*
 Japanese cornelian: *Cornus officinalis.*
 Japanese flowering: *Prunus serrulata, P. yedoensis.*
 Jerusalem: *Solanum Pseudocapsicum.*
 Madden: *Maddenia hypoleuca.*
 Morello: *Prunus Cerasus* var. *austera.*
 Naden: *P. serrulata* cv. 'Takasago'.
 Nanking: *P. tomentosa.*
 North Japanese hill: *P. Sargentii.*
 Oregon: *P. emarginata.*
 Oriental: *P. serrulata.*
 Perfumed: *P. Mahaleb.*
 Pie: *P. Cerasus.*
 Pin: *P. pensylvanica.*
 Potomac: *P. yedoensis.*

Cherry—*Continued*
 Prairie: *P. gracilis.*
 Purple ground: *Physalis lobata.*
 Purple-leaf sand: *Prunus* ✕*cistena.*
 Rosebud: *P. subhirtella.*
 Rum: *P. serotina.*
 Sand: *P. Besseyi, P. depressa, P. pumila, P. susquehanae.*
 Sargent: *P. Sargentii.*
 Sour: *P. Cerasus.*
 Spanish: *Mimusops Elengi.*
 St. Lucie: *Prunus Mahaleb.*
 Surinam: *Eugenia uniflora.*
 Sweet: *Prunus avium.*
 Taiwan: *P. campanulata.*
 Western sand: *P. Besseyi.*
 West Indian: *Cordia nitida.*
 Wild: *Prunus ilicifolia.*
 Wild black: *P. serotina.*
 Wild red: *P. pensylvanica.*
 Winter: *Cardiospermum Halicacabum, Physalis Alkekengi, P. peruviana.*
 Yoshino: *Prunus yedoensis.*
Cherry-of-the-Rio-Grande: *Eugenia aggregata.*
Cherry-pie: *Heliotropium arborescens.*
Chervil: *Anthriscus Cerefolium.*
 Parsnip: *Chaerophyllum bulbosum.*
 Salad: *Anthriscus Cerefolium.*
 Sweet: *Myrrhis odorata.*
 Turnip-rooted: *Chaerophyllum bulbosum.*
 White: *Cryptotaenia canadensis.*
Chess: *Bromus.*
 Foxtail: *B. rubens.*
 Japanese: *B. japonicus.*
 Rattlesnake: *B. briziformis.*
 Soft: *B. mollis.*
Chestnut: *Castanea.*
 American: *C. dentata.*
 California horse: *Aesculus californica.*
 Cape: *Calodendrum capense.*
 Chinese: *Castanea mollissima.*
 Chinese water: *Eleocharis dulcis.*
 Common horse: *Aesculus Hippocastanum.*
 Dwarf horse: *A. parviflora.*
 Eurasian: *Castanea sativa.*
 European: *C. sativa.*
 European horse: *Aesculus Hippocastanum.*
 Guiana: *Pachira aquatica.*
 Horse: *Aesculus Hippocastanum.*
 Japanese: *Castanea crenata.*
 Japanese horse: *Aesculus turbinata.*
 Moreton Bay: *Castanospermum australe.*
 Red horse: *Aesculus* ✕*carnea.*
 Spanish: *Castanea sativa.*
 Water: *Eleocharis dulcis, Pachira aquatica, Trapa.*
 Wild: *Pachira insignis.*
Chestnut vine: *Tetrastigma Voinieranum.*
Chia: *Salvia columbariae.*
Chicken-claws: *Salicornia europaea.*
Chicken-gizzard: *Iresine Herbstii.*
Chicken-toes: *Corallorhiza odontorhiza.*
Chickweed: *Paronychia, Stellaria, S. Media.*
 Field mouse-ear: *Cerastium arvense.*
 Forked: *Paronychia candensis.*
 Great: *Stellaria pubera.*
 Mouse-ear: *Cerastium.*
 Star: *Stellaria pubera.*
 Water: *Callitriche.*
Chicory: *Cichorium.*
 Common: *C. Intybus.*
Chicot: *Gymnocladus dioica.*
Chicozapote: *Manilkara Zapota.*
Chigger flower: *Asclepias tuberosa.*
Chilean nut: *Gevuina Avellana.*
Chile-bells: *Lapageria.*
Chilicothe: *Marah macrocarpus.*
China, wild: *Sapindus marginatus.*
Chinaberry: *Melia Azedarach.*
China tree: *Koelreuteria paniculata, Melia Azedarach.*
Chincherinchee: *Ornithogalum thyrsoides.*
 Giant: *O. Saundersiae.*
Chinese evergreen: *Aglaonema modestum.*
Chinese-hat plant: *Holmskioldia sanguinea.*
Chinese-houses: *Collinsia heterophylla.*

Chinese-jade: *Crassula arborescens.*
Chinese-lantern: *Abutilon hybridum, Physalis Alkekengi.*
Chinese-lantern plant: *Physalis Alkekengi.*
Chinquapin: *Castanea pumila, Castanopsis.*
　　Bush: *Castanea alnifolia, Castanopsis sempervirens.*
　　Downy: *Castanea alnifolia.*
　　Giant: *Castanopsis chrysophylla.*
　　Japanese: *Castanopsis cuspidata.*
　　Water: *Nelumbo lutea.*
Chirimoya: *Annona Cherimola.*
Chittamwood: *Bumelia lanuginosa, Cotinus obovatus.*
Chive: *Allium Schoenoprasum.*
　　Chinese: *A. tuberosum.*
　　Garlic: *A. tuberosum.*
Chloris, Uruguay: *Chloris Berroi.*
Chocolate, Indian: *Geum rivale.*
Chocolate plant: *Pseuderanthemum alatum.*
Chocolate-root: *Geum rivale.*
Chocolate vine: *Akebia quinata.*
Chokeberry: *Aronia, A. arbutifolia.*
　　Black: *A. melanocarpa.*
　　Purple: *A. floribunda.*
　　Red: *A. arbutifolia.*
Chokecherry: *Prunus virginiana.*
Cholla: *Opuntia.*
　　Jumping: *O. prolifera.*
Chorogi: *Stachys affinis.*
Choyote: *Sechium edule.*
Christmas-bells: *Sandersonia aurantiaca.*
Christmas berry: *Heteromeles.*
Christmasberry tree: *Schinus terebinthifolius.*
Christmas bush, Victorian: *Prostanthera lasianthos.*
Christmas-candle: *Cassia alata.*
Christmas-cheer: *Sedum rubrotinctum.*
Christmas flower: *Euphorbia pulcherrima.*
Christmas-jewels: *Aechmea Racinae.*
Christmas-star: *Euphorbia pulcherrima.*
"Christmas tree": Most commonly used for this purpose in N. Amer.
　　are: *Abies balsamea, Picea Abies, Pinus silvestris, Pseudotsuga Menziesii.*
Christmas tree: *Metrosideros excelsa.*
　　New Zealand: *M. excelsa, M. robusta.*
Christ plant: *Euphorbia Milii.*
Christophine: *Sechium edule.*
Christ vine: *Porana paniculata.*
Chrysanthemum: *Chrysanthemum.*
　　Corn: *C. segetum.*
　　Daisy: *C. maximum.*
　　Florist's: *C. ×morifolium.*
　　Garland: *C. coronarium.*
　　Max: *C. maximum.*
　　Nippon: *C. nipponicum.*
　　Portuguese: *C. lacustre.*
　　Tansy: *C. macrophyllum.*
　　Tricolor: *C. carinatum.*
Chufa: *Cyperus esculentus* var. *sativus.*
Chulta: *Dillenia indica.*
Chuparosa: *Anisacanthus Thurberi, Justicia californica.*
Cibotium, poor-man's: *Pteris tremula.*
Ciboule: *Allium fistulosum.*
Cicely
　　Hairy sweet: *Osmorhiza Claytonii.*
　　Smooth sweet: *O. longistylis.*
　　Sweet: *Myrrhis odorata, Osmorhiza.*
　　Woolly sweet: *Osmorhiza Claytonii.*
Cider tree: *Eucalyptus Gunnii.*
Cigar flower: *Cuphea ignea.*
Cigar tree: *Catalpa speciosa.*
Cinderella-slippers: *Sinningia regina.*
Cineraria: *Senecio ×hybridus.*
　　Florist's: *S. ×hybridus.*
Cinnamon: *Cinnamomum zeylanicum.*
　　Wild: *Canella Winterana.*
Cinnamon tree: *Cinnamomum myrianthum.*
Cinnamon vine: *Dioscorea Batatas.*
Cinquefoil: *Potentilla.*
　　Hoary: *P. argentea.*
　　Marsh: *P. palustris.*
　　Old-field: *P. simplex.*
　　Rock: *P. rupestris.*
　　Shrubby: *P. fruticosa.*
　　Silvery: *P. argentea.*

Cinquefoil—*Continued*
　　Tall: *P. arguta.*
　　Three-toothed: *P. tridentata.*
Cipollino: see *Muscari comosum.*
Cissus: *Cissus.*
　　Begonia: *C. discolor.*
　　Pink: *C. adenopoda.*
Citrange: ×*Citroncirus Webberi.*
Citron: *Citrullus lanatus* var. *citroides, Citrus medica.*
　　Etrog: *Citrus medica* cv. 'Etrog'.
Citronella: *Collinsonia canadensis.*
Cive: *Allium Schoenoprasum.*
Clary: *Salvia Sclarea.*
　　Meadow: *S. pratensis.*
　　Wild: *S. Verbenaca.*
Clearing nut: *Strychnos potatorum.*
Clearweed: *Pilea fontana, P. pumila.*
Cleavers: *Galium.*
Cleft-stone: *Pleiospilos Nelii.*
Clematis: *Clematis.*
　　Curly: *C. crispa.*
　　Marsh: *C. crispa.*
Cleome: *Cleome.*
　　Golden: *C. lutea.*
　　Yellow: *C. lutea.*
Cliff-green: *Paxistima Canbyi.*
Climbing-beauty: *Aeschynanthus pulcher.*
Clock vine: *Thunbergia grandiflora.*
　　Bengal: *T. grandiflora.*
　　Bush: *T. erecta.*
Clotbur: *Arctium.*
Crocus, cloth-of-gold: *Crocus angustifolia.*
Cloudberry: *Rubus Chamaemorus.*
Clove: *Syzygium aromaticum.*
Clover: *Trifolium.*
　　Alsike: *T. hybridum.*
　　Alyce: *Alysicarpus.*
　　Bukhara: *Melilotus alba.*
　　Bur: *Medicago hispida.*
　　Bush: *Lespedeza.*
　　Cow hop: *Trifolium procumbens.*
　　Crimson: *T. incarnatum.*
　　Elk: *Aralia californica.*
　　European water: *Marsilea quadrifolia.*
　　Holy: *Onobrychis viciifolia.*
　　Hop: *Medicago lupulina, Trifolium agrarium.*
　　Hubam: *Melilotus alba* var. *annua.*
　　Hungarian: *Trifolium pannonicum.*
　　Indoor: *Alternanthera dentata* cv. 'Rubiginosa'.
　　Italian: *Trifolium incarnatum.*
　　Japanese: *Lespedeza striata.*
　　Korean: *L. stipulacea.*
　　Kura: *Trifolium ambiguum.*
　　Ladino: *T. repens* forma *lodigense.*
　　Large hop: *T. campestre.*
　　Low: *T. campestre.*
　　Lucky: *Oxalis Deppei.*
　　Mammoth: *Trifolium pratense* var. *perenne.*
　　Mexican: *Richardia scabra.*
　　Musk: *Erodium moschatum.*
　　Owl's: *Orthocarpus.*
　　Persian: *Trifolium resupinatum.*
　　Pin: *Erodium cicutarium.*
　　Prairie: *Petalostemon.*
　　Red: *Trifolium pratense.*
　　Reversed: *T. resupinatum.*
　　Silky prairie: *Petalostemon villosum.*
　　Small hop: *Trifolium procumbens.*
　　Stinking: *Cleome serrulata.*
　　Strawberry: *Trifolium fragiferum.*
　　Strawberry-headed: *T. fragiferum.*
　　Subterranean: *T. subterraneum.*
　　Sweet: *Melilotus.*
　　Tick: *Desmodium.*
　　Toothed bur: *Medicago hispida.*
　　Water: *Marsilea.*
　　White: *Trifolium repens.*
　　White Dutch: *T. repens.*
　　White prairie: *Petalostemon candidum.*
　　White sweet: *Melilotus alba.*
　　Yellow: *Trifolium agrarium, T. procumbens.*
　　Yellow sweet: *Melilotus officinalis.*

Cloveroot: *Geum urbanum.*
Clubmoss: see Moss, Club.
Coach-whip: *Fouquieria splendens.*
Coat flower: *Petrorhagia Saxifraga.*
Cobana: *Stahlia monosperma.*
Cobnut: *Corylus Avellana* cv. 'Grandis'.
Cobra plant: *Darlingtonia californica.*
Coca: *Erythroxylum Coca.*
  Wild: *Pachira aquatica.*
Cocaine plant: *Erythroxylum Coca.*
Coccoon plant: *Senecio Haworthii.*
Cochineal plant: *Nopalea cochenillifera.*
Cockle: *Vaccaria pyramidata.*
  Corn: *Agrostemma, A. Githago.*
  Purple: *A. Githago.*
  Sticky: *Silene noctiflora.*
  White: *S. alba.*
Cocklebur: *Agrimonia, Huernia Pillansii.*
Cockroach berry: *Solanum aculeatissimum.*
Cockscomb: *Celosia cristata.*
  Green: *Sedum dendroideum* subsp. *praealtum* cv. 'Cristatum'.
Cock's-eggs: *Salpichroa origanifolia.*
Cock's-foot: *Dactylis glomerata.*
Cockspur: *Crataegus Crus-galli.*
Coco
  Ground: *Eulophia alta.*
  Wild: *E. alta.*
Cocoa-shade, Nicaraguan: *Gliricidia sepium.*
Coco-de-mer: *Lodoicea maldivica.*
Coconut: *Cocos nucifera.*
  Double: *Lodoicea, L. maldivica.*
Coconut plant: *Kalanchoe Houghtonii.*
Coffee: *Coffea, C. arabica.*
  Arabian: *C. arabica.*
  Arabica: *C. arabica.*
  Common: *C. arabica.*
  Liberian: *C. liberica.*
  Liberica: *C. liberica.*
  Robusta: *C. canephora.*
  Wild: *Colubrina arborescens, Polyscias Guilfoylei, Psychotria, P. nervosa, P. Sulzneri, Triosteum aurantiacum, T. perfoliatum.*
  Wild robusta: *Coffea canephora.*
  Zanzibar: *C. zanguebariae.*
Coffeeberry: *Rhamnus californica.*
Coffee plant, Arabian: *Coffea arabica.*
Coffee tree: *Polyscias Guilfoylei.*
  Kentucky: *Gymnocladus dioica.*
Cohosh: *Actaea.*
  Black: *Cimicifuga racemosa.*
  Blue: *Caulophyllum thalictroides.*
  Summer: *Cimicifuga americana.*
  White: *Actaea pachypoda.*
Cokernut, little: *Jubaea chilensis.*
Cola, abata: *Cola acuminata.*
Cola nut: *Cola acuminata.*
Cola tree: *Cola acuminata.*
Cole: *Brassica; B. oleracea,* Acephala Group.
  Red: *Armoracia rusticana.*
Coleus: *Coleus.*
  Brazilian: *Plectranthus Oertendahlii.*
  Butterfly: *Coleus Blumei* var. *Verschaffeltii.*
  Flowering bush: *C. thyrsoideus.*
  Prostrate: *Plectranthus, P. Oertendahlii.*
Colewort: *Brassica oleracea,* Acephala Group; *Crambe cordifolia.*
Colicroot: *Aletris.*
  Yellow: *A. aurea.*
Collard: *Brassica oleracea,* Acephala Group.
  Marsh: *Nuphar.*
  Water: *Nuphar.*
Coltsfoot: *Galax urceolata, Tussilago Farfara.*
  Sweet: *Petasites.*
Columbine: *Aquilegia.*
Columbo: *Frasera.*
Column-of-pearls: *Haworthia Chalwinii.*
Colza: *Brassica Napus.*
Comfrey: *Symphytum.*
  Common: *S. officinale.*
  Prickly: *S. asperum.*
  Russian: *S.* ×*uplandicum.*
Compass plant: *Silphium laciniatum.*
Comptie: *Zamia floridana, Z. integrifolia, Z. pumila.*
Conchita: *Centrosema.*

Coneflower: *Dracopsis amplexicaulis, Rudbeckia.*
  California: *Rudbeckia.*
  Prairie: *Ratibida.*
  Purple: *Echinacea.*
Conehead: *Cycas.*
  Bedding: *Strobilanthes isophyllus.*
Cone plant: *Conophytum.*
Confederate vine: *Antigonon leptopus.*
Consumption weed: *Baccharis halimifolia.*
Convulsion root: *Monotropa uniflora.*
Cooba: *Acacia salicina.*
Cool-tankard: *Borago officinalis.*
Coolwort: *Mitella diphylla, Pilea fontana, P. pumila.*
Coontie: *Zamia floridana. Z. integrifolia, Z. pumila.*
Copal
  East African: *Hymenaea verrucosa.*
  Zanzibar: *H. verrucosa.*
Copal tree: *Ailanthus altissima.*
Copey: *Clusia rosea.*
Copihue: *Lapageria.*
Copperleaf: *Acalypha, A. Wilkesiana, Alternanthera.*
Copperleaves: *Anacampseros telephiastrum.*
Coquillo: *Eleutherine bulbosa.*
Coral-bead plant: *Abrus precatorius, Nertera granadensis.*
Coral-beads: *Cocculus carolinus, Sedum Stahlii.*
Coralbells: *Heuchera sanguinea.*
Coralberry: *Aechmea fulgens, Ardisia crenata, Symphoricarpos orbiculatus.*
Coralblow: *Russelia.*
Coralbush: *Templetonia retusa.*
Coral-drops: *Bessera elegans.*
Coral-gem: *Lotus Berthelotii.*
Corallita: *Antigonon leptopus.*
  White: *Porana paniculata.*
Coral plant: *Jatropha multifida, Russelia, R. equisetiformis.*
Coralroot: *Corallorhiza.*
  Autumn: *C. odontorhiza.*
  Large: *C. maculata.*
  Late: *C. odontorhiza.*
  Small: *C. odontorhiza.*
  Spotted: *C. maculata.*
  Striped: *C. striata.*
  Western: *C. Mertensiana.*
Coral tree: *Erythrina, Macaranga grandifolia.*
  Cockspur: *E. crista-galli.*
  Naked: *E. coralloides.*
Coral vine: *Antigonon leptopus.*
Coralwood: *Adenanthera pavonina.*
Corazón-de-Jesús: *Begonia foliosa* var. *miniata.*
Coriander: *Coriandrum sativum.*
  Roman: *Nigella sativa.*
Corkscrew: *Euphorbia mamillaris.*
Corkscrew flower: *Vigna Caracalla.*
Cork tree: *Phellodendron.*
Corkwood: *Leitneria floridana, Ochroma pyramidale.*
  Gray: *Erythrina vespertilio.*
Corn: *Zea Mays.*
  Broom: see Broomcorn.
  Crow: *Aletris farinosa.*
  Dent: *Zea Mays* var. *indentata.*
  Egyptian: *Sorghum vulgare.*
  Flint: *Zea Mays* var. *indurata.*
  Indian: *Z. Mays.*
  Kafir: *Sorghum bicolor,* Caffrorum Group.
  Pod: *Zea Mays* var. *tunicata.*
  Rice: *Sorghum vulgare.*
  Sand: *Zigadenus paniculatus.*
  Squirrel: *Dicentra canadensis.*
  Sugar: *Zea Mays* var. *saccharata.*
  Sweet: *Z. Mays* var. *saccharata.*
  Turkey: *Dicentra eximia.*
Cornel: *Cornus.*
  Dwarf: *C. canadensis.*
  Japanese: *C. officinalis.*
Cornflower: *Centaurea Cyanus.*
Corn plant: *Dracaena fragrans* cv. 'Massangeana'.
Corn-salad: *Valerianella.*
  Common: *V. Locusta.*
  Italian: *V. eriocarpa.*
Coroa: *Sicana odorifera.*
Corpse plant: *Monotropa uniflora.*
Correosa: *Rhus microphylla.*
Corsican-curse: *Soleirolia Soleirolii.*

Cosmetic-bark tree: *Murraya paniculata.*
Cosmos: *Cosmos.*
  Orange: *C. sulphureus.*
  Yellow: *C. sulphureus.*
Costmary: *Chrysanthemum Balsamita.*
Cotoneaster: *Cotoneaster.*
  Cranberry: *C. apiculata.*
  Rock: *C. horizontalis.*
Cotton: *Gossypium.*
  Arizona wild: *G. Thurberi.*
  Bog: *Eriophorus.*
  Kidney: *Gossypium barbadense* var. *braziliense.*
  Lavender: *Santolina Chamaecyparissus.*
  Levant: *Gossypium herbaceum.*
  Sea Island: *G. barbadense.*
  Tree: *G. arboreum, G. barbadense.*
  Upland: *G. hirsutum.*
  Wild: *Hibiscus Moscheutos.*
Cotton-ball: *Espostoa lanata.*
Cottonweed: *Froelichia, Otanthus maritimus.*
Cottonwood: *Populus, P. deltoides.*
  Black: *P. heterophylla, P. trichocarpa.*
  Fremont: *P. Fremontii.*
  Great Plains: *P. Sargentii.*
  Jack's: *P. Jackii.*
  Rio Grande: *P. Fremontii* var. *Wislizenii.*
  Swamp: *P. heterophylla.*
  Wislizenus: *P. Fremontii* var. *Wislizenii.*
Cotula, stinking: *Anthemis Cotula.*
Council tree: *Ficus altissima.*
Cowbane, spotted: *Cicuta maculata.*
Cowbells: *Uvularia.*
Cowberry: *Viburnum Lentago, Vaccinium Vitis-idaea.*
Cow herb: *Vaccaria pyramidata.*
Cow-itch: *Campsis radicans, Rhus radicans.*
Cowpea: *Vigna unguiculata.*
Cow's-horn: *Euphorbia grandicornis.*
Cowslip: *Caltha palustris, Mertensia virginica, Primula veris.*
  American: *Dodecatheon.*
  Cape: *Lachenalia.*
  Jerusalem: *Pulmonaria officinalis.*
  Virginia: *Mertensia virginica.*
Coyote brush: *Baccharis pilularis.*
Crab: see Apple.
Crab's-eye: *Abrus precatorius.*
Crackeberry: *Cornus canadensis.*
Crakeberry: *Empetrum nigrum.*
Crampbark: *Viburnum trilobum.*
Cranberry: *Vaccinium, V. macrocarpon, V. Vitis-idaea.*
  American: *V. macrocarpon.*
  Australian: *Astroloma humifusum.*
  European: *Vaccinium Oxycoccos.*
  Highbush: *Viburnum trilobum.*
  Hog: *Arctostaphylos Uva-ursi.*
  Large: *Vaccinium macrocarpon.*
  Mountain: *V. Vitis-idaea* var. *minus.*
  Rock: *V. Vitis-idaea* var. *minus.*
  Small: *V. Oxycoccos.*
  Tree: *Viburnum trilobum.*
Cranberry bush: *Viburnum Opulus, V. trilobum.*
  European: *V. Opulus.*
Cranberry tree: *Viburnum trilobum, V. Opulus.*
Crane flower: *Strelitzia reginae.*
Cranesbill: *Geranium.*
  Dove's-foot: *G. molle.*
  Spotted: *G. maculatum.*
  Square-stalk: *Pelargonium tetragonum.*
  Wild: *Geranium maculatum.*
Crassula: *Crassula.*
  Flowering: *C. lactea.*
  Miniature trailing: *C. spathulata.*
  Moss: *C. lycopodioides.*
  Pyramid: *C. pyramidalis.*
  Rattail: *C. lycopodioides.*
  Rattlesnake: *C. teres.*
  Sausage: *Senecio articulatus.*
  Trailing: *Crassula marginalis.*
Crawley-root: *Corallorhiza odontorhiza.*
Crazyweed: *Oxytropis.*
Creambush: *Holodiscus discolor.*
Creamcups: *Platystemon.*
Cream nut: *Bertholletia excelsa.*
Creashak: *Arctostaphylos Uva-ursi.*

Creeping berries: *Senecio radicans.*
Creeping Charlie: *Lysimachia Nummularia, Pilea nummulariifolia.*
Creeping Jennie: *Lysimachia Nummularia.*
Creeping-sailor: *Saxifraga stolonifera.*
Creme-de-menthe plant: *Mentha Requienii.*
Creosote bush: *Larrea.*
Cress
  American: *Barbarea verna.*
  Belle Isle: *B. verna.*
  Blister: *Erysimum.*
  Early winter: *Barbarea verna.*
  Garden: *Lepidium sativum.*
  Garlic: *Peltaria alliacea.*
  Indian: *Tropaeolum majus.*
  Land: *Barbarea verna.*
  Lebanon: *Aethionema coridifolium.*
  Meadow: *Cardamine pratensis.*
  Mountain rock: *Arabis alpina.*
  Mouse-ear: *Arabidopsis.*
  Penny: *Thlaspi.*
  Persian stone: *Aethionema grandiflorum.*
  Rock: *Arabis.*
  Stone: *Aethionema.*
  Upland: *Barbarea, B. verna, Lepidium sativum.*
  Wall rock: *Arabis caucasica.*
  Winter: *Barbarea, B. vulgaris.*
  Yellow: *Rorippa.*
Crest-lip, rose: *Pogonia ophioglossoides.*
Crimson-cup: *Neoregelia farinosa.*
Crinklebush: *Lomatia silaifolia.*
Crinkle-leaf plant: *Adromischus cristatus.*
Crinum, southern swamp: *Crinum americanum.*
Crippled-cranefly: *Tipularia discolor.*
Crocus
  Autumn: *Colchicum, C. autumnale.*
  Celandine: *Crocus Korolkowii.*
  Chilean: *Tecophilaea cyanocrocus.*
  Dutch: *Crocus vernus.*
  Fall: *Colchicum autumnale.*
  Iris-flowered: *Crocus byzantinus.*
  Saffron: *C. sativus.*
  Scotch: *C. biflorus.*
  Tropical: *Kaempferia rotunda.*
  Wild: *Anemone Nuttalliana.*
Crocodile-jaws: *Aloe humilis.*
Crosnes-du-Japon: *Stachys affinis.*
Cross vine: *Bignonia capreolata.*
Crosswort: *Crucianella.*
Croton: *Codiaeum.*
  Garden: *C. variegatum.*
Croton-oil plant: *Croton Tiglium.*
Crowberry: *Empetrum.*
  Black: *E. nigrum.*
  Broom: *Corema.*
Crowfoot: *Ranunculus.*
  Bulbous: *R. bulbosus.*
  Creeping: *R. repens.*
  Early: *R. fascicularis.*
  European: *Aquilegia vulgaris.*
  Fremont's: *Clematis Fremontii.*
  Garden: *Aquilegia vulgaris.*
  Yellow water: *Ranunculus flabellaris.*
Crown-beard: *Verbesina.*
  Golden: *V. encelioides.*
Crown-beauty: *Hymenocallis.*
Crown-jewels: *Lopezia coronata.*
Crown-imperial: *Fritillaria imperialis.*
Crown-of-thorns: *Euphorbia Milii.*
Crown plant: *Calotropis gigantea, Campsis.*
Cruel plant: *Cynanchum ascyrifolium.*
Cry-baby tree: *Erythrina crista-galli.*
Cryptanthus, pink: *Cryptanthus bromelioides.*
Cryptocoryne, African: *Anubias Afzelii.*
Crystalwort: *Riccia fluitans.*
Cuachilote: *Parmentiera edulis.*
Cuban bast: *Hibiscus elatus.*
Cubeb: *Piper Cubeba.*
Cuckold: *Arctium Lappa.*
Cuckoo flower: *Cardamine pratensis, Lychnis Flos-cuculi.*
Cuckoopint: *Arum maculatum.*
Cucumber: *Cucumis sativus.*
  African horned: *C. metuliferus.*
  Bitter: *Momordica Charantia*

Cucumber—*Continued*
 Bur: *Cucumis Anguria, Sicyos angulatus.*
 Mock: *Echinocystis lobata.*
 Prickly: *E. lobata.*
 Serpent: *Trichosanthes Anguina.*
 Squirting: *Ecballium Elaterium.*
 Star: *Sicyos angulatus.*
 Wild: *Cucumis Anguria, Echinocystis lobata.*
Cucumber root, Indian: *Medeola.*
Cucumber tree: *Magnolia acuminata, Averrhoa Bilimbi*
 Large-leaved: *M. macrophylla.*
 Yellow: *M. acuminata* var. *cordata.*
Cudweed: *Artemisia ludoviciana, Gnaphalium.*
Cuipo: *Cavanillesia platanifolia.*
Culcas: *Colocasia esculenta* var. *antiquorum.*
Culver's physic: *Veronicastrum.*
Culver's root: *Veronicastrum virginicum.*
Cumin: *Cuminum Cyminum.*
 Black: *Nigella sativa.*
Cup-and-saucer: *Campanula Medium* cv. 'Calycanthema'.
Cup-and-saucer plant: *Holmskioldia.*
Cup-and-saucer vine: *Cobaea scandens.*
Cupey: *Clusia rosea.*
Cupflower: *Nierembergia.*
 Tall: *N. scoparia.*
Cuphea, clammy: *Cuphea petiolata.*
Cupid's-bower: *Achimenes.*
Cup-of-gold: *Solandra guttata.*
Cup plant: *Silphium laciniatum.*
Curiosity plant: *Cereus peruvianus* cv. 'Monstrosus'.
Curlew berry: *Empetrum nigrum.*
Curlflower: *Clematis crispa.*
Curly-heads: *Clematis ochroleuca.*
Currant: *Ribes.*
 Alpine: *R. alpinum.*
 American black: *R. americanum.*
 Black: *R. nigrum.*
 Bristly black: *R. lacustre.*
 Buffalo: *R. aureum, R. odoratum.*
 Californian black: *R. bracteosum.*
 Chaparral: *R. malvaceum.*
 Cherry: *R. sativum* cv. 'Macrocarpum'.
 Common: *R. sativum.*
 European black: *R. nigrum.*
 Fetid: *R. glandulosum.*
 Garden: *R. sativum.*
 Indian: *Symphoricarpos orbiculatus.*
 Missouri: *Ribes aureum, R. odoratum.*
 Mountain: *R. alpinum.*
 Northern black: *R. hudsonianum.*
 Northern red: *R. rubrum.*
 Red: *R. rubrum, R. sativum.*
 Sierra: *R. nevadense.*
 Skunk: *R. glandulosum.*
 Squaw: *R. cereum.*
 Stink: *R. bracteosum.*
 Swamp red: *R. triste.*
 White-flowered: *R. cereum, R. indecorum.*
 Wild black: *R. americanum.*
Curry-leaf: *Murraya Koenigii.*
Curry-leaf tree: *Murraya Koenigii.*
Curtain plant: *Kalanchoe pinnata.*
Curua: *Sicana odorifera.*
Curubá: *Passiflora mollissima, Sicana odorifera.*
Cushaw: *Cucurbita mixta.*
Cush-cush: *Dioscorea trifida.*
Cushionbush: *Calocephalus Brownii.*
Cutch: *Acacia Catechu.*
 Black: *A. Catechu.*
Cutgrass: *Leersia.*
 Rice: *L. oryzoides.*
Cut-tail: *Eucalyptus fastigiata.*
Cycad, Cycas
 Modjadji: *Encephalartos transvenosus.*
 Prickly: *E. Altensteinii.*
 Sago: *Cycas, Zamia integrifolia, Z. pumila.*
Cycads: *Cycadaceae, Stangeriaceae, Zamiaceae.*
Cyclamen: *Cyclamen.*
 Baby: *C. hederifolium.*
 Florist's: *C. persicum.*
Cypress: *Cupressus, Taxodium.*
 African: *Widdringtonia.*
 Arizona: *Cupressus arizonica.*

Cypress—*Continued*
 Bald: *Taxodium distichum.*
 Berg: *Widdringtonia cupressoides.*
 Bhutan: *Cupressus torulosa.*
 Chinese swamp: *Glyptostrobus lineatus.*
 Cuyamaca: *Cupressus Stephensonii.*
 False: *Chamaecyparis.*
 Golf-ball: *Chamaecyparis obtusa* cv. 'Minima'.
 Gowen: *Cupressus Goveniana.*
 Guadalupe: *Cupressus guadalupensis.*
 Hinoki: *Chamaecyparis obtusa.*
 Hinoki false: *Chamaecyparis obtusa.*
 Italian: *Cupressus sempervirens.*
 Japanese false: *Chamaecyparis obtusa.*
 Lawson: *Chamaecyparis Lawsoniana.*
 MacNab: *Cupressus Macnabiana.*
 Mendocino: *Cupressus pygmaea.*
 Mexican: *Cupressus lusitanica.*
 Modoc: *Cupressus Bakeri.*
 Monterey: *Cupressus macrocarpa.*
 Montezuma: *Taxodium mucronatum.*
 Mourning: *Chamaecyparis funebris, C. Lawsoniana.*
 Nootka: *Chamaecyparis nootkatensis.*
 Piute: *Cupressus nevadensis.*
 Pond: *Taxodium distichum* var. *nutans.*
 Portuguese: *Cupressus lusitanica.*
 Red summer: *Kochia scoparia* var. *culta.*
 Rough-barked Arizona: *Cupressus arizonica.*
 Santa Cruz: *Cupressus Abramsiana.*
 Sargent: *Cupressus Sargentii.*
 Sawara: *Chamaecyparis pisifera.*
 Siskiyou: *Cupressus Bakeri* subsp. *Mathewsii.*
 Smooth-barked Arizona: *Cupressus glabra.*
 Standing: *Ipomopsis rubra.*
 Summer: *Kochia scoparia.*
 Tecate: *Cupressus Forbesii.*
 Tennis-ball: *Chamaecyparis obtusa* cv. 'Juniperoides'.
 Toy: *Crassula lycopodioides.*
Cypress vine: *Ipomoea Quamoclit.*
Cypress-turpentine: *Pistacia Terebinthus.*
Cytherea: *Calypso bulbosa.*

Daffodil: *Narcissus, N. pseudonarcissus.*
 Hoop-petticoat: *N. Bulbocodium.*
 Peruvian: *Hymenocallis narcissiflora.*
 Petticoat: *Narcissus Bulbocodium.*
 Sea: *Hymenocallis, Pancratium maritimum.*
 Winter: *Sternbergia lutea.*
Dagger plant: *Yucca aloifolia.*
Dahl: *Cajanus Cajan.*
Dahlia: *Dahlia*
 Bedding: *D. Merckii.*
 Bell tree: *D. imperialis.*
 Candelabra: *D. imperialis.*
 Common: see under *D. pinnata.*
 Garden: see under *D. pinnata.*
 Sea: *Coreopsis maritima.*
 Tree: *Dahlia imperialis.*
Dahoon: *Ilex Cassine.*
Daily-dew: *Drosera.*
Daisy: *Bellis, Chrysanthemum frutescens, C. Leucanthemum.*
 African: *Arctotis, Gerbera Jamesonii, Lonas annuus.*
 Barberton: *Gerbera Jamesonii.*
 Blue: *Felicia amelloides.*
 Blue-eyed African: *Arctotis stoechadifolia.*
 Boston yellow: *Chrysanthemum frutescens* cv. 'Chrysaster'.
 Butter: *Ranunculus repens, Verbesina encelioides.*
 Cape: *Venidium fastuosum.*
 Clanwilliam: *Euryops Athanasiae.*
 Crown: *Chrysanthemum coronarium.*
 Dahlberg: *Dyssodia tenuiloba.*
 Double orange: *Erigeron aurantiacus.*
 Easter: *Townsendia exscapa.*
 Engelmann: *Engelmannia pinnatifida.*
 English: *Bellis perennis.*
 Giant: *Chrysanthemum serotinum.*
 Globe: *Globularia trichosantha.*
 High: *Chrysanthemum serotinum.*
 Kingfisher: *Felicia Bergerana.*
 Lazy: *Aphanostephus.*
 Livingstone: *Dorotheanthus bellidiformis.*

Daisy—*Continued*
  Michaelmas: many leafy-stemmed, autumn-flowering species of
    Aster, especially *A. laevis, A. novi-angliae, A. novi-belgii,* and
    A. Tradescantii.
  Mountain: *Arenaria groenlandica.*
  Namaqualand: *Venidium.*
  Nippon: *Chrysanthemum nipponicum.*
  Oxeye: *C. Leucanthemum.*
  Painted: *C. coccineum.*
  Panamint: *Enceliopsis Covillei.*
  Paris: *Chrysanthemum frutescens.*
  Portuguese: *C. lacustre.*
  Seaside: *Erigeron glaucus.*
  Shasta: *Chrysanthemum ✕superbum.*
  Sleepy: *Xanthisma.*
  Swan River: *Brachycome iberidifolia.*
  Tahoka: *Machaeranthera tanacetifolia.*
  Transvaal: *Gerbera Jamesonii.*
  Turfing: *Tripleurospermum Tchihatchewii.*
  Veldt: *Gerbera Jamesonii.*
  White: *Chrysanthemum Leucanthemum.*
Daisybush: *Olearia.*
Dame's-rocket: *Hesperis matronalis.*
Damson: *Prunus insititia.*
Dandelion: *Taraxacum.*
  Common: *T. officinale.*
  Dwarf: *Krigia.*
  Russian: *Taraxacum Kok-saghyz.*
Danewort: *Sambucus Ebulus.*
Dangleberry: *Gaylussacia frondosa.*
Danthonia, Australian: *Danthonia semiannularis.*
Daphne: *Daphne.*
  February: *D. Mezereum.*
  October: *Sedum Sieboldii.*
  Purple-leaved: *Daphne Houtteana.*
  Twin-flowered: *D. pontica.*
  Winter: *D. odora.*
Dasheen: *Colocasia esculenta.*
Date: *Phoenix dactylifera.*
  Canary Island: *P. canariensis.*
  Ceylon: *P. zeylanica.*
  Chinese: *Zizyphus jujuba.*
  Cliff: *Phoenix rupicola.*
  Jerusalem: *Bauhinia monandra.*
Datil: *Yucca baccata.*
Dattock: *Detarium senegalense.*
Datura, sacred: *Datura inoxia.*
Dawn flower, blue: *Ipomoea acuminata.*
Dayflower: *Commelina.*
Daylily: *Hemerocallis, Hosta.*
  Dwarf yellow: *Hemerocallis minor.*
  Fulvous: *H. fulva.*
  Lemon: *H. Lilioasphodelus.*
  Orange: *H. fulva.*
  Tawny: *H. fulva.*
  Yellow: *H. Lilioasphodelus.*
Dead-rat tree: *Adansonia digitata.*
Deerberry: *Vaccinium caesium, V. stamineum.*
Deerbush: *Ceanothus integerrimus.*
Deerbrush: *Ceanothus integerrimus.*
Deerfoot: *Achlys triphylla.*
Degame: *Calycophyllum candidissimum.*
Deodar: *Cedrus Deodara.*
Derris: *Derris elliptica.*
Desert-candle: *Eremurus.*
Deu: *Coriaria ruscifolia.*
Devil flower: *Tacca Chantrieri.*
Devil's-backbone: *Kalanchoe Daigremontiana, Pedilanthus tithymal-*
  oides.
Devil's-bit: *Chamaelirium, Succisa.*
Devil's-club: *Oplopanax horridus.*
Devil's-darning-needle: *Clematis virginiana.*
Devil's-paintbrush: *Hieracium aurantiacum.*
Devil's-paw: *Notocactus submammulosus* var. *pampeanus.*
Devil's-shoestrings: *Viburnum alnifolium.*
Devil's-tongue: *Amorphophallus, A. Rivieri, Ferocactus latispinus,*
  Sansevieria, Tacca Chantrieri.
Devil's-walking-stick: *Aralia spinosa.*
Devil tree: *Alstonia scholaris.*
Devilweed: *Osmanthus.*
Devilwood: *Osmanthus americanus.*

Dewberry: *Rubus macropetalus.*
  American: *R. flagellaris.*
  European: *R. dumetorum.*
  Pacific: *R. ursinus.*
  Swamp: *R. hispidus.*
Dewflower: *Drosanthemum speciosum.*
  Showy: *D. speciosum.*
Dew-thread: *Drosera filiformis.*
Diamond flower: *Ionopsidium.*
Dill: *Anethum graveolens.*
Dioon, chestnut: *Dioon edule.*
Dittany: *Cunila, Dictamnus albus.*
  American: *Cunila origanoides.*
  Common: *C. origanoides.*
  Crete: *Origanum Dictamnus.*
Divi-divi: *Caesalpinia coriaria.*
Divine flower: *Dianthus Caryophyllus.*
Dock: *Rumex.*
  Bur: see Burdock.
  Giant water: *R. hydrolapathum.*
  Golden: *R. maritimus.*
  Green: *R. conglomeratus.*
  Patience: *R. patientia.*
  Prairie: *Silphium terebinthinaceum.*
  Purple-wen: *Brasenia Schreberi.*
  Sour: *Rumex Acetosa, R. crispus.*
  Spinach: *R. patientia.*
  Tanner's: *R. hymenosepalus.*
  Western: *R. occidentalis.*
Dockmackie: *Viburnum acerifolium.*
Dogbane: *Apocynum.*
  Common: *A. androsaemifolium.*
  Hemp: *A. cannabinum.*
  Rocky Mountain: *A. pumilum.*
  Spreading: *A. androsaemifolium.*
Dogberry: *Cornus sanguinea, Ribes cynosbati, Sorbus americana,*
  Viburnum alnifolium.
Dog-bone tree: *Polyscias nodosa.*
Dog-hobble: *Leucothoe Fontanesiana, Viburnum alnifolium.*
Dogtail: *Cynosurus.*
  Crested: *C. cristatus.*
Dogwood: *Cornus.*
  American: *C. stolonifera.*
  Blood-twig: *C. sanguinea.*
  Brown: *C. glabrata.*
  Chinese: *C. Kousa.*
  Creek: *C. californica.*
  False: *Sapindus Saponaria.*
  Flowering: *Cornus florida.*
  Giant: *C. controversa.*
  Golden-twig: *C. stolonifera* cv. 'Flaviramea'.
  Jamaican: *Piscidia piscipula.*
  Mountain: *Cornus Nuttallii.*
  Pagoda: *C. alternifolia.*
  Panicled: *C. racemosa.*
  Poison: *Rhus Vernix.*
  Red-osier: *Cornus stolonifera.*
  Round-leaved: *C. rugosa.*
  Siberian: *C. alba* cv. 'Sibirica'.
  Silky: *C. Amomum, C. Purpusii.*
  Stiff: *C. stricta.*
  Tartarian, Tatarian: *C. alba.*
  West Indian: *Piscidia piscipula.*
  White Mountain: *Viburnum alnifolium.*
Dogweed: *Dyssodia.*
Dollar plant: *Crassula argentea.*
Doll's-eyes: *Actaea pachypoda.*
Dominoes: *Opuntia erectoclada.*
Donkey's-tail: *Sedum Morganianum.*
Dove flower: *Peristeria elata.*
Dove's-dung: *Ornithogalum umbellatum.*
Dove tree: *Davidia involucrata.*
Doveweed: *Eremocarpus setigerus.*
Dracaena, Dracena: *Cordyline, Dracaena.*
  Blue: *Cordyline indivisa.*
  Fountain: *C. australis.*
  Giant: *C. australis.*
  Gold-dust: *Dracaena surculosa.*
  Spotted: *D. surculosa.*
  Striped: *D. deremensis* cv. 'Warneckei'.
  Tree: *D. arborea.*
  Umbrella: *Dianella ensifolia.*
Dragon-bones: *Euphorbia lactea.*

Dragon flower: *Huernia*.
  Kenya: *H. keniensis*.
  Red: *H. Schneiderana*.
Dragonhead: *Dracocephalum*.
  False: *Physostegia*.
Dragon-mouth: *Horminum pyrenaicum*.
Dragonroot: *Arisaema Dracontium, A. triphyllum*.
Dragon's-claw: *Corallorhiza odontorhiza*.
Dragon's-mouth: *Arethusa bulbosa*.
Dragon tree: *Dracaena Draco*.
Drake: *Avena fatua*.
Dropseed: *Sporobolus*.
  Sand: *S. cryptandrus*.
Drop-tongue: *Schismatoglottis*.
  Painted: *Aglaonema crispum*.
Dropwort: *Filipendula vulgaris*.
Drunkard's-dream: *Hatiora salicornioides*.
Duck's-meat: *Lemna*.
Duckweed: *Lemna, Spirodela*.
  Common: *Lemna minor*.
  Great: *Spirodela polyrhiza*.
  Lesser: *Lemna minor*.
  Star: *L. trisulca*.
Duckwheat: *Fagopyrum tataricum*.
Dumb plant: *Dieffenbachia*.
Durian: *Durio zibethinus*.
Durra
  Brown: *Sorghum bicolor*, Durra Group.
  White: *S. bicolor*, Cernuum Group.
Dusty-miller: *Artemisia Stellerana, Centaurea Cineraria, C. gymnocarpa, C. ragusina, Chrysanthemum ptarmiciflorum, Lychnis Coronaria, Senecio Cineraria, S. Vira-vira*.
Dutchman's-breeches: *Dicentra Cucullaria*.
Dutchman's-pipe: *Aristolochia durior, Epiphyllum oxypetalum*.
Dutch-mice: *Lathyrus tuberosus*.
Dutch-wings: *Gasteria*.
Dyckia, pineapple: *Dyckia brevifolia*.
Dye root: *Lachnanthes caroliana*.

Eagle-claws: *Echinocactus horizonthalonius*.
Earth nut: *Arachis hypogaea*.
Earth-star: *Cryptanthus*.
Easter-herald's-trumpet: *Beaumontia grandiflora*.
Easter-lily vine: *Beaumontia grandiflora*.
Ebony: *Diospyros Ebenum*.
  East Indian: *D. Ebenum*.
  Green: *Jacaranda*.
  Macassar: *Diospyros Ebenum*.
  Mountain: *Bauhinia Hookeri, B. variegata*.
  Queensland: *B. Carronii*.
  Texas: *Pithecellobium flexicaule*.
Echeveria: *Echeveria*.
  Baby: *E. amoena, E. Derenbergii*.
  Copper-leaf: *E. multicaulis*.
  Coral: *E. carnicolor*.
  Hairy: *E. pilosa*.
  Peacock: *E. Peacockii*.
  Pearl: *E. elegans*.
  Red: *E. Harmsii*.
Eddo: *Colocasia esculenta*.
Edelweiss: *Leontopodium alpinum*.
  Brazilian: *Sinningia leucotricha*.
  New Zealand: *Leucogenes*.
Eggfruit: *Pouteria campechiana*.
Eggplant: *Solanum Melongena* var. *esculentum*.
  Snake: *S. Melongena* var. *serpentinum*.
  Tomato-fruited: *S. integrifolium*.
Eglantine: *Rosa Eglanteria*.
Einkorn: *Triticum monococcum*.
Elder, Elderberry: *Sambucus*.
  American: *S. canadensis*.
  American red: *S. pubens*.
  Blue: *S. caerulea*.
  Box: *Acer Negundo*.
  Dwarf: *S. Ebulus, Aralia hispida*.
  European: *Sambucus nigra*.
  European red: *S. racemosa*.
  Ground: *Aegopodium Podagraria*.
  Pacific Coast red: *Sambucus callicarpa*.
  Poison: *Rhus Vernix*.
  Red-berried: *Sambucus pubens*.
  Stinking: *S. pubens*.

Elder—*Continued*
  Sweet: *S. canadensis*.
  Yellow: *Tecoma stans*.
Elaeagnus: *Elaeagnus*.
  Cherry: *E. multiflora*.
  Thorny: *E. pungens*.
Elecampane: *Inula Helenium*.
Elemi, gum: *Bursera Simaruba*.
Elephant bush: *Portulacaria afra*.
Elephant-ear, velvet: *Kalanchoe beharensis*.
Elephant-foot tree: *Beaucarnea recurvata*.
Elephant-heads: *Pedicularis groenlandica*.
Elephant's-ear: *Caladium, Colocasia, Enterolobium cyclocarpum*.
Elephant's-ear plant: *Alocasia, Colocasia*.
Elephant's-foot: *Dioscorea elephantipes*.
Elephant tree: *Bursera microphylla*.
Eleven-o'clock: *Portulaca grandiflora*.
Elfin herb: *Cuphea hyssopifolia*.
Elfin-spur: *Tipularia discolor*.
Elkhorn: *Euphorbia lactea* cv. 'Cristata', *Hereroa Dyeri*.
Elkhorns: *Rhombophyllum Nelii*.
Elk's-horn: *Platycerium Hillii*.
Elm: *Ulmus*.
  American: *U. americana*.
  Belgian: *U. hollandica* cv. 'Belgica'.
  Bush: *U. hollandica* cv. 'Nana'.
  Camperdown: *U. vegeta* cv. 'Camperdownii'.
  Cedar: *U. crassifolia*.
  Chichester: *U. vegeta*.
  Chinese: *U. parvifolia*.
  Cork: *U. Thomasii*.
  Cornish: *U. angustifolia* var. *cornubiensis*.
  Dutch: *U. hollandica*.
  Dwarf: *U. pumila*.
  English: *U. procera*.
  European white: *U. laevis*.
  Exeter: *U. glabra* cv. 'Exoniensis'.
  Fern-leaf: *U. glabra* cv. 'Crispa'.
  Globe: *U. carpinifolia* cv. 'Umbraculifera'.
  Guernsey: *U. sarniensis*.
  Holland: *U. hollandica*.
  Horned: *U. glabra* cv. 'Cornuta'.
  Huntingdon: *U. vegeta*.
  Japanese: *U. Davidii* var. *japonica*.
  Jersey: *U. sarniensis*.
  Moline: *U. americana* cv. 'Moline'.
  Red: *U. rubra, U. serotina*.
  Rock: *U. Thomasii*.
  Scotch: *U. glabra*.
  September: *U. serotina*.
  Siberian: *U. pumila*.
  Slippery: *U. rubra*.
  Small-leaved: *U. alata*.
  Smooth-leaf: *U. carpinifolia*.
  Tabletop: *U. glabra* cv. 'Horizontalis'.
  Vase: *U. americana* cv. 'Vase'.
  Wahoo: *U. alata*.
  Water: *U. americana, Planera, P. aquatica*.
  Wheatley: *Ulmus sarniensis*.
  White: *U. americana*.
  Willow: *U. viminalis*.
  Winged: *U. alata*.
  Wych: *U. glabra*.
Emblic: *Phyllanthus Emblica*.
Emerald-feather: *Asparagus densiflorus* cv. 'Sprengeri'.
Emerald-idol: *Opuntia cylindrica*.
Emmer: *Triticum turgidum*, Dicoccon Group.
Empress-of-Germany: *Nopalxochia phyllanthoides*.
Endive: *Cichorium Endivia*.
Epaulette tree: *Pterostyrax*.
Epidendrum, Booth's: *Epidendrum Boothianum*.
Episcia, Canal Zone yellow: *Episcia cupreata* cv. 'Tropical Topaz'.
Eranthemum, purple false: *Pseuderanthemum atropurpureum*.
Eriogonum, red: *Eriogonum grande* var. *rubescens*.
Ervil: *Vicia Ervilia*.
Eryngo: *Eryngium*.
  Sea: *E. maritimum*.
Escarole: *Cichorium Endivia*.
Escobita: *Orthocarpus purpurascens*.
Esmeralda: *Arachnis Clarkei*.
Esparcet: *Onobrychis viciifolia*.
Esparto: *Stipa tenacissima*.
Espino cavan: *Acacia Caven*.

Estragon: *Artemisia Dracunculus.*
Ettercap: *Pogonia ophioglossoides.*
   Crested: *P. ophioglossoides.*
Eucalypt, Eucalyptus: *Eucalyptus.*
   Spiral: *E. cinerea.*
Eulalia: *Miscanthus sinensis.*
Eumong: *Acacia stenophylla.*
Euptelea, Japanese: *Euptelea polyandra.*
Euphorbia: *Euphorbia.*
   Abyssinian: *E. trigona.*
   Big-tooth: *E. grandidens.*
   Crested: *E. lactea* cv. 'Cristata'.
   Hedge: *E. neriifolia.*
   Oleander: *E. neriifolia.*
   Rubber: *E. Tirucalli.*
Euryops: *Euryops.*
   Gray-leaved: *E. pectinatus.*
   Wax-leaf: *E. spathaceus.*
Evening-snow: *Linanthus dichotomus.*
Everlasting: *Anaphalis, Antennaria, Gnaphalium, Helichrysum, Helipterum.*
   Pearly: *Anaphalis margaritacea.*
   Swan River: *Helipterum Manglesii.*
   White-leaf: *Helichrysum angustifolium.*
   Winged: *Ammobium alatum.*
Eye-leaves: *Ophthalmophyllum.*

Fair-maids-of-France: *Saxifraga granulata.*
Fairy-bells: *Disporum, D. Hookeri, Melasphaerula ramosa.*
Fairy-castles: *Opuntia clavarioides.*
Fairy-duster: *Calliandra.*
Fairy-elephant's-feet: *Frithia.*
Fairy-fans: *Clarkia Breweri.*
Fairy-fringe: *Habenaria psycodes.*
Fairy-lantern: *Calochortus albus, Disporum Smithii.*
   Golden: *Calochortus amabilis.*
Fairy-lanterns: *Echeveria Weingartii.*
Fairy-needles: *Opuntia Soehrensii.*
Fairy-slipper: *Calypso bulbosa.*
Fairy-wand: *Chamaelirium luteum.*
Fairy-washboard: *Haworthia limifolia.*
Falling-stars: *Campanula isophylla.*
Fameflower: *Talinum, T. paniculatum.*
Fanwort: *Cabomba, C. caroliniana.*
Farewell-to-spring: *Clarkia.*
Fat-hen: *Chenopodium Bonus-Henricus.*
Fatsia, Japanese: *Fatsia japonica.*
Fat Solomon: *Smilacina racemosa* var. *amplexicaulis.*
Feather-bells: *Stenanthium gramineum.*
Feather-fleece: *Stenanthium gramineum* var. *robustum.*
Feather flower: *Verticordia.*
Featherfoil: *Hottonia.*
Feathertop: *Pennisetum villosum.*
Felon herb: *Artemisia vulgaris.*
Feltbush: *Kalanchoe beharensis.*
Fennel: *Foeniculum vulgare.*
   Common dog: *Anthemis Cotula.*
   Common giant: *Ferula communis.*
   Dog: *Anthemis.*
   Florence: *Foeniculum vulgare* var. *azoricum.*
   Wild: *Nigella, N. arvensis, N. damascena.*
Fennel flower: *Nigella.*
Fenugreek: *Trigonella Foenum-graecum.*
Fern
   Adder's: *Polypodium vulgare.*
   Adder's-tongue: *Ophioglossum.*
   Air: not a plant but an animal, a dead, dyed bryozoan, *Bugula turrita.*
   Alabama lip: *Cheilanthes alabamensis.*
   Aleutian maidenhair: *Adiantum pedatum* var. *aleuticum.*
   American maidenhair: *A. pedatum.*
   American parsley: *Cryptogramma crispa* var. *acrostichoides.*
   American wall: *Polypodium virginianum.*
   Anderson's holly: *Polystichum Andersonii.*
   Asparagus: *Asparagus setaceus.*
   Australian maidenhair: *Adiantum formosum, A. hispidulum.*
   Australian tree: *Alsophila australis, Sphaeropteris Cooperi.*
   Ball: *Davallia Mariesii, D. trichomanoides.*
   Bamboo: *Coniogramme japonica.*
   Barbados maidenhair: *Adiantum tenerum* cv. 'Farleyense'.
   Basket: *Nephrolepis pectinata.*
   Beard: *Vittaria lineata.*
   Bear-foot, Bear's-foot: *Humata Tyermannii.*

Fern—*Continued*
   Bear's-paw: *Aglaomorpha Meyenianum.*
   Beech: *Thelypteris hexagonoptera.*
   Bermuda maidenhair: *Adiantum bellum.*
   Berry bladder: *Cystopteris bulbifera.*
   Bird's-nest: *Asplenium nidus, A. serratum.*
   Black-stemmed tree: *Sphaeropteris medullaris.*
   Black tree: *S. medullaris.*
   Bladder: *Cystopteris.*
   Blond tree: *Cibotium splendens.*
   Blue: *Polypodium aureum* cv. 'Mandaianum'.
   Boott's wood: *Dryopteris Boottii.*
   Boston: *Nephrolepis exalta* cv. 'Bostoniensis'.
   Boulder: *Dennstaedtia punctilobula.*
   Braun's holly: *Polystichum Braunii.*
   Brittle: *Cystopteris fragilis.*
   Brittle maidenhair: *Adiantum tenerum.*
   Broad beech: *Thelypteris hexagonoptera.*
   Bulblet: *Cystopteris bulbifera.*
   Bulblet bladder: *C. bulbifera.*
   Button: *Pellaea rotundifolia, Tectaria cicutaria.*
   California: *Conium maculatum.*
   California cloak: *Notholaena californica.*
   California gold: *Pityrogramma triangularis.*
   California holly: *Polystichum californicum.*
   California lip: *Cheilanthes californica.*
   California maidenhair: *Adiantum Jordanii.*
   Carrot: *Davallia.*
   Chain: *Woodwardia.*
   Christmas: *Polystichum acrostichoides.*
   Cinnamon: *Osmunda cinnamomea.*
   Claw: *Onychium.*
   Cleveland's lip: *Cheilanthes Clevelandii.*
   Climbing: *Lygodium, L. palmatum, Stenochlaena palustris.*
   Climbing bird's-nest: *Polypodium punctatum.*
   Clinton's wood: *Dryopteris cristata* var. *Clintoniana.*
   Cloak: *Notholaena.*
   Coastal wood: *Dryopteris arguta.*
   Coffee: *Pellaea andromedifolia.*
   Common cup: *Dennstaedtia cicutaria.*
   Common staghorn: *Platycerium bifurcatum.*
   Cotton: *Notholaena Newberryi.*
   Coville's lip: *Cheilanthes Covillei.*
   Crested: *Pyrrosia lingua* cv. 'Corymbifera', *Dryopteris cristata.*
   Crested felt: *Pyrrosia lingua* cv. 'Corymbifera'.
   Crested wood: *Dryopteris cristata.*
   Cup: *Dennstaedtia.*
   Cuplet: *D. bipinnata.*
   Dagger: *Polystichum acrostichoides.*
   Daisy-leaved grape: *Botrychium matricariifolium.*
   Deer: *Blechnum Spicant.*
   Deer-tongue: *Phyllitis Scolopendrium.*
   Deer's-foot: *Davallia canariensis.*
   Delta maidenhair: *Adiantum Raddianum.*
   Dish: *Pteris.*
   Dissected grape: *Botrychium dissectum.*
   Downy wood: *Thelypteris dentata.*
   Dudley's holly: *Polystichum Dudleyi.*
   Dudley's shield: *P. Dudleyi.*
   Duff's sword: *Nephrolepis Duffii.*
   Dwarf asparagus: *Asparagus setaceus* cv. 'Nanus'.
   Dwarf Boston: *Nephrolepis exalta* cv. 'Compacta'.
   East Indian holly: *Arachniodes aristatum.*
   Eaton's shield: *Polystichum scopulinum.*
   Elephant-ear, Elephant's-ear: *Elaphoglossum crinitum, Platycerium angolense.*
   Elk's-horn: *Platycerium.*
   Emerald: *Asparagus densiflorus* cv. 'Sprengeri'.
   English hedge: *Polystichum setiferum.*
   Erect sword: *Nephrolepis cordifolia.*
   European chain: *Woodwardia radicans.*
   European parsley: *Cryptogramma crispa.*
   Fancy: *Dryopteris austriaca* var. *spinulosa.*
   Fan maidenhair: *Adiantum tenerum.*
   Farley maidenhair: *Adiantum tenerum* cv. 'Farleyense'.
   Feather: *Nephrolepis exalta* cv. 'Whitmanii'.
   Fée's lip: *Cheilanthes Feei.*
   Felt: *Pyrrosia.*
   Fendler's cloak: *Notholaena Fendleri.*
   Fendler's lip: *Cheilanthes Fendleri.*
   Fire: *Oxalis hedysaroides* cv. 'Rubra'.
   Fishtail: *Nephrolepis biserrata* cv. 'Furcans'.
   Five-finger: *Adiantum pedatum.*

Fern—*Continued*

Floating: *Ceratopteris, C. pteridoides.*
Florida ribbon: *Vittaria lineata.*
Florist's: *Dryopteris austriaca* var. *spinulosa.*
Flowering: *Anemia, Osmunda, O. regalis.*
Fragile: *Cystopteris fragilis.*
Fragrant: *Dryopteris fragrans, Polypodium pustulatum.*
Fragrant cliff: *Dryopteris fragrans.*
Giant chain: *Woodwardia fimbriata.*
Giant holly: *Polystichum munitum.*
Giant maidenhair: *Adiantum trapeziforme.*
Glade: *Diplazium pycnocarpon.*
Glory: *Adiantum tenerum* cv. 'Farleyense'.
Glossy cup: *Dennstaedtia bipinnata.*
Gold: *Pityrogramma, P. calomelanos* var. *aureo-flava, P. chryso-phylla.*
Golden-back: *P. triangularis.*
Golden cloak: *Notholaena aurea.*
Golden tree: *Dicksonia fibrosa.*
Goldie's: *Dryopteris Goldiana.*
Goldie's wood: *D. Goldiana.*
Grape: *Botrychium.*
Grass: *Vittaria.*
Hacksaw: *Doodia aspera.*
Hairy lip: *Cheilanthes lanosa, C. vestita.*
Halberd: *Tectaria heracleifolia.*
Hammock: *Blechnum occidentale.*
Hand: *Doryopteris pedata.*
Hare's-foot: *Polypodium aureum.*
Hartford: *Lygodium palmatum.*
Hart's-tongue: *Phyllitis Scolopendrium.*
Hawaiian tree: *Cibotium Chamissoi, C. splendens.*
Hay-scented: *Dennstaedtia punctilobula.*
Hedge: *Polystichum aculeatum, P. setiferum.*
Hen-and-chickens: *Asplenium bulbiferum.*
Holly: *Cyrtomium falcatum, Polystichum Lonchitis.*
Imbricate sword: *Polystichum munitum* var. *imbricans.*
Interrupted: *Osmunda Claytoniana.*
Iron: *Rumohra adiantiformis.*
Jamaica gold: *Pityrogramma sulphurea.*
Japanese climbing: *Lygodium japonicum.*
Japanese felt: *Pyrrosia lingua.*
Japanese holly: *Cyrtomium falcatum, Dryopteris varia.*
Japanese lady: *Diplazium japonicum.*
Japanese shield: *Dryopteris erythrosora.*
Java staghorn: *Platycerium Willinckii.*
King: *Marattia fraxinea.*
King-and-queen: *Asplenium bulbiferum.*
Lace: *Asparagus setaceus, Cheilanthes gracillima, Nephrolepis exaltata* cvs. 'Smithii' and 'Whitmanii'.
Ladder: *Nephrolepis cordifolia.*
Lady: *Athyrium Filix-femina.*
Lady ground: *Dennstaedtia davallioides.*
Leather: *Acrostichum aureum, A. daneifolium, Rumohra adianti-formis.*
Leatherleaf: *Rumohra adiantiformis.*
Leatherwood: *Dryopteris marginalis.*
Leathery grape: *Botrychium multifidum.*
Licorice: *Polypodium glycyrrhiza.*
Limestone oak: *Gymnocarpium Robertianum.*
Lip: *Cheilanthes.*
Long beech: *Thelypteris Phegopteris.*
Maidenhair: *Adiantum, A. pedatum.*
Malay climbing: *Lygodium circinatum.*
Male: *Dryopteris Filix-mas.*
Man: *Cibotium splendens.*
Man tree: *C. splendens.*
Marginal shield: *Dryopteris marginalis.*
Marsh: *Thelypteris palustris.*
Meadow: *Myrica Gale, Thelypteris palustris* var. *pubescens.*
Mexican tree: *Cibotium Schiedei.*
Mosquito: *Azolla.*
Moss: *Selaginella pallescens.*
Mother: *Asplenium bulbiferum.*
Mountain bladder: *Cystopteris montana.*
Mountain holly: *Polystichum Lonchitis.*
Mountain parsley: *Cryptogramma crispa.*
Mountain wood: *Thelypteris Oreopteris.*
Narrow beech: *Thelypteris Phegopteris.*
Narrow-leaved strap: *Polypodium angustifolium.*
Nebraska: *Conium maculatum.*
Nest: *Asplenium nidus.*
Netted chain: *Woodwardia areolata.*

Fern—*Continued*

New York: *Thelypteris noveboracensis.*
Northern holly: *Polystichum Lonchitis.*
Northern lady: *Athyrium Filix-femina* var. *Michauxii.*
Northern maidenhair: *Adiantum pedatum.*
Northern oak: *Gymnocarpium Robertianum.*
Oak: *Gymnocarpium Dryopteris.*
Oak-leaved: *Drynaria quercifolia.*
Ostrich: *Matteuccia.*
Para: *Marattia fraxinea.*
Parry's cloak: *Notholaena Parryi.*
Parsley: *Asplenium bulbiferum, Cryptogramma crispa* var. *acrostichoides.*
Peacock: *Selaginella Willldenovii.*
Pine: *Anemia adiantifolia.*
Plume: *Polystichum setiferum* cv. 'Proliferum'.
Prickly shield: *Polystichum aculeatum.*
Prince-of-Wales: *Leptopteris superba.*
Pursh's holly: *Polystichum Braunii* var. *Purshii.*
Rabbit's-foot: *Davallia fejeensis, Polypodium aureum.*
Rainbow: *Selaginella uncinata.*
Rattlesnake: *Botrychium virginianum.*
Resurrection: *Polypodium polypodioides.*
Ribbon: *Polypodium phyllitidis.*
Rough maidenhair: *Adiantum hispidulum.*
Royal: *Osmunda regalis.*
Sago: *Sphaeropteris medullaris.*
Savannah: *Gleichenia linearis.*
Saw: *Blechnum serrulatum.*
Scented oak: *Gymnocarpium Robertianum.*
Sensitive: *Onoclea sensibilis.*
Shield: *Dryopteris, Polystichum, P. Braunii.*
Shoestring: *Vittaria lineata.*
Sierra water: *Thelypteris nevadensis.*
Silver: *Pityrogramma, P. calomelanos, Pteris quadriaurita* cv. 'Argyraea'.
Silver-back: *Pityrogramma triangularis* var. *viscosa.*
Silver-king tree: *Alsophila tricolor.*
Silver-lace: *Pteris quadriaurita* cv. 'Argyraea'.
Silver-leaf: *P. ensiformis* cv. 'Victoriae'.
Silver tree: *Alsophila tricolor.*
Slender lip: *Cheilanthes Feei.*
Snuffbox: *Thelypteris palustris* var. *pubescens.*
Soft tree: *Alsophila Smithii.*
Southern lady: *Athyrium Filix-femina* var. *asplenioides.*
Southern maidenhair: *Adiantum Capillus-Veneris.*
Spinulose wood: *Dryopteris austriaca* var. *spinulosa.*
Squirrel-foot, Squirrel's-foot: *Davallia Mariesii, D. trichomanoides.*
Staghorn: *Platycerium.*
Strap: *Polypodium phyllitidis.*
Strawberry: *Hemionitis palmata.*
Swamp: *Acrostichum, Blechnum serrulatum.*
Sweet: *Comptonia peregrina.*
Sword: *Nephrolepis, N. biserrata, N. cordifolia.*
Table: *Pteris.*
Tasmanian tree: *Dicksonia antarctica.*
Tassel maidenhair: *Adiantum Raddianum* cv. 'Grandiceps'.
Tongue: *Pyrrosia lingua.*
Toothed sword: *Nephrolepis pectinata.*
Tracy's maidenhair: *Adiantum ×Tracyi.*
Trailing maidenhair: *A. caudatum.*
Tree: *Alsophila, Cibotium, Cyathea, Nephelea, Sphaeropteris.*
Triangle water: *Ceratopteris Richardii.*
Triangular staghorn: *Platycerium Stemaria.*
Turnip: *Angiopteris.*
Upside-down: *Arachniodes Standishii.*
Vegetable: *Diplazium esculentum.*
Venushair, Venus's-hair: *Adiantum Capillus-Veneris.*
Virginia chain: *Woodwardia virginica.*
Viscid lip: *Cheilanthes viscida.*
Walking: *Adiantum caudatum, Camptosorus, C. rhizophyllus.*
Walking leaf: *Camptosorus.*
Walking maidenhair: *Adiantum philippense.*
Wall: *Polypodium vulgare.*
Wart: *P. scolpendria.*
Water: *Azolla, Ceratopteris, C. thalictroides.*
Wavy cloak: *Notholaena sinuata.*
Western holly: *Polystichum scopulinum.*
Western sword: *P. munitum.*
West Indian tree: *Cyathea arborea.*
Whisk: *Psilotum nudum.*
Wild bird's-nest: *Asplenium serratum.*
Winter: *Conium maculatum.*

Fern—*Continued*
  Wood: *Dryopteris.*
  Woolly lip: *Cheilanthes lanosa.*
  Woolly tree: *Dicksonia fibrosa.*
Fernbush: *Chamaebatiaria.*
Fescue: *Festuca.*
  Alta: *F. arundinacea.*
  Blue: *F. ovina* var. *glauca.*
  Chewing: *F. rubra* var. *commutata.*
  Giant: *F. gigantea.*
  Hair: *F. capillata.*
  Hard: *F. ovina* var. *duriuscula.*
  Meadow: *F. elatior.*
  Red: *F. rubra.*
  Reed: *F. arundinacea.*
  Shade: *F. rubra.*
  Sheep: *F. ovina.*
Feterita: *Sorghum bicolor,* Caudatum Group.
Fetterbush: *Leucothoe, Pieris floribunda.*
Feverfew: *Chrysanthemum Parthenium.*
Feverroot: *Triosteum perfoliatum.*
Fever tree: *Pinkneya pubens.*
Feverwort: *Triosteum.*
Fiddleheads: *Osmunda cinnamomea.*
Fiddle-leaf: *Ficus lyrata.*
Fiddleneck: *Phacelia tanacetifolia.*
Fiddlewood: *Citharexylum fruticosum, C. spinosum.*
Fiesta flower: *Pholistoma auritum.*
Fig: *Ficus.*
  Barbary: *Opuntia vulgaris.*
  Bush: *Ficus capensis.*
  Cape: *F. capensis.*
  Cedar: *F. superba* var. *Henneana.*
  Climbing: *F. pumila.*
  Clown: *F. aspera.*
  Cluster: *F. racemosa.*
  Common: *F. carica.*
  Congo: *F. Dryepondtiana.*
  Creeping: *F. pumila.*
  Devil's: *Solanum hispidum.*
  Dracaena: *Ficus pseudopalma.*
  East Indian: *F. benghalensis.*
  Exotic: *F. benjamina* cv. 'Exotica'.
  Fiddle-leaf: *F. lyrata.*
  Glossy-leaf: *F. retusa.*
  Golden: *F. aurea.*
  Hottentot: *Carpobrotus acinaciformis, C. edulis.*
  Indian: *Opuntia Ficus-indica, O. Tuna.*
  Java: *Ficus benjamina.*
  Kaffir: *F. Nekbudu.*
  Keg: *Diospyros Kaki.*
  Little-leaf: *Ficus rubiginosa.*
  Mistletoe: *F. deltoidea, F. diversifolia.*
  Moreton Bay: *F. macrophylla.*
  Mulberry: *F. Sycomorus.*
  Mysore: *F. mysorensis.*
  Oak-leaf: *F. montana.*
  Philippine: *F. pseudopalma.*
  Port Jackson: *F. rubiginosa.*
  Rusty: *F. rubiginosa.*
  Sacred: *F. religiosa.*
  Sea: *Carpobrotus chilensis.*
  Small-leaved Moreton Bay: *Ficus platypoda.*
  Spotted: *F. virens.*
  Strangler: *F. aurea.*
  Sycamore: *F. Sycomorus.*
  Weeping: *F. benjamina.*
  West Indian laurel: *F. perforata.*
  Zulu: *F. Nekbudu.*
Fig tree: *Ficus carica.*
Figwort: *Scrophularia.*
Filaree: *Erodium.*
  Red-stemmed: *E. cicutarium.*
  White-stemmed: *E. moschatum.*
Filbert: *Corylus.*
  American: *C. americana.*
  Beaked: *C. cornuta.*
  Chinese: *C. chinensis.*
  European: *C. Avellana.*
  Giant: *C. maxima.*
  Mildred: *C. mildredensis.*
  Turkish: *C. Colurna.*
Fingernail plant: *Neoregelia spectabilis.*

Finger-of-God: *Aechmea orlandiana.*
Finger tree: *Euphorbia Tirucalli.*
Finocchio: *Foeniculum vulgare* var. *azoricum.*
Fir: *Abies.*
  Algerian: *A. numidica.*
  Alpine: *A. lasiocarpa.*
  Azure: *A. magnifica* cv. 'Glauca'
  Balsam: *A. balsamea.*
  Bristle-cone: *A. bracteata.*
  Cascade: *A. amabilis.*
  China: *Cunninghamia.*
  Cork: *Abies lasiocarpa* var. *arizonica.*
  Douglas: *Pseudotsuga Menziesii.*
  Dwarf Nikko: *Abies homolepis* cv. 'Scottiae'.
  Fraser: *A. Fraseri.*
  Giant: *A. grandis.*
  Greek: *A. cephalonica.*
  Himalayan: *A. spectabilis.*
  Japanese: *A. firma.*
  Joint: *Ephedra.*
  Korean: *Abies koreana.*
  Lowland: *A. grandis.*
  Momi: *A. firma.*
  Needle: *A. holophylla.*
  Nikko: *A. homolepis.*
  Noble: *A. procera.*
  Pacific silver: *A. amabilis.*
  Plum: *Podocarpus andinus.*
  Red: *Abies magnifica.*
  Sakhalin: *A. sachalinensis.*
  Santa Lucia: *A. bracteata.*
  Scotch: *Pinus sylvestris.*
  Shasta red: *Abies magnifica* var. *shastensis.*
  Silver: *A. alba.*
  Southern: *A. Fraseri.*
  Southern balsam: *A. Fraseri.*
  Spanish: *A. Pinsapo.*
  Summer: *Artemisia Gmelinii* cv. 'Viridis'.
  White: *Abies concolor.*
Firebird: *Heliconia Bihai.*
Firebrush, Chilean: *Embothrium coccineum.*
Firebush: *Hamelia patens, Streptosolen Jamesonii, Kochia scoparia* var. *culta.*
Firecracker, floral: *Dichelostemma Ida-Maia.*
Firecracker flower: *Crossandra, Dichelostemma Ida-Maia.*
Firecracker plant: *Cuphea ignea, Echeveria setosa.*
Firecracker vine: *Manettia cordifolia, M. inflata.*
Fire-dragon: *Acalypha Wilkesiana.*
Fire-on-the-mountain: *Euphorbia cyathophora.*
Fire plant, Mexican: *E. cyathophora, E. heterophylla.*
Fire thorn: *Pyracantha.*
Fire tree, Chilean: *Embothrium coccineum.*
Fireweed: *Epilobium, E. angustifolium.*
Firewheel: *Grevillea Wilsonii.*
Firewheel tree: *Stenocarpus sinuatus.*
Fishbone: *Euphorbia polyacantha.*
Fishhooks: *Mammillaria bocosana.*
Fistula, purging: *Cassia fistula.*
Fitsroot: *Monotropa uniflora.*
Fittonia: *Fittonia.*
  Silver: *F. Verschaffeltii.*
  White-leaf: *F. Verschaffeltii.*
Five-finger: *Potentilla.*
  Marsh: *P. palustris.*
Five-fingers: *Neopanax arboreus, Syngonium auritum.*
Five-spot: *Nemophila maculata.*
  Desert: *Eremalche rotundifolia.*
Flag: *Iris, I. ×germanica.*
  Beachhead: *I. setosa* var. *canadensis.*
  Blue: *I. versicolor, I. virginica.*
  Corn: *Gladiolus, G. segetum.*
  Crimson: *Schizostylis.*
  False: *Neomarica.*
  Grass-leaved sweet: *Acorus gramineus.*
  Morning: *Orthrosanthus.*
  Myrtle: *Acorus Calamus.*
  Poison: *Iris versicolor.*
  Slender blue: *I. prismatica.*
  Soft: *Typha angustifolia.*
  Southern blue: *Iris virginica.*
  Spiral: *Costus, C. Malortieanus.*
  Sweet: *Acorus Calamus.*
  Water: *Iris Pseudacorus.*

Flag—*Continued*
  Western blue: *I. missouriensis.*
  Yellow: *I. Pseudacorus.*
Flagroot: *Acorus Calamus.*
Flamboyant: *Delonix regia.*
Flamebush, Mexican: *Calliandra Tweedii.*
Flame creeper: *Combretum microphyllum.*
Flame flower: *Pyrostegia venusta.*
Flamegold: *Koelreuteria Henryi.*
Flameleaf, Mexican: *Euphorbia pulcherrima.*
Flame-of-the-forest: *Butea monosperma, Spathodea campanulata.*
Flame-of-the-woods: *Ixora coccinea.*
Flame tree: *Delonix, Brachychiton australis.*
Flame vine: *Pyrostegia venusta.*
  Mexican: *Senecio confusus.*
Flamingo flower: *Anthurium Scherzeranum.*
Flamingo plant: *Hypoestes phyllostachya, Justicia carnea.*
Flaming-sword: *Vriesia splendens.*
Flaming-trumpet: *Pyrostegia venusta.*
Flannelbush: *Fremontodendron.*
Flannel flower: *Actinotus helianthi.*
Flannel plant: *Verbascum Thapsus.*
Flaver: *Avena fatua.*
Flawn: *Zoysia Matrella.*
Flax: *Linum, L. usitatissimum.*
  Flowering: *L. grandiflorum.*
  Golden: *L. flavum.*
  Mountain: *Phormium Colensoi.*
  New Zealand: *P. tenax.*
  Perennial: *Linum perenne.*
  Yellow: *Reinwardtia indica.*
Flaxseed, water: *Spirodela polyrhiza.*
Fleabane: *Erigeron.*
  Daisy: *E. annuus.*
  Himalayan: *E. multiradiatus.*
  Running: *E. flagellaris.*
  Western: *E. Bellidiastrum.*
Fleawort: *Plantago Psyllium.*
Fleece flower: *Polygonum.*
  Bukhara: *P. baldschuanicum.*
Fleece vine, China: *Polygonum Aubertii.*
Fleur-d'amour: *Tabernaemontana divaricata* cv. 'Flore Pleno'.
Fleur-de-lis: *Iris, I. ×germanica.*
Floating heart: *Nymphoides.*
  Yellow: *N. peltata.*
Floppers: *Kalanchoe pinnata.*
Floradora: *Stephanotis floribunda.*
Flossflower: *Ageratum.*
Floss-silk tree: *Chorisia.*
Flower-fence: *Caesalpinia pulcherrima.*
  Barbados: *C. pulcherrima.*
  Peacock: *Adenanthera pavonia.*
Flowering-quartz: *Gibbaeum.*
Flowering-stones: *Dinteranthus, Lithops.*
Flower-of-an-hour: *Hibiscus Trionum.*
Flower-of-Jove: *Lychnis Flos-Jovis.*
Flower-of-love: *Tabernaemontana divaricata.*
Fly-catcher: *Befaria racemosa.*
Fly-poison: *Amianthium muscitoxicum.*
Foamflower: *Tiarella cordifolia.*
Foliage flower: *Breynia disticha, Phyllanthus angustifolius, P. arbuscula.*
Foolproof plant: *Billbergia pyramidalis.*
Footsteps-of-spring: *Sanicula arctopoides.*
Forget-me-not: *Myosotis.*
  Alpine: *Eritrichium.*
  Chinese: *Cynoglossum amabile.*
  Creeping: *Omphalodes verna.*
  Garden: *Myosotis sylvatica.*
  White: *Cryptantha.*
Fountain bush: *Russelia equisetiformis.*
Fountain plant: *Amaranthus tricolor* var. *salicifolius, Russelia equisetiformis.*
Four-o'clock: *Mirabilis Jalapa.*
Foxberry: *Vaccinium Vitis-idaea.*
Foxglove: *Digitalis.*
  Common: *D. purpurea.*
  Downy false: *Aureolaria virginica.*
  False: *A. pedicularia.*
  Grecian: *Digitalis lanata.*
  Mexican: *Tetranema roseum.*
  Rusty: *Digitalis ferruginea.*

Foxglove—*Continued*
  Willow-leaved: *D. obscura.*
  Yellow: *D. grandiflora.*
Fox's-brush: *Centranthus ruber.*
Foxtail: *Acalypha hispida, Alopecurus.*
  Creeping: *Alopecurus arundinaceus.*
  Meadow: *A. pratensis.*
  Reed: *A. arundinaceus.*
Framboise: *Rubus idaeus.*
Frangipani: *Plumeria, P. rubra.*
Franklin tree: *Franklinia Alatamaha.*
Fraxinella: *Dictamnus albus.*
Freckle-face: *Hypoestes phyllostachya.*
Fremontia: *Fremontodendron.*
Fret-lip, purple: *Habenaria peramoena.*
Friar's-cap: *Aconitum Napellus.*
Friendship plant: *Billbergia nutans, Pilea involucrata.*
Frijol: *Phaseolus vulgaris.*
Frijolito: *Sophora secundiflora.*
Frilled-fan: *Euphorbia lactea* cv. 'Cristata'.
Frilled-panties: *Protea.*
Fringe-bell: *Shortia soldanelloides.*
Fringecups: *Tellima grandiflora.*
Fringepod: *Thysanocarpus.*
Fringe tree: *Chionanthus.*
Fritillary: *Fritillaria.*
  Narrow-leaved: *F. lanceolata.*
  Pink: *F. pluriflora.*
  Scarlet: *F. recurva.*
  White: *F. liliacea.*
  Yellow: *F. pudica.*
Frog-arrow, white: *Habenaria nivea.*
Frogfruit: *Phyla.*
  Common: *P. nodiflora.*
  Northern: *P. lanceolata.*
Frog's-bit: *Hydrocharis Morsus-ranae.*
  American: *Limnobium.*
Frog-spear: *Habenaria nivea.*
Frog-spike: *Habenaria clavellata.*
Frost flower: *Aster.*
Frostweed: *Helianthemum canadense.*
Fruit-salad plant: *Monstera deliciosa.*
Frying-pans: *Eschscholzia Lobbii.*
Fuchsia: *Fuchsia.*
  California: *Zauschneria.*
  Cape: *Phygelius capensis.*
  Hardy: *Fuchsia magellanica.*
  Honeysuckle: *F. triphylla.*
  Tree: *F. arborescens, F. excorticata, Schotia brachypetala.*
Fuki: *Petasites japonicus.*
Fumewort: *Corydalis bulbosa.*
Fumitory, climbing: *Adlumia fungosa.*
Funnel creeper: *Macfadyena Unguis-cati.*
Funnel-crest: *Cleistes divaricata.*
Furze: *Ulex europaeus.*
  Dwarf: *U. minor.*
Fustic: *Cecropia tinctoria.*
Fuzzy-ears: *Cyanotis somaliensis.*

Galax: *Galax urceolata.*
  Fringed: *Shortia soldanelloides.*
Galaxy: *Galax urceolata.*
Gale, sweet: *Myrica Gale.*
Galingale: *Cyperus.*
Gallberry: *Ilex glabra.*
  Bitter: *I. glabra.*
  Large: *I. coriacea.*
  Sweet: *I. coriacea.*
Gall bush, bay: *Ilex coriacea.*
Galleta: *Hilaria Jamesii.*
  Big: *H. rigida.*
Gampi: *Lychnis coronata.*
Gandergoose: *Orchis morio.*
Garbanzo: *Cicer arietinum.*
Gardener's-garters: *Phalaris arundinacea* var. *picta.*
Gardenia: *Gardenia.*
  Butterfly: *Tabernaemontana divaricata* cv. 'Flore Pleno'.
  Crape: *T. divaricata.*
Garget: *Phytolacca americana.*
Garland flower: *Daphne Cneorum, Hedychium coronarium.*
Garlic: *Allium sativum.*
  Bear's: *A. ursinum.*
  Crow: *A. vineale.*

Garlic—*Continued*
  Daffodil: *A. neapolitanum.*
  False: *Nothoscordum.*
  Field: *Allium vineale, A. oleraceum.*
  Fragrant-flowered: *A. ramosum.*
  Giant: *A. Scorodoprasum.*
  Grace: *Nothoscordum.*
  Great-headed: *Allium Ampeloprasum,* Ampeloprasum Group.
  Hog's: *A. ursinum.*
  Levant: *A. Ampeloprasum,* Ampeloprasum Group.
  Mouse: *A. angulosum.*
  Oriental: *A. tuberosum.*
  Round-headed: *A. sphaerocephalum.*
  Serpent: see under *A. sativum.*
  Society: *Tulbaghia violacea.*
  Spanish: *Allium Scorodoprasum.*
  Stag's: *A. vineale.*
  Striped: *A. Cuthbertii.*
  Sweet: *Tulbaghia fragrans.*
  Wild: *Allium candense.*
Garlic vine: *Cydista aequinoctialis.*
Gas plant: *Dictamnus albus.*
Gasteria: *Gasteria.*
  Pencil-leaf: *G. caespitosa.*
  Rice:*G. verrucosa.*
  Wart: *G. verrucosa.*
Gay-feather: *Liatris.*
Gean: *Prunus avium.*
Geiger tree: *Cordia Sebestena.*
Genip: *Genipa.*
Genipap: *Genipa americana.*
Genipe: *Melicoccus bijugatus.*
Genista (of florists): *Cytisus canariensis.*
Gentian: *Gentiana.*
  Alpine: *G. Newberryi.*
  Blind: *G. clausa.*
  Bottle: *G. Andrewsii, G. clausa.*
  Catesby's: *G. Catesbaei.*
  Closed: *G. Andrewsii, G. clausa, G. linearis, G. rubricaulis.*
  Crested: *G. septemfida.*
  Fringed: *Gentianopsis.*
  Green: *Frasera.*
  Horse: *Triosteum.*
  Mendocino: *Gentiana setigera.*
  Pine-barren: *G. autumnalis.*
  Prairie: *Eustoma grandiflorum.*
  Sierra: *Gentianopsis holopetala.*
  Soapwort: *Gentiana Saponaria.*
  Spurred: *Halenia.*
  Stemless: *Gentiana acaulis.*
  Yellow: *G. lutea.*
Geranium: *Geranium, Pelargonium, P. ×hortorum.*
  Almond: *Pelargonium quercifolium.*
  Alpine: *Erodium chamaedryoides.*
  Apple: *Pelargonium odoratissimum.*
  Apricot: *P. scabrum.*
  Bedding: *P. ×hortorum.*
  Beefsteak: *Begonia* Rex-Cultorum Hybrids (see *B. ×rex-cultorum*), *Saxifraga stolonifera.*
  Black-flowered: *Pelargonium ×glaucifolium.*
  Cactus: *P. echinatum.*
  California: *Senecio Petasitis.*
  Coconut: *Pelargonium grossularioides.*
  Crowfoot: *P. radens.*
  English finger-bowl: *P. ×limoneum.*
  Fancy: *P. ×domesticum.*
  Feather: *Chenopodium Botrys.*
  Fern-leaf: *Pelargonium denticulatum* cv. 'Filicifolium'.
  Fish: *P. ×hortorum.*
  Gooseberry: *P. grossularioides.*
  Grape-leaved *P. vitifolium.*
  Hanging: *P. peltatum.*
  Herb-scented: *P. tomentosum.*
  Horseshoe: *P. ×hortorum.*
  House: *P. ×hortorum.*
  Ivy: *P. peltatum.*
  Jungle: *Ixora coccinea.*
  Knotted: *Pelargonium gibbosum.*
  Lady Washington: *P. ×domesticum.*
  Lemon: *P. crispum.*
  Lime: *P. nervosum.*
  Little-leaf rose: *P. ×glaucifolium.*
  Maple-leaved: *P. acerifolium.*

Geranium—*Continued*
  Martha Washington: *P. ×domesticum.*
  Mint: *Chrysanthemum Balsamita.*
  Mint-scented rose: *Pelargonium ×graveolens* cv. 'Variegatum'.
  Nutmeg: *P. fragrans.*
  Oak-leaved: *P. quercifolium.*
  (of florists): *Pelargonium.*
  Orange: *P. ×citrosum.*
  Pansy-flowered: *P. ×domesticum.*
  Peppermint: *P. tomentosum.*
  Pheasant's-foot: *P. glutinosum, P. jatrophifolium.*
  Pine: *P. denticulatum.*
  Polecat: *Lantana montevidensis.*
  Regal: *Pelargonium ×domesticum.*
  Rock: *Heuchera americana.*
  Rose: *Pelargonium graveolens.*
  Rose-scented: *P. capitatum.*
  Show: *P. ×domesticum.*
  Silver-leaved: *Geranium argenteum.*
  Southernwood: *Pelargonium abrotanifolium.*
  Strawberry: *P. scabrum, Saxifraga stolonifera.*
  Sweetheart: *P. echinatum.*
  Sweet-scented: *P. graveolens.*
  Village-oak: *P. quercifolium.*
  Wild: *Geranium maculatum.*
  Zonal: *Pelargonium ×hortorum.*
Gerardia: *Agalinus.*
Germander: *Teucrium.*
  American: *T. canadense.*
  Tree: *T. fruticans.*
  Wood: *T. Scorodonia.*
Gherkin: *Cucumis Anguria,* also *C. sativus.*
  Bur: *C. Anguria.*
  West Indian: *C. Anguria.*
Ghost plant: *Graptopetalum paraguayense.*
Ghostweed: *Euphorbia marginata.*
Giant-club: *Cereus peruvianus* cv. 'Monstrosus'.
Gifboli: *Boophone disticha.*
Gilia
  Granite: *Leptodactylon pungens.*
  Scarlet: *Ipomopsis aggregata.*
Gill-over-the-ground: *Glecoma hederacea.*
Gillyflower: *Matthiola incana.*
Gimlet
  Bastard: *Eucalyptus diptera.*
  Two-winged: *E. diptera.*
Ginger: *Zingiber, Z. officinalis.*
  Butterfly: *Hedychium coronarium.*
  Canton: *Zingiber officinale.*
  Common: *Z. officinale.*
  Crape, Crepe: *Costus speciosus.*
  Kahili: *Hedychium Gardneranum.*
  Orchid: *Alpinia mutica.*
  Red: *A. purpurata.*
  Shell: *A. Zerumbet.*
  Small shell: *A. mutica.*
  Spiral: *Costus afer, C. Malortieanus.*
  Torch: *Nicolaia elatior.*
  Variegated: *Alpinia Sanderae, A. vittata, Zingiber Darceyi.*
  White: *Hedychium coronarium.*
  Wild: *Asarum, A. canadense, Costus speciosus.*
  Yellow: *Hedychium flavescens.*
Gingerbread tree: *Hyphaene thebaica.*
Ginseng: *Panax, P. pseudoginseng, P. quinquefolius.*
  American: *P. quinquefolius.*
  Dwarf: *P. trifolius.*
Girasole: *Helianthus tuberosus.*
Gladiolus, garden: *Gladiolus ×hortulanus.*
Gladwin: *Iris foetidissima.*
  Stinking: *I. foetidissima.*
Glasswort: *Salicornia.*
Globeflower: *Trollius, T. europaeus.*
  Spreading: *T. laxus.*
Glory-bower: *Clerodendrum.*
  Bleeding: *C. Thomsoniae.*
Glorybush: *Tibouchina, T. semidecandra.*
Glory flower: *Eccremocarpus.*
Glory-of-Texas: *Thelocactus bicolor.*
Glory-of-the-snow: *Chionodoxa.*
Glory-of-the-sun: *Leucocoryne ixioides.*
Glory plant, purple: *Sutera grandiflora.*
Glory tree: *Clerodendrum Thomsoniae.*
  Purple: *Tibouchina Urvilleana.*

Glory vine, crimson: *Vitis Coignetiae.*
Gloxinia: *Sinningia speciosa.*
  Brazilian: *S. speciosa.*
  Canterbury-bells: *Gloxinia perennis.*
  Creeping: *Asarina erubescens.*
  (of florists): *Sinningia speciosa,* Fyfiana Group.
  Slipper: see *S. speciosa,* Maxima Group.
  Tree: *Kohleria.*
  Violet slipper: *Sinningia regina, S. speciosa.*
Gnome's-throne: *Opuntia clavarioides.*
Goat nut: *Simmondsia chinensis.*
Goatsbeard: *Aruncus, Tragopogon.*
  False: *Astilbe biternata.*
Goat's-horns: *Cheiridopsis candidissima.*
Gobo: *Abelmoschus esculentus, Arctium Lappa.*
Godetia: *Clarkia.*
Gold-and-silver flower: *Lonicera japonica.*
Goldback: *Pityrogramma triangularis.*
Gold-blossom tree: *Barklya syringifolia.*
Goldcrest: *Lophiola americana.*
Goldcup: *Solandra guttata.*
Gold-dust: *Aurinia saxatilis.*
Gold-dust plant: *Aucuba japonica* cv. 'Variegata'.
Gold-dust tree: *Aucuba japonica* cv. 'Variegata'.
Golden-ball: *Echinocactus Grusonii.*
Golden-barrel, South American: *Lobivia Bruchii.*
Golden-bells: *Emmenanthe penduliflora, Forsythia.*
Golden-buttons: *Tanacetum vulgare.*
Golden-carpet: *Sedum acre.*
Golden-chain: *Laburnum.*
Golden-chain tree: *Laburnum.*
Golden-club: *Orontium aquaticum.*
Golden-column: *Trichocereus Spachianus.*
Golden creeper: *Stigmaphyllon ciliatum.*
Golden-crest: *Lophiola.*
Golden-cup: *Hunnemannia fumariifolia.*
Golden-dewdrop: *Duranta repens.*
Golden-drop: *Onosma taurica.*
Golden-eardrops: *Dicentra chrysantha.*
Golden-feather: *Chrysanthemum Parthenium* cv. 'Aureum'.
Golden-fleece: *Dyssodia tenuiloba.*
Golden-glow: *Rudbeckia laciniata* cv. 'Hortensia'.
Golden-lace: *Mammillaria elongata.*
Golden-rain: *Cassia fistula.*
Golden-rain tree: *Koelreuteria.*
Goldenrod: *Solidago.*
  Blue-stem: *S. caesia.*
  California: *S. californica.*
  European: *S. Virgaurea.*
  Seaside: *S. sempervirens.*
  Sweet: *S. odora.*
  White: *S. bicolor.*
  Wreath: *S. caesia.*
Goldenseal: *Hydrastis canadensis.*
Golden-shower: *Cassia fistula, Pyrostegia venusta.*
Golden-slipper: *Cypripedium Calceolus* var. *pubescens.*
  Small: *C. Calceolus* var. *parviflorum.*
Golden-spines: *Cephalocereus chrysacanthus.*
Golden-stars: *Bloomeria crocea.*
Goldentop: *Lamarckia aurea.*
Golden-trumpet: *Allamanda cathartica.*
Golden vine, Brazilian: *Stigmaphyllon ciliatum.*
Golden-wonder: *Cassia splendida.*
Goldfields: *Lasthenia chrysostoma.*
Gold flower: *Hypericum ×Moseranum.*
Gold-flower-of-Chile: *Solenomelus chilensis.*
Goldilocks: *Aster Linosyris.*
Goldplush: *Opuntia microdasys.*
Goldspire: *Azara integrifolia.*
Goldthread: *Coptis.*
Gold vine, Guinea: *Hibbertia.*
Goldwire: *Hypericum concinnum.*
Golf-ball, gingham: *Euphorbia obesa.*
Gombo: *Abelmoschus esculentus.*
Goober: *Arachis hypogaea.*
Good-King-Henry: *Chenopodium Bonus-Henricus.*
Good-luck leaf: *Kalanchoe pinnata, Oxalis Deppei.*
Good-luck plant: *Cordyline terminalis, Oxalis Deppei, Sansevieria.*
  Hawaiian: *Cordyline terminalis.*
Goora nut: *Cola acuminata.*
Gooseberry: *Ribes.*
  Barbados: *Pereskia aculeata, Physalis peruviana.*
  Canyon: *Ribes Menziesii.*

Gooseberry—*Continued*
  Cape: *Physalis peruviana.*
  Ceylon: *Dovyalis hebecarpa.*
  Chinese: *Actinidia chinensis.*
  Country: *Averrhoa Carambola.*
  Dwarf Cape: *Physalis pruinosa.*
  English: *Ribes uva-crispa.*
  European: *R. uva-crispa.*
  Fuchsia-flowered: *R. speciosum.*
  Gummy: *R. Lobbii.*
  Hawthorn-leaved: *R. oxycanthoides.*
  Hedge: *R. alpestre.*
  Hill: *Rhodomyrtus tomentosa.*
  Kiwiberry: *Actinidia chinensis.*
  Missouri: *Ribes missouriense, R. setosum.*
  Otaheite: *Phyllanthus acidus.*
  Prickly: *Ribes cynosbati.*
  Sierra: *R. Roezlii.*
  Swamp: *R. lacustre.*
Gooseberry tree: *Phyllanthus acidus.*
Goosefoot: *Chenopodium, C. Bonus-Henricus.*
  White: *C. album.*
Gorgon: *Euryale ferox.*
Gorse: *Ulex europaeus.*
Gourd: *Cucurbita, C. Pepo.*
  Ash: *Benincasa hispida.*
  Bitter: *Momordica Charantia.*
  Bottle: *Lagenaria siceraria.*
  Calabash: *L. siceraria.*
  Club: *Trichosanthes Anguina.*
  Dipper: *Lagenaria siceraria.*
  Dishcloth: *Luffa, L. aegyptiaca.*
  Fig-leaf: *Cucurbita ficifolia.*
  Goareberry: *Cucumis Anguria.*
  Gooseberry: *C. Anguria.*
  Hedgehog: *C. dipsaceus.*
  Hercules'-club: *Lagenaria siceraria.*
  Ivy: *Coccinia cordifolia.*
  Knob-kerrie: *Lagenaria siceraria.*
  Malabar: *Cucurbita ficifolia.*
  Missouri: *C. foetidissima.*
  Rag: *Luffa.*
  Scarlet-fruited: *Coccinia cordifolia.*
  Serpent: *Trichosanthes Anguina.*
  Silver-seed: *Cucurbita mixta.*
  Snake: *Trichosanthes Anguina, T. cucumeroides.*
  Sponge: *Luffa aegyptiaca.*
  Sugar-trough: *Lagenaria siceraria.*
  Teasel: *Cucumis dipsaceus.*
  Trumpet: *Lagenaria siceraria.*
  Viper's: *Trichosanthes Anguina.*
  Wax: *Benincasa hispida.*
  White: *B. hispida.*
  (White-flowered): *Lagenaria siceraria.*
  (Yellow-flowered): *Cucurbita Pepo* var. *ovifera.*
Goutweed: *Aegopodium Podagraria.*
Gowan, yellow: *Ranunculus repens.*
Gram: *Cicer arietinum.*
  Black: *Vigna Mungo.*
  Golden: *V. radiata.*
  Green: *V. radiata.*
  Red: *Cajanus Cajan.*
Grama: *Bouteloua.*
  Black: *B. eriopoda.*
  Blue: *B. gracilis.*
  Hairy: *B. hirsuta.*
  Side-oats: *B. curtipendula.*
  Slender: *B. repens.*
Granadilla: *Passiflora quadrangularis.*
  Giant: *P. quadrangularis.*
  Purple: *P. edulis.*
  Red: *P. coccinea.*
  Sweet: *P. ligularis.*
  Yellow: *P. laurifolia.*
Granadina: *Passiflora subpeltata.*
Grape: *Vitis.*
  African: *Rhoicissus.*
  African tree: *Cissus Bainesii.*
  Amur: *Vitis amurensis.*
  Bear's: *Arctostaphylos Uva-ursi.*
  Blue: *Vitis aestivalis* var. *argentifolia.*
  Bullace: *V. rotundifolia.*
  Bunch: *V. aestivalis.*

Grape—*Continued*
  Bush: *V. acerifolia, V. rupestris.*
  Canyon: *V. arizonica.*
  Cape: *Rhoicissus capensis.*
  Cat: *Vitis palmata.*
  Catbird: *V. palmata.*
  Chicken: *V. vulpina.*
  European: *V. vinifera.*
  Evergreen: *Rhoicissus capensis.*
  Frost: *Vitis riparia, V. vulpina.*
  Javan: *Tetrastigma.*
  Miller: *Vitis vinifera* cv. 'Incana'.
  Mountain: *Mahonia Aquifolium, Vitis monticola, V. rupestris.*
  Oregon: *Mahonia Aquifolium, M. nervosa.*
  Panhandle: *Vitis acerifolia.*
  Pigeon: *V. aestivalis.*
  Possum: *Cissus incisa, C. trifoliata, Vitis Baileyana.*
  Red: *Vitis palmata.*
  River-bank: *V. riparia.*
  Rock: *V. rupestris.*
  Sand: *V. rupestris.*
  Sea: *Coccoloba uvifera.*
  Silver-leaf: *Vitis aestivalis* var. *argentifolia.*
  Southern fox: *V. rotundifolia.*
  Spanish: *V. Berlandieri.*
  Sugar: *V. rupestris.*
  Summer: *V. aestivalis.*
  Sweet mountain: *V. monticola.*
  Tail: *Artabotrys.*
  Veldt: *Cissus quadrangula.*
  Wine: *Vitis vinifera.*
  Winter: *V. vulpina.*
Grapefruit: *Citrus ×paradisi.*
Grass
  African Bermuda: *Cynodon transvaalensis.*
  Aleppo: *Sorghum halepense.*
  Alkali: *Zigadenus elegans.*
  American beach: *Ammophila breviligulata.*
  Amur silver: *Miscanthus sacchariflorus.*
  Angleton: *Dichanthium aristatum.*
  Annual beard: *Polypogon monspeliensis.*
  Arrow: *Triglochin.*
  Australian feather: *Stipa elegantissima.*
  Australian rye: *Lolium multiflorum.*
  Australian windmill: *Chloris ventricosa.*
  Bahia: *Paspalum notatum.*
  Barn: *Echinochloa crus-galli.*
  Basket: *Oplismenus hirtellus.*
  Beach: *Ammophila.*
  Bear: *Dasylirion, Nolina, Xerophyllum tenax, Yucca Smalliana.*
  Beard: *Andropogon.*
  Beavertail: *Calochortus coeruleus.*
  Bengal: *Setaria italica.*
  Bent: *Agrostis.*
  Bermuda: *Cynodon Dactylon.*
  Big quaking: *Briza maxima.*
  Billion-dollar: *Echinochloa crus-galli.*
  Blue: see Bluegrass.
  Bluebunch wheat: *Agropyron spicatum.*
  Blue conch: *Digitaria didactyla.*
  Blue-eyed: *Sisyrinchium.*
  Blue finger: *Digitaria didactyla.*
  Blue love: *Eragrostis chloromelas.*
  Boer love: *E. chloromelas.*
  Brahman: *Dichanthium annulatum.*
  Branched cup: *Eriochloa aristata.*
  Bristle: *Setaria.*
  Brome: *Bromus;* see also Brome as a primary entry.
  Buffalo: *Buchloe dactyloides, Stenotaphrum secundatum.*
  Buffel: *Pennisetum ciliare.*
  California blue-eyed: *Sisyrinchium bellum.*
  Canary: *Phalaris, P. canariensis.*
  Carib: *Eriochloa polystachya.*
  Carpet: *Axonopus affinis, Phyla nodiflora.*
  Centipede: *Eremochloa ophiuroides.*
  Chee: *Stipa splendens.*
  China: *Boehmeria nivea.*
  Citronella: *Cymbopogon Nardus.*
  Cloud: *Agrostis nebulosa.*
  Common carpet: *Axonopus affinis.*
  Common rye: *Lolium multiflorum.*
  Cord: *Spartina.*
  Crab: *Digitaria.*

Grass—*Continued*
  Creeping windmill: *Chloris truncata.*
  Crested wheat: *Agropyron cristatum.*
  Crinkled hair: *Deschampsia flexuosa.*
  Cup: *Eriochloa.*
  Curly: *Schizaea pusilla.*
  Cut: see Cutgrass.
  Dallis: *Paspalum dilatatum.*
  Deer: *Rhexia.*
  Desert wheat: *Agropyron sibiricum.*
  Ditch: *Ruppia.*
  Dog: *Agropyron.*
  Domestic rye: *Lolium multiflorum.*
  Dudder: *Adiantum Capillus-Veneris.*
  Dwarf meadow: *Poa annua.*
  Eel: *Vallisneria.*
  Elephant: *Pennisetum purpureum.*
  Elk: *Xerophyllum tenax.*
  English rye: *Lolium perenne.*
  Esparto: *Stipa tenacissima.*
  European beach: *Ammophila arenaria.*
  European dune: *Elymus arenarius.*
  European feather: *Stipa pennata.*
  Fairway crested wheat: *Agropyron cristatum.*
  False wheat: *Elymus chinensis.*
  Feather love: *Eragrostis amabilis.*
  Fever: *Cymbopogon citratus.*
  Finger: *Chloris.*
  Fish: *Cabomba caroliniana.*
  Fountain: *Pennisetum setaceum.*
  Gallow: *Cannabis sativa.*
  Giant finger: *Chloris Berroi.*
  Golden-eyed: *Sisyrinchium californicum.*
  Goose: *Eleusine, E. indica, Potentilla Anserina.*
  Green needle: *Stipa viridula.*
  Guinea: *Panicum maximum.*
  Hair: *Deschampsia, Eleocharis acicularis.*
  Hairy crab: *Digitaria sanguinalis.*
  Hairy cup: *Eriochloa villosa.*
  Harding: *Phalaris tuberosa* var. *stenoptera.*
  Hare's-tail: *Lagurus ovatus.*
  Himalaya fairy: *Miscanthus nepalensis.*
  Hungarian: *Setaria italica.*
  Indian: *Sorghastrum nutans.*
  Indian basket: *Xerophyllum tenax.*
  Indian rice: *Oryzopsis hymenoides.*
  Intermediate wheat: *Agropyron intermedium.*
  Italian rye: *Lolium multiflorum.*
  Japanese carpet: *Zoysia Matrella.*
  Japanese lawn: *Z. japonica.*
  Japanese love: *Eragrostis amabilis.*
  Japanese sedge: *Carex Morrowii* var. *expallida.*
  Johnson: *Sorghum halepense.*
  Kleberg: *Dichanthium annulatum.*
  Korean: *Zoysia japonica.*
  Korean lawn: *Z. japonica.*
  Korean velvet: *Z. tenuifolia.*
  Kuma bamboo: *Sasa Veitchii.*
  Lace: *Eragrostis capillaris.*
  Lazy-man's: *Eremochloa ophiuroides.*
  Lehmann love: *Eragrostis Lehmanniana.*
  Lemon: see Lemongrass.
  Little quaking: *Briza minor.*
  Love: *Eragrostis.*
  Lyme: *Elymus arenarius.*
  Malojilla: *Eriochloa polystachya.*
  Manila: *Zoysia Matrella.*
  Mascarene: *Z. tenuifolia.*
  Mat: *Phyla nodiflora.*
  Means: *Sorghus halepense.*
  Mediterranean salt: *Aeluropus littoralis.*
  Melic: *Melica.*
  Mexican everlasting: *Eriochloa aristata.*
  Molasses: *Melinis minutiflora.*
  Mondo: *Ophiopogon, O. japonicus.*
  Moor: *Molinia coerulea.*
  Napier: *Pennisetum purpureum.*
  Nard: *Cymbopogon Nardus.*
  Natal: *Rhynchelytrum repens.*
  Nepal silver: *Miscanthus nepalensis.*
  Nut: *Cyperus esculentus, C. rotundus.*
  Oat: *Arrhenatherum, Danthonia.*
  Oil: *Cymbopogon.*

Grass—*Continued*
  Orange: *Hypericum gentianoides.*
  Orchid: *Dactylis glomerata.*
  Oregon rye: *Lolium multiflorum.*
  Pacey's English rye: *L. perenne.*
  Palm: *Curculigo capitulata, Setaria palmifolia.*
  Pampas: *Cortaderia.*
  Pangola: *Digitaria decumbens.*
  Para: *Panicum purpurascens.*
  Paraguay Bahia: *Paspalum notatum* var. *Saurae.*
  Pensacola Bahia: *P. notatum* var. *Saurae.*
  Pentz finger: *Digitaria Pentzii.*
  Perennial rye: *Lolium perenne.*
  Perennial veldt: *Ehrharta calycina.*
  Pin: *Erodium cicutarium.*
  Plains bristle: *Setaria macrostachya.*
  Plume: *Erianthus.*
  Poiret bristle: *Setaria Poiretiana.*
  Poverty: *Corema Conradii, Hudsonia tomentosa.*
  Prairie cord: *Spartina pectinata.*
  Pubescent wheat: *Agropyron trichophorum.*
  Pudding: *Hedeoma pulegioides.*
  Purple-eyed: *Sisyrinchium Douglasii.*
  Quack: *Agropyron repens.*
  Quaking: *Briza.*
  Rabbit-foot: *Polypogon monspeliensis.*
  Rabbit-tail: *Lagurus ovatus.*
  Rancheria: *Elymus arenarius.*
  Ravenna: *Erianthus ravennae.*
  Reed canary: *Phalaris arundinacea.*
  Ree wheat: *Agropyron intermedium.*
  Rescue: *Bromus unioloides.*
  Rhodes: *Chloris Gayana.*
  Rib: see Ribgrass.
  Ribbon: *Phalaris arundinacea* var. *picta.*
  Rice: *Oryzopsis.*
  Ringed beard: *Dichanthium annulatum.*
  Ripple: see Ripplegrass.
  Rush: *Sporobolus.*
  Rye: *Lolium.*
  Saint Augustine: *Stenotaphrum secundatum.*
  Sand love: *Eragrostis trichodes.*
  Scorpion: *Myosotis.*
  Scurvy: *Barbarea verna, Cochlearia, C. officinalis, Crambe maritima, Oxalis enneaphylla.*
  Sea lyme: *Elymus arenarius.*
  Sedge: *Carex pendula.*
  Serpent: *Polygonum viviparum.*
  Shave: *Equisetum hyemale.*
  Shore: *Littorella uniflora.*
  Siberian wheat: *Agropyron sibiricum.*
  Signal: *Brachiaria.*
  Silk: *Pityopsis graminifolia, P. nervosa.*
  Slender wheat: *Agropyron trachycaulum.*
  Smilo: *Oryzopsis miliacea.*
  Spike: *Desmazeria sicula, Uniola paniculata.*
  Squaw: *Xerophyllum tenax.*
  Squirreltail: *Hordeum jubatum.*
  Standard crested wheat: *Agropyron sibiricum.*
  Star: *Aletris, Chloris truncata, Hypoxis.*
  Starry: *Cerastium arvense.*
  St. Augustine: *Stenotaphrum secundatum.*
  Stiff-hair wheat: *Agropyron trichophorum.*
  Sudan: *Sorghum sudanense.*
  Sweet vernal: *Anthoxanthum odoratum.*
  Switch: *Panicum virgatum.*
  Sword: *Scirpus americanus.*
  Tall oat: *Arrhenatherum elatius.*
  Tall wheat: *Agropyron elongatum.*
  Tape: *Vallisneria.*
  Texas needle: *Stipa leucotricha.*
  Texas winter: *S. leucotricha.*
  Tobosa: *Hilaria mutica.*
  Transvaal dog-tooth: *Cynodon transvaalensis.*
  Tuber oat: *Arrhenatherum elatius* var. *bulbosum.*
  Tufted hair: *Deschampsia caespitosa.*
  Uva: *Gynerium sagittatum.*
  Vasey: *Paspalum Urvillei.*
  Velvet: *Holcus lanatus.*
  Vernal: *Anthoxanthum.*
  Viper's: *Scorzonera hispanica.*
  Wallaby: *Danthonia setacea.*
  Washington: *Cabomba caroliniana.*

Grass—*Continued*
  Water star: *Heteranthera dubia.*
  Weeping love: *Eragrostis curvula.*
  Western rye: *Lolium multiflorum.*
  Western wheat: *Agropyron Smithii.*
  Wheat: *Agropyron.*
  White: *Leersia.*
  Widgeon: *Ruppia occidentalis.*
  Wilmington Bahia: *Paspalum notatum* var. *Saurae.*
  Witch: *Panicum capillare.*
  Worm: *Spigelia, S. marilandica.*
  Yard: *Eleusine.*
  Yellow-eyed: *Xyris.*
  Yellow nut: *Cyperus esculentus.*
  Zebra: *Miscanthus sinensis* cv. 'Zebrinus'.
  Zoysia: *Zoysia Matrella.*
Grass nut: *Arachis hypogaea, Triteleia laxa.*
Grass-of-Parnassus: *Parnassia.*
Grass tree: *Xanthorrhoea.*
Grass-widow: *Sisyrinchium Douglasii.*
Grassy-bell: *Dierama pendulum.*
Grassy-bells: *Edraianthus.*
Graybeard: *Tillandsia usneoides.*
Greasewood: *Adenostoma fasciculatum, Sarcobatus, Salvia apiana.*
Grecian-vase: *Quesnelia marmorata.*
Green-and-gold-crown: *Aloe nobilis.*
Greenbrier: *Smilax.*
  Bristly: *S. hispida.*
  Common: *S. rotundifolia.*
  Laurel-leaved: *S. laurifolia.*
  Red-berried: *S. Walteri.*
Green-dragon: *Arisaema Dracontium.*
Green-eyes: *Berlandiera.*
Green-feather: *Hedera Helix* cv. 'Meagheri'.
Greengage: *Prunus insititia* var. *italica.*
Greenweed, dyer's: *Genista tinctoria.*
Grevillea, holly-leaved: *Grevillea Aquifolium.*
Grizzly-bear: *Opuntia erinacea* var. *ursina.*
Gromwell: *Lithospermum.*
Groundnut: *Apios americana, Arachis hypogaea, Panax trifolius.*
  Bambara: *Voandzeia subterranea.*
Groundsel: *Senecio.*
  Balsam: *S. pauperculus.*
  Giant: *Ligularia Wilsoniana.*
  Golden: *Senecio aureus.*
  Velvet: *S. Petasitis.*
Groundselbush: *Baccharis halimifolia.*
Groundsel tree: *Baccharis halimifolia.*
Grouseberry: *Vaccinium scoparium, Viburnum trilobum.*
Gru-gru: *Acrocomia Totai.*
Grumixameira: *Eugenia brasiliensis.*
Guajilote: *Parmentiera edulis.*
Guanabana: *Annona muricata.*
Guar: *Cyamopsis tetragonoloba.*
Guava: *Psidium, P. guineense.*
  Apple: *P. Guajava.*
  Cattley: *P. littorale* var. *longipes.*
  Chilean: *Ugni Molinae.*
  Common: *Psidium Guajava.*
  Costa Rican: *P. Friedrichsthalianum.*
  Pineapple: *Feijoa Sellowiana.*
  Purple: *Psidium littorale* var. *longipes.*
  Purple strawberry: *P. littorale* var. *longipes.*
  Strawberry: *P. littorale.*
  Yellow: *P. Guajava.*
  Yellow Cattley: *P. littorale* var. *littorale.*
  Yellow strawberry: *P. littorale* var. *littorale.*
Guave, hill: *Rhodomyrtus tomentosa.*
Guayabo hormiguero: *Triplaris surinamensis.*
Guayule: *Parthenium argentatum.*
Guinea plant, gold: *Hibbertia scandens.*
Gum
  American sweet: *Liquidambar Styraciflua.*
  Apple: *Eucalyptus clavigera.*
  Australian: *Eucalyptus.*
  Barbary: *Acacia gummifera.*
  Black: *Nyssa sylvatica.*
  Blakely's red: *Eucalyptus Blakelyi.*
  Blue: *E. Globulus.*
  Blue weeping: *E. sepulcralis.*
  Cabbage: *E. amplifolia, E. clavigera, E. pauciflora.*
  Candle-bark: *E. rubida.*
  Cape: *Acacia horrida.*

Gum—*Continued*
Cider: *Eucalyptus Gunnii.*
Coral: *E. torquata.*
Cotton: *Nyssa aquatica.*
Cup: *Eucalyptus cosmophylla.*
Deane's: *E. Deanei.*
Desert: *E. rudis.*
Forest red: *E. tereticornis.*
Formosan: *Liquidambar formosana.*
Fuchsia: *Eucalyptus Forrestiana.*
Giant: *E. regnans.*
Gimlet: *E. salubris.*
Gray: *E. punctata.*
Gully: *E. Smithii.*
Heart-leaved silver: *E. cordata.*
Karri: *E. diversicolor.*
Lehmann's: *E. Lehmannii.*
Lemon-scented: *E. citriodora.*
Maiden's: *E. Maidenii.*
Manna: *E. viminalis.*
Morocco: *Acacia gummifera.*
Mountain: *Eucalyptus Dalrympleana.*
Murray red: *E. camaldulensis.*
Omeo round-leaved: *E. neglecta.*
Oriental sweet: *Liquidambar orientalis.*
Red: *Eucalyptus calophylla, Liquidambar Styraciflua.*
Red-flowering: *Eucalyptus ficifolia.*
Red-spotted: *E. mannifera.*
Rose: *E. grandis.*
Rough-barked manna: *E. Huberana.*
Round-leaved snow: *E. Perriniana.*
Salmon: *E. salmonophloia.*
Salmon white: *E. Lane-Poolei.*
Scarlet: *E. phoenicia.*
Scarlet-flowering: *E. ficifolia.*
Scribbly: *E. haemastoma.*
Silver-dollar: *E. polyanthemos.*
Silver-leaved mountain: *E. pulverulenta.*
Small-leaved: *E. parvifolia.*
Snappy: *E. racemosa.*
Snow: *E. niphophila.*
Sour: *Nyssa sylvatica.*
Spinning: *Eucalyptus Perriniana.*
Spotted: *E. maculata.*
Steedman's: *E. Steedmanii.*
Strickland's: *E. Stricklandii.*
Sugar: *E. cladocalyx.*
Swamp: *E. ovata.*
Sweet: *Liquidambar, L. Styraciflua.*
Sydney blue: *Eucalyptus saligna.*
Tasmanian blue: *E. Globulus.*
Tasmanian snow: *E. coccifera.*
Timor white: *E. alba.*
Tumble-down: *E. dealbata.*
Tupelo: *Nyssa aquatica.*
Urn-fruited: *Eucalyptus urnigera.*
Yellow-flowered: *E. Woodwardii.*
Gum arabic, Sudan: *Acacia Senegal.*
Gum-arabic tree: *Acacia Senegal, A. Seyal, A. nilotica.*
Gumbo: *Abelmoschus esculentus.*
Gumbo-limbo: *Bursera Simaruba.*
Gum-elastic: *Bumelia lanuginosa.*
Gumi: *Elaeagnus multiflora.*
Gum-lac: *Schleichera oleosa.*
Gum plant: *Grindelia.*
Gum tree: *Eucalyptus.*
Gumweed: *Grindelia.*
Curly-cup: *G. squarrosa.*
Gypsyweed: *Veronica officinalis.*
Gypsywort: *Lycopus.*

Habbel: *Juniperus drupacea.*
Hackberry: *Celtis.*
Japanese: *C. sinensis.*
Mediterranean: *C. australis.*
Mississippi: *C. laevigata.*
Hackmatack: *Larix laricina, Populus balsaminifera.*
Hagberry: *Prunus Padus.*
Hagbrier: *Smilax hispida.*
Handkerchief tree: *Davidia involucrata.*
Hand plant, Mexican: *Chiranthodendron pentadactylon.*
Hanover salad: *Brassica Napus,* Pabularia Group.
Hapuu: *Cibotium splendens.*

Hapuu-ii: *Cibotium Chamissoi.*
Harbinger-of-spring: *Erigenia bulbosa.*
Hardhack: *Spiraea tomentosa.*
Golden: *Potentilla fruticosa.*
Hardheads: *Centaurea nigra.*
Harebell: *Campanula rotundifolia, Endymion non-scriptus.*
Common: *Campanula rotundifolia.*
Southern: *C. divaricata.*
Hare's-ear: *Bupleurum falcatum.*
Hare's-tail: *Lagurus ovatus.*
Haricot: *Phaseolus vulgaris.*
Harlock: *Arctium majus.*
Hartshorn plant: *Anemone Nuttalliana.*
Hart's-tongue: *Phyllitis Scolopendrium.*
Harvest-lice: *Agrimonia.*
Hat tree: *Brachychiton discolor.*
Haw: *Viburnum, V. nudum.*
Black: *Bumelia lanuginosa, Viburnum Lentago, V. prunifolium.*
Blue: *Viburnum rufidulum.*
Poison: *V. molle.*
Possum: *Ilex decidua, Viburnum acerifolium, V. nudum.*
Red: *Crataegus.*
Southern black: *Viburnum rufidulum.*
Summer: *Crataegus flava.*
Swamp: *Viburnum cassinoides, V. nudum.*
Sweet: *V. prunifolium.*
Hawkweed: *Hieracium.*
Mouse-ear: *H. Pilosella.*
Narrow-leaved: *H. umbellatum.*
Orange: *H. aurantiacum.*
Shaggy: *H. villosum.*
Haworthia: *Haworthia.*
Lace: *H. setata.*
Window: *H. cymbiformis, H. magnifica.*
Zebra: *H. fasciata.*
Hawthorn: *Crataegus.*
English: *C. laevigata, C. monogyna.*
Indian: *Raphiolepis indica.*
Water: *Aponogeton distachyus.*
Yeddo: *Raphiolepis umbellata.*
Haybells: *Uvularia.*
Hazel: *Corylus.*
American: *C. americana.*
Buttercup winter: *Corylopsis pauciflora.*
Chile: *Gevuina Avellana.*
Chinese: *Corylus chinensis.*
Chinese witch: *Hamamelis mollis.*
European: *Corylus Avellana*
Japanese: *Corylus Sieboldiana.*
Japanese witch: *Hamamelis japonica.*
Spike winter: *Corylopsis spicata.*
Tree: *Corylus Colurna.*
Turkish: *Corylus Colurna.*
Winter: *Corylopsis.*
Witch: *Hamamelis.*
Hazelnut: *Corylus.*
American: *C. americana.*
Beaked: *C. cornuta.*
Chinese: *C. chinensis.*
European: *C. Avellana.*
Japanese: *C. Sieboldiana.*
Turkish: *C. Colurna.*
Heal-all: *Habenaria orbiculata, Prunella vulgaris.*
Healing herb: *Symphytum officinale.*
Heart nut: *Juglans ailanthifolia var. cordiformis.*
Heart-of-flame: *Bromelia Balansae, B. serra* cv. 'Variegata'.
Heart-of-Jesus: *Caladium bicolor.*
Hearts-and-honey vine: *Ipomoea ✕multifida.*
Heartsease: *Viola ✕Wittrockiana.*
Heartseed: *Cardiospermum.*
Hearts-entangled: *Ceropegia Woodii.*
Hearts-on-a-string: *Ceropegia Woodii.*
Heart vine: *Ceropegia Woodii.*
Heath: *Erica.*
Berry: *E. baccans.*
Besom: *E. scoparia.*
Cornish: *E. vagans.*
Cranberry: *Astroloma humifusum.*
Cross-leaved: *Erica Tetralix.*
Dorset: *E. ciliaris.*
Fringed: *E. ciliaris.*
Irish: *Daboecia cantabrica, Erica mediterranea.*
Otago: *Leucopogon Fraseri.*

Heath—*Continued*
  Scotch: *Erica cinerea.*
  Spanish: *E. lusitanica.*
  Spike: *Bruckenthalia spiculifolia.*
  Spring: *Erica carnea.*
  Tree: *E. arborea.*
  Twisted: *E. cinerea.*
Heather: *Calluna;* see also *Erica.*
  Beach: *Hudsonia.*
  Bell: *Erica cinerea.*
  Bog: *E. Tetralix.*
  Christmas: *E. canaliculata.*
  Corsican: *E. terminalis.*
  Everblooming French: *E. doliiformis.*
  False: *Cuphea hyssopifolia.*
  French: *Erica hyemalis.*
  Golden: *Hudsonia ericoides.*
  Mediterranean: *Erica mediterranea.*
  Mountain: *Phyllodoce.*
  Red: *P. Breweri.*
  Scotch: *Calluna vulgaris.*
  Snow: *Erica carnea.*
  White: *Cassiope Mertensiana.*
  White winter: *Erica hyemalis.*
Heavenly-twins: *Crassula perforata* cv. 'Gigantea'.
Hedgehog: *Agave stricta, Aloe humilis.*
Hedge plant: *Ligustrum.*
Hegari: *Sorghum bicolor,* Caffrorum Group.
Heliconia, beefsteak: *Heliconia Mariae.*
Heliotrope: *Heliotropium.*
  Garden: *Valeriana officinalis.*
  Seaside: *Heliotropium curassavicum.*
  Winter: *Petasites fragrans.*
  Yellow: *Streptosolen Jamesonii.*
Hellebore: *Helleborus.*
  American white: *Veratrum viride.*
  European white: *V. album.*
  False: *Veratrum.*
  White: *V. viride.*
Helleborine: *Epipactis.*
  Bastard: *E. Helleborine.*
  Broad-leaved: *E. Helleborine.*
  Giant: *E. gigantea.*
Hellfetter: *Smilax hispida.*
Helmet flower: *Aconitum Napellus, Sinningia cardinalis.*
Hemlock: *Conium maculatum, Tsuga.*
  Canada: *Tsuga canadensis.*
  Carolina: *T. caroliniana.*
  Dwarf: *T. canadensis* cv. 'Nana'.
  Ground: *Taxus canadensis.*
  Japanese: *Tsuga diversifolia, T. Sieboldii.*
  Mountain: *T. Mertensiana.*
  Poison: *Conium maculatum.*
  Siebold: *Tsuga Sieboldii.*
  Spotted: *Conium maculatum.*
  Water: *Cicuta.*
  Western: *Tsuga heterophylla.*
Hemp: *Cannabis sativa.*
  African: *Sparmannia africana.*
  African bowstring: *Sansevieria hyacinthoides.*
  Bog: *Boehmeria cylindrica.*
  Bowstring: *Calotropis gigantea, Sansevieria.*
  Ceylon bowstring: *Sansevieria zeylanica.*
  Colorado River: *Sesbania macrocarpa.*
  Cuban: *Furcraea hexapetala.*
  Deccan: *Hibiscus cannabinus.*
  Deckaner: *H. cannabinus.*
  Indian: *H. cannabinus, Apocynum cannabinum.*
  Indian bowstring: *Sansevieria Roxburghiana.*
  Manila: *Musa textilis.*
  Mauritius: *Furcraea foetida.*
  New Zealand: *Phormium tenax.*
  Sisal: *Agave sisalina.*
Hemp plant: *Agave sisalina, Sansevieria.*
Hemp tree: *Vitex Agnus-castus.*
Hemp vine, climbing: *Mikania scandens.*
Hempweed, climbing: *Mikania scandens.*
Hen-and-chickens: *Echeveria, Sempervivum soboliferum, S. tectorum.*
Henbane: *Hyoscyamus niger.*
  Black: *H. niger.*
Henequen: *Agave fourcroydes.*
Henna: *Lawsonia inermis.*
Herald's-trumpet: *Beaumontia grandiflora.*

Herb bennet: *Geum urbanum.*
Herb Gerard: *Aegopodium Podagraria.*
Herb-of-grace: *Ruta graveolens.*
Herb patience: *Rumex patientia.*
Herb Robert: *Geranium Robertianum.*
Hercules'-club: *Aralia spinosa, Lagenaria siceraria, Zanthoxylum clava-Herculis.*
Herniary: *Herniaria.*
Heron's-bill: *Erodium.*
Hibiscus: *Hibiscus.*
  Chinese: *H. Rosa-sinensis.*
  Hawaiian: *H. Rosa-sinensis.*
  Japanese: *H. schizopetalus.*
Hickory: *Carya.*
  Broom: *C. glabra.*
  Chinese: *C. cathayensis.*
  Mockernut: *C. tomentosa.*
  Mountain: *Acacia penninervis.*
  Pale: *Carya pallida.*
  Pignut: *C. glabra.*
  Sand: *C. pallida.*
  Shagbark: *C. ovata.*
  Shellbark: *C. ovata, C. laciniosa.*
  Small-fruited: *C. glabra.*
  Swamp: *C. cordiformis.*
  Water: *C. aquatica.*
  White-heart: *C. tomentosa.*
Hierba-de-vibora: *Ibervillea Lindheimeri.*
Hiedra: *Rhus Toxicodendron.*
Hills-of-snow: *Hydrangea arborescens.*
Himalaya berry: *Rubus procerus.*
Hindu-rope: *Hoya carnosa* cv. 'Krinkle Kurl'.
Hippo, wild: *Euphorbia corollata.*
Hobblebush: *Viburnum alnifolium.*
Hogweed, giant: *Heracleum Mantegazzianum.*
Holly: *Ilex.*
  African: *Solanum giganteum.*
  American: *Ilex opaca.*
  Box: *Ruscus aculeatus.*
  Box-leaved: *Ilex crenata.*
  Canary Island: *I. Perado* var. *platyphylla.*
  Chinese: *I. cornuta, Osmanthus heterophyllus.*
  Costa Rican: *Olmediella Betschlerana.*
  Cuban: *Begonia cubensis.*
  Desert: *Atriplex hymenelytra.*
  Dune: *Ilex opaca* var. *arenicola.*
  Dutch: *I.* ✕*altaclarensis* cv. 'Belgica'.
  Dwarf: *Malpighia coccigera.*
  English: *Ilex Aquifolium.*
  European: *I. Aquifolium.*
  False: *Osmanthus heterophyllus.*
  Furin: *Ilex geniculata.*
  Georgia: *I. longipes.*
  Gold hedgehog: *I. Aquifolium* cv. 'Ferox Aurea'.
  Hedgehog: *I. Aquifolium* cv. 'Ferox'.
  Highclere: *I.* ✕*altaclarensis* cv. 'Altaclerensis'.
  Horned: *I. cornuta.*
  Japanese: *I. crenata.*
  Kashi: *I. chinensis.*
  Kurogane: *I. rotunda.*
  Large-leaved: *I. ambigua* var. *montana.*
  Luster-leaf: *I. latifolia.*
  Madeira: *I. Perado* var. *Perado.*
  Miniature: *Malpighia coccigera.*
  Moonlight: *Ilex Aquifolium* cv. 'Flavescens'.
  Mountain: *I. ambigua* var. *montana, Nemopanthus, Prunus ilicifolia.*
  Myrtle-leaved: *Ilex myrtifolia.*
  Oregon: *I. Aquifolium.*
  Porcupine: *I. Aquifolium* cv. 'Ferox'.
  Puerto Rican. *Olmediella Betschlerana.*
  Sarvis: *Ilex Amelanchier.*
  Screw-leaved: *I. Aquifolium* cv. 'Crispa'.
  Sea: *Eryngium maritimum.*
  Silver hedgehog: *Ilex Aquifolium* cv. 'Ferox Argentea'.
  Singapore: *Malpighia, M. coccigera.*
  Smooth-leaved: *Ilex* ✕*altaclarensis* cv. 'Laurifolia'.
  Soyogo: *I. pedunculosa.*
  Summer: *Comarostaphylis diversifolia.*
  Swamp: *Ilex Amelanchier.*
  Tsuru: *I. rugosa.*
  West Indian: *Leea coccinea.*

Hollyhock: *Alcea.*
  Common: *A. rosea.*
  Sea: *Hibiscus Moscheutos* subsp. *palustris.*
Holm, sea: *Eryngium maritimum.*
Holy Ghost flower: *Peristeria elata.*
Honesty: *Lunaria, L. annua.*
  Perennial: *L. rediviva.*
Honewort: *Cryptotaenia canadensis.*
Honeybells: *Hermannia verticillata.*
Honeyberry: *Celtis australis, Melicoccus bijugatus.*
Honey-bunny: *Opuntia microdasys* cv. 'Albispina'.
Honeybush: *Melianthus.*
Honey flower: *Lambertia formosa, Protea mellifera, Melianthus major.*
Honey plant: *Hoya carnosa.*
Honeyshuck: *Gleditsia triacanthos.*
Honeysuckle: *Aquilegia canadensis, Justicia californica, Lonicera, Rhododendron prinophyllum.*
  Arizona: *Lonicera arizonica.*
  Bush: *Diervilla.*
  Cape: *Tecomaria capensis.*
  Chaparral: *Lonicera interrupta.*
  Coral: *L. sempervirens.*
  Desert: *Anisacanthus Thurberi.*
  European fly: *Lonicera Xylosteum.*
  Fly: *L. canadensis, L. Xylosteum.*
  French: *Hedysarum coronarium.*
  Giant: *Lonicera Hildebrandiana.*
  Giant Burmese: *L. Hildebrandiana.*
  Grape: *L. prolifera.*
  Hairy: *L. hirsuta.*
  Hall's Japanese: *L. japonica* cv. 'Halliana'.
  Himalaya: *Leycesteria formosa.*
  Jamaica: *Passiflora laurifolia.*
  Japanese: *Lonicera japonica.*
  Long-flowered: *L. longiflora.*
  Purple: *Rhododendron nudiflorum.*
  South African: *Turraea obtusifolia.*
  Swamp: *Rhododendron viscosum.*
  Swamp fly: *Lonicera oblongifolia.*
  Tartarian, Tatarian: *L. tatarica.*
  Trumpet: *Campsis radicans, Lonicera sempervirens.*
  Yellow: *Lonicera flava.*
  Yellow cape: *Tecomaria capensis* cv. 'Aurea'.
Honeywort: *Cerinthe.*
Honolulu-queen: *Hylocereus undatus.*
Hop: *Humulus.*
  Common: *H. Lupulus.*
  European: *H. Lupulus.*
  False: *Justicia Brandegeana.*
  Japanese: *Humulus japonicus.*
  Wild: *Bryonia dioica.*
Hopbush: *Dodonaea cuneata.*
Hop tree: *Ptelea.*
Horsemint: *Mentha longifolia, Monarda, M. punctata.*
  Sweet: *Cunila origanoides.*
Horehound: *Marrubium.*
  Black: *Ballota nigra.*
  Common: *Marrubium vulgare.*
  Water: *Lycopus.*
  White: *Marrubium vulgare.*
Hormigo: *Triplaris.*
Hornbeam: *Carpinus.*
  American: *C. caroliniana.*
  American hop: *Ostrya virginiana.*
  European: *Carpinus Betulus.*
  European hop: *Ostrya carpinifolia.*
  Hop: *Ostrya.*
Horncone, Mexican: *Ceratozamia mexicana.*
Horn-of-plenty: *Datura Metel, Fedia cornucopiae.*
Hornwort: *Ceratophyllum.*
Horsefly: *Baptisia tinctoria.*
Horsefly weed: *Baptisia tinctoria.*
Horseradish: *Armoracia rusticana.*
Horseradish tree: *Moringa pterygosperma.*
Horse's-tail: *Sedum Morganianum.*
Horsetail: *Equisetum.*
  Common: *E. hyemale.*
  Variegated: *E. variegatum.*
Horsetail tree: *Casuarina equisetifolia.*
Horseweed: *Collinsonia.*
Hortensia: *Hydrangea macrophylla* subsp. *macrophylla* var. *macrophylla.*

Hottentot-bread: *Dioscorea elephantipes.*
Hound's-tongue: *Cynoglossum.*
Houseleek: *Sempervivum.*
  Cobweb: *S. arachnoideum.*
  Common: *S. tectorum.*
  Roof: *S. tectorum.*
  Spiderweb: *S. arachnoideum.*
Huamuchil: *Pithecellobium dulce.*
Huanuco: *Cinchona micrantha.*
Huckleberry: *Gaylussacia, Vaccinium.*
  Black: *Gaylussacia baccata.*
  Blue: *Vaccinium membranaceum.*
  Box: *Gaylussacia brachycera.*
  California: *Vaccinium ovatum.*
  Dwarf: *Gaylussacia dumosa, G. frondosa.*
  Evergreen: *Vaccinium ovatum.*
  Garden: *Solanum melanocerasum.*
  Hairy: *Vaccinium hirsutum.*
  He: *Cyrilla racemiflora, Lyonia ligustrina.*
  Little-leaf: *Vaccinium scoparium.*
  (of florists): *V. ovatum.*
  Red: *V. parvifolium.*
  Shot: *V. ovatum.*
  Squaw: *V. caesium, V. stamineum.*
  Sugar: *V. vacillans.*
  Thin-leaf: *V. membranaceum.*
Huisache: *Acacia Farnesiana.*
Humble plant: *Mimosa pudica.*
Hunter's-horn: *Sarracenia flava.*
Hunter's-robe: *Epipremnum aureum.*
  Golden: *E. aureum.*
Huntsman's-cup: *Sarracenia purpurea.*
Hurricane plant: : *Monstera deliciosa.*
Hyacinth: *Hyacinthus, H. orientalis.*
  Common: *H. orientalis.*
  Common grape: *Muscari botryoides.*
  Dutch: *Hyacinthus orientalis.*
  Feather: *Muscari comosum* cvs. 'Monstrosum' and 'Plumosum'.
  Garden: *Hyacinthus orientalis.*
  Grape: *Muscari.*
  Meadow: *Camassia scilloides.*
  Musk: *Muscari racemosum.*
  Nutmeg: *M. racemosum.*
  Peacock: *Eichhornia azurea.*
  Pine: *Clematis Baldwinii.*
  Roman: *Hyacinthus orientalis* var. *albulus.*
  Star: *Scilla amoena.*
  Starry: *S. autumnalis.*
  Summer: *Galtonia candicans.*
  Tassel: *Muscari comosum.*
  Water: *Eichhornia crassipes.*
  Wild: *Camassia scilloides, Dichelostemma multiflorum, D. pulchellum, Triteleia hyacinthina.*
  Wood: *Endymion.*
Hyacinth-of-Peru: *Scilla peruviana.*
Hydrangea: *Hydrangea.*
  Climbing: *Decumaria barbara, Hydrangea anomala* subsp. *petiolaris.*
  French: *Hydrangea macrophylla.*
  Peegee: *H. paniculata* cv. 'Grandiflora'.
  Wild: *H. arborescens, Rumex venosus.*
Hydrangea vine, Japanese: *Schizophragma hydrangeoides.*
Hyssop: *Hyssopus, H. officinalis.*
  Anise: *Agastache Foeniculum.*
  Blue giant: *A. Foeniculum.*
  Fennel giant: *A. Foeniculum.*
  Fragrant giant: *A. Foeniculum.*
  Giant: *Agastache.*
  Mexican giant: *A. mexicana.*
  Nettle-leaf: *A. urticifolia.*
  Purple giant: *A. scrophulariifolia.*
  Water: *Bacopa, B. Monnieri.*
  Wrinkled giant: *Agastache rugosa.*
  Yellow giant: *A. nepetoides.*

Icaco: *Chrysobalanus Icaco.*
Ice plant: *Mesembryanthemum, M. crystallinum.*
Icicle plant: *Mesembryanthemum.*
Iigiri tree: *Idesia polycarpa.*
Ilama: *Annona diversifolia.*
Ilang-ilang: *Cananga odorata.*
  Climbing: *Artabotrys hexapetalus.*
Illyarie: *Eucalyptus erythrocorys.*

Immortelle: *Helichrysum, Xeranthemum annuum.*
  Mountain: *Erythrina Poeppigiana.*
  Swamp: *E. fusca.*
Inch plant: *Callisia, Zebrina pendula.*
  Fern-leaf: *Tripogandra multiflora.*
  Flowering: *Tradescantia Blossfeldiana.*
  Giant white: *T. albiflora* cv. 'Albo-vittata'.
  Striped: *Callisia elegans.*
Inchworm: *Senecio pendula.*
Incienso: *Encelia farinosa.*
Indian-comb: *Pachycereus pecten-aboriginum.*
Indian-cup: *Sarracenia purpurea.*
Indian-paint: *Chenopodium capitatum, Lithospermum canescens.*
Indian-physic: *Gillenia trifoliata.*
Indian-pipe: *Monotropa, M. uniflora.*
Indian-salad: *Hydrophyllum virginianum.*
Indian's-dream: *Cheilanthes siliquosa.*
Indian-shoe, yellow: *Cypripedium Calceolus* var. *pubescens.*
Indian-shot: *Canna indica.*
Indian-spice: *Vitex Agnus-castus.*
Indian-warrior: *Pedicularis densiflora.*
Indigo: *Indigofera.*
  Bastard: *Amorpha fruticosa.*
  Blue false: *Baptisia australis.*
  False: *Amorpha, A. fruticosa, Baptisia.*
  Fragrant false: *Amorpha nana.*
  Plains wild: *Baptisia leucophaea.*
  Prairie false: *B. leucantha.*
  White false: *B. leucantha.*
  Wild: *Baptisia, B. tinctoria.*
  Wild blue: *B. australis.*
Indigo bush: *Amorpha fruticosa, Dalea.*
Inkberry: *Ilex glabra.*
Innocence: *Collinsia verna, Hedyotis caerulea.*
Insect flower
  Dalmatian: *Chrysanthemum cinerariifolium.*
  Persian: *C. coccineum.*
Inside-out flower: *Vancouveria planipetala.*
Inula, Caucasian: *Inula orientalis.*
Ipecac: *Cephaelis Ipecacuanha.*
  American: *Gillenia stipulata.*
  Carolina: *Euphorbia ipecacuanhae.*
  False: *Psychotria emetica.*
  Wild: *Euphorbia ipecacuanhae.*
Ipomoea, star: *Ipomoea coccinea.*
Irids: *Iridaceae.*
Iris: *Iris.*
  African: *Dietes vegeta.*
  Beachhead: *Iris setosa* var. *canadensis.*
  Bearded: see Classification of Irises under *Iris.*
  Beardless: see Classification of Irises under *Iris.*
  Butterfly: *Iris spuria, Moraea.*
  Copper: *I. fulva.*
  Crested: *Iris cristata;* see also Classification of Irises under *Iris.*
  Crested dwarf: *I. cristata.*
  Dutch: see *I. Xiphium.*
  Dwarf: *I. verna.*
  Dwarf crested: *I. cristata.*
  English: *I. xiphioides.*
  Evansia: see Classification of Irises under *Iris.*
  Fan: *Neomarica.*
  German: see Classification of Irises under *Iris.*
  House: *Neomarica.*
  Japanese: *Iris Kaempferi.*
  Lamance: *I. brevicaulis.*
  Mourning: *I. susiana.*
  Orchid: *I. orchidoides.*
  Palestine: *I. susiana.*
  Peacock: *Moraea neopavonia.*
  Persian: *Iris persica.*
  Prairie: *Nemastylis acuta.*
  Red: *Iris fulva.*
  Roof: *I. tectorum.*
  Scarlet-seeded: *I. foetidissima.*
  Siberian: *I. sibirica.*
  Sierra: *I. Hartwegii.*
  Snake's-head: *Hermodactylus tuberosus.*
  Spanish: *Iris Xiphium.*
  Spuria: *I. spuria.*
  Stinking: *I. foetidissima.*
  Sword-leaved: *I. ensata.*
  Violet: *I. verna.*

Iris—*Continued*
  Walking: *Neomarica.*
  Wall: *Iris tectorum.*
  Wild: *I. versicolor.*
  Yellow: *I. Pseudacorus.*
Irish-lace: *Tagetes filifolia.*
Irish-mittens: *Opuntia vulgaris.*
Ironbark: *Eucalyptus.*
  Broad-leaved red: *E. fibrosa.*
  Gray: *E. paniculata.*
  Narrow-leaved: *E. crebra.*
  Red: *E. sideroxylon.*
  White: *E. leucoxylon.*
Iron plant: *Aspidistra elatior.*
Iron tree: *Metrosideros.*
Ironweed: *Vernonia.*
  Western: *V. Baldwinii.*
  Yellow: *Verbesina alternifolia.*
Ironwood: *Bumelia lycioides, Carpinus, Cliftonia monophylla, Cyrilla racemiflora, Eugenia confusa, Mesua ferrea, Ostrya virginiana.*
  Brazilian: *Caesalpinia ferrea.*
  Catalina: *Lyonothamnus.*
  Desert: *Olneya Tesota.*
  Morocco: *Argania spinosa.*
  South Sea: *Casuarina equisetifolia.*
Islay: *Prunus ilicifolia.*
Isu tree: *Distylium racemosum.*
Itchweed: *Veratrum viride.*
Ivry-leaves: *Gaultheria procumbens.*
Ivy: *Cissus, Hedera, Kalmia latifolia.*
  Algerian: *Hedera canariensis.*
  American: *Parthenocissus quinquefolia.*
  Aralia: ✕*Fatshedera.*
  Baby: *Hedera Helix* cv. 'Walthamensis'.
  Baltic: *H. Helix* cv. 'Baltica'.
  Bird's-foot: *H. Helix* cv. 'Pedata'.
  Boston: *Parthenocissus tricuspidata.*
  Canary: *Hedera canariensis.*
  Colchis: *H. colchica.*
  Coliseum: *Cymbalaria muralis.*
  Devil's: *Epipremnum aureum.*
  English: *Hedera Helix.*
  Fan: *H. Helix* cv. 'Crenata'.
  Five-leaved: *Parthenocissus quinquefolia.*
  Fragrant: *H. colchica.*
  German: *Senecio mikanioides.*
  Ghost tree: *Hedera canariensis* cv. 'Variegata Arborescens'.
  Gloire-de-Marengo: *H. canariensis* cv. 'Variegata'.
  Grape: *Cissus.*
  Ground: *Glecoma hederacea.*
  Hagenburger's: *H. canariensis* cv. 'Variegata'.
  Heart-leaf: *H. Helix* cv. 'Scutifolia'.
  Irish: *H. Helix* var. *hibernica.*
  Italian: *H. Helix* cv. 'Poetica'.
  Japanese: *H. Helix* cv. 'Conglomerata', *H. rhombea, Parthenocissus tricuspidata.*
  Kenilworth: *Cymbalaria muralis.*
  Madeira: *Hedera canariensis.*
  Marine: *Cissus incisa.*
  Mexican: *Cobaea scandens.*
  Minature grape: *Cissus striata.*
  Nepal: *Hedera nepalensis.*
  Parlor: *Philodendron scandens* subsp. *oxycardium, Senecio mikanioides.*
  Parsley: *Hedera Helix* cv. 'Parsley Crested'.
  Persian: *H. colchica.*
  Poison: *Rhus radicans, R. Toxicodendron.*
  Red: *Hemigraphis alternata.*
  Red-flame: *H. alternata.*
  Solomon Island: *Epipremnum aureum.*
  Spider: *Chlorophytum comosum.*
  Swedish: *Plectranthus.*
  Switch: *Leucothoe Fontanesiana.*
  Tree: ✕*Fatshedera.*
  Variegated: *Hedera canariensis* cv. 'Variegata'.
  Water: *Senecio mikanioides.*
Ivybush: *Kalmia latifolia.*
Ivy tree: ✕*Fatshedera.*

Jaboncillo: *Sapindus Saponaria.*
Jaboticaba: *Myrciaria cauliflora.*

Jacinth
Japanese: *Scilla scilloides.*
Peruvian: *S. peruviana.*
Spanish: *Endymion hispanicus.*
Jackfruit: *Artocarpus heterophyllus.*
Jack-go-to-bed-at-noon: *Tragopogon pratensis.*
Jack-in-the-pulpit: *Arisaema triphyllum.*
Jackwood: *Cordia dentata.*
Jacob's-coat: *Acalypha Wilkesiana.*
Jacob's-ladder: *Pedilanthus tithymaloides* subsp. *tithymaloides, Polemonium, P. caeruleum, Smilax herbacea.*
Jacob's-rod: *Asphodeline.*
Jacob's-staff: *Fouquieria splendens.*
Jade plant, silver: *Crassula arborescens.*
Jade tree: *Crassula argentea.*
Jade Vine: *Strongylodon macrobatus.*
Jalap, wild: *Podophyllum peltatum.*
Jamberry: *Physalis ixocarpa.*
Jambolan: *Syzygium cumini.*
Jambool: *Syzygium cumini.*
Jambos: *Syzygium malaccense.*
Jambosa: *Syzygium samarangense.*
Jambu: *Syzygium cumini.*
Jamestown weed: *Datura Stramonium.*
Japanese-lantern: *Hibiscus schizopetalus, Physalis Alkekengi.*
Jarrah: *Eucalyptus marginata.*
Jasmine: *Jasminum;* see also Jessamine.
Angel-wing: *Jasminum nitidum.*
Arabian: *J. Sambac.*
Blue: *Clematis crispa.*
Cape: *Gardenia jasminoides.*
Carolina: *Gelsemium.*
Catalonian: *Jasminum grandiflorum.*
Chilean: *Mandevilla laxa.*
Cinnamon: *Hedychium coronarium.*
Confederate: *Trachelospermum jasminoides, Jasminum nitidum.*
Crape: *Tabernaemontana divaricata.*
Italian: *Jasminum humile* cv. 'Revolutum'.
Japanese: *J. Mesnyi.*
Madagascar: *Stephanotis floribunda.*
Night: *Nyctanthes Arbor-tristis.*
Orange: *Murraya paniculata.*
Paraguay: *Brunfelsia australis.*
Pinwheel: *Jasminum gracillimum.*
Primrose: *J. Mesnyi.*
Rock: *Androsace.*
Royal: *Jasminum grandiflorum.*
Spanish: *J. grandiflorum.*
Star: *J. gracillimum, J. multiflorum, J. nitidum, Trachelospermum jasminoides.*
Windmill: *Jasminum nitidum.*
Yellow: *J. Mesnyi.*
Jatropha, spicy: *Jatropha integerrima.*
Jaundice berry: *Berberis vulgaris.*
Javillo: *Hura crepitans.*
Jelly-bean plant: *Sedum pachyphyllum.*
Jelly-beans: *Sedum pachyphyllum.*
Jerusalem-cross: *Lychnis chalcedonica.*
Jessamine: *Jasminum;* see also Jasmine.
Carolina yellow: *Gelsemium.*
Day: *Cestrum diurnum.*
Night: *C. nocturnum.*
Night-blooming: *C. nocturnum.*
Orange: *Murraya paniculata.*
Poet's: *Jasminum officinale.*
Willow-leaved: *Cestrum Parqui.*
Yellow: *Gelsemium.*
Jesuit nut: *Trapa natans.*
Jetbead: *Rhodotypos.*
Jewbush: *Pedilanthus tithymaloides.*
Jewel-leaf plant: *Graptopetalum amethystinum.*
Jewelled-crown: ×*Pachyveria Scheideckeri* cv. 'Cristata'.
Jewel plant: ×*Pachyveria Haagei, Titanopsis calcarea.*
Giant: *Aloinopsis Malherbei.*
Jewels-of-Opar: *Talinum paniculatum.*
Jewel vine: *Derris.*
Malay: *D. scandens.*
Jewelweed: *Impatiens, I. capensis, I. pallida.*
Jew's-beard: *Tacca Chantrieri.*
Jim brush: *Ceanothus sorediatus.*
Jim bush: *Ceanothus sorediatus.*
Jimsonweed: *Datura Stramonium.*
Jobo: *Spondias Mombin.*

Job's-tears: *Coix Lacryma-Jobi.*
Jocote: *Spondias purpurea.*
Joe-Pye weed: *Eupatorium maculatum, E. purpureum.*
Green-stemmed: *E. purpureum.*
Sweet: *E. purpureum.*
John-go-to-bed-at-noon: *Tragopogon pratensis.*
Johnny-jump-up: *Viola pedunculata, V. tricolor.*
Jointweed: *Polygonella.*
Jointwood: *Cassia nodosa.*
Jojoba: *Simmondsia chinensis.*
Jonquil: *Narcissus Jonquilla.*
Campernelle: *N.* ×*odorus.*
Joseph's coat: *Alternanthera, Amaranthus tricolor.*
Joshua tree: *Sedum multiceps, Yucca brevifolia.*
Baby: *Sedum multiceps.*
Little: *S. multiceps.*
Miniature: *S. multiceps.*
Joyweed, shoofly: *Alternanthera ficoidea* cv. 'Amoena'.
Judas tree: *Cercis, C. Siliquastrum.*
Jujube: *Ziziphus.*
Chinese: *Z. Jujuba.*
Common: *Z. Jujuba.*
Cottony: *Z. mauritiana.*
Indian: *Z. mauritiana.*
Jumrool: *Syzygium samarangense.*
Juneberry: *Amelanchier.*
Jungle-flame: *Ixora coccinea.*
Juniper: *Juniperus.*
African: *J. procera.*
Alligator: *J. Deppeana* var. *pachyphlaea.*
Ashe: *J. Ashei.*
Blue-spire: *J. communis* cv. 'Erecta Glauca'.
California: *J. occidentalis.*
Canary Island: *J. Cedrus.*
Cherrystone: *J. monosperma.*
Common: *J. communis.*
Creeping: *J. horizontalis.*
Drooping: *J. recurva.*
Greek: *J. excelsa.*
Ground: *J. communis* var. *depressa.*
Himalayan: *J. recurva.*
Incense: *J. thurifera.*
Irish: *J. communis* cv. 'Hibernica'.
Mountain: *J. communis* var.*montana.*
Needle: *J. rigida.*
Plum: *J. drupacea.*
Polish: *J. communis* cv. 'Cracovia'.
Prickly: *J. Oxycedrus.*
Prostrate: *J. communis* var. *depressa.*
Red-berry: *J. Pinchotii.*
Rocky Mountain: *J. scopulorum.*
Sargent: *J. chinensis* var. *Sargentii.*
Shore: *J. conferta.*
Sierra: *J. occidentalis.*
Sweet-fruited: *J. Deppeana* var. *pachyphlaea.*
Syrian: *J. drupacea.*
Waukegan: *J. horizontalis* cv. 'Douglasii.'
Jupiter's beard: *Centranthus ruber.*
Jupiter's distaff: *Salvia glutinosa.*
Justicia, red: *Justicia secunda.*
Jute: *Corchorus capsularis.*
Bastard: *Hibiscus cannabinus.*
Bimli: *H. cannabinus.*
Bimlipatum: *H. cannabinus.*
China: *Abutilon Theophrasti.*
Tossa: *Corchorus olitorius.*
White: *C. capsularis.*

Kadam tree: *Anthocephalus Cadamba.*
Kafir: *Sorghum bicolor,* Caffrorum Group.
Kahika: *Podocarpus dacrydioides.*
Kaki: *Diospyros Kaki.*
Kalanchoe: *Kalanchoe.*
Christmas-tree: *K. laciniata.*
Fir-tree: *K. laciniata.*
Flame: *K. integra.*
Kale: *Brassica oleracea,* Acephala Group.
Cabbage: *B. oleracea,* Acephala Group.
Chinese: *B. oleracea,* Alboglabra Group.
Decorative: *B. oleracea,* Acephala Group.
Dwarf Siberian: *B. fimbriata.*
Flowering: *B. oleracea,* Acephala Group.
Indian: *Xanthosoma Lindenii.*

Kale—*Continued*
  Italian: *Brassica Rapa*, Rapifera Group.
  Kitchen: *B. oleracea*, Acephala Group.
  Ornamental: *B. oleracea*, Acephala Group.
  Ornamental-leaved: *B. oleracea*, Acephala Group.
  Portuguese: *B. oleracea*, Tronchuda Group.
  Ruvo: *B. Rapa*, Ruvo Group.
  Scotch: *B. oleracea*, Acephala Group.
  Sea: *Crambe maritima.*
  Siberian: *Brassica Napus*, Pabularia Group.
  Tall: *B. oleracea*, Acephala Group.
  Tree: *B. oleracea*, Acephala Group.
  Tronchuda: *B. oleracea*, Tronchuda Group
Kalmia, bog: *Kalmia poliifolia.*
Kalo: *Colocasia esculenta.*
Kamani: *Terminalia Catappa.*
Kangaroo-paw: *Anigozanthos.*
Kangaroo vine: *Cissus antarctica.*
Kapok tree: *Ceiba pentandra.*
Karanda: *Carissa Carandas.*
Karo: *Pittosporum crassifolium.*
Karri tree: *Paulownia tomentosa.*
Karum tree: *Pongamia pinnata.*
  Kashmir-bouquet: *Clerodendrum.*
Kassod tree: *Cassia siamea.*
Kat: *Catha edulis.*
Katsura tree: *Cercidiphyllum japonicum.*
Kauri: *Agathis, A. australis.*
  Queensland: *A. robusta.*
Kava: *Piper methysticum.*
Kava-kava, kawa-kawa: *Macropiper excelsum, Piper methysticum.*
Kaya: *Torreya nucifera.*
Kenaf: *Hibiscus cannabinus.*
Kerria, white: *Rhodotypos.*
Khair: *Acacia Catechu.*
Khas-khas: *Vetiveria zizanioides.*
Khat: *Catha edulis.*
Khus-khus: *Vetiveria zizanioides.*
Kimono plant: *Achimenes.*
Kingcup: *Caltha palustris.*
King-devil: *Hieracium aurantiacum.*
King nut: *Carya laciniosa.*
King-of-bromeliads: *Vriesia hieroglyphica.*
King-of-Siam: *Citrus ×nobilis* cv. 'King'.
King-of-the-forest: *Anoectochilus.*
King-of-the-meadow: *Thalictrum polygamum.*
King-of-the-night: *Selenicereus pteranthus.*
King's crown: *Justicia carnea.*
King's mantle: *Thunbergia erecta.*
King's-solomon's-seal: *Polygonatum commutatum.*
King's spear: *Asphodeline lutea, Eremurus.*
Kinnikinick: *Arctostaphylos Uva-ursi.*
Kino: *Coccoloba uvifera.*
  West African: *Pterocarpus erinaceus.*
Kiss-me-over-the-garden-gate: *Polygonum orientale.*
Kitchingia: *Kalanchoe uniflora.*
Ketembilla: *Dovyalis hebecarpa.*
Kitten-tails: *Besseya.*
Kittul tree: *Caryota urens.*
Kleinia, gooseberry: *Senecio gomphophylla.*
Knackaway: *Ehretia Anacua.*
Knapweed: *Centaurea.*
  Black: *C. nigra.*
  Brown: *C. Jacea.*
Knawel: *Scleranthus.*
Knesheneka: *Rubus stellatus.*
Knotroot: *Stachys affinis.*
Knotweed: *Polygonum.*
  Giant: *P. sachalinense.*
  Japanese: *P. cuspidatum.*
Koa: *Acacia Koa.*
Kohlrabi: *Brassica oleracea*, Gongylodes Group.
Kokio: *Kokia drynarioides.*
Konjac: *Amorphophallus Rivieri* cv. 'Konjac'.
Korakan: *Eleusine coracana.*
Kousa: *Cornus Kousa.*
Kowhai: *Sophora tetraptera.*
  Red: *Clianthus puniceus.*
Krishna-bor: *Ficus benghalensis* cv. 'Krishnae'.
Kudzu: *Pueraria lobata.*
  Tropical: *P. phaseoloides.*
Kudzu vine: *Pueraria lobata.*

Kumquat: *Fortunella.*
  Australian desert: *Eremocitrus.*
  Marumi: *Fortunella japonica.*
  Nagami: *F. margarita.*
  Oval: *F. margarita.*
  Round: *F. japonica.*
Kurrajong: *Brachychiton populneus.*
  Desert: *B. Gregoryi.*
Kurrat: see *Allium Ampeloprasum*, Kurrat Group.

Lablab: *Dolichos Lablab.*
Laburnum
  East African: *Calpurnia aurea.*
  Indian: *Cassia fistula.*
  Scotch: *Laburnum alpinum.*
Lacebark: *Hoheria, H. Lyallii, H. populnea.*
  Queensland: *Brachychiton discolor.*
Lace flower, blue: *Trachymene coerulea.*
Lace-flower vine: *Episcia dianthiflora.*
Laceleaf: *Aponogeton madagascariensis.*
Lace plant, Madagascar: *Aponogeton madagascariensis.*
Lacepod: *Thysanocarpus.*
Lace shrub: *Stephanandra incisa.*
Lacquer tree: *Rhus verniciflua.*
  Japanese: *Rhus verniciflua.*
Lac tree: *Schleichera oleosa.*
Ladies'-delight: *Viola ×Wittrockiana.*
Ladies'-eardrops: *Fuchsia.*
Ladies'-fingers: *Anthyllis Vulneraria.*
Ladies'-tobacco: *Antennaria.*
Ladies'-tresses: *Spiranthes.*
  Common: *S. cernua.*
  Giant: *S. praecox.*
  Grass-leaved: *S. praecox*
  Hooded: *S. Romanzoffiana.*
  Little: *S. Grayi.*
  Nodding: *S. cernua.*
  Romanzoff's: *S. Romanzoffiana.*
  Slender: *S. gracilis.*
  Southern slender: *S. gracilis.*
Ladybells: *Adenophora.*
Ladyfinger: *Mammillaria elongata.*
Lady-of-the-night: *Brassavola nodosa, Brunfelsia americana.*
Lady's-eardrops: *Fuchsia.*
Lady's-earrings: *Impatiens capensis.*
Lady's finger: *Abelmoschus esculentus.*
Lady's fingers: *Anthyllis Vulneraria.*
Lady-slipper: see Lady's-slipper.
Lady's-mantle: *Alchemilla.*
  Alpine: *A. alpina.*
Lady's-slipper, Lady-slipper: *Cypripedium, Paphiopedilum, Phragmipedium.*
  Large yellow: *Cypripedium Calceolus* var. *pubescens.*
  Mountain: *C. montanum.*
  Pink: *C. acaule.*
  Ram's-head: *C. arietinum.*
  Showy: *C. reginae.*
  Small white: *C. candidum, C. passerinum.*
  Small yellow: *C. Calceolus* var. *parviflorum.*
  Two-leaved: *C. acaule.*
Lady's-smock: *Cardamine pratensis.*
Lady's-sorrel, creeping: *Oxalis corniculata.*
La-kwa: *Momordica Charantia.*
Lambkill: *Kalmia angustifolia.*
Lamb's-ears: *Stachys byzantina, S. olympica.*
Lamb's-quarters: *Chenopodium album.*
Lamb's-tail: *Sedum Morganianum.*
Lamb's-tongue: *Stomatium agninum.*
Lancepod: *Lonchocarpus.*
Lancewood: *Pseudopanax crassifolius.*
Lantana: *Lantana.*
  Trailing: *L. montevidensis.*
  Weeping: *L. montevidensis.*
Lantern plant: *Physalis Alkekengi.*
Larch: *Larix.*
  American: *L. laricina.*
  Black: *L. laricina.*
  Chinese: *L. Potaninii.*
  Dahurian: *L. Gmelinii.*
  Dunkeld: *L. ×eurolepis.*
  European: *L. decidua.*
  Golden: *Pseudolarix.*
  Japanese: *Larix Kaempferi.*

Larkspur: *Consolida, Delphinium.*
  Dwarf: *Delphinium tricorne.*
  Rocket: *Consolida ambigua.*
  Tall: *Delphinium exaltatum.*
Lasiandra: *Tibouchina semidecandra.*
Latan: *Latania.*
  Blue: *L. Loddigesii.*
  Red: *L. lontaroides.*
  Yellow: *L. Verschaffeltii.*
Latticeleaf: *Aponogeton madagascariensis, Goodyera.*
Laudanum: *Cistus ladaniferus.*
Laurel: *Cordia alliodora, Ficus benjamina, Kalmia, Laurus, L. nobilis.*
  Alexandrian: *Calophyllum inophyllum, Danae racemosa.*
  Alpine: *Kalmia microphylla.*
  American: *Kalmia.*
  Australian: *Pittosporum Tobira.*
  Black: *Gordonia Lasianthus.*
  Bog: *Kalmia polifolia.*
  California: *Umbellularia californica.*
  Cherry: *Prunus caroliniana, P. Laurocerasus.*
  Chinese: *Antidesma Bunius.*
  Drooping: *Leucothoe Fontanesiana.*
  Dwarf: *Kalmia angustifolia.*
  English: *Prunus Laurocerasus.*
  Great: *Rhododendron maximum.*
  Ground: *Epigaea.*
  Himalaya: *Aucuba.*
  Indian: *Calophyllum inophyllum, Ficus retusa.*
  Japanese: *Aucuba japonica.*
  Mountain: *Kalmia latifolia.*
  (of antiquity): *Laurus nobilis.*
  Pale: *Kalmia poliifolia.*
  Pig: *K. angustifolia.*
  Portugal: *Prunus lusitanica.*
  Purple: *Rhododendron catawbiense.*
  Red-twig: *Leucothoe recurva.*
  Sheep: *Kalmia angustifolia.*
  Sierra: *Leucothoe Davisiae.*
  Spurge: *Daphne Laureola.*
  Tasmanian: *Anopterus glandulosus.*
  Tropic: *Ficus benjamina.*
  Variegated: *Codiaeum.*
  Weeping: *Ficus benjamina.*
  Western: *Kalmia microphylla.*
Laurel negro: *Cordia alliodora.*
Laurel tree: *Persea Borbonia.*
Laurelwood: *Calophyllum inophyllum.*
Laurustinus: *Viburnum Tinus.*
Lavatera, tree: *Lavatera Olbia.*
Lavender: *Lavandula.*
  Desert: *Hyptis Emoryi.*
  English: *Lavandula angustifolia.*
  French: *L. dentata, L. Stoechas.*
  Sea: *Limonium.*
  Spanish: *Lavandula Stoechas.*
  Spike: *L. angustifolia* subsp. *angustifolia.*
Lavender-scallops: *Kalanchoe Fedtschenkoi.*
Lawnleaf: *Dichondra carolinensis.*
Lawyer's-tongue: *Gasteria.*
Lead plant: *Amorpha canescens.*
Leadwort: *Plumbago.*
  Cape: *P. auriculata.*
Leather flower: *Clematis, C. versicolor, C. Viorna, C. virginiana.*
Leatherleaf: *Chamaedaphne calyculata, Viburnum Wrightii.*
  (of florists): *Vaccinium ovatum.*
Leatherroot: *Psoralea macrostachya.*
Leatherwood: *Cyrilla racemiflora, Dirca.*
Lebbek tree: *Albizia Lebbek.*
Leechee: *Litchi chinensis.*
Leek: see *Allium Ampeloprasum,* Porrum Group.
  Lady's: *Allium cernuum.*
  Lily: *A. Moly.*
  Meadow: *A. canadense.*
  Rose: *A. canadense.*
  Sand: *A. Scorodoprasum.*
  Wild: *A. Ampeloprasum, A. tricoccum.*
Lemandarin: *C. ×limonia.*
Lemon: *Citrus Limon.*
  American wonder: *C. Limon* cv. 'Ponderosa'.
  Chinese dwarf: *C. Limon* cv. 'Meyer'.
  Dwarf: *C. Limon* cv. 'Meyer'.
  Dwarf Chinese: *C. Limon* cv. 'Meyer'.

Lemon—*Continued*
  Garden: *Cucumis Melo,* Chito Group.
  Giant: *Citrus Limon* cv. 'Ponderosa'.
  Meyer: *C. Limon* cv. 'Meyer'.
  Water: *Passiflora laurifolia.*
  Wild: *Podophyllum peltatum.*
  Wild water: *Passiflora foetida.*
  Wonder: *Citrus Limon* cv. 'Ponderosa'.
Lemonade berry: *Rhus integrifolia.*
Lemon ball: *Mammillaria Pringlei, Notocactus submammulosus.*
Lemongrass: *Cymbopogon citratus.*
  West Indian: *C. citratus.*
Lemonleaf: *Gaultheria Shallon.*
Lemon vine: *Pereskia aculeata.*
Lens-scale: *Atriplex lentiformis.*
Lentil: *Lens culinaris.*
Lentisco: *Pistacia texana, Rhus virens.*
Leopard flower: *Belamcanda chinensis.*
Leopard plant: *Ligularia tussilaginea* cv. 'Aureo-maculata'.
Leopard's-bane: *Doronicum, Senecio Doronicum.*
Lespedeza: *Lespedeza.*
  Chinese: *L. cuneata.*
  Common: *L. striata.*
  Korean: *L. stipulacea.*
Lettuce: *Lactuca.*
  Asparagus: see under *Lactuca.*
  Chalk: *Dudleya pulverulenta.*
  Common lamb's: *V. Locusta.*
  Cos: see *Lactuca sativa.*
  Frog's: *Potamogeton densus.*
  Garden: *Lactuca sativa.*
  Lamb's: *Valerianella.*
  Miner's: *Montia, M. perfoliata.*
  Prickly: *Lactuca Serriola.*
  Romaine: see *Lactuca sativa.*
  Water: *Pistia stratiotes.*
Leverwood: *Ostrya virginiana.*
Lichi: *Litchi chinensis.*
Licorice: *Glycyrrhiza glabra.*
  Indian: *Abrus precatorius.*
  Wild: *A. precatorius.*
Licorice plant: *Helichrysum petiolatum.*
Licorice vine: *Abrus precatorius.*
Life-everlasting: *Anaphalis.*
Life-of-man: *Aralia racemosa.*
Life plant: *Biophytum sensitivum, Kalanchoe pinnata.*
Lightwood: *Acacia implexa.*
Lignum-vitae: *Guaiacum.*
Ligularia, parsley: *Ligularia tussilaginea* cv. 'Crispata'.
Lilac: *Syringa.*
  Catalina mountain: *Ceanothus arboreus.*
  Chinese: *Syringa ×chinensis.*
  Common: *S. vulgaris.*
  Cut-leaf: *S. laciniata.*
  Himalayan: *S. emodi.*
  Hungarian: *S. Josikaea.*
  Indian: *Melia Azedarach.*
  Japanese tree: *Syringa reticulata.*
  Late: *S. villosa.*
  Persian: *S. persica, Melia Azedarach.*
  Summer: *Buddleia Davidii.*
  Vine: *Hardenbergia violacea.*
  Wild: *Ceanothus sanguineus.*
Lilac-sunbonnet: *Langloisia punctata.*
Lilly-pilly: *Acmena Smithii.*
  Blue: *Syzygium coolminianum.*
Lily: *Lilium.*
  Adobe: *Fritillaria pluriflora.*
  African: *Agapanthus africanus.*
  African blood: *Haemanthus.*
  African corn: *Ixia.*
  Alligator: *Hymenocallis Palmeri.*
  Alp: *Lloydia.*
  Alpine: *Lilium parvum.*
  Amazon: *Eucharis grandiflora.*
  Amazon water: *Victoria amazonica.*
  American Turk's cap: *Lilium superbum.*
  Arum: *Zantedeschia aethiopica.*
  Atamasco: *Zephyranthes Atamasco.*
  Australian water: *Nymphaea gigantea.*
  Avalanche: *Erythronium grandiflorum.*
  Aztec: *Sprekelia formosissima.*
  Backhouse hybrid: *Lilium ×Backhousei.*

Lily—*Continued*

Barbados: *Hippeastrum.*
Bell: *Lilium Grayi.*
Belladonna: *Amaryllis Belladonna.*
Bellingham Hybrid: *Lilium* ×*pardaboldtii.*
Bermuda: *L. longiflorum* var. *eximium.*
Bermuda Easter: *L. longiflorum* var. *eximium.*
Blackberry: *Belamcanda chinensis.*
Blood: *Haemanthus.*
Blue African: *Agapanthus africanus.*
Bluebead: *Clintonia borealis.*
Blue funnel: *Androstephium coeruleum.*
Boat: *Rhoeo spathacea.*
Bugle: *Watsonia.*
Butterfly: *Hedychium coronarium.*
Calla: *Zantedeschia, Z. aethiopica.*
Canada: *Lilium canadense.*
Candlestick: *L.* ×*hollandicum, L. pensylvanicum.*
Cape blue water: *Nymphaea capensis.*
Cape Cod pink water: *N. odorata* var.*rosea.*
Carolina: *Lilium Michauxii.*
Caucasian: *L. monadelphum.*
Celestial: *Nemastylis.*
Chamise: *Lilium rubescens.*
Chaparral: *L. rubescens.*
Checker: *Fritillaria lanceolata.*
Checkered: *F. Meleagris.*
Chinese-lantern: *Sandersonia aurantiaca.*
Chinese sacred: *Narcissus Tazetta* var. *orientalis.*
Chinese white: *Lilium leucanthum.*
Climbing: *Gloriosa.*
Coast: *Lilium maritimum.*
Cobra: *Arisaema speciosum, Darlingtonia californica.*
Columbia: *Lilium columbianum.*
Corn: *Clintonia borealis, Ixia, Veratrum californicum.*
Cow: *Nuphar.*
Crane: *Strelitzia reginae.*
Crinum: *Crinum.*
Cuban: *Scilla peruviana.*
Day: see Daylily.
Desert: *Hesperocallis undulata.*
Dwarf ginger: *Kaempferia Roscoeana.*
Easter: *Lilium longiflorum* var. *eximium.*
Egyptian water: *Nymphaea Lotus.*
Eucharist: *Eucharis grandiflora.*
Eureka: *Lilium occidentale.*
European white water: *Nymphaea alba.*
Fairy: *Zephyranthes.*
Fairy water: *Nymphoides aquatica.*
Fawn: *Erythronium, E. californicum.*
Fire: *Cyrtanthus, Xerophyllum tenax, Zephyranthes tubiflora.*
Flamingo: *Anthurium Andreanum.*
Flax: *Dianella, Phormium.*
Fragrant plantain: *Hosta plantaginea.*
Fragrant water: *Nymphaea odorata.*
Garland: *Hedychium.*
Giant water: *Victoria.*
Ginger: *Alpinia, Hedychium, H. coronarium.*
Globe: *Calochortus albus.*
Globe spear: *Doryanthes excelsa.*
Gloriosa: *Gloriosa.*
Glory: *Gloriosa.*
Gold-banded: *Lilium auratum.*
Golden hurricane: *Lycoris africana.*
Golden-rayed: *Lilium auratum.*
Golden spider: *Lycoris africana.*
Gray's: *Lilium Grayi.*
Guernsey: *Nerine sarniensis.*
Herb: *Alstroemeria haemantha.*
Hidden: *Curcuma.*
Humboldt; *Lilium Humboldtii.*
Ifafa: *Cyrtanthus ochroleucus, C. Mackenii.*
India red water: *Nymphaea rubra.*
Jacobean: *Sprekelia formosissima.*
Japanese: *Lilium japonicum.*
Japanese Turk's-cap: *L. Hansonii.*
Josephine's: *Brunsvigia Josephinae.*
Kaffir: *Clivia, Schizostylis.*
Kamchatka: *Fritillaria camschatcensis.*
Lavender globe: *Allium tanguticum.*
Lemon: *Hemerocallis Lilioasphodelus, Lilium Parryi.*
Leopard: *Lilium Catesbaei, L. pardalinum.*
Lesser Turk's-cap: *L. pomponium.*

Lily—*Continued*

Little Turk's-cap: *L. pomponium.*
Long's red: *L. Catesbaei* var. *Longii.*
Madonna: *L. candidum, Eucharis grandiflora.*
Magic: *Lycoris squamigera.*
Magnolia water: *Nymphaea tuberosa.*
Marhan: see *Lilium* ×*Backhousei.*
Mariposa: *Calochortus.*
Martagon: *Lilium Martagon.*
Meadow: *L. canadense.*
Michigan: *L. michiganense.*
Midsummer plantain: *Hosta undulata* cv. 'Erromena'.
Milk-and-wine: *Crinum latifolium* var. *zeylanicum.*
Minor Turk's-cap: *Lilium pomponium.*
Mountain: *Leucocrinum, Lilium auratum.*
Naked-lady: ×*Amarygia Parkeri, Amaryllis Belladonna.*
Nankeen: *Lilium* ×*testaceum.*
Narrow-leaved plantain: *Hosta lancifolia.*
Natal: *Moraea.*
One-day: *Tigridia.*
Orange: *Lilium bulbiferum.*
Orange-bell: *L. Grayi.*
Orange-cup: *L. philadelphicum.*
Oregon: *L. columbianum.*
Palm: *Cordyline australis, Yucca gloriosa.*
Palmer spear: *Doryanthes Palmeri.*
Panther: *Lilium pardalinum.*
Paradise: *Paradisea Liliastrum.*
Perfumed fairy: *Chlidanthus fragrans.*
Peruvian: *Alstroemeria.*
Pig: *Zantedeschia aethiopica.*
Pine: *Lilium Catesbaei.*
Pineapple: *Eucomis.*
Pinewoods: *Eustylis purpurea.*
Pink Easter: *Echinopsis multiplex.*
Pink porcelain: *Alpinia Zerumbet.*
Plantain: *Hosta.*
Pond: *Nymphaea odorata.*
Pot-of-gold: *Lilium iridollae.*
Prickly water: *Euryale ferox.*
Pygmy water: *Nymphaea tetragona.*
Queen: *Curcuma petiolata.*
Rain: *Zephyranthes.*
Red ginger: *Hedychium coccineum.*
Red spider: *Lycoris radiata.*
Redwood: *Lilium rubescens.*
Regal: *L. regale.*
Resurrection: *Kaempferia rotunda, Lycoris squamigera.*
Roan: *Lilium Grayi.*
Rock: *Dendrobium speciosum.*
Royal: *Lilium regale.*
Royal water: *Victoria amazonica* var. *Randii.*
Saint . . . : see St. . . .
Sand: *Leucocrinum.*
Santa Cruz water: *Victoria Cruziana.*
Scarborough: *Vallota speciosa.*
Scarlet ginger: *Hedychium coccineum.*
Scarlet Turk's-cap: *Lilium chalcedonicum.*
Seersucker plantain: *Hosta Sieboldiana.*
Sego: *Calochortus, C. Nuttallii.*
Shasta: *Lilium Washingtonianum* var. *minus.*
Showy: *L. speciosum.*
Showy Japanese: *L. speciosum.*
Siberian: *Ixiolirion tataricum.*
Sierra: *Lilium parvum.*
Small tiger: *L. parvum.*
Snake: *Dichelostemma volubile.*
Solomon's: *Arum palaestinum.*
Southern red: *Lilium Catesbaei.*
Spear: *Doryanthes.*
Speckled wood: *Clintonia unbellata.*
Spider: *Crinum, Hymenocallis, Lycoris radiata.*
St. Bernard's: *Anthericum Liliago, Chlorophytum.*
St. Bruno's: *Paradisea Liliastrum.*
St. James's: *Sprekelia formosissima.*
St. Joseph's: *Hippeastrum* ×*Johnsonii.*
Star: *Leucocrinum, Lilium concolor, Zigadenus Fremontii.*
Sunset: *Lilium pardalinum* cv. 'Giganteum'.
Swamp: *L. superbum, Saururus cernuus.*
Sword: *Gladiolus.*
Tartar: *Ixiolirion tataricum.*
Thimble: *Lilium Bolanderi.*
Tiger: *L. Catesbaei, L. lancifolium.*

Lily—*Continued*
Toad: *Tricyrtis.*
Toad-cup: *Neomarica.*
Torch: *Kniphofia.*
Triplet: *Triteleia laxa.*
Trout: *Erythronium, E. americanum.*
Trumpet: *Lilium longiflorum, Zantedeschia aethiopica.*
Tuberous water: *Nymphaea tuberosa.*
Turban: *Lilium Martagon, L. pomponium.*
Turk's-cap: *L. Martagon, L. Michauxii, L. superbum.*
Voodoo: *Sauromatum guttatum.*
Washington: *Lilium Washingtonianum.*
Water: *Nymphaea.*
Western: *Lilium occidentale.*
Western orange-cup: *L. pardalinum* var. *andinum.*
Wheel: *L. medeoloides.*
White trumpet: *L. longiflorum.*
White water: *Nymphaea odorata.*
Wild orange-red. *Lilium philadelphicum.*
Wild yellow: *L. canadense.*
Wood: *L. philadelphicum.*
Yellow: *L. canadense.*
Yellow-bell: *L.. canadense.*
Yellow pond: *Nuphar.*
Yellow Turk's-cap: *Lilium pyrenaicum.*
Yellow water: *Nuphar luteum, Nymphaea mexicana.*
Zephyr: *Zephyranthes.*
Lily-of-China: *Rohdea japonica.*
Lily-of-the-Altai: *Ixiolirion.*
Lily-of-the-Amazon: *Eucharis grandiflora.*
Lily-of-the-field: *Anemone, Sternbergia lutea.*
Lily-of-the-Incas: *Alstroemeria.*
Lily-of-the-Nile: *Agapanthus africanus.*
Lily-of-the-palace: *Hippeastrum aulicum.*
Lily-of-the-valley: *Convallaria.*
False: *Maianthemum.*
Star-flowered: *Smilacina stellata.*
Wild: *Maianthemum canadense, Pyrola elliptica, P. rotundifolia.*
Lily-of-the-valley bush: *Pieris japonica.*
Lily royal: *Lilium superbum.*
Lilyturf: *Liriope, Ophiopogon.*
Creeping: *Liriope spicata.*
Dwarf: *Ophiopogon japonicus.*
Jaburan: *O. Jaburan.*
White: *O. Jaburan.*
Lime: *Citrus aurantiifolia.*
Australian desert: *Eremocitrus.*
Australian finger: *Microcitrus australasica.*
Australian round: *M. australis.*
Australian wild: *Microcitrus.*
Key: *Citrus aurantiifolia.*
Mandarin: *C. ×limonia.*
Mexican. *C. aurantiifolia.*
Persian: *C. aurantiifolia* cv. 'Tahiti'.
Rangpur: *C. ×limonia.*
Spanish: *Melicoccus bijugatus.*
West Indian: *Citrus aurantiifolia.*
Wild: *Zanthoxylum Fagara.*
Limeberry: *Triphasia trifolia.*
Limequat: *× Citrofortunella floridana, ×C. Swinglei;* see also under *Citrus aurantiifolia.*
Lime tree: *Tilia.*
Linaria: *Linaria.*
Dull-colored: *L. tristis.*
Sad-colored: *L. tristis.*
Linden: *Tilia.*
American: *T. americana.*
Crimean: *T. ×euchlora.*
Indoor: *Sparmannia.*
Japanese: *Tilia japonica.*
Large-leaved: *T. platyphyllos.*
Manchurian: *T. mandshurica.*
Mongolian: *T. mongolica.*
Pendent silver: *T. petiolaris.*
Small-leaved European: *T. cordata.*
Ling: *Calluna, Trapa natans.*
Lingen: *Vaccinium Vitis-idaea* var. *minus.*
Lingberry: *Vaccinium Vitis-idaea* var. *minus.*
Lingenberry, Lingonberry: *Vaccinium Vitis-idaea* var. *minus.*
Linkleaf: *Schlumbergera truncata.*
Link plant: *Rhipsalis paradoxa.*
Link vine: *Vanilla barbellata.*
Lion's-beard: *Anemone Nuttalliana.*

Lion's-ear: *Leonotis, L. Leonurus.*
Lion's-heart: *Physostegia.*
Lion's-tongue: *Opuntia Schickendantzii.*
Lipstick plant: *Aeschynanthus pulcher, A. radicans.*
Lipstick tree: *Bixa orellana.*
Liquorice: *Glycyrrhiza glabra.*
Litchi: *Litchi chinensis.*
Little-candles: *Mammillaria prolifera.*
Little-pickles: *Othonna capensis.*
Little-stars: *Sutera fastigiata.*
Little Virgin: *Caularthron bilamellatum.*
Live-and-die: *Mimosa pudica.*
Live-forever: *Sedum Telephium, Sempervivum.*
Liverberry: *Streptopus amplexifolius* var. *americanus.*
Liverleaf: *Hepatica.*
Living-baseball: *Euphorbia obesa.*
Living-rock: *Ariocarpus fissuratus* var. *fissuratus, Pleiospilos.*
African: *Pleiospilos Bolusii.*
Living-stones: *Lithops.*
Living-vase: *Aechmea.*
Lizard plant: *Tetrastigma Voinieranum.*
Lizard-tail: *×Gastrolea Beguinii.*
Lizard's-tail: *Eriophyllum staechadifolium, Saururus.*
Lobelia: *Lobelia.*
Edging: *L. Erinus.*
Great: *L. siphilitica.*
Pale-spike: *L. spicata.*
Water: *L. Dortmanna.*
Lobster-claw: *Heliconia humilis.*
Lobster-claws: *Cheiridopsis Pillansii, Vriesia carinata.*
Lobster plant: *Euphorbia pulcherrima.*
Loco, purple: *Oxytropis Lambertii.*
Locoweed: *Oxytropis, O. Lambertii.*
Locust: *Robinia.*
African: *Parkia biglobosa.*
Alleghany moss: *Robinia Kelseyi.*
Black: *R. Pseudoacacia.*
Bristly: *R. hispida.*
Clammy: *R. viscosa.*
Honey: *Gleditsia, G. triacanthos.*
Moss: *Robinia hispida.*
Mossy: *R. hispida.*
Ship-mast: *R. Pseudoacacia* cv. 'Rectissima'.
South American: *Hymenaea Courbaril.*
Swamp: *Gleditsia aquatica.*
Sweet: *G. triacanthos.*
Water: *G. aquatica.*
West Indian: *Hymenaea Courbaril.*
Yellow: *Robinia Pseudoacacia.*
Locust tree: *Hymenaea Courbaril.*
Loganberry: *Rubus ursinus* var. *loganobaccus* cv. 'Logan'.
Logwood: *Haematoxylum campechianum.*
London-pride: *Lychnis chalcedonica, Saxifraga umbrosa.*
Longan: *Euphorbia Longan.*
Long John: *Triplaris americana, T. surinamensis.*
Longroot: *Arenaria caroliniana.*
Long-thatch: *Calyptronoma occidentalis.*
Long-tresses: *Spiranthes gracilis.*
Loofah: *Luffa.*
Angled: *L. acutangula.*
Smooth: *L. aegyptiaca.*
Looking-glass plant: *Coprosma repens.*
Loosestrife: *Lysimachia, Lythrum.*
False: *Ludwigia.*
Garden: *Lysimachia punctata, L. vulgaris.*
Gooseneck: *L. clethroides.*
Purple: *Lythrum Salicaria.*
Spiked: *L. Salicaria.*
Swamp: *Decodon verticillatus.*
Tufted: *Lysimachia thyrsiflora.*
Loquat: *Eriobotrya japonica.*
Lords-and-ladies: *Arum maculatum.*
Lord's-candlestick: *Yucca gloriosa.*
Lote tree: *Celtis australis.*
Lotus: *Nelumbo, Nymphaea Lotus.*
American: *Nelumbo lutea.*
Blue: *Nymphaea caerulea, N. stellata.*
East Indian: *Nelumbo nucifera.*
Egyptian: *Nymphaea caerulea, N. Lotus.*
Sacred: *Nelumbo nucifera.*
Water: *Nelumbo.*
White: *Nymphaea Lotus.*

Lousewort: *Pedicularis.*
  Common: *P. canadensis.*
Lovage: *Levisticum officinale.*
Love-charm: *Clytostoma callistegioides.*
Love-in-a-mist: *Nigella damascena, Passiflora foetida.*
Lovejoy: *Episcia.*
Love-lies-bleeding: *Amaranthus caudatus.*
Love plant: *Anacampseros telephiastrum.*
  Mexican: *Kalanchoe pinnata.*
Love tree: *Cercis Siliquastrum.*
Love vine: *Antigonon leptopus.*
Lucerne: *Medicago sativa.*
Lucky nut: *Thevetia peruviana.*
Lucky plant: *Sansevieria.*
Lulo: *Solanum quitoense.*
Lungan: *Euphorbia Longan.*
Lungwort: *Mertensia, Pulmonaria.*
  Blue: *Pulmonaria officinalis.*
  Golden: *Hieracium murorum.*
Lupine: *Lupinus.*
  Blue: *L. hirsutus.*
  Carolina: *Thermopsis caroliniana.*
  False: *Thermopsis.*
  Field: *Lupinus albus.*
  Sundial: *L. perennis.*
  Tree: *L. arboreus.*
  White: *L. albus.*
  Wild: *L. perennis.*
  Yellow: *L. luteus.*
Lustwort: *Drosera rotundifolia.*
Lychee: *Litchi chinensis.*
Lychnis, evening: *Silene alba.*

Macadamia nut: *Macadamia integrifolia, M. tetraphylla.*
  Rough-shell: *M. tetraphylla.*
Macaw-fat: *Elaeis guineensis.*
Macaw flower: *Heliconia Bihai, H. distans.*
Mace, sweet: *Tagetes lucida.*
Madder: *Rubia tinctorum.*
Mad-dog weed: *Alisma Plantago-aquatica.*
Madeira nut: *Juglans regia.*
Madeira vine: *Anredera cordifolia.*
Madia, common: *Madia elegans.*
Madia-oil plant: *Madia sativa.*
Madre: *Gliricidia sepium.*
Madroffo: *Andromeda Menziesii.*
Madrona, Madrone, Madrono, Madroño: *Arbutus Menziesii.*
Madwort: *Alyssum, Aurinia.*
  Goldentuft: *Aurinia saxatilis.*
  Rock: *A. saxatilis.*
Magic flower: *Achimenes, Cantua buxifolia.*
Magic-flower-of-the Incas: *Cantua buxifolia.*
Magician's flower: *Tacca Chantrieri.*
Magnolia: *Magnolia.*
  Ashe: *M. Ashei.*
  Chinese: *M. sinensis, M. ×Soulangiana.*
  Great-leaved: *M. macrophylla.*
  Saucer: *M. ×Soulangiana.*
  Southern: *M. grandiflora*
  Star: *M. stellata.*
  Umbrella: *M. tripetala.*
Magnolia vine: *Schisandra.*
Maguey: *Agave americana.*
Maguey-del-cumbre: *Agave atrovirens.*
Ma-hai: *Eleocharis dulcis.*
Mahala-mat: *Ceanothus prostratus.*
Mahaleb: *Prunus Mahaleb.*
Mahoe: *Hibiscus elatus, H. tiliaceus,*
  (of New Zealand) *Melicytus ramiflorus.*
Mahogany: *Swietenia.*
  African: *Khaya.*
  Big-leaf: *Swietenia macrophylla.*
  Florida: *Persea Borbonia.*
  Honduras: *Swietenia Candollea.*
  Mountain: *Betula lenta, Cercocarpus.*
  Nyasaland: *Khaya nyasica.*
  Red: *Eucalyptus resinifera.*
  Senegal: *Khaya senegalensis.*
  Spanish: *Swietenia Mahagoni.*
  Swamp: *Eucalyptus robusta.*
  Venezuelan: *Swietenia Candollea.*
  West Indian: *S. Mahagoni.*
  White: *Eucalyptus umbra, E. acmenioides.*

Mahonia, holly: *Mahonia Aquifolium.*
Maidenhair: *Adiantum;* see under Fern.
Maidenhair berry: *Gaultheria hispidula.*
Maidenhair tree: *Ginkgo biloba.*
Maidenhair vine: *Muehlenbeckia complexa.*
Maiden's-tears: *Silene vulgaris.*
Maikoa: *Brugmansia arborea.*
Maize: *Zea Mays.*
  Flint: *Z. Mays* var. *indurata.*
  Water: *Victoria amazonica.*
Makola: *Afzelia cuanzensis.*
Malanga: *Xanthosoma.*
Malaxis, green: *Malaxis unifolia.*
Male berry: *Lyonia ligustrina*
Mallee: *Eucalyptus;* see also Mallet.
  Bell-fruited: *E. Preissiana.*
  Blue mountain; *E. stricta.*
  Burracoppin: *E. burracoppinensis.*
  Coarse-leaved: *E. grossa.*
  Congo: *E. dumosa.*
  Desmond: *E. desmondensis.*
  Ewart's: *E. Ewartiana.*
  Gooseberry: *E. calycogona.*
  Horned: *E. eremophila.*
  Kruse's: *E. Kruseana.*
  Lerp: *E. incrassata.*
  Oldfield's: *E. Oldfieldii.*
  Pear-fruited: *E. pyriformis.*
  Red-flowered: *E. erythronema.*
  Ridge-fruited: *E. incrassata.*
  Rose: *E. rhodantha.*
  Round-leaved: *E. orbifolia.*
  Southern-cross silver: *E. crucis.*
  Square-fruited: *E. tetraptera.*
  Stoward's: *E. Stowardii.*
Mallet: *Eucalyptus;* see also Mallee.
  Brown: *E. astringens.*
  Swamp: *E. spathulata.*
Mallow: *Hibiscus, Malva.*
  Chaparral: *Malacothamnus.*
  Common rose: *Hibiscus Moscheutos.*
  Curled: *Malva verticillata* var. *crispa.*
  Desert rose: *Hibiscus Farragei.*
  False: *Sphaeralcea.*
  Giant: *Hibiscus.*
  Glade: *Napaea.*
  Globe: *Sphaeralcea.*
  Great rose: *Hibiscus grandiflorus.*
  Halberd-leaved: *H. militaris.*
  High: *Malva sylvestris.*
  Indian: *Abutilon, A. Theophrasti.*
  Jew's: *Corchorus olitorius.*
  Musk: *Abelmoschus moschatus, Malva, M. moschata.*
  Poppy: *Callirhoe, C. involucrata.*
  Prairie: *Sphaeralcea coccinea.*
  Red false: *S. coccinea.*
  Rose: *Hibiscus.*
  Seashore: *Kosteletzkya.*
  Sleepy: *Malvaviscus.*
  Soldier rose: *Hibiscus militaris.*
  Swamp rose: *H. Moscheutos.*
  Trailing: *Sphaeralcea Philippiana.*
  Tree: *Lavatera, L. arborea.*
  Virginia: *Sida hermaphrodita.*
  Wax: *Malvaviscus arboreus.*
  White: *Althaea officinalis.*
Maltese-cross: *Lychnis chalcedonica.*
Malu creeper: *Bauhinia Vahlii.*
Mamane: *Sophora chrysophylla.*
Mamey: *Mammea americana.*
Mamey colorado: *Pouteria Sapota.*
Mammee: *Mammea americana.*
Mammillaria, thimble: *Mammillaria fragilis.*
Mamoncillo: *Melicoccus bijugatus.*
Manac: *Calyptronoma.*
  Cuban: *C. dulcis.*
  Jamaican: *C. occidentalis.*
Manacá: *Brunfelsia uniflora.*
Mandarin
  King: *Citrus ×nobilis* cv. 'King'.
  Nodding: *Disporum maculatum.*
  Rose: *Streptopus roseus.*

Mandarin—*Continued*
  White: *S. amplexifolius.*
  Yellow: *Disporum lanuginosum.*
Mandarin's-hat: *Holmskioldia sanguinea.*
Mandrake: *Mandragora, Podophyllum peltatum.*
Mangel: *Beta vulgaris,* Crassa Group.
Mangelwurzel: *Beta vulgaris,* Crassa Group.
Mango: *Mangifera indica.*
Mangold: *Beta vulgaris.*
Mangosteen: *Garcinia Mangostana.*
  African: *G. Livingstonei.*
Mangrove: *Rhizophora.*
  American: *R. Mangle.*
  Button: *Conocarpus.*
Man-in-a-boat: *Rhoeo spathacea.*
Manioc: *Manihot esculenta.*
Manjack, red: *Cordia nitida.*
Manna plant: *Tamarix gallica.*
Man-of-the-earth: *Ipomoea leptophylla, I. pandurata.*
Manroot: *Marah, Ipomoea leptophylla.*
Manuka: *Leptospermum scoparium.*
Many-fingers: *Sedum pachyphyllum.*
Manzanita: *Arctostaphylos.*
  Big-berry: *A. glauca.*
  Brittle-leaf: *A. crustacea.*
  Del Norte: *A. cinerea.*
  Dune: *A. pumila.*
  Eastwood: *A. glandulosa.*
  Fort Bragg: *A. Nummularia.*
  Green-leaf: *A. patula.*
  Hairy: *A. columbiana.*
  Heart-leaf: *A. Andersonii.*
  Hoary: *A. canescens.*
  Ione: *A. myrtifolia.*
  Island: *A. insularis.*
  Little Sur: *A. Edmundsii.*
  Mariposa: *A. Mariposa.*
  Mexican: *A. pungens.*
  Monterey: *A. Hookeri.*
  Morro: *A. morroensis.*
  Otay: *A. otavensis.*
  Pajaro: *A. pajaroensis.*
  Parry: *A. Manzanita.*
  Pecho: *A. pechoensis.*
  Pine-mat: *A. nevadensis.*
  Pink-bracted: *A. Pringlei* var. *drupacea.*
  Serpentine: *A. obispoensis.*
  Shagbark: *A. rudis.*
  Silver-leaf: *A. silvicola.*
  Sonoma: *A. densiflora.*
  Stanford: *A. Stanfordiana.*
  White-leaf: *A. viscida.*
  Woolly: *A. tomentosa.*
Manzanote: *Olmediella Betschlerana.*
Maple: *Acer.*
  Amur: *A. Ginnala.*
  Ash-leaved: *A. Negundo.*
  Balkan: *A. Heldreichii.*
  Big-leaf: *A. macrophyllum.*
  Big-tooth: *A. saccharum* subsp. *grandidentatum.*
  Black: *A. saccharum* subsp. *nigrum.*
  Canyon: *A. macrophyllum.*
  Chalk: *A. saccharum* subsp. *leucoderme.*
  Drummond: *A. rubrum* var. *Drummondii.*
  Eagle-claw: *A. platanoides* cv. 'Laciniatum'.
  Field: *A. campestre.*
  Florida: *A. barbatum.*
  Flowering: *Abutilon.*
  Full-moon: *Acer japonicum.*
  Hard: *A. saccharum.*
  Hawthorn: *A. crataegifolium.*
  Hedge: *A. campestre.*
  Hornbeam: *A. carpinifolium.*
  Japanese: *A. japonicum, A. palmatum.*
  Montpellier: *A. monspessulanum.*
  Mountain: *A. glabrum* subsp. *Douglasii* var. *Torreyi, A. spicatum.*
  Nikko: *A. Maximowiczianum.*
  Norway: *A. platanoides.*
  Oregon: *A. macrophyllum.*
  Paperbark: *A. griseum.*
  Parlor: *Abutilon.*
  Pennsylvania: *Acer pensylvanicum.*
  Persian: *A. velutinum.*

Maple—*Continued*
  Red: *A. rubrum.*
  River: *A. saccharinum.*
  Rock: *A. saccharum.*
  Rocky Mountain: *A. glabrum.*
  Rocky Mountain sugar: *A. saccharum* subsp. *grandidentatum.*
  Scarlet: *A. rubrum.*
  Schwedler: *A. platanoides* cv. 'Schwedleri'.
  Shantung: *A. truncatum.*
  Sierra: *A. glabrum* subsp. *Douglasii* var. *Torreyi.*
  Silver: *A. saccharinum.*
  Soft: *A. rubrum, A. saccharinum.*
  Southern sugar: *A. barbatum.*
  Striped: *A. pensylvanicum.*
  Sugar: *A. saccharum.*
  Swamp: *A. rubrum.*
  Sycamore: *A. pseudoplatanus.*
  Tartarian, Tatarian: *A. tataricum.*
  Trident: *A. Buergeranum.*
  Vine: *A. circinatum.*
  White: *A. saccharinum.*
Marañon: *Anacardium occidentale.*
Marbleleaf: *Peristrophe hyssopifolia* cv. 'Aureo-variegata'.
Marble plant: *Neoregelia marmorata.*
Mare's-tail: *Hippuris, H. vulgaris.*
Marguerite: *Chrysanthemum frutescens, C. Leucanthemum.*
  Blue: *Felicia amelloides.*
  Golden: *Anthemis tinctoria.*
  Hardy: *A. tinctoria* cv. 'Kelwayi'.
  White: *Chrysanthemum frutescens.*
Maria: *Calophyllum brasiliense.*
Marigold: *Tagetes.*
  African: *T. erecta.*
  Aztec: *T. erecta.*
  Big: *T. erecta.*
  Bur: *Bidens.*
  Cape: *Dimorphotheca.*
  Corn: *Chrysanthemum segetum.*
  Desert: *Baileya multiradiata.*
  Fetid: *Dyssodia.*
  Field: *Calendula arvensis.*
  Fig: *Glottiphyllum depressum, Mesembryanthemum.*
  French: *Tagetes patula.*
  Marsh: *Caltha, C. palustris.*
  Pot: *Calendula officinalis.*
  Signet: *Tagetes tenuifolia.*
  Sweet-scented: *T. lucida.*
  Water: *Bidens.*
  Wild: *Baileya multiradiata.*
Marijuana: *Cannabis sativa.*
Mariposa: *Calochortus.*
  Desert: *C. Kennedyi.*
  Golden-bowl: *C. concolor.*
  Green-banded: *C. macrocarpus.*
  Lilac: *C. splendens.*
  Weed's: *C. Weedii.*
  White: *C. venustus.*
  Yellow: *C. luteus.*
Marjoram: *Origanum, O. vulgare.*
  Annual: *O. Majorana.*
  Hop: *O. Dictamnus.*
  Pot: *Origanum heracleoticum, O. Onites, O. vulgare.*
  Sweet: *O. Majorana.*
  Wild: *O. vulgare.*
  Winter: *O. heracleoticum.*
  Winter sweet: *O. heracleoticum.*
Marking-nut tree: *Semecarpus Anacardium.*
Markry: *Rhus radicans.*
Marlberry: *Ardisia escallonioides, A. japonica.*
Marlock: *Eucalyptus.*
  Forrest's: *E. Forrestiana.*
  Long-flowered: *E. macrandra.*
  White-leaved: *E. tetragona.*
Marmalade bush: *Streptosolen Jamesonii.*
Marmalade fruit: *Pouteria Sapota.*
Marri: *Eucalyptus calophylla.*
Marrow: *Cucurbita Pepo.*
Marsh mallow: *Althaea officinalis, Hibiscus Moscheutos* subsp.
    palustris.
Marvel-of-Peru: *Mirabilis Jalapa.*
Mask flower: *Alonsoa, A. Warcsewiczii.*
Masterwort: *Angelica atropurpurea, Astrantia, Heracleum Sphon-*
    dylium subsp. *montanum.*

Mastic tree: *Pistacia Lentiscus.*
  Chios: *P. Lentiscus.*
  Mount Atlas: *P. atlantica.*
  Peruvian: *Schinus Molle.*
Ma-tai: *Eleocharis dulcis.*
Matasano: *Casimiroa tetrameria.*
Matchbrush: *Gutierrezia.*
Match-me-if-you-can: *Acalypha Wilkesiana.*
Matchweed: *Gutierrezia.*
Maté: *Ilex paraguariensis.*
Mathers: *Vaccinium ovalifolium.*
Matricary: *Matricaria.*
Matrimony vine: *Lycium.*
  Chinese: *L. chinense.*
  Common: *L. halimifolium.*
Mattress vine: *Muehlenbeckia complexa.*
Maya: *Miconia dodecandra.*
Mayapple: *Podophyllum peltatum.*
  Himalayan: *P. hexandrum.*
May-blob: *Caltha palustris.*
Mayflower: *Cardamine pratensis, Epigaea repens, Maianthemum.*
Maypop: *Passiflora incarnata.*
Mayten: *Maytenus Boaria.*
Mayweed: *Anthemis Cotula.*
Mazzard: *Prunus avium.*
Meadow-beauty: *Rhexia.*
Meadow-bright: *Caltha palustris.*
Meadow-foam: *Limnanthes.*
Meadowsweet: *Filipendula, Spiraea alba, S. latifolia.*
Mealberry: *Arctostaphylos Uva-ursi.*
Measles plant: *Hypoestes phyllostachya.*
Medic, Medick: *Medicago.*
  Black: *M. lupulina.*
Medicine plant: *Aloe barbadensis.*
Medick: see Medic.
Medlar: *Mespilus, Mimusops Elengi.*
  Japanese: *Eriobotrya japonica.*
Medusa's-head: *Euphorbia caput-medusae.*
Meeting-houses: *Aquilegia canadensis.*
Melic: *Melica.*
  Siberian: *M. altissima.*
  Silky spike: *M. ciliata.*
Melilot: *Melilotus, M. officinalis.*
  White: *M. alba.*
  Yellow: *M. officinalis.*
Melist: *Melilotus officinalis.*
Melon
  Casaba: *Cucumis Melo,* Inodorus Group.
  Chinese preserving: *Benincasa hispida.*
  Dudaim: *Cucumis Melo,* Dudaim Group.
  Honeydew: *C. Melo,* Inodorus Group.
  Mango: *C. Melo,* Chito Group.
  Netted: *C. Melo,* Reticulatus Group.
  Nutmeg: *C. Melo,* Reticulatus Group.
  Orange: *C. Melo,* Chito Group.
  Oriental pickling: *C. Melo,* Conomon Group.
  Pear: *Solanum muricatum.*
  Persian: *Cucumis Melo,* Reticulatus Group.
  Pomegranate: *C. Melo,* Dudaim Group.
  Preserving: *Citrullus lanatus* var. *citroides.*
  Queen Anne's pocket: *Cucumis Melo,* Dudaim Group.
  Serpent: *C. Melo,* Flexuosus Group.
  Snake: *C. Melo,* Flexuosus Group.
  Stink: *C. Melo,* Dudaim Group.
  Winter: *C. Melo,* Inodorus Group.
Melongene: *Solanum Melongena* var. *esculenta.*
Melon shrub: *Solanum muricatum.*
Melon tree: *Carica Papaya.*
Menow weed: *Ruellia tuberosa.*
Menthella: *Mentha Requienii.*
Mercury: *Chenopodium Bonus-Henricus, Rhus radicans.*
  Three-seeded: *Acalypha.*
  Vegetable: *Brunfelsia uniflora.*
Mermaid weed: *Proserpinaca.*
Merrit: *Eucalyptus Flocktoniae.*
Merrybells: *Uvularia.*
Merryhearts: *Zigadenus Nuttallii.*
Mescal: *Agave Parryi.*
Mescal-button: *Lophophora.*
Mesquite: *Prosopis glandulosa, P. juliflora, P. laevigata.*
  Curly: *Hilaria Belangeri.*
  Honey: *Prosopis glandulosa* var. *glandulosa.*

Mesquite—*Continued*
  Mock: *Calliandra.*
  Vine: *Panicum obtusum.*
  Western honey: *Prosopis glandulosa* var. *Torreyana.*
Mesquitilla: *Calliandra.*
Metake: *Pseudosasa japonica.*
Mexican creeper: *Antigonon leptopus.*
Mexican-firecracker: *Echeveria setosa.*
Mexican-gem: *Echeveria elegans.*
Mexican-giant: *Cephalocereus fulviceps, Pachycereus Pringlei.*
Mexican-star: *Milla biflora.*
Mezereum: *Daphne Mezereum.*
Miami-mist: *Phacelia Purshii.*
Mickey-Mouse plant: *Ochna serrulata.*
Mignonette: *Reseda.*
  Common: *R. odorata.*
  White upright: *R. alba.*
Mignonette tree: *Lawsonia inermis.*
Mignonette vine: *Anredera cordifolia.*
Mile tree: *Casuarina equisetifolia.*
Milfoil: *Achillea Millefolium, Myriophyllum.*
  Red water: *Myriophyllum hippuroides.*
  Water: *Myriophyllum.*
  Western: *M. hippuroides.*
Milk-barrel: *Euphorbia cereiformis, E. heptagona.*
Milkbush: *Euphorbia Tirucalli.*
  African: *Synadenium Grantii.*
Milkmaids: *Dentaria californica.*
Milk tree, African: *Euphorbia trigona.*
Milkweed: *Asclepias.*
  Horsetail: *A. verticillata.*
  Purple: *A. purpurascens.*
  Swamp: *A. incarnata.*
Milkwort: *Polygala.*
  Yellow: *P. lutea.*
Millet: *Panicum miliaceum.*
  African: *Eleusine coracana, Pennisetum glaucum.*
  Barnyard: *Echinochloa crus-galli.*
  Browntop: *Panicum ramosum.*
  Finger: *Eleusine coracana.*
  Foxtail: *Setaria italica.*
  Hog: *Panicum miliaceum.*
  Indian: *Pennisetum glaucum.*
  Italian: *Setaria italica.*
  Japanese: *Echinochloa crus-galli, Setaria italica.*
  Japanese barnyard: *Echinochloa crus-galli* var. *frumentacea.*
  Pearl: *Pennisetum glaucum.*
  Sanwa: *Echinochloa crus-galli* var. *frumentacea.*
Milo: *Sorghum bicolor,* Subglabrescens Group.
Mimicry plant: *Lithops, Pleiospilos Bolusii, P. Nelii.*
  Stone: *Pleiospilos.*
Mimosa: *Acacia dealbata, Albizia Julibrissin.*
  Egyptian: *Acacia nilotica.*
  Golden: *A. Baileyana.*
  Prairie: *Desmanthus illinoensis.*
  Texas: *Acacia Greggii.*
Mimosa tree: *Albizia Julibrissin.*
Mind-your-own-business: *Soleirolia Soleirolii.*
Ming aralia: *Polyscias fruticosa.*
Minniebush: *Menziesia pilosa.*
Mint: *Mentha.*
  Apple: *M. rotundifolia.*
  Bergamot: *M. piperita* var. *citrata.*
  Corsican: *M. Requienii.*
  Coyote: *Monardella villosa.*
  Creeping: *Meehania cordata.*
  Dog: *Clinopodium vulgare.*
  Dotted: *Monarda punctata.*
  Field: *Mentha arvensis.*
  Japanese: *M. arvensis* var. *piperascens.*
  Lemon: *M. aquatica* var. *citrata, Monarda citriodora.*
  Meehan's: *Meehania, M. cordata.*
  Mountain: *Pycnanthemum.*
  Orange: *Mentha aquatica* var. *citrata.*
  Pineapple: *M. rotundifolia* cv. 'Variegata'.
  Red: *M.* ✕*gentilis.*
  Scotch: *M.* ✕*gentilis.*
  Stone: *Cunila origanoides.*
  Water: *Mentha aquatica.*
  Wood: *Blephilia hirsuta.*
Missey-moosey: *Sorbus americana.*
Mist flower: *Eupatorium coelestinum.*

Mintbush: *Prostanthera.*
  Round-leaf: *P. rotundifolia.*
  Snowy: *P. nivea.*
Mint shrub: *Elsholtzia Stauntonii.*
Mirabelle: *Prunus insititia* var. *syriaca.*
Miracle leaf: *Kalanchoe pinnata.*
Miraculous fruit: *Synsepalum dulcificum.*
Mirasol: *Helianthus annuus.*
Miro: *Podocarpus ferrugineus.*
Mirror-of-Venus: *Ophrys speculum.*
Mirror plant: *Coprosma repens.*
Mistletoe: *Arceuthobium, Phoradendron, Viscum;* see under Loran-
  thaceae.
  American: *Phoradendron serotinum.*
  Dwarf: *Arceuthobium pusillum,* see under Loranthaceae.
  False: *Phoradendron.*
Miterwort: *Mitella.*
  False: *Tiarella.*
Mitsumata: *Edgeworthia papyrifera.*
Moccasin flower: *Cypripedium, C. acaule.*
  Large yellow: *C. Calceolus* var. *pubescens.*
  Small yellow: *C. Calceolus* var. *parviflorum.*
Mochi tree: *Ilex integra.*
Mockernut: *Carya tomentosa.*
Mohintli: *Justicia spicigera.*
Molded-wax: *Echeveria agavoides.*
Mole plant: *Euphorbia heterophylla, E. Lathyrus.*
Molka: *Rubus Chamaemorus.*
Molle: *Schinus Molle.*
Mombin: *Spondias.*
  Purple: *S. purpurea.*
  Red: *S. purpurea.*
  Yellow: *S. Mombin.*
Monarch-of-the-East: *Sauromatum guttatum.*
Monardella: *Monardella.*
  Mountain: *M. odoratissima.*
  Yellow: *M. nana.*
Monastery-bells: *Cobaea scandens.*
Money plant: *Lunaria.*
Money tree: *Eucalyptus pulverulenta.*
Moneywort: *Lysimachia Nummularia.*
Monkey-apple tree: *Clusia rosea.*
Monkey-bread tree: *Adansonia digitata.*
Monkeycomb: *Pithecoctenium.*
Monkey flower: *Mimulus.*
  Alleghany: *M. ringens.*
  Bush: *M. aurantiacus.*
  Common: *M. guttatus.*
  Scarlet: *M. cardinalis.*
Monkey jack: *Artocarpus Lakoocha.*
Monkey nut: *Arachis hypogaea, Lecythis Zabucayo.*
Monkey-pistol: *Hura crepitans.*
Monkey plant: *Ruellia Makoyana.*
Monkeypod: *Samanea Saman.*
Monkey-puzzle: *Araucaria araucana.*
Monkey-puzzle tree: *Araucaria araucana.*
Monkeytail: *Ruschia crassa.*
Monkey's-dinner-bell: *Hura crepitans.*
Monkshood: *Aconitum, Astrophytum myriostigma.*
  Garden: *Aconitum Napellus.*
  Ornamental: *Astrophytum ornatum.*
  Wild: *Aconitum uncinatum.*
Monox: *Empetrum nigrum.*
Montbretia: *Crocosmia.*
Moonah: *Melaleuca lanceolata.*
Moonflower: *Ipomoea alba.*
  Bush: *I. leptophylla.*
Moonseed: *Menispermum.*
  Carolina: *Cocculus carolinus.*
  Red: *C. carolinus.*
  Red-berried: *C. carolinus.*
Moon-set: *Habenaria orbiculata.*
Moonstones: *Pachyphytum oviferum.*
Moonwort: *Botrychium, B. Lunaria, Lunaria.*
Moorberry: *Vaccinium uliginosum.*
Moort: *Eucalyptus.*
  Red-flowered: *E. nutans.*
  Round-leaved: *E. platypus.*
Mooseberry: *Viburnum alnifolium, V. pauciflorum.*
Moose bush: *Viburnum alnifolium.*
Moosewood: *Acer pensylvanicum, Dirca palustris, Viburnum
  alnifolium.*
Morel, petty: *Aralia racemosa.*

Morell, red: *Eucalyptus longicornis.*
Morning flower: *Orthrosanthus.*
Morning-glory: *Calystegia, Convolvulus, Ipomoea.*
  Beach: *Ipomoea Pes-caprae.*
  Brazilian: *I. setosa.*
  Ceylon: *Merremia tuberosa.*
  Common: *Ipomoea purpurea.*
  Dwarf: *Convolvulus tricolor.*
  Imperial Japanese: *Ipomoea Nil.*
  Red: *I. coccinea.*
  Silver: *Argyreia splendens.*
  Wild: *Calystegia sepium.*
  Woolly: *Argyreia nervosa.*
  Yellow: *Merremia tuberosa.*
Morning-noon-and-night: *Brunfelsia australis, B. pauciflora* cv.
  'Eximia'.
Mortinia: *Vaccinium Mortinia.*
Mosaic plant: *Fittonia Verschaffeltii.*
Moschatel: *Adoxa Moschatellina.*
Moses-in-a-boat: *Rhoeo spathacea.*
Moses-in-the-bulrushes: *Rhoeo spathacea.*
Moses-in-the-cradle: *Rhoeo spathacea.*
Moses-on-a-raft: *Rhoeo spathacea.*
Mosquito-bills: *Dodecatheon Hendersonii.*
Mosquito flower: *Lopezia hirsuta.*
Mosquito plant: *Agastache cana, Azolla caroliniana, Cynanchum
  ascyrifolium.*
Moss: see article on Mosses and Liverworts.
  Ball: *Tillandsia recurvata.*
  Basket spike: *Selaginella apoda.*
  Broom: *Dicranum;* see article on Mosses and Liverworts.
  Bunch: *Tillandsia recurvata.*
  Club: *Lycopodium.*
  Coral: *Nertera granadensis.*
  Cushion: *Selaginella Kraussiana* cv. 'Brownii'.
  Ditch: *Anacharis canadensis, Elodea.*
  Douglas's spike: *Selaginella Douglasii.*
  Dwarf club: *S. Kraussiana* cv. 'Brownii'.
  Fairy: *Azolla.*
  Floating: *Salvinia rotundifolia.*
  Flowering: *Pyxidanthera barbulata.*
  Fountain: *Fontinalis.*
  Gold: *Sedum acre.*
  Haircap: *Polytrichum;* see article on Mosses and Liverworts.
  Irish: *Selaginella Kraussiana* cv. 'Brownii', *Soleirolia Soleirolii.*
  Japanese: *Soleirolia Soleirolii.*
  Little club: *Selaginella.*
  Mat spike: *S. Kraussiana.*
  Meadow spike: *S. apoda.*
  Peacock: *S. uncinata.*
  Pincushion: *Leucobryum glaucum;* see article on Mosses and Liver-
    worts.
  Rose: *Portulaca grandiflora.*
  Scotch: *Selaginella Kraussiana* cv. 'Brownii'.
  Shining club: *Lycopodium lucidulum.*
  Spanish: *Tillandsia usneoides.*
  Spike: *Selaginella.*
  Spring: *Fontinalis.*
  Treelet spike: *Selaginella Braunii.*
  Water: *Fontinalis.*
  Willdenow's spike: *Selaginella Willdenovii.*
Mother-in-law: *Kalanchoe pinnata.*
Mother-in-law plant: *Caladium, Dieffenbachia Seguine.*
Mother-in-law's-tongue: *Gasteria, Sansevieria trifasciata.*
Mother-in-law's-tongue plant: *Dieffenbachia.*
Mother-of-pearl plant: *Graptopetalum paraguayense.*
Mother-of-thousands: *Saxifraga stolonifera.*
Mother-of-thyme: *Thymus praecox* subsp. *arcticus.*
Mother's-tears: *Achimenes.*
Motherwort: *Leonurus.*
Mottled-cranefly: *Tipularia discolor.*
Mountain-devil: *Lambertia formosa.*
Mountain-fleece: *Polygonum amplexicaule.*
Mountain-fringe: *Adlumia fungosa.*
Mountain-lover: *Paxistima Canbyi.*
Mountain-misery: *Chamaebatia.*
Mountain-pride: *Penstemon Newberryi.*
Mountain sumac: *Rhus copallina.*
Mountainsweet: *Ceanothus americanus.*
Mourning-bride: *Scabiosa atropurpurea.*
Mouse plant: *Arisarum proboscideum.*
Msasa: *Brachystegia spiciformis.*
Mud-baby, Texas: *Echinodorus cordifolius.*

Mud-midget: *Wolffiella floridana.*
Mugwort: *Artemisia, A. vulgaris.*
  Western: *A. ludoviciana.*
  White: *A. lactiflora.*
Muku tree: *Aphananthe aspera.*
Mulberry: *Morus.*
  Aino: *M. australis.*
  American: *M. rubra.*
  Black: *M. nigra.*
  French: *Callicarpa americana.*
  Indian: *Morinda citrifolia.*
  Paper: *Broussonetia papyrifera.*
  Red: *Morus rubra.*
  Russian: *M. alba* var. *tatarica.*
  Silkworm: *M. alba* var. *multicaulis.*
  White: *M. alba.*
Mule-fat: *Baccharis viminea.*
Mule's-ears: *Opuntia Schickendantzii.*
Mulga: *Acacia aneura.*
  Gray: *A. brachybotrya.*
Mullein: *Verbascum.*
  Common: *V. Thapsus.*
  Cretan: *Celsia cretica.*
  Moth: *Verbascum Blattaria.*
  Purple: *V. phoeniceum.*
  Turkey: *Eremocarpus setigerus.*
  White: *Verbascum lychnitis.*
Mum: *Chrysanthemum* ✕*morifolium.*
Munj: *Saccharum bengalense.*
Mu-oil: *Aleurites montana.*
Muscadine: *Vitis rotundifolia.*
Musk, wild: *Erodium cicutarium.*
Musk flower: *Mimulus moschatus.*
  Scarlet: *Nyctaginia capitata.*
Muskmelon: *Cucumis Melo*, Reticulatus Group.
Musk plant: *Mimulus moschatus.*
Muskrat weed: *Thalictrum polygamum.*
Muskroot: *Adoxa Moschatellina.*
Musquash root: *Cicuta maculata.*
Mustard: *Brassica.*
  Black: *B. nigra.*
  Broad-beaked: *B. narinosa.*
  Broad-leaved: *B. juncea* var. *foliosa.*
  Brown: *B. juncea.*
  Celery: *B. Rapa*, Chinensis Group.
  Chinese: *B. Rapa*, Chinensis Group.
  Curled: *B. juncea* var. *crispifolia.*
  Field: *B. campestris, B. Rapa.*
  Hill: *Bunias orientalis.*
  Indian: *Brassica juncea.*
  Leaf: *B. juncea.*
  Southern curled: *B. juncea* var. *crispifolia.*
  Spinach: *B. Rapa*, Perviridis Group.
  Tower: *Arabis glabra.*
  White: *Brassica hirta.*
Mustard greens: *Brassica juncea.*
Mustard tree: *Nicotiana glauca.*
Muster-John-Henry: *Tagetes minuta.*
Mu tree: *Aleurites montana.*
Myall: *Acacia.*
  Coastal: *A. binervia.*
  Dalby: *A. stenophylla.*
  Fragrant: *A. homalophylla.*
  Gidgee: *A. homalophylla.*
  Weeping: *A. pendula.*
Myallwood: *Acacia homalophylla.*
Myriad leaf: *Myriophyllum verticillatum.*
Myrobalan: *Phyllanthus Emblica, Terminalia bellirica, T. Catappa, T. Chebula.*
Myrrh: *Myrrhis.*
Myrtle: *Cyrilla racemiflora, Myrtus, M. communis, Umbellularia californica, Vinca minor.*
  Alleghany sand: *Leiophyllum buxifolium* var. *prostratum.*
  Australian willow: *Agonis flexuosa.*
  Bog: *Myrica Gale.*
  Box sand: *Leiophyllum buxifolium.*
  Bracelet honey: *Melaleuca armillaris.*
  California wax: *Myrica californica.*
  Candleberry: *M. Faya.*
  Cape: *Myrsine africana.*
  Classic: *Myrtus communis.*
  Crape, crepe: *Lagerstroemia indica.*
  Downy: *Rhodomyrtus tomentosa.*

Myrtle—*Continued*
  Dwarf: *Myrtus communis* cv. 'Microphylla'.
  German: *M. communis* cv. 'Microphylla'.
  Greek: *M. communis.*
  Gum: *Angophora.*
  Honey: *Melaleuca, M. Huegelii.*
  Jew's: *Ruscus aculeatus.*
  Oregon: *Umbellularia californica.*
  Polish: *Myrtus communis* cv. 'Microphylla'.
  Queen's crape: *Lagerstroemia speciosa.*
  Running: *Vinca minor.*
  Sand: *Leiophyllum.*
  Sand-verbena: *Backhousia.*
  Scent: *Darwinia.*
  Sea: *Baccharis halmifolia.*
  Swedish: *Myrtus communis.*
  Wax: *Myrica cerifera.*
  Western tea: *Melaleuca nesophila.*
  Willow: *Agonis.*
Mysteria: *Colchicum autumnale.*

Naegelia: *Smithiantha multiflora.*
Nagoonberry: *Rubus stellatus.*
Naiad: *Najas.*
Nail-rod: *Typha latifolia.*
Nailwort: *Paronychia.*
Naio: *Myoporum sandwicense.*
Nanmu: *Phoebe Nanmu.*
Nannyberry: *Viburnum Lentago, V. nudum, V. prunifolium.*
  Rusty: *V. rufidulum.*
Nap-at-noon: *Ornithogalum umbellatum.*
Naranjilla: *Solanum quitoense.*
Narcissus: *Narcissus.*
  Leedsii: see *N.* ✕*incomparabilis.*
  Paper-white: *N. Tazetta.*
  Poetaz: *N.* ✕*poetaz.*
  Poet's: *N. poeticus.*
  Polyanthus: *N. Tazetta.*
  Primrose peerless: *N. biflorus.*
  Trumpet: *N. Pseudonarcissus.*
Naseberry: *Manilkara Zapota.*
Nashi: *Pyrus pyrifolia* var. *culta.*
Nasturtium: *Tropaeolum.*
  Dwarf: *T. minus.*
  Garden: *T. majus.*
  Tall: *T. majus.*
Naupaka, beach: *Scaevola frutescens.*
Navelseed: *Omphalodes.*
Navelwort: *Hydrocotyle, Omphalodes, Umbilicus rupestris.*
Nealie, dwarf: *Acacia Bynoeana.*
Necklace tree: *Ormosia.*
Necklace vine: *Crassula rupestris, Muehlenbeckia complexa.*
Necklaceweed: *Actaea.*
Nectarine: *Prunus Persica* var. *nucipersica.*
Needle-and-thread: *Stipa comata.*
Needle-flower tree: *Posoqueria latifolia.*
Nelumbo, yellow: *Nelumbo lutea.*
Nenta: *Cotyledon cacaloides, C. Wallichii.*
Nephthytis: *Syngonium podophyllum.*
Nerve plant: *Fittonia Verschaffeltii.*
Nerveroot: *Cypripedium acaule, C. Calceolus* var. *pubescens.*
Netbush: *Calothamnus.*
  Giles: *C. Gilesii.*
  Rough: *C. asper.*
  Woolly: *C. villosus.*
Netleaf: *Goodyera repens* var. *ophioides.*
Nettle: *Urtica.*
  Dead: *Lamium, L. album.*
  Dumb: *L. album.*
  False: *Boehmeria.*
  Flame: *Coleus.*
  Hedge: *Stachys.*
  Hemp: *Galeopsis.*
  Horse: *Solanum carolinense.*
  Painted: *Coleus Blumei.*
  Rock: *Eucnide.*
  Roman: *Urtica pilulifera.*
  Spotted dead: *Lamium maculatum.*
  Spurge: *Cnidoscolus, C. urens.*
  Stinging: *C. texanus, Urtica dioica.*
  Western horse: *Solanum dimidiatum.*
  White dead: *Lamium album.*

Nettle tree: *Celtis, C. occidentalis.*
  European: *C. australis.*
Never-never plant: *Ctenanthe Oppenheimiana* cv. 'Tricolor'.
New Guinea creeper: *Mucuna Bennettii.*
Nicker tree: *Gymnocladus dioica.*
Niger: *Guizotia abyssinica.*
Nightshade: *Solanum Dulcamara.*
  Ball: *S. carolinense.*
  Black: *S. nigrum.*
  Common: *S. nigrum.*
  Deadly: *S. Dulcamara, Atropa Belladonna.*
  Enchanter's: *Circaea.*
  Malabar: *Basella.*
  Melon-leaf: *Solanum citrullifolium.*
  Poisonous: *S. Dulcamara.*
  Soda-apple: *S. aculeatissimum.*
  Sticky: *S. sisymbriifolium.*
  Stinking: *Hyoscyamus niger.*
Ninebark: *Physocarpus.*
Nipa: *Nypa fruticans.*
Nipplefruit: *Solanum mammosum.*
Nippon-bells: *Shortia uniflora.*
Nispero: *Manilkara Zapota.*
Noah's-ark: *Cypripedium Calceolus* var. *pubescens.*
None-so-pretty: *Silene Armeria.*
Nonesuch: *Medicago lupulina.*
Nose-bleed: *Achillea Millefolium.*
Nosegay: *Plumeria rubra.*
Nut-gall tree: *Rhus chinensis.*
Nutmeg: *Myristica fragrans.*
  African: *Monodora.*
  California: *Torreya californica.*
  Jamaica: *Monodora Myristica.*
Nutmeg flower: *Nigella sativa.*
Nux-vomica tree: *Strychnos Nux-vomica.*
Nymphea: *Nymphaea.*

Oak: *Quercus.*
  Arkansas: *Q. arkansana.*
  Austrian turkey: *Q. cerris.*
  Ballota: *Q. Ilex* var. *rotundifolia.*
  Bartram: *Q. heterophylla.*
  Basket: *Q. Michauxii, Q. prinus.*
  Bear: *Q. ilicifolia.*
  Belloot, Belote: *Q. Ilex* var. *rotundifolia.*
  Black: *Q. velutina.*
  Blackjack: *Q. marilandica.*
  Blue: *Q. Douglasii.*
  Bluejack: *Q. incana.*
  Bur: *Q. macrocarpa.*
  California black: *Q. Kelloggii.*
  California field: *Q. agrifolia.*
  California live: *Q. agrifolia.*
  California scrub: *Q. dumosa.*
  California white: *Q. lobata.*
  Canyon: *Q. chrysolepis.*
  Catesby: *Q. laevis.*
  Ceylon: *Schleichera oleosa.*
  Chestnut: *Quercus Muehlenbergii, Q. prinus.*
  Chinquapin: *Q. prinoides.*
  Cork: *Q. Suber.*
  Cow: *Q. Michauxii.*
  Daimyo: *Q. dentata.*
  Darlington: see *Q. laurifolia.*
  Deer: *Q. Sadlerana.*
  Durmast: *Q. petraea.*
  Dwarf chestnut: *Q. prinoides.*
  Emory: *Q. Emoryi.*
  Engelmann: *Q. Engelmannii.*
  English: *Q. robur.*
  Flowering: *Chorizema cordatum.*
  Gambel: *Quercus Gambelii.*
  Gander: *Q. Ganderi.*
  Georgia: *Q. georgiana.*
  Havard: *Q. Havardii.*
  High-ground willow: *Q. incana.*
  Holly: *Q. Ilex.*
  Holm: *Q. Ilex.*
  Huckleberry: *Q. vacciniifolia.*
  Indian: *Barringtonia acutangula.*
  Interior live: *Quercus Wislizenii.*
  Island: *Q. tomentella.*

Oak—*Continued*
  Italian: *Q. Frainetto.*
  Jack: *Q. ellipsoidalis, Q. marilandica.*
  Japanese evergreen: *Q. acuta.*
  Japanese red: *Q. acuta.*
  Jerusalem: *Chenopodium Botrys.*
  Kellogg: *Quercus Kelloggii.*
  Kermes: *Q. coccifera.*
  Konara: *Q. glandulifera.*
  Laurel: *Q. imbricaria, Q. laurifolia.*
  Laurel-leaved: *Q. laurifolia.*
  Leather: *Q. durata.*
  Lebanon: *Q. libani.*
  Live: *Q. virginiana.*
  Maul: *Q. chrysolepis.*
  McDonald: *Q. Macdonaldii.*
  Mongolian: *Q. mongolica.*
  Mossy-cup: *Q. macrocarpa.*
  Northern pin: *Q. ellipsoidalis.*
  Northern red: *Q. rubra.*
  Oregon: *Q. Garryana.*
  Oriental white: *Q. aliena.*
  Overcup: *Q. lyrata.*
  Pin: *Q. palustris.*
  Poison: *Rhus diversiloba, R. radicans, R. Toxicodendron.*
  Possum: *Quercus nigra.*
  Post: *Q. stellata.*
  Pubescent: *Q. pubescens.*
  Red: *Q. rubra.*
  Ring-cupped: *Q. glauca.*
  Rock chestnut: *Q. prinus.*
  Rocky Mountain scrub: *Q. undulata.*
  Scarlet: *Q. coccinea.*
  Scrub: *Q. ilicifolia.*
  She: *Casuarina.*
  Shingle: *Quercus imbricaria.*
  Shinnery: *Q. Havardii.*
  Shumard's red: *Q. Shumardii.*
  Silk: *Grevillea robusta.*
  Southern live: *Quercus virginiana.*
  Spanish: *Q. falcata, Q. palustris.*
  Spanish red: *Q. falcata.*
  Swamp chestnut: *Q. Michauxii, Q. prinus.*
  Swamp post: *Q. lyrata.*
  Swamp white: *Q. bicolor, Q. Michauxii.*
  Tanbark: *Lithocarpus densiflorus.*
  Texas red: *Quercus texana.*
  Truffle: *Q. robur.*
  Turkey: *Q. cerris, Q. incana, Q. laevis.*
  Turner: *Q. Turneri.*
  Ubame: *Q. phillyraeoides.*
  Valley: *Q. lobata.*
  Water: *Q. nigra.*
  Western: *Q. Garryana.*
  White: *Q. alba.*
  Willow: *Q. phellos.*
  Yellow: *Q. Muehlenbergii.*
  Yellow-barked: *Q. velutina.*
  Yellow chestnut: *Q. Muehlenbergii.*
Oat, Oats: *Avena, A. sativa.*
  Animated: *A. sterilis.*
  Potato: *A. fatua.*
  Sea: *Uniola paniculata.*
  Slender wild: *Avena barbata.*
  Tartarian: *A. fatua.*
  Wild: *A. fatua, Chasmanthium latifolium, Uvularia sessilifolia.*
Obedience: *Physostegia, P. virginiana.*
Obedience plant: *Maranta arundinacea.*
Obedient plant: *Physostegia.*
Oca: *Oxalis tuberosa,* see under *Oxalis.*
Ocean-spray: *Holodiscus discolor.*
Oconee-bells: *Shortia galacifolia.*
Ocotillo: *Fouquieria splendens.*
October flower: *Polygonella polygama.*
October plant: *Sedum Sieboldii.*
Octopus plant: *Aloe arborescens.*
Octopus tree: *Brassaia actinophylla.*
Ocumo: *Xanthosoma.*
Oilcloth flower: *Anthurium Andraeanum.*
Okra: *Abelmoschus esculentus.*
  Wild: *Viola palmata.*
Old-lady-of-Mexico: *Mammillaria Hahniana.*

Old-maid: *Catharanthus roseus.*
Old-man: *Artemisia Abrotanum.*
  Bald: *Cephalocereus Palmeri, Pilocereus polylophus.*
  Golden: *Cephalocereus chrysacanthus.*
  Lesser: *Echinocereus Delaetii.*
  Peruvian: *Espostoa lanata.*
  South American: *Borzicactus Celsianus.*
  Yellow: *Cephalocereus Palmeri.*
Old-man-and-woman: *Sempervivum tectorum.*
Old-man-of-the-Andes: *Borzicactus Trollii.*
Old-man-of-the-mountains: *Borzicactus Celsianus.*
Old-man's-beard: *Chionanthus virginicus, Vittaria lineata.*
Old-plainsman: *Hymenopappus scabiosaeus* var. *corymbosus.*
Old-woman: *Artemisia Stellerana.*
Oleander: *Nerium.*
  Common: *N. Oleander.*
  Water: *Decodon verticillatus.*
  Yellow: *Thevetia peruviana.*
Oleaster: *Elaeagnus angustifolia, E. latifolia.*
Olive: *Olea europaea.*
  American: *Osmanthus americanus.*
  Black: *Bucida buceras.*
  Californian: *Umbellularia californica.*
  Common: *Olea europaea.*
  Desert: *Forestiera neomexicana.*
  False: *Cassine orientalis.*
  Fragrant: *Osmanthus fragrans.*
  Holly: *O. heterophyllus.*
  Russian: *Elaeagnus angustifolia.*
  Spurge: *Cneorum tricoccon.*
  Sweet: *Osmanthus fragrans.*
  Tea: *O. fragrans.*
  Wild: *Elaeagnus angustifolia, E. latifolia, Halesia carolina, Osmanthus americanus.*
Olivewood: *Cassine orientalis.*
Olive-wood bark, Bermuda: *Cassine Laneana.*
Ololiuqui: *Turbina corymbosa.*
Onion: *Allium, A. Cepa.*
  Catawissa: see *A. Cepa,* Proliferum Group.
  Climbing: *Bowiea volubilis.*
  Egyptian: see *Allium Cepa,* Proliferum Group.
  Ever-ready: see *A. Cepa,* Aggregatum Group.
  False sea: *Ornithogalum caudatum.*
  Flowering: *Allium neapolitanum.*
  German: *Ornithogalum caudatum.*
  Gypsy: *Allium ursinum.*
  Japanese bunching: *A. fistulosum.*
  Multiplier: see *A. Cepa,* Aggregatum Group.
  Nodding: *A. cernuum.*
  Potato: see *A. Cepa,* Aggregatum Group.
  Prairie: *A. stellatum.*
  Red-skinned: *A. haematochiton.*
  Sea: *Ornithogalum caudatum, Scilla verna, Urginea maritima.*
  Spanish: *Allium fistulosum.*
  Swamp: *A. validum.*
  Top: see *A. Cepa,* Proliferum Group.
  Tree: see *A. Cepa,* Proliferum Group.
  Two-bladed: *A. fistulosum.*
  Welsh: *A. fistulosum.*
  Wild: *A. canadense, A. cernuum.*
Ookow: *Dichelostemma congestum.*
Opiuma: *Pithecellobium dulce.*
Opopanax: *Acacia Farnesiana.*
Opossumwood: *Halesia carolina.*
Opuntia: *Opuntia.*
  Crested: *O. clavarioides.*
  Little tree: *O. vilis.*
  Old-man: *O. vestita.*
  Paper-spined: *O. articulata* cv. 'Syringacantha'.
  Velvet: *O. velutina.*
Orach: *Atriplex, A. hortensis.*
  Garden: *A. hortensis.*
  Sea: *A. Halimus.*
Orange
  African cherry: *Citropsis.*
  Bergamot: *Citrus Aurantium* subsp. *Bergamia.*
  Bitter: *C. Aurantium.*
  Blood: *C. sinensis.*
  Chinese box: *Severinia buxifolia.*
  Common: see *Citrus sinensis.*
  Hardy: *Poncirus trifoliata.*
  House-blooming mock: *Pittosporum Tobira.*

Orange—*Continued*
  Jamaica mandarin: *Glycomis pentaphylla.*
  King: *Citrus* ×*nobilis* cv. 'King'.
  Mandarin: *C. reticulata.*
  Mediterranean: *C. sinensis.*
  Mexican: *Choisya ternata.*
  Mock: *Bumelia lycioides, Murraya, Philadelphus, Pittosporum Tobira, P. undulatum, Prunus caroliniana, Styrax americanus.*
  Natal: *Strychnos spinosa.*
  Navel: *Citrus sinensis.*
  Osage: *Maclura pomifera.*
  Otaheite: see under *Citrus* ×*limonia.*
  Panama: ×*Citrofortunella mitis.*
  Satsuma: *Citrus reticulata.*
  Seville: *C. Aurantium.*
  Sour: *C. Aurantium.*
  Spanish: *C. sinensis.*
  Sweet: *C. sinensis.*
  Tachibana: *C. Tachibana.*
  Temple: *C.* ×*nobilis* cv. 'Temple'.
  Trifoliate: *Poncirus trifoliata.*
  Vegetable: *Cucumis Melo,* Chito Group.
  Wild: *Prunus caroliniana.*
Orange-crest: *Habenaria cristata.*
Orange-fringe: *Habenaria ciliaris.*
Orangeglow vine: *Senecio confusus.*
Orange-plume: *Habenaria ciliaris.*
Orangeroot: *Hydrastis, H. canadensis.*
Orchid
  Alaskan: *Habenaria unalascensis.*
  Baby: *Epidendrum* ×*Obrienianum.*
  Bamboo: *Arundina graminifolia.*
  Bat: *Coryanthes speciosa.*
  Bee: *Ophrys apifera.*
  Bee-swarm: *Cyrtopodium punctatum.*
  Black: *Coelogyne pandurata, Trichoglottis philippinensis* var. *brachiata.*
  Blue: *Vanda caerulea.*
  Blunt-leaf: *Habenaria obtusata.*
  Bottle: *Physosiphon tubatus.*
  Butterfly: *Epidendrum* ×*Obrienianum, E. tampense, Habenaria psycodes, Oncidium Krameranum, O. papilio.*
  Buttonhole: *Epidendrum.*
  Chain: *Dendrochilum.*
  Chocolate: *Epidendrum phoeniceum.*
  Christmas: *Cattleya Trianaei.*
  Cigar: *Cyrtopodium punctatum.*
  Clam-shell: *Epidendrum cochleatum.*
  Cobra: *Darlingtonia californica.*
  Cockle-shell: *Epidendrum cochleatum.*
  Cooktown: *Dendrobium bigibbum.*
  Coral: *Rodriguezia secunda.*
  Cow-horn: *Cyrtopodium punctatum, Schomburgkia.*
  Cradle: *Anguloa.*
  Cranefly: *Tipularia discolor.*
  Crested fringed: *Habenaria cristata.*
  Crested rein: *H. cristata.*
  Crested yellow: *H. cristata.*
  Dancing-doll: *Oncidium flexuosum.*
  Dancing-lady: *Oncidium.*
  Dollar: *Epidendrum Boothianum.*
  Dove: *Peristeria elata.*
  Downy rattlesnake: *Goodyera pubescens.*
  Early spider: *Ophrys aranifera.*
  Easter: *Cattleya Mossiae.*
  Fen: *Liparis Loeselii.*
  Five-leaved: *Isotria.*
  Florida butterfly: *Epidendrum tampense.*
  Fly: *Ophrys insectifera.*
  Fried-egg: *Dendrobium chrysotoxum.*
  Fringed: *Habenaria.*
  Giant: *Epipactis gigantea.*
  Golden chain: *Dendrochilum filiforme.*
  Golden fringed: *Habenaria cristata.*
  Golden swan: *Cycnoches Edgertonianum* var. *aureum.*
  Gold-lace: *Haemaria.*
  Greater purple fringed: *Habenaria psycodes* var. *grandiflora.*
  Green-fly: *Epidendrum conopseum.*
  Green fringed: *Habenaria lacera.*
  Green rein: *H. clavellata.*
  Green swan: *Cycnoches ventricosum* var. *Warscewiczii.*
  Green-winged: *Orchis morio.*
  Green woodland: *Habenaria clavellata.*

Orchid—*Continued*

Hay-scented: *Dendrochilum glumaceum.*
Helmet: *Coryanthes, Galeandra lacustris.*
Hooker's: *Habenaria Hookeri.*
Hyacinth: *Arpophyllum.*
Jewel: *Anoectochilus.*
Jumping: *Catasetum macrocarpum.*
Large butterfly: *Habenaria psycodes* var. *grandiflora.*
Large purple fringed: *H. psycodes* var. *grandiflora.*
Late spider: *Ophrys fuciflora.*
Leafy northern green: *Habenaria hyperborea.*
Leafy white: *H. dilatata.*
Lesser butterfly: *H. bifolia.*
Lesser purple fringed: *H. psycodes.*
Lily-of-the-valley: *Odontoglossum pulchellum.*
Little club-spur: *Habenaria clavellata.*
Mirror: *Ophrys speculum.*
Monkey: *Coryanthes macrantha.*
Moth: *Phalaenopsis.*
Northern green: *Habenaria hyperborea.*
Northern small bog: *H. obtusata.*
Nun: *Lycaste virginalis* (white-fld. form).
Nun's: *Phaius Tankervilliae.*
Nun's-hood: *Phaius Tankervilliae.*
Nut: *Achimenes.*
One-leaf rein: *Habenaria obtusata.*
Pansy: *Miltonia.*
Peacock: *Acidanthera bicolor.*
Pigeon: *Dendrobium crumenatum.*
Pink scorpion: *Arachnis ✕Maingayi.*
Pink slipper: *Calypso bulbosa.*
Poor-man's: *Schizanthus.*
Purple fringeless: *Habenaria peramoena.*
Purple-hooded: *Orchis spectabilis.*
Purple-spire: *Habenaria peramoena.*
Ragged: *H. lacera.*
Ragged fringed: *H. lacera.*
Rainbow: *Epidendrum prismatocarpum.*
Rattlesnake: *Pholidota imbricata.*
Rein: *Habenaria.*
Rosebud: *Cleistes divaricata.*
Round-leaved: *Habenaria orbiculata.*
Salep: *Orchis morio.*
Savannah: *Habenaria nivea.*
Sawfly: *Ophrys tenthredinifera.*
Scarlet: *Epidendrum ✕Obrienianum.*
Scorpion: *Arachnis.*
Shower: *Congea tomentosa.*
Showy: *Orchis spectabilis.*
Sierra rein: *Habenaria dilatata* var. *leucostachys.*
Slender bog: *H. saccata.*
Small purple fringed: *H. psycodes.*
Small round-leaved: *Orchis rotundifolia.*
Snowy: *Habenaria blephariglottis, H. nivea.*
Soldier: *Orchis militaris.*
Southern rein: *Habenaria clavellata.*
Southern small white: *H. nivea.*
Spice: *Epidendrum atropurpureum.*
Spider: *Arachnis flos-aeris, A. ✕Maingayi.*
Stream: *Epipactis gigantea.*
Swan: *Cycnoches.*
Tall white bog: *Habenaria dilatata.*
Tiger: *Odontoglossum grande.*
Virgin: *Caularthron bicornutum.*
Virgin Mary: *C. bicornutum.*
Water: *Spiranthes cernua* var. *odorata.*
White butterfly: *Polyradicion Lindenii.*
White-flowered bog: *Habenaria dilatata* var. *leucostachys.*
White fringed: *H. blephariglottis.*
White nun: *Lycaste virginalis* (white-fld. form).
White rein: *Habenaria nivea.*
Widow: *Pleurothallis macrophylla.*
Windmill: *Bulbophyllum refractum.*
Woodland: *Orchis spectabilis.*
Yellow fringed: *Habenaria ciliaris.*
Orchid tree: *Bauhinia purpurea, B. variegata.*
Orchid vine: *Stigmaphyllon ciliatum.*
Orchis: see Orchid.
Organy: *Origanum vulgare.*
Origano: *Origanum vulgare.*
Orpine: *Sedum, S. Telephium.*
Evergreen: *S. Anacampseros.*
Orris: *Iris ✕germanica* var. *florentina, I. pallida.*

Osier: *Salix, S. viminalis.*
Common: *S. viminalis.*
Green: *Cornus alternifolia.*
Purple: *Salix purpurea.*
Osmanthus, holly: *Osmanthus heterophyllus.*
Osoberry: *Oemleria cerasiformis.*
Ostrich-plume: *Brassica juncea* var. *crispifolia.*
Our-Lady's-bedstraw: *Galium verum.*
Our-Lord's-candle: *Yucca Whipplei.*
Owl-eyes: *Huernia zebrina.*
Little: *H. zebrina.*
Oxalis: *Oxalis.*
Blue: *Parochetus communis.*
Creeping: *Oxalis corniculata.*
Tree: *O. Ortgiesii.*
Oxeye: *Buphthalmum, Heliopsis.*
Oxlip: *Primula elatior.*
Ox-tongue: *Gasteria.*
Oyster plant: *Rhoeo spathacea, Tragopogon porrifolius.*
Black: *Scorzonera hispanica.*
Spanish: *Scolymus hispanicus.*

Pacaya: *Chamaedorea Tepejilote.*
Pachysandra: *Pachysandra.*
Alleghany: *P. procumbens.*
Japanese: *P. terminalis.*
Padauk, Padouk: *Pterocarpus indicus.*
Paeony: see Peony.
Pagoda flower: *Clerodendrum paniculatum, C. speciosissimum.*
Pagoda tree: *Plumeria rubra* forma *acutifolia.*
Japanese: *Sophora japonica.*
Weeping: *S. japonica* cv. 'Pendula'.
Pai: *Alocasia macrorhiza.*
Paintbrush: *Castilleja.*
Indian: *Asclepias tuberosa, Castilleja californica, C. coccinea.*
Natal: *Haemanthus natalensis.*
Scarlet: *Castilleja coccinea, Crassula falcata.*
Painted-cup: *Castilleja.*
Seaside: *C. latifolia.*
Woolly: *C. foliolosa.*
Painted-feather: *✕Guzvriesea magnifica,* see under *Vriesea ✕Mariae.*
Painted-fingernail: *Neoregelia spectabilis.*
Painted-lady: *Echeveria Derenbergii.*
Painted leaf: *Euphorbia cyathophora, E. heterophylla, E. pulcherrima.*
Painted leaves: *Coleus.*
Painted-tongue: *Salpiglossis sinuata, Schismatoglottis picta.*
Paintleaf: *Euphorbia heterophylla.*
Paint root: *Lachnanthes caroliana.*
Pak-choi: *Brassica Rapa,* Chinensis Group.
False: *B. parachinensis.*
Pala: *Marattia Douglasii.*
Pali-mara: *Alstonia scholaris.*
Palm
African oil: *Elaeis guineensis.*
Alexander: *Ptychosperma elegans.*
Alexandra: *Archontophoenix Alexandrae.*
American oil: *Elaeis oleifera.*
Areca: *Chrysalidocarpus lutescens.*
Areng: *Arenga saccharifera.*
Arikury: *Arikuryroba.*
Assai: *Euterpe oleracea.*
Australian cabbage: *Livistona australis.*
Australian fan: *L. australis.*
Australian ivy: *Brassaia actinophylla.*
Australian nut: *Cycas media.*
Bamboo: *Chamaedorea erumpens, Rhapis excelsa.*
Barbel: *Acanthophoenix.*
Barrel: *Colpothrinax Wrightii.*
Belmore sentry: *Howea Belmoreana.*
Betel: *Areca Catechu.*
Betel nut: *Areca Catechu.*
Black: *Normanbya Normanbyi.*
Black-fiber: *Arenga pinnata.*
Bottle: *Beaucarnea, Colpothrinax Wrightii, Hyophorbe amaricaulis.*
Bread: *Cycas.*
Broom: *Coccothrinax argentea.*
Burmese fishtail: *Caryota mitis.*
Butterfly: *Chrysalidocarpus lutescens.*
Cabbage: *Livistona australis.*
Calappa: *Actinorhytis calapparia.*
Canary date: *Phoenix canariensis.*

Palm—*Continued*

Cane: *Chrysalidocarpus lutescens.*
Caribbee royal: *Roystonea oleracea.*
Carnauba: *Copernicia prunifera.*
Cherry: *Pseudophoenix.*
Chilean wine: *Jubaea chilensis.*
Chinese fan: *Livistona chinensis.*
Chinese fountain: *L. chinensis.*
Chinese windmill: *Trachycarpus Fortunei.*
Christmas: *Veitchia Merrillii.*
Clustered fishtail: *Caryota mitis.*
Coconut: *Cocos nucifera.*
Cohune: *Orbignya Cohune.*
Common princess: *Dictyosperma album.*
Coquito: *Jubaea chilensis.*
Coyoli: *Acrocomia mexicana.*
Cuban belly: *Colpothrinax Wrightii.*
Cuban royal: *Roystonea regia.*
Cucurite: *Maximiliana Maripa.*
Curly: *Howea Belmoreana.*
Date: *Phoenix, P. dactylifera.*
Desert fan: *Washingtonia filifera.*
Doom, doum: *Hyphaene thebaica.*
Doub: *Borassus flabellifer.*
Dwarf fan: *Chamaerops humilis.*
East Indian wine: *Phoenix sylvestris.*
Egyptian doum: *Hyphaene thebaica.*
European fan: *Chamaerophe humilis.*
Everglades: *Acoelorraphe Wrightii.*
Fan: *Chamaerops, Coccothrinax, Livistona, Trachycarpus;* also, any palm with palmate leaves.
Feather: any palm with pinnate leaves.
Feather-duster: *Rhopalostylis sapida.*
Fern: *Cycas circinalis.*
Fiji fan: *Pritchardia pacifica.*
Fishtail: *Caryota.*
Florida royal: *Roystonea elata.*
Florida silver: *Coccothrinax argentata.*
Florida thatch: *Thrinax parviflora.*
Forster sentry: *Howea Forsterana.*
Franceschi: *Brahea elegans.*
Funeral: *Cycas.*
Gebang: *Corypha elata.*
Gingerbread: *Hyphaene, H. thebaica.*
Gippsland: *Livistona australis.*
Golden feather: *Chrysalidocarpus lutescens.*
Gomuti: *Arenga pinnata.*
Good luck: *Chamaedorea elegans, Cordyline terminalis, Oxalis Deppei.*
Grass: *Cordyline australis.*
Gru-gru: *Acrocomia.*
Guadalupe: *Brahea edulis.*
Hair: *Chamaerops humilis.*
Hemp: *Trachycarpus Fortunei.*
Hesper: *Brahea.*
Hispaniolan royal: *Roystonea hispaniolana.*
Honey: *Jubaea chilensis.*
Hurricane: *Ptychosperma Macarthurii.*
Inaja: *Maximiliana Maripa.*
India date: *Phoenix sylvestris.*
Ita: *Mauritia flexuosa.*
Ivory: *Palandra, Phytelephas macrocarpa.*
Ivory-nut: *Phytelephas macrocarpa.*
Jaggery: *Caryota urens.*
Jelly: *Butia capitata, B. Yatay.*
Kentia: *Howea Forsterana.*
Key: *Thrinax microcarpa.*
King: *Archontophoenix.*
Lady: *Rhapis.*
Latan: *Latania.*
Leopard: *Amorphophallus Rivieri.*
Licuri: *Syagrus coronata.*
Macarthur: *Ptychosperma Macarthurii.*
Manac: *Calyptronoma.*
Mangrove: *Nypa fruticans.*
Manila: *Veitchia Merrillii.*
Mazari: *Nannorrhops Ritchiana.*
Mexican: *Echeveria coccinea* cv. 'Recurvata'.
Mexican blue: *Brahea armata.*
Mexican Washington: *Washingtonia robusta.*
Miniature date: *Phoenix Roebelenii.*
Miniature fan: *Rhapis humilis.*

Palm—*Continued*

Morass royal: *Roystonea princeps.*
Moriche: *Mauritia.*
Needle: *Rhapidophyllum hystrix, Yucca filamentosa.*
Nibung: *Oncosperma tigillarium.*
Nikau: *Rhopalostylis, R. sapida.*
Nipa: *Nypa fruticans.*
Northern bangalow: *Archontophoenix Alexandrae.*
Nut: *Cycas media.*
Nypa: *Nypa fruticans.*
Oil: *Elaeis guineensis.*
Ouricouri: *Syagrus coronata.*
Overtop: *Rhyticocos amara.*
Palmyra: *Borassus flabellifer.*
Panama-hat: *Carludovica palmata.*
Pandanus: *Pandanus tectorius.*
Parlor: *Chamaedorea elegans.*
Peaberry: *Thrinax.*
Peach: *Bactris Gasipaes.*
Petticoat: *Copernicia macroglossa, Washingtonia filifera.*
Piccabeen: *Archontophoenix Cunninghamiana.*
Piccabeen bangalow: *Archontophoenix Cunninghamiana.*
Pignut: *Hyophorbe.*
Porcupine: *Rhapidophyllum hystrix.*
Prickly: *Bactris major.*
Princess: *Dictyosperma.*
Puerto Rican hat: *Sabal causiarum.*
Puerto Rican royal: *Roystonea borinquena.*
Pygmy date: *Phoenix Roebelenii.*
Queen: *Arecastrum australe.*
Raffia: *Raphia farinifera.*
Rattan: *Calamus.*
Rock: *Brahea.*
Roebelin: *Phoenix Roebelenii.*
Royal: *Roystonea.*
Ruffle: *Aiphanes caryotifolia.*
Sagisi: *Heterospathe elata.*
Sago: *Caryota urens, Cycas revoluta, C. circinalis.*
San Jose hesper: *Brahea Brandegeei.*
Saw cabbage: *Acoelorrhaphe Wrightii.*
Sealing-wax: *Cyrtostachys Lakka, C. Renda.*
Senegal date: *Phoenix reclinata.*
Sentry: *Howea, H. Forsterana.*
Silver: *Coccothrinax, C. argentata.*
Silver saw: *Acoelorrhaphe Wrightii.*
Slender lady: *Rhapis humilis.*
Snake: *Amorphophallus, A. Rivieri.*
Solitaire: *Ptychosperma elegans.*
South American royal: *Roystonea oleracea.*
Spindle: *Hyophorbe Verschaffeltii.*
Spine: *Aiphanes caryotifolia.*
Spiny-club: *Bactris.*
Step: *Archontophoenix Alexandrae* var. *Beatricae.*
Sugar: *Arenga pinnata.*
Syrup: *Jubaea chilensis.*
Tala: *Borassus flabellifer.*
Talipot: *Corypha umbraculifera.*
Thatch: *Coccothrinax crinita, Thrinax.*
Thatch-leaf: *Howea Forsterana.*
Thread: *Washingtonia robusta.*
Toddy: *Borassus flabellifer, Caryota urens.*
Traveler's: *Ravenala madagascariensis.*
Tufted fishtail: *Caryota mitis.*
Umbrella: *Cyperus alternifolius, Hedyscepe Canterburyana.*
Walking-stick: *Linospadix monostachya.*
Washington: *Washingtonia.*
Wax: *Ceroxylon andicola.*
Weddell: *Microcoelum Weddellianum.*
Wild date: *Phoenix sylvestris.*
Windmill: *Chamaerops humilis, Trachycarpus Fortunei.*
Wine: *Borassus flabellifer, Caryota urens.*
Woolly butia: *Butia eriospatha.*
Yatay: *Butia Yatay.*
Yellow: *Chrysalidocarpus lutescens.*
Yellow butterfly: *C. lutescens.*
Yellow princess: *Dictyosperma aureum.*
Zombi: *Zombia.*

Palma Christi: *Ricinus communis.*
Palma corcho: *Microcycas calocoma.*
Palma pita: *Yucca Treculeana.*
Palm-Beach-bells: *Kalanchoe.*
Palmella: *Yucca elata.*

Palmetto: *Chamaerops humilis, Sabal.*
  Bermuda: *Sabal bermudana.*
  Blue: *S. Palmetto, Rhapidophyllum hystrix.*
  Bush: *Sabal minor.*
  Cabbage: *S. Palmetto.*
  Dwarf: *S. minor.*
  Jamaican: *S. jamaicensis.*
  Saw: *Serenoa repens.*
  Scrub: *Sabal Etonia, S. minor, Serenoa repens.*
  Sonoran: *Sabal uresana.*
  Texas: *S. mexicana.*
Palmetto thatch: *Thrinax parviflora.*
Palm-polly: *Polyradicion Lindenii.*
Palo borracho: *Chorisia insignis.*
Palo santo: *Triplaris americana.*
Palo verde: *Cercidium floridum.*
  Mexican: *Parkinsonia aculeata.*
Palta: *Persea americana.*
Panama-hat plant: *Carludovica palmata.*
Panamiga: *Pilea involucrata.*
  Black-leaf: *P. repens.*
  Silver-leaf: *P. pubescens* cv. 'Liebmannii'.
Panda-bear plant: *Kalanchoe tomentosa.*
Pandang: *Pandanus odoratissimus.*
Panda plant: *Kalanchoe tomentosa, Philodendron bipennifolium.*
Panicum: *Panicum.*
  Blue: *P. antidotale.*
  Bulb: *P. bulbosum.*
  Giant: *P. antidotale.*
Pansy: *Viola* ×*Wittrockiana.*
  European wild: *V. tricolor.*
  Field: *V. tricolor, V. Rafinesquii.*
  Garden: *V.* ×*Wittrockiana.*
  Japanese: *Achimenes.*
  Miniature: *Viola tricolor.*
  Monkey-faced: *Achimenes.*
  Orchid: *Achimenes.*
  Wild: *Viola pedunculata.*
Papaw: *Carica Papaya.*
Papaya: *Carica, C. Papaya.*
  Mountain: *C. pubescens.*
Paperbark, swamp: *Melaleuca ericifolia, M. raphiophylla.*
Paperbark tree: *Melaleuca quinquenervia.*
Paperbush: *Edgeworthia papyrifera.*
Paper flower: *Bougainvillea glabra.*
Paper plant: *Cyperus Papyrus, Fatsia japonica.*
  Glossy-leaved: *Fatsia japonica.*
Paper tree, red: *Albizia rhodesica.*
Papooseroot: *Caulophyllum thalictroides.*
Papyrus: *Cyperus Papyrus.*
  Dwarf: *C. isocladus.*
  Miniature: *C. isocladus.*
Parachute plant: *Ceropegia Sandersonii.*
Paradise flower: *Solanum Wendlandii.*
Paradise nut: *Lecythis Zabucayo.*
Paradise plant: *Justicia carnea.*
Paradise tree: *Melia Azedarach, Simarouba glauca.*
Parakeet flower: *Heliconia psittacorum.*
Para nut: *Bertholletia excelsa.*
Para-para: *Pisonia umbellifera.*
Parasol tree, Chinese: *Firmiana simplex.*
Parilla, yellow: *Menispermum canadense.*
Parrotleaf: *Alternanthera ficoidea* cv. 'Amoena'.
Parrot's-beak: *Clianthus puniceus, Lotus Berthelotii.*
Parrot's-bill: *Clianthus puniceus.*
Parrot's-feather: *Myriophyllum aquaticum.*
Parrot's flower: *Heliconia psittacorum.*
Parrot's plantain: *Heliconia psittacorum.*
Parsley: *Petroselinum crispum.*
  Chinese: *Coriandrum sativum.*
  Horse: *Smyrnium Olusatrum.*
  Italian: *Petroselinum crispum* var. *neapolitanum.*
  Turnip-rooted: *P. crispum* var. *tuberosum.*
Parsley-piert: *Alchemilla microcarpa.*
Parsnip: *Pastinaca, P. sativa.*
  American cow: *Heracleum Sphondylium* subsp. *montanum.*
  Bladder: *Lomatium utriculatum.*
  Buck: *L. triternatum.*
  Cow: *Heracleum.*
  Pestle: *Lomatium nudicaule.*
  Water: *Sium latifolium, S. suave.*
  Wild: *Angelica Archangelica.*
Partridgeberry: *Mitchella repens.*

Partridge-breast: *Aloe variegata.*
Pascuita: *Euphorbia leucocephala.*
Paspalum: *Paspalum.*
  Peruvian: *P. racemosum.*
  Ribbed: *P. malacophyllum.*
Pasqueflower: *Anemone Nuttalliana, A. patens, A. Pulsatilla.*
Passionflower: *Passiflora.*
  Bat-leaf: *P. coriacea.*
  Blue: *P. caerulea.*
  New Zealand: *Tetrapathaea.*
  Red: *Passiflora coccinea, P. manicata.*
  Wild: *P. incarnata.*
Passion fruit: *Passiflora edulis.*
  Banana: *P. antioquiensis, P. mollissima.*
  New Zealand: *Tetrapathaea.*
Passion vine, purple: *Gynura aurantiaca* cv. 'Purple Passion'.
Patience: *Rumex patientia.*
  Garden: *R. patientia.*
Patience plant: *Impatiens Wallerana.*
Patient Lucy: *Impatiens Wallerana.*
Pawpaw: *Asimina triloba, Carica Papaya.*
Pea: *Pisum, P. sativum.*
  Angola: *Cajanus Cajan.*
  Asparagus: *Psophocarpus tetragonolobus.*
  Australian: *Dolichos lignosus.*
  Australian flame: *Chorizema cordatum.*
  Austrian winter: *Lathyrus hirsutus.*
  Beach: *L. japonicus, L. littoralis.*
  Black-eyed: *Vigna unguiculata* subsp. *unguiculata.*
  Butterfly: *Centrosema, Clitoria.*
  Caley: *Lathyrus hirsutus.*
  Canada: *Vicia Cracca.*
  Catjang: *Cajanus Cajan.*
  Chaparral: *Pickeringia.*
  Chick: *Cicer arietinum.*
  Congo: *Cajanus Cajan.*
  Coral: *Adenanthera pavonina, Hardenbergia violacea, Kennedia.*
  Darling: *Swainsona galegifolia.*
  Desert: *Clianthus formosus.*
  Earthnut: *Lathyrus tuberosus.*
  Edible-podded: *Pisum sativum* var. *macrocarpon.*
  Egyptian: *Cicer arietinum.*
  English: *Pisum sativum.*
  Everlasting: *Lathyrus grandiflorus, L. latifolius, L. sylvestris.*
  Field: *Pisum sativum* var. *arvense.*
  Flat: *Lathyrus sylvestris.*
  Garden: *Pisum sativum.*
  Glory: *Clianthus formosus, C. puniceus.*
  Green: *Pisum sativum.*
  Heart: *Cardiospermum Halicacabum.*
  Heath: *Lathyrus japonicus.*
  Hoary: *Tephrosia.*
  Jerusalem: *Vigna unguiculata* subsp. *cylindrica.*
  Love: *Abrus precatorius.*
  Marble: *Vigna unguiculata* subsp. *cylindrica.*
  No-eye: *Cajanus Cajan.*
  Partridge: *Cassia fasciculata.*
  Perennial: *Lathyrus latifolius, L. sylvestris.*
  Pigeon: *Cajanus Cajan.*
  Princess: *Psophocarpus tetragonolobus.*
  Rabbit's: *Tephrosia virginiana.*
  Rough: *Lathyrus hirsutus.*
  Rosary: *Abrus precatorius.*
  Seaside: *Lathyrus japonicus.*
  Scurfy: *Psoralea.*
  Shamrock: *Parochetus communis.*
  Singletary: *Lathyrus hirsutus.*
  Snow: *Pisum sativum* var. *macrocarpon.*
  Sturt desert: *Clianthus formosus.*
  Sugar: *Pisum sativum* var. *macrocarpon.*
  Sweet: *Lathyrus odoratus.*
  Two-flowered: *L. grandiflorus.*
  Wild: *Lathyrus.*
  Wild winter: *L. hirsutus.*
  Winged: *Lotus Berthelotii, L. tetragonolobus.*
  Winter: *Lathyrus hirsutus.*
  Winter sweet: *Swainsona galegifolia.*
Peace-in-the-home: *Soleirolia Soleirolii.*
Peach: *Prunus Persica.*
  Desert: *P. Andersonii.*
  Vine: *Cucumis Melo,* Chito Group.
  Wild: *Prunus fasciculata.*
Peach-bells: *Campanula persicifolia.*

Peacock flower: *Delonix regia.*
Peacock plant: *Calathea Makoyana, Kaempferia atrovirens, K. Roscoeana.*
Peanut: *Arachis hypogaea.*
  Common: *A. hypogaea.*
  Hog: *Amphicarpaea.*
Pear: *Pyrus, P. communis.*
  Alligator: *Persea americana.*
  Asian: *Pyrus pyrifolia.*
  Balsam: *Momordica Charantia.*
  Birch-leaved: *Pyrus betulifolia.*
  Blind: *Opuntia microdasys* var. *rufida.*
  Butter: *Persea americana.*
  Chinese: *Pyrus pyrifolia, P. ussuriensis* var. *ovoidea.*
  Common: *P. communis.*
  Evergreen: *P. Kawakamii.*
  Garlic: *Crateva.*
  Japanese: *Pyrus pyrifolia.*
  Melon: *Solanum muricatum.*
  Oriental: *Pyrus pyrifolia.*
  Paper-spined: *Opuntia articulata* cv. 'Syringacantha'.
  Prickly: *Opuntia,* especially species of section *Opuntia.*
  Sacred garlic: *Crateva religiosa.*
  Sand: *Pyrus pyrifolia, P. ussuriensis* var. *ovoidea.*
  Vinegar: *Passiflora laurifolia.*
  Willow-leaved: *Pyrus salicifolia.*
Pear fruit: *Margyricarpus setosus.*
Pearlberry: *Margyricarpus setosus.*
Pearlbush: *Exochorda.*
Pearl fruit: *Margyricarpus setosus.*
Pearl plant: *Haworthia margaritifera.*
Pearl-twist: *Spiranthes.*
  Green: *S. gracilis.*
  Little: *S. Grayi.*
Pearlwort: *Sagina.*
Pearly-dots: *Haworthia papillosa.*
Pea shrub: *Caragana.*
  Russian: *C. frutex.*
  Shag-spine: *C. jubata.*
Pea tree: *Caragana.*
  Siberian: *C. arborescens.*
Pebble plant: *Mesembryanthemum.*
Pecan: *Carya illinoinensis.*
  Bitter: *C. aquatica.*
Peepul: *Ficus religiosa.*
Pegwood: *Cornus sanguinea.*
Pejibaye: *Bactris Gasipaes.*
Pelican flower: *Aristolochia grandiflora.*
Pelican's-beak: *Lotus Berthelotii.*
Pellionia, satin: *Pellionia pulchra.*
Pencil tree: *Euphorbia Tirucalli.*
Pennisetum: *Pennisetum.*
  Chinese: *P. alopecuroides.*
  Uruguay: *P. latifolium.*
Pennyroyal: *Mentha Pulegium.*
  American: *Hedeoma pulegioides.*
  Bastard: *Trichostema dichotomum.*
  Mock: *Hedeoma pulegioides.*
Pennywort: *Cymbalaria muralis, Umbilicus rupestris.*
  Lawn water: *Hydrocotyle sibthorpioides.*
  Water: *Hydrocotyle.*
Pen-wiper: *Kalanchoe marmorata.*
Peony, Paeony: *Paeonia.*
  Chinese: *P. lactiflora.*
  Chinese tree: *P. suffruticosa.*
  Common garden: *P. lactiflora.*
  Majorcan: *P. Cambessedesii.*
  Tibetan: *P. lobata* var. *Ludlowii.*
  Tree: *P. suffruticosa;* see also *P. Delavayi, P. lutea, P. Potaninii.*
Peperomia: *Peperomia.*
  Coin-leaf: *P. polybotrya.*
  Emerald-ripple: *P. caperata.*
  Flowering: *P. Fraseri.*
  Green-ripple: *P. caperata.*
  Ivy: *P. griseo-argentea.*
  Ivy-leaf: *P. griseo-argentea.*
  Leather: *P. crassifolia.*
  Little fantasy: *P. caperata.*
  Platinum: *P. griseo-argentea.*
  Prayer: *P. dolabriformis.*
  Red-edge: *P. clusiifolia.*
  Silver-edge: *P. obtusifolia* cv. 'Albo-marginata'.
  Silver-leaf: *P. griseo-argentea.*

Peperomia—*Continued*
  Vining: *P. Dahlstedtii.*
  Watermelon: *P. argyreia.*
Pepino: *Solanum muricatum.*
Pepper: *Capsicum, Piper.*
  Australian: *Schinus Molle.*
  Baby: *Rivina humilis.*
  Bell: *Capsicum annuum,* Grossum Group.
  Betle: *Piper Betle.*
  Bird: *Capsicum annuum* var. *glabriusculum.*
  Black: *Piper nigrum.*
  Capsicum: *Capsicum annuum,* Longum Group.
  Cayenne: *C. annuum,* Longum Group.
  Celebes: *Piper ornatum.*
  Cherry: *Capsicum annuum,* Cerasiforme Group.
  Chili: *Capsicum; C. annuum,* Longum Group.
  Cluster: *C. annuum,* Fasciculatum Group.
  Cone: *C. annuum,* Conoides Group.
  Cubeb: *Piper Cubeba.*
  Green: *Capsicum; C. annuum,* Grossum Group.
  Japan: *Xanthoxylum piperitum.*
  Long: *Capsicum annuum,* Longum Group.
  Mild water: *Polygonum hydropiperoides.*
  Mountain long: *Piper sylvaticum.*
  Red: *Capsicum; C. annuum,* Longum Group.
  Red cluster: *C. annuum,* Fasciculatum Group.
  Sweet: *C. annuum,* Grossum Group.
  Tabasco: *C. frutescens.*
  Tabasco-sauce: *C. frutescens.*
  White: *Piper nigrum.*
  Wild: *Vitex Agnus-castus.*
Pepper-and-salt: *Erigenia bulbosa.*
Pepperbush, sweet: *Clethra alnifolia.*
Pepper-face: *Peperomia obtusifolia.*
Peppergrass: *Lepidium.*
Pepperidge: *Nyssa sylvatica.*
Peppermint: *Mentha* ✕*piperita.*
  Black: *Eucalyptus amygdalina.*
  Blackbutt: *E. Smithii.*
  Broad-leaved: *E. dives.*
  Gray: *E. radiata.*
  Mount Wellington: *E. coccifera.*
  Narrow-leaved black: *E. Nicholii.*
  Nichol's willow-leaved: *E. Nicholii.*
  River: *E. elata.*
  Robertson's: *E. Robertsonii.*
  Silver: *E. Risdonii, E. tenuiramis.*
  Sydney: *E. piperita.*
  White: *E. pulchella.*
Peppermint tree: *Agonis flexuosa.*
Pepper plant: *Piper nigrum.*
Pepperroot: *Dentaria.*
Pepper tree: *Drimys lanceolata, Macropiper excelsum, Schinus Molle.*
  Brazilian: *Schinus terebinthifolius.*
  California: *S. Molle.*
  Monk's: *Vitex Agnus-castus.*
  Peruvian: *Schinus Molle.*
Pepper vine: *Ampelopsis arborea.*
Pepperwood: *Zanthoxylum clava-Herculis.*
Pepperwort: *Marsilea.*
Peregrina: *Jatropha integerrima.*
Perfume plant: *Matthiola longipetala.*
Periwinkle: *Catharanthus, Vinca.*
  Common: *Vinca minor.*
  Greater: *V. major.*
  Lesser: *V. minor.*
  Madagascar: *Catharanthus roseus.*
  Rose: *C. roseus.*
Permanent-wave plant: *Billbergia leptopoda.*
Peronil: *Ormosia panamensis.*
Persian-shield: *Strobilanthes Dyeranus.*
Persimmon: *Diospyros.*
  Black: *D. texana.*
  Common: *D. virginiana.*
  Japanese: *D. Kaki.*
Pe-tsai: *Brassica Rapa,* Pekinensis Group.
Petunia: *Petunia.*
  Common garden: *P.* ✕*hybrida.*
  Large white: *P. axillaris.*
  Mexican: *Strobilanthes.*
  Seaside: *Petunia parviflora.*
  Violet-flowered: *P. violacea.*
  Wild: *P. parviflora.*

Peyote: *Lophophora, L. Williamsii.*
Phanera: *Bauhinia corymbosa.*
Pheasant's-eye: *Adonis, Narcissus poeticus.*
Pheasant-wings: *Aloe variegata.*
Philippine-medusa: *Acalypha hispida.*
Philodendron: *Philodendron.*
  Black-gold: *P. melanochrysum.*
  Blushing: *P. erubescens.*
  Common: *P. scandens* subsp. *oxycardium.*
  Cut-leaf: *Monstera deliciosa.*
  Dubia: *Philodendron radiatum.*
  Fiddle-leaf: *P. bipennifolium.*
  Giant: *P. giganteum.*
  Heart-leaf: *P. cordatum, P. scandens.*
  Horsehead: *P. bipennifolium.*
  Leather-leaf: *P. guttiferum.*
  Red-leaf: *P. erubescens.*
  Spade-leaf: *P. domesticum.*
  Split-leaf: *Monstera deliciosa.*
  Variegated: *Epipremnum aureum.*
  Velvet-leaf: *Philodendron scandens* subsp. *scandens* forma *micans.*
Phlox: *Phlox.*
  Annual: *P. Drummondii.*
  Blue: *P. divaricata.*
  Creeping: *P. stolonifera.*
  Drummond: *P. Drummondii.*
  Fall: *P. paniculata.*
  Moss: *P. subulata.*
  Mountain: *P. ovata, P. subulata.*
  Perennial: *P. paniculata.*
  Prickly: *Leptodactylon californicum.*
  Sand: *Phlox bifida.*
  Smooth: *P. glaberrima.*
  Star: *P. Drummondii* cv. 'Twinkle'.
  Summer perennial: *P. paniculata.*
  Sword-leaf: *P. Buckleyi.*
  Thick-leaf: *P. carolina.*
  Trailing: *P. nivalis.*
Phoenix tree: *Firmiana simplex.*
Photinia, Japanese: *Photinia glabra.*
Physic nut: *Jatropha Curcas, J. multifida.*
Pia: *Tacca Leontopetaloides.*
Pickaback plant: *Tolmiea Menziesii.*
Pickerel weed: *Pontederia cordata.*
Pickle plant: *Trichodiadema barbatum.*
Pie-marker: *Abutilon Theophrasti.*
Pie plant: *Rheum Rhabarbarum.*
  Red-veined: *R. australe.*
Pigeon berry: *Duranta repens, Phytolacca americana.*
Pigeon-foot: *Salicornia europaea.*
Pigeon-wings: *Clitoria.*
Piggyback plant: *Tolmiea Menziesii.*
Pignut: *Carya cordiformis, C. glabra.*
Pig's-face: *Carpobrotus aequilaterus.*
Pigtail plant: *Anthurium Scherzeranum.*
Pigweed: *Amaranthus hybridus, A. retroflexus, Chenopodium, C. album.*
Pilea, watermelon: *Pilea Cardierei.*
Pilewort: *Ranunculus Ficaria.*
Pillwort: *Pilularia.*
Pimbina: *Viburnum trilobum.*
Pimento: *Capsicum annuum,* Grossum Group; *Pimenta dioica.*
Pimpernel: *Anagallis.*
  Common: *A. arvensis.*
  Scarlet: *A. arvensis.*
  Water: *Samolus.*
  Yellow: *Taenidia integerrima.*
Pinang: *Areca Catechu.*
Pincushion: *Leucospermum, Mammillaria.*
  Blue: *Brunonia australis.*
  Nodding: *Leucospermum nutans.*
  Rocket: *L. reflexum.*
  Snowball: *Mammillaria candida.*
Pincushion flower: *Leucospermum, Scabiosa.*
Pincushions: *Scabiosa atropurpurea.*
Pincushion tree: *Hakea.*
Pindar: *Arachis hypogaea.*
Pine: *Pinus.*
  African fern: *Podocarpus gracilior.*
  Air: *Aechmea.*
  Aleppo: *Pinus halepensis.*
  Amboina: *Agathis Dammara.*
  Apache: *Pinus Engelmannii.*

Pine—*Continued*
  Australian: *Araucaria heterophylla, Casuarina.*
  Austrian: *Pinus nigra.*
  Beach: *P. contorta.*
  Benguet: *P. insularis.*
  Bhutan: *P. Wallichiana.*
  Big-cone: *P. Coulteri.*
  Bishop: *P. muricata.*
  Black cypress: *Callitris Endlicheri.*
  Blue: *Pinus Wallichiana.*
  Brazilian: *Araucaria angustifolia.*
  Bristle-cone: *Pinus aristata.*
  Buddhist: *Podocarpus macrophyllus.*
  Bunya-bunya: *Agathis Bidwillii.*
  Calabrian: *Pinus halepensis* var. *brutia.*
  Canary Island: *P. canariensis.*
  Cedar: *P. glabra.*
  Celery: *Phyllocladus trichomanoides.*
  Chilean: *Araucaria auracana.*
  Chilghoza: *Pinus Gerardiana.*
  Chinese: *Crassula tetragona, Pinus tabuliformis.*
  Chinese water: *Glyptostrobus lineatus.*
  Chir: *Pinus Roxburghii.*
  Cluster: *P. Pinaster.*
  Common screw: *Pandanus utilis.*
  Cow's-tail: *Cephalotaxus Harringtonia* var. *drupacea.*
  Cuban: *Pinus caribaea.*
  Cypress: *Callitris.*
  Dammar: *Agathis.*
  Digger: *Pinus Sabiniana.*
  Dwarf Siberian: *P. pumila.*
  Dwarf stone: *P. pumila.*
  Eastern white: *P. Strobus.*
  Emodi: *P. Roxburghii.*
  Formosa: *P. taiwanensis.*
  Frankincense: *P. Taeda.*
  Georgia: *P. palustris.*
  Gerard's: *P. Gerardiana.*
  Giant: *P. Lambertiana.*
  Gray: *P. Banksiana.*
  Ground: *Lycopodium clavatum, L. complanatum, L. obscurum.*
  Hickory: *Pinus aristata.*
  Himalayan white: *P. Wallichiana.*
  Hoop: *Araucaria Cunninghamii.*
  House: *A. heterophylla.*
  Huon: *Dacrydium Franklinii.*
  Imou: *D. cupressinum.*
  Italian stone: *Pinus pinea.*
  Jack: *P. Banksiana.*
  Japanese black: *P. Thunbergiana.*
  Japanese red: *P. densiflora.*
  Japanese umbrella: *P. densiflora* cv. 'Umbraculifera', *Sciadopitys verticillata.*
  Japanese white: *Pinus parviflora.*
  Jersey: *P. virginiana.*
  Jerusalem: *P. halepensis.*
  Jointed: *Polypodium subauriculatum.*
  Kauri: *Agathis australis.*
  Knob-cone: *Pinus attenuata.*
  Korean: *P. koraiensis.*
  Lace-bark: *P. Bungeana.*
  Limber: *P. flexilis.*
  Loblolly: *P. Taeda.*
  Lodgepole: *P. contorta* var. *latifolia.*
  Longleaf: *P. oocarpa, P. palustris.*
  Long-tag: *P. echinata.*
  Macedonian: *P. Peuce.*
  Mahogany: *Podocarpus Totara.*
  Mallee: *Callitris Preissii* subsp. *verrucosa.*
  Mexican stone: *Pinus cembroides.*
  Mexican white: *P. Ayacahuite.*
  Mexican yellow: *P. patula.*
  Monterey: *Pinus radiata.*
  Moreton Bay: *Araucaria Cunninghamii.*
  Mountain: *Pinus Mugo.*
  Mueller's cypress: *Callitris Muelleri.*
  Nepal nut: *Pinus Gerardiana.*
  New Caledonian: *Araucaria columnaris.*
  Norfolk Island: *A. heterophylla.*
  Norway: *Pinus resinosa.*
  Nut: *P. edulis, P. monophylla.*
  Old-field: *P. Taeda.*
  Oyster Bay: *Callitris rhomboidea.*

Pine—*Continued*
  Paraná: *Araucaria angustifolia.*
  Parry pinyon: *Pinus quadrifolia.*
  Pinyon: *P. edulis.*
  Pitch: *P. rigida.*
  Port Jackson: *Callitris rhomboidea.*
  Poverty: *Pinus virginiana.*
  Prickly: *P. pungens.*
  Prince's: *Chimaphila, C. umbellata* var. *cisatlantica.*
  Princess: *Crassula pseudolycopodioides, Lycopodium obscurum.*
  Red: *Dacrydium cupressinum, Pinus resinosa.*
  Red cypress: *Callitris Endlicheri.*
  Rocky Mountain yellow: *Pinus ponderosa* var. *scopulorum.*
  Rottnest Island: *Callitris Preissii.*
  Rough-barked Mexican: *Pinus Montezumae.*
  Running: *Lycopodium clavatum.*
  Scotch, Scots: *Pinus sylvestris.*
  Screw: *Pandanus.*
  Scrub: *Pinus Banksiana, P. virginiana.*
  Shore: *P. contorta.*
  Shortleaf: *P. echinata.*
  Single-leaf pinyon: *P. monophylla.*
  Slash: *P. Elliottii.*
  Soledad: *P. Torreyana.*
  Southern yellow: *P. palustris.*
  Spruce: *P. glabra, P. virginiana.*
  Stone: *P. monophylla, P. pinea.*
  Sugar: *P. Lambertiana.*
  Swiss mountain: *P. Mugo.*
  Swiss stone: *P. Cembra.*
  Table Mountain: *P. pungens.*
  Tenasserim: *P. Merkusii.*
  Thatch screw: *Pandanus tectorius.*
  Torrey: *Pinus Torreyana.*
  Totara: *Podocarpus Totara.*
  Twisted-leaf: *Pinus Teocote.*
  Two-leaved nut: *P. edulis.*
  Umbrella: *P. pinea, Sciadopitys verticillata.*
  Veitch screw: *Pandanus Veitchii.*
  Western white: *Pinus monticola.*
  Western yellow: *P. ponderosa.*
  White-bark: *P. albicaulis.*
  White: *P. Strobus, Podocarpus dacrydioides.*
  Yellow: *Pinus echinata, P. palustris.*
Pineapple: *Ananas comosus.*
  Red: *A. bracteatus.*
  Wild: *A. bracteatus, Tillandsia fasciculata.*
Pineapple flower: *Eucomis comosa.*
Pineapple shrub: *Calycanthus floridus.*
Pineapple weed: *Matricaria matricarioides.*
Pine-barren-beauty: *Pyxidanthera barbulata.*
Pinedrops: *Pterospora.*
Pinesap: *Monotropa, M. uniflora.*
Pine tree, miniature: *Crassula tetragona.*
Pineweed: *Hypericum gentianoides.*
Piney: *Paeonia officinalis* subsp. *officinalis.*
Pinguin: *Bromelia Pinguin.*
Pink: *Dianthus.*
  Button: *D.* ✕*latifolius.*
  California Indian: *Silene californica.*
  Cameo: *Chamaelaucium ciliatum.*
  Cheddar: *Dianthus gratianopolitanus.*
  Childing: *Petrorhagia prolifera.*
  Clove: *Dianthus Caryophyllus.*
  Cluster-head: *D. carthusianorum.*
  Cottage: *D. plumarius.*
  Cushion: *Silene acaulis.*
  Dairy: *Vaccaria pyramidata.*
  Deptford: *Dianthus Armeria.*
  Election: *Rhododendron nudiflorum, R. prinophyllum.*
  Fire: *Silene virginica.*
  Fringed Indian: *S. laciniata.*
  Grass: *Calopogon, Dianthus plumarius.*
  Ground: *Linanthus dianthiflorus.*
  Indian: *Lobelia Cardinalis, Silene laciniata, Spigelia marilandica.*
  Kirtle: *Orchis spectabilis.*
  Maiden: *Dianthus deltoides.*
  Marsh: *Sabatia stellaris.*
  Moss: *Phlox subulata.*
  Mullein: *Lychnis Coronaria.*
  Pine: *Bletia purpurea.*
  Rainbow: *Dianthus chinensis.*
  Rose: *Sabatia angularis.*

Pink—*Continued*
  Sea: *Armeria, Sabatia stellaris.*
  Spotted kirtle: *Orchis rotundifolia.*
  Swamp: *Arethusa bulbosa, Calopogon, Helonias bullata.*
  Wild: *Arethusa bulbosa, Silene caroliniana.*
Pink-and-white-shower: *Cassia nodosa.*
Pink-buttons: *Crassula marginalis.*
Pink-dot: *Hypoestes phyllostachya.*
Pink-polka-dot: *Hypoestes phyllostachya.*
Pinkroot: *Spigelia, S. marilandica.*
Pink-shower: *Cassia grandis.*
Pink vine: *Antigonon leptopus.*
Pinwheel: *Aeonium Haworthii.*
Pinwheel flower: *Tabernaemontana divaricata.*
Pinxter, Florida: *Rhododendron canescens.*
Pinxterbloom: *Rhododendron periclymenoides.*
Pinxter flower: *Rhododendron nudiflorum.*
Pinyon: *Pinus edulis.*
Pipe plant: *Aeschynanthus pulcher.*
Piperia, Alaska: *Habenaria unalascensis.*
Pipe vine: *Aristolochia durior.*
Pipewort: *Eriocaulon.*
Piprage: *Berberis vulgaris.*
Pipsissewa: *Chimaphila, C. umbellata* var. *cisatlantica.*
Pirul: *Schinus Molle.*
Pistachio: *Pistacia, P. vera.*
  American: *P. texana.*
Pistacia nut: *Pistacia vera.*
Pitanga: *Eugenia Pitanga, E. uniflora.*
Pitaya: *Echinocereus.*
Pitcher plant: *Darlingtonia californica, Nepenthes, Sarracenia.*
  California: *Darlingtonia californica.*
  Common: *Sarracenia purpurea.*
  Hooded: *S. minor.*
  Southern: *S. purpurea* var. *venosa.*
  Sweet: *S. purpurea, S. rubra.*
  Yellow: *S. flava.*
Pitcher sage: *Lepechinia calycina, Salvia spathacea.*
Pitchforks: *Bidens.*
Pitomba: *Eugenia Luschnathiana.*
Pittosporum: *Pittosporum.*
  Cape: *P. viridiflorum.*
  Japanese: *P. Tobira.*
  Narrow-leaved: *P. phillyraeoides.*
  Queensland: *P. rhombifolium.*
  Willow: *P. phillyraeoides.*
Plane: *Platanus.*
  American: *P. occidentalis.*
  London: *P.* ✕*acerifolia.*
  Mock: *Acer pseudoplatanus.*
  Oriental: *Platanus orientalis.*
Plane tree: *Platanus.*
Planer tree: *Planera.*
Plantain: *Musa acuminata, M.* ✕*paradisiaca, Plantago.*
  Checkered rattlesnake: *Goodyera tesselata.*
  Common: *Plantago major.*
  Dwarf rattlesnake: *Goodyera repens.*
  English: *Plantago lanceolata.*
  False: *Heliconia Bihai.*
  Giant rattlesnake: *Goodyera oblongifolia.*
  Lesser rattlesnake: *G. repens.*
  Menzies' rattlesnake: *G. oblongifolia.*
  Mud: *Heteranthera.*
  Narrow-leaved: *Plantago lanceolata.*
  Northern rattlesnake: *Goodyera repens.*
  Poor Robin's: *Erigeron pulchellus, Hieracium venosum.*
  Rattlesnake: *Goodyera.*
  Robin's: *Erigeron pulchellus.*
  Smooth rattlesnake: *Goodyera tesselata.*
  Water: *Alisma.*
  White-blotched rattlesnake: *Goodyera repens* var. *ophioides.*
  Wild: *Heliconia Bihai, H. caribaea.*
Platter dock: *Nymphaea alba.*
Platterleaf: *Coccoloba uvifera.*
Pleatleaf, purple: *Eustylis purpurea.*
Pleroma: *Tibouchina Urvilleana.*
Pleurisy root: *Asclepias tuberosa.*
Plover-eggs: *Adromischus Cooperi.*
Plum
  Alleghany: *Prunus alleghaniensis.*
  American: *P. americana.*
  Apricot: *P. Simonii.*
  Assyrian: *Cordia Myxa.*

Plum—*Continued*
  August: *Prunus americana.*
  Batoko: *Flacourtia indica.*
  Beach: *Prunus maritima.*
  Black: *Syzygium cumini.*
  Burdekin: *Pleiogynium cerasiferum.*
  Canada: *Prunus nigra.*
  Cherry: *P. cerasifera.*
  Chickasaw: *P. angustifolia.*
  Coco: *Chrysobalanus Icaco.*
  Common: *Prunus domestica.*
  Damson: *P. insititia.*
  Damson (of Jamaica): *Chrysophyllum oliviforme.*
  Date: *Diospyros Kaki, D. Lotus, D. virginiana.*
  European: *Prunus domestica.*
  Goose: *P. americana.*
  Governor's: *Flacourtia indica.*
  Ground: *Astragalus crassicarpus.*
  Hog: *Prunus americana, P. Reverchonii.*
  Hortulan: *P. hortulana.*
  Indian: *Oemleria cerasiformis.*
  Jambolan: *Syzygium cumini.*
  Japanese: *Eriobotrya japonica, Prunus japonica, P. salicina.*
  Java: *Syzygium cumini.*
  Kaffir: *Harpephyllum caffrum.*
  Madagascar: *Flacourtia indica.*
  Malabar: *Syzygium Jambos.*
  Marmalade: *Pouteria Sapota.*
  Moxie: *Gaultheria hispidula.*
  Myrobalan: *Prunus cerasifera.*
  Nanny: *Viburnum Lentago.*
  Natal: *Carissa grandiflora.*
  Oklahoma: *Prunus gracilis.*
  Pacific: *P. subcordata.*
  Pigeon: *Coccoloba diversifolia.*
  Queensland hog: *Pleiogynium cerasiferum.*
  Sand: *Prunus angustifolia, P. angustifolia var. Watsonii.*
  Shore: *P. maritima.*
  Sierra: *P. subcordata.*
  Simon: *P. Simonii.*
  Sisson: *P. subcordata var. Kelloggii.*
  Spanish: *Spondias purpurea.*
  Wickson: *Prunus ×sultana.*
  Wild: *P. americana.*
  Wild-goose: *P. hortulana, P. Munsoniana.*
Plumbago, Chinese: *Ceratostigma Willmottiana.*
Plume flower: *Justicia carnea.*
Plume plant: *Justicia carnea.*
Plume-royal: *Habenaria psycodes var. grandiflora.*
Plush plant: *Echeveria pulvinata, Kalanchoe tomentosa.*
Pocan: *Phytolacca americana.*
Pochote: *Ceiba aesculifolia.*
Pocketbook flower: *Calceolaria.*
Podocarpus: *Podocarpus.*
  Broadleaf: *P. Nagi.*
  Fern: *P. elongatus.*
  Weeping: *P. elongatus.*
Pogonia
  Adder's-tongue-leaved: *Pogonia ophioglossoides.*
  Lily-leaved: *Cleistes divaricata.*
  Rose: *Pogonia ophioglossoides.*
  Spreading: *Cleistes divaricata.*
  Whorled: *Isotria.*
Poha: *Physalis peruviana.*
Poinciana: *Delonix.*
  Dwarf: *Caesalpinia pulcherrima.*
  Royal: *Delonix regia.*
  Yellow: *Peltophorum pterocarpum.*
Poinsettia: *Euphorbia pulcherrima.*
  Annual: *E. heterophylla.*
  Japanese: *E. heterophylla, Pedilanthus tithymaloides.*
Point Reyes creeper: *Ceanothus gloriosus.*
Poison berry: *Solanum nigrum.*
Poison bulb: *Crinum asiaticum.*
Poison shrub: *Acokanthera.*
Poison tree: *Acokanthera.*
Poke: *Phytolacca americana.*
  Indian: *P. acinosa, Veratrum viride.*
  Virginian: *Phytolacca americana.*
Pokeberry: *Phytolacca.*
Poker plant: *Kniphofia, K. Uvaria.*
Polecat bush: *Rhus aromatica.*
Polecat weed: *Symplocarpus foetidus.*

Polisandro: *Stahlia monosperma.*
Polka-dot plant: *Hypoestes phyllostachya.*
Pollyanna vine: *Soleirolia Soleirolii.*
Polly-Prim: *Soleirolia Soleirolii.*
Polyanthus: *Primula ×polyantha.*
Polygala, fringed: *Polygala paucifolia.*
Polypody: *Polypodium.*
  Ash-leaf: *P. fraxinifolium.*
  California: *P. californicum.*
  European: *P. vulgare.*
  Golden: *P. aureum.*
  Leathery: *P. Scouleri.*
  Limestone: *Gymnocarpium Robertianum.*
  Rock: *Polypodium virginianum.*
  Wall: *P. vulgare.*
  Western: *P. hesperium.*
Pomegranate: *Punica Granatum.*
  Dwarf: *P. Granatum* cv. 'Nana'.
Pomelo: *Citrus maxima.*
Pomerac: *Syzygium malaccense.*
Pomme blanche: *Psoralea esculenta.*
Pomme-de-liane: *Passiflora laurifolia.*
Pommelo: *Citrus maxima.*
Pompelmous: *Citrus maxima.*
Pond nuts: *Nelumbo lutea.*
Pond-spice: *Litsea aestivalis.*
Pondweed: *Potamogeton.*
  Cape: *Aponogeton distachyus.*
  Horned: *Zannichellia.*
Ponytail: *Beaucarnea recurvata.*
Poonga-oil tree: *Pongamia pinnata.*
Poor-man's-weatherglass: *Anagallis arvensis.*
Pop, running: *Passiflora foetida.*
Popcorn: *Zea Mays var. everta.*
Popcorn flower: *Plagiobothrys.*
Popinac: *Acacia Farnesiana.*
  White: *Leucaena glauca.*
Poplar: *Populus, Liriodendron Tulipifera.*
  Balsam: *Populus balsamifera.*
  Black: *P. nigra.*
  Carolina: *P. canadensis.*
  Chinese white: *P. tomentosa.*
  Downy: *P. heterophylla.*
  Eugene: *P. canadensis* cv. 'Eugenei'.
  Gray: *P. canescens.*
  Lombardy: *P. nigra* cv. 'Italica'.
  Necklace: *P. deltoides.*
  Queensland: *Homalanthus populifolius.*
  Silver-leaved: *Populus alba.*
  Tulip: *Liriodendron Tulipifera.*
  Western balsam: *Populus trichocarpa.*
  White: *P. alba.*
  Yellow: *Liriodendron Tulipifera.*
Popolo, yellow: *Solanum sodomeum.*
Poppy: *Papaver.*
  Arctic: *P. nudicaule.*
  Asiatic: *Meconopsis.*
  Blue: *M. betonicifolia.*
  Bush: *Dendromecon.*
  California: *Eschscholzia, E. californica.*
  California tree: *Romneya Coulteri.*
  Celandine: *Stylophorum diphyllum.*
  Corn: *Papaver Rhoeas.*
  Desert: *Arctomecon Merriamii.*
  Field: *Papaver Rhoeas.*
  Flaming: *Stylomecon heterophylla.*
  Flanders: *Papaver Rhoeas.*
  Harebell: *Meconopsis quintuplinervia.*
  Horned: *Glaucium.*
  Iceland: *Papaver nudicaule.*
  Island tree: *Dendromecon rigida* subsp. *Harfordii.*
  Matilija: *Romneya.*
  Mexican: *Argemone mexicana.*
  Mexican tulip: *Hunnemannia fumariifolia.*
  Opium: *Papaver somniferum.*
  Oriental: *P. orientale.*
  Plume: *Macleaya cordata.*
  Prickly: *Argemone.*
  Satin: *Meconopsis napaulensis.*
  Sea: *Glaucium.*
  Shirley: *Papaver Rhoeas.*
  Snow: *Eomecon.*
  Tree: *Dendromecon.*

Poppy—*Continued*
  Tulip: *Papaver glaucum.*
  Water: *Hydrocleys nymphoides.*
  Welsh: *Meconopsis cambrica.*
  Western: *Papaver californicum.*
  Wind: *Stylomecon heterophylla.*
  Wood: *Stylophorum diphyllum.*
  Yellow chinese: *Meconopsis integrifolia.*
Porcelain flower: *Hoya.*
Portia tree: *Thespesia populnea.*
Possumwood: *Diospyros virginiana.*
Potato: *Solanum tuberosum.*
  Air: *Dioscorea bulbifera.*
  Duck: *Sagittaria latifolia.*
  Irish: *Solanum tuberosum.*
  Prairie: *Psoralea esculenta.*
  Swamp: *Sagittaria, S. sagittifolia.*
  Swan: *S. sagittifolia.*
  Sweet: *Ipomoea Batatas.*
  Telinga: *Amorphophallus campanulatus.*
  White: *Solanum tuberosum.*
  Wild: *Chlorogalum pomeridianum.*
  Zulu: *Bowiea volubilis.*
Potato bush, blue: *Solanum Rantonnetii.*
Potato creeper, giant: *Solanum Wendlandii.*
Potato tree: *Solanum macranthum.*
  Brazilian: *S. macranthum.*
Potato vine: *Solanum jasminoides, S. Wendlandii.*
  Wild: *Ipomoea pandurata.*
Pothos: *Epipremnum aureum.*
  Golden: *E. aureum.*
Pothos vine: *Epipremnum aureum.*
Pouch flower: *Calceolaria.*
Poui: *Tabebuia.*
  Pink: *T. rosea.*
  Yellow: *T. serratifolia.*
Powderpuff: *Calliandra.*
  Red: *C. haematocephala.*
Prairie-smoke: *Anemone Nuttalliana.*
Prairie tea: *Croton monanthogynus, Potentilla rupestris.*
Prayer-beads: *Abrus precatorius.*
Prayer plant: *Maranta leuconeura.*
Pretty-face: *Triteleia ixioides.*
Prickleweed: *Desmanthus illinoensis.*
Prickly Moses: *Acacia verticillata.*
Prickly-pole: *Bactris guineensis.*
Pride-of-Barbados: *Caesalpinia pulcherrima.*
Pride-of-Bolivia: *Tipuana Tipu.*
Pride-of-California: *Lathyrus splendens.*
Pride-of-China: *Melia Azedarach.*
Pride-of-India: *Koelreuteria paniculata, Lagerstroemia speciosa, Melia Azedarach.*
Pride-of-the-peak: *Habenaria peramoena.*
Prim: *Ligustrum vulgare.*
Primavera: *Cybistax Donnell-Smithii.*
Primrose: *Primula, P. vulgaris.*
  Baby: *P. Forbesii, P. malacoides.*
  Beach evening: *Oenothera cheiranthifolia.*
  Bird's-eye: *Primula farinosa, P. laurentiana, P. mistassinica.*
  Buttercup: *P. floribunda.*
  Cape: *Streptocarpus, S. ×hybridus.*
  Chinese: *Primula sinensis.*
  Desert evening: *Oenothera deltoides.*
  English: *Primula vulgaris.*
  Evening: *Oenothera biennis.*
  Fairy: *Primula malacoides.*
  German: *P. obconica.*
  Mexican evening: *Oenothera Berlandieri, O. speciosa.*
  Poison: *Primula obconica.*
  Star: *P. sinensis* cv. 'Stellata'.
  White evening: *Oenothera speciosa.*
Prince-of-Wales-plume: *Leptopteris superba.*
Prince's-feather: *Amaranthus cruentus, A. hybridus* var. *erythrostachys, Polygonum orientale.*
Prince's-plume: *Stanleya.*
Princess-feather: *Polygonum orientale.*
Princess flower: *Tibouchina Urvilleana.*
Princess-of-the-night: *Selenicereus pteranthus.*
Princess tree: *Paulownia tomentosa.*
Princess vine: *Cissus sicyoides.*
Privet: *Ligustrum.*
  Amur: *L. amurense.*
  California: *L. ovalifolium.*

Privet—*Continued*
  Chinese: *L. lucidum.*
  Common: *L. vulgare.*
  Glossy: *L. lucidum.*
  Japanese: *L. japonicum.*
  Nepal: *L. lucidum.*
  Regel's: *L. obtusifolium* var. *Regelianum.*
  Swamp: *Forestiera acuminata.*
  Wax-leaf: *Ligustrum japonicum, L. lucidum.*
Proboscis flower: *Proboscidea louisianica.*
Propeller flower: *Eustylis purpurea.*
Propeller plant: *Crassula cultrata, C. falcata.*
Prophet flower: *Echioides longiflorum.*
Proso: *Panicum miliaceum.*
Protea: *Protea.*
  Giant: *P. cynaroides.*
  Honey: *P. mellifera.*
  King: *P. cynaroides.*
  Oleander-leaved: *P. neriifolia.*
  Peach: *P. grandiceps.*
Provision tree: *Pachira aquatica.*
Psyllium, Spanish: *Plantago Psyllium.*
Puccoon: *Lithospermum, L. canescens.*
  Red: *Sanguinaria canadensis.*
  Yellow: *Hydrastis.*
Puddingberry: *Cornus canadensis.*
Pudding-pipe tree: *Cassia fistula.*
Puka: *Meryta Sinclairii.*
Pumelo, Pummelo: *Citrus maxima.*
Pumpkin: *Cucurbita, C. maxima, C. mixta, C. moschata.*
  Autumn: *C. maxima, C. Pepo.*
  Bush: *C. Pepo* var. *Melopepo.*
  Canada: *C. moschata.*
  Field: *C. Pepo* var. *Pepo.*
  Fetid wild: *C. foetidissima.*
  Summer: *C. Pepo.*
  White: *Benincasa hispida.*
  Winter: *Cucurbita maxima.*
Puncture vine: *Tribulus terrestris.*
Punk tree: *Melaleuca quinquenervia.*
Puriri: *Vitex lucens.*
Purple-and-gold-crown: *Aloe mitriformis.*
Purple-crown: *Aloe mitriformis.*
Purple-heart: *Setcreasea pallida* cv. 'Purple Heart'.
Purple-wreath: *Petrea.*
Purslane: *Portulaca, P. oleracea.*
  Kitchen-garden: *P. oleracea* var. *sativa.*
  Rock: *Calandrinia.*
  Shaggy garden: *Portulaca pilosa.*
  Siberian: *Montia sibirica.*
  Water: *Ludwigia palustris, Peplis.*
  Winter: *Montia perfoliata.*
Pusley: *Portulaca oleracea.*
Pussy-ears: *Calochortus Tolmiei, Cyanotis somaliensis, Kalanchoe tomentosa.*
Pussy-foot: *Ageratum.*
Pussy-paws: *Calyptridium umbellatum.*
Pussy-toes: *Antennaria.*
Puttyroot: *Aplectrum hyemale.*
Pyramid tree: *Lagunaria Patersonii.*
Pyrethrum: *Chrysanthemum cinerariifolium, C. coccineum.*
  Dalmatia: *C. cinerariifolium.*
Pyrola: *Pyrola.*
  Arctic: *P. grandiflora.*
  One-flowered: *Moneses uniflora.*
  One-sided: *Pyrola secunda.*
  Pink: *P. asarifolia.*
Pyxie: *Pyxidanthera barbulata.*

Qat: *Catha edulis.*
Quailbush: *Atriplex lentiformis.*
Quaker-ladies: *Hedyotis coerulea.*
Quamash: *Camassia Quamash.*
Quarter vine: *Bignonia capreolata.*
Quassia, Surinam: *Quassia amara.*
Quebrahacha: *Caesalpinia punctata.*
Queen-Anne's-lace: *Daucus Carota* var. *Carota.*
Queencup: *Clintonia uniflora.*
Queen-of-orchids: *Grammatophyllum speciosum.*
Queen-of-Sheba vine: *Podranea Brycei.*
Queen-of-the-meadow: *Filipendula Ulmaria.*
Queen-of-the-night: *Hylocereus undatus, Nyctocereus serpentinus, Selenicereus grandiflorus, S. Macdonaldiae.*

Queen-of-the-prairie: *Filipendula rubra.*
Queen's-delight: *Stillingia sylvatica.*
Queen's-jewels: *Antigonon leptopus.*
Queen's-lace: *Daucus Carota* var. *Carota.*
Queensland-messmate: *Eucalyptus Cloeziana.*
Queensland nut: *Macadamia integrifolia.*
  Rough-shell: *M. tetraphylla.*
  Small-fruited: *M. ternifolia.*
Queen's root: *Stillingia sylvatica.*
Queen's-tears: *Billbergia nutans.*
Queen's-wreath: *Antigonon leptopus, Petrea, P. volubilis.*
Quercitron: *Quercus velutina.*
Quickbeam: *Sorbus Aucuparia.*
Quicksilver weed: *Thalictrum dioicum.*
Quillwort: *Isoetes.*
Quilted-taffeta plant: *Hoffmannia refulgens.*
Quince: *Cydonia.*
  Berigal: *Aegle Marmelos.*
  Common: *Cydonia oblonga.*
  Flowering: *Chaenomeles, C. speciosa.*
  Japanese: *C. speciosa.*
  Lesser flowering: *C. japonica.*
Quinine: *Cinchona.*
Quinoa, Quinua: *Chenopodium Quinoa.*
Quiverleaf: *Populus tremuloides.*

Raab, broccoli: *Brassica Rapa,* Ruvo Group.
Rabbitbrush: *Chrysothamnus.*
Rabbit-ears: *Opuntia microdasys.*
Rabbit's-foot: *Maranta leuconeura* var. *Kerchoviana, Polypogon monspeliensis.*
Rabbit-tracks: *Maranta leuconeura* var. *Kerchoviana.*
R'accacha: *Arracacia xanthorrhiza.*
Raccoon berry: *Podophyllum peltatum.*
Radish: *Raphanus sativus.*
  Chinese: *R. sativus* cv. 'Longipinnatus'.
  Rat-tailed: *R. sativus* cv. 'Caudatus'.
Ragged-robin: *Lychnis Flos-cuculi.*
Ragi: *Eleusine coracana.*
Ragweed: *Ambrosia.*
Ragwort: *Senecio Jacobaea.*
  Golden: *S. aureus.*
  Purple: *S. elegans.*
  Tansy: *S. Jacobaea.*
Railroad vine: *Ipomoea Pes-caprae.*
Rainbow plant: *Billbergia Saundersii.*
Rainbow-star: *Cryptanthus bromelioides* var. *tricolor.*
Rainbow vine: *Pellionia pulchra.*
Rainhat-trumpet: *Sarracenia minor.*
Rain tree: *Brunfelsia undulata, Samanea Saman.*
Raisin, wild: *Viburnum cassinoides, V. Lentago.*
Raisin tree, Japanese: *Hovenia dulcis.*
Rakkyo: *Allium Bakeri, A. chinense.*
Rambutan, smooth: *Alectryon subcinereus.*
Ramie: *Boehmeria nivea.*
Ramona: *Salvia.*
Ramontchi: *Flacourtia indica.*
Ramp: *Allium tricoccum.*
Rampion: *Campanula Rapunculus.*
  German: *Oenothera biennis.*
  Horned: *Phyteuma.*
  Spiked: *P. spicatum.*
Ram's-horn: *Proboscidea louisianica.*
Ramsons: *Allium ursinum.*
Ramtil: *Guizotia abyssinica.*
Ramtilla: *Guizotia abyssinica.*
Rangoon creeper: *Quisqualis indica.*
Rangpur: *Citrus* ✕*limonia.*
Ranunculus, Persian: *Ranunculus asiaticus.*
Rape: *Brassica Napus.*
  California: *B. Kaber.*
Rapini: *Brassica Rapa,* Rapifera Group.
Raspberry: *Rubus idaeus.*
  American red: *R. idaeus* var. *strigosus.*
  Black: *R. occidentalis.*
  Dwarf: *R. pubescens.*
  European: *R. idaeus.*
  Flowering: *R. odoratus.*
  Hill: *R. niveus.*
  Mauritius: *R. rosifolius.*
  Mysore: *R. niveus.*
  Purple: see under *R. idaeus.*
  Purple-flowering: *R. odoratus.*

Raspberry—*Continued*
  Red: *R. idaeus.*
  Rocky Mountain: *R. deliciosus.*
  Rocky Mountain flowering: *R. deliciosus.*
Raspberry-jam tree: *Acacia acuminata.*
Rattan: see *Calamus, Daemonorops.*
Rattan vine: *Berchemia.*
Rattlebox: *Crotalaria, C. spectabilis, Ludwigia alternifolia, Rhinanthus Crista-galli.*
Rattlesnake-master: *Eryngium yuccifolium.*
Rattlesnake plant: *Calathea insignis.*
Rattlesnake root: *Prenanthes.*
Rattlesnake weed: *Hieracium venosum.*
Rattletop: *Cimicifuga.*
Rattleweed: *Baptisia tinctoria.*
Rayflower, gray: *Anthocercis albicans.*
Red-bead vine: *Abrus precatorius.*
Redberry: *Rhamnus crocea.*
Redbird flower: *Pedilanthus tithymaloides.*
Redbud: *Cercis, C. canadensis.*
  Chinese: *C. chinensis.*
Red-bugle vine: *Aeschynanthus pulcher.*
Red-cloak, Brazilian: *Megaskepasma erythrochlamys.*
Red-crown: *Rebutia minuscula.*
Red-flame: *Oxalis hedysaroides* cv. 'Rubra'.
Red-heart: *Ceanothus spinosus.*
Red-hot-poker: *Kniphofia.*
Redleaf: *Philodendron cruentum.*
  Giant: *Acalypha Wilkesiana* cv. 'Musaica'.
Red-maids: *Calandrinia ciliata.*
Red-ribbons: *Clarkia concinna.*
Red Robin: *Geranium Robertianum.*
Redroot: *Amaranthus retroflexus, Ceanothus, Lachnanthes caroliana.*
Redshanks: *Adenostoma sparsifolium.*
Redtop: *Agrostis gigantea.*
Red-water tree: *Erythrophleum guineense.*
Red-white-and-blue flower: *Cuphea ignea.*
Redwood: *Adenanthera pavonina, Sequoia sempervirens.*
  Coast: *Sequoia sempervirens.*
  Dawn: *Metasequoia glyptostroboides.*
  Giant: *Sequoiadendron giganteum.*
  Madeira: *Swietenia Mahagoni.*
Reed
  Bur: *Sparganium.*
  Burma: *Neyraudia Reynaudiana.*
  Common: *Phragmites australis.*
  Giant: *Arundo Donax.*
  Mauritania vine: *Ampelodesmos maurtianicus.*
  Vine: *Ampelodesmos.*
Reed-mace: *Typha.*
Reefwood: *Stenocarpus salignus.*
Reina-de-la-noche: *Peniocereus Greggii.*
Resinweed: *Gutierrezia.*
Rest-harrow: *Ononis.*
Resurrection plant: *Anastatica hierochuntica, Selaginella lepidophylla.*
Retinospora: *Chamaecyparis.*
Rex-begonia vine: *Cissus discolor.*
Rhapis: *Rhapis.*
  Fern: *R. excelsa.*
  Reed: *R. humilis.*
Rhea: *Boehmeria nivea* var. *tenacissima.*
Rhododendron: *Rhododendron.*
  Bluet: *R. intricatum.*
  Carolina: *R. carolinianum.*
  Catawba: *R. catawbiense.*
  Caucasian: *R. caucasicum.*
  Chapman's: *R. Chapmanii.*
  Fortune's: *R. Fortunei.*
  Fringed: *R. ciliatum.*
  Fujiyama: *R. brachycarpum.*
  Honey-bell: *R. campylocarpum.*
  Indian: *Melastoma malabathricum.*
  Lapland: *Rhododendron lapponicum.*
  Leather-leaf: *R. Metternichii.*
  Piedmont: *R. minus.*
  Silvery: *R. grande.*
  Smirnow: *R. Smirnowii.*
  Tree: *R. arboreum.*
  West Coast: *R. macrophyllum.*
  Willow-leaved: *R. lepidotum.*
  Yunnan: *R. yunnanense.*
Rhodora: *Rhododendron canadense.*

Rhubarb: *Rheum, R. Rhabarbarum.*
  Garden: *R. Rhabarbarum.*
  Monk's: *Rumex alpinus, R. patientia.*
  Mountain: *Rumex alpinus.*
  Sikkim: *Rheum acuminatum, R. nobile.*
  Spinach: *Rumex abyssinicus.*
  Wild: *R. hymenosepalus.*
Ribbonbush: *Homalocladium platycladum.*
Ribbon plant: *Chlorophytum comosum.*
Ribbonwood: *Adenostoma sparsifolium, Hoheria sexstylosa, Plagianthus regius.*
Ribgrass: *Plantago lanceolata.*
Ribwort: *Plantago.*
Rice: *Oryza, O. sativa.*
  Annual wild: *Zizania aquatica.*
  Indian: *Z. aquatica.*
  Mountain: *Oryzopsis.*
  Pampas: *Sorghum vulgare.*
  Tennessee: *S. vulgare.*
  Wild: *Zizania.*
Riceflower: *Pimelea.*
Rice-paper plant: *Tetrapanax papyriferus.*
  Chinese: *T. papyriferus.*
Rice tree, Formosa: *Fatsia japonica.*
Richweed: *Collinsonia canadensis, Pilea fontana, P. pumila.*
Rimu: *Dacrydium cupressinum.*
  Mountain: *D. laxifolium.*
Ripplegrass: *Plantago lanceolata.*
River-beauty: *Epilobium latifolium.*
Roanoke-bells: *Mertensia virginica.*
Robin-redbreast bush: *Melaleuca lateritia.*
Robin-run-away: *Dalibarda repens.*
Rocambole: *Allium sativum, A. Scorodoprasum.*
Rockberry: *Empetrum Eamesii.*
Rocket: *Barbarea vulgaris, Diplotaxis, Hesperis, Eruca vesicaria* subsp. *sativa.*
  Dyer's: *Reseda luteola.*
  Turkish: *Bunias orientalis.*
  Yellow: *Barbarea vulgaris.*
Rocket-salad: *Eruca vesicaria* subsp. *sativa.*
Rockfoil: *Saxifraga.*
Rock-fringe: *Epilobium obcordatum.*
Rock-harlequin: *Corydalis sempervirens.*
Rohuhu: *Pittosporum tenuifolium.*
Roman-candle: *Yucca gloriosa.*
Romero: *Trichostema lanatum.*
Root-blossom, scarlet: *Agalmyla parasitica.*
Ropebark: *Dirca palustris.*
Roquette: *Eruca vesicaria* subsp. *sativa.*
Rosary plant: *Crassula rupestris.*
Rosary vine: *Ceropegia Woodii, Crassula rupestris.*
Rose: *Rosa.*
  Alpine: *Rhododendron ferrugineum, Rosa pendulina.*
  Baby: *Rosa multiflora.*
  Baby sun: *Aptenia cordifolia.*
  Banksia: *Rosa Banksiae.*
  Bog: *Arethusa bulbosa.*
  Bourbon: *Rosa* ×*borboniana.*
  Briar, Brier: *Rosa canina, Rubus coronarius.*
  Burgundy: *Rosa centifolia* cv. 'Parvifolia'.
  Burnet: *R. spinosissima.*
  Cabbage: *R. centifolia.*
  California: *Calystegia hederacea* cv. 'Flore Pleno'.
  Champney: *Rosa* ×*Noisettiana.*
  Cherokee: *R. laevigata.*
  Chestnut: *R. Roxburghii.*
  China: *Hibiscus Rosa-sinensis, Rosa chinensis.*
  Chinquapin: *Rosa Roxburghii.*
  Christmas: *Helleborus niger.*
  Cinnamon: *Rosa cinnamomea.*
  Climbing: *R. setigera.*
  Cluster: *R. pisocarpa.*
  Confederate: *Hibiscus mutabilis.*
  Copper: *Echeveria multicaulis.*
  Cotton: *Hibiscus mutabilis.*
  Damask: *Rosa damascena.*
  Desert: *Adenium obesum, Echeveria rosea, Trichodiadema densum.*
  Dog: *Rosa canina.*
  Evergreen: *R. sempervirens.*
  Fairy: *R. chinensis* cv. 'Minima'.
  Field: *R. arvensis.*
  French: *R. gallica.*

Rose—*Continued*
  Giant velvet: *Aeonium canariense.*
  Gold: *Rosa odorata* cv. 'Pseudindica'.
  Green Mexican: *Echeveria gilva.*
  Ground: *R. spithamea.*
  Guelder: *Viburnum Opulus.*
  Hairy alpine: *Rhododendron hirsutum.*
  Hawaiian wood: *Merremia tuberosa.*
  Himalayan musk: *Rosa Brunonii.*
  Hybrid Bourbon: see *R.* ×*borboniana.*
  Hybrid Perpetual: see *R.* ×*borboniana.*
  Hybrid tea: see *R. odorata;* see also article on Rose.
  Japanese: *Kerria, Rosa rugosa.*
  Karroo: *Lapidaria Margaretae.*
  Lenten: *Helleborus orientalis.*
  Mallow: *Hibiscus Moscheutos.*
  Malva: *Lavatera assurgentiflora.*
  Manetti: *Rosa* ×*Noisettiana* cv. 'Manettii'.
  McCartney: *R. bracteata.*
  Memorial: *R. Wichuriana.*
  Moss: *Portulaca:* see *Rosa centifolia* and article on Rose.
  Mountain: *Antigonon leptopus.*
  Musk: *Rosa moschata.*
  Noisette: *R.* ×*Noisettiana.*
  Nootka: *R. nutkana.*
  Ophir: *R. odorata* cv. 'Pseudindica'.
  Pasture: *R. carolina.*
  Persian yellow: *R. foetida.*
  Polyantha: *R.* ×*Rehderana.*
  Prairie: *R. setigera.*
  Pygmy: *R. chinensis* cv. 'Minima'.
  Rambler: see article on Rose.
  Remontant: see *Rosa* ×*borboniana.*
  Rock: *Cistus, Helianthemum.*
  Rush: *Helianthemum scoparium.*
  Sand: *Anacampseros telephiastrum.*
  Scotch: *Rosa spinosissima.*
  Seven-sisters: *R. multiflora* cv. 'Platyphylla'.
  Shaggy rock: *Cistus villosus.*
  Sturt's desert: *Gossypium Sturtianum.*
  Sun: *Helianthemum, Lampranthus roseus.*
  Swamp: *Rosa palustris.*
  Tea: *R. odorata.*
  Turkestan: *R. rugosa.*
  Underwater: *Samolus parviflorus.*
  Velvet: *Aeonium canariense.*
  Wax: *Pereskia Bleo.*
  White Mexican: *Echeveria elegans.*
  Wood: *Rosa gymnocarpa, Merremia tuberosa.*
  York-and-Lancaster: *Rosa damascena* cv. 'Versicolor'.
Rosebay: *Nerium Oleander, Rhododendron maximum.*
  Broad-leaved: *Tabernaemontana divaricata.*
  California: *Rhododendron macrophyllum.*
  East Indian: *Tabernaemontana divaricata.*
  Lapland: *Rhododendron lapponicum.*
  Mountain: *R. catawbiense.*
Roselle: *Hibiscus Sabdariffa.*
Rosemary: *Ceratiola ericoides, Rosmarinus, R. officinalis.*
  Bog: *Andromeda, A. glaucophylla.*
  Marsh: *Limonium.*
  Wild: *Ledum palustre.*
Rose-of-China: *Hibiscus Rosa-sinensis.*
Rose-of-heaven: *Lychnis coeli-rosa.*
Rose-of-Jericho: *Anastatica hierochuntica, Selaginella lepidophylla.*
Rose-of-Sharon: *Hibiscus syriacus, Hypericum calycinum.*
Rose-of-Venezuela: *Brownea grandiceps.*
Rose-pincushion: *Mammillaria Zeilmanniana.*
Roseroot: *Sedum Rosea.*
Rosewood: *Tipuana Tipu.*
  Burmese: *Pterocarpus indicus.*
  Ceylon: *Albizia odoratissima.*
  Senegal: *Pterocarpus erinaceus.*
Rosilla: *Helenium puberulum.*
Rosinweed: *Grindelia, Silphium.*
Rouge plant: *Rivina humilis.*
Roundwood: *Sorbus americana.*
Rowan: *Sorbus Aucuparia.*
Royal-cross: *Mammillaria Karwinskiana.*
Royal climber: *Oxera.*
Royoc: *Morinda Royoc.*
Rubber (see also Rubber plant and Rubber tree)
  Assam: *Ficus elastica.*
  Panama: *Castilla elastica.*

Rubber plant: *Ficus elastica.*
  American: *Peperomia obtusifolia.*
  Baby: *P. obtusifolia.*
  Broad-leaved India: *Ficus elastica* cv. 'Decora'.
  Chinese: *Crassula argentea.*
  Creeping: *Ficus pumila.*
  Dwarf: *Crassula argentea.*
  Japanese: *C. argentea.*
  Mistletoe: *Ficus deltoidea.*
  Small-leaved: *F. benjamina.*
Rubber tree: *Schefflera.*
  Castilla: *Castilla elastica.*
  India: *Ficus elastica.*
  Para: *Hevea brasiliensis.*
  West African: *Ficus Vogelii.*
Rubber vine: *Cryptostegia, C. grandiflora.*
Ruby-dumpling: *Mammillaria tetracantha.*
Rue: *Ruta.*
  Alpine meadow: *Thalictrum alpinum.*
  Bush: *Cneoridium dumosum.*
  Common: *Ruta graveolens.*
  Early meadow: *Thalictrum dioicum.*
  Goat's: *Galega officinalis, Tephrosia virginiana.*
  Lady: *Thalictrum clavatum.*
  Meadow: *Thalictrum.*
  Tall meadow: *T. polygamum.*
  Wall: *Asplenium Ruta-muraria.*
Rugula: *Eruca vesicaria* subsp. *sativa.*
Runaway Robin: *Glecoma hederacea.*
Rupturewort: *Herniaria, H. glabra.*
Rush: *Juncus.*
  Bog: *Juncus.*
  Chair-maker's: *Scirpus americanus.*
  Common scouring: *Equisetum hyemale.*
  Common wood: *Luzula campestris.*
  Dwarf scouring: *Equisetum hyemale.*
  Field wood: *Luzula campestris.*
  Flowering: *Butomus umbellatus.*
  Grassy: *B. umbellatus.*
  Greater wood: *Luzula sylvatica.*
  Japanese-mat: *Juncus effusus.*
  Least spike: *Eleocharis acicularis.*
  Salt: *Juncus Lesueurii.*
  Scouring: *Equisetum.*
  Slender spike: *Eleocharis acicularis.*
  Soft: *Juncus effusus.*
  Spike: *Eleocharis.*
  Variegated scouring: *Equisetum variegatum.*
  Wood: *Luzula.*
Rush nut: *Cyperus esculentus* var. *sativus.*
Russet-witch: *Liparis Loeselii.*
Rustyleaf: *Menziesia ferruginea.*
Rutabaga: *Brassica Napus,* Napobrassica Group.
Rutland-beauty: *Calystegia sepium.*
Rye: *Secale.*
  Altai wild: *Elymus angustus.*
  Aral wild: *E. aralensis.*
  Blue wild: *E. glaucus.*
  Canada wild: *E. canadensis.*
  Chinese wild: *E. chinensis.*
  Common: *Secale cereale.*
  Giant: *Triticum* ✕*turgidum,* Polonicum Group.
  Giant wild: *Elymus condensatus.*
  Russian wild: *E. junceus.*
  Siberian wild: *E. sibiricus.*
  Virginia wild: *E. virginicus.*
  Volga wild: *E. racemosus.*
  Wild: *Elymus.*

Sabicu: *Lysiloma latisiliqua.*
Sacahuista: *Nolina microcarpa.*
Sacaline: *Polygonum sachalinense.*
Sacred-flower-of-Peru: *Cantua buxifolia.*
Sacred-flower-of-the-Incas: *Cantua buxifolia.*
Sacred-lily-of-China: *Rohdea japonica.*
Safflower: *Carthamus tinctorius.*
Saffron
  Bastard: *Carthamus tinctorius.*
  False: *C. tinctorius.*
  Meadow: *Colchicum autumnale.*
  Spring meadow: *Bulbocodium vernum.*
Saffron-spike: *Aphelandra squarrosa.*

Sage: *Salvia.*
  Autumn: *S. Greggii.*
  Baby: *Salvia microphylla.*
  Bethlehem: *Pulmonaria saccharata.*
  Black: *Salvia mellifera.*
  Bladder: *Salazaria.*
  Blue: *Eranthemum pulchellum, Salvia azurea, S. Clevelandii.*
  Bog: *S. uliginosa.*
  Common: *S. officinalis.*
  Creeping: *S. sonomensis.*
  Desert: *S. eremostachya.*
  Garden: *S. officinalis.*
  Gentian: *S. patens.*
  Gray: *S. leucophylla.*
  Gray ball: *S. Dorrii.*
  Jerusalem: *Phlomis fruticosa, Pulmonaria officinalis, Salvia hierosolymitana.*
  Lilac: *Salvia verticillata.*
  Mealy-cup: *S. farinacea.*
  Mexican bush: *S. leucantha.*
  Pineapple-scented: *S. elegans.*
  Purple: *S. leucophylla.*
  Rose: *S. pachyphylla.*
  Rose-leaf: *S. involucrata.*
  Sand: *Artemisia filifolia.*
  Scarlet: *Salvia coccinea, S. splendens.*
  Silver: *S. argentea.*
  Spanish: *S. Barrelieri, S. lavandulifolia.*
  Texas: *S. coccinea.*
  Thistle: *S. carduacea.*
  Vervain: *S. Verbenaca.*
  White: *Artemisia ludoviciana, Salvia apiana.*
  Wood: *Teucrium canadense, T. Scorodonia.*
  Yellow: *Lantana Camara.*
Sagebrush: *Artemisia.*
  Basin: *A. tridentata.*
  California: *A. californica.*
  Common: *A. tridentata.*
  Low: *A. arbuscula.*
Sage tree: *Vitex Agnus-castus.*
Sago, queen: *Cycas circinalis.*
Saguaro, Sahuaro: *Carnegiea gigantea.*
Sailor-caps: *Dodecatheon Hendersonii.*
Sainfoin: *Onobrychis viciifolia.*
Saint: see St.
Salal: *Gaultheria Shallon.*
Salep: *Tacca Leontopetaloides.*
Saligot: *Trapa natans.*
Sallow: *Salix caprea.*
Sally: *Eucalyptus.*
  Black: *E. stellulata.*
  Broad-leaved: *E. camphora.*
Salmonberry: *Rubus Chamaemorus, R. parviflorus, R. spectabilis.*
Salsify: *Tragopogon porrifolius.*
  Black: *Scorzonera hispanica.*
  Spanish: *S. hispanica.*
Saltbush: *Atriplex.*
  Four-wing: *A. canescens.*
  Spiny: *A. confertifolia.*
Salt tree: *Halimodendron.*
Saman: *Samanea Saman.*
Saman tree: *Samanea Saman.*
Samohu: *Chorisia speciosa.*
Samphire: *Crithmum maritimum, Salicornia, S. europaea.*
Sandalwood: *Santalum.*
  Bastard: *Myoporum sandwicense.*
  Red: *Pterocarpus santalinus.*
  White: *Santalum album.*
Sandalwood tree: *Adenanthera pavonina.*
  Red: *A. pavonina.*
Sandberry: *Arctostaphylos Uva-ursi.*
Sandbox tree: *Hura crepitans.*
Sand-dollar: *Astrophytum asterias.*
Sanderswood, red: *Pterocarpus santalinus.*
Sand jack: *Quercus incana.*
Sandpiper vine: *Petrea.*
Sandweed: *Hypericum fasciculatum.*
Sandwort: *Arenaria.*
  Corsican: *A. balearica.*
  Mountain: *A. groenlandica.*
  Pine-barren: *A. caroliniana.*
  Pink: *A. purpurascens.*

Sandwort—*Continued*
  Rock: *A. stricta.*
  Thyme-leaved: *A. serpyllifolia.*
Sanguinary: *Achillea Millefolium.*
Sanicle: *Sanicula.*
  Purple: *S. bipinnatifida.*
  White: *Eupatorium rugosum.*
Sansevieria: *Sansevieria.*
  Bird's-nest: *S. trifasciata* cv. 'Hahnii'.
  Blue: *S. Ehrenbergii.*
  Hahn's: *S. trifasciata* cv. 'Hahnii'.
  Red-edge: *S. subspicata.*
  Seleb: *S. Ehrenbergii.*
Santa Maria: *Calophyllum brasiliense.*
Sapodilla: *Manilkara Zapota.*
Sapota, Sapote: *Pouteria Sapota.*
  Black: *Diospyros digyna.*
  Mamey, Mammee: *Pouteria Sapota.*
  White: *Casimiroa edulis.*
Sapote amarillo: *Pouteria campechiana.*
Sapote borracho: *Pouteria campechiana.*
Sappanwood: *Caesalpinia Sappan.*
Sapphire berry: *Symplocos paniculata.*
Sapphire flower: *Browallia speciosa* cv. 'Major'.
Sapucaia nut: *Lecythis Zabucayo.*
Sarcococca: *Sarcococca.*
  Fragrant: *S. ruscifolia.*
  Willow-leaf: *S. saligna.*
Sarsaparilla
  Bristly: *Aralia hispida.*
  Wild: *A. nudicaulis, Schisandra coccinea, Smilax glauca.*
Sarviceberry: *Amelanchier.*
Sasanqua: *Camellia Sasanqua.*
Sassafras: *Sassafras albidum.*
Satin flower: *Clarkia amoena, Lunaria.*
Satinleaf: *Chrysophyllum oliviforme.*
Satinwood: *Chloroxylon, Murraya paniculata.*
  East Indian: *Chloroxylon Swietenia.*
Saucer plant: *Aeonium undulatum.*
Sausage tree: *Kigelia pinnata.*
Savin: *Juniperus Sabina.*
  Creeping: *J. horizontalis.*
Savory: *Micromeria, M. Juliana, Satureja.*
  Summer: *Satureja hortensis.*
  Winter: *S. montana.*
Sawbrier: *Smilax glauca.*
Sawwort: *Serratula.*
Saxifrage: *Saxifraga.*
  Alpine brook: *S. rivularis.*
  Early: *S. virginiensis.*
  Golden: *Chrysosplenium.*
  Golden-eye: *Saxifraga tennesseensis.*
  Magic-carpet: *S. stolonifera* cv. 'Tricolor'.
  Meadow: *S. granulata.*
  Purple mountain: *S. oppositifolia.*
  Swamp: *S. pensylvanica.*
  Yellow mountain: *S. aizoides.*
Scabiosa, shepherd's: *Jasione perennis.*
Scabious: *Scabiosa.*
  Sweet: *S. atropurpurea, Erigeron annuus.*
Scammony: *Convolvulus Scammonia.*
Scarlet-bugler: *Cleistocactus Baumannii, Penstemon centranthifolius.*
Scarlet bush: *Hamelia patens.*
Scarlet-lightning: *Lychnis chalcedonica.*
Scarlet-plume: *Euphorbia fulgens.*
Scent-bottle: *Habenaria dilatata.*
Schnittlauch: *Allium Schoenoprasum.*
Scholar tree, Chinese: *Sophora japonica.*
Scoke: *Phytolacca americana.*
Scootberry: *Streptopus amplexifolius* var. *americanus.*
Scorpion weed: *Phacelia.*
Scotch-attorney: *Clusia rosea.*
Screw-augur: *Spiranthes cernua.*
Scrofula weed: *Goodyera pubescens.*
Scupernong: *Vitis rotundifolia.*
Scutcheon
  Olive: *Liparis Loeselii.*
  Purple: *L. liliifolia.*
Scythian-lamb: *Cibotium Barometz.*
Sea-coral: *Opuntia clavarioides.*
Sea-urchin, violet: *Acanthocalycium violaceum.*

Sedge: *Carex.*
  Fraser's: *Cymophyllus Fraseri.*
  Nut: *Cyperus esculentus.*
  Umbrella: *Cyperus, C. alternifolius.*
  Yellow nut: *C. esculentus.*
Sedum: *Sedum.*
  Golden: *S. Adolphi.*
  Silver: *S. Treleasei.*
Seedbox: *Ludwigia alternifolia.*
Seersucker plant: *Geogenanthus undatus.*
Selaginella: *Selaginella.*
  Basket: *S. apoda.*
  Blue: *S. uncinata.*
  Trailing: *S. Kraussiana, S. uncinata.*
Self-heal: *Prunella, P. vulgaris.*
Selu: *Cordia Myxa.*
Seminole-bread: *Zamia floridana, Z. integrifolia, Z. pumila.*
Senecio: *Senecio.*
  Bush: *S. Douglasii.*
  String-of-beads: *S. Rowleyanus.*
Senita: *Lophocereus Schottii.*
Senna: *Cassia.*
  Alexandrian: *C. acutifolia.*
  Apple-blossom: *C. javanica.*
  Bladder: *Colutea.*
  Candlestick: *Cassia alata.*
  Coffee: *C. occidentalis.*
  Prairie: *C. fasciculata.*
  Scorpion: *Coronilla Emerus.*
  Wild: *Cassia hebecarpa, C. marilandica.*
  Wormwood: *C. artemisioides.*
Sensitive plant: *Mimosa pudica.*
  Wild: *Cassia nictitans.*
Sequoia, Giant: *Sequoiadendron giganteum.*
Serviceberry: *Amelanchier.*
Service tree: *Sorbus domestica.*
  Wild: *S. torminalis.*
Sesame: *Sesamum indicum.*
Sevenbark: *Hydrangea arborescens.*
Seven-stars: *Ariocarpus retusus.*
Shad: *Amelanchier.*
Shadbush: *Amelanchier.*
Shaddock: *Citrus maxima.*
Shadscale: *Atriplex confertifolia.*
Shallon: *Gaultheria Shallon.*
Shallot: *Allium Cepa,* Aggregatum Group.
Shallu: *Sorghum bicolor,* Roxburghii Group.
Shame plant: *Mimosa pudica.*
Shamrock, Irish shamrock: *Oxalis Acetosella, Trifolium procumbens, T. repens* forma *minus.*
Shaving-brush tree: *Pachira.*
Shawnee-salad: *Hydrophyllum virginianum.*
Sheepberry: *Viburnum Lentago, V. prunifolium.*
Sheepfat: *Atriplex confertifolia.*
Sheep's-bit: *Jasione perennis.*
Sheep's-tongue: *Stomatium agninum.*
Shellbark, big: *Carya laciniosa.*
Shellflower: *Alpinia Zerumbet, Molucella laevis, Pistia stratiotes, Tigridia.*
Shepherd's-clock: *Anagallis arvensis.*
Shieldwort: *Peltaria.*
Shingle plant: *Marcgravia, Monstera acuminata, Raphidophora celatocaulis.*
Shingle tree: *Acrocarpus fraxinifolius.*
Shinleaf: *Pyrola, P. elliptica.*
  One-flowered: *Moneses uniflora.*
  White-veined: *Pyrola picta.*
Shittimwood: *Bumelia lanuginosa, B. lycioides, Halesia carolina.*
Shoo-fly plant: *Nicandra Physalodes.*
Shooting-star: *Dodecatheon, D. Meadia.*
  Alpine: *D. alpinum.*
  Lowland: *D. Clevelandii.*
  Sierra: *D. Jeffreyi.*
Shoreweed: *Littorella uniflora.*
Shower tree: *Cassia.*
Shrimp bush: *Justicia Brandegeana.*
Shrimp plant: *Justicia Brandegeana.*
  Mexican: *J. Brandegeana.*
Sibipiruna: *Caesalpinia peltophoroides.*
Sickle plant: *Crassula falcata.*
Sicklepod: *Cassia Tora.*
Side-saddle flower: *Sarracenia purpurea.*

Silk-cotton tree: *Ceiba pentandra, Cochlospermum religiosum.*
 Red: *Bombax Ceiba.*
 White: *Ceiba pentandra.*
Silk plant, Chinese: *Boehmeria nivea.*
Silk-tassel: *Garrya.*
Silk-tassel bush: *Garrya.*
Silk tree: *Albizia Julibrissin.*
Silk vine: *Periploca.*
Silkweed: *Ascelpias.*
Silver-beads: *Crassula deltoidea.*
Silver-bell: *Halesia.*
Silver-bell tree: *Halesia.*
Silverberry: *Elaeagnus argentea, E. commutata.*
Silverbush: *Convolvulus Cneorum, Sophora tomentosa.*
Silver-crown: *Cotyledon undulata.*
Silver-dollar: *Astrophytum asterias, Crassula arborescens.*
Silver-dollar tree: *Eucalyptus cinerea, E. polyanthemos.*
Silver-lace: *Chrysanthemum ptarmiciflorum.*
Silver-lace vine: *Polygonum Aubertii.*
Silverling: *Baccharis halimifolia, Paronychia argyrocoma.*
Silver-nerve: *Fittonia Verschaffeltii.*
Silver-net plant: *Fittonia Verschaffeltii.*
Silverrod: *Solidago bicolor.*
Silver-ruffles: *Cotyledon undulata.*
Silver-skin: *Argyroderma octophyllum.*
Silver-star: *Cryptanthus Lacerdae.*
Silver thatch: see *Thatch.*
Silver-threads: *Fittonia Verschaffeltii.*
Silver-tip: *Lemaireocereus Beneckei.*
Silver-torch: *Cleistocactus Straussii.*
Silver tree: *Concarpus erectus* var. *sericeus, Leucodendron argenteum.*
Silver vine: *Actinidia polygama.*
Silverweed: *Potentilla Anserina.*
Simal: *Bombax Ceiba.*
Simpler's-joy: *Verbena hastata.*
Sing-kwa: *Luffa cylindrica.*
Sirin: *Conostegia xalapensis.*
Siris tree: *Albizia Lebbek.*
Sisal, false: *Agave decipiens.*
Siskiyou-mat: *Ceanothus pumilus.*
Sissoo: *Dalbergia Sissoo.*
Skinny-fingers: *Crassula lycopodioides* var. *pseudolycopodioides.*
Skirret: *Sium Sisarum.*
Skullcap: *Scutellaria.*
Skunkbush: *Rhus trilobata.*
Skyflower: *Duranta repens, Thunbergia grandiflora.*
 Blue: *Thunbergia grandiflora.*
 Brazilian: *Duranta repens.*
Skyrocket: *Ipomopsis aggregata.*
Sky vine: *Thunbergia grandiflora.*
Sleekwort, mauve: *Liparis liliifolia.*
Slim Solomon: *Smilacina sessilifolia.*
Slipper flower: *Calceolaria, Pedilanthus tithymaloides.*
Slipper plant: *Pedilanthus tithymaloides.*
Slipperwort: *Calceolaria.*
Sloe: *Prunus alleghaniensis, P. americana, P. spinosa.*
Smartweed: *Polygonum.*
 Water: *P. coccineum.*
Smilax: *Smilax.*
 Baby: *Asparagus asparagoides* cv. 'Myrtifolius'.
 (of florists): *A. asparagoides.*
Smokebush: *Cotinus, C. Coggygria.*
Smoke plant: *Cotinus Coggygria.*
Smoke tree: *Cotinus, C. Coggygria, Dalea spinosa.*
 American: *C. obovatus.*
Smokeweed: *Eupatorium maculatum.*
Snail flower: *Vigna Caracalla.*
Snailseed: *Coccoloba diversifolia, Cocculus carolinus.*
Snail vine: *Vigna Caracalla.*
Snakebeard: *Ophiopogon Jaburan.*
Snakeberry: *Actaea rubra.*
Snakebush: *Hemiandra pungens.*
Snakehead: *Chelone, C. glabra.*
Snake-mouth: *Pogonia ophioglossoides.*
Snake plant: *Sansevieria trifasciata.*
Snakeroot: *Asarum canadense, Sanicula.*
 Black: *Cimicifuga racemosa, Sanicula.*
 Button: *Eryngium yuccifolium, Liatris.*
 Sampson's: *Gentiana Catesbaei, G. villosa.*
 Seneca: *Polygala Senega.*
 Virginia: *Aristolochia Serpentaria.*
 White: *Eupatorium rugosum.*
Snake's-head: *Fritillaria Meleagris.*

Snake vine: *Hibbertia scandens.*
Snakeweed: *Gutierrezia, Polygonum Bistorta.*
Snakewood tree: *Cecropia palmata.*
Snapdragon: *Antirrhinum.*
 Common: *A. majus.*
 Dwarf: *Chaenorrhinum.*
 Garden: *Antirrhinum majus.*
 Lesser: *A. Orontium.*
 Spurred: *Linaria.*
 Wild: *L. vulgaris.*
 Withered: *Antirrhinum multiflorum.*
Snapweed: *Impatiens.*
 Pale: *I. pallida.*
Sneezeweed: *Achillea Ptarmica, Helenium.*
Sneezewort: *Achillea Ptarmica.*
Snowball: *Alternanthera ficoidea* cv. 'Versicolor', *Viburnum Opulus* cv. 'Roseum'.
 Chinese: *Viburnum macrocephalum* forma *macrocephalum.*
 Japanese: *V. plicatum* forma *plicatum.*
 Mexican: *Echeveria elegans.*
 Peruvian: *Espostoa lanata.*
 Wild: *Ceanothus americanus.*
Snowball bush: *Viburnum Opulus* cv. 'Roseum'.
Snowbell: *Styrax.*
 Fragrant: *S. Obassia.*
 Japanese: *S. japonicus.*
Snowberry: *Chiococca, Symphoricarpos, S. albus.*
 Creeping: *Gaultheria hispidula.*
Snowbush: *Breynia disticha, Ceanothus cordulatus.*
Snow creeper: *Porana paniculata.*
Snowdrop: *Galanthus.*
 Common: *G. nivalis.*
 Giant: *G. Elwesii.*
Snowdrop bush: *Styrax officinalis* var. *californica.*
Snowdrop tree: *Halesia.*
Snowflake: *Lamium album, Leucojum.*
 Giant: *Leucojum aestivum.*
 Spring: *L. vernum.*
 Summer: *L. aestivum, Ornithogalum umbellatum.*
 Tropical: *Trevesia palmata* cv. 'Micholitzii'.
 Water: *Nymphoides indica.*
Snowflake plant: *Trevesia palmata* cv. 'Micholitzii'.
Snowflake tree: *Trevesia palmata* cv. 'Micholitzii'.
Snowflower: *Spathiphyllum floribundum.*
Snow-in-summer: *Cerastium tomentosum.*
Snow-in-the-jungle: *Porana paniculata.*
Snow-lover: *Chionophila.*
Snow-on-the-mountain: *Euphorbia marginata.*
Snow-wreath: *Neviusia.*
Soap-bark tree: *Quillaja Saponaria.*
Soapberry: *Sapindus, S. Saponaria, Shepherdia canadensis.*
 Chinese: *Sapindus Mukorossi.*
Soap plant: *Chlorogalum, C. pomeridianum.*
Soap tree: *Yucca elata.*
Soapweed: *Yucca elata, Y. glauca.*
Soapwell: *Yucca glauca.*
Soapwort: *Saponaria.*
Soldier's-cap: *Aconitum Napellus.*
Soldier's-plume: *Habenaria psycodes.*
Solomon's-feather: *Smilacina.*
Solomon's-plume: *Smilacina.*
Solomon's-seal: *Polygonatum.*
 False: *Smilacina.*
 Great: *Polygonatum commutatum.*
 Small: *P. biflorum.*
 Two-leaved: *Maianthemum canadense.*
Solomon's-zigzag: *Smilacina racemosa.*
Sorbet: *Cornus mas.*
Sorghum: *Sorghum bicolor.*
 Grass: *S. halepense, S. sudanense.*
 Sugar: *S. bicolor,* Saccharatum Group.
 Sweet: *S. bicolor,* Saccharatum Group.
Sorgo: *Sorghum bicolor,* Saccharatum Group.
Sorrel: *Rumex.*
 Common: *R. Acetosella.*
 Dock: *Rumex.*
 European wood: *Oxalis Acetosella.*
 French: *Rumex scutatus.*
 Garden: *R. Acetosa, R. scutatus.*
 Indian: *Hibiscus Sabdariffa.*
 Jamaican: *H. Sabdariffa.*
 Lady's: *Oxalis.*
 Mountain: *Oxyria.*

Sorrel—*Continued*
  Red: *Rumex Acetosella.*
  Redwood: *Oxalis oregona.*
  Sheep: *Rumex Acetosella.*
  Tree: *Averrhoa Bilimbi.*
  Violet wood: *Oxalis violacea.*
  Wood: *Oxalis.*
Sorrel tree: *Oxydendrum arboreum.*
Sorrowless tree: *Saraca indica.*
Sotol: *Dasylirion.*
Sourberry: *Rhus integrifolia.*
Sour greens: *Rumex venosus.*
Soursop: *Annona muricata.*
  Mountain: *A. montana.*
  Wild: *A. montana.*
Sourwood: *Oxydendrum arboreum.*
Southernwood: *Artemisia Abrotanum.*
Sowbread: *Cyclamen.*
Spadic: *Erythroxylum Coca.*
Spaniard, Colenso's: *Aciphylla Colensoi.*
Spanish-bayonet: *Yucca aloifolia, Y. baccata.*
Spanish-buttons: *Centaurea nigra.*
Spanish-dagger: *Yucca carnerosana, Y. gloriosa, Y. Treculeana.*
Spanish-needles: *Bidens.*
Spanish nut: *Gynandriris Sisyrinchium.*
Spanish-shawl: *Heterocentron elegans.*
Spanish-stopper: *Eugenia foetida.*
Spathe flower: *Spathiphyllum.*
Spatterdock: *Nuphar.*
  Common: *N. advena.*
Spearhead: *Senecio kleiniiformis.*
Spearmint: *Mentha spicata.*
Spectacle pod: *Dithyrea.*
Speedwell: *Veronica.*
  Common: *V. officinalis.*
  Germander: *V. Chamaedrys.*
  Marsh: *V. scutellata.*
  Thyme-leaved: *V. serpyllifolia.*
Spelt: *Triticum aestivum,* Spelta Group.
  Two-grained: *T. turgidum,* Dicoccon Group.
Spiceberry: *Ardisia crenata.*
Spicebush: *Lindera Benzoin.*
Spider flower: *Cleome Hasslerana, Grevillea.*
Spider plant: *Anthericum, Chlorophytum comosum, Cleome.*
Spider-wisp: *Cleome gynandra.*
Spiderwort: *Tradescantia.*
  Blue: *Commelina coelestis.*
  Common: *Tradescantia virginiana.*
  Purple-leaved: *Rhoeo spathacea.*
  Queen's: *Dichorisandra reginae.*
Spike bush: *Eleocharis.*
Spikenard: *Aralia racemosa.*
  American: *A. racemosa.*
  False: *Smilacina racemosa.*
Spinach: *Spinacia oleracea.*
  Cuban: *Montia perfoliata.*
  Indian: *Basella alba.*
  Malabar: *B. alba.*
  Mountain: *Atriplex hortensis.*
  New Zealand: *Tetragonia tetragonioides.*
  Prickly-seeded: *Spinacia oleracea* var. *oleracea.*
  Round-seeded: *S. oleracea* var. *inermis.*
  Wild: *Chenopodium Bonus-Henricus.*
Spindle tree: *Euonymus, E. japonica.*
  European: *E. europaea.*
  Japanese: *E. japonica.*
  Winged: *E. alata.*
Spiraea, Spirea: *Astilbe, Spiraea.*
  Blue: *Caryopteris incana.*
  False: *Sorbaria.*
  Japanese: *Spiraea japonica.*
  (of florists): *Astilbe japonica.*
  Perennial: *Astilbe.*
  Reeves: *Spiraea cantoniensis.*
  Rock: *Holodiscus dumosus, Petrophytum.*
  Tosa: *Spiraea nipponica.*
Spiral plant: *Costus pulverulentus.*
Spirea: see Spiraea.
Spleenwort: *Asplenium.*
  Black-stem: *A. resiliens.*
  Bradley's: *A. Bradleyi.*
  Ebony: *A. platyneuron.*
  Green: *A. viride.*

Spleenwort—*Continued*
  Little ebony: *A. resiliens.*
  Lobed: *A. pinnatifidum.*
  Maidenhair: *A. Trichomanes.*
  Mother: *A. bulbiferum.*
  Mountain: *A. montanum.*
  Narrow-leaved: *Diplazium pycnocarpon.*
  Pinnatifid: *Asplenium pinnatifidum.*
  Silvery: *Diplazium pycnocarpon.*
  Western: *Asplenium vespertinum.*
Split-rock: *Pleiospilos Nelii.*
Sponge tree: *Acacia Farnesiana.*
Spoon flower: *Dasylirion Wheeleri, Xanthosoma Lindenii.*
Spoonwood: *Kalmia latifolia.*
Spoonwort: *Cochlearia officinalis.*
Spotted-beauty: ×*Gastrolea.*
Spotted evergreen: *Aglaonema costatum.*
Sprengeri: *Asparagus densiflorus* cv. 'Sprengeri'.
Spring-beauty: *Claytonia, C. virginica.*
Spring-gold: *Lomatium utriculatum.*
Sprouting leaf: *Kalanchoe pinnata.*
Sprouts: *Brassica oleracea,* Gemmifera Group.
Spruce: *Picea.*
  Alberta: *P. glauca* var. *albertiana.*
  Big-cone: *Pseudotsuga macrocarpa.*
  Black: *Picea mariana.*
  Black Hills: *P. glauca* cv. 'Densata'.
  Blue: *P. pungens* cv. 'Glauca'.
  Bog: *P. mariana.*
  Cat: *P. glauca.*
  Colorado: *P. pungens.*
  Colorado blue: *P. pungens.*
  Double: *P. mariana.*
  Finnish: *P. obovata* var. *fennica.*
  Hemlock: *Tsuga.*
  Himalayan: *Picea Smithiana.*
  Hondo: *P. jezoensis* var. *hondoensis.*
  Japanese bush: *P. Maximowiczii.*
  Norway: *P. Abies.*
  Red: *P. rubens.*
  Sakhalin: *P. Glehnii.*
  Siberian: *P. obovata.*
  Sitka: *P. sitchensis.*
  Snake: *P. rubens* cv. 'Virgata'.
  Tiger-tail: *P. Torano.*
  White: *P. glauca.*
  Yeddo: *P. jezoensis.*
Spruce-cones: *Opuntia articulata* cv. 'Inermis'.
Spur flower: *Plectranthus.*
Spurge: *Euphorbia, Pachysandra.*
  Alleghany: *Pachysandra procumbens.*
  Caper: *Euphorbia Lathyrus.*
  Cypress: *E. Cyparissias.*
  Fiddler's: *E. cyathophora.*
  Flowering: *E. corollata.*
  Indian tree: *E. Tirucalli.*
  Ipecac: *E. ipecacuanhae.*
  Japanese: *Pachysandra terminalis.*
  Leafy: *Euphorbia Esula.*
  Melon: *E. meloformis.*
  Mottled: *E. lactea.*
  Myrtle: *E. Lathyrus.*
  Seaside: *E. polygonifolia.*
  Slipper: *Pedilanthus.*
  Tramp's: *Euphorbia corollata.*
Spurry, Spurrey: *Spergula.*
  Corn: *S. arvensis.*
  Sand: *Spergularia.*
Squarenut: *Carya tomentosa.*
Squash: *Cucurbita.*
  Acorn: *C. Pepo* var. *Pepo.*
  Autumn: *C. maxima, C. Pepo.*
  Banana: *C. maxima.*
  Boston marrow: *C. maxima.*
  Bush: *C. Pepo* var. *Melopepo.*
  Canada crookneck: *C. moschata.*
  Cocozelle: *C. Pepo* var. *Melopepo* cv. 'Cocozelle'.
  Crookneck: *C. moschata.*
  Hubbard: *C. maxima.*
  Pattypan: *C. Pepo* var. *Melopepo* cv. 'White Bush Scallop'.
  Scallop: *C. Pepo* var. *Melopepo* cv. 'White Bush Scallop'.
  Summer: *C. Pepo.*
  Summer crookneck: *C. Pepo* var. *Melopepo* cv. 'Crookneck'.

Squash—*Continued*
   Turban: *C. maxima* cv. 'Turbaniformis'.
   Winter: *C. maxima, C. mixta, C. moschata.*
   Winter crookneck: *C. moschata.*
Squawberry: *Mitchella repens.*
Squawbush: *Rhus trilobata* var. *malacophylla, Viburnum trilobum.*
Squawroot: *Perideridia Gairdneri, Trillium erectum.*
Squaw vine: *Mitchella repens.*
Squill: *Scilla, Urginea maritima.*
   Autumn: *Scilla autumnalis.*
   Bell-flowered: *Endymion hispanicus.*
   Chinese: *Scilla scilloides.*
   Common blue: *Endymion non-scriptus.*
   Dwarf: *Scilla monophyllos.*
   Hyacinth: *S. hyacinthoides.*
   Indigo: *Camassia scilloides.*
   Italian: *Endymion italicus.*
   Red: *Urginea maritima.*
   Siberian: *Scilla siberica.*
   Spring: *S. verna.*
Squirrel-ear: *Goodyera repens* var. *ophioides.*
St.-Andrew's-cross: *Hypericum hypericoides.*
St.-Catherine's-lace: *Eriogonum giganteum.*
St.-John's-bread: *Ceratonia Siliqua.*
St.-John's-wort: *Hypericum.*
   Blue Ridge: *H. Mitchellianum.*
   Creeping: *H. calycinum.*
   Shrubby: *H. prolificum.*
St.-Peter's-wort: *Hypericum stans.*
St. Thomas tree: *Bauhinia tomentosa.*
Staff vine: *Celastrus scandens.*
Stagbush: *Viburnum prunifolium.*
Staggerbush: *Lyonia mariana.*
Staggerweed: *Dicentra eximia.*
Stapelia: *Stapelia.*
   Giant: *S. gigantea.*
   Shaggy: *S. hirsuta.*
Star-cluster: *Pentas lanceolata.*
   Egyptian: *P. lanceolata.*
Starfish flower: *Stapelia.*
   Hairy: *S. hirsuta.*
Starfish plant: *Cryptanthus acaulis, Stapelia.*
Starflower: *Smilacina stellata, Stapelia variegata, Trientalis, T. borealis.*
   Spring: *Ipheion uniflorum.*
Star-glory: *Ipomoea Quamoclit.*
Starleaf: *Brassaia actinophylla, Schefflera.*
Star-of-Bethlehem: *Campanula isophylla, Ornithogalum arabicum, O. pyrenaicum, O. umbellatum.*
Stars-of-Persia: *Allium Christophii.*
Starwort: *Aster, Stellaria media.*
   Water: *Callitriche.*
Star vine, bay: *Schisandra coccinea.*
Statice: *Limonium.*
Steeplebush: *Spiraea tomentosa.*
Steer's-head: *Dicentra uniflora.*
Stepladder plant: *Costus Malortieanus.*
Stepmother's flower: *Viola ×Wittrockiana.*
Stevia: *Piqueria trinervia.*
Stewartia, Japanese: *Camellia pseudocamellia.*
Stickseed: *Hackelia, Lappula.*
Stick-tights: *Bidens.*
Sticky-heads: *Grindelia.*
Stinking Benjamin: *Trillium erectum.*
Stinking weed: *Cassia occidentalis.*
Stitchwort: *Stellaria media.*
   Greater: *S. Holostea.*
Stock: *Matthiola, M. incana.*
   Brampton: *M. incana.*
   Evening: *M. longipetala.*
   Imperial: *M. incana.*
   Malcolm: *Malcolmia.*
   Ten-weeks: *Matthiola incana* cv. 'Annua'.
   Virginia: *Malcolmia maritima.*
Stonecrop: *Sedum.*
Stoneface: *Lithops.*
Stoneroot: *Collinsonia canadensis.*
Stonewort: *Nitella.*
Stopper: *Eugenia.*
   Red: *E. confusa.*
   White: *E. axillaris.*
Storax: *Styrax.*

Storksbill: *Erodium, Pelargonium.*
   Knotted: *Pelargonium gibbosum.*
Stove-brush, giant: *Haemanthus magnifica.*
Strainer vine: *Luffa.*
Stramonium: *Datura Stramonium.*
Strap flower: *Anthurium crystallinum.*
Strawbell: *Uvularia perfoliata.*
Strawberry: *Fragaria.*
   Barren: *Waldsteinia fragarioides.*
   Beach: *Fragaria chiloensis.*
   Garden: *F. ×Ananassa.*
   Indian: *Duchesnea.*
   Mock: *Duchesnea.*
   Sow-teat: *Fragaria vesca.*
   Virginia: *F. virginiana.*
   Woodland: *F. vesca.*
Strawberry bush: *Euonymus americana.*
   Running: *E. obovata.*
Strawberry shrub: *Calycanthus floridus.*
Strawberry tree: *Arbutus, A. Unedo.*
Strawflower: *Helichrysum bracteatum, Helipterum.*
String-of-buttons: *Crassula perforata.*
String-of-hearts: *Ceropegia Woodii.*
Stringybark: *Eucalyptus.*
   Blaxland's: *E. Blaxlandii.*
   Blue-leaved: *E. agglomerata.*
   Brown: *E. capitellata.*
   Grampian: *E. alpina.*
   Mealy: *E. cinerea.*
   Messmate: *E. obliqua.*
   Red: *E. macrorhyncha.*
   White: *E. globoidea.*
   Yellow: *E. Muellerana.*
Strongback: *Bourreria ovata.*
Strychnine: *Strychnos Nux-vomica.*
Stypticweed: *Cassia occidentalis.*
Succory: *Cichorium Intybus.*
Sugarberry: *Celtis, C. laevigata, C. occidentalis.*
Sugarbush: *Protea mellifera, Rhus ovata.*
Sugarcane: *Saccharum officinarum.*
Sugarplum: *Amelanchier.*
Sugar-scoop: *Tiarella unifoliata.*
Sugar tree: *Acer barbatum.*
Sulphur flower: *Eriogonum umbellatum.*
Sultana: *Impatiens Wallerana.*
Sumac: *Rhus.*
   Desert: *R. microphylla.*
   Dwarf: *R. copallina.*
   Elm-leaved: *R. coriaria.*
   Evergreen: *R. virens.*
   Fragrant: *R. aromatica.*
   Laurel: *R. laurina.*
   Lemon: *R. aromatica.*
   Lemonade: *R. integrifolia.*
   Poison: *R. Vernix.*
   Scarlet: *R. glabra.*
   Scrub: *R. microphylla.*
   Shining: *R. copallina.*
   Sicilian: *R. coriaria.*
   Small-leaved: *R. microphylla.*
   Smooth: *R. glabra.*
   Staghorn: *R. typhina.*
   Sugar: *R. ovata.*
   Swamp: *R. Vernix.*
   Sweet-scented: *R. aromatica.*
   Tanner's: *R. coriaria.*
   Tobacco: *R. virens.*
   Velvet: *R. typhina.*
   Venetian: *Cotinus Coggygria.*
   Virginian: *Rhus typhina.*
   Wing-rib: *Rhus copallina.*
Summerberry: *Viburnum trilobum.*
Summer-sweet: *Clethra, C. alnifolia.*
Sunberry: *Solanum Burbankii.*
Suncup: *Oenothera bistorta, O. heterantha.*
Sundew: *Drosera.*
   Dwarf: *D. brevifolia.*
   Pink: *D. capillaris.*
   Portuguese: *Drosophyllum lusitanicum.*
   Round-leaved: *Drosera rotundifolia.*
   Thread-leaved: *D. filiformis.*
Sundrops: *Oenothera fruticosa, O. perennis, O. pilosella.*

Sunflower: *Balsamorhiza, Helianthus.*
  Ashy: *Helianthus mollis.*
  Common: *H. annuus.*
  Cucumber-leaf: *H. debilis* subsp. *cucumerifolius.*
  Dark-eye: *H. atrorubens.*
  Desert: *Geraea canescens.*
  Giant: *Helianthus giganteus.*
  Maximilian: *H. Maximiliani.*
  Mexican: *Tithonia.*
  Oregon: *Balsamorhiza sagittata.*
  Showy: *Helianthus lactiflorus.*
  Stiff: *H. rigidus.*
  Swamp: *H. angustifolius.*
  Thin-leaf: *H. decapetalus.*
Sunn: *Crotalaria juncea.*
Sun plant: *Portulaca grandiflora.*
Sunray: *Enceliopsis.*
  Panamint: *E. Covillei.*
Suntwood: *Acacia nilotica.*
Supplejack: *Berchemia, B. scandens.*
Swallowwort, black: *Cynanchum nigrum.*
Swan flower: *Swainsona galegifolia.*
Sweat plant: *Selaginella pallescens.*
Swede: *Brassica Napus,* Napobrassica Group.
Sweetbells: *Leucothoe racemosa.*
Sweetberry: *Viburnum Lentago.*
Sweetbrier: *Rosa Eglanteria.*
Sweetcup: *Passiflora maliformis.*
Sweet-hurts: *Vaccinium angustifolium.*
Sweet jarvil, Sweet javril: *Osmorhiza Claytonii.*
Sweetleaf: *Symplocos.*
  Asiatic: *S. paniculata.*
Sweet-potato tree: *Manihot esculenta.*
Sweet-potato vine: *Ipomoea Batatas.*
  Wild: *I. pandurata.*
Sweet shrub: *Calycanthus.*
Sweetsop: *Annona squamosa.*
Sweetspire: *Itea virginica.*
Sweet-sultan: *Centaurea moschata.*
Sweet William: *Dianthus barbatus.*
  Wild: *Phlox divaricata, P. maculata.*
Sweetwood: *Glycyrrhiza glabra.*
Swiss-cheese plant: *Monstera deliciosa.*
Sword plant: *Echinodorus.*
  Amazon: *E. paniculatus, E. tenellus.*
  Dwarf Amazon: *E. magdalenensis.*
  Pygmy chain: *E. intermedia.*
Sycamore: *Acer pseudoplatanus, Platanus.*
  Eastern: *Platanus occidentalis.*
  Egyptian: *Ficus Sycomorus.*
  (of the Bible): *Ficus Sycomorus.*
Syringa: *Philadelphus.*
Sze-kwa: *Luffa aegyptiaca.*

Tabog: *Swinglea.*
Tacamahac: *Populus balsaminifera.*
Taffeta plant: *Hoffmannia refulgens.*
Tagua: *Palandra, Phytelephas macrocarpa.*
Tailflower: *Anthurium.*
Tailor's-patch: *Crassula lactea.*
Talewort: *Borago officinalis.*
Tallow tree: *Detarium senegalense.*
  Chinese: *Sapium sebiferum.*
Tallowwood: *Eucalyptus microcorys.*
Tamarack: *Larix laricina.*
Tamarind: *Tamarindus indica.*
  Manila: *Pithecellobium dulce.*
  Sierra Leone: *Dialium guineense.*
  Velvet: *D. guineense.*
Tamarindo: *Tamarindus indica.*
Tamarind-of-the-Indies: *Vangueria edulis.*
Tamarisk: *Tamarix.*
  False: *Myrciaria.*
  French: *Tamarix gallica.*
Tampala: *Amaranthus tricolor.*
Tangelo: *Citrus ×Tangelo.*
Tangerine: *Citrus reticulata.*
Tanglefoot: *Viburnum alnifolium.*
Tangle-legs: *Viburnum alnifolium.*
Tangor: *Citrus ×nobilis.*
Tania: see Tannia.
Tanier: *Xanthosoma.*
Tanner's tree: *Coriaria nepalensis.*

Tannia, Tania: *Xanthosoma.*
Tansy: *Tanacetum.*
  Common: *T. vulgare.*
  Goose: *Potentilla Anserina.*
Tanyah: *Xanthosoma.*
Tanyosho: *Pinus densiflora* cv. 'Umbraculifera'.
Tapa-cloth tree: *Broussonetia papyrifera.*
Tapeworm: *Senecio pendula.*
Tapeworm plant: *Homalocladium platycladum.*
Tapioca: *Manihot esculenta.*
Tara: *Caesalpinia spinosa.*
Tara vine: *Actinidia arguta.*
Tarajo: *Ilex latifolia.*
Tarata: *Pittosporum eugenioides.*
Tare: *Vicia, V. sativa.*
Tarflower: *Befaria racemosa.*
Taro: *Alocasia macrorrhiza, Colocasia esculenta.*
  Blue: *Xanthosoma violaceum.*
  Chinese: *Alocasia cucullata.*
  Egyptian: *Colocasia esculenta* var. *antiquorum.*
  Imperial: *C. esculenta* var. *illustris.*
  Violet-stemmed: *C. esculenta* var. *Fontanesii, Xanthosoma violaceum.*
Taro vine: *Epipremnum aureum.*
Tarragon: *Artemisia Dracunculus.*
Tartogo: *Jatropha podagrica.*
Tarweed: *Cuphea petiolata, Grindelia, Madia.*
  Chile: *Madia sativa.*
  Common: *M. elegans.*
Tassel flower: *Amaranthus caudatus, Brickellia.*
Tassel-white: *Itea virginica.*
Tawhiwhi: *Pittosporum tenuifolium.*
Tea: *Camellia sinensis.*
  African: *Catha edulis.*
  Appalachian: *Ilex glabra, Viburnum cassinoides.*
  Arabian: *Catha edulis.*
  Ceylon: *Cassine glauca.*
  Crystal: *Ledum palustre.*
  Labrador: *Ledum groenlandicum.*
  Mexican: *Chenopodium ambrosioides.*
  Mountain: *Gaultheria procumbens.*
  New Jersey: *Ceanothus americanus.*
  Oswego: *Monarda didyma.*
  Paraguay: *Ilex paraguariensis.*
  Philippine: *Ehretia microphylla.*
  Siberian: *Bergenia crassifolia.*
  Spanish: *Chenopodium ambrosioides.*
Teaberry: *Gaultheria procumbens, Viburnum cassinoides.*
Teak: *Tectona grandis.*
  Rhodesian: *Baikiaea plurijuga.*
Tea-of-heaven: *Hydrangea macrophylla* subsp. *serrata.*
Tea-oil plant: *Camellia oleifera.*
Tea plant: *Camellia sinensis, Viburnum Lentago.*
Teasel: *Dipsacus.*
  Common: *D. fullonum*
  Fuller's: *D. sativus.*
  Wild: *D. fullonum*
Tea tree: *Leptospermum lanigerum, L. scoparium, Melaleuca quinquenervia.*
  Australian: *Leptospermum laevigatum.*
  New Zealand: *L. scoparium.*
  River: *Melaleuca Leucadendron.*
  Swamp: *M. Leucadendron, M. quinquenervia.*
  Weeping: *M. Leucadendron.*
  Woolly: *Leptospermum lanigerum.*
Teddy-bear plant: *Cyanotis kewensis.*
Teddy-bear vine: *Cyanotis kewensis.*
Teff: *Eragrostis Tef.*
Telegraph plant: *Desmodium motorium.*
Temazcal: *Rhus terebinthifolia.*
Temple-bells: *Smithiantha.*
Temple plant: *Hygrophila stricta.*
Temple tree: *Plumeria.*
Temu: *Luma apiculata.*
Ten-commandments: *Maranta leuconeura.*
Tendergreen: *Brassica Rapa,* Perviridis Group.
Tenderwort: *Malaxis unifolia.*
  Adder's-tongue: *M. unifolia.*
Teosinte: *Zea mexicana.*
Tetterbush: *Lyonia lucida.*
Thatch: *Thrinax.*
  Bull: *Sabal jamaicensis.*
  Silver: *Coccothrinax argentea.*

Thick plant: *Pachyphytum compactum.*
Thimbleberry: *Rubus occidentalis, R. odoratus, R. parviflorus.*
Thimbleweed: *Anemone cylindrica, A. riparia, A. virginiana.*
Thistle: *Cirsium.*
  Acanthus-leaved: *Carlina acanthifolia.*
  Argentine: *Onopordum Acanthium.*
  Blessed; *Cnicus, Silybum Marianum.*
  Bull: *Cirsium vulgare.*
  Canada: *C. arvense.*
  Cotton: *Onopordum Acanthium.*
  Fishbone: *Cirsium diacantha.*
  Globe: *Echinops.*
  Golden: *Scolymus hispanicus.*
  Great globe: *Echinops sphaerocephalus.*
  Holy: *Silybum Marianum.*
  Milk: *S. Marianum.*
  Mountain: *Acanthus montanus.*
  Mountain sow: *Lactuca alpina.*
  Oat: *Onopordum Acanthium.*
  Plume: *Cirsium.*
  Plumeless: *Carduus.*
  Scotch: *Onopordum Acanthium.*
  Silver: *O. Acanthium.*
  Small globe: *Echinops Ritro.*
  Star: *Centaurea calcitrapa.*
  St. Mary's: *Silybum Marianum.*
  Thornless: *Centaurea americana.*
  White: *Atriplex lentiformis.*
Thorn: *Crataegus.*
  Box: *Bursaria spinosa, Lycium, L. europaeum.*
  Camel: *Acacia giraffae.*
  Christ: *Euphorbia Milii, Paliurus Spina-Christi.*
  Cockspur: *Crataegus crus-galli.*
  Crucifixion: *Holacantha Emoryi.*
  Egyptian: *Acacia nilotica.*
  Hedge: *Carissa bispinosa.*
  Jerusalem: *Paliurus Spina-Christi, Parkinsonia aculeata.*
  Kangaroo: *Acacia armata.*
  Karroo: *A. Karroo.*
  Lily: *Catesbaea spinosa.*
  Mysore: *Caesalpinia sepiaria.*
  Paper-bark: *Acacia Woodii.*
  Pear: *Crataegus Calpodendron.*
  Quick-set: *C. laevigata.*
  Sallow: *Hippophae rhamnoides.*
  Sickle: *Asparagus falcatus.*
  Thirsty: *Acacia Seyal.*
  Washington: *Crataegus Phaenopyrum.*
  White: *C. laevigata.*
  Winter: *Acacia albida.*
  Yellow-fruited: *Crataegus flava.*
Thoroughwax: *Bupleurum.*
Thoroughwort: *Eupatorium, E. perfoliatum.*
Thousand-mothers: *Tolmiea Menziesii.*
Thousand-seal: *Achillea Millefolium.*
Three-birds-flying: *Linaria triornithophora.*
Three-men-in-a-boat: *Rhoeo spathacea.*
Thrift: *Armeria.*
  Prickly: *Acantholimon.*
Throatwort: *Campanula Trachelium, Trachelium.*
Thyme: *Thymus.*
  Basil: *Acinos thymoides.*
  Caraway: *Thymus Herba-barona.*
  Common: *T. vulgaris.*
  Garden: *T. vulgaris.*
  Golden: *T. vulgaris* cv. 'Aureus'.
  Lemon: *T. Serpyllum.*
  Spanish: *Coleus amboinicus.*
  Water: *Elodea.*
  Wild: *Thymus Serpyllum.*
Ti: *Cordyline terminalis.*
Tickseed: *Bidens, Coreopsis.*
Tidy-tips: *Layia platyglossa.*
Ti-es: *Pouteria campechiana.*
Tiger flower: *Tigridia, T. Pavonia.*
Tiger-jaws: *Faucaria.*
Tiger nut: *Cyperus esculentus* var. *sativus.*
Tiger's-jaw: *Faucaria tigrina.*
Tillandsia, pot-bellied: *Tillandsia circinnata.*
Timothy: *Phleum.*
  Alpine: *P. alpinum.*
Tinker's-weed: *Triosteum perfoliatum.*
Tipu tree: *Tipuana.*

Tisswood: *Persea Borbonia.*
Titi: *Cliftonia monophylla, Cyrilla racemiflora, Oxydendrum arboreum.*
  Black: *Cliftonia monophylla, Cyrilla racemiflora.*
  Red: *Cyrilla racemiflora.*
  White: *C. racemiflora.*
Toadflax: *Linaria, Spergula arvensis.*
  Bastard: *Comandra.*
  Cloven-lip: *Linaria bipartita.*
  Common: *L. vulgaris.*
  Old-field: *L. canadensis.*
  Purple-net: *L. reticulata.*
  Striped: *L. repens.*
Toad plant: *Stapelia variegata.*
  Giant: *S. gigantea.*
  Hairy: *S. hirsuta.*
Toadshade: *Trillium sessile.*
Tobacco: *Nicotiana, N. rustica, N. Tabacum.*
  Flowering: *N. alata.*
  Indian: *Lobelia inflata.*
  Jasmine: *Nicotiana alata.*
  Long-flowered: *N. longiflora.*
  Tree: *N. glauca.*
  Wild: *N. rustica, Solanum mauritianum.*
Tolguacha: *Datura inoxia.*
Tomatillo: *Physalis ixocarpa.*
Tomato: *Lycopersicon, L. Lycopersicum.*
  Cherry: *L. Lycopersicum* var. *cerasiforme, Physalis peruviana.*
  Currant: *L. pimpinellifolium.*
  Gooseberry: *Physalis peruviana.*
  Husk: *Physalis.*
  Mexican husk: *P. ixocarpa.*
  Pear: *Lycopersicon Lycopersicum* var. *pyriforme.*
  Strawberry: *Physalis Alkekengi, P. peruviana, P. pruinosa, P. pubescens.*
  Tree: *Cyphomandra betacea.*
Tomato tree: *Cyphomandra betacea.*
Tom-thumb: *Parodia aureispina.*
  Golden: *P. aureispina.*
Tongueleaf: *Glottiphyllum.*
Toog: *Bischofia javanica.*
Toothache tree: *Zanthoxylum americanum.*
Tooth-cup: *Rotala.*
Toothwort: *Dentaria.*
Torch flower: *Kniphofia Uvaria.*
Torch plant: *Aloe arborescens, A. ×spinosissima.*
Tormentil: *Potentilla erecta.*
Tornillo: *Prosopis pubescens.*
Torote: *Bursera microphylla.*
Torreya, Japanese: *Torreya nucifera.*
Tortuguero: *Polygala Cowellii.*
Torus herb: *Dorstenia Contrajerva.*
Touch-me-not: *Impatiens, I. Noli-tangere, Mimosa pudica.*
  Pale: *Impatiens pallida.*
  Spotted: *I. capensis.*
Tous-les-mois: *Canna edulis.*
Toyon: *Heteromeles.*
Trapa nut: *Trapa natans.*
Traveler's tree: *Ravenala madagascariensis.*
Treacleberry: *Smilacina racemosa.*
Tread-softly: *Cnidoscolus, C. urens.*
Treasure flower: *Gazania ringens.*
Treebine, Venezuela: *Cissus rhombifolia.*
Tree ivy, Soledad: *Hedera canariensis* cv. 'Variegata Arborescens'.
Tree-of-gold: *Tabebuia argentea.*
Tree-of-heaven: *Ailanthus altissima.*
Tree-of-kings: *Cordyline terminalis.*
Tree-of-life: *Mauritia flexuosa.*
Tree-of-sadness: *Nyctanthes Arbor-tristis.*
Trefoil: *Trifolium.*
  Bird's-foot: *Lotus corniculatus.*
  Broadleaf bird's-foot: *L. corniculatus* var. *arvensis.*
  Marsh: *Menyanthes trifoliata.*
  Narrowleaf bird's-foot: *Lotus corniculatus* var. *tenuifolium.*
  Shrubby: *Ptelea.*
  Tick: *Desmodium.*
  Yellow: *Medicago lupulina.*
Trigger plant: *Stylidium.*
Trillium: *Trillium.*
  Dwarf white: *T. nivale.*
  Nodding: *T. cernuum.*
  Painted: *T. undulatum.*
  Purple: *T. erectum, T. recurvatum.*

Trillium—*Continued*
  Snow: *T. nivale.*
  Wood: *T. viride.*
Trip-toe: *Viburnum alnifolium.*
Triteleia, long-rayed: *Triteleia peduncularis.*
Tritoma: *Kniphofia.*
Trumpet bush: *Tecoma.*
Trumpet creeper: *Campsis radicans.*
  Chinese: *C. grandiflora.*
Trumpet flower: *Bignonia capreolata, Campsis.*
  Chinese: *Campsis grandiflora.*
  Evening: *Gelsemium sempervirens.*
  Nepal: *Beaumontia.*
Trumpetleaf: *Sarracenia flava.*
Trumpet plant: *Solandra guttata.*
Trumpets: *Sarracenia flava.*
Trumpet tree: *Cecropia peltata, Tabebuia.*
  Cuban pink: *Tabebuia pallida.*
  Paraguayan silver: *T. argentea.*
  Rosy: *T. rosea.*
  Silver: *T. argentea.*
Trumpet vine: *Campsis radicans.*
  Argentine: *Clytostoma callistegioides.*
  Blue: *Thunbergia grandiflora.*
  Pink: *Podranea Ricasoliana.*
Tuba root: *Derris elliptica.*
Tubeflower: *Clerodendrum, C. indicum.*
Tuberroot: *Asclepias tuberosa.*
Tuberose: *Polianthes tuberosa.*
Tuckahoe: *Peltandra virginica.*
Tucuma: *Astrocaryum aculeatum.*
Tuftroot: *Dieffenbachia.*
Tulip: *Tulipa.*
  Butterfly: *Calochortus.*
  Common early garden: see under *Tulipa suaveolens.*
  Common late garden: see under *T. Gesnerana.*
  Globe: *Calochortus.*
  Golden globe: *C. amabilis.*
  Guinea-hen: *Fritillaria Meleagris.*
  Lady: *Tulipa Clusiana.*
  Purple globe: *Calochortus amoenus.*
  Sierra star: *C. nudus.*
  Star: *Calochortus.*
  Turkish: *Tulipa acuminata.*
  Water-lily: *T. Kaufmanniana.*
Tulip tree: *Liriodendron, Spathodea campanulata.*
  African: *Spathodea campanulata.*
  American: *Liriodendron Tulipifera.*
  Chinese: *L. chinense.*
Tumbleweed: *Amaranthus albus.*
Tumeric: see Turmeric.
Tuna: *Opuntia.*
  Orange: *O. elata.*
  Rose: *O. basilaris.*
  Thimble: *O. sphaerica.*
Tung: *Aleurites montana.*
Tung-oil tree: *Aleurites Fordii.*
Tunic flower: *Petrorhagia Saxifraga.*
Tunka: *Benincasa hispida.*
Tupelo: *Nyssa.*
  Large: *N. aquatica.*
  Upland: *N. sylvatica.*
Turkeybeard: *Xerophyllum asphodeloides.*
Turkey-tangle: *Phyla nodiflora.*
Turkish-rugging: *Chorizanthe staticoides.*
Turk's-cap: *Aconitum Napellus, Lilium Martagon, L. superbum, Malvaviscus arboreus* var. *mexicanus.*
Turk's-head: *Ferocactus hamatacanthus.*
Turk's-turban: *Clerodendrum indicum.*
Turmeric: *Curcuma domestica, Hydrastis canadensis.*
Turnip: *Brassica Rapa,* Rapifera Group.
  Indian: *Arisaema triphyllum, Psoralea esculenta.*
  Italian: *Brassica Rapa,* Ruvo Group.
  Seven-top: *B. Rapa,* Rapifera Group.
  Swedish: *B. Napus,* Napobrassica Group.
Turnsole: *Heliotropium.*
Turpentine tree: *Syncarpia glomulifera.*
Turpentine weed: *Gutierrezia.*
Turtlehead: *Chelone, C. glabra.*
Tutsan: *Hypericum Androsaemum.*
Twayblade: *Liparis, Listera.*
  Bog: *Liparis Loeselii.*
  Broad-leaved: *Listera convallarioides.*

Twayblade—*Continued*
  Broad-lipped: *L. convallarioides.*
  Heart-leaf: *L. cordata.*
  Large: *Liparis liliifolia.*
  Loesel's: *L. Loeselii.*
  Yellow: *L. Loeselii.*
Twelve-apostles: *Neomarica.*
Twinberry: *Mitchella repens, Lonicera involucrata.*
Twinflower: *Linnaea.*
Twining-firecracker: *Manettia inflata.*
Twinleaf: *Jeffersonia diphylla.*
Twinspur: *Diascia Barberae.*
Twisted-stalk: *Streptopus.*
Twistwood: *Viburnum Lantana.*
Two-eyed berry: *Mitchella repens.*
Two-men-in-a-boat: *Rhoeo spathacea.*

Udo: *Aralia cordata.*
Ulluco: *Ullucus tuberosus* (see *Basellaceae*).
Umbilroot: *Cypripedium Calceolus* var. *pubescens.*
Umbrella flower: *Ceropegia Sandersonii.*
Umbrella leaf: *Diphylleia cymosa.*
Umbrella plant: *Cyperus alternifolius, Eriogonum, E. Allenii, Peltiphyllum peltatum.*
  Dwarf: *Cyperus alternifolius* cv. 'Gracilis'.
Umbrella tree: *Magnolia tripetala, Schefflera.*
  Australian: *Brassaia actinophylla.*
  Ear-leaved: *Magnolia Fraseri.*
  Queen's: *Brassaia actinophylla.*
  Queensland: *B. actinophylla.*
  Texas: *Melia Azedarach.*
Umbrella-trumpets: *Sarracenia flava.*
Umbrellawort: *Mirabilis.*
Unicorn flower: *Proboscidea.*
  Common: *P. louisianica.*
Unicorn plant: *Proboscidea.*
Unicorn root: *Aletris farinosa.*
Upas tree: *Antiaris toxicaria.*
Urd: *Vigna Mungo.*
Urn plant: *Aechmea fasciata.*

Vagabond plant: *Vriesia vagans.*
Valerian: *Valeriana.*
  African: *Fedia cornucopiae.*
  American: *Cypripedium Calceolus* var. *pubescens.*
  Common: *Valeriana officinalis.*
  Greek: *Polemonium, P. caeruleum.*
  Long-spurred: *Centranthus macrosiphon.*
  Red: *C. ruber.*
Vanilla: *Vanilla planifolia.*
  Pompona: *V. Pompona.*
  West Indian: *V. Pompona.*
Vanilla leaf: *Achlys triphylla.*
Varnish tree: *Ailanthus glandulosa, Aleurites moluccana, Koelreuteria paniculata, Rhus verniciflua, Semecarpus Anacardium.*
  Japanese: *Firmiana simplex.*
Vase plant: *Billbergia.*
Vase vine: *Clematis, C. Viorna.*
Vegetable-humming-bird: *Sesbania grandiflora.*
Vegetable marrow: *Cucurbita Pepo* var. *Pepo, Persea americana.*
Vegetable-oyster: *Tragopogon porrifolius.*
Vegetable-sheep: *Haastia pulvinaris.*
Vegetable-sponge: *Luffa.*
Vegetable-tallow: *Sapium sebiferum.*
Velvet-bells: *Bartsia alpina.*
Velvetleaf: *Abutilon Theophrasti, Kalanchoe beharensis.*
Velvet plant: *Gynura aurantiaca, Verbascum Thapsus.*
  Purple: *Gynura aurantiaca.*
  Royal: *G. aurantiaca.*
  Trailing: *Ruellia Makoyana.*
Venushair, Venus's-hair: *Adiantum Capillus-Veneris.*
Venus's-shoe: *Cypripedium Calceolus* var. *pubescens.*
Venus's-flytrap: *Dionaea muscipula.*
Venus's-looking-glass: *Legousia Speculum-Veneris.*
Verbena: *Verbena.*
  Beach sand: *Abronia umbellata.*
  Clump: *Verbena canadensis.*
  Common garden: *V.* ×*hybrida.*
  Desert sand: *Abronia villosa.*
  Lemon: *Aloysia triphylla.*
  Mojave sand: *Abronia pogonantha.*
  Moss: *Verbena tenuisecta.*
  Pink sand: *Abronia umbellata.*

Verbena—*Continued*
Red sand: *A. maritima.*
Rose: *Verbena canadensis.*
Sand: *Abronia.*
Shrub: *Lantana.*
Yellow sand: *Abronia latifolia.*
Vertical leaf: *Senecio crassissimus.*
Vervain: *Verbena, V. lasiostachys, V. rigida.*
Blue: *V. hastata.*
Creeping: *V. canadensis* cv. 'Grandiflora'.
Dakota: *V. bipinnatifida.*
Hoary: *V. stricta.*
Prostrate: *V. bracteata.*
Rose: *V. canadensis.*
White: *V. urticifolia.*
Vetch: *Vicia.*
Bard: *V. monantha.*
Bird: *V. Cracca.*
Bitter: *V. Ervillia.*
Common: *V. angustifolia.*
Cow: *V. Cracca.*
Crown: *Coronilla, C. varia.*
Hairy: *Vicia villosa.*
Horseshoe: *Hippocrepis.*
Hungarian: *Vicia pannonica.*
Kidney: *Anthyllis Vulneraria.*
Large Russian: *Vicia villosa.*
Milk: *Astragalus.*
Narbonne: *Vicia narbonensis.*
Purple: *V. benghalensis.*
Sitka: *V. gigantea.*
Smooth: *V. dasycarpa* var. *glabrescens.*
Spring: *V. sativa.*
Tufted: *V. Cracca.*
Winter: *V. villosa.*
Woolly-pod: *V. dasycarpa.*
Vetchling: *Lathyrus.*
Spring: *L. vernus.*
Tuberous: *L. tuberosus.*
Yellow: *L. pratensis.*
Vetiver: *Vetiveria zizanioides.*
Vi: *Spondias cytherea.*
Viburnum: *Viburnum.*
Double-file: *V. plicatum* forma *tomentosum.*
Maple-leaved: *V. acerifolium.*
Naked: *V. nudum.*
Sweet: *V. Lentago, V. odoratissimum.*
Victory plant: *Cheiridopsis candidissima.*
Vinegar tree: *Rhus glabra.*
Vinegar weed: *Trichostema lanceolatum.*
Viola: *Viola cornuta.*
Violet: *Viola.*
African: *Saintpaulia.*
Alaska: *Viola Langsdorffii.*
Alpine: *Cyclamen.*
Alpine marsh: *Viola palustris.*
American dog: *V. conspersa.*
Arrow-leaved: *V. sagittata.*
Australian: *V. hederacea.*
Bird-foot: *V. pedata.*
Bush: *Browallia.*
California golden: *Viola pedunculata.*
Canada: *V. canadensis.*
Coast: *V. Brittoniana.*
Common African: *Saintpaulia ionantha.*
Confederate: see *Viola sororia.*
Cream: *V. striata.*
Crowfoot: *V. pedata.*
Dame's: *Hesperis matronalis.*
Dog: *Viola canina, V. Riviniana.*
Dog-tooth: *Erythronium, E. Dens-canis.*
Downy yellow: *Viola pubescens.*
Early blue: *V. palmata.*
Early yellow: *V. rotundifolia.*
Eastern water: *V. lanceolata.*
English: *V. odorata.*
Evergreen: *V. sempervirens.*
False: *Dalibarda.*
Flame: *Episcia cupreata, E. reptans.*
Florist's: *Viola odorata.*
Garden: *V. odorata.*
German: *Exacum affine.*
Great Basin: *Viola Beckwithii.*

Verbena—*Continued*
Great-spurred: *V. Selkirkii.*
Green: *Hybanthus.*
Halberd-leaved: *Viola hastata.*
Hook-spur: *V. adunca.*
Horned: *V. cornuta.*
Ivy-leaved: *V. hederacea.*
Kidney-leaved: *V. renifolia.*
Labrador: *V. labradorica.*
Lance-leaved: *V. lanceolata.*
Large-leaved white: *V. incognita.*
Larkspur: *V. pedatifida.*
Long-spurred: *V. rostrata.*
Marsh: *V. palustris.*
Marsh blue: *V. cucullata.*
Mexican: *Tetranema roseum.*
Missouri: *Viola missouriensis.*
Northern blue: *V. septentrionalis.*
Northern bog: *V. nephrophylla.*
Northern downy: *V. fimbriatula.*
Northern white: *V. renifolia.*
Olympic: *V. Flettii.*
Pale: *V. striata.*
Pansy: *V. pedata.*
Persian: *Cyclamen, Exacum affine.*
Philippine: *Barleria cristata.*
Pine: *Viola purpurea.*
Plains: *V. viarum.*
Primrose-leaved: *V. primulifolia.*
Purple prairie: *V. pedatifida.*
Red: *Episcia reptans.*
Redwood: *Viola sempervirens.*
Rock: *V. Flettii.*
Round-leaved yellow: *V. rotundifolia.*
Sagebrush: *V. trinervata.*
Scarlet: *Episcia reptans.*
Smooth yellow: *Viola pubescens* var. *eriocarpa.*
Southern coast: *V. septemloba.*
Strap-leaved: *V. vittata.*
Stream: *V. glabella.*
Striped: *V. striata.*
Sweet: *V. odorata.*
Sweet white: *V. blanda.*
Tall white: *V. canadensis.*
Trailing: *V. hederacea.*
Triangle-leaved: *V. emarginata.*
Tree: *Baphia racemosa.*
Two-eyed: *Viola ocellata.*
Water: *Hottonia.*
Western dog: *Viola adunca.*
Western round-leaved: *V. orbiculata.*
Western sweet white: *V. Macloskeyi.*
White dog-tooth: *Erythronium albidum.*
Wood: *Viola Raviniana.*
Woolly blue: *V. sororia.*
Yellow prairie: *V. Nuttallii.*
Yellow wood: *V. lobata.*
Violeta: *Polygala Cowellii.*
Violet tree: *Polygala Cowellii.*
Violetwood: *Acacia homalophylla.*
Virgilia: *Cladrastis lutea.*
Virginia creeper: *Parthenocissus quinquefolia.*
Virgin's-bower: *Clematis, C. virginiana.*
Visnaga: *Ferocactus.*
Volador: *Triplaris.*

Wadalee-gum tree: *Acacia Catechu.*
Wahoo: *Euonymus atropurpurea.*
Waiawi: *Psidium littorale* var. *littorale.*
Wait-awhile vine: *Calamus.*
Wake-robin: *Trillium, T. sessile.*
Purple: *T. recurvatum.*
Rosy: *T. Catesbaei.*
Virginian: *Peltandra virginica.*
White: *Trillium grandiflorum.*
Walking leaf: *Camptosorus.*
Wallflower: *Cheiranthus Cheiri, Erysimum.*
Beach: *Erysimum suffrutescens.*
Coast: *E. capitatum.*
English: *Cheiranthus Cheiri.*
Winter: *C. kewensis.*
Wallflower-crown: *Rebutia pseudodeminuta.*
Wallowa: *Acacia calamifolia.*

Wallwort: *Sambucus Ebulus.*
Walnut: *Juglans.*
  Arizona: *J. major.*
  Black: *J. nigra.*
  California: *J. californica.*
  Carpathian: *J. regia.*
  Chinese: *J. cathayensis.*
  Country: *Aleurites moluccana.*
  English: *Juglans regia.*
  Indian: *Aleurites moluccana.*
  Japanese: *Juglans ailanthifolia.*
  Little: *J. microcarpa.*
  Manchurian: *J. mandshurica.*
  Otaheite: *Aleurites moluccana.*
  Persian: *Juglans regia.*
  River: *J. microcarpa.*
  West Indies: *J. jamaicensis.*
  White: *J. cinerea.*
Wampi: *Clausena Lansium.*
Wandering Jew: *Tradescantia albiflora, T. fluminensis, Zebrina pendula.*
Wandflower: *Dierama, Galax urceolata, Sparaxis.*
Wand plant: *Galax urceolata.*
Waratah: *Telopea speciosissima.*
  Tasmanian: *T. truncata.*
Wart plant: *Haworthia.*
Watapo: *Sagittaria cuneata, S. latifolia.*
Watch-chain: *Crassula lycopodioides.*
  Giant's: *C. imperialis.*
Watches: *Sarracenia flava.*
Water-carpet: *Chrysosplenium americanum.*
Watercress: *Nasturtium, N. officinale.*
Water-dragon: *Calla palustris, Saururus cernuus.*
Water-feather: *Myriophyllum aquaticum.*
Water-filter nut: *Strychnos potatorum.*
Water-fringe: *Nymphoides peltatum.*
Water gladiolus: *Butomus umbellatus.*
Waterleaf: *Hydrophyllum.*
  Virginia: *H. virginianum.*
Water-mat: *Chrysosplenium americanum.*
Water-meal: *Wolffia.*
Watermelon: *Citrullus lanatus.*
  Chinese: *Benincasa hispida.*
Water-motie: *Baccharis glutinosa.*
Water nut: *Trapa.*
Water-nymph: *Najas, Nymphaea.*
  Common: *Najas guadalupensis.*
Water-platter: *Victoria.*
  Amazon: *V. amazonica.*
  Santa Cruz: *V. Cruziana.*
Water-shield: *Brasenia, B. Schreberi, Cabomba.*
Water-soldier: *Stratiotes.*
Water-tresses: *Spiranthes praecox.*
Water-trumpet: *Cryptocoryne.*
Water-wally: *Baccharis glutinosa.*
Waterweed: *Elodea, E. canadensis.*
  Brazilian: *E. densa.*
Waterwort: *Elatine.*
Wattle: *Acacia.*
  Black: *A. Mearnsii.*
  Blue-leaf: *A. cyanophylla.*
  Bramble: *A. Victoriae.*
  Broom: *A. calamifolia.*
  Buffalo: *A. Kettlewelliae.*
  Cedar: *A. terminalis.*
  Cinnamon: *A. leprosa.*
  Coastal: *A. cyclopis.*
  Cootamundra: *A. Baileyana.*
  Frosty: *A. pruinosa.*
  Glory: *A. spectabilis.*
  Golden: *A. pycnantha.*
  Golden-rain: *A. prominens.*
  Graceful: *A. decora.*
  Green: *A. decurrens* var. *mollis.*
  Hairy: *A. pubescens.*
  Mount Morgan: *A. podalyriifolia.*
  Mudgee: *A. spectabilis.*
  Needle-bush: *A. rigens.*
  Orange: *A. cyanophylla.*
  Oven's: *A. pravissima.*
  Peppermint-tree: *A. terminalis.*
  Prickly: *A. juniperina.*
  Queensland silver: *A. podalyriifolia.*

Wattle—*Continued*
  Red-leaved: *A. rubida.*
  Sally: *A binervia.*
  Screw-pod: *A. implexa.*
  Silver: *A. dealbata.*
  Sticky: *A. Howittii.*
  Sunshine: *A. paniculata.*
  Swamp: *A. elongata.*
  Sydney golden: *A. longifolia.*
  Wallangarra: *A. accola.*
  Weeping: *A. saligna.*
  Wyalong: *A. cardiophylla.*
Waxberry: *Gaultheria hispida, Myrica cerifera, Symphoricarpos albus.*
Waxflower: *Chamaelaucium, Chimaphila, Stephanotis floribunda.*
  Geraldton: *Chamaelaucium uncinatum.*
  Philippine: *Nicolaia elatior.*
Wax plant: *Hoya carnosa.*
  Geraldton: *Chamaelaucium uncinatum.*
  Miniature: *Hoya bella.*
Wax-rosette: *Echeveria gilva.*
Wax tree: *Rhus succedanea.*
  White: *Ligustrum lucidum.*
Wax vine: *Hoya.*
  Variegated: *Senecio macroglossus* cv. 'Variegatus'.
Waxweed, blue: *Cuphea petiolata.*
Waxwork: *Celastrus scandens.*
Wayfaring tree: *Viburnum Lantana.*
  American: *V. alnifolium.*
Weatherglass, golden: *Hypoxis hygrometrica.*
Weather plant: *Abrus precatorius.*
Weather vine: *Abrus precatorius.*
Weld: *Reseda luteola.*
Wheat: *Triticum.*
  Alaska: *T. turgidum,* Turgidum Group.
  Club: *T. aestivum,* Compactum Group.
  Common: *T. aestivum,* Aestivum Group.
  Durum: *T. turgidum,* Durum Group.
  Dwarf: *T. aestivum,* Compactum Group.
  English: *T. turgidum,* Turgidum Group.
  German: *T. turgidum,* Dicoccon Group.
  Hedgehog: *T. aestivum,* Compactum Group.
  India: *Fagopyrum tataricum.*
  Mediterranean: *Triticum turgidum,* Turgidum Group.
  One-grained: *T. monococcum.*
  Polish: *T. turgidum,* Polonicum Group.
  Poulard: *T. turgidum,* Turgidum Group.
  Rice: *T. turgidum,* Dicoccon Group.
  River: *T. turgidum,* Turgidum Group.
  Starch: *T. turgidum,* Dicoccon Group.
  Two-grained: *T. turgidum,* Dicoccon Group.
Wheatgrass, beardless: *Agropyron spicatum* var. *inerme.*
Wheel-of-fire: *Stenocarpus sinuatus.*
Wheel tree: *Trochodendron aralioides.*
Whin: *Ulex europaeus.*
Whinberry: *Vaccinium Myrtillus.*
Whippoorwill flower: *Trillium cuneatum.*
Whippoorwill-shoe: *Cypripedium Calceolus* var. *pubescens.*
Whispering-bells: *Emmenanthe penduliflora.*
Whistlewood: *Acer pensylvanicum.*
Whistling tree: *Acacia Seyal.*
Whitecup: *Nierembergia repens.*
White-gossamer: *Tradescantia sillamontana.*
White-jewel: *Titanopsis Schwantesii.*
White-man's-foot: *Plantago major.*
White nun: *Lycaste virginalis* (white-fld. form).
White-plush plant: *Echeveria leucotricha.*
White-top: *Erigeron annuus.*
White-velvet: *Tradescantia sillamontana.*
Whiteweed: *Chrysanthemum Leucanthemum.*
Whitewood: *Liriodendron Tulipifera, Tabebuia riparia, Tilia, T. americana.*
Whitlavia: *Phacelia minor.*
Whitlowwort: *Paronychia.*
  Silver: *P. argyrocoma.*
Whitten tree: *Viburnum Opulus.*
Whorlflower: *Morina longifolia.*
Whortleberry: *Vaccinium corymbosum, V. Myrtillus.*
Wickup: *Epilobium angustifolium.*
Wicky: *Kalmia angustifolia.*
  White: *K. cuneata.*
Wicopy: *Dirca palustris.*
Widdy: *Potentilla fruticosa.*

Widow's-frill: *Silene stellata.*
Widow's-tears: *Achimenes, Tradescantia virginiana.*
Wig tree: *Cotinus Coggygria.*
Williwilli: *Erythrina tahitensis.*
Willow: *Salix.*
  Arctic: *S. arctica.*
  Arroyo: *S. lasiolepis.*
  Basket: *S. purpurea, S. viminalis.*
  Bay: *S. pentandra.*
  Bay-leaved: *S. pentandra.*
  Bearberry: *S. Uva-ursi.*
  Black: *S. nigra.*
  Brittle: *S. fragilis.*
  Bush: *Combretum erythrophyllum.*
  Crack: *Salix fragilis.*
  Creeping: *S. repens.*
  Cricket-bat: *S. alba* var. *calva.*
  Desert: *Chilopsis linearis.*
  Dragon-claw: *Salix Matsudana* cv. 'Tortuosa'.
  False: *Baccharis angustifolia.*
  Florist's: *Salix caprea.*
  Flowering: *Chilopsis linearis.*
  Goat: *Salix caprea.*
  Golden: *Acacia cyanophylla, Salix alba* var. *vitellina.*
  Gray: *Salix cinerea, S. humilis.*
  Green-scaled: *S. chlorolepis.*
  Halberd-leaved: *S. hastata.*
  Heart-leaved: *S. cordata.*
  Large pussy: *S. discolor.*
  Laurel: *S. pentandra.*
  Niobe: *S. blanda.*
  Peach-leaved: *S. amygdaloides.*
  Pekin: *S. Matsudana.*
  Polished: *S. laevigata.*
  Port Jackson: *Acacia cyanophylla.*
  Prairie: *Salix humilis.*
  Pussy: *S. caprea, S. discolor.*
  Puzzle: *S. ambigua.*
  Red: *Cornus Amomum, Salix laevigata.*
  Sandbar: *Salix interior.*
  Scouler: *S. Scoulerana.*
  Seep: *Baccharis glutinosa.*
  Shining: *Salix lucida.*
  Silky: *S. sericea.*
  Small pussy: *S. humilis.*
  Sprouting: *S. stolonifera.*
  Virginia: *Itea virginica.*
  Water: *Baccharis glutinosa, Decodon verticillatus, Justicia.*
  Weeping: *Salix babylonica.*
  White: *S. alba.*
  Wisconsin weeping: *S. blanda.*
  Woolly: *S. lanata.*
  Yellow: *S. alba* var. *vitellina.*
Willow herb: *Epilobium.*
  Great: *E. angustifolium.*
Windflower: *Anemone.*
Windowleaf: *Monstera.*
Window plant: *Fenestraria, Haworthia cymbiformis, Monstera deliciosa.*
Wineberry: *Rubus phoenicolasius.*
  New Zealand: *Aristotelia racemosa.*
Wine plant: *Rheum Rhabarbarum.*
Wingnut: *Pterocarya.*
  Caucasian: *P. fraxinifolia.*
  Chinese: *P. stenoptera.*
Wingstem: *Verbesina alternifolia.*
Winterberry: *Ilex glabra, I. verticillata.*
  Common: *I. verticillata.*
  Japanese: *I. serrata.*
  Mountain: *I. ambigua* var. *montana.*
  Smooth: *I. laevigata.*
Winter creeper: *Euonymus radicans.*
Wintergreen: *Chimaphila, Gaultheria procumbens, Pyrola.*
  Alpine: *Gaultheria humifusa.*
  Arctic: *Pyrola grandiflora.*
  Chickweed: *Trientalis.*
  Flowering: *Polygala paucifolia.*
  One-sided: *Pyrola secunda.*
  Pink: *P. asarifolia.*
  Spotted: *Chimaphila maculata.*
Winter's-bark: *Drimys Winteri.*
Wintersweet: *Acokanthera oblongifolia, Chimonanthus praecox.*

Wire plant: *Muehlenbeckia.*
Wire vine: *Muehlenbeckia complexa.*
Wirilda: *Acacia retinodes.*
Wishbone flower: *Torenia.*
Wishbone plant: *Torenia.*
Wistaria, Wisteria: *Wisteria.*
  Chinese: *W. sinensis.*
  Japanese: *W. floribunda.*
  Pink: *W. floribunda* cv. 'Rosea'.
  Rhodesian: *Bolusanthus speciosus.*
  Silky: *Wisteria venusta.*
  Water: *Hygrophila difformis.*
  Wild: *Bolusanthus speciosus.*
Wistaria tree, scarlet: *Sesbania grandiflora, S. Tripetii.*
Witch hazel: see under Hazel.
Witch-hobble: *Viburnum alnifolium.*
Withe-rod: *Viburnum cassinoides, V. nudum.*
  Smooth: *V. nudum.*
Witloof: *Cichorium Intybus.*
Wi tree: *Spondias cytherea.*
Woad: *Isatis.*
  Dyer's: *I. tinctoria.*
Woadwaxen: *Genista tinctoria.*
Wolfsbane: *Aconitum Lycoctonum.*
  Garden: *A. Napellus.*
  Trailing: *A. reclinatum.*
Wolf bean: *Lupinus albus.*
Wolfberry: *Symphoricarpos occidentalis.*
Wolffia, common: *Wolffia columbiana.*
Wolf's-milk: *Euphorbia Esula.*
Woman's-tongue tree: *Albizia Lebbek.*
Wonderberry: *Solanum Burbankii.*
Wonder bulb: *Colchicum autumnale.*
Wonder flower: *Ornithogalum thyrsoides.*
  African: *O. thyrsoides.*
Wonder tree: *Ricinus communis.*
Wonga-wonga vine: *Pandorea pandorana.*
Wonkapin: *Nelumbo lutea.*
Woodbine: *Clematis virginiana, Lonicera Periclymenum, Parthenocissus, P. quinquefolia.*
  Dutch: *Lonicera Periclymenum* var. *belgica.*
  Italian: *L. Caprifolium.*
  Spanish: *Merremia tuberosa.*
Wood-oil tree: *Aleurites.*
  China: *A. Fordii.*
  Japan: *A. cordata.*
Woodroof: *Galium odoratum.*
Woodruff: *Asperula, Galium odoratum.*
  Dyer's: *Asperula tinctoria.*
  Sweet: *Galium odoratum.*
Woodsia: *Woodsia.*
  Blunt-lobed: *W. obtusa.*
  Cathcart's: *W. Cathcartiana.*
  Common: *W. obtusa.*
  Fragrant: *W. ilvensis.*
  Large: *W. obtusa.*
  Mexican: *W. mexicana.*
  Northern: *W. alpina.*
  Oregon: *W. oregana.*
  Rocky Mountain: *W. scopulina.*
  Rusty: *W. ilvensis.*
  Smooth: *W. glabella.*
Wood-vamp: *Decumaria barbara.*
Woodwaxen: *Genista tinctoria.*
Woolflower: *Celosia.*
Woolly-bear: *Begonia leptotricha.*
Woollybutt: *Eucalyptus longifolia.*
  Camden: *E. Macarthurii.*
  Darwin: *E. miniata.*
Woolly-sheep: *Opuntia floccosa.*
Wormseed: *Artemisia maritima, Chenopodium ambrosioides.*
  American: *Chenopodium ambrosioides.*
Worm vine: *Vanilla barbellata.*
Wormwood: *Artemisia, Vanilla barbellata.*
  Alpine: *Artemisia laxa.*
  Beach: *A. Stellerana.*
  Common: *A. Absinthium.*
  Roman: *Corydalis sempervirens.*
  Russian: *Artemisia Gmelinii.*
  Sweet: *A. annua.*
Woundwort: *Anthyllis Vulneraria, Stachys.*
  Downy: *Stachys germanica.*

Yam: *Dioscorea, Ipomoea Batatas.*
    Attoto: *Dioscorea ✕cayenensis.*
    Chinese: *D. Batatas.*
    Negro: *D. ✕cayenensis.*
    Water: *Aponogeton fenestrale, Dioscorea alata.*
    White: *Dioscorea alata.*
    Wild: *D. hirticaulis, D. quaternata, D. villosa.*
    Yellow: *D. ✕cayenensis.*
Yampah: *Perideridia.*
Yampee: *Dioscorea trifida.*
Yang-tao: *Actinidia arguta, A. chinensis.*
Yanquapin: *Nelumbo lutea.*
Yarran: *Acacia homalophylla.*
Yarrow: *Achillea.*
    Common: *A. Millefolium.*
    Fern-leaf: *A. filipendulina.*
    Sweet: *A. Ageratum.*
    Woolly: *A. tomentosa.*
Yate: *Eucalyptus.*
    Bushy: *E. Lehmannii.*
    Flat-topped: *E. occidentalis.*
    Warted: *E. megacornuta.*
Yate tree: *Eucalyptus cornuta.*
Yaupon: *Ilex Cassine, I. vomitoria.*
Yautia: *Xanthosoma.*
Yellowbells: *Emmenanthe penduliflora, Tecoma, T. stans.*
Yellowberry: *Rubus Chamaemorus.*
Yellow-flame: *Peltophorum pterocarpum.*
Yellow-rattle: *Rhinanthus.*
Yellowroot, shrub: *Xanthorhiza.*
Yellow-trumpets: *Sarracenia alata.*
Yellowwood: *Cladrastis lutea, Rhodosphaera rhodanthema.*
    African: *Podocarpus elongatus.*
Yerba buena: *Satureja Douglasii.*
Yerba-de-maté: *Ilex paraguariensis.*
Yerba-de-selva: *Whipplea modesta.*
Yerba linda: *Peperomia rotundifolia.*
Yerba mansa: *Anemopsis californica.*
Yerba maté: *Ilex paraguariensis.*
Yerba santa: *Eriodictyon.*
Yertchuk: *Eucalyptus Consideniana.*
Yesterday-and-today: *Brunfelsia australis, B. pauciflora.* cv. 'Eximia'.
Yesterday-today-and-tomorrow: *Brunfelsia australis, B. pauciflora* cv. 'Eximia'.

Yew: *Taxus.*
    American: *T. canadensis.*
    Chinese: *T. chinensis.*
    Chinese plum: *Cephalotaxus Fortunei.*
    English: *Taxus baccata.*
    Florida: *T. floridana.*
    Golden: *T. baccata* cv. 'Aurea'.
    Harrington plum: *Cephalotaxus Harringtonia.*
    Irish: *Taxus baccata* cv. 'Stricta'.
    Japanese: *Podocarpus macrophyllus, Taxus cuspidata.*
    Japanese plum: *Cephalotaxus Harringtonia* var. *drupacea.*
    Plum: *Cephalotaxus.*
    Plum-fruited: *C. Harringtonia* var. *drupacea.*
    Prince Albert: *Saxegothaea conspicua.*
    Southern: *Podocarpus macrophyllus.*
    Western: *Taxus brevifolia.*
Ylang-ylang: see ilang-ilang.
Youngberry: *Rubus ursinus* cv. 'Young'.
Youth-and-old-age: *Aichryson domesticum, Zinnia elegans.*
Youth-on-age: *Tolmiea Menziesii.*
Yuca: *Manihot esculenta.*
Yucca: *Yucca.*
    Banana: *Y. baccata.*
    Blue: *Y. baccata.*
    San Angelo: *Y. Reverchonii.*
    Spineless: *Y. elephantipes.*
    Twisted-leaf: *Y. rupicola.*
Yulan: *Magnolia heptapeta.*

Zamang: *Samanea Saman.*
Zapote blanco: *Casimiroa edulis.*
Zebra plant: *Aphelandra squarrosa, Calathea zebrina, Cryptanthus zonatus.*
Zedoary: *Curcuma Zedoaria*
Zelkova: *Zelkova.*
    Japanese: *Z. serrata.*
    Saw-leaf: *Z. serrata.*
Zinnia: *Zinnia.*
    Common: *Z. elegans.*
    Mexican: *Z. Haageana.*
Zit-kwa: *Benincasa hispida.*
Zucchini: *Cucurbita Pepo* var. *Melopepo* cv. 'Zucchini'.
Zulu-giant: *Stapelia gigantea.*
Zulu nut: *Cyperus esculentus* var. *sativus.*
Zygadene: *Zigadenus.*
    Star: *Z. Fremontii.*

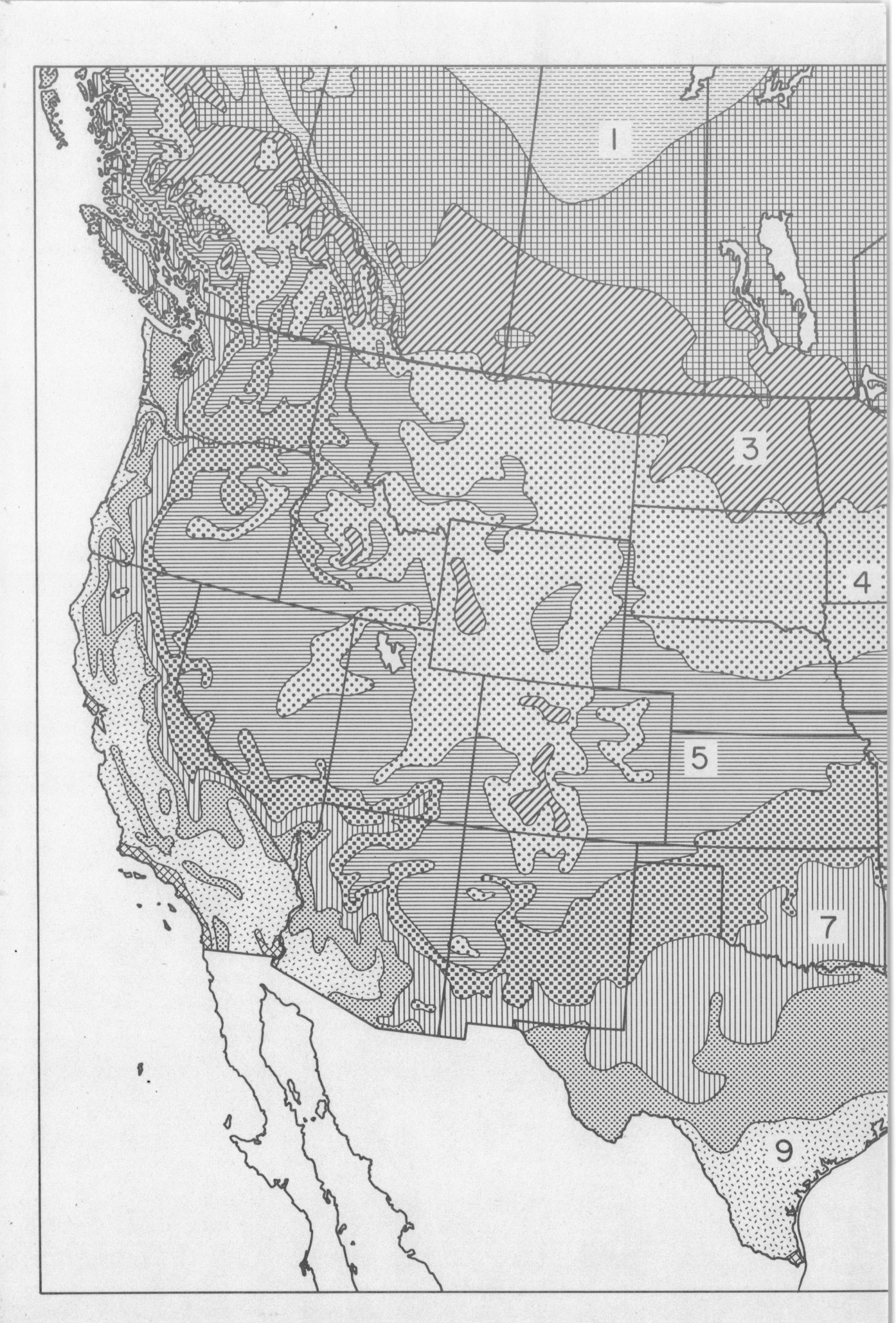